DIGESTED SUMMARY

AND

ALPHABETICAL LIST OF PRIVATE CLAIMS

WHICH HAVE BEEN

PRESENTED TO THE HOUSE OF REPRESENTATIVES

FROM THE FIRST TO THE THIRTY-FIRST CONGRESS,

EXHIBITING

THE ACTION OF CONGRESS ON EACH CLAIM,

WITH

REFERENCES TO THE JOURNALS, REPORTS, BILLS, &c.,

ELUCIDATING ITS PROGRESS.

COMPILED BY ORDER OF THE HOUSE OF REPRESENTATIVES.

VOL. I.

From A to G inclusive.

GENEALOGICAL PUBLISHING CO., INC.
Baltimore 1970

Originally Printed for the
House of Representatives of the United States
32d Congress, 1st Session
as House Miscellaneous Documents, unnumbered, Series 653-655
Washington, D. C., 1853

Reprinted with added Publisher's Preface
Genealogical Publishing Company
Baltimore, 1970

Library of Congress Catalog Card Number 79-135476
International Standard Book Number 0-8063-0447-2

The publisher gratefully acknowledges
the loan of the original of this book
by the
George Peabody Branch
Enoch Pratt Free Library
Baltimore, Maryland

NOTICE

This work was reproduced by the photo-offset process from the original edition. A characteristic of this copy, from which the offset printer worked, was that the image was uneven. Every effort has been made by our photo-offset printer to produce as fine a reprint of the original edition as possible.

Genealogical Publishing Company

Made in the United States of America

Publisher's Preface

The following information concerning the locations of the original Private Claims indexed in the *Digested Summary and Alphabetical List* was supplied to us by Mr. Mark G. Eckhoff, Director of the Legislative, Judicial and Diplomatic Records Division of the National Archives and Records Service, Washington, D. C.:

> "Records relating to the private claims indexed in the *Alphabetical List of Private Claims . . . Presented to the House of Representatives*, 1st-31st Congress, are found in the records of the House of Representatives (Record Group 233) in the National Archives. The types of records will most often include the original petition sent by the claimant; the bill, if any, introduced on his behalf to grant the claim; and the report of the committee in charge of the claim. In addition papers in support of the claim, such as depositions to corroborate an officer's service, may be filed with the petition. A rough estimate is that such supporting papers are present with perhaps one-third of petitions submitted during this period. It should be noted that because of the burning of the Capitol in 1814, and other misfortunes, there are gaps in the records of the House; almost no petitions are found before the 6th Congress (1799), nor original House bills before the 12th Congress (1811). All records of the House of Representatives in the National Archives remain subject to the orders of the House, and authorization to see or have copies made of any unpublished House records must be obtained from the Clerk of the House, the Honorable W. Pat Jennings. Applications for this authorization is usually made through the office of a Congressman.
>
> "Similar series of private claims records are present in the records of the United States Senate (Record Group 46) in the National Archives. These claims are also listed in a series of index volumes similar to [the *Alphabetical List of Private Claims*]. The earliest index is entitled *List of Private Claims Brought Before the Senate of the United States*, and covers the period 1815-1881 (14th-46th Congress); this index was published originally as Senate Miscellaneous Document 14, 46th Congress, 3d Session. No prior authorization is necessary for researchers wishing to view or have copies made of these Senate records."

Additionally, the following information was supplied to us by Mr. James D. Walker, Acting Genealogical and Local History Specialist of the National Archives and Records Service:

> "As an addenda to their reply I think it is important to note that additional records relating to the claimants and their claims appearing in Senate and House lists of private claims are frequently among the records of other Federal Executive agencies that are in the National Archives. An illustration of this would be pension claims approved after 1815, pension claims approved or disapproved after 1832, land claims (private) after 1804, approved bounty-land claims after 1812, approved and disapproved bounty-land claims after 1832, and various miscellaneous claims for pay, service, supplies, equipment, etc. Such records likely to contain additional data would generally be found among the records of the Veterans Administration, the Bureau of Land Management, and the Treasury Department."

Genealogical Publishing Company

Baltimore, Maryland
September, 1970

IN THE HOUSE OF REPRESENTATIVES U. S.,
January 27, 1848.

Resolved, That the Clerk of the House be directed to cause to be prepared an Alphabetical List of Private Claims which have been before the House of Representatives from the commencement of the First Congress to the close of the Twenty-ninth Congress, with the proceedings of the House of Representatives and Senate thereon: showing the names of the claimants; the nature or object of each claim; at what session, and in what manner, it was brought before the House; to what committee it was referred; the nature of the report, and the number of the report if printed, and, if not, the date of the report; the number of the bills, distinguishing between the Senate and House bills; the manner in which the claim was disposed of in the House, and, in cases where it passed both Houses, the date of the act of Congress:—the whole to be compiled from the Journals of the House of Representatives, and by reference, when necessary, to the Journals of the Senate, the reports of committees, the bills of the two Houses, and the laws of the United States. And that the Clerk be authorized to employ James Young, of the city of Washington, with a compensation not exceeding the sum now paid the engrossing clerks of this House, to be paid out of the contingent fund of the House; and that the Clerk of the House furnish such aid, by the clerks in his office, as may not be inconsistent with the discharge of their ordinary duties.

IN THE HOUSE OF REPRESENTATIVES U. S.,
September 2, 1850.

Resolved, That the more effectually to carry out the intention of the House, as expressed in a resolution passed on the 27th day of January, 1848, the Clerk of this House be, and he is hereby, directed to employ such number of experienced clerks (in addition to his own clerks, whose duty it shall be to assist thereat, without additional compensation, when not otherwise officially employed) as will insure the completion, within twelve months, of an alphabetical list of all claims submitted to this House from the day of its organization to the end of the present Congress, according to the plan indicated in the above resolution. Their compensation shall be the same as that allowed the engrossing clerks of the House. The Clerk shall cause the work to be printed as a public document, and, to insure *accuracy*, shall take care to have the clerks carefully compare the proofsheets with their manuscript copy.

IN THE HOUSE OF REPRESENTATIVES U. S.,
December 22, 1851.

Resolved, That the Clerk of this House be, and he is hereby, directed to have completed, in the shortest possible time consistent with accuracy, the digest of claims authorized by the resolutions of the House of the 27th of January, 1848, and the 2d of September, 1850, in the manner and at the rate of compensation therein authorized to the extra clerks employed upon the same; and that he pay the compensation due for services already performed on the work, which has been withheld in consequence of the restriction as to time in the resolution of 1850.

Resolved, further, That the Clerk be, and he is hereby, required to withhold the work from the press until the whole of it shall have been completed and subjected to a re-examination with the journals, reports, laws, &c.; and to have reprinted so much of that now printed as shall, by the discovery of errors in it, connected with that now incomplete or otherwise, be deemed necessary; and that the work, when ready for the press, be printed by the printer now engaged upon it.

An Alphabetical list of Private Claims presented to the House of Representatives of the United States from the commencement of the 1st to the close of the 31st Congress.

Names of claimants.	Nature or object of the claim.	Congress.	Session.	How brought before the House of Reps.	Page of journal.	To what committee of the House referred.	No. or date of the report.	Nature of the report.	No. of the bill.	How disposed of by the House of Reps.	How disposed of by the Senate.	Date of the act of Congress, and remarks.
Aarons, Wm. James	Correction of a land entry	24	2	Petition	47	Public Lands	16	Favorable	773	Referred to Committee Whole House.		
Aarons, Wm. James	Correction of a land entry	25	2	Petition	87	Public Lands	94	Favorable	111	Passed	Passed	App'd June 28, 1838
Abadie, Eugene H.	Compensation for medical services in Florida.	28	2	Petition	485	Claims.						
Abadie, Eugene H.	Compensation for medical services in Florida.	30	2	Petition	120	Claims.						
Abbey, Hezekiah	Pension for revolutionary services.	16	2	Petition	188	Rev. Pensions	Feb. 15, 1821	Adverse		Laid on the table.		
Abbey, Hezekiah	Pension for revolutionary services.	21	1	Petition	46	Military Pensions	Mar. 4, 1830	Adverse		Laid on the table.		
Abbey, Horace B.	Arrears of pension	25	2	Petition	587	Invalid Pensions				Discharged.		
Abbey, Horace B.	Arrears of pension	26	1	Petition	160	Invalid Pensions	350	Favorable	329	Referred to Committee Whole House.		
Abbey, Horace B.	Arrears of pension	27	2	Petition	377	Invalid Pensions	626	Adverse		Laid on the table.		
Abbey, Horace B.	Arrears of pension	27	3	Petition	205	Invalid Pensions	195	Adverse		Laid on the table.		
Abbott, Edward	Compensation for revolutionary services.	14	2	Resolution	67	Pens. & Rev. Cl'ms.						
Abbott, Elias	Pension	21	2	Petition	188	Military Pensions.						
Abbott, Elisha	Pension	28	2	Petition	135	Invalid Pensions				Discharged; leave to withdraw.		
Abbott, Isaac	Pension	10	2	Pension bill	499	Whole House	Feb. 20, 1809	With amend.	158	Passed	Passed	Statutes at Large, vol. 6, p. 81.
Abbott, Isaac	Increase of pension	30	1	Petition	635	Rev. Claims				Discharged; laid on the table.		
Abbott, James	(See Reuben Attwater and others.)	10	2		367							
Abbott, James	Indemnity for property taken for public use.	17	1	Petition	61	Claims	Jan. 28, 1822	Adverse		Laid on the table.		
Abbott, James	Indemnity for property taken for public use.	20	2	Petition	143	Claims.						
Abbott, James	Indemnity for property taken for public use.	21	1	Petition	93	Claims	55	Favorable		Passed	Passed	App'd May 10, 1830
Abbott, James	Pension	28	2	Petition	485	Invalid Pensions.						
Abbott, James, heirs of	Indemnity for his land sold by the United States.	18	2	Petition	42	Public Lands.						
Abbott, James, heirs of	Indemnity for his land sold by the United States.	23	1	Petition	249	Priv. Land Claims.	236	Favorable	262	Referred to Committee Whole House.		
Abbott, James, heirs of	Indemnity for his land sold by the United States.	23	2	Report of Committee Whole.	300			With't amend.	262	Passed	Passed.	
Abbott, James, heirs of	Indemnity for his land sold by the United States.	24	1	Senate bill	639	Public Lands	April 29, 1836	With't amend.	S. 57	Passed	Passed	App'd July 2, 1836
Abbott, Joel, jr.	Compensation for horse lost in public services.	18	2	Resolution	99	Claims	25	Favorable	271	Passed	Passed	App'd March 3, 1825
Abbott, John	Compensation for revolutionary services.	14	2	Resolution	67	Pens. & Rev. Cl'ms.						

List of private claims presented to the House of Representatives of the United States from the 1st to the 31st Congress, inclusive—**Continued.**

Names of claimants.	Nature or object of the claim.	Congress.	Session.	How brought before the House of Reps.	Page of journal.	To what committee of the House referred.	No. or date of the report.	Nature of the report.	No. of the bill.	How disposed of by the House of Reps.	How disposed of by the Senate.	Date of the act of Congress, and remarks.
Abbott, Josiah	(See heirs of E. Peterson)	19	1		57							
Abbott, J. C.	Indemnity for French spoliation prior to 1800.	31	1	Petition	225	Foreign Affairs	355	General bill	318	Referred to Committee Whole House.		
Abbott, Mary	(See heir of Nathaniel Fox)	23	1		41							
Abbott, Matthew	Revolutionary pension	27	2	Petition	524	Rev. Pensions	784	Adverse		Laid on the table.		
Abbott, Nancy	Continuation of pension	28	1	Petition	950	Whole House.						
Abbott, Robert	(See Capt. B. Johnson, U. S. N.)	17	2		278							
Abbott, Robert	(See heirs of James Abbott)	18	2		42							
Abbott, Robert	Compensation for forage and provisions.	21	1	Petition	235	Claims	April 9, 1830	Adverse		Laid on the table.		
Abbott, Robert	Indemnity for depredations by Indians.	29	2	Memorial	149	Indian Affairs.						
Abbott, Samuel	(See heirs of George Makepeace)	23	2		307							
Abbott, Samuel, and others	Compensation for revolutionary services.	4	2	Petition	703	Claims	Feb. 21, 1797	Favorable		Referred to Committee Whole House.		
Abbott, Samuel, and others.	Compensation for revolutionary services.	5	2	Petition	89	Claims.						
Abbott, Samuel P., administrator of.	Remission of penalty for violating non-importation act.	13	2	Petition	389	Ways and Means	April 18, 1814	Adverse		Leave to withdraw.		
Abbott, Samuel P., administrator of.	Remission of penalty for violating non-importation act.	13	3	Petition	707	Ways and Means				Leave to withdraw.		
Abbott, Samuel P., administrator of.	Remission of penalty for violating non importation act.	15	1	Petition	140	Claims				Discharged		Leave to withdraw 2d session.
Abbott, Seth	Compensation for supplies furnished revolutionary army.	14	1	Petition	59	Pens. & Rev. Cl'ms.				Discharged; laid on the table.		
Abbott, Seth	Compensation for supplies furnished revolutionary army.	14	2	Petition	336	Pens. & Rev. Cl'ms.				Discharged; laid on the table.		
Abbott, Thomas	Compensation for military services in 1794.	29	1	Petition	103	Militia.						
Abbott, William T., and others.	Indemnity for a house destroyed by the enemy.	15	2	Petition	172	Claims.						
Abbott, William T., and others.	Indemnity for a house destroyed by the enemy.	18	2	Petition	186	Claims.						
Abbott, William T., and others.	Indemnity for a house destroyed by the enemy.	20	2	Petition	205	Claims				Discharged; laid on the table.		
Abbott, William T., and others.	Indemnity for a house destroyed by the enemy.	21	1	Petition	201	Claims	Feb. 1, 1830	Adverse		Laid on the table.		
Abbott, William T., and others.	Indemnity for a house destroyed by the enemy.	24	1	Petition	405	Claims	538	Adverse		Laid on the table.		
Abeel, Garrett, and others.	Compensation for services as assessors.	7	2	Petition	291	Claims	Jan. 26, 1803	Adverse		Referred to Committee Whole House.		
Abeel, Garrett	Compensation for forage furnished revolutionary army.	19	1	Petition	408	Rev. Claims.						
Abeel, Garrett	Compensation for forage furnished revolutionary army.	19	2	Petition	82	Rev. Claims	Jan. 20, 1827	Adverse		Laid on the table.		
Abeel, G. B.	(See J. Lenox and others)	18	1		193							
Abeel, G. B., & Co.	Payment due from Ottawa Indians.	29	1	Memorial	160	Indian Affairs	287	Adverse.				
Abeel, James S.	Increase of compensation as military storekeeper.	31	2	Petition	158	Military Affairs				Discharged; laid on the table.		
Abell, Jesse	Release as surety for tax collector.	12	1	Petition	108	Select.						
Abell, John, widow of	Revolutionary pension	27	2	Petition	524	Rev. Pensions	784	Adverse		Laid on the table.		
Abell, John, widow of	Revolutionary pension	30	1	Petition	117	Rev. Pensions	27	Adverse		Laid on the table.		

List of private claims presented to the House of Representatives of the United States from the 1st to the 31st Congress, inclusive—Continued.

Names of claimants.	Nature or object of the claim.	Congress.	Session.	How brought before the House of Reps.	Page of journal.	To what committee of the House referred.	No. or date of the report.	Nature of the report.	No. of the bill.	How disposed of by the House of Reps.	How disposed of by the Senate.	Date of the act of Congress, and remarks.
Abell, John, widow of	Revolutionary pension	30	2	Petition	445	Rev. Pensions				Leave to withdraw.		
Abel, Joseph	Compensation for a boat taken for public use.	21	1	Petition	83	Claims	Dec. 30, 1829	Adverse		Laid on the table.		
Abel, Joseph	Compensation for a boat taken for public use.	23	1	Petition	208	Claims.						
Abell, Mosely W	Indemnity for property destroyed by the enemy.	22	1	Petition	188	Claims	Feb. 6, 1832	Adverse		Laid on the table.		
Abel, Peggy	(See heirs of Elijah Green)	24	1		433				645			
Abel, Phebe	(See widow of Alexander Torrence.)	28	1		72							
Abell, Thomas, widow of	Pension for revolutionary services	25	3	Petition	447	Rev. Pensions				Discharged.		
Abell, Thomas, widow of	Pension for revolutionary services	26	1	Petition	170	Rev. Pensions				Discharged.		
Abell, Zebediah	Pension	22	1	Petition	671	Invalid Pensions.						
Abell, ——	(See Swain, Abell, and Simmons.)	28	1		317							
Abelino, schooner	(See Joshua Atwood, jr)	25	2		349							
Abernithie, James M	Confirmation of title to lands in Missouri.	15	1	Petition	157	Priv. Land Claims.						
Abernithie, John T	Confirmation of title to lands in Missouri.	15	1	Petition	157	Priv. Land Claims.						
Abernithie, Washington	Confirmation of title to lands in Missouri.	15	1	Petition	157	Priv. Land Claims.						
Aborn, Joseph	Increase of compensation as a revenue officer.	11	3	Petition	515	Com. and Manufac.						
Aborn, Joseph	Increase of compensation as a revenue officer.	18	1	Petition	38	Ways and Means.						
Aborn, Samuel	Compensation for revolutionary services, &c.	3	1	Petition	52					Referred to Secretary Treasury.		
Aborn, Samuel	Compensation for revolutionary services, &c.	3	2	Rep. of Secretary of Treasury.	284	Claims	March 2, 1795	Adverse		Laid on the able		Leave to withdraw, 4, 1, p. 600.
Aborn, Samuel, executor of.	Compensation for supplies furnished revolutionary army.	25	2	Petition	391	Rev. Claims	1033	Adverse		Laid on the table.		
Abraham, A. H., and others.	Remission of certain duties	27	2	Petition	526	Commerce	892	Adverse		Laid on the table.		
Abraham, Joseph	Balance due for mail service	6	1	Petition	624					Referred to Postmaster General.		
Abro, Benijah	Pension	15	2	Pension bill	231	Whole House	March 3, 1819	With amend.	308	Passed	Postponed.	
Acken, Julia	(See heirs of William Yool)	28	1		434							
Acken, William D	For certain credits in settling his accounts.	21	1	Petition	200	Naval Affairs.						
Acken, William D	For certain credits in settling his accounts.	21	2	Senate bill	384	Naval Affairs	March 2, 1831	Adverse	S. 118	Laid on the table.		
Acken, William D	For certain credits in settling his accounts.	22	1	Petition	26	Claims	443	Favorable	546	Referred to Committee Whole House.		
Acken, William D	For certain credits in settling his accounts.	23	1	Senate bill	844	Claims	June 27, 1834	With amend.	S. 113	Passed	Passed with amendment.	App'd June 30, 1834
Acken, William D	(See heirs of William Yool)	28	1		434							
Acker, Henry	Increase of compensation as land officer.	31	1	Memorial	724	Public Lands.						
Acker, Jacob	Indemnity for losses and injuries in revolutionary war.	1	2	Petition and rep. Sec. of War.	179, 221					Laid on the table.		
Acker, Joel M	Reimbursement of advances on public account	31	1	Petition		Military Affairs	436	Adverse		Referred to Committee Whole House.		

List of private claims presented to the House of Representatives of the United States from the 1st *to the* 31st *Congress, inclusive*—Continued.

Names of claimants.	Nature or object of the claim.	Congress.	Session.	How brought before the House of Reps.	Page of journal.	To what committee of the House referred.	No. or date of the report	Nature of the report.	No. of the bill.	How disposed of by the House of Reps.	How disposed of by the Senate.	Date of the act of Congress, and remarks.
Ackerly, Daniel	(See Daniel Sickles,) alias	27	2		426							
Ackerman, David	Compensation for wood furnished on public account.	4	1	Rep. of Secretary Treasury.	388	Claims	74	Adverse		Laid on the table.		
Ackerman, Isaac	Increase of pension	15	1	Petition	199	Pens. & Rev. Clm's.				Discharged.		
Ackerman, Isaac	Increase of pension	19	2	Petition	307	Military Pensions.						
Ackerman, Isaac	Increase of pension	31	1	Petition	323	Invalid Pensions.						
Ackerman, John	Pension	21	1	Petition	568	Military Pensions.						
Ackerman, John	Pension	21	2	Resolution	157	Military Pensions.						
				Petition	230	Military Pensions.						
Ackerman, John Davis	Confirmation of title to land in Illinois.	28	1	Petition	369	Priv. Land Claims.						
Ackerman, John Davis	Confirmation of title to land in Illinois.	28	2	Petition	216	Priv. Land Claims.	Feb. 25, 1845	Adverse		Laid on the table.		
Ackley, Ely and others	Indemnity for Indian depredations.	25	2	Petition	87	Claims	351	Adverse		Laid on the table.		
Ackley, Ely and others	Indemnity for Indian depredations.	30	1	Petition	77	Claims	52	Adverse		Laid on the table.		
Ackley, John	(See Canadian Refugees.)											
Ackley, Morgan	(See Wm. Baker, assignee, &c.)	22	1		288							
Acklin, J. A. S	Compensation for professional services.	29	1	Appropriat'n bill.								Statutes at Large, vol. 9, p. 34.
Ackling, Francis	Liquidation and settlement of claim against United States.	1	3	Petition and rep. Sec. of War.	330							
					393					Laid on the table.		
Acosta, Roque	Confimation of title to land at Terre aux Bœuffs.	22	1	House bill	107	Whole House	Mar. 23, 1832	With't amend.	125	Passed	Passed	App'd June 25, 1832.
Acre, George	Compensation for military property lost in public service.	23	1	Petition	305	Claims	298	Adverse		Laid on the table.		
Acre, Samuel	Confimation of title to land in Mobile.	15	1	Petition	302	Priv. Land Claims.						
"Active," Revenue Cutter.	(See Henry Cahoone, and others.)	14	2		223							
Acuna, Joseph, agent of	Indemnity for a seizure of a vessel and cargo.	13	2	Petition	177	Ways and Means.	59	Adverse.				
Adair, Abner J	(See administrator of Wyatt Adkins.)	25	3		562							
Adair, Catharine	(See John Adair, widow of.)	31	1		519		254					
Adair, Elisha	Pension for revolutionary services.	28	1	Petition	357	Rev. Pensions.						
Adair, G. W	Compensation for property taken for public use, &c.	22	1	Resolution	943	Indian Affairs.						
Adair, G. W	Compensation for property taken for public use, &c.	22	2	Resolution	79	Indian Affairs.						
Adair, John, widow of	Arreas for revolutionary pension	29	1	Petition	198	Rev. Pensions	526	Adverse		Laid on the table.		
Adair, John, widow of	Arreas for revolutionary pension	29	2	Petition	133	Rev. Pensions				Discharged; laid on the table.		
Adair, John, widow of	Arreas for revolutionary pension	31	1	Petition	519	Rev. Pensions	254	Adverse		Laid on the table.		
Adair, Joseph, executors of.	Redemption of Continental money or equivalent in land.	23	1	Petition	221	Rev. Claims.						
Adair, Joseph, executors of.	Indemnity for loss on Continental money.	25	1	Petition	49					Laid on the table		
Adair, Joseph, executors of.	Indemnity for loss on Continental money.	25	2	Petition	81	Rev. Claims	914	Adverse		Laid on the table.		
Adair, Joseph, executors of.	Indemnity for loss on Continental money.	28	1	Petition	357	Rev. Pensions.						
Adair, Robert	Compensation for improvements on land erreneously entered.	25	2	Petition	868	Priv. Land Claims.	861	Adverse		Laid on the table.		
Adam, Mary	(See John Dunlap, heirs of.)	30	1		118							

List of private claims presented to the House of Representatives of the United States from the 1st to the 31st Congress, inclusive—Continued.

Names of claimants.	Nature or object of the claim.	Congress.	Session.	How brought before the House of Reps.	Page of journal.	To what committee of the House referred.	No. or date of the report.	Nature of the report.	No. of the bill.	How disposed of by the House of Reps.	How disposed of by the Senate.	Date of the act of Congress, and remarks.
Adams, Aaron	Arrears of pension	26	1	Petition	326	Invalid Pensions	665	Adverse	......	Laid on the table.		
Adams, Aaron	Arrears of pension	27	2	Petition and docs.	182	Rev. Pensions.						
Adams, Aaron	Arrears of pension	27	3	Petition and docs.	73	Claims	110	Adverse	......	Laid on the table.		
Adams, Aaron	Compensation for horse lost in public service	27	2	Memorial	1023	Claims.						
Adams, Abraham	Correction of error in entry of lands.	22	2	Petition	114	Public Lands	Jan. 7, 1833	Favorable	661	Passed	Passed	App'd Feb. 19, 1833
Adams, Benjamin, widow of.	Pension—husband died in public service.	16	1	Petition	27	Naval Affairs.						
Adams, Benjamin, & Co.	Reimbursement of excessive duties.	23	2	Petition	182	Commerce.						
Adams, Benjamin, & Co.	Reimbursement of excessive duties.	24	1	Petition	382	Ways and Means	392	Favorable	399	Referred to Committee Whole House.		
Adams, Benjamin, & Co.	Reimbursement of excessive duties.	25	2	Petition	42	Ways and Means	....	....	......	Discharged; laid on the table.		
Adams, Benjamin, & Co.	Reimbursement of excessive duties.	26	1	Petition	178	Ways and Means	6	Favorable	23	Referred to Committee Whole House.		
Adams, Benjamin, & Co.	Reimbursement of excessive duties	26	2	Report of Committee Whole.	165	....	....	With't amend.	23			
Adams, Benjamin, & Co.	Reimbursement of excessive duties.	27	2	Memorial	321	Ways and Means.						
Adams, Benjamin, & Co.	Reimbursement of excessive duties.	28	1	Senate bill	1010	Commerce	June 14, 1844	With't amend.	S. 107	Referred to Committee Whole House.		
Adams, Benjamin, & Co.	Reimbursement of excessive duties.	29	1	Senate bill	972	Ways and Means	Aug. 1, 1846	With amend.	S. 30	Referred to Committee Whole House.		
Adams, Benjamin, & Co.	Reimbursement of excessive duties.	30	1	Senate bill	957	Ways and Means	July 12, 1848	With't amend.	S. 142	Passed	Passed	App'd Aug. 14, 1848
Adams, Catharine	(See Francis Zock, heirs of.)	29	1	....	178	....	336					
Adams, Charles, widow of.	Arrears of pay due deceased for military services.	18	1	Petition	129	Military Affairs	....	....	......	Discharged; leave to withdraw.		
Adams, Charles, widow of.	Arrears of pay due deceased for military services.	18	2	Petition	81	Claims	Jan. 21, 1825	Favorable	289	Passed	Passed	App'd Mar. 3, 1825
Adams, Christopher	(See John Thompson, and others.)	19	1	....	413							
Adams, David	Pension	20	1	Petition	310	Military Pensions	....	....	......	Discharged; laid on the table.		
Adams, David	Pension	20	2	Petition	175	Military Pensions.						
Adams, David	Pension	21	1	Petition	260	Military Pensions.						
Adams, Elizabeth	(See A Poor, and others.)	20	2	....	280							
Adams, Elizabeth M.	(See Wm. H. Adams, widow of.)	29	1	....	474	....	705	....	480			
Adams & Folwell	Relief: they having purchased a land warrant fraudently obtained from government.	31	1	Petition	640	Public Lands.						
Adams & Folwell	Relief: they having purchased a land warrant fraudently obtained from government.	31	2	Petition	132	Priv. Land Claims.						
Adams, Francis	Reimbursement of the amount of a certain judgment.	8	2	Memorial	49	Claims.						
Adams, Francis	Reimbursement of the amount of a certain judgment.	9	1	Memorial	209	Claims	Jan. 7, 1806	Adverse.				
Adams, Francis, surety of	Release from liability	20	2	Memorial	26	Judiciary	....	....	......	Discharged; referred to Fifth Auditor.		
Adams, Francis, surety of.	Release from liability	21	1	Petition	39	Judiciary.						
Adams, Francis, surety of.	Release from liability	21	2	Petition	46	Judiciary.						
Adams, Francis, surety of.	Release from liability	22	1	Senate bill	119	Judiciary	Jan. 6, 1832	With't amend.	S. 17	Passed	Passed	App'd July 13, 1832
Adams, Francis	Pension for revolutionary services.	19	1	Resolution	55	Military Pensions	164	Adverse	......	Laid on the table.		
Adams, Francis	Pension for revolutionary services.	22	1	Petition	56	Rev. Pensions.						

List of private claims presented to the House of Representatives of the United States from the 1st to the 31st Congress, inclusive—Continued.

Names of claimants.	Nature or object of the claim.	Congress.	Session.	How brought before the House of Reps.	Page of journal.	To what committee of the House referred.	No. or date of the report.	Nature of the report.	No. of the bill.	How disposed of by the House of Reps.	How disposed of by the Senate.	Date of the act of Congress, and remarks.
Adams, Francis	Permission to enter and locate certain land.	23	2	Petition	277	Public Lands.						
Adams, Francis	Permission to enter and locate certain land.	25	2	Petition	418	Priv. Land Claims.				Discharged.		
Adams, Francis	Permission to enter and locate certain land.	26	1	Petition	340	Claims.						
Adams, Francis	Permission to enter and locate certain land.	27	2	Petition	749	Public Lands				Discharged.		
Adams, Francis	Permission to enter and locate certain land.	28	1	Petition	361	Public Lands.						
Adams, George, widow of.	Payment of moneys due deceased.	29	1	Petition	316	Judiciary.						
Adams, George, and others.	Reimbursement of costs in defending certain suits.	26	1	Petition	712	Ways and Means.						
Adams, George, and others.	Reimbursement of costs in defending certain suits.	27	2	Petition	95	Ways and Means	329	Adverse		Laid on the table.		
Adams, George	Invalid pension	9	2	Petition	589	Claims.						
Adams, George	Invalid pension	12	1	Pension bill	361	Whole House	June 15, 1812	With amend.	138	Passed	Passed	App'd July 5, 1812
Adams, George	(See Dr. William Adams, administrator of.)	24	2		91							
Adams, George P.	Compensation for horse lost in public service.	25	2	Documents.	273	Claims	546	Adverse		Laid on the table.		
Adams, Henry, widow of.	Pension for revolutionary services.	25	3	Petition	216	Rev. Pensions.						
Adams, Henry, widow of.	Pension for revolutionary services.	26	1	Petition	173	Rev. Pensions.						
Adams, Henry, widow of.	Pension for revolutionary services.	27	2	Petition	97	Rev. Pensions	119	Favorable	165	Passed	Passed	App'd July 27, 1842
Adams, J. S	(See H. Silliman)	12	1		98							
Adams, Jacob	Pensions for revolutionary services.	25	3	Resolution	158	Rev. Pensions	Feb. 25, 1839	Favorable	1170	Referred to Committee Whole House.		
Adams, Jacob	Pensions for revolutionary services.	26	1	Petition	170	Rev. Pensions	139	Favorable	149	Passed	Indef. postp'd.	
Adams, Jacob, (Md.)	Indemnity for French spoliations prior to 1800.	26	1	Memorial	182	Foreign Affairs	343	Favorable	319	Referred to Committee Whole House.		
Adams, James	Compensation for revolutionary services and injuries.	1	3	Petition	396					Referred to Secretary War.		
Adams, James	Indemnity for damages in a certain prosecution.	15	1	Petition	433	Claims.						
Adams, James	Compensation for boats taken for public use.	23	2	Petition	165	Public Lands.						
Adams, James	Compensation for boats taken for public use.	24	1	Memorial	50	Claims	418	Adverse		Laid on the table.		
Adams, Jane	Payment of a lost prize certificate.	4	2	Petition	629	Claims	Jan. 30, 1797	Adverse.				
Adams, Jeremiah	Pension for revolutionary services.	19	2	Petition	64	Military Pensions.						
Adams, Jeremiah	Pension for revolutionary services.	20	1	Resolution	583	Military Pensions.						
Adams, Jeremiah	Pension for revolutionary services.	20	2	Pension bill	55	Whole House	Jan. 15, 1829	With amend.	311	Passed.		
Adams, Jeremiah	Pension for revolutionary services.	21	1	Petition	47	Military Pensions				Discharged; laid on the table.		
Adams, Jeremiah	Pension for revolutionary services.	21	2	Petition	189	Military Pensions.						
Adams, Jeremiah	Pension for revolutionary services.	22	1	Petition	193	Invalid Pensions	391	Favorable	486	Referred to Committee Whole House.		
Adams, Jeremiah	Pension for revolutionary services.	24	2	Memorial	84	Rev. Pensions				Discharged; laid on the table.		
Adams, Jeremiah	Pension for revolutionary services.	26	1	Resolution	386	Rev. Pensions	664	Adverse		Laid on the table.		

List of private claims presented to the House of Representatives of the United States from the 1st to the 31st Congress, inclusive—Continued.

Names of claimants.	Nature or object of the claim.	Congress.	Session.	How brought before the House of Reps.	Page of journal.	To what committee of the House referred.	No. or date of the report.	Nature of the report.	No. of the bill.	How disposed of by the House of Reps.	How disposed of by the Senate.	Date of the act of Congress, and remarks.
Adams, John G., widow of.	Pension	22	1	Petition	261	Invalid Pensions.						
Adams, John G., widow of.	Pension	23	1	Petition	308	Military Affairs	328	Favorable	355	Referred to Committee Whole House.		
Adams, John, (Va.)	Compensation for horse lost in the public service.	10	1	Memorial	188	Claims.						
Adams, John, (Va.)	Compensation for horse lost in the public service.	10	2	Memorial	417	Claims.						
Adams, John, (Va.)	Compensation for horse lost in the public service.	11	2	Petition	268	Claims	Mar. 24, 1810	Adverse.				
Adams, John, (Ky.)	Compensation for horse lost in the public service.	18	2	Petition	70	Claims.						
Adams, John, (Ky.)	Compensation for horse lost in the public service.	19	1	Resolution	182	Claims	55	Favorable	75	Passed	Passed with amendment.	App'd May 20, 1826
Adams, John	Pension for revolutionary services.	20	1	Petition	337	Military Pensions	Mar. 18, 1828	Adverse.				
Adams, John	Pension for revolutionary services.	28	2	Petition	187	Rev. Pensions						
Adams, John	Pension for revolutionary services.	31	1	Petition	788	Rev. Pensions	374	Favorable	322	Referred to Committee Whole House.		
Adams, John	Pension for revolutionary services.	31	2	Petition	277					Leave to withdraw.		
Adams, John	Payment of award for extra work on Cumberland road.	14	2	Petition	117	Roads and Canals	Mar. 1, 1817	Adverse		Claim rejected.		
Adams, John	Payment of award for extra work on Cumberland road.	17	1	Petition	238	Roads and Canals	Mar. 5, 1822	Adverse.				
Adams, John	Payment of award for extra work on Cumberland road.	18	1	Petition	198	Roads and Canals.						
Adams, John & John, Jr.	Remission of fine for breach of revenue laws.	28	1	Petition	240	Claims	494	Favorable	377	Referred to Committee Whole House.		
Adams, John & John, Jr.	Remission of fine for breach of revenue laws.	28	2	Report of Committee Whole.	343			With't amend.	377	Passed	Passed	App'd Feb. 27, 1845
Adams, John J.	Extension of a patent	30	1	Petition	807	Patents.						
Adams, John J.	Extension of a patent	30	1	Petition	109	Patents	Jan. 4, 1848	Favorable	30	Laid on the Table.		
Adams, Jonas	Pension for revolutionary services.	3	2	Rep. of Secretary of War.	278	Claims	Feb. 28, 1795	Favorable, and bill ordered.	130	Passed	Postponed.	
Adams, Jonas	Pension for revolutionary services.	4	1	Rep. of Secretary of War.	447	Claims	Feb. 18, 1796	Pension bill	156	Passed	Passed	App'd April 20, 1796
Adams, Jonas	Increase of pension	11	2	Pension bill	283	Whole House	April 9, 1810	With amend.	107	Passed	Passed	App'd April 27, 1810
Adams, Joseph, widow of.	Payment for revolutionary services.	3	1	Petition	58					Referred to Secretary of War.		
Adams, Joseph	Pension for revolutionary services.	25	2	Petition	230	Rev. Pensions				Discharged; laid on the table.		
Adams, Joseph	See surety of James Nichols	15	1		394							
Adams, Moses	Arrears of pension	21	1	Resolution	246	Military Pensions	402	Adverse		Referred to Committee Whole House.		
Adams, Nathan	Reimbursement of money expended in Mexican war.	31	1	Senate bill	970	Claims	Sep. 2, 1850	With't amend.	S. 241	Passed	Passed	App'd Sept. 20, 1850
Adams, Nathan, heirs of.	Bounty land for revolutionary services.	24	1	Petition	204	Rev. Claims	808	Favorable	725	Referred to Committee Whole House.		
Adams, Nathan, heirs of.	Bounty land for revolutionary services.	25	2	Petition	39	Rev. Claims	104	Favorable	122	Referred to Committee Whole House.		
				Senate bill	508	Rev. Claims	Mar. 6, 1838	With't amend.	S. 35	Passed	Passed	App'd April 20, 1838
Adams, Nathaniel, (Mass.)	Pension	19	1	Petition	98	Military Pensions	164	Adverse		Laid on the table.		
Adams, Nathaniel, (Mass.)	Pension	21	2	Petition	110	Military Pensions.						
Adams, Nathaniel, heirs of.	Pension for revolutionary services.	24	1	Petition	404	Rev. Claims.						

List of private claims presented to the House of Representatives of the United States from the 1*st to the* 31*st Congress, inclusive*—Continued.

Names of claimants.	Nature or object of the claim.	Congress.	Session.	How brought before the House of Reps.	Page of journal.	To what committee of the House referred.	No. or date of the report.	Nature of the report.	No. of the bill.	How disposed of by the House of Reps.	How disposed of by the Senate.	Date of the act of Congress, and remarks.
Adams, Nathaniel, daughter of	Pension for revolutionary services.	25	3	Petition	562	Rev. Pensions.						
Adams, Peter, heirs of	(See heirs of Nathan Adams.)	24	1		204		80		725			
Adams, Rhoda	Continuation of pension	28	1	Petition	72	Rev. Pensions.						
Adams, Richard M.	Compensation for horse lost in Mexican War.	30	1	Petition	146	Claims	428	Adverse		Laid on the table.		
Adams, Samuel	Reimbursement of duties paid at Castine.	17	1	Petition	235	Whole House.						
Adams, Samuel	Reimbursement of duties paid at Castine.	18	1	Petition	27	Ways and Means	Jan. 15, 1824	General bill	60	Passed	Passed	App'd May 19, 1824
Adams, Samuel G., Capt.	Settlement of claim of company commanded by him in late war.	16	1	Petition	24	Claims	Dec. 15, 1819	Adverse		Laid on the table.		
Adams, Sarah	(See widow of Henry Adams)	26	1		173							
Adams, Sarah	(See widow of John Green)	26	1		282							
Adams, Seth and Joseph Loring, Jr.	Indemnity for French Spoliations prior 1800.	9	1	Petition	226	Com. and Manufac.						
Adams, Seth and Joseph Loring, Jr.	Indemnity for French Spoliations prior 1800.	26	1	Memorial	182	Foreign Affairs	343	Favorable	319	Referred to Committee Whole House.		
Adams, Shubael	Pension for disibilities in war of 1812.	31	2	Petition	155	Invalid Pensions.						
Adams, Susan	To be placed on the pension roll	25	2	Resolution	616	Rev. Pensions.						
Adams, Titus	Pension	22	1	Petition	35	Rev. Pensions	Dec. 19, 1831	Adverse.				
Adams, William	Compensation for services as surgeon in revolutionary war.	8	1	Petition	411	Claims	Nov. 2, 1803	Adverse		Referred to Committee Whole House.		
Adams, William, administrator of.	Commutation pay for revolutionary services.	24	2	Petition	91	Rev. Claims.						
Adams, William	(See sureties of Wm. B. Ferguson.)	25	2		921							
Adams, William	Pension for revolutionary services.	1	3	Petition	396					Referred to Secretary of War.		
Adams, William, heirs of.	(See heirs of Nathan Adams)	24	1		204		808		725			
Adams, William	Pension for wounds while on duty as artificer.	27	2	Petition	377	Invalid Pensions.						
Adams, William B	Indemnity for baggage adandoned on a march.	16	1	Petition	148	Claims	Jan. 22, 1820	Adverse		Laid on the table.		
Adams, William B	Arrears of pension	28	1	Petition	827	Invalid Pensions.						
Adams, William B	Arrears of pension	28	2	Petition	72	Invalid Pensions				Discharged; laid on the table.		
Adams, William H., widow of.	Pension for naval services.	29	1	Petition	474	Naval Affairs	705	Favorable	480	Referred to Committee Whole House.		
Adams, William H., widow of.	Pension for naval services.	29	2	House bill	212				480	Passed	Passed	App'd March 3, 1847
See "Addoms."												
Adamson, John	Increase of compensation as postmaster.	15	1	Petition	206	P. O. & P. Roads.						
Adamson, John	Extension of patent for a dry-dock.	21	2	Senate bill	387	Judiciary	Mar. 2, 1831	With't amend.	S. 128	Passed	Passed	App'd March 2, 1831
Addie, Robert	Correction of an erroneous entry of land.	25	2	Petition	721	Priv. Land Claims.						
Addison, Jacob	Increase of pension	28	2	Petition	64	Rev. Pensions				Leave to withdraw.		
Addison, John, Attorney of.	Compensation for revolutionary services and expenditures.	6	1	Petition	676	Claims	May 3, 1800	Adverse		Leave to withdraw.		
Addison, John	(See Samuel Smallwood.)	24	2		266							
Addison, John	(See representatives of Andrew Leitch.)	23	1		189							

List of private claims presented to the House of Representatives of the United States from the 1st to the 31st Congress, inclusive—Continued.

Names of claimants.	Nature or object of the claim.	Congress.	Session.	How brought before the House of Reps.	Page of journal.	To what committee of the House referred.	No. or date of the report.	Nature of the report.	No. of the bill.	How disposed of by the House of Reps.	How disposed of by the Senate.	Date of the act of Congress, and remarks.
Addison, Sarah	(See reps. of Andrew Leitch.)	23	1		189							
Addison, Dr. S. R.	Compensation for services as assistant surgeon in the navy.	31	1	Petition	1179	Naval Affairs.						
Addison, William or William H., widow of.	Pension for loss of husband in naval service.	24	1	Petition	945	Naval Affairs				Discharged; laid on the table.		
Addison, William or William H., widow of.	Pension for loss of husband in naval service.	25	2	Petition	987	Invalid Pensions.						
Addison, William or William H., widow of.	Pension for loss of husband in naval service.	25	3	Petition	89	Invalid Pensions	Jan. 22, 1839	Adverse		Laid on the table.		
Addoms, John	Indemnity for damages to farm by U. S. troops.	15	1	Petition	25	Claims				Discharged; laid on the table.		
Addoms, John	Indemnity for damages to farm by U. S. troops.	17	1	Petition	92	Claims				Discharged; laid on the table.		
Addoms, John, Executor of.	Indemnity for damages to farm by U. S. troops.	24	1	Petition	507	Claims	520	Favorable	515	Referred to Committee Whole House.		
Addoms, John, Executor of.	Indemnity for damages to farm by U. S. troops.	24	2	Documents	72	Claims.						
Addoms, John, Executor of.	Indemnity for damages to farm by U. S. troops.	25	2	Petition	36	Claims	24	Favorable	36	Passed	Indef. postp'd.	
Addoms, John, Executor of.	Indemnity for damages to farm by U. S. troops.	25	3	Petition	87	Claims	Jan. 9, 1839	Favorable	1009	Passed.		
Addoms, John, Executor of.	Indemnity for damages to farm by U. S. troops.	26	1	Petition	167	Claims	27	Favorable	46	Passed	Passed	App'd May 8, 1840
Addoms, John, widow of.	Balance of pension	26	1	Petition	936	Rev. Pensions	714	Adverse		Laid on the table.		
Addoms, John, widow of.	Balance of pension	26	2	Petition	78	Rev. Pensions	Feb. 12, 1841	Adverse		Laid on the table.		
Addoms, John, widow of.	Balance of pension	27	2	Petition	153	Rev. Pensions	784	Adverse		Laid on the table.		
Addoms, John T.	(See executor of John Addoms)	24	1		507							
Adger, James	(See administrat'r of Wm. Price, jr.)	22	1		484							
Adkins, Elizabeth	(See widow of James Adkins)	26	1		385							
Adkins, Isaac	Indemnity in land for injuries in public service.	28	1	Petition	265	Public lands				Discharged; laid on the table.		
Adkins, Isaiah	Balance of bounty due him as recruiting sergeant.	16	2	Petition	113	Claims.						
Adkins, James, widow of.	Revolutionary pension	26	1	Resolution	385	Rev. Pensions.						
Adkins, Wyatt, administrator of.	Indemnity for depredations by Osage Indians.	25	3	Petition	562	Indian Affairs.						
Adkins, Wyatt, administrator of.	Indemnity for depredations by Osage Indians.	26	1	Petition	180	Claims.						
Adle, John, representatives of.	Confirmation of title to a Spanish grant in Louisiana.	31	1	Petition	277	Priv. Land Claims.						
Adlington, John	Increase of Pension	25	2	Petition	587	Rev. Pensions				Discharged; laid on the table.		
Adlum, John	Increase of pay and pension as revolutionary corporal.	23	1	Petition	333	Rev. Pensions.						
Adolph, Peter R.	(See Canadian refugees.)											
Agace, Armand	To exchange location of his preemption right.	23	1	Petition	567	Public Lands.						
Agee, William R.	(See sureties of H. H. B. Hayes.)	26	1	Petition	306	Claims.						
Ager, Robert, heirs of.	Bounty land and pay for revolutionary services.	11	3	Petition	515	Claims.						
Ager, Robert, heirs of.	Bounty land and pay for revolutionary services of deceased.	15	1	Petition	178	Pens. & Rev. Cl'ms.	May 14, 1818	Adverse		Claim rejected.		
Agness, Jean Arnauld	Confirmation of title to land in Louisiana.	22	1	Petition	42	Priv. Land Claims.						

List of private claims presented to the House of Representatives of the United States from the 1st to the 31st Congress, inclusive—Continued.

Names of claimants.	Nature or object of the claim.	Congress.	Session.	How brought before the House of Reps.	Page of journal.	To what committee of the House referred.	No. or date of the report.	Nature of the report.	No. of the bill.	How disposed of by the House of Reps.	How disposed of by the Senate.	Date of the act of Congress, and remarks.
Agness, Jean Arnauld....	Confirmation of title to land in Louisiana.	23	1	Petition	81	Priv. Land Claims.	Feb. 11, 1834	Adverse	......	Leave to withdraw.		
Agnew, George, representatives of.	Indemnity for property destroyed by United States troops.	18	1	Resolution	139	Claims.						
Agnew, George, representatives of.	Indemnity for property destroyed by the enemy.	22	2	Petition	32	Claims..........	49	Adverse	......	Laid on the table.		
Agnew, George, representatives of.	Indemnity for property destroyed by the enemy.	24	2	Petition	172	Claims	Jan. 6, 1837	Adverse	......	Laid on the table.		
Agnew, Robert..........	Pension for revolutionary services.	22	1	Petition	671	Rev. Pensions.						
Aguirre & Galway.......	Release from liability on a bond..	31	1	Petition	1084	Commerce	Sept. 16, 1850	Favorable....	396	Passed............	Reported without amend.	
Ahl, John P., widow of...	Pension for revolutionary services.	20	1	Petition	228	Military Pensions..	Feb. 28, 1828	Adverse	......	Laid on the table.		
Ahl, John P., widow of..	Pension for revolutionary services.	23	1	Petition	137	Invalid Pensions.						
Ahrenfeldt, Charles, and Voght.	Reimbursement of excessive duties paid on prisms.	30	1	Petition	387	Claims	405	Favorable	355	Passed............	Reported without amend.	
Ahrenfeldt, Charles, and Voght.	Reimbursement of excessive duties paid on prisms.	31	1	Petition	213	Claims	3	Favorable	5	Passed.		
Aiken, Andrew	Pension for revolutionary services.	3	2	Rep. of Sec. War.	278	Claims	Feb. 28, 1795	Pension bill..	130	Passed............	Postponed.	
Aiken, Andrew	Pension for revolutionary services	4	1	Rep. of Sec. War.	445	Claims	Mar. 14, 1796	Pension bill ..	156	Passed............	Passed	App'd April 20, 1796
Aiken, David, heirs of....	Renewal of bounty land patent...	25	2	Petition	84	Priv. Land Claims.	....	....	......	Dis., and laid on table.		
Aiken, James...........	Renewal of lost land patent......	25	2	Petition	249	Priv. Land Claims.	350	Adverse	......	Laid on the table.		
Aikin, Martin S., and others	Rifles for military services of his company.	17	1	Resolution	359	Military Affairs....	Mar. 22, 1822	Favorable	R. —	Passed............	Indef. postp'd.	
Aikin, Martin S., and others	Rifles for military services of his company.	17	2	Resolution	32	Military Affairs ...	Dec. 21, 1822	Favorable	R. 3	Ref. to Com. Whole.		
Aikin, Martin S., and others	Rifles for military services of his company.	19	1	Resolution	49	Military Affairs ...	Mar. 7, 1826	Favorable	R. —	Passed............	Passed.......	App'd May 20, 1826
Aikin, Solomon	Pension for revolutionary services.	18	2	Resolution	245	Rev. Pensions	....	....	......	Leave to withdraw.		
Aikman, James and Sam'l	Relief from the effect of an erroneous survey.	15	1	Petition	28	Public Lands......	Dec. 17, 1817	Favorable	11	Passed............	Passed with amendment.	App'd Jan. 14, 1818
Ailes, Amos, and others ..	Confirmation of title to land north west of the Ohio.	4	2	Petition	627	Select............	Jan. 3, 1797	Adverse......	......	Report postponed.		
Ailshites, Henry.........	Compensation for revolutionary services.	24	2	Petition	....	Rev. Claims.						
Airs, George............	Pension for revolutionary services.	3	1	Rep. of Sec. War.	131	Select	May 26, 1791	Pension bill ..	62	Passed............	Passed	App'd June 7, 1794
Aisquith, W. E..........	(See Louis F. Beeler and others.)	30	1	....	115	....	482					
Aken, Captain...........	Reimbursement of advances on public account.	31	1	....	....	Military Affairs ...	436	Adverse......	......	Ordered to be printed.		
Akenford, Endymion R., widow of.	Pension	31	1	Petition	628	Invalid Pensions.						
Aker, George...........	Arrears of pension............	22	1	Petition	288	Invalid Pensions.						
Akerman, or Ackerman, John.	Pension	21	2	Resolution	157	Military Pensions.						
Akers, Larkin N........	Pension for disabilities received in war of 1812.	18	1	Resolution	272	Pens. & Rev. Cl'ms.	Mar. 8, 1824	Adverse				
Akins, Elizabeth	Pension	28	2	Resolution	132	Rev. Pensions.						
Akison, David..........	Pension	27	2	Memorial.......	443	Invalid Pensions...	801	Favorable.....	455	Ordered to a 3d reading.		
Akison, David..........	Pension	27	3	House bill......	88	....	....	....	455	Passed.		
Akison, David..........	Pension	28	1	Petition	514	Invalid Pensions...	297	Favorable.....	207	Passed.		
Alabama, Baldwin county.	See Mobile and Baldwin counties.	18	1	....	89							

List of private claims presented to the House of Representatives of the United States from the 1st to the 31st Congress, inclusive—Continued.

Names of claimants.	Nature or object of the claim.	Congress.	Session.	How brought before the House of Reps.	Page of journal.	To what committee of the House referred.	No. or date of the report.	Nature of the report.	No. of the bill.	How disposed of by the House of Reps.	How disposed of by the Senate.	Date of the act of Congress, and remarks.
Alabama, Mobile county	Compensation for supplies taken for public use.	15	2	Petition	24	Claims	Nov. 26, 1818	Adverse	......	Laid on the table.		
Alabama, Mobile and Baldwin counties.	Compensation for supplies taken for public use.	18	1	Petition	89	Claims.						
Alabama, Mobile	Reimbursement of expenditures during the Creek war.	24	2	Petition	160	Military Affairs						
				Senate bill	260	Claims	304	Bill	S. 15	Rejected.		
Alabama, inhabitants of Irwinton county.	Indemnity for Indian depredations.	25	2	Petition	770	Claims	June 12, 1838	Adverse	......	Laid on the table.		
Alabama, inhabitants of Irwinton county.	Indemnity for Indian depredations.	26	1	Petition	340	Claims.						
Alabama, State of	Indemnity for Indian depredations.	21	1	Petition	111	Indian Affairs.						
Alabama, State of	Indemnity for Indian depredations.	21	2	Petition	45	Claims	Dec. 21, 1830	Adverse	......	Laid on the table.		
Alabama, State of	Indemnity for Indian depredations.	22	2	Petition	75	Indian Affairs	127	Favorable	761	Ref. to Com. Whole.		
Alabama, State of	Indemnity for Indian depredations.	24	1	Petition	153	Indian Affairs.						
Alabama. State of	Indemnity for Indian depredations.	25	2	Memorial	255	Claims	932	Adverse	......	Laid on the table.		
				Pres. Message	323	Claims	1028	Favorable	865	Ref. to Com. Whole.		
Alabama, State of	Indemnity for Indian depredations.	26	1	Petition	388	Claims.						
Alabama, State of	Reimbursement of certain moneys paid for land.	22	1	Petition	34	Public Lands	Dec. 23, 1831	Adverse	......	Laid on the table.		
Alabama, State of	Indemnity for Indian depredations.	29	1	Petition	176	Indian Affairs.						
Alabama, State of	Indemnity for loss of land sold by United States.	19	2	Memorial of legislature.	287	Public Lands.						
Alabama, State of	Remission of duties on University library.	21	1	Resolution of legislature.	260	Ways and Means.						
Alabama, State of	Indemnity for depredations of Creek Indians.	21	1	Memorial of legislature.	262	Indian Affairs.						
Alabama, State of	Indemnity for depredations of Creek Indians.	24	2	Memorial of legislature.	208	Claims.						
Alabama, State of	Indemnity for depredations of Creek Indians.	25	2	Memorial of legislature.	397	Claims.						
Alabama, State of	Indemnity for depredations of Creek Indians.	26	1	Memorial of legislature.	340	Claims.						
				Resolution of legislature.	597	Claims.						
				Resolution of legislature.	613	Military Affairs.						
Alabama, State of	Reimbursement of advances on account of Creek war.	30	1	Memorial of legislature.	595	Claims.						
Alabama, State of	Interest on advances to suppress Indian hostilities.	30	1	Senate bill	794	Ways and Means	Jan. 19, 1848	With amend.	S. 33	Ref. to Com. Whole.		
Alabama, State of	Interest on advances to suppress Indian hostilities.	30	2	Senate bill	102	Claims	Jan. 3, 1849	With amend.	S. 351	Passed with amend'mt	Passed as am'd.	App'd Jan 30, 1849
Alabama, State of	Surrender of two per cent. of reserved fund.	25	2	Memorial of legislature.	93	Roads and Canals	....	....	......	Discharged.		
Alabama, State of	Surrender of two per cent. of reserved fund.	26	1	Memorial of legislature.	608	Public Lands.						
				Senate bill	581	Public Lands	April 4, 1840	With't amend.	S. 11	Ref. to Com. Whole.		
Alabama, State of	Surrender of two per cent. of reserved fund.	26	2	Senate bill	98	Public Lands	Jan. 7, 1841	With amend.	S. 11	Ref. to Com. Whole.		
Alabama, State of	Settlement of certain claims	26	2	Senate bill	213	Claims	....	....	S. 151			
Alabama, State of	Settlement of certain claims	27	2	Senate bill	680	Claims	July 21, 1842	With amend.	S. 53	Passed with amendm't	Passed as am'd	App'd Aug. 17, 1842
Alabama, State of	Settlement of certain claims	29	1	Rep. of Sec. War.	94	Claims	Jan. 20, 1846	Favorable	127	Passed	Passed	App'd Aug. 10, 1846

List of private claims presented to the House of Representatives of the United States from the 1st to the 31st Congress, inclusive—Continued.

Names of claimants.	Nature or object of the claim.	Congress.	Session.	How brought before the House of Reps.	Page of journal.	To what committee of the House referred.	No. or date of the report.	Nature of the report.	No. of the bill.	How disposed of by the House of Reps.	How disposed of by the Senate.	Date of the act of Congress, and remarks.
Alabama, State of	Reimbursement of advances to Mexican volunteers.	31	1	Memorial	909	Military Affairs.						
Alabama, registers and receivers at Huntsville.	Extra compensation for locating land warrants.	31	2	Petition	69	Public Lands.						
				Petition	122	Public Lands.						
Alabama, registers and receivers at Lebanon.	Extra compensation for locating land warrants.	31	2	Petition	77	Public Lands.						
Alabama, registers and receivers at Sparta.	Extra compensation for locating land warrants.											
Alabama volunteers	Compensation for horses lost in Indian wars.	26	1	Document	639	Military Affairs.						
Alabatcha, (an Indian)	(See W. W. Browning & others.)	28	1		75							
Alba, Peter	Confirmation of title to land in Florida.	20	2	Petition	145	Public Lands.						
Alba, Peter	Confirmation of title to land in Florida.	22	2	Petition	171	Public Lands.						
Alba, Peter	Confirmation of title to land in Florida.	23	1	Petition	291	Priv. Land Claims.	403	Favorable	421	Passed	Am'd and laid on the table.	
Alba, Peter	Confirmation of title to land in Florida.	23	2	Petition	146	Public Lands	65	Favorable	685	Ref. to Com. Whole.		
Alba, Peter	Confirmation of title to land in Florida.	24	1	Petition	58	Public Lands	136	Favorable	396	Ref. to Com. Whole.		
Alba, Peter, heirs of	Confirmation of title to land in Florida.	25	2	Petition	41	Public Lands	309	Favorable	346	Ref. to Com. Whole.		
Alba, Peter	Confirmation of title to land in Florida.	25	3	Report of Committee Whole.	377				346	Passed	Passed	App'd Mar. 3, 1839
Albain, Robert	(See Samuel Gilman)	27	2		244		361		295			
Albaugh, William	(See executors of Henry Crowell.)	2	1		464							
Albert, Christian, widow of	Pension	14	2	Petition	71	Claims				Ref. to Com. Whole.		
Albert, Christian, widow of	Pension	17	1	Petition	206	Claims.						
Alberson, John	Pension for revolutionary services.	3	1	Petition	22							
				Rep. of Sec. War	93	Select.						
Albert, James, representatives of.	Bounty land for services in late war.	18	1	Resolution	76	Priv. Land Claims.						
"Albion," schooner, owners of.	(See Joseph Bowden, jr.)	31	2		193							
Albrecht, Martin, widow of	Pension for revolutionary services.	29	1	Petition	189	Rev. Pensions.						
Albrecht, Martin, widow of	Pension for revolutionary services.	29	2	Petition	150	Rev. Pensions	13	Adverse		Laid on the table.		
Albright, Jacob W., widow of.	Settlement of accounts as paymaster United States army.	18	1	Petition	176	Claims	Feb. 13, 1824	Adverse		Leave to withdraw.		
Albright, Jacob W., widow of.	Settlement of accounts as paymaster United States army.	18	2	Petition	210	Claims.						
Albright, Jacob W., widow of.	Settlement of accounts as paymaster United States army.	19	1	Petition	45	Claims	Jan. 6, 1826	Adverse		Laid on the table.		
Albright, Jacob W., widow of.	Settlement of accounts as paymaster United States army.	22	1	Petition	63	Priv. Land Claims.	Dec. 23, 1831	Adverse		Laid on the table.		
Albro, Clark	Pension for revolutionary services	3	1	Rep. of Sec. War.	131	Select	May 26, 1794	Res. to refer to Sec. of War.	R. 12	Passed	Passed	App'd June 9, 1794
Albro, Clark	Pension for revolutionary services.	3	2	Rep. of Sec. War.	337	Claims	Feb. 28, 1795	Pension bill	130	Passed	Postponed.	
Albro, Clark	Pension for revolutionary services.	4	1	Res. and Doc.	445	Claims	Mar. 4, 1796	Pension bill	156	Passed	Passed	App'd April 20, 1796
Alburger, William, widow of.	Pension for loss of husband in public service.	30	2	Memorial	193	Naval Affairs.						

List of private claims presented to the House of Representatives of the United States from the 1st to the 31st Congress, inclusive—Continued.

Names of claimants.	Nature or object of the claim.	Congress.	Session.	How brought before the House of Reps.	Page of journal.	To what committee of the House referred.	No. or date of the report.	Nature of the report.	No. of the bill.	How disposed of by the House of Reps.	How disposed of by the Senate.	Date of the act of Congress, and remarks.
Alcock, Robert	Pension	20	2	Petition	262	Military Pensions.						
Alcock, Robert	Pension	21	1	Petition	231	Military Pensions	May 4, 1830	Adverse	.....	Laid on the table.		
Alcorn, James	Grant of land for naval services	22	2	Petition	219	Priv. Land Claims.						
Alcott, Samuel	Payment due from Ottowa Indians	29	1	Memorial	160	Indian Affairs	287	Adverse.				
Alden, George	To be restored to pension roll	17	1	Petition	256	Rev. Pensions.						
Alden, Horatio, and wife	(See Silas Deane)	23	2	....	196	....	270	....	818			
Alden, James	(See Exploring Expedition)	27	3	....	149							
Alden, John, and others	Remission of duty on salt	6	2	Petition	807							
Alden, John, and J. Paine	Bounty on fishing schr. Traveller	17	1	Petition	32	Commerce.						
Alden, John, and J. Paine	Bounty on fishiug schr. Traveller	17	2	Petition	118	Commerce.						
Alden, Judah	Renewal of lost land warrant	17	2	Petition	207	Priv. Land Claims.						
Alden, Judah	Renewal of lost land warrant	18	1	Petition	157	Priv. Land Claims.	72	Favorable	133	Passed	Laid on table.	
Alden, Judah	Bounty land for revolutionary services.	20	1	Resolution	176	Rev. Claims	106	Favorable	118	Passed	Laid on table.	
Alden, Judah	Bounty land for revolutionary services.	20	2	Resolution	243	Rev. Claims	Feb. 12, 1829	Favorable	435	Passed	Reported without amend't.	
Alden, Judah	Bounty land for revolutionary services.	21	1	Petition	68	Rev. Claims	90	Favorable	124	Passed	Passed	App'd May 28, 1830
Alden, Judah, executors of	Commutation pay for revolutionary services.	29	2	Petition	131	Rev. Claims.						
Alden, Roger	Compensation for services rendered Congress.	1	2	Petition	149	Select	Feb. 4, 1790	Favorable	.....	....	....	Statutes at Large, vol. 1, p. 105.
Alden, Roger	(See agent of Holland Land Company.)	7	2	....	260							
Alden & Williams	Compensation for bakery taken for public use.	31	1	Petition	433	Military Affairs	200	Favorable	207	Referred to Committee Whole House.		
Alden & Williams	Compensation for bakery taken for public use.	31	2	Rep. Committee Whole House.	181	....	....	....	207	Passed.		
Alder, Frederick	Pension	21	2	Res. Indiana legislature.	209	Military Pensions.						
Alders, Thomas	Compensation for horse lost in Seminole war.	23	1	Documents	154	Claims.						
Alders, Thomas	(See William H. Bedford, agent)	28	1	....	262							
Aldeseta, Juan	Confirmation of land title in Missouri, &c.	19	2	....	....	....	....	....	.....	....	....	(See H. bill No. 378.)
Aldred, Henry	Compensation for revolutionary services.	26	1	Petition	45	Military Pensions.						
Aldrich, Caleb	Pension for revolutionary services.	3	2	Rep. of Secretary of War.	350	Claims	Feb. 28, 1795	Pension bill	130	Passed	Postponed.	
Aldrich, Caleb	Pension for revolutionary services.	4	1	Rep. of Secretary of War.	445	Claims	March 4, 1796	Pension bill	156	Passed	Passed	App'd April 20, 1796
Aldrich, Clark, widow of	Pension for revolutionary services.	30	1	Petition	104	Rev. Pensions	519	Pension bill	447	Referred to Committee Whole House.		
Aldrich, Clark, widow of	Pension for revolutionary services.	30	2	Rep. Committee Whole House	318	....	....	....	447	Passed	Passed	App'd March 3, 1849
Aldrich, Gustavus	Increase of pension	4	1	Petition	396	Claims	Jan. 26, 1796	Adverse	.....	Leave to withdraw.		
Aldrich, Gustavus	Increase of pension	9	1	Petition	234	Claims	April 11, 1806	Statem't of facts	.....	Indef. postponed.		
Aldrich, Gustavus	Increase of pension	9	2	Pension bill	608	Whole House	Feb. 28, 1807	Favorable	216	Passed	Passed	App'd March 3, 1807
Aldrich, Gustavus	Increase of pension	12	1	Pension bill	361	Whole House	June 15, 1812	Favorable	138	Passed	Passed	App'd July 5, 1812
Aldrich, Gustavus	Pension	15	1	Petition	35	Pens. & Rev. Cl'ms.	....	....	.....	Discharged; leave to withdraw.		
Aldrich, Gustavus	Increase of pension	15	2	Petition	31	Pens. & Rev. Cl'ms.	Feb. 5, 1819	Pension bill	308	Postponed.		

List of private claims presented to the House of Representatives of the United States from the 1st to the 31st Congress, inclusive—Continued.

Names of claimants.	Nature or object of the claim.	Congress.	Session.	How brought before the House of Reps.	Page of journal.	To what committee of the House referred.	No. or date of the report.	Nature of the report.	No. of the bill.	How disposed of by the House of Reps.	How disposed of by the Senate.	Date of the act of Congress, and remarks.
Aldrich, Gustavus	Increase of pension	17	1	Petition	109	Pens. & Rev. Cl'ms.						
Aldrich, Gustavus, widow of.	Pension for revolutionary services.	25	2	Petition	47	Rev. Pensions.....	....	....	......	Discharged; laid on the table.		
Aldrich, Gustavus, widow of.	Pension for revolutionary services.	28	1	Petition	116	Rev. Pensions.....	....	....	......	Discharged; laid on the table.		
Aldrich, Gustavus, widow of.	Pension for revolutionary services.	28	2	Petition	68	Rev. Pensions.						
Aldrich, Gustavus, widow of.	Pension for revolutionary services.	29	1	Petition	118	Rev. Pensions.....	528	Adverse	......	Laid on the table.		
Aldrich, H. T..........	Bounty land for services.	31	1	Petition	537	Public Lands.						
Aldrich, Luke...........	Increase of pension	12	1	Pension bill	361	Whole House.....	June 15, 1812	With amend..	138	Passed............	Passed with amendment.	App'd July 5, 1812
Aldrich, Timothy........	Release from liabilities in a government suit.	17	2	Petition	224	Judiciary.						
Alexander, Carnes.......	Authority to enter a certain tract of land.	25	3	House bill......	277	Whole House.....	Jan. 25, 1839	....	328	Passed............	Passed.......	App'd March 3, 1839
"Alert," brig, owners of ..	Indemnity for French spoliations prior to 1800.	26	1	Memorial.......	182	Foreign Affairs....	343	Favorable.....	319	Referred to Committee Whole House.		
Alexander, Charles.......	Compensation for supplies furnished revolutionary army.	21	1	Petition	295	Rev. Claims.						
Alexander, Charles	Compensation for supplies furnished revolutionary army.	22	1	Documents	733	Rev. Claims.						
Alexander, Columbus, and Theodore Barnard.	Compensation for printing for Navy Department.	30	1	Senate bill	976	Claims	....	....	S. 173			
Alexander, Columbus, and Theodore Barnard.	Compensation for printing for Navy Department.	30	2	Report of Com..	82	Whole House.....	....	....	S. 173			
Alexander, David........	Indemnity for French spoliations prior to 1800.	26	1	Memorial	182	Foreign Affairs....	343	Favorable	319	Referred to Committee Whole House.		
Alexander, Edward B....	(See Charles Thomas and others).	28	1	....	196	....	....	....	......	....	....	Statutes at Large, vol. 5, p. 698.
Alexander, Esther.......	Continuation of pension.........	30	1	Petition	229	Rev. Pensions.....	Jan. 25, 1848	Adverse......	......	Laid on the table.		
Alexander, Francis	Confirmation of title to land in Mississippi Territory.	13	2	Petition	176	Public Lands	....	....	......	Discharged.		
Alexander, Gabriel, widow of.	Relief for loss of husband in public service.	20	2	Petition of inhabitants.	79	P. Of. & P. Roads.	....		......	Discharged; laid on the table.		
Alexander, George, and others.	Right of pre emption to a mill seat.	28	2	Petition........	461	Public Lands.						
Alexander, George, and others.	Right of pre emption to a mill seat.	29	1	Petition	395	Public Lands.						
Alexander, Dr. George....	Commutation pay for revolutionary services.	24	1	Petition	274	Rev. Claims......	March 3, 1836	Adverse......	......	Laid on the table.		
Alexander, Hugh, & others.	Release from liabilities on a judgment.	7	2	Petition	267	Ways and Means..	Jan. 13, 1803	Favorable	77	Passed.		
Alexander, James........	Compensation for revolutionary services.	1	3	Petition .... Rep. of Secretary of War.	342 385	....	....	....	......	Laid on the table.		
Alexander, James, widow of.	Pension for revolutionary services.	31	1	Petition	306	Rev. Pensions....	217	Adverse......	......	Laid on the table.....	....	Leave to withdraw 2d session.
Alexander, James, heirs of	Confirmation of title to land in Florida.	21	1	Petition........	202	Priv. Land Claims.						
Alexander, James........	Compensation for horses, &c., lost in Seminole War.	23	1	Documents.....	154	Claims.						

List of private claims presented to the House of Representatives of the United States from the 1st to the 31st Congress, inclusive—Continued.

Names of claimants.	Nature or object of the claim.	Congress.	Session.	How brought before the House of Reps.	Page of journal.	To what committee of the House referred.	No. or date of the report.	Nature of the report.	No. of the bill.	How disposed of by the House of Reps.	How disposed of by the Senate.	Date of the act of Congress, and remarks.
Alexander, James	Indemnity for Indian depredations	24	1	Petition	....	Indian Affairs	131	Favorable	141	Passed	Passed	App'd July 1, 1836
Alexander, James	Correction of an entry of land	25	2	Petition	283	Public Lands	585	Favorable	567	Referred to Committee Whole House.		
Alexander, James	Correction of an entry of land	25	3	Rep. Committee Whole House.	380			With't amend.	567	Passed	Adverse report.	
Alexander, James	Correction of an entry of land	26	1	Petition and docs.	177	Public Lands	76	Favorable	64	Passed	Passed	App'd May 2, 1840
Alexander, James	(See Wm. H. Bedford, agent, &c.)	28	1		262							
Alexander, Jane Deborah	Continuation of pension	28	1	Petition	849	Rev. Pensions.						
Alexander, John	(See James Washburn, and J. A.)	13	1		37							
Alexander, John	Pension	24	1	Resolution	276	Invalid Pensions	659	Adverse		Laid on table.		
Alexander, John, widow of	Arrears of pension	29	1	Petition	279	Invalid Pensions				Discharged; laid on table.		
Alexander, John E	Compensation for detecting counterfeiters.	25	2	Petition	200	Claims	Mar. 2, 1838	Favorable; (recommitt'd for amendm'nt.)	599			
				Amended bill	893	Whole House			599			
Alexander, John E	Compensation for detecting counterfeiters.	25	3	Rep. Committee Whole House.	380			With't amend.	599	Passed	Passed	App'd Mar. 2, 1839
Alexander, John E	Additional compensation for detecting counterfeiters.	26	1	Resolution	359	Claims	539	Favorable	439	Referred to Committee Whole House.		
Alexander, John E	Additional compensation for detecting counterfeiters.	27	2	Petition	94	Claims	48	Favorable	83	Passed	Passed	App'd July 27, 1842
Alexander, Lucy	(See heirs of Dr. Laurence Brook.)	24	1		61							
Alexander, Milton K	(See William H. Bedford.)	28	1		262							
Alexander Mira M	(See daughter of George Madison.)	25	3		618							
Alexander, Morgan, heirs of.	Commutation pay for revolutionary services.	23	2	Petition	106	Rev. Claims.						
Alexander, Morgan, heirs of.	Commutation pay for revolutionary services.	25	2	Petition	392	Rev. Claims	1008	Adverse		Laid on table.		
Alexander, Morgan, heirs of.	Commutation pay for revolutionary services.	25	3	Petition	221	Rev. Claims				Discharged.		
Alexander, Morgan, heirs of.	Commutation pay for revolutionary services.	27	2	Petition	154	Claims	365	Adverse		Laid on table.		
Alexander, Nathaniel	Compensation for revolutionary services and losses.	1	3	Petition	352							
				Rep. of Secretary War.	380					Laid on table.		
Alexander, Philip	To be restored to pension roll	17	1	Petition	98	Rev. Pension				Leave to withdraw.		
Alexander, Richard B	Compensation for a slave who died in public service.	25	2	Petition	120	Claims.						
Alexander, Richard B	Compensation for a slave who died in public service.	26	1	Resolution	167	Claims.						
Alexander, Robert	Compensatiom for labor at navy-yard.	9	2	Petition	485	Claims.						
Alexander, Robert	Increase of pension	21	1	Petition	377	Military Pensions.						
Alexander, Robert	Increase of pension	22	1	Petition	165	Rev. Pensions	212	Favorable	283	Passed	Passed with amendment.	App'd July 14, 1832
Alexander, Sarah	(See Wm. Alexander, Lord Stirling, heirs of.)	5	2		81							
Alexander, Thomas	Increase of pension	1	3	Petition	338					Referred to Secretary of War.		
Alexander, Thomas	Increase of pension	3	1	Rep. of Secretary War.	131	Select	May 26, 1794	Resolution to refer to Sec. War.	R. 12	Passed	Passed	App'd June 9, 1794

List of private claims presented to the House of Representatives of the United States from the 1st to the 31st Congress, inclusive—Continued.

Names of claimants.	Nature or object of the claim.	Congress.	Session.	How brought before the House of Reps.	Page of journal.	To what committee of the House referred.	No. or date of the report.	Nature of the report.	No. of the bill.	How disposed of by the House of Reps.	How disposed of by the Senate.	Date of the act of Congress, and remarks.
Alexander, Thomas	Increase of pension	3	2	Petition	311	Claims.						
				Rep. of Secretary War.	337	Claims	Feb. 28, 1795	Pension bill	130	Passed	Postponed.	
Alexander, Thomas	Increase of pension	4	1	Res. and docs.	445	Claims	Mar. 4, 1796	Pension bill	156	Passed	Passed	App'd April 20, 1796
Alexander, Thomas, & wife.	(See heirs of Mary Updegraff.)	27	3	....	394							
Alexander, William	Compensation for services as geographical surveyor.	4	2	Petition	627	Claims	Jan. 9, 1797	Favorable.	......	Referred to Committee Whole House.		
Alexander, William	Compensation for services as geographical surveyor.	5	2	Memorial	122	Whole House	Jan. 19, 1798	Favorable.	42	Passed	Passed	App'd Feb. 27, 1798
Alexander, William	Compensation for labor and materials on Cumberland road.	23	1	Res. and docs.	589	Claims	455	Adverse	......	Laid on table	....	(See Report No. 449)
Alexander, William	Compensation for revolutionary services and advances on public account.	21	1	Petition	70	Rev. Claims	Dec. 29, 1829	Adverse	......	Laid on table.		
Alexander, William	Indemnity for losses on Continental money.	25	2	Petition	916	Rev. Claims	....	....	......	Discharged; laid on table.		
Alexander, William, Lord Stirling, heirs of.	Bounty land for revolutionary services.	5	2	Petition	81	Claims	Jan. 2, 1798	Adverse	......	Referred to Committee Whole House.		
Alexander, William, Lord Stirling, &c.	Bounty land for revolutionary services.	22	1	Memorial	142	Rev. Claims.						
Alexander, William, Lord Stirling &c.	Bounty land for revolutionary services.	23	1	Memorial	306	Rev. Claims.						
Alexander, William, Lord Stirling, &c.	Compensation for revolutionary services.	23	1	Memorial	305	Rev. Claims.						
Alexander, William, Lord Stirling, &c.	Payment of a loan office certificate	23	1	Senate bill	754	Rev. Claims	June 21, 1834	With't amend.	107	Passed	Passed	App'd June 30, 1834
Alexander, William, Lord Stirling, &c.	Balance due deceased for revolutionary services.	24	1	Memorial	104	Rev. Claims						
Alexandré, (French ship).	Reimbursement of duties paid at Newport.	26	1	Pres. message	157	Foreign Affairs	106	Favorable	110	Referred to Committee Whole House.		
				Senate bill	1032	Ways and Means	....	....	S. 219			
Alexandré, (French ship).	Reimbursement of duties paid at Newport.	26	2	Senate bill	203	Foreign Affairs	Feb. 12, 1841	With't amend.	S. 204	Passed	Passed	App'd Mar. 3, 1841
Alexandria	(See District of Columbia.)											
Alexis, Lewis	Confirmation of title to land in Misoruri.	14	2	Petition	485	Public Lands.						
Alfonso, Catalina	Confirmation of title to land in Terre aux Bœuff.	22	1	House bill	107	Whole House	Mar. 23, 1832	With't amend.	125	Passed	Passed	App'd June 25, 1832
Alfonso, Francisco	Confirmation of title to land in Terre aux Bœuff.	22	1	House bill	107	Whole House	Mar. 23, 1832	With't amend.	125	Passed	Passed	App'd June 25, 1832
Alfonso, Juan	Confirmation of title to land in Terre aux Bœuff.	22	1	House bill	107	Whole House	Mar. 23, 1832	With't amend.	125	Passed	Passed	App'd June 25, 1832
Alford, Amasa	Pensions for revolutionary services as "minute man."	25	2	Petition	115	Rev. Pensions.						
Alford, Benedict	Pension for revolutionary services.	21	1	Resolution	484	Military Pensions.						
Alford, Benedict	Pension for revolutionary services.	23	1	Petition	46	Rev. Pensions	177	Favorable	196	Passed	Indef. postp'nd.	
Alford, Benedict	Pension for revolutionary services.	24	1	Petition	56	Rev. Pensions	136	Favorable	475	Passed	Passed	App'd May 14, 1836
Alford, Elisha, or Elijah, heirs of.	Pension for revolutionary services.	27	3	Petition	260	Rev. Pensions	....	....	......	Discharged; leave to withdraw.		
Alford, Elisha, or Elijah, heirs of.	Pension for revolutionary services.	29	1	Petition	939	Rev. Claims.						
Alford, Elisha, or Elijah, heirs of.	Pension for revolutionary services.	29	2	Petition	85	Rev. Claims.						

List of private claims presented to the House of Representatives of the United States from the 1st to the 31st Congress, inclusive—Continued.

Names of claimants.	Nature or object of the claim.	Congress.	Session.	How brought before the House of Reps.	Page of journal.	To what committee of the House referred.	No. or date of the report.	Nature of the report.	No. of the bill.	How disposed of by the House of Reps.	How disposed of by the Senate.	Date of the act of Congress, and remarks.
3 Alford, Elisha, or Elijah, heirs of.	Pension for revolutionary services of deceased.	30	1	Petition........	405	Rev. Claims.......	....	....	......	Discharged; laid on table.		
Alford, Elisha, or Elijah, heirs of.	Pension for revolutionary services of deceased.	30	2	Petition........	117	Rev. Claims.						
Alford, Elisha, or Elijah, heirs of.	Pension for revolutionary services of deceased.	31	1	Petition........	348	Rev. Claims.						
Alford, George..........	To be restored to pension roll....	28	2	Petition	83	Rev. Pensions.						
Alford, George..........	To be restored to pension roll....	29	1	Petition	341	Rev. Pensions.						
Alford, George..........	To be restored to pension roll....	29	2	Petition	150	Rev. Pensions	19	Adverse	......	Laid on table.		
Algerine vessels, captors of	Indemnity for captured property restored.	14	1	House bill......	498	Whole House	Mar. 29, 1816	With amend..	135	Passed	Passed	App'd April 27, 1816
Aliur, James	(See Wm. H. Bedford, agent, &c.)	28	1	....	262							
Allain, Valerian.........	Confirmation of a land claim.....	26	1	Petition	365	Priv. Land Claims.						
Allain, Valerian.........	Confirmation of a land claim.....	26	2	Petition	134	Priv. Land Claims.	122	Favorable	627	Referred to Committee Whole.		
Allain, Valerian.........	Confirmation of a land claim.....	27	2	Petition	99	Public Lands.						
				Senate bill	580	Priv. Land Claims.	831	With't amend.	S. 65	Passed	Passed	App'd Aug. 11, 1842
Allan, Chilton, and wife..	(See heirs of James Sympson)....	26	1	....	200	....	98	....	94			
Allard, Gabriel N........	Confirmation of title to land in Terre aux Bœuff.	22	1	House bill......	107	Whole House	Mar. 23, 1832	With't amend.	125	Passed	Passed	App'd June 25, 1832
Allaways, Joseph, assignee of.	Arrears of pay for military services	18	1	Petition.	432	Claims.						
Allaways, Joseph, assignee of.	Arrears of pay for military services	19	1	Petition	407	Claims	165	Favorable	217	Passed	Passed with amendment.	
Allaways, Joseph, assignee of.	Arrears of pay for military services	19	2	Petition	82	Claims	Dec. 22, 1826	Favorable	313	Passed	Passed	App'd Feb. 22, 1827
Allbright, John S........	(See Louis F. Beeler, and others)	30	1	....	115	....	482					
Allcorn, James..........	(See Reuben E. Gentry, & others)	23	1	....	130	....	....	....	......	....	....	"Inhabitants Cote sans Dessein."
Allcorn, James, widow of.	Pension for injuries received in the public service.	31	1	Petition	449	Invalid Pensions.						
Allen, Abel, guardian of..	Pension, (applicant insane)	21	1	Petition	35	Military Pensions..	May 8, 18[illegible]	Favorable....	464	Passed	Passed	App'd May 29, 1830
Allen, Abraham, heir of..	Pension for revolutionary services of deceased.	31	1	Petition	815	Rev. Pensions	310	Adverse	......	Laid on table.		
Allen, Alborne..........	Compensation for boat built for revenue service.	28	1	Petition	73	Claims	89	Favorable....	104	Passed.		
Allen, Alborne..........	Compensation for boat built for revenue service.	29	1	Petition	106	Claims	105	Favorable....	117	Rejected.		
Allen, Alborne..........	Compensation for boat built for revenue service.	30	1	Petition	70	Claims	42	Favorable....	39	Passed	Passed	App'd Aug. 11, 1848
Allen, Alexander........	(See administratrix of Elijah Cook, and others.)	21	2	....	99							
Allen, Amos	Pension for revolutionary services	22	1	Petition	218	Rev. Pensions	Mar. 26, 1832	Pension bill ..	512	Referred to Committee Whole.		
Allen, Amos	Arrears of Pension............	25	2	Petition	349	Rev. Pensions	....	....	......	Discharged; laid on the table.		
Allen, Andrew..........	Pension for revolutionary services	3	1	Rep. of Secretary War.	131	Select...........	Mar. 26, 1794	Res. to refer to Sec. War.	R. 12	Passed	Passed	App'd June 9, 1794
Allen, Arnold	To be restored to pension roll....	22	1	Resolution	137	Rev. Pensions	365	Favorable....	460	Passed	Indef. postp'd.	
Allen, Barnabas, widow of	Pension for revolutionary services of deceased.	26	1	Resolution	950	Rev. Pensions.						
Allen, Benjamin	Pension for disabilities in war of 1812.	28	1	Petition	820	Invalid Pensions.						

List of private claims presented to the House of Representatives of the United States from the 1st to the 31st Congress, inclusive—**Continued.**

Names of claimants.	Nature or object of the claim.	Congress.	Session.	How brought before the House of Reps.	Page of journal.	To what committee of the House referred.	No. or date of the report.	Nature of the report.	No. of the bill.	How disposed of by the House of Reps.	How disposed of by the Senate.	Date of the act of Congress, and remarks.
Allen, Benjamin	Pension for disabilities in war of 1812.	28	2	Petition	176	Invalid Pensions	42	Favorable	516	Passed	Adverse report.	
Allen, Benjamin	Pension for disabilities in war of 1812.	29	1	Petition	209	Invalid Pensions	473	Favorable	351	Passed	Passed	App'd Aug. 8, 1846
Allen, Benjamin, sen.	Indemnity for Indian depredations	29	2	Petition	92	Rev. Pensions.						
Allen, Benjamin F.	(See heirs of Richard C. Allen)	29	1				548		370			
Allen, Beverly, and wife	(See heirs of F. Valle)	19	1		133							
Allen, Charles	Compensation for slaves set free by the British.	28	1	Petition	278	Claims.						
Allen, Charles	Pension for services in war of 1812	31	1	Petition	194	Invalid Pensions	17	Adverse		Laid on the table.		
Allen, Charles R.	Compensation for services rendered Indian commissioners.	27	3	Petition	366	Claims.						
Allen, Charles R.	Compensation for services rendered Indian commissioners.	28	1	Petition	901	Claims.						
Allen, Charles R.	Compensation for services rendered Indian commissioners.	28	2	Petition	71	Claims	52	Favorable	532	Passed.		
Allen, Charles R.	Compensation for services rendered Indian commissioners.	29	1	Petition	873	Claims.						
Allen, Charles R.	Compensation for services rendered Indian commissioners.	30	1	Memorial	440	Claims	410	Favorable	360	Passed.		
Allen, Clark	Compensation for property lost in public service.	17	2	Petition	69	Military Affairs.						
Allen, Clark	Compensation for property lost in public service.	18	2	Petition	37	Claims	Dec. 20, 1824	Adverse		Laid on table.		
Allen, Clark	Compensation for property lost in public service.	23	1	Petition	34	Claims.						
Allen, Clark	Compensation for property lost in public service.	23	2	Petition	37	Claims	Jan. 28, 1835	Adverse		Laid on table.		
Allen, Clark	Compensation for property lost in public service.	24	1	Petition	49	Claims	65	Favorable	78	Passed	Indef. postp'd.	
Allen, Clark	Compensation for property lost in public service.	25	2	Petition	36	Claims	906	Referred to 3d Auditor.		Report adopted.		
Allen, Clark	Compensation for property lost in public service.	26	1	Documents	702	Claims.						
Allen, Clark	Compensation for property lost in public service.	27	2	Petition	56	Claims.						
Allen, Clark	Compensation for property lost in public service.	27	3	Petition	43	Claims	168	Adverse.				
Allen, Daniel	To be restored to pension roll	17	1	Petition	60	Rev. Pensions.						
Allen, Daniel, widow of	Pension for revolutionary services of deceased.	26	2	Resolution	117	Rev. Pensions.						
Allen, Daniel, widow of	Pension for revolutionary services of deceased.	27	2	Petition	153	Rev. Pensions	784	Adverse		Laid on table.		
Allen, Daniel, widow of	Pension for revolutionary services of deceased.	27	3	Petition	188	Rev. Pensions	295	Adverse		Laid on table.		
Allen, Daniel, widow of	Pension for revolutionary services of deceased.	28	1	Petition	79	Rev. Pensions.						
Allen, Daniel, widow of	Pension for revolutionary services of deceased.	28	2	Petition	119	Rev. Pensions				Discharged; laid on the table.		
Allen, David	Compensation for revolutionary services.	3	1	Petition	60					Referred to Secretary of War.		
Allen, David	Compensation for services as surgeon in revolutionary war.	23	1	Petition	188	Rev. Claims.						

List of private claims presented to the House of Representatives of the United States from the 1st to the 31st Congress, inclusive—Continued.

Names of claimants.	Nature or object of the claim.	Congress.	Session.	How brought before the House of Reps.	Page of journal.	To what committee of the House referred.	No. or date of the report.	Nature of the report.	No. of the bill.	How disposed of by the House of Reps.	How disposed of by the Senate.	Date of the act of Congress, and remarks.
Allen, David, widow of	Compensation for services as surgeon in revolutionary war.	23	2	Petition	94	Rev. Claims.						
Allen, Diarca	Pension	20	2	Petition	39	Military Pensions	Jan. 15, 1829	Adverse	......	Laid on table.		
Allen, Diarca	Pension	21	1	Petition	144	Military Pensions	May 4, 1830	Adverse	......	Laid on table.		
Allen, Ebenezer	Reimbursement of advances to American prisoners.	2	1	Petition	554	....	....	....	......	Referred to Secretary of the Treasury.		
Allen, Edmond	Pension	21	1	Petition	498	Military Pensions	May 4, 1830	Adverse	......	Laid on table.		
Allen, Edmond	Pension	22	1	Resolution	512	Rev. Pensions.						
Allen, Eleazer	Pension for revolutionary services	25	2	Petition	403	Invalid Pensions.						
Allen, Eleazer	Pension for revolutionary services	25	3	Petition	88	Rev. Pensions	....	....	......	Discharged; laid on the table.		
Allen, Eleazer	Pension for revolutionary services	26	1	Petition	170	Rev. Pensions	....	....	......	Discharged; laid on the table.		
Allen, Ethan, heirs of	Payment of pensions due widow of of deceased.	26	1	Petition	625	Rev. Pensions	714	Adverse	......	Laid on table.		
Allen, Ezra	Pension for revolutionary services	21	2	Resolution	165	Military Pensions.						
Allen, Ezra	Pension for revolutionary services	22	1	Petition	329	Rev. Pensions	Mar. 26, 1832	Favorable	511	Referred to Committee Whole.		
Allen, Frederick P.	(See Martin S. Aiken, and others)	17	1	....	359							
Allen, Gabriel	Renewal of a lost certificate	1	2	Petition	145	....	....	....	......	Ref. to Sec'y Treas'y.		
		2	2	Rep. Sec. Treas.								
Allen, Gabriel	Renewal of a lost certificate	2	2	Petition	662	Whole House.						
Allen, Gabriel	Commutation pay for revolutionary services, &c.	15	1	Petition	293	Pens. & Rev. Cl'ms.						
Allen, George	(See representatives of John Reynolds.)	21	1	....	37							
Allen, George W. and Reuben.	Confirmation of title to land	27	2	Documents	139	Priv. Land Claims.						
Allen, George W. and Reuben.	Confirmation of title to land	27	2	House bill	140	Priv. Land Claims.	408	Adverse	......	Laid on table.		
Allen, George W. and Reuben.	Confirmation of title to land	28	1	Petition	141	Priv. Land Claims.	121	Favorable	52	Passed	Passed	App'd June 15, 1844
Allen, Hannah	Benefit of the act of July 4, 1836.	25	2	Petition	311	Rev. Pensions	Jan. 25, 1838	Favorable	456	Ref. to Com. Whole.		
Allen, Heman	Equitable settlement of his claim as Marshal of Vermont.	22	1	Senate bill	892	Judiciary	June 21, 1831	With amend.	S. 41	Passed with amend	Passed as am'd.	App'd July 14, 1832
Allen, Henry, widow of	Pension for revolutionary services of deceased.	25	2	Petition	177	Rev. Pensions	569	Favorable	559	Passed	Adverse report.	
Allen, Henry, widow of	Pension for revolutionary services of deceased.	25	3	Petition	87	Rev. Pensions	73	Favorable	951	Passed	Adverse report.	
Allen, Henry, widow of	Pension for revolutionary services of deceased.	26	1	Petition	170	Rev. Pensions	118	Favorable	128	Passed	Indef. postp'd.	
Allen, Henry, widow of	Pension for revolutionary services of deceased.	26	2	Petition	34	Rev. Pensions	44	Favorable	573	Ref. to Com. Whole.		
Allen, Henry, widow of	Pension for revolutionary services of deceased.	27	2	Petition	59	Rev. Pensions	292	Favorable	260	Passed	Indef. postp'd.	
Allen, Holden	Indemnity for property destroyed by the enemy.	15	2	Petition	148	Claims	Jan. 16, 1819	Adverse	......	Laid on table.		
Allen, Ira, administrator of	Indemnity for seizure of ship "Olive Branch."	18	1	Memorial	525	Foreign Affairs.						
Allen, Ira, administrator of	Indemnity for seizure of ship "Olive Branch"	19	1	Memorial	132	Foreign Affairs	218	Adverse	......	Laid on table.		
Allen, Isaac	Invalid Pension	25	2	Petition	722	Invalid Pensions.						
Allen, Isaac	Invalid Pension	25	3	Petition	349	Invalid Pensions.						

List of private claims presented to the House of Representatives of the United States from the 1st to the 31st Congress, inclusive—Continued.

Names of claimants.	Nature or object of the claim.	Congress.	Session.	How brought before the House of Reps.	Page of journal.	To what committee of the House referred.	No. or date of the report.	Nature of the report.	No. of the bill.	How disposed of by the House of Reps.	How disposed of by the Senate.	Date of the act of Congress, and remarks.
Allen, Isaac	Invalid Pension	26	1	Petition	160	Invalid Pensions	522	Favorable	419	Ref. to Com. Whole.		
Allen, Isaac	Invalid Pension	27	2	Petition	47	Invalid Pensions	209	Adverse	......	Laid on table.		
Allen, Isaac	Invalid Pension	28	1	Petition	131	Invalid Pensions.						
Allen, Isaac	Invalid Pension	28	2	Petition	58	Invalid Pensions	10	Favorable	460	Passed	Passed	App'd Mar. 3, 1845
Allen, James	Pension	14	1	Pension bill	622	Whole House	April 23, 1816	With amend.	171	Passed	Passed with amendment.	App'd April 30, 1816
Allen, James	Pension	20	2	Petition	31	Military Pensions.						
Allen, James	Pension	24	2	Petition	86	Invalid Pensions	....	....	......	Discharged; laid on table.		
Allen, James	Pension	25	2	Petition	85	Invalid Pensions	287	Adverse	......	Laid on table.		
Allen, James	Pension	25	3	Petition	129	Invalid Pensions	....	....	......	Discharged; laid on tale.		
Allen, James, widow of	Pension for revolutionary services of deceased.	28	1	Resolution	315	Rev. Pensions.						
Allen, James, widow of	Pension for loss of husband in Mexican war.	31	1	Petition	762	Invalid Pensions.						
Allen, James, heirs of	Pension for revolutionary services of deceased.	27	3	Petition	260	Rev. Pensions	....	....	......	Discharged; laid on table.		
Allen, James T	Right of pre-emption as New Orleans Br. Pilot.	28	1	Petition	77	Priv. Land Claims.	9	Favorable	35	Passed	Passed	App'd June 17, 1844
Allen, Jeremiah	Payment of certain bills of credit.	3	1	Memorial	68	....	....	....	......	Referred to Secretary of Treasury.		
Allen, Jeremiah	Payment of certain bills of credit.	4	2	Memorial	632	Claims.						
Allen, Jeremiah	Payment of certain bills of credit.	5	2	Memorial	....	Claims	Feb. 26, 1798	Adverse	......	Leave to withdraw.		
Allen, Job	Arrears of pension	25	2	Petition	52	Rev. Pensions	....	....	......	Discharged; laid on table.		
Allen, John	(See Canadian refugees.)											
Allen, John	Bounty on fishing brigantine "Polly."	8	1	Petition	571	Com. and Manufac.	Feb. 17, 1804	Adverse.				
Allen, John	Correction of an erroneous entry of land.	14	2	Petition	107	Public Lands	Jan. 16, 1817	Favorable	59	Passed	Passed	App'd March 3, 1817
Allen, John	Pension	19	1	Petition	52	Military Pensons	April 1, 1826	Adverse.				
Allen, John	Pension	22	1	Petition	381	Rev. Pensions.						
Allen, John	Pension	22	2	Petition	27	Invalid Pensions	113	Favorable	748	Referred to Committee Whole House.		
Allen, John	Pension	23	1	Petition	46	Invalid Pensions	1	Favorable	1	Passed	Passed with amendment.	App'd June 25, 1834
Allen, John	Pay and clothing for revolutionary services.	20	1	Resolution	460	Rev. Claims.						
Allen, John, (Ind.)	Right of pre emption	23	1	Documents	215	Public Lands	Feb. 4, 1834	Favorable	272	Passed	Passed	App'd March 3, 1817
Allen, John	Compensation for services and injuries received at Brooklyn Navy Yard.	27	2	Petition	686	Invalid Pensions	965	Adverse	......	Laid on table.		
Allen, John L.	Reimbursement of moneys paid on public account.	21	1	Petition	264	Claims.						
Allen, John L.	Reimbursement of moneys paid on public account.	25	2	Petition	426	Indian Affairs	760	Favorable	719	Referred to Committee Whole House.		
Allen, John L.	Reimbursement of moneys paid on public account.	25	3	Report of Committee Whole.	380	....	....	With't amend.	719	Passed	Passed	App'd March 3, 1839
Allen, John L.	Arrears of pension	29	1	Petition	175	Invalid Pensions	80	Adverse	......	Laid on table.		
Allen, John R.	Compensation for horse lost in public service.	25	2	Petition	397	Claims	....	....	......	Discharged; laid on table.		
Allen, John R.	Compensation for horse lost in public service.	26	1	Petition	167	Claims	63	Adverse	......	Laid on table.		

List of private claims presented to the House of Representatives of the United States from the 1st to the 31st Congress, inclusive—Continued.

Names of claimants.	Nature or object of the claim.	Congress.	Session.	How brought before the House of Reps.	Page of journal.	To what committee of the House referred.	No. or date of the report.	Nature of the report.	No. of the bill.	How disposed of by the House of Reps.	How disposed of by the Senate.	Date of the act of Congress, and remarks.
Allen, John, widow of	Pension for revolutionary services of deceased.	27	2	Petition	612	Rev. Pensions	784	Adverse		Laid on table.		
Allen, Joseph	(See guardian of Abel Allen)	21	1		35							
Allen, Joseph	Exchange of location of military bounty land.	25	2	Petition	420	Public Lands	March 6, 1838	Adverse		Laid on table.		
Allen, Jonathan, heirs of	Pension for revolutionary services of deceased.	27	3	Petition	260	Rev. Pensions				Discharged; leave to withdraw.		
Allen, Justice, widow of	Pension for military services of deceased.	14	2	Petition	398	Millitary Affairs.						
Allen, Lathrop, representatives of.	Commutation pay for revolutionary services of deceased.	22	1	Petition	559	Rev. Claims	498	Favorable	605	Referred to Committee Whole House.		
Allen, Lathrop, representatives of.	Commutation pay for revolution ary services of deceased.	23	1	Petition	39	Rev. Claims.						
Allen, Lathrop, representatives of.	Commutation pay for revolutionary services of deceased.	24	1	Petition	104	Rev. Claims	139	Favorable	183	Passed	Indef. postp'd.	
Allen, Lathrop, representatives of.	Commutation pay for revolution ary services of deceased.	24	2	Petition	94	Rev. Claims	91	Favorable	835	Referred to Committee Whole House.		
Allen, Lathrop, representatives of.	Commutation pay for revolutionary services of deceased.	25	2	Petition	39	Rev. Claims	131	Favorable	149	Passed	Reported with't amendment.	
Allen, Lathrop, representatives of.	Commutation pay for revolutionary services of deceased.	25	3	Petition	84	Rev. Claims	16	Favorable	914	Referred to Committee Whole House.		
Allen, Lathrop, representatives of.	Indemnity for revolutionary losses and expenditures.	25	3	Petition	216	Rev. Claims				Discharged; laid on table.		
Allen, Lathrop, representatives of.	Indemnity for revolutionary losses and expenditures.	26	1	Petition	163	Rev. Claims	619	Adverse		Laid on table.		
Allen, Lathrop, widow of	Pension for revolutionary services of deceased.	26	1	Petition	170	Rev. Pensions	619	Adverse		Laid on table.		
Allen, Lathrop, representatives of.	Commutation pay for revolutionary services of deceased.	27	2	Petition	784	Rev. Claims	868	Adverse		Laid on table.		
Allen, Lathrop, representatives of.	Commutation pay for revolutionary services of deceased.	29	1	Petition	107	Rev. Claims	139	Adverse		Laid on table.		
Allen, Lathrop, representatives of.	Commutation pay for revolutionary services of deceased.	29	2	Petition	85	Rev. Claims.						
Allen, Lathrop, representatives of.	Commutation pay for revolutionary services of deceased.	30	1	Petition	109	Rev. Claims.						
Allen, Lathrop, representatives of.	Commutation pay for revolutionary services of deceased.	30	2	Petition	127	Rev. Claims.						
Allen, Lathrop, representatives of.	Commutation pay for revolutionary services of deceased.	31	1	Petition	486	Rev. Claims.						
Allen, Lucius B	Extra services as clerk Navy Department.	31	1	Petition	409	Ways and Means.						
Allen, Lydia	Pension	18	1	Resolution	39	Naval Affairs.						
Allen, Madison	Renewal of a destroyed land war rant.	29	1	Senate bill	307	Public Lands	Feb. 16, 1847	With't amend.	S. 63	Referred to Committee Whole House.		
Allen, Moses	Pension	21	1	Resolution	351	Military Pensions.						
Allen, Moses	Pension	21	2	Petition	110	Military Pensions.						
Allen, Nathaniel	Credit for disbursement on public account.	16	2	Senate bill	287	Claims	March 1, 1821	With't amend.	S. 44	Passed	Passed	App'd March 3, 1821
Allen, Peter L	Pension for disabilities war of 1812	23	2	Petition	76	Invalid Pensions.						
Allen, Peter L	Pension for disabilities war of 1812	24	1	Petition	98	Invalid Pensions	Feb. 10, 1836	Favorable	312	Passed	Passed	App'd June 28, 1836
Allen, Peter L	(Repeal of act granting pension)	29	1	Documents	93	Invalid Pensions	465	For repeal of the act.	343	Referred to Committee Whole House.		
Allen, Philip	Remission of certain tonnage duties	3	1	Petition	119	Select	April 22, 1794	Resolution		Claim rejected.		

List of private claims presented to the House of Representatives of the United States from the 1st to the 31st Congress, inclusive—Continued.

Names of claimants.	Nature or object of the claim.	Congress.	Session.	How brought before the House of Reps.	Page of journal.	To what committee of the House referred.	No. or date of the report.	Nature of the report.	No. of the bill.	How disposed of by the House of Reps.	How disposed of by the Senate.	Date of the act of Congress, and remarks.
Allen, Philip, (R. I.)	Indemnity for French Spoliation prior to 1800.	23	1	Memorial	273	Foreign Affairs.						
Allen, Philip, (R. I.)	Indemnity for French Spoliation prior to 1800.	26	1	Memorial	182	Foreign Affairs	343	Favorable	319	Referred to Committee Whole House.		
Allen, Philip, (R. I.)	Indemnity for French Spoliation prior to 1800.	30	1	Memorial	113	Foreign Affairs	Jan. 4, 1848	General bill	21	Referred to Committee Whole House.		
Allen, Phineas	Arrears of pension	26	1	Petition	284	Rev. Pensions	490	Adverse.				
				Recommitted	1012	Rev. Pensions	714	Adverse		Laid on table.		
Allen, Reuben	(See George W. & Reuben Allen.)	27	2		139							
Allen, Richard, executor of.	Payment of pension due deceased.	24	2	Petition	97	Rev. Claims	78	Adverse		Laid on table.		
Allen, Richard C.	Compensation for locating Seminole lands.	21	1	Resolution	345	Public Lands	Mar. 23, 1830	Adverse		Laid on table.		
Allen, Richard C., administrator of.	Compensation for locating Seminole lands.	28	2	Petition	216	Public Lands.						
Allen, Richard C., administrator of.	Compensation for locating Seminole lands.	29	1	House bill	633	Whole House	June 5, 1846	With't amend.	370	Passed	Passed	App'd Aug. 10, 1846
Allen, Richard C.	Indemnity for land included in "Forbes's purchase."	25	2	Petition	417	Public Lands				Discharged.		
Allen, Richard C.	Indemnity for land included in "Forbes's purchase."	25	3	Petition	93	Public Lands				Discharged; laid on table.		
Allen, Richard C., heirs of.	Indemnity for land included in "Forbes's purchase."	29	1	Petition		Public Lands	518	Favorable	370	Passed	Passed	App'd Aug. 10, 1846
Allen, Rhoda	(See heirs of Consider Williston).	31	2		87							
Allen, Samuel	Pension	12	1	House bill	361	Whole House	June 8, 1812	Favorable	138	Passed	Passed	App'd July 5, 1812
Allen, Samuel	Compensation for revolutionary services.	15	1	Petition	83	Pens. & Rev. Cl'ms.	Feb. 10, 1818	Adverse		Claim rejected.		
Allen, Sam'l, and J. H. L.	Indemnity for change in a naval contract.	17	1	Petition	388	Claims.						
Allen, Samuel, and others.	Indemnity for change in a naval contract.	17	2	Petition	30	Claims	Jan. 16, 1823	Adverse		Laid on table.		
Allen, Samuel, and others.	Indemnity for change in a naval contract.	18	1	Petition	114	Claims	Jan. 23, 1824	Adverse		Laid on table.		
Allen, Samuel, and others.	Indemnity for change in a naval contract.	20	1	Petition	397	Claims	April 29, 1828	Adverse		Leave to withdraw.		
Allen, Samuel, (Jane,) widow of.	Pension for revolutionary services of deceased.	26	1	Senate bill	837	Rev. Pensions	May 25, 1840	With amend.	S. 293	Referred to Committee Whole House.		
Allen, Samuel, (Jane,) widow of.	Pension for revolutionary services of deceased.	26	2	Senate bill	297				S. 187			
Allen, Samuel, (Jane,) widow of.	Pension for revolutionary services of deceased.	27	2	Senate bill	1390	Rev. Pensions	Aug. 30, 1842	Adverse	S. 9	Laid on table.		
Allen, Samuel, (Ann H.,) widow of.	Increase of pension	30	1	Memorail	340	Invalid Pensions	462	Adverse		Laid on table.		
Allen, Samuel, (Va.)	Pension for revolutionary services.	21	1	Resolution	281	Military Pensions	May 3, 1830	Pension bill	454	Referred to Committee Whole House.		
Allen, Samuel S.	Commissions on certain duties	26	2	Petition	121	Commerce.						
Allen, Samuel S.	Commissions on certain duties	28	1	Petition	90	Commerce.						
Allen, Samuel S.	Commissions on certain duties	28	2	Petition	45	Commerce.						
Allen, Samuel S.	Commissions on certain duties	29	1	Petition	92	Commerce.						
Allen, Samuel S.	Commissions on certain duties	29	2	Petition	100	Commerce.						
Allen, Samuel S.	Commissions on certain duties	31	1	Petition	518	Commerce.						
Allen, Sarah	(See Samuel Drew, mother of)	16	1		32							
Allen, Sarah	(See heirs of Michael De Graff)	29	2		54		40					

List of private claims presented to the House of Representatives of the United States from the 1st to the 31st Congress, inclusive—Continued.

Names of claimants.	Nature or object of the claim.	Congress.	Session.	How brought before the House of Reps.	Page of journal.	To what committee of the House referred.	No. or date of the report.	Nature of the report.	No. of the bill.	How disposed of by the House of Reps.	How disposed of by the Senate.	Date of the act of Congress, and remarks.
Allen, Seth, widow of	Pension for revolutionary services of deceased.	26	2	Petition	133	Rev. Pensions	Jan. 7, 1841	Adverse	......	Laid on table.		
Allen, Shubael	Indemnity for Indian depredations.	23	1	Resolution	515	Indian Affairs	May 6, 1834	Adverse	......	Laid on table.		
Allen, Spartan	Compensation for horse lost in public service.	26	1	Documents	336	Claims	680	Adverse	......	Laid on table.		
Allen, Squire	Indemnity for Indian depredations.	21	2	Documents	89	Military Affairs.						
Allen, Stephen	(See heir of Abraham Allen)	31	1	....	815							
Allen, Stephen	Compensation for forage furnished in 1813.	21	1	Petition	235	Claims	Mar. 17, 1830	Adverse	......	Laid on table.		
Allen, Stephen	Compensation for forage furnished in 1813.	23	1	Petition	384	Claims	374	Adverse	......	Laid on table.		
Allen, Thomas	Compensation for printing "Blue Book."	27	2	Petition	535	Claims	....	....	......	....	....	(See Blair & Rives.)
Allen, Thomas	Additional compensation for printing Biennial Register.	29	2	Memorial	67	Claims.						
Allen, Thomas	Compensation for printing Compendium of Sixth Census.	28	1	Memorial	358	Claims.						
Allen, Thomas	Compensation for printing Compendium of Sixth Census.	28	2	Memorial	71	Claims	2	Favorable	451	Referred to Committee Whole House.		
Allen, Thomas	Compensation for printing Compendium of Sixth Census.	29	1	Memorial	67	Claims.						
				Memorial, (2)	510	Claims.						
Allen, Thomas	Compensation for printing Compendium of Sixth Census.	30	1	Petition	154	Claims.						
Allen, Thomas	Compensation for printing Compendium of Sixth Census.	30	2	Petition	116	Claims.						
Allen, Thomas	Compensation for printing Compendium of Sixth Census.	31	1	Petition	311	Claims.						
Allen, Vincent, widow of	Pension for revolutionary services of deceased.	25	3	Resolution	402	Rev. Pensions	....	....	......	Discharged.		
Allen, Vincent, widow of	Pension for revolutionary services of deceased.	26	1	Petition	170	Rev. Pensions	March 5, 1840	Adverse	......	Laid on table.		
Allen, Wade	Compensation for transporting United States mail.	29	2	Senate bill	380	P. Of. and P. Roads.	Feb. 24, 1847	With't amend.	S. 116	Referred to Committee Whole House.		
Allen, Wade	Indemnity for annulment of mail contract.	31	2	Petition	95	P. Of. and P. Roads.						
Allen, Weston, and others	Reimbursement of duty on rum found at sea.	22	1	Petition	132	Ways and Means.						
Allen, Weston, and others	Reimbursement of duty on rum found at sea.	23	1	Petition	186	Ways and Means	Jan. 21, 1834	Adverse	......	Laid on table.		
Allen, William	(See William Bell)	5	2	....	116							
Allen, William	Compensation for naval services, &c., in 1808.	25	3	Petition	225	Naval Affairs.						
Allen, William	Compensation for naval services, &c., in 1808.	26	1	Petition	179	Naval Affairs.						
Allen, William	Compensation for naval services, &c., in 1808.	27	2	Petition	64	Naval Affairs	560	....	355	Ordered to 3d reading.		
Allen, William	Compensation for naval services, &c., in 1808.	27	3	House bill	87	....	....	....	355	Passed	Passed with amendment.	App'd March 1, 1843
Allen, William	Compensation for naval services, &c., in 1808.	28	1	Petition	143	Invalid Pensions	234	Adverse	......	Laid on table.		
				Petition (2)	655	Invalid Pensions.						

List of private claims presented to the House of Representatives of the United States from the 1st to the 31st Congress, inclusive—Continued.

Names of claimants.	Nature or object of the claim.	Congress.	Session.	How brought before the House of Reps.	Page of journal.	To what committee of the House referred.	No. or date of the report.	Nature of the report.	No. of the bill.	How disposed of by the House of Reps.	How disposed of by the Senate.	Date of the act of Congress, and remarks.
Allen, William	Compensation for naval services, &c., in 1808.	28	2	Petition	119	Invalid Pensions	44	Adverse		Laid on table.		
Allen, William H., administrator of.	Compensation for capture and destruction of enemy's property.	14	1	Petition	340	Naval Affairs				Discharged; leave to withdraw.		
Allen, William H., administrator of.	Compensation for capture and destruction of enemy's property.	14	2	Petition	41	Naval Affairs	20	Adverse		Referred to Committee Whole House.		
Allen, William H., administrator of.	Half-pay pension for 5 years	17	2	Resolution	33	Naval Affairs	59	Favorable	208	Referred to Committee Whole House.		
Allen, William H., administrator of.	Prize money.	21	1	Petition	233	Naval Affairs.						
Allen, William H	Allowance for office rent and fuel.	21	1	Petition	361	Public Lands.						
Allen, William H	Compensation as land commissioner, Florida.	22	1	Resolution	159	Public Lands	Mar. 29, 1832	Adverse		Leave to withdraw.		
Allen, Zachariah	Remission of certain tonnage duties.	3	1	Petition	119	Select	April 22, 1794	Resolution		Claim rejected.		
Allen, Zeno	(See John Perkins and others)	16	2		216							
Allen, Zeno	(See assignees of Thomas Tupper.)	22	2		142		115					
Allega, James	Bounty land for services in war of 1812.	19	2	Petition	157	Military Affairs.						
Allega, James	Bounty land for services in war of 1812.	20	1	Petition	126	Military Affairs	Jan. 24, 1828	Adverse		Laid on table.		
Alleghany, ship	(See Bowie & Kurtz and others).	13	2		176				S. 94			
Allers, Francis	Confirmation of title to land in Missouri.	15	1	Petition	102	Priv. Land Claims.						
Allers, Francis	Confirmation of title to land in Missouri.	16	1	Petition	72	Priv. Land Claims.						
Allers, Francis	Confirmation of title to land in Missouri.	17	1	Petition	53	Public Lands.						
Allers, Francis	Confirmation of title to land in Missouri.	18	1	Petition	53	Public Lands	Jan. 16, 1824	Favorable	65	Passed	Passed	App'd May 26, 1824
Alley, John	Pension	27	2	Petition	458	Rev. Pensions	784	Adverse		Laid on table.		
Alley, John H., sureties of.	Release from liability	17	1	Petition	129	Ways and Means.						
Alley, Joshua O., heirs of.	Pension for naval services	26	1	Petition	199	Naval Affairs.						
Alley, Moses	Compensation for horse taken for public use.	13	3	Petition	486	Claims	Oct. 29, 1814	Adverse		Leave to withdraw.		
Alley, Moses	Compensation for horse taken for public use.	14	1	Petition	249	Claims.						
Alley, Reuben	Drawback and bounty on fishing vessels.	9	2	Petition	503	Com. and Man.	Jan. 6, 1807	Adverse		Claim rejected.		
Alley, William	Right of pre-emption to a quarter section of land.	24	2	Petition	269	Public Lands.						
Allgood, William	Pension and bounty land for revolutionary services.	26	1	Petition	1332					Laid on table.		
Alling, Lieut. Stephen	Compensation for revolutionary services.	10	1	Memorial	87	Select.						
Alling, Lieut. Stephen	Compensation for revolutionary services.	10	2	Memorial	459	Whole House.						
Alling, Lieut. Stephen	Compensation for revolutionary services.	11	1	Petition	79	Claims.						
Alling, Lieut. Stephen	Compensation for revolutionary services.	11	2	Petition	131	Claims	Feb. 23, 1810	Adverse		Claim rejected.		
Alling, Lieut. Stephen	Commutation pay and bounty land	12	1	Petition	51	Claims	May 7, 1812	Adverse.				
Alling, Lieut. Stephen	Commutation pay and bounty land	12	2	Petition	610	Claims.						

List of private claims presented to the House of Representatives of the United States from the 1st to the 31st Congress, inclusive—Continued.

Names of claimants.	Nature or object of the claim.	Congress.	Session.	How brought before the House of Reps.	Page of journal.	To what committee of the House referred.	No. or date of the report.	Nature of the report.	No. of the bill.	How disposed of by the House of Reps.	How disposed of by the Senate.	Date of the act of Congress, and remarks.
Alling, Lieut. Stephen	Commutation pay and bounty land	13	2	Petition	190	Pensions	Mar. 28, 1814	Favorable		Referred to Committee Whole.		
Alling, Lieut. Stephen	Commutation pay and bounty land	15	1	Petition	38	Pens. & Rev. Cl'ms.				Discharged; leave to withdraw.		
Allis, Henry, administratrix of.	Reimbursement of advances on public account, &c.	2	1	Petition	461					Referred to Secretary War.		
Allis, Henry, administratrix of.	Reimbursement of advances on public account, &c.	2	2	Petition	702	Select.						
Allis, Lemuel	Pension for revolutionary services.	15	2	Petition	300	Rev. Pensions.						
Allis, Randall	(See Timothy Twitchell)	22	1		33							
Allison, Amey	Indemnity for damage to her property, &c.	4	1	Rep. of Secretary Treasury.	388	Claims	74	Adverse		Laid on table.		
Allison, Burgess	For renewal of a patent	14	2	Petition	354	Select.						
Allison, Jeremiah	Pension for revolutionary services.	24	2	Petition	390	Public Lands.						
Allison, John	Pension for services in Indian war.	31	1	Petition	298	Rev. Pensions.						
Allison, Lieut. John	Pension	25	2	Documents	85	Invalid Pensions	678	Favorable	657	Passed	Adverse report.	
Allison, Lieut. John	Pension	26	1	Resolution	160	Invalid Pensions	219	Favorable	231	Passed	Indef. postp'd.	
Allison, Major John	Indemnity for losses and compensation for revolutionary services.	21	2	Resolut'n Indiana Legislature.	209	Military Pensions.						
Allison, Major John	Indemnity for losses and compensation for revolutionary services.	22	1	Petition	294	Public Lands.						
Allison, Col. John, representatives of.	Commutation pay due deceased for revolutionary services.	23	1	Petition	110	Rev. Claims.						
Allison, Joseph	Compensation for revolutionary supplies (wood.)	4	1	Rep. of Secretary Treasury.	388	Claims	74	Adverse		Laid on table.		
Allison, Robert	Pension and pay for revolutionary services.	16	1	Petition	38	Rev. Pensions	April 22, 1820	Adverse		Laid on table.		
Allison, Robert	Bounty land for revolutionary services.	23	2	Petition	56	Priv. Land Claims.	105	Favorable	733	Referred to Committee Whole.		
Allison, Robert	Bounty land for revolutionary services.	24	1	Petition	121	Priv. Land Claims.	110	Favorable	126	Referred to Committee Whole.		
Allison, Robert	Bounty land for revolutionary services.	24	2	Rep. Committee Whole.	62			With amend.	126	Rejected.		
Allison, Robert, heirs of	Increase of pension	29	1	Petition	812	Rev. Pensions.						
Allison, Robert, heirs of	Increase of pension	29	2	Petition	150	Rev. Pensions	11	Adverse		Laid on table.		
Allison, Robert, heirs of	Increase of pension	30	1	Petition	676	Rev. Pensions.						
Allison, Samuel	(See William H. Bedford, agent, &c.)	28	1		262							
Allman, Lawrence	Compensation for revolutionary services.	1	3	Petition	351							
				Rep. of Secretary War.	380					Laid on table.		
Allmand, Harrison, jr.	(See Administrator of James R. Barnett.)	18	1		70							
Allmand, Samuel H.	(See Assignee of Jesse Bolling)	18	2		223							
Al-lo-lah, (Indian,) heirs of.	Confirmation of title to a section of land.	31	1	Petition	599	Indian Affairs	277	Favorable	256	Passed	Passed	App'd Aug. 30, 1850
Allspach, David	Release of judgment in favor of United States.	26	1	Petition	352	Judiciary	327	Favorable	294	Referred to Committee Whole.		
Allspach, David	Release of judgment in favor of United States.	27	2	Petition	100	Judiciary	251	Favorable	217	Passed	Adverse report.	
Allspach, David	Release of judgment in favor of United States.	27	3	Petition	44	Judiciary	11	Favorable	632	Passed.		

List of private claims presented to the House of Representatives of the United States from the 1st to the 31st Congress, inclusive—Continued.

Names of claimants.	Nature or object of the claim.	Congress.	Session.	How brought before the House of Reps.	Page of journal.	To what committee of the House referred.	No. or date of the report.	Nature of the report.	No. of the bill.	How disposed of by the House of Reps.	How disposed of by the Senate.	Date of the act of Congress, and remarks.
Allspach, David	Release of judgment in favor of U. S.	28	1	Petition	79	Judiciary	317	Favorable	224	Passed	Passed	App'd June 17, 1844
Allstadt, John C.	Payment for materials furnished for New York custom-house.	28	2	Petition	421	Claims.						
Allsup, Halsey	Pension for disability in naval service.	24	1	Petition	661	Naval Affairs	....	....	......	Discharged; laid on the table.		
Allyn, Captain Francis	Compensat'n for expenses in bringing Lafayette to this country in 1824.	22	2	Petition and docs	31	Foreign Affairs.						
Allyn, Captain Francis	Compensat'n for expenses in bringing Lafayette to this country in 1824.	23	2	Petition	37	Foreign Affairs.						
Allyn, Captain Francis	Compensat'n for expenses in bringing Lafayette to this country in 1824.	24	1	Senate bill	928	Naval Affairs	June 4, 1836	Adverse	S. 135	Laid on table.		
Allyn, Captain Francis	Compensat'n for expenses in bringing Lafayette to this country in 1824.	24	2	Senate bill	552	Claims	326	Adverse	S. 122	Referred to Committee Whole.		
Allyn, Captain Francis	Compensat'n for expenses in bringing Lafayette to this country in 1824.	26	1	Memorial	293	Claims.						
Allyn, Captain Francis	Compensat'n for expenses in bringing Lafayette to this country in 1824.	26	2	Petition	135	Claims.						
Allyn, Captain Francis	Compensat'n for expenses in bringing Lafayette to this country in 1824.	27	2	Petition	56	Claims	56	Favorable	91	Referred to Committee Whole.		
Allyn, Captain Francis	Compensat'n for expenses in bringing Lafayette to this country in 1824.	28	1	Petition	98	Claims	74	Favorable	96	Referred to Committee Whole.		
Allyn, Captain Francis	Compensat'n for expenses in bringing Lafayette to this country in 1824.	29	1	Petition	90	Claims	17	Favorable	31	Referred to Committee Whole.		
Allyn, Captain Francis	Compensat'n for expenses in bringing Lafayette to this country in 1824.	30	1	Petition	154	Claims.						
Allyn, Captain Francis	Compensat'n for expenses in bringing Lafayette to this country in 1824.	30	2	Petition	87	Claims	12	Favorable	705	Referred to Committee Whole.		
Allyn, Captain Francis	Compensat'n for expenses in bringing Lafayette to this country in 1824.	31	1	Petition	283	Claims.						
Allyn, Robert, heirs of	Indemnity for French spoliations prior to 1800.	31	1	Petition	284	Foreign Affairs	355	General bill	318	Referred to Committee Whole.		
Almon, John and George Woolsey.	Permission to exchange an entry of land.	24	1	Petition	599	Public Lands	April 5, 1836	Favorable	526	Passed	Passed with amendment.	App'd July 2, 1836
Almy, William	(See John H. Dexter)	24	1	....	382							
Alpuente, Edward, successors of.	Confirmation of title to land at Terre aux Bœuff.	22	1	House bill	107	Whole House	May 23, 1832	With't amend.	125	Passed	Passed	App'd June 25, 1832
Alricks, William	Extra pay as Clerk in Treasury Department.	3	1	Petition	88	Select	47	Adverse	......	Laid on table.		
Alsbury, Thomas	Compensation for a mare lost in the public service.	18	1	Resolution	220	Claims	Mar. 3, 1824	Adverse	......	Laid on table.		

List of private claims presented to the House of Representatives of the United States from the 1st to the 31st Congress, inclusive—Continued.

Names of claimants.	Nature or object of the claim.	Congress.	Session.	How brought before the House of Reps.	Page of journal.	To what committee of the House referred.	No. or date of the report.	Nature of the report.	No. of the bill.	How disposed of by the House of Reps.	How disposed of by the Senate.	Date of the act of Congress, and remarks.
Alshouse, David	Comp. for revolutionary services	2	1	Petition	510					Referred to Sec. War.		
Alshouse, David	Increase and arrears of pension	4	2	Petition	631	Claims	Jan. 23, 1797	Adverse.				
Alsop, Benjamin	(See Carey M. Wood, an orphan)	9	1		247							
Alstoll, John	Pension for revolutionary services	17	2	Petition	224	Pens. & Rev. Cl'ms.						
Alstoll, John	Pension for revolutionary services	18	1	Petition	196	Rev. Claims	Mar. 24, 1824	Adverse		Laid on table.		
Alston, Joseph J., executors of.	(See executors of John B. Mebane)	18	1		61				214			
Alston, William M.	(See John Earle and others)	10	1		212							
Alsworth, Andrew	Pension for revolutionary services	20	2	Resolution	186	Military Pensions.						
Alsworth, Andrew	Pension for revolutionary services	21	1	Resolution	432	Military Pensions.						
Alsworth, Andrew	Pension for revolutionary services	21	2	Resolution	77	Military Pensions.						
Alsworth, Andrew	Pension for revolutionary services	22	1	Petition	46	Rev. Pensions.						
Alva, Peter and Fr. Bonel.	Indemnity for vessel condemned at Mobile.	17	2	Petition	166	Judiciary	Feb. 15, 1823	General bill	297	Ref. to Com. Whole.		
Alvarez, Manuel, (agent)	Drawback on goods exported in original packages.	27	2	Petition	418	Commerce.						
Alvarez, Manuel, (agent)	Drawback on goods exported in original packages.	28	1	Petition	240	Commerce.						
Alverson, George	Pension	15	2	Petition	46	Pens. & Rev. Cl'ms.	Jan. 5, 1819	Adverse		Laid on table.		
Alverson, John	Pension	3	1	Rep. of Sec. War.	131	Select	May 26, 1794	Pension bill	62	Passed	Passed	App'd June 7, 1794
Alvey, John Durham, widow of.	Pension for revolutionary services of deceased.	26	1	Petition	285	Rev. Pensions.						
Alvis, John, widow of	Pension for revolutionary services of deceased.	30	1	Petition	874	Rev. Pensions.						
Alvis, John, widow of	Pension for revolutionary services of deceased.	30	2	Petition	289	Rev. Pensions				Leave to withdraw.		
Alvis, Zachariah C	Comp. for horse lost in Creek war.	18	1	Resolution	232	Claims	April 24, 1824	Adverse		Laid on table.		
Alvord, Benedict	Pension for revolutionary services	23	1	Resolution	434							See Note, Jour. p. 434
Alvord, Eliab	Pension for revolutionary services	15	2	Petition	300	Rev. Pensions.						
Alvord, Job, son of	Bounty land due deceased for revolutionary services.	21	1	Petition	37	Rev. Pensions	102	Favorable	140	Referred to Committee Whole.		
Alvord, Job, son of	Bounty land due deceased for revolutionary services.	22	1	Petition	114	Rev. Pensions	89	Favorable	172	Passed.		
Alward, Henry	Compensation for apprehending deserters.	18	1	Resolution	77	Claims	Jan. 12, 1824	Adverse		Laid on table.		
Alway, Isaac	Pension	30	2	Petition	541	Invalid Pensions.						
Alway, Isaac	Pension	31	1	Petition	348	Invalid Pensions	390	Adverse		Laid on table.		
Ama, Antonio	Proceeds of certain forfeited merchandise.	11	1	Petition	52	Com. and Manufac.						
Amberson, William	Continuation of pension for revolutionary services.	16	2	Petition	47	Pens. and Revolutionary Claims.	Feb. 15, 1821	Adverse		Leave to withdraw.		
Amberson, William	To be restored to pension roll	17	1	Petition	155	Rev. Pensions.						
Amberson, William	Pension for revolutionary services	19	1	Petition	149	Military Pensions	April 1, 1826	Adverse		Leave to withdraw.		
Amberson, William	Commutation pay for revolutionary services.	24	1	Resolution	342	Rev. Claims.						
Amberson, William, administrator of.	Commutation pay for revolutionary services.	29	1	Petition	510	Rev. Claims.						
Amberson, William, administrator of.	Commutation pay for revolutionary services.	29	2	Petition	85	Rev. Claims.						
Amberson, William, administrator of.	Commutation pay for revolutionary services.	30	1	Petition	111	Rev. Claims.						
Ambler, Charles P.	(See Squire Ambler, widow of)	28	1		99							
Ambler, Franklin P.	(See Squire Ambler, widow of)	28	1		99		218		172			

List of private claims presented to the House of Representatives of the United States from the 1st to the 31st Congress, inclusive—Continued.

Names of claimants.	Nature or object of the claim.	Congress.	Session.	How brought before the House of Reps.	Page of journal.	To what committee of the House referred.	No. or date of the report.	Nature of the report.	No. of the bill.	How disposed of by the House of Reps.	How disposed of by the Senate.	Date of the act of Congress, and remarks.
Ambler, James	Pension for revolutionary services.	16	1	Petition	51	Rev. Pensions	April 5, 1820	Adverse	......	Leave to withdraw.		
Ambler, James	Pension for revolutionary services.	22	1	Petition	566	Rev. Pensions.						
Ambler, John	Compensation for revolutionary services.	19	1	Petition	78	Rev. Claims	Jan. 24, 1826	Adverse	......	Claim rejected.		
Ambler, Peter	Pension	25	2	Petition	400	Invalid Pensions.						
Ambler, Peter	Pension	26	1	Resolution	161	Invalid Pensions	291	Adverse	......	Laid on the table.		
Ambler, Peter	Pension	29	1	Petition	309	Invalid Pensions.						
Ambler, Squire, widow of.	Pension for revolutionary services of deceased.	25	3	Petition	217	Rev. Pensions	247	Faborable	1118	Referred to Committee Whole.		
Ambler, Squire, widow of.	Pension for revolutionary services of deceased.	26	1	Petition	513	Rev. Pensions	Mar. 5, 1840	Adverse	......	Laid on the table.		
Ambler, Squire, widow of.	Pension for revolutionary services of deceased.	28	1	Petition	99	Rev. Pensions	218	Favorable	172	Passed	No amend.	
Ambrozine, John	Compensation for surrender of a patent.	29	1	Petition	178	Public Lands	218	General bill	213	Referred to Committee Whole.		
Ambrozine, John	Compensation for surrender of a patent.	30	1	Memorial	199	Public Lands	812	Adverse	......	Laid on the table.		
Amelung, Ferdinand L.	Release from liabilities for public money of which he was robbed.	13	3	Petition	519	Ways and Means	....	....	......	Discharged.		
Amelung, T. L. E.	(See Albert Seecamp, administrator of.)	26	1	....	182	....	343	....	319			
American Academy of Fine Arts.	(See New York.)	22	2	....	86							
American Colonization Society.	Indemnity for support of recaptured Africans.	31	1	Senate bill	1447	Claims	....	....	S. 4			
American Colonization Society.	Indemnity for support of recaptured Africans.	31	2	Rep. of committee	46	....	2	With't amend.	S. 4	Passed	Passed	App'd March 3, 1851
American Fur Company	Permission to import merchandise from Canada.	12	1	Petition	269	Com. and Manuf.						
Ames, David	Further compensation as superintendent, Springfield, Mass.	5	2	Petition	82	....	....	....	......	Referred to Secretary of War.		
Ames, David	Pension	21	2	Petition	73	Military Pensions.						
Ames, David A.	Pension	22	1	Petition	219	Rev. Pensions	426	Favorable	528	Passed	Passed with amendment.	
Ames, David A.	Pension	23	1	Petition	46	Invalid Pensions	Dec. 13, 1833	Pension bill	42	Passed	Passed with amendment.	App'd June 25, 1834
Ames, David	Increase of rations as artificer at Springfield armory.	5	2	Petition	82	....	....	....	......	Referred to Secretary of War.		
Ames, John	Renewal of patent for making paper.	23	1	Petition	569	Patents.						
Ames, John	Renewal of patent for making paper.	24	1	Petition	211	Judiciary.						
Ames, L.	(See assignees of Thomas Tupper)	22	2	....	142							
Ames, Richard	Arrears of pay and bounty land	30	1	Petition	644	Claims	656	Adverse	......	Laid on the table.		
Ames, Robert	Pension	9	2	House bill	608	Whole House	Feb. 28, 1807	Favorable	216	Passed	Passed	App'd March 3, 1807
Ames, Rufus	Payment of certificate barred by statute of limitations.	6	1	Petition	643	Claims	Mar. 31, 1800	Adverse	......	Claim rejected.		
Ames, Smith	Right of pre-emption	26	1	Petition	608	Public Lands.						
Ames, Spafford	Pension for revolutionary services	3	1	Rep. of Secretary War.	131	Select	May 26, 1794	Res. to refer to Sec. War.	R. 12	Passed	Passed	App'd June 9, 1794
Ames, Spafford	Pension for revolutionary services	3	2	Rep. of Secretary War.	337	Claims.						
Ames, Spafford	Pension for revolutionary services	9	1	Petition	277	Claims	Mar. 28, 1806	Indefinite	......	Leave to withdraw.		

List of private claims presented to the House of Representatives of the United States from the 1*st to the* 31*st Congress, inclusive*—Continued.

Names of claimants.	Nature or object of the claim.	Congress.	Session.	How brought before the House of Reps.	Page of journal.	To what committee of the House referred.	No. or date of the report.	Nature of the report.	No. of the bill.	How disposed of by the House of Reps.	How disposed of by the Senate.	Date of the act of Congress, and remarks.
Ames, Spafford	Pension for revolutionary services	9	2	Pension bill	608	Whole House	Feb. 28, 1807	With amend.	216	Passed	Passed	App'd March 3, 1807
Ammons, Joshua	Compensation for services as clerk in Adjutant General's office.	23	1	Petition	222	Military Affairs	Feb. 4, 1834	Adverse	.....	Laid on the table.		
"Amistad," schooner, owners of.	Indemnity	28	1	President's message.	299	Foreign Affairs	425	Favorable	328	Referred to Committee Whole.		
Amity Association	(See Iowa)	27	3		349							
Amory, Charles	Indemnity for French spoliations prior to 1800.	26	1	Memorial	182	Foreign Affairs	343	Favorable	319	Referred to Committee Whole House.		
Amory, Francis	Remission of duties on cargo of ship "Astrea."	9	1	Petition	230	Com. and Manuf.	Feb. 3, 1806	Adverse.				
Amory, Francis	Indemnity for French spoliations prior to 1800.	26	1	Memorial	182	Foreign Affairs	343	Favorable	319	Referred to Committee Whole House.		
Amory & Callender	Release from a judgment in favor of United States.	10	1	Petition	150	Com. and Manuf.						
Amory, Jonathan	(See Bordman & Pope, and others)	12	1		136							
Amory, Jonathan	(See William Gray, and others)	18	1		238							
Amory, Jonathan, jr.	(See sureties for George Scott)	15	1		30							
Amory, Nathaniel	(See assignees of Baron de Bastrop)	15	2		44							
Amory, Thomas C., representatives of.	(See sureties of George Scott)	15	1		30							
Amory, Thomas C., representatives of.	(See Nathaniel Goddard, & others)	16	1		27							
Amory, Thomas C. & Co.	(See William Gray, and others)	18	1		238							
Amsden, Benjamin	Pension for revolutionary services	22	1	Resolution	510	Rev. Pensions.						
Amsden, Benjamin	Pension for revolutionary services	23	1	Petition	308	Rev. Pensions.						
Amsden, Joel	Indemnity for destruction of property by the enemy.	21	1	Petition	318	Claims	Mar. 2, 1830	Adverse	.....	Laid on the table.		
Ansden, Silas	Pension	3	1	Rep. of Sec. War.	131	Select	May 26, 1794	Pension bill	62	Passed	Passed	App'd June 7, 1794
Anacostia Bridge Company	(See District of Columbia)	13	3		688							
Anders, John and wife	(See administrators of Jas. White.)	6	1		619							
Anderson, Abraham	(See Thomas Ringlang and others)	31	2		155							
Anderson, Alexander	Renewal of a patent	14	2	Petition	75	Select	.....	.....	.....	Discharged.		
Anderson, Alexander, and others, assignee of.	Payment of contract price for removing Indians.	30	1	Memorial	288	Indian Affairs.						
Anderson, Alexander, and others, assignee of.	Payment of contract price for removing Indians.	31	2	Memorial	165	Indian Affairs.						
				Senate bill	350	.....	.....	.....	S. 432			
Anderson, Andrew	Right of pre-emption as New Orleans Br. pilot.	28	1	Petition	77	Priv. Land Claims.	9	Favorable	35	Passed	Passed	App'd June 17, 1844
Anderson, Anne	(See representatives of William Anderson.)	23	2		68							
Anderson, Barker T	Compensation for horse, &c., lost in public service.	20	2	Petition	24	Claims.						
Anderson, Barker T	Compensation for horse, &c., lost in public service.	21	1	Resolution	78	Claims.						
Anderson, Barker T	Compensation for horse, &c., lost in public service.	21	2	Resolution	39	Claims.						
Anderson, Benjamin	(See Thomas Ringlang and others)	31	2		155							
Anderson, Charles	Exchange of a tract of land	19	1	Resolution	236	Priv. Land Claims.	80	Favorable	110	Passed	Passed	App'd May 16, 1826
Anderson, Charles C., mother of.	Pension for loss of son in Mexico.	31	1	Petition	270	Invalid Pensions.						

List of private claims presented to the House of Representatives of the United States from the 1st to the 31st Congress, inclusive—Continued.

Names of claimants.	Nature or object of the claim.	Congress.	Session.	How brought before the House of Reps.	Page of journal.	To what committee of the House referred.	No. or date of the report.	Nature of the report.	No. of the bill.	How disposed of by the House of Reps.	How disposed of by the Senate.	Date of the act of Congress, and remarks.
Anderson, Charles E	Additional compensation for diplomatic services.	25	2	Memorial	407	Foreign Affairs				Dis.; laid on table.		
Anderson, Elbert	Credits in settlement of accounts as contractor.	18	2	Petition	59	Claims.						
Anderson, Elbert	Credits in settlement of accounts as contractor.	19	1	Petition	44	Claims	13	Adverse		Laid on table.		
Anderson, Elbert	Credits in settlement of accounts as contractor.	20	1	Resolution	90	Claims	Mar. 19, 1828	Adverse		Laid on table.		
Anderson, Elbert, administrator of.	Equitable settlement of the accounts of deceased.	21	2	Petition	45	Claims	57	Adverse		Laid on table.		
Anderson, Elbert, administrator of.	Equitable settlement of the accounts of deceased.	22	1	Petition	133	Claims	465	Favorable	562	Ref. to Com. Whole.		
Anderson, Elbert, administrator of.	Equitable settlement of the accounts of deceased.	23	1	Petition	33	Claims	27	Favorable	27	Passed	Passed with amendment.	App'd June 18, 1834
Anderson, Elbert, administrator of.	Extra allowance for whiskey	25	3	Petition	461	Claims.						
Anderson, Elbert, representatives of.	Indemnity for loss on contracts	26	1	Petition	167	Claims	692	Adverse		Laid on table.		
Anderson, Elbert, representatives of.	Indemnity for loss on contracts	30	1	Petition	618	Claims.						
Anderson, Enoch, widow of	Pension	18	2	Petition	107	Pens. & Rev. Cl'ms.				Dis.; leave to withd'w.		
Anderson, Ezekiel, widow of.	Pension for revolutionary services of deceased.	25	2	Petition	913	Rev. Pensions				Dis.; laid on table.		
Anderson, Ezekiel, widow of.	Pension for revolutionary services of deceased.	26	1	Petition	170	Rev. Pensions.						
Anderson, George	Reimbursement of duties paid on certain merchandise.	20	2	Petition	64	Ways and Means	Jan. 19, 1829	Favorable	378	Ref. to Com. Whole.		
Anderson, George	Reimbursement of duties paid on certain merchandise.	21	1	Petition	50	Ways and Means	Jan. 4, 1830	Favorabte	67	Passed	Passed	App'd April 7, 1830
Anderson, George	Indemnity for depredation of Seminole Indians.	24	2	Documents	308	Claims.						
Anderson, George	Indemnity for depredation of Seminole Indians.	25	2	Petition	93	Claims	896	Adverse		Laid on table.		
Anderson, George	Indemnity for depredation of Seminole Indians.	26	1	Petition	624	Claims.						
Anderson, Mrs. George	Compensation for a negro killed at Durlawton.	25	2	Documents	541	Claims.						
Anderson, Hugh A	Exchange of an entry of land	19	1	Petition	89	Public Lands.						
Anderson, Isaac	Pension for revolutionary services.	21	1	Resolution	328	Military Pensions	April 13, 1830	Adverse		Laid on table.		
Anderson, Isaac	Pension for revolutionary services.	21	2	Petition	127	Military Pensions.						
Anderson, Isaac	Pension for revolutionary services.	23	2	Petition	289	Invalid Pensions.						
Anderson, Jacob	Indemnity for property lost in the public service.	24	2	Petition	394	Claims.						
Anderson, Jacob	Indemnity for property lost in the public service.	27	2	Petition	613	Claims	691	Adverse		Laid on table.		
Anderson, James	Reimbursement of advances on public account.	12	1	Petition	11	Claims	Jan. 3, 1812	Favorable		Leave to withdraw.		
Anderson, James	Reimbursement of advances on public account.	12	2	Petition	550	Claims	Dec. 4, 1812	Favorable	206			
Anderson, James	Reimbursement of advances on public account.	13	2	Petition	198	Claims	Jan. 19, 1814	Adverse		Leave to withdraw.		
Anderson, James	Indemnity for depredations of Seminole Indians.	24	2	Documents	308	Claims.						

List of private claims presented to the House of Representatives of the United States from the 1st to the 31st Congress, inclusive—Continued.

Names of claimants.	Nature or object of the claim.	Congress.	Session.	How brought before the House of Reps.	Page of journal.	To what committee of the House referred.	No. or date of the report.	Nature of the report.	No. of the bill.	How disposed of by the House of Reps.	How disposed of by the Senate.	Date of the act of Congress, and remarks.
Anderson, James	Indemnity for depredations of Seminole Indians.	25	2	Petition	93	Claims	896	Adverse		Laid on table.		
Anderson, James	Indemnity for depredations of Seminole Indians.	26	1	Petition	624	Claims.						
Anderson, James, (Iowa)	Permission to purchase a sixteenth section.	25	3	Petition	564	Public Lands.						
Anderson, James, (Iowa)	Permission to purchase a sixteenth section.	26	1	Petition	177	Public Lands.						
				Petition (2)	364	Public Lands	318	Favorable	283	Referred to Committee Whole House.		
Anderson, James, (Iowa)	Permission to purchase a sixteenth section.	28	1	Petition	631	Public Lands	348	Favorable	249	Passed	Passed	App'd June 17, 1844
Anderson, James, administrator of.	Permission to perfect entry of sixteenth section.	29	1	Petition	117	Public Lands	165	Favorable	173	Passed	Passed	App'd Aug. 8, 1846
Anderson, James C	Permission to purchase certain lands.	23	2	Petition	201	Public Lands.						
Anderson, James W	Indemnity for property confiscated in Canada.	17	1	Petition	306	Claims	Mar. 27, 1822	Adverse		Laid on table.		
Anderson, James W	Compensation for horse lost in public service.	25	2	Documents	396	Claims				Discharged; laid on table.		
Anderson, James W	Compensation for horse lost in public service.	25	3	Petition	207	Claims.						
Anderson, James W	Compensation for horse lost in public service.	26	1	Petition	167	Claims	428	Adverse		Laid on table.		
Anderson, Jane M	(See heirs of William Lewis)	27	2		62		37					
Anderson, Jasper	(See son of Richard Anderson)	13	1		21							
Anderson, John, assignee of.	Confirmation of title to land in Missouri.	15	2	Petition	67	Priv. Land Claims.						
Anderson, John, assignee of.	Confirmation of title to land in Missouri.	17	1	Petition	53	Priv. Land Claims				Committee discharged; laid on table.		
Anderson, John, assignee of.	Confirmation of title to land in Missouri.	18	1	Petition	53	Priv. Land Claims.						
Anderson, John, representatives of.	Balance due deceased withheld by Second Auditor.	26	2	Petition	81	Claims	31	Adverse		Laid on table.		
Anderson, John, representatives of.	Balance due deceased withheld by Second Auditor.	27	2	Petition	155	Claims	167	Adverse		Laid on table.		
Anderson, John	Indemnity for property destroyed by the enemy in late war.	15	1	Petition	48	Claims	24	Favorable	22	Passed	Postponed.	
Anderson, John	Indemnity for property destroyed by the enemy in late war.	15	2	Senate bill	325	Whole House			S. 72			
Anderson, John	Indemnity for property destroyed by the enemy in late war.	17	1	Resolution	78	Claims	Feb. 12, 1822	Favorable	85	Passed	Passed	App'd April 17, 1822
Anderson, John	Indemnity for property destroyed by the enemy in late war.	19	1	Petition	67	Claims	Jan. 18, 1826	Adverse		Laid on table.		
Anderson, John	Indemnity for property destroyed by the enemy in late war.	19	2	Petition	217	Claims.						
Anderson, John	Indemnity for property destroyed by the enemy in late war.	20	1	Petition	47	Claims	Jan. 25, 1828	Adverse		Laid on table.		
Anderson, John	Indemnity for property destroyed by the enemy in late war.	22	1	Petition	133	Claims	492	Adverse.				
Anderson, John	Indemnity for property destroyed by the enemy in late war.	22	2	Petition	33	Claims	Dec. 21, 1832	Adverse		Laid on table.		
Anderson, John	Indemnity for property destroyed by the enemy in late war.	27	2	Petition	613	Claims	692	Adverse		Laid on table.		

List of private claims presented to the House of Representatives of the United States from the 1st to the 31st Congress, inclusive—Continued.

Names of claimants.	Nature or object of the claim.	Congress.	Session.	How brought before the House of Reps.	Page of journal.	To what committee of the House referred.	No. or date of the report.	Nature of the report.	No. of the bill.	How disposed of by the House of Reps.	How disposed of by the Senate.	Date of the act of Congress, and remarks.
Anderson, John	Indemnity for property destroyed by the enemy in late war.	27	3	Petition	73	Claims.						
Anderson, John, administrator of.	Indemnity for property destroyed by the enemy in late war.	29	1	Petition	262	Claims	277	Adverse	......	Laid on table.		
Anderson, John, and others.	Indemnity for property destroyed in late war.	15	1	Report of commissioner claims.	195	Claims.						
Anderson, John, and others.	Indemnity for property destroyed in late war.	16	1	Resolution	85	Claims.						
Anderson, John, and others.	Indemnity for property destroyed in late war.	17	1	Resolution	78	Claims	Jan. 17, 1822	Adverse	......	Referred to Committee Whole House.		
Anderson, John, and others.	Indemnity for property destroyed in late war.	17	2	Resolution	83	Whole House.						
Anderson, John, (N. Y.)	Pension	19	1	Petition	128	Military Pensions	164	Adverse.				
Anderson, John, (N. Y.)	Pension	19	2	Petition	132	Military Pensions.						
Anderson, John, (N. Y.)	Pension	28	1	Petition	272	Rev. Pensions.						
Anderson, John	(See assignee of John B. Jerome.)	22	1	Petition	294	....	....	....	540			
Anderson, John	(See Wm. H. Bedford, agent, &c.)	28	1	....	262							
Anderson, John, (Ind.)	Bounty land for military services.	28	1	Petition	326	Public Lands.						
Anderson, John	(See assignee of Geo. McDougall).	22	1	....	294	....	....	....	540			
Anderson, John	(See Archibald B. Lord and others.)	15	2	....	178							
Anderson, John, and others.	Confirmation of title to land in Michigan.	22	1	Petition	294	Public Lands.						
Anderson, John, (Mo.)	Reimbursement of erroneous payment for rents.	28	2	Petition	164	Claims.						
Anderson, John, (Mo.)	Reimbursement of erroneous payment for rents.	29	1	House bill	190	Claims	27	Favorable	33	Rejected.		
Anderson, John, (Mo.)	Reimbursement of erroneous payment for rents.	30	1	Petition	154	Claims	39	Favorable	36	Passed	Passed	App'd Aug. 5, 1848
Anderson, John	Indemnity for a recovery against him for his official acts.	15	1	House bill	91	Whole House	Dec. 31, 1817	With't amend.	19	Passed	Postponed.	
Anderson, John	(See Anderson & Moody)	24	2	....	273							
Anderson, John, widow of.	Pension for revolutionary services of deceased.	27	2	Petition	238	Rev. Pensions	784	Adverse	......	Laid on table.		
Anderson, John	(See Ira Harris and others)	17	2	....	209							
Anderson, John H	(See attorney of Wm. Harris and others.)	20	1	....	51	....	77	....	......	....	....	(See H. P. Cathell, attorney.)
Anderson, John, *et al*	(See Anderson & Moody)	26	1	....	182	....	343	....	319			
Anderson, John P	Indemnity for French spoliations prior to 1800.	29	2	Memorial	113	Foreign Affairs.						
Anderson, John R	Release of a judgment in favor of United States.	24	1	Petition	537	Judiciary	....	....	......	Discharged; laid on table.		
Anderson, Joseph	Compensation for services and supplies, revolutionary war.	1	3	Petition	349							
				Rep. of Secretary War.	378	....	....	....	......	Laid on table.		
Anderson, Joseph	Pension for revolutionary services.	15	2	Petition	55	Rev. Pensions	Jan. 5, 1819	Adverse	......	Laid on table	....	Leave to withdraw.
Anderson, Joseph	Pension for revolutionary services.	16	1	Petition	27	Rev. Pensions.						
Anderson, Joseph	Pension for disability in Indian wars.	24	2	Petition	120	Invalid Pensions	Jan. 19, 1837	Adverse	......	Laid on table.		
Anderson, Joseph, assignee	Confirmation of title to land in Alabama.	24	2	Petition	83	Priv. Land Claims.	....	....	......	Discharged; laid on table.		
Anderson, Rev. Joseph	Credit for forfeited land payment.	14	1	Senate bill	122	Public Lands	Jan. 9, 1816	With't amend.	......	Passed	Passed	App'd Jan. 22, 1816

List of *private claims presented to the House of Representatives of the United States from the* 1st *to the* 31st *Congress, inclusive*—Continued.

Names of claimants.	Nature or object of the claim.	Congress.	Session.	How brought before the House of Reps.	Page of journal.	To what committee of the House referred.	No. or date of the report.	Nature of the report.	No. of the bill.	How disposed of by the House of Reps.	How disposed of by the Senate.	Date of the act of Congress, and remarks.
Anderson, Josiah, widow of	Reimbursement of advances on public account.	19	1	Petition	251	Rev. Claims	Mar. 22, 1826	Adverse		Laid on table		
Anderson, Josiah, executor of.	Credit for revolutionary claims of deceased.	24	2	Petition	95	Rev. Claims.						
Anderson, Josiah, representative of.	Credit for revolutionary claims of deceased.	25	2	Petition	111	Rev. Claims	619	Adverse		Laid on table.		
Anderson, J. D	(See Exploring Expedition)	27	3		149		270		818			
Anderson, Lewis	Compensation for revolutionary services and supplies.	2	1	Petition	455					Referred to Secretary War.		
Anderson, Lewis	Compensation for revolutionary services.	2	2	Petition	692					Referred to Secretary War.		
Anderson, Lewis	Compensation for a horse taken by Indians.	21	1	Petition	69	Claims.						
Anderson, Lewis	Compensation for a horse taken by Indians.	21	2	Petition	74	Claims	8	Favorable	506	Referred to Committee Whole.		
Anderson, Lewis	Compensation for a horse taken by Indians.	22	1	Petition	26	Claims	Dec. 19, 1831	Favorable	31	Passed	Passed	App'd Jan. 13, 1832
Anderson, Lieut. Colonel.	Balance due him	23	1	Appropriat'n bill.	146	Whole House	Jan. 9, 1834	Amended	110	Passed	Passed	App'd Jan. 24, 1834
Anderson & Moody, representative of.	Indemnity for French spoliations prior to 1800.	24	2	Petition	273	Foreign Affairs.						
Anderson & Moody, representative of.	Indemnity for French spoliations prior to 1800.	26	1	Memorial	182	Foreign Affairs	343	Favorable	319	Referred to Committee Whole House.		
Anderson, Peter	Compensation for military services.	22	1	Petition	29	Rev. Claims	Jan. 10, 1832	Adverse		Laid on table.		
Anderson, Richard, son of.	Bounty land for revolutionary services.	13	1	Petition	21	Public Lands.						
Anderson, Richard, son of.	Bounty land for revolutionary services.	13	2	Petition	222	Select	90	Recom. general provision.		Referred to Committee Whole.		
Anderson, Richard, heirs of.	Arrears of pension	24	1	Senate bill	811	Invalid Pensions	June 2, 1836	With't amend.	S. 197	Passed	Passed	App'd June 15, 1836
Anderson, Richard, agent of.	New patent for bounty land	24	1	Memorial	409	Public Lands				Discharged; laid on table.		
Anderson, Richard, agent of.	New patent for bounty land	24	2	Documents	390	Public Lands.						
Anderson, Robert	Indemnity for land lost by Choctaw treaty.	24	1	Petition	57	Public Lands	208	Favorable	208	Referred to Committee Whole.		
Anderson, Robert	(See sureties of Peyton A. Southall.)	27	2		807		928		546			
Anderson, Robert	(See administrator of Alexander Macauley.)	26	1		182		343		319			
Anderson, Robert M., and others.	Compensation for services as attorneys.	24	1	Resolution	676	Indian Affairs.						
Anderson, Captain R	Arrearages of pay for services in Black Hawk war.	28	1	Appropriat'n bill.								Statutes at Large, vol. 5, p. 695.
Anderson, Samuel	(See Samuel Sanderson)	24	2		199							
Anderson, Samuel B	(See Wm. and Sam'l B. Anderson.)	25	2		425							
Anderson, Samuel P	Compensation for slave killed in Florida war.	24	2	Petition	144	Claims	Feb. 22, 1837	Adverse		Laid on table.		
Anderson, Samuel S	Pension for disability in naval service.	29	1	Memorial	91	Naval Affairs	207	Favorable	201	Referred to Committee Whole.		
Anderson, Samuel S	Pension for disability in naval service.	30	1	Petition	115	Naval Affairs	364	Favorable	R. 20			
Anderson, Samuel S	Pension for disability in naval service.	30	2	Rep. Committee Whole.	143			With't amend.	R. 20	Passed.		

List of private claims presented to the House of Representatives of the United States from the 1st to the 31st Congress, inclusive—Continued.

Names of claimants.	Nature or object of the claim.	Congress.	Session.	How brought before the House of Reps.	Page of journal.	To what committee of the House referred.	No. or date of the report.	Nature of the report.	No. of the bill.	How disposed of by the House of Reps.	How disposed of by the Senate.	Date of the act of Congress, and remarks.
Anderson, Samuel T.....	Equitable adjustment of his accounts.	16	1	Petition	485	Claims.						
Anderson, Samuel T.....	Equitable adjustment of his accounts.	16	2	Petition	173	Claims	74	Favorable	223	Referred to Committee Whole.		
Anderson, Samuel T.....	Equitable adjustment of his accounts.	23	1	Petition	66	Naval Affairs.						
Anderson, Samuel T.....	Equitable adjustment of his accounts.	24	1	Memorial	94	Ways and Means.						
Anderson, Samuel T.....	Indemnity for loss on treasury notes.	21	1	Petition	199	Ways and Means..	Feb. 1, 1830	Adverse	......	Laid on table.		
Anderson, Samuel T.....	Indemnity for loss on treasury notes.	24	1	Petition	93	Claims.						
Anderson, Samuel T.....	Indemnity for loss on treasury notes.	24	2	Petition	81	Claims	....	....	......	Discharged; laid on table.		
Anderson, Samuel T.....	Compensation for services, war of 1812.	25	2	Petition	172	Ways and Means..	987	Favorable	848	Referred to Committee Whole.		
Anderson, Samuel T.....	Compensation for services, war of 1812.	25	3	House bill	432	Whole House.....	....	....	848			
Anderson, Samuel T.....	Compensation for services, war of 1812.	26	1	Petition	178	Claims.						
Anderson, Samuel T.....	Compensation for services, war of 1812.	26	2	Petition	80	Claims	27	Adverse	......	Laid on table.		
Anderson, Samuel T.....	Compensation for services, war of 1812.	27	2	Petition	228	Military Affairs.						
Anderson, Samuel T.....	Compensation for services, war of 1812.	27	3	Petition	73	Claims	142	Adverse	......	Laid on table.		
Anderson, Samuel T.....	Compensation for services, war of 1812.	28	1	Petition	145	Claims.						
Anderson, Samuel T.....	Compensation for services, war of 1812.	31	1	Petition	326	Naval Affairs.....	266	Adverse	......	Laid on table.		
Anderson, Sarah P.......	Compensation for a slave killed by Indians.	25	2	Petition	120	Claims.						
Anderson, Sarah P.......	Compensation for a slave killed by Indians.	25	3	Petition	87	Claims.						
Anderson, Sarah P.......	Compensation for a slave killed by Indians.	26	2	Petition	135	Claims.						
Anderson, Sarah P.......	Compensation for a slave killed by Indians.	29	1	Petition	630	Claims.						
Anderson, Susanna......	Indemnity for depredations of Caddo Indians.	20	1	Petition	226	Indian Affairs.						
Anderson, Thomas	Pension	12	1	Petition	89	Claims.						
Anderson, Thomas	Reimbursement of office rent, revolutionary war.	12	2	Petition	617	Claims.						
Anderson, Thomas	Reimbursement of office rent, revolutionary war.	13	1	Petition	49	Claims.						
Anderson, Thomas	Reimbursement of office rent, revolutionary war.	13	2	Petition	173	Pensions.						
Anderson, Thomas B....	Indemnity for French spoliations prior to 1800.	26	1	Memorial	182	Foreign Affairs....	343	Favorable	319	Referred to Committee Whole.		
Anderson, Thomas D....	Equitable adjustment of his accounts.	24	1	Petition	202	Foreign Affairs....	....	....	......	Discharged; laid on table.		
Anderson, Thomas O.....	(See widow of Stephen Decatur and others.)	20	1	....	295							

List of private claims presented to the House of Representatives of the United States from the 1st to the 31st Congress, inclusive—Continued.

Names of claimants.	Nature or object of the claim.	Congress.	Session.	How brought before the House of Reps.	Page of journal.	To what committee of the House referred.	No. or date of the report.	Nature of the report.	No. of the bill.	How disposed of by the House of Reps.	How disposed of by the Senate.	Date of the act of Congress, and remarks.
Anderson, Timothy	(See Ira Harris and others)	17	2		209							
Anderson, Walter G., widow of.	Indemnity for loss of husband in public service.	17	2	Petition	251	Naval Affairs				Discharged; leave to withdraw.		
Anderson, Wm. E., widow of.	Continuation of the pension of deceased.	25	2	Petition	111	Rev. Pensions				Discharged; leave to withdraw.		
Anderson, William S.	Compensation for horse lost in public service.	22	1	Petition	63	Claims	360	Favorable	459	Referred to Committee Whole House.		
Anderson, William S.	Compensation for horse lost in public service.	23	1	Petition	34	Claims	7	Favorable	7	Passed	Passed	App'd May 11, 1834
Anderson, Wm. S., widow of.	Pension for naval services of deceased.	25	2	Petition	576	Naval Affairs.						
Anderson, Wm. S., widow of.	Pension for naval services of deceased.	25	3	Petition	368	Naval Affairs.						
Anderson, Wm. S., widow of.	Pension for naval services of deceased.	26	1	Petition	179	Naval Affairs.						
Anderson, William, representatives of.	Indemnity for depredations of Cherokee Indians.	23	2	Petition	68	Claims.						
Anderson, William, representatives of.	Indemnity for depredations of Cherokee Indians.	24	1	Petition	95	Indian Affairs	252	Favorable	263	Referred to Committee Whole House.		
Anderson, William, representatives of.	Indemnity for depredations of Cherokee Indians.	24	2	House bill	176	Indian Affairs			263	Rejected.		
Anderson, William, representatives of.	Indemnity for depredations of Cherokee Indians.	25	2	Resolution	77	Indian Affairs.						
Anderson, William, representatives of.	Indemnity for depredations of Cherokee Indians.	25	3	Resolution	160	Indian Affairs	284	Favorable	1147	Referred to Committee Whole.		
Anderson, William	Invalid pension	3	1	Rep. of Secretary of war.	131	Select	May 26, 1794	Res. to refer to Sec'y War.	J. R. 12	Passed	Passed	App'd June 9, 1794
Anderson, Wm. and S. P.	Indemnity for money lost in the mail.	25	2	Petition	425	P. O. & P. Roads.	628	Adverse		Laid on table.		
Anderson, Wm. and S. P.	Indemnity for money lost in the mail.	27	2	Petition	70	P. O. & P. Roads.	190	Adverse		Laid on table.		
Anderson, William P.	Confirmation of title to land in Missouri.	16	1	Petition	396	Priv. Land Claims.						
Anderson, William, heirs of.	Indemnity for Indian depredations.	26	1	Petition	180	Claims.						
Anderson, William	Pension for revolutionary services.	12	1	Petition	188	Claims	June 12, 1812	Adverse		Laid on table		Leave to withdraw.
Anderson, William	Pension for revolutionary services.	18	1	Petition	65	Pens. & Rev. Cl'ms.	Jan. 2, 1824	Adverse		Laid on table		(See Report May 7, 1844.)
Anderson, William	Pension for revolutionary services.	20	1	Petition	226	Claims	Feb. 1, 1828	Adverse		Laid on table.		
Anderson, William	Pension for revolutionary services.	21	1	Petition	59	Claims	Dec. 28, 1829	Adverse		Laid on table.		
Anderton, John	(See John A. Barnes.)	22	1		562							
Andrew, Antonia	(See F. M. Arredondo and others.)	19	1		252							
Andrews, Abner	Increase of pension	10	2	Pension bill	499	Whole House	Feb. 20, 1809	With amend.	158	Passed	Passed with amendment.	App'd Mar. 3, 1809
Andrews, Ammi	Pensions for revolutionary services.	17	1	Petition	98	Rev. Pensions				Discharged; leave to withdraw.		
Andrews, Ammi	Pension for revolutionary services.	24	1	Petition	456	Invalid Pensions				Discharged; laid on table.		
Andrews, Amos	Pension	20	2	Petition	99	Military Pensions	Feb. 13, 1829	Pension bill	440	Passed.		
Andrews, Amos	Pension	21	1	Petition	49	Military Pensions	Jan. 5, 1830	Favorable	72	Passed	Passed	App'd May 20, 1830
Andrews, Andrew	Pension	21	1	Petition	35	Military Pensions				Discharged; laid on table.		
Andrews, Andrew	Pension	21	2	Petition	127	Military Pensions.						

List of private claims presented to the House of Representatives of the United States from the 1st to the 31st Congress, inclusive—Continued.

Names of claimants.	Nature or object of the claim.	Congress.	Session.	How brought before the House of Reps.	Page of journal.	To what committee of the House referred.	No. or date of the report.	Nature of the report.	No. of the bill.	How disposed of by the House of Reps.	How disposed of by the Senate.	Date of the act of Congress, and remarks.
Andrews, Asa	Credit for fishing bounties paid by him.	10	2	Memorial	414	Com. and Manuf	Feb. 10, 1809	Favorable	162	Referred to Committee Whole.		
Andrews, Asa	Credit for fishing bounties paid by him.	11	1	Memorial	17	Com. and Manuf						
Andrews, Asa	Compensation for services as collector at Ipswich.	24	1	Petition	533	Commerce.						
Andrews, Asa	Payment of sum recovered in suit with United States.	28	1	Senate bill	1097	Judiciary	....	....	S. 142			
Andrews, Asa	Payment of sum recovered in suit with United States.	28	2	Senate bill	220	Judiciary	105	Adverse	S. 37	Referred to Committee Whole.		
Andrews, Caleb	Drawback on silk re-exported	22	2	Petition	63	Commerce.						
Andrews, ———, Capt.	(See Wm. H. Bedford, agent, &c.)	28	1	....	262							
Andrews, Clement	Pension	22	2	Petition	82	Invalid Pensions.						
Andrews, Clement	Pension	23	2	Petition	198	Invalid Pensions.						
Andrews, Colin	Pension	31	1	Petition	623	Invalid Pensions	479	Favorable	376	Referred to Committee Whole.		
Andrews, Colin	Pension	31	2	House bill	418	....	....	....	376	Passed.		
Andrews, Elisha, widow of.	Pension for disability in naval service.	25	3	Petition	225	Naval Affairs.						
Andrews, Elisha, widow of.	Pension for disability in naval service.	26	1	Petition	179	Naval Affairs.						
Andrews, Elisha, widow of.	Pension for disability in naval service.	26	2	Petition	212	Naval Affairs.						
Andrews, Elisha, widow of.	Pension for disability in naval service.	27	2	Petition	85	Naval Affairs	597	Adverse	......	Leave to withdraw.		
Andrews, Elizabeth	(See Sam'l W. and Eliza Andrews.)	11	3	Petition	494	Claims.						
Andrews, Henry	Pension	21	2	Petition	188	Military Pensions.						
				Petition (2)	208	Military Pensions.						
Andrews, Henry W	Indemnity for depredations of Indians in Florida.	30	1	Petition	235	Claims	244	Adverse	......	Laid on lable.		
Andrews, Israel	(See widow of John Andrews.)	29	1	....	510							
Andrews, James	Pension	15	1	Resolution	40	Pens. & Rev. Cl'ms.						
Andrews, James	Pension	15	2	Resolution	112	Pens. & Rev. Cl'ms.	Feb. 5, 1819	Pension bill	308	Postponed.		
Andrews, James	Pension	16	1	Petition	54							
				Rep. of Secretary War.	350	....	....	....	......	Laid on table.		
Andrews, James	(See Wyatt, Singleton, and others.)	22	1	....	133							
Andrews, Dr. James H	Compensation for public services in Louisiana.	26	1	Documents.	940	Claims.						
Andrews, Dr. James H	Compensation for public services in Louisiana.	26	2	Petition	182	Claims.						
Andrews, Dr. James H	Compensation for public services in Louisiana.	27	2	Petition	155	Claims	322	Adverse	......	Leave to withdraw.		
Andrews, John	Bounty land	18	1	Petition	158	Military Affairs.						
Andrews, John	Bounty land	18	2	Petition	37	Claims	Feb. 22, 1825	Adverse	......	Leave to withdraw.		
Andrews, John	Pension for revolutionary services.	22	1	Petition	77	Rev. Pensions.						
Andrews, John, widow of.	Continuation of pension	27	2	Petition	239	Rev. Pensions	784	Adverse	......	Laid on table.		
Andrews, John, widow of.	Pension for revolutionary services of deceased.	29	1	Petition	510	Rev. Pensions.						
Andrews, John, widow of.	Pension for revolutionary services of deceased.	29	2	Petiton	150	Rev. Pensions	18	Adverse	......	Laid on table.		
Andrews, John H	(See Samuel Page, heirs of.)	26	1	Memorial	182	Foreign Affairs	343	Favorable	319	Referred to Committee Whole House.		

List of private claims presented to the House of Representatives of the United States from the 1st to the 31st Congress, inclusive—Continued.

Names of claimants.	Nature or object of the claim.	Congress.	Session.	How brought before the House of Reps.	Page of journal.	To what committee of the House referred.	No. or date of the report.	Nature of the report.	No. of the bill.	How disposed of by the House of Reps.	How disposed of by the Senate.	Date of the act of Congress, and remarks.
Andrews John P	Indemnity for French spoliations prior to 1800.	29	2	Memorial	113	Foreign Affairs.						
Andrews, Mary	Remission of tax on distillery	14	1	Petition	34	Ways and Means				Laid on table.		
Andrews, Mary	(See Oliver Norton, heirs of)	29	2		54							
Andrews, Phineas	Compensation for services in United States army.	16	1	Petition	129	Claims	Jan. 28, 1820	Adverse		Claim rejected		Leave to withdraw.
Andrews, P	Compensation for militia services.	14	1	Petition	33	Claims				Discharged; referred to Sec. War.		
Andrews, Sally	(See Haym M. Solomon, heirs of.)	30	1		899							
Andrews, Samuel	Pension for revolutionary services.	3	1	Rep. of Secretary War.	131	Select	May 26, 1794	Res. to refer to Sec. War.	R. 12	Passed	Passed	App'd June 9, 1794
Andrews, Samuel	Pension	16	1	Petition	235	Rev. Pensions.						
Andrews, Sam. W, and E.	Payment of a loan office certificate.	11	3	Petition	494	Claims.						
Andrews, Syrenus	Arrears of pension	31	1	Petition	542	Invalid Pensions.						
Andrews, Thomas	Pension	21	2	Petition	43	Military Pensions.						
Andrews, William	To be restored to pension roll	24	2	Resolution	76	Rev. Pensions.						
				Documents	97	Rev. Pensions				Discharged; laid on the table.		
Andrews, William	To be restored to pension roll	25	2	Resolution	108	Rev. Pensions	539	Fevorable	532	Passed.		
Andrews, William	To be restored to pension roll	25	3	Resolution	88	Rev. Pensions	Jan. 9, 1839	Favorable	994	Passed.		
Andrews, William	To be restored to pension roll	26	1	Resolution	170	Rev. Pensions	163	Favorable	173	Passed	Passed	App'd July 20, 1840
Andross, John P	Indemnity for property plundered by the enemy.	23	1	Petition	34	Claims	Dec. 19, 1833	Adverse		Laid on table.		
Andross, Theodore (See Theodore Andrus.)	Pension for revolutionary services.	3	1	Petition	106					Referred to Secretary of War.		
Andrus, Abraham H.	Increase of compensation as clerk in district court, Louisiana.	23	1	Petition	567	Judiciary.						
Andrus, Clement	Pension	3	1	Rep. of Secretary War.	131	Select	May 26, 1794	Res. to refer to Sec. War.	R. 12	Passed	Passed	App'd June 9, 1794
Andrus, Clement	Pension	24	1	Petition	507	Invalid Pensions	July 1, 1836	Adverse		Laid on table.		
Andrus, Henry	Pension for revolutionary services of deceased father.	26	2	Petition	507	Rev. Pensions	209	Adverse		Laid on table.		
Andrus, Samuel, jr.	Compensation for revolutionary services.	2	1	Petition	491					Referred to Secretary of War.		
Andrus, Samuel	Pension for revolutionary services.	3	2	Rep. of Secretary War.	337	Claims	Feb. 28, 1795	Pension bill	130	Passed	Postponed.	
Andrus, Samuel	Pension for revolutionary services.	4	1	Resolution	445	Claims	Mar. 4, 1796	Pension bill	156	Passed	Passed with amendment.	App'd April 20, 1796
Andrus, Samuel	Pension for revolutionary services.	10	2	Pension bill	499	Whole House	Feb. 20, 1809	Pension bill	158	Passed	Passed with amendment.	App'd March 3, 1809
Andrus, Theodore	Pension for revolutionary services.	3	1	Rep. of Secretary War.	131	Select	May 26, 1794	Res. to refer to Sec. War.	R. 12	Passed	Passed	App'd June 9, 1794
Andrus, Theodore	Pension for revolutionary services.	4	1	Resolution	445	Claims	Mar. 4, 1796	Pension bill	156	Passed	Passed	App'd April 20, 1796
Angel, Matthias	Pension	25	3	Petition	129	Invalid Pensions.						
Angel, Matthias	Pension	26	1	Petition	160	Invalid Pensions.						
Angel, Sarah	(See heirs of Benjamin King)	24	1		1055							
Angell, Zaddock	(See Zaddock Ingell)	22	1		330							
Angle, David	Compensation for arms furnished on public account.	25	3	Petition	462	Claims.						
Angle, David	Compensation for arms furnished on public account.	26	1	Petition	306	Claims.						
Anglea, William	Pension for revolutionary services.	25	2	Petition	75	Invalid Pensions.						

List of private claims presented to the House of Representatives of the United States from the 1st to the 31st Congress, inclusive—Continued.

Names of claimants.	Nature or object of the claim.	Congress.	Session.	How brought before the House of Reps.	Page of journal.	To what committee of the House referred.	No. or date of the report.	Nature of the report.	No. of the bill.	How disposed of by the House of Reps.	How disposed of by the Senate.	Date of the act of Congress, and remarks.
Anglea, William	Pension for revolutionary services.	25	3	Petition	87	Rev. Pensions				Discharged; laid on the table.		
Anglea, William	Pension for revolutionary services.	26	1	Petition	170	Rev. Pensions				Discharged; laid on the table.		
Anglea, William	Pension for revolutionary services.	26	2	Petition	106	Rev. Pensions				Laid on table.		
Anglea, William	Pension for revolutionary services.	27	2	Petition	97	Rev. Pensions				Laid on table.		
Anglea, William	Pension for revolutionary services.	27	3	Petition	43	Rev. Pensions	295	Adverse		Laid on table.		
Anglea, William	Pension for revolutionary services.	29	1	Petition	149	Rev. Pensions	292	Adverse		Laid on table.		
Angleton, Sarah	(See widow of John Robinson)	26	1		950							
Angus, Samuel, widow of.	Naval pension	27	2	Memorial	224	Commerce.						
Angus, Samuel, widow of.	Naval pension	27	3	Petition	107	Naval Affairs	37	Favorable	664	Passed	Indef. postp'd.	
Angus, Samuel, widow of.	Naval pension	28	1	Petition	217	Naval Affairs.						
Angus, Samuel, widow of.	Naval pension	29	1	Petition	487	Naval Affairs	836	Favorable	553	Referred to Committee Whole.		
Angus, Samuel, widow of.	Naval pension	30	1	Petition	99	Naval Affairs	74	Favorable	59	Passed	Passed (2d session.)	App'd Jan. 9, 1849
Anmar, Thomas, heirs of.	(See Thomas Armor, heirs of)	29	1		750							
"Ann," Boat	(See Jonah Morse)	27	3		274		275		821			
Annin, Samuel	Compensation as paymaster	14	1	Petition	193	Claims	Feb. 19, 1816	Adverse		Laid on table		Leave to withdraw.
Annis, Phineas, heir of.	Pension for revolutionary services	30	1	Petition	606	Rev. Pensions	638	Adverse		Laid on table.		
Ansart, Lewis, widow of.	Compensation for revolutionary services as engineer.	8	2	Petition	151	Claims.						
Ansart, Lewis, widow of.	Compensation for revolutionary services as engineer.	9	1	Petition	314	Claims	Mar. 17, 1806	Adverse		Leave to withdraw.		
Ansart, Lewis, widow of.	Compensation for revolutionary services as engineer.	25	2	Petition	664	Rev. Pensions.						
Ansart, Lewis, widow of.	Compensation for revolutionary services as engineer.	26	1	Petition	282	Rev. Pensions	490	Adverse		Laid on table.		
Ansman, Abraham	Pension	28	2	Petition	103	Invalid Pensions.						
Ansman, Abraham	(See Abrham Ausman)	29	1		93							
Anspach, Peter	(See T. Pickering)	1	2		254							
Anspach, Peter	Payment of revolutionary certificate.	4	1	Rep. of Secretary Treasury.	388	Claims	74	Adverse		Laid on table.		
Anspach, Philip	Arrears of pension	25	2	Petition	400	Invalid Pensions				Discharged; laid on the table.		
Anspach, Philip	Arrears of pension	26	2	Petition	119	Invalid Pensions	222	Adverse		Laid on the table.		
Anstill, Jeremiah	(See Jeremiah Austill)	22	1		124							
Anthony, Bennington	Increase of compensation as marshal of Rhode Island.	20	1	Petition	397	Judiciary.						
Anthony, Charles	Indemnity for land taken by United States.	29	2	Petition	295	Public Lands.						
Anthony, Joseph R., and others.	Remmission of duties on oil, &c.	26	1	Petition	289	Commerce.						
Anthony, Michael	Pension	21	2	Petition	159	Military Pensions.						
Anthony, Michael	Pension	22	1	Petition	80	Rev. Pensions.						
Anthony, Michael	Pension	22	2	Petition	26	Invalid Pensions.						
Anthony, Michael	Pension	23	1	Petition	89	Invalid Pensions	Feb. 21, 1834	Adverse		Laid on table.		
Antill, Edward	Bounty land as a Nova Scotia refugee.	12	1	House bill	242	Whole House	Mar. 20, 1812	With amend.	85	Passed	Passed with amendment.	App'd April 23, 1812
Apelatche Indians	(See Indians)	24	2		88							
Apling & Co.	(See Lequeux, Apling & Co.	16	1		70							
Apperson, Richard, representatives of.	Commutation pay for revolutionary services.	24	1	Petition	259	Rev. Claims	319	Adverse		Laid on table.		

List of private claims presented to the House of Representatives of the United States from the 1st to the 31st Congress, inclusive—Continued.

Names of claimants.	Nature or object of the claim.	Congress.	Session.	How brought before the House of Reps.	Page of journal.	To what committee of the House referred.	No. or date of the report.	Nature of the report.	No. of the bill.	How disposed of by the House of Reps.	How disposed of by the Senate.	Date of the act of Congress, and remarks.
Apperson, Richard, representatives of.	Commutation pay for revolutionary services.	24	2	Petition	216	Rev. Claims.						
Apperson, Richard, representatives of.	Commutation pay for revolutionary services.	25	2	Petition	82	Rev. Claims.						
Apperson, Richard, representatives of.	Commutation pay for revolutionary services.	25	3	Petition	221	Rev. Claims.						
Apperson, Richard, representatives of.	Commutation pay for revolutionary services.	26	1	Petition	163	Rev. Claims	235	Adverse		Laid on table.		
Apperson, Richard, representatives of.	Commutation pay for revolutionary services.	27	2	Petition	132	Rev. Claims	366	Adverse		Laid on table.		
Appleby, George	(See William Thompson, of Va.)	19	1		312							
Appleby, Stephen	Pension for services; war of 1812.	24	2	Petition	42	Invalid Pensions				Discharged; laid on table.		
Appleby, Stephen	Pension for services; war of 1812.	25	2	Petition	401	Invalid Pensions	643	Favorable	619	Passed	Adverse report.	
Appleby, Stephen	Pension for services; war of 1812.	25	3	Petition	90	Invalid Pensions	132	Favorable	999	Passed	Adverse report.	
Appleby, Stephen	Pension for services; war of 1812.	26	1	Petition	160	Invalid Pensions	181	Favorable	193	Passed	Indef. postp'd.	
Applegate, Hezekiah	(See William Baker, assignee, &c.)	22	1		288							
Appleton, C. H.	(See Nath'l W. and C. H. Appleton.)	17	1		110							
Appleton, Daniel, widow of	Pension for naval services of dec'd.	19	2	Petition	216	Naval Affairs	69	Favorable	420	Referred to Committee Whole.		
Appleton, Daniel, widow of	Pension for naval services of dec'd.	20	1	Petition	278	Naval Affairs	148	Favorable	171	Passed	Reported with amendment.	
Appleton, Daniel, widow of	Pension for naval services of dec'd.	20	2	Petition	127	Naval Affairs.						
Appleton, Daniel, widow of	Pension for naval services of dec'd.	21	1	Petition	39	Naval Affairs.						
Appleton, Daniel, widow of	Pension for naval services of dec'd.	23	1	Petition	73	Naval Affairs.						
Appleton, Daniel, widow of	Continuation of naval pension	24	2	Petition	260	Naval Affairs	180	Favorable	897	Passed	Passed	App'd Mar. 3, 1837
Appleton, Daniel, widow of	Continuation of naval pension	28	1	Petition	374	Naval Affairs.						
Appleton, Daniel, widow of	Continuation of naval pension	28	2	Petition	72	Naval Affairs.						
Appleton, Daniel, widow of	Continuation of naval pension	29	1	Petition	1038	Naval Affairs.						
Appleton, Daniel, widow of	Pension for loss of husband; war of 1812.	31	1	Petition	827	Naval Affairs.						
Appleton, Ebenezer	(See Daniel P. Parker)	13	1		91							
Appleton, John	Comp. as an assessor in Mass.	13	3	Petition	503					Referred to Secretary of the Treasury.		
Appleton, Nathan	(See Daniel P. Parker, *et al*)	13	1		91							
Appleton, Nathaniel	Reimbursement of expenses incurred as commissioner of loans.	3	2	Memorial	249	Select	Jan. 13, 1795	Favorable		Report disagreed to.		
Appleton, Nathaniel	Increase of compensation as commissioner of loans.	4	1	Memorial	385	Select.						
Appleton, Nathaniel	Increase of compensation as commissioner of loans.	4	2	Memorial	623	Select.						
Appleton, Nathaniel W.	Remission of duties on imports to Castine while it was in possession of the British.	15	1	Petition	165	Ways and Means.						
Appleton, Nath'l W. and C. H.	Remission of duties on imports to Castine while it was in possession of the British.	17	1	Petition	110	Ways and Means	Feb. 1, 1822	General bill	69	Laid on table.		
Appleton, Nath'l W. and C. H.	Remission of duties on imports to Castine while it was in possession of the British.	18	1	Petition	27	Ways and Means	Jan. 15, 1824	General bill	60	Passed	Passed	App'd May 19, 1824
Appleton, Thomas	Interest on certain expenditures at Naples.	15	1	Petition	349	Claims.						

List of private claims presented to the House of Representatives of the United States from the 1st to the 31st Congress, inclusive—Continued.

Names of claimants.	Nature or object of the claim.	Congress.	Session.	How brought before the House of Reps.	Page of journal.	To what committee of the House referred.	No. or date of the report.	Nature of the report.	No. of the bill.	How disposed of by the House of Reps.	How disposed of by the Senate.	Date of the act of Congress, and remarks.
Appling, Daniel, sister of	Payment for captured gun-boats	16	1	Petition	66	Military Affairs	12	Favorable	21	Claim rejected.		
Apsley, John and Sarah	Compensation for attendance on sick soldiers.	23	1	Petition	141	Claims	Jan. 10, 1834	Adverse	......	Laid on table.		
Arbuckle, Matthew	Patent for conf. Spanish grants of land.	22	1	Resolution	219	Judiciary.						
Arbuckle, Matthew	Patent for conf. Spanish grants of land.	23	1	Petition	57	Public Lands.						
Arbuckle, Matthew	Patent for conf. Spanish grants of land.	23	2	Petition	85	Public Lands.						
Arbuckle, Matthew	Patent for conf. Spanish grants of land.	24	1	Documents	58	Public Lands.						
Arbuckle, Matthew	Patent for conf. Spanish grants of land.	25	2	Senate bill	952	Public Lands	949	With't amend.	S. 188	Referred to Committee Whole House.		
Arbuster, or Armbriester, Matthias.	Comp. for revolutionary services	2	1	Petition	467	Claims	Jan. 11, 1811	Adverse	......	Referred to Secretary of War.		
Arbuster, or Armbriester, Matthias.	Comp. for revolutionary services	11	3	Petition	439	....	....	....	......	Claim rejected.		
Arbuthnot, James	Confirmation of title to land in La.	29	1	Petition	461	Priv. Land Claims.						
Arbuthnot, William	Indemnity for destruction of property on Niagara frontier.	15	2	Petition	148	Claims	Jan. 16, 1819	Adverse	......	Laid on table.		
Arbuthnot, William	Indemnity for destruction of property on Niagara frontier.	19	2	Petition	159	Claims	Jan. 29, 1827	Adverse	......	Laid on table.		
Arbuthnot, William	Indemnity for destruction of property on Niagara frontier.	22	1	Petition	54	Claims	285	Adverse	......	Laid on table.		
Arbuthnot, William	Indemnity for destruction of property on Niagara frontier.	23	1	Petition	74	Claims.						
Archer, Hugh	Compensation as clerk House of Representatives, Florida.	28	1	Petition	319	Territories.						
Archer, James	Indem. for loss on contin'l money.	19	1	Resolution	230	Rev. Claims	Mar. 1, 1826	Adverse	......	Laid on table.		
Archer, James	Comp. for revolutionary services	20	1	Petition	417	Rev. Claims.						
Archer, Moses	Pension	23	1	Senate bill	811	Invalid Pensions	June 26, 1834	With amend.	S. 162	Passed with amendm't.	Passed as am'd.	App'd June 30, 1834
Archer, Moses	Increase of pension	23	2	Petition	41	Invalid Pensions	Jan. 22, 1835	Adverse	......	Laid on table.		
Archer, Moses	Increase of pension	25	2	Petition	494	Invalid Pensions.						
Archer, Moses	Increase of pension	26	1	Petition	603	Invalid Pensions	570	Adverse	......	Laid on table.		
Archer, Moses	Increase of pension	26	2	Petition	55	Invalid Pensions	233	Adverse	......	Laid on table.		
Archer, Richard F	Right of pre-emption to land in Mississippi.	23	1	Petition	450	Priv. Land Claims.						
Archer, Richard F	Right of pre-emption to land in Mississippi.	23	2	Petition	68	Priv. Land Claims.	32	Favorable	614	Passed	Passed	App'd Mar. 3, 1835
Archer, Thomas	(See T. Graham, heirs of)	26	1	....	182	....	343	....	319			
Arden, John	Confirmation of title to land in Mississippi.	13	3	Petition	720	Public Lands	....	....	......	Discharged.		
Arden, John	Confirmation of title to land in Mississippi.	14	1	Petition	75	Public Lands.						
Arden, John	Confirmation of title to land in Mississippi.	14	2	Petition	51	Priv. Land Claims.						
Arden, John D. S	Permission to enter certain land at minimum price.	26	1	....	947	Priv. Land Claims.						
Arden, John D. S	Permission to enter certain land at minimum price.	26	2	Petition	248	Priv. Land Claims.						
Arden, John D. S	Permission to enter certain land at minimum price.	27	3	Petition	317	Public Lands.						

List of private claims presented to the House of Representatives of the United States from the 1st to the 31st Congress, inclusive—Continued.

6

Names of claimants.	Nature or object of the claim.	Congress.	Session.	How brought before the House of Reps.	Page of journal.	To what committee of the House referred.	No. or date of the report.	Nature of the report.	No. of the bill.	How disposed of by the House of Reps.	How disposed of by the Senate.	Date of the act of Congress, and remarks.
Ardis, John S., guardian of the children of.	Renewal of a naval pension......	29	1	Petition	510	Naval Affairs.						
Ardis, John S., guardian of the children of.	Renewal of a naval pension......	31	1	Petition	827	Naval Affairs.						
Arendell, Bridges........	Increase of comp. as collector N. C.	15	1	Petition	258	Ways and Means.						
Arendell, Bridges........	Increase of comp. as collector N. C.	15	2	Petition	169	Commerce & Manufactures.						
Arey, Crosby	Bounty on fishing sch'r "Burr" .	21	1	Petition	169	Commerce	April 3, 1830	Favorable	405	Referred to Committee Whole.		
Arey, Crosby	Bounty on fishing sch'r "Burr" .	22	1	Petition	162	Commerce	Jan. 12, 1832	Favorable	251	Referred to Committee Whole.		
Arey, Crosby	Bounty on fishing sch'r "Burr" .	22	2	....	92	....	Dec. 22, 1832	....	251	Passed	Passed	App'd Feb. 19, 1833
Arey, Crosby	Bounty on fishing sch'r "Burr" .	23	1	Petition	32	Commerce.						
Argabright, Alfred.......	(See Albert C. Bryan and others)	30	1	....	146							
"Argus," Brig	(See Wm. H. Allen, administrator of.)	14	1	....	340							
Argyle, John W	Increase of compensation for locating land warrants.	30	2	Petition	193	Public Lands.						
Arheart, Robert	Pay and bounty land for military services.	26	2	Petition	76	Public Lands.						
Arickson, Samuel C	Pension	13	2	Pension bill	344	Whole House	Mar. 30, 1814	With amend .	166	Passed	Passed with amendment.	App'd April 18, 1814
Arkabright, Alfred.......	(See Alfred Argabright)	30	1	....	146							
Arkansas, agent of State..	Comp'n for selecting public grants.	21	2	Resolution	157	Public Lands.						
Arkansas, inhabitants of ..	Right of pre emption against Indian claims.	16	1	Petition	130	Public Lands.						
				Petition	177	Public Lands.						
Arkansas, inhabitants of ..	Right of pre-emption to lands they reside on.	16	1	Petition	285	Public Lands.						
Arkansas, inhabitants of ..	Right of pre-emption to lands they reside on.	22	2	Petition	246	Public Lands.						
Arkansas, inhabitants of ..	Indemnity for Osage depredations.	20	2	Senate bill	148	Indian Affairs	Jan. 26, 1829	With't amend.	S. 51	Laid on table.		
Arkansas, inhabitants of ..	Indemnity for Osage depredations.	21	2	Senate bill	87	Indian Affairs	Dec. 29, 1829	With't amend.	S. 8	Passed	Passed	App'd Mar. 25, 1830
Arkansas, inhabitants of ..	Indemnity for Osage depredations.	23	1	House bill	358	Whole House	....	....	323			
Arkansas, inhabitants of ..	Indemnity for loss of improvements by Choctaw treaty.	24	1	Memorial of Legislature.	57	Public Lands	208	Favorable....	208	Referred to Committee Whole House.		
Arkanses, inhabitants of ..	Indemnity for loss of improvements by Choctaw treaty.	24	1	Petition	914	Whole House.						
Arkansas, inhabitants of ..	Indemnity for loss of improvements by Choctaw treaty.	25	2	Senate bill	455	Public Lands	629	With amend..	S. 43	Referred to Committee Whole House.		
Arkansas, inhabitants of ..	Indemnity for loss of improvements by Choctaw treaty.	25	3	Senate bill	245	Public Lands	Jan. 23, 1839	With amend..	S. 29	Referred to Committee Whole House.		
Arkansas, inhabitants of ..	Indemnity for loss of improvements by Choctaw treaty.	26	1	Senate bill	802	Priv. Land Claims.	Jan. 21, 1840	With't amend.	S. 72			
Arkansas, inhabitants of ..	Indemnity for loss of improvements by Choctaw treaty.	26	2	Senate bill	106	Public Lands.....	....	....	S. 26			
Arkansas, inhabitants of ..	Indemnity for loss of improvements by Choctaw treaty.	27	2	Senate bill	409	Public Lands	601	With amend..	S. 70	Laid on table.		
Arkansas, inhabitants of ..	Indemnity for loss of improvements by Choctaw treaty.	27	3	Senate bill	115	Whole House.....	....	....	S. 17	Referred to Committee Whole House.		
Arkansas, registers and receivers.	Compensation for extra services...	20	1	House bill......	539	Whole House.....	....	....	265			
Arkansas, registers and receivers.	Compensation for extra services...	20	2	Report of Committee Whole.	285	....	....	With't amend.	265	Passed.		

List of private claims presented to the House of Representatives of the United States from the 1st to the 31st Congress, inclusive—Continued.

Names of claimants.	Nature or object of the claim.	Congress.	Session.	How brought before the House of Reps.	Page of journal.	To what committee of the House referred.	No. or date of the report.	Nature of the report.	No. of the bill.	How disposed of by the House of Reps.	How disposed of by the Senate.	Date of the act of Congress, and remarks.
Arkansas, volunt'rs, mounted.	Pay while in service of United States.	21	1	House bill......	517	Whole House.						
Armand, Brigider General	(See heirs of General Duportail)..	26	2	....	119							
Armas, Joseph De.......	(See Joseph De Armas.)											
Armbriester, Mathias.....	(See Matthias Arbuster)........	11	3	....	439							
Armbrister, Michael......	Confirm'n of title to Creek lands..	24	2	Petition	275	Whole House.						
Armbrister, Michael......	Confirm'n of title to Creek lands..	25	2	Senate bill	763	Indian Affairs	888	With amend..	S. 181	Referred to Committee Whole House.		
Armbrister, Michael......	Confirm'n of title to Creek lands..	25	3	House bill ..... Senate bill	375 557	Whole House .... Public Lands	Jan. 25, 1839	With't amend.	167 S. 28	Passed	Passed	App'd March 3, 1839
Armington, Asa.........	Remission of duties on cargo molasses.	23	1	Petition	89	Ways and Means..	233	Favorable....	259	Referred to Committee Whole House.		
Armington, Asa.........	Remission of duties on cargo molasses.	23	2	Report of Committee Whole.	291	....	....	With't amend.	259			
Armington, Asa.........	Remission of duties on cargo molasses.	24	1	Petition	95	Ways and Means..	112	Favorable....	128	Referred to Committee Whole House.		
Armington, Asa.........	Remission of duties on cargo molasses.	24	2	Petition	76	Ways and Means..	45	Favorable....	791	Referred to Committee Whole House.		
Armington, Asa.........	Remission of duties on cargo molasses.	25	2	Petition	42	Ways and Means..	....	....	......	Discharged; laid on table.		
Armington, Asa.........	Remission of duties on cargo molasses.	27	2	Petition	55	Ways and Means.						
Armington, Asa.........	Remission of duties on cargo molasses.	27	3	Petition	112	Ways and Means..	....	....	......	Discharged; laid on table.		
Armington, Asa.........	Remission of duties on cargo molasses.	29	1	Petition	115	Commerce	60	Favorable....	57	Rejected.		
Armington, Asa.........	(See surety of Armington and Burrough.)	26	1	....	945							
Armington, Asa and others	(See surety of Armington and Burrough.)	25	3	....	546	....	....	....	S. 93			
Armington and Burrough .	Remission of duties on cargo molasses.	21	2	Petition	110	Ways and Means.						
Armington and Burrough .	Remission of duties on cargo molasses.	22	1	Petition	24	Ways and Means.						
Armington and Burrough, sureties of.	Release from custom-house bonds.	25	3	Senate bill	546	Whole House	....	....	S. 93			
Armington & Burrough, sureties of.	Release from custom house bonds.	26	1	Petition	945	Ways and Means.						
Armington & Burrough, sureties of.	Release from custom house bonds.	26	2	Petition	35	Ways and Means.						
Armington & Burrough, sureties of.	Release from custom-house bonds.	28	1	Petition	73	Ways and Means.						
Armistead, Francis A., widow of.	Pension for services as a marine officer.	28	1	Petition	718	Naval Affairs.						
Armistead, Geo., widow of.	Remission of a balance due......	17	1	Petition	248	Military Affairs.						
Armistead, Sharkey, executor of.	Release of a satisfied judgment...	30	2	Senate bill......	167	Judiciary	Jan. 31, 1849	With't amend.	S. 359	Passed............	Passed......	App'd Feb. 2, 1849
Armistead, Theodorick ...	Permission to enter a cargo of brandy.	9	1	House bill......	197	Com. and Manuf..	Dec. 13, 1805	With't amend.	76	Passed............	Rejected.	
Armistead, Walter K.....	Equitable settlement of his accounts.	19	1	Senate bill......	510	Claims	May 8, 1826	With't amend.	S. 126	Passed............	Passed	App'd May 22, 1826
Armistead, Walter K., heirs of.	Equitable settlement of his accounts.	31	1	Senate bill......	1539	....	....	....	S. 360			

List of private claims presented to the House of Representatives of the United States from the 1st to the 31st Congress, inclusive—Continued.

Names of claimants.	Nature or object of the claim.	Congress.	Session.	How brought before the House of Reps.	Page of journal.	To what committee of the House referred.	No. or date of the report.	Nature of the report.	No. of the bill.	How disposed of by the House of Reps.	How disposed of by the Senate.	Date of the act of Congress, and remarks.
Armistead, Walter K., heirs of.	Equitable settlement of his accounts.	31	2	Senate bill.....	170	Military Affairs....	Feb. 18, 1851	With't amend.	S. 360	Passed............	Passed	App'd Feb. 27, 1851
Armistead, William......	Extension of time for the payment of a judgment.	9	1	Petition	262	Claims	Feb. 12, 1806	Adverse.				
Armon, Nancy..........	Payment of loan office certificate No. 490.	14	2	Petition	149	Pens. & Rev. Cl'ms.	Feb. 3, 1817	Favorable	96	Referred to Committee Whole House.		
Armon, Nancy..........	Payment of loan office certificate No. 490.	17	1	Petition	391	Whole House.						
Armon, Nancy..........	Payment of loan office certificate No. 490.	17	2	Resolution	89	Pens. & Rev. Cl'ms.						
Armor, Edward.........	Increase of pension...........	30	1	Petition	457	Invalid Pensions.						
Armor, G. M. and others.	Bounty on fishing schooner Three Brothers.	26	1	Petition	710	Commerce.						
Armor, James	Compensation for horses taken for public use.	3	2	Petition	334	Claims.						
Armor, James	Compensation for horses taken for public use.	4	1	Petition	373	Claims	Jan. 6, 1796	Adverse.				
Armor, Thomas, executor of.	Compensation for revolutionary services and reimbursement of advances.	3	1	Petition	50	....	....	....	......	Referred to Secretary Treasury.		
Armor, Thomas, executor of.	Compensation for revolutionary services and reimbursement of advances.	3	2	Rep. of Secretary Treasury.	284	....	....	....	......	Laid on the table.		
Armor, Thomas, heirs of..	Compensation for revolutionary services and reimbursement of advances.	25	2	Petition	722	Rev. Claims......	....	....	......	Discharged; laid on table.		
Armor, Thomas, heirs of..	Compensation for revolutionary services and reimbursement of advances.	26	1	Petition	360	Rev. Claims.						
Armor, Thomas, heirs of..	Compensation for revolutionary services and reimbursement of advances.	26	2	Petition	36	Rev. Claims.						
Armor, Thomas, heirs of..	Compensation for revolutionary services and reimbursement of advances.	27	2	Petition	268	Rev. Claims......	359	Adverse	......	Leave to withdraw.		
Armor, Thomas, heirs of..	Compensation for revolutionary services and reimbursement of advances.	29	1	Petition	172	Rev. Claims......	....	....	......	Discharged; laid on table.		
Armor, Thomas, heirs of..	Compensation for revolutionary services and reimbursement of advances.	29	2	Petition	54	Rev. Claims.						
Armor, Thomas, heirs of..	Compensation for revolutionary services and reimbursement of advances.	31	1	....	1178	Rev. Claims.						
Armory, Harper's Ferry, officers at.	Increase of compensation........	24	1	Petition	200	Military Affairs.						
Armroyd, George, & Co..	Drawback on merchandise exported	11	2	Petition	165	Com. and Manuf..	Feb. 21, 1810	Favorable.				
Armroyd, George, & Co..	Drawback on merchandise exported	11	3	Petition	437	Com. and Manuf..	Dec. 10, 1810	Favorable	153	Passed............	Passed	App'd Jan. 21, 1811
Armroyd, George, & Co..	Restoration of vessel seized under non-importation act.	12	1	Petition	11	Com. and Manuf.						
Arms, Lemuel..........	Indemnity for destruction of building at Sackett's Harbor.	17	1	Petition	46	Claims.						

List of private claims presented to the House of Representatives of the United States from the 1st to the 31st Congress, inclusive—**Continued.**

Names of claimants.	Nature or object of the claim.	Congress.	Session.	How brought before the House of Reps.	Page of journal.	To what committee of the House referred.	No. or date of the report.	Nature of the report.	No. of the bill.	How disposed of by the House of Reps.	How disposed of by the Senate.	Date of the act of Congress, and remarks.
Arms, Lemuel	Indemnity for destruction of building at Sackett's Harbor.	18	1	Petition	37	Claims	50	Favorable	96	Passed	Passed	App'd May 18, 1824
Arms, Thomas	Benefit of act for Canadian refugees.	18	2	Petition	101	Priv. Land Claims.	Jan. 18, 1825	Adverse	......	Rejected.		
Armstead, William, assignee of.	Land scrip in lieu of original grant.	31	1	Petition	234	Priv. Land Claims.						
Armsley, William	Extension of patent for ship building.	26	2	Petition	50	Patents.						
Armstrong, Amos	Pension for disabilities in war of 1812.	29	1	Memorial	541	Invalid Pensions	813	Favorable	538			
Armstrong, Amos	Pension for disabilities in war of 1812.	30	1	Petition	120	Invalid Pensions	553	Favorable	453			
Armstrong, Amos	Pension for disabilities in war of 1812.	30	2	....	318	....	....	....	453			
Armstrong, Amos	Pension for disabilities in war of 1812.	31	1	Petition	284	Invalid Pensions.						
Armstrong, Andrew	Equitable settlement of his accounts.	23	1	Senate bill	755	Naval Affairs	536	With amend.	S. 146	Passed with amend'mt	Passed as am'd	App'd June 30, 1834
Armstrong, Andrew	Further credits in settlement of account.	24	1	Senate bill	1128	Claims	833	With't amend.	S. 226	Referred to Committee Whole House.		
Armstrong, Andrew	Further credits in settlement of account.	25	2	Senate bill	197	Naval Affairs	Jan. 18, 1838	With't amend.	S. 53	Referred to Committee Whole House.		
Armstrong, Andrew	Adjustment of account as navy agent.	27	2	Petition	73	Claims	693	Adverse	......	Laid on table.		
Armstrong, Andrew C.	Adjustment of accounts as navy agent, Lima.	28	1	Petition	104	Naval Affairs.						
Armstrong, Andrew C.	Adjustment of accounts as navy agent, Lima.	29	1	Petition	258	Naval Affairs	791	Favorable	520	Referred to Committee Whole House.		
Armstrong, Andrew C.	Adjustment of accounts as navy agent, Lima.	30	1	Petition	148	Naval Affairs	274	Favorable	269	Referred to Committee Whole House.		
Armstrong, Andrew C.	Adjustment of accounts as navy agent, Lima.	31	1	Petition	214	Claims.						
Armstrong & Barnewall	Remission of duties on iron ordnance.	5	2	Petition	319	Com. and Manufac.						
Armstrong, Edward	Pension for revolutionary services.	7	1	Petition	21	Claims	Dec. 30, 1801	Adverse.				
Armstrong, Elijah	Arrears of pension	31	1	Petition	193	Invalid Pensions	100	Adverse	......	Laid on table.		
Armstrong, Elizabeth	(See heirs of Josiah Fletcher)	21	2	....	143							
Armstrong, Francis W.	Compensation for horses lost in public service.	19	1	Petition	292	Claims.						
Armstrong, Francis W.	Compensation for keeping fifty-three negroes.	19	1	Memorial	371	Claims.						
Armstrong, Francis W.	Compensation for keeping negroes.	21	2	Appropriat'n bill.	....	....	....	....	......	....	....	App'd Feb. 25, 1831
Armstrong, George	(See Wm. Baker, assignee, &c.).	22	1	....	288							
Armstrong, George	Pension	25	2	Petition	74	Invalid Pensions.						
Armstrong, George	Pension	26	1	Petition	160	Invalid Pensions	473	Favorable	387	Referred to Committee Whole House.		
Armstrong, George	Pension	27	2	Petition	60	Invalid Pensions	Feb. 9, 1842	Adverse	......	Laid on table.		
Armstrong, George	Pension	27	3	Petition	72	Invalid Pensions	266	Adverse	......	Laid on table.		
Armstrong, George	Pension	28	1	Memorial	160	Invalid Pensions	180	Adverse	......	Laid on table.		
Armstrong, George	Indemnity for property destroyed in war of 1812.	31	1	Petition	627	Claims	239	Favorable	237	Referred to Committee Whole House.		
Armstrong, James	Revolutionary pension	9	1	Petition	277	Claims	Mar. 28, 1806	Adverse	......	Indef. postponed	....	Leave to withdraw.
Armstrong, James	Pension for revolutionary services.	12	1	Pension bill	361	Whole House	June 15, 1812	With amend.	138	Passed	Passed	App'd July 5, 1812

List of private claims presented to the House of Representatives of the United States from the 1st to the 31st Congress, inclusive—Continued.

Names of claimants.	Nature or object of the claim.	Congress.	Session.	How brought before the House of Reps.	Page of journal.	To what committee of the House referred.	No. or date of the report.	Nature of the report.	No. of the bill.	How disposed of by the House of Reps.	How disposed of by the Senate.	Date of the act of Congress, and remarks.
Armstrong, James, heirs of.	Commutation pay due for revolutionary services.	23	1	Petition	42	Rev. Claims	Jan. 10, 1834	Adverse	......	Laid on table.		
Armstrong, Jas., widow of	Pension for revolutionary services.	29	1	Memorial	283	Rev. Pension.						
Armstrong, Jas., widow of	Pension for revolutionary services	29	2	Memorial	150	Rev. Pensions	26	Adverse	......	Laid on table.		
Armstrong, James, and J. Carter.	Reimbursement of payment for quarters in Mexico.	31	1	Petition	755	Military Affairs	399	Adverse	......	Laid on table.		
Armstrong, James F., widow of.	Provision for widows of revolutionary officers and soldiers.	20	2	....	290	....	....	....	......	....	....	(See 21st Cong. 2d sess., report No. 4.)
Armstrong, James S	Remission of duty on distillery license.	14	1	Petition	449	Ways and Means.						
Armstrong, Jeremiah	(See John & Jeremiah Armstrong)	23	2	....	67							
Armstrong, John	Payment of bills drawn as minister to France.	10	1	Senate bill	270	Whole House	April 23, 1808	With amend.	S. 16	Passed with amendm't	Passed as am'd	App'd April 25, 1808
Armstrong, John	(See trustees of Frances L. Taney)	10	1	....	216							
Armstrong, John	Commissons on internal revenue collected.	14	1	Petition	40	Claims	Dec. 21, 1815	Adverse	......	Claim rejected.		
Armstrong, John	Compensation for horse, &c., taken for public use.	17	1	Petition	417	Claims.						
Armstrong, John	Compensation for horse, &c., taken for public use.	17	2	Petition	225	Claims.						
Armstrong, John	Compensation for horse, &c., taken for public use.	18	1	Petition	66	Claims	Jan. 30, 1824	Adverse	......	Laid on table	....	Leave to withdraw, 2d Session.
Armstrong, John	Confirmation of title to land in Louisiana.	19	1	Report of register and receiver.	64	Public lands	33	Favorable	254	Referred to Committee Whole House.		
Armstrong, John	Location of a confirmed claim in Louisiana.	23	2	Petition	27	Priv. Land Claims.	Jan. 9, 1835	Adverse	......	Laid on table.		
Armstrong, John	Location of a confirmed claim in Louisiana.	24	1	Petition	121	Priv. Land Claims.	June 12, 1836	Adverse	......	Laid on table.		
Armstrong, John	Location of a confirmed claim in Louisiana.	25	2	Petition	374	Priv. Land Claims.	945	Adverse	......	Laid on table.		
Armstrong, John, heirs of.	Payment of two loan office certificates.	14	1	Petition	47	Pens. & Rev. Cl'ms.						
Armstrong, John, heirs of.	Payment of two loan office certificates.	14	2	Petition	87	Pens. & Rev. Cl'ms.	Feb. 3, 1817	Favorable	96	Referred to Committee Whole House.		
Armstrong, John, brother of.	Commutation pay and bounty land for revolutionary services.	9	1	Petition	277	Claims	Mar. 28, 1806	Adverse	......	Indef. postponed	....	Leave to withdraw.
Armstrong, John, attorney, &c.	Bounty land claims of sundry soldiers.	6	2	Petition and rep. of Sec. War.	619 636	Select.						
Armstrong, John	(See heirs of Richard McCarty)	11	1	....	33							
Armstrong, John and Silas	(See Wyandot Indians)	27	3	....	259	....	160	....	776			
Armstrong, John and Jeremiah.	Bounty land in consideration of their long captivity among the Indians.	23	2	Petition	67	Public Lands.						
Armstrong, John and Jeremiah.	Bounty land in consideration of their long captivity among the Indians.	24	1	Petition	96	Indian Affairs	....	....	......	Discharged; laid on table.	....	Leave to withdraw, 2d Session.
Armstrong, John and Jeremiah.	Bounty land in consideration of their long captivity among the Indians.	25	2	Petition	282	Priv. Land Claims.						
Armstrong, J. Y., and others.	Increase of compensation as Post Office clerks.	31	2	Petition	192	P. Of. and P. Roads.						
				Petition (2)	204	P. Of. and P. Roads.						
				Petition (3)	215	P. Of. and P. Roads.						

List of private claims presented to the House of Representatives of the United States from the 1st to the 31st Congress, inclusive—Continued.

Names of claimants.	Nature or object of the claim.	Congress.	Session.	How brought before the House of Reps.	Page of journal.	To what committee of the House referred.	No. or date of the report.	Nature of the report.	No. of the bill.	How disposed of by the House of Reps.	How disposed of by the Senate.	Date of the act of Congress, and remarks.
Armstrong, Robert and William.	Compensation for services as Indian spies.	25	2	Petition	396	Claims	742	Adverse	......	Laid on table.		
Armstrong, Samuel	Indemnity for injuries in public service.	1	2	Petition	163							
				Rep. of Secretary War.	169	......	......	......	......	Laid on table.		
				Petition	213							
				Rep. of Secretary War.	221	......	......	......	......	Laid on table.		
Armstrong, Samuel	Indemnity for injuries in public service.	2	1	Resolution	450	Whole House	Nov. 7, 1791	Adverse.				
Armstrong, Thomas	(See heirs of Josiah Fletcher)	21	2	......	143							
Armstrong, William	(See Robert & Wm. Armstrong)	25	2	......	396							
Armstrong, William	Indemnity for loss by steamboat explosion.	28	2	......	....	......	......	......	......	......	......	Statutes at Large, vol. 5, p. 776.
Armstrong, William, representatives of.	Compensation for extra services as Choctaw agent.	30	1	Memorial	666	Indian Affairs	771	Favorable	605	Referred to Committee Whole House.		
Armstrong, William, representatives of.	Compensation for extra services as Cherokee agent.	31	1	Petition	199	Indian Affairs.						
Armstrong, William, representatives of.	Compensation for extra services as Cherokee agent.	31	2	Petition	206	Indian Affairs	17	Adverse	......	Laid on table.		
Armstrong, William M	Indemnity for French spoliations prior to 1800.	26	1	Memorial	182	Foreign Affairs	343	Favorable	319	Referred to Committee Whole House.		
Army	(See officers, &c.)											
Army, Officers of	(See Amos Stoddard and others)	10	1	......	69							
Army of the revolution	(See officers, &c.)											
Army, soldiers of 4th regiment.	Bounty land for services; war of 1812.	25	2	Documents	461	Invalid Pensions.						
Army, soldiers of 4th regiment.	Bounty land for services; war of 1812.	26	1	Resolution	372	Select	232	Favorable	245	Referred to Committee Whole House.		
Army, soldiers of 4th regiment.	Bounty land for services; war of 1812.	27	2	Petition	255	Select	322	Favorable	291	Referred to Committee Whole House.		
Army, enlisted men, Ordinance Department.	Same land as troops of the line.	30	1	Senate bill	343	Invalid Pensions	Feb. 29, 1848	With amend.	124	Passed with amendm't.	Passed as am'd.	App'd July 10, 1848
				Memorial	675	Military Affairs.						
Army, clerks in Paymaster's Department.	Increase of compensation	30	1	Petition	807	Military Affairs	......	......	......	Discharged; laid on table.		
Army, clerks in Adjutant General's office.	Increase of compensation	31	1	Petition	787	Military Affairs.						
Arnan, Stephen	Compensation for property destroyed by United States volunteers.	25	2	Petition	274	Claims.						
Arnan, Stephen	Compensation for property destroyed by United States volunteers.	26	1	Petition	167	Claims	44	Adverse	......	Laid on table.		
Arnan, Stephen	Compensation for property destroyed by United States volunteers.	26	2	Petition	125	Claims.						
Arnan, Stephen	Compensation for property destroyed by United States volunteers.	27	2	Petition	94	Claims	498	Adverse	......	Laid on table.		
Arnaud, John P	Pension	21	2	Resolution	68	Military Pensions.						
Arnaud, John P	Pension	22	1	Resolution	73	Rev. Pensions.						
Arnauld, Jean	Confirmation of title to land in Louisiana.	23	1	Resolution	314	Priv. Land Claims.	......	......	......	Laid on table.		
Arndt, John P	Indemnity for depredation of Pottawatomie Indians.	20	1	Petition	195	Claims	Mar. 21, 1828	Adverse	......	Laid on table.		

List of private claims presented to the House of Representatives of the United States from the 1st to the 31st Congress, inclusive—Continued.

Names of claimants.	Nature or object of the claim.	Congress.	Session.	How brought before the House of Reps.	Page of journal.	To what committee of the House referred.	No. or date of the report.	Nature of the report.	No. of the bill.	How disposed of by the House of Reps.	How disposed of by the Senate.	Date of the act of Congress, and remarks.
Arndt, John P.	Confirmation of title to land in Michigan.	21	1	Petition	68	Priv. Land Claims.						
Arndt, John P.	(See Daniel Whitney and others).	23	1		450							
Arndt, John P.	Compensation for outfit of Menominie Indians.	28	2	Petition	317	Military Affairs.						
Arnell, William	Indemnity for destruction of property by United States troops.	26	1	Petition	946	Rev. Claims.						
Arnell, William	Indemnity for destruction of property by United States troops.	27	2	Petition	346	Rev. Claims.						
Arnet, William S	Bounty land for military services	25	3	Petition	461	Invalid Pensions.						
Arnold, Alexander F. and W. Napton.	Reimbursement of advances on public account.	30	1	Memorial Legislature of N. J.	627					Laid on table.		
Arnold, Anthony	Pension	26	1	Petition	602	Invalid Pensions.						
Arnold, Aza	Renewal of patent for "Double Speeder."	24	1	Petition	724	Select.						
Arnold, Caleb	Increase of pension	23	1	Petition	88	Rev. Pensions	Dec. 23, 1833	Adverse		Laid on table.		
Arnold, David, (R. I.)	Pension	21	1	Resolution	353	Military Pensions	Feb. 13, 1830	Declaratory bill	248	Passed	Indef. postp'd.	
Arnold, David, (N. C.)	Pension	21	1	Resolution	434	Military Pensions.						
Arnold, David	Pension	21	2	Resolution	165	Military Pensions.						
Arnold, Elias	(See Raphael Paine & E. A.)	22	2		441				S. 93			
Arnold, Jacob, jr.	(See adminis's of Mahlon Ford.)	17	2		81							
Arnold, James, and others	Increase of compensation as revenue officer, (R. I.)	4	2	Memorial	656	Whole House.						
Arnold, James	(See Wm. H. Bedford, agent, &c.)	28	1		262							
Arnold, John	Invalid pension	20	1	Resolution	153	Military Pensions.						
Arnold, John, administrator of.	Extension of a patent for manufacturing cloth.	30	2	Petition	317	Patents	88	Favorable	784	Referred to Committee Whole House.		
Arnold, John, administrator of.	Extension of a patent for manufacturing cloth.	31	1	Petition	503	Patents	151	Favorable	169	Referred to Committee Whole House.		
Arnold, John, administrator of.	Extension of a patent for manufacturing cloth.	31	2	House bill	422				169			
Arnold, Remington, jr., & others.	Bounty on fishing schooner "Admiral."	22	1	Petition	441	Commerce	404	Favorable	501			
Arnold, Remington, jr., & others.	Bounty on fishing schooner "Admiral."	23	1	Petition	79	Commerce	Dec. 31, 1833	Favorable	117	Passed	Passed	App'd June 30, 1834
Arnold, Thomas	Drawback on coffee exported in 1798.	5	3	Petition	472	Com. and Manufac.	Jan. 4, 1799	Favorable	168	Referred to Committee Whole House.		
Arnold, Thomas	Drawback on coffee exported in 1798.	6	1	Petition	588	Com. and Manufac.	Feb. 18, 1800	Favorable	208	Passed.		
Arnold, Thomas	(See Joseph Stewart, and others)	13	3		751							
Arnold, Thomas, heirs of	Indemnity for French spoliations prior to 1800.	31	1	Petition	196	Foreign Affairs	355	General bill	318	Referred to Committee Whole House.		
Arnold, William	Renewal of loan office certificate	2	1	Petition Rep. of Secretary of Treasury.	461 583	 Select.						
Arnold, William	Renewal of loan office certificate	13	3	Petition	468	Pensions	Nov. 11, 1814	Favorable	257	Passed	Passed	App'd Feb. 2, 1815
Arnold, William	Pension	14	2	Petition	106	Pensions and Revolutionary Claims.	Jan. 29, 1817	Pension bill	91	Passed	Passed with amendment.	App'd March 3, 1817
Arnold, William	Increase of pension	15	1	Documents.	136	Pensions and Revolutionary Claims.						
Arnold, William	Increase of pension	15	2	Pension bill Pension bill	231 41	Whole House	March 3, 1819	With't amend.	208 203	Passed Passed	Postponed. Passed with amendment.	 App'd March 3, 1819

List of private claims presented to the House of Representatives of the United States from the 1st to the 31st Congress, inclusive—Continued.

Names of claimants.	Nature or object of the claim.	Congress.	Session.	How brought before the House of Reps.	Page of journal.	To what committee of the House referred.	No. or date of the report.	Nature of the report.	No. of the bill.	How disposed of by the House of Reps.	How disposed of by the Senate.	Date of the act of Congress, and remarks.
Arnold, William, heirs of	Quarter section of land for military services.	28	1	Petition	73	Priv. Land Claims.						
		29	1	Petition	119	Public Lands				Discharged; laid on table.		
Arntz, H. P. P.	Increase of pension	31	2	Petition	112	Invalid Pensions.						
Arny William	Increase of revolutionary pension	25	2	Petition	722	Rev. Pensions				Discharged; laid on table.		
Arredondo, F. M., & others	Adjustment of claims under Florida treaty.	19	1	Memorial	252	Foreign Affairs	112	Adverse		Laid on table.		
Arredondo, F. M., & others	Adjustment of claims under Florida treaty.	19	2	Memorial	108	Judiciary	Feb. 13, 1826	Indefinite		Discharged.		
Arredondo, F. M., & others	Adjustment of claims under Florida treaty.	20	1	Resolution	35	Judiciary	16	Adverse		Laid on table.		
Arredondo, F. M., & others	Adjustmeut of claims under Florida treaty.	20	2	Petition	61	Foreign Affairs	99	Favorable		Referred to Committee Whole House.		
Arredondo, F. M., & others	Adjustment of claims under Florida treaty.	21	1	Petition	51	Foreign Affairs	176	Favorable	221	Referred to Committee Whole House.		
Arredondo, F. M., & others	Adjustment of claims under Florida treaty.	21	2	Petition	235	Public Lands.						
Arredondo, F. M., & others	Adjustment of claims under Florida treaty.	22	1	Petition	32	Foreign Affairs	223	Favorable	297	Referred to Committee Whole House.		
				Resolution	39	Foreign Affairs.						
Arredondo, F. M., & others	Adjustment of claims under Florida treaty.	22	2	Rep. Committee Whole House.	171			Enact'g clause stricken out.	297	Referred to Committee Whole House.		
Arredondo, F. M., & others	Adjustment of claims under Florida treaty.	23	1	Petition	67	Foreign Affairs	368	Favorable	395	Passed	Passed	App'd June 26, 1834
Arredondo, J. M.	(See F. M. Arredondo, and others)											
Arrell, David, heirs of	Commutation pay for revolutionary services.	24	1	Petition	432	Rev. Claims						
Arrell, David, heirs of	Commutation pay for revolutionary services.	24	2	Petition	40	Rev. Claims.						
Arrell, David, heirs of	Commutation pay for revolutionary services.	25	2	Petition	70	Rev. Claims	622	Adverse		Laid on table.		
Arrington, Thomas	Pension for revolutionary services	24	2	Petition	133	Rev. Pensions				Discharged; laid on table.		
Artacho, Gregoire	Confirmation of title to land in Louisiana.	21	1	Petition	51	Priv. Land Claims.						
Arthur, John	Pension	20	1	Petition	242	Military Pensions	Feb. 19, 1828	Adverse.				
Arthur, John	Back peusion	22	1	Resolution	126	Rev. Pensions.						
Arthur, John	Pensions for revolutionary services	27	2	Petition	936	Rev. Pensions				Discharged; laid on table.		
Arthur, Martin H.	(See Samuel Davis, and others)	25	3		98							
Artman, Justice	Pension for revolutionary services.	24	1	Petition	107	Rev. Pensions.						
Artman, Justice	Pension for revolutionary services.	25	2	Petition	729	Rev. Pensions				Discharged; laid on table.		
Artmen, Justice	Pension for revolutionary services.	26	1	Petition	170	Rev. Pensions				Discharged; laid on table.		
Arundel, Robert, widow of.	Indemnity for loss of husband in the public service.	12	2	Petition	664	Claims.						
Arundel, Robert, widow of.	Indemnity for loss of husband in the public service.	13	1	Petition	12	Claims				Discharged.		
Arundel, Robert, widow of.	Continuance of pension	15	1	Petition	187	Naval Affairs.						
Arundel, Willliam, representatives of.	Indemnity for Indian depredations.	26	1	Petition	353	Claims.						

List of private claims presented to the House of Representatives of the United States from the 1st to the 31st Congress, inclusive—Continued.

Names of claimants.	Nature or object of the claim.	Congress.	Session.	How brought before the House of Reps.	Page of journal.	To what committee of the House referred.	No. or date of the report.	Nature of the report.	No. of the bill.	How disposed of by the House of Reps.	How disposed of by the Senate.	Date of the act of Congress, and remarks.
Asbury, Samuel M.	Pension	23	1	Petition	459	Invalid Pensions	388	Favorable	405	Referred to Committee Whole House.		
Asbury, Samuel M.	Pension	23	2	Rep. Committee Whole House.	336			With amend.	405	Passed	Passed with amendment.	
Asbury, Samuel M.	Pension	24	1	Petition	260	Invalid Pensions	558	Favorable	550	Passed	Passed	App'd June 28, 1836
Asbury, Samuel M.	Pension	24	2	Petition	398	Invalid Pensions				Leave to withdraw.		
Asbury, Samuel M.	Increase of pension	25	2	Resolution	77	Invalid Pensions	297	Favorable	337	Passed	Indef. postp'd.	
Asbury, Samuel M.	Increase of pension	25	3	Resolution	89	Invalid Pensions	76	Favorable	954	Passed	Adverse report.	
Asbury, Samuel M.	Increase of pension	26	1	Resolution	160	Invalid Pensions	176	Favorable	187	Passed	Indef. postp'd.	
Asbury, Samuel M.	Increase of pension	27	3	House bill	91	Whole House	Dec. 23, 1842	Favorable	571	Passed	Passed	App'd March 3, 1843
Asbury, Samuel M.	Increase of pension	28	1	Petition	261	Invalid Pensions				Discharged; laid on table.		
Asbury, Samuel M.	Increase of pension	29	1	Petition	872	Invalid Pensions.						
Asbury, Samuel M.	Increase of pension	29	2	Petition	92	Invalid Pensions.						
Asbury, Henry	Relating to a land warrant	21	1	Documents	327	Priv. Land Claims				Discharged; leave to withdraw.		
Asevedo, Manuel	Confimation of title to land at Terre aux Bœuff.	22	1	House bill	107	Whole House	Mar. 23, 1832	With't amend.	125	Passed	Passed	App'd June 25, 1832
Ash, Christain	(See Christain Ish.)	21	2		67							
Ash, George	Confirmation of title to land North West Territory.	7	1	Petition	76	Select				Discharged; referred to Committee Whole House.		
Ash, George	Confirmation of title to land North West Territory.	8	2	Petition	53	Claims.						
Ash, George	Confirmation of title to land North West Territory.	9	1	Petition	227	Public Lands				Discharged; referred to Committee Whole House.		
Ash, George	Confirmation of title to land North West Territory.	9	2	Petition	571	Public Lands				Discharged; referred to Committee Whole House.		Statutes at Large, vol. 2, p. 449.
Ash, George	Indemnity for property destroyed by the enemy.	15	2	Petition	148	Claims.						
Ash, George	Indemnity for property destroyed by the enemy.	25	3	Petition	120	Claims	62	Adverse		Laid on table.		
Ash, John B., representatives of.	Commutation pay for revolutionary services.	23	2	Petition	48	Rev. Claims.						
Ash, John B., representatives of.	Commutation pay for revolutionary services.	24	1	Petition	63	Rev. Claims	364	Favorable	367	Referred to Committee Whole House.		
Ash, John B., representatives of.	Commutation pay for revolutionary services.	25	2	Petition	39	Rev. Claims	122	Favorable	140	Passed	Passed	App'd July 7, 1838
Ashard, William K.	Compensation for canon lock, &c.	30	1	Memorial	460	Naval Affairs	717	Favorable	562	Referred to Committee Whole House.		
Ashbridge, Joseph	Pension for revolutionary services.	21	1	Petition	91	Military Pensions.						
Ashbridge, Joshua	Compensation for property taken for public use.	1	3	Petition	355					Referred to Secretary Treasury.		
Ashbridge, Joshua	Compensation for property taken for public use.	2	2	Rep. of Secretary Treasury.	626	Whole House.						
Ashbridge, Joshua	Compensation for property taken for public use.	3	2	Petition	309	Claims.						
Ashbridge, Joshua	Compensation for property taken for public use.	4	1	Petition	373	Claims	Jan. 4, 1796	Adverse		Leave to withdraw.		
Ashbrook, John	(See Carruthers and Ashbrook.)	25	2		594							
Ashburn, Lewis, agent of.	Compensation for military services	18	2	Senate bill	284	Military Affairs	Mar. 1, 1825	With't amend.	S. 41	Passed	Passed	App'd Mar. 3, 1825

List of private claims presented to the House of Representatives of the United States from the 1st to the 31st Congress, inclusive—Continued.

Names of claimants.	Nature or object of the claim.	Congress.	Session.	How brought before the House of Reps.	Page of journal.	To what committee of the House referred.	No. or date of the report.	Nature of the report.	No. of the bill.	How disposed of by the House of Reps.	How disposed of by the Senate.	Date of the act of Congress, and remarks.
Ashbury, Samuel	Pension for disability in the war of 1812.	24	2	Petition	48	Invalid Pensions.	....	....	....	Disch'd; laid on table.		
Ashby, James A., widow of	Pension for disability of deceased in Florida war.	29	1	Petition	1203	Invalid Pensions.						
Ashby, James A., widow of	Pension for disability of deceased in Florida war.	31	1	Petition	1279	Invalid Pensions.						
Ashby, Capt. John	Appropriation to satisfy Virginia land warrant.	31	2	Petition	177	Priv. Land Claims						
Ashby, Nathan	Increase of revolutionary pension	27	2	Petition	377	Invalid Pensions.						
				Documents	515	Invalid Pensions	....	....	....	Disch'd; laid on table.		
Ashby, Nathan	Increase of revolutionary pension	29	1	Petition	104	Rev. Pensions	78	Adverse	....	Laid on table.		
				Memorial	162	Invalid Pensions	....	....	....	Disch'd; laid on table.		
Ashby, Nathaniel, heirs of	Compensation for revolutionary services.	25	3	Petition	361	Rev. Claims.	....	....	....	Discharged.		
Ashby, Nathaniel, heirs of	Compensation for revolutionary services.	27	2	Documents	376	Rev. Claims	526	Adverse	....	Laid on table.		
Ashby, Nathaniel, heirs of	Compensation for revolutionary services.	28	1	Petition	183	Rev. Claims	....	....	....	Disch'd; laid on table.		
Ashby, Nathaniel, heirs of	Compensation for revolutionary services.	28	2	Petition	140	Claims.						
Ashby, Peter, heirs of	Compensation for revolutionary services.	30	2	Memorial	204	Rev. Pensions.						
Ashby, Peter, heirs of	Compensation for revolutionary services.	31	1	Memorial	214	Rev. Pensions	126	Adverse	....	Laid on table.		
Ashcroft, John, heir of	Right of pre-emption	21	2	Petition	272	Public Lands.						
Ashe, John B., heir of	Commutation pay for revolutionary services.	23	1	Petition	189	Rev. Claims.						
Ashe, John B., heir of	Commutation pay for revolutionary services.	23	2	Petition	48	Rev. Claims.						
Ashe, John B., heir of	Commutation pay for revolutionary services.	24	1	Petition	63	Rev. Claims	364	Favorable	367	Referred to Committee Whole House.		
Ashe, John B., representatives of	Commutation pay for revolutionary services.	25	2	Petition	39	Rev. Claims	122	Favorable	140	Passed	Passed	App'd July 9, 1838
Ashe, Samuel,	(See sureties of Timothy Bloodworth.)	11	2	....	226							
Ashe, Samuel P.	(See heir of John B. Ashe)	23	1	....	189							
Ashley, James P.	(See surety of N. P. Robinson)	26	1	....	619							
Ashley, Nathaniel, heirs of	Compensation for revolutionary services.	25	2	Petition	546	Rev. Claims.						
Ashley, Nathaniel, heirs of	Compensation for revolutionary services.	25	3	Petition	361	Rev. Claims.						
Ashley, Robert & others	Confirmation of sundry Spanish claims in Mississippi.	5	2	Memorial	158	Select.						
Ashley, Samuel, jr.	Additional compensation for taking 5th census.	22	1	Petition	288	Claims.						
Ashley, Warren, executors of.	Indemnity for French spoliations prior to 1800.	26	1	Memorial	182	Foreign Affairs	343	Favorable	319	Referred to Committee Whole House.		
Ashley, Warren, executors of.	Commutation pay for revolutionary services.	23	1	Memorial	157	Rev. Claims.						
Ashley, Warren, executors of.	Commutation pay for revolutionary services.	23	2	Memorial	138	Rev. Claims	Jan. 19, 1835	Adverse	....	Laid on table.		
Ashley, Warren, executors of.	Commutation pay for revolutionary services.	24	1	Memorial	102	Rev. Claims	March 3, 1831	Adverse	....	Laid on table.		

List of private claims presented to the House of Representatives of the United States from the 1st to the 31st Congress, inclusive—Continued.

Names of claimants.	Nature or object of the claim.	Congress.	Session.	How brought before the House of Reps.	Page of journal.	To what committee of the House referred.	No. or date of the report.	Nature of the report.	No. of the bill.	How disposed of by the House of Reps.	How disposed of by the Senate.	Date of the act of Congress, and remarks.
Ashley, Warren, executors of.	Separation of interest, &c., in case of the brig Bayard.	25	3	Petition	119	Foreign Affairs.				Discharged.		
Ashley, Warren, executors of.	Separation of interest, &c., in case of the brig Bayard.	26	1	Petition	350	Foreign Affairs.						
Ashley, Warren, executors of.	Separation of interest, &c., in case of the brig Bayard.	26	2	Petition	181	Foreign Affairs.						
Ashley, William	Pension	21	1	Petition	91	Military Pensions.				Discharged; laid on the table.		
Ashly, William	(See as signeeof Grant Weed.)	23	1		385							
Ashton, Henry	Compensation as marshal of District of Columbia.	23	1	Petition	337	Dist. of Columbia.						
Ashton, Henry & others	Compensation as Inspectors of Penitentiary, District of Columbia.	23	1	Petition	337	Dist. of Columbia.						
Ashton, Henry, surety of	Release from liability	27	2	Petition	106	Judiciary	Feb. 9, 1842	Favorable Bill.	116	Passed	Passed	App'd July 27, 1842
Ashton, James	Compensation as watchman to jail of District of Columbia.	24	1	Petition	853	Dist. of Columbia.						
Ashton, Jacob, (Mass.)	Indemnity for French spoliations prior to 1800.	26	1	Memorial	182	Foreign Affairs	343	Favorable	319	Referred to Committee Whole House.		
Ashton, John	Pay and emoluments as lieutenant in revolutionary war.	2	2	Petition	683							
				Report Secretary War.	735					Laid on table.		
Ashton, John	Compensation for revolutionary services.	8	1	Petition	540	Claims				Referred to Committee Whole House.		
Ashton, John	Pension	16	2	Petition	92	Pens. & Rev. Clm's.				Referred to Secretary War.		
Ashton, John	Pension	17	1	Petition	67	Rev. Pensions				Leave to withdraw.		
Ashton, John	Pension	23	1	Petition	332	Invalid Pensions	442	Favorable	460	Referred to Committee Whole House.		
Ashton, John	Pension	23	2	Rep't Committee Whole House.	336			With't amend.	460	Passed	Passed	App'd March 3, 1835
Ashton, John	Increase of pension	28	1	Petition	440	Invalid Pensions.						
Askins, Robert	Pension for revolutionary services.	17	2	Petition	117	Pens. & Rev. Cl'ms.						
Askins, Robert	Pension for revolutionary services.	19	1	Petition	149	Military Pensions.	April 1, 1826	Adverse		Laid on table.		
Askins, Robert, heirs of	Compensation for revolutionary services.	21	2	Resolution	85	Rev. Claims.						
Askins, Robert, heirs of	Compensation for revolutionary services.	22	1	Petition	46	Rev. Pensions	Mar. 6, 1832	Adverse		Laid on table.		
Askins, Robert, widow of.	Compensation for revolutionary services.	20	1	Petition	78	Rev. Claims				Discharged; leave to withdraw.		
Askins, Robert, widow of	Compensation for revolutionary services.	25	3	Petition	216	Rev. Pensions				Discharged; laid on table.		
Askins, Rebert, widow of.	Compensation for revolutionary services.	26	1	Petition	172	Rev. Pensions				Discharged; laid on table.		
Askins, Robert, widow of.	Compensation for revolutionary services.	26	2	Petition	78	Rev. Pensions				Discharged; laid on table.		
Askins, Robert, widow of.	Compensation for revolutionary services.	29	1	Petition	856	Rev. Pensions	826	Adverse		Laid on table.		
Asop, Samuel	Renewal of a lost certificate	2	1	Petition	540					Referred to Secretary Treasury.		
Aspinwall, Augustus	Drawback on sugar exported	19	2	Petition	187	Ways and Means.				Discharged.		
Aspinwall, Augustus	Drawback on sugar exported	20	1	Petition	92	Ways and Means.	155	Favorable	179			
Aspinwall, Augustus	Drawback on sugar exported	20	2	Rep't Committee Whole House.	174			With't amend.	179	Passed	Passed	App'd Feb. 24, 1829

List of private claims presented to the House of Representatives of the United States from the 1st to the 31st Congress, inclusive—**Continued.**

Names of claimants.	Nature or object of the claim.	Congress.	Session.	How brought before the House of Reps.	Page of journal.	To what committee of the House referred.	No. or date of the report.	Nature of the report.	No. of the bill.	How disposed of by the House of Reps.	How disposed of by the Senate.	Date of the act of Congress, and remarks.
Aspinwall, Gilbert	Drawback on merchandise exported	14	1	Petition	386	Com. and Manuf.	April 12, 1816	Favorable		Indef. postponed.		
Aspinwall, Gilbert	Drawback on merchandise exported	14	2	Petition	101	Com. and Manuf.	Dec. 31, 1816	Favorable	36	Passed	Passed	App'd March 3, 1817
Aspinwall, John	Indemnity for French spoliations prior to 1800.	26	1	Memorial	182	Foreign Affairs	343	Favorable	319	Referred to Committee Whole House.		
Aspinwall, Thomas	Reimbursement of contingent expenses as consul.	23	2	House bill	36	Foreign Affairs	7	With't amend.	571	Referred to Committee Whole House.		
Aspinwall, Thomas	Reimbursement of contingent expenses as consul.	24	1	Memorial	115	Foreign Affairs.						
Aspinwall, Thomas	Reimbursement of contingent expenses as consul.	24	1	Senate bill	146	Foreign Affairs	119	With't amend.	S. 110	Passed	Passed	App'd Jan. 19, 1836
Assessors under act of 1813	Additional compensation in certain cases.	15	2	Resolution	260	Ways and Means	Feb. 27, 1819	Favorable	329	Referred to Committee Whole House.		
Astachio, Gregorie	Confirmation of title to land in Louisiana.	20	1	Petition	343	Priv. Land Claims.						
Astley, Thomas	(See Phillips, Crammond, & Co., attorney of.)	26	1		182		343		319			
Aston, John	Pension for disability, war of 1812	25	2	Petition	267	Invalid Pensions				Discharged; laid on table.		
Aston, John	Pension for disability, war of 1812	25	3	Petition	128	Invalid Pensions.						
Aston, John	Pension for disability, war of 1812	26	1	Petition	162	Invalid Pensions	Mar. 5, 1840	Adverse		Laid on table.		
Aston, John	Pension for disability, war of 1812	26	2	Petition	36	Invalid Pensions	225	Adverse		Laid on table.		
Aston, John	Pension for disability, war of 1812	29	1	Petition	265	Invalid Pensions	291	Adverse		Laid on table.		
Astor, John Jacob	Confirmation of title to land in Michigan.	18	2	Petition	32	Public Lands.						
Astor, John Jacob	Release of United States title to Fort Gansevoort.	22	1	House bill	391	Whole House			401			
Atalanta brig, owners of	Indemniy for French spoliations prior to 1800.	26	1	Memorial	182	Foreign Affairs	343	Favorable	319	Referred to Committee Whole House.		
Atchison, John	Release from judgment in favor of United States.	28	1	Senate bill	697	Judiciary	May 15, 1844	With't amend.	S. 67	Passed	Passed	App'd June 17, 1844
Atchison, Joseph T.	Compensation for services, war of 1812.	29	1	Petition	270	Claims	276	Adverse		Laid on table.		
Atchison, Samuel	Indemnity for injuries received in public service.	25	3	Petition	452	Public Buildings				Discharged; laid on table.		
Atchison, Samuel	Indemnity for injuries received in public service.	26	1	Petition	182	Public Buildings				Discharged; laid on table.		
Atchison, Samuel	Indemnity for injuries received in public service.	26	2	Petition	79	Dist. of Columbia.						
Atherton, Caleb	Pension	16	1	Resolution	268	Pens. & Rev. Cl'ms.						
Atherton, Caleb	Pension	22	2	Petition	82	Invalid Pensions.						
Atherton, Charles H.	Reimbursement of payments for public lands.	26	1	Petition	960	Claims.						
Atherton, Charles H.	Reimbursement of payments for public lands.	26	2	Petition	38	Claims.						
Atherton, Charles H.	Reimbursement of payments for public lands.	27	2	Petition	55	Claims	266	Favorable	224	Passed	Passed with amendment.	App'd June 22, 1842
Atherton, Charles H.	Reimbursement of payments for public lands.	31	1	Petition	1227	Claims.						
Atherton, John	Pension for revolutionary services.	26	1	Petition	324	Rev. Pensions				Discharged; laid on table.		
Atkins, Ambrose, heirs of	Indemnity for French spoliations prior to 1800.	31	1	Petition	224	Foreign Affairs	355	General bill	318	Referred to Committee Whole House.		
Atkins, George	(See Cephas Carpenter and others.)	27	2		247							
Atkins, Hampton	Pension	21	1	Petition	377	Military Pensions.						

List of private claims presented to the House of Representatives of the United States from the 1st to the 31st Congress, inclusive—Continued.

Names of claimants.	Nature or object of the claim.	Congress.	Session.	How brought before the House of Reps.	Page of journal.	To what committee of the House referred.	No. or date of the report.	Nature of the report.	No. of the bill.	How disposed of by the House of Reps.	How disposed of by the Senate.	Date of the act of Congress, and remarks.
Atkins, Isaac	Section of land for disability in public service.	25	3	Petition	135	Public Lands	59	Adverse	......	Laid on table.		
Atkins, Joseph	Bounty on fishing schooner Hannah.	4	1	Petition	536	....	....	....	......	Laid on table.		
Atkins, Mary	Indemnity for property destroyed by the enemy.	15	2	Petition	148	Claims.						
Atkins, Quintus F.	Reimbursement of wages, &c., for servant.	15	1	Petition	326	Millitary Affairs.						
Atkinson, Amos, executor of.	Indemnity for French spoliations prior to 1800.	26	1	Memorial	182	Foreign Affairs	343	Favorable	319	Referred to Committee Whole House.		
Atkinson, Benjamin	Right of pre-emption	27	2	Documents	75	Public Lands	504	Adverse	......	Laid on table.		
Atkinson, George	(See Alexander Campbell, heirs of, attorney.)	26	1	....	182	....	343	....	319			
Atkinson, Jesse	Bounty land for services in war of 1812.	28	1	Petition	326	Claims.						
Atkinson, Theodore	Increase of pension	24	2	Petition	346	Rev. Claims	....	....	......	Discharged; laid on table.		
Atkinson, Thomas	(See heirs of Wm. Nelson)	23	1	....	524							
Atkinson, Thomas, executors of.	(See surety for Richard Bean)	25	2	....	279							
Atkinson, Thomas	(See Wm. H. Bedford, agent, &c.)	28	1	....	262							
Atkinson, Wm., widow of.	Pension for revolutionary services.	14	2	Petition	213	Pens. & Rev. Cl'ms.	Jan. 29, 1817	Adverse	......	Rejected.		
Atkinson, William	Extension of patent for India-rubber cloth.	31	1	Petition	1282	Patents.						
Atlee, William A., administrator of.	Balance due as commissary of prisoners in revolutionary war.	28	1	Petition	195	Claims	72	Favorable	94	Passed	Reported with't amendment.	
Atlee, William A., administrator of.	Balance due as commissary of prisoners in revolutionary war.	29	1	Petition	679	Claims.						
Atlee, William A., administrator of.	Balance due as commissary of prisoners in revolutionary war.	30	1	Petition	110	Rev. Claims.						
Atlee, William A., administrator of.	Balance due as commissary of prisoners in revolutionary war.	30	2	Petition	239	Rev. Claims.						
Atlee, William A., administrator of.	Balance due as commissary of prisoners in revolutionary war.	31	1	Petition	391	Claims	418	Adverse	......	Laid on table.		
Atset, Joseph	Pension	16	2	Petition	249	Rev. Pensions	Feb. 28, 1821	Adverse	......	Laid on table.		
Atset, Joseph	Pension	18	1	Resolution	280	Rev. Pensions	....	....	......	Discharged; leave to withdraw.		
Atwater, Caleb	Compensation for attendance on Committee of Ways and Means.	24	2	Documents	391	Indian Affairs.						
Atwater, Caleb	Compensation for attendance on Committee of Ways and Means.	25	2	Documents	398	Claims	832	Adverse	......	Laid on table.		
Atwater, Caleb	Compensation for services as Indian agent.	27	3	Petition	53	Indian Affairs	151	Adverse	......	Laid on table.		
Atwater & Daggett, and others.	Remission of extra tonnage duty	22	1	Petition	30	Commerce	Jan. 11, 1832	Adverse	......	Laid on table.		
Atwater & Daggett, and others.	Remission of extra tonnage duty	23	1	Petition	107	Commerce	102	Favorable	106	Passed	Passed	App'd June 30, 1834
Atwater, Elnathan, & others	Arrest of proceedings against ship Ann Maria.	12	1	Petition	50	Com. and Manufac.						
Atwater, Elnathan, & others	Indemnity for French spoliations prior to 1800.	26	1	Memorial	182	Foreign Affairs	343	Favorable	319	Referred to Committee Whole House.		
Atwater, Elnathan, & others	Indemnity for French spoliations prior to 1800.	29	2	Memorial	83	Foreign Affairs.						

List of private claims presented to the House of Representatives of the United States from the 1st to the 31st Congress, inclusive—Continued.

Names of claimants.	Nature or object of the claim.	Congress.	Session.	How brought before the House of Reps.	Page of journal.	To what committee of the House referred.	No. or date of the report.	Nature of the report.	No. of the bill.	How disposed of by the House of Reps.	How disposed of by the Senate.	Date of the act of Congress, and remarks.
Atwater, J. M.	Indemnity for French spoliations prior to 1800.	26	1	Memorial	182	Foreign Affairs	343	Favorable	319	Referred to Committee Whole House.		
Atwater, Reuben	Compensation for services as secretary, &c., Michigan.	12	2	Senate bill	655	Claims	Feb. 5, 1813	With't amend.	S. 56	Passed	Passed	App'd Feb. 24, 1813
Atwater, Reuben	Compensation as acting Governor, &c., Michigan.	18	2	Petition	158	Ways and Means.						
Atwater, Reuben	Compensation as acting Governor, &c., Michigan.	19	1	Petition	407	Ways and Means				Discharged; leave to withdraw.		
Atwater, Russell	Pension	21	2	Petition	209	Military Pensions.						
Atwater, Russell	Pension	22	1	Petition	56	Rev. Pensions.						
Atwater, Russell	Back pension	23	1	Resolution	107	Rev. Pensions.						
Atwater, Russell	Back pension	24	2	Resolution	71	Rev. Pensions.						
Atwell, Ebenezer	Payment of prize money due him	28	2	Petition	205	Naval Affairs				Discharged; laid on table.		
Atwell, Ebenezer	Payment of prize money due him	29	1	Petition	90	Claims	32	Adverse		Laid on table.		
Atwell, Jos., & E. Hayden	Indemnity for illegal seizure of pork.	23	1	Petition	246	Claims.						
Atwell, Jos., & E. Hayden	Indemnity for illegal seizure of pork.	23	2	Petition	59	Claims.						
Atwell, Jos., & E. Hayden	Indemnity for illegal seizure of pork.	24	1	Documents	264	Claims	296	Adverse		Laid on table.		
Atwell, Jos., & E. Hayden	Indemnity for illegal seizure of pork.	24	2	Documents	395	Claims.						
Atwell, Jos., & E. Hayden	Indemnity for illegal seizure of pork.	25	2	Petition	88	Claims	Jan. 17, 1838	Adverse		Laid on table.		
Atwell, Jos., & E. Hayden	Indemnity for loss on contract for pork.	26	2	Petition	52	Claims.						
Atwood, Asenah	Two sections of land in Iowa	26	1	Petition	935	Public Lands.						
Atwood, John	Pension for wounds in naval service.	23	1	Petition	273	Invalid Pensions	Feb. 21, 1834	Adverse		Laid on table.		
Atwood, Joshua, jr.	Bounty on fishing schooner Abelino.	25	2	Petition	349	Commerce				Discharged; laid on table.		
Atwood, Joshua, jr.	Bounty on fishing schooner Abelino.	25	3	Petition	189	Commerce				Discharged.		
Atwood, Joshua, jr.	Bounty on fishing schooner Abelino.	26	1	Petition	176	Commerce.						
Atwood, Joshua, jr.	Bounty on fishing schooner Abelino.	26	2	Petition	107	Commerce.						
Atwood, Joshua, jr.,	Bounty on fishing schooner Abelino.	27	2	Petition	96	Commerce	63	Favorable	98	Passed	Passed	App'd July 27, 1842
Atwood, Moses	Pension for revolutionary services	22	1	Resolution	87	Rev. Pensions.						
Atwood, Tisdale	Pension for services in Indian wars	24	2	Petition	72	Rev. Pensions				Discharged; laid on table.		
Atwood, William, administrator of.	Claim as Postmaster, Alabama	26	1	Documents	1162	P. O. & P. Roads.						
Auchinclops, Hugh	(See James Stewart, executor of)	26	1		182		343		319			
Auberry, James	Compensation for horses, &c., lost in Seminole war.	23	1	Document	154	Claims.						
Auberry, James	Compensation for horses, &c., lost in Seminole war.	28	1	Petition	262	Claims.						
Auberry, Noland	(See Wm. H. Bedford, agent, &c.)	28	1		262							

List of private claims presented to the House of Representatives of the United States from the 1st to the 31st Congress, inclusive—Continued.

Names of claimants.	Nature or object of the claim.	Congress.	Session.	How brought before the House of Reps.	Page of journal.	To what committee of the House referred.	No. or date of the report.	Nature of the report.	No. of the bill.	How disposed of by the House of Reps.	How disposed of by the Senate.	Date of the act of Congress, and remarks.
Aubin, Joshua	(See William Whitehead, and others.)	16	2		300				S. 56			
Aud, Joseph	Exchange of a land entry	26	1	Petition	356	Public Lands.						
Audebert, Philip, and others	Increase of salaries as clerks in War Department.	3	1	Petition	40	Select.						
				Memorial	93	Select	54	Favorable	69	Passed	Rejected.	
Audebert, Philip, and others	Extra compensation as clerk in War Department.	4	2	Memorial	636	Claims.						
Audrain, Peter	Compensation as clerk to Land Commissioners, Michigan.	11	2	Petition	144	Claims	Feb. 14, 1810	Favorable	83	Referred to Committee Whole House.		
Audrain, Peter	Compensation as clerk to Land Commissioners, Michigan.	11	3	Petition	441	Claims	Jan. 9, 1811	Favorable	171	Passed	Passed	App'd Feb. 26, 1811
Audrain, Peter	Compensation as clerk and interpreter, &c.	12	1	Petition	66	Claims.						
Audrain, Peter	Compensation as clerk and interpreter, &c.	13	2	Petition	182	Claims				Discharged.		
Audrain, Peter	Compensation as clerk and interpreter, &c.	13	3	Petition	640	Claims	Feb. 27, 1815	Adverse		Referred to Committee Whole House.		
Audrain, Peter	Compensation as clerk and interpreter, &c.	14	1	Petition	93	Claims	Feb. 19, 1816	Favorable	84	Passed	Passed with amendment.	App'd April 30, 1816
Audubon, John S	Remission of duty on his work on the birds of North America.	22	1	Petition	383	Ways and Means.						
Audubon, John S	Remission of duty on his work on the birds of North America.	22	2	Petition	44	Ways and Means.						
Auger, W	Compensation for bust of Chief Justice Ellsworth.)	24	2	Appropriation bill								Statutes at Large, vol. 5, p. 173.
Augusta, city of	(See Georgia.)											
Augur, Felix, widow of	Pension for revolutionary services.	27	2	Petition	737	Rev. Pensions	917	Favorable	531	Ordered to 3d reading.		
Augur, Felix, widow of	Pension for revolutionary services.	27	3	House bill	89				531	Passed	Laid on table.	
Augustus, Alex'r F	(See heirs of Count De Grasse)	28	1	Memorial	90	Rev. Claims.						
Augustus, David	Refunding fine imposed for violation of law in relation to distilleries.	18	1	Petition	109	Ways and Means.						
Augustus, David	Refunding fine imposed for violation of law in relation to distilleries.	19	1	Petition	36	Ways and Means				Discharged; laid on table.		
Auld, Colin	(See John Ramsey, executor of.)	26	1		182		343		319			
Auld, John	Indemnity for French spoliations prior to 1800.	26	1	Memorial	182	Foreign Affairs	343	Favorable	319	Referred to Committee Whole House.		
Aulick, John H	Compensation for extra duties; captain United States navy.	23	1	Petition	621	Naval Affairs	June 3, 1834	Favorable	507	Referred to Committee Whole House.		
Aulick, John H	Compensation for extra duties; captain United States navy.	24	1	Petition	61	Naval Affairs.						
Aulick, John H	Compensation for extra duties; captain United States navy.	24	2	Petition	46	Naval Affairs				Discharged; laid on table.		
Auner, Peter G., widow of	Bounty land for military services.	13	1	Petition	87					Laid on table.		
Auner, Peter G., widow of	Bounty land for military services.	13	2	Petition	189	Claims.						
Aupoix, Peter	Debenture on exported merchandise	5	2	Petition	108	Com. and Manuf.	Jan. 2, 1798	Favorable	82	Passed	Indef. postp'd.	
Aurora, ship, owners of	Reimbursement of certain duties.	28	1	Petition	325	Commerce.						
Ausburn, Ebenezer	Bounty land for services under General Clarke.	19	1	Resolution	102	Priv. Land Claims.	Feb. 21, 1826	Adverse		Laid on table.		
Ausement, William D	Pension for bounty land	28	1	Petition	687	Claims.						

List of private claims presented to the House of Representatives of the United States from the 1st to the 31st Congress, inclusive—Continued.

Names of claimants.	Nature or object of the claim.	Congress.	Session.	How brought before the House of Reps.	Page of journal.	To what committee of the House referred.	No. or date of the report.	Nature of the report.	No. of the bill.	How disposed of by the House of Reps.	How disposed of by the Senate.	Date of the act of Congress, and remarks.
Ausement, William D.	Pension for bounty land	29	1	Resolution	129	Claims	116	Adverse		Laid on table		Leave to withdraw 31st Cong. 2d sess.
Ausley, John	Compensation for transporting American prisoners.	14	1	Petition	43	Claims				Discharged; laid on table.		
Ausman, Abraham	Pension	29	1	Petition	93	Invalid Pensions	471	Favorable	349	Passed	Passed	App'd Aug. 8, 1846
Ausman, Abraham	Pension	30	2	Petition	239	Invalid Pensions	96	Adverse		Discharged.		
Austell, Jeremiah, (Mobile)	Release of liabilities in consequence of the loss of vouchers by fire.	25	2	Petition	274	Claims	April 20, 1838	Adverse		Laid on table.		
Austell, Jeremiah	Indemnity for loss on mail contract.	21	2	Petition	206	P. Of. and P. Roads.	Mar. 1, 1831	Adverse		Laid on table.		
Austell, Jeremiah	Indemnity for loss on mail contract.	22	1	Petition	124	P. Of. and P. Roads.	Jan. 20, 1832	Adverse		Laid on table.		
Austell, Jeremiah	Indemnity for loss on mail contract.	22	2	Petition	75	P. Of. and P. Roads.						
Austell, Jeremiah	Indemnity for loss on mail contract.	23	1	Senate bill	165	P. Of. and P. Roads.			S. 12			
Austell, Jeremiah, & others.	Compensation for opening mail road.	23	2	Petition	147	P. Of. and P. Roads.						
Austell, Jeremiah, & others.	Compensation for opening mail road.	24	2	Senate bill	279				S. 200			
Austell, Jeremiah, & others.	Compensation for opening mail road.	25	2	Senate bill	301	P. Of. and P. Roads.	745	Adverse	S. 20	Laid on table.		
Austell, Jeremiah, & others.	Compensation for opening mail road.	26	1	Senate bill	227	P. Of. and P. Roads.	July 21, 1840	Adverse	S. 29			
Austin, Benjamin	Compensation for extra services as commissioner of loans.	15	2	Petition	225	Claims.						
Austin, Caleb	Pension for revolutionary services.	3	2	Report Secretary War.	278	Claims.	Feb. 28, 1795	Pension bill	130	Passed	Postponed.	
Austin, Caleb	Pension for revolutionary services.	4	1	Report Secretary War.	445	Claims	Feb. 18, 1796	Pension bill	156	Passed	Passed with amendment.	App'd April 20, 1796
Austin, Daniel	(See Thomas Russell and others).	3	1		67							
Austin, David	(See Haggerty & Austin)	21	2		128							
Austin, Eusebius	Continuation of pension	16	2	Petition	164	Rev. Pensions	Feb. 15, 1821	Adverse		Leave to withdraw.		
Austin, Eusebius	Continuation of pension	17	2	Petition	82	Whole House				Discharged; leave to withdraw.		
Austin, Eusebius	Arrears of pension	19	1	Petition	149	Military Pensions	April 1, 1826	Adverse		Laid on table.		
Austin, Isaac	Pension for revolutionary services.	24	2	Resolution	76	Rev. Pensions.						
Austin, Isaac	Pension for revolutionary services.	24	2	Documents	97	Rev. Pensions	145	Favorable	875			
Austin, Isaac	Pension for revolutionary services.	25	2	Resolution	37	Rev. Pensions	155	Favorable	180	Adverse report.		
Austin, Isaac	Pension for revolutionary services.	26	1	Petition	170	Rev. Pensions	159	Favorable	169	Passed	Indef. postp'd.	
Austin, James	Confirmation of title to land in Missouri.	15	1	Petition	312	Priv. Land Claims.						
Austin, James	Confirmation of title to land in Missouri.	16	1	Petition	71	Priv. Land Claims.						
Austin, James	Confirmation of title to land in Missouri.	17	1	Petition	53	Priv. Land Claims.						
Austin, James	Confirmation of title to land in Missouri.	18	1	Petition	53	Public Lands	Jan. 16, 1824	Favorable	65	Passed	Passed	App'd May 26, 1824
Austin, John	To be restored to pension roll	21	1	Resolution	88	Military Pensions.						
Austin, John	To be restored to pension roll	21	2	Resolution	77	Military Pensions.						
Austin, John	Pension	23	1	Petition	53	Rev. Pensions.						
Austin, John P.	(See Austin & Tailer)	23	2		304							
Austin, John T.	Right of pre emption	25	3	Rep't Committee	243		112	Adverse		Laid on table.		

List of private claims presented to the House of Representatives of the United States from the 1st to the 31st Congress, inclusive—Continued.

Names of claimants.	Nature or object of the claim.	Congress.	Session.	How brought before the House of Reps.	Page of journal.	To what committee of the House referred.	No. or date of the report.	Nature of the report.	No. of the bill.	How disposed of by the House of Reps.	How disposed of by the Senate.	Date of the act of Congress, and remarks.
Austin, Joseph	Compensation for horse lost in public service.	24	2	Petition	93	Indian Affairs.						
Austin, Joseph	Compensation for horse lost in public service.	25	2	Petition	97	Indian Affairs				Discharged.		
Austin, Joseph	(See Reuben E. Gentry and others.)	23	1		130							
Austin, Loring	Indemnity on account of a certain judgment.	15	1	Petition	21	Claims	60	Favorable	52	Passed	Passed	App'd April 20, 1818
Austin, Loring, and G. Wells.	Amendatory of act of last session.	15	2	Resolution	282	Claims.						
Austin, Nathaniel	Increase of compensation as collector at New York.	2	2	Memorial	628					Referred to Secretary Treasury.		
Austin, Nathaniel	Pension	11	3	Pension bill	604	Whole House	Mar. 2, 1811	With amend.	218	Passed	Passed with amendment.	App'd March 3, 1811
Austin, Richard, widow of.	Pension for revolutionary services.	29	1	Petition	266	Rev. Pensions	459	Favorable	336	Passed	Passed	App'd Aug. 8, 1846
Austin, Samuel, jr.	Reimbursement of certain duties on hemp.	24	1	Memorial	94	Ways and Means	Jan. 27, 1836	By Bill	233	Referred to Committee Whole House.		
Austin & Tailer	Indemnity for loss on contract with Engineer Department.	23	2	Memorial	304	Military Affairs.						
Austin & Tailer	Indemnity for loss on contract with Engineer Department.	24	1	Petition	201	Claims	694	Favorable	652	Referred to Committee Whole House.		
Austin & Tailer	Indemnity for loss on contract with Engineer Department.	25	2	Memorail	36	Claims	49	Favorable	61	Passed	Passed	App'd June 7, 1838
Austin, William	(See Hugh McMahon, heirs of)	21	1		264							
Austin, William	Pension	27	2	Petition	48	Naval Affairs	579	Adverse		Laid on table.		
Autery, Alexander	Benefit of act of March 2, 1821	18	2	Petition	24	Public Lands.						
Avart, Robert, representatives of.	Indemnity for property destroyed by United States troops.	22	1	Petition	266	Claims	339	Favorable	431	Referred to Committee Whole House.		
Avart, Robert, representatives of.	Indemnity for property destroyed by United States troops.	23	1	Petition	34	Claims	5	Favorable	5	Passed	Passed	App'd Jan. 24, 1834
Aver, John	(See Louis F. Beeler)	30	1		115		482					
Averill, Calvin K.	Compensation for public services.	27	2	Petition	247	Judiciary.						
Averill, Canfield	Pension for disability, war of 1812	30	1	Petition	980	Invalid Pensions	803	Favorable	624	Referred to Committee Whole House.		
Averill, Canfield	Pension for disability, war of 1812	30	2	Rep't Committee Whole House.	363			With't amend.	624	Passed.		
Averill, Canfield	Pension for disability, war of 1812	31	1	Petition	275	Invalid Pensions	51	Favorable	81	Passed	Passed	App'd Aug. 30, 1850
Averill, Daniel	Pension for revolutionary services	13	3	Petition	712	Rev. Claims	Feb. 20, 1815	Pension bill	303	Passed	Passed	App'd March 3, 1815
Averill, Daniel	Pension for revolutionary services	16	1	Petition	32	Pens. & Rev. Cl'ms.						
Averill, Ebenezer	Indemnity for damage to property by United States troops.	16	1	Petition	447	Claims.						
Averill, Ebenezer	Indemnity for damage to property by United States troops.	16	2	Petition	152	Claims.						
Averill, Ebenezer	Indemnity for damage to property by United States troops.	17	1	Petition	39	Claims	Jan. 22, 1822	Adverse		Laid on table.		
Averill, Ebenezer	Indemnity for damage to property by United States troops.	18	1	Petition	130	Claims	Feb. 2, 1824	Adverse.				
Averill, Ebenezer	Indemnity for damage to property by United States troops.	18	2	Petition	46	Claims	8	Favorable	249	Passed	Passed	App'd March 3, 1825
Averill, Eliphalet	Remission of tax on distillery	14	2	Petition	211	Ways and Means.						
Averill, E. & H. & Co.	To import British goods	12	1	Petition	95	Com. and Manuf.						
Averill, Henry K.	(See Martin S. Aiken and others.)	17	1		359							
Averill, James, jr., and others.	Permission to import card wire	12	1	Petition	85	Com. and Manuf.						

List of private claims presented to the House of Representatives of the United States from the 1st to the 31st Congress, inclusive—**Continued.**

Names of claimants.	Nature or object of the claim.	Congress.	Session.	How brought before the House of Reps.	Page of journal.	To what committee of the House referred.	No. or date of the report.	Nature of the report.	No. of the bill.	How disposed of by the House of Reps.	How disposed of by the Senate.	Date of the act of Congress, and remarks.
Averill, Joseph K.	Additional compensation as witness against White.	25	2	Petition	1123	Claims	981	Favorable	841	Referred to Committee Whole House.		
Averill, Joseph K.	Additional compensation as witness against White.	26	1	Petition	167	Claims.						
Averill, Nathan, jr.	Indemnity for destruction of property at Plattsburgh.	13	3	Petition	723	Claims	Feb. 15, 1815	Favorable	297	Passed	Passed	App'd March 3, 1815
Avery, Amos	Increase of pension	10	2	Pension bill	499	Whole House	Feb. 20, 1809	With amend.	158	Passed	Passed with amendment.	App'd Mar. 3, 1809
Avery, Amos	(See David Hull and others)	20	2		147							
Avery, A., and others	Release from payment of two notes.	25	2	Resolution	478	Claims	930	Adverse		Laid on table.		
Avery, Charles, widow of	Pension for revolutionary services.	27	2	Petition	238	Rev. Pensions	784	Adverse		Laid on table.		
Avery, David	(See John Avery and others.)	8	1		410							
Avery, Rev. D., heirs of	Pension for services as chaplain in revolutionary army.	28	2	Petition	111	Rev. Pensions.						
Avery, Rev. D., heirs of	Pension for services as chaplain in revolutionary army.	29	1	Petition	399	Rev. Pensions	607	Adverse		Laid on table.		
Avery, Rev. D., heirs of	Pension for services as chaplain in revolutionary army.	30	1	Memorial	936	Rev. Pensions	788	Adverse.		Laid on table.		
Avery, Ebenezer	Increase of pension	10	2	Pension bill	499	Whole House	Feb. 20, 1809	With amend.	158	Passed	Passed	App'd March 3, 1809
Avery, Ebenezer	Pension	21	2	Petition	52	Military Pensions.						
Avery, Ebenezer	Pension	22	1	Petition	67	Rev. Pensions.						
Avery, Elisha, and others	Bounty on a fishing vessel	23	2	Memorial	320	Commerce.						
Avery, Griswold	Pension for revolutionary services.	25	3	Resolution	291	Rev. Pensions.						
Avery, Griswold	Pension for revolutionary services.	26	1	Petition	170	Rev. Pensions.						
				Petition (2.)	284	Rev. Pensions.						
Avery, Henry and Hannah.	(See Hugh McClannon, heir of.)	30	1		67		172					
Avery, James	(See Canadian Refugees.)											
Avery, John, and others	Indemnity for infringement of their patent.	8	1	Petition	410	Claims				Discharged; leave to withdraw.		
Avery, John H	(See Justice Forbes and others)	24	1		914							
Avery, John J.	Indemnity for damage to his land in the late war.	23	1	Petition	74	Claims	240	Favorable	267	Referred to Committee Whole House.		
Avery, John J.	Indemnity for damage to his land in the late war.	23	2	Rep't Committee Whole House.	300			With't amend.	267	Passed	Passed	App'd March 3, 1835
Avery, Park	Increase of pension	10	2	Pension bill	499	Whole House	Feb. 20, 1809	With amend.	158	Passed	Passed with amendment.	App'd March 3, 1809
Avery, Park	Further increase of pension	15	2	Petition	43	Pens. & Rev. Cl'ms.						
Avery, Park	Further increase of pension	16	1	Petition	323	Pens. & Rev. Cl'ms.						
Avery, Saltmarsh, & Co.	Indemnity for Indian depredations.	24	2	Documents	85	P. O. & P. Roads.						
				Documents (2)	214	P. O. & P. Roads.	280	Favorable	958	Referred to Committee Whole House.		
Avery, Saltmarsh, & Co.	Indemnity for Indian depredations.	25	2	Documents	457	P. O. & P. Roads.	561	Favorable	550	Referred to Committee Whole House.		
Avery, Saltmarsh, & Co.	Indemnity for Indian depredations.	25	3	Rep't Committee Whole House.	380			With't amend.	550			
Avery, Saltmarsh, & Co.	Indemnity for Indian depredations.	26	2	Senate bill	203	P. O. & P. Roads.	Feb. 12, 1841	With't amend.	S. 18	Passed	Passed	App'd March 3, 1841
Avery, Samuel	(See John Avery and others)	8	1		410							
Avery, Samuel	Redemption of Continental money.	31	1	Petition	815	Claims.						
Avery, Thatcher	Remission of duties on importations at Castine, while in the possesion of the British.	16	2	Petition	101	Ways and Means.	Feb. 13, 1821	Favorable	251	Referred to Committee Whole House.		
Avery, Thatcher	Remission of duties on imports to Castine.	17	1	House bill	214	Whole House	May 4, 1822	With't amend.	69	Laid on table.		

List of private claims presented to the House of Representatives of the United States from the 1st to the 31st Congress, inclusive—Continued.

Names of claimants.	Nature or object of the claim.	Congress.	Session.	How brought before the House of Reps.	Page of journal.	To what committee of the House referred.	No. or date of the report.	Nature of the report.	No. of the bill.	How disposed of by the House of Reps.	How disposed of by the Senate.	Date of the act of Congress, and remarks.
Avery, Thatcher	Remission of duties on imports to Castine.	17	2	House bill	76	....	....	....	....	Referred to Committee Whole House.		
Avery, Thatcher	Remission of duties on imports to Castine.	18	1	Petition	214	Ways and Means	29	General bill	60	Passed	Passed	App'd May 19, 1824
Avery, Lieut. Thomas	Increase of pension for revolutionary services.	8	2	Petition	143	Claims.						
Avery, Lieut. Thomas	Increase and arrears of pension	9	1	Petition	190	Claims.						
Avery, Lieut. Thomas	Increase and arrears of pension	9	2	Pension bill	608	Whole House	Feb. 28, 1807	With't amend.	216	Passed	Passed	App'd March 3, 1807
Avery, William, administrator of.	Commutation pay for revolutionary services.	23	2	Petition	177	Rev. Claims.						
Avery, William, administrator of.	Commutation pay for revolutionary services.	24	1	Petition	104	Rev. Claims.						
Avila, Joseph, attorney of.	Indemnity for seizure of a cargo of slaves.	11	3	Petition	574	Com. and Manuf.						
Awkward, Henry	Indemnity for injuries at burning of the Treasury.	23	1	Petition	187	Dist. of Columbia	417	Favorable	438	Referred to Committee Whole House.		
Awkward, Henry	Indemnity for injuries at burning of the Treasurey.	23	2	House bill	162	....	....	....	438	Passed	Passed	App'd March 3, 1835
Axson, Dr. Samuel J.	Commutation pay and bounty land.	15	2	Petition	132	Pens. & Rev. Cl'ms.	Dec. 30, 1818	Adverse	....	Claim rejected.		
Axson, Dr. Samuel J., heirs of.	Commutation pay and bounty land.	22	1	Resolution	562	Rev. Claims	436	Favorable	531	Passed	Passed	App'd June 15, 1832
Axson, Dr. Samuel J., heirs of.	Full pay as surgeon in revolutionary war.	25	2	Petition	1118	Rev. Claims	....	....	....	Discharged; laid on table.		
Axson, Dr. Samuel J., heirs of.	Full pay as surgeon in revolutionary war.	26	2	Petition	84	Rev. Claims	Feb. 12, 1841	Adverse	....	Laid on table.		
Axton, Jeremiah	Compensation for rent of a house, &c.	23	1	Petition	217	Claims	212	Adverse	....	Laid on table.		
Ayer, Elijah	(See Canadian refugees.)											
Ayer, Elijah, jr.	(See Canadian refugees.)											
Ayer, Obadiah	(See Canadian refugees.)											
Ayers, Jonathan	Pay as lieutenant, revolutionary army.	3	1	Petition	93	....	....	....	....	Referred to Secretary War.		
Ayers, Jonathan	Pay as lieutenant, revolutionary army.	3	2	Rep. of Secretary of War.	278	....	....	....	....	Laid on table.		
Ayers, Thomas	(See Canadian refugees.)											
Ayers, Reuben	Pension for disabilities received in revolutionary war.	12	2	Petition	553	Claims	Feb. 26, 1813	Adverse	....	Laid on table.		
Aylet, Col. Wm., heirs of.	Half-pay for revolutionary services.	31	1	Petition	234	Rev. Claims.						
Aylette, William, heirs of.	Compensation for services, war of 1812.	27	2	Petition	73	Rev. Claims	204	Adverse	....	Laid on table.		
Aylward, James	(See James O'Brien)	4	2	....	716							
Ayot, Alexis	Pension for injuries in Fremont's expedition.	29	1	Senate bill	1108	Invalid Pensions	July 25, 1846	With't amend.	S. 174	Passed	Passed	App'd Aug. 10, 1846
Ayott, Lewis	Compensation for supplies furnished revolutionary army.	3	1	Petition	98	Select	50	Favorable	....	Laid on table.		
Ayres, Anne	Indemnity for French Spoliations prior 1800.	26	1	Memorial	182	Foreign Affairs	343	Favorable	319	Referred to Committee Whole House.		
Ayres, Henry	Half-pay as a revolutionary officer.	15	1	Petition	102	Pens. & Rev. Cl'ms.	....	....	....	Discharged.		

List of private claims presented to the House of Representatives of the United States from the 1st to the 31st Congress, inclusive—Continued.

Names of claimants.	Nature or object of the claim.	Congress.	Session.	How brought before the House of Reps.	Page of journal.	To what committee of the House referred.	No. or date of the report.	Nature of the report.	No. of the bill.	How disposed of by the House of Reps.	How disposed of by the Senate.	Date of the act of Congress, and remarks.
Babb, Seth, widow of	Arrears of pension due for revolutionary services.	29	1	Petition	219	Rev. Pensions.						
Babbit, Amey	Pension	27	2	Senate bill	1126	Rev. Pensions	Aug. 20, 1842	With't amend.	S. 228	Passed	Passed	App'd Aug. 29, 1842
Babbit, Almon W.	Compensation as Delegate from Utah.	31	1	Defic'y bill, pay and mileage.	1434	...	...	...	...	...	...	Stat. at large, vol. 9, p. 616.
Babbit, Charles W.	Compensation as acting carpenter in United States Navy.	29	2	Petition	56	Naval Affairs.						
Babbit, Charles W.	Compensation as acting carpenter in United States Navy.	30	1	Petition	99	Naval Affairs	108	General bill	97	Referred to Committee Whole House.		
Babbit, Charles W.	Compensaiion as acting carpenter in United States Navy.	31	1	Petition	371	Naval Affairs.						
Babbit, Edward B.	Extra pay, &c., while commanding Gurrier.	22	2	Senate bill	441	Whole House	Mar. 2, 1833	With't amend.	S. 87	Passed	Passed	App'd March 2, 1833
Babbit, Elijah C.	Pension	28	1	Petition	103	Invalid Pensions	39	Adverse	...	Laid on table.		
Babbit, Elijah C.	Pension	29	1	Petition	59	Invalid Pensions	155	Favorable	158	Passed	Passed	App'd Aug. 8, 1846
Babbit, Fitz H., mother of	Pension for naval services	21	2	Senate bill	387	Naval Affairs	Mar. 2, 1831	Adverse	S. 171	Laid on table.		
Babbit, Fitz H., mother of	Pension for naval services	22	2	Senate bill	211	Naval Affairs	Feb. 8, 1833	With amend.	S. 50	Passed	Passed	App'd March 2, 1833
Babbit, Fitz H., mother of	Extension of her pension	24	1	Resolution	339	Naval Affairs.						
				Senate bill	1157	Naval Affairs	July 1, 1836	With't amend.	S. 257	Passed	Passed	App'd July 2, 1836
Babbit, Fitz H., mother of	Further extension of pension	26	2	Petition	52	Naval Affairs.						
Babbit, Fitz H., mother of	Further extension of pension	27	2	Petition	690	Naval Affairs	597	Adverse	...	Laid on table.		
Babbit, Jacob & J. Dennis	Remission of duties on sugar destroyed.	14	1	Senate bill	410	Com. and Manuf.	April 12, 1816	With't amend.	S. 15	Indef. postponed.		
Babbit, Jacob	Remission of duties on sugar destroyed.	16	1	Senate bill	524	Whole House	...	...	S. 124			
Babbit, Jacob	Remission of duties on sugar destroyed.	17	1	Senate bill	374	Ways and Means	Mar. 21, 1822	With't amend.	S. 52	Laid on table.		
Babbit, Jacob	Remission of duties on sugar destroyed.	17	2	Senate bill	67	Ways and Means	Dec. 27, 1822	With't amend.	S. 7	Laid on table.		
Babbit, Jacob	Release from interest on bond for duties.	18	1	Petition	30	Ways and Means	3	Faborable	12	Passed	Passed	App'd Jan. 19, 1824
Babbit, James	Grant of land for military services	14	2	Petition	46	Military Affairs	Feb. 21, 1817	Adverse	...	Laid on table.		
Babbit, James	Grant of land for military services	15	1	Petition	22	Military Affairs.						
Babbit, James	Grant of land for military services	23	2	Resolution	115	Priv. Land Claims.						
Babbit, Joel	Increase of pension	17	1	Petition	567	...	...	...	...	Laid on table.		
Babbit, Joel	Increase of pension	17	2	Petition	165	Pension and Revolutionary Claims.						
Babbit, Lieut., widow of	Pension for loss of husband in U. S. service.	27	3	Petition	61	Naval Affairs	...	...	...	Discharged; laid on tale.		
Babbit, Mary Jane	(See mother of Fitz H. Babbitt)	21	2	...	387							
Babbit, Nathan	Compensation for revolutionary services.	10	1	Petition	15	Select.						
Babbit, Nathan	Componsation for revolutionary services.	10	2	Resolution	380	Select.						
Babbit, Nathan	Compensation for revolutionary services.	19	1	Resolution	51	Rev. Claims	Jan. 11, 1826	Adverse	...	Laid on table.		
Babbit, Thomas, widow of	Pension for services United States Navy.	19	2	Petition	154	Naval Affairs.						
Babbit, William D., widow of.	Pension for services United States Navy.	19	2	Petition	104	Naval Affairs.						
Babbit, William D., widow of.	Pension for services United States Navy.	23	1	Petition	128	Naval Affairs.						

List of private claims presented to the House of Representatives of the United States from the 1st to the 31st Congress, inclusive—Continued.

Names of claimants.	Nature or object of the claim.	Congress.	Session.	How brought before the House of Reps.	Page of journal.	To what committee of the House referred.	No. or date of the report.	Nature of the report.	No. of the bill.	How disposed of by the House of Reps.	How disposed of by the Senate.	Date of the act of Congress, and remarks.
Babbit, William D., widow of.	Pension for servtces United States Navy.	28	1	Petition	102	Naval Affairs.						
Babcock, Caleb, administrator of.	Compensation for military services	22	1	Petition (2)....	115	Naval Affairs.						
				Petition	288	Claims	480	Adverse	......	Referred to Committee Whole House.		
Babcock, Henry, assignee of.	Reimbursement of advances on public account.	18	1	Petition	432	Claims.						
Babcock, Henry, assignee of.	Reimbursement of advances on public account.	19	1	Petition	407	Claims..........	165	Favorable....	217	Passed	Reported with amendment.	
Babcock, Henry, assignee of.	Reimbursement of advances on public account.	19	2	Petition	82	Claims	Dec. 22, 1826	Favorable....	313	Passed	Passed.......	App'd Feb. 22, 1827
Babcock, Latham........	Indemnity for property destroyed at Dog Island.	28	1	Petition	442	Commerce........	....	....	......	Discharged; laid on table.		
Babcock, Phineas	Compensation for property taken for public use.	16	2	Petition	112	Pen. & Rev. Claims	Jan. 15, 1821	Adverse	......	Claim rejected.		
Babcock, Phineas, widow of.	Compensation for property taken for public use.	20	1	Petition	243	Rev. Claims.						
Babcock, Phineas, widow of.	Compensation for property taken for public use.	23	2	Petition	66	Rev. Claims......	Jan. 12, 1835	Adverse	......	Laid on table.		
Babcock, Samuel	Balance due on account..........	23	1	Appropriation bill	283	Whole House.....	....	Amendment..	283	Passed	Passed	App'd June 27, 1834
Babcock, Samuel H......	(See executor of John Brazer)...	26	1	....	182	....	343	....	319			
Babcock, William	Pension	19	2	Petition	186	Military Pensions.						
Babin, Pierre	Confirmation of title to land in Louisiana.	25	3	Senate bill.....	478	Priv. Land Claims.	....	....	S. 255			
Babin, Pierre	Confirmation of title to land in Louisiana.	26	1	Senate bill	420	Priv. Land Claims.	July 21, 1840	With't amend.	62			
Babin, Pierre	Confirmation of title to land in Louisiana.	26	2	Senate bill	225	Priv. Land Claims.	....	....	117			
Babson, Mary D.........	(See heir of Nathaniel Haradon).	25	2	....	1209							
Bache, George W., widow of.	Indemnity for property washed overboard.	30	1	Petition	165	Naval Affairs.						
Bache, George W., widow of.	Indemnity for property washed overboard.	30	2	Petition	345	Naval Affairs.						
Bache, George W., widow of.	Indemnity for property washed over board.	31	1	Petition	362	Naval Affairs.						
Bachelder, John.........	(See John Batchelder)..........	21	2	....	299							
Bachelder, Samuel.......	(See Samuel Batchelder)											
Back, Theophilus & Chas. McEvers.	Indemnity for French spoliations prior to 1800.	26	1	Memorial	182	Foreign Affairs ...	343	Favorable....	319	Referred to Committee Whole House.		
Backus, Charles D.......	Indemnity for destruction of property at Plattsburgh.	13	3	Petition	723	Claims	Feb. 15, 1815	Favorable	297	Passed............	Passed.......	App'd March 3, 1815
Backus, Electus, widow of	Continuance of half-pay pension..	17	2	Resolution	67	Military Affairs.						
Backus, Electus, widow of	Continuance of half pay pension..			Documents	145	Military Affairs.						
Backus, Electus, widow of	Continuance of half-pay pension..	18	2	Petition	58	Rev. Pensions....	Jan. 4, 1825	Adverse......	......	Laid on table.		
Backus, Electus, widow of	Continuance of half-pay pension..	20	2	Petition	70	Military Pensions..	Jan. 13, 1829	Adverse......	......	Laid on the table.		
Backus, Electus, widow of	Continuance of half-pay pension..	21	1	Petition	59	Military Pensions.						
Backus, Electus, widow of	Continuance of half-pay pension..	23	2	Petition	77	Military Affairs.						
Backus, Electus, widow of	Continuance of half-pay pension..	24	1	Petition	97	Invalid Pensions...	....	....	......	Discharged; laid on table.		
Backus, Gurdon & others.	Release from a judgment........	3	1	Petition	163	Select...........	May 29, 1794	Adverse......	......	Laid on the table.		
Backus, Gurdon & others.	Release from a judgment........	4	1	Petition	439	Com. and Manuf..	April 5, 1796	Adverse......	......	Leave to withdraw.		

List of private claims presented to the House of Representatives of the United States from the 1st to the 31st Congress, inclusive—Continued.

Names of claimants.	Nature or object of the claim.	Congress.	Session.	How brought before the House of Reps.	Page of journal.	To what committee of the House referred.	No. or date of the report.	Nature of the report.	No. of the bill.	How disposed of by the House of Reps.	How disposed of by the Senate.	Date of the act of Congress, and remarks.
Bacon, Abel	Arrears of Pension	21	1	Petition	260	Military Pensions	May 4, 1830	Adverse	......	Laid on table.		
Bacon, Andrew	Pension	20	1	Petition	310	Military Pensions	April 29, 1828	Pension Bill	283	Passed.		
Bacon, Andrew	Pension	21	1	Petition	47	Military Pensions	Jan. 5, 1830	Pension Bill	72	Passed	Passed, with amendment.	App'd May 20, 1830
Bacon, Ebenezer	(See Benjamin Hallett & others)	18	1	....	235							
Bacon, Frederich A., widow of.	Relief for loss of husband in U. S. service.	26	2	Petition	52	Naval Affairs	198	Adverse	......	Laid on table.		
Bacon, Frederick H	(See Exploring Expedition)	27	3	....	149	....	270	....	818			
Bacon, Henry	Compensation for revolutionary services.	2	2	Petition	618							
				Rep. of Secretary War.	696	....		....	......	Laid on table.		
Bacon, Henry, widow of	Compensation for revolutionary services.	25	3	Petition	334	Rev. Claims.						
Bacon, Henry, widow of	Compensation for revolutionary services.	26	1	Petition	166	Rev. Claims.						
Bacon, Israel	Pension for disability in revolutionary war.	13	1	Petition	107	Military Affairs.						
Bacon, Jacob	Indemnity for loss on Continental money.	3	1	Petition	57							
				Rep. of Secretary of War.	93	Select.						
Bacon, Josiah	Pension for revolutionary services.	16	1	Petition	172	....	....	....	......	Discharged; referred to Secretary of War.		
Bacon, Judah, widow of	Indemnity for French spoliations prior to 1800.	28	1	Petition	87	Foreign Affairs.						
Bacon, Richard, attorney of.	Indemnity for French spoliations prior to 1800.	26	1	Memorial	182	Foreign Affairs	343	Favorable	319	Referred to Committee Whole House.		
Bacon, Samuel	Pension for revolutionary services.	22	1	Petition	218	Rev. Pensions	371	Favorable	466	Passed	Indef. postp'd.	
Bacot, Thomas W	Increase of compensation as postmaster at Charleston, S. C.	4	2	Petition	612	Select.						
Bacot, Thomas W	Reimbursement of expenses for apprehending mail robber.	17	1	Petition	213	P. Of. & P. Roads.						
				Senate bill	445	P. Of. & P. Roads.	April 17, 1822	With't amend.	S. 71	Referred to Committee Whole House.		
Bacot, Thomas W	Reimbursement of expenses for apprehending mail robber.	17	2	Petition	252	P. Of. & P. Roads.	Feb. 24, 1823	Favorable	312	Referred to Committee Whole House.		
Bacot, Thomas W	Reimbursement of expenses for apprehending mail robber.	18	1	Petition	59	P. Of. & P. Roads.	4	Favorable	13	Passed	Passed	App'd Jan. 7, 1824
Bacot, Thomas W., widow of.	Reimbursement of expenditure on public account.	23	2	Petition	354	Select	117	Favorable	751	Referred to Committee Whole House.		
Bacot, Thomas W., widow of.	Reimbursement of expenditure on public account.	24	1	Petition	111	Claims	531	Favorable	525	Referred to Committee Whole House.		
Bacot, Thomas W., representatives of.	Reimbursement of expenditure on public account.	25	2	Petition	36	Claims	25	Favorable	37	Passed	Passed	App'd Mar. 28, 1838
Bacot, Thomas W., representatives of.	Amendment to law of last session.	25	3	Petition	206	Claims.						
Bacot, Thomas W., representatives of.	Amendment to law of last session.	26	1	Petition	168	Claims	368	Adverse	......	Laid on table.		
Baden, William	Pension	22	1	Petition	260	Invalid Pensions.						
Baden, William	Pension	23	1	Resolution	509	Invalid Pensions	438	Favorable	459	Referred to Committee Whole House.		
Baden, William	Pension	23	2	Rep't Committee Whole House.	336	....	....	With't amend.	459	Passed	Passed	App'd March 3, 1835
Badger, Joseph	Compensation for laying out a military road.	24	1	Petition	943	Claims.						

List of private claims presented to the House of Representatives of the United States from the 1st to the 31st Congress, inclusive—Continued.

Names of claimants.	Nature or object of the claim.	Congress.	Session.	How brought before the House of Reps.	Page of journal.	To what committee of the House referred.	No. or date of the report.	Nature of the report.	No. of the bill.	How disposed of by the House of Reps.	How disposed of by the Senate.	Date of the act of Congress, and remarks.
Badger, Nehemiah W	Increase of pension	22	1	Petition	37	Invalid Pensions	210	Pension bill	228	Passed	Passed	App'd July 14, 1832; name of the petitioner omitted.
Badger, Nehemiah W	Increase of pension	22	2	Petition	109	Invalid Pensions	Feb. 15, 1833	Pension bill	738	Referred to Committee Whole House.		
Badger, Thomas	Pension	28	1	Petition	406	Invalid Pensions.						
Badger, Thomas	Pension	29	1	Petition	298	Invalid Pensions.						
Badger, Thomas	Pension	29	2	Petition	141	Invalid Pensions				Discharged; laid on table.		
Badger, Thomas	Pension	30	1	Petition	82	Invalid Pensions	139	Favorable	128	Passed	Passed, 2d sess.	App'd Jan. 26, 1849
Badollett, John	Increase of compensation as register of land office.	18	2	Petition	96	Public Lands.						
Badon, Cattelina, heirs of.	To relocate their land patent	31	2	Petition	123	Priv. Land Claims.						
Badon, Joseph, heirs of	Confirmation of title to land	20	1	Petition	168	Public Lands.						
Baggott, James	To be restored to pension roll	20	2	Resolution	68	Military Pensions.						
Baggott, John	Pension	26	1	Petition	1186	Invalid Pensions.						
Baggott, John	Pension	26	2	Petition	212	Invalid Pensions.						
Baggs, John	Compensation for revolutionary services.	2	1	Petition	492					Referred to Secretary of War.		
Baggs, John	Compensation for revolutionary services.	3	1	Rep. of Secretary War.	131	Select	May 26, 1794	Res. to refer to Sec. War.	R. 12	Passed	Passed	App'd June 9, 1794
Baggs, John	Compensation for revolutionary services.	4	1	Resolution	373	Claims	Feb. 18, 1796	Pension bill	156	Passed	Passed with amendment.	App'd April 20, 1796
Bagley, Abner S	(See John Bagley and others)	5	2		113							
Bagley, Azor	Payment of certain final settlement certificates.	5	2	Petition	96	Claims	Dec. 22, 1797	Adverse		Referred to Committee Whole House.		
Bagley, Benjamin	(See Lyman Spalding	10	2		484							
Bagley, Jacob	Compensation for revolutionary services.	11	2	Petition	249	Claims	Mar. 14, 1810	Adverse		Laid on table.		
Bagley, John, and others	Reimbursement of certain tonnage duties.	5	2	Petition	113	Com. and Manuf.	Jan. 8, 1798	Adverse		Leave to withdraw.		
Bagley, John & Son	Indemnity for French spoliations prior to 1800.	26	1	Memorial	182	Foreign Affairs	343	Favorable	319	Referred to Committee Whole House.		
Bagley, Samuel	(See Eliphalet, Lord, and S. B.)											
Bagnal, Richard	(See executor of James B. Vaughn.)	21	2		45							
Bahin, John	Pension for revolutionary services.	22	1	Petition	165	Rev. Pensions	369	Favorable	464	Referred to Committee Whole House.		
Bailey, Anselm	Pension	20	1	Petition	163	Military Pensions	April 29, 1828	Pension bill	283	Passed.		
Bailey, Anselm	Pension	21	1	Petition	47	Military Pensions	Jan. 5, 1830	Pension bill	72	Passed	Passed with amendment.	App'd May 20, 1830
Bailey, Anselm	Arrears of pension	27	2	Petition	69	Rev. Pensions	123	Favorable	169	Passed	Rejected.	
Bailey, Benjamin, & others	Indemnity for loss by fall of a monument erected under contract with United States.	19	1	Petition	98	Commerce.						
Bailey, Benjamin, & others	Indemnity for loss by fall of a monument erected under contract with United States.	19	2	Petition	83	Commerce				Discharged; leave to withdraw.		
Bailey, Benjamin, & others	Indemnity for loss by fall of a monument erected under contract with United States.	20	1	Petition	56	Commerce	Jan. 2, 1828	Adverse		Laid on table.		
Bailey, Benjamin, & others	Reimbursement of duty on brandy for exportation.	10	2	Petition	482	Com. and Manuf.						
Bailey, Christopher C	(See Christopher T. Bayley)	24	1		735							

List of private claims presented to the House of Representatives of the United States from the 1st to the 31st Congress, inclusive—Continued.

Names of claimants.	Nature or object of the claim.	Congress.	Session.	How brought before the House of Reps.	Page of journal.	To what committee of the House referred.	No. or date of the report.	Nature of the report.	No. of the bill.	How disposed of by the House of Reps.	How disposed of by the Senate.	Date of the act of Congress, and remarks.
Bailey, Daniel	Pension for revolutionary services.	14	1	Petition	260	Pens. & Rev. Cl'ms.	April 11, 1816	Favorable	171	Passed	Passed	App'd April 30, 1816
Bailey, Daniel R. J.	(See Robert Eldred, and others)	24	2		124							
Bailey, David	Drawback on wine for exportation.	15	1	Petition	258	Ways and Means	Feb. 27, 1818	Adverse		Claim rejected.		
Bailey, David	Confirmation of title to land in Missouri.	15	2	Petition	210	Priv. Land Claims.						
Bailey, David	Confirmation of title to land in Missouri.	24	2	Petition	314	Priv. Land Claims.						
Bailey, David	Confirmation of title to land in Missouri.	25	2	Petition	282	Priv. Land Claims.	Jan. 20, 1838	Adverse		Laid on table.		
Bailey, Dixon	(See Margaret Bailey.)											
Bailey, Elijah, and others.	Bounty on fishing sloop Lucy Anne.	17	2	Petition	56	Commerce.						
Bailey, Elijah, and others.	Bounty on fishing sloop Lucy Anne.	18	1	Petition	47	Commerce.						
Bailey, Elijah, and others.	Bounty on fishing sloop Lucy Anne.	18	2	House bill	207	Whole House	Feb. 26, 1825	With't amend.	319	Passed	Passed	App'd March 3, 1825
Bailey, Ephraim	Pension for revolutionary services.	3	2	Report of Secretary of War.	337	Claims.						
Bailey, Ephraim	Pension for revolutionary services.	4	1	Report of Secretary of War.	447	Claims	Feb. 18, 1796	Pension bill	156	Passed	Passed with amendment.	App'd April 20, 1796
Bailey, Ephraim	Increase of pension	9	2	House bill	608	Whole House	Feb. 28, 1807	With amend.	216	Passed	Passed	App'd March 3, 1807
Bailey, Henry	Pay as revolutionary seamen	22	1	Resolution	58	Rev. Claims.						
Bailey, Henry	Compensation for revolutionary services.	23	1	Petition	157	Rev. Claims.						
Bailey, Hezekiah	Pension for revolutionary services.	12	1	Pension bill	361	Whole House	June 15, 1812	With amend	138	Passed	Passed with amendment.	App'd July 5, 1812
Bailey, Hezekiah	Increase of pension.	13	2	Pension bill	344	Whole House	March 3, 1814	With amend.	166	Passed	Passed with amendment.	App'd April 18, 1814
Bailey, Hortense	Amount due her under Chicago treaty.	30	2	Petition	380	Judiciary.						
Bailey, Jacob	Compensation and settlement of claims for revolutionary services.	1	2	Petition	221					Referred to Secretary of Treasury.		
Bailey, Jacob	Compensation and settlement of claims for revolutionary services.	3	1	Rep. of Secretary Treasury.	77					Laid on table.		
Bailey, Jacob	Compensation and settlement of claims for revolutionary services.	4	1	Resolution	427	Claims	May 7, 1796	Adverse.				
Bailey, Jacob	Pension for revolutionary services.	17	1	Petition	30	Rev. Pensions.						
Bailey, James	Pension	25	2	Petition	57	Invalid Pensions	354	Favorable	382	Read third time and postponed.		
Bailey, James	Pension	25	3	House bill	156				382	Laid on table.		
Bailey, James	Pension	26	1	Petition	161	Invalid Pensions	190	Favorable	192	Passed	Indef. postp'd.	
Bailey, James	Pension	26	2	Petition and docs.	61	Invalid Pensions	229	Adverse		Laid on table.		
Bailey, James W.	Pension for revolutionary services.	16	1	Petition	194	Claims				Discharged; referred to Secretary of War.		
				Rep. of Secretary War.	350					Laid on table.		
Bailey, Jesse	Pension for revolutionary services.	24	1	Petition	951	Rev. Pensions				Discharged; laid on table.		
Bailey, Jesse	Pension for revolutionary services.	24	2	Petition	217	Rev. Pensions.				Discharged; laid on table.		
Bailey, John	Pension for revolutionary services.	3	2	Rep. of Secretary War.	337	Claims.						
Bailey, John	Right of pre-emption as New Orleans Branch pilot.	28	1	Petition	77	Priv. Land Claims.	9	Favorabte	35	Passed	Passed	App'd June 17, 1844

List of private claims presented to the House of Representatives of the United States from the 1st to the 31st Congress, inclusive—Continued.

Names of claimants.	Nature or object of the claim.	Congress.	Session.	How brought before the House of Reps.	Page of journal.	To what committee of the House referred.	No. or date of the report.	Nature of the report.	No. of the bill.	How disposed of by the House of Reps.	How disposed of by the Senate.	Date of the act of Congress, and remarks.
9 Bailey, John	Pension	24	1	Petition	136	Rev. Pensions.						
Bailey, Jonathan	Indemnity for depreciation of paper money.	3	1	Petition	29	Select.						
Bailey, Jonathan	Indemnity for depreciation of paper money.	3	2	Petition	353	Claims	March 2, 1795	Adverse		Laid on table.		
Bailey, Jonathan	Pension	4	1	Rep. of Secretary War.	598	Claims	May 31, 1796	Adverse		Laid on table.		
Bailey, Jonathan	Remission of foreign tonnage duty, schooner Astrea.	10	2	Petition	415	Com. and Manuf.						
Bailey, Jona'an N., (N. Y.)	Reimbursement of an over-payment of duties.	17	1	Petition	99	Ways and Means	Jan. 30, 1822	Favorable	66	Passed	Passed	App'd April 17, 1822
Bailey, Jonathan N., (Ill.)	Indemnity for losses in war of 1812.	22	1	Petition	471	Priv. Land Claims.	Mar. 23, 1832	Adverse		Laid on table.		
Bailey, Joseph	Pension for revolutionary services.	25	2	Petition	117	Rev. Pensions	587	Favorable	574	Passed.		
Bailey, Joseph	Pension for revolutionary services.	26	1	Petition	171	Rev. Pensions	127	Favorable	137	Passed	Indef. postp'd.	
Bailey, Joshua	Pension for revolutionary services.	25	2	Petition	587	Rev. Pensions						
Bailey, Joshua	Pension for revolutionary services.	26	1	Petition	173	Rev. Pensions						
Bailey, Joshua, (Penn.)	Indemnity for French spoliations prior to 1800.	26	1	Memorial	182	Foreign Affairs	343	Favorable	319	Referred to Committee Whole House.		
Bailey, Littleton	Confirmation of title to land in Louisiana.	22	1	Petition	133	Priv. Land Claims.	Jan. 13, 1832	Adverse		Laid on table.		
Bailey, Littleton	Confirmation of title to land in Louisiana.	23	1	Petition	76	Priv. Land Claims.						
Bailey, Littleton	Confirmation of title to land in Louisiana.	25	2	Petition	631	Priv. Land Claims.	726	Adverse		Laid on table.		
Bailey, Littleton	Confirmation of title to land in Louisiana.	27	3	Petition	482					Leave to withdraw.		
Bailey, Loudon	Pension	19	1	Petition	203	Military Pensons	April 1, 1826	Adverse		Laid on table.		
Bailey, Major, widow of	Pension for loss of husband in public service.	22	2	Petition	347	Commerce.						
Bailey, Margaret	Indemnity for losses in Indian wars.	14	2	Petition	71	Claims.						
Bailey, Margaret	Confirmation of land title	14	2	Petition	72	Public Lands.						
Bailey, Margaret	Confirmation of land title	15	1	Petition	56	Priv. Land Claims.	Jan. 20, 1818	Favorable	49	Passed	Passed with amendment.	App'd April 20, 1818
Bailey, Martha	(See administrator of Elbert Anderson.)	21	2		45							
Bailey, Michael	Pension	31	1	Petition	880	Invalid Pensions.						
Bailey, Nancy	Indemnity for losses in Creek war.	14	2	Petition	71	Claims.						
Bailey, Nancy, *et al.*	Confirmation of land title.	14	2	Petition	72	Public Lands.						
Bailey, Nathaniel	Pension for revolutionary services.	29	2	Petition	215	Rev. Pensions.						
Bailey, Nathaniel	Pension for revolutionary services.	30	1	Petition	676	Rev. Pensions				Discharged; laid on table.		
Bailey, Nathaniel	Pension for revolutionary services.	30	2	Petition	314	Rev. Pensions.						
Bailey, Noah	Pension for revolutionary services.	12	1	Petition	201	Claims	June 12, 1812	Adverse		Laid on table.		
Bailey, O. W.	Compensation for horse lost in Creek war.	28	1	Petition	216	Claims	558	Adverse		Laid on table.		
Bailey, Peggy	(See Margaret Bailey.)	15	1		56							
Bailey, Peter	To be restored to pension roll	25	2	Petition	271	Rev. Pensions.						
Bailey, Rebecca	(See heirs of Edward Lloyd)	23	1		381							
Bailey, Richard	Pension for revolutionary services.	27	2	Petition	375	Rev. Pensions	784	Adverse		Laid on table.		
Bailey and Rinker, surviving partner of.	Indemnity for damages to property by United States troops.	16	1	Petition	323	Claims	April 3, 1820	Adverse		Referred to Committee Whole House.		
Bailey and Rinker, surviving partner of.	Indemnity for damages to property by United States troops.	19	2	Petition	44	Claims	Jan. 8, 1827	Adverse		Laid on table.		

List of private claims presented to the House of Representatives of the United States from the 1st to the 31st Congress, inclusive—Continued.

Names of claimants.	Nature or object of the claim.	Congress.	Session.	How brought before the House of Reps.	Page of journal.	To what committee of the House referred.	No. or date of the report.	Nature of the report.	No. of the bill.	How disposed of by the House of Reps.	How disposed of by the Senate.	Date of the act of Congress, and remarks.
Bailey and Rinker, surviving partner of.	Indemnity for damages to property by United States troops.	20	1	Petition	64	Claims	Dec. 27, 1827	Adverse	......	Referred to Committee Whole House.		
Bailey, Robert	Pension for revolutionary services.	4	1	Rep. of Secretary of War.	447	Claims	Feb. 18, 1796	Pension bill	156	Passed	Passed with amendment.	App'd April 20, 1796
Bailey, Samuel	Confirmation of title to land in Missouri.	15	2	Petition	210	Priv. Land Claims.						
Bailey, Samuel	Confirmation of title to land in Missouri.	24	2	Petition	314	Priv. Land Claims.						
Bailey, Samuel	Confirmation of title to land in Missouri.	25	2	Petition	282	Priv. Land Claims.	Jan. 20, 1838	Adverse	......	Laid on table.		
Bailey, Samuel A.	(See heirs of Edward Lloyd)	23	1	....	381							
Bailey, Theodorus, widow of.	(See admimintrator of Elbert Anderson.)	21	2	....	45							
Bailey, Thomas	Pension for revolutionary services.	15	1	Petition	49	Pens. & Rev. Cl'ms.						
Bailey, Thomas	Pension for revolutionary services.	15	2	Pension bill	41	....	....	....	203	Passed	Passed, with amendment.	App'd March 3, 1819
Bailey & Torrey	Payment of claim under Spanish treaty.	20	1	Resolution	67	Foreign Affairs	262	Adverse.	......	Laid on table.		
Bailey, William, (Conn.).	Pension for revolutionary services.	4	1	Rep. of Secretary War.	447	Claims	Feb. 18, 1796	Pension bill	156	Passed	Passed, with amendment.	App'd Apr. 20, 1796
Bailey, William, (Conn.).	Increase of Pension	11	3	Pension bill	604	Whole House	Mar. 2, 1811	With amend.	218	Passed	Passed, with amendment.	App'd Mar. 3, 1811
Bailey, William	(See Bailey & Delord)	23	2	....	83							
Bailey, William, assignees of.	Reimbursement of money paid for lands in District of Columbia.	23	1	Petition	219	Dist. of Columbia.	June 5, 1834	Favorable	515	Rep. by Com. Whole House with't amend.		
Bailey, William, assignees of.	Reimbursement of money paid for lands in District of Columbia.	23	2	House bill	162	....	....	....	515	Passed	Passed	App'd Mar. 3, 1835
Bailey, Maj. William, heirs of.	Balance due for revolutionary services.	23	2	Petition	165	Rev. Claims.						
Railey, Maj. William, heirs of.	Compensation for revolutionary services.	24	1	Petition Recom. with doc's	105 508	Rev. Claims Rev. Claims.	Jan. 27, 1836	Adverse.				
Bailey & Bogert	Extension of credit on Custom House bond.	8	2	Petition	89	Com. and Manuf						
Bailey & Bogert	Remission of duty on goods destroyed by fire.	8	2	Petition	76	Com. and Manuf	Feb. 27, 1805	Favorable	35	Laid on table.		
Bailey & Delord	Compensation for supplies furnished on bublic account.	23	2	Petition	83	Claims.						
Bailey & Delord	Compensation for supplies furnished on public account.	24	1	Petition	141	Claims	359	Favorable	364	Referred to Committee Whole House.		
Bailey & Delord	Compensation for supplies furnished on public account.	24	2	Documents	308	Claims	192	Res. to refer to Com. of W. H.		Referred to Committee Whole House.		
Bailey & Delord	Compensation for supplies furnished on public account.	25	2	Petition	36	Claims	9	Favorable	21	Passed	Indef. postpo'd	
Bailey & Delord	Compensation for supplies furnished on public account.	26	1	Petition	168	Claims	24	Favorable	43	Passed	Indef. postpo'd	
Bailey & Delord	Compensation for supplies furnished on public account.	26	2	Petition	80	Claims	33	Favorable	566	Referred to Committee Whole House.		
Bailey & Delord	Compensation for supplies furnished on public account.	27	2	Petition	56	Claims.						
Bailey & Delord	Compensation for supplies furnished on public account.	28	1	Petition	70	Claims.						
Bailey & Delord	Compensation for supplies furnished on public account.	30	1	Petition	581	Claims.						
Bailey & Delord	Compensation for supplies furnished on public account.	31	1	Petition	519	Claims.						

List of private claims presented to the House of Representatives of the United States from the 1st to the 31st Congress, inclusive—Continued.

Names of claimants.	Nature or object of the claim.	Congress.	Session.	How brought before the House of Reps.	Page of journal.	To what committee of the House referred.	No. or date of the report.	Nature of the report.	No. of the bill.	How disposed of by the House of Reps.	How disposed of by the Senate.	Date of the act of Congress, and remarks.
Bailie, Alexander........	Release from indebtedness to United States.	10	1	Petition	112	Select...........	Jan. 14, 1808	Favorable....	34	Referred to Committee Whole House.		
Bailie, Alexander........	Release from indebtedness to United States.	10	2	Resolution......	424	Select...........	Jan. 13, 1809	Favorable....	144	Referred to Committee Whole House.		
Bailie, Alexander........ (See Bayley & Bayly.)	Release from indebtedness to United States.	11	2	Petition	118	Select.						
Bain, James............	Pension for revolutionary services.	23	1	Petition	289	Rev. Pensions.						
Bain, John.............	Pension for revolutionary services.	20	2	Resolution	201	Military Pensions.						
Baillio, Paul...........	Payment of claims against Kanzas Indians.	19	1	Appropr'n bill..	378	Whole House.....	May 18, 1826	With't amend.	179	Passed............	Passed.......	App'd May 20, 1826
Bain, John, (Pa.).......	Increase of pension............	26	1	Petition	322	Rev. Pensions.....	424	Adverse		Laid on table.		
Bain, John, (Pa.).......	Increase of pension............	31	1	Petition	880	Rev. Pensions	363	Adverse		Laid on table.		
Baine, Betsey...........	(See widow of Job Kenniston)....	29	1	....	532							
Bainbridge, Joseph	Equitable settlement of accounts with Navy Department.	17	1	Petition	150	Naval Affairs.....	....	....	......	Discharged; leave to withdraw.		
				Petition, (2)....	339	Naval Affairs.....	Mar. 21, 1822	Favorable....	132	Passed	Passed.......	App'd May 7, 1822
Bainbridge, Joseph	(See widow of Stephen Decatur, and others.)	20	1	Petition	295	....	201	....	S. 50			
Bainbridge, Joseph, widow of.	Naval pension	25	3	Petition	360	Naval Affairs.						
Bainbridge, Joseph, widow of.	Naval pension	26	1	Petition	180	Naval Affairs.						
Bainbridge, Joseph, widow of.	Naval pension	27	3	Petition	309	Naval Affairs.....	....	....	......	Discharged; laid on table.		
Bainbridge, Joseph, widow of.	Naval pension	28	1	Petition	1020	Naval Affairs.						
Bainbridge, Joseph, widow of.	Balance due	26	1	Memorial	330	Naval Affairs.						
Bair, John.............	Pensions for revolutionary services	12	1	Pension bill	361	Whole House	June 15, 1812	With amend..	138	Passed	Passed with amendment.	App'd July 5, 1812
Bair, Thomas	Indemnity for deficit in land	15	1	Petition	344	Priv. Land Claims.						
Baird, Absalom.........	Half-pay as revolutionary surgeon	3	1	Petition	50	Select.						
Baird, Absalom.........	Half-pay as revolutionary surgeon	3	2	Petition	247	Claims..........	Feb. 25, 1795	Adverse	......	Referred to Committee Whole House.		
Baird, Absalom.........	Half-pay as revolutionary surgeon	4	2	Petition	626	Claims..........	Dec. 21, 1796	Adverse	......	Leave to withdraw.		
Baird, Absalom, heirs of..	Commutation pay and bounty land	15	1	Petition	242	Pens. & Rev. Cl'ms.	Mar. 6, 1818	Adverse	......	Laid on table.		
Baird, Absalom, heirs of..	Commutation pay and bounty land	19	1	Petition	136	Rev. Claims......	Jan. 18, 1826	Adverse	......	Laid on table.		
Baird, Absalom, heirs of..	Commutation pay and bounty land	19	2	Resolution	76	Rev. Claims.						
Baird, Absalom, heirs of..	Commutation pay and bounty land	21	1	Petition	122	Rev. Claims.						
Baird, Absalom, heirs of..	Commutation pay and bounty land	22	1	Petition	386	Rev. Claims.						
				Petition, (2)....	416							
Baird, Absalom, heirs of..	Commutation pay and bounty land	22	2	Petition	30	Rev. Claims.						
Baird, Absalom, heirs of..	Commutation pay and bounty land	23	1	Petition	39	Rev. Claims.						
Baird, Absalom, heirs of..	Commutation pay and bounty land	23	2	Petition	84	Rev. Claims......	136	Favorable....	771	Referred to Committee Whole House.		
Baird, Absalom, heirs of..	Commutation pay and bounty land	24	1	Petition	63	Rev. Claims......	63	Favorable....	83	Passed	Passed	App'd June 23, 1836
Baird, Absalom, heirs of..	Interest on commutation pay, &c.	25	2	Petition	48	Rev. Claims......	640	Favorable....	617	Postponed.		
Baird, Absalom, heirs of..	Interest on commutation pay, &c.	31	1	Petition	396	Rev. Claims......	....	....	......	Discharged; laid on table.		
Baird, Henry, and others..	Indemnity in land for loss of situation.	24	2	Petition	94	Indian Affairs.						
Baird, Henry, and others..	Indemnity in land for loss of situation.	25	2	Petition	173	Indian Affairs.....	Jan. 12, 1838	Adverse	......	Laid on table.		

List of private claims presented to the House of Representatives of the United States from the 1st to the 31st Congress, inclusive—Continued.

Names of claimants.	Nature or object of the claim.	Congress.	Session.	How brought before the House of Reps.	Page of journal.	To what committee of the House referred.	No. or date of the report.	Nature of the report.	No. of the bill.	How disposed of by the House of Reps.	How disposed of by the Senate.	Date of the act of Congress, and remarks.
Baird, Henry S., Michigan	Compensation for services as U. S. attorney.	21	1	Petition	298	Judiciary	Mar. 13, 1830	Adverse	......	Laid on table.		
Baird, John, (Alabama)	Payment of claims arising from Seminole war.	21	2	Petition	74	Claims	Dec. 31, 1830	Adverse	......	Laid on table.		
Baird, John, (Alabama)	Payment of claims arising from Seminole war.	26	1	Petition	336	Claims.						
Baird, Robert	Pension for services under General Wayne.	7	1	Petition	83	Claims	Feb. 10, 1802	Adverse	......	Leave to withdraw.		
Baird, Robert	Pension for services under General Wayne.	8	1	Petition	540	Claims						
Baird, Robert	Pension for services under General Wayne.	10	1	Petition	230	Claims.						
Baird, Robert	Pension for services under General Wayne.	11	2	Pension bill	283	Whole House	Mar. 24, 1810	With amend.	107	Passed	Passed with amendment	App'd April 27, 1810
Baird, Thomas	(See heirs of Absalom Baird)	15	1	....	242							
Baisdell, John	Pension	21	2	Petition	299	Military Pensions.						
Baker, Abel, (N. Y.)	Pension for revolutionary services.	18	2	Petition	135	Rev. Pensions	Jan. 24, 1825	Adverse	......	Laid on table.		
Baker, Abel, (N. Y.)	Pension for revolutionary services.	19	2	Petition	132	Rev. Pensions.						
Baker, Absalom	Pension for revolutionary services.	20	1	Resolution	514	Military Pensions.						
Baker, Absalom	Pension for revolutionary services.	21	1	Petition	47	Military Pensions.	Feb. 13, 1830	Pension bill.	72	Passed	Passed with amendment.	App'd May 20, 1820
Baker, Artemas	Compensation for work on Cumberland road.	23	1	Resolution	589	Claims	456	Statement of facts.	......	....	....	See Report No. 449.
Baker, Barnabas	(See Joseph Baker and others)	27	2	....	822							
Baker, Benjamin F.	Indemnity for Indian depredations.	25	2	Petition	213	Indian Affairs.						
Baker, Charles H.	(See Godfrey, Haga, & Co., attorney of.)											
Baker, Daniel B.	Pension	26	1	Petition	288	Invalid Pensions	268	Adverse	......	Laid on table.		
Baker, Daniel B.	Pension	28	1	Documents	513	Invalid Pensions.						
Baker, David, heir of widow	Arrears of pension	25	2	Petition	54	Rev. Pensions.						
Baker, Elijah, (Ky.)	Pension	20	2	Petition	229	Military Pensions.						
Baker, Elijah, (Ky.)	Pension	21	2	Petition	81	Military Pensions.						
Baker, Elijah, (Ky.)	Pension	22	1	Petition	90	Rev. Pensions.						
Baker, Frederick	Pension	31	1	Petition	898	Invalid Pensions.						
Baker, George E., (N. Y.)	Additional compensation for taking census.	31	2	Petition	193	Judiciary.						
Baker, Glover	Pension for revolutionary services.	14	2	Rep. of Sec. War	349	Pens. & Rev. Cl'ms.	Jan. 29, 1817	Pension bill	91	Passed	Passed	App'd March 3, 1817
Baker, Harriet De la P.	(See heir of F. H. Weissenfels)	25	3	....	81							
Baker, Henry Cleland	Increase of pension for revolutionary services.	2	2	Petition	653	....	....	....	......	Rejected Dec. 24, 1792		
Baker, Isaac	(See Isaac Barker)	23	1	....	135							
Baker, Isaiah	(See Isaiah Parker)	29	1	....	118							
Baker, Jacob	Right of pre-emption as New Orleans branch pilot.	28	1	Petition	77	Priv. Land Claims.	9	Favorable	35	Passed	Passed	App'd June 17, 1844
Baker, Jacob	Pension	31	1	Petition	369	Invalid Pensions.						
Baker, Jacob	Remission of duties on wrecked goods.	25	2	Petition	409	Commerce.						
Baker, Jacob	Remission of duties on wrecked goods.	25	3	Petition	348	Commerce.						
Baker, Jacob	Remission of duties on wrecked goods.	26	1	Petition	176	Commerce.						
Baker, James	Compensation for property furnished on public account.	24	1	Petition	92	Claims	414	Favorable	425	Referred to Committee Whole House.	....	See Report No. 769.

List of private claims presented to the House of Representatives of the United States from the 1st to the 31st Congress, inclusive—Continued.

Names of claimants.	Nature or object of the claim.	Congress.	Session.	How brought before the House of Reps.	Page of journal.	To what committee of the House referred.	No. or date of the report.	Nature of the report.	No. of the bill.	How disposed of by the House of Reps.	How disposed of by the Senate.	Date of the act of Congress, and remarks.
Baker, James	Compensation for property furnished on public account.	25	2	Petition	35	Claims	16	Favorable	28	Passed	Passed	App'd Mar. 19, 1838
Baker, Jane	(See Thomas Baker, widow of)	16	2		69							
Baker, Jane	(See heir of D. Ochiltree)	23	1		41							
Baker, Jesse	Bounty land for military services	30	1	Petition	617	Priv. Land Claims.						
Baker, John (Mississippi)	Confirmation of title under a Spanish grant.	10	1	Petition	18	Public Lands.						
Baker, John (Mississippi)	Confirmation of title under a Spanish grant.	11	2	Petition	116	Public Lands.						
Baker, John (Mississippi)	Confirmation of title under a Spanish grant.	11	3	Petition	457	Public Lands.						
Baker, John (Mississippi)	Confirmation of title under a Spanish grant.	12	1	Petition	13	Public Lands.						
Baker, John (Mississippi)	Referrence of claim to certain land commissioners.	9	1	Petition	315	Public Lands.						
Baker, John (Mississippi)	Referrence of claim to certain land commissioners.	9	2	Petition	479	Public Lands.						
Baker, John, representatives of (Mississippi.)	Referrence of claim to certain land commissioners.	15	1	Petition	226	Priv. Land Claims.	Feb. 18, 1818	Favorable	92	Passed	Passed with amendment.	App'd April 9, 1818
Baker, John (Pa.)	Arrears of pension	27	2	Petition	525	Invalid Pensions.						
Baker, John (Pa.)	Arrears of pension	27	3	Petition	151	Invalid Pensions	267	Adverse		Laid on table.		
Baker, John (Ky.)	Pension for revolutionary services	18	1	Petition	74	Pens. & Rev. Clm's.	Feb. 18, 1824	Adverse		Laid on table.		
Baker, John (Ky.)	Increase of pension	28	1	Petition	322	Invalid Pensions	193	Adverse		Laid on table.		
Baker, John, heirs of (Ala.)	Confirmation of title to land	15	1	Petition	212	Priv. Land Claims.	Mar. 10, 1818	Favorable	131	Referred to Committee Whole House.		
Baker, John, heirs of (Ala.)	Confirmation of title to land	15	2	House bill	131	Whole House			131			
Baker, John, heirs of (Ala.)	Confirmation of title to land	27	3	Petition	76	Priv. Land Claims.	Feb. 28, 1843	Favorable	825	Referred to Committee Whole House.		
Baker, John, heirs of (Ala.)	Confirmation of title to land	28	1	Petition	405	Priv. Land Claims.	357	Favorable	270	Passed	Passed	App'd June 17, 1844
Baker, John	Indemnity for loses, &c., during Maine difficulties.	25	2	Appropriat'n bill	294	Whole House			412	Passed	Passed	App'd July 9, 1838
Baker, John (Ohio)	Right of pre-emption to land in Ohio.	25	3	Petition	211	Public Lands.						
Baker, John (Ohio)	Payment of money lost in the mail	26	1	Petition	617	P. Of. and P. Roads.	548	Adverse		Laid on table.		
Baker, John (Ohio)	Payment of money lost in the mail	27	3	House bill	89				489	Passed	Passed	App'd Feb. 24, 1843
Baker, John	(See John Lawson, administrators of.)	29	1		824							
Baker, John H	Drawback of duties on coffee	7	2	Petition	245	Com. and Manuf.	Jan. 18, 1803	Adverse		Leave to withdraw.		
Baker, John H	Drawback of duties on coffee	8	1	Petition	410	Com. and Manuf.	Nov. 27, 1803	Adverse		Leave to withdraw.		
Baker, John H. (N. Y.)	Reimbursement of ransom paid for American seamen.	29	2	House bill	324	Commerce			652			
				Petition	326	Commerce				Discharged; laid on table.		
Baker, John H. (N. Y.)	Reimbursement of ransom paid for American seamen.	30	1	Petition	263	Claims	479	Favorable	400	Passed	Reported without amend't.	
Baker, John H. (N. Y.)	Reimbursement of ransom paid for American seamen.	31	1	Petition	647	Claims	401	Favorable	338	Referred to Committee Whole House.		
Baker, John M., widow of.	(See F. H. Weissenfels, heirs of.)	25	3		81							
Baker, John Martin	Compensation for diplomatic services in Brazil.	25	3	Petition	125	Foreign Affairs.						
Baker, John Martin	Compensation for diplomatic services in Brazil.	26	1	Petition	182	Foreign Affairs	276	Adverse		Laid on table.		

List of private claims presented to the House of Representatives of the United States from the 1st to the 31st Congress, inclusive—Continued.

Names of claimants.	Nature or object of the claim.	Congress.	Session.	How brought before the House of Reps.	Page of journal.	To what committee of the House referred.	No. or date of the report.	Nature of the report.	No. of the bill.	How disposed of by the House of Reps.	How disposed of by the Senate.	Date of the act of Congress, and remarks.
Baker, John Martin, widow of.	Compensation for diplomatic services in Brazil.	27	2	Petition	298	Foreign Affairs.						
Baker, John Martin, widow of.	Compensation for diplomatic services in Brazil.	30	1	Petition	865	Foreign Affairs....	Aug. 8, 1848	Favorable	644	Referred to Committee Whole House.		
Baker, John Martin, widow of.	Compensation for diplomatic services in Brazil.	31	1	Petition	370	Foreign Affairs.						
Baker, Joseph and others.	Bounty on fishing schooner Union.	27	2	Petition	822	Commerce........	1022	Favorable	595	Referred to Committee Whole House.		
Baker, Joseph and others.	Bounty on fishing schooner Union.	27	3	Rep. Committee Whole House.	91	....	....	With't amend.	595	Passed	Indef. postp'd.	
Baker, Joseph and others.	Bounty on fishing schooner Union.	28	1	Petition	449	Commerce	411	Favorable	316	Passed.		
Baker, Joseph and others.	Bounty on fishing schooner Union.	28	2	Petition	73	Commerce	59	Favorable	538	Referred to Committee Whole House.		
Baker, Joseph and others.	Bounty on fishing schooner Union.	29	1	Petition	106	Commerce	265	Favorable	227	Referred to Committee Whole House.		
Baker, Joseph and others.	Bounty on fishing schooner Union.	30	1	Petition	288	Commerce	259	Favorable....	252	Referred to Committee Whole House.		
Baker, Joseph	(See William Robinson *et al.*)...	13	3	....	455	....	15	....	248			
Baker, Josiah, widow of ..	Pension for revolutionary services.	28	1	Petition........	443	Rev. Pensions.						
Baker, Josiah, widow of ..	Pension for revolutionary services.	28	2	Petition........	119	Rev. Pensions.						
Baker, Lewis, administrator of.	Compensation for military services.	22	2	Petition.........	288	Claims	480	Adverse	......	Referred to Committee Whole House.		
Baker, Lois	Indemnity for destruction of property at Plattsburgh.	13	3	Petition	723	Claims	Feb. 15, 1815	Favorable	297	Passed............	Passed......	App'd March 3, 1815
Baker, Malyn, (Ohio)....	Pension for revolutionary services.	14	2	Petition	83	Pens. & Rev. Cl'ms.	Jan. 29, 1817	Pension bill...	91	Passed............	Passed with amendment.	App'd March 3, 1817
Baker, Martin	Naval pension	26	1	Petition........	713	Naval Affairs.						
Baker, Mehitabel........	(See widow of Obediah Newton) .	4	2	....	645							
Baker, Melchior, and others	Compensation for services against the Indians in 1781.	2	2	Petition	686	Whole House.						
Baker, Melchior, and others	Compensation for services against the Indians in 1781.	16	2	Petition	50	Pens. & Rev. Cl'ms.						
Baker, Melchior, and others	Compensation for services against the Indians in 1781.	17	1	Petition	145	Pens. & Rev. Cl'ms.	Jan. 25, 1822	Adverse	......	Laid on table.		
Baker, Melchior, and others	Compensation for services against the Indians in 1781.	17	2	Petition	53	Pens. & Rev. Cl'ms.						
Baker, Melchior, and others	Compensation for services against the Indians in 1781.	19	1	Resolution	266	Rev. Claims......	April 5, 1826	Adverse	......	Laid on table.		
Baker, Melchior, and others	Compensation for services against the Indians in 1781.	22	1	Resolution	534	Claims.						
Baker, Polly	(See widow of Andrew McGahee)	20	2	....	142							
Baker, Reuben, (Mass.) ..	Pension....................	19	1	Petition	149							
Baker, Robert, heirs of ...	Indemnity for losses by non-fulfilment of contract by government	30	1	Petition	676	Indian Affairs.						
Baker, Robert, heirs of ...	Indemnity for losses by non-fulfilment of contract by government.	31	1	Petition	599	Indian Affairs.						
Baker, Robert, heirs of ...	Indemnity for losses by non-fulfilment of contract by government.	31	2	Petition........	445	Indian Affairs.....	87	Adverse	......	Laid on table.		
Baker, Major R. L	Payment and emolument for brevet rank.	30	2	S. Resolution ...	162	Military Affairs ...	Feb. 8, 1849	With't amend.	S.R.43	Referred to Committee Whole House.		
Baker, Samuel..........	Pension for revolutionary services.	31	1	Petition	232	Rev. Pensions.						
Baker, Solomon, (Ind.) ..	Exchange of location of land	20	1	Petition	245	Public Lands.						
Baker, Stephen	(See Thomas Miller & S. Baker.)	14	1	Petition	491							
Baker, Thomas, (Md.) ...	Bounty land for revolut'y services.	9	1	Petition	207	Claims.						

List of private claims presented to the House of Representatives of the United States from the 1st to the 31st Congress, inclusive—Continued.

Names of claimants.	Nature or object of the claim.	Congress.	Session.	How brought before the House of Reps.	Page of journal.	To what committee of the House referred.	No. or date of the report.	Nature of the report.	No. of the bill.	How disposed of by the House of Reps.	How disposed of by the Senate.	Date of the act of Congress, and remarks.
Baker, Thomas, (Md.)	Indemnity for disabilities in revolutionary war.	10	1	Petition	54	Whole House.						
Baker, Thomas, (Ky.)	Compensation for revolutionary services.	19	2	Petition	133	Military Pensions.						
Baker, Thomas, (Ky.)	Compensation for revolutionary services.	20	1	Resolution	464	Military Pensions.						
Baker, Thomas, (Ky.)	Compensation for revolutionary services.	20	2	Resolution	126	Military Pensions				Discharged; laid on table.		
Baker, Thomas, (Ky.)	Compensation for revolutionary services.	25	2	Petition	1030	Invalid Pensions.						
Baker, Thomas, (Ky.)	Compensation for revolutionary services.	25	3	Petition	89	Invalid Pensions.						
Baker, Thomas, widow of	Continuance of pension	16	2	Petition	69	Pens. & Rev. Cl'ms.	Dec. 20, 1820	Adverse		Laid on table.		
Baker, Thomas, widow of	Continuance of pension	18	1	Petition	81	Rev. Pensions	Jan. 12, 1824	Adverse		Laid on table.		
Baker, Thomas, widow of	Continuance of pension	20	1	Petition	128	Naval Affairs	Feb. 21, 1828	Adverse		Laid on table.		
Baker, Thomas, widow of	Continuance of pension	21	1	Petition	567	Naval Affairs.						
Baker, Thomas, widow of	Continuance of pension	21	2	Petition	56	Naval Affairs.						
Baker, Thomas, widow of	Continuance of pension	22	1	Petition	387	Naval Affairs.						
Baker, Thomas, widow of	Continuance of pension	22	2	Petition	217	Naval Affairs.						
Baker, Thomas, widow of	Continuance of pension	28	2	Petition	188	Naval Affairs	113	Adverse		Laid on table.		
Baker, Thomas, widow of	Continuance of pension	29	1	Petition	226	Naval Affairs.						
Baker, Thomas Marshall	Compensation for revolutionary services.	2	1	Petition						Referred to Secretary of War.		
Baker, Thomas Marshall	Compensation for revolutionary services.	2	2	Rep. of Secretary of War.	735					Laid on table.		
Baker, Thomas Marshall	Pension for revolutionary services	3	2	Rep. of Secretary of War.	337	Claims.						
Baker, Thomas Marshall	Pension for revolutionary services	4	1	Resolution	373	Claims.						
Baker, Thomas Marshall	Pension for revolutionary services	4	2	Resolution	614	Claims.						
Baker, Thomas Marshall	Pension for revolutionary services	8	1	Petition	454	Claims	Mar. 13, 1804	(Indefinite.)		Postponed.		
Baker, Thomas Marshall	Pension for revolutionary services	8	2	Petition	64	Claims				Discharged; referred to Com. Whole House.		
Baker, Thomas Marshall	Pension for revolutionary services	9	2	Pension bill	608	Whole House	Feb. 28, 1807	With amend.	216	Passed	Passed	App'd March 3, 1807
Baker, William	Renewal of lost loan office certificate.	2	1	Petition	517							
				Rep. of Secretary Treasury.	583	Select.						
Baker, William	Additional compensation for mail service.	31	1	Petition	666	P. Of. & P. Roads.	168	Adverse		Laid on table.		
Baker, William, (N. Y.)	Payment of his accounts against certain deceased soldiers.	22	1	Petition	288	Claims	480	Adverse		Referred to Committee Whole House.		
Baker, William, (N. Y.)	Indemnity for damage to property at Sackett's Harbor.	23	1	Petition	355	Claims	424	Favorable	450	Referred to Committee Whole House.		
Baker, William, (N. Y.)	Indemnity for damage to property at Sackett's Harbor.	24	1	Petition	50	Claims	12	Favorable	12	Passed	Passed	App'd Feb. 17, 1836
Baker, William, (N. Y.)	Additional allowance for damage, &c.	24	2	Petition	38	Claims	4	Adverse.				
Baker, William, (L. I)	Confirmation of title to land in Florida.	24	1	Petition	282	Priv. Land Claims.						
Baker, William, (L. I.)	Confirmation of title to land in Florida.	24	2	Petition	102	Priv. Land Claims.				Discharged; laid on table.		
Baker, William, (Maine)	Pension	24	1	Petition	98	Invalid Pensions				Discharged; laid on table.		

List of private claims presented to the House of Representatives of the United States from the 1st to the 31st Congress, inclusive—Continued.

Names of claimants.	Nature or object of the claim.	Congress.	Session.	How brought before the House of Reps.	Page of journal.	To what committee of the House referred.	No. or date of the report.	Nature of the report.	No. of the bill.	How disposed of by the House of Reps.	How disposed of by the Senate.	Date of the act of Congress, and remarks.
Baker, William, (Maine)	Pension	26	1	Petition	162	Invalid Pensions	411	Adverse		Laid on table.		
Baker, William, (Tenn.)	Pension	25	3	Petition	570	Invalid Pensions.						
Baker, William	(See Tuttle & Baker)	22	2		177							
Baker, Dr. Wm., (D. C.)	Compensation for medical services to British prisoners.	23	1	Petition	304	Claims	452	Favorable	469	Referred to Committee Whole House.		
Baker, Dr. Wm., (D. C.)	Compensation for medical services to British prisoners.	24	1	Petition	50	Claims	13	Favorable	13	Passed	Passed	App'd Feb. 17, 1836
Baker, William A	(See heirs of John Baker)	27	3		76							
Baker, William R	(See heir of Robert Baker)	30	1		676							
Balastier, J., & Co. and others.	Drawback on Spanish playing cards exported.	19	1	Petition	93	Ways and Means	April 28, 1826	Favorable	240	Passed	Referred with't amendment.	
Balastier, J., & Co. and others.	Drawback on Spanish playing cards exported.	19	2	Senate bill	81	Ways and Means	Dec. 26, 1826	With't amend.	S. 13	Passed	Passed	App'd March 3, 1827
Balch, John	Indemnity for French spoliations prior to 1800.	26	1	Memorial	182	Foreign Affairs	343	Favorable	319	Referred to Committee Whole House.		
Balch, John, jr	Payment for property saved from a British wreck.	24	2	Petition	301	Judiciary.						
Balch, John, jr	Payment for property saved from a British wreck.	25	2	Petition	119	Judiciary	443	Favorable	447	Referred to Committee Whole House.		
Balch, John, jr	Payment for property saved from a British wreck.	25	3	House bill	378	Whole House	June 25, 1839	No amendm't.	447	Passed	Amended and passed.	App'd Mar. 3, 1839
Balch, John, jr	Compensation for property erroneously seized at Boston.	26	1	Petition	336	Claims	366	Adverse		Laid on table.		
Balch, Samuel Y	Increase of pension	14	2	Petition	45	Pen. & Rev. Claims						
Balcom, Ebenezer	Pension	20	1	Petition	74	Military Pensions	April 5, 1828	Adverse		Laid on table.		
Bald, John R	Increase of pension	27	3	Petition	154	Invalid Pensions	139	Adverse		Laid on table.		
Balden, Bartholomew, and others.	Indemnity for improvements lost by re-survey.	30	2	Petition	313	Claims.						
Baldock, Levi	Additional compensation for mail service.	28	1	Petition	515	Claims.						
Baldridge, Eli, sureties of	Release from payment of bond	14	2	Petition	76	Ways and Means	Feb. 4, 1817	Adverse		Petition rejected.		
Baldridge, Isabella	(See Cap. John Baldridge, widow of.)	28	1		632							
Baldridge, James	Confirmation of title to land	23	2	Petition	234	Public Lands	Feb. 25, 1835	Favorable	765	Referred to Committee Whole House.		
Baldridge, James	Confirmation of title to land	24	1	Petition	114	Public Lands	Jan. 27, 1835	Favorable	218	Passed	Passed	App'd July 2, 1836
Baldridge, John	Indemnity for improvement on lands surrendered to Cherokees.	24	1	Petition	509	Indian Affairs	April 12, 1836	Favorable	548	Referred to Committee Whole House.		
Baldridge, John	Indemnity for improvement on lands surrendered to Cherokees	25	2	Petition	43	Indian Affairs	Jan. 30, 1838	Favorable	494	Referred to Committee Whole House.		
Baldridge, John	Indemnity for improvement on lands surrendered to Cherokees.	25	3	Rep. of Committee Whole.	379			With't amend.	494	Passed	Adverse report.	
Baldridge, John	Indemnity for improvement on lands surrendered to Cherokees.	26	1	Petition	180	Claims.						
Baldridge, Captain John, widow of.	Pension for revolutionary services.	28	1	Petition	632	Rev. Pensions	Jan. 7, 1844	Favorable	413	Referred to Committee Whole House.		
Baldridge, Captain John, widow of.	Pension for revolutionary services.	28	2	Rep. of Committee Whole.	344				413	Passed	Reported with't amendment.	
Baldridge, Captain John, widow of.	Pension for revolutionary services.	29	1	Petition	87	Rev. Pensions	151	Favorable	154	Passed	Passed	App'd July 18, 1846
Baldridge, Thomas	Pension for revolutionary services.	25	3	Petition	360	Rev. Pensions.						
Baldridge, Thomas	Pension for revolutionary services.	26	1	Petition	173	Rev. Pensions				Discharged; laid on table.		

List of private claims presented to the House of Representatives of the United States from the 1st to the 31st Congress, inclusive—Continued.

Names of claimants.	Nature or object of the claim.	Congress.	Session.	How brought before the House of Reps.	Page of journal.	To what committee of the House referred.	No. or date of the report.	Nature of the report.	No. of the bill.	How disposed of by the House of Reps.	How disposed of by the Senate.	Date of the act of Congress, and remarks.
Baldwin, Aaron	Release of a vessel and cargo from seizure.	12	1	Petition	24	Com. and Manuf.						
Baldwin, Alfred, (N. Y.)	Pension	20	2	Petition	49	Military Pensions	Jan. 21, 1829	Adverse		Laid on table.		
Baldwin, Alfred, (N. Y.)	Pension	21	2	Petition	127	Military Pensions.						
Baldwin, Alfred, (N. Y.)	Pension	22	1	Petition	67	Invalid Pensions	278	Favorable	360	Passed.		
Baldwin, Alfred, (N. Y.)	Pension	23	1	Petition	128	Invalid Pensions	Jan. 3, 1834	Favorable bill.	128	Passed	Passed	App'd June 30, 1834
Baldwin, Alfred, widow of	Continuation of pension	29	1	Petition	83	Invalid Pensions	305	Adverse		Laid on table.		
Baldwin, Anne Maria	Additional compensation for services as a witness.	26	1	Petition	622	Claims.						
Baldwin, Anne Maria	Additional compensation for services as a witness.	29	2	Petition	99	Claims.						
Baldwin, Anne Maria	Additional compensation for services as a witness.	30	1	Petition	566	Claims	760	Adverse		Laid on table.		
Baldwin, Augustus S.	(See Exploring Expedition)	27	3	Petition	149							
Baldwin, Benjamin	Bounty land for revolutionary services.	13	2	Petition	297	Pen. & Rev. Claims	Mar. 30, 1814	Adverse		Laid on table.		
Baldwin, Brackett, widow of.	Bounty land and arrears of pay	25	2	Petition	657	Military Affairs	871	Adverse		Laid on table.		
Baldwin, Brackett, widow of.	Bounty land and arrears of pay	25	3	Petition	454	Military Affairs	285	Adverse.				
Baldwin, Cornelius	Compensation for services as a revolutionary surgeon.	10	1	Petition	232	Claims.						
Baldwin, Cornelius	Compensation for services as a revolutionary surgeon.	15	1	Petition	94	Pens. & Rev. Cl'ms.	Feb. 16, 1818	Adverse		Laid on table.		
Baldwin, David	Compensation for services as surveyor of revenue.	9	2	Petition	495	Claims				Discharged.		
				Rep. of Secretary Treasury.	592	Claims.						
Baldwin, David A.	Pension	25	2	Petition	268	Invalid Pensions.						
Baldwin, David A.	Pension	26	1	Petition	161	Invalid Pensions	218	Favorable	230	Passed.		
Baldwin, David A.	Pension	26	2	Petition	107	Invalid Pensions	41	Favorable	569	Referred to Committee Whole House.		
Baldwin, David A.	Pension	27	2	Petition	60	Invalid Pensions.						
Baldwin, Daniel	Compensation for revolutionary services.	8	1	Petition	539	Whole House.						
Baldwin, Daniel	Compensation for revolutionary services.	12	1	Petition	99	Claims	June 12, 1812	Adverse		Laid on table.		
				Petition	233	Whole House.						
Baldwin, Daniel, widow of.	Continuation of pension	14	1	Petition	134	Pens. & Rev. Cl'ms.						
Baldwin, Elijah, (Vt.)	Pension	20	2	Petition	49	Military Pensions	Jan. 21, 1829	Adverse		Laid on table.		
Baldwin, Enoch, and others	Reimbursement of tonnage duty on brig Despatch.	23	2	Senate bill	428	Commerce	130	Adverse	S. 45	Laid on table.		
Baldwin, Enoch, and others	Reimbursement of tonnage duty on brig Despatch.	24	1	Senate bill	146	Commerce	June 23, 1836	Adverse	S. 35	Referred to Committee Whole House.		
Baldwin, Enoch, and others	Reimbursement of tonnage duty on brig Despatch.	25	2	Senate bill	508	Commerce	Feb. 28, 1838	No amendm't.	S. 120	Referred to Committee Whole House.		
Baldwin, Enoch, and others	Reimbursement of tonnage duty on brig Despatch.	25	3	Senate bill	149	Commerce	109	No amendm't.	S. 56	Passed		App'd Feb. 6, 1839
Baldwin, Enoch, and others	Reimbursement of tonnage duty on brig Despatch.	26	1	Senate bill	811	Commerce	June 17, 1840	No amendm't.	S. 158	Referred to Committee Whole House.		
Baldwin, Enoch, and others	Reimbursement of tonnage duty on brig Despatch.	28	2	Petition	141	Commerce						Leave to withdraw, 30th Cong. 1st sess.
Baldwin, George, heirs of.	Bounty land for military services.	24	2	Petition	121	Military Affairs.						

List of private claims presented to the House of Representatives of the United States from the 1st to the 31st Congress, inclusive—Continued.

Names of claimants.	Nature or object of the claim.	Congress.	Session.	How brought before the House of Reps.	Page of journal.	To what committee of the House referred.	No. or date of the report	Nature of the report.	No. of the bill.	How disposed of by the House of Reps.	How disposed of by the Senate.	Date of the act of Congress, and remarks.
Baldwin, George, heirs of.	Bounty land for military services.	25	2	Petition	249	Military Affairs	Jan. 10, 1838	Adverse		Laid on table.		
Baldwin, George, heirs of.	Bounty land for military services.	25	3	Petition	212	Ways and Means.						
Baldwin, Hezekiah	Pension for revolutionary services.	16	2	Petition	90	Rev. Pensions	Feb. 15, 1821	Adverse		Claim rejected.		
Baldwin, Ira, (Canada vol.)	Compensation and bounty for military services.	21	2	Petition	160	Claims.						
Baldwin, Ira, (Canada vol.)	Compensation and bounty for military services.	25	2	Petition	121	Claims.						
Baldwin, Ira, (Canada vol.)	Compensation and bounty for military services.	26	1	Petition	167	Claims.						
Baldwin, Ira, (Canada vol.)	Compensation and bounty for military services.	26	2	Petition	148	Claims.						
Baldwin, Ira, (Canada vol.)	Compensation and bounty for military services.	27	2	Petition	216	Claims	343	Adverse		Laid on table.		
Baldwin, Ira, (Canada vol.)	Compensation and bounty for military services.	28	1	Petition	73	Priv. Land Claims.	266	Favorable	198	Referred to Committee Whole House.		
Baldwin, Ira, (Canada vol.)	Compensation and bounty for military services.	28	2	Rep't Committee Whole House.	343			With't amend.	198	Passed.		
Baldwin, Ira, (Canada vol.)	Compensation and bounty for military services.	29	1	Petition	123	Priv. Land Claims.	484	Adverse		Laid on table.		
Baldwin, Ira, (Canada vol.)	Compensation and bounty for military services.	30	1	Petition	70	Public Lands.						
Baldwin, Ira, (Canada vol.)	Compensation and bounty for military services.	30	2	Petition	163	Public Lands.						
Baldwin, Ira, (Canada vol.)	Compensation and bounty for military services.	31	1	Petition	214	Claims.						
Baldwin, Isaac	(See Richard Cain and J. Baldwin)	18	2		131							
Baldwin, Isaac, widow of.	Renewal and continuation of pension.	29	2	Petition	236	Naval Affairs.						
Baldwin, Jackomeyer	(See administrators of Harper Brosiers.)	30	1		525							
Baldwin, John	Reimbursement of advances on public account.	12	1	Petition	85	Claims.						
Baldwin, John, and others.	Payment of Mexican certificate of indemnity.	27	2	Petition	215	Foreign Affairs.						
Baldwin, John, and others.	Payment of Mexican certificate of indemnity.	29	1	Petition	425	Foreign Affairs.						
Baldwin, John, and others.	Payment of Mexican certificate of indemnity.	29	2	Memorial	176	Foreign Affairs.						
Baldwin, John, and others.	Payment of Mexican certificate of indemnity.	30	1	Petition	218	Foreign Affairs.						
Baldwin, John	Balance due him on naval contract	31	1	Petition	258	Naval Affairs.						
Baldwin, John	Balance due him on naval contract	31	2	Petition	445	Naval Affairs	105	Adverse		Laid on table.		
Baldwin, John P	Indemnity for vessel burnt by Commodore Dallas.	26	1	Petition	337	Claims	698	Adverse		Laid on table.		
Baldwin, John P	Indemnity for vessel burnt by Commodore Dallas.	26	2	Petition	135	Claims	Jan. 4, 1841	Adverse		Laid on table.		
Baldwin, John P	Indemnity for vessel burnt by Commodore Dallas.	27	2	Petition	94	Claims	695	Adverse		Laid on table.		
Baldwin, Loammi	Compensation for services by request of Secretary Navy.	23	1	Senate bill	845	Naval Affairs	June 27, 1834	With't amend.	S. 134	Rejected.		
Baldwin, Luther	Indemnity for revolutionary injuries and reimbursement of advances.	3	1	Report of Secretary of War.	93	Select.						
Baldwin, Nathan	Pension for revolutionary services.	25	3	Petition	127	Rev. Pensions.						

List of private claims presented to the House of Representatives of the United States from the 1st to the 31st Congress, inclusive—Continued.

Names of claimants.	Nature or object of the claim.	Congress.	Session.	How brought before the House of Reps.	Page of journal.	To what committee of the House referred.	No. or date of the report.	Nature of the report.	No. of the bill.	How disposed of by the House of Reps	How disposed of by the Senate.	Date of the act of Congress, and remarks.
Baldwin, Nathan	Pension for revolutionary services	26	1	Petition	170	Rev. Pensions	136	Favorable	146	Passed	Indef. postp'd.	
Baldwin, Nathan	Pension for revolutionary services	26	2	Petition	148	Rev. Pensions	131	Favorable	642			
Baldwin, Nathan	Pension for revolutionary services	27	2	Petition	238	Rev. Pensions	298	Favorable	266	Passed	Indef. postp'd.	
Baldwin, Russell, & others	Remission of duty on sword for McDonough.	17	1	Petition	50	Ways and Means	Jan. 22, 1822	Favorable	53	Passed	Passed	App'd April 17, 1822
Baldwin, Silas	Pension	3	1	Report of Secretary of War.	131	Select	May 26, 1794	Res. to refer to Sec. of War.	R. 12	Passed	Passed	App'd June 9, 1794
Baldwin, Thomas	Pension	4	1	Report of Secretary of War.	447	Claims	Feb. 18, 1796	Pension bill	156	Passed	Passed with amendment.	App'd April 20, 1796
Baldwin, Thomas O	Pension	14	1	Petition	47	Pens. & Rev. Cl'ms.	April 11, 1816	Pension bill	171	Passed	Passed	App'd April 30, 1816
Baldwin, Thomas O	Increase of pension	18	1	Petition	137	Pens. & Rev. Cl'ms.				Discharged, referred to Secretary of War.		
Baldwin, Thomas P., surety of.	Discharge from liability	19	2	Petition	37							
Baldwin, Thomas P., surety of.	Discharge from liability	20	1	Resolution	30	Claims	3	Adverse.				
				Recommitted	111	Claims	95	Favorable	105	Passed	Passed	App'd May 24, 1828
Baldwin, Waterman	Pension for revolutionary services and sufferings.	10	1	Pension bill	232	Select	May 17, 1808	Pension bill	81	Passed	Passed with amendment.	App'd April 25, 1808
Baldwin, William, widow of.	Pension for naval services	16	1	Petition	141	Naval Affairs	Feb. 10, 1820	Adverse		Laid on table.		
Baldwin, William, widow of.	Pension for naval services	24	2	Petition	399	Naval Affairs.						
Baldy, John	Indemnity for loss on treasury notes, &c.	15	1	Petition	258	Claims.						
Baldy, John	Indemnity for loss on treasury notes, &c.	17	2	Petition	120	Claims.						
Baldy, John	Indemnity for loss on treasury notes, &c.	18	1	Petition	236	Claims.						
Baldy, John	Indemnity for loss on treasury notes, &c.	18	2	Petition	145	Claims	Jan. 19, 1825	Adverse		Laid on table.		
Baley, Henry	Pension	21	1	Petition	448	Rev. Claims.						
Balfour, John	Indemnity for land taken by government.	23	2	Resolution	243	Public Lands	79	General bill	696	Postponed.		
Ball, Anna	Pension for military services of husband.	26	1	Petition	173	Rev. Pensions	490	Adverse		Laid on table.		
Ball, Anna	Pension for military services of husband.	28	2	Petition	163	Rev. Pensions.						
Ball, Burgess	Compensation for supplies furnished revolutionary army.	25	2	Petition	391	Rev. Claims.						
Ball, Burgess	Compensation for supplies furnished revolutionary army.	25	3	Petition	85	Rev. Claims.						
Ball, Burgess	Compensation for supplies furnished revolutionary army.	26	1	Petition	166	Rev. Claims	443	Adverse		Laid on table.		
Ball, Burgess	Compensation for supplies furnished revolutionary army.	27	2	Petition	93	Rev. Claims.						
Ball, Daniel	Pension for revolutionary services	9	2	Pension bill	608	Whole House	Feb. 28, 1807	With't amend.	216	Passed	Passed	App'd March 3, 1807
Ball, E	(See assignees of Thomas Tupper.)	22	2		142							
Ball, Gideon	Pension for revolutionary services	18	2	Resolution	223	Rev. Pensions.						
Ball, Hannah	Continuation of pension of husband	28	1	Petition	849	Rev. Pensions.						
Ball, Jane	(See heirs of Samuel Wise)	2	1		459							
Ball, John, (N. Y.)	Commutation pay for revolutionary services.	10	1	Petition	216	Claims.						

List of private claims presented to the House of Representatives of the United States from the 1st to the 31st Congress, inclusive—Continued.

Names of claimants.	Nature or object of the claim.	Congress.	Session.	How brought before the House of Reps.	Page of journal.	To what committee of the House referred.	No. or date of the report.	Nature of the report.	No. of the bill.	How disposed of by the House of Reps.	How disposed of by the Senate.	Date of the act of Congress, and remarks.
Ball, John, (N. Y.)	Commutation pay for revolutionary services.	15	1	Petition	265	Pens. & Rev. Cl'ms.						
Ball, John, (N. Y.)	Commutation pay for revolutionary services.	22	2	Petition	30	Rev. Claims	Jan. 4, 1833	Adverse	......	Laid on table.		
Ball, John, (N. Y.)	Commutation pay for revolutionary services.	23	1	Petition	43	Rev. Claims	Dec. 20, 1833	Adverse	......	Laid on table.		
Ball, John, (N. Y.)	Commutation pay for revolutionary services.	2	2	Petition	215	Rev. Claims.						
Ball, John, (N. Y.)	Pension for revolutionary services.	24	1	Petition	404	Rev. Claims.						
Ball, John, (N. Y.)	Pension for revolutionary services.	26	1	Petition	285	Rev. Pensions	490	Adverse	......	Laid on table.		
Ball, John, (I. L.) executor of.	Set-off his claims against United States.	1	3	Petition	380	....	....	....	......	Referred to Secretary Treasury.		
Ball, John, (I. L.) executor of.	Set off his claims against United States.	2	1	Rep. of Secretary War.	625	....	....	....	......	Laid on table.	....	Leave to withdraw, p. 733
Ball, John T.	Compensation for extra services in Clerk's office, House Represen's	28	1	Petition	434	Accounts.						
Ball, John T.	Compensation for extra servces in Clerk's office, House Represent's	28	2	Petition	192	Accounts.						
Ball, John T.	Compensation for extra services in Clerk's office, House Represent's	29	2	Petition	356	Accounts.						
Ball, John T.	Compensation for extra services in Clerk's office, House Represent's	30	2	Petition	217	Claims	....	....	......	Discharged; laid on table.		
Ball, Joseph	(See heirs of Samuel Wise)	2	1	....	459							
Ball, Joseph	Payment of certain bills of credit.	4	1	Rep. of Secretary of Treasury.	388	Claims	May 31, 1796	Adverse	......	Laid on table.		
Ball, Joseph	Payment of certain bills of credit.	4	2	Memorial	629	Claims.						
Ball, Joseph	Payment of certain bills of credit.	5	2	Petition	91	....	Feb. 26, 1798	Adverse	......	Leave to withdraw.		
Ball, J. E. & G. I. Wasson	Compensation for special mail service.	30	1	Petition	379	Claims	423	Adverse	......	Laid on table.		
Ball, Mottram, (Va.)	Indemnity for property destroyed by the enemy.	15	1	Report of Committee Claims.	37	Claims	146	Favorable	125	Referred to Committee Whole House.		
Ball, Mottram, (Va.)	Indemnity for property destroyed by the enemy.	15	2	Report of Committee Whole.	....	....	....	With't amend.	125	Passed	Passed	App'd Jan. 19, 1819
Ball, Nehemiah, widow of.	Pension	25	3	Petition	219	Invalid Pensions.						
Ball, Nehemiah, widow of.	Pension	26	1	Petition	162	Invalid Pensions	287	Adverse	......	Laid on table.		
Ball, Samuel	Pension for revolutionary services	3	1	Petition	131	Select	May 26, 1794	Res. to refer to Sec'y War.	R. 12	Passed	Passed	App'd June 9, 1794
Ball, Samuel	Pension for revolutionary services.	4	1	Rep. of Secretary War.	373	Claims.						
Ball, Thomas, (D. C.)	Arrears of pension	22	1	Petition	188	Invalid Pensions	289	Favorable	377	Passed.		
Ball, Thomas, (D. C.)	Arrears of pension	22	2	Petition	118	Invalid Pensions	Feb. 15, 1833	Favorable	738	Referred to Committee Whole House.		
Ball, Thomas, (D. C.)	Arrears of pension	23	1	Petition	184	Invalid Pensions	Feb. 7, 1834	Favorable	287	Referred to Committee Whole House.		
Ball, Thomas, (D. C.)	Arrears of pension	23	2	Rep't. Committee Whole House.	300	....	....	With't amend.	287	Passed	Passed	App'd March 3, 1835
Ball, Thomas	(See heir of William Ball)	22	2	....	86							
Ball, Wait	Compensation for revolutionary services.	23	1	Petition	220	Rev. Claims.						
Ball, William	Arrears of pension & bounty land.	25	2	Memorial	197	Rev. Pensions.						
Ball, William	Arrears of pension & bounty land.	26	1	Petition	162	Invalid Pensions	558	Adverse	......	Laid on table.		
Ball, William, (Va.)	Compensation for revolutionary services.	19	2	Petition	91	Rev. Claims	Jan. 23, 1827	Adverse	......	Laid on table.		

List of private claims presented to the House of Representatives of the United States from the 1st to the 31st Congress, inclusive—Continued.

Names of claimants.	Nature or object of the claim.	Congress.	Session.	How brought before the House of Reps.	Page of journal.	To what committee of the House referred.	No. or date of the report.	Nature of the report.	No. of the bill.	How disposed of by the House of Reps.	How disposed of by the Senate.	Date of the act of Congress, and remarks.
Ball, William, heir of	Commutation pay for revolutionary services.	22	2	Petition	86	Rev. Claims.						
Ballance, Charles	Right of pre-emption	24	1	Petition	257	Public Lands.						
Ballantine, David	Payment of forfeited land certificate	25	2	Resolution	522	Priv. Land Claims.	Mar. 28, 1838	Favorable	701	Referred to Committee Whole House.		
Ballantine, David	Payment of forfeited land certificate	25	3	Rep't Committee Whole House	...	...	...	With't amend.	701	Passed	Passed	App'd March 3, 1839
Ballantine and Mechan	Compensation for work and material on Cumberland road.	23	1	Resolution	589	Claims	455	Adverse	...	Laid on table	...	See Report No. 449
Ballard, Benjamin	Comfirmation of title to land	29	1	Senate bill	1075	Priv. Land Claims.	July 17, 1846	With't amend.	S. 81	Passed	Passed	App'd July 21, 1846
Ballard, Ebenezer	Pension for naval services	29	1	Senate bill	1075	Naval Affairs	July 24, 1846	With't amend.	S. 84	Passed	Passed	App'd August 6, 1846
Ballard, Eliza	(See heir of widow of David Baker)	25	2	...	54							
Ballard, William, assignee of.	Permission to locate a military land warrant.	7	1	Petition	109	...	...	...	...	Laid on table.		
Ballard, William H.	Pension for revolutionary services.	12	1	Petition	187	Claims	June 12, 1812	Adverse	...	Laid on table.		
Ballinger, John	Pension	20	2	Petition	204	Rev. Claims.						
Ballowe, Robert	(See Moses Brown and others)	9	2	...	555							
Balster, John	Pension	26	1	Memorial	713	Naval Affairs.						
Balthoope, John	Compensation for a plan for supplying public buildings at Washington with water.	21	2	Petition	162	Whole House.						
Baltimore Bible Society	(See Bible Society, Baltimore)	14	1	...	533							
Bamper, Jacob, (N. J.)	Pension	19	1	Petition	93	Military Pensions.	April 1, 1826	Adverse	...	Laid on table.		
Bancroft, Ebenezer	Increase of pension	9	2	Pension bill	608	Whole House	Oct. 28, 1807	With amend.	216	Passed	Passed	App'd March 3, 1807
Bancroft, James, (Mass.)	Pension	20	1	Petition	223	Military Pensions.	...	...	...	Discharged; leave to withdraw.		
Bancroft, Laysel	Release from a judgment	12	2	Petition	598	Ways and Means.	March 1, 1813	Adverse	...	Claim rejected.		
Bancroft, Laysel	Release from a judgment	13	1	Petition	12	Ways and Means.						
Bancroft, Laysel	Release from a judgment	13	2	House bill	337	Ways and Means.	Mar. 11, 1814	Favorable	162	Passed	Passed	App'd April 18, 1814
Bancroft, Robert	Pension for revolutionary services.	3	1	Rep. of Secretary War.	131	Select	May 26, 1794	Res. to refer to Sec. War.	R. 12	Passed	Passed	App'd June 9, 1794
Bancroft, Robert	Pension for revolutionary services.	4	1	Rep. Committee Claims.	447	Whole House	...	...	156	Passed	Passed with amendment.	App'd April 20, 1796
Bane, John	Pension for revolutionary services.	18	2	Petition	81	Rev. Pensions.						
Banfield, George	Pension for revolutionary services.	17	1	Petition	31	Rev. Pensions.						
Bangs, Dean	Bounty on fishing schooners	4	2	Petition	615	...	...	...	...	Referred to Secretary Treasury.		
Bangs, George P., & others	Remission of duties on goods destroyed by fire.	19	1	Petition	130	Ways and Means.	166	Favorable	215	Postponed.		
Bangs, George P., & others	Remission of duties on goods destroyed by fire.	20	1	House bill	107	Whole House	...	...	38	Laid on table.		
Bangs, George P., & others	Remission of duties on goods destroyed by fire.	21	1	Petition	68	Ways and Means.	44	Favorable	66	Bill rejected.		
Bangs, Isaac	(See George P. Bangs, and others)	19	1	...	130							
Bangs, William	(See George P. Bangs, and others)	19	1	...	130							
Banister, W. B.	(See Moses Brown, attorney of)	26	1	...	182	...	343	...	319			
Banks, Abijah, widow of	Pension for revolutionary services.	28	1	Petition	318	Rev. Pensions	...	...	...	Discharged; laid on table.		
Banks, Bartholomew	(See heir of John Banks)	28	1	...	451							
Banks, David	(See Gould & Banks)	22	1	...	54							
Banks, Elizabeth	(See widow of Joseph Potter)	19	1	...	365							
Banks, G. W.	Release from costs and damages in a suit.	18	1	Resolution	289	P. Of. & P. Roads.	April 30, 1824	Adverse	...	Laid on table.		
Banks, Henry	(See J. Banks & Co)	21	2	...	217							

List of private claims presented to the House of Representatives of the United States from the 1st to the 31st Congress, inclusive—Continued.

Names of claimants.	Nature or object of the claim.	Congress.	Session.	How brought before the House of Reps.	Page of journal.	To what committee of the House referred.	No. or date of the report.	Nature of the report.	No. of the bill.	How disposed of by the House of Reps.	How disposed of by the Senate.	Date of the act of Congress, and remarks.
Banks, John	(See Henry Hill, *et al.*)				83							
Banks, John	(See Harris & Blachford)	2	2		615							
Banks, John, heir of	Indemnity for French spoliations prior to 1800.	28	1	Petition	451	Foreign Affairs.						
Banks, Joseph	(See Louis F. Beeler, *et al*)	30	1		115		482					
Banks, J., & Co	Compensation for revolutionary supplies.	21	2	Memorial	216	Claims.						
Banks, J., & Co	Compensation for revolutionary supplies.	22	1	Memorial	62	Rev. Claims	March 6, 1832	Adverse		Laid on table.		
Banks, J., & Co	Compensation for revolutionary supplies.	24	1	Memorial	218	Rev. Claims	Feb. 4, 1836	Adverse		Laid on table.		
Banks, Richard T.	Indemnity for loss on contract for removing Indians.	25	2	Senate bill	1058	Indian Affairs	July 2, 1838	With't amend.	S. 340	Referred to Committee Whole House.		
Banks, Richard T.	Indemnity for loss on contract for removing Indians.	26	1	Documents.	1009	Priv. Land Claims.						
				Senate bill	189	Claims			S. 24			
Banks, Richard T., representatives of.	Indemnity for loss on contract for removing Indians.	26	2	Senate bill	113	Claims			S. 54			
Banks, Richard T., representatives of.	Indemnity for loss on contract for removing Indians.	27	2	Senate bill	680	Indian Affairs	May 4, 1842	With't amend.	139	Passed	Passed	App'd Aug. 11, 1842
Bank of the United States	(See Williamson Smith, assignee of.)	27	2		514							
Bankson, Benjamin	Extra compensation as clerk in State Department.	3	1	Petition	93	Select	54	General bill	69	Passed	Rejected.	
Bankson, Mary	Increase of compensation for revolutionary services of husband.	20	2	Petition	142	Military Pensions.						
Bankston, Ignatius	Indemnity for land seized by officers of government.	23	2	Resolution	243	Public Lands	79	General bill	696	Postponed.		
Banneau, Timothy N.	Pension for revolutionary services.	23	2	Petition	288	Rev. Pensions	Jan. 28, 1835			Discharged; laid on table.		
Bannister, S. B.	(See Exploring Expedition)	27	3		149							
Bannon, Andrew O., heirs of.	Compensation for revolutionary services.	31	1	Petition	714	Rev. Claims.						
Bannon, Jeremiah	Restoration of pension	17	1	Petition	77	Rev. Pensions.						
Banta, Andrew	Arrears of pension	25	2	Petition	588	Invalid Pensions.						
Banta, Andrew	Compensation for horse lost in public service.	24	1	Petition	429	Claims	568	Adverse		Laid on table.		
Banta, Jacob	(See Abraham Chapline, assignee of.)	31	1		1215							
Barbarick, John	Increase of pension	10	2	House bill	499	Whole House	Feb. 20, 1809	Pension bill	158	Passed	Passed with amendment.	App'd March 3, 1809
Barbarick, John	Increase of pension	18	1	Petition	155	Pens. & Rev. Cl'ms.						
Barbaric, Otto Vantuyl	(See devisees of Robert Farman)	11	2		149							
Barbee, Daniel, (Ky.)	Increase of comp'n as postmaster	15	1	Petition	122	P. Of. & P. Roads.						
Barber, Benjamin	(See executor of Charles Marsh)	26	1		169							
Barber, Daniel	Pension for revolutionary services.	22	2	Petition	176	Rev. Pensions.						
Barber, Henry	Pension for revolutionary services.	22	1	Resolution	138	Rev. Pensions.						
Barber, Job L.	Reimbursement of forfeiture in United States court.	25	2	Petition	50	Judiciary.						
Barber, Joseph	Compensation for supplies, &c., on public account.	26	1	Petition	623	Claims.						
Barber, Joseph	Compensation for supplies, &c., on public account.	26	2	Petition	80	Claims.						
Barber, Joseph	Compensation for supplies, &c., on public account.	31	1	Petition	533	Claims.						

List of private claims presented to the House of Representatives of the United States from the 1st to the 31st Congress, inclusive—Continued.

Names of claimants.	Nature or object of the claim.	Congress.	Session.	How brought before the House of Reps.	Page of journal.	To what committee of the House referred.	No. or date of the report.	Nature of the report.	No. of the bill.	How disposed of by the House of Reps.	How disposed of by the Senate.	Date of the act of Congress, and remarks.
Barber, Moses, widow of..	Pension for revolutionary services.	26	1	Petition	283	Rev. Pensions	424	Adverse	......	Laid on table.		
Barber, Moses, widow of..	Pension for revolutionary services.	26	2	Petition	212	Rev. Pensions.						
Barber, Noyes..........	Bounty on fishing schooner Lucy Anne.	17	2	Petition	56	Commerce.						
Barber, Noyes..........	Bounty on fishing schooner Lucy Anne.	18	1	Petition	47	Commerce.						
Barber, Noyes, representatives of.	Bounty on fishing schooner Lucy Anne.	18	2	House bill	207	Whole House.....	Feb. 26, 1825	With't amend.	319	Passed	Passed	App'd March 3, 1825
Barber, Robert..........	Remission of duty on distillery...	7	2	Memorial	363	Claims	Feb. 26, 1803	Indefinite	......	Postponed.		
Barber, Robert, jr........	(See George Schnabel)	27	2	....	534							
Barber, Uriah, and others.	Exchange of a location of land...	14	1	Petition	257	Public Lands	....	....	......	Discharged; leave to withdraw.		
Barber, Uriah, and others.	Exchange of a location of land...	14	2	Petition	117	Priv. Land Claims.						
Barber, Uriah, and others.	Exchange of a location of land...	15	2	Petition	220	Public Lands	....	....	......	Discharged; leave to withdraw.		
Barber, William, heirs of..	Commutation pay for revolutionary services.	11	2	Petition	120	Claims	Feb. 7, 1810	Adverse	......	Rejected.		
Barber, William	(See administrator of Conrad Laub)	15	1	....	114							
Barber, Zachariah	Pension for revolutionary services	31	1	Resolution	419	Rev. Pensions	99	Adverse	......	Laid on table.		
Barbin, L. P.	Increase of compensation as clerk in land office, Louisiana.	15	1	Petition	151	Claims.						
Barbour, James, jr.	(See William B. Lawrence, and others.)	21	1	....	326	....	....	....	275			
Barbour, Philip, heir of ..	Indemnity for bounty land sold by government.	15	2	Petition	21	Priv. Land Claims.	16	Favorable	213	Referred to Committee Whole House.		
Barbour, Philip, heir of ..	Indemnity for bounty land sold by government.	16	1	Petition	30	Priv. Land Claims.	8	Favorable	12	Passed	Passed	App'd Jan. 14, 1820
Barbour, Philip, heir of ..	Indemnity for bounty land sold by government.	24	2	Petition	122	Priv. Land Claims.	Jan. 13, 1837	Favorable	812	Referred to Committee Whole House.		
Barbour, Philip, heir of ..	Indemnity for bounty land sold by government.	25	2	Petition	43	Priv. Land Claims.	495	Favorable	492	Referred to Committee Whole House.		
Barbour, Philip, heir of ..	Indemnity for bounty land sold by government.	25	3	Rep. of Committee Whole.	379	....	....	With't amend.	492	Postponed.		
Barbour, Philip, heir of ..	Confirmation of title to land.....	25	2	Senate bill	1166	Priv. Land Claims.	June 27, 1838	With't amend.	S. 293	Referred to Committee Whole House.		
Barbour, Philip, heir of ..	Confirmation of title to land.....	26	1	Senate bill	1097	Priv. Land Claims.	....	....	S. 112			
Barbrick, John, daughter of	Arrears of pension.............	29	1	Petition	227	Rev. Pensions	....	....	......	Discharged; laid on table.		
Barby, Henry...........	Certificate of debenture on goods exported.	18	2	Petition	294	....	....	....	......	Referred to Secretary Treasury.		
Barckley, Margaret	(See heirs of John O'Connor)....	14	1	....	60							
Barclay, James..........	Increase of pension	31	1	Petition	323	Invalid Pensions.						
Barclay, Joseph.........	Compensation for services in the war of 1812.	24	1	Petition	64	Military Affairs....	....	....	......	Discharged; laid on table.		
Barclay, Joseph.........	Compensation for services in the war of 1812.	25	2	Petition	96	Military Affairs....	Mar. 30, 1838	Adverse	......	Laid on table		
Barclay, Joseph.........	Compensation for services in the war of 1812.	25	3	Petition	454	Military Affairs....	....	....	......	Discharged; laid on table.		
Barclay, Joseph.........	Compensation for services in the war of 1812.	28	1	Petition	435	Military Affairs.						
Barclay & Livingston	Reimbursement of overpaid duties	29	2	Memorial	146	Claims	54	Favorable	656	Referred to Committee Whole House.		
Barclay & Livingston....	Reimbursement of overpaid duties	30	1	Petition	79	Commerce	65	Favorable	47	Passed	Passed	App'd June 28, 1848

List of private claims presented to the House of Representatives of the United States from the 1st to the 31st Congress, inclusive—Continued.

Names of claimants.	Nature or object of the claim.	Congress.	Session.	How brought before the House of Reps.	Page of journal.	To what committee of the House referred.	No. or date of the report.	Nature of the report.	No. of the bill.	How disposed of by the House of Reps.	How disposed of by the Senate.	Date of the act of Congress, and remarks.
Barclay, Robert, (Mo.)	Indemnity for a Spanish grant sold by government.	20	1	Senate bill	332	Priv. Land Claims	Feb. 26, 1828	With't amend.	S. 57	Referred to Committee Whole House.		
Barclay, Robert, (Mo.)	Indemnity for a Spanish grant sold by government.	29	1	Senate bill	1075	Priv. Land Claims	July 17, 1846	With't amend.	S. 129	Passed	Passed	App'd July 21, 1846
Barclay, Stephen, widow of	Pension for military services	31	2	Petition	118	Invalid Pensions.						
Barclay, Thomas	Credit for depreciation of paper money, &c.	1	3	Petition	376	Select				Discharged; referred to Secretary of Treas.		
Barclay, Thomas	Credit for depreciation of paper money, &c.	2	2	Rep. of Secretary Treasury.	625					Laid on table.		
Barclay, Thomas	Compensation for services as public agent.	1	1	Petition	120					Laid on table.		
Barclay, Thomas	Compensation for services as public agent.	1	2	Petition	163	Select	July 28, 1790	Favorable	91	Passed	Passed with amendment.	
Barclay, Thomas, widow of.	Compensation for services as public agent.	9	2	Petition	574	Claims.						
Barclay, Thomas, widow of.	Compensation for services as public agent.	10	1	Petition	37	Claims	Jan. 8, 1808	Favorable	51	Passed	Passed	App'd April 18, 1808
Barclay, Thomas, assignee of.	Set off claim for services prior to May 16, 1791.	2	2	Petition	652					Referred to Secretary of Treasury.		
Barclay, Thomas, assignee of.	Set-off claim for services prior to May 16, 1791.	4	2	Petition	443	Claims	Feb. 18, 1797	Favorable		Referred to Committee Whole House.		
Bard, Archibald	(See executors of Robert Johnston.)	19	1		44							
Bard, Ebenezer, widow of.	(See surety of William Bard)	21	2		160							
Bard, Samuel	(See administrator of John Kerlin)	19	1		131							
Bard, William, surety of.	Release from suretyship	21	2	Petition	160	Claims	Jan. 26, 1831	Adverse		Laid on table.		
Barden, Elijah	(See Elijah Borden).											
Barden, Henry	To be restored to pension roll	30	1	Petition	201	Rev. Pensions				Discharged; laid on table.		
Bardin, James	Confirmation of title to land in Louisiana	22	2	Petition	264	Priv. Land Claims.						
Bardin, James	Confirmation of title to land in Louisiana.	23	2	Petition	284	Priv. Land Claims.						
Bardin, William	(See F. M. Arredondo, *et al.*)	19	1		252							
Bardstown, Bishop of	(See Benedict Joseph Flaget)	19	1		99							
Bare, William, heirs of	Confirmation of title to land in Louisiana.	21	1	Petition	298	Priv. Land Claims.						
Bargelo, Lorenzo, administrator of.	Compensation for military services	22	1	Petition	288	Claims	480	Adverse		Referred to Committee Whole House.		
Bargrain, A. S	(See heirs of Joseph Masi)	27	2		369							
Bargy, Peter, jr., & others	Extra compensation for making dam on Savannah river.	21	1	Petition	201	Claims	248	Favorable	307	Referred to Committee Whole House.		
Bargy, Peter, jr., & others	Extra compensation for making dam on Savannah river.	21	2	Rep't Committee Whole House	333			With't amend.	307	Passed	Reported with't amendment.	
Bargy, Peter, jr., & others	Extra compensation for making dam on Savannah river.	22	1	Petition	25	Claims	231	Favorable	309	Referred to Committee Whole House.		
Bargy, Peter, jr., & others	Extra compensation for making dam on Savannah river.	22	2	Rep't Committee Whole House.	336			With't amend.	309	Passed	Passed	App'd March 2, 1833
Bargy, Peter, jr	Indemnity for loss on a certain contract.	25	2	Senate bill	557	Claims	809	With't amend.	S. 125	Referred to Committee Whole House.		
Bargy, Peter, jr	Indemnity for loss on a certain con tract.	25	3	Senate bill	372	Claims	March 2, 1839	With't amend.	S. 81	Passed	Passed	App'd March 3, 1839
Bargy, Peter, jr., assignee of.	Further compensation for work on Pennsylvania avenue.	26	1	Petition	294	Claims.						

List of private claims presented to the House of Representatives of the United States from the 1st to the 31st Congress, inclusive—Continued.

Names of claimants.	Nature or object of the claim.	Congress.	Session.	How brought before the House of Reps.	Page of journal.	To what committee of the House referred.	No. or date of the report.	Nature of the report.	No. of the bill.	How disposed of by the House of Reps.	How disposed of by the Senate.	Date of the act of Congress, and remarks.
Bargy, Peter, jr., assignee of.	Further compensation for work on Pennsylvania avenue.	26	2	Petition	80	Claims	240	Adverse	......	Laid on table.	....	Min'y report favorable.
Bargy, Peter, jr., assignee of.	Further compensation for work on Pennsylvania avenue.	27	2	Petition	154	Claims	488	Adverse	......	Laid on table.		
Bargy, Peter, jr., assignee of.	Further compensation for work on Pennsylvania avenue.	27	3	Petition	167	Claims	....	....	......	Discharged; laid on table.		
Bargy, Peter, jr., assignee of.	Further compensation for work on Pennsylvania avenue.	28	1	Resolution	941	Select	525	Favorable	400	Referred to Committee Whole House.		
Bargy, Peter, jr., assignee of.	Further compensation for work on Pennsylvania avenue.	29	1	Petition	105	Dist. of Columbia	106	Favorable	118	Rejected.		
Bargy, Peter, jr., assignee of.	Further compensation for work on Pennsylvania avenue.	30	1	Petition	258	Dist. of Columbia	594	Favorable	473	Referred to Committee Whole House.		
Bargy, Peter, jr., assignee of.	Further compensation for work on Pennsylvania avenue.	30	1	Senate bill	915	Claims	745	Adverse	S. 151	Referred to Committee Whole House.		
Bargy, Peter, jr., assignee of.	Further compensation for work on Pennsylvania avenue.	30	2	Petition	118	Dist. of Columbia.						
Barham, F. & F., assignee of.	Confirmation of title to land in Louisiana.	20	1	Resolution	448	Priv. Land Claims.	May 9, 1828	Adverse	......	Laid on table.		
Barham, F. & F., assignee of.	Confirmation of title to land in Louisiana.	20	2	Resolution	44	Priv. Land Claims.						
Barham, F. & F., assignee of.	Confirmation of title to land in Louisiana.	22	1	Resolution	173	Priv. Land Claims.	197	Favorable	283	Referred to Committee Whole House.		
Barham, F. & F., assignee of.	Confirmation of title to land in Louisiana.	22	2	Rep't Committee Whole House.	170	....	....	With't amend.	283	Passed.		
Barham, F. & F., assignee of.	Confirmation of title to land in Louisiana.	23	1	Petition	49	Priv. Land Claims.	Dec. 17, 1833	Favorable	43	Passed	Passed	App'd June 18, 1834
Barham, Newson	Pension	14	1	Petition	59	Pens. & Rev. Cl'ms.	April 8, 1816	Adverse	......	Claim rejected.		
Barhyett, Jerome	Compensation for horses, &c., lost in public service.	24	1	Petition	92	Claims	Jan. 5, 1836	Adverse	......	Laid on table.		
Barhyt, Daniel	Pension for revolutionary services.	3	1	Report of Secretary of War.	131	Select	May 26, 1794	Res. to refer to Sec. War.	R. 12	Passed	Passed	App'd June 9, 1794
Baribeau, Pierre	Confirmation of title to land in Illinois territory.	14	2	Petition	276	Public Lands.						
Baribeau, Pierre	Confirmation of title to land in Illinois territory.	15	1	Petition	188	Priv. Land Claims.						
Baribeau, Pierre	Confirmation of title to land in Illinois territory.	15	2	Petition	25	Priv. Land Claims.	....	....	......	Discharged; leave to withdraw.		
Barkelow, Farrington	(See Mary Rapleye, administrators of.)	12	1	....	98							
Barker, Abel	Pension	19	1	Petition	423	Military Pensions	April 20, 1826	Adverse	......	Claim rejected.		
Barker, Abraham	Remission of duties on oil	12	1	Petition	333	Com. and Manuf.						
Barker, Abraham	Remission of duties on oil	12	2	Petition	564	Com. and Manuf.						
Barker, Isaac, (R. I.)	Pension for revolutionary services.	23	1	Petition	135	Rev. Pensions	244	Favorable	278	Referred to Committee Whole House.		
Barker, Isaac, (R. I.)	Pension for revolutionary services.	23	2	House bill	300	....	....	....	278	Postponed.		
Barker, Isaac, widow of, (R. I.)	Pension for revolutionary services.	24	1	Petition	107	Rev. Pensions	243	Favorable	249	Referred to Committee Whole House.		
Barker, Isaac, widow of, (R. I.)	Pension for revolutionary services.	24	2	House bill	198	....	....	....	249	Passed.		
Barker, Isaac, widow of, (R. I.)	Pension for revolutionary services.	25	2	Petition	36	Rev. Pensions	213	Favorable	250	Passed.		
Barker, Isaac, widow of, (R. I.)	Pension for revolutionary services.	26	1	Petition	171	Rev. Pensions	132	Favorable	142	Passed	Indef. postp'd.	

List of private claims presented to the House of Representatives of the United States from the 1st to the 31st Congress, inclusive—Continued.

Names of claimants.	Nature or object of the claim.	Congress.	Session.	How brought before the House of Reps.	Page of journal.	To what committee of the House referred.	No. or date of the report.	Nature of the report.	No. of the bill.	How disposed of by the House of Reps.	How disposed of by the Senate.	Date of the act of Congress, and remarks.
Barker, Isaac, (Illinois)	Increase of pension	28	1	Petition	159	Invalid Pensions	402	Favorable	312	Passed.		
Barker, Isaac, (Illinois)	Increase of pension	28	2	House bill	134				468	Referred to Committee Whole House.		
Barker, Isaac, (Illinois)	Increase of pension	29	1	Petition	83	Invalid Pensions	46	Adverse		Laid on table.		
Barker, Jacob	Withdrawal of suits against endorsers.	14	1	Petition	532	Ways and Means.						
Barker, Jacob	Equitable settlement of claims for loans to United States.	17	1	Petition	100	Claims.						
Barker, Jacob, assignees of	Equitable settlement of claims for loans to United States.	18	2	Memorial	223	Claims.						
Barker, Jacob, assignees of	Equitable settlement of claims for loans to United States.	19	1	Memorial	151	Ways and Means.						
Barker, Jacob, assignees of	Equitable settlement of claims for loans to United States.	23	1	Memorial	311	Judiciary.						
Barker, Jacob, assignees of	Equitable settlement of claims for loans to United States.	23	2	Memorial	423	Judiciary				Discharged; laid on table.		
Barker, Jacob, assignees of	Equitable settlement of claims for loans to United States.	28	1	Petition	861	Judiciary.						
Barker, Jacob, assignees of	Equitable settlement of claims for loans to United States.	28	2	Petition	333	Judiciary.						
Barker, Jacob, assignees of	Equitable settlement of claims for loans to United States.	31	1	Petition	985	Judiciary.						
Barker, James	Pension for revolutionary services.	18	1	Petition	284	Pens. and Revolutionary Claims.						
Barker, James	Pension for revolutionary services.	18	2	Petition	66	Rev. Pensions	50	Favorable	307	Passed	Passed	App'd Mar. 3, 1825
Barker, Joseph	Compensation for a horse lost in public service.	24	1	Petition	206	Claims	Feb. 17, 1836	Adverse		Laid on table.		
Barker, Joshua	Compensation for a horse lost in public service.	25	3	Petition	462	Claims.						
Barker, Josiah	Confirmation of land title	20	2	Petition	119	Public Lands	Feb. 17, 1829	Favorable	447	Referred to Committee Whole House.		
Barker, Josiah	Confirmation of land title	21	2	Petition	83	Priv. Land Claims.	Feb. 24, 1831	By bill	651	Passed.		
Barker, Josiah	Confirmation of land title	22	1	Petition	417	Priv. Land Claims.	Mar. 16, 1832	Favorable	476	Referred to Committee Whole House.		
Barker, Josiah	Confirmation of land title	22	2	House bill	93	Whole House	Dec. 28, 1832	Amended	265	Passed	Passed	App'd Feb. 9, 1833
Barker, Pierre A., sureties of.	Release from liability	27	2	Petition	972	Judiciary.						
Barker, Pierre A., sureties of.	Release from liability	27	3	Petition	44	Judiciary.						
Barker, Samuel	Commutation pay for revolutionary services.	12	1	Petition	238	Claims.						
Barker, Samuel, heirs of	Commutation pay for revolutionary services.	24	1	Petition	105	Rev. Claims.						
Barker, Samuel, heirs of	Commutation pay for revolutionary services.	25	2	Petition	199	Rev. Claims.						
Barker, Stephen, widow of.	Pension for revolutionary services.	30	1	Petition	786	Rev. Pensions.						
Barker, Thomas	Indemnity for his land sold by United States.	19	1	Petition	271	Priv. Land Claims.						
Barker, Thomas	Indemnity for his land sold by United States.	24	1	Petition	853	Priv. Land Claims.						
Barker, Zedekiah, widow of.	Pension for revolutionary services.	26	1	Petition	950	Pev. Pensions.						
Barker, Zedekiah, widow of.	Pension for revolutionary services.	28	1	Petition	436	Rev. Pensions.						
Barker, Zenas	Pension	20	1	Petition	98	Military Pensions	Jan. 30, 1828	Adverse		Laid on table.		

List of private claims presented to the House of Representatives of the United States from the 1st to the 31st Congress, inclusive—Continued.

Names of claimants.	Nature or object of the claim.	Congress.	Session.	How brought before the House of Reps.	Page of journal.	To what committee of the House referred.	No. or date of the report.	Nature of the report.	No. of the bill.	How disposed of by the House of Reps.	How disposed of by the Senate.	Date of the act of Congress, and remarks.
Barkley, George	Pension	22	2	Resolution and petition.	182	Invalid Pensions.						
Barkley, George	Pension	23	1	Petition	92	Invalid Pensions	Dec. 24, 1833	Adverse	......	Laid on table.		
Barkley, George	Pension	24	1	Petition	615	Invalid Pensions	June 4, 1836	Favorable	677	Passed	Adverse report.	
Barkley, George	Pension	25	2	Resolution	38	Invalid Pensions	190	Favorable	216	Passed	Adverse report.	
Barkley, George	Pension	25	3	House bill	449	Whole House	....	....	1094			
Barkley, George	Pension	26	1	Petition	161	Invalid Pensions	353	Favorable	332	Referred to Committee Whole House.		
Barkley, John	(See John Berkley.)	23	1	....	386							
Barks, Jacob	Confirmation of title to land in Missouri.	15	2	Petition	207	Public Lands.						
Barks, Jacob	Confirmation of title to land in Missouri.	17	1	Petition	53	Public Lands.						
Barks, Jacob	Confirmation of title to land in Missouri.	18	1	Petition	53	Public Lands	Jan. 16, 1824	Favorable	65	Passed	Passed	App'd May 26, 1824
Barksdale, Richard H.	Compensation for services in Indian wars.	22	2	Resolution	273	Claims.						
Barlett, Philip	Compensation for revolutionary services.	4	1	Petition	425	Claims.						
Barlett, Philip	Compensation for revolutionary services.	4	2	Petition	614	Claims.						
Barling, Aaron	Land for settling on Lovely's purchase.	22	1	Petition	294	Public Lands.						
Barlow, Joseph	Pension for revolutionary services.	20	1	Resolution	120	Military Pensions	....	Pension bill	283	Passed.		
Barlow, Joseph	Pension for revolutionary services.	21	1	Petition	47	Military Pensions	Feb. 13, 1830	Pension bill	72	Passed	Passed	App'd May 20, 1830
Barmer, John (N. C.)	Pension for revolutionary services.	21	1	Resolution	167	Military Pensions						
Barmon, N. N.	(See James Bruton, sureties of.)	31	2	....	107							
Barnaby, George	(See John N. Stout)	10	1	....	119							
Barnard, Cyprian	Pension	19	1	Petition	9	Military Pensions	April 1, 1826	Adverse.				
Barnard, ———	(See Dodd and Barnard)	20	1	....	111							
Barnard, Edward	(See J. B. Fanning, administrator of.)	18	1	....	175							
Barnard, Frederick	Compensation for services as clerk in Adjutant General's Office.	23	2	Petition	68	Military Affairs	Jan. 23, 1835	Adverse	......	Resolution to refer to Secretary War.		
Barnard, Grove	Pension for revolutionary services.	22	1	Resolution	58	Rev. Pensions	Dec. 21, 1831	Favorable	69	Passed.		
Barnard, John	Indemnity for damage to property by United States troops.	16	2	Petition	101	Claims.						
Barnard, John	Bounty land for revolutionary services	16	2	Petition	188	Claims	Feb. 7, 1821	Adverse	......	Claim rejected.		
Barnard, John, (Penn.)	To be restored to pension roll	17	1	Petition	124	Rev. Pensions.						
Barnard, John, (Penn.)	To be restored to pension roll	19	1	Petition	35	Military Pensions	April 1, 1826	Adverse	......	Laid on table.		
Barnard, Joseph	Compensation for vessel taken by the enemy.	3	1	Memorail	109	....	....	....	......	Referred to Secretary War.		
Barnard, Joseph	Compensation for vessel taken by the enemy.	3	2	Rep. of Secretary War.	278	Claims	Mar. 2, 1795	Adverse	......	Laid on table.		
Barnard, Joseph	Compensation for vessel taken by the enemy.	4	1	Memorial	....	Claims	May 31, 1796	Adverse	......	Laid on table.		
Barnard, Joseph. (See Joseph Bernard.)	Exchange of a confirmed tract of land.	26	1	Senate bill	811	Priv. Land Claims	....	....	S. 163			
Barnard, J. G.	Increase of compensation as an engineer.	30	2	Petition	274	Military Affairs.						
Barnard, Silas, (Maine)	Additional compensation for taking Fifth Census.	22	1	Petition	435	Claims.						

List of private claims presented to the House of Representatives of the United States from the 1st to the 31st Congress, inclusive—Continued.

Names of claimants.	Nature or object of the claim.	Congress.	Session.	How brought before the House of Reps.	Page of journal.	To what committee of the House referred.	No. or date of the report.	Nature of the report.	No. of the bill.	How disposed of by the House of Reps.	How disposed of by the Senate.	Date of the act of Congress, and remarks.
Barnard, Silas, (Maine)	Additional compensation for taking Fifth Census.	22	2	Resolution	153	Claims.						
Barnard, Theodore, & C. A.	Compensation for printing for Navy Department.	30	1	Senate bill	976	Claims			S. 173			
Barnard, Theodore, & C. A.	Compensation for printing for Navy Department.	30	2	Senate bill	82	Whole House			S. 173			
Barner, Harrison	Pension for revolutionary services.	28	1	Petition	318	Rev. Pensions.						
Barnes, Amos	Pension for revolutionary services.	3	1	Rep. of Secretary War.	131	Select	May 26, 1794	Res. to refer to Sec. War.	R. 12	Passed	Passed	App'd June 9, 1794
Barnes, Andrew	Pension for revolutionary services.	11	3	Petition	526	Claims.						
Barnes, Barret, heirs of	Balance of pension due	26	1	Resolution	442	Rev. Pensions	424	Adverse		Laid on table.		
Barnes, Calvin	Pension for revolutionary services.	14	1	Petition	467	Pens. & Rev. Cl'ms.	April 11, 1816	Pension bill	171	Passed	Passed	App'd April 30, 1816
Barnes, Calvin	Reimbursement of expenses of curing his wounds.	14	2	Petition	384	Claims.						
Barnes, Calvin	Reimbursement of expenses of curing his wounds.	15	1	Petition	85	Claims				Discharged; leave to withdraw.		
Barnes, Cæsar, (N. H.)	Arrears of pensions for revolutionary services.	5	2	Petition	87	Claims	Jan. 9, 1798	By bill	38	Passed	Passed	App'd Feb. 2, 1798
Barnes, Cornelius (See Daniel Barns.)	Interest on loan to government U. States.	2	2	Petition	636					Laid on table.		
Barnes, David	Pension for revolutionary disabilities.	3	2	Petition	285	Claims	Mar. 2, 1795	Adverse		Laid on table.		
Barnes, David	Pension for revolutionary disabilities.	4	1	Petition	598	Claims	May 31, 1796	Adverse.		Laid on table.		
Barnes, Edward	Increase of compensation as revenue officer.	6	2	Petition	758	Ways and Means	May 8, 1800	Adverse		Claim rejected.		
Barnes, Edward	Increase of compensation as revenue officer.	7	1	Petition	60	Claims	April 3, 1802	Report.				
Barnes, Edward	Increase of compensation as revenue officer.	7	2	Petition & Rep't	248	Claims	Dec. 22, 1802	Adverse.				
Barnes, Elijah	Pension for revolutionary services	4	1	Rep. of Secretary War.	447	Claims	Feb. 18, 1796	Pension bill	156	Passed	Passed with amendment.	App'd April 20, 1796
Barnes, Elijah, widow of	Pension	26	1	Senate bill	794	Rev. Pensions	May 25, 1840	With't amend.	S. 16	Referred to Committee Whole House.		
Barnes, Elijah, widow of	Pension	26	2	Senate bill	113	Rev. Pensions	Feb. 12, 1841	With amend.	S. 2	Referred to Committee Whole House.		
Barnes, Elijah, widow of	Pension	27	2	Senate bill	131	Rev. Pensions	Feb. 9, 1842	With't amend.	S. 7	Passed	Passed	App'd Mar. 19, 1842
Barnes, Elisha	Pension	21	2	Petition	87	Military Pensions.						
Barnes, Enos, widow of	Pension for revolutionary services	25	2	Petition	403	Rev. Pensions.						
Barnes, Francis	Indemnity for loss on a naval contract.	22	1	Petition	226	Claims	Mar. 6, 1832	Adverse.				
				Recommitted	525	Claims	May 17, 1832	Favorable	577	Referred to Committee Whole House.		
Barnes, Francis	Indemnity for loss on a naval contract.	23	1	Petition	33	Claims	25	Favorable	25	Passed	Passed	App'd June 18, 1834
Barnes, Frederick	(See Reuben E. Gentry, and others)	23	1	Petition	138							
Barnes, Hartwell	Pension for revolutionary services.	3	1	Rep. of Secretary War.	131	Select	May 26, 1794	Res to refer to Sec. War.	R. 12	Passed	Passed	App'd June 9, 1794
Barnes, Henrietta	(See representatives of Lathrop Allen.)	22	1		559							
Barnes, Henry W., and others.	Compensation for clothing for New York volunteers.	30	2	Petition	216	Military Affairs.						
Barnes, Hugh, Rev	Pension for revolutionary services.	13	2	Pension bill	344	Whole House	Mar. 31, 1814	With amend.	166	Passed	Passed	App'd April 18, 1814

List of private claims presented to the House of Representatives of the United States from the 1st *to the* 31st *Congress, inclusive*—Continued.

Names of claimants.	Nature or object of the claim.	Congress.	Session.	How brought before the House of Reps.	Page of journal.	To what committee of the House referred.	No. or date of the report.	Nature of the report.	No. of the bill.	How disposed of by the House of Reps.	How disposed of by the Senate.	Date of the act of Congress, and remarks.
Barnes, Hugh, Rev.	Increase of pension	14	1	Resolution	658	Pens. & Rev. Cl'ms.	April 11, 1816	Pension bill	171	Passed	Passed	App'd April 30, 1816
Barnes, Hugh, Rev.	Arrears of pension	19	2	Petition	333	Military Pensions.						
Barnes, Hugh, Rev.	Arrears of pension	20	1	Petition	310	Military Pensions.						
Barnes, Hugh, Rev.	Arrears of pension	20	2	Petition	82	Military Pensions.						
Barnes, Hugh, Rev.	Arrears of pension	21	1	Senate bill	401	Military Pensions.	May 21, 1830	Adverse	64	Laid on table.		
Barnes, Hugh, Rev.	Arrears of pension	21	2	Senate bill	196	Military Pensions.	Jan. 26, 1831	Adverse	73	Passed	Passed	App'd March 2, 1831
Barnes, James, (Mo.)	(See Reuben E. Gentry, and others)	23	1		138							
Barnes, Joel	Pension for revolutionary services	27	2	Petition	55	Rev. Pensions	784	Adverse.		Laid on table.		
Barnes, John, (D. C.)	Increase of compensation as a revenue officer.	18	1	Peitition	235	Commerce.						
Barnes, John, (D. C.)	Increase of compensation as a revenue officer.	19	1	Petition	35	Commerce.						
Barnes, John, executors of	Proceeds of a certain bond	26	1	Petition	335	Claims	301	Favorable	263	Referred to Committee Whole House.		
Barnes, John, executors of	Proceeds of a certain bond	27	2	Petition	55	Claims	8	Favorable	48	Passed	Passed	App'd July 27, 1842
Barnes, John, heirs of	Commutation pay for revolutionary services.	25	2	Petition	546	Rev. Claims	693	Favorable	666	Passed	Rejected.	
Barnes, John, heirs of	Commutation pay for revolutionary services.	25	3	Petition	84	Rev. Claims	3	Favorable	901	Referred to Committee Whole House.		
Barnes, John, heirs of	Commutation pay for revolutionary services.	26	1	Petition	164	Rev. Claims						See Report 436.
Barnes, John, heirs of	Commutation pay for revolutionary services.	27	2	Petition	55	Rev. Claims	367	Adverse		Laid on table.		
Barnes, John, heirs of	Commutation pay for revolutionary services.	31	1	Petition	1044	Rev. Claims.						
Barnes, John A., (Mi.)	Right of pre-emption	22	1	Resol'n & petit'n	562	Public Lands.						
Barnes, John A., (Mi.)	Right of pre-emption	22	2	Petition	48	Public Lands.						
Barnes, John A., (Mi.)	Right of pre emption	23	1	Petition	138	Priv. Land Claims.	348	Favorable	375	Referred to Committee Whole House.		
Barnes, Lemuel	Pension for revolutionary services.	3	1	Rep. of Secretary of War.	131	Select	May 26, 1794	Res. to refer to Sec. War.	R. 12	Passed	Passed	App'd June 9, 1794
Barnes, Philip	(See assignees of Elizabeth Mason)	22	1		227							
Barnes, Pricilla	(See executrix of George Birch)	31	1		809							
Barnes, Richard, heirs of	Indemnity for French Spoliations prior 1800.	31	1	Petition	450	Foreign Affairs.						
Barnes, Robert	Compensation for horse taken for public use.	14	2	Petition	102	Military Affairs.						
Barnes, Samuel, (Con.)	Pensions for revolutionary services.	21	1	Resolution	64	Military Pensions.						
Barnes, Samuel, (Con.)	Pension for revolutionary services.	22	1	Resolution	116	Military Pensions.	367	Favorable.	462	Passed	Indef. postp'd.	
Barnes, Shadrack	(See Reuben E. Gentry and others)	23	1		138							
Barnes, Sibil	(See Thomas Barnes, widow of)	25	2		93							
Barnes, Thomas, widow of.	Pension for revolutionary services.	25	2	Petition	93	Rev. Pensions	701	Favorable.	675	Passed.		
Barnes, Thomas, widow of.	Pension for revolutionary services.	25	3	Petition	87	Rev. Pensions	68	Favorable.	946	Passed	Passed	App'd March 3, 1839
Barnes, William	(See Joseph Stewart and others)	13	3		751							
Barnes, William	Compensation for horse lost in the public service.	27	2	Petition	534	Claims.						
				Documents	883	Claims	694	Adverse		Laid on table.		
Barnes, William	Compensation for horse lost in the public service.	27	3	Petition	72	Claims	105	Adverse		Laid on table.		
Barnes, William T.	(See William L. Whitfield & W. T. B.)	15	1		356							
Barnes, Willie	Compensation for horses lost in Seminole war.	28	1	Petition	262	Claims.						
Barnett, Charles	Patent for a certain tract of land	27	2	Petition	368	Public Lands	479	Favorable	331	Passed	Passed	App'd Aug. 27, 1842

List of private claims presented to the House of Representatives of the United States from the 1st to the 31st Congress, inclusive—Continued.

Names of claimants.	Nature or object of the claim.	Congress.	Session.	How brought before the House of Reps.	Page of journal.	To what committee of the House referred.	No. or date of the report.	Nature of the report.	No. of the bill.	How disposed of by the House of Reps.	How disposed of by the Senate.	Date of the act of Congress, and remarks.
Barnett, Daniel	(See Barnet Eichelberger assignee)	3	1		107							
Barnett, James	Confirmation of land title	22	2	Petition	124	Priv. Land Claims.						
Barnett, James	Commutation pay due for revolutionary services.	21	1	Petition		Rev. Claims	Jan. 6, 1830	Favorable	161	Passed	Passed	App'd May 28, 1830
Barnett, James	Interest on commutation pay	21	2	Petition	54	Rev. Claims	Feb. 25, 1831	Favorable	653	Referred to Committee Whole House.		
Barnett, James	Interest on commutation pay	22	1	Petition	51	Rev. Claims	Jan. 6, 1832	Favorable	215	Referred to Committee Whole House.		
Barnett, James	Interest on commutation pay	22	2	Petition	67			With't amend.	215	Passed	Passed	App'd March 2, 1833
Barnett, James	Commutation pay for revolutionary services.	23	2	Resolution	110	Rev. Claims.						
Barnett, James	To be restored to pension	25	2	Petition	240	Pensions.						
Barnett, James R., (Va.,) administrator of.	Reimbursement of certain duties	18	1	Petition	70	Ways and Means	Dec. 24, 1823	Adverse.				
Barnett, Oliver	Indemnity for hides taken by the enemy.	3	2	Petition	271	Claims	Feb. 27, 1795	Indefinite.				
Barnett, Oliver	Indemnity for hides taken by the enemy.	4	2	Petition	626	Claims	Dec. 21, 1796	Indefinite		Postponed.		
Barnett, Robert	Compensation for revolutionary services.	2	1	Petition	491					Referred to Secretary of War.		
Barnett, Thompson	Additional compensation for mail service.	31	1	Petition	495	P. Of. and P. Roads.						
Barnett, William	Bounty land for military services	15	2	Petition	75	Military Affairs	Dec. 9, 1818	Adverse		Referred to Committee Whole House.		
Barnett, William	Exchange of bounty land	23	2	Petition	167	Public Lands.						
Barnett, William P	Compensrtion for horse lost in the public service.	24	2	Petition	266	Claims	Feb. 4, 1837	Indefinite		Referred to Third Auditor.		
Barney, Benjamin	Reimbursement of costs and indemnity for land sold by U. States.	22	2	Petition	265	Claims.						
Barney, Harriett	(See Commodore Joshua Barney, widow of.)	15	2		199							
Barney, H. M	Release from liability for money destroyed by fire.	30	1	Petition	346	P. Of. & P. Roads.	326	Favorable	R. 18	Passed	Passed, second session.	App'd Feb. 22, 1849
Barney, Jabez	Compensation for revolutionary services.	4	1	Petition	370	Claims	Jan. 11, 1796	Adverse		Postponed.		
Barney, Jabez	Componsation for revolutionary services.	4	2	Petition	623	Whole House.						
Barney, John	Release from an illegal seizure of goods.	15	1	Petition	151	Ways and Means	Jan. 26, 1818	Adverse		Claim rejected.		
Barney, John	(See executor of Joshua Barney)	29	2		70							
Barney, John H	Pension for revolutionary services	23	1	Petition	216	Rev. Pensions.						
Barney, Joshua	Commutation pay for services in revolutionary navy.	1	3	Petition	353	Select	Jan. 19, 1791	Favorable	127	Rejected.		
Barney, Joshua, widow of.	Continuation of naval pension	15	2	Petition	199	Pension and Revolutionary Claims.						
Barney, Joshua, widow of.	Continuation of naval pension	25	3	Petition	675	Naval Affairs				Discharged; laid on tale.		
Barney, Joshua, widow of.	Continuation of naval pension	26	1	Petition	1021	Naval Affairs	535	Favorable	434	Referred to Committee Whole House.		
Barney, Joshua, widow of.	Pension for disability in 1812	25	3	Petition	147	Invalid Pensions.						
Barney, Joshua, widow of.	Pension for disability in 1812	27	2	Petition	97	Invalid Pensions	597	Adverse		Laid on table.		
Barney, Joshua, widow of.	Pension for disability in 1812	28	1	Petition	141	Invalid Pensions	174	Adverse		Laid on table.		
Barney, Joshua, widow of.	Pension for disability in 1812	30	1	Petition	78	Invalid Pensions	19	Favorable	23	Passed	Passed	App'd May 9, 1848

List of private claims presented to the House of Representatives of the United States from the 1st to the 31st Congress, inclusive—Continued.

Names of claimants.	Nature or object of the claim.	Congress.	Session.	How brought before the House of Reps.	Page of journal.	To what committee of the House referred.	No. or date of the report.	Nature of the report.	No. of the bill.	How disposed of by the House of Reps.	How disposed of by the Senate.	Date of the act of Congress, and remarks.
Barney, Joshua, executor of.	Indemnity for French spoliations prior to 1800.	26	1	Memorial	182	Foreign Affairs	343	Favorable	319	Referred to Committee Whole House.		
Barney, Joshua, executor of.	Indemnity for French spoliations prior to 1800.	29	2	Memorial	70	Foreign Affairs	Feb. 9, 1847	General bill	561	Referred to Committee Whole House.		
Barney, Joshua, executor of.	Indemnity for French spoliations prior to 1800.	31	1	Petition	196	Foreign Affairs.						
				Petition (2)	215	Foreifin Affairs	355	General bill	318	Referred to Committee Whole House.		
Barney, Joshua	Reimbursement of over payment on military road.	30	1	Petition	345	Claims	483	Favorable	401	Passed	Passed, second session.	App'd March 2, 1849
Barney, J. S.	(See administrator of George W. Evans.)	19	1		109							
Barney, Louis	Pension	25	3	Petition	218	Invalid Pensions.						
Barney, Louis	Pension	26	1	Petition	161	Invalid Pensions	283	Adverse		Laid on table.		
Barney, Louis	Pension	27	2	Peiiton	60	Invalid Pensions	231	Adverse		Laid on table.		
Barney, Louis	(See Paul Bentalon, executors of.)	29	2		70							
Barney, Nathaniel	Pension for revolutionary services.	3	1	Rep. of Secretary War.	131	Select	May 26, 1794	Ref. Secretary War.	R. 12	Passed	Passed	App'd June 9, 1794
Barney, Nathaniel	Pension for revolutionary services.	6	1	Petition	556	Claims	April 12, 1800	Adverse		Laid on table.		
Barney, Samuel, widow of.	Pension for revolutionary services.	25	2	Petition	53	Rev. Pensions	420	Favorable	427	Passed	Passed	App'd July 7, 1838
Barnham, Edw'd, surety of.	Release from liability	15	1	Petition	71	Ways and Means.	Jan. 23, 1818	Adverse		Petition rejected.		
Barnhill, Robert (N. C.)	Pension	19	2	Petition	156	Military Pensions.						
Barnitz, George A	(See David Grier, heirs of)	30	1		229				308			
Barnitz, Jacob	Arrears of pension	5	3	Petition	470	Claims	Mar. 1, 1799	Indefinite		Postponed.		
Barnitz, Jacob	Arrears of pension	6	2	Petition	762	Claims	Mar. 2, 1801	Indefinite		Postponed.		
Barnitz, Jacob	Arrears of pension	7	1	Petition	19	Claims	April 8, 1802	Legislation unnecessary.		Leave to withdraw.		
Barnitz, Jacob	Reimbursement of expenditures in curing his wounds.	8	2	Petition	108	Claims.						
Barnitz, Jacob	Reimbursement of expenditures in curing his wounds.	9	1	Petition	193	Claims	Mar. 28, 1806	Indefinite		Indef. postponed		Leave to withdraw.
Barnitz, Jacob	Reimbursement of expenditures in curing his wounds.	10	2	Resolution	413	Select	Jan. 18, 1809	Favorable	147	Passed	Passed	App'd March 3, 1809
Barnitz, Margaret	(See David Grier, heirs of.)	30	1		229				308			
Barns, Daniel	Pension for revolutionary services.	3	1	Rep. of Secretary War.	131	Select	May 26, 1794	Res. to refer to Sec. War.	R. 12	Passed	Passed	App'd June 9, 1794
Barns, Daniel	Pension for revolutionary services.	13	2	Petition	239	Pens. & Rev. Cl'ms.						
Barnum, Abijah & sureties.	Release from payment of public money lost.	8	1	Petition	446	Claims	Dec. 21, 1803	Adverse		Claim rejected.		
Barnum, Abijah & sureties.	Release from payment of public money lost.	8	2	Petition	54	Claims	Jan. 15, 1805	Adverse		Leave to withdraw.		
Barnum, Abijah & sureties.	Release from payment of public money lost.	9	1	Petition	271							
				Rep. of Secretary Treasury.	301	Whole House.						
Barnum, Elihu	(See Abijah Barnum and sureties.)	8	1		446							
Barnum, Enoch	Pension for revolutionary services.	14	2	Petition	422	Pens. & Rev. Cl'ms.	Jan. 29, 1817	Pension bill	91	Passed	Passed	App'd March 3, 1817
Barnum, H. L.	Balance due for surveying mail route.	20	1	Petition	457	Claims	May 5, 1828	Adverse		Leave to withdraw.		
Barnum, Stephen	Pension for revolutionary services.	3	1	Rep. of Secretary of War.	131	Select	May 26, 1794	Res. to refer to Sec. War.	R. 12	Passed	Passed	App'd June 9, 1794
Barnum, Stephen	Pension for revolutionary services.	3	2	Report Secretary War.	262	Claims.						

List of private claims presented to the House of Representatives of the United States from the 1st to the 31st Congress, inclusive—Continued.

Names of claimants.	Nature or object of the claim.	Congress.	Session.	How brought before the House of Reps.	Page of journal.	To what committee of the House referred.	No. or date of the report.	Nature of the report.	No. of the bill.	How disposed of by the House of Reps.	How disposed of by the Senate.	Date of the act of Congress, and remarks.
Barnum, Stephen	Pension for revolutionary services	4	1	Resolution	373	Claims.						
Barnum, Stephen	Pension for revolutionary services	12	1	Pension bill	361	Whole House	June 15, 1812	Pension bill	138	Passed	Passed with amendment.	App'd July 5, 1812
Barnum, Stephen	Pension for revolutionary services	15	1	Petition	160	Pens. & Rev. Cl'ms.	Feb. 16, 1818	Adverse		Claim rejected.		
Barnwell,	(See Robertson and Barnwell)	20	1		419							
Baron, Marguerite	(See J. Pierre Ledoux, widow of.)	23	1		49							
Barr, Alexander	Pension	13	2	Pension bill	344	Whole House	Mar. 31, 1814	With amend.	166	Passed	Passed	App'd April 18, 1814
Barr, Alexander, (Pa.)	Increase of compensation as postmaster.	16	1	Petition	202	P. Of. & P. Roads.	Mar. 3, 1820	Adverse		Laid on table.		
Barr, Frances	Compensation for services of her husband.	26	1	Petition	939	Claims.						
Barr, Frances	Compensation for services of her husband.	26	2	Petition	107	Military Affairs	196	Adverse		Laid on table.		
Barr, James	Pension for revolutionary services	14	1	Petition	504	Pen. & Rev. Claims						
Barr, James	Arrears of Pension	28	1	Petition	193	Invalid Pensions	272	Adverse		Laid on table.		
Barr, James	Compensation for horse lost in Seminole war.	28	1	Petition	262	Claims.						
Barr, James	Pension for naval services	26	1	Petition	713	Naval Affairs.						
Barr, James	Pension for naval services	26	2	Petition	79	Naval Affairs.						
Barr, John, guardian of	Indemnity for French spoliations prior to 1800.	26	1	Memorial	182	Foreign Affairs	343	Favorable	319	Referred to Committee Whole House.		
Barr, John	(See surety of Jacob Weaver)	15	1		44							
Barr, John F., and others	Confirmation of title to land in Indiana.	19	1	Petition	68	Priv. Land Claims.	May 10, 1826	Adverse		Laid on table.		
Barr, John W.	Bounty land for military services	28	1	Petition	432	Military Affairs.						
Barr, Samuel	Pension for revolutionary services	24	1	Petition	406	Rev. Pensions.						
Barr, ——	(See Stewart & Barr)	31	1		298							
Barr, William	(See representatives of Edward Murphy.)	22	1		237				311			
Barranton, Perry J.	Compensation for horse taken for public use.	25	2	Petition	397	Claims	834	Adverse		Laid on table.		
Barraque, Antoine	Indemnity for Indian depredations.	21	1	Senate bill	87	Indian Affairs	Dec. 29, 1829	With't amend.	S. 8	Passed	Passed	App'd Mar. 25, 1830
Barraque, Antoine	Indemnity for Indian depredations.	21	2	Documents	89	Military Affairs.						
Barraque, Antoine	Indemnity for Indian depredations.	23	1	Documents	220	Indian Affairs.						
Barras, or Burras, Geo. G.	(See Nathaniel Hunt, and others)	19	2		242							
Barras, Stephen	Compensation for revolutionary services.	10	2	Petition	577					Laid on table.		
Barray, John	(See heirs of Samuel Barray)	27	3		260							
Barray, Samuel	Pension for revolutionary services.	27	3	Petition	260	Rev. Pensions				Discharged; laid on table.		
Barre, Charles, assignee of	Confirmation of title to land	27	2	Documents	140	Priv. Land Claims.						
Barella, Joaquim, (La.)	Confirmation of title to land	24	1	Petition	671	Priv. Land Claims.				Discharged; laid on table.		
Barret, Beatley, (Va.)	Pension for revolutionary disabilities.	8	2	Petition	51	Whole House						
Barret, Beatley, (Va.)	Pension for revolutionary disabilities.	13	2	Petition	266	Pen. & Rev. Claims				Discharged; leave to withdraw.		
Barrett, Humphrey, heir of	Compensation for property taken for public use.	23	2	Petition	56	Rev. Claims.						
Barrett, Humphrey, heir of	Compensation for property taken for public use.	24	1	Petition	63	Rev. Claims.						
Barrett, Humphrey, heir of	Compensation for property taken for public use.	25	2	Petition	82	Rev. Claims	June 27, 1838	Adverse		Laid on table.		

List of private claims presented to the House of Representatives of the United States from the 1st to the 31st Congress, inclusive—Continued.

Names of claimants.	Nature or object of the claim.	Congress.	Session.	How brought before the House of Reps.	Page of journal.	To what committee of the House referred.	No. or date of the report.	Nature of the report.	No. of the bill.	How disposed of by the House of Reps.	How disposed of by the Senate.	Date of the act of Congress, and remarks.
Barrett, James, (Tenn.)	Confirmation of title to land	24	1	Petition	112	Priv. Land Claims.	June 17, 1836	....	......	Discharged; laid on table.		
Barrett, James, (Tenn.)	Confirmation of title to land	25	2	Petition	828	Priv. Land Claims.	954	Favorable	816	Passed	Passed	App'd June 28, 1838
Barrett, James	Pension for revolutionary services.	26	1	Petition	625	Rev. Pensions	490	Adverse	......	Claim rejected.		
Barrett, John	Pension and payment of prize money.	30	2	Petition	87	Invalid Pensions	....	....	......	Discharged; laid on table.		
Barrett, John	Pension and payment of prize money.	31	1	Petition	1316	Invalid Pensions.						
Barrett, John	Pension and payment of prize money.	31	2	Petition	282	Invalid Pensions.						
Barrett, Mary, (Vt.)	Pension for loss of her son in Indian war.	12	1	Petition	283	Claims.						
Barrett, M. H.	Right of pre-emption	24	1	Petition	65	Indian Affairs.						
Barrett, Richard F.	Authority to perfect his claim to land.	25	2	Resolution	1126	Priv. Land Claims.						
Barrett, Richard F.	Authority to perfect his claim to land.	25	3	Rep. of Secretary War.	149	Priv. Land Claims.						
Barrett, Richard H., (Ga.)	Confirmation of title to land	30	1	Memorial	345	Priv. Land Claims.	56	Favorable	761	Referred to Committee Whole House.		
Barrett, Richard H., (Ga.)	Confirmation of title to land	31	1	Petition	197	Priv. Land Claims.	42	Favorable	71	Passed	Passed	App'd July 29, 1850
Barrett, Samuel, (Mass.)	Payment of balance due him for revolutionary services.	3	1	Petition	131	Select.						
Barrett, Samuel, (Canada)	Restoration of property seized by revenue officers.	12	2	Petition	610	Ways and Means	....	....	......	....	....	See act of Jan. 2, 1813
Barrett, Samuel, (Va.)	Pension for revolutionary services.	22	1	Petition	265	Rev. Pensions	381	Favorable	472	Passed	Indef. postp'd.	
Barrett, Squire	Compensation for horse lost in Seminole war.	28	1	Petition	262	Claims.						
Barrette, Nicholas	(See Nicholas Barth)	12	1	....	361							
Barretts, Francis	(See surety of Joaquin Da Castra.)											
Barron, Ann M.	(See William Barron, heir of)	21	2	....	44							
Barron, Captain	(See Col. Jos. Brown and others.)	27	2	....	94							
Barron, Elias	Increase of pension	11	2	Pension bill	283	Whole House	Mar. 24, 1810	With amend.	107	Passed	Passed with amendment.	App'd April 27, 1810
Barron, Eustace, and others	Indemnity for seizure and confiscation of schooner William.	31	1	Petition	256	Foreign Affairs	16	Adverse	......	Laid on table.		
Barron, James, U. S. N.	Reimbursement of duties paid on certain models.	17	1	Petition	387	Ways and Means	April 9, 1822	Favorable	164	Passed	Passed	App'd May 7, 1822
Barron, James, U. S. N.	Renewal of patent for improvement in corks.	23	1	Petition	74	Judiciary	Dec. 31, 1833	Adverse	......	Laid on table.		
Barron, James, U. S. N.	Renewal of patent for improvement in corks.	23	2	Petition	85	Judiciary.						
Barron, James, U. S. N.	Renewal of patent for improvement in corks.	24	1	Senate bill	124	Judiciary	666	Favorable	S. 26	Passed	Passed	App'd July 2, 1836
Barron, James, U. S. N.	Renewal of patent for improvement in pumps.	23	1	Memorial	74	Judiciary	Dec. 31, 1833	Adverse	......	Laid on table.		
Barron, James, U. S. N.	Renewal of patent for improvement in pumps.	23	2	Memorial	85	Judiciary.						
Barron, James, U. S. N.	Renewal of patent for improvement in pumps.	24	1	Senate bill	124	Judiciary	666	Favorable	S. 26	Passed	Passed	App'd July 2, 1836
Barron, James, U. S. N.	Compensation for code of signal for United States navy.	23	1	Memorial	440	Naval Affairs.						
Barron, James, U. S. N.	Compensation for use of patent for ventilating ships.	23	2	Memorial	85	Naval Affairs	64	Favorable	68	Referred to Committee Whole House.		

List of private claims presented to the House of Representatives of the United States from the 1st to the 31st Congress, inclusive—Continued.

Names of claimants.	Nature or object of the claim.	Congress.	Session.	How brought before the House of Reps.	Page of journal.	To what committee of the House referred.	No. or date of the report.	Nature of the report.	No. of the bill.	How disposed of by the House of Reps.	How disposed of by the Senate.	Date of the act of Congress, and remarks.
Barron, James, U. S. N.	Compensation for use of patent for ventilating ships.	24	1	Petition	99	Naval Affairs	224	Favorable	234	Referred to Committee Whole House.		
Barron, James, U. S. N.	Compensation for use of patent for ventilating ships.	24	2	House bill	62	...	...	...	234			
				Documents	392	Whole House.						
Barron, James, U. S. N.	Compensation for use of patent for ventilating ships.	25	2	Petition	41	Naval Affairs	151	Favorable	174	Referred to Committee Whole House.		
Barron, James, U. S. N.	Compensation for use of patent for ventilating ships.	25	3	Petition	91	Naval Affairs.						
Barron, James, U. S. N., heirs of.	Compensation for use of patent for ventilating ships.	26	1	Petition	179	Naval Affairs.						
Barron, James, U. S. N., heirs of.	Compensation for use of patent for ventilating ships.	26	2	Petition	37	Naval Affairs	199	Adverse	...	Laid on table.		
Barron, John	Balance due him for military services.	14	1	Petition	149	Claims	...	...	...	Discharged; leave to withdraw.		
Barron, John V	Indemnity for losses in the war of 1812.	27	1	Petition	106	Military Affairs.						
Barron, John V	Indemnity for losses in the war of 1812.	27	2	Petition	49	Claims	164	Adverse	...	Laid on table.		
Barrons, Mark	(See Israel Pearce, heirs of.)											
Barron, Marguerite	(See J. Pierre Ledoux)	23	1	...	49							
Barron, Micah	Remission of double duties on alcohol.	23	3	Petition	723	Ways and Means.						
Barron, Oliver, widow of.	Pension for revolutionary services.	26	1	Petition	1115	Invalid Pensions.						
Barron, Samuel, heirs of.	Deficiency of bounty land for revolutionary services.	24	1	Petition	105	Rev. Claims.						
Barron, William, heir of.	Payment of balance due at his death.	21	2	Petition	44	Rev. Claims	46	Favorable	546	Referred to Committee Whole House.		
Barron, William, heir of.	Payment of balance due at his death.	22	1	Petition	295	Rev. Claims	307	Favorable	384	Referred to Committee Whole House.		
Barron, William, heir of.	Payment of balance due at his death.	23	1	Petition	85	Rev. Claims	53	Favorable	61	Passed	Passed	App'd June 30, 1834
Barron, William A	Reimbursement of expenses as captain engineer corps.	8	1	Senate bill	666	Select	Mar. 24, 1804	Adverse	S. 28	Indef. postponed.		
Barron, William A	Reimbursement of expenses as captain engineer corps.	8	2	Petition	47	Claims	Feb. 19, 1805	Favorable; bill ordered.	66	Referred to Committee Whole House.		
Barron, William A	Reimbursement of expenses as captain engineer corps.	9	1	Petition	196	Claims	April 11, 1806	Adverse	...	Indef. postponed.		
Barron, William R	Confirmation of title to land in Louisiana.	26	1	Petition	179	Priv. Land Claims.						
Barrow, Elias,	Increase of Pension	16	1	Resolution	268	Pens. & Rev. Cl'ms.						
Barrow, Matthew	Reimbursement of costs in a certain suit.	15	2	Senate bill	91	Claims	Dec. 16, 1818	With't amend.	S. 8	Referred to Committee Whole House.		
Barrow, Matthew	Reimbursement of costs in a certain suit.	16	1	Senate bill	67	Claims	Dec. 27, 1819	With't amend.	S. 3	Passed	Passed	App'd Jan. 28, 1820
Barrow, William	Confirmation of title to land in Louisiana.	25	3	Petition	133	Priv. Land Claims.						
Barrows, Tillson	Pension	24	1	Petition	51	Invalid Pensions.						
Barrows, Tillson	Pension	24	2	Petition	419	Invalid Pensions	Feb. 16, 1837	Adverse	...	Laid on table.		
Barry, Bartholomew	Increase of pension	13	3	Petition	674	Pens. & Rev. Cl'ms.						
Barry, Cole & Barry	Indemnity for French spoliations prior to 1800.	26	1	Memorial	182	Foreign Affairs	343	Favorable	319	Referred to Committee Whole House.		

List of private claims presented to the House of Representatives of the United States from the 1st to the 31st Congress, inclusive—Continued.

Names of claimants.	Nature or object of the claim.	Congress.	Session.	How brought before the House of Reps.	Page of journal.	To what committee of the House referred.	No. or date of the report.	Nature of the report.	No. of the bill.	How disposed of by the House of Reps.	How disposed of by the Senate.	Date of the act of Congress, and remarks.
Barry, Daniel	(See Louis F. Peeler, *et al.*)	30	1		115		482					
Barry, Edward & I. H.	Indemnity for loss by burning of navy yard.	14	1	Senate bill	252	Naval Affairs.	Feb. 19, 1816	Adverse	S. 13	Laid on table.		
Barry, Edward & I. H.	Indemnity for loss by burning of navy yard.	14	2	Petition	38	Claims	Dec. 20, 1816	Adverse.				
Barry, Edward & I. H.	Indemnity for loss by burning of navy yard.	15	1	Petition	22	Claims	Jan. 5, 1818	Adverse		Laid on table.		
Barry, Edward	Indemnity for loss by burning of navy yard.	16	2	Petition	145	Naval Affairs	Feb. 6, 1821	Adverse		Laid on table.		Leave to withdraw, 17 1 p. 568
Barry, Edward	Indemnity for loss by burning of navy yard.	18	1	Petition	195	Naval Affairs	Mar. 24, 1824	Adverse		Leave to withdraw.		
Barry, Edward	Indemnity for loss by burning of navy yard.	22	1	Senate bill	806	Naval Affairs	June 2, 1832	With't amend.	S. 103	Passed	Passed	App'd July 14, 1832
Barry, G. R., U. S. N.	Set-off accounts as purser	29	1	Senate resolution	1016	Naval Affairs.			S.R. 30			
				Petition		Naval Affairs	718	Favorable	R. 40	Ordered to 3d reading.		
Barry, G. R , U. S. N.	Set-off accounts as purser	29	2	House resolution	212				R. 40	Passed	Passed	App'd March 2, 1847
Barry, Harriet	(See Joshua Barry, administratrix of.)	26	1		182		343		319			
Barry, James, executor of.	Payment of Spanish claim	20	1	Petition	85	Foreign Affairs	262	Adverse		Laid on table.		
Barry, James, executor of.	Indemnity for French spoliations prior to 1800.	26	1	Memorial	182	Foreign Affairs	343	Favorable	319	Referred to Committee Whole House.		
Barry, James, executor of.	Indemnity for French spoliations prior to 1800.	26	2	Memorial	320	Whole House.						
Barry, James, executor of.	Reimbursement of money paid for lot in Washington.	24	2	Memorial	89	Dist. of Columbia.						
Barry, Joshua, administratrix of.	Indemnity for French spoliations prior to 1800.	26	1	Memorial	182	Foreign Affairs	343	Favorable	319	Referred to Committee Whole House.		
Barry, Mary	(See Thomas Barry, widow of)	27	3		78							
Barry, Robert, administrator of.	Indemnity for sinking ship Nancy.	31	1	Recommitted.	193	Claims	32	Favorable	60	Recommitted.		
Barry, Robert	(See Gabriel Wood)			Petition	646	Claims.						
Barry, Thomas	Compensation for improvement in repeating arms.	23	2	Petition	86	Naval Affairs				Discharged; laid on table.		
Barry, Thomas, widow of.	Payment of a balance	27	3	Petition	78	Naval Affairs	44	Favorable	672	Passed	Indef. postp'd.	
Barry, Thomas, widow of.	Payment of a balance	28	1	Petition	361	Naval Affairs	366	Adverse		Laid on table.		
Barry, Thomas, widow of.	Payment of a balance	31	1	Petition	49	Naval Affairs				Discharged; leave to withdraw.		
Barsayline, Lawrence	Pension for naval services	26	2	Petition	90	Naval Affairs.						
Bartam, James	Pension	23	1	Petition	216	Naval Affairs.						
Barteline, Lewis	Confirmation of land title	19	2	Petition	137	Public Lands	60	Favorable	401	Referred to Committee Whole House.		
Bartell, John, (Louisiana.)	Indemnity for land taken from him by United States.	22	2	Petition	32	Claims.						
Bartell, John, (Louisiana.)	Indemnity for land taken from him by United States.	23	1	Petition	38	Judiciary.						
Bartell, John, (Louisiana.)	Indemnity for land taken from him by United States.	23	2	Petition	57	Public Lands.						
Barter, John	Pension for revolutionary services.	4	1	Report of Secretary War.	447	Claims	Feb. 18, 1796	Pension bill	156	Passed	Passed	App'd April 20, 1796
Barth, or Barrette, Nicholas.	Increase of pension	12	1	Pension bill	361	Whole House	June 15, 1812	With amend.	138	Passed	Passed with amendment.	App'd July 5, 1812
Barth, or Barrette, Nicholas.	Arrears of pension	13	1	Petition	12	Claims.						

List of private claims presented to the House of Representatives of the United States from the 1st to the 31st Congress, inclusive—Continued.

Names of claimants.	Nature or object of the claim.	Congress.	Session.	How brought before the House of Reps.	Page of journal.	To what committee of the House referred.	No. or date of the report.	Nature of the report.	No. of the bill.	How disposed of by the House of Reps.	How disposed of by the Senate.	Date of the act of Congress, and remarks.
Barthold, or Bartholet, Lewis.	Compensation for Indian depredations.	24	2	Petition	210	Indian Affairs.						
Barthold, or Bartholet, Lewis.	Compensation for Indian depredations.	25	2	Petition	97	Indian Affairs	212	Favorable	248	Referred to Committee Whole House.		
Bartholett, Henry	(See Gabriel Richard, *et al.*)	17	2		44							
Bartholomew, Leonard	Compensation for revolutionary services.	3	1	Petition	60					Referred to Secretary War.		
Bartholomew, Leonard	Compensation for revolutionary services.	3	2	Report of Secretary War.	278					Laid on table.		
Bartholomew, Riley	(See Anthony Hoffman & others.)	17	1		164							
Bartle, Andrew	Pension for revolutionary services.	6	1	Petition	693					Laid on table.		
Bartle, Andrew	Pension for revolutionary services.	12	1	Pension bill	361	Whole House	June 15, 1812	With amend.	138	Passed	Passed with amendment.	App'd July 5, 1812
Bartle, Andrew	Equitable settlement of accounts; Fort Washington.	15	2	Petition	136	Claims.						
Bartle, Andrew	Equitable settlement of accounts; Fort Washington.	16	2	Petition	105	Claims	Feb. 7, 1821	Adverse		Claim rejected.		
Bartle, Andrew	Equitable settlement of accounts; Fort Washington.	17	1	Petition	178	Claims				Discharged; leave to withdraw.		
Bartle, Andrew	Equitable settlement of accounts; Fort Washington.	17	2	Petition	61	Claims.						
Bartle, Andrew	Equitable settlement of accounts; Fort Washington.	26	1	Petition	340	Claims	370	Adverse		Laid on table.		
Bartleson, Levi	Compensation for supplies furnished on public account.	1	3	Petition	364					Referred to Secretary of the Treasury.		
Bartleson, Levi	Compensation for supplies furnished on public account.	2	1	Report of Secretary Treasury.	580					Laid on table.		
Bartlett, Aaron, widow of.	Pension	25	3	Resolution	160	Rev. Pensions	253	Favorable	1124	Referred to Committee Whole House.		
Bartlett, Adin	Increase of pension	21	2	Petition	231	Military Pensions.						
Bartlett, Adin	Increase of pension	25	2	Petition	588	Invalid Pensions				Discharged; laid on table.		
Bartlett, Adin	Increase of pension	25	3	Petition	12[illegible]	Invalid Pensions	187	Adverse		Referred to Committee Whole House.		
Bartlett, Adin	Increase of pension	27	2	Petition	60	Invalid Pensions	262	Adverse		Laid on table.		
Bartlett, Adin	Bounty land	28	1	Petition	107	Public Lands	114	Adverse		Laid on table.		
Bartlett, Amey	Continuation of pension of husband	28	1	Petition	849	Rev. Pensions.						
Bartlett, Benjamin C	Increase of pension for revolutionary services.	9	2	Petition	593	Claims	Feb. 28, 1807	Pension bill	216	Passed	Passed	App'd March 3, 1807
Bartlett, Benjamin C	Further increase of pension	14	1	Petition	153					Laid on table		Leave to withdraw, 2d session.
Bartlett, David	Compensation for services and reimbursement of advances.	22	2	Petition	28	Claims.						
Bartlett, David	Compensation for services and reimbursement of advances.	23	1	Petition	80	Claims	362	Favorable	389	Referred to Committee Whole House.		
Bartlett, David	Compensation for services and reimbursement of advances.	24	1	Petition	50	Claims	11	Favorable	11	Passed	Passed	App'd Feb. 17, 1836
Bartlett, David	Interest on balance due him on settlement.	25	2	Petition	50	Claims.						
Bartlett, David	Interest on balance due him on settlement.	25	3	Petition	86	Claims	48	Adverse		Laid on table.		
Bartlett, David	Interest on balance due him on settlement.	26	1	Petition	702	Claims	292	Adverse		Laid on table.		

List of private claims presented to the House of Representatives of the United States from the 1st to the 31st Congress, inclusive—Continued.

Names of claimants.	Nature or object of the claim.	Congress.	Session.	How brought before the House of Reps.	Page of journal.	To what committee of the House referred.	No. or date of the report.	Nature of the report.	No. of the bill.	How disposed of by the House of Reps.	How disposed of by the Senate.	Date of the act of Congress, and remarks.
Bartlett, David	Interest on balance due him on settlement.	27	2	Petition	55	Claims	35	Adverse		Laid on table.		
Bartlett, David	Increase of pension	25	3	Petition	129	Invalid Pensions	186	Adverse		Laid on table.		
Bartlett, David	Increase of pension	26	1	Petition	161	Invalid Pensions	292	Adverse		Laid on table.		
Bartlett, David	Increase of pension	26	2	Petition	38	Claims	Jan. 4, 1841	Adverse		Laid on table.		
Bartlett, David	Increase of pension	27	2	Petition	509	Invalid Pensions	424	Adverse		Laid on table.		
Bartlett, David	Increase of pension	27	3	Petition	60	Invalid Pensions.						
Bartlett, David	Increase of pension	28	1	Petition	141	Invalid Pensions	Jan. 31, 1844	Adverse		Laid on table.		
Bartlett, Devereaux D.	(See heir of William Bartlett)	30	1		828							
Bartlett, Edmund	Indemnity for French spoliations prior to 1800.	26	1	Memorial	182	Foreign Affairs	343	Favorable	319	Referred to Committee Whole House.		
Bartlett, Edwin	Compensation for diplomatic services at Lima.	27	2	Petition	549	Foreign Affairs	744	Favorable	422	Ordered to a 3d reading.		
Bartlett, Edwin	Compensation for diplomatic services at Lima.	27	3	House bill	88				422	Passed	Passed	App'd March 3, 1843
Bartlett, Elkanah	Pension as an officer of revolutionary navy.	17	1	Petition	314	Rev. Pensions.						
Bartlett, Enos	Indemnity for lands sold for taxes.	15	1	Petition	132	Ways and Means.						
Bartlett, Esther	(See Moses Bartlett, widow of)	30	1		406							
Bartlett,	(See Everett & Bartlett)	31	1		715							
Bartlett, George W	Compensation for supplies furnished on public account.	18	2	Petition	59	Claims	Jan. 13, 1825	Adverse		Laid on table.		
Bartlett, James	Compensation for passage of American seamen from England.	13	2	Petition	307	Ways and Means.						
Bartlett, John	Pay and rations for services as revolutionary surgeon.	2	2	Petition	622	Select	Dec. 24, 1792	Adverse		Laid on table.		
Bartlett, John	Remission of duty on goods imported to Castine.	16	1	Senate bill	108	Ways and Means	Jan. 14, 1820	With amend.	S. 13	Passed	Passed	App'd April 20, 1820
Bartlett, John	Permission to locate certain land warrants.	26	1	Petition	363	Public Lands				Discharged; laid on table.		
Bartlett, John	Permission to locate certain land warrants.	26	2	Petition	147	Public Lands.						
Bartlett, John	Permission to locate certain land warrants.	27	2	Petition	782	Public Lands.						
Bartlett, John	Pension	25	2	Petition	118	Invalid Pensions.						
Bartlett, John	Pension	27	2	Petition	415	Invalid Pensions				Discharged; laid on table.		
Bartlett, John	Pension	27	3	Petition	346	Invalid Pensions.						
Bartlett, Jones	(See Jeremiah Dale)	25	2		232							
Bartlett, Jonathan	(See Dana, Wheeler & Bartlett)	12	2		696							
Bartlett, Jonathan	(See Jabez Mowry)	14	1		242							
Bartlett, Levi	Pension for revolutionary services	22	1	Petition	558	Rev. Pensions.						
Bartlett, Lydia	(See heir of John Deveriece)	27	2		256							
Bartlett, Moses, widow of.	Pension to be continued	30	1	Petition	406	Rev. Pensions	537	Adverse		Laid on table.		
Bartlett, Nathaniel	To be restored to pension roll	22	1	Resolution	261	Rev. Pensions	365	Favorable	460	Passed	Indef. postp'd.	
Bartlett, Samuel	Pension	3	1	Rep. of Secretary War.	131	Select	May 26, 1794	Res. to refer to Sec. War.	R. 12	Passed	Passed	App'd June 9, 1794
Bartlett, Samuel	Remission of duties on goods imported to Castine.	16	1	Senate bill	108	Ways and Means	Jan. 14, 1820	With amend.	S. 13	Passed	Passed	App'd April 11, 1820
Bartlett, Samuel	Indemnity for French spoliations prior to 1800.	31	1	Petition	285	Foreign Affairs	355	General bill	318	Referred to Committee Whole House.		
Bartlett, Sylvanus, and E. Spooner.	Payment of a revolutionary certificate.	5	2	Petition	145	Select.						

List of private claims presented to the House of Representatives of the United States from the 1st to the 31st Congress, inclusive—Continued.

Names of claimants.	Nature or object of the claim.	Congress.	Session.	How brought before the House of Reps.	Page of journal.	To what committee of the House referred.	No. or date of the report.	Nature of the report.	No. of the bill.	How disposed of by the House of Reps.	How disposed of by the Senate.	Date of the act of Congress, and remarks.
Bartlett, Thomas	Right of pre-emption to land in Missouri.	16	1	Petition	40	Priv. Land Claims.	Jan. 31, 1820	Adverse.	......	Claim rejected.		
Bartlett, Thomas	Indemnity for French spoliations prior to 1800.	26	1	Memorial	182	Foreign Affairs	343	Favorable	319	Referred to Committee Whole House.		
Bartlett, Thomas, reps. of.	Pension for revolutionary services	25	2	Petition	730	Rev. Pensions.						
Bartlett, Thomas, (Boston)	Indemniy for French spoliations prior to 1800.	26	1	Memorial	182	Foreign Affairs	343	Favorable	319	Referred to Committee Whole House.		
Bartlett, William, & others	Bounty on fishing schooner Angler	16	2	Petition	149	Commerce	Feb. 26, 1821	Favorable	248	Referred to Committee Whole House.		
Bartlett, William, & others	Bounty on fishing schooner Angler	17	1	Petition	45	Commerce	Jan. 17, 1822	Favorable	43	Passed	Indef. postp'd.	
Bartlett, William, & others	Bounty on fishing schooner Angler	17	2	Petition	43	Commerce	Jan. 21, 1823	Favorable	241	Referred to Committee Whole House.		
Bartlett, William, & others	Bounty on fishing schooner Angler	18	1	Petition	30	Commerce	Dec. 23, 1823	Favorable	22	Passed	Passed	App'd Jan. 19, 1824
Bartlett, William	(See Jos. Peabody, and others, Neopolitan indemnity.)	25	2	....	172							
Bartlett, William, executors of.	Indemnity for French spoliations prior to 1800.	29	2	Memorial	303	Foreign Affairs.						
Bartlett, William, heir of.	Arrears of pension	30	1	Petition	828	Rev. Pensions.						
Bartlett, William, heir of.	Arrears of pension	31	2	Petition	174	Rev. Pensions	52	Adverse	......	Laid on table.		
Bartlett, Zadock	Pension	21	2	Petition	42	Military Pensions.						
Bartlett, Zadock	Pension	22	1	Petition	93	Rev. Pensions	163	Favorable	237	Referred to Committee Whole House.		
Bartis, Ethel	Arrears of pension	30	1	Petition	217	Invalid Pensions	809	Adverse.	......	Laid on table.		
Bartol, George, jr.	(See executors of Mary Sears.)	23	2	....	199							
Bartoll, Lydia	(See daughter of John Deveriece)	27	2	....	256							
Barton, Azariah	(See Archibald Beard and others)	30	1	....	289	....	597	....	478			
Barton, Benjamin	Indemnity for destruction of property by the enemy.	15	2	Petition	148	Claims.						
Barton, Benjamin	Indemnity for destruction of property by the enemy.	19	2	Petition	240	Claims.						
Barton, Benjamin	(See sureties of J. Harrison)	16	2	....	170							
Barton, George C	Compensation for apprehending deserters.	22	1	Resolution	125	Claims.						
Barton, George C.	Compensation for apprehending deserters.	22	2	Resolution	34	Claims.						
Barton, Henry, (Pa.)	Pension for services in war of 1812	20	1	Resolution	382	Military Pensions	April 25, 1828	Adverse	......	Laid on table.		
Barton, Henry, (Pa.)	Pension for services in war of 1812	21	1	Petition	47	Military Pensions	Jan. 5, 1830	Favorable	72	Passed	Passed with amendment.	App'd May 20, 1830
Barton, Henry, (Pa.)	Increase of pension	25	2	Petition	268	Invalid Pensions	679	Favorable	658	Passed	Passed with amendment.	App'd July 7, 1838
Barton, Job.	Pension for services in war of 1812	17	1	Petition	45	Rev. Pensions	....	....	......	Discharged; referred to Sec. War.		
Barton, Job	Pension for services in war of 1812	18	1	Petition	297	Pens. & Rev. Cl'ms.	April 7, 1824	Adverse.	......	Laid on table.		
Barton, Job	Pension for services in war of 1812	20	1	Petition	388	Military Pensions.						
Barton, Job	Pension for services in war of 1812	23	1	Petition	141	Invalid Pensions	227	Favorable	250	Referred to Committee Whole House.		
Barton, Job.	Pension for services in war of 1812	23	2	Rep. Committee Whole House.	299	....	....	With't amend.	250	Passed.	Passed.	App'd March 3, 1835
Barton, Job.	Increase of pension	25	2	Resolution.	530	Invalid Pensions.	....	....	......	Discharged; laid on table.		
Barton, John B.	(See heirs of General William Barton)	31	2	....	183	....	....	....	S. 423			
Barton, Robert, *et al.*	Bounty on fishing vessels	3	2	Petition	313	Select.	Feb. 18, 1795	Favorable bill.	120	Passed.	Passed.	App'd March 2, 1795

List of private claims presented to the House of Representatives of the United States from the 1st to the 31st Congress, inclusive—Continued.

Names of claimants.	Nature or object of the claim.	Congress.	Session.	How brought before the House of Reps.	Page of journal.	To what committee of the House referred.	No. or date of the report.	Nature of the report.	No. of the bill.	How disposed of by the House of Reps.	How disposed of by the Senate.	Date of the act of Congress, and remarks.
Barton, Rufus, widow of..	Payment of dues as revolutionary commissary.	25	2	Petition	47	Rev. Claims.						
Barton, Rufus, representatives of.	Payment of dues as revolutionary commissary.	25	3	Petition	85	Rev. Claims.						
Barton, Rufus, representatives of.	Payment of dues as revolutionary commissary.	26	1	Petition	165	Rev. Claims......	....	....	......	Discharged; laid on table.		
Barton, Seth, administrator of.	Indemnity for French spoliations prior to 1800.	26	1	Memorial.......	182	Foreign Affairs....	343	Favorable....	319	Referred to Committee Whole House.		
Barton, Seth, administrator of.	Indemnity for French spoliations prior to 1800.	29	2	Memorial......	59	Foreign Affairs....	Dec. 21, 1846	General bill...	561	Referred to Committee Whole House.		
Barton, Thomas B.......	(See Louisa Livingston and others)	29	1	....	339							
Barton, T. B	(See administrator of Seth Barton)	29	2	....	59							
Barton, Thomas P.......	Compensation for diplomatic services in France.	24	1	Documents.....	115	Foreign Affairs....	294	Favorable....	302	Referred to Committee Whole House.	....	See civil & diplomatic bill, July 2, 1836.
Barton, William.........	(See L. Wood and others)	3	1	....	88							
Barton, William and others	Compensation for depreciation of pay for revolutionary services.	9	1	Petition	288	Whole House.						
Barton, William and others	Compensation for depreciation of pay for revolutionary services.	9	2	Petition	486	Claims.						
Barton, William and others	Compensation for depreciation of pay for revolutionary services.	10	1	Petition	100	Whole House.						
Barton, William and others	Compensation for depreciation of pay for revolutionary services.	10	2	Petition	421	Select.						
Barton, William, (Vt.) ..	Compensation for revolutionary services and expenses.	13	2	Petition	328	Pens. & Rev. Cl'ms.	Mar. 28, 1814	Adverse......	......	Referred to Committee Whole House.		
Barton, William, (Vt.)...	Compensation for revolutionary services and expenses.	13	3	Petition	577	Pens. & Rev. Cl'ms.						
Barton, William, (Vt.)...	Bounty land for revolutionary services.	17	2	Petition	40	Military Affairs....	....	....	......	Discharged; referred to Sec. War.		
Barton, William, (Ind.) ..	Exchange of an entry of land....	15	1	Petition	232	Public Lands.....	Feb. 25, 1818	Favorable....	109	Referred to Committee Whole House.		
Barton, William, (Ind.)..	Exchange of an entry of land....	15	2	Report of Committee Whole.	70	....	....	With't amend.	109	Passed............	Passed......	App'd Dec. 28, 1818
Barton, William, (Pa.)...	Increase of naval pension	22	2	Petition	245	Naval Affairs.						
Barton, William, (Pa.)...	Increase of naval pension	23	1	Petition	369	Naval Affairs.						
Barton, General William, heirs of	Arrears of pension............	31	2	Senate bill	183	....	....	....	S. 423			
Barton, Willoughby	Compensation for loss on contract for live oak.	20	1	Senate bill	707	Naval Affairs	May 10, 1828	With't amend.	S. 146	Passed	Passed	App'd May 15, 1828
Bartow, Anthony, executors of.	Compensation for revolutionary supplies.	3	2	Petition	315	Claims.						
Bartow, Anthony, executors of.	Compensation for revolutionary supplies.	4	1	Petition	373	Claims	Jan. 6, 1796	Adverse	......	Laid on table.		
Bartow, Anthony, executors of.	Compensation for revolutionary supplies.	23	1	Petition	71	Rev. Claims......	251	Adverse	......	Laid on table.		
Bartow, Anthony, executors of.	Compensation for revolutionary supplies.	24	1	Petition	63	Rev. Claims......	Jan. 28, 1836	Adverse	......	Laid on table.		
Bartow, Anthony, executors of.	Compensation for revolutionary supplies.	25	2	Petition	48	Rev. Claims......	June 27, 1838	....	......	Discharged; laid on table.		
Bartow, John...........	(See heirs of Thomas Smith)....	29	2	....	136							
Bartram, Job..........	Pension for revolutionary services.	3	1	Rep. of Secretary War.	131	Select	May 26, 1794	Res. to refer to Sec. War.	R. 12	Passed	Passed	App'd June 9, 1794

List of private claims presented to the House of Representatives of the United States from the 1st to the 31st Congress, inclusive—Continued.

Names of claimants.	Nature or object of the claim.	Congress.	Session.	How brought before the House of Reps.	Page of journal.	To what committee of the House referred.	No. or date of the report.	Nature of the report.	No. of the bill.	How disposed of by the House of Reps.	How disposed of by the Senate.	Date of the act of Congress, and remarks.
Bartram, Job	Pension for revolutionary services	3	2	Rep. of Secretary War.	262	Claims	Feb. 28, 1795	Favorable	130	Passed	Postponed.	
Bartram, Job	Pension for revolutionary services	4	1	Rep. of Secretary War.	447	Claims	Feb. 18, 1796	Pension bill	156	Passed	Passed with amendment.	App'd April 20, 1796
Bartram, Job	Increase of pension	11	3	Pension bill	604	Whole House	Mar. 2, 1811	With amend	218	Passed	Passed with amendment.	App'd March 3, 1811
Bashford, Francis	Pension	21	2	Petition	143	Military Pensions.						
Bashford, Francis	Pension	22	1	Petition	143	Rev. Pensions.						
Bashford, Francis	Pension	24	1	Petition	97	Invalid Pensions	148	Favorable	156	Passed	Passed	App'd June 28, 1836
Baskerville, Samuel	To be restored to pension roll	17	1	Petition	238	Whole House.						
Baskerville, Samuel	To be restored to pension roll	17	2	Petition	96	Whole House.						
Baskins, George, (Ohio)	Pension for services as spy in Indian wars.	23	1	Petition	219	Rev. Pensions				Discharged; laid on table.		
Basmarin and Raimbaux, heirs of.	Settlement of claims for revolutionary transactions.	21	2	Memorial	245	Foreign Affairs				Discharged; laid on table.		
Bass, Henry	Renewal of loan office certificate	1	2	Petition	279					Referred to Secretary Treasury.		
Bass, Henry, & Co., surviving partner of.	Indemnity for French spoliations prior to 1800.	26	1	Memorial	182	Foreign Affairs	343	Favorable	319	Referred to Committee Whole House.		
Bass, Henry, & Co., surviving partner of.	Indemnity for French spoliations prior to 1800.	27	2	Memorial	253	Foreign Affairs.						
Bass, Henry, & Co., surviving partner of.	Indemnity for French spoliations prior to 1800.	29	2	Memorial	101	Foreign Affairs.						
Bass, Henry, & Co., surviving partner of.	Indemnity for French spoliations prior to 1800.	31	1	Petition	276	Foreign Affairs	355	General bill	318	Referred to Committee Whole House.		
Bass, Job	Confirmation of title to school lands	22	1	Petition	890	Priv. Land Claims.						
Bass, Job	Confirmation of title to school lands	23	1	Petition	195	Priv. Land Claims.	229	Favorable	252	Referred to Committee Whole House.		
Bass, Job	Confirmation of title to school lands	23	2	Rep't Committee Whole House.	299			With amend	252			
Bass, Job	Confirmation of title to school lands	24	1	Petition	156	Priv. Land Claims.				Dis.; laid on table.		
Bass, Job, assignee of	Confirmation of title to school lands	25	2	Petition	374	Priv. Land Claims.	Mar. 9, 1838	Favorable	639	Passed	Passed	App'd Mar. 28, 1838
Bass, Joseph, (Mass.)	Pension	20	1	Petition	124	Military Pensions.						
Bass, Joseph, (Mass.)	Pension	21	1	Petition	47	Military Pensions.						
Bass, Joseph	(See Joseph Boss.)											
Bass, Joseph, assignee of	Confirmation of land title	23	2	Petition	438	Priv. Land Claims.						
Bass, Joseph, assignee of	Confirmation of land title	24	1	Petition	121	Priv. Land Claims.	142	Favorable	149	Passed	Rejected.	
B ss, Joseph, assignee of	Confirmation of land title	25	2	Petition	374	Priv. Land Claims.	665	Favorable	639	Passed	Passed	App'd Mar. 28, 1838
Bass, Obadiah, (Vt.)	Pension for revolutionary services	15	2	Petition	295					Laid on table.		
Bass, Obadiah, (Mass.)	Pension for services; war of 1812	29	1	Petition	430	Invalid Pensions	666	Adverse		Laid on table.		
Bassett, Christopher	Indemnity for French spoliations prior to 1800.	26	1	Memorial	182	Foreign Affairs	343	Favorable	319	Referred to Committee Whole House.		
Bassett, Edward	Increase of pension	10	2	Pension bill	499	Whole House	Feb. 20, 1809	With amend	158	Passed	Passed with amendment.	App'd March 3, 1809
Basset, Jas., and J. Loomis	Payment of prize money	15	1	Petition	127	Naval Affairs	Mar. 24, 1818	Favorable	158	Referred to Committee Whole House.		
Basset, Jas., and J. Loomis	Payment of prize money	15	2	Rep't Committee Whole House.	181			With amend	158	Passed	Rejected.	
Basset, Jas., and J. Loomis	Payment of prize money	21	1	Petition	50	Naval Affairs	Feb. 12, 1830	Favorable	239	Referred to Committee Whole House.		
Basset, Jas., and J. Loomis	Payment of prize money	25	2	Petition	201	Naval Affairs	Jan. 18, 1838	Favorable	422	Referred to Committee Whole House.		
Basset, Jas., and J. Loomis	Payment of prize money	25	3	Rep't Committee Whole House.	378			With amend	422	Passed	Passed	App'd March 3, 1839

List of private claims presented to the House of Representatives of the United States from the 1st to the 31st Congress, inclusive—Continued.

Names of claimants.	Nature or object of the claim.	Congress.	Session.	How brought before the House of Reps.	Page of journal.	To what committee of the House referred.	No. or date of the report.	Nature of the report.	No. of the bill.	How disposed of by the House of Reps.	How disposed of by the Senate.	Date of the act of Congress, and remarks.
13 Bassett, Joseph	Pension	25	2	Senate bill	1155	Rev. Pensions	July 7, 1838	With't amend.	S. 251	Referred to Committee Whole House.		
Bassett, Joseph	Pension	25	3	Senate bill	546	Rev. Pensions	Feb. 25, 1839	With't amend.	S. 98	Referred to Committee Whole House.		
Bassett, Joseph	Pension	26	1	Senate bill	836	Rev. Pensions	May 25, 1840	With't amend.	S. 115	Referred to Committee Whole House.		
Bassett, Joseph	Pension	26	2	Senate bill	113	Rev. Pensions	Feb. 12, 1841	With't amend.	S. 71	Referred to Committee Whole House.		
Bassett, Joseph	Pension	27	2	Senate bill	122	Rev. Pensions	Feb. 9, 1842	With't amend.	S. 13	Passed	Passed	App'd Mar. 19, 1842
Bassett, Natnaniel	Confirmation of title to land in Arkansas.	16	1	Petition	291	Priv. Land Claims.						
Bassett, Nathaniel	Confirmation of title to land in Arkansas.	22	1	House bill	421				425	Passed	Passed with amendment	App'd June 25, 1832
Bassett, Richard	(See William Tilghman, *et al*)	7	2		307							
Bassett, William H.	Indemnity for breach of contract	19	1	Petition	154	Naval Affairs	187	Favorable	251	Passed	Rep'd without amendment.	
Bassett, William H.	Indemnity for breach of contract	19	2	Petition	96	Naval Affairs.						
Bast & Youce	Confirmation of title to land in Louisiana.	20	2	Resolution	52	Priv. Land Claims.						
Bast & Youce	Confirmation of title to land in Louisiana.	21	1	Petition	51	Priv. Land Claims.	Feb. 22, 1831	Favorable	642	Passed.		
Bast & Youce	Confirmation of title to land in Louisiana.	21	2	Petition	83	Priv. Land Claims.						
Bast & Youce	Confirmation of title to land in Louisiana.	22	1	Petition	75	Priv. Land Claims.						
Bastien, Washington	(See assignee of Joseph Lauligne)	26	1		365							
Bastrop	(See Baron de Bastrop)	17	1		129							
Bastress, Peter	Compensation for discovery of anthracite coal.	23	1	Petition	492	Manufactures	June 20, 1834	Adverse		Laid on table.		
Batchelder, Archelaus	Pension for revolutionary services.	3	2	Rep. of Secretary of war.	278	Claims	Feb. 28, 1795	Pension bill	130	Passed	Postponed.	
Batchelder, Archelaus	Pension for revolutionary services.	4	1	Rep. of Secretary War.	447	Claims	Feb. 18, 1796	Pension bill	156	Passed	Passed with amendment.	App'd April 20, 1796
Batchelder, Archelaus, daughter of.	Pension for revolutionary services.	29	1	Petition	284	Rev. Pensions	490	Adverse		Leave to withdraw.		
Batchelder, Gideon and S.	Compensation for stone, Sandy bay Breakwater.	28	1	Senate bill	942	Claims	Jan. 7, 1844	With't amend.	S. 85	Referred to Committee Whole House.		
Batchelder, Gideon and S.	Compensation for stone, Sandy bay Breakwater.	28	2	Senate bill	131	Claims	Dec. 31, 1844	With't amend.	S. 34	Passed	Passed	App'd Feb. 13, 1845
Batchelder, James	Pension for revolutionary services.	3	2	Rep. of Secretary War.	262	Claims	Feb. 28, 1795	Pension bill	130	Passed	Postponed.	
Batchelder, James	Pension for revolutionary services.	4	1	Rep. of Secretary War.	447	Claims	Feb. 18, 1796	Pension bill	156	Passed	Passed, with amendment.	App'd April 20, 1796
Batchelder, James	Pension for revolutionary services.	17	1	Petition Rep. of Secretary War.	113 279	Pens. & Rev. Cl'ms.	March 1, 1822	Adverse		Leave to withdraw.		
Batchelder, John	Pension	21	2	Petition	299	Military Pensions.						
Batchelder, John Adams	Pension for revolutionary services.	13	3	Petition	459	Pens. & Rev. Cl'ms.	Nov. 4, 1814	Adverse		Leave to withdraw.		
Batchelder, John Adams	Pension for revolutionary services.	19	1	Petition	52	Military Pensions	April 1, 1826	Adverse		Laid on table.		
Batchelder, Josiah	Increase of salary as port surveyor	3	2	Petition	248	Select	Jan. 26, 1795	General bill	75	Passed	Passed with amendment.	App'd Feb. 14, 1795
Batchelder, Shadrach	(See Gideon & S. Batchelder	28	1		942							
Bate, John	Extension of lease of United States salines.	14	1	Petition	94	Select	Jan. 11, 1816	Favorable	29	Passed	Passed	App'd April 24, 1816

List of private claims presented to the House of Representatives of the United States from the 1st to the 31st Congress, inclusive—Continued.

Names of claimants.	Nature or object of the claim.	Congress.	Session.	How brought before the House of Reps.	Page of journal.	To what committee of the House referred.	No. or date of the report.	Nature of the report.	No. of the bill.	How disposed of by the House of Reps	How disposed of by the Senate.	Date of the act of Congress, and remarks.
Bate, John	Release from rent for salines	14	2	Petition	132	Select	Jan. 28, 1817	Favorable	86	Referred to Committee Whole House.		
Bate, John	Release from rent for salines	15	1	Petition	22	Select	Dec. 8, 1817	Favorable	2	Passed	Passed	App'd April 3, 1818
Bateman, Henry	Pay and pension for military services.	13	3	Petition of Leg. of Indiana.	463	Pens. & Rev. Cl'ms.	Feb. 20, 1815	Pension bill	303	Passed	Passed	App'd March 3, 1815
Bateman, M. W.	(See G. W. Waters & M. W. B.)	22	1		264							
Bateman, Nicholas	Indemnity for damage to property by United States troops.	14	1	Petition	94	Select	Jan. 17, 1816	Favorable	29	Passed	Passed	App'd April 24, 1816
Bateman, Smith	(See Martin S. Aikin, *et al.*)	17	1		359							
Bateman, Thomas	Pension for revolutionary services	23	1	Petition	639	Rev. Pensions.						
Bates, Alexander, (Tenn)	Indemnity for damages, &c., in a certain suit.	18	1	Petition	130	Claims.						
Bates, Ambrose	Pension	20	1	Petition	637	Military Pensions.						
Bates, Cornelius	Increase of pension	30	2	Petition	316	Rev. Pensions.						
Bates, David G, and others	Reimbursement of rent paid for lead mines.	30	1	Petition	124	Claims	....	....	....	Discharged; laid on table.		
Bates, Drury	Compensation for horses lost in public service.	15	2	Petition	139	Claims.						
Bates, Elias, and others	Remission of duties on goods at Eastport.	15	2	Petition	109	Ways and Means.						
Bates, Eliphalet	Pension	16	1	Petition	147	Pens. & Rev. Clm's.						
				Rep. of Secretary War.	350	....	....	....	....	Laid on table.		
Bates, Elizur	Increase of pay as master armorer	24	1	Petition	200	Millitary Affairs.						
Bates, Fleming C.	(See James A. Bates and others)	24	2		88							
Bates, Frederick	Compensation for bearing report of land commissioners.	14	1	Petition	377	Public Lands	Mar. 14, 1816	Favorable	128	Passed	Passed with amendment.	App'd April 29, 1816
Bates, George C.	(See Orville B. Dibble)	30	1		359							
Bates, George, (Boston)	Indemnity for French spoliations prior to 1800.	26	1	Memorial	182	Foreign Affairs	373	Favorable	319	Referred to Committee Whole House.		
Bates, Hickey	Pension	27	2	Petition	525	Rev. Pensions	784	Adverse	....	Laid on table.		
Bates, Iris W.	Compensation for extra tonage of two public vessels.	31	1	Petition	1111	Claims	496	Adverse	....	Laid on table.		
Bates, Israel	Pension	19	2	Petition	111	Military Pensions.						
Bates, James	Pension	21	2	Petition	126	Military Pensions.						
Bates, James	Pension	22	1	Petition	80	Military Pensions.						
Bates, James and others	To enter land on Choctaw reservations in lieu of pre-emption.	24	2	Petition	88	Public Lands.						
Bates, James M.	Compensation for services in the Florida war.	30	1	Petition	435	Claims	....	....	....	Leave to withdraw.		
Bates, James M.	Compensation for services in the Florida war.	30	2	Petition	123	Claims.						
Bates, John	Compensation as boatswain United States navy.	31	1	Petition	579	Naval Affairs.						
Bates, Joseph	To locate a confirmed Spanish grant.	14	1	Petition	49	Public Lands.						
Bates, Joseph	To locate a confirmed Spanish grant.	14	2	Petition	50	Priv. Land Claims.						
Bates, Joseph	Pension for revolutionary services.	3	1	Rep. of Secretary War.	131	Select	May 26, 1794	Res. to refer to Sec. War.	R. 12	Passed	Passed	App'd June 9, 1794
Bates, Joshua, widow of	Pension for revolutionary services.	26	1	Petition	283	Rev. Pensions	714	Adverse	....	Laid on table.		
Bates, Joshua, widow of	Benefit of a certain pension act	27	2	Petition	97	Rev. Pensions	580	Favorable	376	Ordered to 3d reading.		
Bates, Joshua, widow of	Benefit of a certain pension act	27	3	House bill	....	....	....	....	376	Passed	Indef. postp'd.	

List of private claims presented to the House of Representatives of the United States from the 1st to the 31st Congress, inclusive—Continued.

Names of claimants.	Nature or object of the claim.	Congress.	Session.	How brought before the House of Reps.	Page of journal.	To what committee of the House referred.	No. or date of the report	Nature of the report.	No. of the bill.	How disposed of by the House of Reps.	How disposed of by the Senate.	Date of the act of Congress, and remarks.
Bates, Levi, widow of....	Compensation for loss of husband in public service.	11	1	Petition.........	34	Claims...........	June 6, 1809	Adverse	......	Claim rejected.		
Bates, Lewis H. & Co...	Indemnity for damages in a certain suit.	23	1	Petition........	48	Ways and Means .	289	Favorable	325	Referred to Committee Whole House.		
Bates, Lewis H. & Co...	Indemnity for damages in a certain suit.	24	1	Petition........	215	Ways and Means .	286	Favorable	289	Referred to Committee Whole House.		
Bates, Lewis H. & Co...	Indemnity for damages in a certain suit.	25	2	Petition.........	60	Ways and Means. .	527	Favorable	518	Referred to Committee Whole House.		
Bates, Lewis H. & Co...	Indemnity for damages in a certain suit.	25	3	Rep't Committee Whole House.	379	....	....	With't amend.	518	Rejected.		
Bates, Lewis H. & Co...	Indemnity for damages in a certain suit.	26	1	Petition.........	178	Ways and Means. .	4	Favorable	20	Passed	Indef. postpn'd	
Bates, Lewis H. & Co...	Indemnity for damages in a certain suit.	27	2	Petition........	55	Ways and Means.						
Bates, Lewis H. & Co...	Indemnity for damages in a certain suit.	28	1	Petition.........	183	Ways and Means.						
Bates, Lewis H. & Co...	Indemnity for damages in a certain suit.	29	1	Petition........	69	Commerce........	....	....	......	Discharged; laid on table.		
Bates, Lewis H. & Co...	Indemnity for damages in a certain suit.	30	1	Petition.........	110	Commerce........	729	Favorable	570	Referred to Committee Whole House.		
Bates, Lewis H. & Co...	Indemnity for damages in a certain suit.	30	2	Rep't Committee Whole House.	319	....	....	With't amend.	570	Passed.		
Bates, Lewis H. & Co...	Indemnity for damages in a certain suit.	31	1	Petition	284	Commerce.						
Bates, Noble E	(See Weston, Allen, and others)..	22	1	....	132							
Bates, Robert, widow of..	Continuation of pension........	15	2	Petition	36	Naval Affairs.						
Bates, Robert H. A. T....	(See James A. Bates and others).	24	2	....	88							
Bates, Roswell (Illinois)..	Pension	29	2	Documents.....	53	Invalid Pensions ..	....	....	......	Discharged; laid on table.		
Batherson, William......	Increase of compensation as postmaster.	23	1	Petition	437	P. Of. and P. Roads.						
Bathurst & Thompson....	(See Kantzow & Biel)	18	2	....	136							
Batman, Henry.........	Patent for land purchased.......	15	2	Petition	211	Public Lands.....	Feb. 12, 1819	Favorable	319	Passed............	Passed.......	App'd March 3, 1819
Baton Rouge...........	(See Louisiana)...............	18	1	....	428							
Batson, James.........	Pension	11	3	House bill......	604	Whole House.....	Mar. 2, 1811	Favorable	218	Passed............	Passed.......	App'd March 3, 1811
Battelle	(See Everett & Battelle)........	30	1	....	1057							
Battelle, Jonathan	Remission of duty on goods destroyed by fire.	15	2	Petition	155	Com. and Manuf.						
Battelle, Jonathan	Remission of duty on goods destroyed by fire.	16	1	Petition	215	Commerce.						
Battelle, Jonathan	Remission of duty on goods destroyed by fire.	17	1	Petition	73	Ways and Means. .	25	Adverse	......	Referred to Committee Whole House.		
Batterson, George	Pension for revolutionary services.	15	2	Petition	26	Rev. Pensions	Jan. 5, 1819	Adverse	......	Laid on table.		
Battey, John	(See John Carr and others)	27	3	....	423							
Battle, Isaac L., heirs of..	Release from a judgment........	30	1	Petition	679	P. Of. & P. Roads.	....	....	......	Discharged; laid on table.	....	Leave to withdraw, 2d Session.
Battle, Ithiel...........	Compensation for revolutionary services.	19	2	Petition	25	Rev. Claims.						
Battle, Ithiel...........	Compensation for revolutionary services.	20	1	Petition	45	Rev. Claims.						
Baty, John............	Compensation for horse lost in Seminole war.	28	1	Petition	262	Claims.						
Baucker, James	Arrears of pension.............	29	2	Memorial	58	Rev. Pensions.						

List of private claims presented to the House of Representatives of the United States from the 1st to the 31st Congress, inclusive—Continued.

Names of claimants.	Nature or object of the claim.	Congress.	Session.	How brought before the House of Reps.	Page of journal.	To what committee of the House referred.	No. or date of the report.	Nature of the report.	No. of the bill.	How disposed of by the House of Reps.	How disposed of by the Senate.	Date of the act of Congress, and remarks.
Baudin, Lewis and others	Compensation for cattle taken for public use.	15	2	Petition	33	Claims	Nov. 27, 1818	Adverse	......	Claim rejected.		
Baudin, Lewis and others	Compensation for cattle taken for public use.	18	1	Petition	486	Claims	May 4, 1824	Adverse	......	Leave to withdraw.		
Baudin, Nicholas, heirs of	Confirmation of title to land	18	1	Senate bill	187	Priv. Land Claims.	Feb. 10, 1824	Adverse	S. 27	Referred to Committee Whole House.		
Baudouin, A. & A. D. R.	Indemnity for loss of boat and cargo by collision with a public vessel.	29	2	Petition	56	Claims.						
Baudouin, A. & A. D. R.	Indemnity for loss of boat and cargo by collision with a public vessel.	30	1	Petition	102	Claims	459	Favorable	389	Referred to Committee Whole House.		
Baudouin, A. & A. D. R	Indemnity for loss of boat and cargo by collision with a public vessel.	30	2	Rep't Committee Whole House.	318	....	....	With't amend.	389	Passed.		
Baudouin, A. & A. D. R.	Indemnity for loss of boat and cargo by collision with a public vessel.	31	1	Petition	390	Claims	76	Favorable	91	Referred to Committee Whole House.		
Baudouin, A. & A. D. R.	Indemnity for loss of boat and cargo by collision with a public vessel.	31	2	Rep't Committee Whole House.	154	....	....	With't amend.	91	Passed.		
Baugh, Jacob	Pension	25	2	Petition	115	Rev. Pensions	Mar. 10, 1838	Favorable	641	Passed	Adverse report.	
Baugh, Jacob	Pension	25	3	Petition	87	Rev. Pensions	Dec. 21, 1838	Favorable	441	Passed	Adverse report.	
Baugh, Jacob	Pension	26	1	Petition	171	Rev. Pensions	362	Favorable	341	Referred to Committee Whole House.		
Baugh, Joseph	Pension	28	1	Petition	124	Rev. Pensions	....	....	......	Discharged; laid on table.		
Baughan, Augustine	(See Joshua Harvey and others)	7	2	....	343							
Baughman, George, widow of.	Arrears of pension for revolutionary services.	30	1	Petition	786	Rev. Pensions.						
Baum, Martin	Resale of certain public lands	17	1	Petition	511	....	....	....	......	Laid on table.		
Baum, Martin	Resale of certain public lands	17	2	Petition	31	Public Lands	....	....	......	Laid on table.		
Baur, Matthias	Pension for injuries received in public service.	29	1	Petition	679	Invalid Pensions.						
Baury, Louis, widow of	Pension for revolutionary services.	31	1	Petition	711	Rev. Pensions.						
Baury, Louis, widow of	Pension for revolutionary services.	31	2	Petition	431	Rev. Pensions	49	Adverse	......	Laid on table.		
Baury, Mary	(See Louis Baury, widow of.)	31	1	....	711							
Bauvais, Jean B	(See heirs of Francis Vallé.)	15	2	....	47							
Baxter, Abigail	(See widow of Ebenezer Wild.)	25	2	....	913							
Baxter, Chester, & others	Patents for certain lots in Louisiana.	27	3	Resolution	68	Priv. Land Claims.	95	Favorable	717	Passed	Passed	App'd Mar. 3, 1843
Baxter, Francis	Pension for revolutionary services.	3	1	Rep. of Secretary War.	131	Select	May 26, 1794	Res. to refer to Sec. War.	R. 12	Passed	Passed	App'd June 9, 1794
Baxter, Francis	Pension for revolutionary services.	4	1	Rep. of Secretary War.	373	Claims	Feb. 18, 1796	Pension bill	156	Passed	Passed	App'd Apr. 20, 1796
Baxter, Israel	Pension for revolutionary services.	23	1	Petition	639	Rev. Pensions.						
Baxter, John	To be restored to pension roll	17	2	Petition	99	Whole House.						
Baxter, John W. C	(See Jabez Mowry & others.)	14	1	Petition	242	....	....	....	......	....	....	App'd Apr. 29, 1816
Baxter, Stephen	Equitable settlement of accounts as paymaster.	16	1	Petition	163	Claims	61	Favorable	67	Passed	Passed	App'd May 8, 1820
Baxter, William, (Pa.)	Bounty land for military services.	17	1	Petition	266	Military Affairs.	....	....	......	Discharged; leave to withdraw.		
Baxter, William, widow of	Compensation for revolutionary services.	4	1	Petition	470	Claims	May 31, 1796	Adverse	......	Laid on table.		
Baxter, Zebulon	Bounty land as Canada volunteer.	23	2	Petition	176	Priv. Land Claims.	41	Favorable	625	Referred to Committee Whole House.		
Baxter, Zebulon	Bounty land as Canada volunteer.	24	1	Petition	664	Priv. Land Claims.						
Baxter, Zebulon	Bounty land as Canada volunteer.	25	2	Petition	59	Priv. Land Claims.	284	Favorable	327	Referred to Committee Whole House.		

List of private claims presented to the House of Representatives of the United States from the 1st to the 31st Congress, inclusive—Continued.

Names of claimants.	Nature or object of the claim.	Congress.	Session.	How brought before the House of Reps.	Page of journal.	To what committee of the House referred.	No. or date of the report.	Nature of the report.	No. of the bill.	How disposed of by the House of Reps.	How disposed of by the Senate.	Date of the act of Congress, and remarks.
Baxter, Zebulon	Bounty land as Canada volunteer	25	3	Rep't Committee Whole House.	377	....	....	With't amend.	327	Passed	Passed	App'd March 3, 1839
Bay, Andrew	Pension	21	1	Petition	254	Military Pensions.						
Bay, Elihu, Hall & others	Confirmation of title to land in Louisaina.	16	1	Petition	182	Select.						
Bay, Elihu, Hall & others	Confirmation of title to land in Louisiana.	17	1	Petition	389	Public Lands.						
Bay, Elihu, Hall & others	Confirmation of title to land in Louisiana.	17	2	Petition	150	Public Lands.						
Bay, Elihu, Hall & others	Confirmation of title to land in Louisiana.	18	2	Petition	70	Priv. Land Claims.						
Bay, Elihu, Hall & others	Confirmation of title to land in Louisiana.	19	2	Petition	92	Priv. Land Claims.						
Bay, Elihu, Hall & others	Confirmation of title to land in Louisiana.	20	1	Petition	33	Priv. Land Claims.						
Bay, Elihu, Hall & others	Confirmation of title to land in Louisiana.	21	1	Petition	40	Priv. Land Claims.						
Bay, Elihu, Hall & others	Confirmation of title to land in Louisiana.	22	1	Senate bill	902	Judiciary	July 14, 1832	With't amend.	S. 78	Referred to Committee Whole House.		
Bay, Elihu, Hall & others	Confirmation of title to land in Louisiana.	22	2	Petition	162	Priv. Land Claims.	54	Adverse		Laid on table.		
Bay, Elihu, Hall & others	Confirmation of title to land in Louisiana.	24	1	Petition	112	Priv. Land Claims.	197	Favorable	199	Referred to Committee Whole House.		
Bay, Elihu Hall	Confirmation of title to land in Louisiana.	25	2	Petition	1272	Priv. Land Claims.	1059	Adverse	......	Referred to Committee Whole House.		
Bay, Elihu Hall, heirs of	Indemnity for land taken by government United States.	28	1	Petition	75	Priv. Land Claims.						
Bay, Robert	Compensation for services as a military officer.	15	1	Petition	294	Claims.						
Bay, Robert	Compensation for services as a military officer.	15	2	Petition	52	Claims.						
Bay, Robert	Compensation for services as a military officer.	16	1	Petition	92	Claims	Dec. 31, 1819	Adverse	......	Laid on table.		
Bayard, Andrew	Indemnity for French spoliations prior to 1800.	26	1	Memorial	182	Foreign Affairs	343	Favorable	319	Referred to Committee Whole House.		
Bayard, A. W., (Pa.)	Pension	25	2	Petition	400	Invalid Pensions	....	....	......	Discharged; laid on table.		
Bayard, A. W., (Pa.)	Back pension from 1817 to 1844	29	1	Petition	225	Invalid Pensions	335	Favorable	270	Referred to Committee Whole House.		
Bayard, A. W., (Pa.)	Back pension from 1817 to 1844	30	1	Petition	78	Invalid Pensions	21	Favorable	25	Passed.		
Bayard, A. W., (Pa.)	Back pension from 1817 to 1844	31	1	Petition	467	Invalid Pensions	141	Favorable	157	Referred to Committee Whole House.		
Bayard, John, executor of	Payment of lost loan office certificates.	22	2	Petition	229	Rev. Claims.						
Bayard, John, executor of	Payment of lost loan office certificates.	23	1	Petition	42	Rev. Claims	157	Favorable	172	Passed	Passed	App'd June 28, 1834
Bayard, ...	(See Pettit & Bayard)	26	1	....	182	....	343	....	319			
Bayard, Samuel	(See executors of John Bayard)	22	2	....	229							
Bayard, Samuel J.	Release from liability for public money stolen.	30	1	Petition	415	Claims	Mar. 15, 1848	....	......	Discharged; laid on table.		
Bayard, Samuel J.	Release from liability for public money stolen.	30	2	Petition	176	Claims	....	....	......	Discharged; leave to withdraw.		

List of private claims presented to the House of Representatives of the United States from the 1st to the 31st Congress, inclusive—Continued.

Names of claimants.	Nature or object of the claim.	Congress.	Session.	How brought before the House of Reps.	Page of journal.	To what committee of the House referred.	No. or date of the report.	Nature of the report.	No. of the bill.	How disposed of by the House of Reps.	How disposed of by the Senate.	Date of the act of Congress, and remarks.
Bayard, William, & others	Payment of certain three per cent. stocks.	16	1	Memorial	271	Ways and Means	95	Adverse	......	Laid on table.		
Bayard, William	(See Thomas L. Ogden and others)	17	1	....	38							
Bayles, David	Compensation for revolutionary services.	25	2	Resolution	155	Rev. Claims.						
Bayles, Nathaniel, administrator of.	Compensation for services in revolutionary navy.	4	1	Petition	370	Claims	Jan. 20, 1796	Adverse	......	Claim rejected	....	Leave to withdraw.
Bayless, Israel	Pension for disability, war of 1812	29	2	Petition	184	Invalid Pensions.						
Bayless, Israel	Pension for disability, war of 1812	30	1	Petition	339	Invalid Pensions	451	Favorable	381	Passed	Reported without amend't.	
Bayley, Christopher T.	Compensation for medical services in St. Domingo.	23	1	Petition	239	Commerce	342	Adverse	......	Laid on table.		
Bayley, Christopher T.	Compensation for medical services in St. Domingo.	23	2	Senate bill	318	Commerce	101	Adverse	S. 93	Laid on table.		
Bayley, Christopher T.	Compensation for medical services in St. Domingo.	24	1	Petition	200	Commerce.						
Bayley, Christopher T.	Compensation for medical services in St. Domingo.	24	1	Senate bill	735	Commerce	....	....	S. 86			
Bayley, Samuel	(See Eliphalet Loud & S. B.)	18	2	....	209							
Bayley, Samuel, executor of	Indemnity for French spoliations prior to 1800.	26	1	Memorial	182	Foreign Affairs	343	Favorable	319	Referred to Committee Whole House.		
Bayley, Major William	Compensation for revolutionary services.	2	1	Petition	482	....	....	....	......	Laid on table.		
Baylies, Nehemiah	Pension	16	1	Petition	26							
Baylies, Samuel	Payment of reward for apprehending deserters.	18	2	Petition	42	Claims	9	Favorable	250	Passed	Passed	App'd March 3, 1825
				Rep. of Secretary War.	350	....	....	....	......	Laid on table.		
Baylis, William, (Ky.)	Increase of pension for revolutionary services.	21	2	Petition	127	Military Pensions.						
Baylis, William, (Ky.)	Increase of pension for revolutionary services.	22	1	Petition	113	Rev. Pensions.						
Baylis, William, (Ky.)	Increase of pension for revolutionary services.	23	1	Petition	426	Invalid Pensions	April 4, 1834	Adverse	......	Laid on table.		
Bayliss, Hodijah	Increase of salary as collector of customs.	4	1	Petition	446	Com. and Manuf.						
Baylis, Platt, heirs of.	Compensation for revolutionary services.	9	1	Petition	351	....	....	....	......	Laid on table.		
Baylis, Platt, heirs of.	Compensation for revolutionary services.	12	1	Petition	176	Claims.						
Baylis, Samuel	(See heirs of Platt Baylis)	12	1	....	176							
Baylis, Zephaniah	(See heirs of Platt Bayliss)	12	1	....	176							
Baylor, Ann D.	(See John Walker Baylor, widow of.)											
Baylor, George, executor of.	Settlement of accounts	1	2	Memorial	178							
				Report Secretary of War.	255	Select	July 16, 1790	Res. to refer to Sec. of War.	......	Referred to Secretary War.		
Baylor, George, executor of.	Settlement of accounts	1	3	Report Secretary of War.	385	....	....	....	......	Laid on table.		
Baylor, George, heirs of.	Balance due for revolutionary services.	19	1	Petition	34	Pens. & Rev. Cl'ms.	52	Favorable	72	Passed	Passed	App'd May 20, 1826
Baylor, George, heirs of.	Balance due for revolutionary services.	19	2	Resolution	101	Rev. Claims	Jan. 25, 1827	Adverse	......	Laid on table.		

List of private claims presented to the House of Representatives of the United States from the 1st to the 31st Congress, inclusive—Continued.

Names of claimants.	Nature or object of the claim.	Congress.	Session.	How brought before the House of Reps.	Page of journal.	To what committee of the House referred.	No. or date of the report.	Nature of the report.	No. of the bill.	How disposed of by the House of Reps.	How disposed of by the Senate.	Date of the act of Congress, and remarks.
Baylor, George, heirs of..	Payment of revolutionary certificates	21	1	Petition	235	Rev. Claims......	237	Favorable....	296	Passed	Passed......	App'd May 29, 1830
Baylor, George, heirs of..	Commutation pay for revolutionary services.	21	2	Petition........	44	Rev. Claims......	5	Favorable....	504	Referred to Committee Whole House.		
Baylor, George, heirs of..	Commutation pay for revolutionary services.	22	1	Petition	28	Rev. Claims......	78	Favorable....	154	Passed............	Passed.......	App'd May 25, 1832
Baylor, George, heirs of..	Interest on claim allowed for revolutionary services.	27	2	Petition	525	Rev. Claims......	527	Adverse......	......	Laid on table.		
Baylor, George, heirs of..	Balance of interest due on revolutionary certificates.	29	1	Petition	319	Rev. Pensions.....	....	....	......	....	....	See 26, 1 Rep., No. 436.
Baylor, John	(See executor of George Baylor)..	1	2	....	178							
Baylor, John G., surety of.	Release from payment of a judgment.	18	1	Petition	132	Ways and Means..	Jan. 16, 1824	Adverse	......	Laid on table.		
Baylor, John G., surety of.	Release from payment of a judgment.	19	2	Petition	288	Claims.						
Baylor, John Walker, widow of.	(See heirs of George Baylor)	21	1	....	235							
Baylor, John W., (Ky.)..	Release from judgment for lost public money.	17	2	Petition	30	Claims...........	Jan. 3, 1823	Adverse	......	Laid on table.		
Baylor, John W., (Ky.)..	Release from judgment for lost public money.	18	1	Petition	159	Claims...........	Feb. 4, 1824	Adverse	......	Laid on table.		
Baylor, Robert T........	(See surety of John G. Baylor) ..	18	1	....	132							
Baylor, Walker.........	Increase of pension.............	11	2	Pension bill	283	Whole House.....	Mar. 24, 1810	With amend..	107	Passed............	Passed.......	App'd April 27, 1810
Baylor, Walker	Further compensation for revolutionary services.	12	2	Petition	568	Claims.						
Baylor, Walker.........	Further compensation for revolutionary services.	13	2	Petition	175	Pens. & Rev. Cl'ms.	50	Adverse......	......	Laid on table.		
Baylor, Walker, assignees of.	For the amount of pension due and assigned by him.	12	1	Petition	139	....	....	....	......	Referred to Secretary War.		
Bayly, Mountjoy........	Compensation and bounty land for revolutionary services.	11	3	Petition	491	Claims.						
Bayly, Mountjoy........	Compensation and bounty land for revolutionary services.	12	2	Petition	591	Public Lands.						
Bayly, Mountjoy........	Compensation and bounty land for revolutionary services.	14	2	Petition	205	Pens. & Rev. Cl'ms.	....	....	......	Discharged; referred to Sec. War.		
Bayly, Mountjoy........	Commutation pay for revolutionary services.	21	1	Senate bill	271	Rev. Claims.......	Feb. 19, 1830	With't amend.	S. 52	Passed............	Passed.......	App'd May 26, 1830
Bayly, Mountjoy........	Commutation pay for revolutionary services.	21	2	Gen. app'n bill..	128	Whole House	....	....	528	Passed	Passed	App'd Mar. 2, 1831
Bayly, Henry...........	Pension	21	1	Petition	448	Rev. Pensions	....	....	......	Disch'd; laid on table.		
Bayne, Betsy	(See widow of Job Kenniston) ...	29	1	....	532							
Baynham, William	Interest on revolutionary certificates	11	2	Petition	257	Ways and Means..	Mar. 13, 1810	Favorable....	100	Passed	Passed.......	App'd April 20, 1810
Bayse, Jeremiah	Compensation for revolutionary services of his brothers.	23	1	Petition	55	Rev. Claims.......	Dec. 30, 1833	Adverse	.....	Laid on table.		
Baytop, Thomas, heirs of.	Commutation pay for revolutionary services.	23	1	Petition	65	Rev. Claims.						
Baptop, Thomas, heirs of.	Commutation pay for revolutionary services.	23	2	Petition	239	Rev. Claims.						
Baytop, Thomas, heirs of.	Commutation pay for revolutionary services.	24	1	Petition	104	Rev. Claims......	355	Favorable	361	Referred to Committee Whole House.		
Baytop, Thomas, heirs of.	Commutation pay for revolutionary services.	25	2	Petition	39	Rev. Claims......	478	Adverse	......	Laid on table.		
Baytop, Thomas, heirs of.	Commutation pay for revolutionary services.	29	1	Petition	823	Rev. Claims.						

List of private claims presented to the House of Representatives of the United States from the 1st to the 31st Congress, inclusive—Continued.

Names of claimants.	Nature or object of the claim.	Congress.	Session.	How brought before the House of Reps.	Page of journal.	To what committee of the House referred.	No. or date of the report.	Nature of the report.	No. of the bill.	How disposed of by the House of Reps.	How disposed of by the Senate.	Date of the act of Congress, and remarks.
Baytop, Thomas, heirs of.	Commutation pay for revolutionary services.	31	1	Petition	917	Rev. Claims.						
Bazadone, Laurent	Compensat'n for supplies furnished in revolutionary war.	14	1	Petition	393	Claims.						
Bazadone, Laurent	Compensat'n for supplies furnished in revolutionary war.	14	2	Petition	90	Claims	Jan. 13, 1817	Adverse		Rejected.		
Bazadone, Laurent, administrators of.	Compensat'n for supplies furnished in revolutionary war.	24	1	Petition	942	Rev. Claims.						
Bazadone, Laurent, executors of.	Compensat'n for supplies furnished in revolutionary war.	24	1	Memorial	1062	Rev. Claims.						
Bazadone, Laurent, executors of.	Compensat'n for supplies furnished in revolutionary war.	24	2	Petition	92	Rev. Claims.						
Bazadone, Laurent, executors of.	Compensat'n for supplies furnished in revolutionary war.	25	2	Petition	49	Rev. Claims.						
Bazadone, Laurent, executors of.	Compensat'n for supplies furnished in revolutionary war.	25	3	Petition	84	Rev. Claims.						
Bazadone, Laurent, executors of.	Compensat'n for supplies furnished in revolutionary war.	26	1	Petition	164	Rev. Claims.						
Bazard, Anthony	Pension	28	1	Petition	414	Invalid Pensions.						
Bazier, Daniel	Pension for services, war of 1812.	24	1	Petition	98	Invalid Pensions.						
Beach, Deborah	(See widow of Lieut. James Coon)	2	1		455							
Beach, Edmond	Pension	19	1	Petition	423	Military Pensions.	April 20, 1826	Adverse		Rejected.		
Beach, Edmond	Pension	19	2	Petition	132	Military Pensions.						
Beach, Harvey and Hiram.	Right of pre-emption to a certain tract of land.	26	1	Petition	611	Public Lands	July 21, 1840	Favorable	509	Referred to Committee Whole House.		
Beach, Israel	Pension	21	2	Petition	299	Military Pensions.						
Beach, Israel	Pension	22	1	Petition	56	Rev. Pensions	38	Favorable	83	Passed	Indef. postp'd.	
Beach, Jesse	Pension	14	1	Resolution	451	Pens. & Rev. Cl'ms.	April 23, 1816	General bill	171	Passed	Passed	App'd April 30, 1816
Beach, John	(See J. Harrison, sureties of)	16	2		170							
Beach, John, heirs of	Indemnity for property destroyed by the enemy.	19	2	Petition	240	Claims.						
Beach, Julius	Pension	21	1	Petition	197	Military Pensions.	May 18, 1830	Adverse		Laid on table.		
Beach, Julius	Pension	21	2	Petition	127	Military Pensions.						
Beach, Michael	Pension	21	1	Resolution	255	Military Pensions.						
Beach, Nathaniel	Pension for revolutionary services	3	1	Rep. of Secretary War.	131	Select	May 26, 1794	Res. to refer to Sec. War.	R. 12	Passed	Passed	App'd June 9, 1794
Beach, Robert, (Vt.)	Pension for revolutionary services	24	2	Petition	74	Rev. Pensions				Discharged; laid on table.		
Beach, Robert, (Vt.)	Increase of pension	30	1	Petition	674	Rev. Pensions.						
Beach, Robert, (Vt.)	Increase of pension	30	2	Petition	345	Rev. Pensions.						
Beach, Robert, (Vt.)	Increase of pension	31	1	Petition	194	Rev. Pensions	22	Adverse		Laid on table.		
Beach, Samuel, heirs of	Half-pay for revolutionary services	30	2	Petition	92	Rev. Claims	7	Adverse		Laid on table.		
Beach, William	Renewal of patent	27	2	Petition	530	Patents.						
Beach, William	Renewal of patent	28	1	Petition	267	Patents	487	Adverse		Laid on table.		
Beacham, John, heir of	Indemnity for property destroyed during revolution.	26	2	Petition	48	Rev. Claims.						
Beacham, John, heir of	Indemnity for property destroyed during revolution.	30	2	Petition	86	Rev. Claims.						
Beacham, John, heir of	Indemnity for property destroyed during revolution.	31	1	Petition	672	Rev. Claims.						
Beacham, Sarah	Indemnity for damage to property during revolution.	3	1	Petition	19					Referred to Secretary of War.		

List of *private claims presented to the House of Representatives of the United States from the* 1*st to the* 31*st Congress, inclusive*—Continued.

Names of claimants.	Nature or object of the claim.	Congress.	Session.	How brought before the House of Reps.	Page of journal.	To what committee of the House referred.	No. or date of the report.	Nature of the report.	No. of the bill.	How disposed of by the House of Reps.	How disposed of by the Senate.	Date of the act of Congress, and remarks.
Beacham, Sarah	Indemnity for damage to property during revolution.	3	2	Rep. of Secretary War.	278	Claims	Mar. 2, 1795	Adverse		Laid on table.		
Beacham, Sarah	Indemnity for damage to property during revolution.	4	1	Petition		Claims	May 31, 1796	Adverse		Laid on table.		
Beacham, Thomas, heirs of	Indemnity for property destroyed by the enemy.	22	1	Petition	472	Claims.						
Beacham, Thomas, heirs of	Indemnity for property destroyed by the enemy.	22	2	Petition	33	Claims.						
Beacham, Thomas, heirs of	Indemnity for property destroyed by the enemy.	23	1	Petition	33	Claims.						
Beacham, Thomas, heirs of	Indemnity for property destroyed by the enemy.	23	2	Petition	59	Claims	108	Favorable	737	Referred to Committee Whole House.		
Beacham, Thomas, heirs of	Indemnity for property destroyed by the enemy.	24	1	Resolution	51	Claims	37	Favorable	37	Passed	Passed	App'd Feb. 17, 1836
Beagle, William	Release from a judgment	15	1	Petition	84	Claims.						
Beal, John H.	Compensation for services as surgeon U. S. N.	31	1	Petition	495	Claims.						
Beal, William	(See heirs of John Wilson)	27	1		100							
Beale, George, sen., administrator of.	Indemnity for property destroyed at navy yard.	23	1	Petition	437	Claims	436	Adverse		Laid on table.		
Beale, George	(See administrators of C. B. C. Thompson.)	23	1		129							
Beale, Joseph	Indemnity for revolutionary injuries and losses.	1	2	Petition	193					Referred to Secretary Treasury.		
Beale, Levi, agent of	New patent for military bounty land.	24	1	Petition	409	Public Lands.						
Beale, Levi, agent of	New patent for military bounty land.	24	2	Documents	390	Public Lands.						
Beale, Richard C.	Reimbursement of expenses incurred in public service.	9	1	Petition	188	Claims	Dec. 13, 1805	Adverse		Laid on table.		
Beales rifle company	(See Beverly Chew, and others.)	26	1		962							
Beale, Robert, heirs of	Depreciation pay for revolutionary services.	10	2	Petition	367	Claims.						
Beale, Robert, heirs of	Depreciation pay for revolutionary services.	11	2	Petition	108	Claims	Dec. 21, 1809	Adverse		Claim rejected.		
Beale, Robert, heirs of	Depreciation pay for revolutionary saivices.	11	3	Petition	450	Claims						
Beale, Robert, heirs of	Depreciation pay for revolutionary services.	12	1	Petition	142	Claims.						
Beale, Robert, heirs of	Depreciation pay for revolutionary services.	13	2	Petition	304	Pens. & Rev. Cl'ms.	92	Adverse		Referred to Committee Whole House.		
Beale, Robert	(See Geo. Beale, administrator of.)	23	1		437							
Beale, Robert, sen. and jr.	(See G. L. Turberville, heirs of.)	22	2		46							
Beale, Robert	Reimbursement of expenses to Virginia.	30	2	Appropriation bill	157	Whole House		Amendments	692	Passed	Passed	App'd March 3, 1849
Beale, Samuel Brooke	Renewal of revolutionary certificates.	4	1	Petition	477	Claims.						
Beale, Samuel Brooke	Renewal of revolutionary certificates.	4	2	Resolution	614	Claims	Feb. 7, 1797	Adverse		Postponed.		
Beale, Samuel Brooke	Renewal of revolutionary certificates.	5	2	Report of commissioner claims.	232	Whole House	Mar. 22, 1798	With amend.		Claim rejected.		
Beale, Samuel Brooke	Renewal of revolutionary certificates.	7	1	Petition	34	Claims	April 1, 1802	Adverse		Referred to Committee Whole House.		

List of private claims presented to the House of Representatives of the United States from the 1st to the 31st Congress, inclusive—Continued.

Names of claimants.	Nature or object of the claim.	Congress.	Session.	How brought before the House of Reps.	Page of journal.	To what committee of the House referred.	No. or date of the report.	Nature of the report.	No. of the bill.	How disposed of by the House of Reps.	How disposed of by the Senate.	Date of the act of Congress, and remarks.
Beale, Samuel Brooke....	Renewal of revolutionary certificates.	8	2	Petition........	58	Whole House.						
				Resolution	131	Select.						
Beale, Samuel Brooke....	Renewal of revolutionary certificates.	9	1	Petition	222	Whole House.						
Beale, Samuel Brooke....	Renewal of revolutionary certificates.	9	2	Petition	524	Whole House.						
Beale, Samuel Brooke....	Renewal of revolutionary certificates.	10	1	Petition	31	Select.						
Beale, Samuel Brooke....	Renewal of revolutionary certificates.	15	1	Petition	223	Whole House.						
Beale, Samuel Brooke....	Renewal of revolutionary certificates.	15	2	Petition.......	46	Pen. & Rev. Cl'ms.	Jan. 15, 1819	Favorable....	275	Referred to Committee Whole House.		
Beale, Samuel Brooke....	Renewal of revolutionary certificates.	16	1	Petition	23	Pen. & Rev. Cl'ms.	Jan. 14, 1820	Favorable....	42	Passed	Passed	App'd May 11, 1820
Beale, Samuel B	To be restored to pension roll....	19	1	Resolution	461	Military Pensions.						
Beale, William..........	Indemnity for damages and costs in a certain suit.	20	2	Petition	289	Ways and Means.						
Beall, Alexander, representatives of.	Compensation for land granted by proclamation of the King of England in 1663.	8	2	Petition	49	Claims	Dec. 14, 1804					
Beall, Benjamin L.......	Compensation for extra services in the Pension Office.	23	1	Petition	335	Claims..........	378	Adverse......	......	Laid on table.		
Beall, Elijah	(See Alexander Beall, representatives of.)	8	2	....	49							
Beall, Isaac.............	(See Capt. Thomas Beall, son of.)	29	1	....	576							
Beall, Thomas (Md.)	Payment of revolutianary certificate.	10	1	Petition........	59	Select.						
Beall, Thomas (Geo.)....	Compensation for horse lost in Creek war.	24	2	Petition	266	Claims..........	Feb. 24, 1837	Adverse......	......	Laid on table.		
Beall, Thomas, son of....	Compensation for revolutionary services.	29	1	Petition	576	Rev. Claims.						
Beall, Thomas, son of....	Compensation for revolutionary services.	30	1	Petition	156	Rev. Claims......	....	....	......	Discharged; leave to withdraw.		
				Memorial.......	571	Rev. Claims.						
Beall, Thomas, son of....	Compensation for revolutionary services.	30	2	Petition	124	Rev. Claims......	128	Favorable....	806	Referred to Committee Whole House.		
Beall, Thomas, son of....	Compensation for revolutionary services.	31	1	Petition	620	Rev. Claims.						
Beall, William Dent.....	Compensation for revolutionary services.	11	3	Petition	457	Claims	Jan. 23, 1811	Favorable....	185	Passed	Postponed.	
Beall, William Dent.....	Compensation for revolutionary services.	12	1	Petition	38	Claims	Feb. 7, 1812	Favorable....	63	Passed	Passed.	App'd June 24, 1812
Beall, William Dent.....	Compensation for revolutionary services.	12	2	Petition	373	Claims.						
Beall, William Dent.....	Compensation for revolutionary services.	13	1	Petition	20	Claims.						
Beall, William Dent.....	Compensation for revolutionary services.	13	2	Petition	226	Pens. & Rev. Cl'ms.	Feb. 16, 1814	Adverse	......	Referred to Committee Whole House.		
Beall, William Dent.....	Compensation for revolutionary services.	13	3	Petition	472	Pens. & Rev. Cl'ms	Jan. 21, 1816	Adverse	......	Claim rejected.		
Beall, William Dent.....	Compensation for revolutionary services.	14	1	Petition	100	Pens. & Rev. Cl'ms.						

List of private claims presented to the House of Representatives of the United States from the 1st to the 31st Congress, inclusive—Continued.

Names of claimants.	Nature or object of the claim.	Congress.	Session.	How brought before the House of Reps.	Page of journal.	To what committee of the House referred.	No. or date of the report.	Nature of the report.	No. of the bill.	How disposed of by the House of Reps.	How disposed of by the Senate.	Date of the act of Congress, and remarks.
Beall, William Dent	Compensation for revolutionary services.	14	2	Petition	75	Pens. & Rev. Cl'ms.						
Beall, William Dent	Compensation for revolutionary services.	15	1	Petition	76	Pens. & Rev. Cl'ms.	Feb. 12, 1818	Adverse	......	Claim rejected.		
Beall, William Dent	Compensation for revolutionary services.	15	2	Petition	121	Pens. & Rev. Cl'ms.	Jan. 18, 1819	Adverse	......	Claim rejected.		
Beall, William Dent	Compensation for revolutionary services.	16	1	Petition	38	Pens. & Rev. Cl'ms.	Jan. 7, 1820	Adverse	......	Claim rejected.		
Beall, William Dent	Compensation for revolutionary services.	17	1	Petition	50	Pens. & Rev. Cl'ms.	Jan. 2, 1822	Adverse	......	Claim rejected.		
Beall, William Dent	Compensation for revolutionary services.	17	2	Petition	53	Pens. & Rev. Cl'ms.	Jan. 24, 1823	Adverse	......	Laid on table.		
				Petition (2)	75	Pens. & Rev. Cl'ms.						
Beall, William Dent	Compensation for revolutionary services.	18	1	Petition	156	Pens. & Rev. Cl'ms.						
Beall, William Dent	Compensation for revolutionary services.	22	1	Petition	582	Rev. Claims.						
Bealle, Richard, R. S.	(See representatives of Rob't Bealle)											
Bealle, Robert, representatives of.	Commutation pay for revolutionary services.	22	2	Senate bill	458	Rev. Claims	Mar. 2, 1833	With't amend.	S. 100	Laid on table.		
Bealle, Robert, representatives of.	Commutation pay for revolutionary services.	24	1	Petition	475	Rev. Claims.						
Bealle, Robert, representatives of.	Commutation pay for revolutionary services.	24	2	Petition	308	Rev. Claims.						
Bealle, Robert, representatives of.	Commutation pay for revolutionary services.	25	2	Petition	49	Rev. Claims	405	Favorable	416			
				Recommitted	1017	Rev. Claims	June 13, 1828	Adverse	......	Laid on table.		
Bealle, Robert, representatives of.	Commutation pay for revolutionary services.	25	3	Petition	221	Rev. Claims.						
Bealle, Robert, representatives of.	Commutation pay for revolutionary services.	26	1	Petition	164	Rev. Claims.						
Bealle, Robert, representatives of.	Commutation pay for revolutionary services.	27	2	Petition	60	Rev. Claims.	368	Adverse	......	Laid on table.		
Bealle, Robert, representatives of.	Commutation pay for revolutionary services.	28	1	Resolution	305	Rev. Claims						
Beals, Peter B.	Additional compensation for mail service.	18	2	Petition	209	P. Of. & P. Roads.	....	....	......	Discharged; laid on table.		
Beam, Conrad, widow of	Pension for revolutionary services.	28	1	Petition	204	Rev. Pensions	....	....	......	Discharged; laid on table.		
Beam, Jane	(See Conrad Beam, widow of.)	28	1	....	204							
Beaman, Joel	Compensation for extra mail service.	25	2	Petition	424	P. O. & P. Roads.						
Beaman, Joel	Compensation for extra mail service.	25	3	Petition	91	P. O. & P. Roads.						
Beaman, Joel	Compensation for extra mail service.	26	1	Petition	301	P. Of. & P. Roads.	399	Adverse	......	Laid on table.		
Beaman, Joel	Compensation for extra mail service.	28	1	Petition	105	P. Of. & P. Roads.						
Beaman, Nathan	(See Nathan Beman)	26	1	....	281							
Beamish, Henry	Remission of forfeiture incurred under revenue laws.	22	1	Petition	220	Commerce.						
Beamish, Henry	Remission of forfeiture incurred under revenue laws.	23	1	Petition	163	Commerce.						

List of private claims presented to the House of Representatives of the United States from the 1st to the 31st Congress, inclusive—Continued.

Names of claimants.	Nature or object of the claim.	Congress.	Session.	How brought before the House of Reps.	Page of journal.	To what committee of the House referred.	No. or date of the report.	Nature of the report.	No. of the bill.	How disposed of by the House of Reps.	How disposed of by the Senate.	Date of the act of Congress, and remarks.
Beamish, Henry	Remission of forfeiture incurred under revenue laws.	24	1	Petition	612	Commerce	643	Favorable	618	Referred to Committee Whole House.		
Beamish, Henry	Remission of forfeiture incurred under revenue laws.	25	2	Petition	40	Commerce	78	Favorable	93	Passed	Indef. postp'd.	
Beamish, Henry	Remission of forfeiture incurred under revenue laws.	25	3	Petition	457	Commerce.						
Beamish, Henry	Remission of forfeiture incurred under revenue laws.	26	1	Petition	292	Commerce.						
Beams, Betsey	(See John McGilbry & others.)	22	1		264							
Bean, Benjamin	To be restored and continued on pension roll.	17	1	Petition	30	Rev. Pensions.						
Bean, Charles, and others	Compensation for enforcing embargo act.	11	2	Petition	215	Claims	April 9, 1810	Favorable	132	Referred to Committee Whole House.		
Bean, Charles, and others	Compensation for enforcing embargo act.	11	3	Petition	456	Claims.						
Bean, Ebenezer	Pension	4	1	Report of Secretary of War.	447	Claims	Feb. 18, 1796	Favorable	156	Passed	Passed with amendment.	App'd April 20, 1796
Bean, Ebenezer	Increase of pension	13	1	Pension bill	56	Whole House	July 20, 1813	Pension bill	31	Passed	Passed with amendment.	App'd Aug. 2, 1813
Bean, Elizabeth	(See widow of Job Kenniston)	23	1		127							
Bean, James	Increase of pension	24	2	Petition	117	Invalid Pensions	Jan. 5, 1837	Adverse		Laid on table.		
Bean, John, (Me.)	Pension for revolutionary services.	3	1	Report of Secretary of War.	131	Select	May 26, 1794	Pension bill	62	Passed	Passed	App'd June 7, 1794
Bean, John, (Md.)	Pension for revolutionary services.	3	2	Rep. of Secretary War.	262	Claims	Feb. 28, 1795	Pension bill	130	Passed	Postponed.	
Bean, John, (Md.)	Pension for revolutionary services.	4	1	Rep. of Secretary of War.	445	Claims	Feb. 18, 1796	Pension bill	156	Passed	Passed with amendment.	App'd April 20, 1796
Bean, Jonathan L.	Compensation for establishing Indian boundary lines.	24	2	Petition	160	Claims	Feb. 16, 1837	Adverse		Laid on table.		
Bean, Jonathan L.	Compensation for establishing Indian boundary lines.	24	2	Appropriat'n bill	100	Whole House	Jan. 31, 1837	Amended	757	Passed	Passed	App'd March 3, 1837
Bean, Jonathan, widow of	(See Jonathan Been).											
Bean, Mark & R. H.	Compensation for supplies to Creek Indians.	21	1	House bill	685				480	Referred to Committee Whole House.		
Bean, Mark & R. H.	Compensation for supplies to Creek Indians.	21	2	House bill	142				480	Passed	Passed	App'd Jan. 27, 1831
Bean, Nicholas G.	Bounty land for military services	21	1	Petition	71	Military Affairs				Discharged; laid on table.		
Bean, Oliver	Pension	24	1	Petition	188	Invalid Pensions	June 23, 1836	Adverse		Laid on table.		
Bean, Rhoda	Continuation of pension	25	2	Resolution	107	Rev. Pensions				Disch'd, and ref. to C. W. H. on bill 456.		
Bean, Richard, surety of	Release from liability	25	2	Petition	279	Judiciary	Feb. 6, 1838	Adverse, verbal		Laid on table.		
Bean, Sarah	(See William Bean, widow of)	26	1		283							
Bean, Thomas	Pension	21	1	Petition	498	Military Pensons.						
Bean, William, widow of	To be restored to pension roll	26	1	Petition	283	Rev. Pensions				Discharged; leave to withdraw.		
Bear, John	(See assignee of J. Anderson)	15	2		67							
Bear, John	(See heirs of Francis Valle)	15	2		47							
Bear, Michael, assignees of	Reimbursement of duty on stills	17	2	Petition	100	Ways and Means.						
Beard, Archibald, & others	Compensation for use of horses; Florida war.	30	1	Petition	239	Claims	597	Favorable	478	Passed	Passed, with amendment.	App'd Aug. 7, 1848
Beard, Archibald, & others	To extend provisions of act of 1848	31	2	Resolution	64	Military Affairs	32	Favorable	304	Referred to Committee Whole House.		

List of private claims presented to the House of Representatives of the United States from the 1st to the 31st Congress, inclusive—Continued.

Names of claimants.	Nature or object of the claim.	Congress.	Session.	How brought before the House of Reps.	Page of journal.	To what committee of the House referred.	No. or date of the report.	Nature of the report.	No. of the bill.	How disposed of by the House of Reps.	How disposed of by the Senate.	Date of the act of Congress, and remarks.
Beard, Betty H.	(See heirs of Dr. John Gray)	25	2		120							
Beard, David, and others	Compensation for gun-powder, &c. at Detroit.	14	1	Petition	125	Ways and Means.						
Beard, David, and others	Compensation for gun-powder, &c. at Detroit.	15	1	Petition	272	Ways and Means.						
Beard, David, and others	Compensation for gun powder, &c. at Detroit.	16	1	Petition	141	Ways and Means				Discharged; leave to withdraw.		
Beard, David, and others	Compensation for gun-powder, &c. at Detroit.	16	2	Petition	63	Ways and Means.						
Beard, David, and others	Compensation for gun-powder, &c. at Detroit.	17	2	Petition	121	Ways and Means.						
Beard, David, and others	Compensation for gun-powder, &c. at Detroit.	19	1	Petition	150	Ways and Means	April 20, 1826	Adverse		Laid on table.		
Beard, David, assignee of	Compensation for gun-powder, &c. at Detroit.	24	1	Petition	851	Claims	713	Adverse		Laid on table.		
Beard, David, assignee of	Compensation for gun-powder, &c. at Detroit.	25	2	Petition	121	Claims.						
Beard, David, assignee of	Compensation for gun-powder, &c. at Detroit.	25	3	Petition	86	Claims	49	Adverse		Laid on table.		
Beard, David, assignee of	Compensation for gun-powder, &c. at Detroit.	26	1	Petition	168	Claims	41	Adverse		Laid on table.		
Beard, David, assignee of	Compensation for gun-powder, &c., at Detroit.	27	2	Petition	268	Claims	764	Adverse		Laid on table.		
Beard, David	Indemnity for illegal seizure of goods.	18	1	Petition	132	Claims	85	Favorable	158	Passed	Passed	App'd May 17, 1824
Beard, David	Balance due for illegal seizure of goods.	21	1	Senate bill	646	Ways and Means	April 26, 1830	With't amend.	S. 112	Passed	Passed	App'd May 31, 1830
Beard, David	Indemnity for property illegally condemned.	23	2	Senate bill	428	Judiciary	Feb. 24, 1835	With amend.	S. 95	Referred to Committee Whole House.		
Beard, David	Indemnity for property illegally condemned.	24	1	Senate bill Memorial	320 407	Judiciary Judiciary.	July 2, 1836	Adverse	S. 59	Referred to Committee Whole House.		
Beard, Eliza	(See David Beard)	24	1		407							
Beard, Harriet	(See James, Beard, widow of)	25	2		176							
Beard, Henry, *et al.*	Confirmation of title to Indian lands.	18	2	Petition	252	Indian Affairs				Discharged; laid on table.		
Beard, Hugh	Correction of an entry of land	22	1	Petition	190	Priv. Land Claims.	229	Favorable	307	Referred to Committee Whole House.		
Beard, Hugh	Correction of an entry of land	22	2	Rep't Committee Whole House	336			With't amend.	307	Passed	Passed	App'd Mar. 2, 1833
Beard, James, widow of	Indemnity for property destroyed; war of 1812.	25	2	Petition	176	Claims.						
Beard, James, widow of	Indemnity for property destroyed; war of 1812.	26	1	Petition	168	Claims	367	Adverse		Laid on table.		
Beard, Matilda W.	(See Wm. C. Beard, widow of)	30	2		126							
Beard, Moses	Pension for revolutionary services	22	1	Resolution	249	Rev. Pensions.						
Beard, Nathan	Redemption of Continental money	27	3	Petition	394	Rev. Claims.						
Beard, Nathan	Redemption of Continental money	28	1	Petition	72	Rev. Claims.						
Beard, Nathan	Redemption of Continental money	29	1	Petition	58	Rev. Claims	May 4, 1846	Adverse		Laid on table.		
Beard, Nathan	Redemption of Continental money	29	2	Petition	150	Rev. Claims.						
Beard, Nathan	Redemption of Continental money	30	1	Petition	239	Rev. Claims	360	Adverse		Laid on table.		
Beard, Nathan	Redemption of Continental money	31	1	Petition	632	Rev. Claims.						
Beard, Parthenia	(See assignee of David Beard)	24	1		851							
Beard, Samuel	(See assignee of David Beard)											

List of private claims presented to the House of Representatives of the United States from the 1st to the 31st Congress, inclusive—Continued.

Names of claimants.	Nature or object of the claim.	Congress.	Session.	How brought before the House of Reps.	Page of journal.	To what committee of the House referred.	No. or date of the report.	Nature of the report.	No. of the bill.	How disposed of by the House of Reps.	How disposed of by the Senate.	Date of the act of Congress, and remarks.
Beard, Stephen	(See heirs of Dr. John Gray)	25	2		120							
Beard, William	Indemnity for property destroyed by the enemy.	17	1	Petition	161	Claims.						
Beard, William	Indemnity for property destroyed by the enemy.	18	1	Petition	131	Claims	Jan. 28, 1824	Adverse		Recommitted.		
Beard, William	Pension for revolutionary services.	24	1	Petition	513	Rev. Pensions				Discharged; laid on table.		
Beard, William	Pension for revolutionary services.	27	2	Petition	139	Rev. Pensions	784	Adverse		Laid on table.		
Beard, William	Pension for revolutionary services.	29	1	Memorial	326	Rev. Pensions	271	Favorable	238	Rejected.		
Beard, William C.	Pension	21	1	Petition	523	Military Pensions.						
Beard, William C.	Pension	22	1	Petition	569	Invalid Pensions.						
Beard, William C.	Pension	22	2	Petition	124	Invalid Pensions.						
Beard, William C.	Pension	23	1	Petition	368	Invalid Pensions				Discharged; laid on table.		
Beard, William C.	Pension	23	2	Petition	198	Invalid Pensions	73	Favorable	693	Passed	Adverse report.	
Beard, William C.	Pension	24	1	Petition	275	Invalid Pensions	336	Favorable	351	Referred to Committee Whole House.		
Beard, William C.	Pension	24	2	House bill	198				351	Passed	Passed	App'd March 3, 1837
Beard, William C., widow of.	Extension of pension	30	2	Memorial	126	Rev. Pensions	Feb. 13, 1849	Adverse		Laid on table.		
Beardon, John, heirs of	Indemnity for property destroyed by United States troops.	30	1	Senate bill	361	Judiciary	Feb. 29, 1848	With't amend.	S. 48	Laid on table.		
Beardon, John, heirs of	Indemnity for property destroyed by United States troops.	30	2	Senate bill	625	Whole House	Mar. 3, 1849	With amend.	S. 48	Passed with amendm't	Passed as am'd.	App'd March 3, 1849
Beardsley, Ichabod	Pension for revolutionary services.	24	1	Petition	944	Rev. Pensions.						
Beardsley, Ichabod	Pension for revolutionary services.	24	2	Petition	217	Rev. Pensions	158	Favorable	885	Referred to Committee Whole House.		
Beardsley, Ichabod	Pension for revolutionary services.	25	2	Petition	37	Rev. Pensions	170	Favorable	195	Passed	Adverse report.	
Beardsley, Ichabod	Pension for revolutionary services.	25	3	Petition	87	Rev. Pensions	67	Favorable	945	Passed	Adverse report.	
Beardsley, Ichabod	Pension for revolutionary services.	26	1	Petition	170	Rev. Pensions	138	Favorable	148	Passed	Passed	App'd July 20, 1840
Beardsley, Jerome J	Compensation for military services.	26	1	Petition	711	Military Affairs.						
Beardsley, Jerome J	Compensation for military services.	26	-2	Petition	36	Military Affairs.						
Beardsley, John jr.,	Increase of pension	10	1	Pension bill	232	Whole House	April 19, 1808	With amend.	78	Passed	Passed with amendment.	App'd April 25, 1808
Beardsley, Moses	Pension for revolutionary services.	25	2	Petition	586	Rev. Pensions				Discharged; laid on table.		
Beare, Thomas	(See Bernard Rogan and others)	17	1		55							
Beares, Henry	Indemnity for loss on a contract	30	1	Petition	959	Claims.						
Beares, Henry	Indemnity for loss on a contract	30	2	Petition	270	Claims.						
Bearing, James	Confirmation of title to land in Missouri.	15	2	Petition	207	Priv. Land Claims.						
Bearing, James	Confirmation of title to land in Missouri.	17	1	Petition	53	Priv. Land Claims.						
Bearly, Henry	Compensation for revolutionary services.	15	2	Petition	190	Rev. Pensions	Jan. 21, 1819	Adverse		Claim rejected.		
Bearsticker, Andrew	Extra pay as revolutionary artificer	4	1	Petition	447	Claims	May 11, 1796	Adverse		Laid on table.		
Beatey, Alexander	Pension for revolutionary services.	16	1	Petition	221	Rev. Pensions	April 22, 1820	Adverse		Laid on table.		
Beaty, Adam	Exchange of a land entry	24	1	Petition	215	Public Lands				Discharged; laid on table.		
Beatty, Charles A.	Special act of insolvency	7	1	Petition	153	Select	April 1, 1802	Favorable		Referred to Committee Whole House.		
Beatty, C. C.	(See administrator of James Vanuxen.)	29	2		235							
Beatty, Edward	Permission to purchase land with Treasury certificates.	25	2	Petition	1030	Public Lands	July 6, 1838	Favorable	R. 26	Referred to Committee Whole House.		

List of private claims presented to the House of Representatives of the United States from the 1st to the 31st Congress, inclusive—Continued.

Names of claimants.	Nature or object of the claim.	Congress.	Session.	How brought before the House of Reps.	Page of journal.	To what committee of the House referred.	No. or date of the report.	Nature of the report.	No. of the bill.	How disposed of by the House of Reps.	How disposed of by the Senate.	Date of the act of Congress, and remarks.
Beatty, Edward	Permission to purchase land with Treasury certificates.	25	3	Rep't Committee Whole House.	433	With't amendm't.	....	....	R. 26	Passed	Passed	App'd March 3, 1839
Beatty, Francis G	Indemnity for injuries received at Treasury building.	28	1	Petition	149	Dist. of Columbia.						
Beatty, Francis G.	Indemnity for injuries received at Treasury building.	29	1	Petition	701	Claims.						
Beatty, Hecter St. John.	Pension	31	1	Resolution	491	Invalid Pensions.						
Beatty, Henry	Pension for revolutionary services.	24	1	Petition	433	Rev. Pensions	....	....	......	Discharged; laid on table.		
Beatty, John	(See heirs of John Carr)	29	1	....	91							
Beatty, John, (Ky.)	Increase of pension for revolutionary services.	25	3	Resolution	275	Rev. Pensions.						
Beatty, Thomas, agent of.	Compensation for horse lost in Seminole war.	28	1	Petition	262	Claims						
Beatty, William, heirs of.	Half pay for revolutionary services	23	1	Petition	377	Rev. Claims.						
Beatty, Zacheus A	Right of pre-emption.	20	1	Petition	244	Whole House.						
Beaubien, Jean Marie	Indemnity for property destroyed by the enemy.	19	2	Petition	159	Claims	....	....	......	Discharged; laid on table.		
Beaubien, Josette and children.	Permission to locate certain lands.	23	2	Petition	138	Priv. Land Claims.						
Beaubien, Josette and children.	Permission to locate certain lands.	24	1	Petition	65	Priv. Land Claims.						
				Senate bill	899	Indian Affairs	June 18, 1836	With't amend.	127	Passed	Passed	App'd July 2, 1836
Beaubien, J. B. and others	Confirmation of claim to military reservation at Fort Dearborn.	25	3	Document	305	....	....	....	......	Laid on table.		
Beaudreaux, Catharine, heirs of.	Confirmation of land title.	13	3	Petition	674	Public Lands.						
Beaudreaux, Jean B., heirs of.	Confirmation of title to land in Missouri territory.	13	3	Petition	674	Public Lands.						
Beaudreaux, Jean B., heirs of	Confirmation of title to land in Missouri territory.	14	1	Petition	55	Public Lands.						
Beaudreaux, Jean B., heirs of.	Confirmation of title to land in Missouri territory.	14	2	Petition	51	Public Lands.						
Beaudreaux, Jean B., heirs of.	Confirmation of title to land in Missouri territory.	15	1	Petition	115	Priv. Land Claims.						
Beaudreaux, Jean B., heirs of.	Confimation of title to land in Missouri territory.	17	1	Petition	361	Public Lands.						
Beaudreaux, Jeau B., heirs of.	Confirmation of title to land in Missouri territory.	17	2	Petition	27	Priv. Land Claims.						
Beaudreaux, Jean B., heirs of.	Confirmation of title to land in Missouri territory.	18	1	Petition	28	Priv. Land Claims.	Jan. 2, 1824	Adverse	......	Laid on table.		
Beaudreaux, Jean B., heirs of.	Confirmation of title to land in Missouri territory.	20	1	Petition	312	Priv. Land Claims.						
Beauford, Thomas	(See Thomas Buford)	16	2	....	27							
Beaugrand, John B	(See Gabrial Godfroy, *et al.*)	21	1	....	62							
Beaugrond, Jean B	Indemnity for property destroyed by the enemy.	15	1	Petition	195	Claims.						
Beaugrond, Jean B	Indemnity for property destroyed by the enemy.	16	1	Petition	106	Claims.						
Beaugrond, Jean B	Indemnity for property destroyed by the enemy.	16	2	Petition	120	Claims	33	Adverse	......	Referred to Committee Whole House.		
Beaugrond, Jean B	Indemnity for property destroyed by the enemy.	17	1	Petition	47	Claims.						
Beaugrond, Jean B	Indemnity for property destroyed by the enemy.	20	2	Petition	66	Claims.						

List of private claims presented to the House of Representatives of the United States from the 1st to the 31st Congress, inclusive—Continued.

Names of claimants.	Nature or object of the claim.	Congress.	Session.	How brought before the House of Reps.	Page of journal.	To what committee of the House referred.	No. or date of the report.	Nature of the report.	No. of the bill.	How disposed of by the House of Reps.	How disposed of by the Senate.	Date of the act of Congress, and remarks.
Beaugrond, Jean B	Indemnity for property destroyed by the enemy.	21	1	Petition	93	Claims.						
Beaugrond, Jean B	Indemnity for property destroyed by the enemy.	21	2	Petition	62	Claims	35	Favorable	556	Referred to Committee Whole House.		
Beaugrond, Jean B	Indemnity for property destroyed by the enemy.	22	1	Petition	26	Claims	Jan. 4, 1832	Favorable	199	Referred to Committee Whole House.		
Beaugrond, Jean B.	Indemnity for property destroyed by the enemy.	22	2	Rep't Committee Whole House.	66			With't amend.	199	Passed	Passed	App'd Feb. 9, 1833
Beaugrond, J. B., heirs of.	Execution of 6th article Wyandot treaty.	30	1	Petition	214	Indian Affairs.						
Beaulieu, Lewis Joseph	Pension for revolutionary services.	3	1	Petition	20							
				Rep. of Secretary War.	93	Select.	April 22, 1794	Adverse		Laid on table.		
Beaulieu, Lewis Joseph	Pension for revolutionary services.	4	1	Petition	387	Claims.	Jan. 26, 1796	Adverse		Leave to withdraw.		
Beaulieu, Lewis Joseph	Pension for revolutionary services.	14	2	Document	316	Pens. & Rev. Cl'ms.	Jan. 31, 1817	Adverse		Leave to withdraw.		
Beaulieu, Lewis Joseph	Pension for revolutionary services.	15	2	Petition	103	Rev. Pensions.	Jan. 21, 1819	Favorable	289	Laid on table.		
Beaulieu, Lewis Joseph	Pension for revolutionary services.	16	1	Petition		Rev. Pensions	5	Favorable	6	Passed	Rejected.	
Beaulieu, Lewis Joseph	Pension for revolutionary services.	18	1	Petition	28	Pens. & Rev. Cl'ms.	Feb. 19, 1824	Adverse		Laid on table.		
Beaulieu, Lewis Joseph	Ten years commutation of pension	4	1	Petition	454	Claims	May 31, 1796	Adverse		Laid on table.		
Beaulieu, Lewis Joseph	Indemnity for wounds received in revolutionary war.	20	2	Pet'n and Doc'nt	240					Laid on table.		
Beaumarchais, Amelie E.	(See heir of Caron de Beaumarchais.)	9	1		212							
Beaumont, Edmund	Release from imprisonment	10	2	Petition	364	Select	Dec. 27, 1808	Favorable	127	Passed	Passed	App'd Jan. 30, 1809
Beaumont, Isaiah	Pension for revolutionary services.	3	1	Rep. of Secretary War.	131	Select	May 26, 1794	Res. to refer to Sec'y War.	R. 12	Passed	Passed	App'd June 9, 1794
Beaumont, Margaret	Indemnity for destruction of property at Plattsburgh.	13	3	Petition	723	Claims	Feb. 15, 1815	Favorable	297	Passed	Passed	App'd March 3, 1815
Beauregarde, Gab. Emil.	(See widow of De Beauregarde)	18	1		28							
Beauvais, Jean Baptiste	(See heirs of Francis Valle)	15	2		28							
Beauvais, St. Jemme	(See heirs of Francis Valle)	15	2		28							
Beauvois, Antoine	Confirmation of title to land in Arkansas.	22	2	House bill	421				425	Passed	Passed	App'd June 25, 1832
Beauvois, St. Jam	Confirmation of title to land at Kaskaskia.	1	3	Senate bill	352				S. 15	Passed	Passed	App'd March 3, 1791
Beaver, Black	Compensation for services of Indian volunteers.	31	1	Petition	197	Military Affairs	Jan. 22, 1850	Favorable	6	Passed	Passed	App'd Sept. 28, 1850
Beaver, Daniel	Compensation for supplies furnished on public account.	30	1	Petition	656	Military Affairs.						
Beaver, John	Reimbursement of an over payment for land.	21	2	Petition	211	Public Lands	Feb. 21, 1831	Adverse		Laid on table.		
Beaver, Matthias	(See Joseph F. Law.)	30	2		296							
Bebee, Silas, *et al.*	Fishing bounty	20	2	Petition	48	Commerce	Jan. 26, 1829	Adverse		Laid on table.		
Beck, Charles	Pension for disability incurred in United States Navy.	29	1	Petition	1031	Invalid Pensions.						
Beck, Hannah W.	(See John Barbrick, daughter of).	29	1		227							
Beck, Jacob	Pension for revolutionary services.	3	2	Petition	332	Claims.						
Beck, Jacob	Pension for revolutionary services.	4	1	Resolution	373	Claims	Jan. 8, 1796	Adverse		Laid on table.		
Beck, John	Pension for revolutionary services.	25	2	Resolution	213	Rev. Pensions.						
Beck, John	Pension for revolutionary services.	25	3	Resolution	88	Rev. Pensions.						
Beck, John	Pension for revolutionary services.	26	1	Petition	172	Rev. Pensions				Discharged; laid on table.		

List of private claims presented to the House of Representatives of the United States from the 1st to the 31st Congress, inclusive—Continued.

Names of claimants.	Nature or object of the claim.	Congress.	Session.	How brought before the House of Reps.	Page of journal.	To what committee of the House referred.	No. or date of the report.	Nature of the report.	No. of the bill.	How disposed of by the House of Reps.	How disposed of by the Senate.	Date of the act of Congress, and remarks.
Beck, John	To be restored to pension roll	27	3	Petition	131	Rev. Pensions	162	Favorable	778	Referred to Committee Whole House.		
Beck, John J.	Compensation for horse killed at Tippecanoe.	24	1	Petition	264	Claims	361	Adverse	......	Laid on table.		
Beck, John J.	Compensation for horse killed at Tippecanoe.	28	1	Petition	74	Claims	44	Adverse	......	Laid on table.		
				Documents	279	Claims	136	Adverse	......	Laid on table.		
Beck, Joseph W.	Compensation as assistant postmaster Ho. of Representatives.	26	1	Resolution	1325	....	....	....	......	Rejected.		
Beck, Paul, and J. Harvey	Reimbursement of duties paid on copper.	15	2	Petition	94	Com. and Manufac.						
Beck, Paul, and J. Harvey	Reimbursement of duties paid on copper.	16	1	Petition	29	Commerce	Dec. 16, 1819	Favorable	10	Passed	Passed	App'd May 8, 1820
Beck, Paul, jr.	Indemnity for French spoliations prior to 1800.	26	1	Memorial	182	Foreign Affairs	343	Favorable	319	Referred to Committee Whole House.		
Beck, Richard	Compensation for services at Monterey, Mexico.	31	1	Petition	1215	Claims.						
Beck, Samuel	Compensation for rifles furnished on public account.	24	1	Petition	912	Indian Affairs.						
Beck, Samuel	Compensation for rifles furnished on public account.	24	2	Petition	392	Indian Affairs.						
Beck, Samuel	Compensation for rifles furnished on public account.	25	2	Petition	595	Indian Affairs	....	....	......	Discharged; laid on table.		
Becker, Henry	Pension	21	1	Senate bill	646	Military Pensions	Mar. 21, 1830	With amend.	136	Referred to Committee Whole House.		
Becker, Henry	Pension	21	2	Senate bill	106	Military Pensions	Dec. 31, 1830	With amend.	27	Passed	Passed	App'd Mar. 2, 1831
Becker, Jacob	To be restored to pension roll	25	2	Petition	231	Rev. Pensions	607	Favorable	587	Passed.		
Becker, Jacob	To be restored to pension roll	26	1	Petition	171	Rev. Pensions	110	Favorable	121	Passed	Passed	App'd July 20, 1840
Becker, John	(See heirs of A. Briggs)	23	1	....	215							
Becker, John P.	Pension	24	1	Petition	56	Rev. Pensions	376	Favorable	378	Referred to Committee Whole House.		
Becker, John P.	Pension	24	2	House bill	198	....	....	....	378	Passed	Passed with amendment	App'd Mar. 3, 1837
Becker, John P.	Increase of pension	25	2	Resolution	101	Rev. Pensions	....	....	......	Discharged; laid on table.		
Becker, John P.	Increase of pension	6	1	Petition	307	Rev. Pensions	714	Adverse	......	Laid on table.		
Becker, Maria B.	(See widow of Joel Brown)	30	1	....	460							
Becker, Thankful T.	(See widow of Jeduthan Thompson.)	27	2	....	105							
Beckett, Charles	Pension	20	1	Petition	440	Military Pensions.						
Beckett, Humphrey	Pension for revolutionary services	10	1	Pension bill	232	Whole House	Mar. 17, 1808	With amend.	81	Passed	Passed	App'd April 25, 1808
Beckett, Humphrey	Increase of pension	17	1	Petition	238	Pens. & Rev. Cl'ms.	Mar. 1, 1822	Adverse	......	Leave to withdraw.		
Beckett, Humphrey	Increase of pension	18	2	Petition	159	Pens. & Rev. Cl'ms.	....	....	......	Discharged; laid on table.		
Beckett, Humphrey	Increase of pension	20	1	Petition	37	Military Pensions.						
Beckett, Humphrey	Increase of pension	21	1	Petition	47	Military Pensions	Feb. 13, 1830	Pension bill	72	Passed	Passed, with amendment.	App'd May 20, 1830
Beckett, Humphrey	Arrears of pension	21	2	Petition	85	Military Pensions	50	Favorable	582	Passed.		
Beckett, Humphrey	Arrears of pension	22	1	Petition	58	Rev. Pensions	Dec. 21, 1831	Favorable	66	Passed	Indef. postp'd.	
Beckett, Humphrey, widow of.	Arrears of pension	23	2	Petition	345	Rev. Claims.						
Beckett, Humphrey	Bounty land for revolutionary services.	11	3	Petition	505	Claims.						

List of private claims presented to the House of Representatives of the United States from the 1st to the 31st Congress, inclusive—Continued.

Names of claimants.	Nature or object of the claim.	Congress.	Session.	How brought before the House of Reps.	Page of journal.	To what committee of the House referred.	No. or date of the report.	Nature of the report.	No. of the bill.	How disposed of by the House of Reps.	How disposed of by the Senate.	Date of the act of Congress, and remarks.
Beckett, Humphrey	Bounty land for revolutionary services.	13	3	Petition	652	Public Lands				Discharged; laid on table.		
Beckett, Humphrey	Bounty land for revolutionary services.	18	2	Petition	159	Public Lands.						
Becket, William	Compensation for horses lost in Black Hawk war.	25	3	Petition	205	Claims	207	Adverse		Laid on table.		
Beckford, Benjamin, and others.	Location of land in lieu of sixteenth section.	26	1	Petition	608	Public Lands.						
Beckham, Armistead	Increase of compensation as armorer at Harper's Ferry.	19	2	Petition	189	Military Affairs.						
Beckham, Armistead	Increase of compensation as armorer at Harper's Ferry.	20	1	Petition	57	Military Affairs.						
Beckham, William, widow of.	Pension	20	1	Resolution	49	Military Pensions	232	Favorable	259	Passed	Passed	App'd May 24, 1828
Beckham, Rebecca	(See widow of William Gray)	26	1		322							
Beckit, Humphrey	Pension	21	1	Pension bill	130	Whole House	Feb. 12, 1830	With amend.	72	Passed	Passed with amendment.	App'd May 20, 1830
Beckley, Philippina, heirs of.	Right of pre-emption	11	2	Petition	227	Public Lands	Mar. 20, 1810	Adverse		Rejected.		
Becktle	(See Riddle, Becktle & Headington)	23	1		259							
Beckwith, Abner	Pension	16	1	Petition	139							
				Report of Secretary of War.	350					Laid on table.		
Beckwith, Benjamin	Pension	2[illegible]	2	Petition	53	Military Pensions.						
Beckwith, Gurden, widow of.	Bounty land and arrears of pay	24	1	Petition	662	Public Lands	766	Adverse to arrears of pay.				
Beckwith, Gurden, widow of.	Bounty land and arrears of pay	25	2	Petition	174	Public Lands.						
Beckwith, Wealthy	(See Gurden Beckwith, widow of)	24	1		662							
Bedel, Hazen	Exchange of an entry of land	21	1	Petition	140	Priv. Land Claims.						
Bedel, Hazen	Exchange of an entry of land	21	2	Petition	189	Priv. Land Claims.						
Bedford, Drayton P	Confirmation of title to land in Louisiana.	22	1	Petition	417	Priv. Land Claims.	Mar. 1, 1832	Adverse		Laid on table.		
Bedford, Drayton P	(See heir of Thomas B. Bedford)	25	2		281							
Bedford, John	Compensation for military services.	15	1	Petition	247	Claims				Discharged; laid on table.		
Bedford, Joseph	Compensation for public services	1	2	Petition	221					Referred to Secretary Treasury.		
Bedford, Joseph	Compensation for public services	3	1	Rep. of Secretary of Treasury.	77					Laid on table.		
Bedford, Robert	Compensation for horses lost in public service.	18	2	Petition	36	Claims	15	Adverse		Laid on table.		
Bedford, Thos. B., heirs of	Confirmation of land title	25	2	Petition	281	Priv. Land Claims.	600	Adverse		Laid on table.		
Bedford, William H., agent	Compensation for horses lost in Seminole war.	28	1	Petition	262	Claims.						
Bedinger, Daniel	Increase of compensation as armorer at Harper's Ferry.	22	2	Petition	138	Military Affairs.						
Bedinger, George M	Pension for revolutionary services.	25	2	Resolution	525	Rev. Pensions.						
Bedinger, George M	Pension for revolutionary services.	26	1	Petition	172	Rev. Pensions	464	Favorable	378	Referred to Committee Whole House.		
Bedinger, George M	Pension for revolutionary services.	27	2	Petition	328	Rev. Pensions	154	Favorable	201	Passed	Passed	App'd July 27, 1842
Bedinger, Henry	Arrears of pay, &c., as revolutionary officer.	16	1	Petition	106	Pens. & Rev. Cl'ms	53	Adverse		Laid on table.		

List of private claims presented to the House of Representatives of the United States from the 1st to the 31st Congress, inclusive—Continued.

Names of claimants.	Nature or object of the claim.	Congress.	Session.	How brought before the House of Reps.	Page of journal.	To what committee of the House referred.	No. or date of the report.	Nature of the report.	No. of the bill.	How disposed of by the House of Reps.	How disposed of by the Senate.	Date of the act of Congress, and remarks.
Bedinger, Henry	Arrears of pay, &c., as revolutionary officer.	21	1	Petition	320	Rev. Claims.						
Bedinger, Henry	Arrears of pay, &c., as revolutionary officer.	21	2	Petition	137	Rev. Claims.						
Bedinger, Henry	Arrears of pay, &c., as revolutionary officer.	22	1	Petition	107	Rev. Claims				Discharged; laid on table.		
Bedinger, Henry	Arrears of pay, &c., as revolutionary officer.	23	2	Petition	106	Rev. Claims.						
Bedinger, Henry	Arrears of pay, &c., as revolutionary officer.	24	1	Petition	138	Rev. Claims				Discharged; laid on table.		
Bedinger, Henry	Arrears of pay, &c., as revolutionary officer.	24	2	Petition	126	Rev. Claims.						
Bedinger, Henry	Arrears of pay, &c., as revolutionary officer.	27	2	Petition	936	Rev. Claims	971	Adverse		Laid on table.		
Bedinger, Henry	(See W. Somerville, surety of.)	19	1		129							
Beddinger, James	Compensation as fireman on board public steamer.	31	1	Petition	255	Claims	410	Adverse		Laid on table.		
Bedlow, William	Eextension of time on a judgment favor United States.	1	2	Petition	171	Select.						
Bedsole, Rebecca	(See Seth Sterling, heirs of.)	30	1	Petition	807	Rev. Pensions.						
Bee, Hamilton P.	Reimbursement of money expended on public account.	31	1	Petition		Military Affairs				Discharged; laid on table.		
Beebe, Bezaleel	Pension	16	1	Petition	65	Rev. Pensions	Jan. 14, 1820	Adverse		Laid on table.		
Beebe, Ezekiel	To be restored to pension roll	17	1	Petition	37	Rev. Pensions.						
Beebe, Ezekiel	To be restored to pension roll	17	2	Petition	59	Rev. Pensions.						
Beebe, Jason	Increase of pension	8	1	Petition	435	Claims	Feb. 28, 1804	Adverse.		Leave to withdraw.		
Beebe, Jason, widow of	Pension for revolutionary services.	26	2	Petition	82	Rev. Pensions.						
Beebe, Jason, widow of	Pension for revolutionary services.	27	2	Petition	60	Invalid Pensions.	1008	Adverse.		Laid on table.		
Beebe, Paul	Pension	13	1	Pension bill	56	Whole House	July 20, 1813	With amend.	31	Passed	Passed with amendment.	App'd Aug. 2, 1813
Beebe, Samuel	Liquidation of certificate of public debt.	8	2	Petition	6	Ways and Means.						
Beebe, Samuel	Liquidation of certificate of public debt.	9	1	Petition	196	Ways and Means.	Jan. 8, 1806	Favorable		Referred to Committee Whole House.		
Beebe, Samuel	Liquidation of certificate of public debt.	9	2	Petition	513	Ways and Means.	Jan. 2, 1807	Favorable	180	Indefinite postponed.		
Beebe, Samuel	Liquidation of certificate of public debt.	10	1	Petition	14	Ways and Means.	Jan. 15, 1808	Favorable	38	Passed	Passed with amendment	App'd March 11, 1808
Beebe, Silas and others	Bounty on fishing schooner	20	2	Petition	48	Commerce	Jan. 21, 1829	Adverse.		Laid on table.		
Beebe, Thaddeus	Indemnity for revolutionary injuries.	1	2	Petition	267					Referred to Secretary of War.		
Beebe, Thaddeus	Indemnity for revolutionary injuries.	1	3	Rep. of Secretary War.	393					Laid on table.		
Beebe, Thaddeus	Indemnity for revolutionary injuries.	3	1	Report of Secretary of War.	131	Select.	May 26, 1794	Res. to refer to Sec. War.	R. 12	Passed	Passed	App'd June 9, 1794
Beebe, Thaddeus	Indemnity for revolutionory injuries.	4	1	Report of Secretary of War.	373	Claims.						
Beebe, Washington T. or S.	Indemnity for property lost in Mexico.	30	1	Petition	718	Claims.						
Beebe, Washington T or S.	Indemnity for property lost in Mexico.	30	2	Petition	302	Claims	41	Favorable	731	Referred to Committee Whole House.		
Beecher, Thankful T.	(See Thankful T. Becker.)	27	2		105							
Beechy, Elizabeth W.	(See M. McDonald, daughter of.)	27	2		220							

List of private claims presented to the House of Representatives of the United States from the 1st to the 31st Congress, inclusive—Continued.

Names of claimants.	Nature or object of the claim.	Congress.	Session.	How brought before the House of Reps.	Page of journal.	To what committee of the House referred.	No. or date of the report.	Nature of the report.	No. of the bill.	How disposed of by the House of Reps.	How disposed of by the Senate.	Date of the act of Congress, and remarks.
Beekes, Benjamin, widow of.	Pension for revolutionary services.	29	1	Petition	462	Rev. Pensions	618	Adverse		Laid on table.		
Beekham Armstead	Increase of compensation as armorer Harper's Ferry.	19	2	Petition	189	Military Affairs.						
Beekham Armstead	Increase of compensation as armorer Harper's Ferry.	20	1	Petition	57	Military Affairs.						
Beekham, Wm., widow of	Pension for revolutionary services.	19	2	Resolution	150	Military Pensions.						
Beekman, Rebecca	(See widow of William Gray)	26	2		148							
Beekman, Samuel, widow of.	Compensation for revolutionary services.	25	2	Petition	632	Rev. Claims.						
Beekman, Theophilus E.	Pension	23	2	Documents	198	Invalid Pensions.						
Beekman, Theophilus E.	Pension	24	1	Petition	98	Invalid Pensions.	129	Favorable	139	Passed	Passed	App'd June 28, 1836
Beeler George	Pension for revolutionary services.	22	1	Resolution	301	Rev. Claims.	410	Favorable	510	Referred to Committee Whole House.		
Beeler, Louis F., and others	Mileage as volunteers in Mexican war.	30	1	Petition	115	Claims	482	Adverse		Laid on table.		
Beeman, Ebenezer	Pension	20	1	Petition	396	Military Pensions.						
Beeman, Ebenezer	Pension	21	1	Petition	47	Military Pensions	Jan. 5, 1830	Favorable	72	Passed	Passed with amendment.	App'd May 20, 1830
Beeman, Joseph	Compensation for services in the war of 1812.	20	1	Petition	255	Claims	Feb. 6, 1828	Adverse		Laid on table.		
Beeman, Joseph	Compensation for services in the war of 1812.	21	1	Petition	291	Claims	Mar. 5, 1830	Adverse		Laid on table.		
Beeman, Joseph	Compensation for services in the war of 1812.	25	2	Petition	177	Claims	April 17, 1838	Adverse		Laid on table.		Leave to withdraw 3d Session.
Beeman, Nathan	Land for revolutionary services	28	1	Petition	123	Rev. Claims.						
Beeman, Nathan	Land for revolutionary services	29	1	Petition	330	Rev. Claims.						
Beeman, Nathan	Land for revolutionary services	30	1	Petition	491	Rev. Claims.						
Beeman, Nathan	Land for revolutionary services	31	1	Petition	534	Rev. Claims.						
Beeman, Trueman	Pension for revolutionary services.	22	1	Petition	533	Rev. Pensions.						
Been, Jonathan	Pension	21	2	Petition	270	Military Pensions.						
Been, Jonathan	Pension	22	1	Petition	120	Invalid Pensions	177	Favorable	253	Passed	Laid on table.	
Been, Jonathan	Pension	22	2	Petition	52	Invalid Pensions	Dec. 19, 1832	Favorable	626	Passed	Rejected.	
Been, Jonathan	Pension	24	2	Petition	72	Invalid Pensions				Discharged; laid on table.		
Been, Jonathan	Pension	25	2	Petition	168	Invalid Pensions	Jan. 18, 1838	Adverse		Laid on table.		
				Petition, (2)	722	Invalid Pensions				Discharged; laid on table.		
Been, Jonathan	Pension	26	1	Petition	326	Invalid Pensions	July 21, 1840	Adverse		Laid on table		
Been, Jonathan	Pension	26	2	Petition	77	Invalid Pensions	148	Favorable	659	Referred to Committee Whole House.		
Been, Jonathan	Pension	27	2	Petition	60	Invalid Pensions	158	Adverse		Laid on table.		
Been, Jonathan	Pension	28	1	Petition	103	Invalid Pensions	13	Favorable	40	Rejected.		
				House bill	656	Invalid Pensions	April 12, 1844	With amend.	257	Passed.		
Been, Jonathan, widow of	Pension	28	2	Petition	250	Invalid Pensions.						
Been, Jonathan, widow of.	Pension	29	1	Petition	200	Invalid Pensions	828	Adverse		Laid on table		Leave to withdraw 31st Cong. 2d sess.
Been, Lydia	(See Jonathan Been, widow of)	28	2		250							
Beenees, Mercy	(See Mercy Bemis)	27	3		365							
Beern, Daniel S.	Compensation for horse lost in public service.	2	2	Petition	541	Claims.						
Beern, Daniel S.	Compensation for horse lost in public service.	25	3	Petition	207	Claims.						

List of private claims presented to the House of Representatives of the United States from the 1st to the 31st Congress, inclusive—Continued.

Names of claimants.	Nature or object of the claim.	Congress.	Session.	How brought before the House of Reps.	Page of journal.	To what committee of the House referred.	No. or date of the report.	Nature of the report.	No. of the bill.	How disposed of by the House of Reps.	How disposed of by the Senate.	Date of the act of Congress, and remarks.
Beers, Daniel	Pension for revolutionary services	20	1	Resolution	314	Military Pensions.						
Beers, Isaac	To be restored to pension roll	17	2	Petition	142	Whole House.						
Beers, James	Compensation for revolutionary services, &c.	2	1	Petition	444					Referred to Secretary War.		
Beers, James	Pension	3	1	Rep. of Secretary War.	131	Select	May 26, 1794	Res. to refer to Sec. War.	R. 12	Passed	Passed	App'd June 9, 1794
Beers, John	Arrears of pension	20	2	Petition	229	Military Pensions.						
Beers, John	Arrears of pension	21	1	Petition	294	Military Pensions	April 2, 1830	Adverse		Laid on table.		
Beers, Samuel	Compensation for recruiting services.	13	3	Petition	694	Claims.						
Beesley, Maurice, (Pa.)	Reimbursement of money paid in a certain suit.	5	2	Petition	271	Claims	July 13, 1798	Indefinite		Postponed.		
Beesley, Maurice, (Pa.)	Reimbursement of money paid in a certain suit.	5	3	Petition	421	Claims	Mar. 2, 1799	Indefinite		Postponed.		
Beeson, J. & W.	Compensation for supplies in Black Hawk war.	23	2	Senate bill	179	Military Affairs	Jan. 28, 1835	With amend.	S. 34	Referred to Committee Whole House.		
Beeson, J. & W.	Compensation for supplies in Black Hawk war.	25	3	Senate bill	653				S. 132			
Beetly, Hector St. J.	Arrears of pension	29	1	Petition	189	Invalid Pensions	82	Adverse		Laid on table.		
Beewalk, James, widow of.	Pension for revolutionary services	27	3	Petition	125	Rev. Pensions.						
Begbic, Wiseman, & Co.	Reimbursement of excessive duties	30	2	Petition	76	Claims	34	Favorable	726	Referred to Committee Whole House.		
Begbic, Wiseman, & Co.	Reimbursement of excessive duties	31	1	Petition	213	Claims.						
Begley, John, attorney of.	Compensation for revolutionary services.	10	1	Petition	140							
				Rep. of Secretary War.	166	Whole House			20	Laid on table.		
Behn, James B.	(See heir of John H. Behn)	29	2		330							
Behn, John H.	(See Mannhardt, Behn & Co.)	7	2		264							
Behn, John H, heir of.	Indemnity for French spoliations prior to 1800.	29	2	Petition	330	Claims.						
Behney, Peter, widow of.	Continuation of pension	27	3	Petition	70	Rev. Pensions				Discharged; laid on table.		
Beise, Frederick	(See John D. Needham and others)	15	1		136							
Belcher, Andrew	(See heir of Jeremiah Belcher)	19	1		128							
Belcher & Brothers	Reimbursement of duties on goods lost.	31	2	Petition	321	Commerce.						
Belcher, Fuller, administrator of.	Indemnity for French spoliations prior to 1800.	29	2	Petition	136	Foreign Affairs.						
Belcher, Jeremiah, heir of.	Compensation for revolutionary services.	19	1	Petition	128	Military Pensions	April 1, 1826	Adverse		Laid on table.		
Belcher, N., and others	Patents for land entered at Galena	27	2	Petition	132	Public Lands.						
Belcher, William, & others	Indemnity for a vessel destroyed by the enemy.	18	2	Petition	185	Naval Affairs.						
Belcher, William, & others	Indemnity for a vessel destroyed by the enemy.	19	1	Petition	67	Naval Affairs	Jan. 16, 1826	Adverse		Laid on table.		
Belden, Ebenezer	Indemnity for property destroyed by the enemy.	15	2	Petition	148	Claims	Jan. 16, 1819	Adverse		Laid on table.		
Belden, Thomas	Compensation for two vessels built on public account.	21	2	Resolution	101	Claims	92	Adverse		Laid on table.		
Belding, David	(See heirs of Moses Belding)	31	1		409							
Belding, Godfrey H.	Increase of pension	21	1	Petition	120	Military Pensions				Discharged; laid on table.		

List of private claims presented to the House of Representatives of the United States from the 1st to the 31st Congress, inclusive—Continued.

Names of claimants.	Nature or object of the claim.	Congress.	Session.	How brought before the House of Reps.	Page of journal.	To what committee of the House referred.	No. or date of the report.	Nature of the report.	No. of the bill.	How disposed of by the House of Reps.	How disposed of by the Senate.	Date of the act of Congress, and remarks.
Belding, Moses, heirs of	Compensation for revolutionary services.	31	1	Petition	409	Rev. Claims.						
Belding, Samuel	(See sureties of M. W. Bostwick.)	23	1		160							
Belew, Bennett, heirs of	Grant of land	24	1	Petition	62	Private Lands				Discharged; laid on table.		
Belew, Solomon	Remission of distillery duties	15	1	Petition	71	Ways and Means	Jan. 23, 1818	Adverse		Claim rejected.		
Belfort, Jean Baptiste	Confirmation of title to land in Missouri.	15	1	Petition	102	Priv. Land Claims.						
Belfort, Jean Baptiste	Confirmation of title to land in Missouri.	16	1	Petition	71	Priv. Land Claims.						
Belfort, Jean Baptiste	Confirmation of title to land in Missouri.	17	1	Petition	53	Public Lands.						
				Senate bill	482	Public Lands			S. 84			
Belfort, Jean Baptiste	Confirmation of title to land in Missouri.	18	1	Senate bill	53	Public Lands	July 16, 1824	General bill	65	Passed	Passed	App'd May 26, 1824
Belgar, Juan	Permission to locate a confirmed grant.	25	2	Senate bill	1155	Priv. Land Claims.	July 2, 1838	With't amend	S. 261	Referred to Committee Whole House.		
Belgar, Juan	Permission to locate a confirmed grant.	25	3	Senate bill	478	Priv. Land Claims.	Feb. 16, 1839	With amend.	S. 164	Referred to Committee Whole House.		
Belgar, Juan	Permission to locate a confirmed grant.	26	1	Senate bill	443	Priv. Land Claims.	April 14, 1840	With't amend.	S. 58	Referred to Committee Whole House.		
Belgar, Juan	Permission to locate a confirmed grant.	26	2	Senate bill	221	Priv. Land Claims.			S. 115			
Belgar, Juan	Permission to locate a confirmed grant.	27	2	Senate bill	1126	Priv. Land Claims.	990	Adverse	S. 84	Laid on table.		
Belger, James	Pension	21	1	Senate bill	401	Military Pensions.	May 21, 1830	Adverse	S. 63	Laid on table.		
Belger, James	Pension	21	2	Senate bill	384	Military Pensions.	March 2, 1831	With't amend.	S. 119	Passed	Passed	App'd March 2, 1831
Belknap, Ebenezer	Pension for revolutionary services.	21	2	Petition	209	Military Pensions.						
Belknap, Ebenezer	Pension for revolutionary services.	22	1	Petition	441	Rev. Pensions.						
Belknap, Ebenezer, (N. Y.)	Arrears or increase of pension	25	2	Petition	629	Rev. Pensions				Dis.; laid on table.		
Belknap, Ebenezer, (N. Y.)	Arrears or increase of pension	27	2	Petition	613	Rev. Pensions	July 21, 1842	Adverse		Laid on table.		
Belknap, Isaac and others	(See John P. Coxe)	13	3		570							
Belknap, Isaac	Pension for revolutionary services.	28	2	Petition	208	Rev. Pensions.						
Belknap, Isaac, widow of	Pension for revolutionary services.	29	1	Petition	370	Rev. Pensions	492	Adverse		Laid on table.		
Belknap, John, heirs of	Compensation for revolutionary services.	25	2	Petition	390	Rev. Claims				Discharged; laid on table.		
Belknap, Jonas	Pension for revolutionary services.	3	1	Report of Secretary of War.	131	Select	May 26, 1794	Pension bill	62	Passed	Passed	App'd June 7, 1794
Belknap, Samuel and other	Balance due on certain bills of credit.	3	1	Petition	67					Referred to Secretary Treasury.		
Belknap, Susan	(See Isaac Belknap, widow of	29	1		370							
Belknap, Wm. G	Permission to locate a certain land claim.	25	2	Petition	373	Priv. Land Claims.	March 7, 1838	Favorable	632	Referred to Committee Whole House.		
Belknap, Wm. G	Permission to locate a certain land claim.	25	3	Rep't Committee Whole House.	376			With amend.	632	Passed	Passed	App'd Mar. 3, 1839
Bell, Aaron	Settlement of account against Post Office Department.	19	1	Petition	53	P. Of. & P. Roads.	Jan. 4, 1826	Adverse.		Laid on table.		
Bell, Abraham.	Bounty land for revolutionary services.	6	1	Petition	643	Select	April 2, 1800	Adverse		Referred to Committee Whole House.		
Bell, A. W.	Indemnity for French spoliations prior to 1800.	26	1	Memorial	182	Foreign Affairs	343	Favorable	319	Referred to Committee Whole House.		
Bell, Alexander	Remission of duties on goods destroyed by fire.	10	1	Petition	150	Com. and Manuf.	Mar. 16, 1808	Adverse		Claim rejected.		

List of private claims presented to the House of Representatives of the United States from the 1st to the 31st Congress, inclusive—Continued.

Names of claimants.	Nature or object of the claim.	Congress.	Session.	How brought before the House of Reps.	Page of journal.	To what committee of the House referred.	No. or date of the report.	Nature of the report.	No. of the bill.	How disposed of by the House of Reps.	How disposed of by the Senate.	Date of the act of Congress, and remarks.
Bell, Caleb	(See administrator of Matthew Bell)	29	1		275							
Bell, Cuthbert T	Compensation for horse lost in Florida war.	28	1	Petition	262	Claims.						
Bell, David	(See heirs of Jesse Bell)	31	1		306							
Bell, Elijah S	Compensation for buildings at Fort Macon.	22	1	Petition	387	Claims	Mar. 21, 1832	Adverse		Laid on table.		
Bell, Elijah S	Compensation for buildings at Fort Macon.	25	2	Petition	655	Claims	850	Indefinite		Discharged; referred to Secretary War.		
Bell, Elijah S	Compensation for buildings at Fort Macon.	25	3	Rep. of Secretary War.	201	Claims	Mar. 2, 1839	Adverse		Laid on table.		
Bell, Elijah S	Compensation for buildings at Fort Macon.	26	1	Petition	939	Claims.						
Bell, Elijah S	Compensation for buildings at Fort Macon.	26	2	Petition	53	Claims	29	Adverse		Laid on table.		
Bell, Elijah S	Compensation for buildings at Fort Macon.	27	2	Petition	154	Claims	697	Adverse		Laid on table.		
Bell, Elijah S	Compensation for buildings at Fort Macon.	27	3	Petition	106	Claims	202	Adverse		Laid on table.		
Bell, Elijah S	Compensation for buildings at Fort Macon.	28	1	Petition	513	Claims	502	Adverse		Laid on table.		
Bell, Elijah S	Compensation for buildings at Fort Macon.	28	2	Petition	214	Claims.						
Bell, Elijah S	Compensation for buildings at Fort Macon.	29	1	Petition and docs.	810	Claims.						
Bell, Elijah S	Compensation for buildings at Fort Macon.	29	2	Petition	74					Laid on table.		
Bell, Elijah S	Compensation for buildings at Fort Macon.	31	1	Petition	432	Commerce.						
Bell, Frederick M., heirs of.	Commutation pay for revolutionary services.	25	2	Resolution	534	Rev. Claims.						
Bell, Frederick M., heirs of.	Duplicate land warrant for one lost	25	2	Resolution	160	Priv. Land Claims.	347	Favorable	378			
				Recommitted	1058	Priv. Land Claims.	June 13, 1838	Favorable	R. 22	Passed	Reported with't amendment.	
Bell, Frederick M., heirs of.	Duplicate land warrant for one lost	25	3	Petition	188	Priv. Land Claims.	Jan. 11, 1839	Favorable	R. 35	Passed	Passed	App'd March 3, 1839
Bell, Guy H	Additional compensation as land office clerk in Louisiana.	14	2	Petition	224	Claims.						
Bell, Henry	Prize money for sale of Algerine frigate.	23	1	Petition	303	Naval Affairs	Mar. 4, 1834	Favorable	335	Referred to Committee Whole House.		
Bell, Isaac	(See Samuel & Isaac Bell)	25	2		88							
Bell, I	(See N. Rogers & J. Bell)	26	1		182		343		319			
Bell, Jacob	Reimbursement of duties improperly collected.	1	3	Petition	330					Referred to Secretary Treasury.		
Bell, Jacob	Reimbursement of duties improperly collected.	2	2	Rep. of Secretary Treasury.	625	Whole House	Feb. 5, 1793	Fav. and bill ordered.	230	Passed	Rejected.	
Bell, James	Compensation for revolutionary services and advances.	3	1	Petition	91	Select	April 23, 1794	Favorable	42	Rejected.		
Bell, James	Compensation for revolutionary services and advances.	6	1	Petition	622	Claims	Mar. 26, 1800	Adverse		Claim rejected.		
Bell, James	Compensation for revolutionary services and advances.	7	1	Petition	95		April 3, 1802					
				Rep. of Secretary Treasury.	111	Whole House.						

List of private claims presented to the House of Representatives of the United States from the 1st to the 31st Congress, inclusive—Continued.

Names of claimants.	Nature or object of the claim.	Congress.	Session.	How brought before the House of Reps.	Page of journal.	To what committee of the House referred.	No. or date of the report.	Nature of the report.	No. of the bill.	How disposed of by the House of Reps.	How disposed of by the Senate.	Date of the act of Congress, and remarks.
Bell, James	Compensation for revolutionary services and advances.	7	2	Petition	247	Claims	Feb. 19, 1803	Adverse		Claim rejected.		
Bell, James	Compensation for revolutionary services and advances.	11	2	Petition	206	Claims.						
Bell, James, heirs of	Compensation for revolutionary services and advances.	23	1	Petition	70	Rev. Claims	184	Favorable	203	Passed	Passed with amendment.	App'd June 30, 1834
Bell, James, heirs of	Interest on claim allowed as above.	24	1	Senate bill	1084	Rev. Claims	July 2, 1836	With amend.	S. 125	Referred to Committee Whole House.		
Bell, James, heirs of	Interest on claim allowed as above.	28	2	Senate bill	304	Rev. Claims	Feb. 25, 1845	With't amend	S. 88	Referred to Committee Whole House.		
Bell, James, heirs of	Interest on claim allowed as above.	30	1	Memorial	459	Rev. Claims.						
Bell, James, heirs of	Interest on claim allowed as above.	30	2	Memorial	117	Rev. Claims	54	Favorable	758	Referred to Committee Whole House.		
Bell, James, heirs of	Interest on claim allowed as above.	31	1	Memorial	391	Rev. Claims.						
Bell, James, heirs of	Interest on claim allowed as above.	31	2	Memorial	183	Rev. Claims				Discharged; leave to withdraw.		
Bell, James, heirs of	(See assignee of Thomas Tupper.)	22	2		142							
Bell, James, (Pa.)	Compensation for team taken for public use.	7	1	Petition	147	Claims	April 3, 1802	Indefinite		Postponed.		
Bell, James, (Pa.)	Compensation for team taken for public use.	7	2	Petition	247	Claims	Feb. 26, 1803	Indefinite		Postponed.		
Bell, James, (Pa.)	Compensation for team taken for public use.	8	1	Petition	468	Claims	Jan. 30, 1804	Adverse		Leave to withdraw.		
Bell, James	(See represent's of Joseph Webb)	26	2		60							
Bell, James	Arrears of pension	18	1	Petition	108	Naval Affairs	Jan. 13, 1804	Adverse		Laid on table.		
Bell, James L., and others	(See assignees of Jonathan Carver)	18	1		48							
Bell, Jane	(See J. R. Bell, widow of)	27	3		69							
Bell, Jesse, (N. Y.)	Pension for revolutionary services.	18	2	Petition	65	Pens. & Rev. Cl'ms.				Discharged; laid on table.		
Bell, Jesse, (N. Y.)	Pension for revolutionary services.	20	1	Petition	37	Military Pensions	Feb. 8, 1828	Adverse		Laid on table.		
Bell, Jesse, (N. Y.)	Pension for revolutionary services.	20	2	Report of last session.	65	Military Pensions				Discharged; laid on table.		
Bell, Jesse, (Mi.)	Indemnity for land covered by a Spanish grant.	22	1	Petition	388	Public Lands	388	Favorable	480	Passed	Passed	App'd July 14, 1832
Bell, Jesse, heir of	Pro-rata share of pension	31	1	Petition	306	Rev. Pensions				Discharged; laid on table.		
Bell, John	Pension for revolutionary services.	3	1	Rep. of Secretary War.	131	Select	May 26, 1794	Res. to refer to Sec. War.	R. 12	Passed	Passed	App'd June 9, 1794
Bell, John	Pension for revolutionary services.	3	2	Rep. of Secretary War.	350	Claims	Mar. 2, 1795	Pension bill	130	Passed	Postponed.	
Bell, John	Pension for revolutionary services.	4	1	Rep. of Secretary War.	447	Claims	Feb. 18, 1796	Favorable	156	Passed	Passed	App'd April 20, 1796
Bell, John	Pension for revolutionary services.	13	3	Documents	484	Pens. & Rev. Cl'ms.	Feb. 20, 1815	Pension bill	303	Passed	Passed	App'd Mar. 3, 1815
Bell, John, (N. Y.)	Pension for revolutionary services.	22	1	Resolution	228	Rev. Pensions.						
Bell, John	Right of pre-emption to land in Louisiana.	22	1	Petition	400	Priv. Land Claims.						
Bell, John	(See Joseph Stewart, and others)	13	3		159							
Bell, John	(See sureties of Hillary Langlois)	9	2		497							
Bell, John, administrator of	Indemnity for French spoliations prior to 1800.	31	1	Petition	270	Foreign Affairs	355	General bill	318	Referred to Committee Whole House.		
Bell, John, widow of	Extension of the term of lease of salt works.	9	2	Petition	561	Claims.						
Bell, John, widow of	Extension of the term of lease of salt works.	10	2	Petition	385	Claims.						
Bell, John D.	Right of pre-emption to certain lands.	24	1	Petition	478	Public Lands.						

List of private claims presented to the House of Representatives of the United States from the 1st to the 31st Congress, inclusive—Continued.

Names of claimants.	Nature or object of the claim.	Congress.	Session.	How brought before the House of Reps.	Page of journal.	To what committee of the House referred.	No. or date of the report.	Nature of the report.	No. of the bill.	How disposed of by the House of Reps.	How disposed of by the Senate.	Date of the act of Congress, and remarks.
Bell, John D.	Right of pre-emption to certain lands.	24	2	Petition	313	Public Lands.						
Bell, John D.	Right of pre-emption to certain lands.	25	2	Petition	421	Public Lands.						
Bell, John W.	Compensation for horse lost in Mexico.	30	1	Petition	147	Claims	234	Adverse	......	Laid on table.		
Bell, J. G.	(See Exploring expedition)	27	3	....	149							
Bell, J. R., widow of	Pension for revolutionary services.	27	3	Petition	69	Rev. Pensions	....	....	......	Discharged; laid on table.		
Bell, Joseph, (Ky.)	Pension for revolutionary services.	22	1	Petition	711	Rev. Claims.						
Bell, Joseph, (Tenn.)	Pension for disability, war of 1812	29	1	Petition	175	Invalid Pensions.						
				Documents	193	Invalid Pensions	183	Adverse	......	Laid on table.		
Bell, Joseph, (Tenn.)	Pension for disability, war of 1812	31	1	Petition	433	Invalid Pensions.						
Bell, Maria C.	(See Richard H. Bell, widow of).	25	2	....	267							
Bell, Maria, *et al.*	(See Joseph Webb, represent's of)	26	2	....	60							
Bell, Matthew, administrator of.	Balance due for services as United States dragoon.	29	1	Petition	275	Claims	398	Adverse	......	Laid on table.		
Bell, Matthew, administrator of.	Balance due for services as United States dragoon.	29	2	Petition	99	Claims.						
Bell, Matthew, administrator of.	Balance due for services as United States dragoon.	30	1	Petition	169	Claims	486	Adverse	......	Laid on table.		
Bell, Nicholas	Indemnity for schooner taken by the enemy.	25	2	Pension	175	Claims	548	Adverse	......	Laid on table.		
Bell, Patterson	Pension for revolutionary services.	20	2	Resolution	212	Military Pensions.						
Bell, Phineas	Compensation for revolutionary services.	25	2	Petition	270	Rev. Claims	....	....	......	Discharged; laid on table.		
Bell, Phineas	Compensation for revolutionary services.	26	1	Petition	284	Rev. Pensions	714	Adverse	......	Laid on table.		
Bell, Phineas	Compensation for revolutionary services.	27	2	Petition	153	Rev. Pensions	784	Adverse	......	Laid on table.		
Bell, Polly, *alias* Collins	Authority to locate certain land	19	2	Senate bill	227	Priv. Land Claims.	Mar. 1, 1827	With amend.	S. 54	Passed	Passed	App'd March 2, 1827
Bell, Richard H., widow of	Compensation for superintending lead mines.	23	2	Senate bill	456	Claims	Mar. 2, 1835	With't amend.	S. 146	Referred to Committee Whole House.		
Bell, Richard H., widow of	Pension for disability, war of 1812	25	2	Petition	267	Invalid Pensions						
Bell, Richard H., widow of	Pension for disability, war of 1812	26	1	Petition	162	Invalid Pensions	358	Favorable	337	Referred to Committee Whole House.		
Bell, Robert	Confirmation of title to land	23	2	Petition	276	Priv. Land Claims.						
Bell, Sampson	(See heirs of Thomas Bell)	11	2	....	169							
Bell, Samuel and Isaac	Compensat'n for supplies furnished on public account.	25	2	Documents	88	Claims	491	Adverse	......	Laid on table.		
Bell, Samuel and Isaac	Compensat'n for supplies furnished on public account.	25	3	Documents	122	Claims	60	Adverse	......	Laid on table.		
Bell, Samuel W.	Compensation for services in Seminole treaty.	29	2	Senate bill	374	Indian Affairs	80	Adverse	S. 83	Laid on table.		
Bell, Samuel W.	Compensation for services in Seminole treaty.	30	1	Senate bill	684	Indian Affairs	May 17, 1848	With't amend.	S. 97	Passed	Passed	App'd May 31, 1848
Bell, Thomas	(See Joshua T. Jones and others).	30	1	....	66							
Bell, Thomas, heirs of	Restoration of lands taken for public use.	11	2	Petition	169	Claims	Jan. 24, 1810	....	......	Discharged; referred to Secretary of War.		
Bell, Thomas, heirs of	Restoration of lands taken for public use.	11	3	Rep. of Secretary War.	436	....	....	....	......	Laid on table	....	Leave to withdraw, 14th Con., 1st sess., p. 294.
Bell, Thomas	Extra allowance for services in Exploring Expedition.	28	2	Petition & mem	70	Naval Affairs.						

List of private claims presented to the House of Representatives of the United States from the 1st to the 31st Congress, inclusive—**Continued.**

Names of claimants.	Nature or object of the claim.	Congress.	Session.	How brought before the House of Reps.	Page of journal.	To what committee of the House referred.	No. or date of the report.	Nature of the report.	No. of the bill.	How disposed of by the House of Reps.	How disposed of by the Senate.	Date of the act of Congress, and remarks.
Bell, Thomas	(See Exploring Expedition)	27	3		149		270		818			
Bell, Thomas, and others	Claim under treaty of Ghent	20	2	Memorial	231	Foreign Affairs	79	Adverse		Laid on table.		
Bell, William	(See sureties of Hillary Langlois)	9	2		497							
Bell, William	(See heirs of James Bell)	23	1		70							
Bell, William	Payment of revolutionary certificate.	4	1	Rep. of Secretary Treasury.	388	Claims	74	Adverse		Laid on table.		
Bell, William, (Phila.)	Release from judgment and imprisonment.	5	2	Petition	82	Com. and Manuf.	Jan. 4, 1798			Discharged, and to Select.		
Bell, William	(See sureties for Wm. Whitsitt)	17	2		228							
Bell, William, widow of	Pension for revolutionary services.	18	1	Petition	330	Pens. & Rev. Cl'ms.	Mar. 31, 1824	Adverse		Laid on table.		
Bell, William H.	Extra compensation for services at Delaware breakwater.	23	2	Petition	489	Claims.						
Bell, William H.	Extra compensation for services at Delaware breakwater.	24	1	Petition	264	Claims	Mar. 3, 1836	Favorable	383	Referred to Committee Whole House.		
Bell, William H.	Extra compensation for services at Delaware breakwater.	25	2	Petition	36	Claims	11	Favorable	23	Passed	Indef. postp'd.	
Bell, William H.	Extra compensation for services at Delaware breakwater.	26	1	Petition	168	Claims.						
Bell, William H.	Compensation for invention in pointing and firing cannon.	24	1	Petition	151	Military Affairs	Feb. 23, 1836	Favorable.	376	Referred to Committee Whole House.		
				Senate bill	956	Military Affairs	June 9, 1836	With't amend.	S. 174	Passed	Passed	App'd July 4, 1836
Bellamy, Aaron	Indemnity for vessel lost in the public service.	14	2	Petition	416	Claims.						
Bellamy, Aaron	Indemnity for vessel lost in the public service.	15	2	Petition	80	Claims.						
Bellamy, Aaron	Indemnity for vessel lost in the public service.	16	1	Resolution	64	Claims	Jan. 5, 1820	Adverse		Rejected.		
Bellamy, Aaron	Indemnity for vessel lost in the public service.	16	2	Petition	211	Claims.						
Bellamy, Aaron	Indemnity for vessel lost in the public service.	22	1	Petition	93	Claims.						
Bellamy, Aaron	Indemnity for vessel lost in the public service.	22	2	Petition	45	Claims.	93	Favorable	735	Referred to Committee Whole House.		
Bellamy, Aaron	Indemnity for vessel lost in the public service.	23	1	Petition	33	Claims.	38	Favorable	44	Passed.	Passed	App'd June 18, 1844
Bellamy, Justus	Indemnity for vessel captured by the enemy.	13	3	Petition	740	Ways and Means.						
Bellew, Peter	Indemnity for revolutionary injuries and compensation, &c.	2	1	Petition	447					Referred to Secretary War.		
Bellew, Solomon	Confirmation of land title	24	1	Senate bill	564	Public Lands	April 22, 1836	With amend.	2	Passed	Passed	App'd July 4, 1836
Bellinger, Frederick, heirs of.	Commutation pay for revolutionary services.	30	1	Petition	229	Rev. Claims.						
Bellinger, John	Reimbursement of expenses attending the sickness and death of four sons in the public service.	15	1	Petition	172	Claims	Mar. 3, 1818	Adverse.		Rejected.		
Bellinger, Peter	Reimbursement of money paid for land by mistake.	31	1	Petition	384	Priv. Land Claims.						
				Petition (2)	624	Priv. Land Claims.	425	Adverse		Leave to withdraw.		
Bellinger, Peter P.	Pension for revolutionary services.	30	1	Petition	936	Rev. Pensions.						
Bellows, Ezra	Pension for revolutionary services.	3	2	Rep. of Secretary War.	337	Claims.						
Bellows, Ezra	Pension for revolutionary services.	4	1	Resolution	373	Claims.						

List of private claims presented to the House of Representatives of the United States from the 1st to the 31st Congress, inclusive—Continued.

Names of claimants.	Nature or object of the claim.	Congress.	Session.	How brought before the House of Reps.	Page of journal.	To what committee of the House referred.	No. or date of the report.	Nature of the report.	No. of the bill.	How disposed of by the House of Reps.	How disposed of by the Senate.	Date of the act of Congress, and remarks.
Bellows, Ezra	Pension for revolutionary services.	4	2	Resolution	614	Claims.						
Bellows, Ezra	Pension for revolutionary services.	13	2	Pension bill	344	Whole House	Mar. 30, 1814	With amend.	160	Passed	Passed with amendment.	App'd April 18, 1814
Bellows, Isaac	Pension for revolutionary services.	3	2	Rep. of Secretary War.	337	Claims.						
Bellows, Josiah	(See David Stone and others)	13	2		386							
Bellows, Levi	Remission of distillery duties	14	2	Petition	453	Claims	Jan. 23, 1818					
Bellows, Levi	Remission of distillery duties	15	1	Petition	59	Ways and Means.						
Bellows, Levi	Remission of distillery duties	16	1	Petition	252	Ways and Means.						
Bellows, Levi	Remission of distillery duties	16	2	Petition	154	Ways and Means.						
Bellows, Levi	Remission of distillery duties	17	1	Petition	117	Ways aud Means	Jan. 17, 1822	Adverse		Laid on lable.		
Belsha, Robert	Indemnity for lost pre-emption right.	23	2	Petition	278							
Belt, Benjamin M	(See Langley and Belt)	18	1		422				S. 80			
Belt, Carlton	Compensation for a gun furnished for public use.	24	1	Petition	92	Claims.						
Belt, Joseph C	Indemnity for property lost, war of 1812.	20	2	Resolution	238	Claims.						
Belt, Joseph C	Indemnity for property lost, war of 1812.	21	2	Petition	38	Claims	19	Adverse		Referred to Committee Whole House.		
Belt, Joseph C	Indemnity for property lost, war of 1812.	23	1	Petition	384	Claims	April 1, 1834	Adverse.				
Belt, Joseph S., heirs of	Pension due	25	2	Petition	181	Rev. Pensions				Discharged; laid on table.		
Belt, Joseph S., heirs of	Pension due	25	3	Petition	88	Rev. Pensions				Discharged; laid on table.		
Belt, William M	(See J. H. Trenholm and W. M. B[illegible])	31	1		1509				334			
Beltzhoover, Jacob	Pension for revolutionary services.		2	Petition	267	Claims	Feb. 27, 1795	Adverse		Laid on table.		
Beltzhoover, Jacob	Pension for revolutionary services.	4	2	Petition	626	Claims	Dec. 21, 1797	Adverse		Leave to withdraw.		
Beman, Nathan	Compensation for revolutionary services.	26	1	Petition	281	Rev. Claims.						
Beman, Nathan	Compensation for revolutionary services.	26	2	Petition	35	Rev. Claims.						
Bement, Ebenezer	Compensation for revolutionary services.	2	1	Petition	528					Referred to Secretary of War.		
Bement, Ebenezer	Pension for revolutionary services.	3	1	Rep. of Secretary of War.	131	Select	May 26, 1794	Res. to refer to Sec. War.	R. 12	Passed	Passed	App'd June 9, 1794
Bemis, Albert G	(See Henry S. Bemis, heirs of)	18	1		314							
Bemis, Anna	(See Daniel Morley, heirs of.)	25	3		455							
Bemiss, Ezra H	Bounty land as Canadian volunteer.	16	1	Petition	197	Claims.						
Bemis, Henry S., heirs of.	Bounty land and half-pay	18	1	Petition	314	Military Pensions.						
Bemis, Isaac	Pension	16	1	Resolution	63	Rev. Pensions	Jan. 14, 1820	Adverse		Laid on table.		
Bemis, Jonas	Compensation for revolutionary services.	20	1	Petition	278	Rev. Claims.						
Bemis, Joseph	(See Henty S. Bemis, heirs of.)	18	1		314							
Bemis, Mercy	(See Buckminister White, widow of.)	27	3		365							
Bempton, Captain, agent of.	Compensation for horse lost in Florida war.	28	1	Petition	262	Claims	167	General bill	19	Passed	Passed	App'd June 15, 1844
Beneker, Benjamin	Indemnity for losses under Choctaw treaty.	24	1	Memorial	57	Public Lands	208	Favorable	208	Referred to Committee Whole House.		

List of private claims presented to the House of Representatives of the United States from the 1st to the 31st Congress, inclusive—**Continued.**

Names of claimants.	Nature or object of the claim.	Congress.	Session.	How brought before the House of Reps.	Page of journal.	To what committee of the House referred.	No. or date of the report.	Nature of the report.	No. of the bill.	How disposed of by the House of Reps.	How disposed of by the Senate.	Date of the act of Congress, and remarks.
Bend William B	Reimbursement of duties on goods destroyed by fire.	30	1	Petition	682	Commerce.						
Bender, Major George	Double rations and commission on disbursement.	23	1	Petition	384	Claims	475	Favorable	491	Referred to Committee Whole House.		
Bender, Major George	Double rations and commission on disbursements.	24	1	Petition	50	Claims	16	Favorable	16	Passed	Passed	App'd June 23, 1836
Bender, George	Compensation for constructing Delaware breakwater.	24	1	Petition	49	Claims.						
Bender, John, widow of	Pension for revolutionary services.	26	2	Petition	82	Rev. Pensions.						
Bender, Magaret	(See John Bender, widow of.)	26	2		82							
Bendure, Elizabeth	(See daughter of Louden Trotter)	27	2		936							
Benedict, Cyrus	(See representatives of John Robinson.)	23	1		54							
Benedict, George	Pension for revolutionary services.	11	2	Pension bill	283	Whole House	Mar. 24, 1810	With amend.	107	Passed	Passed with amendment.	App'd April 27, 1810
Benedict, Jared	Pension	23	2	Petition	276	Invalid Pensions	Feb. 24, 1835	Adverse	......	Laid on table.		
Benedict, Joseph, son of	Pension for revolutionary services.	28	2	Petition	57	Rev. Claims.						
Benedict, Joseph, son of	Pension for revolutionary services.	29	1	Petition	648	Rev. Claims.						
Benedict, Lewis	Authority to locate an Indian land claim.	30	1	Petition	103	Priv. Land Claims.	127	Favorable	118	Passed.		
Benedict, Noble, and others	Depreciation of pay and emolument for revolutionary services.	3	2	Petition	299	Claims.						
Benedict, Noble, and others	Depreciation of pay and emolument for revolutionary services.	4	1	Petition	373	Claims	Dec. 28, 1795	Adverse	......	Postponed.		
Benedict, Stephen	(See son of Joseph Benedict)	28	2		57							
Benedict, Thomas P.	Indemnity for property destroyed by the enemy.	13	2	Petition	201	Claims	Jan. 19, 1814	Adverse	......	Claim rejected.		
Benedict, Thomas P., widow of.	Indemnity for property destroyed by the enemy.	23	1	Petition	384	Claims	371	Adverse	......	Laid on table.		
Benedict, Timothy	Pension	19	2	Petition	143	Military Pensions.						
Benedict, Timothy	Pension	20	1	Petition	45	Military Pensions.						
Benedict, Timothy	Pension	21	1	Petition	47	Military Pensions	Jan. 5, 1830	Pension bill	72	Passed	Passed	App'd May 20, 1830
Benezet, Anthony	(See heirs of Daniel Benezet)	8	2		131							
Benezete, Daniel, heirs of	Release from a judgment	8	2	Petition	131	Ways and Means	Feb. 22, 1805	Adverse	......	Laid on table.		
Benezete, Daniel, heirs of	Release from a judgment	9	1	Petition	191	Ways and Means.						
Benezete, Daniel, heirs of	Release from a judgment	9	2	Petition	486	Ways and Means	Jan. 2, 1807	Favorable	162	Recommitted.		
Benezete, Daniel, heirs of	Release from a judgment	10	1	Petition	104	Claims.						
Benge, Obadiah M.	Pension for revolutionary services.	28	1	Petition	857	Rev. Pensions.						
Benguine, R.	Increase of compensation for locating land warrants.	30	2	Petition	126	Public Lands.						
Benjamin, Charlotte C.	(See representatives of P. Surgett and others.)	22	1		205				S. 45			
Benjamin, Isaac	Compensation for revolutionary services and supplies.	2	1	Petition	483				......	Referred to Secretary War.		
Benjamin, Isaac	Compensation for revolutionary services and supplies.	2	2	Rep. of Secretary War.	696				......	Laid on table.		
Benjamin, Joseph, widow of.	Pension	20	1	Petition	310	Military Pensions	April 18, 1828	Adverse	......	Laid on table.		
Benjamin, Meigs D., & Co.	Reimbursement of duties on damaged goods.	26	1	Petition	292	Commerce	31	Favorable	50	Passed	Passed	App'd May 2, 1840
Benjamin, Roger	Pension for revolutionary services.	22	1	Petition	509	Rev. Pensions	June 16, 1832	Adverse	......	Laid on table.		
Benjamin, Samuel	Additional compensation for revolutionary services.	25	2	Petition	270	Rev. Claims	866	Adverse	......	Laid on table.		

List of private claims presented to the House of Representatives of the United States from the 1st to the 31st Congress, inclusive—Continued.

Names of claimants.	Nature or object of the claim.	Congress.	Session.	How brought before the House of Reps.	Page of journal.	To what committee of the House referred.	No. or date of the report.	Nature of the report.	No. of the bill.	How disposed of by the House of Reps.	How disposed of by the Senate.	Date of the act of Congress, and remarks.
Bennerville, Daniel de....	(See Daniel DeBennerville)......	2	1	Petition	492							
Bennett, Aaron, (Vt.)....	Pension for revolutionary services.	26	1	Petition	936	Rev. Pensions....	714	Adverse	......	Laid on table.		
Bennett, Aaron, (N. J.)..	(See sureties of Joseph B. Hughes)	25	2	....	203							
Bennett, Benjamin	Permission to correct error in entry of land.	24	1	Petition	113	Public Lands.....	Feb. 7, 1836	Favorable....	540	Passed	Passed	App'd May 14, 1836
Bennett, Charles	Reimbursement of duties on certain goods.	23	1	Petition	186	Ways and Means.						
Bennett, Elijah	Compensation for revolutionary services.	3	1	Rep. of Secretary War.	131	Select	May 26, 1794	Res. to refer to Sec. War.	R. 12	Passed	Passed	App'd June 9, 1794
Bennett, Elijah	Compensation for revolutionary services.	3	2	Rep. of Secretary War.	278	Claims	Feb. 28, 1795	Favorable....	130	Passed	Postponed.	
Bennett, Elijah	Compensation for revolutionary services.	4	1	Resolution	373	Claims	Feb. 18, 1796	Favorable....	156	Passed	Passed with amendment.	App'd April 20, 1796
Bennett, Elisha	Compensation for revolutionary naval services.	4	1	Petition	389	Claims	Jan. 29, 1796	Adverse	......	Leave to withdraw.		
Bennett, Elisha	Compensation for revolutionary naval services.	7	1	Petition	63	Claims	Mar. 24, 1802	Adverse	......	Claim rejected.		
Bennett, Elizabeth.......	Pension for revolutionary services.	21	2	Petition	120	Military Pensions..	....	....	......	Discharged; laid on table.		
Bennett, Ezekiel, heirs of.	Change of a location of land	23	1	Petition	499	Public Lands.						
Bennett, George, widow of.	Pension for military services.....	20	1	Petition	278	Military Pensions..	....	....	......	Discharged; laid on table.		
Bennett, George W......	Correction of an erroneous land entry.	24	1	Petition	113	Public Lands.....	April 7, 1836	Favorable....	540	Passed	Passed	App'd May 14, 1836
Bennett, Henry, and others	Indemnity for loss on a rescinded mail contract.	18	1	Memorial	432	P. O. & P. Roads.						
Bennett, Henry, and others	Indemnity for loss on a rescinded mail contract.	18	2	Petition	209	P. O. & P. Roads.						
Bennett, Henry, and others	Indemnity for loss on a rescinded mail contract.	19	1	Petition	254	P. O. & P. Roads.						
Bennett, Isaac	Pension for revolutionary services.	3	1	Rep. of Secretary War.	131	Select	May 26, 1794	Res. to refer to Sec. War.	R. 12	Passed	Passed	App'd June 9, 1794
Bennett, Isaac	Increase of pension	11	2	Pension bill	283	Whole House	Mar. 24, 1810	Pension bill ..	107	Passed	Passed with amendment.	App'd April 27, 1810
Bennett, James	(See Andrew Young, and others).	18	1	....	214							
Bennett, James	Pension for revolutionary services.	22	1	Petition	130	Rev. Pensions.						
Bennett, Jasper	(See assignee of Theodore Wood)	15	2	....	117	....	67	....	260			
Bennett, John	Payment of revolutionary certificates.	2	1	Petition	539	....	....	....	......	Referred to Secretary of War.		
Bennett, John	Payment of revolutionary certificates.	4	2	Rep. of Secretary War.	709	Claims	Feb. 21, 1797	Favorable....	......	Referred to Committee Whole House.		
Bennett, John	Payment of revolutionary certificates.	5	2	Rep. of Comm'r Claims.	89	Whole House	Mar. 19, 1798	Res. favorable.	......	Resolution rejected.		
Bennett, John, and others.	Compensation for use of ferry, &c.	3	1	Rep. of Secretary War.	93	Select	April 22, 1794	Adverse	......	Laid on table.		
Bennett, John, and others.	Compensation for use of ferry, &c.	3	2	Rep. of Secretary War.	250	Claims	Feb. 25, 1795	Adverse	......	Referred to Committee Whole House.		
Bennett, John, (Del.)....	Pension	15	2	Petition	177	Pen. & Rev. Claims	Jan. 15, 1819	Adverse	......	Laid on table.		
Bennett, John, (Va.)	Pension	23	1	Petition	112	Invalid Pensions ..	....	....	......	Discharged; laid on table.		
Bennett, John, (Va.)	Pension	24	1	Petition	98	Invalid Pensions ..	Jan. 28, 1836	Favorable....	253	Passed	Passed	App'd June 28, 1836
Bennett, John, (Ky.)....	Compensation for revolutionary services.	21	1	Petition	205	Rev. Claims.						

List of private claims presented to the House of Representatives of the United States from the 1st to the 31st Congress, inclusive—Continued.

Names of claimants.	Nature or object of the claim.	Congress.	Session.	How brought before the House of Reps.	Page of journal.	To what committee of the House referred.	No. or date of the report	Nature of the report.	No. of the bill.	How disposed of by the House of Reps.	How disposed of by the Senate.	Date of the act of Congress, and remarks.
Bennett, John, (N. C.)	Pension for revolutionary services	29	2	Petition	172	Rev. Pensions.						
Bennett, John, widow of	Pension for services	26	1	Documents	626	Whole House.						
Bennett, John S., (S. C.)	(See Thomas Napier, and others)	17	2		142							
Bennett, Joseph	Redemption of Congressional bills of credit.	2	2	Petition	653					Referred to Secretary of Treasury.		
Bennett, Joseph	Redemption of Congressional bills of credit.	3	1	Rep. of Secretary Treasury.	77					Laid on table.		
Bennett, Joseph, (Penn.)	Pension	21	1	Petition	66	Military Pensions	Dec. 31, 1829	Adverse		Laid on table.		
Bennett, Joshua	Compensation for horse lost in the public service.	17	1	Petition	96	Claims	Feb. 4, 1822	Favorable	75	Passed	Rejected.	
Bennett, Joshua	Compensation for horse lost in the public service.	17	2	Petition	86	Claims	Jan. 3, 1823	Favorable	212	Referred to Committee Whole House.		
Bennett, Joshua	Compensation for horse lost in the public service.	18	1	Petition	198	Claims	53	Favorable	102	Passed	Passed	App'd May 19, 1824
Bennett, Mary	(See George Bennett, widow of	20	1		278							
Bennett, Malcolm	(See assignee of Theodore Wood.)	15	2		117							
Bennett, Martin	Compensation for horse lost in the public service.	15	2	Petition	33	Claims	Dec. 1, 1818	Adverse		Claim rejected.		
Bennett, Martha	(See Rufus Bennett, widow of)	28	1		238							
Bennett & Morte creditors of.	Payment of balance for erecting fortification.	21	1	Senate bill	552	Whole House	May 21, 1830	With't amend.	104	Passed	Passed	App'd May 26, 1830
Bennett, Patrick	Arrears of pay as revolutionary quartermaster.	1	1	Petition	83					Referred to Secretary of War.		
Bennett, Patrick	Arrears of pay as revolutionary quartermaster.	1	2	Report of Secretary War.	141					Laid on table.		
Bennett, Patrick	Depreciation pay as forage master	3	1	Report of Seere tary of War.	18	Select	April 22, 1794	Adverse		Laid on table.		
Bennett, Rufus, widow of.	Pension for revolutionary services	28	1	Petition	238	Rev. Pensions.						
Bennett, Samuel	Pension for revolutionary services	3	1	Report of Secretary of War.	131	Select	May 26, 1794	Adverse		Referred to Committee Whole House.		
Bennett, Samuel	Pension for revolutionary services	4	1	Resolution	373	Claims.						
Bennett, Samuel	Pension for revolutionary services	4	2	Resolution	614	Claims	Feb. 6, 1797	Pension bill	224	Passed	Indef. postp'd.	
Bennett, Samuel	Pension for revolutionary services	15	2	Petition	32	Pens. & Rev. Cl'ms.	Jan. 19, 1819	Pension bill	286	Referred to Committee Whole House.		
Bennett, Samuel	Pension for revolutionary services	19	2	Petition	285	Military Pensions.						
Bennett, Samuel	Pension for revolutionary services	22	1	Resolution	176	Rev. Pensions.						
Bennett, Stephen	Pension for revolutionary services	20	2	Petition	228	Military Pensions.						
Bennett, Stephen	Pension for revolutionary services	21	1	Petition	67	Military Pensions	Feb. 13, 1830	Pension bill	72	Passed	Passed with amendment.	App'd May 20, 1830
Bennett, Stephen	Bounty land for revolutionary services.	24	1	Petition	203	Rev. Claims	600	Adverse		Laid on table.		
Bennett, Stephen	Bounty land for revolutionary services.	25	2	Petition	178	Rev. Claims	Jan. 18, 1818	Adverse		Laid on table.		
Bennett, Thomas, (Stratford.)	Pension for revolutionary services	25	2	Petition	54	Rev. Pensions.						
Bennett, Thomas, (Stratford.)	Pension for revolutionary services	26	1	Petition	173	Rev. Pensions	150	Favorable	160	Passed	Passed	App'd July 20, 1840
Bennett, Thomas, (Rome.)	To be restored to pension roll	26	1	Petition	936	Rev. Pensions.						
Bennett, William	Pension for revolutionary services	21	1	Petition	66	Military Pensions.						
Bennett, William	Pension for revolutionary services	28	1	Petition	567	Rev. Pensions.						
Bennett, William P.	Release from imprisonment	13	3	Petition	732	Ways and Means	Feb. 18, 1815	Favorable	301	Passed	Passed	App'd March 3, 1815
Benning, Thomas C., and others.	Right of pre emption	29	2	Petition	177	Public Lands.						

List of private claims presented to the House of Representatives of the United States from the 1st to the 31st Congress, inclusive—Continued.

Names of claimants.	Nature or object of the claim.	Congress.	Session.	How brought before the House of Reps.	Page of journal.	To what committee of the House referred.	No. or date of the report.	Nature of the report.	No. of the bill.	How disposed of by the House of Reps.	How disposed of by the Senate.	Date of the act of Congress, and remarks.
Benns, Charles	Indemnity for illegal custom house seizure.	22	2	Petition	67	Claims	27	Statement of the case.	.....	Referred to Secretary of Treasury.		
Benns, Charles	Indemnity for illegal custom house seizure.	23	1	Report of Secretary Treasury.	140	Claims.						
Benns, Charles	Indemnity for illegal custom house seizure.	24	1	Petition	93	Claims.						
Benns, Charles	Indemnity for illegal custom house seizure.	24	2	Petition	73	Claims.	324	Favorable	973	Referred to Committee Whole House.		
Benns, Charles	Indemnity for illegal custom house seizure.	25	2	Petition	36	Claims.	76	Favorable	88	Passed	Indef. postp'd.	
Benns, Charles	Indemnity for illegal custom house seizure.	25	3	Petition	86	Claims	219	Favorable	1074	Passed	Adverse report.	
Benns, Charles	Indemnity for illegal custom house seizure.	26	1	Petition	168	Claims.						
Benns, Charles	Indemnity for illegal custom house seizure.	26	2	Petition	80	Claims.						
Benns, Charles	Indemnity for illegal custom house seizure.	28	2	Petition	235	Claims.						
Benns, Charles	Indemnity for illegal custom house seizure.	29	1	Petition	67	Claims	2	Favorable	17	Passed	Reported without amend.	
Benns, Charles	Indemnity for illegal custom house seizure.	30	1	Petition	136	Claims	70	Favorable	52	Passed	Passed 2d session, amend.	App'd March 3, 1849
Benny, John	Pay for revolutionary service	16	1	Petition	....	Rev. Pensions	Jan. 14, 1820	Adverse	......	Leave to withdraw.		
Benson, A. S. and A. W.	Equitable settlement of his accounts	30	2	Senate resolution	573	....	....	....	J. R. 66	Passed	Passed	App'd March 3, 1849
Benson and Blodget	Remission of duties imposed at Castine.	16	1	Senate bill	108	Ways and Means	Jan. 14, 1820	With amend.	S. 13	Passed	Passed	App'd April 11, 1820
Benson, Egbert	Restoration of original compensation as United States Judge.	7	2	Petition	307	Whole House	Jan. 27, 1803	Adverse	......	Claim rejected	....	Leave to withdraw.
Benson, George	Right of pre-emption as New Orleans branch pilot.	28	1	Petition	77	Priv. Land Claims.	9	Favorable	35	Passed	Passed	App'd June 17, 1844
Benson, John	Remission of duties imposed at Castine	16	1	Senate bill	108	Ways and Means.	Jan. 14, 1820	With amend.	S. 13	Passed	Passed	App'd April 11, 1820
Benson, Joseph	(See Cephas Carpenter and others)	27	2	....	648							
Benson, William	Balance of depreciation pay for revolutionary services.	7	2	Petition	321	Claims	Feb. 23, 1803	Adverse	......	Referred to Committee Whole House.		
Benson, Zachariah	Compensation for horses lost in Black Hawk war.	25	3	Petition	205	Claims	207	Adverse	......	Laid on table.		
Bent, Lemuel	Settlement of accounts as paymaster United States army.	18	1	Petition	52	Claims.						
Bent, St. Vrain, & Co.	Compensation for provisions furnished on public account.	28	2	Senate resolution Petition Documents	180 187 206	Military Affairs. Military Affairs. Military Affairs	Jan. 24, 1845	With't amend.	S. R. 4	Referred to Committee Whole House.		
Bent, St. Vrain, & Co.	Compensation for provisions furnished on public account.	29	1	Senate bill	1041	Military Affairs	Aug. 10, 1846	With't amend.	77	Referred to Committee Whole House.		
Bent, St. Vrain, & Co.	Compensation for provisions furnished on public account.	30	1	Petition	154	Claims	37	Favorable	34	Passed	Passed	App'd Aug. 5, 1848
Bent, St. Vrain, & Co.	Indemnity for goods taken by Pawnee Indians.	28	2	Petition	187	Indian Affairs	194	Adverse	......	Laid on table.		
Bentalon, Paul	(See attorney of Paul Louis Celeron.)	12	1	....	39							
Bentalon, Paul and others	Indemnity for illegal detention of ship "Flora."	6	2	Memorial	733	Com. and Manuf.	....	....	......	Discharged; leave to withdraw.		

List of private claims presented to the House of Representatives of the United States from the 1st to the 31st Congress, inclusive—Continued.

Names of claimants.	Nature or object of the claim.	Congress.	Session.	How brought before the House of Reps.	Page of journal.	To what committee of the House referred.	No. or date of the report.	Nature of the report.	No. of the bill.	How disposed of by the House of Reps.	How disposed of by the Senate.	Date of the act of Congress, and remarks.
Bentalon, Paul, executor of.	Indemnity for French spoliations prior to 1800.	26	1	Memorial	182	Foreign Affairs	343	Favorable	319	Referred to Committee Whole House.		
Bentalon, Paul, executor of.	Indemnity for French spoliations prior to 1800.	29	2	Memorial	70	Foreign Affairs.						
Bentalon, Paul, executor of.	Indemnity for French spoliations prior to 1800.	31	1	Memorial	196	Foreign Affairs	355	General bill	318	Referred to Committee Whole House.		
Bentham, Robert	(See administ'r of Simeon Theus).	21	1	....	145							
Bentley, Benjamin, heirs of.	Compensation for wood taken for public use.	19	1	Petition	223	Claims.						
Bentley, Benjamin, heirs of.	Compensation for wood taken for public use.	19	2	Petition	154	Claims.						
Bentley, Benjamin, heirs of.	Indemnity for damage to farm by United States troops.	23	2	Petition	60	Claims	58	Favorable	663	Referred to Committee Whole House.		
Bentley, Benjamin, heirs of.	Indemnity for damage to farm by United States troops.	24	1	Petition	51	Claims	June 7, 1836	Adverse	......	Laid on table.		
Bentley, Benjamin, heirs of.	Indemnity for damage to farm by United States troops.	27	3	Petition	106	Claims	291	Adverse	......	Laid on table.		
Bentley, Benjamin, heirs of.	Indemnity for damage to farm by United States troops.	31	1	Petition	628	Claims.						
Bentley, Elisha	Pension for revolutionary services.	25	2	Petition	404	Rev. Pensions	707	Favorable	681	Passed.		
Bentley, Elisha	Pension for revolutionary services.	25	3	Petition	457	Rev. Pensions	302	Favorable	1171	Referred to Committee Whole House.		
Bentley, Gideon	Compensation for revolutionary services.	31	1	Petition	194	Rev. Claims	59	Adverse	......	Laid on table.		
Bentley, John	Compensation for corn taken for public use.	23	1	Petition	74	Claims.						
Bentley, John A., heirs of.	Pension for revolutionary services.	21	1	Petition	66	Military Pensions	....	....	......	Discharged; laid on table.		
Bentley, Richard	Pension for revolutionary services.	14	2	Petition	86	Pens. & Rev. Cl'ms.						
Bentley, Robert	(See heirs of Benjamin Bentley)	19	1	....	223							
Bentley, Thomas	Compensation for horses lost in public service.	22	1	Petition	333	Claims	Feb. 20, 1832	Adverse	......	Laid on table.		
Bentley, William, heirs of	Compensation for revolutionary services.	22	1	Petition	55	Rev. Claims.						
Bentley, William, widow of.	Pension for revolutionary services.	29	1	Petition	520	Rev. Pensions	786	Adverse	......	Laid on table.		
Benton, Job	Pension for revolutionary services.	23	1	Petition	242	Rev. Pensions	....	....	......	Discharged; laid on table.		
Benton, John, (N. C.)	Pension for revolutionary services.	3	1	Rep. of Secretary War.	131	Select	May 26, 1794	Favorable.				
Benton, John, (N. C.)	Pension for revolutionary services.	4	1	Rep. of Secretary War.	447	Claims	Feb. 18, 1796	Pension bill	156	Passed	Passed	App'd April 20, 1796
Benton, John, (Ga.)	Pension	21	2	Resolution	172	Military Pensions.						
Benton, John, (Ga.)	Pension	22	1	Resolution	85	Rev. Pensions.						
Benton, Lemuel	(See attorney of Joseph Long)	4	1	....	373							
Benton, Samuel H., & Co.	Release from guarantee on mail contract.	25	2	Petition	1259	P. Of. and P. Roads.	1051	Adverse	......	Laid on table.		
Benton, Selah	Pension for revolutionary services.	12	1	Petition	25	Claims	Jan. 31, 1812	Favorable	55	Passed	Passed	App'd Feb. 21, 1812
Benton, Selah, widow of.	Arrears of pension	12	2	Petition	607	Claims.						
Benton, Selah, widow of.	Arrears of pension	13	2	Petition	287	Pensions	92	Adverse	......	Leave to withdraw.		
Benton, Selah, widow of.	Arrears of pension	18	2	Petition	41	Pens. & Rev. Cl'ms.	20	Adverse	......	Laid on table.		

List of private claims presented to the House of Representatives of the United States from the 1st to the 31st Congress, inclusive—Continued.

Names of claimants.	Nature or object of the claim.	Congress.	Session.	How brought before the House of Reps.	Page of journal.	To what committee of the House referred.	No. or date of the report.	Nature of the report.	No. of the bill.	How disposed of by the House of Reps.	How disposed of by the Senate.	Date of the act of Congress, and remarks.
Benton, Selah, widow of..	Arrears of pension............	19	1	Petition	204	Military Pensions..	April 1, 1826	Adverse.				
Bents, Francis..........	Compensation for revolutionary services.	20	2	Petition	40	Rev. Claims......	Jan. 22, 1829	Adverse	......	Laid on table.		
Bentson, John..........	(See Stephen Decatur, widow of, and others.)	18	2	....	54							
Bentout, Josiah	Indemnity for French Spoliations prior 1800.	26	1	Memorial	182	Foreign Affairs....	343	Favorable....	319	Referred to Committee Whole House.		
Bequette, Charles	Confirmation of title to land in Missouri.	15	1	Petition	226	Priv. Land Claims.						
Bequette, Charles	Confirmation of title to land in Missouri.	16	1	Petition	71	Priv. Land Claims.						
Bequette, Charles	Confirmation of title to land in Missouri.	17	1	Petition	53	Public Lands.						
Bequette, Charles	Confirmation of title to land in Missouri.	18	1	Petition	53	Public Lands.	Jan. 16, 1824	General bill ..	65	Passed	Passed.......	App'd May 26, 1824
Bequette, Henry	Permission to enter a 16th section of land.	28	1	Petition	181	Public Lands.	181	Adverse......	......	Laid on table.		
Berard, Baptiste, widow of.	Confirmation of title to land in Louisiana.	28	1	Petition	550	Priv. Land Claims.	460	Favorable and bill.	356	Passed	Passed.......	App'd June 17, 1844
Bergen, Elizabeth	Annuity........	6	2	General appropriation bill.	752	....	....	....	277	Passed............	Passed.......	App'd March 3, 1801
Bergen, W.............	(See exploring expedition.)......	27	3	....	149							
Bergen, W.............	(See James Tilton and others.)..	30	1	....	328	....	....	....	S. 118			
Berger, Peter, heirs of....	Permission to locate certain land warrants.	24	2	Petition	273	Priv. Land Claims.	....	....	......	Discharged; laid on table.		
Bergin, John	(See O. Shedlate, surety of)....	15	2	Petition	103	Judiciary	Dec. 29, 1818	Adverse.	......	Claim rejected.		
Bergure, Jean Charles....	Land claim (no paper on file)....	25	2	Documents.....	548	Public Lands .						
Berham, Francis and Fielding, representatives of.	Confirmation of title to land in Louisiana.	20	1	Resolution	448	Priv. Land Claims.	May 9, 1828	Adverse	......	Laid on table.		
Berham, Francis and Fielding, representatives of	Confirmation of title to land in Louisiana.	20	2	Resolution	44	Priv. Land Claims.						
Berham, Francis and Fielding, representatives of.	Confirmation of title to land in Louisiana.	22	1	Resolution	173	Priv. Land Claims.	197	Favorable....	283	Referred to Committee Whole House.		
Berins, Edward, assignee of.	Permission to locate land warrants No. 27.115.	26	1	Resolution......	951	Priv. Land Claims.						
Berkhammer, Henry.....	Pension for revolutionary services.	23	1	Petition	112	Rev. Pensions.						
Berkhammer, Henry	Pension for revolutionary services.	24	1	Petition	274	Rev. Pensions	....	....	......	Discharged; laid on table.		
Berkley, John	Indemnity for dificiency in public land purchase.	23	1	Petition	386	Priv. Land Claims.	June 24, 1834	Adverse	......	Laid on table		
Berkley, John	Indemnity for deficiency in public land purchase.	23	2	Petition	95	Priv. Land Claims.	Feb. 13, 1835	Favorable....	734	Referred to Committee Whole House.		
Berkley, John	Indemnity for deficiency in public land purchase.	24	1	Petition	112	Priv. Land Claims.	115	Favorable....	132	Passed.		
Bernard, Hyacinthe......	Confirmation of title to land in Louisiana.	15	1	Petition	173	Priv. Land Claims.						
Bernard, Hyacinthe......	Confirmation of title to land in Louisiana.	20	1	Petition	343	Priv. Land Claims.						
Bernard, Hyacinthe......	Confirmation of title to land in Louisiana.	20	2	Petition	34	Public Lands	22	Favorable	339	Referred to Committee Whole House.		
Bernard, Hyacinthe......	Confirmation of title to land in Louisiana.	21	1	Petition	40	Priv. Land Claims.	Dec. 28, 1829	Favorable	42	Passed............	Passed	App'd March 23, 1830

List of private claims presented to the House of Representatives of the United States from the 1st to the 31st Congress, inclusive—Continued.

Names of claimants.	Nature or object of the claim.	Congress.	Session.	How brought before the House of Reps.	Page of journal.	To what committee of the House referred.	No. or date of the report.	Nature of the report.	No. of the bill.	How disposed of by the House of Reps.	How disposed of by the Senate.	Date of the act of Congress, and remarks.
Bernard, Joseph	Compensation for revolutionary services and loses.	1	2	Petition	160					Laid on table.		
Bernard, Joseph, representatives of.	Permission to locate certain land	26	1	Senate bill	811	Priv. Land Claims			S. 163			
Bernard, John, (Pa.)	To be restored to pension roll	19	1	Petition	35	Rev. Pensions	April 1, 1826	Adverse		Laid on table.		
Bernard, John, heirs of (N. C.)	Compensation for revolutionary services.	23	2	Petition	165	Rev. Claims.						
Bernard	(See Dodd & Bernard)	20	1		249							
Bernhisel, John M.	Compensation for services as agent of Utah.	31	2	Petition	120	Territories	Feb. 6, 1851	Favorable	452	Laid on table.		
Berri, Emm'l, and J. H. Keese.	Reimbursement of duties on damaged goods.	29	1	House bill	273	Commerce	Jan. 30, 1846	With amend.	132	Passed	Indef. postp'd.	
Berri, Emm'l, and J. H. Keese.	Reimbursement of duties on damaged goods.	30	1	Memorial	436	Commerce	319	Favorable	296	Passed		
Berrian, George	To correct error in the issue of a land warrant.	21	1	Petition	121	Priv. Land Claims	Jan. 18, 1830	Adverse		Laid on table.		
Berrian, Dr. John, heirs of.	Compensation for medical services, revolutionary army.	23	1	Petition	39	Rev. Claims	100	Favorable	105	Passed	Passed	App'd June 19, 1834
Berrian, Samuel, & others.	Remission of penalty for violation of revenue laws.	4	1	Petition	528	Com. and Manuf.						
Berrian, Samuel, & others.	Remission of penalty for violation of revenue laws.	4	2	Petition	629	Com. and Manuf.	105	Adverse		Rejected.		
Berringer, George, widow of.	Pension for loss in public service	31	1	Petition	417	Invalid Pensions.						
Berry, Abigail	Payment of certain bills of credit	4	1	Report Secretary of Treasury.	388	Claims	May 31, 1796	Adverse		Laid on table.		
Berry, Bartholomew	Pension for revolutionary services.	10	2	Pension bill	499	Whole House	Feb. 20, 1809	With amend.	158	Passed	Passed with amendment.	App'd Mar. 3, 1809
Berry, Benjamin, & others, attorney of.	Exchange of location of certain Virginia land warrants.	14	1	Petition	409	Public Lands.						
Berry, Benjamin, (Me)	Payment for transportation of goods from a wreck.	15	1	Petition	38	Claims	68	Favorable	65	Passed	Passed	App'd April 20, 1818
Berry, Benjamin, (Md)	Pension	21	2	Petition	270	Military Pensions.						
Berry, David	Compensation for services as interpreter to Indians.	15	2	Petition	173	Public Lands.						
Berry, E. M.	(See Louis F. Beeler, *et al*)	30	1		115		482					
Berry, Elisha	Pension	23	1	Petition	241	Rev. Pensions	Feb. 18, 1834	Adverse		Laid on table.		
Berry, Jabez	Pension for revolutionary services.	21	2	Petition	80	Military Pensions.						
Berry, Jabez	Pension for revolutionary services.	22	1	Petition	219	Rev. Pensions				Discharged; laid on table.		
Berry, James	Pension for revolutionary services.	11	2	Pension bill	283	Whole House	Mar. 10, 1810		107	Passed	Passed	App'd April 27, 1810
Berry, James, (Va)	Compensation for horse lost in the public service.	22	2	Petition	32	Claims	Dec. 26, 1832	Adverse		Laid on table.		
Berry, James, (Ohio)	Pension for revolutionary services.	29	2	Petition	133	Rev. Pensions.						
Berry, John	Pension for revolutionary services.	9	2	Pension bill	608	Whole House	Feb. 28, 1807	With amend.	216	Passed	Passed with amendment.	App'd Mar. 3, 1807
Berry, John, (Mass)	Arrears of pension	10	1	Petition	117	Select.						
Berry, John	Pension for revolutionary services.	13	2	Pension bill	377	Whole House	Mar. 31, 1814	With amend.	166	Passed	Passed with amendment.	App'd April 18, 1814
Berry, John, (Va.)	Pension for revolutionary services.	7	2	Petition	291	Claims.						
Berry, John, (Va.)	Pension for revolutionary services.	16	1	Petition	32	Pens. & Rev. Cl'ms.						
Berry, John, (Va.)	Bounty land for revolutionary services.	15	2	Petition	125	Pens. & Rev. Cl'ms.	Dec. 28, 1818	Adverse		Claim rejected.		

List of private claims presented to the House of Representatives of the United States from the 1st to the 31st Congress, inclusive—Continued.

Names of claimants.	Nature or object of the claim.	Congress.	Session.	How brought before the House of Reps.	Page of journal.	To what committee of the House referred.	No. or date of the report.	Nature of the report.	No. of the bill.	How disposed of by the House of Reps.	How disposed of by the Senate.	Date of the act of Congress, and remarks.
Berry, John	(See Reuben E. Gentry, & others)	24	1		291		266		273			
Berry, John	(See heir of Alexander Gillespie)	6	2		756							
Berry, Lt. Joseph	Indemnity for damages recovered against him.	15	1	Petition	344	Claims.						
Berry, Mary Ann	(See heirs of John Briggs)	26	1		360							
Berry, Peletiah, widow of.	Continuation of pension	27	2	Petition	47	Rev. Pensions	784	Adverse		Laid on table.		
Berry, Peletiah, widow of.	Continuation of pension	28	2	Petition	119	Rev. Pensions.						
Berry, Taylor	Permission to exchange a location of land.	17	2	Senate bill	278	Priv. Land Claims.			S. 52			
Berry, William	Pension	13	3	Pension bill	740	Whole House	Mar. 1, 1805	With amend.	303	Passed	Passed with amendment.	App'd March 3, 1815
Berry, William	Pension	25	2	Senate bill	1155	Rev. Pensions	July 7, 1838	With't amend.	S. 288			
Berry, Lt. Wm., widow of	Half-pay for services	24	1	Petition	408	Naval Affairs.						
Berryhill, John	Pension	21	1	Petition	265	Military Pensions	May 3, 1830	Favorable	453	Referred to Committee Whole House.		
Berryhill, John	Pension	21	2	Rep't Committee Whole House	315			With't amend.	453	Passed.		
Berryman, Charles	(See widow of Stephen Decatur, others.)											
Berryman, Newton	Compensation for services as clerk in Navy Department.	22	2	Senate bill	441	Claims	Mar. 1, 1833	With't amend.	S. 89	Passed	Passed	App'd March 2, 1833
Berta, Marianna S.	(See Gabriel W. Perpall, & others)	21	1		150							
Berthiaume, Francis J.	Confirmation of title to land in Missouri.	15	2	Petition	230	Priv. Land Claims.						
Berthiaume, Francis J.	Confirmation of title to land in Missouri.	17	1	Petition	53	Public Lands.						
Berthiaume, Francis J.	Confirmation of title to land in Missouri.	18	1	Petition	53	Public Lands	July 16, 1824	General bill	65	Passed	Passed	App'd May 26, 1824
Bertier & Co.	Release of goods seized by revenue officers.	1	2	Petition	199					Laid on table.		
Berzat, Gabriel, widow of.	Confirmation of title to land in Louisiana.	16	1	Senate bill	429	Priv. Land Claims.			S. 76	Discharged; laid on table.		
Berzat, Gabriel, widow of.	Confirmation of title to land in Louisiana.	16	2	Senate bill	102	Priv. Land Claims.	Jan. 3, 1821	With amend	S. 11	Referred to Committee Whole House.		
Berzat, Gabriel, widow of.	Confirmation of title to land in Louisiana.	17	1	Petition	290	Priv. Land Claims.	49	Favorable	96	Passed	Passed	App'd May 7, 1822
Berzat, Susan	(See Gabriel Berzat, widow of)	16	1		429							
Besley, Sarah	(See widow of Henry Adams)	25	3		216							
Besiah, (an Indian)	Permission to locate land	28	1	House bill	508	Public Lands	542	Adverse	184	Laid on table.		
Bessee, Anthony	Permission to locate an uncontested claim.	29	1	Petition	384	Priv. Land Claims.	654	Favorable	436	Referred to Committee Whole House.		
Bessee, Anthony	Permission to locate an uncontested claim.	30	1	Petition	109	Priv. Land Claims.	128	Favorable	119	Passed	Passed 2d sess.	App'd Jan. 10, 1849
Besse, Claudius, heirs of.	Indemnity for French spoliations prior to 1800.	29	2	Petition	163	Foreign Affairs.						
Besse, Claudius, heirs of.	Indemnity for French spoliations prior to 1800.	31	1	Petition	271	Foreign Affairs	355	General bill	318	Referred to Committee Whole House.		
Bessee, John, widow of	Indemnity for French spoliations prior to 1800.	31	1	Petition	471	Fareign Affairs	355	General bill	318	Referred to Committee Whole House.		
Bessinger, Lieutenant, widow, &c., of.	Half-pay for services in Florida	24	1	Petition	260	Invalid Pensions	415	Favorable	426	Passed	Passed	App'd July 4, 1836
Bessom, Philip	Indemnity for a French capture in 1797.	20	2	Petition	289	Foreign Affairs.						

List of private claims presented to the House of Representatives of the United States from the 1st to the 31st Congress, inclusive—Continued.

Names of claimants.	Nature or object of the claim.	Congress.	Session.	How brought before the House of Reps.	Page of journal.	To what committee of the House referred.	No. or date of the report.	Nature of the report.	No. of the bill.	How disposed of by the House of Reps.	How disposed of by the Senate.	Date of the act of Congress, and remarks.
Bessom, Philip	Indemnity for a French capture in 1797.	21	1	Petition	50	Foreign Affairs.						
				Petition (2)	198	Foreign Affairs				Discharged; laid on table.		
Bessom, Philip	Indemnity for a French capture in 1797.	22	2	Petition	40	Foreign Affairs	Feb. 19, 1853	Favorable	742	Referred to Committee Whole House.		
Bessom, Philip	Compensation for transporting American seamen from France.	21	2	Petition	53	Foreign Affairs				Discharged; laid on table.		
Bessom, Philip	Compensation for transporting American seamen from France.	22	1	Petition	115	Foreign Affairs.						
Bessom, Philip	Compensation for transporting American seamen from France.	23	1	Memorial	37	Foreign Affairs	92	Favorable	31	Passed	Passed	App'd June 26, 1834
Besson, Julien, representatives of.	Confirmation of title to land in Opelousas, Louisiana.	19	2	Rep. of Secretary Treasury.	50	Public Lands	49	Favorable	378	Referred to Committee Whole House.		
Besson, Julien, representatives of.	Confirmation of title to land in Opelousas, Louisiana.	24	1	Rep. of Secretary Treasury.	362	Priv. Land Claims.	93	Statement of facts.				
Besson, Pierre, representatives of.	Confirmation of title to land in Opelousas, Louisiana.	19	2	Rep. of Secretary Treasury.	50	Public	49	Favorable	378	Referred to Committee Whole House.		
Besson, Pierre, representatives of.		24	1	Rep. of Secretary Treasury.	362	Priv. Land Claims.	93	Statement of facts.				
Best, George	Compensation for work on Cumberland road.	23	1	Resolution	589	Claims	455	Adverse		Laid on table.		
Best, Isaac, attorney of	Indemnity for Indian depredations.	19	2	Petition	134	Indian Affairs	51	Favorable		Referred to Committee Whole House.		
Bethall, Gilley C	(See heirs of Christopher Miller)	28	1		113							
Bethamy, Matthew	Confirmation of title to land in Louisiana.	20	1	Petition	245	Priv. Land Claims.						
Bethel, William	Indemnity for French spoliations prior to 1800.	26	1	Memorial	182	Foreign Affairs	343	Favorable	319	Referred to Committee Whole House.		
Bethell, William C	Indemnity for Indian depredations.	26	2	Documents	124	Claims.						
Bethman & sons, agent of.	Remission of duties on wines	4	2	Petition	633	Com. and Manuf	Jan. 3, 1797	Adverse		Claim rejected.		
Bethune, Farq	(See F. M. Arredondo)	19	1		252							
Betsey, brig, owners of	Compensrtion for vessel sunk in Baltimore harbor.	21	1	Memorial	82	Commerce	Feb. 2, 1830	Favorable	191	Passed	Passed	App'd May 29, 1830
Betton, Solomon	Settlement of accounts as assessor of Creek Indians' property.	22	1	Resolution	319	Indian Affairs	April 6, 1832	Adverse		Laid on table.		
Betton, Solomon D, sureties of.	Release from judgment	27	2	Senate bill	1126	Judiciary	Aug. 20, 1842	Bill amended.	S. 266	Passed	Concurred in	App'd Aug. 26, 1842
Betterton, Benjamin	Compensation for extra services as clerk in War Department.	3	1	Petition	93	Select	54	Favorable	69	Passed	Rejected.	
Bettincourt, Antonio	Compensation for naval services	28	2	Petition	354	Naval Affairs.						
Bettes, Jeremiah	Increase of pension	14	1	Petition	346	Pens. & Rev. Cl'ms.				Discharged: laid on table.		
Bettes, Jeremiah	Increase of pension	15	1	Petition	80	Pens. & Rev. Cl'ms.				Dischargad; laid on table.		
Bettes, Jeremiah	Increase of pension	15	2	Petition	70	Pens. & Rev. Cl'ms.				Discharged; laid on table.		
Betto, Peter	Bounty land for revolutionary services.	15	2	Petition	118	Pens. & Rev. Cl'ms.				Discharged; referred to Secretary of War.		
Betts, Hannah	(See administratrix of Jesse Raymond.)	29	1		625							
Betts, James	Compensation for revolutionary services.	4	1	Petition	554	Claims.						

List of private claims presented to the House of Representatives of the United States from the 1st to the 31st Congress, inclusive—Continued.

Names of claimants.	Nature or object of the claim.	Congress.	Session.	How brought before the House of Reps.	Page of journal.	To what committee of the House referred.	No. or date of the report.	Nature of the report.	No. of the bill.	How disposed of by the House of Reps.	How disposed of by the Senate.	Date of the act of Congress, and remarks.
Betts, James	Compensation for revolutionary services.	4	2	Petition	614	Claims	Jan. 3, 1797	Adverse	......	Claim rejected.		
Betts, John	Compensation for horse lost in Seminole war.	23	1	Petition	155	Claims.						
Betts, Joseph or Josiah T.	(See Felix St. Vrain, sureties of).	25	2									
Betts, Peter	Indemnity for loss on paper currency.	2	2	Memorial	678	....	....	....	.....	Laid on table.		
Betts, Solomon	Indemnity for French spoliations prior to 1800.	26	1	Memorial	182	Foreign Affairs	343	Favorable	319	Referred to Committee Whole House.		
Betts, Stephen	Pension for revolutionary services.	15	1	Petition	211	Pens. & Rev. Cl'ms.	....	....	......	Discharged; laid on table.		
Betts, Timothy	Pension for revolutionary services.	19	1	Resolution	326	Military Pensions	May 5, 1826	Favorable.				
Betts, Timothy	Pension for revolutionary services.	19	2	Petition	66	Military Pensions	....	....	......	Discharged; laid on table.		
Betts, Tophar	Pension for revolutionary services.	21	2	Resolution	65	Military Pensions.						
Betz, Preserved, widow of.	Pension for revolutionary services.	28	2	Petition	198	Rev. Pensions.						
Betz, Preserved, widow of.	Pension for revolutionary services.	29	1	Documents	120	Rev. Pensions	458	Favorable	335	Passed	Passed	App'd Aug. 8, 1846
Bevan, Joseph	Remission of duties on steam engine.	15	1	Petition	135	Ways and Means	Jan. 23, 1818	Adverse	......	Claim rejected.		
Beverly, Robert	Indemnity for depredations of French armed vessels.	7	1	Memorial	219	....	....	....	......	Laid on table.		
Beverly, Robert	Indemnity for depredations of French armed vessels.	24	1	Petition	202	Foreign Affairs.						
Beverly, Robert	Indemnity for depredations of French armed vessels.	26	1	Memorial	182	Foreign Affairs	343	....	319			
Bevins, Ebenezer	Pension for revolutionary services.	4	1	Resolution	373	Claims.						
Bevins, Ebenezer	Pension for revolutionary services.	4	2	Resolution	614	Claims.						
Bevoise, Hannah	(See John Johnson and others)	15	1	....	247							
Beyer, George T.	Indemnity for property taken by the enemy.	20	2	Petition	33	Foreign Affairs	25	Adverse	......	Laid on table.		
Beyer, George T	Indemnity for property taken by the enemy.	23	1	Petition	299	Foreign Affairs.						
Beyer, George T	Indemnity for property taken by the enemy.	24	1	Petition	143	Foreign Affairs	529	Adverse	......	Laid on table.		
Beyer, George T	Indemnity for property taken by the enemy.	28	1	Petition	483	Claims	343	Adverse	......	Laid on table.		
Beyer, George T	Indemnity for property taken by the enemy.	29	1	Petition	92	Claims	225	Adverse	......	Laid on table.		
Beyer, George T	Indemnity for property taken by the enemy.	30	1	Petition	682	Foreign Affairs.						
Beziah, (Indian woman)	Grant of land in Indiana	28	1	House bill	508	Public Lands	542	Adverse	184	Laid on table.		
Beziers, Captain F.	Compensation for rescue of Americans from a wreck.	25	2	Pres. Message & Documents.	607							
Beziers, Captain F.	Compensation for rescue of Americans from a wreck.	26	1	Documents.	182	Foreign Affairs.						
Beziers, Captain F.	Compensation for rescue of Americans from a wreck.	26	2	Documents	118	Foreign Affairs.						
Beziers, Captain F.	Compensation for rescue of Americans from a wreck.	27	2	Pres. Message	251	Foreign Affairs.						
Beziers, Captain F.	Compensation for rescue of Americans from a wreck.	27	3	Documents	223	Foreign Affairs.						
Bezior, Benjamin, widow of	Indemnity for property taken by British and Indians.	23	1	Petition	438	Claims	437	Adverse	......	Laid on table.		

List of private claims presented to the House of Representatives of the United States from the 1st to the 31st Congress, inclusive—Continued.

Names of claimants.	Nature or object of the claim.	Congress.	Session.	How brought before the House of Reps.	Page of journal.	To what committee of the House referred.	No. or date of the report.	Nature of the report.	No. of the bill.	How disposed of by the House of Reps.	How disposed of by the Senate.	Date of the act of Congress, and remarks.
Biays, James, trustees of.	Indemnity for French spoliations prior to 1800.	26	1	Memorial	182	Foreign Affairs	343	Favorable	319	Referred to Committee Whole House.		
Biays, James, trustees of.	Indemnity for French spoliations prior to 1800.	31	1	Petition	1076	Foreign Affairs	355	General bill	318	Referred to Committee Whole House.		
Bibb, John G.	Compensation for horse lost in public service.	25	2	Petition	177	Rev. Claims.						
Bibb, John G.	Compensation for horse lost in public service.	26	1	Petition	170	Claims	679	Adverse	......	Laid on table.		
Bibb, John G.	Compensation for horse lost in public service.	26	2	Resolution	62	Claims.						
Bibb, John G.	Compensation for horse lost in public service.	27	2	Petition	55	Claims	342	Adverse	......	Laid on table.		
Bibbans, Benjamin	Pension for revolutionary services.	23	1	Petition	490	Rev. Pensions.						
Bibbans, Benjamin	Pension for revolutionary services.	23	2	Petition	237	Rev. Pensions	....	....	......	Discharged; laid on table.		
Bibbans, Benjamin	Pension for revolutionary services.	24	1	Petition	213	Rev. Pensions	....	....	......	Discharged; laid on table.		
Bibbans, Benjamin	Pension for revolutionary services.	25	3	Petition	127	Rev. Pensions	....	....	......	Discharged; laid on table.		
Bible, Adam, widow of.	Increase of pension	27	2	Petition	684	Rev. Pensions	784	Adverse	......	Laid on table.		
Bible Society, Baltimore	Remission of duties on stereotype plates.	14	1	Senate bill	533	Whole House	April 15, 1816	No amendm't.	......	Passed	....	App'd April 20, 1816
Bible Society, British and Foreign.	Remission of duty on books sent to Canada.	26	1	Petition	297	Ways and Means	....	....	.....	Discharged; laid on table.		
Bible Society, Massachusetts.	Debenture on drawback of duties.	14	1	Senate bill	533	Whole House	April 15, 1816	No amendm't.	......	Passed	....	App'd April 20, 1816
Bible Society of Philadelphia.	Remission of duties on stereotype plates.	12	2	House bill	621	Whole House	Jan. 19, 1813	No amendm't.	232	Passed.		
Bible Society of Philadelphia.	Remission of duties on stereotype plates.	12	2	Senate bill	623	Whole House	....	No amendm't.	S. 51	Passed	....	App'd Feb. 2, 1813
Bickham, Armistead	(See Armistead Beckham)	19	2	....	189							
Bickham, William, widow of.	(See widow of William Beckham)	20	1	....	49							
Bickley & Clark, representatives of.	Payment of exchange drawn by J. Armstrong.	15	2	Petition	24	Ways and Means	Dec. 18, 1818	Favorable	236	Referred to Committee Whole House.		
Bickley & Clark, representatives of.	Payment of exchange drawn by J. Armstrong.	16	1	Petition	164	Ways and Means	April 8, 1820	Favorable	132	Passed	Passed	App'd May 6, 1820
Bicknell, Joshua, widow of	Continuation of pension	25	2	Petition	230	Rev. Pensions	Jan. 25, 1838	General bill	456	Referred to Committee Whole House.		
Biddle, Augustine	Renewal of a lost revolutionary certificate.	3	2	Memorial	315	Select.						
Biddle, Augustine	Renewal of a lost revolutionary certificate.	4	1	Memorial	428	Claims.						
Biddle, Augustine	Renewal of a lost revolutionary certificate.	4	2	Memorial	683	Claims	Feb. 7, 1797	Adverse	......	Postponed.		
Biddle, Augustine	Renewal of a lost revolutionary certificate.	5	2	Resolution	232	Whole House.						
Biddle, Clement	To fund certain revolutionary certificates.	5	2	Petition	143	Whole House.						
Biddle, Clement	To fund certain revolutionary certificates.	6	2	Appropriat'n bill.	752	Whole House	Feb. 17, 1801	Amendments	277	Passed	Passed	App'd March 3, 1801
Biddle, Edward	(See sureties of Aaron M. Wright.)	21	1	....	69							
Biddle, Edward, and William Mitchell.	Indemnity for loss resulting from acts of Indian agent.	21	1	Petition	146	Judiciary.						

List of private claims presented to the House of Representatives of the United States from the 1st to the 31st Congress, inclusive—Continued.

Names of claimants.	Nature or object of the claim.	Congress.	Session.	How brought before the House of Reps.	Page of journal.	To what committee of the House referred.	No. or date of the report.	Nature of the report.	No. of the bill.	How disposed of by the House of Reps.	How disposed of by the Senate.	Date of the act of Congress, and remarks.
Biddle, Edward, and William Mitchell.	Reimbursement of land payment	24	1	Appropriat'n bill	1012	Ways and Means	Jan. 15, 1836	Amendments	695	Passed	Passed	App'd July 2, 1836
Biddle, James, *et al.*	Prize-money for sloop of war Penguin.	14	1	House bill	94	Whole House	Feb. 12, 1816	Bill amended		Passed	Passed	App'd Feb. 28, 1816
Biddle, Jesse	Pension	29	1	Petition	146	Invalid Pensions	84	Adverse		Laid on table.		
Biddle, John, (Mich.)	Compensation as clerk to land commissioners.	19	1	Appropriat'n bill	142				42	Passed	Amended, and passed.	App'd Mar. 14, 1826
Biddle, John	Compensation for extra services in land office at Detroit.	31	1	Petition	193	Claims.						
Biddle, Richard	(See administ'r of John Wilkins, jr.)	16	1		198				S. 81			
Biddle, Samuel	Indemnity for impressment by the British.	10	1	Petition	10					Referred to Secretary of State.		
Biddle, Samuel	Pension	19	2	Petition	333	Military Pensions				Discharged; laid on table.		
Biddle, Sophia	Reimbursement of land payment	24	1	Appropriat'n bill	1012	Ways and Means	Jan. 15, 1836	Amendments	695	Passed	Passed	App'd July 2, 1836
Biddle, Thomas	(See Andrew Summers, assignee of.)	26	1		182		343		319			
Biel	(See agents of Kantzow and Biel)	18	2		136							
Bienvenue, Antoine	Indemnity for property destroyed by United States troops.	14	2	Petition	142	Claims	Feb. 3, 1817	Favorable	99	Passed	Rejected.	
Bienvenue, Antoine	Indemnity for negro carried off by the enemy.	14	2	Petition	306					Referred to Secretary State.		
Bienvenue, Antoine	Indemnity for negro carried off by the enemy.	15	1	Referred to Secretary State.	46	Claims	Dec. 23, 1817	Adverse		Leave to withdraw.		
Bienvenu, Brothers	Comfirmation of title to land in Louisiana, (Terre aux Bœuff.)	22	1	Petition	64	Priv. Land Claims	62	Favorable	125	Passed	Passed	App'd June 25, 1832
Bierce, William	Pension	16	2	Petition	248	Rev. Pensions	Feb. 28, 1821	Adverse		Leave to withdraw.		
Bierwith, Leopold	(See Conrad Faber and others)	31	1		256							
Bigelow, Isaac	Compensation for property lost by burning of ship "Missouri."	28	2	Petition	46	Naval Affairs				Discharged; laid on table.		
Bigelow, Jacob, administrator.	Compensation for revolutionary supplies.	29	1	Petition	276	Rev. Claims.						
Bigelow, Taylor or Tyler	(See representatives of General William Hull.)	19	1		223							
Bigelow, Hardin	Indemnity for damage by illegal seizure of iron.	28	1	Memorial	430					Laid on table.		
Bigelow, Hopestill	Arrears of pension	26	1	Petition	287	Invalid Pensions	405	Adverse		Laid on table.		
Bigelow, Hopestill	Arrears of pension	27	2	Petition	485	Invalid Pensions	814	Adverse		Laid on table.		
Bigers, Joseph	Compensation for military services	14	1	Petition	74	Claims.						
Biggs, Benjamin, widow of	Pension for revolutionary services	27	2	Petition	458	Rev. Pensions	784	Adverse		Laid on table.		
Biggs, Jeremiah	Duplicate land warrant	31	1	Petition	1255	Public Lands.						
Biggs, Joseph	Pension for revolutionary services	3	1	Petition	111	Select	May 14, 1794	Favorable		Laid on table.		
Biggs, Joseph	Pension for revolutionary services	4	1	Petition	384	Claims.						
Biggs, Joseph	Pension for revolutionary services	4	2	Petition	614	Claims	Jan. 24, 1797	Adverse		Laid on table.		
Biggs, Joseph	Pension for revolutionary services	19	2	Petition	133	Rev. Claims	Jan. 31, 1827	Adverse		Laid on table.		
Biggs, Joseph	Pension for revolutionary services	20	1	Petition	311	Rev. Claims	Feb. 26, 1828	Adverse		Laid on table.		
Biggs, Randolph, widow of	Pension for revolutionary services	26	1	Resolution	385	Rev. Pensions	664	Adverse		Laid on table.		
Biggs, Robert	Confirmation of title to land in Indiana.	21	1	Documents	298	Public Lands.						
Biggs, William	Bounty land for revolutionary services.	10	1	Petition	156	Public lands	April 23, 1808	Adverse		Leave to withdraw.		
Biggs, William	Bounty land for revolutionary services.	10	2	Petition	375	Public Lands.						

List of private claims presented to the House of Representatives of the United States from the 1st to the 31st Congress, inclusive—Continued.

Names of claimants.	Nature or object of the claim.	Congress.	Session.	How brought before the House of Reps.	Page of journal.	To what committee of the House referred.	No. or date of the report.	Nature of the report.	No. of the bill.	How disposed of by the House of Reps.	How disposed of by the Senate.	Date of the act of Congress, and remarks.
Biggs, William	Bounty land for revolutionary services.	13	3	Petition	45	Public Lands				Discharged.		
Biggs, William	Bounty land for revolutionary services.	14	1	Petition	66	Public Lands.						
Biggs, William	Bounty land for revolutionary services.	16	1	Resolution	200	Public Lands.						
Biggs, William	Bounty land for revolutionary services.	17	1	Petition	146	Public Lands	April 5, 1822	Favorable	156	Referred to Committee Whole House.		
Biggs, William	Bounty land for revolutionary services.	18	1	Documents	316	Public Lands.						
Biggs, William	Bounty land for revolutionary services.	18	2	Petition	119	Public Lands.						
Biggs, William	Bounty land for revolutionary services.	19	1	Petition	53	Public Lands.						
				Resolution	468	Public Lands.						
				Senate bill	547	Public Lands	May 16, 1826	With't amend.	143	Passed	Passed	App'd May 22, 1826
Bigham, Agnes	(See heirs of Thomas Armor)	25	2		722							
Bigham, Margaret	(See heirs of Thomas Armor)	25	2		722							
Bigham, Robert	(See executors of Thomas Armor.)	3	1		50							
Bigham, Thomas	(See Thomas Bingham)	28	1		449							
Bigham, William W.	Correction of an entry of land	25	2	Petition	86	Public Lands	Jan. 4, 1838	Favorable	295	Referred to Committee Whole House.		
Bigham, William W.	Correction of an entry of land	25	3	Rep't Committee Whole House.	376			With't amend.	295	Passed	Passed	App'd Mar. 3, 1839
Bilcher, Joshua	Reimbursement of payment to Indian interpreter.	24	1	Petition	96	Indian Affairs.						
Bill, Benijah	Pension for revolutionary services.	22	1	Petition	219	Rev. Pensions.				Discharged; laid on table.		
Bill, Daniel	Increase of pension	10	2	Pension bill	499	Whole House	Feb. 20, 1809	With amend.	158	Passed	Passed	App'd Mar. 3, 1809
Bill, Jabez	Compensation for revolutionary services.	1	3	Rep. of Secretary War.	393					Laid on table.		
Bill, Jabez	Compensation for revolutionary services.	9	2	Petition	569	Claims.						
Bill, Jabez	Compensation for revolutionary services.	10	2	Petition	377	Select.						
Bill, James	(See Thomas Tupper, assignee of.	22	2		142							
Bill, Joshua	Pension for revolutionary services.	18	1	Resolution	201	Pens. & Rev. Cl'ms.	May 21, 1824	Adverse		Laid on table.		
Bill, Joshua	Pension for revolutionary services.	20	2	Petition	31	Military Pensions.						
Bill, Joshua	Pension for revolutionary services.	21	1	Pension bill	130	Whole House	Feb. 13, 1830	With amend.	72	Passed.	Passed with amendment.	App'd May 20, 1830
Bill, Joshua	Arrears of pension	24	2	Petition	71	Invalid Pensions	Dec. 30, 1836	Adverse		Laid on table.		
Bill, Joshua	Arrears of pension	25	2	Petition	19	Rev. Claims.				Discharged; laid on table.		
Bill, Joshua	Arrears of pension	26	1	Petition	172	Rev. Pensions.						
Bill, Joshua	Arrears of pension	26	2	Petition	134	Invalid Pensions				Discharged; laid on table.		
Bille, John H. D.	Extra compensation as paymaster Washington arsenal.	30	2	Petition	274	Military Affairs.						
Billiette, John Baptiste	Confirmation of title to land in Arkansas.	22	1	Petition	421	Public Lands	Feb. 28, 1832	General bill	425	Passed.	Passed with amendment.	App'd June 25, 1832
Billings, Alpheus, heirs of.	Indemnity for French spoliations prior to 1800.	29	2	Petition	87	Foreign Affairs.						
Billings, John	Pension for revolutionary services.	22	1	Petition	533	Rev. Pensions				Discharged; laid on table.		

List of private claims presented to the House of Representatives of the United States from the 1st to the 31st Congress, inclusive—Continued.

Names of claimants.	Nature or object of the claim.	Congress.	Session.	How brought before the House of Reps.	Page of journal.	To what committee of the House referred.	No. or date of the report.	Nature of the report.	No. of the bill.	How disposed of by the House of Reps.	How disposed of by the Senate.	Date of the act of Congress, and remarks.
Billings, John S.	Increase of pension	25	2	Senate bill	1155	Invalid Pensions			S. 349	Discharged; laid on table.		
Billings, John S.	Increase of pension	25	3	Senate bill	657				S. 157			
Billings, John S	Increase of pension	26	1	Senate bill	836	Invalid Pensions	661	Adverse	S. 117	Referred to Committee Whole House.		
Billings, John S.	Increase of pension	27	2	Senate bill	238	Invalid Pensions	Feb. 9, 1842	With't amend.	S. 104	Passed	Passed	App'd April 14, 1842
Billings, Samuel	Bounty on fishing schooner Lurana.	26	1	Petition	957	Commerce.						
Billings, Samuel	Bounty on fishing schooner Lurana.	26	2	Petition	181	Commerce.						
Billings, Samuel	Bounty on fishing schooner Lurana.	27	2	Petition	57	Commerce	875	Favorable	499	Ordered to a 3d reading.		
Billings, Samuel	Bounty on fishing schooner Lurana.	27	3	House bill	89				499	Passed.		
Billings, Samuel	Bounty on fishing schooner Lurana.	29	1	Petition	461	Commerce	582	Favorable	400	Referred to Committee Whole House.		
Billings, Stephen, widow of	Pension for revolutionary services	25	3	Petition	562	Rev. Pensions				Discharged.		
Billings, William	(See T. Pillsbury, and others)	18	2		157							
Bills, Alanson	Pension for services in Indian wars	28	1	Petition	687	Rev. Pensions				Discharged; laid on table.		
Bills, Alanson	Pension for services in Indian wars	29	2	Petition	159	Rev. Pensions	6	Adverse		Laid on table.		
Bills, Alanson	Pension for revolutionary services	28	1	Petition	794	Rev. Pensions.						
Bills, Alanson	Pension for revolutionary services	28	2	Petition	68	Rev. Pensions.						
Bills, Alanson, widow of	Pension for revolutionary services	29	1	Petition	118	Rev. Pensions.						
Bills, Alanson, widow of	Pension for revolutionary services	29	2	Rep't Committee Whole House.	150	Rev. Pensions	6	Adverse		Laid on table.		
Bills, John	Confirmation of title to land	22	1	Petition	424	Priv. Land Claims.	340	Favorable	432	Referred to Committee Whole House.		
Bills, John	Confirmation of title to land	23	1	Petition	49	Priv. Land Claims.	23	Favorable	23	Passed	Passed with amendment.	App'd April 15, 1834
Bills, Thomas, heirs of	Confirmation of title to land	18	2	Petition	38	Public Lands.						
Bills, Thomas, heirs of	Confirmation of title to land	19	2	Petition	60	Priv. Land Claims.	Jan. 5, 1827	Adverse		Leave to withdraw.		
Bills, Thomas, heirs of	Confirmation of title to land	20	1	Petition	281	Priv. Land Claims.						
Bills, Thomas, heirs of	Confirmation of title to land	20	2	Petition	75	Priv. Land Claims.						
Billsland, William	Pension for wound received in Indian war.	23	1	Resolution	335	Invalid Pensions				Discharged; laid on table.		
Billsland, William, widow of.	Pension for wound received in Indian war.	28	1	Petition	371	Invalid Pensions.						
Billsland, William, widow of.	Pension for wound received in Indian war.	29	1	Petition	477	Invalid Pensions.						
Billups, Josie	(See heirs of W. Respass, jr.)	29	2		100							
Billups, B. C.	Patent for a certain quarter section of land.	27	2	Petition	368	Public Lands	479	General bill	331	Passed	Passed	App'd Aug. 27, 1843
Bindon, Joseph	Indemnity for losses as a Canadian refugee.	2	1	Petition	465	Select.						
Bindon, Joseph	Indemnity for losses as a Canadian refugee.	2	2	Petition	619	Select	Feb. 19, 1793	Favorable		Referred to Committee Whole House.		
Bindon, Joseph	Indemnity for losses as a Canadian refugee.	4	1	Petition	430	Select.						
Bindon, Joseph	(See Canadian refugees)	4	2		614							
Bingey, John W	(See representatives of Alexander Young.)	17	1		248							
Bingey, John W.	Increase of compensation as revenue officer.	23	1	Petition	443	Commerce.						

List of private claims presented to the House of Representatives of the United States from the 1st to the 31st Congress, inclusive—Continued.

Names of claimants.	Nature or object of the claim.	Congress.	Session.	How brought before the House of Reps.	Page of journal.	To what committee of the House referred.	No. or date of the report.	Nature of the report.	No. of the bill.	How disposed of by the House of Reps.	How disposed of by the Senate.	Date of the act of Congress, and remarks.
Bingey, John W.	Increase of compensation as revenue officer.	24	1	Petition	199	Commerce.						
Bingey, Thomas	Increase of compensation as watchman, Navy Department.	25	2	Petition	923	Naval Affairs.						
Bingey, Thomas	Increase of compensation as watchman, Navy Department.	26	1	Petition	180	Naval Affairs	544	Adverse	......	Laid on table.		
Bingham, Eleazer	Compensation for property impressed for public use.	17	1	Petition	228	Claims.						
Bingham, Eleazer	Compensation for property impressed for public use.	19	1	Petition	204	Claims	Feb. 1, 1826	Adverse	......	Laid on table.		
Bingham, Eleazer	Compensation for property impressed for public use.	26	1	Petition	294	Claims.						
Bingham, Eleazer	Compensation for property impressed for public use.	26	2	Petition	38	Claims.						
Bingham, Eleazer	Compensation for property impressed for public use.	27	2	Petition	56	Claims	184	Adverse	......	Laid on table.		
Bingham, James and others.	Increase of salarys as guagers at New York.	3	1	Petition	93	Select	April 3, 1794	Does not appear.	......	Laid on table.		
Bingham, John	(See A. Tracy and others.)											
Bingham, Luther	Release from imprisonment	14	2	Petition	47	Select	Dec. 16, 1816	Favorable	10	Passed	Rejected.	
Bingham, Thomas	Bounty land for military services	28	1	Petition	449	Claims	522	Favorable	397	Referred to Committee Whole House.		
Bingham, William, agent of.	Release from a payment of a judgment.	7	1	Petition	90	Claims	April 3, 1802	Adverse	......	Postponed.		
Bingley, William B.	Additional compensation for site of dry dock at Gosport.	25	3	Petition	283	Naval Affairs.						
Bingley, William B.	Additional compensation for site of dry dock at Gosport.	26	1	Petition	180	Naval Affairs.						
Bingley, William B.	Additional compensation for site of dry dock at Gosport.	31	1	Petition	326	Naval Affairs	....	....	......	Discharged; laid on table.		
Bingley, William B.	Additional compensation for site of dry dock at Gosport.	31	2	Petition	119	Naval Affairs.						
Bingaman, Adam L.	(See P. C. and C. Surget, representatives of.)	22	1									
Binkley, Adam.	Pension	20	1	Petition	110	Military Pensions	....	....	......	Discharged; laid on table.		
Binney, Amos	Credit for depreciation on treasury notes.	20	2	Petition	27	Naval Affairs	Dec. 30, 1828	Favorable	342	Referred to Committee Whole House.		
Binney, Archibald & J. R.	Reimbursement of duties paid on antimony.	6	2	Petition	782	Com. and Manuf.	Feb. 19, 1801	Adverse	......	Claim rejected.		
Binney, Archibald & J. R.	Reimbursement of duties paid on antimony.	7	1	Petition	42	Com. and Manuf.						
Binnion, John	Exchange of an erroneous entry of land.	11	3	Petition	475	Public Lands.						
Binnion, John	Exchange of an erroneous entry of land.	12	1	Petition	85	Public Lands.						
Binnion, John	Exchange of an erroneous entry of land.	12	2	Petition	577	Public Lands	Jan. 7, 1813	Favorable	223	Passed	Passed	App'd Jan. 29, 1813
Binns, Charles	(See John A. Binns, surety of.)	25	2	....	396							
Binns, Henrietta M.	Right of pre-emption	23	2	Petition	437	Public Lands.						
Binns, John A., surety of.	Release from a judgment	25	2	Petition	396	Claims	839	Adverse	......	Laid on table.		
Binns, John A., surety of.	Release from a judgment	25	3	Petition	86	Claims	38	Adverse	......	Laid on table.		

List of private claims presented to the House of Representatives of the United States from the 1st to the 31st Congress, inclusive—Continued.

Names of claimants.	Nature or object of the claim.	Congress.	Session.	How brought before the House of Reps.	Page of journal.	To what committee of the House referred.	No. or date of the report.	Nature of the report.	No. of the bill.	How disposed of by the House of Reps.	How disposed of by the Senate.	Date of the act of Congress, and remarks.
Binns, John A	Settlement of accounts as an officer U. S. army.	18	2	Petition	186	Claims.						
Binns, John A	Settlement of accounts as an officer U. S. army.	19	1	Petition	269	Claims	April 14, 1826	Adverse	......	Laid on table.		
Binns, John A	Settlement of accounts as an officer U. S. army.	21	1	Petition	597	Claims	May 11, 1830	Adverse	......	Laid on table.		
Binns, Reuben	Bounty land for services war of 1812.	15	1	Petition	243	Claims.						
Biquett, Joseph	Patent for a Spanish grant of land.	22	1	Petition	263	Priv. Land Claims.	Feb. 17, 1832	Favorable	380	Referred to Committee Whole House.		
Birch, George, executrix of.	Compensation for extra serivces.	31	1	Petition	809	Claims.						
Birch, Thomas E	Pension for revolutionary services.	15	2	Petition	172	Rev. Pensions	Feb. 11, 1819	Adverse	......	Laid on table.		
Birch, Major	Compensation for a survey of Red river.	21	2	Appropriation bill	194	....	....	....	566	Passed	Passed	App'd March 2, 1831
Birchmore, Wm., widow of	Pension for services of deceased as surgeon United States navy.	22	1	Petition	29	Naval Affairs.						
Birchmore, Wm., widow of	Pension for services of deceased as surgeon United States navy.	22	2	Petition	28	Naval Affairs.						
Birchmore, Wm., widow of	Pension for services of deceased as surgeon United States navy.	23	1	Petition	74	Naval Affairs.						
Birchmore, Wm., widow of	Pension for services of deceased as surgeon United States navy.	27	3	Petition	61	Naval Affairs	....	....	......	Discharged; laid on table.		
Birchmore, Wm., widow of	Pension for services of deceased as surgeon United States navy.	28	1	Petition	181	Invalid Pensions	172	Adverse	......	Laid on table.		
Birchmore, Wm., widow of	Pension for services of deceased as surgeon United States navy.	28	2	Petition	73	Invalid Pensions.						
Birchmore, Wm., widow of	Pension for services of deceased as surgeon United States navy.	29	1	Petition	118	Invalid Pensions	41	Adverse	......	Laid on table.		
Birchmore, Julianna	(See Wm. Birchmore, widow of.)	22	1	....	29							
Birckhead & Pearce	Remission of duty on guano	28	2	Petition	353	Ways and Means.						
Bird, Benjamin	Renewal of a lost revolutionary certificate.	1	2	Petition	142	....	....	....	......	Laid on table.		
Bird, Benjamin	Renewal of a lost revolutionary certificate.	6	1	Petition	547	Claims	April 22, 1800	Adverse	......	Referred to Committee Whole House.		
Bird, Benjamin	Renewal of a lost revolutionary certificate.	6	2	Petition	731	Claims	Jan. 26, 1801	Adverse.				
Bird, Benjamin, representatives of.	Renewal of a lost revolutionary certificate	23	1	Resolution	42	Rev. Claims	126	Favorable	135	Passed	Passed	App'd June 28, 1834
Bird, Benjamin	Pension	18	1	Petition	336	Pens. & Rev. Cl'ms.	....	....	......	Discharged; leave to withdraw.		
Bird, Daniel	Compensation for horse taken for public use.	25	2	Petition	397	Claims	837	Adverse	......	Laid on table.		
Bird, Gustavus A	(See Martin S. Aikin and others.)	17	1	....	359							
Bird, Herman	Pension for revolutionary services.	5	2	Pension bill	127	Whole House	Jan. 11, 1798	With amend.	38	Passed	Passed with amendment.	App'd Feb. 2, 1798
Bird, Joseph	Pension for revolutionary services.	2	1	Petition	476	....	....	....	......	Laid on table.		
Bird, Joseph	Pension for revolutionary services.	8	1	Petition	506	Claims	Mar. 13, 1804	Adverse.				
Bird, Joseph	Pension for revolutionary services.	10	1	Pension bill	232	Whole House	April 19, 1808	With amend.	78	Passed	Passed with amendment.	App'd April 25, 1808
Bird, Nathaniel	Compensation for revolutionary services.	20	2	Petition	43	Rev. Claims	Jan. 15, 1829	Adverse	......	Laid on table.		

List of private claims presented to the House of Representatives of the United States from the 1st to the 31st Congress, inclusive—Continued.

Names of claimants.	Nature or object of the claim.	Congress.	Session.	How brought before the House of Reps.	Page of journal.	To what committee of the House referred.	No. or date of the report.	Nature of the report.	No. of the bill.	How disposed of by the House of Reps.	How disposed of by the Senate.	Date of the act of Congress, and remarks.
Bird, Nathaniel	Compensation for revolutionary services.	21	1	Petition	295	Rev. Claims	286	Favorable	340	Referred to Committee Whole House.		
Bird, Nathaniel	Compensation for revolutionary services.	21	2	Rep't Committee Whole House.	361	....	....	With't amend.	340	Passed.		
Bird, Nathaniel	Compensation for revolutionary services.	22	1	Petition	442	Rev. Claims.						
Bird, Nathaniel	Compensation for revolutionary services.	23	1	Petition	65	Rev. Claims.						
Bird, Nathaniel	Compensation for revolutionary services.	23	2	Petition	120	Rev. Claims.						
Bird, Nathaniel	Compensation for revolutionary services.	24	1	Petition	102	Rev. Claims.						
Bird, Nathaniel	Compensation for revolutionary services.	24	2	Petition	95	Rev. Pensions	....	....	.....	Discharged; laid on table.		
Bird, Nathaniel	Compensation for revolutionary services.	25	2	Petition	112	Rev. Claims	576	Adverse	.....	Laid on table.		
Bird, Nathaniel	Compensation for revolutionary services.	29	1	Petition	172	Rev. Pensions	93	Favorable	112	Passed.		
Bird, Nathaniel, (N. Y.)	Arrears of pension	24	2	Petition	261	Whole House.						
Bird, Nathaniel, (N. Y.)	Arrears of pension	25	2	Petition	55	Rev. Pensions.						
Bird, Nathaniel, (N. Y.)	Arrears of pension	29	1	Petition	168	Rev. Pensions	236	Adverse	.....	Laid on table.		
Bird, Nathaniel	Compensation for the services of G. M. Fowle.	25	2	Petition	51	Claims.						
Bird, Nathaniel	Compensation for the services of G. M. Fowle.	26	1	Petition	168	Claims.						
Birdsall, Benjamin	Indemnity for wounds received at Fort Erie.	15	1	Petition	172	Military Affairs	Jan. 27, 1818	Favorable	59	Passed	Passed	App'd April 20, 1818
Birdsall, D. H	Increase of compensation as postmaster.	30	1	Petition	558	P. Of. and P. Roads.						
Birdseye, Nat. G., and D. Booth.	Relinquishment of title acquired by judgment and execution.	15	2	Senate bill	316	Judiciary	Mar. 2, 1819	With't amend.	62	Passed	Passed	App'd March 3, 1819
Birdsong, John, widow of.	Compensation for revolutionary services.	12	2	Petition	669	Claims.						
Birely, John, assignee of.	Reimbursement of money erroneously paid by order of Navy Department.	31	2	Petition	123	Naval Affairs.						
Biren, John	Location of a military land warrant.	26	1	Petition	1004	Public Lands.						
Bisbee, Elisha, widow of.	Increase of pension	26	2	Petition	88	Rev. Pensions	....	....	.....	Discharged; laid on table.		
Biscoe, George W	Indemnity for destruction of property by the enemy.	22	1	Petition	556	Claims	April 13, 1832	Adverse.	.....	Laid on table.		
Biscoe, George W	Indemnity for destruction of property by the enemy.	30	1	Petition	577	Claims.	....	....	.....	Discharged; laid on table.		
Biscoe, George W	Indemnity for schooner Speedwell captured by the enemy.	25	2	Petition	233	Foreign Affairs	533	Adverse	.....	Laid on table.		
Biscoe, George W	Indemnity for schooner Speedwell captured by the enemy.	31	1	Petition	863	Claims.						
Biscoe, Josiah	Compensation for revolutionary services.	26	1	Petition	630	Rev. Claims.						
Biscoe, Josiah	Compensatian for revolutionary services.	26	2	Petition	77	Rev. Claims	184	Adverse	.....	Laid on table.		
Bisente, Sardina	Confirmation of title to land in Louisiana, (Terre aux Bœuff)	22	1	Petition	64	Priv. Land Claims.	62	Favorable	125	Passed	Passed	App'd June 25, 1832

List of private claims presented to the House of Representatives of the United States from the 1st to the 31st Congress, inclusive—Continued.

Names of claimants.	Nature or object of the claim.	Congress.	Session.	How brought before the House of Reps.	Page of journal.	To what committee of the House referred.	No. or date of the report.	Nature of the report.	No. of the bill.	How disposed of by the House of Reps.	How disposed of by the Senate.	Date of the act of Congress, and remarks.
Bishop, Aquilla	Indemnity for losses on a government contract.	24	1	Petition	264	Claims	Mar. 3, 1836	Adverse		Laid on table.		
Bishop, Benoni, widow of.	Pension for revolutionary services.	26	2	Petition	133	Rev. Pensions	133	Favorable	641	Referred to Committee Whole House.		
Bishop, Charles	Pension	3	1	Rep. of Secretary War.	131	Select	May 26, 1794	Res. to refer to Sec. War.	R. 12	Passed	Passed	App'd June 9, 1794
Bishop, Colin, widow of	Compensation for extra services as postmaster, Tuscaloosa.	26	1	Senate bill	811	P. Of. & P. Roads.	April 30, 1840	With't amend.	S. 91	Referred to Committee Whole House.		
Bishop, Colin, widow of	Compensation for extra services as postmaster, Tuscaloosa.	26	2	Senate bill	229	P. Of. & P. Roads.			S. 32			
Bishop, Colin, widow of	Compensation for extra services as postmaster, Tuscaloosa.	27	2	Petition	391	P. Of. & P. Roads.						
Bishop, Colin, widow of	Compensation for extra services as postmaster, Tuscaloosa.	27	3	Petition	175	P. Of. & P. Roads.				Discharged; leave to withdraw.		
Bishop, Elizabeth	(See Benoni Bishop, widow of.)	26	2		133		133		641			
Bishop, Francis	Pension for revolutionary services.	24	1	Petition	506	Rev. Claims.						
Bishop, George	Bounty land for military services.	15	1	Petition	184	Public Lands				Discharged.		
Bishop, George G	(See administrator of John Arnold)	30	2		317		88		784			
Bishop, Henry	Arrears due him as messenger in Patent Office.	23	1	Petition	307	Patents.						
Bishop, James	Payment for an ox slaughtered for public use.	19	1	Resolution	186	Claims	Feb. 1, 1826	Adverse		Laid on table.		
Bishop, James, (Conn)	Pension	21	1	Resolution	227	Military Pensions				Discharged; laid on table.		
Bishop, John	Pay for revolutionary service	16	1	Petition		Rev. Pensions	Jan. 14, 1820	Adverse		Leave to withdraw.		
Bishop, John	Pension for revolutionary services.	23	1	Petition	308	Rev. Pensions.						
Bishop, John	Pension for revolutionary services.	24	1	Petition	213	Rev. Pensions	Jan. 29, 1836	Adverse		Laid on table.		
Bishop, John	Pension for revolutionary services.	24	2	Petition	74	Rev. Pensions				Discharged; laid on table.		
Bishop, John, administratrix of.	Benefit of a certain act	18	1	Petition	199	Public Lands				Discharged; leave to withdraw.		
Bishop, Joseph	Pension for revolutionary services.	11	2	Petition	115	Claims				Discharged; referred to Secretary War.		
				Rep. of Secretary of War.	306					Laid on table.		
Bishop, Joshua, heirs of	Indemnity for horses stolen by Indians.	25	2	Petition	426	Indian Affairs.						
Bishop, Joshua, heirs of	Indemnity for horses stolen by Indians.	26	1	Petition	180	Claims.						
Bishop, Levi	Pension for loss of arm in battle.	13	1	Petition	107	Military Affairs				Discharged; leave to withdraw.		
Bishop, Levi	Pension for loss of arm in battle.	13	2	Petition	378	Whole House	Mar. 31, 1814	Favorable	166	Passed	Passed	App'd April 18, 1814
Bishop, William	Arrears of pay due deserters	19	2	Petition	157	Claims.						
Bishop, William	Arrears of pay due deserters	20	1	Petition	30	Claims	Dec. 18, 1827	Adverse		Laid on table.		
Bispham, Lieut. John E.	An award for capture of a piratical vessel.	26	1	Senate bill	588	Naval Affairs	May 25, 1840	With't amend.	S. 213	Referred to Committee Whole House.		
Bispham, Lieut. John E.	An award for capture of a piratical vessel.	26	2	Senate bill	176	Claims	Jan. 16, 1841	With't amend.	S. 192	Passed	Passed.	App'd March 2, 1841
Bispham, Lieut. John E.	Reimbursement of expenses in a certain prosecution.	30	2	Petition	75	Judiciary	50	Favorable	748	Referred to Committee Whole House.		
Bispham, Lieut. John E., executor of.	Reimbursement of expenses in a certain prosecution.	31	1	Petition	584	Judiciary	May 22, 1850	Favorable	301	Referred to Committee Whole House.		

List of private claims presented to the House of Representatives of the United States from the 1st to the 31st Congress, inclusive—Continued.

Names of claimants.	Nature or object of the claim.	Congress.	Session.	How brought before the House of Reps.	Page of journal.	To what committee of the House referred.	No. or date of the report.	Nature of the report.	No. of the bill.	How disposed of by the House of Reps.	How disposed of by the Senate.	Date of the act of Congress, and remarks.
Bissell, Daniel	Compensation for secret services in revolutionary war.	4	1	Petition	406	Claims	Jan. 26, 1796	Adverse	......	Leave to withdraw.		
Bissell, Daniel, jr.	Compensation for revolutionary services.	9	1	Petition	280	Claims.						
Bissell, Daniel, jr.	Compensation for revolutionary services.	10	2	Petition	468	Claims.						
Bissell, Lewis	Indemnity for depredations upon his timber lands.	24	2	Petition	394	Claims	283	Adverse	......	Laid on table.		
Bissell, Lewis	Indemnity for depredations upon his timber lands.	25	2	Petition	176	Claims	900	Adverse	......	Laid on table.		
Bissell, Lewis	Indemnity for depredations upon his timber lands.	25	3	Documents	462	Claims.						
Bissell, Lewis	Indemnity for depredations upon his timber lands.	26	1	Documents	168	Claims	50	Adverse	......	Laid on table.		
Bissell, Nathaniel C.	Indemnity for French spoliations prior to 1800.	26	1	Memorial	182	Foreign Affairs	343	Favorable	319	Referred to Committee Whole House.		
Bissell, Samuel, widow of.	Pension for revolutionary services.	29	1	Petition	233	Rev. Pensions	527	Adverse	......	Laid on table.		
Bissell, Thomas & Son	Indemnity for French spoliations prior to 1800.	26	1	Memorial	182	Foreign Affairs	343	Favorable	319	Referred to Committee Whole House.		
Bissett, Benjamin, & others	Indemnity for French spoliations prior to 1800.	26	2	Memorial	161	Whole House.						
Bissett, Benjamin, & others	Indemnity for French spoliations prior to 1800.	27	2	Petition	308	Whole House.						
Bitton, Solomon D., sureties of.	Reimbursement of moneys illegally recovered.	27	2	Petition	70	P. O. & P. Roads.						
Biven, John	Bounty land for services, war of 1812.	27	2	Petition	75	Priv. Land Claims.						
Bixby, Adonijah	Pension	21	2	Petition	57	Military Pensions.						
Bixby, Elias	To be restored to pension roll	17	1	Petition	51	Rev. Pensions.						
Bixby, Samuel	Compensation for revolutionary services and losses.	19	2	Petition	32	Rev. Claims	Dec. 19, 1826	Adverse	......	Laid on table.		
Bixby, Samuel	Compensation for revolutionary services and losses.	24	2	Petition	269	Rev. Claims	Feb. 28, 1837	Adverse	......	Laid on table.		
Bixby, Samuel	Compensation for revolutionary services and losses.	25	2	Petition	112	Rev. Pensions	542	Adverse	......	Referred to Committee Whole House.		
Bixby, Samuel	Compensation for revolutionary services and losses.	27	2	Petition	255	Rev. Claims	522	Adverse	......	Laid on table.		
Blachford, Joseph	(See surviving partner of Harris and Blatchford.)	2	2	....	615							
Black, Alexander	Pension for revolutionary services.	24	2	Petition	399	Rev. Pensions.						
Black, Anthony	Permission to locate a land claim.	23	2	Petition	201	Public Lands.						
Black, Anthony	Permission to locate a land claim.	24	1	Petition.	114	Public Lands.						
Black, Catharine	Pension	19	1	Petition.	....	Military Pensions.	April 1, 1826	Adverse	......	Laid on table.		
Black, Charles	Pension for revolutionary wounds and disabilities.	13	3	Petition	643	Pen. & Rev. Claims						
Black, Charles, (Tex.)	Indemnity for seizure of a vessel.	31	1	Petition	502	Commerce.						
Black, Charles, (Tex.)	Indemnity for seizure of a vessel.	31	2	Petition	75	Commerce.						
Black, David	Increase of pension	30	1	Petition	369	Rev. Pensions	381	Adverse	......	Laid on table.		
Black, Hugh	Pension for revolutionary serveics	18	1	Petition	210	Rev. Pensions	Mar. 9, 1824	Adverse	......	Laid on table.		
Black, Jacob	Confirmation of title to land in Louisiana.	21	2	Petition	338	Priv. Land Claims.						
Black, Jacob	Confirmation of title to land in Louisiana.	22	1	Petition	65	Priv. Land Claims.	Dec. 27, 1831	Favorable	141	Passed	Passed	App'd July 14, 1832

List of private claims presented to the House of Representatives of the United States from the 1st to the 31st Congress, inclusive—Continued.

Names of claimants.	Nature or object of the claim.	Congress.	Session.	How brought before the House of Reps.	Page of journal.	To what committee of the House referred.	No. or date of the report.	Nature of the report.	No. of the bill.	How disposed of by the House of Reps.	How disposed of by the Senate.	Date of the act of Congress, and remarks.
Black, James, (Ala.)	Pension for revolutionary services	21	2	Petition	118	Military Pensions.						
Black, James, (Ohio)	Pensions for revolutionary services	25	2	Petition	1274	....	....	....	....	Laid on table.		
Black, James, (Ark.)	Indemnity for cession of mill site to Choctaws.	24	1	Petition	58	Public Lands	....	....	....	Discharged; laid on table.		
Black, John	(See executors of Caleb Newbold)	2	2	Petition	706							
Black, John, (S. C.)	Compensation for revolutionary services.	4	2	....	707	Claims.						
Black, John, (S. C.)	Compensation for revolutionary services.	5	2	Petition	....	Claims	Dec. 19, 1797	Adverse	....	Rejected.		
Black, John	Pension for revolutionary services	15	2	Petition	23	Pens. & Rev. Cl'ms.	Nov. 25, 1818	Adverse	....	Laid on table.		
Black, John, (Geo.)	To be restored to pension roll	25	2	Resolution	525	Rev. Pensions	820	Favorable	760	Passed.		
Black, John, (Geo.)	To be restored to pension roll	26	1	Petition	171	Rev. Pensions	160	Favorable	170	Passed	Indef. postp'd.	
Black, John, (Geo.)	To be restored to pension roll	26	2	Petition	148	Rev. Pensions	142	Favorable	648	Referred to Committee Whole House.		
Black, John, (Geo.)	To be restored to pension roll	27	2	Petition	97	Rev. Pensions	107	Favorable	153	Passed	Indef. postp'd.	
Black, John	Compensation for diplomatic services, &c.	30	1	Senate bill	434	Foreign Affairs	443	With't amend.	S. 82	Passed	Passed	App'd May 9, 1848
Black, Joseph	Pension	21	2	Petition	188	Military Pensions.						
Black, Mary	Indemnity for damages occasioned by Choctaw Indians.	24	1	Petition	66	Indian Affairs	....	....	....	Discharged; laid on table.		
Black, Ruth	Continuation of pension	28	1	Petition	72	Rev. Pensions.						
Black, Samuel, heirs of	Payment for revolutionary certificates.	14	1	Petition	40	Claims.						
Black, Samuel, heirs of	Payment for revolutionary certificates.	14	2	Petition	101	Pens. & Rev. Cl'ms	Feb. 3, 1817	Favorable	96	Referred to Committee Whole House.		
Black, Samuel, heirs of	Payment for revolutionary certificates.	15	1	Petition	35	Pens. & Rev. Cl'ms.	....	....	....	Discharged; leave to withdraw.		
Black, Samuel	Pension	16	1	Petition	89	Rev. Pensions	Jan. 14, 1820	Adverse	....	Laid on table.		
Black, Samuel	Pension	16	2	Petition	113	Rev. Pensions	Feb. 15, 1821	Adverse	....	Leave to withdraw.		
Black, Samuel	Pension	17	1	Petition	165	Whole House.						
Black, Samuel	Pension	17	2	Petition	209	Rev. Pensions	....	....	....	Discharged; laid on table.		
Black, William	(See Exploring Expedition)	27	3	....	149							
Black, William	Extra compensation as boatswain Exploring Expedition.	31	1	Petition	191	Naval Affairs.						
Black, William	Pension	21	1	Petition	377	Military Pensions	....	....	....	Discharged; laid on table.		
Black, William	Pension	22	1	Petition	51	Rev. Pensions.						
Black, William	(See John L. Phillips and others)	30	1	....	740							
Blackburn, Benjamin	Pension	11	3	Pension bill	604	Whole House	Mar. 2, 1811	With amend.	218	Passed	Passed	App'd March 3, 1811
Blackburn, Elizabeth L.	(See widow of Felix G. Bosworth)	31	1	....	1430							
Blackburn, James	To locate land warrant in Alabama or Mississippi.	23	1	Petition	385	Priv. Land Claims.						
Blackburn, James	To locate land warrant in Alabama or Mississippi.	23	2	Petition	95	Priv. Land Claims.						
Blackburn, Lemuel A.	Pension for services in war of 1812.	29	1	Petition	161	Invalid Pensions.						
Blackburn, Thomas, heirs of.	Balance of pension due for revolutionary service.	23	1	Petition	639	Invalid Pensions.						
Blackburn, Thomas, heirs of.	Full pay and bounty land.	24	1	Petition	204	Rev. Claims.						
Blackburn, Thomas, heirs of.	Full pay and bounty land	24	2	Petition	147	Rev. Claims.						

List of p ivate claims presented to the House of Representatives of the United States from the 1*st to the* 31*st Congress, inclusive*—Continued.

Names of claimants.	Nature or object of the claim.	Congress.	Session.	How brought before the House of Reps.	Page of journal.	To what committee of the House referred.	No. or date of the report.	Nature of the report.	No. of the bill.	How disposed of by the House of Reps.	How disposed of by the Senate.	Date of the act of Congress, and remarks.
Blackburn	(See Houston and Blackburn)	19	1		369							
Blackden, Samuel	Bounty land and commutation pay	6	2	Memorial	739	Claims	Dec. 18, 1801	Adverse		Rejected.		
Blackden, Samuel, widow of.	Compensation for revolutionary services.	7	1	Petition	44	Claims	Mar. 8, 1802	Adverse		Leave to withdraw.		
Blackden, Samuel, widow of.	Compensation for revolutionary services.	8	2	Petition	51	Claims.						
Blackford, William M	Salary as chargé to New Granada	29	1	Petition	257	Foreign Affairs.						
Blackford, William M	Salary as chargé to Mew Granada	30	1	Petition	114	Foreign Affairs	336	Favorable	314	Passed.		
Blackford, William M	Salary as chargé to New Granada	30	1	Appropr'n bill	523	Whole House		Amendments	298	Passed	Passed	App'd Aug. 12, 1848
Black fox, (Indian chief)	Annuity	9	2	House bill	609	Whole House	Mar. 2, 1807	No amendment	217	Passed	Passed	App'd March 3, 1807
Blackledge, Richard	Compensation for supplies to North Carolina troops.	1	3	Petition	358					Referred to Secretary Treasury.		
Blackledge, Richard	Compensation for supplies to North Carolina troops.	2	2	Rep. of Secretary Treasury.	592					Laid on table.		
Blackledge, Richard, executor of.	Compensation for revolutionary supplies.	3	1	Petition	68	Select	Mar. 19, 1794	Adverse		Laid on table.		
Blackledge, Richard, executor of.	Compensation for revolutionary supplies.	4	2	Petition	636	Claims	Feb. 14, 1797	Adverse		Laid on table.		
Blackman Daniel	Pension for revolutionary services	21	1	Petition	228	Military Pensions				Discharged; laid on table.		
Blackman, David J	(See Josiah Blackman)	29	1		624							
Blackman, David	Pension for revolutionary services	3	1	Rep. of Secretary War.	131	Select	May 26, 1794	Res. to refer to Sec. War.	R. 12	Passed	Passed	App'd June 9, 1794
Blackman, David	Pension for revolutionary services	3	2	Rep. of Secretary War.	262	Claims	Feb. 28, 1795	Favorable	130	Passed	Indef. postp'd.	
Blackman, David	Pension for revolutionary services	4	1	Rep. of Secretary War.	447	Claims	Feb. 18, 1796	Favorable	156	Passed	Passed with amendment.	App'd April 20, 1796
Blackman, Josiah	Releaf under a mail contract	29	1	Petition	624	P. Of. & P. Roads.				Discharged; laid on table.		
Blackman William S	(See Josiah Blackman)	29	1		624							
Blackmore, George D	Pension for revolutionary services	21	2	Petition	53	Military Pensions.						
Blackmore, George D, widow of.	Pension for revolutionary services	28	1	Petition	370	Rev. Pensions	262	Favorable	194	Passed	Passed	App'd May 23, 1844
Blackmore, Sarah	(See George D. Blackmore, widow of.)	28	1		370							
Blacksheare, Joseph	(See Francis Tennille, heirs of.)	20	2		101							
Blackshire, Ebenezer	Pension for revolutionary services	19	2	Resolution	89	Rev. Claims				Discharged; laid on table.		
Blackshire, Ebenezer	Pension for revolutionary services	20	1	Resolution	640	Military Pensions				Discharged; laid on table.		
Blackshire, Ebenezer, widow of.	Pension for revolutionary services	26	2	Petition	100	Rev. Pensions	211	Adverse		Laid on table.		
Blackney, William	Pension for revolutionary services	11	2	Petition	147	Claims	Jan. 27, 1810	Adverse.				
Blackstone, John	(See Thomas Durham, and J. B.)	26	2		229							
Blackwell, Ann or Agatha	(See Edwin Hall, widow of.)	24	1		274							
Blackwell, Capt. C	(See Captain B. F. Hill *et al.*	31	1		1012				331			
Blackwell, David	Payment of revolutionary certificate.	11	1	Petition	53	Claims.						
Blackwell, David	Payment of revolutionary certificate.	11	2	Petition	127	Claims	Feb. 20, 1810	Favorable	108	Passed	Rejected.	
Blackwell, David	Payment of revolutionary certificate.	12	1	Petition	120	Claims.						

List of private claims presented to the House of Representatives of the United States from the 1st to the 31st Congress, inclusive—Continued.

Names of claimants.	Nature or object of the claim.	Congress.	Session.	How brought before the House of Reps.	Page of journal.	To what committee of the House referred.	No. or date of the report.	Nature of the report.	No. of the bill.	How disposed of by the House of Reps.	How disposed of by the Senate.	Date of the act of Congress, and remarks.
Blackwell, Francis	Indemnity for French spoliations prior to 1800.	26	1	Memorial	182	Foreifin Affairs	343	Favorable	319	Referred to Committee Whole House.		
Blackwell, Jacob A., attorney of.	Reimbursement of excessive tonnage duties, brig Prospect.	17	2	Petition	118	Commerce.						
Blackwell, Jacob A., attorney of.	Reimbursement of excessive tonnage duties, brig Prospect.	18	1	Petition	284	Commerce.						
Blackwell, Jacob A., attorney of.	Reimbursement of excessive tonnage duties, brig Prospect.	18	2	Petition	120	Ways and Means	Jan. 24, 1825	Favorable	291	Passed	Passed	App'd Mar. 3, 1825
Blackwell, Jesse	Confirmation of title to land in Missouri.	15	1	Petition	52	Priv. Land Claims.						
Blackwell, Thomas	Commutation pay for revolutionary services.	20	1	Petition	311	Rev. Claims	199	Favorable	231			
Blackwell, Thomas	Commutation pay for revolutionary services.	20	2	Petition	177	Rev. Claims.						
				Recommitted	475	Rev. Claims	....	....	......	Discharged; leave to withdraw.		
Blackwell, Thomas	Commutation pay for revolutionary services.	21	1	Petition	50	Rev. Claims	129	Favorable	173	Passed	Passed	App'd May 29, 1830
Blackwell, Thomas, heirs of.	Interest on commutation pay	22	2	Petition	40	Rev. Claims.						
Blackwell, Thomas, heirs of.	Interest on commutation pay	23	1	Petition	54	Rev. Claims	68	Favorable	78	Recommitted.		
Blackwell, Capt. William, heir of.	Bounty land for revolutionary services.	22	1	Petition	263	Public Lands.	....	....	......	Discharged; laid on table.		
Blackwell, Capt. William, heir of.	Bounty land for revolutionary services.	22	1	Senate bill	806	Rev. Claims.	June 26, 1832	No amendm't.	110	Passed	....	App'd July 14, 1832
Blackwood, Samuel, widow of.	Compensation for revolutionary services.	11	3	Petition	547	Claims.						
Blackwood, Samuel, widow of.	Compensation for revolutionary services.	12	1	Petition	60	Claims.						
Blagden, George	Compensotion for work and materials on the Capitol.	12	1	Petition	236	Ways and Means	April 24, 1812	General bill	114	Passed	Passed	App'd July 6, 1812
Blagge, Benjamin	(See Samuel Blagge, heirs of)	29	2	....	136							
Blagge, Samuel, heirs of	Indemnity for French spoliations prior to 1800.	29	2	Petition	136	Foreign Affairs.						
Blagge, Samuel, heirs of	Indemnity for French spoliations prior to 1800.	31	1	Petition	256	Foreign Affairs	355	General bill	318	Referred to Committee Whole House.		
Blagrove, Henry B	(See William Duvall, representatives of.)	27	2	....	253							
Blagrove, William	Compensation for services as clerk in Navy Department.	17	1	Petition	459	Naval Affairs.						
Blagrove, William	Compensation for services as clerk in Navy Department.	17	2	Petition	47	Naval Affairs	....	....	......	Discharged; leave to withdraw.		
Blagrove, William	Credit on judgment for balance due him for services.	18	1	Petition	66	Naval Affairs	Jan. 13, 1824	Favorable	55	Passed	Passed	App'd May 18, 1824
Blaine, Ephraim, executors of.	Compensation for revolutionary services in Commissary Department	9	1	Petition	268	Claims	....	....	......	Indef. postponed.		
Blaine, Ephraim, executors of.	Compensation for revolutionary services in Commissary Department	9	2	Petition	570	Claims.						
Blaine, James	(See executors of Ephraim Blaine)	9	1	....	268							
Blaine, Robert	(See executors of Ephraim Blaine)	9	1	....	268							
Blair, Francis P	(See surety of S. B. Crockett.)	25	2	....	1028							
Blair, James C	Confirmation of title to land	24	2	Petition	....	Priv. Land Claims.	....	....	......	....	....	**Omitted on journal.**

List of private claims presented to the House of Representatives of the United States from the 1st to the 31st Congress, inclusive—Continued.

Names of claimants.	Nature or object of the claim.	Congress.	Session.	How brought before the House of Reps.	Page of journal.	To what committee of the House referred.	No. or date of the report.	Nature of the report.	No. of the bill.	How disposed of by the House of Reps.	How disposed of by the Senate.	Date of the act of Congress, and remarks.
Blair, James C.	Indemnity for clothing sunk with the Mississippi.	25	3	Petition	462	Claims.						
Blair, James L.	(See Exploring Expedition)	27	3		149							
Blair, John	Compensation for revolutionary services.	22	1	Petition	29	Rev. Claims	Jan. 3, 1832	Adverse		Laid on table.		
Blair, John	Compensation for revolutionary services.	22	2	Petition	143	Rev. Claims	Jan. 24, 1833	Adverse		Laid on table.		
Blair, Joshua	Compensation for property applied to public use.	18	1	Petition	89	Military Affairs				Discharged; leave to withdraw.		
Blair, Peter	Compensation for revolutionary services.	22	1	Petition	29	Rev. Claims	Jan. 3, 1832	Adverse		Laid on table.		
Blair, Peter	Compensation for revolutionary services.	22	2	Petition	143	Rev. Claims	Jan. 24, 1833	Adverse		Laid on table.		
Blair, Phineas	(See attorney of James Homer.)	16	2		177							
Blair & Rives	Compensation for printing Compendium Sixth Census.	27	2	Memorial	108	Select	45	Adverse		Laid on table.		
Blair & Rives	Compensation for printing Compendium Sixth Census.	28	1	Petition	1009	Claims.						
Blair & Rives	Compensation for printing Compendium Sixth Census.	28	2	Petition	71	Claims.						
Blair & Rives	Compensation for printing Compendium Sixth Census.	29	1	Petition	208	Claims.						
Blair & Rives	Compensation for printing Compendium Sixth Census.	29	2	Petition	82	Claims.						
Blair & Rives	Printing Sixth Census, &c.	27	2	Documents	421	Claims				Discharged.		
				Memorial	447	Select	1009	Favorable	584	Referred to Committee Whole House.		
Blair & Rives	Allowance of fifteen per cent. deducted from their accounts.	30	1	Petition	915	Ways and Means.						
Blair, Robert L.	Reimbursement of advances on public account.	31	1	Senate bill	1498	Military Affairs			S. 353	Motion to reconsider pending.		
Blair, Robert L.	Reimbursement of advances on public account	31	2	Motion to reconsider.	425					Laid on table.		
Blair, William, (Pa.)	Pension for revolutionary services.	18	1	Petition	42	Pens. & Rev. Cl'ms.	Dec. 19, 1823	Adverse		Laid on table.		
Blair, William, (Pa.)	Pension for revolutionary services.	19	1	Resolution	170	Military Pensions	April 1, 1826	Adverse		Laid on table.		
Blair, William K.	Compensation for services as pension agent.	27	2	Petition	375	Rev. Pensions.						
Blair, William K.	Compensation for services as pension agent.	31	1	Petition	810	Rev. Pensions	448	Adverse		Laid on table.		
Blair, William K.	Compensation for services as pension agent.	31	2	Petition	58	Rev. Pensions	45	Adverse		Laid on table.		
Blairran, ship	(See Peter A. Guestier and others)	8	2		100							
Blaisdell, Enoch	Pension	23	1	Petition	241	Invalid Pensions	321	Favorable	352	Referred to Committee Whole House.		
Blaisdell, Enoch	Pension	23	2	Rep't Committee Whole House	336			With't amend.	352	Passed	Adverse report.	
Blaisdell, Enoch	Pension	24	1	Petition	52	Invalid Pensions	46	Favorable	58	Passed.	Passed	App'd May 14, 1836
Blaisdell, Jonathan M.	Release from a judgment	20	2	Petition	25	Ways and Means.	6	Adverse		Laid on table.		
Blaisdell, Jonathan M.	Release from a judgment	21	1	Petition	50	Ways and Means	138	Adverse		Referred to Committee Whole House.		
Blaisdell, Jonathan M.	Release from a judgment	23	1	Senate bill	873	Ways and Means.	Jan. 28, 1834	With't amend.	S. 142	Passed	Passed	App'd June 30, 1834
Blake, A	(See Chester Baxter, and others)	27	3		68							
Blake, Alphonso T. A.	(See heir of Wm. Carmichael)	24	1		202							

List of private claims presented to the House of Representatives of the United States from the 1st to the 31st Congress, inclusive—Continued.

Names of claimants.	Nature or object of the claim.	Congress.	Session.	How brought before the House of Reps.	Page of journal.	To what committee of th House referred.	No. or date of the report	Nature of the report.	No. of the bill.	How disposed of by the House of Reps.	How disposed of by the Senate.	Date of the act of Congress, and remarks.
Blake, Andrew	Bounty on fishing schooner Two Brothers.	28	1	Petition	182	Commerce........	384	Favorable	282	Passed.		
Blake, Andrew	Bounty on fishing schooner Two Brothers.	28	2	Petition	136	Commerce	60	Favorable	539	Referred to Committee Whole House.		
Blake, Andrew	Bounty on fishing schooner Two Brothers.	29	1	Petition	152	Commerce........	266	Favorable	228	Referred to Committee Whole House.		
Blake, Andrew	Bounty on fishing schooner Two Brothers.	30	1	Petition	70	Commerce.						
Blake, Andrew	Bounty on fishing schooner Two Brothers.	31	1	Petition	299	Commerce.						
Blake, Charles..........	Pension for services as surgeon's mate.	24	1	Petition	281	Invalid Pensions...	404	Favorable	412	Passed............	Passed	App'd June 28, 1836
Blake, David, (N. Y.)....	Pension for revolutionary services.	22	1	Petition	219	Rev. Pensions ..	....	....	......	Discharged; laid on table.		
Blake, Ebenezer	Balance of pay due him for revolutionary services.	7	2	Petition	301	Claims	Feb. 26, 1803					
Blake, Ebenezer	Balance of pay due him for revolutionary services.	9	1	Petition	271	Whole House.						
Blake, Edward, jr	Permission to import certain English goods.	10	2	Petition	413	Com. and Manuf.						
Blake, Edward, executors of.	Amount due on judgment *vs.* the United States.	24	1	Petition	102	Judiciary	May 17, 1836	By bill......	644	Referred to Committee Whole House.		
Blake, Edward, executors of.	Amount due on judgment *vs.* the United States.	25	2	Petition	41	Judiciary	344	Favorable	374	Referred to Committee Whole House.		
Blake, Edward, executors of.	Amount due on judgment *vs.* the United States.	25	3	Rep't Committee Whole House.	378	....	....	With't amend.	374	Passed	Passed	App'd March 3, 1839
Blake, Eleazer..........	Pension for revolutionary services.	17	1	Petition	98	Rev. Pensions.						
Blake, Eleazer..........	Increase of pension	29	1	Petition	120	Rev. Claims......	....	....	......	Discharged; laid on table.		
Blake, George	(See widow of David Stearns)...	19	2	....	156							
Blake, George E	(See administrator of J. Edmund Blake.)	30	1	....	259							
Blake, Henry...........	To be restored to pension roll....	17	2	Petition	81	Rev. Pensions	....	....	......	Discharged; leave to withdraw.		
Blake, Henry J.........	Equitable settlement of accounts; vouchers lost.	17	1	Petition	98	Rev. Pensions.						
Blake, John............	(See administrator of Daniel Tucker.)	3	2	....	286							
Blake, John............	Reimbursement of advances and compensation for supplies.	2	1	....	459	....	....	....	......	Laid on table.		
Blake, John............	Indemnity for losses as a Canadian refugee.	2	1	Petition	465	Select.						
Blake, John............	Indemnity for losses as a Canadian refugee.	2	2	Petition	619	Select	Feb. 19, 1793	....	......	Referred to Committee Whole House.		
Blake, John............	Indemnity for losses as a Canadian refugee.	4	1	Resolution	430	Select						
Blake, John............	(See Canadian refugees)	4	2	....	614							
Blake, John, (Maine)....	Pension for revolutionary services.	18	1	Petition	234	Pens. & Rev. Cl'ms.	....	....	......	Discharged; leave to withdraw.		
Blake, John, (Maryland).	Pension for revolutionary services.	20	1	Petition	57	Select	....	....	......	Discharged; laid on table.		
Blake, John, (N. H.)....	Pension	20	2	Petition	31	Military Pensions..	....	....	......	Discharged; laid on table.		

List of private claims presented to the House of Representatives of the United States from the 1st to the 31st Congress, inclusive—Continued.

Names of claimants.	Nature or object of the claim.	Congress.	Session.	How brought before the House of Reps.	Page of journal.	To what committee of the House referred.	No. or date of the report.	Nature of the report.	No. of the bill.	How disposed of by the House of Reps.	How disposed of by the Senate.	Date of the act of Congress, and remarks.
Blake, John	Pension for revolutionary services	22	1	Senate bill	779	Rev. Pensions	May 24, 1832	With't amend.	S. 129	Laid on table.		
Blake, Joseph, heirs of	Grant of land for revolutionary services.	11	3	Petition	495	Claims.						
Blake, Joseph, representatives of.	Compensation for revolutionary services.	20	1	Petition	51	Rev. Claims	Jan. 11, 1828	Adverse	......	Laid on table.		
Blake, Joseph, representataves of.	Bounty land for revolutionary services.	21	2	Petition	337	Rev. Claims.						
Blake, Joseph, representatives of.	Bounty land for revolutionary services.	22	1	Petition	164	Rev. Claims.						
Blake, J., Edmund administrator of.	Reimbursement of money stolen from him.	30	1	Petition	259	Military Affairs	623	Adverse	......	Laid on table.		
Blake, Nathaniel	Drawback on molasses	19	2	Petition	30	Ways and Means.						
Blake, Nathaniel	Drawback on molasses	20	1	Petition	68	Ways and Means	Jan. 4, 1828	Favorable	53	Passed.		
Blake, Nathaniel	Drawback on molasses	20	2	Petition	25	Ways and Means	Dec. 31, 1828	Favorable	352	Referred to Committee Whole House.		
Blake, Nathaniel	Drawback on molasses	21	1	Petition	142	Ways and Means.						
Blake, Nathaniel	Drawback on molasses	21	2	Petition	44	Ways and Means.						
Blake, Nathaniel	Drawback on molasses	22	1	House bill	101	Whole House	....	....	118	Passed	Rejected.	
Blake, Nathaniel	Drawback on molasses	22	2	Petition	28	Ways and Means	Dec. 27, 1832	Favorable	643	Passed	Rejected.	
Blake, Nathaniel	Drawback on molasses	23	1	Petition	58	Ways and Means	....	....	......	Discharged; laid on table.		
Blake, Thomas	Extra compensation for revolutionary services.	22	2	Petition	40	Rev. Claims.						
Blake, William	Increase of pension, &c.	29	1	Petition	233	Invalid Pensions.						
Blake, William	Increase of pension, &c.	29	2	Petition	89	Invalid Pensions.						
Blake, William	Increase of pension, &c.	30	1	Petition	65	Invalid Pensions	192	Favorable	202	Referred to Committee Whole House.		
Blake, William	Increase of pension, &c.	30	2	Rep't Committee Whole House.	143	....	....	With amend.	202	Passed	Adverse report.	
Blake, William	Increase of pension, &c.	31	2	Petition	141	Invalid Pensions.						
Blakely, Johnston, widow of.	Support for self and daughter in consideration of the loss of husband in the Wasp.	14	1	Petition	168	Select.						
Blakely, Johnston, widow of.	Pensions to legal representatives of those lost in the Wasp.	14	1	Senate bill	500	Naval Affairs	Mar. 25, 1816	With't amend.	......	Passed with amend'mt	Passed as am'd.	App'd April 16, 1853
Blakely, Johnston, heirs of	Settlement of accounts	17	2	Senate bill	278	Naval Affairs	Mar. 1, 1823	With't amend.	S. 55	Passed	Passed	App'd Mar. 3, 1823
Blakely, Josiah, representatives of.	Confirmation of title to land on Blakely's island.	27	2	Petition	365	Priv. Land Claims	249	Favorable	215	Passed	Passed	App'd July 9, 1842
Blakely, Josiah, heirs of	Confirmation of title to land in Northwest territory.	30	1	Senate bill	913	Priv. Land Claims	....	....	S. 147	Referred to Committee Whole House.		
Blakely, Josiah, heirs of	Confirmation of title to land in Northwest territory.	30	2	Rep't Committee Whole House.	119	....	....	With't amend.	S. 147	Passed	Passed	App'd Dec. 21, 1848
Blakely, Robert	Payment of a bill drawn by deputy quartermaster general.	13	1	Petition	125	Ways and Means.						
Blakemore, George, (Ten.)	Grant of land for public services	22	1	Petition	417	Public Lands	Mar. 6, 1832	Adverse	......	Laid on table.		
Blakemore, George	Pension for revolutionary services	20	2	Petition	27	Rev. Claims	Feb. 18, 1828	Adverse	......	Laid on table.		
Blakemore, George	Pension for revolutionary services	21	1	Petition	236	Rev. Claims.						
Blakemore, George, widow of.	Pension for revolutionary services	28	1	Petition	370	Rev. Pensions	262	Favorable	194	Passed	Passed	App'd May 23, 1844
Blakemore, Joseph, widow of.	Pension for services of husband and self as Indian fighters.	23	2	Petition	394	Claims.						
Blakeny, Abel	Pension for revolutionary services	16	1	Petition	89	Rev. Pensions	Jan. 14, 1820	Adverse	......	Laid on table.		

List of private claims presented to the House of Representatives of the United States from the 1st to the 31st Congress, inclusive—Continued.

Names of claimants.	Nature or object of the claim.	Congress.	Session.	How brought before the House of Reps.	Page of journal.	To what committee of the ouse referred.	No. or date of the report.	Nature of the report.	No. of the bill.	How disposed of by the House of Reps.	How disposed of by the Senate.	Date of the act of Congress, and remarks.
Blakeny, Abel	Pension for revolutionary services	22	1	Resolution	378	Rev. Pensions				Discharged; laid on table.		
Blakeny, Abel	Increase of pension	24	2	Petition	273	Rev. Pensions				Discharged; laid on table.		
Blakeny, Abel	Increase of pension	25	2	Petition	72	Rev. Pensions				Discharged; laid on table.		
Blakeny, Abel, widow of	Restoration of pension	26	1	Petition	937	Rev. Pensions.						
Blakeny, Abel, widow of	Restoration of pension	27	2	Petition	58	Rev. Pensions.						
Blakeny, Abel, widow of	Restoration of pension	29	1	Petition	658	Rev. Pensions	606	Adverse		Laid on table.		
Blakeny, Abel, widow of	Restoration of pension	30	1	Petition	491	Rev. Pensions	371	Adverse		Laid on table.		
Blakeny, Mary	(See Abel Blakeny, widow of)	26	1		937							
Blakeslee, Abel	(See Abel Blakeny.)											
Blakely, Abel	(See Abel Blakeny.)											
Blakeslee, S., sureties of	Release from liability	15	1	Petition	211	Ways and Means				Discharged; laid on table.		
Blakeslee, S., sureties of	Release from liability	15	2	Petition	267	Ways and Means				Discharged; laid on table.		
Blakesley, Enos	Pension for revolutionary services	3	1	Rep. of Secretary War.	131	Select	May 26, 1794	Res. to refer to Sec. War.	R. 12	Passed	Passed	App'd June 9, 1794
Blakesley, Enos	Pension for revolutionary services	3	2	Rep. of Secretary War.	262	Claims	Feb. 28, 1795	Pension bill	130	Passed	Indef. postp'd.	
Blakesley, Enos	Pension for revolutionary services	4	1	Rep. of Secretary War.	447	Claims	Feb. 18, 1796	Pension bill	156	Passed	Passed with amendment.	App'd April 20, 1796
Blambo, Gideon	Pension for revolutionary services	14	1	Petition	260	Pens. & Rev. Cl'ms.						
Blanc, John	Renewal of a patent	25	2	Petition	74	Patents	666	Favorable	642	Referred to Committee Whole House.		
Blanc, John	Renewal of a patent	25	3	Rep't Committee Whole House.	380			With't amend.	642	Passed	Passed	App'd March 3, 1839
Blanchard, Albert G., and others.	Compensation for extra services in Mexican war.	30	2	Petition	285	Military Affairs				Discharged; laid on table.		
Blanchard, Albert G., and others.	Compensation as acting commis sary of subsistence.	31	2	Petition	72	Claims.						
Blanchard, Cost	(See Louis F. Beeler, *et al.*)	30	1		115		482					
Blanchard, Edward, agent of.	Compensation for services as a truckman	2	1	Petition	492					Referred to Secretary Treasury.		
Blanchard, Edward, agent of.	Compensation for services as a truckman.	2	2	Rep. of Secretary Treasury.	625					Laid on table.		
Blanchard, Edward, agent of.	Compensation for services as a truckman.	3	1	Resolution	135	Select	May 14, 1794	Favorable		Referred to Committee Whole House.		
Blanchard, Edward, agent of.	Compensation for services as a truckman.	3	2	Resolution	246	Whole House	Dec. 3, 1794	Fav. and bill ordered.	80	Passed	Passed	App'd Dec. 18, 1794
Blanchard, George	(See agent of Edward Blanchard.)	3	1		135							
Blanchard, Harrison R.	Permission to enter land in Florida.	25	3	Petition	134	Public Lands.						
Blanchard, Harrison R.	Permission to enter land in Florida.	26	1	Petition	178	Public Lands	80	Adverse		Laid on table.		
Blanchard, James	(See agent of Edward Blanchard.)	2	1		492							
Blanchard, Jeremiah	Pension	21	2	Petition	299	Military Pensions.						
Blanchard, Thomas	(See represent's of Chas. Thomas.)	5	2		283							
Blanchard, Thomas, (Ky.)	Compensation for horse lost in public service.	21	1	Resolution	255	Claims	Feb. 12, 1830	Adverse		Laid on table.		
Blanchard, Thomas, (Ky.)	Compensation for horse lost in public service.	21	2	Resolution	56	Claims	Dec. 31, 1830	Adverse		Laid on table.		
Blanchard, Thomas, (N.Y.)	Compensation for the use of inventions by government.	25	3	Petition	206	Claims.						

List of private claims presented to the House of Representatives of the United States from the 1st to the 31st Congress, inclusive—Continued.

Names of claimants.	Nature or object of the claim.	Congress.	Session.	How brought before the House of Reps.	Page of journal.	To what committee of the House referred.	No. or date of the report.	Nature of the report.	No. of the bill.	How disposed of by the House of Reps.	How disposed of by the Senate.	Date of the act of Congress, and remarks.
Blanchard, Thomas, (N. Y.)	Compensation for the use of inventions by government.	26	1	Petition	168	Claims.						
Blanchard, Thomas, (N. Y.)	Renewal of patent	23	1	Petition	160	Patents	397	Favorable	417	Passed	Passed	App'd June 30, 1834
Blanchard, Thomas, (N. Y.)	Amendatory act	25	3	Senate bill	245	Patents	Jan. 22, 1839	With amend.	S. 177	Passed with amendm't.	Passed	App'd Feb. 6, 1839
Blanchard, Thomas, (N. Y.)	Renewal of patent	29	1	Petition	494	Patents	713	Favorable	488	Referred to Committee Whole House.		
Blanchard, Thomas, (N. Y.)	Renewal of patent	29	2	Senate bill	317				S. 74	Passed	Passed	App'd Feb. 15, 1847
Blanchard, Thomas, (N. Y.)	Protection of his patent right	31	1	Petition	258	Judiciary	April 24, 1850	General bill	254	Referred to Committee Whole House.		
Blanchard, William	Pension	13	2	Pension bill	344	Whole House	Mar. 31, 1814	With amend.	166	Passed	Passed	App'd April 18, 1814
Blanchard, William, (Vt.)	Pension for revolutionary services.	19	1	Petition	149	Military Pensions	April 1, 1826	Adverse		Laid on table.		
Blanchard, William, (Vt.)	Pension for revolutionary services.	19	2	Petition	132	Military Pensions				Discharged; laid on table.		
"Blanche," brig, owners of	Indemnity for vessel sunk in defence of Baltimore.	21	1	Petition	....	Commerce	Feb. 2, 1830	Favorable	191	Passed	Passed	App'd May 29, 1830
Blanco, Manuel	Patent for land under Spanish grant.	22	1	Petition	263	Priv. Land Claims.	Feb. 17, 1832	Favorable	380	Referred to Committee Whole House.		
Bland, Edward	Indemnity for property destroyed at Navy Yard, Washington.	13	3	Senate bill	768	Whole House	March 3, 1815	With't amend.	S. 97	Passed	Passed	App'd March 3, 1815
Blane, Thomas	(See assignees of T. Williams and J. Carey.)	9	2		607							
Blaney, Aaron	Compensation for revolutionary services and supplies.	17	1	Petition	165	Pens. & Rev. Cl'ms.	Jan. 25, 1822	Adverse		Rejected.		
Blaney, Aaron	Compensation for revolutionary services and supplies.	18	1	Petition	113	Pens. & Rev. Cl'ms.						
Blaney, Aaron	Compensation for revolutionary services and supplies.	18	2	Rep. of Committee Whole.	288		March 1, 1825	Adverse		Laid on table.		
Blaney, Aaron	Indemnity for French spoliations prior to 1800.	26	1	Memorial	182	Foreign Affairs	343	Favorable	319	Referred to Committee Whole House.		
Blaney, John	Increase and arrears of revolutionary services.	5	2	Petition	147	Claims	Feb. 1, 1798	Adverse.				
Blaney, Samuel	Pension	15	1	Petition	160	Pens. & Rev. Cl'ms.	Feb. 14, 1818	Adverse		Leave to withdraw.		
Blankenship, George	Indemnity for French spoliations prior to 1800.	20	1	Petition	196	Foreign Affairs	264					
Blankenship, Henry	Pension for revolutionary services.	22	1	Petition	36	Invalid Pensions	46	Favorable	51	Passed	Indef. postp'd.	
Blanks, James	Compensation for horse, &c., lost in Seminole war.	23	1	Petition	154	Claims.						
Blanton, William	Indemnity for loss of pre-emption right.	23	2	Petition	278							
Blasdell, Nicholas	(See Stephen Waite and others)	12	2		643							
Blassingham, Wade	Exchange of an entry of land	25	2	Petition	1182	Priv. Land Claims.						
Blas-ingham, Wade	Exchange of an entry of land	28	1	Petition	784	Public Lands.						
Blassingham, Wade	Exchange of an entry of land	28	2	Petition	228	Public Lands.						
Blatchley, M. and J. Scranton.	Indemnity for French spoliations prior to 1800.	22	1	Memorial	671	Foreign Affairs.						
Blatchley, Martin	Indemnity for French spoliations prior to 1800.	26	1	Memorial	182	Foreign Affairs	343	Favorable bill.	319	Referred to Committee Whole House.		
Blauvelt, Abraham	Pension for revolutionary services.	3	1	Rep. of Secretary War.	131					Laid on table.		
Blauvelt, Abraham	Pension for revolutionary services.	4	1	Rep. of Secretary War.	373	Claims	Feb. 18, 1796	Pension bill.	156	Passed	Passed with amendment.	App'd April 20, 1796
Blauvelt, Garret	(See executors of Hendrick Oblenis)	14	2		90							

List of private claims presented to the House of Representatives of the United States from the 1st to the 31st Congress, inclusive—Continued.

Names of claimants.	Nature or object of the claim.	Congress.	Session.	How brought before the House of Reps.	Page of journal.	To what committee of the House referred.	No. or date of the report.	Nature of the report.	No. of the bill.	How disposed of by the House of Reps.	How disposed of by the Senate.	Date of the act of Congress, and remarks.
Blay, Joseph	Patent for lands (old mines) in Missouri.	22	1	Petition	263	Priv. Land Claims.	308	Favorable	380	Referred to Committee Whole House.		
Blean, Robert	Compensation for property taken for public use.	17	1	Petition	47	Claims	Jan. 2, 1822	Adverse	......	Rejected.		
Blean, Robert	Compensation for property taken for public use.	18	1	Petition	71	Claims	Mar. 22, 1824	Favorable	174	Passed	Passed	App'd May 19, 1824
Bledsoe, Elijah	Compensation for services in Indian campaign of 1793.	9	2	Petition	506	Claims.						
Bledsoe, George	Pension for revolutionary services.	3	2	Report of Secretary of War.	337	Claims	Feb. 28, 1795	Favorable.				
Bledsoe, George	Pension for revolutionary services.	4	1	Report of Secretary of War.	373	Claims	Feb. 18, 1796	Pension bill	156	Passed	Passed with amendment.	App'd April 20, 1796
Bledsoe, G., (N. C.)	Increase of pension	19	1	Petition	130	Military Pensions	April 1, 1826	Adverse	......	Laid on table.		
Bleecker, A. L., executors of.	Indemnity for French spoliations prior to 1800.	26	1	Memorial	182	Foreign Affairs	343	Favorable	319	Referred to Committee Whole House.		
Bleecker, Major Leonard	Compensation for revolutionary services.	22	2	Petition	132	Rev. Claims.						
Bleecker, Major Leonard	Compensation for revolutionary services.	23	1	Petition	60	Rev. Pensions.						
Bleecker, Major Leonard	Pension for revolutionary services.	23	2	Petition	78	Rev. Pensions.						
Bleecker, Major Leonard	Pension for revolutionary services.	24	1	Petition	107	Rev. Pensions	Jan. 19, 1836	Adverse	......	Laid on table.		
Blessingham, Wade	(See Wade Blassingham.)											
Blever, James	Increase of pension	10	2	Pension bill	499	Whole House	Feb. 20, 1809	With amend.	158	Passed	Passed with amendment.	App'd March 3, 1809
Blevin, Samuel	Pension for revolutionary services.	3	1	Report of Secretary of War.	131	Select	May 26, 1794	Res. to refer to Sec. War.	R. 12	Passed	Passed	App'd June 9, 1794
Blevins, Henry, widow of.	Pension for revolutionary services.	21	1	Petition	938	Rev. Pensions.						
Blew, Abijah	Pension for revolutionary services.	16	1	Petition	45	Rev. Pensions	....	....	......	Discharged; leave to withdraw.		
Blick, James	Additional compensation for revolutionary services.	22	2	Petition	74	Claims.						
Blight, Charles	(See heirs of Robert Fulton.)											
Blight, John, and others	Increase of pay as officers United States army.	26	1	Petition	304	Naval Affairs.						
Blight, Julia	(See heirs of Robert Fulton.)											
Blight, Peter, assignees of.	Indemnity for French spoliations prior to 1800.	26	1	Memorial	182	Foreign Affairs	343	Favorable	319	Referred to Committee Whole House.		
Blincoe, John, (Va.)	Pension	21	1	Petition	67	Military Pensions	....	....	......	Discharged; laid on table.		
Bliss, Huldah	(See Thomas Theodore Bliss, widow of.)	16	1	....	51							
Bliss, James	(See Casper P. Cooke and others)	26	1	....	702							
Bliss, John	Pension	20	1	Petition	396	Military Pensions	April 5, 1828	Adverse	......	Laid on table.		
Bliss, John	Pension	21	1	Petition	318	Military Pensions	....	....	......	Discharged; laid on table.		
Bliss, John	Pension	21	2	Petition	64	Military Pensions.						
Bliss, John	Pension	22	1	Petition	288	Rev. Pensions	....	....	......	Discharged; laid on table.		
Bliss, Moses	Compensation for services as deputy marshal of Vermont.	23	2	Petition	83	Claims	17	Favorable	594	Referred to Committee Whole House.		
Bliss, Moses	Compensation for services as deputy marshal of Vermont.	24	1	House bill	77	Whole House	Jan. 18, 1836	With't amend.	29	Passed	Passed	App'd June 7, 1836
Bliss, Samuel	Pension for revolutionary services.	21	2	Petition	40	Military Pensions.						
Bliss, Samuel	Pension for revolutionary services.	22	1	Petition	35	Rev. Pensions	161	Favorable	237	Referred to Committee Whole House.		

List of private claims presented to the House of Representatives of the United States from the 1st to the 31st Congress, inclusive—Continued.

Names of claimants.	Nature or object of the claim.	Congress.	Session.	How brought before the House of Reps.	Page of journal.	To what committee of the House referred.	No. or date of the report.	Nature of the report.	No. of the bill.	How disposed of by the House of Reps.	How disposed of by the Senate.	Date of the act of Congress, and remarks.
Bliss, Samuel	Pension for revolutionary services	22	2	House bill	123				237	Laid on table.		
Bliss, Thomas Theodore, widow of.	Pension for revolutionary services	16	1	Petition	51	Rev. Pensions	April 22, 1820	Adverse		Laid on table.		
Bliven, James	Pension for revolutionary services	3	1	Report Secretary of War.	131	Select	May 26, 1794	Res. to refer to Sec'y War.	R. 12	Passed	Passed	App'd June 9, 1794
Blocker, Michael B.	Pension	22	1	Petition	509	Invalid Pensions	April 11, 1832	Adverse		Laid on table.		
Blodget, Bliss, and others	Restoration of a vessel and cargo seized.	12	2	Petition	620	Ways and Means	May 1, 1813	Adverse		Rejected.		
Blodget, Elijah, (Ct.)	Pension	22	2	Petition	26	Invalid Pensions.						
Blodget, Elijah, (Ct.)	Pension	23	1	Petition	44	Invalid Pensions	Feb. 4, 1834	Adverse		Laid on table.		
Blodget, Elijah, (Ct.)	Pension	23	2	Petition	198	Invalid Pensions	84	Favorable	703	Passed.		
Blodget, Elijah, (Ct.)	Pension	24	1	Petition	140	Invalid Pensions	July 1, 1836	Adverse		Laid on table.		
Blodget, Elijah, (Ct.)	Pension	24	2	Petition	41	Invalid Pensions.						
Blodget, Elijah, (Ct.)	Pension	25	2	Petition	57	Invalid Pensions	573	Favorable	563	Passed	Adverse report.	
Blodget, Elijah, (Ct.)	Pension	25	3	Petition	90	Invalid Pensions	74	Favorable	952	Passed	Adverse report.	
Blodget, Elijah, (Ct.)	Pension	26	1	Petition	161	Invalid Pensions	178	Favorable	189	Passed	Indef. postpn'd	
Blodget, Elijah, (Ct.)	Pension	26	2	Petition	36	Invalid Pensions.						
Blodget, Elijah, (Ct.)	Pension	27	2	Petition	60	Invalid Pensions	446	Adverse		Laid on table.		
Blodget, Elijah, (Ct.)	Pension	27	3	Petition	44	Invalid Pensions.						
Blodget, Elijah, (Ct.)	Pension	28	1	Petition	82	Invalid Pensions	229	Favorable	186	Passed	Adverse report.	
Blodget, Elijah, (Ct.)	Pension	28	2	Petition	57	Invalid Pensions	11	Favorable	461	Passed	Indef. postpn'd	
Blodget, Elijah, (Ct.)	Pension	29	1	Petition	101	Invalid Pensions	45	Adverse		Leave to withdraw.		
Blodget, Harry	Pension	15	1	Petition	156	Pens. & Rev. Cl'ms.						
Blodget, Henry	Pension	22	1	Petition	51	Invalid Pensions	233	Favorable	344	Passed	Laid on table.	
Blodget, Henry	Pension	22	2	Petition	82	Invalid Pensions	Feb. 15, 1833	Favorable	738	Referred to Committee Whole House.		
Blodget, Newcomb	Pension for revolutionary services	16	2	Petition	188	Rev. Pensions	Feb. 15, 1821	Adverse		Rejected.		
Blodget, Newcomb	Pension for revolutionary services	25	2	Petition	913	Rev. Pensions				Discharged; laid on table.		
Blodget, Newcomb	Pension for revolutionary services	26	1	Petition	173	Rev. Pensions				Discharged; laid on table.		
Blodget, Rebecca	(See Samuel Blodget, widow of.)	19	1	Petition	271							
Blodget, Rufus	Compensation for revolutionary services.	2	2	Petition	618							
				Rep. of Secretary War.	735					Laid on table.		
Blodget, Rufus	Compensation for revolutionary services.	3	1	Petition	72	Whole House				Leave to withdraw.		
Blodget, Samuel	Release from judgment as a lottery manager.	7	2	Petition	264	Select.						
Blodget, Samuel, widow of	Compensation for right of dower	19	1	Petition	271	Dist. of Columbia	Mar. 31, 1826	Favorable	193	Passed	Passed	App'd May 20, 1826; referred to Att'y. Gen.
Blodget, Samuel, widow of	Compensation for right of dower	19	2	Petition	224	Judiciary.						
Blodget, Samuel, widow of	Compensation for right of dower	20	1	Petition	197	Judiciary	157	Favorable	180	Passed	Passed	App'd May 19, 1828; conditional.
Blodget, Samuel, widow of	Compensation for right of dower	22	1	Senate bill	844	Judiciary	June 12, 1832	With't amend.	S. 195	Passed	Passed	App'd July 14, 1832
Blodget, Sardis	Pension	16	1	Petition	210	Rev. Pensions	April 6, 1820	Adverse		Laid on table.		
Blodget, Sylvanus	Pension for disability, war of 1812	29	1	Petition	303	Invalid Pensions				Discharged; laid on table.		
Blodget, Sylvanus	Pension for disability, war of 1812	30	1	Petition	136	Invalid Pensions	779	Favorable	616	Referred to Committee Whole House.		
Blodget, Sylvanus	Pension for disability, war of 1812	30	2	Rep't Committee Whole House.	362			With't amend.	616	Passed.		

List of private claims presented to the House of Representatives of the United States from the 1st *to the* 31st *Congress, inclusive*—Continued.

Names of claimants.	Nature or object of the claim.	Congress.	Session.	How brought before the House of Reps.	Page of journal.	To what committee of the House referred.	No. or date of the report.	Nature of the report.	No. of the bill.	How disposed of by the House of Reps.	How disposed of by the Senate.	Date of the act of Congress, and remarks.
Blodget, Sylvanus	Pension for disability, war of 1812	31	1	Petition	194	Invalid Pensions	305	Favorable	275	Referred to Committee Whole House.		
Blodget, Sylvanus	Pension for disability, war of 1812	31	2	Rep't Committee Whole House.	182			With amend.	275	Passed.		
Blood, Francis	Pension for revolutionary services.	10	1	Pension bill	232	Whole House	April 19, 1808	With amend.	78	Passed	Passed with amendment.	App'd April 25, 1808
Blood, Hosea	Pension	14	1	Petition	449	Pens. & Rev. Cl'ms.						
Blood, Dr. Hosea, administrator of.	Indemnity for property burnt on brig Detroit.	19	1	Petition	311	Claims	April 4, 1826	Adverse		Laid on table.		
Blood, John	(See administrator of Dr. Hosea Blood.)	19	1		311							
Bloodgood, Abraham	Pension for naval services	25	2	Petition	723	Naval Affairs				Discharged; laid on table.		
Bloodgood, John	(See sureties of Thomas H. Smith and son.)	20	2		142							
Bloodworth, Timothy, sureties of.	Extension of time for payment of bond.	11	2	Petition	226	Ways and Means.						
Bloom, George and Henry S.	Right of pre-emption	30	1	Petition	218	Public Lands	323	Adverse.				
Bloom, Peter, heirs of	Confirmation of title to land in Missouri.	24	1	Senate bill	365	Priv. Land Claims.	June 15, 1836	Adverse	S. 24	Referred to Committee Whole House.		
Bloom, Peter, heirs of	Confirmation of title to land in Missouri.	24	2	Senate bill	250	Priv. Land Claims.			S. 30	Discharged; laid on table.		
Bloom, Peter, heirs of	Confirmation of title to land in Missouri.	25	2	Senate bill	197	Priv. Land Claims.	Jan. 5, 1838	With't amend.	S. 66	Referred to Committee Whole House.		
Bloom, Peter, heirs of	Confirmation of title to land in Missouri.	26	1	Senate bill	443	Priv. Land Claims.	April 4, 1840	With't amend	S. 68	Referred to Committee Whole House.		
Bloom, Peter, heirs of	Confirmation of title to land in Missouri.	27	2	Senate bill	521	Priv. Land Claims.	July 27, 1842	With't amend.	S. 48	Passed	Passed	App'd Aug. 11, 1842
Bloomer, William	Sergeant's allowance of one year's clothing.	25	2	Petition	84	Military Affairs	604	Favorable	584	Referred to Committee Whole House.		
Bloomfield, Ann	(See Thomas Bloomfield, widow of.)	25	2		37							
Bloomfield, James	Pension	21	2	Petition	80	Military Pensions.						
Bloomfield, Joseph	(See New Jersey—College)	8	2		19							
Bloomfield, Joseph E	(See Richard S. Hackley)	15	2		177							
Bloomfield, Thomas	Pension for revolutionary services.	20	2	Petition	203	Military Pensions.				Discharged; laid on table.		
Bloomfield, Thomas	Pension for revolutionary services.	21	1	Petition	67	Military Pensions.	Feb. 13, 1830	Pension bill	72	Passed	Passed with amendment.	App'd May 20, 1830
Bloomfield, Thomas	Pension for revolutionary services.	21	2	Resolution	71	Military Pensions.						
Bloomfield, Thomas, heirs of.	Continuation of pension	24	2	Petition	216	Rev. Pensions	234	Favorable	937			
Bloomfield, Thomas, widow of.	Continuation of pension	25	2	Petition	37	Rev. Pensions	272	Favorable	315	Passed.		
Bloomfield, Thomas, widow of.	Continuation of pension	26	1	Petition	171	Rev. Pensions	153	Favorable	163	Passed	Indef. postp'd.	
Blooming Youth, schooner.	(See Israel Goodridge, and others.)	26	2		99							
Bloss, Richard	(See sureties of Thaddeus P. Haskell.)	29	2		375				S. 97			
Bloss, Timothy K.	(See heirs of Martin L. Patterson.)	30	1		77							
Blossom, Joseph	Compensation for revolutionary services and settlement of accounts.	9	1	Petition	267							
				Rep. of Secretary War.	287					Claim rejected.		

20

List of private claims presented to the House of Representatives of the United States from the 1st to the 31st Congress, inclusive—**Continued.**

Names of claimants.	Nature or object of the claim.	Congress.	Session.	How brought before the House of Reps.	Page of journal.	To what committee of the House referred.	No. or date of the report.	Nature of the report.	No. of the bill.	How disposed of by the House of Reps.	How disposed of by the Senate.	Date of the act of Congress, and remarks.
Blossom, Joseph	Bounty land for services under Wayne.	24	2	Petition	47	Rev. Pensions				Discharged; laid on table.		
Blount, James K.	Indemnity for failure of title to public lands.	29	1	Petition	380	Claims	322	Adverse		Laid on table.		
Blount, James S.	(See surety of Isaac Smith)	25	3		465							
Blount, John G., & others	Indemnity for French spoliations prior to 1800.	18	1	Memorial	101					Laid on table.		
Blount, John G., & others	Indemnity for French spoliations prior to 1800.	26	1	Memorial	182	Foreign Affairs	343	Favorable	319	Referred to Committee Whole House.		
Blount, Willie	Settlement of his account for services, war of 1812.	17	2	Petition	144	Claims.						
Blount, Willie	Settlement of his account for services, war of 1812.	18	1	Memorial	61	Select	Feb. 24, 1824	Adverse		Recommitted.		
Blount, Willie	Settlement of his account for services, war of 1812.	18	2	Petition	46	Select	Feb. 1, 1825	Favorable	312	Laid on table.		
Blount, Willie	Settlement of his account for services, war of 1812.	19	1	Petition	251	Select	121	Favorable	161	Passed.		
Blount, Willie	Settlement of his account for services, war of 1812.	19	2	Resolution	88	Select	Jan. 3, 1827	Favorable	340	Passed	Laid on table.	
Blount, Willie	Settlement of his account for services, war of 1812.	21	1	Petition	122	Select	362	Favorable	421	Referred to Committee Whole House.		
Blount, Willie	Settlement of his account for services, war of 1812.	22	1	Petition	43	Claims.						
Blount, Willie	Settlement of his account for services, war of 1812.	23	1	Petition	80	Claims	559	Favorable	556	Referred to Committee Whole House.		
Blount, Willie, representatives of.	Settlement of his account for services, war of 1812.	24	1	Petition	51	Claims	27	Favorable	27	Passed	Passed	App'd Feb. 17, 1836
Blow, Henry, heirs of	Arrears of pension	30	1	Petition	664	Invalid Pensions	833	Adverse		Laid on table.		
Blow, Henry, heirs of	Arrears of pension	31	1	Petition	996	Invalid Pensions.						
Bludget, Phineas, sen.	Bounty land for military services.	24	1	Petition	409	Public Lands.						
Bludget, Phineas, sen.	Bounty land for military services.	24	2	Petition	390	Public Lands.						
Bludget, Phineas, sen.	Bounty land for military services.	25	2	Petition	233	Public Lands	595	Adverse		Laid on table.		
Bludget, Phineas, jr.	Bounty land for military services.	24	1	Petition	409	Public Lands.						
Bludget, Phineas, jr.	Bounty land for military services.	24	2	Petition	390	Public Lands.						
Bludget, Phineas, jr.	Bounty land for military services.	25	2	Petition	233	Public Lands	595	Adverse		Laid on table.		
Blue Eyes, (Indian)	(See William Parker, and others).	17	1		135							
Blue Jacket, (Indian)	Confirmation of title to land in Ohio.	23	1	Petition	249	Private Land Clm's						
Blue Jacket, (Indian)	Confirmation of title to land in Ohio.	23	2	Petition	239	Priv. Land Claims.						
Blue Jacket, (Indian)	(See James W. Stewart)	24	1	Petition	426							
Blue, John, widow of	Pension	28	1	Petition	217	Invalid Pensions	Mar. 7, 1844	Adverse		Laid on table.		
Blue, John, widow of	Pension	29	1	Petition	648	Invalid Pensions.						
Blue, John, widow of	Pension	30	1	Petition	271	Invalid Pensions	393	Favorable	345	Passed		
Blue, John, widow of	Pension	31	1	Resolution	493	Invalid Pensions	149		165	Referred to Committee Whole House.		
Blundel, Absalom	Pension for revolutionary services.	25	2	Resolution	522	Rev. Pensions				Discharged; laid on table.		
Blunt, Robert, heirs of	Indemnity for French spoliations prior to 1800.	26	1	Memorial	182	Foreign Affairs	343	Favorable	319	Referred to Committee Whole House.		
Blunt, S. F.	(See Exploring expedition)	27	3		149							
Blunt, Lieut., U. S. Navy	Increase of pay to officers on coast of California.	31	1	Petition	756	Naval Affairs.						

List of private claims presented to the House of Representatives of the United States from the 1st to the 31st Congress, inclusive—Continued.

Names of claimants.	Nature or object of the claim.	Congress.	Session.	How brought before the House of Reps.	Page of journal.	To what committee of the House referred.	No. or date of the report.	Nature of the report.	No. of the bill.	How disposed of by the House of Reps.	How disposed of by the Senate.	Date of the act of Congress, and remarks.
Blye, John F. or W.	Indemnity for loss of clothing on frigate Philadelphia.	24	1	Petition	273	Naval Affairs.						
Blye, John F. or W.	Indemnity for loss of clothing on frigate Philadelphia.	24	2	Petition	85	Naval Affairs.	27	Adverse		Leave to withdraw.		
Blye, John F. or W.	Indemnity for loss of clothing on frigate Philadelphia.	25	2	Petition	723	Naval Affairs.				Disch'd; laid on table.		
Blythe, Calvin	(See executors of Jesse D. Elliott)	30	1		807							
Blythe, Samuel	Pension	19	1	Petition	175	Military Pensions	April 1, 1826	Adverse		Leave to withdraw.		
Blythe, Samuel	Pension	20	1	Petition	92	Military Pensions	Jan. 3, 1828	Favorable	46	Passed	Laid on table.	
Blythe, Samuel	Pension	20	2	Petition	124	Military Pensions				Discharged; leave to withdraw.		
Boand, Jean	Reimbursement of excessive tonage duties.	1	2	Petition	209	Select.						
Board, Patrick	Pension for revolutionary services.	22	1	Petition	300	Rev. Pensions.						
Boardman, Elijah	Pension for revolutionary services.	3	1	Rep. of Secretary War.	131	Select	May 26, 1794	Res. to refer to Sec. War.	R. 12	Passed	Passed	App'd June 9, 1794
Boardman, Elijah	Pension for revolutionary services.	4	1	Report of Secretary of War.	373	Claims	Feb. 18, 1796	Favorable	156	Passed	Passed	App'd Apr. 20, 1796
Boardman, Elijah	Indemnity for property lost in the public service.	16	2	Petition	89	Claims	Jan. 8, 1821	Adverse		Laid on table.		
Boardman, George	(See Elisha Dunham and George Boardman.)	24	2		75							
Boardman, George	Indemnity for French spoliations prior to 1800.	26	1	Memorial	182	Foreign Affairs	343	Favorable	319	Referred to Committee Whole House.		
Boardman, John	Permission to enter public land	19	2	Senate bill	348	Public Lands	Mar. 2, 1827	With amend.	S. 76	Passed with amendm't	Passed as am'd	App'd Mar. 2, 1827
Boardman, John	Payment of a revolutionary bill of credit.	24	2	Petition	158	Rev. Claims.						
Boardman, Moses	Pension for revolutionary services.	3	1	Report of Secretary of War.	131	Select	May 26, 1794	Res. to refer to Sec. War.	R. 12	Passed	Passed	App'd June 9, 1794
Boardman, Moses	Pension for revolutionary services.	4	1	Rep. of Secretary War.	373	Claims.						
Boardman, Moses	Pension for revolutionary services.	4	2	Rep. of Secretary War.	614	Claims.						
Boardman and Pope and others.	(See Bordman.)											
Boardman, Richard, widow of.	Pension	18	1	Petition	284	Pens. & Rev. Cl'ms.	Mar. 12, 1824	Adverse		Laid on table.		
Boardman, Samuel	Compensation for medical services in Florida.	31	1	Petition	909	Claims.						
Boardman, Samuel	Indemnity for French Spoliations prior to 1800.	26	1	Memorial	182	Foreign Affairs	343	Favorable	319	Referred to Committee Whole House.		
Boardman, Sarah	(See Joseph Irwin, heirs of.)	25	2		373							
Boardman, Seth	Pension for revolutionary disability.	1	2	Petition		Select	July 16, 1790	Pension bill	88	Passed	Passed	App'd Aug. 11, 1790
Boardman, William, administrator of.	Indemnity for French spoliations prior to 1800.	26	1	Memorial	182	Foreign Affairs	343	Favorable	319	Referred to Committee Whole House.		
Boase, Hardy	Compensation for a gun taken for public use.	23	1	Petition	195	Claims.						
Bock, George	Pension for revolutionary services.	30	1	Petition	274	Rev. Pensions	682	Adverse		Laid on table.		
Bock, William	Pension for revolutionary services.	26	1	Petition	173	Rev. Pensions				Discharged; laid on table.		
Bockover, B. T.	(See T. N. Hathaway, administrator of.)	31	1		413							

List of private claims presented to the House of Representatives of the United States from the 1st to the 31st Congress, inclusive—Continued.

Names of claimants.	Nature or object of the claim.	Congress.	Session.	How brought before the House of Reps.	Page of journal.	To what committee of the House referred.	No. or date of the report.	Nature of the report.	No. of the bill.	How disposed of by the House of Reps.	How disposed of by the Senate.	Date of the act of Congress, and remarks.
Boden, James	Pension for revolutionary services	10	1	Pension bill	232	Whole House	April 19, 1808	With amend	78	Passed	Passed with amendment.	App'd Apr. 25, 1808
Boden, Moses	(See F. M. Arredono *et al.*)	19	1		252							
Boden, Sarah	Compensation for naval services of her son.	25	2	Petition	114	Naval Affairs				Discharged; laid on table.		
Bodey, Samuel	(See heirs of John W. Bush.)	31	1		256							
Bodfish, William, widow of.	Pension for revolutionary services	29	1	Petition	765	Rev. Pensions	786	Adverse		Laid on table.		
Bodley, A. D. W	Pension	26	1	Petition	628	Invalid Pensions	487	Adverse		Laid on table.		
Bodley, A. D. W	Pension	28	1	Petition	84	Invalid Pensions	299	Favorable	209	Passed	Adverse report; laid on table.	
Bodley, A. D. W	Pension	29	1	Petition	381	Invalid Pensions	786	Adverse		Laid on table.		
Bodwell, Elijah	(See John Matthews and Elijah Bodwell.)	3	1		41							
Bodwell, Solomon	Confirmation of title to land in Arkansas.	16	1	Petition	291	Priv. Land Claims.						
Bodwell, Solomon, assign's of.	Confirmation of title to land in Arkansas.	22	1	Petition	64	Public Lands	62	Favorable bill	425	Passed	Passed with amendment.	App'd June 25, 1832
Bœrum, William	Pay as flag captain	25	3	Memorial	563	Naval Affairs.						
Bœrum, William	Pay as flag captain	26	1	Petition	180	Naval Affairs	542	Adverse		Laid on table.		
Bogard, Cornelius	Compensation for horses lost in public service.	28	1	Petition	75	Claims	64	Adverse		Laid on table.		
Bogardus, Archibald R	That his pension bear even date with disability.	30	2	Petition	121	Naval Affairs.						
Bogardus, Everardus	Indemnity for revolutionary damages.	3	1	Petition	218					Referred to Secretary of War.		
Bogardus, Everardus	Indemnity for revolutionary damages.	8	2	Rep. of Secretary War.	278					Laid on table.		
Bogardus, Henry	(See heirs of Peter Bogardus)	29	1		90		33					
Bogardus, James	Extension of patent	29	1	Senate bill	214	Patents	Jan. 10, 1846	With't amend.	S. 33	Passed	Passed	App'd Jan. 14, 1846
Bogardus, James	Reimbursement of fee for patent never issued.	27	1	Petition	107	Claims.						
Bogardus, John L	Indemnity for Indian depredations	24	1	Petition	575	Claims	April 9, 1836	Adverse		Laid on table.		
Bogardus, John L	Indemnity for Indian depredations	25	2	Petition	107	Claims.						
Bogardus, Peter, heirs of	Indemnity for destruction of property by the enemy.	29	1	Petition	90	Claims	33	Adverse		Laid on table.		
Bogart, W	Release from liability as surety on custom-house bond.	20	1	Petition	218	Judiciary				Discharged; laid on table.		
Bogert, Abraham, widow of.	Bounty land as Canadian refugee	6	2	Refugee bill	766	Whole House	Jan. 26, 1801	With amend	280	Passed	Passed	App'd Feb. 18, 1801
Bogert, Gilbert	Bounty land for military services	25	2	Petition	59	Priv. Land Claims.	289	Adverse		Laid on table.		
Bogert, James	(See Benjamin Bailey and others)	10	2		484							
Bogert, John G	Reimbursement of payment for lots purchased at marshal's sale.	15	1	Petition	157	Claims	Feb. 9, 1818	Adverse		Rejected.		
				Senate bill	393	Claims	April 1, 1818	Adverse	S. 50	Referred to Committee Whole House.		
Bogert, John G	Reimbursement of payment for lots purchased at marshal's sale.	16	1	Petition	27	Claims	Jan. 12, 1820	Adverse		Referred to Committee Whole House.		
Bogert, John G	Reimbursement of payment for lots purchased at marshal's sale.	16	2	Rep't. Committee Whole House.	74			Adverse report adopted.		Rejected; leave to withdraw.		
Bogert, John G	Reimbursement of payment for lots purchased at marshal's sale.	17	1	Petition	361	Claims	Mar. 27, 1822	Adverse		Laid on table.		

List of private claims presented to the House of Representatives of the United States from the 1st to the 31st Congress, inclusive—Continued.

Names of claimants.	Nature or object of the claim.	Congress.	Session.	How brought before the House of Reps.	Page of journal.	To what committee of the House referred.	No. or date of the report.	Nature of the report.	No. of the bill.	How disposed of by the House of Reps.	How disposed of by the Senate.	Date of the act of Congress, and remarks.
Bogert, John G.	Reimbursement of payment for lots purchased at marshal's sale.	17	2	Report of Committee Claims.	71	Whole House.						
Bogert & Kneeland, and others.	Aid in settlement of claims against Venezuela.	29	2	Petition	142	Foreign Affairs				Discharged; referred to Secretary State.		
Bogert & Kneeland, and others.	Aid in settlement of claims against Venezuela.	30	1	Petition	461	Foreign Affairs.						
Bogert & Kneeland, and others.	Aid in setttlement of claims against Venezuela.	30	2	Petition	550	Foreign Affairs				Discharged; laid on table.		
Bogert, Nicholas N., heir of.	Commutation pay	31	1	Memorial	307	Rev. Claims	185	Adverse		Laid on table.		
Bogert, Rudolph	(See New York, United Insurance Company of.)	26	1		182		343		319			
Bogert, Theunis, widow of	Compensation for services and supplies.	4	1	Memorial	467	Claims	May 31, 1796	Adverse		Laid on table.		
Boggess, Giles S.	Indemnity for loss in express mail service.	25	2	Petition	540	P. Of. and P. Roads.	805	Adverse		Laid on table.		
Boggess, Giles S.	Indemnity for loss in express mail service.	28	2	Petition	283	P. Of. and P. Roads.						
Boggess, Giles S.	Indemnity for loss in express mail service.	29	2	Petition	183	P. Of. and P. Roads.						
Boggs, Elliott	Compensation for horse lost in Black Hawk war.	25	2	Petition	275	Claims.						
Boggs, John, widow of	Pension for revolutionary services.	29	1	Petition	718	Rev. Pensions	826	Adverse		Laid on table.		
Boggs, John, widow of	Pension for revolutionary services.	29	2	Petition	86	Rev. Pensions.						
Boggs, John, widow of	Pension for revolutionary services.	30	1	Petition	117	Rev. Pensions	773	Favorable	609	Referred to Committee Whole House.		
Boggs, John, widow of	Pension for revolutionary services.	30	2		362				609	Passed	Passed	App'd March 3, 1849
Boggs, Joseph, *et al.*	Indemnity for Indian depredations.	22	2	Resolution	122	Indian Affairs	91	Adverse		Laid on table.		
Boggs, Joseph	(See Reuben E. Gentry & others.)	23	1		138							
Boggs & Thompson	Drawback on goods exported	14	1	Petition	511	Com. and Manuf.						
Boggs & Thompson	Drawback on goods exported	14	2	Petition	91	Com. and Manuf.						
Boggs & Thompson	Drawback on goods exported	26	1	Petition	292	Commerce	30	Favorable	49	Passed	Passed	App'd July 20, 1840
Bogle, Joseph	Pension for revolutionary services.	22	1	Petition	35	Rev. Pensions.						
Bogle, Robert	(See administrator of Robert Boyd)	22	2		131							
Bogle, William	Pension for revolutionary services.	22	1	Petition	476	Rev. Pensions.						
Bogy, Joseph	Compensation for supplies to recruiting party.	18	1	Petition	387	Claims.						
Bogy, Joseph	Compensation for supplies to recruiting party.	21	2	Petition	232	Claims	87	Favorable	635	Referred to Committee Whole House.		
Bogy, Joseph	Compensation for supplies to recruiting party.	22	1	Petition	26	Claims	Dec. 19, 1831	Favorable	48	Passed	Passed	App'd May 19, 1832
Bogy, Joseph	Amount of draft in favor of J. Placey.	23	1	Senate bill	846	Rev. Claims			S. 139			
Bogy, Joseph	Indemnity for Indian depredations.	22	1	Petition	413	Indian Affairs.						
Bogy, Joseph	Indemnity for Indian depredations.	23	1	Petition	73	Indian Affairs.						
				Rep. of 3d Auditor	146	Indian Affairs	Dec. 31, 1833	General bill	108	Passed	Passed	App'd June 30, 1834
Bogy, Joseph	Indemnity for Indian depredations.	24	1	Senate bill	956	Indian Affairs	June 9, 1836	With't amend.	S. 169	Passed	Passed	App'd July 2, 1836
Bogy, Joseph, (Ark.)	Confirmation of title to land in Arkansas.	15	1	Petition	60	Priv. Land Claims.						
Bogy, Joseph, (Ark.)	Confirmation of title to land in Arkansas.	22	1	Petition	425	Public Lands	Feb. 28, 1832	General bill	425	Passed	Passed	App'd June 25, 1832
Bogy, Joseph, (Ark.)	Amendatory act	25	2	Senate bill	197	Priv. Land Claims.	Jan. 5, 1838	With't amend.	S. 64	Referred to Committee Whole House.		

List of private claims presented to the House of Representatives of the United States from the 1st to the 31st Congress, inclusive—Continued.

Names of claimants.	Nature or object of the claim.	Congress.	Session.	How brought before the House of Reps.	Page of journal.	To what committee of the House referred.	No. or date of the report.	Nature of the report.	No. of the bill.	How disposed of by the House of Reps.	How disposed of by the Senate.	Date of the act of Congress, and remarks.
Bogy, Joseph, (Ark.)	Amendatory act	25	3	Senate bill	447	Priv. Land Claims.			S. 49			
Bogy, Joseph, (Ark.)	Amendatory act	26	1	Senate bill	443	Priv. Land Claims.	June 23, 1840	With't amend.	S. 67	Referred to Committee Whole House.		
Bogy, Joseph, (Ark.)	Amendatory act	26	2	Senate bill	178	Priv. Land Claims.	Feb. 12, 1841	With't amend.	S. 78	Passed with amendm't.	Passed as am'd.	App'd March 3, 1841
Bogy, Joseph	(See Joseph Placey)	24	2		250				S. 22			
Bogy, Louis	Indemnity for Indian depredations.	23	1	Documents	220	Indian Affairs				Discharged; laid on table.		
Bohanan, Stephen	Pension for disability, war of 1812	24	1	Senate bill	811	Invalid Pensions	May 31, 1836	Witht' amend.	S. 244	Passed	Passed	App'd June 15, 1836
Bohler & Borie	Reimbursement of duties on brandy.	27	3	Petition	95	Ways and Means.						
Bohler & Borie	Reimbursement of duties on brandy.	28	1	Petition	84	Ways and Means.	378	Adverse		Laid on table.		
Bohler & Borie	Reimbursement of duties on brandy.	29	1	Petition	106	Commerce.						
Bohlen, B. & J	Indemnity for French spoliations prior to 1800.	26	1	Memorial	182	Foreign Affairs	343	Favorable	319	Referred to Committee Whole House.		
Bohlen, John	(See Ross & Surison, assignee of.)	26	1		182		343		319			
Bohlen, John	(See I. G. Wacksmith, executor of)	26	1		182		343		319			
Bohon, William	Pension	24	1	Petition	201	Invalid Pensions	Feb. 16, 1836	Adverse		Laid on table.		
Boilieu, James	(See Jacques Porlier and others.)	23	1		450		396		415			
Boilvin, Nicholas	Indemnity for Indian depredations.	15	1	Petition	254	Claims	Feb. 24, 1818	Adverse		Rejected.		
Boilvin, Nicholas, heirs of.	Indemnity for Indian depredations.	22	2	Petition	246	Indian Affairs.						
Boilvin, Nicholas, heirs of.	Balance due for services as Indian agent.	23	1	Petition	98	Indian Affairs.						
Boilvin, Nicholas	Grant of land to complete Indian reservation.	28	1	Petition	853	Priv. Land Claims.						
Boilvin, Nicholas	Grant of land to complete Indian reservation.	29	1	Petition	160	Indian Affairs.						
Boilvin, Nicholas	Grant of land to complete Indian reservation.	31	1	Petition	433	Public Lands.						
Boilvin, Nicholas	Grant of land to complete Indian reservation.	31	2	Petition	445	Public Lands	101	Adverse		Laid on lable.		
Boisdorē, Louis, heirs of	Confirmation of title to land in Louisiana.	23	1	Petition	139	Priv. Land Claims.						
Boisgervais, James H.	Indemnity for damage to property by United States troops.	14	2	Petition	142	Claims	Feb. 3, 1817	Favorable	98	Passed	Passed	App'd March 3, 1817
Boislandry, R. C., trustee of.	Indemnity for French spoliations prior to 1800.	26	1	Memorial	182	Foreign Affairs	343	Favorable	319	Referred to Committee Whole House.		
Boislandry, R. C., executors of.	Indemnity for French spoliations prior to 1800.	31	1	Petition	271	Foreign Affairs	355	General bill	318	Referred to Committee Whole House.		
Boker, William	Compensation for mail service	31	1	Petition	275	P. Of. & P. Roads.						
Bold, John R.	Increase of pension	27	3	Petition	309	Invalid Pensions.						
Bold, John R.	Increase of pension	28	2	Petition	172	Invalid Pensions.						
Bold, John R.	Increase of pension	29	1	Petition	466	Invalid Pensions.						
Bolduc, Etienne	(See heirs of Prudhomme Bolduc)	15	2		28							
Bolduc, Louis, heirs of	Confirmation of title to land in Missouri.	15	2	Petition	28	Priv. Land Claims.						
Bolduc, Prudhomme, heirs of.	Confirmation of title to land in Missouri.	15	2	Petition	28	Priv. Land Claims.						
Bolen, Edward	Compensation for public services in Florida.	27	3	Petition	101	Claims.						
Bolen, Edward	Compensation for public services in Florida.	28	1	Petition	526	Claims.						
Bolen, Edward	Compensation for public services in Florida.	29	1	Senate bill	1108	Claims			S. 158			

List of private claims presented to the House of Representatives of the United States from the 1st to the 31st Congress, inclusive—Continued.

Names of claimants.	Nature or object of the claim.	Congress.	Session.	How brought before the House of Reps.	Page of journal.	To what committee of the House referred.	No. or date of the report.	Nature of the report.	No. of the bill.	How disposed of by the House of Reps.	How disposed of by the Senate.	Date of the act of Congress, and remarks.
Bolen, Edward	Compensation for public services in Florida.	30	1	Senate bill	366	Claims	Feb. 9, 1848	With't amend.	S. 65	Passed	Passed	App'd May 31, 1848
Boles, Absalom	Exchange of an entry of land	22	2	Senate bill	441	Public Lands	March 2, 1833	With't amend	S. 98	Passed	Passed	App'd March 2, 1833
Bollermann, Anthony	Reimbursement of duties paid on damaged goods.	22	1	Petition	332	Commerce	350	Favorable	447	Referred to Committee Whole House.		
Boley, John	(See Zebulon Pike and companions)	10	1		189							
Boley, Lawrence	(See Conrad Houseman, administrator of.											
Bolling, Dulany, attorney of.	Indemnity for Indian depredations.	19	2	Petition	134	Indian Affairs	51	Favorable		Referred to Committee Whole House.		
Bolling, Jesse, assignee of.	Compensation for military services.	18	2	Petition	223	Claims.						
Bollinger, John	Confirmation of title to land	15	2	Petition	149	Priv. Land Claims.						
Bollinger, Matthias	Confirmation of title to land	15	1	Petition	267	Priv. Land Claims.						
Bolon, Amable	(See heirs of Antoine Marie.)	11	2		146							
Bolon, Gabriel J.	(See heirs of Antoine Marie.)	11	2		146							
Bolster, Isaac	Renewal of lost revolutionary certificate.	2	1	Petition	578					Referred to Secretary Treasury.		
Bolster, Isaac	Renewal of lost revolutionary certificate.	4	1	Petition	472					Referred to Secretary Treasury.		
Bolton, Abijah T.	Pension for disabilities in war of 1812.	29	1	Petition	666	Invalid Pensions	July 25, 1846	Adverse		Laid on table.		
Bolton, Abijah T.	Pension for disabilities in war of 1812.	29	2	Petition	86	Invalid Pensions.						
Bolton, Abijah T.	Pension for disabilities in war of 1812.	30	1	Petition	457	Invalid Pensions.						
Bolton, Abijah T.	Pension for disabilities in war of 1812.	30	2	Petition	116	Invalid Pensions	100	Adverse		Laid on table.		
Bolton, Abijah T.	Pension for disabilities in war of 1812.	31	1	Petition	298	Invalid Pensions	68	Adverse		Laid on table.		
Bolton, Aquilla M.	(See executor of John J. Yarnall)	14	2		460							
Bolton, Curtis	Indemnity for French spoliations prior to 1800.	31	1	Petition	196	Foreign Affairs	355	General bill	318	Referred to Committee Whole House.		
Bon, Jaques, and Alexander Coleman.	Location of a confirmed tract of land in Missouri.	26	2	Senate bill	329				S. 196			
Bon, Jaques, and Alexander Coleman.	Location of a confirmed tract of land in Missouri.	27	2	Senate bill	521	Priv. Land Claims			S. 49			
Bonabel, Marcellin	Permission to register land claims.	20	2	Petition	50	Public Lands	Dec. 21, 1828	Favorable bill.	240	Referred to Committee Whole House.		
Bonani, Peter, executor of	Compensation for designs for public buildings.	18	1	Petition	70	Public Buildings				Discharged; leave to withdraw.		
Bonchard, Joseph	(See Isaac Laurence, *et al.*)	14	1		386							
Bond, George	(See Leighton Wood and others).	3	1		88							
Bond, Hance	Compensation for revolutionary supplies.	2	1	Petition	530					Referred to Secretary of War.		
Bond, Hance	Compensation for revolutionary supplies.	2	2	Rep. of Secretary War.	696					Laid on table.		
Bond, John	Compensation for revolutionary services.	9	1	Petition	321	Public Lands				Leave to withdraw.		
Bond, John	Compensation for naval services.	14	1	Petition	33	Claims.						
Bond, John R.	Compensation for services as purser	31	2	Petition	69	Naval Affairs.						
Bond, Lewis	Confirmation of title to land in Michigan.	21	1	Petition	202	Priv. Land Claims.						
Bond, Lewis	Grant of adjoining land	22	1	Petition	474	Public Lands.						

List of private claims presented to the House of Representatives of the United States from the 1st to the 31st Congress, inclusive—Continued.

Names of claimants.	Nature or object of the claim.	Congress.	Session.	How brought before the House of Reps.	Page of journal.	To what committee of the House referred.	No. or date of the report.	Nature of the report.	No. of the bill.	How disposed of by the House of Reps.	How disposed of by the Senate.	Date of the act of Congress, and remarks.
Bond, Lewis	Compensation for services as Indian agent.	22	1	Petition	514	Public Lands.						
Bond, Lucy	(See Col. William Bond, widow of)											
Bond, Mary Ann	(See heirs of Hugh Smith)	18	1		82							
Bond, Nathan	To fund certain bills of credit	4	1	Petition	387	Ways and Means.						
Bond, Richard	(See Isaiah Rogers and Richard Bond.)	25	3		335							
Bond, Robert	Right of pre-emption in Florida	22	1	Resolution	134	Public Lands	94	Favorable	184	Passed	Passed	App'd July 14, 1832
Bond, Shandrach, heirs of	Compensation for revolutionary services.	26	1	Resolution	359	Rev. Claims.						
Bond, Sylvia	Extension of pension laws	26	1	Petition	830	Rev. Pensions				Discharged; laid on table.		
Bond, William	Pension for revolutionary services.	13	3	Petition	511	Pens. & Rev. Cl'ms.	Feb. 20, 1815	Favorable	303	Passed	Passed	App'd March 3, 1815
Bond, Colonel Wm., widow of.	Payment of claims for revolutionary services.	2	1	Petition	445							
				Rep. of Secretary War.	459	Select				Laid on table.		
Bond, Colonel Wm., heirs of.	Half-pay for revolutionary services.	23	1	Resolution	42	Rev. Claims	138	General bill	149	Passed	Passed with amendment.	App'd June 30, 1834
Bond, Colonel Wm., representatives of.	Interest on half-pay	23	2	Petition	109	Rev. Claims.						
				Senate bill	335	Rev. Claims	Feb. 13, 1835	With't amend.	S. 96	Referred to Committee Whole House.		
Bond, Colonel Wm., representatives of.	Interest on half-pay	24	1	Senate bill	745	Rev. Claims	May 10, 1836	With't amend.	S. 111	Referred to Committee Whole House.		
Bond, Colonel Wm., representatives of.	Interest on half pay	24	2	Senate bill	579				S. 158			
Bondie, or Boidie, Antoine.	Indemnity for property destroyed by Indians.	15	1	Petition	222	Claims	Feb. 16, 1818	Adverse		Claim rejected.		
Bonds, Nelson	(See H. McMahon, and others).											
Bonell, Francisco	(See Peter Alva, and others)	17	2		166							
Bones, John	Permission to withdraw land entry.	15	1	Senate bill	245	Public Lands	Feb. 18, 1818	Favorable, and bill.	23	Passed	Passed	App'd March 9, 1818
Bonhomme, Pierre, representatives of.	Confirmation of title to land in Michigan.	26	1	Senate bill	837	Priv. Land Claims.	June 23, 1840	With't amend.	S. 264	Referred to Committee Whole House.		
Bonhomme, Pierre, representatives of.	Confirmation of title to land in Michigan.	26	2	Senate bill	229	Priv. Land Claims.			S. 76			
Bonnabel, Antoine	Confirmation of title to land in Louisiana.	19	2	Petition	286	Priv. Land Claims.						
Bonnabel, Antoine	Confirmation of title to land in Louisiana.	20	1	Petition	40	Priv. Land Claims.						
Bonnabel, Antoine, representatives of.	Confirmation of title to land in Louisiana.	21	1	Petition	51	Priv. Land Claims.						
Bonnabel, Antoine, representatives of.	Confirmation of title to land in Louisiana.	21	2	Petition	83	Priv. Land Claims.	Feb. 19, 1831	Favorable	641	Passed.		
Bonnabel, Antoine, assignee of.	Confirmation of title to land in Louisiana.	21	2	Petition	111	Priv. Land Claims.	106	Favorable	657	Referred to Committee Whole House.		
Bonnabel, Antoine, representatives of.	Confirmation of title to land in Louisiana.	22	1	Petition	32	Priv. Land Claims.	Dec. 19, 1831	Favorable	46	Passed	Passed	App'd Mar. 15, 1832
Bonne, Michael and others, agents of.	Reservation of certain confirmed lands.	16	1	Petition	177					Laid on table.		
Bonnefield, Samuel	Pension for revolutionary services.	23	2	Petition	95	Rev. Claims.						

List of private claims presented to the House of Representatives of the United States from the 1st to the 31st Congress, inclusive—Continued.

Names of claimants.	Nature or object of the claim.	Congress.	Session.	How brought before the House of Reps.	Page of journal.	To what committee of the House referred.	No. or date of the report.	Nature of the report.	No. of the bill.	How disposed of by the House of Reps.	How disposed of by the Senate.	Date of the act of Congress, and remarks.
Bonnefils, Peter	Payment of award under Spanish treaty.	21	1	Petition	356	Foreign Affairs	284	Adverse		Laid on table.		
Bonnel, Lewis	(See administrator of I. Hammell.)	18	2		188							
Bonnell, James	Release from imprisonment for debt.	3	1	Petition	73	Whole House.						
Bonnell, James	Renewal of a lost revolutionary certificate.	8	2	Petition	75	Select.						
Bonnell, James	Renewal of a lost revolutionary certificate.	9	1	Petition	209	Claims				Discharged.		
Bonnell, James	Renewal of a lost revolutionary certificate.	9	2	Petition	589	Whole House.						
Bonnell, James	Renewal of a lost revolutionary certificate.	10	1	Petition	38	Select.						
Bonnell, John	(See executors of John Calhoun).	19	2		213							
Bonnell, Joseph	Pension	27	2	Petition	219	Invalid Pensions	578	Favorable	374	Ordered to 3d reading.		
Bonnell, Joseph	Pension	27	3	House bill	88				374	Passed.		
Bonnell, Joseph	Pension	28	1	Petition	101	Rev. Pensions	92	Favorable	108	Passed	Passed	App'd May 23, 1844
Bonnell, Paul	Pension for wounds received at Fort Meigs.	14	1	Resolution	527	Pens. & Rev. Clm's.	April 11, 1816	Favorable	171	Passed	Passed	App'd April 30, 1816
Bonnet, Joseph, widow of.	Pension for revolutionary services.	24	2	Petition	44	Rev. Pensions				Discharged; laid on table.		
Bonnett, Jacob	Pension	22	2	Petition	26	Invalid Pensions.						
Bonnet, Samuel	Pension	22	2	Petition	26	Invalid Pensions.						
Bonneveillon, Pierre	Confirmation of title to land in Louisiana.	20	1	Petition	343	Priv. Land Claims.						
Bonneveillon, Pierre	Confirmation of title to land in Louisiana.	21	1	Petition	51	Priv. Land Claims.	Mar. 23, 1830	Adverse		Laid on table.		
Bonney, James	Compensation for revolutionary services.	4	1	Petition	379	Claims	Jan. 20, 1796	Adverse		Laid on table.		
Bonney, John	Pension	21	1	Petition	490	Military Pensions.	April 2, 1830	Adverse		Laid on table.		
Bonney, John	Pension	22	1	Resolution	228	Rev. Pensions	378	Favorable	469	Referred to Committee Whole House.		
Bonney, John B.	Pension	20	2	Petition	288	Military Pensions.				Discharged; laid on table.		
Bonney, William, attorney of.	Bounty land for services war of 1812.	24	1	Petition	409	Public Lands.						
Bonney, William, attorney of.	Bounty land for services war of 1812.	24	2	Documents	390	Public Lands.						
Bonney, William, attorney of.	Bounty land for services war of 1812.	25	2	Petition	233	Public Lands	595	Adverse		Laid on table.		
Bonsal, Caleb	Indemnity for French Spoliations prior to 1800.	26	1	Memorial	182	Foreign Affairs	343	Favorable	319	Referred to Committee Whole House.		
Bonval, Nicholas	Patent for land at Old mines, Missouri.	22	1	Petition	263	Priv. Land Claims.	Feb. 17, 1832	Favorable	380	Referred to Committee Whole House.		
Boody, Henry H	(See James Rackliff and others.)	20	1		162							
Boody, Henry H	(See Caleb S. Carter and others.)	26	1		710							
Booker, Edmund	(See James and Robert Foster, heirs of.)	17	2		35							
Booker, Richard and others.	Reimbursement of expense of uniforms.	25	2	Petition	1118	Claims	990	Favorable	849	Referred to Committee Whole House.		
Booker, Richard and others.	Reimbursement of expense of uniforms.	25	3	Rep't Committee Whole House.	432			With't amend.	849	Passed	Adverse report.	

List of p ivate claims presented to the House of Representatives of the United States from the 1st to the 31st Congress, inclusive—Continued.

Names of claimants.	Nature or object of the claim.	Congress.	Session.	How brought before the House of Reps.	Page of journal.	To what committee of the House referred.	No. or date of the report.	Nature of the report.	No. of the bill.	How disposed of by the House of Reps.	How disposed of by the Senate.	Date of the act of Congress, and remarks.
Booker, Richard and others.	Reimbursement of expense of uniforms.	26	1	Petition	168	Claims	12	Favorable	31	Passed	Passed	App'd May 2, 1840
Bool, W. H.	Indemnity for French spoliations prior to 1800.	26	1	Memorial	182	Foreign Affairs	343	Favorable	319	Referred to Committee Whole House.		
Booley, Hubert H.	Pension for disability, Florida war.	30	1	Petition	482	Invalid Pensions	556	Favorable	456	Referred to Committee Whole House.		
Booley, Hubert H.	Pension for disability, Florida war.	31	1	Petition	233	Invalid Pensions	221	Favorable	113	Referred to Committee Whole House.		
Booley, Hubert H.	Pension for disability, Florida war.	31	2	Senate bill	106	Whole House			S. 93	Passed	Passed	App'd March 3, 1851
Boom, Nicholas	Pension	14	1	Pension bill	622	Whole House	April 23, 1816	Amendments	171	Passed	Passed	App'd Apr. 29, 1816—petition's name omitted.
Boomer, David	Arrears of privateer's pension	25	3	Petition	51	Naval Affairs.						
Boomer, David	Increase of pension	31	1	Petition	537	Invalid Pensions	Aug. 1, 1850	Adverse		Laid on table.		
Boomer Ephraim	Bounty land for revolutionary services.	25	2	Petition	200	Rev. Claims.						
Boon, Baptiste	Confirmation of title to land under Quapaw treaty.	19	2	Petition	137	Public Lands	60	Favorable	401	Referred to Committee Whole House.		
Boone, Daniel	Confirmation of title to Spanish grant in Louisiana.	10	1	Petition	55	Public Lands.						
Boone, Daniel	Confirmation of title to Spanish grant in Louisiana.	11	2	Petition	166	Select	Feb. 1, 1810	Does not appear.		Referred to Committee Whole House.		
Boone, Daniel	Confirmation of title to Spanish grant in Louisiana.	12	1	Petition	132	Public Lands.						
				Res. legislature of Kentucky.	219	Public Lands.						
Boone, Daniel	Confirmation of title to Spanish grant in Louisiana.	12	2	Petition	624	Select.	Jan. 29, 1813	Does not appear.		Referred to Committee Whole House.		
Boone, Daniel	Confirmation of title to Spanish grant in Louisiana.	13	2	Petition	168	Public Lands	10	Favorable	71	Passed.	Passed	App'd Feb. 10, 1814
Boone, Daniel, heirs of	Compensation for military services.	24	1	Petition.	673	Select.						
Boone, Daniel, heirs of	Compensation for military services.	24	2	Resolution	110	Select.						
Boone, Daniel, heirs of	Compensation for military services.	25	2	Petition	98	Select.	1039	Favorable	872	Referred to Committee Whole House.		
Boone, Daniel, heirs of	Compensation for military services.	25	3	Rep't Committee Whole House.	432			With't amend.	872	Passed	Adverse report.	
Boone, Daniel, heirs of	Compensation for military services.	31	1	Petition.		Invalid Pensions	472	Adverse		Laid on table.		
Boone, Elisha	Bounty land for revolutionary services.	26	1	Petition	609	Public Lands				Discharged; laid on table.		
Boone, Hampton L.	Compensation for services in land office, Missouri.	20	1	Senate bill	187	Claims	Jan. 18, 1828	With't amend.	S. 43	Passed	Passed	App'd Feb. 21, 1828
Boone, Hawkins, heirs of.	Commutation pay for revolutionary services.	26	1	Petition	359	Rev. Claims	596	Favorable	454	Referred to Committee Whole House.		
Boone, Hawkins, heirs of.	Commutation pay for revolutionary services.	27	2	Petition	61	Rev. Claims	15	Favorable	56	Passed	Indef. postp'd.	
Boone, Hawkins, heirs of.	Commutation pay for revolutionary services.	29	1	Petition	89	Rev. Claims.						
Boone, Hawkins, heirs of.	Commutation pay for revolutionary services.	31	1	Petition	624	Rev. Claims.						

List of private claims presented to the House of Representatives of the United States from the 1*st to the* 31*st Congress, inclusive*—Continued.

Names of claimants.	Nature or object of the claim.	Congress.	Session.	How brought before the House of Reps.	Page of journal.	To what committee of the House referred.	No. or date of the report.	Nature of the report.	No. of the bill.	How disposed of by the House of Reps.	How disposed of by the Senate.	Date of the act of Congress, and remarks.
Boone, John, (Md.)	Compensation for revolutionary services.	21	1	Petition	231	Military Pensions..	350	Favorable	451	Referred to Committee Whole House.		
Boone, John, (Md.)	Compensation for revolutionary services.	21	2	Rep't Committee Whole House.	321	....	....	With't amend.	451	Passed.		
Boone, John, (Md.)	Compensation for revolutionary services.	22	1	Petition	219	Rev. Claims	368	Favorable	463	Passed	Indef. postp'd.	
Boone, John, (Md.)	Compensation for revolutionary services.	24	1	Petition	406	Rev. Pensions	Mar. 2, 1836	Favorable....	464	Passed	Passed	App'd June 28, 1836
Boone, John, (Md.)	Commutation pay for revolutionary services.	23	2	Petition	120	Rev. Claims.						
Boone, John, (Illinois)...	Indemnity for property destroyed in Black Hawk war.	21	1	Documents.....	206	Claims.						
Boon, John, ...	Confirm'n of title to a Spanish grant	18	1	Petition	105	Public Lands.						
Boone, Jonathan, (Mo.)..	The correction of a land entry....	24	1	Petition	57	Public Lands	76	Favorable	92	Passed	Indef. postp'd.	
Boone, Jonathan, (Mo.)..	The correction of a land entry....	24	2	Resolution	107	Public Lands	56	Favorable.....	806	Referred to Committee Whole House.		
Boone, Jonathan, (Mo.)..	The correction of a land entry....	25	2	Petition	42	Public Lands	207	Favorable	242	Referred to Committee Whole House.		
Boone, Jonathan. (Mo.)..	The correction of a land entry....	25	3	Rep't Committee Whole House	376	....	....	....	242	Passed.		
Boone, Jonathan, (Mo.)..	The correction of a land entry....	26	1	Petition	177	Public Lands	July 21, 1840	Favorable	507	Referred to Committee Whole House.		
Boone, Robert H.	(See Erasmus Chapman and R. H. Boone, assignees of)	19	1	....	209	....	63	....	S. 31			
Boone, Squire	Increase of pension	11	2	Pension bill	283	Whole House.....	Mar. 24, 1810	Favorable	107	Passed	Passed	App'd April 27, 1810
Boone, Squire	Arrears of pension..............	12	1	Petition	14	Claims	Dec. 24, 1811	Adverse	......	Leave to withdraw.		
Boone, William, & Co. ..	Compensation for pork furnished for public use.	19	2	Petition	91	Claims	Jan. 22, 1827	Adverse	......	Leave to withdraw.		
Boorhen, John..........	Comp'n for revolutionary services.	9	2	Petition	506	Claims.						
Boorman & Johnston	Debenture on goods exported to Leghorn.	18	2	Petition	80	Ways and Means..	....	....	......	Discharged; referred to Secretary of Treas.		
Boorman & Johnston	(See agents of Kantzow & Biel.)											
Booth, Benj. W., widow of	Pension for revolutionary services.	20	2	Petition	60	Naval Affairs.....	103	Adverse	......	Laid on table.		
Booth, Benj. W., widow of	Pension for revolutionary services.	21	2	Petition	114	Naval Affairs.						
Boothe, Benjamin, heirs of	Pecuniary aid for loss of ancestor	23	2	Petition	147	Naval Affairs.						
Boothe, Benjamin, heirs of	Pecuniary aid for loss of ancestor	24	1	Petition	260	Priv. Land Claims.						
Boothe, Betsey..........	(See devisee of John Harris)	10	1	....	121							
Boothe, Daniel..........	(See Birdseye & Boothe)	15	2	....	316							
Boothe, Fox............	Permission to enter certain land ..	31	2	Petition	173	Public Lands.						
Boothe, George	Bounty land for revolutionary services.	16	2	Petition	248	....	....	....	......	Referred to Secretary War.		
Boothe, Isaac	Pension for revolutionary services.	22	1	Petition	287	Rev. Pensions.						
Boothe, Joseph, (Va.) ...	Pension for revolutionary services.	19	1	Petition	149	Military Pensions..	April 1, 1826	Adverse	......	Laid on table.		
Boothe, Joseph, (Va.) ...	Pension for revolutionary services.	20	1	Petition	124	Military Pensions.						
Boothe, Joseph, (Va.) ...	Pension for revolutionary services.	21	1	Petition	197	Military Pensions..	Feb. 13, 1830	Favorable....	72	Passed	Passed.......	App'd May 20, 1830
Booth, Michael, heir of...	Location of a Virginia military land warrant.	28	2	Petition	234	Priv. Land Claims.	....	....	......	Discharged; laid on table.		
Booth, Michael, heir of....	Location of a Virginia military land warrant.	29	1	Petition	502	Priv. Land Claims.						
Boothe, Mordecai, & others	Provision for heirs of persons lost in U. S. schooner "Wild Cat."	21	1	Memorial	447	Naval Affairs.....	May 18, 1830	Favorable	473	Referred to Committee Whole House.		
Boothe, Mordecai, & others	Provision for heirs of persons lost in U. S. schooner "Wild Cat."	21	1	Senate bill	685	....	....	....	S. 158	Referred to Committee Whole House.		

List of private claims presented to the House of Representatives of the United States from the 1st to the 31st Congress, inclusive—Continued.

Names of claimants.	Nature or object of the claim.	Congress.	Session.	How brought before the House of Reps.	Page of journal.	To what committee of the House referred.	No. or date of the report.	Nature of the report.	No. of the bill.	How disposed of by the House of Reps.	How disposed of by the Senate.	Date of the act of Congress, and remarks.
Boothe, Mordecai, & others	Provision for heirs of persons lost in U. S. schooner "Wild Cat."	23	1	Memorial	247	Naval Affairs.						
Boothe, Mordecai, & others	Provision for heirs of persons lost in U. S. schooner "Wild Cat."	24	1	Memorial	100	Naval Affairs	Jan. 19, 1836	Favorable	178	Passed	Laid on table.	
Boothe, Nathaniel	Arrears of pension for revolutionary services.	20	2	Petition	100	Rev. Claims	Jan. 22, 1829	Adverse		Laid on table.		
Boothe, Walker	Pension for revolutionary services.	18	1	Resolution	119	Rev. Pensions.						
Boothe, W. L	(See heirs of Ben. W. Boothe)	23	2		147							
Boothroyd, Jabez	(See William Patterson and others)	16	1		85							
Bootman, Thomas	Pension for revolutionary services.	26	1	Petition	1021	Rev. Pensions	551	Adverse		Laid on table.		
Booz, Richard	Pension for revolutionary services.	24	1	Petition	506	Rev. Pensions.						
Booz, Richard	Pension for revolutionary services.	24	2	Petition	158	Rev. Pensions	Jan. 10, 1831	Adverse		Laid on table.		
Booz, Richard	Pension for revolutionary services.	25	2	Petition	730	Rev. Pensions				Discharged; laid on table.		
Borden, Benjamin	(See Joseph Borden, executor of)	26	1		182		343		319			
Borden, Elijah	Arrears of pension	24	1	Petition	403	Rev. Pensions				Discharged; laid on table.		
Borden, Elijah	Arrears of pension	24	2	Petition	130	Rev. Pensions	Jan. 24, 1837	Favorable	876			
Borden, Elijah	Arrears of pension	25	2	Resolution	37	Rev. Pensions				Discharged; laid on table.		
Borden, Elijah	Arrears of pension	26	1	Resolution	558	Rev. Pensions				Discharged; laid on table.		
Borden, James W., heirs of.	Indemnity for French spoliations prior to 1800.	24	2	Petition	214	Foreign Affairs.						
Borden, James W., heirs of.	Indemnity for French spoliations prior to 1800.	25	1	Petition	80	Foreign Affairs				Laid on table.		
Borden, Joshua, widow of.	Pension for revolutionary services.	27	3	Petition	223	Rev. Pensions	295	Adverse		Laid on table.		
Borden, John	Pension for revolutionary services.	23	1	Petition	436	Rev. Pensions.						
Borden. Joseph, executor of.	Indemnity for French spoliations prior to 1800.	26	1	Memorial	182	Foreign Affairs	343	Favorable	319	Referred to Committee Whole House.		
Borden, Josiah, widow of.	Continuation of pension	25	3	Petition	562	Rev. Pensions				Discharged; laid on table.		
Borden, Josiah, widow of.	Continuation of pension	26	1	Petition	172	Rev. Pensions				Discharged; laid on table.		
Borden, Samuel	Bounty land for services in the war of 1812.	23	1	Petition	380	Public Lands.						
Borden, William & Joshua, representatives of.	Indemnity for a vessel captured by the French.	28	1	Petition	1066	Foreign Affairs.						
Bordman, John	Permission to enter a certain tract of land.	19	2	Senate bill	348	Public Lands	Mar. 2, 1827	With amend.	76	Passed	Passed	App'd March 2, 1827
Bordman and Pope, and others.	Remission of penalty under non intercourse act, incurred by ship "American Hero."	12	1	Petition	136	Com. and Manuf.						
Bordman and Pope, and others.	Remission of penalty under non intercourse act, incurred by ship "American Hero."	12	2	Petition	552	Ways and Means				Discharged; laid on table.		
Bordoishe, company of rangers.	Indemnity for depredations of Indians.	22	1	Resolution	338	Claims.						
Borel, Eugene	Confirmation of title to land in Louisiana.	20	1	Petition	312	Priv. Land Claims.						
Borel, Eugene	Confirmation of title to land in Louisiana.	20	2	Petition	34	Priv. Land Claims.						

List of private claims presented to the House of Representatives of the United States from the 1st to the 31st Congress, inclusive—Continued.

Names of claimants.	Nature or object of the claim.	Congress.	Session.	How brought before the House of Reps.	Page of journal.	To what committee of the House referred.	No. or date of the report.	Nature of the report.	No. of the bill.	How disposed of by the House of Reps.	How disposed of by the Senate.	Date of the act of Congress, and remarks.
Borel, Eugene	Confirmation of title to land in Louisiana.	21	1	Petition	40	Priv. Land Claims.	199	Favorable	253	Referred to Committee Whole House.		
Borel, Eugene	Confirmation of title to land in Louisiana.	21	2	Rep't Committee Whole House.	265			With't amend.	253	Passed.		
Borel, Eugene	Confirmation of title to land in Louisiana.	22	1	Petition	75	Priv. Land Claims.	91	Favorable	176	Referred to Committee Whole House.		
Borel, Eugene	Confirmation of title to land in Louisiana.	22	2	Rep't Committee Whole House.	66			With't amend.	176	Passed	Passed	App'd Jan. 14, 1833
Borel, Eugene	Confirmation of title to land in Louisiana.	27	2	Petition	140	Priv. Land Claims.	297	Favorable	245	Passed.		
Boreman, John, widow of.	Revolutionary pension	29	1	Report			784	Adverse		Laid on table.		
Borey, John	Permission to correct a land entry	24	1	Petition	207	Priv. Land Claims.	Feb. 4, 1836	Favorable	278	Referred to Committee Whole House.		
Borey, John	Permission to correct a land entry	25	2	Petition	43	Priv. Land Claims.	255	Favorable	298	Referred to Committee Whole House.		
Borey, John	Permission to correct a land entry	25	3	Rep't Committee Whole House.	376			With't amend.	298	Passed	Passed	App'd March 3, 1839
Borgstrom, John	Bounty land and extra pay	30	2	Petition	122	Rev. Pensions	32	Adverse		Laid on table.		
Borie	(See Bohler & Borie)	27	3		95							
Boring, Abraham	Survey and sale of certain public land.	23	1	Petition	567	Public Lands.						
Boring, Abraham	Survey and sale of certain public land.	23	2	Petition	67	Public Lands.						
Boring, Joseph	Confirmation of title to land	15	1	Petition	52	Priv. Land Claims.						
Borley, Hubert H	(See Hubert H. Booley.)											
Borrowdale, John	(See James Sanderson and others)	14	1		292							
Borrows, John	Increase of compensation as messenger at Washington.	9	2	Petition	600	Ways and Means.						
Borst, John, jr	Pension for services, war of 1812.	27	3	Petition	85	Invalid Pensions.						
Borum, Edward	Pension	14	1	Pension bill	622	Whole House	April 11, 1816	With amend.	171	Passed	Passed with amendment.	App'd April 30, 1816
Boss, Daniel C., widow of	Pension	27	3	Petition	205	Invalid Pensions	226	Adverse		Laid on table.		
Boss, Elliott	(See heirs of J. F. & N. G. Boss)	29	2		292							
Boss, J. F. & N. G., heirs of.	Indemnity for French spoliations prior to 1800.	29	2	Petition	292	Foreign Affairs.						
Boss, Joseph, (N. J.)	Pension	21	1	Petition	36	Military Pensions.						
				Documents	203	Military Pensions	April 6, 1830	Adverse		Laid on table.		
				Senate amendm't	664				72	Passed	Passed	App'd May 20, 1830
Boss, Joseph, (N. J.)	Increase of pension	21	2	Petition	61	Military Pensions.						
Bosseler, John, heirs of	Confirmation of title to land	21	2	Petition	341	Priv. Land Claims.	Feb. 22, 1831	Favorable	642	Passed.		
Bosseler, John, heirs of	Confirmation of title to land	22	1	Petition	75	Priv. Land Claims.						
Bostick, Nathaniel	Prize-money for Captain of the Hermes.	19	1	Petition	110	Naval Affairs	Jan. 23, 1826	Adverse		Leave to withdraw.		
Bostick, Oliver	Increase of pension	10	2	House bill	499	Whole House	Feb. 28, 1809	No amendm't.	158	Passed	Passed	App'd March 3, 1809
Boston, Jacob	Pension	20	1	Petition	223	Military Pensions.						
Boston, Jacob	Pension	22	1	Petition	259	Naval Affairs.						
Boston, Jacob	Pension	23	1	Petition	159	Naval Affairs.						
Boston, Jacob	Pension	23	2	Petition	343	Naval Affairs.						
Boston, Jacob	Pension	24	1	Petition	509	Naval Affairs.						
Boston, Jacob	Pension	25	3	Petition	218	Naval Affairs.						
Boston, Jacob	Pension	26	1	Petition	180	Naval Affairs.						
Boston, Jacob	Pension	27	2	Documents	73	Naval Affairs.						

List of private claims presented to the House of Representatives of the United States from the 1st to the 31st Congress, inclusive—Continued

Names of claimants	Nature or object of the claim.	Congress.	Session.	How brought before the House of Reps.	Page of journal.	To what committee of the House referred.	No. or date of the report.	Nature of the report.	No. of the bill.	How disposed of by the House of Reps.	How disposed of by the Senate.	Date of the act of Congress, and remarks.
Boston, Jacob	Pension	28	1	Petition	853	Naval Affairs	509	Favorable	384	Referred to Committee Whole House.		
Boston, Jacob	Pension	28	2	Rep't Committee Whole House.	343			With't amend.	384	Passed.		
Boston, Jacob	Pension	29	1	Petition	464	Naval Affairs.						
Boston, Jacob	Pension	30	1	Petition	581	Naval Affairs	772	Favorable	607	Referred to Committee Whole House.		
Boston, Jacob	Pension	30	2	Rep't Committee Whole House.	362			With't amend.	607	Passed.		
Boston, Jacob	Pension	31	1	Petition	298	Invalid Pensions.						
Boston, Joshua	Pension for revolutionary services.	15	2	Petition	300	Rev. Pensions.						
Boston, Solomon	Remission of fine for breach of revenue laws.	6	2	Petition	750	Select	Jan. 15, 1801	Favorable	283	Passed	Passed	App'd Jan. 30, 1801
Boston, United States ship, officers of.	Compensation for depreciation of their pay.	24	1	Senate bill	978	Claims	June 27, 1836	Adverse	S. 181	Referred to Committee Whole House.		
Boston, United States ship, officers of.	Compensation for depreciation of their pay.	24	2	Senate bill	250	Naval Affairs	278	Adverse	S. 29	Laid on table.		
Bostwick, Elijah	Reimbursement of costs in a suit on public account.	2	1	Petition	469	Select.						
Bostwick, Elijah	Reimbursement of costs in a suit on public account.	2	2	Petition.	632	Select	Jan. 14, 1793	Favorable	231	Passed	Passed	App'd March 2, 1793
Bostwick, Elizur	Pension for revolutionary services.	21	1	Petition	319	Military Pensions.						
Bostwick, Elizur	Compensation for services as revolutionary teamster.	29	1	Petition	540	Rev. Claims.						
Bostwick, Melancton W., surety of.	Release from liability	23	1	Petition.	160	Naval Affairs	Feb. 14, 1834	Favorable	306	Referred to Committee Whole House.		
Bostwick, Melancton W., surety of.	Settlement of accounts as purser of Epervier.	25	3	Resolution	517	Naval Affairs.						
Bostwick, Melancton W., surety of.	Settlement of accounts as purser of Epervier.	26	1	Petition.	179	Naval Affairs	105	Favorable	109	Passed	Passed	App'd July 20, 1840
Bostwick, Oliver	Pension for revolutionary services.	3	1	Rep. of Secretary of War.	131	Select	May 26, 1794	Favorable	62	Passed	Passed	App'd June 7, 1794
Bostwick, Oliver	Increase of pension	10	2	Pension bill	499	Whole House	Feb. 20, 1809	With amend.	158	Passed	Passed with amendment.	App'd Mar. 3, 1809
Boswell, H., and others	Increase of compensation as receivers of public money.	18	2	Petition	55	Public Lands.						
Boswell, H., and others	Increase of compensation as receivers of public money.	19	1	Petition	64	Public Lands.						
Boswell, H., and others	Increase of compensation as receivers of public money.	19	2	Petition	137	Public Lands.						
Boswell, Joseph	To be restored to pension roll	18	1	Petition	88	Rev. Pensions	Jan. 9, 1824	Adverse		Laid on table.		
Boswell, Thomas P.	(See Louis F. Beeler, *et al.*)	30	1		115		482					
Boswell, William E.	(See surety of Robert G. Respass.)	18	1		176							
Bosworth, Felix G., widow of.	Release from a judgment	31	1	Senate bill	1430	Judiciary			S. 207			
Bosworth, Jacob	Duplicate land warrant	21	2	Resolution	225	Rev. Claims.						
Bosworth, Jacob	Duplicate land warrant	22	1	Petition	386	Rev. Claims.						
Bosworth, Jacob	Duplicate land warrant	22	2	Petition	63	Rev. Claims	Dec. 22, 1832	Favorable	232	Passed	Passed	App'd Feb. 1, 1833
Bosworth, John	Pension.	24	1	Petition	852	Invalid Pensions	July 1, 1836	Adverse.		Laid on table.		
Bosworth, John	Pension	24	2	Petition	42	Invalid Pensions.	7	Favorable	764	Referred to Committee Whole House.		
Bosworth, John	Pension	25	2	Petition	38	Invalid Pensions.	183	Favorable	209	Passed	Adverse report.	

List of private claims presented to the House of Representatives of the United States from the 1st to the 31st Congress, inclusive—Continued.

Names of claimants.	Nature or object of the claim.	Congress.	Session.	How brought before the House of Reps.	Page of journal.	To what committee of the House referred.	No. or date of the report.	Nature of the report.	No. of the bill.	How disposed of by the House of Reps.	How disposed of by the Senate.	Date of the act of Congress, and remarks.
Bosworth, Samuel, widow of.	Pension for revolutionary services.	24	2	Petition	125	Rev. Pensions	132	Favorable	861	Referred to Committee Whole House.		
Bott, James	Increase of pension	15	1	Petition	23	Pens. & Rev. Cl'ms.						
Bott, James	Payment of a loan office certificate.	15	2	House bill	146	Whole House	Jan. 5, 1819	With amend.	154	Rejected.		
Bott, James	Payment of a loan office certificate.	19	2	Petition	63	Rev. Claims	Jan. 16, 1827	Adverse	......	Laid on table.		
Bouce, Henry	Pension for revolutionary services.	3	1	Rep. of Secretary War.	131	Select	May 26, 1794	Favorable	62	Passed	Passed	App'd June 7, 1794
Bouchand, Joseph	(See Ebenezer Stevens & Co., and others.)	16	2	......	30							
Bouchand, Joseph	(See surety of John S. Roulet)	25	2	Petition	408	Commerce.						
Bouchand, Joseph	(See Isaac Lawrence and others)	14	2	......	101							
Bouche, Benjamin	Indemnity for loss as a Canadian refugee.	14	2	Petition	428	Claims.						
Bouchell, Sluyter	Compensation for revolutionary supplies.	2	1	Petition	554	......	......	......	......	Referred to Secretary Treasury.		
Bouchell, Sluyter	Compensation for revolutionary supplies.	3	2	Rep. of Secretary of Treasury.	284	......	......	......	......	Laid on table.		
Boucher, John	Pension	28	1	Petition	189	Invalid Pensions.						
Bouck, Abraham	Pension in consideration of Indian captivity.	29	1	Petition	275	Rev. Claims	488	Adverse	......	Laid on table.		
Boudreau, Jean Charles	Confirmation of title to land in Louisiana.	22	1	Petition	471	Priv. Land Claims.	385	Favorable	477	Referred to Committee Whole House.		
Boudreau, Jean Charles	Confirmation of title to land in Louisiana.	23	2	Petition	138	Priv. Land Claims.	42	Favorable	627	Referred to Committee Whole House.		
Bouyage, John, and others.	Compensation for cattle taken for public use.	15	1	Petition	243	Claims	Feb. 25, 1818	Adverse	......	Laid on table.		
Bougard, Claudius	Confirmation of title to land in Mississippi.	11	3	Petition	461	Public Lands.						
Bougard, Claudius	(See John F. Carmichael)	20	1	......	33	......	......	......	R. 5			
Bougard, Don Claudia, assignee of.	Confirmation of title to a Spanish grant.	17	2	Petition	225	Priv. Land Claims.	......	......	......	Discharged; leave to withdraw.		
Boughan, Alex'r, widow of.	Compensation for revolutionary services.	2	1	Petition	447	......	......	......	......	Referred to Secretary War.		
Boughan, Alex'r, widow of.	Compensation for revolutionary services.	2	2	Rep. of Secretary War.	696	......	......	......	......	Laid on table.		
Boughman, Paul	Pension for revolutionary services.	8	2	Petition	134	Whole House.						
Boughten, Hannah	(See heirs of Daniel Mills)	27	2	......	62							
Boughten, Matthew	Pension for revolutionary services.	26	2	Petition	49	Rev. Pensions	Feb. 12, 1841	Adverse	......	Laid on table.		
Bogue, Francis	Indemnity for property destroyed by the enemy.	19	1	Petition	365	Claims	April 18, 1826	Adverse	......	Laid on table.		
Bogue, Francis	Indemnity for property destroyed by the enemy.	20	1	Petition	582	Claims.						
Bouligny, widow of	Confirmation of title to land in New Orleans.	17	1	Resolution	282	Priv. Land Claims.						
Boultber, Horatio	Indemnity for destruction of property by United States troops.	31	1	Petition	985	Military Affairs.						
Boultber, Horatio	Indemnity for destruction of property by United States troops.	31	2	Petition	239	Military Affairs	22	Favorable	454	Referred to Committee Whole House.		
Bountree, Francis	Additional compensation for certain mail service.	25	2	Petition	277	P. Of. & P. Roads.	......	......	......	Discharged; laid on table.		
Boure, Louis, widow of	Indemnity for depredations of Indians.	20	1	Resolution	152	Claims	93	Adverse	......	Laid on table.		

List of private claims presented to the House of Representatives of the United States from the 1st to the 31st Congress, inclusive—Continued.

Names of claimants.	Nature or object of the claim.	Congress.	Session.	How brought before the House of Reps.	Page of journal.	To what committee of the House referred.	No. or date of the report.	Nature of the report.	No. of the bill.	How disposed of by the House of Reps.	How disposed of by the Senate.	Date of the act of Congress, and remarks.
Boure, Louis, widow of	Indemnity for depredations of Indians.	20	2	Resolution	71	Claims	Jan. 12, 1829	Adverse	......	Laid on table.		
Boure, Louis, widow of	Indemnity for depredations of Indians.	21	1	Resolution	246	Claims	May 17, 1830	Adverse	......	Laid on table.		
Bourg, John Baptiste	Confirmation of title to land, (Terre aux Bœuff.)	22	1	Petition	64	Priv. Land Claims.	62	Favorable	125	Passed	Passed	App'd June 25, 1835
Bourgeat, Margaret A.	(See James Fort Muse)	27	2	....	155	....	....	....	247			
Bourgoud, Antoine and J. Dozet.	Indemnity for destruction of property by United States troops.	15	2	Senate bill	316	Claims	Feb. 27, 1819	With amend.	S. 65			
Bourgoud, Antoine and J. Dozet.	Indemnity for destruction of property by United States troops.	18	2	Senate bill	278	Claims	Mar. 1, 1825	With't amend.	S. 39	Passed	Passed	App'd March 3, 1825
Bourguin, Edward	Right of pre-emption as New Orleans branch pilot.	28	1	Petition	77	Priv. Land Claims.	9	Favorable	35	Passed	Passed	App'd June 17, 1844
Bourke, Edward	(See heir of James Williams)	31	1	....	279							
Bourlin, Joseph	(See Joseph Bowlen)	27	3	....	101							
Bourne, Benjamin	(See William Tilghman, *et al.*)	7	2	....	307							
Bourne, Benjamin	Bounty on fishing schooner	21	1	Petition	82	Commerce.						
Bourne, Benjamin	Bounty on fishing schooner	21	2	Petition	95	Commerce.						
Bourne, Elisha	(See Josiah Holmes and others)	26	1	....	290							
Bourne, George S	Compensation for services and expenses in the public service.	22	2	Petition	216	Foreign Affairs.						
Bourn, Shearjashub, widow of.	Continuation of pension	27	2	Petition	239	Rev. Pensions.						
Bourne, Sylvanus	Reimbursement of advances on public account.	4	1	Petition	520	Com. and Manuf.	May 6, 1796	Favorable	186	Passed	Passed	App'd May 30, 1796
Bouslog, John	Reimbursement of duties on spirits destroyed.	6	2	Petition	727	Com. and Manuf.	Dec. 9, 1800	Adverse	......	Leave to withdraw.		
Bouslog, John	Reimbursement of duties on spirits destroyed.	7	1	Petition	89	Claims	Mar. 5, 1802	Adverse	......	Laid on table.		
Bouten, or Bowton, Samuel and others.	Indemnity for destruction of property by United States troops.	15	1	Petition	247	Claims.						
Bouten, or Bowton, Samuel and others.	Indemnity for destruction of property by United States troops.	15	2	Petition	40	Claims	Jan. 5, 1819	Adverse	......	Laid on table.		
Bouten, or Bowton, Samuel and others.	Indemnity for destruction of property by United States troops.	18	2	Petition	160	Claims.						
Bouton, Daniel	Increase of pension	12	1	Pension bill	361	Whole House	June 15, 1812	With't amend.	138	Passed	Passed	App'd July 5, 1812
Bouton, Richard M.	Compensation for use of patent for percussion caps.	30	1	Petition	338	Claims	748	Favorable	587	Referred to Committee Whole House.		
Bouton, Richard M.	Compensation for use of patent for percussion caps.	31	1	Petition	197	Military Affairs	197	Favorable	204	Referred to Committee Whole House.		
Boutwell, Abraham E.	Pension	23	1	Resolution	587	Invalid Pensions	544	Favorable	550	Referred to Committee Whole House.		
Boutwell, Abraham E.	Pension	23	2	Rep't Committee Whole House.	336	....	....	With't amend.	550	Passed	Passed	App'd March 3, 1835
Boutwell, Lt. E. D.	Compensation as bearer of despatches.	27	2	Petition	73	Claims.						
Bovey, John	(See John Borey.)											
Bowden, Joseph, jr.	Bounty on fishing schooner Albion	31	2	Petition	193	Commerce.						
Bowell, Basil	Compensation for horse lost in the public service.	25	2	Petition	396	Claims.						
Bowell, Basil	Compensation for horse lost in the public service.	25	3	Petition	207	Claims.						
Bowen, Deborah	(See mother of Benjamin Hillman)	25	3	....	463							

List of private claims presented to the House of Representatives of the United States from the 1st to the 31st Congress, inclusive—Continued.

Names of claimants.	Nature or object of the claim.	Congress.	Session.	How brought before the House of Reps.	Page of journal.	To what committee of the House referred.	No. or date of the report.	Nature of the report.	No. of the bill.	How disposed of by the House of Reps.	How disposed of by the Senate.	Date of the act of Congress, and remarks.
Bowen, Dijah	(See Pierre Gideon)	27	2	Petition	254							
Bowen, Ephraim	Additional compensation for revolutionary services.	22	2	Petition	29	Rev. Claims.						
Bowen, Ephraim	Additional compensation for revolutionary services.	23	1	Petition	243	Rev. Claims.						
Bowen, Ephraim	Additional compensation for revolutionary services.	23	2	Petition	66	Rev. Claims.						
Bowen, Ephraim	Additional compensation for revolutionary services.	25	2	Petition	232	Rev. Claims				Discharged; laid on table.		
Bowen, Ephraim	Additional compensation for revolutionary services.	25	3	Petition	85	Rev. Claims				Discharged: laid on table.		
Bowen, Ephraim	Additional compensation for revolutionary services.	26	1	Petition	166	Rev. Claims.						
Bowen, Ephraim	Additional compensation for revolutionary services.	26	2	Petition	35	Rev. Claims	171	Adverse		Laid on table.		
Bowen, Ephraim	Additional compensation for revolutionary services.	27	2	Petition	62	Rev. Claims	360	Adverse		Laid on table.		
Bowen, George	Additional compensation for certain mail service.	21	1	Resolution	275	P. Of. and P. Roads.	April 3, 1830	Favorable	403	Referred to Committee Whole House.		
Bowen, George	Additional compensation for certain mail service.	22	1	Petition	331	P. Of. and P. Roads.	354	Favorable	453	Referred to Committee Whole House.		
Bowen, George	Additional compensation for certain mail service.	23	1	Petition	177	P. Of. and P. Roads.	162	Favorable	176	Passed	Passed	App'd June 30, 1834
Bowen, Jabez	Reimbursement of expenses for clerk hire, &c., while commissioner of loans for Rhode Island.	2	1	Report of Secretary War.	526	Select	Mar. 16, 1792	Favorable	194	Passed	Passed	App'd May 8, 1794
Bowen, Jabez	Increase of compensation as commissioner of loans.	4	1	Petition	422	Select.						
Bowen, John	Pension for revolutionary services.	22	1	Petition	165	Rev. Pensions.						
Bowen, John, heirs of	Pension for revolutionary services.	25	2	Petition	115	Rev. Pensions.						
Bowen, John, (Pa.)	Location of a Virginia military land warrant.	28	1	Documents	753	Claims.						
Bowen, John, (Pa.)	Location of a Virginia military land warrant.	28	2	Petition	89	Rev. Claims.						
Bowen, Stephen, widow of	Pension for revolutionary services.	28	1	Petition	124	Rev. Pensions.						
Bowen, Sally	(See widow of Wm. Gardner)	15	2		148							
Bowen, Sayles J.	Compensation for extra services as clerk in Treasury Department.	29	2	Petition	132	Ways and Means				Discharged; laid on table.		
Bowen, Sayles J.	Compensation for extra services as clerk in Treasury Department.	30	2	Petition	76	Claims	40	Favorable	730	Passed.		
Bowen, Sayles J.	Compensation for extra services as clerk in Treasury Department.	31	1	Petition	337	Claims	77	Favorable	92	Referred to Committee Whole House.		
Bowen, Sayles J.	Compensation for extra services as clerk in Treasury Department.	31	2	Rep't Committee Whole House.	154			With't amend.	92	Passed	Passed	App'd Feb. 27, 1851
Bowen, Lieutenant Seth	Depreciation pay for revolutionary services.	8	1	Petition	523					Ref. to Com. Whole House, on bill 184.		
Bowen, Lieutenant Seth	Depreciation pay for revolutionary services.	8	2	Petition	78					Ref. to Com. Whole House, on bill 11.		
Bowen, Lieutenant Seth	Depreciation pay for revolutionary services.	13	2	Petition	302	Pens. & Rev. Cl'ms.	92	Adverse		Leave to withdraw.		
Bowen, Oliver	Interest on advances during revolutionary war.	2	2	Petition	704					Referred to Secretary Treasury.		

List of private claims presented to the House of Representatives of the United States from the 1st to the 31st Congress, inclusive—Continued.

Names of claimants.	Nature or object of the claim.	Congress.	Session.	How brought before the House of Reps.	Page of journal.	To what committee of the House referred.	No. or date of the report.	Nature of the report.	No. of the bill.	How disposed of by the House of Reps.	How disposed of by the Senate.	Date of the act of Congress, and remarks.
Bowen, Oliver	Interest on advances during revolutionary war.	3	1	Rep. of Secretary Treasury.	77					Laid on table.		
Bowen, William	Pension for revolutionary services.	18	1	Resolution	232	Rev. Pensions	Mar. 10, 1824	Adverse.		Laid on table.		
Bower, Henry	Renewal of lost revolutionary certificate.	3	1	Petition	103					Laid on table.		
Bower, Henry	Renewal of lost revolutionary certificate.	4	1	Petition	485	Claims.						
Bower, Henry	Renewal of lost revolutionary certificate.	4	2	Petition	614	Claims	Jan. 31, 1797	Adverse		Laid on table.		
Bowerman, Peter	Pension for revolutionary services.	23	2	Resolution	223	Rev. Pensions.						
Bowers, Balaam	Pension for revolutionary services.	24	1	Petition	273	Rev. Pensions	May 11, 1836	Favorable	621	Passed	Passed	App'd June 28, 1836
Bowers, David	Pension for revolutionary services.	15	1	Petition	211	Pens. & Rev. Cl'ms.	Feb. 20, 1818	Indefinite		Leave to withdraw.		
Bowers, Henry, and others	Bounty on fishing schooner Joanna	25	2	Petition	923	Commerce				Discharged; laid on table.		
Bowers, Henry, and others	Bounty on fishing schooner Joanna	26	1	Petition	710	Commerce.						
Bowers, Jerathmeel, heirs of.	Indemnity for French spoliations prior to 1800.	29	2	Petition	101	Foreign Affairs.						
Bowers, John, (Mass.)	Bounty on fishing schooners George, &c.	8	2	Petition	80	Com. and Manuf.						
Bowers, John, administrator of.	Indemnity for French spoliations prior to 1800.	26	1	Memorial	182	Foreign Affairs	343	Favorable	319	Referred to Committee Whole House.		
Bowers, John, and others.	Indemnity for French spoliations prior to 1800.	29	2	Petition	100	Foreign Affairs.						
Bowers, Jonathan	Pension for revolutionary services.	3	1	Rep. of Secretary War.	131	Select	May 26, 1794	Res. to refer to Sec. War.	R. 12	Passed	Passed	App'd June 9, 1794
Bowers, Jonathan	Pension for revolutionary services.	4	1	Report Secretary of War.	373	Claims	Feb. 18, 1796	Pension bill	156	Passed	Passed	App'd April 20, 1796
Bowers, Jonathan	Increase of pension	10	2	Pension bill	499	Whole House	Feb. 28, 1809	With amend.	158	Passed	Passed with amendment.	App'd March 3, 1809
Bowers, Jonathan	Increase of pension	15	1	Petition	23	Pens. & Rev. Cl'ms.				Leave to withdraw.		
Bowers, Mary	(See Samuel Bowers, adminis'r of.)	29	1		58							
Bowers, Samuel	Pension for revolutionary services.	15	2	Petition	160	Rev. Pensions.						
Bowers, Samuel, administrator of.	Compensation for timber furnished United States.	29	1	Petition	58	Claims	115	Adverse.		Laid on table.		
Bowers, Sarah	Continuation of pension	28	1	Petition	849	Rev. Pensions.						
Bowhay, William	Compensation for the public use of his invention.	31	2	Petition	180	Claims.						
Bowhay, William P.	Indemnity for French spoliations prior to 1800.	24	2	Petition	273	Foreign Affairs.						
Bowhay, William P.	Indemnity for French spoliations prior to 1800.	26	1	Memorial	182	Foreign Affairs	343	Favorable	319	Referred to Committee Whole House.		
Bowie & Kurtz, and others	Indemnity for seizure and condemnation of schooner Alleghany.	13	2	Petition	176	Claims				Discharged; leave to withdraw.		
Bowie & Kurtz, and others	Indemnity for seizure and condemnation of schooner Alleghany.	13	3	Senate bill	732	Claims	Feb. 27, 1815	With't amend.	S. 81	Indef. postponed.		
Bowie & Kurtz, and others	Indemnity for seizure and condemnation of schooner Alleghany.	14	1	Petition	347	Claims	Mar. 30, 1816	Favorable	156	Indef. postponed.		
Bowie & Kurtz, and others	Indemnity for seizure and condemnation of schooner Alleghany.	14	2	Petition	39	Claims	35	Adverse.		Referred to Committee Whole House.		
Bowie & Kurtz, and others	Indemnity for seizure and condemnation of schooner Alleghany.	15	1	Petition	94	Claims.						
Bowie & Kurtz, and others	Indemnity for seizure and condemnation of schooner Alleghany.	15	2	Petition	33	Claims	35	Adverse.		Referred to Committee Whole House.		

List of private claims presented to the House of Representatives of the United States from the 1st to the 31st Congress, inclusive—Continued.

Names of claimants.	Nature or object of the claim.	Congress.	Session.	How brought before the House of Reps.	Page of journal.	To what committee of the House referred.	No. or date of the report.	Nature of the report.	No. of the bill.	How disposed of by the House of Reps.	How disposed of by the Senate.	Date of the act of Congress, and remarks.
Bowie & Kurtz, and others	Indemnity for seizure and condemnation of schooner Alleghany.	16	1	Senate bill	251	Claims	Mar. 6, 1820	Adverse	S. 35	Laid on table.		
Bowie & Kurtz, and others	Indemnity for seizure and condemnation of schooner Alleghany.	16	2	Petition	34	Claims	28	Favorable	183	Referred to Committee Whole House.		
Bowie & Kurtz, and others	Indemnity for seizure and condemnation of schooner Alleghany.	19	1	Petition	150	Claims	....	....	......	Discharged; laid on table.		
Bowie & Kurtz, and others	Indemnity for seizure and condemnation of schooner Alleghany.	20	1	Petition	52	Claims.						
Bowie & Kurtz, and others	Indemnity for seizure and condemnation of schooner Alleghany.	20	2	Petition	40	Claims	75	Favorable	431	Referred to Committee Whole House.		
Bowie & Kurtz, and others	Indemnity for seizure and condemnation of schooner Alleghany.	21	1	Petition	84	Foreign Affairs	100	Favorable	138	Passed	Passed	App'd May 29, 1830
Bowie & Kurtz, and others	Indemnity for seizure and condemnation of schooner Alleghany.	25	2	Senate bill	301	Foreign Affairs	Mar. 6, 1838	With't amend.	S. 94	Referred to Committee Whole House.		
Bowie & Kurtz, and others	Indemnity for seizure and condemnation of schooner Alleghany.	26	1	Petition	168	Claims	573	Adverse	......	Laid on table.		
Bowier, William	Pension for revolutionary services.	26	1	Resolution	385	Rev. Claims	664	Adverse	......	Laid on table.		
Bowlen, Joseph	Pension	25	3	Petition	218	Invalid Pensions.						
Bowlen, Joseph	Pension	26	2	Petition	222	Invalid Pensions.						
Bowlen, Joseph	Pension	27	2	Petition	60	Invalid Pensions	228	Adverse	......	Laid on table.		
Bowlen, Joseph	Pension	27	3	Petition	101	Invalid Pensions	115	Adverse	......	Laid on table.		
Bowlen, Joseph	Pension	28	1	Petition	106	Invalid Pensions.						
Bowlen, Joseph	Pension	28	2	Petition	46	Invalid Pensions	12	Adverse	......	Laid on table.		
Bowler, Sarah	(See heir of John Brothers)	31	1	....	349							
Bowles, Absalom	Correction of entry of land	20	1	Petition	557	Public Lands.						
Bowles, Alexander, mother of.	Arrears of pay for services	30	1	Petition	276	Claims	122	Favorable and bill.	112	Referred to Committee Whole House.		
Bowles, Elizabeth	(See heirs of William Scott	14	2	....	285							
Bowles, John	To be restored to pension roll	17	1	Petition	45	Rev. Pensions.						
Bowling, Wm., and others	Correction of an error in the location of land.	24	2	Senate bill	553	Priv. Land Claims	....	....	S. 137			
Bowling, Wm. J., widow of.	Five months' pension	17	1	Petition	270	Rev. Pensions.						
Bowling, Wm. J., widow of.	Five months' pension	17	2	Petition	56	Rev. Pensions.						
Bowman, Abraham	Commutation pay for revolutionary services.	23	1	Petition	42	Rev. Claims	154	Adverse	......	Laid on table.		
Bowman, Abraham, heirs of.	Commutation pay for revolutionary services.	23	2	Petition	239	Rev. Claims.						
Bowman, Abraham, heirs of.	Commutation pay for revolutionary services.	24	1	Petition	431	Rev. Claims	601	Adverse	......	Laid on table.		
Bowman, Abraham, heirs of.	One year's pay under act November, 1778.	29	1	Petition	336	Rev. Claims	442	Favorable	315	Referred to Committee Whole House.		
Bowman, Abraham, heirs of.	One year's pay under act November, 1778.	30	1	Petition	575	Rev. Claims.						
Bowman, Abraham, heirs of.	One year's pay under act November, 1778.	30	2	Petition	174	Rev. Claims.						
Bowman, Abraham, heirs of.	One year's pay under act November, 1778.	31	1	Petition	472	Rev. Claims.						
Bowman, Charles	Pension for revolutionary services.	3	1	Petition	136	....	....	....	......	Referred to Secretary War.		
Bowman, Charles	Pension for revolutionary services.	3	2	Rep. of Secretary War.	278	....	....	....	......	Laid on table.		

List of private claims presented to the House of Representatives of the United States from the 1st to the 31st Congress, inclusive—Continued.

Names of claimants.	Nature or object of the claim.	Congress.	Session.	How brought before the House of Reps.	Page of journal.	To what committee of the House referred.	No. or date of the report.	Nature of the report.	No. of the bill.	How disposed of by the House of Reps.	How disposed of by the Senate.	Date of the act of Congress, and remarks.
Bowman, Charles	Pension for revolutionary services	15	2	Petition	103	Pens. & Rev. Cl'ms.	Dec. 18, 1818	Adverse	......	Rejected.		
Bowman, Dorothy	(See Samuel Bowman, widow of)	26	1	....	962							
Bowman, Frederick, former widow of.	Compensation as messenger in Treasury Department.	4	1	Petition	486	Claims.						
Bowman, Frederick, former widow of.	Compensation as messenger in Treasury Department.	4	2	Petition	614	Claims.						
Bowman, John	Indemnity for property destroyed by Osage Indians.	21	1	Senate bill	87	Indian Affairs	Dec. 29, 1829	With amend.	S. 8	Passed	Passed	App'd Mar. 25, 1830
Bowman, John, and T. Ney.	To change location of a land warrant.	26	1	Petition	608	Public Lands.						
Bowman, John L., and others.	Bounty on fishing schooner George.	26	1	Petition	199	Commerce	74	Favorable	61	Passed	Passed	App'd July 20, 1840
Bowman, J. H. D.	(See Anthony Hutchins & others.)	25	3	....	133							
Bowman, Lieut., widow of.	Half-pay; husband killed in Indian wars.	24	1	Petition	430	Claims.						
Bowman, Paul	Pension for revolutionary disabilities.	1	3	Petition	392	....	....	....	......	Referred to Secretary of War.		
Bowman, Samuel, widow of.	Arrears of pension	26	1	Petition	962	Rev. Pensions.						
Bowman, Samuel, widow of.	Arrears of pension	26	2	Petition	195	Rev. Pensions.						
Bowman, Samuel, widow of.	Arrears of pension	27	2	Petition	59	Rev. Pensions	120	Favorable	166	Passed	Passed	App'd Aug. 27, 1842
Bowman, Thankful	Pension for revolutionary services.	28	1	Petition	839	Whole House.						
Bowman, William, (Mo.).	Pension	22	2	Petition	246	Invalid Pensions.						
Bowman, William, (Mo.).	Pension	23	1	Petition	92	Invalid Pensions	April 8, 1834	Adverse	......	Laid on table.		
Bowman, William, (Mo.).	Pension	24	2	Petition	87	Invalid Pensions	130	Favorable	859	Referred to Committee Whole House.		
Bowman, William, (Mo.).	Pension	25	2	Petition	38	Invalid Pensions	223	Favorable	261	Passed.		
Bowman, William, (Mo.).	Pension	26	1	Petition	161	Invalid Pensions	216	Favorable	228	Passed	Passed	App'd July 20, 1840
Bowman, William, (Inda.)	Exchange of an entry of land	23	2	Resolution	256	Priv. Land Claims.	Jan. 26, 1835	Favorable	677			
Bowman, William, (Inda.)	Exchange of an entry of land	24	1	Petition	65	Priv. Land Claims.	53	Favorable	66	Passed	Passed	App'd June 28, 1836
Bowne, Michael, representatives of.	Confirmation of land title	16	1	Petition	177	Public Lands	....	....	......	Discharged; laid on table.		
Bowne, Robert, executors of.	Indemnity for French spoliations prior to 1800.	26	1	Memorial	182	Foreign Affairs	343	Favorable	319	Referred to Committee Whole House.		
Bowne, Robert	(See assignees of Robinson & Hartshorn.)	12	1	....	295	....	....	....	......	....	....	(See Ho. bill No. 46.)
Bowne, Robert	(See Isaac Laurence, *et al*)	14	1	....	386							
Bowne, Robert H.	(See Isaac Laurence, *et al*)	14	1	....	386							
Bowne, R. H. & J. L.	(See Robert Bowne, executors of.)	26	1	....	182	....	343	....	319			
Bowyer, William	Pension	14	1	Resolution	451	Pens. & Rev. Cl'ms.	April 23, 1816	Favorable bill.	171	Passed	Passed	App'd April 30, 1816
Boxwell, Joseph	(See Joseph Boswell)	18	1	....	127							
Boxwell, Joseph	Pension	21	1	Petition	604	Military Pensions	May 4, 1830	Adverse	......	Laid on table.		
Boxwell, Robert	To be restored to pension roll	17	2	Petition	43	Rev. Pensions	....	....	......	Discharged; leave to withdraw.		
Boyce, Abraham	Pension	21	1	Petition	66	Military Pensions	April 29, 1830	Adverse	......	Laid on table.		
Boyce, Abraham	Pension	23	2	Petition	435	Rev. Pensions.						
Boyce, Abraham	Pension	24	2	Petition	271	Rev. Pensions			......	Disch'd; laid on table.		
Boyce, Abraham	Pension	25	2	Petition	178	Rev. Claims.						
Boyce, Joseph P	Bounty land for services in United States army.	30	1	Petition	259	Military Affairs			......	....	....	Leave to withdraw 2d session.
Boyce, Purnell, heir of	Payment of prize money due	22	1	Petition	42	Claims	Feb. 24, 1832	Favorable	414	Referred to Committee Whole House.		
Boyce, William	Confirmation of title to land under Virginia grant.	5	3	Petition	421	Claims	....	....	......	Discharged; laid on table.		

List of private claims presented to the House of Representatives of the United States from the 1st to the 31st Congress, inclusive—Continued.

Names of claimants.	Nature or object of the claim.	Congress.	Session.	How brought before the House of Reps.	Page of journal.	To what committee of the House referred.	No. or date of the report.	Nature of the report.	No. of the bill.	How disposed of by the House of Reps.	How disposed of by the Senate.	Date of the act of Congress, and remarks.
Boyce, William	Confirmation of title to land under Virginia grant.	6	1	Petition	535	Claims	Feb. 25, 1800	Adverse	......	Leave to withdraw.		
Boyce, William	Confirmation of title to land under Virginia grant.	10	2	Petition	357	Select.						
Boyce, William, representatives of.	Compensation for revolutionary services.	23	1	Resolution	250	Rev. Claims.						
Boyce, William, representatives of.	Compensation for revolutionary services.	23	2	Petition	262	Rev. Claims.	....	....	......	Discharged; leave to withdraw.		
Boyce, William, representatives of.	Compensation for revolutionary services.	24	1	Resolution	64	Rev. Claims.	May 3, 1836	Favorable	390	Referred to Committee Whole House.		
Boyce, William, representatives of.	Compensation for revolutionary services.	25	2	Resolution	39	Rev. Claims.	481	Adverse	......	Referred to Committee Whole House.		
Boyd, Alexander	Confirmation of title to land in Louisiana.	20	2	Resolution	52	Priv. Land Claims.						
Boyd, Alexander	Confirmation of title to land in Louisiana.	21	1	Petition	51	Priv. Land Claims.	86	Favorable	94	Laid on table.		
Boyd, Alexander	Confirmation of title to land in Louisiana.	22	1	Petition	75	Priv. Land Claims.	144	Favorable	219	Referred to Committee Whole House.		
Boyd, Alexander	Confirmation of title to land in Louisiana.	22	2	Rep. Committee Whole House.	·67	....	....	With't amend.	219	Passed	Laid on table.	
Boyd, Alexander	Confirmation of title to land in Louisiana.	23	1	Petition	48	Priv. Land Claims.	28	Favorable	28	Passed	Passed	App'd June 18, 1834
Boyd, Benjamin	Compensation for revolutionary services and supplies.	4	1	Petition	466	Claims	May 31, 1796	Adverse	......	Laid on table.		
Boyd, Benjamin	Compensation for revolutionary services and supplies.	10	1	Petition	89	Select.						
Boyd, Benjamin	Compensation for revolutionary services and supplies.	13	1	Petition	20	Claims	....	....	......	Discharged; laid on table.		
Boyd, Doctor, (M. A.) widow of.	To be restored to pension roll	27	3	Petition	....	Naval Affairs	....	....	......	Discharged; laid on table.		
Boyd, Elijah	Compensation for horse lost in the war of 1812.	18	2	Petition	87	Claims	Jan. 10, 1825	Adverse	......	Leave to withdraw.		
Boyd, George (Mich.)	(See Aaron M. Wright, sureties of.)	21	1	....	69							
Boyd, Col. George	Compensation for services as Indian agent.	29	1	Petition	309	Indian Affairs	Aug. 10, 1846	Favorable	554	Referred to Committee Whole House.		
Boyd, Col. George, heirs of.	Settlement of accounts with the United States.	30	1	Petition	199	Claims	....	....	......	Discharged; laid on table.		
Boyd, Hugh	(See Barent J. Staats, executors of.)											
Boyd, Isaac	Pension	25	2	Petition	56	Invalid Pensions	300	Favorable	340	Passed	Adverse report.	
Boyd, Isaac	Pension	25	3	Petition	88	Invalid Pensions	85	Favorable	964	Passed	Adverse report.	
Boyd, Isaac	Pension	26	1	Petition	160	Invalid Pensions	215	Favorable	227	Passed	Indef. postp'd.	
Boyd, Isaac	Pension	27	2	Petition	459	Invalid Pensions	620	Adverse	......	Laid on table.		
Boyd, James	Settlement of account for revolutionary services.	2	2	Petition	674	....	....	....	......	Referred to Secretary Treasury.		
Boyd, James	Settlement of account for revolutionary services.	3	2	Rep. of Secretary Treasury.	284	....	....	....	......	Laid on table.		
Boyd, James	(See Canadian refugees.)	6	2	....	733							
Boyd, James (Va.)	Pension for revolutionary services.	21	1	Resolution	350	Military Pensions	May 3, 1830	Adverse	......	Laid on table.		
Boyd, James (Va.)	Pension for revolutionary services.	24	2	Petition	133	Rev. Pensions	....	....	......	Discharged; laid on table.		
Boyd, James (Va.)	Pension for revolutionary services.	25	2	Resolution	117	Rev. Pensions	419	Favorable	425	Passed	Passed	App'd July 9, 1838

List of private claims presented to the House of Representatives of the United States from the 1st to the 31st Congress, inclusive—Continued.

Names of claimants.	Nature or object of the claim.	Congress.	Session.	How brought before the House of Reps.	Page of journal.	To what committee of the House referred.	No. or date of the report.	Nature of the report.	No. of the bill.	How disposed of by the House of Reps.	How disposed of by the Senate.	Date of the act of Congress, and remarks.
Boyd, James, (Va.) widow of.	Pension for revolutionary services.	29	2	Petition	69	Rev. Pensions	72	Favorable	682	Referred to Committee Whole House.		
Boyd, James, (Augusta) widow of.	Compensation for horse killed in public service.	31	2	Petition	111	Military Affairs.						
Boyd, James	(See Louis F. Beeler, *et al.*	30	1		115		482					
Boyd, James, (Ohio)	Increase of pension	27	2	Petition	799	Rev. Pensions						Leave to withdraw, 3d session.
Boyd, John	Remission of duty on distillery	15	1	Petition	24	Ways and Means				Discharged; leave to withdraw.		
Boyd, John, (Mass.)	Pension	21	2	Petition	188	Military Pensions.						
Boyd, John, (Mass.)	Pension	22	1	Petition	124	Rev. Pensions.						
Boyd, John, (Mass.)	Pension	25	3	Petition	215	Rev. Pensions				Discharged; laid on table.		
Boyd, John, (Mass.)	Pension	26	1	Petition	172	Rev. Pensions				Discharged; laid on table.		
Boyd, John, (Ala.)	Reimbursement of money paid for erroneous land entry.	28	2	Petition	65	Public Lands	63	Favorable	545	Passed	Indef. postp'd.	
Boyd, John, (Ala.)	Reimbursement of money paid for erroneous land entry.	29	1	Petition	523	Public Lands.						
Boyd, John, widow of, (Pa.)	Pension for revolutionary services.	29	1	Petition	1074	Rev. Pensions.						
Boyd, John, widow of, (Pa.)	Pension for revolutionary services.	29	1	Petition	487	Rev. Pensions	525	Adverse		Laid on table.		
Boyd, John, widow of, (Pa.)	Pension for revolutionary services.	30	1	Petition	394	Rev. Pensions	437	Adverse		Laid on table.		
Boyd, Joseph	(See widow of Stephen Decatur, and others.)											
Boyd, Joseph Coffin	Credit for public money accidentally lost.	14	2	Petition	242	Claims.						
Boyd, Joseph Coffin	Credit for public money accidentally lost.	17	1	Senate bill	430	Military Affairs	May 7, 1822	With't amend.	S. 65	Laid on table.		
Boyd, Joseph Coffin	Credit for public money accidentally lost.	17	2	Petition	77	Claims	Feb. 26, 1823	Adverse		Laid on table.		
Boyd, Joseph Coffin	Credit for public money accidentally lost.	18	1	Senate bill	138	Claims	Jan. 28, 1824	With't amend.	S. 7	Passed	Passed	App'd May 4, 1824
Boyd, Joseph K.	Prize money as a recaptor of frigate Philadelphia.	22	1	Petition	537	Naval Affairs.						
Boyd, Joseph K.	Prize money as a recaptor of frigate Philadelphia.	22	2	Petition	31	Naval Affairs	43	Adverse		Laid on table.		
Boyd, Joseph K.	Prize money as a recaptor of frigate Philadelphia.	25	2	Petition	201	Naval Affairs				Discharged; laid on table.		
Boyd, Joseph K.	Prize money as a recaptor of frigate Philadelphia.	26	1	Memorial	626	Naval Affairs.						
Boyd, Joseph K.	Prize money as a recaptor of frigate Philadelphia.	28	1	Petition	429	Naval Affairs				Discharged; laid on table.		
Boyd, Joseph K.	Prize money as a recaptor of frigate Philadelphia.	31	1	Petition	192	Naval Affairs	14	Favorable	17	Laid on table.		
Boyd, Joseph, sureties of.	Release from liability	31	1	Petition	1095	Judiciary.						
Boyd, Joseph, sureties of.	Release from liability	31	2	Petition	165	Judiciary	5	Adverse		Laid on table.		
Boyd, Patrick	Compensation for shoeing horses for Lee's legion.	15	2	Petition	226	Pens. & Rev. Cl'ms.						
Boyd, Patrick	Compensation for shoeing horses for Lee's legion.	16	1	Petition	96	Pens. & Rev. Cl'ms.	Jan. 3, 1820	Adverse		Laid on table.		

List of private claims presented to the House of Representatives of the United States from the 1st to the 31st Congress, inclusive—Continued.

Names of claimants.	Nature or object of the claim.	Congress.	Session.	How brought before the House of Reps.	Page of journal.	To what committee of the House referred.	No. or date of the report	Nature of the report.	No. of the bill.	How disposed of by the House of Reps.	How disposed of by the Senate.	Date of the act of Congress, and remarks.
Boyd, Patrick	Compensation for shoeing horses for Lee's legion.	17	1	Petition	253	Pens. & Rev. Cl'ms.	Feb. 12, 1822	Adverse	......	Leave to withdraw.		
Boyd, Rebecca	(See John Boyd, widow of)	29	1	Petition	487							
Boyd, Robert, administrator of.	Compensation for horses impressed into public service.	22	2	Petition	131	Claims	Jan. 11, 1833	Adverse	......	Laid on table.		
Boyd, Robert	(See Valerian Allain)	26	1	....	365							
Boyd, R. W.	Compensation for extra services in surveyor general's office, La.	28	2	Petition	235	Public Lands.						
Boyd, Samuel	Settlement of accounts for revolutionary services.	[illegible]	[illegible]	Petition	674	....	....	....	......	Referred to Secretary War.		
Boyd, Spencer	Pension for revolutionary services.	20	2	Petition	351	Rev. Pensions.						
Boyd, Thomas	Pension for revolutionary disabilities.	1	2	Petition	175	....	....	....	......	Laid on table.		
Boyd, Thomas	Pension for revolutionary disabilities.	1	3	Petition	354							
				Rep. of Secretary War.	393	....	....	....	......	Laid on table.		
Boyd, Thomas	Pension for revolutionary disabilities.	3	1	Petition	103	....	....	....	......	Referred to Secretary of War.		
Boyd, Thomas	Pension for revolutionary disabilities.	3	2	Rep. of Secretary War.	278	....	....	....	......	Laid on table.		
Boyd, Thomas	Indemnity for loss on continental money.	3	2	Rep. of Secretary War.	305	Claims.						
Boyd, Thomas	Indemnity for loss on continental money.	4	1	Petition	373	Claims	Dec. 28, 1795	Adverse	......	Leave to withdraw.		
Boyd, Thomas, (Ohio,)	To make valid a patent for land	27	3	Petition	....	....	....	....	......	Laid on table.		
Boyd, William	Pension for revolutionary services.	3	2	Petition	259	Claims	Feb. 25, 1795	Indefinite	......	Referred to Committee Whole House.	....	Leave to withdraw, 4, 1, p. 602.
Boyd, William, administrator of.	Indemnity for French spoliations prior to 1800.	26	1	Memorial	182	Foreign Affairs	343	Favorable	319	Referred to Committee Whole House.		
Boyden, Josiah, widow of.	Pension for revolutionary services.	25	2	Petition	913	Rev. Pensions	....	....	......	Discharged; laid on table.		
Boyer, Cecille (Indian)	Grant of public land	20	1	Petition	197	Indian Affairs	127	Favorable	146	Passed.		
Boyer, Cecille (Indian)	Grant of public land	20	2	Petition	41	Indian Affairs	Dec. 15, 1828	Favorable	315	Referred to Committee Whole House.		
Boyer, Charles	Patent for a Spanish grant of "old mines."	22	1	Petition	263	Priv. Land Claims.	Feb. 17, 1832	Favorable	380	Referred to Committee Whole House.		
Boyer, Frederick	Arrears of pension	24	2	Petition	48	Invalid Pensions	....	....	......	Disch'd; laid on table.		
Boyer, Frederick	Arrears of pension	27	2	Petition	1049	Rev. Pensions	....	....	......	Discharged; leave to withdraw.		
Boyer, Joseph	Patent for Spanish grant of "old mines," Missouri.	22	1	Petition	263	Priv. Land Claims.	Feb. 17, 1832	Favorable	380	Referred to Committee Whole House.		
Boyer, Joseph	(See heirs of Francis Vallé)	15	2	....	67							
Boyer, Levi	Reimbursement of over-payment for public land.	13	3	Petition	454	Public Lands	....	....	......	Discharged; laid on table.		
Boyer, Louis	Patent for Spanish grant of "old mines," Missouri.	22	1	Petition	263	Priv. Land Claims.	Feb. 17, 1832	Favorable	380	Referred to Committee Whole House.		
Boyer, Peter	(See heirs of Francis Vallé)	15	2	....	67							
Boyer, Pierre	Patent for Spanish grant of "old mines," Missouri.	22	1	Petition	263	Priv. Land Claims.	Feb. 17, 1832	Favorable	380	Referred to Committee Whole House.		
Boyer, William	Pension	14	1	Petition	64	Pens. & Rev. Cl'ms.	April 11, 1816	Favorable	171	Passed	Passed	App'd April 30, 1816
Boyers, Louis	Bounty land for revolutionary services.	23	2	Petition	48	Rev. Claims	Jan. 22, 1835	Adverse	......	Laid on table.		

List of private claims presented to the House of Representatives of the United States from the 1st to the 31st Congress, inclusive—Continued.

Names of claimants.	Nature or object of the claim.	Congress.	Session.	How brought before the House of Reps.	Page of journal.	To what committee of the House referred.	No. or date of the report.	Nature of the report.	No. of the bill.	How disposed of by the House of Reps.	How disposed of by the Senate.	Date of the act of Congress, and remarks.
Boyes, Genet	Revolutionary pension	28	1	Petition	839	Whole House.						
Boyington, Josiah	Indemnity for French spoliations prior to 1800.	27	2	Petition	527	Foreign Affairs.						
Boylan, James	Pension for revolutionary services.	24	1	Petition	634	Rev. Pensions	802	Favorable	718	Referred to Committee Whole House.		
Boylan, James	Pension for revolutionary services.	25	2	Petition	37	Rev. Pensions	326	Favorable	368	Passed.		
Boylan, James	Pension for revolutionary services.	25	3	Petition	348	Rev. Pensions	287	Favorable	1151	Referred to Committee Whole House.		
Boylan, James	Pension for revolutionary services.	26	1	Petition	171	Rev. Pensions	133	Favorable	143	Passed	Indef. postp'd.	
Boyle, Andrew, (Ky.)	Compensation for horse lost in public service.	20	2	Resolution	187	Claims				Leave to withdraw.		
Boyle, Andrew, (Ky.)	Compensation for horse lost in public service.	21	1	Petition	51	Claims	Feb. 11, 1830	Adverse		Laid on table.		
Boyle, Andrew, (Ky.)	Compensation for horse lost in public service.	22	1	Petition	226	Claims	280	Adverse		Laid on table.		
Boyle, John	Compensation for property taken for public use.	30	1	Petition	159	Public Buildings & Grounds.						
Boyle, John	Compensation for property taken for public use.	30	2	Petition	115	Public Buildings & Grounds.						
Boyle, John	Compensation for property taken for public use.	31	1	Petition	415	Public Buildings & Grounds.						
Boyles, John	(See widow of Stephen Decatur and others.)											
Boyle, John	(See Jeremiah D. Hayden, sureties of.)	22	1		943							
Boyle & McGirth	Compensation for horses lost in Seminole war.	18	2	Senate bill	259	Claims	Feb. 28, 1825	With't amend.	S. 26	Passed	Passed	App'd March 3, 1825
Boyle, Robert	Pension	16	1	Petition	32	Pens. & Rev. Cl'ms.				Discharged; referred to Secretary War.		
Boyle, Thomas H., daughter of.	Compensation for revolutionary services.	15	1	Petition	136	Pens. & Rev. Cl'ms.	Feb. 10, 1818	Adverse.				
Boyle, Thomas H., heirs of.	Seven years half-pay	25	2	Resolution	405	Rev. Claims	692	Favorable	665	Passed	Passed	App'd July 7, 1838
Boyle, Thomas H., widow of.	Indemnity for land ceded to Indians.	17	1	Petition	176	Public Lands.						
Boyle, Thomas H., representatives of.	Indemnity for land ceded to Indians.	22	2	Senate bill	277	Priv. Land Claims.			S. 60			
Boyle, Thomas H., representatives of.	Indemnity for land ceded to Indians.	23	1	Petition	195	Priv. Land Claims.						
				Senate bill	390	Public Lands	May 27, 1834	With't amend.	S. 49	Passed.	Passed	App'd June 30, 1834
Boyle, Thomas H., widow of.	Location of land to include improvements.	18	1	Petition	49	Priv. Land Claims.						
Boyles, Thomas H	Compensation for secret services, &c.	14	1	Petition	163	Select	Feb. 10, 1816	Favorable	75	Passed	Passed	App'd April 27, 1816
Boynton, Betty	Continuation of pension	28	1	Petition	849	Rev. Pensions.						
Boynton, Daniel, (Vt.)	Arrears of pension	15	1	Petition	23	Pens. & Rev. Cl ms.				Discharged; leave to withdraw.		
Boynton, Daniel, (Vt.)	Arrears of pension	22	2	Petition	206	Invalid Pensions.						
Boynton, Daniel, (Vt.)	Arrears of pension	23	1	Petition	44	Invalid Pensions	1	Favorable	1	Passed	Passed with amendment.	App'd June 25, 1834
Boynton, Isaac	Pension	20	2	Petition	319	Military Pensions.						
Boynton, Isaac	Pension	21	1	Petition	143	Military Pensions.						
Boynton, Isaac	Pension	21	2	Petition	73	Military Pensions.						
Boynton, Isaac	Pension	23	1	Petition	44	Invalid Pensions	Feb. 26, 1834	Adverse		Laid on table.		

List of private claims presented to the House of Representatives of the United States from the 1st to the 31st Congress, inclusive—Continued.

Names of claimants.	Nature or object of the claim.	Congress	Session.	How brought before the House of Reps.	Page of journal.	To what committee of the House referred.	No. or date of the report.	Nature of the report.	No. of the bill.	How disposed of by the House of Reps.	How disposed of by the Senate.	Date of the act of Congress, and remarks.
Boreman, John	Pension for revolutionary services	29	1	Petition	....	Rev. Pensions	784	Adverse	......	Laid on table.		
Bozman, Joseph	Release from a judgment	3	2	Petition	296	Select	Feb. 28, 1795	Favorable	......	Referred to Committee Whole House.		
Brabrook, Walter	Indemnity for damage to vessel in public service.	15	2	Petition	84	Claims	....	....	......	Discharged; leave to withdraw.		
Brace, Stephen	Compensation for time lost while prisoner of war.	17	2	Petition	143	Claims	Feb. 12, 1823	Favorable	291	Referred to Committee Whole House.		
Brace, Stephen	Compensation for time lost while prisoner of war.	18	1	Petition	81	Claims	Jan. 30, 1824	Favorable	92	Passed	Passed	App'd May 17, 1824
Bracken, Charles	Permission to enter land at minimum price.	28	1	Petition	1069	Public Lands.						
Bracken, Charles	Permission to enter land at minimum price.	28	2	Petition	239	Public Lands.						
Brackenridge, Jane	Pension in consideration of Indian captivity.	28	1	Petition	840	Rev. Pensions.						
Brackett, Heard	Pension	22	1	House bill	206	Whole House	July 4, 1832	No amendm't.	288	Passed	Passed	App'd July 13, 1832—petition's name omitted
Brackett, Heard	Pension	22	2	Petition	63	Invalid Pensions	Dec. 19, 1832	Favorable	626	Passed	Passed with amendment.	App'd March 2, 1833
Brackett, Samuel	Pension	21	2	Petition	208	Military Pensions.						
Brackett, Samuel	Pension	22	1	Petition	35	Rev. Pensions.						
Brackett, Wm	Pension	22	1	Petition	435	Invalid Pensions	425	Favorable	524	Passed	Laid on table.	
Brackett, Wm	Pension	22	2	Petition	172	Invalid Pensions	Feb. 15, 1833	Favorable	738	Referred to Committee Whole House.		
Brackett, Wm	Pension	23	1	Petition	44	Invalid Pensions	1	Favorable	1	Passed.	Passed	App'd June 25, 1834—petition's name omitted
Bradbury, Francis	Indemnity for French spoliations prior to 1800.	26	1	Memorial	182	Foreign Affairs	343	Favorable	319	Referred to Committee Whole House.		
Bradbury, Jeremiah	(See heirs of Ivory Sherman)	16	1	....	285							
Bradbury, J., and others	Indemnity for libeled merchandise released by act of Congress.	29	1	Memorial	279	Commerce.						
Braddock, John D	Confirmation of title to land in Florida.	23	2	Petition	167	Public Lands.						
Braden, Elizabeth	(See George Braden, mother of)	16	1	....	285							
Braden, George, mother of	Pay and bounty land due	16	1	Petition	285	Public Lands	Mar. 25, 1820	Favorable	119	Passed	Passed	App'd April 24, 1820
Bradford, Alden	(See A. Ogden and others).											
Bradford, Augustus	Arrears of pension	25	2	Petition	588	Invalid Pensions.						
Bradford, Augustus	Arrears of pension	25	3	Petition	219	Invalid Pensions	....	....	......	Discharged; laid on table.		
Bradford, Augustus	Arrears of pension	28	1	Petition	827	Invalid Pensions.						
Bradford, Carpenter	(See Noah Miller and others)	16	1	....	118							
Bradford, Charles, representatives of.	Pension due at his death	18	1	Petition	173	Pens. & Rev. Cl'ms	59	Favorable	108	Passed	Passed	App'd May 19, 1824
Bradford, Lieut'nt Colonel	Bounty land as Canadian refugee	6	2	House bill	733	Select	Jan. 19, 1801	Favorable	280	Passed	Passed	App'd Feb. 18, 1801
Bradford, Duncan	Compensation for time lost waiting orders.	30	2	Petition	75	Naval Affairs.						
Bradford, Duncan	Compensation for time lost waiting orders.	31	1	Petition	720	Naval Affairs	437	Adverse	......	Laid on table.		
Bradford, Duncan	Four months extra pay	30	2	Memorial	389	Claims.						
Bradford, Dunscomb, representatives of.	Compensation for services as acting consul at Paris.	25	2	Documents	112	Foreign Affairs	924	Favorable	810	Referred to Committee Whole House.		
Bradford, Dunscomb, representatives of.	Compensation for services as acting consul at Paris.	25	3	Rep't Committee Whole House.	433	....	....	With't amend.	810	Passed	Passed	App'd March 3, 1839
Bradford, Esek	(See James Averill, jr., and others)	12	1	....	85							

List of private claims presented to the House of Representatives of the United States from the 1st to the 31st Congress, inclusive—Continued.

Names of claimants.	Nature or object of the claim.	Congress.	Session.	How brought before the House of Reps.	Page of journal.	To what committee of the House referred.	No. or date of the report.	Nature of the report.	No. of the bill.	How disposed of by the House of Reps.	How disposed of by the Senate.	Date of the act of Congress, and remarks.
Bradford, Frederick	(See Elijah Cook, admin'x of, *et al.*)	21	2		99							
Bradford, George	Increase of pension	2	1	Petition	560					Laid on table.		
Bradford, George	Increase of pension	2	2	Petition	621	Select.						
Bradford, George	Increase of pension	5	2	Petition	321	Claims	June 5, 1798	Favorable		Referred to Committee Whole House.		
Bradford, George	Increase of pension	9	2	Pension bill	608	Whole House	Feb. 28, 1807	With amend.	216	Passed	Passed	App'd March 3, 1807
Bradford, Henry	(See Charles Collins, attorney of)	26	1		182		343		319			
Bradford, Henry	Confirmation of title to land	21	1	Petition	207	Priv. Land Claims.						
Bradford, James, widow of	Pension	4	1	Petition	485	Claims	May 31, 1796	Adverse		Laid on table.		
Bradford, James	Confirmation of title to land in Louisiana.	21	1	Petition	202	Priv. Land Claims.	297	Favorable	356	Referred to Committee Whole House.		
Bradford, James	Confirmation of title to land in Louisiana.	22	1	Petition	32	Priv. Land Claims.	274	Favorable	352	Referred to Committee Whole House.		
Bradford, James	Confirmation of title to land in Louisiana.	23	1	Petition	617	Priv. Land Claims.	457	Favorable	475	Referred to Committee Whole House.		
Bradford, James	Confirmation of title to land in Louisiana.	24	1	Petition	276	Priv. Land Claims.	March 3, 1836	Favorable	392	Passed	Passed	App'd July 2, 1836
Bradford, James	Confirmation of title to land in Louisiana.	25	2	Petition	43	Priv. Land Claims.	Dec. 22, 1837	Adverse		Laid on table.		
Bradford, James H.	Pension	25	2	Petition	58	Invalid Pensions	227	Favorable	265	Passed	Passed	App'd July 9, 1838
Bradford, James H.	Pension	28	1	Petition	541	Invalid Pensions.						
Bradford, John	Right of pre emption to land in Mississippi.	14	2	Petition	112	Public Lands	Jan. 18, 1817	Adverse		Laid on table.		
Bradford, John, (Pa.)	Increase of compensation as post master.	15	1	Petition	203	P. Of. & P. Roads.						
Bradford, John, (Ky.)	Reimbursement of ransom money paid Indians.	18	1	Petition	173	Pens. & Rev. Cl'ms.	59	Favorable	108	Passed	Passed	App'd May 19, 1824
Bradford, John, executor of.	Compensation for revolutionary supplies, &c.	1	1	Petition	467	Claims	May 31, 1796	Adverse		Laid on table.		
Bradford, Joseph	Compensation for horse lost in public service.	23	2	Petition	267	Claims.						
Bradford, Peabody	Pension	22	1	Resolution	240	Rev. Pensions.						
Bradford, Perez	Increase of pension	16	1	Petition	202	Pens. & Rev. Clm's.				Discharged; referred to Secretary War.		
				Rep. of Secretary War.	350					Laid on table		Leave to withdraw.
Bradford, Perez	Increase of pension	16	2	Petition	137	Pens. & Rev. Cl'ms.				Discharged; referred to Secretary of War.		
Bradford, Robert	Indemnity for horse, &c., lost in the public service.	23	1	Documents	154	Claims.						
Bradford, Robert, agent of.	Compensation for horse lost in Florida war.	28	1	Petition	262	Claims	167	General bill	19	Passed	Passed	App'd June 15, 1844
Bradford, Samuel	(See Zachariah McGirt.)											
Bradford, Samuel	(See executor of John Bradford)	4	1		467							
Bradford, Samuel K., heirs of.	Commutation pay for revolutionary services.	21	1	Petition	261	Rev. Claims.						
Bradford, Thomas O.	Pension	21	1	Resolution	207	Military Pensions.						
Bradford, Thomas H.	Compensation for horse lost in the public service.	18	2	Petition	42	Claims	Dec. 17, 1824	Adverse		Laid on table.		
Bradford, Thomas H.	Compensation for horse lost in the public service.	19	1	Petition	104	Claims	90	Adverse		Referred to Committee Whole House.		Leave to withdraw, 2d session.
Bradford, Wm. J. A.	Compensation for reporting decisions of Supreme Court.	28	2	Petition	65	Claims.						

List of private claims presented to the House of Representatives of the United States from the 1st to the 31st Congress, inclusive—Continued.

Names of claimants.	Nature or object of the claim.	Congress.	Session.	How brought before the House of Reps.	Page of journal.	To what committee of the House referred.	No. or date of the report.	Nature of the report.	No. of the bill.	How disposed of by the House of Reps.	How disposed of by the Senate.	Date of the act of Congress, and remarks.
Bradford, Wm. J. A.	Compensation for reporting decisions of Supreme Court.	29	1	Petition	146	Claims.						
Bradford, Wm. J. A.	Compensation for reporting decisions of Supreme Court.	30	1	Petition	338	Claims	247	Adverse		Laid on table.		
Bradish, David, heirs of	Pension for revolutionary services.	25	3	Petition	217	Rev. Pensions.						
Bradish, David, heirs of	Commutation pay for revolutionary services.	28	1	Petition	712	Rev. Claims.						
Bradley, Aner	Pension	3	1	Rep. of Secretary War.	131	Select	May 26, 1794	Res. to refer to Sec. War.	R. 12	Passed	Passed	App'd June 9, 1794
Bradley, Aner	Pension	4	1	Rep. of Secretary War.	447	Claims	Feb. 18, 1796	Pension bill	156	Passed	Passed	App'd April 20, 1796
Bradley, Daniel	Indemnity for horse killed in the revolutionary service.	6	1	Petition	652	Claims	April 24, 1800	Adverse		Leave to withdraw.		
Bradley, Daniel	Indemnity for horse killed in the revolutionary service.	11	1	Petition	52	Claims.						
Bradley, Daniel	Indemnity for horse killed in the revolutionary service.	11	2	Petition	173	Claims	Jan. 17, 1810	Indefinite		Referred to Secretary of War.		
Bradley, Edward, widow of.	Mileage from Michigan to Washington.	30	1	Resolution	287					Adopted.		
Bradley, Gilbert	Pension for revolutionary services.	23	1	Petition	144	Rev. Pensions.						
Bradley, Henry	Reimbursement of expenses while sick.	14	2	Petition	242	Military Affairs	Feb. 21, 1817	Adverse		Laid on table.		
Bradley, Nathan	Pension	3	1	Rep. of Secretary War.	131	Select.						
Bradley, Nathaniel	Increase of pension	10	1	Pension bill	231	Whole House	April 19, 1808	With amend.	78	Passed	Passed with amendment.	App'd April 25, 1808
Bradley, Nathaniel, (N. Y.)	Pension for revolutionary services.	26	1	Petition	625	Rev. Pensions	July 10, 1840	Adverse		Laid on table.		
Bradley, Peter, (Conn.)	Commissions on disbursement and pay as captain.	16	1	Petition	375	Claims	April 17, 1820	Adverse		Laid on table.		
Bradley, Peter, (Conn.)	Commissions on disbursement and pay as captain.	17	2	Petition	164	Claims				Discharged; leave to withdraw.		
Bradley, Peter, (Vt.)	Pension	22	1	Resolution	433	Invalid Pensions	426	Favorable	528	Passed	Passed	App'd July 16, 1832
Bradley, Philip B.	Compensation for revolutionary services.	21	1	Documents	559	Military Pensions.						
Bradley, Samuel	(See Zebulon Pike & Companions)	10	1		189							
Bradley, Timothy	Indemnity for loss resulting from error in settlement.	2	1	Petition	478					Referred to Secretary Treasury.		
Bradley, Timothy	Compensation for revolutionary services and supplies.	2	2	Petition	688					Referred to Secretary Treasury.		
Bradley, Timothy	Compensation for revolutionary services and supplies.	3	2	Rep. of Secretary Treasury.	284	Claims	May 2, 1795	Adverse		Laid on table.		
Bradley, Timothy	Compensation for revolutionary services and supplies.	4	1	Rep. of Secretary Treasury.	598	Claims	May 31, 1796	Adverse		Laid on table.		
Bradley, Walter	Additional compensation as collector of customs.	24	1	Petition	1062	Claims.						
Bradley, Walter	Additional compensation as collector of customs.	24	2	Petition	396	Ways and Means.						
Bradley, Walter	Additional compensation as collector of customs.	25	2	Petition	204	Ways and Means	1016	Adverse		Laid on table.		
Bradley, Walter	Additional compensation as collector of customs.	26	1	Petition	297	Ways and Means.						
Bradshaw, George, widow of.	Continuation of pension	24	1	Petition	273	Rev. Pensions				Discharged; laid on table.		

List of private claims presented to the House of Representatives of the United States from the 1st to the 31st Congress, inclusive—Continued.

Names of claimants.	Nature or object of the claim.	Congress.	Session.	How brought before the House of Reps.	Page of journal.	To what committee of the House referred.	No. or date of the report.	Nature of the report.	No. of the bill.	How disposed of by the House of Reps.	How disposed of by the Senate.	Date of the act of Congress, and remarks.
Bradshaw, George, widow of.	Continuation of pension	24	2	Petition	45	Rev. Pensions				Discharged; laid on table.		
Bradshaw, George, widow of.	Continuation of pension	25	2	Petition	70	Rev. Pensions				Discharged; laid on table.		
Bradshaw, James	(See representatives of Jacob Odom)	15	1		312							
Bradshaw, John	Pension for revolutionary services	22	1	Petition	46	Rev. Claims	Dec. 31, 1831	Favorable	110	Passed	Indef. postp'd.	
Bradstreet, Dudley	Compensation for revolutionary services.	2	1	Petition	587					Referred to Secretary War.		
Bradstreet, Dudley	Compensation for revolutionary services.	3	1	Rep. of Secretary War.	131	Select	Mar. 26, 1794	Pension bill	62	Passed	Passed with amendment.	App'd June 7, 1794
Bradstreet, Mary, & others, attorney of.	Bounty on fishing schooner Mary	27	2	Petition	549	Commerce	1020	Favorable	593	Referred to Committee Whole House.		
Bradstreet, Mary, & others, attorney of.	Bounty on fishing schooner Mary	27	3	Rep't Committee Whole House.	91			With't amend.	593	Passed	Indef. postp'd.	
Bradstreet, Mary, & others, attorney of.	Bounty on fishing schooner Mary	28	1	Petition	827	Commerce.						
Bradstreet, William	(See attorney of Mary Bradstreet and others.)	27	2		549							
Bradt, Henry	Pension for revolutionary services	3	1	Rep. of Secretary War.	131	Select	May 26, 1794	Pension bill	62	Passed	Passed with amendment.	App'd June 7, 1794
Bradwell, Nathan or Nathaniel, heirs of.	Commutation pay for revolutionary services.	23	1	Petition	376	Rev. Claims.						
Brady, Abner	Pension	4	1	Rep. of Secretary of war.	447	Claims	Feb. 18, 1796	Favorable	156	Passed	Passed with amendment.	App'd April 20, 1796
Brady, Freeman	Balance due on contract, Cumberland road.	24	2	Petition	132	Claims	122	Favorable	850	Referred to Committee Whole House.		
Brady, Freeman	Balance due on contract, Cumberland road.	25	2	Petition	36	Claims	62	Favorable	74	Passed	Passed	App'd April 20, 1838
Brady Guards	(See Michigan)	27	3		71							
Brady, James	Duplicate revolutionary land warrants.	16	2	Petition	88	Priv. Land Claims	41	Favorable	202	Passed	Passed	App'd March 2, 1821
Brady, John	Compensation for work and materials on Cumberland road.	23	1	Petition and docs.	589	Claims	455	Adverse		Laid on table		See report No. 449.
Brady, John	Pension for services in Indian war	29	1	Petition	362	Invalid Pensions				Discharged; laid on table.		
Brady, John, widow of	Pension for revolutionary services	31	1	Petition	415	Rev. Pensions	125	Adverse		Laid on table.		
Brady, Nicholas, & others	Compensation for services at New Orleans.	31	2	Petition	216	Claims.						
Brady, Robert	Compensation for schooner taken for public use.	26	1	Petition	335	Claims.						
Brady, Robert	Compensation for schooner taken for public use.	28	1	Petition	513	Claims.						
Brady, Robert	Compensation for schooner taken for public use.	29	1	Petition	75	Claims	104	Adverse		Laid on table.		
Brady, Samuel	Confirmation of title to land in Ohio.	3	2	Memorial	291	Select.						
Brady, Samuel	Confirmation of title to land in Ohio.	4	1	Memorial	381	Select				Discharged; referred to Com. Whole House.		
Brady, Samuel W.	Pension for wounds and disabilities in Mexican war.	31	2	Petition	87	Invalid Pensions.						
Brady, William P.	Pension for disability, war of 1812	30	1	Petition	114	Invalid Pensions	199	Favorable	209	Passed	Passed	App'd May 19, 1848
Bragdon, Elijah, widow of	Balance of pay and bounty land	29	1	Petition	102	Military Affairs	760	Favorable	499	Ordered to 3d reading		
Bragdon, Elijah, widow of	Balance of pay and bounty land	29	2	House bill	212				499	Passed.		

List of private claims presented to the House of Representatives of the United States from the 1st to the 31st Congress, inclusive—Continued.

Names of claimants.	Nature or object of the claim.	Congress.	Session.	How brought before the House of Reps.	Page of journal.	To what committee of the House referred.	No. or date of the report.	Nature of the report.	No. of the bill.	How disposed of by the House of Reps.	How disposed of by the Senate.	Date of the act of Congress, and remarks.
Bragdon, Elijah, widow of	Balance of pay and bounty land	30	1	Petition	571	Claims	414	Favorable	365	Passed.		
Bragdon, Samuel, & others	Bounty on fishing schooner "Halcyon."	23	1	Petition	185	Commerce	Jan. 16, 1834	Favorable	204	Referred to Committee Whole House.		
Bragdon, Samuel, & others	Bounty on fishing schooner "Halcyon."	23	2	Rep't Committee Whole House.	82	....	....	With't amend.	204	Passed	Passed	App'd Jan. 27, 1835
Brahan, John, and J. Read	Remission of interest on purchase of public lands.	20	2	Senate bill	349	Public Lands	Feb. 28, 1829	With't amend.	S. 69	Referred to Committee Whole House.		
Brahan, John, and J. Read	Remission of interest on purchase of public land.	21	1	Senate bill	108	Public Lands	....	....	S. 22			
Brahan, John, and J. Read	Remission of interest on purchase of public land.	21	2	Senate bill	134	Public Lands	Feb. 24, 1831	Adverse	S. 28	Laid on table.		
Brahan, John	Reimbursement of expenditure for clerk hire.	20	1	Senate bill	410	Public Lands	April 24, 1828	With't amend.	S. 76	Passed	Passed	App'd May 26, 1828
Brahan, John	Equitable settlement of his accounts	21	1	Petition	473	Public Lands.						
Brahan, John	Equitable settlement of his accounts	21	2	Petition	63	Claims	Feb. 11, 1831	Adverse	......	Laid on table.		
Brahan, John	Equitable settlement of his accounts	22	1	Petition	134	Public Lands	Jan. 20, 1832	Adverse	......	Laid on table.		
Brahan, John, heirs of	Equitable settlement of his accounts	23	2	Petition	85	Public Lands	45	Favorable	631	Referred to Committee Whole House.		
Brahan, John, heirs of	Equitable settlement of his accounts	24	1	Petition	114	Public Lands	Jan. 12, 1836	Favorable	124	Passed	Adverse report.	
Brahan, John, heirs of	Equitable settlement of his accounts	24	2	Petition	47	Public Lands	2	Favorable	761	Referred to Committee Whole House.		
Brahan, John, heirs of	Equitable settlement of his accounts	25	2	Petition	42	Public Lands	240	Favorable	280	Referred to Committee Whole House.		
Brahan, John, heirs of	Equitable settlement and release of interest.	25	2	Senate bill	1249	Public Lands	July 6, 1838	With amend.	S. 258	Laid on table.		
Brahan, John, heirs of	Equitable settlement and release of interest.	25	3	Senate bill	98	Public Lands	Jan. 8, 1839	With amend.	S. 5	Passed with amendm't	Passed as am'd.	App'd Feb. 9, 1839
Brahany, James	Release from imprisonment	13	3	Petition	573	Ways and Means	Jan. 7, 1815	Favorable	252	Passed	Passed	App'd Feb. 2, 1815
Braidfoot, Rev. John, heirs of.	Half pay under resolve of Congress	23	1	Petition	157	Rev. Claims.						
Braidfoot, Rev. John, heirs of.	Half-pay under resolve of Congress	23	2	Petition	138	Rev. Claims.						
Braidfoot, Rev. John, heirs of.	Half-pay under resolve of Congress	24	1	Petition	138	Rev. Claims	Jan. 19, 1836	Adverse	......	Laid on table.		
Braidfoot, Rev. John, heirs of.	Half-pay under resolve of Congress	25	2	Petition	270	Rev. Claims	479	Adverse	......	Laid on table.		
Brainard, Asahel	Increase of pension	27	3	Senate bill	413	....	....	....	S. 132	Passed	Passed	App'd Feb. 24, 1843
Brainard, Asahel	Increase of pension	28	2	Petition	150	Invalid Pensions.						
Brainard, Asahel	Arrears of pension	28	2	Senate bill	243	Invalid Pensions	Jan. 28, 1845	With't amend.	S. 62	Passed	Passed	App'd Feb. 5, 1845
Brainard, Elijah	Pension for revolutionary disabilities.	8	2	Petition	71	Whole House.						
Brainard, Elijah	Pension for revolutionary disabilities.	10	1	Petition	100	Select.						
Brainard, Elijah	Pension for revolutionary disabilities.	11	2	Pension bill	283	Whole House	Mar. 24, 1810	With amend.	107	Passed	Passed with amendment.	App'd April 27, 1810
Brainard, Elijah	Pension for revolutionary disabilities.	11	3	Petition	474	Claims.						
Brainard, Elijah	Arrears of pension	8	2	Petition	251	Pens. & Rev. Cl'ms.						
Brainard, Elijah	Arrears of pension	19	3	Petition	129	Military Pensions	April 1, 1826	Adverse	......	Laid on table.		
Brainard, John and others	Extra compensation for taking census of Connecticut.	7	1	Petition	63	Claims	Jan. 29, 1802	Favorable	......	Postponed.		
Brainard, John, 2d	(See George W. Clark and others)	28	1	....	415							

List of private claims presented to the House of Representatives of the United States from the 1st to the 31st Congress, inclusive—Continued.

Names of claimants.	Nature or object of the claim.	Congress.	Session.	How brought before the House of Reps.	Page of journal.	To what committee of the House referred.	No. or date of the report.	Nature of the report.	No. of the bill.	How disposed of by the House of Reps.	How disposed of by the Senate.	Date of the act of Congress, and remarks.
Braman, Benjamin, widow of.	Continuation of pension........	25	2	Petition	587	Rev. Pensions....	....	....	.....	Discharged; laid on table.		
Bramble, Charles, widow of	Prize money due	22	1	Petition	431	Whole House.						
Bramble, George	Indemnity for French spoliations prior to 1800.	26	1	Memorial......	182	Foreign Affairs....	343	Favorable	319	Referred to Committee Whole House.		
Bramble, John, administrator of.	Indemnity for French spoliations prior to 1800.	31	1	Petition	471	Foreign Affairs....	355	Favorable....	318	Referred to Committee Whole House.		
Bramin, Daniel	(See Daniel Braman)	18	2	....	210							
Bramlette, Ambrose S	(See Thomas Elliott, heirs of....	29	2	....	169							
Branch, Elijah, widow of.	Pension for revolutionary services.	26	2	Petition	122	Rev. Pensions.....	....	....	.....	Discharged; laid on table.		
Branch, Elijah, widow of.	Pension for revolutionary services.	27	2	Petition	60	Rev. Pensions	784	Adverse	.....	Laid on table.		
Branch, Elizabeth........	Pension for revolutionary services of husband.	31	2	Petition	68	Rev. Pensions.						
Branch, Hugh B........	Bounty land for services in Mexican war.	30	1	Petition	80	Military Affairs.						
Branch, Olive	Redemption of Continental money.	27	2	Petition	376	Rev Claims......	942	Adverse	.....	Laid on table.		
Branch, Palmer.........	Pension for services in the war of 1812.	24	2	Petition	41	Invalid Pensions...	Jan. 3, 1837	Adverse	.....	Laid on table.		
Branch, Palmer.........	Pension for services in the war of 1812.	25	2	Petition	118	Invalid Pensions...	Jan. 18, 1838	Adverse	.....	Laid on table.		
Branch, Palmer.........	Pension for services in the war of 1812.	25	3	Petition	348	Invalid Pensions.						
Branch, Palmer.........	Pension for services in the war of 1812.	26	1	Petition	197	Invalid Pensions ..	284	Adverse	.....	Laid on table.		
Branch, Palmer.........	Pension for services in the war of 1812.	26	2	Petition	197	Invalid Pensions ..	224	Adverse	.....	Laid on table.		
Branch, Palmer.........	Pension for services in the war of 1812.	27	2	Petition	97	Invalid Pensions ..	161	Adverse	.....	Laid on table.		
Branch, Palmer.........	Pension for services in the war of 1812.	28	1	Petition	117	Invalid Pensions ..	Jan. 31, 1814	Adverse	.....	Laid on table.		
Branch, Palmer.........	Pension for services in the war of 1812.	28	2	Petition	214	Invalid Pensions.						
Branch, Palmer.........	Pension for services in the war of 1812.	29	1	Petition	209	Invalid Pensions ..	503	Adverse	.....	Laid on table.		
				Petition (2)....	701	Invalid Pensions.						
Branch, Palmer.........	Pension for services in the war of 1812.	29	2	Petition	169	Invalid Pensions.						
Branch, Palmer.........	Pension for services in the war of 1812.	30	2	Petition	95	Invalid Pensions ..	85	Favorable....	781	Referred to Committee Whole House.	....	Leave to withdraw, 31st Con., 1st sess.
Brand, George W.......	Compensation for use of building by United States' agent.	24	1	Petition	631	Indian Affairs.						
Brand, George W.......	Compensation for use of building by United States' agent.	24	2	Senate bill	251	Indian Affairs.....	Feb. 24, 1837	With't amend	S. 91	Referred to Committee Whole House.		
Brand, Godfroid.........	Reimbursement of money paid for public land, &c.	30	1	Petition	980	Judiciary.						
Brand, Godfroid.........	Reimbursement of money paid for public land, &c.	30	2	Petition	235	Judiciary.						
Brand, O..............	(See F. Denon and others)......	27	3	....	274							
Brandon, George, (Tenn.)	Compensation for property lost in public service.	23	1	Resolution	513	Claims.						
Brandon, John..........	Payment of a claim against United States.	1	2	Petition	250	....	....	....	.....	Referred to Secretary Treasury.		

List of private claims presented to the House of Representatives of the United States from the 1st to the 31st Congress, inclusive—Continued.

Names of claimants.	Nature or object of the claim.	Congress.	Session.	How brought before the House of Reps.	Page of journal.	To what committee of the House referred.	No. or date of the report.	Nature of the report.	No. of the bill.	How disposed of by the House of Reps.	How disposed of by the Senate.	Date of the act of Congress, and remarks.
Brandon, John	Payment of a claim against United States.	3	1	Rep. of Secretary Treasury.	77					Laid on table.		
Brandon, Peter	(See Zebulon Pike, and companions.)	10	1		189							
Brandrum, Samuel	(See assignees of T. Williams and J. Carey.)	9	2		607							
Brandt, Adam, (Ohio)	Compensation for horse lost in public service.	22	1	Petition	73	Claims.						
Brandt, Adam, (Ohio)	Compensation for horse lost in public service.	22	2	Petition	35	Claims	71	Adverse		Laid on table.		
Brandt, Adam, (Ohio)	Compensation for horse lost in public service.	23	1	Petition	33	Claims	Dec. 16, 1833	Adverse		Laid on table.		
Brandt, Joackim Jacob	Indemnity for disability in naval revolutionary service.	2	1	Petition	461					Referred to Secretary of War.		
Brandt, Joackim Jacob	Pension	3	1	Report of Secretary of War.	131	Select	May 26, 1794	Res. to refer to Sec. War.	R. 12	Passed	Passed	App'd June 9, 1794
Brandt, Joackim Jacob, administrators of.	Arrears of pension	3	2	Petition	264	Claims	Feb. 27, 1795	Adverse		Laid on table.		
Brandt, Joackim Jacob, administrators of.	Arrears of pension	4	1	Resolution	373	Claims.						
Brandt, Joackim Jacob, administrators of.	Arrears of pension	4	2	Resolution	614	Claims	Jan. 18, 1797	Adverse		Leave to withdraw.		
Brandt, William, & Co.	Reimbursement of duties paid at New York.	18	1	Petition	431	Ways and Means.						
Brandt, William, & Co.	Reimbursement of duties paid at New York.	18	2	Petition	80	Ways and Means	Feb. 25, 1825	Adverse		Laid on table.		
Branham, Ebenezer, and others.	Indemnity for horses killed, insurrection in Pennsylvania.	3	2	Petition	340	Claims.						
Branham, Ebenezer, and others.	Indemnity for horses killed, insurrection in Pennsylvania.	4	1	Petition	373	Claims	Feb. 18, 1796	Adverse		Leave to withdraw.		
Branham, George C.	Reimbursement of advances to a public contractor.	29	1	Petition	270	Judiciary.						
Branneau, Timothy N.	Pension for revolutionary services.	23	2	Petition	238	Rev. Pensions.						
Brannin, James W.	Confirmation of title to land in Missouri.	21	1	Petition	41	Priv. Land Claims.	409	Favorable	482	Referred to Committee Whole House.		
Brannin, James W.	Confirmation of title to land in Missouri.	22	1	Petition	388	Priv. Land Claims.	Mar. 6, 1832	Adverse		Laid on table.		
Brannin, Richard	Indemnity for Indian depredations	22	2	Resolution	122	Indian Affairs	91	Adverse		Laid on table.		
Brannin, Richard	Indemnity for Indian depredations.	23	1	Petition	450	Indian Affairs.						
Brannin, Richard	Indemnity for Indian depredations.	24	2	Petition	144	Indian Affairs				Discharged; laid on table.		
Brannin, Richard	Indemnity for Indian depredations	25	2	Petition	279	Indian Affairs.						
Brannin, Richard	Indemnity for Indian depredations.	25	3	Petition	91	Indian Affairs				Discharged; laid on table.		
Brannin, Richard	Compensation for horses lost in Black Hawk war.	25	3	Petition	205	Claims	207	Adverse		Laid on table.		
Branson, Nathan	Reimbursement of duties twice paid	16	1	Petition	58	Commerce.						
Branson, Nathan	Reimbursement of duties twice paid	17	1	Petition	44	Ways and Means	Jan. 17, 1822	Favorable	44	Passed	Rejected.	
Branson, Nathan	Reimbursement of duties twice paid	17	2	Petition	22	Ways and Means	Dec. 12, 1822	Favorable	189	Passed	Passed	App'd Mar. 1, 1823
Branson, Sarah	(See heirs of Hugh McMahon)	21	1		264							
Brant, Simeon	Pension for revolutionary services.	22	1	Petition	287	Rev. Pensions.						
Brantley, John	(See A. M. Mintor & J. Brantley)	21	1		172							
Branu, Robert Peter	Drawback on platillas exported	7	2	Petition	266	Com. and Manuf.	Jan. 10, 1803	Adverse		Leave to withdraw.		

List of private claims presented to the House of Representatives of the United States from the 1st to the 31st Congress, inclusive—Continued.

Names of claimants.	Nature or object of the claim.	Congress.	Session.	How brought before the House of Reps.	Page of journal.	To what committee of the House referred.	No. or date of the report.	Nature of the report.	No. of the bill.	How disposed of by the House of Reps.	How disposed of by the Senate.	Date of the act of Congress, and remarks.
Branu, Robert Peter	Drawback on platillas exported	10	2	Petition	366	Com. and Manuf.	Feb. 16, 1809	Adverse	......	Leave to withdraw.		
Brasher, Thomas R.	Permission to enter part of a 16th section.	28	1	Petition	181	Public Lands	181	Adverse	......	Laid on table.		
Brashears, Ann	Confirmation of title to land in Mississippi.	11	3	Petition	510	Public Lands.						
Brashears, Ann	Confirmation of title to land in Mississippi.	14	1	Petition	361	Public Lands.						
Brashears, Ann	Confirmation of title to land in Mississippi.	14	2	Petition	50	Priv. Land Claims.						
Brashears, Ann	Confirmation of title to land in Mississippi.	15	2	Petition	25	Priv. Land Claims.	Jan. 11, 1819	Adverse	......	Claim rejected.		
Brashears, Ann	Confirmation of title to land in Mississippi.	18	2	Petition	70	Priv. Land Claims.						
Brashears, Ann	Confirmation of title to land in Mississippi.	19	2	Petition	112	Priv. Land Claims.						
Brashears, Ann	Confirmation of title to land in Mississippi.	20	1	Petition	100	Priv. Land Claims.	142	Favorable	163	Passed.		
Brashears, Ann	Confirmation of title to land in Mississippi.	21	1	Petition	52	Priv. Land Claims.	101	Favorable	139	Passed	Passed	App'd May 28, 1830
Brashears, Ann, heirs of	Exchange of confirmed tract	22	1	Senate bill	502	Priv. Land Claims.	469	Adverse	S. 59	Rejected.		
Brashears, Ann, heirs of	Exchange of confirmed tract	22	2	Senate bill	112	Public Lands	51	Adverse	S. 51	Referred to Committee Whole House.		
Brashears, Samuel	Confirmation of title to land	19	1	Petition	45	Public Lands	Jan. 4, 1826	Favorable	36	Passed	Passed	App'd May 16, 1826
Brasington, Samuel	Compensation for revolutionary services.	21	1	Petition	261	Rev. Claims.						
Braswell, Henry	Pension	22	1	Petition	120	Rev. Pensions.						
Braswell, Richard, widow of	Pension for revolutionary services	28	1	Petition	362	Rev. Pensions.						
Braswell, Samson, widow of	Pension for revolutionary services	27	2	Petition	219	Rev. Pensions	784	Adverse	......	Laid on table.		
Braswell, Samson, widow of	Pension for revolutionary services	28	1	Petition	257	Rev. Pensions.						
Bratton, William	(See Lewis & Clark and companions.)	9	2									
Brawn, Daniel	Pension	3	2	Rep. of Secretary War.	278	Claims.						
Brawn, Daniel	Pension	4	1	Rep. of Secretary War.	373	Claims	Feb. 18, 1796	Favorable	156	Passed	Passed	App'd April 20, 1796
Brawner, Lawrence	Compensation for revolutionary services and reimbursement of advances.	2	1	Petition	554	....	....	....	......	Referred to Secretary Treasury.		
Brawner, William	Compensation for revolutionary services and reimbursement of advances.	9	1	Petition	296	Whole House.						
Brawner, William	Compensation for revolutionary services and reimbursement of advances.	9	2	Petition	480	Whole House.						
Brawner, William	Compensation for revolutionary services and reimbursement of advances.	10	1	Petition	73	Whole House.						
Brawner, William	Compensation for revolutionary services and reimbursement of advances.	1[illegible]	1	Petition	344	Pens. & Rev. Cl'ms.	....	....	......	Discharged; laid on table.		
Bray, James	Compensation for revolutionary services.	2	1	Petition	483	....	....	....	......	Referred to Secretary of War.		

List of private claims presented to the House of Representatives of the United States from the 1st to the 31st Congress, inclusive—Continued.

Names of claimants.	Nature or object of the claim.	Congress.	Session.	How brought before the House of Reps.	Page of journal.	To what committee of the House referred.	No. or date of the report.	Nature of the report.	No. of the bill.	How disposed of by the House of Reps.	How disposed of by the Senate.	Date of the act of Congress, and remarks.
Bray, John	(See Bordman & Pope and others)	12	1		136							
Bray, John	(See Philip Lefavor and others)	16	1		271							
Bray, Thomas	Remission of duty on old copper	10	1	Petition	86	Com. and Manuf.						
Bray, Thomas	Remission of duty on old copper	11	2	Petition	216	Com. and Manuf.						
Bray, Thomas	Remission of duty on old copper	11	3	Petition	510	Com. and Manuf.						
Bray, Timothy	Increase of pension	17	1	Petition	263					Referred to Secretary of War.		
				Rep. of Secretary War.	548					Laid on table.		
Brayman, Daniel	Indemnity for property destroyed by United States troops.	18	2	Petition	210	Claims.						
Brayman, Daniel	Indemnity for property destroyed by United States troops.	19	1	Resolution	92	Claims	Jan. 11, 1826	Adverse.				
Brayman, Daniel	Indemnity for property destroyed by United States troops.	21	1	Petition	262	Claims	Feb. 19, 1830	Adverse.				
Brayman, Daniel	Indemnity for property destroyed by United States troops.	22	2	Resolution	185	Claims	59	Adverse.				
Brayman, Daniel	Indemnity for property destroyed by United States troops.	23	1	Petition	33	Claims	Dec. 18, 1833	Adverse.				
Brayman, Daniel	Indemnity for property destroyed by United States troops.	23	2	Petition	37	Claims.						
Brayman, Daniel	Indemnity for property destroyed by United States troops.	27	2	Petition	382	Claims	337	Adverse.				
Brayman, Daniel	Indemnity for property destroyed by United States troops.	28	1	Petition	101	Claims	337	Adverse				Leave to withdraw, 31st Cong., 2d sess.
Braynard, Samuel D.	Pension for disability, war of 1812	25	3	Petition	449	Invalid Pensions.						
Braynard, Samuel D.	Pension for disability, war of 1812	26	1	Petition	162	Invalid Pensions	257	Adverse		Laid on table.		
Brayton, James W.	Pension for military services	21	1	Petition	46	Military Pensions.						
Brazeau, August	Confirmation of title to land in Missouri.	15	2	Petition	21	Priv. Land Claims.						
Brazeau, August	Confirmation of title to land in Missouri.	24	1	Petition	65	Priv. Land Claims.	Jan. 6, 1836	Adverse		Laid on table.		
Brazeaux, Louis, representatives of.	Confirmation of title to land in Missouri.	25	2	Petition	418	Priv. Land Claims.				Discharged; laid on table.		
Brazer, John, executor of.	Indemnity for French spoliations prior to 1800.	26	1	Memorial	182	Foreign Affairs	343	Favorable	319	Referred to Committee Whole House.		
Brazer, John, executor of.	Indemnity for French spoliations prior to 1800.	29	2	Petition	101	Foreign Affairs.						
Brazer, John, executor of.	Indemnity for French spoliations prior to 1800.	31	1	Petition	276	Foreign Affairs	355	General bill	318	Referred to Committee Whole House.		
Bread, Daniel, & J. Cornelius.	Payment of their share of annuity	31	2	Petition	118	Indian Affairs	18	Favorable	450	Referred to Committee Whole House.		
Bready, John	(See Conrad Houseman, *et al.*)											
Brean, Constant	Right of pre-emption	21	2	Petition	46	Priv. Land Claims.	Feb. 23, 1831	Adverse		Laid on table.		
Brean, Constant	Right of pre emption	22	1	Petition	75	Priv. Land Claims.	Dec. 30, 1831	Adverse		Laid on table.		
Brearly, David, (Indian ag't)	Indemnity for loss by removal from office.	22	2	Petition	269	Indian Affairs	125	Favorable	760	Referred to Committee Whole House.		
Brearly, David, (Indian ag't)	Indemnity for loss by removal from office.	23	1	Petition	73	Indian Affairs.						
Brearly, David, (Indian ag't)	Indemnity for loss by removal from office.	23	2	Petition	86	Indian Affairs.						
Brearly, David, (Indian ag't)	Equitable settlement of account for purchases.	24	1	Petition	672	Indian Affairs.						

List of private claims presented to the House of Representatives of the United States from the 1*st to the* 31*st Congress, inclusive*—Continued.

Names of claimants.	Nature or object of the claim.	Congress.	Session.	How brought before the House of Reps.	Page of journal.	To what committee of the House referred.	No. or date of the report.	Nature of the report.	No. of the bill.	How disposed of by the House of Reps.	How disposed of by the Senate.	Date of the act of Congress, and remarks.
Brearly, David, (Indian ag't)	Equitable settlement of account for purchases.	24	1	Appropriat'n bill.	129	....	....	....	70	Passed	Passed	App'd June 14, 1836
Brearly, Joseph Henry....	Confirmation of title to land in Arkansas.	26	1	Petition	610	Priv. Land Claims.	496	Favorable....	396	Referred to Committee Whole House.		
Breasha, Phebe	(See widow of John Lang)......	29	1	....	533							
Breathitt, John..........	(See sureties of William Whitsitt)	17	2	....	228							
Breck, Daniel	(See Nathaniel Sawyier and others)	14	1	....	153							
Breck, Joseph	(See attorney of George Brown)..	30	2	....	284							
Breck, Samuel	(See executors of John Ross)....	14	1	....	53							
Breck, William, jr.......	Compensation for sea stores furnished S. Bruce.	7	2	Petition	328	Claims	Feb. 22, 1803	Favorable....	......	Referred to Committee Whole House.		
Breck, William, jr.......	Compensation for sea stores furnished S. Bruce.	8	2	Petition	82	Claims	Feb. 13, 1805	Favorable....	......	Referred to Committee Whole House.		
Breck, William, jr.......	Compensation for sea stores furnished S. Bruce.	9	1	Petition	197	Claims	Dec. 30, 1805	Favorable, bill ordered.				
Breckenridge, Henry M..	Compensation for public services in Florida.	19	1	Resolution	186	Ways and Means..	Feb. 20, 1826	Favorable....	108	Passed.		
Breckenridge, Henry M..	Compensation for public services in Florida.	19	2	Documents.....	31	Ways and Means..	Dec. 29, 1826	Favorable....	321	Passed	Passed	App'd March 3, 1827
Breckenridge, Henry M..	Reconveyance of certain lands in Florida.	20	2	Petition........	27	Naval Affairs.....	....	....	......	Leave to withdraw.		
Bree, Ides	Indemnity for French spoliations prior to 1800.	26	1	Memorial	182	Foreign Affairs....	343	Favorable....	319	Referred to Committee Whole House.		
Breed, Ebenezer, jr., and John.	Restoration of ship seized for violation of embargo.	12	2	Petition	691	Ways and Means..	Mar. 1, 1813	Adverse	......	Laid on table.		
Breed, Ebenezer.........	Remission of duty on wine destroyed by fire.	21	1	Petition	412	Ways and Means..	Mar. 27, 1830	Adverse	......	Laid on table.		
Breed, Ebenezer.........	Remission of duty on wine destroyed by fire.	21	2	Petition........	160	Ways and Means.						
Breed, Ebenezer.........	Remission of duty on wine destroyed by fire.	22	1	Petition........	24	Commerce	Mar. 19, 1832	Adverse	......	Laid on table.		
Breed, Ebenezer.........	Remission of duty on wine destroyed by fire.	23	1	Petition........	32	Ways and Means..	Feb. 10, 1830	Favorable....	293	Referred to Committee Whole House.		
Breed, Ebenezer.........	Remission of duty on wine destroyed by fire.	23	2	Rep't. Committee Whole House.	300	....	....	Witht' amend.	293	Passed.		
Breed, Ebenezer.........	Remission of duty on wine destroyed by fire.	24	1	Petition	143	Ways and Means..	60	Favorable....	121	Referred to Committee Whole House.		
Breed, Ebenezer.........	Remission of duty on wine destroyed by fire.	24	2	House bill	256	....	....	....	121	Passed	Passed	App'd March 3, 1837
Breed, Ebenezer, & Co...	Indemnity for loss on sugar detained by collector.	22	2	Petition	63	Commerce.						
Breed, Ebenezer, & Co...	Indemnity for loss on sugar detained by collector.	23	1	Petition	32	Ways and Means.						
Breeding, William.......	Compensation for horse lost in Florida war.	28	1	Petition	262	Claims.						
Breeding, William	Pension for disability, war of 1812	31	2	Petition	286	Invalid Pensions.						
Breedlove, James W., collector at New Orleans.	Allowance for spurious coin received.	27	2	Petition	319	Ways and Means..	1036	Adverse	......	Laid on table.		
Breedlove, James W., collector at New Orleans.	Allowance for spurious coin received.	30	1	Petition	116	Claims.						
Breedlove, James W., collector at New Orleans.	Reimbursement of the amount of judgment recovered against him as a public officer.	31	1	Petition	192	Claims.						

List of private claims presented to the House of Representatives of the United States from the 1st to the 31st Congress, inclusive—Continued.

Names of claimants.	Nature or object of the claim.	Congress.	Session.	How brought before the House of Reps.	Page of journal.	To what committee of the House referred.	No. or date of the report.	Nature of the report.	No. of the bill.	How disposed of by the House of Reps.	How disposed of by the Senate.	Date of the act of Congress, and remarks.
Breeze, Robert	Compensation for military services in 1811.	13	2	Petition	315	Military Affairs				Discharged; referred to Paymaster.		
Brenan, E	Indemnity for detention of whiskey by United States officers.	31	1	Memorial	839	Claims.						
Brenan, John F	Reimbursement of payment for distillery license.	13	3	Petition	662	Ways and Means				Discharged; laid on table.		
Brenan, John F	Reimbursement of payment for distillery license.	14	2	Petition	233	Ways and Means.						
Brenan, Robert	Compensation for use of his patent paint.	31	2	Petition	155	Military Affairs				Discharged; laid on table.		
Brenneman, Henry	Pension for disability in Harrison's army.	13	2	Petition	322	Pensions	Mar. 29, 1814	Favorable	166	Passed	Passed	App'd April 18, 1814
Brenner, Elizabeth	(See admin'x of John B. Church.)	31	1		196							
Brent, Daniel	Compensation for extra services as consul at Paris.	24	1	Resolution	545	Foreign Affairs.						
Brent, Daniel	Pay and emoluments same as consul at London.	24	2	Petition	46	Foreign Affairs.						
Brent, Daniel	Pay and emoluments same as consul at London.	25	2	Petition	50	Foreign Affairs				Discharged; laid on table.		
Brent, Daniel, heirs of	Compensation for diplomatic services.	27	2	Petition	738	Foreign Affairs	742	Favorable	420	Referred to Committee Whole House.		
Brent, Daniel, heirs of	Compensation for diplomatic services.	27	3	Rep't Committee Whole House.	90			With't amend.	420	Passed	Passed	App'd March 3, 1843
Brent, George, representatives of.)	Pension	28	2	Memorial	118	Rev. Claims.						
Brent, George, representatives of.)	Pension	29	1	Memorial	91	Rev. Claims.						
Brent, George, representatives of.)	Pension	29	2	Memorial	85	Rev. Claims	46	Minority report favorable.		Discharged; laid on table.		
Brent, George, representatives of.)	Pension	30	1	Memorial	79	Rev. Claims	354	Adverse		Laid on table		Leave to withdraw, 30th Con., 2d sess.
Brent, George Lee	Compensation as bearer of despatches.	30	1	Appropriat'n bill.	523	Whole House		Amendments.	298	Passed	Passed	App'd Aug. 12, 1848
Brent, John, (collector of customs.)	Release from judgment for seizure of a vessel.	11	1	Petition	59	Com. and Manuf.						
Brent, John, (collector of customs.)	Release from judgment for seizure of a vessel.	11	2	Petition	274	Com. and Manuf.						
Brent, John, heirs of	Half pay for revolutionary services.	26	1	Petition	361	Rev. Claims.						
Brent, John, heirs of	Half pay for revolutionary services.	26	2	Petition	106	Rev. Claims.						
Brent, John, heirs of	Half pay for revolutionary services.	27	2	Petition	96	Rev. Claims	202	Adverse		Laid on lable.		
Brent, John, heirs of	Half pay for revolutionary services.	27	3	Petition	44	Rev. Claims	233	Adverse		Laid on table.		
Brent, John, heirs of	Half-pay for revolutionary services.	28	1	Petition	190	Rev. Claims.						
Brent, John, heirs of	Half pay for revolutionary services.	29	1	Petition	148	Rev. Claims.						
Brent, Lucy P	(See representatives of Col. George Baylor.)	29	1		319							
Brent, McKnight, & Wood	Indemnity for destruction of flour by United States troops.	30	1	Petition	236	Claims	243	Adverse		Laid on table.		
Brent, Robert	Increase of compensation as pay master general.	11	2	Petition	179	Ways and Means.						

List of private claims presented to the House of Representatives of the United States from the 1st to the 31st Congress, inclusive—Continued.

Names of claimants.	Nature or object of the claim.	Congress.	Session.	How brought before the House of Reps.	Page of journal.	To what committee of the House referred.	No. or date of the report.	Nature of the report.	No. of the bill.	How disposed of by the House of Reps.	How disposed of by the Senate.	Date of the act of Congress, and remarks.
Brent, Robert	Increase of compensation as pay master general.	13	2	Petition	368	Ways and Means	April 7, 1814	Favorable	186	Referred to Committee Whole House.		Statutes at Large, vol. 3, p. 128.
Brent, Robert Carroll, administrator of.	(See George Brent)	28	2		118							
Brent, Thomas L. L.	Reimbursement of expenses as chargé to Portugal.	24	1	Petition	425	Foreign Affairs	May 17, 1836	Favorable	634	Amendment to bill No. 214; passed.	Passed	App'd July 2, 1836
Brent, Thomas L. L.	Outfit as acting chargé to Madrid.	27	2	Petition	171	Foreign Affairs	957	Adverse		Laid on table.		
Brent, Thomas L. L.	Outfit as acting chargé to Madrid.	28	2	Petition	177	Foreign Affairs.						
Brent, Thomas L. L.	Outfit as acting chargé to Madrid.	30	1	Petition	535	Ways and Means.						
Brent, William	(See Daniel Carroll and others)	17	1		428							
Brenton, David	(See sureties of James Bruton)	31	2		107							
Brereton, Amelia	(See John A. Brereton, widow of.)	29	1		101							
Brereton, John A, widow of.	Balance of pay due	29	1	Petition	101	Claims	379	Favorable	287	Referred to Committee Whole House.		
Brereton, John A., widow of.	Balance of pay due	30	1	Petition	153	Claims	57	Favorable	42	Passed	Adverse report.	
Brereton, Stephen	Pension	29	1	Petition	600	Invalid Pensions.						
Bressie, Thomas, representatives of.	Commutation pay for revolutionary services.	30	1	Memorial	879	Rev. Claims.						
Bressie, Thomas, representatives of.	Commutation pay for revolutionary services.	30	2	Memorial	254	Rev. Claims				Discharged; leave to withdraw.		
Brest, John	Confirmation of title to land in Louisiana.	19	1	Petition	493	Priv. Land Claims.						
Brest, John	Confirmation of title to land in Louisiana.	19	2	Petition	37	Priv. Land Claims.	Dec. 22, 1826	Adverse		Laid on table.		
Brest, John	Confirmation of title to land in Louisiana.	20	1	Petition	33	Priv. Land Claims.	34	Adverse.				
Brest, John	Confirmation of title to land in Louisiana.	20	2	Petition	55	Priv. Land Claims.	33	Favorable	349			
Brest, John	Confirmation of title to land in Louisiana.	21	1	Petition	40	Priv. Land Claims.	21	Favorable	80	Passed	Passed	App'd March 23, 1830
Bretigny, Francis de	Pay, &c., due him for revolutionary services.	2	2	Petition	682					Referred to Secretary of War.		
Brett, John	Pension	21	2	Petition	299	Military Pensions.						
Brett, Edmund, (marine)	Same pay and emolument as a soldier of United States army.	13	2	Petition	270	Claims				Leave to withdraw.		
Bretty, Mary	Pension	16	1	Petition	92	Pens. & Rev. Cl'ms				Discharged; referred to Sec. War.		
Breuil, Francis, heirs of	Indemnity for French spoliations prior to 1800.	26	1	Memorial	182	Foreign Affairs	343	Favorable	319	Referred to Committee Whole House.		
Breuil, C. F	(See Francis Breuil, heirs of)	26	1		182		343		319			
Brevard, Joseph	Payment of revolutionary certificate.	3	2	Petition	295					Laid on table.		
Brevard, Joseph	Payment of revolutionary certificate.	4	1	Petition	409	Claims.						
Brevard, Joseph	Payment of revolutionary certificate.	4	2	Resolution	614	Claims	Feb. 2, 1797	Adverse		Leave to withdraw.		
Brevard, Joseph	Payment of revolutionary certificate.	11	2	Petition	305	Claims.						
Brevard, Joseph	Payment of revolutionary certificate.	13	2	Senate bill	370	Pens. & Rev. Cl'ms.	Mar. 30, 1814	With't amend.	S. 42	Passed	Passed	App'd April 13, 1814
Brevelle, Jean Baptiste	Confirmation of title to land in Louisiana.	22	2	Petition	41	Priv. Land Claims.						

List of private claims presented to the House of Representatives of the United States from the 1st to the 31st Congress, inclusive—Continued.

Names of claimants.	Nature or object of the claim.	Congress.	Session.	How brought before the House of Reps.	Page of journal.	To what committee of the House referred.	No. or date of the report.	Nature of the report.	No. of the bill.	How disposed of by the House of Reps.	How disposed of by the Senate.	Date of the act of Congress, and remarks.
Brevelle, Jean Baptiste...	Confirmation of title to land in Louisiana.	23	1	Petition	586	Priv. Land Claims.						
Brevelle, Jean Baptiste...	Confirmation of title to land in Louisiana.	23	2	Petition	49	Priv. Land Claims.						
Brevoort, Abraham N. ...	Pension for disability in public service.	25	3	Petition	460	Invalid Pensions.						
Brevoort, Abraham N. ...	Pension for disability in public service.	26	1	Petition	162	Invalid Pensions...	250	Adverse	......	Laid on table.		
Brevoort, Henry	(See Thomas L. Ogden & others)	17	1	....	38							
Brevoort, Henry B.......	Compensation for lumber taken for public use.	17	1	Petition	82	Claims	Feb. 7, 1822	Adverse	......	Referred to Committee Whole House.		
Brevoort, Henry B.......	Compensation for lumber taken for public use.	18	1	Petition	114	Claims.						
Brevoort, Henry B.......	Compensation for lumber taken for public use.	20	1	Petition	52	Public Lands.						
Brevoort, Henry B.......	Compensation for lumber taken for public use.	23	1	Resolution	643	Claims	June 23, 1834	Adverse	......	Laid on table.		
Brevoort, Henry B.......	Compensation for lumber taken for public use.	23	2	Petition	59	Claims.						
Brevoort, Henry, jr.......	Deduction of 30 per cent. on certain duties.	14	1	Petition	562	Com. and Manuf..	....	....	......	Discharged; laid on table.		
Brevoort, John W.	Release from judgment for an escape.	10	1	Petition	146	Claims.						
Brewer, Aaron..........	Compensation for loss by fire while light-house keeper.	27	2	Petition	535	Claims...........	698	Adverse	......	Laid on table.		
Brewer, Barrett	Pension for revolutionary services.	28	1	Petition	204	Rev. Pensions	....	....	......	Discharged; laid on table.		
Brewer, Eliab, surety of...	Release from liability on bond to United States.	8	2	Petition	145	Claims.						
Brewer, F. W...........	Location of a certain claim on public land.	24	1	Petition	425	Priv. Land Claims.	....	....	......	Discharged; laid on table.		
Brewer, F. W...........	Location of a certain claim on public land.	25	2	Petition	374	Priv. Land Claims.	....	....	......	Discharged; laid on table.		
Brewer, George	Confirmation of title to land	12	1	Petition	13	Public Lands.						
Brewer, George	Location of a Spanish grant......	14	1	Petition	49	Public Lands.						
Brewer, George	Location of a Spanish grant......	14	2	Petition	50	Public Lands.						
Brewer, George	Confirmation of title to land in Alabama territory.	15	1	Petition	226	Priv. Land Claims.	Feb. 18, 1818	Favorable....	92	Passed	Passed	App'd April 9, 1818
Brewer, George	(See Richard S. Bryan and G. B.)	9	1	....	296							
Brewer, James, (Ohio.)...	Reimbursement of money paid for public land.	24	1	Resolution	485	Public Lands	466	Favorable....	473	Referred to Committee Whole House.		
Brewer, James, (Ohio.)...	Reimbursement of money paid for public land.	25	2	Resolution	42	Public Lands.						
Brewer, James, (Ohio.)...	Reimbursement of money paid for public land.	26	1	Petition	178	Public Lands.....	77	Favorable....	65	Passed	Passed	App'd May 2, 1840
Brewer, James, (Ohio.)...	Indemnity for land purchased patented to another.	26	1	Petition	610	Priv. Land Claims.	April 4, 1840	Adverse	......	Laid on table.		
Brewer, James H.	Indemnity for loss in arresting pirates.	22	1	Petition	43	Judiciary	409	Favorable....	509	Referred to Committee Whole House.		
Brewer, James H.	Indemnity for loss in arresting pirates.	23	1	Petition	34	Claims	9	Favorable....	9	Passed.............	Passed	App'd Feb. 5, 1834
Brewer, John..........	Pension for revolutionary services	23	1	Petition	46	Rev. Claims.						

List of private claims presented to the House of Representatives of the United States from the 1st to the 31st Congress, inclusive—**Continued.**

Names of claimants.	Nature or object of the claim.	Congress.	Session.	How brought before the House of Reps.	Page of journal.	To what committee of the House referred.	No. or date of the report.	Nature of the report.	No. of the bill.	How disposed of by the House of Reps.	How disposed of by the Senate.	Date of the act of Congress, and remarks.
Brewer, John	Compensation for horse, &c., lost in public service.	24	1	Petition	430	Claims.						
Brewster, Caleb	Pension for wounds, and reimbursement of expenses, Revolution.	1	2	Rep. of Secretary War.	193	Select	July 16, 1790	Pension bill	88	Passed	Passed	App'd April 11, 1790
Brewster, Caleb	Compensation for special revolutionary services.	19	1	Petition	291	Rev. Claims	April 5, 1826	Adverse		Laid on table.		
Brewster, Daniel	Pension for disabilities in war of 1812.	21	1	Resolution	90	Military Pensions.						
Brewster, F. & W., and others.	Reimbursement of advances on Indian goods.	21	1	Petition	151	Indian Affairs.						
Brewster, Henry, (N. Y.)	Pension	20	1	Petition	337	Military Pensions	Mar. 18, 1828	Adverse		Laid on table.		
Brewster, Timothy	Compensation for revolutionary supplies.	7	2	Petition	285	Claims	Feb. 23, 1803	Favorable		Referred to Committee Whole House.		Leave to withdraw, 8th Con., 1st sess.
Brian, Stephen	Pension for disability in war of 1812.	29	1	Memorial	466	Invalid Pensions	664	Adverse		Laid on table.		
Briant, Joseph	Reimbursement of duties on importation to Castine.	16	1	Senate bill	108	Ways and Means	Jan. 14, 1820	With't amend	S. 13	Passed	Passed	App'd April 11, 1820
Brice, Henry	Pension for disability in war of 1812.	24	1	Petition	275	Invalid Pensions				Discharged; laid on table.		
Brice, Henry	Pension for disability in war of 1812.	24	2	Documents	311	Invalid Pensions				Discharged; laid on table.		
Brice, Henry	Pension for disability in war of 1812.	25	2	Petition	71	Invalid Pensions				Discharged; laid on table.		
Brice, Henry	Pension for disability in war of 1812.	28	2	Petition	337	Invalid Pensions.						
Brice, Howell	(See assignees of Henry Davis)	21	1		85							
Brice, James	(See Benjamin Wells and others)	13	3		521							
Brice, John	(See assignees of Henry Davis)	21	1		85							
Brice, John M	(See George B. Russell, *et al.*)											
Brice, Lawson S	Remission of duties on goods reimported.	22	1	Petition	74	Commerce	172	Adverse		Laid on table.		
Brickell, J. J	Indemnity for French spoliations prior to 1800.	26	1	Memorial	182	Foreign Affairs	343	Favorable	319	Referred to Committee Whole House.		
Brickel, John	(See surety of John Hain)	15	1		307							
Brickel, Joseph, executor of.	Indemnity for French spoliations prior to 1800.	26	1	Memorial	182	Foreign Affairs	343		319	Referred to Committee Whole House.		
Brickel, Sarah	Indemnity for French spoliations prior to 1800.	24	2	Petition	154	Foreign Affairs.						
Brickel, Thomas, (N. C.)	Indemnity for revolutionary injuries.	8	2	Petition	151	Claims.						
Brickel, Thomas, (N. C.)	Indemnity for revolutionary injuries.	11	2	Petition	136	Claims	Dec. 20, 1809	Adverse		Laid on table.		
Brickhouse, John N	(See administrator of Covington Simkins.)	31	1		196							
Brickley, John	Right of pre emption to land in Missouri.	14	2	Petition	76	Public Lands.						
Brickley, John	Right of pre-emption to land in Missouri.	15	1	Petition	115	Priv. Land Claims.						
Brident, Alexander	Confirmation of title to land in Missouri.	15	1	Petition	371	Priv. Land Claims.						
Bridge, Nathan	(See Thomas K. Jones and others)	9	1		324							
Bridges, Frances Ann	Pension for revolutionary services of husband.	19	1	Resolution	76	Military Pensions	April 1, 1826	Adverse		Laid on table.		

List of p ivate claims presented to the House of Representatives of the United States from the 1st to the 31st Congress, inclusive—Continued.

Names of claimants.	Nature or object of the claim.	Congress.	Session.	How brought before the House of Reps.	Page of journal.	To what committee of the House referred.	No. or date of the report.	Nature of the report.	No. of the bill.	How disposed of by the House of Reps.	How disposed of by the Senate.	Date of the act of Congress, and remarks.
Bridget, James	Pension for revolutionary services	12	1	Pension bill	361	Whole House	June 15, 1812	With't amend.	138	Passed	Passed	App'd July 5, 1812
Bridgwood, Samuel	Release from imprisonment	14	2	Petition	184	Ways and Means.						
Brien, Nathaniel M	Compensation for horses lost in public service.	18	2	Petition	229	Claims.						
Brigance, James, (Ten.)	Compensation for services in Indian wars.	22	1	Petition	288	Claims	March 1, 1832	Adverse	......	Laid on table.		
Brigg, Sally	Compensation for revolutionary services of husband.	24	2	Petition	153	Rev. Pensions.						
Briggs, Abiezer, (Mass.)	Pension	16	1	Petition	32	Pens. & Rev. Cl'ms.						
Briggs, Abiezer, (Mass.)	Pension	21	1	Petition	46	Military Pensions	April 7, 1830	Adverse	......	Laid on table.		
Briggs, Abraham, heirs of	Balance of pension	23	1	Petition	215	Rev. Pension.						
Briggs, Abraham, widow of	Continuation of pension	27	2	Petition	238	Rev. Pensions	784	Adverse	......	Laid on table.		
Briggs, Arnold, widow of	Pension for revolutionary services	28	2	Petition	193	Rev. Pensions.						
Briggs, Benjamin	Pension for revolutionary services	24	1	Resolution	822	Rev. Pensions	....	....	......	Discharged; laid on table.		
Briggs, Benjamin	Pension for revolutionary services	24	2	Resolution	56	Rev. Pensions	....	....	......	Discharged; laid on table.		
Briggs, Burton	Pension for revolutionary services	3	1	Rep. of Secretary War.	131	Select	May 26, 1794	Res. to refer to Sec. War.	R. 12	Passed	Passed	App'd June 9, 1794
Briggs, Darius	Pension for revolutionary services	21	1	Resolution	254	Military Pensions.						
Briggs, Darius	Pension for revolutionary services	22	1	Petition	412	Rev. Pensions.						
Briggs, David	Compensation for services in Indian wars.	17	1	Petition	234	Pens. & Rev. Cl'ms.	Feb. 15, 1822	Adverse	......	Rejected.		
Briggs, David	Compensation for services in Indian wars.	19	2	Petition	78	Rev. Claims	Jan. 4, 1821	Adverse	......	Laid on table.		
Briggs, David	Compensation for services in Indian wars.	21	2	Petition	106	Military Pensions.						
Briggs, Douglass	Pension	24	1	Petition	426	Invalid Pensions	April 15, 1836	Adverse	......	Laid on table.		
Briggs, Edmund	Bounty on fishing sch'r "Phebe"	8	1	Petition	860	Com. and Manuf.						
Briggs, Edmund	Bounty on fishing sch'r "Phebe"	8	2	Petition	89	Com. and Manuf.	Feb. 15, 1805	Favorable	62	Passed	Passed	App'd March 3, 1805
Briggs, Edmund	Bounty on fishing sch'r "Phebe"	10	.	Petition	208	Com. and Manuf.	....	....	.....	Discharged; referred to Sec. Treasury.		
				Rep. of Secretary Treasury.	287	....	....	....	......	Laid on table.		
Briggs, Edmund	Bounty on fishing sch'r "Phebe"	10	2	Rep. of Secretary Treasury.	476	Com. and Manuf	....	....	......	Discharged; leave to withdraw.		
Briggs, Edmund	Revisal of act for relief of Robert Patton and others.	9	1	Petition	192	Com. and Manuf.						
Briggs, Edmund	Revisal of act for relief of Robert Patton and others.	9	2	Petition	481	Com. and Manuf.	Jan. 8, 1807	Favorable	170	Passed	Passed	App'd Feb. 10, 1807
Briggs, Edmund	Pension	21	2	Petition	87	Military Pensions.						
Briggs, Gideon	To be restored to pension roll	17	1	Petition	5	Rev. Pensions.						
Briggs, Isaac	Compensation for exploring mail route.	8	2	Petition	153	Ways and Means.						
Briggs, Isaac	Compensation for exploring mail route.	9	1	Resolution	293	P. O. & P. Roads.						
Briggs, Isaac	Compensation for exploring mail route.	9	2	Petition	569	Claims	Feb. 20, 1807	Favorable	210	Referred to Committee Whole House.		
Briggs, Isaac	Compensation for exploring mail route.	10	1	Petition	158	Claims	Mar. 28, 1808	Favorable	81	Referred to Committee Whole House.		
Briggs, Isaac	Compensation for exploring mail ronte.	10	2	Petition	455	Claims	Jan. 23, 1809	Favorable	153	Referred to Committee Whole House.		

List of private claims presented to the House of Representatives of the United States from the 1st to the 31st Congress, inclusive—Continued.

Names of claimants.	Nature or object of the claim.	Congress.	Session.	How brought before the House of Reps.	Page of journal.	To what committee of the House referred.	No. or date of the report.	Nature of the report.	No. of the bill.	How disposed of by the House of Reps.	How disposed of by the Senate.	Date of the act of Congress, and remarks.
Briggs, Isaac	Compensation for exploring mail route.	11	2	Petition	165	Claims	Jan. 17, 1810	Favorable	64	Rejected.		
Briggs, Isaac	Compensation for exploring mail route.	14	2	Senate bill	553					Laid on table.		
Briggs, Isaac	Compensation for exploring mail route.	15	1	Senate bill	190	Claims	Feb. 11, 1818	With't amend	S. 14	Passed	Passed	App'd Apr. 18, 1818
Briggs, Jehoshaphat	Pension for services in the war of 1812.	26	1	Petition	836	Rev. Pensions	225	Favorable	237	Referred to Committee Whole House.		
Briggs, Jehoshaphat	Pension for services in the war of 1812.	27	2	Petition	60	Invalid Pensions	256	Favorable	222	Passed	Passed	App'd Aug. 23, 1842
Briggs, John, heirs of	Pension for revolutionary services.	26	1	Petition	360	Rev. Claims				Discharged; laid on table.		
Briggs, John (Ohio)	Reimbursement of an erroneous land payment.	25	2	Memorial	1119	Priv. Land Claims.						
Briggs, John (Ohio)	Reimbursement of an erroneous land payment.	26	1	Memorial	179	Priv. Land Claims.						
Briggs, Dr. John P.	Pension for naval services	24	1	Petition	1035	Invalid Pensions.						
Briggs, Dr. John P.	Pension for naval services	24	2	Petition	48	Naval Affairs	148	Favorable	872	Passed	Passed	App'd Mar. 3, 1837
Briggs, Joseph	Pension for revolutionary services.	4	1	Petition	284	Claims.						
Briggs, Joseph	Pension for revolutionary services.	4	2	Petition	614	Claims	Jan. 29, 1797	Adverse		Laid on table.		
Briggs, Lemuel	Pension for revolutionary services.	15	1	Petition	43	Pens. & Rev. Cl'ms.				Discharged; referred to Secretary of War.		
Briggs, Leonard	To be restored to pension roll	17	1	Petition	67	Rev. Pensions.						
Briggs, Nathaniel	Remission of penalty for violation of revenue law.	20	1	Petition	110	Commerce	96	Favorable	107	Passed	Passed	App'd May 24, 1828
Briggs, Solomon	Arrears of pension.	27	2	Petition	836	Rev. Pensions				Discharged; laid on table.		
Briggs, Tobias	(See Israel Pearce, heir of)	30	1		422							
Briggs, Zacheus, and others.	Increase of compensation as receivers of public monies.	8	1	Petition	500	Select				Discharged; laid on table.		
Brigham, Abraham	Pension for revolutionary services.	18	2	Resolution	218	Rev. Pensions	Feb. 24, 1825	Adverse		Laid on table.		
Brigham, Ebenezer	Right of pre-emption to mineral land, Michigan.	23	1	Petition	499	Public Lands.						
Brigham, James H.	Confirmation of title to land in Louisiana.	29	1	Petition	255	Priv. Land Claims.						
Brigham, James H.	(See Sarah Caldwell)	29	1		1031							
Brigham, Jonathan	Pension	20	2	Petition	26	Military Pensions				Discharged; referred to Com. Whole House.		
Brigham, Jonathan	Pension	21	1	Petition	47	Military Pensions	May 4, 1830	Adverse		Laid on table.		
Brigham, Lemuel	Right of pre-emption to land in Michigan.	23	1	Petition	568	Public Lands.						
Brigham, Lydia	Pension for revolutionary services of husband.	28	1	Petition	849	Rev. Pensions.						
Brigham, Robert	Exchange of military bounty land.	19	1	Petition	94	Public Lands	54	Favorable	77	Passed	Passed	App'd May 22, 1826
Brigham, Wm, widow of.	Pension for revolutionary services.	12	1	Petition	299	Claims.						
Bright, Charles	(See heirs of Robert Fulton)	26	1	Petition	293	Claims.						
Bright, Henry	Confirmation of title to land in Mobile.	23	1	Petition	499	Priv. Land Claims.						
Bright, Henry	Confirmation of title to land in Mobile.	23	2	Petition	68	Priv. Land Claims.	9	Favorable	579	Referred to Committee Whole House.		
Bright, John H.	(See heir of William Bright)	31	2		69							
Bright, William, heirs of.	Bounty land for revolutionary services.	31	2	Petition	69	Priv. Land Claims.						

List of private claims presented to the House of Representatives of the United States from the 1st to the 31st Congress, inclusive—Continued.

Names of claimants.	Nature or object of the claim.	Congress.	Session.	How brought before the House of Reps.	Page of journal.	To what committee of the House referred.	No. or date of the report.	Nature of the report.	No. of the bill.	How disposed of by the House of Reps.	How disposed of by the Senate.	Date of the act of Congress, and remarks.
25 Bright, Washington	(See Exploring Expedition)	27	3		149		270		818			
Bright, Washington	Extra allowance for services in Exploring Expedition.	28	2	Memorial	70	Naval Affairs.						
Brightwell, Alexander	Pension	27	2	Petition	348	Invalid Pensions	162	Adverse		Laid on table.		
Brightwell, Alexander	Pension	27	3	Petition	306	Invalid Pensions				Discharged; laid on table.		
Brightwell, Alexander	Pension	28	2	Petition	284	Invalid Pensions.						
Brightwell, Alexander	Pension	29	1	Petition	847	Invalid Pensions				Discharged; laid on table.		
Brightwell, Alexander	Increase and arrears of pension	31	2	Petition	157	Invalid Pensions.						
Brightwell, Theodore, administrator of.	Adjustment of accounts as marshal of Mississippi Territory.	19	2	Resolution	57	Ways and Means.						
Brightwell, Theodore, administrator of.	Adjustment of accounts as marshal of Mississippi Territory.	20	1	Resolution	279	Claims	April 23, 1828	Adverse		Laid on table.		
Brightwell, Theodore, administrator of.	Adjustment of accounts as marshal of Mississippi Territory.	20	2	Resolution	75	Judiciary.						
Brightwell, Theodore, administrator of.	Adjustment of accounts as marshal of Mississippi Territory.	21	1	Resolution	415	Judiciary.						
Brimfield, Richard B	(See Richard B. Brumfield.)											
Brimmer, Andrew	Payment of certain bills of credit.	4	1	Rep. of Secretary Treasury.	388	Claims	74	Adverse		Laid on table.		
Brimmer, Herman	Payment of certain bills of credit.	4	1	Rep. of Secretary Treasury.	388	Claims	74	Adverse		Laid on table.		
Brinck, Aaron	Pension	11	2	Pension bill	283	Whole House	Mar. 24, 1810	With amend.	107	Passed	Passed with amendment.	App'd April 27, 1810
Brindle, Jacob	Pension	25	2	Petition	167	Invalid Pensions.						
Brindle, Jacob	Pension	25	3	Petition	89	Invalid Pensions.						
Bringham, John	Location of a certain land claim	23	2	Petition	201	Public Lands.						
Bringham, Nancy	(See John Whitsitt)	29	1		353		311		249			
Bringier, Louis	Confirmation of title to land in Louisiana.	14	1	Petition	164	Public Lands.						
Bringman, Daniel	Pension for disability, war of 1812	30	1	Petition	980	Invalid Pensions.						
Bringman, Daniel	Pension for disability, war of 1812	30	2	Petition	203	Invalid Pensions.				Discharged; laid on table.		
Bringman, Daniel	Pension for disability, war of 1812	31	1	Petition	588	Invalid Pensions.						
Brink, Abigail	Pension for sufferings in Indian captivity.	23	1	Petition	110	Rev. Claims	Jan. 24, 1834	Adverse		Laid on table.		
Brink, John, widow of	Pension for revolutionary services.	29	1	Petition	1001	Rev. Pensions				Discharged; leave to withdraw.		
Brinker, Abram	(See Jacob Brinker, heir of)	28	1		441							
Brinker, Jacob, heir of	Payment of a revolutionary certificate.	28	1	Petition	441	Rev. Claims.						
Brinker, Jacob, heir of	Payment of a revolutionary certificate.	30	1	Petition	344	Rev. Claims	621	Adverse		Laid on table.		
Brinkerhoff, George	(See Joseph Howland, assignee of.)	26	1		182		343		319			
Brinkley, Capt. William	Commutation pay for revolutionary services.	25	2	Petition	392	Rev. Claims	1022	Adverse		Laid on table.		
Brinsfield, William	Pension for revolutionary services.	3	2	Rep. of Secretary of War.	337	Claims.						
Brinton, Anson, assignee of.	Compensation for forage on public account.	24	1	Petition	91	Claims.						
Brinton, John E	(See represent's of Lewis Clarke).											
Brisban, James	Duplicate land warrant	16	1	Petition	91	Priv. Land Claims				Disch'd; laid on table.		

List of private claims presented to the House of Representatives of the United States from the 1st to the 31st Congress, inclusive—Continued.

Names of claimants.	Nature or object of the claim.	Congress.	Session.	How brought before the House of Reps.	Page of journal.	To what committee of the House referred.	No. or date of the report.	Nature of the report.	No. of the bill.	How disposed of by the House of Reps.	How disposed of by the Senate.	Date of the act of Congress, and remarks.
Brisban, James	Duplicate land warrant	17	1	Petition	100	Priv. Land Claims.	39	Favorable	89	Passed	Passed	App'd May 7, 1822
Brisban, John	Pension	4	1	Petition	507	Claims	May 31, 1796	Adverse	......	Laid on table.		
Brisbois, Bernard W	Confirmation of title to land in Wisconsin.	27	2	Petition	1204	Public Lands.						
Brisbois, Michael	Indemnity for destruction of property by the enemy.	21	1	Petition	547	Claims	April 24, 1830	Adverse	......	Laid on table.		
Brisbois, Michael	Compensation for property taken for public use.	22	1	Petition	596	Claims.						
Brisbois, Michael	Compensation for property taken for public use.	23	2	Petition	59	Claims.						
Brisbois, Michael	Compensation for property taken for public use.	25	2	Petition	655	Claims	827	Adverse	......	Laid on table.		
Brisbois, Michael, representatives of.	Compensation for property taken for public use.	26	1	Petition	623	Claims.						
Brisbois, Michael, representatives of.	Compensation for property taken for public use.	26	2	Petition	167	Claims.						
Briscoe, Eliza	(See heirs of Peter B. Bruen)	29	1	....	233							
Briscoe, George W	(See George W. Biscoe.)											
Briscoe, Gerrard	Reimbursement of expenses incurred in recruiting.	6	2	Petition	805	Claims	....	....	......	Discharged; leave to withdraw.		
Briscoe, John H	Compensation for services as revolutionary surgeon.	26	1	Petition	960	Rev. Claims.						
Briscoe, John H	Compensation for services as revolutionary surgeon.	26	2	Petition	79	Claims.						
Briscoe, Samuel	(See James Corrie and others)	26	1	....	182							
Briscoe, William	(See heirs of Peter B. Bruen)	29	1	....	233							
Brish, David	Further provision for his support	21	1	Petition	295	Military Pensions.						
Brisland, John	Confirmation of title to land in Mississippi.	14	1	Petition	504	Public Lands.						
Brisland, John	Confirmation of title to land in Mississippi.	14	2	Petition	50	Priv. Land Claims.	....	....	......	....	....	Leave to withdraw, 18th Cong., 1st sess.
Brison, Hugh	Pension	20	1	Petition	223	Military Pensions.						
Brister, Aaron, widow of	Pension for revolutionary services.	29	1	Petition	1012	Rev. Pensions	....	....	......	Leave to withdraw.		
Bristol, Charles B	Payment of judgment against collector of Oswego.	24	1	Petition	405	Claims.						
Bristol, Charles B	Payment of judgment against collector of Oswego.	24	2	Petition	81	Claims	233	Adverse	......	Laid on table.		
Bristol, Dan	Indemnity for property destroyed by the enemy.	22	1	Petition	188	Claims	Feb. 6, 1832	Adverse	......	Laid on table.		
Bristol, John S	Pension for revolutionary services.	15	2	Petition	143	Pens. & Rev. Cl'ms.	....	....	......	Discharged; referred to Secretary of War.		
Bristol, Lyman	Pension	25	3	Petition	128	Invalid Pensions.						
Bristol, Lyman	Pension	26	1	Petition	160	Invalid Pensions	199	Favorable	211	Passed	Passed	App'd July 20, 1840
Bristol, Thomas	Increase of pension	10	1	Pension bill	232	Whole House	....	With amend.	78	Passed	Passed with amendment.	App'd April 25, 1808
Briston, William	Benefit of a certain act	17	1	Petition	33	Public Lands.						
Britt, Daniel	Compensation for supplies to revolutionary army.	6	1	Petition	571	Claims.						
Britt, Thomas	Remission of penalty as surety for collector, Edenton.	6	1	Petition	593	Com. and Manufac.						
Brittain, Jonathan	Pension for revolutionary services.	27	2	Petition	46	Rev. Pensions	106	Favorable	152	Passed	Indef. postp'd.	
Brittain, Jonathan	Pension for revolutionary services.	27	3	Petition	43	Rev. Pensions	7	Favorable	628	Passed	Passed	App'd March 3, 1843
Britten, James	Indemnity for goods seized under revenue laws.	15	2	Petition	55	Ways and Means.						

List of private claims presented to the House of Representatives of the United States from the 1*st to the* 31*st Congress, inclusive*—Continued.

Names of claimants.	Nature or object of the claim.	Congress.	Session.	How brought before the House of Reps.	Page of journal.	To what committee of the House referred.	No. or date of the report.	Nature of the report.	No. of the bill.	How disposed of by the House of Reps.	How disposed of by the Senate.	Date of the act of Congress, and remarks.
Britten, James	Indemnity for goods seized under revenue laws.	17	1	Petition	176	Ways and Means	Feb. 28, 1822	Favorable	99	Passed	Passed	App'd May 7, 1822
Brittingham, J. P.	Indemnity for seizure of brig Opher by Mexico.	31	1	Petition	742	Foreign Affairs	....	....	......	Leave to withdraw.		
Britton, Job	Pension for revolutionary services.	3	2	Rep. of Secretary War.	350	Claims.						
Britton, Job	Pension for revolutionary services.	4	1	Rep. of Secretary War.	373	Claims	Feb. 18, 1796	Pension bill	156	Passed	Passed	App'd April 20, 1796
Britton, Joseph	Arrears of pension	20	2	Resolution	72	Military Pensions.						
Broadbury, Hezekiah	Pension	21	2	Petition	53	Military Pensions.						
Broadfoot, William	(See Wm. Boyd, administrator of.)	26	1	....	182	....	343	....	319			
Broadfoot, William, heirs of	Indemnity for French spoliations prior to 1800.	29	2	Petition	87	Foreign Affairs.						
Broadus, James, heirs of	Commutation pay for revolutionary services.	22	1	Petition	62	Rev. Claims.						
Broadus, James, heirs of	Commutation pay for revolutionary services.	22	2	Petition	29	Rev. Claims.						
Broadus, James, heirs of	Commutation pay for revolutionary services.	23	1	Petition	334	Rev. Claims.						
Broadus, James, heirs of	Commutation pay for revolutionary services.	23	2	Petition	199	Rev. Claims.						
Broadus, James, heirs of	Commutation pay for revolutionary services.	24	2	Petition	39	Rev. Claims	276	Adverse	......	Laid on table.		
Broadus, James, heirs of	Commutation pay for revolutionary services.	25	2	Petition	72	Rev. Claims	670	Favorable	648	Passed	Adverse report.	
Broadus, James, heirs of	Commutation pay for revolutionary services.	25	3	Petition	188	Rev. Claims	105	Favorable	980	Referred to Committee Whole House.		
Broadus, James, heirs of	Commutation pay for revolutionary services.	26	1	Petition	165	Rev. Claims.						
Broadus, James, heirs of	Commutation pay for revolutionary services.	26	2	Petition	134	Rev. Claims.						
Broadus, James, heirs of	Commutation pay for revolutionary services.	27	2	Petition	96	Rev. Claims	773	Adverse	......	Laid on table.		
Broadus, James, heirs of	Commutation pay for revolutionary services.	31	1	Petition	256	Rev. Pensions	128	Adverse	......	Laid on table.		
Broadus, Martha R	Revolutionary pension	31	2	Petition	145	Rev. Pensions.						
Broadus, William, (Va.)	Compensation for revolutionary services.	18	1	Petition	60	Pens. & Rev. Cl'ms.	Dec. 23, 1823	Adverse	......	Laid on table.		
Broadus, William, (Va.)	Increase of compensation as military storekeeper, Harper's Ferry.	18	2	Petition	41	Military Affairs.						
Broadus, William, sureties of.	Release from liability	22	2	Petition	397	Claims.						
Broadwater, Charles L	Increase of pension	25	2	Petition	547	Rev. Pensions	....	....	......	Discharged; laid on table.		
Broadwater, Charles L	Increase of pension	26	1	Petition	171	Rev. Pensions	....	....	......	Discharged; laid on table.		
Broadwater, Charles L	Increase of pension	27	2	Petition	58	Rev. Pensions	784	Adverse	......	Laid on table.		
Broadwill, Noah	Indemnity for destruction of property at Plattsburgh.	13	3	Petition	723	Claims	Feb. 15, 1815	Favorable	297	Passed	Passed	App'd March 3, 1815
Broadwood, James	Compensation for revolutionary services.	2	1	Petition	489	....	....	....	......	Referred to Secretary War.		
Brobson, James, deceased, sureties of.	Equitable settlement of accounts as Marshal, District of Columbia.	24	1	Senate bill	601	Claims	April 5, 1836	With amend.	166	Passed with amendm't	Passed as am'd.	App'd July 2, 1836

List of private claims presented to the House of Representatives of the United States from the 1st to the 31st Congress, inclusive—Continued.

Names of claimants.	Nature or object of the claim.	Congress.	Session.	How brought before the House of Reps.	Page of journal.	To what committee of the House referred.	No. or date of the report.	Nature of the report.	No. of the bill.	How disposed of by the House of Reps.	How disposed of by the Senate.	Date of the act of Congress, and remarks.
Brobson, James, *et al.*	Indemnity for French spoliations prior to 1800.	26	1	Memorial	182	Foreign Affairs	343	Favorable	319	Referred to Committee Whole House.		
Brock, Samuel, widow of.	Pension	26	1	Petition	1115	Invalid Pensions.						
Brockenbrough, Austin	Compensation for horses taken for public use.	25	2	Petition	200	Claims.						
Brockenbrough, Austin	Compensation for horses taken for public use.	26	1	Petition	169	Claims	369	Adverse	......	Laid on table.		
Brockenbrough, Austin	Compensation for horses taken for public use.	29	1	Petition	647	Claims.						
Brockway, Benjamin	Pension for revolutionary services.	13	1	Pension bill	56	Whole House	July 20, 1813	With amend.	31	Passed	Passed with amendment.	App'd Aug. 2, 1813
Brockway, W. H	(See administrator of John and Susan Johnston.)	30	1	....	685	....	677					
Brockwell, Archibald	Pension	25	2	Petition	588	Invalid Pensions	April 10, 1830	Adverse	......	Laid on table.		
Brodhead, Colonel Daniel, heirs of.	Commutation pay for revolutionary services.	31	2	Petition	36	Rev. Claims.						
Brodhead, Daniel, heirs of.	Commutation pay for revolutionary services.	31	2	Petition	44	Rev. Claims.						
Brodhead, Daniel D., assignee of.	Reimbursement of amount paid for apprehending deserters.	26	1	Petition	702	Claims	655	Favorable	492	Referred to Committee Whole House.		
Brodhead, John M	(See assignee of Daniel D. Brodhead.)	26	1	....	702							
Brodhead, Luke	Arrears of pension for revolutionary services.	6	2	Petition	757	Claims	Jan. 19, 1801	Adverse.				
Brodhead, Luke, widow of.	Pension for revolutionary services.	9	2	Petition	559	Claims.						
Brodhead, Luke, widow of.	Pension for revolutionary services.	11	2	Petition	165	Claims	Feb. 7, 1810	Favorable	......	Referred to Committee Whole House.		
Brodie, Alexander O	(See agent of Louis Mark)	21	1	....	170	....	160	....	204			
Brodie, Charles D	Compensation for a naval invention.	18	2	Petition	137	Naval Affairs	Feb. 4, 1825	Favorable	318	Passed	Passed	App'd March 3, 1825
Brodock, Bartholomew, heirs of.	Pension for revolutionary services.	29	1	Petition	85	Rev. Pensions	687	Adverse	......	Laid on table.		
Brokan, Richard	Pension	21	2	Petition	43	Military Pensions.						
Bromaghin, William	Pension	28	1	Petition	788	Invalid Pensions.						
Bronaugh, John B. administrator of.	Indemnity for French spoliations prior to 1800.	26	1	Memorial	182	Foreign Affairs	343	Favorable	319	Referred to Committee Whole House.		
Bronaugh, John T., and A. Fleming.	Extra compensation for mail services.	27	2	Petition	747	P. Of. & P. Roads.	....	....	......	Discharged; leave to withdraw.		
Bronaugh, John W., widow of.	Release of a certain judgment	25	3	Petition	456	Foreign Affairs.						
Bronaugh, John W., widow of.	Release of a certain judgment	26	1	Petition	182	Foreign Affairs	343	General bill	319	Referred to Committee Whole House.		
Bronaugh, John W., widow of.	Release of a certain judgment	26	2	Petition	36	Foreign Affairs	....	....	......	Discharged; laid on table.		
Bronaugh, John W., widow of.	Release of a certain judgment	27	2	Petition	63	Judiciary	....	....	......	Discharged; laid on table.		
Bronaugh, John W., widow of.	Release of a certain judgment	28	1	Petition	514	Judiciary.						
Bronaugh, John W., widow of.	Release of a certain judgment	28	2	Petition	87	Judiciary.						
Bronaugh, John W., administrator of.	Indemnity for French spoliations prior to 1800.	24	1	Memorial	202	Foreign Affairs.						
Bronaugh, John W., administrator of.	Indemnity for French spoliations prior to 1800.	26	1	Memorial	182	Foreign Affairs	343	Favorable	319	Referred to Committee Whole House.		

List of private claims presented to the House of Representatives of the United States from the 1st to the 31st Congress, inclusive—Continued.

Names of claimants.	Nature or object of the claim.	Congress.	Session.	How brought before the House of Reps.	Page of journal.	To what committee of the House referred.	No. or date of the report.	Nature of the report.	No. of the bill.	How disposed of by the House of Reps.	How disposed of by the Senate.	Date of the act of Congress, and remarks.
Bronaugh, J. W., and J. Talbot.	Extension of their patent	19	2	Resolution	226	Judiciary.						
Bronaugh, J. W., and J. Talbot.	Extension of thelr patent	20	1	Petition	128	Judiciary.						
Bronaugh, Thomas	Pension	25	2	Petition	920	Invalid Pensions.						
Bronough, Thomas	Pension	25	3	Petition	218	Invalid Pensions.						
Bronaugh, Thomas	Pension	26	1	Petition	326	Invalid Pensions	July 21, 1840	Adverse	......	Laid on table.		
Bronaugh, Thomas	Pension	28	2	Petition	193	Invalid Pensions	77	Favorable	561	Passed	Passed	App'd March 3, 1845
Bronson, Alwin, & others	Indemnity for vessels impressed and captured.	15	1	Petition	433	Claims.						
Bronson, Alwin, & others	Indemnity for vessels impressed and captured.	16	1	Petition	23	Claims	81	Adverse	......	Referred to Committee Whole House.		
Bronson, Alwin, & others	Indemnity for vessels impressed and captured.	16	2	Petition	40	Claims	39	Adverse	......	Referred to Committee Whole House.		
Bronson, Alwin, & others	Indemnity for vessels impressed and captured.	17	1	Petition	106	Claims	40	Adverse	......	Rejected.		
Bronson, Alwin, & others	Indemnity for vessels impressed and captured.	18	1	Petition	47	Claims	Jan. 7, 1824	Favorable	40	Passed	Passed	App'd May 17, 1824
Bronson, Frederick	Reimbursement of duties erroneously paid.	26	1	Petition	712	Ways and Means.						
Bronson, Frederick	Reimbursement of duties erroneously paid.	26	2	Petition	120	Ways and Means.						
Bronson, Frederick	Reimbursement of duties erroneously paid.	27	2	Petition	55	Ways and Means	907	Adverse	......	Laid on table.		
Bronson, Isaac	Commutation pay for revolutionary services.	24	2	Senate bill	250	Rev. Claims	259	Adverse	S. 51	Referred to Committee Whole House.		
Bronson, Isaac	Commutation pay for revolutionary services.	25	2	Senate bill	605	Rev. Claims	May 11, 1838	With amend.	S. 134	Referred to Committee Whole House.		
Bronson, John	Indemnity for property taken by the enemy.	29	2	Senate bill	380	Claims	Feb. 26, 1847	With amend.	S. 141	Referred to Committee Whole House.		
Bronson, Samuel	Compensation for timber taken for public use.	13	2	Petition	299	Claims	Mar. 7, 1814	Favorable	......	Laid on table.		
Bronson, Townsend, & Co.	(See Rufus Spalding and others)	15	2	....	148							
Brooke, Edmund	Depreciation pay and compensation for revolutionary services.	5	2	Petition	123	Claims	April 18, 1798	Adverse.				
Brooke, Edmund	Depreciation pay and compensation for revolutionary services.	7	2	Petition	316	Claims	Feb. 26, 1803	....	......	Postponed.		
Brooke, Edmund	Depreciation pay and compensation for revolutionary services.	8	1	Petition	458	Whole House.						
Brooke, Edmund	Depreciation pay and compensation for revolutionary services.	8	2	Petition	6	Claims.						
Brooke, Edmund	Depreciation pay and compensation for revolutionary services.	9	1	Petition	189	Claims	Mar. 28, 1806	Indefinite	......	Leave to withdraw.		
Brooke, Edmund	Depreciation pay and compensation for revolutionary services.	10	1	Petition	52	Select.						
Brooke, Edmund	Depreciation pay and compensation for revolutionary services.	11	2	Petition	277	Claims	April 9, 1810	Favorable	......	Referred to Committee Whole House.		
Brooke, Edmund	Depreciation pay and compensation for revolutionary services.	11	3	Petition	439	Claims	Jan. 19, 1811	Favorable	......	Referred to Committee Whole House.		
Brooke, Edmund	Depreciation pay and compensation for revolutionary services.	12	1	Petition	32	Claims.						
Brooke, Edmund	Depreciation pay and compensation for revolutionary services.	15	1	Petition	24	Pens. & Rev. Clm's.	Dec. 23, 1817	Adverse	......	Laid on table.		

List of private claims presented to the House of Representatives of the United States from the 1st to the 31st Congress, inclusive—Continued.

Names of claimants.	Nature or object of the claim.	Congress.	Session.	How brought before the House of Reps.	Page of journal.	To what committee of the House referred.	No. or date of the report.	Nature of the report.	No. of the bill.	How disposed of by the House of Reps.	How disposed of by the Senate.	Date of the act of Congress, and remarks.
Brooke, Edmund	Pay and commutation for revolutionary services.	18	2	Resolution	38	Pens. & Rev. Cl'ms.	19	Adverse	......	Referred to Committee Whole House.		
Brooke, Edmund	Pay and commutation for revolutionary services.	19	1	Petition	204	Military Pensions.	227	Favorable	278	Referred to Committee Whole House.		
Brooke, Edmund	Pay and commutation for revolutionary services.	20	1	Petition	39	Rev. Claims	107	Adverse	......	Laid on table.		
Brooke, Edmund	Pay and commutation for revolutionary services.	21	1	Petition	50	Rev. Claims	236	Favorable	295	Referred to Committee Whole House.		
Brooke, Edmund	Pay and commutation for revolutionary services.	21	2	House bill	340	....	....	....	295	Passed.		
Brooke, Edmund	Pay and commutation for revolutionary services.	22	1	Petition	29	Rev. Claims	219	Favorable	291	Passed	Passed	App'd May 25, 1832
Brooke, F. J.	Compensation for horse taken by Indians.	21	2	Senate bill	245	Military Affairs	Feb. 8, 1831	With't amend.	S. 102	Passed	Passed	App'd March 3, 1831
Brooke, George	Indemnity for property destroyed by the enemy.	18	1	Resolution	208	Claims.						
Brooke, George M.	Equitable settlement of his accounts.	15	2	Petition	250	Claims	Feb. 23, 1819	Favorable	328	Passed	Passed	App'd March 3, 1819
Brooke, George M., agent of.	Half of judgment against Walden and others.	20	1	Senate bill	604	Ways and Means.	May 24, 1828	With't amend.	S. 136	Passed	Passed	App'd May 26, 1827
Brooke, James, and others.	Remission of the penalty on a certain bond.	15	1	Petition	367	Ways and Means.						
Brooke, James, and others.	Remission of the penalty on a certain bond.	17	2	Petition	74	Claims.						
Brooke, James, and others.	Release from judgment on a contract.	17	2	Petition	82	Claims.						
Brooke, James, and others.	Additional compensation for arms furnished on contract.	17	1	Petition	156	Claims.						
Brooke, James, and others.	Additional compensation for arms furnished on contract.	18	1	Petition	198	Claims	April 28, 1824	Favorable	207	Passed	Passed	App'd May 19, 1824
Brooke, Jehu	(See James Brooke and others)	15	1	....	367							
Brooke, Lawrence	Commutation pay as revolutionary surgeon.	7	1	Petition	160	Claims	April 3, 1802	Favorable	......	Postponed.		
Brooke, Lawrence, heirs of	Prize-money as surgeon to Paul Jones.	24	1	Petition	61	Naval Affairs.						
Brooke, Lawrence, heirs of	Prize-money as surgeon to Paul Jones.	24	2	Petition	40	Rev. Claims.						
Brooke, Lawrence, heirs of	Prize-money as surgeon to Paul Jones.	25	2	....	199	Foreign Affairs	389	Favorable	......	Referred to President United States.		
Brooke, Lawrence, heirs of	Prize-money as surgeon to Paul Jones.	25	3	Petition	90	Foreign Affairs.						
Brooke, Lawrence, heirs of	Prize-money as surgeon to Paul Jones.	26	1	Petition	182	Foreign Affairs.						
Brooke, Lawrence, heirs of	Prize-money as surgeon to Paul Jones.	26	2	Petition	99	Rev. Claims.						
Brooke, Lawrence, heirs of	Prize-money as surgeon to Paul Jones.	27	2	Petition	60	Rev. Claims	1058	Adverse	......	Laid on table.		
Brooke, Lawrence, heirs of	Prize-money as surgeon to Paul Jones.	28	1	Petition	216	Rev. Pensions.						
Brooke, Lawrence, heirs of	Prize-money as surgeon to Paul Jones.	29	1	Petition	939	Naval Affairs.						
Brooke, Nathaniel	(See James Brooke and others)	15	1	....	367							
Brooke, Robert	(See heirs of Michael Fenwick)	19	1	....	131							

List of private claims presented to the House of Representatives of the United States from the 1st to the 31st Congress, inclusive—Continued.

Names of claimants.	Nature or object of the claim.	Congress.	Session.	How brought before the House of Reps.	Page of journal.	To what committee of the House referred.	No. or date of the report.	Nature of the report.	No. of the bill.	How disposed of by the House of Reps.	How disposed of by the Senate.	Date of the act of Congress, and remarks.
Brooke, Samuel B	Pension for wounds in naval service	15	1	Petition	144	Naval Affairs	Mar. 9, 1818	Adverse		Laid on table.		
Brooke, Thomas	Pension for naval services	31	2	Petition	281	Invalid Pensions.						
Brooke, William	Pension for revolutionary services.	23	1	Resolution	161	Rev. Pensions.						
Brookfield, N	(See Rasselas Whitcomb & others)	25	2		1047		960					
Brookhouser, Mary	Revolutionary pension	26	1	Resolution	662	Rev. Pensions.						
				Documents	737	Rev. Pensions.						
Brookhouser, Mary	Revolutionary pension	27	2	Petition	153	Rev. Pensions	784	Adverse		Laid on table.		
Brookings, Henry	Reimbursement of penalty for violation of revenue laws.	26	1	Petition	199	Commerce.						
Brookon, John	Pension	29	1	Petition	275	Invalid Pensions.						
Brookover, Jacob	Pension	27	2	Petition	699	Invalid Pensions.						
Brooks, Alexander S	Payment of certain emoluments	23	1	Petition	36	Military Affairs.						
Brooks, Almarin	To be restored to pension roll	17	1	Petition	51	Rev. Pensions.						
Brooks, Almarin	To be restored to pension roll	17	2	Petition	99	Whole House				Leave to withdraw.		
Brooks, Almarin, widow of	Pension for revolutionary services.	21	1	Petition	99	Military Pensions.						
Brooks, Bartemas	(See Martin S. Aikin *et al.*)	17	1		359							
Brooks, Benjamin, child of.	Commutation pay for revolutionary services.	27	2	Memorial	441	Rev. Claims	640	Adverse		Laid on table.		
Brooks, Caleb	Indemnity in land for forfeiture in Canada.	15	2	Petition	58					Referred to Secretary War.		
Brooks, Caleb D	Compensation for horse lost in the Florida war.	28	1	Petition	262	Claims.						
Brooks, Christopher	Additional compensation for prosecuting mail robbers.	20	2	Petition	264	Claims.						
Brooks, Christopher	Additional compensation for prosecuting mail robbers.	22	1	Senate bill	715	Claims	May 21, 1832	With't amend.	S. 81	Passed	Passed	App'd July 14, 1832
Brooks, Cornelius (N. Y.)	Compensation for masts furnished navy.	9	1	Petition	190	Secretary of Navy.	Dec. 13, 1805			Adverse.		
				Rep. of Secretary Navy.	197					Claim rejected.		
Brooks, Cornelius (N. Y.)	Compensation for masts furnished navy.	19	2	Petition	84	Claims	Feb. 2 1827	Adverse		Laid on table.		
Brooks, Cornelius (N. Y.)	Pension	19	2	Petition	104	Military Pensions.						
Brooks, Cornelius (N. Y.)	Pension	21	1	Petition	260	Military Pensions.						
Brooks, Cornelius (N. Y.)	Pension	22	1	Petition	188	Rev. Pensions.						
Brooks, David	Pension for revolutionary services.	21	1	Petition	197	Military Pensions.	353	Favorable	417	Passed	Passed	App'd May 29, 1830
Brooks, David	Arrears of pension	21	2	Petition	88	Military Pensions.	Jan. 18, 1831	Adverse		Referred to Committee Whole House.		
Brooks, David	Arrears of pension	22	1	Petition	131	Rev. Pensions	273	Favorable	351	Passed	Passed	App'd July 4, 1832
Brooks, David	Commutation pay for revolutionary services.	23	1	Petition	71	Rev. Claims.						
Brooks, David	Commutation pay for revolutionary services.	23	2	Petition	113	Rev. Claims				Discharged; leave to withdraw.		
Brooks, David, widow of.	Pension for revolutionary services.	27	2	Petition	524	Rev. Pensions	799	Favorable	453	Ordered to 3d reading.		
Brooks, David, widow of.	Pension for revolutionary services.	27	3	House bill	88				453	Passed	Indef. postp'd.	
Brooks, David	(See Daniel Neil, heirs of.)	22	1		288		309		389			
Brooks, Ebenezer	Compensation for revolutionary services.	2	1	Petition	467					Referred to Secretary of War.		
Brooks, Ebenezer	Compensation for revolutionary services.	3	2	Rep. of Secretary War.	337	Claims.						
Brooks, Ebenezer	Compensation for revolutionary services.	4	1	Rep. of Secretary War.	373	Claims.						

List of private claims presented to the House of Representatives of the United States from the 1st to the 31st Congress, inclusive—Continued.

Names of claimants.	Nature or object of the claim.	Congress.	Session.	How brought before the House of Reps.	Page of journal.	To what committee of the House referred.	No. or date of the report.	Nature of the report.	No. of the bill.	How disposed of by the House of Reps.	How disposed of by the Senate.	Date of the act of Congress, and remarks.
Brooks, Ebenezer	Compensation for revolutionary services.	4	2	Rep. of Secretary War.	614	Claims.						
Brooks, Edward	Pension for naval services, revolutionary war.	25	2	Petition	729	Rev. Pensions.						
Brooks, Edward	Pension for naval services, revolutionary war.	25	3	Petition	217	Rev. Pensions.						
Brooks, Edward	Pension for naval services, revolutionary war.	26	1	Petition	283	Rev. Pensions.						
Brooks, Edward	Pension for naval services, revolutionary war.	26	2	Petition	35	Rev. Pensions	Feb. 12, 1834	Adverse		Laid on table.		
Brooks, Edward	Pension for naval services, revolutionary war.	27	2	Petition	97	Invalid Pensions	1068	Adverse		Laid on table.		
Brooks, Jacob R.	Exchange of location of land	23	1	Petition	300	Public Lands.						
Brooks, John	Pension for revolutionary services.	16	1	Petition	32	Pens. & Rev. Cl'ms.	Dec. 20, 1819	Adverse		Leave to withdraw.		
Brooks, John, executor of.	Compensation for revolutionary services.	13	1	Petition	15	Claims				Discharged; laid on table.		
Brooks, John, executor of.	Compensation for revolutionary services.	16	1	Petition	114	Pens. & Rev. Cl'ms.				Discharged; referred to Sec. War.		
Brooks, John, executor of.	Compensation for revolutionary services.	20	1	Petition	196	Rev. Claims.						
Brooks, John, heirs of	Commutation pay due as revolutionary officer.	23	2	Petition	165	Rev. Claims.						
Brooks, John, heirs of	Commutation pay due as revolutionary officer.	24	1	Petition	103	Rev. Claims.						
Brooks, John, heirs of	Commutation pay due as revolutionary officer.	25	2	Senate bill	605	Rev. Claims	May 11, 1838	Adverse	S. 144	Laid on table.		
Brooks, John, heirs of	Commutation pay due as revolutionary officer.	26	1	Petition	282	Rev. Claims.						
Brooks, John, heirs of	Commutation pay due as revolutionary office.	27	2	Res. and Docs.	73	Rev. Claims.						
Brooks, John, (Mass.,) executor of.	Commutation pay for revolutionary services.	31	1	Petition	680	Rev. Claims	340	Adverse		Laid on table.		
Brooks, John S.	Extra compensation for mail service, Mississippi.	28	1	Petition	608	P. Of. and P. Roads.	550	Adverse		Laid on table.		
Brooks, John, and N. Peed	Reimbursement of costs on a certain judgment.	8	1	Petition	565	Claims	March 7, 1804	Adverse		Leave to withdraw.		
Brooks, Jonathan	(See J. McCready and J. B.)	14	1		722							
Brooks, Joseph B.	Pension for revolutionary services.	25	2	Petition	586	Rev. Pensions				Discharged; leave to withdraw.		
Brooks, Joseph B.	Pension for revolutionary services.	26	1	Petition	173	Rev. Pensions.				Discharged; leave to withdraw.		
Brooks, Lemuel, widow of.	Pension for revolutionary services.	26	1	Petition	936	Rev. Pensions.						
Brooks, Martin	(See Noah Miller and others.)											
Brooks, Nathan	(See administrator of Samuel Burr)	22	1	Petition	332							
Brooks, P. C., *et al.*	Indemnity for French spoliations prior to 1800.	26	1	Memorial	182	Foreign Affairs	343	Favorable	319	Referred to Committee Whole House.		
Brooks, Samuel	Compensation for horse lost in Florida war.	28	1	Petition	262	Claims.						
Brooks, Thomas	Pension for revolutionary services.	3	1	Rep. of Secretary War.	131					Laid on table.		
Brooks, Thomas	Pension for revolutionary services.	3	2	Rep. of Secretary War.	350	Claims	Feb. 28, 1795	Favorable	130	Passed	Indef. postp'd.	

List of private claims presented to the House of Representatives of the United States from the 1st to the 31st Congress, inclusive—Continued.

Names of claimants.	Nature or object of the claim.	Congress.	Session.	How brought before the House of Reps.	Page of journal.	To what committee of the House referred.	No. or date of the report.	Nature of the report.	No. of the bill.	How disposed of by the House of Reps.	How disposed of by the Senate.	Date of the act of Congress, and remarks.
26 Brooks, Thomas	Pension for revolutionary services.	4	1	Report of Secretary of War.	447	Claims	Feb. 18, 1796	Favorable	156	Passed	Passed with amendment.	App'd April 20, 1796
Brooks, Thomas, (N. J.)	Pension	21	2	Petition	299	Military Pensions.						
Brooks, William, and others	Indemnity for Indian depredations.	25	2	Petition	87	Claims	351	Adverse.	......	Laid on table.		
Brooks, William, and others	Indemnity for Indian depredations.	30	1	Petition	77	Claims	13	Adverse.	......	Laid on table.		
Brooks, Zachariah	Remission of a license penalty	15	2	Petition	281	Ways and Means.						
Brookshire, Mauring	Pension for revolutionary services.	27	2	Petition	833	Rev. Pensions	....		......	Discharged; laid on table.		
Broome, John	Indemnity for property destroyed by the enemy.	24	1	Memorial	507	Claims	April 12, 1836	Adverse	......	Laid on table.		
Broome, John	Indemnity for property destroyed by the enemy.	24	2	Memorial	395	Claims	260	Adverse	......	Laid on table.		
Broome, John	Indemnity for property destroyed by the enemy.	25	2	Memorial	485	Claims	1064	Adverse	......	Laid on table.		
Broome, John	Indemnity for property destroyed by the enemy.	25	3	Memorial	121	Claims	115	Adverse	......	Laid on table.		
Broome, John, heirs of	Indemnity for property destroyed by the enemy.	27	2	Memorial	226	Rev. Claims	1077	Adverse	......	Laid on table.		
Broome, John, heirs of	Indemnity for property destroyed by the enemy.	31	1	Memorial	671	Claims.						
Broome, Thomas R	Equitable settlement of accounts as paymaster.	18	2	Senate bill	284	Military Affairs	March 1, 1825	With't amend.	S. 28	Passed	Passed	App'd March 3, 1825
Brophy, James	(See A. G. Higgins and others)	29	1	....	152							
Brophy, John	Compensation for horse lost in public service.	23	2	Petition	165	Claims	75	Adverse	......	Laid on table.		
Brophy, John	Compensation for horse lost in public service.	24	1	Petition	50	Claims	Jan. 5, 1836	Adverse	......	Laid on table.		
Brosiers, Harper, administrator of.	(See assignee of William Kingsbury.	30	1	....	525	....	837	....	650			
Brother, Henry	Indemnity for losses on Niagara frontier.	14	2	Resolution	67	Claims.						
Brother, Henry	Indemnity for losses on Niagara frontier.	15	2	Documents	235	Claims.						
Brother, Henry	Indemnity for losses on Niagara frontier.	16	1	Petition	184	Claims	Jan. 31, 1820	Adverse	......	Laid on table.		
Brother, Henry	Indemnity for losses on Niagara frontier.	16	2	Petition	84	Claims	Dec. 20, 1820	Adverse	......	Claim rejected.		
Brothers, Coster & Co.	Drawback on merchandise exported	3	2	Petition	303	Select	Feb. 25, 1795	Favorable.				
Brothers, Elijah	Right of pre-emption	28	2	Petition	199	Public Lands.						
Brothers, John, heir of	Indemnity for losses by depreciation of continental money.	31	1	Petition	349	Rev. Claims	57	Adverse.	......	Laid on table.		
Brotherton, James	Compensation for revolutionary services.	4	2	Petition	677	Claims	Feb. 8, 1797	Adverse.	......	Laid on table.		
Brotherton, Robert	(See surety of John Crabb)	18	1	....	331	....	....	....	213			
Brotherton, Thomas	Pension for revolutionary services.	21	1	Resolution	255	Military Pensions.						
Brotherton, Thomas	Pension for revolutionary services.	21	2	Resolution	49	Military Pensions.						
Brough, William	Pension for revolutionary services.	15	1	Petition	129	Pens. & Rev. Cl'ms.	Feb. 13, 1818	Adverse	......	Leave to withdraw.		
Brough, William	Pension for revolutionary services.	17	1	Petition	27	Pens. & Rev. Cl'ms.	Dec. 18, 1821	Adverse	......	Leave to withdraw.		
Brough, William	Pension for revolutionary services.	18	1	Petition	343	Pens. & Rev. Cl'ms.	April 13, 1824	Adverse	......	Laid on table.		
Brough, William	Pension for revolutionary services.	19	2	Resolution	291	Military Pensions.						
Brough, William	Pension for revolutionary services.	20	1	Resolution	387	Military Pensions.						
Brough, William	Pension for revolutionary services.	21	1	Petition	98	Rev. Claims	Feb. 15, 1830	Adverse	......	Laid on table.		

List of private claims presented to the House of Representatives of the United States from the 1st to the 31st Congress, inclusive—Continued.

Names of claimants.	Nature or object of the claim.	Congress.	Session.	How brought before the House of Reps.	Page of journal.	To what committee of the House referred.	No. or date of the report.	Nature of the report.	No. of the bill.	How disposed of by the House of Reps.	How disposed of by the Senate.	Date of the act of Congress, and remarks.
Brough, William	Increase of compensation as postmaster, Hampton, Va.	15	1	Petition	129	P. Of. & P. Roads.						
Brough, William	Increase of compensation as postmaster, Hampton, Va.	16	1	Petition	181	P. Of. & P. Roads.	Mar. 3, 1820	Adverse	......	Laid on table.		
Brougham, Nathan, surety of.	Remission of duty on distillery	15	1	Petition	264	Ways and Means.						
Brougher, Christian	Pension for revolutionary services.	25	3	Resolution	163	Rev. Pensions	304	Favorable	1173	Referred to Committee Whole House.		
Brougher, Christian	Pension for revolutionary services.	26	1	Petition	171	Rev. Pensions	164	Favorable	174	Passed	Indef. postp'd.	
Brougher, Christian	Pension for revolutionary services.	27	2	Petition	97	Rev. Pensions.						
Broughton, Bartholomew.	Pension for revolutionary disabilities.	12	1	Petition	38	Claims	......	......	......	Leave to withdraw.		
Broughton, Bartholomew.	Pension for revolutionary disabilities.	13	3	Petition	467	Pens. & Rev. Cl'ms.	......	......	......	Discharged; leave to withdraw.		
Broughton, Glover	Bounty on fishing schooner Union.	22	1	Petition	162	Commerce.						
Broughton, Glover	Bounty on fishing schooner Union.	22	2	Petition	40	Commerce	Dec. 21, 1832	Favorable	634	Passed	Passed	App'd Feb. 27, 1833
Broughton, Glover	Bounty on fishing schooner Tancred.	28	2	Petition	300	Commerce.						
Broughton, Glover	Bounty on fishing schooner Tancred.	29	1	Petition	177	Commerce	94	Favorable	113	Passed	Passed	App'd Aug. 8, 1846
Broughton, Nicholas	Bounty on a lost fishing schooner.	19	2	Petition	213	Commerce.						
Brouillett, Michael	Compensation for services as Indian interpreter.	19	2	Petition	82	Indian Affairs	Jan. 27, 1827	Adverse	......	Laid on table.		
Brouillett, Michael	Compensation for horse lost at Tippecanoe.	20	1	Resolution	54	Claims	April 16, 1828	Adverse	......	Laid on table.		
Brouillett, Michael	Compensation for horse lost at Tippecanoe.	23	1	Petition	92	Claims	June 26, 1834	Adverse	......	Laid on table.		
Brouillett, Michael	Compensation for horse lost at Tippecanoe.	23	2	Petition	106	Claims.						
Brouillett, Michael	Compensation for horse lost at Tippecanoe.	25	2	Petition	275	Claims.						
Brouillett, Michael	Compensation for horse lost at Tippecanoe.	26	1	Petition	169	Claims.						
Broutin, Narcissus	Confirmation of title to land in Missouri.	15	1	Petition	207	Priv. Land Claims.	Feb. 18, 1818	Favorable	92	Passed	Passed	App'd April 3, 1818
Browder, Isham	Reimbursement of money paid on public lands.	19	1	Petition	642	Public Lands	......	......	......	Discharged; leave to withdraw.		
Browder, Isham, heirs of.	Reimbursement of money paid on public lands.	21	2	Petition	68	Public Lands.						
Browder, Isham, heirs of.	Reimbursement of money paid on public lands.	22	1	Petition	334	Public Lands.						
Brower, Adolphus	Indemnity for losses and injuries in revolutionary war.	1	2	Petition	179	......	......	......	......	Referred to Secretary Treasury.		
Brower, Adolphus	Indemnity for losses and injuries in revolutionary war.	2	1	Rep. of Secretary Treasury.	580	......	......	......	......	Laid on table.		
Brower, Jeremiah, heirs of.	Indemnity for destruction of property by revolutionary army.	15	2	Petition	36	Pens. & Rev. Cl'ms	Nov. 13, 1818	Adverse	......	Rejected.		
Brower, John	Revolutionary pension	25	3	Petition	460	Rev. Pensions.						
Brower, John	Revolutionary pension	26	1	Petition	171	Rev. Pensions	......	......	......	Discharged; leave to withdraw.		
Brower, John	Revolutionary pension	27	2	Petition	428	Rev. Pensions.						
Brower, Mary	(See heir of Jeremiah Brower)	15	2	......	36							
Browers & Brown, surviving partner of.	Remission of duties on glass destroyed by fire.	7	1	Petition	105	Com. and Manuf.	Mar. 8, 1802	Adverse	......	Leave to withdraw.		

List of private claims presented to the House of Representatives of the United States from the 1st to the 31st Congress, inclusive—Continued.

Names of claimants.	Nature or object of the claim.	Congress.	Session.	How brought before the House of Reps.	Page of journal.	To what committee of the House referred.	No. or date of the report.	Nature of the report.	No. of the bill.	How disposed of by the House of Reps.	How disposed of by the Senate.	Date of the act of Congress, and remarks.
Brown, Aaron	(See representatives of Larned S. Brown.)	22	2		52							
Brown, Abiel	Pension for revolutionary services.	18	1	Petition	105	Rev. Pensions	Jan. 12, 1824	Adverse		Laid on table.		
Brown, Abiel	Pension for revolutionary services.	19	1	Petition	52	Military Pensions	April 1, 1826	Adverse		Laid on table.		
Brown, Abiel	Pension for revolutionary services.	20	1	Resolution	265	Military Pensions.						
Brown, Abiel	Pension for revolutionary services.	21	1	Petition	47	Whole House	Feb. 13, 1830	Favorable	72	Passed	Passed	App'd May 20, 1830
Brown, Adam	Confirmation of title to land in Missouri.	15	1	Petition	102	Priv. Land Claims.						
Brown, Adam, representatives of.	Indemnity for losses on treasury notes.	24	1	Senate bill	956	Claims	Jan. 8, 1836	With't amend.	S. 161	Passed	Passed	App'd July 2, 1836
Brown, A. J	Settlement of accounts and release from imprisonment.	20	1	Petition	223	Ways and Means.				Discharged; referred to President U. States.		
Brown, Alexander & Sons.	Permission to import linen from Liverpool.	10	2	Petition	375	Com. and Manuf.						
Brown, Amasa	Pension	28	1	Petition	414	Invalid Pensions	432	Adverse		Laid on table.		
Brown, Amos W	Compensation in land for services as Canadian volunteer.	22	1	Petition	189	Priv. Land Claims.	253	Favorable	339	Referred to Committee Whole House.		
Brown, Amos W	Compensation in land for services as Canadian volunteer.	23	1	Petition	125	Priv. Land Claims.	91	Favorable	99	Passed	Passed	App'd June 30, 1834
Brown, Amos W	Compensation in land for services as Canadian volunteer.	23	2	Petition	174	Military Affairs.						
Brown, Amos W	Compensation in land for services as Canadian volunteer.	24	1	Petition	474	Claims	467	Adverse		Laid on table.		
Brown, Amy	(See daughter of Nathan'l Adams.)	25	3		562							
Brown, Arabia, *et al.*	Correction of an entry of land	31	1	Petition	234	Public Lands	336	Favorable	296	Referred to Committee Whole House.		
Brown, Aris, widow of	Pension for revolutionary services.	30	2	Petition	274	Rev. Pensions						Leave to withdraw 31st Cong. 1st sess.
Brown, Basil	Compensation for horses furnished for public use.	24	1	Petition	153	Indian Affairs	605	Favorable	591	Referred to Committee Whole House.		
Brown, Basil	Compensation for horses furnished for public use.	25	2	Petition	43	Indian Affairs	524	Adverse		Recommitted.		
Brown, Benjamin	Settlement of claim against United States.	1	2	Petition	285					Referred to Secretary Treasury.		
Brown, Benjamin	Settlement of claim against United States.	2	2	Rep. of Secretary Treasury.	625					Laid on table.		
Brown, Bennett C	Additional compensation for taking census in Missouri.	31	2	Petition	143	Judiciary				Discharged; laid on table.		
Brown, Burnett	(See surviving partner of Browers & Brown.)	7	1		105							
Brown, Catharine	(See Arabia Brown, *et al.*)	31	1		234							
Brown, Charles, (surgeon)	Pension for wounds received in Indian wars.	8	1	Petition	564	Claims	Mar. 13, 1804			Postponed.		
Brown, Charles, (Va.)	Pension	16	1	Petition	126	Pens. & Rev. Cl'ms.				Discharged; referred to Secretary War.		
				Rep. of Secretary War.	350					Laid on table.		
Brown, Charles, (Ky.)	Pension for revolutionary services.	21	1	Petition	37	Military Pensions	94	Favorable	128	Passed	Passed	App'd May 29, 1830
Brown, Charles, N. Y.)	Bounty land for services, war of 1812.	25	2	Petition	577	Military Affairs.						
Brown, Charles	(See executor of Moses Brown)	29	2		129							
Brown, Charles, (S. C.,) heirs of.	Commutation pay for revolutionary services.	24	1	Petition	106	Rev. Claims	Jan. 27, 1836	Adverse		Laid on table.		

List of private claims presented to the House of Representatives of the United States from the 1st to the 31st Congress, inclusive—Continued.

Names of claimants.	Nature or object of the claim.	Congress.	Session.	How brought before the House of Reps.	Page of journal.	To what committee of the House referred.	No. or date of the report.	Nature of the report.	No. of the bill.	How disposed of by the House of Reps.	How disposed of by the Senate.	Date of the act of Congress, and remarks.
Brown, Charles, (S. C.,) heirs of.	Duplicate for a lost revolutionary land warrant.	25	2	Petition	983	Priv. Land Claims.	Jan. 6, 1838	Favorable	R. 17	Passed.		
Brown, Charles, (S. C.,) heirs of.	Duplicate for a lost revolutionary land warrant.	25	3	Petition	184	Priv. Land Claims.	Jan. 2, 1839	Favorable	R. 33	Passed	Passed	App'd March 2, 1833
Brown, Charles, (S. C.,) heirs of.	Duplicate for a lost revolutionary land warrant.	26	1	Petition	179	Priv. Land Claims.				Discharged; laid on table.		
Brown, Christopher T	(See Robert B. Carter)	23	2		275							
Brown, Clement C	Extra pay for clerical services, Philadelphia.	3	1	Memorial	88	Select	47	Favorable	69	Passed	Rejected.	
Brown, Conrad, heir of	Compensation for property taken for public use.	23	1	Petition	98	Rev. Claims.						
Brown, Conrad, heir of	Compensation for property taken for public use.	23	2	Petition	138	Rev. Claims	139	Adverse		Laid on table.		
Brown, Conrad, heir of	Compensation for property taken for public use.	26	1	Petition	946	Rev. Claims.						
Brown, Conrad, heir of	Compensation for property taken for public use.	26	2	Petition	77	Rev. Claims	175	Adverse		Laid on table.		
Brown, Conrad, heir of	Compensation for property taken for public use.	27	2	Petition	96	Rev. Claims.						
				Petition (2)	236	Rev. Claims	513	Adverse		Laid on table.		
Brown, Colonel, and others.	Compensation for military services.	26	2	Petition	124	Claims.						
Brown, Colonel, and others.	Compensation for military services.	27	2	Petition	94	Claims.						
Brown, Cyrus	Bounty on fishing schooner Dolphin.	24	2	Petition	345	Commerce.						
Brown, Cyrus	Bounty on fishing schooner Dolphin.	25	2	Petition	412	Commerce				Discharged; laid on table.		
Brown, Daniel	Increase of pension	12	1	Pension bill	361	Whole House	June 15, 1812	With amend.	138	Passed	Passed with amendment.	App'd July 5, 1812
Brown, Daniel	Payment of the award of a jury	20	1	Petition	598	Claims				Discharged; leave to withdraw.		
Brown, Daniel	Payment of the award of a jury	20	2	Petition	32	Claims.						
Brown, Daniel	Payment of the award of a jury	21	1	Petition	98	Claims	Jan. 11, 1830	Adverse		Laid on table.		
Brown, Daniel	Payment of the award of a jury	22	1	Petition	54	Claims	Jan. 25, 1832	Adverse		Laid on table.		
Brown, Daniel	Payment of the award of a jury	23	1	Resolution	125	Claims.						
Brown, Daniel	Payment of the award of a jury	29	1	Memorial	383	Claims.						
Brown, Daniel	Payment of the award of a jury	30	1	Memorial	116	Claims	62	Adverse		Laid on table.		
Brown, Daniel	Compensation for property lost in public service.	30	1	Petition	116	Claims	96	Adverse		Laid on table.		
Brown, Daniel, widow of.	Pension for revolutionary services.	23	1	Petition	135	Rev. Pensions.						
Brown, David	Compensation for revolutionary services.	2	1	Petition	483					Referred to Secretary War.		
Brown, Ebenezer, (Conn.)	Compensation for revolutionary services.	23	1	Petition	39	Rev. Claims.						
Brown, Ebenezer, (Mass.)	Pension for revolutionary disabilities.	8	2	Petition	50	Claims.						
Brown, Ebenezer, (Mass.)	Pension for revolutionary disabilities.	9	1	Petition	193	Claims	Mar. 28, 1806	Indefinite		Indef. postponed		Leave to withdraw.
Brown, Ebenezer, (Mass.)	Pension for revolutionary disabilities.	10	1	Petition	97	Select.						
Brown, Ebenezer, (Mass.)	Pension for revolutionary disabilities.	11	3	Petition	493	Claims	Mar. 24, 1810	Favorable	218	Passed	Passed	App'd March 3, 1811
Brown, Ebenezer, (Mass.)	Commutation pay for revolutionary services.	12	1	Petition	60	Whole House.						

List of *private claims presented to the House of Representatives of the United States from the* 1*st to the* 31*st Congress, inclusive*—Continued.

Names of claimants.	Nature or object of the claim.	Congress.	Session.	How brought before the House of Reps.	Page of journal.	To what committee of the House referred.	No. or date of the report.	Nature of the report.	No. of the bill.	How disposed of by the House of Reps.	How disposed of by the Senate.	Date of the act of Congress, and remarks.
Brown, Ebenezer, (Mass.)	Commutation pay for revolutionary services.	12	2	Petition	591	Claims.						
Brown, Ebenezer, (Mass.)	Commutation pay for revolutionary services.	13	2	Petition	319	Pens. & Rev. Cl'ms.	Mar. 28, 1814	Favorable		Referred to Committee Whole House.		
Brown, Ebenezer, (Mass.)	To be restored to pension roll	24	1	Petition	136	Rev. Claims.						
Brown, Edwin C	(See heirs of James Craine.)											
Brown, Eleanor	(See heirs of Thomas Brown)	12	2		571							
Brown, Eli	Bounty land for revolutionary services.	11	2	Petition	354	Claims.						
Brown, Eli	Pension for revolutionary services.	21	1	Petition	101	Military Pensions.						
Brown, Elijah	Reimbursement of money paid for license.	15	2	Petition	74	Ways and Means.	Dec. 16, 1818	Adverse		Referred to Committee Whole House.		
Brown, Elijah, representatives of.	Compensation for revolutionary services.	29	1	Petition	284	Rev. Claims				Discharged; laid on table.		
Brown, Elijah, representatives of.	Compensation for revolutionary services.	30	1	Petition	887	Rev. Claims.				Discharged; laid on table.		
Brown, Elijah W	(See representatives of Elijah Brown.)	29	1		284							
Brown, Elkanah	Pension for revolutionary services.	22	1	Petition	130	Rev. Pensions.						
Brown, Elijah	Compensation for horse lost in Florida war.	28	1	Petition	262	Claims.						
Brown, Eliphas C	Pension for disability in Florida war.	29	1	Petition	82	Invalid Pensions				Discharged; laid on table.		
Brown, Eliphas C	Pension for disability in Florida war.	30	1	Petition	606	Invalid Pensions	559	Favorable	459	Passed.		
Brown, Eliphas C	Pension for disability in Florida war.	31	1	Petition	214	Invalid Pensions	52	Favorable	82	Passed	Passed	App'd Aug. 17, 1850
Brown, Elizabeth	(See sister of James Farrell)	27	2		221							
Brown, Ellery	(See heirs of Daniel Harris)	26	1		282							
Brown, Enos	Indemnity for revolutionary injuries.	1	2	Rep. of Secretary War.	221					Laid on table.		
Brown, Ezekiel	To be restored to pension roll	17	1	Petition	72	Rev. Pensions.						
				Petition	118	Rev. Pensions.						
Brown, Fielding G	Pension	28	1	Petition	372	Invalid Pensions	276	Adverse		Laid on table.		
Brown, Fielding G	Pension	29	1	Petition	396	Invalid Pensions	663	Adverse		Laid on table.		
Brown, Fielding G	Pension	29	2	Petition	292	Invalid Pensions.						
Brown, Fielding G	Pension	30	1	Petition	207	Invalid Pensions	628	Favorable	503	Passed.		
Brown, Fielding G	Pension	31	1	Petition	257	Invalid Pensions	238	Favorable	233	Referred to Committee Whole House.		
Brown, Fielding G	Pension	31	2	Rep. Committee Whole House.	182			With amend.	233	Passed.		
Brown, Francis	Pension for revolutionary services.	24	1	Petition	944	Rev. Pensions.						
Brown & Francis	Reimbursement of excessive duties	1	3	Petition	391					Referred to Secretary Treasury.		
Brown & Francis	Reimbursement of excessive duties	2	2	Rep. of Secretary of Treasury.	625					Laid on table.		
Brown & Francis	Remission of duty on teas destroyed by fire.	3	1	Petition	156					Referred to Secretary Treasury.		
Brown & Francis	Remission of duty on teas destroyed by fire.	3	2	Rep. of Secretary of Treasury.	284					Laid on table.		
Brown & Francis	Drawback on gin and codfish exported.	2	2	Petition	687					Referred to Secretary Treasury.		
Brown, Frederick	Equitable settlement of accounts	14	1	Petition	503	Claims.						

List of private claims presented to the House of Representatives of the United States from the 1st to the 31st Congress, inclusive—Continued.

Names of claimants.	Nature or object of the claim.	Congress.	Session.	How brought before the House of Reps.	Page of journal.	To what committee of the House referred.	No. or date of the report.	Nature of the report.	No. of the bill.	How disposed of by the House of Reps.	How disposed of by the Senate.	Date of the act of Congress, and remarks.
Brown, Frederick	Equitable settlement of accounts	15	1	Petition	24	Military Affairs	Mar. 19, 1818	Favorable	151	Passed	Indef. postp'd.	
Brown, Frederick	Equitable settlement of accounts	15	2	Petition	66	Military Affairs	Dec. 8, 1818	Favorable	218	Passed	Passed	App'd Jan. 19, 1819.
Brown, George	(See James Collingsworth *et al.*)	9	2		563							
Brown, George	(See widow of Stephen Decatur and others.)											
Brown, George	(See sureties of Wm. Whitsitt)	17	2		228							
Brown, George, attorney of, (La.)	Three months' extra pay	30	2	Petition	284	Invalid Pensions	70	Adverse		Laid on table.		
Brown, George, (Ky.)	Pension	20	2	Petition	262	Military Pensions.						
Brown, George, (R. I.)	Additional compensation as surveyor of customs.	21	2	Petition	89	Commerce.						
Brown, George, and others, (Pa.)	Compensation for services in Indian wars.	2	2	Petition	686	Select.						
Brown, George, and others, (Pa.)	Compensation for services in Indian wars.	3	1	Petition	49	Select.						
Brown, George, and others, (N. Y.)	Reimbursement of foreign tonnage duties.	22	1	Petition	253	Commerce	April 13, 1832	Adverse		Laid on table.		
Brown, George, widow of.	Pecuniary aid for diplomatic services.	30	1	Petition	70	Claims	7	Adverse		Laid on table.		
Brown, George, sureties of	Release from liability and commissions on collections.	21	1	Petition	132	Judiciary	250	Favorable	309	Referred to Committee Whole House.		
Brown, George, sureties of	Release from liability and commissions on collections.	21	2	Rep't Committee Whole House.	333			With't amend.	309	Passed.		
Brown, George, sureties of	Commissions on money recovered.	22	1	Senate bill	816	Claims	June 7, 1832	With't amend.	82	Passed	Passed	App'd July 14, 1832
Brown, George, sureties of	Release from liability	23	1	Petition	338	Judiciary.						
Brown, George F	Additional compensation for services in Algiers.	22	2	Appropriat'n bill.	145	Whole House	Feb. 5, 1833	Amendments	669	Passed	Passed	App'd March 2, 1833
Brown, George F	Further compensation for services in Algiers.	24	1	Petition	727	Foreign Affairs	Jan. 26, 1836	Favorable	214	Passed	Passed	App'd July 2, 1836
Brown, George H	Pension for revolutionary services.	15	1	Petition	129	Pens. & Rev. Cl'ms.						
Brown, Gilbert	Right of pre-emption	23	2	Petition	309	Priv. Land Claims.						
Brown, G. H	Payment of claim against Ottawa Indians.	29	1	Petition	160	Indian Affairs	287	Adverse.				
Brown, Harriet	(See George Brown, widow of)	30	1		70							
Brown, Harvey	Indemnity for losses and costs in certain suits.	22	1	Memorial	54	Judiciary	74	Favorable	142	Passed	Passed	App'd July 14, 1832
Brown, Harvey	Reimbursement of money paid on public account.	22	1	Petition	121	Military Affairs	Jan. 21, 1832	Favorable	302	Referred to Committee Whole House.		
Brown, Harvey	Reimbursement of money paid on public account.	22	2	Rep't Committee Whole House.	336			With't amend.	302	Passed	Passed	App'd March 2, 1833
Brown & Havens	(See Noah Brown and others)	15	1		183							
Brown, Hector	Bounty land for services in war of 1812.	31	1	Petition	711	Claims.						
Brown, Henry D	Revolutionary pension for services in Rhode Island brigade.	14	2	Petition	283	Pens. & Rev. Cl'ms.						
Brown, Henry D	Revolutionary pension for services in Rhode Island brigade.	23	2	Memorial	67	Select	Feb. 25, 1835	By Bill	769	Referred to Committee Whole House.		
Brown, Henry D	Revolutionary pension for services in Rhode Island brigade.	24	1	Documents	136	Select	337	By bill	352	Referred to Committee Whole House.		
Brown, Henry	Pension for disability, war of revolution.	15	2	Petition	23	Rev. Pensions				Discharged; leave to withdraw.		
Brown, Henry	Pension for disability, war of revolution.	16	1	Petition	38	Rev. Pensions				Discharged; leave to withdraw.		

List of private claims presented to the House of Representatives of the United States from the 1*st to the* 31*st Congress, inclusive*—Continued.

Names of claimants.	Nature or object of the claim.	Congress.	Session.	How brought before the House of Reps.	Page of journal.	To what committee of the House referred.	No. or date of the report.	Nature of the report.	No. of the bill.	How disposed of by the House of Reps.	How disposed of by the Senate.	Date of the act of Congress, and remarks.
Brown, Henry	Arrears and increase of pension	31	2	Petition	282	Invalid Pensions.						
Brown, Hubbard	Pension for revolutionary services	21	1	Petition	57	Rev. Claims	Dec. 31, 1829	Adverse		Laid on table.		
Brown, Hubbard	Pension for revolutionary services	21	2	Resolution	166	Military Pensions.						
Brown, Isaac, widow of	Pension for revolutionary services	25	2	Petition	53	Rev. Pensions.						
Brown, Israel, representatives of.	Drawback on merchandise exported	20	1	Petition	217	Commerce	Jan. 26, 1828	Favorable	112	Passed	Passed	App'd May 24, 1828
Brown, Jabez, representatives of.	Pension for revolutionary services	28	1	Petition	284	Rev. Pensions.						
Brown, Jacob, (N. J.)	Indemnity for loss of time while in public service.	19	1	Petition	89	Claims	Jan. 11, 1826	Adverse		Claim rejected		Leave to withdraw.
Brown, Jacob, (Tenn.)	Pension for services, war of 1812	25	2	Petition	406	Invalid Pensions	Mar. 10, 1838	Adverse		Laid on table.		
Brown, Jacob, (Ark.)	Confirmation of title and patent for land.	25	2	Senate bill	1039	Public Lands	June 12, 1838	With amend.	S. 172	Passed with amendm't.	Passed as am'd.	App'd July 5, 1838
Brown, Jacob, (Mass.)	Pension for revolutionary services	20	2	Petition	82	Military Pensions	Feb. 16, 1829	Adverse		Laid on table.		
Brown, Jacob, (Mass.)	Pension for revolutionary services	22	1	Petition	509	Rev. Pensions				Discharged; laid on table.		
Brown, Jacob, widow of (Ms.)	Pension for revolutionary services	29	1	Petition	1074	Rev. Claims	825	Favorable	550	Referred to Committee Whole House.		
Brown, Jacob, widow of (Ms.)	Pension for revolutionary services	30	1	Petition	79	Rev Claims	4	Favorable	4	Passed	Passed	App'd May 29, 1848
Brown, General Jacob	Indemnity for damages recovered against him.	15	1	Petition	198	Claims	Feb. 9, 1818	Favorable	71	Passed	Passed	App'd April 18, 1818
Brown, Gen. Jacob, widow of.	Certain allowances	20	1	Senate bill	455	Military Affairs	Mar. 31, 1828	With't amend.	S. 111	Passed	Passed	App'd April 3, 1828
Brown, Gen. Jacob, widow of.	Half pay	25	2	Petition	57	Invalid Pensions	402	Favorable	411	Read 3d time and postponed.		
Brown, Gen. Jacob, widow of.	Half-pay	25	3	House bill	156				411	Passed.		
Brown, Gen. Jacob, widow of.	Half pay	26	1	Petition	161	Invalid Pensions	201	Favorable	213	Referred to Committee Whole House.		
Brown, Gen. Jacob, widow of.	Half-pay	27	2	Petition	60	Invalid Pensions.						
Brown, James, (N. Y.)	Compensation for revolutionary supplies.	5	2	Petition	165	Claims	Mar. 9, 1798	Adverse		Laid on table.		
Brown, James, (N. Y.)	Pension for revolutionary services	16	1	Petition	26	Pens. & Rev. Cl'ms.						
Brown, James, (N. Y.)	Pension for revolutionary services	16	2	Petition	152	Pens. & Rev. Cl'ms.				Disch'd; laid on table.		
Brown, James, (Lee's Legion.)	Bounty land and pay due him	16	2	Petition	155	Pens. & Rev. Cl'ms.	Jan. 29, 1821	Adverse		Laid on table.		
Brown, James, (Pa.)	Pension for revolutionary services	18	1	Petition	388					Laid on table.		
Brown, James, (Pa.)	Pension for revolutionary services	19	2	Resolution	127	Military Pensions.						
				Petition	131	Military Pensions.						
Brown, James, (Pa.)	Pension for revolutionary services	20	1	Resolution	160	Military Pensions.						
Brown, James, (N. J.)	Pension	20	1	Petition	680	Military Pensions	May 13, 1828	Adverse		Laid on table.		
Brown, James, 2d	Bounty land for revolutionary services.	16	1	Petition	117	Pens. & Rev. Cl'ms	Jan. 19, 1820	Adverse		Claim rejected.		
Brown, James, 2d	Bounty land for revolutionary services.	22	1	Petition	107	Priv. Land Claims.						
Brown, James	(See Louis F. Beeler, *et al.*)	30	1		115		482					
Brown, James	(See executors of John Doyle)	22	1		512							
Brown, James, heirs of	Indemnity for negroes taken by Cherokee Indians.	11	2	Petition	240	Select.						
Brown, James, heirs of	Indemnity for negroes taken by Cherokee Indians.	11	3	Petition	461	Whole House.						

List of private claims presented to the House of Representatives of the United States from the 1st to the 31st Congress, inclusive—Continued.

Names of claimants.	Nature or object of the claim.	Congress.	Session.	How brought before the House of Reps.	Page of journal.	To what committee of the House referred.	No. or date of the report.	Nature of the report.	No. of the bill.	How disposed of by the House of Reps.	How disposed of by the Senate.	Date of the act of Congress, and remarks.
Brown, James, heirs of...	Indemnity for negroes taken by Cherokee Indians.	17	1	Petition	68	Indian Affairs....	Jan. 21, 1827	Adverse	......	Claim rejected.		
Brown, James, heirs of...	Indemnity for negroes taken by Cherokee Indians.	21	2	Petition	75	Indian Affairs.						
Brown, James, heirs of...	Indemnity for negroes taken by Cherokee Indians.	22	1	Petition	50	Indian Affairs	311	Favorable	391	Referred to Committee Whole House.		
Brown, James, heirs of...	Indemnity for negroes taken by Cherokee Indians.	23	1	Petition	67	Indian Affairs	175	Favorable	194	Passed	Passed	App'd June 30, 1834
Brown, James, heirs of...	Interest on claim allowed by 23d Congress.	24	1	Resolution	268	Indian Affairs	....	....	......	Discharged; laid on table.		
Brown, James, heirs of...	Interest on claim allowed by 23d Congress.	25	2	Resolution.....	186	Indian Affairs	685	Adverse	......	Laid on table.		
Brown, James, heirs of...	Payment of amount allowed by act of June 30, 1834.	30	1	Petition........	99	Claims	10	Favorable	12	Passed	Passed	App'd June 26, 1848
Brown, James, (Cherokee).	Indemnity for certain improvements on land.	21	1	Petition	360	Indian Affairs.						
Brown, James, (Cherokee).	Indemnity for certain improvements on land.	22	1	Petition	387	Indian Affairs.						
Brown, James, (Cherokee).	Indemnity for certain improvements on land.	22	2	Petition	79	Indian Affairs	73	Favorable	717	Referred to Committee Whole House.		
Brown, James, (Cherokee).	Indemnity for certain improvements on land.	23	1	Petition	50	Indian Affairs.						
Brown, James, (Cherokee).	Indemnity for certain improvements on land.	23	2	Resolution	74	Indian Affairs.						
Brown, James, (Cherokee).	Indemnity for certain improvements on land.	24	1	Resolution	268	Indian Affairs	Feb. 5, 1836	Favorable	292	Referred to Committee Whole House.		
Brown, James, (Cherokee).	Indemnity for certain improvements on land.	24	2	Rep't Committee Whole House.	200	....	....	With't amend.	292	Passed	Passed	App'd March 3, 1837
Brown, James, (Cherokee).	Interest on claim allowed by act of March 3, 1837.	26	1	Petition	946	Indian Affairs.						
Brown & Jarvis, surviving partner of.	Reimbursement of excessive duties.	24	1	Petition	143	Ways and Means.						
Brown, Jedediah	Pension for revolutionary services.	2	1	Petition	444	....	....	....	......	Referred to Secretary War.		
Brown, Jedediah........	Pension for revolutionary services.	3	1	Rep. of Secretary War.	131	Select.						
Brown, Jedediah	Pension for revolutionary services.	3	2	Rep. of Secretary War.	262	Claims.						
Brown, Jedediah	Pension for revolutionary services.	4	1	Petition	373	Claims	Feb. 18, 1796	Pension bill ..	156	Passed	Passed with amendment.	App'd April 20, 1796
Brown, Jedediah	Increase of pension	11	2	Pension bill	283	Whole House	Mar. 24, 1810	With amend..	107	Passed	Passed with amendment.	App'd April 27, 1810
Brown, Jeptha..........	Pension for injuries in public service.	13	2	Petition	175	Pens. & Rev. Cl'ms.	....	....	......	Discharged; referred to Com. Whole House.		
Brown, Jeptha..........	Pension for injuries in public service.	14	2	Petition	105	Pens. & Rev. Cl'ms.	Jan. 29, 1817	Favorable	91	Passed	Passed	App'd March 3, 1817
Brown, Jeptha..........	Increase of pension	15	1	Petition........	97	Pens. & Rev. Cl'ms.	Feb. 13, 1818	Adverse.......	......	Rejected.		
Brown, Jesse..........	Pension for revolutionary services.	15	1	Petition	279	Pens. & Rev. Cl'ms.	....	....	......	Discharged; referred to Secretary of War.		
Brown, Jesse, daughter of.	Pension for revolutionary services.	30	2	Petition	92	Rev. Claims.						
Brown, Joel, widow of...	Pension for services, war of 1812.	30	1	Petition	460	Rev. Pensions.						

List of p ivate claims presented to the House of Representatives of the United States from the 1st to the 31st Congress, inclusive—Continued.

Names of claimants.	Nature or object of the claim.	Congress.	Session.	How brought before the House of Reps.	Page of journal.	To what committee of the House referred.	No. or date of the report.	Nature of the report.	No. of the bill.	How disposed of by the House of Reps.	How disposed of by the Senate.	Date of the act of Congress, and remarks.
Brown, John	Pension for revolutionary services.	3	1	Rep. of Secretary War.	131	Select.						
Brown, John	Pension for revolutionary services.	4	2	Petition	660	Claims	Feb. 14, 1797	Adverse	......	Laid on table.		
Brown, John	(See Zebulon Pike and companions.)	10	1	....	189							
Brown, John, (R. I.)	Drawback on glass ware exported.	4	2	Petition	700	Com. and Manuf.	Feb. 25, 1797	Favorable	239	Passed	Passed	App'd March 3, 1797
Brown, John	(See Moses Brown and others....	9	2	....	555							
Brown, John	Pension for revolutionary services.	11	3	Pension bill	604	Whole House	Mar. 2, 1811	With amend.	218	Passed	Passed with amendment.	App'd March 3, 1811
Brown, John, (Mass.)	Pension for revolutionary services.	15	1	Petition	190	Pens. & Rev. Cl'ms.						
Brown, John, (Ky.)	Confirmation of title to land in Missouri.	15	2	Petition	118	Priv. Land Claims.						
Brown, John, (Penn.)	To be restored to pension roll	18	2	Petition	117	Rev. Pensions	Jan. 17, 1825	Adverse.	......	Laid on table.		
Brown, John, (N. Y.)	Pension	21	2	Petition	208	Military Pensions.						
Brown, John	Indemnity for damages occasioned by United States troops.	9	2	Petition	555	Claims	....	....	......	Discharged; laid on table.		
Brown, John	Indemnity for damages occasioned by United States troops.	10	1	Petition	177	Claims	Feb. 25, 1808	Favorable	......	Referred to Committee Whole House.		
Brown, John	Indemnity for damages occasioned by United States troops.	10	2	Petition	350	Claims	Nov. 18, 1808	Favorable	106	Passed.		
Brown, John	Indemnity for damages by United States troops.	13	3	Petition	455	Claims	15	Favorable	248	Passed	Passed	App'd Jan. 28, 1815
Brown, John, (Md.)	Indemnity for property destroyed, war of 1812.	25	2	Petition	72	Claims.						
Brown, John, (Ohio)	Pension for services, war of 1812.	25	2	Petition	588	Invalid Pensions	777	Favorable	730	Passed	Adverse report.	
Brown, John, (Ohio)	Pension for services, war of 1812.	26	1	Petition	161	Invalid Pensions	229	Favorable	241	Passed	Indef. postp'd.	
Brown, John, (Ohio)	Pension for services, war of 1812.	29	1	Petition	503	Invalid Pensions	July 25, 1846	Adverse	......	Laid on table.		
Brown, John, (Indiana)	Compensation for horse lost in removing Indians.	26	1	Petition	335	Claims	705	Adverse	......	Laid on table.		
Brown, John, (Cherokee)	Compensation for improvement on lands relinquished.	21	1	Petition	318	Indian Affairs.						
Brown, John, (Cherokee)	Compensation for improvement on lands relinquished.	21	2	Petition	163	Indian Affairs.						
Brown, John, (Cherokee)	Compensation for improvement on lands relinquished.	22	1	Petition	387	Indian Affairs.						
Brown, John, (Cherokee)	Compensation for improvement on lands relinquished.	22	2	Petition	79	Indian Affairs	73	Favorable	717	Referred to Committee Whole House.		
Brown, John, (Cherokee)	Compensation for improvement on lands relinquished.	23	1	Petition	50	Indian Affairs.						
Brown, John, (Cherokee)	Compensation for improvement on lands relinquished.	24	1	Petition	96	Indian Affairs	Feb. 5, 1836	Favorable	292	Referred to Committee Whole House.		
Brown, John, (Cherokee)	Compensation for improvement on lands relinquished.	24	2	Rep't Committee Whole House.	200	....	....	With't amend.	292	Passed	Passed	App'd March 3, 1837
Brown, John, (Cherokee)	Interest on claim allowed by act of March 3, 1837.	26	1	Petition	946	Indian Affairs.						
Brown, Rev. John, (S. C.)	Remission of duty on books imported.	6	1	Petition	626	Com. and Manuf.	Mar. 18, 1800	Adverse	......	Leave to withdraw.		
Brown, John G	Remission of duties on goods illegally seized.	14	2	Petition	95	Ways and Means	Jan. 2, 1817	Adverse	......	Rejected.		
Brown, John G	Reimbursement of a remitted forfeiture.	14	2	Petition	415	Ways and Means.						
Brown, John G	Reimbursement of a remitted forfeiture.	15	1	Petition	302	Claims.						

List of private claims presented to the House of Representatives of the United States from the 1st to the 31st Congress, inclusive—Continued.

Names of claimants.	Nature or object of the claim.	Congress.	Session.	How brought before the House of Reps.	Page of journal.	To what committee of the House referred.	No. or date of the report.	Nature of the report.	No. of the bill.	How disposed of by the House of Reps.	How disposed of by the Senate.	Date of the act of Congress, and remarks.
Brown, John G	Reimbtrsement of a remitted forfeiture.	15	2	Appropriation bill	211	Whole House		Amendments	294	Passed	Passed	App'd March 3, 1819
Brown, John D	Indemnity for illegal acts of government officers.	21	1	Petition	471	Naval Affairs.						
Brown, John H	(See John R. Brown and others)	24	1		753							
Brown, John P	Compensation as interpreter at Constantinople.	31	1	Petition	311	Foreign Affairs.						
Brown, John P	Compensation as interpreter at Constantinople.	31	2	Petition	101	Foreign Affairs						Statutes at Large, vol. 9, p. 615.
Brown, John R	Pension for revolutionary services.	17	1	Petition	195	Pens. & Rev. Cl'ms.	Feb. 19, 1822	Adverse		Leave to withdraw.		
Brown, John R	Right of pre-emption as New Orleans branch pilot.	28	1	Petition	77	Priv. Land Claims.	9	Favorable	35	Passed	Passed	App'd June 17, 1844
Brown, John R., & others.	Indemnity for ship taken by the French.	24	1	Petition	753	Foreign Affairs	July 4, 1836	Adverse		Laid on table.		
Brown, John W., & others.	Right of pre-emption to land in Louisiana.	23	1	Petition	93	Priv. Land Claims.						
Brown, John, & Co	Compensation for extra mail service.	24	2	Petition	47	P. Of. & P. Roads.						
Brown, John, & Co	Compensation for extra mail service.	25	2	Petition	74	P. Of. and P. Roads.	594	Favorable	581	Referred to Committee Whole House.		
Brown, John, & Co	Compensation for extra mail service.	25	3	Rep't Committee Whole House.	431			With't amend.	581	Passed	Passed	App'd March 3, 1839
Brown, Col. John, widow of.	Compensation for revolutionary services.	3	1	Memorial	70	Select	Mar. 11, 1794	Adverse		Laid on table.		
Brown, John, widow of	Pension for loss of husband in public service.	13	2	Petition	185	Pen. & Rev. Cl'ms.	31	Adverse		Laid on table.		
Brown, John, widow of	Pension for loss of husband in public service.	13	3	Petition	709	Pens. & Rev. Cl'ms	Mar. 3, 1815	Adverse		Laid on table.		
Brown, John, executrix of	Equitable settlement of accounts	25	2	Petition	395	Claims.						
Brown, John, heirs of	Confirmation of title to land in Louisiana.	26	1	Petition	611	Priv. Land Claims.	598	Favorable	456	Referred to Committee Whole House.		
Brown, John, heirs of	Confirmation of title to land in Louisiana.	27	2	Petition	155	Priv. Land Claims.	83	Favorable	123	Passed.		
Browne, John	Pension for revolutionary services.	3	1	Rep. of Secretary War.	131	Select.						
Browne, John	Pension for revolutionary services.	5	2	Petition	179	Claims.						
Brown, Jonathan, (R. I.)	Increase of pension	16	2	Petition	50	Pens. & Rev. Cl'ms.						
Brown, Jonathan, (N. Y.)	Pension for revolutionary services.	21	1	Petition	546	Military Pensions.						
Brown, Jonathan, (N. Y.)	Pension for revolutionary services.	21	2	Petition	231	Military Pensions.						
Brown, Jonathan, (N. Y.)	Pension for revolutionary services.	27	2	Petition	749	Rev. Pensions	784	Adverse		Laid on table.		
Brown, Jonathan, (N. Y.)	Pension for revolutionary services.	29	1	Petition	370	Rev. Pensions	455	Favorable	332	Passed	Indef. postp'd.	
Brown, Jonathan, (N. Y.)	Pension for revolutionary services.	29	2	Petition	74	Rev. Pensions	71	Favorable	681	Referred to Committee Whole House.		
Brown, Jonathan W	Reimbursement of an overpayment for land.	20	1	Senate bill	414	Public Lands	Mar. 24, 1828	With't amend.	S. 82	Referred to Committee Whole House.		
Brown, Joseph	Increase of pension	10	2	Pension bill	499	Whole House	Feb. 28, 1809	With amend.	158	Passed	Passed with amendment.	App'd March 3, 1809
Brown, Joseph, (Miss.)	Correction of an error in land entry	22	1	Petition	51	Public Lands.						
Brown, Joseph, (Ky.)	Pension for services in the war of 1812.	23	1	Resolution	512	Invalid Pensions.						
Brown, Joseph, (Ky.)	Pension for services in the war of 1812.	25	3	Petition	218	Invalid Pensions.						

List of private claims presented to the House of Representatives of the United States from the 1st to the 31st Congress, inclusive—Continued.

Names of claimants.	Nature or object of the claim.	Congress.	Session.	How brought before the House of Reps.	Page of journal.	To what committee of the House referred.	No. or date of the report.	Nature of the report.	No. of the bill.	How disposed of by the House of Reps.	How disposed of by the Senate.	Date of the act of Congress, and remarks.
Brown, Joseph	Balance due him as assignee of sundry persons for property lost in the Seminole war.	24	2	Resolution	78	Claims	Feb. 22, 1837	Adverse	......	Laid on table.		
Brown, Joseph	Balance due him as assignee of sundry persons for property lost in the Seminole war.	25	2	Resolution	475	Claims	729	Adverse	......	Laid on table.		
Brown, Joseph	Balance due him as assignee of sundry persons for property lost in the Seminole war.	26	2	Petition	124	Claims.						
Brown, Joseph	Balance due him as assignee of sundry persons for property lost in the Seminole war.	27	2	Petition	94	Claims.						
Brown, Joseph, (Vt.)	Arrears of pension	25	3	Petition	571	Invalid Pensions.						
Brown, Joseph, (Vt.)	Arrears of pension	26	1	Petition	161	Invalid Pensions	294	Adverse	......	Laid on table.		
Brown, Joseph, (Tenn.)	Indemnity for losses as collector of direct tax.	26	1	Petition	336	Claims.						
Brown, Joseph, (Tenn.)	Indemnity for losses as collector of direct tax.	26	2	Petition	248	Claims.						
Brown, Joseph, (Tenn.)	Indemnity for losses as collector of direct tax.	27	2	Petition	76	Claims.						
				Documents	948	Claims.						
Brown, Joseph, (Tenn.)	Indemnity for losses as collector of direct tax.	28	1	Petition	743	Claims.						
Brown, Joseph, (C. C., Pa.)	Pension for services in the war of 1812.	27	2	Petition	218	Invalid Pensions	941	Adverse	......	Leave to withdraw.		
Brown, Joseph, (E. C., Pa.)	Arrears of pension	28	1	Petition	113	Invalid Pensions	....	....	......	Discharged; laid on table.		
Brown, Joseph, (E. C., Pa.)	Arrears of pension	30	1	Petition	495	Invalid Pensions	583	Adverse	......	Laid on table.		
Brown, Joseph	(See heirs of James Brown)	11	2	....	240							
Brown, Joseph C	Payment of balance due for public services.	22	2	Resolution	156	Claims	102	Favorable	743	Recommitted.		
Brown, Joseph C	Payment of balance due for public services.	22	2	Gen. app'n bill	240	Ways and Means	Jan. 26, 1833	Amended	714	Passed	Passed	App'd March 2, 1833
Brown, Joseph C	Payment of balance due for public services.	23	1	Petition	34	Ways and Means	19	Favorable	19	Referred to Committee Whole House.		
Brown, Joseph, widow of.	Continuation of pension	26	1	Petition	283	Rev. Pensions	490	Adverse	......	Laid on table.		
Brown, Joseph R	Reimbursement of expenses in arresting Indian offenders.	30	1	Petition	414	Claims	317	Adverse	......	Laid on table.		
Brown, Josiah	Renewal of letters patent	23	2	Petition	39	Judiciary.						
Brown, Josiah H	Pension for services in the war of 1812.	23	1	Petition	332	Invalid Pensions	308	Favorable	343	Referred to Committee Whole House.		
Brown, Josiah H	Pension for services in the war of 1812.	23	2	Rep't Committee Whole House.	336	....	....	With't amend.	343	Passed.		
Brown, Josiah H	Pension for services in the war of 1812.	24	1	Petition	53	Invalid Pensions	46	Favorable	58	Passed	Passed	App'd May 14, 1836
Brown, Laban	Pension for services in United States army.	18	2	Petition	65	Pens. & Rev. Clm's.						
Brown, Laban	Pension for services in United States army.	19	1	Petition	175	Military Pensions	April 1, 1828	Adverse	......	Laid on table.		
Brown, Laban	Pension for services in United States army.	20	1	Petition	38	Military Pensions.						
Brown, Larned S., representatives of.	Reimbursement of medical expenses, attendance, &c.	22	2	Petition	52	Invalid Pensions	Jan. 15, 1833	Adverse	......	Laid on table.		

List of private claims presented to the House of Representatives of the United States from the 1st to the 31st Congress, inclusive—Continued.

Names of claimants.	Nature or object of the claim.	Congress.	Session.	How brought before the House of Reps.	Page of journal.	To what committee of the House referred.	No. or date of the report.	Nature of the report.	No. of the bill.	How disposed of by the House of Reps.	How disposed of by the Senate.	Date of the act of Congress, and remarks.
Brown, Levi, (N. Y.)	Pension	22	1	Petition	288	Invalid Pensions	Feb. 15, 1832	Favorable bill.	377	Passed.		
Brown, Levi, (N. Y.)	Pension	23	1	Petition	72	Invalid Pensions	Dec. 23, 1833	Favorable bill.	79	Passed	Passed	App'd June 30, 1834
Brown, Levi, (Ohio)	Pension for services; war of 1812	28	1	Petition	352	Invalid Pensions	232	Adverse		Laid on table.		
Brown, Low	Bounty land for services in Indian wars.	20	2	Petition	119	Priv. Land Claims.						
Brown, Low	Bounty land for services in Indian wars.	21	1	Petition	98	Rev. Claims	Feb. 3, 1830	Adverse		Laid on table.		
Brown, Lucretia	(See widow of Joseph Brown)	26	1		283							
Brown, Luther	Compensation for horse lost in Florida war.)	28	1	Petition	262	Claims.						
Brown, Marcus	(See heir of Conrad Brown)	23	1		98							
Brown, Margaret C.	(See widow of Thomas Murray, jr.)	29	1		175		446					
Brown, Mary	(See widow of Samuel Brown)	3	1		22							
Brown, Mary	(See widow of Jacob Brown)	29	1		1074							
Brown, Morgan	Compensation for horse killed in Creek war.	16	2	Senate bill	67	Claims	Dec. 20, 1820	Adverse	S. 10	Referred to Committee Whole House.		
Brown, Morgan	Compensation for horse killed in Creek war.	17	1	Petition	92	Claims	30	Adverse		Referred to Committee Whole House.		
Brown, Moses, and others	Indemnity for damage by United States troops.	9	2	Petition	555	Claims				Discharged; laid on table.		
Brown, Moses, and others	Indemnity for damage by United States troops.	10	1	Petition	177	Claims	Feb. 25, 1808	Favorable		Referred to Committee Whole House.		
Brown, Moses, and others	Indemnity for damage by United States troops.	10	2	Petition	350	Claims	Nov. 18, 1808	Favorable	106	Passed.		
Brown, Moses, and others	Indemnity for damage by United States troops.	11	2	Memorail	177	Claims	Dec. 26, 1809	Favorable	51	Referred to Committee Whole House.		
Brown, Moses, and others	Indemnity for damage by United States troops.	13	3	Petition	455	Claims	15	Favorable	242	Passed	Passed	App'd Jan. 28, 1815
Brown, Moses, and others	Drawback on merchandise exported	3	1	Senate bill	179	Whole House			S. 16	Passed	Passed	App'd June 4, 1794
Brown, Moses, attorney of	Indemnity for French spoliations prior to 1800.	26	1	Memorial	182	Foreign Affairs	343	Favorable	319	Referred to Committee Whole House.		
Brown, Moses, executor of	Indemnity for French Spoliations prior to 1800.	26	1	Memorial	182	Foreign Affairs	343	Favorable	319	Referred to Committee Whole House.		
Brown, Moses, executor of	Indemnity for French spoliations prior to 1800.	29	2	Petition	129	Foreign Affairs.						
Brown, Mrs.	Payment of certain bills of credit	4	1	Report Secretary of Treasury.	388	Claims	74	Adverse		Laid on table.		
Brown, Mrs.	(See daughter of Sergeant Jasper.)	25	2	Petition Petition (2)	525 707	Rev. Pensions. Rev. Pensions.						
Brown, Nathaniel	(See David Jackson, and N. B.)	18	2		228							
Brown, Napoleon	(See Arabia Brown, *et al*)	31	1		234							
Brown, Nicholas	Pension for revolutionary services.	14	1	Petition	105	Pens. & Rev. Cl'ms.						
Brown, Nicholas	(See widow of Stephen Decatur, and others.)	18	2		55							
Brown, Nicholas, *et al*	Indemnity for French spoliations prior to 1800.	23	1	Memorial	273	Foreign Affairs.						
Brown, Nicholas, *et al.*	Indemnity for French spoliations prior to 1800.	26	1	Memorial	182	Foreign Affairs	343	Favorable	319	Referred to Committee Whole House.		
Brown, Nicholas	(See surviving partner of Brown & Jarvis.)	24	1		143							
Brown, Noah, and others.	Proceeds of the sale of a capture by their brig.	15	1	Petition	183	Judiciary	Feb. 28, 1818	Adverse		Referred to Committee Whole House.		

List of private claims presented to the House of Representatives of the United States from the 1st to the 31st Congress, inclusive—Continued.

Names of claimants.	Nature or object of the claim.	Congress.	Session.	How brought before the House of Reps.	Page of journal.	To what committee of the House referred.	No. or date of the report.	Nature of the report.	No. of the bill.	How disposed of by the House of Reps.	How disposed of by the Senate.	Date of the act of Congress, and remarks.
Brown, Noah, and others.	Proceeds of the sale of a capture by their brig.	17	2	Petition	251	Commerce.						
Brown, Noah, and others.	Proceeds of the sale of a capture by their brig.	18	1	Petition	197	Ways and Means..	Feb. 20, 1824	Adverse	......	Laid on table.		
Brown, Noah, and others.	Proceeds of the sale of a capture by their brig.	20	1	Petition	417	Judiciary.						
Brown, Noah, and others.	Proceeds of the sale of a capture by their brig.	21	1	Petition	234	Judiciary	Feb. 8, 1830	Adverse	......	Laid on table.		
Brown, Noah, and others.	Proceeds of the sale of a capture by their brig.	22	1	Petition	286	Ways and Means.						
Brown, Noah, and others.	Proceeds of the sale of a capture by their brig.	23	1	Petition	111	Ways and Means..	....	....	......	Discharged; laid on table.		
Brown, Noah, and others.	Proceeds of the sale of a capture by their brig.	23	2	Petition	199	Ways and Means..	....	....	......	Discharged; leave to withdraw.		
Brown, Noah, and others.	Proceeds of the sale of a capture by their brig.	24	1	Memorial	214	Ways and Means..	June 7, 1836	Favorable....	682	Referred to Committee Whole House.		
Brown, Noah, and others.	Proceeds of the sale of a capture by their brig.	25	2	Memorial.......	42	Ways and Means..	986	Favorable	847	Referred to Committee Whole House.		
Brown, Noah, and others.	Proceeds of the sale of a capture by their brig.	25	3	Rep. of Committee Whole.	432	....	....	With't amend.	847	Passed.		
Brown, Noah, and others.	Proceeds of the sale of a capture by their brig.	26	1	Petition	298	Judiciary.						
Brown, Noah, and others.	Proceeds of the sale of a capture by their brig.	27	2	Petition	240	Ways and Means..	877	Favorable....	501	Ordered to 3d reading.		
Brown, Noah, and others.	Proceeds of the sale of a capture by their brig.	27	3	House bill......	89	....	....	....	501	Passed	Indef. postp'd.	
Brown, Noah, widow of..	Reimbursement of expenditure on light-house.	27	2	Petition	246	Claims.						
				Documents.....	413	Claims...........	165	Adverse	......	Laid on table.		
Brown, Noah	Indemnity for losses on Treasury notes.	24	1	Senate bill	956	Claims...........	June 8, 1836	With't amend.	S. 161	Passed	Passed	App'd July 2, 1836
Brown, Obediah	Pension for revolutionary services.	3	2	Rep. of Secretary War.	278	Claims.						
Brown, Obediah	Pension for revolutionary services.	5	2	Petition	179	Claims	April 19, 1798	Favorable	84	Passed	Passed	App'd May 4, 1798
Brown, Obediah	Increase of pension	12	1	Petition	139	Claims	June 12, 1812	Adverse	......	Laid on table.		
Brown, Oliver	Pension for disability, war of 1812	31	2	Petition	50	Invalid Pensions.						
Brown, Orris	(See Elijah White, *at al.*)......	29	1	....	1016							
Brown, Pamela	(See widow of Gen. Jacob Brown)	25	2	....	57							
Brown, Phebe	(See William Brown, widow of)	30	1	....	78							
Brown, Rebecca	(See heirs of George D. McMahon)	24	2	....	119							
Brown, Return B	Release from a judgment........	23	1	Petition	299	Judiciary.........	....	....	......	Discharged; laid on table.		
Brown, Return B	Release from a judgment........	24	1	Petition	106	Judiciary	739	Favorable	684	Referred to Committee Whole House.		
Brown, Return B	Release from a judgment........	25	2	Petition	41	Judiciary	376	Favorable....	400	Referred to Committee Whole House.		
Brown, Return B	Release from a jndgment........	25	3	Rep. of Committee Whole.	378	....	....	With't amend.	400	Passed	Passed	App'd March 3, 1839
Brown, Return B	Indemnity for losses sustained in public service.	27	1	Petition	99	Claims.						
Brown, Return B	Indemnity for losses sustained in public service.	27	2	Petition	93	Claims	186	Adverse	......	Laid on table.		
Brown, Reuben.........	Compensation for horse lost in Florida war.	28	1	Petition	262	Claims.						

List of private claims presented to the House of Representatives of the United States from the 1st to the 31st Congress, inclusive—Continued.

Names of claimants.	Nature or object of the claim.	Congress.	Session.	How brought before the House of Reps.	Page of journal.	To what committee of the House referred.	No. or date of the report.	Nature of the report.	No. of the bill.	How disposed of by the House of Reps.	How disposed of by the Senate.	Date of the act of Congress, and remarks.
Brown, Richard	Compensation for running Creek boundary.	18	2	Documents	160	Claims.						
Brown, Richard	Compensation for running Creek boundary.	19	1	Petition	36	Claims	Dec. 16, 1825	Adverse		Laid on table.		
Brown, Richard, sen., and others.	Exchange of an erroneous land entry.	28	1	Petition	744	Public Lands.						
Brown, Robert	Compensation for revolutionary services.	2	1	Petition	507					Referred to Secretary War.		
Brown, Robert	Right of pre emption to mill seat	12	1	Petition	43	Public Lands.						
Brown, Robert, (Pa.)	Compensation for services as deputy assessor.	19	2	Petition	242	Ways and Means.						
Brown, Robert T.	(See heirs of Francis Vallé)	19	1		133							
Brown, Sampson	Pension for revolutionary services.	2	1	Petition	447					Referred to Secretary of War.		
Brown, Sampson	Pension for revolutionary services.	3	1	Rep. of Secretary War.	131	Select	May 26, 1794	Res. to refer to Sec. War.	R. 12	Passed	Passed	App'd June 9, 1794
Brown, Sampson	Pension for revolutionary services.	3	2	Report of Secretary of War.	262	Claims.						
Brown, Sampson (Mass.)	Pension for services in the war of 1812.	27	3	Petition	58	Invalid Pensions	84	Favorable	712	Passed.		
Brown, Sampson (Mass.)	Pension for services in the war of 1812.	28	1	Petition	183	Invalid Pensions	111	Adverse		Laid on table.		
Brown, Sampson (Mass,)	Pension for services in the war of 1812.	29	1	Petition	162	Invalid Pensions	152	Favorable	155	Passed	Passed	App'd July 15, 1846
Brown, Samuel and others.	Bounty on fishing schooner Betsy.	4	1	Petition	370	Com. and Manuf.	90	Favorable	181	Passed	Rejected.	
Brown, Samuel, widow of (Va.)	Pension for loss of hasband killed in battle.	3	1	Petition	22					Laid on table.		
Brown, Samuel, widow of.	Reimbursement of money erroneously paid for land.	22	2	Petition	246	Public Lands.						
Brown, Samuel, widow of.	Reimbursement of money erroneously paid for land.	23	1	Petition	132	Public Lands	Jan. 2, 1834	Favorable	124	Passed.		
Brown, Samuel, widow of.	Reimbursement of money erroneously paid for land.	23	2	House bill	148				596	Postponed.		
Brown, Samuel, widow of.	Reimbursement of money erroneously paid for land.	24	1	Petition	114	Public Lands	191	Favorable	196	Passed.		
Brown, Samuel, (Boston.)	Indemnity for French spoliations prior to 1800.	26	1	Memorial	182	Foreign Affairs	343	Favorable	319	Referred to Committee Whole House.		
Brown, Samuel, attorney of.	Compensation for revolutionary services.	6	1	Petition	530	Claims	Mar. 25, 1800	Favorable		Referred to Committee Whole House.		
Brown, Samuel	(See Thomas Tupper, assignees of.)	22	2		142							
Brown, Samuel, jr., administrator of.	Indemnity for French spoliations prior to 1800.	26	1	Memorial	182	Foreign Affairs	343	Favorable	319	Referred to Committee Whole House.		
Brown, Samuel (Me.)	Pension	24	1	Petition	822	Invalid Pensions	Jan. 23, 1800	Favorable	727	Referred to Committee Whole House.		
Brown, Samuel (Me.)	Pension	25	2	Petition	38	Invalid Pensions	184	Favorable	210	Passed.	Adverse report.	
Brown, Samuel (Me.)	Pension	26	1	Petition	198	Invalid Pensions	213	Favorable	225	Passed.	Indef. postp'd.	
Brown, Samuel (R. I.)	Compensation for services as United States assessor.	24	2	Documents	37	Claims	140	Adverse		Laid on table.		
Brown, Samuel (R. I.)	Increase of compensation for services as naval officer.	26	1	Petition	709	Commerce.						
Brown, Samuel (R. I.)	Indemnity for French spoliations prior to 1800.	29	2	Petition	161	Foreign Affairs.						

List of private claims presented to the House of Representatives of the United States from the 1st to the 31st Congress, inclusive—Continued.

Names of claimants.	Nature or object of the claim.	Congress.	Session.	How brought before the House of Reps.	Page of journal.	To what committee of the House referred.	No. or date of the report.	Nature of the report.	No. of the bill.	How disposed of by the House of Reps.	How disposed of by the Senate.	Date of the act of Congress, and remarks.
Brown, Samuel	Pension for injuries received in public service.	27	2	Petition	60	Invalid Pensions	159	Adverse	......	Laid on table.		
Brown, Samuel, heir of	Pension for revolutionary services.	31	2	Petition	74	Rev. Claims.						
Brown, Samuel W	(See Theodore Stanwood and others.)	21	2	....	54							
Brown, Sarah	Indemnity for property taken by the enemy.	14	1	Petition	74	Rev. Claims.						
Brown, Silas & Co	Reimbursement of excessive duties	21	1	Petition	232	Ways and Means	Feb. 17, 1830	Adverse	......	Laid on table.		
Brown, Simon	Compensation for manuscript list of private claims.	30	1	Memorial	379	Accounts.						
Brown, Stark	Pension for revolutionary services.	3	1	Petition	103	....	....	....	......	Referred to Secretary of War.		
Brown Stewart	(See Falls and Brown.)	26	1	....	182	....	343	....	319			
Brown, Stephen	Compensation for horse lost in Florida war.	28	1	Petition	262	Claims.						
Brown, Tarlton	Commutation pay for revolutionary services.	24	1	Petition	475	Rev. Claims.						
Brown and Tarbox	Compensation for mail services in Texas.	31	1	Petition	214	P. Of. & P. Roads.	37	Favorable	65	Passed	Passed	App'd May 6, 1850
Brown, Thomas	(See representatives of H. L. Gaskins.)											
Brown, Thomas, (Tenn.)	Pension for revolutionary services.	22	1	Resolution	589	Rev. Pensions.						
Brown, Thomas, (N. J.)	Pension for revolutionary services.	23	1	Petition and docs.	617	Rev. Pensions.						
Brown, Thomas, (N. Y.)	Pension for revolutionary services.	25	2	Petition	585	Rev. Pensions	....	....	......	Discharged; laid on table.		
Brown, Thomas	Compensation for surveying public lands.	25	2	Petition	1047	Claims	960	Res. to refer to Sec. Treas'y.	......	Referred to Secretary Treasury.		
Brown, Thomas, heirs of.	Payment of revolutionary certificate.	12	2	Petition	571	Claims.	Feb. 12, 1813	Adverse	......	Laid on table.		
Brown, Thomas, heirs of.	Payment of revolutionary certificate.	13	2	Petition	329	Pensions	Mar. 14, 1814	Adverse	......	Laid on table.		
Brown, Thomas, executor of.	Indemnity for French spoliations prior to 1800.	26	1	Memorial	182	Foreign Affairs	343	Favorable	319	Referred to Committee Whole House.		
Brown, Thomas, heirs of.	Indemnity for French spoliations prior to 1800.	29	2	Petition	101	Foreign Affairs.						
Brown, Thomas, and others.	Additional compensation for flour at Indian treaty.	20	1	Senate bill	186	Claims	Feb. 6, 1828	Favorable	S. 41	Passed	Passed	App'd May 19, 1828
Brown, Thomas, 3d, (N. Y.)	Increase of pension	26	2	Petition	50	Rev. Pensions	....	....	......	Discharged; laid on table.		
Brown, Thomas G., (Tenn.)	Pension for disability, war of 1812.	31	2	Petition	132	Invalid Pensions.						
Brown, Thomas H., (Md.)	Bounty land for services, war of 1812.	27	2	Memorial	1437	Invalid Pensions.						
Brown, Thomas H., (Md.)	Bounty land for services, war of 1812.	27	3	Memorial	71	Public Lands	111	Favorable	731	Passed	Indef. postp'd.	
Brown, Thomas H., (Md.)	Bounty land for services, war of 1812.	28	1	Memorial	295	Public Lands.						
Brown, Thomas H., (Md.)	Bounty land for services, war of 1812.	28	2	Memorial	68	Public Lands.						
Brown, Thomas H., (Md.)	Bounty land for services, war of 1812.	29	1	Memorial	117	Public Lands	47	Adverse	......	Laid on table.		
Brown, Thomas H., (D. C.)	Pension for disability, war of 1812.	28	1	Memorial	240	Invalid Pensions	285	Adverse	......	Laid on table.		
Brown, Thomas H., (D. C.)	Pension for disability, war of 1812.	28	2	Petition	66	Invalid Pensions.						

List of private claims presented to the House of Representatives of the United States from the 1st to the 31st Congress, inclusive—Continued.

Names of claimants.	Nature or object of the claim.	Congress.	Session.	How brought before the House of Reps.	Page of journal.	To what committee of the House referred.	No. or date of the report.	Nature of the report.	No. of the bill.	How disposed of by the House of Reps.	How disposed of by the Senate.	Date of the act of Congress, and remarks.
Brown, Vernon	(See Ebenezer Breed & Co.)											
Brown, William	Indemnity for revolutionary losses and services.	4	2	Petition	635	Claims.						
Brown, William	Indemnity for revolutionary losses and services.	5	2	Petition	132	Claims	Jan. 12, 1798	Adverse	......	Laid on table.		
Browne, William	Balance due for services, Northeastern boundary commission.	24	1	Appropriat'n bill.	239	Whole House	April 15, 1836	Amendments	216	Passed	Passed	App'd May 9, 1836
Brown, William	(See James Collingsworth.)											
Brown, William, (Mich.)	Compensation for medical services among Indians.	10	2	Petition	489	Public Lands.						
Brown, William, (Mich.)	Indemnity for property sacrificed in Canada.	22	1	Petition	414	Public Lands.						
Brown, William, (Mich.)	Indemnity for property sacrificed in Canada.	22	2	Petition	64	Public Lands.						
Brown, William	Compensation for surveying State of Tennessee.	19	2	Resolution	75	Public Lands	21	Favorable	324	Referred to Committee Whole House.		
Brown, William	Compensation for surveying State of Tennessee.	20	1	Resolution	43	Public Lands.						
Brown, William	(See assignee of John Dwiggins)	25	2	....	543							
Brown, William, (N. Y.)	Pension	21	1	Petition	197	Military Pensions.						
Brown, William, (Tenn.)	Arrears of pension	28	1	Petition	633	Invalid Pensions.						
Brown, William, (Mo.)	(See Samuel Davis and others)	25	3	....	98							
Brown, William, (Ohio)	Bounty land	25	3	Petition	130	Priv. Land Claims.	....	....	......	Discharged; laid on table.		
Brown, William, (Ohio)	Bounty land	26	1	Petition	600	Public Lands.						
Brown, William, widow of	Pension for revolutionary services.	30	1	Petition	78	Rev. Pensions	218	Adverse	......	Laid on table.		
Brown, William, heirs of	Commutation pay for revolutionary services.	26	1	Petition	337	Claims.						
Brown, William, (Maine)	Pension for wounds in naval service.	28	1	Senate bill	1010	Naval Affairs	Jan. 7, 1844	With't amend.	S. 181	Referred to Committee Whole House.		
Brown, William, (Maine)	Pension for wounds in naval service.	29	1	Petition	82	Invalid Pensions	....	....	......	Discharged; laid on table.		
Brown, William, & others	Compensation for services as U. S. assessor, Tennesee.	14	1	Petition	232	Ways and Means.						
Brown, William D	Compensation for improvements on land sold by U. S.	21	2	Memorial	272	Public Lands.						
Brown, William D	Compensation for improvements on land sold by U. S.	23	1	Petition	383	Public Lands.						
Brown, W. S	Right of pre-emption to land in Louisiana.	23	1	Petition	93	Priv. Land Claims.						
Brown, William T	(See heirs of Charles Brown)	25	2	....	983							
Brownell, Jeremiah	Release from imprisonment at suit of United States.	15	1	Petition	24	Ways and Means.						
Brownell, Thomas	Pension for disability, in naval service.	27	2	Senate bill	1064	Naval Affairs	Aug. 20, 1842	With't amend.	S. 194	Passed	Passed	App'd Aug. 29, 1842
Brownell, Thomas	Continuation of pension	28	2	Petition	332	Naval Affairs	168	Favorable	636	Referred to Committee Whole House.		
Brownell, Thomas	Continuation of pension	29	1	Petition	89	Naval Affairs.						
				Senate bill	1075	Naval Affairs	July 24, 1846	With't amend.	S. 118	Rejected.		
Brownell, Thomss	Continuation of pension	29	2	Senate bill	306	Naval Affairs	Feb. 16, 1847	With't amend.	S. 34	Passed	Passed	App'd Feb. 18, 1847
Brownell, Thomas	Reimbursement of amount paid for medical services at Sackett's Harbor.	29	2	Senate bill	374	Naval Affairs	Feb. 24, 1847	With't amend.	S. 76	Referred to Committee Whole House.		

List of private claims presented to the House of Representatives of the United States from the 1st to the 31st Congress, inclusive—Continued.

Names of claimants.	Nature or object of the claim.	Congress.	Session.	How brought before the House of Reps.	Page of journal.	To what committee of the House referred.	No. or date of the report.	Nature of the report.	No. of the bill.	How disposed of by the House of Reps.	How disposed of by the Senate.	Date of the act of Congress, and remarks.
28 Brownell, Thomas	Reimbursement of amount paid for medical services at Sackett's Harbor.	30	1	Senate bill	683	Naval Affairs	May 18, 1848	With't amend.	S. 88	Passed	Passed	App'd May 31, 1848
Brownell, Wilbur	Bounty on fishing vessel	16	1	Petition	27	Ways and Means	Dec. 27, 1819	Adverse		Rejected.		
Browner, William	Indemnity for revolutionary losses.	2	1	Petition	554					Referred to Secretary War.		
Browner, William	Indemnity for revolutionary losses.	2	2	Rep. of Secretary War.	625					Laid on table.		
Brownfield, Robert	Pension for revolutionary services.	25	2	Petition	587	Rev. Pensions				Discharged; laid on table.		
Brownfield, Robert	Pension for revolutionary services.	25	3	Petition	460	Rev. Pensions.						
Brownfield, Robert	Pension for revolutionary services	26	1	Petition	173	Rev. Pensions	481	Adverse		Laid on table.		
Brownfield, Robert	Pensions for revolutionary services	26	2	Petition	962	Rev. Pensions	714	Adverse		Laid on table.		
Browning, David	Exchange of location of land	24	1	Petition	57	Public Lands	75	Favorable	91	Passed	Passed	App'd June 23, 1836
Browning, Elijah, & others	Compensation for team lost in public service.	13	3	Petition	455	Claims	Nov. 14, 1814	Favorable	228	Passed	Indef. postp'd.	
Browning, Elijah, & others	Compensation for teaml ost in public service.	14	1	Petition	54	Claims.						
Browning, Joshua	Compensatisn for mule taken for public use.	16	2	Petition	35	Claims	Dec. 19, 1820	Adverse		Rejected.		
Browning, Joshua	Compensation for mule taken for public use.	22	1	Petition	333	Claims	Feb. 27, 1832	Adverse		Laid on table.		
Browning, Meshack	Compensation for horse lost in public service.	20	1	Petition	342	Claims.						
Browning, Meshack	Compensation for horse lost in public service.	21	1	Petition	230	Claims	155	Favorable	198	Passed	Passed	App'd May 29, 1830
Browning, Lewright	(See Robert L. Browning, widow of.)	31	1		1249							
Browning, Robert L., widow of.	Pension for naval services	31	1	Petition	1249	Rev. Claims.						
				Senate bill	1414				S. 319	Passed	Passed	App'd Sept. 30, 1850
Browning, Samuel	Indemnity for property captured by the British.	20	1	Petition	438	Claims	April 2, 1828	Adverse		Laid on table.		
Browning, Samuel	Extension of patent right	21	2	Senate bill	278	Judiciary	Feb. 11, 1831	With't amend.	S. 106	Passed	Passed	App'd Mar. 3, 1831
Browning, W. W. & J. S. S.	Confirmation of title to land in Mississippi.	28	1	Petition	75	Indian Affairs	36	Favorable	66	Passed	Passed	App'd Mar. 26, 1844
Brownlee, Alexander, son of.	Commutation pay; killed in battle	21	2	Petition	190	Rev. Claims.						
Brownlee, Alexander, son of.	Commutation pay; killed in battle	22	1	Petition	51	Rev. Claims	142	Favorable	216	Referred to Committee Whole House.		
Brownlee, Alexander, son of.	Commutation pay; killed in battle	22	2	Rep't Committee Whole House.	67			With amend.	216	Passed	Passed	App'd Feb. 9, 1833
Brownlee, Alexander, son of.	Arrears of pay for revolutionary services.	23	1	Petition	306	Rev. Claims.						
Brownlee, Alexander, son of.	Arrears of pay for revolutionary services.	23	2	Petition	138	Rev. Claims.						
Brownlee, Alexander, son of.	Arrears of pay for revolutionary services.	24	1	Petition	138	Rev. Claims	Feb. 19, 1836	Adverse		Laid on table.		
Brownlee, Alexadner, son of.	Arrears of pay for revolutionary ervices.	26	1	Petition	360	Rev. Claims.						
Brownlee, Alexarder, son of.	Duplicate revolutionary land warrant.	29	2	Petition	92	Public Lands				Discharged; laid on table.		
Brownlee, Alexander, son of.	Duplicate revolutionary land warrant.	30	1	Petition	228	Public Lands				Discharged; laid on table.		

List of private claims presented to the House of Representatives of the United States from the 1st *to the* 31*st Congress, inclusive*—Continued.

Names of claimants.	Nature or object of the claim.	Congress.	Session.	How brought before the House of Reps.	Page of journal.	To what committee of the House referred.	No. or date of the report.	Nature of the report.	No. of the bill.	How disposed of by the House of Reps.	How disposed of by the Senate.	Date of the act of Congress, and remarks.
Brownlee, James	(See son of Alexander Brownlee)	21	2		190							
Brownlee, John	(See agents of Thomas Knox)	20	1		338							
Brownlee, William	Compensation for services; war of 1812.	22	1	Resolution	262	Claims	Feb. 15, 1832	Adverse		Rejected.		
Brownlow, John	Pension for revolutionary services	14	1	Documents	36	Pens. & Rev. Cl'ms.	Nov. 30, 1818	Adverse		Rejected.		
Brownson, Abraham	Compensation for revolutionary services.	20	1	Petition	243	Rev. Claims.						
Brownson, Abraham	Compensation for revolutionary services.	20	2	Petition	264	Rev. Claims.						
Brownson, Abraham	Compensation for revolutionary services.	21	1	Petition	75	Rev. Claims	Feb. 18, 1830	Adverse		Laid on table.		
				Senate bill	685	Military Affairs	May 22, 1830	With't amend.	S. 169	Passed	Passed	App'd May 26, 1830
Brownson, Gideon	Pension for revolutionary disabilities.	2	2	Petition	694					Referred to Secretary of War.		
Brownson, Gideon	Pension for revolutionary disabilities.	3	1	Rep. of Secretary War.	131	Select	May 26, 1794	Res. to refer to Sec. War.	R. 12	Passed	Passed	App'd June 9, 1794
Brownson, Gideon	Pension for revolutionary disiabilities.	3	2	Rep. of Secretary War.	262	Claims	Feb. 28, 1795	Pension bill	130	Passed	Indef. postp'd.	
Brownson, Gideon	Pension for revolutionary disabilities.	4	1	Rep. of Secretary War.	447	Claims	Feb. 18, 1796	Pension bill	156	Passed	Passed with amendment.	App'd April 20, 1796
Brownson, Gideon	Arrears of pay for revolutionary services.	2	2	Petition	706					Referred to Secretary of War.		
Brownson, Hector, & others	Additional bounty land for military services.	15	2	Petition	154	Military Affairs.						
Brownson, Hector, & others	Additional bounty land for military services.	16	1	Petition	32	Military Affairs	Jan. 3, 1820	Adverse		Rejected.		
Brownson, Timothy	Correction of an erroneous land entry.	20	1	Petition	309	Public Lands.						
Bronwson, William	Right of pre-emption as New Orleans branch pilot.	28	1	Petition	77	Priv. Land Claims.	9	Favorable	35	Passed	Passed	App'd June 17, 1844
Bruce, Benjamin B.	Pension	21	1	Petition	168	Military Pensions	April 13, 1830	Adverse		Laid on table.		
Bruce, Benjamin B.	Pension	21	2	Petition	260	Military Pensions.						
Bruce, Benjamin B.	Pension	22	1	Petition	389	Invalid Pensions	April 11, 1832	Adverse		Laid on table.		
Bruce, Benjamin B.	Pension	22	2	Petition	69	Indian Affairs.						
Bruce, Charles	(See John and Charles Bruce)	29	2		52							
Bruce, Hannah	Continuation of pension	27	2	Petition	256	Rev. Pensions.						
Bruce, Hannah	Continuation of pension	28	1	Petition	541	Rev. Pensions.						
Bruce, Henry, and others	Prize money for capture of a slaver	29	1	Petition	591	Naval Affairs						Leave to withdraw, 2d session.
Bruce, John (Tenn.)	Commutation of pension for land	28	1	Petition	433	Public Lands	335	Adverse		Laid on table.		
Bruce, John, (Ky.)	Indemnity for suspension of contract.	22	1	Resolution	511	Claims.						
Bruce, John, (Ky.)	Indemnity for suspension of contract.	22	2	Petition	79	Claims				Discharged; referred to Chief Engineer.		
Bruce, John, (Ky.)	Indemnity for suspension of contract.	23	1	Report of Chief Engineer.	26	Claims	193	Favorable	213	Passed	Passed	App'd June 30, 1834
Bruce, John	Pension for revolutionary services	14	1	Pension bill	622	Whole House	April 23, 1816	With amend.	171	Passed	Passed with amendment.	App'd April 30, 1816
Bruce, John and Charles	Renewal of letters patent	29	2	Petition	52	Patents	Jan. 20, 1847	Favorable	52	Passed	Passed	App'd Feb. 22, 1847
Bruce, John	(See administrator of Philip Bush)	19	2		308							
Bruce, Joseph	Compensation for horse lost in public service.	15	2	Petition	270	Claims.						

List of private claims presented to the House of Representatives of the United States from the 1st to the 31st Congress, inclusive—Continued.

Names of claimants.	Nature or object of the claim.	Congress.	Session.	How brought before the House of Reps.	Page of journal.	To what committee of the House referred.	No. or date of the report.	Nature of the report.	No. of the bill.	How disposed of by the House of Reps.	How disposed of by the Senate.	Date of the act of Congress, and remarks.
Bruce, Joseph	Compensation for horse lost in public service.	16	1	Petition	286	Claims	Mar. 6, 1820	Favorable	99	Passed	Passed	App'd May 8, 1820
Bruce, Matilda	Continuation of pension	28	1	Petition	849	Rev. Pensions.						
Bruce, Stephen	(See William Breck, jr.)	7	2		328							
Bruce, Stephen	(See Stephen Brace)	17	2		143							
Bruce, William	Confirmation of title to land in Ohio.	13	3	Petition	662	Public Lands.						
Bruce, William	Confirmation of title to land in Ohio.	14	1	Petition	43	Public Lands	35	Favorable	58	Passed	Passed	App'd April 27, 1816
Bruen, Matthias	(See sureties of Thomas H. Smith and Son.)	20	2		142							
Bruen, Peter Bryan	Confirmation of title to land in Louisiana.	12	2	Petition	621	Public Lands.						
Bruen, Peter Bryan	Confirmation of title to land in Louisiana.	16	1	Petition	47	Priv. Land Claims.	Mar. 8, 1820	Adverse		Rejected.		
Bruce, Peter Bryan, heirs of.	Arrears of pension for revolutionary services.	29	1	Petition	233	Rev. Pensions	618	Adverse		Laid on table.		
Bruen, Timothy	Compensation for horse taken for public use.	21	1	Resolution	476	Claims.						
Bruen, Timothy	Compensation for horse taken for public use.	21	2	Petition	40	Claims	Dec. 15, 1830	Adverse		Laid on table.		
				Recommitted	218	Claims.						
Bruff, James	Pension	10	1	Pension bill	232	Whole House	April 19, 1808	With amend.	78	Passed	Passed with amendment.	App'd April 25, 1808
Brum, Philip, widow of	Increase of pension	25	2	Petition	400	Naval Affairs				Discharged; laid on table.		
Brum, Philip, widow of	Increase of pension	25	3	Petition	189	Naval Affairs				Discharged; laid on table.		
Brum, Philip, widow of	Increase of pension	26	1	Petition	180	Naval Affairs.						
Brum, Philip, widow of	Increase of pension	27	2	Petition	861	Naval Affairs	759	Favorable	443	Ordered to 3d reading.		
Brum, Philip, widow of	Increase of pension	27	3	House bill	88				443	Passed	Indef. postpo'd.	
Brum, Philip, widow of	Increase of pension	28	1	Petition	788	Naval Affairs.						
Brum, Philip, widow of	Increase of pension	29	1	Petition	279	Naval Affairs	601	Favorable	424	Ordered to 3d reading.		
Brum, Philip, widow of	Increase of pension	29	2	House bill	210				424	Passed	Passed	App'd March 3, 1847
Brumfield, Richard B.	(See Samuel H. Brumfield, heir of)	24	1		64							
Brumfield, Samuel H., heir of.	Remuneration for military services.	24	1	Petition	64	Military Affairs.						
Brumfield, Samuel H., heir of.	Remuneration for military services.	25	3	Petition	461	Invalid Pensions.						
Brumfield, Samuel H., heir of.	Remuneration for military services.	26	1	Petition	162	Invalid Pensions.						
Brumfield, Samuel H., heir of.	Remuneration for military services.	27	2	Petition	154	Invalid Pensions.						
Brumfield, Samuel H., heir of.	Remuneration for military services.	27	3	Petition	72	Invalid Pensions	193	Adverse		Laid on table.		
Brumley, Preserved	Pension for services, war of 1812.	29	2	Petition	470					Laid on table.		
Brumley, Preserved	Pension for services, war of 1812.	31	1	Petition	496	Invalid Pensions				Discharged; laid on table.		
Bruner, Mary Ann	Compensation in land for services of husband.	25	2	Petition	418	Priv. Land Claims.						
Bruner, Mary Ann	Reimbursement of payment for land without title.	28	1	Petition	357	Public Lands	204	Adverse		Referred to Committee Whole House.		

List of private claims presented to the House of Representatives of the United States from the 1st to the 31st Congress, inclusive—Continued.

Names of claimants.	Nature or object of the claim.	Congress.	Session.	How brought before the House of Reps.	Page of journal.	To what committee of the House referred.	No. or date of the report.	Nature of the report.	No. of the bill.	How disposed of by the House of Reps.	How disposed of by the Senate.	Date of the act of Congress, and remarks.
Bruner, Mary Ann	Reimbursement of payment for land without title.	28	2	House bill	133	Public Lands	153	With amend.	464	Referred to Committee Whole House.		
Bruner, Mary Ann	Reimbursement of payment for land without title.	29	1	Petition	117	Public Lands.						
				Petition (2)	125	Public Lands	63	Favorable	60	Referred to Committee Whole House.		
Bruner, Martin	Right of pre-emption	24	1	Petition	913	Public Lands.						
Brunot, Elizabeth	(See Felix Brunot, widow of)	27	3		349							
Brunot, Felix, widow of	Pension for revolutionary services.	27	3	Memorial	349	Rev. Pensions.						
Brunot, Felix, wibow of	Pension for revolutionary services.	28	1	Memorial	811	Rev. Pensions	536	Favorable	412	Referred to Committee Whole House.		
Brunot, Felix, widow of	Pension for revolutionary services.	29	1	Petition	472	Rev. Pensions	462	Favorable	339	Referred to Committee Whole House.		
Brunot, Felix, widow of	Pension for revolutionary services.	30	1	Petition	279	Rev. Pensions	636	Adverse		Laid on table.		
Brunot, Felix, widow of	Pension for revolutionary services.	31	1	Petition	194	Rev. Pensions.						
Brunson, John	Indemnity for property destroyed by the enemy.	20	1	Petition	226	Claims	Feb. 15, 1828	Adverse		Laid on table.		
Brunson, John	Indemnity for property destroyed by the enemy.	21	1	Senate bill	502	Claims	May 17, 1830	Adverse	S. 93	Referred to Committee Whole House.		
Brunson, John	Indemnity for property destroyed by the enemy.	21	2	Senate bill	90	Claims	Feb. 25, 1831	Adverse	S. 13	Laid on table.		
Brunson, John	Indemnity for property destroyed by the enemy.	22	1	Senate bill	455	Claims	Mar. 26, 1832	With't amend.	S. 62	Passed with amendm't	Passed as am'd	App'd July 11, 1832
Brunson, John	Indemnity for property destroyed by the enemy.	23	1	Petition	132	Claims	147	Adverse		Laid on table.		
Brunson, John	Indemnity for property destroyed by the enemy.	23	2	Petition	59	Claims.						
Brunson, Stout	Compensation for revolutionary services.	20	1	Petition	278	Rev. Claims.						
Brush, Elijah, widow of	Indemnity for property destroyed by the enemy.	17	2	Petition	26	Claims	Dec. 18, 1822	Adverse		Laid on table.		
Brush, Elijah, widow of	Indemnity for property destroyed by the enemy.	18	1	Petition	61	Claims	43	Favorable	84	Passed	Passed	App'd May 17, 1824
Brush, John C	Compensation for fire place in the hall of Representatives.	17	1	Petition	299	Public Buildings				Discharged; laid on table.		
Brush, John C., widow of.	Compensation for fire place in the hall of Representatives.	17	2	Petition	87	Public Buildings				Leave to withdraw.		
Brush, John C., widow of.	Compensation for fire place in the hall of Representatives.	24	1	Petition	432	Dis. of Col.						
Brush, John C., widow of.	Compensation for fire place in the hall of Representatives.	25	2	Memorial	1029	Dis. of Col.						
Brush, John C., widow of.	Pension	21	1	Petition	546	Military Pensions	May 7, 1830	Adverse		Laid on table.		
Brush, John M	(See Nehemiah Brush, executors of)	29	1		465							
Brush, Nathaniel, widow of.	Release from balance claimed by United States.	8	2	Petition	96	Claims.						
Brush, Nehemiah	Pension	21	2	Petition	270	Military Pensions.						
Brush, Nehemiah	Pension	30	2	Senate bill	240	Invalid Pensions	Feb. 13, 1849	With't amend.	S. 259	Passed	Passed	App'd Feb. 22, 1849
Brush, Nehemiah, executors of (Florida.)	Indemnity for property destroyed in Seminole war.	28	2	Petition	144	Claims.						
Brush, Nehemiah, executors of (Florida.)	Indemnity for property destroyed in Seminole war.	29	1	Petition	465	Military Affairs.						
Brush, Nehemiah, executors of (Florida.)	Indemnity for property destroyed in Seminole war.	30	2	Senate bill	518	Claims	Mar. 3, 1849	With't amend.	S. 237	Referred to Committee Whole House.		

List of private claims presented to the House of Representatives of the United States from the 1st to the 31st Congress, inclusive—Continued.

Names of claimants.	Nature or object of the claim.	Congress.	Session.	How brought before the House of Reps.	Page of journal.	To what committee of the House referred.	No. or date of the report.	Nature of the report.	No. of the bill.	How disposed of by the House of Reps.	How disposed of by the Senate.	Date of the act of Congress, and remarks.
Brush, Platt	Compensation for extra services as register land office.	22	1	Petition	514	Public Lands.						
Brush, Platt	Compensation for extra services as register land office.	22	2	Petition	178	Public Lands.						
Brush, Platt	Compensation for extra services as register land office.	23	1	Petition	637	Public Lands.						
Brush, Platt	Compensation for extra services as register land office.	24	1	Petition	946	Public Lands.						
Brush, Robert	Pension for revolutionary services.	23	1	Resolution	114	Rev. Pensions	178	Favorable	196	Passed	Indef. postp'd.	Enrolled, and approved by mistake.
Brush, Robert	Pension for revolutionary services.	23	2	Resolution	434	Rev. Pensions.						
Brush, Robert	Pension for revolutionary services	24	1	Resolution	470	Rev. Pensions.	Mar. 24, 1836	Favorable	475	Passed	Passed	App'd May 14, 1836
Brush, Thomas, jr	Pension for revolutionary disabilities.	1	3	Petition	392					Referred to Secretary War.		
Brush, Thomas, jr	Pension for revolutionary disabilities.	4	1	Rep. of Secretary War.	447	Claims	Feb. 18, 1796	Favorable bill.	156	Passed	Passed	App'd April 20, 1796
Brussel, Joseph	Annuity.	6	2	Appropriat'n bill.	752				277	Passed.	Passed	App'd Mar. 3, 1801
Bruton, James, sureties of.	Discharged from obligation	31	2	Petition	107	Judiciary				Discharged; laid on table.		
Bry, H. M	Confirmation of title to land	27	2	Petition	685	Priv. Land Claims.						
Bry, H. M	Confirmation of title to land	27	3	Petition	45	Priv. Land Claims.						
Bryan, Albert C., *et al*	Compensation for horses lost in public service.	30	1	Petition	146	Claims	409	Favorable	359	Passed	Passed 2d sess.	App'd March 3, 1849
Bryan, Barrick, widow of.	Continuation of pension	28	1	Petition	685	Rev. Pensions.						Statutes at Large, vol. 5, p. 680.
Bryan	(See Clements, Bryan & Co.)	26	1		794							
Bryan, Edward, and others.	Depreciation pay and other emoluments for revolutionary services.	5	2	Petition	207	Claims	April 26, 1798	Adverse		Rejected.		
Bryan, Ellen P	Confirmation of title to land in Arkansas.	28	2	Petition	531	Priv. Land Claims.						
Bryan, George W	Indemnity for French spoliations prior to 1800.	26	1	Memorial	182	Foreign Affairs	343	Favorable	319	Referred to Committee Whole House.		
Bryan, John	Pension for disability, war of 1812.	18	2	Petition	41	Pens. & Rev. Cl'ms.						
Bryan, John	Pension for disability, war of 1812.	19	2	Petition	186	Military Pensions.						
Bryan, John	Pension for disability, war of 1812.	21	1	Petition	498	Military Pensions.						
Bryan, John A	Compensation as commissioner to treat with Indians.	28	1	Petition	108	Indian Affairs	359	Favorable	272	Referred to Committee Whole House.		
Bryan, John A	Compensation as commissioner to treat with Indians.	29	1	Petition	250	Indian Affairs	700	Favorable	475	Referred to Committee Whole House.		
Bryan, John A	Compensation as commissioner to treat with Indians.	30	1	Petition	80	Indian Affairs	93	Adverse		Laid on table.		
Bryan, J. R	(See administrator of Isaac Garretson.)	28	1		335							
Bryan, Joseph and others.	Confirmation of title to land in Alabama.	27	2	Senate bill	1395	Priv. Land Claims.			S. 310			
Bryan, Joseph and others.	Confirmation of title to land in Alabama.	27	3	Senate bill	477	Indian Affairs	March 2, 1843	With't amend.	S. 10			
Bryan, Joseph and others.	Confirmation of title to land in Alabama.	28	1	Senate bill	743	Indian Affairs	June 7, 1844	With't amend	S. 87	Passed	Passed	App'd June 12, 1844
Bryan, Joseph	Compensation as commissioner to take testimony.	31	1	Appropriat'n bill.	643	Whole House	Mar. 22, 1850	With amend's.	154	Passed	Passed	App'd May 15, 1850
Bryan, Joseph	Compensation for purchasing and distributing stock animals among Cherokee Indians.	29	1	Indian appropriation bill.	205	Whole House	Feb. 19, 1846	With amend's.	48	Passed	Passed	App'd June 27, 1846

List of private claims presented to the House of Representatives of the United States from the 1st to the 31st Congress, inclusive—Continued.

Names of claimants.	Nature or object of the claim.	Congress.	Session.	How brought before the House of Reps.	Page of journal.	To what committee of the House referred.	No. or date of the report.	Nature of the report.	No. of the bill.	How disposed of by the House of Reps.	How disposed of by the Senate.	Date of the act of Congress, and remarks.
Bryan, Joseph, purser U. States navy.	Credit for certain disbursements	29	1	Memorial	400	Naval Affairs.						
Bryan, Joseph, purser U. States navy.	Credit for certain disbursements	29	2	Memorial	193	Naval Affairs	35	Favorable	620	Referred to Committee Whole House.		
Bryan, Joseph, purser U. States navy.	Credit for certein disbursements	30	1	Memorial	115	Naval Affairs	188	Favorable	198	Passed	Passed 2d sess.	App'd Jan. 26, 1849
Bryan, Lloyd, J	Increase of pension	27	2	Petition	361	Naval Affairs	560	Favorable	356	Ordered to 3d reading.		
Bryan, Lloyd, J	Increase of pension	27	3	House bill	87				356	Passed	Indef. postp'd.	
Bryan, Manypenny & Co.	Extra compensation for mail service, &c.	27	3	Petition	156	P. Of. and P. Roads.						
Bryan, Manypenny & Co.	Extra compensation for mail service, &c.	28	1	Petition	405	P. Of. and P. Roads.						
Bryan, Manypenny & Co.	Extra compensation for mail service, &c.	28	2	Petition	177	P. Of. and P. Roads.						
Bryan, Manypenny & Co.	Extra compensation for mail service, &c.	29	1	Petition	890	P. Of. and P. Roads.						
Bryan, Manypenny & Co.	Extra compensation for mail ser vice, &c.	29	2	Petition	90	P. Of. and P. Roads.						
Bryan, Manypenny & Co.	Extra compensation for mail service, &c.	30	1	Petition	260	P. Of. and P. Roads.						
Bryan, Mona and others	Settlement of claims for revolutionary services.	3	1	Petition	115	Select.						
Bryan, Richard S. & G. Brewer.	Extension of time to enter land certificates.	9	1	Petition	296	Public Lands	Mar. 18, 1806	Favorable	135	Passed	Passed	App'd April 21, 1806
Bryan, Samuel J.	Indemnity for losses on a public contract.	28	1	Petition	222	Claims.						
Bryan, Samuel J.	Indemnity for losses on a public contract.	23	2	Petition	199	Claims.						
Bryan, Thomas	Compensation for a horse lost in public service.	30	1	Petition	146	Claims	235	Adverse		Laid on table.		
Bryan, William, assignees of.	Confirmation of title to land in Arkansas.	28	2	Petition	531	Priv. Land Claims.						
Bryan, William, (Pa.)	Indemnity for baggage lost in public service.	30	2	Petition	236	Military Affairs.						
Bryan, William P.	(See attorney for John Rice Jones)	13	1		20							
Bryan, Wm. A., and A. Herron.	Permission to enter eertain land at minimum price.	27	2	Resolution	682	Public Lands.						
Bryant, Edward	Pension for revolutionary services.	3	2	Petition	308	Claims.						
Bryant, Edward	Pension for revolutionary services.	4	1	Petition	373	Claims	Jan. 4, 1796	Adverse		Leave to withdraw.		
Bryant, Gridley	(See Jonathan Newcomb, & others)	22	1		257							
Bryant, John	Pension for revolutionary services.	3	1	Rep. of Secretary of war.	93					Laid on table.		
Bryant, John, (Va.)	Pension for services; war of 1812	21	1	Resolution	574	Military Pensions.						
Bryant, John	Pension	22	1	Senate bill	883	Invalid Pensions	June 22, 1832	With't amend.	S. 146	Passed	Passed	App'd July 9, 1832
Bryant, John, (N. H.)	Pension	23	2	Petition	40	Invalid Pensions	27	Favorable	607	Passed	Passed	App'd March 3, 1835
Bryant, Joseph	(See Jonathan L. Stephens, and others.)											
Bryant, Philip	Indemnity for damage to property by the enemy.	15	1	Petition	143	Claims	Feb. 24, 1818	Adverse		Rejected		Leave to withdraw.
Bryant, Philip	Indemnity for damage to property by the enemy.	17	1	Petition	281	Claims.						
Bryant, Philip	Indemnity for damage to property by the enemy.	19	1	Petition	312	Claims	April 26, 1826	Adverse		Laid on lable.		

List of private claims presented to the House of Representatives of the United States from the 1st to the 31st Congress, inclusive—Continued.

Names of claimants.	Nature or object of the claim.	Congress.	Session.	How brought before the House of Reps.	Page of journal.	To what committee of the House referred.	No. or date of the report.	Nature of the report.	No. of the bill.	How disposed of by the House of Reps.	How disposed of by the Senate.	Date of the act of Congress, and remarks.
Bryant, Philip	Indemnity for damage to property by the enemy.	22	2	Petition	119	Claims	Jan. 18, 1833	Adverse	......	Laid on table.		
Bryant, Thomas	Pension for revolutionary services.	26	1	Petition	171	Rev. Pensions	....	....	......	Discharged; laid on table.		
Bryant, Thomas S.	Compensation for property taken for public use.	31	1	Petition	611	Claims.						
Bryant, Thomas, widow of	Pension for revolutionary services.	25	3	Petition	564	Rev. Pensions.						
Bryant, William Geo.	Arrears of pension	22	2	Petition	342	Rev. Pensions.						
Bryce, Henry	Remission of penalty for importing British goods.	13	1	Petition	36	Ways and Means.						
				Senate bill	82	Whole House	July 22, 1813	With amend.	S. 20	Passed with amend't.	Passed as am'd	App'd July 29, 1813
Bryden, William	Compensation for horse taken for public use.	23	1	Petition	192	Claims	373	Adverse	......	Laid on table.		
Bryden, William	Compensation for horse taken for public use.	23	2	Petition	210	Claims	Feb. 2, 1835	Adverse	......	Laid on table.		
Bryden, William	Compensation for horse taken for public use.	25	2	Petition	770	Claims.						
Bryden, William	Compensation for horse taken for public use.	26	1	Petition	168	Claims	37	Adverse	......	Laid on table.		
Brydia, David	Pension for revolutionary services.	3	1	Rep. of Secretary War.	131	Select	May 26, 1794	Res. to refer to Sec. War.	12	Passed	Passed	App'd June 9, 1794
Brydia, David	Pension for revolutionary services.	4	1	Rep. of Secretary War.	447	Claims	Feb. 18, 1796	Pension bill	156	Passed	Passed with amendment.	App'd April 20, 1796
Bryne, Matthew	(See Edward Simpson and others.)	4	1	....	428							
Bryson, Elisha	(See Isaac Bryson)	27	2	....	1056							
Bryson, Isaac	Bounty land	27	2	Senate bill	1056	Public Lands	....	....	S. 161			
Bryson, Samuel, heirs of.	Compensation for revolutionary services.	27	2	Petition	226	Rev. Claims	222	Adverse	......	Laid on table.		
Buchanan, Alexander	Location of a grant of the British Crown.	4	2	Petition	696	Claims.						
Buchanan, Alexander	Location of a grant of the British Crown.	5	2	Petition	145	Claims	Jan. 22, 1798	Adverse	......	Laid on table.		
Buchanan, Andrew	(See John Ross, of Baltimore, and others.)	11	2	....	235							
Buchanan, Andrew, trustee of.	Indemnity for French spoliations prior to 1800.	26	1	Memorial	182	Foreign Affairs	343	Favorable	319	Referred to Committee Whole House.		
Buchanan, Benjamin	Pension for revolutionary services.	15	1	Petition	49	Pens. & Rev. Cl'ms.						
Buchanan, Elijah	Pension for services, war of 1812.	29	1	Petition	168	Invalid Pensions	79	Adverse	......	Laid on table.		
Buchanan, George A.	(See Buchanan & Young)	26	1	....	182							
Buchanan, George, assignee of.	Duplicate of forfeited land scrip	22	1	Petition	173	Public Lands	Feb. 17, 1832	Favorable	385	Passed	Passed	App'd Mar. 31, 1832
Buchanan, James, (Ky.)	Extension of time for locating land.	17	2	Petition	70	Whole House.						
Buchanan, James	Compensation for diplomatic services, &c.	29	1	Appropriat'n bill.	206	Whole House	....	Amendments	50	Passed	Passed	App'd Aug. 10, 1846
Buchanan, James, (Ga.)	Pension	21	1	Petition	59	Military Pensions.						
Buchanan, John	To exchange location of military land.	15	2	Petition	163	Public Lands	Jan. 15, 1819	Adverse	......	Rejected.		
Buchanan, McKean	Commissions on exchange as purser in United States navy.	23	1	Petition	568	Naval Affairs.						
Buchanan, McKean	Commissions on exchange as purser in United States navy.	23	2	Senate bill	194	Naval Affairs	....	....	S. 26			
Buchanan, McKean	Commissions on exchange as purser in United States navy.	24	1	Senate bill	956	Naval Affairs	June 24, 1836	Adverse	S. 173	Referred to Committee Whole House.		

List of private claims presented to the House of Representatives of the United States from the 1st to the 31st Congress, inclusive—Continued.

Names of claimants.	Nature or object of the claim.	Congress.	Session.	How brought before the House of Reps.	Page of journal.	To what committee of the House referred.	No. or date of the report.	Nature of the report.	No. of the bill.	How disposed of by the House of Reps.	How disposed of by the Senate.	Date of the act of Congress, and remarks.
Buchanan, McKean	Commissions on exchange as purser in United States navy.	25	2	Petition	56	Naval Affairs	......	......	......	Discharged; laid on table.		
Buchanan, Richard	Pension for services, war of 1812.	28	2	Petition	300	Invalid Pensions.						
Buchanan, Richard	Ponsion for services, war of 1812.	29	1	Petition	93	Invalid Pensions	178	Adverse	......	Laid on table.		
Buchanan, Robert	Indemnity for property destroyed while in public use.	13	2	Petition	399	......	......	......	......	Referred to Secretary of War.		
Buchanan, Robert	Indemnitv for property destroyed while in public use.	14	1	Petition	534	Claims.						
Buchanan, William, (Ky.)	Bounty land for services, war of 1812.	23	1	Petition	65	Priv. Land Claims.						
Buchanan, William, (Ky.)	Bounty land for services, war of 1812.	28	1	Petition	223	Public Lands.						
Buchanan, William, (Ky.)	Pension for services, war of 1812.	29	1	Petition	655	Invalid Pensions	......	......	......	Discharged; laid on table.		
Buchanan, Wm. W	Pension for revolutionary services.	28	1	Petition	927	Rev. Pensions.						
Buchanan, Wm. W	Pension for revoiutionary services.	28	2	Petition	284	Rev. Pensions.						
Buchanan & Young	Indemnity for French spoliations prior to 1800.	26	1	Memorial	182	Foreign Affairs	343	Favorable	319	Referred to Committee Whole House.		
Buchel, Augustus	Compensation for services as interpreter in Mexico.	31	1	Petition	234	Military Affairs	......	......	......	Discharged; laid on table.		
Buchel, Augustus	Compensation for services as interpreter in Mexico.	31	2	Petition	291	Military Affairs	26	Favorable	470	Referred to Committee Whole House.		
Buck, Anthony	(See Canadian refugees.)	8	2	......	90	......	......	......	64			
Buck, Anthony	(See surety for James A. Stewart.)	11	2	......	115							
Buck, Charles N	Reimbursement of certain discriminating duties.	19	1	Memorial	152	Ways and Means	175	Favorable	225	Referred to Committee Whole House.		
Buck, Daniel	Compensation for revolutionary services.	9	2	Petition	598	Claims.						
Buck, Daniel	Compensation for revolutionary services.	10	1	Petition	22	Claims	Mar. 17, 1808	Pension bill	78	Passed	Passed with amendment.	App'd April 25, 1808
Buck, Daniel	(See Gurdon and Daniel Buck)	12	1	......	21							
Buck, Daniel	(See executor of Josiah Hempsted)	29	2	......	53							
Buck, Ebenezer, widow of	Pension for revolutionary services.	28	2	Petition	346	Rev. Pensions.						
Buck, Ebenezer, widow of	Pension for revolutionary services	29	1	Petition	219	Rev. Pensions	234	Adverse	......	Laid on table.		
Buck, Fbenezer, widow of	Pension for revolutionary services.	30	1	Petition	598	Rev. Pensions	689	Favorable	548	Referred to Committee Whole House.		
Buck, Ebenezer, widow of	Pension for revolutionary services	30	2	Rep't Committee Whole House.	319	......	......	With't amend.	548	Passed	Passed	App'd March 3, 1849
Buck, Gurdon and Daniel	Permission to import British merchandise.	12	1	Petition	21	Com. and Manuf.						
Buck, Joel	Arrears of pension	21	2	Petition	73	Military Pensions.						
Buck, Joel	Arrears of pension	22	1	Petition	219	Rev. Pensions	......	......	......	Discharged; laid on table.		
Buck, Joel	Arrears of pension	22	2	Petition	151	Rev. Pensions.						
Buck, John	Remission of duty on goods imported to Castine.	16	1	Senate bill	108	Ways and Means	Jan. 14, 1820	With amend	S. 13	Passed	Passed	App'd April 11, 1820
Buck, Marcus C	Increase of compensation as military store-keeper.	24	1	Petition	447	Military Affairs						
Buck, Mary	(See Ebenezer Buck, widow of).	28	2	......	346							
Buck, Philip	Compensation for impressment into naval service.	1	3	Petition	344	......	......	......	......	Referred to Secretary War.		
				Rep. of Secretary War.	393	......	......	......	......	Laid on table.		

List of private claims presented to the House of Representatives of the United States from the 1st to the 31st Congress, inclusive—Continued.

Names of claimants.	Nature or object of the claim.	Congress.	Session.	How brought before the House of Reps.	Page of journal.	To what committee of the House referred.	No. or date of the report.	Nature of the report.	No. of the bill.	How disposed of by the House of Reps.	How disposed of by the Senate.	Date of the act of Congress, and remarks.
Buck, Robert	(See Hezekiah Pierpont & others)	18	1		213							
Buck, Samuel	(See John Ross, executors of.)											
Buck, William O	Compensation for revolutionary services.	21	2	Petition	302	Rev. Claims.						
Buck, William O	Compensation for horse lost in public service.	23	2	Resolution	276	Claims.						
Buck, Winthrop	Bounty on certain fish exported	22	1	Petition	25	Ways and Means.						
Buck, Winthrop	Bounty on certain fish exported	22	2	Petition	265	Ways and Means.						
Buckhouse, John N	(See Covington Simpkins)	29	2		100							
Buckingham, Isaac	(See administrator of Thomas Vowell.)	31	1		256							
Buckingham, Jared	Pension	22	1	Petition	260	Invalid Pensions.						
Buckingham, Jared	Pension	23	1	Petition	44	Invalid Pensions	Jan. 7, 1834	Favorable	154	Passed.		
Buckingham, Jared	Pension	23	2	Petition	109	Invalid Pensions	30	Favorable	610	Passed	Indef. postp'd.	
Buckingham, Jared	Pension	24	1	Petition	53	Invalid Pensions	46	Favorable	58	Passed	Passed	App'd May 14, 1836
Buckingham, Jared	Arrears of pension	24	2	Petition	120	Invalid Pensions	Jan. 19, 1837	Adverse		Laid on table.		
Buckingham, Jared	Arrears of pension	26	1	Petition	1254	Invalid Pensions				Discharged; laid on table.		
Buckingham, Jared	Arrears of pension	28	2	Petition	240	Invalid Pensions.						
Buckingham, Jared	Arrears of pension	29	1	Petition	823	Invalid Pensions.						
Buckley, A. M. & W., assignees of.	Release of balance due for duties on imports.	12	1	Petition	174	Com. and Manuf.						
Buckley, A. M. & W., assignees of.	Release of balance due for duties on imports.	12	2	Petition	548	Com. and Manuf.	Jan. 20, 1813	Adverse		Leave to withdraw.		
Buckley, A. M. & W., assignees of.	Release of balance due for duties on imports.	13	2	Petition	359	Com. and Manuf.						
Buckley, Chauncey	Compensation for certain clerical services.	26	1	Petition	1251	Elections	July 10, 1840	Favorable.				
Buckley, Elijah	Remission of forfeiture of public land.	19	1	Senate bill	258	Priv. Land Claims.	Feb. 21, 1826	With't amend.	S. 35	Passed	Passed	App'd March 3, 1816
Buckley, James S.	Compensation for services as draw-keeper of public bridge.	31	2	Rep't. Committee Whole House.	444		90	Favorable	488	Referred to Committee Whole House.		
Buckley, Jeremiah, heirs of	Confirmation of title to land in Indiana.	19	1	Petition	61	Priv. Land Claims.						
Buckley, Jeremiah, heirs of	Confirmation of title to land in Indiana.	19	2	Petition	65	Priv. Land Claims.	85	Favorable	441	Referred to Committee Whole House.		
Buckley, Jeremiah, heirs of	Confirmation of title to land in Indiana.	20	1	Resolution	189	Priv. Land Claims.						
Buckley, Jeremiah, heirs of	Confirmation of title to land in Indiana.	21	1	Petition	212	Priv. Land Claims.	316	Favorable	374	Referred to Committee Whole House.		
Buckley, Jeremiah, heirs of	Confirmation of title to land in Indiana.	22	1	Petition	64	Priv. Land Claims.	71	Favorable	139	Passed	Passed	App'd July 14, 1832
Buckley, Reuben	Compensation for revolutionary supplies.	14	1	Petition	48	Pens. & Rev. Cl'ms.	Feb. 21, 1816	Adverse		Rejected.		
Buckley, William	(See assignees of A. M. & W. Buckley.)	12	1		174							
Bucklin, Oliver, heirs of	Compensation for revolutionary services.	26	1	Petition	280	Rev. Claims.						
Buckman, Benj., widow of	Pension for revolutionary services.	29	1	Petition	168	Rev. Pensions	527	Adverse		Laid on table.		
Buckmaster, C. W	Compensation for work, &c., on Cumberland road.	23	1	Resolution	589	Claims	455	Adverse		Laid on table.		
Buckmaster, George	Compensation for a whale boat built for United States.	14	2	Petition	296	Claims	Feb. 7, 1817	Favorable	109	Passed	Passed	App'd March 3, 1817

List of private claims presented to the House of Representatives of the United States from the 1st to the 31st Congress, inclusive—Continued.

Names of claimants.	Nature or object of the claim.	Congress.	Session.	How brought before the House of Reps.	Page of journal.	To what committee of the House referred.	No. or date of the report.	Nature of the report.	No. of the bill.	How disposed of by the House of Reps.	How disposed of by the Senate.	Date of the act of Congress, and remarks.
Buckminster, Thomas, administrator of.	Equitable settlement of accounts.	16	1	Petition	28	Claims	Dec. 28, 1819	Favorable	25	Passed	Passed	App'd Feb. 28, 1820
Buckner, Dorothea B.	(See widow of Wm. McWilliams)	25	2		70							
Buckner, Reuben	Pension for revolutionary services.	22	1	Petition	44	Rev. Pensions.						
Buckner, Richard	(See William Jones, administrator of.)	5	2		160							
Buckner, Simeon	Compensation for removing Chickasaw Indians.	29	1	Petition	798	Indian Affairs.						
Buckner, Simeon	Compensation for removing Chickasaw Indians.	30	1	Petition	459	Indian Affairs.						
Buckner, Simeon	Compensation for removing Chickasaw Indians.	30	2	Petition	164	Indian Affairs.						
Buckner, Simeon	Compensation for removing Chickasaw Indians.	31	1	Petition	299	Indian Affairs.						
Buckner, Simeon	Compensation for removing Chickasaw Indians.	30	2	Petition	447	Indian Affairs				Discharged; laid on table.		
Buckner, William W.	(See executor of John J. Bulow, jr.)	30	1		270							
Budd, John B., and others	Payment of certain Texas bonds.	31	1	Petition	669	Judiciary.						
Budd, John C.	Compensation for revolutionary services.	28	1	Petition	99	Rev. Pensions				Discharged; laid on table.		
Budd, John D.	Payment of a certificate of debenture.	28	1	Petition	482	Commerce.						
Budd, Thomas A.	(See Exploring Expedition)	27	3		149							
Budlong, Hannah	(See widow of Elias Hyde)	24	1		474							
Buel, Elias	Pension for revolutionary services.	15	2	Petition	211	Rev. Pensions	Feb. 11, 1819	Adverse		Laid on table.		
Buel, Elias	Pension for revolutionary services.	16	1	Petition	137	Rev. Pensions	Jan. 14, 1821	Adverse		Laid on table.		
Buel, Samuel	Release from imprisonment and settlement of accounts.	17	2	Senate bill	198	Judiciary	Feb. 11, 1823	With't amend.	32	Passed	Passed	App'd Feb. 21, 1823
Buel, Samuel	Examination of his claim against United States.	18	2	Petition	46	Judiciary				Discharged; leave to withdraw.		
Buel, Samuel	Examination of his claim against United States.	21	2	Petition	120	Judiciary.						
Buel, Solomon	Pension for revolutionary services.	15	2	Petition	213	Rev. Pensions	Feb. 11, 1819	Adverse		Laid on table.		
Buell, Dillon	Reimbursement of money paid for patent right.	20	1	Senate bill	471	Claims	228	Adverse	108	Referred to Committee Whole House.		
Buell, Ezra	Pension	21	2	Petition	113	Military Pensions.						
Buell, Ezra	Pension	22	1	Petition	45	Rev. Pensions	Dec. 22, 1831	Adverse		Referred to Committee Whole House.		
Buell, Isaac	Pension for revolutionary services.	3	1	Rep. of Secretary War.	131	Select	May 26, 1794	Res. to refer to Sec. War.	R. 12	Passed	Passed	App'd June 9, 1794
Buell, Isaac	Pension for revolutionary services.	3	2	Rep. of Secretary War.	262	Claims.						
Buell, Isaac	Pension for revolutionary services.	4	1	Rep. of Secretary War.	445	Claims	Feb. 18, 1796	Pension bill.	156	Passed	Passed with amendment.	App'd April 20, 1796
Buell, Isaac	Increase of pension	12	1	Petition	42					Referred to Secretary War.		
				House bill	361	Whole House	June 17, 1812	With't amend.	138	Passed	Passed with amendment.	App'd July 5, 1812
Buell, Matthew	(See Nathaniel Gates, and others)	13	2		185							
Buell, Samuel	Indemnity for building destroyed by the enemy.	13	3	Petition	692					Referred to Secretary Treasury.		
Buell, Samuel	Indemnity for building destroyed by the enemy.	15	1	Petition	135							
				Rep. of Secretary Treasury.	181	Ways and Means	Feb. 25, 1818	Adverse		Leave to withdraw.		

List of private claims presented to the House of Representatives of the United States from the 1st to the 31st Congress, inclusive—Continued.

Names of claimants.	Nature or object of the claim.	Congress.	Session.	How brought before the House of Reps.	Page of journal.	To what committee of the House referred.	No. or date of the report.	Nature of the report.	No. of the bill.	How disposed of by the House of Reps.	How disposed of by the Senate.	Date of the act of Congress, and remarks.
Buell, Samuel	Indemnity for building destroyed by the enemy.	15	2	Petition	193	Ways and Means.						
Buffalo, schooner	(See Isaac Champlin, and others)	[illegible]7		....	485							
Buffenberger, Semington	Indemnity for loss of public land purchased of United States.	29		Petition	1[illegible]	Public Lands	7	Favorable	19	Passed	Passed	App'd July 15, 1846
Buffinton, Samuel	(See Francis S. Delevere)	1	3	....	342							
Buford, Jane	(See widow of Thomas Quirk)	26	1	....	808							
Buford, Thomas, (Ky.)	Additional compensation as deputy commissary.	16	2	Petition	27	Claims	Nov. 28, 1820	Adverse	......	Laid on table.		
Buford, Thomas, (Ky.)	Additional compensation as deputy commissary.	19	2	Petition	96	Military Affairs.						
Buford, Thomas, (Ky.)	Additional compensation as deputy commissary.	20		Petition	83	Claims	71	Adverse	......	Laid on table.		
Buford, Thomas, (Ky.)	Additional compensation as deputy commissary.	21	1	Petition	6[illegible]	Military Affairs	43	Favorable	65	Passed	Passed	App'd Mar. 25, 1830
Buford, Thomas, (Ky.)	Compensation for services and reimbursement of expenditures.	22	1	Petition	64	Military Affairs	422	Favorable	522	Referred to Committee Whole House.		
Buford, Thomas, (Ky.)	Compensation for services and reimbursement of expenditures.	23	1	Petition	31[illegible]	Military Affairs.						
Buford, Thomas, (Ky.)	Compensation for services and reimbursement of expenditures.	23	2	Petition	39	Military Affairs	2	Favorable	561	Passed	Passed	App'd March 3, 1835
Buford, Thomas, (Ky.)	Compensation for services and reimbursement of expenditures	24	1	Petition	206	Claims.						
Buford, Thomas, (Ky.)	Compensation for services and reimbursement of expenditures.	24	2	Petition	81	Claims	Jan. 10, 1837	Adverse	......	Laid on table.		
Buford, Thomas, (Ky.)	Compensation for services and reimbursement of expenditures.	25	2	Petition	88	Claims	Jan. 4, 1838	Adverse	......	Laid on table.		
Buford, William M.	(See sureties of Goodman Oldham)	20	1	....	365							
Bugbee, Peter, widow of	To be restored to pension roll	27	2	Petition	320	Rev. Pensions.						
Bugbee, Peter, widow of	To be restored to pension roll	27	3	Petition	365	Rev. Pensions.						
Bugbee, Peter, widow of	To be restored to pension roll	28	1	Petition	839	Whole House.						
Bugbee, Peter, widow of	To be restored to pension roll	30	1	Petition	229	Rev. Pensions	Jan. 25, 1848	Adverse	......	Laid on table.		
Buhler, John	Confirmation of title to land in Louisiana.	17	2	Senate bill	230	Public Lands	....	....	S. 21			
Buhler, John	Confirmation of title to land in Louisiana.	18	1	Petition	136	Priv. Land Claims.	Feb. 3, 1824	Adverse	......	Laid on table.		
Buhler, John	Confirmation of title to land in Louisiana.	18	2	Petition	52	Priv. Land Claims.	Dec. 29, 1824	Adverse	......	Laid on table.		
Buhler, John	Confirmation of title to land in Louisiana.	19	1	Petition	109	Priv. Land Claims.						
Buhler, John	Confirmation of title to land in Louisiana.	21	1	Petition	51	Priv. Land Claims.	198	Favorable	250	Referred to Committee Whole House.		
Buhler, John	Confirmation of title to land in Louisiana.	21	2	Rep't Committee Whole House.	265	....	Feb. 4, 1831	With't amend.	250	Passed.		
Buhler, John	Confirmation of title to land in Louisiana.	22	1	Petition	32	Priv. Land Claims.	81	Favorable	161	Passed	Passed	App'd July 14, 1832
Buhler, John	(See Wm. McFarland, administrator of.)	27	3	....	52							
Buisson, Lewis	Confirmation of title to land in Illinois.	17	1	Petition	86	Public Lands.						
Buker, Israel H.	Reimbursement of money paid for public land.	25	2	Memorial	1128	Claims.						

List of private claims presented to the House of Representatives of the United States from the 1st to the 31st Congress, inclusive—Continued.

Names of claimants.	Nature or object of the claim.	Congress.	Session.	How brought before the House of Reps.	Page of journal.	To what committee of the House referred.	No. or date of the report.	Nature of the report.	No. of the bill.	How disposed of by the House of Reps.	How disposed of by the Senate.	Date of the act of Congress, and remarks.
Buker, Israel H	Reimbursement of money paid for public land.	26	1	Memorial	169	Claims	Feb. 29, 1840	Favorable		Refered to Secretary Treas'y for paym'nt.		
Bukey, Drusilla	(See Hezekiah Bukey, widow of.)	29	2		146							
Bukey, Hezekiah, widow of.	Pension for services of husband in Indian war.	29	2	Petition	146	Rev. Pensions.						
Bukey, Hezekiah, widow of.	Pension for services of husband in Indian war.	30	1	Petition	637	Rev. Pensions	528	Adverse		Laid on table.		
Bulfinch, Charles	Compensation for services as United States architect.	21	1	Petition	170	Public Buildings.						
Bulfinch, Charles	Compensation for services as United States architect.	21	2	Amendm'nt to appropriation bill.	353				407	Passed	Passed	App'd March 2, 1831
Bulfinch, Charles and others	Confirmation of title to land in Oregon.	26	1	Petition	202	Foreign Affairs.						
Bulfinch, Charles and others	Confirmation of title to land in Oregon.	27	3	Petition	350	Foreign Affairs.						
Bulfinch, Charles and others	Confirmation of title to land in Oregon.	30	1	Petition	587	Territories				Discharged; laid on table.		
Bulgin, James	(See McFarland and Player, assignees of.)	7	2		258							
Bulgin, James M	Compensation for naval services, war of 1812.	15	2	Petition	40	Naval Affairs	Dec. 3, 1818	Adverse		Rejected.		
Bulkley, Asa	Release from a recognizance	15	1	Petition	179	Ways and Means.	Feb. 3, 1818	Adverse		Rejected		Leave to withdraw.
Bulkley, Asa and L. Dewing.	Reimbursement of damages collected from them.	18	1	Petition	115	Ways and Means.						
Bulkley, Asa and L. Dewing.	Reimbuasement of damages collected from them.	20	1	Petition	51	Ways and Means	14	Adverse		Laid on table.		
Bulkley, Chauncey	Indemnity for French spoliations prior to 1800.	26	1	Memorial	182	Foreign Affairs	343	Favorable	319	Referred to Committee Whole House.		
Bulkley, Francis, attorney of.	Indemnity for French spoliations prior to 1800.	26	1	Memorial	182	Foreign Affairs	343	Favorable	319	Referred to Committee Whole House.		
Bulkley, Jonathan	Pension for disability in naval service.	23	1	Petition	57	Naval Affairs	Jan. 27, 1834	Adverse		Laid on table.		
Bulkley, Jonathan	Pension for disability in naval service.	26	1	Petition	330	Naval Affairs.						
Bull, Amos	Pension	26	1	Petition	602	Invalid Pensions	507	Adverse		Laid on table.		
Bull, Amos	Pension	29	1	Petition	70	Invalid Pensions	820	Favorable	545	Referred to Committee Whole House.		
Bull, Amos	Pension	30	1	Petition	162	Invalid Pensions	552	Favorable	452	Passed.		
Bull, Archibald and L. S. Finch.	Compensation for detecting a public criminal.	29	1	Petition	524	Claims	583	Favorable	401	Referred to Committee Whole House.		
Bull, Archibald and L. S. Finch.	Compensation for detecting a public criminal.	30	1	Petition	154	Claims	150	Favorable	129	Passed	Passed, second session.	App'd Jan. 8, 1849
Bull, John, sen., heir of	Balance of pension due	27	3	Petition	59	Invalid Pensions	189	Adverse		Laid on table.		
Bull, John, sen., heir of	Balance of pension due	28	1	Petition	71	Rev. Pensions	21	Adverse		Laid on table.		
Bull,	(See Stocking and Bull)	15	2		148							
Bull, William G	(See represen's of Josiah Blakely.)	27	2		365							
Bullard, Aaron	To be restored to pension roll	17	1	Petition	51	Rev. Pensions.						
Bullard, Isaac	Pension for revolutionary services.	22	1	Petition	381	Rev. Pensions	410	Favorable	510	Referred to Committee Whole House.		
Bullard, Reuben N	Compensation for horse taken for public use.	22	2	Petition	74	Claims	24	Adverse		Laid on table.		
Bullard, Reuben N	Compensation for horse taken for public use.	23	1	Petition	60	Claims.						

List of private claims presented to the House of Representatives of the United States from the 1st to the 31st Congress, inclusive—Continued.

Names of claimants.	Nature or object of the claim.	Congress.	Session.	How brought before the House of Reps.	Page of journal.	To what committee of the House referred.	No. or date of the report.	Nature of the report.	No. of the bill.	How disposed of by the House of Reps.	How disposed of by the Senate.	Date of the act of Congress, and remarks.
Bullard, Reuben N	Compensation for horse taken for public use.	23	2	Petition	68	Claims	Jan. 3, 1835	Adverse	......	Laid on table.		
Bullard, Reuben N	Compensation for horse taken for public use.	24	1	Petition	50	Claims	88	Adverse	......	Laid on table.		
Bullion, John, agent of...	Compensation for horse lost in Florida war.	28	1	Petition........	262	Claims						
Bullion, Thomas, agent of.	Compensation for horse lost in Florida war.	28	1	Petition	262	Claims.						
Bullitt, Benjamin........	Confirmation of title to land in Louisiana.	21	2	Petition	302	Priv. Land Claims.						
Bullitt, Benjamin........	Confirmation of title to land in Louisiana.	22	2	Petition	65	Priv. Land Claims.	72	Favorable	140	Passed	Passed.......	App'd July 14, 1832
Bullitt, Celeste..........	(See heirs of Francis Vallé).....	15	2	....	67							
Bullitt, C. & F.........	(See sureties of Chas. M. Taylor.)	20	1	....	168							
Bullett, Thomas, heirs of..	Compensation for revolutionary services.	23	1	Resolution	189	Rev. Claims.						
Bullett, Thomas, heirs of..	Compensation for revolutionary services.	23	2	Resolution	196	Rev. Claims.						
Bullett, Thomas, heirs of..	Compensation for revolutionary services.	24	1	Petition	475	Rev. Claims......	Jan. 15, 1836	Adverse	......	Laid on table.		
Bullitt, Colonel, heirs of..	Land scrip to satisfy Virginia land warrant.	27	3	Petition	155	Rev. Claims.						
Bulley, Benjamin	Pension for revolutionary services.	20	2	Petition	142	Whole House.						
Bulloch, Archibald S. and others.	Part of the forfeiture of a slave vessel.	17	1	Petition	151	Claims	63	Adverse	......	Referred to Committee Whole House.		
Bulloch, Israel..........	Release from a certain bond......	9	1	Petition	231	Com. and Manuf..	....	....	......	Leave to withdraw.		
Bulloch, Israel..........	Pension for revolutionary services.	21	2	Resolution	258	Military Pensions.						
Bulloch, Israel..........	Pension for revolutionary services.	22	1	Petition	187	Rev. Pensions.....	365	Favorable	460	Passed	Indef. postp'd.	
Bulloch, James S........	(See Arch'd S. Bulloch and others.)	17	1	....	151							
Bulloch, James	Commutation pay for revolutionary services.	21	1	Resolution	437	Rev. Claims	May 10, 1836	Adverse	......	Laid on table.		
Bulloch, Josias..........	Indemnity for acts of United States agent.	11	3	Petition	510	Public Lands.						
Bulloch, Josias..........	Indemnity for acts of United States agent.	14	1	Petition........	186	Public Lands.						
Bulloch, Josias..........	Indemnity for acts of United States agent.	15	1	Petition	133	Priv. Land Claims.	Jan. 28, 1818	Favorable....	......	Rejected.		
Bulloch, Josias..........	Indemnity for acts of United States agent.	16	1	Petition	223	Priv. Land Claims.						
Bulloch, Nathaniel	Increase of compensation as collector Rhode Island.	22	1	Petition........	560	Commerce.						
Bulloch, Simeon	Pension	21	2	Petition	159	Military Pensions.						
Bulloch, Simeon	Pension	22	1	Petition	80	Rev. Pensions	124	Favorable....	194	Referred to Committee Whole House.		
Bulloch, Simeon	Pension......................	22	2	House bill......	66	....	....	....	194	Laid on table.		
Bullus, Oscar...........	Pension for naval services	26	1	Petition	713	Naval Affairs.						
Bulow, C. W. and J., guardian of.	Confirmation of title to land in Florida.	30	2	Petition	361	Priv. Lands Claim.						
Bulow, John J., jr.......	Indemnity for Indian depredations.	24	1	Petition	751	Claims.						
Bulow, John J., jr.......	Indemnity for Indian depredations.	21	2	Petition	47	Claims	....	....	......	Discharged; laid on table.		
				Senate bill	579	....	....	....	S. 173			
Bulow, John J., jr.......	Indemnity for Indian depredations.	25	2	Petition	51	Claims	....	....	......	Disch'd; laid on table.		

List of private claims presented to the House of Representatives of the United States from the 1st to the 31st Congress, inclusive—Continued.

Names of claimants.	Nature or object of the claim.	Congress.	Session.	How brought before the House of Reps.	Page of journal.	To what committee of the House referred.	No. or date of the report.	Nature of the report.	No. of the bill.	How disposed of by the House of Reps.	How disposed of by the Senate.	Date of the act of Congress, and remarks.
Bulow, John J., jr	Indemnity for Indian depredations	25	3	Senate bill	633				S. 231			
Bulow, John J., jr	Indemnity for Indian depredations.	26	1	Petition	167	Claims.						
Bulow, John J., jr	Indemnity for Indian depredations.	26	2	Petition	36	Indian Affairs.						
Bulow, John J., jr.	Indemnity for Indian depredations	27	2	Petition	56	Claims.						
Bulow, John J., jr., executors of.	Indemnity for Indian depredations	27	3	Memorial	139	Claims	176	Adverse		Laid on table.		
Bulow, John J., jr., executors of.	Indemnity for Indian depredations.	28	1	Petition	267	Claims.						
Bulow, John J., jr., executors of.	Indemnity for Indian depredations	30	1	Petition	270	Claims				Discharged; laid on table.		
Bulow, John J., jr., executors of	Indemnity for Indian depredations	32	2	Petition	217	Claims.						
Bulow, John J., jr., executors of.	Indemnity for Indian depredations	31	1	Petition	232	Claims.	403	Favorable	340	Referred to Committee Whole House.		
Bulsan, Alexander	Compensation for revolutionary supplies.	4	1	Petition	38	Claims	74	Adverse		Laid on table.		
Button, Joseph	Increase of pension	20	2	Petition	99	Military Pensions.	Jan. 20, 1829	Adverse		Laid on table.		
Buman, Joseph, (Vt.)	Credit for disbursement on public account.	19	1	Petition	130	Claims	Feb. 1, 1826	Adverse		Laid on table.		
Buman, Joseph, (Vt.)	Credit for disbursement on public account.	20	1	Petition	196	Claims	Feb. 6, 1828	Adverse		Laid on table.		
Bumbough, James	Invalid pension	29	1	Petition	82	Invalid Pensions	22	Adverse		Laid on table.		
Bumford, Geoage	Compensation under act March 2, 1819.	31	1	Petition	671	Claims.						
Bumgardner, George	Pension	14	1	Petition	309	Pens. & Rev. Cl'ms.	Mar. 13, 1816	Adverse		Rejected.		
Bumgardner, George	Pension	15	1	Petition	14	Pens. & Rev. Cl'ms.						
Bumgardner, William	Pension for revolutionary services.	17	1	Petition	67	Rev. Pensions.						
Bump, Asa	To be restored to pension roll	17	1	Petition	13	Rev. Pensions.						
Bump, Rebecca	Extension of revolutionary pension law.	30	1	Petition	460	Rev. Pensions.						
Bump, Samuel	Compensation for disability in public service.	29	1	Petition	162	Invalid Pensions	176	Adverse		Laid on table.		
Bunce, Asa	Pension for revolutionary services.	3	1	Report Secretary of War.	131	Select	May 26, 1794	Res. to refer to Sec. War.	R. 12	Passed	Passed	App'd June 9, 1794
Bunce, Asa	Pension for revolutionary services.	3	2	Rep of Secretary War.	262	Claims.						
Bunce, David	Pension for revolutionary services.	18	1	Petition	31	Rev. Claims	Jan. 12, 1824	Adverse		Laid on table.		
Bunce, Eve	(See heir of Henry Sheafe)	7	1	Petition	11	Claims				Leave to withdraw.		
Bunce, Isaiah	Pension for revolutionary services.	3	1	Rep. of Secretary War.	131	Select	May 26, 1794	Res. to refer to Sec. War.	R. 12	Passed	Passed	App'd June 9, 1794
Bunce, Isaiah	Pension for revolutionary services.	3	2	Rep. of Secretary War.	262	Claims.						
Bunce, Russel	(See executors of Nathan Sage)	25	2		165							
Bunce, William, administrator of.	Indemnity for damage to property in Florida.	28	2	Petition	214	Claims.						
Bunce, William, administrator of.	Indemnity for damage to property in Florida.	29	1	Petition	215	Claims	194	Favorable	185	Referred to Committee Whole House.		
Bunce, William, administrator of.	Indemnity for damage to property in Florida.	29	2	Rep't Committee Whole House.	305			With't amend.	185	Passed	Passed	App'd March 3, 1847
Bunce, Zeph. W	Permission to erect mill on public land.	19	1	Petition	226	Public Lands.						
Bunch, David	Pension for revolutionary services.	18	1	Petition	31	Rev. Pensions	Jan. 12, 1824	Adverse		Laid on table.		

List of private claims presented to the House of Representatives of the United States from the 1st to the 31st Congress, inclusive—Continued.

Names of claimants.	Nature or object of the claim.	Congress.	Session.	How brought before the House of Reps.	Page of journal.	To what committee of the House referred.	No. or date of the report.	Nature of the report.	No. of the bill.	How disposed of by the House of Reps.	How disposed of by the Senate.	Date of the act of Congress, and remarks.
Bunch, Samuel H., surety of.	Release from liability for stolen money.	30	1	Petition	738	Indian Affairs.						
Bunch, Samuel H., surety of.	Release from liability for stolen money.	30	2	Petition	121	Indian Affairs.						
Bunch, Samuel H., surety of.	Release from liability for stolen money.	30	1	Petition	384	Indian Affairs	98	Adverse	......	Laid on table.		
Bunch, Samuel H., surety of.	Relesae from liability for stolen money.	31	2	Petition	206	Indian Affairs	15	Adverse	......	Laid on table.		
Bunker, Benjamin	Pension for revolutionary services.	24	1	Petition	474	Rev. Pensions	....	....	......	Discharged; laid on table.		
Bunker, George	Indemnity for French spoliations prior to 1800.	26	1	Memorial	182	Foreign Affairs	343	Favorable	319	Referred to Committee Whole House.		
Bunker, Job	Pension for revolutionary services.	15	2	Petition	21	Rev. Pensions	Feb. 11, 1819	Adverse	......	Laid on table.		
Bunker, Zachariah	Increase of pension	18	1	Petition	343	Whole House.						
Bunker, Zachariah	Increase of pension	18	1	Senate bill	309	Pens. & Rev. Cl'ms.	Mar. 24, 1824	No amendm't.	S. 46	Passed	....	App'd May 21, 1824
Bunnell, Cata	(See mother of Abden Turrill)	15	1	....	388	....	....	....	S. 40			
Bunnell, Joseph	To be restored to pension roll	17	1	Petition	285	Whole House	....	....	......	Leave to withdraw.		
Bunner, Jacob, widow of	Compensation for revolutionary supplies.	13	2	Petition	345	Pens. & Rev. Cl'ms.	92	Adverse	......	Leave to withdraw.		
Bunner, Jacob, widow of	Compensation for revolutionary supplies.	24	1	Petition	536	Rev. Claims.						
Bunner, Jacob, widow of	Compensation for revolutionary supplies.	24	2	Petition	95	Rev. Claims	209	Adverse	......	Laid on table.		
Bunner, Jacob, widow of	Compensation for revolutionary supplies.	25	2	Petition	370	Rev. Claims.						
Buntin, Robert	(See executors of Laurent Bazadone.)	21	1	....	1062							
Buntin, Robert	Compensation for surveying public lands.	16	2	Petition	143	Public Lands	Jan. 17, 1821	Favorable	207	Passed	Passed	App'd March 2, 1821
Bunting, Thomas	Remission of a forfeiture	21	1	Petition	293	Commerce.						
Bunting, Thomas	Remission of a forfeiture	21	2	Petition	62	Commerce.						
Bunting, Wm. B., heirs of.	Commutation pay for revolutionary services.	23	1	Petition	40	Rev. Claims.						
Bunting, Wm. B., heirs of.	Commutation pay for revolutionary services.	23	2	Petition	114	Rev. Claims.						
Bunting, Wm. B., heirs of.	Commutation pay for revolutionary services.	24	1	Petition	103	Rev. Claims	598	Favorable	582	Referred to Committee Whole House.		
Bunting, Wm. B., heirs of.	Commutation pay for revolutionary services.	25	2	Petition	39	Rev. Claims	115	Favorable	133	Passed	Passed	App'd July 7, 1838
Buntling, C. C.	Extra compensation for naval services.	30	1	Senate bill	328	Naval Affairs	Feb. 29, 1848	With't amend.	S. 118	Referred to Committee Whole House.		
Burbank, John, heirs of	Prize-money as master-at arms under Paul Jones.	30	1	Petition	344	Rev. Claims	....	....	......	Discharged; laid on table.		
Burbanks, Moore	Confirmation of title to land in Missouri.	15	2	Petition	210	Priv. Land Claims.						
Burbeck, Henry, widow of	Pension for revolutionary services.	30	2	Petition	77	Rev. Claims.						
Burbeck, Henry, widow of	Pension for revolutionary services.	31	1	Petition	284	Rev. Claims.						
Burbridge, Benjamin, widow of.	Pension for revolutionary services.	16	1	Petition	190	Pens. & Rev. Cl'ms.	Feb. 7, 1820	Adverse	......	Laid on table.		
Burbridge, Benjamin, widow of.	Pension for revolutionary services.	17	1	Petition	99	Pens. & Rev. Cl'ms.	Jan. 8, 1822	Adverse	......	Rejected.		
Burbridge, Thomas	Pension for revolutionary services.	3	1	Petition	131	Select.						
Burch, Benjamin	Pension for revolutionary services.	22	1	Resolution	509	Rev. Pensions.						

List of private claims presented to the House of Representatives of the United States from the 1st to the 31st Congress, inclusive—Continued.

Names of claimants.	Nature or object of the claim.	Congress.	Session.	How brought before the House of Reps.	Page of journal.	To what committee of the House referred.	No. or date of the report.	Nature of the report.	No. of the bill.	How disposed of by the House of Reps.	How disposed of by the Senate.	Date of the act of Congress, and remarks.
Burch, Benjamin, widow of.	Pension for revolutionary services.	25	2	Petition	637	Rev. Claims	939	Favorable	820	Passed	Adverse report.	
Burch, Erskine	(See Thomas E. Birch.)	15	2		173							
Burch, Stanislaus	Compensation for horse lost in war of 1812.	17	2	Petition	163	Claims	Feb. 7, 1823	Adverse		Laid on table.		
Burcham, John	Pension for services in Indian wars	27	2	Petition	771	Rev. Pensions	914	Adverse		Laid on table.		
Burchmore, George	Indemnity for olive oil seized by Bey of Tunis.	12	1	Memorial	206					Referred to Secretary State.		
Burckle, Christian J.	Drawback of duties on certain merchandise.	18	2	Petition	210	Ways and Means	Feb. 25, 1825	Favorable	360	Passed	Passed	App'd March 3, 1825
Burden, Timothy	Pension for revolutionary services.	23	1	Petition	307	Rev. Pensions.						
Burdett, Mary	Renewal of pension	26	1	Petition	304	Naval Affairs.						
Burdett, Mary	Renewal of pension	27	2	Petition	330	Naval Affairs	603	Adverse		Laid on table.		
Burdett, Mary	Renewal of pension	28	1	Petition	177	Naval Affairs.						
Burdge, Jonathan, administrator of.	Reimbursement of the amount of two judgments.	18	1	Petition	196	Ways and Means.						
Burdge, Michael	To be restored to pension roll	17	1	Petition	30	Rev. Pensions				Discharged; leave to withdraw.		
Burdick, Isaac	Compensation for horse taken for public use.	18	2	Petition	75	Claims.						
Burdick, Peleg, administrator of.	Compensation for military services.	22	1	Petition	288	Claims	480	Adverse		Referred to Committee Whole House.		
Burdick, Perry	Pension for revolutionary services.	27	3	Petition	205	Rev. Pensions.						
Burdick, Perry	Pension for revolutionary services.	28	1	Petition	275	Rev. Pensions.						
Burdick, Perry	Pension for revolutionary services.	28	2	Petition	68	Rev. Pensions.						
Burdick, Walter	Increase of pension	10	2	Pension bill	499	Whole House	Feb. 20, 1809	With amend.	158	Passed	Passed with amendment.	App'd March 3, 1809
Burdick, William A.	(See John Rogers and others)	14	1		416							App'd April 27, 1816
Burdin, John	Pension for revolutionary services.	24	1	Petition	137	Rev. Pensions				Discharged; laid on table.		
Burdyne, Amos	Confirmation of title to land in Missouri.	26	1	Petition	961	Priv. Land Claims.	June 23, 1840	Adverse		Laid on table.		
Burdine, Lieut., assignee of	Payment of an account for public services.	23	1	Petition	567	Claims	469	Favorable	483	Referred to Committee Whole House.		
Burdine, Lieut., assignee of	Payment of an account for public services.	24	1	Petition	50	Claims	14	Favorable	14	Passed	Passed	App'd Feb. 17, 1836
Burdsall, Barnett	Arrears of pension	25	2	Petition	587	Invalid Pensions.						
Burdsall, Barnett	Arrears of pension	25	3	Petition	89	Invalid Pensions	289	Favorable	1153	Referred to Committee Whole House.		
Burdsall, Barnett	Arrears of pension	26	1	Petition	161	Invalid Pensions	527	Favorable	423	Referred to Committee Whole House.		
Burdsall, Barnett	Arrears of pension	27	2	Petition	60	Invalid Pensions	23	Favorable	64	Passed	Passed	App'd July 9, 1842
Burdwin, Samuel	Pension for revolutionary services.	3	1	Rep. of Secretary War.	131	Select.	1794					
Burdwin, Samuel	Pension for revolutionary services.	3	2	Rep. of Secretary War.	262	Claims.						
Burdwin, Samuel	Pension for revolutionary services.	4	1	Rep. of Secretary War.	373	Claims.						
Burdwin, Samuel	Pension for revolutionary services.	4	2	Rep. of Secretary War.	614	Claims.						
Burdwin, Samuel	Increase of pension	10	2	Pension bill	499	Whole House	Feb. 20, 1809	With amend.	158	Passed	Passed with amendment.	App'd March 3, 1809
Burck, Anthony	(See Canadian refugees)	4	2		614							

List of private claims presented to the House of Representatives of the United States from the 1st to the 31st Congress, inclusive—Continued.

Names of claimants.	Nature or object of the claim.	Congress.	Session.	How brought before the House of Reps.	Page of journal.	To what committee of the House referred.	No. or date of the report.	Nature of the report.	No. of the bill.	How disposed of by the House of Reps.	How disposed of by the Senate.	Date of the act of Congress, and remarks.
30 Burfort, Mary E.	(See executrix of John Clark)	29	1		316							
Burford, John	Confirmation of title to land in Alabama.	15	1	Petition	56	Priv. Land Claims.						
Burgan, Isaiah, heirs of	Correction of misnomer in land patent.	29	1	Petition	485	Public Lands.						
Burgan, James	(See heirs of Isaiah Burgan)	29	1		485							
Burgess, Abiel, widow of	Pension for revolutionary services.	25	2	Petition	729	Rev. Pensions				Discharged; laid on table.		
Burgess, Abiel, widow of	Pension for revolutionary services.	26	1	Petition	173	Rev. Pensions				Discharged: laid on table.		
Burgess, Jane	(See Abiel Burgess, widow of)	25	2		729							
Burgess, Demsey	Renewal of a loan office certificate.	4	1	Petition	497	Claims.						
Burgess, Demsey	Renewal of a loan office certificate.	4	2	Petition	614	Claims	Feb. 7, 1797	Adverse		Postponed.		
Burgess, Demsey	Renewal of a loan office certificate.	5	1	Petition	232	Claims.						
Burgess, Edward	Reimbursement of expenses on recruiting service.	23	1	Petition	388	Claims	April 1, 1834	Adverse		Laid on table.		
Burgess, Edward	Reimbursement of expenses on recruiting service.	24	1	Petition	141	Claims	344	Favorable	355	Referred to Committee Whole House.		
Burgess, Edward	Reimbursement of expenses on recruiting service.	25	2	Petition	36	Claims	6	Favorable	19	Passed	Passed	App'd March 7, 1838
Burgess, John, daughter of	Pension for revolutionary services of father.	28	1	Petition	947	Rev. Pensions.						
Burgess, Saunders	(See John Jarrott, representatives of.)	30	1		236							
Burgess, Vachel	Pension for revolutionary services.	10	1	Petition	193	Select.						
Burgess, Vachel	Pension for revolutionary services.	23	1	Petition	580	Rev. Pensions.						
Burgess, William, administrator of.	Compensation for military services.	22	1	Petition	288	Claims	480	Adverse		Referred to Committee Whole House.		
Burgess, William G.	(See administrator of Rane C. Rayland.)	27	2		1186							
Burgevin, Henry	Compensation for services as page in House of Representatives.	28	2	Resolution	138	Accounts.						
Burgh, William	(See William Brough.)											
Burghart, Adolphus, heirs of.	Settlement of his accounts	15	1	Petition	27	Military Affairs	Mar. 14, 1818	Favorable	140	Referred to Committee Whole House.		
Burghart, Adolphus, heirs of.	Settlement of his accounts	15	2	Rep't Committee Whole House	70			With't amend.	140	Passed	Indef. postp'd.	
Burghart, Adolphus, heirs of.	Settlement of his accounts	16	2	Petition	109	Military Affairs	Jan. 12, 1821	Favorable	190	Referred to Committee Whole House.		
Burghart, Adolphus, heirs of.	Settlement of his accounts	21	1	Petition	170	Claims	Jan. 26, 1830	Adverse		Laid on table.		
Burghart, Adolphus, heirs of.	Settlement of his accounts	26	1	Petition	658	Claims.						
Burgin, John	(See surety of Oliver Shead)	14	1		722							
Burk, Anthony, heirs of	Bounty land as Canadian refugee.	12	1	House bill	242	Whole House	Mar. 20, 1812	With't amend.	85	Passed	Passed with amendment.	App'd April 23, 1812
Burk, Anthony, heirs of	Renewal of grant per act of April 23, 1812.	15	2	Petition	132	Priv. Land Claims.						
Burk, Anthony, heirs of	Renewal of grant per act of April 23, 1812.	16	1	Petition	31	Priv. Land Claims.	Dec. 23, 1819	Favorable	19	Passed	Passed	App'd Feb. 18, 1820
Burkart, Frederick	Pension	20	1	Petition	369	Military Pensions.						
Burkart, Frederick	Pension	21	2	Petition	305	Military Pensions.						
Burkart, Frederick	Pension	22	1	Petition	51	Rev. Pensions.						
Burkart, Frederick	Pension	26	1	Petition	937	Rev. Pensions.						

List of private claims presented to the House of Representatives of the United States from the 1*st to the* 31*st Congress, inclusive*—Continued.

Names of claimants.	Nature or object of the claim.	Congress.	Session.	How brought before the House of Reps.	Page of journal.	To what committee of the House referred.	No. or date of the report.	Nature of the report.	No. of the bill.	How disposed of by the House of Reps.	How disposed of by the Senate.	Date of the act of Congress and remarks.
Burke, Edmund	Pension....................	19	1	Petition	265	Rev. Claims.						
Burke, Glendy	Exchange of a land location	27	2	Petition	738	Public Lands.						
Burke, James M	Compensation as clerk Treasury Department.	27	2	Petition	745	Claims	1040	Adverse.	......	Laid on table.		
Burke, John, (Ky.)......	Pension for revolutionary services.	22	1	Petition	105	Rev. Pensions.						
Burke, John, (Ind.)	Pension for revolutionary services.	21	2	Memorial.......	209	Military Pensions.						
Burke, John, (Ind.)	Pension for revolutionary services.	28	1	Petition	114	Rev. Pensions.						
Burke, John, (Va.)......	Indemnity for destruction of property by the enemy.	23	2	Petition	200	Claims.						
Burke, John, (Va.)......	Indemnity for destruction of property by the enemy.	24	1	Petition	93	Claims	267	Adverse	......	Laid on table.		
Burke, John, (Va.)......	Indemnity for destruction of property by the enemy.	25	3	Senate bill	657	....	....	....	S. 179			
Burke, John, (Va.)......	Indemnity for destruction of property by the enemy.	27	3	Petition	134	Claims	203	Adverse	......	Laid on table.		
Burke, John, administrator of.	Indemnity for French spoliations prior to 1800.	29	2	Petition	87	Foreign Affairs.						
Burke, Thomas	Pension	18	1	Petition	315	Pens. & Rev. Cl'ms.						
Burke, Thomas	Pension	18	2	Petition	30	Pens. & Rev. Cl'ms.						
Burke, Thomas	Pension	19	1	Petition	368	Military Affairs ...	May 5, 1826	Favorable	......	Leave to withdraw.		
Burke, William, heirs of .	Exchange of land location.......	12	1	Petition	26	Public Lands.						
Burke, William, heirs of .	Exchange of land location.......	12	2	Petition	550	Public Lands.						
Burke, William	Pension for revolutionary services.	11	3	Pension bill	604	Whole House	Mar. 2, 1811	Favorable	218	Passed	Passed	App'd March 3, 1811
Burke, William, (Mo.) ..	Pension	24	1	Petition	852	Invalid Pensions ..	July 1, 1836	Adverse	......	Laid on table.		
Burke, William, (Md) heirs of.	Pension for revolutionary services.	28	2	Petition	221	Rev. Pensions.						
Burke, William, & others	Bounty land and indemnity for losses, Florida war.	31	1	Petition	996	Public Lands.						
Burkham, Charles, and others.	Compensation as spies on frontier of Arkansas.	23	1	Senate bill	592	Claims	May 9, 1834	With't amend.	S. 70	Passed	Passed	App'd June 24, 1834
Burland, Thomas M.	Patent for public land purchased..	23	1	Petition	214	Public Lands......	Feb. 3, 1835	Favorable	697	Referred to Committee Whole House.		
Burland, Thomas M.	Patent for public land purchared..	24	1	Petition	121	Public Lands.....	709	Favorable	662	Referred to Committee Whole House.		
Burland, Thomas M	Patent for public land purchased..	24	2	House bill......	62	....	....	....	662			
Burland, Thomas M.....	Patent for public land purchased..	25	2	Petition	41	Priv. Land Claims.						
Burland, Thomas M.....	Patent for public land purchased..	25	3	Petition	133	Priv. Land Claims.	158	Favorable	1027	Passed	Passed	App'd March 3, 1839
Burley, Elizabeth	Continuance of pension	28	1	Petition	849	Rev. Pensions.						
Burlison, John	Pension	28	1	Petition	328	Invalid Pensions...	103	Adverse	......	Laid on table.		
Burlingame, Benjamin ...	Pension	22	1	Petition	36	Invalid Pensions...	186	Favorable	266	Passed.		
Burlingame, Benjamin ...	Pension	22	2	Petition	27	Invalid Pensions...	Dec. 19, 1832	Favorable	626	Passed	Passed with amendment.	Name stricken out.
Burlingame, Benjamin ...	Pension	23	1	Petition	44	Invalid Pensions ..	1	Favorable	1	Passed	Passed	App'd June 25, 1834
Burlingame, Solomon	Arrears of pension	21	1	Petition	377	Military Pensions.						
Burn, Joseph	Title to land under Quapaw treaty	19	2	Petition	137	Public Lands	60	Favorable	401	Laid on table.		
Burnell, Frederick A.....	(See Ebenezer Stevens)	16	2	....	30							
Burner, Abraham, heir of.	Pension for revolutionary services.	29	1	Petition	679	Rev. Pensions	785	Adverse	......	Laid on table.		
Burner, Jacob H........	(See heirs of Abraham Burner)..	29	1	....	679							
Burnett, Charles A	Compensation for work and material on President's house.	19	2	Petition	84	Public Buildings ..	57	Favorable	396	Referred to Committee Whole House		
Burnett, Charles A	Compensation for work and material on President's house.	20	1	Petition	245	Public Buildings ..	Feb. 25, 1828	Favorable	192	Referred to Committee Whole House.		

List of private claims presented to the House of Representatives of the United States from the 1st to the 31st Congress, inclusive—Continued.

Names of claimants.	Nature or object of the claim.	Congress.	Session.	How brought before the House of Reps.	Page of journal.	To what committee of the House referred.	No. or date of the report.	Nature of the report.	No. of the bill.	How disposed of by the House of Reps.	How disposed of by the Senate.	Date of the act of Congress, and remarks.
Burnett, Charles A	Compensation for work and material on President's house.	20	2	Rep. of Secretary of War.	198			With't amend.	192	Passed	Passed	App'd March 3, 1829
Burnett, Daniel	Confirmation of title to land in Mississippi territory.	12	1	Petition	214	Public Lands.						
Burnett, Daniel	Confirmation of title to land in Mississippi territory.	14	1	Petition	250	Public Lands.						
Burnett, Daniel	Confirmation of title to land in Mississippi territory.	14	2	Petition	34	Priv. Land Claims.						
Burnett, Daniel	Confirmation of title to land in Mississippi territory.	15	1	Petition	192	Priv. Land Claims.	Feb. 18, 1818	Favorable	94	Passed	Passed	App'd April 11, 1818
Burnett, Elisha	Location of a military land warrant.	27	2	Senate bill	1063	Public Lands	Aug. 20, 1842	With't amend.	S. 189	Passed	Passed	App'd Aug. 30, 1842
Burnett, James	Confirmation of title to land in Michigan.	20	2	Petition	71	Indian Affairs	Dec. 20, 1828	Adverse		Laid on table.		
Burnett, John, sen	Confirmation of title to land in Mississippi territory.	14	2	Petition	34	Public Lands.						
Burnett, John, sen	Confirmation of title to land in Mississippi territory.	15	1	Petition	115	Priv. Land Claims.						
Burnett, John S	Reimbursement of certain costs of suit.	25	3	Petition	132	P. Of. & P. Roads.	228	Adverse		Laid on table.		
Burnett, Joseph	Indemnity for property taken by the enemy.	20	1	Petition	366	Foreign Affairs	198	Adverse		Laid on table.		
Burnett, Salmon	Increase of pension	25	3	Petition	130	Rev. Pensions				Discharged; laid on table.		
Burnett, Samuel M	Release of mail contract	26	1	Petition	619	P. Of. & P. Roads.	477	Adverse		Laid on table.		
Burnett, Ward B	Additional compensation as civil engineer. Philadelphia.	31	1	Petition	745	Naval Affairs.						
Burnett, William	Compensation for horse lost in Seminole war	19	1	Petition	114	Claims.						
Burnett, William	Compensation for horse lost in Seminole war.	22	1	Petition	575	Claims.						
Burnett, William	Compensation for horse lost in Seminole war.	23	1	Petition	120	Claims.						
Burney, David	Confirmation of title to lands in Mississippi territory.	12	1	Petition	128	Public Lands.						
Burney, David	Confirmation of title to lands in Mississippi territory.	14	1	Petition	147	Public Lands.						
Burney, David	Confirmation of title to lands in Mississippi territory.	14	2	Petition	50	Priv. Land Claims.						
Burney, David	Confirmation of title to lands in Mississippi territory	15	1	Petition	192	Priv. Land Claims.						
Burney, David	Pension for revolutionary services.	24	1	Resolution	218	Rev. Pensions.						
Burney, Thomas	Confirmation of title to land in Mississippi territory.	13	3	Petition	762					Laid on table.		
Burnham, Asa	Payment of a revolutionary certificate.	23	1	Petition	305	Rev. Claims.						
Burnham, Barbara	(See John Burnham, widow of)	25	3		126							
Burnham, Catharine	(See daughter of Guy Young)	24	1	Petition	137	Rev. Claims	Jan. 21, 1836	Adverse		Laid on table.		
Burnham, Caty	Pension for revolutionary services.	30	1	Petition	606	Rev. Pensions	638	Adverse		Leave to withdraw.		
Burnham, Elias	(See Zophar Robinson)	25	2		721							
Burnham, Ezekiel	Invalid Pension	24	2	Resolution	129	Invalid Pensions	82	Adverse		Laid on table.		
Burnham, Hiram	Compensation for capturing Indian murderers.	28	1	Petition	854	Claims.						

List of private claims presented to the House of Representatives of the United States from the **1st** *to the* **31st** *Congress, inclusive*—**Continued.**

Names of claimants.	Nature or object of the claim.	Congress.	Session.	How brought before the House of Reps.	Page of journal.	To what committee of the House referred.	No. or date of the report.	Nature of the report.	No. of the bill.	How disposed of by the House of Reps.	How disposed of by the Senate.	Date of the act of Congress, and remarks.
Burnham, Hiram	Compensation for services as surveyor.	28	1	Petition	854	Claims.						
Burnham, Isaac	Pension	10	1	Pension bill	232	Whole House	April 19, 1808	With amend.	78	Passed	Passed with amendment.	App'd April 25, 1808
Burnham, Isaac	Arrears of pension	16	2	Petition	240	Pens. & Rev. Cl'ms.	Feb. 23, 1821	Adverse	......	Laid on table.		
Burnham, James	Compensation for medical aid to wounded seamen.	13	3	Petition	692	Naval Affairs	Feb. 1, 1815	Favorable	280	Passed	Passed	App'd Feb. 24, 1815
Burnham, Jeremiah	Increase of pension	15	2	Pension bill	41	....	....	....	203	Passed	Passed as am'd.	App'd March 3, 1819
Burnham, John	Reimbursement of ransom paid Algerines.	4	1	Appropriat'n bill.	83	....	....	....	19	Passed	Passed	App'd May 30, 1796
Burnham, John	Indemnity for losses, &c., in Algerine captivity.	7	1	Petition	95	....	....	....	......	Referred to Secretary State.		
Burnham, John	Indemnity for losses, &c., in Algerine captivity.	7	2	Rep. of Secretary State.	307	Claims.						
Burnham, John	Indemnity for losses, &c., in Algerine captivity.	12	1	Petition	24	Select	Nov. 25, 1811	Favorable	12	Passed	Passed	App'd Jan. 10, 1812
Burnham, John	Reimbursement of ransom money to British consul.	15	2	Petition	88	Claims.						
Burnham, John	Reimbursement of ransom money to British consul.	16	1	Petition	130	Claims	Jan. 31, 1820	Adverse	......	Laid on table.		
Burnham, John	Reimbursement of ransom money to British consul.	20	2	Petition	109	Foreign Affairs	102	Favorable	461	Referred to Committee Whole House.		
Burnham, John	Reimbursement of ransom money to British consul.	21	1	Petition	51	Foreign Affairs	19	Favorable	26	Passed	Passed	App'd April 7, 1830
Burnham, John	Reimbursement of ransom money to British consul.	21	2	Petition	99	Foreign Affairs	45	Favorable	575	Referred to Committee Whole House.		
Burnham, John	Reimbursement of ransom money to British consul.	22	1	Petition	30	Foreign Affairs	Dec. 19, 1831	Favorable	44	Passed	Passed with amendment.	App'd May 25, 1832
Burnham, John	Indemnity for property taken by the Algerines.	23	1	Petition	74	Foreign Affairs.						
Burnham, John	Revolutionary pension	25	3	Petition	126	Rev. Pensions	Feb. 6, 1839	Adverse	......	Laid on table.		
Burnham, John	Revolutionary pension	28	2	Petition	59	Rev. Pensions.						
Burnham, Joshua, (Mass.)	Pension	21	1	Petition	120	Military Pensions.						
Burnham, Joshua, (Mass.)	Pension	2[illegible]	1	Petition	34	Rev. Pension.						
Burnham, Mark	(See representatives of Robert Rogers.)	26	2	....	196							
Burnham, Oliver	Pension for revolutionary services.	4		Report Secretary of War.	447	Claims	Feb. 18, 1796	Pension bill.	156	Passed	Passed with amendment.	App'd April 20, 1796
Burnham, Ruhannah	Continuation of pension	28	1	Petition	849	Rev. Pensions.						
Burnham, Samuel	Portion of the proceeds of a capture.	13	2	Petition	384	....	....	....	......	Laid on table.		
Burnham, Sylvanus	Pension for revolutionary disability	31	2	Petition	58	Rev. Pensions.						
Burnham, Thomas	Bounty on fishing sloop Cyrus	10	1	Petition	213							
				Rep. of Secretary Treasury.	230	....	....	....	......	Laid on table.		
Burnham, Wolcott	Arrears of pension	30	1	Petition	508	Rev. Pensions	696	Adverse	......	Laid on table.		
Burnley, Garland, representatives of.	Commutation pay for revolutionary services.	22	2	Petition	142	Rev. Claims.						
Burnley, Garland, representatives of.	Commutation pay for revolutionary services.	23	1	Petition	41	Rev. Claims.						
Burnley, Garland, representatives of.	Commutation pay for revolutionary services.	23	2	Petition	56	Rev. Claims.						

List of private claims presented to the House of Representatives of the United States from the 1st to the 31st Congress, inclusive—Continued.

Names of claimants.	Nature or object of the claim.	Congress.	Session.	How brought before the House of Reps.	Page of journal.	To what committee of the House referred.	No. or date of the report.	Nature of the report.	No. of the bill.	How disposed of by the House of Reps.	How disposed of by the Senate.	Date of the act of Congress, and remarks.
Burnley, Garland, representatives of.	Commutation pay for revolutionary services.	24	1	Petition	62	Rev. Claims	220	Favorable	229	Referred to Committee Whole House.		
Burnley, Garland, representatives of.	Commutation pay for revolutionary services.	24	2	House bill	62	....	....	....	229			
Burnley, Garland, representatives of.	Commutation pay for revolutionary services.	25	2	Petition	70	Rev. Claims	243	Favorable	284	Passed.		
Burnley, Garland, representatives of.	Commutation pay for revolutionary services.	25	3	Petition	84	Rev. Claims.						
Burnley, Garland, representatives of.	Commutation pay for revolutionary services.	26	1	Petition	164	Rev. Claims	239	Adverse	......	Laid on table.		
Burnley, Garland, representatives of.	Commutation pay for revolutionary services.	27	2	Petition	60	Rev. Claims	369	Adverse	......	Laid on table	....	See 26th Cong. 1st sess., Rep. No. 436.
Burns, Andrew	Confirmation of title to land in Missouri.	15	2	Petition	28	Priv. Land Claims.						
Burns, Garrett	Pension	31	1	Petition	582	Invalid Pensions.						
Burns, Gerrard	Pension	15	1	Petition	136	Pens. & Rev. Cl'ms.						
Burns, James	Pension for disability in naval service.	30	1	Petition	165	Invalid Pensions	358	Adverse	......	Laid on table.		
Burns, James, and others.	Right of pre-emption to lands in Missouri.	15	1	Petition	279	Public Lands.						
Burns, James, and others.	Right of pre-emption to lands in Missouri.	15	2	Petition	118	Public Lands.						
Burns, John	Pension	15	1	Petition	140	Pens. & Rev. Cl'ms.						
Burns, Malachi	Confirmation of title to land in Louisiana.	18	1	Petition	78	Priv. Land Claims.	48	Favorable	91	Passed	Laid on table.	
Burns, Malachi	Confirmation of title to land in Louisiana.	18	2	Petition	42	Priv. Land Claims.	Dec. 21, 1824	Favorable	241	Passed	Passed	App'd March 3, 1825
Burns, Otway	Release from judgment on custom house bond.	19	1	Senate bill	458	Whole House	May 19, 1826	With't amend.	62	Passed	Passed	App'd May 20, 1826
Burns, Otway	Indemnity for loss on contract for brick.	22	1	Petition	333	Claims	Mar. 21, 1832	Adverse	.....	Laid on table.		
Burns, Samuel	(See represent's of John Payett)	30	1	Petition	236	Priv. Land Claims.						
Burns, Thomas, administrator of.	Compensation for supplies, war of 1812.	16	1	Petition	229	Claims.						
Burns, William	Pension	26	2	Petition	118	Invalid Pensions.						
Burns, William	Pension	27	2	Petition	154	Invalid Pensions.						
Burnside, Josiah, & others.	Increase of salary as clerks, Treasury Department.	3	1	Petition	185	Whole House.						
Burnside, Robert	Indemnity for an illegal seizure of goods.	14	2	Petition	129	Ways and Means	58	Favorable	89	Passed	Passed	App'd March 3, 1817
Burnside, Robert	Interest on payment pursuant to act.	15	1	Petition	90	Ways and Means	Feb. 3, 1818	Adverse	......	Rejected.		
Burnside, Thomas	(See Catharine Hogg & T. B.)	24	1	....	662							
Burnside, James	Pension	15	1	Petition	23	Pens. & Rev. Cl'ms.	Dec. 29, 1817	Adverse	......	Leave to withdraw.		
Burpee, Elijah	Compensation for revolutionary services.	22	2	Petition	118	Rev. Claims.						
Burr, Aaron, witnesses against.	(See Return J. Megs and others.)	10	1	....	23							
Burr, David H.	Remission of duties on maps	27	2	Petition	49	Ways and Means.	550	Adverse	......	Laid on table.		
Burr, David H.	Reimbursement of expenditures in the publication of certain maps.	28	1	Petition	79	P. Of. and P. Roads.	....	....	......	Discharged; laid on table.		
Burr, Ephraim W. and N. P. Smith.	Remission of duty on linseed oil	26	2	Petition	99	Ways and Means	Feb. 12, 1841	Favorable	677	Referred to Committee Whole House.		

List of private claims presented to the House of Representatives of the United States from the 1st to the 31st Congress, inclusive—Continued.

Names of claimants.	Nature or object of the claim.	Congress.	Session.	How brought before the House of Reps.	Page of journal.	To what committee of the House referred.	No. or date of the report.	Nature of the report.	No. of the bill.	How disposed of by the House of Reps.	How disposed of by the Senate.	Date of the act of Congress, and remarks.
Burr, Ephraim W. and N. P. Smith.	Remission of duty on linseed oil.	27	2	Petition	95	Ways and Means	906	Favorable	524	Ordered to 3d reading.		
Burr, Ephraim W. and N. P. Smith.	Remission of duty on linseed oil.	27	3	House bill	89				524	Passed	Passed	App'd Jan. 20, 1843
Burr, James (Conn.)	Indemnity for French spoliations prior to 1800.	26	1	Memorial	182	Foreign Affairs	343	Favorable	319	Referred to Committee Whole House.		
Burr, James	Renewal of patent	22	1	Petition	292	Judiciary.						
Burr, Levi	Reimbursement of expenditures in recruiting.	17	2	Petition	74	Claims.						
Burr, Levi	Reimbursement of expenditures in recruiting.	18	1	Petition	286	Military Affairs.						
Burr, Levi	Pension for wounds, war of 1812	18	1	Petition	497	Pens. & Rev. Cl'ms.	May 22, 1824	Adverse		Laid on table.		
Burr, Nathan	Pension for revolutionary services.	4	1	Report of Secretary of War.	447	Claims	Feb. 18, 1796	Pension bill	156	Passed	Passed with amendment.	App'd April 20, 1796
Burr, Salmon	Pension for revolutionary disabilities.	1	2	Petition	142							
				Rep. of Secretary Treasury.	153					Laid on table.		
Burr, Salmon	Pension for revolutionary disabilities.	3	1	Rep. of Secretary Treasury.	131	Select	May 26, 1794	Res. to refer to Sec. War.	R. 12	Passed	Passed	App'd June 9, 1794
Burr, Samuel	Payment of loan office certificate.	15	1	Petition	293	Pens. & Rev. Cl'ms	165	Favorable	158	Referred to Committee Whole House.		
Burr, Samuel	Payment of loan office certificate.	15	2	Rep't Committee Whole House	158			Adverse	158	Rejected.		
Burr, Samuel, administrator of.	Payment of loan office certificate.	22	1	Petition	332	Rev. Claims.						
Burr, Samuel, administrator of.	Payment of loan office certificate.	23	1	Petition	329	Rev. Claims.						
Burr, Samuel, administrator of.	Payment of loan office certificate.	24	1	Petition	403	Rev. Claims.						
Burr, Samuel, administrator of.	Payment of loan office certificate.	30	1	Petition	69	Rev. Claims.						
Burr, Samuel, administrator of.	Payment of loan office certificate.	30	2	Petition	328	Rev. Claims.						
Burr, Thaddeus	Payment of revolutionary certificate.	4	1	Petition	388	Claims	74	Adverse		Laid on table.		
Burr, Timothy	Credit for money stolen from agent.	13	2	Petition	298	Claims	Feb. 23, 1814	Adverse		Laid on table.		
Burras, George G.	(See Nathaniel Hunt and others.)	19	2		242							
Burras, George G.	Compensation as inspector of customs New York.	28	1	Petition	98	Claims.						
Burras, George G.	Compensation as inspector of customs New York.	28	2	Petition	118	Claims.						
Burrell, Ebenezer, widow of.	Pension for revolutionary services.	26	1	Petition	936	Rev. Pensions.						
Burrell, William	Pension	19	1	Petition	203	Military Pensions	April 1, 1826	Adverse		Laid on table.		
Burrett, Samuel	Pension for revolutionary services.	26	1	Petition	759	Rev. Pensions	424	Adverse		Laid on table.		
Burriss, Elijah, agent of.	Compensation for horse lost in Florida war.	28	1	Petition	262	Claims.						
Burriss, Elizabeth, heirs of.	Confirmation of title to land in Arkansas.	27	2	Petition	406	Priv. Land Claims.	555	Favorable	347	Passed.		
Burriss, Elizabeth, heirs of.	Confirmation of title to land in Arkansas.	27	3	Petition	223	Priv. Land Claims.	Jan. 31, 1843	Favorable	741	Passed	Indef. postpn'd	

List of private claims presented to the House of Representatives of the United States from the 1st to the 31st Congress, inclusive—Continued.

Names of claimants.	Nature or object of the claim.	Congress.	Session.	How brought before the House of Reps.	Page of journal.	To what committee of the House referred.	No. or date of the report.	Nature of the report.	No. of the bill.	How disposed of by the House of Reps.	How disposed of by the Senate.	Date of the act of Congress, and remarks.
Burriss, Elizabeth, heirs of.	Confirmation of title to land in Arkansas.	28	1	Petition	372	Priv. Land Claims.				Discharged; laid on table.		
Burriss, Elizabeth, heirs of.	Confirmation of title to land in Arkansas.	29	1	Petition	498	Priv. Land Claims.	698	Favorable	473	Referred to Committee Whole House.		
Burriss, Elizabeth, heirs of.	Confirmation of title to land in Arkansas.	30	1	Petition	109	Priv. Land Claims.	181	Favorable	191	Passed	Passed 2d sess.	App'd Jan. 10, 1849
Burris, William	Exchange of an erroneous land entry.	21	1	Petition	237	Priv. Land Claims.	Feb. 22, 1830	Adverse.		Laid on table.		
Burris, William	Exchange of an erroneous land entry.	21	2	Senate bill	217	Priv. Land Claims.	Feb. 8, 1831	With't amend.	S. 79	Passed	Passed	App'd Feb. 19, 1831
Burris, William	Amendatory act	23	1	Senate bill	833	Priv. Land Claims.	June 27, 1834	With't amend.	S. 109	Passed	Passed	App'd June 30, 1834
Burritt, Andrew	Pension for revolutionary services.	24	1	Petition	506	Rev. Pensions				Discharged; laid on table.		
Burritt, William	Pension for revolutionary services.	4	1	Rep. of Secretary War.	447	Claims	Feb. 18, 1796	Favorable	156	Passed	Passed with amendment.	App'd April 20, 1796
Burritt, William	Increase of pension	7	2	Petition	254	Claims	Jan. 11, 1803	Adverse.				
Burritt, William	Increase of pension	9	2	Pension bill	608	Whole House	Feb. 28, 1807	With amend.	216	Passed	Passed	App'd March 3, 1807
Burroughs, ———	(See Armington & Burroughs.)	21	2		110							
Burroughs, Daniel	Pension	20	2	Petition	203	Military Pensions.						
Burroughs, Daniel	Pension	21	1	Petition	75	Military Pensions.						
Burroughs, Robert S., & S. H.	Increase of compensation as custom-house officers.	4	1	Petition	449	Com. and Manuf.						
Burroughs, Robert S., & S. H.	Increase of compensation as custom-house officers.	6	2	Petition	786	Com. and Manuf.				Postponed.		
Burroughs, Robert S., & S. H	Increase of compensation as custom-house officers.	10	1	Petition	180	Com. and Manuf.						
Burroughs, Robert S., & S. H.	Increase of compensation as custom-house officers.	10	2	Petition	366	Com. and Manuf.						
Burroughs, Robert S., & S. H.	Increase of compensation as custom-house officers.	11	2	Petition	147	Com. and Manuf.						
Burroughs, Robert S., & S. H.	Increase of compensation as custom-house officers.	11	3	Petition	570	Com. and Manuf.						
Burroughs, Robert S., & S. H.	Increase of compensation as custom-house officers.	12	1	Petition	122	Com. and Manuf.						
Burroughs, Robert S., & S. H., administrator of	Payment of certain fees	31	1	Petition	754	Claims	324	Favorable	281	Referred to Committee Whole House.		
Burroughs, Robert S., & S. H., administrator of.	Payment of certain fees	31	2	Rep't Committee Whole House.	181			With't amend.	281	Passed	Passed	App'd Feb. 27, 1851
Burrows, Asa	Pension	21	2	Petition	103	Military Pensions.						
Burrows, Daniel	Increase of compensation as surveyor of customs.	19	2	Petition	98	Commerce.						
Burrows, Eden	Additional compensation for revolutionary services.	11	3	Petition	461	Select.						
Burrows, Eden	Additional compensation for revolutionary services.	12	1	Petition	110	Select.				Discharged; referred to Com. Whole House.		
Burrows, Eden, widow of.	Continuation of pension	19	1	Petition	35	Rev. Pensions	April 1, 1826	Adverse		Laid on table.		
Burrows, John, heir of	Pension for revolutionary services.	26	1	Petition	359	Rev. Claims.						
Burrows, Joseph	Pension for revolutionary services.	3	1	Rep. of Secretary War.	131	Select	May 6, 1794	Pension bill	62	Passed	Passed	App'd June 7, 1794
Burrows, Nathaniel	Pension for revolutionary services.	22	1	Petition	287	Rev. Pensions.						
Burrows, Richard	Pension	21	2	Petition	299	Military Pensions.						
Burrows, Tillson	Pension	24	2	Petition	267	Invalid Pensions.						
Burrows, Tillson	Pension	25	2	Petition	57	Invalid Pensions.						

List of private claims presented to the House of Representatives of the United States from the 1st to the 31st Congress, inclusive—Continued.

Names of claimants.	Nature or object of the claim.	Congress.	Session.	How brought before the House of Reps.	Page of journal.	To what committee of the House referred.	No. or date of the report.	Nature of the report.	No. of the bill.	How disposed of by the House of Reps.	How disposed of by the Senate.	Date of the act of Congress, and remarks.
Burrows, Willard	(See Rasselas Whitcomb & others)	25	2		1047		960					
Burrows, William	Increase of pension	10	2	Pension bill	499	Whole House	Feb. 20, 1809	With amend.	158	Passed	Passed with amendment.	App'd March 3, 1809
Burseil, James	Pension	15	1	Petition	....	Pens. & Rev. Cl'ms.	Dec. 29, 1817	Adverse	......	Referred to Committee Whole House.		
Burseil, Moses	Pension for revolutionary services	16	1	Petition	23	Pens. & Rev. Cl'ms.						
				Rep. of Secretary War.	350	Pens. & Rev. Cl'ms.						
Burseil, Moses	Pension for revolutionary services	17	1	Petition	25	Pens. & Rev. Cl'ms.	Jan. 25, 1822	Adverse	......	Leave to withdraw.		
				Reconsidered	190	Pens. & Rev. Cl'ms.	....	....	......	Discharged; referred to Secretary of War.		
				Rep. of Secretary War.	548	....	....	....	......	Laid on table.		
Burseil, Moses	Pension for revolutionary services	17	2	Rep. of Secretary War.	28	Pens. & Rev. Cl'ms.						
Burseil, Moses	Pension for revolutionary services	18	1	Petition	74	Pens. & Rev. Cl'ms.	Dec. 23, 1823	Pension bill	35	Passed	Passed	App'd May 19, 1824, petition's name omitted
Burt, Enoch	Renewal of a patent	31	2	Petition	147	Patents.						
Burt, Joel	Release from judgment for seizures by authority.	12	1	Petition	199	Com. and Manuf.						
Burt, Joel	Payment by government of judgment against him.	24	1	Petition	140	Claims	255	Adverse	......	Laid on table.		
Burt, Joel, widow of	Reimbursement of expenditure in the public service.	26	1	Petition	295	Claims.						
Burt, Joel, widow of	Reimbursement of expenditure in the public service.	27	2	Petition	309	Claims.						
Burt, John M., administrator of.	Indemnity for French spoliations prior to 1800.	24	2	Memorial	315	Foreign Affairs.						
Burt, John M., administrator of.	Indemnity for French spoliations prior to 1800.	26	1	Memorial	182	Foreign Affairs	343	Favorable	319	Referred to Committee Whole House.		
Burt, John M., administrator of.	Indemnity for French spoliations prior to 1800.	31	1	Memorial	215	Foreign Affairs	355	General bill	318	Referred to Committee Whole House.		
Burt, Martin	Pension for revolutionary services	27	2	Petition	401	Rev. Pensions	784	Adverse	......	Laid on table.		
Burtch, Billings	Pension for revolutionary services	20	2	Resolution	107	Military Pensions	....	....	......	Discharged; referred to Com. Whole House.		
Burtch, Billings	Pension for revolutionary services	21	1	Petition	67	Military Pensions	April 2, 1830	Adverse	......	Laid on table.		
Burtch, Billings	Pension for revolutionary services	22	1	Petition	534	Rev. Pensions.						
Burton, Amelia	Balance due husband as surgeon general.	29	1	Petition	101	Claims.						
Burton, Benjamin	(See John Burton and others)	19	1		334							
Burton, George	Increase of pension	18	1	Petition	74	Pens. & Rev. Cl'ms.						
Burton, James, widow of.	Commutation pay for revolutionary services.	22	2	Petition	142	Rev. Claims.						
Burton, James, widow of.	Commutation pay for revolutionary services.	23	1	Petition	97	Rev. Claims.						
Burton, James, widow of.	Commutation pay for revolutionary services.	24	1	Petition	138	Rev. Claims	428	Favorable	434	Referred to Committee Whole House.		
Burton, James, widow of.	Commutation pay for revolutionary services.	25	2	Petition	70	Rev. Claims	244	Favorable	285	Passed.		
Burton, James, widow of.	Commutation pay for revolutionary services.	25	3	Petition	85	Rev. Claims	10	Favorable	907	Referred to Committee Whole House.		
Burton, James, representatives of.	Half-pay for revolutionary services.	26	1	Petition	163	Rev. Claims.						

List of private claims presented to the House of Representatives of the United States from the 1st to the 31st Congress, inclusive—Continued.

Names of claimants.	Nature or object of the claim.	Congress.	Session.	How brought before the House of Reps.	Page of journal.	To what committee of the House referred.	No. or date of the report.	Nature of the report.	No. of the bill.	How disposed of by the House of Reps.	How disposed of by the Senate.	Date of the act of Congress, and remarks.
Burton, John	Pension for revolutionary services	3	1	Rep. of Secretary War.	131	Select	May 26, 1794	Res. to refer to Sec. War.	R. 12	Passed	Passed	App'd June 9, 1794
Burton, John, and others	Remission of the forfeiture of the schooner Volante.	19	1	Petition	334	Ways and Means	204	Favorable	265	Referred to Committee Whole House.		
Burton, John, and others	Remission of the forfeiture of the schooner Volante.	20	1	Petition	125	Ways and Means	147	Favorable	170	Passed.		
Burton, John, and others	Remission of the forfeiture of the schoonor Volante.	20	2	Petition	25	Ways and Means	Dec. 10, 1828	Favorable	308	Referred to Committee Whole House.		
Burton, John, and others	Remission of the forfeiture of the schooner Volante.	21	1	Petition	39	Ways and Means	Jan. 5, 1830	Favorable	73	Passed	Passed	App'd April 24, 1830
Burton, John, (Ark.)	Indemnity for improvements lost by Cherokee treaty.	23	2	Petition	256	Public Lands.						
Burton, Robert	(See administrator of Wm. Scott)	21	2		157							
Burton, Salah, (Ohio)	Pension	20	1	Petition	223	Military Pensions.						
Burton, Samuel	Pension	10	2	Pension bill	499	Whole House	Feb. 20, 1809	With amend.	158	Passed	Passed with amendment.	App'd March 3, 1809
Burton, Simon	Bounty land for services, war of 1812.	24	2	Petition	314	Priv. Land Claims.	190	Adverse		Laid on table.		
Burton, Stephen	Arrears of pension	29	1	Petition	161	Invalid Pensions				Discharged; laid on table.		
Burton, Thomas	(See John Burton and others)	19	1		334							
Burton, Thomas, (Md.)	Pension for revolutionary services.	22	1	Petition	632	Rev. Pensions.						
Burwell, Jonathan	Pension for revolutionary services.	3	1	Rep. of Secretary War.	131	Select	May 26, 1794	Pension bill	62	Passed	Passed with amendment.	App'd June 7, 1794
Burzette, Charles, widow of	Bounty land for revolutionary services.	24	2	Petition	397	Rev. Claims.						
Burzette, Charles, widow of	Bounty land for revolutionary services.	25	2	Petition	48	Rev. Claims	868	Adverse		Laid on table.		
Burzette, Charles, widow of	Bounty land for revolutionary services.	26	1	Petition	701	Priv. Land Claims.	629	Adverse		Laid on table.		
Busby, James	Increase of pension	23	1	Petition	436	Rev. Pensions.						
Busey, Frederick	Pension	14	1	Petition	84	Pens. & Rev. Cl'ms.	April 11, 1816	Favorable	171	Referred to Committee Whole House.		
Busey, Frederick	Pension	14	2	Resolution	103	Pens. & Rev. Clm's.						
Busey, Frederick	Pension	15	2	Petition	61	Pens. & Rev. Cl'ms.						
Bush, Daniel	Pension	21	1	Petition	573	Military Pensions.						
Bush, Daniel	Pension	21	2	Petition	126	Military Pensions.						
Bush, Daniel	Pension	22	1	Resolution	594	Rev. Pensions.						
Bush, Daniel B	Exchange of a land entry	24	1	Petition	112	Priv. Land Claims.	Jan. 27, 1836	Favorable	221	Passed	Adverse report; indef. post'd.	
Bush, Daniel B.	Exchange of a land entry	24	2	Senate bill	578				S. 73			
Bush, Daniel B.	Exchange of a land entry	25	2	Senate bill	159	Priv. Land Claims.	Jan. 5, 1838	With't amend.	S. 23	Referred to Committee Whole House.		
Bush, Daniel B.	Exchange of a land entry	25	3	Senate bill	657				S. 143			
Bush, Daniel B.	Exchange of a land entry	26	1	Senate bill	813	Public Lands	July 11, 1840	With't amend.	S. 226	Referred to Committee Whole House.		
Bush, Daniel B.	Exchange of a land entry	27	2	Senate bill	1126	Public Lands	July 27, 1842	With't amend.	S. 250	Passed	Passed	App'd Aug. 11, 1842
Bush, Edward	(See widow of Stephen Decatur and others.)											
Bush, Frank, widow of	Land under act of August 4, 1842	28	1	Petition	839	Public Lands.						
Bush, Henry, (N. Y.)	Pension for revolutionary services.	22	1	Petition	632	Rev. Pensions.						
Bush, Henry, (N. Y.)	Pension for revolutionary services.	25	2	Petition	404	Rev. Pensions	761	Favorable	720	Passed	Adverse report.	
Bush, Henry,)N. Y.)	Pension for revolutionary services.	26	1	Petition	171	Rev. Pensions	154	Favorable	164	Passed.		
Bush, Hezekiah	Pension	21	2	Petition	208	Military Pensions.						

List of private claims presented to the House of Representatives of the United States from the 1st to the 31st Congress, inclusive—**Continued.**

Names of claimants.	Nature or object of the claim.	Congress.	Session.	How brought before the House of Reps.	Page of journal.	To what committee of the House referred.	No. or date of the report.	Nature of the report.	No. of the bill.	How disposed of by the House of Reps.	How disposed of by the Senate.	Date of the act of Congress, and remarks.
Bush, Isaac, and others	Compensation for services and supplies in Florida war.	30	1	Petition	740	Claims.						
Bush, Isaac, and others	Compensation for services in Florida war.	30	1	Petition	838	Military Affairs	740	Favorable	582	Referred to Committee Whole House.		
Bush, Isaac, and others	Compensation for services in Florida war.	31	1	Petition	338	Military Affairs.						
Bush, Isaac, and others	Compensation for services in Florida war.	31	2	Petition	241	Military Affairs	Feb. 6, 1851	Favorable	456	Referred to Committee Whole House.		
Bush, John	Indemnity for revolutionary disabilities.	2	1	Petition	447					Referred to Secretary War.		
				Report of Secretary of War.	459	Select	Nov. 25, 1791	Pension bill	152	Passed	Passed	App'd Mar. 27, 1792
Bush, John Wesley	Claim for land under act of 1824.	18	2	Petition	138	Priv. Land Claims.						
Bush, John W., heirs of	Pension for services, &c., in Mexico.	31	1	Petition	256	Rev. Pensions	133	Favorable	150	Referred to Committee Whole House.		
Bush, John W., heirs of	Pension for services, &c., in Mexico.	31	2	Rep't Committee Whole House.	103			With't amend.	150	Passed.		
Bush, Matthias, assignee of	Compensation for supplies to revolutionary prisoners.	1	3	Petition	396					Referred to Secretary of the Treasury.		
Bush, Matthias, assignee of	Compensation for supplies to revolutionary prisoners.	3	1	Rep. of Secretary Treasury.	77					Laid on table.		
Bush, Philip	Renewal of lost loan certificate	2	1	Petition	456					Referred to Secretary Treasury.		
Bush, Philip	Renewal of lost loan certificate	3	2	Rep. of Secretary Treasury.	290	Select.						
Bush, Philip	Renewal of lost loan certificate	4	2	Petition	649	Claims	Feb. 7, 1797	Adverse		Laid on table.		
Bush, Philip	Renewal of lost loan certificate	5	2	Petition	188	Claims	Mar. 19, 1798	Adverse		Laid on table.		
Bush, Philip	Renewal of lost loan certificate	6	1	Petition	614	Claims	April 12, 1800	Adverse		Laid on table.		
Bush, Philip	Renewal of lost loan certificate	6	2	Petition	731	Claims	Jan. 26, 1801	Adverse		Rejected.		
Bush, Philip	Renewal of lost loan certificate	8	2	Petition	58	Whole House.						
Bush, Philip, executor of	Renewal of lost loan certificate	15	2	Petition	138	Rev. Claims.						
Bush, Philip, executor of	Renewal of lost loan certificate	16	1	Petition	119	Rev. Claims	35	Adverse		Laid on table.		
Bush, Philip, executor of	Renewal of lost loan certificate	19	1	Petition	154	Rev. Claims.						
Bush, Philip, administrator of.	Renewal of lost loan certificate	19	2	Petition	308	Rev. Claims.						
Bush, Philip, administrator of.	Renewal of lost loan certificate	20	1	Petition	85	Rev. Claims	159	Adverse		Laid on table.		
				Recommitted	249	Rev. Claims	Feb. 23, 1828	Adverse		Referred to Committee Whole House.		
Bush, Philip, administrator of.	Renewal of lost loan certificate	21	1	Petition	199	Rev. Claims	243	Favorable	306	Referred to Committee Whole House.		
Bush, Philip, administrator of.	Renewal of lost loan certificate	21	2	Rep't Committee Whole House.	340			With't amend.	306	Passed	Laid on table.	
Bush, Philip, administrator of.	Renewal of lost loan certificate	22	1	Petition	55	Rev. Claims	150	Favorable	229	Referred to Committee Whole House.		
Bush, Philip, administrator of.	Renewal of lost loan certificate	22	2	Rep't Committee Whole House.	92			With't amend.	229	Passed	Passed	App'd March 2, 1833
Bush, Philip, administrator of.	Further allowance under act of 2d March, 1833.	23	1	Petition	97	Rev. Claims.						
Bush, Philip, administrator of.	Further allowance under act of 2d March, 1833.	23	2	Petition	56	Rev. Claims.						
Bush, Sarah A.	(See heirs of John W. Bush)	31	1		256				150			
Bush William	Indemnity for Indian depredations.	22	1	Memorial	385	Claims	Mar. 12, 1832	Adverse		Laid on table.		

List of private claims presented to the House of Representatives of the United States from the 1st to the 31st Congress, inclusive—Continued.

Names of claimants.	Nature or object of the claim.	Congress.	Session.	How brought before the House of Reps.	Page of journal.	To what committee of the House referred.	No. or date of the report.	Nature of the report.	No. of the bill.	How disposed of by the House of Reps.	How disposed of by the Senate.	Date of the act of Congress, and remarks.
Bush, William F.	Compensation for horse lost in public services.	27	2	Petition	951	Claims.						
Bushart	Pension	28	2	Resolution	132	Rev. Pensions.						
Bushnell, Handy	Pension	16	1	Petition	288	Rev. Pensions	April 22, 1820	Adverse	......	Laid on table.		
Buskirk, Betsey, D.	Pension	26	2	Petition	100	Invalid Pensions	Feb. 12, 1841	Adverse	......	Laid on table.		
Bussell, Daniel	Increase of pension	10	2	Pension bill	499	Whole House	Feb. 20, 1809	With amend.	158	Passed	Passed with amendment.	App'd March 3, 1809
Busten, James, executor of.	Commutation pay for revolutionary services.	23	1	Resolution	99	Rev. Claims.						
Buster, General Joshua	Reimbursement of expenditure on public account.	24	2	Resolution	221	Claims.						
Buster, General Joshua	Reimbursement of expenditure on public account.	25	2	Resolution	77	Claims	999	Adverse	......	Laid on table.		
Butcher, Bartholomew	(See Sebastian Butcher and others.)	24	1	....	365							
Butcher, Michael	(See Sebastian Butcher and others.)	24	1	....	365							
Butcher, Sebastian & others	Confirmation of title to land	24	1	Senate bill	365	Priv. Land Claims.	June 15, 1836	Adverse	S. 24	Referred to Committee Whole House.		
Butcher, Sebastian & others	Confirmation of title to land	24	2	Senate bill	250	Priv. Land Claims.	....	....	S. 30	Discharged; laid on table.		
Butcher, Sebastian & others	Confirmation of title to land	25	2	Senate bill	197	Priv. Land Claims.	Jan. 5, 1838	With't amend.	S. 66	Referred to Committee Whole House.		
Butcher, Sebastian & others	Confirmation of title to land	25	3	Senate bill	477	Priv. Land Claims.	March 2, 1839	With amend.	S. 50	Referred to Committee Whole House.		
Butcher, Sebastian & others	Confirmation of title to land	26	1	Senate bill	68	Priv. Land Claims.	April 4, 1840	With't amend.	S. 68	Referred to Committee Whole House.		
Butcher, Sebastian & others	Confirmation of title to land	26	2	Senate bill	282	....	....	....	S. 80			
Butcher, Sebastian & others	Confirmation of title to land	27	2	Senate bill	521	Priv. Land Claims.	July 27, 1842	With't amend.	S. 48	Passed	Passed	App'd Aug. 11, 1842
Butler, Amos	Compensation for advertising official notices.	23	1	Petition	190	Judiciary	250	Adverse	......	Laid on table.		
Butler, Amos	Compensation for advertising official notices.	23	2	Petition	198	Judiciary.						
Butler, Amos	Compensation for advertising official notices.	24	1	Petition	53	Judiciary	....	....	......	Discharged; laid on table.		
Butler, Amos	Compensation for advertising official notices.	25	2	Petition	403	Judiciary	....	....	......	Discharged; laid on table.		
Butler, Charles	(See Elizabath Swain, attorney of.)	26	1	....	182	....	343	....	319			
Butler, Cyrus	Indemnity for French spoltations prior to 1800.	26	1	Memorial	182	Foreign Affairs	343	Favorable	319	Referred to Committee Whole House.		
Butler, David	Compensation for extra services at Little Rock.	31	1	Petition	827	Military Affairs.						
		31	1	Appropriat'n bill.	1467	Whole House	....	Amendments	390	Passed	Passed	App'd Sept. 28, 1850
Butler, Edward	Compensation as bearer of Cherokee treaty.	7	1	Petition	190	Claims	April 14, 1802	Adverse	......	Leave to withdraw.		
Butler, Edward	Compensation as bearer of Cherokee treaty.	8	1	Petition	457	Claims	Dec. 6, 1803	Adverse.				
Butler, Eleazer	Compensation for revolutionary services.	26	1	Petition	727	Rev. Claims.						
Butler, Eleazer	Compensation for revolutionary services.	27	2	Petition	96	Rev. Claims	528	Adverse	......	Laid on table.		
Butler, Eleazer	Compensation for revolutionary services.	27	3	Petition	70	Rev. Claims	234	Adverse	......	Laid on table.		
Butler, Jacob	Compensation for horses lost in public service.	19	1	Petition	94	Claims	132	Favorable	173	Passed.		

List of private claims presented to the House of Representatives of the United States from the 1st to the 31st Congress, inclusive—**Continued.**

Names of claimants.	Nature or object of the claim.	Congress.	Session.	How brought before the House of Reps.	Page of journal.	To what committee of the House referred.	No. or date of the report.	Nature of the report.	No. of the bill.	How disposed of by the House of Reps.	How disposed of by the Senate.	Date of the act of Congress, and remarks.
Butler, Jacob	Compensation for horses lost in public service.	19	2	Petition	50	Claims	Dec. 15, 1826	Favorable	294	Passed	Passed	App'd March 2, 1827
Butler, James, (Md.)	Pension	19	2	Petition	111	Naval Affairs	Jan. 17, 1827	Adverse		Laid on table.		
Butler, James, (Md.)	Pension	20	1	Petition	58	Naval Affairs	Feb. 15, 1828	Adverse		Laid on table.		
Butler, James, (Penn.)	Pension for disability in naval service.	28	1	Petition	101	Invalid Pensions	Jan. 31, 1844	Adverse		Laid on table.		
Butler, James, (Penn.)	Pension for disability in naval service.	31	1	Petition	542	Invalid Pensions	379	Favorable	327	Referred to Committee Whole House.		
Butler, James, (N. Y.)	Pension for revolutionary services.	25	2	Petition	198	Rev. Pensions.						
Butler, James, (N. Y.)	Pension for revolutionary services.	26	1	Petition	173	Rev. Pensions.						
Butler, James and others	Right of pre-emption to lands in Missouri.	25	2	Petition	97	Public Lands.						
Butler, James and others	Right of pre-emption to lands in Missouri.	25	3	Petition	92	Public Lands.						
Butler, John, heirs of	Pension for revolutionary services.	26	1	Petition	173	Rev. Pensions				Discharged; laid on table.		
Butler, John W	Confirmation of title to land in Louisiana.	23	2	Petition	230	Priv. Land Claims.						
Butler, Mary	Confirmation of title to land in Louisiana.	28	1	Petition	416	Priv. Land Claims.						
Butler, Medad	Pension for revolutionary services.	28	1	Petition	338	Rev. Pensions.						
Butler, Norman	Payment of revolutionary certificate.	4	1	Petition	388	Claims	74	Adverse		Laid on table.		
Butler, Paul D	Right of pre-emption to land in Ohio.	12	1	Petition	14	Public Lands.						
Butler, Paul D	Compensation for corn applied to public use.	14	1	Petition	410	Claims	Mar. 8, 1816	Favorable		Passed	Passed with amendment.	App'd April 27, 1816
Butler, Pierce M	Release from balance due United States as Indian commissioner.	31	1	Senate resolution.	870	Indian Affairs	July 31, 1850	With't amend.	R. 12	Passed	Passed	App'd Aug. 10, 1850
				Senate resolution.	1403				R. 31	Passed	Passed	App'd Sept. 16, 1850
Butler, Reuben, heirs of	Commutation pay for revolutionary services.	24	1	Petition	275	Rev. Claims	May 17, 1836	Adverse		Laid on table.		
Butler, Rueben, heirs of	Commutation pay for revolutionary services.	24	2	Petition	92	Rev. Claims	101	Adverse		Laid on table.		
Butler, Richard, executor of.	Compensation for revolutionary services.	2	1	Petition	537	Whole House.						
Butler, Richard, executor of.	Compensation for revolutionary services.	3	2	Petition	295	Claims.						
Butler, Richard, executor of.	Compensation for revolutionary services.	4	1	Petition	373	Claims	May 10, 1796	Favorable		Referred to Committee Whole House.		
Butler, Richard, widow of.	Compensation for revolutionary services.	4	1	Petition	402	Claims	Mar. 4, 1796	Favorable	162	Passed	Rejected.	
Butler, Robert	Grant of land	19	2	Petition	27	Public Lands.						
Butler, Robert	Indemnity for loss of improvements.	27	2	Memorial	617	Claims	696	Adverse		Laid on table.		
Butler, Robert	Indemnity for loss of improvements.	28	1	Memorial	132	Priv. Land Claims.						
Butler, Robert	Indemnity for loss of improvements.	29	1	Memorial	199	Priv. Land Claims.						
Butler, Robert	Indemnity for loss of improvements.	29	2	Memorial	132	Claims				Discharged; laid on table.		
Butler, Samuel	Pension	25	2	Petition	167	Invalid Pensions	Jan. 30, 1838	Adverse		Laid on table.		
				Recommitted	953	Invalid Pensions.						

List of private claims presented to the House of Representatives of the United States from the 1st to the 31st Congress, inclusive—Continued.

Names of claimants.	Nature or object of the claim.	Congress.	Session.	How brought before the House of Reps.	Page of journal.	To what committee of the House referred.	No. or date of the report.	Nature of the report.	No. of the bill.	How disposed of by the House of Reps.	How disposed of by the Senate.	Date of the act of Congress, and remarks.
Butler, Samuel	Pension	25	3	Petition	81	Invalid Pensions	Jan. 16, 1839	Adverse		Laid on table.		
Butler, Samuel	Pension	26	1	Petition	287	Invalid Pensions	406	Adverse		Laid on table.		
Butler, Samuel	Pension	27	2	Petition	545	Invalid Pensions	674	Adverse		Laid on table.		
Butler, Samuel	Pension	27	3	Petition	223	Invalid Pensions	Feb. 3, 1843	Adverse		Laid on table.		
				Recommitted	411	Invalid Pensions.						
Butler, Samuel	Pension	28	1	Petition	143	Invalid Pensions	221	Favorable	175	Passed.		
Butler, Samuel	Pension	28	2	Petition	145	Invalid Pensions				Discharged; laid on table.		
Butler, Samuel	Pension	29	1	Petition	149	Invalid Pensions.						
Butler, Samuel	Pension	30	1	Petition	203	Invalid Pensions.						
Butler, Samuel	Pension	30	2	Petition	366	Invalid Pensions	88	Favorable	783	Referred to Committee Whole House.		
Butler, Samuel	Pension	31	1	Petition	433	Invalid Pensions.						
Butler, Samuel	Compensation for team taken for public use.	16	1	Petition	447	Claims.						
Butler, Samuel	Compensation for team taken for public use.	20	2	Resolution	160	Claims.						
Butler, Samuel	Compensation for team taken for public use.	21	2	Resolution	108	Claims.						
Butler, Samuel	Compensation for team taken for public use.	22	1	Resolution	59	Claims.						
Butler, Samuel	Compensation for team taken for public use.	22	2	Resolution	168	Claims.						
Butler, Samuel	Compensation for team taken for public use.	23	1	Resolution	228	Claims	220	Favorable	237	Referred to Committee Whole House.		
Butler, Samuel	Compensation for team taken for public use.	23	2	Rep. Committee Whole House.	299			With amend	237	Passed	Passed	App'd March 3, 1835
Butler, Samuel	Release from suretyship on certain bonds.	13	3	Petition	729	Ways and Means				Discharged; laid on table.		
Butler, Thomas	Resurvey and indemnity for deficiency in public land.	4	2	Petition	707	Select	March 3, 1797			Discharged; laid on table.		
Butler, Thomas C.	(See Andrew Ogden & T. C. B.)	15	1		90							
Butler, Walter	Compensation for house occupied by Legislature of Iowa Territory	27	2	Petition	714	Claims	1041	Adverse		Laid on table.		
Butler, William, (Pa.)	To be restored to pension roll	17	1	Petition	155	Whole House.						
Butler, William, (Va.)	Pension for revolutionary disabilities.	17	1	Petition	96	Rev. Pensions.						
Butler, William, (Del.)	Pension for disability in public service.	30	1	Petition	280	Invalid Pensions	278	Favorable	274	Passed	Adverse report, 2d session.	
Butler, Zebulon, heirs of	Commutation pay, &c., for revolutionary services.	23	1	Petition	65	Rev. Claims.						
Butman, Richard	Reimbursement of certain tonnage duties.	23	1	Petition	411	Ways and Means	Mar. 18, 1834	Favorable	380	Referred to Committee Whole House.		
Butman, Richard	Reimbursement of certain tonnage duties.	23	2	Rep't Committee Whole House.	299			With't amend.	380	Passed	Passed	App'd March 3, 1835
Butman, Thomas	Pension for revolutionary services.	26	1	Petition	707	Rev. Pensions.						
Butman, Thomas	Pension for revolutionary services.	26	2	Petition	181	Rev. Pensions	Feb. 12, 1841	Adverse		Laid on table.		
Butrick, John, administrator of.	Compensation for military services.	22	1	Petition	288	Claims	480	Adverse		Referred to Committee Whole House.		
Butt, William	(See executor of Warren Ashley.)	25	3		119							
Butterfield, Charles	Reimbursement of land payment.	24	1	Appropriat'n bill.	1012				695	Passed	Passed	App'd July 2, 1836
Butterfield, James	Pension for disability in the public service.	17	1	Petition	106	Pens. & Rev. Cl'ms.						

List of private claims presented to the House of Representatives of the United States from the 1st to the 31st Congress, inclusive—Continued.

Names of claimants.	Nature or object of the claim.	Congress.	Session.	How brought before the House of Reps.	Page of journal.	To what committee of the House referred.	No. or date of the report.	Nature of the report.	No. of the bill.	How disposed of by the House of Reps.	How disposed of by the Senate.	Date of the act of Congress, and remarks.
Butterfield, Justin	(See assignees of Thomas Tupper)	22	2		142							
Butterfield, Shubael	(See representatives of Kendall & Butterfield.)	19	2		348							
Butterfield, William	Pension	25	2	Petition	400	Invalid Pensions				Discharged; laid on table.		
Butterfield, William	Pension	25	3	Petition	89	Invalid Pensions.						
Butterfield, William	Pension	26	1	Petition	162	Invalid Pensions	209	Favorable	221	Passed	Indef. postp'd.	
Butterfield, William	Pension	26	2	Petition	119	Invalid Pensions	159	Favorable	665	Referred to Committee Whole House.		
Butterfield, William	Pension	27	2	Petition	60	Invalid Pensions	163	Adverse		Laid on table.		
Butterfield, William	Pension	28	1	Petition	60	Invalid Pensions	57	Adverse		Laid on table.		
Butterfoss, Andrew	Pension	21	1	Petition	318	Military Pensions.						
Butterfoss, Andrew	Pension	21	2	Petition	231	Military Pensions.						
Buttolph, George	Pension for revolutionary services.	3	2	Rep. of Secretary War.	278	Claims.						
Buttolph, George	Pension for revolutionary services.	4	1	Rep. of Secretary War.	373	Claims	Feb. 18, 1796	Pension bill	156	Passed	Passed with amendment.	App'd April 20, 1796
Button, Elisha	(See assignee of Anson Brinton)	24	1		91							
Button, Elisha	Indemnity for property destroyed, war of 1812.	25	2	Petition	121	Claims.						
Button, Elisha	Indemnity for property destroyed, war of 1812.	26	1	Petition	169	Claims	66	Adverse		Laid on table.		
Button, Elisha	Indemnity for property destroyed, war of 1812.	31	1	Petition	519	Claims	406	Adverse		Laid on table.		
Butts, James R.	(See Charles Day and J. R. Butts)	24	2		316							
Butts, John	(See heirs of Hawkins Boone)	26	1		359							
Butts, Sherebiah	Pension for revolutionary services.	22	1	Resolution	512	Rev. Pensions.						
Buxenstein, Charles H.	Increase of pension	31	1	Petition	976	Invalid Pensions.						
Buxenstein, Charles H.	Increase of pension	31	2	Petition	334	Invalid Pensions.						
Buxton, James	Pension for revolutionary services.	11	2	Pension bill	283	Whole House	Mar. 24, 1810	Favorable	107	Passed	Passed with amendment.	App'd April 27, 1810
Buxton, Peter	Pension for revolutionary services.	22	1	Petition	36	Rev. Pensions	6	Favorable	51	Passed	Indef. postp'd.	
Buyat, Louis, and others	(See Missouri, inhabitants of St. Genevieve.)	17	1	Petition	93	Public Lands.						
Buzzle, Noah, widow of	Redemption of Continental money	25	2	Petition	405	Rev. Pensions.						
Byam, Sarah	Continuation of pension	28	1	Petition	849	Rev. Pensions.						
Byarly, James H., *et al.*	Pension	31	1	Petition	730	Rev. Pensions	216	Adverse		Laid on table.		
Byers, Ebenezer	Pension for services in Indian wars	26	1	Petition	936	Rev. Pensions.						
Byers, Ebenezer	Pension for services in Indian wars	27	2	Petition	851	Rev. Pensions	784	Adverse		Laid on table.		
Byers, James and John	Indemnity for depreciation United States funds.	16	2	Petition	57	Claims	Jan. 8, 1821	Adverse		Leave to withdraw.		
Byers, James and John	Settlement of account for provisions for United States army.	17	1	Petition	26	Claims	11	Favorable	31	Passed	Indef. postp'd.	Leave to withdraw.
Byers, James and John	Settlement of account for provisions for United States army.	18	2	Senate bill	93	Claims	Jan. 8, 1823	With't amend.	10	Passed	Passed	App'd March 3, 1823
Byers, John H.	Indemnity for loss of a pre-emption right.	23	2	Petition	278					Laid on table.		
Byers, Dr. John	Compensation for services as revolutionary surgeon.	2	1	Petition	464	Select.						
Byers, Robert	Compensation for team lost in public service.	2	1	Petition	493					Referred to Secretary War.		
Byers, Robert	Compensation for team lost in public service.	2	2	Report of Secretary of War.	696					Laid on table.		

List of private claims presented to the House of Representatives of the United States from the 1st to the 31st Congress, inclusive—Continued.

Names of claimants.	Nature or object of the claim.	Congress.	Session.	How brought before the House of Reps.	Page of journal.	To what committee of the House referred.	No. or date of the report.	Nature of the report.	No. of the bill.	How disposed of by the House of Reps.	How disposed of by the Senate.	Date of the act of Congress, and remarks.
Byers, Samuel	Pension	22	1	Resolution	251	Invalid Pensions.						
Byers, Samuel	Pension	22	2	Resolution	57	Invalid Pensions.						
Byers, William W., and others.	Indemnity for loss of a pre-emption right.	23	2	Petition	278	....	....	....	......	Laid on table.		
Byington, Abraham	(See surety of Robert Gilmore)	15	1	....	48							
Byington, Joel	Indemnity for damage to premises by United States troops.	15	1	Petition	25	Claims.						
Byington, Joel	Indemnity for damage to premises by United States troops.	17	1	Petition	92	Claims	Feb. 6, 1822	Adverse	......	Referred to Committee Whole House.		
Byington, Joel	Indemnity for damage to premises by United States troops.	19	2	Petition	72	Claims.						
Byington, Joel	Indemnity for damage to premises by United States troops.	20	1	Petition	75	Claims	224	Favorable	266	Referred to Committee Whole House.		
Byington, Joel	Indemnity for damage to premises by United States troops.	20	2	Rep't Committee Whole House.	285	....	....	With't amend.	266	Passed.		
Byington, Joel	Indemnity for damage to premises by United States troops.	21	1	Petition	35	Claims	6	Favorable	6	Passed	Passed	App'd Jan. 30, 1830
Byington, Joel	Additional compensation for damage, &c.	22	1	Resolution	442	Claims	497	Favorable	604	Referred to Committee Whole House.		
Byington, Joel	Additional compensation for damage, &c.	23	1	Resolution	107	Claims	59	Favorable	69	Passed	Passed	App'd June 27, 1834
Byington, Joel	Additional compensation for damage, &c.	24	1	Resolution	912	Claims.						
Byington, Joel	Additional compensation for damage, &c.	24	2	Resolution	108	Claims.						
Byington, Joel	Additional compensation for damage, &c.	25	2	Resolution	78	Claims.						
Byington, Joel	Additional compensation for damage, &c.	26	1	Petition	168	Claims	47	Adverse	......	Laid on table.		
Byington, Joel	Additional compensation for damage, &c.	31	1	Petition	438	Claims	499	Adverse	......	Laid on table.		
Bylee, J. N. & E. H.	Relief as representatives of De Lafayette Roane.	18	2	Resolution	219	Claims.						
Byles, Nathaniel, administratrix of.	Indemnity for losses in public service.	4	1	Petition	370	Claims	Jan. 19, 1796	Adverse	......	Rejected	....	Leave to withdraw.
Byrd, Baylor, widow of	Pension for revolutionary services.	27	2	Petition	329	Rev. Pensions	527	Favorable	368	Ordered to 3d reading.		
Byrd, Baylor, widow of	Pension for revolutionary services.	27	3	House bill	87	....	....	....	368	Passed	Indef. postp'd.	
Byrd, Baylor, widow of	Pension for revolutionary services.	29	1	Petition	666	Rev. Pensions.						
Byrd, Baylor, widow of	Pension for revolutionary services.	30	1	Petition	780	Rev. Pensions	....	....	......	Discharged; laid on table.		
Byrd, Jacob, sen.	Pension	23	2	Petition	128	Invalid Pensions	Jan. 21, 1835	Adverse	......	Laid on table.		
Byrd, John	Confirmation of title to land	31	1	Petition	235	Priv. Land Claims.						
Byrd, Nancy	(See Baylor Byrd, widow of)	27	2	....	329							
Byrd, Otway	Bounty land for revolutionary services.	6	2	Petition	646	Whole House.						
Byrd, Otway, widow of	Balance of pension	29	1	Petition	104	Rev. Pensions	618	Adverse	......	Laid on table.		
Byrd, Otway, widow of	Balance of pension	30	1	Petition	156	Rev. Pensions	....	....	......	Discharged; laid on table.		
Byrne, Bernard M.	Compensation for medical services.	25	3	Documents	205	Claims	213	Adverse	......	Laid on table.		
Byrnes, Daniel	Revolutionary supplies	3	2	Petition	24	Claims	Feb. 27, 1795	Adverse	......	Laid on table	....	Leave to withdraw.
Byrnes, Matthew	(See Edward Simpson *et al.*)	4	1	....	428							
Byrnside, James, attorney of.	Indemnity for Indian depredations.	19	2	Petition	134	Indian Affairs	51	Favorable	......	Referred to Committee Whole House.		

List of private claims presented to the House of Representatives of the United States from the 1st to the 31st Congress, inclusive—Continued.

Names of claimants.	Nature or object of the claim.	Congress.	Session.	How brought before the House of Reps.	Page of journal.	To what committee of the House referred.	No. or date of the report.	Nature of the report.	No. of the bill.	How disposed of by the House of Reps.	How disposed of by the Senate.	Date of the act of Congress, and remarks.
Caban, William W	Pension	19	1	Petition	52	Military Pensions	164	Adverse	......	Laid on table.		
Cabanne, John P	(See Charles Gratiot, administrators of.)											
Cabanne, Jonh P	(See Jacques Clamorgan, executors of)											
Cabanne, John P	(See P. F. Devolsey, assignee of.)											
Cabanne, John P	(See Francis Coleman, assignee of.)											
Caberly, Joseph	(See Joseph Coberly.)											
Cabet, Peter, widow of	Five years' half pay, in lieu of land, for services of husband in war of 1812.	21	1	Petition	144	Military Affairs	99	Rep. & bill for minor child'n	134	Passed	Indef. postp'd.	
Cable, Jared	(See Jos Lauligne, assignee of.)											
Cable, Jared and others	Confirmation of title to land in Louisiana.	26	1	Petition	365	Priv. Land Claims	July 21, 1840	....	......	Laid on table.		
Cable, Jared and others	Confirmation of title to land in Louisana.	27	2	Petition	58	Priv. Land Claims.						
Cable, Thomas and Abraham Scribner.	Payment for a vessel impressed in United States service and lost in 1776.	1	2	Petition	214	....	....	....	......	Referred to Secretary War.		
Cable, Thomas and Abraham Scribner.	Payment for vessel impressed in United States service and lost in 1776.	2	2	Rep. of Secretary War.	636	....	....	....	......	Laid on table.		
Cabos, John	Pension	19	1	Petition	221	Military Pensions	Feb. 23, 1826	By Bill	119	Passed	Ref. and committee disc'd.	
Cabos, John	Pension	19	2	Petition	66	Military Pensions	Dec. 22, 1826	By bill	315	Passed	Reported with amend't and indef. post'd.	
Cabot, Joseph S	Indemnity for French spoliations prior to 1800.	26	1	Memorial	182	Foreign Affairs	343	Favorable bill.	319	Referred to Committee Whole House.		
Cadbury, H	Damages by closing the port of New Orleans, in 1803, and a legal subdivision of land purchased by him.	9	2	Petition	616	....	....	....	......	Laid on table.		
Cadwell, Mathew	Release as surety for Edward Barnham.	15	1	Petition	71	Ways and Means	Jan. 23, 1818	Rep. and res. adverse.	......	Resolution adopted	....	Leave to withdraw.
Cadwell, Moses	Payment and bounty land for services as a soldier in the war of 1812.	16	1	Petition	42	Claims	Feb. 2, 1820	Adverse	......	Laid on table.		
Cadwell, Moses	Payment and bounty land for services as a soldier in the war of 1812.	18	1	Petition	314	Claims.						
Cadwell, Peter, and James Britten.	Proceeds of property sold by the United States, for violation of non-importation act.	15	2	Petition	55	Ways and Means	....	....	......	Discharged; laid on table.		
Cadwell, Peter, and James Britten.	Proceeds of property sold by the United States, for violation of non-importation act.	16	2	Petition	....	Ways and Means	Feb. 5, 1821	Rep. and res. adverse.	......	Resolution adopted.		
Cadwell, Peter, and James Britten.	Proceeds of property sold by the United States, for violation of non-importation act.	17	1	Petition	176	Ways and Means	Feb. 28, 1822	By bill	99	Passed	Passed	App'd May 7, 1822

List of private claims presented to the House of Representatives of the United States from the 1st to the 31st Congress, inclusive—Continued.

Names of claimants.	Nature or object of the claim.	Congress.	Session.	How brought before the House of Reps.	Page of journal.	To what committee of the House referred.	No. or date of the report.	Nature of the report.	No. of the bill.	How disposed of by the House of Reps.	How disposed of by the Senate.	Date of the act of Congress, and remarks.
Cady, Abijah	Invalid pension	3	1	Rep. of Secretary War.	131	Select	May 26, 1794	Referred to Sec. with inst'on.	R. 12	Passed.	Passed	App'd June 9, 1794
Cady, Abijah	Invalid pension	9	1	Petition	285	Claims	Mar. 28, 1806	Indef. postp'd.		Report adopted.		
Cady, David	Repayment of amount expended in curing a wound received in revolutionary war.	11	3	Petition	547	Claims.						
Cady, Heman	Payment for services as deputy marshal in reference to the Canadian troubles of 1837 and 1838.	25	2	Pres. message	1057	Foreign Affairs.						
Cady, Heman	Payment for services as deputy marshal in reference to the Canadian troubles of 1837 and 1838.	26	1	Petition	182	Foreign Affairs				Discharged; laid on table.		
Cady, Jeremiah	Revolutionary pension	24	1	Petition	402	Rev. Pensions.						
Cady, Jeremiah	Revolutionary pension	25	2	Petition	586	Rev. Pensions				Discharged; laid on table.		
Cady, Jeremiah	Revolutionary pension	25	3	Petition	460	Rev. Pensions				Discharged.		
Cady, Jeremiah	Revolutionary pension	26	1	Petition	173	Rev. Pensions	714	Adverse		Laid on table.		
Cady, Squire	Revolutionary pension	21	2	Resolution	65	Military Pensions				Laid on table.		
Cady, Squire	Revolutionary pension	22	1	Resolution	137	Rev. Pensions.						
Cæsar, Julius	Revolutionary pension	27	2	Resolution	401	Rev. Pensions	784			Discharged; laid on table.		
Caffey, Medford	Compensation for horse lost in Seminole war.	30	1	Petition	120	Claims	153	Report and bill	132	Passed.	Ref. to Com. Claims.	
Cahel, John	Compensation for four horses lost in United States service.	16	2	Petition	216	Claims				Discharged; laid on table.		
Cahel, John	Compensation for four horses lost in United States service.	17	1	Petition	145	Claims				Discharged; laid on table.		
Cahel, John	Compensation for four horses lost in United States service.	17	2	Petition	69	Claims	Jan. 10, 1823	Adverse		Laid on table.		
Cahill, James	Increase of pension	31	2	Petition	50	Rev. Claims	44	Adverse		Laid on table.		
Cahoon, Samuel, by Ebenezer Hazard.	Compensation for wood furnished in revolutionary war.	4	1	Rep. of Secretary of Treasury.	388	Claims	May 31, 1796	Adverse		Laid on table.		
Cahoone, Benjamin J.	Allowance of amount paid Mr. Fleming for services as purser's clerk.	30	1	Petition and Senate bill.	111, 826	Naval Affairs	June 14, 1848	Sen. bill; with amendment.	109	Passed	Passed	App'd Aug. 14, 1848
Cahoone, Henry, & others	Increase of compensation as officers of revenue cutter Active.	14	2	Petition	223	Ways and Means				Discharged; laid on table.		
Cahoone, Henry, & others	Increase of compensation as officers of revenue cutter Active.	15	1	Petition	225	Ways and Means				Discharged; laid on table.		
Cahoone, Henry, & others	Increase of compensation as officers of revenue cutter Active.	16	1	Petition	91	Commerce				Discharged; laid on table.		
Cahoone, Joseph	(See John Earle, jr., and others)											
Cahoone, John, and others	Reward for capturing privateer Wasp.	13	2	Senate bill	309	Naval Affairs	Feb. 26, 1814	With't amend.	36	Passed.	Passed	App'd April 11, 1814
Cahuawago, (an Indian,)	(See Thomas Williams)	14	1		157							
Cain, David	Pension	22	2	Petition	26	Invalid Pensions.						
Cain, Henry	Payment for horse lost in United States service, war of 1812.	16	1	Resolution	58	Claims	Jan. 14, 1820	Adverse		Referred to Committee Whole House.		
Cain, Henry	Payment for horse lost in United States service, war of 1812.	16	2	Resol'n and docs.	22	Claims	Jan. 15, 1821	Report and bill	201	Referred to Committee Whole House.		

List of private claims presented to the House of Representatives of the United States from the 1st to the 31st Congress, inclusive—Continued.

Names of claimants.	Nature or object of the claim.	Congress.	Session.	How brought before the House of Reps.	Page of journal.	To what committee of the House referred.	No. or date of the report.	Nature of the report.	No. of the bill.	How disposed of by the House of Reps.	How disposed of by the Senate.	Date of the act of Congress, and remarks.
Cain, John, (Ia.)	Compensation for horses, &c., lost in an Indian expedition, 1832.	24	1	Petition	430	Claims.						
Cain, John, (Ala.)	To apply an amount claimed of U. States to the entry of land.	27	2	Petition	76	Priv. Land Claims				Leave to withdraw.		
Cain, John, widow of	Revolutionary pension	27	3	Petition	190	Rev. Pensions				Leave to withdraw.		
Cain, Michael	Pension for revolutionary services.	27	2	Petition	541	Claims.						
Cain, Richard, and Issac Baldwin.	Patent for land purchased at Marietta, Ohio.	18	2	Senate bill	131	Public Lands	Feb. 17, 1825	With't amend.	17	Passed	Passed	App'd March 3, 1825
Cain, William, of Ala., by sundry inhabitants of Jefferson county.	Pension for services as an officer in revolutionary army.	17	2	Petition	229	Pens. & Rev. Cl'ms				Discharged; laid on table.		
Cain, William, (Pa.)	Pension for services in war of 1812.	26	1	Petition	796	Invalid Pensions.						
Cake, Philip	100 acres of land in lieu of revolutionary bounty land to which he is entitled.	19	1	Resolution	387	Priv. Land Claims				Discharged; laid on table.		
Cairn, ——	(See Potash & Cairn.)											
Cairns, William	(See David Henderson, jr.)											
Calderwood, Thomas	Arrearages of pension	18	1	Petition	193	Pens. & Rev. Cl'ms.	Mar. 10, 1824	Adverse		Laid on table.		
Caldwell, Adam	Release from imprisonment for violation of laws of trade.	1	2	Petition	243	Select	Aug. 6, 1790	By bill	99	Passed	Postponed to next session.	
Caldwell, Alexander & Thomas Hunter.	Release from judgment of United States court of Kentucky.	28	1	Petition	325	Judiciary	205	Report and bill.	160	Passed	Passed	App'd June 17, 1844
Caldwell, Andrew	Liquidation of a revolutionary quartermaster's certificate.	4	1	Rep. of Secretary Treasury.	388	Claims	May 31, 1796	Adverse		Laid on table.		
Caldwell, Andrew, (Penn.,) heir of.	Indemnity for losses on Continental money.	26	1	Petition	360	Rev. Claims.						
Caldwell, A. M.	Compensation for services and expenses as an officer of Tennessee volunteers in 1836.	25	2	Petition	776	Military Affairs				Discharged; laid on table.		
Caldwell, Billy	Annuity under treaty with Apalachicola Indians of 1832.	22	2	Senate bill	441	Ways and Means	March 1, 1833	With't amend.	128	Passed	Passed	App'd March 2, 1833
Caldwell, Bratton	(See Isaac Smith.)											
Caldwell, Charles	Pre-emption to land in Arkansas	23	2	Petition	107	Public Lands	Jan. 9, 1835	By bill	622	Passed	Amendm't reported.	
Caldwell, Charles	Pre-emption to land in Arkansas	24	2	Petition	120	Public Lands.						
Caldwell, David & Charles J. Ingersoll.	Payment of accounts as clerk and attorney of U. S. court for eastern district of Pennsylvania.	23	1	Petition	636	Judiciary.						
Caldwell, David & Charles J. Ingersoll.	Payment of accounts as clerk and attorney of U. S. court for eastern district of Pennsylvania.	24	1	Petition	53	Claims	834	Discharged		Laid on table.		
Caldwell, David, executor of.	Payment of $3,724 due deceased for fees, and $792 38 for certified allowances as clerk of U. S. court in Pennsylvania.	24	1	Petition	49	Claims	390	Report and bill.	397	Referred to Committee Whole House.		
Caldwell, David, legal representatives of.	Payment of $4,496 38 for fees, &c., due deceased as clerk of U. S. court for eastern district of Pennsylvania.	24	1	Senate bill	1097	Claims	June 27, 1836	With't amend.	231	Passed	Passed	App'd July 2, 1836
Caldwell, David, executor of.	Payment of $3,724 due deceased for fees, and $792 38 for certified allowances as clerk of U. S. court for eastern district of Pennsylvania.	25	2	Petition	36	Claims	12	Report and bill.	24	Passed	Indef. postp'd.	It would appear to have passed the House the second time. See act of 1836.

List of private claims presented to the House of Representatives of the United States from the 1st to the 31st Congress, inclusive—Continued.

Names of claimants.	Nature or object of the claim.	Congress.	Session.	How brought before the House of Reps.	Page of journal.	To what committee of the House referred.	No. or date of the report.	Nature of the report.	No. of the bill.	How disposed of by the House of Reps.	How disposed of by the Senate.	Date of the act of Congress, and remarks.
Caldwell, Elias B., heirs of.	Compensation for law liabrary destroyed by the British, war of 1812.	28	1	Petition	583	Claims.						
Caldwell, Elizabeth	Pension for services of husband in revolutionary war.	24	1	Petition	433	Rev. Pensions				Discharged; laid on table.		
Caldwell, Harry & Amasa Jackson.	Relief for condemnation of a vessel brought to New Orleans with slaves expelled from Cuba.	11	2	Petition	122	Select	Dec. 22, 1809	By bill	50	Passed	Passed	App'd Feb. 6, 1810
Caldwell, James	Remission of duties on snuff destroyed by fire.	3	2	Petition	286	Select.						
Caldwell, James	Payment for supplies furnished United States army in 1792.	14	2	Petition	411	Claims				Discharged; laid on table.		
Caldwell, James	Payment for supplies furnished United States army in 1792.	15	1	Petition	179	Claims				Discharged.		
Caldwell, James	Payment for supplies furnished United States army in 1792.	16	1	Petition	65	Claims				Discharged; laid on table.		
Caldwell, James, heirs of.	Indemnity for property destroyed by British in revolutionary war.	22	1	Petition	224	Rev. Claims.						
Caldwell, James H., (N.O.)	Remission of duties on imported gas-pipes.	24	1	Petition	156	Ways and Means				Discharged; laid on table.		
Caldwell, James H., (N.O.)	Remisssion of duties on imported gas-pipes.	26	1	Petition	358	Ways and Means.						
Caldwell, James H., (N.O.)	Remission of duties on imported gas-pipes.	28	1	Petition	113	Ways and Means.						
Caldwell, John	(See Thomas Sloo & J. Caldwell.)	16	2		200							
Caldwell, John	Indemnity for property burnt at Plattsburg by order of General Macomb.	14	2	Petition	142	Claims				Discharged.		
Caldwell, John	Indemnity for property burnt at Plattsburg by order of General Macomb.	15	2	Petition	155	Claims				Discharged; laid on table.		
Caldwell, John	Indemnity for property burnt at Plattsburg by order of General Macomb.	16	1	Petition	37	Claims	Jan. 14, 1820	Adverse		Laid on table.		
Caldwell, John, (Conn.)	Payment of final settlement certificate for services in revolutionary army.	22	1	Resolution	227	Rev. Claims	310	Report and bill.	390	Referred to Committee Whole House.		
Caldwell, John, (Conn.)	Indemnity for French spoliations prior to 1800.	26	1	Memorial	182	Foreign Affairs	343	Favorable; bill.	319	Referred to Committee Whole House.		
Caldwell, John, (Ohio.)	Compensation for services in Indian war of 1795.	29	1	Petition	673	Rev. Pensions	826	Adverse		Laid on table.		
Caldwell, John, (Ohio.)	Compensation for services in Indian war of 1795.	29	2	Petition	86	Rev. Pensions.						
Caldwell, John, (Ohio.)	Compensation for services in Indian war of 1795.	30	1	Petition	406	Rev. Pensions				Discharged; laid on table.		
Caldwell, John, (Ohio.)	Compensation for services in Indian war of 1795.	31	1	Petition	424	Rev. Pensions	319	Adverse		Laid on table.		
Caldwell, John F., (N. Y.)	Revolutionary pension	21	1	Petition	46	Military Pensions				Discharged; laid on table.		
Caldwell, John F., (N. Y.)	Revolutionary pension	22	1	Petition	120	Rev. Pensions				Disch'd; laid on table.		
Caldwell, Joseph, or Josiah F. (Va.)	Indemnity for losses on mail contract changed by Postmaster General.	23	2	Petition	83	P. Of. and P. Roads.						

List of private claims presented to the House of Representatives of the United States from the 1st to the 31st Congress, inclusive—Continued.

Names of claimants.	Nature or object of the claim.	Congress.	Session.	How brought before the House of Reps.	Page of journal.	To what committee of the House referred.	No. or date of the report.	Nature of the report.	No. of the bill.	How disposed of by the House of Reps.	How disposed of by the Senate.	Date of the act of Congress, and remarks.
Caldwell, Joseph, or Josiah F. (Va.)	Indemnity for losses on mail contract changed by Postmaster General.	24	1	Petition	59	P. Of. and P. Roads.						
Caldwell, Joseph, or Josiah F. (Va.)	Indemnity for losses on mail contract changed by Postmaster General.	24	2	Petition	46	P. Of. & P. Roads.						
Caldwell, Joseph, or Josiah F. (Va.)	Indemnity for losses on mail contract changed by Postmaster General.	25	2	Petition	120	P. Of. & P. Roads.	961 988	Adverse; re-committed; Rep. and bill.	850	Ref'd to Com. W. H.		
Caldwell, Joseph, or Josiah F. (Va.)	Indemnity for losses on mail contract changed by Postmaster General.	25	3	Bill of last sess.	432	Whole House.....	Feb. 1, 1839	With't amend.	850	Passed	Adverse report.	
Caldwell, Joseph, or Josiah F. (Va.)	Indemnity for losses on mail contract changed by Postmaster General.	26	1	Petitions.......	183, 341	P. Of. & P. Roads.						
Caldwell, Joseph, or Josiah F. (Va.)	Indemnity for losses on mail contract changed by Postmaster General.	26	2	Petition	57	P. Of. and P. Roads.						
Caldwell, Joseph, or Josiah F. (Va.)	Indemnity for losses on mail contract changed by Postmaster General.	27	2	Petition	339	P. Of. and P. Roads.	75	Report and bill	111	Passed	Passed with amendment.	App'd Aug. 16, 1842
Caldwell, Joseph, or Josiah F. (Va.)	Indemnity for losses on mail contract changed by Postmaster General.	27	3	Petition	156	P. Of. and P. Roads.						
Caldwell, Joseph, or Josiah F. (Va.)	Indemnity for losses on mail contract changed by Postmaster General.	28	1	Petition	60	P. Of. and P. Roads.	186	Adverse	......	Laid on table.		
Caldwell, Joseph, or Josiah F. (Va.)	$1167 due for mail service on routes Nos. 1984 and 2080 in Virginia	29	2	Senate bill	375	P. Of. and P. Roads.	Feb. 26, 1847	With't amend.	107	Referred to Committee Whole House.		
Caldwell, Joseph, or Josiah F. (Va.)	$1167 due for mail service on routes Nos. 1984 and 2080 in Virginia	30	1	Senate bill	683	P. Of. and P. Roads.	607	With't amend.	83	Referred to Committee Whole House.		
Caldwell, Joseph, or Josiah F. (Va.)	$1167 due for mail service on routes Nos. 1984 and 2080 in Virginia	30	2	Senate bill	319	Whole House.....	Jan. 26, 1849	With't amend.	83	Passed	Passed	App'd Feb. 1, 1849
Caldwell, Joseph, or Josiah F. (Va.)	Interest on amount allowed per act of 1st February, 1849.	31	1	Petition	413	P. Of. and P. Roads.	109	Adverse	......	Laid on table.		
Caldwell, Robert, widow of.	Pension for revolutionary services.	28	1	Petition	405	Rev. Pensions.						
Caldwell, Samuel	(See John Taggart)...........	8	1	....	429							
Caldwell, Gen. Samuel ...	Compensation for services as an officer of Kentucky militia in service of United States, war of 1812.	21	2	Petition	111	Claims	114	Adverse	......	Laid on table.		
Caldwell, Sarah D., by James H. Brigham.	Confirmation of title to land in Louisiana.	29	1	Petition	1031	Priv. Land Claims.						
Caldwell, Sarah D., by James H. Brigham.	Confirmation of title to land in Louisiana.	30	1	Petition	240	Priv. Land Claims.	333	Report and bill.	310	Passed	Reported with't amendment.	
Caldwell, Sarah D., by James H. Brigham.	Confirmation of title to land in Louisiana.	30	2	Bill of last session amended by Senate.	237	Priv. Land Claims.	Feb. 8, 1849	Concurrence in Sen. amendments.	310	Passed	Passed	App'd Feb. 9, 1849
Caldwell, Thomas	(See John Wilmot and others)...	11	2	....	350							
Caldwell, William.......	Commutation pay, &c., due as a captain in revolutionary army.	4	1	Memorial.......	564	Claims.						
Caldwell, William.......	Commutation pay, &c., due as a captain in revolutionary army.	4	2	Memorial	614	Claims..........	Jan. 3, 1797	Adverse	......	Rejected.		

List of private claims presented to the House of Representatives of the United States from the 1st to the 31st Congress, inclusive—Continued.

Names of claimants.	Nature or object of the claim.	Congress.	Session.	How brought before the House of Reps.	Page of journal.	To what committee of the House referred.	No. or date of the report.	Nature of the report.	No. of the bill.	How disposed of by the House of Reps.	How disposed of by the Senate.	Date of the act of Congress, and remarks.
Caldwell, Wm., and others.	Compensation for extra work on Cumberland bridge over Simon's creek.	24	1	Petition	851	Claims	714	Adverse	......	Laid on table.		
Caldwell, William A.	(See John P. White)	11	2	....	169							
Caldwell, William M., widow of.	Arrearages of pension for naval services.	24	1	Petition	798	Naval Affairs.						
Caldwell, Wm. M., widow of	Increase of pension	24	2	Petition	45	Naval Affairs.						
Calef, John, by Achseh Calef, legal representative of.	Payment for rope-walk and contents destroyed at Baltimore by order of United States officers.	13	3	Petition	529	Claims	Dec. 5, 1814	Report and bill.	235	Passed	Passed	App'd Feb. 27, 1815
Calhoun, Benjamin	Pension	22	1	Petition	161	Invalid Pensions	426	Report and bill.	528	Passed	Passed	App'd July 16, 1832
Calhoun, Chauncey	$305 due for services as a carpenter in 1816.	25	2	Petition	121	Claims	....	....	......	Discharged.		
Calhoun, Chauncey	$305 due for services as a carpenter in 1816.	25	3	Petition	86	Claims	151	Report and bill.	1018	Passed	Passed	App'd March 3, 1839
Calhoun, Chauncey	Amendment to act of March, 1839, authorizing payment.	26	1	Petition	295	Claims	17	Report and bill.	36	Passed	Adverse report; postponed.	
Calhoun, Chauncey	Amendment to act of March, 1839, authorizing payment.	26	2	Petition	38	Claims	8	Report and bill.	546	Referred to Committee Whole House.		
Calhoun, Chauncey	Amendment to act of March, 1839, authorizing payment.	27	2	Petition	55	Claims	7	Report and bill.	47	Passed	Passed	App'd July 9, 1842
Calhoun, George, heirs and representatives of.	Further allowance for services as captain in United States army, 1789.	21	1	Petition	472	Rev. Claims	....	....	......	Discharged; laid on table.		
Calhoun, James S.	Indemnity for detention of steamboat and barges in U. States service after expiration of contract.	25	2	Petition	273	Claims	1034	Adverse	......	Laid on table.		
Calhoun, James S.	Indemnity for detention of steamboat and barges in United States service after expiration of contract.	25	3	Amendm't to bill No. 1048, reported by Com. on Commerce.	560	Whole House	....	....	1048			
Calhoun, James S.	Indemnity for detention of steamboat and barges in United States service after expiration of contract.	26	1	Petition	339	Claims	654	Report and bill.	490	Referred to Committee Whole House.		
Calhoun, James S.	Indemnity for detention of steamboat and barges in United States service after expiration of contract.	27	2	Petition	94	Claims	1015	Report and bill.	588	Referred to Committee Whole House.		
Calhoun, James S.	Indemnity for detention of steamboat and barges in United States service after expiration of contract.	27	3	Bill of last sess.	91	Whole House	Dec. 23, 1842	With't amend.	588	Passed	Passed amen'd.	App'd March 3, 1843
Calhoun, John	Increase of pension	11	2	Petition	350	Select	April 16, 1810	Report and bill.	138	Referred to Committee Whole House.		
Calhoun, John	Increase of pension	11	3	Petition	441	Claims	Jan. 7, 1811	Favorable; bill ordered.	218	Passed	Passed	App'd March 3, 1811
Calhoun, John, widow of.	Pension for revolutionary services.	28	1	Petition	217	Rev. Pensions	219	Report and bill.	173	Passed	Passed	App'd May 23, 1844
Calhoun, John, executors of.	Payment for two negroes drowned while aiding him as keeper of a light house.	19	2	Petition	213	Commerce	....	....	......	Discharged; laid on table.		
Califfe, Stephen	Compensation for losses and injuries in service of United States	1	2	Petition, and rep't of Sec. of War.	186	Select	July 16, 1790	By bill	88	Passed	Passed	App'd Aug. 11, 1790
California, claimants in Territy of.	Payment for liabilities of the military and civil governments under Stockton and Frémont.	30	1	Senate bill	748	Military Affairs	817	With't amend.	158	Referred to Committee Whole House.		

List of private claims presented to the House of Representatives of the United States from the 1st to the 31st Congress, inclusive—Continued.

Names of claimants.	Nature or object of the claim.	Congress.	Session.	How brought before the House of Reps.	Page of journal.	To what committee of the House referred.	No. or date of the report.	Nature of the report.	No. of the bill.	How disposed of by the House of Reps.	How disposed of by the Senate.	Date of the act of Congress, and remarks.
California, sundry merchants in State of.	Repayment of duties illegally exacted.	31	1	Petition	1539	Ways and Means.						
Calkins, Eleanor	(See David Stark, widow of)	24	2		72							
Calkins, Elizabeth	(See Silas Winans, late widow of.)											
Call, Jacob	(See Samuel Rosebrough.)											
Call, Richard K.	(See Edmond Doyle, executors of)											
Call, Richard K.	(See Isabella Valverdi, attorney for)											
Call, Oris	Pension as a soldier in war of 1812	25	2	Petition	400	Invalid Pensions				Discharged; laid on table.		
Call, Oris	Pension as a soldier in war of 1812	25	3	Petition	129	Invalid Pensions				Discharged; laid on table.		
Callaghan, Bryan	Compensation for goods destroyed by U. S. troops by Col. Harney.	30	1	Petition	108	Claims.						
Callaghan, Bryan	Compensation for goods destroyed by U. S. troops by Col. Harney.	30	2	Senate bill	202	Claims	March 3, 1849	With't amend.	310	Laid on table.		
Callaghan, Charles	Indemnity for losses from illegal and oppressive acts of officers of the government of Mexico.	23	1	Petition	450	Foreign Affairs				Discharged; laid on table.		
Callaghan, Daniel, heirs of	Confirmation of title to land in Louisiana.	14	2	Petition	96	Priv. Land Claims				Discharged; laid on table.		
Callaghan, Daniel, heirs of	Confirmation of title to land in Louisiana.	15	1	Petition	173	Priv. Land Claims				Discharged.		
Callahan, Daniel	Invalid pension	3	1	Rep. of Secretary War.	131	Select	May 26, 1794	To refer to Sec. with instruc.	R. 12	Passed	Passed	App'd June 9, 1794
Callahan, George	Invalid pension	23	1	Petition	309	Invalid Pensions				Discharged; laid on table.		
Callahan, George	Invalid pension	24	1	Petition	603	Invalid Pensions				Discharged; laid on table.		
Callahan, George	Invalid pension	27	2	Petition	526	Invalid Pensions	822	Adverse		Laid on table.		
Callahan, J. R.	Payment of expenses of sickness and burial of discharged United States soldier.	30	2	Petition	127	Claims	45	Adverse		Laid on table.		
Callahan, William, by attorney.	Indemity for Indian depredations	19	2	Petition	134	Indian Affairs	51	Favorable		Referred to Committee Whole House.		
Callamore, Lebbeus	Compensation for services as lieutenant in the war of 1812.	15	2	Petition	228	Military Affairs				Discharged; laid on table.		
Callan, James	Compens'n for services as draughtsman in General Land Office.	24	1	Petition	140	Claims	195	Adverse		Laid on table.		
Callan, James	Compens'n for services as draughtsman in General Land Office.	24	2	Petition	103	Claims	244	Report and bill	943	Referred to Committee Whole House.		
Callan, James	Compens'n for services as draughtsman in General Land Office.	25	2	Petition	36	Claims	65	Report and bill	77	Passed	Passed	App'd April 20, 1838
Callan, John F.	(See James Green, represent've of)	30	1		270							
Callan, Patrick	Equitable settlement of his account as lieut. in the war of 1812.	15	2	Petition	109	Military Affairs	51	Report and bill	237	Passed	Passed	App'd March 3, 1819
Callaway, Charles	Pension	21	1	Petition	116	Military Pensions				Discharged; laid on table.		
Callender, Catharine W.	(See Wm. Callender, widow of.)											
Callender, Samuel	Revolutionary pension	19	2	Res. and petition	89, 91	Military Pensions.						
Callender, Samuel	Revolutionary pension	20	1	Resolution	160	Military Pensions	Mar. 10, 1828	Adverse		Laid on table.		
Callender, Silas	(See David Hull and others)	20	2		147							
Callender, Silas, widow of	Pension for revolutionary services.	25	2	Petition	775	Rev. Pensions				Discharged; laid on table.		

List of private claims presented to the House of Representatives of the United States from the 1st to the 31st Congress, inclusive—Continued.

Names of claimants.	Nature or object of the claim.	Congress.	Session.	How brought before the House of Reps.	Page of journal.	To what committee of the House referred.	No. or date of the report.	Nature of the report.	No. of the bill.	How disposed of by the House of Reps.	How disposed of by the Senate.	Date of the act of Congress, and remarks.
Callender, Silas, widow of	Pension for revolutionary services	26	1	Petition	173	Rev. Pensions	....	....	....	Discharged; laid on table.		
Callender, William, widow of.	Extension of pension act of July, 1838, for her benefit.	26	1	Petition	727	Rev. Pensions.						
Callender, William, widow of.	Extension of pension act of July, 1838, for her benefit.	27	2	Petition	97	Rev. Pensions	305	Report and bill.	274	Passed	Indef. postp'd.	
Callender, William, widow of.	Extension of pension act of July, 1838, for her benefit.	27	3	Petition	74	Rev. Pensions.						
Caller, Jacob	Indemnity for French spoliations prior to 1800.	26	1	Petition	182	Foreign Affairs	343	Favorable; bill	319	Referred to Committee Whole House.		
Caller, James	Confirmation of title to land in Mississippi Territory.	12	2	Petition	575	Public Lands.						
Caller, James	Confirmation of title to land in Mississippi Territory.	13	3	Petition	720	Public Lands	....	....	....	Discharged.		
Caller, James	Confirmation of title to land in Mississippi Territory.	14	1	Petition	75	Public Lands	....	....	....	Discharged; laid on table.		
Caller, James	Confirmation of title to land in Mississippi Territory.	14	2	Petition	50	Priv. Land Claims.	....	....	....	Discharged; laid on table.		
Caller, James, heirs of	(See Isabella Trouillet, assignee of.)											
Caller, James, heirs of	(See Thomas Frazier, assignee of.)											
Caller, James, heirs of	(See Joseph Anderson, assignee of.)	24	2	....	83							
Caller, James, heirs of	(See William Hartley, assignee of.)											
Calleway, John	(See Jonathan D. Owsley, heir of.)	15	1	....	232							
Calley, Elizabeth	Pension for revolutionary services of husband.	28	1	Petition	950	Whole House, on bill No. 7.	....	....	....	....	....	See act June 17, 1844
Callier, James	Relief from injuries sustained by decision of commissioners to settle land title.	9	1	Petition	212	Public Lands.						
Callier, James	Relief from injuries sustained by decision of commissioners to settle land title.	9	2	Petition	479	Public Lands.						
Callier, James	Relief from injuries sustained by decision of commissioners to settle land title.	10	1	Petition	18	Public Lands.						
Calliot, John P	Confirmation of title to land in Territory of Arkansas.	22	1	Memorial	62, 108	Public Lands	Feb. 28, 1832	By bill	425	Passed	Passed	App'd June 25, 1832
Callis, Otho W	Equitable settlement of accounts as captain in United States army.	16	1	Petition	35	Claims	....	....	....	Discharged; leave to withdraw.		
Callis, Otho W	Equitable settlement of accounts as captain in United States army.	16	2	Petition	119	Claims	Jan. 22, 1821	Adverse	....	Laid on table; leave to withdraw.		
Callis, Otho W	Equitable settlement of accounts as captain in United States army.	17	1	Petition	73	Claims	Feb. 18, 1822	Adverse	....	Laid on table.		
Callis, Otho W	Equitable settlement of accounts as captain in United States army.	18	1	Petition	198	Claims	Mar. 5, 1824	Adverse	....	Laid on table.		
Callis, Otho W	Equitable settlement of accounts as captain in United States army.	19	1	Petition	292	Claims	Mar. 17, 1826	Adverse	....	Laid on table.		
Calloway, James, Henry, William, and John.	(See James Steptoe, sen., & others.)											
Calloway, John, and others	Grant of land	27	2	Petition	378	Priv. Land Claims.						
Calman, Joseph, & Co., trustees of.	Indemnity for French spoliations prior to 1800.	26	1	Memorial	182	Foreign Affairs	343	Favorable; bill	319	Referred to Committee Whole House.		
Calmese, George	Compensation for wagon and team taken for public use in 1780.	3	1	Petition	23	....	....	....	....	Laid on table.		

List of private claims presented to the House of Representatives of the United States from the 1st to the 31st Congress, inclusive—Continued.

Names of claimants.	Nature or object of the claim.	Congress.	Session.	How brought before the House of Reps.	Page of journal.	To what committee of the House referred.	No. or date of the report.	Nature of the report.	No. of the bill.	How disposed of by the House of Reps.	How disposed of by the Senate.	Date of the act of Congress, and remarks.
Calmese, George	Compensation for wagon and team taken for public use in 1780.	3	2	Petition	258	Claims	Feb. 25, 1795	Adverse	......	Referred to Committee Whole House.		
Calmese, George	Compensation for wagon and team taken for public use in 1780.	4	2	Resolution	624	Claims	Dec. 29, 1796	Adverse	......	Rejected.		
Calmese, George, heirs of.	Commutation pay and land for services as an officer in the revolutionary war.	23	2	Resolution	309	Rev. Claims.						
Calverly, John	Naval pension	27	2	Petition	526	Invalid Pensions.						
Calvert, Samuel	(See Elisha Winter & Sons, representatives of.)	19	2	......	159							
Calvin, Bartholomew, and Rowland Gardner.	Confirmation of title to land in Michigan.	21	1	Petition	68	Priv. Land Claims	......	......	......	Discharged; laid on table.		
Calvin, Jacob	Pension for wounds and services as a spy in Indian battles of 1789, 1790, and 1791.	28	1	Petition	428	Invalid Pensions	433	Adverse	......	Laid on table.		
Calvin, James, (Indiana)	Change of land entry	24	1	Petition	113	Public Lands	April 7, 1836	By bill	540	Passed	Passed	App'd May 14, 1836
Calvin, James, (Indiana)	Invalid pension	23	1	Petition	131	Invalid Pensions	......	......	......	Discharged; laid on table.		
Calvin, James, (Indiana)	Invalid pension	23	2	Petition	110	Invalid Pensions	93	Report and bill.	718	Referred to Committee Whole House.		
Calvin, James, (Indiana)	Invalid pension	24	1	Petition	52	Invalid Pensions	46	Report and bill.	58	Passed	Passed	App'd May 14, 1836
Calvit, Thomas	Confirmation of title to land in Louisiana.	16	2	Petition	95	Priv. Land Claims	......	......	......	Discharged; laid on table.		
Calvit, Thomas	Confirmation of title to land in Louisiana.	18	1	Petition	137	Priv. Land Claims.						
Cameron, Alexander	Revolutionary pension	8	2	Senate bill	165	Whole House	Mar. 3, 1805	With't amend.	14	Passed	Passed	App'd March 3, 1805
Cameron, Charles, heir of.	Commutation of half-pay due for services as lieutenant in revolutionary army.	23	1	Petition	439	Rev. Claims.						
Cameron, Daniel, and wife.	(See James Bell, heirs of.)	23	1	......	70							
Cameron, George, heirs of.	Indemnity for French spoliations prior to 1800.	26	1	Memorial	182	Foreign Affairs	343	Favorable bill.	319	Referred to Committee Whole House.		
Cameron, George, heirs of.	Indemnity for French spoliations prior to 1800.	31	1	Petition	255	Claims	355	Rep. and bill.	318	Referred to Committee Whole House.		
Cameron, John	(See John McKown, and others.)	22	2	......	397							
Cameron, John, by Christie, widow of.	Public support of family of husband, who died of disease contracted in United States service.	14	2	Petition	80	......	......	......	......	Referred to Committee Whole House on bill 14.		
Cameron, John, (of N. C.) by Magaret, widow of.	Payment for provisions, &c., taken from husband for the revolutionary army.	23	1	Petition	81	Rev. Claims.						
Cameron, Joseph	Bounty land for twenty-one years service in United States army.	18	1	Petition	199	Public Lands	......	......	......	Discharged; leave to withdraw.		
Cameron, Margaret	(See James Bell, heirs of.)	23	1	......	70							
Camfield, Isaac	(See Stephen Decatur, widow of, and others.)											
Cammack, John, representatives of.	Amount due as an invalid pensioner.	25	2	Petition	1209	Invalid Pensions.						
Cammack, John, representatives of.	Amount due as an invalid pensioner.	25	3	Petition	88	Rev. Pensions.						
Cammack, John, representatives of.	Amount due as an invalid pensioner.	26	1	Petitions	173, 289	Invalid Pensions	296	Adverse	......	Laid on table.		

List of private claims presented to the House of Representatives of the United States from the 1st to the 31st Congress, inclusive—Continued.

33

Names of claimants.	Nature or object of the claim.	Congress.	Session.	How brought before the House of Reps.	Page of journal.	To what committee of the House referred.	No. or date of the report.	Nature of the report.	No. of the bill.	How disposed of by the House of Reps.	How disposed of by the Senate.	Date of the act of Congress, and remarks.
Cammack, John, representatives of.	Amount due as an invalid pensioner.	27	2	Petition	1060	Invalid Pensions.						
Cammack, William	Pension	17	2	Petition	223	Pens. & Rev. Cl'ms.				Dischargd, referred to Com. Whole House on bill 195.		
Cammack, William	Pension	18	1	Petition	173	Pens. & Rev. Cl'ms.	Feb. 2, 1824	Adverse		Laid on table.		
Cammack, William, representatives of.	Pension due at the time of his death.	25	2	Petition	1209	Invalid Pensions				Discharged.		
Cammack, William, executors of.	Indemnity for French spoliations prior to 1800.	26	1	Memorial	182	Foreign Affairs	343	Favorable bill.	319	Referred to Committee Whole House.		
Camp, Amos	Invalid pension	3	1	Rep. of Secretary War.	131	Select	May 26, 1794	Favorable; bill ordered.	62	Passed	Passed	App'd June 7, 1794
Camp, Amos, and Amos Minor.	Arrears of pension	3	2	Petition	323	Claims	Mar. 2, 1795	To discharge, & postpone.		Laid on table.		
Camp, Amos, and Amos Minor.	Arrears of pension	4	1	Petition	373	Claims	Jan. 6, 1796	Adverse		Leave to withdraw.		
Camp, Jesse	Revolutionary pension	17	2	Petition	87	Rev. Pensions	Jan. 13, 1823	Adverse		Laid on table.		
Camp, Jesse	Revolutionary pension	19	1	Petition	269	Military Pensions	164	Adverse		Laid on table.		
Camp, Jesse	Revolutionary pension	22	1	Petition	52	Rev. Pensions						
Camp, Joel	Invalid pension	3	1	Rep. of Secretary War.	131	Select	May 26, 1794	Favorable; bill ordered.	62	Passed	Passed	App'd June 7, 1794
Camp, John	Revolutionary pension	24	1	Resolution	343	Rev. Pensions	Feb. 19, 1836	Adverse		Laid on table.		
Camp, John G	Settlement of accounts as Deputy Quartermaster General, the vouchers for which were captured by the enemy.	14	1	Petition	138	Claims	Jan. 13, 1816	Report and bill.		Passed	Passed	App'd Feb. 1, 1816
Camp, John G	Reimbursement of $63 paid on account of United States.	21	1	Petition	619	Claims	May 24, 1830	Adverse		Laid on table.		
Camp, Thomas	Revolutionary pension	16	1	Petition	89	Rev. Pensions	Jan. 14, 1820	Adverse		Referred to Committee Whole House.		
Camp, William, heirs of.	Compensation for houses and other property destroyed and used by American troops in 1777.	2	2	Petition	699					Laid on table.		
Camp, William, heirs of.	Commutation pay as an officer of revolutionary army.	23	1	Petition	189	Rev. Claims.						
Camp, William, heirs of.	Commutation pay as an officer of revolutionary army.	23	2	Petition	165	Rev. Claims.						
Camp, William, heirs of.	Commutation pay as an officer of revolutionary army.	24	1	Petition	138	Rev. Claims.	June 2, 1836	Adverse		Laid on table.		
Camp, William, heirs of.	Commutation pay as an officer of revolutionary army.	24	2	Petition	95	Rev Claims	102	Adverse		Laid on table.		
Campau, Jacques	(See Michigan, rector of St. Ann's Church.)											
Campau, Joseph	Compensation for horse lost in services of U. S., war of 1812.	15	2	Petition	33	Claims	Dec. 1, 1818	Rep. and res. adverse.		Resolution adopted.		
Campau, Joseph	Compensation for damages to property by United States troops, and for supplies furnished in 1814.	21	2	Petition	104	Claims.						
Campau, Joseph	Patent certificate for land on Lake St. Clair.	26	1	Senate bill	420	Priv. Land Claims.	April 25, 1840	With't amend.	64	Referred to Committee Whole House.		
Campau, Joseph	Patent certificate for land on Lake St. Clair.	28	1	Senate bill	868	Public Lands	May 25, 1844	With't amend.	78	Passed	Passed	App'd June 17, 1844

List of private claims presented to the House of Representatives of the United States from the **1st** *to the* **31st** *Congress, inclusive*—**Continued.**

Names of claimants.	Nature or object of the claim.	Congress.	Session.	How brought before the House of Reps.	Page of journal.	To what committee of the House referred.	No. or date of the report.	Nature of the report.	No. of the bill.	How disposed of by the House of Reps.	How disposed of by the Senate.	Date of the act of Congress, and remarks.
Campau, Joseph	Patent for a tract of Indian reservation of Grand Traverse, as assignee of Taw-cum e-go-qua.	26	1	Senate bill	581	Priv. Land Claims.	April 4, 1840	With't amend.	65	Referred to Committee Whole House.		
Campau, Joseph	Patent for a tract of Indian reservation of Grand Traverse, as assignee of Taw cum e go-qua.	26	2	Senate bill......	282	....	....	....	88			
Campau, Joseph	Patent for a tract of Indian reservation of Grand Traverse, as assignee of Taw-cum-e go-qua.	28	1	Senate bill	868	Priv. Land Claims.	June 14, 1844	With't amend.	79	Passed	Passed	App'd June 15, 1844
Campbell, Alexander, heirs of, by attorney.	Indemnity for French spoliations prior to 1800.	26	1	Memorial	182	Foreign Affairs....	343	Favorable	319	Referred to Committee Whole House.		
Campbell, Andrew, (Mass.) children of.	Compensation for services as an officer of the revolutionary army.	25	3	Petition	217	Rev. Pensions	....	....	.....	Discharged.		
Campbell, Andrew, (Mass.) children of.	Compensation for services as an officer of the revolutionary army.	26	1	Petition	173	Rev. Pensions	....	....	.....	Discharged; laid on table.		
Campbell, Archibald S., (Lieut. in U. S. Navy.)	Compensation for services as naval storekeeper at Pensacola.	21	2	Petition	160	Claims	Feb. 2, 1831	Adverse	.....	Laid on table.		
Campbell, Archibald S., (Lieut. in U. S. Navy.)	Compensation for services as naval storekeeper at Pensacola.	22	1	Petition	292	Naval Affairs.						
Campbell, Archibald S., (Lieut. in U. S. Navy.)	Compensation for services as naval storekeeper at Pensacola.	23	1	Senate bill	654	Naval Affairs.....	....	....	88			
Campbell, Archibald, administrator of.	Indemnity for French spoliations prior to 1800.	26	1	Memorial	182	Foreign Affairs ...	343	Favorable bill.	319	Referred to Committee Whole House.		
Campell, Archibald, (N. Y.) daughter of.	Compensation for services as a soldier under Wayne from 1792 to 1802.	28	1	Petition........	194	Claims	134	Adverse	.....	Laid on table.		
Campbell, Arthur L......	Payment for merchandise furnished United States at Highwassie.	12	2	Petition	554	Claims.						
Campbell, Arthur L......	Payment for merchandise furnished United States at Highwassie.	13	2	Petition	303	Claims	Feb. 28, 1814	Rep. and res. adverse.	.....	Resolution abopted.		
Campbell, Arthur L......	Payment for merchandise furnished United States at Highwassie.	14	2	Petition	410	....	....	....	.....	Referred to Secretary War.		
Campell, Asenath	(See James Miller, late widow of.)											
Campbell, Cassandra.....	(See Henry Miller, heirs of.)											
Campbell, Charles, (Pa.)..	To be exempt from payment of judgment for money deposited with him as paymaster of militia in 1792.	13	2	Petition	188	Claims...........	....	....	.....	Discharged.		
Campbell, Charles, (Pa.)..	To be exempt from payment of judgment for money deposited with him as paymaster of militia in 1792.	13	3	Petition	573	Claims...........	....	....	.....	Discharged.		
Campbell, Charles, (Pa.)..	To be exempt from payment of judgment for money deposited with him as paymaster of militia in 1792.	14	1	Petition	351	Claims...........	....	....	.....	Discharged; laid on table.		
Campbell, Charles, (Pa.)..	To be exempt from payment of judgment for money deposited with him as paymaster of militia in 1792.	14	2	Petition	75	Claims	....	....	.....	Discharged; laid on table.		
Campbell, Charles, (Pa.)..	Settlement of his accounts in equity as paymaster of Pennsylvania militia, 1792-'93.	17	1	Petition	256	Judiciary	Mar. 1, 1822	By bill	101	Passed	Passed	App'd May 7, 1822

List of p ivate claims presented to the House of Representatives of the United States from the 1*st to the* 31*st Congress, inclusive*—Continued.

Names of claimants.	Nature or object of the claim.	Congress.	Session.	How brought before the House of Reps.	Page of journal.	To what committee of the House referred.	No. or date of the report.	Nature of the report.	No. of the bill.	How disposed of by the House of Reps.	How disposed of by the Senate.	Date of the act of Congress, and remarks.
Campbell, Charles, (Pa.)	Pension	21	1	Petition	59	Military Pensions				Discharged; laid on table.		
Campbell, Charles, (Ala.)	Bounty land for services as a soldier in revolutionary army.	24	2	Petition	270	Rev. Claims.						
Campbell, Cornelius, and others.	Pre-emption to certain inundated lands in Louisiana.	24	2	Petition	389	Public Lands.						
Campbell, Cornelius, and others.	Pre emption to certain inundated lands in Louisiana.	25	2	Petition	95	Public Lands.						
Campbell, Cornelius, and others.	Pre-emption to certain inundated lands in Louisiana.	25	3	Petition	92	Public Lands	97	Adverse		Laid on table.		
Campbell, David S., (Ky.)	Payment for rifle gun lost in the service of United States, war of 1812.	23	2	Petition	37	Claims	22	Report and bill	603	Referred to Committee Whole House.		
Campbell, David S., (Ky.)	Payment for rifle gun lost in the service of United States, war of 1812.	21	1	Petition	50	Claims	30	Report and bill	30	Passed	Passed	App'd Feb. 17, 1836
Campbell, David G., widow of, (N. Y.)	Bounty land for service in war of 1812.	28	2	Petition	272	Claims.						
Campbell, Donald	Compensation for services in revolutionary war.	1	2	Petition	154	Select	April 20, 1790	Favorable		Rejected.		
Campbell, Donald	Compensation for services in revolutionary war.	1	3	Petition	355					Rejected.		
Campbell, Duncan	Compensation for money advanced United States in revolutionary war.	1	1	Petition	36					Referred to Secretary Treasury.		
Campbell, Duncan	Invalid pension	2	2	Petition	627	Select.						
Campbell, Duncan	Invalid pension	3	2	Rep. of Secretary War.	278	Claims	Feb. 28, 1795	Favorable bill.	130	Passed	Posp'd to next session.	
Campbell, Duncan	Invalid pension	4	1	Rep. of Secretary War.	445	Claims	Feb. 18, 1796	Favorable bill.	156	Passed	Passed	App'd April 20, 1796
Campbell, Duncan	Compensation for injuries received in revolutionary army.	4	1	Petition	422	Claims	May 31, 1796	Adverse		Laid on table.		
Campbell, Duncan	Compensation for losses and injuries as a Canadian refugee, revolutionary war.	6	1	Petition	578	Claims	Feb. 13, 1800	Adverse		Rejected.		
Campbell, Duncan	Nine years arrearages of half-pay as lieutenant in revolutionary army.	8	2	Petition	143	Claims.						
Campbell, Duncan P.	(See Thomas L. Ogden, & others)	16	1		444							
Campbell, Duncan P.	(See New York Insuranre Company.)	26	1		182							
Campbell, Eleanor	Revolutionary pension	28	1	Petition	839	Whole House						See act June 17, 1844
Campbell, Ethan	Revenue steamer Dallas, per contract of Secretary Treasury.	31	1	Amendment to House bill.					334	Passed	Passed	App'd Sept. 30, 1850
Campbell, George	Compensation for services as captain of artificers in revolutionary army.	3	2	Petition	226	Claims	Feb. 25, 1795	Adverse		Referred to Committee Whole House.		
Campbell, George	Compensation for services as captain of artificers in revolutionary army.	4	2	Petition	614	Claims	Dec. 29, 1796	Adverse		Rejected.		
Campbell, George W	(See Eilis Richardson)											
Campbell, Gustavus, heirs of.	Pension for wounds in United States army.	13	2	Petition	387	Pensions	April 13, 1814	Rep. and res.; adverse.		Resolution adopted.		

List of private claims presented to the House of Representatives of the United States from the 1st to the 31st Congress, inclusive—Continued.

Names of claimants.	Nature or object of the claim.	Congress.	Session.	How brought before the House of Reps.	Page of journal.	To what committee of the House referred.	No. or date of the report.	Nature of the report.	No. of the bill.	How disposed of by the House of Reps.	How disposed of by the Senate.	Date of the act of Congress, and remarks.
Campbell, Harry W	Refunding of money deposited for extension of patent.	27	2	Petition	507	Claims.						
Campbell, Isabel Narbonne.	(See Peter Trouillet, heirs of.)											
Campbell, Jacob	Revolutionary pension	22	1	Resolution	82	Rev. Pensions	167	Report and bill.	244	Passed		Its passage as per House Journal is probably a mistake.
Campbell, Jacob	Revolutionary pension	22	2	Bill of last session.	123				244	Laid on table.		
Campbell, James, (Conn.)	Invalid pension	3	1	Rep. of Secretary War.	131	Select	May 26, 1794	Res. to refer to Sec. of War.	12	Passed	Passed	App'd June 9, 1794
Campbell, James, (Mass.)	Invalid pension	4	1	Rep. of Committee on Claims	457	Whole House	March 7, 1796	Favorable; bill ordered.	156	Passed	Passed	App'd April 20, 1796
Campbell, James, (Mass.)	Arrears of pension	5	3	Petition	467	Claims	March 2, 1799	Adverse		Laid on table.		
Campbell, James, (Mass.)	Increase of pension	10	1	House bill	232	Whole House	April 19, 1808	Favorable	78	Passed	Passed	App'd April 25, 1808
Campbell, James, (Vt.)	Invalid pension	4	1	Rep. of Committee on Claims.	457	Whole House	March 7, 1796	Favorable; bill ordered.	156	Passed	Passed	App'd April 20, 1796
Campbell, James	Increase of pension	14	1	Petition	42	Pens. & Rev. Cl'ms				Discharged; laid on table.		
Campbell, James	Increase of pension	15	1	House bill	405	Whole House	April 17, 1818	Favorable	172	Passed	Postponed.	
Campbell, James	Increase of pension	15	2	House bill	231	Whole House	March 3, 1819	Favorable	308	Passed	Passed	App'd March 3, 1819
Campbell, James, executor of.	Arrears of pension	19	2	House bill	85	Whole House	Feb. 2, 1827	Favorable	314	Passed	Passed	App'd March 3, 1827
Campbell, James, (N. C.)	Compensation for services as captain in revolutionary army.	9	2	Petition	580	Claims				Referred to Committee Whole House.		
Campbell, James, (N. C.)	Compensation for services as captain in revolutionary army.	10	1	Petition	38	Select.						
Campbell, James, (N. C.)	Compensation for services as captain in revolutionary army.	11	2	Petition	215	Claims	Mar. 24, 1810	Adverse		Laid on table.		
Campbell, James, (N. C.)	Compensation for services as captain in revolutionary army.	11	3	Petition	445	Claims.						
Campbell, James	Bounty land for services as drum major in revolutionary army.	15	2	Petition	182	Pens. & Rev. Cl'ms.				Discharged; laid on table.		
Campbell, James, (Ohio)	Provision for support as a soldier in revolutionary war.	20	2	Petition	261	Rev. Claims				Discharged; laid on table.		
Campbell, James, (Ohio)	Provision for support as a soldier in revolutionary war.	21	1	Petition	57	Military Pensions.				Discharged; laid on table.		
Campbell, James, (Ind.)	Pension for services as a soldier in war of 1812.	25	2	Petition	920	Invalid Pensions				Discharged.		
Campbell, James, (Ind.)	Pension for services as a soldier in war of 1812.	25	3	Petition	416	Invalid Pensions	Feb. 16, 1839	Adverse.		Laid on table.		
Campbell, James, (Ind.)	Pension for services as a soldier in war of 1812.	26	1	Petition	327	Invalid Pensions	554	Adverse		Laid on table.		
Campbell, James, (Ind.)	Pension for services as a soldier in war of 1812.	27	2	Petition	790	Invalid Pensions	936	Adverse		Laid on table.		
Campbell, James, (Ind.)	Pension for services as a soldier in war of 4812.	29	1	Petition	83	Invalid Pensions	307	Adverse.		Laid on table.		
Campbell, James, widow of.	Revolutionary pension	26	1	Resolution	950	Rev. Pensions.						
Campbell, James S	(See Samuel Campbell, deceased representative of.)											
Campbell, James S., (New York.)	Release from judgment against him as surety of Stephen Matther.	21	1	Petition	173	Judiciary				Discharged; laid on table.		
Campbell, Jesse	Pension for disabilities in war of 1812.	28	1	Petition	622	Invalid Pensions.						

List of private claims presented to the House of Representatives of the United States from the 1st to the 31st Congress, inclusive—Continued.

Names of claimants.	Nature or object of the claim.	Congress.	Session.	How brought before the House of Reps.	Page of journal.	To what committee of the House referred.	No. or date of the report.	Nature of the report.	No. of the bill.	How disposed of by the House of Reps.	How disposed of by the Senate.	Date of the act of Congress, and remarks.
Campbell, Jesse	Pension for disabilities in war of 1812.	28	2	Petition	83	Invalid Pensions.						
Campbell, Jesse	Pension for disabilities in war of 1812.	29	1	Petition	107	Invalid Pensions	662	Adverse	.....	Laid on table.		
Campbell, John, (Ky.)	Compensation for timber and wood furnished United States dragoons in 1793.	5	2	Memorial	134	Claims	Mar. 21, 1798	Adverse	......	Leave to withdraw		
Campbell, John, (Ky.)	Land and pension for disabilities contracted in the army.	13	2	Petition	315	Pens. & Rev. Cl'ms.	....	....	......	Leave to withdraw.		
Campbell, John, and Alvin Day.	Compensation to company of volunteers in the service of United States, war of 1812.	15	2	Petition	306	Claims	....	....	......	Discharged; laid on table.		
Campbell, John, and Alvin Day.	Compensation to company of volunteers in the service of United States, war of 1812.	16	1	Petition	175	Claims	Jan. 31, 1820	Adverse	......	Laid on table.		
Campbell, John, by Joseph Rolette, assignee of the heirs of.	Possession of all the land in Michigan granted to Campbell by act of February 21, 1823.	23	1	Petition	249	Priv. Land Claims.	332	Report and bill.	360	Referred to Committee Whole House.		
Campbell, John, heirs of	Possession of all the land in Michigan granted to Campball by act of February 21, 1823.	24	2	Documents	210	Priv. Land Claims.	153	Report and bill.	881	Referred to Committee Whole House.		
Campbell, John, heirs of	Possession of all the land in Michigan granted to Campbell by act of February 21, 1823.	25	2	Petition	43	Priv. Land Claims.	....	....	......	Discharged; laid on table.		
Campbell, John, heirs of	Possession of all the land in Michigan granted to Campbell by act of February 21, 1823.	27	2	Petition	132	Public Lands	69	Report and bill.	105	Passed	Passed	App'd July 27, 1842
Campbell, John, (N. Y.,) heirs of.	Settlement of accounts as a deputy quartermaster general in revolutionary army.	21	1	Petition	295	Rev. Claims	273	Report and bill.	323	Referred to Committee Whole House.		
Campbell, John, (N. Y.,) heirs of.	Settlement of accounts as a deputy quartermaster general in revolutionary army.	21	2	Bill of last sess.	340	Whole House	Feb. 22, 1831	With't amend.	323	Passed	Reported with amendment.	
Campbell, John, (N. Y.,) heirs of.	Settlement of accounts as a deputy quartermaster general in revolutionary army.	22	1	Petition	165	Rev. Claims	220	Report and bill.	292	Referred to Committee Whole House.		
Campbell, John, (N. Y.,) heirs of.	Settlement of accounts as a deputy quartermaster general in revolutionary army.	22	2	Bill of last sess.	171	Whole House	Jan. 11, 1833	With't amend.	292	Passed	Passed	App'd March 2, 1833
Campbell, John, (N. Y.,) heirs of.	Interest on amount allowed per act of March 2, 1833.	23	1	Petition	127	Rev. Claims.						
Campbell, John, (N. Y.,) heirs of.	Interest on amount allowed per act of March 2, 1833.	24	1	Petition	62	Rev. Claims	160	Adverse	......	Laid on table.		
Campbell, John, (N. Y.,) heirs of.	Interest on amount allowed per act of March 2, 1833.	25	2	Petition	391	Rev. Claims	673	Report and bill.	651	Referred to Committee Whole House.		
Campbell, John, (N. Y.,) heirs of.	Interest on amount allowed per act of March 2, 1833.	25	3	Bill of last sess	380	Whole House	....	....	651			
Campbell, John, (N. Y.,) heirs of.	Interest on amount allowed per act of March 2, 1833, and whatever else may be found due.	26	1	Petition	165, 281	Rev. Claims	440	Report and bill.	359	Referred to Committee Whole House.		
Campbell, John, (N. Y.,) heirs of.	Interest on amount allowed per act of March 2, 1833, and whatever else may be found due.	27	2	Petition	62	Rev. Claims	36 860	Adverse Adverse	....	Recommitted. Laid on table.		

List of private claims presented to the House of Representatives of the United States from the 1st to the 31st Congress, inclusive—Continued.

Names of claimants.	Nature or object of the claim.	Congress.	Session.	How brought before the House of Reps.	Page of journal.	To what committee of the House referred.	No. or date of the report.	Nature of the report.	No. of the bill.	How disposed of by the House of Reps.	How disposed of by the Senate.	Date of the act of Congress, and remarks.
Campbell, John, (Mo.)...	(See Richard Campbell, heirs of.)											
Campbell, John, (Mo.)...	Compensation for property destroyed by Indians in war of 1812.	24	1	Petition	206	Claims.						
Campbell, John, (Tenn.,) and others.	(See William Williams, sen., heirs of.)	25	3	....	135							
Campbell, John, (Penn.,) widow of.	Revolutionary pension..........	26	1	Petition	322	Rev. Pensions	468	Report and bill.	382	Referred to Committee Whole House.		
Campbell, John, (Penn.,) widow of.	Revolutionary pension..........	27	2	Petition	59	Rev. Pensions	94	Report and bill.	140	Passed	Adverse report; Indef. postp'nd.	
Campbell, John, (Penn.,) widow of.	Revolutionary pension..........	27	3	Petition	145	Rev. Pensions	....	....	......	Referred to Commissioner Pensions.		
Campbell, John, (Penn.,) widow of.	Revolutionary pension..........	29	1	Petition	337	Rev. Pensions	424	Report and bill.	299	Passed	Passed	App'd Aug. 8, 1846
Campbell, John, (Maine).	Pension as a soldier in war of 1812	26	1	Petition	708	Invalid Pensions.						
Campbell, John, (Maine).	Pension as a soldier in war of 1812	27	2	Petition	154	Invalid Pensions ..	425	Adverse	......	Laid on table.		
Campbell, John, (Maine).	Pension as a soldier in war of 1812	28	2	Petition	199	Invalid Pensions.						
Campbell, John, (Maine).	Pension as a soldier in war of 1812	29	1	Petition	146	Invalid Pensions ..	469	Report and bill.	347	Passed	Passed	App'd Aug. 8, 1846
Campbell, John, (Maine).	Arrears of pension.............	30	1	Petition	280	Invalid Pensions ..	289	Report and bill.	285	Referred to Committee Whole House.		
Campbell, John, (Maine).	Arrears of pension.............	30	2	Bill of last sess.	142	Whole House.....	Dec. 22, 1848	With't amend.	285	Passed	Passed	App'd March 3, 1849
Campbell, John, (Maine).	Arrears of pension.............	31	1	Petition	863	Invalid Pensions ..	482	Adverse as to arrears, but by bill for increase.	379	Referred to Committee Whole House.		
Campbell, John, & Co., (Florida.)	Compensation for subsistence of United States troops.	30	1	Petition	695	Military Affairs ...	....	....	......	Discharged; laid on table.		
Campbell, John B., widow of.	Indemnity for expenses of suit instituted by United States, for money adjudged not to be due by husband, and release from payment of a sum for which she is threatened with another suit.	17	1	Petition	474	Claims	....	....	......	Discharged; laid on table.		
Campbell, John B., widow of.	Indemnity for expenses of suit instituted by United States, for money adjudged not to be due by husband, and release from payment of a sum for which she is threatened with another suit.	17	2	Petition	74	Claims	Feb. 17, 1823	Report and bill.	300	Passed	Passed	App'd March 3, 1823
Campbell, John P.......	Credit of $200 on a treasurer's receipt disallowed by government.	27	2	Petition	76	Claims	9	Report and bill.	46	Passed	Passed as am'd	App'd July 27, 1842
Campbell, John S.......	Revolutionary pension..........	23	1	Petition	46	Rev. Pensions.						
Campbell, John S.......	Revolutionary pension..........	23	2	Petition	101	Rev. Claims......	....	....	......	Discharged; laid on table.		
Campbell, John S.......	Revolutionary pension..........	24	1	Petition	274	Rev. Pensions	....	....	......	Discharged; laid on table.		
Campbell, John W......	Compensation as pension agent in Tennessee.	27	2	Petition	226	Claims...........	330	Adverse	......	Laid on table.		
Campbell, John W......	Compensation as pension agent in Tennessee.	31	1	Petition	762	Rev. Pensions	445	Adverse	......	Laid on table.		
Campbell, Naomi	Pension for revolutionary services of husband.	28	1	Petition	950	Whole House, on bill No. 7.	....	....	......	....	....	See act June 17, 1844
Campbell, Patrick.......	Relief for wounds, &c., received in revolutionary war.	2	2	Petition and report Sec. War.	621	....	....	....	......	Laid on table.		

List of private claims presented to the House of Representatives of the United States from the 1st to the 31st Congress, inclusive—Continued.

Names of claimants.	Nature or object of the claim.	Congress.	Session.	How brought before the House of Reps.	Page of journal.	To what committee of the House referred.	No. or date of the report.	Nature of the report.	No. of the bill.	How disposed of by the House of Reps.	How disposed of by the Senate.	Date of the act of Congress, and remarks.
Campbell, Patrick, heirs of.	Pension for revolutionary services.	30	1	Petition	566	Rev. Pensions....	529	Adverse	.....	Laid on table.		
Campbell, Patrick, heirs of.	Pension for revolutionary services.	31	1	Petition	890	Rev. Pensions....	362	Adverse	.....	Laid on table.		
Cambell, Polly..........	(See William Beckham, widow of)	20	1									
Campbell, Richard, heirs of.	Half-pay due as colonel in Virginia line, revolutionary war.	24	1	Petition	205	Rev. Claims.....	464	Report and bill.	471	Referred to Committee Whole House.		
Campbell, Richard, heirs of.	Half pay due as colonel in Virginia line, revolutionary war.	24	2	Bill of last sess.	62	Whole House....	....	....	471			
Campbell, Richard, heirs of.	Half-pay due as colonel in Virginia line, revolutionary war.	25	2	Petition	39	Rev. Claims......	108	Report and bill.	126	Passed	Passed	App'd July 7, 1838
Campbell, Robert........	(See Bartholomew Yates, administrator of.											
Campbell, Robert, & George B. Cumming.	(See Richard Henry Wilde.)											
Campbell, Robert, widow and children of.	Annuity in consideration of husband having been killed in United States military service.	13	3	Petition	705	Military Affairs.						
Campbell, Samuel, (N. Y.) representatives of.	Payment for property destroyed at Cherry valley by British forces in revolutionary war.	21	2	Petition	54	Rev. Claims.....	96	Adverse	.....	Laid on table.		
Campbell, Samuel, (N. Y.) representatives of.	Payment for property destroyed at Cherry valley by British forces in revolutionary war.	22	2	Petition	94	Claims.						
Campbell, Samuel, (N. Y.) representatives of.	Payment for property destroyed at Cherry valley by British forces in revolutionary war.	28	1	Petition	85	Rev. Claims.....	573	Report and bill.	428	Referred to Committee Whole House.		
Campbell, Samuel, (N. Y.) representatives of.	Payment for property destoyed at Cherry valley by British forces in revolutionary war.	28	2	Bill of last sess.	344	Whole House....	Feb. 7, 1845	With't amend.	428	Laid on table.		
Campbell, Samuel, (N. Y.) representatives of.	Settlement of accounts for services as an officer in revolutionary army.	21	2	Petition	161	Rev. Claims.						
Campbell, Samuel (Ohio.)	Revolutionary pension..........	25	2	Petition	271	Rev. Pensions....	....	....	.....	Discharged.		
Campbell, Samuel (Ohio.)	Revolutionary pension..........	25	3	Petition	130	Rev. Pensions....	....	....	.....	Discharged.		
Campbell, Samuel (Ohio.)	Revolutionary pension..........	26	1	Petition	165	Rev. Pensions....	Mar. 5, 1840	Adverse	.....	Laid on table.		
Campbell, Samuel (Ohio.)	Revolutionary pension..........	26	2	Petition	133	Rev. Pensions....	210	Adverse	.....	Laid on table.		
Campbell, Samuel (Ind.)	Pension for disability incurred in Indian war of 1794.	31	1	Petition	692	Invalid Pensions ..	Aug. 2, 1850	Adverse	.....	Laid on table.		
Campbell, Scott.........	An amount equal to an annuity and grant of land from Sioux Indians, rejected by Senate from treaty of 1837.	30	2	Petition	458	Claims.						
Campbell, Susan........	(See Colonel William Campbell, heirs of.											
Campbell, Thomas.......	(See James Sharp.)...........	4	1	....	388							
Campbell, Thomas (Penn.)	Invalid pension..............	1	3	Petition	392	....	....	....	.....	Referred to Secretary War.		
Campbell, Thomas (Penn.)	Invalid pension..............	2	1	Rep. of Secretary War.	466	....	....	Embraced by amendment.	153	Passed...........	Passed	App'd Dec. 16, 1791
Campbell, Thomas (Penn.)	Compensation for services, &c., in addition to that provided in act of December 16, 1791.	7	1	Petition	163	....	....	....	.....	Laid on table	....	Leave to withdraw.

List of private claims presented to the House of Representatives of the United States from the 1st to the 31st Congress, inclusive—Continued.

Names of claimants.	Nature or object of the claim.	Congress.	Session.	How brought before the House of Reps.	Page of journal.	To what committee of the House referred.	No. or date of the report.	Nature of the report.	No. of the bill.	How disposed of by the House of Reps.	How disposed of by the Senate.	Date of the act of Congress, and remarks.
Campbell, Thomas (Penn.)	Commutation of revolutionary pay surrendered under act of December 16, 1791, refunded.	8	1	Petition	576	Claims	Mar. 13, 1804	Discharged and postponed.	......	Report adopted.		
Campbell, Thomas (Penn.)	Commutation of revolutionary pay surrendered under act of December 16, 1791, refunded.	8	2	Petition	56	Claims.						
Campbell, Thomas (Penn.)	Commutation of revolutionary pay surrendered under act of December 16, 1791, refunded.	9	1	Petition	205	Claims	Feb. 26, 1806	Leave to withdraw.	......	Laid on table.		
Campbell, Thomas (Penn.)	Relief for wounds received in revolutionary war.	10	1	Petition	221	Select.						
Campbell, Thomas (Penn.)	Relief for wounds receieed in revolutionary war.	11	2	Petition	203	Select	Feb. 27, 1810	Favorable	......	Referred to Committee Whole House.		
Campbell, Thomas (Penn.)	Relief for wounds received in revolutionary war.	11	3	Petition	461	Select	Jan. 7, 1811	Rep. and res. for relief.	......	Referred to Committee Whole House.		
Campbell, Thomas (Penn.)	Relief for wounds received in revolutionary war.	11	3	Senate bill	513	Whole House.....	....	....	55			
Campbell, Thomas (Penn.)	Relief for wounds received in revolutionary war.	12	1	Petition	50	Claims.						
Campbell, Triphey	(See Jacob Taylor, late widow of.)	29	1	....	341							
Campbell, Gen. Wm., heirs of, (Va.)	Land due for military services in the revolutionary war.	10	2	Petition	381	Public Lands.						
Campbell, Gen. Wm., heirs of, (Va.)	Land due for military services in the revolutionary war.	15	1	Petition	238	Select	....	....	......	Discharged; laid on table.		
Campbell, Gen. Wm., heirs of, (Va.)	Land due for military services in the revolutionary war.	19	1	Petition	408	Public Lands	192	Report and bill	253	Referred to Committee Whole House.		
Campbell, Gen. Wm., heirs of, (Va.)	Land due for military services in the revolutionary war.	20	1	Petition	224	Priv. Land Claims.	207	Report and bill	236	Referred to Committee Whole House.		
Campbell, Gen. Wm., heirs of, (Va.)	Land due for military services in the revolutionary war.	20	2	Bill of last sess'n	227	Whole House.....	Feb. 6, 1829	With amend..	236	Passed	Reported without amend..	
Campbell, Gen. Wm., heirs of, (Va.)	Land due for military services in the revolutionary war.	21	1	Senate bill	271	Priv. Land Claims.	234	With't amend.	29	Referred to Committee Whole House.		
Campbell, Gen. Wm., heirs of, (Va.)	Seven years half-pay under resolution of August 24, 1780.	23	1	Petition	620	Rev. Claims.						
Campbell, Gen. Wm., heirs of, (Va.)	Seven years half-pay under resolution of August 24, 1780.	23	1	Senate bill	847	Rev. Claims......	....	....	189	Discharged; laid on table.		
Campbell, Col. Wm., heirs of, (Va.)	Pension for revolutionary services.	29	1	Petition	126	Rev. Claims......	285	Adverse	......	Laid on table.		
Campbell, Col. Wm., heirs of, (Va.)	Pension for revolutionary services.	30	1	Petition	407	Rev. Claims......	545	Adverse	......	Laid on table.		
Campbell, Col. Wm., heirs of, (Va.)	Pension for revolutionary services.	30	2	Petition	344	Rev. Claims.						
Campbell, William, (Va.)	Commutation pay as an officer of the revolutionary army, and land and compensation due for services of his brothers Joseph and James, who died in the service.	12	1	Petition	43	Select.						
Campbell, Wm., (Ind.) ..	Patent for land, having expended means for additional payments by being driven off by Indians, and in consideration of revolutionary services.	19	2	Petition	85	Public Lands	....	....	......	Discharged; laid on table.		

List of private claims presented to the House of Representatives of the United States from the 1st to the 31st Congress, inclusive—Continued.

34

Names of claimants.	Nature or object of the claim.	Congress.	Session.	How brought before the House of Reps.	Page of journal.	To what committee of the House referred.	No. or date of the report.	Nature of the report.	No. of the bill.	How disposed of by the House of Reps.	How disposed of by the Senate.	Date of the act of Congress, and remarks.
Campbell, William, (Mo.)	Reimbursement of money over paid to United Statee as assistant superintendent of lead mines, and for a quantity of lead.	23	1	Petition	438	Claims	464	Adverse	......	Laid on table.		
Campbell, Wm., heirs of	Indemnity for French spoliations prior to 1800.	26	1	Memorial	182	Foreign Affairs	343	Favorable; bill	319	Referred to Committee Whole House.		
Campbell, Wm. L., (Ill.)	Compensation for horse lost in U. S. service.	24	1	Resolution	1102	Claims.						
Campbell, William R., and others.	Bounty land and extra pay for services in Mexican war.	30	2	Senate bill	358	Military Affairs	....	....	407			
Campbell, William R., and others.	Bounty land and extra pay for services in Mexican war.	31	1	Petition	215	Military Affairs	....	....	......	....	....	See Resolution H. R., No. 15.
Campeau, John, atto'ny of	Compensation for provisions, &c., for use of troops in 1814.	16	1	Petition	49	Claims.						
Campeau, Rene	Confirmation of title to land in Indiana.	12	2	House bill	609	Whole House	Jan. 18, 1813	With't amend.	222	Passed	Passed	App'd Feb. 13, 1813
Campin, James	Invalid pension	11	3	House bill	604	Whole House	Mar. 2, 1811	Favorable	218	Passed	Passed	App'd March 3, 1811
Canada, Nathaniel	Compensation for bridge destroyed by the British at Niantic, Conn.	19	2	Petition	132	Claims.						
Canada, Nathaniel	Compensation for bridge destroyed by the British at Niantic, Conn.	20	1	Petition	38	Claims	Dec. 19, 1827	Adverse	......	Laid on table.		
Canada, Nathaniel, representatives of.	Compensation for bridge destroyed by the British at Niantic, Conn	24	1	Senate bill	940	Claims	June 7, 1836	With't amend.	154	Passed	Passed	App'd July 2, 1836
Canadian refugees	Compensation for revolutionary services.	4	2	Reports and petitions.	614	Whole House	Dec. 29, 1796	Favorable; bill ordered.	209	Referred to Committee Whole House.		
Canadian refugees	Compensation for revolutionary services.	5	2	Bill of last Cong.	83	Select	Dec. 27, 1997	By bill	30	Recommitted.		
					88	....	Jan. 10, 1798	By bill	40	Passed	Passed with amendment.	App'd April 7, 1798
Canadian refugees	Land in satisfaction of claims for revolutionary services.	6	1	Resolution	603	Select	May 8, 1800	By bill	265	Passed	Amended	Postponed by House.
Canadian refugees	Land in satisfaction of claims for revolutionary services.	6	1	Report of Commissioners.	703	Select	May 9, 1800	Favorable	......	Ref. to Com. Whole House, on bill 265.		
Canadian refugees	Land in satisfaction of claims for revolutionary services.	6	2	Report of Commissioners.	748	Select	Jan. 19, 1801	By bill	280	Passed	Passed	App'd Feb. 18, 1801
Canadian refugees	Extension of time, per act of 1798, for proving claims.	7	1	Resolution	16	Claims	Jan. 12, 1802	Adverse	......	Referred to Committee Whole House.		
Canadian refugees	Land for unsatisfied claims for revolutionary services.	7	2	Report of Commissioners.	361	Select	Feb. 24, 1803	By bill	123	Passed	Passed	App'd March 3, 1803
Canadian refugees	Revival for two years of act 1798.	8	1	Resolution	....	Claims	Feb. 22, 1804	By bill	189	Passed with amendm't	Passed	App'd Mar. 16, 1804
Canadian refugees	Land for unsatisfied claims for revolutionary services.	8	2	Resolution	90	Select	Feb. 19, 1805	By bill	64	Referred to Committee Whole House.		
Canadian refugees	Land for unsatisfied claims for revolutionary services.	9	1	Report of Commissioners.	194	Select	Dec. 13, 1805	By bill	75	Passed.		
Canadian refugees	Land for unsatisfied claims for revolutionary services.	9	2	Report of Commissioners.	480	Select	Dec. 17, 1806	By bill	150	Passed	Postponed.	
Canadian refugees	Revival of act of 1798 for relief of.	9	2	House bill	490	Whole House	....	....	153			
Canadian refugees	Land for unsatisfied claims for revolutionary services.	10	1	Report of Commissioners.	42	Select	Dec. 22, 1807	Report and bill.	21	Referred to Committee Whole House.		
Canadian refugees	Land for unsatisfied claims for revolutionary services.	11	2	Report of Commissioners.	137	Public Lands	Jan. 3, 1810	By bill	57	Referred to Committee Whole House.		
Canadian refugees	Revival of act of 1798 for relief of.	11	2	Resolution	120	Public Lands	Dec. 11, 1809	By bill	35	Passed with amendm't	Further am'd and passed.	App'd Feb. 24, 1810

List of private claims presented to the House of Representatives of the United States from the 1st to the 31st Congress, inclusive—**Continued.**

Names of claimants.	Nature or object of the claim.	Congress.	Session.	How brought before the House of Reps.	Page of journal.	To what committee of the House referred.	No. or date of the report.	Nature of the report.	No. of the bill.	How disposed of by the House of Reps.	How disposed of by the Senate.	Date of the act of Congress, and remarks.
Canadian refugees	Land for unsatisfied claims for revolutionary services.	12	1	Report of Commissioners.	215	Public Lands	Mar. 11, 1812	By bill	85	Passed with amendm't	Passed	App'd April 22, 1812
Canadian refugees	Further provision for claimants	12	1	Senate bill	369	Public Lands	June 20, 1812	With't amend.	40	Referred to Committee Whole House.		
Canadian refugees, widows of sundry.	Pension for services of deceased in Col. Hazen's regiment in revolutionary war.	23	1	Petition	491	Rev. Pensions	....	....	......	Discharged; laid on table.		
Canadian volunteers	Land for services and sacrifices in war of 1812.	14	1	Petition	98	Select	30	Report and bill.	51	Passed	Passed	App'd March 5, 1816
Canby, Israel T.	(See Ann Sprigg, represent's of.)											
Canby, Israel T.	(See John H. Piatt, represent's of.)											
Canely, William J.	Revolutionary pension	22	2	Petition	30	Rev. Pensions.						
Canez, Ferdinand Y.	Possession of nine acres of land near New Orleans.	11	3	Petition	443	Public Lands.						
Canez, Ferdinand Y.	Possession of nine acres of land near New Orleans.	12	1	Petition	11	Public Lands.						
Canfield, Ezekiel	Revolutionary pension	16	2	Petition	152	Rev. Pensions	Feb. 15, 1821	Rep't and res.; adverse.	......	Resolution adopted.		
Canfield, Ezekiel	Revolutionary pension	21	2	Senate bill	196	Military Pensions	Feb. 2, 1831	Adverse	72	Laid on table.		
Canfield, Ithamar	Bounty land as assignee of E. and J. Tomlinson and Abr. Shelby, revolutionary soldiers.	6	1	Senate bill	649	Select	May 7, 1800	With't amend.	59	Passed	Passed	App'd May 10, 1800
Canfield, Lizur B.	Invalid pension, war of 1812	30	1	Resolution	123	Invalid Pensions	286	Report and bill.	282	Passed	Passed 2d sess.	App'd March 2, 1849
Canney, Asenath	(See Nathaniel Nayson, late widow of.)	29	1	....	865	....	....	....	S. 166			
Canning, Peter	Indemnity for Indian depredations in Florida.	28	2	Petition	84	Claims.						
Cannon, Hugh	Grant of land for services in revolutionary war.	18	1	Petition	234	Rev. Pensions.						
Cannon, Hugh	Pension	23	2	Petition	296	Rev. Pensions	....	....	......	Discharged; laid on table.		
Cannon, Hugh	Pension	24	1	Petition	260	Rev. Pensions	....	....	......	Discharged; laid on table.		
Cannon, Hugh	Additional compensation for disability incurred in revolutionary war.	25	2	Petition	663	Rev. Pensions	....	....	......	Discharged; laid on table.		
Cannon, Hugh	Additional compensation for disability incurred in revolutionary war.	25	3	Petition	458	Rev. Claims	....	....	......	Discharged: laid on table.		
Cannon, Hugh	Additional compensation for disability incurred in revolutionary war	26	1	Petition	166	Invalid Pensions	668	Adverse	......	Laid on table.		
Cannon, James	Pension	16	1	Report of Committee.	137	Rev. Pensions	Jan. 14, 1820	Adverse	......	Laid on table.		
Cannon, James	Pension	20	2	Petition	142	....	....	....	......	Ref. to Com. Whole House, on bill 311.		
Cannon, James, of Tenn., widow of.	Compensat'n for wagons and teams furnished United States in war of 1812.	28	1	Petition	567	Claims						
Cannon, James, of Tenn., widow of.	Compensat'n for wagons and teams furnished United States in war of 1812.	28	2	Petition	333	Claims.						
Cannon, James, of Tenn., widow of.	Compensat'n for wagons and teams furnished United States in war of 1812.	29	1	Petition	161	Claims	719	Adverse	......	Laid on table.		
Cannon, Joseph S.	Naval pension	21	2	Senate bill	181	Naval Affairs	73	With amend.	66	Passed with amendm't.	Passed	App'd March 3, 1831

List of private claims presented to the House of Representatives of the United States from the 1*st to the* 31*st Congress, inclusive*—Continued.

Names of claimants.	Nature or object of the claim.	Congress.	Session.	How brought before the House of Reps.	Page of journal.	To what committee of the House referred.	No. or date of the report.	Nature of the report.	No. of the bill.	How disposed of by the House of Reps.	How disposed of by the Senate.	Date of the act of Congress, and remarks.
Cannon, Joseph S., widow of.	Pension from naval pension fund.	23	1	Petition	303	Naval Affairs.						
Cannon, Joseph S., widow of.	Pension from naval pension fund.	23	2	Petition	309	Naval Affairs.						
Cannon, Joseph S., widow of.	Pension from naval pension fund.	24	1	Petition	139	Naval Affairs	Feb. 4, 1836	Adverse		Laid on table.		
Cannon, Joshua	Bounty land for services in war of 1812.	17	1	Amend't to House bill.	559				72	Passed	Passed	App'd May 8, 1822
Cannon, Luke, heirs of	Commutation of half-pay due as an officer in revolutionary naval service.	22	2	Petition	332	Rev. Claims.						
Cannon, Luke, heirs of	Commutation of half-pay due as an officer in revolutionary naval service.	23	1	Petition	65	Rev. Claims.						
Cannon, Luke, heirs of	Commutation of half-pay due as an officer in revolutionary naval service.	23	2	Petition	147	Rev. Claims.						
Cannon, Luke, heirs of	Commutation of half-pay due as an officer in revolutionary naval service.	24	1	Petition	138	Rev. Claims.						
Cannon, Luke, heirs of	Commutation of half-pay due as an officer in revolutionary naval service.	24	2	Petition	126	Rev. Claims.						
Cannon, Luke, heirs of	Commutation of half-pay due as an officer in revolutionary naval service.	25	2	Petition	70	Rev. Claims	444	Adverse		Laid on table.		
Cannon, Matthew	Pension for disability contracted in United States service in 1808.	24	2	Petition	139	Invalid Pensions				Discharged; laid on table.		
Cannon, Thomas	Correction of entry of land	24	2	Senate bill	260	Public Lands	Feb. 1, 1837	With't amend.	114	Referred to Committee Whole House.		
Cannon, William, & others of Gillespie company of Texas volunteers.	Compensation for horses lost in United States service in 1846.	29	2	Petition	149	Military Affairs.						
Canny, Thomas	(See Jere. Prescott and Thomas Canny, heirs of.)											
Canoe, Twenty, (Indian).	Pension for wounds received in war of 1812.	21	1	Resolution	600	Military Pensions				Discharged; laid on table.		
Canous	(See John Nicholas *alias* Canous)	19	2		43							
Canter, David	(See David Carter.)											
Canter, James	Compansation for services as a volunteer in Cherokee country, in 1838.	26	1	Petition	340	Claims				Discharged; laid on table.		
Canter, James	Compensation for services as a volunteer in Cherokee country, in 1838.	26	2	Petition	205	Claims.						
Canter, James	Compensation for services as a volunteer in Cherokee country, in 1838.	27	2	Petition	94	Claims	1017	Favorable bill.	590	Referred to Committee Whole House.		
Canter, James	Compensation for services as a volunteer in Cherokee country, in 1838.	27	3	Bill of last sess.	91	Whole House	Dec. 23, 1842	With't amend.	590	Passed	Passed	App'd Jan. 20, 1843
Canterbury, John	Revolutionary pension	26	1	Petition	962	Rev. Pensions.						
Cantney, Josias	Compensation for supplies furnished revolutionary army.	12	1	Petition	265	Claims.						

List of private claims presented to the House of Representatives of the United States from the 1st to the 31st Congress, inclusive—Continued.

Names of claimants.	Nature or object of the claim.	Congress.	Session.	How brought before the House of Reps.	Page of journal.	To what committee of the House referred.	No. or date of the report.	Nature of the report.	No. of the bill.	How disposed of by the House of Reps.	How disposed of by the Senate.	Date of the act of Congress, and remarks.
Cantney, Josias,	Compensation for supplies furnished revolutionary army.	13	2	Petition	307	Pens. & Rev. Cl'ms.						
Cantrall, Levi, attorney for.	Compensation for horse lost in U. S. service in 1813.	16	1	Petition	250	Claims	April 24, 1820.	Adverse		Laid on table.		
Cantrill, Stephen & others.	Compensation for services of self & co., against Cherokees in 1795.	5	2	Petition and rep. Sec. War.	89	Whole House	April 23, 1798.	Favorable: bill ordered.	85	Passed	Passed	App'd May 8, 1798
Cantwell, Thomas	Compensaiion for property destroyed by the British at Plattsburg, war of 1812.	17	2	Petition	186	Claims				Discharged; leave to withdraw.		
Cantwell, Thomas	Compensation for property destroyed by the British at Plattsburg, war of 1812.	18	1	Petition	32	Claims.						
Capella, Andrew, administrator of.	Indemnity for losses from marauding parties of U. S. troops, in investment of St. Augustine, 1813.	28	2	Petition	532	Judiciary.						
Capella, Andrew, administrator of.	Adjudication, under act of 26th June, 1834, of claim for losses.	29	2	Senate bill	307	Judiciary	Feb. 24, 1847	With't amend.	66	Laid on table.		
Capella, Andrew, administrator of.	Adjudication, under act of 26th June, 1834, of claim for losses.	30	1	Senate bill	361	Judiciary	Feb. 29, 1848	With't amend.	48	Referred to Committee Whole House.		
Capella, Andrew, administrator of.	Adjudication, under act of 26th June, 1834, of claim for losses.	30	2	Bill of last sess.	625	Whole House	Mar. 3, 1849	With't amend.	48	Passed	Passed	App'd March 3, 1849
Capen, James	Revolutionary pension	31	1	Petition	311	Invalid Pensions.						
Capen, Phineas	(See John Cox, heirs of.)											
Capen, Samuel	Pension	21	2	Petition	158	Military Pensions				Discharged; laid on table.		
Capen, Samuel	Pension	22	1	Resolution	93	Rev. Pensions				Disch'd; laid on table.		
Capen, Theophilus	Indemnity for loss in remitting $200 to supervisor of direct taxes.	8	1	Petition	460	Claims	Dec. 21, 1803	Adverse		Rejected.		
Caperton, George	(See Hardy Doyal.)											
Caplinger, Adam	Compensation for services as an artificer in a corps of Kentucky militia, war of 1812.	22	2	Senate bill	405	Claims	Mar. 2, 1833	With't amend.	78	Passed	Passed	App'd March 2, 1833
Caplinger, John, widow of	Payment for a gun lost in United States service, 1813.	15	2	Petition	139	Claims				Discharged; laid on table.		
Capo, John	Adjudication per act of 26th June, 1834, of claim for losses by U. S. troops in Florida.	29	2	Senate bill	307	Judiciary	Feb. 24, 1847	With't amend.	66	Laid on table.		
Capo, John	Adjudication per act of 26th June, 1834, of claim for losses by U. S. troops in Florida.	30	1	Senate bill	361	Judiciary	Feb. 29, 1848	With't amend.	48	Referred to Committee Whole House.		
Capo, John	Adjudication per act of 26th June, 1834, of claim for losses by U. S. troops in Florida.	30	2	Bill of last sess'n	625	Whole House	Mar. 3, 1849	With't amend.	48	Passed	Passed	App'd March 3, 1849
Cappel, Charles	Confirmation of title to land in Louisiana.	28	2	Petition	337	Priv. Land Claims.	146	Adverse		Laid on table.		
Cappel, Charles	Confirmation of title to land in Louisiana.	29	1	Petition	348	Priv. Land Claims.	595	Report and bill	414	Referred to Committee Whole House.		
Cappel, Charles	Confirmation of title to land in Louisiana.	30	1	Petition	99	Priv. Land Claims.	Feb. 29, 1848	By bill	266	Passed	Passed	App'd Aug. 5, 1848
Capron, Elisha	Invalid pension	11	3	House bill	604	Whole House	Mar. 2, 1811	Favorable	218	Passed	Passed	App'd March 3, 1811
Capron, Seth	Pension	21	1	Petition	573	Military Pensions				Discharged.		
Capron, Seth	Further compensation for services as a soldier in revolutionary army.	22	2	Petition	46	Rev. Claims.						

List of private claims presented to the House of Representatives of the United States from the 1st to the 31st Congress, inclusive—Continued.

Names of claimants.	Nature or object of the claim.	Congress.	Session.	How brought before the House of Reps.	Page of journal.	To what committee of the House referred.	No. or date of the report.	Nature of the report.	No. of the bill.	How disposed of by the House of Reps.	How disposed of by the Senate.	Date of the act of Congress, and remarks.
Capron, Seth, and others, (N. Y.)	Benefit of act of 1828, as "three years' men" in revolutionary army.	23	1	Memorial	135	Rev. Pensions.						
Caramelli, Hamet	Relief for services and sufferings in war with Tripoli.	9	1	Presid'ts message	232, 260	Select.						
Caramelli, Hamet	Relief for services and sufferings in war with Tripoli.	9	1	Senate bill	410	Whole House	April 21, 1806	With't amend.	35	Passed	Passed	App'd April 21, 1806
Caramelli, Hamet	Further relief for sufferings, &c., in war with Tripoli.	10	1	Memorial	16	Select	Dec. 18, 1807	Favorable	......	Referred to Committee Whole House.		
Carabaugh, Peter........	Pension	20	1	Petition	30	Military Pensions..	....	....	.....	Discharged; laid on table.		
Caradine, John Jose	Extension of time to file proof of title to land in Louisiana.	19	2	Rep. of Secretary Treasury.	50	Priv. Land Claims.	49	Report and bill	378	Referred to Committee Whole House.		
Carberry, Thomas	Compensation for planning and superintending erection of penitentiary in District of Columbia.	22	2	House bill	274	Whole House.....	Feb. 26, 1833	With't amend.	721	Passed	Passed	App'd March 2, 1833
Carberry, Thomas.......	(See Henry Ashton and others.)											
Carboneux, Amable and Pieriche.	(See James Vieux, jr., and others).	21	1	....	68							
Carby, Thaddeus, mother of.	Bounty land and pay due as a soldier in war of 1812.	17	1	Petition	269	Public Lands	April 2, 1822	By bill	145	Passed	Passed	App'd May 7, 1822
Card, Henry	Compensation for extra work on Cumberland road.	24	2	Petition	72	Claims...........	18	Adverse	......	Laid on table.		
Card, Potter	(See Israel Pearce, heir of.)											
Cardelli, Peter..........	Patent for certain models and casts.	16	1	Petition	258	Judiciary	April 2, 1820	By bill	130	Referred to Committee Whole House.		
Carden, Anselm L	(See John Hooker, assignee of)..	31	1	....	681							
Carder, Jacob	Pension for wounds received in war of 1812.	31	1	Petition	857	Invalid Pensions...	Aug. 1, 1850	Adverse	......	Laid on table.		
Cardiff, John	Compensation for services in the army of the Revolution.	1	3	Pet. and rep. of Sec. of War.	357	....	....	....	......	Laid on table.		
Cardiff, John	Invalid pension...............	3	2	Rep. of Secretary of War.	278	Claims	Feb. 28, 1795	Favorable; bill ordered.	130	Passed............	Postponed.	
Cardiff, John	Invalid pension...............	4	1	Rep. of Secretary of War.	445	Claims	Feb. 18, 1796	Favorable; bill ordered.	156	Passed	Passed	App'd April 20, 1796
Cardin, Joseph W	Benefit of act of 1821 relative to purchase of public land.	18	2	Res. and Doc....	100	Public Lands.						
Cardinal, Charles	(See Reuben E. Gentry & others.)											
Cardinal, Francois.......	Confirmation of title to land in Indiana.	12	2	House bill	609	Whole House	Jan. 18, 1813	With't amend.	222	Passed	Passed	App'd Feb. 13, 1813
Cardozo, David, widow of.	Arrears of pension due for revolutionary services, and a pension for herself.	28	1	Petition	484	Rev. Pensions.						
Cardozo, Jacob N	Reduction of debt due to United States, and extension of time for payment.	21	1	Petition	39	Ways and Means..	360	Report and bill.	361	Referred to Committee Whole House.		
Cardozo, Jacob N	Reduction of debt due to United States, and extension of time for payment.	21	1	Senate bill	615	Whole House	....	....	130			
Cardozo, Jacob N	Reduction of debt due to United States, and extension of time for payment.	21	2	Senate bill	204	Ways and Means.	Jan. 28, 1831	With't amend.	49	Passed	Passed	App'd March 2, 1831
Cardwell, Sally	Revolutionary pension..........	28	2	Petition	73	Rev. Pensions.						

List of private claims presented to the House of Representatives of the United States from the 1st to the 31st Congress, inclusive—Continued.

Names of claimants.	Nature or object of the claim.	Congress.	Session.	How brought before the House of Reps.	Page of journal.	To what committee of the House referred.	No. or date of the report.	Nature of the report.	No. of the bill.	How disposed of by the House of Reps.	How disposed of by the Senate.	Date of the act of Congress, and remarks.
Care, Philip, executor of heirs of.	Indemnity for French spoliations prior to 1800.	31	1	Petition	233	Foreign Affairs	355	Favorable; bill.	318	Referred to Committee Whole House.		
Care, William, executors of.	Indemnity for French spoliations prior to 1800.	26	1	Memorial	182	Foreign Affairs	343	Favorable; bill.	319	Referred to Committee Whole House.		
Careeno, Charles	Compensation out of Indian annuity for injuries inflicted by a Chippewa Indian.	31	1	Petition	1039	Indian Affairs.						
Careuthers, Wilson T	(See James Walker and others)	24	2		579							
Carey	(See Cary)											
Cargill, Charles C.	Pension for disability from exposure in Mexican war.	30	2	Petition	216	Invalid Pensions	35	Adverse		Laid on table.		
Cargill, Charles C	Pension for disability from exposure in Mexican war.	31	1	Petition	348	Invalid Pensions.						
Carhart, John and others	Restoration of pensions	24	2	Resolution	222	Rev. Pensions				Disch'd; laid on table.		
Carhart, Thomas	Compensation for services in revolutionary war.	2	1	Petition	455					Referred to Secretary War.		
Carhart, Thomas	Invalid pension	3	1	Rep. of Secretary War.	131	Select	May 26, 1794	Favorable; bill ordered.	62	Passed	Passed	App'd June 7, 1794
Carhart, Thomas	Increase of pension	11	2	House bill	283	Whole House	May 24, 1810	Adverse	108	Passed	Passed	App'd April 27, 1810
Carl, Asahel T	Pension for disability incurred in the war of 1812.	31	1	Petition	956	Invalid Pensions.						
Carlan, Elizabeth	(See William Carlan, guardian of the heirs of.)											
Carlan, William, guardian of the heirs of.	Pension and arrearages of pay due.	16	2	Petition	105	Military Affairs				Discharged; laid on table.		
Carle, Francis	Confirmation of title to land in Louisiana.	22	1	Petition	64	Priv. Land Claims.	62	Rep. and bill	125	Passed	Passed	App'd June 25, 1832
Carle, Peter	Arrears of pension as a soldier in the war of 1812.	29	2	Petition	59	Invalid Pensions.						
Carle, Peter	Arrears of pension as a soldier in the war of 1812.	31	1	Petition	362	Invalid Pensions.						
Carleth, Susan	Restoration of pension	30	1	Petition	188	Naval Affairs.						
Carleton, Ebenezer	Invalid pension	3	2	Report of Secretary of War.	278	Claims	Feb. 28, 1795	Favorable; bill ordered.	130	Passed	Postponed to next session.	
Carleton, Ebenezer	Invalid pension	4	1	Report of Secretary of War.	445	Claims	Feb. 18, 1796	Favorable; bill ordered.	156	Passed	Passed	App'd April 20, 1796
Carleton, Ebenezer	Increase of pension	12	1	House bill	361	Whole House	June 15, 1812	Favorable	138	Passed	Passed	App'd July 5, 1812
Carleton, Samuel	Compensation for losses and injuries in U. S. service in revolutionary war.	1	2	Pet. & Report of Sec. of War.	177					Laid on table.		
Carley, Jonathan	Renewal of pension granted per act of March, 1814.	16	2	Petition	240	Rev. Pensions				Discharged; laid on table.		
Carlin, William	Compensation for damage to house occupied by U. S. troops in 1777.	6	2	Petition	830					Laid on table.		
Carlin, William, heirs of	Compensation for damage to house occupied by U. S. troops in 1777	23	1	Petition	307	Rev. Claims.						
Carlisle, James M	Additional compensation as clerk to committee on elections.	26	2	Resolution	191					Laid on table.		
Carlisle, John and others	Release from judgments as sureties for Jos. Kerr.	20	1	Petition	368	Judiciary				Discharged; laid on table.		
Carlisle, John and others	Release from judgments as sureties for Jos. Kerr.	21	1	Petition	264	Judiciary	Apr. 12, 1830	Res. to dis. and leave to withdraw.		Resolution adopted.		

List of private claims presented to the House of Representatives of the United States from the 1st to the 31st Congress, inclusive—Continued.

Names of claimants.	Nature or object of the claim.	Congress.	Session.	How brought before the House of Reps.	Page of journal.	To what committee of the House referred.	No. or date of the report.	Nature of the report.	No. of the bill.	How disposed of by the House of Reps.	How disposed of by the Senate.	Date of the act of Congress, and remarks.
Carlock, Abraham	Donation of, or pre-emption to, land for services to his country.	17	2	Petition	27	Public Lands	....	....	......	Discharged; leave to withdraw.		
Carlon, James	Compensation for services as clerk to Captain of United States late brig Vixen.	13	2	Petition	263	Claims	March 7, 1814	Res. for leave to withdraw.	......	Resolution adopted.		
Carlton, Isaac	Bounty on fishing vessel and cargo lost.	17	1	Petition	280	Commerce	....	....	......	Discharged; laid on table.		
Carlton, Isaac	Bounty on fishing vessel and cargo lost.	17	2	Petition	163	Commerce	....	....	......	Discharged; laid on table.		
Carlton, Isaac	Bounty on fishing vessel and cargo lost.	18	1	Petition	172	Commerce.						
Carlton, Israel	Revolutionary pension	23	1	Petition	53	Rev. Pensions.						
Carlton, James P.	Release from liability for revenue lost by the burning of the post office at Cumberland, Maryland.	24	1	Petition	852	Judiciary.						
Carlton, James P.	Release from liability for revenue lost by the burning of the post office at Cumberland, Maryland.	24	2	Petitions	48, 314	Judiciary	Feb. 25, 1837	By bill	960	Referred to Committee Whole House.		
Carlton, James P.	Release from liability for revenue lost by the burning of the post office at Cumberland, Maryland	25	2	Petition	41	Judiciary	Jan. 9, 1838	By bill	351	Referred to Committee Whole House.		
Carlton, James P.	Release from liability for revenue lost by the burning of the post office at Cumberland, Maryland.	25	3	Bill of last sess.	377	Whole House	Jan. 25, 1839	With't amend.	351	Passed; reconsidered and laid on table.		
Carlton, James P.	Release from liability for revenue lost by the burning of the post office at Cumberland, Maryland.	26	1	Petition	175	Judiciary	393	Adverse	......	Laid on table.		
Carlton, John	Pension	15	1	Petition	250	Pens. & Rev. Cl'ms.	....	....	......	Discharged; referred to Secretary of War.		
Carlton, John	Pension	19	1	Petition	66	Military Pensions	164	Adverse	......	Laid on table.		
Carlton, John	Pension	19	2	Petition	43	Military Pensions.						
Carlton, John	Pension	20	1	Resolution	90	Military Pensions	....	....	......	Discharged; laid on table.		
Carlton, John	Pension	20	2	House bill	55	Whole House	Jan. 15, 1829	Favorable	311	Passed	Laid on table.	
Carlton, John	Pension	21	1	Petition	46	Military Pensions	Jan. 15, 1830	By bill	72	Passed	Passed	App'd May 20, 1830
Carlton, Moses	Indemnity for French spoliations prior to 1800.	26	1	Memorial	182	Foreign Affairs	343	Favorable; bill	319	Referred to Committee Whole House.		
Carlton, Moses, and others.	Indemnity for French spoliations prior to 1800.	29	2	Petition	58	Foreign Affairs.						
Carlton, Moses, and others.	Indemnity for French spoliations prior to 1800.	31	1	Petition	407	Commerce	355	Rep. and bill.	318	Referred to Committee Whole House.		
Carlton, Washington	Indemnity for loss by mail of $110 of post office funds.	31	2	Petition	204	P. Of. & P. Roads.						
Carly, Simon	Revolutionary pension	25	2	Petition	....	Rev. Pensions	....	....	......	Disch'd; laid on table.		
Carly, Simon	Revolutionary pension	26	1	Petition	324	Rev. Pensions	714	Adverse	......	Laid on table.		
Carly, Simon	Revolutionary pension	26	2	Petition	51	Rev. Pensions.						
Carly, Simon	Revolutionary pension	27	2	Petition	58	Rev. Pensions	784	Adverse	......	Laid on table.		
Carly, Simon	Revolutionary pension	27	3	Petition	43	Rev. Pensions	295	Adverse	......	Laid on table.		
Carlyle, Ebenezer, son of.	Pension for services in revolutionary war.	28	1	Petition	944	Rev. Pensions.						
Carmack, Cornelius, (Ala.)	Compensation to volunteers under his command for services in Creek Indian war.	24	2	Petition	160	Military Affairs.						

List of private claims presented to the House of Representatives of the United States from the 1st to the 31st Congress, inclusive—Continued.

Names of claimants.	Nature or object of the claim.	Congress.	Session.	How brought before the House of Reps.	Page of journal.	To what committee of the House referred.	No. or date of the report.	Nature of the report.	No. of the bill.	How disposed of by the House of Reps.	How disposed of by the Senate.	Date of the act of Congress, and remarks.
Carmack, Isaac	Compensation for horse lost in United States service, war of 1812.	26	1	Petition	1009	Claims	706	Adverse	......	Laid on table.		
Carmack, Isaac	Compensation for horse lost in United States service, war of 1812.	27	3	Petition	73	Claims	91	Adverse	......	Laid on table.		
Carmack, John	Revolutionary pension	23	1	Resolution	115	Rev. Pensions	259	Rep. and bill	296	Referred to Committee Whole House.		
Carmack, John	Revolutionary pension	23	2	Bill of last sess.	300	Whole House	Jan. 31, 1835	With't amend.	296	Postponed.		
Carman, Benjamin	Pension	21	1	Petition	149	Military Pensions	Mar. 3, 1830	By bill	454	Referred to Committee Whole House.		
Carman, Benjamin	Pension	21	2	Bill of last sess.	318	Whole House	Feb. 16, 1831	With't amend.	454	Passed	Amendm't reported.	
Carman, Benjamin	Pension	22	1	Petition	174	Rev. Pensions	369	Report and bill.	464	Referred to Committee Whole House.		
Carman, Daniel	Pension	16	1	Petition	26	Pens. & Rev. Cl'ms.	Dec. 17, 1819	Rep. and res.; adverse.	......	Resolution adopted.		
Carman, Henry	Compensation for losses and services in revolutionary war.	1	2	Petition and rep't Sec. of War.	160	....	....	....	......	Laid on table.		
Carman, Henry	Invalid pension	3	1	Rep. of Secretary War.	175	....	....	....	......	Laid on table.		
Carman, Henry	Invalid pension	3	2	Rep. of Secretary War.	262	Claims	Feb. 28, 1795	Favorable; bill ordered.	130	Passed	Postponed to next session.	
Carman, Henry	Invalid pension	4	1	Rep. of Secretary War.	445	Claims	Feb. 18, 1796	Favorable; bill ordered.	......	....	....	Does not appear in law of April 20, 1796.
Carman, John, assignee of	Payment of certificate No. 12,171, signed T. Pickering, Quartermaster General, January 1, 1782, with interest.	15	2	Resolution	167	Pens. & Rev. Cl'ms.	....	....	......	Discharged; laid on table.		
Carman, John, assignee of	Payment of certificate No. 12,171, signed T. Pickering, Quartermaster General, January 1, 1782, with interest.	22	2	Resolution	185	Rev. Claims.						
Carman, John, assignee of	Payment of certificate No. 12,171, signed T. Pickering, Quartermaster General, January 1, 1782, with interest.	23	1	Petition	188	Rev. Claims.						
Carman, John, assignee of	Payment of certificate No. 12,171, signed T. Pickering, Quartermaster General, January 1, 1782, with interest.	23	2	Resolution	134	Rev. Claims.						
Carman, John, (N. Y.)	Pension	16	1	Petition	26	Pens. & Rev. Cl'ms.	Dec. 17, 1819	Rep. and res.; adverse.	......	Resolution adopted.		
Carman, Joseph	Relief for error in a land entry	31	1	Petition	862	Public Lands.						
Carmichael, John	Invalid pension	9	2	Petition	529	Claims.						
Carmichael, John	Invalid pension	10	2	Petition	351	Claims	Jan. 30, 1809	By bill	158	Passed	Passed	App'd March 3, 1809
Carmichael, John, (Tenn.)	Compensat'n for damages sustained as United States mail contractor.	19	1	Petition	78	P. Of. and P. Roads.	Jan. 12, 1826	Adverse	......	Laid on table.		
Carmichael, John F	Confirmation of title to land in Mississippi Territory.	20	1	Petition	33	Priv. Land Claims.	57	Rep. and res.	R. 5	Passed	Passed	App'd May 19, 1828
Carmichael, John F	Confirmation of title to land in Mississippi Territory.	20	2	Report of register and receiver.	...	....	....	....	......	Laid on table.		

List of private claims presented to the House of Representatives of the United States from the 1st to the 31st Congress, inclusive—Continued.

Names of claimants.	Nature or object of the claim.	Congress.	Session.	How brought before the House of Reps.	Page of journal.	To what committee of the House referred.	No. or date of the report.	Nature of the report.	No. of the bill.	How disposed of by the House of Reps.	How disposed of by the Senate.	Date of the act of Congress, and remarks.
35 Carmichael, John F.	Confirmation of title to land in Mississippi Territory.	21	1	Senate bill	615	Public Lands	May 29, 1830	With't amend.	116	Passed	....	App'd May 31, 1830
Carmichael, Robert	Arrears of pension	12	1	Petition	51	Claims	May 5, 1812	Rep. and res.; adverse.	......	Resolution adopted.		
Carmichael, William, widow of.	Compensation for services as chargé d'affaires to Spain.	4	1	Memorial	449	....	....	....	......	Referred to Secretary of State.		
Carmichael, William, widow of.	Compensation for services as chargé d'affaires to Spain.	4	2	Report of Secretary State.	715	....	....	....	......	Referred to Committee Whole House.		
Carmichael, William, widow of.	Compensation for services as chargé d'affaires to Spain.	5	2	Report of Secretary State.	83	Whole House	Nov. 28, 1797	Favorable; bill ordered.	22	Passed	Passed	App'd Jan. 15, 1798
Carmichael, William, legal representatives of.	Balance found due per settlement of accounts.	5	2	Resolution	231	Whole House	Mar. 20, 1798	Favorable; bill ordered.	70	Passed	Passed	App'd April 27, 1798
Carmichael, William, heir of.	Re-examination of accounts and payment of such sum as may be found due.	24	1	Petition	202	Foreign Affairs.						
Carmichael, William, heir of.	Re-examination of accounts and payment of such sum as may be found due.	24	2	Petition	90	Foreign Affairs.						
Carmichael, William, heir of.	Re-examination of accounts and payment of such sum as may be found due.	25	2	Petition	74	Foreign Affairs	....	....	......	Discharged.		
Carmichael, William, heir of.	Re-examination of accounts and payment of such sum as may be found due.	26	1	Petition	182	Foreign Affairs	634	Majority, adverse; minority, to refer to Sec. of State for examination.	......	Referred to Committee Whole House.		
Carmichael, William, heir of.	Re-examination of accounts and payment of such sum as may be found due.	27	2	Petition	63	Foreign Affairs.						
Carmody, John	Revolutionary pension	21	1	Resol'n and report Sec. of War.	353, 281	Military Pensions	....	....	......	Discharged; laid on table.		
Carmouche, Narcisse	Confirmation of title to land in Louisiana.	26	1	Petition	947	Priv. Land Claims.						
Carmouche, Narcisse	Confirmation of title to land in Louisiana.	26	2	Petition	134	Priv. Land Claims.	191	Adverse	......	Laid on table.		
Carmouche, Narcisse, and others.	Confirmation of title to land in Louisiana.	31	1	Petition	1227	Priv. Land Claims.						
Carnaghan, John	Compensation for services, &c., in the revolutionary army.	2	1	Petition and rep't Sec. of War.	483	....	....	....	......	Laid on table.		
Carne, Daniel	Compensation for services as a soldier in revolutionary army.	13	1	Petition	28	Claims	....	....	......	Discharged.		
Carne, Daniel	Compensation for services as a soldier in revolutionary army.	13	2	Petition	177	Pens. & Rev. Cl'ms.						
Carnes, Edward, executors of.	Payment of a liquidated debt due estate by United States.	1	2	Petition	152	....	....	....	......	Referred to Secretary Treasury.		
Carnes, Edward, executors of.	Payment of a liquidated debt due estate by United States.	2	1	Rep. of Secretary Treasury.	523	Whole House.						
Carnes, Edward, executors of.	Payment of a liquidated debt due estate by United States.	2	2	Report Secretary of Treasury.	628	Select	Dec. 7, 1792	Favorable; gen. bill ordered.	211	Passed	Passed	App'd Feb. 12, 1793
Carnes, Peter A.	(See Wm. Duval & P. A. Carnes.)											
Carnes, Peter A.	Indemnity for losses sustained as sutler to United States army.	30	2	Petition	126	Claims	42	Adverse	......	Laid on table.		

List of private claims presented to the House of Representatives of the United States from the 1st to the 31st Congress, inclusive—Continued.

Names of claimants.	Nature or object of the claim.	Congress.	Session.	How brought before the House of Reps.	Page of journal.	To what committee of the House referred.	No. or date of the report.	Nature of the report.	No. of the bill.	How disposed of by the House of Reps.	How disposed of by the Senate.	Date of the act of Congress, and remarks.
Carnes, Thomas Jenners	Pay, &c., as lieutenant in revolutionary army under resolutions of late Congress.	3	1	Petition	65					Referred to Secretary War.		
Carnes, Thomas Jenners	Pay, &c., as lieutenant in revolutionary army under resolutions of late Congress.	3	2	Rep. of Secretary War.	278					Laid on table.		
Carney, Arthur	(See John McGilbry and others.)											
Carney, John, (Ind.)	Compensation for services under Gen. St. Clair in 1791.	23	2	Petition	389	Rev. Pensions.						
Carney, John, of Ohio, widow of.	Pension for revolutionary services.	26	1	Petition	324	Rev. Pensions	490	Adverse		Laid on table.		
Carney, John, of Ohio, widow of.	Pension for revolutionary services.	26	2	Petition	168	Rev. Pensions.						
Carney, John, of Ohio, widow of.	Pension for revolutionary services.	27	2	Petition	459	Rev. Pensions				Discharged; laid on table.		
Carney, John, of Ohio, widow of.	Pension for revolutionary services.	30	1	Petition	782	Rev. Pensions						Leave to withdraw, 31st Cong., 2d sess.
Carney, Josiah, and John F. McGrew.	Further time to prove title to land in Mississippi Territory.	14	2	Petition	200	Priv. Land Claims.	Feb. 11, 1817	By bill	123	Referred to Committee Whole House.		
Carney, Josiah, and John F. McGrew.	Further time to prove title to land in Mississippi Territory.	15	1	Petition	39	Priv. Land Claims.						
Carney, Josiah	Confirmation of title to land in Alabama.	15	1	Petition	212	Priv. Land Claims.	Feb. 18, 1818	By bill	92	Passed	Passed	App'd April 4, 1818
Carney, Stephen J.	(See John Owens, heirs of.)											
Carney, Thomas B.	Payment for a slave drowned while in service of United States.	19	2	Petition	105	Claims	Jan. 17, 1827	Adverse		Laid on table.		
Carnith, Thomas	(See James Price.)											
Carnochan, John, and Peter Mitchell.	Remission of duties on damaged merchandise.	14	1	Petition	558	Ways and Means				Discharged; laid on table.		
Caro, Joseph E.	Additional compensation for translating public archives in Florida.	21	1	Petition	128	Claims	Jan. 15, 1830	Adverse		Laid on table.		
Caro, Joseph E.	Additional compensation for translating public archives in Florida.	27	2	Memorial	85	Judiciary.						
Caro, Joseph E.	Additional compensation for translating public archives in Florida.	27	3	Petition	106	Claims	127	Adverse		Laid on table.		
Caro, Joseph E.	Additional compensation for translating public archives in Florida.	28	1	Petition	133	Claims	128	Adverse.		Laid on table.		
Caro, Joseph E.	Additional compensation for translating public archives in Florida.	29	2	Petition	161, 397	Claims.						
Carothers, Robert	(See J. N. Porter, executors of.)											
Carpender, William, widow of.	Pension in consideration of death of husband of disease contracted in U. S. service.	16	1	Petition	343	Pens. & Rev. Cl'ms.				Discharged; laid on table.		
Carpenter, Benajah, widow of.	Invalid pension	3	1	Petition	68					Referred to Secretary of War.		
Carpenter, Benajah, widow of.	Invalid pension	3	2	Rep. of Secretary War.	278	Claims						
Carpenter, Benajah, widow of.	Invalid pension	4	1	Rep. of Secretary War.	373	Claims	Jan. 8, 1796	Adverse		Leave to withdraw.		
Carpenter, Benjamin	(See Hopkins Rice.)											
Carpenter, Benjamin	Compensation for services as a soldier in revolutionary army.	23	1	Petition	144	Rev. Pensions				Discharged; laid on table.		

List of private claims presented to the House of Representatives of the United States from the 1st to the 31st Congress, inclusive—Continued.

Names of claimants.	Nature or object of the claim.	Congress.	Session.	How brought before the House of Reps.	Page of journal.	To what committee of the House referred.	No. or date of the report.	Nature of the report.	No. of the bill.	How disposed of by the House of Reps.	How disposed of by the Senate.	Date of the act of Congress, and remarks.
Carpenter, Cephus, & others	Compensation for services in defence of Plattsburg.	27	2	Petition	247	Claims	490	Adverse		Laid on table.		
Carpenter, Cephus, & others	Compensation for services in defence of Plattsburg.	28	1	Petition	216	Claims				Discharged; laid on table.		
Carpenter, David	Pension for services as an Indian spy.	27	2	Petition	524	Rev. Pensions	784	Adverse		Laid on table.		
Carpenter, Elias	Arrears of pension	23	1	Petition	45	Invalid Pensions	Jan. 24, 1834	Adverse		Laid on table.		
Carpenter, Elias	Arrears of pension	23	2	Petition	47	Invalid Pensions	Feb. 3, 1835	Adverse		Laid on table.		
Carpenter, Elias	Arrears of pension	25	2	Petition	198	Invalid Pensions	Jan. 30, 1838	Adverse		Laid on table.		
Carpenter, Elias	Arrears of pension	25	3	Petition	81	Invalid Pensions	Jan. 16, 1839	Adverse		Laid on table.		
Carpenter, Elias	Increase of pension	28	1	Petition	245	Invalid Pensions	185	Adverse		Laid on table.		
Carpenter, Elias	Arrears of pension	28	2	Petition	69	Invalid Pensions.						
Carpenter, Elias	Arrears of pension	29	1	Petition	120	Invalid Pensions	83	Adverse		Laid on table.		
Carpenter, Elizabeth	(See Dothick Hewitt, daughter of)											
Carpenter, Guy	Compensation for expenses incurred in the Black Hawk war.	27	3	Petition	210	Claims	206	Adverse		Laid on table.		
Carpanter, Guy	Compensation for expenses incurred in the Black Hawk war.	28	1	Petition	429	Claims.						
Carpenter, Guy	Compensation for expenses incurred in the Black Hawk war.	29	1	Petition	489	Claims	396	Adverse		Laid on table.		
Carpenter, Ira	Compensation for use of a house and for injury of a horse, &c., by U. S. troops, war of 1812.	24	2	Petition	394	Claims.						
Carpenter, Ira	Compensation for use of a house and for injury of a horse, &c., by U. S. troops, war of 1812.	25	2	Petition	176	Claims	392	Adverse		Laid on table.		
Carpenter, Ira	Compensation for use of a house and for injury of a horse, &c., by U. S. troops, war of 1812.	26	1	Petition	622	Claims.						
Carpenter, Ira	Compensation for use of a house and for injury of a horse, &c., by U. S. troops, war of 1812.	27	2	Petition	470	Claims.						
Carpenter, Ira	Compensation for use of a house and for injury of a horse, &c., by U S. troops, war of 1812.	27	3	Petition	72	Claims	150	Adverse		Laid on table.		
Carpenter, Ira	Compensation for use of a house and for injuries of a horse, &c., by United States troops in war of 1812.	28	1	Petition	333	Claims	247	Adverse		Laid on table.		
Carpenter, Ira	Compensation for use of a house and for injuries of a horse, &c., by United States troops in war of 1812.	29	1	Petition	323	Claims	171	Adverse		Laid on table.		
Carpenter, Ira	Compensation for use of a house and for injuries of a horse, &c., by United States troops in war of 1812.	31	1	Petition	510	Claims	164	Adverse		Laid on table.		
Carpenter, Ira	Compensation for use of a house and for injuries of a horse, &c., by United States troops in war of 1812.	31	2	Petition	308	Claims.						
Carpenter, Isaac	Pension	19	1	Petition	66	Military Pensions	Feb. 23, 1826	By bill	118	Passed	Referred, com. discharged.	

List of private claims presented to the House of Representatives of the United States from the 1st to the 31st Congress, inclusive—**Continued.**

Names of claimants.	Nature or object of the claim.	Congress.	Session.	How brought before the House of Reps.	Page of journal.	To what committee of the House referred.	No. or date of the report.	Nature of the report.	No. of the bill.	How disposed of by the House of Reps.	How disposed of by the Senate.	Date of the act of Congress, and remarks.
Carpenter, Isaac	Pension	19	2	House bill	85	Whole House	Feb. 2, 1827	Favorable	314	Passed	Passed	App'd March 3, 1827
Carpenter, Jacob, widow of.	Pension for naval services	30	1	Petition	340	Naval Affairs	444	Report and bill.	375	Referred to Committee Whole House.		
Carpenter, Jeremiah	Additional compensation on contract for a sea wall at Sackett's harbor.	29	1	Petition	369	Claims	402	Adverse		Laid on table.		
Carpenter, Jeremiah	Additional compensation on contract for a sea-wall at Sackett's harbor.	30	1	Petition	355	Claims	758	Adverse		Laid on table.		
Carpenter, Jeremiah	Additional compensation on contract for a sea-wall at Sackett's harbor.	30	2	Petition	120	Claims	110	Adverse		Laid on table.		
Carpenter, Jesse	Refunding purchase money on a tract of land.	26	2	Senate bill	339				209			
Carpenter, Jesse	Refunding purchase money on a tract of land.	27	2	Senate bill	409	Public Lands	April 1, 1842	With't amend.	93	Passed	Passed	App'd Jan. 27, 1842
Carpenter, Miles, widow of.	Pension—husband killed in Indian fight 1791.	16	1	Petition	70	Pens. & Rev. Cl'ms.	Jan. 3, 1820	Adverse		Laid on table.		
Carpenter, Shubael	Pension	14	1	Petition	32	Pens. & Rev. Cl'ms.				Discharged.		
Carpenter, Stephen	(See Francis Porie.)											
Carpenter, Stephen, administrator of.	Indemnity for French spoliations prior to 1800.	21	1	Petition	171	Foreign Affairs				Discharged; laid on table.		
Carpenter, Stephen, administrator of.	Indemnity for French spoliations prior to 1800.	26	1	Memorial	182	Foreign Affairs	343	Favorable bill.	319	Referred to Committee Whole House.		
Carpenter, Stephen, administrator of.	Indemnity for French spoliations prior to 1800.	31	1	Petition	413	Foreign Affairs	355	Favorable bill.	318	Referred to Committee Whole House.		
Carpenter, Susanah	(See James French, representatives of.)											
Carpenter, Thomas	(See Leffert Lefferts.)											
Carpenter, Thomas (N. Y.)	Invalid pension	24	1	Petition	140	Invalid Pensions	Jan. 28, 1836	Adverse		Laid on table.		
Carpenter, Thomas (N. Y.)	Invalid pension	24	2	Petition	42	Invalid Pensions				Discharged; laid on table.		
Carpenter, Thomas (N. Y.)	Invalid pension	27	2	Petition	536	Invalid Pensions	812	Adverse		Laid on table.		
Carpenter, Uriah, widow of.	Revolutionary pension	25	2	Petition	54	Rev. Pensions				Discharged; laid on table.		
Carpentier, Lewis A	(See Stephen Monot and others.)											
Carpentier, Lewis D	Drawback on duties on merchandise shiped to the Isle of France in the Venus.	10	1	Memorial	241	Com. and Manuf.						
Carpentier, Lewis D	Drawback on duties on merchandise shiped to the Isle of France in the Venus.	12	1	Petition	180	Com. and Manuf.				Discharged; leave to withdraw.		
Carr, Allen	Indemnity for depredations by Seminole Indians.	23	1	Petition	196	Indian Affairs				Discharged; laid on table.		
Carr, Benjamin	Pension for injuries sustained in war of 1812.	17	1	Petition	165	Military Affairs	Feb. 20, 1822	Adverse		Leave to withdraw.		
Carr, Charles	Credit for residue of judgment against him as late paymaster of Kentucky malitia.	17	2	Petition	144	Claims	Feb. 21, 1823	Report and bill.	807	Passed	Passed	App'd March 3, 1823
Carr, Daniel	Pension	14	1	Petition	152	Pens. & Rev. Cl'ms.				Discharged; laid on table.		
Carr, Elijah	Relief: he having relinquished certain improved lands by mistake.	20	2	Petition	34	Public Lands	4	Report and bill.	316	Referred to Committee Whole House.		

List of private claims presented to the House of Representatives of the United States from the 1st to the 31st Congress, inclusive—Continued.

Names of claimants.	Nature or object of the claim.	Congress.	Session.	How brought before the House of Reps.	Page of journal.	To what committee of the House referred.	No. or date of the report.	Nature of the report.	No. of the bill.	How disposed of by the House of Reps.	How disposed of by the Senate.	Date of the act of Congress, and remarks.
Carr, Elijah	Relief: he having relinquished certain improved lands by mistake	21	1	Petition	41	Public Lands	7	Report and bill.	12	Passed	Passed	App'd Jan. 13, 1830
Carr, James	Pension	16	2	Petition	109	Pens. & Rev. Cl'ms.	Jan. 9, 1821	Adverse		Leave to withdraw.		
Carr, James	Pension	19	1	Petition	364	Military Pensions	164	Adverse		Laid on table.		
Carr, John, (Delaware)	Renewal of pension	2	1	Petition	518					Referred to Secretary of War.		
Carr, John, (Delaware)	Renewal of pension	3	1	Rep. of Secretary War.	186					Referred to Committee Whole House.		
Carr, John, (Delaware)	Renewal of pension	3	2	Rep. of Secretary War.	262	Claims.						
Carr, John, (Delaware)	Renewal of pension	4	1	Rep. of Secretary War.	373	Claims	Feb. 18, 1796	Ref. to Secretary, with instructions.	R. 16	Passed	Passed	App'd April 18, 1796
Carr, John, (Maryland)	Pay and emoluments as lieutenant in revolutionary army.	3	1	Petition	68	Select	April 22, 1794	Favorable		Laid on table.		
Carr, John, (Maryland)	Pay and emoluments as lieutenant in revolutionary army.	4	1	Report	583	Whole House.						
Carr, John, (Maryland)	Pay and emoluments as lieutenant in revolutionary army.	4	2	Report	640	Whole House.						
Carr, John, (Maryland)	Pay and emoluments as lieutenant in revolutionary army.	5	2	Report	100	Claims	Jan. 17, 1798	Adverse		Referred to Committee Whole House.		
Carr, John, (Maryland)	Pay and emoluments as lieutenant in revolutionary army.	5	3	Report	441	Whole House.						
Carr, John, (Maryland)	Pay and emoluments as lieutenant in revolutionary army.	7	1	Petition & report.	48	Claims	Jan. 27, 1802	Adverse		Rejected.		
Carr, John, (Maryland)	Pay and emoluments as lieutenant in revolutionary army.	9	1	Petition	226	Claims				Discharged.		
Carr, John, (Maryland)	Pay and emoluments as lieutenant in revolutionary army.	14	2	Petition	224	Pens. & Rev. Cl'ms.				Discharged; laid on table.		
Carr, John, (Maryland)	Pay and emoluments as lieutenant in revolutionary army.	15	1	Petition	24	Pens. & Rev. Cl'ms.	Jan. 13, 1818	Adverse		Laid on table.		
Carr, John, (New York)	Revolutionary pension	21	1	Petition	143	Military Pensions	May 18, 1830	Adverse		Laid on table.		
Carr, John, (New York)	Revolutionury pension	22	1	Resolution	308	Rev. Pensions				Disch'd; laid on table.		
Carr, John, (New York)	Increase of pension	25	3	Petition	571	Invalid Pensions.						
Carr, John	Compensation for work and material furnished as contractor on Cumberland road.	23	1	Res. and papers.	589	Claims	456	Favorable		Referred to Secretary War.		
Carr, John, (Va.,) daughter of.	Pension due from 1818 to 1831 for services as a revolutionary soldier.	25	2	Petition	70	Rev. Pensions	536	Report and bill.	529	Passed	Adverse report.	
Carr, John, (Va.,) daughter of.	Pension due from 1818 to 1831 for services as a revolutionary soldier.	25	3	Petition	87	Rev. Pensions	28	Report and bill.	928	Passed	Adverse report.	
Carr, John, (Va.,) daughter of.	Pension due from 1818 to 1831 for services as a revolutionary soldier.	26	1	Petition	171	Rev. Pensions	116	Report and bill.	126	Referred to Committee Whole House.		
Carr, John, (Va.,) daughter of.	Pension due from 1818 to 1831 for services as a revolutionary soldier.	26	2	Bill of last sess	194	Whole House	Jan. 16, 1841	With't amend.	126	Laid on table.		
Carr, John, (Va.,) daughter of.	Pension due from 1818 to 1831 for services as a revolutionary soldier.	27	2	Petition	58	Rev. Pensions	22	Report and bill.	63	Passed	Indef. postp'd.	

List of private claims presented to the House of Representatives of the United States from the 1st to the 31st Congress, inclusive—Continued.

Names of claimants.	Nature or object of the claim.	Congress.	Session.	How brought before the House of Reps.	Page of journal.	To what committee of the House referred.	No. or date of the report.	Nature of the report.	No. of the bill.	How disposed of by the House of Reps.	How disposed of by the Senate.	Date of the act of Congress, and remarks.
Carr, John, (Va.,) daughter of.	Pension due from 1818 to 1831 for services as a revolutionary soldier.	27	3	Petition	43	Rev. Pensions	....	....	......	Discharged; laid on table.		
Carr, John, (Va.,) daughter of.	Pension due from 1818 to 1831 for services as a revolutionary soldier.	28	1	Petition	105	Rev. Pensions	51	Report and bill.	74	Passed	Indef. postp'd.	
Carr, John, (Va..) daughter of.	Pension due from 1818 to 1831 for services as a revolutionary soldier.	28	2	Petition	59	Rev. Pensions	6	Report and bill.	456	Referred to Committee Whole House.		
Carr, John, (Va.,) daughter of.	Pension due from 1818 to 1831 for services as a revolutionary soldier.	29	1	Petition	91	Rev. Pensions	14	Report and bill.	28	Rejected.		
Carr, John, (Va.,) daughter of.	Pension due from 1818 to 1231 for services as a revolutionary soldier.	30	1	Senate bill	683	Rev. Pensions	767	Adverse	91	Laid on table.		
Carr, John, (Va.,) daughter of.	Pension due from 1818 to 1831 for services as a revolutionary soldier.	31	2	Senate bill	190	....	....	....	94	Laid on table.		
Carr, John and others	Compensation for detention as witnesses in a case of mutiny.	27	3	Petition	423	Claims.						
Carr, Jonn and others	Compensation for detention as wit nesses in a case of mutiny.	28	2	Petition	301	Claims	126	Report and bill.	611	Referred to Committee Whole House.		
Carr, John and others	Compensation for detention as witnesses in a case of mutiny.	29	1	Petition	440	Claims	434	Report and bill.	302	Passed	Passed	App'd Aug. 8, 1846
Carr, Jonathan	Revolutionary pension	21	1	Resolution	255	Military pensions	....	....	......	Discharged; laid on table.		
Carr, Joseph, (Tenn.)	Payment for a gun, &c., lost in the service of the United States.	19	1	Petition	248	Claims	April 19, 1826	Adverse	......	Laid on table.		
Carr, Joseph, (Tenn.)	Payment for a gun, &c., lost in the service of the United States.	20	1	Petition	38	Claims	Jan. 25, 1828	Adverse	......	Laid on table.		
Carr, Joseph, (Tenn.)	Payment for a gun, &c., lost in the service of the United States.	21	1	Petition	51	Claims	....	....	......	Discharged; laid on table.		
Carr, J. Wingate	(See John Pearson, executors of.)	28	1	....	245							
Carr, Kinchen, administrator of.	Release from liability as surety for J. W. Walker.	28	2	Petition	239	P. Of. & P. Roads.						
Carr, Margarett	Arrears of pension	12	2	Petition	633	Claims	Feb. 26, 1813	Adverse	......	Laid on table.		
Carr, Overton	(See Exploring Expedition.)											
Carr, Resolved	Fishing bounty	10	1	Pet. and rep. of Sec. Treasury.	132, 238	Com. and Manuf.						
Carr, Richard, widow of	Bounty land due as a soldier in the United States service.	22	2	Resolution	70	Public Lands	Jan. 7, 1833	By bill	662	Passed	Passed	App'd Feb. 20, 1833
Carr, Richard, sister and legal representatives of.	Bounty land due as a soldier in the United States service.	27	3	Petition	60	Public Lands.						
Carr, Robert, alias Cars	Invalid pension	3	1	Report Secretary of War.	131	Select	May 26, 1794	To refer to Sec. with instruc.	R. 12	Passed	Passed	App'd June 9, 1794
Carr, Robert, alias Cars	Invalid pension	3	2	Report Secretary of War.	337	Claims	Feb. 28, 1795	Favorable; bill ordered.	130	Passed	Postponed to next session.	
Carr, Robert, alias Cars	Invalid pension	4	1	Report Secretary of War.	445	Claims	Feb. 18, 1796	Favorable; bill ordered.	156	Passed	Passed	App'd April 20, 1796
Carr, Robinson, & Co	(See John Jones, of Del., & others.)											
Carr, Samuel and William	Relief in consequence of the sale of their lands for direct taxes.	15	1	Petition	132	Ways and Means	....	....	......	Discharged.		

List of private claims presented to the House of Representatives of the United States from the 1st to the 31st Congress, inclusive—Continued.

Names of claimants.	Nature or object of the claim.	Congress.	Session.	How brought before the House of Reps.	Page of journal.	To what committee of the House referred.	No. or date of the report.	Nature of the report.	No. of the bill.	How disposed of by the House of Reps.	How disposed of by the Senate.	Date of the act of Congress, and remarks.
Carr, Sarah	(See Richard Carr, widow of.)											
Carr, Thomas, and others.	Compensation for land in Mississippi territory, granted by State of Georgia prior to its cession to United States.	14	1	Petition	194	Public Lands	Mar. 27, 1816	Report not of record.	......	Indef. postponed.		
Carr, Thomas, and others.	Compensation for land in Mississippi territory, granted by State of Georgia prior to its cession to United States.	14	2	Petition	297	Public Lands	......	......	......	Discharged; laid on table.		
Carr, Thomas, and others.	Compensation for land in Mississippi territory, granted by State of Georgia prior to its cession to United States.	15	1	Petition	185	Select	86	Report and bill.	74	Laid on table.		
Carr, Thomas, and others.	Compensation for land in Mississippi territory, granted by State of Georgia prior to its cession to United States.	15	2	Report, former	59	Select	31	Report and bill.	225	Referred to Committee Whole House.		
Carr, Thomas, and others.	Compensation for land in Mississippi territory, granted by State of Georgia prior to its cession to United States.	16	1	Petition	30	Select	2	Report and bill.	5	Recommitted.		
						Priv. Land Claims.	62	Adverse	......	Referred to Committee Whole House.		
Carr, Thomas, and others.	Compensation for land in Mississippi territory, granted by State of Georgia prior to its cession to United States.	17	1	Senate bill	465	Public Lands	April 25, 1822	With't amend.	36	Laid on table.		
Carr, Thomas, and others.	Compensation for land in Mississippi territory, granted by State of Georgia prior to its cession to United States.	17	2	Senate bill	117	Public Lands	Jan. 30, 1823	With amend.	11	Laid on table.		
Carr, Thomas, and others.	Compensation for land in Mississippi territory, granted by State of Georgia prior to its cession to United States.	18	1	Petition & papers	48, 56	Public Lands	......	Embraced by amendm't in bill.	73	Rejected.		
Carr, Thomas, and others.	Compensation for land in Mississippi territory, granted by State of Georgia prior to its cession to United States.	18	1	Senate bill	518	Public Lands	May 20, 1824	With amend.	106	Passed	Passed	App'd May 24, 1824
Carr, William	Invalid pension	10	2	House bill	499	Whole House	Feb. 20, 1809	Favorable	158	Passed	Passed	App'd March 3, 1809
Carrell, Eli H.	Relief for loss on building purchased at Harper's Ferry.	31	1	Petition	977	Claims.						
Carrere, John	(See De Bastrop, Baron, assig's of.)											
Carrere, John	Indemnity for French spoliations prior to 1800.	26	1	Memorial	182	Foreign Affairs	343	Favorable; bill	319	Referred to Committee Whole House.		
Carrier, Elizabeth	Restoration of pension	27	2	Petition	320	Rev. Pensions.						
Carrier, Hannah	(See Guy Dodd, widow of.)											
Carrier, John	(See Henry Missioner, exec'rs of)	26	1	......	182							
Carrier, Jonathan D.	Pension	14	1	Resolution	158	Pens. & Rev. Cl'ms.	......	......	......	Discharged; leave to withdraw.		
Carrier, Jonathan D.	Pension	14	2	Petition	141	Pens. & Rev. Cl'ms.	Jan. 29, 1817	By bill	91	Passed	Passed	App'd March 3, 1817
Carrier, Jonathan D.	Increase of pension	15	2	Rep. of Secretary War.	48	Pens. & Rev. Cl'ms.	Feb. 3, 1819	By bill	308	Passed	Postponed.	

List of private claims presented to the House of Representatives of the United States from the 1st to the 31st Congress, inclusive—Continued.

Names of claimants.	Nature or object of the claim.	Congress.	Session.	How brought before the House of Reps.	Page of journal.	To what committee of the House referred.	No. or date of the report.	Nature of the report.	No. of the bill.	How disposed of by the House of Reps.	How disposed of by the Senate.	Date of the act of Congress, and remarks.
Carrington, Henry	(See Edward Read, executor of late widow of.)											
Carrington, Timothy W.	Incaease of compensation as postmaster at Aldie, Va.	14	2	Resolution	142	P. Of. and P. Roads.				Discharged.		
Carroll, Charles W.	Compensation for unjust imprisonment by officers of United States army.	31	1	Petition	956	Military Affairs.						
Carroll, Daniel, and others	Indemnity for damage to house occupied by Congress from 1815 to 1819.	17	1	Senate bill	428	Claims	April 27, 1822	With't amend.	60	Referred to Committee Whole House.		
Carroll, Daniel, and others	Repair of building lately occupied by Congress.	17	2	Petition	57	Claims	Jan. 8, 1823	By bill	220	Referred to Committee Whole House.		
Carroll, Daniel, and others	Repair of building lately occupied by Congress.	18	1	Petition	61	Claims	Dec. 22, 1823	By bill rejected, reconsidered, and recommitted.	17			
							Feb. 27, 1824	By bill: without amendment.	17	Passed	Passed	App'd May 19, 1824
Carroll, David	Revolutionary pension	26	1	Petition	324	Rev. Pensions	424	Adverse		Laid on table.		
Carroll, Dennis	Additional price on naval contract for beef and pork.	13	3	Petition	738	Claims				Leave to withdraw.		
Carroll, Hamilton	Pension for wounds received in war 1812.	30	2	Petition	139	Invalid Pensions.						
Carroll, Hamilton	Increase of pension	31	1	Resolution	493	Invalid Pensions	237	Report and bill	232	Referred to Committee Whole House.		
Carroll, John, widow of	Relief—husband killed in revolutionary war.	2	1	Petition	560					Referred to Secretary War.		
Carroll, John, widow of	Relief—husband killed in revolutionary war.	2	2	Rep. of Secretary War.	696					Laid on table.		
Carroll, Malachi	Revolutionary pension	22	1	Petition	106	Rev. Pensions.						
Carroll, Martin	Revolutionary pension	14	1	Res. and Docs.	450	Pens. & Rev. Cl'ms.	April 11, 1816	By bill	171			Bill became a law, omitting Carroll's name.
Carroll, Michael B.	Share of any grant made for the destruction of frigate Philadelphia.	20	1	Petition	245	Naval Affairs	201	Adverse		Referred to Committee Whole House.		
Carroll, Samuel	Payment for a horse lost in war of 1812.	16	1	Petition	369	Claims	April 7, 1820	Adverse		Laid on table.		
Carroll, William	(See Louis F. Beeler and others.)											
Carroll, William T.	Payment of account for writing up records of United States Supreme Court.	20	2	Petition	176	Ways and Means				Discharged; laid on table.		
Carroll, William T.	Payment of account for writing up records of United States Supreme Court.	21	1	Petition	260	Ways and Means	Jan. 24, 1830	By bill	286	Referred to Committee Whole House.		
Carroll, William T.	Payment of account for writing up records of United States Supreme Court.	21	2	Bill of last sess.	239	Whole House	Feb. 21, 1831	With't amend.	286	Passed	Passed	App'd March 3, 1831
Carruth, Adam, sureties of	Release from liability, and for stoppage of legal proceedings.	17	2	Petition	225	Military Affairs	Feb. 25, 1823	Adverse		Laid on table.		

List of private claims presented to the House of Representatives of the United States from the 1st to the 31st Congress, inclusive—Continued.

Names of claimants.	Nature or object of the claim.	Congress.	Session.	How brought before the House of Reps.	Page of journal.	To what committee of the House referred.	No. or date of the report.	Nature of the report.	No. of the bill.	How disposed of by the House of Reps.	How disposed of by the Senate.	Date of the act of Congress, and remarks.
Carruth, Thomas	Compensation for wounds received in revolutionary war.	2	1	Petition	487	....	....	....	....	Referred to Secretary of War.		
Carruthers, G. M., & John Ashbrook.	Pre-emption right to a tract of land.	25	2	Petition	594	Public Lands	....	....	....	Discharged.		
Carryl, Patrick	Compensation for services in revolutionary war.	3	1	Petition	103	....	....	....	....	Referred to Secretary of War.		
Carryl, Patrick	Compensation for services in revolutionary war.	3	2	Rep. of Secretary War.	278	....	....	....	....	Laid on table.		
Carryl, Patrick	Compensation for services in revolutionary war.	11	2	Petition	302	Claims.						
Carson, Alfred T.	Confirmation of title to land in Mississippi.	23	2	Petition	346	Priv. Land Claims.						
Carson, Charles C.	(See James Dysart, heirs of.)											
Carson, Daniel	Increase of pension	24	1	Petition	433	Rev. Claims	....	....	....	Discharged; laid on table.		
Carson, James	Compensation for services in revolutionary war.	2	1	Petition	500	....	....	....	....	Referred to Secretary of War.		
Carson, James G.	Pre-emption right to land in Louisiana.	29	1	Petition	395	Claims.						
Carson, James G.	Pre-emption right to land in Louisiana.	29	2	Petition	70	Priv. Land Claims.	50	Report and bill	642	Referred to Committee Whole House.	....	Leave to withdraw.
Carson, James G.	Pre-emption right to land in Louisiana.	30	1	Senate bill	976	Priv. Land Claims.	....	....	185			
Carson, James C.	Pre-emption right to land in Louisiana.	30	2	Bill of last sess.	180	Priv. Land Claims.	Jan. 3, 1849	With't amend.	185	Passed	Passed	App'd March 3, 1849
Carson, Jane	Compensation for transportation of troops over Tombigbee river.	14	1	Petition	497	Claims	April 15, 1816	Rep. and res. adverse.	....	Resolution adopted.		
Carson, Joseph	(See John D. Matthews and others.)											
Carson, J.	(See Anthony Hutchins and others.)											
Carson, Samuel	Permission, as an alien, to hold title to land in District of Columbia.	8	2	Petition	16	Select	Dec. 6, 1804	Favorable; bill ordered.	15	Referred to Committee Whole House.		
Carson, Samuel	Permission, as an alien, to hold title to land in District of Columbia.	10	2	Petition	459	Dist. of Columbia.						
Carson, Samuel	Permission, as an alien, to hold title to land in District of Columbia.	11	1	Petition	41	Dist. of Columbia.						
Carson, William	Invalid pension	27	1	Petition	108	Invalid Pensions.						
Carswell, David	Revolutionary pension	18	1	Petition	344	Rev. Pensions	May 17, 1824	Adverse	....	Laid on table.		
Carswell, David	Revolutionary pension	18	2	Rep., former	61	....	....	....	....	Referred to Committee Whole House.		
Carswell, David	Revolutionary pension	19	1	Petition	62	Military Pensions	164	Adverse	....	Laid on table.		
Carswell, David	Revolutionary pension	20	1	Petition	193	Military Pensions	April 29, 1828	By bill	283	Passed	Ref. and Com. discharged.	
Carswell, David	Revolutionary pension	20	2	House bill	55	Whole House	Jan. 15, 1829	Favorable	311	Passed	Laid on table.	
Carswell, David	Revolutionary pension	21	1	Petition	47	Military Pensions	Jan. 5, 1830	By bill	72	Passed	Passed	App'd May 20, 1830
Carswell, David	Arrears of pension	24	2	Petition	90	Rev. Pensions	....	....	....	Disch'd; laid on table.		
Carswell, David	Arrears of pension	25	2	Petition	546	Rev. Pensions	....	....	....	Disch'd; laid on table.		
Carswell, David	Arrears of pension	25	3	Petition	173, 226	Rev. Pensions	....	....	....	Discharged; laid on table.		
Carswell, David	Arrears of pension	26	1	Petition	624	Rev. Pensions.						
Cartanos, Juan Jose	Compensation for money advanced to American sailors and others to enable them to return to their country.	31	1	Petition	815	Claims.						

List of private claims presented to the House of Representatives of the United States from the 1st to the 31st Congress, inclusive—Continued.

Names of claimants.	Nature or object of the claim.	Congress.	Session.	How brought before the House of Reps.	Page of journal.	To what committee of the House referred.	No. or date of the report.	Nature of the report.	No. of the bill.	How disposed of by the House of Reps.	How disposed of by the Senate.	Date of the act of Congress, and remarks.
Carter, Alfred	Pre-emption right to land in Iowa	26	1	Petition	364	Public Lands	July 21, 1840	By bill	512	Referred to Committee Whole House.		
Carter, Alfred M.	(See Landon Carter, heirs of.)											
Carter, A. R.	Compensation for locating Choctaw land certificates.	31	2	Petition	184	Public Lands.						
Carter, Barnabas	Arrears of pension	20	2	Resolution	92	Military Pensions	...	...	...	Discharged; laid on table.		
Carter, Braxton	Invalid pension	12	2	Petition	560	Claims.						
Carter, Braxton	Invalid pension	13	1	House bill	56	Whole House	July 20, 1813	Favorable	31	Passed	Passed	App'd Aug. 2, 1813
Carter, Caleb S., and others	Incidental expenses paid by them as United States weighers, guagers and measurers at Portland, Maine	26	1	Petition	710	Commerce.						
Carter, Calvin, sureties of.	Release from liability	27	2	Petition	792	P. Of. & P. Roads	...	...	...	Discharged; laid on table.		
Carter, Calvin, sureties of.	Release from liability	29	2	Petition	183	P. Of. and P. Roads.						
Carter, Calvin, sureties of.	Release from liability	30	1	Petition	439	Claims	379	Adverse	...	Laid on table.		
Carter, Charles	(See Charles Lewis, representatives of.)	23	1	...	42							
Carter, Charles	(See John Carter, heir of.)											
Carter, Charles	Compensation for services in war of 1812.	24	1	Petition	752	Invalid Pensions	...	...	...	Discharged; laid on table.		
Carter, Charles	Compensation for services in war of 1812.	25	2	Petition	71	Invalid Pensions	...	...	...	Discharged; laid on table.		
Carter, Charles	Compensation for services in war of 1812.	27	2	Petition	96	Invalid Pensions	Feb. 9, 1842	Adverse	...	Laid on table.		
Carter, Charles	Compensation for services in war of 1812.	27	3	Petition	72	Invalid Pensions.						
Carter, Chauncey	Mileage from Indiana to seat of government to adjust accounts as Indian agent.	26	1	Resolution	565	Claims.						
Carter, David	Payment of bill of exchange drawn by United States consul at St. Bart's for provisions for U. S.	18	2	Memorial	36	Claims	Jan. 10, 1825	Adverse	...	Laid on table.		
Carter, Esther	(See John Beacham, heir of.)											
Carter, Farish	Equitable settlement of accounts for military supplies.	22	1	Senate bill	1020	Claims	...	...	171			
Carter, Farish	Equitable settlement of accounts for military supplies.	22	2	Senate bill	281	Claims	March 2, 1833	With't amend.	57	Passed	Passed	App'd March 2, 1833
Carter, Farish, as assignee.	Patent for land for which he holds certificates of purchase.	23	1	Petition	211	Priv. Land Claims.	270	Rep. and bill.	307	Referred to Committee Whole House.		
Carter, Farish, as assignee.	Patent for land for which he holds certificates of purchase.	24	1	Petition	65	Priv. Land Claims.	72	Rep. and bill.	88	Passed	Amend'nt rep.; laid on table.	
Carter, Farish, as assignee.	Patent for land for which he holds certificates of purchase.	25	2	Petition	109	Priv. Land Claims.	Dec. 22, 1837	By bill	159	Referred to Committee Whole House.		
Carter, Farish, as assignee.	Patent for land for which he holds certificates of purchase.	25	3	Bill of last sess.	375	Whole House	Jan. 25, 1839	With't amend.	159	Passed	Passed	App'd March 3, 1839
Carter, Francis	(See Jesse Kent, late widow of.)	22	1	...	556							
Carter, Hezekiah	Donation right for six hundred and forty acres of land.	12	1	Petition	100	Public Lands.						
Carter, Hezekiah	Donation right for six hundred and forty acres of land.	12	2	Petition	550	Public Lands.						
Carter, Hezekiah	Confirmation of title to land in Mississippi Territory.	14	2	Petition	200	Priv. Land Claims.						

List of private claims presented to the House of Representatives of the United States from the 1st to the 31st Congress, inclusive—Continued.

Names of claimants.	Nature or object of the claim.	Congress.	Session.	How brought before the House of Reps.	Page of journal.	To what committee of the House referred.	No. or date of the report.	Nature of the report.	No. of the bill.	How disposed of by the House of Reps.	How disposed of by the Senate.	Date of the act of Congress, and remarks.
Carter, Hugh, (Tenn.)	Benefit of act of June 7, 1832, for revolutionary services.	24	1	Resolution	437	Rev. Pensions				Discharged; laid on table.		
Carter, Hugh, (Tenn.)	Benefit of act of June 7, 1832, for revolutionary services.	24	2	Petition	147	Invalid Pensions				Discharged; laid on table.		
Carter, Isaac	Pension	23	1	Petition	352	Invalid Pensions	447	Rep. and bill.	465	Referred to Committee Whole House.		
Carter, Isaac	Pension	23	2	Bill of last sess.	336	Whole House	Feb. 6, 1835	With't amend.	465	Passed	Adverse report.	
Carter, Isaac	Pension	21	1	Petition	53	Invalid Pensions	46	Rep. and bill.	58	Passed	Passed	App'd May 14, 1830
Carter, Jacob	(See Zebulon M. Pike and companions.											
Carter, James	(See James Canter.)											
Carter, James, of Va., heirs of.	Compensation for revolutionary services.	12	1	Petition	120	Claims.						
Carter, James, (N. C.)	Revolutionary pension	22	1	Resolution	400	Rev. Pensions				Discharged; laid on table.		
Carter, James, (Ga.)	Compensation for damages by invasion of Seminole Indians.	26	1	Petition	341	Claims.						
Carter, James, (Ky.)	Pension for services as a soldier in revolutionary war.	29	1	Petition	348	Rev. Pensions.						
Carter, Jeremiah	Invalid pension, war of 1812	29	1	Petition	82	Invalid Pensions				Discharged; laid on table.		
Carter, John, heirs of	Compensation for services in revolutionary war.	24	1	Petition	752	Rev. Claims.						
Carter, John, heirs of	Compensation for services in revolutionary war.	25	2	Petition	71	Invalid Pensions				Discharged; laid on table.		
Carter, John, heirs of	Compensation for services in revolutionary war.	27	2	Petition	96	Invalid Pensions	Feb. 9, 1842	Adverse		Laid on table.		
Carter, John, heirs of	Compensation for services in revolutionary war.	27	3	Petition	72	Invalid Pensions.						
Carter, John, heirs of	Compensation for services in revolutionary war.	28	1	Petition	509	Invalid Pensions.						
Carter, John Drummond	Restoration of property seized under non-importation act.	12	2	Petition	583	Ways and Means				Discharged.		
Carter, John Drummond	Restoration of property seized under non importation act.	15	1	Petition	191	Ways and Means				Discharged.		
Carter, John Drummond	Restoration of property seized under non-importation act.	15	2	House bill	187	Whole House			276			
Carter, John Drummond	Restoration of property seized under non-importation act.	16	1	House bill	160	Whole House	April 7, 1820	With't amend.	56	Passed	Passed	App'd May 8, 1820
Carter, John K., lieutenant United States navy.	Allowance for discount paid on depreciated United States funds.	18	1	Petition	236	Naval Affairs	April 28, 1824	Report and bill.	208	Passed	Passed	App'd May 21, 1824
Carter, Joseph	Revolutionary pension	28	2	Petition	53	Rev. Pensions	172	Report and bill.	642	Referred to Committee Whole House.		
Carter, Joseph	Revolutionary pension	29	1	Petition	353	Rev. Pensions.						
Carter, Joseph	Revolutionary pension	29	2	Petition	59	Rev. Pensions.						
Carter, Joseph	Revolutionary pension	30	1	Petition	78	Rev. Pensions	88	Adverse		Laid on table.		
Carter, Joseph	Revolutionary pension	31	1	Petition	232	Rev. Pensions	451	Adverse		Laid on table.		
Carter, Joshua, assignee of.	Indemnity for French spoliations prior to 1800.	26	1	Memorial	182	Foreign Affairs	343	Favorable bill.	319	Referred to Committee Whole House.		
Carter, Josiah	Pension under act March 18, 1818.	15	2	Petition	160	Rev. Pensions.						
Carter, Landon, heirs of	Payment of an unliquidated loan office certificate for $500.	14	2	Senate bill	107	Pens. & Rev. Cl'ms.	Jan. 2, 1817	With amends.	1	Laid on table.		

List of private claims presented to the House of Representatives of the United States from the 1st to the 31st Congress, inclusive—Continued.

Names of claimants.	Nature or object of the claim.	Congress.	Session.	How brought before the House of Reps.	Page of journal.	To what committee of the House referred.	No. or date of the report.	Nature of the report.	No. of the bill.	How disposed of by the House of Reps.	How disposed of by the Senate.	Date of the act of Congress, and remarks.
Carter, Landon, heirs of..	Payment of an unliquidated loan office certificate for $500.	15	1	Senate bill.....	68	Pens. & Rev. Cl'ms.	April 4, 1818	With amends.	1	Indefinite postponed.		
Carter, Landon N.......	Payment of rent for quarters as lieutenant of marines.	24	1	Petition	139	Naval Affairs.....	420	Adverse	......	Referred to Committee Whole House.		
Carter, Mansfield	Compensation for services as blacksmith to Sacs and Fox Indians.	31	1	Senate bill	970	Indian Affairs.....	Jan. 29, 1851 (2d sess.)	With't amend.	171	Passed	Passed	App'd March 3, 1851
Carter, Margaret, & others, of Illinois.	(See Bennet Belew, heirs of.)											
Carter, Mary	Pension for revolutionary services of husband.	28	1	Petition	950	Whole House on bill No. 7.	....	....	......	....	....	See act June 17, 1844
Carter, Nathaniel, widow of.	Pension for husband who died in United States naval service.	18	1	Petition	88	Naval Affairs	Dec. 30, 1823	Report and res. to refer to commis'ners naval pension fund.	......	Resolution adopted.		
Carter, Nathaniel, widow of.	Pension for husband who died in United States naval service.	22	1	Petition	187	Naval Affairs.						
Carter, Nathaniel, widow of.	Renewal of pension heretofore granted.	23	1	Petition........	213	Naval Affairs.						
Carter, Nathaniel, widow of.	Renewal of pension heretofore granted.	28	1	Petition	61	Naval Affairs.						
Carter, Nathaniel, widow of.	Renewal of pension heretofore granted.	29	2	Petition	74	Rev. Pensions.						
Carter, Randolph........	Pension for services and wounds in engagements with the Indians under Wayne.	25	2	Petition	84	Invalid Pensions .	229	Report and bill.	267	Passed	Adverse report.	
Carter, Randolph........	Pension for services and wounds in engagements with the Indians under Wayne.	25	3	Petition........	461	Invalid Pensions...	292	Report and bill.	1156	Referred to Committee Whole House.		
Carter, Randolph........	Pension for services and wounds in engagements with the Indians under Wayne.	26	1	Petition........	161	Invalid Pensions.						
Carter, Randolph........	Pension for services and wounds in engagements with the Indians under Wayne.	26	2	Petition........	148	Invalid Pensions...	94	Report and bill.	600	Referred to Committee Whole House.		
Carter, Randolph........	Pension for services and wounds in engagements with the Indians under Wayne.	27	2	Petition	97	Invalid Pensions ..	131	Report and bill.	177	Passed	Passed	App'd Aug. 26, 1842
Carter, Reuben, (Ohio) ..	Pension	20	2	Petition	64	Military Pensions..	Feb. 13, 1829	By bill	440	Passed	Reported with't amendment.	
Carter, Reuben, (Ohio) ..	Pension.....................	21	1	Petition	49	Military Pensions..	Jan. 5, 1830	By bill	72	Passed	Passed	App'd May 20, 1830
Carter, Robert	Grant of land as further compensation for services as an officer in the war of 1812.	22	2	Petition	30	Public Lands......	....	....	......	Discharged; laid on table.		
Carter, Rrbert B., administrator of.	Settlement of accounts of deceased and others for army supplies in war of 1812, and participation in proceeds of contracts entered into by James Roddy and dec'd.	23	2	Petitions.......	275, 447	Claims	Feb. 28, 1835	Rep. & res. to refer to 3d Auditor.	......	Resolution adopted.		
Carter, Robert B., administrator of.	Settlement of accounts of deceased and others for army supplies in war of 1812, and participation in proceeds of contracts entered into by James Roddy and dec'd.	24	1	Report of Third Auditor.	69	Claims.						

List of private claims presented to the House of Representatives of the United States from the 1st to the 31st Congress, inclusive—Continued.

Names of claimants.	Nature or object of the claim.	Congress.	Session.	How brought before the House of Reps.	Page of journal.	To what committee of the House referred.	No. or date of the report.	Nature of the report.	No. of the bill.	How disposed of by the House of Reps.	How disposed of by the Senate.	Date of the act of Congress, and remarks.
Carter, Robert B., administrator of.	Settlement of accounts of deceased and others for army supplies in war of 1812, and participation in proceeds of contracts entered into by James Roddy and dec'd.	27	2	Petition	56	Claims.						
Carter, Robert B., administrator of.	Settlement of accounts of deceased and others for army supplies in war of 1812, and participation in proceeds of contracts entered into by James Roddy and dec'd.	27	3	Petition	73	Claims	128	Report and bill	750	Referred to Committee Whole House.	....	Feb. 27, 1843; House directed Sec. Treas. to state the accounts.
Carter, Robert B., administrator of.	Settlement of accounts of deceased and others for army supplies in war of 1812, and participation in proceeds of contracts entered into by James Roddy and dec'd.	28	1	Rep. of Secretary of Treasury.	408	Claims.						
Caster, Samuel, and Ransom McElroy.	Pre-emption right to land on which they reside.	23	1	Petition	332	Public Lands	318	Adverse	......	Laid on table.		
Carter, Samuel, (Fla.)	Compensation for mare lost in U. S. service.	26	1	Petition	621	Claims	682	Adverse	......	Laid on table.		
Carter, Seth	Revolutionary pension	20	1	Petition	223	Military Pensions	Feb. 13, 1828	By bill	166	Passed	Referred and Com. dis.	
Carter, Seth	Revolutionary pension	20	2	House bill	55	Whole House	Jan. 15, 1829	Favorable	311	Passed	Laid on table.	
Carter, Seth	Revolutionary pension	21	1	Petition	116	Military Pensions	April 13, 1830	Adverse	......	Laid on table.		
Carter, Seth	Revolutionary pension	22	1	Petition	68	Rev. Pensions	Dec. 28, 1831	Adverse	......	Laid on table.		
Carter, Stanly	Revolutionary pension	27	2	Petition	374	Rev. Pensions	784	Adverse	......	Laid on table.		
Carter. Stephen	Invalid pension	12	1	House bill	361	Whole House	June 15, 1812	Favorable	138	Passed	Passed	App'd July 5, 1812
Carter, Thomas, (Va.) heirs of.	Additional compensation for services as surgeon in revolutionary war.	25	2	Senate bill	605	Rev. Claims	Mar. 22, 1838	With't amend.	136	Passed	Passed	App'd May 25, 1838
Carter, Thomas, (Va.) heirs of.	Interest on half pay allowed him	26	1	Petition	361	Rev. Claims.						
Carter, Thomas, (Va.) heirs of.	Interest on half-pay allowed him	26	2	Petition	35	Rev. Claims.						
Carter, Thomas, (Va.) heirs of.	Interest on half pay allowed him	27	2	Petition	470	Rev. Claims	529	Adverse	......	Laid on table.		
Carter, Thomas, (Maine)	Arrears of pension as a soldier in war of 1812.	25	3	Petition	219	Invalid Pensions.						
Carter, Thomas, (Mass.)	Indemnity for French spoliations prior to 1800.	26	1	Memorial	182	Foreign Affairs	343	Favorable; bill	319	Referred to Committee Whole House.		
Carter, William, executors of.	Patent for 6,000 acres of land located in Ohio by Virginia military warrant No. 4,569.	8	1	Petition	489	Select.						
Carter, William, executors of.	Patent for 6,000 acres of land located in Ohio by Virginia military warrant No. 4,569.	8	2	Petition	14	Claims.						
Carter, William, executors of.	Patent for 6,000 acres of land located in Ohio by Virginia military warrant No. 4,569.	9	1	Petition	193	Public Lands	April 14, 1806	Indef. postp'd.	......	Laid on table.		
Carter, William, executors of.	Patent for 6,000 acres of land located in Ohio by Virginia military warrant No. 4,569.	9	2	Petition	480	Public Lands.						
Carter, William	Pension	14	2	Resolution	209	Pens. & Rev. Cl'ms.	Jan. 29, 1817	By bill	91	Passed	Passed	App'd March 3, 1817

List of private claims presented to the House of Representatives of the United States from the 1st to the 31st Congress, inclusive—Continued.

Names of claimants.	Nature or object of the claim.	Congress.	Session.	How brought before the House of Reps.	Page of journal.	To what committee of the House referred.	No. or date of the report.	Nature of the report.	No. of the bill.	How disposed of by the House of Reps.	How disposed of by the Senate.	Date of the act of Congress, and remarks.
Carter, William (N. C.)	Relief from an act of the Territorial Legislature of Florida, depriving him of wife, children, and property.	20	2	Petition	319	Judiciary				Discharged; laid on table.		
Carter, William, heirs of	Five years' full pay for services as surgeon in revolutionary army.	21	1	Petition	98	Rev. Claims	332	Report and bill	391	Referred to Committee Whole House.		
Carter, William, heirs of	Five years' full pay for services as surgeon in revolutionary army.	22	1	Petition	51	Rev. Claims	56	Report and bill	107	Passed	Passed	App'd May 25, 1832
Carter, William B	(See James Carter, heir of.)											
Carter, William B., heirs of.	Relief in consideration of his death in U. States service, war of 1812.	14	2	Senate bill	534					Laid on table.		
Carter, William B., widow of.	Bounty land for services, war of 1812.	16	1	Petition	235	Priv. Land Claims.				Discharged; laid on table.		
Carter, William B., widow of.	Bounty land for services, war of 1812.	18	1	Petition	156	Pens. & Rev. Cl'ms.				Discharged; laid on table.		
Carter, William B., widow of.	Bounty land for services, war of 1812.	19	1	Petition	62	Claims	Jan. 9, 1826	Adverse		Laid on table.		
Carteret, John	(See Joseph Snelling and others).	5	3		452							
Carteret, John	Balance due for services in Commissary's Department at Boston, in revolutionary war.	10	1	Petition	17	Select.						
Carthy, John	Payment of a lost certificate for supplies furnished the United States in 1781.	6	1	Petition	636	Claims	May 1, 1800	Adverse		Rejected.		
Cartmell, Joseph, mother of.	Compensation for his maintenance while disabled by injuries received as an artificer in U. States service.	23	2	Petition	115	Military Affairs.				Discharged; laid on table.		
Carty, Mary	Compensation for horse lost by her son, who was killed at Buena Vista.	30	1	Petition	147	Claims	238	Report and bill.	238	Referred to Committee Whole House.		
Carusi, Gætano	Provision for return of himself and family to Italy, per contract.	21	2	Petition	81	Naval Affairs	Feb. 4, 1831	Adverse		Laid on table.		
Carusi, Gætano	Provision for his return to Italy and compensation as leader of marine band.	22	1	Petition	54	Claims.						
Carusi, Gætano	Provision for return of himself and family to Italy, per contract.	22	2	Petition	123	Naval Affairs.						
Carusi, Gætano	Provision for return of himself and family to Italy, per contract.	23	1	Petition	56	Naval Affairs	180	Report and bill.	198	Recommitted.		
Carusi, Gætano	Provision for return of himself and family to Italy, per contract	23	1	Petition	59	Naval Affairs.	May 2, 1834	Bill, with am't	198	Referred to Committee Whole House.		
Carusi, Gætano	Provision for return of himself and family to Italy, per contract.	24	1	Petition	61	Naval Affairs	86	Rep. and bill.	102	Passed.	Laid on table.	
Carusi, Gætano	Provision for return of himself and family to Italy, per contract.	24	2	Petition	46	Naval Affairs.						
Carusi, Gætano	Compensation as instructor to U. States band of music.	26	1	Petition	622	Claims.						
Carusi, Gætano	Compensation as instructor to U. States band of music.	29	1	Petition	146	Naval Affairs	745	Adverse		Laid on table		Leave to withdraw, 2d sess., 30th Cong.
Caruthers, Richard E	(See Wm. Findley, executors of.)											
Caruthers, Wilson T	(See Thomas Rhodes and others.)											
Caruthers, Wilson T	(See Walker, Kinkle, and others).	25	2		301							
Carver, Benjamin	(See Wm. H. Bedford, agent, &c.)	28	1		262							

List of private claims presented to the House of Representatives of the United States from the 1st to the 31st Congress, inclusive—Continued.

Names of claimants.	Nature or object of the claim.	Congress.	Session.	How brought before the House of Reps.	Page of journal.	To what committee of the House referred.	No. or date of the report.	Nature of the report.	No. of the bill.	How disposed of by the House of Reps.	How disposed of by the Senate.	Date of the act of Congress, and remarks.
Carver, Elial	Compensation as surveyor of lands in Louisiana.	24	1	Resolution	636	Claims	616	Adverse		Laid on table.		
Carver, Hiram	Increase of compensation as postmaster at Providence, Va.	18	2	Petition	184	P. Of. and P. Roads.				Discharged; laid on table.		
Carver, Jonathan	Confirmation of title to land near falls of St. Anthony.	17	1	Resolution and Pres. Message.	192, 493	Public Lands				Discharged; laid on table.		
Carver, Jonathan	Confirmation of title to land near falls of St. Anthony.	18	1	Petition	48	Priv. Land Claims.				Discharged; laid on table.		
Carver, Jonathan, daughter of.	Confirmation of title to land and recovery of estate in America.	18	1	Petition	252	Public Lands				Discharged; laid on table.		
Carver, Jonathan, assignee of.	Confirmation of title to land near falls of St. Anthony.	18	2	Petition	74	Priv. Land Claims.	44	Adverse		Referred to Committee Whole House.		
Carver, Jonathan, heir of.	Confirmation of title to land near falls of St. Anthony.	31	1	Petition	545	Priv. Land Claims.						
Carver, Nathan	(See John M. Grant, administrator of.)	15	1		371							
Carver, Nathan	Indemnity for property lost in United States service, war of 1812.	22	1	Petition	387	Claims	342	Report and bill.	439	Referred to 3d Auditor.		
Carver, Nathan	Compensation for use of house by United States troops in 1814, and damages to his property.	23	1	Petition	80	Claims.						
Carver, Nathan, widow of.	Compensation for medical services and for property lost in war of 1812.	29	2	Petition	352	Claims.						
Carver, Nathan, widow of.	Compensation for medical services and for property lost in war of 1812.	30	1	Petition	68	Claims.						
Carver, Nathan, widow of.	Compensation for medical services and for property lost in war of 1812.	30	2	Petition	76	Claims	39	Report and bill.	729	Referred to Committee Whole House.		
Carver, Nathan, widow of.	Compensation for medical services and for property lost in war of 1812.	31	1	Petition	486	Claims	152	Report and bill.	170	Referred to Committee Whole House.		
Carver, Nathan, widow of.	Compensation for medical services and for property lost in war of 1812.	31	2	Bill of last sess.	103	Whole House	Jan. 3, 1851	With't amend.	170	Passed	Ref. to Com. Claims.	
Carver, Nathaniel	Fishing bounty on vessel and cargo lost at sea.	16	2	Petition	203	Commerce	Feb. 20, 1821	By bill	259	Referred to Committee Whole House.		
Carver, Nathaniel	Fishing bounty on vessel and cargo lost at sea.	17	1	Petition	45	Commerce	Jan. 17, 1822	By bill	43	Passed	Indef. postp'd.	
Carver, Nathaniel	Fishing bounty on vessel and cargo lost at sea.	17	2	Petition	43	Commerce	Jan. 21, 1823	By bill	241	Referred to Committee Whole House.		
Carver, Nathaniel	Fishing bounty on vessel and cargo lost at sea.	18	1	Petition	30	Commerce	Dec. 23, 1823	By bill	22	Passed	Passed	App'd Jan. 19, 1824
Carver, Rufus	Compensation for services in revolutionary war.	19	2	Petition	240	Rev. Claims				Discharged.		
Cary, Barnabas	Pension as a soldier in war of 1812.	25	3	Petition	128	Invalid Pensions.						
Cary, Barnabas	Pension as a soldier in war of 1812.	27	2	Petition	130	Invalid Pensions	430	Adverse		Laid on table.		
Cary, Barnabas	Pension as a soldier in war of 1812.	28	1	Petition	122	Invalid Pensions.						

List of private claims presented to the House of Representatives of the United States from the 1st to the 31st Congress, inclusive—Continued.

Names of claimants.	Nature or object of the claim.	Congress.	Session.	How brought before the House of Reps.	Page of journal.	To what committee of the House referred.	No. or date of the report.	Nature of the report.	No. of the bill.	How disposed of by the House of Reps.	How disposed of by the Senate.	Date of the act of Congress, and remarks.
Cary, Christopher	Pension	20	1	Petition	310	Military Pensions	April 29, 1828	By bill	283	Passed	Ref'd, & com. discharged.	
Cary, Christopher	Pension	20	2	House bill	55	Whole House	Jan. 15, 1829	Favorable	311	Passed	Laid on table.	
Cary, Christopher	Pension	21	1	Petition	47	Military Pensions	Jan. 5, 1830	By bill	72	Passed	Passed	App'd May 20, 1830
Cary, Elnathan	(See Joseph Pierce, heirs of, &c.)											
Cary, John, (Pa.)	Compensation for services and injuries in revolutionary war.	3	1	Petition and rep't Sec'y of War.	39	Select.						
Cary, John, (Pa.)	Invalid pension	3	1	Rep. of Secretary War.	131	Select	May 26, 1794	Favorable; bill ordered.	62	Passed	Passed	App'd June 7, 1794
Cary, John, (Pa.)	Revolutionary pension	19	2	Resolution	69	Military Pensions.						
Carey, John, heirs of, (N. Y.)	Location of bounty land in Illinois	24	1	Petition	409	Public Lands.						
Carey, John, heirs of, (N. Y.)	Location of bounty land in Illinois	24	2	Documents	390	Public Lands.						
Carey, John, heirs of, (N. Y.)	Location of bounty land in Illinois	25	2	Petition	233	Public Lands	595	Adverse		Laid on table.		
Cary, John, (colored)	Pension as a servant to General Washington in revolut'ary war.	27	3	Resolution	218	Rev. Pensions	133	Report and bill.	755	Passed	Indef. postp'd.	
Cary, John P., representatives of, (Georgia.)	Allowance for payments to officers and soldiers rejected by the Treasury.	17	1	Petition	110	Claims.						
Cary, John P., representatives of, (Georgia.)	Allowance for payments to officers and soldiers rejected by the Treasury.	17	2	Petition	95, 150	Claims	Jan. 31, 1823	Adverse		Laid on table		Leave to withdraw.
Cary, John P., representatives of, (Georgia.)	Allowance for payments to officers and soldiers rejected by the Treasury.	20	1	Petition	279	Claims	153	Adverse		Referred to Committee Whole House.		
Cary, John P., representatives of, (Georgia.)	Allowance for payments to officers and soldiers rejected by the Treasury.	20	2	Report, former	115	Whole House.						
Carey, Joseph	(See Thomas Williams and Joseph Carey.)											
Cary, Joseph H.	Revolutionary pension	21	2	Resolution	70	Military Pensions				Discharged.		
Carey, Matthew	Exonerated from payment of duties on books, maps, and charts exported.	9	1	Petition	308	Com. and Manuf.						
Carey, Samuel	Relief for losses and injuries sustained, and services rendered, in revolutionary war.	3	1	Petition	71					Referred to Secretary of War.		
Carey, Samuel	Relief for losses and injuries sustained, and services rendered, in revolutionary war.	3	2	Rep. of Secretary War.	278					Laid on table.		
Caryl, Benjamin	(See Lucius Storrs and others.)											
Casbott, Robert	Pension	22	1	Petition	329	Rev. Pensions.						
Case, A. Ludlow	(See Exploring Expedition.)											
Case, Henry	Patent for land in Indiana	20	1	Senate bill	746	Public Lands	May 24, 1828	With't amend.	148	Referred to Committee Whole House.		
Case, Henry	Patent for land in Indiana	20	2	Senate bill	94	Priv. Land Claims	Jan. 12, 1829	Adverse	11	Laid on table.		
Case, James, (Vt.,) widow of.	Continuation of pension	24	2	Petition	271	Rev. Pensions	222	Report and bill.	929	Referred to Committee Whole House.		

List of private claims presented to the House of Representatives of the United States from the 1st to the 31st Congress, inclusive—Continued.

37

Names of claimants.	Nature or object of the claim.	Congress.	Session.	How brought before the House of Reps.	Page of journal.	To what committee of the House referred.	No. or date of the report	Nature of the report.	No. of the bill.	How disposed of by the House of Reps.	How disposed of by the Senate.	Date of the act of Congress, and remarks.
Case, James, (Vt.,) widow of.	Continuation of pension	25	2	Petition	37	Rev. Pensions	177	Report and bill.	202	Passed	Adverse report.	
Case, James, (Vt.,) widow of.	Continuation of pension	26	1	Petition	171	Rev. Pensions	140	Report and bill.	150	Passed	Indef. postp'd.	
Case, Joseph	Pension for wounds received in war of 1812.	19	1	Resolution	147	Military Pensions	164	Adverse		Laid on table.		
Case, Loudon	Compensation for oxen impressed in United States service, war of 1812.	17	1	Petition	233	Claims	March 8, 1822	Report and bill.	110	Passed	Rejected.	
Case, Loudon	Compensation for oxen impressed in United States service, war of 1812.	17	2	Petition	86	Claims	Jan. 20, 1823	Report and bill.	240	Referred to Committee Whole House.		
Case, Loudon	Compensation for oxen impressed in United States service, war of 1812.	18	1	Petition	75	Claims	Dec. 22, 1823	By bill	19	Passed	Passed	App'd Jan. 7, 1824
Case, Solomon	Pension	23	2	Resolution	205	Invalid Pensions	80	Report and bill.	700	Passed	Passed	App'd March 3, 1835
Case, William	Invalid pension	3	1	Rep. of Secretary War.	131	Select	May 26, 1794	Ref. to Secretary, with instructions.	R. 12	Passed	Passed	App'd June 9, 1794
Casety, James	Indemnity for sufferings and loss of property as a Canadian refugee in revolutionary war.	15	1	Petition	371	Claims				Discharged.		
Casey, John	Invalid pension	23	1	Petition	249	Invalid Pensions	282	Report and bill.	319	Referred to Committee Whole House.		
Casey, John	Invalid pension	23	2	Bill of last sess.	336	Whole House	Feb. 6, 1835	With't amend.	319	Passed	Passed am'd.	Laid on table in House.
Casey, John	Invalid pension	24	1	Petition	151	Invalid Pensions	330	Report and bill.	345	Passed	Indef. postp'd.	
Casey, John	Invalid pension	24	2	Petition	212	Invalid Pensions	Feb. 24, 1837	By bill	878	Referred to Committee Whole House.		
Casey, John	Invalid pension	25	2	Petition	38	Invalid Pensions	461	Report and bill.	464	Passed	Adverse report.	
Casey, John	Invalid pension	26	1	Petition	385	Rev. Pensions	664	Adverse		Laid on table.		
Casey, Robert	Pension as a soldier in war of 1812.	25	2	Petition	56	Invalid Pensions	318	Report and bill.	360	Passed	Passed	App'd June 28, 1838
Casey, Robert	Bounty land and extra pay for services in war of 1812.	25	3	Petition	132	Priv. Land Claims.	166	Adverse		Laid on table.		
Casey, Robert	Bounty land and extra pay for services in war of 1812.	26	1	Petition	278	Priv. Land Claims.	450	Report and bill.	362	Referred to Committee Whole House.		
Casey, William	Increase of pension for revolutionary services.	28	1	Petition	296	Rev. Pensions.						
Cash, David	(See Giles U. Ellis.)											
Casler, Nicholas	Expenses incurred in suit in United States court in New York.	31	1	Petition	971	Claims.						
Casper, David	Pension as a soldier in war of 1812.	31	1	Petition	1269	Invalid Pensions.						
Cass, Jonas	Relief—land sold for direct tax	15	1	Petition	132	Ways and Means				Discharged.		
Cass, Moses	Invalid pension	3	1	Rep. of Secretary War.	131	Select	May 26, 1794	Favorable; bill ordered.	62	Passed	Passed	App'd June 7, 1794
Cassady, George, (Pa.)	Increase of pension as a soldier in war 1812.	25	2	Petition	699	Invalid Pensions	July 2, 1838	By bill	871	Referred to Committee Whole House.		
Cassady, George, (Pa.)	Increase of pension as a soldier in war 1812.	25	3	Bill of last sess'n.	432	Whole House	Feb. 1, 1839	With't amend.	871	Passed	Adversely reported on.	
Cassady, George, (Pa.)	Increase of pension as a soldier in war 1812.	26	1	Petition	161	Invalid Pensions	412	Adverse		Laid on table.		
Cassady, George, (Pa.)	Increase of pension as a soldier in war 1812.	27	2	Petition	219	Invalid Pensions	440	Adverse		Laid on table.		

List of private claims presented to the House of Representatives of the United States from the 1st to the 31st Congress, inclusive—Continued.

Names of claimants.	Nature or object of the claim.	Congress.	Session.	How brought before the House of Reps.	Page of journal.	To what committee of the House referred.	No. or date of the report.	Nature of the report.	No. of the bill.	How disposed of by the House of Reps.	How disposed of by the Senate.	Date of the act of Congress, and remarks.
Cassady, George, (Ohio)	Pension for disability by fall from his horsee while at drill.	30	1	Petition	264	Invalid Pensions	577	Adverse		Laid on table.		
Cassady, George, (Ohio)	Pension for disability by fall from his horse while at drill.	30	2	Petition	118	Invalid Pensions				Discharged; laid on table.		
Cassady, George, (Ohio)	Pension for disability by fall from his horse while at drill.	31	1	Petition	276, 424	Invalid Pensions	47	Report and bill.	77	Passed	Rep. on without amend't.	
Cassady, John	Compensation for injuries incurred for reporting misconduct of naval constructor Barker.	28	2	Petition	337	Naval Affairs.						
Cassady, John	Compensation for injuries incurred for reporting misconduct of naval constructor Barker.	30	1	Petition	939	Naval Affairs.						
Cassady, John	Compensation for injuries incurred for reporting misconduct of naval constructor Barker.	31	2	Petition	173	Naval Affairs.						
Cassanova, Gabriel	Confirmation of title to land in Louisiana.	22	1	Petition	64	Priv. Land Claims.	62	Report and bill.	125	Passed	Passed	App'd July 25, 1832
Cassanova, Juan	Confirmation of title to land in Louisiana.	22	1	Petition	64	Priv. Land Claims.	62	Report and bill.	125	Passed	Passed	App'd July 25, 1832
Cassedy, Charles	Compensation for services as clerk to United States land commissioner, Coffee, in 1814.	21	1	Rep. of Secretary War.	602	Claims	394	Report and bill.	460	Referred to Committee Whole House.		
Cassedy, Charles	Compensarion for services as clerk to United States land commissioner, Coffee, in 1814.	22	1	Petition	43	Claims	Dec. 19, 1831	By bill	28	Passed	Passed	App'd Jan. 18, 1832
Cassell, Henry R	Pre-emption right to tract of land.	24	1	Petition	154	Public Lands				Discharged; laid on table.		
Cassell, Henry R	Pre-emption right to tract of land.	24	2	Petition	95	Public Lands.						
Cassell, Michael	Land in lieu of a tract entered by mistake.	25	2	Senate bill	639	Public Lands.	Mar. 28, 1838	With't amend.	103	Passed	Passed	App'd April 4, 1838
Cassety, Mathew W	Release as surety for J. French, postmaster at Pomfret, N. Y.	19	1	Petition	363	P. Of. and P. Roads.						
Cassin, Patrick, widow and administratrix of.	Payment of certificates, held by her, issued to soldiers in war of 1812.	16	1	Petitions	271, 312	Claims				Discharged; laid on table.		
Cassin, Patrick, widow and administratrix of.	Payment of certificates, held by her, issued to soldiers in war of 1812.	16	1	Senate bill	309	Claims	Mar. 17, 1820	With't amend.	54	Passed	Passed	App'd April 5, 1820
Casso, Peter	Payment for groceries furnished sick soldiers, in the revolutionary war.	11	3	Petition	510	Select.						
Casson, Philip	Invalid pension	4	2	Rep. of Secretary War.	651	Claims	Feb. 6, 1797	Favorable; bill ordered.	224	Passed	Postponed to next session.	
Casson, Philip	Invalid pension	5	2	House bill	127	Whole House	Jan. 11, 1798	Favorable	38	Passed	Passed	App'd Feb. 2, 1798
Cassont, Antoine, heirs of.	Land and money due from Virginia, for services in Clark's regiment revolutianary war.	26	1	Resolution	359	Rev. Claims.						
Casteel, David	Payment for a rifle gun impressed in United States service.	20	1	Resolution	382	Claims	Mar. 19, 1828	Adverse		Laid on table.		
Casteel, David	Payment for a rifle gun impressed in United States service.	21	1	Petition	201	Claims	Feb. 24, 1830	Adverse		Laid on table.		
Casteline, Loammi, widow of.	Pension for revolutionary services.	28	1	Petition	754	Rev. Pensions.						

List of private claims presented to the House of Representatives of the United States from the 1st to the 31st Congress, inclusive—Continued.

Names of claimants.	Nature or object of the claim.	Congress.	Session.	How brought before the House of Reps.	Page of journal.	To what committee of the House referred.	No. or date of the report.	Nature of the report.	No. of the bill.	How disposed of by the House of Reps.	How disposed of by the Senate.	Date of the act of Congress, and remarks.
Casten, Samuel, heir of	Pension for revolutionary services	31	1	Petition	234	Rev. Claims.						
Castille, John	Discharge from imprisonment at suit of United States.	13	2	Petition	297	Ways and Means	April 5, 1814	By bill	182	Referred to Committee Whole House.		
Castille, John	Discharge from imprisonment at suit of United States.	13	3	Petition	486	Ways and Means	210	Report and bill.	210	Passed	Passed	App'd Dec. 1, 1814
Castle, Anthony	Pension for services in war of 1812	31	2	Petition	106	Invalid Pensions.						
Castleman, John	Compensation for services as captain in revolutionary war.	4	1	Petition	423	Claims	May 7, 1796	Adverse	......	Laid on table.		
Castor, Vincent	Revolutionary pension	21	2	Resolution	56	Military Pensions	....	....	......	Disch'd ; laid on table.		
Castor, Vincent	Revolutionary pension	22	1	Petition	105	Rev. Pensions	....	....	......	Discharged ; laid on table.		
Caswell, Richard G	Pension for injuries received in service of United States at navy-yard.	31	1	Petition	432	Invalid Pensions	392	To be disch'ed.	......	Laid on table.		
Caswell, Richard G	Pension for injuries received in service of United States at navy-yard.	31	2	Petition	74	Invalid Pensions.						
Caswell, Simeon	Pension as a soldier in war of 1812	27	2	Petition	91	Invalid Pensions	234	Adverse	......	Laid on table.		
Caswell, Simeon	Pension as a soldier in war of 1812	28	1	Petition	143	Invalid Pensions	98	Report and bill	114	Passed	Adverse report: indef. post'd.	
Caswell, Simeon	Pension as a soldier in war of 1812	29	1	Petition	227	Invalid Pensions	509	To be disch'ed.	......	Laid on table.		
Catalona, Salvadore	Compensation for piloting ketch Intrepid in harbor of Tripoli.	9	1	Petition	194	Claims	Dec. 31, 1805	Leave to withdraw.	......	Report adopted.		
Catalona, Salvadore	$1,297 for chamber money while sailing master in United States navy.	19	1	Petition	52	Naval Affairs	Feb. 9, 1826	Adverse	......	Laid on table.		
Catalona, Salvadore	$1,297 for chamber money while sailing master in United States navy.	22	2	Petition	137	Naval Affairs.						
Catalona, Salvadore	$1,297 for chamber money while sailing master in United States navy.	23	1	Petition	132	Naval Affairs.						
Catalona, Salvadore	$1,297 for chamber money while sailing master in United States navy.	23	2	Petition	86	Naval Affairs.						
Catalona, Salvadore	$1,297 for chamber money while sailing master in United States navy.	24	1	Petition	214	Naval Affairs	325	Adverse	......	Laid on table.		
Catalona, Salvadore	(See Stephen Decatur, widow of, and others.)											
Catching, Harriet L	Relinquishment of a judgment of United States court for district of Mississippi.	29	1	Senate bill	1075	Judiciary	July 24, 1846	With't amend.	114	Passed	Passed	App'd July 29, 1846
Catching, Silas M	Refunding of money paid to a land officer by mistake.	26	1	Petition	608	Public Lands	....	....	......	Discharged ; laid on table.		
Cates, Thomas	Compensation for services as a soldier in revolutionary army.	12	1	Petition	22	Claims.						
Cathcart, James L., by agent.	Remission of duties on an American vessel.	12	1	Petition	361	Com. and Manuf.						
Cathcart, James Leander	Payment for services and reimbursement of money expended for other American captives in Algiers.	15	1	Petition	426	....	....	....	......	Referred to Secretary State.		

List of private claims presented to the House of Representatives of the United States from the 1st to the 31st Congress, inclusive—Continued.

Names of claimants.	Nature or object of the claim.	Congress.	Session.	How brought before the House of Reps.	Page of journal.	To what committee of the House referred.	No. or date of the report.	Nature of the report.	No. of the bill.	How disposed of by the House of Reps.	How disposed of by the Senate.	Date of the act of Congress, and remarks.
Cathcart, James Leander..	Payment for services and reimbursement of money expended for other American captives in Algiers.	16	1	Petition, and rep't of Sec. State.	28, 45	Claims..........	Feb. 4, 1820	Adverse	.....	Leave to withdraw.		
Cathcart, James Leander..	Payment for services and reimbursement of money expended for other American captives in Algiers.	16	1	Senate bill	492	Claims..........	May 10, 1820	With't amend.	114	Passed	Passed	App'd May 15, 1820
Cathcart, James Leander..	An act explanatory, allowing claim as stated by himself.	16	2	Senate bill	174	Claims..........	Feb. 28, 1821	With't amend.	22	Referred to Committee Whole House.		
Cathcart, James Leander..	An act explanatory, allowing claim as stated by himself.	17	1	Senate bill	103	Claims..........	Mar. 7, 1822	With amend..	5	Passed	Passed	App'd May 8, 1822
Cathcart, James Leander..	Payment in full satisfaction of all his claims against the U. States.	24	1	Senate bill	1077	Foreign Affairs....	July 1, 1836	With't amend.	213	Passed	Passed	App'd July 2, 1836
Cathell, H. P..........	(See William Harris and others)..	20	1	....	51							
Cation, James	Pension.....................	16	1	Petition and rep't of Sec. War.	284	....	....	....	......	Laid on table.		
Catlett, Charles J.......	Compensation for tobacco taken for military breastwork in war of 1812.	20	2	Petition	27	Claims..........	....	....	......	Discharged; laid on table.		
Catlett, Charles J.......	Compensation for tobacco taken for military breastwork in war of 1812.	22	1	Petition	195	Claims..........	413	Adverse	......	Laid on table.		
Catlett, Charles J.......	Compensation for tobacco taken for military breastwork in war of 1812.	24	1	Senate bill	1097	Claims..........	June 28, 1836	With't amend.	95	Passed	Passed	App'd July 2, 1836
Catlett, Charles J.......	Compensation for property taken by British forces at Alexandria, Va., war of 1812.	23	1	Petition	59	Claims..........	....	....	......	Discharged; leave to withdraw.		
Catlett, Hanson, surg'n U. S. army.	Compensa'n for negro slave drowned while in service, war of 1812.	15	2	Petition	117	Claims..........	....	....	......	Discharged; laid on table.		
Catlett, Hanson, widow of.	Reimbursement of amount paid for hospital steward at Pittsburg, from June, 1816, to January, 1820.	20	1	Petition	164	Claims..........	Feb. 11, 1828	Adverse	......	Laid on table	....	Leave to withdraw.
Catlett, Hanson, widow of.	Reimbursement of amount paid for hospital steward at Pittsburg, from June, 1816, to January, 1820.	21	2	Petition	45	Claims..........	47	Report and bill.	576	Referred to Committee Whole House.		
Catlett, Hanson, widow of.	Reimbursement of amount paid for hospital steward at Pittsburg, from June, 1816, to January, 1820.	22	1	Petition	43	Claims..........	Dec. 19, 1831	By bill	37	Passed............	Passed	App'd Feb. 24, 1832
Catlett, James	Compensation for negro and horse impressed by United States in Pennsylvania rebellion.	4	1	Petition	486	Claims..........	May 31, 1796	Adverse	......	Laid on table.		
Catlett, Peter, widow of..	Compensation for services as an officer in revolutionary war.	25	2	Petition	181	Rev. Pensions.....	....	....	......	Discharged; laid on table.		
Catlett, Peter, widow of..	Compensation for services as an officer in revolutionary war.	26	1	Petition	173, 385	Rev. Pensions.....	664	Adverse	......	Laid on table	....	Leave to withdraw, 2d session, 30th Cong.
Catlin, George	Exemption of duties on certain books published by him in London.	27	2	Petition	327	Ways and Means..	636	Adverse	......	Laid on table.		

List of private claims presented to the House of Representatives of the United States from the 1st to the 31st Congress, inclusive—Continued.

Names of claimants.	Nature or object of the claim.	Congress.	Session.	How brought before the House of Reps.	Page of journal.	To what committee of the House referred.	No. or date of the report.	Nature of the report.	No. of the bill.	How disposed of by the House of Reps.	How disposed of by the Senate.	Date of the act of Congress, and remarks.
Catlin, Peoples & Co....	Compensation for Creek Indian depredations.	26	1	Petition	623	Claims.						
Catlin, Peoples & Co....	Compensation for Creek Indian depredations.	29	1	Petition	630	Indian Affairs.						
Catlin, Peoples & Co....	Compensation for Creek Indian depredations.	31	1	Petition	191	Indian Affairs.						
Catner, Philip	To exchange land located by mistake.	25	2	Petition	661	Public Lands.						
Catner, Philip	To exchange land located by mistake.	25	3	Petition	93	Public Lands	155	Report and bill.	1022	Passed	Passed	App'd March 3, 1839
Caton, Benjamin, (Mo.)..	(See Reuben E. Gentry, & others.)											
Caton, Charles W., dec'd, by William.	Payment of amount as a seaman U. S. navy.	23	1	Petition	304	Claims	322	Adverse	......	Laid on table.		
Caton, Richard, sureties of	Remission of interest on bond....	8	2	Rep. of Secretary Treasury.	132	Com. and Manuf.						
Caton, Richard, sureties of	Remission of interest on bond....	9	1	Petition	191	Com. and Manuf..	Feb. 11, 1806	Favorable, in part, bill.	104	Referred to Committee Whole House.		
Caton, Richard..........	(See Joshua Harvey, and others.)											
Caton, Richard..........	Indemnity for French spoliations prior to 1800.	26	1	Memorial	182	Foreign Affairs....	343	Favorable; bill	319	Referred to Committee Whole House.		
Caton, Joseph	(See Joseph Stewart, and others.)											
Catt, John	(See Melchoir Baker, and others.)											
Caubarreux, V..........	(See H. Fredieu, and others.)											
Cauchois, Lambert	Payment of money alleged to be due by United States.	19	2	Petition	217	Claims	....	....	......	Discharged.		
Caulfield, Col...........	(See Alabama volunteers against Creeks and Seminole Indians.)											
Caulfield, James.........	Confirmation of title to land in Alabama.	21	2	Petition	39	Priv. Land Claims.	Jan. 5, 1831	Adverse	......	Laid on table.		
Caulfield, James.........	Confirmation of title to land in Alabama.	22	1	Petition	400	Priv. Land Claims.	336	Report and bill	429	Referred to Committee Whole House.		
Caulfield, James.........	Confirmation of title to land in Alabama.	23	1	Petition	138	Priv. Land Claims.	Jan. 8, 1834	Adverse.	......	Recommitted.		
							408	Report and bill	424	Referred to Committee Whole House.		
Caulfield, James.........	Confirmation of title to land in Alabama.	24	1	Petition	65	Priv. Land Claims.	77	Report and bill	93	Passed	Passed	App'd June 23, 1836
Caulk, Richard..........	Confirmation of title to land in Missouri Territory.	15	2	Petition	21	Priv. Land Claims.	....	....	......	Discharged; laid on table.		
Caulk, Richard..........	Confirmation of title to land in Missouri Territory.	17	1	Petition	53	Public Lands	....	....	......	Discharged; laid on table.		
Caulk, Richard..........	Confirmation of title to land in Missouri Territory.	18	1	Petition	53	Public Lands	Jan. 16, 1824	By bill	65	Passed	Passed	App'd May 26, 1824
Caulk, Thomas	Confirmation of title to land in Missouri Territory.	15	2	Petition	21	Priv. Land Claims.	....	....	......	Discharged; laid on table.		
Caulk, Thomas	Confirmation of title to land in Missouri Territory.	17	1	Petition	53	Public Lands.....	....	....	......	Discharged; laid on table.		
Caulk, Thomas	Confirmation of title to land in Missouri Territory.	18	1	Petition	53	Public Lands.....	Jan. 16, 1824	By bill	65	Passed	Passed	App'd May 26, 1824
Causeby, William	(See Wm. H. Bedford, agent, &c.)	28	1	....	262							
Causey, William	Invalid pension, war of 1812....	29	1	Petition	397	Invalid Pensions...	657	Report and bill	440	Reported from Com. Whole House and laid on table.		

List of private claims presented to the House of Representatives of the United States from the 1st to the 31st Congress, inclusive—Continued.

Names of claimants.	Nature or object of the claim.	Congress.	Session.	How brought before the House of Reps.	Page of journal.	To what committee of the House referred.	No. or date of the report.	Nature of the report.	No. of the bill.	How disposed of by the House of Reps.	How disposed of by the Senate.	Date of the act of Congress, and remarks.
Causey, William	Invalid pension, war of 1812	29	2	Bill of last sess'n	211				440	Passed	Passed	App'd March 3, 1847
Causin, Eliza	(See John H. Stone, heirs of.)											
Causin, Nathaniel P.	(See John H. Stone, heirs of.)											
Causten, Isaac	Indemnity for French spoliations prior to 1800.	26	1	Memorial	182	Foreign Affairs	343	Foreign Affairs	319	Referred to Committee Whole House.		
Causten, Isaac, widow of.	Indemnity for French spoliations prior to 1800.	29	2	Petition	161	Foreign Affairs.						
Causten, James H.	Compensation for vessel taken by United States military forces at Baltimore for harbor defence.	13	3	Petition	712					Referred to Secretary War.		
Causten, James H.	Further compensation for vessel taken by United States military forces at Baltimore for harbor defence.	16	1	Petition	218	Claims				Discharged; laid on table.		Leave to withdraw.
Causten, James H.	(See Maryland, sundry merchants of Baltimore.)											
Causten, James H.	(See Mexican claimants under convention of 1839.)											
Cavalier, Anthony, & Peter Petit.	Confirmation of title to land in Louisiana.	15	1	Senate bill	440	Priv. Land Claims.	April 11, 1818	With't amend.	71	Laid on table.		
Cavalier, Anthony, & Peter Petit.	Confirmation of title to land in Louisiana.	15	2	Senate bill	252	Priv. Land Claims.			32			
Cavalier, Anthony, & Peter Petit.	Confirmation of title to land in Louisiana.	16	1	Senate bill	207	Priv. Land Claims.	Feb. 18, 1820	With't amend.	21	Passed	Passed	App'd Feb. 28, 1820
Cavalier, A. & Z.	Refunding of duties exacted on certain merchandise.	20	1	Petition	167	Ways and Means.	162	Adverse		Laid on table.		
Cavalier, A. & Z.	Refunding of duties exacted on certain merchandise.	22	1	Petition	105	Commerce				Discharged; laid on table.		
Cavalier, A. & Z.	Refunding of duties exacted on certain merchandise.	22	2	Petition	89	Commerce.						
Cavan, Timothy	Invalid pension	26	1	Petition	1001	Invalid Pensions				Discharged; laid on table.		
Cavan, Timothy	Invalid pension	30	2	Senate bill	325				406	Passed	Passed	App'd Feb. 2, 1849
Cavan, Timothy	Arrears of pension	31	1	Petition	1044	Invalid Pensions.						
Cavana, Patrick, son of	Compensation for two wagons and nine horses impressed and lost in United States service, revolutionary war.	25	2	Petition	177	Rev. Claims	596	Adverse		Laid on table.		
Cavana, Patrick, son of	Compensation for two wagons and nine horses impressed and lost in United States service, revolutionary war.	27	2	Petition	1371	Rev. Claims	1060	Adverse		Laid on table.		
Cavana, Patrick, son of	Compensation for two wagons and nine horses impressed and lost in United States service, revolutionary war.	28	1	Petition	122	Rev. Claims.						
Cavenaugh, James, and Matthew Cottril.	Interposition of United States with France to procure payment of a claim.	16	2	Petition	244	Foreign Affairs				Discharged; referred to Sec. State.		
Cavenaugh, Edward	Compensation for services in revolutionary war.	2	1	Petition	474					Referred to Secretary of War.		
Cavenaugh, John	Invalid pension	3	1	Rep. of Secretary War.	131	Select	May 26, 1794	Favorable; bill ordered.	62	Passed	Passed	App'd June 7, 1794

List of private claims presented to the House of Representatives of the United States from the 1st to the 31st Congress, inclusive—Continued.

Names of claimants.	Nature or object of the claim.	Congress.	Session.	How brought before the House of Reps.	Page of journal.	To what committee of the House referred.	No. or date of the report.	Nature of the report.	No. of the bill.	How disposed of by the House of Reps.	How disposed of by the Senate.	Date of the act of Congress, and remarks.
Cavenaugh, John	Increase of pension	9	2	House bill	608	Whole House	Feb. 28, 1807	Favorable	216	Passed	Passed	App'd March 3, 1807
Caveny, Patrick	Invalid pension	5	2	Petition	127	Claims	April 17, 1798	Adverse	......	Laid on table.		
Caveny, Patrick	Invalid pension	5	3	Report, former	432	Whole House.						
Cavitt, Joseph	Grant of land for erection of a mill	21	1	Petition	473	Public Lands	....	....	......	Discharged; laid on table.		
Cawood, Berry	Pay and bounty land as a revolutionary soldier under Gen. G. R. Clark against the Indians.	17	1	Petition	238	Pens. & Rev. Cl'ms.	Feb. 22, 1822	Rep. and res.; adverse.	......	Resolution adopted.		
Caxillo, Jose.	Confirmation of title to land in Mississippi.	29	1	Petition	192	Priv. Land Claims.	445	Report and bill	318	Passed	Passed	App'd Aug. 8, 1846
Cayford, John	Reimbursement of expenses to England to procure mechanics for government.	24	2	Petition	208	Claims	176	Adverse	......	Laid on table.		
Cayford, John	Payment for services in erection of arsenal in Florida.	25	2	Petition	983	Military Affairs	July 7, 1838	Adverse	......	Laid on table.		
Caze, James, and John Richaud.	Recovery of a ship taken by British in violation of treaty, and compensation for suit of sails burnt with frigate John Adams.	14	1	Petition	171	Claims	....	....	......	Discharged; laid on table.		
Caze, James, and John Richaud.	Recovery of a ship taken by British in violation of treaty, and compensation for suit of sails burnt with frigate John Adams.	14	2	Petition	58	Claims	Jan. 6, 1817	By bill	41	Passed	Postponed.	
Caze, James, and John Richaud.	Recovery of a ship taken by British in violation of treaty.	15	1	Petition and report Sec. State.	63	....	....	....	......	Laid on table.		
Caze, James, and John Richaud.	Recovery of a ship taken by British in violation of treaty.	15	2	Petition	52	Claims.						
Caze, James, and John Richaud.	Compensation for suit of sails burnt with frigate John Adams.	15	1	Petition	64	Claims	....	....	......	Discharged; laid on table.		
Caze, James, and John Richaud.	Compensation for suit of sails burnt with frigate John Adams.	15	2	Petition	52	Claims	Jan. 13, 1819	Adverse	......	Laid on table.		
Caze, James, and John Richaud.	Compensation for suit of sails burnt with frigate John Adams.	16	1	Petition	197	Claims.						
Caze, James, and John Richaud.	Compensation for suit of sails burnt with frigate John Adams.	17	1	Petition	253	Claims	60	Adverse	......	Referred to Committee Whole House.	....	Leave to withdraw.
Caze, James, and John Richaud.	Compensation for suit of sails burnt with frigate John Adams.	21	2	Petition	128	Claims	Jan. 18, 1831	Adverse	......	Laid on table.		
Caze, James, and John Richaud.	Compensation for suit of sails burnt with frigate John Adams.	23	1	Petition	37	Claims	114	Adverse	......	Laid on table.		
Caze, James, and John Richaud.	Compensation for suit of sails burnt with frigate John Adams.	24	1	Petition	48	Claims	Jan. 5, 1836	Adverse	......	Laid on table.		
Cazeau, Francis	Settlement of claims for various services in revolutionary war.	7	1	Memorial	48	Claims	Jan. 20, 1802	Adverse	......	Leave to withdraw.	....	See act Feb. 18, 1801
Cazeau, Francis	Compensation for losses and injuries sustained as a Canadian refugee.	7	1	Memorial	189	....	....	....	......	Postp'd to next sess.		
Cazeau, Francis, by Charles Cazeau.	Balance due on account of supplies furnished the revolutionary army.	9	1	Petition	321	Claims	....	....	......	Discharged; laid on table.		
Cazeau, Francis, legal representatives of.	Compensation for services and sacrifices in revolutionary war.	14	2	Senate bill	451	Pens. & Rev. Cl'ms.	Feb. 27, 1817	With't amend.	43	Passed	Passed	App'd March 3, 181~
Cazeau, Francis, legal representatives of.	Relief: money granted by act of March 3, 1817, was fraudulently obtaiaed by one F. Corbeaux.	15	1	Petition	360	Ways and Means	....	....	......	Discharged.		

List of private claims presented to the House of Representatives of the United States from the 1st to the 31st Congress, inclusive—Continued.

Names of claimants.	Nature or object of the claim.	Congress.	Session.	How brought before the House of Reps.	Page of journal.	To what committee of the House referred.	No. or date of the report.	Nature of the report.	No. of the bill.	How disposed of by the House of Reps.	How disposed of by the Senate.	Date of the act of Congress, and remarks.
Cazeau, Francis, legal representatives of.	$42,737 in full satisfaction of all claims.	24	2	Senate bill	552	Whole House	....	....	130			
Cazeau, Francis, legal representatives of.	$60,655 in full for supplies furnished revolutionary army.	25	2	Senate bill	301	Judiciary	April 13, 1838	With amend.	92	Postponed.		
Cazeau, Francis, legal representatives of.	$60,655 in full for supplies furnished revolutionary army.	26	1	Senate bill	966	Judiciary	....	....	208			
Cazeau, Francis, legal representatives of.	Amount granted by act of 1817, fraudulently obtained by F. Corbeaux.	28	1	Petition	177	Judiciary	355	Report and bill.	268	Passed	Passed	App'd June 15, 1844
Cazeau, Francis, administrator of.	Additional remuneration for advances, supplies, &c., in revolutionary war.	29	1	Petition	276	Judiciary	694	Report and bill.	467	Referred to Committee Whole House.	....	The report at this session makes no reference to the act of 1844.
Cazeau, Francis, administrator of.	Additional remuneration for advances, supplies, &c., in revolutionary war.	30	1	Petition	81	Judiciary	270	Report and bill.	263	Referred to Committee Whole House.		
Cazeau, Francis, administrator of.	Additional remuneration for advances, supplies, &c, in revolutionary war.	31	1	Petition	194	Judiciary.						
Cazenove, A. C. & Co.	(See Charles Bennett)	23	1	....	186							
Cazlard, Peter	Indemnity for damage to his property in New Orleans by United States troops.	14	2	Petition	142	Claims	Feb. 3, 1817	Report and bill.	100	Passed	Passed	App'd March 3, 1817
Celeron, Paul Louis, attorney for.	Bounty land as a French officer in revolutionary war.	12	1	Petition	39	....	....	....	....	Referred to Secretary War.		
Center, George	Losses sustained in Seminole war of 1836.	28	2	Petition	144	Claims.						
Center, George	Losses sustained in Seminole war of 1836.	29	1	Petition	69	Military Affairs	204	Report and bill.	198	Rejected.		
Center, George	Losses sustained in Seminole war of 1836.	30	1	Senate bill.	1209	Claims.	....	....	107			
Center, George	Losses sustained in Seminole war of 1836.	30	2	Bill of last sess.	105	Claims.	Dec. 18, 1849	With't amend.	107	Passed	Passed	App'd March 3, 1849
Center, John P., mother of.	Pension for services in Florida war.	25	2	Petition	534, 612	Invalid Pensions.	....	....	....	Discharged.		
Center, John P., mother of.	Pension for services in Florida war.	25	3	Petition	348	Invalid Pensions.						
Center, John P., mother of.	Pension for services in Florida war	26	1	Petition	162	Rev. Pensions.	....	....	....	Discharged; laid on table.		
Center, Willis S	Compensation for extra mail service.	29	2	Petition	232	P. Of. & P. Roads.						
Chabot	(See Watson, Chabot & Co.)											
Chace	(See Chase.)											
Chacherie, Louis	Compensation as translator to Board of Land Commissioners in Orleans territory.	12	1	Petition	272	Claims.	April 28, 1812	By bill	117	Referred to Committee Whole House.	....	Dec. 1, 1812, leave to withdraw.
Chacherie, Louis	Compensation as translator to Board of Land Commissioners in Orleans territory.	12	2	Senate bill.	612	Claims	Feb. 10, 1813	With't amend.	53	Passed	Passed	App'd March 3, 1813
Chadbourn, Levi	Invalid pension	3	1	Report of Secretary of War.	131	Select	May 26, 1794	Favorable; bill ordered.	62	Passed	Passed	App'd June 7, 1794
Chadbourn, Levi	Increase of pension	12	1	House bill.	361	Whole House	June 15, 1812	Favorable	138	Passed	Passed	App'd July 5, 1812
Chadowen, John	Grant of land	22	1	Petition	337	Public Lands.						

List of private claims presented to the House of Representatives of the United States from the 1st to the 31st Congress, inclusive—Continued.

Names of claimants.	Nature or object of the claim.	Congress.	Session.	How brought before the House of Reps.	Page of journal.	To what committee of the House referred.	No. or date of the report.	Nature of the report.	No. of the bill.	How disposed of by the House of Reps.	How disposed of by the Senate.	Date of the act of Congress, and remarks.
Chadwick, Caleb	Invalid pension	1	3	Petition and report Sec. War.	352	...	...	...	...	Laid on table.		
Chadwick, Caleb	Invalid pension	3	1	Rep. of Secretary War.	131	Select	May 26, 1794	To refer to Sec. with instrucs.	R. 12	Passed	Passed	App'd June 9, 1794
Chadwick, Caleb	Invalid pension	4	1	Report of Com. on Claims.	457	Whole House	Mar. 7, 1796	Favorable: bill ordered.	156	Passed	Passed	App'd April 20, 1796
Chadwick, David	Bounty land for services as a soldier, war of 1812.	24	1	Petition	405	Claims.						
Chadwick, Ebenezer	(See John C. Jones, executors of.)	26	1	...	182							
Chadwick, Isaac	Revolutionary pension	22	1	Petition	44	Rev. Claims.						
Chadwick, John	Compensation for services, supplies, and losses in revolutionary war.	1	3	Petition and rep. Sec. War.	352	...	...	...	...	Laid on table.		
Chadwick, John, (Ky.)	Increase of pension	25	3	Resolution	275	Rev. Pensions	...	...	...	Discharged.		
Chadwick, Levi	Renewal of revolutionary bounty land warrant lost.	16	2	Petition	141	Priv. Land Claims	...	...	...	Discharged; leave to withdraw.		
Chadwick, Levi	Renewal of revolutionary bounty land warrant lost.	24	1	Petition	432	Rev. Claims	720	Report and bill.	668	Referred to Committee Whole House.		
Chadwick, Levi	Renewal of revolutionary bounty land warrant lost.	25	2	Petition	39	Rev. Claims	129	Report and bill.	147	Passed	Reported without amend.	
Chadwick, Levi	Renewal of revolutionary bounty land warrant lost.	25	3	House bill	141	...	...	...	910	Passed	Passed	App'd March 2, 1839
Chadwick, Mary	Continuation of pension	28	1	Petition	850	Rev. Pensions.						
Chadwick, Peter	Equitable settlement of his accounts as captain United States army.	17	1	Petition	314	Claims.						
Chaffee, John	Compensation as military storekeeper and paymaster at Springfield, Massachusetts.	25	3	Petition	206	Claims.						
Chaffee, John	Compensation as military storekeeper and paymaster at Spring field, Massachusetts.	26	1	Petition	169	Claims.						
Chaffee, John	Compensation as military store keeper and paymaster at Spring field, Massachusetts.	27	2	Petition	94	Claims	339	Adverse	...	Laid on table.		
Chaffee, John	Compensation as military store keeper and paymaster at Spring field, Massachusetts.	27	3	Petition	155	Claims	201	Adverse	...	Laid on table.		
Chaffee, John	Compensation as military storekeeper and paymaster at Spring field, Massachusetts.	29	1	Petition	336	Claims	397	Adverse	...	Laid on table.		
Chaffee, Joseph	Relief on claim against Wyandotte Indians.	30	1	Petition	740	Indian Affairs	...	...	...	Discharged; laid on table.		
Chaffer, Joseph	Pre-emption to land in Ohio	29	1	Petition	297	Public Lands.						
Chalaire	(See Debouchelle & Chalaire.)											
Challer, Henry	Increase of pension	25	2	Petition	56	Invalid Pensions	680	Report and bill.	659	Passed	Passed	App'd July 7, 1838
Chalmers, Andrew, widow of.	Pension for services as revolutionary soldier.	25	1	Petition	78	...	...	...	...	Laid on table.		
Chalmers, Charles B	(See John Chalmers & Son.)											
Chalmers, James	Revolutionary pension	24	2	Petition	45	Rev. Pensions	...	...	...	Discharged; laid on table.		
Chalmers, James	Revolutionary pension	25	2	Petition	71	Rev. Pensions	...	...	...	Disch'd; laid on table.		
Chalmers, John, jr.	Compensation for tar destroyed by order of United States officer.	13	3	Petition	487	Claims	16	Report and bill.	208	Passed	Passed	App'd Nov. 21, 1814

List of private claims presented to the House of Representatives of the United States from the **1st** *to the* **31st** *Congress, inclusive*—Continued.

Names of claimants.	Nature or object of the claim.	Congress.	Session.	How brought before the House of Reps.	Page of journal.	To what committee of the House referred.	No. or date of the report.	Nature of the report.	No. of the bill.	How disposed of by the House of Reps.	How disposed of by the Senate.	Date of the act of Congress, and remarks.
Chalmers, John, jr.	Compensation for rope walk destroyed at time of the invasion of Washington city by the British in 1814.	14	2	Petition	275	Claims				Discharged; laid on table.		Leave to withdraw.
Chalmers, John, jr.	Compensation for rope walk destroyed at time of the invasion of Washington city by the British in 1814.	15	1	Rep. of Com'r of Claims.	225	Claims	Feb. 25, 1818	Adverse		Laid on table.		
Chalmers, John, jr.	Compensation for rope walk destroyed at time of the invasion of Washington city by the British in 1814.	16	1	Petition	101	Claims	Jan. 4, 1820	Adverse		Laid on table.		
Chalmers, John, jr.	Compensation for rope walk destroyed at time of the invasion of Washington city by the British in 1814.	16	2	Petition and rep.	72	Claims	Jan. 8, 1821	Adverse.		Laid on table.		
Chalmers, John, jr.	Compensation for rope walk destroyed at time of the invasion of Washington city by the British in 1814.	17	1	Petition	331	Claims	Mar. 18, 1822	Adverse.		Laid on table.		
Chalmers, John, jr.	Compensation for rope walk destroyed at time of the invasion of Washington city by the British in 1814.	18	1	Petition	236	Claims	79	Adverse.		Laid on table.		March 3, 1825; leave to withdraw.
Chalmers, John, heirs of.	Compensation for rope walk destroyed at time of the invasion of Washington city by the British in 1814.	24	1	Petition	92	Claims	Jan. 5, 1836	Adverse.		Laid on table.		
Chalmers, John, heirs of.	Compensation for rope walk destroyed at time of the invasion of Washington city by the British in 1814.	24	2	Petition	126	Claims	Jan. 10, 1837	Adverse.		Laid on table.		
Chalmers, John, heirs of.	Compensation for rope walk destroyed at time of the invasion of Washington city by the British in 1814.	26	1	Petition	436	Claims.						
Chalmers, John, heirs of.	Compensation for rope walk destroyed at time of the invasion of Washington city by the British in 1814.	26	2	Petition	148	Claims.						
Chalmers, John, heirs of.	Compensation for rope walk destroyed at time of the invasion of Washington city by the British in 1814.	27	2	Petition	327	Claims.						
Chalmers, John, & Son.	Indemnity for French spoliations prior to 1800.	24	2	Memorial	155	Foreign Affairs.						
Chalmers, John, & Son.	Indemnity for French spoliations prior to 1800.	26	1	Memorial	182	Foreign Affairs.	343	Favorable; bill	319	Referred to Committee Whole House.		
Chalmers, John, of Md., heirs of.	Indemnity for French spoliations prior to 1800.	31	1	Petition	816	Foreign Affairs.	355	Report and bill.	318	Referred to Committee Whole House.		
Chalmers, John, sen.	Indemnity for French spoliations prior to 1800.	26	1	Memorial	182	Foreign Affairs.	345	Favorable; bill	319	Referred to Committee Whole House.		

List of private claims presented to the House of Representatives of the United States from the 1st to the 31st Congress, inclusive—Continued.

Names of claimants.	Nature or object of the claim.	Congress.	Session.	How brought before the House of Reps.	Page of journal.	To what committee of the House referred.	No. or date of the report.	Nature of the report.	No. of the bill.	How disposed of by the House of Reps.	How disposed of by the Senate.	Date of the act of Congress, and remarks.
Chalmers, John, (N. Y.,) heirs of.	Indemnity for French spoliations prior to 1800.	31	1	Petition	502	Foreign Affairs	355	Report and bill.	318	Referred to Committee Whole House.		
Chalmers, Samuel	Indemnity for French spoliations prior to 1800.	31	1	Petition	816	Foreign Affairs	355	Report and bill.	318	Referred to Committee Whole House.		
Chamard, Andrew	Confirmation of title to land in Louisiana.	26	1	Petition	365	Priv. Land Claims.						
Chamard, Andrew	Confirmation of title to land in Louisiana.	28	1	Petition	132	Priv. Land Claims				Discharged.		
Chamberlain, Charles	Pension	22	1	Petition	441	Invalid Pensions	381	Report and bill.	472	Passed	Indef. postpn'd	
Chamberlain, Ebenezer	Renewal of pension	17	2	Petition	142					Referred to Committee Whole House on bill 207.		See act March 1, 1823
Chamberlain, Edward, son of.	Pension for revolutionary services.	26	1	Petition	625	Rev. Pensions	490	Adverse		Laid on table.		
Chamberlain, Elias	Pension	22	1	Petition	441	Rev. Pensions	381	Report and bill.	472	Passed	Indef. postp'd.	
Chamberlain, Emanuel	Bounty land as a soldier in United States army.	15	2	Petition	228	Military Affairs				Discharged; laid on table.		
Chamberlain, E. M	(See S. P. Simonton.)											
Chamberlain, John (Mass.)	Principal and interest of a certain loan office certificate barred by the Statute of Limitations.	8	1	Memorial	610					Referred to Committee Whole House.		
Chamberlain, John (Mass.)	Principal and interest of a certain loan office certificate barred by the Statute of Limitations.	8	2	Memorial	63	Claims.						
Chamberlain, John (N. Y.)	Revolutionary pension	21	1	Petition	663	Rev. Pensions				Discharged; laid on table.		
Chamberlain, John, (N. C.) widow of.	Continuation of pension	27	2	Petition	219	Invalid Pensions	784	Adverse		Laid on table.		
Chamberlain, John, (N. H.)	Pension for wounds received in war of 1812.	28	2	Petition	222	Invalid Pensions.						
Chamberlain, Joseph	Arrearages of pension	22	1	Senate bill	129	Invalid Pensions	Jan. 10, 1832	With't amend.	24	Passed	Passed	App'd July 9, 1832
Chamberlain, Joseph, (Pa.)	Pension	22	1	Petition	189	Invalid Pensions	229	Report and bill.	344	Passed	Rep. on without amend't, and laid on table.	
Chamberlain, Joseph, (Pa.)	Pension	22	2	Petition	62	Invalid Pensions	7	Report and bill.	626	Passed	Rejected.	
Chamberlain, Joseph, (Pa.)	Pension	23	1	Petition	72	Invalid Pensions	69	Report and bill.	79	Passed	Passed	App'd June 30, 1834
Chamberlain, Moses M.	(See Josiah Tuttle, administrator of.)											
Chamberlain, Moses	Renewal of pension	19	2	Resolution	40	Military Pensions				Discharged.		
Chamberlain, Solomon K.	(See Aldrich Wiley, heirs of.)											
Chamberlain, Thomas	Remission of penalty for violation of license law, or suspension until his accounts for suppplies furnished in 1812 are settled.	15	1	Petition	389					Referred to Secretary Treasury.		
Chamberlayne, Byrd, representatives of.	Bounty land and half-pay for services as lieutenant in revolutionary army.	27	2	Petition	545	Rev. Claims.	865	Adverse		Laid on table.		
Chamberlayne, William Byrd.	(See William Moseby, heirs of.)											
Chamberlin, Freedom	Pension	16	1	Petition	45	Rev. Pensions	April 22, 1820	Rep't and res.: leave to withdraw.		Resolution adopted.		

List of private claims presented to the House of Representatives of the United States from the 1st to the 31st Congress, inclusive—Continued.

Names of claimants.	Nature or object of the claim.	Congress.	Session.	How brought before the House of Reps.	Page of journal.	To what committee of the House referred.	No. or date of the report.	Nature of the report.	No. of the bill.	How disposed of by the House of Reps.	How disposed of by the Senate.	Date of the act of Congress, and remarks.
Chamberlin, James L.	(See John C. Edwards, and others.)											
Chamberlin, Solomon	(See Aldrich Wiley, heirs of.)											
Chambers, Alexander	Pension under act of 7th June, 1832	26	2	Petition	122	Rev. Pensions.						
Chambers, Alexander	Pension for revolutionary services.	31	2	Petition	266	Rev. Pensions.						
Chambers, David	Credit of $320 paid on land forfeited in the purchase of other land	17	1	Petition	196	Priv. Land Claims.	Feb. 15, 1822	Adverse		Laid on table.		
Chambers, David	Credit of $320 paid on land forfeited in the purchase of other land.	18	2	Petition	47	Public Lands	68	Adverse		Laid on table.		
Chambers, David	Credit of $320 paid on land forfeited in the purchase of other land.	19	1	Petition	37	Public Lands	Dec. 27, 1825	Adverse		Laid on table		Leave to withdraw, 1st sess., 20th Con.
Chambers, David S.	(See Titan Kimble, assignee of.)											
Chambers, James, (Md.)	Renewal of pension	20	1	Resolution	112	Military Pensions.				Discharged: laid on table.		
Chambers, James, (Va.)	Allowance of pension prior to June, 1839.	26	1	Resolution	663, 857	Invalid Pensions.						
Chambers, James W.	Indemnity for French spoliations prior to 1800.	31	1	Petition	323	Foreign Affairs	355	Report and bill.	318	Referred to Committee Whole House.		
Chambers, John, (Pa.)	Invalid pension and bounty land	12	1	Petition	123	Claims	June 12, 1812	Adverse		Laid on table.		
Chambers, John, (Pa.)	Arrears of pension	27	2	Resolution	791	Invalid Pensions.						
Chambers, John	Pre-emption to land in Mississippi territory.	14	2	Petition	65	Public lands				Discharged; laid on table.		
Chambers, Joseph	Revolutionary pension	24	1	Petition	56	Invalid Pensions	April 15, 1836	Adverse		Laid on table.		
Chambers, Joseph	Revolutionary pension	24	2	Petition	217	Invalid Pensions	Feb. 22, 1837	Adverse		Laid on table.		
Chambers, Landon G.	Money lost in transmission by mail	30	1	Petition	259	P. Of. & P. Roads				Discharged; laid on table.		
Chamblin, Turner	Payment for horse and equipments lost in Florida war.	25	2	Documents	542	Claims				Discharged.		
Chamblin, Turner	Payment for horse and equipments lost in Florida war.	26	1	Petition	168	Claims	702	Adverse		Laid on table.		
Chamblin, Turner	Payment for horse and equipments lost in Florida war.	28	1	Petition	515	Claims.						
Champ, John, heirs of	Renewal of a bounty land warrant	31	2	Senate bill	191				110			
Champaigne, Margaret G. C.	(See Stephen Monot and others.)											
Champayne, John R., administrix of.	Indemnity for French spoliations prior to 1800.	26	2	Petition	131	Whole House, on bill No. 319.						
Champayne, John R., administrix of.	Indemnity for French spoliations prior to 1800.	29	2	Petition	70	Foreign Affairs.						
Champayne, John R., administrix of.	Indemnity for French spoliations prior to 1800.	31	1	Petition	348	Foreign Affairs	355	Report and bill.	318	Referred to Committee Whole House.		
Champe, John, heirs of	Grant of land, &c., for a highly important secret service under General Washington.	15	1	Petition	353	Pens. & Rev. Cl'ms.				Discharged.		
Champe, John, widow and heirs of.	Pension and grant of land for highly important secret service under General Washington.	15	2	Petition	186	Rev. Pensions	Feb. 6, 1819	Rep. and res.; adverse.		Resolution adopted.		
Champe, John, heirs of	Grant of land, &c., for important secret service under General Washington.	16	1	Petition	177	Priv. Land Claims.				Discharged; referred to Secretary War.		
Champe, John, heirs of	Grant of land, &c., for important secret service under General Washington.	20	2	Petition	101	Public Lands				Discharged; laid on table.		

List of private claims presented to the House of Representatives of the United States from the 1st to the 31st Congress, inclusive—Continued.

Names of claimants.	Nature or object of the claim.	Congress.	Session.	How brought before the House of Reps.	Page of journal.	To what committee of the House referred.	No. or date of the report.	Nature of the report.	No. of the bill.	How disposed of by the House of Reps.	How disposed of by the Senate.	Date of the act of Congress, and remarks.
Champe, John, heirs of	Grant of land, &c., for important secret service under General Washington.	22	1	Petition	78	Rev. Claims.						
Champe, John, heirs of	Commutation pay for revolutionary services.	24	1	Petition	105	Rev. Claims	180	Adverse	......	Laid on table.		
Champe, John, heirs of	Commutation pay for revolutionary services.	24	2	Petition	79	Military Affairs.						
Champe, John, heirs of	Compensation for hazardous attempt to secure General Arnold after his treason.	26	1	Petition	359	Rev. Claims.						
Champe, John, heirs of	Compensation for hazardous attempt to secure General Arnold after his treason.	27	2	Petition	96	Rev. Claims	486	Report and bill.	342	Referred to Committee Whole House.		
Champe, John, heirs of	Compensation for hazardous attempt to secure General Arnold after his treason.	28	1	Petition	828	Rev. Claims.						
Champe, John, heirs of	Compensation for hazardous attempt to secure General Arnold after his treason.	28	2	Bill and petititon	133, 150	Rev. Claims	....	....	463			
Champe, John, heirs of	Compensation for hazardous attempt to secure General Arnold after his treason.	29	1	Petition	68	Rev. Claims	326	Report and bill.	261	Reported from Com. Whole House, and laid on table.		
Champe, John, heirs of	Compensation for hazardous attempt to secure General Arnold after his treason.	29	2	Bill of last sess.	71	....	....	....	261	Passed	Passed	App'd March 3, 1847
Champe, John, widow of	Revolutionary pension	25	2	Petition	271	Rev. Pensions	568	Report and bill.	558	Passed	Passed	App'd July 7, 1838
Champe, Nathan	Civil or military appointment for services in war of 1812.	16	1	Petition	177	Priv. Land Claims.	....	....	......	Discharged; referred to Secretary of War.		
Champenois, William	Invalid pension	3	1	Rep. of Secretary War.	175	....	....	....	......	Laid on table.		
Champenois, William	Invalid pension	3	1	Rep. of Secretary War.	262	Claims	Feb. 28, 1795	Favorable; bill ordered.	130	Passed	Postp'd to next session.	
Champenois, William	Invalid pension	4	1	Rep. of Secretary War.	445	Claims	Feb. 8, 1796	Favorable; bill ordered.	156	Passed	Passed	App'd April 20, 1796
Champion, Robert H.	(See Philip F. Dering.)											
Champion, Silas	Invalid pension	31	1	Petition	519	Invalid Pensions.						
Champlain, Oliver	Increase of compensation as surveyor of customs.	14	2	Petition	216	Ways and Means	....	....	......	Discharged; laid on table.		
Champlain, Oliver	Increase of compensation as surveyor of customs.	15	1	Petition	84	Ways and Means	....	....	......	Discharged; laid on table.		
Champlain, Oliver	Increase of compensation as surveyor of customs.	15	2	Petition	88	Com. and Manuf.	....	....	......	Discharged; laid on table.		
Champlain, Oliver	Increase of compensation as surveyor of customs.	16	1	Petition	58	Commerce	....	....	......	Discharged; laid on table.		
Champlain, Oliver	Increase of compensation as surveyor of customs.	19	2	Petition	37	Commerce	....	....	......	Discharged.		
Champlain, Oliver	Increase of compensation as surveyor of customs.	20	1	Petition	104	Commerce	....	....	......	Discharged; laid on table.		
Champlin, Charles, D.	(See Jesse Wood, heirs of.)											
Champlin, Isaac	Revolutionary pension	16	1	Petition	208	Rev. Pensions	April 6, 1820	Adverse	......	Laid on table	....	Leave to withdraw.
Champlin, Isaac, and others	Fishing bounty on schooner Buffalo	23	2	Petition	220	Commerce	55	Report and bill.	654	Referred to Committee Whole House.		
Champlin, Isaac, and others	Fishing bounty on schooner Buffalo	24	1	Petition	78	Commerce	43	Report and bill	45	Passed	Indef. postp'd.	

List of private claims presented to the House of Representatives of the United States from the 1st to the 31st Congress, inclusive—Continued.

Names of claimants.	Nature or object of the claim.	Congress.	Session.	How brought before the House of Reps.	Page of journal.	To what committee of the House referred.	No. or date of the report.	Nature of the report.	No. of the bill.	How disposed of by the House of Reps.	How disposed of by the Senate.	Date of the act of Congress, and remarks.
Champlin, Isaac, and others	Fishing bounty on schooner Buffalo	25	2	Petition	40	Commerce	....	....	......	Discharged.		
Champlin, Isaac, and others	Fishing bounty on schooner Buffalo	25	3	Petition	213	Commerce	....	....	......	Discharged.		
Champlin, Isaac, and others	Fishing bounty on schooner Buffalo	26	1	Petition	176	Commerce	69	Report and bill.	56	Passed	Indef. postp'd.	
Champlin, Isaac, and others	Fishing bounty on schooner Buffalo	27	2	Petition	485	Commerce	738	Report and bill.	415	Engrossed.		
Champlin, Isaac, and others	Fishing bounty on schooner Buffalo	27	3	Bill of last sess.	88	....	....	....	415	Passed	Adverse report; indef. postp'd.	
Champlin, Jabez	Liquidation and settlement of claims against the United States.	1	2	Petition	255	....	....	....	......	Referred to Secretary Treasury.		
Champlin, Jabez	Liquidation and settlement of claims against the United States.	3	1	Rep. of Secretary of Treasury.	77	....	....	....	......	Laid on table.		
Champlin, John T.	(See John Thurston, executors of)	26	1	....	182							
Champlin, John T.	(See William Minturn, executors of.)	26	1	....	182							
Champlin, Jonathan	Renewal of pension	20	1	Resolution	370	Military Pensions.	....	....	......	Discharged; laid on table.		
Champlin, Jonathan	Renewal of pension	20	2	Petition	31	Military Pensions.	....	....	......	Discharged; laid on table.		
Champlin & Minturn	(See Minturn & Champlin.)	23	1	....	175							
Champlin, Samuel, sureties of.	Release from judgment	21	1	Petition	146	Judiciary.						
Champlin, Samuel, sureties of.	Release from judgment	24	1	Petition	211	Judiciary.						
Champlin, Samuel, sureties of.	Release from judgment	24	2	Petition	266	Judiciary	187	Adverse	......	Laid on table.		
Champlin, Samuel, sureties of.	Release from judgment	25	2	Petition	89	Judiciary.						
Champlin, Samuel, sureties of.	Release from judgment	25	3	Petition (2) Petition	173 86	Judiciary. Judiciary.						
Champlin, Samuel, sureties of.	Release from judgment	26	1	Petition (2) Petition	450 175	Judiciary. Judiciary	July 21, 1840	Favorable	519	Referred to Committee Whole House.		
Champlin, Samuel, sureties of.	Release from judgment	27	2	Petition	390	Judiciary	April 12, 1842	Favorable	397	Referred to Committee Whole House.		
Champlin, Samuel, sureties of.	Release from judgment	27	3	Rep't Committee Whole House.	90	....	....	....	397	Passed	Passed	App'd Feb. 15, 1843
Champlin, Stephen, (Lieut. U. S. N.)	Compensation for being robbed by British officers when his vessel was captured on Lake Erie.	14	2	Petition	427	Naval Affairs	Feb. 27, 1817	Rep. and res. adverse.	......	Resolution adopted.		
Champlin, Stephen	Arrears of pension	24	1	Petition	507	Naval Affairs.						
Champlin, Stephen	Pension withheld from 1838 to 1844	29	2	Petition	99	Naval Affairs	34	Report and bill.	618	Referred to Committee Whole House.		
Champlin, Stephen	Pension withheld from 1838 to 1844	30	1	Petition	79	Naval Affairs	98	Report and bill.	77	Passed	Passed second session.	App'd Jan. 26, 1849
Champlin, William	Compensation for losses and services in revolutionary war.	29	1	Petition	939	Rev. Claims.						
Champlin, William	Compensation for losses and services in revolutionary war.	29	2	Petition	177	Rev. Claims.						
Champlin, William	Compensation for losses and services in revolutionary war.	30	1	Petition	173	Rev. Claims	....	....	......	Discharged; leave to withdraw.		
Champman, Sidney F.	(See Lincefield Sharpe, heirs of)											
Champney, Robert	Revolutionary pension	16	1	Petition	117	Rev. Pensions	April 6, 1820	Adverse	......	Laid on table.		
Champney, Wm., widow of.	Pension for accidental death of husband at navy yard, Mass.	25	2	Petition	201	Naval Affairs	488	Report and bill.	485	Passed	Adverse.	

List of private claims presented to the House of Representatives of the United States from the 1st to the 31st Congress, inclusive—Continued.

Names of claimants.	Nature or object of the claim.	Congress.	Session.	How brought before the House of Reps.	Page of journal.	To what committee of the House referred.	No. or date of the report.	Nature of the report.	No. of the bill.	How disposed of by the House of Reps.	How disposed of by the Senate.	Date of the act of Congress, and remarks.
Champney, Wm., widow of.	Pension for accidental death of husband at navy-yard, Mass.	25	3	Petition	103	Naval Affairs.						
Champney, Wm., widow of.	Pension for accidental death of husband at navy-yard, Mass.	26	1	Petition	179	Naval Affairs	532	Report and bill.	431	Referred to Committee Whole House.		
Champney, Wm., widow of.	Pension for accidental death of husband at navy-yard, Mass.	27	2	Petition	268	Naval Affairs.						
Chance, John Joseph	Refunding of duty on bell	31	1	Petition	992	Ways and Means						Provided for per app. act of Sept. 30, 1850.
Chance, Vincent	Compensation for services as a soldier in revolutionary army.	21	2	Petition	209	Rev. Claims.						
Chance, Vincent	Compensation for services as a soldier in revolutionary army.	22	1	Petition	73	Rev. Pensions				Discharged; laid on table.		
Chandler, Benjamin	Pension for services as a soldier, war of 1812.	25	3	Petition	570	Invalid Pensions.						
Chandler, Benjamin	Pension for services as a soldier, war of 1812.	27	2	Petition	255	Invalid Pensions.						
Chandler, Carter B.	Revolutionary pension	24	1	Petition	944	Rev. Pensions.						
Chandler, Carter B.	Revolutionary pension	24	2	Petition	126	Rev. Pensions	Jan. 7, 1837	Adverse		Laid on table.		
Chandler, Carter B.	Revolutionary pension	26	2	Petition	133	Rev. Pensions				Discharged; laid on table.		
Chandler, Carter B.	Revolutionary pension	27	2	Petition	459	Rev. Pensions	569	Report and bill.	365	Engrossed.		
Chandler, Carter B.	Revolutionary pension	27	3	Bill of last sess.	87				365	Passed	Adverse rep't; indef. post'd.	
Chandler, Carter B.	Revolutionary pension	28	1	Petition	144	Rev. Pensions				Discharged; laid on table.		
Chandler, Carter B.	Revolutionary pension	28	2	Petition	88	Rev. Pensions				Discharged; laid on table.		
Chandler, Daniel, widow of	Revolutionary pension	25	2	Resolution	187	Rev. Pensions	552	Report and bill.	539	Passed	Adverse.	
Chandler, Daniel, widow of	Revolutionary pension	26	1	Petition	385	Rev. Pensions	664	Adverse		Laid on table.		
Chandler, David	Revolutionary pension	25	2	Petition	267	Rev. Pensions				Discharged; laid on table.		
Chandler, Green	(See Wm. H. Bedford, agent, &c.)	28	1		262							
Chandler, Isaac	Revolutionary pension	22	1	Petition	594	Rev. Pensions				Discharged; laid on table.		
Chandler, Joel	To change an entry of land	23	1	Petition	568	Public Lands.						
Chandler, Joel	To change an entry of land	24	1	Petition	433	Public Lands	504	Report and bill.	504	Referred to Committee Whole House.		
Chandler, Joel	To change an entry of land	25	2	Petition	87	Public Lands	96	Report and bill.	113	Passed	Passed	App'd June 28, 1838
Chandler, John	Invalid pension	3	1	Rep. of Secretary War.	131	Select	May 26, 1794	Res. to refer to Sec. with instructions.	R. 12	Passed	Passed	App'd June 9, 1794
Chandler, John, and Wm. Johnston.	Refunding of money paid as sureties for J. B. Griffin.	22	1	Senate bill	892	Claims			S. 39			
Chandler, John, and Wm. Johnston.	Refunding of money paid as sureties for J. B. Griffin.	23	1	Senate bill	692	P. Of. & P. Roads.	June 20, 1834	With't amend.	S. 13	Passed	Passed	App'd June 30, 1834
Chandler, Jonathan	Revolutionary pension	23	1	Petition	80	Rev. Pensions.						
Chandler, Jonathan	Revolutionary pension	24	1	Petition	107	Rev. Pensions				Discharged; laid on table.		
Chandler, Jonathan	Revolutionary pension	25	2	Petition	106	Rev. Pensions				Discharged; laid on table.		
Chandler, Jonathan, widow of.	Revolutionary pension	26	1	Petition	285	Rev. Pensions	424	Adverse		Laid on table.		

List of private claims presented to the House of Representatives of the United States from the 1st to the 31st Congress, inclusive—Continued.

Names of claimants.	Nature or object of the claim.	Congress.	Session.	How brought before the House of Reps.	Page of journal.	To what committee of the House referred.	No. or date of the report.	Nature of the report.	No. of the bill.	How disposed of by the House of Reps.	How disposed of by the Senate.	Date of the act of Congress, and remarks.
Chandler, Jonathan, widow of.	Revolutionary pension	28	1	Petition	273	Rev. Pensions				Discharged; laid on table.		
Chandler, Joseph R	Relief as surety for Wm. C. Graham.	27	2	Memorial	613	Claims.						
Chandler, Joseph R	Relief as surety for Wm. C. Graham.	27	3	Petition	43	Claims	5	Report and bill	623	Passed	Passed	App'd March 3, 1843
Chandler, Lewis	Revolutionary pension	26	1	Petition	284	Rev. Pensions	424	Adverse		Laid on table.		
Chandler, Martin	Arrearages of pay as a revolutionary soldier.	19	2	Resolution	291	Military Pensions	Feb. 27, 1827	Adverse		Laid on table.		
Chandler, Martin, & others, revolutionary soldiers.	A footing similar to that of commissioned officers of revolutionary army when disbanded, and a continuance of pensions.	24	1	Petition	258	Rev. Claims	396	Adverse		Laid on table.		
Chandler, Martin, widow of.	Arrearages of pension	31	1	Petition	396	Rev. Pensions	64	Adverse		Laid on table.		
Chandler, Moses, widow of.	Pension for revolutionary services.	31	1	Petition	762	Rev. Pensions.						
Chandler, Stephen	(See Archibald Beard and others).											
Chandler, Thomas	Compensation for services, &c., in revolutionary war.	2	1	Petition	483					Referred to Secretary War.		
Chandler, Walter S., and Samuel Ward.	Payment of final settlement certificate burnt in 1790.	18	1	Senate bill	240	Pens. & Rev. Cl'ms.	Mar. 26, 1824	Adverse	29	Laid on table.		
Chandler, Walter S., and Samuel Ward.	Payment of final settlement certificate burnt in 1790.	18	2	Petition	38	Select	37	Report and bill.	294	Passed	Passed	App'd March 3, 1825
Chandonet, Margaret	Payment of expense of wound inflicted by a United States soldier, and for pension.	22	2	Petition	45	Invalid Pensions.						
Chaney, Jacques	Land and money due from Virginia for revolutionary services in Clark's Illinois regiment.	26	1	Petition	359	Rev. Claims.						
Chaney, John	Revolutionary pension	25	2	Petition	52	Rev. Pensions				Discharged.		
Chaney, John	Revolutionary pension	28	2	Petition	273	Rev. Pensions.						
Chaney, John	Revolutionary pension	29	1	Petition	510	Rev. Pensions	605	Adverse		Laid on table.		
Chaney, Richard, (Iowa)	Indemnity for being deprived of pre-emption to land.	27	2	Petition	84	Public Lands.						
Chaney, Richard, (Iowa)	Indemnity for being deprived of pre emption to land.	29	1	Petition	58	Public Lands.						
Chaney, Richard, (Illinois.)	Compensation for services in war of 1812.	31	1	Petition	595	Claims.						
Chaney, Thomas	Allowance of extra compensation granted him as an attendant on House of Representatives, 25th Congress, 1st session.	27	3	Petition	349	Claims.						
Chaney, Thomas	Payment for painting, glazing, &c., for House of Representatives.	30	1	Petition	355	Claims	602	Adverse		Laid on table		Leave to withdraw, Dec. 18, 1849
Chaney, Thomas	Extra compensation for services as a painter, after adjournment of 3d session 25th Congress.	30	2	Petition	269	Accounts.						
Channing, Walter, surviving partner of Gibbs & Channing.	Remission of duties on salt-petre, and refunding amount already paid.	8	2	Petition	30	Com. and Manuf	Jan. 30, 1805	Adverse		Referred to Committee Whole House.		
Channing, Walter, surviving partner of Gibbs & Channing.	Remission of duties on salt-petre, and refunding amount already paid.	10	1	Petition	82	Com. and Manuf.						

List of private claims presented to the House of Representatives of the United States from the 1st to the 31st Congress, inclusive—Continued.

Names of claimants.	Nature or object of the claim.	Congress.	Session.	How brought before the House of Reps.	Page of journal.	To what committee of the House referred.	No. or date of the report.	Nature of the report.	No. of the bill.	How disposed of by the House of Reps.	How disposed of by the Senate.	Date of the act of Congress, and remarks.
Channing, Walter, surviving partner of Gibbs & Channing.	Remission of duties on salt-petre, and refunding amount already paid.	16	1	Senate bill	283	Ways and Means	April 3, 1820	With't amend.	42	Passed	Passed	App'd April 11, 1820
Chapaton, Louis	Payment for forage taken by United States troops, war of 1812.	20	1	Resolution	78	Claims				Discharged; laid on table.		
Chapaton, Louis	Payment for forage taken by United States troops, war of 1812.	21	1	Petition	472	Claims	April 6, 1830	Adverse		Laid on table.		
Chapell, Lucy	(See Daniel Starr, children of.)											
Chapell, Prudence	(See Thomas Weakly, widow of.)											
Chapin, Benjamin, heirs of.	Location of a Virginia revolutionary warrant for naval services on any vacant land in Ohio.	15	2	Petition	163	Priv. Land Claims.	Jan. 11, 1819	Adverse		Laid on table.		
Chapin, Benjamin, heirs of.	Location of a Virginia revolutionary warrant for naval services on any vacant land in Ohio.	16	1	Petition	393	Priv. Land Claims.				Discharged; laid on table.		
Chapin, Benjamin, heir of.	Compensation for revolutionary services.	26	2	Petition	131	Rev. Claims				Discharged; laid on table.		
Chapin, Cyrenus	Pension for wounds received while commanding militia in war of 1812.	20	1	Resolution	95	Military Pensions				Discharged; laid on table.		
Chapin, Cyrenus	Pension	20	2	House bill	55	Whole House	Jan. 15, 1829	Favorable	311	Passed	Laid on table.	
Chapin, Cyrenus	Equitable compensation for services as a colonel in war of 1812.	21	1	Petition	377	Military Affairs	Mar. 15, 1830	Adverse		Laid on table.		
Chapin, Cyrenus	Share of prize money for capturing British brigs Caledonia and Adams, war of 1812.	21	1	Petition	378	Naval Affairs.						
Chapin, David S.	Grant of land in Michigan as a United States pensioner.	18	2	Petition	210	Pens. & Rev. Cl'ms.				Discharged; laid on table.		
Chapin, Gurden, heirs of	(See Benjamin Chapin, heirs of.)											
Chapin, Luther	Compensation for a vessel captured on Lake Erie, by the British, while in United States service.	16	1	Petition	42	Claims	Jan. 7, 1820	Adverse		Referred to Committee Whole House.		
Chapin, Luther	Compensation for a vessel captured on Lake Erie, by the British, while in United States service.	18	1	Petition	32	Claims	Mar. 15, 1824	Adverse		Referred to Committee Whole House.		
Chapin, Luther	Compensation for a vessel captured on Lake Erie, by the British, while in United States service.	19	1	Petition	78	Claims	70	Report and bill.	98	Passed	Amendm't reported.	
Chapin, Luther	Compensation for a vessel captured on Lake Erie, by the British, while in United States service.	19	2	Petition	92	Claims	73	Report and bill.	427	Passed	Amendm't reported.	
Chapin, Luther	Compensation for a vessel captured on Lake Erie, by the British, while in United States service.	20	1	Petition	68	Claims	152	Report and bill.	175	Passed	Amendm't reported.	
Chapin, Luther	Compensation for a vessel captured on Lake Erie, by the British, while in United States service.	20	2	Petition	55	Claims	14	Report and bill.	330	Referred to Committee Whole House.		
Chapin, Luther	Compensation for a vessel captured on Lake Erie, by the British, while in United States service.	21	1	Petition	35	Claims	39	Report and bill.	52	Passed	Passed	App'd April 23, 1830
Chapin, Luther	Fifty dollars for transporting Ohio volunteers across Lake Erie after the surrender by General Hull.	18	2	Resolution	67	Claims	Jan. 28, 1825	Report and bill.	304	Passed	Passed	App'd March 3, 1825

List of *private claims presented to the House of Representatives of the United States from the* 1*st to the* 31*st Congress, inclusive*—Continued.

Names of claimants.	Nature or object of the claim.	Congress.	Session.	How brought before the House of Reps.	Page of journal.	To what committee of the House referred.	No. or date of the report.	Nature of the report.	No. of the bill.	How disposed of by the House of Reps.	How disposed of by the Senate.	Date of the act of Congress, and remarks.
Chapin, Lydia	Continuation of pension	28	1	Petition	827	Whole House on bill No. 7.						See act June 17, 1844
Chapin, Myron	Pension for injuries sustained in marching to Plattsburg, war of 1812.	25	2	Petition	118	Invalid Pensions	281	Report and bill.	324	Passed	Indef. postp'd.	
Chapin, Myron	Pension for injuries sustained in marching to Plattsburg, war of 1812.	25	3	Petition	90	Invalid Pensions	79	Report and bill.	957	Passed	Adverse report.	
Chapin, Myron	Pension for injuries sustained in marching to Plattsburg, war of 1812.	26	1	Petition	161	Invalid Pensions	197	Report and bill.	209	Passed	Indef. postp'd.	
Chapin, Seth	Compensation for services as a spy in revolutionary war.	7	2	Petition	280	Claims	Feb. 23, 1803	Adverse		Referred to Committee Whole House.		
Chapin, Seth	Compensation for services as a spy in revolutionary war.	9	1	Petition	234	Claims				Referred to Committee Whole House on bill 108.		Feb. 18, 1807, leave to withdraw.
Chapin, Seth, heir of	Pension for services as a spy in revolutionary war.	26	1	Petition	283	Rev. Pensions	471	Report and bill.	385	Referred to Committee Whole House.		
Chapin, Seth, heir of	Pension for services as a spy in revolutionary war.	27	2	Petition	59	Rev. Pensions	126	Report and bill.	172	Passed	Indef. postp'd.	
Chapin, Seth, heir of	Pension for services as a spy in revolutionary war.	27	2	Petition	43	Rev. Pensions.						
Chapin, Seth, heir of	Pension for services as a spy in revolutionary war.	28	1	Petition	417	Rev. Pensions	535	Report and bill.	411	Referred to Committee Whole House.		
Chapin, Seth, heir of	Pension for services as a spy in revolutionary war.	29	1	Petition	91	Rev. Pensions	247	Adverse		Laid on table.		
Chapin, Sylva, late Holmes.	Indemnity for property destroyed by the British, war of 1812.	15	2	Petition	148	Claims	Jan. 16, 1819	Report and res.; adverse.		Laid on table.		
Chapin, Sylva, late Holmes.	Indemnity for property destroyed by the British, war of 1812.	17	1	Petition	46	Claims	Jan. 25, 1822	Adverse		Laid on table.		
Chapline, Abraham, Capt.	Location of Virginia military land warrants on any vacant lands northwest of Ohio river.	14	1	Petition	172	Pens. & Rev. Cl'ms.				Discharged; laid on table.		
Chapline, Abraham, assignee of.	Permission to locate revolutionary land warrants.	31	1	Petition	1215	Claims.						
Chapline, Abraham, assignee of.	Permission to locate revolutionary land warrants.	31	2	Petition	175	Priv. Land Claims.	11	Favorable	447	Passed.		
Chaplin, David	Revolutionary pension	22	1	Resolution	89	Rev. Pensions.						
Chaplin, David	Renewal of pension	22	1	Senate bill	205	Rev. Pensions	Jan. 21, 1832	With't amend.	48	Rejected.		
Chaplin, Ebenezer	Revolutionary pension	21	2	Petition	43	Military Pensions.						
Chaplin, Ebenezer	Revolutionary pension	22	1	Petition	35	Rev. Pensions	Dec. 21, 1831	Adverse		Laid on table.		
Chapline, James	Pension	16	1	Petition	101	Rev. Pensions	Apr. 22, 1830	Adverse		Laid on table.		
Chaplin, Joseph	Revolutionary pension	20	1	Petition	92	Military Pensions.	Feb. 13, 1828	By bill	166	Passed.		
Chaplin, Joseph	Revolutionary pension	20	2	House bill	55	Whole House	Jan. 15, 1829	Favorable	311	Passed	Laid on table.	
Chaplin, Joseph	Revolutionary pension	21	1	Petition	47	Military Pensions.	Jan. 15, 1830	By bill	72	Passed	Passed	App'd May 20, 1830
Chaplin, Philip	Invalid pension	9	1	Petition	311	Claims	Mar. 28, 1806	Indef. postp'd.		Leave to withdraw.		
Chapman, Albert	Invalid pension	10	1	House bill	232	Whole House	April 19, 1808	Favorable	78	Passed	Passed	App'd April 26, 1808

List of private claims presented to the House of Representatives of the United States from the 1st to the 31st Congress, inclusive—Continued.

Names of claimants.	Nature or object of the claim.	Congress.	Session.	How brought before the House of Reps.	Page of journal.	To what committee of the House referred.	No. or date of the report.	Nature of the report.	No. of the bill.	How disposed of by the House of Reps.	How disposed of by the Senate.	Date of the act of Congress, and remarks.
Chapman, Albert	Increase of pension	15	1	Petition	140	Pens. & Rev. Cl'ms.	April 1, 1818	By bill	172	Passed	Indef. postp'd.	
Chapman, Albert	Increase of pension	16	1	Petition	45	Pens. & Rev. Cl'ms.				Discharged; laid on table.		
Chapman, Asenath	(See Peter Chapman, widow of.)											
Chapman, Barnabus	Invalid pension	3	1	Rep. of Secretary War.	131	Select	May 26, 1794	To refer to Secretary, with instructions.	R. 12	Passed	Passed	App'd June 9, 1794
Chapman, Barnabus	Invalid pension	4	1	Rep. Committee Claims.	457	Whole House	Mar. 7, 1796	Favorable; bill ordered.	156	Passed	Passed	App'd April 20, 1796
Chapman, Benjamin	Revolutionary pension	26	1	Resolution	561	Rev. Pensions	423	Discharged		Laid on table.		
Chapman, Benjamin	Arrears of pension	26	1	Petition	707	Rev. Pensions	639	Report and bill.	472	Referred to Committee Whole House.		
Chapman, B. A.	Compensation for horse lost in Mexican war.	30	1	Petition	146	Claims	409	Report and bill.	359	Passed	Committed to claims.	
Chapmam Christain	Payment for ropewalk and contents destroyed by fire, at Baltimore, by order of U. S. officers.	13	3	Petition	555	Claims	Dec. 5, 1814	Report and bill.	235	Passed	Passed	App'd Feb. 27, 1815
Chapman, Constant	Revolutionary pension	16	2	Petition	173	Rev. Pensions	Feb. 15, 1821	Rep. and res. adverse.		Resolution adopted.		
Chapman, Daniel, and others, (Conn.)	Bounty on certain vessels engaged in the cod fishery.	8	1	Petition	553	Com. and Manuf.	Feb. 17, 1804	Adverse		Rejected.		
Chapman, Daniel (N. Y.)	Payment for certain revolutionary services.	25	2	Petition	391	Rev. Claims	613	Adverse		Laid on table.		
Chapman, Daniel (N. Y.)	Payment for certain revolutionary services.	25	3	Petition	221	Rev. Claims				Discharged.		
Chapman, Daniel (N. Y.)	Payment for certain revolutionary services.	26	1	Petition	165	Rev. Claims.						
Chapman, Daniel (N. Y.)	Payment for certain revolutionary services.	27	2	Petition	309	Rev. Claims	528	Adverse		Laid on table.		
Chapman, Edward D.	Bounty land for services in Mexican war.	31	1	Petition	451	Priv. Land Claims.						
Chapman, Erasmus and R. H. Boon, by Wilkins Tannehill, assignee of.	Compensation for services with teams in war of 1812.	19	1	Senate bill	209	Claims	63	Adverse	31	Laid on table.		
Chapman, Erasmus and R H. Boon, by Wilkins Tannehill, assignee of.	Compensation for services with teams in war of 1812.	19	2	Senate bill	276	Claims	March 3, 1827	Adverse	67	Laid on table.		
Chapmam, Erasmus and R. H. Boon, by Wilkins Tannehill, assignee of.	Compensation for services with teams in war of 1812.	20	1	Senate bill	96	Claims			14			
Chapman, Erasmus and R H Boon, by Wilkins Tannehill, assignee of.	Compensation for services with teams in war of 1812.	21	1	Petition	170	Claims	107	Report and bill.	147	Passed	Passed	App'd May 28, 1830
Chapman, Erasmus	Revolutionary pension	27	2	Petition	70	Rev. Pensions	784	Adverse		Laid on table.		
Chapman, Ezekiel	(See Daniel Pettibone and others.)											
Chapman, Ezra	Commutation pay for revolutionary services.	31	1	Petition	310	Rev. Claims	191	Report and bill.	197	Referred to Committee Whole House.		
Chapman, Isaac, & others.	Bounty land as soldiers in the war of 1812.	24	2	Petition	312	Public Lands.						
Chapman, Isaac, & others.	Bounty land as soldiers in the war of 1812.	25	2	Petition	577	Military Affairs				Discharged.		
Chapman, Isaac, & others.	Bounty land and three months' extra pay.	26	1	Petition	295	Claims.						

List of private claims presented to the House of Representatives of the United States from the 1st to the 31st Congress, inclusive—Continued.

Names of claimants.	Nature or object of the claim.	Congress.	Session.	How brought before the House of Reps.	Page of journal.	To what committee of the House referred.	No. or date of the report.	Nature of the report.	No. of the bill.	How disposed of by the House of Reps.	How disposed of by the Senate.	Date of the act of Congress, and remarks.
Chapman, James, late widow of.	Revolutionary pension	26	1	Petition	171	Rev. Pensions				Discharged; laid on table.		
Chapman, James, (Maine)	Bounty land and money for services in war of 1812.	30	1	Petition	136	Public Lands	145	Adverse		Laid on table.		
Chapman, Jeremiah	(See John Rogers and others.)											
Chapman, John A	Compensation for horse lost in the Creek war.	22	1	Resolution	149	Claims	Feb. 6, 1832	Adverse		Laid on table.		
Chapman, John B	Balance of appropriation on contract for improvement of Choctawhatchie river.	29	1	Petition	304, 450	Naval Affairs. Claims.						
Chapman, John B	Authority for Secretary of War to issue certificate for his claim against the Chippewa and other Indians.	30	1	Petition	298	Indian Affairs	442	Report and bill.	374	Referred to Committee Whole House.		
Chapman, Jonathan	Debenture on rum exported to Palermo.	20	1	Senate bill	625	Ways and Means	April 29, 1828	With't amend.	129	Referred to Committee Whole House.		
Chapman, Jonathan	Debenture on rum exported to Palermo.	20	2	Senate bill	130	Ways and Means	Feb. 4, 1829	With't amend.	42	Referred to Committee Whole House.		
Chapman, Jonathan	Debenture on rum exported to Palermo.	21	1	Senate bill	258	Ways and Means	Feb. 22, 1830	With't amend.	9	Passed	Passed	App'd May 26, 1830
Chapman, Levi	Payment for three horses lost in U. States service, war of 1812.	15	2	Petition	55	Claims	Dec. 30, 1818	Rep. and res.; adverse.		Resolution adopted.		
Chapman, Levi	Payment for three horses lost in U. States service, war of 1812.	16	1	Petition	213	Claims	Feb. 18, 1820	Adverse.		Laid on table.		
Chapman, M. S.	(See Elijah White and others.)											
Chapman, Martha	Extension of pension act of June 17, 1844.	30	1	Petition	229	Rev. Pensions	Jan. 25, 1848	Adverse.		Laid on table.		
Chapman, Nathan	Compensation for time he was prisoner to the British, revolutionary war.	19	1	Petition	153	Rev. Claims	Feb. 17, 1826	Adverse.		Laid on table.		
Chapman, Nathan	Increase of pension	22	1	Petition	133	Invalid Pensions.						
Chapman, Nathan	Increase of pension	22	2	Petition	39	Invalid Pensions				Discharged; laid on table.		
Chapman, Nathan	Increase of pension	23	1	Petition	54	Invalid Pensions				Discharged; leave to withdraw.		
Chapman, Peter, (N. Y.)	(See Isaac Chapman and others.)											
Chapman, Peter, widow of, (Mass.)	Revolutionary pension	26	1	Petition	728	Rev. Pensions	714	Adverse		Laid on table.		
Chapman, Peter, widow of, (Mass.)	Revolutionary pension	27	2	Petition	97	Rev. Pensions	784	Adverse		Laid on table.		
Chapman, Peter, widow of, (Mass.)	Revolutionary pension	27	3	Petition	43	Rev. Pensions	295	Adverse		Laid on table.		
Chapman, Reuben	Invalid pension	3	1	Rep. of Secretary War.	131	Select	May 26, 1794	To refer to Sec. with instructions.	R. 12	Passed	Passed	App'd June 9, 1794
Chapman, Reuben, heirs of	Commutation of half-pay as captain in the revolutionary army.	23	1	Petition	110	Rev. Claims.						
Chapman, Reuben, heirs of	Commutation of half-pay as captain in the revolutionary army.	23	2	Petition	66	Rev. Claims.						
Chapman, Reuben, heirs of	Commutation of half-pay as captain in the revolutionary army.	24	1	Petition	103	Rev. Claims	423	Adverse		Laid on table.		
Chapman, Reuben, heirs of	Commutation of half-pay as captain in the revolutionary army.	24	2	Petition	94	Rev. Claims	67	Adverse		Laid on table.		

List of private claims presented to the House of Representatives of the United States from the 1st to the 31st Congress, inclusive—Continued.

Names of claimants.	Nature or object of the claim.	Congress.	Session.	How brought before the House of Reps.	Page of journal.	To what committee of the House referred.	No. or date of the report.	Nature of the report.	No. of the bill.	How disposed of by the House of Reps.	How disposed of by the Senate.	Date of the act of Congress, and remarks.
Chapman, Rodman	Compensation for articles furnished military storekeeper at Vergennes, Vermont.	31	1	Petition	754	Claims.						
Chapman, Shadrack, widow of.	Revolutionary pension	27	2	Petition	329	Rev. Pensions	784	Adverse		Laid on table.		
Chapman, Shadrack, widow of.	Revolutionary pension	27	3	Petition	74	Rev. Pensions	295	Adverse		Laid on table.		
Chapman, Shadrack, widow of.	Revolutionary pension	29	1	Petition	619	Rev. Pensions.						
Chapman, Sidney F.	(See Lincefield Sharpe, heirs of.)											
Chapman, S. F.	Additional compensation for taking the Census in Dist. of Columbia.	27	2	Petition	680	Claims.						
Chapman, S. F.	Additional compensation for taking the Census in Dist. of Columbia.	27	3	Petition	139	Claims.						
Chapman, S. F.	Additional compensation for taking the Census in Dist. of Columbia.	28	1	Petition	84	Claims.						
Chapman, S. F.	Additional compensation for taking the Census in Dist. of Columbia.	28	2	Petition	166	Claims.						
Chapman, S. F.	Additional compensation for taking the Census in Dist. of Columbia.	29	1	Petition	207	Claims	416	Adverse		Laid on table.		
Chapman, Stephen	Compensation for horse and equipage lost in Seminole war of 1818.	23	1	Documents	154	Claims.						
Chapman, Thomas	Proportion of proceeds of a vessel and cargo libelled in district of Georgetown, S C., of which he is collector.	15	2	Petition	27	Claims	Dec. 2, 1818	Rep. and res.; adverse.		Resolution adopted.		
Chapman, Thomas, executors of.	Remission of forfeiture incurred under revenue act.	17	1	Petition	83	Ways and Means				Discharged; laid on table.		
Chapman, Thomas, executors of.	Remission of forfeiture incurred under revenue act.	17	2	Petition	78	Ways and Means				Discharged.		
Chapman, Thomas, executors of.	Remission of forfeiture incurred under revenue act.	18	1	Petition	115	Judiciary				Discharged; laid on table.		Dec. 23, 1824, leave to withdraw.
Chapman, Thomas, executors of.	Remission of forfeiture incurred under revenue act.	22	1	Resolution	567	Judiciary	494	Report and bill.	602	Referred to Committee Whole House.		
Chapman, Thomas, executors of.	Remission of forfeiture incurred under revenue act.	23	1	Petition	92	Judiciary	320	Report and bill.	351	Referred to Committee Whole House.		
Chapman, Thomas, executors of.	Remission of forfeiture incurred under revenue act.	24	1	Petition	106	Judiciary				Discharged; laid on table.		
Chapman, Thomas, executors of.	Remission of forfeiture incurred under revenue act.	25	2	Petition	95	Ways and Means	403	Adverse		Recommitted.		
							July 6, 1838	Report, former, with't amend.		Laid on table.		
Chapman, Thomas, executors of.	Remission of forfeiture incurred under revenue act.	26	1	Petition	175	Judiciary	602	Adverse		Laid on table.		
Chapman, Thomas, executors of.	Remission of forfeiture incurred under revenue act.	27	2	Petition	223	Judiciary.						
Chapman, Thomas J.	(See Primeau & Chapman.)											
Chapman, Wm., heirs of.	Relief for land forfeited after three-fourths of the purchase money had been paid.	19	1	Petition	206	Committee Whole House, bill 32.						Provided for by act of May 4, 1826.
Chappell, Amazian	Increase of pension	13	1	House bill	56	Whole House	July 20, 1813	Favorable	31	Passed	Passed	App'd Aug. 2, 1813
Chappell, Benjamin, heirs of.	Arrears of pension	25	2	Petition	664	Rev. Pensions				Discharged; laid on table.		

List of p ivate claims presented to the House of Representatives of the United States from the 1st to the 31st Congress, inclusive—Continued.

Names of claimants.	Nature or object of the claim.	Congress.	Session.	How brought before the House of Reps.	Page of journal.	To what committee of the House referred.	No. or date of the report.	Nature of the report.	No. of the bill.	How disposed of by the House of Reps.	How disposed of by the Senate.	Date of the act of Congress, and remarks.
Chappell, Benjamin, heirs of.	Arrears of pension	25	3	Petition	188	Rev. Pensions	Jan. 16, 1839	Adverse		Laid on table.		
Chappell, Benjamin, heirs of.	Arrears of pension	26	1	Petition	173	Rev. Pensions				Discharged; laid on table.		
Chappell, Benjamin, heirs of.	Arrears of pension	27	2	Petition	58	Rev. Pensions	784	Adverse		Laid on table.		
Chappell, Benjamin, heirs of.	Arrears of pension	27	3	Petition	73	Rev. Pensions				Discharged; laid on table.		
Chappel, David	Bounty land as a Canadian volunteer, war of 1812.	29	1	Petition	1018	Priv. Land Claims.						
Chappel, David	Bounty land as a Canadian volunteer, war of 1812.	30	1	Petition	617	Priv. Land Claims.						
Chappel, David	Bounty land as a Canadian volunteer, war of 1812.	31	1	Petition	534	Priv. Land Claims.						
Chappel, Isaac Newton	Damages for illegal seizure and detention of his vessel in 1818.	19	1	Petition	268	Commerce				Discharged; laid on table.		
Chappel, John	Invalid pension	1	2	Pet. and rep. of Sec. of War.	244					Laid on table.		
Chappel, John	Invalid pension	3	1	Rep. of Secretary War.	131	Select	May 26, 1794	To refer to Secretary, with instructions.	R. 12	Passed	Passed	App'd June 9, 1794
Chappel, John	Invalid pension	3	2	Rep. of Secretary War.	278	Claims.						
Chappel, John	Invalid pension	4	1	Rep. of Secretary War.	445	Claims	Feb. 18, 1796	Favorable; bill ordered.	156	Passed	Passed	App'd April 20, 1796
Chappel, Robert	Indemnity for losses by acts of United States troops in the Cherokee nation.	22	1	Resol'n and docs.	52	Indian Affairs.						
Chappel, Robert	Indemnity for losses by acts of United States troops in the Cherokee nation.	23	1	Petition	138	Indian Affairs				Discharged; laid on table.		
Chappel, Robert	Indemnity for losses by acts of United States troops in the Cherokee nation.	23	2	Petition	102	Indian Affairs				Discharged; laid on table.		
Chappell, Russell	Invalid pension	4	1	Rep. of Secretary War.	445	Claims	Feb. 18, 1796	Favorable; bill ordered.	156	Passed	Passed	App'd April 20, 1796
Chappel, William	Bounty land as a Canadian volunteer, war of 1812.	29	1	Petition	1018	Priv. Land Claims.						
Chappel, William	Bounty land as a Canadian volunteer, war of 1812.	30	1	Petition	617	Priv. Land Claims.						
Chappel, William	Bounty land as a Canadian volunteer, war of 1812.	31	1	Petition	534	Priv. Land Claims.						
Chappen, Paul	Pension for services as a soldier in revolutionary war.	29	1	Memorial	283	Rev. Pensions.						
Chapu, Michael	Invalid pension	14	1	Petition	416	Pens. & Rev. Cl'ms.	April 11, 1816	By bill	171	Passed	Passed	App'd April 30, 1816
Charbenon, German, assignee of.	Confirmation of title to land in Louisiana.	22	1	Petition	62, 108	Public Lands	Feb. 28, 1832	By bill	425	Passed	Passed	App'd June 25, 1832
Charbono, Tousaint	(See Lewis & Clarke, and their companions.)											
Charles, James	Pension for injuries received in war of 1812.	30	1	Petition	560	Invalid Pensions				Discharged; laid on table.		
Charles, Joel	Payment for property destroyed by U. States militia, war of 1812.	22	1	Petition	42	Claims	Jan. 23, 1832	Adverse		Laid on table.		

List of private claims presented to the House of Representatives of the United States from the 1st to the 31st Congress, inclusive—Continued.

Names of claimants.	Nature or object of the claim.	Congress.	Session.	How brought before the House of Reps.	Page of journal.	To what committee of the House referred.	No. or date of the report.	Nature of the report.	No. of the bill.	How disposed of by the House of Reps.	How disposed of by the Senate.	Date of the act of Congress, and remarks.
Charles, Reuben	Grant of land in Florida in consideration of Indian depredations.	19	1	Petition	99	Public Lands				Discharged; laid on table.		
Charles, Stephen, (N. C.)	Increase of compensation as collector of customs.	23	1	Petition	244	Commerce.						
Charlesworth, John M.	Compensation for services or losses in revolutionary war	1	3	Petition and rep't Sec. of War.	350					Laid on table.		
Charlesworth, John M.	Invalid pension	3	1	Rep. of Secretary War.	131	Select	May 26, 1794	To refer to Sec. with instruc.	R. 12	Passed	Passed	App'd June 9, 1794
Charleville, François, heirs of.	Land and money due by Virginia for services in Clark's Illinois regiment, revolutionary war.	26	1	Petition	359	Rev. Claims.						
Charlout, Peter	Invalid pension	3	1	Rep. of Secretary War.	131	Select	May 26, 1794	To refer to Sec. with instruc	R. 12	Passed	Passed	App'd June 9, 1794
Charlton, Charles	Pension for wounds received in revolutionary war.	17	1	Petition	118	Rev. Pensions				Discharged; laid on table.		
Charlton, James jr.,	Time to discharge judgments against him, and allowance of certain credits.	16	1	Resolution	201	Ways and Means				Discharged.		
Charlton, Sarah M., and others, (Cherokee Inds.)	Commutation, subsistence, and transportation of themselves and families.	26	2	Senate bill	329				194			
Charpenkie, François, *alias* Le Blanc.	Confirmation of title to land in Illinios.	18	1	Petition	177	Public Lands	Mar. 12, 1824	By bill	155	Indefinitely postponed.		
Charpenkie, François, *alias* Le Blanc.	Confirmation of title to land in Illinois.	19	1	Petition and res.	331	Priv. Land Claims.	April 28, 1826	By bill	241	Passed	Reported without amend.	
Charpenkie, François, *alias* Le Blanc.	Confirmation of title to land in Illinois.	19	2	Petition and res.	136	Priv. Land Claims.				Discharged; laid on table.		
Charpenkie, François, *alias* Le Blanc.	Confirmation of title to land in Illinois.	20	1	Petition and res.	154	Priv. Land Claims.						
Charter, William	(See Wm. H. Bedford, agent, &c.)	28	1		262							
Chartier, J. B., by Isidore Moore, assignee of.	Patent on a New Madrid land certificate.	19	1	Petition	134	Public Lands	86	Report and bill.	123	Rejected.		
Chartier, J. B., by Isidore Moore, assignee of.	Patent on a New Madrid land certificate.	19	2	Petition	32	Public Lands	5	Report and bill.	286	Referred to Committee Whole House.		
Chartier, J. B., by Isidore Moore, assignee of.	Patent on a New Madrid land certificate.	21	1	Petition	51	Priv. Land Claims.				Discharged; laid on table.		
Chase, Benjamin, widow of	Pension for revolutionary services.	25	2	Petition	58	Invalid Pensions				Discharged; laid on table.		
Chase, Cyrus, and others	Increase of compensation as revenue inspector at Salem, Mass.	26	1	Petition	710	Commerce.						
Chase, Daniel	Invalid pension	26	2	Resolution	87	Invalid Pensions	145	Report and bill.	656	Referred to Committee Whole House.		
Chase, Daniel	Invalid pension	27	2	Petition	60	Invalid Pensions	143	Report and bill.	190	Passed	Passed	App'd July 27, 1842
Chase, David	(See Samuel Bragdon.)											
Chase, Enoch	(See New York, sundry inhabitants of Plattsburg.)											
Chase, Gideon	Compensation for services, &c., in revolutionary war.	20	1	Petition	75	Rev. Claims	Jan. 3, 1828	Adverse		Laid on table.		
Chace, Grindal	Pension	21	2	Petition	159	Military Pensions.						
Chace, Grindal	Pension	22	1	Petition	80	Rev. Pensions	411	Report and bill.	511	Referred to Committee Whole House.		
Chace, Jabez, heirs of	Compensation for revolutionary services.	24	2	Petition	38	Rev. Claims.						

List of private claims presented to the House of Representatives of the United States from the 1st to the 31st Congress, inclusive—Continued.

Names of claimants.	Nature or object of the claim.	Congress.	Session.	How brought before the House of Reps.	Page of journal.	To what committee of the House referred.	No. or date of the report.	Nature of the report.	No. of the bill.	How disposed of by the House of Reps.	How disposed of by the Senate.	Date of the act of Congress, and remarks.
Chase, James, administrator of.	Indemnity for property captured by the French prior to 1800.	23	1	Memorial	246	Foreign Affairs.						
Chase, James, administrator of.	Indemnity for property captured by the French prior to 1800.	26	1	Memorial	182	Foreign Affairs	343	Favorable bill.	319	Referred to Committee Whole House.		
Chase, James, widow of.	Indemnity for property captured by the French prior to 1800.	29	2	Memorials	129, 163	Foreign Affairs.						
Chase, James, heirs of.	Indemnity for property captured by the French prior to 1800.	31	1	Petition	323	Foreign Affairs	355	Report and bill.	318	Referred to Committee Whole House.		
Chase, Joel	Bounty land and other allowance for services in revolutionary war.	10	1	Petition	30	Select.						
Chase, Joel	Bounty land and other allowance for services in revolutionary war.	15	1	Petition	93	Pens. & Rev. Cl'ms.				Discharged.		
Chase, Jonathan	Further compensation for services as an officer of the revolutionary army.	16	2	Petition	230	Rev. Pensions	Feb. 23, 1821	Adverse		Laid on table.		
Chase, Joseph, and Jared Gardner, and others.	Exemption of ship Manilla and cargo from certain penalties.	10	1	Senate bill	176	Whole House	April 25, 1808	With't amend.	7	Passed	Passed	App'd April 25, 1808
Chase, Joseph	Additional compensation for taking the fifth census in Maine.	22	1	Petition	732	Claims.						
Chase, Joseph	Additional compensation for taking the fifth census in Maine.	22	2	Petition	74	Claims	20	Adverse		Laid on table.		
Chase, Joseph, (N. H.,) widow of.	Revolutionary pension	27	2	Petition	320	Rev. Claims.						
Chase, Joseph, (N. H.,) widow of.	Revolutionary pension	27	3	Petition	365	Rev. Pensions.						
Chase, Joshua T., and others	Bounty on a fishing voyage	20	1	Petition	29	Commerce	Dec. 18, 1827	By bill	11	Passed	Passed	App'd Mar. 10, 1828
Chase, Mary	Pension for revolutionary services of husband.	28	1	Petition	850	Rev. Pensions.						
Chase, Mary	Extension of pension act of June 17, 1844.	30	1	Petition	230	Rev. Pensions	Jan. 25, 1848	Adverse		Laid on table.		
Chase, Nathaniel, 2d, and others.	Fishing bounty on schooner George & Alfred.	30	2	Petition	262	Commerce.						
Chase, Parker	Pension	24	1	Senate bill	1084	Invalid Pensions	July 1, 1836	With't amend.	305	Passed	Passed	App'd July 2, 1836
Chase, Paul, and his security, Samuel Clark.	Exoneration from the payment of duties on goods carried off by the British, war of 1812.	18	1	Petition	253	Ways and Means.						
Chase, Paul, and his security, Samuel Clark.	Exoneration from the payment of duties on goods carried off by the British, war of 1812.	18	2	Petition		Ways and Means	27	Report and bill.	276	Passed	Passed	App'd March 3, 1825
Chase, ——, (Bishop of Ohio.)	Remission of duties on contributions to the P. E. church seminary.	19	1	Petition	175	Ways and Means				Discharged; laid on table.		
Chase, Philander, (Bishop of P. E. church, in Ill.)	Pre-emption right to land in Peoria for a religious institution.	21	2	Petition	87	Public Lands.						
Chase, Philander, (Bishop of P. E. church, in Ill.)	Pre-emption right to land in Peoria for a religious institution.	25	2	Petition	770	Public Lands				Discharged.		
Chase, Philip	Indemnity for French spoliations prior to 1800.	26	1	Memorial	182	Foreign Affairs	343	Favorable; bill	319	Referred to Committee Whole House.		
Chase, Polly	Pension for revolutionary services of husband.	28	1	Petition	839	Whole House, on bill No. 7.						See act June 17, 1844
Chase, Richard	Invalid pension	4	1	Report of Committee Claims.	457	Whole House	Mar. 7, 1796	Favorable; bill ordered.	156	Passed	Passed	App'd April 20, 1796
Chase, Richard	Increase of pension	20	2	Petition	59	Military Pensions				Discharged; laid on table.		

List of private claims presented to the House of Representatives of the United States from the 1st to the 31st Congress, inclusive—Continued.

40

Names of claimants.	Nature or object of the claim.	Congress.	Session.	How brought before the House of Reps.	Page of journal.	To what committee of the House referred.	No. or date of the report.	Nature of the report.	No. of the bill.	How disposed of by the House of Reps.	How disposed of by the Senate.	Date of the act of Congress, and remarks.
Chase, Richard	Increase of pension	21	1	Petition	168	Military Pensions				Discharged; laid on table.		
Chase, Samuel, administrator of.	Indemnity for French spoliations prior to 1800.	26	1	Memorial	182	Foreign Affairs	343	Foreign Affairs	319	Referred to Committee Whole House.		
Chase, Samuel	Increase of salary as judge of the Orphans' Court, Washington, D. C.	22	1	Memorial	261	Dist. of Columbia				Discharged; leave to withdraw.		
Chase, Sill, & Co	Payment due from Ottowa Indians	29	1	Memorial	160	Indian Affairs	287	Adverse				
Chase, Simeon	Pension	21	2	Petition	159	Military Pensions.						
Chase, Simeon	Pension	22	1	Petition	80	Rev. Pensions	116	Report and bill.	193	Referred to Committee Whole House.		
Chase, Simeon	Pension	22	2	Bill of last sess.	66				193	Laid on table.		
Chase, Simeon	Revolutionary pension	25	2	Resolution	466	Rev. Pensions				Discharged; laid on table.		
Chase, Solomon, widow of	Revolutionury pension	25	2	Resolution	466	Rev. Pensions				Discharged; laid on table.		
Chase, Solomon, widow of	Revolutionary pension	26	1	Petition	173	Rev. Pensions	482	Adverse		Laid on table.		
Chase, Stephen	Benefit of act of 18 March, 1818, for revolutionary services.	15	2	Petition	160	Rev. Pensions				Discharged; laid on table.		
Chase, Stephen, administrator of.	Indemnity for French spoliations prior to 1800.	26	1	Memorial	182	Foreign Affairs	343	Favorable bill.	319	Referred to Committee Whole House.		
Chase, Theodore	Indemnity for French spoliations prior to 1800.	26	1	Memorial	182	Foreign Affairs	343	Favorable bill.	319	Referred to Committee Whole House.		
Chase, William H	Payment of claim per decision of Second Comptroller.	31	1	House bill	1034	Whole House	Aug. 26, 1850	Favorable	334	Passed	Passed	App'd Sept. 30, 1850
Chase, William	(See Stephen Chase, administrator of.)	26	1		182							
Chase, William, (N. H.,)	Indemnity for French spoliations prior to 1800.	26	1	Memorial	182	Foreign Affairs	343	Favorable bill.	319	Referred to Committee Whole House.		
Chasseaud, John	Compensation as consul at Syria and Palestine.	29	1	House bill	403	Commerce	May 4, 1846	Bill amendat'y	233	Passed	Passed	App'd Aug. 3, 1846
Chastang, Joseph, heirs of.	Confirmation of title to land	18	1	Senate bill	187	Priv. Land Claims.	Feb. 10, 1824	Adverse	27	Recommitted.		
							Mar. 26, 1824	Adverse	27	Referred to Committee Whole House.		
Chastelain, Julien, and Eli Ponvert.	Remission of duties on goods burnt on ship-board.	22	1	Petition	90	Commerce	134	Report and bill.	203	Referred to Committee Whole House.		
Chastelain, Julien, and Eli Ponvert.	Remission of duties on goods burnt on ship board.	22	2	Bill of last session.	66	Whole House	Dec. 15, 1832	With amend.	203	Passed with amendm't	Reported with amendment.	
Chastelain, Julien, and Eli Ponvert.	Remission of duties on goods burnt on ship-board.	23	1	Petition	79	Ways and Means	49	Report and bill.	54	Passed	Ref. to Finance	
Chastelain, Julien, and Eli Ponvert.	Remission of duties on goods burnt on ship-board.	23	2	Petition	139	Ways and Means	38	Report and bill.	621	Referred to Committee Whole House.		
Chastelain, Julien, and Eli Ponvert.	Remission of duties on goods burnt on ship board.	24	1	Petition	277	Ways and Means	285	Report and bill.	288	Referred to Committee Whole House.		
Chastelain, Julien, and Eli Ponvert.	Remission of duties on goods burnt on ship-board.	24	2	Bill of last sess.	200	Whole House			288			
Chastelain, Julien, and Eli Ponvert.	Remission of duties on goods burnt on ship board.	25	2	Petition	42	Ways and Means	1	Report and bill.	12	Passed	Indef. postp'd.	
Chastelain, Julien, and Eli Ponvert.	Remission of duties on goods burnt on ship-board.	25	3	House bill	105	Whole House	Jan. 25, 1839	With't amend.	894	Passed	Adverse report.	
Chastelain, Julien, and Eli Ponvert.	Remission of duties on goods burnt on ship-board.	26	1	Petition	178	Ways and Means	8	Report and bill.	27	Passed	Passed with amendment.	App'd July 21, 1840
Chatfield, Joel, widow of.	Pension for revolutionary services.	29	1	Petition	385	Rev. Pensions	527	Adverse		Laid on table.		

List of private claims presented to the House of Representatives of the United States from the 1st to the 31st Congress, inclusive—**Continued.**

Names of claimants.	Nature or object of the claim.	Congress.	Session.	How brought before the House of Reps.	Page of journal.	To what committee of the House referred.	No. or date of the report.	Nature of the report.	No. of the bill.	How disposed of by the House of Reps.	How disposed of by the Senate.	Date of the act of Congress, and remarks.
Chatfield, Joel, widow of	Pension for revolutionary services	30	2	Petition	296	Rev. Pensions.						
Chatfield, Silas	Pension for wounds received in war of 1812.	28	2	Petitions	472, 547	Invalid Pensions.						
Chatfield, Silas	Pension for wounds received in war of 1812.	29	1	Memorial	327	Invalid Pensions	712	Report and bill.	487	Laid on table.		
Chatfield, Silas	Pension for wounds received in war of 1812.	29	2	Bill of last sess.	212				487	Passed	Passed	App'd March 3, 1847
Chatfield, Silas	Arrears of pension	30	1	Petition	647	Invalid Pensions	834	Adverse		Laid on table.		
Chaudonia, John B., heirs of.	Land in consideration of services in war of 1812.	28	1	Petition	541	Public Lands.						
Chaudonia, John B., heirs of.	Land in consideration of services in war of 1812.	29	1	Petition	297	Public Lands	653	Report and bill.	433	Laid on table.		
Chaudonia, John B., heirs of.	Land in consideration of services in war of 1812.	29	2	Bill of last sess.	211				433	Passed	Passed	App'd March 3, 1847
Chauncey, Wolcott	Indemnity for depreciation of Treasury notes.	23	1	Senate bill	654	Claims	527	With't amend.	89	Passed	Passed	App'd June 30, 1834
Cheatham, L. P	Indemnity for failure of U. States in contract for removal of Cherokee Indians.	28	1	Petition	358	Indian Affairs.						
Cheatham, L. P	Indemnity for failure of U. States in contract for removal of Cherokee Indians.	29	1	Petition	147	Indian Affairs	734	Adverse		Laid on table.		
Cheatham, L. P	Indemnity for failure of U. States in contract for removal of Cherokee Indians.	29	2	Petition	133	Claims.						
Cheatham, L. P	Indemnity for failure of U. States in contract for removal of Cherokee Indians.	30	1	Petition	188	Claims				Discharged; laid on table.		Leave to withdraw, 2d session.
Check, Amos	(See Exploring Expedition.)											
Cheears, James H., representatives of.	Compensation for services as assistant surgeon to troops in Florida.	25	2	Resolution	936	Claims	928	Report and bill.	811	Referred to Committee Whole House.		
Cheears, James H., representatives of.	Compensation for services as assistant surgeon to troops in Florida.	25	3	Bill of last sess'n	431	Whole House	Feb. 1, 1839	With't amend.	811	Passed	Passed	App'd March 3, 1839
Cheek, James	Compensation for horses lost in United States service in 1794.	23	2	Petition	106	Claims	Jan. 3, 1835	Adverse		Laid on table.		
Cheek, James	Compensation for horses lost in United States service in 1794.	24	1	Petition	50	Claims	55	Adverse		Laid on table.		
Cheek, James	Compensation for horses lost in United States service in 1794.	27	2	Petition	107	Claims	335	Adverse		Laid on table.		
Cheeseborough, Asa	Revolutionary pension	25	2	Petition	913	Rev. Pensions				Disch'd; laid on table.		
Cheeseborough, Edward	Exoneration from payment of two duty bonds.	14	2	Petition	136	Ways and Means	Feb. 4, 1817	Rep. and res. adverse.		Resolution adopted.		
Cheeseman, Thomas, heirs of.	Grant of land in satisfaction of a Virginia military land warrant.	27	3	Petition	77	Rev. Claims	232	Adverse		Laid on table.		
Cheever, Abijah	Commutation pay as surgeon's mate in revolutionary army.	23	1	Petition	368	Rev. Claims.						
Cheever, Abijah	Commutation pay as surgeon's mate in revolutionary army.	25	2	Petition	49	Rev. Claims.						
Cheever, Abijah	Commutation pay as surgeon's mate in revolutionary army.	25	3	Petition	84	Rev. Claims.						
Cheever, James	(See Benjamin Crowninshields and others.)											

List of private claims presented to the House of Representatives of the United States from the 1st to the 31st Congress, inclusive—Continued.

Names of claimants.	Nature or object of the claim.	Congress.	Session.	How brought before the House of Reps.	Page of journal.	To what committee of the House referred.	No. or date of the report.	Nature of the report.	No. of the bill.	How disposed of by the House of Reps.	How disposed of by the Senate.	Date of the act of Congress, and remarks.
Cheever, Joseph	Renewal and continuation of pension.	16	2	Petition	205	Rev. Pensions	Feb. 15, 1820	Report and res. for leave to withdraw.	......	Resolution adopted.		
Cheever, Mary	Public support in consideration of loss of two sons in engagement between Constitution and Java.	13	2	Petition	177	Pens. & Rev. Cl'ms.	43	Adverse; bill ordered.	148	Passed	Passed	App'd April 12, 1814
Cheever, Nathaniel, and others.	Reimbursement of money paid in error as sureties of Daniel Evans, collector of internal revenue.	21	2	Senate bill	382	Ways and Means	Mar. 2, 1831	With't amend.	116	Passed	Passed	App'd March 2, 1831
Cheever, William D., representatives of.	Indemnity for loss sustained on treasury notes paid for services in 1814.	25	2	Petition	51	Claims	....	....	......	Discharged.		
Cheever, William D., representatives of.	Indemnity for loss sustained on treasury notes paid for services in 1814.	25	3	Petition	86	Claims.						
Cheever, William D., representatives of.	Indemnity for loss sustained on treasury notes paid for services in 1814.	26	1	Petition	167	Claims.						
Cheever, William D., representatives of.	Indemnity for loss sustained on treasury notes paid for services in 1814.	26	2	Petition	38	Claims	35	Report and bill.	563	Referred to Committee Whole House.		
Cheever, William D., representatives of.	Indemnity for loss sustained on treasury notes paid for services in 1814.	27	2	Petition	56	Claims	4	Report and bill.	43	Passed	Passed	App'd Aug. 30, 1842
Cheever, William D., executors of.	Indemnity for loss sustained on treasury notes paid for services in 1814.	28	1	Memorial	602	Claims	311	Report and bill.	219	Referred to Committee Whole House.		
Cheever, William D., representatives of.	$21,231 for loss on treasury notes paid on contract for army supplies, war of 1812.	28	2	Senate bill	473	Claims	Mar. 3, 1845	With't amend.	71	Referred to Committee Whole House.		
Cheever, William D., representatives of.	$21,231 for loss on treasury notes paid on contract for army supplies, war of 1812.	29	1	Petition and Sen. bill.	92, 411	Claims	Feb. 24, 1846	With't amend.	18	Referred to Committee Whole House.		
Cheever, William D., representatives of.	$21,231 for loss on treasury notes paid on contract for army supplies, war of 1812.	29	2	Senate bill	373	Judiciary	Feb. 24, 1847	With't amend	75	Referred to Committee Whole House.		
Cheever, William D., representatives of.	$21,231 for loss on treasury notes paid on contract for army supplies, war of 1812.	30	1	Petition	316	Claims	232	Report and bill	236	Referred to Committee Whole House.		
Cheever, William D., representatives of.	$21,231 for loss on treasury notes paid on contract for army supplies, war of 1812.	30	1	Senate bill	683	Whole House	....	....	43			
Cheever, William D., representatives of.	$21,231 for loss on treasury notes paid on contract for army supplies, war of 1812.	30	2	Bill of last sess.	368	Whole House	Feb. 3, 1849	With't amend.	43	Passed	Passed	App'd Feb. 10, 1849
Chelsey, John, or Chesley	Indemnity for loss of property at the battle of North Point.	15	2	Petition	161	....	....	....	......	Laid on table.		
Chelsey, John	Indemnity for loss of property at the battle of North Point.	21	1	Petition	235	Claims	Feb. 5, 1830	Adverse	......	Laid on table.		
Cheney, Beley	Confirmation of title to land in Mississippi Territory.	13	2	Petition	168	Public Lands	....	....	......	Discharged.		
Cheney, Beley	Confirmation of title to land in Alabama.	15	1	House bill	387	Whole House on bill No. 70.	....	....	160			

List of private claims presented to the House of Representatives of the United States from the 1st to the 31st Congress, inclusive—Continued.

Names of claimants.	Nature or object of the claim.	Congress.	Session.	How brought before the House of Reps.	Page of journal.	To what committee of the House referred.	No. or date of the report.	Nature of the report.	No. of the bill.	How disposed of by the House of Reps.	How disposed of by the Senate.	Date of the act of Congress, and remarks.
Cheney, Beley	Confirmation of title to land in Alabama.	16	1	Petition	204	Priv. Land Claims.	64	Report and bill.	69	Passed	Passed	App'd May 8, 1820
Cheney, Beley	(See Richard Cravat and others.)											
Cheney, Benjamin	Payment of balance due on property furnished and services rendered United States at Green Bay.	19	2	Resolution	87	Claims				Discharged.		
Cheney, Betsey	Pension for revolutionary services of husband.	28	1	Petition	950	Whole House on bill No. 7.						See act June 17, 1844
Cheney, Ebenezer, executor of.	Compensation for house and fuel used by troops of revolutionary army.	3	2	Petition	296	Claims	March 2, 1795	Adverse		Laid on table.		
Cheney, Ebenezer, executor of.	Compensation for house and fuel used by troops of revolutionary army.	4	1	Petition	373	Claims	May 31, 1796	Adverse		Laid on table.		
Cheney, Elijah	Revolutionary pension	25	2	Resolution	535	Invalid Pensions				Discharged; laid on table.		
Cheney, Richard	Restoration to pension roll	17	1	Petition	348	Whole House on bill No. 37.						
Cheney, Samuel	Compensation for use of cart and horse impressed in United States service.	14	1	Petition	253	Claims				Discharged; leave to withdraw.		
Cheney, Samuel	Pension for disability in naval service.	14	2	Petition	448	Naval Affairs				Discharged; laid on table.		
Cheney, Samuel	Pension for disability in naval service.	15	1	Petition and rep't Sec. of Navy.	336, 380					Laid on table.		
Cheney, Samuel	Pension for wounds received in revolutionary war.	17	1	Petition	128	Pens. & Rev. Cl'ms.	Jan. 15, 1822	Rep. and res. adverse.		Resolution adopted.		
Cheney, Solomon	Pension for wounds received in war of 1812.	31	2	Petition	106	Invalid Pensions.						
Chenowith, James	Pension for services in western Indian war.	31	1	Petition	214	Invalid Pensions						Leave to withdraw, 2d sess.
Chenowith, Richard	(See Richard Chinowith.)											
Chepauney, (Creek Indian)	Means to remove from Georgia to the Indian territory.	31	1	Petition	349	Indian Affairs.						
Cherino, Antonio	Confirmation of title to land in Louisiana.	27	2	Petition	75	Priv. Land Claims.	284	Report and bill.	250	Passed	Reported without amend.	
Cherino, Antonio	Confirmation of title to land in Louisiana.	28	1	Petition	132	Priv. Land Claims.	320	Report and bill.	228	Passed	Referred, com. discharged.	
Cheriot, Henry	Remission of duties on wines destroyed by fire at New York.	5	2	Petition	82	Com. and Manuf.	Dec. 4, 1797	Rep. and res. adverse.		Resolution adopted.		Leave to withdraw.
Cherrier, Oliver	Confirmation of title to land in Michigan.	17	1	Petition	184	Public Lands				Discharged; laid on table.		
Cherry, Henry, widow of.	Benefit of act of July, 1838, granting half-pay and pension.	27	2	Petition	458	Rev. Pensions.	784	Adverse		Laid on table.		
Cherry, Peter	Renewal of pension	17	2	Petition	209	Rev. Pensions.				Leave to withdraw		See act March 1, 1823
Cherry, William, heirs of	Revolutionary pension	28	2	Petition	89	Rev. Pensions.						
Cherry, William, heirs of	Full pay and interest for one year, due for services as captain in revolutionary army.	29	1	Petition	268	Rev. Claims.	408	Adverse		Laid on table.		
Cherry, William, heirs of	Full pay and interest for one year, due for services as captain in revolutionary army.	30	1	Petition	575	Rev. Claims.	832	Adverse		Laid on table.		

List of private claims presented to the House of Representatives of the United States from the 1st to the 31st Congress, inclusive—Continued.

Names of claimants.	Nature or object of the claim.	Congress.	Session.	How brought before the House of Reps.	Page of journal.	To what committee of the House referred.	No. or date of the report.	Nature of the report.	No. of the bill.	How disposed of by the House of Reps.	How disposed of by the Senate.	Date of the act of Congress, and remarks.
Cherry, William, heirs of	Full pay and interest for one year, due for services as captain in revolutionary army.	31	1	Petition	472	Rev. Claims	341	Adverse	......	Laid on table.		
Chesley, Francis H.	(See Cuthbert Harrison, heir of.)											
Chesley, John	(See John Chelsey.)											
Chesnutt, Samuel	Compensation for a horse lost in United States service in war of 1812.	19	1	Petition	151	Claims	195	Adverse	......	Recommitted.		
							May 5, 1826	Report and bill	255	Passed.	Amendm'nt reported.	
Chesnutt, Samuel	Compensation for a horse lost in United States service in war of 1812.	19	2	Petition	132	Claims	Jan. 10, 1827	Report and bill	360	Passed	Amendm'nt reported.	
Chesnutt, Samuel	Compensation for a horse lost in United States service in war of 1812.	20	1	Petition	311	Claims	158	Report and bill.	181	Referred to Committee Whole House.		
Chesnutt, Samuel	Compensation for a horse lost in United States service in war of 1812.	20	2	Bill of last sess.	174	Whole House	Jan. 17, 1829	With't amend.	181	Passed	Passed	App'd March 3, 1829
Chesnut, William R.	Compensation for flour furnished troops in Florida war 1837.	31	2	Petition	199	Claims.						
Chess, Mary	(See James Alexander, widow of.)	31	1	....	306							
Chesson, John B.	(See William Ross, heirs of.)											
Chester, Jacob	(See Joseph Dunham, and others.)	24	2	....	324							
Chester, James, or John	Pension for long services in army, and for death of a son by fulminating powder.	30	1	Petition	560	Invalid Pensions	....	....	......	Discharged; laid on table.		
Chester, John	Credit of $551 24 as supervisor of internal taxes.	9	2	Senate bill	575	Claims	Feb. 13, 1807	With't amend.	45	Passed	Passed	App'd March 3, 1807
Chester, Samuel	Compensation for services, &c., in revolutionary war.	2	1	Petition	539	....	....	....	......	Referred to Secretary War.		
Chester, Samuel	Compensation for services, &c., in revolutionary war.	2	2	Rep. of Secretary War.	696	....	....	....	......	Laid on table.		
Chester, Samuel	Compensation for services, &c., in revolutionary war.	4	2	Petition	612	Claims	Jan. 20, 1797	Adverse	......	Rejected.		
Chester, Simeon	Compensation for services, &c., in revolutionary war.	2	1	Petition	528	....	....	....	......	Referred to Secretary of War.		
Chester, Simeon	Compensation for services, &c., in revolutionary war.	2	2	Report of Secretary of War.	733	....	....	....	......	Laid on table.		
Chester, Simeon	Compensation for services, &c., in revolutionary war.	3	1	Report former	29	Select	April 1, 1794	Favorable	......	Referred to Committee Whole House.		
Chester, Simeon, heirs of	(See Canadian refugees.)											
Chevallie, J. A.	(See A. E. De Beaumarchais.)											
Chevers, William, widow of.	Continuation of pension	24	2	Petition	84	Rev. Pensions	....	....	......	Discharged; laid on table.		
Chew, Ann Maria B.	(See Benjamin Brooks, child of.)											
Chew, Beverly, and others.	Portion of proceeds of a cargo of negroe slaves sold for violation of act 1807.	19	1	Memorial	336	....	....	....	......	Ref. to Com. Whole House, on S. bill 109.		
Chew, Beverly, and others.	Portion of proceeds of a cargo of negro slaves sold for violation of act 1807.	19	1	Senate bill	478	Ways and Means	May 5, 1826	With't amend.	109	Laid on table.		

List of private claims presented to the House of Representatives of the United States from the 1st *to the* 31st *Congress, inclusive*—Continued.

Names of claimants.	Nature or object of the claim.	Congress.	Session.	How brought before the House of Reps.	Page of journal.	To what committee of the House referred.	No. or date of the report	Nature of the report.	No. of the bill.	How disposed of by the House of Reps.	How disposed of by the Senate.	Date of the act of Congress, and remarks.
Chew, Beverly, and others.	Portion of proceeds of a cargo of negro slaves sold for violation of act 1807.	21	1	Senate bill	552	Judiciary	....	....	96			
Chew, Berverly, and others.	Portion of proceeds of a cargo of negro slaves sold for violation of act 1807.	21	2	Senate bill	384	Judiciary	Mar. 2, 1831	With't amend.	22	Passed	Passed.......	App'd March 3, 1831
Chew, Beverly, and others, survivors of Beal's rifle company.	Compensation in land in Louisiana for services in the war of 1812.	24	1	Petition	151	Public Lands.						
Chew, Beverly, and others, survivors of Beal's rifle company.	Compensation in land in Louisiana for services in the war of 1812.	26	1	Petition	962	Priv. Land Claims.						
Chew, Beverly, and others, survivors of Beal's rifle company.	Compensation in land in Louisiana for services in the war of 1812.	28	1	Petition	406	Military Affairs.						
Chew, John, (Md.)......	Increase of compensation as surveyor of customs.	27	3	Petition	471	Commerce........	212	Report and bill.	808	Referred to Committee Whole House.		
Chew, Nathaniel, widow of.	Pension for revolutionary services of husband.	28	1	Petition	983	Rev. Pension.						
Chew, Nathaniel, widow of.	Pension for revolutionary services of husband.	28	2	Petition	110	Rev. Claims.						
Chew, Nathaniel, widow of.	Pension for revolutionary services of husband.	29	1	Petition	463	Rev. Claims.						
Chew and Relfe.........	(See De Maison Rouge, marquis of.)											
Chew, Robert, and others .	(See De Maison Rouge, marquis of.)											
Chew, William W......	Payment of difference of compensation between that of chargé and secretary of legation at St. Petersburg.	26	2	Petition	55	Foreign Affairs.						
Chew, William W......	Payment of difference of compensation between that of chargé and secretary of legation at St. Petersburg.	27	3	Petition	77	Foreign Affairs.						
Chew, William W......	Allowance of outfit as chargé at Russia.	28	2	Petition	216	Foreign Affairs.						
Chezum, James H.......	Additional compensation for repair of warf near penitentiary, D. C.	30	1	Petition	414	Claims...........	481	Adverse	......	Laid on table.		
Chiapella, Celestin	Confirmation of title to land in Louisiana.	22	1	Petition	46	Priv. Land Claims.	33	Report and bill.	78	Passed	Passed	App'd May 19, 1832
Chick, Nathaniel........	Revolutionary pension..........	29	2	Petition	402	Rev. Pensions.						
Chickering, John and John M. Noyes.	Indemnity for cargo seized by United States—the claimants' being ignorant of the law.	16	1	Petition	160	Claims...........	Jan. 31, 1820	Adverse	......	Laid on table.		
Child, Farr & Co.	Remission of duties on goods destroyed by fire.	31	1	Petition	641	Commerce........	329	Report and bill.	286	Laid on table.		
Child, Farr & Co.	Remission of duties on goods destroyed by fire.	31	2	Bill of last sess..	181	Whole House.....	Jan. 24, 1851	With't amend.	286	Passed	Rep'd without amendment.	
Child, John T...........	Indemnity for French spoliations prior to 1800.	26	1	Memorial	182	Foreign Affairs....	343	Favorable ; bill	319	Referred to Committee Whole House.		
Child, Joseph...........	(See John Earle, jr., and others.)											

List of private claims presented to the House of Representatives of the United States from the 1st to the 31st Congress, inclusive—Continued.

Names of claimants.	Nature or object of the claim.	Congress.	Session.	How brought before the House of Reps.	Page of journal.	To what committee of the House referred.	No. or date of the report.	Nature of the report.	No. of the bill.	How disposed of by the House of Reps.	How disposed of by the Senate.	Date of the act of Congress, and remarks.
Child, Thomas	Indemnity for French spoliations prior to 1800.	26	1	Memorial	182	Foreign Affairs	343	Favorable; bill	319	Referred to Committee Whole House.		
Childers, Edwin H.	(See John P. Hickman, administrator of.)											
Childers, Isom	Increase of pension	27	3	Petition	77	Rev. Pensions	295	Adverse		Laid on table.		
Childers, Nathaniel	Reimbursement of money advanced as forage master, U. S. A.	15	1	Petition	190	Claims				Discharged		April 25, 1820, leave to withdraw.
Childers, Nathaniel	Additional compensation for taking 4th Census of Norfolk, Va.	17	1	Petition	119	Claims	35	Adverse		Referred to Committee Whole House.		
Childers, Nathaniel	Additional compensation for taking 4th Census of Norfolk, Va.	17	2	Petition, report former.	28	Claims	Feb. 3, 1823	Adverse		Referred to Committee Whole House.		
Childers, Nathaniel	Additional compensation for taking 4th Census of Norfolk, Va.	18	1	Petition	37	Claims	47	Adverse		Referred to Committee Whole House.		
Childers, Nathaniel	Additional compensation for taking 4th Census of Norfolk, Va.	19	1	Petition	151	Claims	161	Adverse		Referred to Committee Whole House.		
Childers, Nathaniel	Additional compensation for taking 4th Census of Norfolk, Va.	20	1	Petition	195	Claims	Feb. 1, 1828	Adverse		Referred to Committee Whole House.		
Childers, Nathaniel	Additional compensation for taking 4th Census of Norfolk, Va.	21	1	Petition	34	Claims	121	Adverse		Recommitted.		
							335	Report and bill.	395	Passed	Passed	App'd May 29, 1830
Childress, David	Amount due for services as a soldier in revolutionary war.	22	1	Petition	55	Rev. Claims				Discharged; laid on table.		
Childress, David	Amount due for services as a soldier in revolutionary war.	25	2	Petition	271	Rev. Pensions	864	Adverse		Laid on table.		
Childress, David	Amount due for services as a soldier in revolutionary war.	26	1	Petition	360	Rev. Claims.						
Childress, David	Amount due for services as a soldier in revolutionary war.	27	2	Petition	154	Rev. Claims	224	Adverse		Laid on table.		
Childress, Edward H.	(See John P. Hickman, administrator of.)											
Childs, Aaron, (N. Y.)	Indemnity for property destroyed by British, war of 1812.	19	2	Petition	240	Claims				Discharged.		
Childs, Aaron, (N. Y.)	Indemnity for property destroyed by British, war of 1812.	21	1	Petition	147	Claims	Jan. 22, 1830	Adverse		Laid on table.		
Childs, Aaron, (N. Y.)	Indemnity for property destroyed by British, war of 1812.	22	1	Petition	104	Claims	Jan. 13, 1832	Adverse		Laid on table.		
Childs, Aaron, (N. Y.)	Indemnity for property destroyed by British, war of 1812	23	2	Petition	83	Claims	Jan. 12, 1835	Adverse		Laid on table.		
Childs, Aaron, (N. Y.)	Indemnity for property destroyed by British, war of 1812.	25	2	Petition	234	Claims	Mar. 28, 1838	Adverse		Laid on table.		
Childs, Caleb	Revolutionary pension	15	1	Petition	265	Pens. & Rev. Cl'ms.				Referred to Secretary of War.		
Childs, Caleb	Revolutionary pension	17	2	Petition	20	Pens. & Rev. Cl'ms.	Dec. 16, 1822	Adverse.		Ref. to Com. Whole House, on bill 195.		
Childs, Charles B.	Allowance of naval pay whilst cooperating with the navy.	27	2	Petition	377	Claims.						
Childs, Charles B.	Allowance of naval pay whilst cooperating with the navy.	27	3	Petition	319	Claims.						
Childs, Charles B.	Allowance of naval pay whilst cooperating with the navy.	28	1	Petition	159	Claims.						
Childs, Charles W.	Payment for steamboat lost indirectly in public service.	25	2	Petition	770	Claims	843	Adverse		Laid on table.		

List of private claims presented to the House of Representatives of the United States from the 1st to the 31st Congress, inclusive—Continued.

Names of claimants.	Nature or object of the claim.	Congress.	Session.	How brought before the House of Reps.	Page of journal.	To what committee of the House referred.	No. or date of the report.	Nature of the report.	No. of the bill.	How disposed of by the House of Reps.	How disposed of by the Senate.	Date of the act of Congress, and remarks.
Childs, Ebenezer	Patent for land entered under pre-emption act of 1834.	25	2	Resolution	1176	Priv. Land Claims.				Discharged; laid on table.		
Childs, Ebenezer	Patent for land entered under pre-emption act of 1834.	26	1	Senate bill	1105	Public Lands	July 21, 1840	With't amend.	57	Laid on table.		
Childs, Ebenezer	Patent for land entered under pre-emption act of 1834.	26	2	Senate bill	178	Public Lands			90			
Childs, Evander	(See Henry Remsen.)											
Childs, Evander	Refunding amount paid to United States marshal of N. Y., for certain bounty land sold to another.	27	2	Petition	375	Rev. Claims	701	Adverse		Laid on table.		
Childs, Evander	Refunding amount paid to United States marshal of N. Y., for certain bounty land sold to another.	27	3	Petition	70	Claims.						
Childs, Evander	Refunding amount paid to United States marshal of N. Y., for certain bounty land sold to another.	29	1	Petition	517	Claims	839	Adverse		Laid on table.		
Childs, Ezra	Compensation for revolutionary services in war of 1812.	15	2	Petition	104	Military Affairs	59	Report and bill.	250	Referred to Committee Whole House.		
Childs, Ezra	Compensation for revolutionary services in war of 1812.	16	1	Petition	42	Claims	Jan. 24, 1820	Adverse		Laid on table.		
Childs, Ezra	Compensation for revolutionary services in war of 1812.	16	2	Report, former	147	Claims	Feb. 2, 1821	Rep. and res. adverse.		Resolution adopted.		
Childs, Henry	Pension for disabilities incurred in military service.	30	1	Petition	759	Invalid Pensions	710	Rep. and bill.	555	Referred to Committee Whole House.		
Childs, Henry	Pension for disabilities incurred in military service.	30	2	Bill of last sess.	319	Whole House	Jan. 26, 1849	With't amend.	555	Passed	Adverse report.	
Childs, Henry	Pension for disabilities incurred in military service.	31	1	Petition	270	Invalid Pensions.						
Childs, Timothy, widow of	Pension for revolutionary services.	29	1	Petition	255	Rev. Pensions	240	Adverse		Laid on table.		
Chiles, Thomas	Invalid pension	4	1	Rep. of Comm'r Claims.	457	Whole House	Mar. 7, 1796	Favorable; bill ordered.	156	Passed	Passed	App'd April 20, 1796
Chilson, Samuel W.	Compensation for failure of government to execute mail contract.	27	2	Petition	1024	P. Of. and P. Roads.						
Chilson, Samuel W.	Compensation for failure of government to execute mail contract.	27	3	Petition	44	P. Of. and P. Roads.						
Chilson, Samuel W.	Compensation for failure of government to execute mail contract.	28	1	Petition	811	P. Of. and P. Roads.						
Chilson, Samuel W.	Compensation for failure of government to execute mail contract.	28	2	Petition	110	P. Of. and P. Roads.						
Chilton, John, heirs of.	Seven years half pay as captain in revolutionary army, killed at Brandywine.	23	2	Petition	38	Rev. Claims	Feb. 16, 1835	Adverse		Laid on table.		
Chilton, John, heirs of	Seven years half-pay as captain in revolutionary army, killed at Brandywine.	24	1	Petition	259	Rev. Claims	388	Rep. and bill.	395	Referred to Committee Whole House.		
Chilton, John, heirs of	Seven years half-pay as captain in revolutionary army, killed at Brandywine.	25	2	Petition	39	Rev. Claims	109	Report and bill.	127	Passed	Passed	App'd July 7, 1838
Chiminoaquat, (Indian,) trustee of.	Six thousand four hundred dollars in lieu of a section of land.	24	1	House bill	1012	Whole House	Jan. 30, 1836	Favorable	695	Passed	Passed	App'd July 2, 1836
Chinn, Edward	Grant of land for revolutionary services as a Canadian refugee.	6	2	House bill	766	Whole House	Jan. 26, 1801	Favorable	280	Passed	Passed	App'd Feb. 18, 1801

List of private claims presented to the House of Representatives of the United States from the 1st to the 31st Congress, inclusive—Continued.

Names of claimants.	Nature or object of the claim.	Congress.	Session.	How brought before the House of Reps.	Page of journal.	To what committee of the House referred.	No. or date of the report.	Nature of the report.	No. of the bill.	How disposed of by the House of Reps.	How disposed of by the Senate.	Date of the act of Congress, and remarks.
Chinn, George	Allowance of extra undrawn rations as lieutenant of revenue cutter Search.	22	1	Petition	221	Claims	306	Report and bill.	383	Referred to Committee Whole House.		
Chinn, George	Allowance of extra undrawn rations as lieutenant of revenue cutter Search.	23	1	Petition	34	Claims	3	Report and bill.	3	Passed	Passed	App'd Jan. 24, 1834
Chinn, Thomas W	Confirmation of title to land in Louisiana.	26	1	Petition	610	Priv. Land Claims.	495	Report and bill.	395	Referred to Committee Whole House.		
Chinn, Thomas W	Confirmation of title to land in Louisiana.	27	2	Petition	58	Priv. Land Claims.	283	Report and bill.	249	Passed	Rep. on without amend't	
Chinn, Thomas W	Confirmation of title to land in Louisiana.	27	3	Petition	45	Priv. Land Claims.						
Chinn, Thomas W., Micajah Courtney and others.	Release from judgment against them as sureties of T. G. Morgan, collector at New Orleans.	30	1	Petition	685	Judiciary.						
Chinn, Thomas W., Micajah Courtney and others.	Release from judgment against them as sureties of T. G. Morgan, collector at New Orleans.	30	2	Senate bill	162	Claims	March 3, 1849	With amend.	301	Amended and passed.	Passed	App'd March 3, 1849
Chinowith, Richard	Compensation for services and work on behalf of Virginia in revolutionary war.	2	2	Petition	619	Select	Feb. 1, 1793	Adverse & res.; leave to withdraw.	......	Resolution adopted.		
Chinoworth, Robert, alias Richard Chinoweth, heirs of.	Compensation for services in erecting a garrison on the Ohio river in revolutionary war.	24	2	Petition	91	Rev. Claims.						
Chinoworth, Robert, alias Richard Chinoweth, heirs of.	Compensation for services in erecting a garrison on the Ohio river in revolutionary war.	25	2	Petition	82	Rev. Claims	....	....	......	Discharged; laid on table.		
Chinoworth, Robert, alias Richard Chinoweth, heirs of.	Compensation for services in erecting a garrison on the Ohio river in revolutionary war.	26	1	Petition	361	Rev. Claims.						
Chinoweth, Richard, heirs of.	Compensation for services in erecting a garrison on the Ohio river in revolutionary war.	26	2	Petition	106	Rev. Claims	183	Adverse	......	Laid on table.		
Chipman, Henry, and William Woodbridge.	Compensation for adjusting claims to lots in Detroit.	22	1	Petition	514	Public Lands.						
Chipman, Henry, and William Woodbridge.	Compensation for adjusting claims to lots in Detroit.	22	2	Petition	42	Judiciary	....	....	......	Discharged; laid on table.		
Chipman, Henry, and William Woodbridge.	Compensation for adjusting claims to lots in Detroit.	23	1	Senate bill	845	Judiciary	June 27, 1834	Adverse	124	Laid on table.		
Chipman, Henry, and William Woodbridge.	Compensation for adjusting claims to lots in Detroit.	23	2	Petition	59	Territories.						
Chipman, Henry, and William Woodbridge.	Compensation for adjusting claims to lots in Detroit.	30	1	Senate bill	913	Judiciary	July 19, 1848	With't amend.	146	Referred to Committee Whole House.		
Chipman, Henry, and William Woodbridge.	Compensation for adjusting claims to lots in Detroit.	31	1	Petition	216	Judiciary	176	Report and bill.	189	Referred to Committee Whole House.		
Chipman, Henry, and William Woodbridge.	Compensation for adjusting claims to lots in Detroit.	31	2	Bill of last sess.	103	Judiciary	Jan. 3, 1851	With't amend.	189	Passed	Referred to Judiciary.	
Chipman, Levi	(See Levi Chapman.)											
Chisholm, Alexander	(See Robert Farquar, heir of.)											
Chisholm, James P	Payment for plantation ceded to U. S. by Cherokee Indians.	23	2	Petition	276	Indian Affairs	....	....	......	Discharged; laid on table.		
Chisholm, James P	Payment for plantation ceded to U. S. by Cherokee Indians.	24	1	Petition	265	Indian Affairs	....	....	......	Discharged; laid on table.		

List of private claims presented to the House of Representatives of the United States from the 1st to the 31st Congress, inclusive—Continued.

Names of claimants.	Nature or object of the claim.	Congress.	Session.	How brought before the House of Reps.	Page of journal.	To what committee of the House referred.	No. or date of the report.	Nature of the report.	No. of the bill.	How disposed of by the House of Reps.	How disposed of by the Senate.	Date of the act of Congress, and remarks.
Chisholm, John L.	Payment for a horse lost in United States service.	22	1	Petition	49	Claims	281	Adverse	......	Laid on table.		
Chism, William	Amount expended by mounted gunmen for shoeing their horses.	14	2	Petition	79	Claims	Jan. 27, 1817	Report and bill.	79	Passed	Passed	App'd March 3, 1817
Chittenden, James	Confirmation of claim to two islands on river Detroit.	18	2	Petition	137	Priv. Land Claims.						
Chittenden, James	Indemnity for property destroyed by British in war of 1812.	21	1	Petition	201	Claims	Feb. 3, 1830	Adverse	......	Laid on table.		
Chittenden, Noah	Pension	22	2	Petition	264	Invalid Pensions.						
Chittenden, Noah	Pension	23	1	Petition	54	Invalid Pensions	228	Adverse	......	Recommitted.		
							Jan. 28, 1834	Report and bill.	251	Referred to Committee Whole House.		
Chittenden, Noah	Pension	23	2	Bill of last sess.	299	Whole House	Jan. 31, 1835	With amend.	251	Passed.	Adverse report.	
Chittenden, Noah, widow of	Pension	25	2	Petition	167	Invalid Pensions	497	Report and bill.	500	Passed	Passed	App'd July 7, 1838
Chittim, John	Pension	14	1	House bill	622	Whole House	April 23, 1816	Favorable	171	Passed	Passed	App'd April 30, 1816
Chitwood, John, widow of.	Pension for husband, who died after return from expedition against the Indians, war of 1812.	15	2	Petition	31	Pens. & Rev. Cl'ms.						
Chitwood, John, widow of.	Benefit of acts for relief of widows of those who died in U. States military service.	18	1	Petition	36	Pens. & Rev. Cl'ms.	Dec. 23, 1823	By bill	25	Passed	Indef. postp'd.	
Chitwood, John, widow of.	Benefit of acts for relief of widows of those who died in U. States military service.	19	1	Petition	102	Military Pensions	164	Adverse	......	Laid on table.		
Chitwood, John, widow of.	Benefit of acts for relief of widows of those who died in U. States military service.	20	1	Petition	50	Military Pensions	117	Report and bill.	135	Passed	Passed	App'd May 24, 1828
Choate, Francis and Isaac.	Compensation for losses and injuries as prisoners to the Muskingum Indians.	2	1	Petition	441	Select	Nov. 3, 1791	Adverse	......	Rejected.		
Chotard, Sarah F.	(See Henry Willis, widow of.)											
Chouteau, Auguste	Confirmation of title to land in Missouri Territory.	15	1	Petition	238	Priv. Land Claims.	......	......	......	Discharged.		
Chouteau, Auguste	Confirmation of title to land in Missouri Territory.	16	1	Petition	71	Priv. Land Claims.	......	......	......	Discharged; laid on table.		
Chouteau, Auguste	Confirmation of title to land in Missouri Territory.	17	1	Petition	53	Public Lands	......	......	......	Discharged; laid on table.		
Chouteau, Auguste	Confirmation of title to land in Missouri Territory.	18	1	Petition	53	Public Lands	Jan. 16, 1824	By bill	65	Passed.	Passed.	App'd May 26, 1824
Chouteau, Auguste, representatives of.	(See Antoine Soulard, widow of.)											
Chouteau, Auguste P.	Payment of debt due from Kanzas Indians under treaty of 1825.	19	1	House bill	378	Whole House	May 18, 1826	With't amend.	179	Passed.	Passed	App'd May 20, 1826
Chouteau, Auguste P.	Expenses of mission to the wild Indians of the southwest.	25	2	House bill	213	Whole House	July 5, 1838	Favorable	269	Passed	Passed	App'd July 7, 1838
Chouteau, Demun, & Co.	Indemnity for having been captured and imprisoned by Spanish government.	15	1	Resolution and Pres. message.	319, 471	......	......	......	......	Laid on table	......	See Ex. Doc. No. 197
Chouteau, Francis G.	Payment of debt due from Kanzas Indians under treaty of 1825.	19	1	House bill	378	Whole House	May 18, 1826	With't amend.	179	Passed	Passed	App'd May 20, 1826
Chouteau, Pierre, sen.	(See Don Jacques Clamorgan, assignee of.)											
Chouteau, Pierre, jr.	(See Julien Dubuque, heirs of.)											

List of private claims presented to the House of Representatives of the United States from the 1st to the 31st Congress, inclusive—Continued.

Names of claimants.	Nature or object of the claim.	Congress.	Session.	How brought before the House of Reps.	Page of journal.	To what committee of the House referred.	No. or date of the report.	Nature of the report.	No. of the bill.	How disposed of by the House of Reps.	How disposed of by the Senate.	Date of the act of Congress, and remarks.
Chouteau, Pierre, jr., & Co	Payment of Shawnee Indians draft on Commissioner of Indian Affairs out of their trust fund.	29	2	Petition	172	Indian Affairs.						
Chouteau, Pierre, jr., & Co.	Payment of Shawnee Indians draft on Commissioner of Indian Affairs out of their trust fund.	30	2	Senate bill	279	Indian Affairs	Feb. 8, 1849	With't amend.	212	Passed	Passed	App'd March 3, 1849
Chretien, Louis, heirs of, by Gerard and Hypolite Chretien.	Refunding of $14,806 27 illegally collected from him as surety for John Thompson.	19	1	Petition	78	Claims	9	Favorable bill.	22	Passed	Passed	App'd March 3, 1826
Chretien, Francis	Confirmation of title to land in Louisiana.	28	1	Petition	550	Priv. Land Claims.	460	Favorable bill.	356	Passed	Passed	App'd June 17, 1844
Christian, Edmund	(See William Gregory, heirs of.)											
Christian, James	Invalid pension	3	2	Rep. of Secretary War.	350	Claims	Feb. 23, 1795	Favorable; bill ordered.	130	Passed	Postponed to next session.	
Christian, James	Invalid pension	4	1	Rep. of Secretary War.	445	Claims	Feb. 18, 1796	Favorable; bill ordered.	156	Passed	Passed	App'd April 20, 1796
Christian, Rawleigh C.	Pension	15	1	Petition	97	Pens. & Rev. Cl'ms.	Feb. 5, 1819	By bill	308	Passed	Postponed.	
Christian, Valentine	Revolutionary pension	22	1	Petition	556	Rev. Pensions				Discharged; laid on table.		
Christian, William A.	Payment of amount paid to warrant officers of ship Princeton.	29	2	Senate bill	381	Naval Affairs	Feb. 24, 1847	With't amend.	154	Referred to Committee Whole House.		
Christian, William A.	Payment of amount paid to warrant officers of ship Princeton.	30	1	Petition	111	Naval Affairs.						
Christian, William, heirs of.	Commutation pay due for revolutionary services.	31	1	Petition	891	Rev. Claims	417	Adverse		Laid on table.		
Christie, John W.	Extra pay as inspector at Philadelphia during the yellow fever in 1793.	4	1	Petition	493	Claims.						
Christie, John W.	Extra pay as inspector at Philadelphia during the yellow fever in 1793.	4	2	Petition	614	Claims.						
Christler, Daniel, widow of	Revolutionary pension	26	1	Petition	385	Rev. Claims	664	Adverse		Laid on table.		
Christman, Frederick	Revolutionary pension	28	2	Petition	70	Rev. Pensions				Discharged; leave to withdraw.		
Christophers, Joseph, widow and heirs of.	Indemnity for property captured by French prior to 1800.	22	1	Petition	186	Foreign Affairs.						
Christophers, Joseph, widow and heirs of.	Indemnity for property captured by French prior to 1800.	26	1	Petition	182	Foreign Affairs	343	Favorable bill.	319	Referred to Committee Whole House.		
Christophers, Joseph, heirs of.	Indemnity for property captured by French prior to 1800.	31	1	Petition	225	Foreign Affairs	355	Report and bill.	318	Referred to Committee Whole House.		
Christopher, William G., legal representatives of.	Confirmation of title to land in Florida.	22	1	Petition	227	Priv. Land Claims.	271	Report and bill.	349	Referred to Committee Whole House.		
Christopher, William G., legal representatives of.	Confirmation of title to land in Florida.	23	1	Petition	158	Priv. Land Claims.	173	Report and bill.	189	Passed	Passed	App'd June 30, 1834
Christy, David	Invalid pension	24	1	Petition	473	Invalid Pensions	April 12, 1836	Adverse		Laid on table.		
Christy, James	Revolutionary pension	25	3	Resolution	275	Rev. Pensions				Discharged.		
Christy, James	Revolutionary pension	28	1	Petition	742	Rev. Pensions.						
Christy, William	Confirmation of title to land in Missouri territory.	15	1	Petition	232	Priv. Land Claims.				Discharged.		
Christy, William	Confirmation of title to land in Missouri territory.	16	1	Petition	71	Priv. Land Claims.				Discharged; laid on table.		

List of private claims presented to the House of Representatives of the United States from the 1st to the 31st Congress, inclusive—Continued.

Names of claimants.	Nature or object of the claim.	Congress.	Session.	How brought before the House of Reps.	Page of journal.	To what committee of the House referred.	No. or date of the report.	Nature of the report.	No. of the bill.	How disposed of by the House of Reps.	How disposed of by the Senate.	Date of the act of Congress, and remarks.
Christy, William	Confirmation of title to land in Missouri territory.	17	1	Petition	53	Public Lands				Discharged; laid on table.		
Christy, William	Confirmation of title to land in Missouri territory.	18	1	Petition	53	Public Lands	Jan. 16, 1824	By bill	65	Passed	Passed	App'd May 26, 1824
Christy, William, (Ind.)	Pension for wounds received in engagement with Indians under Wayne, in 1794.	21	2	Senate bill	145	Military Pensions	Jan. 13, 1831	Adverse	55	Laid on table.		
Christy, William, (Ind.)	Pension for wounds received in engagement with Indians under Wayne, in 1794.	25	2	Petition	181	Rev. Pensions				Discharged; laid on table.		
Christy, William, (La.)	Relief from judgment against him as paymaster U. S. infantry, and an equitable settlement of his accounts.	23	2	Petition	49	Claims.						
Christy, William, (La.)	Relief from judgment against him as paymaster U. S. infantry, and an equitable settlement of his accounts.	24	1	Petition	93	Claims	271	Report and bill.	277	Referred to Committee Whole House.		
Christy, William, (La.)	Relief from judgment against him as paymaster U. S. infantry, and an equitable settlement of his accounts.	24	2	Bill of last sess'n	199	Whole House	Jan. 13, 1837	With't amend.	277	Passed	Passed	App'd March 3, 1837
Chromister, James	(See Wm. H. Bradford, agent, &c.)	28	1		262							
Chryselius, Adolph, & John B. Ward.	Compensation for services, &c., in revolutionary war.	3	1	Petition	131	Select.						
Chubbuck, Levi	Invalid pension	3	2	Rep. of Secretary War.	278	Claims	Feb. 28, 1795	Favorable; bill ordered.	130	Passed	Postp'd to next session.	
Chubbuck, Levi	Invalid pension	4	1	Rep. of Secretary War.	445	Claims	Feb. 18, 1796	Favorable; bill ordered.	156	Passed	Passed	App'd April 20, 1796
Chubbuck, Levi	Increase of pension	10	1	House bill	232	Whole House	April 19, 1808	Favorable	78	Passed	Passed	App'd April 25, 1808
Chudwick, Peter	(See S. Hersey)	12	1		137							
Church, Benjamin	Pension	22	1	Petition	51	Rev. Pensions				Discharged; laid on table.		
Church, Caleb	Revolutionary pension	22	1	Resolution	82	Rev. Pensions	170	Report and bill.	244	Passed		Its passage, as per Ho. Journal, is probably a mistake.
Church, Caleb	Revolutionary pension	22	2	Bill of last sess'n.	123				244	Laid on table.		
Church, Charles	Pension	21	2	Petition	299	Military Pensions.						
Church, Constant	Revolutionary pension	21	1	Resolution	550	Military Pensions				Discharged; laid on table.		
Church, Daniel W.	Compensation for horses impressed in United States service, war of 1812.	26	1	Petition	294	Claims.						
Church, Daniel W.	Compensation for horses impressed in United States service, war of 1812.	26	2	Petition	38	Claims.						
Church, Daniel W.	Pension for militia services in war of 1812.	26	1	Petition	938	Invalid Pensions	669	Adverse		Laid on table.		
Church, Daniel W	Pension for militia services in war of 1812.	26	2	Petition	36	Invalid Pensions	57	Adverse		Laid on table.		
Church, Daniel W	Pension for militia services in war of 1812.	28	1	Petition	130	Invalid Pensions	436	Report and bill	333	Passed	Passed	App'd June 17, 1844
Church, Jabez	Invalid pension	10	1	House bill	232	Whole House	April 19, 1808	Favorable	78	Passed	Passed	App'd April 25, 1808

List of private claims presented to the House of Representatives of the United States from the 1st to the 31st Congress, inclusive—Continued.

Names of claimants.	Nature or object of the claim.	Congress.	Session.	How brought before the House of Reps.	Page of journal.	To what committee of the House referred.	No. or date of the report.	Nature of the report.	No. of the bill.	How disposed of by the House of Reps.	How disposed of by the Senate.	Date of the act of Congress, and remarks.
Church, Jabez	Invalid pension	19	1	Petition	98	Military Pensions	164	Adverse		Laid on lable.		
Church, John, (Maine)	Pension	22	1	Petition	287	Rev. Pensions.						
Church, John, and others, descendants of those who fell at Wyoming.	Remuneration for losses and sufferings of their ancestors in revolutionary war.	25	2	Petition	391	Rev. Claims	1032	Adverse		Laid on table.		
Church, John, widow of, (Ohio.)	Pension for revolutionary services.	28	2	Petition	145	Rev. Pensions.						
Church, John, widow of, (Ohio.)	Pension for revolutionary services.	29	1	Petition	118	Rev. Pensions.	528	Adverse		Laid on table.		
Church, John B., administrator of.	Indemnity for French spoliations prior to 1800.	31	1	Petition	196	Foreign Affairs	355	Report and bill.	318	Referred to Committee Whole House.		
Church, Nathaniel	Increase of pension	10	1	House bill	232	Whole House	April 19, 1808	Favorable	78	Passed	Passed	App'd April 25, 1808
Church, Nathaniel	Invalid pension	10	2	House bill	499	Whole House	Feb. 20, 1809	Favorable	158	Passed	Passed	App'd March 3, 1809
Church, Nathaniel	Arrearages of pension up to 1808.	15	2	Petition	94	Pens. & Rev. Cl'ms.	Dec. 18, 1818	Rep. and res.; adverse.		Resolution adopted.		
Church, Ozias S.	Compensation for services as assistant marshal in New York.	27	2	Petition	76	Claims.						
Church, Reuben	Renewal of pension	17	2	Petition	142					Referred to Committee Whole House on bill No. 207.		See act Mar. 1, 1823
Church, Samuel	Revolutionary pension	22	1	Petition	631	Rev. Pensions.						
Chuch, jr., Thomas, (N. Y.)	Compensation for recapturing sch'r Lively, war of 1812.	21	1	Petition	122	Naval Affairs	Jan. 22, 1830	Adverse		Laid on table.		
Church, Thomas, of Mass., heirs of.	Legislative relief respecting the pension of deceased.	24	1	Petition	56	Rev. Pensions				Discharged; laid on table.		
Church, Willard	Renewal of pension	17	1	Petition	92	Rev. Pensions				Discharged; laid on table.		
Churchman, John	Exclusive right of vending spheres, maps, and tables made on principles of magnetism invented by him.	1	1	Petition	14	Select	April 20, 1789	Fav'rable; general bill ordered.	10	Postponed to next session.		
Churchill, Benjamin K.	Restoration of pension	27	2	Petition	254	Naval Affairs	603	Adverse		Laid on table.		
Churchill, Benjamin K.	Restoration of pension	28	1	Petition	104	Naval Affairs	518	Report and bill.	393	Referred to Committee Whole House.		
Churchill, Cadwallader	(See Bryant R. Young and others.)											
Churchill, Charles, widow of.	Pension for services as a soldier in the war of 1812.	26	1	Petition	708	Invalid Pensions	565	Adverse		Laid on table.		
Churchill, Sylvester	Allowance for extraordinary services as inspector general with the army in Florida.	25	3	Resolution	156	Military Affairs				Discharged; laid on table.		
Churchill, Sylvester	Allowance for extraordinary services as inspector general with the army in Florida.	26	1	Resolution	557	Claims.						
Churchill, Sylvester	Allowance for extraordinary services as inspector general with the army in Florida.	26	2	Petition	80	Claims	23	Adverse		Laid on table.		
Churchill, Thomas J.	Relief from liability as commissary, having lost vouchers for his accounts.	31	1	Petition	37	Military Affairs	30	Adverse		Laid on table.		
Churchill, William H., widow of.	Expences as acting commissary of subsistence in Mexican war.	31	1	Petition	392	Military Affairs				Discharged; laid on table.		
Churchman, Samuel W.	Refunding of duties on mahogany.	27	3	Petition	76	Ways and Means.						

List of private claims presented to the House of Representatives of the United States from the 1st to the 31st Congress, inclusive—Continued.

Names of claimants.	Nature or object of the claim.	Congress.	Session.	How brought before the House of Reps.	Page of journal.	To what committee of the House referred.	No. or date of the report.	Nature of the report.	No. of the bill.	How disposed of by the House of Reps.	How disposed of by the Senate.	Date of the act of Congress, and remarks.
Churchwell, George W	(See Robt. M. Anderson and others.)											
Chute, Richard	Reimbursed for clothing furnished Winnebago Indians.	29	2	Petition	228	Indian Affairs						Provided for in Indian appropriation act of 30th Sept., 1850.
Chute, Thomas, guardian of the widow of.	Pension for services as a revolutionary soldier.	25	3	Petition	675					Laid on table.		
Chute, Thomas, guardian of the widow of.	Pensoin for services as a revolutionary soldier.	26	1	Petition	707	Rev. Pensions.						
Cicot, Francois	Compensation for property destroyed by Indians at Detroit.	28	1	Petition	853	Claims.						
Cicot, Francois	Compensation for property destroyed by Indians at Detroit.	31	1	Petition	213	Claims	267	Adverse		Laid on table.		
Cicot, Francois	Compensation for services in Michigan militia, war of 1812.	31	1	Petition	695	Claims.						
Cilley, Jonathan, and others	Allowance for depreciation of pay as officers of New Hampshire regiments.	3	1	Petition	57					Referred to Secretary of War.		
Cilley, Jonathan, and others	Allowance for depreciation of pay as officers of New Hampshire regiments.	3	2	Rep. of Secretary of War.	278					Laid on table.		
Cisné, James, assignee of	Confirmation of title to land in Michigan Territory.	23	1	Petition	338	Priv. Land Claims.	458	Report and bill	476	Referred to Committee Whole House.		
Cisné, James, assignee of	Confirmation of title to land in Michigan Territory.	24	1	Senate bill	1077	Priv. Land Claims.	July 1, 1836	With't amend.	210	Passed	Passed	App'd July 2, 1836
Cisné, James, assignee of	Confirmation of title to land in Michigan Territory.	30	1	Petition	759	Priv. Land Claims.						
Cisné, James, assignee of	Confirmation of title to land in Michigan Territory.	30	2	Petition	91	Priv. Land Claims.	55	Report and bill	760	Referred to Committee Whole House.		
Cisné, James, assignee of.	Confirmation of title to land in Michigan Territory.	31	1	Petition	425	Priv. Land Claims.	344	Report and bill.	305	Referred to Committee Whole House.		
Cissna, Charles, Lieut., widow of.	Half pay pension for five years	20	2	Resolution	225	Military Pensions				Discharged; laid on table.		
Cissna, Charles, Lieut., widow of.	Half pay pension for five years	21	1	Petition	294	Military Pensions	April 2, 1830	Adverse		Laid on table.		
Clackner, Adam	Restoration to revolutionary pension roll.	18	1	Petition	116	Rev. Pensions	Jan. 14, 1824	Adverse		Laid on table.		
Claflin, George S	Indemnity for injuries, &c., sustained as prisoner at Halifax, war of 1812.	30	1	Petition	589	Claims	707	Report and bill.	552	Referred to Committee Whole House.		
Claflin, George S	Indemnity for injuries, &c., sustained as prisoner at Halifax, war of 1812.	30	2	Bill of last sess.	319	Whole House	Jan. 26, 1849	With't amend.	552	Passed	With't amend.	
Claflin, George S	Indemnity for injuries, &c., sustained as prisoner at Halifax, war of 1812.	31	1	Petition	231	Invalid Pensions	293	Report and bill.	166	Referred to Committee Whole House.		
Claflin, George S	Indemnity for injuries, &c., sustained as prisoner at Halifax, war of 1812.	31	2	Bill of last sess.	104	Whole House	Jan. 3, 1851	With amend.	166	Passed with amend't.	Adverse.	
Clagatt, R. H.	(See J. Ramay, administrators of.)											
Claggett, Samuel, representatives of.	Commutation pay due	25	2	Petition	69	Rev. Claims				Discharged; laid on table.		
Claggett, Samuel, representatives of.	Commutation pay due	26	1	Petition	164	Rev. Claims.						

List of private claims presented to the House of Representatives of the United States from the 1*st to the* 31*st Congress, inclusive*—Continued.

Names of claimants.	Nature or object of the claim.	Congress.	Session.	How brought before the House of Reps.	Page of journal.	To what committee of the House referred.	No. or date of the report.	Nature of the report.	No. of the bill.	How disposed of by the House of Reps.	How disposed of by the Senate.	Date of the act of Congress, and remarks.
Claggett, Thomas, and Horatio Judson, agent of.	Remission of duties on goods imported in ship Termagant and destroyed by fire.	2	1	Memorial	511	....	....	....	.....	Referred to Secretary Treasury.		
Claggett, Thomas, and Horatio Judson, agent of.	Remission of duties on goods imported in ship Termagant and destroyed by fire.	3	1	Rep. of Secretary Treasury.	78	....	....	....	.....	Laid on table.		
Claghorn, George	Compensation for extra services in building and fitting out frigate Constitution.	13	1	Petition	37	Claims	....	....	.....	Discharged.		
Claghorn, George	Pension for revolutionary services.	16	1	Petition	32	Pens. & Rev. Cl'ms.	Dec. 20, 1819	Report & res. adverse.	.....	Resolution adopted.		
Claghorn, George	Pension for revolutionary services.	17	2	Petition	186	Pens. & Rev. Cl'ms.	....	....	.....	Discharged; laid on table.		
Claghorn, James	(See James Miller, late widow of.)											
Claiborne, Augustin	(See A. O. Frazer, executors of.)	20	1	....	408							
Claiborne, Buller, heir of.	Commutation of half-pay due as an officer in revolutionary army.	23	1	Petition	40	Rev. Claims......	43	Report and bill.	48	Passed	Passed	App'd June 30, 1834
Claiborne, M. G. L......	(See Exploring Expedition.)											
Claiborne, Richard, (La.).	Extension of patent for propelling boats.	14	1	Petition	347	Com. and Manuf..	....	....	.....	Discharged; laid on table.		
Claiborne, Richard, (La.).	Extension of patent for propelling boats.	14	2	Petition	112	Judiciary	Jan. 6, 1817	Rep. and res.; adverse.	.....	Resolution adopted.		
Claiborne, Richard, (La.).	Extension of patent for propelling boats.	15	1	Petition	247	Judiciary	Mar. 13, 1818	Rep. and res.; leave to withdraw.	.....	Resolution adopted.		
Claiborne, Richard, (Penn.) widow of.	Pension for revolutionary services.	31	1	Petition	369	Rev. Pensions....	65	Adverse	.....	Laid on table.		
Clair, Godfrey	Revolutionary pension..........	26	1	Petition	285	Rev. Pensions.						
Clamberg, Philip, and others	Compensation for services, &c., in revolutionary war.	3	1	Pet. & Report of Sec. of War.	43	Select.						
Clamorgan, Don Jacques, representatives of.	Confirmation of title to land in Territory of Missouri.	15	1	Petition	144	Priv. Land Claims.	Feb. 11, 1818	By bill	83	Referred to Committee Whole House.		
Clamorgan, Don Jacques, executors of.	Confirmation of title to land in Territory of Missouri.	15	1	Petition	312	Priv. Land Claims.						
Clamorgan, Don Jacques, executors of.	Confirmation of title to land in Territory of Missouri.	16	1	Petition	72	Priv. Land Claims.	....	....	.....	Discharged; laid on table.		
Clamorgan, Don Jacques, executors of.	Confirmation of title to land in Territory of Missouri.	17	1	Petition	53	Public Lands.....	....	....	.....	Discharged; laid on table.		
Clamorgan, Don Jacques, executors of.	Confirmation of title to land in Territory of Missouri.	18	1	Petition........	53	Public Lands.....	Jan. 16, 1824	By bill	65	Passed	Passed	App'd May 26, 1824, extended per act 17th June, 1844.
Clamorgan, Don Jacques, Pierre Chauteau, sr., assignee of.	Confirmation of title to land in Missouri.	24	2	Petition	84	Priv. Land Claims.						
Clamorgan, Don Jacques, representatives of.	Removal of restriction in act 17th June, 1844, and permission to enter other land in lieu of that claimed.	29	1	Petition	311	Priv. Land Claims.						
Clamorgan, Don Jacques, heirs of.	Permission to enter other land in lieu of that claimed.	30	1	Petition	638	Priv. Land Claims.	506	Report and bill.	427	Referred to Committee Whole House.		
Clan, Michael G........	Pre emption right to certain lands.	30	2	Memorial	91	Public Lands.....	115	Favorable	793	Referred to Committee Whole House.		
Clapham, Josias.........	Renewal of certain loan office certificates destroyed by fire.	2	1	Pet. and rep. of Sec. Treasury.	450	Select.						

List of private claims presented to the House of Representatives of the United States from the 1st *to the* 31st *Congress, inclusive*—Continued.

Names of claimants.	Nature or object of the claim.	Congress.	Session.	How brought before the House of Reps.	Page of journal.	To what committee of the House referred.	No. or date of the report.	Nature of the report.	No. of the bill.	How disposed of by the House of Reps.	How disposed of by the Senate.	Date of the act of Congress, and remarks.
Clapier, L.	Indemnity for French spoliations prior to 1800.	26	1	Memorial	182	Foreign Affairs	343	Favorable; bill	319	Referred to Committee Whole House.		
Clapp, Daniel, daughter of	Revolutionary pension	27	3	Petition	283	Rev. Pensions.						
Clapp, Daniel, daughter of	Revolutionary pension	28	1	Petition	122	Rev. Pensions	215	Favorable; bill	169	Passed	Adverse report.	
Clapp, Daniel, daughter of	Revolutionary pension	28	2	Petition	88	Rev. Pensions				Discharged; laid on table.		
Clapp, David, (N. Y.)	Pension for disabilities incurred as a soldier in war of 1812.	21	2	Petition	188	Military Pensions.						
Clapp, David, (N. Y.)	Pension for disabilities incurred as a soldier in war of 1812.	22	1	Resolution	176	Invalid Pensions	204	Report and bill.	288	Passed	Rejected.	
Clapp, David, (N. Y.)	Pension for disabilities incurred as a soldier in war of 1812.	22	2	Resolution	138	Invalid Pensions	Feb. 15, 1833	Report and bill.	738	Referred to Committee Whole House.		
Clapp, David, (N. Y.)	Pension for disabilities incurred as a soldier in war of 1812.	23	1	Petition	332	Invalid Pensions	Mar. 15, 1834	Report and bill.	367	Referred to Committee Whole House.		
Clapp, David, (N. Y.)	Pension for disabilities incurred as a soldier in war of 1812.	23	2	Bill of last sess.	336	Whole House	Feb. 6, 1835	With't amend.	367	Passed	Referred.	
Clapp, David, (N. Y.)	Pension for disabilities incurred as a soldier in war of 1812.	24	1	Petition	634	Invalid Pensions	June 22, 1836	Adverse		Laid on table.		
Clapp, David, (N. Y.)	Pension for disabilities incurred as a soldier in war of 1812.	24	2	Petition	42	Invalid Pensions	Dec. 30, 1836	Adverse		Laid on table.		
Clapp, D., and others	Compensation for locating bounty land warrants.	31	1	Petition	198	Public Lands.						
Clapp, Eliakim	Revolutionary pension	20	2	Resolution	104	Military Pensions				Discharged; laid on table.		
Clapp, Eliakim	Revolutionary pension	21	1	Petition	49	Military Pensions	Jan. 5, 1830	By bill	72	Passed	Passed	App'd May 20, 1830
Clapp, Frederick	(See Samuel Clapp's administrator)	26	1		182							
Clapp, Preserved	Compensation for preparing spiked cannon for use.	5	2	Petition	239	Claims	April 9, 1798	Adverse		Rejected.		
Clapp, Preserved, heirs of	Compensation for preparing spiked cannon for use.	25	2	Petition	658, 827	Rev. Claims				Discharged; laid on table.		
Clapp, Rowland	Pre-emption to land on which he resides.	19	1	Petition	44	Priv. Land Claims	Dec. 20, 1825	Adverse		Laid on table.		
Clapp, Rowland C., widow of.	Retention out of any money due Harris & Farrow, contractors for fortifications on Dauphin Island, of an amount due by them.	21	1	Petition	414	Claims				Discharged; laid on table.		
Clapp, Rowland C., widow of.	Payment of claim against Harris & Farrow, on the plea that the Secretary has failed to execute act of 3d March, 1825.	21	1	Petition	524	Claims				Discharged; laid on table.		
Clapp, Rowland C., widow of.	Payment of claim against Harris & Farrow, on the plea that the Secretary has failed to execute act of 3d March, 1825.	21	2	Petition	62	Claims.						
Clapp, Samuel, administrator of.	Indemnity for French spoliations prior to 1800.	26	1	Memorial	182	Foreign Affairs	343	Favorable; bill	319	Referred to Committee Whole House.		
Clapp, Silas	Renewal of pension	25	2	Petition	180	Rev. Pensions				Disch'd; laid on table.		
Clapp, Stephen	Settlement of claim against United States.	1	3	Petition and rep't Sec'y of War.	342					Laid on table.		
Clapp, Stephen	Commutation of half-pay as an officer in revolutionary army.	15	1	Petition	122	Pens. & Rev. Cl'ms.	March 2, 1818	Adverse		Laid on table		Leave to withdraw.
Clapp, Stephen, executor of	Commutation of half-pay as an officer in revolutionary army.	31	2	Petition	286	Rev. Claims.						

List of private claims presented to the House of Representatives of the United States from the 1st to the 31st Congress, inclusive—Continued.

Names of claimants.	Nature or object of the claim.	Congress.	Session.	How brought before the House of Reps.	Page of journal.	To what committee of the House referred.	No. or date of the report.	Nature of the report.	No. of the bill.	How disposed of by the House of Reps.	How disposed of by the Senate.	Date of the act of Congress, and remarks.
Clapper, George, widow of.	Pension for revolutionary services.	29	1	Petition	1139	Rev. Pensions.						
Clapper, George, widow of.	Pension for revolutionary services.	29	2	Petition	69	Rev. Pensions.						
Clapper, George, widow of.	Pension for revolutionary services.	30	1	Petition	100	Rev. Pensions	18	Report and bill.	22	Passed		
Clapperton, Louis	(See Louis Chapaton.)											
Claidy, A. N.	Compensation for horse and equipments lost in Seminole campaign of 1818.	23	1	Documents	154	Claims.						
Clark, Absalom	Remission of duties on distillery destroyed by fire.	14	2	Petition	468					Laid on table.		
Clark, Allen	Drawback of duty on exported merchandise withheld for a mistake in his entry.	15	1	Petition	83	Com. and Manuf.	Dec. 30, 1817	Res. for leave to withdraw.		Resolution adopted.		
Clark, Ambrose, administrator of.	Indemnity for French spoliations prior to 1800.	26	1	Petition	715	Foreign Affairs	343	Favorable; bill	319	Referred to Committee Whole House.		
Clark, Ambrose, administrator of.	Indemnity for French spoliations prior to 1800.	31	1	Petition	271	Foreign Affairs	355	Report and bill.	318	Referred to Committee Whole House.		
Clark, Andrew, (N. Y.)	Revolutionary pension	22	1	Petition	255	Rev. Pensions				Discharged; laid on table.		
Clark, Andrew, (Tenn.)	Payment for horse and equipments lost in Seminole campaign of 1818.	23	1	Documents	154	Claims.						
Clark, Andrew, of Mich., late widow of.	Payment for property destroyed at river Huron, war of 1812.	22	1	Petition	366	Claims	March 9, 1822	Adverse		Laid on table.		
Clark, Andrew, of Mich., late widow of.	Payment for property destroyed at river Huron, war of 1812.	23	1	Petition	217	Claims	382	Adverse		Laid on table.		
Clark, Anna	(See Stephen Thayer, late widow of.)											
Clark, Archibald, (Ga.)	Indemnity for amount of judgment against him as collector at St. Mary's.	18	1	House bill	438	Whole House	April 24, 1829	With't amend.	200	Passed	Passed	App'd May 19, 1824
Clark, Archibald	(See Robert Seagrave, administrator of, and others.)											
Clark, Archibald, heirs of, (N. C.)	Payment for provisions and clothing taken for use of revolutionary army.	23	1	Petition	81	Rev. Claims.						
Clark, Asa, (Mass.)	Wages due for services in revolutionary war.	25	3	Petition	103	Rev. Claims				Discharged.		
Clark, Asa, (Mass.)	Wages due for services in revolutionary war.	26	1	Petition	164	Rev. Claims	612	Adverse		Laid on table.		
Clark, Asa, (Mass.)	Wages due for services in revolutionary war.	27	2	Petition	376	Rev. Claims	974	Adverse		Laid on table.		
Clark, Asa, (Florida)	Refunding of money deposited with receiver of land office in Florida.	28	2	Petition	85	Public Lands.						
Clark, Ashael	Costs, &c., growing out of of suits and judgments against him in supreme court New York.	15	1	Senate bill	358	Military Affairs	Dec. 25, 1818	With't amend.	43	Passed	Passed	App'd April 11, 1818
Clarke, Audly	Indemnity for French spoliations prior to 1800.	26	1	Memorial	182	Foreign Affairs	343	Favorable; bill	319	Referred to Committee Whole House.		
Clarke, Audly	(See Caleb Gardner, executors of.)											
Clarke, Bailey L., heirs of.	Refunding of money paid for Washington city lots previously sold.	23	1	Petition	219	Dist. of Columbia.	515	Report and bill.	515	Referred to Committee Whole House.		
Clarke, Bailey L., heirs of.	Refunding of money paid for Washington city lots previously sold.	23	2	Bill of last sess.	162				515	Passed	Passed	App'd March 3, 1835

List of private claims presented to the House of Representatives of the United States from the 1st to the 31st Congress, inclusive—Continued.

Names of claimants.	Nature or object of the claim.	Congress.	Session.	How brought before the House of Reps.	Page of journal.	To what committee of the House referred.	No. or date of the report.	Nature of the report.	No. of the bill.	How disposed of by the House of Reps.	How disposed of by the Senate.	Date of the act of Congress, and remarks.
Clark, Benjamin	Pre-emption right to land on which his mills are erected.	16	1	Petition	365	Public Lands				Discharged; laid on table.		
Clark, Benjamin	Increase of compensation as postmaster at Sandy Hill, (N. Y.)	20	1	Petition	58	P. Of. and P. Roads.				Discharged; laid on table.		
Clark, Benjamin, administrators of.	Compensation for wagon and team destroyed in war of 1812.	19	2	Petition	190	Claims				Discharged.		
Clark, Benjamin, administrators of.	Compensation for wagon and team destroyed in war of 1812.	20	1	Petition	419	Claims				Discharged; laid on table.		
Clark, Benjamin, administrators of.	Compensation for wagon and team destroyed in war of 1814.	21	1	Petition	57	Claims	16	Report and bill.	23	Passed	Passed	App'd Feb. 11, 1830
Clark & Connor and others.	Permission to fund bills of credit issued by Congress in certificates of public debt.	4	1	Petition	387	Ways and Means.						See report of Secretary Treasury, December 23, 1795.
Clark & Connor, by Joseph Perkins.	Liquidation of certain revolutionary quartermaster's certificates.	4	1	Rep. of Secretary Treasury.	388	Claims	May 31, 1796	Adverse		Laid on table.		
Clark, Carey	Pension	22	1	Petition	114	Invalid Pensions	213	Report and bill.	288	Passed	Rejected.	
Clark, Carey	Pension	24	1	Senate bill	811	Invalid Pensions.	June 9, 1836	With't amend.	176	Passed	Passed	App'd June 15, 1836
Clark, Catharine	(See John Clark, deceased, administratrix of.)											
Clark, Charles	Allowance for depreciation of revolutionary pay.	4	1	Petition	422	Claims	Jan. 29, 1796	Adverse		Referred to Committee Whole House.		
Clark, Charles G	Revolutionary pension	21	2	Resolution	142	Military Pensions.						
Clark, Charles G	Revolutionary pension	22	1	Resolution	70	Rev. Pensions	Dec. 29, 1831	Adverse		Laid on table.		
Clark, Charles Alexander.	Pre-emption right to four square miles of Grand prarie, Missouri.	23	1	Petition	76	Public Lands.						
Clark, Christopher, (N. Y.)	Indemnity for losses and expenses incurred in war of 1812.	23	2	Petition	220	Claims						
Clark, Christopher, (N. Y.)	Indemnity for losses and expenses incurred in war of 1812.	24	1	Petition	49, 670	Claims	172	Adverse		Recommitted.		
							May 6, 1836	Favorable; bill.	608	Referred to Committee Whole House.		
Clark, Christopher, (N. Y.)	Indemnity for losses and expenses incurred in war of 1812.	25	2	Petition	36	Claims	40	Report and bill.	52	Passed	Passed	App'd April 20, 1838
Clark, Daniel P	(See New York, sundry inhabitants of Plattsburgh.)											
Clark, Daniel, (Salem, Massachusetts.)	Restoration of property taken by consul at Cuba, or its equivalent.	8	2	Petition	128	Claims.						
Clark, Daniel, (Salem, Massachusetts.)	Restoration of property taken by consul at Cuba, or its equivalent.	9	1	Petition	212	Claims.						
Clark, Daniel, (Salem, Massachusetts.)	Restoration of real estate on payment of tax for which it passed to United States.	19	1	Petition	52	Judiciary	6	Report and bill.	14	Passed	Passed	App'd May 16, 1826
Clark, Daniel C., assignee of.	Compensation for horses furnished United States for Florida war.	25	2	Petition	397	Claims	836	Adverse		Laid on table.		
Clarke, David, widow of.	Revolutionary pension	27	3	Petition	401	Rev. Pensions.						
Clark, Dennis	Return of money paid on land reverted to the United States.	13	2	Petition	190	Public Lands.	18	Favorable; bill ordered.	168	Passed	Passed	App'd April 18, 1814
Clark, Eaton and others	Fishing bounty on schooner Susan.	23	2	Petition	272	Commerce.						
Clark, Edward	Invalid pension	3	2	Rep. of Secretary War.	350	Claims	Mar. 3, 1795	To discharge and postp'e.		Laid on table.		
Clark, Edward	Invalid pension	4	1	Rep. of Secretary War.	445	Claims	Feb. 18, 1796	Favorable; bill ordered.	156	Passed	Passed	App'd April 20, 1796

List of private claims presented to the House of Representatives of the United States from the 1st to the 31st Congress, inclusive—Continued.

Names of claimants.	Nature or object of the claim.	Congress.	Session.	How brought before the House of Reps.	Page of journal.	To what committee of the House referred.	No. or date of the report.	Nature of the report.	No. of the bill.	How disposed of by the House of Reps.	How disposed of by the Senate.	Date of the act of Congress, and remarks.
Clark, Edward, and others	Compensation for services, &c., in revolutionary war.	4	1	Petition	396	Claims	Mar. 32, 1796	Adverse	......	Laid on table.		
Clark, Edward	Pre emption right to land as a New Orleans branch pilot.	28	1	Petition	77	Priv. Land Claims.	9	Favorable; bill	35	Passed	Passed	App'd June 17, 1844
Clark, Eleanor	(See Ambrose Clark, administrator of.)											
Clarke, Elijah L	Confirmation of title to land in Louisiana.	18	2	Petition	253	Priv. Land Claims.	....	....	......	Laid on table.		
Clarke, Elijah L.	Confirmation of title to land in Louisiana.	19	1	Petition	44	Priv. Land Claims.						
Clarke, Elijah L	Confirmation of title to land in Louisiana.	19	2	Petition	53	Priv. Land Claims.	28	Report and bill.	330	Referred to Committee Whole House.		
Clarke, Elijah L	Confirmation of title to land in Louisiana.	20	1	Petition	224	Priv. Land Claims.	April 1, 1828	Report and bill.	251	Referred to Committee Whole House.		
Clarke, Elijah L	Confirmation of title to land in Louisiana.	20	2	Bill of last sess.	284	Whole House	Feb. 13, 1829	With't amend.	251	Passed		
Clarke, Elijah L	Confirmation of title to land in Louisiana.	21	1	Senate bill	87	Priv. Land Claims.	Jan. 4, 1830	With't amend.	3	Passed with amendm't	Passed	App'd Feb. 27, 1830
Clark, Elisha	Invalid pension	3	1	Rep. of Secretary War.	131	Select	May 26, 1794	Ref. to Sec. with instruc.	R. 12	Passed	Passed	App'd June 9, 1794
Clark, Elisha	Invalid pension	3	2	Rep. of Secretary War.	337	Claims	Feb. 28, 1795	Favorable; bill ordered.	130	Passed	Postp'd to next session.	
Clark, Elisha	Invalid pension	4	1	Rep. of Secretary War.	445	Whole House	Mar. 7, 1796	Favorable; bill ordered.	156	Passed	Passed	App'd April 20, 1796
Clark, Elisha	Increase of pension	10	2	House bill	499	Whole House	Feb. 20, 1809	Favorable	158	Passed	Passed	App'd March 3, 1809
Clark, Elisha, widow of	Arrears of pension	29	1	Petition	292	Rev. Pensions	214	Report and bill	208	Referred to Committee Whole House.	....	Leave to withdraw.
Clarke, Elizabeth	Revolutionary pension	27	2	Petition	845	Rev. Pensions	....	....	......	Discharged; laid on table.		
Clark, Ephraim	Compensation for services and injuries as a mariner in the frigate Alliance.	10	2	Petition	358	Select.						
Clark, Ephraim	Prize money due him as a seaman in frigate Alliance.	28	2	Petition	328	Rev. Claims.						
Clark, Ephraim	Prize money due him as a seaman in frigate Alliance.	29	1	Petition	202	Rev. Claims.						
Clark, Ephraim	Prize money due him as a seaman in frigate Alliance.	29	2	Petition	233	Rev. Claims.						
Clark, Fphraim, heirs of	Prize money due him as a seaman in frigate Alliance.	30	1	Petition	344	Rev. Claims	....	....	......	Discharged; laid on table.		
Clark, Ezra, widow of	Arrears of pension	21	1	Petition	128	Military Pensions.	May 4, 1830	Adverse	......	Laid on table.		
Clark, Ezra, widow of	Arrears of pension	22	2	Petition	67	Rev. Pensions	....	....	......	Discharged; laid on table.		
Clark, Ezra, widow of	Arrears of pension	23	1	Petition	54	Rev. Pensions	....	....	......	Discharged; laid on table.		
Clark, Ezra, widow of	Arrears of pension	24	1	Petition	136	Rev. Pensions.						
Clark, Ezra, widow of	Arrears of pension	25	2	Petition	63	Rev. Pensions	....	....	......	Discharged; laid on table.		
Clark, Ezra, widow of	Arrears of pension	26	2	Resolution	87	Rev. Pensions.						
Clark, Ezra, widow of	Arrears of pension	27	2	Petition	59	Rev. Pensions	784	Adverse	......	Laid on table.		
Clark, Ezra, widow of	Arrears of pension	29	2	Petition	54	Rev. Pensions.						
Clark, Ezra, widow of	Arrears of pension	30	1	Petition	625	Rev. Pensions	637	Adverse	......	Laid on table	....	Leave to withdraw, 2d session.
Clarke, Flavel	Revolutionary pension	19	1	Petition	128	Military Pensions.	164	Adverse	......	Laid on table.		
Clarke, Flavel	Revolutionary pension	27	2	Petition	669	Rev. Pensions	784	Adverse	......	Laid on table.		

List of private claims presented to the House of Representatives of the United States from the 1st to the 31st Congress, inclusive—Continued.

Names of claimants.	Nature or object of the claim.	Congress.	Session.	How brought before the House of Reps.	Page of journal.	To what committee of the House referred.	No. or date of the report.	Nature of the report.	No. of the bill.	How disposed of by the House of Reps.	How disposed of by the Senate.	Date of the act of Congress, and remarks.
Clarke, Ferdinand, (Cuba)	Refunding of tonnage duty paid on brig Conde de Villanueva wrecked.	24	2	Petition	43	Commerce	64	Report and bill.	813	Referred to Committee Whole House.		
Clarke, Ferdinand, (Cuba)	Refunding of tonnage duty paid on brig Conde de Villanueva wrecked.	25	2	Petition	40	Commerce	88	Report and bill.	104	Passed	Indef. postp'd.	
Clarke, Ferdinand, (Cuba)	Refunding of tonnage duty paid on brig Conde de Villanueva wrecked.	26	1	Petition	176	Commerce	....	....	......	Discharged; laid on table.		
Clarke, Ferdinand, (Cuba)	Refunding of tonnage duty paid on brig Conde de Villanueva wrecked.	29	2	Memorial	185	Commerce.						
Clarke, Ferdinand, (Cuba)	Refunding of tonnage duty paid on brig Conde de Villanueva wrecked.	30	1	Petition	163	Commerce	Jan. 25, 1848	Adverse	......	Laid on table	....	Leave to withdraw, 2d session.
Clarke, Frederick	Refundment of certain tonnage duties.	31	1	Petition	720	Commerce.						
Clark, Gershom	Invalid pension	3	1	Rep. of Secretary War.	131	Select	Feb. 26, 1794	Favorable; bill ordered.	62	Passed	Passed	App'd June 7, 1794
Clark, Gershom	Increase of pension	10	1	House bill	232	Whole House	April 19, 1808	Favorable	78	Passed	Passed	App'd April 25, 1808
Clark, George Rogers	Confirmation of title to land conveyed by Piankeshaw Indians.	9	1	Petition	209	Public Lands	Dec. 23, 1805	Rep. and res.; adverse.	......	Resolution adopted.		
Clark, George R., of United States army.	Compensation for medical aid to inhabitants of Fort Gilliland, Florida.	26	1	Petition	331	Military Affairs.						
Clark, George, (Tenn.)	Revolutionary pension	21	1	Resolution	550	Military Pensions	....	....	......	Discharged; laid on table.		
Clark, George F	(See F. M. Arredondo and others.)	19	1	....	252							
Clark, George, lieutenant in revenue service.	Pay and emoluments of a lieutenant in navy while co-operating with naval forces in Florida.	26	1	Petition	331	Naval Affairs	July 2, 1840	By bill	462	Referred to Committee Whole House.		
Clark, George W	(See Exploring Expedition.)											
Clark, George W., and others.	Payment for stone furnished for Fort Adams.	28	1	Petition	415	Claims	200	Report and bill.	157	Passed	Passed	App'd June 17, 1844
Clark, George, of Pa., heirs of.	Compensation for revolutionary services.	28	1	Petition	868	Rev. Claims.						
Clark, Gibson	Confirmation of title to land in Territory of Mississippi.	14	1	Petition	250	Public Lands	....	....	......	Discharged; laid on table.		
Clark, Gibson	Confirmation of title to land in Territory of Mississippi.	14	2	Petition	50	Priv. Land Claims.						
Clark, Gibson	Confirmation of title to land in Territory of Mississippi.	15	1	Petition	192	Priv. Land Claims.	Feb. 18, 1818	Report and bill.	94	Passed	Passed	App'd April 11, 1818
Clark, Gowin T	(See Alex'r KcKnight, heirs of.)											
Clark, Greenleaf, widow of.	Pension for services as a captain in revolutionary army.	25	2	Petition	198	Rev. Pensions	551	Report and bill.	538	Passed	Adverse report.	
Clark, Greenleaf, widow of.	Pension for services as a captain in revolutionary army.	26	1	Petition	171	Rev. Pensions	462	Report and bill.	376	Referred to Committee Whole House.		
Clark, Hannah	Revolutionary pension	27	3	Petition	394	Rev. Pensions.						
Clark, Henry	(See Daniel Walker, heirs of.)											
Clark, Henry	(See Isaac Champlin and others.)											
Clark, Henry	Indemnity for French spoliations prior to 1800.	26	1	Memorial	182	Foreign Affairs	343	Favorable; bill.	319	Referred to Committee Whole House.		

List of p ivate claims presented to the House of Representatives of the United States from the 1st to the 31st Congress, inclusive—Continued.

Names of claimants.	Nature or object of the claim.	Congress.	Session.	How brought before the House of Reps.	Page of journal.	To what committee of the House referred.	No. or date of the report.	Nature of the report.	No. of the bill.	How disposed of by the House of Reps.	How disposed of by the Senate.	Date of the act of Congress, and remarks.
Clark, Hezekiah, deceased, heirs of.	Grant of land to which he would have been entitled as surgeon's mate in revolutionary war, had he served to the close of the war.	22	1	Resolution	122	Rev. Claims.						
Clark, Isaac, colonel, (Vt.)	Value of arms, horses, &c., captured at Missisque, Canada, for his command.	14	1	Petition	574	Claims				Discharged: laid on table.		
Clark, Isaac, colonel, (Vt.)	Value of arms, horses, &c., captured at Missisque, Canada, for his command.	14	2	Petition	75	Claims.						
Clark, Isaac, colonel, (Vt.)	Value of arms, horses, &c., captured at Missisque, Canada, for his command.	15	1	Petition	98	Claims				Discharged; laid on table.		
Clark, Isaac, colonel, (Vt.)	Value of arms, horses, &c., captured at Missisque, Canada, for his command.	15	2	Petition	33	Claims	28	Report and bill.	220	Referred to Committee Whole House.		
Clark, Isaac, colonel, (Vt.)	Pension for services in revolutionary war.	15	2	Petition	132	Pens. & Rev. Cl'ms.	Feb. 11, 1818	Adverse		Laid on table.		
Clark, Isaac, (Vt.)	Pension for wounds, &c., received in war of 1812.	29	1	Petition	269	Invalid Pensions.	July 25, 1846	Adverse		Laid on table.		
Clark, Isaac, (Vt.)	Arrears of pension	29	2	Petition	151	Invalid Pensions.						
Clark, Israel, and others	Fishing bounty on schooner Codhook.	25	3	Petition	571	Commerce				Discharged.		
Clarke, Jacob B	Return of duties on imported wool	29	2	Memorial	141	Claims.						
Clark, James	Payment for work on Treasury Department per contract.	6	2	Petition	745	Claims	Jan. 9, 1801	Rep. and res. adverse.		Recommitted.		
							Jan. 20, 1801	Rep. and res. adverse.		Resolution adopted		Leave to withdraw.
Clark, James, (Ohio.)	Payment for services as an officer United States militia, 1812.	15	1	Petition	294	Claims				Discharged; laid on table.		
Clark, James, (Ohio.)	Payment for services as an officer United States militia, 1812.	15	2	Petition	52	Claims				Discharged; laid on table.		
Clark, James	(See Noble Benedict and others.)											
Clark, James, (Va.)	Interest on $944 due him from 1800 to 1818.	15	2	Petition	88	Claims				Discharged; laid on table.		
Clark, James, (Pa.)	Increase of pension	26	1	Petition	937	Rev. Pensions.						
Clark, James, executor of	Indemnity for French spoliations prior to 1800.	26	1	Memorial	182	Foreign Affairs	343	Favorable	319	Referred to Committee Whole House.		
Clarke, James, (Md.,) administrator of.	Indemnity for French spoliations prior to 1800.	29	2	Memorial	129	Foreign Affairs.						
Clark, James A	Pre-emption right to land in Missouri.	25	2	Petition	86	Public Lands				Discharged.		
Clark, James A	Pre-emption right to land in Missouri.	25	3	Petition	92	Public Lands	94	Adverse		Laid on table.		
Clark, James H	Credit as purser U. S. N. for money of which he was robbed.	15	2	Senate bill	232	Claims	Feb. 19, 1819	With't amend.	23	Referred to Committee Whole House.		
Clark, James H	Credit as purser U. S. N. for money of which he was robbed.	16	1	Petition	203	Claims				Discharged; laid on table.		
Clark, James H	Credit as purser U. S. N. for money of which he was robbed.	16	2	Petition		Claims	Feb. 5, 1821	Adverse		Laid on table.		
Clark, James H	Credit as purser U. S. N. for money of which he was robbed.	17	1	Senate bill	359	Naval Affairs	Mar. 25, 1822	With't amend.	22	Laid on table.		

List of private claims presented to the House of Representatives of the United States from the 1st to the 31st Congress, inclusive—Continued.

Names of claimants.	Nature or object of the claim.	Congress.	Session.	How brought before the House of Reps.	Page of journal.	To what committee of the House referred.	No. or date of the report.	Nature of the report.	No. of the bill.	How disposed of by the House of Reps.	How disposed of by the Senate.	Date of the act of Congress, and remarks.
Clark, James H.........	Credit as purser U. S. N. for money of which he was robbed.	17	2	Petition	52	Naval Affairs.....	68	Report and bill.	244	Passed	Passed	App'd March 3, 1823
Clark, James H.........	Three thousand and sixty one dollars in full for all claims against United States to April, 1830.	26	1	Senate bill	1237	....	....	....	281			
Clark, James H.........	Credit as purser U. S. N. for items disallowed by department.	28	1	Petition	987	Naval Affairs.						
Clark, James H.........	Credit as purser U. S. N. for items disallowed by department.	28	2	Petition	....	Naval Affairs.....	135	Report and bill	618	Referred to Committee Whole House.		
Clark, James H.........	Credit as purser U. S. N. for items disallowed by department.	29	1	Petition	178	Naval Affairs.....	May 4, 1846	By bill	419	Reported from Com. Whole House without amendment.		
Clark, James H.........	Credit as purser U. S. N. for items disallowed by department.	29	2	Bill of last sess.	211	....	....	....	419	Passed	Passed	App'd March 3, 1847
Clark, Jane	Relief: husband and father killed by Indians in revolutionary war.	3	1	Petition	82	....	....	....	.....	Laid on table.		
Clark, Jesse	Revolutionary pension..........	22	1	Petition	131	Rev. Pensions.....	395	Report and bill.	494	Referred to Committee Whole House.		
Clarke, Job, widow of....	Pension for revolutionary services.	30	1	Petition	571	Rev. Pensions.						
Clark, John............	Redemption of continental bills, old mission.	4	1	Rep. of Secretary Treasury.	388	Claims...........	May 31, 1796	Adverse	.....	Laid on table.		
Clark, John, (Penn.)	Compensation as auditor of army accounts revolutionary war.	3	1	Petition	54	....	....	....	.....	Referred to Secretary Treasury.		
Clark, John, (Penn.)....	Compensation as auditor of army accounts revolutionary war.	3	2	Rep. of Secretary Treasury.	284	Claims	Mar. 2, 1795	Adverse	.....	Laid on table.	....	Dec. 9, 1795, leave to withdraw.
Clark, John, (Penn.)	Compensation as auditor of army accounts revolutionary war.	12	1	Petition	270	Claims.						
Clark, John, (Penn.)	Compensation for revolutionary services as stipulated, with board of treasury.	15	2	Senate bill	249	Public Lands.....	Feb. 12, 1819	With't amend.	27	Passed............	Passed.......	App'd Feb. 20, 1819
Clark, John, (Penn.) administrator of, and Daniel Bickley.	Payment of bill of exchange (15,000 francs) drawn by American minister, under Louisiana treaty, and frudulently sold by American consul and lost.	15	2	Petition	24	Ways and Means..	Dec. 18, 1818	By bill	236	Referred to Committee Whole House.		
Clark, John, (Penn.) administrator of, and Daniel Bickley.	Payment of bill of exchange (15,000 francs) drawn by American minister, under Louisiana treaty, and fraudulently sold by American consul and lost.	16	1	Petition	164	Ways and Means..	April 8, 1820	By bill	132	Passed	Passed	App'd May 8, 1820
Clark, John, (Penn.) heirs of.	Pay and bounty land due as an ensign in revolutionary army.	19	1	Resolution	362	Rev. Claims.......	April 5, 1826	Adverse	.....	Laid on table.		
Clark, John, (Penn.) heirs of.	Commutation of half-pay due....	24	1	Petition	203	Rev. Claims......	599	Adverse	.....	Laid on table.		
Clark, John, (Penn.)	Pension for wound, &c., received at the battle of Queenstown in war of 1812.	24	1	Petition	407	Invalid Pensions ..	750	Report and bill.	691	Passed	Laid on table.	
Clark, John, (Penn.)	Pension for wound, &c., received at the battle of Queenstown in war of 1812.	25	3	Petition	129	Invalid Pensions...	135	Report and bill.	1002	Passed	Passed	App'd March 3, 1839
Clark, John............	Invalid pension................	10	1	House bill	232	Whole House.....	April 19, 1808	Favorable....	78	Passed	Passed	App'd April 25, 1801

List of private claims presented to the House of Representatives of the United States from the 1*st to the* 31*st Congress, inclusive*—Continued.

Names of claimants.	Nature or object of the claim.	Congress.	Session.	How brought before the House of Reps.	Page of journal.	To what committee of the House referred.	No. or date of the report.	Nature of the report.	No. of the bill.	How disposed of by the House of Reps.	How disposed of by the Senate.	Date of the act of Congress, and remarks.
Clark, John, (Mass.)	Compensation for services and property lost while an officer in revolutionary army.	15	2	Petition	61	Pens. & Rev. Cl'ms.	27	Adverse		Laid on table.		
Clark, John, widow of	Continuation of pension	18	1	Petition	108	Pens. & Rev. Cl'ms.	Jan. 12, 1824	Adverse		Laid on table.		
Clark, John, widow of	Continuation of pension	19	1	Petition	176	Rev. Claims.				Discharged; laid on table.		
Clark, John, (Va.)	Commutation of half-pay as a cornet in revolutionary army.	23	1	Petition	71	Rev. Claims.						
Clark, John, (Va.)	Commutation of half-pay as a cornet in revolutionary army.	23	2	Petition	77	Rev. Claims.						
Clark, John, (Va.)	Commutation of half-pay as a cornet in revolutionary army.	24	1	Petition	103	Rev. Claims.	306	Report and bill.	320	Referred to Committee Whole House.		
Clark, John, (Va.)	Commutation of half-pay as a cornet in revolutionary army.	24	2	Bill of last sess.	201	Whole House			320			
Clark, John, (Va.)	Commutation of half-pay as a cornet in revolutionary army.	55	2	Petition	39	Rev. Claims.	196	Report and bill.	222	Passed	Adverse report.	
Clark, John, (Va.)	Commutation of half-pay as a cornet in revolutionrry army.	26	1	Petition	164	Rev. Claims.						
Clark, John, (Va.)	Commutation of half-pay as a cornet in revolutionary army.	27	2	Petition	60	Rev. Claims.	370	Adverse		Laid on table.		
Clark, John, (Va.) widow and heirs of.	Commutation of half-pay as a cornet in revolutionary army.	31	1	Petition	433	Rev. Claims.						
Clark, John, (Va.) widow and heirs of.	Commutation of half pay as a cornet in revolutionary army.	31	2	Petition	50	Rev. Claims.						
Clark, John, (Va.)	Pension for services as a revolutionary soldier.	28	1	Petition	332	Rev. Pensions				Discharged; laid on table.		Leave to withdraw.
Clark, John, (Va.) executrix of.	Payment for cannon furnished government.	29	1	Petition	316	Claims.						
Clark, John, (Va.) executrix of.	Payment for cannon furnished government.	30	1	Petition	219	Claims.				Discharged; laid on table.		
Clark, John, (Va.) executrix of.	Payment for cannon furnished government.	31	1	Petition	470	Claims.						
Clark, John, Rev. (Va.) widow of.	Pension for services as an officer in revolutionary army.	29	1	Petition	472	Rev. Pensions.						
Clark, John, Rev. (Va.) widow of.	Pension for services as an officer in revolutionary army.	29	2	Petition	....	Rev. Pensions	23	Adverse		Laid on table.		
Clark, John, Rev. (Va.) widow of.	Pension for services as an officer in revolutionary army.	30	1	Petition	714	Rev. Pensions	686	Adverse		Laid on table.		
Clark, John, (Vt.)	Revolutionary pension	26	1	Petition	936	Rev. Pensions.						
Clark, John,)Vt.)	Revolutionary pension	26	2	Petition	77	Rev. Pensions	207	Adverse		Laid on table.		
Clark, John, (Maine)	Pension as a soldier in war of 1812	29	1	Senate bill	1108	Invalid Pensions	Aug. 4, 1846	With't amend.	171	Referred to Committee Whole House.		
Clark, John, (Maine)	Pension as a soldier in war of 1812	29	2	Senate bill	306	Invalid Pensions	Feb. 24, 1847	With't amend.	7	Laid on table.		
Clark, John, (Maine)	Pension as a soldier in war of 1812	30	1	Senate bill	913	Invalid Pensions	July 25, 1848	With't amend.	145	Passed	Passed	App'd Aug. 14, 1848
Clark, John, by Agnes, widof.	Renewal of acts for widows of revolutionary pensioners.	30	1	Petition	264	Rev. Pensions	309	Legislation unnecssary.		Laid on table		See act of Feb. 1, 1848
Clark, John C.	Increase of pay as clerk to naval captain.	27	3	Petition	61	Naval Affairs.						
Clark, John G., legatees of	Indemnity for French spoliations prior to 1800.	29	2	Memorial	90	Foreign Affairs.						
Clark, John Innes	Remission of duty on tea imported at Providence, R. I., in ship Ann and Hope, and destroyed by fire.	6	2	House bill	825	Whole House				Discharged; bill passed	Passed	App'd March 3, 180[illegible]

List of private claims presented to the House of Representatives of the United States from the 1st to the 31st Congress, inclusive—Continued.

Names of claimants.	Nature or object of the claim.	Congress.	Session.	How brought before the House of Reps.	Page of journal.	To what committee of the House referred.	No. or date of the report.	Nature of the report.	No. of the bill.	How disposed of by the House of Reps.	How disposed of by the Senate.	Date of the act of Congress, and remarks.
Clark, John and George, (Mich.)	(See Shadrach Gilbert, and others)											
Clark, John L.	(See Andrew Summers, assignee of)	26	1		182							
Clark, Johnson	Compensation for property destroyed by U. S. troops at Baltimore.	13	3	Petition	598	Claims				Discharged		March 9, 1816; leave to withdraw.
Clark, Jonas	Compensation for horse lost in Creek Indian war.	16	1	Petition	59	Claims				Discharged; laid on table.		
Clarke, Jonathan, widow of	Compensation for services in revolutionary war.	20	1	Petition	78	Military Pensions	Feb. 20, 1828	Adverse		Laid on table.		
Clark, Jonathan, (Conn.)	Repayment of $30 paid with a view to a patent which he has abandoned.	24	1	Resolution	926	Claims.						
Clark, Jonathan, (Conn.)	Repayment of $30 paid with a view to a patent which he has abandoned.	25	2	Resolution	107	Claims				Discharged.		
Clark & Jones	Indemnity for French spoliations prior to 1800.	26	1	Memorial	182	Foreign Affairs	343	Favorable; bill	319	Referred to Committee Whole House.		
Clark, ——	(See Tufts & Clark.)											
Clark, Joseph	(See James W. Stewart & others.)											
Clarke, Joseph, representatives of.	Balance due as loan officer for State of Rhode Island.)	4	1	Rep't Committee Ways & Means.	411	Whole House	Jan. 15, 1796	Favorable; bill ordered.	142	Passed	Passed	App'd Feb. 5, 1796
Clark, Joseph and others	Relief from penalties incurred on importation of goods from St. Domingo.	13	2	Petition	305	Ways and Means				Discharged; leave to withdraw.		
Clarke, Joseph, (Va.)	Compensation for military services of son, who died during war of 1812, and for loss of property.	16	1	Petition	188	Claims				Discharged; laid on table.		
Clark, Joseph, (Mass.)	Revolutionary pension	21	1	Resolution	430	Military pensions				Disch'd; laid on table.		
Clark, Joseph, (Mass.)	Revolutionary pension	21	2	Resolution	85	Military Pensions.						
Clark, Joseph, (N. Y.,) widow of.	Pension for wounds received at the battle of Tripoli.	30	1	Petition	105	Naval Affairs	28	Adverse		Laid on table.		
Clark, Joseph, (N. Y.,) widow of.	Pension for wounds received at the battle of Tripoli.	30	1	Petition	713	Invalid Pensions	708	Report and bill.	553	Passed	Passed 2d sess.	App'd March 3, 1849
Clark, Joseph, (N. Y.,) widow of.	Pension for wounds received at the battle of Tripoli.	31	1	Petition	410	Invalid Pensions	480	Report and bill.	377	Referred to Committee Whole House.		The Committee do not seem to be aware of the *act* of 1849.
Clark, Joseph, (Penn.)	Pension	31	1	Petition	449	Rev. Pensions.						
Clark, Joshua	(See Isaac Champlin and others.)											
Clark, Joshua	Release from liability as paymaster for money of which he was robbed.	14	2	Petition	234	Claims				Discharged; laid on table.		
Clark, Joshua	Belease from liability as paymaster for money of which he was robbed.	15	1	Petition	24	Claims				Discharged.		
Clark, Josiah	Revolutionary pension	21	2	Resolution	165	Military Pensions.						
Clark, Josiah	Revolutionary pension	22	1	Resolution	70	Rev. Pensions.						
Clark, Josiah	Revolutionary pension	24	2	Petition	74	Rev. Pensions	114	Report and bill.	847	Referred to Committee Whole House.		
Clark, Josiah	Revolutionary pension	25	2	Petition	37	Rev. Pensions	174	Report and bill.	199	Passed	Passed	App'd June 28, 1838
Clark, Lardner	Confirmation of title to mill-seat near Kaskaskia.	6	1	Petition	533	Select	Feb. 4, 1800	Adverse		Rejected		March 24, 1804; leave to withdraw.
Clark, Leonard	Relief for injuries sustained in revolutionary war.	12	2	Petition	579	Claims.						

List of private claims presented to the House of Representatives of the United States from the 1st to the 31st Congress, inclusive—Continued.

Names of claimants.	Nature or object of the claim.	Congress.	Session.	How brought before the House of Reps.	Page of journal.	To what committee of the House referred.	No. or date of the report.	Nature of the report.	No. of the bill.	How disposed of by the House of Reps.	How disposed of by the Senate.	Date of the act of Congress, and remarks.
Clark, Leonard	Invalid pension	13	1	House bill	56	Whole House	July 20, 1813	Favorable	31	Passed	Passed	App'd Aug. 2, 1813
Clarke, Lewis, representatives of.	Confirmation of title to land in Louisiana.	18	2	Petition	253	Priv. Land Claims.						
Clarke, Lewis, representatives of.	Confirmation of title to land in Louisiana.	19	1	Petition	44	Priv. Land Claims.						
Clarke, Lewis, representatives of.	Confirmation of title to land in Louisiana.	19	2	Petition	53	Priv. Land Claims.	28	Report and bill.	331	Referred to Committee Whole House.		
Clarke, Lewis, representatives of.	Confirmation of title to land in Louisiana.	20	1	Petition	224	Priv. Land Claims.	April 1, 1828	Report and bill.	250	Referred to Committee Whole House.		
Clarke, Lewis, representatives of.	Confirmation of title to land in Louisiana.	20	2	Bill of last sess.	284	Whole House	Feb. 13, 1829	With't amend.	250	Passed	Ref. to Private Land Cl'ms.	
Clarke, Lewis, representatives of.	Confirmation of title to land in Louisiana.	21	1	Senate bill	87	Priv. Land Claims.	Jan. 4, 1830	With't amend.	3	Amended and passed.	Passed	App'd Feb. 27, 1830
Clark, Lorenzo N	Indemnity for losses on contract for emigrating Creek Indians.	24	2	Petition	98	Claims.						
Clark, Lorenzo N	Indemnity for losses on contract for emigrating Creek Indians.	25	2	Petition	88	Claims				Discharged.		
Clark, Lorenzo N	Indemnity for losses on contract for emigrating Creek Indians.	26	1	Petition	169	Claims	503	Adverse		Laid on table.		
Clark, Marston G	Release as surety for A. D. Thorn, collector of internal taxes, Territory of Indiana.	18	2	Resolution	224	Ways and Means.						
Clark, Marston G	Release as surety for A. D. Thorn, collector of internal taxes, Territory of Indiana.	19	1	Res. and mem.	113, 176	Ways and Means.				Discharged; laid on table.		
Clark, Marston G	Release as surety for A. D. Thorn, collector of internal taxes, Territory of Indiana.	19	2	Memorial	50	Judiciary				Discharged; laid on table.		
Clark, Marston G	Equitable settlement of accounts as Indian agent.	27	2	Senate bill	1126	Indian Affairs	July 27, 1842	With't amend.	156	Passed	Passed	App'd Aug. 11, 1842
Clark, Martin	Pension for injuries as United States seaman.	23	2	Petition	436	Invalid Pensions.						
Clark, M. M	Settlement of accounts as Assistant Quartermaster General.	30	2	Resolution	158	Judiciary	Jan. 3, 1849	Report and bill.	706	Referred to Committee Whole House.		Provided for in appropriation act of Sept. 30, 1850.
Clark, Matthew St. Clair.	(See Georgia, agent of the State of.)	24	1		259							
Clark, Nathaniel	Pension	14	1	House bill	622	Whole House	April 23, 1816	Favorable	171	Passed	Passed	App'd April 30, 1816
Clark, Nathaniel, (Mass.)	Increase of pension	20	1	Petition	163	Military Pensions.				Discharged; laid on table.		
Clark, Nathaniel, (N. H.)	Increase of pension	22	1	Petition	56	Invalid Pensions.	Jan. 11, 1832	Adverse		Laid on table.		
Clark, Nathaniel, (N. H.)	Increase of pension	22	2	Petition	118	Invalid Pensions.						
Clark, Nathaniel, (Ind.)	To relinquish certain bounty land and locate other land in Indiana.	19	2	Petition	78	Public Lands				Discharged.		
Clark, Nathaniel, (Ind.)	To relinquish certain bounty land and locate other land in Indiana.	20	1	Petition	116	Public Lands				Discharged; laid on table.		
Clark, Noah	Revolutionary pension	29	1	Petition	85	Invalid Pensions	516	Adverse		Laid on table.		
Clark, Noah	Revolutionary pension	30	1	Petition	576	Rev. Pensions	439	Adverse		Laid on table.		
Clark & Nightingale	(See Nathaniel West and others.)											
Clark, Parker	(See Canadian refugees)	6	2									
Clarke, Peleg	Compensation for services, &c., in United States navy.	24	1	Petition	481	Naval Affairs.						
Clarke, Peleg	Compensation for services, &c., in United States navy.	25	2	Petition	399	Naval Affairs				Discharged; laid on table.		

List of private claims presented to the House of Representatives of the United States from the 1st to the 31st Congress, inclusive—Continued.

Names of claimants.	Nature or object of the claim.	Congress.	Session.	How brought before the House of Reps.	Page of journal.	To what committee of the House referred.	No. or date of the report.	Nature of the report.	No. of the bill.	How disposed of by the House of Reps.	How disposed of by the Senate.	Date of the act of Congress, and remarks.
Clarke, Peleg	Allowance for wages while a prisoner.	26	1	Petition	303	Naval Affairs.						
Clark, Peter, administratrix of.	Indemnity for French spoliations prior to 1800.	30	1	Petition	118	Foreign Affairs	Jan. 4, 1848	By bill	21	Referred to Committee Whole House.		
Clark, Ransom	Increase of pension for many wounds received at Dade's massacre in Florida.	24	1	Petition	1102	Invalid Pensions	June 27, 1836	Report and bill.	729	Passed	Adverse report.	
Clark, Richard, (N. Y.)	Revolutionary pension	17	1	Petition	266	Whole House, on bill No. 37.						
Clark, Richard, (N. Y.)	Compensation for services and supplies in revolutionary war.	19	1	Petition	67	Rev. Claims				Discharged; laid on table.		
Clark, Richard, (N. Y.)	Compensation for services and supplies in revolutionary war.	19	2	Petition	112	Rev. Claims	Jan. 30, 1827	Adverse		Laid on table.		
Clark, Richard, (N. Y.)	Revolutionary pension	21	1	Petition	377	Military Pensions	May 4, 1830	Adverse		Laid on table.		
Clark, Richard, (N. Y.)	Revolutionary pension	22	1	Petition	72	Invalid Pensions				Discharged; laid on table.		
Clark, Richard, (Mass.)	Revolutionary pension	21	2	Petition	159	Military Pensions.						
Clark, Richard, (Mass.)	Revolutionary pension	22	1	Petition	80	Rev. Pensions	117	Report and bill.	193	Referred to Committee Whole House.		
Clark, Richard, (Mass.)	Revolutionary pension	22	2	Bill of last sess.	66				193	Laid on table.		
Clarke, Richard, (Maine)	Revolutionary pension	25	2	Petition	327	Rev. Pensions				Discharged; laid on table.		
Clark, Robert, (Tenn.)	Revolutionary pension	23	1	Petition	191	Rev. Pensions	Feb. 21, 1834	Adverse		Laid on table.		
Clark, Robert, (Tenn.)	Revolutionary pension	23	2	Petition	48	Rev. Pensions	Feb. 10, 1835	Adverse		Laid on table.		
Clark, Robert, (La.)	Permission to enter a tract of land.	28	1	Petition	372	Public Lands.						
Clark, Robert	(See Menzies Gillespie.)											
Clark, Samuel, (Ga.)	(See Paul Chase.)											
Clark, Samuel M. D	Confirmation of title to land in Louisiana.	20	2	Petition	119	Public Lands				Discharged; laid on table.		
Clark, Samuel M. D	Confirmation of title to land in Louisiana.	21	1	Petition	41	Public Lands	Dec. 29, 1829	Adverse		Laid on table.		
Clark, Samuel, (N. Y.)	Revolutionary pension	22	1	Petition	381	Rev. Pensions	479	Report and bill.	580	Referred to Committee Whole House.		
Clark, Samuel, (Pa.)	Revolutionary pension	23	2	Petition	164	Rev. Pensions				Discharged; laid on table.		
Clark, Samuel, (Pa.,) by Catharine, widow of.	Compensation for revolutionary services.	23	2	Petition	308	Rev. Claims.						
Clark, Samuel, (Ohio)	Arrears of pension for services in war of 1812.	27	2	Petition	377	Invalid Pensions				Discharged; laid on table.		
Clark, Samuel, (Ohio)	Arrears of pension for services in war of 1812.	28	1	Petition	300	Invalid Pensions.						
Clark, Samuel, (Ohio)	Arrears of pension for services in war of 1812.	29	1	Petition	541	Invalid Pensions.						
Clark, Samuel	Confirmation of title to land in Florida.	31	1	Petition	511	Priv. Land Claims.						
Clark, Samuel J	(See Atwater, Daggett, and others)											
Clarke, Satterlee	Settlement of accounts as late paymaster U. S. A. as per verdict of United States court in N. York.	19	2	Petition	317	Judiciary				Discharged.		
Clarke, Satterlee	Settlement of accounts as late paymaster U. S. A. as per verdict of United States court in N. York.	21	1	Petition	273	Claims.						

List of private claims presented to the House of Representatives of the United States from the 1st to the 31st Congress, inclusive—Continued.

Names of claimants.	Nature or object of the claim.	Congress.	Session.	How brought before the House of Reps.	Page of journal.	To what committee of the House referred.	No. or date of the report	Nature of the report.	No. of the bill.	How disposed of by the House of Reps.	How disposed of by the Senate.	Date of the act of Congress, and remarks.
Clarke, Satterlee	Settlement of accounts as late paymaster U. S. A. as per verdict of United States court in N. York.	24	2	Petition	73	Claims	164	Adverse		Laid on table.		
Clarke, Satterlee	Settlement of accounts as late paymaster U. S. A. as per verdict of United States court in N. York.	29	1	Petition	67	Claims						Leave to withdraw.
Clarke, Satterlee	Settlement of accounts as late paymaster U. S. A. as per verdict of United States court in N. York.	29	2	Petition	232	Claims.						
Clarke, Satterlee	Settlement of accounts as late paymaster U. S. A. as per verdict of United States court in N. York.	30	1	Petition	116, 169	Claims	727	Report and bill.	568	Referred to Committee Whole House.		
Clarke, Satterlee	Settlement of accounts as late paymaster U. S. A. as per verdict of United States court in N. York.	30	2	Bill of last sess.	319	Whole House	Jan. 26, 1849	With't amend.	568	Passed	Passed	App'd March 3, 1849
Clark, Seth, and Andrew Newell.	Settlement of accounts as assistant commissary of issues.	1	1	Petition	26					Laid on table.		
Clark, Shadrach, heirs of.	To locate bounty land on any public land.	25	2	Petition	596	Priv. Land Claims				Discharged; laid on table.		
Clark, Silas	Increase of pension	4	1	Petition	387	Claims	Jan. 26, 1796	Adverse		Leave to withdraw.		
Clark, Stephen	(See Charles M. Davis and others)											
Clark, Thaddeus	(See assignees of Thomas Tupper)											
Clark, Thomas B.	(See James Cisné, assignee of.)											
Clark, Thomas, widow of.	Compensation for revolutionary services and reimbursement of money recovered from his estate by suit for services of a negro in revolutionary war.	3	1	Petition	31	Select	Jan. 22, 1794	Favorable; bill ordered.	9	Referred to Committee Whole House.		
Clark, Thomas, widow of.	Compensation for revolutionary services and reimbursement of money recovered from his estate by suit for services of a negro in revolutionary war.	4	2	Petition	636	Claims.						
Clark, Thomas, widow of.	Compensation for revolutionary services and reimbursement of money recovered from his estate by suit for services of a negro in revolutionary war.	5	2	Petition	89	Claims	Jan. 18, 1798	Adverse as to services; favorable as to money.	45	Passed	Rejected.	
Clark, Thomas M.	Indemnity for French spoliations prior to 1800.	26	1	Memorial	182	Foreign Affairs	[illegible]	Favorable; bill	319	Referred to Committee Whole House.		
Clark & Vanuxem	Indemnity for French spoliations prior to 1800.	26	1	Memorial	182	Foreign Affairs	[illegible]	Favorable; bill	319	Referred to Committee Whole House.		
Clark, William	(See Samuel Mims.)											
Clark, William, (Miss.)	Invalid pension	4	2	Petition	612	Claims	Jan. 19, 1797	Rep. and res.; adverse.		Resolution adopted.		
Clark, William, (Md.)	Invalid pension	20	1	Petition	64	Military Pensions	Feb. 13, 1828	By bill	166	Passed	Discharged.	
Clark, William, (Md.)	Invalid pension	20	2	House bill	55	Whole House	Jan. 15, 1829	Favorable	311	Passed	Laid on table.	
Clark, William, (Md.)	Invalid pension	21	1	Petition	47	Military Pensions	Jan. 5, 1830	By bill	72	Passed	Passed	App'd May 20, 1830
Clark, William, (Md.)	Increase of pension	21	2	Petition	110	Military Pensions				Discharged; laid on table.		
Clark, William, (Pa.)	**Compensation for services as a soldier in revolutionary war.**	**21**	**2**	**Petition**	**337**	**Rev. Claims.**						

List of private claims presented to the House of Representatives of the United States from the 1st to the 31st Congress, inclusive—Continued.

Names of claimants.	Nature or object of the claim.	Congress.	Session.	How brought before the House of Reps.	Page of journal.	To what committee of the House referred.	No. or date of the report.	Nature of the report.	No. of the bill.	How disposed of by the House of Reps.	How disposed of by the Senate.	Date of the act of Congress, and remarks.
Clark, Wlliam, (Pa.)	Compensation for services as a soldier in revolutionary war.	22	1	Petition	90	Rev. Claims	Jan. 10, 1832	Adverse		Laid on table.		
Clark, William, (N. Y.)	Bounty land for services in war of 1812.	24	1	Petition	664	Priv. Land Claims.	726	Adverse		Laid on table.		
Clark, William, (N. Y.)	Bounty land for services in war of 1812.	25	2	Petition	59	Priv. Land Claims.	283	Report and bill.	326	Referred to Committee Whole House.		
Clark, William, (N. Y.)	Bounty land for services in war of 1812.	25	3	Bill of last sess.	377	Whole House	Jan. 25, 1839	With't amend.	326	Passed with amendm't.	Passed	App'd March 3, 1839
Clark, William, (Ind.)	Pension for services as a soldier in war of 1812.	29	1	Petition	904	Invalid Pensions.						
Clark, William, of Ky., widow of.	Pension for services in revolutionary war.	30	2	Petition	361	Rev. Pensions.						
Clark, William, of Ky., widow of.	Pension for services in revolutionary war.	31	1	Petition	214	Rev. Pensions	124	Adverse		Laid on table		Leave to withdraw, 2d session.
Clarke, William	(See Lewis & Clarke, and companions.)											
Clarkson, Matthew, Thos., and Levinnus.	Redress for seizure of merchandise in Holland by the French in 1808.	18	1	Memorial	172	Foreign Affairs	127	Rep. and res. for inform'n from President.		Resolution adopted		See President's message to House, Dec. 23, 1824.
Clarkson, Randolph	Invalid pension	12	1	Petition	256	Claims	June 8, 1812	By bill	138	Passed	Passed	App'd July 5, 1812
Clarkson, Randolph	Increase of pension	21	2	Petition	81	Military Pensions.						
Clarkson, Randolph	Reimbursement of money advanced to United States in revolutionary war.	12	1	Petition	256	Claims.						
Clarkson, Samuel	Refunding of duties paid on copper in 1806.	12	1	Petition	44	Whole House on bill No. 2.						
Clarkson, Samuel	Refunding of duties paid on copper in 1806.	16	2	Petition	25	Commerce	Jan. 23, 1821	Report and bill.	217	Referred to Committee Whole House.		
Clarkson, Samuel	Refunding of duties paid on copper in 1806.	17	1	Petition	23	Commerce	Dec. 18, 1821	By bill	6	Passed	Passed	App'd Jan. 11, 1822
Clarkson, Samuel, & others.	Indemnity for cargo of brig Sea Nymph, captured by a British frigate in 1796.	4	1	Memorial	520	Whole House.						
Clarkson & Van Horne	Indemnity for French spoliations prior to 1800.	26	1	Memorial	182	Foreign Affairs	343	Favorable; bill	319	Referred to Committee Whole House.		
Clason, Isaac	Drawback on sugar and coffee exported in 1793.	3	1	Petition	175					Laid on table.		
Clason, Isaac	Drawback on sugar, (1424 boxes)	9	1	Petition	198	Com. and Manuf.	Dec. 24, 1805	Favorable		Referred to Committee Whole House.		
Clason, Isaac	Drawback on sugar, (1424 boxes)	9	2	Petition	490, 509	Com. and Manuf.						
Clason, Isaac	Drawback on sugar, (1424 boxes)	10	1	Senate bill	277	Whole House			20	Indefinitely postponed.		
Clason, Isaac	Drawback on sugar, (1424 boxes)	10	2	Petition	351	Com. and Manuf.						
Clason, Isaac	Drawback on sugar, (1424 boxes)	11	1	Petition	19					Referred to Committee Whole House, on bill 2.		
Clason, Isaac	Drawback on sugar, (1424 boxes)	11	2	Petition	135	Com. and Manuf.	Dec. 19, 1809	By bill	42	Referred to Committee Whole House.		
Clason, Isaac	Drawback on sugar, (1424 boxes)	11	3	Petition	444	Com. and Manuf.	Dec. 14, 1810	By bill	146	Passed	Postponed to next session.	
Clason, Isaac	Drawback on sugar, (1424 boxes)	12	1	Petition	21	Com. and Manuf.	Dec. 2, 1811	By bill	14	Referred to Committee Whole House.		
Clason, Isaac	Drawback on sugar, (1424 boxes)	12	2	Petition	620	Com. and Manuf.						

List of private claims presented to the House of Representatives of the United States from the 1st to the 31st Congress, inclusive—Continued.

Names of claimants.	Nature or object of the claim.	Congress.	Session.	How brought before the House of Reps.	Page of journal.	To what committee of the House referred.	No. or date of the report.	Nature of the report.	No. of the bill.	How disposed of by the House of Reps.	How disposed of by the Senate.	Date of the act of Congress, and remarks.
Clason, Isaac	Drawback on sugar, (1424 boxes)	13	2	Senate bill	228	Com. and Manuf	Jan. 22, 1814	With't amend.	27	Passed	Passed	App'd Mar. 24, 1814
Clason, Isaac, executors of	Indemnity for French spoliations prior to 1800.	26	1	Memorial	182	Foreign Affairs	343	Favorable bill.	319	Referred to Committee Whole House.		
Class, Frederick	Compensation for revolutionary services.	31	1	Petition	215	Rev. Claims.						
Claxton, Alexander, U. S. N.	Salvage out of duties paid on cargo of British ship James Mitchell, and amount of costs, &c., incurred in a suit for the same.	20	2	Petition	60	Naval Affairs	48	Report and bill.	373	Referred to Committee Whole House.		
Claxton, Alexander, U. S. N.	Salvage out of duties paid on cargo of British ship James Mitchell, and amount of costs, &c., incurred in a suit for the same.	21	1	Petition	129	Naval Affairs	61	Report and bill.	84	Passed	Passed	App'd May 28, 1830
Claxton, Alexander, U. S. N.	Additional appropriation to defray expenses intended to be provided for in act of May, 1830.	22	2	Senate bill	405	Naval Affairs	Feb. 27, 1833	With't amend.	75	Passed	Passed	App'd March 2, 1833
Claxton, Alexander, U. S. N.	(See George Hervy, attorney, &c.)											
Claxton, Alexander, widow of.	Extension of certain naval pension acts.	29	1	Petition	124	Naval Affairs	147	Report and bill.	151	Referred to Committee Whole House.		
Claxton, Alexander, widow of.	Extension of certain naval pension acts.	29	2	Petition	169	Naval Affairs.						
Claxton, Alfred B	(See Benjamin Homans and A. B. Claxton.)											
Claxton, Roger	Benefit of act of July, 1820, for relief of purchasers of land.	17	2	Petition	87	Public Lands	Feb. 5, 1823	By bill	271	Passed	Passed	App'd March 3, 1823
Claxton, Thomas	Additional compensation as doorkeeper to House Representatives.	1	3	Petition	399					Laid on table.		
Claxton, Thomas	Additional compensation as doorkeeper to House Representatives.	2	1	Petition	528	Select	Mar. 8, 1792	Res to allow $100.		Resolution adopted.		
Claxton, Thomas	Allowance for services of a laborer in the office of doorkeeper.	3	1	Memorial	25					Allowed by resolution, January 3, 1794.		
Claxton, Thomas	Compensation for extra services as doorkeeper.	4	1	Resolution	601					Resolution adopted.		
Claxton, Thomas	(See James Mathers)	5	2		219							
Clay, Cassius M	Compensation for watch, clothes, horses, &c., lost in Mexican war.	30	1	Petition	355	Claims	365	Report and bill.	331	Referred to Committee Whole House.		
Clay, Cassius M	Reimbursement of amount paid on judgment for trespass committed under military orders.	30	2	Petition	175	Claims	131	Report and bill.	811	Referred to Committee Whole House.		
Clay, David	(See Isaac Richmond, and others.)											
Clay, Henry	(See James Morrison, executors of)	21	1		122							
Clay, Jefferson	(See Isaac Richmond, and others.)											
Clay, Jeremiah, and wife	Grant of land in Louisiana as an old settler.	24	1	Petition	112	Priv. Land Claims.				Discharged; laid on table.		
Clay, Jeremiah, and wife	Grant of land in Louisiana as an old settler.	25	3	Petition	223	Priv. Land Claims.						
Clay, John Randolph	$7,200 for services as chargé d'affaires 1 year and 7 months.	22	2	Senate amendm't to House bill.	477	Whole House	Mar. 2, 1823	With't amend.	669	Passed	Passed	App'd March 2, 1833
Clay, John Randolph	Balance due as chargé d'affaires at Russia.	23	2	Amend't to House bill.	251				616	Passed	Passed	App'd March 3, 1835
Clay, John Randolph	Salary and expenses as acting chargé at Russia.	24	1	Petition	59	Foreign Affairs	212	Report and bill.	214	Passed	Passed	App'd July 2, 1836

List of private claims presented to the House of Representatives of the United States from the 1st to the 31st Congress, inclusive—Continued.

Names of claimants.	Nature or object of the claim.	Congress.	Session.	How brought before the House of Reps.	Page of journal.	To what committee of the House referred.	No. or date of the report.	Nature of the report.	No. of the bill.	How disposed of by the House of Reps.	How disposed of by the Senate.	Date of the act of Congress, and remarks.
Clay, John Randolph....	Additional compensation as minister *ad interim* at Russia.	25	2	Petition.......	172	Foreign Affairs....	534	Report and bill.	526	Referred to Committee Whole House.		
Clay, John Randolph....	Additional compensation as minister *ad interim* at Russia.	25	3	Bill of last sess.	379	Whole House.....	Jan. 25, 1839	With't amend.	526	Passed............	Passed......	App'd March 2, 1839
Clay, John Randolph....	Outfit and salary as chargé at Vienna.	27	3	Petition.......	60	Foreign Affairs....	21	Report and bill.	647	Passed............	Passed......	App'd March 3, 1843
Clay, John Randolph....	Outfit and salary as chargé at St. Petersburgh.	30	1	Petition.......	81	Foreign Affairs....	....	Embraced by amd't in civ. & dip. bill.	298	Passed............	Passed......	App'd Aug. 12, 1848
Clay, Joseph, administrator of.	Amount of seven revolutionary loan office certificates.	15	1	Petition.......	165	Pens. & Rev. Cl'ms.	....	....	......	Discharged; leave to withdraw.		
Clay, Richard, and James Lowell.	Refunding of duties on sugar and molasses destroyed by fire.	24	2	Petition.......	40	Ways and Means..	208	Adverse......	......	Laid on table.		
Clay, Richard, and James Lowell.	Refunding of duties on sugar and molasses destroyed by fire.	25	2	Petition.......	112	Ways and Means..	522	Adverse......	.....	Laid on table.		
Clay, Thomas, executor of	Relocation of certain land warrants for revolutionary services.	26	1	Petition.......	1009	Priv. Land Claims.						
Clay, Thomas, executor of	Relocation of certain land warrants for revolutionary services.	27	1	Petition.......	160	Public Lands.						
Claycomb, Frederick.....	Compensation for horse lost in U. S. service.	25	2	Petition.......	121	Claims..........	....	....	......	Discharged.		
Claypoole, William......	(See Louis F. Beeler, and others.)											
Clayton, Henry, widow of	Difference in amount of a private's and lieutenant's pension.	29	1	Petition.......	....	Rev. Pensions.....	771	Report and bill.	486	Rept'd from C. W. H. with't amend't, and laid on table.		
Clayton, Henry, widow of	Difference in amount of a private's and lieutenant's pension.	29	2	Bill of last sess.	212	....	....	....	486	Passed............	Passed......	App'd March 3, 1847
Clayton, John G.........	Payment for horse lost in United States service, war of 1812.	25	2	Petition.......	921	Claims..........	....	....	......	Discharged.		
Clayton, John G.........	Payment for horse lost in United States service, war of 1812.	25	3	Petition.......	461	Claims.						
Clayton, John G.........	Payment for horse lost in United States service, war of 1812.	26	1	Petition.......	306	Claims.						
Clayton, John G.........	Payment for horse lost in United States service, war of 1812.	26	2	Petition.......	38	Claims.						
Clayton, John G.........	Payment for horse lost in United States service, war of 1812.	27	2	Petition.......	55	Claims..........	342	Adverse......	......	Laid on table.		
Clayton & Mitchell......	$48 advanced to William Kemplin upon an informal power of attorney.	26	1	Petition.......	323	Rev. Pensions.....	714	Adverse......	......	Laid on table.		
Clayton, William........	Indemnity for property taken for use of revolutionary army.	14	1	Petition.......	170	Pens. & Rev. Cl'ms.	Mar. 13, 1816	Rep't and res. adverse.	......	Resolution adopted.		
Clayton, William........	Indemnity for property taken for use of revolutionary army.	14	2	Petition.......	29	Claims..........	....	....	......	Discharged; laid on table.		
Clayton & Randall......	(See Margaret Dowell.)											
Clearland, Moses, widow of	Revolutionary pension..........	25	3	Petition.......	127	Rev. Pensions....	....	....	......	Discharged.		
Cleaveland, Aquilla, widow of.	Revolutionary pension..........	25	3	Petition.......	127	Rev. Pensions....	Jan. 16, 1839	Adverse......	......	Laid on table.		
Cleer, Peter............	Pension as a soldier in French revolutionary corps.	16	1	Petition.......	293	Rev. Pensions.....	April 22, 1820	Rep. and res. for leave to withdraw.	......	Resolution adopted.		
Cleer, Peter............	Pension as a soldier in French revolutionary corps.	19	1	Petition.......	66	Military Pensions..	Feb. 23, 1826	By bill......	119	Passed............	Discharged.	

List of private claims presented to the House of Representatives of the United States from the 1st to the 31st Congress, inclusive—Continued.

Names of claimants.	Nature or object of the claim.	Congress.	Session.	How brought before the House of Reps.	Page of journal.	To what committee of the House referred.	No. or date of the report.	Nature of the report.	No. of the bill.	How disposed of by the House of Reps.	How disposed of by the Senate.	Date of the act of Congress, and remarks.
Cleer, Peter	Pension as a soldier in French revolutionary corps.	19	2	Petition	64	Military Pensions	Dec. 22, 1826	By bill	315	Passed	Indef. postp'd.	
Cleer, Peter	Pension as a soldier in French revolutionary corps.	20	1	Petition	98	Military Pensions	April 29, 1828	By bill	283	Passed	Discharged.	
Cleer, Peter	Pension as a soldier in French revolutionary corps.	20	2	House bill	55	Whole House	Jan. 15, 1829	Favorable	311	Passed	Laid on table.	
Cleer, Peter	Pension as a soldier in French revolutionary corps.	21	1	Petition	47	Military Pensions				Discharged; laid on table.		
Cleer, Peter	Pension as a soldier in French revolutionary corps.	21	2	Senate bill	387	Military Pensions	March 2, 1831	Adverse	160	Passed	Passed	App'd March 2, 1831
Cleftan, William	Indemnity for impressment of wagon and team in United States service, war of 1812.	18	1	Resolution	364	Claims.						
Cleghorn, John	Benefit of the act of March 3, 1791, granting land to settlers.	9	1	Petition	343	Public Lands	April 10, 1806	To postpone indefinitely.		Report adopted.		
Cleghorn, Joseph	Compensation for revolutionary services.	20	1	Petition	78	Military Pensions				Discharged; laid on table.		
Cleghorn, Joseph	Compensation for revolutionary services.	20	2	Petition	176	Claims				Discharged; laid on table.		
Cleghorn, Joseph	Pension	21	1	Petition	46	Military Pensions	April 2, 1830	Adverse		Laid on table.		
Cleghorn, Joseph	Pension	21	1	Petition	546	Military Pensions				Discharged; laid on table.		
Cleghorn, Joseph	Pension	22	1	Petition	56	Military Pensions				Discharged; laid on table.		
Clelland, James	(See Sarah M. Charlton and others.)											
Clem, Michael G.	(See David A. Ely)	30	2		91							
Clemens, Christian	Compensation for services as lieutenant colonel in war of 1812.	21	1	Petition	170	Claims	Jan. 22, 1830	Adverse		Laid on table.		
Clemens, Christian	Compensation for services as lieutenant colonel in war of 1812.	23	1	Petition	335	Claims.						
Clemens, Reuben	Compensation for services in war of 1812.	31	1	Petition	715	Military Affairs.						
Clemens, Jacob	Compensation for supplies, or for property impressed in revolutionary service.	2	1	Petition	521					Referred to Secretary Treasury.		
Clemens, Jacob	Compensation for supplies, or for property impressed in revolutionary service.	3	2	Rep. of Secretary Treasury.	284					Laid on table.		
Clemens, Jacob	(See John Neiler, heirs of.)											
Clement, Jacob C	Compensation for two vessels chartered by United States for Venezuela, and lost.	13	1	Petition	18	Com. and Manuf.						
Clement, Jacob C	Compensation for two vessels chartered by United States for Venezuela, and lost.	13	2	Petition	201	Ways and Means				Discharged; leave to withdraw.		
Clement, Jacob C	Compensation for two vessels chartered by United States for Venezuela, and lost.	14	1	Petition	59	Claims	Jan. 10, 1816	Rep. and res.; adverse.		Resolution adopted.		
Clement, Jacob C	Compensation for two vessels chartered by United States for Venezuela, and lost.	17	1	Petition	263	Claims				Discharged; leave to withdraw.		

List of private claims presented to the House of Representatives of the United States from the 1st to the 31st Congress, inclusive—Continued.

Names of claimants.	Nature or object of the claim.	Congress.	Session.	How brought before the House of Reps.	Page of journal.	To what committee of the House referred.	No. or date of the report.	Nature of the report.	No. of the bill.	How disposed of by the House of Reps.	How disposed of by the Senate.	Date of the act of Congress, and remarks.
Clement, Jacob, assignees of	Compensation for two vessels chartered by United States for Venezuela, and lost.	19	1	Petition & doc's.	312, 365	Commerce	April 27, 1826	By bill	234	Passed	....	Leave to withdraw.
Clement, Jacob, assignees of	Compensation for two vessels chartered by United States for Venezuela, and lost.	20	1	Petition	56	Commerce	41	Report and bill.	35	Passed	Rejected	Dec. 16, 1828; leave to withdraw.
Clement, Jacob, assignees of	Compensation for two vessels chartered by United States for Venezuela, and lost.	23	1	Petition	334	Commerce	290	Adverse	......	Laid on table.		
Clement, Jacob, assignees of	Compensation for two vessels chartered by United States for Venezuela, and lost.	23	2	Petition	121	Commerce.						
Clement, Jacob, assignees of	Compensation for two vessels chartered by United States for Venezuela, and lost.	24	1	Petition	200	Commerce.						
Clement, Jacob, assignees of	Compensation for two vessels chartered by United States for Venezuela, and lost.	24	2	Petition	43	Commerce.						
Clement, Jacob, assignees of	Compensation for two vessels chartered by United States for Venezuela, and lost.	25	2	Petition	46	Commerce	1047	Report and bill.	881	Referred to Committee Whole House.		
Clement, Jacob, assignees of	Compensation for two vessels chartered by United States for Venezuela, and lost.	25	3	Bill of last sess.	432	Whole House	Feb. 1, 1839	With't amend.	881	Passed	Passed	App'd March 3, 1839
Clement, Vachel	Revolutionary pension	23	1	Resolution	333	Invalid Pensions.						
Clements, Bryan & Co.	Equitable allowance for loss on contract for removal and subsistence of Cherokee Indians.	26	1	Senate bill	794	Claims	July 21, 1840	Adverse	278	Laid on table.		
Clements, Bryan & Co.	Equitable allowance for loss on contract for removal and subsistence of Cherokee Indians	26	2	Senate bill	151	Claims	137	With't amend.	97	Referred to Committee Whole House.		
Clements, Bryan & Co.	Equitable allowance for loss on contract for removal and subsistence of Cherokee Indians.	26	2	Senate amend't to House bill.	351	Whole House	March 3, 1841	Favorable	685	Passed	Passed	App'd March 3, 1841
Clements, Bryan & Co.	Additional compensation for loss on contract for removal of Indians.	29	1	Memorial	352	Judiciary	284	Adverse	......	Laid on table.		
Clements, Francis	Pension	21	2	Petition	336	Military Pensions.						
Clements, Jacob	Indemnity for French spoliations prior to 1800.	26	1	Memorial	182	Foreign Affairs	343	Favorable; bill.	319	Referred to Committee Whole House.		
Clements, R. A.	(See J. N. Mullican, administrator of.)											
Clements, William	Indemnity for damage to house by United States troops.	14	2	Petition	29	Claims	....	....	......	Discharged; laid on table.		
Clements, William	Indemnity for damage to house by United States troops.	15	1	Petition	28	Claims	Dec. 22, 1817	Rep. and res.; adverse.	......	Resolution adopted.		
Clementson, John, widow of	Allowance for house rent, &c., due as a sail-maker at navy-yard in Massachusetts.	23	1	Petition	246	Claims	Feb. 4, 1834	Adverse	......	Laid on table.		
Clementson, John, widow of	Allowance for house rent, &c., due as a sail-maker at navy-yard in Massachusetts.	23	2	Petition	308	Claims	Feb. 6, 1835	Adverse	......	Laid on table.		
Clemm, John, (Tenn.)	Revolutionary pension	24	1	Petition	260	Rev. Pensions	....	....	......	Discharged; laid on table.		

List of private claims presented to the House of Representatives of the United States from the 1st to the 31st Congress, inclusive—Continued.

Names of claimants.	Nature or object of the claim.	Congress.	Session.	How brought before the House of Reps.	Page of journal.	To what committee of the House referred.	No. or date of the report.	Nature of the report.	No. of the bill.	How disposed of by the House of Reps.	How disposed of by the Senate.	Date of the act of Congress, and remarks.
Clemmons, Benjamin	Pension	21	2	Petition	126	Military Pensions.						
Clemmons, Thomas, heirs of.	Compensation as an artificer in Kentucky militia, war of 1812.	23	1	Resolution	84	Claims	242	Report and bill.	273	Referred to Committee Whole House.		
Clemmons, Thomas, heirs of.	Compensation as an artificer in Kentucky militia, war of 1812.	23	2	Bill of last sess.	300	Whole House	Jan. 3, 1835	With't amend.	273	Passed	Passed	App'd March 3, 1835
Clemons, Willis, and Joab Griffin.	Release from judgment against them as sureties for J. B. Southmayd.	24	1	Petition	476	Judiciary.						
Clemson, Henry A.	(See Exploring Expedition.)											
Clency, George	Revolutionary pension	19	2	Resolution	203	Military Pensions.	....	....	.....	Discharged.		
Clendenin, Samuel M.	Compensation for services in Iowa as clerk to Lieut. D. Ruggles.	28	1	Petition	622	Claims.						
Clendenning, Thomas	Release from judgment against him as surety for M. Denny, postmaster at Denton, Maryland.	19	1	Petition	291	P. Of. & P. Roads.	....	....	.....	Discharged; laid on table.		
Clendenning, Thomas	Release from judgment against him as surety for M. Denny, postmaster at Denton, Maryland.	25	2	Petition	931	P. Of. & P. Roads.	....	....	.....	Discharged.		
Clendenning, Thomas	Release from judgment against him as surety for M. Denny, postmaster at Denton, Maryland.	26	1	Petitions	183, 341	P. Of. & P. Roads.						
Clendenning, William	Additional compensation for hauling timber at Harper's Ferry.	26	2	Petition	52	Claims	109	Adverse	.....	Laid on table.		
Clendenning, William	Additional compensation for hauling timber at Harper's Ferry.	27	2	Petition	268	Claims.						
Clendenning, William	Additional compensation for hauling timber at Harper's Ferry.	27	3	Petition	72	Claims	149	Adverse	.....	Laid on table.		
Cler, Peter	(See Peter Cleer.)											
Cler, Jean Daniel	Compensation for money and services applied to sick emigrants on their passage from Switzerland.	18	1	Petition	37	Priv. Land Claims.	Jan. 2, 1824	Adverse	.....	Laid on table.		
Clerk, James	Reimbursement of duties on certain stills.	7	1	Petition	32	Claims	Jan. 7, 1802	Adverse	.....	Laid on table.		
Clerks in executive offices, chief.	Increase of salaries	3	1	Petition	24	Select	Mar. 11, 1794	Discriminating	.....	Laid on table.		
Clerks of State, Treasury, and War Departments principal.	Increase of salaries	3	1	Senate bill	180	Whole House	June 5, 1794	With't amend.	17	Passed	Passed	App'd June 7, 1794
Clerks in executive offices.	Increase of compensation	15	1	Memorial	459	Whole House	April 17, 1818	By bill	127	Passed	Passed	App'd April 20, 1818
Clerks in executive offices.	Increase of compensation	24	1	Petition	610	Ways and Means.	641	Report and bill.	616	Referred to Committee Whole House.		
Clerks in executive offices.	Increase of compensation	24	2	Memorials	....	Ways and Means.	161	Report and bill.	886	Referred to Committee Whole House.	....	Provided for in civil appropriation act of March 3, 1837.
Clerks on the Sixth Census.	Additional compensation	27	2	Petition	221	Select	....	....	.....	Disch'd; laid on table.		
Clerks of district courts of United States.	Additional compensation for returns under bankrupt act.	29	2	Resolution	109	Ways and Means.						
Clerks of district courts of United States.	Additional compensation for returns under bankrupt act.	30	1	Resolution	123	Ways and Means.	....	....	.....	....	....	Provided for in civil appropriation act of August 12, 1848.
Clermont, Pierre, heirs of.	Confirmation of title to land in Louisiana.	30	2	Petition	379	Priv. Land Claims.						
Clermont, Pierre, heirs of.	Confirmation of title to land in Louisiana.	31	1	Petition	224	Priv. Land Claims.						

List of private claims presented to the House of Representatives of the United States from the 1st to the 31st Congress, inclusive—Continued.

Names of claimants.	Nature or object of the claim.	Congress.	Session.	How brought before the House of Reps.	Page of journal.	To what committee of the House referred.	No. or date of the report.	Nature of the report.	No. of the bill.	How disposed of by the House of Reps.	How disposed of by the Senate.	Date of the act of Congress, and remarks.
Cleveland, Jeremiah, (N.Y.)	Pension	21	2	Petition	159	Military Pensions						
Cleveland, Jeremiah, (N.Y.)	Pension	22	1	Petition	188	Rev. Pensions.						
Cleveland, John	Pension	19	1	Petition	221	Military Pensions	164	Adverse		Laid on table.		
Cleveland, Joseph, (N. Y.)	Further compensation for services as a revolutionary soldier.	22	1	Petition	29	Rev. Pensions.						
Cleveland, Palma	(See Lucius Storrs and others.)											
Cleveland, jr., Samuel, (Vt.)	Invalid pension and bounty land for disabilities incurred, war of 1812.	18	1	Petition	158	Claims	104	Report and bill.	189	Passed	Passed	App'd May 26, 1824
Cleveland, jr., Samuel, (Vt.)	Bounty land as a soldier in war of 1812.	24	1	Resolution	285	Military Affairs.						
Cleveland, jr., Samuel, (Vt.)	Pension as a soldier in war of 1812.	24	1	Petition	140	Invalid Pensions	Mar. 3, 1836	Adverse		Laid on table.		
Cleveland, jr., Samuel, (Vt.)	Pension as a soldier in war of 1812.	24	2	Petition	73	Invalid Pensions	Jan. 19, 1837	Adverse		Laid on table.		
Clewet, James R.	(See Bartholomew Balden and others.)											
Clicke, Henry, (Tenn.)	Pension	22	1	Petition	226	Invalid Pensions	263	Report and bill.	344	Passed	Laid on table.	
Clicke, Henry, (Tenn.)	Pension	22	2	Petition	....	Invalid Pensions	7	Report and bill.	626	Passed	Passed	App'd March 2, 1833
Clicke, Henry, (Tenn.)	Increase of pension	30	1	Bill and petition	437, 440	Invalid Pensions	706	With't amend.	230	Referred to Committee Whole House.		
Clicke, Henry, (Tenn.)	Increase of pension	30	2	Bill of last sess.	319	Whole House	Jan. 26, 1849	With't amend.	230	Passed	With't amend.	
Clicke, Henry, (Tenn.)	Increase of pension	31	1	Petition	276	Invalid Pensions	146	Report and bill.	162	Referred to Committee Whole House.		
Clicke, Henry, (Tenn.)	Increase of pension	31	2	Bill of last sess.	104	Whole House	Jan. 3, 1851	With't amend.	162	Passed with amendm't	Ref'd to Com on Pensions.	
Cliff, Hiram	(See John Davlin, representatives of.)											
Clifford, John and Thomas, and others.	Refunding duties on copper	11	3	Petition	509	Com. and Manuf.	Feb. 9, 1811	By bill	203	Referred to Committee Whole House.		
Clifford, John and Thomas, and others.	Refunding duties on copper	12	1	Petition	12	Com. and Manuf.	Nov. 13, 1811	By bill	2	Recommitted.		
Clifford, John and Thomas, and others.	Refunding duties on copper	13	3	Petition	522	Com. and Manuf.	Feb. 1, 1815	By bill	277	Referred to Committee Whole House.		
Clifford, John and Thomas, and others.	Refunding duties on copper	14	1	Petition	47	Com. and Manuf.	Dec. 19, 1815	By bill		Passed	Rejected.	
Clifford, John and Thomas, and others.	Refunding duties on copper	14	2	Petition	136	Com. and Manuf.	Jan. 10, 1817	By bill	45	Passed	Rejected.	
Clifford, John and Thomas, and others.	Refunding duties on copper	15	1	Petition	90	Com. and Manuf.	Jan. 20, 1818	By bill	46	Passed	Passed	App'd April 20, 1818
Clifford, John, and others.	Restoration of schooner Jefferson and cargo, seized under the non-importation act.	12	1	Petition	43	Com. and Manuf.						
Clifford, Michael	Pension	20	2	Petition	143	Military Pensions				Discharged; laid on table.		
Clifford, Michael	Pension	21	1	Petition and res.	67, 277	Military Pensions				Discharged; laid on table.		
Clifford, Michael	Pension	21	2	Petition	159	Military Pensions.						
Clifford, Pierson D.	(See Wm. H. Bedford, agent, &c.)	28	1		262							
Clifford, Thomas, & Son.	(See John and Thomas Clifford.)											
Clift, Joseph	(See John Davlin, representatives of.)											
Clift, Lemuel	Arrears of pension	31	1	Petition	542	Rev. Pensions	135	Adverse		Laid on table.		
Clifton, Andrew J.	Salvage on cargo of quartermaster's stores saved from wreck at Tampico.	30	2	Petition	139	Claims.						

List of private claims presented to the House of Representatives of the United States from the 1st to the 31st Congress, inclusive—Continued.

Names of claimants.	Nature or object of the claim.	Congress.	Session.	How brought before the House of Reps.	Page of journal.	To what committee of the House referred.	No. or date of the report.	Nature of the report.	No. of the bill.	How disposed of by the House of Reps.	How disposed of by the Senate.	Date of the act of Congress, and remarks.
Clifton, Andrew J.......	Salvage on cargo of quartermaster's stores saved from wreck at Tampico.	31	1	Petition	308	Claims.						
Clifton, Joshua	Invalid pension................	10	2	Petition	489	Claims.						
Clinch, Duncan L.......	Confirmation of title to land in Florida.	23	1	Petition	638	Public Lands.						
Clinch, Duncan L.......	Pre emption right to land on which he has settled upon, and surrender of land confirmed to him as assignee of G. F. Clark.	23	2	Senate bill	341	Public Lands	Feb. 10, 1835	With't amend.	37	Postponed.		
Clinch, Duncan L.......	Pre-emption right to land on which he has settled upon, and surrender of land confirmed to him as assignee of G. F. Clark.	24	1	Senate bill......	735	Priv. Land Claims.	June 9, 1836	With't amend.	11	Passed	Passed	App'd July 2, 1836
Clinch, Duncan L.......	Payment of account for forage, &c., furnished United States forces in Florida.	25	3	Resolution	176	Claims.						
Clinch, Duncan L.......	Payment of account for forage, &c., furnished United States forces in Florida.	26	1	Petition	335	Claims	303	Report and bill.	265	Recommitted.		
							April 24, 1840	Bill.........	265	Passed.	Passed	App'd June 19, 1794
Clinch, Duncan L.......	Indemnity for damages and loss of property during Indian hostilities in Florida.	27	3	Senate bill......	495	Claims	....	....	87	Discharged; laid on table.		
Clinch, James...........	(See Solomon T. Nicoll, & Co.)											
Cline, Anthony	(See Richard Skimmer, and others)											
Cline, Jesse............	Pension as a soldier in war of 1812.	28	1	Petition	609	Invalid Pensions...	....	....	......	Discharged; laid on table.		
Cline, Jesse	Pension as a soldier in war of 1812.	28	2	Petition	216	Invalid Pensions.						
Cline, John L. (lieutenant of Tennessee volunteers.)	Relief from costs and judgment against him for dispossessing Sherwood Robinson of an improvement, under orders.	26	1	Petition	623	Claims.						
Cline, John L. (lieutenant of Tennessee volunteers.)	Relief from costs and judgment against him for dispossessing Sherwood Robinson of an improvement, under orders.	26	2	Petition	38	Claims	36	Report and bill.	564	Referred to Committee Whole House.		
Cline, John L. (lieutenant of Tennessee volunteers.)	Relief from cost and judgment against him for dispossessing Sherwood Robinson of an improvement, under orders.	27	2	Petition	55	Claims	1	Report and bill.	40	Passed	Passed	App'd July 9, 1842
Clingen, Charles	Compensation for services, &c., in revolutionary war.	1	3	Petition	378	....	....	....	......	Referred to Secretary of War.		
Clingen, Charles	Compensation for services, &c., in revolutionary war.	2	2	Report of Secretary of War.	735	....	....	....	......	Laid on table.		
Clingen, Charles	Compensation for services, &c., in revolutionary war.	3	2	Rep. of Secretary War.	278	....	....	....	......	Laid on table.		
Clinginsmith, Daniel, and others.	Confirmation of title to land in territory of Missouri.	15	2	Petition	207	Priv. Land Claims.	....	....	......	Discharged; laid on table.		
Clinginsmith, Daniel, and others.	Confirmation of title to land in territory of Missouri.	17	1	Petition	53	Public Lands.	....	....	......	Discharged; laid on table.		

List of private claims presented to the House of Representatives of the United States from the 1st to the 31st Congress, inclusive—Continued.

Names of claimants.	Nature or object of the claim.	Congress.	Session.	How brought before the House of Reps.	Page of journal.	To what committee of the House referred.	No. or date of the report.	Nature of the report.	No. of the bill.	How disposed of by the House of Reps.	How disposed of by the Senate.	Date of the act of Congress, and remarks.
Clinginsmith, Daniel, and others.	Confirmation of title to land in territory of Missouri.	18	1	Petition	53	Public Lands	Jan. 16, 1824	By bill	65	Passed	Passed	App'd May 26, 1824
Clingman, John	(See Uriah Barber, and others.)											
Clinton, Joseph	Compensation for services in revolutionary war.	4	1	Petition	379	Claims	Jan. 20, 1796	Res. adverse		Resolution adopted.		
Clinton, Patty	Pension for revolutionary services of three brothers.	28	1	Petition	946	Rev. Claims.						
Clitherall, George C., widow of.	Amount of expenses for rent of quarters as surgeon United States army.	23	1	Petition	379	Military Affairs	363	Report and bill	390	Referred to Committee Whole House.		
Clitherall, George C., widow of.	Amount of expenses for rent of quarters as surgeon United States army.	24	1	Petition	64	Military Affairs				Discharged; laid on table.		
Clitherall, George C., widow of.	Amount of expenses for rent of quarters as surgeon United States army.	24	2	Senate bill	250	Military Affairs	Feb. 14, 1837	With't amend.	23	Referred to Committee Whole House.		
Clitherall, George C., widow of.	Amount of expenses for rent of quarters as surgeon United States army.	25	2	Senate bill	301	Claims	526	Adverse	72	Referred to Committee Whole House.		
Clitherall, George C., widow of.	Amount of expenses for rent of quarters as surgeon United States army.	27	2	Senate bill	411	Military Affairs	362	Adverse	2	Rejected.		
Clitherall, George C., widow of.	Amount of expenses for rent of quarters as surgeon United States army.	28	1	Senate bill	733	Military Affairs	May 2, 1844	Adverse	13	Referred to Committee Whole House.		
Close, Elijah	Pension for injuries from exposure in war of 1812.	31	2	Petition	131	Invalid Pensions						
Close, J.	(See Charles Barre, assignee of.)	27	2		140							
Close, William	(See Benjamin F. Hart, executors of.)											
Closeau, Louis and Gilbert.	(See Antoine Prudhomme, and others.)											
Closs and Stouffer	Indemnity for French spoliations prior to 1800.	26	1	Memorial	182	Foreign Affairs	343	Favorable; bill.	319	Referred to Committee Whole House.		
Clossey, Miles F.	Extra compensation as clerk in Treasury Department, in Philadelphia, during the yellow fever in 1793.	3	1	Petition	88	Select	April 17, 1794	Favorable: bill ordered.	69	Passed	Rejected.	
Closson, Wilber	Pension	20	1	Petition	30	Military Pensions.	Jan. 28, 1828	Adverse		Laid on table.		
Cloud, Caleb W., widow of.	Increase of pension	25	2	Petition	594	Naval Affairs				Discharged.		
Cloud, Martin	(See William Carlan, heirs of.											
Clough, Abigail	Pension as widow of two revolutionary soldiers.	22	2	Petition	118	Rev. Pensions				Laid on table.		
Clough, John	Invalid pension	3	1	Rep. of Secretary War.	131	Select	May 26, 1794	To refer to Sec. with instruc	R. 12	Passed	Passed	App'd June 9, 1794
Clough, Noah	Invalid pension	3	1	Rep. of Secretary War.	131	Select	May 26, 1794	Favorable; bill ordered.	62	Passed	Passed	App'd June 7, 1794
Clough, Polly	(See Jonathan Hilliard, widow of.)											
Cloutier, A.	Confirmation of title to land in Louisiana.	26	1	Petition	365	Priv. Land Claims.						
Cloutman, Thomas	Compensation for services and sacrifices in revolutionary war.	25	2	Petition						Laid on table.		

List of private claims presented to the House of Representatives of the United States from the 1st to the 31st Congress, inclusive—Continued.

Names of claimants.	Nature or object of the claim.	Congress.	Session.	How brought before the House of Reps.	Page of journal.	To what committee of the House referred.	No. or date of the report.	Nature of the report.	No. of the bill.	How disposed of by the House of Reps.	How disposed of by the Senate.	Date of the act of Congress, and remarks.
Cloutman, Thomas	Compensation for services and sacrifices in revolutionary war.	25	3	Petition	221	Rev. Claims	....	....	......	Discharged.		
Cloutman, Thomas	Compensation for services and sacrifices in revolutionary war.	26	1	Petition	282	Rev. Claims.						
Clower, Jonathan	Pension	22	1	Resolution	171	Rev. Pensions	....	....	......	Discharged.		
Clower, William	Additional compensation for carrying the mail between Greenville and Fayette, Mississippi.	21	1	Resolution	339	P. Of. and P. Roads.	371	Report and bill.	431	Referred to Committee Whole House.		
Clower, William	Additional compensation for carrying the mail between Greenville and Fayette, Mississippi.	21	2	Bill of last sess	340	Whole House	Feb. 22, 1831	With amend.	431	Passed	Passed	App'd March 2, 1831
Cloyd, William	Relief from a military fine, the duty being performed by a substitute.	19	2	Petition	50	Claims	13	Report and bill.	306	Referred to Committee Whole House.		
Cloyd, William	Relief from a military fine, the duty being performed by a substitute.	20	1	Petition	38	Claims	4	Report and bill.	5	Passed	Passed	App'd Mar. 10, 1828
Cloyd, James	Pension	23	1	Petition	493	Rev. Pensions	....	....	......	Discharged; laid on table.		
Cluff, John	Arrears of pension	22	1	Petition	412	Rev. Pensions	....	....	......	Discharged; laid on table.		
Cluff, Matthew	(See Barney Tisdale and others.)											
Clum, Philip, late widow of.	Revolutionary pension	25	2	Petition	531	Rev. Pensions	793	Report and bill.	742	Passed	Adverse report.	
Clum, Philip, late widow of.	Revolutionary pension	25	3	Petition	88	Rev. Pensions	Jan. 9, 1839	By bill	993	Passed	Adverse report.	
Clum, Philip, late widow of.	Revolutionary pension	26	1	Petition	171	Rev. Pensions	161	Report and bill.	171	Passed	Indef. postp'd.	
Clusky, Charles B	Compensation for plans and estimates for custom-house at Savannah, Georgia.	30	1	Petition	849	Commerce	752	Report and bill.	591	Referred to Committee Whole House.		
Clute, Frederick	Revolutionary pension	24	1	Petition	751	Rev. Pensions.						
Clutes, John, & Jacob Hart, assignee of.	Compensation for services as teamsters at Fort Macomb, Florida.	27	3	Petition	101	Claims.						
Clutes, John, & Jacob Hart, assignee of.	Compensation for services as teamsters at Fort Macomb, Florida.	28	1	Petition	451	Claims.						
Clutes, John, & Jacob Hart, assignee of.	Compensation for services as teamsters at Fort Macomb, Florida.	28	2	Petition	71	Claims.						
Clutes, John, & Jacob Hart, assignee of.	Compensation for services as teamsters at Fort Macomb, Florida.	30	2	Senate bill	518	Claims	Mar. 3, 1849	With't amend.	223	Referred to Committee Whole House.		
Clutes, John, & Jacob Hart, assignee of.	Compensation for services as teamsters at Fort Macomb, Florida.	31	1	Senate bill	1414	Claims	....	....	36			
Clutter, Simeon	Revolutionary pension	24	1	Resolution	437	Rev. Pensions	585	Adverse	......	Laid on table.		
Clyman, James	Grant of land in consideration of injuries sustained from the Menomonee Indians.	24	1	Memorial	430	Claims	468	Adverse	......	Laid on table.		
Coates, Frederick	Compensation for horse killed in U. S. service, war of 1812.	16	2	Petition	197	Claims	Feb. 8, 1821	Adverse	......	Laid on table.		
Coates, Frederick	Compensation for horse killed in U. S. service, war of 1812.	17	1	Petition	119	Claims	Feb. 25, 1822	Adverse	......	Laid on table.		
Coats, James	Confirmation of title to land in Louisiana.	19	1	Report Secretary of Treasury.	64	Public Lands	33	Adverse	......	Recommitted.		
							May 5, 1826	By bill	254	Laid on table.		
Coates, John	(See Clark, Conner, and others.)											

List of private claims presented to the House of Representatives of the United States from the 1st to the 31st Congress, inclusive—Continued.

Names of claimants.	Nature or object of the claim.	Congress.	Session.	How brought before the House of Reps.	Page of journal.	To what committee of the House referred.	No. or date of the report.	Nature of the report.	No. of the bill.	How disposed of by the House of Reps.	How disposed of by the Senate.	Date of the act of Congress, and remarks.
Coates, John	Invalid pension	3	1	Rep. of Secretary War.	131	Select	May 26, 1794	Res. to refer to Sec. with instructions.	R. 12	Passed	Passed	App'd June 9, 1794
Coates, John	Invalid pension	4	1	Rep. of Secretary War.	445	Claims	Feb. 18, 1796	Res. to refer to Sec. with instructions.	R. 16	Passed	Passed	App'd April 18, 1796
Coates, John	Invalid pension	4	2	Rep. of Secretary War.	651	Claims.						
Coates, John, (Ohio)	Compensation for extra services as receiver of public moneys.	30	2	Petition	78	Claims	18	Adverse	......	Laid on table.		
Coats, Moses H.	(See John Mitchell, and others.)	31	2	....	74							
Coats, Nathan	Allowance for certain disbursements in 1837 as quartermaster to volunteers in Creek war.	26	1	Petition	336	Claims	575	Adverse	......	Laid on table.		
Coats & Howel	(See Howel & Coats)											
Coates, Reynell	Settlement of claim for expenses and damages incurred in South Arctic Exploring Expedition.	25	3	Petition	564	Naval Affairs.						
Coates, Reynell	Indemnity for being detached from Exploring Expedition, after relinquishing other business.	26	1	Petition	330	Naval Affairs.						
Coates, Reynell, and others	Indemnity for losses claimed as members of scientific corps of Exploring Expedition.	26	1	Senate bill	1121	Claims	....	....	240			
Coates, Reynell, and others	Indemnity for losses claimed as members of scientific corps of Exploring Expedition.	26	2	Senate bill	231	Naval Affairs	....	....	164			
Coates, Reynell, and others	Indemnity for losses claimed as members of scientific corps of Exploring Expedition.	27	2	Petition	227	Claims.						
Coates, Reynell, and others	Indemnity for losses claimed as members of scientific corps of Exploring Expedition.	27	2	Senate bill	782	Claims	832	With amend.	141	Laid on table.		
Coates, Reynell, and others	Indemnity for losses claimed as members of scientific corps of Exploring Expedition.	28	1	Senate bill	942	Naval Affairs	June 7, 1844	With't amend.	96	Referred to Committee Whole House.		
Coats, Thomas	Pension for services as a soldier in war of 1812.	31	1	Petition	663	Invalid Pensions	147	Report and bill.	163	Referred to Committee Whole House.		
Cobb, Charles, widow of	Pension for injuries from exposure in naval service.	31	1	Petition	632	Invalid Pensions	....	....	.....	Discharged; leave to withdraw.		
Cobb, Daniel	Revolutionary pension	24	1	Resolution	776	Rev. Pensions	736	Report and bill.	679	Passed	Passed	App'd June 28, 1836
Cobb, David, widow of	Revolutionary pension	26	1	Resolution	596	Rev. Pensions	663	Adverse	......	Laid on table.		
Cobb, Elkanah, widow of, (Pa.)	Patent for certain inventions	15	2	Petition	144	Judiciary	Jan. 5, 1818	Rep't and res. adverse.	......	Resolution adopted.		
Cobb, Elkanah, (Mass.)	Revolutionary pension	23	2	Petition	105	Rev. Pensions	....	....	......	Disch'd; laid on table.		
Cobb, Enos, as attorney	Pensions for sundry revolutionary officers and soldiers in Maine.	21	2	Petition	42	Military Pensions.						
Cobb, Enos, as attorney	Pensions for sundry revolutionary officers and soldiers in Maine.	22	1	Petition	45	Rev. Pensions.						
Cobb, Etheldred	Invalid pension	12	1	House bill	361	Whole House	Jan. 15, 1812	Favorable	138	Passed	Passed	App'd July 5, 1812
Cobb, Francis	Revolutionary pension	22	1	Resolution	261	Rev. Pensions	365	Report and bill.	460	Passed	Indef. postp'd.	
Cobb, Francis	Revolutionary pension	27	2	Petition	374	Rev. Pensions	784	Adverse	......	Laid on table	....	Feb. 11, 1843; leave to withdraw.

List of private claims presented to the House of Representatives of the United States from the 1st to the 31st Congress, inclusive—Continued.

Names of claimants.	Nature or object of the claim.	Congress.	Session.	How brought before the House of Reps.	Page of journal.	To what committee of the House referred.	No. or date of the report.	Nature of the report.	No. of the bill.	How disposed of by the House of Reps.	How disposed of by the Senate.	Date of the act of Congress, and remarks.
Cobb, Isaac	Pension for injuries, &c., in war of 1812.	29	1	Memorial	533	Invalid Pensions	....	....	....	Discharged; laid on table.		
Cobb, Isaac	Pension for injuries, &c., in war of 1812.	31	1	Petition	731	Rev. Pensions	296	Report and bill.	265	Referred to Committee Whole House.		
Cobb, Isaac	Pension for injuries, &c., in war of 1812.	31	2	Bill of last sess.	182	Whole House	Jan. 24, 1851	With amend.	265	Amendment rejected and bill passed.	Ref'd to Com. on Pensions.	
Cobb, James D	Pay as an army officer from the date of his dismissal to that of disbanding his corps.	18	2	Petition	209	Military Affairs	....	....	....	Discharged; leave to withdraw.		
Cobb, James D	Pay as an army officer from the date of his dismissal to that of disbanding his corps.	20	2	Petition	129	Military Affairs	67	Report and bill.	411	Referred to Committee Whole House.		
Cobb, James D.	Pay as an army officer from the date of his dismissal to that of disbanding his corps.	31	1	Petition	50	Military Affairs	18	Report and bill.	25	Passed	Passed	App'd Feb. 11, 1830
Cobb, Jonathan, widow of.	Pension for services, &c., in U. S. army.	30	1	Petition	229	Invalid Pensions.						
Cobb, Jonathan H.	Grant of land for a silk factory	22	2	Petition	33	Agriculture.						
Cobb, Justus	Pension	23	2	Resolution	89	Invalid Pensions	66	Report and bill.	687	Passed	Passed	App'd March 3, 1835
Cobb, Oliver E	(See Peter and John S. Crary & Co.)											
Cobb, Phœbe	Extension of pension act of 17th June, 1844.	30	1	Petition	229	Rev. Pensions	June 25, 1848	Adverse	....	Laid on table.		
Cobb, Samuel, heirs of	Five years' full pay in lieu of half-pay for life as a Lieut. in revolutionary army.	23	1	Petition	97	Rev. Claims	....	....	....	Discharged; laid on table.		
Cobb, Surranus	Pension for disabilities incurred in war of 1812.	29	1	Memorial	275	Invalid Pensions	466	Report and bill.	344	Passed	Passed	App'd Aug. 8, 1846
Cobb, Sylvester, widow of.	Pension for revolutionary services.	31	2	Petition	99	Rev. Pensions.						
Cobb, Thomas, widow of.	Continuation of pension	29	2	Petition	302	Rev. Pensions.						
Cobb, Thomas, widow of.	Continuation of pension	30	1	Petition	230	Rev. Pensions.						
Cobbs, Waddy V	Pay as major while commanding as such.	24	2	Petition	37	Claims.						
Cobbs, Waddy V., widow of.	Pension for loss of deceased from exposure in U. S. service.	30	1	Petition	759	Invalid Pensions	801	Report and bill.	622	Referred to Committee Whole House.		
Cobbs, Waddy V., widow of.	Pension for loss of deceased from exposure in U. S. service.	30	2	Bill of last sess.	363	Whole House	Feb. 2, 1849	With't amend.	622	Passed	Passed	App'd March 3, 1849
Cobbett, Philip	(See John Cox, heirs of.)											
Coberly, Joseph	Invalid pension	26	1	Petition	326	Invalid Pensions	....	....	....	Discharged; laid on table.		
Coberly, Joseph	Invalid pension	27	2	Petition	526	Invalid Pensions	632	Adverse	....	Laid on table.		
Coberly, Joseph	Invalid pension	27	3	Petition	259	Invalid Pensions	167	Adverse	....	Laid on table.		
Coberly, Joseph	Invalid pension	30	1	Petition	82	Invalid Pensions	33	Adverse	....	Laid on table	....	Leave to withdraw, 2d session.
Cobey, James	Increase of pension	11	2	House bill	283	Whole House	Mar. 24, 1810	Favorable	108	Passed	Passed	App'd April 27, 1810
Cobler, John	Compensation for two horses lost in Florida for want of forage.	18	2	Resolution	248	Claims.						
Coburn, Abigail	Pension for revolutionary services of husband.	28	1	Petition	839	Committee Whole House, bill No. 7.	....	....	....	....	....	See act June 17, 1844
Coburn, Abigail	Extension of act of 17th June, 1844.	30	1	Petition	230	Rev. Pensions	June 25, 1848	Adverse	....	Laid on table.		
Coburn, Morrell	Invalid pension	3	2	Rep. of Secretary War.	350	Claims	Mar. 3, 1795	To discharge and postp'd.	....	Laid on table.		

List of private claims presented to the House of Representatives of the United States from the 1st to the 31st Congress, inclusive—Continued.

Names of claimants.	Nature or object of the claim.	Congress.	Session.	How brought before the House of Reps.	Page of journal.	To what committee of the House referred.	No. or date of the report.	Nature of the report.	No. of the bill.	How disposed of by the House of Reps.	How disposed of by the Senate.	Date of the act of Congress, and remarks.
Coburn, Morrell	Invalid pension	4	1	Rep. of Secretary War.	445	Claims	Feb. 18, 1796	Favorable; bill ordered.	156	Passed	Passed	App'd April 20, 1796
Coburn, Moses B	Increase of pension	25	2	Petition	350	Rev. Claims	May 24, 1838	Adverse		Laid on table.		
Coburn, Nathaniel, widow of.	Allowance of half-pay, under act of 16th April, 1816.	24	1	Resolution	286	Military Affairs				Discharged; laid on table.		
Coburn, Samuel	Confirmation of title to land in Mississippi.	21	2	Senate bill	185	Priv. Land Claims	Feb. 1, 1831	Adverse		Recommitted.		
							Feb. 22, 1831	With amends.	69	Passed	Passed	App'd March 3, 1831
Cochran, Charles B	Relief for non-compliance with conditions by navy officers in taking his property.	13	2	Petition	172	Claims				Discharged.		
Cochran, Charles B	Relief for non-compliance with conditions by navy officers in taking his property.	13	3	Petition	589	Claims				Discharged.		
Cochran, George	Compensation for certain clothing furnished United States army in 1815.	28	1	Petition	114	Claims.						
Cochran, George	Compensation for certain clothing furnished United States army in 1815.	28	1	Petition	310	Judiciary.						
Cochran, George	Compensation for certain clothing furnished United States army in 1815.	30	1	Petition	260	Claims	162	Adverse		Laid on table		Leave to withdraw.
Cochran, George W	(See Sam'l Washburne & G. W. C.)	25	3		135							
Cochran, James	(See John Grant, jr., and others.)											
Cochran, James	Arrears of pension	30	2	Petition	239	Invalid Pensions	97	Adverse		Laid on table.		
Cochran, James D	Pension for injuries received in Mexican war.	31	1	Petition	692	Invalid Pensions.						
Cochran, James L.	Permission to avail himself of a pre-emption act.	24	1	Petition	215	Public Lands	Feb. 12, 1836	By bill	335	Referred to Committee Whole House.		
Cochran, James L	Permission to avail himself of a pre-emption act.	24	2	Bill of last sess.	62	Whole House			335			
Cochran, James L	Permission to avail himself of a pre emption act.	25	2	Petition	42	Public Lands	Mar. 6, 1838	By bill	612	Referred to Committee Whole House.		
Cochran, James L	Permission to avail himself of a pre-emption act.	25	3	Bill of last sess.	380	Whole House	Jan. 25, 1839	With amend.	612	Passed with amendm't.	Adverse report.	
Cochran, James L	Permission to avail himself of a pre-emption act.	26	1	Petition	177	Public Lands	Mar. 4, 1840	By bill	71	Passed	Passed with amendment.	App'd June 1, 1840
Cochran, John, (N. Y.)	Extra compensation as receiver of Continental taxes and commissioner of loan office.	1	2	Petition and rep't Sec. of War.	141					Laid on table.		
Cochran, John, (N. Y.)	Restoration of pension	17	1	Petition	51	Rev. Pensions	Jan. 15, 1822	General bill	37	Passed	Rejected	See act March 1, 1823
Cochran, Joseph	Pre-emption right to land in Missouri.	25	2	Senate bill	1166	Public Lands	July 6, 1838	With't amend	338	Referred to Committee Whole House.		
Cochran, Joseph	Pre emption right to land in Missouri.	25	3	Senate bill	477	Priv. Land Claims			154			
Cochran, Joseph	Pre-emption right to land in Missouri.	26	1	Senate bill	419	Priv. Land Claims	Mar. 5, 1840	With't amend.	54	Passed	Passed	App'd May 27, 1840
Cochran, Richard E., heirs of.	Compensation for horse lost at Resaca de la Palma, May 9, 1846.	29	2	Memorial	182	Claims.						
Cochran, Richard E., heirs of.	Compensation for horse lost at Resaca de la Palma, May 9, 1846.	30	1	Petition	345	Claims	499	Report and bill.	413	Passed	Committed to Claims.	

List of private claims presented to the House of Representatives of the United States from the 1st to the 31st Congress, inclusive—Continued.

Names of claimants.	Nature or object of the claim.	Congress.	Session.	How brought before the House of Reps.	Page of journal.	To what committee of the House referred.	No. or date of the report.	Nature of the report.	No. of the bill.	How disposed of by the House of Reps.	How disposed of by the Senate.	Date of the act of Congress, and remarks.
Cochran, Robert E	Release from imprisonment on judgment of United States.	13	2	Petition	172	Judiciary	41	Report and res.; adverse.		Resolution adopted.		
Cochran, Robert, (N. C.)	Reimbursement of money expended for sick and disabled seamen.	13	2	Petition	185	Claims				Discharged.		
Cochran, Robert	Confirmation of title to land in Mississippi.	22	2	Petition	105	Priv. Land Claims.	Dec. 29, 1832	Adverse		Laid on table.		
Cochran, Samuel, (Tenn.)	Pension	21	1	Resolution	254	Military Pensions.				Discharged; laid on table.		
Cochran, Samuel, (Tenn.)	Pension	21	2	Petition	110	Military Pensions.						
Cochran, Samuel, (N. Y.)	Pension for injuries received in war of 1812.	29	1	Petition	74	Invalid Pensions	81	Adverse.		Laid on table.		
Cochran, William, administrator of.	(See Worden Pope and others)	20	1		168							
Cock, James, (N. Y.,) widow of.	Pension for revolutionary services.	31	1	Petition	1467	Rev. Pensions.						
Cock, James, (N. Y.,) widow of.	Pension for revolutionary services.	31	2	Petition	431	Rev. Pensions	62	Adverse		Laid on table.		
Cock, John, (Tenn.)	Revolutionary pension	15	2	Petition	27	Pens. & Rev. Cl'ms.				Discharged; referred to Secretary of War.		
Cock, Simon	(See Daniel Wheeler.)	15	1		261							
Cockburn, Walter	Release from a payment on land purchased, and pre-emption to other land.	22	1	Senate bill	816	Claims	July 3, 1832	With't amend.	117	Passed	Passed	App'd July 13, 1832
Cocke, John, (Tenn.)	Credit for money advanced as commissioner to Cherokee Indians, and release from judgment against him.	25	3	Petition	352	Claims.						
Cocke, John, (Tenn.)	Credit for money advanced as commissioner to Cherokee Indians, and release from judgment against him.	26	1	Petition	168	Claims	304	Report and bill.	266	Referred to Committee Whole House.		
Cocke, John, (Tenn.)	Credit for money advanced as commissioner to Cherokee Indians, and release from judgment against him.	27	2	Petition	757	Claims.						
Cocke, John, (Tenn.)	Credit for money advanced as commissioner to Cherokee Indians, and release from judgment against him.	28	1	Petition	1042	Claims.						
Cocke, Joseph	Restoration of pension	17	1	Petition	109	Rev. Pensions.	Jan. 15, 1822	General bill	37	Passed	Rejected	See act March 1, 1823
Cocke, Pleasant B	(See Charles W. Roberts, assignee of.)											
Cocke, Sterling	(See William C. Ellis, heirs of.)											
Cocke, William	Six hundred and forty acres of land for extraordinary services to U. States, in war of 1812.	18	1	Petition	237	Military Affairs	105	Report and bill	191	Passed	Passed	App'd May 18, 1824
Cocke, William H., widow of.	Pension: husband killed in United States naval service.	27	3	Resolution	241	Naval Affairs.						
Cockerille, William S	Confirmation of title to land in Louisiana.	23	1	Petition	76	Priv. Land Claims.	152	Report and bill.	162	Passed	Laid on table.	
Cockle, John	Amount of his proportion of certain bills drawn in France on United States, under convention of April 30, 1803.	11	2	Petition	244	Com. and Manuf.						

List of private claims presented to the House of Representatives of the United States from the 1*st to the* **31***st Congress, inclusive*—Continued.

Names of claimants.	Nature or object of the claim.	Congress.	Session.	How brought before the House of Reps.	Page of journal.	To what committee of the House referred.	No. or date of the report.	Nature of the report.	No. of the bill.	How disposed of by the House of Reps.	How disposed of by the Senate.	Date of the act of Congress, and remarks.
Cockle, John	Amount of his proportion of certain bills drawn in France on United States, under convention of April 30, 1803.	12	1	Petition	248	Claims.						
Cockle, John	Amount of his proportion of certain bills drawn in France on United States, under convention of April 30, 1803.	21	1	Petition	100	Foreign Affairs				Discharged; laid on table.		
Cockley, John	Bounty land for military services	1	3	Petition	360					Referred to Secretary of War.		
Cocks, Robert	Confirmation of title to land in Mississippi Territory.	12	1	Petition	26, 87	Public Lands.						
Cocks, Robert	Confirmation of title to land in Mississippi Territory.	12	2	Petition	550	Public Lands.						
Cocks, Robert	Confirmation of title to land in Mississippi Territory.	13	2	Petition	294	Public Lands				Discharged.		
Cocks, William T.	Pension	21	1	Petition	231	Military Affairs	April 2, 1830	Adverse		Laid on table.		
Coctlogon, Count of	(See M. A. Marquis, *et al.*)	20	1		728							
Coddington, Benjamin	Invalid pension	12	1	House bill	361	Whole House	June 15, 1812	Favorable	138	Passed	Passed	App'd July 5, 1812
Coddington, Robert	Increase of pension	11	3	House bill	604	Whole House	Mar. 2, 1811	Favorable	218	Passed	Passed	App'd March 3, 1811
Codman, John, executors of.	Indemnity for French spoliations prior to 1800.	26	1	Memorial	182	Foreign Affairs	343	Favorable; bill.	319	Referred to Committee Whole House.		
Codman, Stephen	Indemnity for French spoliations prior to 1800.	26	1	Memorial	182	Foreign Affairs	343	Favorable; bill.	319	Referred to Committee Whole House.		
Codmas, Andrew	Grant and conveyance of certain land in New Jersey.	7	1	Senate bill	111	Whole House	Mar. 24, 1802	With't amend.	3	Passed	Passed	App'd Mar. 30, 1802
Coe, Benjamin	Pension	21	1	Petition	471	Military Affairs	April 13, 1830	Adverse		Laid on table.		
Coe, Benjamin	Pension	22	1	Petition	130	Rev. Claims				Discharged; laid on table.		
Coe, Benjamin	Pension	25	2	Petition	180	Rev. Claims				Discharged; laid on table.		
Coe, Ebenezer	Increase of pension	9	2	House bill	608	Whole House	Feb. 28, 1807	Favorable	216	Passed	Passed	App'd March 3, 1807
Coe, James	Pension for wounds, &c., received in war of 1812.	29	1	Memorial	440	Invalid Pensions.						
Coe, James	Pension for wounds, &c., received in war of 1812.	29	2	Petition	162	Invalid Pensions.						
Coe, James	Pension for wounds, &c., received in war of 1812.	30	1	Petition	482	Invalid Pensions	576	Adverse		Laid on table.		
Coe, Samuel	Compensation for services as wagon master in revolutionary war.	4	1	Petition	424	Claims	May 7, 1796	Adverse		Leave to withdraw.		
Coffee, G	(See D. W. Haley and others)	26	1		605							
Coffee, James	Revolutionary pension	22	1	Petition	733	Rev. Pensions.						
Coffee, John, (Penn.)	Invalid pension	8	2	Petition	98	Claims.						
Coffee, John, (Alabama)	Allowance for clerk hire as surveyor general of public lands in Alabama.	16	2	Senate bill	174	Public Lands	Feb. 6, 1821	With't amend.	19	Referred to Committee Whole House.		
Coffee, John, (Alabama)	Allowance for clerk hire as surveyor general of public lands in Alabama.	17	1	Senate bill	126	Public Lands	Jan. 31, 1832	With't amend.	3	Laid on table.		
Coffee, John, (Alabama)	Allowance for clerk hire as surveyor general of public lands in Alabama.	17	2	Papers, &c.	92	Public Lands	Feb. 15, 1823	By bill	295	Passed	Passed	App'd March 3, 1823
Coffee, William	Revolutionary pension	24	1	Resolution	666	Rev. Pensions				Discharged; laid on table.		

List of private claims presented to the House of Representatives of the United States from the 1st to the 31st Congress, inclusive—Continued.

Names of claimants.	Nature or object of the claim.	Congress.	Session.	How brought before the House of Reps.	Page of journal.	To what committee of the House referred.	No. or date of the report.	Nature of the report.	No. of the bill.	How disposed of by the House of Reps.	How disposed of by the Senate.	Date of the act of Congress, and remarks.
Coffee, William J	Compensation for a design for ornament to the Capitol of U. States.	19	1	Petition	154	Public Buildings	Feb. 23, 1826	Adverse	.....	Laid on table.		
Coffey, Eli	Revolutionary pension	27	2	Petition	107	Rev. Pensions	784	Adverse	.....	Laid on table.		
Coffin, Catharine	(See Lemuel Coffin, widow of.)											
Coffin, Charles	Pension for services in war of 1812.	24	2	Petition	41	Invalid Pensions	92	Favor'ble & bill	837	Referred to Committee Whole House.		
Coffin, Charles	Pension for services in war of 1812.	25	2	Petition	38	Invalid Pensions	188	Report and bill.	214	Passed	Passed	App'd June 28, 1838
Coffin, David	(See Samuel Rodman and others.)	14	1		82							
Coffin, David	Indemnity for French spoliations prior to 1800.	26	1	Memorial	182	Foreign Affairs	343	Favorable; bill.	319	Referred to Committee Whole House.		
Coffin, David, assignee of.	Indemnity for French spoliations prior to 1800.	29	2	Memorial	57	Foreign Affairs.						
Coffin, Edmund, agent of.	Indemnity for French spoliations prior to 1800.	26	1	Memorial	182	Foreign Affairs	343	Favorable; bill.	319	Referred to Committee Whole House.		
Coffin, James J	Pension for revolutionary services.	24	1	Petition	136	Rev. Pensions	322	Report and bill.	336	Passed	Postp'd to next session.	
Coffin, James J	Pension for revolutionary services.	24	2	Petition	97	Rev. Pensions	59	Report and bill.	809	Referred to Committee Whole House.		
Coffin, James J	Pension for revolutionary services.	25	2	Petition	37	Rev. Pensions	449	Report and bill.	452	Passed	Adverse report.	
Coffin, James J	Pension for revolutionary services.	26	1	Petition	171	Rev. Pensions	146	Report and bill.	156	Passed	Indef. postp'd.	
Coffin, John	(See Samuel Coffin, heirs of)	26	1		182							
Coffin, Jonathan	(See Tristram Coffin, representatives of.)											
Coffin, Lemuel	Allowance for depreciation of pay for revolutionary services.	9	1	Petition	222	Claims	.....	.....	.....	Discharged; referred to Com. Whole House on bill No. 108.		
Coffin, Lemuel	Allowance for depreciation of pay for revolutionary services.	11	2	Petition	278	Claims.						
Coffin, Lemuel	Allowance for depreciation of pay for revolutionary services.	12	1	Petition	142	Claims	Mar. 10, 1812	Rep. and res.; adverse.	.....	Resolution adopted.		
Coffin, Lemuel	Allowance for depreciation of pay for revolutionary services.	15	1	Petition	132	Pens. & Rev. Cl'ms.	.....	.....	.....	Discharged; leave to withdraw.		
Coffin, Lemuel	Pension	20	2	Petition	99	Military Pensions	.....	.....	.....	Discharged; laid on table.		
Coffin, Lemuel, widow of.	Continuation of pension	25	2	Petition	273	Rev. Pensions	.....	.....	.....	Discharged; laid on table.		
Coffin, Lemuel, widow of.	Continuation of pension	26	1	Petition	282	Rev. Pensions.						
Coffin, Samuel, heirs of.	Indemnity for French spoliations prior to 1800.	26	1	Memorial	182	Foreign Affairs	343	Favorable; bill.	319	Referred to Committee Whole House.		
Coffin, Stephen, administrator of.	Indemnity for French spoliations prior to 1800.	26	1	Memorial	182	Foreign Affairs	343	Favorable; bill.	319	Referred to Committee Whole House.		
Coffin, Tristram	Compensation for vessel impressed by United States, and burnt by the enemy.	1	1	Petition	54	.....	.....	.....	.....	Referred to Secretary Treasury.		
Coffin, Tristram	Compensation for vessel impressed by United States, and burnt by the enemy.	3	1	Memorial	42	.....	.....	.....	.....	Referred to Secretary Treasury.		
Coffin, Tristram	Compensation for vessel impressed by United States, and burnt by the enemy.	3	2	Rep. of Secretary Treasury.	284	Claims	Mar. 2, 1795	To be disch'd.	.....	Laid on table.		
Coffin, Tristram	Compensation for vessel impressed by United States, and burnt by the enemy.	4	1	Petition and rep't Sec. Treasury.	373	Claims	Dec. 28, 1795	Adverse	.....	Leave to withdraw.		

List of private claims presented to the House of Representatives of the United States from the 1st to the 31st Congress, inclusive—Continued.

Names of claimants.	Nature or object of the claim.	Congress.	Session.	How brought before the House of Reps.	Page of journal.	To what committee of the House referred.	No. or date of the report.	Nature of the report.	No. of the bill.	How disposed of by the House of Reps.	How disposed of by the Senate.	Date of the act of Congress, and remarks.
Coffin, Tristram, representatives of.	Compensation for vessel impressed by United States and burnt by the enemy.	21	1	Petition	199	Rev. Claims	Feb. 15, 1830	Adverse		Laid on table.		
Coffin, Tristram, representatives of.	Compensation for vessel impressed by United States and burnt by the enemy.	21	2	Petition	88	Rev. Claims				Discharged; laid on table.		
Coffin, Tristram, representatives of.	Compensation for vessel impressed by United States and burnt by the enemy.	22	1	Petition	55	Rev. Claims	198	Adverse		Referred to Committee Whole House.		
Coffin, Tristram, representatives of.	Compensation for vessel impressed by United States and burnt by the enemy.	22	2	Petition	53	Rev. Claims.						
Coffin, Tristram, representatives of.	Compensation for vessel impressed by United States and burnt by the enemy.	23	2	Petition	100	Rev. Claims	92	Report and bill.	714	Referred to Committee Whole House.		
Coffin, Tristram, representatives of.	Compensation for vessel impressed by United States and burnt by the enemy.	24	1	Petition	102	Rev. Claims	146	Report and bill.	153	Referred to Committee Whole House.		
Coffin, Tristram, representatives of.	Compensation for vessel impressed by United States and burnt by the enemy.	24	2	Bill of last sess.	62	Whole House	Dec. 25, 1836	To strike out enact'g clause.	153	Report adopted.		
Coffin, Tristram, representatives of.	Compensation for vessel impressed by United States and burnt by the enemy.	25	2	Petition	112	Rev. Claims	1012	Adverse		Laid on table.		
Coffin, Tristram, representatives of.	Compensation for vessel impressed by United States and burnt by the enemy.	26	1	Petition	280	Rev. Claims.						
Coffin, Tristram, representatives of.	Compensation for vessel impressed by United States and burnt by the enemy.	26	2	Petition	134	Rev. Claims.						
Coffin, Tristram, representatives of.	Compensation for vessel impressed by United States and burnt by the enemy.	27	2	Petition	96	Rev. Claims	530	Adverse		Laid on table.		
Coffin, William, and others.	Drawback of duties on exported whale oil.	15	1	Petition	97	Ways and Means				Discharged; laid on table.		
Coffin, William, and others.	Drawback of duties on exported whale oil.	15	2	Resolution	53	Ways and Means	53	Report and bill.	243	Referred to Committee Whole House.		
Coffin, William, and others.	Drawback of duties on exported whale oil.	16	1	Resolution	31	Ways and Means	21	Report and bill.	27	Passed	Passed	App'd May 4, 1820
Coffin, William	Indemnity for French spoliations prior to 1800.	26	1	Memorial	182	Foreign Affairs	343	Favorable; bill.	319	Referred to Committee Whole House.		
Cofren, Robert	Pension for services in revolutionary war.	23	2	Petition	271	Rev. Pensions				Discharged; laid on table.		
Cofren, Robert	Pension for services in revolutionary war.	24	1	Petition	1049	Rev. Pensions.						
Cogbill, John	Compensation as storekeeper to an assistant deputy Quartermaster General.	3	1	Petition	57	Select	Jan. 3, 1794	Adverse		Laid on table.		
Co-ge-e-coy-hee (a Cherokee.)	Compensation for negroes forcibly taken from him by one Joseph Brown.	24	1	Petition	537	Indian Affairs.						
Cogswell, Amos	(See Samuel Wallingsford, late widow of.)											

List of p ivate claims presented to the House of Representatives of the United States from the 1st to the 31st Congress, inclusive—Continued.

Names of claimants.	Nature or object of the claim.	Congress.	Session.	How brought before the House of Reps.	Page of journal.	To what committee of the House referred.	No. or date of the report.	Nature of the report.	No. of the bill.	How disposed of by the House of Reps.	How disposed of by the Senate.	Date of the act of Congress, and remarks.
Cogswell, Amos	Allowance for depreciation pay as an officer of revolutionary army.	15	1	Petition	309	Pens. & Rev. Cl'ms.				Discharged.		
Cogswell, Amos	Restoration of pension	17	1	Petition	155	Rev. Pensions	Jan. 15, 1822	By bill	37	Passed	Rejected.	See act March 1, 1823
Cogswell, Amos	Pension, or an allowance for depreciation of pay.	17	2	Petition	186	Pens. & Rev. Cl'ms.				Discharged; laid on table.		
Cogswell, Amos	Revolutionary pension	18	1	Petition	173	Rev. Pensions	Feb. 23, 1824	Adverse		Laid on table.		
Cogswell, Amos	A just consideration and allowance for revolutionary services.	19	1	Petition	109	Select Military Pensions	Jan. 3, 1826 May 8, 1826	Report and bill. With amend.	33 33	Recommitted. Referred to Committee Whole House.		See act May 15, 1828
Cogswell, E. B	Compensation for services, &c., as blacksmith, to Texas Indians	30	1	Petition	228	Indian Affairs	618	Report and bill.	497	Referred to Committee Whole House.		
Cogswell, E. B	Compensation for services, &c., as blacksmith, to Texas Indians.	30	2	Bill of last sess.	318	Whole House	Jan. 26, 1849	With't amend.	497	Passed	Passed	App'd March 2, 1849
Cogswell, Joseph	Pension as as-istant surgeon in revolutionary army.	29	2	Petition	67	Rev. Pensions.						
Cogswell, Joseph	Pension as assistant surgeon in revolutionary army.	30	1	Petition	394	Rev. Pensions	693	Adverse		Laid on table.		
Cogswell, Lydia	(See Samuel Wallingsford, late widow of.)											
Cogswell, Nathaniel	Indemnity for vessel and money captured by Spanish ship.	12	1	Petition	187					Referred to Secretary State.		
Cogswell, Nathaniel, administrator of.	Indemnity for vessel and money captured by Spanish ship.	27	2	Petition	46	Claims.						
Cogswell, Nathaniel, administrator of.	Indemnity for vessel and money captured by Spanish ship.	27	3	Petition	43	Claims.						
Cogswell, Nathaniel, administrator of.	Indemnity for vessel and money captured by Spanish ship.	28	2	Petition	55	Claims.						
Cogswell, Pearson	Compensation for carrying a mail.	20	1	Petition	194	P. Of. & P. Roads.	Feb. 18, 1828	Adverse		Laid on table.		
Cogswell, Pearson	Settlement of his accounts as United States marshal, district of New Hampshire.	26	1	Petition	201	Claims.						
Cogswell, Pearson	Settlement of his accounts as United States marshal, district of New Hampshire.	26	2	Petition	80	Claims	163	Report and bill.	678	Referred to Committee Whole House.		
Cogswell, Pearson	Settlement of his accounts as United States marshal, district of New Hampshire.	27	3	Petition	95	Claims.						
Cogswell, Pearson	Balance awarded him by circuit court of United States of New Hampshire.	28	1	Petition	257	Judiciary	504	Adverse		Laid on table.		
Cogswell, Pearson	Balance awarded him by circuit court of United States of New Hampshire.	29	2	Senate bill	380	Judiciary			142			
Cogswell, Pearson	Balance awarded him by circuit court of United States of New Hampshire.	30	2	Petition	120	Claims	132	Report and bill.	812	Referred to Committee Whole House.		
Cogswell, William (N. H.)	Invalid pension	3	2	Report of Secretary of War.	278	Claims	March 2, 1795	Res. to refer to Sec. of War, with instructions.		Resolution adopted.		
Cogswell, William, heirs of.	Commutation of pay as a revolutionary army surgeon, as per resolution of March, 1783.	23	2	Resolution	89	Rev. Claims	Jan. 2, 1835	Adverse		Laid on table.		

List of private claims presented to the House of Representatives of the United States from the 1st to the 31st Congress, inclusive—Continued.

Names of claimants.	Nature or object of the claim.	Congress.	Session.	How brought before the House of Reps.	Page of journal.	To what committee of the House referred.	No. or date of the report.	Nature of the report.	No. of the bill.	How disposed of by the House of Reps.	How disposed of by the Senate.	Date of the act of Congress, and remarks.
Cogswell, William, heirs of.	Commutation of pay as a revolutionary army surgeon, as per resolution of March, 1783.	24	2	Senate bill	251	Rev. Claims	259	Adverse	59	Referred to Committee Whole House.		
Cogswell, William, heirs of.	Commutation of pay as a revolutionary army surgeon, as per resolution of March, 1783.	25	2	Senate bill	763	Rev. Claims	May 11, 1838	With amend; disagreed to by House	186	Passed	Passed	App'd June 12, 1838
Cogswell, William	Indemnity for property confiscated in Canada for his engaging in United States service, war of 1812.	15	2	Petition	182	Military Affairs				Discharged; laid on table.		
Cogswell, William	Indemnity for property confiscated in Canada for his engaging in United States service, war of 1812.	16	1	Petition		Military Affairs	Feb. 18, 1820	Rep. and res. adverse.		Resolution adopted.		
Cohen, Jacob, heirs of	Five years' full pay as a captain in revolutionary army.	26	1	Petition	164	Rev. Claims	233	Adverse		Laid on table.		
Cohen, Jacob, heirs of	Five years' full pay as a captain in revolutionary army.	26	2	Petition	77	Rev. Claims.						
Cohen, Jacob, heirs of	Five years' full pay as a captain in revolutionary army.	27	2	Petition	62	Rev. Claims	371	Adverse		Laid on table.		
Cohen, Jacob, heirs of	Five years' full pay as a captain in revolutionary army.	28	2	Petition	118	Rev. Claims.						
Cohen, Jacob, heirs of	Five years' full pay as a captain in revolutionary army.	29	1	Petition	435	Rev. Claims				Discharged; laid on table.		
Cohen, Jacob, heirs of	Five years' full pay as a captain in revolutionary army.	30	1	Petition	422	Rev. Claims.						
Cohen, William, heirs of	Compensation for revolutionary services.	28	2	Petition	120	Rev. Claims.						
Cohoon, John C.	(See Francis B. Gamble, administrator of widow of.)											
Coil, James	Pension	21	2	Resolution	204	Military Pensions.						
Coil, James	Pension	22	1	Petition	412	Rev. Pensions.						
Coil, Patrick, widow of	Pension for loss of husband from exposure in war of 1812.	31	1	Petition	731	Invalid Pensions.						
Coit, Benjamin	Revolutionary pension	24	1	Resolution	286	Rev. Pensions	516	Report and bill.	511	Passed	Passed	App'd June 28, 1836
Coit, Benjamin	Indemnity for French spoliations prior to 1800.	26	1	Memorial	182	Foreign Affairs	343	Favorable; bill	319	Referred to Committee Whole House.		
Coit, Daniel	Renewal of a patent for medicine	15	1	Petition	179	Judiciary	Jan. 28, 1818	Adverse		Laid on table.		
Coit, Isaac	Revolutionary pension	21	2	Resolution	165	Military Pensions.						
Coit, Levi	Indemnity for French spoliations prior to 1800.	26	1	Memorial	182	Foreign Affairs	343	Favorable; bill	319	Referred to Committee Whole House.		
Coit, Thomas	Exonerated from payment of duties collected at Norwich, Connecticut, and lost by fire.	2	2	Petition	706					Referred to Secretary Treasury.		
Coit, Thomas	Exonerated from payment of duties collected at Norwich, Connecticut, and lost by fire.	3	2	Petition and rep. Sec. of Treas.	312					Leave to withdraw.		
Coit, Thomas	Compensation as surgeon's mate in garrison, from 1808 to 1814.	21	1	Petition	471	Military Affairs				Discharged; laid on table.		
Coit, Thomas	Compensation as surgeon's mate in garrison, from 1808 to 1814.	21	2	Petition	190	Military Affairs	Jan. 26, 1831	Adverse		Laid on table.		
Coit, Thomas	Compensation as surgeon's mate in garrison, from 1808 to 1814.	25	3	Resolution	291	Claims.						

Names of claimants.	Nature or object of the claim	Congress.	Session.	How brought before the House of Reps.	Page of journal.	To what committee of the House referred.	No. or date of the report.	Nature of the report.	No. of the bill.	How disposed of by the House of Reps.	How disposed of by the Senate.	Date of the act of Congress, and remarks.
Coit, Thomas	Compensation as surgeon's mate in garrison, from 1808 to 1814.	26	1	Petition	168	Claims	55	Adverse		Laid on table.		
Coit, Woolsey & Howland	Indemnity for French spoliations prior to 1800.	26	1	Memorial	182	Foreign Affairs	343	Favorable; bill	319	Referred to Committee Whole House.		
Coke, Richard, jr., & others	Release from liability as sureties for P. A. Southall.	27	2	Petition	807	Judiciary	928	Report and bill.	546	Engrossed.		
Coke, Richard, jr., & others	Release from liability as sureties for P. A. Southall.	27	3	Bill of last sess.	89				546	Passed	Passed	App'd March 3, 1843
Coker, Charles, widow of.	Pension for services in Mexican war.	31	1	Petition	496	Invalid Pensions.						
Coker, Thomas W.	Payment for horse lost in United States service.	25	2	Petition	922	Claims				Discharged.		
Coker, Thomas W.	Payment for horse lost in United States service.	26	1	Petition	306	Claims	693	Adverse		Laid on table.		
Colbert, George, a Chickasaw chief.	Compensation for supplies furnished an expedition against Creek Indians in 1794.	4	2	Petition	633	Claims	Feb. 3, 1797	Adverse		Referred to Committee Whole House.		
Colbert, George, a Chickasaw chief.	Indemnity under treaty of July, 1805.	9	2	Resolution	517	Whole House	Jan. 22, 1807	Favorable; bill ordered.	187	Passed	Passed	App'd March 3, 1807
Colbert, Pitman and others, Chickasaw Indians.	Compensation for military services rendered in war with the Creek Indians.	22	2	Petition	269	Indian Affairs.						
Colborn, John	Pension as provided for others under act of 18th March, 1818.	15	2	Petition	160	Rev. Pensions.						
Colborn, Jonathan	Pension as provided for others under act of 18th March, 1818.	15	2	Petition	160	Rev. Pensions.						
Colborn, Nathan	Pension as provided for others under act of 18th March, 1818.	15	2	Petition	160	Rev. Pensions.						
Colborn, Reuben, (Maine).	Compensation for furnishing batteau and other supplies in revolutionary war.	3	2	Petition	311	Claims	March 2, 1795	To discharge & postpone.		Laid on table.		
Colborn, Reuben, (Maine).	Compensation for furnishing batteau and other supplies in revolutionary war.	4	1	Petition	373	Claims	Jan. 15, 1796	Adverse		Referred to Committee Whole House.		
Colborn, Reuben, (Maine).	Compensation for furnishing batteau and other supplies in revolutionary war.	4	2	Rep. of last sess.	623	Claims	Feb. 20, 1797	Adverse		Referred to Committee Whole House.		
Colborn, Reuben, (Maine).	Compensation for furnishing batteau and other supplies in revolutionary war.	6	1	Petition	551	Claims	Jan. 14, 1800	Adverse		Laid on table.		
Colborn, Reuben, (Maine).	Compensation for furnishing batteau and other supplies in revolutionary war.	9	1	Petition	191	Claims				Discharged; referred to Com. Whole House on bill No. 108.		
Colborn, Reuben, (Maine).	Compensation for furnishing batteau and other supplies in revolutionary war.	9	2	Petition	576	Claims				Discharged; referred to Com. Whole House.		
Colborn, Reuben, (Maine).	Compensation for furnishing batteau and other supplies in revolutionary war.	10	1	Petition	17	Select.						
Colborn, Reuben, (Maine).	Compensation for furnishing batteau and other supplies in revolutionary war.	11	2	Petition	150	Select.						

List of private claims presented to the House of Representatives of the United States from the 1st to the 31st Congress, inclusive—Continued.

Names of claimants.	Nature or object of the claim.	Congress.	Session.	How brought before the House of Reps.	Page of journal.	To what committee of the House referred.	No. or date of the report.	Nature of the report.	No. of the bill.	How disposed of by the House of Reps.	How disposed of by the Senate.	Date of the act of Congress, and remarks.
Colborn, Reuben, (Maine).	Compensation for furnishing batteau and other supplies in revolutionary war.	15	2	Resolution	130	Pens. & Rev. Cl'ms.	Jan. 15, 1819	Rep. and res.; adverse.	......	Resolution adopted.		
Colborn, Reuben, heirs of.	Compensation for furnishing batteau and other supplies in revolutionary war.	21	2	Res. and docs ..	64	Rev. Claims......	....	....	......	Discharged; laid on table.		
Colborn, Reuben, heirs of.	Compensation for furnishing batteau and other supplies in revolutionary war.	22	1	Resolution	87	Rev. Claims.						
Colborn, Reuben, heirs of.	Compensation for furnishing batteau and other supplies in revolutionary war.	22	2	Resolution	33	Rev. Claims.						
Colburn, Benaiah & others.	Compensation for materials deposited for breakwater at Rockport, Massachusetts.	27	2	Petition	613	Claims	700	Adverse	......	Laid on table.		
Colburn, Benaiah & others.	Compensation for materials deposited for breakwater at Rockport, Massachusetts.	28	1	Petition	100	Claims.						
Colburn, Charles	Compensation for services in navy.	30	1	Petition	1163	Naval Affairs.						
Colburn, Charles	Compensation for services in navy.	30	2	Petition	430	Claims.						
Colburn, Charles	Compensation for services in navy.	31	1	Petition	285, 437	Naval Affairs.						
Colburn, John	Invalid pension	3	2	Rep. of Secretary War.	350	Claims	March 3, 1795	To discharge & postpone.	.....	Laid on table.		
Colburn, John	Invalid pension	4	1	Rep. of Secretary War.	445	Claims.						
Colburn, Nathaniel, widow of.	Pension for services in war of 1812	28	1	Petition	101	Military Affairs....	....	....	......	Discharged; laid on table.		
Colburn, Nathaniel, widow of.	Pension for services in war of 1812.	28	2	Petition	381	Military Affairs ...	March 3, 1845	Adverse	......	Laid on table.		
Colburn, Reuben	Refunding of fine for illegally clearing a vessel from Pittston, Maine.	23	2	Petition	82	Commerce	Jan. 23, 1835	By bill	675	Referred to Committee Whole House.		
Colburn, Reuben	Refunding of fine for illegally clearing a vessel from Pittston, Maine.	24	1	Petition	54	Commerce	Dec. 21, 1835	By bill	44	Passed	Passed	App'd May 14, 1836
Colbourn, lieutenant-colonel, widow of.	Pension: husband killed in revolutionary war.	15	1	Petition	143	Rev. Claims......	....	....	......	Discharged; laid on table.		
Colby, Charles	Invalid pension	22	1	Petition	631	Invalid Pensions.						
Colbey, Christopher John.	Bounty land for revolutionary services.	24	2	Petition	266	Rev. Claims.						
Colbey, Christopher John.	Bounty land for revolutionary services.	25	2	Petition	575	Rev. Claims......	786	Adverse	......	Laid on table.		
Colby, Eben	Increase of pension	27	2	Petition	47	Rev. Pensions	784	Adverse	......	Laid on table.		
Colby, Joseph	Revolutionary pension..........	16	1	Resolution	254	Rev. Pensions	....	....	......	Discharged; laid on table.		
Colby, Lydia...........	Restoration of pension..........	27	2	Petition	320	Rev. Pensions.						
Colby, Lydia	Restoration of pension..........	28	1	Petition	849	Rev. Pensions.						
Colby, Sylvanus, widow of	Continuation of pension	25	2	Petition	349	Rev. Pensions	....	....	......	Discharged; laid on table.		
Colby, Sylvanus, widow of	Continuation of pension	26	1	Petition	173	Rev. Pensions	....	....	......	Disch'd; laid on table.		
Colby, Theophilus.......	Invalid pension	11	2	Petition	145	Claims	Jan. 24, 1810	Rep. and res. adverse.	......	Resolution adopted.		
Coldwell, Robert	Invalid pension................	3	2	Rep. of Secretary War.	350	Claims	Mar. 3, 1795	To discharge and postp'e.	......	Laid on table.		

List of private claims presented to the House of Representatives of the United States from the 1st to the 31st Congress, inclusive—Continued.

Names of claimants.	Nature or object of the claim.	Congress.	Session.	How brought before the House of Reps.	Page of journal.	To what committee of the House referred.	No. or date of the report.	Nature of the report.	No. of the bill.	How disposed of by the House of Reps.	How disposed of by the Senate.	Date of the act of Congress, and remarks.
Coldwell, Robert	Invalid pension	4	1	Rep. of Secretary War.	445	Claims	Feb. 18, 1796	Ref. to Sec. with instruc.	R. 16	Passed	Passed	App'd April 18, 1796
Cole, Abigail	(See Daniel Wheelwright, heir of.)											
Cole, Ambrose	(See Canadian refugees.)											
Cole, Andrew	Revolutionary pension	24	2	Petition	217	Rev. Pensions	....	....	.....	Discharged; laid on table.		
Cole, Asa	Revolutionary pension	22	1	Petition	44	Rev. Pensions.						
Cole, A. H	Equitable settlement of debts due him as army suttler in Florida by deceased and discharged soldiers.	30	2	Senate bill	518	Claims	Mar. 3, 1849	With't amend.	224	Referred to Committee Whole House.		
Cole, Barry, and Barry	(See Barry Cole and Barry)	26	1	....	182							
Cole, Benjamin, late widow of.	Pension for services in revolutionary war.	31	2	Petition	155	Rev. Pensions	Mar. 3, 1851	Adverse	.....	Laid on table.		
Cole, Captain, (Onondaga Indian.)	Pension for wound received in U. S. service, war of 1812.	22	1	Resolution	571	Invalid Pensions	474	Report and bill.	576	Passed	Laid on table.	
Cole, Captain, (Onondaga Indian.)	Pension for wound received in U. S. service, war of 1812.	22	2	Resolution	96	Invalid Pensions	Feb. 15, 1833	Report and bill.	738	Referred to Committee Whole House.		
Cole, Captain, (Onondaga Indian.)	Pension for wound received in U. S. service, war of 1812.	23	2	Petition	41	Invalid Pensions	52	Report and bill	647	Passed	Passed	App'd March 3, 1835
Cole, David	(See Captain Cole.)											
Cole, Ebenezer	(See William Jessup, and others.)											
Cole, Edith	Pension for revolutionary services of husband.	28	1	Petition	829	Whole House, on bill No. 7.						
Cole, Edward	(See Canadian refugees.)											
Cole, Edward	Increase of pension	30	1	Petition	482	Invalid Pensions	705	Report and bill	551	Referred to Committee Whole House.		
Cole, Edward	Increase of pension	30	2	Bill of last sess.	319	Whole House	Jan. 26, 1849	With't amend.	551	Passed.		
Cole, Eldridge	Compensation for horse lost in U. S. service.	25	2	Petition	541	Claims	....	....	.....	Discharged.		
Cole, Hamblin	Pension	20	1	Resolution	43	Military Pensions	April 29, 1828	By bill	283	Passed.		
Cole, Hamblin	Pension	20	2	House bill	55	Whole House	Jan. 15, 1829	By bill	311	Passed.	Laid on table.	
Cole, Hamblin	Pension	21	1	Res. and petition	48, 65	Military Pensions	Jan. 5, 1830	By bill	72	Passed	Passed	App'd May 20, 1830
Cole, Hannah, by attorney	Indemnity for Indian depredations.	19	2	Petition	134	Indian Affairs	51	Favorable	.....	Referred to Committee Whole House.		
Cole, Hannah	(See Samuel Cole, widow of.)											
Cole, Jacob, son and heir of	Land and money due deceased for services as lieutenant in revolutionary army.	29	1	Petition	939	Rev. Claims.						
Cole, Jacob, son and heir of	Land and money due deceased for services as lieutenant in revolutionary army.	29	2	Petition	85	Rev. Pensions.						
Cole, Jacob, son and heir of	Land and money due deceased for services as lieutenant in revolutionary army.	30	1	Petition	405	Rev. Claims.						
Cole, Jacob, son and heir of	Land and money due deceased for services as lieutenaat in revolutionary army.	30	2	Petition	117	Rev. Claims.						
Cole, Jacob, son and heir of	Land and money due deceased for services as lieutenant in revolutionary army.	31	1	Petition	348	Rev. Claims.						

List of private claims presented to the House of Representatives of the United States from the 1st to the 31st Congress, inclusive—**Continued.**

Names of claimants.	Nature or object of the claim.	Congress.	Session.	How brought before the House of Reps.	Page of journal.	To what committee of the House referred.	No. or date of the report.	Nature of the report.	No. of the bill.	How disposed of by the House of Reps.	How disposed of by the Senate.	Date of the act of Congress, and remarks.
Cole, James	Grant of land for services as revolutionary Canadian refugee.	6	2	House bill	766	Whole House	Jan. 26, 1801	With amend'ts	280	Passed	Passed	App'd Feb. 18, 1801
Cole, James, (N. Y.,)	Invalid pension	3	1	Rep. of Secretary of War.	131	Select	May 26, 1794	Favorable; bill ordered.	62	Passed	Passed	App'd June 7, 1794
Cole, James, (Mass.,)	Invalid pension	9	1	Petition	321	Claims	Mar. 28, 1806	Indef. postp'd.	......	Report adopted	....	Leave to withdraw.
Cole, John, administrators of, (Pa.)	Revolutionary pension	2	2	Petition	668	....	....	....	......	Referred to Secretary of War.		
Cole, John, administrators of, (Pa.)	Revolutionary pension	3	1	Rep. of Secretary War.	93	Select.						
Cole, John, son of, (Va.)	Commutation of half-pay as an officer in revolutionary army.	23	2	Petition	38	Rev. Claims	Dec. 23, 1835	Adverse	......	Laid on table.		
Cole, John, son of, (Va.)	Commutation of half-pay as an officer in revolutionary army.	24	1	Petition	104	Rev. Claims	Jan. 28, 1836	Adverse	......	Laid on table.		
Cole, John, (Mo)	Pre emption right to land improved by him.	25	3	Petition	451	Public Lands.						
Cole, John, (Mo.)	Pre-emption right to land improved by him.	26	1	Petition	178	Public Lands	85	Adverse	......	Laid on table.		
Cole, John, (N. Y.)	Increase of pension	26	1	Petition	288	Invalid Pensions.						
Cole, John, (N. Y.)	Increase of pension	27	2	Petition	154	Invalid Pensions	413	Adverse	......	Laid on table.		
Cole, Martin, (Miss.)	Change of entry of a tract of land	13	2	Petition	233	Public Lands	....	....	......	Discharged.		
Cole, Martin, (Miss.)	Change of entry of a tract of land	13	3	Petition	627	Public Lands	....	....	......	Discharged.		
Cole, Martin, (Miss.)	Change of entry of a tract of land	14	1	Petition	66	Public Lands	Jan. 4, 1816	By bill	......	Passed	Passed	App'd Feb. 6, 1816
Cole, Mary	Public support, having lost two husbands and a son in United States service.	14	2	Petition	29	Pens. & Rev. Cl'ms.	....	....	......	Discharged; laid on table.		
Cole, Mehitabel	(See John Fairfield, mother of.)											
Cole, Nathaniel, jr.	Pension for injuries received in war of 1812.	29	1	Petition	225	Invalid Pensions.						
Cole, Robert, (a Choctaw Indian.)	Annuity under treaty of 1825	19	1	House bill	378	Whole House	May 18, 1826	With't amend.	179	Passed	Passed	App'd May 20, 1826
Cole, Robert, (a Choctaw Indian.)	Annuity under treaty of 1825	22	1	House bill	418	Whole House	May 21, 1832	With't amend.	417	Passed	Passed	App'd June 4, 1832
Cole, Samuel, (Pa.)	Pension for services in war of 1812	19	1	Res. and petition.	92, 108, 221	Military Pensions	164	Adverse	......	Laid on table.		
Cole, Samuel, (Pa.)	Pension for services in war of 1812	24	1	Petition	98	Invalid Pensions	258	Report and bill.	266	Passed	Passed	App'd June 28, 1836
Cole, Samuel, widow of (Ohio.)	Bounty land for services in Mexican war.	30	2	Petition	92	Public Lands	123	Adverse	......	Laid on table.		
Cole, Siney, alias Perry	(See Jacob Thompson)	22	1	....	388							
Cole, Thomas	Invalid pension	1	2	Pet. & Report of Sec. of War.	173	....	....	....		Laid on table.		
Cole, Thomas, heirs of	Commutation of half-pay as a captain in revolutionary army.	24	1	Petition	104	Rev. Claims.						
Cole, Thomas, heirs of	Commutation of half-pay as a captain in revolutionary army.	24	2	Petition	216	Rev. Claims.						
Cole, Thomas, heirs of	Bounty land for revolutionary services.	24	1	Petition	664	Priv. Land Claims	....	....	......	Discharged; laid on table.		
Cole, William, (N. Y.)	Revolutionary pension	18	1	Petition	74	Rev. Pensions	May 18, 1824	Adverse	......	Laid on table	....	Leave to withdraw.
Cole, William, (N. Y.)	Revolutionary pension	18	2	Petition	95	Rev. Pensions	Jan. 21, 1825	Adverse	......	Laid on table	....	Leave to withdraw.
Cole, William, (N. Y.)	Revolutionary pension	19	1	Petition	225	Rev. Claims	May 3, 1826	Report & res. adverse.	......	Resolution adopted.		

List of private claims presented to the House of Representatives of the United States from the 1st to the 31st Congress, inclusive—Continued.

Names of claimants.	Nature or object of the claim.	Congress.	Session.	How brought before the House of Reps.	Page of journal.	To what committee of the House referred.	No. or date of the report.	Nature of the report.	No. of the bill.	How disposed of by the House of Reps.	How disposed of by the Senate.	Date of the act of Congress, and remarks.
Cole, William, (N. Y.)	Revolutionary pension	20	1	Petition	243	Military Pensions	April 29, 1828	By bill	283	Passed	Ref., and com. discharged.	
Cole, William, (N. Y.)	Revolutionary pension	20	2	House bill	55	Whole House	Jan. 15, 1829	Favorable	311	Passed	Laid on table.	
Cole, William, (N. Y.)	Revolutionary pension	21	1	Petition	236	Whole House	Feb. 12, 1830	Amend't to bill	72	Passed	Passed	App'd May 20, 1830
Cole, William, (N. Y.)	Arrears of pension	22	2	Petition	397	Rev. Pensions.						
Cole, William, 2d, (N. Y.)	Pension	22	1	Petition	329	Rev. Pensions	479	Report and bill.	580	Referred to Committee Whole House.		
Cole, William, executors of	Indemnity for French spoliations prior to 1800.	26	1	Memorial	182	Foreign Affairs	343	Favorable; bill	319	Referred to Committee Whole House.		
Coleman, Alexander	(See Jacques Bon.)											
Coleman, Alexander	Location of a Missouri confirmed mine concession claim on other land.	29	1	Petition	756	Priv. Land Claims.						
Coleman, Daniel	Pension	20	1	Petition	278	Military Pensions	May 6, 1828	Adverse		Laid on table.		
Coleman, Daniel	Pension	21	1	Petition	197	Military Pensions				Discharged; laid on table.		
Coleman, Edward	Revolutionary pension	22	1	Petition	219	Rev. Pensions.						
Coleman, Elijah	Compensation for services as surgeon, and for losses in war of 1812.	15	2	Petition	306	Claims				Discharged; laid on table.		
Coleman, Elijah	Compensation for services as surgeon, and for loss of horse in war of 1812.	19	1	Petition	446	Claims	April 18, 1826	Adverse		Resolution adopted.		
Coleman, Francis, assignee of.	Confirmation of title to land in territory of Missouri.	15	2	Petition	207	Priv. Land Claims.				Discharged; laid on table.		
Coleman, Francis, assignee of.	Confirmation of title to land in territory of Missouri.	16	1	Petition	71	Priv. Land Claims.				Discharged; laid on table.		
Coleman, Francis, assignee of	Confirmation of title to land in territory of Missouri.	17	1	Petition	53	Public Lands.				Discharged; laid on table.		
Coleman, Francis, assignee of.	Confirmation of title to land in territory of Missouri.	18	1	Petition	53	Public Lands	Jan. 16, 1824	By bill	65	Passed	Passed	App'd May 26, 1824
Coleman, Henry	Indemnity for damages sustained by contract for erecting arsenal at Liberty, Missouri.	25	2	Petition	192	Claims	388	Adverse		Laid on table.		
Coleman, John	Bounty land as a revolutionary soldier.	19	1	Petition	98	Rev. Claims	Feb. 26, 1826	Adverse		Laid on table.		
Coleman, John, representatives of.	Prize money due as one of the captors of the British fleet on Lake Champlain, 1814.	21	1	Petition	472	Naval Affairs				Discharged; laid on table.		
Coleman, John, representatives of.	Prize money due as one of the captors of the British fleet on Lake Champlain, 1814.	21	2	House bill	367				655	Referred to Committee Whole House.		
Coleman, John, representatives of.	Prize money due as one of the captors of the British fleet on Lake Champlain, 1814.	22	1	Petition	259	Naval Affairs	319	Report and bill.	400	Referred to Committee Whole House.		See act July 14, 1832
Coleman, John, representatives of.	Prize money due as one of the captors of the British fleet on Lake Champlain, 1814.	23	1	Petition	190	Naval Affairs	188	Report and bill.	208	Referred to Committee Whole House.		See act June 30, 1834
Coleman, Joseph	(See Missouri, inhabitants of Old Mines.)											
Coleman, Nathaniel	Revolutionary pension	23	1	Petition	379	Rev. Claims				Discharged; laid on table.		
Coleman, Nicholas D.	(See Amos Hill, assignee of the widow of.)											

List of private claims presented to the House of Representatives of the United States from the 1st *to the* 31st *Congress, inclusive*—Continued.

Names of claimants.	Nature or object of the claim.	Congress.	Session.	How brought before the House of Reps.	Page of journal.	To what committee of the House referred.	No. or date of the report.	Nature of the report.	No. of the bill.	How disposed of by the House of Reps.	How disposed of by the Senate.	Date of the act of Congress, and remarks.
Coleman, Patrick	Invalid pension	12	1	Petition	96	Claims	June 12, 1812	Adverse	......	Laid on table	....	Provided for by act of July 5, 1812.
Coleman, Philip	Pension for wound received at Fort Meigs.	24	1	Petition	97	Invalid Pensions	Jan. 13, 1836	Adverse	......	Laid on table.		
Coleman, Sarah	(See John Coleman, representative of.)											
Coleman, Thomas, (N. C.)	Indemnity for loss of $75 of public money by robbery.	8	1	Memorial	581	Claims	Feb. 18, 1804	Adverse	......	Rejected	....	Leave to withdraw.
Coleman, Thomas, (N. Y.)	Revolutionary pension	21	1	Petition	197	Military Pensions	....	....	......	Disch'd; laid on table.		
Coleman, Thomas, (N. Y.)	Revolutionary pension	22	1	Petition	164	Invalid Pensions.						
Coleman, Vinere	(See Missouri, inhabitants of Old Mines.)											
Coleman, William	Confirmation of title to land	8	2	Petition	149	....	....	....	......	Laid on table.		
Coleman, William	Relief from injuries sustained by decision of commissioners to settle the land titles.	9	1	Petition	296	Public Lands.						
Coleman, William	Relief from injuries sustained by decision of commissioners to settle the land titles.	9	2	Petition	479	Public Lands.						
Coleman, William	Authority for court of Mississippi Territory to revise decision of land commissioners on his claim.	9	2	Petition	548	Public Lands.						
Coleman, William	Authority for court of Mississippi Territory to revise decision of land commissioners on his claim.	10	1	Petition	18	Public Lands.						
Coleman, William	Authority for court of Mississippi Territory to revise decision of land commissioners on his claim.	11	3	Petition	457	Public Lands	Jan. 3, 1811	Favorable; bill ordered.	170	Passed	Passed	Vetoed by President.
Coleman, William	Authority for court of Mississippi Territory to revise decision of land commissioners on his claim.	11	3	Senate bill	612	....	....	....	68	Passed	Passed	App'd March 3, 1811
Coleman, William	Permission to locate land warrant east of Pearl river.	12	2	Petition	623	Public Lands.						
Coleman, William	Permission to locate land warrant east of Pearl river.	13	2	Petition	203	Public Lands	Mar. 22, 1814	Rep. and res. adverse.	......	Resolution adopted.		
Coleman, William	Location of any public land in Alabama in satisfaction of act of March 3, 1811.	19	1	Resolution	373	Public Lands	....	....	......	Discharged; laid on table.		
Coleman, William	Grant of land in lieu of that of which he has been deprived by United States.	21	2	Petition	47	Priv. Land Claims.						
Coleman, William	Grant of land in lieu of that of which he has been deprived by United States.	22	1	Petition	32	Priv. Land Claims.						
Coleman, William	Grant of land in lieu of that of which he has been deprived by United States.	22	2	Petition	69	Priv. Land Claims.						
Coleman, William	Grant of land in lieu of that of which he has been deprived by United States.	23	1	Petition	139	Public Lands.						
Coleman, William	Grant of land in lieu of that of which he has been deprived by United States.	23	2	Petition	121	Priv. Land Claims.						

List of private claims presented to the House of Representatives of the United States from the 1st to the 31st Congress, inclusive—Continued.

Names of claimants.	Nature or object of the claim.	Congress.	Session.	How brought before the House of Reps.	Page of journal.	To what committee of the House referred.	No. or date of the report.	Nature of the report.	No. of the bill.	How disposed of by the House of Reps.	How disposed of by the Senate.	Date of the act of Congress, and remarks.
Coler, George	(See David R. Denham and others.)											
Coles, Coleman	(See Jacob Thompson)	22	1	....	388							
Coles, Jesse	Compensation for secret service in revolutionary war.	3	2	Petition	306	Claims	Mar. 2, 1795	To discharge & postpone.	......	Laid on table.		
Coles, Jesse	Compensation for secret service in revolutionary war.	4	1	Petition	373	Claims	Dec. 28, 1795	Adverse	......	Leave to withdraw.		
Coles, Jesse	Compensation for services in revolutionary war.	24	1	Petition	404	Rev. Claims	April 21, 1836	Adverse	......	Laid on table.		
Coles, John	Damages for detention of ship Grand Turk by agent of United States at Gibraltar and Tunis.	7	2	Memorial	310	Claims	Feb. 26, 1803	To discharge & postpone.	......	Report adopted.		
Coles, John	Damages for detention of ship Grand Turk by agent of United States at Gibraltar and Tunis.	8	1	Memorial	468	Claims	Dec. 21, 1803	Favorable; bill ordered.	151	Passed	Passed	App'd Jan. 14, 1804
Coles, Willett	Release from imprisonment at suit of United States.	14	1	Petition	563	Ways and Means	....	....	......	Discharged; laid on table.		
Coles, Willett	Release from imprisonment at suit of United States.	14	2	Petition	242	Ways and Means	....	....	......	Discharged; laid on table.		
Coley, James	Revolutionary pension	22	1	Resolution	261	Rev. Pensions.						
Coley, William	Increase of pension	24	2	Senate bill	579	....	....	....	195	Laid on table.		
Coley, William	Increase of pension	25	2	Senate bill	1155	Rev. Pensions	....	....	342			
Colfax, Jonathan & Robert, widow of.	Revolutionary pension	26	1	Petition	285	Rev. Pensions.						
Colfax, Jonathan & Robert, widow of.	Revolutionary pension	26	2	Petition	34	Rev. Pensions.						
Colfax, Jonathan & Robert, widow of.	Revolutionary pension	27	2	Petition	428	Rev. Pensions	293	Report and bill.	261	Passed	Passed	App'd Aug. 26, 1842
Colfield, William	(See Don Claudia Bougaud.)											
Colgan, Harvey H	Pre-emption right in the purchase of land.	25	2	Petition	86	Public Lands	....	....	......	Discharged.		
Colgan, Harvey H	Pre-emption right in the purchase of land.	25	3	Petition	98	Public Lands.						
Colgan, Harvey H	Pre-emption right in the purchase of land.	26	1	Petition	178	Public Lands	....	....	......	Discharged; laid on table.		
Colegate, Robert	(See George P. Pollen.)											
Colhoun, E. Ross	Compensation as captain's clerk in ship Marion.	29	1	Memorial	208	Naval Affairs.						
Colhoun, Hugh and Gustavus.	Relief in a case of claret wine sold in error by a district court of the United States.	5	2	Petition	148	Com. and Manuf.	April 18, 1798	Favorable	......	Recommitted.		
Colhoun, Hugh and Gustavus.	Half the proceeds of certain merchandise sold irregularly on account of United States.	9	1	Petition	281	Com. and Manuf.						
Colhouse, Dowthy	(See Henry Schrœder and others.)											
Colles, Christopher	Invention for counting revolutions or vibrations of wheels.	1	1	Petition	70	....	....	....	......	Laid on table.		
Colles, Christopher	Commission for life on relinquishing his patent right to a new species of telegraphing.	14	1	Petition	149	Military Affairs	Feb. 20, 1816	Adverse	......	Laid on table.		
Collet, John	Register for an American vessel rebuilt in England.	6	1	Petition	612	Com. and Manf.	Mar. 19, 1800	By bill	220	Passed	Rejected.	
Collet, John, (Ky.)	Pension	20	2	Petition	26	Military Pensions	Jan. 8, 1829	Adverse	......	Laid on table.		

List of private claims presented to the House of Representatives of the United States from the 1st to the 31st Congress, inclusive—Continued.

Names of claimants.	Nature or object of the claim.	Congress.	Session.	How brought before the House of Reps.	Page of journal.	To what committee of the House referred.	No. or date of the report.	Nature of the report.	No. of the bill.	How disposed of by the House of Reps.	How disposed of by the Senate.	Date of the act of Congress, and remarks.
Collier, Ann	(See James Marshall, heirs and representatives of)											
Collier, Charles M	Compensation for boat impressed and lost in service of U. States.	17	1	Petition	26	Claims	....	....	......	Discharged; leave to withdraw.		
Collier, Charles M	Compensation for boat impressed and lost in service of U. States.	17	2	Petition	22	Claims	Dec. 23, 1822	Adverse	301	Recommitted.		
							Feb. 17, 1823	Report and bill with't amend.	301	Referred to Committee Whole House.		
Collier, Charles M	Compensation for boat impressed and lost in service of U. States.	18	1	Petition	49	Claims	Dec. 11, 1823	Report and bill.	3	Passed	Passed	App'd Jan. 7, 1824
Collier, Coleman A	Pension for injury received in war of 1812.	24	1	Petition	52	Invalid Pensions	329	Report and bill.	344	Passed	Passed	App'd July 2, 1836
Collier, George, and others.	Indemnity for non-payment of a draft of Commissioner of Indian Affairs.	26	1	Petition	623	Claims.						
Collier, George, and others	Indemnity for non-payment of a draft of Commissioner of Indian Affairs.	26	2	Petition	182	Claims.						
Collier, George, and others.	Indemnity for non-payment of a draft of Commissioner of Indian Affairs.	27	2	Petition	94	Claims	334	Adverse	......	Laid on table.		
Collier, George, and others.	Indemnity for non-payment of a draft of Commissioner of Indian Affairs.	30	2	Petition	416	Claims.						
Collier, George, and others.	Indemnity for non-payment of a draft of Commissioner of Indian Affairs.	31	1	Petition	349	Claims	74	Report and bill.	89	Passed	Reported with't amendment.	
Collier, James, and others.	Fishing bounty on schooner Little Sarah lost at sea.	18	1	Petition	133	Commerce.						
Collier, James, and others.	Fishing bounty on schooner Little Sarah lost at sea.	18	2	Petition	117	Commerce.						
Colliér, James	Compensation for services as an army spy in 1794.	24	1	Petition	92	Claims	127	Adverse	......	Laid on table.		
Collier, Nathaniel	(See William Baker and others)	22	1	....	288							
Colligan, John	(See Antoine Vasques and others, representatives of.)											
Collingsworth, James	Grant of land in Mississippi Territory upon which he has erected a mill.	9	2	Petition	563	Public Lands.						
Collingsworth, James, and William and Geo. Brown.	Confirmation of title to land in Mississippi Territory.	9	2	Petition	563	Public Lands.						
Collingsworth, James, and William and Geo. Brown.	Confirmation of title to land in Mississippi Territory.	10	1	Petition	18	Public Lands.						
Collingsworth, Edmund G., Geo. M., Jas. B., Margaret Anne, Mary B., and William C.	(See James Brown, heirs of.)											
Collins, Benjamin	Exoneration from a judgm't against him as surety for the postmaster at St. Francisville, Louisiana.	22	2	Petition	265	Claims	110	Adverse	......	Laid on table.		
Collins, Benj., and Charles G. Johnson.	Indemnity for services in taking and holding the fort at Baton Rouge for the United States until 1810.	23	1	Petition	307	Military Affairs.						

List of private claims presented to the House of Representatives of the United States from the 1st to the 31st Congress, inclusive—Continued.

Names of claimants.	Nature or object of the claim.	Congress.	Session.	How brought before the House of Reps.	Page of journal.	To what committee of the House referred.	No. or date of the report.	Nature of the report.	No. of the bill.	How disposed of by the House of Reps.	How disposed of by the Senate.	Date of the act of Congress, and remarks.
Collins, Benj., and Charles G. Johnson.	Indemnity for services in taking and holding the fort at Baton Rouge for the United States until 1810.	23	2	Petition	58	Public Lands	....	....	.....	Discharged; laid on table.		
Collins, Benj., and Charles G. Johnson.	Indemnity for services in taking and holding the fort at Baton Rouge for the United States until 1810.	25	2	Petition	719	Public lands	....	....	.....	Discharged.		
Collins, Charles	Compensation for naval services to the United States.	1	3	Petition	357	....	....	....	.....	Laid on table.		
Collins, Charles	A moiety of the forfeiture of the vessel Nedeshda condemned by him while collector at Bristol, Rhode Island.	20	2	Petition	59	Ways and Means	....	....	.....	Discharged; laid on table.		
Collins, Charles	A moiety of the forfeiture of the vessel Nedeshda condemned by him while collector at Bristol, Rhode Island.	21	1	Petition	50	Ways and Means	136	Report and bill.	182	Passed	Passed	App'd May 29, 1830
Collins, Charles	Indemnity for French spoliations prior to 1800.	26	1	Memorial	182	Foreign Affairs	182	Favorable	319	Referred to Committee Whole House.		
Collins, Charles, administratrix of.	Indemnity for French spoliations prior to 1800.	31	1	Petition	197	Foreign Affairs	355	Rep. and bill.	318	Referred to Committee Whole House.		
Collins, Chedor	Pension	20	2	Petition	89	Military Pensions	Jan. 21, 1829	Adverse	.....	Laid on table.		
Collins, Claramont	(See Samuel Higdon.)											
Collins, Daniel	Compensation for services as a soldier in revolutionary war.	16	2	Petition	212	Rev. Pensions	....	....	.....	Discharged; laid on table.		
Collins, Dempsey	Payment for horse lost in United States service.	25	2	Petition	397	Claims	967	Adverse	.....	Laid on table.		
Collins, Elizabeth	Permission to pay for certain land and for a certificate of purchase.	12	1	Petition	151	Public Lands.						
Collins, Elizabeth	Permission to pay for certain land, and for a certificate of purchase.	12	2	Petition	550	Public Lands.						
Collins, Elizabeth	Permission to pay for certain land, and for a certificate of purchase.	13	2	Petition	316	Public Lands	....	....	.....	Discharged.		
Collins, Elizabeth	Confirmation of title to land in Mississippi Territory.	13	3	Petition	720	Public Lands	....	....	.....	Discharged.		
Collins, Elizabeth	Confirmation of title to land in Mississippi Territory.	14	1	Petition	75	Public Lands	....	....	.....	Discharged; laid on table.		
Collins, E. K. & Co	Additional compensation under steam mail contract between New York and Liverpool.	31	2	Petition	217	Naval Affairs	36	Adverse	.....	Laid on table.		
Collins, George, (Indian).	Invalid pension	10	2	Petition	495	Claims.						
Collins, George, (Virginia).	Revolutionary pension	22	1	Petition	574	Rev. Claims.						
Collins, George H	Repayment of purchase money on a tract of land.	28	1	Petition	361	Public Lands.	252	Adverse	.....	Laid on table.		
Collins, Henry	Arrears of pension	21	2	Petition	61	Military Pensions.						
Collins, Henry	Arrears of pension	22	1	Petition	383	Invalid Pensions	....	....	.....	Disch'd; laid on table.		
Collins, Henry	Arrears of pension	22	2	Petition	114	Invalid Pensions	....	....	.....	Discharged; laid on table.		
Collins, Jabez	Restoration of pension	25	2	Petition	729	Rev. Pensions.						
Collins, Jabez	Restoration of pension	26	1	Petition	173	Rev. Pensions	111	Report and bill.	122	Passed	Indef. postp'd.	
Collins, Jabez	Restoration of pension	26	2	Petition	36	Rev. Pensions	19	Report and bill.	560	Referred to Committee Whole House.		

List of private claims presented to the House of Representatives of the United States from the 1st to the 31st Congress, inclusive—Continued.

Names of claimants.	Nature or object of the claim.	Congress.	Session.	How brought before the House of Reps.	Page of journal.	To what committee of the House referred.	No. or date of the report.	Nature of the report.	No. of the bill.	How disposed of by the House of Reps.	How disposed of by the Senate.	Date of the act of Congress, and remarks.
Collins, Jabez	Restoration of pension	27	2	Petition	59	Rev. Pensions	784	Adverse		Laid on table.		
Collins, James	(See Thomas Talbot and others)	20	2		312							
Collins, James L	Compensation for losses and for imprisonment while in United States service in Mexican war.	31	1	Petition	1251	Military Affairs.						
Collins, John	(See Lewis & Clarke, and their companions.)											
Collins, John	(See George Crowninshield and others)											
Collins, John, (Maine)	Renewal of pension	17	2	Petition	162	Whole House on bill No. 207.						See act March 1, 1823
Collins, John, (Miss.)	Confirmation of title to land in Mississippi.	19	2	Petition	223	Priv. Land Claims.						See act May 28, 1830
Collins, John, (Ohio)	Revolutionary pension	22	1	Petition	174	Invalid Pensions	April 11, 1832	Adverse		Laid on table.		
Collins, John, (Mass.)	Revolutionary pension	24	1	Petition	136	Rev. Pensions	276	Report and bill	283	Passed	Passed	App'd June 28, 1836
Collins, John	Compensation for services as boat swain in U. S. ship Cyane.	31	1	Petition	271	Naval Affairs.						
Collins, John, and others	Extension of act of 3d March, 1807, to them as members of Lewis & Clark's expedition.	10	2	Petition	480	Public Lands.						
Collins, J. P.	(See Archibald Beard and others.)											
Collins, John G	(See Theophilus Collins, heirs of.)											
Collins, John T.	(See George Spalding and others.)	23	1		47							
Collins, John W	(See John Braidfoot.)											
Collins, Joseph D	(See Reuben Young, administrator of.)											
Collins, Lyman	(See John McGilbry and others.)											
Collins, Lysander	Pension for services as a soldier in war of 1812.	26	2	Petition	118	Invalid Pensions.						
Collins, Madison	Invalid pension	23	1	Petition	121	Invalid Pensions	April 8, 1834	Adverse		Laid on table.		
Collins, Madison	Invalid pension	25	1	Petition	133					Laid on table.		
Collins, Madison	Invalid pension	25	2	Petition	85	Invalid Pensions	Jan. 25, 1838	Adverse		Laid on table.		
Collins, Madison	Invalid pension	25	3	Petition	89	Invalid Pensions.						
Collins, Madison	Invalid pension	26	1	Resolution	392	Invalid Pensions	675	Adverse		Laid on table.		
Collins, Madison	Invalid pension	26	1	Petition	962	Invalid Pensions	July 21, 1840			Laid on table.		
Collins, Nancy	Confirmation of title to land in Mississippi.	19	2	Petition	45	Priv. Land Claims.				Discharged.		
Collins, Nancy	Confirmation of title to land in Mississippi.	20	1	Petition	100	Priv. Land Claims.				Discharged; laid on table.		See act May 28, 1830
Collins, Patrick, attorney of.	Compensation for injuries sustained in revolutionary war.	2	1	Petition	494					Referred to Secretary of War.		
Collins, Patrick, attorney of.	Compensation for injuries sustained in revolutionary war.	3	2	Rep. of Secretary War.	278					Laid on table.		
Collins, Patrick, attorney of.	Compensation for injuries sustained in revolutionary war.	4	1	Rep. of Secretary War.	383	Claims	Jan. 6, 1796	Adverse		Leave to withdraw.		
Collins, Pitman	Payment for vessel impressed by United States, and taken by the enemy.	1	2	Petition	172					Referred to Secretary Treasury.		
Collins, Pitman	Payment for vessel impressed by United States, and taken by the enemy.	2	2	Rep. of Secretary Treasury.	625					Laid on table.		
Collins, Polly	(See Polly Bell.)											
Collins, Samuel	Revolutionary pension	25	3	Senate bill	636				138			

List of private claims presented to the House of Representatives of the United States from the 1st to the 31st Congress, inclusive—Continued.

Names of claimants.	Nature or object of the claim.	Congress.	Session.	How brought before the House of Reps.	Page of journal.	To what committee of the House referred.	No. or date of the report.	Nature of the report.	No. of the bill.	How disposed of by the House of Reps.	How disposed of by the Senate.	Date of the act of Congress, and remarks.
Collins, Samuel	Revolutionary pension	26	1	Senate bill	882	Rev. Pensions	Mar. 25, 1840	With't amend.	116	Referred to Committee Whole House.		
Collins, Samuel	Revolutionary pension	26	2	Senate bill	113	Rev. Pensions	Feb. 12, 1841	With't amend.	70	Referred to Committee Whole House.		
Collins, S. L. & Co.	Payment due from Ottawa Indians	29	1	Memorial	160	Indian Affairs	287	Adverse.				
Collins, Solomon	Revolutionary pension	22	1	Petition	105	Rev. Pensions.						
Collins, Solomon, heirs of.	Arrears of pension	27	2	Petition	69	Rev. Pensions	784	Adverse		Laid on table.		
Collins, Theophilus, heirs of.	Confirmation of title to land in Louisiana.	21	1	Petition	298	Priv. Land Claims.				Discharged; laid on table.		
Collins, Theophilus, heirs of.	Confirmation of title to land in Louisiana.	21	2	Petition	76	Priv. Land Claims.	Jan. 12, 1831	Adverse		Laid on table.		
Collins, Theophilus, heirs of.	Confirmation of title to land in Louisiana.	23	1	Petition	586	Priv. Land Claims.						
Collins, Theophilus, heirs of.	Confirmation of title to land in Louisiana.	23	2	Petition	48	Priv. Land Claims.						
Collins, Thomas, (Pa.)	Compensation for money advanced for equipment of a company of volunteers in war of 1812.	17	1	Petition	349	Claims				Discharged; laid on table.		
Collins, Thomas, (Pa.)	Compensation for money advanced for equipment of a company of volunteers in war of 1812.	17	2	Petition	143	Claims	Feb. 12, 1823	By bill	290	Referred to Committee Whole House.		
Collins, Thomas, (Pa.)	Compensation for money advanced for equipment of a company of volunteers in war of 1812.	18	1	Petition	75	Judiciary	Jan. 9, 1824	Adverse; recommitted;		Discharged; laid on table.		
Collins, Thomas, (Pa.)	Compensation for money advanced for equipment of a company of volunteers in war of 1812.	18	2	Res. and petition	150, 160	Claims.						
Collins, Thomas, (Pa.)	Compensation for money advanced for equipment of a company of volunteers in war of 1812.	19	1	Resolution	50	Claims	Feb. 26, 1826	Adverse		Laid on table.		
Collins, Thomas, (Pa.)	Release from United States judgment against him, and allowance for money advanced, &c.	19	1	Resolution	316	Ways and Means	Mar. 15, 1826	By bill	273	Passed	Amendm'nt reported.	
Collins, Thomas, (Pa.)	Release from United States judgment against him, and allowance for money advanced, &c.	19	2	Resolution	48	Ways and Means	Jan. 5, 1827	By bill	346	Passed	Passed	App'd March 3, 1827
Collins, Thomas, (Pa.) heirs of.	Indemnity to estate for certain money expended in United States service, war of 1812.	20	1	Resolution	186	Claims	Jan. 23, 1828	Adverse		Laid on table.		
Collins, Thomas, (Pa.) heirs of.	Indemnity to estate for certain money expended in United States service, war of 1812.	21	1	Petition	83	Claims	Jan. 4, 1830	Adverse		Laid on table.		
Collins, Thomas, (Pa.) heirs of.	Indemnity to estate for certain money expended in United States service, war of 1812.	22	1	Petition	534	Claims	April 13, 1832	Adverse		Laid on table.		
Collins, Thomas, (Tenn.)	Relief for disabilities incurred in war of 1812.	24	2	Petition	86	Invalid Pensions	Dec. 30, 1836	Adverse		Recommitted.		
							93	Favorable; bill	838	Referred to Committee Whole House.		
Collins, Thomas, (Tenn.)	Relief for disabilities incurred in war of 1812.	25	2	Petition	85	Invalid Pensions	181	Report and bill	207	Passed	Adverse report.	
Collins, Thomas (Tenn.)	Relief for disabilities incurred in war of 1812.	25	3	Petition	89	Invalid Pensions	75	Report and bill.	953	Passed	Adverse report.	

List of private claims presented to the House of Representatives of the United States from the 1st to the 31st Congress, inclusive—**Continued.**

Names of claimants.	Nature or object of the claim.	Congress.	Session.	How brought before the House of Reps.	Page of journal.	To what committee of the House referred.	No. or date of the report.	Nature of the report.	No. of the bill.	How disposed of by the House of Reps.	How disposed of by the Senate.	Date of the act of Congress, and remarks.
Collins, Thomas, (Tenn.)	Relief for disabilities incurred in war of 1812.	26	1	Petition	162	Invalid Pensions	179	Report and bill.	190	Passed	Indef. postp'd.	
Collins, Thomas, (Tenn.)	Relief for disabilities incurred in war of 1812.	26	2	Petition	36	Invalid Pensions	21	Report and bill.	562	Referred to Committee Whole House.		
Collins, Thomas, (Tenn.)	Relief for disabilities incurred in war of 1812.	27	2	Petition	68	Invalid Pensions	129	Report and bill.	175	Passed	Passed	App'd July 27, 1842
Collins, Thomas J	Additional compensation for transporting the mail.	25	3	Resolution	173	P. Of. and P. Roads.				Discharged.		
Collins, William, (N. Y.)	Pension	22	2	Petition	26	Invalid Pensions	Feb. 15, 1833	Report and bill.	738	Referred to Committee Whole House.		
Collins, William, (N. Y.)	Pension	23	1	Petition	72	Invalid Pensions	69	Report and bill.	79	Passed	Passed	App'd June 30, 1834
Collins, William	Confirmation of title to land in Mississippi Territory.	13	2	Petition	297	Public Lands				Discharged.		
Collins, William	Confirmation of title to land in Mississippi Territory.	13	3	Petition	720	Public Lands				Discharged.		
Collins, William	Confirmation of title to land in Mississippi Territory.	14	1	Petition	75	Public Lands				Discharged; laid on table.		
Collins, William	Confirmation of title to land in Mississippi Territory.	14	2	Petition	50	Priv. Land Claims.				Discharged; laid on table.		
Collins, William	Confirmation of title to land in Mississippi Territory.	15	2	Petition	25	Priv. Land Claims.	Jan. 8, 1819	Adverse		Laid on table.		
Collins, William	Confirmation of title to land in Mississippi Territory.	16	2	Petition	173	Priv. Land Claims.				Discharged; laid on table.		
Collins, William	Confirmation of title to land in Mississippi Territory.	17	2	Petition	225	Priv. Land Claims.				Discharged; leave to withdraw.		See act May 28, 1830
Collins, William L	Confirmation of title to two tracts of land in Louisiana.	14	2	Petition	96	Priv. Land Claims.				Discharged; laid on table.		
Collins, William L	Confirmation of title to two tracts of land in Louisiana.	15	1	Petition	173	Priv. Land Claims.				Discharged.		
Collins, William	Pension	14	1	House bill	622	Whole House	April 23, 1816	Favorable	171	Passed	Passed	App'd April 30, 1816
Collins, William, (Tenn.)	Invalid pension	24	1	Petition	566	Invalid Pensions	June 23, 1796	Adverse		Laid on table.		
Collins, William, (Tenn.)	Invalid pension	24	2	Petition	86	Invalid Pensions	48	Report and bill.	795	Referred to Committee Whole House.		
Collins, William, (Tenn.)	Invalid pension	25	2	Petition	82	Invalid Pensions	498	Report and bill.	501	Passed	Passed	App'd July 7, 1838
Collins, William	(See Wm. H. Bedford, agent, &c.)	28	1		262							
Collins, W	(See James Tilton and others.)											
Collis, Solomon	Indemnity for French spoliations prior to 1800.	26	1	Memorial	182	Foreign Affairs	343	Favorable; bill	319	Referred to Committee Whole House.		
Collomy, Daniel	Pension	14	1	Petition	63	Pens. & Rev. Cl'ms.				Discharged; laid on table.		
Collomy, Daniel	Pension	14	2	Petition	95	Pens. & Rev. Cl'ms.	Jan. 29, 1817	By bill	91	Passed	Passed	App'd March 3, 1817
Collyer, Isaac, and others.	Fishing bounty on schooner Dove, lost at sea.	17	1	Petition	50	Commerce	Feb. 7, 1822	By bill	80	Passed	Indef. postp'd.	
Collyer, Isaac, and others.	Fishing bounty on schooner Dove, lost at sea.	17	2	Petition	95	Commerce	Jan. 21, 1823	By bill	241	Referred to Committee Whole House.		
Collyer, Isaac, and others.	Fishing bounty on schooner Dove, lost at sea.	18	1	Petition	104	Commerce	Jan. 6, 1824	By bill	39	Passed	Passed	App'd May 19, 1824
Colman, Charles	Compensation for services in war of 1812.	27	3	Petition	76	Claims	92	Adverse		Laid on table.		
Colmesnil, John D., & Co.	Extra compensation for mail service between Louisville and New Orleans.	31	1	Petition	298	P. Of. and P. Roads.	252	Report and res.	R. 12	Referred to Committee Whole House.		

List of private claims presented to the House of Representatives of the United States from the 1st to the 31st Congress, inclusive—Continued.

Names of claimants.	Nature or object of the claim.	Congress.	Session.	How brought before the House of Reps.	Page of journal.	To what committee of the House referred.	No. or date of the report.	Nature of the report.	No. of the bill.	How disposed of by the House of Reps.	How disposed of by the Senate.	Date of the act of Congress, and remarks.
Colmesnil, John D., & Co.	Extra compensation for mail service between Louisville and New Orleans.	31	2	Res. of last sess.	181	Whole House	Jan. 24, 1851	With't amend.	R. 12	Passed	Passed	App'd Feb. 27, 1851
Colmus, Levi	Pension for services in war of 1812	25	2	Petition	181	Invalid Pensions	645	Report and bill.	621	Passed	Adverse report.	
Colmus, Levi	Pension for services in war of 1812	25	3	Petitions	129, 348	Invalid Pensions	259	Report and bill.	1130	Referred to Committee Whole House.		
Colmus, Levi	Pension for services in war of 1812	26	1	Petition	161	Invalid Pensions	220	Report and bill.	232	Passed	Referred, and Com. disch'd	
Colmus, Levi	Pension for services in war of 1812	26	2	Petition	77	Invalid Pensions	77	Report and bill.	592	Referred to Committee Whole House.		
Colmus, Levi	Pension for services in war of 1812	27	2	Petition	97	Invalid Pensions	138	Report and bill.	184	Laid on table.		
Colmus, Levi	Pension for services in war of 1812	27	3	Petition	43	Rev. Pensions.						
Colmus, Levi	Pension for services in war of 1812	28	1	Petition	105	Invalid Pensions	96	Report and bill.	112	Passed	Passed	App'd May 23, 1844
Colmus, Levi	Pension from 1814 to 1844	29	1	Petition	199	Invalid Pensions.						
Colmus, Levi	Pension from 1814 to 1844	30	1	Petition	299	Invalid Pensions	456	Report and bill.	386	Passed	Adverse report.	
Colmus, Levi	Pension from 1814 to 1844	31	1	Petition	869	Invalid Pensions.						
Colonization Society	(See American Colonization Society.)											
Colony, Richard	Invalid pension	3	2	Report Secretary of War.	278	Claims	Feb. 28, 1795	Favorable; bill ordered.	130	Passed	Postponed to next session.	
Colony, Richard	Invalid pension	4	1	Report Secretary of War.	445	Claims	Feb. 18, 1796	Favorable; bill ordered.	156	Passed	Passed	App'd April 20, 1796
Colquhoun, Robert & Walter.	Relief from payment of duties on goods lost or damaged at Norfolk, Virginia.	6	1	Petition	538	Com. and Manuf.	....	....	......	Leave to withdraw.		
Colquhoun, William S., lieutenant.	Compensation for extra services in the commissary's department.	24	1	Memorial	64	Military Affairs	320	Report and bill.	333	Referred to Committee Whole House.		
Colquhoun, William S., lieutenant.	Compensation for extra services in the commissary's department.	25	2	Memorial	41	Military Affairs	352	Report and bill.	381	Referred to Committee Whole House.		
Colquhoun, William S., lieutenant.	Compensation for extra services in the commissary's department.	25	3	Bill of last sess.	378	Whole House	Jan. 25, 1839	With't amend.	381	Passed	Passed	App'd March 3, 1839
Colquoun, William S	Repayment of $590 in Continental bills.	26	1	Petition	631	....	....	....	......	Laid on table.		
Colson, David	Renewal of pension	20	2	Petition	82	Military Pensions	Feb. 13, 1829	By bill	440	Passed	Rep'd without amendment.	
Colson, David	Renewal of pension	21	1	Petition	49	Military Pensions	Jan. 5, 1830	By bill	72	Passed	Passed	App'd May 20, 1830
Colson, John	Pension for services as a revolutionary soldier.	29	1	Petition	887	Rev. Pensions.						
Colson, Samuel, heir of	One year's pay for services in revolutionary army, and interest.	29	1	Memorial	199	Invalid Pensions.						
Colson, Samuel, heir of	One year's pay for services in revolutionary army, and interest.	30	1	Petition	575	Rev. Claims.						
Colson, Samuel, heir of	One year's pay for services in revolutionary army, and interest.	31	1	Petition	472	Rev. Claims.						
Colston, Josiah	Sundry allowances as purser United States navy.	29	1	Memorial	1038	Naval Affairs.						
Colston, Josiah	Sundry allowances as purser United States navy.	29	2	Petition	99	Naval Affairs.						
Colston, Josiah	Sundry allowances as purser United States navy.	30	1	Petition	459	Naval Affairs.						
Colt, Samuel, & B. F. Morse.	Reimbursement of duties paid on presents from the Sultan of Turkey.	31	1	Senate resolution	998	Ways and Means	....	....	R. 19			

List of private claims presented to the House of Representatives of the United States from the 1st to the 31st Congress, inclusive—Continued.

Names of claimants.	Nature or object of the claim.	Congress.	Session.	How brought before the House of Reps.	Page of journal.	To what committee of the House referred.	No. or date of the report.	Nature of the report.	No. of the bill.	How disposed of by the House of Reps.	How disposed of by the Senate.	Date of the act of Congress, and remarks.
Colt, William, & Wm Donaldson.	Payment of money lost by robbery of the mails, and expenses.	25	2	Petition	200	Claims	528	Report and bill.	519	Referred to Committee Whole House.		
Colt, William, & Wm. Donaldson.	Payment of money lost by robbery of the mails, and expenses.	25	3	Bill of last sess.	379	Whole House	Jan. 25, 1839	With't amend.	519	Passed	Passed	App'd March 2, 1839
Colter, John	(See Lewis & Clarke, and their companions.)											
Coltman, Robert & others.	Additional compensation for damage in a contract for marine hospital at Charleston, S. C.	23	1	Petition	418	Claims	Jan. 10, 1834	Adverse		Laid on table.		
Coltman, Robert, son of.	Arrears of pay due for revolutionary services.	31	1	Petition	233	Rev. Claims	207	Adverse.		Laid on table.		
Coltman, Thomas E. H.	Pre-emption right to land in Louisiana.	27	1	Petition	99	Priv. Land Claims.						
Colton, Andrew, & Lydia.	Compensation for services, or for supplies or losses in U. S. service.	1	3	Petition	349					Referred to Secretary of War.		
Colton, Alpheus	Compensation for services as a soldier in revolutionary war.	15	2	Petition	154	Pens. & Rev. Cl'ms.	Jan. 13, 1819	Rep. and res.; adverse.		Resolution adopted.		
Colton, John	Restoration to pension roll	17	2	Petition	43	Rev. Pensions.	Dec. 27, 1822	By bill	207	Passed	Passed	App'd March 1, 1823
Colton, Julius, widow of.	Arrearages of pension	25	2	Petition	230	Rev. Pensions				Discharged; laid on table.		
Colton, Samuel	Pension	21	2	Petition	61	Military Pensions.						
Colton, Walter	(See Exploring Expedition.)											
Colton, Walter	Compensation for services as acting governor of a portion of California, in Mexican war.	31	1	Petition	487	Judiciary.						
Colton, Walter	Compensation for services as acting governor of a portion of California, in Mexican war.	31	1	Senate bill	1403	Judiciary.	Dec. 12, 1850, (2d session.)	With't amend.	127	Referred to Committee Whole House.		
Colton, Warren	(See Thomas W. Phelps.)											
Columbia, Dist. of, inspectors of customs at Alexandria.	Increase of compensation	9	1	Petition	242	Ways and Means.						
Columbia, Dist. of, inspectors of customs at Alexandria.	Increase of compensation	9	2	Petition	482	Ways and Means.						
Columbia, Dist. of, Washington Bridge Company.	Compensation for destruction of bridge by U. S. military forces.	13	3	Petition	455	Claims				Discharged.		
Columbia, Dist. of, Eastern Branch Bridge Comp'y.	Compensation for destruction of bridge by U. S military forces.	13	3	Pet. & Reps. Secs. War & Navy.	455	Claims	Feb. 11, 1815	Report and bill.	293	Passed	Passed	App'd March 3, 1815
Columbia, Dist. of, Anacosta Bridge Company, by Thos. Ewell, agent.	Compensation for destruction of bridge by U. S. military forces.	13	3	Petition	513	Claims	Jan. 26, 1815	Report and bill.	273	Passed	Passed	App'd March 3, 1815
Columbia, Dist. of, sundry employees at the Navy Yard.	Compensation for tools destroyed by the burning of the navy yard buildings.	13	3	Petition	475	Claims				Discharged.		
Columbia, Dist. of, Potomac Bridge Company.	Appropriation to alter bridge and draw of.	21	1	Senate bill	159	Dist. of Columbia.	Jan. 26, 1830	With't amend.	40	Passed	Passed	App'd May 14, 1830
Columbia, Dist. of, Washington Bridge Comp'y.	Appropriation to purchase bridge, and render it free.	22	1	Senate bill	427	Dist. of Columbia.	Mar. 14, 1832	Adverse	8	Passed	Passed	App'd July 14, 1832
Columbia, Dist. of, sundry merchants of Alexandria.	Indemnity for French spoliations prior to 1800.	14	2	Petition	132	Foreign Affairs				Discharged; leave to withdraw.		
Columbia, Dist of, sundry merchants of Alexandria.	Indemnity for French spoliations prior to 1800.	15	1	Petition	130	Select				Discharged; laid on table.		

List of private claims presented to the House of Representatives of the United States from the 1st to the 31st Congress, inclusive—Continued.

Names of claimants.	Nature or object of the claim.	Congress.	Session.	How brought before the House of Reps.	Page of journal.	To what committee of the House referred.	No. or date of the report.	Nature of the report.	No. of the bill.	How disposed of by the House of Reps.	How disposed of by the Senate.	Date of the act of Congress, and remarks.
Columbia, Dist. of, sundry merchants of Alexandria.	Indemnity for French spoliations prior to 1800.	18	1	Petition	115	Judiciary	....	....	......	Discharged; laid on table.		
Columbia, Dist. of, Marine Ins. Co, Alexandria.	Indemnity for French spoliations prior to 1800.	25	2	Petition	75	Dist. of Columbia.						
Columbia, Dist. of, sundry inh. city of Washington.	Authority for sale of certain lots in U. S. reservation, No. 10.	14	2	Senate bill	214	Dist. of Columbia.	Feb. 13, 1817	With amend..	......	Passed	Passed	App'd Feb. 22, 1817
Columbia, Dist. of, sundry persons of Washington.	Compensation for attendance as witnesses in criminal cases.	19	1	Memorial	129	Judiciary	Feb. 24, 1826	Report and bill.	121	Passed	Passed	App'd May 20, 1826
Columbia, Dist. of, George town college.	Pecuniary aid in support of......	22	2	Memorial	110	Dist. of Columbia.	Jan. 2, 1833	Report and bill.	651	Passed	Passed	App'd March 2, 1833
Columbia, Dist. of, sundry citizens of Georgetown.	Appropriation to improve the river Potomac, and for the purchase of Little Falls bridge.	22	2	Senate bill	277	Dist. of Columbia.	Feb. 7, 1833	With amend..	62	Passed...........	Passed	App'd March 2, 1833
Columbia, Dist. of, Judges of circuit court.	(See Wm. Cranch, and others.)											
Columbia, Dist. of, Judges of circuit court.	Increase of Salary	15	1	Senate bill	280	Judiciary	Mar. 5, 1818	With't amend.	16	Passed	Passed	App'd April 20, 1818
Columbia, Dist. of, Orphan Asylums of Washington.	Pecuniary aid in support of......	22	1	Senate bill	779	Dist. of Columbia.	May 29, 1832	With amend..	149	Passed	Passed	App'd July 14, 1832
Columbia, Dist. of, Judges of Orphans' court.	Increase of compensation........	16	1	Senate bill	407	Dist. of Columbia.	April 18, 1820	With amend..	52	Passed	Passed	App'd May 1, 1820
Columbia, Dist. of, Judge of Orphans' court, Alexandria.	Compensation of $500 per annum in lieu of the present.	20	1	Senate bill	730	Dist. of Columbia.	May 14, 1828	With't amend.	121	Passed	Passed	App'd May 19, 1828
Columbia, Dist. of, Corporation of Washington.	Authority to drain low ground around public reservations, and to improve the same.	17	1	Senate bill	465	Dist. of Columbia.	April 18, 1822	With't amend.	80	Passed	Passed	App'd May 7, 1822
Columbia, Dist. of, Corporation of Washington.	Permission to introduce into their authorized lotteries certain land prizes.	19	2	Senate bill	276	Dist. of Columbia.	Feb. 10, 1827	With't amend.	84	Passed	Passed	App'd Feb. 22, 1827
Columbia, Dist. of, Corporation of Washington.	To be invested with the rights, &c., of the Washington Canal Company, and grant reservation of land along the canal in aid thereof.	22	1	Memorial	....	Dist. of Columbia.	May 19, 1832	By bill	492	Passed	Passed	App'd May 31, 1832
Columbia, Dist. of, Corporation of Washington.	Commutation of the land granted by act of 31st May, 1832, to money.	22	2	Resolution	64	Public Buildings ..	63	Report and bill.	706	Passed	Passed	App'd March 2, 1833
Columbia, Dist. of, Corporation of Washington.	Relief by the U. States assuming their subscription to the Chesapeake and Ohio canal stock.	23	1	Memorial	245	Dist. of Columbia.	Mar. 25, 1834	Report and bill.	394	Laid on table.		
Columbia, Dist. of, corporate cities in.	Relief by the U. States assuming their subscription to the Chesapeake and Ohio canal stock.	24	1	Senate bill	564	Dist. of Columbia.	April 1, 1836	With't amend.	112	Passed	Passed	App'd May 20, 1836
Columbia, Dist of, Corporation of Washington.	Appropriation of $70,000 for extinguishing interest on city debt.	23	1	Senate bill	847	Dist. of Columbia.	Jan. 27, 1834	With't amend.	203	Passed	Passed	App'd June 28, 1834
Columbia, Dist. of, Mayor, &c, of Washington.	Additional payment for that part of City Hall bought by U. S.	19	1	Petition	61	Dist. of Columbia.	....	....	......	Discharged; laid on table.		
Columbia, Dist. of, Christ Church of Washington parish.	Appropriation to enclose burial ground.	18	1	Senate bill	430	Dist. of Columbia.	April 22, 1824	With't amend.	65	Passed	Passed	App'd May 4, 1824
Columbia, Dist. of, vestry of Washington parish.	Aid in building keeper's house to burial ground.	22	1	Petition	295	Dist. of Columbia.	Feb. 7, 1832	Report and bill.	356	Passed	Passed	App'd May 25, 1832

List of private claims presented to the House of Representatives of the United States from the 1st to the 31st Congress, inclusive—Continued.

Names of claimants.	Nature or object of the claim.	Congress.	Session.	How brought before the House of Reps.	Page of journal.	To what committee of the House referred.	No. or date of the report.	Nature of the report.	No. of the bill.	How disposed of by the House of Reps.	How disposed of by the Senate.	Date of the act of Congress, and remarks.
Columbia, Dist. of, Washington Canal Company.	To alter plan of canal, and collect tolls and wharfage at deep water places only.	19	1	Petition	365	Dist. of Columbia.	Mar. 30, 1826	By bill	191	Passed	Passed	App'd May 20, 1826
Columbia, Dist. of, Alexandria Canal Company.	Aid in construction of their canal.	22	1	Memorial	50	Dist. of Columbia.	Mar. 30, 1832	Report and bill.	520	Passed	Passed	App'd June 25, 1832
Columbia, Dist. of, city corporations of.	Sanction to subscriptions to Chesapeake and Ohio canal stock, and to tax and pledge property for redemption of.	20	1	Memorial	111	Roads and Canals.	112	Report and bill.	128	Passed.	Passed	App'd May 24, 1828
Columbia, Dist. of, Turnpike Road Company.	Damages by branch of Ohio railroad.	21	2	Memorial	138	...	...	...	...	Laid on table.		
Columbian Institute, in District of Columbia.	To be invested with the use of five acres of public ground for building.	16	1	Petition	54	Dist. of Columbia.	Jan. 11, 1820	By bill	36	Passed	Passed	App'd May 8, 1820
Columbian Institute, in District of Columbia.	Compensation for improvements on ground granted, but resumed for enlargement of Capitol grounds.	24	2	Memorial	180	Public Buildings	226	Report and bill.	934	Referred to Committee Whole House.		
Columbian College, in District of Columbia.	Aid of Congress to relieve from pecuniary embarrassments.	20	1	Senate bill	325	Dist. of Columbia.	Feb. 23, 1828	With't amend.	7	Passed	Passed	App'd Mar. 19, 1828
Columbian College, in District of Columbia.	Endowment in lots of ground in Washington.	22	1	Senate bill	779	Dist. of Columbia.	May 25, 1832	With amend.	150	Passed	Passed	App'd July 14, 1832
Columbia, Dist. of, Marine Insurance Company of.	Indemnity for French spoliations prior to 1800.	26	1	Memorial	180	Foreign Affairs	343	Favorable; bill	319	Referred to Committee Whole House.		
Colver, Esther	(See Esther Culver.)											
Colville, Charles	Reimbursement of amount paid for ransom from Algerine slavery, and for travelling expenses.	2	1	Petition and report Sec. State.	449	...	...	...	...	Laid on table.		
Colville, Charles, and John Robertson, (*alias* William.)	Reimbursement of amount paid for ransom from Algerine slavery, and for travelling expenses.	2	1	Petition	580	Select	April 25, 1792	Favorable	...	Ref. to Com. Whole House, on bill 188.		
Colville, Charles	Reimbursement of amount paid for ransom from Algerine slavery, and for travelling expenses.	4	1	Petition, and report Sec. State.	515	Whole House	May 10, 1796	Favorable; bill ordered.	140	Passed	Passed	App'd May 30, 1796
Colvin, James	(See James Calvin.)											
Colvin, Patrick	Compensation for losses and injuries committed on his property by revolutionary army.	1	3	Petition	349	...	...	...	...	Referred to Secretary Treasury.		
Colvin, Patrick	Compensation for losses and injuries committed on his property by revolutionary army.	2	2	Rep. of Secretary Treasury.	625	...	...	...	...	Referred to Committee Whole House.		
Colvocorresses, G. M.	(See Exploring Expedition.)											
Colwell, Stephen	(See William T. Smith, executor of.)											
Combs, Charles, and wife.	Confirmation of title to land in Louisiana.	20	1	Petition	312	Priv. Land Claims.	...	...	...	Discharged; laid on table.		
Combs, Charles, and wife.	Confirmation of title to land in Louisiana.	20	2	Petition	34	Priv. Land Claims.	...	...	...	Discharged; laid on table.		
Combs, Charles, and wife.	Confirmation of title to land in Louisiana.	21	1	Petition	40	Priv. Land Claims.	186	Report and bill.	232	Referred to Committee Whole House.		
Combs, Charles, and wife.	Confirmation of title to land in Louisiana.	21	2	Bill of last sess.	264	Whole House	Feb. 4, 1831	With't amend.	232	Passed	Reported with amendment.	
Combs, Charles, and wife.	Confirmation of title to land in Louisiana.	22	1	Petition	75	Priv. Land Claims.	131	Report and bill.	201	Referred to Committee Whole House.		

List of private claims presented to the House of Representatives of the United States from the 1st to the 31st Congress, inclusive—Continued.

Names of claimants.	Nature or object of the claim.	Congress.	Session.	How brought before the House of Reps.	Page of journal.	To what committee of the House referred.	No. or date of the report.	Nature of the report.	No. of the bill.	How disposed of by the House of Reps.	How disposed of by the Senate.	Date of the act of Congress, and remarks.
Combs, Charles, and wife	Confirmation of title to land in Louisiana.	22	2	Bill of last sess.	66	Whole House	Dec. 15, 1832	With't amend.	201	Passed	Passed	App'd July 14, 1833
Combs, Elijah	Extra compensation for services as mail contractor.	28	1	Petition	346	P. Of. and P. Roads.						
Combs, Elijah	Extra compensation for services as mail contractor.	29	1	Petition	446	P. Of. and P. Roads.	....	....	.....	Discharged; laid on table.		
Combs, George	(See Cornelius Manning, exec'r of.)											
Combs, Leslie	Pay for a company of spies under his command in the Northwestern army.	13	3	Petition	521	Military Affairs.						
Combs, Leslie	Pension for wound received in war of 1812.	22	2	Resolution	90	Invalid Pensions	Feb. 15, 1833	By bill	738	Referred to Committee Whole House.		
Combs, Leslie	Pension for wound received in war of 1812.	23	1	Petition	54	Invalid Pensions	37	Report and bill.	42	....	....	Bill became a law, omitting claimant's name.
Combs, Leslie	Invalid pension	24	1	Senate bill	871	Invalid Pensions	June 9, 1836	With't amend	221	Passed	Passed	App'd June 15, 1836
Combs, Leslie	Payment of bonds of the Republic of Texas held by him.	30	1	Petition	146	Claims.						
Combs, Leslie	Payment of bonds of the Republic of Texas held by him.	30	2	Petition	379	Claims.						
Combs, Leslie	Payment of bonds of the Republic of Texas held by him.	31	1	Petition	192, 194	Claims.						
Combs, Philip, and others.	Fishing bounty on schooner John, lost at sea.	20	1	Petition	162	Commerce	Jan. 22, 1828	By bill	101	Passed	Passed	App'd May 24, 1828
Combs, William	(See Elias De Butts and others.)											
Comeau, Alexander	Confirmation of title to land in Louisiana.	26	1	Petition	365	Priv. Land Claims.	96	Report and bill.	92	Passed	Passed	App'd July 20, 1840
Comeau, Jean Baptiste	Land in lieu of that granted to him but sold by United States.	26	1	Senate bill	836	Priv. Land Claims.	July 21, 1840	With't amend	263	Referred to Committee Whole House.		
Comeau, Jean Baptiste	Land in lieu of that granted to him but sold by United States.	26	2	Senate bill	225	Priv. Land Claims.	Feb. 12, 1841	With't amend.	121	Passed	Passed	App'd March 2, 1841
Comeau, Jean Baptiste	Land in lieu of that granted to him but sold by United States.	27	2	Senate bill	1126	Priv. Land Claims.	April 6, 1842	With't amend.	235	Amended and passed.	Passed	App'd Aug. 29, 1842
Comegys, Cornelius	Liquidation of certain revolutionary quartermasters' certificates.	4	1	Rep. of Secretary Treasury.	388	Claims	May 31, 1796	Adverse	.....	Laid on table.		
Comer, James	Benefit of act of May 15, 1828, for relief of revolutionary officers and soldiers.	22	1	Resolution	228	Rev. Pensions	....	....	.....	Discharged; laid on table.		
Comery, Peter	(See William Baker and others.)	22	1	....	288							
Comins, Jonas	Revolutionary pension	24	1	Resolution	285	Rev. Pensions	499	Report and bill.	499	Passed	Passed	App'd June 28, 1836
Comley, Rebecca	(See Isaac Worrell, heir of.)											
Commager, Henry S.	Payment of certain claims against Ottawa Indians.	28	1	Petition	275	Indian Affairs	424	Report and bill.	326	Passed	Passed	App'd June 17, 1844
Commissary, Abraham	Maintenance while educating for the ministry as the son of an Onondaga Indian killed in U. States service at the battle of Chippewa.	15	2	Petition	234	Pens. & Rev. Cl'ms.	....	....	.....	Discharged; laid on table.		
Commissioners to treat with Southern Indians.	(See Benjamin Lincoln & others.)											
Comparé, Cecile	Title to land under Kanzas Indian treaty of June, 1825.	23	1	Petition	300	Public Lands	....	....	.....	Discharged; laid on table.		
Comparet, Francis, *alias* Jean B.	Payment of $500, as per treaty with the Pottawatomies.	21	1	Petition	83	Indian Affairs	38	Report and bill.	51	Passed	Passed	App'd March 25, 1830

List of private claims presented to the House of Representatives of the United States from the 1st to the 31st Congress, inclusive—Continued.

Names of claimants.	Nature or object of the claim.	Congress.	Session.	How brought before the House of Reps.	Page of journal.	To what committee of the House referred.	No. or date of the report.	Nature of the report.	No. of the bill.	How disposed of by the House of Reps.	How disposed of by the Senate.	Date of the act of Congress, and remarks.
Compere, Pierre S	Confirmation of title to land in Louisiana.	22	2	Petition	41	Priv. Land Claims.	53	Report and bill.	696	Referred to Committee Whole House.		
Compere, Pierre S	Confirmation of title to land in Louisiana.	23	1	Petitions	76, 93	Priv. Land Claims.	June 8, 1834	To be disch'd	......	Laid on table.		
Compton, Alexander	Release from imprisonment at suit of United States, and permission to discharge his debt by instalments.	17	1	Petition	234	P. Of. and P. Roads.	....	....	......	Discharged; laid on table.		
Compton, Henderson	(See Archibald Beard and others.)											
Compton, Henry T	(See Alexander Trueman, children of.)											
Compton, John & Leonard	(See William Miller and others.)											
Compton, John	(See Garriguez Flaujac, assignee of.)											
Compton, Joseph	(See Wm. H. Bedford, agent, &c.)	28	1	....	262							
Compton, Levi	Confirmation of land title	26	1	Petition	178	Public Lands.						
Compton, Zachariah	(See Archibald Beard and others.)											
Comstock, James	(See Daniel Webb and James Comstock.)											
Comstock, Nathan	Revolutionary pension	22	1	Petition	714	Rev. Pensions.						
Conant, Artemas, guardian of.	Arrears of pension	30	1	Petition	387	Invalid Pensions	279	Report and bill.	275	Passed.		
Conant, Artemas, guardian of.	Arrears of pension	31	1	Petition	1226	Invalid Pensions.						
Conant, Ebenezer	Revolutionary pension	24	2	Petition	73	Rev. Pensions	41	Adverse	......	Laid on table.		
Conant, Ebenezer	Revolutionary pension	26	1	Petition	286	Rev. Pensions	424	Adverse	......	Laid on table.		
Conant, Ebenezer	Revolutionary pension	26	2	Petition	76	Rev. Pensions.						
Conant, Ebenezer	Revolutionary pension	29	1	Petition	104	Rev. Pensions	272	Report and bill.	239	Passed	Passed	App'd Aug. 8, 1846
Conant, James	Arrearages of revolutionary pension.	20	1	Resolution	584	Military Pensions	....	....	......	Discharged; laid on table.		
Conant, James	Arrearages of revolutionary pension.	24	2	Petition	74	Rev. Pensions	....	....	......	Discharged; laid on table.		
Conant, James	Arrearages of revolutionary pension.	25	2	Petition	182	Rev. Pensions	....	....	......	Discharged; laid on table.		
Conant, John	Revolutionary pension	28	1	Petition	708	Rev. Pensions.						
Conant, Luther	Restoration to pension roll	17	2	Petition	163	....	....	....	......	Referred to Committee Whole House on bill No. 207.	....	See act Mar. 1, 1823
Conant, Shubael	(See John S. Langham, sureties of.)	22	1	....	473							
Conant, Shubael	(See Stephen Mack.)											
Conant, Shubael	Remission of duties on goods taken from N. York to Detroit, through Canada.	16	1	Petition	172	Ways and Means.	....	....	......	Discharged; laid on table.		
Conant, Shubael	Money advanced for forage to troops at Detroit, war of 1812.	23	1	Petition	246	Claims	246	Report and bill.	281	Referred to Committee Whole House.		
Conant, Shubael	Money advanced for forage to troops at Detroit, war of 1812.	23	2	Bill of last sess.	300	Whole House	Jan. 31, 1835	With't amend.	281	Passed	Passed	App'd March 3, 1835
Conant, Shubael	Remission of interest on amount of liability as surety for John S. Langham.	23	1	Petition	448	Claims	493	Adverse	......	Laid on table.		
Conard, Elizabeth	(See Abraham Nanna, heirs of.)											
Conard, John	Aid in discharging judgment against him as United States marshal in Pennsylvania.	21	1	Pres. Message	394	Judiciary	323	Report and bill.	379	Passed	Passed	App'd May 29, 1830

List of private claims presented to the House of Representatives of the United States from the 1st to the 31st Congress, inclusive—Continued.

Names of claimants.	Nature or object of the claim.	Congress.	Session.	How brought before the House of Reps.	Page of journal.	To what committee of the House referred.	No. or date of the report.	Nature of the report.	No. of the bill.	How disposed of by the House of Reps.	How disposed of by the Senate.	Date of the act of Congress, and remarks.
Conard, John	Fees as United States marshal for executing a *fi. fa.* against Ed. Thompson.	21	2	Petition	192	Judiciary.						
Conard, John	Fees as United States marshal for executing a *fi. fa.* against Ed. Thompson.	22	2	Petition	45	Judiciary				Discharged; laid on table.		
Conard, John	(See New York, insurance companies of the city of.)											
Concklin, George	(See Joseph Falconer, executors of.)	20	2		42							
Concklin, John, and Jedediah Frost.	Indemnity for damage to farm by United States troops in revolutionary war.	4	1	Petition	437	Claims	May 31, 1796	Adverse		Laid on table.		
Concklin, John, and Jedediah Frost.	Indemnity for damage to farm by United States troops in revolutionary war.	6	1	Petition	592	Claims	May 6, 1800	Adverse		Report adopted.		
Concklin, Timothy	Compensation for a pair of oxen taken by the enemy.	3	2	Petition	285	Claims	Mar. 2, 1795	Adverse		Laid on table		Leave to withdraw.
Conckling, Josiah	Invalid pension	4	1	Rep. of Secretary War.	445	Claims	Feb. 18, 1796	Favorable; bill ordered.	156	Passed	Passed	App'd April 20, 1796
Concle, John, jr.,	(See John Couch, jr.)											
Condy, Jeremiah, and William.	(See Leffert Lefferts.)											
Condy, Thomas Hollis	Compensation for services, losses, or injuries sustained in revolutionary war.	1	2	Petition and rep't of Sec. War.	213					Laid on table.		
Condy, Thomas Hollis	Compensation for services, losses, or injuries sustained in revolutionary war.	2	1	Petition and rep't of Sec. War.	450					Claim rejected.		
Condy, Thomas Hollis	Compensation for services, losses, or injuries sustained in revolutionary war.	11	1	Petition	32	Claims.						
Condy, Thomas Hollis	Compensation for services, losses, or injuries sustained in revolutionary war.	11	2	Petition	124	Claims.						
Cone, Giles	Increase of pension	17	1	Petition	567					Laid on table.		
Cone, Giles	Increase of pension	17	2	Petition	165					Referred to Secretary War.		
Cone, Henry	Invalid pension	3	1	Rep. of Secretary War.	175					Laid on table.		
Cone, Henry	Invalid pension	3	2	Rep. of Secretary War.	262	Claims	Feb. 28, 1795	Favorable; bill ordered.	130	Passed	Postponed.	
Cone, Henry	Invalid pension	4	1	Rep. of Secretary War.	445	Claims	Feb. 18, 1796	Favorable; bill ordered.	156	Passed	Passed	App'd April 20, 1796
Cone, Henry	Increase of pension	11	2	House bill	283	Whole House	Mar. 24, 1810	Favorable	108	Passed	Passed	App'd April 27, 1810
Cone, Jared	Pension	21	1	Petition	411	Military Pensions	May 26, 1830	By bill	491	Referred to Committee Whole House.		
Cone, Jared	Pension	21	2	Bill of last sess.	318	Whole House	Feb. 16, 1831	With't amend.	491	Passed	Amendm't reported.	
Cone, Jared	Pension	22	1	Petition	51	Rev. Pensions	5	Report and bill.	50	Passed	Passed	App'd Feb. 18, 1832
Cone, Jared, widow of	Pension for revolutionary services.	28	1	Petition	357	Rev. Pensions.						
Cone, Jared, widow of	Pension for revolutionary services.	30	1	Petition	116	Rev. Pensions	209	Adverse		Laid on table.		

List of private claims presented to the House of Representatives of the United States from the 1st to the 31st Congress, inclusive—Continued.

Names of claimants.	Nature or object of the claim.	Congress.	Session.	How brought before the House of Reps.	Page of journal.	To what committee of the House referred.	No. or date of the report.	Nature of the report.	No. of the bill.	How disposed of by the House of Reps.	How disposed of by the Senate.	Date of the act of Congress, and remarks.
Cone, Joseph	Grant of land as a Canadian refugee, and for revolutionary ser vices.	6	2	House bill	766	Whole House	Jan. 26, 1801	With amend.	280	Passed	Passed	App'd, Feb. 18, 1801
Coney, Samuel	Invalid pension, war of 1812	29	1	Petition	59	Invalid Pensions	296	Adverse	.....	Laid on table.		
Coney, Samuel	Invalid pension, war of 1812	30	1	Petition	229	Invalid Pensions	197	Report and bill.	207	Passed	Passed	App'd Aug. 11, 1848
Coney, William	Moity of forfeiture of a vessel paid into United States treasury.	19	2	Petition	63	Commerce	Jan. 19, 1827	Adverse	.....	Laid on table.		
Congdon, John	Pension	21	2	Petition	126	Military Pensions.						
Congdon, John	Pension	22	1	Petition	80	Military Pensions	.....	.....	.....	Discharged; laid on table.		
Congdon, Jonathan	Pension	21	2	Petition	127	Military Pensions.						
Congdon, Jonathan	Pension	22	1	Petition	80	Military Pensions.						
Conger, John S.	(See Amos Hedden, assignee of.)											
Conger, Stephen M.	Pension	14	1	House bill	622	Whole House	April 23, 1816	Favorable	171	Passed	Passed	App'd April 30, 1816
Conger, Zachariah S.	Pension	20	1	Petition	243	Military Pensions	Feb. 15, 1828	Adverse	.....	Recommitted.		
							April 29, 1828	By bill	283	Passed.		
Conger, Zachariah S.	Pension	20	2	House bill	55	Military Pensions	Jan. 15, 1829	Favorable	311	Passed	Laid on table.	
Conger, Zachariah S.	Pension	21	1	Petition	47	Military Pensions	Jan. 5, 1830	By bill	72	Passed	Passed	App'd May 20, 1830
Congleton, Moses, widow of.	Revolutionary pension	26	1	Petition	323	Rev. Pensions.						
Congleton, Moses, widow of.	Revolutionary pension	26	2	Petition	195	Rev. Pensions.						
Congleton, Moses, widow of.	Revolutionary pension	27	2	Petition	59	Rev. Pensions	125	Report and bill.	171	Passed	Adverse report.	
Congleton, Moses, widow of.	Revolutionary pension	28	1	Petition	436	Rev. Pensions.						
Coningham, Grove	(See William Jessup and others.)											
Conkey, Robert	Compensation for revolutionary services.	4	1	Petition	425	Claims	May 31, 1796	Adverse	.....	Laid on table.		
Conkey, Samuel T., attorney of.	Bounty land in Illinois for services in war of 1812.	24	1	Petition	409	Public Lands	.....	.....	.....	Discharged; laid on table.		
Conkey, Samuel T., attorney of.	Bounty land in Illinois for services in war of 1812.	25	2	Petition	233	Public Lands	595	Adverse	.....	Laid on table.		
Conkin, John	Revolutionary pension	23	1	Petition	308	Invalid Pensions	309	Report and bill.	343	Referred to Committee Whole House.		
Conkin, John	Revolutionary pension	23	2	Bill of last sess.	336	Whole House	Feb. 6, 1835	With't amend.	343	Passed	Adverse report.	
Conkin, John	Revolutionary pension	24	1	Petition	260	Invalid Pensions	316	Report and bill.	329	Passed	Passed	App'd June 28, 1836
Conkin, John	Increase of pension	26	2	Petition	60	Invalid Pensions	.....	.....	.....	Discharged; laid on table.		
Conkin, John	Increase of pension	30	2	Petition	252	Invalid Pensions.						
Conkin, John	Increase of pension	31	1	Petition	276	Invalid Pensions.						
Conklin, Enoch, widow of.	Renewal of pension from privateer fund.	21	1	Petition	295	Naval Affairs	.....	.....	.....	Discharged; laid on table.		
Conklin, Enoch, widow of.	Renewal of pension from privateer fund.	25	2	Petition	400	Invalid Pensions	.....	.....	.....	Discharged; laid on table.		
Conklin, Enoch, widow of.	Relief additional to that afforded by act of 19th June, 1834.	25	3	Petition	454	Naval Affairs.						
Conklin, Enoch, widow of.	Relief additional to that afforded by act of 19th June, 1834.	26	1	Petition	304	Naval Affairs.						
Conklin, Enoch, widow of.	Relief additional to that afforded by act of 19th June, 1834.	27	2	Petition	236	Naval Affairs	603	Adverse	.....	Laid on table.		
Conklin, Ezekiel, & others of Orange county, N. Y.	Indemnity for damage to property in revolutionary war.	1	2	Petition	372	.....	.....	.....	.....	Referred to Secretary Treasury.		

List of private claims presented to the House of Representatives of the United States from the 1st to the 31st Congress, inclusive—Continued.

Names of claimants.	Nature or object of the claim.	Congress.	Session.	How brought before the House of Reps.	Page of journal.	To what committee of the House referred.	No. or date of the report.	Nature of the report.	No. of the bill.	How disposed of by the House of Reps.	How disposed of by the Senate.	Date of the act of Congress, and remarks.
Conklin, Ezekiel, & others, of Orange county, N. Y.	Indemnity for damage to property in revolutionary war.	2	2	Rep. of Secretary Treasury.	625	Whole House.						
Conklin, Ezekiel	Indemnity for damage to his farm in 1779–'80.	4	1	Rep. of Secretary Treasury.	388	Claims	May 31, 1796	Adverse		Laid on table.		
Conklin, Isaac	Indemnity for damage to his property in 1779 and 1780.	4	1	Rep. of Secretary of Treasury.	388	Claims	May 31, 1796	Adverse		Laid on table.		
Conklin, John, (N. Y.)	Revolutionary pension	21	1	Petition	143	Military Pensions				Discharged; laid on table.		
Conklin, John, (N. Y.)	Revolutionary pension	21	2	Petition	53	Military Pensions.						
Conklin, John, (N. Y.)	Revolutionary pension	22	1	Petition	120	Rev. Pensions	410	Report and bill.	510	Referred to Committee Whole House.		
Conklin, William	Compensation for wood furnished to revolutionary army.	4	1	Rep. of Secretary of Treasury.	388	Claims	May 31, 1796	Adverse		Laid on table.		
Conklin, William, heirs of.	Pension for services as a revolutionary soldier.	29	1	Petition	463	Rev. Claims	826	Adverse		Laid on table.		
Conklin, William, heirs of.	Pension for services as a revolutionary soldier.	29	2	Petition	68	Rev. Pensions.						
Conkling, Aurelian	Compensation for services as deputy clerk of U. S. court for northern district of New York, under resolution of House of Representatives.	30	1	Petition	68	Claims	97	Adverse		Laid on table.		
Conkling, John A.	Reimbursement of fine imposed by authorities at Rio Janeiro.	29	1	Petition	589	Naval Affairs.						
Conkling, Robert H. and Catharine.	(See Joseph Webb, heirs of.)											
Conley, Arthur, widow of.	Revolutionary pension	26	1	Petition	385	Rev. Pensions	663	Adverse		Laid on table.		
Conley, Arthur, widow of.	Revolutionary pension	26	2	Petition	272	Rev. Pensions.						
Conly, Isaac	Pension for wounds received in United States service.	25	2	Petition	400	Invalid Pensions	984	Report and bill.	844	Referred to Committee Whole House.		
Conly, Isaac	Pension for wounds received in United States service.	25	3	Bill of last sess.	432	Whole House	Feb. 1, 1839	With't amend.	844	Passed	Passed	App'd March 3, 1839
Conley, J	(See James Tilton and others.)											
Conley, James H.	Compensation as acting carpenter in ship Princeton.	29	1	Memorial	339	Naval Affairs	764	Report and bill.	503	Laid on table.		
Conley, James H.	Compensation as acting carpenter in ship Princeton.	29	2	Bill of last sess.	212				503	Passed	Passed	App'd March 3, 1847
Conley, James H.	Additional compensation as acting carpenter.	30	1	Petition	79	Naval Affairs	78	Report and bill.	63	Passed	Passed second session.	App'd Jan. 26, 1849
Conley, Michael, widow of.	Balance of pay and bounty land due as a soldier in U. S. army.	23	1	Petition	438	Claims	April 30, 1834	Rep. and res. to refer to 3d Auditor.		Resolution adopted.		
Conly, Thomas	Invalid pension	27	2	Petition	845	Invalid Pensions.						
Connecticut, State of, sundry citizens of New Haven	Indemnity for property taken by British vessels in revolutionary war.	4	1	Memorial	444	Whole House.						
Connecticut, State of, sundry merchants of Hartford.	Indemnity for capture of property by French cruisers.	7	1	Memorial	111	Select	April 22, 1802	Adverse		Referred to Committee Whole House.		
Connecticut, State of, sundry merchants of Middlesex county.	Indemnity for capture of property by French cruisers.	7	1	Memorial	134	Select	April 22, 1802	Adverse		Referred to Committee Whole House.		

List of private claims presented to the House of Representatives of the United States from the 1st to the 31st Congress, inclusive—Continued.

Names of claimants.	Nature or object of the claim.	Congress.	Session.	How brought before the House of Reps.	Page of journal.	To what committee of the House referred.	No. or date of the report.	Nature of the report.	No. of the bill.	How disposed of by the House of Reps.	How disposed of by the Senate.	Date of the act of Congress, and remarks.
Connecticut, State of, sundry citizens of New London county.	Indemnity for capture of property by French cruisers.	7	1	Memorial......	136	Select..........	April 22, 1802	Adverse	.....	Referred to Committee Whole House.		
Connecticut, State of, sundry citizens of New London county.	Indemnity for capture of property by French cruisers.	7	1	Memorial	127	Select..........	April 22, 1802	Adverse	.....	Referred to Committee Whole House.		
Connecticut, State of, sundry inhabitants of Norwich and New Haven.	Indemnity for capture of property by French cruisers.	7	1	Memorial	153	Select..........	April 22, 1802	Adverse	.....	Referred to Committee Whole House.		
Connecticut, sundry citizens of the State of.	Indemnity for French spoliations prior to 1800.	22	1	Petition	43	Foreign Affairs.						
Connecticut, sundry citizens of the State of.	Indemnity for French spoliations prior to 1800.	23	2	Petition	346, 347	Foreign Affairs.						
Connecticut, sundry citizens of the State of.	Indemnity for French spoliations prior to 1800.	26	1	Memorial	182	Foreign Affairs....	343	Favorable; bill.	319	Referred to Committee Whole House.		
Connecticut, State of, sundry merchants of New Haven.	Relief from penalties incurred by imported British manufactures.	12	2	Petition	549	Ways and Means..	Nov. 25, 1812	Favorable; bill ordered.	239	Rejected..........	....	See acts Jan. 2, and Feb. 27, 1813.
Connecticut, State of, sundry non-commissioned officers, privates, &c., war of 1812.	(See Hector Brownson and others.)											
Connecticut, sundry inhabitants of the State of.	(See Charles Dolph, heirs of.)											
Connecticut, sundry inhabitants of the State of.	Payment for capture of midshipman and two marines, war of 1812.	14	2	Petition	211	Naval Affairs.....	....	....	.....	Discharged; laid on table.		
Connecticut, sundry inhabitants of the State of.	Payment for capture of midshipman and two marines, war of 1812.	15	1	Petition	312	Naval Affairs.....	....	....	.....	Discharged; laid on table.		
Connecticut, State of.....	Payment of sum allowed by resolution of Congress, 17th June, 1777, for a monument to General D. Wooster.	18	2	Resolution	166	Select..........	Feb. 17, 1825	By bill	343	Referred to Committee Whole House.		
Connecticut, State of.....	Payment of expenses of militia, &c., in war of 1812.	22	1	Resol'n and report Sec. of War.	137	Military Affairs. ..	March 1, 1832	By bill	433	Referred to Committee Whole House.		
Connecticut, State of.....	Payment of expenses of militia, &c., in war of 1812.	23	1	Resol'n and report Sec. of War.	65	Military Affairs....	Dec. 19, 1833	By bill	57	Referred to Committee Whole House.		
Connecticut, State of.....	Payment of expenses of militia, &c., in war of 1812.	24	1	Resol'n and report Sec. of War.	160	Military Affairs....	Feb. 5, 1836	By bill	297	Referred to Committee Whole House.		
Connecticut, State of.....	Payment of expenses of militia, &c., in war of 1812.	24	2	Resol'n of State Assembly.	147	....	....	....	.....	Laid on table.		
Connecticut, Derby Fishing Company of.	Remission of penalties, &c., incurred on certain importations from Great Britain.	12	1	Petition	72	Com. and Manuf.						
Connecticut, Derby Fishing Company of.	Remission of penalties, &c., incurred on certain importations from Great Britain.	13	1	Petition	19	Ways and Means.						
Connell, Benoni, widow of	Revolutionary pension..........	27	2	Petition	48	Rev. Pensions	784	Adverse	.....	Laid on table.		
Connell, James..........	Relief for injuries sustained at the navy yard, New York.	11	1	Petition	53	Claims.						
Connell, John	Indemnity for losses on naval contract.	11	2	Petition	227	....	....	....	.....	Referred to Secretary Navy.		

List of private claims presented to the House of Representatives of the United States from the 1st to the 31st Congress, inclusive—Continued.

Names of claimants.	Nature or object of the claim.	Congress.	Session.	How brought before the House of Reps.	Page of journal.	To what committee of the House referred.	No. or date of the report.	Nature of the report.	No. of the bill.	How disposed of by the House of Reps.	How disposed of by the Senate.	Date of the act of Congress, and remarks.
Connell, John	Indemnity for losses on naval contract.	11	3	Rep. of Secretary Navy.	495	Claims.						
Connell, John	Indemnity for losses on naval contract.	12	1	Petition	21	Claims	Dec. 30, 1811	Adverse	......	Referred to Committee Whole House.	....	Leave to withdraw.
Connelly, John G.	(See Cincinnatus Trousdale.)											
Connelly, Alexander	Refunding of certain money collected by him for Post Office Department.	28	1	Petition	73	P. Of. and P. Roads.						
Connelly, Michael	(See William Copeland and others)											
Connelsky, *alias* Chalenge, *alias* Connooluskee, *alias* Connelsky, Jones, (a Cherokee Indian.)	(See William Wilson and others.) (See Catharine Riley and others.) (See Joseph Elliott and others.)	7	2	....	295							
Conaleskee, *alias* Chalenge, &c.	Permission to dispose of land secured to him for life by treaty.	21	1	Petition	60	Public Lands	69	Report and bill.	97	Passed	Passed	App'd May 29, 1830
Conner, Benjamin, (N. H.)	Restoration to rank as captain of Topographical Engineers, and arrears of pay.	19	1	Petition	130	Military Affairs	....	....	......	Discharged; laid on table.		
Conner, Benjamin, (N. H.)	Revolutionary pension	21	1	Petitions	294, 695	Military Pensions	....	....	......	Discharged; laid on table.		
Conner, Benjamin, (N. H.)	Revolutionary pension	21	2	Petition	53	Military Pensions	....	....	......	Discharged; referred to Com. Rev. Claims.		
Conner, Benjamin, (N. H.)	Revolutionary pension	22	1	Memorial	198	Rev. Pensions	....	....	......	Discharged; laid on table.		
Conner, Henry, (Mich.)	Compensation for services in war of 1812.	19	2	Petition	240	Claims.						
Conner, Henry, (Mich.)	Compensation for services in war of 1812.	20	1	Petition	105	Claims	Jan. 11, 1828	Adverse	......	Laid on table.		
Conner, Henry, (Mich.)	Land to complete quantity granted by act of May 11, 1820.	23	1	Petition	158	Priv. Land Claims.						
Conner, James	Compensation for horse taken by the British in war of 1812.	15	1	Petition	265	Claims	March 9, 1818	Adverse	......	Laid on table.		
Conner, John, heirs of	Confirmation of title to land in Mississippi.	15	2	Petition	230	Priv. Land Claims.	....	....	......	Discharged; laid on table.		
Conner, John	(See David Gould, administrator of the heir of.)											
Conner, Joseph	Revolutionary pension	19	1	Resolution	523	Military Pensions	May 9, 1826	Favorable	......	Referred to Committee Whole House on bill No. 119.		
Conner, Joseph	Revolutionary pension	19	2	Resolution	48	Military Pensions	Dec. 22, 1826	By bill	315	Passed.	Indef. postp'd.	
Conner, Noah	Invalid pension	26	1	Petition	198	Invalid Pensions	247	Adverse	......	Laid on table.		
Conner, Patrick	(See John McElroy and others.)											
Conner, Patrick, (Md.)	Arrears of pension	20	1	Petition	310	Military Pensions	....	....	......	Discharged; laid on table.		
Conner, Patrick, (Md.)	Arrears of pension	20	2	House bill	55	Whole House	Jan. 15, 1829	Favorable	311	Passed	Laid on table.	
Conner, Patrick, heirs of.	Arrears of pension	21	1	House bill	130	Whole House	Feb. 12, 1830	Amended	72	Passed.	Passed	App'd May 20, 1830
Conner, Patrick, widow of	Arrears of pension	21	2	Petition	209	Military Pensions.						
Conner, Patrick, widow of.	Arrears of pension	22	1	Resolution	71	Invalid Pensions.						
Conner, Samuel	(See Canadian refugees.)											
Conner, William Jackson, heirs of.	Allowance for depreciation of pay and other emoluments due for revolutionary services.	5	2	Petition	150	Claims	Feb. 8, 1798	Adverse	......	Rejected.		

List of private claims presented to the House of Representatives of the United States from the 1st to the 31st Congress, inclusive—Continued.

Names of claimants.	Nature or object of the claim.	Congress.	Session.	How brought before the House of Reps.	Page of journal.	To what committee of the House referred.	No. or date of the report.	Nature of the report.	No. of the bill.	How disposed of by the House of Reps.	How disposed of by the Senate.	Date of the act of Congress, and remarks.
Conner, William, (Ind.)	Grant of land at Delaware towns, Indiana, to Conner and wife (an Indian woman) and children.	17	1	Senate bill	374	Public Lands	Mar. 28, 1822	With't amend.	50	Passed	Passed	App'd May 7, 1822
Conner, William, (Ind.)	That the patent for land granted to him and family, jointly, may issue in severalty.	18	1	Resolution	182	Public Lands	....	....	......	Discharged; laid on table.		
Conner, William, (Ind.)	That the patent for land granted to him and family, jointly, may issue in severalty.	18	2	Resolution	233	Public Lands.						
Conner, William, (Ind.)	Amendment to act of May 7, 1822, vesting a fee simple title to the land granted in him.	20	1	Senate bill	585	Judiciary	May 24, 1828	With't amend.	77	Laid on table.		
Conner, William, (Conn.)	Increase of compensation as surveyor of customs.	20	1	Petition	221	Commerce.						
Conner, William, (Ky.,) heirs of.	Five years full pay or commutation for services of deceased as ensign in revolutionary war.	25	2	Petition	81	Rev. Claims	741	Adverse	......	Laid on table.		
Connolly, Hugh	Revolutionary pension	14	1	Petition	512	Pens. & Rev. Cl'ms.	....		......	Discharged; laid on table.	....	Referred to Secretary War, December 23, 1816.
Connolly, Owen	Compensation for injuries received from a fall while watchman at the Capitol.	31	1	Petition	909	Public Buildings.						
Connolly, Robert	Compensation for loss of sight and other injuries sustained in revolutionary war.	1	2	Petition	283	....	....	....	......	Referred to Secretary War.		
Connolly, Robert	Compensation for loss of sight and other injuries sustained in revolutionary war.	1	3	Rep. of Secretary War.	393	....	....	....	......	Laid on table.		
Connolly, Robert	Invalid pension	3	2	Rep. of Secretary War.	278	Claims.						
Connolly, Robert	Invalid pension	4	1	Rep. of Secretary War.	445	Claims.						
Connolly, Robert	Invalid pension	9	1	Petition	210	Claims	Mar. 28, 1806	To indef. postpone & leave to withdraw.	......	Report adopted.		
Connor, Benjamin	Compensation for use of his patent for jointing planks in United States navy yards.	18	2	Petition	161	Judiciary	....	....	......	Discharged; leave to withdraw.		
Connor, Betsy	Compensation for services as hospital nurse at Fort Constitution.	27	1	Petition	106	Military Affairs.						
Connor, Betsy	Compensation for services as hospital nurse at Fort Constitution.	27	2	Petition	53	Claims	699	Adverse	......	Laid on table.		
Connor, Edward	Pension as an officer in revolutionary army.	16	1	Petition	163	Rev. Pensions	April 6, 1820	Adverse	......	Laid on table.		
Connor, Morgan, heirs of.	Allowance for depreciation of pay and arrears due for services as lieutenant colonel in revolutionary war.	11	2	Petition	176	Claims	Jan. 31, 1810	Adverse	......	Laid on table.		
Conover, Thomas D. heirs of.	Pension for revolutionary services.	28	1	Petition	288	Rev. Pensions.						

List of private claims presented to the House of Representatives of the United States from the 1st to the 31st Congress, inclusive—Continued.

Names of claimants.	Nature or object of the claim.	Congress.	Session.	How brought before the House of Reps.	Page of journal.	To what committee of the House referred.	No. or date of the report.	Nature of the report.	No. of the bill.	How disposed of by the House of Reps.	How disposed of by the Senate.	Date of the act of Congress, and remarks.
Constable, William, & Co.	Drawback of duty on teas exported to France.	2	2	Petition	622	....	....	....	.....	Referred to Secretary Treasury.		
Constable, William, & Co.	Drawback of duty on teas exported to France.	3	2	Rep. of Secretary Treasury.	284	....	....	....	.....	Laid on table.		
Constable, William and James.	Liquidation of bills of credit of certain States under act of March 18, 1780.	4	1	Rep. of Secretary Treasury.	388	Claims..........	May 31, 1796	Adverse	.....	Laid on table.		
Constable, William and James.	Liquidation of bills of credit of certain States under act of March 18, 1780.	4	2	Petition	629	Claims.						
Constable, William and James.	Liquidation of bills of credit of certain States under act of March 18, 1780.	5	2	Petition	....	Claims..........	Feb. 26, 1798	Adverse	.....	Report adopted.		
Constable, William and James, excutors of.	Indemnity for French spoliations prior to 1800.	26	1	Memorial	182	Foreign Affairs....	343	Favorable; bill.	319	Referred to Committee Whole House.		
Constantine, Thomas	Compensation for furnishing with desks for the House, two hundred inks and sands, not in the contract.	16	1	Petition	333	Accounts........	Mar. 31, 1820	Rep. and res., to pay $250.	.....	Resolution adopted.		
Constitution, United States frigate.	(See Charles Stewart *et al.*)	14	1	....	116							
Contractors, for the manufacture of arms.	Extra allowance over contract price.	13	2	Petition	389	....	....	....	.....	Laid on table.		
Conture, Jean Baptiste ...	Indemnity for property destroyed by British in war of 1812.	15	1	Report of Com. of Claims.	195	Claims..........	....	....	.....	Discharged.		
Conture, Jean Baptiste. ..	Indemnity for property destroyed by British in war of 1812.	16	1	Report former...	106	Claims	....	....	.....	Discharged; laid on table.		
Conture, Jean Baptiste ...	Indemnity for property destroyed by British in war of 1812.	16	2	Report, former..	....	Claims	33	Adverse	.....	Referred to Committee Whole House.	....	Leave to withdraw.
Conture, Jean Baptiste, administrator of.	Indemnity for property destroyed by British in war of 1812.	17	1	Petition	47	Claims	34	Adverse	.....	Referred to Committee Whole House.		
Conture, Jean Baptiste, administrator of.	Indemnity for property destroyed by British in war of 1812.	18	1	Petition	159	Claims.						
Conture, Jean Baptiste, administrator of.	Indemnity for property destroyed by British in war of 1812.	20	1	Petition	57	Claims	....	....	.....	Discharged; laid on table.		
Conture, Jean Baptiste, administrator of.	Indemnity for property destroyed by British in war of 1812.	20	2	Petition	40	Claims	51	Report and bill	380	Referred to Committee Whole House.		
Conture, Jean Baptiste, administrator of.	Indemnity for property destroyed by British in war of 1812.	21	1	Petition	....	Claims..........	33	Report and bill.	45	Passed	Passed......	App'd April 7, 1830
Conture, Medad.........	Compensation for a horse &c., lost at the surrender of Detroit in war of 1812.	23	1	Petition	59	Claims.						
Converse, Daniel	Compensation for horse impressed in U. S service, war of 1812.	15	2	Petition	62	Claims	....	....	.....	Discharged; laid on table.		
Converse, Daniel........	Compensation for horse impressed in U. S. service, war of 1812.	16	1	Petition	....	Claims..........	Feb. 21, 1820 Mar. 22, 1820	Report and bill. Report and bill.	84 112	Recommitted. Passed	 Passed	 App'd May 8, 1820
Converse, John P., and Henry J. Reese.	Interest on certain protested drafts on Post Office department.	24	2	Petition	394	Claims	246	Report and bill.	945	Referred to Committee Whole House.		
Converse, John P., and Henry J. Reese.	Interest on certain protested drafts on Post Office department.	25	2	Petition	37	Claims..........	67	Report and bill.	79	Passed.		
Converse, John P., and Henry J. Reese.	Interest on certain protested drafts on Post Office department.	26	1	Senate bill	811	P. Of. and P. Roads.	July 21, 1840	With't amend.	168	Laid on table.		

List of private claims presented to the House of Representatives of the United States from the 1st to the 31st Congress, inclusive—Continued.

Names of claimants.	Nature or object of the claim.	Congress.	Session.	How brought before the House of Reps.	Page of journal.	To what committee of the House referred.	No. or date of the report.	Nature of the report.	No. of the bill.	How disposed of by the House of Reps.	How disposed of by the Senate.	Date of the act of Congress, and remarks.
Converse, John P., and Henry J. Reese.	Interest on certain protested drafts on Post Office department.	26	2	Petition	38	P. Of. & P. Roads.						
Converse, John P., and Henry J. Reese.	Interest on certain protested drafts on Post Office department.	26	2	Senate bill	334	....	....	....	207			
Converse, John P., and Henry J. Reese.	Interest on certain protested drafts on Post Office department.	27	2	Petition	334	Claims	47	Report and bill	82	Passed	Passed	App'd Aug. 1, 1842
Converse, John P	Payment of expenses in settling judgment against him as United States mail contractor.	28	1	Petition	80	Claims	314	Report and bill.	221	Passed	Adverse report.	
Converse, John P	Payment of expenses in settling judgment against him as United States mail contractor.	28	2	Petition	144	Claims	54	Report and bill.	534	Passed	With't amend.	
Converse, John P	Payment of expenses in settling judgment against him as United States mail contractor.	29	1	Petition	67	Claims	373	Adverse	....	Laid on table.		
Converse, Jonn P	Payment of expenses in settling judgment against him as United States mail contractor.	30	1	Petition	214	Claims	100	Report and bill.	90	Recommitted.		
							July 12, 1848	With amend.	90	Referred to Committee Whole House.		
Converse, John P	Payment of expenses in settling judgment against him as United States mail contractor.	31	1	Petition	324	Claims	165	Adverse	....	Laid on table.		
Converse, John P	Payment of expenses in settling judgment against him as United States mail contractor.	31	2	Petition	67	P. Of. and P. Roads.						
Converse, Josiah, widow of	Bounty land due deceased as an ensign in revolutionary war.	23	1	Petition	329	Rev. Claims.						
Converse, Josiah, widow of	Bounty land due deceased as an ensign in revolutionary war.	23	2	Petition	230	Rev. Claims.						
Converse, Josiah, widow of	Bounty land due deceased as an ensign in revolutionary war.	24	2	Petition	....	Rev. Claims.						
Converse, Josiah, widow of	Bounty land due deceased as an ensign in revolutionary war.	25	3	Petition	221	Rev. Claims	....	....	....	Discharged.		
Converse, Josiah, widow of	Bounty land due deceased as an ensign in revolutionary war.	26	1	Petition	282	Rev. Claims.						
Converse, Josiah, widow of	Bounty land due deceased as an ensign in revolutionary war.	26	2	Petition	36	Rev. Claims.						
Converse, Josiah, widow of	Bounty land due deceased as an ensign in revolutionary war.	28	1	Petition	100	Rev. Claims.						
Converse, Josiah, widow of	Bounty land due deceased as an ensign in revolutionary war.	29	1	Petition	126	Rev. Claims	593	Report and bill.	412	Laid on table.		
Converse, Josiah, widow of	Bounty land due deceased as an ensign in revolutionary war.	29	2	Bill of last sess.	382	....	....	....	412	Passed.		
Converse, Josiah, widow of	Bounty land due deceased as an ensign in revolutionary war.	30	1	Petition	156	Rev. Claims	272	Report and bill.	265	Passed.		
Converse, Josiah, widow of	Bounty land due deceased as an ensign in revolutionary war.	31	1	Petition	276	Rev. Claims.						
Converse, Royal	Release from imprisonment at suit of United States.	12	2	Petition	577	Select	Dec. 30, 1812	By bill	219	Passed	Passed	App'd Feb. 25, 1813
Converse, Wright	Payment for slaves placed on board a ship of war in 1783 and captured by the British.	23	1	Petition	40	Rev. Claims.						

List of private claims presented to the House of Representatives of the United States from the 1st to the 31st Congress, inclusive—Continued.

49

Names of claimants.	Nature or object of the claim.	Congress.	Session.	How brought before the House of Reps.	Page of journal.	To what committee of the House referred.	No. or date of the report.	Nature of the report.	No. of the bill.	How disposed of by the House of Reps.	How disposed of by the Senate.	Date of the act of Congress, and remarks.
Converse, Wright	Payment for slaves placed on board a ship of war in 1783, and captured by the British.	23	2	Petition	59	Rev. Claims				Discharged; laid on table.		
Conway, Edwin, widow of	Extension of pension	30	1	Petition	274	Naval Affairs	444	Report and bill.	375	Referred to Committee Whole House.		
Conway, Henry	To file in land office in Alabama evidence of his title to land.	15	1	Petition	45	Priv. Land Claims				Discharged; laid on table.		
Conway, Henry	(See Wm. Tarvin, heirs of.)											
Conway, Henry, heirs of	Commutation pay due as a captain in revolutionary army.	23	1	Petition	40, 100	Rev. Claims.						
Conway, Henry, heirs of	Commutation pay due as a captain in revolutionary army.	24	1	Petition	104	Rev. Claims.						
Conway, Henry, heirs of	Commutation pay due as a captain in revolutionary army.	24	2	Petition	40	Rev. Claims.						
Conway, James, heirs of	Seven years' half pay as lieutenant in revolutionary army.	24	1	Petition	753	Rev. Claims	635	Report and bill.	614	Referred to Committee Whole House.		
Conway, James, heirs of	Seven years' half-pay as lieutenant in revolutionary army.	25	2	Petition	39	Rev. Claims	191	Report and bill.	217	Passed.		
Conway, James, heirs of	Seven years' half-pay as lieutenant in revolutionary army.	25	3	Petition	84	Rev. Claims	9	Report and bill.	906	Referred to Committee Whole House.		
Conway, James, heirs of	Seven years' half-pay as lieutenant in revolutionary army.	26	1	Petition	165	Rev. Claims.						
Conway, James, heirs of	Seven years' half-pay as lieutenant in revolutionary army.	26	2	Petition	36	Rev. Claims.						
Conway, James, heirs of	Seven years' half pay as lieutenant in revolutionary army.	27	2	Petition	73	Rev. Claims.	276	Report and bill.	242	Referred to Committee Whole House.		See report No. 777.
Conway, James, heirs of	Seven years' half-pay as lieutenant in revolutionary army.	28	2	Petition	112	Rev. Claims.						
Conway, James, heirs of	Seven years' half pay as lieutenant in revolutionary army.	29	1	Petition	257	Rev. Claims.						
Conway, James, heirs of	Seven years' half-pay as lieutenant in revolutionary army.	30	1	Petition	298	Rev. Claims.						
Conway, James, heirs of	Seven years' half-pay as lieutenant in revolutionary army.	31	1	Petition	616	Rev. Claims	338	Adverse		Laid on table.		
Conway, James S	Release from a judgment of United States court for Arkansas.	29	2	Senate bill	381	Judiciary	Feb. 24, 1847	With't amend.	149	Passed	Passed	App'd Feb. 25, 1847
Conway, Samuel	Remission of balance due on land in consideration of services as a revolutionary soldier.	17	2	Petition	144	Priv. Land Claims.	Jan. 29, 1823	Adverse		Laid on table.		
Conway, Samuel	Grant of land for services in revolutionary army.	18	1	Petition	215	Priv. Land Claims.						
Conway, Samuel	Grant of land for services in revolutionary army.	18	2	Petition	142	Priv. Land Claims.	Jan. 18, 1825	Report and res.; adverse.		Resolution adopted.		
Conway, Samuel	Grant of land for services in revolutionary army.	19	1	Petition	78	Rev. Claims	Feb. 1, 1826	Adverse		Laid on table.		
Conway, Samuel	Revolutionary pension	19	1	Resolution	232	Military Pensions	164	Advers		Laid on table.		
Conway, Samuel	Revolutionary pension	19	2	Petition	91	Rev. Claims	Jan. 16, 1827	Adverse		Laid on table.		
Conway, William, heirs of	Land in lieu of that sold by government to which they held claim.	24	1	Senate bill	932	Priv. Land Claims.	Jan. 9, 1836	With't amend.	144	Passed	Passed	App'd July 2, 1836
Conway, William, heirs of	Permission to locate any United States land in Louisiana, under act for their relief.	24	2	Petition	49	Priv. Land Claims				Discharged; laid on table.		

List of private claims presented to the House of Representatives of the United States from the 1st to the 31st Congress, inclusive—Continued.

Names of claimants.	Nature or object of the claim.	Congress.	Session.	How brought before the House of Reps.	Page of journal.	To what committee of the House referred.	No. or date of the report.	Nature of the report.	No. of the bill.	How disposed of by the House of Reps.	How disposed of by the Senate.	Date of the act of Congress, and remarks.
Conway, William, heirs of.	Permission to locate any United States land in Louisiana, under act for their relief.	25	3	Senate bill	478	Priv. Land Claims.			254			
Conway, William, heirs of.	Permission to locate any United States land in Louisiana, under act for their relief.	26	1	Senate bill	420	Priv. Land Claims.	June 23, 1840	With't amend.	61	Referred to Committee Whole House.		
Conway, William, heirs of.	Permission to locate any United States land in Louisiana, under act for their relief.	26	2	Senate bill	221	Priv. Land Claims.			116			
Conway & Whittle, surviving partner of.	Repayment of money erroneously paid under French treaty of 1831.	25	2	Senate bill	675	Ways and Means.	Mar. 30, 1838	With't amend.	283	Passed	Passed	App'd April 4, 1838
Conyne, Peter	Invalid pension	11	2	House bill	283	Whole House	Mar. 24, 1810	Favorable	108	Passed	Passed	App'd April 27, 1810
Conyngham, D. H	Indemnity for French spoliations prior to 1800.	26	1	Memorial	182	Foreign Affairs	343	Favorable; bill.	319	Referred to Committee Whole House.		
Conyngham, D. H. executor of.	Indemnity for French spoliations prior to 1800.	31	1	Petition	196	Foreign Affairs	355	Report and bill.	318	Referred to Committee Whole House.		
Conyngham, Gustavus	Compensation for naval services in revolutionary war.	2	1	Petition	446					Referred to Secretary Treasury.		
Conyngham, Gustavus	Compensation for naval services in revolutionary war.	3	2	Report of Secretary Treasury.	284					Laid on table.		
Conyngham, Nesbitt, & Co.	Indemnity for French spoliations prior to 1800.	26	1	Memorial	182	Foreign Affairs	343	Favorable; bill	319	Referred to Committee Whole House.		
Coody, Charles H	(See Wm. H. Bedford, agent, &c.)	28	1		262							
Coodey, William S	(See Indians, Cherokee, agent of.)	21	2		233							
Coody, Susan, and others.	Settlement of claims for property destroyed by United States troops at Fort Gibson in 1845.	30	2	Senate resolution.	573					Laid on table.		
Cook, Aaron	Relief for wounds received in revolutionary war.	2	1	Petition	470					Referred to Secretary of War.		
Cook, Aaron	Invalid pension	3	1	Rep. of Secretary War.	131	Select	May 26, 1794	Ref. to Secretary, with instructions.	R. 12	Passed	Passed	App'd June 9, 1794
Cook, Aaron	Invalid pension	3	2	Rep. of Secretary War.	278	Claims.						
Cook, Aaron	Invalid pension	4	1	Rep. of Secretary War.	445	Claims.						
Cook, Abraham	Revolutionary pension	27	2	Petition	524	Rev. Pensions	784	Adverse		Laid on table.		
Cook, Alston	Pension	14	1	Petition	574	Pens. & Rev. Cl'ms.	April 11, 1816	By bill	171	Passed	Passed	App'd April 30, 1816
Cook, Anthony, Mahon, and others.	Indemnity for treasury notes stolen from the mail.	30	1	Senate bill	826	Judiciary	July 19, 1848	With't amend.	S. 113	Passed		App'd Aug. 14, 1848
Cook, Archibald	Revolutionary pension	22	1	Petition	470	Rev. Pensions				Discharged; laid on table.		
Cooke, Bates	(See Rufus Spalding and others.)											
Cooke, Bates	(See Alexander Watson, administrator of.)											
Cook, Benjamin, widow of.	Revolutionary pension	26	1	Petition	962	Rev. Claims.						
Cook, Caroline M	(See John Nelson, heir of.)											
Cook, Casper B., & others.	Compensation for services as musicians in war of 1812.	26	1	Petition	702	Claims.						
Cook, Casper B., & others.	Compensation for services as musicians in war of 1812.	27	2	Petition	154	Claims	501	Adverse		Laid on table.		
Cook, Casper B., & others.	Compensation for services as musicians in war of 1812.	29	1	Petition	218	Military Affairs	241	Adverse		Laid on table.		
Cook, Casper B., & others.	Compensation for services as musicians in war of 1812.	30	1	Petition	272	Claims	245	Report and bill.	241	Referred to Committee Whole House.		

List of private claims presented to the House of Representatives of the United States from the 1st to the 31st Congress, inclusive—Continued.

Names of claimants.	Nature or object of the claim.	Congress.	Session.	How brought before the House of Reps.	Page of journal.	To what committee of the House referred.	No. or date of the report.	Nature of the report.	No. of the bill.	How disposed of by the House of Reps.	How disposed of by the Senate.	Date of the act of Congress, and remarks.
Cooke, Cassius D.	Compensation for services and property lost in war of 1812.	23	2	Petition	163	Claims.						
Cook, Daniel	Invalid pension	6	1	Petition	562	Claims	Feb. 11, 1800	Adverse		Rejected.		
Cook, Daniel, (Vt.)	Invalid pension	13	2	Petition	336	Pens. & Rev. Cl'ms.	Mar. 28, 1814	Report not extant.		Referred to Committee Whole House, on bill No. 166.		
Cook, Daniel	Restoration of pension	19	1	Resolution	429	Military Pensions	May 3, 1826	Rep. and res.; adverse.		Resolution adopted.		
Cook, Daniel, (N. Y.)	Increase of pension	27	2	Petition	239	Invalid Pensions	417	Adverse		Laid on table.		
Cook, David	Compensation for services in revolutionary war.	1	2	Petition and rep't Sec. of War.	162	Select	April 5, 1790	By bill	53	Engrossment ordered.		
Cook, David	Compensation for services in revolutionary war.	1	3	Petition and rep't Sec. of War.	378	Select	Mar. 2, 1791	By bill	140	Read once.		
Cook, David	Compensation for services in revolutionary war.	2	1	Petition	448	Select	Nov. 25, 1791	Report and bill.	153	Passed	Passed	App'd Dec. 16, 1791
Cooke, David, (Pa.)	Payment for gunpowder furnished United States in 1814.	23	2	Petition and rep't Sec. of War.	59	Claims.						
Cooke, David, (Pa.)	Payment for gunpowder furnished United States in 1814.	24	1	Petition	93	Claims	Jan. 23, 1836	Adverse		Laid on table.		
Cooke, David, (Pa.)	Payment for gunpowder furnished United States in 1814.	25	2	Petition	398	Claims	789	Adverse		Laid on table.		
Cooke, David, (Pa.)	Payment for gunpowder furnished United States in 1814.	27	3	Petition	210	Judiciary	223	Adverse		Laid on table.		
Cooke, David, (Pa.)	Payment for gunpowder furnished United States in 1814.	28	1	Petition	275	Judiciary	249	Adverse		Laid on table.		
Cooke, David, (Pa.)	Payment for gunpowder furnished United States in 1814.	30	1	Petition	187	Claims	472	Adverse		Laid on table.		
Cook, Edward P.	Pension	21	1	Petition	411	Military pensions	April 13, 1830	Adverse		Laid on table.		
Cook, Edward P.	Pension	21	2	Petition	336	Military Pensions.						
Cook, Elijah	Award of proceeds of prize captured to officers and men of privateer armed schooner Madison.	13	3	Petition	678	Ways and Means				Discharged.		
Cook, Elijah	Award of proceeds of prize captured to officers and men of privateer armed schooner Madison.	15	2	Petition	249	Claims				Discharged; laid on table.		
Cook, Elijah	Award of proceeds of prize captured to officers and men of privateer armed schooner Madison.	18	2	Petition	134	Claims.						
Cook, Elijah	Award of proceeds of prize captured to officers and men of privateer armed schooner Madison.	19	1	Petition	152	Ways and Means	Jan. 18, 1826 May 5, 1826	Adverse Adverse		Recommitted. Referred to Committee Whole House.		
Cook, Elijah	Award of proceeds of prize captured to officers and men of privateer armed schooner Madison.	19	2	Petition and rep't of last session.	99	Claims	Jan. 3, 1827	Adverse		Laid on table.		
Cook, Elijah	Award of proceeds of prize captured to officers and men of privateer armed schooner Madison.	20	1	Petition	222	Ways and Means				Discharged; laid on table.		
Cook, Elijah	Award of proceeds of prize captured to officers and men of privateer armed schooner Madison.	21	1	Petition	39	Ways and Means	Jan. 27, 1830	Adverse		Laid on table.		
Cook, Elijah, administratrix of, and others.	Award of proceeds of prize captured to officers and men of privateer armed schooner Madison.	21	2	Petition	99	Ways and Means	Jan. 11, 1831	Adverse		Laid on table.		

List of private claims presented to the House of Representatives of the United States from the 1st to the 31st Congress, inclusive—**Continued.**

Names of claimants.	Nature or object of the claim.	Congress.	Session.	How brought before the House of Reps.	Page of journal.	To what committee of the House referred.	No. or date of the report.	Nature of the report.	No. of the bill.	How disposed of by the House of Reps.	How disposed of by the Senate.	Date of the act of Congress, and remarks.
Cook, Elijah, administratrix of, and others.	Award of proceeds of prize captured to officers and men of privateer armed schooner Madison.	22	1	Petition	41	Ways and Means	....	....	....	Discharged; laid on table.		
Cook, Eliza, (half breed Indian.)	Land under treaty with Ottawas and Chippewas of 1836.	24	1	House bill	1012	Whole House	June 30, 1836	With't amend.	695	Passed	Passed	App'd July 2, 1836
Cook, Foster	(See John McAllister.)											
Cook, George	Confirmation of title to land in Territory of Missouri.	15	1	Petition	312	Priv. Land Claims.	....	....	....	Discharged; laid on table.		
Cook, George	Confirmation of title to land in Territory of Missouri.	16	1	Petition	72	Priv. Land Claims.	....	....	....	Discharged; laid on table.		
Cook, George	Confirmation of title to land in Territory of Missouri.	17	1	Petition	53	Public Lands	....	....	....	Discharged; laid on table.		
Cook, George	Confirmation of title to land in Territory of Missouri.	18	1	Petition	53	Public Lands	Jan. 16, 1824	By bill	65	Passed	Passed	App'd May 26, 1824
Cook, George, of Tenn., widow of.	Pension, husband having died in U. S. service, war of 1812.	16	1	Petition	232	Claims	April 5, 1820	Adverse	....	Laid on table.		
Cook, George, of Tenn., widow of.	Compensation for wagon and five horses lost in U. S. service.	25	2	Petition	921	Claims	1007	Adverse	....	Laid on table.		
Cook, George, of Tenn., widow of.	Compensation for wagon and five horses lost in U. S. service.	28	1	Petition	1009	Claims.						
Cook, George, of Tenn., widow of.	Compensation for wagon and five horses lost in U. S. service.	29	1	Petition	493	Claims	....	....	....	Discharged; laid on table.		
Cook, George, of Tenn., widow of.	Compensation for wagon and five horses lost in U. S. service.	30	1	Petition & add'l evidence.	360	Claims.						
Cook, George, of Tenn., widow of.	Compensation for wagon and five horses lost in U. S. service.	31	1	Petition	695	Claims.						
Cook, George, of Md., heirs of.	Compensation for services as a revolutionary soldier.	25	2	Petition	231	Rev. Pensions	....	....	....	Discharged: laid on table.		
Cook, George, of Md., heirs of.	Compensation for services as a revolutionary soldier.	26	2	Petition	35	Rev. Claims						
Cook, G. B.	Indemnity for French spoliations prior to 1800.	26	1	Memorial	182	Foreign Affairs	343	Favorable; bill	319	Referred to Committee Whole House.		
Cook, George K.	Pension	24	1	Petition	97	Invalid Pensions	Feb. 4, 1836	Adverse	....	Laid on table.		
Cook, Harris	(See John W. Clarke and others.)											
Cook, Henry	(See John McCormick, heirs of.)											
Cook, Isaac	Grant of an improved quarter section of land on an Indian reservation in Ohio.	24	2	Memorial	312	Public Lands.						
Cook, Isaac, and others, (Ohio.)	Compensation for schooner Tempest, impressed in United States service in 1814.	25	3	Petition	121	Claims.						
Cook, Isaac, and others, (Ohio.)	Compensation for schooner Tempest, impressed in United States service in 1814.	26	1	Petition	337	Claims.						
Cook, Isaac, and others, (Ohio.)	Compensation for schooner Tempest, impressed in United States service in 1814.	26	2	Petition	38	Claims.						
Cook, Isaac, and others, (Ohio.)	Compensation for schooner Tempest, impressed in United States service in 1814.	27	2	Petition	94	Claims	495	Adverse	....	Laid on table.		
Cook, Isaac, and others, (Ohio.)	Compensation for schooner Tempest, impressed in United States service in 1814.	29	1	Petition	638	Claims	723	Adverse	....	Laid on table.		

List of private claims presented to the House of Representatives of the United States from the 1st to the 31st Congress, inclusive—Continued.

Names of claimants.	Nature or object of the claim.	Congress.	Session.	How brought before the House of Reps.	Page of journal.	To what committee of the House referred.	No. or date of the report.	Nature of the report.	No. of the bill.	How disposed of by the House of Reps.	How disposed of by the Senate.	Date of the act of Congress, and remarks.
Cook, Isaac, and others, (Ohio.)	Compensation for schooner Tempest, impressed in United States service in 1814.	30	1	Petition	270	Claims.						
Cook, Isaac, and others, (Ohio.)	Compensation for schooner Tempest, impressed in United States service in 1814.	30	2	Petition	322	Claims	136	Adverse		Laid on table.		
Cook, Isaac, and others, (Ohio.)	Compensation for schooner Tempest, impressed in United States service in 1814.	31	1	Petition	711	Claims	327	Report and bill.	284	Referred to Committee Whole House.		
Cook, Isaac, and others, (Ohio.)	Compensation for schooner Tempest, impressed in United States service in 1814.	31	2	Bill of last sess.	181	Whole House	Jan. 24, 1851	With't amend.	284	Passed	Ref. to Com. on Claims.	
Cook, James	(See Elijah Cook, administrator of)											
Cook, James	(See James Devereaux and others)											
Cook, James	(See James McLaughlin, assignee of.)											
Cook, John	(See Kennedy, Lampas & Co., assignee of.)											
Cook, John	(See William & Kennedy Lampas, assignee of.)											
Cook, John	(See Miles King, heirs of.)											
Cook, John, widow of	Revolutionary pension	30	1	Petition	798	Rev. Pensions				Discharged; laid on table.		
Cook, John, heirs of	Compensation for services as commander of ship Defence in the revolutionary war, and for property seized by the British.	23	1	Petition	439	Rev. Claims.						
Cook, John, heirs of	Compensation for services as commander of ship Defence in the revolutionary war, and for property seized by the British.	23	2	Petition	67	Rev. Claims.						
Cook, John, heirs of	Compensation for services as commander of ship Defence in the revolutionary war, and for property seized by the British.	27	2	Petition	268	Rev. Claims.						
Cook, John, heirs of	Compensation for services as commander of ship Defence in the revolutionary war, and for property seized by the British.	28	1	Petition	60	Rev. Claims				Discharged; laid on table.		
Cook, John, and others	Fishing bounty on schooner Fox, lost at sea.	19	1	Petition	222	Commerce				Discharged; laid on table.		
Cooke, John K.	Indemnity for losses, &c., as consul at Xibara, Cuba.	28	1	Petition	880	Foreign Affairs.						
Cooke, John K.	Indemnity for losses, &c., as consul at Xibara, Cuba.	28	2	Petition	205	Foreign Affairs	170	Report and bill.	638	Referred to Committee Whole House.		
Cooke, John K.	Indemnity for losses, &c., as consul at Xibara, Cuba.	29	1	Petition	498	Foreign Affairs.						
Cook, John P.	(See Caspar B. Cook and others.)											
Cook, John R.	Additional compensation as postmaster at Rains' Tavern, Va.	25	2	Resolution	761	P. Of. & P. Roads.	May 17, 1838	Adverse.				
Cook, John R.	Additional compensation as postmaster at Rains' Tavern, Va.	25	3	Resolution	91	P. Of. & P. Roads.				Discharged.		
Cook, John W.	Pension	21	2	Petition	113	Military Pensions.						

List of private claims presented to the House of Representatives of the United States from the 1st to the 31st Congress, inclusive—Continued.

Names of claimants.	Nature or object of the claim.	Congress.	Session.	How brought before the House of Reps.	Page of journal.	To what committee of the House referred.	No. or date of the report.	Nature of the report.	No. of the bill.	How disposed of by the House of Reps.	How disposed of by the Senate.	Date of the act of Congress, and remarks.
Cook, John W.	Pension	22	1	Petition	80	Rev. Pensions	411	Report and bill.	511	Referred to Committee Whole House.		
Cook, Johnson	Revolutionary pension	14	1	Petition	84	Pens. & Rev. Cl'ms.				Discharged; laid on table.		
Cook, Johnson	Revolutionary pension	14	2	Petition	80	Pens. & Rev. Cl'ms.	Jan. 29, 1817	By bill	91	Passed	Passed	App'd March 3, 1817
Cook, Johnson	Increase of pension	15	1	Petition	143	Pens. & Rev. Cl'ms.				Discharged; laid on table.		
Cook, Johnson	Increase of pension	17	1	Petition	89	Pens. & Rev. Cl'ms.	Dec. 28, 1821	Rep. and res. to withdraw.		Resolution adopted.		
Cook, Johnson	Restoration of pension	18	1	Petition	93	Pens. & Rev. Cl'ms	Mar. 9, 1824	Adverse		Laid on table.		
Cook, Johnson	Increase of pension	19	2	Petition	187	Military Pensions.						
Cook, Johnson	Restoration of pension	21	1	Petition	59	Military Pensions.	May 3, 1830	Adverse		Laid on table.		
Cook, Johnson	Arrears of pension	21	2	Petition	209	Military Pensions.						
Cook, Johnson	Arrears of pension	22	1	Petition	189	Invalid Pensions	Feb. 2, 1832	Adverse		Laid on table.		
Cook, Johnson	Arrears of pension	22	2	Petition	206	Invalid Pensions.						
Cook, Johnson	Arrears of pension	23	1	Petition	639	Invalid Pensions.						
Cooke, Jonah	Invalid pension	3	1	Rep. of Secretary War.	131	Select	May 26, 1794	To refer to Secretary, with instructions.	R. 12	Passed	Passed	App'd June 9, 1794
Cooke, Jonah	Invalid pension	3	2	Rep. of Secretary War.	278	Claims	Feb. 28, 1795	Favorable; bill ordered.	130	Passed	Postp'd to next session.	
Cooke, Jonah	Invalid pension	4	1	Rep. of Secretary War.	445	Claims	Feb. 18, 1796	Favorable; bill ordered.	156	Passed	Passed	App'd April 20, 1796
Cooke, Jonah	Increase of pension	10	1	House bill	232	Whole House	April 19, 1808	Favorable	78	Passed	Passed	App'd April 25, 1808
Cook, Lemuel, (Mass.)	Restoration of pension	22	1	Resolution	137	Military Pensions.				Discharged; laid on table.		
Cook, Lemuel, (N. Y.)	(See Rufus Spalding, and others.)											
Cook, Lemuel, (N. Y.)	Compensation for property destroyed at Lewiston by the British in war of 1812.	19	2	Petition	159	Claims	Jan. 23, 1827	Adverse		Laid on table.		
Cook, Lemuel, (N. Y.)	Compensation for property destroyed at Lewiston by the British in war of 1812.	20	1	Petition	279	Claims	Feb. 26, 1828	Adverse		Laid on table.		
Cook, Lemuel, (N. Y.)	Compensation for property destroyed at Lewiston by the British in war of 1812.	21	1	Petition	215	Claims	Jan. 27, 1830	Adverse		Laid on table.		
Cook, Lemuel, (N. Y.)	Compensation for property destroyed at Lewiston by the British in war of 1812.	22	1	Petition	49	Claims	228	Adverse		Referred to Committee Whole House.		
Cook, Lemuel, (N. Y.)	Compensation for property destroyed at Lewiston by the British in war of 1812.	22	2	Report of last session.	171	Whole House	Jan. 11, 1833	Concurrence in adv. report.		Recommit'd to Claims.		
Cook, Lemuel, (N. Y.)	Compensation for property destroyed at Lewiston by the British in war of 1812.	23	1	Petition	33	Claims	338	Adverse		Referred to Committee Whole House.		
Cook, Lyman N.	Pension for injuries received in war of 1812.	24	1	Petition	275	Invalid Pensions	June 2, 1836	Adverse		Laid on table.		
Cook, Lyman N.	Pension for injuries received in war of 1812.	25	2	Petition	269	Invalid Pensions				Discharged.		
Cook, Lyman N.	Pension for injuries received in war of 1812.	26	1	Petition	162	Invalid Pensions	208	Report and bill.	220	Passed	Indef. postp'd.	
Cook, Lyman N.	Pension for injuries received in war of 1812.	26	2	Petition	36	Invalid Pensions	158	Report and bill.	670	Referred to Committee Whole House.		

List of private claims presented to the House of Representatives of the United States from the 1st to the 31st Congress, inclusive—Continued.

Names of claimants.	Nature or object of the claim.	Congress.	Session.	How brought before the House of Reps.	Page of journal.	To what committee of the House referred.	No. or date of the report.	Nature of the report.	No. of the bill.	How disposed of by the House of Reps.	How disposed of by the Senate.	Date of the act of Congress, and remarks.
Cook, Lyman N.	Pension for injuries received in war of 1812.	27	2	Petition	756	Invalid Pensions	805	Report and bill	459	Engrossed.		
Cook, Lyman N.	Pension for injuries received in war of 1812.	27	3	Bill of last sess.	89				459	Passed	Passed	App'd March 3, 1843
Cook, Lyman N.	Increase of pension	28	1	Petition	428	Invalid Pensions	375	Adverse		Laid on table.		
Cook, Medad	Pension for services in the war of 1812.	25	3	Petition	460	Invalid Pensions.						
Cook, Medad	Pension for services in the war of 1812.	26	1	Petition	161	Invalid Pensions.	198	Report and bill.	210	Passed	Passed	App'd July 20, 1840
Cook, Moses, heirs of	Money advanced as captain of artificers in revolutionary war.	27	2	Petition	1372	Rev. Claims	1087	Adverse		Laid on table.		
Cook, Moses, heirs of	Money advanced as captain of artificers in revolutionary war.	28	2	Petition	144	Rev. Claims.						
Cook, Moses, heirs of	Money advanced as captain of artificers in revolutionary war.	29	1	Petition	298	Rev. Claims	624	Adverse		Laid on table.		
Cook, Moses, heirs of	Money advanced as captain of artificers in revolutionary war.	30	1	Petition	565	Rev. Claims.						
Cook, Nathaniel	Invalid pension	3	1	Rep. of Secretary War.	131	Select	May 26, 1794	Favorable: bill ordered.	62	Passed	Passed	App'd June 7, 1794
Cook, Nathan, widow of.	Continuation of pension	27	2	Petition	612	Rev. Claims	784	Adverse		Laid on table.		
Cooke, Noah	Compensation for services in revolutionary war.	2	1	Petition	500					Referred to Secretary War.		
Cooke, Noah	Compensation for services in revolutionary war.	3	2	Rep. of Secretary War.	278					Laid on table.		
Cooke, Noah	Revolutionary pension	20	2	Resolution	76					Referred to Committee Whole House, on bill No. 317.		
Cooke, Noah	Revolutionary pension	21	2	Resolution	165	Military Pensions.						
Cook, Orchard, and Abiel Wood, jr.	Remission of duties on rum lost in schooner Mary in 1796.	4	2	Petition	727	Com. and Manuf.						
Cook Orchard, and Abiel Wood, jr.	Remission of duties on rum lost in schooner Mary in 1796.	5	2	Petition	92	Com. and Manuf.	Dec. 18, 1797	Adverse		Recommitted.		
							Dec. 29, 1797	Adverse		Referred to Committee Whole House.		
Cook, Orville	Release from a United States judgment against him, or other reasonable relief.	17	2	Petition	210	Ways and Means.				Discharged; leave to withdraw.		
Cook, Peter	Pension	23	1	Petition	308	Invalid Pensions	June 28, 1834	Adverse		Laid on table.		
Cook, Peter	Pension	24	1	Petition	140	Invalid Pensions	221	Report and bill.	230	Passed	Passed	App'd June 28, 1836
Cook, Raines, heirs of	Money due as a captain in revolutionary army, and interest thereon.	24	2	Petition	91	Rev. Claims.						
Cook, Raines, heirs of	Money due as a captain in revolutionary army, and interest thereon.	25	2	Petition	82	Rev. Claims	912	Adverse		Laid on table.		
Cook, Raines, heirs of	Money due as a captain in revolutionary army, and interest thereon.	26	1	Petition	359	Rev. Claims.						
Cook, Raines, heirs of	Money due as a captain in revolutionary army, and interest thereon.	26	2	Petition	35	Rev. Claims.						
Cook, Rhoda	(See Elijah Cook, administra'x of.)											
Cook, Richard D., heirs of.	Commutation pay for revolutionary services.	25	3	Resolution	512	Rev. Claims.						

List of private claims presented to the House of Representatives of the United States from the 1st to the 31st Congress, inclusive—Continued.

Names of claimants.	Nature or object of the claim.	Congress.	Session.	How brought before the House of Reps.	Page of journal.	To what committee of the House referred.	No. or date of the report	Nature of the report.	No. of the bill.	How disposed of by the House of Reps.	How disposed of by the Senate.	Date of the act of Congress, and remarks.
Cook, Richard D., heirs of.	Commutation pay for revolutionary services.	26	1	Petition	166	Rev. Claims.						
Cook, Rudolph	Invalid pension	3	1	Rep. of Secretary War.	131	Select	May 26, 1794	Ref. to Sec. with instruc.	R. 12	Passed	Passed	App'd June 9, 1794
Cook, Samuel	(See James Devereaux and others.)											
Cook, Seaborn J., deceased, brother of.	Payment of bounty land, and pay due for the benefit of infant heirs.	31	1	Petition	311	Invalid Pensions	387	Adverse		Laid on table.		
Cook, Solomon, administrator of.	Indemnity for French spoliations prior to 1800.	29	1	Memorial	101	Foreign Affairs.						
Cook, Solomon, administrator of.	Indemnity for French spoliations prior to 1800.	31	1	Petition	196	Foreign Affairs	355	Report and bill.	318	Referred to Committee Whole House.		
Cook, Susan	(See Christopher Lambert, heir of.)											
Cook, Sylvanus	Increase of pension	4	1	Petition	370	Claims	Jan. 11, 1796	Adverse		Leave to withdraw.		
Cook, Thomas	Invalid pension	3	1	Report of Secretary of War.	131	Select	May 26, 1794	Referred to Sec. with instructions.	R. 12	Passed	Passed	App'd June 9, 1794
Cook, Thomas	Increase of compensation as collector at Edgartown, Massachusetts.	14	2	Petition	68	Ways and Means	Feb. 7, 1817	By bill	112	Passed	Passed	App'd March 3, 1817
Cooke, Thomas, (Virginia,) heirs of.	Commutation of half pay due as captain in revolutionary army.	23	2	Petition	308	Rev. Claims.						
Cooke, Thomas, (Virginia,) heirs of.	Commutation of half-pay due as captain in revolutionary army.	24	1	Petition	103	Rev. Claims	211	Report and bill.	213	Referred to Committee Whole House.		
Cooke, Thomas, (Virginia,) heirs of.	Commutation of half-pay due as captain in revolutionary army.	24	2	Bill of last sess.	62	Whole House			213			
Cooke, Thomas, (Virginia,) heirs of.	Commutation of half-pay due as captain in revolutionary army.	25	2	Petition	39	Rev. Pensions	245	Report and bill.	286	Passed	Rep'd without amendment.	
Cooke, Thomas, (Virginia,) heirs of.	Commutation of half pay due as captain in revolutionary army.	25	3	Petition	84	Rev. Claims	11	Report and bill.	908	Referred to Committee Whole House.		
Cooke, Thomas, (Virginia,) heirs of.	Commutation of half-pay due as captain in revolutionary army.	26	1	Petition	164	Rev. Claims.						
Cooke, Thomas, (Virginia,) heirs of.	Commutation of half-pay due as captain in revolutionary army.	26	2	Petition	36	Rev. Claims.						
Cooke, Thomas, (Virginia,) heirs of.	Commutation of half-pay due as captain in revolutionary army.	27	2	Petition	61	Rev. Claims	372	Adverse		Laid on table.		
Cooke, Thomas, (Virginia,) heirs of.	Commutation of half pay due as captain in revolutionary army.	31	2	Petition	87	Rev. Claims.						
Cook, Timothy, (Ohio)	Compensation for loss of equipments, &c., in war of 1812.	26	1	Petition	337	Claims.						
Cook, Timothy, (Ohio)	Compensation for loss of equipments, &c., in war of 1812.	27	2	Petition	56	Claims	185	Adverse		Laid on table.		
Cook, Timothy, (Ohio)	Compensation for loss of equipments, &c., in war of 1812.	27	3	Petition	132	Claims	208	Adverse		Laid on table.		
Cook, Timothy, (Mass.)	Increase of pension	29	1	Petition	65	Invalid Pensions.						
Cook, William	Renewal of lost Pennsylvania loan office certificate.	1	3	Petition	349					Laid on table.		
Cooke, William	(See Canadian refugees.)											
Cook, William	Invalid pension	13	3	Amended bill					302	Passed	Passed	App'd March 3, 1815
Cook, William, (Kentucky)	Pension for services in revolutionary army.	16	2	Petition	170	Rev. Pensions	Feb. 15, 1821	Rep. and res.; leave to withdraw.		Resolution adopted.		
Cook, William, (Penn.)	Allowance for office rent in his accounts as quartermaster in United States army, war of 1812.	17	1	Petition	100	Claims				Discharged; laid on table.		

List of private claims presented to the House of Representatives of the United States from the 1st to the 31st Congress, inclusive—Continued.

Names of claimants.	Nature or object of the claim.	Congress.	Session.	How brought before the House of Reps.	Page of journal.	To what committee of the House referred.	No. or date of the report.	Nature of the report.	No. of the bill.	How disposed of by the House of Reps.	How disposed of by the Senate.	Date of the act of Congress, and remarks.
50 Cook, William, (Mass.)	Indemnity for French spoliations prior to 1800.	26	1	Memorial	182	Foreign Affairs	343	Favorable; bill.	319	Referred to Committee Whole House.		
Cook, William, (Mass.)	Pension for wounds, &c., received in naval service.	30	2	Petition	430	Invalid Pensions.						
Cook, William H	Confirmation of title to land in Louisiana.	28	1	Petition	115	Priv. Land Claims.	100	Discharged		Laid on table.		
Cook, Zebedee	Indemnity for French spoliations prior to 1800.	26	1	Memorial	182	Foreign Affairs	343	Favorable; bill.	319	Referred to Committee Whole House.		
Cookers, Elizabeth	Pension	25	2	Petition	70	Rev. Pensions				Referred to Committee Whole House on bill No. 456.		
Cookers, Hermanus	Compensation for grain furnished revolutionary army, and for grinding.	15	1	Petition	179	Claims				Discharged; laid on table.		
Cookers, Hermanus	Compensation for grain furnished revolutionary army, and for grinding.	17	1	Petition	274	Pens. & Rev. Cl'ms.	Mar. 5, 1822	Rep. and res.; adverse.		Resolution adopted.		
Cookers, Hermanus, heirs of.	Compensation for grain furnished revolutionary army, and for grinding.	22	1	Resolution	83	Rev. Claims	Mar. 22, 1832	Adverse		Laid on table.		
Cookerly, Benjamin	(See Benjamin Price, heirs of.)											
Cookerly, Eleanore	(See Benjamin Price, daughter of.)											
Cookerly, John P	(See Benjamin Price, heirs of.)											
Cooksey, Theophilus	Compensation for horse and equipments lost in United States service, in war of 1812.	17	2	Petition	186	Pens. & Rev. Clm's.				Discharged; laid on table.		
Cooksey, Theophilus	Compensation for horse and equipments lost in United States service, in war of 1812.	20	2	Petition	50	Claims	16	Report and bill.	335	Referred to Committee Whole House.		
Cooksey, Theophilus	Compensation for horse and equipments lost in United States service, in war of 1812.	21	1	Petition	51	Claims	Dec. 21, 1829	Report and bill.	10	Passed	Passed	App'd Jan. 30, 1830
Cooley, Aaron	Restoration of pension	17	1	Petition	30	Rev. Claims	Jan. 15, 1822	General bill	37	Passed	Rejected.	See act March 1, 1823
Cooley, Ebenezer	Compensation for loss of improvements on land granted to General Lafayette.	19	1	Petition	154	Priv. Land Claims.				Discharged; laid on table.		
Cooley, Ebenezer	Compensation for loss of improvements on land granted to General Lafayette.	19	2	Petition	32					Referred to Secretary Treasury.		
Cooley, Ebenezer	Compensation for loss of improvements on land granted to General Lafayette.	20	1	Rep. of Secretary Treasury.	171	Public Lands				Discharged; laid on table.		
Cooley, Ebenezer	Compensation for loss of improvements on land granted to General Lafayette.	20	2	Petition	34	Public Lands	28	Report and bill	350	Referred to Committee Whole House.		
Cooley, Ebenezer	Compensation for loss of improvements on land granted to General Lafayette.	21	1	Petition	41	Public Lands	Jan. 15, 1830	Adverse		Laid on table.		
Cooley, Ebenezer	Compensation for loss of improvements on land granted to General Lafayette.	22	1	Petition	120	Public Lands	Jan. 3, 1832	Adverse		Laid on table.		
Cooley, George	(See William H. Bedford, agent &c.)	28	1		262							

List of private claims presented to the House of Representatives of the United States from the 1st to the 31st Congress, inclusive—Continued.

Names of claimants.	Nature or object of the claim.	Congress.	Session.	How brought before the House of Reps.	Page of journal.	To what committee of the House referred.	No. or date of the report.	Nature of the report.	No. of the bill.	How disposed of by the House of Reps.	How disposed of by the Senate.	Date of the act of Congress, and remarks.
Cooley, Randolph M.	(See Henry W. Barnes.)											
Cooley, Richard	(See William H. Bedford, agent, &c.)	28	1	....	262							
Cooley, William	Indemnity for property destroyed by Indians in Florida.	26	1	Petition	961	Claims	695	Adverse	......	Laid on table.		
Cooley, William	Indemnity for property destroyed by Indians in Florida.	26	2	Petition	125	Claims.						
Cooley, William	Indemnity for property destroyed by Indians in Florida.	27	2	Petition	94	Claims	770	Adverse	......	Laid on table.		
Cooley, William S.	(See John Ross and others.)											
Coolidge, Cornelius	(See William Osborne, representative of.)											
Coolidge, Dorothy, heirs of	Payment of quartermasters certificate for five years use of property in Watertown, Massachusetts, in revolutionary war.	15	2	Petition	253	Pens. & Rev. Cl'ms.	....	....	......	Discharged; laid on table.		
Coolidge, Jonathan, heirs of	Indemnity for French spoliations prior to 1800.	26	1	Memorial	182	Foreign Affairs	343	Favorable; bill.	319	Referred to Committee Whole House.		
Coolidge, Thomas B.	(See Nathaniel Cheever & others.)											
Coolidge, Uriah	Compensation for expenses, &c., for wounded seamen, placed in his care.	13	3	Petition	668	Naval Affairs	Feb. 1, 1815	By bill	280	Passed	Passed	App'd Feb. 24, 1815
Coombe, Griffith	Liquidation of a revolutionary quartermaster's certificate.	4	1	Rep. of Secretary Treasury.	388	Claims	May 31, 1796	Adverse	......	Laid on table.		
Coombe, Griffith	(See Danial Carroll and others.)											
Coombe, Griffith, and John P. Ingle.	Compensation for use of brick capitol building by commissioners under Danish convention.	25	2	Petition	574	Claims	....	....	......	Discharged.		
Coombe, Griffith, and John P. Ingle.	Compensation for use of brick capitol building by commissioners under Danish convention.	25	3	Petition	....	Claims	1	Report and bill.	899	Passed	Passed	App'd March 3, 1839
Coombe, Philip	(See John Pearson and others.)											
Coombes, Hosea	Invalid pension	6	1	Petition	608	Claims	Mar. 17, 1800	Adverse	......	Leave to withdraw.		
Coombs, Philip	Indemnity for French spoliations prior to 1800.	28	1	Petition	124	Foreign Affairs.						
Coombs, William, administrator of.	Indemnity for French spoliations prior to 1800.	26	1	Memorial	182	Foreign Affairs	343	Favorable; bill	319	Referred to Committee Whole House.		
Coomley, Philip	Indemnity for French spoliations prior to 1800.	26	1	Memorial	182	Foreign Affairs	343	Favorable; bill	319	Referred to Committee Whole House.		
Coon, Elias	Fishing bounty on schooner Congress lost at sea.	29	1	Petition	674	Commerce	652	Report and bill.	432	Referred to Committee Whole House.		
Coon, Elias	Fishing bounty on schooner Congress lost at sea.	30	1	Petition	79	Commerce	259	Report and bill.	252	Referred to Committee Whole House.		
Coon, Farley F.	Pension for injuries received in war of 1812.	31	1	Petition	647	Invalid Pensions.						
Coon, Henry	(See William Baker and others)	22	1	....	288							
Coon, James, deceased, late widow of.	Compensation for services as lieutenant in revolutionary army.	2	1	Petition	455	....	....	....	......	Referred to Secretary of War.		
Coon, Peter	Increase of pension	25	2	Petition	775	Rev. Pensions	....	....	......	Discharged; laid on table.		
Coon, Ross	Pension	19	2	Petition	156	Military Pensions.						
Coone, Christian	Compensation for horses in United States service.	2	1	Petition	448	....	....	....	......	Referred to Secretary War.		

List of private claims presented to the House of Representatives of the United States from the 1st to the 31st Congress, inclusive—Continued.

Names of claimants.	Nature or object of the claim.	Congress.	Session.	How brought before the House of Reps.	Page of journal.	To what committee of the House referred.	No. or date of the report.	Nature of the report.	No. of the bill.	How disposed of by the House of Reps.	How disposed of by the Senate.	Date of the act of Congress, and remarks.
Coone, Christian	Compensation for horses in United States service.	2	2	Rep. of Secretary of War.	696	....	....	....	......	Laid on table.		
Cooney, James	Invalid pension	3	1	Rep. of Secretary of War.	131	Select	May 26, 1794	To refer to Sec. with instrucs.	R. 12	Passed	Passed	App'd June 9, 1794
Cooper, Adam	Pension for revolutionary wounds and services.	17	1	Petition	96	Pens. & Rev. Cl'ms.	Jan. 4, 1822	Rep. and res to withdraw.	......	Resolution adopted.		
Cooper, Adam	Pension for revolutionary wounds and services.	18	1	Petition	42	Pens. & Rev. Cl'ms.	Dec. 31, 1823	By bill	35	....	....	Bill became a law May 19, 1824, omitting claimant's name.
Cooper, Adam	Pension for revolutionary wounds and services.	18	2	Petition	118	Pens. & Rev. Cl'ms.						
Cooper, Adam	Pension for revolutionary wounds and services.	19	1	Petition	73	Military Pensions.	194	Favorable	......	Referred to Committee Whole House on bill No. 118.		
Cooper, Adam	Pension for revolutionary wounds and services.	19	2	House bill	85	Whole House	Feb. 2, 1827	Favorable	314	Passed	Passed	App'd March 3, 1827
Cooper, Albert G	Compensation for horse lost in Mexican war.	30	1	Petition	305	Claims	420	Legislation unnecssary.	......	Laid on table.		
Cooper, Apollos, late widow of.	Pension for revolutionary services.	15	2	Petition	220	Pens. & Rev. Cl'ms.						
Cooper, Apollos, heirs of.	Commutation of half-pay for services as a revolutionary officer.	24	1	Petition	274	Rev. Claims	848	Report and bill.	748	Referred to Committee Whole House.		
Cooper, Apollos, heirs of.	Commutation of half-pay for services as a revolutionary officer.	25	2	Petition	39	Rev. Claims	126	Report and bill.	144	Passed.		
Cooper, Apollos, heirs of.	Commutation of half pay for services as a revolutionary officer.	25	3	Petition	86	Rev. Claims	111	Report and bill.	986	Referred to Committee Whole House.		
Cooper, Apollos, heirs of.	Commutation of half-pay for services as a revolutionary officer.	26	1	Petition	166	Rev. Claims	510	Report and bill.	411	Referred to Committee Whole House.		
Cooper, Apollos, heirs of.	Commutation of half-pay for services as a revolutionary officer.	27	2	Petition	62	Rev. Claims	81	Report and bill.	121	Referred to Committee Whole House.	....	See report No. 777.
Cooper, Apollos, heirs of.	Commutation of half-pay for services as a revolutionary officer.	28	1	Petition	247	Rev. Pensions	....	....	......	Discharged; laid on table.		
Cooper, Apollos, heirs of.	Commutation of half-pay for services as a revolutionary officer.	29	1	Petition	219	Rev. Claims.						
Cooper, Apollos, heirs of.	Commutation of half-pay for services as a revolutionary officer.	29	2	Petition	85	Rev. Claims.						
Cooper, Apollos, heirs of.	Commutation of half-pay for services as a revolutionary officer.	30	1	Petition	156	Rev. Claims.						
Cooper, Apollos, heirs of.	Commutation of half-pay for services as a revolutionary officer.	30	2	Petition	420	Rev. Claims.						
Cooper, Apollos, heirs of.	Commutation of half-pay for services as a revolutionary officer.	31	1	Petition	310	Rev. Claims.						
Cooper, Augustus	Pension for injuries received from exposure in military service of United States.	31	2	Petition	225	Invalid Pensions.						
Cooper, David	Compensation for chimney and plank taken for United States barracks at Fort Shelby.	16	2	Resolution	58	....	....	....	......	Rejected.		
Cooper, David	Compensation for chimney and plank taken for United States barracks at Fort Shelby.	17	1	Senate bill	483	Claims	....	....	86	Discharged; laid on table.		
Cooper, David	Compensation for chimney and plank taken for United States barracks at Fort Shelby.	18	1	Petition	131	Claims	Mar. 10, 1824	Report and bill.	152	Passed	Passed	App'd May 17, 1824

List of private claims presented to the House of Representatives of the United States from the 1st to the 31st Congress, inclusive—Continued.

Names of claimants.	Nature or object of the claim.	Congress.	Session.	How brought before the House of Reps.	Page of journal.	To what committee of the House referred.	No. or date of the report.	Nature of the report.	No. of the bill.	How disposed of by the House of Reps.	How disposed of by the Senate.	Date of the act of Congress, and remarks.
Cooper, Enoch, widow of.	Pension for five years' service as lieutenant United States army.	20	1	Petition	120	Invalid Pensions				Discharged; laid on table.		
Cooper, Francis, (Mo.)	(See Reuben E. Gentry & others.)	24	1	Petition	153							
Cooper, George, (D. C.)	Compensation for four horses lost in United States military service.	13	3	Petition	493	Claims	Nov. 14, 1814	By bill	228	Passed	Indef. postp'd.	
Cooper, George, (Pa.)	Restoration of pension	17	1	Petition	155	Whole House on bill No. 37.						See act March 1, 1823
Cooper, Jacob	Land of equal value to that which he purchased and improved, and was then deprived.	15	2	Petition	89	Public Lands	Dec. 17, 1818	Rep't and res. to reject.		Resolution adopted		Leave to withdraw.
Cooper, James, jr	Repayment of difference between American and foreign duties on imports, in the case of the sch'r Ann Eliza.	10	1	Memorial	97	Com. and Manuf.						
Cooper, James, jr	Repayment of difference between American and foreign duties on imports, in the case of the sch'r Ann Eliza.	10	2	Memorial	350	Com. and Manuf.						
Cooper, James, (Pa.)	Renewal of a lost bounty land warrant, No. 12,966.	24	2	Petition	49	Priv. Land Claims	Jan. 10, 1837	By bill	823	Referred to Committee Whole House.		
Cooper, James, (Pa.)	Renewal of a lost bounty land warrant, No. 12,966.	25	2	Petition	43	Priv. Land Claims.	254	Report and bill.	297	Referred to Committee Whole House.		
Cooper, James, (Pa.)	Renewal of a lost bounty land warrant, No. 12,966.	25	3	Bill of last sess.	376	Whole House	Jan. 25, 1839	With't amend.	297	Passed	Passed	App'd March 3, 1839
Cooper, James, (Ind.)	Payment for horse lost in United States service.	25	2	Documents	396	Claims				Discharged.		
Cooper, James, (Ind.)	Payment for horse lost in United States service.	25	3	Petition	207	Claims.						
Cooper, James C	Compensation for horse lost in the Mexican war.	30	1	Petition	305	Claims	238	Report and bill.	238	Referred to Committee Whole House.		
Cooper, John, (Va.)	(See William Estis, sureties of.)											
Cooper, John, (N. J.)	Compensation for services in revolutionary war.	2	1	Petition	446					Referred to Secretary of War.		
Cooper, John, (N. J.)	Invalid pension	3	1	Rep. of Secretary War.	131	Select	May 26, 1794	To refer to Sec. with instructions.	R. 12	Passed	Passed	App'd June 9, 1794
Cooper, John, (N. J.)	Invalid pension	3	2	Rep. of Secretary War.	350	Claims	May 3, 1795	To discharge & postpone.		Laid on table.		
Cooper, John, (N. J.)	Invalid pension	4	1	Rep. of Secretary War.	445	Claims.						
Cooper, John, (N. J.)	Invalid pension	21	1	Petition	120	Military Pensions	April 24, 1830	Adverse		Laid on table.		
Cooper, John, (N. J.)	Invalid pension	21	2	Petition	53	Military Pensions				Discharged; laid on table.		
Cooper, John, (N. J.)	Invalid pension	22	1	Petition	174	Rev. Pensions				Discharged; laid on table.		
Cooper, John, (N. J.)	Invalid pension	25	2	Petition	403	Rev. Pensions	822	Adverse		Laid on table.		
Cooper, John, (N. Y.)	Compensation for services as sergeant in revolutionary army.	23	2	Petition	303	Rev. Pensions				Discharged; laid on table.		
Cooper, John, (N. Y.)	Compensation for services as sergeant in revolutionary army.	24	1	Petition	107	Rev. Pensions				Discharged; laid on table.		
Cooper, John, (N. Y.)	Compensation for services as sergeant in revolutionary army.	30	2	Petition	534	Rev. Pensions.						

List of private claims presented to the House of Representatives of the United States from the 1st to the 31st Congress, inclusive—Continued.

Names of claimants.	Nature or object of the claim.	Congress.	Session.	How brought before the House of Reps.	Page of journal.	To what committee of the House referred.	No. or date of the report.	Nature of the report.	No. of the bill.	How disposed of by the House of Reps.	How disposed of by the Senate.	Date of the act of Congress, and remarks.
Cooper, John, (N. Y.)	Arrears of pension for disability in war of 1812.	27	2	Petition	360	Invalid Pensions	625	Adverse		Laid on table.		
Cooper, John, heir of	Indemnity for French spoliations prior to 1800.	26	1	Memorial	182	Foreign Affairs	343	Favorable; bill	319	Referred to Committee Whole House.		
Cooper, John B	Compensat'n for property destroyed by British while in service of United States.	20	2	Petition	74	Claims	Dec. 29, 1828	Adverse		Laid on table.		
Cooper, John B	Compensat'n for property destroyed by British while in service of United States.	21	1	Petition	56	Claims	May 19, 1830	Adverse		Laid on table.		
Cooper, John B	Compensat'n for property destroyed by British while in service of United States.	30	1	Petition	724	Claims				Discharged; laid on table.		
Cooper, John B	Compensat'n for property destroyed by British while in service of United States.	30	2	Petition	196	Claims	108	Adverse		Laid on table.		
Cooper, John B	Compensat'n for property destroyed by British while in service of United States.	31	1	Petition	519	Claims.						
Cooper, John Batts, as heir	Indemnity for French spoliations prior to 1800.	29	2	Memorial	235	Foreign Affairs.						
Cooper, Joseph	Indemnity for losses by failure of United States to pay for beef, per contract.	23	1	Petition	217	Claims	280	Report and bill.	318	Referred to Committee Whole House.		
Cooper, Joseph	Indemnity for losses by failure of United States to pay for beef, per contract.	24	1	Petition	50	Claims	3	Report and bill.	3	Passed	Passed	App'd Feb. 17, 1836
Cooper, Joshua	(See Reuben E. Gentry and others.)											
Cooper, Leonard	Payment of a lost certificate for revolutionary services.	16	1	Petition	49	Pens. & Rev. Cl'ms.	Jan. 3, 1820	Adverse		Laid on table.		
Cooper, Leonard, heirs of.	Commutation of half pay	23	1	Petition	97	Rev. Claims.						
Cooper, Leonard, heirs of.	Commutation of half pay	28	1	Petition	132	Rev. Claims.						
Cooper, Margaret	(See John Campbell, heirs of.)											
Cooper, Mark A	Compensation for loss of a horse in Florida war.	24	1	Resolution	675	Claims.						
Cooper, Peter	(See William Baker and others.)	22	1		288							
Cooper, Rebecca G	Restoration of pension, and for arrears of pension.	29	1	Petition	476	Rev. Pensions.						
Cooper, Robert	Pre-emption right to land as a New Orleans branch pilot.	28	1	Petition	77	Priv. Land Claims.	9	Favorable; bill.	35	Passed	Passed	App'd June 17, 1844
Cooper, Samuel, late widow of.	Revolutionary pension	26	1	Resolution	386	Rev. Pensions	664	Adverse		Laid on table.		Leave to withdraw, 2d Sess. 30th Cong.
Cooper, Samuel, (Pa.)	Pension for services in war of 1812	30	2	Petition	194	Invalid Pensions				Discharged; laid on table.		
Cooper, Samuel, (Mass.,) son of.	Compensation for revolutionary services of deceased on board United States ship Alliance.	31	1	Petition	610	Rev. Claims.						
Cooper, Samuel, (Mass.,) son of.	Compensation for revolutionary services of deceased on board United States ship Alliance.	31	2	Petition		Rev. Claims	7	Adverse		Laid on table.		
Cooper, Sarthal, administrators of.	Remuneration for Indian depredations.	24	1	Petition	265	Indian Affairs.						
Cooper, Sarthal, administrators of.	Remuneration for Indian depredations.	24	2	Petition	93	Indian Affairs.						

List of private claims presented to the House of Representatives of the United States from the 1st to the 31st Congress, inclusive—Continued.

Names of claimants.	Nature or object of the claim.	Congress.	Session.	How brought before the House of Reps.	Page of journal.	To what committee of the House referred.	No. or date of the report.	Nature of the report.	No. of the bill.	How disposed of by the House of Reps.	How disposed of by the Senate.	Date of the act of Congress, and remarks.
Cooper, Sarthal, administrators of.	Remuneration for Indian depredations.	25	2	Petition	97	Indian Affairs	212	Report and bill.	248	Referred to Committee Whole House.		
Cooper, Solomon, representative of.	Permission to locate 2560 acres of revolutionary bounty land granted to deceased, but from which he is barred by limitation.	25	2	Petition	178	Priv. Land Claims.	....	....	.....	Discharged.		
Cooper, Thomas	Redress for fine and imprisonment under alien and sedition act.	7	1	Petition	226	....	....	....	.....	Postponed to next session.		
Cooper, Thomas	Redress for fine and imprisonment under alien and sedition act.	19	1	Petition	74	Judiciary.........	16	Adverse	.....	Laid on table.		
Cooper, Thomas	Redress for fine and imprisonment under alien and sedition act.	21	1	Petition	234	Judiciary	....	....	.....	Discharged; laid on table.		
Cooper, Thomas	Redress for fine and imprisonment under alien and sedition act.	21	2	Petition	46	Judiciary.						
Cooper, Thomas	Redress for fine and imprisonment under alien and sedition act.	22	1	Petition	224	Judiciary.........	244	Report and bill.	332	Referred to Committee Whole House.		
Cooper, Thomas	Redress for fine and imprisonment under alien and sedition act.	23	1	Petition	38	Judiciary	473	Report and bill.	485	Referred to Committee Whole House.		
Cooper, Thomas	Redress for fine and imprisonment under alien and sedition act.	24	1	Petition	157	Judiciary	303	Report and bill.	317	Referred to Committee Whole House.		
Cooper, Thomas	Redress for fine and imprisonment under alien and sedition act.	24	1	Senate bill	1077	Judiciary	June 28, 1836	With't amend.	85	Recommitted.		
						Whole House	July 1, 1836	To strike out the enacting clause.	85	Laid on table.		
Cooper, Thomas	Redress for fine and imprisonment under alien and sedition act.	24	2	Ho. bill last sess.	200	Whole House.....	....	....	317			
Cooper, Thomas	Redress for fine and imprisonment under alien and sedition act.	25	2	Petition	41	Judiciary	343	Report and bill.	373	Referred to Committee Whole House.		
Cooper, Thomas	Redress for fine and imprisonment under alien and sedition act.	25	2	Senate bill	746	Judiciary	April 20, 1838	With't amend.	162	Referred to Committee Whole House.		
Cooper, Thomas	Redress for fine and imprisonment under alien and sedition act.	25	3	Ho. bill last sess.	378	Whole House.....	....	....	373			
Cooper, Thomas, executor of.	Redress for fine and imprisonment under alien and sedition act.	26	1	Petition	340	Claims.						
Cooper, Thomas, executor of.	Redress for fine and imprisonment under alien and sedition act.	26	1	Senate bill	1147	Judiciary	....	....	251			
Cooper, Thomas, executor of.	Redress for fine and imprisonment under alien and sedition act.	26	2	Petition	79	Judiciary.						
Cooper, Thomas, executor of.	Redress for fine and imprisonment under alien and sedition act.	26	2	Senate bill	210	Judiciary	....	....	124			
Cooper, Thomas, executor of.	Redress for fine and imprisonment under alien and sedition act.	27	3	Res. of Leg. of S. Carolina.	111, 126	Judiciary.						
Cooper, Thomas, executor of.	Redress for fine and imprisonment under alien and sedition act.	28	1	Petition	101	Judiciary.						
Cooper, Thomas, executor of.	Redress for fine and imprisonment under alien and sedition act.	29	1	Petition	192	Judiciary.						
Cooper, Thomas, executor of.	Redress for fine and imprisonment under alien and sedition act.	29	2	Petition	59	Judiciary	37	Report and bill	625	Referred to Committee Whole House.		
Cooper, Thomas, executor of.	Redress for fine and imprisonment under alien and sedition act.	31	1	Petition	362	Judiciary	11	Report and bill.	13	Passed	Passed	App'd July 29, 1850
Cooper, Warren.........	(See A. G. Higgins and others.)											

List of private claims presented to the House of Representatives of the United States from the 1st to the 31st Congress, inclusive—Continued.

Names of claimants.	Nature or object of the claim.	Congress.	Session.	How brought before the House of Reps.	Page of journal.	To what committee of the House referred.	No. or date of the report.	Nature of the report.	No. of the bill.	How disposed of by the House of Reps.	How disposed of by the Senate.	Date of the act of Congress, and remarks.
Cooper, William	Compensation for horse, &c., lost in Seminole war, 1818.	23	1	Documents	154	Claims.						
Cooper, William	(See William H. Bedford, agent, &c.)	28	1		262							
Coopman, Francis	(See Stephen Zacharie and others.)											
Coopman, Zachariah, trustees of.	Indemnity for French spoliations prior to 1800.	26	1	Memorial	182	Foreign Affairs	343	Favorable; bill	319	Referred to Committee Whole House.		
Cooprider, John	Change an entry of land	20	1	Petition	40	Public Lands				Discharged; laid on table.		
Coots, Thomas	Pension for injuries received in war of 1812.	31	1	Petition	410	Invalid Pensions.						
Copeland, Jesse, heirs of	Equitable settlement of accounts as captain in U. S. army.	24	1	Petition	671	Military Affairs	619	Report and bill.	606	Referred to Committee Whole House.		
Copeland, Jesse, heirs of	Equitable settlement of accounts as captain in U. S. army.	25	2	Petition	41	Military Affairs	Dec. 28, 1837	By bill	249	Referred to Committee Whole House.		
Copeland, Jesse, heirs of	Equitable settlement of accounts as captain in U. S. army.	25	3	Bill of last sess.	376	Whole House	Jan. 25, 1839	With't amend.	249	Passed	Passed	App'd March 2, 1839
Copeland, John	Pension	20	2	Petition	106	Military Pensions				Disch'd; laid on table.		
Copeland, John	Pension	21	1	Petition	143	Military Pensions.						
Copeland, Thomas	Balance due for services at arsenal, Alleghany, Pa.	27	2	Petition	883	Military Affairs	895	Report and bill.	518	Engrossed.		
Copeland, Thomas	Balance due for services at arsenal, Alleghany, Pa.	27	3	Bill of last sess.	89				518	Passed	Indef. postp'd.	
Copeland, Thomas	Balance due for services at arsenal, Alleghany, Pa.	29	2	Petition	89	Claims						Leave to withdraw.
Copeland, Thomas	Balance due for services at arsenal, Alleghany, Pa.	30	1	Petition	272	Claims				Discharged; laid on table.		
Copeland, William, and others, attorney for.	Compensation for services, &c., in revolutionary war.	1	3	Petition	378					Referred to Secretary War.		
Copeland, William, and others, attorney for.	Compensation for services, &c., in revolutionary war.	3	2	Rep. of Secretary War.	278					Laid on table.		
Copeland Zaccheus	Compensation for services as a revolutionary soldier.	23	1	Petition	440	Rev. Claims.						
Copeland, Zaccheus	Compensation for services as a revolutionary soldier.	24	1	Petition	740	Claims	644	Adverse		Laid on table.		
Copenrath, Frederic, heirs of.	Legalization of a transfer of bounty land warrant, No. 7943.	30	1	Petition		Public Lands	261	Report and bill.	256	Referred to Committee Whole House.		
Copes, Thomas P.	Conditional pre-emption to certain inundated land in Missouri.	24	1	Petition	435	Public Lands.						
Copes, Thomas P.	Conditional pre-emption to certain inundated land in Missouri.	25	2	Petition	95	Public Lands.						
Copes, Thomas P.	Conditional pre-emption to certain inundated land in Missouri.	25	3	Petition	92	Public Lands	114	Adverse		Laid on table.		
Copes, Thomas P.	(See Cornelius Campbell, and others.)											
Copes, Thomas P.	Relocation of his New Madrid land claim—displaced by a French and Spanish grant.	25	2	Petition	418	Priv. Land Claims.				Discharged.		
Copes, Thomas P.	Relocation of his New Madrid land claim—displaced by a French and Spanish grant.	26	1	Senate bill	837	Priv. Land Claims.	June 23, 1840	With't amend.	313	Referred to Committee Whole House.		
Copes, Thomas P.	Relocation of his New Madrid land claim—displaced by a French and Spanish grant.	26	2	Senate bill	178	Public Lands			79			

List of private claims presented to the House of Representatives of the United States from the 1st to the 31st Congress, inclusive—Continued.

Names of claimants.	Nature or object of the claim.	Congress.	Session.	How brought before the House of Reps.	Page of journal.	To what committee of the House referred.	No. or date of the report.	Nature of the report.	No. of the bill.	How disposed of by the House of Reps.	How disposed of by the Senate.	Date of the act of Congress, and remarks.
Copin, John and Samuel, administrator of.	Bounty land due as revolutionary soldiers.	23	1	Petition	639	Rev. Claims.						
Copin, John and Samuel, administrator of.	Bounty land due as revolutionary soldiesr.	24	1	Petition	261	Priv. Land Claims.						
Copin, John and Samuel, administrator of.	Bounty land due as revolutionary soldiers.	25	2	Petition	84	Rev. Claims	Jan. 5, 1838	Adverse		Laid on table.		
Coplin, Benjamin	Pension	22	2	Petition	26	Invalid Pensions				Discharged; laid on table.		
Copp, Ebenezer	Invalid pension	3	1	Rep. of Secretary War.	131	Select	May 26, 1794	To refer to Sec. with instructions.	R. 12	Passed	Passed	App'd June 9, 1794
Copp, Ebenezer	Invalid pension	4	1	Rep't Committee on Claims.	457	Whole House	May 7, 1796	Favorable; bill ordered.	156	Passed	Passed	App'd April 20, 1796
Copp, Michael	Compensation for gun impressed into U. S. service.	19	1	Petition	94	Claims	12	Report and bill.	27	Passed	Passed	App'd May 16, 1826
Copp, Timothy	(See Canadian refugees.)											
Coppernoll, Richard	Compensation for mill burnt by the British, and for wheat, &c., taken for the garrison at Fort Paris, 1780.	3	1	Petition	70	Select	Mar. 11. 1794	Adverse		Laid on table.		
Coppedge, William	Revolutionary pension	23	1	Petition	600	Rev. Pensions.						
Coppinger, Francis	(See Monsieur Reliquet.)											
Cohpinger, Francis, assignee of.	Indemnity for French spoliations prior to 1800.	26	1	Memorial	182	Foreign Affairs	343	Favorable; bill.	319	Referred to Committee Whole House.		
Coquillard, Alexander, and others.	Payment of claims due by Pottawatamie Indians.	29	1	Petition	346	Indian Affairs.						
Coquillard, Alexander, and others.	Payment of claims due by Pottawatamie Indinns.	30	1	Petition	397	Indian Affairs	442	Report and bill.	374	Referred to Committee Whole House.		
Corbett, John	Increase of pension	7	1	Petition	16	Claims	Dec. 16, 1801	Adverse		Rejected.		
Corbin, Bluford	Pension for injuries received in war of 1812.	31	1	Petition	1189	Invalid Pensions.						
Corbin, David, widow of.	Revolutionary pension	30	1	Petition	68	Rev. Pensions	295	Adverse		Laid on table.		
Corbin, George L.	(See William Tee, and others.)											
Corbin, Isaiah	Invalid pension	9	2	Petition	498	Claims.						
Corbin, Isaiah	Invalid pension	10	2	House bill	499	Whole House	Feb. 20, 1809	Favorable	158	Passed	Passed	App'd March 3, 1809
Corbin, James	Invalid pension	23	1	Petition	112	Invalid Pensions				Discharged; laid on table.		
Corbin, James	Invalid pension	23	2	Petition	391	Invalid Pensions.						
Corbin, James	Invalid pension	24	2	Petition	213	Invalid Pensions				Discharged; laid on table.		
Corbin, James	Invalid pension	25	2	Petition	85	Invalid Pensions				Discharged; laid on table.		
Corbin, Patience	Revolutionary pension	29	1	Petition	340	Rev. Pensions.						
Corbin, Patience	Revolutionary pension	30	1	Petition	240	Rev. Pensions				Discharged; laid on table.		Leave to withdraw.
Corbitt, Peter, widow of.	Five years' half-pay in lieu of land for services in war of 1812.	21	1	Petition	144	Military Affairs	99	Rep't & bill for minor children.	134	Passed	Indef. postp'd.	
Corbitt, Thomas	Restoration of pension	17	1	Petition	128	Rev. Claims	Jan. 15, 1822	General bill	37	Passed	Rejected.	
Corbitt, Thomas	Restoration of pension	17	2	Petition	43	Rev. Pensions	Dec. 27, 1822	General bill	207	Passed	Passed	App'd March 1, 1823
Corby, Thomas M.	Indemnity for French spoliations prior to 1800.	26	1	Memorial	182	Foreign Affairs	343	Favorable; bill.	319	Referred to Committee Whole House.		

List of private claims presented to the House of Representatives of the United States from the 1st to the 31st Congress, inclusive—Continued.

51

Names of claimants.	Nature or object of the claim.	Congress.	Session.	How brought before the House of Reps.	Page of journal.	To what committee of the House referred.	No. or date of the report.	Nature of the report.	No. of the bill.	How disposed of by the House of Reps.	How disposed of by the Senate.	Date of the act of Congress, and remarks.
Corby, Thomas M.	Indemnity for French spoliations prior to 1800.	29	2	Memorial	136	Foreign Affairs.						
Corby, Thomas M., widow of.	Indemnity for French spoliations prior to 1800.	31	1	Petition	225	Foreign Affairs	355	Report and bill.	318	Referred to Committee Whole House.		
Corcoran, James	(See Louis F. Beeler, and others)											
Cordell, John, son of	Commutation of pay and land for services in Virginia revolutionary line.	31	2	Petition	141	Rev. Claims.						
Corder, Bolus, heirs of	Tract of land in Louisiana	25	2	Petition	281	Priv. Land Claims.	446	Rep. and res. adverse.		Laid on table.		
Corder, Henry	(See Joseph Stewart, and others.)											
Core, John	Payment for a horse lost in United States service.	14	2	Petition	184	Claims				Discharged; laid on table.		
Core, John	Payment for a horse lost in United States service.	21	2	Petition	338	Claims.						
Core, John	Payment for a horse lost in United States service.	27	2	Petition	333	Claims	468	Report and bill.	318	Passed.		
Core, John	Peyment for a horse lost in United States service.	27	3	Petition	43	Claims	2	Report and bill.	620	Passed	Passed	App'd March 1, 1843
Core, Margaret and William.	(Sve William B. Bunting, heirs of.)											
Corey, Nathan	Pension for revolutionary services.	31	1	Petition	194	Rev. Pensions	19	Adverse		Laid on table.		
Corkle, John	Indemnity for French spoliations prior to 1800.	26	1	Memorial	182	Foreign Affairs	343	Favorable; bill	319	Referred to Committee Whole House.		
Corl, Leonard	Restoration of pension	20	1	Resolution	634	Military Pensions				Discharged; laid on table.		
Corl, Leonard	Pension	20	2	House bill	55	Whole House	Jan. 8, 1829	Favorable	311	Passed	Laid on table.	
Corl, Leonard	Restoration of pension	21	1	Petition	47	Military Pensions	Jan. 5, 1830	By bill	72	Passed	Passed	App'd May 20, 1830
Corl, Leonard	Arrears of pension	24	2	Petition	271	Rev. Pensions				Discharged; laid on table.		
Corlette, Edward, widow of	Renewal of naval pension	29	2	Petition	70	Naval Affairs.						
Corley, Dudley	Compensation for horse, &c., lost Seminole campaign of 1818.	23	1	Documents	154	Claims.						
Corley, Dudley	(See William H. Bedford, agent, &c.)	28	1		262							
Corliss, Emerson	Pension	19	1	Petition	334	Military Pensions	164	Adverse		Laid on table.		
Corliss, Samuel	Bounty land and additional pay as sergeant in 11th U. S. infantry.	17	1	Resolution	192	Military Pensions	Feb. 9, 1822	Adverse		Laid on table		Leave to withdraw.
Corlis, John and others	Remission of duty on tea imported at Providence, Rhode Island, in ship Resource, and destroyed by fire.	6	2	House bill	825	Whole House			320	Disch'd; bill passed	Passed	App'd March 3, 1801
Cormack, Isaac	(See Isaac Carmack.)											
Cormyn & McAlister	Compensation for work on Cumberland road.	23	1	Resolution	589	Claims	456	Favorable		Referred to Secretary War.		
Corn, George	Revolutionary pension	22	1	Resolution	561	Rev. Pensions				Discharged; laid on table.		
Cornec, Oliver	Continuation of pension	16	2	Petition	90	Rev. Pensions	Feb. 15, 1821	Rep. and res adverse.		Resolution adopted.		
Cornelius, Daniel	Pre-emption right to land on which he resides.	15	1	Petition	380	Public Lands				Discharged.		
Cornelius, Jacob	(See Daniel Bread.)											
Cornelius, Jesse	Public support for services as a revolutionary soldier.	18	2	Petition	91	Rev. Pensions	Jan. 17, 1825	Adverse		Laid on table		Leave to withdraw.

List of private claims presented to the House of Representatives of the United States from the 1st to the 31st Congress, inclusive—Continued.

Names of claimants.	Nature or object of the claim.	Congress.	Session.	How brought before the House of Reps.	Page of journal.	To what committee of the House referred.	No. or date of the report.	Nature of the report.	No. of the bill.	How disposed of by the House of Reps.	How disposed of by the Senate.	Date of the act of Congress, and remarks.
Cornelius, Joseph	Confirmation of title to land in Illinois.	15	2	Petition	200	Priv. Land Claims				Discharged; laid on table.		
Cornelius, Joseph	(See John Swaggart and others.)											
Cornell, Benjamin	Revolutionary pension	23	2	Resol'n and docs.	114, 143	Rev. Pensions				Discharged; laid on table.		
Cornell, George	Grant of land for services in Colonial army from 1758 to 1765.	9	1	Petition	262	Public Lands	April 9, 1806	Indef. postp'd.		Report adopted.		
Cornell, George	Grant of land for services in Colonial army from 1758 to 1765.	9	2	Petition	486	Public Lands.						
Cornell, James	Indemnity for losses in Creek Indian war.	14	2	Petition	71	Ways and Means	Jan. 29, 1817	Report and bill.	93	Passed	Passed	App'd March 3, 1817
Cornell, James	Fee simple title to a tract of land in Alabama.	14	2	Petition	72	Public Lands				Discharged; laid on table.		
Cornell, James	Fee simple title to a tract of land in Alabama.	15	1	Petition	56	Priv. Land Claims				Discharged; laid on table.		
Cornell, Stephen	Pay, &c., of a lieutenant in navy while co-operating with naval forces in Florida.	26	1	Petition	303	Naval Affairs	July 2, 1840	By bill	462	Referred to Committee Whole House.		
Cornell, Stephen	Pay, &c., of a lieutenant in navy while co-operating with naval forces in Florida.	27	2	Petition	63	Naval Affairs.						
Cornell, Thomas F	Compensation for services as district attorney *pro tem.* in East Florida.	20	1	Petition and res.	93, 154	Territories	105	Report and bill.	117	Passed	Laid on table.	
Cornell, Thomas F	Compensation for services as district attorney *pro tem.* in East Florida.	20	2	Resolution	126	Territories	Jan. 16, 1829	Report and bill.	372	Passed	Amendm't reported.	
Cornell, Thomas F	Compensation for services as district attorney *pro tem.* in East Florida.	21	1	Petition	296	Territories	208	Report and bill.	258	Referred to Committee Whole House.		
Cornell, Thomas F	Compensation for services as district attorney *pro tem.* in East Florida.	21	2	Bill of last sess.	265	Whole House	Feb. 4, 1831	With't amend.	258	Passed	Amendm't reported.	
Cornell, Thruston	Revolutionary pension	25	2	Petition	403	Rev. Pensions	794	Report and bill.	743	Passed	Ref., and com. discharged.	
Cornell, Thruston	Revolutionary pension	25	3	Petition	126	Rev. Pensions	Jan. 9, 1839	By bill	995	Passed	Adverse report.	
Cornell, Thruston	Revolutionary pension	26	1	Petition	171	Rev. Pensions	142	Report and bill.	152	Passed	Indef. postp'd.	
Cornell, William	Indemnity for damage to his property by establishing a military garrison near it in Brooklyn, New York.	16	2	Petition	115	Claims				Discharged; laid on table.		
Cornell, William	Indemnity for damage to his property by establishing a military garrison near it in Brooklyn, New York.	17	2	Petition	164	Military Affairs				Discharged; laid on table.		
Cornell, William	Indemnity for damage to his property by establishing a military garrison near it in Brooklyn, New York.	18	1	Petition	135	Military Affairs				Discharged; leave to withdraw.		
Corning, Erastus	(See Edward C. Delavan & others.)											
Corning, Malachi	Release from imprisonment on judgment for money disbursed as paymaster of the 11th regiment.	17	1	Petition	309	Claims				Discharged; laid on table.		

List of private claims presented to the House of Representatives of the United States from the 1st to the 31st Congress, inclusive—Continued.

Names of claimants.	Nature or object of the claim.	Congress.	Session.	How brought before the House of Reps.	Page of journal.	To what committee of the House referred.	No. or date of the report.	Nature of the report.	No. of the bill.	How disposed of by the House of Reps.	How disposed of by the Senate.	Date of the act of Congress, and remarks.
Cornish, Gabriel	Location of military land warrant in Michigan.	23	1	Petition	568	Public Lands.						
Cornochan, John	Compensation for sugar works, &c., destroyed by Indians in Florida.	21	1	Petition	235	Indian Affairs.						
Cornover, Sylvester	Compensation for horse lost in Mexican war.	30	1	Petition	147	Claims	427	Adverse	......	Laid on table.		
Cornwall, Adamson	(See George Alexander and others.)											
Cornwall, Amos	Revolutionary pension	25	2	Petition	729	Rev. Pensions	885	Adverse	......	Laid on table.		
Cornwall, William A.	Compensation for loss of time whilst lieutenant in Stevenson's regiment, New York volunteers.	29	2	Petition	50, 89	Millitary Affairs.						
Cornwell, Samuel	Pension for injuries received in war of 1812.	31	1	Petition	647	Invalid Pensions.						
Corneyn	(See McAllister & Cornyn.)											
Cornyn, Peter	Compensation for materials and work on Cumberland road.	23	1	Resolution	589	Claims	455	Adverse	......	Laid on table.		
Cornyn, Peter, and Arthur Taggart.	Settlement of accounts for materials and work on Cumberland road.	24	1	Resolution	349	Claims	540	Adverse	......	Recommitted.		
Cornyn, Peter	Compensation for work and materials on Cumberland road.	25	2	Petition	88	Claims.						
Cornyn, Peter	Compensation for work and materials on Cumberland road.	30	1	Petition	370	Claims.						
Corp, Samuel	Payment of certificates of debenture on account of goods landed at New Orleans.	7	1	Petition	154	Com. and Manuf.	April 16, 1802	Postponed to next session.	......	Report adopted.		
Corp, Samuel	Payment of certificates of debenture on account of goods landed at New Orleans.	7	2	Petition	248	Com. and Manuf.	Dec. 16, 1802	Adverse	......	Recommitted.		
							Jan. 26, 1803	Favorable; bill ordered.	102	Passed	Rejected	Oct. 31, 1803, leave to withdraw.
Corp, Samuel	Payment of certificates of debenture on account of goods landed at New Orleans.	8	1	Petition	533	Com. and Manuf.	Jan. 23, 1804	Favorable; bill ordered.	169	Passed	Passed	App'd Feb. 25, 1804
Correar, John	Invalid pension	10	2	House bill	499	Whole House.	Feb. 20, 1809	Favorable	158	Passed	Passed	App'd March 3, 1809
Correll, Nicholas	Revolutionary pension	23	1	Petition	308	Rev. Pensions	......	......	......	Discharged; laid on table.		
Corrie, James, and others.	Settlement for services as deputy quartermaster clerks in Deleware and Michigan in revolutionary war.	4	2	Petition	630	Claims	Jan. 13, 1797	Rep. and res.; adverse.	......	Resolution adopted.		
Corrier, James, representatives of.	(See Alexander Mactier & others.)											
Corrier, James, representatives of.	Indemnity for French spoliations prior to 1800.	26	1	Memorial	182	Foreign Affairs.	343	Favorable; bill.	319	Referred to Committee Whole House.		
Corse, John	Pension and land for wounds, and services as an officer in revolutionary war.	15	1	Petition	89	Pens. & Rev. Cl'ms.	April 1, 1818	By bill	172	Passed	Indef. postp'd.	
Corser, Solomon T	(See David Shaw.)											
Corson, David	Increase of pension	25	3	Petition	81	Rev. Pensions	......	......	......	Disch'd; laid on table.		
Cortwite, Charles	Increase of pension	29	1	Petition	275	Invalid Pensions	242	Adverse	......	Laid on table.		
Cortwite, Charles	Increase of pension	31	1	Petition	537	Invalid Pensions.						
Corvan, George R.	(See David Shaver, sen., & others.)											
Corwin, Ezra	Compensation for property taken by British in revolutionary war.	24	2	Petition	209	Rev. Claims.						

List of private claims presented to the House of Representatives of the United States from the 1st to the 31st Congress, inclusive—Continued.

Names of claimants.	Nature or object of the claim.	Congress.	Session.	How brought before the House of Reps.	Page of journal.	To what committee of the House referred.	No. or date of the report.	Nature of the report.	No. of the bill.	How disposed of by the House of Reps.	How disposed of by the Senate.	Date of the act of Congress, and remarks.
Corwin, Gershom, widow of.	Pension for revolutionary services.	28	2	Petition	169	Rev. Pensions.						
Corwin, Gershom, widow of.	Pension for revolutionary services.	29	1	Petition	59, 178	Rev. Pensions	526	Adverse		Laid on table.		
Corwin, Jedediah, widow of.	Pension for revolutionary services.	30	1	Petition	136	Rev. Pensions	23	Adverse		Laid on table.		
Cory, Benedict	Revolutionary pension	22	1	Resolution	534	Rev. Pensions				Discharged; laid on table.		
Cory, Elnathan	(See Joseph Pierce, heirs of.)											
Cory, Samuel	Pension	21	1	Petition and res.	36, 90	Military Pensions	April 27, 1830	Adverse		Laid on table.		
Cory, Samuel	Pension	22	1	Resolution	250	Rev. Pensions				Discharged; laid on table.		
Cory, Stephen A	Arrears of pension	30	1	Petition	65	Invalid Pensions	719	Adverse		Laid on table.		
Cory, Stephen A	Arrears of pension	31	1	Petition	579	Invalid Pensions	384	Adverse		Laid on table.		
Coryell, Lewis S	A just award in his claim against Navy department.	19	2	Petition	190	Naval Affairs.						
Coryell, Lewis S	A just award in his claim against Navy department.	20	1	Petition	92	Naval Affairs						Leave to withdraw.
Cossly, George W	(See J. P. Landerneau, heirs of).	28	1		366		248					
Coste, N. D. lieutenant in revenue service.	Compensation for extra service on coast of Florida in 1837.	29	1	Petition	572	Claims.						
Costigan, Lewis J	Compensation for services as an officer in revolutionary war.	1	2	Petition and rep't Sec. of War.	213					Laid on table.		
Costigan, Lewis J	Compensation for services as an officer in revolutionary war.	3	1	Memorial & rep't Sec. of War.	25	Select.						
Costigan, Lewis J	Compensation for services as an officer in revolutionary war.	15	1	Petition	114	Select	Mar. 21, 1818	Rep. and res. to be discharg'd.		Resolution adopted.		
Costin, Benjamin	(See Reuben E. Gentry & others.)											
Coston, William	(See George Brown, sureties of.)											
Cot, Thomas	Arrears of short pay as surgeon's mate at Fort Trumbull, Conn.	25	3	Resolution	291	Claims.						
Cotheall, Robert	Increase of pension	11	3	House bill	604	Whole House	Mar. 2, 1811	Favorable	218	Passed	Passed	App'd March 3, 1811
Cotheal & Hoff, (N. Y.)	Drawback on gin exported to West Indies.	14	1	Petition	248	Com. and Manuf.				Discharged; laid on table.		
Cotheal & Hoff, (N. Y.)	Drawback on gin exported to West Indies.	26	1	Petition	292	Commerce	30	Report and bill.	49	Passed	Passed	App'd July 20, 1840
Cotheal, Henry and David, and A. S. Hallet.	Redress for the capture and condemnation of their vessel and cargo in a Spanish port.	18	1	Petition	77	Foreign Affairs	22	Action inexpedient, & res. to withdraw.		Laid on table.		
Cotheal, Henry and David.	Drawback on Spanish playing cards exported.	24	1	Petition	277	Ways and Means	Feb. 10, 1836	By bill	309	Referred to Committee Whole House.		
Cotheal, Henry and David.	Drawback on Spanish playing cards exported.	24	2	Bill of last sess.	200	Whole House	Jan. 13, 1837	With't amend.	309	Passed	Passed	App'd March 3, 1837
Cott, Isaac	(See Rufus Spalding and others.)											
Cottineau, Dennis, widow of.	Pension for services as captain of ship Pallas in revolutionary war.	15	2	Petition	23	Pens. & Rev. Cl'ms.	Nov. 25, 1818	Rep. and res.; adverse.		Resolution adopted.		
Cottle, Almond, and others.	Confirmation of title to land in Territory of Missouri.	15	2	Petition	210	Priv. Land Claims				Discharged; laid on table.		
Cottle, Almond, and others	Confirmation of title to land in Territory of Missouri.	17	1	Petition	53	Public Lands				Discharged; laid on table.		
Cottle, Almond, and others.	Confirmation of title to land in Territory of Missouri.	18	1	Petition	53	Public Lands	Jan. 16, 1824	By bill	65	Passed	Passed	App'd May 26, 1824

List of private claims presented to the House of Representatives of the United States from the 1st to the 31st Congress, inclusive—Continued.

Names of claimants.	Nature or object of the claim.	Congress.	Session.	How brought before the House of Reps.	Page of journal.	To what committee of the House referred.	No. or date of the report.	Nature of the report.	No. of the bill.	How disposed of by the House of Reps.	How disposed of by the Senate.	Date of the act of Congress, and remarks.
Cottle, Almond, widow of.	Confirmation of title to land in Territory of Missouri.	24	2	Petition	314	Priv. Land Claims.						
Cottle, Almond, widow of.	Confirmation of title to land in Territory of Missouri.	25	2	Petition	282	Priv. Land Claims.	Jan. 20, 1838	Adverse	......	Laid on table.		
Cottle, Ira	(See Reuben E. Gentry & others)											
Cottle, Robert	Pension	15	1	Petition	23	Pens. & Rev. Cl'ms.						
Cottle, Robert	Pension	15	2	Resolution	90	Rev. Pensions	Dec. 24, 1818	Rep. and res for leave to withdraw.	......	Resolution adopted.		
Cottle, William	Compensation for military services in revolutionary war.	1	3	Petition and rep't Sec. of War.	342	....	....	....	......	Laid on table.		
Cotton, Daniel	Damages for detention by Bey of Tunis of ship Ann Maria, chartered by United States.	8	2	Memorial	5	Claims.						
Cotton, Daniel	Damages for detention by Bey of Tunis of ship Ann Maria, chartered by United States.	9	1	Memorial	222	Claims	Mar. 25, 1806	Leave to withdraw.	......	Report adopted.		
Cotton, Daniel	Damages for detention by Bey of Tunis of ship Ann Maria, chartered by United States.	9	1	Petition	380	Claims	April 14, 1806	Indef. postp'd.	......	Report adopted.		
Cotton, Daniel	Damages for detention by Bey of Tunis of ship Ann Maria, chartered by United States.	9	2	Petition	503	Claims	Feb. 19, 1807	Favorable	......	Referred to Committee Whole House.		
Cotton, Daniel	Damages for detention by Bey of Tunis of ship Ann Maria, chartered by United States.	10	1	Memorial	188	Claims	Mar. 7, 1808	Favorable	......	Referred to Committee Whole House.		
Cotton, Daniel	Damages for detention by Bey of Tunis of ship Ann Maria, chartered by United States.	10	2	Memorial	351	Claims	Nov. 18, 1808	Favorable; bill ordered.	123	Passed	Passed	App'd Feb. 28, 1809
Cotton, Benjamin	Invalid pension	11	2	House bill	283	Whole House	Mar. 24, 1810	Favorable	108	Passed	Passed	App'd April 27, 1810
Cotton, Elisha	Pension	16	1	Resolution	63	Rev. Pensions	Jan. 14, 1820	Adverse; & res. to withdraw.	......	Laid on table.		
Cotton, M. T., and others, of Alabama.	Indemnity for French spoliations prior to 1800.	23	2	Petition	346	Foreign Affairs.						
Cotton, M. T	(See John Smith, administrator of.)	26	1	....	182							
Cotton, Rowland	Pension	14	2	Petition	377	Pens. & Rev. Cl'ms.	....	....	......	Discharged; laid on table.		
Cotton, Samuel	Revolutionary pension	22	1	Petition	97	Rev. Pensions	....	....	......	Discharged; laid on table.		
Cotton, William	Revolutionary pension	28	1	Petition	547	Rev. Pensions	April 12, 1844	Adverse	......	Laid on table.		
Cotton, William	Revolutionary pension	28	2	Petition	145	Rev. Pensions.						
Cottrill, John	Restoration to pension roll	25	2	Petition	231	Rev. Pensions	....	....	......	Discharged; laid on table.		
Cottrill, John	Restoration to pension roll	25	3	Petition	88	Rev. Pensions	....	....	......	Discharged.		
Cottrill, John	Restoration to pension roll	26	1	Petition	173	Rev. Pensions	....	....	......	Discharged; laid on table.		
Cottrill, John	Restoration to pension roll	29	1	Petition	309	Rev. Pensions	826	Adverse	......	Laid on table.		
Cottrill, Mahlon	(See Ira Day and M. Cottrill)	23	1	....	191							
Cottrill, Matthew	(See James Cavanaugh.)											
Cottrill, Richard, *alias* Cottriall, (Va.)	Invalid pension	23	2	Petition	116	Invalid Pensions	Jan. 20, 1835	Adverse	......	Laid on table.		
Cottrill, Richard, *alias* Cottriall, (Va.)	Invalid pension	24	1	Petition	661	Invalid Pensions	650	Adverse	......	Laid on table.		

List of private claims presented to the House of Representatives of the United States from the 1st to the 31st Congress, inclusive—Continued.

Names of claimants.	Nature or object of the claim	Congress.	Session.	How brought before the House of Reps.	Page of journal.	To what committee of the House referred.	No. or date of the report.	Nature of the report.	No. of the bill.	How disposed of by the House of Reps.	How disposed of by the Senate.	Date of the act of Congress, and remarks.
Cottrill, Richard, *alias* Cottriall, (Va.)	Invalid pension	24	2	Resolution	78	Rev. Claims.						
Cottrill, Richard, *alias* Cottriall, (Va.)	Invalid pension	26	2	Petition	101	Invalid Pensions	87	Adverse		Laid on table.		
Cottrill, Richard, (Ala.)	Compensation for forage furnished United States troops in war of 1812.	23	2	Petition	275	Claims.						
Cottrill, Richard, (Ala.)	Compensation for forage furnished United States troops in war of 1812.	24	1	Petition	611	Claims	696	Adverse		Laid on table.		
Couch, jr., John, *alias* Concle.	Pension	22	2	Petition	124	Invalid Pensions	Feb. 15, 1833	By bill	738	Referred to Committee Whole House.		
Couch, jr., John, *alias* Concle.	Pension	23	1	Petition	44	Invalid Pensions	1	Report and bill.	1	Passed	Passed	App'd June 25, 1834
Couch, John, widow of	Revolutionary pension	27	2	Petition	525	Rev. Pensions	797	Report and bill.	451	Engrossed.		
Couch, John, widow of	Revolutionary pension	27	3	Bill of last sess.	88				451	Passed	Indef. postp'd.	
Couch, Timothy	Pension	21	2	Petition	158	Military Pensions.						
Couch, Timothy	Pension	22	1	Petition	23	Rev. Pensions.						
Couch, William	Pension for services in revolutionary war.	28	2	Petition	136	Rev. Pensions	118	Report and bill.	597	Referred to Committee Whole House.		
Coughran, James	Compensation for wounds received while a soldier under General Wayne.	11	2	Petition	182					Referred to Secretary of War.		
Couliard, Francis	Invalid pension	21	1	Petition	188	Invalid Pensions				Discharged; laid on table.		
Coulon, Paul, a citizen of the French Republic.	Payment for two prize vessels and cargoes seized by the collector at Wilmington, N. C., and for damages.	7	1	Petition	29	Claims	Feb. 1, 1802 March 7, 1802	Adverse. Favorable; bill ordered.	 56	Recommitted. Passed	 Rejected.	
Coulon, Paul, a citizen of the French Republic.	Payment for two prize vessels and cargoes seized by the collector at Wilmington, N. C., and for damages.	7	2	Memorial	339	Claims	Feb. 16, 1803	Favorable; bill ordered.	130	Passed	Postponed.	
Coulon, Paul, a citizen of the French Republic.	Payment for two prize vessels and cargoes seized by the collector at Wilmington, N. C., and for damages.	8	1	Memorial	435	Claims	Nov. 16, 1803 Dec. 13, 1803	Favorable Favorable; bill ordered.	 146	Recommitted. Passed	 Passed	 App'd Jan. 26, 1804
Coulon, Paul, a citizen of the French Republic.	Permission to institute suit against United States for value of two prize vessels and cargoes seized in 1798 by collector at Wilmington, N. C.	8	1	Petition	660					Laid on table.		
Coulter, James	(See James Armstrong.)											
Coulter, Mifflin, children of.	Pension for services as surgeon in navy.	31	1	Petition	1226	Invalid Pensions				Leave to withdraw.		
Count, James, administrators of.	Indemnity for French spoliations prior to 1800.	26	1	Memorial	182	Foreign Affairs	343	Favorable; bill	319	Referred to Committee Whole House.		
Countee, John R.	(See Jacob Thompson.)											
Courtney, Buchanan, & Co.	Indemnity for French spoliations prior to 1800.	26	1	Memorial	182	Foreign Affairs	343	Favorable	319	Referred to Committee Whole House.		
Courtney, Francis	Invalid pension	3	1	Rep. of Secretary of War.	131	Select	May 26, 1794	Ref. to Sec. with instruc.	R. 12	Passed	Passed	App'd June 9, 1794

List of private claims presented to the House of Representatives of the United States from the 1st to the 31st Congress, inclusive—Continued.

Names of claimants.	Nature or object of the claim.	Congress.	Session.	How brought before the House of Reps.	Page of journal.	To what committee of the House referred.	No. or date of the report.	Nature of the report.	No. of the bill.	How disposed of by the House of Reps.	How disposed of by the Senate.	Date of the act of Congress, and remarks.
Courtney, George	Pension, land, money, and pay for clothing, to which he conceives he is entitled as a soldier.	14	1	Petition	139	Pens. & Rev. Cl'ms	April 11, 1816	By bill	171			Bill became a law April 30, 1816, omitting Courtney's name.
Courtney, John T., and Samuel Harrison.	Compensation for services in extinguishing fire applied by British to schooner Asp.	13	2	Petition	263	Naval Affairs	Mar. 15, 1814	Res. to refer to Sec. Navy.		Resolution adopted		Secretary's report of April 16, laid on table.
Courtney, John T., and Samuel Harrison.	Compensation for services in extinguishing fire applied by British to schooner Asp.	13	3	Petition	472	Naval Affairs.						
Courtney, John T., and Samuel Harrison.	Compensation for services in extinguishing fire applied by British to schooner Asp.	14	1	Petition	83	Naval Affairs	Feb. 19, 1816	By bill	87	Passed	Passed	App'd April 26, 1816
Courtney, Micajah	(See Thomas W. Chinn and others.)											
Courtney, Philip, heirs of.	Payment of amount due as ensign in revolutionary war.	27	3	Petition	76	Rev. Claims	231	Adverse		Laid on table.		
Courtney, Philip, heirs of.	Payment of amount due as ensign in revolutionary war.	29	1	Petition	1124	Rev. Claims.						
Courtney, Philip, heirs of.	Payment of amount due as ensign in revolutionary war.	31	1	Petition	816	Rev. Claims.						
Courtney, Robert, administrator of.	Indemnity for French spoliations prior to 1800.	26	1	Memorial	182	Foreign Affairs	343	Favorable; bill	319	Referred to Committee Whole House.		
Courtney, Robert, administrator of.	Indemnity for French spoliations prior to 1800.	31	1	Petition	216	Foreign Affairs	355	Report and bill.	318	Referred to Committee Whole House.		
Courtney, Thomas	Pension for services rendered U. S. in 1780.	24	1	Petition	942	Invalid Pensions				Discharged; laid on table.		
Courtney, William	Compensation for house and other property destroyed by American troops in revolutionary war.	4	1	Petition	373	Claims	Jan. 20, 1796	Adverse; leave to withdraw.		Report adopted.		
Courtois, Louis	Confirmation of title to land in Missouri.	15	1	Petition	326	Priv. Land Claims				Discharged.		
Courtois, Louis	Confirmation of title to land in Missouri.	16	1	Petition	36	Priv. Land Claims				Discharged; laid on table.		
Courtois, Louis	Confirmation of title to land in Missouri.	17	1	Petition	53	Public Lands				Discharged; laid on table.		See act May 26, 1824
Courts, Richard Henly	Compensation as surgeon's mate in United States hospital.	2	1	Petition and report Sec. War.	497					Laid on table.		
Courts, Richard Henly	Compensation as surgeon's mate in United States hospital.	9	2	Petition	594	Whole House.						
Courts, Richard H. widow of.	Compensation for services of husband as surgeon's mate in U. S. hospital.	20	2	Petition	33	Rev. Claims				Discharged; laid on table.		
Courts, Richard H. widow of.	Compensation for services of husband as surgeon's mate in U. S. hospital.	21	1	Petition	107	Rev. Claims	240	Report and bill.	302	Referred to Committee Whole House.		
Courts, Richard H. widow of.	Compensation for services of husband as surgeon's mate in U. S. hospital.	21	2	Bill of last sess.	340	Whole House	Feb. 22, 1831	With't amend.	302	Passed	Laid on table.	
Courts, Richard H. widow of.	Compensation for services of husband as surgeon's mate in U. S. hospital.	22	2	Senate bill	166	Rev. Claims	Jan. 10, 1833	With't amend.	36	Passed	Passed	App'd March 2, 1833

List of private claims presented to the House of Representatives of the United States from the 1st to the 31st Congress, inclusive—Continued.

Names of claimants.	Nature or object of the claim.	Congress.	Session.	How brought before the House of Reps.	Page of journal.	To what committee of the House referred.	No. or date of the report.	Nature of the report.	No. of the bill.	How disposed of by the House of Reps.	How disposed of by the Senate.	Date of the act of Congress, and remarks.
Cousens, Nathaniel	Pension	16	1	Petition	26	Rev. Pensions	Jan. 14, 1820	Adverse; res. to withdraw.		Laid on table.		
Cousins, François	Confirmation of title to land in Louisiana.	19	2	Petition	245	Priv. Land Claims.						
Cousot, François	(See James Scull and others.)	19	2		137							
Couture, Jean Baptiste	(See Jean Baptiste Conture.)											
Couvillion, Amelia	(See Zenon St. Romain, wife of.)											
Covel, David	Compensation for services in navy of the revolution.	4	1	Petition	457	Claims	May 31, 1796	Adverse		Laid on table.		
Covel, Ebenezer, (Mass.)	Restoration of pension	17	1	Petition	67	Rev. Pensions	Jan. 15, 1822	General bill	37	Passed	Rejected.	See act March 1, 1823
Covel, Joseph	Pension	21	1	Petition	411	Military Pensions				Discharged; laid on table.		
Covenhoven, Albert	Compensation for services in the revolutionary army.	21	1	Documents	203	Military Pensions				Discharged; laid on table.		
Covenhoven, Nicholas, and others, of King's county, N. Y.	Compensation for subsistence of American officers (prisoners) in revolutionary war.	1	2	Petition	167	Select	April 21, 1790	Favorable		Pet. and rep. referred to Sec. Treasury.		
Covenhoven, Nicholas, and others, of King's county, N. Y.	Compensation for subsistence of American officers (prisoners) in revolutionary war.	2	2	Rep. of Secretary Treasury.	625					Laid on table.		
Covenhoven, Peter	Increase of pension, and amount of expenses incurred in confinement with wounds received in revolutionary war.	2	1	Petition	510					Referred to Secretary of War.		
Covenhoven, Peter	Increase of pension, and amount of expenses incurred in confine ment with wounds received in revolutionary war.	2	2	Report Secretary of War.	711					Laid on table.		
Covenhoven, Peter	Increase of pension, and amount of expenses incurred in confinement with wounds received in revolutionary war.	3	2	Report Secretary of War.	225	Whole House	Nov. 13, 1794	Favorable; bill ordered.	70	Passed	Passed	App'd Jan'y 1, 1795
Covenhoven, Peter	Invalid pension	12	1	Petition	61	Claims	June 12, 1812	Adverse; leave to withdraw.		Laid on table.		
Covenhoven, Peter	Increase of pension	16	1	Petition	153	Pens. & Rev. Cl'ms.				Discharged; laid on table.		
Covenhoven, William	Pension	21	2	Petition	209	Military Pensions.						
Covenhoven, William	Pension	22	1	Petition	73	Rev. Pensions				Discharged; laid on table.		
Covil, Ebenezer, (N. Y.)	Pension	21	2	Petition	43	Military Pensions.						
Coville, Peter	Invalid pension	28	2	Petition	216	Invalid Pensions.						
Coville, Peter	Invalid pension	29	1	Petition	330	Invalid Pensions.						
Coville, Peter	Invalid pension	30	1	Petition	82	Invalid Pensions	34	Adverse		Laid on table.		
Cowan, George R.	(See David Shaver, sen., & others.)											
Cowan, John	Compensation to his company of mounted gun-men for expenses in horse shoeing, &c.	15	1	Petition	84	Claims	126	Adverse		Referred to Committee Whole House.		
Cowan, John	Compensation to his company of mounted gun-men for expenses in horse shoeing, &c.	15	2	Rep. of last sess.	83	Whole House	Dec. 10, 1818	Favorable; bill ordered.	227	Referred to Committee Whole House.		
Cowan, John	Compensation to his company of mounted gun-men for expenses of horse shoeing, &c.	16	1	Petition	42	Claims	25	Report & res. adverse.		Referred to Committee Whole House.		

List of private claims presented to the House of Representatives of the United States from the 1st to the 31st Congress, inclusive—Continued.

Names of claimants.	Nature or object of the claim.	Congress.	Session.	How brought before the House of Reps.	Page of journal.	To what committee of the House referred.	No. or date of the report.	Nature of the report.	No. of the bill.	How disposed of by the House of Reps.	How disposed of by the Senate.	Date of the act of Congress, and remarks.
Cowan, John	Compensation to his company of mounted gun-men for expenses of horse shoeing, &c.	16	2	Rept. and res. of last session.	34	Whole House	Nov. 24, 1820	With't amend.		Resolution adopted.		
Cowan, J. Epes	(See Antoine Vasques, and others, representatives of.)											
Cowan, Thomas, & others	Remission of tax on salt-works destroyed by the sea.	14	1	Petition	134	Ways and Means				Discharged; laid on table.		
Cowan, William	(See Virginia Yazoo Company, agent of.)											
Cowden, David	Pension for wounds received at battle of Queenstown.	30	1	Petition	215	Invalid Pensions.						
Cowden, David	Pension for wounds received at battle of Queenstown.	31	1	Petition	863	Invalid Pensions	Aug. 1, 1850	Adverse		Laid on table.		
Cowdery, Augustus A.	Remuneration for room rent for U. S. court at Norfolk, Va.	29	1	Petition	588	Claims	637	Adverse		Laid on table.		
Cowdry, Jonathan	Revolutionary pension	22	1	Petition	219	Rev. Pensions				Discharged; laid on table.		
Cowell, John G., widow of	Relief; husband killed in frigate Essex, war of 1812.	28	1	Petition	98	Claims.						
Cowell, Ebenezer	Allowance of account for gunsmith's work, and reimbursement of money advanced on contract for same.	2	1	Petition	482	Select	Feb. 3, 1792	Adverse		Laid on table.		
Cowell, Ebenezer	Allowance of account for gunsmith's work, and reimbursement of money advanced on contract for same.	2	2	Report, former	660					Rejected.		
Cowell, Samuel	Pension	21	1	Petition	217	Military Pensions	May 4, 1830	Adverse		Laid on table.		
Cowgill, Valentine	Release from service in U. S. army	26	1	Petition	331	Military Affairs	243	Adverse		Laid on table.		
Cowing, James	Revolutionary pension	18	1	Petition	210	Rev. Pensions				Leave to withdraw.		
Cowing, James	Revolutionary pension	18	2	Petition	59	Rev. Pensions	Jan. 19, 1825	Adverse		Laid on table		
Cowles, Noah	Pension	21	2	Petition	103	Military Pensions.						
Cowles, Phineas	Pension	21	1	Petition	143	Military Pensions				Discharged; laid on table.		
Cowls, Elias	(See Samuel Langdon, and others)	12	1	Petition	138							
Cowper & Co.	Indemnity for French spoliations prior to 1800.	26	1	Memorial	182	Foreign Affairs	343	Favorable; bill	319	Referred to Committee Whole House.		
Cowper, John	(See Warren Ashley, executor of.)											
Cowper, John, (Va.)	Commissions as agent for claimants under Florida treaty.	23	2	Petition	114	Claims	106	Report and bill.	736	Referred to Committee Whole House.		
Cowper, John, (Va.)	Commissions as agent for claimants under Florida treaty.	24	1	Petition	94	Claims	151	Report and bill.	159	Passed	Passed	App'd July 4, 1836
Cowper, John	(See Cowper & Co.)	26	1		182							
Cowper, John	Indemnity for French spoliations prior to 1800.	26	1	Memorial	182	Foreign Affairs	343	Favorable; bill	319	Referred to Committee Whole House.		
Cowper, John, (Va.,) agent for sundry citizens.	Indemnity for French spoliations prior to 1800.	27	2	Petition	306	Whole House, on bill No. 57.						
Cowperthwait, Joseph	Release from liability for public money of which he was robbed while acting navy agent.	5	2	Petition	159	Claims	May 16, 1798	Adverse.		Laid on table.		
Cowtzer, Philip	(See Abraham Mosser and others.)											
Cox, Abraham	Settlement of his claims as quartermaster United States army.	27	2	Petition	383	Claims	649	Adverse		Laid on table.		

List of private claims presented to the House of Representatives of the United States from the 1st to the 31st Congress, inclusive—Continued.

Names of claimants.	Nature or object of the claim.	Congress.	Session.	How brought before the House of Reps.	Page of journal.	To what committee of the House referred.	No. or date of the report.	Nature of the report.	No. of the bill.	How disposed of by the House of Reps.	How disposed of by the Senate.	Date of the act of Congress, and remarks.
Cox, Barney	Compensation for services, &c., in revolutionary war.	2	1	Petition	456					Referred to Secretary of War.		
Cox, Bartley	Compensation for horse lost in the Seminole camp, 1818.	22	1	Petition	32	Claims	Dec. 30, 1831	Adverse		Laid on table.		
Cox, Benjamin, (Maine,) widow of.	Revolutionary pension	22	1	Petition	329	Rev. Pensions				Discharged; laid on table.		
Cox, Benjamin, (Vt.)	Revolutionary pension	24	1	Petition and res.	635, 662	Rev. Pensions				Discharged; laid on table.		
Cox, Benjamin, (Vt.)	Revolutionary pension	24	2	Petition	73	Rev. Claims				Discharged; laid on table.		
Cox, Benjamin, (Vt.)	Revolutionary pension	25	2	Petition	459	Rev. Pensions	Feb. 17, 1838	To ref. to Com. W. Ho. on bill No. 176		Report adopted.		
Cox, Benjamin, (Vt.)	Revolutionary pension	26	1	Petition	173	Rev. Pensions	714	Adverse		Laid on table.		
Cox, Benjamin, (Vt.)	Revolutionary pension	26	1	Resolution	407	Rev. Pensions	663	Adverse		Laid on table.		
Cox, Daniel W., and others	Drawback of duties on foreign merchandise exported from Philadelphia.	7	1	Petition	42	Com. and Manuf.	Jan. 26, 1802	Report and bill.	16	Rejected.		
Cox, Daniel W.	(See De Maison Rouge, Marquis of.)											
Cox, Daniel W.	Indemnity for French spoliations prior to 1800.	26	1	Memorial	182	Foreign Affairs	343	Favorable; bill	319	Referred to Committee Whole House.		
Cox, David	Pension	21	1	Petition	36	Military Pensions.	April 2, 1830	Adverse		Laid on table.		
Cox, Ebenezer	Pension	25	2	Petition	638	Rev. Pensions.				Discharged; laid on table.		
Cox, Elizabeth	(See Thomas Bills, heirs of.)											
Cox, Ellen	Revolutionary pension	25	2	Petition	180	Rev. Pensions.				Discharged; laid on table.		
Cox, George	Revolutionary pension	24	1	Resolution	647	Rev. Pensions.				Discharged; laid on table.		
Cox, Good	(See Wm. H. Bedford, agent, &c.)	28	1		262							
Cox, Gover	Compensation for horse lost in the Seminole camp, 1818.	23	1	Documents	154	Claims.						
Cox, Isaac	Compensation for wood furnished in revolutionary war.	4	1	Rep. of Secretary Treasury.	388	Claims	May 31, 1796	Adverse		Laid on table.		
Cox, James	Pension for injuries by a fall in frigate Constellation.	25	2	Petition	657	Claims				Discharged; laid on table.		
Cox, James	Pension for injuries by a fall in frigate Constellation.	25	3	Petition	460	Invalid Pensions.						
Cox, James	Pension for injuries by a fall in frigate Constellation.	26	1	Petition	162	Invalid Pensions	285	Adverse		Laid on table.		
Cox, James, (Penn.)	Fees as crier of court allowed in the marshal's account, but not paid him.	25	2	Petition	723	Claims	902	Report and bill.	796	Referred to Committee Whole House.		
Cox, James, (Penn.)	Fees as crier of court allowed in the marshal's account, but not paid him.	25	3	Bill of last sess.	431	Whole House	Feb. 1, 1839	With't amend.	796	Passed	Adverse report.	
Cox, James, (Penn.)	Fees as crier of court allowed in the marshal's account, but not paid him.	26	1	Petition	168	Claims	16	Report and bill.	35	Passed	Indef. postp'd.	
Cox, James, (Penn.)	Fees as crier of court allowed in the marshal's account, but not paid him.	26	2	Petition	101	Claims	12	Report and bill.	550	Referred to Committee Whole House.		

List of private claims presented to the House of Representatives of the United States from the 1st to the 31st Congress, inclusive—Continued.

Names of claimants.	Nature or object of the claim.	Congress.	Session.	How brought before the House of Reps.	Page of journal.	To what committee of the House referred.	No. or date of the report.	Nature of the report.	No. of the bill.	How disposed of by the House of Reps.	How disposed of by the Senate.	Date of the act of Congress, and remarks.
Cox, James	(See William H. Bedford, agent, &c.)	28	1	....	262							
Cox, James H	(See John B. Crozier & Co., of Tennessee volunteers.)											
Cox, John	(See Joseph Falconer, heirs of.)											
Cox, John	Compensation as a wagoner in United States service in 1812.	24	2	Documents	215	Military Affairs.						
Cox, John	Compensation as a wagoner in United States service in 1812.	29	1	Documents	353	Military Affairs.						
Cox, John, (Mass.,) heirs of.	Payment to Phineas Capen of amount due per books of treasury.	29	1	Petition	275	Claims	538	Report and bill.	360	Passed.		
Cox, John, (Mass.,) heirs of.	Payment to Phineas Capen of amount due per books of treasury.	30	1	Petition	69	Claims	3	Report and bill.	3	Passed	Passed	App'd June 26, 1848
Cox, John Palmer	Credit in his account as paymaster of New York militia for moneys of which he was robbed.	13	3	Petition	770	Claims	63	Adverse	......	Indef. postponed.		
Cox, John Palmer	Credit in his account as paymaster of New York militia for moneys of which he was robbed.	17	2	Petition	82	Claims	....	....	......	Leave to withdraw.		
Cox, John Palmer	Credit in his account as paymaster of New York militia for moneys of which he was robbed.	18	1	Petition	214	Claims	80	Adverse	......	Referred to Committee Whole House.		
Cox, Pohn Palmer, widow of.	Release of his estate from judgment of United States.	19	1	Petition	89	Claims	114	Report and bill.	153	Passed	Amendm't reported.	
Cox, John Palmer, widow of.	Release of his estate from judgment of United States.	19	2	Petition	64	Claims	Jan. 10, 1827	Report and bill.	361	Rejected.		
Cox, John Palmer, widow of.	Release of his estate from judgment of United States.	20	1	Petition	38	Claims	52	Report and bill.	52	Rejected.		
Cox, John Palmer, representatives of.	Release of his estate from judgment of United States.	21	1	Senate bill	118	Claims	52	With't amend.	25	Referred to Committee Whole House.		
Cox, John Palmer, widow of.	Release of his estate from judgment of United States.	22	1	Petition	73	Claims	467	Report and bill.	565	Referred to Committee Whole House.		
Cox, John, (Va.)	Indemnity for French spoliations prior to 1800.	26	1	Memorial	182	Foreign Affairs	343	Favorable; bill	319	Referred to Committee Whole House.		
Cox, John Redman	Reimbursement of duties on minerals, and chemical, and philosophical apparatus.	14	1	Petition	71	Com. and Manuf	Jan. 4, 1816	By bill	......	Passed	Passed	App'd Feb. 28, 1816
Cox, John and Samuel	Confirmation of title to land in Territory of Missouri.	15	1	Petition	157	Priv. Land Claims	....	....	......	Discharged	....	See act May 26, 1824
Cox, John W	Pension	23	1	Petition	423	Invalid Pensions	533	Report and bill.	539	Referred to Committee Whole House.		
Cox, John W	Pension	23	2	Bill of last sess.	336	Whole House	Feb. 6, 1835	With't amend.	539	Passed	Adverse report.	
Cox, John W	Pension	25	2	Petition	193	Invalid Pensions	779	Adverse	......	Referred to Committee Whole House.		
Cox, John W	Pension	26	1	Petition	327	Invalid Pensions	475	Report and bill.	389	Referred to Committee Whole House.		
Cox, John W	Pension	27	2	Petition	410	Invalid Pensions	607	Adverse	......	Laid on table.		
Cox, Joseph	Commutation of five years half-pay for revolutionary services.	1	3	Petition	392	....	....	....	......	Referred to Secretary War.		
Cox, Joseph	Compensation for services, &c., in revolutionary war.	4	1	Petition	470	Claims	May 31, 1796	Adverse	......	Laid on table.		

List of private claims presented to the House of Representatives of the United States from the 1st to the 31st Congress, inclusive—Continued.

Names of claimants.	Nature or object of the claim.	Congress.	Session.	How brought before the House of Reps.	Page of journal.	To what committee of the House referred.	No. or date of the report.	Nature of the report.	No. of the bill.	How disposed of by the House of Reps.	How disposed of by the Senate.	Date of the act of Congress, and remarks.
Cox, Joseph	Invalid pension	3	1	Rep. of Secretary War.	131	Select	May 26, 1794	Res. to refer to Sec. of War, with instructions.	R. 12	Passed	Passed	App'd June 9, 1794
Cox, Joseph	Invalid pension	3	2	Rep. of Secretary War.	278	Claims	Feb. 28, 1795	Favorable; bill ordered.	130	Passed	Postponed to next session.	
Cox, Joseph	Invalid pension	4	1	Rep. of last sess.	445	Claims	Feb. 18, 1796	Favorable; bill ordered.	156	Passed	Passed	App'd April 20, 1796
Cox, Joseph, and Elias Thomas.	Refunding of duties on sugar intended for exportation, and burnt.	7	2	Petition	283	Com. and Manuf.	Jan. 18, 1803	Res. adverse, & for leave to withdraw.	......	Resolution adopted.		
Cox, Nathaniel	(See William Nott and others.)											
Cox, Nathaniel, widow of.	(See Samuel Elkins, administrator of.)											
Cox, Nathaniel, widow and executrix of.	Payment of balance due deceased as navy agent at New Orleans.	29	2	Petition	56	Claims	29	Report and bill.	608	Referred to Committee Whole House.		
Cox, Nathaniel, widow and executrix of.	Payment of balance due deceased as navy agent at New Orleans.	30	1	Petition	102	Claims	66	Report and bill.	48	Recommitted.		
							362	Adverse	48	Laid on table.		
Cox, Phineas	Invalid pension	3	1	Rep. of Secretary War.	131	Select	May 26, 1794	Res. to refer to Sec. of War, with instructions.	R. 12	Passed	Passed	App'd June 9, 1794
Cox, Robert J.	Bounty land for services, &c., in Mexican war.	30	1	Petition	874	Claims.						
Cox, Robert J.	Bounty land for services, &c., in Mexican war.	31	1	Petition	649	Claims	....	....	......	Discharged; laid on table.		
Cox, Richard S.	(See David Beard, assignee of.)											
Cox, Richard S	(See Mexican claimants.)											
Cox, Richard S., agent of.	(See John Baldwin, and others.)											
Cox, Richard S	Compensation for services as attorney for Post Office department.	29	1	Senate bill	1075	Judiciary	July 24, 1846	With't amend.	113	Referred to Committee Whole House.		
Cox, Richard S.	Compensation for services as attorney for Post Office department.	29	2	Senate bill	199	Judiciary	Feb. 24, 1847	With't amend.	48	Referred to Committee Whole House.		
Cox, Richard S.	Compensation for services as attorney for Post Office department.	30	1	Senate bill	361	Judiciary	Feb. 29, 1848	With't amend.	55	Referred to Committee Whole House.		
Cox, Samuel	Compensation for wood furnished in revolutionary war.	4	1	Rep. of Secretary Treasury.	338	Claims	May 31, 1796	Adverse	......	Laid on table.		
Cox, Samuel, (Ala.)	Compensation for horse lost in U. S. service for want of forage.	17	2	Petition	40	Claims	....	....	......	Leave to withdraw.		
Coxe, Stinson, and others.	Compensation for locating bounty land warrants.	31	1	Petition	284	Public Lands.						
Cox, Thomas	Invalid pension	4	2	Petition	701	Claims.						
Cox, Thomas	Invalid pension	5	3	Petition	89	Claims	April 17, 1798	Adverse	......	Referred to Committee Whole House.		
Cox, Thomas	Invalid pension	5	2	Rep. of last sess.	432	Whole House.						
Cox, Thomas, and Dudley Palmer.	Increase of pension of certain pensioners assembled in Washington, D. C.	18	1	Petition	105	Rev. Pensions	54	Adverse	......	Laid on table.		
Cox & Tunno	Indemnity for French spoliations prior to 1800.	26	1	Memorial	182	Foreign Affairs	343	Favorable; bill.	319	Referred to Committee Whole House.		
Cox, William, (D. C.)	Allowance for damage to house and store in use of United States after conflagration of Treas'y building.	24	1	Petition	429	Claims	472	Adverse	......	Laid on table.		

List of private claims presented to the House of Representatives of the United States from the 1st to the 31st Congress, inclusive—Continued.

Names of claimants.	Nature or object of the claim.	Congress.	Session.	How brought before the House of Reps.	Page of journal.	To what committee of the House referred.	No. or date of the report.	Nature of the report.	No. of the bill.	How disposed of by the House of Reps.	How disposed of by the Senate.	Date of the act of Congress, and remarks.
Cox, William, (D. C.)	Allowance for damage to house and store in use of United States after conflagration of Treas'y building.	24	2	Petition	73	Rev. Claims.						
Cox, William, (Vt.)	Revolutionary pension	24	1	Petition	662	Rev. Pensions				Discharged; laid on table.		
Cox, Zachariah	Redress of injuries sustained from United States judicial and military authorities at Natchez and Nashville, in 1798.	8	1	Mem'l and President's message.	434	Select	Nov. 28, 1803	Adverse		Rejected.		
Cox, Zachariah	Redress of injuries sustained from United States judicial and military authorities at Natchez and Nashville, in 1798.	19	1	Petition	248	Claims	April 20, 1826	Adverse		Laid on table.		
Cox, Zachariah	Redress of injuries sustained from United States judicial and military authorities at Natchez and Nashville, in 1798.	20	1	Petition	58	Claims	Feb. 7, 1828	Adverse		Laid on table.		
Cox, Zachariah	Redress of injuries sustained from United States judicial and military authorities at Natchez and Nashville, in 1798.	20	2	Petition	32	Claims				Discharged; laid on table.		
Cox, Zachariah	Redress of injuries sustained from United States judicial and military authorities at Natchez and Nashville, in 1798.	21	1	Petition	235	Claims	Feb. 5, 1830	Adverse		Laid on table.		
Coy, Christopher, widow of.	Pension for services in war of 1812.	28	1	Petition	527	Rev. Pensions.						
Coy, Christopher, widow of.	Pension for services in war of 1812.	29	1	Petition	310	Rev. Claims.						
Coyle, James, deceased, son of.	Payment for revolutionary services and for that of his horse and teams.	25	2	Petition	696	Rev. Claims				Discharged; laid on table.		
Coyle, James, deceased, son of.	Payment for revolutionary services and for that of his horse and teams.	25	3	Petition	84	Rev. Claims				Discharged.		
Coyle, James, deceased, son of.	Payment for revolutionary services and for that of his horse and teams.	26	1	Petition	163	Rev. Claims	238	Adverse		Laid on table.		
Coyle, James, deceased, son of.	Payment for revolutionary services and for that of his horse and teams.	27	2	Petition	357	Rev. Claims	655	Adverse		Laid on table.		
Coyle, James, deceased, son of.	Payment for revolutionary services and for that of his horse and teams.	28	1	Petition	129	Rev. Claims.						
Coyle, John, sr., and John, jr., and others.	Increase of compensation as clerks in office of First Auditor.	18	2	Petition	158	Ways and Means				Discharged; laid on table.		
Coyle, Manesseh	Revolutionary pension	15	2	Petition	258	Rev. Pensions	Feb. 11, 1819	Adverse		Laid on table.		
Cozac, Jacob	Change of entry of a tract of land to which a prior claim exists.	10	2	Petition	538							
Cozad, Jacob	Reimbursement of amount paid for ransom of his children from Indian captivity.	4	2	Memorial	666	Select	Feb. 6, 1797	Adverse, & res. to withdraw.		Resolution adopted.		
Cozad, Samuel	Compensation for suffering Indian captivity in 1794.	23	2	Petition	390	Rev. Claims.						

List of private claims presented to the House of Representatives of the United States from the 1st to the 31st Congress, inclusive—Continued.

Names of claimants.	Nature or object of the claim.	Congress.	Session.	How brought before the House of Reps.	Page of journal.	To what committee of the House referred.	No. or date of the report.	Nature of the report.	No. of the bill.	How disposed of by the House of Reps.	How disposed of by the Senate.	Date of the act of Congress, and remarks.
Cozad, Samuel	Compensation for suffering Indian captivity in 1794.	24	1	Petition	50	Claims	54	Adverse	......	Laid on table.		
Cozad, Samuel	Compensation for suffering Indian captivity in 1794.	24	2	Petition	95	Claims	213	Adverse	......	Laid on table.		
Cozzens, William B.	Compensation for horses taken from him at Point Isabel in 1847.	31	2	Petition	125	Claims.						
Crabb, Horatio N.	Portions of pay and emoluments as lieutenant in U. S. N., stopped by 4th Auditor.	21	1	Petition	547	Naval Affairs	....	....	......	Discharged; laid on table.		
Crabb, Horatio N.	Allowance for services and expenses as commanding marine officer.	24	2	Senate resolution.	527	Whole House	....	....	R. 10			
Crabb, Horatio N.	Restoration of pay, &c., withheld by accounting officers.	26	1	Petition	330	Naval Affairs.						
Crabb, Horatio N.	Restoration of pay, &c., withheld by accounting officers.	26	2	Petition	107	Naval Affairs.						
Crabb, Horatio N.	Restoration of pay, &c., withheld by accounting officers.	27	2	Petition	63	Claims	333	Adverse	......	Laid on table.		
Crabb, Horatio N.	Restoration of pay, &c., withheld by accounting officers.	27	3	Petition	112	Claims.						
Crabb, Horatio N.	Restoration of pay, &c., withheld by accounting officers.	29	1	Petition	303	Naval Affairs.						
Crabb, Horatio N.	Restoration of pay, &c., withheld by accounting officers.	30	1	Petition	607	Naval Affairs.						
Crabb, Horatio N.	Restoration of pay, &c., withheld by accounting officers.	30	2	Petition	295	Naval Affairs.						
Crabb, Horatio N.	Restoration of pay, &c., withheld by accounting officers.	31	1	Petition	258	Naval Affairs	117	Report and bill.	137	Referred to Committee Whole House.		
Crabb, Horatio N.	Compensation for extra services as assistant quartermaster of marine corps.	22	2	Petition	30	Naval Affairs	47	Report and bill.	691	Referred to Committee Whole House.		
Crabb, Horatio N.	Compensation for extra services as assistant quartermaster of marine corps.	23	1	Petition	36	Naval Affairs	29	Report and bill.	33	Passed	Passed	App'd June 30, 1834
Crabb, Horatio N.	Reimbursement of private funds expended in Creek campaign of 1836.	28	1	Petition	239	Claims.						
Crabb, Jesse	Bounty land for services in war of 1812.	29	1	Petition	739	Invalid Pensions.						
Crabb, John, surety of	Release from liability	18	1	Petition	331	Judiciary	April 30, 1824	By bill	213	Passed	Passed	App'd May 19, 1824
Crabb, Philip	Invalid pension	22	2	Resolution	150	Invalid Pensions	....	....	......	Discharged: laid on table.		
Crabb, Robert	To fund a certificate barred by the act of limitations.	3	2	Petition	277	Claims	Mar. 2, 1795	Adverse	......	Laid on table.		
Crabb, Robert	To fund a certificate barred by the act of limitations.	4	1	Petition	373	Claims	May 31, 1796	Adverse	......	Laid on table.		
Crabb, Thomas	Extra pay, &c., as acting 1st lieutenant at Washington navy yard.	23	1	Petition	56	Naval Affairs.						
Crabtree, Haynes	Compensation for horses lost in Seminole war, 1818.	17	1	Petition	349	Claims	....	....	......	Discharged; laid on table.		
Crabtree, Haynes	Compensation for horses lost in Seminole war, 1818.	20	1	Petition	100	Claims	....	....	......	Discharged; laid on table.		

List of private claims presented to the House of Representatives of the United States from the 1st to the 31st Congress, inclusive—Continued.

Names of claimants.	Nature or object of the claim.	Congress.	Session.	How brought before the House of Reps.	Page of journal.	To what committee of the House referred.	No. or date of the report.	Nature of the report.	No. of the bill.	How disposed of by the House of Reps.	How disposed of by the Senate.	Date of the act of Congress, and remarks.
Crabtree, Haynes	Compensation for horses lost in Seminole war, 1818.	20	2	Petition	40	Claims				Discharged; laid on table.		
Crabtree, Haynes	Compensation for wagon and two horses lost in Seminole war of 1818.	21	1	Petition	104	Claims				Discharged; laid on table.		
Crabtree, Haynes	Compensation for wagon and two horses lost in Seminole war of 1818.	21	2	Petition	74, 233	Claims.						
Crabtree, Haynes	Compensation for wagon and two horses lost in Seminole war of 1818.	22	1	Petition	25	Claims	Jan. 16, 1832	Adverse		Laid on table.		
Crabtree, Jacob	(See William H. Bedford, agent, &c.)	28	1		262							
Crabtree, James	Compensation for services as commissary, &c., in revolutionary war.	4	1	Petition	394	Claims	Jan. 26, 1796	Res. adv.; leave to withdraw.		Resolution adopted.		
Crabtree, Littleton	Pension for services in war of 1812	28	2	Petition	64	Invalid Pensions.						
Crabtree, Littleton	Pension for services in war of 1812	29	1	Petition	303	Invalid Pensions	290	Adverse		Laid on table.		
Crackbon, Lemuel	(See Jabez Mowry, and others.)											
Crader, Abraham	Confirmation of title to land in Territory of Missouri.	15	1	Petition	267	Priv. Land Claims				Discharged.		
Crader, Abraham	Confirmation of title to land in Territory of Missouri.	16	1	Petition	72	Priv. Land Claims				Discharged; laid on table.		
Crader, Abraham	Confirmation of title to land in Territory of Missouri.	17	1	Petition	53	Public Lands				Discharged; laid on table.		
Crader, Abraham	Confirmation of title to land in Territory of Missouri.	18	1	Petition	53	Public Lands	Jan. 16, 1824	By bill	65	Passed	Passed	App'd May 26, 1824
Craddock, John H.	Compensation for property destroyed by order of Colonel J. T. Lane, in 1836.	26	1	Sen. amendment to Ho. bill.	1343	Whole House	July 21, 1840	Favorable	27	Passed	Passed	App'd July 21, 1840
Craddock, Robert	(See Bartholomew Tardiveau, devisee for the heirs of.)											
Craddock, Robert	Compensation for services as an officer of revolutionary army.	23	2	Petition	147	Rev. Claims.						
Craddock, Robert	Compensation for services as an officer of revolutionary army.	24	1	Petition	152	Rev. Claims	421	Adverse		Laid on table.		
Craddock, Robert	Compensation for services as an officer of revolutionary army.	24	2	Petition	106	Rev. Claims				Discharged; laid on table.		
Craford, James	Compensation for services and losses as a refugee from Nova Scotia, in revolutionary war.	4	2	Petition	614	Whole House, on bill No. 209.						
Craft, Jacob	Compensation for services, &c., in revolutionary war.	2	1	Petition	517					Laid on table		Leave to withdraw, May 7, 1794.
Crafts, Charles	Compensation for services in revolutionary war.	19	2	Petition	243	Rev. Claims				Discharged.		
Crafts, Charles	Compensation for services in revolutionary war.	20	1	Petition	440	Military Pensions				Discharged; laid on table.		
Crafts, Charles	Compensation for services in revolutionary war.	21	1	Petition	59	Military Pensions	May 4, 1830	Adverse		Laid on table.		
Crafts, Charles	Compensation for services in revolutionary war.	22	1	Petition	67	Rev. Pensions				Discharged; laid on table.		
Crafts, Charles	Compensation for services in revolutionary war.	23	1	Petition	158	Rev. Pensions				Discharged; laid on table.		

List of private claims presented to the House of Representatives of the United States from the 1st to the 31st Congress, inclusive—Continued.

Names of claimants.	Nature or object of the claim.	Congress.	Session.	How brought before the House of Reps.	Page of journal.	To what committee of the House referred.	No. or date of the report.	Nature of the report.	No. of the bill.	How disposed of by the House of Reps.	How disposed of by the Senate.	Date of the act of Congress, and remarks.
Crafts, Harriet & Margaret	(See William Crafts, heirs of.)	26	1	....	182							
Crafts, William, heirs of.	Indemnity for French spoliations prior to 1800.	26	1	Memorial	182	Foreign Affairs	343	Favorable; bill	319	Referred to Committee Whole House.		
Craghead, George, & others	Allowance for military stores captured and delivered to General Smallwood in revolutionary war.	3	1	Memorial	42	....	....	....	.....	Referred to Secretary Treasury.		
Craghead, George, & others	Allowance for military stores captured and delivered to General Smallwood in revolutionary war.	3	2	Rep. of Secretary Treasury.	284	....	....	....	.....	Laid on table.		
Craghead, George, & others	Allowance for military stores captured and delivered to General Smallwood in revolutionary war.	4	1	Rep. of Secretary Treasury.	385	Claims	May 31, 1796	Adverse	.....	Laid on table.		
Craig, Andrew	Compensation as a mail contractor.	26	1	Petition	547	P. Of. and P. Roads.	401	Adverse	.....	Laid on table.		
Craig, Elijah	(See Hugh Alexander and others.)	7	2	....	262							
Craig, Hector, and others.	Compensation for services and expenses as commissioners of insolvency for southern district of N. York.	22	1	Petition	447	Judiciary	....	....	.....	Discharged; laid on table.		
Craig, Isaac, and others	Relief as purchasers of land deficient in quantity.	5	1	Petition	49	....	....	....	.....	Referred to Secretary Treasury.		
Craig, James, heirs of	Half pay promised by Virginia to officers in her Continental line.	24	2	Petition	96	Rev. Claims	Feb. 28, 1837	Adverse	.....	Laid on table.		
Craig, James, heirs of	Pension due under act of 1838.	28	1	Petition	729	Rev. Pensions.						
Craig, James, (Ill.)	Compensation for services in protecting inhabitants, near the Upper Mississippi, from the Indians	27	2	Petition	807	Claims.						
Craig, John, (Pa.)	Restoration of pension	10	1	Petition	129	Claims.						
Craig, John, (Pa.)	Restoration of pension	11	3	Petition	490	Select	Jan. 24, 1811	Rep. and res.; favorable.	.....	Laid on table.		
Craig, John, (Pa.)	Restoration of pension	13	2	Petition	196	Pens. & Rev. Cl'ms.	Jan. 10, 1814	Rep. and res.; adverse.	.....	Resolution adopted.		
Craig, John, executors of.	Indemnity for French spoliations prior to 1800.	26	1	Memorial	182	Foreign Affairs	343	Favorable; bill	319	Referred to Committee Whole House.		
Craig, John D.	Credit in his accounts as Superintendent of Patent Office for $160 embezzled by a messenger.	22	2	Petition	131	Claims.						
Craig, Lewis	(See Philemon Thomas and others)											
Craig, Lewis S.	Payment of certificates of deposite issued by Treasury Department, and assigned him by Commercial Bank of Cincinnati.	25	2	Resolution	1182	Ways and Means	....	....	.....	Discharged.		
Craig, Peter, heirs of	Pension	24	2	Senate bill	553	Whole House	....	....	167			
Craig, Robert, heir of	Compensation for revolutionary services.	27	2	Petition	181	Rev. Claims	205	Adverse	.....	Laid on table.		
Craig, Thomas, representative of.	Commutation pay for services as an officer in revolutionary army.	23	2	Petition	84	Rev. Claims	Dec. 29, 1834	Adverse	.....	Laid on table.		
Craig, William	(See Henry Saddler & Co.)	26	1	....	182							
Craig, William	(See Hugh Pollock, assignee of.)	26	1	....	182							
Craighead, Robert	Pension	15	1	House bill	405	Whole House	April 17, 1818	Favorable	172	Passed	Postponed.	
Craighead, Robert	Pension	1[illegible]	2	House bill	231	Whole House	Mar. 3, 1819	Favorable	308	Passed	Passed	App'd March 3, 1819
Craigmiles, Joseph	Invalid pension, war of 1812	2[illegible]	[illegible]	Petition	281	Invalid Pensions	74	Report and bill.	558	Passed	Adverse report; indef. postp'd	

List of private claims presented to the House of Representatives of the United States from the 1st to the 31st Congress, inclusive—Continued.

Names of claimants.	Nature or object of the claim.	Congress.	Session.	How brought before the House of Reps.	Page of journal.	To what committee of the House referred.	No. or date of the report.	Nature of the report.	No. of the bill.	How disposed of by the House of Reps.	How disposed of by the Senate.	Date of the act of Congress, and remarks.
53 Craigmiles, Joseph	Invalid pension, war of 1812	29	1	Petition	161, 353	Invalid Pensions	184	Adverse	......	Laid on table.		
Craine, Ezra	Pension	14	2	Resolution	322	Pens. & Rev. Cl'ms.						
Craine, James, legal representatives of.	Commutation of five years' full pay for services as captain in revolutionary army.	16	2	Petition	505	Whole House on bill No. 129.						
Craine, James, legal representatives of.	Commutation of five years' full pay for services as captain in revolutionary army.	11	2	Petition	141	Claims	Mar. 16, 1810	Adverse	......	Rejected.		
Craine, James, legal representatives of.	Commutation of five years' full pay for services as captain in revolutionary army.	11	3	Petition	473	Claims	Jan. 9, 1811	Adverse	......	Recommitted.		
Craine, James, legal representatives of.	Commutation of five years' full pay for services as captain in revolutionary army.	12	1	Petition	176	Claims	Mar. 6, 1812	Rep. and res.; adverse.	......	Recommitted.		
Craine, James, legal representatives of.	Commutation of five years' full pay for services as captain in revolutionary army.	12	2	Petition	591	Claims.						
Craine, James, legal representatives of.	Commutation of five years' full pay for services as captain in revolutionary army.	13	3	Petition	519	Pens. & Rev. Cl'ms.	Jan. 21, 1815	Rep. and res.; adverse.	......	Resolution adopted.		
Craine, James, legal representatives of.	Commutation of five years' full pay for services as captain in revolutionary army.	14	1	Petition	71	Pens. & Rev. Cl'ms.						
Craine, James, legal representatives of.	Commutation of five years' full pay for services as captain in revolutionary army.	14	2	Petition	29	Claims	....	....	......	Discharged; laid on table.		
Craine, James, legal representatives of.	Commutation of five years' full pay for services as captain in revolutionary army.	15	1	Petition	331	Claims	....	....	......	Discharged; laid on table.		
Craine, James, legal representatives of.	Commutation of five years' full pay for services as captain in revolutionary army.	15	2	Petition	24	Pens. & Rev. Cl'ms.	11	Adverse	......	Laid on table.		
Craine, James, legal representatives of.	Commutation of five years' full pay for services as captain in revolutionary army.	22	2	Petition	94	Rev. Claims.						
Craine, James, legal representatives of.	Commutation of five years' full pay for services as captain in revolutionary army.	23	1	Petition	41	Rev. Claims	70	Report and bill.	80	Passed	Passed	App'd June 30, 1834
Craine, James, legal representatives of.	Commutation of five years' full pay for services as captain in revolutionary army.	25	2	Petition	1079	Rev. Claims	....	....	......	Discharged; laid on table.		
Craine, James, legal representatives of.	Commutation of five years' full pay for services as captain in revolutionary army.	25	3	Petition	85	Rev. Claims	....	....	......	Discharged.		
Craine, John	Renewal of lost loan office certificate.	2	1	Petition and rep. Sec. of Treas.	158	Select.						
Craine, John	Payment of final settlement certificate issued in 1784.	15	1	Petition	132	Pens. & Rev. Cl'ms.	....	....	......	Discharged.		
Craine, John	Payment of final settlement certificate issued in 1784.	16	1	Petition	20	Pens. & Rev. Cl'ms.	Jan. 14, 1820	Adverse	......	Laid on table.		
Craine, John	Payment of final settlement certificate issued in 1784.	17	1	Petition	83	Pens. & Rev. Cl'ms.	....	....	......	Discharged; laid on table.		

List of private claims presented to the House of Representatives of the United States from the 1st to the 31st Congress, inclusive—Continued.

Names of claimants.	Nature or object of the claim.	Congress.	Session.	How brought before the House of Reps.	Page of journal.	To what committee of the House referred.	No. or date of the report.	Nature of the report.	No. of the bill.	How disposed of by the House of Reps.	How disposed of by the Senate.	Date of the act of Congress, and remarks.
Craine, John	Payment of final settlement certificate issued in 1784.	17	2	Petition	43	Rev. Pensions	Jan. 24, 1823	Report and bill.	251	Referred to Committee Whole House.		
Craine, John	Payment of final settlement certificate issued in 1784.	18	1	Petition	113	Pens. & Rev. Cl'ms.	......	......	......	Discharged; laid on table.		
Craine, John	Payment of final settlement certificate issued in 1784.	18	2	Petition	197	Select	55	Report and bill.	314	Passed	Passed	App'd March 3, 1825
Cramer.	(See Hagedorn and Cramer.)											
Cramer, Charles & George, and others.	A moiety of forfeiture of their vessel to U. S.	21	1	Petition	375	Ways and Means	279	Adverse; recommited.	......	Discharged; laid on table.		
Cramer, Charles, and others	A moiety of forfeiture of their vessels to U. S.	21	2	Petition	81	Ways and Means.						
Cramer, Charles, and others	A moiety of forfeiture of their vessel to U. S.	22	1	Petition	41	Ways and Means	......	......	......	Discharged; laid on table.		
Cramer, Charles, and others	A moiety of forfeiture of their vessel to U. S.	23	1	Petition	96	Ways and Means	170	Report and bill.	186	Passed	Passed	App'd June 30, 1834
Cramer, Henry	Pension	21	2	Petition	270	Military Pensions.						
Cramer, Jacob	Restoration of pension	20	1	Petition	464	Military Pensions	April 29, 1828	By bill	283	Passed.		
Cramer, Jacob	Pension	20	2	Resolution	29	Military Pensions	Dec. 12, 1828	By bill	311	Passed.	Laid on table.	
Cramer, Jacob	Pension	21	1	House bill	130	Whole House	Feb. 13, 1830	Favorable	72	Passed	Passed	App'd May 20, 1830
Cramer, John	Invalid pension	10	2	House bill	499	Whole House	Feb. 20, 1809	Favorable	158	Passed	Passed	App'd March 3, 1809
Cramer, Sarah	Pension for revolutionary services of husband.	27	3	Petition	59	Rev. Pensions	295	Adverse	......	Laid on table.		
Cramond, and Philips	Indemnity for French spoliations prior to 1800.	26	1	Memorial	182	Foreign Affairs	343	Favorable; bill.	319	Referred to Committee Whole House.		
Crampersey, John	Increase of pension	14	1	Petition	44	Pens. & Rev. Cl'ms.	Feb. 15, 1816	Amendment to Sen. bill.	......	Passed	Passed	App'd Feb. 22, 1816
Cranch, William and others	Increase of compensation as judges of the circuit court of the District of Columbia.	11	3	Petition	496	Dist. of Columbia.	Jan. 31, 1811	By bill	193	Passed	Passed	App'd March 3, 1811, see act of April 20, 1818, for further increase.
Cranch, William	Compensation for his code of jurisprudence for District of Columbia.	15	2	Letter and code.	29	Select	Jan. 28, 1819	By bill	296	Referred to Committee Whole House.	......	Provided for in appropriation act March 2, 1831.
Crandall, Abraham	Invalid pension, war of 1812.	28	1	Petition	869	Invalid Pensions.						
Crandall, Abraham C	Compensation for staves, &c., destroyed by United States troops at Fort Oswego.	29	1	Petition	638	Claims	640	Adverse	......	Laid on table.		
Crandall, Abraham C.	Compensation for staves, &c., destroyed by United States troops at Fort Oswego.	31	1	Petition	628	Claims.						
Crandall, P. M.	(See Marcellus Eells, and others.)											
Crander, Ralph E.	(See Ralph Crunden, devisee of.)											
Cranhon, John, (Ia.)	Pension for naval services	21	2	Petition	230	Military Pensions.						
Crandon, John, (Ia.)	Pension fer naval services	22	1	Petition	265	Invalid Pensions.						
Crandon, John, (Ia.)	Pension for naval services	23	2	Petition	391	Invalid Pensions.						
Crandon, John, (Ia.)	Pension for naval services	24	1	Petition	99	Invalid Pensions	Mar. 25, 1836	Adverse	......	Laid on table.		
Crandon, John, (Ia.)	Pension for naval services	24	2	Petition	48	Invalid Pensions	......	......	......	Disch'd; laid on table.		
Crandon, John, (Ia.)	Pension for naval services	25	2	Petition	269	Invalid Pensions	......	......	......	Discharged; laid on table.	......	Leave to withdraw.
Crandon, John, widow of.	Pension for naval services of husband.	27	2	Petition	376	Invalid Pensions	935	Adverse	......	Laid on table.		
Crandon, John, widow of.	Pension for naval services of husband.	28	1	Petition	429	Rev. Claims.						

List of private claims presented to the House of Representatives of the United States from the 1st to the 31st Congress, inclusive—Continued.

Names of claimants.	Nature or object of the claim.	Congress.	Session.	How brought before the House of Reps.	Page of journal.	To what committee of the House referred.	No. or date of the report.	Nature of the report.	No. of the bill	How disposed of by the House of Reps.	How disposed of by the Senate.	Date of the act of Congress, and remarks.
Crane, Aaron	Invalid pension	10	1	House bill	232	Whole House	April 19, 1808	Favorable	78	Passed	Passed	App'd April 25, 1808
Crane, Abijah	Revolutionary pension	22	1	Senate bill	745	Rev. Pensions	May 23, 1832	With't amend.	95	Laid on table.		
Crane, Albert	(See John Perkins and others.)											
Crane, Caleb, widow of	Invalid pension	25	2	Petition	236	Invalid Pensions				Discharged; laid on table.		
Crane, Elisha	Revolutionary pension	22	1	Petition	219	Rev. Pensions				Discharged; laid on table.		
Crane, Henry	Compensation for services, &c., in revolutionary war.	2	1	Petition	447					Referred to Secretary War.		
Crane, Jabez	Increase of pension	23	2	Petition	343	Invalid Pensions.						
Crane, Jabez	Increase of pension	24	1	Petition	406	Invalid Pensions				Discharged; laid on table.		
Crane, John, (Mass.)	Invalid pension	3	1	Rep. of Secretary War.	131	Select	May 26, 1794	Res. to refer to Sec. with instructions.	R. 12	Passed	Passed	App'd June 9, 1794
Crane, John, (N. Y.) widow of.	Revolutionary pension	25	2	Petition	327	Rev. Pensions	March 3, 1838	By bill	603	Passed	Passed	App'd July 7, 1838
Crane, John W	(See Lewis Crane, son of.)											
Crane, Lewis, son of	Indemnity for depredations by Creek Indians.	27	3	Petition	112	Claims	200	Adverse		Laid on table.		
Crane, Lewis, son of	Indemnity for depredations by Creek Indians.	28	1	Petition	117	Claims	30	Adverse		Laid on table.		
Crane, Lewis, son of	Indemnity for depredations by Creek Indians.	29	1	Petition	190	Claims	514	Adverse		Laid on table.		
Crane, Orson, sureties of	Release from judgment	25	2	Petition	51	Claims	544	Favorable; bill	535	Referred to Committee Whole House.		
Crane, Orson, sureties of	Release from judgment	25	3	Bill of last sess.	379	Whole House	Jan. 25, 1839	With't amend.	535	Passed	Passed	App'd March 3, 1839
Crane, Peter, widow of	Arrears of pension due him, and continuance to her.	25	2	Petition	349	Whole House on bill No. 456.						
Crane, William	Invalid pension	3	1	Rep. of Secretary War.	131	Select	May 26, 1794	Res. to refer to Sec. with instructions.	R. 12	Passed	Passed	App'd June 9, 1794
Crane, William	Invalid pension	3	2	Rep. of Secretary War.	262	Claims	Feb. 28, 1795	Favorable; bill ordered.	130	Passed	Postponed to next session.	
Crane, William	Invalid pension	4	1	Rep. of Secretary, March 2, 1795.	445	Claims	Feb. 18, 1796	Favorable: bill ordered.	156	Passed	Passed	App'd April 20, 1796
Crannall, Cornelius, widow of.	Revolutionary pension	27	2	Petition	69	Invalid Pensions	784	Adverse		Laid on table.		
Cranston, Peleg	Pension	23	1	Petition	190	Rev. Pensions.						
Cranston, William, mother of.	Pension for naval services, killed in war of 1812.	24	2	Petition	45	Naval Affairs	26	Adverse		Laid on table.		
Crapin, Samuel	Pension for wounds received in war of 1812.	24	2	Petition	132	Invalid Pensions	Jan. 5, 1837	Adverse		Laid on table.		
Crapin, Samuel	Pension for wounds received in war of 1812.	25	2	Senate bill	1155	Rev. Pensions			348			
Crapin, Samuel	Pension for wounds received in war of 1812.	26	1	Senate bill	813	Rev. Pensions	April 25, 1840	With't amend.	113	Referred to Committee Whole House.		
Crapin, Samuel	Pension for wounds received in war of 1812.	26	2	Senate bill	327				188			
Crapin, Samuel	Pension for wounds received in war of 1812.	27	2	Senate bill	101	Invalid Pensions	Feb. 9, 1842	With't amend.	20	Passed	Passed	App'd Mar. 19, 1842
Crapin, Samuel	Increase of pension	30	2	Petition	476	Invalid Pensions				Discharged; laid on table.		

List of private claims presented to the House of Representatives of the United States from the 1st to the 31st Congress, inclusive—Continued.

Names of claimants.	Nature or object of the claim.	Congress.	Session.	How brought before the House of Reps.	Page of journal.	To what committee of the House referred.	No. or date of the report.	Nature of the report.	No. of the bill.	How disposed of by the House of Reps.	How disposed of by the Senate.	Date of the act of Congress, and remarks.
Crapin, Samuel	Increase of pension	31	1	Petition	537	Invalid Pensions.						
Crapo, Samuel A.	(See Thomas William Tucker.)											
Crary, Allen, or Crosy	Revolutionary pension	24	1	Resolution	666	Rev. Pensions				Discharged; laid on table.		
Crary, Archibald, for self and others, of Rhode Island brigade.	Pay, &c., granted others of same grade in service during revolutionary war.	1	2	Petition	249					Referred to Secretary War.		
Crary, Christopher	Revolutionary pension	27	3	Petition	133	Rev. Pensions	295	Adverse		Laid on table.		
Crary, Peter, and John S. & Co.	Drawback of duties on foreign goods exported to South America.	21	1	Petition	38	Commerce	Dec. 29, 1829	Report and bill.	40	Passed	Passed	App'd April 15, 1830
Crary, John S.	(See Philetus Havens, executors of,)	26	1		182							
Cravath, Lemuel	Compensation for injuries sustained in revolutionary war.	1	2	Petition	142					Referred to Secretary Treasury.		
Cravath, Lemuel	Compensation for injuries sustained in revolutionary war.	2	2	Report Secretary Sec. Treasury.	625					Laid on table.		
Cravat, Richard	Confirmation of title to land in Territory of Mississippi.	13	2	Petition	168	Public Lands				Discharged.		
Cravat, Richard	Confirmation of title to land in Territory of Mississippi.	15	1	House bill	387				160	Referred to Committee Whole House.		
Cravat, Richard	Confirmation of title to land in Territory of Mississippi.	16	1	Petition	204	Priv. Land Claims.	64	Report and bill.	69	Passed	Passed	App'd May 8, 1820
Cravat, Richard and others.	Land in lieu of that confirmed by act of May, 1820, which was sold by United States.	25	2	Senate bill	994	Priv. Land Claims.	June 27, 1838	With't amend.	216	Passed	Passed	App'd July 5, 1838
Craven, Thomas T.	(See Exploring Expedition.)											
Crawford, Alexander	Remission of duties on distillery, destroyed by fire.	14	2	Petition	384	Ways and Means				Discharged; laid on table.		
Crawford, Andrew	Pension	23	2	Petition	237	Invalid Pensions.						
Crawford, Andrew	Pension	24	1	Petition	1099	Invalid Pensions.						
Crawford, Angus M. A.	Compensation for horse lost in United States service, 1837.	26	1	Petition	621	Claims.						
Crawford, Angus M. A.	Compensation for horse lost in United States service, 1837.	26	2	Petition	135	Claims.						
Crawford, Angus M. A.	Compensation for horse lost in United States services, 1837.	27	2	Petition	94	Claims	336	Adverse		Laid on table.		
Crawford, Ann	(See William Haslett, heirs of.)											
Crawford, Benjamin	Indemnity for losses, &c., consequent on breaking up of his trading establishment in Creek Indians nation by U. S. officer.	29	1	Petition	93	Judiciary	297	Adverse		Laid on table.		
Crawford, David	(See Job Gard.)											
Crawford, David Ross, widow of.	Compensation for loss of husband in attempt to save a drowning seaman.	27	2	Petition	224	Naval Affairs	564	Report and bill.	359	Engrossed.		
Crawford, David Ross, widow of.	Compensation for loss of husband in attempt to save a drowning seaman.	27	3	Bill of last sess	87				359	Passed	Passed	App'd March 1, 1843
Crawford, George	(See Stephen Decatur, widow of, and others.)											
Crawford, George W	Compensation for provisions furnished Texas volunteers.	30	1	Petition	229	Military Affairs				Discharged; laid on table.		

List of private claims presented to the House of Representatives of the United States from the 1st to the 31st Congress, inclusive—Continued.

Names of claimants.	Nature or object of the claim.	Congress.	Session.	How brought before the House of Reps.	Page of journal.	To what committee of the House referred.	No. or date of the report.	Nature of the report.	No. of the bill.	How disposed of by the House of Reps.	How disposed of by the Senate.	Date of the act of Congress, and remarks.
Crawford, Hannah	Relief: her husband killed by Indians in revolutionary war.	8	2	Petition	56	Claims.						
Crawford, Hannah	Relief: her husband killed by Indians in revolutionary war.	9	1	Petition	194	Claims				Discharged; referred to Com. Whole House on bill No. 108.		
Crawford, Hardy W	Compensation for horse, &c., lost in Seminole campaign of 1818.	23	1	Documents	154	Claims.						
Crawford, Henry	Invalid pension	3	1	Rep. of Secretary War.	131	Select	May 26, 1794	Favorable; bill ordered.	62	Passed	Passed	App'd June 7, 1794
Crawford, Ingoldsby W	Compensation for superintending light-houses, erection of custom-house, &c., from 1831 to 1837.	26	1	Resolution	372	Commerce.						
Crawford, Ingoldsby W	Compensation for superintending light houses, erection of custom-house, &c., from 1831 to 1837.	26	2	Resolution	134	Commerce.						
Crawford, Ingoldsby W	Compensation for superintending light-houses, erection of custom house, &c., from 1831 to 1837.	27	2	Resolution	57	Commerce	64	Report and bill.	99	Passed	Amended and passed.	App'd July 27, 1842
Crawford, Ingoldsby W	Compensation for superintending light-houses, erection of custom house, &c., from 1831 to 1837.	28	1	Petition	528	Commerce				Discharged; laid on table.		
Crawford, James	(See Hendrick Henderson, consignee of.)	3	1	Petition	131	Select.						
Crawford, James, & others	Remission of duties on goods imported into Castine, Maine, while occupied by the British in war of 1812.	16	2	Petition	101	Ways and Means	Feb. 13, 1821	By bill	251	Referred to Committee Whole House.		
Crawford, James, & others	Remission of duties on goods imported into Castine, Maine, while occupied by the British in war of 1812.	17	1	Petition	114	Ways and Means	Feb. 1, 1822	By bill	69	Laid on table.		
Crawford, James, & others	Remission of duties on goods imported into Castine, Maine, while occupied by the British in war of 1812.	17	2	Bill of last sess.	76	Whole House			69			
Crawford, James, & others	Remission of duties on goods imported into Castine, Maine, while occupied by the British in war of 1812.	18	1	Petition	27	Ways and Means	Jan. 15, 1824	By bill	60	Passed	Passed	App'd May 19, 1824
Crawford, James	Grant of land for revolutionary services as a Canadian refugee.	6	2	House bill	766	Whole House	Jan. 26, 1801	With amend.	280	Passed	Passed	App'd Feb. 18, 1801
Crawford, James, (Pa.)	Invalid pension	11	3	Petition	49	Claims.						
Crawford, James, (Pa.)	Invalid pension	12	1	Petition	85	Claims	June 8, 1812	By bill	138	Passed	Passed	App'd July 5, 1812
Crawford, James, (Pa.)	Increase of pension	12	2	Petition	554	Claims	Feb. 26, 1813	Adverse; leave to withdraw.		Laid on table.		
Crawford, James, (Ohio)	Relief from payment of $8 per acre for land partly paid for at $5 per acre.	12	1	Petition	385							
Crawford, James, (Ohio)	Relief from payment of $8 per acre for land partly paid for at $5 per acre.	13	2	Petition	199	Public Lands	Feb. 14, 1814	By bill	121	Passed	Passed	App'd March 9, 1814
Crawford, James, (Tenn.)	Revolutionary pension	19	2	Resolution	160	Military Pensions				Discharged.		
Crawford, James, (Tenn.)	Revolutionary pension	31	1	Petition	168	Military Pensions.						

List of private claims presented to the House of Representatives of the United States from the 1st to the 31st Congress, inclusive—Continued.

Names of claimants.	Nature or object of the claim.	Congress.	Session.	How brought before the House of Reps.	Page of journal.	To what committee of the House referred.	No. or date of the report.	Nature of the report.	No. of the bill.	How disposed of by the House of Reps.	How disposed of by the Senate.	Date of the act of Congress, and remarks.
Crawford, James, (Tenn.)	Revolutionary pension	21	2	Resolution	199	Military Pensions.						
Crawford, James	Compensation for horse, &c., lost in Seminole camp, 1818.	23	1	Documents	154	Claims.						
Crawford, James, (Pa.)	Money in lieu of land due his son, killed in war of 1812.	22	1	Petition	513	Priv. Land Claims.	April 6, 1832	Adverse	......	Laid on table.		
Crawford, James, (Pa.)	Money in lieu of land due his son, killed in war of 1812.	22	2	Petition	138	Priv. Land Claims.	Jan. 7, 1833	Adverse	......	Laid on table.		
Crawford, James, (Pa.)	Money in lieu of land due his son, killed in war of 1812.	29	2	Petition	303	Priv. Land Claims.						
Crawford, James, (Pa.)	Money in lieu of land due his son, killed in war of 1812.	30	1	Petition	457	Priv. Land Claims.						
Crawford, James, (Pa.)	Money in lieu of land due his son, killed in war of 1812.	30	2	Petition	204	Priv. Land Claims.						
Crawford, James, (Pa.)	Money in lieu of land due his son, killed in war of 1812.	31	1	Petition	362	Priv. Land Claims.	....	....	......	Discharged; laid on table.		
Crawford, James, (N. Y.)	Revolutionary pension	28	1	Petition	415	Rev. Pensions	263	Report and bill.	195	Passed	Adverse report.	
Crawford, James, (N. Y.)	Revolutionary pension	28	2	Petition	59	Rev. Pensions.						
Crawford, James	Indemnity for French spoliations prior to 1800.	26	1	Memorial	182	Foreign Affairs	343	Favorable; bill	319	Referred to Committee Whole House.		
Crawford, James, of Maine, executors of.	Indemnity for French spoliations prior to 1800.	31	1	Petition	225	Foreign Affairs	355	Report and bill.	318	Referred to Committee Whole House.		
Crawford, James	(See William H. Bedford, agent).	28	1	....	262							
Crawford, Joel	(See Sureties of T. F. Green)	23	1									
Crawford, John, (Del.)	Invalid pension	8	2	Petition	13	Claims	....	....	......	Discharged; referred to Com. Whole House on bill No. 28.	....	See act March 3, 1805
Crawford, John	Arrearages of pension	16	1	Petition	329	Rev. Pensions	....	....	......	Discharged; laid on table.		
Crawford, John, (Va.)	Pension	19	2	Petition	215	Military Pensions	Feb. 14, 1827	By bill	436	Referred to Committee Whole House.		
Crawford, John, (Va.)	Pension	20	1	Petition	50	Military Pensions	....	....	......	Discharged; laid on table.		
Crawford, John, (N. H.)	Invalid pension	25	2	Petition	350	Invalid Pensions	....	....	......	Discharged; laid on table.		
Crawford, John, (Miss.)	Location of F. L. stock in Louisiana instead of Mississippi.	30	2	Senate bill	524	Priv. Land Claims.	....	....	345			
Crawford, John	(See Archibald Beard and others.)											
Crawford, Jonathan	Invalid pension	22	1	Resolution	240	Invalid Pensions	Feb. 15, 1832	Adverse	......	Laid on table.		
Crawford, Richard, widow of.	Pension for services as a soldier in revolutionary army.	25	3	Petition	126	Rev. Pensions	....	....	......	Discharged.		
Crawford, Richard, widow of.	Pension for services as a soldier in revolutionary army.	26	1	Petition	173	Rev. Pensions	....	....	......	Discharged; laid on table.		
Crawford, Smith, & others, Missouri and Indiana volunteers.	Payment for services against Indians in 1832.	24	1	Senate bill	810	Claims	May 17, 1836	With't amend.	131	Passed	Passed	App'd July 2, 1836
Crawford, Thomas, and Samuel Jones.	Payment of claim against United States.	1	2	Petition and rep't Sec. of War.	193	....	....	....	......	Laid on table.		
Crawford, William	(See Israel Pickins.)											
Crawford, William, and others, of Alabama.	Compensation for services as land commission'r west of Pearl river.	14	1	Petition	44	Public Lands	Mar. 14, 1816	By bill	128	Passed	Passed	App'd Feb. 22, 1816
Crawford, William, and others, of Alabama.	Confirmation of title to land	24	1	Senate bill	1078	Public Lands	July 1, 1836	With't amend.	227	Passed	Passed	App'd July 2, 1836

List of private claims presented to the House of Representatives of the United States from the 1st to the 31st Congress, inclusive—Continued.

Names of claimants.	Nature or object of the claim.	Congress.	Session.	How brought before the House of Reps.	Page of journal.	To what committee of the House referred.	No. or date of the report.	Nature of the report.	No. of the bill.	How disposed of by the House of Reps.	How disposed of by the Senate.	Date of the act of Congress, and remarks.
Crawford, William, (Ind.)	Exoneration from judgment against him as surety for Andrew P. Hay.	22	1	Petition	558	Judiciary				Discharged; laid on table.		
Crawford, William, (Ind.)	Exoneration from judgment against him as surety for Andrew P. Hay.	22	2	Petition	31	Judiciary				Discharged; laid on table.		
Crawford, William, (Ind.)	Exoneration from judgment against him as surety for Andrew P. Hay.	23	1	Petition	38	Judiciary	101	Adverse		Laid on table.		
Crawford, William, (Ind.)	Exoneration from judgment against him as surety for Andrew P. Hay.	24	1	Petition	425	Judiciary.						
Crawford, William, (Ind.)	Exoneration from judgment against him as surety for Andrew P. Hay.	24	2	Petition	89	Judiciary.						
Crawford, William	(See William Baker and others)	22	1		288							
Crawford, William, heirs of.	Seven years half-pay, as colonel in Virginia line, was burnt by Indians at Sandusky, 1782.	23	2	Resolution	166	Rev. Claims	127	Report and bill.	768	Referred to Committee Whole House.		
Crawford, Wilson	Compensation for work done on U. States arsenal at Pittsburg.	21	1	Petition	318	Claims				Discharged; laid on table.		
Crawford, Wilson	Compensation for work done on U. States arsenal at Pittsburg.	22	1	Petition	104	Claims	Jan. 20, 1832	Adverse		Laid on table.		
Crawford, Wilson	Compensation for work done on U. States arsenal at Pittsburg.	23	1	Petition	192	Claims.						
Crayton, Thomas, heirs of.	Renewal of lost loan office certificate.	2	1	Petition	573					Referred to Secretary Treasury.		
Creamer, George	(See Charles Cramer and others.)											
Creamer, John	Invalid pension	3	1	Rep. of Secretary of War.	131	Select	May 26, 1794	To refer to Sec. with instrucs.	R. 12	Passed	Passed	App'd June 9, 1794
Creamer, John	Invalid pension	3	2	Rep. of Secretary of War.	350	Claims	Mar. 3, 1795	To discharge & postpone.		Laid on table.		
Creamer, John	Invalid pension	4	1	Rep. of Secretary War.	445	Claims	Feb. 18, 1796	To refer to Sec. with instrucs.	R. 16	Passed	Passed	App'd April 18, 1796
Crease, Anthony	Permission to hold land in his own name, he being an alien.	12	1	Petition	19	Dist. of Columbia.	Nov. 22, 1811	By bill	10	Rejected.		
Crecy, William, sr	Compensation for revolutionary services.	27	2	Petition	560	Rev. Claims	657	Adverse		Laid on table.		
Creel, George L. father of.	Bounty land for services in Mexican war.	31	1	Petition	544	Public Lands.						
Creel, Simon	Compensation for a horse lost in U. S. service, war of 1812.	22	1	Petition	49	Claims	Dec. 29, 1831	Adverse		Laid on table.		
Creeth, Samuel	(See Canadian refugees.)											
Creesy, Josiah P. and others.	Fishing bounty on vessel lost at sea.	21	2	Petition	62	Commerce	Jan. 6, 1831	By bill	540	Referred to Committee Whole House.		
Creesy, Josiah P. and others.	Fishing bounty on vessel lost at sea.	22	1	Petition	114	Commerce	Jan. 4, 1831	By bill	198	Referred to Committee Whole House.		
Creesy, Josiah P. and others.	Fishing bounty on a vessel lost at sea.	22	2	Bill of last sess.	66	Whole House	Dec. 15, 1832	With't amend.	198	Passed	Passed	App'd, Feb. 27, 1833
Creighton, James, jr	Drawback of duties on merchandise shipped to Havana.	10	1	Memorial	113	Com. and Manuf.						
Creighton, James, jr	Drawback of duties on merchandise shipped to Havana.	10	2	Memorial	360	Com. and Manuf.	Feb. 16, 1809	Adverse & res. leave to withdraw.		Resolution adopted.		
Creighton, Jeremiah	(See Joseph Stuart and others.)											
Creighton, Samuel	(See Joseph Stuart and others.)											
Crely, Joseph	Confirmation of title to land in Michigan.	17	1	Petition	184	Public Lands				Discharged; laid on table.		

List of private claims presented to the House of Representatives of the United States from the 1st to the 31st Congress, inclusive—Continued.

Names of claimants.	Nature or object of the claim.	Congress.	Session.	How brought before the House of Reps.	Page of journal.	To what committee of the House referred.	No. or date of the report.	Nature of the report.	No. of the bill.	How disposed of by the House of Reps.	How disposed of by the Senate.	Date of the act of Congress, and remarks.
Cremeens, Moses	Pension	22	1	Petition	509	Invalid Pensions	474	Report and bill.	576	Passed	Reported with't amendment.	
Cremeens, Moses	Pension	22	2	Petition	91	Invalid Pensions	Dec. 22, 1832	Report and bill	626	Passed	Passed	App'd March 2, 1833
Cresap, Daniel, heirs of	Compensation for services as an officer in revolutionary army.	24	1	Petition	708	Rev. Claims	647	Adverse	......	Laid on table.		
Cresap, Daniel, heirs of	Compensation for services as an officer in revolutionary army.	24	2	Petition	119	Claims.						
Cress, George	Invalid pension	11	2	House bill	283	Whole House	Mar. 24, 1810	Favorable	108	Passed	Passed	App'd April 27, 1810
Cress, Henry, executors of,	Compensation for house used by U. S. troops in 1777.	2	2	Petition	678	....	....	....	......	Laid on table.		
Cressy, Benjamin, N. H.	Restoration of pension	17	1	Petition	37	Rev. Pensions	....	....	......	Discharged; laid on table.	....	See act March 1, 1823
Cressy, Benjamin, (Me.)	Pension for sufferings as a British prisoner, war of 1812.	28	2	Petition	327	Invalid Pensions.						
Cressy, Benjamin, (Me.)	Pension for sufferings as a British prisoner, war of 1812.	29	1	Petition	199	Invalid Pensions.						
Cressy, Benjamin, (Me.)	Pension for sufferings as a British prisoner, war of 1812.	29	2	Petition	233	Naval Affairs.						
Cressy, Benjamin, (Me.)	Pension for sufferings as a British prisoner, war of 1812.	30	1	Petition	637	Naval Affairs	513	Report and bill.	440	Referred to Committee Whole House.		
Cressy, Benjamin, (Me.)	Pension for sufferings as a British prisoner, war of 1812.	31	1	Petition	236	Naval Affairs	231	Report and bill	226	Referred to Committee Whole House.		
Cressy, Benjamin, (Me.)	Pension for sufferings as a British prisoner, war of 1812.	31	2	Bill of last sess.	182	Naval Affairs	Jan. 24, 1851	With amend.	226	Amendment rejected, and bill passed.	Ref. to Com. on Naval Affairs.	
Cressy, Daniel	(See William Baker and others)	22	1	....	288							
Cressy, Jonathan	Pension and bounty land for revolutionary services.	15	1	Petition	320	Pens. & Rev. Cl'ms.	....	....	......	Discharged; laid on table.		
Cresy, Manuel	Pension	22	1	Petition	72	Invalid Pensions	294	Report and bill.	377	Passed	Ref'd to Com. on Pensions.	
Cresy, Manuel	Pension	22	2	Petition	88	Invalid Pensions	Feb. 15, 1833	Report and bill.	738	Referred to Committee Whole House.		
Cresy, Manuel	Pension	23	1	Petition	92	Invalid Pensions	69	Report and bill.	79	Passed	Passed	App'd June 30, 1834
Crew, Caleb, guardian of the children of.	Pension for services as assistant surgeon in frigate Macedonian.	20	2	Petition	54	Naval Affairs	103	To be disch'd.	......	Laid on table.		
Crew, Caleb, guardian of the children of.	Pension for services as assistant surgeon in frigate Macedonian.	21	1	Petition	84	Naval Affairs	....	....	......	Discharged; laid on table.		
Crews, Thomas	(See James Franklin, executor of.)											
Crews, William B	Wages due as a soldier in United States army in 1837 and 1838.	27	3	Petition	252	Claims.						
Crews, William B	Wages due as a soldier in United States army in 1837 and 1838.	28	1	Petition	239	Claims.						
Crews, William B	Wages due as a soldier in United States army in 1837 and 1838.	28	2	Petition	229	Claims.						
Crews, William B	Wages due as a soldier in United States army in 1837 and 1838.	30	1	Petition	338	Claims	....	....	......	Discharged; laid on table.		
Crews, William B	Wages due as a soldier in United States army in 1837 and 1838.	30	2	Petition	101	Claims	43	Report and bill.	732	Referred to Committee Whole House.		
Crews, William B	Wages due as a soldier in United States army in 1837 and 1838.	31	1	Petition	255	Claims	2	Report and bill.	4	Passed	Passed	App'd July 18, 1850
Crigier, Thomas	Compensation for services and for supplies furnished in revolutionary war.	4	1	Petition	384	Claims	Jan. 20, 1796	Adverse, and for leave to withdraw.	......	Report adopted by resolution.		
Cripps, John S., administrator of.	(See Robert Hazlehurst, assignees of.)											

List of private claims presented to the House of Representatives of the United States from the 1st to the 31st Congress, inclusive—Continued.

Names of claimants.	Nature or object of the claim.	Congress.	Session.	How brought before the House of Reps.	Page of journal.	To what committee of the House referred.	No. or date of the report.	Nature of the report.	No. of the bill.	How disposed of by the House of Reps.	How disposed of by the Senate.	Date of the act of Congress, and remarks.
54 Cripps, John	Bounty land and revolutionary pension.	28	1	Petition	879	Rev. Pensions.						
Cripps, John	Bounty land and revolutionary pension.	29	1	Petition	592	Priv. Land Claims.						
Cripps, John	Bounty land and revolutionary pension.	29	2	Petition	87	Priv. Land Claims.						
Cripps, John	Benefit of pension act of June 7, 1832.	30	1	Petition	535	Rev. Pensions	690	Adverse		Laid on table.		
Cripps, Michael	Invalid pension, war of 1812	24	1	Petition	187	Invalid Pensions	Feb. 5, 1836	Adverse		Laid on table.		
Cripps, Michael	Invalid pension, war of 1812	25	2	Petition	588	Invalid Pensions				Discharged.		
Crites, Abraham, & Daniel	Confirmation of title to land in Territory of Missouri.	15	2	Petition	89	Priv. Land Claims.				Discharged; laid on table.		
Crites, Abraham, & Daniel	Confirmation of title to land in Territory of Missouri.	17	1	Petition	53	Public Lands				Discharged; laid on table.		
Crites, Abraham, & Daniel	Confirmation of title to land in Territory of Missouri.	18	1	Petition	53	Public Lands	Jan. 16, 1824	By bill	65	Passed	Passed	App'd May 26, 1824
Crites, Devault, heir of	Confirmation of title to land in Territory of Missouri.	15	1	Petition	180	Priv. Land Claims.				Discharged; laid on table.		
Crites, Devault, heir of	Confirmation of title to land in Territory of Missouri.	16	1	Petition	72	Priv. Land Claims.				Discharged; laid on table.		
Crites, Devault, heir of	Confirmation of title to land in Territory of Missouri.	17	1	Petition	53	Public Lands				Discharged; laid on table.		
Crites, Devault, heir of	Confirmation of title to land in Territory of Missouri.	18	1	Petition	53	Public Lands	Jan. 16, 1824	By bill	65	Passed	Passed	App'd May 26, 1824
Crites, Peter	Confirmation of title to land in Territory of Missouri.	15	2	Petition	89	Priv. Land Claims.				Discharged; laid on table.		
Crites, Peter	Confirmation of title to land in Territory of Missouri.	17	1	Petition	53	Public Lands				Discharged; laid on table.		
Crites, Peter	Confirmation of title to land in Territory of Missouri.	18	1	Petition	53	Public Lands.	Jan. 16, 1824	By bill	65	Passed	Passed	App'd May 26, 1824
Crittenton, Nathaniel	Restoration of pension	17	1	Petition	88	Rev. Pensions				Leave to withdraw.		
Crittenton, Nathaniel	Restoration of pension	17	2	Petition	163	Whole House on bill No. 207.				Leave to withdraw		See act March 1, 1823
Crittenden, Robert, assignee of.	Compensation for two horses lost in Seminole campaign, 1818.	21	1	Resolution	464	Claims	339	Report and bill.	399	Passed	Passed	App'd May 29, 1830
Crittenden, Stephen	Payment for land conveyed to U. S. for a custom house at Middletown, Connecticut.	23	2	Petition	119	Claims	44	Report and bill.	630	Referred to Committee Whole House.		
Crittenden, Stephen	Payment for land conveyed to U. S. for a custom-house at Middletown, Connecticut.	24	1	Petition	51	Claims	34	Report and bill.	34	Passed	Passed	App'd Feb. 25, 1836
Crittenden, Sevier, and Searcy.	(See German Charbenau, assignees of.)											
Crocker, Benjamin	Invalid pension	3	2	Rep. of Secretary War.	278	Claims.						
Crocker, Benjamin	Invalid pension	4	1	Rep. of Secretary War.	445	Claims.						
Crocker, D	(See Crocker, Hichboon, and Wright.)											
Crocker, David	(See Benjamin Hallet and others.)											
Crocker, Hichboon, and Wright.	Indemnity for French spoliations prior to 1800.	26	1	Memorial	182	Foreign Affairs	343	Favorable; bill	319	Referred to Committee Whole House.		
Crocker, Jonathan	Restoration of pension	21	2	Senate bill	121	Military Pensions	20	With't amend.	42	Passed	Passed	App'd March 2, 1831

List of private claims presented to the House of Representatives of the United States from the 1st to the 31st Congress, inclusive—Continued.

Names of claimants.	Nature or object of the claim.	Congress.	Session.	How brought before the House of Reps.	Page of journal.	To what committee of the House referred.	No. or date of the report.	Nature of the report.	No. of the bill.	How disposed of by the House of Reps.	How disposed of by the Senate.	Date of the act of Congress, and remarks.
Crocker, James	Pension for wounds received in war of 1812.	31	2	Petition	199	Invalid Pensions.						
Crocker, Sally S	(See Jonathan Stark, heir of.)											
Crockett, Anthony	(See Robert McAfee.)											
Crockett, Daniel H	Invalid pension, war of 1812	24	1	Resolution	810	Invalid Pensions.						
Crockett, Daniel H	Invalid pension, war of 1812	24	2	Petition	71	Invalid Pensions	Jan. 13, 1837	Adverse		Laid on table.		
Crockett, Daniel H	Invalid pension, war of 1812	25	2	Petition	118	Invalid Pensions	676	Report and bill.	655	Passed	Passed	App'd July 7, 1838
Crockett, John	(See William H. Bedford, agent, &c.)	28	1		262							
Crockett, Joseph, surety of	Release from liability	18	2	Resolution	223	Judiciary	81	Favorable	357	Passed.		
Crockett, Joseph, surety of	Release from liability	19	1	Resolution	40	Judiciary	Feb. 1, 1826	Favorable	86	Passed	Passed	App'd May 20, 1826
Crockett, Joseph	Commutation of half-pay as an officer in revolutionary army.	15	2	Petition	78	Pens. & Rev. Cl'ms.				Discharged; laid on table.		
Crockett, Joseph	Pension as major in revolutionary army.	19	2	Resolution	70	Military Pensions				Discharged.		
Crockett, Joseph, heirs of.	Compensation for revolutionary services, without reference to apparant balance against him as United States marshal.	26	1	Petition	352	Judiciary.						
Crockett, Joseph, heirs of.	Relief in relation to claim and account of deceased.	30	1	Petition	909	Claims						Leave to withdraw, 2d session.
Crockett, Joseph, heirs of.	Compensation for land granted by North Carolina, but lost by boundary dispute between said State and Kentucky.	26	1	Petition	332	Judiciary						Leave to withdraw, 16th May, 1842.
Crockett, Joseph, heirs of.	Change the location of 1000 acres of land.	27	2	Petition	833	Judiciary.						
Crockett, Samuel B	Credit in his account as postmaster at Frankfort for notes of the bank of Kentucky, received by him before its failure.	18	1	Petition	89	P. Of. & P. Roads.	Mar. 24, 1824	Adverse		Laid on table.		
Crockett, Samuel B	Credit of his account as postmaster at Frankfort for notes of the bank of Kentucky, received by him before its failure.	19	1	Petition	149	P. Of. & P. Roads.	62	Adverse.		Laid on table.		
Crockett, Samuel B., sureties of.	Release from libilities	25	2	Memorial	1028	Select.						
Crode, John T. and Robert C.	(See Freeborn Sisson and others.)											
Crofford, James	(See Canadian refugees.)											
Crofoot, Benjamin	Revolutionary pension	22	1	Petition	46	Rev. Claims	36	Report and bill.	81	Passed	Indef. postp'd.	
Crofts, John	Revolutionary pension	24	1	Petition	56	Rev. Pensions	Jan. 23, 1836	Adverse		Laid on table.		
Crofts, John	Revolutionary pension	24	2	Petition	154	Rev. Pensions				Discharged; laid on table.		
Crofts, John	Revolutionary pension	25	2	Petition	111	Rev. Pensions				Discharged; laid on table.		
Crofts, John	Revolutionary pension	25	3	Petition	216	Rev. Pensions				Discharged; laid on table.		
Crofts, John	Revolutionary pension	26	1	Petition	171	Rev. Pensions				Discharged, laid on table.		
Crombie, James	Invalid pension	3	1	Rep. of Secretary War.	131	Select	May 26, 1794	To refer to Secretary, with instructions.	R. 12	Passed	Passed	App'd June 9, 1794

List of private claims presented to the House of Representatives of the United States from the 1st to the 31st Congress, inclusive—Continued.

Names of claimants.	Nature or object of the claim.	Congress.	Session.	How brought before the House of Reps.	Page of journal.	To what committee of the House referred.	No. or date of the report.	Nature of the report.	No. of the bill.	How disposed of by the House of Reps.	How disposed of by the Senate.	Date of the act of Congress, and remarks.
Crombie, James	Invalid pension	3	2	Rep. of Secretary War.	350	Claims	Mar. 3, 1795	Discharged and postponed.	.....	Laid on table.		
Crombie, James	Invalid pension	4	1	Rep. of Secretary War.	445	Claims	Feb. 18, 1796	Favorable; bill ordered.	156	Passed	Passed	App'd April 20, 1796
Crome, Christian	Relief for wounds received in revolutionary war.	2	1	Petition	510	.....	.....	.....	.....	Laid on table.		
Crommelin, Charles, (Ala.)	Pre-emption right to land on which he resides.	22	1	Petition	711	Public Lands.						
Cromwell, Dawson, heirs of	Lands under treaties betw'n France and Spain, and France and the United States.	30	1	Petition	718	Priv. Land Claims.						
Cronk, Dennis	Pension	21	2	Petition	43	Military Pensions.						
Cronk, Dennis	Pension	22	1	Petition	67	Rev. Pensions	.....	.....	.....	Discharged; laid on table.		
Cronk, John, *alias* Cronkhite, widow of.	Revolutionary pension	27	2	Resolution	333	Rev. Pensions	784	Adverse	.....	Laid on table.		
Cronk, John, *alias* Cronkhite, widow of.	Revolutionary pension	28	1	Petition	122	Rev. Pensions	158	Report and bill.	147	Passed	Passed with amendment.	App'd May 31, 1844
Crook, Joseph	Increase of compensation as late collector at New York.	2	2	Memorial	628	.....	.....	.....	.....	Referred to Secretary Treasury.		
Crook, Joseph	Increase of compensation as late collector at New York.	3	2	Rep. of Secretary Treasury.	284	Select	Jan. 26, 1795	By bill	75	Passed	Passed	App'd Feb. 14, 1795
Crook, Peter	Compensation for two horses lost in Seminole campaign, 1818.	16	1	Petition	174	Claims	April 26, 1820	By bill	141	Passed	Passed	App'd May 15, 1820
Crooke, Robert, jr., administrator of.	Compensation for services in revolutionary war.	2	1	Petition	446	.....	.....	.....	.....	Referred to Secretary War.		
Crooke, Robert, jr., administrator of.	Compensation for services in revolutionary war.	2	2	Rep. of Secretary War.	735	.....	.....	.....	.....	Laid on table.		
Crook, William	Possession of land due for services as revolutionary soldier.	14	1	Petition	243	Pens. & Rev. Cl'ms.	April 9, 1816	Rep't and res. adverse.	.....	Resolution adopted	.....	Leave to withdraw.
Crooks, William, (Canada)	Compensation for lumber taken for U. S. service in 1812.	23	1	Petition	74	Claims	129	Adverse	.....	Recommitted.		
Crooks, William, (Canada)	Compensation for lumber taken for U. S. service in 1812.	23	2	Petition	109	Claims.						
Crooks, William and James	Indemnity for illegal capture of schooner Lord Nelson in war of 1812.	23	1	Memorial	672	Foreign Affairs.						
Crooks, William and James	Indemnity for illegal capture of schooner Lord Nelson in war of 1812.	24	1	Petition	143	Claims	814	Rep. & res. for Sec. Navy to take testim'y	.....	Resolution adopted.		
Crooks, William and James	Indemnity for illegal capture of schooner Lord Nelson in war of 1812.	24	2	Rep. of Secretary Navy.	379	Claims	243	Report and bill.	942	Referred to Committee Whole House.		
Crooks, William and James	Indemnity for illegal capture of schooner Lord Nelson in war of 1812.	25	2	Petition	36	Claims	64	Report and bill.	76	Passed	Rejected.	
Crooks, William and James	Indemnity for illegal capture of schooner Lord Nelson in war of 1812.	25	3	Petition	86	Claims.						
Crooks, William and James	Indemnity for illegal capture of schooner Lord Nelson in war of 1812.	27	2	Petition	1207	Claims.						

List of private claims presented to the House of Representatives of the United States from the 1st to the 31st Congress, inclusive—Continued.

Names of claimants.	Nature or object of the claim.	Congress.	Session.	How brought before the House of Reps.	Page of journal.	To what committee of the House referred.	No. or date of the report.	Nature of the report.	No. of the bill.	How disposed of by the House of Reps.	How disposed of by the Senate.	Date of the act of Congress, and remarks.
Crooks, William and James	Indemnity for illegal capture of schooner Lord Nelson in war of 1812.	27	3	Petition	43	Claims.						
Crooks, William and James	Indemnity for illegal capture of schooner Lord Nelson in war of 1812.	30	1	Petition	425	Claims	426	Adverse	......	Recommitted.		
Crooks, William and James	Indemnity for illegal capture of schooner Lord Nelson in war of 1812.	31	1	Petition	337	Foreign Affairs.						
Crooks, William and James	Indemnity for illegal capture of schooner Lord Nelson in war of 1812.	31	2	Petition	....	Foreign Affairs ...	108	Adverse	......	Laid on table.		
Crookshank, George	Compensation for batteau taken for public use by General Green in 1776.	3	2	Petition	268	Claims..........	Feb. 27, 1795	Adverse	......	Laid on table.		
Crookshank, George	Compensation for batteau taken for public use by General Green in 1776.	4	2	Petition	614	Claims	Dec. 26, 1796	Adverse	......	Leave to withdraw.		
Crookshanks, John	Invalid pension................	11	2	House bill	283	Whole House.....	Mar. 24, 1810	Favorable....	108	Passed	Passed	App'd April 27, 1810
Crookshanks, John	Increase of pension	14	1	Petition	309	Pens. & Rev. Cl'ms.	....	....	......	Discharged; leave to withdraw.		
Crookshanks, Nathaniel ..	(See Robert Forrester, administrator of.)											
Croop, Lucy T..........	(See Richard Noel, heirs of.)											
Cropper, John, heirs of...	Commutation of half-pay due as an officer in revolutionary army.	23	1	Petition	157	Rev. Claims.						
Cropper, John, heirs of...	Commutation of half-pay due as an officer in revolutionary army.	24	1	Petition	204	Rev. Claims.						
Cropper, John, heirs of...	Commutation of half pay due as an officer in revolutionary army.	24	2	Petition	95	Rev. Claims.						
Crosby, Andrew D., heirs of.	Credit as purser for payments to warrant officers of U. S. ship Ontario.	29	2	Senate bill	381	Naval Affairs.....	Feb. 24, 1847	With't amend.	153	Referred to Committee Whole House.		
Crosby, Andrew D., administrator of.	Five years' pension for benefit of heirs of.	30	1	Petition	104	Naval Affairs.						
Crosby, David, heirs of...	Compensation for revolutionary services.	28	1	Petition........	868	Rev. Claims.						
Crosby, Eliakim	Grant of land as a Canadian refugee.	20	1	Petition	40	Priv. Land Claims.	249	Report and bill.	295	Referred to Committee Whole House.		
Crosby, Eliakim	Grant of land as a Canadian refugee.	21	1	Petition	40	Priv. Land Claims.	262	Report and bill.	319	Referred to Committee Whole House.		
Crosby, Eliakim	Grant of land as a Canadian refugee.	21	2	Bill of last sess..	333	Whole House.....	Feb. 19, 1831	With't amend.	319	Passed	Amendment.	
Crosby, Eliakim	Grant of land as a Canadian refugee.	22	1	Petition	55	Priv. Land Claims.	55	Report and bill.	106	Passed	Passed	App'd June 4, 1832
Crosby, Enoch, widow of.	Pension for revolutionary services.	28	1	Petition	526	Rev. Pensions.						
Crosby, James..........	Remission of duties on distillery destroyed by fire.	6	2	Petition	787	Com. and Manuf..	Feb. 23, 1801	Adverse	......	Leave to withdraw.		
Crosby, John, and John, jr.	Compensation for the burning of wharf, warehouse, and goods in firing U. S. ship John Adams, by Capt. Morris.	13	3	Petition	467	Claims	....	....	......	Discharged.		

List of private claims presented to the House of Representatives of the United States from the 1st to the 31st Congress, inclusive—Continued.

Names of claimants.	Nature or object of the claim.	Congress.	Session.	How brought before the House of Reps.	Page of journal.	To what committee of the House referred.	No. or date of the report.	Nature of the report.	No. of the bill.	How disposed of by the House of Reps.	How disposed of by the Senate.	Date of the act of Congress, and remarks.
Crosby, John, and John, jr.	Compensation for the burning of wharf, warehouse, and goods in firing U. S. ship John Adams, by Capt. Morris.	14	1	Petition	425	Claims	April 1, 1816	Favor'ble & bill	......	Passed	Passed	App'd April 26, 1816
Crosby, John	Indemnity for French spoliations prior to 1800.	26	1	Memorial	182	Foreign Affairs	343	Favorable; bill.	319	Referred to Committee Whole House.		
Crosby, John, heirs of	Indemnity for French spoliations prior to 1800.	31	1	Petition	971	Foreign Affairs	355	Favorable, and bill.	318	Referred to Committee Whole House.		
Crosby, Joshua	Revolutionary pension	21	2	Petition	106	Military Pensions.						
Crosby, Joshua	Revolutionary pension	22	1	Resolution	70	Rev. Pensions	119	Report and bill.	194	Referred to Committee Whole House.		
Crosby, Joshua	Revolutionary pension	22	2	Bill of last sess.	66	....	....	....	194	Laid on table.		
Crosby, Nathan	Pension	14	2	Petition	406	Pens. & Rev. Cl'ms.	....	Dischargd, and embraced in bill.	91	Passed	Passed	App'd March 3, 1817
Crosby, Oliver, and others	Fishing bounty on the Oliver Cromwell, captured by the British.	15	1	Petition	211	Com. and Manuf.	....	....	......	Discharged; laid on table.		
Crosby, Orris	Pension for wounds received in war of 1812.	29	1	Petition	189	Invalid Pensions	154	Report and bill.	157	Passed	Passed	App'd Aug. 8, 1846
Crosby, Sampson	(See Frederick Guion.)											
Crosby, Simon	Invalid pension	3	1	Rep. of Secretary War.	131	Select	May 26, 1794	To refer to Sec. with instructions.	R. 12	Passed	Passed	App'd June 9, 1794
Crosby, Simon	Invalid pension	4	1	Rep't Committee on Claims.	457	Whole House	May 7, 1796	Favorable; bill ordered.	156	Passed	Passed	App'd April 20, 1796
Crosby, Simon	Increase of pension	11	2	House bill	283	Whole House	Mar. 24, 1810	Favorable	108	Passed	Passed	App'd April 27, 1810
Croskey, Joseph, & others, agent for.	Indemnity for losses from non-performance of stipulations of United States with them in Florida war of 1836.	25	2	Petition	398	Claims	957	Adverse	......	Laid on table.		
Croskey, Joseph, & others, agent for.	Indemnity for losses from non-performance of stipulations of United States with them in Florida war of 1836.	26	1	Petition	339	Claims	700	Adverse	......	Laid on table.		
Croskey, Joseph, & others, agent for.	Indemnity for losses from non-performance of stipulations of United States with them in Florida war of 1836.	26	2	Petition	125	Claims.						
Cross, James	Pay and land for services as a soldier in war of 1812.	15	2	Petition	165	Military Affairs	....	....	......	Discharged; laid on table.		
Cross, James, (Pa.)	Reimbursement of money expended in support of militia insurrection of 1794.	23	1	Petition	304	Claims	471	Adverse	......	Laid on table.		
Cross, John	Pension for wounds received in the French revolutionary corps.	17	1	Petition	89	Pens. & Rev. Cl'ms.	Dec. 28, 1821	Rep. and res.; adverse.	......	Resolution adopted	....	Leave to withdraw.
Cross, Joseph	Certain credits in settlement of his accounts as Lieut. U. S. Navy.	18	1	Petition	109	Naval Affairs	Feb. 24, 1824	Adverse	......	Laid on table.		
Cross, Joseph, heirs of	Value of brig Friendship and cargo, captured by the French prior to 1800.	22	1	Petition	435	Foreign Affairs.						
Cross, Joseph, heirs of	Value of brig Friendship and cargo, captured by the French prior to 1800.	26	1	Petition	182	Foreign Affairs	343	Favorable; bill.	319	Referred to Committee Whole House.		

List of private claims presented to the House of Representatives of the United States from the 1st to the 31st Congress, inclusive—Continued.

Names of claimants.	Nature or object of the claim.	Congress.	Session.	How brought before the House of Reps.	Page of journal.	To what committee of the House referred.	No. or date of the report.	Nature of the report.	No. of the bill.	How disposed of by the House of Reps.	How disposed of by the Senate.	Date of the act of Congress, and remarks.
Cross, Joseph, (Va.)	Pension for services in war of 1812	31	1	Petition	256	Invalid Pensions	Aug. 1, 1850	Adverse	......	Laid on table.		
Cross, Middleton, heir of	Pay and land due as an enlisted soldier.	15	1	Petition	294	......	......	......	......	Referred to Secretary War.		
Cross, Moses	Restoration of pension	17	1	Petition	37	Rev. Pensions	......	......	......	Discharged; laid on table.	......	See act March 1, 1823
Cross, Nathaniel	Indemnity for losses and services as consul at Matanzas.	27	3	Petition	53	Foreign Affairs.						
Cross, Osborne	Release from liability for public money of which he was unlawfully deprived.	30	1	Petition	711	Claims.						
Cross, Osborne	Release from liability for public money of which he was unlawfully deprived.	31	2	Petition	37	Claims	81	Report and bill.	485	Referred to Committee Whole House.		
Cross, Samuel	Compensation for services against Indians in 1779.	27	2	Petition	374	Rev. Claims	654	Adverse	......	Laid on table.		
Cross, Thomas	Pre-emption right to land as a New Orleans branch pilot.	28	1	Petition	77	Priv. Land Claims.	9	Favorable; bill.	35	Passed	Passed	App'd June 17, 1844
Cross, Thomas	(See Louis F. Beeler and others.)											
Cross, Thomas, (N. Y.)	Pension	22	1	Petition	36	Rev. Pensions	40	Report and bill	81	Passed	Indef. postp'd.	
Cross, Trueman	(See Archibald Stewart)	26	1	Memorial	182	Foreign Affairs	343	Favorable; bill	319	Referred to Committee Whole House.		
Cross, Trueman	(See William McCreery, attorney for the administratrix of.)											
Cross, Trueman	Compensation for services as acting quartermaster general U. S. A.	24	1	Petition	142	Military Affairs	443	Report and bill.	458	Referred to Committee Whole House.		
Cross, Trueman	Compensation for services as acting quartermaster general U. S. A.	25	2	Memorial	41	Military Affairs	......	......	......	Discharged.		
Cross, Trueman	Compensation for services as acting quartermaster general U. S. A.	28	1	Memorial	604	Military Affairs	334	Adverse	......	Laid on table.		
Crossman, Samuel	Pension	21	1	Petition	143	Military Pensions	April 2, 1830	Adverse	......	Laid on table.		
Crossman, William, widow of.	Pension for revolutionary services.	30	1	Petitions	340, 406	Rev. Pensions	681	Report and bill.	544	Referred to Committee Whole House.		
Crossman, William, widow of.	Pension for revolutionary services.	30	2	Bill of last sess.	318	Whole House	Jan. 26, 1849	Adverse	544	Laid on table	......	Leave to withdraw.
Crosy, Allen	(See Allen Crary.)											
Crouch, Hazel W., administrator of.	Compensation for medical attendance by him to persons at United States ordnance depot, Charleston, South Carolina.	25	2	Petition	629	Claims	849	Report and bill.	765	Referred to Committee Whole House.		
Crouch, Hazel W., administrator of.	Compensation for medical attendance by him to persons at United States ordnance depôt, Charleston, South Carolina.	25	3	Bill of last sess.	431	Whole House	Feb. 1, 1839	With't amend.	765	Passed	Passed	App'd March 3, 1839
Crouch, Richard	Increase of pension	11	2	House bill	283	Whole House	Mar. 24, 1810	Favorable	108	Passed	Passed	App'd April 27, 1810
Crouse, Peter	Grant of a mile square of land for sufferings in the Revolution as a prisoner with Indians.	29	1	Petition	474	Indian Affairs	......	......	......	Discharged; laid on table.		
Crousillat, Lewis	Indemnity for Spanish spoliations on his property in 1795.	19	1	Memorial	153	Foreign Affairs	......	......	......	Discharged; leave to withdraw.		
Crousillat, Lewis	Indemnity for Spanish spoliations on his property in 1795.	26	1	Memorial	182	Foreign Affairs	343	Favorable; bill	319	Referred to Committee Whole House.		
Crow, Albion T	Compensation for property lost in Indian war.	23	2	Resolution	282	Claims.						

List of private claims presented to the House of Representatives of the United States from the 1st to the 31st Congress, inclusive—Continued.

Names of claimants.	Nature or object of the claim.	Congress.	Session.	How brought before the House of Reps.	Page of journal.	To what committee of the House referred.	No. or date of the report.	Nature of the report.	No. of the bill.	How disposed of by the House of Reps.	How disposed of by the Senate.	Date of the act of Congress, and remarks.
Crow, Albion T	Compensation for property lost in Indian war.	24	1	Petition	92	Claims	491	Report and bill	493	Referred to Committee Whole House.		
Crow, Albion T	Compensation for property lost in Indian war.	25	2	Petition	98	Claims	22	Report and bill.	34	Passed	Passed	App'd March 2, 1838
Crow, George	Allowance for depreciation of pay, &c., for services in revolutionary army.	3	1	Petition	71					Referred to Secretary War.		
Crow, George	Allowance for depreciation of pay, &c., for services in revolutionary army.	3	2	Rep. of Secretary War.	278					Laid on table.		
Crow, Isaac, assignee of	Confirmation of title to land in Louisiana.	27	2	Petition &c	140, 622	Priv. Land Claims.						
Crow, Jonathan	Pension	25	2	Senate bill	1012	Invalid Pensions	July 2, 1838	With't amend.	243	Referred to Committee Whole House.		
Crow, Peter	Compensation for services as spy or ranger in 1792.	13	3	Petition	652	Claims				Discharged; leave to withdraw.		
Crow, Walter	(See Bernard Rogan and others.)											
Crowell, A. P	Indemnity for French spoliations prior to 1800.	26	1	Memorial	182	Foreign Affairs	343	Favorable; bill.	319	Referred to Committee Whole House.		
Crowell, Elias B. & others.	(See clerks of 6th Census.)											
Crowell, George	(See Winthrop Sears and others.)											
Crowell, Henry, executors of.	Renewal of lost loan office certificate.	2	1	Petition and rep. Sec. Treasury.	464	Select.						
Crowell, John	Compensation as clerk to naval office in Philadelphia, 1828 and 1829.	22	2	Memorial	397	Ways and Means.						
Crowell, John	Compensation as clerk to naval office in Philadelphia, 1828 and 1829.	23	1	Memorial	56	Ways and Means.						
Crowell, John	Equitable settlement of accounts as agent for Creek Indians.	29	1	Senate bill	1034	Indian Affairs	July 24, 1846	With amend.	67	Amended and passed.	Passed	App'd Aug. 6, 1846
Crowell, John, legal representatives of.	Compensation for services and losses as Indian agent.	30	1	Petition	892	Indian Affairs.						
Crowell, John, legal representatives of.	Compensation for services and losses as Indian agent.	30	2	Petition	164	Indian Affairs	144	Adverse		Laid on table.		
Crowell, Samuel	(See Joseph Baker and others.)											
Crowell, Sylvanus	Fishing bounty on schooners Jerusha, Phebe, and Ruth.	5	2	Petition	157	Com. and Manuf.	Feb. 13, 1798	Favorable; bill ordered.	54	Passed	Passed	App'd Mar. 19, 1798
Crowell, Thomas	Invalid pension	3	2	Rep. of Secretary War.	337	Claims	Feb. 28, 1795	Favorable; bill ordered.	130	Passed	Postponed.	
Crowell, Thomas	Invalid pension	4	1	Rep. of Secretary War.	445	Claims	Feb. 18, 1796	Favorable; bill ordered.	156	Passed	Passed	App'd April 20, 1796
Crown, Jeremiah, & others	Additional compensation as laborers in Treasury Department.	31	2	Petition	78	Ways and Means.						
Crown, Thomas	Compensation for losses on contract for brick for Oak Island fort, N. Carolina.	20	1	Petition	195	Claims				Discharged; laid on table.		
Crown, Thomas	Compensation for losses on contract for brick for Oak Island fort, N. Carolina.	20	2	Petition	231					Referred to Secretary of War.		
Crown, Thomas	Compensation for losses on contract for brick for Oak Island fort, N. Carolina.	21	1	Petition and rep't Sec. of War.	74, 211	Claims	Mar. 31, 1830	Adverse		Laid on table.		

List of private claims presented to the House of Representatives of the United States from the 1st to the 31st Congress, inclusive—Continued.

Names of claimants.	Nature or object of the claim.	Congress.	Session.	How brought before the House of Reps.	Page of journal.	To what committee of the House referred.	No. or date of the report.	Nature of the report.	No. of the bill.	How disposed of by the House of Reps.	How disposed of by the Senate.	Date of the act of Congress, and remarks.
Crown, Thomas	Compensation for losses on contract for brick for Oak Island fort, N. Carolina.	22	1	Petition	98	Claims	Jan. 30, 1832	Adverse	......	Laid on table.		
Crown, Thomas	Compensation for losses on contract for brick for Oak Island fort, N. Carolina.	23	1	Petition	192	Claims	Jan. 28, 1834	Adverse	......	Laid on table.		
Crown, Thomas	Compensation for losses on contract for brick for Oak Island fort, N. Carolina.	24	1	Petition	93	Claims.						
Crown, Thomas	Compensation for losses on contract for brick for Oak Island fort, N. Carolina.	24	2	Petition	209	Claims.						
Crown, Thomas	Compensation for losses on contract for brick for Oak Island fort, N. Carolina.	25	2	Petition	73	Claims	Jan. 27, 1838	Adverse	......	Laid on table.		
Crown, Thomas	Compensation for losses on contract for brick for Oak Island fort, N. Carolina.	26	1	Petition	167	Claims	54	Adverse	......	Laid on table.		
Crown, Thomas	Compensation for losses on contract for brick for Oak Island fort, N. Carolina.	27	3	Petition	43	Claims	53	Adverse	......	Laid on table.		
Crown, Thomas	Compensation for losses on contract for brick for Oak Island fort, N. Carolina.	28	1	Petition	319	Claims	557	Adverse	......	Laid on table.		
Crown, Thomas	Compensation for losses on contract for brick for Oak Island fort, N. Carolina.	28	2	Petition	215	Claims.						
Crown, Thomas	Compensation for losses on contract for brick for Oak Island fort, N. Carolina.	29	1	Petition	125	Claims	645	Report and bill	428	Referred to Committee Whole House.		
Crown, Thomas	Compensation for losses on contract for brick for Oak Island fort, N. Carolina.	30	1	Petition	77	Claims	366	Report and bill	332	Referred to Committee Whole House.		
Crown, Thomas	Compensation for losses on contract for brick for Oak Island fort, N. Carolina.	31	1	Petition	223	Claims	244	Report and bill	241	Referred to Committee Whole House.		
Crowninshield, Benjamin, and others.	Indemnity for French spoliations prior to 1800.	22	1	Petition	186	Foreign Affairs.						
Crowninshield, George, and others.	Compensation for vessel and cargo captured (having a double set of papers) by United States ship Confederacy.	3	1	Petition	19	....	....	....	......	Referred to Secretary Treasury.		
Crowninshield, George, and others.	Compensation for vessel and cargo captured (having a double set of papers) by United States ship Confederacy.	3	2	Petition and rep't Sec. Treasury.	284	Claims	Mar. 2, 1795	Adverse	......	Laid on table.		
Crowninshield, George, and others.	Compensation for vessel and cargo captured (having a double set of papers) by United States ship Confederacy.	4	1	Petition and rep't Sec. Treasury.	373	Claims	Mar. 31, 1796	Adverse	......	Laid on table.		
Crowninshield, Jacob, guardian of the children of.	Renewal of a lost loan office certificate.	13	2	Petition	337	Ways and Means	April 5, 1814	By bill	188	Passed	Passed	App'd April 18, 1814

List of private claims presented to the House of Representatives of the United States from the 1st to the 31st Congress, inclusive—Continued.

Names of claimants.	Nature or object of the claim.	Congress.	Session.	How brought before the House of Reps.	Page of journal.	To what committee of the House referred.	No. or date of the report.	Nature of the report.	No. of the bill.	How disposed of by the House of Reps.	How disposed of by the Senate.	Date of the act of Congress, and remarks.
55 Crowninshield, John, and others.	Increase of compensation as appraisers in Boston.	23	1	Petition	32	Commerce.						
Crowninshield, John, and others.	Increase of compensation as appraisers in Boston.	23	2	Petition	56	Commerce.						
Crowninshield, William, widow of.	Continuation of pension granted to late husband.	16	1	Petition	312	Rev. Pensions	April 22, 1820	Adverse	......	Laid on table.		
Crowther, Stephen.......	(See Andrew Leitch.)											
Croxall, Charles.........	Compensation for services in revolutionary war.	2	1	Petition	451	....	....	....	......	Referred to Secretary War.		
Croxall, Charles	Compensation for services in revolutionary war.	2	2	Rep. of Secretary War.	735	....	....	....	......	Laid on table.		
Croxall, Charles	Commutation of half-pay, &c., due for services as captain in revolutionary war.	8	2	Petition	69	Claims.						
Croxall, Charles	Commutation of half-pay, &c., due for services as captain in revolutionary war.	11	2	Petition	350	Claims.						
Croxall, Charles	Further compensation for services in revolutionary army.	14	1	Petition	376	Pens. & Rev. Cl'ms.	....	....	......	Discharged; laid on table.		
Croxall, Charles	Further compensation for services in revolutionary army.	14	2	Petition	75	Pens. & Rev. Cl'ms.	....	....	......	Discharged; laid on table.		
Croxall, Charles.........	Further compensation for services in revolutionary army.	15	1	Petition	211	Pens. & Rev. Cl'ms.	....	....	......	Discharged; laid on table.		
Croxall, Charles.........	Reimbursement of money advanced to officers in revolutionary war.	19	1	Petition	205	Rev. Claims......	....	....	......	Discharged; laid on table.		
Croxall, Charles, heirs of..	Reimbursement of money advanced to officers in revolutionary war.	31	1	Petition	810	Rev. Claims.						
Croxford, Daniel, or David.	Pension	21	2	Petition	113	Military Pensions..	....	....	......	Discharged; laid on table.		
Crozier, Anthony........	Credit in his account as postmaster at Anderson, Tenn., for money lost by the burning of his house.	18	1	Petition	253	P. Of. and P. Roads.						
Crozier, John B., and companions of mounted Tennessee volunteers.	Indemnity for expenses of rendezvous in 1836.	25	3	Resolution	408	Claims.						
Crozier, John B., and companions of mounted Tennessee volunteers.	Indemnity for expenses of rendezvous in 1836.	28	1	Petition	706	Military Affairs.						
Crozier, John B., and companions of mounted Tennessee volunteers.	Indemnity for expenses of rendezvous in 1836.	28	2	Petition	83	Military Affairs ...	72	Report and bill.	555	Passed.		
Crozier, John B., and companions of mounted Tennessee volunteers.	Indemnity for expenses of rendezvous in 1836.	29	1	House bill	397	Whole House	July 5, 1846	With't amend.	230	Passed	Referred to Military Affairs.	
Crozier, Matthew, & others.	Co[illegible] in Pennsylvania militia, revolutionary war.	10	2	Petition	363	Select.						
Crozier, R. G...........	Indemnity for goods taken from him by United States soldiers in Mexico.	30	2	Petition	416	Military Affairs ...	....	....	......	Discharged; laid on table.		
Crozier, R. G...........	Indemnity for goods taken from him by United States soldiers in Mexico.	31	1	Petition	672	Military Affairs.						

List of private claims presented to the House of Representatives of the United States from the 1st to the 31st Congress, inclusive—Continued.

Names of claimants.	Nature or object of the claim.	Congress.	Session.	How brought before the House of Reps.	Page of journal.	To what committee of the House referred.	No. or date of the report.	Nature of the report.	No. of the bill.	How disposed of by the House of Reps.	How disposed of by the Senate.	Date of the act of Congress, and remarks.
Cruff, William	(See Philip Lefavour and others.)											
Cruger, Henry N	(See David R. Denham and others.)											
Cruger, Henry N	(See William De Peyster.)											
Cruger, Nicholas, executors of.	Indemnity for French spoliations prior to 1800.	26	1	Memorial	182	Foreign Affairs	343	Favorable; bill.	319	Referred to Committee Whole House.		
Cruise, Walter	Compensation for services, &c., in revolutionary war.	3	2	Petition	271, 305	Claims	Feb. 27, 1795	Adverse	......	Laid on table.		
Cruise, Walter	Compensation for services, &c., in revolutionary war.	4	2	Petition	614	Claims	Jan. 18, 1797	Adverse	......	Leave to withdraw.		
Cruise, Walter	Compensation for services, &c., in revolutionary war.	7	1	Petition	311	Claims	....	....	......	Discharged; leave to withdraw.		
Crum, David	Change location of land in Mississippi.	14	2	Petition	41	Public Lands	Dec. 23, 1816	Rep. and res.; adverse.	......	Resolution adopted	....	Leave to withdraw.
Crum, Tobias	Change location of land in Indiana.	24	1	Petition	599	Priv. Land Claims.	April 2, 1836	By bill	522	Passed	Passed	App'd July 2, 1836
Crummitt, James	Invalid pension	3	1	Rep. of Secretary War.	131	Select	May 26, 1794	Favorable; bill ordered.	62	Passed	Passed	App'd June 7, 1794
Crummitt, James	Increase of pension	12	1	House bill	361	Whole House	June 15, 1812	Favorable	138	Passed	Passed	App'd July 5, 1812
Crump, Benjamin, heir of.	Compensation for revolutionary services.	31	1	Petition	752	Rev. Claims.						
Crump, Abner and William.	(See James Steptoe, sen., & others.)											
Crump, Joshua and Polly.	(See Thomas Patterson, heirs of.)											
Crumpton, John	Compensation for supplies furnished in revolutionary war.	2	1	Rep. of Secretary Treasury.	580	....	....	....	......	Laid on table.		
Crumvine, Peter	Compensation for work and materials for Cumberland road.	23	1	Res. and papers	589	Claims	455	Adverse	......	Laid on table.		
Crunden, Ralph, devisee of	Pay, &c., for services as surgeon in revolutionary war.	10	2	Petition	376	Select	Dec. 28, 1808	By bill	129	Referred to Committee Whole House.		
Crunden, Ralph, devisee of	Pay, &c., for services as surgeon in revolutionary war.	11	1	Petition	52	Claims.						
Crunden, Ralph, devisee of	Pay, &c., for services as surgeon in revolutionary war.	11	2	Petition	154	Claims	Mar. 14, 1810	Report & res.; adverse.	......	Resolution adopted.		
Crus, Santiago	Extension of time to file proof of title to land in Louisiana.	19	2	Rep. of Secretary Treasury.	50	Priv. Land Claims.	49	Report and bill	378	Referred to Committee Whole House.		
Cruse, Englehart	Extension of privilege to construct and vend a new steam engine.	1	1	Petition	35	Select	June 24, 1789	By bill	10	Postponed.		
Cruse, Samuel	(See Benjamin S. Pope.)											
Crush, Michael	Compensation for services, &c., in revolutionary war.	8	1	Petition	472	Claims	Mar. 13, 1804	To discharge and postp'e.	......	Report adopted.		
Crutcher, John, & Thomas Rawlings.	Compensation for horses, &c., lost in United States service, war of 1812.	15	2	Petition	24	Claims	Nov. 23, 1818	Adverse	......	Laid on table.		
Crutcher, John, & Thomas Rawlings.	Compensation for horses, &c., lost in United States service, war of 1812.	16	1	Petition	142	Claims	Jan. 17, 1820	Adverse	......	Laid on table.		
Crutchlow, James, widow of.	Arrears of pension withheld under acts of May, 1820.	24	2	Petition	90	Rev. Pensions	....	....	......	Discharged; laid on table.		
Crute, John	Invalid pension	10	2	House bill	499	Whole House	Feb. 20, 1809	Favorable	158	Passed	Passed	App'd March 3, 1809
Crute, John	Renewal of a lost final settlement certificate of the issue of 1784.	14	1	Petition	253	Pens. & Rev. Cl'ms.	April 8, 1816	Rep. and res.; adverse.	......	Resolution adopted.		
Crute, John	Renewal of a lost final settlement certificate of the issue of 1784.	15	2	Petition	204	Pens. & Rev. Clm's.	....	....	......	Discharged; laid on table.	....	Leave to withdraw, 2d March, 1820.
Crute, John	Renewal of a lost final settlement certificate of the issue of 1784.	16	2	House bill	109	Whole House	....	....	185			

List of private claims presented to the House of Representatives of the United States from the 1st to the 31st Congress, inclusive—Continued.

Names of claimants.	Nature or object of the claim.	Congress.	Session.	How brought before the House of Reps.	Page of journal.	To what committee of the House referred.	No. or date of the report.	Nature of the report.	No. of the bill.	How disposed of by the House of Reps.	How disposed of by the Senate.	Date of the act of Congress, and remarks.
Crute, John	Renewal of a lost final settlement certificate of the issue of 1784.	17	1	Petition	86	Pens. & Rev. Cl'ms.	Feb. 5, 1822	By bill	77	Passed	Passed	App'd May 7, 1822
Crutchett, James	Compensation for gas-light, &c., to Capitol and grounds.	30	1	House bill	268	Whole House	May 26, 1848	To lay on table	103	Report adopted	....	Provided for per acts of March 3, 1847, and March 27, 1848.
Crutchett, James	Compensation for gas light, &c., to Capitol and grounds.	30	1	Senate bill	343	Whole House	May 26, 1848	To lay on table	121	Report adopted.		
Cruttenden, Joel	Indemnity for losses and services as disbursing agent of Cherokee commission.	31	1	Petition	307	Indian Affairs	278	Legislation unnecessary.	......	Leave to withdraw.		
Cruzat, Anthony, and L. P. Deverges.	Indemnity for property destroyed near New Orleans, by order of Gen. Jackson.	14	2	Senate bill	146	Claims	Jan. 10, 1817	With't amend.	......	Passed	Passed	App'd March 1, 1817
Cruzat, Antoine	Confirmation of title to land in Louisiana.	22	1	Petition	133	Public Lands	234	Report and bill.	314	Referred to Committee Whole House.		
Cruzat, Antoine	Confirmation of title to land in Louisiana.	23	1	Petition	132	Public Lands	105	Report and bill.	113	Passed	Passed	App'd June 30, 1834
Cruzat, Manuel	Refunding of amount of certain judgments paid by him to United States.	26	1	Petition	353	Judiciary	....	....	......	Discharged; laid on table.		
Cruzat, Manuel	Refunding of amount of certain judgments paid by him to United States.	27	3	Petition	319	Judiciary	264	Adverse	......	Laid on table.		
Cruzat, Manuel	Refunding of amount of certain judgments paid by him to United States.	28	1	Petition	142	Judiciary	....	....	......	Discharged; laid on table.		
Cruzat, Manuel, widow of.	Refunding of amount of certain judgments paid by him to U. S.	31	1	Petition	653	Claims	328	Report and bill.	285	Referred to Committee Whole House.		
Cruzat, Manuel, widow of.	Refunding of amount of certain judgments paid by him to U. S.	31	2	Bill of last sess.	181	Whole House	July 24, 1851	With't amend.	285	Passed	Ref'd to Com. Claims.	
Cruzatte, Pierre	(See Lewis & Clarke, and their companions.)											
Cryder, Michael, heirs of.	Compensation for supplies furnished in revolutionary war.	27	2	Petition	376	Rev. Claims	656	Adverse	......	Laid on table.		
Cryder, Michael, heirs of.	Compensation for supplies furnished in revolutionary war.	28	1	Petition	787	Rev. Claims.						
Cryder, Michael, heirs of.	Compensation for supplies furnished in revolutionary war.	29	1	Memorial	476	Rev. Claims	724	Adverse	......	Laid on table.		
Cryder, Michael, heirs of.	Compensation for supplies furnished in revolutionary war.	30	1	Petition	369	Rev. Claims.						
Crygier, Simon	Pension	19	1	Petition	57	Military Pensions.	Feb. 23, 1826	By bill	118	Passed	Ref., and Com. discharged.	
Crygier, Simon	Pension	19	2	House bill	85	Whole House	Feb. 2, 1827	Favorable	314	Passed	Passed	App'd March 3, 1837
Crysell, Jeremiah	Revolutionary pension	21	1	House bill	130	Whole House	Feb. 12, 1830	Adverse	72	Passed.	Passed	App'd May 20, 1830, omitting claimants name.
Crysell, Jeremiah, widow of	Arrears of pension	26	1	Petition	625	Rev. Pensions	551	Adverse	......	Laid on table.		
Crysell, Jeremiah, widow of	Arrears of pension	28	1	Petition	668	Rev. Pensions.						
Crysell, Jeremiah, widow of	Arrears of pension	29	1	Petition	91	Rev. Pensions	726	Adverse	......	Laid on table.		
Cubbage, George	Indemnity for Indian depredations in Black Hawk war of 1832.	24	1	Petition	206	Claims	569	Adverse	......	Laid on table.		
Cubbage, George	(See Illinois, sundry settlers on the frontiers of.)											

List of private claims presented to the House of Representatives of the United States from the 1st to the 31st Congress, inclusive—Continued.

Names of claimants.	Nature or object of the claim.	Congress.	Session.	How brought before the House of Reps.	Page of journal.	To what committee of the House referred.	No. or date of the report.	Nature of the report.	No. of the bill.	How disposed of by the House of Reps.	How disposed of by the Senate.	Date of the act of Congress, and remarks.
Cuddeback, William A.	Pension for services as a soldier in revolutionary war.	25	2	Resolution	162	Rev. Pensions	778	Report and bill.	731	Passed	Ref., and Com. discharged.	
Cuddeback, William A.	Pension for services as a soldier in revolutionary war.	25	3	Petition	88	Rev. Pensions	125	Report and bill.	992	Passed	Adverse report.	
Cuddeback, William A.	Pension for services as a soldier in revolutionary war.	26	1	Petition	170	Rev. Pensions	124	Report and bill.	134	Passed	Indef. postp'd.	
Cuddy, James	Compensation for services as an artificer in revolutionary war.	24	1	Petition	61	Rev. Claims				Discharged; laid on table.		
Cudney, Elizabeth	Relief; husband died in captivity.	4	1	Petition	384	Claims	Jan. 20, 1796	Adverse; leave to withdraw.		Resolution adopted.		
Cudworth, Nathaniel, heirs of.	Commutation of pay for revolutionary services.	31	2	Petition	141	Rev. Claims.						
Culberly, Joseph	Invalid pension, war of 1812	28	1	Petition	114	Invalid Pensions.						
Culberly, Joseph	Invalid pension, war of 1812	29	1	Petition	511	Invalid Pensions.						
Culbertson, John	Compensation as interpreter to U. S. court in Louisiana.	20	1	Petition	168, 197	Judiciary	Jan. 28, 1828	By bill	113	Referred to Committee Whole House.		
Culbertson, John	Compensation as interpreter to U. S. court in Louisiana.	20	1	Senate bill	401	Whole House			69			
Culbertson, John	Compensation as interpreter to U. S. court in Louisiana.	20	2	Senate bill	88	Judiciary	Feb. 13, 1829	With amend's.	27	Referred to Committee Whole House.		
Culbertson, John	Compensation as interpreter to U. S. court in Louisiana.	21	1	Senate bill	97	Judiciary	Mar. 13, 1830	With't amend.	15	Referred to Committee Whole House.		
Culbertson, John	Compensation as interpreter to U. S. court in Louisiana.	21	2	Senate bill	384	Judiciary	March 2, 1831	With't amend.	136	Passed	Passed	App'd March 3, 1831
Culbertson, Joseph	Pension	19	1	Petition	108	Military Pensions	Feb. 23, 1826	By bill	118	Passed	Discharged.	
Culbertson, Joseph	Pension	19	2	House bill	85	Whole House			314			Bill became a law, Mar. 3, 1827, omitting petitioners name
Culbertson, Joseph	Pension	20	1	Petition	124	Military Pensions				Discharged; leave to withdraw.		
Culbertson, Josiah	Pension	20	2	Petition	229	Military Pensions				Discharged; referred to Com. Whole House on bill No. 317.		
Culbertson, Josiah	Pension	21	1	Petition	99	Military Pensions	April 7, 1830	Adverse		Laid on table.		
Culbertson, Samuel, widow of.	Compensation for occupation of farm as a hospital in 1777.	6	2	Petition	810	Claims	March 2, 1801	To discharge and postp'd.		Resolution adopted.		
Culbertson, Samuel, widow of.	Compensation for occupation of farm as a hospital in 1777.	7	1	Petition	105	Claims	March 8, 1802	Rep. and res. adverse.		Resolution adopted.		
Culley, Armstead	Pension	21	2	Petition	209	Military Pensions.						
Cullins, John	Special act for a revolutionary pension.	23	1	Petition	242	Rev. Pensions	268	Report and bill.	304	Referred to Committee Whole House.		
Cullins, John	Special act for a revolutionary pension.	23	2	Bill of last sess.	336	Rev. Pensions	Feb. 6, 1835	With't amend.	304	Passed	Passed	App'd March 3, 1835
Cullumber, Joshua	Compensation for vessel impressed in United States service, war of 1812, and lost.	23	1	Petition	637	Claims.						
Cullumber, Joshua	Compensation for vessel impressed in United States service, war of 1812, and lost.	23	2	Petition	146	Claims	35	Report and bill.	618	Referred to Committee Whole House.		
Cullumber, Joshua	Compensation for vessel impressed in United States service, war of 1812, and lost.	24	1	Petition	51	Claims	38	Report and bill.	38	Passed	Passed	App'd Feb. 17, 1836

List of private claims presented to the House of Representatives of the United States from the 1st to the 31st Congress, inclusive—Continued.

Names of claimants.	Nature or object of the claim.	Congress.	Session.	How brought before the House of Reps.	Page of journal.	To what committee of the House referred.	No. or date of the report.	Nature of the report.	No. of the bill.	How disposed of by the House of Reps.	How disposed of by the Senate.	Date of the act of Congress, and remarks.
Culp, John	(See Samuel Dixon, administrator of.)											
Culver, Aaron, heirs of the late widow of.	Arrears of pension	29	1	Petition	520	Invalid Pensions.						
Culver, Daniel	Invalid pension	1	2	House bill	271	Whole House	July 19, 1790	Favorable	88	Passed	Passed	App'd Aug. 11, 1790
Culver, Dan	Increase of pension	11	3	House bill	604	Whole House	Mar. 2, 1811	Favorable	218	Passed	Passed	App'd March 3, 1811
Culver, Esther	(See Moses Jones, widow of.)											
Culver, William	Compensation for losses under contract for building custom-house at New London, Connecticut.	25	2	Petition	46	Commerce	306	Report and bill.	343	Referred to Committee Whole House.		
Culver, William	Compensation for losses under contract for building custom house at New London, Connecticut.	25	3	Bill of last sess.	377	Whole House	Jan. 25, 1839	With't amend.	343	Passed.		
Culver, William	Compensation for losses under contract for building custom-house at New London, Connecticut.	26	1	Petition	176	Commerce.						
Culver, William	Compensation for losses under contract for building custom house at New London, Connecticut.	26	2	Petition	212	Commerce.						
Culver, William	Compensation for losses under contract for building custom-house at New London, Connecticut.	27	2	Petition	57	Claims.						
Culver, William	Compensation for losses under contract for building custom-house at New London, Connecticut.	27	3	Petition	73	Claims.						
Culver, William	Compensation for losses under contract for building custom house at New London, Connecticut.	28	1	Petition	100	Claims.						
Culver, William	Compensation for losses under contract for building custom-house at New London, Connecticut.	28	1	Petition	206	Claims.						
Culver, William	Compensation for losses under contract for building custom-house at New London, Connecticut.	29	1	Petition	92	Claims	58	Report and bill.	55	Passed	Reported with't amendment.	
Culver, William	Compensation for losses under contract for building custom-house at New London, Connecticut.	29	2	Petition	150	Claims	4	Report and bill.	598	Referred to Committee Whole House.		
Culver, William	Compensation for losses under contract for building custom-house at New London, Connecticut.	30	1	Petition	116	Claims	6	Report and bill.	10	Passed	Passed	App'd Aug. 5, 1848
Cumberland College, (Te.) trustees of.	Indemnity in land for certain losses under act of April, 1806.	19	1	Memorial	443	Public Lands.						
Cummings, Alexander	Pay of lieutenant colonel U. S. army, while acting as such.	24	2	Petition	89	Military Affairs.						
Cummings, Alexander	Pay of lieutenant colonel U. S. army, while acting as such.	25	2	Memorial	171	Military Affairs	Jan. 18, 1838	Adverse	......	Laid on table.		
Cumming, Alexander M.	Compensation for carrying the mail.	28	2	Petition	103	P. Of. & P. Roads.	28	Rep. and res.	R. 62	Referred to Committee Whole House.		
Cumming, Alexander M.	Compensation for carrying the mail.	29	1	Petition	68	P. Of. & P. Roads.	169	Rep. and res.	R. 12	Reported from Com. Whole House with amendment.		
Cumming, Alexander M.	Compensation for carrying the mail.	29	2	Res. of last sess.	68	....	....	....	R. 12	Amended and passed.	Passed	App'd Feb. 19, 1847

List of private claims presented to the House of Representatives of the United States from the 1st to the 31st Congress, inclusive—Continued.

Names of claimants.	Nature or object of the claim.	Congress.	Session.	How brought before the House of Reps.	Page of journal.	To what committee of the House referred.	No. or date of the report.	Nature of the report.	No. of the bill.	How disposed of by the House of Reps.	How disposed of by the Senate.	Date of the act of Congress, and remarks.
Cummins, Charles B	Extension of a saw-mill patent.	24	1	Petition	754	Select.						
Cumming, David, (Pa.)	Equitable settlement of account as captain United States army.	17	1	Petition	31	Claims	Jan. 17, 1822	Report and bill.	42	Passed	Passed	App'd May 7, 1822
Cumming, David, (Pa.)	Allowance of items of account rejected by Treasury Department.	21	2	Petition	145	Claims.						
Cumming, David, (Pa.)	Allowance of items of account rejected by Treasury Department.	25	2	Petition	234	Claims	....	....	....	Discharged.		
Cumming, David, (Pa.)	Allowance of items of account rejected by Treasury Department.	26	1	Petition	169	Claims.						
Cumming, David, (Pa.)	Allowance of items of account rejected by Treasury Department.	26	2	Petition	80	Claims.						
Cumming, David, (Pa.)	Allowance of items of account rejected by Treasury Department.	28	1	Petition	983	Claims.						
Cumming, David, (Pa.)	Allowance of items of account rejected by Treasury Department.	28	2	Petition	111	Claims.						
Cummings, David, (Pa.)	Extension to him of acts for relief of purchasers of public lands.	18	1	Petition	69	Public Lands	....	....	....	Discharged	Leave to withdraw.	
Cummings, David, (Pa.)	Refunding money paid on tract of land.	19	1	Resolution	65	Public Lands	....	....	....	Discharged.		
Cummings, David, (Pa.)	Refunding money paid on tract of land.	19	2	Resolution	151	Public Lands	....	....	....	Discharged.		
Cummins, D	(See Thos. Perkins, executors of).	26	1	....	182							
Cummings, E. H	Compensation for furnishing census tables to members of the House	22	2	Resolution	462	....	....	....	....	Resolution adopted.		
Cumming, George B	(See Richard Henry Wilde.)											
Cummings, Isaac	Pension as a soldier in war of 1812.	25	2	Petition	327	Invalid Pensions	Feb. 6, 1838	Adverse	....	Laid on table.		
Cumming, Jacob	Revolutionary pension	21	1	Petition	356	Military Pensions	....	....	....	Discharged; laid on table.		
Cumming, Jacob	Revolutionary pension	22	1	Resolution	251	Military Pensions	....	....	....	Discharged; laid on table.		
Cumming, James, (Tenn.)	Pay as chaplain to Tennessee volunteers in service against the Cherokees.	25	2	Petition	406	Military Affairs	686	Adverse	....	Laid on table.		
Cummings, James, (N. Y.)	Pension as a soldier in war of 1812.	25	3	Petition	128	Invalid Pensions.						
Cummings, James, (N. Y.)	Pension as a soldier in war of 1812.	26	1	Petition	162	Invalid Pensions	188	Report and bill.	200	Passed	Indef. postp'd.	
Cummins, John, (Ohio)	Repayment of purchase money for certain land.	24	1	Senate bill	1128	Public Lands	July 1, 1836	With't amend.	183	Passed	Passed	App'd July 2, 1836
Cummins, John, sergeant United States army.	Additional compensation as assistant commissary of subsistence.	30	2	Petition	282	Military Affairs.						
Cummins, John, sergeant United States army.	Additional compensation as assistant commissary of subsistence.	31	1	Petition	768, 836	Military Affairs.						
Cumming, John N., widow of.	(See Andrew Hunter, widow of, and others.)											
Cumming, Josiah	Pension for services as a soldier in revolutionary war.	15	2	Petition	58	Rev. Pensions	Jan. 5, 1819	Adverse	....	Laid on table.		
Cumming, Robert	Relief from penalties incurred by importing British manufactures.	12	2	Petition	562	Ways and Means	Nov. 25, 1812	Favorable; bill ordered.	239	Rejected.	....	See acts Jan. 2, and Feb. 27, 1813.
Cumming, Samuel, widow of.	Payment, &c., due as a soldier killed in an Indian fight, Nov. 4, 1791.	7	1	Petition	12	Claims	Dec. 16, 1801	Adverse	....	Leave to withdraw.		

List of private claims presented to the House of Representatives of the United States from the 1st to the 31st Congress, inclusive—Continued.

Names of claimants.	Nature or object of the claim.	Congress.	Session.	How brought before the House of Reps.	Page of journal.	To what committee of the House referred.	No. or date of the report.	Nature of the report.	No. of the bill.	How disposed of by the House of Reps.	How disposed of by the Senate.	Date of the act of Congress, and remarks.
Cummins, Stewart	Extra compensation as a clerk in Treasury Department in Piladilphia, during the yellow fever, in 1793.	3	1	Petition	88	Select	April 17, 1796	Adverse	......	Rejected.		
Cumming, Thomas	(See Joseph Clay, administrator of.)											
Cumming, Thomas	Pre emption right to land on which he resides.	15	1	Petition	386	Public Lands	....	....	......	Discharged; laid on table.		
Cummings, Thomas W.	(See Exploring Expedition.)											
Cumming, William	Revolutionary pension	25	2	Resolution	189	Rev. Pensions	....	....	......	Discharged; laid on table.		
Cumming, William	Revolutionary pension	25	3	Resolution	168	Rev. Pensions	....	....	......	Discharged.		
Cumming, William	Revolutionary pension	26	1	Petition	173	Rev. Pensions.						
Cumming, William	Revolutionary pension	28	1	Petition	769	Rev. Pensions.						
Cumming, William	Revolutionary pension	28	2	Petition	150	Rev. Pensions.						
Cummings and Spyker	Compensation for loss of $2,000 by robbery of the mail.	25	2	Resolution	760	P. Of. and P. Roads.	May 17, 1838	Adverse	......	Laid on table.		
Cumpston, Eliza	Benjamin Flowers, heir of the late widow of.)											
Cundiff, John	(See Benjamin Parker.)											
Cunitz, John and Sebastian	Compensation for services, &c., in revolutionary war.	2	1	Petition	474	....	....	....	......	Referred to Secretary of War.		
Cunitz, John and Sebastian	Compensation for services, &c., in revolutionary war.	3	1	Petition and rep't Sec. of War.	19	Select.						
Cunning, John, mother of.	Money in lieu of land due as a soldier, war of 1812.	23	1	Petition	567	Public Lands.						
Cunningham, Alexander	Military bounty land	20	2	Senate bill	209	Public Lands	78	Adverse	60	Referred to Committee Whole House.		
Cunningham, A. and O. (Mass.)	Reimbursement of duties on merchandise purchased prior to date of tariff of 1828.	24	1	Petition	94	Ways and Means	Jan. 27, 1836	By bill	233	Referred to Committee Whole House.		
Cunningham, Christopher	Pension for wound received at the battle of Buena Vista.	30	1	Senate bill	678	Invalid Pensions	588	With't amend.	213	Passed	Passed	App'd May 9, 1848
Cunningham, Hezekiah	$814 in full for mail services in Indiana and Illinois.	26	1	Senate bill	813	P. Of. and P. Roads.	....	....	200			
Cunningham, Hezekiah	$843 in full for mail services in Indiana and Illinois.	27	2	Senate bill	482	P. Of. and P. Roads.	May 25, 1842	With't amend.	108	Passed	Passed	App'd Aug. 23, 1842
Cunningham, Hugh	Compensation for services as wagon master in revolutionary war.	2	1	Petition	498	....	....	....	......	Referred to Secretary Treasury.		
Cunningham, Hugh	Compensation for services as wagon master in revolutionary war.	2	2	Rep. of Secretary Treasury.	625	....	....	....	......	Laid on table.		
Cunningham, James	Revolutionary pension	22	1	Petition	89	Rev. Pensions.						
Cunningham, Jesse	Invalid pension	21	2	Petition	230	Military Pensions.						
Cunningham, Jesse	Invalid pension	22	1	Petition	51	Rev. Pensions	202	Report and bill.	288	Passed	Rejected.	
Cunningham, Jesse	Invalid pension	22	2	Petition	26	Invalid Pensions	7	Report and bill.	626	Passed	Passed	App'd March 2, 1833
Cunningham, Jesse	Invalid pension	23	1	Petition	45	Invalid Pensions	69	By bill	79	Passed	Rejected	For motion to repeal the above act, see p. 901, 25th Cong., 2d sess.
Cunningham, John, (Ga.)	Pension as a brevet major in revolutionary army.	20	1	Resolution	174	Military Pensions	May 13, 1828	Adverse	......	Laid on table.		
Cunningham, John, (Ga.)	Pension as a brevet major in revolutionary army.	20	2	Petition	55	Military Pensions	Jan. 20, 1829	Report and bill.	384	Referred to Committee Whole House.		

List of private claims presented to the House of Representatives of the United States from the 1st to the 31st Congress, inclusive—Continued.

Names of claimants.	Nature or object of the claim.	Congress.	Session.	How brought before the House of Reps.	Page of journal.	To what committee of the House referred.	No. or date of the report.	Nature of the report.	No. of the bill.	How disposed of by the House of Reps.	How disposed of by the Senate.	Date of the act of Congress, and remarks.
Cunningham, John, (Va.)	Compensation for services of his father as a pilot to the French fleet in revolutionary war.	21	2	Petition	44	Rev. Claims......	....	....	......	Discharged; laid on table.		
Cunningham, John, heirs of.	Commutation of half-pay for services as a lieutenant in Virginia line, revolutionary war.	23	2	Documents.....	48	Rev. Claims.						
Cunninghom, John A....	(See Caleb Loring, and others.)											
Cunningham, John B.....	Pension	31	1	Petition	....	Invalid Pensions...	....	....	......	Discharged; leave to withdraw.		
Cunningham, J. B.......	Indemnity for French spoliations prior to 1800.	26	1	Memorial	182	Foreign Affairs....	343	Favorable; bill.	319	Referred to Committee Whole House.		
Cunningham, Joseph, (Va.)	Pension	23	1	Petition	113	Indian Affairs	....	....	......	Discharged; laid on table.		
Cunningham, Joseph, (Ill.)	Indemnity for Indian depredations.	25	2	Petition	87	Claims	351	Adverse	......	Laid on table.		
Cunningham, Joseph H...	Discharge from liability as surety for P. D. Spencer.	15	2	Petition	190	Judiciary	....	....	......	Discharged; referred to Sec. Treasury.		
Cunningham, Joseph H...	Discharge from liability as surety for P. D. Spencer.	16	1	Petition	130	Judiciary........	....	....	......	Discharged; referred to Sec. Treasury.		
Cunningham, M.........	Allowance of money withheld on contract for transportation of ordnance.	27	2	Petition	228	Claims	767	Adverse	......	Laid on table.		
Cunningham, Obadiah....	Payment of loan office certificate, issued December 21, 1779, to Robert Hoops or bearer.	14	2	Resolution	440	Pens. & Rev. Cl'ms.	....	....	......	Discharged; laid on table.		
Cunningham, Patrick, (O.)	Pension	19	1	Petition	492	Military Pensions..	193	Favorable; embraced in bill	119	Passed.		
Cunningham, Patrick, (O.)	Pension	19	2	Petition	67	Military Pensions..	Dec. 22, 1826	By bill	315	Passed.............	Indef. postp'd.	
Cunningham, Patrick, (Ill.)	Indemnity for Indian depredations.	29	1	Petition	....	Claims...........	3	Adverse	.....	Laid on table.		
Cunningham, Patrick, (Ill.)	Indemnity for Indian depredations.	30	1	Petition	77	Claims	15	Adverse	......	Laid on table.		
Cunningham, Richard....	Pension as a soldier in revolutionary war.	20	1	Resolution	267	Military Pensions..	May 6, 1828	Adverse	......	Laid on table.		
Cunningham, Robert, heir of.	Indemnity of estate for losses on Continental money.	26	1	Petition	360	Rev. Claims.						
Cunningham, William, representative of.	Commutation of half-pay for revolutionary services.	24	1	Petition and res..	62, 218	Rev. Claims......	May 11, 1836	Rep. and res. to refer to Sec. War for settlement.	......	Resolution adopted.		
Cunningham, William, representative of.	Commutation of half-pay for revolutionary services.	24	1	Rep. of Secretary War.	1011	Rev. Pensions.						
Cunningham, William, representative of.	Commutation of half-pay for revolutionary services.	24	2	Memorial	39	Rev. Claims.						
Cunningham, William, representative of.	Commutation of half-pay for revolutionary services.	25	2	Resolution	77	Rev. Claims......	Feb. 8, 1838	Adverse	......	Laid on table.		
Cunningham, Wm., (N. C.)	Compensation for services as wagon master in removal of Cherokees.	26	2	Resolution	62	Claims	....	....	......	Discharged; laid on table.		
Cunningham, William H..	Refunding of money collected of him by Post Office Department.	28	1	Petition	297	P. Of. and P. Roads.						
Cunow, John G.........	(See United Brethren, Society of.)											
Curd, John B., & Cyrenus Wait.	Release from liability as sureties for a postmaster in Kentucky.	24	2	Petition	146	P. Of. and P. Roads.						
Curd, John B., & Cyrenus Wait.	Release from liability as sureties for a postmaster in Kentucky.	25	2	Petition	93	P. Of. and P. Roads.	Dec. 28, 1837	Adverse	......	Laid on table.		
Curd, John.............	Arrears of pension.............	19	1	Petition	221	Military Pensions..	164	Adverse	......	Laid on table.		

List of private claims presented to the House of Representatives of the United States from the 1st to the 31st Congress, inclusive—Continued.

Names of claimants.	Nature or object of the claim.	Congress.	Session.	How brought before the House of Reps.	Page of journal.	To what committee of the House referred.	No. or date of the report.	Nature of the report.	No. of the bill.	How disposed of by the House of Reps.	How disposed of by the Senate.	Date of the act of Congress, and remarks.
Curd, John	Arrears of pension	21	1	Petition	82	Military Pensions	April 24, 1830	Adverse		Laid on table.		
Curd, Samuel H.	(See Fidelis C. Sharp and others.)											
Cure, Louis	Confirmation of title to land in Louisiana.	22	1	Petition	64	Priv. Land Claims.	62	Report and bill.	125	Passed	Passed	App'd July 25, 1832
Curle, John	(See John Valentine.)											
Curle, Portland	(See George E. Harris, assignee of)											
Curley, John	Compensation for services, &c., in revolutionary war.	2	1	Petition	475					Referred to Secretary of War.		
Curley, John	Compensation for services, &c., in revolutionary war.	4	1	Petition	444	Claims.						
Curley, John	Compensation for services, &c., in revolutionary war.	4	2	Petition	614	Claims	Jan. 24, 1797	Adverse		Rejected.		
Curman, Daniel	Pension	21	2	Petition	103	Military Pensions						
Curren, Timothy	Compensation for occupancy of his house in Philadelphia as an hospital.	14	2	Petition	284	Claims				Discharged; laid on table.		
Curren, Timothy	Compensation for occupancy of his house in Philadelphia as an hospital.	18	1	Petition	197	Claims	Mar. 12, 1824	Adverse		Laid on table.		
Curren, Timothy	Compensation for occupancy of his house in Philadelphia as an hospital.	19	1	Petition	248	Claims				Discharged; laid on table.		
Curren, Timothy	Compensation for occupancy of his house in Philadelphia as an hospital.	20	1	Petition	243	Claims	Feb. 8, 1828	Adverse		Laid on table.		
Curren, Timothy, administrator of.	Compensation for occupancy of his house in Philadelphia as an hospital.	25	2	Petition	655	Claims	846	Adverse		Laid on table.		
Currie, Samuel	Pension	21	2	Resolution	165	Military Pensions.						
Currier, David	Invalid pension	30	1	Petition	826	Invalid Pensions	June 20, 1848	With't amend.	134	Passed	Passed	App'd Aug. 14, 1848
Currier, Elizabeth	Pension for revolutionary services of husband.	28	1	Petition	849	Rev. Pensions.						
Currier, Henry	Invalid pension	3	2	Rep. of Secretary War.	278	Claims.						
Currier, Henry	Invalid pension	4	1	Rep. of Secretary War.	445	Claims	Feb. 13, 1796	To refer to Secretary, with instructions.	R. 16	Passed	Passed	App'd April 18, 1796
Currier, Henry	Invalid pension	4	2	Rep. of Secretary War.	651	Claims.						
Currier, Solomon H.	Commissions on bonds taken as collector at Newburyport, Mass.	24	1	Petition	198	Commerce.						
Currier, Solomon H.	Commissions on bonds taken as collector at Newburyport, Mass.	24	2	Petition	75	Commerce.						
Currier, Solomon H.	Commissions on bonds taken as collector at Newburyport, Mass.	25	2	Petitions	46, 165	Commerce	394	Rep. and res.; adverse.		Laid on table.		
Currier, Solomon H.	Commissions on bonds taken as collector at Newburyport, Mass.	25	2	Petition	165	Commerce	394	Adverse		Laid on table.		
Currier, S. H.	(See James Price, executors of)	26	1		182							
Currill, Nicholas, heirs of.	Commutation of half-pay due as a revolutionary officer.	23	1	Petition	121	Rev. Claims.						
Currill, Nicholas, heirs of.	Commutation of half-pay due as a revolutionary officer.	23	2	Petition	77	Rev. Claims.						

List of private claims presented to the House of Representatives of the United States from the 1st to the 31st Congress, inclusive—Continued.

Names of claimants.	Nature or object of the claim.	Congress.	Session.	How brought before the House of Reps.	Page of journal.	To what committee of the House referred.	No. or date of the report.	Nature of the report.	No. of the bill.	How disposed of by the House of Reps.	How disposed of by the Senate.	Date of the act of Congress, and remarks.
Currill, Nicholas, heirs of.	Commutation of half-pay due as a revolutionary officer.	24	1	Petition	103	Rev. Claims	April 1, 1836	Adverse	......	Laid on table.		
Currier, William	(See Edward Toppan)	8	2		96							
Currier, William and Solomon H.	(See Elnathan Attwater and others.)											
Currin, Edward	Pension	20	1	Petition	396	Military Pensions	April 29, 1818	By bill	283	Passed	Ref. to Com. on Pensions.	
Currin, Edward	Pension	20	2	House bill	55	Whole House	Jan. 15, 1829	Favorable	311	Passed	Laid on table.	
Currin, Edward	Pension	21	1	Petition	48	Military Pensions	Jan. 15, 1830	By bill	72	Passed	Passed	App'd May 20, 1830
Curry, Benjamin F	(See George B. Russell and others.)											
Curry, Cæsar J	To locate a Spanish grant upon certain lands in Louisiana.	22	1	Petition	115	Priv. Land Claims	Jan. 6, 1832	Adverse	......	Laid on table.		
Curry, James, heirs of	Land and money due for services in Clark's (Illinois) regiment.	26	1	Petition	359	Rev. Claims.						
Curry, Joseph, heir of	Confirmation of title to land in Florida.	17	2	Petition	112	Priv. Land Claims	Jan. 17, 1823	Rep. and res.; adverse.	......	Resolution adopted	....	Leave to withdraw.
Curry, Robert	Pension	20	1	Petition	557	Military Pensions	....	....	......	Discharged; laid on table.		
Curry, Robert	Pension	20	2	House bill	55	Whole House	Jan. 15, 1829	Favorable	311	Passed	Laid on table.	
Curry, Robert	Pension	21	1	Petition	48	Military Pensions	Jan. 5, 1830	By bill	72	Passed	Passed	App'd May 20, 1830
Curter, Henry, assignee of.	Confirmation of title to land in Territory of Arkansas.	16	1	Petition	291	Priv. Land Claims	....	....	......	Discharged; laid on table.		
Curtis, Abner	Pension	15	1	Petition	195	Select	Mar. 21, 1818	Rep. and res. to be disch'd.	......	Resolution adopted.		
Curtis, Abner	Compensation for vessel captured while conveying timber for United States navy.	15	1	Petition	389	Claims	....	....	......	Discharged.		
Curtis, Abner	Compensation for vessel captured while conveying timber for United States navy.	15	2	Petition	237	Naval Affairs	....	....	......	Discharged; laid on table.		
Curtis, Bartholomew, brother of.	Payment of revolutionary pension for supporting him twenty years, while deaf and dumb.	17	1	Petition	387	Rev. Pensions	....	....	......	Discharged; laid on table.		
Curtis, Chauncy	Pension	15	1	Petition	195	Select	Mar. 21, 1818	Rep. and res. to be disch'd.	......	Resolution adopted.		
Curtis, Ebenezer	Invalid pension	3	1	Report of Secretary of War.	131	Select	May 26, 1794	To refer to Secretary, with instructions.	R. 12	Passed	Passed	App'd June 9, 1794
Curtis, Elisha, and others.	Payment of claim against United States.	1	2	Petition	191	....	....	....	......	Referred to Secretary of War.		
Curtis, Henry D. & Charles	Redress for the capture of brig Adventure by a French cruizer.	12	1	Petition	328	....	....	....	......	Referred to Secretary of State.		
Curtis, Isaac	Pension for disability incurred in war of 1812.	25	2	Petition	167	Invalid Pensions	....	....	......	Discharged.		
Curtis, Isaac	(See Israel Pearce, heir of.)											
Curtis, James	Pension	19	1	Petition	203	Military Pensions	164	Adverse	......	Laid on table.		
Curtis, John	Revolutionary pension	19	1	Resolutions	163, 368	Military Pensions	164	Adverse	......	Laid on table.		
Curtis, John	Revolutionary pension	20	2	Resolution	224	Military Pensions	....	....	......	Discharged; referred to Com. Whole House on bill No. 317.		
Curtis, John	Revolutionary pension	24	1	Resolution	692	Rev. Pensions.						
Curtis, John	Revolutionary pension	24	2	Petition	50	Rev. Pensions.						

List of private claims presented to the House of Representatives of the United States from the 1st to the 31st Congress, inclusive—Continued.

Names of claimants.	Nature or object of the claim.	Congress.	Session.	How brought before the House of Reps.	Page of journal.	To what committee of the House referred.	No. or date of the report.	Nature of the report.	No. of the bill.	How disposed of by the House of Reps.	How disposed of by the Senate.	Date of the act of Congress, and remarks.
Curtis, Josiah	Invalid pension	24	1	Petition	473	Invalid Pensions	April 15, 1836	By bill	564	Passed	Passed	App'd June 28, 1836
Curtis, Jotham	Arrearages of pension, and bounty land.	27	2	Petition	908	Rev. Claims	869	Adverse		Laid on table.		
Curtis, Nathan W.	Compensation for property confiscated in Canada, for his attachment to the American cause.	15	1	Petition	248	Claims				Discharged; leave to withdraw.		
Curtis, Nathan W.	Compensation for property confiscated in Canada, for his attachment to the American cause.	15	2	Petition	78	Military Affairs				Discharged; leave to withdraw.		
Curtice, Thomas	Compensation for services in revolutionary war.	3	2	Petition	249	Claims	Feb. 25, 1795	Adverse		Referred to Committee Whole House.		
Curtice, Thomas	Compensation for services in revolutionary war.	4	2	Petition	614	Claims	Dec. 27, 1796	Adverse		Leave to withdraw.		
Curtis, Thomas	(See Caleb Loring, and others.)											
Curtis, William	Invalid pension	3	2	Rep. of Secretary War.	350	Claims	May 3, 1795	Discharged and postponed.		Laid on table.		
Curtis, William	Invalid pension	4	1	Rep. of Secretary War.	445	Claims	Feb. 18, 1796	Favorable; bill ordered.	156	Passed	Passed	App'd April 20, 1796
Curtis, William	Increase of pension	10	2	House bill	499	Whole House	Feb. 20, 1809	Favorable	158	Passed	Passed	App'd March 3, 1809
Curwen, Joseph	(See Willing & Curwen.)											
Cushing, Billy	(See William Baker, and others)	22	1		288							
Cushing, Charles, sen.	(See Jos. Sheafe, executors of.)	26	1		182							
Cushing, John	Pension	21	2	Petition	61	Military Pensions.						
Cushing, Nathaniel, attorney of.	Location of certain land warrants in the Northwest Territory.	4	2	Petition	654	Select	Feb. 3, 1797	Adverse		Laid on table.		
Cushing, Thomas P.	(See Benjamin Adams & Co., and others.)											
Cushing, Thomas P.	(See Wm. and S. Lawrence, and others.)											
Cushing, Thomas	Fishing bounty on schooner Germantown.	24	1	Petition	796	Commerce	804	Report and bill.	720	Referred to Committee Whole House.		
Cushing, Thomas	Fishing bounty on schooner Germantown.	25	2	Petition	40	Commerce	89	Report and bill.	105	Passed	Passed	App'd April 20, 1838
Cushing, Thomas	Fishing bounty on schooner Commerce.	25	2	Petition	199	Commerce	754	Report and bill.	714	Referred to Committee Whole House.		
Cushing, Thomas	Fishing bounty on schooner Commerce.	25	3	Bill of last sess.	380	Whole House	Jan. 26, 1839	With't amend.	714	Passed	Passed with amendment.	App'd March 3, 1839
Cushing, William	Invalid pension	12	1	House bill	361	Whole House	June 15, 1812	Favorable	138	Passed	Passed	App'd July 5, 1812
Cushman, Andrew	Pension	19	1	Petition	127	Military Pensions	164	Adverse		Laid on table.		
Cushman, Daniel	Pension	19	1	Petition	175	Military Pensions	164	Adverse		Laid on table.		
Cushman, Ephraim	Restoration of pension	17	1	Petition	77	Rev. Pensions				Discharged; laid on table.		See act March 1, 1823
Cushman, George	Restoration of pension	17	1	Petition	67	Rev. Pensions				Discharged; laid on table.		See act March 1, 1823
Cushman, Lemuel	(See Lemuel Parker, son of the late widow of.)											
Cushman, Obed	Revolutionary pension	20	2	Resolution	201	Military Pensions.						
Cushman, Obed	Revolutionary pension	21	1	Petition	49	Military Pensions	Jan. 5, 1830	By bill	72	Passed	Passed	App'd May 20, 1830
Custer, John W.	Payment for horse lost in Seminole campaign of 1836.	28	1	Petition	406	Claims	245	Adverse		Laid on table		March 25, 1844; recommitted to Judiciary.
Custis, Thomas, heir of	Commutation of pay as an officer in revolutionary army.	23	1	Petition	306	Rev. Claims.						
Custis, Thomas, heir of	Commutation of pay as an officer in revolutionary army.	23	2	Petition	84	Rev. Claims.						

List of private claims presented to the House of Representatives of the United States from the 1st to the 31st Congress, inclusive—Continued.

Names of claimants.	Nature or object of the claim.	Congress.	Session.	How brought before the House of Reps.	Page of journal.	To what committee of the House referred.	No. or date of the report.	Nature of the report.	No. of the bill.	How disposed of by the House of Reps.	How disposed of by the Senate.	Date of the act of Congress, and remarks.
Custis, Thomas, heir of...	Commutation of pay as an officer in revolutionary army.	24	1	Petition	103	Rev. Claims......	Jan. 14, 1836	Adverse	......	Laid on table.		
Custis, Thomas, heir of...	Commutation of pay as an officer in revolutionary army.	24	2	Petition	95	Rev. Claims......	189	Adverse	......	Laid on table.		
Cutaw, Angelica, (*alias* Mu-ta-ma-go-quo, Chippewa Indian.)	Grant of land..................	20	1	Petition	197	Indian Affairs.....	127	Report and bill.	146	Passed	Amendm't reported.	
Cutaw, Angelica, (*alias* Mu-ta-ma-go-quo, Chippewa Indian.)	Grant of land..................	20	2	Petition	41	Indian Affairs.....	Dec. 15, 1828	Report and bill.	315	Referred to Committee Whole House.		
Cutbush, Edward, & S. R. Marshall.	Increase of pay, &c., of surgeons and assistants in U. S. navy.	14	2	Petition	163	Naval Affairs.....	....	....	......	Discharged; laid on table.		
Cutcheon, James........	(See James McCutcheon.)											
Cutchlow, James.........	Revolutionary pension..........	21	2	Resolution	166	Military Pensions.						
Cutler, Abraham	Payment for whiskey furnished U. S. army in Canada, war of 1812.	14	2	Petition	46	Claims	....	....	......	Discharged; laid on table.		
Cutler, Enos	Exoneration from judgment against him for acts in discharge of duty as lieut. colonel U. S. army.	21	1	Petition	144	Military Affairs....	Jan. 20, 1830	Report and bill.	135	Passed	Passed	App'd May 29, 1830
Cutler, Jervis...........	Pay and travelling expenses as captain in U. S. army.	11	3	Petition and rep't Sec. of War.	463	Claims.						
Cutler, Jervis...........	Pay and travelling expenses as captain in U. S. army.	12	1	Petition	132	Claims.						
Cutler, Jervis...........	Pay and travelling expenses as captain in U. S. army.	12	2	Petition	579	Claims.						
Cutler, Jervis...........	Pay and travelling expenses as captain in U. S. army.	13	2	Petition	190	Claims	Feb. 28, 1814	Report and bill.	143	Passed	Passed	App'd April 18, 1814
Cutler, Joseph..........	Increase of pension	13	2	House bill	244	Whole House	Mar. 31, 1814	Favorable	166	Passed	Passed	App'd April 18, 1814
Cutler, Joseph, (N. Y.)..	Revolutionary pension..........	21	1	Resolution	431	Military Pensions..	....	....	......	Discharged; laid on table.		
Cutler, Joseph, (N. Y.)..	Revolutionary pension..........	21	2	Petition	68	Military Pensions.						
Cutler, Joseph, (N. Y.)..	Revolutionary pension..........	22	1	Petition	130	Rev. Claims.						
Cutler, Rachel	Pension for services of husband...	28	1	Petition	849	Rev. Pensions.						
Cutter, A. W...........	Indemnity for French spoliations prior to 1800.	26	1	Memorial	182	Foreign Affairs ...	343	Favorable; bill.	319	Referred to Committee Whole House.		
Cutter, Charles W	Allowance for office rent as clerk United States court, district of New Hampshire.	23	2	Petition	389	Judiciary.						
Cutter, Charles W	Allowance for office rent as clerk United States court, district of New Hampshire.	25	2	Petition	719	Judiciary	....	....	......	Discharged.		
Cutter, Charles W	Allowance for office rent as clerk United States court, district of New Hampshire.	26	1	Petition	175	Judiciary	437	Adverse	......	Laid on table.		
Cutter, Daniel and Jacob..	Indemnity for French spoliations prior to 1800.	26	1	Memorial	182	Foreign Affairs....	343	Favorable; bill.	319	Referred to Committee Whole House.		
Cutter, John.	Bounty land and extra pay as a soldier, war of 1812.	15	2	Petition	27	Military Affairs....	15	Adverse	......	Referred to Committee Whole House.		
Cutter, Nathaniel	Remission of duties on merchandise shipped at Portsmouth, N. H., for Surinam, but returned.	5	2	Petition	115	Com. and Manuf..	Jan. 8, 1798	Adverse	......	Referred to Committee Whole House.		

List of private claims presented to the House of Representatives of the United States from the 1st to the 31st Congress, inclusive—Continued.

Names of claimants.	Nature or object of the claim.	Congress.	Session.	How brought before the House of Reps.	Page of journal.	To what committee of the House referred.	No. or date of the report.	Nature of the report.	No. of the bill.	How disposed of by the House of Reps.	How disposed of by the Senate.	Date of the act of Congress, and remarks.
Cutter, Nathaniel	Remission of duties on merchandise shipped at Portsmouth, N. H., for Surinam, but returned.	5	3	Petition and rep., former.	406	Com. and Manuf.	Dec. 17, 1798	Rep. and res.; adverse.		Resolution adopted.		
Cutter, William, and Wm. Woodbury.	Repayment of forfeit incurred in reference to crew of brig Harriet, at Boston.	24	1	Petition	127	Commerce.						
Cutter, Levi	(See Elisha Gardner.)											
Cutting, Earl	Restoration of pension	17	1	Petition	106	Rev. Pensions.				Discharged; laid on table.		
Cutting, Earl	Pension	19	1	Petition	98	Military Pensions.	164	Adverse		Laid on table.		
Cutting, John Brown	Reimbursement of money expended for use of government.	2	1	Presid'ts message	503	Select	Feb. 22, 1792	Report and bill.	192	Passed	Passed	App'd May 8, 1792
Cutting, John Brown	Reimbursement of money expended for relief of impressed American seamen.	5	3	Rep. of Secretary State.	497					Laid on table.		
Cutting, Nathaniel	Grant of land for long and faithful public service.	15	1	Petition	94	Public Lands	Jan. 7, 1818	Rep. and res.; adverse.		Resolution adopted.		
Cutting, Nathaniel	Increase of compensation as chief clerk on bounty lands, War Department.	15	2	Petition	258	Claims				Discharged; laid on table.		
Cutting, Nathaniel	Increase of compensation as clerk on bounty lands, War Department, and extra pay for services rendered.	16	1	Petition	89	Ways and Means.	Feb. 3, 1820	Rep't and res.; leave to withdraw.		Resolution adopted.		
Cutts, Dominicus	(See Samuel P. Abbott and others.)											
Cutts, Edward, (N. H.)	Indemnity for French spoliations prior to 1800.	26	1	Memorial	182	Foreign Affairs	343	Favorable; bill.	319	Referred to Committee Whole House.		
Cutts, Edward, administrator of.	Indemnity for French spoliations prior to 1800.	26	1	Memorial	182	Foreign Affairs	343	Favorable; bill.	319	Referred to Committee Whole House.		
Cutts, Hampden	(See Edw. Cutts, administrator of.)											
Cutts, Hampden	(See Samuel Cutts, heirs of.)											
Cutts, Joseph	Compensation for rotting of ship by detention at Norfolk under embargo act of 1812.	14	1	Petition	339	Claims				Discharged; laid on table.		
Cutts, Joseph	Compensation for rotting of ship by detention at Norfolk under embargo act of 1812.	15	1	Petition	122	Claims				Discharged; laid on table.		
Cutts, Joseph	Compensation for rotting of ship by detention at Norfolk under embargo act of 1812.	16	1	Petition	33	Com. and Manuf.				Discharged: laid on table.		
Cutts, Joseph	Relief from judgment on bonds partly paid to collector at York, Mass., who has absconded.	14	1	Petition	360	Claims	Mar. 15, 1816	Rep. and res.; adverse.		Laid on table.		
Cutts, Joseph	Relief from judgment on bonds partly paid to collector at York, Mass., who has absconded.	15	1	Petition	122	Claims	Jan. 29, 1818	Rep. and res.; adverse.		Laid on table.		
Cutts, Noah	Revolutionary pension	21	1	Resolution	270	Military Pensions.				Disch'd; laid on table.		
Cutts, Samuel, heirs of	Indemnity for French spoliations prior to 1800.	26	1	Memorial	182	Foreign Affairs	343		319	Referred to Committee Whole House.		
Cutts, Thomas, jr.	Repayment of amount paid for sch'r sold by United States, of which he has been dispossessed by decree of supreme court of Mass.	13	2	Petition	168	Claims	82	Rep. and res.; adverse.		Resolution adopted.		

List of private claims presented to the House of Representatives of the United States from the 1st to the 31st Congress, inclusive—Continued.

Names of claimants.	Nature or object of the claim.	Congress.	Session.	How brought before the House of Reps.	Page of journal.	To what committee of the House referred.	No. or date of the report.	Nature of the report.	No. of the bill.	How disposed of by the House of Reps.	How disposed of by the Senate.	Date of the act of Congress, and remarks.
Cutts, Thomas, jr.......	Repayment of amount paid for sch'r sold by United States, of which he has been dispossessed by decree of supreme court of Mass.	13	3	Petition	454	Claims..........	4	Rep. and res.; adverse.	......	Resolution adopted.		
Cutts, Thomas, jr.......	Repayment of amount paid for sch'r sold by United States, of which he has been dispossessed by decree of supreme court of Mass.	15	2	Petition........	113	Claims	....	....	......	Discharged; laid on table.		
Cutts, Thomas, jr.......	Repayment of amount paid for sch'r sold by United States, of which he has been dispossessed by decree of supreme court of Mass.	16	1	Petition	....	Claims	April 17, 1820	Adverse	......	Laid on table.		
Cutts, Thomas, jr.......	Repayment of amount paid for sch'r sold by United States, of which he has been dispossessed by decree of supreme court of Mass.	18	1	Petition	114	Claims	Jan. 33, 1824	Adverse	......	Laid on table.		
Cutts, Thomas, jr.......	Repayment of amount paid for sch'r sold by United States, of which he has been dispossessed by decree of supreme court of Mass.	19	1	Petition	79	Claims..........	59	Adverse	......	Referred to Committee Whole House.		
Cutts, Thomas, jr.......	Repayment of amount paid for sch'r sold by United States, of which he has been dispossessed by decree of supreme court of Mass.	24	2	Petition	266	Claims.						
Cutts, Thomas, jr.......	Payment of loan office prize certificate, No. 228, for $500.	20	1	Resolution	176	Rev. Claims......	Feb. 12, 1828	By bill	161	Referred to Committee Whole House.		
Cutts, Thomas, jr.......	Payment of loan office prize certificate, No. 228, for $500.	20	2	Bill of last sess..	58	Whole House.....	Dec. 15, 1828	With't amend.	161	Passed	Referred to Finance.	
Cutts, Thomas, jr.......	Payment of loan office prize certificate, No. 228, for $500.	21	1	Petition	35	Judiciary.........	Jan. 4, 1830	Adverse	......	Laid on table.		
Cutts, Thomas, jr.......	Payment of loan office prize certificate, No. 228, for $500.	21	2	Resolution	130	Rev. Claims......	....	....	......	Discharged; laid on table.		
Cutts, Thomas, jr.......	Payment of loan office prize certificate, No. 228, for $500.	22	1	Petition	226	Rev. Claims......	310	Report and bill.	390	Referred to Committee Whole House.		
Cutts, Thomas, jr., legal representatives of.	Payment of loan office prize certificate, No. 228, for $500.	23	1	Resolution	89	Rev. Claims......	....	....	......	Discharged; laid on table.		
Cyelder, Sally	Continuation of pension	28	1	Petition	72	Rev. Pensions.						
Cypress, Andrew........	Pension	20	1	Petition	45	Military Pensions..	Jan. 31, 1828	Adverse	......	Laid on table.		

List of private claims presented to the House of Representatives of the United States from the 1st to the 31st Congress, inclusive—Continued.

Names of claimants.	Nature or object of the claim.	Congress.	Session.	How brought before the House of Reps.	Page of journal.	To what committee of the House referred.	No. or date of the report.	Nature of the report.	No. of the bill.	How disposed of by the House of Reps.	How disposed of by the Senate.	Date of the act of Congress, and remarks.
Dabney, Colonel Charles, heirs of.	Commutation pay for services in revolutionary war.	25	2	Petition	579	Rev. Pensions	....	....	......	Discharged; laid on table.		
Dabney, Col. Charles, heirs of.	Commutation pay for services in revolutionary war.	25	3	Petition	84	Rev. Claims.						
Dabney, Col. Charles, heirs of.	Commutation pay for services in revolutionary war.	26	1	Petition	164	Rev. Claims.						
Dabney, Col, Charles, heirs of.	Commutation pay for services in revolutionary war.	26	2	Petition	134	Rev. Claims.						
Dabney, Col. Charles, heirs of.	Commutation pay for services in revolutionary war.	27	2	Petition	61	Rev. Claims	531	Adverse	......	Laid on table.		
Dabney, James W	Compensation for losses sustained in Florida war by Indians.	26	1	Petition	621	Claims.						
Dabney, James W	Compensation for losses sustained in Florida war by Indians.	26	2	Petition	135	Claims.						
Dabney, James W	Compensation for losses sustained in Florida war by Indians.	27	2	Petition	94	Claims	351	Adverse	......	Laid on table.		
Dabney, James W	Compensation for losses sustained in Florida by Indians.	29	1	Petition	574	Military Affairs.						
Dabney, John B	For difference in exchange, expenses, &c., at Fayal, while consul of the United States at Azores.	14	1	Petition	592	Select.						
Dabney, John B	For differences in exchange, expenses, &c., at Fayal, while consul of the United States at Azores.	14	2	Petition	377	Ways and Means.						
Dabney, John B	For difference in exchange, expenses, &c., at Fayal, while consul of the United States at Azores.	15	1	Petition	114	Ways and Means	Feb. 13, 1818	Favorable; bill.	85	Passed	Passed	App'd April 20, 1818
Daboll, John	Pension	10	2	House bill	499	Whole House	Jan. 30, 1809	Favorable; bill	158	Passed	Passed	App'd March 3, 1809
Daboll, John, widow of	Pension	25	2	Petition	755	Rev. Pensions	....	....	......	Discharged.		
Daboll, John, widow of	Pension	26	1	Petition	173	Rev. Pensions	490	Adverse	......	Laid on table.		
Dacus, Lewis	For horse and equipments lost in Seminole war.	23	1	Documents	154	Claims.						
Dacus, Lewis, agent of	For horse and equipments lost in Seminole war.	28	1	Petition	262	Claims.						
Dade, Francis	Compensation for military services in revolutionary war.	1	2	Petition	285	....	....	....	......	Referred to Secretary War.		
Dade, Francis	Compensation for military services in revolutionary war.	3	2	Petition and report Sec. War.	278	Claims.						
Dade, Major Francis L., widow of.	Renewal of pension	26	1	Petition	1001	Invalid Pensions	669	Adverse	......	Laid on table.		
Dade, Major Francis L., widow of.	Renewal of pension	30	1	Petition	236	Rev. Pensions	532	Adverse	......	Laid on table.		
Dade, Major Francis L., widow of.	Renewal of pension	31	1	Senate bill	1530	Whole House	....	....	S. 167	Laid on table.		
Dade, Major Francis L., widow of.	Renewal of pension	31	2	Senate bill	169	Rev. Pensions	....	....	S. 167			
Dade, Major Francis L., widow and children of.	For half-pay, loss of husband and father in Florida war.	24	1	House bill	457	Whole House	415	Favorable; bill	426	Passed	Passed	App'd July 4, 1836

List of private claims presented to the House of Representatives of the United States from the 1st to the 31st Congress, inclusive—Continued.

Names of claimants.	Nature or object of the claim.	Congress.	Session.	How brought before the House of Reps.	Page of journal.	To what committee of the House referred.	No. or date of the report.	Nature of the report.	No. of the bill.	How disposed of by the House of Reps.	How disposed of by the Senate.	Date of the act of Congress, and remarks.
Dade Jane *et al.*	(See William Rumney, representatives of.)	27	3		140							
Dade Institute of Florida	Grant of land	26	1	Petition	177	Public Lands	93	Favorable; bill	89	Referred to Committee Whole House.		
Dade, William	Invalid pension	1	3	Petition	364					Referred to Secretary War.		
Daffon, George, assignee of	For money advanced for use of army in 1815.	18	1	Petition	432	Claims.						
Daffon, George, assignee of	For money advanced for use of army in 1815.	19	1	Petition	407	Claims	165	Favorable; bill	217	Passed	Ref. to Com. on Military Affairs.	
Daffon, George, assignee of	For money advanced for use of army in 1815.	19	2	Petition	82	Claims	Dec. 22, 1826	Favorable; bill	313	Passed	Passed	App'd Feb. 22, 1827
Daggett,	(See Atwater and Daggett *et al.*).	22	1		30							
Daggett, E. M	Indemnity for horse lost in Mexican war.	31	2	Petition	111	Military Affairs.						
Daggett, F., jr	Indemnity for French spoliations prior to 1800.	26	1	Memorial	182	Foreign Affairs	343	Favorable; bill	319	Referred to Committee Whole House.		
Dagget, Henry, jr	Indemnity for French spoliations prior to 1800.	18	1	Petition	526					Laid on table.		
Daggett, Jacob, heirs of	(See Jacob Doggett, heirs of.)	18	1		53							
Daggett, Nathan, heirs of.	Remuneration for revolutionary services of ancestor.	25	2	Petition	326	Rev. Claims	683	Adverse		Discharged; laid on table.		
Daggett, Nathan, heirs of.	Remuneration for revolutionary services of ancestor.	25	3	Petition	51	Rev. Claims				Discharged.		
Daggett, Nathan, heirs of.	Remuneration for revolutionary services of ancestor.	26	1	Petition	201	Rev. Claims.						
Daggett, Nathan, heirs of.	Remuneration for revolutionary services of ancestor.	27	2	Petition	96	Rev. Claims	524	Adverse		Laid on table.		
Daggett, Samuel	Revolutionary pension	27	2	Petition	823	Rev. Pensions	784	Adverse		Laid on table.		
Daggett, Sarah	(See Charles Earnest, widow of.)	15	1		156							
Daggett, Tristram	Revolutionary pension	20	1	Resolution	599	Military Pensions	April 29, 1828	Favorable; bill	283	Passed.		
Daggett, Tristram	Revolutionary pension	20	2	House bill	55	Military Pensions	Dec. 12, 1828	Favorable; bill	311	Passed	Laid on table.	
Daggett, Tristram	Revolutionary pension	21	1	Petition	48	Military Pensions	Jan. 5, 1830	Favorable; bill	72	Passed	Passed	App'd May 20, 1830
Daggett, William	Revolutionary pension	21	2	Petition	159	Military Pensions.						
Daggett, William	Revolutionary pension	22	1	Petition	80	Rev. Pensions.						
Daggs, Hezekiah	Settlement of acconnts for undrawn rations.	12	1	Petition	180	Claims				Leave to withdraw.		
Daguette, Pierre	Permission to lay certain proofs before land commissioners.	12	1	Petition	51	Public Lands.						
Dahling, John O	Pre-emption right to land	25	3	Petition	135	Public Lands.						
Dahling, John O	Pre-emption right to land	26	1	Petition	177	Public Lands.						
Dahling, John O	Pre emption right to land	26	2	Petition	37	Public Lands.						
Dahling, John O	Pre-emption right to land	27	2	Petition	63	Public Lands	505	Adverse		Laid on table.		
Dahlgren, C. G	Permission to pay for land in treasury notes.	27	2	Petition	971	Public Lands.						
Dahlgren, John A	Naval pension	25	3	Petition	570	Invalid Pensions.						
Dahlgren, John A	Naval pension	26	1	Petition	162	Invalid Pensions				Discharged; laid on table.		
Daigre, Francis	Confirmation of land title	21	2	Petition	46	Priv. Land Claims.	52	Favorable; bill	587	Referred to Committee Whole House.		
Daigre, Francis	Confirmation of land title	22	1	Petition	75	Priv. Land Claims.	82	Favorable; bill	162	Passed	Passed	App'd July 14, 1832
Daily, Dennis	Pension	19	1	Petition	93	Military Pensions	164	Adverse		Laid on table.		

List of private claims presented to the House of Representatives of the United States from the 1st to the 31st Congress, inclusive—Continued.

57

Names of claimants.	Nature or object of the claim.	Congress.	Session.	How brought before the House of Reps.	Page of journal.	To what committee of the House referred.	No. or date of the report.	Nature of the report.	No. of the bill.	How disposed of by the House of Reps.	How disposed of by the Senate.	Date of the act of Congress, and remarks.
Daily, *alias* Daly John, (Canada.)	Indemnity for property confiscated by British government, and for losses by fire in Newark.	14	2	Petition	47	Select	33	Favorable		Laid on table.		
Daily, *alias* Daly John, (Canada.)	Indemnity for property confiscated by British government, and for losses by fire in Newark.	15	1	Petition	231	Select	191	Favorable; bill	182	Rejected.		
Daily, *alias* Daly John, (Canada.)	Indemnity for property confiscated by British government, and for losses by fire in Newark.	16	2	Petition & docs.	30	Select	May 11, 1820	Adverse		Laid on table.		
Daily, *alias* Daly John, (Canada.)	Compensation for supplies furnished, and services rendered United States army, and for losses of property on Niagara frontier.	21	2	Senate bill	202	Claims	Feb. 16, 1831	Favorable; bill	76	Passed	Passed	App'd March 2, 1831
Daily *alias* Daly John, (Canada.)	Further allowance for losses sustained.	22	1	Petition	431	Claims.						
Daily, James, children of	Bounty land	15	2	Petition	78	Military Affairs				Discharged; laid on table.		
Daily, John S	Pension	16	2	Petition	50	Pens. & Rev. Cl'ms.				Discharged; laid on table.		
Daily, John S	Pension	17	1	Petition	320	Secretary of War	May 3, 1822	Report		Laid on table.		
Daily, Lawrence	(See Lawrence Daly)	30	1		146							
Dakin, Jonathan	Bounty land for revolutionary services.	19	1	Petition	74	Rev. Claims	Jan. 23, 1826	Adverse		Laid on table.		
Dakin, Jonathan, heir of	Money in lieu of bounty land	27	2	Petition	535	Claims	707	Adverse		Laid on table.		
Dal, John	Revolutionary pension	23	1	Petition	353	Rev. Pensions	365	Favorable; bill	392	Referred to Committee Whole House.		
Dal, John	Revolutionary pension	23	2	Rep't Committee Whole House.	337			With't amend.	392	Passed	Indef. postp'd.	
Dal, John	Revolutionary pension	24	1	Petition	107	Rev. Pensions	184	Favorable; bill	189	Passed	Passed	App'd June 28, 1836
Dalby, William	Invalid pension	3	1	Rep. of Secretary of War.	131	Select	May 26, 1794	Res. to refer to Sec. with instructions.	J. R. 12	Passed	Passed	App'd June 9, 1794
Dalck, Andrew	Compensation for horse lost in war of 1812.	16	2	Petition	245	Claims				Discharged; laid on table.		
Dale, J. D	(See Exploring Expedition)	27	3		149							
Dale, Jeremiah, heirs of	Compensation for revolutionary services.	25	2	Petition	232	Rev. Claims	530	Adverse		Laid on table.		
Dale, Richard	Compensation for certain revolutionary naval services.	1	3	Petition	369	Report of Secretary Treasury.	April 25, 1792	Report.				
Dale, Commodore Richard, representatives of.	Prize money on vessels captured in revolutionary war.	20	2	Memorial	372	Naval Affairs.						
Dale, Richard	Relief from charge of $862 70 by Secretary of Navy.	7	2	Petition	320	Claims	Feb. 26, 1803	Report		Postponed.		
Dale, Richard	Relief from charge of $862 70 by Secretary of Navy.	11	3	Petition	463	Claims.						
Dale, Richard	Relief from charge of $862 70 by Secretary of Navy.	12	1	Petition	11	Claims	Feb. 13, 1813	Favorable; bill	131	Referred to Committee Whole House.		
Dale, Richard	Relief from charge of $862 70 by Secretary of Navy.	12	2	Petition	568	Claims.						
Dale, Richard	Relief from charge of $862 70 by Secretary of Navy.	13	1	Petition	22	Claims				Discharged.		
Dale, Richard	Relief from charge of $862 70 by Secretary of Navy.	13	2	Petition	172	Claims	5	Favorable; bill	59	Passed	Passed	App'd Jan. 11, 1814

List of private claims presented to the House of Representatives of the United States from the 1st to the 31st Congress, inclusive—Continued.

Names of claimants.	Nature or object of the claim.	Congress.	Session.	How brought before the House of Reps.	Page of journal.	To what committee of the House referred.	No. or date of the report.	Nature of the report.	No. of the bill.	How disposed of by the House of Reps.	How disposed of by the Senate.	Date of the act of Congress, and remarks.
Dale, Samuel	Compensation for coffee illegally sold in 1813.	14	2	Petition	280					Refered to Secretary of Treasury.		Leave to withdraw.
Dale, Samuel	Compensation for coffee illegally sold in 1813.	15	2	Petition	155	Claims				Discharged; laid on table.		
Dale, Samuel	Compensation for coffee illegally sold in 1813.	16	1	Petition	119	Claims	36	Adverse		Laid on table.		
Dale, Samuel	Compensation for coffee illegally sold in 1813.	16	2	Petition and rep.	36	Claims	Dec. 11, 1820	Adverse		Laid on table.		
Dale, Samuel	Compensation for coffee illegally sold in 1813.	17	1	Petition	180	Ways and Means	Mar. 27, 1822			Discharged; laid on table.		
Dale, Col. Samuel, (Ala.)	Compensation for services in Creek Indian war in 1812.	15	2	Petition	144	Military Affairs.						
Dale, Col. Samuel, (Ala.)	Compensation for services in Creek Indian war in 1812.	16	1	Report	32	Public Lands	Dec. 23, 1819	Report		Laid on table.		
Dale, Col. Samuel, (Ala.)	Compensation for services and supplies furnished troops.	17	1	Memorial	177, 181	Military Affairs.						
Dale, Col. Samuel, (Ala.)	Compensation for services and supplies furnished troops.	17	2	Petition	120	Military Affairs	Feb. 13, 1823	Adverse		Laid on table.		
Dale, Col. Samuel, (Ala.)	Compensation for services and supplies furnished troops.	18	1	Petition	315	Claims.						
Dale, Col. Samuel, (Ala.)	Compensation for services and supplies furnished troops.	18	2	Petition	92	Claims	75	Favorable; bill	345	Passed	Passed	App'd March 3, 1825
Dale, Col. Samuel, (Ala.)	Equitable settlement of accounts for forage supplies, &c.	19	1	Petition	43	Claims.						
Dale, Col. Samuel, (Ala.)	Equitable settlement of accounts for forage supplies, &c.	19	2	Petition	37	Claims				Discharged.		
Dale, Col. Samuel, (Ala.)	Equitable settlement of accounts for forage supplies, &c.	20	1	Petition	137	Claims	Jan. 9, 1828	Adverse		Laid on table.		
Dale, Col. Samuel, (Ala.)	Equitable settlement of accounts for forage supplies, &c.	21	1	Petition	116	Claims				Discharged; laid on table.		
Dale, Col. Samuel, (Ala.)	Equitable settlement of accounts for forage supplies, &c.	21	2	Petition	45	Claims	79	Favorable; bill	627	Referred to Committee Whole House.		
Dale, Col. Samuel, (Ala.)	Equitable settlement of accounts for forage supplies, &c.	22	1	Petition	79	Claims	Dec. 28, 1831	Favorable; bill	151	Passed	Passed	App'd July 4, 1832
Daley, John	(See John Daily, of Canada)	21	2		434							
Dalgarn, James, (Ohio)	Pension	21	2	Petition	143	Military Pensions.						
Dalien, Joseph	Confirmation of land title	19	2	Petition	137	Public Lands	60	Favorable; bill	401	Referred to Committee Whole House.		
Dallam, Richard	Relief from certain suits by, and balance due to the United States	3	1	Petition	52	Select	Feb. 21, 1794	Favorable		Referred to Committee Whole House.		
Dallas, Alexander J	Balance standing to credit of Dallas at Treasury Department; amount to be paid to use of the State of Pennsylvania.	19	1	Resolution	158	Ways and Means.						
Dallas, James, and John N. Taylor, heirs of.	Confirmation of land title	15	1	Petition	226	Priv. Land Claims.						
Dalliez, Maria J	(See Peter Luc, wife of)	5	2		225							
Dallinar, Richard, heirs of.	Compensation for revolutionary services.	26	1	Petition	360	Rev. Claims.						
Dallinar, Richard, heirs of.	Compensation for revolutionary services.	26	2	Petition	152					Leave to withdraw.		

List of private claims presented to the House of Representatives of the United States from the 1st to the 31st Congress, inclusive—Continued.

Names of claimants.	Nature or object of the claim.	Congress.	Session.	How brought before the House of Reps.	Page of journal.	To what committee of the House referred.	No. or date of the report.	Nature of the report.	No. of the bill.	How disposed of by the House of Reps.	How disposed of by the Senate.	Date of the act of Congress, and remarks.
Dallum, Francis J.	Compensation for services as assistant quartermaster Maryland militia, in 1814.	14	2	Petition	123	Claims				Discharged; leave to withdraw.		
Dallum & Hamburg	Indemnity for Indian depredations.	26	2	Petition	135	Claims	111	Adverse		Laid on table.		
Dally, Gifford	Compensation as assistant Doorkeeper House of Representatives.	1	2	Petition	170	Select	Mar. 8, 1790	Favorable; bill	47	Passed	Passed	App'd Mar. 26, 1790
Dally, Gifford	Rate of compensation assigned him as Doorkeeper House of Representatives.	2	1	Petition	489	Select	Jan. 11, 1792	Res.; favorable				
Dally, Gifford	Reimbursement of expenses incurred in performing menial services.	2	2	Petition	620	Whole House	Feb. 13, 1793	Favorable.				
Dally, Gifford	Relief from the payment of public money used by self.	3	2	Petition	357					Laid on table.		
Dalrymple, Alexander	That certain duties on merchandise be refunded.	15	1	Petition	84	Ways and Means.						
Dalrymple, Joseph	Increase of naval pension	23	2	Petition	128	Naval Affairs	Feb. 25, 1835	Adverse		Laid on table.		
Dalton, Isaac	Revolutionary pension	21	2	Resolution	165	Military Pensions.						
Dalton, Isaac	Revolutionary pension	22	1	Petition	56	Rev. Pensions	52	Favorable; bill	104	Passed	Passed	App'd June 15, 1832
Dalton, Thomas	Pay for pension stolen from United States mail.	25	2	Petition	405	Rev. Pensions				Discharged; laid on table.		
Dalton, William	Pay for pension stolen from United States mail	25	2	Petition	405	Rev. Pensions				Discharged; laid on table.		
Daly, Lawrence	Pay for horse lost in the Mexican war.	30	1	Petition	146	Claims	406	Favorable; bill	356	Referred to Committee Whole House.		
Dalzell, William	(See William Delzell.)	20	1		264							
Daman, Stephen	Pension	20	2	Petition	99	Military Pensions.				Dis.; referred to Com. Whole House.		
Dameron, Charles, widow of.	Revolutionary pension	29	1	Memorial	319	Rev. Pensions	463	Favorable; bill	340	Passed	Indef. postp'd.	
Dameron, Charles, widow of.	Revolutionary pension	30	1	Petition	865	Rev. Pensions	683	Favorable; bill	545	Referred to Committee Whole House.		
Dameron, Charles, widow of.	Revolutionary pension	30	2	Rep't Committee Whole House.	319			No amendm'nt	545	Passed	Passed	App'd March 3, 1849
Dameron, Martha	(See Lieut. Christopher Tompkins, widow of.)	26	1		323							
Dameron, G. B., and Wm. Houzie.	Compensation for services performed in adjusting and locating land claims.	20	1	Resolution	202	Public Lands	Mar. 31, 1828	By bill	246	Referred to Committee Whole House.		
Dameron, G. B., and Wm. Houzie.	Allowance for office rent and fuel in military service.	21	2	Senate bill	217	Claims	Feb. 11, 1831	Amended	S. 90	Passed	Passed	App'd March 3, 1831
Dameron, G. B., and Wm. Houzie.	Extra allowance as register and receiver at land office, Mississippi.	22	1	Senate bill	806	Public Lands	July 3, 1832	By bill	S. 107	Rejected.		
Damerville, Madame Maria	(See Bouligny, widow of.)	17	1		282							
Dana, Anderson, and William Ross.	(See Wyoming sufferers.)	26	1		630							
Dana, Daniel	Indemnity for loss of certain treasury notes, and compensation for property destroyed by United States army in late war.	17	1	Petition	31	Claims	Jan. 15, 1832	Adverse		Laid on table.		
Dana, Daniel	Relief from charge of $3200 in treasury department.	18	2	Petition	186	Claims.						

List of private claims presented to the House of Representatives of the United States from the 1st to the 31st Congress, inclusive—Continued.

Names of claimants.	Nature or object of the claim.	Congress.	Session.	How brought before the House of Reps.	Page of journal.	To what committee of the House referred.	No. or date of the report.	Nature of the report.	No. of the bill.	How disposed of by the House of Reps.	How disposed of by the Senate.	Date of the act of Congress, and remarks.
Dana, Daniel	Relief from imprisonment on execution in favor of United States.	19	1	Petition	269	Claims discharged, and to Judiciary, and to 3d Auditor in part.	May 13, 1826	Adverse by Judiciary.	......	Leave to withdraw.		
Dana, Edmund	Compensation for clothing furnished United States army.	14	1	Petition	249	Claims	Feb. 16, 1816	Adverse	......	Rejected.		
Dana, James	Indemnity for losses sustained by wreck of United States ship Peacock.	28	1	Petition	515	Naval Affairs	427	Report	......	Laid on table.		
Dana, Joseph	Revolutionary pension	30	1	Petition	849	Rev. Pensions	775	Favorable; bill	611	Referred to Committee Whole House.		
Dana, Joseph	Revolutionary pension	30	2	Rep't Committee Whole House.	362	....	....	With't amend.	611	Passed	Amended.	
Dana, Joseph	Revolutionary pension	31	1	Petition	1467	....	....	....	......	Leave to withdraw.		
Dana, Maria	Indemnity for French spoliations prior to 1800.	26	1	Memorial	182	Foreign Affairs	343	Favorable; bill	319	Referred to Committee Whole House.		
Dana, N. and L., & Co	Remission of duties on a cargo of salt.	22	1	Petition	285	Ways and Means	326	Favorable; bill	409	Referred to Committee Whole House.		
Dana, N. and L., & Co.	Remission of duties on a cargo of salt.	23	1	Petition	88	Ways and Means.						
Dana, M. and L., & Co.	Remission of duties on a cargo of salt.	24	1	Petition	95	Ways and Means	99	Favorable; bill	114	Referred to Committee Whole House.		
Dana, N. and L., & Co	Remission of duties on a cargo of salt.	24	2	House bill	203	Whole House	....	....	114	Rejected		
Dana, N. and L., & Co	Remission of duties on a cargo of salt.	28	1	Petition	325	Commerce.						
Dana, N. and L., & Co	Remission of duties on a cargo of salt.	29	1	Petition	323	Commerce	420	Favorable; bill	167	Passed	Indef. postp'd.	
Dana, N. and Z., & Co	Return of forfeiture incurred under misapprehension of law.	24	1	Petition	127	Ways and Means	....	....	......	Discharged, referred to Com. on Commerce.		
Dana, Wheeler and Bartlett.	Remission of penalties incurred by importing plaster of Paris.	12	2	Petition	696	Ways and Means	Mar. 1, 1813	Adverse	......	Laid on table.		
Dana, Wheeler and Bartlett.	Remission of penalties incurred by importing plaster of Paris.	14	1	Petition	242	Select	57	Favorable	J.R. 56	Passed	Passed with amendment.	App'd April 27, 1816
Dana, William	Payment of certain bills of credit	4	2	Memorial	629	Claims.						
Dana, William	Payment of certain bills of credit	5	2	Memorial & rep.	202	Whole House	Mar. 12, 1798	Adverse	......	Leave to withdraw.		
Danby, James	Payment of bounty money awarded in revolutionary war.	23	2	Petition	84	Rev. Claims.						
Dandridge, John, widow of	Commutation pay for revolutionary services of husband.	21	1	Petition	98	Rev. Claims	182	Favorable; bill	229	Passed	Indef. postp'd.	
Daney, Joseph, heirs of	For land and money due from Virginia for revolutionary services.	26	1	Petition	359	Rev. Claims.						
Danforth, Eli	Indemnity for property destroyed by Indians, late war.	15	1	Petition	212	Select	....	....	......	Discharged; laid on table.		
Danforth, Elkannah	Restoration of pension	17	2	Petition	142	Whole House	Jan. 27, 1822	Favorable; bill	207	Passed	Passed	App'd March 1, 1823
Danforth, Elkannah	Restoration of pension	18	1	Petition	155	Rev. Pensions	Mar. 10, 1824	Adverse	......	Laid on table.		
Danforth, Henry	Invalid pension	3	2	Rep. of Secretary War.	278	Claims	Feb. 28, 1795	Favorable; bill	130	Passed	Postponed.	
Danforth, Henry	Invalid pension	4	1	Rep. of Secretary War.	447	Claims	Feb. 18, 1796	Favorable; bill	156	Passed	Passed	App'd April 20, 1796
Danforth, Joseph	Revolutionary pension	24	1	Petition	433	Rev. Pensions	431	Favorable; bill	443	Passed	Passed	App'd June 28, 1836
Danforth, Joshua	(See Gad Worthington)	15	1	....	440							

List of private claims presented to the House of Representatives of the United States from the 1st to the 31st Congress, inclusive—Continued.

Names of claimants.	Nature or object of the claim.	Congress.	Session.	How brought before the House of Reps.	Page of journal.	To what committee of the House referred.	No. or date of the report.	Nature of the report.	No. of the bill.	How disposed of by the House of Reps.	How disposed of by the Senate.	Date of the act of Congress, and remarks.
Danforth, Mary	Revolutionary pension	28	1	Petition	956	Whole House.						
Dangerfield, Bathurst	Increase of compensation as surveyor of customs.	17	2	Petition	57	Ways and Means.	....	....	......	Discharged; leave to withdraw.		
Dangerfield, Dr. William A. widow of.	Payment of money due the estate of her husband.	27	2	Petition	92	Claims	174	Adverse	......	Laid on table.		
Daniels, Amos	Invalid pension	24	2	Petition	219	Invalid Pensions	....	....	......	Discharged; laid on table.		
Daniels, Amos	Invalid pension	25	2	Petition	401	Invalid Pensions	....	....	......	Discharged; laid on table.		
Daniels, Amos	Invalid pension	26	1	Petition	288	Invalid Pensions.						
Daniels, Amos	Invalid pension	28	1	Petition	372	Invalid Pensions	282	Adverse	......	Laid on table.		
Daniels, Amos	Invalid pension	28	2	Petition	150	Invalid Pensions.						
Daniels, Benjamin	Invalid pension	13	2	Petition	336	Invalid Pensions	Mar. 15, 1814	Favorable; bill	166	Passed	Passed	App'd April 18, 1814
Daniels, David, widow of.	Revolutionary pension	28	1	Petition	214	Rev. Pensions.						
Daniel, Henry	(See Triplett & Daniel)	27	2	....	1169							
Daniel, James	Indemnity for losses in Creek war.	28	1	Petition	337	Claims.						
Daniels, Job	Revolutionary pension	23	1	Resolution	618	Rev. Pensions	....	....	......	Discharged; laid on table.		
Daniels, Job	Revolutionary pension	24	1	Resolution	279	Rev. Pensions	509	Favorable; bill	506	Passed	Passed	App'd June 28, 1836
Daniels, John, (Pa.)	Invalid pension	5	3	Petition	402	Claims	Dec. 18, 1798	Adverse	......	Laid on table.		
Daniels, John, (N. Y.)	Pension	21	1	Petition	197	Military Pensions	April 7, 1830	Adverse	......	Laid on table.		
Daniel, John	Indemnity for losses on depreciated bank notes received for public land.	29	1	Memorial	1124	Judiciary.						
Daniels, Margaret	(See Leonard Repshere, former widow of.)	18	1	....	130							
Daniel, Samuel, (N. Y.)	Pension	22	1	Petition	329	Rev. Pensions.						
Daniel, William	Confirmation of Spanish land title.	12	1	Petition	315	Public Lands.						
Daniel, William	Confirmation of Spanish land title.	12	2	Petition	550	Public Lands.						
Daniel, William	Confirmation of Spanish land title.	14	1	Petition	157	Public Lands	....	....	......	Discharged; laid on table.		
Daniel, William	Confirmation of Spanish land title.	14	2	Petition	49	Priv. Land Claims.	Jan. 29, 1817	Favorable; bill	92	Referred to Committee Whole House.		
Daniel, William	Confirmation of Spanish land title.	15	1	Petition	56	Priv. Land Claims.	Jan. 6, 1818	Favorable; bill	30	Passed	Postponed	Leave to withdraw.
Daniel, William	Confirmation of Spanish land title.	15	2	Petition	25	Priv. Land Claims.	....	....	......	Discharged; laid on table.	....	Leave to withdraw.
Danielson, Levi	Revolutionary pension	16	1	Petition	26	Rev. Claims	Dec. 15, 1819	Adverse	......	Rejected.		
Danish Brigantine Henrick	Indemnity for losses by U. States officers.	7	2	Pres. message	363	Claims	Feb. 28, 1803	By bill	132	Referred to Committee Whole House.		
Danish Brigantine Henrick	Indemnity for losses by U. States officers.	8	1	Resolution	428	Claims	Dec. 22, 1803	Report Com. W. House.	......	Recommitted.		
Danish Brigantine Henrick	Indemnity for losses by U. States officers.	8	1	Resolution	498	Claims	Jan. 13, 1804	Supplem'l bill.	161	Passed	Passed.	
Danish Brigantine Henrick	Indemnity for losses by U. States officers.	8	2	Pres. message	119	Claims	Feb. 20, 1805	Report	......	Referred to Committee Whole House.		
Danish Brigantine Henrick	Indemnity for losses by U. States officers.	9	1	Resolution	198	Whole House	Feb. 19, 1806	Favorable; bill	107	Passed	Rejected.	
Danish Brigantine Henrick	Indemnity for losses by U. States officers.	13	1	Resolution	181	Claims	April 5, 1814	On leave by bill	......	....	....	Bill not found.
Danish Brigantine Henrick	Indemnity for losses by U. States officers.	16	1	Pres. message	82	Foreign Affairs	Feb. 8, 1820	Adverse	......	Referred to Committee Whole House.		
Danish Brigantine Henrick	Indemnity for losses by U. States officers.	21	2	Petition	207	Foreign Affairs	Feb. 23, 1831	Adverse	......	Laid on table.		

List of private claims presented to the House of Representatives of the United States from the 1st *to the* 31st *Congress, inclusive*—Continued.

Names of claimants.	Nature or object of the claim.	Congress.	Session.	How brought before the House of Reps.	Page of journal.	To what committee of the House referred.	No. or date of the report.	Nature of the report.	No. of the bill.	How disposed of by the House of Reps.	How disposed of by the Senate.	Date of the act of Congress, and remarks.
Danish Brigantine Henrick	Indemnity for losses by U. States officers.	27	3	Memorial	109	Foreign Affairs.						
Danks, Benoni, widow of.	Compensation for property destroyed by U. S. army.	3	1	Memorial	71					Laid on table.		
Danks, Isaac	For 640 acres of land as a refugee	6	2	Resolution	733	Select	Jan. 19, 1801	Favorable; bill	280	Passed	Passed	App'd Feb. 18, 1801
Danley, James, (N. Y.)	Reimbursement of bounty money advanced in revolutionary war.	20	2	Petition	27	Rev. Claims	Dec. 18, 1828	Adverse		Laid on table.		
Danley, James, (N. Y.)	Reimbursement of bounty money advanced in revolutionary war.	21	1	Petition	235	Rev. Claims	Mar. 8, 1830	Adverse		Laid on table.		
Danley, James, (N. Y.)	Reimbursement of bounty money advanced in revolutionary war.	21	2	Petition	137	Rev. Claims				Discharged; laid on table.		
Darby, John F.	Confirmation of land title	24	1	Petition	435	Public Lands.						
Darby, Richard, widow of.	Revolutionary pension	30	2	Memorial	127	Rev. Pensions	Jan. 17, 1849	Favorable; bill	723	Passed	Passed	App'd Feb. 1, 1849
Darby, William	Compensation for use of maps for boundary line, France and U. States.	30	1	Petition	276	Claims	154	Adverse.				
Darby, William	Compensation for use of maps for boundary line, France and U. States.	31	1	Senate bill	840	Claims			S. 39			
Darden, David, by Amy, widow of.	Compensation for horse lost in service of the United States.	3	1	Petition	75					Laid on table.		
Darden, David, by Amy, widow of.	Compensation for horse lost in service of the United States.	4	1	Petition	386	Claims	Jan. 26, 1796	Adv. to Com. W. House.		Recommitted.		
Darden, David, by Amy, widow of.	Compensation for horse lost in service of the United States.	4	2	Resolution	614	Claims	Feb. 24, 1797	Favorable		Referred to Committee Whole House.		
Darden, David, by Amy, widow of.	Compensation for horse lost in service of the United States.	5	2	Resolution	112	Whole House	Feb. 19, 1798	Adverse.				
Darden, David, by Amy, widow of.	Compensation for horse lost in service of the United States.	5	3	Petition	614	Claims	Jan. 8, 1800	Adverse		Leave to withdraw.		
Darden, David, by Amy, widow of.	Compensation for horse lost in service of the United States.	6	1	Petition	571	Claims	Mar. 18, 1800	Adverse		Leave to withdraw.		
Darden, David, by Amy, widow of.	Compensation for horse lost in service of the United States.	7	2	Petition	319	Claims	Feb. 23, 1803	Adverse		Referred to Committee Whole House.		
Darden, David, by Amy, widow of.	Compensation for horse lost in service of the United States.	8	1	Petition	409	Claims	Nov. 25, 1803	Favorable; bill	141	Referred to Committee Whole House.		
Darden, David, by Amy, widow of.	Compensation for horse lost in service of the United States.	8	2	Petition	67	Whole House	Feb. 12, 1805	Favorable; bill	59	Referred to Committee Whole House.		
Darden, David, by Amy, widow of.	Compensation for horse lost in service of the United States.	9	1	Petition	352	Whole House.						
Darden, David, by Amy, widow of.	Compensation for horse lost in service of the United States.	9	2	Petition	497	Select.						
Darden, David, by Amy, widow of.	Compensation for horse lost in service of the United States.	10	1	Petition	86	Select.						
Darden, David, by Amy, widow of.	Compensation for horse lost in service of the United States.	10	2	Petition	358	Claims				Discharged; referred to Select Committee.		
Darden, David, by Amy, widow of.	Compensation for horse lost in service of the United States.	11	1	Petition	28	Claims.						
Darden, David, by Amy, widow of.	Compensation for horse lost in service of the United States.	11	2	Petition	120	Select	34	Favorable; bill	99	Passed	Rejected.	
Darden, David, by Amy, widow of.	Compensation for horse lost in service of the United States.	11	3	Petition	443	Claims	Dec. 27, 1810	Report		Referred to Committee Whole House.		
Darden, David, by Amy, widow of.	Compensation for horse lost in service of the United States.	12	1	Petition	43	Claims	April 10, 1812	Res. and bill	143	Referred to Committee Whole House.		

List of private claims presented to the House of Representatives of the United States from the 1st to the 31st Congress, inclusive—Continued.

Names of claimants.	Nature or object of the claim.	Congress.	Session.	How brought before the House of Reps.	Page of journal.	To what committee of the House referred.	No. or date of the report.	Nature of the report.	No. of the bill.	How disposed of by the House of Reps.	How disposed of by the Senate.	Date of the act of Congress, and remarks.
Darden, David, by Amy, widow of.	Compensation for horse lost in service of the United States.	13	1	Petition	12	Claims	Jan. 12, 1813	....	......	Discharged.		
Darden, David, by Amy, widow of.	Compensation for horse lost in service of the United States.	13	2	Petition	198	Rev. Claims	....	....	......	Discharged.		
Darden, David, by Amy, widow of.	Compensation for horse lost in service of the United States.	13	3	Petition	591	Pensions	46	Favorable; bill	265	Passed	Rejected.	
Darden, David, by Amy, widow of.	Compensation for horse lost in service of the United States.	21	2	Petition	82	Rev. Claims	98	Favorable; bill	647	Referred to Committee Whole House.		
Darden, David, by Amy, widow of.	Compensation for horse lost in service of the United States.	22	1	Petition	55	Rev. Claims	43	Favorable; bill	92	Passed	Passed	App'd June 15, 1832
Darden, David	Compensation for horse lost in Seminole war.	28	1	Pet. and papers	262	Claims.						
Darden, Simeon, and John B. Smith.	Remuneration for arresting a mail robber.	30	1	House bill	556	Claims	508	Favorable; bill	328	Passed	Ref. to Com. on Claims.	
Darden, Simeon, and John B. Smith.	Remuneration for arresting a mail robber.	30	2	Senate amendm't.	127	Whole House	Dec. 22, 1848	Concurred in	328	Passed	Passed	App'd Jan. 10, 1849
Dark, William L.	Compensation for horse lost in Seminole war.	28	1	Pet. and papers.	262	Claims.						
Darley, Daniel, widow of.	Grant of land under act of August 4, 1842.	28	1	Petition	839	Public Lands.						
Darling, Benjamin	Revolutionary pension	21	2	Resolution	64	Military Pensions.						
Darling, Dennison, and B. S. Smoot.	Indemnity for house destroyed by United States army in 1812.	15	2	Petition	139	Claims	....	....	......	Discharged; laid on table.		
Darling, Dennison, and B. S. Smoot.	Indemnity for house destroyed by United States army in 1812.	18	2	Petition	95	Claims.						
Darling, Dennison, and B. S. Smoot.	Indemnity for house destroyed by United States army in 1812.	19	1	Petition	44	Claims	Jan. 30, 1826	Adverse	......	Referred to Committee Whole House.		
Darling, Dennison, and B. S. Smoot.	Confirmation of land title	16	2	Petition	113	Priv. Land Claims	....	....	......	Discharged; leave to withdraw.		
Darling, Eli	Revolutionary pension	24	1	Petition	107	Rev. Pensions	Jan. 14, 1836	Adverse	......	Laid on table.		
Darling, Eli	Relief; wounds received at Brooklyn navy yard in 1834.	24	2	Petition	85	Naval Affairs	23	Adverse	......	Laid on table.		
Darling, Eli	Relief; wounds received at Brooklyn navy yard in 1834.	25	2	Petition	921	Claims	May 25, 1838	Adverse	......	Laid on table.		
Darling, Eli	Relief; wounds received at Brooklyn navy yard in 1834.	25	3	Memorial	224	Naval Affairs.						
Darling, Eli	Relief; wounds received at Brooklyn navy yard in 1834.	26	1	Petition	303	Naval Affairs.						
Darling, Eli	Relief; loss of eyes in naval service of United States.	28	1	Petition	223	Naval Affairs.						
Darling, Eli	Relief; loss of eyes in naval service of United States.	31	1	Petition	271	Naval Affairs	289	Favorable; bill	262	Referred to Committee Whole House.		
Darling, Eli	Relief; loss of eyes in naval service of United States.	31	2	Rep't Committee Whole House	181	....	....	With't amend.	262	Passed	With't amend.	
Darling, Francis	Pension	22	2	House bill	334	Invalid Pensions	Feb. 15, 1833	Favorable; bill	738	Referred to Committee Whole House.		
Darling, Henry	Remission of duties imported into Castine.	16	1	Senate bill	108	Ways and Means	Jan. 14, 1820	Bill amended	S. 13	Passed	Concurred in.	App'd April 11, 1820
Darling, Henry	Payment of a moiety of a certain forfeiture.	22	1	Petition	162	Commerce	361	Favorable; bill	461	Referred to Committee Whole House.		
Darling, Henry	Payment of a moiety of a certain forfeiture.	23	1	Petition	32	Commerce	108	Favorable; bill	118	Passed.		

List of private claims presented to the House of Representatives of the United States from the 1*st to the* 31*st Congress, inclusive*—Continued.

Names of claimants.	Nature or object of the claim.	Congress.	Session.	How brought before the House of Reps.	Page of journal.	To what committee of the House referred.	No. or date of the report.	Nature of the report.	No. of the bill.	How disposed of by the House of Reps.	How disposed of by the Senate.	Date of the act of Congress, and remarks.
Darling, Henry	Payment of a moiety of a certain forfeiture.	24	1	Petition	54	Commerce	44	Favorable; bill.	49	Passed	Passed	App'd June 14, 1836
Darling, John	Pension	16	1	Petition	38	Rev. Pensions	April 22, 1820	Adverse		Laid on table.		
Darling, John O	(See John O. Dahling.)											
Darling, Oliver	Invalid pension	3	2	Rep. of Secretary War.	337	Claims	March 3, 1795	Favorable; bill	130	Passed	Postponed.	
Darling, Oliver	Invalid pension	4	1	Report and docs	447	Claims	Feb. 18, 1796	Favorable; bill	156	Passed	Passed	App'd April 20, 1796
Darling, Oliver	Increase of pension	12	1	House bill	361	Whole House	Jan. 15, 1812	Favorable; bill	138	Passed	Passed	App'd July 5, 1812
Darling & Kennedy, (Fla.)	Indemnity for store burnt by Seminole Indians.	31	1	Petition	1528	Military Affairs.						
Darlington, Abraham	Payment for property used by United States in revolutionary war.	2	1	Petition and rep. Sec. of Treas.	483		April 17, 1792			Laid on table.		
Darlington, Joseph	(See George Wilson, representatives of.)	7	2		303							
Darne, Lucy	Pension for services of husband in revolutionary war.	28	1	Petition	950	Whole House.						
Darnell, John	Settlement of account for rations furnished Maryland militia.	14	1	Petition	266	Claims				Discharged; laid on table.		
Darnell, John	Settlement of account for rations furnished Maryland militia.	14	2	Petition	85	Select	Jan. 23, 1817	Favorable; bill.	71	Indef. postponed.		
Darnell, John	Settlement of account for rations furnished Maryland militia.	15	1	Petition	76	Select	Mar. 27, 1818	Favorable; bill.	163	Referred to Committee Whole House.		
Darnell, Nicholas	Arrears of pension	24	1	Resolution	750	Invalid Pensions	Jan. 4, 1836	Adverse		Laid on table.		
Darnell, Nicholas	Arrears of pension	24	2	Petition	122	Invalid Pensions.						
Darnell, Nicholas	Arrears of pension	26	1	Resolution	383	Invalid Pensions.						
Darnell, Spencer	Pension	13	3	House bill	740	Whole House	Mar. 1, 1815	Bill amended.	303	Passed	Passed	App'd March 3, 1815
Darnin, James *et al.*	(See William Kennedy, representatives of.)	22	2		142							
Daron,	(See Kohn and Daron, & Co.)	27	1		97							
Darra, James, widow of	Arrears of pension	4	1	Petition	409	Claims				Leave to withdraw.		
Darrell, Edward	Compensation for revolutionary services, and settlement of claim.	3	1	Report and letter Sec. Treasury.	77					Laid on table.		
Darrell, Richard	(See Thomas Nelmes, administrator of.)	2	1		539							
Darrell,	(See Smith, Dessassure, and Darrell.)	26	1		182							
Darrow, George, jr., (N. Y.)	Pension	20	2	Petition	99	Military Pensions				Discharged; referred to Com. Whole House.		
Darrow, George, jr., (N. Y.)	Pension	21	1	Petition	46	Military Pensions	April 24, 1830	Adverse		Laid on table.		
Dart, Joseph	Indemnity for French spoliations prior to 1800.	26	1	Memorial	182	Foreign Affairs	343	Favorable; bill	319	Referred to Committee Whole House.		
Dartmouth College	Remission of duties on certain instruments.	30	1	Petition	393	Ways and Means.						
Darwin Thomas C	(See Archibald Beard, *et al.*	30	1		239		597					
Dash, John B. administrator of.	Remission of duties paid on copper bottoms.	17	1	Petition	56	Commerce	Jan. 4, 1822	Favorable; bill	24	Passed	Passed	App'd May 7, 1822
Dashiel, George W., representative of Jas. Corrie.	(See Alexander Mactier.)	17	1		40		32					
Dashiel, George W	(See James Corrier, representatives of.)	26	1		182		343		319			
Dashiel, Henry, widow of.	Indemnity for French spoliations prior to 1800.	29	2	Memorial	75	Foreign Affairs.						

List of private claims presented to the House of Representatives of the United States from the 1st to the 31st Congress, inclusive—Continued.

Names of claimants.	Nature or object of the claim.	Congress.	Session.	How brought before the House of Reps.	Page of journal.	To what committee of the House referred.	No. or date of the report.	Nature of the report.	No. of the bill.	How disposed of by the House of Reps.	How disposed of by the Senate.	Date of the act of Congress, and remarks.
58 Dashiel, Henry, widow of.	Indemnity for French spoliations prior to 1800.	31	1	Petition	196	Foreign Affairs ...	355	Favorable; bill	318	Referred to Committee Whole House.		
Dashnay, Christmas......	For patent and confirmation of land title.	17	1	Petition........	568	....	....	....	......	Laid on table.		
Dashner, John	Invalid pension	13	2	Petition	297	Pens. & Rev. Cl'ms.	....	....	......	Leave to withdraw.		
Daspit, Robert	Confirmation of land title........	31	1	Petition	971	Priv. Land Claims.						
Datamer, John..........	Revolutionary pension..........	21	1	Petition	319	Military Pensions .	....	....	......	Discharged; laid on table.		
Datamer, John..........	Revolutionary pension..........	21	2	Resolution	49	Military Pensions.						
Datamer, John..........	Revolutionary pension..........	22	1	Petition	514	Rev. Pensions.						
Daugherty, Jesse	Compensation for services by impressment at New Orleans.	31	2	Petition	216	Claims.						
Daugherty, Michael......	Compensation for services as an officer in revolutionary war.	13	2	Petition	301	Pens. & Rev. Cl'ms.	92	Adverse	......	Laid on table.		
Dauphin, John, by Jane, widow and adminis'x of.	Remission of forfeiture for violation of embargo act.	18	1	Petition	197	Ways and Means.						
Dauphin, John, by Jane, widow and adminis'x of.	Remission of forfeiture for violation of embargo act.	21	1	Petition and docs.	171	Foreign Affairs....	....	....	......	Discharged; laid on table.		
Dauphin, John, by Jane, widow and adminis'x of.	Remission of forfeiture for violation of embargo act.	21	1	Resolution	310	Foreign Affairs....	301	Adverse......	......	Laid on table.		
Dauphin, John, by Jane, widow and adminis'x of.	Remission of forfeiture for violation of embargo act.	22	1	Petition	62	Foreign Affairs....	140	Favorable; bill.	211	Referred to Committee Whole House.		
Dauphin, John, by Jane, widow and adminis'x of.	Remission of forfeiture for violation of embargo act.	22	2	Rep't Committee Whole House.	66	....	....	With't amend.	211	Passed	Passed	App'd March 2, 1833
Davee, Isaac	(See Isaac Deavee)...........	31	1	....	362							
Davenport, Abbington, by Mary, widow of.	Invalid pension................	26	2	Petition	134	Invalid Pensions ..	....	....	......	Discharged, and to Rev. Pensions.		
Davenport, Ambrose, or A. P.	Confirmation of title to land	20	1	Resolution	28	Claims	42	Favorable; bill.	34	Passed	Passed	App'd April 17, 1828
Davenport, Anthony.....	Indemnity for French spoliations prior to 1800.	26	1	Memorial	182	Foreign Affairs....	343	Favorable; bill.	319	Referred to Committee Whole House.		
Davenport, Anthony, executors of.	Indemnity for French spoliations prior to 1800.	31	1	Petition	337	Foreign Affairs....	355	Favorable; bill.	318	Referred to Committee Whole House.		
Davenport, Adrian H.....	Pre-emption right to land in Wisconsin.	25	2	Petition	422	Public Lands.						
Davenport, Barr, *et al*....	Settlement of land claims........	25	3	Resolution	173	Priv. Land Claims.						
Davenport, Benjamin, by Elizabeth, widow of.	Revolutionary pension..........	27	3	Petition	260	Rev. Pensions.....	....	....	......	Discharged; leave to withdraw.		
Davenport, Edward J	Indemnity for French spoliations prior to 1800.	24	2	Petition	315	Foreign Affairs.						
Davenport, Edward J.....	Indemnity for French spoliations prior to 1800.	26	1	Memorial	182	Foreign Affairs....	343	Favorable; bill.	319	Referred to Committee Whole House.		
Davenport, Franklin.....	Revolutionary pension..........	22	1	Petition	219	Rev. Pensions	....	....	......	Discharged; laid on table.		
Davenport & Farnham ...	(See Farnham & Davenport)....	22	2									
Davenport & Gage	(See Gage & Davenport)........	20	1	....	28	....	42	....	34	....	....	App'd April 17, 1828
Davenport, George, (Ill.).	Pre-emption right to land	22	1	Petition	192	Public Lands	Jan. 30, 1832	Favorable; bill.	337	Referred to Committee Whole House.		
Davenport, George, (Ill.).	Pre-emption right to land	23	1	Petition	300	Public Lands	Feb. 11, 1834	Favorable; bill.	294	Referred to Committee Whole House.		
Davenport, George, (Ill.).	Pre-emption right to land	23	2	Rep't Committee Whole House.	300	....	Jan. 31, 1835	With't amend.	294	Passed............	Passed with amendment.	

List of private claims presented to the House of Representatives of the United States from the 1st to the 31st Congress, inclusive—Continued.

Names of claimants.	Nature or object of the claim.	Congress.	Session.	How brought before the House of Reps.	Page of journal.	To what committee of the House referred.	No. or date of the report.	Nature of the report.	No. of the bill.	How disposed of by the House of Reps.	How disposed of by the Senate.	Date of the act of Congress, and remarks.
Davenport, George, (Ill.)	Pre-emption right to land	25	2	Senate bill	611	Public Lands	April 11, 1838	With't amend.	S. 91	Referred to Committee Whole House.		
Davenport, George, (Ill.)	Pre emption right to land	28	1	Senate bill	440	Public Lands	Feb. 21, 1844	With't amend.	S. 44	Passed	Passed	App'd April 2, 1844
Davenport, Henriette	(See John Davenport, widow of)	26	1		705							
Davenport, Henry	(See Stephen Decatur, heirs of, et al.)	23	1		36		45		50			
Davenport, Hezekiah, heir of.	Remuneration for revolutionary services.	25	2	Petition	52	Rev. Pensions				Discharged; laid on table.		
Davenport, Isaac	(See Joseph Davenport, heir of)	28	2		103							
Davenport, James, heirs of	Arrears of pension	20	1	Resolution	263	Military Pensions	237	Favorable; bill.	277	Referred to Committee Whole House.		
Davenport, James, heirs of	Arrears of pension	20	2	Rep't Committee Whole House.	285			With't amend.	277	Passed	Amended.	
Davenport, James, heirs of	Arrears of pension	21	1	Petition	59	Military Affairs	Jan. 19, 1830	Favorable; bill.	133	Passed	Passed	App'd May 20, 1830
Davenport, James B., *et al.*	(See Samuel Davenport, representative of.)	21	1		297							
Davenport, James B	(See Josiah Davenport, heir of)	29	1		347							
Davenport, John, (Ohio)	Pension	22	1	Petition	265	Rev. Pensions				Disch'd; laid on table.		
Davenport, John, administrator of.	Indemnity for French spoliations prior to 1800.	26	1	Memorial	182	Foreign Affairs	343	Favorable; bill.	319	Referred to Committee Whole House.		
Davenport, John	Continuation of pension	23	2	Resolution	295	Invalid Pensions	March 2, 1825	Adverse		Laid on table		
Davenport, John, widow of	Revolutionary pension	26	1	Petition	705	Rev. Pensions	551	Adverse		Laid on table.		
Davenport, John, (Mo.)	Arrears of pension for services in war of 1812.	29	1	Petition	688	Invalid Pensions				Discharged; laid on table.		
Davenport, John, (Mo.)	Arrears of pension for services in war of 1812.	30	1	Petition	676	Invalid Pensions				Discharged; laid on table.		
Davenport, Jonathan	Revolutionary pension	3	1	Report Secretary of War.	131	Select	May 26, 1794	To refer to Sec. with instructions.	J. R. 12	Passed	Passed	App'd June 9, 1794
Davenport, Jonathan	Revolutionary pension	4	1	Report Secretary of War.	447	Claims	Feb. 18, 1796	Favorable; bill	156	Passed	Passed	App'd April 20, 1796
Davenport, Joseph, heir of	Revolutionary pension	28	2	Petition	103	Rev. Pensions.						
Davenport, Joseph, heir of	Revolutionary pension	29	1	Petition	193	Rev. Pensions	618	Adverse		Laid on table.		
Davenport, Josiah, heir of	Confirmation of title to land in Louisiana.	29	1	Petition	347	Priv. Land Claims.	696	Favorable; bill	470	Referred to Committee Whole House.		
Davenport, Josiah, heir of	Confirmation of title to land in Louisiana.	30	1	Petition	109	Priv. Land Claims.	177	Favorable; bill	187	Passed	With't amend.	
Davenport, Josiah, heir of	Confirmation of title to land in Louisiana.	30	2	Sen. amendment to House bill.	166	Whole House	Jan. 4, 1849	Concurred in.	187	Passed	Passed	App'd Jan. 10, 1849
Davenport, Lewis	(See Samuel Wagstaffe, legal representative of.)	21	1		499							
Davenport, Mary	(See Abbington Davenport, widow of.)	26	2		134							
Davenport, Mary	(See Samuel Brock and Oliver Barron, former widow of.)	26	1		1115							
Davenport, Moses	Indemnity for French spoliations prior to 1800.	26	1	Memorial	182	Foreign Affairs	343	Favorable; bill	319	Referred to Committee Whole House.		
Davenport, Samuel	Confirmation of title to land in Louisiana.	21	1	Petition	297	Priv. Land Claims.						
Davenport, Samuel	Confirmation of title to land in Louisiana.	21	2	Petition	62	Priv. Land Claims.						
Davenport, Samuel	Confirmation of title to land in Louisiana.	22	1	Petition	65	Priv. Land Claims.	Jan. 25, 1832	Favorable, bill	311	Referred to Committee Whole House.		

List of private claims presented to the House of Representatives of the United States from the 1st to the 31st Congress, inclusive—Continued.

Names of claimants.	Nature or object of the claim.	Congress.	Session.	How brought before the House of Reps.	Page of journal.	To what committee of the House referred.	No. or date of the report.	Nature of the report.	No. of the bill.	How disposed of by the House of Reps.	How disposed of by the Senate.	Date of the act of Congress, and remarks.
Davenport, Samuel	Confirmation of title to land in Louisiana.	23	1	Petition	714	Priv. Land Claims.						
Davenport, Sophia	(See Edmund Jones, heir of.)	31	1		598							
Davenport, S. H.	Indemnity for French spoliations prior to 1800.	26	1	Memorial	182	Foreign Affairs	343	Favorable; bill	319	Referred to Committee Whole House.		
Davenport, Capt. Thomas.	Commutation pay and bounty land	22	1	Senate bill	779	Naval Affairs	May 25, 1832	With't amend.	S. 168	Passed	Passed	App'd July 14, 1832
Davenport, William	(See Hezekiah Davenport, heir of.)	25	2		52							
Davenport, Capt. William, heir of.	Commutation pay for services in revolutionary war.	26	1	Petition	961	Rev. Claims	551	Adverse		Laid on table.		
Davenport, Capt. William, heir of.	Commutation pay for services in revolutionary war.	26	2	Petition	212	Rev. Claims.						
Davenport, Capt. William, heirs of.	Commutation pay for services in revolutionary war.	29	1	Memorial	1103	Rev. Claims.						
Davenport, Capt. William, heirs of.	Commutation pay for services in revolutionary war.	30	1	Memorial	156	Rev. Claims.						
Davenport, Capt. William, heirs of.	Commutation pay for services in revolutionary war.	31	1	Petition	534	Rev. Claims	181	Adverse		Laid on table.		
Davezac, Auguste	Difference of pay between secretary of legation and chargé d'affaires.	26	1	Petition	351	Foreign Affairs.						
Davezac, Auguste	Difference of pay between secretary of legation and chargé d'affaires.	26	1	Senate bill	1156	Foreign Affairs			S. 366			
Davezac, Auguste	Difference of pay between secretary of legation and chargé d'affaires.	26	1	Sen. amendment to House bill.	1343	Whole House	July 21, 1840	Concurred in.	27	Passed	Passed	App'd July 21, 1840
David, Francis	Drawback on merchandise exported in 1815.	14	1	Petition	42	Com. and Manuf.	Jan. 22, 1826	Adverse		Leave to withdraw.		
David, John T.	Settlement of accounts as late paymaster.	14	1	Petition	40	Claims	Jan. 22, 1816	Favorable; bill		Laid on table.		
David, John T.	Settlement of accounts as late paymaster.	15	1	Petition	64	Claims	Feb. 27, 1818	Adverse		Rejected.		
David, John T.	Settlement of accounts as late paymaster.	15	2	Petition	110	Claims				Discharged; laid on table.		
David, John T.	Settlement of accounts as late paymaster.	16	1	Petition	181	Claims	Mar. 17, 1820	Adverse		Laid on table.		
Davids, John	Payment for property destroyed by British in 1812.	22	1	Petition	188	Claims	Feb. 6, 1832	Adverse		Laid on table.		
Davids, John	Payment for property destroyed by British in 1812.	22	2	Petition	177	Claims.						
David, Virgil, by Selina, widow of.	Compensation for services of husband as steward of Alleghany arsenal.	26	1	Petition	613	Military Pensions.						
Davidson, Capt. Alexander, representatives of.	Compensation for services of ancestor in revolutionary war.	31	2	Petition	157	Rev. Pensions				Leave to withdraw.		
Davidson, Bracket	Pension	14	1	House bill	622	Pens. & Rev. Cl'ms.	April 11, 1816	With't amend.	171	Passed	Passed	App'd April 30, 1816
Davidson, D. F., and Benjamin Thompson.	Restoration of certain tonnage duties.	30	2	Petition	282	Naval Affairs.						
Davidson, David, (Pa.)	Pension	19	1	Resolution	266	Military Pensions.	164	Adverse.				
Davidson, David	That money expended by him in revolutionary war be refunded, with interest.	14	2	Petition	95	Pens. & Rev. Cl'ms.	Dec. 30, 1816	Adverse		Laid on table.		
Davidson, Eleanor.	(See Henry Davidson, widow of).	31	1		311							
Davidson, Elizabeth	(See John Davidson, widow of, N. York.)											
Davidson, Francis	Pension	10	1	House bill	232	Whole House	Mar. 17, 1808	With't amend.	78	Passed	Passed	App'd April 25, 1808

List of private claims presented to the House of Representatives of the United States from the 1st to the 31st Congress, inclusive—Continued.

Names of claimants.	Nature or object of the claim.	Congress.	Session.	How brought before the House of Reps.	Page of journal.	To what committee of the House referred.	No. or date of the report.	Nature of the report.	No. of the bill.	How disposed of by the House of Reps.	How disposed of by the Senate.	Date of the act of Congress, and remarks.
Davidson, Francis, (Pa.)	Revolutionary pension	28	2	Petition	70	Rev. Pensions.						
Davidson, George L., son of Brig. Gen. Davidson.	Land warrant for 2,000 acres of land in right of his father.	18	1	Resolution	504	Whole House	Feb. 27, 1804	Favorable; bill	194	Passed	Rejected.	
Davidson, Hamilton	Reimbursement of certain duties	23	1	Petition	69	Ways and Means	....	....	.....	Laid on table.		
Davidson, Henry, widow of.	Pension for death of husband in Mexican war.	31	1	Petition	311	Rev. Pensions	130	Favorable; bill	149	Referred to Committee Whole House.		
Davidson, Henry, widow of.	Pension for death of husband in Mexican war.	31	2	Rep't Committee Whole House.	103	Whole House	Jan. 3, 1851	With't amend.	149	Passed	Ref'd to Com. on Pensions.	
Davidson, James	Pay and rations whilst prisoner among Indians.	17	1	Petition	140	Claims	Feb. 11, 1842	Adverse	.....	Laid on table.		
Davidson, James, (Md.)	Pension	20	1	Petition	338	Military Pensions	April 29, 1828	Favorable; bill	283	Passed.		
Davidson, James, (Md.)	Pension	20	2	House bill	55	Military Pensions	Dec. 12, 1828	Favorable; bill	311	Passed	Laid on table.	
Davidson, James, (Md.)	Pension	21	1	Petition	48	Military Pensions	Jan. 5, 1830	Favorable; bill	72	Passed	Passed	App'd May 20, 1830
Davidson, James	Revolutionary pension	22	1	Resolution	454	Rev. Pensions	....	....	.....	Discharged; laid on table.		
Davidson, James, (Tenn.)	Invalid pension for services in war of 1812.	28	1	Petition	602	Invalid Pensions.						
Davidson, James, (Tenn.)	Invalid pension for services in war of 1812.	28	2	Petition	353	Invalid Pensions	144	Favorable; bill	625	Referred to Committee Whole House.		
Davidson, James, (Tenn.)	Invalid pension for services in war of 1812.	29	1	Petition	83	Invalid Pensions	16	Favorable; bill	30	Passed	Passed	App'd July 15, 1846
Davidson, James H	(See John Gillock, guardian of son.)	4	1	....	385							
Davidson, Lieut. J. W	Release from refunding government funds stolen from him in California.	31	2	Petition	111	Millitary Affairs.						
Davidson, John, widow of.	Revolutionary pension	25	2	Resolution	764	Rev. Pensions.						
Davidson, John, widow of.	Revolutionary pension	25	3	Resolution	162	Rev. Pensions	....	....	.....	Discharged.		
Davidson, John, widow of.	Revolutionary pension	26	1	Petition	172	Rev. Pensions	109	Favorable; bill	119	Passed	Passed	App'd July 20, 1840
Davidson, John	Permission to fund lost certificate.	10	1	Petition	14	Ways and Means	Nov. 23, 1807	Favorable; bill	38	Passed	Passed with amendment.	App'd Mar. 11, 1808
Davidson, John O	(See Samuel Ragsdale)	20	1	....	342							
Davidson, John, former widow of.	Revolutionary pension	26	1	Documents	624	Rev. Pensions	490	Adverse	.....	Laid on table.		
Davidson, John	Relief from duties on salt destroyed.	1	2	Petition	256	Select	July 27, 1790	Favorable; bill	90	Passed	Passed	App'd August 4, 1790
Davidson, Joseph	Invalid pension	13	1	House bill	56	Whole House	July 20, 1813	Favorable; bill	31	Passed	Passed	App'd August 2, 1813
Davidson, Joseph, heir of.	Revolutionary pension	28	2	Petition	64	Rev. Pensions	....	....	.....	Discharged; laid on table.		
Davidson, Josiah	Revolutionary pension	25	2	Petition	984	Rev. Pensions	....	....	.....	Discharged.		
Davidson, Josiah	Revolutionary pension	26	1	Petition	175	Rev. Pensions	....	....	.....	Discharged; laid on table.		
Davidson, Joshua	Invalid pension	3	1	Rep. of Secretary of War.	131	Select	May 26, 1794	Res. to refer to Sec. with instructions.	J. R. 12	Passed	Passed	App'd June 9, 1794
Davidson, Joshua	Invalid pension	3	2	Rep. of Secretary of War.	350	Claims	Mar. 3, 1795	Res. to refer to Sec. with instructions.	.....	Resolution adopted.		
Davidson, Joshua	Invalid pension	5	2	House bill	127	Whole House	Jan. 9, 1798	Favorable; bill	38	Passed	Passed	App'd Feb. 2, 1798
Davidson, Richard	Compensation for medicine, and attendance on officers and crew of gunboat No. 11 in revolutionary war.	10	2	Petition	498	Claims.						

List of private claims presented to the House of Representatives of the United States from the 1st to the 31st Congress, inclusive—Continued.

Names of claimants.	Nature or object of the claim.	Congress.	Session.	How brought before the House of Reps.	Page of journal.	To what committee of the House referred.	No. or date of the report.	Nature of the report.	No. of the bill.	How disposed of by the House of Reps.	How disposed of by the Senate.	Date of the act of Congress, and remarks.
Davidson, Richard......	Compensation for medicine, and attendance on officers and crew of gunboat No. 11 in revolutionary war.	11	2	Petition and rep't Sec. of Navy.	167	Claims..........	....	....	......	Discharged; referred to Sec. Navy.		
Davidson, Robert........	Confirmation of land title	30	1	Petition	187	Public Lands.						
Davidson, Robert........	Confirmation of land title	31	1	Petition	197	Priv. Land Claims.	84	Favorable; bill	104	Referred to Committee Whole House.		
Davidson, Robert........	Confirmation of land title	31	2	Rep't Committee Whole House.	154	Whole House.....	Jan. 18, 1851	With't amend.	104	Passed	Adverse.	
Davidson, Samuel, by agent	Indemnity for loss of horse and equipments in Seminole war.	23	1	Documents.....	154	Claims.						
Davidson, Samuel, by agent	Indemnity for loss of horse and equipments in Seminole war.	28	1	Petition	262	Claims.						
Davidson, Samuel C	Compensation for carrying mail..	27	3	House bill	120	Whole House.....	Dec. 31, 1842	With't amend.	804	Passed	Passed	App'd March 3, 1843
Davidson, Thomas.......	Compensation for services in revolutionary war.	2	2	Petition	618	Referred to Sec. of War.	March 2, 1793	Report	......	Laid on table.		
Davidson, Thomas G., (register.)	Increase of salary..............	21	2	Petition	232	Public Lands.						
Davidson, Thomas G., (register.)	Increase of salary..............	22	1	Petition	75	Public Lands.....	....	....	......	Discharged; laid on table.		
Davidson, William	Compensation for services as marshal of Florida.	18	1	Resolution	420	Ways and Means..	May 6, 1824	Favorable; bill	221	Passed	Passed	App'd May 26, 1824
Davidson, William, assignee of.	Indemnity for French spoliations prior to 1800.	26	1	Memorial	182	Foreign Affairs....	343	Favorable; bill	319	Referred to Committee Whole House.		
Daviess, James..........	Compensation as agent of Chickasaw Indians, &c.	21	1	Petition	294	Claims	Mar. 2, 1830	Favorable; bill	308	Referred to Committee Whole House.		
Daviess, James..........	Compensation as agent of Chickasaw Indians, &c.	21	2	Rep't Committee Whole House.	333	Whole House.....	249	With't amend.	308	Passed	With't amend.	
Daviess, James..........	Compensation as agent of Chickasaw Indians, &c.	22	1	Petition	43	Claims	Dec. 19, 1831	Favorable; bill	9	Passed	Passed	App'd Jan. 23, 1832
Davison, James.........	Extra compensation as clerk in P. O. Department.	3	1	Resolution	209	Select	June 6, 1794	Favorable; bill	69	Passed	Rejected.	
Davison, John..........	Revolutionary pension..........	28	1	Petition	144	Rev. Pensions	....	....	......	Discharged; laid on table.		
Davison, John F., by agent	Indemnity for horse lost in Seminole war.	28	1	Petition	262	Claims.						
Davison, Josiah	Restoration of pension..........	24	2	Petition	84	Rev. Pensions	....	....	......	Discharged; laid on table.		
Davis, A. B.	(See Exploring Expedition)	27	3	....	149							
Davis, Abigail	(See Flint Davis, widow of).....	31	1	....	616							
Davis, Abraham	Increase of pension	14	2	Petition	45	Pens. & Rev. Cl'ms.	....	....	......	Discharged; laid on table.		
Davis, Amasa, assignee of.	Reimbursement of penalty erroneously paid.	19	2	Petition	44	Judiciary	....	....	......	Discharged.		
Davis, Amasa, assignee of.	Reimbursement of penalty erroneously paid.	20	1	Petition	31	Ways and Means..	184	Adverse	......	Recommitted.		
Davis, Amasa, assignee of.	Reimbursement of penalty erroneously paid.	20	1	Report of Com.	399	Ways and Means..	Mar. 10, 1828	Favorable; bill	211	Referred to Committee Whole House.		
Davis, Amasa, assignee of.	Reimbursement of penalty erroneously paid.	20	2	Rep't Committee Whole House.	202	Whole House.....	Jan. 24, 1829	With't amend.	211	Passed	With't amend.	
Davis, Amasa, assignee of.	Reimbursement of penalty erroneously paid.	21	1	Petition	58	Ways and Means..	270	Favorable; bill	322	Referred to Committee Whole House.		
Davis, Amasa, assignee of.	Reimbursement of penalty erroneously paid.	21	2	Rep't Committee Whole House.	340	Whole House.....	Feb. 22, 1831	With't amend.	322	Passed	With't amend.	

List of private claims presented to the House of Representatives of the United States from the 1st to the 31st Congress, inclusive—Continued.

Names of claimants.	Nature or object of the claim.	Congress.	Session.	How brought before the House of Reps.	Page of journal.	To what committee of the House referred.	No. or date of the report.	Nature of the report.	No. of the bill.	How disposed of by the House of Reps.	How disposed of by the Senate.	Date of the act of Congress, and remarks.
Davis, Amasa, assignee of.	Reimbursement of penalty erroneously paid.	22	1	Petition	100	Ways and Means	58	Favorable; bill	112	Passed	Passed	App'd June 25, 1832
Davis, Amos, (Mass.)	Invalid pension	23	1	Petition	436	Invalid Pensions	....	....	......	Discharged; laid on table.		
Davis, Amos, (Mass.)	Invalid pension	27	2	Petition	526	Invalid Pensions	800	Favorable; bill	454	Referred to Committee Whole House.		
Davis, Alexander, *et al.*	Pre-emption right to land	23	1	Petition	387	Public Lands.						
Davis, Asa	Invalid pension	23	1	Petition	436	Invalid Pensions	....	....	......	Discharged; laid on table.		
Davis, Asa	Invalid pension	27	2	Petition	526	Invalid Pensions	800	Favorable; bill	454	Referred to Committee Whole House.		
Davis, Asa	Invalid pension	27	3	Rep't Committee Whole House.	88	Whole House	May 26, 1842	With't amend.	454	Passed	Indef. postp'd.	
Davis, Asa	Invalid pension	28	1	Petition	297	Invalid Pensions	435	Favorable; bill	332	Passed	Passed	App'd Jan. 17, 1844
Davis, Benjamin, widow of	Naval pension	16	1	Petition	27	Naval Affairs	....	....	......	Discharged; laid on table.		
Davis, Benjamin, widow of	Naval pension	21	2	Petition	81	Naval Affairs	....	....	......	Discharged; laid on table.		
Davis, Benjamin, widow of	Naval pension	26	1	Petition	200	Naval Affairs.						
Davis, Benjamin, widow of	Naval pension	26	2	Petition	37	Naval Affairs.						
Davis, Catharine, *et al.*	(See John Watson, heirs of)	15	2	....	40							
Davis, Charles B	(See William N. Esenbeck, *et al*)	11	3	....	570							
Davis, Charles B	Indemnity for loss of furniture burnt by enemy in 1812.	13	3	Petition	511	Claims	Nov. 11, 1814	Adverse.				
Davis, Charles B	Indemnity for loss of furniture burnt by enemy in 1812.	22	1	Petition	226	Claims	Feb. 6, 1832	Adverse	......	Laid on table.		
Davis, Charles B	Indemnity for loss of furniture burnt by enemy in 1812.	23	1	Petition	305	Claims	314	Adverse	......	Laid on table.		
Davis, Charles B., widow of.	Compensation for horse and cart used by enemy in 1814.	26	1	Petition	919	Claims	....	....	......	Discharged; laid on table.		
Davis, Charles B., widow of.	Compensation for horse and cart used by enemy in 1814.	26	2	Petition	130	Claims.						
Davis, Charles B., widow of.	Compensation for horse and cart used by enemy in 1814.	27	2	Petition	55	Claims	177	Adverse	......	Laid on table.		
Davis, Charles B., widow of.	Compensation for horse and cart used by enemy in 1814.	27	3	Petition	152	Claims.						
Davis, Charles M., *et al.*	Pre-emption right to land in Michigan.	21	2	Petition	192	Public Lands.						
Davis, Cornelius, heir of	Compensation for revolutionary services.	29	1	Petition	197	Rev. Claims	....	....	......	Discharged; laid on table.		
Davis, Daniel	Permission to correct error in location of land.	14	1	Resolution	470	Public Lands	....	....	......	Discharged; laid on table.		
Davis, Daniel	Pension	15	2	Rep. of Secretary War.	48	Pens. & Rev. Cl'ms.	Feb. 5, 1819	Favorable; bill.	308	Postponed.		
Davis, Daniel, (Maine)	Revolutionary pension	24	2	Petition	44	Rev. Pensions	61	Favorable; bill.	811	Referred to Committee Whole House.		
Davis, Daniel, (Maine)	Revolutionary pension	25	2	Petition	37	Rev. Pensions	157	Favorable; bill.	182	Rejected.		
Davis, Daniel, (Maine)	Revolutionary pension	28	1	Petition	631	Rev. Pensions.						
Davis, Daniel	Bounty land for revolutionary services.	19	1	Petition	143	Priv. Land Claims.	60	Favorable; bill.	83	Passed	Passed	App'd May 20, 1826
Davis, Daniel, administrator of.	Indemnity for advances to soldiers of United States army on certificates of discharge.	20	1	Petition	366	Claims	April 9, 1828	Adverse	......	Laid on table.		

List of private claims presented to the House of Representatives of the United States from the 1st to the 31st Congress, inclusive—Continued.

Names of claimants.	Nature or object of the claim.	Congress.	Session.	How brought before the House of Reps.	Page of journal.	To what committee of the House referred.	No. or date of the report.	Nature of the report.	No. of the bill.	How disposed of by the House of Reps.	How disposed of by the Senate.	Date of the act of Congress, and remarks.
Davis, Daniel	Bounty of $80, and for value of horse lost in service of United States.	21	1	Petition	53	Claims	Jan. 30, 1830	Adverse as to horse.				
Davis, Daniel	Compensation for horse lost in service of United States.	22	1	Petition	559	Claims	April 12, 1832	Adverse		Laid on table.		
Davis, Daniel	Compensation for horse lost in service of United States.	24	1	Petition	207	Claims	412	Favorable; bill.	424	Referred to Committee Whole House.		
Davis, Daniel	Compensation for horse lost in service of United States.	25	2	Petition	36	Claims	15	Favorable; bill.	27	Passed	Passed	App'd March 28, 1838
Davis, David, widow of	Relief for husband killed in war of 1812.	14	1	Petition	295	Whole House.						
Davis, David, widow of	Relief for husband killed in war of 1812.	19	1	Petition and docs.	569					Leave to withdraw.		
Davis, David, (N. Y.)	Pension	21	1	Petition	120	Military Pensions	May 4, 1830	Adverse		Laid on table.		
Davis, David, (N. H.)	Arrears of pension	21	2	Petition	188	Military Pensions.						
Davis, Deborah	(See Sanford Davis, widow of)	19	1		108							
Davis, Edward E., widow of.	Continuation of pension	25	2	Petition	404	Rev. Pensions	Feb. 17, 1838	Refer. to Com. Whole House on bill 456.				
Davis, Edward E., widow of.	Continuation of pension	28	1	Petition	827	Whole House.						
Davis, Edward E., widow of.	Continuation of pension	30	1	Petition	823	Rev. Pensions.						
Davis, Edward E., widow of.	Continuation of pension	30	2	Petition	333					Leave to withdraw.		
Davis, Edward G., a New Orleans branch pilot.	Authority to enter land at minimum price.	28	1	Petition	77	Priv. Land Claims.	9	Favorable; bill.	35	Passed	Passed	App'd June 17, 1844
Davis, Eli, jr	Compensation for horse lost in Indian war in 1832.	23	1	Petition	384	Claims	476	Adverse		Laid on table.		
Davis, Eli and Brinkley	(See Wallace Rea, sureties of)	23	1		570							
Davis, Elias	Revolutionary pension	15	2	Rep. of Secretary War.	48	Pens. & Rev. Cl'ms.	Feb. 5, 1819	Favorable; bill	308	Postponed.		
Davis, Elijah	Revolutionary pension	16	1	Petition	210	Rev. Pensions	April 6, 1820	Adverse		Laid on table.		
Davis, Elijah	(See Jesse Davis, executors of)	28	2		208							
Davis, Elisha	Revolutionary pension	25	2	Petition	349	Rev. Pensions	700	Favorable; bill	674	Passed	Ref. to Com. on Pensions.	
Davis, Elisha	Revolutionary pension	26	1	Petition	172	Rev. Pensions.						
Davis, Elisha	Revolutionary pension	26	2	Petition	78	Rev. Pensions.						
Davis, Elisha	Revolutionary pension	27	2	Petition	97	Rev. Pensions	302	Favorable; bill	271	Passed	Indef. postp'd.	
Davis, Elizabeth	(See Charles B. Davis, widow of)	26	1		919							
Davis, Elizabeth	Restoration of pension	27	2	Petition	614	Rev. Pensions	May 25, 1842	Adverse.				
Davis, Ephraim	(See Isaac Davis, heir of)	7	1		12							
Davis, Ezra, (Boston)	Indemnity for vessel and cargo seized and sold by French officers in 1809.	18	1	Petition	284	Foreign Affairs	127	Report and res.		Resolution adopted		See President's message to House, December 23, 1824.
Davis, Flint, widow of	Revolutionary pension	31	1	Petition	616	Rev. Pensions	461	Adverse		Laid on table.		
Davis, Hannah	Indemnity for property destroyed by British in 1812.	15	1	Letter from Com'r of Claims.	316	Claims.						
Davis, Hannah	Indemnity for property destroyed by British in 1812.	16	1	Petition	77	Claims	Jan. 10, 1820	Adverse		Laid on table.		
Davis, Hannah	Indemnity for property destroyed by British in 1812.	16	2	Petition and rep.	37	Claims	16	Adverse		Referred to Committee Whole House.		
Davis, Hannah	Indemnity for property destroyed by British in 1812.	18	1	Petition	288	Claims	March 3, 1824	Adverse		Laid on table.		

List of private claims presented to the House of Representatives of the United States from the 1st to the 31st Congress, inclusive—Continued.

Names of claimants.	Nature or object of the claim.	Congress.	Session.	How brought before the House of Reps.	Page of journal.	To what committee of the House referred.	No. or date of the report.	Nature of the report.	No. of the bill.	How disposed of by the House of Reps.	How disposed of by the Senate.	Date of the act of Congress, and remarks.
Davis, Hannah	(See Joseph Davis, mother of)	23	1		140							
Davis, Henry, (N. C.)	Compensation for keeping prisoner by authority of government.	15	1	Petition	27	Claims	Mar. 13, 1818	Favorable; bill	138	Referred to Committee Whole House.		
Davis, Henry, (N. C.)	Compensation for keeping prisoner by authority of government.	15	2	Rep't Committee Whole House.	181	Whole House	Jan. 13, 1819	With't amend.	138	Passed	Passed	App'd Feb. 20, 1819
Davis, Henry, assignees of.	Relief for spoliations on commerce by government of Hayti.	21	1	Memorial	85	Foreign Affairs	Dec. 31, 1829	Adverse		Laid on table.		
Davis, Hester	(See David Davis, widow of)	14	1		295							
Davis, Hugh	Revolutionary pension	25	2	Petition	70	Rev. Pensions				Discharged; laid on table.		
Davis, Hugh	Revolutionary pension	25	3	Petition	87	Rev. Pensions				Discharged.		
Davis, Hugh	Revolutionary pension	26	1	Petition	171	Rev. Pensions	121	Favorable; bill	131	Passed	Indef. postp'd.	
Davis, Isaac	Invalid pension	3	1	Rep. of Secretary War.	131	Select	May 26, 1794	Res. to refer to Sec. with instructions.	J. R. 12	Passed	Passed	App'd June 9, 1794
Davis, Isaac	Invalid pension	3	2	Rep. of Secretary War.	350	Claims	Feb. 28, 1795	Favorable: bill ordered.	130	Passed	Indef. postp'd.	
Davis, Isaac, heir of	Compensation for revolutionary services.	7	1	Petition	12	Claims				Leave to withdraw.		
Davis, Isaac	Invalid pension	18	1	Petition	358	Pens. & Rev. Cl'ms.						
Davis, Isaac, widow of	Invalid pension	27	2	Petition	1043	Invalid Pensions				Discharged; laid on table.		
Davis, Isaac	(See Cornelius Davis, heir of)	29	1		197							
Davis, Isaac, former widow of.	Revolutionary pension	15	1	Petition	156	Rev. Claims.						
Davis, Isaac, former widow of.	Revolutionary pension	26	1	Petition	937	Rev. Pensions	July 10, 1840	Adverse		Laid on table.		
Davis, Isaac P	Indemnity for losses on contract with United States for cordage for frigates.	19	2	Petition and rep't of Sec. War.	130	Naval Affairs	Feb. 27, 1827	Adverse		Laid on table.		
Davis, Jacob	Invalid pension	25	2	Petition	722	Invalid Pensions.						
Davis, James	Compensation as agent of Chicasaw Indians.	21	1	Petition	294	Claims	249	Favorable; bill	308	Referred to Committee Whole House.		
Davis, James, (Va.)	Remission of forfeiture	21	2	Petition	256	Commerce				Discharged; referred to Secretary War.		
Davis, James S	Invalid pension	23	2	Petition	140	Invalid Pensions				Discharged; laid on table.		
Davis, James S	Arrears of pension	24	1	Petition	48	Invalid Pensions	Jan. 28, 1836	Adverse		Laid on table.		
Davis, James S	Arrears of pension	24	2	Petition	98	Invalid Pensions	Dec. 23, 1836	Adverse		Laid on table.		
Davis, James	Indemnity for fishery destroyed by U. S. government.	26	2	Petition	130	Claims.						
Davis, James	Indemnity for fishery destroyed by U. S. government.	27	2	Petition	356	Claims.						
Davis, James	Indemnity for fishery destroyed by U. S. government.	27	3	Petition	72	Claims	56	Adverse		Laid on table.		
Davis, James	Compensation for loss of property by the burning of the steamship Missouri.	28	2	Petition	46	Naval Affairs				Discharged; laid on table.		
Davis, James	(See Levi Davis, administrator of.)	30	2		75							
Davis, James	Compensation for supplies furnished in revolutionary war.	3	2	Petition	277	Claims	Mar. 2, 1795	Adverse		Laid on table.		
Davis, James	Compensation for supplies furnished in revolutionary war.	4	1	Report	598	Claims	May 31, 1796	Adverse		Laid on table.		

List of private claims presented to the House of Representatives of the United States from the 1st to the 31st Congress, inclusive—Continued.

Names of claimants.	Nature or object of the claim.	Congress.	Session.	How brought before the House of Reps.	Page of journal.	To what committee of the House referred.	No. or date of the report.	Nature of the report.	No. of the bill.	How disposed of by the House of Reps.	How disposed of by the Senate.	Date of the act of Congress, and remarks.
Davis, Jane	(See Rezin Gere, heirs of.)	24	2		155							
Davis, Jesse, executor of	Pay due for revolutionary services	28	2	Petition	208	Rev. Claims.						
Davis, Jesse, executor of	Pay due for revolutionary services	29	1	Petition	389	Rev. Claims.						
Davis, Capt. Jesse	Commutation pay for revolutionary services.	15	2	Petition	40	Select				Discharged.		
Davis, Capt. Jesse	Commutation pay for revolutionary services.	16	1	Petition	139	Pens. & Rev. Cl'ms.	Mar. 22, 1820	Adverse		Laid on table.		
Davis, Capt. Jesse, widow and heirs of.	Commutation pay for revolutionary services.	19	1	Resolution	70	Select				Discharged; laid on table.		
Davis, Capt. Jesse, widow and heirs of.	Commutation pay for revolutionary services.	21	1	Petition	523	Rev. Claims	324	Adverse		Laid on table.		
Davis, Capt. Jesse, widow and heirs of.	Commutation pay and bounty land.	21	2	Petition	161	Rev. Claims				Discharged, laid on table.		
Davis, Capt. Jesse, widow and heirs of.	Commutation pay and bounty land.	22	1	Petition	210	Rev. Claims	Feb. 7, 1832	Adverse		Laid on table.		
Davis, Capt. Jesse, widow of.	Commutation pay and bounty land.	25	2	Documents	84	Rev. Pensions				Discharged; laid on table.		
Davis, John	Compensation for services as surgeon in revolutionary war.	2	1	Petition	454					Referred to Secretary War.		
Davis, John	Compensation for services as surgeon in revolutionary war.	2	2	Rep. of Secretary War.	735					Laid on table.		
Davis, John	Compensation for services as surgeon in revolutionary war.	4	1	Petition	385	Claims	April 5, 1796	Adverse		Laid on table		Leave to withdraw.
Davis, John	(See Samuel G. East, representatives of.)	11	2		164							
Davis, John	Compensation for provisions furnished U. S. army.	13	3	Petition	511	Claims				Discharged.		
Davis, John	Compensation for provisions furnished U. S. army.	14	2	Petition	163	Claims				Discharged; leave to withdraw.		
Davis, John, (Mass.)	Indemnity for French spoliations prior to 1800.	26	1	Memorial	182	Foreign Affairs	343	Favorable; bill.	319	Referred to Committee Whole House.		
Davis, John, son and heir of.	Commutation pay and bounty land	24	1	Petition	204	Rev. Claims.						
Davis, John, son and heir of.	Commutation pay and bounty land	24	2	Petition	155	Rev. Claims	69	Adverse		Laid on table		Leave to withdraw.
Davis, John, (Ga.)	Pension	21	2	Resolution	86	Military Pensions				Discharged; laid on table.		
Davis, John, (Ky.)	Pension	21	1	Petition	197	Military Pensions	April 7, 1830	Adverse		Laid on table.		
Davis, John, (Ky.)	Pension	21	2	Petition	218	Military Pensious				Discharged; laid on table.		
Davis, John, (Va.)	Restoration of pension	24	2	Resolution	78	Rev. Pensions.						
Davis, John, (Va.)	Restoration of pension	25	2	Resolution	240	Rev. Pensions	605	Favorable; bill	585	Passed	Rejected.	
Davis, John, (Va.)	Restoration of pension	25	3	Resolution	88	Rev. Pensions	31	Favorable; bill	931	Passed	Rejected.	
Davis, John, (Wisconsin).	Pension for services in war of 1812	25	2	Petition	399	Invalid Pensions	Mar. 7, 1838	Adverse		Laid on table.		
Davis, John	Revolutionary pension	26	1	Petition	171	Rev. Pensions	148	Favorable; bill	158	Passed	Indef. postp'd.	
Davis, John	Prize-money for capture of frigate Philadelphia.	19	2	House bill	98	Naval Affairs	74	With amend.	70	Referred to Committee Whole House.		
Davis, John	Prize-money for capture of frigate Philadelphia.	20	2	House bill	108	Naval Affairs	37	With't amend.	30	Rejected.		
Davis, John	Prize-money for captue of frigate Philadelphia.	21	1	House bill	137	Naval Affairs	Jan. 7, 1830	With't amend.	82	Laid on table.		
Davis, John	Prize-money for capture of frigate Philadelphia.	22	1	Papers on file	29	Naval Affairs	Dec. 23, 1831	Favorable; bill	98	Referred to Committee Whole House.		

List of private claims presented to the House of Representatives of the United States from the 1st to the 31st Congress, inclusive—Continued.

Names of claimants.	Nature or object of the claim.	Congress.	Session.	How brought before the House of Reps.	Page of journal.	To what committee of the House referred.	No. or date of the report.	Nature of the report.	No. of the bill.	How disposed of by the House of Reps.	How disposed of by the Senate.	Date of the act of Congress, and remarks.
Davis, John	Prize-money for capture of frigate Philadelphia.	23	1	Petition	36	Naval Affairs	45	Favorable; bill	50	Laid on table.		
Davis, John, heirs of	Prize-money for capture of Algerine vessels.	30	1	Petition	799	Naval Affairs.						
Davis, John, former widow of.	Revolutionary pension	26	1	Petition	323	Rev. Pensions	500	Favorable; bill	402	Referred to Committee Whole House.		
Davis, John, attorney of.	Indemnity for Indian depredations.	19	2	Petition	134	Indian Affairs	51	Favorable	......	Referred to Committee Whole House.		
Davis, John	(See James Hoge and John Davis.)	21	1	....	70							
Davis, John, administrator of.	Commutation pay for services in revolutionary war.	31	1	Petition	628	Rev. Claims	432	Favorable; bill	360	Referred to Committee Whole House.		
Davis, John B., *et al.*	(See Thomas Latta, administrator of.)	14	1	....	495							
Davis, John M. (Pa.)	Additional compensation for taking Fifth Census.	22	1	Petition	224	Judiciary	....	....	......	Discharged; laid on table.		
Davis, John P.	Indemnity for French spoliations prior to 1800.	26	1	Memorial	182	Foreign Affairs	343	Favorable; bill	319	Referred to Committee Whole House.		
Davis, Jonathan, *et al.*	Restoration of, or remuneration for, merchandise seized under act of July 6, 1812.	13	2	Petition	177, 270	Ways and Means	59	Favorable; bill	115	Passed	Passed	App'd April 6, 1814
Davis, Jonathan, *et al.*	Indemnity for French spoliations prior to 1800.	26	1	Memorial	182	Foreign Affairs	343	Favorable; bill	319	Referred to Committee Whole House.		
Davis, Jonathan, (Pa.)	Indemnity for losses sustained by United States troops in Canada.	22	1	Petition	513	Claims.						
Davis, Jonathan, (Pa.)	Indemnity for losses sustained by United States troops in Canada.	22	2	Petition	67	Claims.						
Davis, Jonathan, (Pa.)	Indemnity for losses sustained by United States troops in Canada.	23	1	Petition	129	Claims.						
Davis, Jonathan, (Pa.)	Indemnity for losses sustained by United States troops in Canada.	24	1	Petition	273	Claims	482	Favorable; bill	486	Referred to Committee Whole House.		
Davis, Jonathan, (Pa.)	Indemnity for losses sustained by United States troops in Canada.	25	2	Petition	36	Claims	21	Favorable; bill	33	Passed	Passed	App'd Mar. 19, 1838
Davis, Jonathan, (Pa.)	Payment for property taken for use of army in war of 1812.	25	2	Petition	51	Claims.						
Davis, Jonathan, (Pa.)	Payment for property taken for use of army in war of 1812.	25	3	Petition	120	Claims	44	Adverse	......	Laid on table.		
Davis, Joseph	Compensation for services as wagoner in revolutionary war.	15	1	Petition	129	Pens. & Rev. Cl'ms.	Feb. 13, 1818	Adverse	......	Rejected.		
Davis, Joseph	Reimbursement of expenses for capturing deserters in the Black Hawk war.	29	1	Petition	630	Claims	627	Adverse	......	Laid on table.		
Davis, Joseph W., administrator of.	Indemnity for fishery destroyed by United States government.	27	2	Petition	356	Claims.						
Davis, Joseph W., administrator of.	Indemnity for fishery destroyed by United States government.	27	3	Petition	72	Claims	56	Adverse	......	Laid on table.		
Davis, Joseph, former widow of.	Revolutionary pension	26	1	Res. and petition	556, 626	Rev. Pensions	423	Adverse	......	Laid on table.		
Davis, Joseph, (N. Y.)	Pension	19	2	Petition	285	Military Pensions	....	....	......	Discharged.		
Davis, Joseph, (Pa.)	Invalid pension	26	1	Documents	325	Invalid Pensions.						
Davis, Joseph, mother of.	Fishing bounty on schooner Mary and Hannah.	23	1	Petition	140	Commerce	Jan. 14, 1834	Favorable; bill.	193	Passed	Passed	App'd June 30, 1834
Davis, Joshua	Restoration of pension	17	2	Petition	119	Whole House.						
Davis, Josiah	Revolutionary pension	22	1	Resolution	450	Rev. Pensions.						

List of private claims presented to the House of Representatives of the United States from the 1st to the 31st Congress, inclusive—Continued.

Names of claimants.	Nature or object of the claim.	Congress.	Session.	How brought before the House of Reps.	Page of journal.	To what committee of the House referred.	No. or date of the report.	Nature of the report.	No. of the bill.	How disposed of by the House of Reps.	How disposed of by the Senate.	Date of the act of Congress, and remarks.
Davis, Lamar	Pension	10	1	House bill	232	Whole House	Mar. 17, 1808	With't amend.	78	Passed	Passed	App'd April 25, 1808
Davis, Levi, administrator of.	Compensation for revolutionary services.	30	2	Petition	75	Rev. Pensions				Discharged; laid on table.		
Davis, Lewis, (Ala.)	Permission to re-enter land	18	1	Petition	178	Public Lands				Laid on table.		
Davis, Lewis, (Tenn.)	Invalid pension	27	2	Petition	67	Invalid Pensions	235	Adverse		Laid on table.		
Davis, Levi, & Farus Forman.	Pay for services as attorneys in the case of United States *vs.* James M. Strode.	25	2	Documents	541	Claims	710	Adverse		Laid on table.		
Davis, Lot	Naval invalid pension	24	2	Petition	41	Naval Affairs	30	Adverse		Laid on table.		
Davis, Lot	Naval invalid pension	28	1	Petition	236	Naval Affairs	532	Favorable; bill	409	Referred to Committee Whole House.		
Davis, Lot	Naval invalid pension	28	2	Rep't Committee Whole House.	344	Whole House	Feb. 7, 1845	With't amend.	409	Passed	Ref. to Com. on Naval Affairs.	
Davis, Lot	Naval invalid pension	29	1	Petition	199	Invalid Pensions.						
Davis, Lot	Naval invalid pension	29	2	Petition	233	Naval Affairs.						
Davis, Lot	Naval invalid pension	30	1	Petition	637	Naval Affairs	512	Favorable; bill	439	Passed	Ref. to Com. on Naval Affairs.	
Davis, Lot	Naval invalid pension	31	1	Petition	233	Naval Affairs	232	Favorable; bill	227	Referred to Committee Whole House.		
Davis, Lot	Naval invalid pension	31	2	Rep't Committee Whole House.	182	Whole House	Jan. 24, 1851	With't amend.	227	Passed	Ref. to Com. on Naval Affairs.	
Davis, Lucy	(See William Davis, widow of, N. Y.)	25	2		37							
Davis, Martha	(See Benjamin Davis, widow of.)	16	1		27							
Davis, Mary	(See Samuel Davis, widow of.)	23	1		140							
Davis, Mary Ann	(See Nathan Speak, heirs of.)	24	1		204							
Davis, Mary	(See Isaac Davis, widow of.)	27	2		104							
Davis, Mary	Indemnity for French spoliations prior to 1800.	26	1	Memorial	182	Foreign Affairs	343	Favorable; bill	319	Referred to Committee Whole House.		
Davis, Mary F	For benefit of act of March 3, 1837, respecting widows of seamen, &c.	29	1	Petition	476	Rev. Pensions.						
Davis, Mary	(See Solomon Davis, heirs of)	17	2		91							
Davis, Michael E	Confirmation of title to land in Louisiana.	29	1	Petition	572	Priv. Land Claims.						
Davis, Morton	Arrears of pension	31	1	Petition	383	Invalid Pensions.						
Davis, Moses, (Pa.)	Revolutionary pension	25	2	Petition	404	Rev. Pensions	Feb. 17, 1828	Adverse		Laid on table.		
Davis, Moses, (N. H.)	Invalid pension	27	3	Petition	85	Invalid Pensions.						
Davis, Moses, (N. H.)	Invalid pension	28	1	Petition	359	Invalid Pensions	231	Adverse		Laid on table.		
Davis, Moses, (N. H.)	Invalid pension	28	2	Petition	54	Invalid Pensions.						
Davis, Moses, (N. H.)	Invalid pension	29	1	Petition	258	Invalid Pensions	533	Adverse		Laid on table		Leave to withdraw.
Davis, Nancy	(See James Moore, heirs of widow of.)	31	1		414							
Davis, Nathan	Invalid pension	3	1	Rep. of Secretary War.	131	Select	May 26, 1794	Favorable; bill ordered.	62	Passed	Passed	App'd June 7, 1794
Davis, Nathan	Compensation for services, supplies, or losses in revolutionary war.	1	3	Petition	350	Referred to Sec. of War.	Feb. 26, 1791	Report		Laid on table.		
Davis, Nathan	Arrears of pension	4	1	Petition	385	Claims	Jan. 27, 1796	Adverse		Leave to withdraw.		
Davis, Nathaniel	Invalid pension	25	2	Petition	71	Invalid Pensions	298	Favorable; bill	338	Passed	Indef. postp'd.	
Davis, Nathaniel	Invalid pension	25	3	Petition	89	Invalid Pensions	81	Favorable; bill	959	Referred to Committee Whole House.		
Davis, Nathaniel	Invalid pension	26	1	Petition	161	Invalid Pensions	186	Favorable; bill	198	Passed	Indef. postp'd.	
Davis, Nathaniel, heirs of.	Invalid pension	26	1	Documents	325	Invalid Pensions.						

List of private claims presented to the House of Representatives of the United States from the 1st to the 31st Congress, inclusive—Continued.

Names of claimants.	Nature or object of the claim.	Congress.	Session.	How brought before the House of Reps.	Page of journal.	To what committee of the House referred.	No. or date of the report.	Nature of the report.	No. of the bill.	How disposed of by the House of Reps.	How disposed of by the Senate.	Date of the act of Congress, and remarks.
Davis, Nathaniel, heirs of.	Invalid pension	26	2	Petition	77	Invalid Pensions	227	Adverse		Laid on table.		
Davis, Nathaniel, heirs of.	Invalid pension	27	2	Petition	60	Invalid Pensions	229	Adverse		Laid on table.		
Davis, Needham	(See Samuel Davis, heir of.)	22	2		264							
Davis, Oliver	Bounty land for services in war of 1812	21	1	Petition	273	Claims				Discharged; referred to Priv. Land Cl'ms.		
Davis, Philip	(See John E. Metcalf, *et al*)	25	2		1052							
Davis, Rachael	Continuation of pension	28	1	Petition	849	Rev. Pensions.						
Davis, Richard, and wife	(See Lieut. Jonathan Dye, heirs of.)	26	1		164							
Davis, Robert, (Ky.)	Compensation for horse and equipage lost in Seminole war.	19	1	Petition	136	Claims	Jan. 20, 1826	Adverse		Laid on table.		
Davis, Robert, (Ky.)	Compensation for horse and equipage lost in Seminole war.	19	2	Petition	31	Claims	Dec. 22, 1826	Adverse		Laid on table.		
Davis, Robert, (Ky.)	Compensation for horse and equipage lost in Seminole war.	20	1	Petition	31	Claims	10	Adverse.				
Davis, Robert, (Ky.)	Compensation for horse and equipage lost in Seminole war.	21	1	Resolution	94	Claims				Discharged; laid on table.		
Davis, Robert, (Ky.)	Compensation for horse and equipage lost in Seminole war.	25	3	Petition	120	Claims	43	Adverse		Laid on table.		
Davis, Robert, (Ky.)	Compensation for horse and equipage lost in Seminole war.	27	2	Petition	382	Claims	467	Favorable; bill	317	Passed	Ref. to Com. on Claims.	
Davis, Robert C.	Pension	14	1	House bill	622	Pens. & Rev. Cl'ms.	April 11, 1816	With't amend.	171	Passed	Passed	App'd April 30, 1816
Davis, Robert, (N. C.)	Compensation for services in revolutionary war.	22	1	Petition	513	Rev. Claims.						
Davis, Richard, (Pa.)	Indemnity for French spoliations prior to 1800.	26	1	Memorial	182	Foreign Affairs	343	Favorable; bill	319	Referred to Committee Whole House.		
Davis, Capt. Richard, heirs of.	Commutation pay and bounty land	23	1	Petition, &c.	395, 571	Rev. Claims.						
Davis, Samuel, (Miss.)	Pre emption right to land	12	1	Petition	128	Public Lands.						
Davis, Samuel, (Miss.)	Pre emption right to land	12	2	Petition	550	Public Lands.						
Davis, Samuel	Revolutionary pension	22	1	Petition	534	Rev. Pensions				Discharged; laid on table.		
Davis, Samuel, heir of	Confirmation of title to land in Florida.	22	2	Petition	264	Priv. Land Claims.						
Davis, Samuel, *et al*, (Mo.)	Pre-emption right to purchase land on which they reside.	25	2	Petition	179	Public Lands.						
Davis, Samuel, *et al*, (Mo.)	Pre-emption right to purchase land on which they reside.	25	3	Petition	98	Public Lands	Jan. 2, 1839	Adverse.				
Davis, Samuel, *et al*, (Mo.)	Pre emption right to purchase land on which they reside.	26	1	Petition	600	Public Lands.						
Davis, Samuel, widow of	Fishing bounty on schooner Mary and Hannah.	23	1	Petition	140	Commerce	Jan. 14, 1834	Favorable; bill	193	Passed	Passed	App'd June 30, 1834
Davis, Samuel	Fishing bounty on schooner Daniel	30	1	Petition	724	Ways and Means				Discharged; referred to Com. Commerce.		
Davis, Sanford, widow of.	Restoration of pension	19	1	Petition	108	Military Affairs.						
Davis, Sarah C.	(See Lieut. Jonathan Dye, heirs of)	29	1		179							
Davis, Sarah	(See Edward E. Davis, widow of)	25	2		404							
Davis, Sarah	(See Wm. Davis, widow of)	27	3		113							
Davis, Sally	(See Wm. Davis, widow of, N. Y.)	28	1		256							
Davis, Simon, *et al.*	(See John Jells, sureties of)	8	1		428							
Davis, Solomon	Permission to correct error in entry of land.	30	1	Petition	398	Public Lands.						
Davis, Solomon	Permission to correct error in entry of land.	30	2	Petition	146	Public Lands	Feb. 27, 1849	Favorable; bill	795	Passed	Passed	App'd March 2, 1849

List of private claims presented to the House of Representatives of the United States from the 1st to the 31st Congress, inclusive—Continued.

Names of claimants.	Nature or object of the claim.	Congress.	Session.	How brought before the House of Reps.	Page of journal.	To what committee of the House referred.	No. or date of the report.	Nature of the report.	No. of the bill.	How disposed of by the House of Reps.	How disposed of by the Senate.	Date of the act of Congress, and remarks.
Davis, Solomon, heirs of..	Payment for Seneca stone to be used at Capitol.	17	2	Petition	91	Public Buildings ..	82	Adverse	......	Laid on table.		
Davis, Stephen B........	Restoration of pension..........	17	1	Petition	288	Whole House.....	....	....	......	Leave to withdraw.		
Davis, Stephen.........	(See Alexander Davis, *et al*)....	23	1	....	387							
Davis, Theodosius......	Invalid pension...............	30	1	Petition	356	Invalid Pensions ..	461	Adverse	......	Laid on table.		
Davis, Thomas Lamar....	Pension	10	1	House bill	232	Whole House.....	Mar. 17, 1808	With't amend.	78	Passed	Passed	App'd April 25, 1808
Davis, Thomas..........	Increase of pension............	29	1	Petition	523	Rev. Pensions.						
Davis, Thomas..........	Invalid pension...............	31	1	Petition	909	Invalid Pensions.						
Davis, Thomas..........	(See Elijah Cook, administrator, *et al.*)	21	2	....	99							
Davis, Thomas N........	(See Solomon Davis, heirs of.)...	17	2	....	91							
Davis, Thomas..........	(See William and Thomas Davis.)	26	1	....	182	....	343	....	319			
Davis, William, (N. Y.)..	Revolutionary pension..........	17	2	Res. and docs...	138	Rev. Pensions.....	....	....	......	Discharged; laid on table.		
Davis, William, (N. Y.)..	Revolutionary pension..........	18	1	Petition and docs	23, 31	Rev. Pensions.....	Jan. 12, 1824	Adverse	......	Laid on table.		
Davis, William, (N. Y.)..	Revolutionary pension....... ..	18	2	Petition	95	Rev. Pensions	Jan. 21, 1825	Adverse	......	Laid on table.		
Davis, William, (N. Y.)..	Revolutionary pension..........	21	1	Petition	47	Military Pensions..	Dec. 31, 1829	Adverse	......	Laid on table.		
Davis, William, (N. Y.)..	Revolutionary pension..........	23	2	Petition	197	Rev. Pensions.						
Davis, William, (N. Y.)..	Revolutionary pension..........	24	1	Petition	107	Rev. Pensions	416	Favorable; bill	384	Passed	Indef. postp'd.	
Davis, William, (N. Y.)..	Revolutionary pension..........	25	2	Petition	37	Rev. Pensions.....	214	Favorable; bill	251	Passed	Rejected.	
Davis, William, widow of	Revolutionary pension..........	26	1	Petition	171	Rev. Pensions	551	Adverse	......	Laid on table.		
Davis, William, widow of.	Revolutionary pension..........	27	2	Petition	684	Rev. Pensions	784	Adverse	......	Laid on table.		
Davis, William, widow of.	Revolutionary pension..........	28	2	Petition	46	Rev. Pensions	117	Favorable; bill	596	Referred to Committee Whole House.		
Davis, William, widow of.	Revolutionary pension..........	29	1	Petition	102	Rev. Pensions	483	Adverse	......	Laid on table.		
Davis, William, jr.......	For debenture certificates on domestic spirits exported.	16	2	Petition	116	Ways and Means..	....	....	......	Discharged; referred to Com. on Commerce.		
Davis, William, jr.......	For debenture certificates on domestic spirits exported.	17	1	Petition	133	Commerce.						
Davis, William	Bounty land under act of September, 1850.	31	2	Petition	179	Public Lands.						
Davis, William	Revolutionary pension..........	22	1	Petition	412	Rev. Pensions	....	....	......	Discharged; laid on table.		
Davis, William	Revolutionary pension..........	25	2	Petition	729	Rev. Pensions	214	Favorable; bill	251	Passed	Adverse.	
Davis, William G., and wife.	Confirmation of title to land in Florida.	22	2	Petition	138	Priv. Land Claims.	Jan. 7, 1833	Adverse	......	Laid on table.		
Davis, William G., and wife.	Confirmation of title to land in Florida.	23	1	Petition	319	Priv. Land Claims.	Feb. 21, 1834	Adverse	......	Laid on table.		
Davis, Wm. G., and Mary Ann.	Compensation for use and occupation of property by United States troops in Seminole war.	29	2	Memorial.......	146	Claims.						
Davis, Wm. G., and Mary Ann.	Compensation for use and occupation of property by United States troops in Seminole war.	29	2	Senate bill	374	Claims	Feb. 26, 1847	With't amend.	S. 81	Referred to Committee Whole House.		
Davis, Wm. G., and Mary Ann.	Compensation for use and occupation of property by United States troops in Seminole war.	30	1	Petition	108	Claims	....	....	......	Discharged; laid on table.		
Davis, Wm. G., and Mary Ann.	Compensation for use and occupation of property by United States troops in Seminole war.	31	1	Petition	383	Claims.						
Davis, William, (Ohio.)..	Bounty land for revolutionary services.	26	1	Petition	333	Public Lands.....	....	....	......	Discharged.		

List of private claims presented to the House of Representatives of the United States from the 1st to the 31st Congress, inclusive—Continued.

Names of claimants.	Nature or object of the claim.	Congress.	Session.	How brought before the House of Reps.	Page of journal.	To what committee of the House referred.	No. or date of the report.	Nature of the report.	No. of the bill.	How disposed of by the House of Reps.	How disposed of by the Senate.	Date of the act of Congress, and remarks.
Davis, William C., (a New Orleans branch pilot.)	Authority to enter certain land at minimum price.	28	1	Petition	77	Priv. Land Claims.	9	Favorable; bill	35	Passed	Passed	App'd June 17, 1844
Davis, William R.	Compensation for services in Indiana militia.	27	2	Senate bill	1056	Claims	July 5, 1842	With't amend.	S. 178	Referred to Committee Whole House.		
Davis, William R.	Compensation for services in Indiana militia.	28	1	Senate bill	868	Claims	May 2, 1844	With't amend.	S. 124	Passed	Passed	App'd Jan. 17, 1844
Davis, William	(See Alexander Davis, *et al.*)	23	1	....	387							
Davis, William F. R., sen.	Revolutionary pension	25	3	Petition	130	Rev. Pensions	....	....	......	Discharged.		
Davis, William, (N. Y.,) widow of.	Revolutionary pension	28	1	Petition	256	Rev. Pensions	....	....	......	Discharged; laid on table.		
Davis, William, (N. Y.,) widow of.	Revolutionary pension	28	2	Petition	176	Rev. Pensions.						
Davis, William, widow of.	For amount due husband as engineer in war of 1812.	27	3	Petition	113	Claims.						
Davis, William, widow of.	For amount due husband as engineer in war of 1812.	29	1	Petition	69	Claims.						
Davis, William	Payment of $365 for books furnished State Department.	24	2	Petition	217	Library.						
Davis, William	Compensation for work done, and materials furnished on Cumberland road.	23	1	Res. and papers.	589	Claims	455	Adverse	......	....	....	See Report No. 449.
Davis, William, administratrix of.	Compensation for services and expenses while in command of U. S. schooner Eufaula.	31	1	Petition	391	Naval Affairs.						
Davis, William & Thomas	Indemnity for French spoliations prior to 1800.	26	1	Memorial	182	Foreign Affairs	343	Favorable; bill	319	Referred to Committee Whole House.		
Davis, Winthrop	Revolutionary pension	21	1	Petition	377	Military Pensions	May 29, 1830	Favorable; bill	499	Referred to Committee Whole House.		
Davis, Winthrop	Revolutionary pension	21	2	Rep. Committee Whole House.	319	Whole House	Feb. 16, 1831	With't amend.	499	Passed	Amended.	
Davis, Winthrop	Revolutionary pension	22	1	Petition	90	Rev. Pensions	118	Favorable; bill	194	Referred to Committee Whole House.		
Davis, Winthrop	Revolutionary pension	22	2	Rep't Committee Whole House.	66	Whole House	Dec. 15, 1832	With't amend.	194	Laid on table.		
Davison, Bracket	(See Bracket Davidson.)											
Davlin, John, representatives of.	To exchange entry of land	23	1	Petition	132	Public Lands	Jan. 7, 1834	Favorable; bill	140	Passed	Indef. postp'd.	
Davlin, John, representatives of.	To exchange entry of land	24	1	Petition	114	Public Lands	Feb. 16, 1836	Favorable; bill	340	Referred to Committee Whole House.		
Davlin, John, representatives of.	To exchange entry of land	25	2	Petition	42	Public Lands	Dec. 28, 1837	Favorable; bill	238	Referred to Committee Whole House.		
Davlin, John, representatives of.	To exchange entry of land	25	3	Rep't Committee Whole House	376	Whole House	Jan. 25, 1839	Favorable; bill	238	Passed	Passed	App'd March 2, 1839
Davlin, John, representatives of.	To revive act of March 2, 1839, to surrender patent.	27	2	Resolution	453	Priv. Land Claims.	850	Favorable; bill	493	Engrossed.		
Davlin, John, representatives of.	To revive act of March 2, 1839, to surrender patent.	27	3	House bill	89	Whole House	Dec. 23, 1842	With't amend.	493	Passed	Passed	App'd March 3, 1843
Davy, Jacob	Remission of duties on property destroyed by fire.	14	1	Petition	171	Ways and Means	....	....	......	Leave to withdraw.		
Davy, Jacob	Remission of duties on property destroyed by fire.	14	2	Petition	101	Ways and Means	Jan. 28, 1817	Adverse.				
Davy, Jacob	Remission of duties on property destroyed by fire.	16	1	Petition	48	Ways and Means	Jan. 17, 1820	Adverse.				

List of private claims presented to the House of Representatives of the United States from the 1st to the 31st Congress, inclusive—Continued.

Names of claimants.	Nature or object of the claim.	Congress.	Session.	How brought before the House of Reps.	Page of journal.	To what committee of the House referred.	No. or date of the report.	Nature of the report.	No. of the bill.	How disposed of by the House of Reps.	How disposed of by the Senate.	Date of the act of Congress, and remarks.
Davy, William, *et al*	For extension of time of oath and remission of forfeiture.	10	1	Memorial	48					Laid on table.		
Davy, William, *et al*	For extension of time of oath and remission of forfeiture.	11	1	Petition	16	Com. and Manuf.						
Daw, John	(See John Dow.)	24	1		433		555		546			App'd June 28, 1836
Daws, Josephus	Allowance of mileage to volunteers in Mexico.	30	1	Petition	115	Claims	482	Adverse		Laid on table.		
Dawkins, Charles, by Elizabeth, widow of.	Invalid pension	27	2	Petition	219	Invalid Pensions	576	Favorable; bill	372	Referred to Committee Whole House.		
Dawkins, Charles, by Elizabeth, widow of.	Invalid pension	27	3	Rep't Committee Whole House.	88	Whole House	Dec. 23, 1842	With't amend	372	Passed	Adverse; laid on table.	
Daws, Mary, *et al*	Pre-emption right to land	22	1	Petition	134	Public Lands	94	Favorable; bill	184	Passed	Passed with amendment.	App'd July 14, 1832
Dawson, A. B	Indemnity for losses sustained by Creek Indians.	31	2	Petition	74	Indian Affairs				Discharged; laid on table.		
Dawson, Deborah	(See Joseph Dawson, widow of.)	22	1		857							
Dawson, Frederick, *et al.*	Indemnity for vessels furnished Republic of Texas transferred to United States.	30	1	Petition	617	Judiciary.						
Dawson, Frederick, *et al.*	Indemnity for vessels furnished Republic of Texas transferred to United States.	30	2	Petition	164	Judiciary	13	Favorable; bill	707	Referred to Committee Whole House.		
Dawson, Frederick, *et al.*	Indemnity for vessels furnished Republic of Texas transferred to United States.	31	1	Petition	224	Judiciary.						
Dawson, George	Compensation for work done on Cumberland road.	24	1	Senate bill	928	Claims	734	With't amend.	S. 134	Passed	Passed	App'd July 2, 1836
Dawson, James L	Reimbursement of money expended in making road to Little Rock, Arkansas.	22	1	Petition	31	Military Affairs	Dec. 28, 1831	Favorable; bill	69	Passed	Rejected.	
Dawson, Jared, (an Indian)	Permission to change location of land.	27	3	Petition	259	Public Lands	160	Favorable; bill	776	Read 1st and 2d time.		
Dawson, John, heirs of	Confirmation of land title	24	1	Petition	635	Priv. Land Claims.						
Dawson, John, heirs of	Confirmation of land title	24	2	Petition	49	Priv. Land Claims.	36	Favorable; bill	783	Referred to Committee Whole House.		
Dawson, John, heirs of	Confirmation of land title	25	2	Petition	43	Priv. Land Claims.	295	Favorable; bill	335	Referred to Committee Whole House.		
Dawson, John, heirs of	Confirmation of land title	25	3	Rep. Committee Whole House.	377	Whole House	Jan. 25, 1839	With't amend.	335	Passed	Passed	App'd March 3, 1839
Dawson, John	Compensation for services as pension agent.	28	2	Petition	229	Claims.						
Dawson, John	Compensation for services as pension agent.	30	1	Petition	276	Claims.						
Dawson, John	(See George B. Russell)	39	1		87							
Dawson, Joseph, widow of	Revolutionary pension	22	1	Petition	857	Rev. Pensions.						
Dawson, Joshua	Increase of pay as clerk in Treasury Department.	3	1	Memorial	88	Select	47	Favorable; bill	69	Passed.	Rejected.	
Dawson, Peter P	Pension	20	1	Resolution	155	Military Pensions.						
Dawson, Peter P	Pension	21	2	Petition	120	Military Pensions				Discharged; laid on table.		
Dawson, Peter P	Compensation for services in United States army in 1792.	24	2	Petition	260	Rev. Pensions				Discharged; laid on table.		
Dawson, Robert	Remission of duties on raw silk	4	1	Petition	473	Com. and Manuf.						

List of private claims presented to the House of Representatives of the United States from the 1st to the 31st Congress, inclusive—Continued.

Names of claimants.	Nature or object of the claim.	Congress.	Session.	How brought before the House of Reps.	Page of journal.	To what committee of the House referred.	No. or date of the report.	Nature of the report.	No. of the bill.	How disposed of by the House of Reps.	How disposed of by the Senate.	Date of the act of Congress, and remarks.
Day, Asa	Compensation for losses sustained in war of 1812.	24	1	Petition	28	Foreign Affairs.						
Day, Asa	Pension for services in revolutionary and late war.	30	1	Petition	685	Rev. Pensions	698	Adverse		Laid on table.		
Day, Lieutenant Alvin	(See John Campbell and Alvin Day.)	15	2		306							
Day, Benjamin	Revolutionary pension	18	2	Petition	54	Rev. Claims	54	Adverse		Laid on table.		
Day, Charles, and J. R. Butts.	Permission to import iron free of duty.	24	2	Memorial	316	Whole House.						
Day, Charles, and J. R. Butts.	Permission to import iron free of duty.	25	2	Senate bill	611	Manufactures	Mar. 14, 1838	With amend.	S. 147	Passed	Passed	App'd July 7, 1838
Day, Chauncey	Pension for services in war of 1812.	29	1	Petition	517	Invalid Pensions.						
Day, Ezekiel	Pension	21	1	Petition	471	Military Pensions.				Discharged; laid on table.		
Day, Ira, and M. Catrell.	Compensation for mail service	23	1	Petition	191	P. Of. and P. Roads.				Discharged; laid on table.		
Day, Ira	Compensation for mail service	31	2	Senate bill	106				S. 89	Referred to Committee Whole House.		
Day, James	Increase of pay as Executive messenger.	29	1	Petition	309	Ways and Means.						
Day, John	(See Canadian refugees)	6	2		733							
Day, John	Arrears of pension	4	1	Petition	544	Claims.						
Day, John	Arrears of pension	4	2	Petition	635	Claims	Jan. 16, 1797	Adverse.				
Day, John, (Ohio)	Pension	19	1	Petition	128	Military Pensions.	164	Adverse		Laid on table.		
Day, John, (Ohio)	Pension	20	1	Petition	38	Military Pensions.	Feb. 13, 1828	Favorable; bill	166	Passed.		
Day, John, (Ohio)	Pension	20	2	House bill	55	Military Pensions.	Dec. 12, 1828	Favorable; bill	311	Referred to Committee Whole House.		
Day, John, (Ohio)	Pension	21	1	Petition	48	Military Pensions.	Jan. 5, 1830	By bill	72	Passed	Passed with amendment.	App'd May 20, 1830; name of petitioner omitted in law.
Day, John, (Ohio)	Pension	22	1	Petition	172	Rev. Pensions.						
Day, John	Naval pension	25	2	Petition	113	Naval Affairs				Discharged; laid on table.		
Day, John	To refund tonnage duty exacted by collector at New Orleans.	29	1	Petition	812	Claims.						
Day, John, heirs of	Relief on account of services in U. States army.	31	1	Petition	595	Rev. Pensions.						
Day, John, heirs of	Bounty land for services in revolutionary war.	31	1	Petition	596	Public Lands.						
Day, John, attorney of	Indemnity for Indian depredations.	22	2	Petition	178	Indian Affairs.						
Day, John, attorney of	Indemnity for Indian depredations.	23	1	Memorial	629	Indian Affairs.						
Day, John, & David Lentry	Compensation for mail services	25	2	Petition	931	P. Of. and P. Roads.						
Day, Joseph	(See Abijah Barnum)	8	1		446							
Day, Capt. Joseph, heirs of.	Commutation pay, and interest thereon.	24	1	Petition	204	Rev. Claims	819	Adverse		Laid on table.		
Day, Lewis	Revolutionary pension	22	1	Resolution	160	Rev. Pensions.						
Day, Robert	Revolutionary pension	23	1	Petition	569	Rev. Claims.						
Day, Samuel	Arrears of pension	25	3	Petition	129	Invalid Pensions	Feb. 6, 1839	Adverse		Laid on table.		
Day, Samuel	Arrears of pension	27	2	Petition	771	Invalid Pensions.						
Day, Samuel	Arrears of pension	27	3	Petition	154	Invalid Pensions.						
Day, Samuel	Arrears of pension	28	1	Petition	509	Invalid Pensions.						
Day, Samuel, by Sally, widow of.	Revolutionary pension	25	3	Petition	562	Rev. Pensions				Discharged.		

List of private claims presented to the House of Representatives of the United States from the 1st to the 31st Congress, inclusive—Continued.

Names of claimants.	Nature or object of the claim.	Congress.	Session.	How brought before the House of Reps.	Page of journal.	To what committee of the House referred.	No. or date of the report.	Nature of the report.	No. of the bill.	How disposed of by the House of Reps.	How disposed of by the Senate.	Date of the act of Congress, and remarks.
60 Day, Samuel, by Sally, widow of.	Revolutionary pension	26	1	Petition	359	Rev. Pensions.						
Day, Samuel, by Sally, widow of.	Revolutionary pension	27	2	Petition	153	Rev. Pensions	304	Favorable; bill	273	Passed	Indef. postp'd.	
Day, Sylvester	Compensation for property destroyed by burning the British brig Detroit.	12	2	Petition	657	Claims				Leave to withdraw.		
Day, Sylvester	Reimbursement of money paid for quarters for sick.	23	2	Petition	197	Military Affairs	111	Favorable; bill	738	Referred to Committee Whole House.		
Day, Sylvester	Reimbursement of money paid for quarters for sick.	24	1	Petition	64	Military Affairs				Discharged; laid on table.		
Day, Sylvester	Reimbursement of money paid for quarters for sick.	24	2	Petition	75	Military Affairs.						
Day, Sylvester	Reimbursement of money paid for quarters for sick.	25	2	Petition	84	Military Affairs	401	Adverse		Laid on table.		
Dayh, Margaret	(See Captain James Bradford, widow of.)	4	1		488							
Dayhoff, Frederick	Permission to correct error in entry of land.	18	1	Petition	116	Public Lands.						
Dayton, John	Release from imprisonment under embargo act.	11	2	Petition	289	Com. and Manuf.						
Dayton, John, by Nancy, widow of.	Renewal of final settlement certificates.	22	2	Resolution	34	Rev. Claims.						
Dayton, Jonathan, by Susan, widow of.	Provision for support	20	2	Memorial	290	Whole House.						
Dayton, Jonathan, by Susan, widow of.	Provision for support	21	1	Petition	37	Rev. Claims.						
Dayton, Jonathan, by Susan, widow of.	Provision for support	22	1	Petition	97	Rev. Pensions				Discharged.		
Dayton, Jonathan, by Susan, widow of.	Provision for support	22	2	Petition	41	Rev. Claims.						
Da Costa, Jose Joaquin, & Da Silva Toas Jose.	Release from imprisonment in New York at suit of the U. States.	5	2	Petition	215	Whole House.						
Da Costa, Jose Joaquin, surety of.	Release from payment of judgment against him.	9	1	Petition	309	Com. and Manuf.	April 2, 1806			Referred to Committee Whole House.		
Da Costa, Jose Joaquin, surety of.	Release from payment of judgment against him.	10	1	Petition	150	Com. and Manuf.	Mar. 21, 1808	Favorable; bill.	80	Recommitted.		
Da Ponte, Lorenzo	Reimbursement of duties paid on books.	20	2	Petition	176	Ways and Means.						
Deadrick, David, executors of.	Remuneration for wagon and horses furnished United States troops in 1813 and 1814.	29	1	Petition	756	Claims.						
Deadrick, George M.	Balance of pay due a certain detachment of troops for services in 1792 and 1793.	8	1	Petition	579	Ways and Means				Leave to report by bill.		
Deagon, George Jacob	Invalid pension	9	1	Petition	235	Claims	Mar. 28, 1806	Report		Leave to withdraw.		
Deal, James	Indemnity for French spoliations prior to 1800.	26	1	Memorial	182	Foreign Affairs	343	Favorable; bill.	319	Referred to Committee Whole House.		
Deal, James, heirs of	Indemnity for French spoliations prior to 1800.	31	1	Petition	1076	Foreign Affairs	365	Favorable; bill.	318	Referred to Committee Whole House.		
Deale, Samuel	Revolutionary pension	24	2	Petition	45	Rev. Pensions				Discharged; laid on table.		
Dealty, James	Increase of pension	26	1	Petition	171	Rev. Pensions	120	Favorable; bill.	130	Passed	Indef. postp'd.	

List of private claims presented to the House of Representatives of the United States from the 1st to the 31st Congress, inclusive—Continued.

Names of claimants.	Nature or object of the claim.	Congress.	Session.	How brought before the House of Reps.	Page of journal.	To what committee of the House referred.	No. or date of the report.	Nature of the report.	No. of the bill.	How disposed of by the House of Reps.	How disposed of by the Senate.	Date of the act of Congress, and remarks.
Deamit, John	Compensation for losses sustained by carrying United States mail.	30	1	Petition	521	P. Of. and P. Roads.						
Deamit, John	Compensation for losses sustained by carrying United States mail.	31	1	Petition	415	P. Of. and P. Roads.	160	Favorable; bill.	180	Referred to Committee Whole House.		
Deamit, John	Compensation for losses sustained by carrying United States mail.	31	2	Rep't Committee Whole House.	103	Whole House	Jan. 3, 1851	With't amend.	180	Passed	With't amend.	
Dean, Benjamin, agent of.	Bounty land for services in revolutionary war.	23	1	Petition	195	Rev. Claims.						
Dean, Benjamin, agent of.	Bounty land for services in revolutionary war.	24	1	Petition	431	Rev. Claims	April 21, 1836	Adverse		Laid on table.		
Dean, Daniel	Bounty land, horse lost, and services in war of 1812.	27	2	Petition	312	Claims	705	Adverse		Laid on table.		
Dean, Daniel	Bounty land, horse lost, and services in war of 1812.	28	1	Petition	194	Claims	82	Favorable; bill.	99	Referred to Committee Whole House.		
Dean, Edward	Pension	15	1	Petition	456	Whole House.						
Dean, Edward	Pension	15	2	Petition	43	Pens. & Rev. Cl'ms.				Discharged; referred to Secretary of War.		
Deane, Edmond	Revolutionary pension	22	1	Petition	470	Rev. Pensions.						
Deane, Edmond	Arrears of pension	25	2	Petition	327	Rev. Pensions				Discharged; laid on table.		
Dean, Ezekiel	Bounty land	27	2	Affidavit	556	Rev. Claims				Discharg'd, and to Public Lands.		
Dean, Gilbert	Compensation for services in revolutionary war.	3	2	Petition	271	Claims				Laid on table.		
Dean, Gilbert	Compensation for services in revolutionary war.	4	2	Report	629	Claims	Dec. 27, 1796	Adverse		Leave to withdraw.		
Dean, James	Invalid pension	3	2	Rep. of Secretary War.	350	Claims	Feb. 28, 1795	Favorable; bill	130	Passed	Indef. postp'd.	
Dean, James	Invalid pension	4	1	Rep. of Secretary of War.	445	Claims	Feb. 18, 1796	Favorable; bill	156	Passed	Passed	App'd April 20, 1796
Dean, John, (N. Y.)	Revolutionary pension	22	1	Petition	574	Rev. Pensions.						
Dean, John, (Ind.)	Invalid pension for services in war of 1812.	25	3	Petition	129	Invalid Pensions.						
Dean, John, (Ind.)	Invalid pension for services in war of 1812.	26	1	Petition	162	Invalid Pensions	259	Adverse		Laid on table.		
Dean, John, (Ind.)	Invalid pension for services in war of 1812.	27	2	Petition	377	Invalid Pensions				Discharged; laid on table.		
Dean, John, (Ind.)	Invalid pension for services in war of 1812.	28	1	Petition	945	Invalid Pensions.						
Dean, John, (Ind.)	Invalid pension for services in war of 1812.	28	2	Petition	199	Invalid Pensions.						
Dean, Joseph, executor of.	Indemnity for French spoliations prior to 1800.	26	1	Memorial	182	Foreign Affairs	343	Favorable; bill	319	Referred to Committee Whole House.		
Dean, Lemuel	Invalid pension	3	2	Rep. of Secretary War.	350	Claims	Feb. 28, 1795	Favorable; bill ordered.	130	Passed	Indef. postp'd.	
Dean, Lemuel	Invalid pension	4	1	Report and docs.	445	Claims	Feb. 18, 1796	Favorable; bill ordered.	156	Passed	Passed	App'd April 20, 1796
Dean, Lemuel	Increase of pension	10	1	House bill	232	Whole House	Mar. 17, 1808	With't amend.	78	Passed	Passed	App'd April 25, 1808
Dean, Olive	Continuation of pension	27	2	Petition	256	Rev. Pensions.						
Deans, Samuel	(See Benjamin Goodwin, administrator of.)	23	1		188							
Dean, Samuel, (Conn.)	Restoration of pension	17	2	Petition	163	Whole House.						
Dean, Samuel, (Conn.)	Restoration of pension	19	1	Petition	221	Military Pensions	164	Adverse		Laid on table.		

List of private claims presented to the House of Representatives of the United States from the 1st to the 31st Congress, inclusive—Continued.

Names of claimants.	Nature or object of the claim.	Congress.	Session.	How brought before the House of Reps.	Page of journal.	To what committee of the House referred.	No. or date of the report.	Nature of the report.	No. of the bill.	How disposed of by the House of Reps.	How disposed of by the Senate.	Date of the act of Congress, and remarks.
Dean, Samuel, (Conn.)	Restoration of pension	19	2	Petition	186	Military Pensions.						
Dean, Samuel, (Conn.)	Restoration of pension	20	1	Petition	56	Military Pensions.						
Dean, Samuel, (Conn.)	Restoration of pension	21	1	Petition	36	Military Affairs.	April 6, 1830	Adverse	......	Laid on table.		
Dean, Samuel, (Conn.)	Restoration of pension	21	2	Petition	67	Military Affairs.						
Dean, Samuel, (Conn.)	Revolutionary pension	24	2	Petition	399	Rev. Pensions.						
Dean, Samuel, (Conn.)	Arrears of pension	25	2	Petition	116	Rev. Pensions.						
Dean, Samuel, (Conn.)	Revolutionary pension	25	3	Petition	460	Rev. Pensions.						
Dean, Samuel, (Conn.)	Revolutionary pension	26	1	Petition	173	Rev. Pensions	....	....	......	Discharged; laid on table.		
Deane, Silas, heirs of	Equitable settlement of accounts	23	2	Petition	196	Rev. Claims.						
Deane, Silas, heirs of	Equitable settlement of accounts	24	1	Petition, &c.,	102	Rev. Claims	....	....	......	Referred to Secretary Treasury.		
Deane, Silas, heirs of	Equitable settlement of accounts	24	2	Petition	216	Rev. Claims.						
Deane, Silas, heirs of	Equitable settlement of accounts	25	2	Memorial	407	Foreign Affairs.						
Deane, Silas, heirs of	Equitable settlement of accounts	27	2	Senate bill	968	Rev. Claims	952	Bill amended	S. 155	Passed	Passed	App'd Aug. 11, 1842
Dean, William	Permission to import merchandise from Great Britain, ordered previous to act of March 2, 1811.	12	1	Petition	12	Com. and Manuf.						
Dean, William A. and F. Koons.	Compensation for goods, &c., furnished volunteers.	30	1	Petition	470	Claims.						
Dean, William A. and F. Koons.	Compensation for goods, &c., furnished volunteers.	30	2	Petition	145	....	....	....	......	Leave to withdraw.		
Deany, Lieut. James A., by Mary, widow of.	Pension on account of services and death of husband in war with Mexico.	31	1	Petition	1040	Rev. Pensions	456	Adverse	......	Laid on table.		
Dearborn, Benjamin	(See Daniel Evans, sureties of)	21	2	....	382							
Dearborn, Enoch	Invalid pension	25	2	Petition	57	Invalid Pensions.						
Dearborn, Enoch	Invalid pension	25	3	Petition	219	Invalid Pensions.						
Dearborn, Enoch	Invalid pension	26	1	Petition	162	Invalid Pensions.						
Dearborn, Sherborn, (Me.)	Revolutionary pension	23	1	Petition	53	Rev. Pensions.						
Deardorff, C.	Compensation for services as an officer in war of 1812.	15	1	Petition	294	Claims.						
Deardorff, C.	Compensation for services as an officer in war of 1812.	15	2	Petition	52	Claims	....	....	......	Discharged; laid on table.		
Deardoff, David, (Ohio)	Pre-emption right to land	26	1	Resolution	822	Public Lands	538	Favorable; bill	407	Referred to Committee Whole House.		
Dearing, Col. Wm. L. S.	For loss of surveying instruments in service of United States.	22	2	Petition	105	Claims	34	Adverse	......	Laid on table.		
Dearing, Col. Wm. L. S.	For loss of surveying instruments in service of United States.	23	1	Petition	136	Claims	128	Adverse	......	Laid on table.		
Dearing, Col. Wm. L. S.	For loss of surveying instruments in service of United States.	23	2	Petition	242	Claims	Jan. 28, 1825	....	......	Laid on table.		
Dearing, Col. Wm. L. S.	For loss of surveying instruments in service of United States.	24	1	Petition	943	Claims	June 9, 1836	Adverse	......	Laid on table.		
Dearing, Col. Wm. L. S.	For loss of surveying instruments in service of United States.	25	3	Petition	462	Claims.						
Dearing, Col. Wm. L. S.	Compensation for extra services as surveyor in Louisiana.	24	1	Petition	257	Public Lands	321	Adverse	......	Laid on table.		
Dearing, Col. Wm. L. S.	Compensation for services as surveyor of public land.	24	1	Petition	264	Claims	341	Adverse	......	Laid on table.		
Dearing, Col. Wm. L. S.	Arrears of pay for surveying public land in Louisiana.	26	1	Petition	336	Claims.						

List of private claims presented to the House of Representatives of the United States from the 1st to the 31st Congress, inclusive—Continued.

Names of claimants.	Nature or object of the claim.	Congress.	Session.	How brought before the House of Reps.	Page of journal.	To what committee of the House referred.	No. or date of the report.	Nature of the report.	No. of the bill.	How disposed of by the House of Reps.	How disposed of by the Senate.	Date of the act of Congress, and remarks.
Dearing, Col. Wm. L. S.	Arrears of pay for surveying public land in Louisiana.	29	1	Petition	383	Claims	842	Adverse	....	Laid on table.		
Dearing, Col. Wm. L. S.	Permission to locate land at minimum price.	25	2	Petition	420	Public Lands.						
Deas, Doctor E. Horry	Compensation for medical services rendered United States troops.	23	2	Resolution	178	Military Affairs	Jan. 22, 1835	Favorable; bill	665	Referred to Committee Whole House.		
Deas, George	Remuneration for injuries received in public service.	30	2	Memorial	76	Military Affairs.						
Deatly, James	Revolutionary pension	25	2	Petition	70	Rev. Pensions	....	....	......	Discharged; laid on table.		
Deatly, James	Revolutionary pension	25	3	Petition	87	Rev. Pensions.						
Deatly, James	Revolutionary pension	26	1	Petition	171	Rev. Pensions	120	Favorable; bill	130	Passed	Indef. postp'd.	
Deatly, James	Revolutionary pension	26	2	Petition	34	Rev. Pensions	4	Favorable; bill	541	Referred to Committee Whole House.		
Deatly, James	Revolutionary pension	27	2	Petition	58	Rev. Pensions	20	Favorable; bill	62	Passed	Indef. postp'd.	
Deausenbury, John	Invalid pension	12	1	Petition	183	....	....	....	......	Referred to Secretary of War.		
Deavee, Isaac	Invalid pension	30	1	Petition	406	Invalid Pensions	Mar. 30, 1848	Adverse	......	Laid on table.		
Deavee, Isaac	Invalid pension	31	1	Petition	362	Invalid Pensions.						
Deaver, Aquilla	Bounty land for services in revolutionary war.	12	2	Petition	598	Claims	Jan. 30, 1813	Favorable; bill	242	Referred to Committee Whole House.		
Deaver, Aquilla	Bounty land for services in revolutionary war.	13	2	Petition	169	Claims	Jan. 31, 1814	Report	......	Discharged; leave to withdraw.		
Deaver, William	Invalid pension	13	1	Petition	46	Claims	....	....	......	Discharged.		
Debelle, John H.	Additional compensation for extra service as clerk to paymaster at Washington arsenal.	30	2	Petition	274	Military Affairs.						
Debleiux, Alexander L.	For land in lieu of land sold	25	2	Petition	373	Priv. Land Claims.	....	....	......	Laid on table.		
Debleiux, Alexander L.	For land in lieu of land sold	25	3	Petition	134	Priv. Land Claims.	150	Adverse	......	Laid on table.		
Deboise, Hannah	(See Hannah De Bevois)	15	1	....	207							
Debrille, Alzira, or Eliza	(See Sam'l Mitchell, daughters of.)	17	1	....	354							
Debouchelle and Chalaire, (brothers.)	Confirmation of land title	22	1	House bill	64	Priv. Land Claims.	62	Favorable; bill	125	Passed	Passed	App'd June 25, 1830
Decamp, Pierre, administrator of.	Renewal of lost loan office certificates.	3	2	Petition	287	Select	Jan. 22, 1795	Favorable; bill	122	Referred to Committee Whole House.		
Decatur, Stephen, by Susan, widow of, *et al.*	Compensation for destruction of the frigate Philadelphia, at Tripoli, in 1804.	18	2	Petition	55	Naval Affairs.						
Decatur, Stephen, by Susan, widow of, *et al.*	Compensation for destruction of the frigate Philadelphia, at Tripoli, in 1804.	19	1	Petition	78	Naval Affairs	48	Favorable; bill	70	Laid on table.		
Decatur, Stephen, by Susan, widow of, *et al.*	Compensation for destruction of the frigate Philadelphia, at Tripoli, in 1804.	19	2	House bill	98	Naval Affairs	74	With amend.	70	Laid on table.		
Decatur, Stephen, by Susan, widow of, *et al.*	Compensation for destruction of the frigate Philadelphia, at Tripoli, in 1804.	20	1	Petition	39	Naval Affairs	....	....	......	Discharged; laid on table.		
Decatur, Stephen, by Susan, widow of, *et al.*	Payment of prize money due recaptors of frigate Philadelphia.	20	1	Senate bill	295	Naval Affairs	201	With't amend.	S. 50	Referred to Committee Whole House.		
Decatur, Stephen, by Susan, widow of, *et al.*	Payment of prize money due recaptors of frigate Philadelphia.	20	2	Petition	32	Naval Affairs	....	....	......	Discharged; laid on table.		
Decatur, Stephen, by Susan, widow of, *et al.*	Payment of prize money due recaptors of frigate Philadelphia.	20	2	Senate bill	108	Naval Affairs	37	With't amend.	S. 30	Rejected.		

List of private claims presented to the House of Representatives of the United States from the 1st to the 31st Congress, inclusive—Continued.

Names of claimants.	Nature or object of the claim.	Congress.	Session.	How brought before the House of Reps.	Page of journal.	To what committee of the House referred.	No. or date of the report.	Nature of the report.	No. of the bill.	How disposed of by the House of Reps.	How disposed of by the Senate.	Date of the act of Congress, and remarks.
Decatur, Stephen, by Susan, widow of, *et al.*	Payment of prize money due recaptors of frigate Philadelphia.	21	1	President's message.	31	Naval Affairs	60	Favorable ; bill	82	Referred to Committee Whole House.		
Decatur, Stephen, by Susan, widow of, *et al.*	Payment of prize money due recaptors of frigate Philadelphia.	21	2	Rep't Committee Whole House.	203	Whole House	Feb. 11, 1831	With amend..	82	Rejected.		
Decatur, Stephen, by Susan, widow of, *et al.*	Payment of prize money due recaptors of frigate Philadelphia.	22	1	Documents.....	29	Naval Affairs.....	Dec. 23, 1831	Favorable ; bill	98	Referred to Committee Whole House.		
Decatur, Stephen, by Susan, widow of, *et al.*	Payment of prize money due recaptors of frigate Philadelphia.	22	2	Memorial	45	Naval Affairs.						
Decatur, Stephen, by Susan, widow of, *et al.*	Payment of prize money due recaptors of frigate Philadelphia.	23	1	Petition	36	Naval Affairs	45	Favorable ; bill	50	Postponed.		
Decatur, Stephen, by Susan, widow of, *et al.*	Payment of prize money due recaptors of frigate Philadelphia.	23	2	House bill	161	Whole House.....	....	....	50	Laid on table.		
Decatur, Stephen, by Susan, widow of, *et at.*	Payment of prize money due recaptors of frigate Philadelphia.	24	1	Petition	100	Naval Affairs.....	237	Favorable ; bill	225	Referred to Committee Whole House.		
Decatur, Stephen, by Susan, widow of, *et al.*	Payment of prize money due recaptors of frigate Philadelphia.	24	1	Senate bill	928	Naval Affairs	June 4, 1836	With't amend.	S. 138	Referred to Committee Whole House.		
Decatur, Stephen, widow of	Naval pension	24	1	Joint resolution .	342	Whole House	Feb. 13, 1836	....	J.R.6 B	Referred to Committee Whole House.		
Decatur, Stephen, widow of	Naval pension	24	2	Joint resolution .	239	Whole House	Jan. 18, 1837	....	J.R.6 B	Passed............	Passed	App'd March 3, 1837
Decatur, Stephen, widow of	Compensation for recapture of frigate Philadelphia.	31	1	Petition	406	Naval Affairs.						
Decreet, Joseph, (Ky.)...	Compensation for services as artillerist in war of 1812.	18	2	Petition	37	Claims	33	Favorable ; bill	290	Passed	Passed	App'd March 3, 1825
Decret, Joseph..........	Bounty land.................	30	2	House bill	125	Military Affairs ...	....	....	683			
Deck, John	Indemnity for Indian depredations.	21	2	Documents.....	89	Military Affairs ...	....	....	......	Discharged ; laid on table.		
Deck, Wilhelm	Invalid pension	1	2	Petition	158	Referred to Secretary of War.	May 24, 1790	Report	......	Ref. to Commissioner on Army Accounts.		
Decker, Samuel, by Sarah, widow of.	Revolutionary pension..........	21	1	Petition	46	Military Pensions..	April 7, 1830	Adverse	......	Laid on table.		
Decker, Samuel, by Sarah, widow of.	Revolutionary pension..........	25	3	Petition	216	Rev. Pensions.....	....	....	......	Discharged.		
Decker, Samuel, by Sarah, widow of.	Revolutionary pension..........	26	1	Petition	173	Rev. Pensions	....	....	......	Discharged: laid on table.		
Decker, Samuel, by Sarah, widow of.	Revolutionary pension..........	26	2	Petition	35	Rev. Pensions	140	Favorable ; bill	647	Referred to Committee Whole House.		
Decker, Samuel, by Sarah, widow of.	Revolutionary pension..........	27	2	Petition	59	Rev. Pensions	93	Favorable; bill	139	Passed	Passed	App'd July 9, 1842
Decker, Everet..........	Revolutionary pension..........	22	1	Petition	339	Rev. Pensions	....	....	......	Discharged ; laid on table.		
Deckert, Jacob..........	(See John M. Maclay, sureties of)	19	2	....	217							
Declue, Alexander.......	Patent for land under Spanish grant.	22	1	Petition	263	Priv. Land Claims.	Feb. 17, 1832	Favorable; bill.	380	Referred to Committee Whole House.		
Dedman, Dixon.........	Revolutionary pension..........	29	1	Petition	86	Rev. Claims.						
Deddolph, Owen	Arrears of pension.............	23	2	Petition	116	Naval Affairs.....	Feb. 25, 1835	Adverse	......	Laid on table.		
Deddolph, Owen	Arrears of pension.............	24	1	Petition	275	Invalid Pensions...	Feb. 11, 1836	....	......	Discharged ; laid on table.		
Deddolph, Owen	Arrears of pension.............	25	2	Petition	198	Invalid Pensions ..	Feb. 20, 1838	Adverse	......	Laid on table.		
Deening, John..........	Indemnity for French spoliations prior to 1800.	26	1	Memorial	182	Foreign Affairs....	343	Favorable; bill.	319	Referred to Committee Whole House.		
Deerick, James, and Chas. S. Pierce.	Reimbursement of duties paid on wool.	22	2	Petition	312	Commerce.						

List of private claims presented to the House of Representatives of the United States from the 1st to the 31st Congress, inclusive—Continued.

Names of claimants.	Nature or object of the claim.	Congress.	Session.	How brought before the House of Reps.	Page of journal.	To what committee of the House referred.	No. or date of the report.	Nature of the report.	No. of the bill.	How disposed of by the House of Reps.	How disposed of by the Senate.	Date of the act of Congress, and remarks.
Defenders of Baltimore, Association of.	Compensation for services in war of 1812.	31	2	Petition	321	Public Lands.						
Deford, Joseph	Arrears of pay for revolutionary services.	11	2	Petition	229	Claims				Leave to withdraw.		
Defore, John	Pension	21	1	Petition	411	Military Pensions				Discharged; laid on table.		
Defiance, schooner	(See Charles S. Stone, *et al.*, owners of.)	29	1		390							
Defrees, Henry	(See John D. Fanning, sureties of.)	26	1		297							
Defries, Moses	Compensation for horse and equipments lost in war of 1812.	23	1	Petition	438	Claims.						
Defries, Moses	Compensation for horse and equipments lost in war of 1812.	23	2	Petition	95	Claims.						
Degarmo, Paul	(See Paul De Garmo)	16	2		176							
Degrand, Peter Paul Francis.	Remission of duties on certain goods from New Orleans.	13	2	Petition	102	Ways and Means	Mar. 11, 1814	Adverse.				
Degroat, John, son and heir of.	Compensation for services in revolutionary war.	29	1	Petition	618	Claims.						
Degroat, John, son and heir of.	Compensation for services in revo lutionary war.	29	2	Petition	69	Claims.						
Degroat, John, son and heir of.	Compensation for services in revolutionary war.	30	1	Petition	288	Claims	377	Adverse		Laid on table.		
Dehetre, Hyacinthe	(See M. P. Laduc)	15	1		102							
Deibler, Mary	Compensation for horse and equipments lost, and husband killed in service of United States.	13	3	Petition	514	Claims	Nov. 14, 1814	Favorable; bill.	228	Passed	Indef. postp'd..	
Deidrick, Robert	Payment of judgment against Swartwout, New York.	26	1	Petition	169	Claims.						
Deisbob, Francis Henry	Compensation for services as quartermaster in revolutionary war.	4	1	Petition	385	Claims	Jan. 20, 1796	Adverse		Laid on table.		
Deiter, George B., & Co.	Indemnity for loss of steamer Colonel Harney.	30	2	Memorial	124	Claims.						
Deiter, George B., & Co.	Indemnity for loss of steamer Colonel Harney.	31	1	Petition	611	Claims.						
Deitrick, Ludwig	Compensation for services in revolutionary war.	13	2	Petition	296	Pens. & Rev. Cl'ms.	Feb. 23, 1814	Adverse		Rejected.		
Deitz, Johan Jost	(See Johan Jost Dietz)	25	2		198		452		454			
Deitz, John	Compensation for services as dragoon in 1811.	13	2	Petition	343					Referred to paymaster United States army.		
Deitz, Margaret	Ransom, &c., of husband, a captive in Algiers.	3	1	Memorial	82					Laid on table.		
Deitz, Capt. Peter, heirs of.	Arrears of pay for revolutionary services.	19	2	Petition	216	Rev. Claims				Discharged.		
Deitz, Capt. Peter, heirs of.	Arrears of pay for revolutionary services.	21	2	Petition	63	Rev. Claims				Discharged; laid on table.		
Deitz, Capt. Peter, heirs of.	Arrears of pay for revolutionary services.	22	1	Resolution	475	Rev. Claims	Mar. 21. 1832	Adverse		Laid on table.		
Deitz, Capt. Peter, heirs of.	Compensation for services in revolutionary war.	24	1	Petition	404	Rev. Claims.						
Dejean, Nicholas	Confirmation of land title	22	1	Petition	64	Priv. Land Claims.	Dec. 27, 1831	Favorable; bill	125	Passed	Passed	App'd June 25, 1832
Delafield, Henry, executor of.	Indemnity for French spoliations prior to 1800.	26	1	Memorial	182	Foreign Affairs	343	Favorable; bill	319	Referred to Committee Whole House.		
Delafield, John, executor of	Indemnity for French spoliations prior to 1800.	26	1	Memorial	182	Foreign Affairs	343	Favorable; bill	319	Referred to Committee Whole House.		

List of private claims presented to the House of Representatives of the United States from the 1st to the 31st Congress, inclusive—Continued.

Names of claimants.	Nature or object of the claim.	Congress.	Session.	How brought before the House of Reps.	Page of journal.	To what committee of the House referred.	No. or date of the report.	Nature of the report.	No. of the bill.	How disposed of by the House of Reps.	How disposed of by the Senate.	Date of the act of Congress, and remarks.
Delafield, John	Payment of certain loan office certificates.	14	1	Petition	105	Select	51	Favorable; bill	86	Referred to Committee Whole House.		
Delafield, John	Payment of certain loan office certificates.	14	2	Petition	32	Select	17	Favorable; bill	34	Referred to Committee Whole House.		
Delafield, John	Payment of certain loan office certificates.	15	1	Petition	106	Pens. & Rev. Cl'ms.	163	Favorable; bill	154	Referred to Committee Whole House.		
Delafield, John	Payment of certain loan office certificates.	15	2	Rep't Committee Whole House.	146	Whole House	134	With't amend.	154	Rejected.		
Deland, Alvoid, by Rufus, father of.	Bounty land, arrears of pay, and for certain expenses incurred.	15	1	Petition	27	Claims				Discharged; referred to War Department.		
Delano, Aaron, by Ann, widow of.	Continuation of pension	24	2	Petition	216	Rev. Pensions				Discharged; laid on table.		
Delano, Aaron, by Ann, widow of.	Continuation of pension	25	2	Petition	180	Rev. Pensions				Discharged; laid on table.		
Delano, James	(See Thomas Delano, heir of.)	26	1		714							
Delano, Jesse	Restoration of pension	17	1	Petition	67	Rev. Pensions				Discharged; laid on table.		
Delano, John V	Allowance of pay, rations, &c.	21	1	Petition	388	Naval Affairs				Discharged; laid on table.		
Delano, Jonathan	Arrears of pension	20	2	Resolution	107	Military Pensions				Discharged; laid on table.		
Delano, Jonathan	Arrears of pension	21	1	Petition	91	Military Pensions	April 7, 1830	Adverse		Laid on table.		
Delano, Seth	Invalid pension	3	1	Rep. of Secretary War.	131	Select	May 26, 1794	Favorable; bill ordered.	62	Passed	Passed	App'd June 7, 1794
Delano, Thomas, heir of	Indemnity for French spoliations prior to 1800.	26	1	Petition	714	Foreign Affairs.						
Delany, Hugh	(See Archibald B. Lord, *et al.*	15	2		178							
Delany, James	Bounty land for revolutionary services.	14	1	Petition	243	Pens. & Rev. Cl'ms.	April 9, 1816	Adverse		Leave to withdraw.		
Delany, John R.	To refund certain moneys expended in Cherokee country.	27	2	Petition	534	Claims	752	Favorable; bill	430	Referred to Committee Whole House.		
Delany, John R.	To refund certain moneys expended in Cherokee country.	27	3	Rep't Committee Whole House.	88	Whole House	4	With't amend.	430	Passed	Passed	App'd Jan. 20, 1843
Delany, William, (Va.)	Compensation as witness at suit of United States government.	18	1	Petition	315	Claims.						
Delany, William, (Pa.)	Arrears of pay as assistant apothecary at military hospital.	2	1	Petition	501					Referred to Secretary Treasury.		
Delany, William, (Pa.)	Pension	20	1	Petition	30	Military Pensions	April 15, 1828	Adverse		Laid on table.		
Delapierre, Bartholomew	(See Bartholomew De la Pierre.)	21	1		265							
Delaplaine, John F.	(See Isaac Clason, executors of.)	26	1		182		343		319			
Delaplaine, John F. & E. P.	(See Otis and Harris Pendleton, *et al.*)	18	1		153							
Delaunay, Alexander, (N. Y.)	Reimbursement of duties paid on books.	23	1	Petition	369	Ways and Means	345	Favorable; bill	372	Referred to Committee Whole House.		
Delaunay, David, (Missouri)	Compensation for services as adjutant general of militia, and for three horses lost.	13	3	Petition	705	Claims	Feb. 27, 1815			Discharged.		
Delaunay, David, (Missouri)	Compensation for services, and property lost in war of 1812.	22	2	Resolution	151	Claims	50	Adverse		Laid on table.		
Delaunay, David, (Missouri)	Confirmation of title to land in Missouri.	15	1	Petition	281	Priv. Land Claims				Discharged.		
Delaunay, David, (Missouri)	Confirmation of title to land in Missouri.	16	1	Petition	36	Priv. Land Claims.						

List of private claims presented to the House of Representatives of the United States from the 1st to the 31st Congress, inclusive—Continued.

Names of claimants.	Nature or object of the claim.	Congress.	Session.	How brought before the House of Reps.	Page of journal.	To what committee of the House referred.	No. or date of the report.	Nature of the report.	No. of the bill.	How disposed of by the House of Reps.	How disposed of by the Senate.	Date of the act of Congress, and remarks.
Delaunay, David, (Missouri)	Confirmation of title to land in Missouri.	17	1	Petition	53	Public Lands.....	....	....	......	Discharged; laid on table.		
Delaunay, David, (Missouri)	Confirmation of title to land in Missouri.	18	1	Petition	53	Public Lands.....	Jan. 16, 1824	By bill	65	Passed with amendm't	Passed	App'd May 26, 1824
Delauriere, Chas. Frimon.	(See Don Jacques Clamorgan) ...	15	1	....	144							
Delassus, Chas. D., (Mo.).	Confirmation of title to land in Missouri.	15	1	Petition	312	Priv. Land Claims.	....	....	......	Discharged; laid on table.		
Delassus, Chas. D., (Mo.).	Confirmation of title to land in Missouri.	16	1	Petition	54	Priv. Land Claims.	....	....	......	Discharged; laid on table.		
Delassus, Chas. D., (Mo.).	Confirmation of title to land in Missouri.	17	1	Petition	53	Public Lands.	....	....	......	Discharged; laid on table.		
Delassus, Chas. D., (Mo.).	Confirmation of title to land in Missouri.	18	1	Petition	53	Public Lands.	Jan. 16, 1824	By bill	65	Passed with amendm't.	Passed	App'd May 26, 1824
Delassus, Chas. D., (Mo.).	Confirmation of title to land in Missouri.	23	1	Opinion Supreme Court U. S.	447							
Delassus, Chas. D., (Mo.).	Confirmation of title to land in Missouri.	24	1	Opinion Supreme Court U. S.	435	Public Lands.						
Delassus, Don Carlos Dehault.	Reimbursement of money, with interest, forcibly taken for use of United States.	19	1	Senate bill	552	Claims	May 19, 1826	Bill amended .	S. 102	Referred to Committee Whole House.		
Delassus, Don Carlos Dehault.	Reimbursement of money, with interest, forcibly taken for use of United States.	22	1	Senate bill	1029	Claims	500	Bill amended .	S. 21	Passed	Passed	App'd July 14, 1832
Delassus, Don Carlos Dehault.	Interest on amount allowed by act of July 14, 1832.	24	1	Senate bill	1055	Claims	June 30, 1836	With't amend.	S. 192	Passed	Passed	App'd July 2, 1836
Delassus, Don Carlos Dehault.	(See Antoine Soulard, widow of, *et al.*)	25	2	....	416	....	....	....	S. 352			
Delawder, Isaac.........	Permission to correct error in entry of land.	19	1	Petition	206	Public Lands.	May 9, 1826	Favorable; bill	260	Passed	Amended.	
Delawder, Isaac.........	Permission to correct error in entry of land.	19	2	Petition	85	Public Lands.	Jan. 3, 1827	Favorable; bill	335	Passed	Passed with amendment.	App'd March 2, 1827
Delaware, State of.......	Amount of interest due.........	19	1	Senate bill	478	Rev. Claims......	May 20, 1826	With't amend.	S. 104	Passed	....	App'd May 20, 1826
Delaware, State of.......	Interest on advances............	20	1	Senate bill	486	Claims	May 5, 1828	With't amend.	S. 101	Referred to Committee Whole House.		
Delaware, State of.......	Interest on certain stocks, and settlement of accounts.	21	1	Resolution	229	Military Affairs....	185	Favorable; bill	231	Referred to Committee Whole House.		
Delaware, State of, inhabitants of Georgetown.	Additional compensation for postmaster in.	15	2	Resolution	210	P. Of. and P. Roads.	....	....	......	Discharged; laid on table.		
Delaware, State of, inhabitants of Georgetown.	Additional compensation for postmaster in.	16	1	Petition	77	P. Of. and P. Roads.	Mar. 3, 1820	Adverse	......	Laid on table.		
Delaware, State of, trustees of Wilmington Academy.	Compensation for use of, and injuries done to, property by United States troops in war of 1812.	1	3	Petition	340	....	....	....	......	Referred to Secretary Treasury.		
Delaware, State of, trustees of Wilmington Academy.	Compensation for use of, and injuries done to, property by United States troops in war of 1812.	2	1	Rep. of Secretary of Treasury.	53	Whole House.....	April 5, 1792	Favorable; bill	176	Passed	Passed	App'd April 13, 1792
Delaware line of the Revolution, officers of.	Compensation equivalent to half-pay for life.	10	2	Memorial	452	Select.						
Delesdernier, William....	(See Stephen Jones and William Delesdernier.)	18	1	....	154							
Delesdernier, Lewis F....	For 960 acres of land as a refugee from Great Britain.	6	2	Resolution	733	Select	Jan. 19, 1801	Favorable; bill	280	Passed	Passed	App'd Feb. 18, 1801
Delesdernier, Lewis F....	Pension	17	2	Petition	186	Pens. & Rev. Clm's.	....	....	......	Disch'd; laid on table.		

List of private claims presented to the House of Representatives of the United States from the 1st to the 31st Congress, inclusive—Continued.

Names of claimants.	Nature or object of the claim.	Congress.	Session.	How brought before the House of Reps.	Page of journal.	To what committee of the House referred.	No. or date of the report.	Nature of the report.	No. of the bill.	How disposed of by the House of Reps.	How disposed of by the Senate.	Date of the act of Congress, and remarks.
Delesdernier, Lewis F...	Pension	18	1	Petition	60	Pens. & Rev. Cl'ms.	Jan. 8, 1824	Adverse	......	Laid on table.		
Delesdernier, Lewis F....	Pension	19	1	Petition	52	Military Pensions..	164	Adverse.				
Delesdernier, Lewis F....	Pension	22	1	Petition	35	Rev. Pensions....	169	Favorable; bill	244	Referred to Committee Whole House.		
Delesdernier, Lewis F....	Pension	22	2	Rep'rt Committee Whole House.	123	Whole House.....	....	....	244	Laid on table.		
Delesdernier, Lewis F., per son William.	Balance of pension due father....	25	2	Petition	405	Rev. Pensions.....	Mar. 13, 1838	Favorable; bill	654	Passed	Passed	App'd July 7, 1838
Delesdernier, Lewis F., by Sophia, widow of.	Continuation of pension	25	3	Petition	562	Rev. Pensions....	....	....	......	Discharged.		
Delesdernier, Lewis F., by Sophia, widow of.	Continuation of pension	26	1	Petition	173	Rev. Pensions.....	....	....	......	Discharged.		
Deletra, L., *et al*	Additional compensation to deputy clerks of naval officer at New Orleans.	28	1	Petition	77	Commerce.						
Delevan, Edward C., *et al.*	Confirmation of certain line of land.	27	2	Memorial	886	Territories.						
Delevere, Francis Suzor, attorney of.	Liquidation and settlement of claim	1	3	Petition	342	Referred to Secretary of War.	Feb. 15, 1791	Rep. favorable.	......	Referred to Committee Whole House.		
Delevere, Francis Suzor, attorney of.	Liquidation and settlement of claim	2	1	House bill	463	Whole House	Jan. 6, 1792	By bill	159	Passed	Passed	App'd Mar. 27, 1792
Delgarn, James..........	Pension	21	2	Petitions	143	Military Pensions.						
Delgarn, James..........	Pension	22	1	Petition	143	Rev. Pensions.						
Delgarn, John	Interest paid on money on house at Harper's Ferry.	25	2	Petition	595	Military Affairs.						
Delgarn, John	Interest paid on money on house at Harper's Ferry.	25	3	Petition	90	Military Affairs ...	....	....	......	Discharged; laid on table.		
Deliesseline, Francis D...	Remission of duties on certain goods lost.	6	2	Petition	769	Com. and Manuf..	....	....	......	Leave to withdraw.		
Deline, Benjamin........	Pension	15	2	Petition	182	Rev. Pensions.....	Feb. 11, 1819	Adverse	......	Laid on table.		
Delino, Ignace Chalmet, heirs of.	Indemnity for property destroyed in Louisiana.	14	1	Senate bill	699	Whole House	April 23, 1816	With't amend.	S. 45	Postponed.		
Delino, Ignace Chalmet, heirs of, *et al.*	Indemnity for property destroyed in Louisiana.	14	2	Senate bill	146	Claims	Jan. 10, 1819	With't amend.	S. 3	Passed	Passed	App'd March 1, 1817
Delisle, Anthony S.......	(See Edward B. Dudley, *et al* ...	16	1	....	207							
Delius, Henry, and others.	To be exonerated from payment of duties on wines destroyed in New York.	22	2	Petition	315	Commerce.						
Dell, Bennett M........	Payment for property used by United States in 1835.	25	2	Petition	392	Claims.						
Dell, Bennett M........	Payment for property used by United States in 1835.	27	3	Petition	101	Claims.						
Dell, Bennett M........	Payment for property used by United States in 1835.	28	1	Petition	137	Claims...........	410	Adverse	......	Laid on table.		
Dell, Bennett M........	Payment for property used by United States in 1835.	28	1	Additional testimony.	1024	Claims	524	Favorable; bill	399	Referred to Committee Whole House.		
Dell, Bennett M........	Payment for property used by United States in 1835.	28	2	Rep't. Committee Whole House.	344	Whole House	Feb. 7, 1845	With't amend.	399	Passed	With't amend-	
Dell, Bennett M........	Payment for property used by United States in 1835.	29	1	Petition	463	Military Affairs....	448	Favorable; bill	322	Referred to Committee Whole House.		
Dell, Bennett M........	Payment for property used by United States in 1835.	30	1	Petition	138	Military Affairs ...	104	Favorable; bill	94	Passed	Passed	App'd Aug. 5, 1848

List of private claims presented to the House of Representatives of the United States from the 1*st to the* 31*st Congress, inclusive*—Continued.

Names of claimants.	Nature or object of the claim.	Congress.	Session.	How brought before the House of Reps.	Page of journal.	To what committee of the House referred.	No. or date of the report.	Nature of the report.	No. of the bill.	How disposed of by the House of Reps.	How disposed of by the Senate.	Date of the act of Congress, and remarks.
Dell, Charles L.	Compensation for services in the Florida war.	30	1	Senate bill	361	Military Affairs	June 2, 1848	With't amend.	S. 51	Passed	Passed	App'd June 13, 1848
Dell, James	Reimbursement of money expended at marine hospital in Florida.	24	1	Petition	751	Claims	....	....	.....	Discharged; referred to Committee on Commerce.		
Delmas, Valentine	Confirmation of title to land in Mississippi.	17	1	Petition	361	Public Lands	....	....	.....	Discharged; laid on table.		
Delmas, Valentine	Confirmation of title to land in Mississippi.	17	2	Petition	27	Priv. Land Claims.	....	....	.....	Discharged; laid on table.		
Delmas, Valentine	Confirmation of title to land in Mississippi.	18	1	Petition	28	Priv. Land Claims.	Jan. 2, 1824	Adverse	.....	Laid on table.		
Deloach, Simon	Pension	22	1	Petition	288	Invalid Pensions	296	Favorable; bill	377	Passed	Ref. to Com. on Pensions.	
Deloach, Simon	Pension	23	1	Petition	54	Invalid Pensions	37	Favorable; bill	42	Passed	Passed	App'd June 30, 1834
Delong, Solomon	Revolutionary pension	22	1	Resolution	301	Rev. Pensions.						
Delord, Henry	Indemnity for property destroyed in war of 1812.	15	1	Petition	114	Claims	....	....	.....	Discharged.		
Delord, Henry	Indemnity for property destroyed in war of 1812.	16	1	Documents	203	Claims.	April 17, 1820	Adverse	.....	Laid on table.		
Delord, Henry	Indemnity for property destroyed in war of 1812.	16	2	Report of Committee.	58	Whole House.						
Delord, Henry	Indemnity for property destroyed in war of 1812.	17	1	Petition	92	Claims.						
Delord, Henry, widow of.	(See Bailey & Delord)	23	2	....	83							
Delozier, D.	Additional compensation as surveyor of port of Baltimore.	11	3	Petition	497	Com. and Manuf.						
Delp, Samuel, representatives of, by attorney.	Compensation for damages by U. S. troops in revolutionary war.	17	1	Petition	86	Pens. & Rev. Cl'ms	Dec. 28, 1821	Adverse.				
Delvare, Joseph	Confirmation of title to land in Michigan.	20	2	Resolution	28	Public Lands	42	Favorable; bill	34	Passed	Passed	App'd April 22, 1828
Delzell, William, (Ohio)	Revolutionary pension	20	1	Petition	264	Military Pensions	April 29, 1828	Favorable; bill	283	Passed	Ref., and Com. discharged.	
Delzell, William, (Ohio)	Revolutionary pension	20	2	Petition	55	Military Pensions	Dec. 12, 1828	Favorable; bill	311	Passed	Laid on table.	
Delzell, William, (Ohio)	Revolutionary pension	21	1	Petition	48	Military Pensions	Dec. 12, 1830	Favorable; bill	72	Passed	Passed	App'd May 20, 1830; pet'rs name omitted.
Deman, O. N. A., administrator of.	Indemnity for French spoliations prior to 1800.	26	1	Memorial	182	Foreign Affairs	343	Favorable	319	Referred to Committee Whole House.		
Demarest, Jane C.	(See Thos. C. Benning and Jane C. Demarest.)	29	2	....	177							
Demarest, John	Pay for wood furnished army in revolutionary war.	4	1	Petition	388	Claims	74	Adverse	.....	Laid on table.		
Demarest, John	Revolutionary pension	22	1	Petition	631	Rev. Pensions	....	....	.....	Discharged; laid on table.		
Demarest, Samuel	Indemnity for property destroyed in late war.	15	2	Petition	297	Claims	....	....	.....	Discharged; laid on table.		
Demarest, Samuel	Indemnity for property destroyed in late war.	16	1	Petition	173	Claims	50	Adverse	.....	Referred to Committee Whole House.		
Demarest, Samuel	Indemnity for property destroyed in late war.	20	1	Petition	344	Priv. Land Claims.	....	....	.....	Discharged; laid on table.		
Demarest, Samuel	Indemnity for property destroyed in late war.	20	2	Petition	40	Claims	Jan. 7, 1829	Adverse	.....	Laid on table.		
Demarest, Samuel	Indemnity for property destroyed in late war.	21	1	Petition	201	Claims	138	Adverse	.....	Laid on table.		

List of private claims presented to the House of Representatives of the United States from the 1st to the 31st Congress, inclusive—Continued.

Names of claimants.	Nature or object of the claim.	Congress.	Session.	How brought before the House of Reps.	Page of journal.	To what committee of the House referred.	No. or date of the report.	Nature of the report.	No. of the bill.	How disposed of by the House of Reps.	How disposed of by the Senate.	Date of the act of Congress, and remarks.
Demarest, Samuel	Indemnity for property destroyed in late war.	22	1	Petition	769	Claims.						
Demarest, Samuel	Revolutionary pension	22	1	Petition	558	Rev. Pensions				Laid on table.		
Demary, Rebecca	Continuation of pension	28	1	Petition	849	Rev. Pensions.						
Demarets, Ursin	(See Eugene Senet, heirs of)	23	1		220							
Demasters, Edward, by Sally, widow of.	Revolutionary pension	29	1	Memorial	1102	Rev. Pensions.						
Demasters, Edward, by Sally, widow of.	Revolutionary pension	30	2	Petition	408					Leave to withdraw.		
Demasters, Foster	To re-locate bounty land warrant.	29	1	Petition	619	Public Lands.						
Demelt, Barnet, (N. Y.)	Revolutionary pension	21	1	Resolution	208	Military Pensions				Discharged; laid on table.		
Demelt, Barnet, (N. Y.)	Revolutionary pension	22	1	Petition	287	Rev. Pensions.						
Dement, John, (Ill.)	Permission to correct error in land, or enter other land.	23	1	Petition	385	Priv. Land Claims.	351	Favorable; bill	379	Referred to Committee Whole House.		
Dement, John, (Ill.)	Permission to correct error in land, or enter other land.	24	1	Petition	58	Public Lands	71	Favorable; bill	86	Passed	Laid on table.	
Dement, Richard	(See John C. Edwards, *et al.*)	22	1		538							
Dement, William	(See Louis F. Beeler, *et al.*)	30	1		115		482					
Deming, Chauncey	Revolutionary pension	25	2	Resolution	618	Rev. Pensions				Discharged; laid on table.		
Deming, Demas	(See Hugh Glen, assignee of)	18	1		335							
Deming, Elisha	Increase of invalid pension	25	3	Petition	81	Invalid Pensions				Discharged; laid on table.		
Deming, Elisha	Increase of invalid pension	26	1	Petition	287	Invalid Pensions				Discharged; laid on table.		
Deming, Elisha	Arrears of pension for services in late war.	29	1	Memorial	168	Invalid Pensions	245	Adverse		Laid on table.		
Deming, George	Indemnity for vessel captured by British, late war.	15	2	Petition	172	Claims				Discharged; laid on table.		
Deming, George	Indemnity for vessel captured by British, late war.	19	2	Petition	245	Claims				Discharged.		
Deming, George	Indemnity for vessel captured by British, late war.	23	1	Petition	34	Claims.						
Deming, Henry	(See Samuel Whiting)	10	1		54							
Deming, James	Indemnity for French spoliations prior to 1800.	26	1	Memorial	182	Foreign Affairs	343	Favorable; bill	319	Referred to Committee Whole House.		
Deming, John J	Extra compensation as clerk of United States court at Detroit.	17	1	Petition	185	Judiciary				Discharged; laid on table.		
Deming, John J	Extra compensation as clerk of United States court at Detroit.	17	2	Petition	44	Judiciary				Discharged; leave to withdraw.		
Deming, John J	Compensation for preparing and publishing maps for the use of Commissioners in Michigan.	20	1	House bill	106	Whole House	Feb. 8, 1828	Bill amended	34	Passed	Passed	App'd April 17, 1828
Deming, Jonathan	Revolutionary pension	16	2	Petition	63	Rev. Pensions	Feb. 15, 1821	Adverse		Leave to withdraw.		
Demmon, Martha	(See Archibald Campbell, daughter of.)	28	1		194							
Demorast, Peter D	Pension for services in revolutionary war, or other relief.	8	2	Petition	131	Claims.						
Demorast, Peter D	Pension for services in revolutionary war, or other relief.	9	1	Petition	296	Claims	Mar. 28, 1806			Leave to withdraw.		
Demorast, Peter D	Pension for services in revolutionary war, or other relief.	9	2	House bill	608	Claims	Feb. 24, 1807	With't amend.	216	Passed	Passed	App'd March 3, 1807
Demorast, Peter D	Increase of pension	11	2	House bill	283	Whole House	Mar. 15, 1810	By bill	107	Passed	Passed	App'd April 27, 1810

List of private claims presented to the House of Representatives of the United States from the 1st to the 31st Congress, inclusive—Continued.

Names of claimants.	Nature or object of the claim.	Congress.	Session.	How brought before the House of Reps.	Page of journal.	To what committee of the House referred.	No. or date of the report.	Nature of the report.	No. of the bill.	How disposed of by the House of Reps.	How disposed of by the Senate.	Date of the act of Congress, and remarks.
Demoyes, Peter	Reimbursement of moneys paid for United States circuit court.	23	2	Petition	391	Claims.						
Dempsey, Dennis	Pension	12	1	Petition	23	Claims	Feb. 25, 1812			Leave to withdraw.		
Dempsey, Dennis, by Mary, widow of.	Continuation of Pension	18	2	Petition	252	Pens. & Rev. Cl'ms.	Feb. 22, 1825	Adverse		Laid on table.		
Dempsey, Peter	Increase of pension	16	1	Petition	110	Pens. & Rev. Cl'ms.				Discharged; referred to Sec. War.		
Dempsey, Timothy	Relief; injuries received in revolutionary war.	11	2	Petition	280	Claims	Mar. 21, 1810	Adverse.				
Denby, Nathaniel, sureties of.	Release from payment of liabilities	30	2	Memorial	350	Naval Affairs.						
Dench, Gilbert	Reimbursement for sums advanced for the transportation of military stores in revolutionary war.	2	1	Petition	471					Referred to Secretary Treasury.		
Dench, Gilbert	Reimbursement for sums advanced for the transportation of military stores in revolutionary war.	3	2	Petition	288	Claims	Jan. 29, 1795	Adverse.				
Dench, Gilbert	Reimbursement for sums advanced for the transportation of military stores in revolutionary war.	4	2	Petition	624	Claims	Jan. 4, 1797	Adverse.				
Dench, Gilbert	Reimbursemsnt for sums advanced for the transportation of military stores in revolutionary war.	6	1	Petition	603	Claims	Mar. 21, 1800	Adverse		Leave to withdraw.		
Dench, Gilbert	Reimbursement for sums advanced for the transportation of military stores in revolutionary war.	8	2	Petition	54	Claims	Dec. 21, 1804	Adverse.				
Dench, Gilbert, heirs of	Compensation for services rendered the United States under contract with quartermaster general.	24	2	Petition	303	Rev. Claims.						
Dench, Gilbert, heirs of	Compensation for services rendered the United States under contract with quartermaster general.	25	3	Petition	178	Rev. Claims				Discharged; laid on table.		
Dench, Gilbert, heirs of	Compensation for services rendered the United States under contract with quartermaster general.	25	3	Petition	85	Rev. Claims				Discharged.		
Dench, Gilbert, heirs of	Compensation for services rendered the United States under contract with quartermaster general.	26	1	Petition	382	Rev. Claims.						
Dench, Gilbert, by William, heir of.	Compensation for services rendered the United States under contract with quartermaster general.	26	2	Petition	35	Rev. Claims.						
Dench, Gilbert, by William, heir of.	Compensation for services rendered the United States under contract with quartermaster general.	27	2	Petition	96	Rev. Claims	314	Adverse		Laid on table.		
Dench, Gilbert, by William, heir of.	Compensation for services rendered the United States under contract with quartermaster general.	28	1	Petition	104	Rev. Claims.						
Denford, William	Authority to enter land at minimum price.	28	1	Petition	77	Priv. Land Claims.	9	Favorable; bill	35	Passed	Passed	App'd June 17, 1844
Denghausen, Haas, & Co.	Indemnity for Mexican spoliations.	31	2	Petition	142	Commerce.						
Denham, A. W	Additional pay for superintending laborers on General Post Office building.	26	2	Petition	83	Public Buildings				Discharged; laid on table.		

List of private claims presented to the House of Representatives of the United States from the 1st to the 31st Congress, inclusive—Continued.

Names of claimants.	Nature or object of the claim.	Congress.	Session.	How brought before the House of Reps.	Page of journal.	To what committee of the House referred.	No. or date of the report.	Nature of the report.	No. of the bill.	How disposed of by the House of Reps.	How disposed of by the Senate.	Date of the act of Congress, and remarks.
Denham, David R., *et al.*	Indemnity for Indian depredations in Florida.	25	3	Petition	121	Claims	162	Adverse	......	Laid on table.		
Denham, Washington	Pension	14	1	Petition	495	Pens. & Rev. Cl'ms.	April 9, 1816	Adverse	......	Leave to withdraw.		
Denham, Washington	Arrears of pension for services in war of 1812.	29	1	Petition	1018	Invalid Pensions.						
Denham, Washington	Arrears of pension for services in war of 1812.	30	2	Petition	271	Invalid Pensions	....	....	......	Discharged; laid on table.		
Denham, Washington	Arrears of pension for services in war of 1812.	31	1	Petition	396	Invalid Pensions	398	Adverse	......	Laid on table.		
Denio, Frederick	Invalid pension	27	3	Petition	285	Invalid Pensions	171	Adverse	......	Laid on table.		
Denio, Frederick	Invalid pension	28	1	Petition	371	Invalid Pensions.						
Denio, Frederick	Invalid pension	28	2	Petition	240	Invalid Pensions.						
Denne, Charles, assignee of	Confirmation of land title	24	2	Petition	49	Priv. Land Claims.	Dec. 22, 1836	Adverse	......	Laid on table.		
Denne, Charles, assignee of	Confirmation of land title	25	2	Documents	179	Priv. Land Claims.	395	Adverse	......	Laid on table.		
Dennen, Job	Indemnity for illegal seizure of vessel by British.	28	2	Petition	73	Foreign Affairs.						
Dennin, Job	Indemnity for illegal seizure of vessel by British.	31	1	Petition	235	Commerce	....	....	......	Discharged; laid on table.		
Dennery, Thomas	Remission of tonnage duties in the case of certain French citizens.	3	2	Memorial	282	Whole House	Jan. 12, 1794	By bill	95	Passed	Passed	App'd Jan. 28, 1795
Dennett, John	Fishing bounty	20	1	Petition	29	Commerce	Dec. 18, 1827	By bill	11	Passed	Passed	App'd Mar. 10, 1828
Dennett, Lemuel	Indemnity for French spoliations prior to 1800.	26	1	Memorial	182	Foreign Affairs	343	Favorable; bill	319	Referred to Committee Whole House.		
Dennet, Lewis	Increase of pension	15	1	Petition	180	Pens. & Rev. Cl'ms.	....	....	......	Discharged; laid on table.		
Denney, James, by Penelope, mother of.	Allowance of $120 for five years, son killed in service of U. States.	17	2	Res. and petition	109, 112	Naval Affairs	62	Favorable; bill	225	Referred to Committee Whole House.		
Denney, James, by Penelope, mother of.	Allowance of $120 for five years, son killed in service of U. States.	18	1	Petition	32	Naval Affairs	6	Favorable; bill	16	Rejected.		
Denney, James, by Penelope, mother of.	Allowance of $120 for five years, son killed in service of U. States.	18	2	Petition	36	Claims.						
Denney, James, by Penelope, mother of.	Allowance of $120 for five years, son killed in service of U. States.	19	1	Petition	52	Naval Affairs	1	Favorable; bill	6	Passed	Passed	App'd May 16, 1826
Denney, James, by Penelope, mother of.	Allowance of $120 for five years, son killed in service of U. States.	20	2	Petition	32	Naval Affairs	103	Report	......	Laid on table.		
Denney, James, by Penelope, mother of.	Allowance of $120 for five years, son killed in service of U. States.	21	1	Petition	50	Naval Affairs	....	....	......	Discharged; laid on table.		
Denney, John, by Penelope, widow of.	Compensation for services as an officer, and for supplies furnished in revolutionary war.	15	2	Petition	61	Pens. & Rev. Cl'ms.	....	....	......	Discharged; laid on table.		
Denney, John, by Penelope, widow of.	Compensation for services as an officer, and for supplies furnished in revolutionary war.	17	1	Petition	25	Pens. & Rev. Cl'ms.	Dec. 28, 1821	Adverse	......	Leave to withdraw.		
Dennie, William	Pension	14	1	House bill	622	Pens. & Rev. Cl'ms.	April 11, 1816	With't amend.	171	Passed	Passed	App'd April 30, 1816
Dennin, Simeon	Pension for services in war of 1812.	28	1	Petition	317	Invalid Pensions	156	Favorable; bill	145	Passed	Passed	App'd Jan. 17, 1844
Denning, William, *et al.*	Interest on certain bills of credit	3	1	Memorial	88	Select	May 16, 1797	Adverse	......	Laid on table.		
Denning, William, *et al.*	Interest on certain bills of credit	3	2	Rep. & memorial.	216	Whole House.						
Dennis, Andrew	Bounty land for services in revolutionary war.	27	2	Petition	1049	Priv. Land Claims.						
Dennis, Andrew	Bounty land for services in revolutionary war.	28	1	Petition	122	Priv. Land Claims.						
Dennis, Andrew	Bounty land for services in revolutionary war.	28	2	Petition	58	Priv. Land Claims.						

List of private claims presented to the House of Representatives of the United States from the 1st to the 31st Congress, inclusive—Continued.

Names of claimants.	Nature or object of the claim.	Congress.	Session.	How brought before the House of Reps.	Page of journal.	To what committee of the House referred.	No. or date of the report.	Nature of the report.	No. of the bill.	How disposed of by the House of Reps.	How disposed of by the Senate.	Date of the act of Congress, and remarks.
Dennis, Andrew	Bounty land for services in revolutionary war.	29	1	Petition	430	Priv. Land Claims.						
Dennis, Andrew	Bounty land for services in revolutionary war.	30	1	Petition	88	Priv. Land Claims.						
Dennis, Anna	(See Stephen Billings, widow of.)	25	3	....	562							
Dennis, Edward	Revolutionary pension	24	1	Resolution	74	Rev. Pensions.						
Dennis, Edward, widow of.	Relief for services as a mariner on board the schooner Industry.	28	2	Petition	188	Naval Affairs	....	....	......	Disch'd, and ref'd to Com. Whole House.		
Dennis, Henry	Compensation for revolutionary services.	30	1	Petition	1025	Rev. Claims.						
Dennis, Henry	Compensation for revolutionary services.	30	2	Petition	196	Rev. Claims.						
Dennis, Henry	Compensation for revolutionary services.	31	1	Petition	988	Rev. Claims.						
Dennis, James, (Pa)	Compensation for use of wagon and team in war of 1812.	23	1	Petition	304	Claims	299	Adverse	......	Laid on table.		
Dennis, James, (Pa)	Compensation for use of wagon and team in war of 1812.	24	1	Petition	273	Claims	627	Adverse	......	Laid on table.		
Dennis, James	Revolutionary pension	11	2	Petition	154	Claims.						
Dennis, John, (R. I)	Remission of duties on coffee	14	1	Senate bill	410	Com. and Manuf.	April 12, 1816	With't amend.; ref'd to Com. Whole Ho.	31	Indefinitely postponed.		
Dennis, John	Invalid pension	26	1	Petition	328	Invalid Pensions.						
Dennis, Patrick, (N. Y.)	Increase of compensation as master of revenue cutter.	2	2	Petition	686	....	....	....	......	Referred to Secretary Treasury.		
Dennis, Patrick, (N. Y.)	Increase of compensation as master of revenue cutter.	3	2	Rep. of Secretary Treasury.	284	....	....	....	......	Laid on table.		
Dennis, Patrick, *et al.* (N.Y)	Increase of compensation as master of revenue cutter.	3	2	Memorial	333	....	....	....	......	Laid on table.		
Dennis, Richard	Indemnity for French spoliations prior to 1800.	26	1	Memorial	182	Foreign Affairs	343	Favorable; bill	319	Referred to Committee Whole House.		
Dennis, Richard	Increase of salary as register of land office in Louisiana.	29	1	Memorial	272	Public Lands.						
Dennis, Richard	Increase of salary as register of land office in Louisiana.	30	1	Petition	111	Public Lands.						
Dennis, Sarah	(See Edward Dennis, widow of).	28	2	....	188							
Dennis, Susannah	Renewal of invalid pension	27	2	Petition	219	Invalid Pensions	784	Adverse	......	Laid on table.		
Dennis, Thomas	Patent for land	22	1	Senate bill	455	Public Lands	Mar. 16, 1832	With't amend.	S. 67	Passed	Passed	App'd Mar. 31, 1832
Dennis, Thomas	Invalid pension	31	1	Petition	231	Naval Affairs	March 6, 1850	Favorable; bill	144	Passed	Passed	App'd Mar. 29, 1850
Dennis, William	Pension	23	1	Petition	388	Invalid Pensions	Mar. 26, 1834	Adverse	......	Laid on table.		
Dennison, Amos, widow of	Compensation for services, and for property destroyed in late war.	31	2	Petition	247	Claims.						
Dennison, Christopher	Revolutionary pension	24	2	Petition	271	Rev. Pensions	198	Favorable; bill	918	Referred to Committee Whole House.		
Dennison, Christopher	Revolutionary pension	25	2	Petition	99	Rev. Pensions	171	Favorable; bill	196	Passed	Passed	App'd June 28, 1838
Dennison, Elijah	(See P. C. Ellis, administrator of)	27	2	....	82	....	....	....	692			
Dennison, Elisha, *et al.*	Indemnity for French spoliations prior to 1800.	26	1	Memorial	182	Foreign Affairs	343	Favorable; bill	319	Referred to Committee Whole House.		
Dennison, Isaac	Compensation for providing for son wounded at Stonington.	14	1	Petition	592	Claims	April 9, 1816	Favorable; bill	55	Passed	Passed	App'd April 29, 1816
Dennison, Leonard, and Elisha Ely.	For transportation of ammunition and naval stores.	20	2	Petition	119	Claims	Jan. 14, 1829	Report	......	Discharged; leave to withdraw.		

List of private claims presented to the House of Representatives of the United States from the 1st *to the* 31st *Congress, inclusive*—Continued.

Names of claimants.	Nature or object of the claim.	Congress.	Session.	How brought before the House of Reps.	Page of journal.	To what committee of the House referred.	No. or date of the report.	Nature of the report.	No. of the bill.	How disposed of by the House of Reps.	How disposed of by the Senate.	Date of the act of Congress, and remarks.
Dennison, Leonard, and Elisha Ely.	For transportation of ammunition and naval stores.	21	1	Petition	294	Claims	329	Favorable; bill	387	Referred to Committee Whole House.		
Dennison, Leonard, and Elisha Ely.	For transportation of ammunition and naval stores.	22	1	Petition	43	Claims	Dec. 19, 1831	Favorable; bill	17	Passed	Passed	App'd Mar. 22, 1832
Dennison, Leonard	(See Thos. L. Tupper, assignees of.)	22	2		142							
Dennison, Lois	(See Amos Dennison, widow of.)	31	2		247							
Dennison, Prince	Invalid pension	3	2	Rep. of Secretary War.	278	Claims	Feb. 28, 1795	Favorable; bill	130	Passed	Postponed.	
Dennison, Prince	Invalid pension	4	1	Documents	445	Claims	Feb. 18, 1796	Favorable; bill ordered.	156	Passed	Passed	App'd April 20, 1796
Denniston, James	Confirmation of military land title.	3	2	Petition	285	Whole House.						
Denniston, James	Confirmation of military land title.	4	1	Petition	379	Select				Dis.; referred to Com. Whole House.		
Denniston, William	Indemnity for property destroyed in Black Hawk war.	30	1	Memor'l and res.	147	Claims	48	Adverse.				
Dennistown, A. and J. & Co.	Reimbursement of duties on goods exported to Havana.	24	1	Senate bill	928	Ways and Means	June 7, 1836	With't amend.	S. 140	Passed	Passed	App'd July 2, 1836
Dennley, James, heirs of	Permission to pay for and to perfect title to land.	12	1	Petition	316	Public Lands.						
Dennley, James, heirs of	Permission to pay for and to perfect title to land.	12	2	Petition	550	Public Lands.						
Dennley, James, heirs of	Permission to pay for and to perfect title to land.	13	2	Petition	191	Public Lands				Discharged.		
Dennley, John, (Miss.)	Permission to change location of land.	12	1	Petition	110	Public Lands.						
Dennley, John, (Miss.)	Permission to change location of land.	14	1	Petition	222	Public Lands				Discharged; laid on table.		
Dennley, John, (Miss.)	Permission to change location of land.	14	2	Petition	49	Priv. Land Claims.						
Dennley, John, (Miss.)	Permission to change location of land.	15	1	Petition	226	Priv. Land Claims.				Discharged; laid on table.		
Denny, James, *et al*	Compensation for undrawn rations furnished Ohio volunteers.	13	2	Petition	210	Military Affairs				Discharged; referred to Secretary of War.		
Denny, Montgomery, surety of.	Release from judgment	19	1	Petition	291	P. Of. and P. Roads.				Discharged; laid on table.		
Denny, Montgomery, surety of.	Release from judgment	25	2	Petition	931	P. Of. and P. Roads.				Discharged; laid on table.		
Denny, Montgomery, surety of.	Release from judgment	26	1	Petition	183, 341	P. Of. and P. Roads.						
Denny, Thomas	Remission on certain fine on card wire.	13	1	Senate bill	66	Ways and Means	July 24, 1813	With't amend.	S. 16	Passed	Passed	App'd July 28, 1813
Denon, F., and others	Confirmation of land title	27	3	Petition	274	Public Lands.						
Denoyes, Francis	(See Reuben E. Gentry, *et al.*)	24	1		294				273			
Denslow, Benjamin	Increase of pension	10	2	House bill	499	Whole House	Jan. 30, 1809	With't amend.	158	Passed	Passed	App'd March 3, 1809
Denslow, Benjamin	Increase of pension	23	1	Petition	234	Invalid Pensions	Jan. 24, 1834	Adverse		Laid on table.		
Denson, Josiah A	(See Francis Moss, heirs of)	25	2		178							
Dent, George W	Indemnity for property destroyed by fire at St. Louis.	27	2	Petition	455	Claims	704	Adverse		Laid on table.		
Dent, George W	Indemnity for property destroyed by fire at St. Louis.	28	1	Petition	122	Claims	86	Adverse		Laid on table.		
Dent, Hatch, executors of	Confirmation of land title	14	2	Petition	148	Public Lands	60	Favorable; bill	90	Rejected.		
Dent, H	Permission to locate certain lands in Missouri.	23	2	Petition	201	Public Lands.						

List of private claims presented to the House of Representatives of the United States from the 1st to the 31st Congress, inclusive—Continued.

Names of claimants.	Nature or object of the claim.	Congress.	Session.	How brought before the House of Reps.	Page of journal.	To what committee of the House referred.	No. or date of the report.	Nature of the report.	No. of the bill.	How disposed of by the House of Reps.	How disposed of by the Senate.	Date of the act of Congress, and remarks.
Dent, H.	Permission to locate certain lands in Missouri.	24	1	Petition	114	Public Lands.						
Dent, Capt. Hatch, heirs of	Commutation pay for services in revolutionary war.	23	2	Petition	165	Rev. Claims.						
Dent, Capt. Hatch, heirs of	Commutation pay for services in revolutionary war.	24	1	Petition	247	Rev. Claims.						
Dent, Capt. Hatch, heirs of	Commutation pay for services in revolutionary war.	24	2	Petition	94	Rev. Claims.						
Dent, John	Payment of loan office certificates.	14	2	Petition	31	Pens. & Rev. Cl'ms.	Feb. 3, 1817	Favorable; bill	96	Referred to Committee Whole House.		
Dent, John	Payment of loan office certificates.	15	1	Petition	21	Pens. & Rev. Cl'ms.	....	....	......	Discharged; leave to withdraw.		
Dentt, Frederick	Confirmation of title and protection of land.	30	2	Memorial	294	Priv. Land Claims.						
Dentt, Frederick	Confirmation of title and protection of land.	31	1	Resolution	474	Priv. Land Claims.						
Denton, Daniel	Remission of duties on distillery destroyed by fire.	15	1	Petition	264	Ways and Means.	....	....	......	Discharged; laid on table.		
Denton, Gabriel W., and others.	Relief from liability on custom-house bonds.	24	1	Petition	153	Claims	April 15, 1836	....	......	Discharged; leave to withdraw.		
Denton, Gabriel W., and others.	Relief from liability on custom-house bonds.	24	1	Senate bill	1018	Claims	June 17, 1836	With't amend.	S. 247	Passed	Passed	App'd July 2, 1836
Denton, John B., & Curtis Humphreys.	Relief from penalties as mail contractors.	28	2	Petition	130	P. Of. & P. Roads.	96	Report	......	Referred to Committee Whole House.		
Denton, John B., & Curtis Humphreys.	Relief from penalties as mail contractors.	29	1	Petition	244	P. Of. & P. Roads.	371	Report	J.R. 23	Passed	Passed	App'd August 8, 1846
Denton, Little, & Co., and H. Hendricks.	Repayment of duties on copper bottoms.	12	1	Petition	22	Com. and Manuf.						
Denton, Little, & Co., and H. Hendricks.	Repayment of duties on copper bottoms.	12	2	Petition	567	Ways and Means.						
Denton, Little, & Co., and H. Hendricks.	Repayment of duties on copper bottoms.	15	2	Petition	32	Ways and Means.	Nov. 30, 1818	Favorable; bill	207	Referred to Committee Whole House.		
Denton, Little, & Co., and H. Hendricks.	Repayment of duties on copper bottoms.	16	1	Petition	24	Ways and Means.	Dec. 13, 1819	Favorable; bill	3	Passed	Passed	App'd Feb. 18, 1820
Denton, Thankful	(See John Winn, heirs of.)	26	1	....	962							
Denton, Hall and Nathan.	For amount of bills drawn by John Armstrong, minister to France, on Secretary of Treasury.	10	1	Petition	173	Referred to Secretary Treasury.	Feb. 22, 1808	Report	......	Referred to Committee on Claims.		
		10	1	Senate bill	270	Whole House	April 16, 1808	With't amend.	S. 16	Passed	Passed	App'd April 25, 1808
Denvers, Nancy	(See Francis Popman, heirs of.)	29	2	....	85							
Deprefontain, John	Invalid pension	26	1	Petition	604	Invalid Pensions.						
Depuy, Benjamin	Revolutionary pension	24	1	Petition	662	Rev. Pensions.	June 7, 1836	Adverse	......	Laid on table.		
Depuy, Benjamin	Revolutionary pension	24	2	Petition	74	Rev. Pensions.						
Depuy, Benjamin	Revolutionary pension	2	2	Petition	55, 404	Rev. Pensions.	....	....	......	Discharged; laid on table.		
Depuy, Benjamin	Revolutionary pension	25	3	Petition	88	Rev. Pensions.	....	....	......	Discharged.		
Depuy, Benjamin	Revolutionary pension	26	1	Petition	307	Rev. Pensions.						
Depuy, Daniel	Pension	20	1	Petition	98	Military Pensions.	April 29, 1828	Favorable; bill.	283	Passed.		
Depuy, Daniel	Pension	20	2	House bill	55	Whole House	Jan. 15, 1829	Favorable; bill	311	Passed	Laid on table.	
Depuy, Daniel	Pension	21	1	Petition	59	Whole House	Jan. 5, 1830	By bill	72	Passed	Passed	App'd May 20, 1830
Depuy, *alias* Depew, John, (N. Y.)	Revolutionary pension	24	2	Petition	399	Rev. Pensions.						

List of private claims presented to the House of Representatives of the United States from the 1st to the 31st Congress, inclusive—Continued.

Names of claimants.	Nature or object of the claim.	Congress.	Session.	How brought before the House of Reps.	Page of journal.	To what committee of the House referred.	No. or date of the report.	Nature of the report.	No. of the bill.	How disposed of by the House of Reps.	How disposed of by the Senate.	Date of the act of Congress, and remarks.
Depuy, *alias* Depew, John (N. Y.)	Restoration of pension	25	3	Petition	127	Rev. Pensions				Discharged.		
Depuy, *alias* Depew, John (N. Y.)	Revolutionary pension	27	3	Petition	499	Rev. Pensions.						
Depuy, *alias* Depew, John (N. Y.)	Restoration of pension	28	2	Petition	104	Rev. Pensions.						
Dequindre, Antoine	Confirmation of title to lands in Michigan.	20	1	Resolution	28	Public Lands	42	Favorable; bill	34	Passed	Passed	App'd April 22, 1828
Dequindre, Antoine	(See Michigan Detroit church of St. Ann, trustee of.)	17	2		44							
Dequindre, Antoine, and R. Smith.	Compensation for services of selves, and volunteers in 1812.	21	1	Petition	318	Claims	268	Favorable; bill	318	Referred to Committee Whole House.		
Dequindre, Antoine, and R. Smith.	Compensation for services of selves, and volunteers in 1812.	21	2	Rep't Committee Whole House	340	Whole House	Feb. 22, 1831	With't amend.	318	Passed.		
Dequindre, Antoine, and R. Smith.	Compensation for services of selves, and volunteers in 1812.	22	1	Petition	25	Claims	Dec. 19, 1831	Favorable; bill.	10	Passed	Passed	App'd Feb. 18, 1832
Dequindre, Louis and Antoine, legal representatives of.	Release from payment of bonds to secure duties on goods.	15	1	Senate bill	397	Ways and Means	April 13, 1818	With't amend.	S. 58	Referred to Committee Whole House.		
Dequindre, Louis and Antoine, legal representatives of.	Release from payment of bonds to secure duties on goods.	15	2	Senate bill	120	Ways and Means	Dec. 22, 1818	With't amend.	S. 13	Referred to Committee Whole House.		
Dequindre, Louis and Antoine, legal representatives of.	Release from payment of bonds to secure duties on goods.	21	2	Senate bill	204	Commerce	Feb. 1, 1831	With't amend.	S. 77	Passed	Passed	App'd March 3, 1831
Derbanne, Joseph	Confirmation of title to land in Louisiana.	22	2	Petition	42	Priv. Land Claims.						
Derbanne, Joseph	Confirmation of title to land in Louisiana.	23	1	Petition	81	Priv. Land Claims.	Feb. 11, 1834	Report		Laid on table.		
Derbanne, Pierre S.	(See Pierre S. Durbanne.)	28	1		107							
Derby, Andrew	(See James Doyle and Andrew Derby.)	15	1		394							
Derby, Elias H.	Relief from payment of duty on a cargo of tea.	1	2	Petition	249	Select	June 28, 1790	Favorable		Referred to Secretary Treasury.		
Derby, Elias H.	Relief from payment of duty on a cargo of tea.	1	2	Rep. of Secretary Treasury.	400		March 2, 1791			Laid on table.		
Derby, Elias H., executors of.	Indemnity for French spoliations prior to 1800.	26	1	Memorial	182	Foreign Affairs	343	Favorable; bill.	319	Referred to Committee Whole House.		
Derby Fishing company	(See Connecticut, State of.)	12	1		72							
Derby, Hannah	Continuation of pension	28	1	Petition	849	Rev. Pensions.						
Derby, John	Indemnity for French spoliations prior to 1800.	26	1	Memorial	182	Foreign Affairs	343	Favorable; bill	319	Referred to Committee Whole House.		
Derby, John, executors of.	Payment for vessel and cargo seized and sold by British government.	23	1	Memorial	186	Foreign Affairs.						
Derby, Samuel G.	Indemnity for French spoliations prior to 1800.	26	1	Memorial	182	Foreign Affairs	343	Favorable; bill	319	Referred to Committee Whole House.		
Derby, Simon	Revolutionary pension	17	1	Petition	31	Rev. Pensions				Disch'd; laid on table.		
Dering, Henry P.	Increase of compensation as collector and inspector.	4	2	Memorial	647	Com. and Manuf.		Merged in general bills.	210, 211	Passed	Passed	App'd March 3, 1797
Dering, Henry P.	Increase of compensation as collector at Sag Harbor.	9	2	Petition	563	Ways and Means.						
Dering, Philip F., & Rob't H. Champion.	Pre-emption right to mineral land.	29	2	Senate bill	381	Public Lands	Feb. 24, 1847	With't amend.	S. 155	Passed	Passed	App'd Feb. 25, 1847

List of private claims presented to the House of Representatives of the United States from the 1st to the 31st Congress, inclusive—Continued.

Names of claimants.	Nature or object of the claim.	Congress.	Session.	How brought before the House of Reps.	Page of journal.	To what committee of the House referred.	No. or date of the report.	Nature of the report.	No. of the bill.	How disposed of by the House of Reps.	How disposed of by the Senate.	Date of the act of Congress, and remarks.
Dermott, James	Indemnity for damage to contract on Cumberland road by freshet.	22	1	Petition	223	Claims	April 13, 1832	Adverse		Laid on table.		
Dermott, James	Indemnity for damage to contract on Cumberland road by freshet.	23	1	Petition	426	Claims	Mar. 21, 1834	Adverse		Laid on table.		
Derrance, Colonel George, former widow of.	Relief for loss of husband, and indemnity for British and Indian depredations in 1778.	2	2	Petition	712					Laid on table.		
Derrick, James	Revolutionary pension and bounty land.	12	2	Petition	552	Claims.						
Derrick, James	Revolutionary pension and bounty land.	13	2	Petition	196	Pens. & Rev. Cl'ms.	12	Adverse		Referred to Committee Whole House, on bill No. 166.		
Derring, Christopher	(See Anthony Selin, orphan children of.)	6	1		636							
Derrington, Asa	Invalid pension	25	1	Petition	49					Laid on table.		
Derrington, Asa	Invalid pension	25	2	Petition	85	Invalid Pensions				Discharged; laid on table.		
Derrington, Asa	Invalid pension	26	2	Petition	284	Invalid Pensions				Discharged; laid on table.		
Derrington, Asa	Invalid pension	31	1	Petition	612	Invalid Pensions	Aug. 1, 1850	Adverse		Laid on table.		
Derry, James	Compensation for military service in revolutionary war.	1	2	Petition	158					Referred to Secretary of War.		
Derry, James	Compensation for military service in revolutionary war.	1	2	Rep. of Secretary War.	250	Claims	July 16, 1790	By bill	88	Passed	Passed with amendment.	App'd Aug. 11, 1790
Derryberry, Andrew	Revolutionary pension	20	1	Resolution	317	Military Pensions				Discharged; laid on table.		
Derryberry, Andrew	Revolutionary pension	21	1	Petition	128	Military Pensions	April 6, 1830	Adverse		Laid on table.		
Derryberry, Andrew	Revolutionary pension	21	2	Resolution	147	Military Pensions				Discharged; laid on table.		
Desdoity, John B.	Drawback on merchandise exported	14	1	Petition	386	Com. and Manuf	April 12, 1816	By bill		Indef. postponed.		
Desdoity, John B.	Drawback on merchandise exported	14	2	Petition	101	Com. and Manuf	Dec. 31, 1816	Favorable; bill	36	Passed	Passed	App'd March 3, 1817
Desdoity, John B., executors of.	Indemnity for French spoliations prior to 1800.	26	1	Memorial	182	Foreign Affairs	343	Favorable; bill	319	Referred to Committee Whole House.		
Desha, Benjamin	(See H. Boswell, *et al.*)	18	2		55							
Desha, Benjamin	(See Bernard Smith & B. Desha)	21	1		378							
Deshields, Joseph D.	Remission of fine imposed by collector at Norfolk.	24	2	Petition	43	Commerce	34	Favorable; bill	780	Referred to Committee Whole House.		
Deshields, Joseph D.	Remission of fine imposed by collector at Norfolk.	25	2	Petition	74	Commerce	86	Favorable; bill	102	Passed	Passed	App'd April 20, 1838
Deshon, Christopher	Indemnity for spoliations by ruler of Island of St. Domingo in 1810.	16	1	Petition	85	Foreign Affairs				Discharged; referred to Secretary State.		
Deslande, George, by Rosalie P., widow of.	Indemnity for use of, and damage to, property by U. S. army in warof 1812.	15	1	Petition	160	Claims.						
Deslande, George, by Rosalie P., widow of.	Indemnity for use of, and damage to, property by U. S. army in war of 1812.	15	2	Senate bill	316	Claims	March 2, 1819	With't amend	S. 59	Referred to Committee Whole House.		
Deslande, George, by Rosalie P., widow of.	Indemnity for use of, and damage to, property by U. S. army in war of 1812.	16	1	Senate bill	309	Claims	Mar. 31, 1820	Adverse	64	Laid on table.		
Deslande, George, by Rosalie P., widow of.	Indemnity for use of, and damage to, property by U. S. army in war of 1812.	16	2	Petition	20	Claims	12	Favorable; bill	167	Passed	Passed	App'd March 2, 1821

List of private claims presented to the House of Representatives of the United States from the 1st to the 31st Congress, inclusive—Continued.

Names of claimants.	Nature or object of the claim.	Congress.	Session.	How brought before the House of Reps.	Page of journal.	To what committee of the House referred.	No. or date of the report.	Nature of the report.	No. of the bill.	How disposed of by the House of Reps.	How disposed of by the Senate.	Date of the act of Congress, and remarks.
Desobry, Benjamin, attorney of.	Drawback on coffee exported to Hamburg.	17	1	Petition	387	Ways and Means	Mar. 28, 1822	Favorable; bill	137	Passed	Rejected.	
Desobry, Benjamin, attorney of.	Drawback on coffee exported to Hamburg.	18	1	Petition	213	Claims	Feb. 17, 1824	Favorable; bill	119	Passed	Passed	App'd May 19, 1824
Despard, John	Indemnity for property destroyed by British in late war.	17	1	Petition	164	Claims				Discharged; laid on table.		
Despard, John	Indemnity for property destroyed by British in late war.	18	1	Petition	130	Claims	Jan. 28, 1824	Adverse		Laid on table.		
Despatch, Brig	(See Enoch Baldwin, *et al*, owners of.)	23	2		428		130		45			
Despeller, Martin	Confirmation of land title	19	2	Letter Sec. Treasury, &c.	50	Public Lands	49	Favorable; bill	378	Referred to Committee Whole House.		
Despeller, Martin	Confirmation of land title	24	1	Docs. and report.	155	Priv. Land Claims.	93	Report		Ordered to be printed.		
Despert, Henry	(See Conrad Houseman, administrator of.)	4	1		373							
Desportes, John, by Catharine, widow of, & children.	Five years' half-pay and bounty land.	18	1	Petition	81	Pens. & Rev. Cl'ms.				Discharged; laid on table.		
Dessassure, ——	(See Smith, Dessassure & Darrel)	26	1		182		343		319			
Destrehan, Noel	(See Edward McCarty, representative of.)	16	2		115				237			
Deterville, Theodore	Confirmation of title to land in Louisiana.	22	2	Petition	41	Priv. Land Claims.						
Detherage, William	(See John Roberts, assignee of)	26	1		753		328		295			
Detchemondy, Paschal	Confirmation of title to land in Missouri.	15	2	Petition	193	Priv. Land Claims.				Discharged; laid on table.		
Detchemondy, Paschal	Confirmation of title to land in Missouri.	17	1	Petition	53	Public Lands				Discharged; laid on table.		
Detchemondy, Paschal	Confirmation of title to land in Missouri.	18	1	Petition	53	Public Lands	Jan. 16, 1824	By bill	65	Amended and passed.	Passed	App'd May 26, 1824
Devane, John, by Ann J., widow of.	Revolutionary pension	27	2	Petition	375	Rev. Pensions.						
Devane, John, by Ann J., widow of.	Revolutionary pension	28	2	Petition	187	Rev. Pensions.						
Devens, Richard	Liquidation of certain bills of credit	4	1	Rep. of Secretary Treasury.	388	Claims	74	Adverse		Laid on table.		
Devenney, James M., *et al*	Relief; lot sold by United States for tax in Baltimore.	10	2	Petition	382	Select.						
Deveraux, James, *et al*	Indemnity for spoliations on brig Osprey by Brazilian government.	20	1	Memorial	222	Foreign Affairs				Discharged; leave to withdraw.		
Deveraux, James, *et al*	Indemnity for spoliations on brig Osprey by Brazilian government	20	2	Petition	49	Foreign Affairs	24	Favorable		Laid on table.		
Devereice, John, daughter of.	Revolutionary pension	27	2	Petition	256	Rev. Pensions	784	Adverse		Laid on table.		
Devereice, John, daughter of.	Revolutionary pension	28	2	Petition	140	Rev. Pensions.						
Devereux, Humphrey	(See Pickering Dodge, exec'rs of)	26	1		182							
Devereux, John	Remission of duty on salt destroyed	4	1	Petition	402	Com. and Manuf.	88	Adverse		Leave to withdraw.		
Devereux, Thomas P.	(See George Pollock, executors of.)	27	3		425							
Deverges, L. P., *et al.*	Indemnity for property destroyed in Louisiana in late war.	14	2	Senate bill	146	Claims	Jan. 10, 1817	With't amend.	S. 3	Passed	Passed	App'd March 1, 1817
Devlin, Henry, and others.	Compensation for work done on Cumberland road.	23	1	Res. and papers.	589	Claims	456	Statem't of facts		Discharged; referred to Secretary War.		See report No. 449.

List of private claims presented to the House of Representatives of the United States from the 1st to the 31st Congress, inclusive—**Continued.**

Names of claimants.	Nature or object of the claim.	Congress.	Session.	How brought before the House of Reps.	Page of journal.	To what committee of the House referred.	No. or date of the report.	Nature of the report.	No. of the bill.	How disposed of by the House of Reps.	How disposed of by the Senate.	Date of the act of Congress, and remarks.
Devlin, John S.	Compensation for extra services as clerk to quartermaster.	21	2	Petition	47	Naval Affairs.						
Devlin, John S.	Compensation for extra services as clerk to quartermaster.	22	1	Petition	163	Naval Affairs	Jan. 17, 1832	Favorable; bill.	280	Referred to Committee Whole House.		
Devlin, John S	Compensation for extra services as clerk to quartermaster.	22	2	Rep't Committee Whole House.	93	Whole House	Jan. 22, 1833	Favorable; bill.	280	Passed	Passed with amendment.	App'd Feb. 27, 1833
Devlin, John S.	An act explanatory of an act for his relief.	23	1	Petition	56	Naval Affairs	294	Favorable; bill.	331	Referred to Committee Whole House.		
Devlin, John S.	An act explanatory of an act for his relief.	24	1	Petition	139	Naval Affairs	154	Favorable; bill.	163	Passed	Passed	App'd July 1, 1836
Devlin, John S.	Benefit of act of March 2, 1819, giving 15 cents per day extra.	24	1	Petition	432	Naval Affairs	453	Adverse	......	Laid on table.		
Devlin, John S.	(See Elijah J. Weed, administrator of.)	28	2	....	299							
Devlin, Lieut. John S.	Compensation for services as acting assist. quartermaster of marines.	28	1	Petition	601	Naval Affairs.						
Devlin, Lieut. John S.	Compensation for services as acting assist. quartermaster of marines.	30	1	Petition	717	Naval Affairs.						
Devlin, Lieut. John S.	Compensation for services as acting assist. quartermaster of marines.	30	2	Petition	192	Naval Affairs.						
Devlin, Lieut. John S.	Compensation for services as acting assist. quartermaster of marines.	31	1	Petition	236	Naval Affairs.						
Devlin, John	Compensation for services in office of Fifth Auditor of Treasury.	29	2	Joint resolution.	381	Claims	Feb. 26, 1847	With't amend.	J.R. 11	Referred to Committee Whole House.		
Devlin, John	Compensation for services in office of Fifth Auditor of Treasury.	31	1	Senate bill	1335	Claims	....	....	S. 245			
Devine, Miles	(See Miles Divine)	30	1	....	594							
Devillings, William	Arrears of pension	31	2	Petition	100	Invalid Pensions.						
Devitt, Edward, *et al.*	Compensation for services as fireman on board United States steamship.	31	1	Petition	255	Claims	410	Adverse	......	Laid on table.		
Devoe, John	Pension or other relief for services in revolutionary war.	8	2	Petition	24	Claims	....	....	......	Discharged; referred to Com. Whole House.		
Devoe, John	Pension or other relief for services in revolutionary war.	9	1	Petition	296	Claims	Mar. 28, 1806	....	......	Leave to withdraw.		
Devoe, John	Pension or other relief for services in revolutionary war.	9	2	Petition	348	Claims	Feb. 25, 1807	By bill	216	Passed	Passed	App'd March 3, 1807
Devoe, John	Increase of pension	10	1	Petition	232	Claims	Mar. 17, 1807	Favorable; bill	78	Passed	Passed	App'd April 25, 1808
Devoe, John	Renewal of pension	22	1	Petition	189	Invalid Pensions.						
Devol, Charles	Compensation for military services in war of 1812.	28	2	Petition	237	Claims	151	Adverse	.....	Laid on table.		
Devolsay, P. F., assignee of.	Confirmation of title to land in Missouri.	15	2	Petition	207	Priv. Land Claims.						
Devolsay, P. F., assignee of.	Confirmation of title to land in Missouri.	16	1	Petition	71	Priv. Land Claims.						
Devolsay, P. F., assignee of.	Confirmation of title to land in Missouri.	17	1	Petition	53	Public Lands.						
Devolsay, P. F., assignee of.	Confirmation of title to land in Missouri.	18	1	Petition	53	Public Lands.						
Devor, William M.	Permission to correct error in entry of land.	19	1	Petition	37	Public Lands	13	Favorable; bill	26	Passed	Passed with amendment.	App'd March 16, 1826
Devore, Timothy	Invalid pension	27	3	Petition	217	Invalid Pensions.						
Devourix, James	Pension	14	1	House bill	622	Pens. & Rev. Cl'ms.	April 11, 1816	By bill	171	Passed	Passed	App'd April 30, 1816

List of private claims presented to the House of Representatives of the United States from the 1st to the 31st Congress, inclusive—Continued.

Names of claimants.	Nature or object of the claim.	Congress.	Session.	How brought before the House of Reps.	Page of journal.	To what committee of the House referred.	No. or date of the report.	Nature of the report.	No. of the bill.	How disposed of by the House of Reps.	How disposed of by the Senate.	Date of the act of Congress, and remarks.
Dewar, Capt. Thomas	(See Thomas Duer.)	30	1		369							
Dewees, Hezekiah	Pension	22	1	Petition	224	Rev. Pensions	April 11, 1822	Adverse		Laid on table.		
Dewees, William, heirs of.	Compensation for losses and injuries received in service of United States.	1	3	Petition	357					Referred to Secretary War.		
Dewees, William, heirs of.	Indemnity for property destroyed by British in revolutionary war.	3	1	Petition	48	Select	39	Favorable		Laid on table.		
Dewees, William, heirs of.	Indemnity for property destroyed by British in revolutionary war.	3	2	Rep't Committee Whole House.	262	Whole House	Dec. 15, 1794	Adverse.				
Dewees, William, by Sarah, widow of.	Indemnity for property destroyed by British in revolutionary war.	12	1	Petition	94	Claims.						
Dewees, William, by Sarah, widow of.	Indemnity for property destroyed by British in revolutionary war.	14	2	Petition	79	Pens. & Rev. Cl'ms.	43	Adverse		Laid on table.		
Dewees, William, by Sarah, widow of.	Indemnity for property destroyed by British in revolutionary war.	15	1	Petition	59	Pens. & Rev. Cl'ms.	Jan. 19, 1818	Favorable; bill	44	Passed	Passed	App'd April 11, 1818
Dewees, William, by Sarah, widow of.	Additional pay for property destroyed by British in revolutionary war.	16	2	Petition	72	Pens. & Rev. Cl'ms.	19	Adverse		Laid on table.		
Dewees, William, by Sarah, widow of.	Additional pay for property destroyed by British in revolutionary war.	17	1	Petition	253	Pens. & Rev. Cl'ms.	Feb. 15, 1822	Adverse		Laid on table.		
Dewees, William, heirs of.	Additional pay for property destroyed by British in revolutionary war.	21	2	Petition	54	Rev. Claims	Jan. 12, 1831	Adverse		Laid on table.		
Dewees, William, heirs of.	Additional pay for property destroyed by British in revolutionary war.	22	1	Petition	197	Rev. Claims	Mar. 2, 1832	Adverse		Laid on table.		
Dewey, Amos, by Sally, widow of.	Commutation pay in lieu of bounty land.	18	1	Petition	286	Military Affairs				Discharged; laid on table.		
Dewey, Daniel	Compensation for horse injured in revolutionary war.	23	1	Petition	334	Rev. Claims.						
Dewey, Daniel	Compensation for horse injured in revolutionary war.	24	1	Petition	404	Rev. Claims.						
Dewey, Ebenezer	Revolutionary pension	24	1	Resolution	285	Rev. Pensions	497	Favorable; bill	497	Passed	Passed	App'd June 28, 1836
Dewey, Ebenezer	Increase of pension	25	2	Resolution	161	Rev. Pensions.						
Dewey, Ebenezer	Increase of pension	26	1	Resolution	407	Rev. Pensions.						
Dewey, Ebenezer	Increase of pension	26	2	Petition	50	Rev. Pensions	52	Favorable; bill	570	Referred to Committee Whole House.		
Dewey, Ebenezer	Increase of pension	27	2	Petition	1240	Rev. Pensions.						
Dewey, Ebenezer	Increase of pension	27	3	Petition	43	Rev. Pensions	181	Favorable; bill	795	Referred to Committee Whole House.		
Dewey, Joseph	Revolutionary pension	28	1	Petition	245	Rev. Pensions.						
Dewey, Martin	Revolutionary pension	30	1	Petition	45	Rev. Pensions	436	Adverse		Laid on table.		
Dewey, Samuel	Revolutionary pension	31	1	Petition	306	Rev. Claims	45	Favorable; bill	75	Passed	Ref. to Com. on Pensions.	
Dewing, Luke	(See Asa Bulkly & Luke Dewing)	18	1		115							
Dews, William	Depreciation of pay and other emoluments.	5	2	Petition	150	Claims	Feb. 8, 1798	Adverse.				
Dexter, Allen	(See L. Hammond and Allen Dexter.)	26	2		123							
Dexter, A. A	Indemnity for French spoliations prior to 1800.	31	1	Petition	633	Foreign Affairs	355	Favorable; bill	318	Referred to Committee Whole House.		
Dexter, David	Revolutionary pension	15	2	Petition	65	Rev. Pensions	Dec. 11, 1818	Adverse		Rejected.		

List of private claims presented to the House of Representatives of the United States from the 1st to the 31st Congress, inclusive—Continued.

Names of claimants.	Nature or object of the claim.	Congress.	Session.	How brought before the House of Reps.	Page of journal.	To what committee of the House referred.	No. or date of the report.	Nature of the report.	No. of the bill.	How disposed of by the House of Reps.	How disposed of by the Senate.	Date of the act of Congress, and remarks.
Dexter, Daniel S.	Release from imprisonment at suit of United States.	9	2	Petition	556	Select	Feb. 9, 1807	Favorable; bill	198	Passed	Passed with amendment.	App'd March 3, 180
Dexter, Daniel	Prize money for capture of vessel in 1812.	14	1	Petition	486	Ways and Means.						
Dexter, Daniel	Prize money for capture of vessel in 1812.	14	2	Petition	111	Ways and Means	Jan. 28, 1817	Adverse.				
Dexter, Daniel L.	Revolutionary pension	14	2	Petition	283	Pens. & Rev. Cl'ms.						
Dexter, Daniel L.	Revolutionary pension	23	2	Memorial	67	Select	Feb. 25, 1835	Favorable; bill	769	Referred to Committee Whole House.		
Dexter, Daniel L.	Revolutionary pension	24	1	Documents	136	Select	337	Favorable; bill	352	Referred to Committee Whole House.		
Dexter, Edward	(See William Mumford and others)	19	2	....	286							
Dexter, Edward, (R. I.)	Indemnity for French spoliations prior to 1800.	20	2	Petition	263	Foreign Affairs	82	Report	......	Laid on table.		
Dexter, Edward, (R. I.)	Indemnity for French spoliations prior to 1800.	22	1	Petition	106	Foreign Affairs.						
Dexter, Edward, (R. I.)	Indemnity for French spoliations prior to 1800.	24	1	Memorial	661	Foreign Affairs.						
Dexter, Edward, (R. I.)	Indemnity for French spoliations prior to 1800.	26	1	Memorial	182	Foreign Affairs	343	Favorable; bill	319	Referred to Committee Whole House.		
Dexter, Edward, (R. I.)	Indemnity for French spoliations prior to 1800.	27	3	Petition	224	Whole House.						
Dexter, Edmund	To cancel bond given for duties on brandy.	31	1	Petition	437	Commerce	158	Favorable; bill	176	Referred to Committee Whole House.		
Dexter, Edmund	To cancel bond given for duties on brandy.	31	2	Rep. Committee Whole House.	103	Whole House	158	With't amend.	176	Passed.		
Dexter, George W.	Indemnity for French spoliations prior to 1800.	26	1	Memorial	182	Foreign Affairs	343	Favorable; bill	319	Referred to Committee Whole House.		
Dexter, Horatio	Compensation for services in Indian department, Florida.	21	1	Petition	41	Indian Affairs	Jan. 19, 1830	Adverse	......	Leave to withdraw.		
Dexter, John H., and William Almy.	Reimbursement of excessive duties.	24	1	Memorial	382	Ways and Means	March 3, 1836	Favorable; bill	399	Referred to Committee Whole House.		
Dexter, John H., and William Almy.	Reimbursement of excessive duties.	30	1	Senate bill	957	Commerce	Jan. 26, 1848	Favorable; bill	S. 142	Passed	Passed	App'd Aug. 14, 1848
Dexter, Phœbe	For benefit of act of July 4, 1836.	25	2	Petition	311	Rev. Pensions	Jan. 25, 1838	Favorable; bill	456	Referred to Committee Whole House.		
Dexter, Samuel	Indemnity for French spoliations prior to 1800.	26	1	Memorial	182	Foreign Affairs	343	Favorable; bill	319	Referred to Committee Whole House.		
Dexter, Samuel, late Secretary of War.	Relief from suit for rent of house for government purposes, and to be indemnified.	7	1	Letter	30	Select	Jan. 13, 1802	Favorable; bill	9	Passed	Passed	App'd April 14, 1802
Dexter, Theodore	Indemnity for French spoliations prior to 1800.	36	1	Memorial	182	Foreign Affairs	343	Favorable; bill	319	Referred to Committee Whole House.		
Dey, Anthony, and James McDonald.	Extension of patent for cleaning unrotted hemp.	17	1	Petition	294	Judiciary	67	Rep. and res.	......	Discharged; laid on table.		
Dezendorff, Andrew	Naval pension	26	1	Memorial	713	Naval Affairs.						
De Amburgeæ, Countess	(See De Rochambeau, heirs of)	22	2	....	406							
De Angelis, Ophelia	(See Martin Hanson, daughter of)	25	2	....	723							
De Angelis, Paschal, C. J.	Revolutionary pension	22	1	Petition	710	Rev. Pensions	....	....	......	Discharged; laid on table.		
De Angelis, Paschal, C. J., widow of.	Revolutionary pension	28	1	Petition	370	Rev. Pensions.						
De Armas, Joseph and Bartole.	Confirmation of land title	22	1	Petition	64	Priv. Land Claims.	62	Favorable; bill	125	Passed	Passed	App'd June 25, 1832

List of private claims presented to the House of Representatives of the United States from the 1st to the 31st Congress, inclusive—Continued.

Names of claimants.	Nature or object of the claim.	Congress.	Session.	How brought before the House of Reps.	Page of journal.	To what committee of the House referred.	No. or date of the report.	Nature of the report.	No. of the bill.	How disposed of by the House of Reps.	How disposed of by the Senate.	Date of the act of Congress, and remarks.
De Auterive, Bernard, heirs of.	Confirmation of land title	25	2	Petition	548	Public Lands.						
De Auterive, Bernard, heirs of.	Confirmation of land title	26	1	Documents	610	Priv. Land Claims.						
De Auterive, Bernard, heirs of.	Confirmation of land title	27	2	Petition	58	Priv. Land Claims.						
De Auterive, Bernard, heirs of.	Confirmation of land title	27	3	Petition	45	Priv. Land Claims.						
De Auterive, Maregny	Compensation for services of negro, and supplies furnished.	18	1	Resolution	239	Claims.						
De Auterive, Maregny	Compensation for services of negro, and supplies furnished.	18	2	Petition	47	Claims.						
De Auterive, Maregny	Compensation for services of negro, and supplies furnished.	19	1	Petition	38	Claims	126	Favorable; bill	166	Referred to Committee Whole House.		
De Auterive, Maregny	Compensation for services of negro, and supplies furnished.	19	2	Rep't Committee Whole House.	338	Whole House	Feb. 27, 1827	With amend.	166	Passed	Ref. to Com. on Claims.	
De Auterive, Maregny	Compensation for services of negro, and supplies furnished.	20	1	Petition	31	Claims	27, 210	Favorable; bill	19	Laid on table.		
De Auterive, Maregny	Compensation for services of negro, and supplies furnished.	21	1	Petition	84	Claims	26	Favorable; bill	34	Passed	Passed	App'd April 2, 1830
De Bastrop, Baron, assignee of.	Confirmation of a Spanish grant of land.	15	2	Petition	44	Priv. Land Claims.						
De Bastrop, Baron, by inhab'ts of Ouachita, La.	Confirmation of a Spanish grant of land.	17	1	Petition	129	Public Lands	....	....	....	Discharged; laid on table.		
De Bastrop, Baron, by inhab'ts of Ouachita, La.	Confirmation of a Spanish grant of land.	17	2	Petition	23	Select	....	....	....	Discharged; leave to withdraw.		
De Bastrop, Baron, by inhab'ts of Ouachita, La.	Authority to institute suit *vs.* United States.	18	1	Petition	31	Priv. Land Claims.						
De Bastrop, Baron, by inhab'ts of Ouachita, La.	Authority to institute suit *vs.* United States.	18	2	Petition	52	Select	21	Favorable; bill.	264	Passed	Laid on table.	
De Bastrop, Baron, by inhab'ts of Ouachita, La.	Authority to institute suit *vs.* United States.	19	1	Petition	43, 75	Judiciary	3	Favorable; bill.	7	Laid on table.		
De Bastrop, Baron, by inhab'ts of Ouachita, La.	Authority to institute suit *vs.* United States.	20	1	Memorial	125	Public Lands	....	....	....	Discharged; laid on table.		
De Bastrop, Baron, by inhab'ts of Ouachita, La.	Authority to institute suit *vs.* United States.	21	1	Senate bill	158	Priv. Land Claims.	April 6, 1830	With't amend.	S. 21	Referred to Committee Whole House.		
De Bastrop, Baron, by inhab'ts of Ouachita, La.	Authority to institute suit *vs.* United States.	22	1	Petition	216	Priv. Land Claims.	232	Favorable; bill.	311	Referred to Committee Whole House.		
De Bastrop, Baron, representatives of.	Authority to institute suit *vs.* United States.	23	2	Resolution	76	Public Lands.						
De Bastrop, Baron, representatives of.	Authority to institute suit *vs.* United States.	24	1	Senate bill	320	Priv. Land Claims.	554	Favorable; bill.	S. 1	Referred to Committee Whole House.		
De Bastrop, Baron, representatives of, *et al.*	For legal adjustment of claim to land under grants and concessions.	24	2	Senate bill	527	Whole House	....	....	S. 49			
De Bastrop, Baron, representatives of, *et al.*	For legal adjustment of claim to land under grants and concessions.	25	2	Senate bill	332	Priv. Land Claims.	Feb. 7, 1838	Adverse	S. 84	Referred to Committee Whole House.		
De Bastrop, Baron, representatives of, *et al.*	For legal adjustment of claim to land under grants and concessions.	25	3	Resolution	173	Priv. Land Claims.						
De Bastrop, Baron, representatives of, *et al.*	For legal adjustment of claim to land under grants and concessions	31	1	Senate bill	1545	Whole House	....	....	S. 156			

List of private claims presented to the House of Representatives of the United States from the 1st to the 31st Congress, inclusive—Continued.

Names of claimants.	Nature or object of the claim.	Congress.	Session.	How brought before the House of Reps.	Page of journal.	To what committee of the House referred.	No. or date of the report.	Nature of the report.	No. of the bill.	How disposed of by the House of Reps.	How disposed of by the Senate.	Date of the act of Congress, and remarks.
De Bastrop, Baron, representatives of, *et al.*	For legal adjustment of claim to land under grants and concessions.	31	2	Senate bill	422	Whole House	Mar. 3, 1851	With't amend.	S. 156	Passed	Passed	App'd March 3, 1851
De Beaulieu, Lewis Joseph	(See Lewis Joseph Beaulieu)	3	1	....	20							
De Beaumarchais, Baron, representatives of.	Indemnity for supplies furnished United States.	9	1	House bill	292	Whole House	Feb. 21, 1806	By bill	110	Passed	Passed	App'd April 18, 1806
De Beaumarchais, Baron, representatives of.	Relief from unjust settlement of account at Treasury for supplies furnished and services rendered United States.	9	1	Petition	212	Claims	....	....	......	Laid on table.		
De Beaumarchais, Baron, representatives of.	Relief from unjust settlement of account at Treasury for supplies furnished and services rendered United States.	9	2	Presid'ts message	569	Claims	....	....	......	Referred to Secretary of State.		
De Beaumarchais, Baron, representatives of.	Relief from unjust settlement of account at Treasury for supplies furnished and services rendered United States.	10	1	Report of Secretary State.	73	Claims	....	....	......	Discharged; laid on table.		
De Beaumarchais, Baron, representatives of.	Relief from unjust settlement of account at Treasury for supplies furnished and services rendered United States.	10	2	Petition and rep't	368	Claims.						
De Beaumarchais, Baron, representatives of.	Relief from unjust settlement of account at Treasury for supplies furnished and services rendered United States.	11	3	Petition	453	Claims.						
De Beaumarchais, Baron, representatives of.	Relief from unjust settlement of account at Treasury for supplies furnished and services rendered United States.	12	1	Petition	20	Claims	Mar. 23, 1812	Adverse	......	Referred to Committee Whole House.		
De Beaumarchais, Baron, representatives of.	Relief from unjust settlement of account at Treasury for supplies furnished and services rendered United States.	12	2	Petition	584	Claims.						
De Beaumarchais, Baron, representatives of.	Relief from unjust settlement of account at Treasury for supplies furnished and services rendered United States.	13	2	Petition	272	Select	84	Report and res.	......	Indef. postponed	....	Leave to withdraw.
De Beaumarchais, Baron, representatives of.	For balance debited to his account by United States.	14	2	Presid'ts message	318	Pens. & Rev. Cl'ms.	....	....	......	Discharged; laid on table.		
De Beaumarchais, Baron, representatives of.	For balence debited to his account by United States.	15	1	Presid'ts message	152	Select	111	Favorable; bill.	105	Referred to Committee Whole House.		
De Beaumarchais, Baron, representatives of.	For balance debited to his account by United States.	15	2	Rep't Committee Whole House.	43	Whole House	Dec. 4, 1818	With't amend.	105	Rejected.		
De Beaumarchais, Baron, representatives of.	For balance debited to his account by United States.	17	1	Presid'ts message	421	Select	....	....	......	Discharged; laid on table.		
De Beaumarchais, Baron, representatives of.	For balance debited to his account by United States.	17	2	Presid'ts message	23	Select	75	Favorable; bill.	258	Referred to Committee Whole House.		
De Beaumarchais, Baron, representatives of.	For balance debited to his account by United States.	18	1	Presid'ts message	91	Select	64	Favorable	......	Laid on table.		
De Beaumarchais, Baron, representatives of.	For balance debited to his account by United States.	19	1	Resolution	414	Foreign Affairs	217	Report	......	Laid on table.		

List of private claims presented to the House of Representatives of the United States from the 1st to the 31st Congress, inclusive—Continued.

Names of claimants.	Nature or object of the claim.	Congress.	Session.	How brought before the House of Reps.	Page of journal.	To what committee of the House referred.	No. or date of the report.	Nature of the report.	No. of the bill.	How disposed of by the House of Reps.	How disposed of by the Senate.	Date of the act of Congress, and remarks.
63 De Beaumarchais, Baron, representatives of.	For balance debited to his account by United States.	20	1	Resolution	317	Foreign Affairs	220	Favorable; bill.	252	Referred to Committee Whole House.		
De Beaumarchais, Baron, representatives of.	For balance debited to his account by United States.	21	1	House bill	311	Judiciary	Feb. 19, 1830	Favorable; bill.	262	Discharged; referred to President U. S.		
De Beaumarchais, Baron, representatives of.	For balance debited to his account by United States.	21	2	House bill	389	Whole House			262	Discharged; referred to President U. S.		
De Bellvue, Francis B.	Invalid pension	27	2	Petition	329	Invalid Pensions	313	Favorable; bill.	282	Passed	Passed	App'd Aug. 29, 1842
De Bellvue, Francis B., widow of.	Pension	28	2	Petition	56	Invalid Pensions.						
De Bellvue, Francis B., widow of.	Pension	29	1	Petition	101	Invalid Pensions				Discharged; referred to Com. on Judiciary.		
De Bellvue, Francis B., widow of.	Pension	31	1	Petition	348	Invalid Pensions.						
De Benneville, Daniel	Compensation for services as surgeon in revolutionary war.	2	1	Petition	492					Referred to Secretary War.		
De Bernoux, Francis G	Commutation of half pay	3	1	Petition	73					Referred to Secretary of War.		
De Bernoux, Francis G	Commutation of half-pay	3	2	Petition and rep't Sec. of War.	278	Claims.						
De Bernoux, Francis G	Commutation of half-pay	4	1	Res. and docs.	372	Claims.						
De Bernoux, Francis G	Commutation of half-pay	4	2	Res. and docs	614	Claims.						
De Bevoise, Hannah, *et al.*	Indemnity for damages to property by troops in late war.	15	1	Petition	247	Claims				Discharged; laid on table.		
De Bevoise, Hannah, *et al*	Indemnity for damages to property by troops in late war.	15	2	Petition	40	Claims	71	Adverse		Laid on table.		
De Bevoise, Hannah, *et al.*	Indemnity for damages to property by troops in late war.	18	2	Petition	160	Claims.						
De Bordes, Lieut. Jean Marie.	Compensation for revolutionary services.	4	1	Petition	396	Claims	Jan. 27, 1796	Adverse		Referred to Committee Whole House.		
De Bretigny, Lieut. Col. Francis.	Pay and emoluments for services rendered, as per resolution of Congress.	2	2	Petition	682					Referred to Secretary of War.		
De Butts, Elias, *et al*	Indemnity for damages to vessel and cargo libelled, &c.	9	2	Petition	616					Laid on table.		
De Butts, Elias, *et al*	Indemnity for damages to vessel and cargo libelled, &c.	10	1	Petition	203	Refer'd to Secretary Treasury.	April 18, 1808	Report		Referred to Committee Whole House.		
De Buys, William	Extra compensation as postmaster at New Orleans under act of appropriation for 1841.	27	2	Senate bill	1194	P. Of. & P. Roads.			S. 284	Referred to Committee Whole House.		
De Buys, William	Reimbursement for repairs and fixtures of post office at New Orleans.	27	3	Senate bill	171	P. Of. & P. Roads.	Feb. 3, 1843	Bill amended.	S. 38	Passed	Passed	App'd Feb. 18, 1843
De Buys, William	Reimbursement of expenses for post office, and increase of pay.	28	1	Senate bill	989	P. O. & P. Roads.			S. 129			
De Buys, William	Increase of compensation as postmaster at New Orleans.	30	1	House bill	255	P. Of. & P. Roads.	316	Favorable; bill	85	Referred to Committee Whole House.		
De Buys, William	Increase of compensation as postmaster at New Orleans.	30	2	Rep't Committee Whole House.	143	Whole House	Dec. 22, 1849	With't amend.	85	Passed	Passed.	App'd Feb. 19, 1849
De Cabrera, Don Joseph	Release from imprisonment under warrant of governor of Pennsylvania.	8	2	Letter & mem'al.	90	Whole House				Leave to withdraw.		
De Camp, Morris	Increase of pension	12	1	House bill	361	Whole House.	June 15, 1812	Amended.	138	Passed	Passed	App'd July 5, 1812

List of private claims presented to the House of Representatives of the United States from the 1st to the 31st Congress, inclusive—Continued.

Names of claimants.	Nature or object of the claim.	Congress.	Session.	How brought before the House of Reps.	Page of journal.	To what committee of the House referred.	No. or date of the report.	Nature of the report.	No. of the bill.	How disposed of by the House of Reps.	How disposed of by the Senate.	Date of the act of Congress, and remarks.
De Cantillon, Richard, and Daniel Lefferts.	Relief in the case of the sloop Union.	4	2	Memorial	613	Com. and Manuf.	Jan. 30, 1797	Rep. and res.	......	Bill ordered.		
De Carpentier, Lewis	Payment of debenture on goods exported.	15	1	Petition	143	Com. and Manuf	....	....	......	Discharged; leave to withdraw.		
De Cassas, Eulogia, heirs of.	Permission to change location of land, and confirmation of title.	18	1	Resolution	336	Military Affairs	April 26, 1824	Favorable; bill	203	Passed	Passed	App'd May 26, 1824
De Castando, John	Indemnity for property destroyed by United States troops in 1812.	14	2	Petition	142	Claims	Feb. 3, 1817	Favorable; bill	......	Passed	Passed	App'd March 3, 1817
De Castor, Julien	Confirmation of title to land in Mississippi.	13	2	Petition	160	Public Lands	....	....	......	Discharged.		
De Castroy, Ferrar B.	Indemnity for property destroyed by United States troops in 1812.	19	1	Memorial	252	Foreign Affairs	112	Adverse	......	Laid on table.		
De Castroy, Ferrar B.	Indemnity for property destroyed by United States troops in 1812.	20	2	Petition	339	Foreign Affairs	99	Favorable; bill	385	Referred to Committee Whole House.		
De Castroy, Ferrar B.	Indemnity for property destroyed by United States troops in 1812.	23	1	Petition	67	Foreign Affairs	368	Favorable; bill	395	Passed	Passed	App'd June 27, 1834
De Clozel, Charles Oliver	Confirmation of land title	28	1	Petition	550	Priv. Land Claims.						
De Cotteneau, Dennis	Prize money on vessels captured by Paul Jones.	9	2	Petition	554	Claims.						
De Cotteneau, Dennis	Prize money on vessels captured by Paul Jones.	10	1	Memorial	168	Claims	....	....	......	Discharged.		
De Eslava, Miguel, heirs of	(See Miguel Eslava, heirs of.)	24	1	....	436							
De Eslava, Miguel	(See Thomas F. Townley, guardian of children of.)	23	1	....	111							
De Ferriet, Baron Lewis, assignee of.	Confirmation of land title	25	3	Senate bill	477	Public Lands	Feb. 16, 1839	With't amend.	S. 116	Referred to Committee Whole House.		
De Ferriet, Baron Lewis, assignee of.	Confirmation of land title	31	1	House bill	456	Priv. Land Claims.	....	....	26			
De Fleury, Colonel, heiress of.	Amount due for services in revolutionary war.	19	1	Memorial	381	Rev. Claims	....	....	......	Discharged; laid on table.		
De Forrest, Ebenezer	Revolutionary pension	22	1	Petition	36	Rev. Pensions	8	Favorable; bill	55	Passed	Indef. postp'd.	
De Forrest, Lockwood	(See Oliver H. Hicks and L. De Forrest.)	11	1	....	491							
De Forrest, Dr. William	Compensation for medical services rendered United States troops in Florida.	25	3	Documents	205	Claims.						
De Forrest, Dr. William	Compensation for medical services rendered United States troops in Florida.	26	1	Petition	170	Claims.						
De Forrest, Dr. William	Compensation for medical services rendered United States troops in Florida.	26	2	Petition	135	Claims.						
De Fougeres, Marquis	Permission to test title to land by suit.	30	1	Senate bill	678	Claims	April 26, 1848	With't amend.	S. 215	Passed	....	App'd July 20, 1848
De Freest, Peter	Compensation for services rendered, and supplies furnished in revolutionary war.	3	2	Petition	323	Claims.						
De Freest, Peter	Compensation for services rendered, and supplies furnished in revolutionary war.	4	1	Res. and docs	373	Claims	Jan. 6, 1796	Adverse	......	Leave to withdraw.		
De Frias, Antonio	Indemnity for illegal capture of slaves by United States revenue cutter.	24	1	Petition	115	Foreign Affairs	209	Adverse	......	Laid on table.		

List of private claims presented to the House of Representatives of the United States from the 1st to the 31st Congress, inclusive—Continued.

Names of claimants.	Nature or object of the claim.	Congress.	Session.	How brought before the House of Reps.	Page of journal.	To what committee of the House referred.	No. or date of the report.	Nature of the report.	No. of the bill.	How disposed of by the House of Reps.	How disposed of by the Senate.	Date of the act of Congress, and remarks.
De Frey, Charles	Half-pay for services as an officer in revolutionary war.	3	2	Memorial	316	Claims.						
De Frey, Charles	Half-pay for services as an officer in revolutionary war.	4	1	Res. and docs.	373	Claims	Jan. 6, 1796	Adverse	......	Leave to withdraw.		
De Garmo, Paul	Revolutionary pension	16	2	Petition	176	Rev. Pensions	Feb. 15, 1821	Adverse.				
De Garmo, Paul	Revolutionary pension	27	2	Petition	386	Invalid Pensions.						
De Garmo, Paul	Revolutionary pension	28	1	Petition	516	Invalid Pensions.						
De Garmo, Paul	Revolutionary pension	29	1	Petition	856	Invalid Pensions	819	Favorable; bill	544	Referred to Committee Whole House.		
De Garmo, Paul	Revolutionary pension	30	1	Petition	78	Invalid Pensions.						
De Garmo, Paul	Revolutionary pension	30	2	Petition	36	Invalid Pensions	Feb. 13, 1849	Adverse	......	Laid on table.		
De Glaubeck, Baron	Compensation for losses and for services in revolutionary war.	1	1	Petition	35, 65	Select	Sept. 21, 1789	Favorable; res.				
De Glaubeck, Baron	Compensation for losses and for services in revolutionary war.	1	1	Senate bill	130	Whole House	Sept. 29, 1789	With't amend.	S. 5	Passed	....	App'd Sept. 29, 1789
De Graff, John J.	(See Jonathan Walton & Co.)	21	1	....	523							
De Graff, Michael, by heirs of Jane, widow of.	Revolutionary pension	29	2	Petition	54	Rev. Pensions	40	Adverse	......	Laid on table.		
De Grand, John A. E.	To refund amount paid to Patent Office.	29	1	Petition	493	Patents.						
De Grasse, Count, heirs of.	For temporary loan of money	3	2	Memorial	324	Select	Feb. 18, 1795	Favorable; bill	119	Passed	Passed	App'd Feb. 27, 1795
De Grasse, Count, heirs of.	For further loan of money	5	2	Memorial	113	Select	Jan. 4, 1798	Favorable; bill	36	Passed	Passed	App'd Jan. 15, 1798
De Grasse, Count, heirs of.	Compensation for revolutionary services.	22	2	Pres. Message	403	Rev. Claims.						
De Grasse, Count, heirs of.	Compensation for revolutionary services.	27	2	Memorial	220	Rev. Claims.						
De Grasse, Count, heirs of.	Compensation for revolutionary services.	28	1	Memorial	90	Rev. Claims.						
De Grasse, Count, heirs of.	Compensation for revolutionary services.	28	2	Petition	66	Rev. Claims.						
De Grasse, Count, heirs of.	Compensation for revolutionary services.	29	1	Memorial	115	Rev. Claims	142	Adverse	......	Laid on table.		
De Haas, John Philip	To refund amount advanced for public service.	1	3	Petition	344	Referred to Sec. of War.	Feb. 28, 1791	Report	......	....	....	Comptroller ordered to adjust accounts.
De Haas, John Philip	To refund amount advanced for public service.	2	1	House bill	463	Whole House	Nov. 19, 1791	By bills	152, 159	Passed	Passed	App'd March 23, 1792
De Hauterive, Joseph Vallerie, heirs of.	Relief in the case of grant of land in Arkansas.	31	2	Petition	270	Judiciary.						
De Haven, Edward J.	(See Exploring Expedition.)	27	3	....	149							
De Hevia, Don Francisco H., attorney of.	Confirmation of title to sundry tracts of land.	18	1	Memorial	177	Priv. Land Claims.	....	....	......	Discharged; leave to withdraw.		
De Hevia, Don Francisco H., attorney of.	Confirmation of title to sundry tracts of land.	21	2	Resolution	57	Priv. Land Claims.						
De Hevia, Don Francisco H., attorney of.	Confirmation of title to sundry tracts of land.	22	1	Petition	32	Priv. Land Claims.	May 1, 1832	Adverse	......	Laid on table.	....	Leave to withdraw, 26th Con., 2d sess.
De Huff, A. A.	Redemption of Continental money.	27	2	Petition	1024	Claims.						
De Jeaumont, Fontenille, *et al.*	Compensation for services, French army in revolutionary war.	22	2	Pres. Message	406	Rev. Claims.						
De Kalb, Baron, children and representatives of	Pay and commutation pay for services in revolutionary war.	16	1	Petition	26	Pens. & Rev. Cl'ms.	63	Adverse	......	Laid on table.		
De Kalb, Baron, children and representatives of.	Pay and commutation pay for services in revolutionary war.	16	2	Petition	47	Pens. & Rev. Cl'ms.	32	Adverse	......	Laid on table.		

List of private claims presented to the House of Representatives of the United States from the 1st to the 31st Congress, inclusive—Continued.

Names of claimants.	Nature or object of the claim.	Congress.	Session.	How brought before the House of Reps.	Page of journal.	To what committee of the House referred.	No. or date of the report.	Nature of the report.	No. of the bill.	How disposed of by the House of Reps.	How disposed of by the Senate.	Date of the act of Congress, and remarks.
De Kalb, Baron, heirs of..	Compensation for services rendered in revolutionary war.	23	1	Petition & Pres. Message.	658	Foreign Affairs.						
De Kalb, Baron, heirs of..	Compensation for services rendered in revolutionary war.	24	1	Petition	735							
De Kalb, Baron, heirs of..	Compensation for services rendered in revolutionary war.	24	2	Petition	307	Rev. Claims.						
De Kalb, Baron, heirs of..	Compensation for services, and interest on loan office certificates.	26	1	Petition	361	Rev. Claims.						
De Kalb, Baron, heirs of..	Compensation for services, and interest on loan office certificates.	26	2	Petition	305	Rev. Claims.						
De Kalb, Baron, heirs of..	Compensation for services, and interest on loan office certificates.	27	2	Petition	504	Rev. Claims	277	Favorable; bill	243	Passed	Laid on table.	
De Kalb, Baron, heirs of..	Compensation for services, and interest on loan office certificates.	27	3	Petition	44	Rev. Claims......	Dec. 23, 1842	By bill	617	Passed	Indef. postp'd.	
De Kalb, Baron, heirs of..	Compensation for services, and interest on loan office certificates.	28	1	Petition	144	Rev. Claims......	508	Favorable; bill	383	Referred to Committee Whole House.		
De Kalb, Baron, heirs of..	Compensation for services, and interest on loan office certificates.	29	1	Memorial	177	Rev. Claims......	364	Favorable; bill	277	Referred to Committee Whole House.		
De Kalb, Baron, heirs of..	Compensation for services, and interest on loan office certificates.	29	2	Additional testimony & House bill.	293	Whole House.....	Feb. 2, 1847	With't amend.	277	Referred to Committee Whole House.		
De Kalb, Baron, heirs of..	Compensation for services, and interest on loan office certificates.	30	1	Petition	136	Rev. Claims.	175	Favorable; bill	185	Referred to Committee Whole House.		
De Kalb, Baron, heirs of..	Compensation for services, and interest on loan office certificates.	30	2	Rep't Committee Whole House.	142	Whole House.....	Dec. 22, 1848	By bill	185	Passed	Amended.	
De Kalb, Baron, heirs of..	Compensation for services, and interest on loan office certificates.	31	1	Petition	234	Rev. Claims......	184	Favorable; bill	193	Referred to Committee Whole House.		
De Kalb, Henri, representatives of.	For transfer of land granted heirs of Baron De Kalb.	25	2	Memorial	1119	Priv. Land Claims.						
De Kalb, Henri, representatives of.	For transfer of land granted heirs of Baron De Kalb.	25	3	Memorial	189	Priv. Land Claims.						
De Kalb, Henri, representatives of.	For transfer of land granted heirs of Baron De Kalb.	26	1	Petition	179	Priv. Land Claims.	July 21, 1840	Adverse	......	Laid on table.		
De Kay, George C.......	Reimbursement for expenses incurred in conveying provisions to the relief of inhabitants of Ireland and Scotland.	30	1	Petition	271	Naval Affairs.....	541	Favorable.....	J. R. 26	Referred to Committee Whole House.	....	Provided for by Civil Diplomatic bill, approved August 12, 1848.
De Kay, George C., by Janet, widow of.	Remuneration for services and expenses of husband for conveying provisions to relief of poor in Ireland.	31	1	Petition	258	Naval Affairs.....	60	Adverse	......	Laid on table.		
De Kermion, Labeydeyere.	Indemnity for property destroyed by United States army in revolutionary war.	15	1	Petition	179	Claims	....	....	......	Discharged; laid on table.		
De Kermion, Labeydeyere.	Indemnity for property destroyed by United States army in revolutionary war.	15	2	Senate bill	334	Whole House.....	Mar. 2, 1819	....	S. 82			
De Kermion, Labeydeyere.	Indemnity for property destroyed by United States army in revolutionary war.	16	1	Senate bill	269	Claims	....	....	S. 46			
De Kermion, Labeydeyere.	Indemnity for property destroyed by United States army in revolutionary war.	16	2	Petition	164	Claims	Jan. 29, 1820	Adverse	......	Laid on table.		

List of private claims presented to the House of Representatives of the United States from the 1st to the 31st Congress, inclusive—Continued.

Names of claimants.	Nature or object of the claim.	Congress.	Session.	How brought before the House of Reps.	Page of journal.	To what committee of the House referred.	No. or date of the report.	Nature of the report.	No. of the bill.	How disposed of by the House of Reps.	How disposed of by the Senate.	Date of the act of Congress, and remarks.
De Kermion, Labeydeyere.	Indemnity for property destroyed by United States army in revolutionary war.	17	1	Petition	47	Claims				Discharged; laid on table.		Leave to withdraw.
De Kersant, Henriette	Remission of duties on goods sent for charitable purposes.	25	3	Petition	212	Ways and Means.						
De Keyser, Lee	Liquidation and settlement of claim as captain and major in Georgia line in revolutionary war.	5	2	Petition	144	Claims	Mar. 20, 1796			Leave to withdraw.		
De Klyn, Barnet	Renewal of loan office certificates stolen.	4	1	Petition	517	Claims.						
De Klyn, Barnet	Renewal of loan office certificates stolen.	4	2	Petition and res.	614	Claims	Feb. 1, 1797	Adverse.				
De Krafft, Frederick C	(See Stephen Decatur, widow of, *et al.*)	19	2		98							
De Krafft, Frederick C	Compensation as surveyor of public lots in the city of Washington, and for annual salary.	21	1	Petition	173	Dist. of Columbia.				Discharged; laid on table.		
De Krafft, Frederick C	Compensation as surveyor of public lots in the city of Washington, and for annual salary.	23	1	Petition	245	Dist. of Columbia.						
De Krafft, Frederick C	Compensation as surveyor of public lots in the city of Washington, and for annual salary.	24	1	Petition	188	Dist. of Columbia.	351	Favorable; bill	357	Passed	Passed	App'd July 4, 1836
De Labigarre, Margaret	Certain lots near New Orleans, or other relief.	10	1	Memorial	268	Whole House, on bill No. 84.						
De Lapperiere, Auge	Compensation for horses lost in Seminole war.	18	1	Petition	85	Claims				Discharged; referred to Military Affairs.		
De Lassize, Jean Vallery	Indemnity for destruction of boat by United States troops.	19	1	Petition	151	Claims	156	Favorable; bill.	207	Passed.		
De Lassize, Jean Vallery	Indemnity for destruction of boat by United States troops.	19	2	Petition	132	Claims				Discharged.		
De Laurriston, J. A. B. L.	(See John Law, heirs of)	20	1		728							
De la Aumont, Nicholas	Revolutionary pension	26	1	Petition	759	Rev. Pensions	424	Adverse		Laid on table.		
De la Aumont, Viscount	Revolutionary pension	25	3	Petition	215	Rev. Pensions				Discharged.		
De la Carrera, Milton, heirs of.	Confirmation of title to land	23	1	Petition	499	Priv. Land Claims.						
De la Carrera, Milton, heirs of.	Confirmation of title to land	23	2	Senate bill	259	Priv. Land Claims.	Feb. 3, 1835	With't amend.	S. 75	Referred to Committee Whole House.		
De la Carrera, Milton, heirs of.	Confirmation of title to land	24	1	Senate bill	390	Priv. Land Claims.	Mar. 26, 1836	With't amend.	S. 68	Passed		App'd July 2, 1836
De la Carrera, William	Permission to return slaves from Cuba.	17	1	Petition	181	Suppression of slave trade.	83	Adverse		Laid on table.		
De la Colombe, Gen., heirs of.	Warrant for bounty land	26	2	Petition	119	Priv. Land Claims.				Discharged; referred to Rev. Claims.		
De la Colombe, Gen., heirs of.	Warrant for bounty land	27	2	Petition	62	Rev. Claims	14	Favorable; bill	55	Passed	Indef. postp'd.	Provided for in House bill No. 26, approved July 27, 1842.
De la Croix, Dussuan	Confirmation of title to land in Mobile.	18	1	Resolution	455	Priv. Land Claims.						
De la Croix, Dussuan	Confirmation of title to land in Mobile.	18	2	Petition	87	Priv. Land Claims.						
De la Croix, Dussuan	Confirmation of title to land in Mobile.	25	3	Petition	463	Priv. Land Claims.						

List of private claims presented to the House of Representatives of the United States from the 1st to the 31st Congress, inclusive—Continued.

Names of claimants.	Nature or object of the claim.	Congress.	Session.	How brought before the House of Reps.	Page of journal.	To what committee of the House referred.	No. or date of the report.	Nature of the report.	No. of the bill.	How disposed of by the House of Reps.	How disposed of by the Senate.	Date of the act of Congress, and remarks.
De la Croix, Dussuan....	Confirmation of title to land in Mobile.	26	1	Petition	179	Priv. Land Claims.						
De la Forrest, Aubin.....	Indemnity for losses sustained in Florida.	12	1	Petition	358	Select.						
De la Francia, Joseph....	Compensation for arms, &c., sold to people in Florida in 1810.	20	1	Petition	440	Ways and Means..	May 1, 1828	Favorable; bill	286	Referred to Secretary State.		
De la Francia, Joseph....	Compensation for arms, &c., sold to people in Florida in 1810.	20	2	Rep. of Secretary State, &c.	225	Ways and Means..	....	....	......	Discharged; laid on table.		
De la Francia, Joseph....	Compensation for arms, &c., sold to people in Florida in 1810.	22	1	Petition	471	Ways and Means.						
De la Francia, Joseph....	Compensation for arms, &c., sold to people in Florida in 1810.	28	2	Petition	89	Claims	189	Favorable; bill	646	Referred to Committee Whole House.		
De la Francia, Joseph....	Compensation for arms, &c., sold to people in Florida in 1810.	29	1	Petition	83	Judiciary	283	Adverse	......	Laid on table.		
De la Francia, Joseph....	Compensation for arms, &c., sold to people in Florida in 1810.	29	2	Senate bill	374	Judiciary	78	With't amend.	S. 62	Rejected.		
De la Francia, Joseph....	Compensation for arms, &c., sold to people in Florida in 1810.	30	1	Senate bill	684	Judiciary	667	With't amend.	S. 122	Passed	....	App'd Aug. 14, 1848
De la Gautrais, Don H, heirs of.	Confirmation of title to land in Louisiana.	18	1	Senate bill	339	Priv. Land Claims.	....	....	S. 59			
De la Gorce, Madame....	(See Count De Rochambeau, heirs of.)	22	2	....	406							
De la Houssaye, Alexander, heirs of.	Confirmation of title to land in Louisiana.	20	1	Petition	40	Priv. Land Claims.	Dec. 27, 1827	Adverse	......	Laid on table.		
De la Houssaye, Alexander, heirs of.	Confirmation of title to land in Louisiana.	20	2	Petition	34	Priv. Land Claims.	Dec. 18, 1828	Adverse	......	Laid on table.		
De la Houssaye, De Peltier.	Confirmation of title to land in Louisiana.	18	1	Report	31	Priv. Land Claims.	....	....	......	Discharged; laid on table.		
De la Houssaye, Louis, heirs of.	Confirmation of title to land in Louisiana.	19	1	Petition	37	Priv. Land Claims.	28	Favorable; bill	138	Passed.		
De la Houssaye, Louis, heirs of.	Confirmation of title to land in Louisiana.	19	2	Petition	45	Priv. Land Claims.	Dec. 19, 1826	Favorable; bill	303	Passed	Passed	App'd March 2, 1827
De la Houssaye, Louis, heirs of.	To change location and confirm title to land.	29	2	Senate bill	380	Priv. Land Claims.	Mar. 1, 1847	With't amend.	S. 124	Passed	....	App'd March 2, 1847
De la Houpoje, Octave, guardian of.	To amend act confirming land to..	30	1	Petition	387	Priv. Land Claims.						
De la Huff, George	Compensation for making axes and hatchets for militia, and for materials furnished for same.	13	3	Petition	706	Claims..........	....	....	......	Leave to withdraw.		
De la Marquisie, Bernard..	Arrears and depreciation of pay...	5	3	Petition	423	Claims	Feb. 11, 1799	Adverse	......	Rejected.		
De la Neuville, Alexander.	Confirmation of title to land in Louisiana.	22	1	Petition	133	Priv. Land Claims.	Jan. 13, 1832	Adverse	......	Laid on table.		
De la Neuville, L. P. L...	Liquidation of claim for services in revolutionary war.	1	2	Petition	212	....	....	....	......	Leave to withdraw.		
De la Pierre, Bartholomew	Pension	19	1	Petition	221	Military Pensions..	Feb. 23, 1826	Favorable; bill	118	Passed.		
De la Pierre, Bartholomew	Pension	19	2	House bill......	85	Military Pensions..	Dec. 22, 1826	With't amend	314	Referred to Committee Whole House.		
De la Pierre, Bartholomew	Pension	20	1	Petition	484	Military Pensions..	....	....	......	Discharged; laid on table.		
De la Pierre, Bartholomew	Pension	21	1	Petition	265	Military Pensions..	391	Favorable; bill	452	Referred to Committee Whole House.		
De la Pierre, Bartholomew	Pension	21	2	House bill......	318	Whole House.....	Feb. 16, 1831	With't amend.	452	Passed.		
De la Pierre, Bartholomew	Pension	22	1	Petition	164	Invalid Pensions ..	201	Favorable; bill	288	Passed	Passed	App'd July 14, 1832

List of private claims presented to the House of Representatives of the United States from the 1st to the 31st Congress, inclusive—Continued.

Names of claimants.	Nature or object of the claim.	Congress.	Session.	How brought before the House of Reps.	Page of journal.	To what committee of the House referred.	No. or date of the report.	Nature of the report.	No. of the bill.	How disposed of by the House of Reps.	How disposed of by the Senate.	Date of the act of Congress, and remarks.
De la Porte, Frederick, administrator of.	Indemnity for French spoliations prior to 1800.	23	1	Petition	637	Claims	....	....	......	Dis.; referred to Com. Foreign Affairs.		
De la Porte, Frederick, administrator of.	Indemnity for French spoliations prior to 1800.	26	1	Memorial	182	Foreign Affairs....	343	Favorable; bill	319	Referred to Committee Whole House.		
De la Roche, George F....	Credit for expenses incurred on account of an order from the Navy Department.	28	2	Memorial	266	Naval Affairs.						
De la Roche, George F...	Credit for expenses incurred on account of an order from the Navy Department.	29	1	Memorial	470	Naval Affairs	367	Favorable; bill	280	Referred to Committee Whole House.		
De la Roche, George F...	Credit for expenses incurred on account of an order from the Navy Department.	29	2	Rep't Committee Whole House.	71	Naval Affairs.....	Dec. 18, 1846	By bill	280	Passed	Passed	App'd March 3, 1847
De la Roche, George F...	Reimbursement of expenses incurred at dry-dock, N. Y.	30	1	Petition	161	Naval Affairs.....	130	Favorable; bill	121	Passed	Passed second session.	App'd Jan. 26, 1849
De la Roche, George F...	See Andrew Buchanan, trustee of)	26	1	....	182	....	343	....	319			
De la Roche, George F...	(See William L. Sountaz & Co., representative of.)	31	1	....	416							
De la Ronde, Pierre Dennis	Indemnity for damages to property by United States troops, late war	15	1	Petition	72	Claims.						
De la Ronde, Pierre Dennis	Indemnity for damages to property by United States troops, late war	15	2	Senate bill	280	Claims	141	Bill amended..	S. 44	Referred to Committee Whole House.		
De la Ronde, Pierre Dennis	Indemnity for damages to property by United States troops, late war	16	1	Senate bill	417	Claims	....	....	S. 73			
De la Ronde, Pierre Dennis	Indemnity for damages to property by United States troops, late war	16	2	Petition	19	Claims	25	Favorable; bill	192	Passed	Passed	App'd March 2, 1821
De la Rue, Amelia Eugenie	(See Caron De Beaumarchais.)...	18	1	....	435							
De Leaumont, Marie Nicholas.	Revolutionary pension..........	26	1	Report & petition.	759	Rev. Pensions	424	....	......	Laid on table.		
De Leisseline, Francis G..	Revolutionary pension..........	29	2	Petition	169	Rev. Pensions.						
De Leisseline, Francis G..	Revolutionary pension	30	1	Petition	261	Rev. Pensions.....	227	Adverse	......	Laid on table.		
De Leon, Juan, representatives of.	Confirmation of land title	19	2	Rep. of Secretary Treasury.	50	Public Lands	49	Favorable; bill	378	Referred to Committee Whole House.		
De Leon, Juan, representatives of.	Confirmation of land title	24	1	Report and docs	155	Priv. Land Claims.	93	Favorable....	......	Ordered to be printed.		
De, Leon, M. H	(See Thomas Cooper, executors of.)	26	1	....	340							
De Lirac, G............	Debenture on goods exported to Canada.	30	1	Petition	276	Claims	156	Favorable; bill	160	Passed.		
De Lirac, G............	Debenture on goods exported to Canada.	31	1	Petition	213	Claims	409	Adverse	......	Laid on table.		
De Lisa, Joaquin........	Confirmation of title to land in Missouri.	15	1	Petition	85	Priv. Land Claims.						
De Lisa, Joaquin........	Confirmation of title to land in Missouri.	16	1	Petition	36	Priv. Land Claims.						
De Lisa, Joaquin........	Confirmation of title to land in Missouri.	17	1	Petition	54	Public Lands	....	....	......	Discharged; laid on table.		
De Lisa, Joaquin........	Confirmation of title to land in Missouri.	18	1	Petition	54	Public lands......	Jan. 16, 1824	By bill	65	Passed with amendm't.	Passed	App'd May 26, 1824
De Lisa, Manuel........	Confirmation of title to land in Missouri.	15	1	Petition	85	Priv. Land Claims.						
De Lisa, Manuel........	Confirmation of title to land in Missouri.	16	1	Petition	36	Priv. Land Claims.						

List of private claims presented to the House of Representatives of the United States from the 1st to the 31st Congress, inclusive—Continued.

Names of claimants.	Nature or object of the claim.	Congress.	Session.	How brought before the House of Reps.	Page of journal.	To what committee of the House referred.	No. or date of the report.	Nature of the report.	No. of the bill.	How disposed of by the House of Reps.	How disposed of by the Senate.	Date of the act of Congress, and remarks.
De Lisa, Manuel	Confirmation of title to land in Missouri.	17	1	Petition	54	Public Lands				Discharged; laid on table.		
De Lisa, Manuel	Confirmation of title to land in Missouri.	18	1	Petition	54	Public Lands	Jan. 16, 1824	By bill	65	Passed with amendm't	Passed	App'd May 26, 1824
De Lord, Henry	(See Henry Delord)											
De Lozeair, Asa	(See John Begley, attorney of)	10	1		140							
De Lothbiniere, De Chartier, Marquis.	Compensation for two manors at head of Lake Superior.	1	1	Petition	97					Rejected.		
De Lusser, Madame, heirs of.	Confirmation of titles to certain lands.	25	2	Senate bill	1166	Priv. Land Claims.			S. 371			
De Lusser, Madame, heirs of.	Confirmation of titles to certain lands.	25	3	Senate bill	478	Priv. Land Claims.	March 2, 1839	With amend.	S. 156	Referred to Committee Whole House.		
De Lusser, Madame, heirs of.	Confirmation of titles to certain lands.	25	3	Senate bill	478	Priv. Land Claims.			S. 263			
De Lusser, Madame, heirs of.	Confirmation of titles to certain lands.	26	1	Senate bill	578	Priv. Land Claims.	April 4, 1840	With't amend.	S. 55	Referred to Committee Whole House.		
De Lusser, Madame, heirs of.	Confirmation of titles to certain lands.	26	2	Senate bill	229	Priv. Land Claims.			S. 156			
De Lusser, Madame, heirs of.	Confirmation of titles to certain lands.	26	2	Senate bill	282				S. 172	Referred to Committee Whole House.		
De Lusser, Madame, heirs of.	Confirmation of titles to certain lands.	27	2	Senate bill	1126	Priv. Land Claims.	July 21, 1842	With't amend.	S. 236	Referred to Committee Whole House.		
De Lusser, Madame, heirs of.	Confirmation of titles to certain lands.	27	3	Memorial	59	Priv. Land Claims.						
De Lusser, Madame, heirs of.	Confirmation of titles to certain lands.	27	3	Senate bill	384	Priv. Land Claims.	Feb. 28, 1842	With't amend.	S. 43	Passed	....	App'd March 1, 1843
De Maison Rouge, Marquis, representatives of.	Confirmation of title to land in Louisiana.	14	2	Petition	164	Public Lands	73	Favorable; bill	118	Referred to Committee Whole House.		
De Maison Rouge, Marquis, representatives of.	Confirmation of title to land in Louisiana.	15	1	Petition	317	Priv. Land Claims.				Discharged.		
De Maison Rouge, Marquis, representatives of.	Confirmation of title to land in Louisiana.	16	2	Memorial	37	Priv. Land Claims.						
De Maison Rouge, Marquis, representatives of.	Confirmation of title to land in Louisiana.	16	2	Senate bill	270	Priv. Land Claims.	Mar. 1, 1821	With't amend.	S. 15	Referred to Committee Whole House.		
De Maison Rouge, Marquis, representatives of.	Confirmation of title to land in Louisiana.	17	1	Senate bill	426	Public Lands	April 10, 1822	With't amend.	S. 17	Laid on table.		
De Maison Rouge, Marquis, representatives of.	Confirmation of title to land in Louisiana.	17	1	Memorial	23	Priv. Land Claims.						
De Maison Rouge, Marquis, representatives of.	Confirmation of title to land in Louisiana.	18	1	Petition and docs.	78, 359	Priv. Land Claims.				Discharged; leave to withdraw.		
De Maison Rouge, Marquis, representatives of.	Confirmation of title to land in Louisiana.	18	1	Res. and docs.	119	Priv. Land Claims.	Feb. 18, 1824	Favorable; bill	128	Passed	Rejected.	
De Maison Rouge, Marquis, representatives of.	Confirmation of title to land in Louisiana.	18	2	Res. and report of Sec. Treasury.	57	Select	18	Favorable; bill	262	Passed	Rejected.	
De Maison Rouge, Marquis, representatives of.	Confirmation of title to land in Louisiana.	19	1	Rep. of Secretary of Treasury.	54	Select	2	Favorable; bill	7	Laid on table.		
De Maison Rouge, Marquis, representatives of.	Confirmation of title to land in Louisiana.	20	1	Res. and report of Sec. Treasury.	55	Public Lands	123	Favorable; bill	143	Referred to Committee Whole House.		
De Maison Rouge, Marquis, representatives of.	Confirmation of title to land in Louisiana.	21	1	Senate bill	158	Priv. Land Claims.	April 6, 1830	With't amend.	S. 21	Referred to Committee Whole House.		
De Maison Rouge, Marquis, representatives of.	Confirmation of title to land in Louisiana.	22	1	Petition	75	Priv. Land Claims.	178	Favorable; bill	254	Referred to Committee Whole House.		

List of private claims presented to the House of Representatives of the United States from the 1st to the 31st Congress, inclusive—Continued.

Names of claimants.	Nature or object of the claim.	Congress.	Session.	How brought before the House of Reps.	Page of journal.	To what committee of the House referred.	No. or date of the report.	Nature of the report.	No. of the bill.	How disposed of by the House of Reps.	How disposed of by the Senate.	Date of the act of Congress, and remarks.
De Maison Rouge, Marquis, representatives of.	Confirmation of title to land in Louisiana.	22	2	Rep't Committee Whole House.	92	Whole House	Dec. 28, 1832	By bill	254	Laid on table.		
De Maison Rouge, Marquis, representatives of.	Confirmation of title to land in Louisiana.	24	1	Senate bill	320	Priv. Land Claims.	554	With amend.	S. 1	Referred to Committee Whole House.		
De Maison Rouge, Marquis, representatives of.	Confirmation of title to land in Louisiana.	24	2	Senate bill	527	Whole House			S. 49			
De Maison Rouge, Marquis, representatives of.	Confirmation of title to land in Louisiana.	25	2	Senate bill	332	Priv. Land Claims.	Feb. 6, 1838	Adverse	S. 84	Discharged; referred to Com. Whole House.		
De Maison Rouge, Marquis, representatives of.	Confirmation of title to land in Louisiana.	25	3	Resolution	173	Priv. Land Claims.						
De Maison Rouge, Marquis, representatives of.	Confirmation of title to land in Louisiana.	27	2	Memorials	614, 681	Priv. Land Claims.						
De Maison Rouge, Marquis, representatives of.	Confirmation of title to land in Louisiana.	31	2	Senate bill	175	Priv. Land Claims.	Jan. 22, 1851	With't amend.	S. 68	Passed		App'd Jan. 27, 1851
De Menou, Count	(See Philip Renaut, heirs of)	27	3		91				555			
De Monbreun, Timothy	Compensation for supplies furnished and services rendered in revolutionary war.	2	2	Memorial	635					Referred to Secretary of War.		Leave to withdraw.
De Motte, Lewis	Naval invalid pension	27	3	Petition	284	Invalid Pensions.						
De Mun, Louis	Confirmation of land title	15	1	Petition	102	Priv. Land Claims.				Discharged.		
De Neven, Gustave	Repayment of money paid for inundated lands.	29	1	Memorial	395	Public Lands	641	Adverse		Laid on table.		
De Neufville, John, by Anna, widow of.	Compensation for services and for losses in revolutionary war.	4	2	Memorial	678	Select	Feb. 7, 1797	Favorable; bill	230	Passed	Passed	App'd March 2, 1797
De Neufville, John, heir of.	Reimbursement for advances made in revolutionary war.	31	1	Petition	1035	Rev. Claims	Sept. 24, 1850	By joint res.	28			
De Neufville, John, heir of.	Reimbursement for advances made in revolutionary war.	31	2	Joint resolution.	196	Whole House	Mar. 3, 1851	With't amend.	J. R. 28	Passed	Passed	App'd March 3, 1851
De Oteza, Celestino	Restoration of brig Patriota, seized for violation of revenue laws.	13	2	Petition	174	Ways and Means	59	Adverse		Referred to Committee Whole House.		
De Passau, George	To enter land in lieu of land deprived of by fraud.	26	1	Senate bill	836	Priv. Land Claims.	June 23, 1840	With't amend.	S. 237	Referred to Committee Whole House.		
De Passau, George	To enter land in lieu of land deprived of by fraud.	26	2	Senate bill	225	Priv. Land Claims.			S. 119			
De Passau, George	To enter land in lieu of land deprived of by fraud.	27	2	Petition	140	Priv. Land Claims.						
De Passau, George	To enter land in lieu of land deprived of by fraud.	27	2	Senate bill	238	Priv. Land Claims.	Feb. 9, 1843	With't amend.	S. 66	Rejected.		
De Pancemont, John F. M.	(See Philip Renaut, heirs of)	14	2		337							
De Pancemont, Madame R. M.	(See Philip Renaut, heirs of)	14	2		337							
De Peyster, Frederick, *et al.*	Indemnity for French spoliations prior to 1800.	19	2	Petition	217	Foreign Affairs				Discharged.		
De Peyster, Frederick, *et al.*	Indemnity for French spoliations prior to 1800.	26	1	Memorial	182	Foreign Affairs	343	Favorable; bill	319	Referred to Committee Whole House.		
De Peyster, George B.	Payment of $18 40 costs incurred in certain suit.	25	2	Petition	574	Claims.						
De Peyster, George B.	Payment of $18 40 costs incurred in certain suit.	25	3	Petition	87	Claims				Discharged; leave to withdraw.		
De Peyster, Jacobus, administrators of.	Settlement of claim for supplies furnished United States in revolutionary war.	4	1	Petition	467	Claims.						

List of private claims presented to the House of Representatives of the United States from the 1st to the 31st Congress, inclusive—Continued.

Names of claimants.	Nature or object of the claim.	Congress.	Session.	How brought before the House of Reps.	Page of journal.	To what committee of the House referred.	No. or date of the report.	Nature of the report.	No. of the bill.	How disposed of by the House of Reps.	How disposed of by the Senate.	Date of the act of Congress, and remarks.
De Peyster, William H., and Henry N. Cruger.	Remuneration for value of slave, (Romeo,) and for his services.	27	2	Senate bill	215	Military Affairs....	....	....	S. 101			
De Peyster, William H., and Henry N. Cruger.	Remuneration for value of slave, (Romeo,) and for his services.	27	3	Senate bill	234	Military Affairs....	146	With amend..	S. 68	Referred to Committee Whole House.		
De Peyster, William H., and Henry N. Cruger.	Remuneration for value of slave, (Romeo,) and for his services.	28	1	Senate bill	539	Claims	March 8, 1844	With't amend.	S. 58	Passed	....	App'd June 17, 1844
De Piernas, Madame Le Compte.	Indemnity for damages, and for articles furnished U. S. army during invasion of Louisiana.	19	1	Resolution	39	Claims..........	April 21, 1826	Adverse	......	Referred to Committee Whole House.		
De Piernas, Madame Le Compte.	Indemnity for damages, and for articles furnished U. S. army during invasion of Louisiana.	19	2	Petition	44	Claims..........	....	....	......	Discharged.		
De Piernas, Madame Le Compte.	Indemnity for damages, and for articles furnished U. S. army during invasion of Lousiaina.	21	2	Petition	143	Claims..........	Jan. 12, 1831	Adverse	......	Laid on table.		
De Repintigny, Chevalier, heirs of.	Confirmation of land title	31	1	Petition	1044	Priv. Land Claims.						
De Rham, H. C	(See Ebenezer Stevens and sons, *et al.*)	16	2	....	30							
De Rochambeau, Marshal Count, heirs of.	Compensation for services in revolutionary war.	22	2	President's message.	406	Rev. Claims.						
De Rochambeau, Marshal Count, heirs of.	Compensation for services in revolutionary war.	23	1	President's message, &c.	658, 807	Foreign Affairs.						
De Rochambeau, Marshal Count, heirs of.	Compensation for services in revolutionary war.	23	2	Memorial	38	Rev. Claims.						
De Rochambeau, Marshal Count, heirs of.	Compensation for services in revolutionary war.	24	1	Petition and docs.	104	Rev. Claims......	307	Favorable ; bill	321	Referred to Committee Whole House.		
De Rochambeau, Marshal Count, heirs of.	Compensation for services in revolutionary war.	24	2	Memorial	110	Rev. Claims.						
De Rochambeau, Marshal Count, heirs of.	Compensation for services in revo lutionary war.	26	1	Petition	165	Rev. Claims.						
De Rochambeau, Marshal Count, heirs of.	Compensation for services in revolutionary war.	27	2	Memorial	226	Rev. Claims......	1071	Adverse	......	Laid on table.		
De Rochambeau, Marshal Count, heirs of.	Compensation for services in revolutionary war.	28	1	Petition	90	Rev. Claims.						
De Rochambeau, Marshal Count, heirs of.	Compensation for services in revolutionary war.	28	2	Petition	66	Rev. Claims.						
De Rochambeau, Marshal Count, heirs of.	Compensation for services in revolutionary war.	29	1	Memorial	115	Rev. Claims......	201	Favorable ; bill	195	Referred to Committee Whole House.		
De Rochambeau, Marshal Count, heirs of.	Compensation for services in revolutionary war.	29	2	Rep't Committee Whole House.	381	Whole House.....	Feb. 19, 1847	By bill	195	Referred to Committee Whole House.		
De Rose, John J., heirs of.	Indemnity for French spoliations prior to 1800.	30	1	Petition	118	Foreign Affairs....	Jan. 4, 1848	By bill	21	Referred to Committee Whole House.		
De Roxas, Jose	Donation of land	26	1	Petition	947	Priv. Land Claims.						
De Russy, G. A	Arrears of salary as acting purser United States navy.	28	2	Petition	215	Claims.						
De Russy, G. A	Arrears of salary as acting purser United States navy.	29	1	Petition	370	Naval Affairs.....	744	Adverse	......	Laid on table.		
De Russy, G. A	Arrears of salary as acting purser United States navy.	31	1	Petition	216	Naval Affairs	203	Favorable ; bill	211	Referred to Committee Whole House.		
De Russy, G. A	Arrears of salary as acting purser United States navy.	31	2	Rep't Committee Whole House.	181	Whole House	Jan. 24, 1851	By bill	211	Passed.		

List of private claims presented to the House of Representatives of the United States from the 1st to the 31st Congress, inclusive—Continued.

Names of claimants.	Nature or object of the claim.	Congress.	Session.	How brought before the House of Reps.	Page of journal.	To what committee of the House referred.	No. or date of the report.	Nature of the report.	No. of the bill.	How disposed of by the House of Reps.	How disposed of by the Senate.	Date of the act of Congress, and remarks.
De Russy, Lewis G.	Relief from judgment on account of loss of public funds.	29	1	Joint Resolution.	826	Military Affairs	July 17, 1846	With't amend.	S. 24	Passed	Passed	App'd July 21, 1846
De Russy, Lieutenant Colonel R. E.	For settlement of accounts, and to be allowed certain credits.	30	1	Petition	1237	Claims.						
De Russy, Lieutenant Colonel R. E.	For settlement of accounts, and to be allowed certain credits.	30	2	Petition	102	Claims	46	Adverse		Laid on table.		
De Saussane, H. A.	(See Alexander Garden, executor of.)	22	1		538		425		530			
De Silva, Joseph	Revolutionary pension	15	2	Petition	196	Rev. Pensions	Feb. 11, 1819	Adverse		Laid on table.		
De Silva, Joseph	Revolutionary pension	19	1	Petition	203	Military Pensions	164	Adverse.				
De Silva, Joseph	Revolutionary pension	20	2	Petition	203	Military Pensions				Discharged; laid on table.		
De Silva, Joseph	Revolutionary pension	21	1	Petition	523	Military Pensions				Discharged; laid on table.		
De Silveira, Gracia Albert.	Remission of duties on vessel and cargo captured by the enemy.	15	2	Petition	300	Ways and Means				Discharged; laid on table.		
Des Jardins, François, by Mary, widow of.	Compensation for military and other services rendered during revolutionary war.	2	1	Petition	581					Referred to Secretary War.		
Des Jardins, François, by Mary, widow of.	Compensation for military and other services rendered during revolutionary war.	2	2	Rep. of Secretary War.	733					Laid on table.		
Des Jardins, François, by Mary, widow of.	Compensation for military and other services rendered during revolutionary war.	3	2	Rep. of Secretary War.	350	Claims.						
De Sogrome, La Mise	(See Colonel De Fleury, heiress of)	19	1		381							
De Steuben, Baron Fredrick William.	Compensation for services in revolutionary war.	1	1	Petition	110					Referred to Secretary Treasury.		
De Steuben, Baron Fredrick William.	Compensation for services in revolutionary war.	1	2	Rep. of Secretary Treasury.	192	Select	May 3, 1790	By bill	60	Passed	Passed	App'd June 4, 1790
De Steuben, Baron Fredrick William.	Annual allowance of $2,500	3	1	Appropr'n bill								App'd Mar. 14, 1794
De Steuben, Baron Frederick William, executor of.	Confirmation of land title	4	1	Petition	545	Select	May 14, 1796	By bill	192	Passed	Rejected.	
De St. Romes, C. D.	For advertising for government	20	1	Petition	598	Claims				Disch'd; laid on table.		
De Torres, Francisco	Confirmation of land title	22	1	Petition	64	Priv. Land Claims.	62	Favorable; bill	125	Passed	Passed	App'd June 25, 1832
De Treville, Jonn, heirs of.	Commutation of half-pay	23	2	Petition	256	Rev. Claims.						
De Treville, John, heirs of	Commutation of half-pay	24	1	Petition	205	Rev. Claims	393	Favorable; bill	400	Referred to Committee Whole House.		
De Treville, John, heirs of.	Commutation of half pay	25	2	Petition	40, 193	Rev. Claims	133	Favorable; bill.	151	Passed.		
De Treville, John, heirs of.	Commutation of half-pay	25	3	Petition	226	Rev. Claims	161	Favorable; bill.	1026	Referred to Committee Whole House.		
De Treville, John, heirs of.	Commutation of half pay	26	1	Petition	165	Rev. Claims.						
De Treville, John, heirs of.	Commutation of half-pay	27	2	Senate bill	1116	Rev. Claims	1029	Adverse	S. 75	Referred to Committee Whole House.		
De Treville, John, heirs of.	Commutation of half-pay	30	1	Resolution	678	Rev. Claims.						
De Treville, John, heirs of.	Commutation of half pay	31	1	Petition	433	Rev. Claims	430	Favorable; bill	358	Referred to Committee Whole House.		
De Utrick, Baron, heirs of.	Release from indemnity bond	16	1	Petition	39	Ways and Means	Jan. 22, 1820	By bill	57	Passed	Passed	App'd May 4, 1820
De Valverde, Augustine, by Isabel O., widow of.	Indemnity for losses sustained by reason of the invasion of Florida by United States army in 1818.	20	1	Memorial	46	Foreign Affairs	49	Adverse		Laid on table.		

List of private claims presented to the House of Representatives of the United States from the 1st to the 31st Congress, inclusive—Continued.

Names of claimants.	Nature or object of the claim.	Congress.	Session.	How brought before the House of Reps.	Page of journal.	To what committee of the House referred.	No. or date of the report.	Nature of the report.	No. of the bill.	How disposed of by the House of Reps.	How disposed of by the Senate.	Date of the act of Congress, and remarks.
De Valverde, Augustine, by Isabel O., widow of.	Indemnity for losses sustained by reason of the invasion of Florida by United States army in 1818.	22	1	Petition	472	Foreign Affairs.						
De Van Brun, John Lavacher, by Ann, widow of.	Commutation pay	24	2	Petition	94	Rev. Claims	302	Favorable; bill	966	Referred to Committee Whole House.		
De Van Brun, John Lavacher, by Ann, widow of.	Commutation pay	25	2	Petition	40	Rev. Claims	1030	Favorable; bill	866	Referred to Committee Whole House.		
De Van Brun, John Lavacher, by Ann, widow of.	Commutation pay	25	3	Rep't Committee Whole House.	432	Whole House	Feb. 1, 1839	By bill	866	Passed	Passed	App'd March 3, 1839
De Veaux, Samuel	Indemnity for property destroyed by British in 1812.	15	2	Petition	148	Claims				Discharged; laid on table.		
De Veaux, Samuel	Indemnity for property destroyed by British in 1812.	17	1	Petition	46	Claims				Discharged; laid on table.		
De Veaux, Samuel	Indemnity for property destroyed by British in 1812.	18	1	Petition	130	Claims	Jan. 28, 1824	Adverse		Laid on table.		
De Vienne, Marquis	Compensation for services in revolutionary war.	8	1	Memorial	484	Claims				Discharged; referred to Com. Whole House.		
De Vienne, Marquis	Compensation for services in revolutionary war.	15	2	Petition	52	Select	29	Favorable; bill	222	Passed	Passed	App'd Feb. 24, 1819
De Vienne, Marquis	Balance due on settlement under act of February 24, 1819.	16	1	House bill	238	Whole House	Feb. 28, 1820	With't amend.	86	Passed	Passed	App'd April 11, 1820
De Villemont, Don Carlos.	Confirmation of title to land in Arkansas.	17	1	Petition	267	Priv. Land Claims.				Discharged; laid on table.		
De Villemont, Don Carlos.	Confirmation of title to land in Arkansas.	17	2	Petition	36	Priv. Land Claims.				Discharged.		
De Villemont, Don Carlos.	Confirmation of title to land in Arkansas.	18	1	Petition	32	Priv. Land Claims.	Jan. 9, 1824	Adverse		Laid on table		Leave to withdraw.
De Villemont, Don Carlos, heirs of.	Confirmation of title to land in Arkansas.	20	1	Resolution	413	Public Lands				Discharged; laid on table.		
De Villemont, Don Carlos, heirs of.	Confirmation of title to land in Arkansas.	22	1	Resolution, &c.	95, 770	Public Lands.						
De Villemont, Don Carlos, heirs of.	Confirmation of title to land in Arkansas.	25	2	Documents	569	Priv. Land Claims.				Discharged; laid on table.		
De Villemont, Don Carlos, heirs of.	Confirmation of title to land in Arkansas.	25	3	Memorial	249	Priv. Land Claims.	244	Favorable; bill	1107	Referred to Committee Whole House.		
De Villemont, Don Carlos, heirs of.	Confirmation of title to land in Arkansas.	26	1	Petition	179	Priv. Land Claims.	97	Favorable; bill	93	Referred to Committee Whole House.		
De Villemont, Don Carlos, heirs of.	Confirmation of title to land in Arkansas.	26	2	Rep't Committee Whole House.	194	Whole House	Jan. 16, 1841	Adverse	93	Rejected.		
De Villemont, Don Carlos, heirs of.	Confirmation of title to land in Arkansas.	28	1	Petition	130	Priv. Land Claims.						
De Villiers, F. D. P., administrator of.	Discharge from judgment as surety on custom house bond.	27	2	Senate bill	1064	Judiciary	July 21, 1842	With't amend.	S. 213	Passed		App'd Aug. 11, 1842
De Villiers, Jumonville	Indemnity for property destroyed by United States troops in 1812.	14	2	Petition	142	Claims	Feb. 3, 1817	Favorable; bill	102	Passed	Passed	App'd March 3, 1817
De Villiers, Jumonville	Indemnity for damages to plantation near New Orleans in 1812.	18	1	Petition	253	Claims.						
De Villiers, Jumonville	Indemnity for damages to plantation near New Orleans in 1812	19	1	Petition	38, 151	Claims	Jan. 18, 1826	Adverse		Laid on table.		
De Villiers, Jumonville	Indemnity for damages to plantation near New Orleans in 1812.	19	2	Petition	44	Claims	Jan. 17, 1827	Adverse		Laid on table.		
De Villiers, Jumonville	Indemnity for damages to plantation near New Orleans in 1812.	20	1	Petition	31	Claims	Dec. 21, 1827	Adverse		Laid on table.		

List of private claims presented to the House of Representatives of the United States from the 1st to the 31st Congress, inclusive—Continued.

Names of claimants.	Nature or object of the claim.	Congress.	Session.	How brought before the House of Reps.	Page of journal.	To what committee of the House referred.	No. or date of the report.	Nature of the report.	No. of the bill.	How disposed of by the House of Reps.	How disposed of by the Senate.	Date of the act of Congress, and remarks.
De Villiers, Jumonville...	Indemnity for damages to plantation near New Orleans in 1812.	21	2	Petition	143	Claims	Jan. 13, 1831	Adverse	......	Laid on table.		
De Villiers, Marcos, *et al*.	Indemnity for illegal arrest and imprisonment by authorities of West Florida.	17	1	Petition	281	Military Affairs.						
De Vobecye, Louis Le Gras.	(See Robert Farmer, heirs of)....	24	1	....	112	....	352	....	358			
De Watts, Eleanor.......	(See John Bowen, heirs of).....	25	2	....	115							
De Witt, Charles G......	(See Hector Craig, *et al*).......	22	1	....	447							
De Witt, James.........	Invalid pension................	19	1	Petition	396	Military Pensions..	May 5, 1826	Favorable....	......	Discharged.		
De Witt, James.........	Invalid pension................	19	2	Petition & papers	53	Military Pensions..	Dec. 22, 1826	Favorable; bill	314	Passed	Passed	App'd March 3, 1827
De Witt, William, (Pa.)..	Invalid pension................	4	1	Rep. of Secretary War.	447	Claims	Feb. 18, 1796	Favorable; bill ordered.	156	Passed	Passed	App'd April 20, 1796
De Witt, William, (N. Y.)	Arrears of pension............	21	1	Petition	46	Military Claims...	April 2, 1830	Adverse	......	Recommitted.		
De Wolf, Charles, *et al*...	(See John Jells, sureties of).....	8	1	....	428							
De Wolf, James.........	Indemnity for vessel and cargo captured by British in 1795.	16	2	Petition	32	Claims	Feb. 5, 1821	Adverse	......	Laid on table.		
De Wolf, James.........	Indemnity for vessel and cargo captured by British in 1795.	17	1	Petition	299	Claims	....	....	......	Discharged; laid on table.		
De Wolf, John, (Bristol, R. I.)	Relief from bond given for duties on spirits exported.	6	2	Petition	783	Com. and Manuf..	....	....	......	Discharged; leave to withdraw.		
De Wolf, John, (Bristol, R. I.)	Relief from bond given for duties on spirits exported.	7	1	Petition	135	Com. and Manuf..	Mar. 15, 1802	Adverse......	......	Laid on table.		
De Wolf, John, (Bristol, R. I.)	Relief from bond given for duties on spirits exported.	7	2	Petition	329	Com. and Manuf..	Feb. 15, 1803	Report.......	......	Leave to withdraw.		
De Wolf, John, (Bristol, R. I.)	Compensation for services as U. S. assessor in 1816 and 1817.	24	2	Documents	37	Claims	141	Adverse	......	Laid on table.		
De Wolf, John, jr., (Bristol, R. I.)	Remuneration for expenses as consul to Nova Scotia.	26	2	Petition	57	Claims.						
De Wolf, John, jr., (Bristol, R. I.)	Remuneration for expenses as consul to Nova Scotia.	27	2	Petition	56	Foreign Affairs....	994	Adverse	......	Laid on table.		
De Wolf, John, jr., (Bristol, R. I.)	Remuneration for expenses as consul to Nova Scotia.	27	3	Petition	72	Foreign Affairs.						
De Wolf, John, jr., (Bristol, R. I.)	Remuneration for expenses as consul to Nova Scotia.	28	1	Petition	84	Foreign Affairs....	43	Adverse	......	Laid on table.		
De Wolf, John, (Portsm'th, R. I.)	Revolutionary pension..........	23	1	Petition	190	Rev. Pensions.						
De Young, Isaac	Arrears of pension............	16	2	Petition	225	Pens. & Rev. Cl'ms.	Feb. 16, 1821	Adverse	......	Laid on table.		
De Young, Isaac	Arrears of pension............	17	1	Petition	145	Pens. & Rev. Cl'ms.	Jan. 22, 1822	Adverse	......	Laid on table.		
Diamond, Eleanor	(See Wm. Scott, administrator of)	3	1	....	131							
Diamond, Rebecca.......	Continuation of pension	28	1	Petition	819	Rev. Pensions.						
Dias, Joseph Lopez	Discharge from judgment of district court, New York.	23	2	Rep. of Secretary Treasury.	255	Judiciary.						
Dias, Joseph Lopez	(See Franklin, Robinson & Co.)..	26	1	....	182	....	343	....	319			
Dibble, Israel	Invalid pension................	4	1	Rep. of Secretary War.	447	Claims	Feb. 18, 1796	Favorable; bill ordered.	156	Passed	Passed	App'd April 20, 1796
Dibble, Israel...........	Increase of pension	12	1	House bill	361	Whole House	Jan. 15, 1812	With't amend.	138	Passed............	Passed	App'd July 5, 1812
Dibble, Israel...........	Increase of pension	13	1	House bill	56	Whole House	July 20, 1803	By bill	31	Passed	Passed	App'd August 2, 1813
Dibble, Israel...........	Increase of pension	15	2	Petition	132	Pens. & Rev. Cl'ms.	Dec. 30, 1818	Adverse	......	Laid on table.		
Dibble, Jonas...........	(See Exploring Expedition).....	27	3	....	149	....	270	....	818			
Dibble, Jonas...........	Extra pay for services on Exploring Expedition.	28	2	Memorial	70	Naval Affairs.						
Dibble, Mary D.	(See Colonel William M. Smith, daughter of.)	28	1	....	305							

List of private claims presented to the House of Representatives of the United States from the 1st to the 31st Congress, inclusive—Continued.

Names of claimants.	Nature or object of the claim.	Congress.	Session.	How brought before the House of Reps.	Page of journal.	To what committee of the House referred.	No. or date of the report.	Nature of the report.	No. of the bill.	How disposed of by the House of Reps.	How disposed of by the Senate.	Date of the act of Congress, and remarks.
Dibble, Orange H.	Pay under contract for building bridge across Potomac.	23	1	Amend't to House bill.	866	Roads and Canals.	Feb. 11, 1834	By bill	303	Passed	Passed	App'd June 30, 1834
Dibble, Orange H.	Pay under contract for building bridge across Potomac.	23	2	Rep. of Secretary Treasury.	42	Claims	142	Joint resolut'n.	21	Passed	Adverse.	
Dibble, Orange H.	Pay under contract for building bridge across Potomac.	24	1	Petition and docs.	284	Claims	792	Joint resolut'n.	17	Postponed.		
Dibble, Orange H.	Pay under contract for building bridge across Potomac.	24	2	Joint resolution	176	Whole House			J.R. 17	Passed	Passed	App'd March 3, 1837
Dibble, Orange H.	Pay under contract for building bridge across Potomac.	25	2	Petition	51	Claims				Discharged.		
Dibble, Orange H.	Pay under contract for building bridge across Potomac.	25	3	Petition	86	Claims.						
Dibble, Orange H.	Pay under contract for building bridge across Potomac.	26	1	Petition	472	Claims	56	Adverse		Laid on table.		
Dibble, Orange H.	Pay under contract for building bridge across Potomac.	28	1	Petition	98	Claims	521	Joint resolut'n.	38	Referred to Committee Whole House.		
Dibble, Orange H.	Pay under contract for building bridge across Potomac.	29	1	Petition	90	Claims	725	Adverse		Laid on table.		
Dibble, Orange H.	Pay under contract for building bridge across Potomac.	30	1	Petition	68	Claims	744	Favorable; bill	585	Referred to Committee Whole House.		
Dibble, Orange H.	Pay under contract for building bridge across Potomac.	31	1	Petition	283	Claims.						
Dibble, Solomon	Indemnity for costs of suit, &c.	22	1	Petition	26	Claims	Dec. 21, 1831	Adverse		Laid on table.		
Dibble, Stephen	(See Jonathan Meeker, administrator of.)	29	1		648							
Dick, Major Alexander, devisee of.	Indemnity for land ceded to Chickasaw Indians.	4	1	Petition	437	Select.						
Dick, Major Alexander, devisee of.	Indemnity for land ceded to Chickasaw Indians.	4	2	Petition	647	Select	Feb. 3, 1797	Adverse		Laid on table.		
Dick, Alexander, heirs of.	Commutation pay	22	1	Petition	44	Rev. Claims	Mar. 9, 1832	Favorable; bill	456	Referred to Committee Whole House.		
Dick, Alexander, heirs of.	Commutation pay	23	1	Petition	97	Rev. Claims.						
Dick, Alexander, heirs of.	Commutation pay	24	1	Petition	275	Rev. Claims				Discharged; laid on table.		
Dick, Alexander, heirs of.	Commutation pay	25	2	Petition	232	Rev. Claims				Discharged; laid on table.		
Dick, Alexander, heirs of.	Commutation pay	25	3	Petition and memorial.	125	Rev. Claims				Discharged; laid on table.		
Dick, Elias D., administrator of.	Release from payment of money due United States.	19	1	Petition	46	Judiciary	Jan. 4, 1826	Adverse		Laid on table.		
Dick, Elias D., administrator of.	Release from payment of money due United States.	19	2	Petition	134	Claims				Discharged.		
Dick, Elias D., administrator of.	Release from payment of money due United States.	20	1	Petition	104	Claims	129	Favorable; bill.	148	Passed.		
Dick, Elias D., administrator of.	Release from payment of money due United States.	20	2	Petition	90	Claims	30	Favorable; bill.	347	Referred to Committee Whole House.		
Dick, Elias D., administrator of.	Release from payment of money due United States.	22	1	Petition	172	Claims	193	Favorable; bill.	273	Referred to Committee Whole House.		
Dick, Elias D., administrator of.	Release from payment of money due United States.	22	2	Rep't Committee Whole House.	93	Whole House	Dec. 28, 1832	With amend.	273	Passed	Ref. to Committee on Judiciary.	
Dick, Elias D., administrator of.	Release from payment of money due United States.											

List of private claims presented to the House of Representatives of the United States from the 1st to the 31st Congress, inclusive—Continued.

Names of claimants.	Nature or object of the claim.	Congress.	Session.	How brought before the House of Reps.	Page of journal.	To what committee of the House referred.	No. or date of the report.	Nature of the report.	No. of the bill.	How disposed of by the House of Reps.	How disposed of by the Senate.	Date of the act of Congress, and remarks.
Dick, Samuel	Patent for land	9	1	Petition	236	Public Lands.						
Dick, Samuel	Patent for land	9	2	Petition	568	Public Lands.						
Dick, Samuel	Confirmation of title to land	13	3	Petition	662	Public Lands	...	...	...	Discharged.		
Dibk, Samuel	Confirmation of title to land	14	1	Petition	43	Public Lands	35	Favorable; bill.	58	Passed	Passed	App'd April 27, 1816
Dickason, John	Compensation for services as acting sailingmaster.	25	3	Petition	334	Naval Affairs.						
Dickason, John	Compensation for services as acting sailingmaster.	26	1	Petition	180	Naval Affairs	546	Adverse	...	Laid on table.		
Dickerson, Benjamin	Pension	16	1	Petition	194	Pens. & Rev. Cl'ms.	...	...	...	Discharged; referred to Secretary of War.	...	Leave to withdraw.
Dickerson, Benjamin	Pension	16	2	Petition	68	Pens. & Rev. Cl'ms.	...	...	...	Leave to withdraw.		
Dickerson, Benjamin	Pension	21	2	Petition	73	Military Pensions.						
Dickerson, Benjamin	Pension	22	1	Petition	288	Rev. Pensions	...	...	...	Discharged; laid on table.		
Dickerson, Braddock	Arrears or increase of pension	25	2	Petition	180	Rev. Pensions	...	...	...	Discharged; laid on table.		
Dickerson, Clark, *et al*	Donation of land	24	2	Petition	94	Indian Affairs.						
Dickerson, David	Compensation for revolutionary services.	25	2	Petition	390	Rev. Claims	...	...	...	Discharged; laid on table.		
Dickerson, Elbert, by legislature of Wisconsin.	Indemnity for provisions consumed by Winnebago Indians in 1839 and 1840.	29	1	Memorial	690	Indian Affairs.						
		29	2	Memorial	428	Indian Affairs.						
Dickerson, Ira	Indemnity for property destroyed by enemy in 1813-'14.	17	1	Petition	46	Claims	...	...	...	Discharged; laid on table.		
Dickerson, Ira, by Matilda, widow of.	Indemnity for property destroyed by enemy in 1813-'14.	26	1	Petition	294	Claims.						
Dickerson, Ira, by Matilda, widow of.	Indemnity for property destroyed by enemy in 1813-'14.	26	2	Petition	148	Rev. Claims.						
Dickerson, Ira, by Matilda, widow of.	Indemnity for property destroyed by ememy in 1813-'14.	27	2	Petition	53	Claims	346	Adverse	...	Laid on table.		
Dickerson, John	(See John Diekason.)	26	1	...	180	...	546					
Dickerson, Nathn'l, (N. Y.)	Pension	21	2	Petition	230	Military Pensions.						
Dickerson, Nathaniel, per Henry.	Commutation pay	24	1	Petition	259	Rev. Claims.						
Dickerson Obediah	Patent for land	21	1	Petition	151	Priv. Land Claims.	May 27, 1830	Favorable; bill	494	Referred to Committee Whole House.		
Dickerson, Samuel, (Ill.)	Permission to correct error in entry of land.	24	1	Petition	215	Public Lands	287	Favorable; bill	290	Referred to Committee Whole House.		
Dickerson, Samuel, (Ill.)	Permission to correct error in entry of land.	24	2	Rep't Committee Whole House.	200	Whole House	Jan. 13, 1837	By bill	290			
Dickerson, Samuel, (Ill.)	Permission to correct error in entry of land.	25	2	Petition	42	Public Lands.	494	Favorable; bill	490	Referred to Committee Whole House.		
Dickerson, Samuel, (Ill.)	Permission to correct error in entry of land.	25	3	Rep. Committee Whole House.	379	Whole House	Jan. 25, 1839	By bill	490	Passed	Passed	App'd March 2, 1839
Dickey, Captain, (an Indian.)	Pension	21	1	Petition	600	Military Affairs	...	...	...	Discharged; laid on table.		
Dickey, Darius	Remuneration for services rendered in capture of the British schooner Industry.	27	3	Petition	271	Claims.						
Dickey, David	For land under general act for relief of refugees.	12	1	House bill	242	Whole House	Mar. 2, 1812	With't amend	85	Passed	Passed	App'd April 23, 1812

List of private claims presented to the House of Representatives of the United States from the 1st to the 31st Congress, inclusive—Continued.

Names of claimants.	Nature or object of the claim.	Congress.	Session.	How brought before the House of Reps.	Page of journal.	To what committee of the House referred.	No. or date of the report.	Nature of the report.	No. of the bill.	How disposed of by the House of Reps.	How disposed of by the Senate.	Date of the act of Congress, and remarks.
Dickey, George	Permission to locate confirmed land claim.	14	1	Petition	222	Public Lands.				Discharged; laid on table.		
Dickey, George	Permission to locate confirmed land claim.	14	2	Petition	50	Priv. Land Claims.				Discharged; laid on table.		
Dickey, John	For moiety of fine collected from William Quick.	30	1	Petition	102	Claims	44	Adverse		Laid on table.		
Dickey, Milus W	Payment as mail contractor	25	3	Resolution	272	Claims	274	Favorable; bill	1143	Referred to Committee Whole House.		
Dickey, Milus W., executor of.	Payment as mail contractor	28	1	Petition	338	Claims	440	Favorable; bill	338	Passed.	Passed	App'd June 17, 1844
Dickey, Robert, (N. Y.)	Drawback on wines exported	19	1	Petition	364	Ways and Means.	May 3, 1826	Adverse		Referred to Committee Whole House.		
Dickey, Robert, (N. Y.)	Drawback on wines exported	23	1	Petition	329	Ways and Means.	Mar. 18, 1834	Favorable; bill	377	Referred to Committee Whole House.		
Dickey, Robert, (N. Y.)	Drawback on wines exported	24	1	Petition	95	Ways and Means.	Jan. 12, 1836	Favorable; bill	108	Passed	Laid on table.	
Dickey, Robert, (N. Y.)	Drawback on wines exported	24	2	Petition	267	Ways and Means.	Jan. 24, 1837	Favorable; bill	870	Referred to Committee Whole House.		
Dickey, Robert, (N. Y.)	Drawback on wines exported	25	2	Petition	42	Ways and Means.	Dec. 14, 1837	Favorable; bill	13	Passed	Passed	App'd March 2, 1838
Dickey, Robert, (Ohio.)	Increase of pension	21	2	Petition	398	Rev. Claims.						
Dickey, Lieut. William, heirs of.	Compensation for revolutionary services.	25	2	Petition	232	Rev. Claims.						
Dickey, Lieut. William, heirs of.	Compensation for revolutionary services.	26	1	Petition	165	Rev. Claims.						
Dickey, Lieut. William, heirs of.	Compensation for revolutionary services.	28	1	Petition	334	Rev. Claims.						
Dickins, Henry, *et al*	Fishing bounty	20	2	Petition	203	Commerce	Feb. 5, 1829	Favorable; bill	415	Referred to Committee Whole House.		
Dickins, Henry, *et al.*	Fishing bounty	21	1	Petition	38	Commerce	Dec. 24, 1829	Favorable; bill	32	Passed	Passed	App'd March 25, 1830
Dickins, Tristram	(See Henry Dickins, *et al.*)	20	2		203				415			
Dickinson, Cadwalader, widow of.	Compensation for board of wounded officers, and for advances made by deceased in revolutionary war.	2	1	Petition	584					Referred to Secretary Treasury.		
Dickinson, David, by Clarissa, daughter of.	Compensation for revolutionary services of deceased.	29	1	Petition	228	Rev. Claims.						
Dickinson, David B	(See Nathaniel Dickinson, son of.)	27	2		375							
Dickinson, Festus	(See Col. William McWilliams, widow of, by administrator of.)	27	2		374		784					
Dickinson, Francis, (N. Y.)	Revolutionary pension	22	1	Petition	35	Rev. Pensions.	Dec. 22, 1831	Adverse		Laid on table.		
Dickinson, Hannah	(See Samuel Dickinson, widow of.)	25	2		272							
Dickinson, H., *et al.*, (Philadelphia.)	(See George Troutman, *et al.*)	17	1		100							
Dickinson, Mary	(See Cadwalader Dickinson, widow of.)	2	1		584							
Dickinson, Nathaniel, son of.	Revolutionary pension	27	2	Petition	375	Rev. Pensions.	784	Adverse		Laid on table.		
Dickinson, Nathaniel, son of.	Revolutionary pension	28	1	Petition	788	Rev. Pensions.						
Dickinson, Samuel, widow of.	Revolutionary pension	25	2	Petition	272	Rev. Pensions				Discharged; laid on table.		
Dickinson, Seth, (N. Y.)	Revolutionary pension	22	1	Petition	35	Rev. Pensions.	42	Favorable; bill	81	Passed	Indef. postp'd.	
Dickinson, Thomas Wells.	Compensation for services as deputy commissioner in revolutionary war.	23	2	Memorial	177	Rev. Claims.						

List of private claims presented to the House of Representatives of the United States from the 1st to the 31st Congress, inclusive—Continued.

Names of claimants.	Nature or object of the claim.	Congress.	Session.	How brought before the House of Reps.	Page of journal.	To what committee of the House referred.	No. or date of the report.	Nature of the report.	No. of the bill.	How disposed of by the House of Reps.	How disposed of by the Senate.	Date of the act of Congress, and remarks.
65 Dickinson, Thomas Wells.	Compensation for services as deputy commissioner in revolutionary war.	24	1	Petition	796	Rev. Claims.						
Dickinson, Thomas Wells.	Compensation for services as deputy commissioner in revolutionary war.	24	2	Memorial	73	Rev. Claims.						
Dickinson, Thomas Wells.	Compensation for services as deputy commissioner in revolutionary war.	25	2	Memorial	48	Rev. Claims......	505	Adverse	......	Laid on table.		
Dickman, John, by Phebe, widow of.	Revolutionary pension..........	25	2	Petition	913	Rev. Pensions	....	....	......	Discharged.		
Dickman, John, by Phebe, widow of.	Revolutionary pension..........	25	3	Petition	226	Rev. Pensions.....	....	....	......	Discharged.		
Dickman, John, by Phebe, widow of.	Revolutionary pension..........	26	1	Petition	171	Rev. Pensions.....	112	Favorable; bill	123	Passed	Indef. postp'd.	
Dickman, John, by Phebe, widow of.	Revolutionary pension..........	27	2	Petition	485	Rev. Pensions.						
Dickman, Samuel	(See Robert Elliott, administrator of.)	23	2	....	47							
Dickson, Alexander......	Indemnity for loss of horse and equipments in Seminole war.	23	1	Documents.....	154	Claims.						
Dickson, Cotton	Revolutionary pension..........	15	2	Petition	300	Rev. Pensions.....	....	....	......	Discharged; laid on table.		
Dickson, Elizabeth......	(See William Dickson, widow of).	28	2	....	84							
Dickson, Ephraim D.....	Compensation for shoeing horses for company of volunteers.	26	2	Senate bill	229	Claims..........	Feb. 12, 1841	With't amend.	S. 61	Referred to Committee Whole House.		
Dickson, Ephraim D.....	Compensation for shoeing horses for company of volunteers.	27	2	Senate bill	409	Claims..........	667	Adverse	S. 38			
Dickson, Ephraim D.....	Compensation for shoeing horses for company of volunteers.	27	3	Senate bill	115	Claims..........	48	With amend..	S. 26	Passed.		
Dickson, Ephraim D.....	Compensation for shoeing horses for company of volunteers.	28	1	Senate bill	868	Claims..........	May 1, 1844	With't amend.	S. 71	Passed	....	App'd June 17, 1844
Dickson, Frederick, *et al.*, by inhabitants of Missouri.	Pre-emption right to land	15	1	Petition	279	Public Lands.						
Dickson, Frederick, *et al.*..	Remuneration in land, or money for services rendered the United States.	27	2	Petition	140	Invalid Pensions ..	615	Adverse	......	Laid on table.		
Dickson, George	Grant of land and pre-emption right.	22	1	Petition	394	Public Lands.....	....	....	......	Discharged; laid on table.		
Dickson, James, attorney of	Relief from certain judgment	12	2	Petition	634	Ways and Means..	....	....	......	Discharged.		
Dickson, James and William.	Remission of forfeiture of ship and cargo.	17	2	Petition	165	Ways and Means..	....	....	......	Discharged; leave to withdraw.		
Dickson, James and William.	Remission of forfeiture of ship and cargo.	18	1	Petition	132	Ways and Means..	44	Adverse	......	Laid on table.		
Dickson, James and William.	Remission of forfeiture of ship and cargo.	19	1	Senate bill	290	Ways and Means..	Mar. 24, 1826	With't amend.	S. 39	Passed	....	App'd May 20, 1826
Dickson, James, (Pa.)....	Pension	21	2	Petition	43	Military Pensions.						
Dickson, James.........	(See John Hogg, trustees of)....	26	1	....	182	....	343	....	319			
Dickson, John..........	Compensation for services in war of 1812.	25	2	Petition	574	Claims.						
Dickson, John, and Isaac Lambert.	Pre-emption for land to erect grist mills.	14	1	Petition	56	Public Lands.						

List of private claims presented to the House of Representatives of the United States from the 1st to the 31st Congress, inclusive—Continued.

Names of claimants.	Nature or object of the claim.	Congress.	Session.	How brought before the House of Reps.	Page of journal.	To what committee of the House referred.	No. or date of the report.	Nature of the report.	No. of the bill.	How disposed of by the House of Reps.	How disposed of by the Senate.	Date of the act of Congress, and remarks.
Dickson, John, surviving partner of Lambert and Dickson.	Balance of judgment against United States by Hugh Glenn.	31	1	Petition	306	Claims	25	Favorable; bill	58	Passed	Ref'd to Com. on Claims.	
Dickson, John, *et al.*	Prize-money for capture of British brigs.	19	2	Petition	105	Claims	Jan. 29, 1827	Adverse	......	Laid on table.		
Dickson, John, *et al.*	Prize-money for capture of British brigs.	23	1	Petition	192	Claims.						
Dickson, John, *et al.*	Prize-money for capture of British brigs.	23	2	Petition	238	Claims.						
Dickson, John, *et al.*	Prize-money for capture of British brigs.	27	2	Petition	829	Claims.						
Dickson, Joseph, (Mich.)	Arrears of pension	24	1	Petition	426	Invalid Pensions	....	....	......	Discharged; laid on table.		
Dickson, Joseph N., (Va.)	Revolutionary pension	23	1	Petition	639	Rev. Pensions	....	....	......	Discharged; laid on table.		
Dickson, Mark	Compensation for carrying mail	30	1	Memorial	928	P. Of. and P. Roads.						
Dickson, Mark	Compensation for carrying mail	30	2	Petition	125	P. Of. and P. Roads.						
Dickson, Peter	Compensation for materials to construct battery.	23	1	Petition	154	Claims	Jan. 21, 1834	Adverse	......	Laid on table.	....	Manuscript report adverse, Feb. 22, 1837, not found on journal.
Dickson, Peter	Compensation for materials to construct battery.	24	1	Petition	345	Claims.						
Dickson, Peter	Compensation for materials to construct battery.	31	2	Petition	142	Claims.						
Dickson, Robert, sureties of.	Release from liability	17	1	Petition	160	P. Of. & P. Roads.	Mar. 8, 1822	Favorable; bill	111	Passed	Passed	App'd May 7, 1822
Dickson, Samuel, (Ky.)	Pension for services rendered in 1791.	28	1	Petition	89	Invalid Pensions.						
Dickson, Samuel, (Ky.)	Pension for services rendered in 1791.	28	2	Petition	172	Invalid Pensions.						
Dickson, Samuel, (Ky.)	Pension for services rendered in 1791.	30	1	Petition	173	Invalid Pensions	357	Adverse	......	Laid on table.		
Dickson, Samuel, (Ky.)	Pension for services rendered in 1791.	31	1	Petition	391	Invalid Pensions.						
Dickson, Thomas, & Co.	(See Thomas Dixon & Co.)	24	1	....	54							
Dickson, William, (N. Y.)	Remission of tonnage duties	5	2	Petition	108	Com. and Manuf.	....	....	......	Laid on table.	....	Leave to withdraw.
Dickson, William	For land in lieu of land resold by United States.	22	1	Senate bill	816	Public Lands	June 8, 1832	With't amend.	S. 122	Passed	....	App'd July 13, 1832
Dickson, William, widow of.	Confirmation of land title	28	2	Memorial	84	Priv. Land Claims.	143	Favorable; bill	624	Referred to Committee Whole House.		
Dickson, William, widow of.	Confirmation of land title	29	1	Petition	123	Priv. Land Claims.	594	Favorable; bill	413	Referred to Committee Whole House.		
Dickson, William	Renewal or payment of three drafts from the acting quartermaster, which were lost.	25	2	Petition	274	Claims	959	Favorable; bill	835	Passed	With't amend.	
Dicy, Samuel	Revolutionary pension	26	2	Petition	118	Invalid Pensions	151	Favorable; bill	662	Referred to Committee Whole House.		
Dicy, Samuel	Revolutionary pension	27	2	Petition	47	Invalid Pensions	140	Favorable; bill	186	Passed	Laid on table.	
Dicy, Samuel	Revolutionary pension	27	3	Senate bill	209	Invalid Pensions	Jan. 20, 1843	With't amend.	S. 65	Passed	....	App'd Feb. 4, 1843
Didlake, George B	(See Benjamin J. Harrison, sureties of.)	27	2	....	77							
Diedrick, Robert	Payment of judgment against S. Swartwout.	25	3	Petition	461	Claims.						
Diedrick, Robert	Payment of judgment against S. Swartwout.	27	2	Petition	94	Claims	345	Adverse	......	Laid on table.		

List of private claims presented to the House of Representatives of the United States from the 1st to the 31st Congress, inclusive—Continued.

Names of claimants.	Nature or object of the claim.	Congress.	Session.	How brought before the House of Reps.	Page of journal.	To what committee of the House referred.	No. or date of the report.	Nature of the report.	No. of the bill.	How disposed of by the House of Reps.	How disposed of by the Senate.	Date of the act of Congress, and remarks.
Dieffendorff, Jacob	Invalid pension	3	2	Rep. of Secretary War.	278	Claims	Feb. 28, 1795	Favorable; bill	130	Passed	Postponed.	
Dieffendorff, Jacob	Invalid pension	4	1	Resol'n and docs.	373	Claims	Mar. 4, 1796	Res. to refer to Sec. with instructions.	J. R. 16	Passed	Passed	App'd April 18, 1796
Dieffendorff, Jacob	Invalid pension	4	2	Resol'n and docs.	614	Claims.						
Diehl, William W.	Increase of pension	31	1	Petition	214	Invalid Pensions.						
Diekamp, Henry, *et al*	Confirmation of land title	30	2	Petition	241	Public Lands.						
Diemar, James	Compensation for services in revolutionary war.	2	1	Petition	490					Referred to Secretary of War.		
Diemer, Dr. James	Compensation for medicines and attendance on British prisoners.	3	1	Petition	73					Referred to Secretary of War.		
Diemer, Dr. James	Compensation for medicines and attendance on British prisoners.	3	2	Petition and rep't of Sec. War.	278					Laid on table.		
Dies, John	Bounty land	30	2	Petition	204	Military Affairs	30	Adverse		Laid on table.		
Dietz, Johan Jost	Restoration of pension	25	2	Petition	198	Rev. Pensions	452	Favorable; bill	454	Passed	Passed	App'd July 7, 183[illegible]
Diffendorffer, John A. and Sarah A.	(See Bernard Todd, heirs of)	29	1		381		157		175			
Diggs, Beverly, *et al.*	(See John Ross, heirs of)	29	2		136							
Diggs, John T.	Spoliations or claims under 1st article of treaty of Ghent.	20	2	Petition	231	Foreign Affairs	79	Adverse		Laid on table.		
Diggs, William W., heirs of.	Compensation for land for site of fort Washington.	21	2	Resolution	97	Military Affairs	Jan. 7, 1831	Favorable; bill	542	Passed	Passed	App'd March 2, 1831
Dike, Calvin	Pension	15	2	Petition	43	Pens. & Rev. Cl'ms.				Discharged; laid on table.		
Dikeman, Jonathan	Revolutionary pension	16	2	Petition	21	Rev. Pensions	Feb. 15, 1821	Adverse		Leave to withdraw.		
Dill, Eliza, *et al.*	(See General Arthur St. Clair, daughters of.)	18	1		37							
Dill, Isaiah	Redemption of bills of credit issued during revolutionary war.	21	2	Petition	269	Rev. Claims.						
Dill, Capt. James, by Helena, widow of.	Confirmation of land title	28	1	Petition	108	Priv. Land Claims.	116	Adverse		Laid on table.		
Dillard, James G., (Ga.)	Restoration of pension	20	1	Resolution	248	Military Pensions	Feb. 13, 1828	Favorable; bill	166	Passed	Ref'd, & com. discharged.	
Dillard, James G., (Ga.)	Restoration of pension	20	2	House bill	55	Military Pensions	Dec. 12, 1828	With't amend.	311	Passed	Laid on table.	
Dillard, James G., (Ga.)	Restoration of pension	21	1	Petition	48	Military Pensions	Dec. 12, 1830	Favorable; bill	72	Passed	Passed	App'd May 20, 1830; petit'rs name omitted in act.
Dillard, James H.	Compensation for services in war with Mexico.	31	1	Petition	501	Military Affairs.						
Dillard, Capt. James, executors of.	Commutation of half-pay	22	2	Petition	88	Rev. Claims.						
Dillard, Capt. James, executors of.	Commutation of half-pay	23	1	Petition	39	Rev. Claims.						
Dillard, Capt. James, executors of.	Commutation of half-pay	23	2	Petition	113	Rev. Claims.						
Dillard, Capt. James, executors of.	Commutation of half-pay	24	1	Petition	63	Rev. Claims	855	Adverse.				
Dillard, Capt. James, executors of.	Commutation of half pay	25	2	Petition	72	Rev. Claims	Jan. 18, 1838	Adverse		Laid on table.		
Dillard, Capt. James, executors of.	Commutation of half-pay	25	3	Petition	85	Rev. Claims				Discharged.		
Dillard, Capt. James, executors of.	Commutation of half-pay	26	1	Petition	360	Rev. Claims.						

List of private claims presented to the House of Representatives of the United States from the 1st to the 31st Congress, inclusive—Continued.

Names of claimants.	Nature or object of the claim.	Congress.	Session.	How brought before the House of Reps.	Page of journal.	To what committee of the House referred.	No. or date of the report.	Nature of the report.	No. of the bill.	How disposed of by the House of Reps.	How disposed of by the Senate.	Date of the act of Congress, and remarks.
Dillard, Lieut. L. H.	(See William H. Bedford, agent.)	28	1		262							
Dillard, Thomas, (Ga.)	Compensation for the loss of three horses in war of 1812.	20	1	Petition	111	Claims	Jan. 16, 1828	Adverse		Laid on table.		
Dillingham, Elisha, (R. I.)	Revolutionary pension	22	1	Petition	35	Rev. Pensions				Discharged; laid on table.		
Dillingham, Elisha, (R. I.)	Arrears of pension	25	3	Petition	126	Rev. Pensions	Jan. 6, 1839	Adverse (verbal.)		Laid on table.		
Dillingham, Elisha, (R. I.)	Arrears of pension	26	1	Petition	173	Rev. Pensions.						
Dillingham, Elisha, (R. I.)	Arrears of pension	26	2	Petition	35	Rev. Pensions.						
Dillinar, Capt. Richard	(See Captain Richard Dallinar.)	26	1		360							
Dillon, John, (Baltimore.)	Indemnity for condemnation and sale of vessel.	12	1	Petition	32	Claims.						
Dillon, John, (Baltimore.)	Indemnity for condemnation and sale of vessel.	12	2	Petition	564	Claims.						
Dillon, John, (Baltimore.)	Indemnity for condemnation and sale of vessel.	13	1	Petition	30	Claims	June 16, 1813	Favorable; bill	24	Referred to Committee Whole House.		Leave to withdraw.
Dillon, John, (Baltimore.)	Indemnity for condemnation and sale of vessel.	15	1	Petition	165	Ways and Means	Feb. 10, 1818	Favorable; bill	78	Passed	Passed	App'd April 20, 1818
Dillon, Josiah H.	Repayment of money advanced for use of army in late war.	27	2	Petition and res.	139	Claims.						
Dillon, Josiah H.	Repayment of money advanced for use of army in late war.	27	3	Petition	43	Claims.						
Dillon, Josiah H.	Repayment of money advanced for use of army in late war.	28	1	Petition	223	Claims	445	Favorable; bill	342	Passed	Passed	App'd June 17, 1844
Dillon, Josiah H.	Repayment of money advanced for use of army in late war.	28	2	Petition	113	Claims.						
Dillon, Josiah H.	Repayment of money advanced for use of army in late war.	29	1	Petition	666	Claims.						
Dillon, Thomas	Confirmation of land title, and other relief.	8	1	Petition	539	Whole House.						
Dilworth, Caleb	Payment for land sold to him by U. States previously patented.	25	2	Petition	771	Priv. Land Claims.						
Dilworth, Caleb	Payment for land sold to him by U. States previously patented.	26	1	Petition	334	Priv. Land Claims				Discharged; referred to Com. on Claims.		
Dimanche, succession of	Confirmation of land title	22	1	Petition	64	Priv. Land Claims.	62	Favorable; bill	125	Passed	Passed	App'd June 25, 1832
Dimick, Peter, (N. Y.)	Revolutionary pension	24	1	Petition	56	Rev. Claims	215	Favorable; bill	222	Passed	Passed	App'd June 28, 1836
Dimock, Davis, widow of	Compensation as late member of Congress to end of term.	27	2	Petition	999	Accounts	930	Favorable; res.				
Dimsdale, George, (N. C.)	Invalid pension for services in war of 1812.	29	1	Petition	82	Invalid Pensions	348	Adverse		Laid on table.		
Dingey, Carle	Invalid pension for services in war of 1812.	29	2	Pet. & declaration	53	Invalid Pensions	Feb. 24, 1847	Adverse		Laid on table.		
Dingman, Daniel W.	(See Wm. T. Wilson and others.)	31	2		266							
Dingman, Daniel W.	(See Samuel Helm.)	27	2		374							
Dingman, Guardus	Pension	11	2	House bill	283	Whole House	Mar. 24, 1810	Favorable; bill	107	Passed	Passed	App'd April 27, 1810
Dinkins, John	Pension, or land in lieu of same	21	1	Memorial Legislature Miss.	53	Public Lands	April 2, 1830	Adverse		Laid on table.		
Dinkins, T. J.	Compensation for supplies furnished troops in Florida in 1836.	24	2	Petition	308	Military Affairs.						
Dinsdale, George	(See George Dimsdale.)	29	1		82		348					
Dinsmore, Robert	Invalid pension for services in war of 1812.	19	1	Resolution	160	Military Pensions	Feb. 23, 1826	Favorable; bill	118	Referred to Committee Whole House.		

List of private claims presented to the House of Representatives of the United States from the 1st to the 31st Congress, inclusive—Continued.

Names of claimants.	Nature or object of the claim.	Congress.	Session.	How brought before the House of Reps.	Page of journal.	To what committee of the House referred.	No. or date of the report.	Nature of the report.	No. of the bill.	How disposed of by the House of Reps.	How disposed of by the Senate.	Date of the act of Congress, and remarks.
Dinsmore, Robert	Invalid pension for services in war of 1812.	19	2	House bill	60	Whole House	Dec. 22, 1826	Favorable; bill	314	Passed	Passed	App'd March 3, 1827
Dinsmore, Silas	Additional compensation as Indian agent.	6	1	Petition	638	Claims	April 14, 1800			Leave to withdraw.		
Dinsmore, Silas	(See John Pitchlynn)	10	1		40							
Dinsmore, Silas	Confirmation of title to land, Indian grant.	17	1	Petition	101	Public Lands				Discharged; laid on table.		
Dinsmore, Silas	Compensation for services as deputy surveyor of public lands.	19	1	Petition	94	Public Lands	Feb. 10, 1816	Adverse		Leave to withdraw.		
Dinsmore, Silas	Compensation for services as deputy surveyor of public lands.	19	2	Petition	240	Claims				Discharged; leave to withdraw.		
Diron, Dominique	Indemnity for loss of vessel destroyed in 1811.	14	1	Petition	416					Referred to Secretary of State.		
Disbrow, Erastus	Pension	14	1	Resolution	158	Pens. & Rev. Cl'ms.	April 11, 1816	Favorable; bill	171	Passed	Passed	App'd April 30, 1816
Disbrow, Henry	Compensation for property destroyed by British in late war.	21	1	Petition	200	Claims	Feb. 3, 1830	Adverse		Laid on table.		
Disbrow, Henry	Compensation for property destroyed by British in late war.	22	1	Petition	677	Claims.						
Disbrow, Henry	Compensation for property destroyed by British in late war.	27	2	Petition	613	Claims	706	Adverse		Laid on table.		
Disbrow, Henry	Compensation for property destroyed by British in late war.	27	3	Petition	88	Claims	224	Adverse		Laid on table.		
Disbrow, Henry	Compensation for property destroyed by British in late war.	28	2	Petition	215	Claims.						
Disbrow, Henry	Compensation for property destroyed by British in late war.	29	1	Petition	297	Claims	223	Adverse		Leave to withdraw.		
Disbrow, Henry	Compensation for property destroyed by British in late war.	31	1	Petition	192	Claims	18	Adverse		Laid on table.		
Disbrow, William	Arrears of pension	22	2	Petition	132	Invalid Pensions.						
Discompte, Pierre dit Labadie.	Confirmation of title to land in Michigan.	20	1	Resolution	28	Public Lands	42	Favorable; bill	34	Passed	Passed	App'd April 22, 1828
Dishough, Reddick, sureties of.	That $228 96, paid on account of default, be refunded.	25	3	Memorial	369	P. Of. and P. Roads.						
Dismal Swamp Land Company.	Reimbursement of money expended for use of United States.	28	1	Petition	430	Roads and Canals.						
Dismal Swamp Land Company.	Reimbursement of money expended for use of United States.	28	2	Petition	59	Claims	47	Favorable; bill	522	Passed	Passed	App'd March 1, 1845
District of Columbia	(See Columbia, District of.)											
Ditcher, Robert	Pension	20	1	Petition	440	Military Pensions	April 29, 1828	Favorable; bill	283	Passed	Referred; Com. discharged.	
Ditcher, Robert	Pension	20	2	House bill	55	Military Pensions	Dec. 12, 1828	Favorable; bill	311	Passed	Laid on table.	
Ditcher, Robert	Pension	21	1	Petition	48	Military Pensions	Jan. 5, 1830	Favorable; bill	72	Passed amended.	Passed	App'd May 20, 1830—name omitted in act.
Ditson, Thomas	Compensation for services in revolutionary war.	2	1	Petition	447					Referred to Secretary War.		
Dittmarr, John M., (N. Y.)	Pension	19	2	Petition	307	Military Pensions.						
Dittmarr, John M., (N. Y.)	Pension	20	1	Petitions	223, 338	Military Pensions	Feb. 28, 1829	Adverse		Laid on table.		
Ditto, Michael, (Ala.)	Ferriage of troops in 1814 and 1815 at Point Rock.	23	1	Petition and docs.	35	Claims	Dec. 20, 1823	Adverse		Laid on table.		
Ditts, Francis	Pension	20	2	Petition	89	Military Pensions	Jan. 28, 1829	Report		Laid on table.		
Ditty, John, sen., (Pa.)	Compensation for services in revolutionary war.	24	1	Resolution	157	Rev. Claims.						

List of private claims presented to the House of Representatives of the United States from the 1st to the 31st Congress, inclusive—Continued.

Names of claimants	Nature or object of the claim.	Congress.	Session.	How brought before the House of Reps.	Page of journal.	To what committee of the House referred.	No. or date of the report.	Nature of the report.	No. of the bill.	How disposed of by the House of Reps.	How disposed of by the Senate.	Date of the act of Congress, and remarks.
Ditty, John, sen., (Pa.)	Compensation for services in revolutionary war.	24	2	Petition and res.	154	Rev. Claims				Discharged; laid on table.		
Ditty, John, sen., (Pa.)	Compensation for services in revolutionary war.	25	2	Petition	270	Rev. Claims				Discharged; laid on table.		
Ditty, John, sen., (Pa.)	Compensation for services in revolutionary war.	25	3	Petition	130	Rev. Claims				Discharged.		
Ditty, John, sen., (Pa.)	Compensation for services in revolutionary war.	26	1	Petition	359	Rev. Claims.						
Ditty, John, sen., (Pa.)	Compensation for services in revolutionary war.	26	2	Petition	84	Rev. Claims.						
Ditty, John, sen., (Pa.)	Compensation for services in revolutionary war.	27	2	Petition	96	Rev. Claims	516	Adverse		Laid on table.		
Ditty, John, sen., (Pa.)	Compensation for services in revolutionary war.	31	2		206					Leave to withdraw.		
Diver, Patrick	(See William Baker)	22	1		288		480					
Divin, W. W., *et al.*	Payment for horses lost in war with Mexico.	30	2	Memorial	46	Claims.						
Divine, Miles	Invalid pension	30	1	Petition	594	Invalid Pensions				Discharged; laid on table.		
Dix, Christopher H.	(See Christopher H. Pix)	31	1									
Dix, Dudley, by Ellen, widow of.	Naval pension	27	3	Petition	422	Naval Affairs.						
Dix, John A.	Compensation for extra services in the United States army.	15	2	Senate bill	248	Military Affairs	Feb. 22, 1819	With't amend.	S. 29	Referred to Committee Whole House.		
Dix, John A	Compensation for extra services in the United States army.	16	1	Senate bill	108	Claims	Feb. 3, 1820	With't amend.	S. 5	Passed		App'd April 5, 1820
Dix, John, by Ellen, widow of.	Continuation of pension	20	2	Petition	32	Naval Affairs	103	Adverse		Laid on table.		
Dix, John, by Ellen, widow of.	Continuation of pension	21	1	Petition	100	Naval Affairs				Discharged; laid on table.		
Dix, John, by Ellen, widow of.	Continuation of pension	21	2	Petition	88	Naval Affairs.						
Dix, John, by Ellen, widow of.	Continuation of pension	23	1	Petition	136	Naval Affairs.						
Dix, Timothy, by Lucy, widow of.	Commutation pay	14	1	Petition	300	Whole House				Discharged; laid on table.		
Dixey, Peter, (Mass.)	Pay for extra undrawn rations	23	1	Petition	187	Naval Affairs.						
Dixey, Peter, (Mass.)	Pay for extra undrawn rations	23	2	Petition	76	Claims	Feb. 16, 1835	Adverse		Laid on table.		
Dixey, Peter, (Mass.)	Pay for extra undrawn rations	24	1	Petition	74	Claims	Dec. 29, 1835	Adverse		Laid on table.		
Dixon, Alexander	(See William H. Bedford, agent.)	28	1		262							
Dixon, Amos, (N. Y.)	Revolutionary pension	22	1	Petition	255	Rev. Pensions.						
Dixon, Frederick M.	Bounty land	26	1	Petition	364	Public Lands.						
Dixon, Col. Henry, heirs of.	Commutation pay	26	1	Petition	1097	Rev. Claims.						
Dixon, Col. Henry, heirs of.	Commutation pay	26	2	Petition, &c.	84, 177	Rev. Claims.						
Dixon, Col. Henry, heirs of.	Commutation pay	27	2	Petition	557	Rev. Claims	973	Adverse		Laid on table.		
Dixon, James	Compensation for work done on court-house in Alexandria, D. C.	27	3	Petition	113	Claims.						
Dixon, James	Compensation for work done on court-house in Alexandria, D. C.	28	1	Petition	115	Dist. of Columbia				Discharged; laid on table.		
Dixon, James	Compensation for work done on court-house in Alexandria, D. C.	28	2	Petition	149	Dist. of Columbia.	69	Favorable; bill	551	Referred to Committee Whole House.		

List of private claims presented to the House of Representatives of the United States from the 1st to the 31st Congress, inclusive—Continued.

Names of claimants.	Nature or object of the claim.	Congress.	Session.	How brought before the House of Reps.	Page of journal.	To what committee of the House referred.	No. or date of the report.	Nature of the report.	No. of the bill.	How disposed of by the House of Reps.	How disposed of by the Senate.	Date of the act of Congress, and remarks.
Dixon, James	Compensation for work done on court-house in Alexandria, D. C.	29	1	Petition	190	Dist. of Columbia.	89	Favorable; bill	107	Recommitted.		
Dixon, James	Compensation for work done on court-house in Alexandria, D. C.	29	1	House bill	470	Dist. of Columbia.	363	With't amend.	107	Referred to Committee Whole House.		
Dixon, James	Compensation for work done on court-house in Alexandria, D. C.	30	1	Petition	136	Dist. of Columbia.	497	Favorable; bill	409	Referred to Committee Whole House.		
Dixon, James	Compensation for work done on court-house in Alexandria, D. C.	31	1	Petition	474	Dist. of Columbia.	85	Favorable; bill	105	Referred to Committee Whole House.		
Dixon, Jared	Invalid pension	2	2	Rep. of Secretary War.	649	Whole House.						
Dixon, Jared	Invalid pension	3	1	Rep. of Secretary War.	131	Select	May 26, 1794	Res. to refer to Sec. with instructions.	J. R. 12	Passed	Passed	App'd June 9, 1794
Dixon, Jared, (Vt.)	Restoration of pension	17	1	Petition	51	Rev. Pensions				Leave to withdraw.		
Dixon, John, (N. J.)	Revolutionary pension	17	1	Petition	50	Rev. Claims	March 1, 1822	Adverse		Leave to withdraw.		
Dixon, John, (Va.)	Bounty land and three months' extra pay.	25	2	Petition	75	Priv. Land Claims.	252	Favorable; bill	293	Referred to Committee Whole House.		
Dixon, John, (Va.)	Bounty land and three months' extra pay.	25	3	Rep't Committee Whole House.	376	Whole House	Dec. 25, 1839	With't amend.	293	Passed	Passed	App'd March 3, 1839
Dixon, John	Additional appropriation of land to satisfy bounty land warrant.	26	1	Petition	332	Public Lands.						
Dixon, John	Additional appropriation of land to satisfy bounty land warrant.	27	2	Petition	98	Public Lands.						
Dixon, John, (Va.)	Pension for invalid services in war of 1812.	27	3	Petition	151	Invalid Pensions	194	Adverse		Laid on table.		
Dixon, John, (Va.)	Pension for invalid services in war of 1812.	28	1	Petition	189	Invalid Pensions	183	Adverse		Laid on table.		
Dixon, John, (Va.)	Pension for invalid services in war of 1812.	29	1	Petition	149	Invalid Pensions	293	Adverse		Laid on table.		
Dixon, John S., (Tenn.)	Indemnity for injury to property by U. S. troops in 1836.	24	2	Petition	308	Claims						Mss. report adverse, dated Feb. 22, 1837, not found on journ'l.
Dixon, John S., (Tenn.)	Indemnity for injury to property by U. S. troops in 1836.	26	1	Petition	940	Claims.						
Dixon, John S., (Tenn.)	Indemnity for injury to property by U. S. troops in 1836.	26	2	Petition	38	Claims.						
Dixon, John S., (Tenn.)	Indemnity for injury to property by U. S. troops in 1836.	28	1	Petition	910	Claims.						
Dixon, John S., (Tenn.)	Indemnity for injury to property by U. S. troops in 1836.	29	1	Petition	340	Claims.						
Dixon, Joseph, (N. Y.)	Revolutionary pension	18	1	Petition	250	Pens. & Rev. Cl'ms.	Mar. 9, 1824	Adverse		Discharged; leave to withdraw.		
Dixon, Joseph, (Maine)	Indemnity for damage to farm by erection of fort.	18	2	Petition	135	Claims.						
Dixon, Joseph, (Maine)	Indemnity for damage to farm by erection of fort.	20	1	Petition	91	Claims	241	Favorable; bill	287	Referred to Committee Whole House.		
Dixon, Joseph, (Maine)	Indemnity for damage to farm by erection of fort.	21	1	Petition	35	Claims	Dec. 21, 1829	Favorable; bill	9	Passed	Passed	App'd Feb. 11, 1830
Dixon, Joseph	Arrears of pension	27	2	Petition	369	Invalid Pensions	939	Adverse		Laid on table.		
Dixon, Joseph	Arrears of pension	28	1	Petition	189	Invalid Pensions.						
Dixon, Lewis	(See William H. Bedford, agent)	28	1		262							
Dixon, Lucy	(See Roger Dixon, widow of)	16	2		364							
Dixon, Luther	Indemnity in case of judgment for costs for punishing a soldier for mutiny.	16	2	Petition	263	Claims				Discharged; laid on table.		

List of private claims presented to the House of Representatives of the United States from the **1st** *to the* **31st** *Congress, inclusive*—Continued.

Names of claimants.	Nature or object of the claim.	Congress.	Session.	How brought before the House of Reps.	Page of journal.	To what committee of the House referred.	No. or date of the report.	Nature of the report.	No. of the bill.	How disposed of by the House of Reps.	How disposed of by the Senate.	Date of the act of Congress, and remarks.
Dixon, Luther	Indemnity in case of judgment for costs for punishing a soldier for munity.	17	1	Petition	184	Claims				Discharged; laid on table.		
Dixon, Luther	Indemnity in case of judgment for costs for punishing a soldier for muriny.	17	2	Petition	120	Claims				Discharged; leave to withdraw.		
Dixon, Luther	Indemnity in case of judgment for costs for punishing a soldier for munity.	18	1	Petition	52	Military Affairs				Discharged; referred to Com. on Claims.		
Dixon, Col. Luther	Compensation for services in late war.	29	2	Petition	56	Claims.						
Dixon, Roger, & John Steele	(See Polser Shilling, executors of)	11	2		116							
Dixon, Roger, widow of	Payment of $329 93, amount of final settlement certificate, with interest.	10	2	Petition	364	Claims				Discharged; referred to Select Committee.		
Dixon, Roger, widow of	Payment of $329 93, amount of final settlement certificate, with interest.	11	1	Petition	52	Claims.						
Dixon, Roger, widow of	Payment of $329 93, amount of final settlement certificate, with interest.	11	2	Petition	132	Claims	Feb. 14, 1810	Favorable; bill	108	Passed	Rejected.	
Dixon, Roger, widow of	Payment of $329 93, amount of final settlement certificate, with interest.	11	3	Petition	457	Claims.						
Dixon, Roger, widow of	Payment of $329 93, amount of final settlement certificate, with interest.	12	1	Petition	20	Claims	230	Adv'se; recommitted, and rep'd by bill.	142	Referred to Committee Whole House on bill No. 141.		
Dixon, Roger, widow of	Payment of $329 93, amount of final settlement certificate, with interest.	12	2	Petition	549	Claims	Dec. 15, 1812	Favorable; bill.	207	Passed	Passed	App'd Feb. 25, 1813
Dixon, Samuel, administrator of.	Arrears of pension	31	1	Petition	583	Military Affairs	213	Adverse		Laid on table.		
Dixon, Thomas & Co.	(See J. P and E. B. Penney)	21	2		44							
Dixon, Thomas & Co.	Remission of penalty incurred for want of consular's certificates on imported woolens.	23	1	Petition	48	Ways and Means	Jan. 28, 1834	Favorable; bill	249	Referred to Committee Whole House.		
Dixon, Thomas & Co.	Remission of penalty incurred for want of consular's certificates on imported woolens.	23	2	Rep't Committee Whole House	299			With't amend.	249	Passed	With't amend.	
Dixon, Thomas & Co.	Remission of penalty incurred for want of consular's certificates on imported woolens.	24	1	Petition	54	Ways and Means	Jan. 5, 1836	Favorable; bill	71	Passed	Passed	App'd June 28, 1836
Dixon, Walter	Pension	14	2	Resolution	424	Pens. & Rev. Cl'ms				Discharged; laid on table.		
Dixon, William	(See Stephen Decatur, heirs of, *et al.*)	23	1		36		45		50			
Dixon, William and James	(See James and William Dickson)	18	1		132							
Dixon, Zachariah, (Miss.)	Pre-emption right to land	22	2	Resolution	59	Public Lands.						
Dixon, Zachariah, (Miss.)	Pre-emption right to land	23	1	Resolution	229	Public Lands				Discharged; laid on table.		
Dixon, Zachariah, (Miss.)	Pre-emption right to land	23	2	Petition	242	Public Lands.						
Dixon, Zachariah, (Miss.)	Pre-emption right to land	24	1	Petition	476	Priv. Land Claims.				Discharged; laid on table.		

List of *private claims presented to the House of Representatives of the United States from the 1st to the 31st Congress, inclusive*—Continued.

Names of claimants.	Nature or object of the claim.	Congress.	Session.	How brought before the House of Reps.	Page of journal.	To what committee of the House referred.	No. or date of the report.	Nature of the report.	No. of the bill.	How disposed of by the House of Reps.	How disposed of by the Senate.	Date of the act of Congress, and remarks.
Do John, Baptiste	Confirmation of title to land in Missouri.	15	2	Petition	210	Priv. Land Claims				Discharged; laid on table.		
Doak, Robert	Compensation for horse lost in service of United States, revolutionary war.	23	1	Petition	524	Rev. Claims.						
Doak, Robert	Compensation for horse lost in service of United States, revolutionary war.	23	2	Petition	196	Rev. Claims.						
Doak, Robert	Compensation for horse lost in service of United States, revolutionary war.	24	1	Petition	205	Rev. Claims.						
Doak, Robert	Compensation for horse lost in service of United States, revolutionary war.	26	1	Petition	360	Rev. Claims.						
Doak, Samuel	Invalid pension	10	1	Petition	30	Claims				Discharged; referred to Select Committee.		
Doak, Samuel	Invalid pension	10	2	Petition	568	Whole House.						
Doak, Samuel	Invalid pension	11	3	Documents	506					Referred to Secretary of War.		
Doak, Samuel	Release from liability to pay duties for license to distil spirits.	13	3	Petition	732	Ways and Means	Feb. 18, 1815	Adverse.				
Doake, William	(See Noble Osborne and Wm. Doake.)	17	1		283				S. 29			
Doane, David, administrator of.	Remuneration for fort built on Dauphin Island.	20	1	Petition	339	Claims.						
Doane, Edwin F.	Permission to change entry of land.	25	3	Petition	463	Priv. Land Claims.						
Doane, Eleazor, by Legislature of Territory of Arkansas.	Donation for losses by Choctaw treaty.	24	1	Petition	57	Public Lands	208	Favorable; bill	208	Referred to Committee Whole House.		
Doane, Elisha	Compensation for services on board United States ships Cyane and Erie.	28	2	Petition	354	Naval Affairs.						
Doane, Jesse	Pension for injuries sustained firing salute on return of army from Mexico.	30	1	Petition	208	Invalid Pensions				Discharged; laid on table.		
Doane, Jesse	Pension for services in war with Mexico.	31	1	Petition	298	Invalid Pensions	91	Favorable; bill.	112	Referred to Committee Whole House.		
Doane, Nathaniel, widow of.	Indemnity for French spoliations prior to 1800.	22	1	Petition	222	Foreign Affairs.						
Doane, Nathaniel, widow of.	Indemnity for French spoliations prior to 1800.	26	1	Memorial	182	Foreign Affairs	343	Favorable; bill	319	Referred to Committee Whole House.		
Doane, Nathaniel, widow of.	Indemnity for French spoliations prior to 1800.	31	1	Petition	437	Commerce	355	Favorable; bill	318	Referred to Committee Whole House.		
Doane, Sturges, & Co., (N. Y.)	(See George Brown, *et al.*)	22	1		253							
Doase, John	Pre-emption right to land	12	1	Petition	26	Public Lands.						
Doase, John	Pre-emption right to land	12	2	Petition	663	Public Lands.						
Dobbins, Caleb, *et al.*	Payment of certain certificates	14	2	Petition	391	Rev. Claims				Discharged; laid on table.		
Dobbins, Caleb, *et al.*	Payment of certain certificates	15	1	Petition	178	Pens. & Rev. Cl'ms.				Discharged		Leave to withdraw.
Dobbin, Daniel, and R. F. Reid.	Compensation for vessel taken for public use.	13	1	Petition	18	Claims				Discharged.		

List of private claims presented to the House of Representatives of the United States from the 1st to the 31st Congress, inclusive—Continued.

Names of claimants.	Nature or object of the claim.	Congress.	Session.	How brought before the House of Reps.	Page of journal.	To what committee of the House referred.	No. or date of the report.	Nature of the report.	No. of the bill.	How disposed of by the House of Reps.	How disposed of by the Senate.	Date of the act of Congress, and remarks.
Dobbin, Daniel, and R. F. Reid.	Compensation for vessel taken for public use.	13	2	Petition	169	Claims				Discharged; leave to withdraw.		
Dobbin, Daniel, and R. F. Reid.	Compensation for vessel taken for public use.	14	1	Petition	138	Claims	Mar. 15, 1816	Favorable; bill	131	Passed	Passed	App'd April 27, 1816
Dobbin, Colonel Hugh W.	Remuneration for services and sufferings in late war.	27	3	Petition	305	Invalid Pensions.						
Dobbin, Colonel Hugh W.	Remuneration for services and sufferings in late war.	28	1	Petition	203	Invalid Pensions.						
Dobbin, Colonel Hugh W.	Compensation for services in late war.	30	1	Petition	114	Claims						
Dobbin, Colonel Hugh W., and Sons.	Remuneration for services and sufferings in late war.	30	1	Petition	236	Invalid Pensions				Discharged; laid on table.		
Dobbin, Colonel Hugh W.	Arrears of pension	30	1	Petitions	215, 261, 289	Invalid Pensions				Discharged; laid on table.		
Dobbin, Colonel Hugh W.	Pension for services in late war	30	1	Petition	300	Naval Affairs				Discharged; referred to Invalid Pensions.		
Dobbin, John	Compensation as superintendent of blacksmith department in Colonel Thomas's regiment in Mexico.	31	2	Petition	101	Military Affairs.						
Dobson, Euphemia	Renewal of privateer pension	25	2	Petition	171	Naval Affairs				Discharged; laid on table.		
Dobson, Euphemia	Renewal of privateer pension	26	1	Petition	304	Naval Affairs.						
Dobson, Euphemia	Renewal of privateer pension	27	2	Petition	330	Naval Affairs	April 12, 1842	Adverse		Laid on table.		
Dobson, Euphemia	Renewal of privateer pension	28	1	Petition	177	Naval Affairs	518	Favorable; bill	393	Referred to Committee Whole House.		
Dobyns, Enoch	Pension	28	2	Petition	87	Invalid Pensions.						
Dobyns, Enoch	Pension	29	1	Petition	124	Invalid Pensions	175	Adverse		Laid on table.		
Dobyns, Enoch	Pension	31	1	Petition	578	Invalid Pensions	475	Adverse		Laid on table.		
Dockery, Matthew	Permission to change entry of land	16	2	Petition	102	Public Lands	30	Favorable; bill	198	Referred to Committee Whole House.		
Dockray, James R.	(See John Robinson, *et al.*)	4	2		636							
Dodd & Bernard	Reimbursement of duties paid on goods in 1821.	20	1	Memorial	111	Ways and Means				Discharged; referred to Com. Whole House.		
Dodd & Bernard	Reimbursement of duties paid on goods in 1821.	20	1	Senate bill	249	Ways and Means	Feb. 8, 1828	With't amend.	S. 52	Passed		App'd May 23, 1828
Dodd, Benjamin	(See Jonathan Merry, administrator of.)	2[illegible]	1		182		343		319			
Dodd, Charles A.	Compensation for horse and equipments lost in service of United States.	25	3	Senate bill	657	Whole House			S. 123			
Dodd, Daniel	Invalid pension	13	2	House bill	344	Whole House	Mar. 31, 1814	With't amend.	166	Passed	Passed	App'd April 18, 1814
Dodd, David	Pension	20	1	Petition	68	Military Pensions	May 13, 1828	Adverse		Laid on table.		
Dodd, Guy, former widow of.	Revolutionary pension	27	2	Petition	268	Rev. Pensions	297	Favorable; bill	265	Passed	Passed	App'd Aug. 30, 1842
Dodd, Jesse	Arrears of pension	25	2	Resolution	1065	Rev. Pensions				Discharged.		
Dodds, Margaret	Revolutionary pension	28	2	Petition	184	Rev. Pensions.						
Dodd, William	Compensation as witness in case of contested seat.	30	2	Petition	77	Accounts.						
Dodds, Zachariah	Revolutionary pension	18	2	Petition	70	Rev. Pensions	Jan. 17, 1825	Adverse		Laid on table.		
Dodds, Zachariah	Revolutionary pension	19	1	Petition	77	Military Pensions	164	Adverse		Laid on table.		
Doddridge, Philip	Money in lieu of land	19	2	Memorial	78	Whole House.						
Doddridge, Philip	Money in lieu of land	21	2	Senate bill	134	Priv. Land Claims.	Jan. 31, 1831	With't amend.	S. 47	Passed		App'd Feb. 12, 1831

List of private claims presented to the House of Representatives of the United States from the 1st to the 31st Congress, inclusive—Continued.

Names of claimants.	Nature or object of the claim.	Congress.	Session.	How brought before the House of Reps.	Page of journal.	To what committee of the House referred.	No. or date of the report.	Nature of the report.	No. of the bill.	How disposed of by the House of Reps.	How disposed of by the Senate.	Date of the act of Congress, and remarks.
Dodge, Capt. Andrew	Reimbursement of expenses incurred in service of United States.	23	1	Petition	355	Claims	470	Favorable; bill.	484	Referred to Committee Whole House.		
Dodge, Capt. Andrew	Reimbursement of expenses incurred in service of United States.	24	1	Petition	50	Claims	15	Favorable; bill.	15	Passed	Passed	App'd Feb. 17, 1836
Dodge, Catharine	Difference in exchange of land	24	1	Petition	57	Public Lands				Discharged; laid on table.		
Dodge, Catharine	Difference in exchange of land	25	2	Petition	719	Public Lands.						
Dodge, Catharine	Difference in exchange of land	25	3	Petition	98	Public Lands	117	Adverse		Laid on table.		
Dodge, Francis	Pension for services in late war	28	2	Petition	141	Invalid Pensions	84	Adverse		Laid on table.		
Dodge, Francis	Pension for services in late war	29	1	Petition	82	Invalid Pensions.						
Dodge, George, *et al.*	(See Jacob Perkins, assignees of.)	9	1		232							
Dodge, Gen. Henry	Compensation for services in certain negotiations with Indians.	21	1	House bill	326	Whole House	Mar. 16, 1830	With amend.	299	Passed	Passed	App'd April 7, 1830
Dodge, John, heirs of	1,280 acres of land as a refugee	6	2	Resolution	733	Select	Jan. 19, 1801	Favorable; bill.	280	Passed	Passed	App'd Feb. 18, 1801
Dodge, John, heirs of, per guardian.	Pension for services in war of 1812	18	1	Petition	343	Pens. & Rev. Cl'ms.	April 8, 1824	Adverse		Laid on table.		
Dodge, John	Remission and repayment of a fine imposed for not doing military duty in late war.	17	1	Petition	73	Military Affairs	Feb. 1, 1822	Adverse.				
Dodge, John	Remission and repayment of a fine imposed for not doing military duty in late war.	17	2	Petition	47	Militia	Feb. 6, 1823	Adverse		Discharged; leave to withdraw.		
Dodge, John	Pre-emption right to land	19	2	Petition	113	Public Lands				Discharged; laid on table.		
Dodge, John	Pre-emption right to land	20	1	Petition	310	Public Lands				Discharged; laid on table.		
Dodge, Joshua	Compensation for services and expenses as special agent.	24	2	Commu'tion from Sec. of State.	292	Commerce	163	Favorable; bill	887	Referred to Committee Whole House.		
Dodge, Joshua	Compensation for services and expenses as special agent.	25	2	House bill	152	Commerce	200	Favorable	231	Referred to Committee Whole House.		
Dodge, Joshua	Compensation for services and expenses as special agent.	29	1	Memorial	320	Foreign Affairs.						
Dodge, Joshua	Compensation for services and expenses as special agent.	29	2	Senate bill	141	Foreign Affairs	Feb. 24, 1847	With't amend.	S. 38	Referred to Committee Whole House.		
Dodge, Joshua	Compensation for services and expenses as special agent.	30	1	Petition	170	Foreign Affairs	589	Favorable; bill	443	Referred to Committee Whole House.		
Dodge, Joshua	Compensation for services and expenses as special agent.	30	2	House bill	318	Whole House	Jan. 26, 1849	Adverse		Laid on table		Provided for in general bill. App'd August 12, 1848.
Dodge, Paul, heirs of	Arrears of pension	24	1	Resolution	752	Rev. Pensions.						
Dodge, Phineas, (N. Y.)	Pension	19	1	Petition	381	Military Pensions	164	Adverse.				
Dodge, Phineas, (N. Y.)	Pension	19	2	Petition	132	Military Pensions				Discharged.		
Dodge, Phineas, (N. Y.)	Pension	20	2	Petition	26	Military Pensions				Discharged; laid on table.		
Dodge, Phineas, (N. Y.)	Pension	21	1	Petition	37	Military Pensions				Discharged; laid on table.		
Dodge, Phineas, (N. Y.)	Pension	21	2	Petition	103	Military Pensions.						
Dodge, Pickering, executor of.	Indemnity for French spoliations prior to 1800.	26	1	Memorial	182	Foreign Affairs	343	Favorable	319	Referred to Committee Whole House.		
Dodge, Pickering, executor of.	Indemnity for French spoliations prior to 1800.	29	2	Memorial	135	Foreign Affairs.						
Dodge, Pickering, executor of.	Indemnity for French spoliations prior to 1800.	31	1	Petition	215	Foreign Affairs	355	Favorable; bill	318	Referred to Committee Whole House.		

List of private claims presented to the House of Representatives of the United States from the 1st to the 31st Congress, inclusive—Continued.

Names of claimants.	Nature or object of the claim.	Congress.	Session.	How brought before the House of Reps.	Page of journal.	To what committee of the House referred.	No. or date of the report.	Nature of the report.	No. of the bill.	How disposed of by the House of Reps.	How disposed of by the Senate.	Date of the act of Congress, and remarks.
Dodge, William, *et al.*	Increase of compensation as measurers of port of New York.	4	2	Petition	696	Whole House	Feb. 6, 1797	By bill	211	Passed	Passed	App'd March 3, 1797
Dodge, William, *et al.*	Increase of compensation as measurers of port of New York.	5	2	Petition	82	Com. and Manuf.						
Dodge, William, *et al.*	Increase of compensation as measurers of port of New York.	5	3	Petition	467	Whole House.						
Dodson, Abigail	(See Abigail Brink)	23	1		110							
Dodson, Beverly	Compensation for horse and equipment lost in Seminole war.	23	1	Documents	154	Claims.						
Dodson, Esau	Invalid pension	17	1	Petition	134	Referred to Sec. of War.	Feb. 19, 1822	Report		Leave to withdraw.		
Dodson, Esau	Invalid pension	17	2	Petition	209	Rev. Pensions				Discharged; leave to withdraw.		
Dodson, Esau	Invalid pension	20	1	Petition	64	Military Pensions				Disch'd; laid on table.		
Dodson, Isham	(See David A. Ely, *et al.*)	30	2		91		115		793			
Dodson, James	(See David A. Ely, *et al.*)	30	2		91		115		793			
Dodson, John	(See David A. Ely, *et al.*)	30	2		91		115		793			
Dodson, Joseph	Compensation for horse lost in public service.	13	3	Petition	654	Committee Whole House, on bill No. 228.						
Dodson, Levi	Compensation for horse and equipments lost in Seminole war.	23	1	Documents	154	Claims.						
Dodson, Samuel	(See William H. Bedford, agent.)	28	1		262							
Dodson, Simeon W	(See David A. Ely, *et al.*)	30	2		91		115		793			
Doft, George	Remuneration for services and work done in late war.	26	1	Petition	355	Claims.						
Doft, George	Remuneration for services and work done in late war.	26	2	Petition	79	Claims.						
Doft, George	Remuneration for services and work done in late war.	27	2	Petition	94	Claims	168	Adverse		Laid on table.		
Doft, George	Remuneration for services and work done in late war.	27	3	Petition	106	Claims	89	Adverse		Laid on table.		
Dogan, Garret	Pension	22	1	Petition	330	Rev. Pensions				Discharged; laid on table.		
Doggett, Jacob, heirs of	Confirmation of title to land in Missouri.	15	2	Petition	28	Priv. Land Claims				Discharged; laid on table.		
Doggett, Jacob, heirs of	Confirmation of title to land in Missouri.	17	1	Petition	53	Public Lands.						
Doggett, Jacob, heirs of	Confirmation of title to land in Missouri.	18	1	Petition	53	Public Lands	Jan. 16, 1824	By bill	65	Passed with amend'mt.	Passed	App'd May 26, 1824
Doggett, William	Revolutionary pension	22	2	Petition	216	Rev. Pensions				Discharged; laid on table.		
Doherty, George, sen	Pension	21	1	Petition	197	Military Pensions				Discharged; laid on table.		
Doherty, George, sen	Pension	22	1	Petition	104	Rev. Pensions.						
Doherty, George, (Tenn.)	Compensation for services as an officer, and for arms furnished government in revolutionary war.	21	2	Petition	128	Rev. Claims.						
Doherty, Henry	Pension	14	2	Resolution	209	Pens. & Rev. Cl'ms.	Jan. 29, 1817	Favorable; bill	91	Passed	Passed with amendment.	App'd March 3, 1817
Dohrman, Arnold Henry, by Rachael, widow of and heirs of.	Additional remuneration for services in revolutionary war.	14	2	Senate bill	345	Pens. & Rev. Cl'ms.	Feb. 13, 1817	With amend.	S. 32	Passed	Concurred in.	App'd March 3, 1817

List of private claims presented to the House of Representatives of the United States from the 1st to the 31st Congress, inclusive—Continued.

Names of claimants.	Nature or object of the claim.	Congress.	Session.	How brought before the House of Reps.	Page of journal.	To what committee of the House referred.	No. or date of the report.	Nature of the report.	No. of the bill.	How disposed of by the House of Reps.	How disposed of by the Senate.	Date of the act of Congress, and remarks.
Dohrman, Arnold Henry, agent of.	Patent for land grant for benefit of creditors.	6	2	Petition	745	Claims	Feb. 24, 1801	Favorable; bill	313	Passed	Passed	App'd Feb. 27, 1801
Dohrman, Arnold Henry, heirs of.	Confirmation of title to land in Ohio.	22	1	Senate bill	745	Priv. Land Claims.	June 6, 1832	Adverse	S. 90	Rejected.		
Dohrman, Arnold Henry, heirs of.	Confirmation of title to land in Ohio.	22	2	Resolution	110	Priv. Land Claims.	96	Favorable; bill.	711	Referred to Committee Whole House.		
Dohrman, Arnold Henry, heirs of.	Confirmation of title to land in Ohio.	23	1	Resolution	82	Priv. Land Claims.	55	Favorable; bill.	64	Passed	Passed	App'd June 28, 1834
Dohrman, Arnold Henry, by Rachael, widow of.	Payment of annuity and grant	27	2	General bill	274	Whole House	Jan. 25, 1842	With't amend.	74	Passed	Passed	App'd May 18, 1842
Dohrman, Arnold Henry, by Rachael, widow of.	Payment of annuity and grant	27	3	General bill	53	Whole House	Dec. 14, 1842	With't amend.	615	Passed	Passed	App'd Dec. 14, 1842
Dohrman, Arnold Henry, by Rachael, widow of.	Payment of annuity and grant	27	3	General bill	394	Whole House	Feb. 17, 1843	With't amend.	804	Passed	Passed	App'd March 3, 1843
Dolan, Nancy	Indemnity for land bought of and sold by United States.	20	1	Petition	93	Public Lands	150	Favorable; bill.	173	Passed	Amended.	
Dolan, Nancy	Indemnity for land bought of and sold by United States.	20	2	House bill	209	Priv. Land Claims.	57	Favorable; bill.	394	Referred to Committee Whole House.		
Dolan, Nancy	Indemnity for land bought of and sold by United States.	21	1	Petition	41	Public Lands	8	Favorable; bill	13	Passed	Passed	App'd Feb. 11, 1830
Dolaway, William, *et al.*	Payment for vessel impressed into service of United States.	15	1	Petition	433	Claims				Discharged; leave to withdraw.		
Dolber, Benjamin	Restoration of pension	17	2	Petition	47	Rev. Pensions.				Discharged; leave to withdraw.		
Dolby, William	Relief for wounds received in revolutionary war.	2	1	Petition	463					Referred to Secretary War.		
Dolby, William	Invalid pension	5	3	Petition	445	Claims.						
Dole, Abigail	(See Jeremiah Dole, widow of)	24	2		260							
Dole, Amos	Restoration of pension	17	1	Petition	98	Rev. Pensions.				Discharged; laid on table.		
Dole, Campbell	Revolutionary pension	25	2	Petition	272	Rev. Pensions				Discharged; laid on table.		
Dole, David	Indemnity for French spoliations prior to 1800.	26	1	Memorial	182	Foreign Affairs	343	Favorable; bill	319	Referred to Committee Whole House.		
Dole, James	Invalid pension	3	1	Rep. of Secretary War.	131	Select	May 26, 1794	Favorable; bill ordered.	62	Passed	Passed	App'd June 7, 1794
Dole, James	Restoration of pension	17	1	Petition	39	Rev. Claims				Referred to Secretary of War.		
Dole, James, heirs of	Commutation pay and bounty land.	24	1	Resolution	511	Rev. Claims.						
Dole, Jeremiah, widow of.	Revolutionary pension	24	2	Petition	260	Rev. Claims.						
Dole, Thomas	Compensation for goods and provisions furnished New York Indians.	28	2	House bill	173	Whole House	Jan. 6, 1845	With't amend.	491	Passed	Passed	App'd March 3, 1845
Dolet, Pierre, heirs of	Confirmation of land title	26	2	Senate bill	282	Whole House			S. 182			
Dolet, Pierre, heirs of	Confirmation of land title	27	2	Senate bill	782	Priv. Land Claims.			81			
Doliber, William, by Abigail, widow of, *et al.*	Fishing bounty on schooner Mary & Hannah.	23	1	Petition	140	Commerce	Jan. 14, 1834	Favorable; bill	193	Passed	Passed	App'd June 30, 1834
Doliver, Louis, and wife Louisa.	Confirmation of title to land in Alabama.	15	1	Petition	213, 226	Priv. Land Claims.				Leave to withdraw.		
Dolive, Louis & Lefroy	Confirmation of title to lots in Mobile.	18	1	Petition	116	Whole House				Leave to withdraw.		
Dolive, Louis & Lefroy	Confirmation of title to lots in Mobile.	18	2	Petition	43	Priv. Land Claims.						

List of private claims presented to the House of Representatives of the United States from the 1st to the 31st Congress, inclusive—Continued.

Names of claimants.	Nature or object of the claim.	Congress.	Session.	How brought before the House of Reps.	Page of journal.	To what committee of the House referred.	No. or date of the report.	Nature of the report.	No. of the bill.	How disposed of by the House of Reps.	How disposed of by the Senate.	Date of the act of Congress, and remarks.
Dolive, Louis, *et al.*	Compensation for cattle taken for use of army in late war.	15	2	Petition	33	Claims	Nov. 27, 1815	Adverse	......	Rejected.		
Dolive, Louis, *et al*, by citizens of Alabama.	Compensation for cattle taken for use of army in late war.	18	1	Petition	80	Claims	May 4, 1824	Adverse	......	Leave to withdraw.		
Doll, Henry	Pension	20	2	Petition	109	Military Pensions	Feb. 13, 1829	Favorable; bill	440	Passed.		
Doll, Henry	Pension	21	1	House bill	130	Whole House	Jan. 5, 1830	With't amend.	72	Passed	Passed	App'd May 20, 1830, petit'rs name omitted in act.
Doll, Martin	Pension	21	2	Petition	88	Military Pensions.						
Dollay, Thomas H.	Compensation for naval and military service rendered U. S.	25	3	Petition	118	Naval Affairs.						
Dollay, Thomas H.	Compensation for naval and military service rendered U. S.	26	1	Petition	180	Naval Affairs.						
Dolman, A. & S.	Compensation for work done on Cumberland road.	23	1	Res. and papers	589	Claims	456	Statem't of facts	......	Discharged; referred to Secretary of War.	....	See Report No. 449.
Dolph, Charles, heirs of	Compensation for capturing prisoners on prize vessels.	14	1	Petition	162	Select	44	Favorable; bill	69	Passed	Passed	App'd April 27, 1816
Dolson, Euphemia	(See Euphemia Dobson)	27	2	....	330							
Doly, Maria	(See Alexander Bowles, mother of)	30	1	....	276							
Doly, Preston	(See Alexander Bowles)	30	1	....	276							
Dolluside, James S.	Additional compensation as lieutenant in war with Mexico.	31	1	Petition	862	Public Lands.						
Dominge, Paul, by Sophia, widow and administratrix of.	....	19	2	Petition	91	Claims	....	....	....	....	....	Nature of claim not on journal; petition and papers not on file in office.
Domingues, Manuel, heirs of.	Remuneration for cattle destroyed by United States troops.	26	1	Petition	337	Claims.						
Domingues, Manuel, heirs of.	Remuneration for cattle destroyed by United States troops.	26	2	Petition	135	Claims.						
Domingues, Manuel, heirs of.	Remuneration for cattle destroyed by United States troops.	27	2	Petition	94	Claims	499	Adverse	......	Referred to Committee Whole House.		
Donahay, James	Invalid pension	28	1	Petition	319	Invalid Pensions	233	Adverse	......	Laid on table.		
Donahay, James	Invalid pension	29	1	Petition	85	Rev. Pensions.						
Donaher, James	Pension and pay for revolutionary services.	14	2	Petition	283	Pens. & Rev. Cl'ms.	....	....	......	Discharged; laid on table.		
Donaher, James	Pension and pay for revolutionary services.	15	1	Petition	165	Pens. & Rev. Cl'ms.	....	....	......	Discharged; leave to withdraw.		
Donahoe, James	Revolutionary pension	10	1	Petition	199	Select.						
Donahoe, James	Revolutionary pension	12	1	Petition	174	Claims	June 12, 1812	Adverse	......	Laid on table.		
Donahoe, James	Revolutionary pension	12	2	Petition	583	Claims	....	....	......	Laid on table.		
Donald, William	(See William Donnal)	22	1	....	164							
Donaldson, Alexander	(See Alexander Donelson)	22	1	....	126							
Donaldson, Handley	(See Handley Donelson)	31	1	....	719	....	316					
Donaldson, James Lowry	Settlement of accounts, and for a credit of $400 money stolen.	29	2	Petition	127	Military Affairs.						
Donaldson, James, & Co.	Indemnity for French spoliations prior to 1800.	26	1	Memorial	182	Foreign Affairs	343	Favorable; bill	319	Referred to Committee Whole House.		
Donaldson, John J.	(See Andrew Buchanan, trustee of)	26	1	....	182	....	343	....	319			
Donaldson, John, representatives of, *et al.*	Compensation for certain land	15	1	Petition	184	Select	86	Favorable; bill	74	Laid on table.		
Donaldson, John, representatives of, *et al.*	Compensation for certain land	15	2	Petition	59	Select	31	Favorable; bill	225	Referred to Committee Whole House.		

List of private claims presented to the House of Representatives of the United States from the 1st to the 31st Congress, inclusive—Continued.

Names of claimants.	Nature or object of the claim.	Congress.	Session.	How brought before the House of Reps.	Page of journal.	To what committee of the House referred.	No. or date of the report.	Nature of the report.	No. of the bill.	How disposed of by the House of Reps.	How disposed of by the Senate.	Date of the act of Congress, and remarks.
Donaldson, John, representatives of, *et al.*	Compensation for certain land	16	1	Petition	30	Priv. Land Claims.	2	Favorable; bill	5	Recommitted.		
Donaldson, John, representatives of, *et al.*	Compensation for certain land	16	1	Petition	....	Priv. Land Claims.	62	Adverse	......	Referred to Committee Whole House.		
Donaldson, John, representatives of, *et al.*	Compensation for certain land	17	1	Senate bill	465	Public Lands	April 25, 1822	With amend.	S. 36	Laid on table.		
Donaldson, John, representatives of, *et al.*	Compensation for certain land	17	2	Senate bill	117	Public Lands	Jan. 30, 1823	With amend.	S. 11	Laid on table.		
Donaldson, John, representatives of, *et al.*	Compensation for certain land	18	1	House bill	162	Public Lands	Jan. 20, 1824	With amend.	73	Rejected.		
Donaldson, John, representatives of, *et al.*	Compensation for certain land	18	1	Senate bill	518	Public Lands	May 20, 1824	With amend.	S. 106	Passed	Concurred in.	App'd May 24, 1824
Donaldson, John, representatives of, *et al.*	To extend and continue in force the act of May 24, 1824.	19	1	Senate bill	547	Public Lands	May 12, 1826	With't amend.	132	Passed	Passed	App'd May 15, 1826
Donaldson, John, representatives of, *et al.*	To extend and continue in force the act of May 24, 1824.	22	1	Petition	173	Public Lands	Jan. 20, 1832	Favorable; bill	299	Passed	Passed with amendment.	App'd May 19, 1832
Donaldson, John, representatives of, *et al.*	To extend and continue in force the act of May 24, 1824.	24	1	Senate bill	320	Public Lands	Feb. 19, 1836	With't amend.	S. 20	Passed	Passed	App'd June 23, 1836
Donaldson, John J.	(See Thorowgood Smith, trustee of)	26	1	....	182	....	343	....	319			
Donaldson, Joseph, heirs of.	Release from payment of claim in favor of United States.	12	1	Petition	112	Claims.						
Donaldson, Lothario, (N. Y.)	Pension	21	2	Petition	212	Military Pensions.						
Donaldson, Lothario, (N. Y.)	Restoration of pension	22	1	Resolution	433	Rev. Pensions	380	Favorable; bill	473	Passed	Indef. postp'd.	
Donaldson, Robert & James	Indemnity for French spoliations prior to 1800.	26	1	Memorial	182	Foreign Affairs	343	Favorable; bill	319	Referred to Committee Whole House.		
Donaldson, Samuel	(See George Grundy, trustee of)	26	1	....	182	....	343	....	319			
Donaldson, Sarah	(See Joseph Donaldson, heirs of)	12	1	....	124							
Donaldson, Stephen F., sureties of.	Release from liability	17	1	Petition	172	Military Affairs	....	....	......	Discharged; laid on table.		
Donaldson, William	(See William Colt)	25	2	....	200	....	528	....	519			
Donaldson, William, attorney of.	Compensation for services and injuries sustained in revolutionary war.	5	3	Petition	492	Claims.						
Donaldson, William, attorney of.	Compensation for services and injuries sustained in revolutionary war.	6	1	Petition	535	Claims	Jan. 1, 1800	Adverse	......	Laid on table.		
Donation, James	(See R. G. Dunlap)	26	1	....	603							
Donden, James	Confirmation of title to land in Missouri.	15	2	Petition	28	Priv. Land Claims.	....	....	......	Discharged; laid on table.		
Donden, James	Confirmation of title to land in Missouri.	17	1	Petition	53	Public Lands	....	....	......	Discharged; laid on table.		
Donden, James	Confirmation of title to land in Missouri.	18	1	Petition	53	Public Lands	Jan. 16, 1824	General bill	65	Passed with amendm't	Passed	App'd May 26, 1824
Doneghy, J. G.	Payment of $137 50 claimed by Post Office Department.	26	2	Petition	56	P. Of. and P. Roads.						
Doneghy, J. G.	Payment of $137 50 claimed by Post Office Department.	29	2	Petition	57	P. Of. and P. Roads.	196	Adverse	......	Laid on table.		
Donelson, Alexander	(See David G. Howard, assignee of)	22	1	....	126	....	188	....	269			
Donelson, Handley	Invalid pension	31	1	Petition	719	Rev. Claims	316	Adverse	......	Laid on table.		
Donelson, John, representatives of.	(See John Donaldson, representatives of.)	24	1	....	320							

List of private claims presented to the House of Representatives of the United States from the 1st to the 31st Congress, inclusive—Continued.

Names of claimants.	Nature or object of the claim.	Congress.	Session.	How brought before the House of Reps.	Page of journal.	To what committee of the House referred.	No. or date of the report.	Nature of the report.	No. of the bill.	How disposed of by the House of Reps.	How disposed of by the Senate.	Date of the act of Congress, and remarks.
Donley, John	Compensation for carrying United States mail.	19	1	Senate bill	474	P. Of. and P. Roads.	April 27, 1826	With't amend.	S. 91	Passed	Passed	App'd May 20, 1826
Donn, John	Compensation for property destroyed by British in 1812.	21	1	Petition	358	Claims	May 12, 1830	Adverse		Laid on table.		
Donn, John	Compensation for property destroyed by British in 1812.	21	2	Petition	161	Claims	Feb. 23, 1831	Adverse		Laid on table.		
Donnal, William	Revolutionary pension	18	2	Petition	183	Rev. Pensions				Discharged; laid on table.		
Donnal, William	Revolutionary pension	22	1	Petition	164	Rev. Pensions				Discharged; laid on table.		
Donnan, Gorshom	(See Gersham Dorman.)	12	1		135							
Donnel, John, executors of	That claim under treaty of Ghent be placed on Commissioners' list	21	1	Petition	52	Judiciary	206	Adverse		Laid on table.		
Donnel, John, executors of	Compensation for property taken for use of United States in late war.	24	1	Memorial	405	Claims.						
Donnel, John, executors of	Compensation for property taken for use of United States in late war.	24	2	Petition	155	Claims.						
Donnel, John, executors of	Compensation for property taken for use of United States in late war.	25	2	Petition	73	Claims.						
Donnel, John, executors of	Compensation for property taken for use of United States in late war.	25	3	Petition	86	Claims	66	Adverse		Laid on table.		
Donnell, John, (Md.)	Indemnity for French spoliations prior to 1800.	26	1	Memorial	182	Foreign Affairs	343	Favorable; bill	319	Referred to Committee Whole House.		
Donnell, John, heirs of	Arrears or balance of pension	28	1	Petition	263	Rev. Pensions	331	Favorable; bill	239	Passed.		
Donnell, John, heirs of	Arrears or balance of pension	29	1	Petition	275	Rev. Pensions				Discharged; laid on table.		
Donnellan, Thomas, (Md.)	Renewal of certificate of indebtedness.	1	2	Petition	168					Referred to Secretary Treasury.		
Donnellan, Thomas, (Md.)	Renewal of certificate of indebtedness.	2	1	Petition	501					Referred to Secretary Treasury.		
Donnellan, Thomas, (Md.)	Renewal of certificate of indebtedness.	3	2	Petition	317	Claims				Discharged; leave to withdraw.		
Donnellan, Thomas, (Md.)	Renewal of certificate of indebtedness.	4	1	Petition	422	Claims.						
Donnellan, Thomas, (Md.)	Renewal of certificate of indebtedness.	4	2	Petition and res.	668	Claims	Jan. 31, 1797	Adverse.				
Donnelly, Charles	Bounty land for services in war of 1812.	31	1	Petition	471	Public Lands	246	Favorable; bill	244	Referred to Committee Whole House.		
Donner, Avery	(See Avery Downer.)	24	1		56							
Donnet, Armand F.	Compensation for services as acting chargé d'affaires.	28	1	Petition	986	Foreign Affairs.						
Donnet, Armand F.	Compensation for services as acting chargé d'affaires.	28	2	Petition	83	Foreign Affairs	91	Favorable; bill	605	Referred to Committee Whole House.		
Donnet, Armand F.	Compensation for services as acting chargé d'affaires.	29	1	Petition	120	Foreign Affairs.						
Donnet, Armand F.	Compensation for services as acting chargé d'affaires.	30	1	Memorial	647	Foreign Affairs	March 9, 1848	General bill	298	Passed	Passed	App'd Aug. 12, 1848
Donnon, Patrick	Compensation for extra services a surveyor in Virginia.	11	3	House bill	487	Whole House	Jan. 17, 1811	With't amend.	177	Passed	Passed	App'd Feb. 20, 1811

List of *private claims presented to the House of Representatives of the United States from the* 1*st to the* 31*st Congress, inclusive*—Continued.

Names of claimants.	Nature or object of the claim.	Congress.	Session.	How brought before the House of Reps.	Page of journal.	To what committee of the House referred.	No. or date of the report.	Nature of the report.	No. of the bill.	How disposed of by the House of Reps.	How disposed of by the Senate.	Date of the act of Congress, and remarks.
67 Donoho, Stephen	(See James Ross and Stephen Donoho.)	20	1	....	92							
Donoho, Thomas, administrator of.	Commutation pay	31	2	Petition	194	Rev. Pensions.						
Donohoe, George, by Rachael, widow of.	Arrears of pay for services in war of 1812.	20	1	Resolution	324	Military Pensions	....	....	......	Discharged; laid on table.		
Donovan, Richard, *et al.*	Remuneration for losses on contract at Treasury building.	26	1	Petition	728	Claims.						
Doogan, George	Pension	20	1	Petition	124	Military Pensions	Feb. 13, 1828	Favorable; bill	166	Passed	Referred, and Com. disch'd.	
Doogan, George	Pension	20	2	House bill	55	Military Pensions	Dec. 12, 1828	Favorable; bill	311	Passed	Laid on table.	
Doogan, George	Pension	21	1	House bill	130	Whole House	Jan. 5, 1830	By bill	72	Passed	Passed with amendment.	App'd May 20, 1830
Dooley, William	Compensation for six horses lost in Seminole war.	17	1	Petition	125	Claims	Feb. 8, 1822	Favorable; bill	81	Passed	Passed	App'd May 7, 1822
Doolford, Daniel	Pension	27	3	Petition	240	Invalid Pensions.						
Doolin, John, representatives of.	(See John Davlin, representatives of.)	23	1	....	132							
Doolin, Patrick	Pension	19	1	Petition	52	Military Pensions	164	Favorable; refer'd to Com. Whole Ho.	......	Discharged.		
Doolin, Patrick	Pension	19	2	Petition	66	Military Pensions	....	....	......	Discharged.		
Doolittle, Hackabiah	Revolutionary pension	10	1	Petition	17	Select	Nov. 12, 1807	Rep. and res.	......	Leave to withdraw.		
Doolittle, Hackabiah	Revolutionary pension	11	2	House bill	283	Whole House	Mar. 15, 1810	With't amend	107	Passed	Passed	App'd April 27, 1810
Dopkins, Nathaniel W.	Pension for services in war of 1812	29	1	Petition	648	Invalid Pensions.						
Doran, Miles	Relief for injuries received in revolutionary war.	11	2	Petition	206	Whole House.						
Doremus, Suydam & Nixen.	(See Cook, Anthony and Mahon, *et al.*)	30	1	....	826							
Dorland, Lambert	Compensation for services in revolutionary war.	3	2	Petition	332	Claims.						
Dorland, Lambert	Compensation for services in revolutionary war.	4	1	Res. and docs	373	Claims	Jan. 6, 1796	Rep't refer'd to Com. Whole House.	......	Leave to withdraw.		
Dorman, Gersham	Invalid pension	3	1	Rep. of Secretary War.	131	Select	May 26, 1794	Res. to refer to Sec. with instructions.	J. R. 12	Passed	Passed	App'd June 9, 1794
Dorman, Gersham	Invalid pension	4	1	Res. and docs	445	Claims	Feb. 18, 1796	Favorable; bill ordered.	156	Passed	Passed	App'd April 20, 1796
Dorman, Gersham	Increase of pension	12	1	House bill	138	Whole House	June 15, 1812	By bill	138	Passed	Passed	App'd July 5, 1812
Dornbach, Anna Maria	Revolutionary pension	25	3	Petition	368	Rev. Pensions	....	....	......	Discharged.		
Dornbach, Anna Maria	Revolutionary pension	26	1	Petition	173	Rev. Pensions.						
Dornbach, Anna Maria	Revolutionary pension	28	1	Petition	79	Rev. Pensions.						
Dorney, Daniel	(See Edward McGuire & D. Dorney.)	15	2	....	62							
Dornin, Lieut. Thomas	Compensation for survey of coast of United States in 1817.	23	1	Petition	440	Naval Affairs	April 24, 1834	Favorable; bill.	445	Referred to Committee Whole House.	....	Provided for in general appropriation bill, app'd June 30, 1834.
Dornin, Thomas A	(See Exploring Expedition)	27	3	....	149							
Dorr, Andrew C., *et al.*	Register for brigantine Frances Eliza.	7	1	Petition	31	Com. and Manuf.	Jan. 11, 1802	Adverse.				
Dorr, Andrew C., by Charlotte, widow of.	Indemnity for French spoliations prior to 1800.	29	2	Memorial	75	Foreign Affairs.						

List of private claims presented to the House of Representatives of the United States from the 1st to the 31st Congress, inclusive—Continued.

Names of claimants.	Nature or object of the claim.	Congress.	Session.	How brought before the House of Reps.	Page of journal.	To what committee of the House referred.	No. or date of the report.	Nature of the report.	No. of the bill.	How disposed of by the House of Reps.	How disposed of by the Senate.	Date of the act of Congress, and remarks.
Dorr, Eben Ritchie	Compensation as chargé d'affaires to Chili.	30	1	Petition	619	Foreign Affairs						Provided for in general appropriation bill, app'd Aug. 12, 1848.
Dorr, Ebenezer, *et al.*	Relief from payment of certain duties.	5	1	Memorial	25	Select	June 13, 1797	By bill	2	Amended and rejected.		
Dorr, Ebenezer, executors of.	Indemnity for French spoliations prior to 1800.	26	1	Memorial	182	Foreign Affairs	343	Favorable; bill.	319	Referred to Committee Whole House.		
Dorr, Capt. Gustavus	Pension	30	1	Senate bill	1205	Whole House		With't amend.	S. 217	Passed	Passed	App'd Aug. 12, 1848
Dorr, Henry	Revolutionary pension	27	1	Petition	101	Rev. Pensions.						
Dorr, Henry	Revolutionary pension	27	2	Petition	59	Rev. Pensions	784	Adverse		Laid on table.		
Dorr, Henry	Revolutionary pension	27	3	Petition	73	Rev. Pensions	295	Adverse		Laid on table.		
Dorr, John	Debenture of drawback on playing cards.	9	1	Petition	196	Com. and Manuf.	Dec. 31, 1805	Report and res.		Leave to withdraw.		
Dorr, John	Debenture of drawback on playing cards.	19	2	Petition	217	Ways and Means				Discharged.		
Dorr, John	Debenture of drawback on playing cards.	20	1	Petition	45	Ways and Means	21	Adverse		Leave to withdraw.		
Dorr, John	(See Ebenezer Dorr, executor of.)	26	1		182		343		319			
Dorr, Joseph H.	(See John Whitney)	13	2		311							
Dorr, Mathias	Pension	25	2	Petition	822	Rev. Pensions				Discharged.		
Dorr, Matthias	Pension	26	1	Petition	631	Rev. Pensions.						
Dorr, Matthias	Pension	27	2	Petition	97	Rev. Pensions	784	Adverse		Laid on table.		
Dorr, Matthew	Remuneration for losses in revolutionary war.	27	3	Petition	113	Rev. Pensions.						
Dorr, Nathaniel	(See William Lambert, executor of.)	26	1		182		343		319			
Dorr & Co.	(See W. & S. Lawrence & others)	21	2		67							
Dorrance, O. B.	Fishing bounty	20	2	Petition	288	Commerce				Discharged; laid on table.		
Dorsett, Fielder	(See Samuel Dorsett, heir of)	29	2		176							
Dorsett, Oliver	Invalid pension	25	2	Petition	167	Invalid Pensions	610	Favorable; bill	590	Passed	Passed	App'd July 7, 1838
Dorsett, Samuel, heir of	Indemnity for French spoliations prior to 1800.	29	2	Memorial	176	Foreign Affairs.						
Dorsett, Samuel, heir of	Indemnity for French spoliations prior to 1800.	31	1	Petition	391	Foreign Affairs	355	Favorable; bill	318	Referred to Committee Whole House.		
Dorsey, John E., administrator of.	Relief on certain contract for anchors.	18	1	Petition	155	Ways and Means	Feb. 19, 1824	Adverse		Laid on table.		
Dorsey, John E., administrator of.	Relief on certain contract for anchors.	19	1	Petition	251	Judiciary	96	Favorable; bill	130	Passed	With amend.	
Dorsey, John E., administrator of.	Relief on certain contract for anchors.	19	2	Petition	60	Judiciary	Dec. 19, 1826	Favorable; bill	301	Passed	Passed, with amendment.	App'd March 2, 1827
Dorsey, John E., executrix of.	Indemnity for French spoliations prior to 1800.	29	2	Memorial	58	Foreign Affairs.						
Dorsey, John E., executrix of.	Indemnity for French spoliations prior to 1800.	31	1	Petition	195, & 6	Foreign Affairs	355	Favorable; bill	318	Referred to Committee Whole House.		
Dorsey, John	Compensation for losses sustained by enemy in 1814.	29	1	Petition	401	Military Affairs	406	Adverse		Laid on table.		
Dorsey, John M.	Reimbursement of costs of suit in favor of United States.	21	1	Petition	83	Claims	Dec. 30, 1829	Adverse		Laid on table.		
Dorsey, Jonathan	Compensation for property destroyed in Black Hawk war.	24	1	Documents	206	Claims.						
Dorsey, Joshua	Discharge from judgment in favor of United States.	13	1	Petition	96	Ways and Means	July 3, 1813	Favorable; bill	56	Passed	Passed	App'd Aug. 2, 1813

List of private claims presented to the House of Representatives of the United States from the 1st to the 31st Congress, inclusive—Continued.

Names of claimants.	Nature or object of the claim.	Congress.	Session.	How brought before the House of Reps.	Page of journal.	To what committee of the House referred.	No. or date of the report.	Nature of the report.	No. of the bill.	How disposed of by the House of Reps.	How disposed of by the Senate.	Date of the act of Congress, and remarks.
Dorsey, Mary Matilda	Indemnity for losses by fire in erecting post office building.	26	1	Petition	619	P. Of. and P. Roads.				Discharged; laid on table.		
Dorsey, Roderick	Permission to correct error in paying members of the House of Representatives.	25	2	Communication.	253	Select	Jan. 31, 1838	Favorable		Laid on table.		
Dos Palacios, Capt. J. J.	Compensation for services as captain of a spy company in war with Mexico.	31	1	Petition	406	Military Affairs.						
Dossett, James, heirs of.	Bounty land services in war of 1812.	30	1	Petition	202	Public Lands	146	Adverse		Laid on table.		
Doty, Elias	Revolutionary pension	27	2	Petition	684	Rev. Pensions	784	Adverse		Laid on table.		
Doty, Elijah	Indemnity for property destroyed by British in late war.	15	2	Petition	148	Claims				Discharged; laid on table.		
Doty, Ephraim	Pension	22	1	Res. of Legis'ture Illinois.	97	Rev. Pensions.				Discharged; laid on table.		
Doty, James Duane	Confirmation of title to lands in Michigan.	20	1	Memorial & res.	28	Claims	42	Favorable; bill.	34	Passed	Passed	App'd April 17, 1828
Doty, James D	Payment of balance due as governor and superintendant of Indian Affairs, Wisconsin Territory.	31	1	House bill	1034	Whole House	June 19, 1850	General bill	334	Passed	Passed	App'd Sept. 30, 1850
Doty, Levi	Pension	23	2	Petition	220	Rev. Pensions.				Discharged; laid on table.		
Doty, Thomas	Invalid pension	24	1	Petition	261	Invalid Pensions	Mar. 24, 1836	Adverse.				
Douberman, Henry	Invalid pension	12	1	Petition	124	Claims	June 12, 1812	Adverse		Laid on table.		
Douberman, Henry	Invalid pension	13	1	Petition	97	Pens. & Rev. Cl'ms.				Discharged; leave to withdraw.		
Doud, Benjamin B	Pension for services in war of 1812.	25	2	Petition	588	Invalid Pensions	803	Favorable; bill	750	Passed	Passed	App'd July 7, 1838
Dougan, James	Revolutionary pension	21	1	Resolution	550	Military Pensions.				Discharged; laid on table.		
Doughty, Abigail	(See Ichabod Doughty, daughter of.)	29	1		675		785					
Doughty, Amos, (Maine.)	Pension	28	2	Resolution	286	Invalid Pensions.						
Doughty, Amos, (Maine.)	Invalid pension	29	1	Petition	82	Invalid Pensions.				Discharged; laid on table.		
Doughty, Christopher	Revolutionary pension	21	1	Resolution	350	Military Pensions.	May 3, 1830	Adverse		Laid on table.		
Doughty, Christopher	Revolutionary pension	21	2	Petition	108	Military Pensions.						
Doughty, Christopher	Revolutionary pension	22	1	Petition	46	Military Pensions.	410	Favorable; bill	510	Referred to Committee Whole House.		
Doughty, Christopher	Revolutionary pension	24	2	Petition	215	Rev. Pensions				Discharged; laid on table.		
Doughty, Christopher	Increase of pension	27	2	Petition	222	Rev. Pensions	784	Adverse		Laid on table.		
Doughty, Christopher	Increase of pension	27	3	Petition	237	Rev. Pensions.						
Doughty, Daniel	Bounty land for services in war of 1812.	16	1	Res. and papers.	81	Priv. Land Claims.	Jan. 27, 1820	Adverse.		Laid on table.		
Doughty, Edward	Bounty land for services in war with Mexico.	30	1	Petition	259	Military Affairs.						
Doughty, Ichabod, daughter of.	Relief on account of services of deceased in revolutionary war.	29	1	Petition	675	Rev. Pensions	785	Adverse		Laid on table.		
Doughty, James	Compensation for services in revolutionary war.	2	1	Petition	474					Referred to Secretary War.		
Doughty, James	Naval pension for services in war of 1812.	29	2	Petition	176	Naval Affairs.						

List of private claims presented to the House of Representatives of the United States from the 1st to the 31st Congress, inclusive—Continued.

Names of claimants.	Nature or object of the claim.	Congress.	Session.	How brought before the House of Reps.	Page of journal.	To what committee of the House referred.	No. or date of the report.	Nature of the report.	No. of the bill.	How disposed of by the House of Reps.	How disposed of by the Senate.	Date of the act of Congress, and remarks.
Doughty, Richard	Pension for injuries received in retreat from Indians.	24	1	Petition	602	Invalid Pensions.	June 17, 1836	Adverse		Laid on table.		
Doughty, Thomas	Prize money on board of Macedonian in 1815.	19	1	Resolution	467	Ways and Means.	April 26, 1826	Favorable; bill	229	Passed	With amend.	
Doughty, Thomas	Prize money on board of Macedonian in 1815.	19	2	Resolution	76	Ways and Means.	Jan. 9, 1827	Favorable; bill	359	Passed	Passed, with amendment.	App'd March 2, 1827
Doughty, William	Payment of certain bonds issued by Territory of Wisconsin.	28	1	Petition	238	Territories	578			Laid on table.		
Dougherty, Bernard	Compensation for work done on Cumberland road, and for materials furnished.	23	1	Petition	305, 539	Claims	456	Report		Referred to Secretary War.		See report No. 449.
Dougherty, John	Revolutionary pension	15	1	Petition	26	Pens. & Rev. Cl'ms	Feb. 10, 1818	Adverse		Leave to withdraw.		
Dougherty, John	Revolutionary pension	15	2	Rep. of Secretary of War.	48	Pens. & Rev. Cl'ms.	Feb. 5, 1819	Favorable; bill	308	Postponed.		
Dougherty, John	Compensation for extra services as Indian agent.	23	2	Petition	376	Indian Affairs.						
Dougherty, John	Equitable settlement of accounts as Indian agent.	23	2	Senate bill	656	Indian Affairs	Feb. 28, 1835	With amend.	S. 166	Passed	Passed	App'd March 3, 1835
Dougherty, John	Confirmation of land title	15	1	Petition	50	Priv. Land Claims.				Discharged; laid on table.		
Dougherty, John	Confirmation of land title	16	1	Petition	72	Priv. Land Claims.				Discharged; laid on table.		
Dougherty, John	Confirmation of land title	17	1	Petition	53	Public Lands				Discharged; laid on table.		
Dougherty, John	Confirmation of land title	18	1	Petition	53	Public Lands	Jan. 16, 1824	General bill	65	Passed with amendm't.	Passed	App'd May 26, 1824
Dougherty, John, (Wis.)	Permission to enter land at minimum price.	25	2	Petition	90	Public Lands	687	Favorable; bill	662	Referred to Committee Whole House.		
Dougherty, John, (Wis.)	Permission to enter land at minimum price.	25	3	Rep't Committee Whole House.	380	Whole House	Jan. 25, 1839	By bill	662	Passed	Passed, with amendment.	App'd March 3, 1839
Dougherty, Joseph	Relief from sale of bounty land for taxes.	22	1	Memorial	836	Priv. Land Claims.				Discharged; laid on table.		
Dougherty, Michael	(See Michael Daugherty.)	13	2		301		92					
Dougherty, Owen, by Margaret, widow of.	Prize money for capture of Algerine vessel.	28	1	Report and bill.	913	Whole House	473	With't amend.	363	Passed	Passed	App'd June 17, 1844
Dougherty, Patrick	Revolutionary pension	2	2	Petition	619	Select.						
Dougherty, Patrick	Invalid pension	3	1	Rep. of Secretary War.	131	Select	May 26, 1794	Favorable; bill ordered.	62	Passed	Passed	App'd June 7, 1794
Dougherty, Susan	(See Moses Oldham, heir of.)	20	1		113							
Dougherty, Thomas	(See Zebulon Pike & companions)	10	1		189				74			
Dougherty, William	Pension	21	1	Petition	149	Military Pensions.	Mar. 26, 1830	Adverse		Laid on table.		
Dougherty, William	Pension	21	2	Petition	73	Military Pensions.						
Dougherty, William	Pension	22	1	Petition	73	Rev. Pensions	367	Favorable; bill	462	Passed	Indef. postp'd.	
Dougherty, William	Pension or other relief	22	2	Petition	29	Rev. Claims.						
Douglass, Achilles	Compensation for service of wagon and team in 1794.	7	2	Petition	435	Claims				Discharged; leave to withdraw.		
Douglass, Alford	Pre-emption right to land in Mississippi.	22	2	Petition	105	Priv. Land Claims.				Discharged; laid on table.		
Douglass, Alford	Pre-emption right to land in Mississippi.	23	1	Petition	138	Priv. Land Claims.	135	Favorable; bill	147	Passed.		
Douglass, Alford	Pre-emption right to land in Mississippi.	23	2	Petition	256	Public Lands	61	Favorable; bill	676	Referred to Committee Whole House.		
Douglass, Alford	Pre-emption right to land in Mississippi.	24	1	Petition	426	Priv. Land Claims.	677	Favorable; bill	636	Referred to Committee Whole House.		

List of private claims presented to the House of Representatives of the United States from the 1st to the 31st Congress, inclusive—Continued.

Names of claimants.	Nature or object of the claim.	Congress.	Session.	How brought before the House of Reps.	Page of journal.	To what committee of the House referred.	No. or date of the report.	Nature of the report.	No. of the bill.	How disposed of by the House of Reps.	How disposed of by the Senate.	Date of the act of Congress, and remarks.
Douglass, Alford	Pre-emption right to land in Mississippi.	25	2	Petition	43	Priv. Land Claims.	198	Adverse		Laid on table.		
Douglass, Charles	Indemnity for loss of goods in Canada in war of 1812.	15	2	Petition	132	Claims				Discharged; laid on table.		
Douglass, Charles	Indemnity for loss of goods in Canada in war of 1812.	17	1	Petition	46	Claims	Dec. 21, 1821	Adverse		Laid on table.		
Douglass, Daniel	(See Elijah Bailey, *et al*	17	2		56							
Douglass, Daniel	Indemnity for French spoliations prior to 1800.	22	1	Memorial	334	Foreign Affairs.						
Douglass, Daniel	Indemnity for French spoliations prior to 1800.	26	1	Memorial	182	Foreign Affairs	343	Favorable; bill	319	Referred to Committee Whole House.		
Douglass, Dennison	Payment for grain, &c, taken for use of United States army in 1812.	18	2	Petition	253	Claims.						
Douglass, Dennison	Payment for grain, &c., taken for use of United States army in 1812.	19	1	Petition	224	Claims	April 24, 1826	Adverse		Laid on table.		
Douglass, Dennison	Payment for grain, &c., taken for use of United States army in 1812.	20	1	Petition	38	Claims	238	Adverse		Referred to Committee Whole House.		
Douglass, Elisha	Pension	19	1	Petition	66	Military Pensions	164	Adverse.				
Douglass, Elisha	Pension	19	2	Petition	43	Military Pensions				Discharged.		
Douglass, Elisha	Pension	20	1	Petition	90	Military Pensions				Discharged; laid on table.		
Douglass, Elisha	Pension	20	2	Petition	55	Military Pensions	Dec. 12, 1828	Favorable; bill	311	Passed	Laid on table.	
Douglass, Elisha	Pension	21	1	Petition	46	Military Pensions	Jan. 5, 1830	General bill	72	Passed	Passed with amendment.	App'd May 20, 1830
Douglass, Elizabeth	(See John Readpath, representatives of.)	3	1		68							
Douglass, Elizabeth	(See Lieut. Daniel Starr, heirs of.)	28	1		99							
Douglass, George, (N. Y.)	Relief for services and injuries in United States army in revolutionary war.	10	1	Petition	120	Claims				Discharged; referred to Select Committee.		
Douglass, George, (N. Y.)	Invalid pension	12	1	Petition	51	Claims	May 7, 1812	Report		Leave to withdraw.		
Douglass, George	Pre-emption right to land	22	2	Petition	105	Priv. Land Claims.				Discharged; laid on table.		
Douglass, George	Pre-emption right to land	23	1	Petition	138	Priv. Land Claims.	135	Favorable; bill	147	Passed.		
Douglass, George	Pre-emption right to land	23	2	Petition	256	Public Lands	61	Favorable; bill	676	Referred to Committee Whole House.		
Douglass, George	Pre-emption right to land	24	1	Petition	416	Priv. Land Claims.	677	Favorable; bill	636	Referred to Committee Whole House.		
Douglass, George	Pre-emption right to land	25	2	Petition	43	Priv. Land Claims.	198	Adverse		Laid on table.		
Douglass, Hannah	(See Col. William Douglass, widow of)	1	2		243							
Douglass, James	(See Ephraim Gilman and others.)	16	1		194							
Douglass, James S., *et al.*	Pre-emption right to land	22	2	Petition	105	Priv. Land Claims.				Discharged; laid on table.		
Douglass, James S., *et al.*	Pre-emption right to land	23	1	Petition	138	Priv. Land Claims.	135	Favorable; bill	147	Passed.		
Douglass, James S., *et al.*	Pre-emption right to land	23	2	Petition	256	Public Lands	61	Favorable; bill	676	Referred to Committee Whole House.		
Douglass, James S., *et al.*	Pre-emption right to land	24	1	Petition	426	Priv. Land Claims.	677	Favorable; bill	636	Referred to Committee Whole House.		
Douglass, James S., *et al.*	Pre-emption right to land	25	2	Petition	43	Priv. Land Claims.	198	Adverse		Laid on table.		

List of private claims presented to the House of Representatives of the United States from the 1st to the 31st Congress, inclusive—Continued.

Names of claimants.	Nature or object of the claim.	Congress.	Session.	How brought before the House of Reps.	Page of journal.	To what committee of the House referred.	No. or date of the report.	Nature of the report.	No. of the bill.	How disposed of by the House of Reps.	How disposed of by the Senate.	Date of the act of Congress, and remarks.
Douglass, Joseph, heirs of.	Pre-emption right to land	22	2	Petition	105	Priv. Land Claims.				Discharged; laid on table.		
Douglass, Joseph, heirs of.	Pre-emption right to land	23	1	Petition	138	Priv. Land Claims.	135	Favorable; bill.	147	Passed.		
Douglass, Joseph, heirs of.	Pre emption right to land	23	2	Petition	256	Public Lands	61	Favorable; bill.	676	Referred to Committee Whole House.		
Douglass, Joseph, heirs of.	Pre-emption right to land	24	1	Petition	426	Priv. Land Claims.	677	Favorable; bill.	636	Referred to Committee Whole House.		
Douglass, Joseph, heirs of.	Pre emption right to land	25	2	Petition	43	Priv. Land Claims.	198	Adverse		Laid on table.		
Douglass & Maguire	Compensation for horses and other property lost in 1832, in an expedition against the Indians.	24	1	Petition	430	Claims.						
Douglass, Stephen	Pre-emption right to land	22	2	Petition	105	Priv. Land Claims.				Discharged: laid on table.		
Douglass, Stephen	Pre emption right to land	23	1	Petition	138	Priv. Land Claims.	135	Favorable; bill.	147	Passed.		
Douglass, Stephen	Pre-emption right to land	23	2	Petition	256	Public Lands	61	Favorable; bill.	676	Referred to Committee Whole House.		
Douglass, Stephen	Pre-emption right to land	24	1	Petition	426	Priv. Land Claims.	677	Favorable; bill.	636	Referred to Committee Whole House.		
Douglass, Stephen	Pre-emption right to land	25	2	Petition	43	Priv. Land Claims.	198	Adverse		Laid on table.		
Douglass, Thomas James	Pension and other compensation for services in revolutionary war.	18	1	Petition	210	Rev. Claims				Discharged; leave to withdraw.		
Douglass, Thomas James	Pension and other compensation for services in revolutionary war.	19	1	Resolution	75	Military Pensions	164	Adverse		Leave to withdraw.		
Douglass, Thomas James	Pension and other compensation for services in revolutionary war.	20	1	Resolution	200	Military Pensions				Discharged; laid on table.		
Douglass, Thomas	Compensation for services as attorney for East Florida.	22	2	House bill	145	Whole House	Jan. 7, 1833	General bill	669	Passed	Passed	App'd March 2, 1833
Douglass, Thomas	Compensation for taking testimony in case of C. F. Sibbald.	25	2	Petition	921	Claims	June 16, 1838	Res ; favorable		Clerk of House directed to pay.		
Douglass, Thomas	Compensation for defending certain suits as district attorney.	29	2	Senate bill	306	Judiciary	Feb. 24, 1847	With't amend.	S. 47	Referred to Committee Whole House.		
Douglass, Thomas	Compensation for defending certain suits as district attorney.	30	1	Petition	422	Judiciary.						
Douglass, Thomas	Compensation for defending certain suits as district attorney.	30	1	Senate bill	684	Judiciary	June 14, 1848	With't amend.	S. 94	Referred to Committee Whole House.		
Douglass, Thomas	Compensation for defending certain suits as district attorney.	30	2	Senate bill	319	Whole House	Jan. 26, 1849	With't amend.	S. 94	Passed	Passed	App'd Feb. 1, 1849
Douglass, William	(See John Readpath, representatives of.)	3	1		68							
Douglass, William, *et al.*	Remission of duties on certain imports.	7	2	Petition	245	Com. and Manuf.	Jan. 18, 1803	Adverse		Discharged; leave to withdraw.		
Douglass, Col. Wm., widow of.	Revolutionary pension	1	2	Petition	243	Referred to Sec. of War.	June 18, 1790	Report		Laid on table.		
Douglass, Col. Wm., widow of.	Revolutionary pension	1	3	Rep. of Secretary War.	393					General bill ordered.		
Douglass, Col. Wm., widow of.	Revolutionary pension	9	1	Petition	199	Claims.						
Douglass, Col. William, representatives of.	Seven years' half-pay	23	1	Petition	42	Rev. Claims	138	Favorable ; bill	149	Passed	Passed	App'd June 30, 1834
Douglass, Col. William, representatives of.	Interest on seven years' half-pay	23	2	Petition	109	Rev. Claims.						
Douglass, Col. William, representatives of.	Interest on seven years' half-pay	23	2	Senate bill	335	Rev. Claims	Feb. 13, 1835	With't amend.	S. 96	Referred to Committee Whole House.		

List of private claims presented to the House of Representatives of the United States from the 1st to the 31st Congress, inclusive—Continued.

Names of claimants.	Nature or object of the claim.	Congress.	Session.	How brought before the House of Reps.	Page of journal.	To what committee of the House referred.	No. or date of the report.	Nature of the report.	No. of the bill.	How disposed of by the House of Reps.	How disposed of by the Senate.	Date of the act of Congress, and remarks.
Douglass, Col. William, representatives of.	Interest on seven years' half-pay	24	1	Senate bill	745	Rev. Claims	May 10, 1836	With't amend.	S. 111	Referred to Committee Whole House.		
Douglass, Col. William, representatives of.	Interest on seven years' half-pay	24	2	Senate bill	579	Whole House	....	....	S. 158			
Douglass, William, *et al.*	Confirmation of land title	30	2	Petition	241	Public Lands.						
Douglass, William	(See Shakers, society of)	16	1	....	33							
Doupart, Barbara	(See Peter King, heirs of)	18	1	....	59							
Dousman, John	Confirmation of title to land in Michigan.	20	1	Resolution	28	Public Lands	42	Favorable; bill	34	Passed	Passed	App'd April 22, 1828
Dousman, Michael	Confirmation of title to land in Michigan.	20	1	Resolution	28	Public Lands	42	Favorable; bill	34	Passed	Passed	App'd April 22, 1828
Dousman, Michael	Patents for certain lots confirmed in 1823 and 1828.	23	1	Petition	450	Priv. Land Claims.	396	Favorable; bill	415	Referred to Committee Whole House.		
Dousman, Michael	Patents for certain lots confirmed in 1823 and 1828.	24	1	Petition	50	Priv. Land Claims.	182	Favorable; bill	172	Referred to Committee Whole House.		
Dousman, Michael	Patents for certain lots confirmed in 1823 and 1828.	24	2	Rep't Committee Whole House.	203	Whole House	....	....	172			
Dousman, Michael	Patents for certain lots confirmed in 1823 and 1828.	25	2	Senate bill	508	Public Lands	782	....	S. 17	Referred to Committee Whole House.		
Dousman, Rosalia	(See La Borde)	20	1	....	28	....	42	....	34			
Douthet, Samuel	(See Malachia Motlon)	14	1	....	231							
Douty, Thomas	(See Thomas Doughty)	19	1	....	467							
Dove, John, *et al.*	Arrears of pay as American masters of vessels, improperly with held from them.	7	2	Memorial	296	Com. and Manuf.	Jan. 24, 1803	Adverse	......	Leave to withdraw.		
Dove, Richard G.	Arrears of salary as assistant messenger in the Third Auditor's Office.	28	2	Petition	82	Claims	30	Adverse	......	Laid on table.		
Dove, schooner	(See Elisha Luce, owners of)	27	3	....	252							
Dove, William	Compensation for gallantry	14	1	Petition	249	Naval Affairs	April 11, 1816	Favorable; bill	......	Passed	Passed	App'd Feb. 8, 1817
Dover, Lieut. Andrew	Compensation for services in revolutionary war.	2	1	Petition	451	....	....	....	......	Referred to Secretary of War.		
Dover, Lieut. Andrew	Compensation for services in revolutionary war.	3	2	Rep. of Secretary War.	278	....	....	....	......	Laid on table.		
Dover, Lieut. Andrew, heirs of.	Commutation pay for revolutionary services.	29	2	Petition	89	Rev. Pensions.						
Dover, Lieut. Andrew, heirs of.	Commutation pay for revolutionary services.	30	1	Petition	566	Rev. Pensions	....	....	......	Discharged; referred to Com. Rev. Claims.		
Dover, Lieut. Andrew, heirs of.	Commutation pay for revolutionary services.	30	2	Resolution	664	....	....	....	......	Leave to withdraw.		
Dow, Abner, heirs of	Pension for services in revolutionary war.	29	1	Petition	1204	Rev. Pensions.						
Dow, Alexander, widow of.	Arrears of pay for services in revolutionary war.	3	1	Petition	42	Referred to Secretary of War.	Mar. 17, 1794	Report	......	Laid on table.		
Dow, Alexander, widow of.	Arrears of pay for services in revolutionary war.	3	2	Memorial	306	Claims	Jan. 6, 1796	Adverse	......	Laid on table.		
Dow, Alexander, widow of.	Arrears of pay for services in revolutionary war.	4	1	Memorial	403	Claims	....	....	......	Leave to withdraw.		
Dow, Benjamin	Invalid pension	22	1	Petition	189	Invalid Pensions	232	Favorable; bill	310	Passed	With amend.	
Dow, Benjamin	Invalid pension	22	2	Petition	27	Invalid Pensions	7	Favorable; bill	626	Passed	Passed, with amendment.	App'd March 2, 1833
Dow, Jesse	Revolutionary pension	16	1	Petition	33	Pens. & Rev. Cl'ms.	Dec. 16, 1819	Adverse	......	Rejected.		

List of private claims presented to the House of Representatives of the United States from the 1st to the 31st Congress, inclusive—Continued.

Names of claimants.	Nature or object of the claim.	Congress.	Session.	How brought before the House of Reps.	Page of journal.	To what committee of the House referred.	No. or date of the report.	Nature of the report.	No. of the bill.	How disposed of by the House of Reps.	How disposed of by the Senate.	Date of the act of Congress, and remarks.
Dow, Jesse E.	Compensation as complainant in the case of W. D. Chesley, &c.	24	1	Petition	153	Claims	343	Favorable; bill	354	Referred to Committee Whole House.		
Dow, Jesse E.	Compensation as complainant in the case of W. D. Chesley, &c.	25	2	Petition	36	Claims	5	Favorable; bill	18	Passed	Passed	App'd Feb. 22, 1838
Dow, Jesse E.	Compensation as bearer of certain despatches.	24	1	Petition	799	Foreign Affairs	....	....	......	Discharged; referred to Com. Nav. Affairs.		
Dow, Jesse E.	Compensation as bearer of certain despatches.	25	2	Petition	201	Naval Affairs	806	Favorable; bill	751	Referred to Committee Whole House.		
Dow, Jesse E.	Compensation as bearer of certain despatches.	25	3	Rep't Committee Whole House	380	Whole House	Jan. 26, 1839	Favorable; bill	751	Passed	Passed	App'd March 2, 1839
Dow, Jesse, attorney for certain mail contractors.	Remuneration for losses sustained.	27	2	Memorial	1067	P. Of. & P. Roads.						
Dow, Jesse, attorney for certain mail contractors.	Remuneration for losses sustained.	28	1	Petition	434	P. Of. & P. Roads.						
Dow, John	Revolutionary pension	24	1	Petition	433	Rev. Pensions	555	Favorable; bill	546	Passed	Passed	App'd June 28, 1836
Dow, Jonathan	Revolutionary pension	24	1	Petition	233	Rev. Pensions	436	Favorable; bill	451	Passed	Passed	App'd June 28, 1836
Dow, Martha	(See Alexander Dow, widow of.)	3	1	....	42							
Dow, Reuben	Revolutionary pension	10	1	House bill	232	Whole House	Mar. 17, 1808	General bill	78	Passed	Passed	App'd April 25, 1808
Dow, S. & F., & Co	To refund duties paid on silk twist.	26	1	Resolution	555	Commerce	309	Favorable; bill	271	Referred to Committee Whole House.		
Dowd, Benjamin B.	(See Benjamin B. Doud)	25	2	....	588	....	803	....	750			
Dowdney, Samuel	Relief for wounds received in revolutionary war.	9	1	Petition	196	Claims	Mar. 28, 1806	Report	......	Leave to withdraw.		
Dowdney, Samuel	Relief for wounds received in revolutionary war.	9	2	House bill	608	Whole House	Feb. 24, 1807	General bill	216	Passed	Passed	App'd March 3, 1807
Dowell, George	Revolutionary pension	25	2	Petition	730	Rev. Pensions	July 2, 1838	Adverse	......	Laid on table.		
Dowell, Margaret, *et al.*	Compensation for vessel destroyed in Captain Barney's flotilla.	14	1	Petition	236	Claims	....	....	......	Discharged; laid on table.		
Dowety, Zachariah	Liquidation of account for wagon hire in revolutionary war.	2	2	Petition	464	Select.						
Dowler, Thomas, assignee of.	For rations, clothing, &c., as a soldier in late war.	24	2	Petition	37	Claims	83	Adverse	......	Laid on table.		
Dowling, Alice	(See Terrence Dowling, widow of)	31	2	....	267							
Dowling, John	(See Lieut. Levin Gale, assignee of.)	23	1	....	449							
Dowling, Michael	Bounty land for services in United States army.	30	1	Petition	259	Military Affairs.						
Dowling, Michael	Bounty land for services in United States army.	30	2	Petition	181	....	....	....	......	Leave to withdraw.		
Dowling, Terrence	Revolutionary pension	19	1	Petition	35	Rev. Pensions	164	Adverse	......	Laid on table.		
Dowling, Terrence, widow of.	Compensation for wounds received by husband in service of United States.	31	2	Petition	267	Naval Affairs.						
Dowling, Terrence, widow of.	Compensation for wounds received by husband in service of United States.	31	2	Memorial	343	Invalid Pensions.						
Downard, Joshua	Compensation for discovery of certain salt springs.	21	1	Petition	145	Claims	Mar. 10, 1830	Adverse	......	Laid on table.		
Downer, Abner P., and E. Sims.	Renewal of patent of George Park.	31	1	Add'al evidence.	955	Patents.						
Downer, Avery	Revolutionary pension	24	1	Petition	56	Rev. Pensions	....	....	......	Discharged; laid on table.		

List of private claims presented to the House of Representatives of the United States from the 1st to the 31st Congress, inclusive—Continued.

Names of claimants.	Nature or object of the claim.	Congress.	Session.	How brought before the House of Reps.	Page of journal.	To what committee of the House referred.	No. or date of the report.	Nature of the report.	No. of the bill.	How disposed of by the House of Reps.	How disposed of by the Senate.	Date of the act of Congress, and remarks.
Downer, Avery	Revolutionary pension	31	1	Petition	284	Rev. Pensions	44	Favorable; bill	74	Passed	Ref. to Com. on Pensions.	
Downer, Eliphalet	Compensation for services in revolutionary war.	2	1	Petition	475					Referred to Committee Whole House.		
Downer, Eliphalet	Compensation for services in revolutionary war.	3	2	Report Secretary of War.	337	Claims	Feb. 28, 1795	Favorable		Bill ordered.		
Downer, John, (Maine.)	Pension	19	2	Petition	156	Military Pensions.						
Downer, John, (Maine.)	Pension	20	1	Petition	45	Military Pensions	Feb. 13, 1828	General bill	166	Passed.		
Downer, John, (Maine.)	Pension	20	2	House bill	55	Military Pensions	Dec. 12, 1828	General bill	311	Passed	Laid on table.	
Downer, John, (Maine.)	Pension	21	1	Petition	48	Military Pensions	Jan. 5, 1830	Favorable; bill ordered.	72	Passed	Passed with amendment.	App'd May 20, 1830
Downer, Robert, and John Bonnell.	(See John Calhoun, Executors of.)	19	2		213							
Downes, Abijah, attorney of	Indemnity for French spoliations prior to 1800.	26	1	Memorial	182	Foreign Affairs	343	Favorable	319	Referred to Committee Whole House.		
Downes, Jesse, by Naomi, widow of.	Revolutionary pension	27	3	Petition	61	Rev. Pensions	295	Adverse		Laid on table.		
Downes, Captain John, U. States navy.	To be credited with money alleged to be twice charged, $723 60.	22	1	Petition	163	Naval Affairs.						
Downes, Captain John, U. States navy.	To be credited with money alleged to be twice charged, $723 60.	23	2	Petition	114	Claims	48	Favorable; bill	638	Referred to Committee Whole House.		
Downes, Captain John, U. States navy.	To be credited with money alleged to be twice charged, $723 60.	24	1	Memorial	49	Claims	33	Favorable; bill	33	Recommitted.		
Downes, Captain John, U. States navy.	To be credited with money alleged to be twice charged, $723 60.	24	1			Claims	728	Favorable; bill	673	Referred to Committee Whole House.		
Downes, Captain John, U. States navy.	To be credited with money alleged to be twice charged, $723 60.	25	2	Petition	50	Claims	53	Favorable; bill	65	Passed	With amend.	
Downes, Captain John, U. States navy.	To be credited with money alleged to be twice charged, $723 60.	25	3	Petition	86	Claims	98	Joint resolut'n.	34	Referred to Committee Whole House.		
Downes, Captain John, U. States navy.	To be credited with money alleged to be twice charged, $723 60.	26	1	Petition	168	Claims	28	Favorable; bill	47	Passed	Passed	App'd July 20, 1840
Downes, Captain John, U. States navy.	Reimbursement of expenses incurred as commander of Pacific squadron.	23	2	Memorial	36	Foreign Affairs	102	Favorable; bill	727	Referred to Committee Whole House.		
Downes, Captain John, U. States navy.	Reimbursement of expenses incurred as commander of Pacific squadron.	23	2	House bill	176	Whole House	Jan. 7, 1835	General bill	616	Passed	Passed	App'd March 3, 1835
Downes, Michael, former widow of.	Revolutionary pension	26	1	Petition	386	Rev. Pensions	664	Adverse		Laid on table		Jan. 22, 1849; leave to withdraw.
Downey, Edward	Pay for work done on Cumberland road, and for materials furnished.	23	1	Res. and papers.	589	Claims	456	Statem't of facts		Discharged; referred to Secretary War.		See report No. 449.
Downey, James	Naval invalid pension	30	1	Petition	714	Naval Affairs.						
Downey, William	Grant of land for services in war of 1812.	23	1	Petition	368	Public Lands.						
Downing, C., (Fa.)	Allowance for fuel and office rent.	21	1	Petition	361	Public Lands				Discharged; laid on table.		
Downing, Jonathan, by Alice, widow of.	Revolutionary pension	25	3	Petition	293	Rev. Pensions				Discharged; laid on table.		
Downing, Jonathan, by Alice, widow of.	Revolutionary pension	27	2	Petition	618	Rev. Pensions	784	Adverse		Laid on table.		
Downing, Michael	Pension	25	2	Petition	85	Invalid Pensions				Disch'd; laid on table.		
Downing, Polly	(See Robert Young, former widow of.)	26	1		324							

List of private claims presented to the House of Representatives of the United States from the 1st to the 31st Congress, inclusive—Continued.

Names of claimants.	Nature or object of the claim.	Congress.	Session.	How brought before the House of Reps.	Page of journal.	To what committee of the House referred.	No. or date of the report.	Nature of the report.	No. of the bill.	How disposed of by the House of Reps.	How disposed of by the Senate.	Date of the act of Congress, and remarks.
Downing, Samuel	(See Leroy Opie, sureties of)	16	2		137							
Downing, Thomas	(See Timothy Downing, surety of)	25	3		621							
Downing, Timothy, surety of.	To refund money paid as surety of.	25	3	Resolution	621	Claims				Discharged.		
Downing, William	Increase of compensation as register of land office in Missouri.	26	1	Petition	608	Public Lands.						
Downman, Captain R. P.	Pay and emoluments due by resolution of Congress.	2	2	Petition and rep. Sec. Treasury.	688	Select				Laid on table.		
Downs, Isaac	Invalid pension	30	1	Petition	859	Invalid Pensions	712	Favorable; bill	557	Referred to Committee Whole House.		
Downs, Isaac	Invalid pension	30	2	Rep't Committee Whole House.	319	Whole House	Jan. 26, 1849	With't amend.	557	Passed	With't amend.	
Downs, Isaac	Invalid pension	31	1	Petition	439	Invalid Pensions	301	Favorable; bill	270	Referred to Committee Whole House.		
Downs, Isaac	Invalid pension	31	2	Rep't Committee Whole House.	182	Whole House	Jan. 24, 1851	With't amend.	270	Passed	Ref. to Com. on Pensions.	
Downs, Jeremiah	Compensation for forage furnished a company of mounted volunteers.	24	1	Petition	943	Claims.						
Downs, John	Compensation for services in revolutionary war.	2	2	Petition	615	Select.						
Downs, John	Compensation for services in revolutionary war.	3	1	Rep. of Secretary War.	131	Select	May 26, 1794	Res. to refer to Sec. with instructions.	J. R. 12	Passed	Passed	App'd June 9, 1794
Downs, John	Compensation for services in revolutionary war.	3	2	Rep. of Secretary War.	337	Claims	Feb. 28, 1795	Favorable; bill ordered.	130	Passed	Postponed.	
Downs, John	Compensation for services in revolutionary war.	5	2	House bill	127	Whole House	Jan. 9, 1798	With amend.	38	Passed	Passed	App'd Feb. 2, 1798
Downs, John	Pension	14	1	Petition	518	Pens. & Rev. Cl'ms.	April 11, 1816	Favorable; bill	171	Passed	Passed	App'd April 30, 1816
Downs, John	Pension for naval and land services.	29	1	Documents	269	Invalid Pensions	494	Adverse		Laid on table.		
Downs, John	Pension for naval and land services.	29	2	Petition	164	Invalid Pensions.						
Downs, Martha L.	Continuation of pension	30	1	Resolution	238	Naval Affairs.						
Downs, William, representatives of.	Confirmation of title to certain land	15	1	Petition	184	Select	86	Favorable; bill	74	Laid on table.		
Downs, William, representatives of.	Confirmation of title to certain land	15	2	Petition	59	Select	31	Favorable; bill	225	Referred to Committee Whole House.		
Downs, William, representatives of.	Confirmation of title to certain land	16	1	Petition	30	Priv. Land Claims.	2	Favorable; bill	5	Recommitted.		
Downs, William, representatives of.	Confirmation of title to certain land	16	1			Priv. Land Claims.	62	Adverse		Referred to Committee Whole House.		
Downs, William, representatives of.	Confirmation of title to certain land	17	1	Senate bill	465	Public Lands	April 25, 1822	With amend.	S. 36	Laid on table.		
Downs, William, representatives of.	Confirmation of title to certain land	17	2	Senate bill	117	Public Lands	Jan. 30, 1823	With amend.	S. 11	Laid on table.		
Downs, William, representatives of.	Confirmation of title to certain land	18	1	House bill	162	Public Lands	Jan. 20, 1824	With amend.	73	Rejected.		
Downs, William, representatives of.	Confirmation of title to certain land	18	1	Senate bill	518	Public Lands	May 20, 1824	With amend.	S. 106	Passed	Concurred in.	App'd May 24, 1824
Downs, William, representatives of.	Additional grant of land	23	2	Petition	174	Priv. Land Claims.				Discharged; laid on table.		
Dowson, John	Confirmation of title to land in Missouri.	15	1	Petition	102	Priv. Land Claims.				Discharged.		

List of private claims presented to the House of Representatives of the United States from the 1st to the 31st Congress, inclusive—Continued.

Names of claimants.	Nature or object of the claim.	Congress.	Session.	How brought before the House of Reps.	Page of journal.	To what committee of the House referred.	No. or date of the report.	Nature of the report.	No. of the bill.	How disposed of by the House of Reps.	How disposed of by the Senate.	Date of the act of Congress, and remarks.
Dowty, James	Confirmation of title to land in Missouri.	15	1	Petition	102	Priv. Land Claims.				Discharged.		
Dowty, James	Confirmation of title to land in Missouri.	16	1	Petition	72	Priv. Land Claims.				Discharged; laid on table.		
Dowty, James	Confirmation of title to land in Missouri.	17	1	Petition	53	Public Lands				Discharged; laid on table.		
Dowty, James	Confirmation of title to land in Missouri.	18	1	Petition	53	Public Lands	Jan. 16, 1824	General bill	65	Passed with amendm't	Passed	App'd May 26, 1824
Dox, Gerret L., sureties of.	Release from judgment on payment of $239 30.	21	1	Memorial	66	P. O. & P. Roads.	109	Favorable; bill	150	Passed	Passed	App'd May 29, 1830
Dox, Jacob	Compensation as commissioner of Niagara claim.	15	2	Letter	35	Claims	18	Favorable; bill.	216	Referred to Committee Whole House.		
Dox, Myndert M.	(See Lucius Storrs, *et al.*)	22	1		220							
Dox, Peter	(See Gerret L. Dox, sureties of)	21	1		66							
Doxy, Joseph C.	Remuneration for losses sustained in war of 1812.	27	2	Petition	53	Claims	350	Adverse		Laid on table.		
Doxy, Joseph C.	Remuneration for losses sustained in war of 1812.	28	1	Petition	513	Claims.						
Doxy, Joseph C.	Remuneration for losses sustained in war of 1812.	29	1	Petition	75	Claims	536	Favorable; bill	358	Referred to Committee Whole House.		
Doxy, Joseph C.	Remuneration for losses sustained in war of 1812.	30	1	Petition	153	Claims	40	Favorable; bill	37	Passed	With't amend.	
Doxy, Joseph C.	Remuneration for losses sustained in war of 1812.	31	1	Petition	283	Claims	408	Adverse		Laid on table.		
Doxy, Samuel H.	Leave to enter and purchase certain lots in Alabama.	23	1	Petition	196	Public Lands	Jan. 29, 1834	Favorable; bill	254	Referred to Committee Whole House.		
Doxy, Samuel H.	Leave to enter and purchase certain lots in Alabama.	23	2	Rep't Committee Whole House.	337	Whole House	Jan. 31, 1835	By bill	254	Passed	Laid on table.	
Doxtator, Peter	Revolutionary pension	23	1	Petition	379	Rev. Pensions.	364	Favorable; bill	391	Referred to Committee Whole House.		
Doxtator, Peter	Revolutionary pension	23	2	House bill	337	Whole House	Feb. 6, 1835	With't amend.	391	Passed	Indef. postp'd.	
Doxtator, Peter	Revolutionary pension	24	1	Petition	57	Rev. Pensions	39	Favorable; bill	73	Passed	Passed	App'd May 14, 1836
Doyal, Hardy, and G. Caperton.	Right of pre-emption to purchase lands on which they have erected mills.	18	1	Petition	216	Public Lands				Laid on table.		
Doyal, Hardy	Claim arising out of transactions in Seminole war.	21	1	Documents	376	Claims				Discharged; laid on table.		
Doyal, Hardy	Claim arising out of transactions in Seminole war.	21	2	Petition	291	Claims.						
Doyal, Hardy	Claim arising out of transactions in Seminole war.	22	1	Petition	570	Claims.						
Doyer, Hendrick	Relief in case of an alleged breach of revenue laws.	4	2	Petition	687	Com. and Manuf				Laid on table.		
Doyle, Andrew	Pension	22	2	Petition	313	Invalid Pensions.						
Doyle, Dennis	Invalid pension	27	2	Petition	845	Invalid Pensions	1007	Adverse		Laid on table.		
Doyle, Dennis	Invalid pension	28	1	Petition	365	Invalid Pensions	274	Adverse		Laid on table.		
Doyle, Edmond	Confirmation of title to land in Florida.	18	2	Petition	96	Priv. Land Claims.	14	Favorable; bill	261	Passed	Laid on table.	
Doyle, Edmond	Confirmation of title to land in Florida.	19	1	Petition	37	Priv. Land Claims.	27	Favorable; bill	4	Passed	Passed	App'd May 16, 1826
Doyle, Edmond	Indemnity for property destroyed by Indians in 1817.	19	1	Petition	270	Claims	Mar. 29, 1826	Adverse		Laid on table.		

List of private claims presented to the House of Representatives of the United States from the 1st to the 31st Congress, inclusive—Continued.

Names of claimants.	Nature or object of the claim.	Congress.	Session.	How brought before the House of Reps.	Page of journal.	To what committee of the House referred.	No. or date of the report.	Nature of the report.	No. of the bill.	How disposed of by the House of Reps.	How disposed of by the Senate.	Date of the act of Congress, and remarks.
Doyle, Edmond	Indemnity for property destroyed by Indians in 1817.	19	2	Petition	45	Claims	Dec. 29, 1826	Adverse	......	Laid on table.		
Doyle, Edmond	Remuneration for improvements made on a plantation ceded by treaty to an Indian.	19	2	Documents	159	Claims.						
Doyle, Edmond, executors of.	Indemnity for losses sustained by reason of invasion of Florida by United States army in 1818.	22	1	Petition	472	Foreign Affairs.						
Doyle, James	Payment for services and expenses in bringing certain criminals to justice.	12	1	Petition	94	Claims.						
Doyle, James	Payment for services and expenses in bringing certain criminals to justice.	12	2	Petition	612	Claims.						
Doyle, James	Payment for services and expenses in bringing certain criminals to justice.	13	2	Petition	295	Claims	66	Favorable; bill	125	Laid on table.		
Doyle, James	Payment for services and expenses in bringing certain criminals to justice.	13	3	Petition	556	Claims	Dec. 15, 1814	Favorable; bill	240	Passed	Rejected.	
Doyle, James	Payment for services and expenses in bringing certain criminals to justice.	14	1	Petition	504	Claims	....	....	......	Discharged; laid on table.		
Doyle, James	Payment for services and expenses in bringing certain criminals to justice.	15	1	Petition	287	Claims	....	....	......	Discharged.		
Doyle, James	Payment for services and expenses in bringing certain criminals to justice.	15	2	Petition	55	Claims	Jan. 11, 1819	Adverse	......	Laid on table.		
Doyle, James	Payment for services and expenses in bringing certain criminals to justice.	16	1	Petition	102	Claims	....	....	......	Discharged; laid on table.		
Doyle, James, and Andrew Derby.	Relief in case of capture of vessel by British.	15	1	Petition	394	Foreign Affairs	....	....	......	Discharged; referred to Secretary State.		
Doyle, John, executors of.	Pay for extra work done on Cumberland road.	22	1	Petition	512	Claims	....	....	......	Leave to withdraw.	....	To settle at Treasury.
Doyle, John	(See William Doyle, heirs of.)	25	2	....	392							
Doyle, John, heirs of	For land and money due for services in revolutionary war.	26	1	Petition	359	Rev. Claims.						
Doyle, Margaret	(See Capt. James Bradford, widow of.)	4	1	....	485							
Doyle, Patrick	(See Wall & Doyle)	25	2	....	172							
Doyle, Richard	Prize-money for capture of frigate Philadelphia.	19	2	House bill	99	Naval Affairs	74	With amend.	70	Referred to Committee Whole House.		
Doyle, Richard	Prize-money for capture of frigate Philadelphia.	20	2	House bill	108	Naval Affairs	37	With't amend.	30	Rejected.		
Doyle, Richard	Prize-money for capture of frigate Philadelphia.	21	1	House bill	137	Naval Affairs	Jan. 7, 1830	General bill	82	Laid on table.		
Doyle, Richard	Prize-money for capture of frigate Philadelphia.	22	1	Papers on file	29	Naval Affairs	Dec. 23, 1831	Favorable; bill	98	Referred to Committee Whole House.		
Doyle, Richard	Prize-money for capture of frigate Philadelphia.	23	1	Petition	36	Naval Affairs	45	Favorable; bill	50	Laid on table.		

List of private claims presented to the House of Representatives of the United States from the 1st to the 31st Congress, inclusive—Continued.

Names of claimants.	Nature or object of the claim.	Congress.	Session.	How brought before the House of Reps.	Page of journal.	To what committee of the House referred.	No. or date of the report.	Nature of the report.	No. of the bill.	How disposed of by the House of Reps.	How disposed of by the Senate.	Date of the act of Congress, and remarks.
Doyle, Thomas	Reimbursement of costs in the case of a deserter.	8	1	Memorial	446	Claims				Discharged; leave to withdraw.		
Doyle, William, heirs of	Compensation for services in revolutionary war.	25	2	Petition	392	Rev. Pensions	March 2, 1838	Adverse		Laid on table.		
Dozet, Joseph, and Antoine Bougoud.	Indemnity for property destroyed in war of 1812.	15	2	Senate bill	316	Claims	Feb. 27, 1819	With amend.	S. 65	Referred to Committee Whole House.		
Dozet, Joseph, and Antoine Bougouud.	Indemnity for property destroyed in war of 1812.	18	2	Senate bill	278	Claims	Mar. 1, 1825	With't amend.	S. 39	Passed	Passed	App'd March 3, 1825
Dozi, Louis	(See Charles Coombs and wife	21	1		40		186		232			
Draggo, William	Confirmation of land title	16	1	Petition	24	Priv. Land Claims.	Dec. 17, 1819	Adverse		Laid on table.		
Dragon, Michael, heirs of.	Confirmation of title to land in Louisiana.	17	1	Petition	361	Public Lands				Discharged; laid on table.		
Dragon, Michael, heirs of.	Confirmation of title to land in Louisiana.	17	2	Petition	27	Priv. Land Claims.				Discharged; leave to withdraw.		
Dragon, Michael, heirs of.	Confirmation of title to land in Louisiana.	18	1	Petition	28	Priv. Land Claims.						
Dragon, Michael, heirs of.	Confirmation of title to land in Louisiana.	24	2	Senate bill	552	Priv. Land Claims.	March 2, 1837	With't amend.	138	Passed	Passed	App'd March 2, 1837
Drake, Gilbert	Release from imprisonment at suit of United States.	9	2	Petition	598	Select	Feb. 24, 1807	Favorable; bill	215	Passed	Passed	App'd March 3, 1807
Drake, N. P.	Money due for work done on L. P. Bay Road, Michigan.	28	1	Petition	239	Claims	131	Favorable; bill	121	Passed	Passed	App'd June 15, 1844
Drake, Reuben, and R. Y. Quarles.	Pre-emption right to land on Red river.	27	3	Petition	141	Public Lands				Discharged; laid on table.		
Drake, Samuel, (Ohio)	Pension	19	2	Petition	31	Military Pensions				Discharged.		
Drake, Simeon	(See John Heard, surety of.)	9	2		542							
Drakeford, William	Additional compensation as assistant marshal taking 4th Census.	17	1	Resolution	406	Claims	April 27, 1822	Adverse		Referred to Committee Whole House.		
Drakeford, William	Additional compensation as assistant marshal taking 4th Census.	17	2	Report	41		16	Adverse		Ordered to be printed.		
Drane, Lieut. Anthony	Amount of judgment and costs obtained against him for repairs of barracks at New Orleans.	24	1	Estimates, &c.	118	Claims	121	Adverse		Laid on table.		
Drane, Capt. G. S.	Pay of company of volunteers, a guard to emigrating Indians.	25	3	Documents, &c.	244	Military Affairs	Jan. 8, 1839	Favorable; bill	987	Referred to Committee Whole House.		
Draper, Daniel	Pre-emption right to land	24	2	Petition	389	Public Lands.						
Draper, Daniel	Pre-emption right to land	26	1	Petition	356	Public Lands	July 21, 1840	Favorable; bill	530	Referred to Committee Whole House.		
Draper, Hannah	(See William Draper, heirs of)	20	1		225							
Draper, Jeremiah	Release from judgment in favor of United States.	22	1	Petition	331	Judiciary				Discharged; laid on table.		
Draper, John F	Increase of pay as postmaster at Salem, Illinois.	25	2	Petition	668	P. Of. & P. Roads.						
Draper, Nathaniel	Revolutionary pension	22	1	Petition	436	Rev. Pensions.						
Draper, Simeon	Pension	20	2	Petition	142	Whole House.						
Draper, Simeon	Additional compensation for services in revolutionary war.	22	2	Petition	46	Rev. Claims.						
Draper, William, (Mass.)	Pension	21	2	Petition	270	Military Pensions				Discharged; laid on table.		
Draper, William, (Mass.)	Pension	22	1	Resolution	93	Rev. Pensions				Discharged; laid on table.		
Drayton, Hannah, *et al.*	(See William Drayton, heirs of)	20	1		225							

List of private claims presented to the House of Representatives of the United States from the 1*st to the* 31*st Congress, inclusive*—Continued.

Names of claimants.	Nature or object of the claim.	Congress.	Session.	How brought before the House of Reps.	Page of journal.	To what committee of the House referred.	No. or date of the report.	Nature of the report.	No. of the bill.	How disposed of by the House of Reps.	How disposed of by the Senate.	Date of the act of Congress, and remarks.
Drayton, Stephen	Compensation for services and for injuries received in revolutionary war.	1	3	Petition	378					Referred to Secretary of War.		
Drayton, Stephen	Compensation for services and for injuries received in revolutionary war.	2	2	Rep. of Secretary War.	735					Laid on table.		
Drayton, Stephen	Reimbursement of amount of debt contracted for government.	5	1	Petition	58					Laid on table.		
Drayton, Stephen	Reimbursement of amount of debt contracted for government.	5	2	Petition	237	Claims	April 6, 1798	Adverse.				
Drayton, William, heirs of.	To release interest of United States in certain lands in East Florida.	20	1	Petition	225, 426	Public lands	200	Favorable; bill	232	Referred to Committee Whole House.		
Drayton, William, heirs of.	To release interest of United States in certain lands in East Florida.	20	2	Rep't Committee Whole House.	227	Whole House	Feb. 2, 1829	With amend.	232	Rejected.		
Drayton, William, heirs of.	To release interest of United States in certain lands in East Florida.	21	1	Petition	100	Priv. Land Claims.				Discharged; laid on table.		
Drenen, William, (Fla.)	Grant of land for services in revolutionary war.	20	1	Petition	419	Public Lands				Discharged; laid on table.		
Drennan, Hugh	Revolutionary pension	25	2	Resolution	807	Rev. Pensions				Discharged.		
Dresboh, Henry	Compensation for services in revolutionary war.	4	1	Petition	385	Claims	Jan. 27, 1796	Adverse		Laid on table.		Leave to withdraw
Dresser, Benjamin	To refund duties paid on distillery.	15	2	Petition	109	Ways and Means.				Discharged; laid on table.		
Dresser, Levi	Pension	21	1	Petition	120	Military Pensions.				Discharged; laid on table.		
Dresser, Thomas	Pension for services in war of 1812	28	1	Petition	61	Invalid Pensions.						
Dresser, Thomas	Pension for services in war of 1812	29	1	Petition	161	Invalid Pensions	244	Adverse		Laid on table.		
Drew, Carter H., heirs of.	Payment of amount due for services in revolutionary war.	22	2	Petition	46	Rev. Claims.						
Drew, Consider	Revolutionary pension	17	1	Petition	326	Rev. Pensions				Discharged; laid on table.		
Drew, George	Indemnity for judgment against him for breach of revenue laws.	16	1	Petition	203	Claims	Feb. 14, 1820	Adverse		Laid on table.		
Drew, Isaac	Revolutionary pension	16	1	Petition	110					Referred to Secretary War.		
Drew, Isaac	Revolutionary pension	21	2	Resolution	256	Military Pensions.				Discharged; laid on table.		
Drew, Isaac	Revolutionary pension	22	1	Petition	113	Rev. Pensions				Discharged; laid on table.		
Drew, John	(See Jean Baptiste Dubois, assignee of.)	20	1		28		42		34			
Drew, John, heirs of	Compensation for services in revolutionary war.	22	2	Resolution	227	Rev. Claims				Discharged; laid on table.		
Drew, John, *et al.*	Liquidation and settlement of claim	22	1	House bill	734	Whole House	Jan. 30, 1832	With amend.	575	Passed	Passed	App'd July 30, 1832
Drew, John, widow of.	Naval pension	18	1	Petition	316	Naval Affairs	Mar. 17, 1824	Adverse		Laid on table.		
Drew, John, widow of.	Naval pension	22	2	Petition	235	Naval Affairs.						
Drew, John, widow of.	For benefit of act of March 3, 1837	29	1	Petition	476	Rev. Pensions.						
Drew, Joshua	To refund $253 paid for supposed violation of revenue laws.	26	1	Petition	290	Commerce.						
Drew, Joshua	To refund $253 paid for supposed violation of revenue laws.	27	2	Petition	95	Commerce	888	Favorable; bill	511	Referred to Committee Whole House.		
Drew, Joshua	To refund $253 paid for supposed violation of revenue laws.	27	3	Rep't Committee Whole House.	89	Whole House	Dec. 23, 1842	By bill	511	Passed	Passed	App'd Jan. 20, 1843

List of private claims presented to the House of Representatives of the United States from the 1st to the 31st Congress, inclusive—Continued.

Names of claimants.	Nature or object of the claim.	Congress.	Session.	How brought before the House of Reps.	Page of journal.	To what committee of the House referred.	No. or date of the report.	Nature of the report.	No. of the bill.	How disposed of by the House of Reps.	How disposed of by the Senate.	Date of the act of Congress, and remarks.
Drew, Nicholas	(See John W. Flowers, *et al*)	22	1		596							
Drew, Sarah	(See John Drew, widow of)	18	1		316							
Drew, Samuel, mother of	Bounty land and pay for services in war of 1812.	16	1	Petition	32	Select	Dec. 21, 1819	Favorable; bill	16	Passed	Passed with amendment.	App'd Jan. 19, 1820
Drew, Samuel	Invalid pension	28	1	Petition	114	Invalid Pensions	190	Adverse		Laid on table.		
Drew, Samuel	Invalid pension	28	2	Petition	227	Invalid Pensions.						
Drew, Samuel	Invalid pension	29	2	Petition	69	Invalid Pensions.						
Drew, Thomas H., heirs of	Commutation pay for services in revolutionary war.	22	1	Petition	190	Rev. Claims	Jan. 27, 1832	Adverse		Laid on table.		
Drew, William	(See John W. Flowers, *et al*)	22	1		596							
Drewry, Thomas W.	Pension for services in war of 1812	27	3	Petition	151	Invalid Pensions	155	Adverse		Laid on table.		
Dreyer, Gustavus, W., attorney of.	Repayment of money paid for land	29	1	Petition	609	Claims	802	Adverse		Laid on table.		
Driggs, Seth	Aid of Government to enable him to recover his claim against Colombia.	25	2	Memorial	584	Foreign Affairs				Discharged; referred to Sec. of State.		
Driggs, Seth	Aid of Government to enable him to recover his claim against Colombia.	26	2	Petition	55	Foreign Affairs.						
Drinker, Catharine	Pension	28	1	Petition	374	Naval Affairs.						
Drinker, Joanna J.	(See Lawrence Montgomery, former widow of.)	30	1		513							
Drinkhouse, Jacob	Revolutionary pension	31	1	Petition	369	Rev. Pensions	89	Favorable; bill	110	Referred to Committee Whole House.		
Drinkwater, Samuel	Pension as pilot of U. S. brig Enterprize.	19	1	Resolution	275	Military Pensions				Discharged; laid on table.		
Drips, James	Reimbursement of $160 paid on forfeited lands.	22	1	Petition	471	Priv. Land Claims.						
Driscoll, Dennis	Invalid pension	8	1	Petition	412	Claims	Nov. 3, 1803	Rep. and res.		Leave to withdraw.		
Driscoll, Dennis	Invalid pension	13	2	Petition	305	Rev. Pensions				Discharged; leave to withdraw.		
Driscoll, Thomas D.	Indemnity for money lost in U. S. mail.	28	2	Petition	429	Claims.						
Driscoll, William	(See Jonathan Low, and others)	13	3		683							
Drish, Charles	(See Christopher Ish, representative of.)	21	1		298		56					
Driskell, William, *et al.*	(See James W. Low, *et al*)	15	1		366							
Dromgoole, Alexander	Compensation for services rendered and expenses incurred in the intercourse between U. States and Cherokee Indians.	18	1	Petition	43	Indian Affairs.						
Drouet, Antoine, & Dillas	For certain lands, and for time to locate.	14	1	Petition	78	Public Lands.						
Drouillard, Jean Baptiste	Confirmation of land title	20	1	Resolution	28	Public Lands	42	Favorable; bill.	34	Passed	Passed	App'd April 22, 1828
Drouillard, Captain Lewis	Invalid pension	29	2	Memorial	375	Invalid Pensions.						
Drouillard, Captain Lewis	Invalid pension	30	1	Petition	104	Invalid Pensions.						
Drouillard, Captain Lewis	Invalid pension	31	2	Petition	102					Leave to withdraw.		
Drout, Susannah	Arrears of pension	28	1	Petition	950	Whole House.						
Drown, Daniel P.	Increase of compensation as collector of customs, New Hampshire.	24	1	Petition	505	Commerce.						
Drown, Frederick, by Martha, widow of.	Revolutionary pension	26	2	Petition	201	Rev. Claims.						
Drown, Captain Jonathan, by Sarah, widow of.	Remuneration for services of deceased in revolutionary war.	24	1	Petition	106	Rev. Pensions				Discharged; laid on table.		

List of private claims presented to the House of Representatives of the United States from the 1st to the 31st Congress, inclusive—Continued.

Names of claimants.	Nature or object of the claim.	Congress.	Session.	How brought before the House of Reps.	Page of journal.	To what committee of the House referred.	No. or date of the report.	Nature of the report.	No. of the bill.	How disposed of by the House of Reps.	How disposed of by the Senate.	Date of the act of Congress, and remarks.
Drubaker, David	Compensation for certain timber	1	3	Petition	376					Laid on table.		
Drude, Francis	Compensation for instruments lost in service of United States.	31	1	Petition	197	Military Affairs				Discharged; laid on table.		
Druit, Micah	Pension	21	2	Petition	42	Military Pensions.						
Drulyard, George	Compensation for services on exploring expedition of Lewis and Clark.	9	1	Pres. Message	284					Laid on table.		
Drulyard, George	Compensation for services on exploring expedition of Lewis and Clark.	9	2	Resolution	507	Select	Jan. 23, 1807	By bill	183	Passed	Passed	App'd March 3, 1807
Drummond, Grieve	Pension	13	3	Resolution	376	Pens. & Rev. Cl'ms.	Feb. 20, 1815	Favorable; bill.	303	Passed	Passed	App'd March 3, 1815
Drummond, Grieve	Arrears of pension	22	1	Petition	56	Invalid Pensions	154	Favorable; bill.	233	Passed	Passed, with amendment.	App'd July 16, 1832
Drummond, John, *et al.*	Relief from penalty incurred on goods imported.	13	1	Petition	18	Com. and Manuf.						
Drummond, Richard	(See Roger Quarles and Richard Drummond.)	14	1		587							
Drummond, Richard, *et al.*	Interest on excess of duties paid on prizes made by schooner Roger.	20	1	Petition	195	Claims	176	Adverse		Leave to withdraw.		
Drummond, Richard, *et al.*	Interest on excess of duties paid on prizes made by schooner Roger.	23	2	Petition	95	Ways and Means.						
Drummond, Richard, *et al.*	Interest on excess of duties paid on prizes made by schooner Roger.	24	1	Petition	95	Ways and Means	July 4, 1836	Adverse		Laid on table.		
Drury, Luther	Bounty land as a Canadian volunteer.	14	2	Petition	256	Whole House.						
Drury, Luther, by Rhoda, widow of.	Pension for services of deceased in revolutionary war.	30	1	Petitions	619	Rev. Pensions				Discharged; laid on table.		
Drury, Matilda	(See William S. Tillard, child of.)	24	1		584							
Drury, Wilfred	Compensation for gallantry	13	3	House bill	665	Whole House	Jan. 13, 1815	By bill	259	Passed	Postponed.	
Drury, Wilfred	Compensation for gallantry	14	1	House bill	249	Whole House	April 11, 1816	With amend.		Passed	Passed	App'd April 29, 1816
Drybread, James, assignee of.	Confirmation of land title	15	2	Petition	21	Priv. Land Claims				Discharged; laid on table.		
Drybread, James, assignee of.	Confirmation of land title	17	1	Petition	54	Public Lands.						
Drybread, James, assignee of.	Confirmation of land title	18	1	Petition	54	Public Lands	Jan. 16, 1824	General bill	65	Passed with amendm't.	Passed	App'd May 26, 1824
Drysdale, John	Compensation for services in Florida war.	27	2	Petition	535	Claims	842	Favorable; bill	485	Referred to Committee Whole House.		
Drysdale, John	Compensation for services in Florida war.	27	3	Rep. Committee Whole House.	89	Whole House	Dec. 23, 1842	By bill	485	Passed	Passed	App'd March 3, 1843
Duene, William	Arrears of pay for public printing.	8	2	Resolution	169	Accounts.						
Duane, Colonel William	Liquidation of his accounts, &c	18	1	Senate bill	442	Claims	April 23, 1824	With't amend.	S. 76	Passed	Passed	App'd May 13, 1824
Duane, Colonel William	Compensation for compiling a system of infantry tactics.	18	2	Petition	86	Claims	13	Favorable; bill	258	Passed	Passed	App'd March 3, 1825
Du Barry, Edmund L.	Pay as surgeon in United States navy whilst out of service.	30	1	Petition	79	Naval Affairs	510	Favorable; bill	437	Referred to Committee Whole House.		
Du Barry, Edmund L.	Pay as surgeon in United States navy whilst out of service.	31	1	Petition	325	Naval Affairs	205	Favorable; bill	213	Referred to Committee Whole House.		
Du Barry, Edward L	Pay as surgeon in United States navy whilst out of service.	31	2	Rep't Committee Whole House.	181	Whole House	Jan. 14, 1851	By bill	213	Postponed.		
Dubay, Joseph	Confirmation of title to land in Michigan.	20	1	Resolution	28	Public Lands	42	Favorable; bill	34	Passed	Passed	App'd April 22, 1828
Bubayle, P	(See A. Gras, heirs of)	20	1		52							

List of private claims presented to the House of Representatives of the United States from the 1st to the 31st Congress, inclusive—Continued.

Names of claimants.	Nature or object of the claim.	Congress.	Session.	How brought before the House of Reps.	Page of journal.	To what committee of the House referred.	No. or date of the report.	Nature of the report.	No. of the bill.	How disposed of by the House of Reps.	How disposed of by the Senate.	Date of the act of Congress, and remarks.
Dube, Alexis	Confirmation of title to land in Michigan.	20	1	Resolution	28	Public Lands	42	Favorable; bill	34	Passed	Passed	App'd April 22, 1828
Dube, Joseph, assignee of.	Confirmation of title to land in Michigan.	20	1	Resolution	28	Public Lands	42	Favorable; bill	34	Passed	Passed	App'd April 22, 1828
Dubernat, John A	Indemnity for French spoliations prior to 1800.	26	1	Memorial	182	Foreign Affairs	343	Favorable; bill	319	Referred to Committee Whole House.		
Dubois, Barent	Revolutionary pension	22	1	Petition	558	Rev. Pensions				Discharged; laid on table.		
Dubois, David, by Hannah, widow of.	Pension	28	1	Petition	884	Invalid Pensions	482	Favorable; bill	369	Passed	Adverse.	
Dubois, David, by Hannah, widow of.	Pension	28	2	Petition	103	Invalid Pensions	40	Favorable; bill	514	Referred to Committee Whole House.		
Dubois, David, by Hannah, widow of.	Pension	29	2	Petition	128	Invalid Pensions	Feb. 24, 1847	Adverse		Laid on table.		
Dubois, Henry	(See Laurent Bazadone, executors of.)	24	1		1062							
Dubois, J. B	(See Henry Duchuquette, representatives of.)	23	2		353				726			
Dubois, Jean Baptiste, assignee of.	Confirmation of title to land in Michigan.	20	1	Resolution	28	Public Lands	42	Favorable; bill	34	Passed	Passed	App'd April 22, 1828
Dubois, John L	Pension	23	2	Petition	303	Invalid Pensions.						
Dubois, John H	(See Matthew Dubois, heirs of)	12	1		141							
Dubois, Lewis	Pension and reimbursement of money advanced in revolutionary war.	3	1	Petition	88	Select	April 3, 1794	Favorable; bill	48	Passed	Passed	App'd June 4, 1794
Dubois, Lewis	Reimbursement of money advanced in revolutionary war.	11	2	Petition	14	Claims.						
Dubois, Matthew, heirs of.	Reimbursement of money advanced in revolutionary war.	12	1	Petition	141	Claims.						
Dubois, Peter	(See Jacobus De Peyster, representatives of.	4	1		467							
Du Bois, Oliver	Compensation for horses lost, and expenses incurred by failure of government to comply with contract.	30	2	Memorial	668	Claims.						
Dubose, Samuel	(See Elias D. Dick, administrator of.)	19	1		46							
Du Bourg, Louis Wm., *et al.*	Confirmation of title to land	15	2	Petition	34	Priv. Land Claims.				Discharged; laid on table.		
Du Bourg, Louis Wm., *et al.*	Confirmation of title to land	17	1	Petition	53	Public Lands				Discharged; laid on table.		
Du Bourg, Louis Wm., *et al.*	Confirmation of title to land	18	1	Petition	53	Public Lands	Jan. 16, 1824	General bill	65	Passed with amendm't.	Passed	App'd May 26, 1824
Dubreuille, Antoine, *et al.*	(See Etienne Parent, heirs of)	15	2		28							
Dubreuille, Antoine	Confirmation of title to land in Missouri.	15	2	Petition	28	Priv. Land Claims.				Discharged; laid on table.		
Dubreuille, Antoine	Confirmation of title to land in Missouri.	17	1	Petition	53	Public Lands				Discharged; laid on table.		
Dubreuille, Antoine	Confirmation of title to land in Missouri.	18	1	Petition	53	Public Lands	Jan. 16, 1824	General bill	65	Passed with amendm't.	Passed	App'd May 26, 1824
Dubreuille, Jean Baptiste	Confirmation of title to land in Missouri.	17	1	Petition	53	Public Lands				Discharged; laid on table.		
Dubreuille, Jean Baptiste	Confirmation of title to land in Missouri.	18	1	Petition	53	Public Lands	Jan. 16, 1824	General bill	65	Passed with amendm't.	Passed	App'd May 26, 1824

69

List of private claims presented to the House of Representatives of the United States from the 1st to the 31st Congress, inclusive—**Continued.**

Names of claimants.	Nature or object of the claim.	Congress.	Session.	How brought before the House of Reps.	Page of journal.	To what committee of the House referred.	No. or date of the report.	Nature of the report.	No. of the bill.	How disposed of by the House of Reps.	How disposed of by the Senate.	Date of the act of Congress, and remarks.
Dubrocar, Benjamin	Release from bond given to secure duties.	12	1	Petition	176	Com. and Manuf.						
Dubrocar, Benjamin	Release from bond given to secure duties.	13	2	Petition	210	Com. and Manuf.	...	...	...	Laid on table.		
Dubrocar, Benjamin	Release from bond given to secure duties.	13	3	Petition	684	Ways and Means.						
Dubrocar, Benjamin	Release from bond given to secure duties.	14	1	Petition	220	Com. and Manuf.	Feb. 2, 1816	Adverse	...	Leave to withdraw.		
Dubrocar, Benjamin	Release from bond given to secure duties.	15	1	Petition	225	Ways and Means.	...	...	...	Discharged; laid on table.		
Dubrocar, Benjamin	Confirmation of title to land in Alabama.	26	1	Senate bill	240	Priv. Land Claims.	Mar. 5, 1840	With't amend.	S. 40	Passed	Passed	App'd May 27, 1840
Dubs, Martin	Compensation for provisions furnished U. S. troops in 1814.	15	1	Petition	237	Claims	Feb. 20, 1818	Adverse.				
Dubuque, Julien, heirs of.	Confirmation of title to land	28	1	Petition	718	Priv. Land Claims.						
Dubuque, Julien, heirs of.	Confirmation of title to land	29	1	Memorial	87	Priv. Land Claims.	675	Favorable	...	Laid on table.		
Dubuque, Julien, heirs of.	Confirmation of title to land	30	1	Petition	109	Priv. Land Claims.						
Duchasin, Antoine	Confirmation of title to land	19	2	Petition	137	Public Lands	60	Favorable; bill	401	Referred to Committee Whole House.		
Duchasin, Joseph	Confirmation of title to land	19	2	Petition	137	Public Lands	60	Favorable; bill	401	Referred to Committee Whole House.		
Duchassin, John B., assignee of.	Confirmation of title to land	22	1	House bill	421	Public Lands	Feb. 28, 1832	Favorable; bill	425	Passed	Passed	App'd June 25, 1832
Ducharme, Paul	Confirmation of title to land in Michigan.	20	2	Petition	101	Public Lands	...	...	...	Discharged; laid on table.		
Ducharme, Paul	Confirmation of title to land in Michigan.	22	1	Petition	476	Public Lands	363	Adverse	...	Laid on table.		
Duchemin, Francis	Drawback on sugars exported	7	1	Petition	81	Com. and Manuf.	May 11, 1802	Adverse	...	Leave to withdraw.		
Duchouquet, Francis	Compensation for relief to sundry captives among Indians, and for money expended.	7	1	Petition	97	Claims	Feb. 19, 1802	Favorable; bill	32	Passed	Passed	App'd Mar. 16, 1802
Duchouquet, Francis, representative of.	Patent for land granted by Shawnee Indians.	23	1	Petition	138	Priv. Land Claims.	330	Favorable; bill	357	Referred to Committee Whole House.		
Duchouquet, Francis, representative of.	Patent for land granted by Shawnee Indians.	24	1	Petition	112	Priv. Land Claims.	114	Favorable; bill	131	Passed	Passed	App'd June 23, 1836
Duchuquette, Henry, representatives of.	Permission to change location of land.	23	2	House bill	353	Public Lands	Feb. 10, 1835	By bill	726	Referred to Committee Whole House.		
Duchuquette, Henry, representatives of.	Permission to change location of land.	24	1	House bill	739	Whole House	April 22, 1836	By bill	586			
Duchuquette, Henry, representatives of.	Permission to change location of land.	25	2	Petition	42	Public Lands	310	Favorable; bill	347	Referred to Committee Whole House.		
Duchuquette, Henry, representatives of.	Permission to change location of land.	25	3	Rep't Committee Whole House	377	Whole House	...	By bill	347	Passed	Rejected.	
Duchuquette, Henry, representatives of.	Permission to change location of land.	26	1	Petition	177	Public Lands.						
Duck, George	Compensation for services in revolutionary war.	2	1	Petition	483	...	...	...	...	Referred to Committee Whole House.		
Duck, George	Compensation for services in revolutionary war.	3	2	Rep. of Secretary War.	278	Claims	...	...	...	Laid on table.		
Duck, George	Compensation for services in revolutionary war.	4	1	Petition	598	Claims	May 31, 1796	Adverse	...	Laid on table.		
Duck, Philip	Compensation for services in revolutionary war.	2	1	Petition	483	...	...	...	...	Referred to Secretary War.		

List of private claims presented to the House of Representatives of the United States from the 1st to the 31st Congress, inclusive—Continued.

Names of claimants.	Nature or object of the claim.	Congress.	Session.	How brought before the House of Reps.	Page of journal.	To what committee of the House referred.	No. or date of the report.	Nature of the report.	No. of the bill.	How disposed of by the House of Reps.	How disposed of by the Senate.	Date of the act of Congress, and remarks.
Duck, Philip	Compensation for services in revolutionary war.	3	2	Petition and rep't of Sec. War.	278	Claims	Mar. 2, 1795	Report		Laid on table.		
Duck, Philip	Compensation for services in revolutionary war.	4	1	Petition	598	Claims	May 31, 1796	Adverse		Laid on table.		
Duck, Philip	Compensation for services in revolutionary war.	4	2	Res. and docs.	614	Claims.						
Ducke'd, William	(See Stephen Decatur, heirs of.)	23	1		36		45		50			
Ducker, Enoch	Invalid pension	13	2	House bill	344	Whole House	Mar. 31, 1814	With't amend	166	Passed	Passed	App'd April 18, 1814
Ducker, Enoch	Increase of pension	20	2	Petition	118	Military Pensions				Disch'd; laid on table.		
Duckwitz, George F	(See Theodore Victor, *et al.*)	25	2		278							
Ducoing, Francis	Pension for services in war of 1812	21	1	Petition	448	Military Pensions	May 25, 1830	Favorable; bill	490	Referred to Committee Whole House.		
Ducoing, Francis	Pension for services in war of 1812	21	2	House bill	319	Whole House	Feb. 16, 1831	With't amend.	490	Passed	With't amend.	
Ducoing, Francis	Pension for services in war of 1812	22	1	Petition	36	Invalid Pensions	157	Favorable; bill	236	Passed	Amended and laid on table.	
Ducoing, Francis	Pension for services in war of 1812	22	2	Petition	88	Invalid Pensions.						
Ducoing, Francis	Pension for services in war of 1812	23	1	Petition	92	Invalid Pensions	69	Favorable; bill	79	Passed	Passed, with amendment.	App'd June 30, 1834
Ducoing, Francis	Pension for services in war of 1812	28	1	Petition	113	Invalid Pensions	235	Adverse		Laid on table.		
Du Commun, Joseph	Invalid pension	22	1	Petition	97	Military Affairs	125	Favorable; bill.	196	Referred to Committee Whole House.		
Du Commun, Joseph	Invalid pension	22	2	Rep'rt Committee Whole House.	66	Whole House	Dec. 15, 1832	With amend.	196	Rejected.		
Ducoste, Jean Pierre	Pre-emption right to land in Louisiana.	21	1	Petition	68	Priv. Land Claims.				Discharged; laid on table.		
Ducoste, Jean Pierre	Pre-emption right to land in Louisiana.	23	2	Petition	138	Priv. Land Claims.						
Ducre, Leander, and Simon	Confirmation of title to land in Louisiana.	19	2	Petition	32	Priv. Land Claims.	Jan. 9, 1827	Adverse		Laid on table.		
Ducre, Leander, and Simon	Confirmation of title to land in Louisiana.	20	1	Petition	40	Priv. Land Claims.	Jan. 3, 1828	Adverse		Laid on table.		
Dudley, Abraham, & wife.	(See John Winn, heirs of.)	26	1		797		575		416			
Dudley, Benjamin W., *et al.*, executors of.	(See Taylor, Morrison & Wilkins)	21	1		122							
Dudley, Christopher, *et al.*	(See Timothy Bloodworth, sureties of.)	11	2		226							
Dudley, Edward B., *et al.*	Relief for alleged violation of laws.	16	1	Senate bill	207	Ways and Means.	Feb. 14, 1820	With amend.	S. 23	Passed	Concurred in.	App'd April 7, 1820
Dudley, Guilford, heirs of.	Compensation for property used, and for services in revolutionary war.	23	1	Resolution	250, 494	Rev. Claims.						
Dudley, Guilford, heirs of.	Compensation for property used, and for services in revolutionary war.	23	2	Petition	120	Rev. Claims	Jan. 26, 1835	Adverse		Laid on table.		
Dudley, Guilford, heirs of.	Compensation for property used, and for services in revolutionary war.	24	1	Petition	259	Rev. Claims.						
Dudley, Guilford, heirs of.	Compensation for property used, and for services in revolutionary war.	28	1	Petition	873	Rev. Claims.						
Dudley, Guilford, heirs of.	Compensat'n for property used, and for services in revolutionary war.	29	1	Petition	487	Rev. Claims.						
Dudley, Lieut. James A., by Mary Helen, mother of	Compensation for property left at Tunis.	25	3	Petition	206	Claims.						

List of private claims presented to the House of Representatives of the United States from the 1st to the 31st Congress, inclusive—Continued.

Names of claimants.	Nature or object of the claim.	Congress.	Session.	How brought before the House of Reps.	Page of journal.	To what committee of the House referred.	No. or date of the report.	Nature of the report.	No. of the bill.	How disposed of by the House of Reps.	How disposed of by the Senate.	Date of the act of Congress, and remarks.
Dudley, Lieut. James A., by Mary Helen, mother of	Compensation for property left at Tunis.	26	1	Petition	169	Claims	....	....	....	Dis.; referred to Com. Naval Affairs.		
Dudley, Paul	Revolutionary pension	28	1	Petition	873	Rev. Pensions.						
Dudley, Sherrel	(See Archibald Beard, *et al.*)	30	1	....	239	....	597					
Dudley, Thomas P.	Invalid pension	31	1	Petition	415	Invalid Pensions.						
Duelos, Francis	Invalid pension, and for depreciation of emoluments.	8	2	Petition	131	Claims.						
Duer, John	(See Theodosius Fowler, representatives of.)	27	3	....	423							
Duer, John and William A.	(See William Alexander, Earl of Stirling.)	23	1	....	305, 306							
Duer, Capt. Thomas	Remuneration for advances made to military company.	30	1	Petition	207	Claims.						
Duer, Capt. Thomas	Remuneration for advances made to military company.	30	2	Memorial	122	Claims	111	Adverse	....	Laid on table.		
Duer, Capt. Thomas	Remuneration for advances made to military company.	31	1	Petition	578	Claims.						
Duer, William	(See Theodosius Fowler.)	6	2	....	783							
Duer, William, administrator of.	Balance due for supplies furnished St. Clair's army.	27	2	Memorial	1004	Claims.						
Duer, William, administrator of.	Balance due for supples furnished St. Clair's army.	28	1	Petition	98	Claims.						
Duer, William, administrator of.	Balance due for supplies furnished St. Clair's army.	28	2	Petition	185	Claims.						
Duer, William, administrator of.	Balance due for supplies furnished St. Clair's army.	29	1	Petition	58	Claims	133	Adverse	....	Laid on table.		
Duer, William, administrator of.	Balance due for supplies furnished St. Clair's army.	30	1	Petition	183	....	....	....	....	Leave to withdraw.		
Duerson, William, jr.	Payment for clothing, and for mule lost in Mexican War.	29	2	Petition	229	Claims.						
Duerson, Capt. William	Compensation as assistant quartermaster in war with Mexico.	31	1	Petition	438	Claims	155	Favorable; bill	173	Referred to Committee Whole House.		
Duerson, Capt. William	Compensation as assistant quartermaster in war with Mexico.	31	2	Rep't Committee Whole House.	103	Whole House	Jan. 3, 1851	By bill	173	Passed	Ref'd to Com. on Claims.	
Dufault, Joseph and Francis.	(See Antoinette Lalonet, assignees of.)	20	1	....	28							
Duff, A. D, surety of	Release from liability	17	1	Petition	310	Ways and Means	....	....	....	Discharged; laid on table.		
Duff, A. D., surety of	Release from liability	18	1	Petition	286	Judiciary	Mar. 16, 1824	....	....	Leave to withdraw.		
Duffey, Bernard	Extra compensation for carrying United States mail.	26	1	Memorial	1003	P. Of. & P. Roads.						
Duffey, Lewis	Arrears of pay due for services in revolutionary war.	20	2	Resolution	126	Military Pensions	....	....	....	Discharged; laid on table.		
Duffey, Terrence	Compensation for service in revolutionary war.	9	1	Petition	226	Claims	Mar. 28, 1806	Indef. postp'd	....	Leave to withdraw.		
Duffie, James	(See Captain William Sloo, executor of.)	15	2	....	154							
Duffield, Jacob, by Hannah, widow of.	Invalid pension	26	1	Petition	603	Invalid Pensions.						
Duffield, John M.	Compensation for services in war with Mexico.	31	1	Petition	809	Claims	....	....	....	Dis'd; referred to Com. on Military Affairs.		
Duffield, Margaretta, *et al.*	Indemnity for damages to property by United States troops.	15	1	Petition	247	Claims	....	....	....	Discharged; laid on table.		

List of private claims presented to the House of Representatives of the United States from the 1st to the 31st Congress, inclusive—Continued.

Names of claimants.	Nature or object of the claim.	Congress.	Session.	How brought before the House of Reps.	Page of journal.	To what committee of the House referred.	No. or date of the report.	Nature of the report.	No. of the bill.	How disposed of by the House of Reps.	How disposed of by the Senate.	Date of the act of Congress, and remarks.
Duffield, Margaretta, *et al.*	Indemnity for damages to property by United States troops.	15	2	Petition	40	Claims	71	Adverse	......	Laid on table.		
Duffield, Margaretta, *et al.*	Indemnity for damages to property by United States troops.	18	2	Petition	160	Claims.						
Duffy, James	Pension	28	1	Senate bill	989	Naval Affairs	June 7, 1844	With't amend.	S. 161	Referred to Committee Whole House.		
Duffy, James	Pension	28	2	Senate bill	92	Naval Affairs	Dec. 19, 1844	With't amend.	S. 9	Passed	Passed	App'd Feb. 13, 1845
Dufossat, Joseph S.	Confirmation of title to land in Louisiana.	22	1	Petition	63	Priv. Land Claims.	32	Favorable; bill	77	Passed	Passed	App'd May 19, 1832
Dufour & Gaudry	(See Gaudry & Duforer)	16	1	....	223							
Dufour, John James, *et al.*	Permission to purchase certain lands.	7	1	Senate bill	140	Whole House	April 30, 1802	With't amend.	S. 4	Passed	Passed	App'd May 1, 1802
Dufour, John James, *et al.*	Extension of time to complete payment for lands.	12	2	Petition	612	Public Lands.						
Dufour, John James, *et al.*	Extension of time to complete payment for lands.	13	1	Petition	19	Public Lands	June 14, 1813	Favorable; bill	22	Passed	Passed	App'd Aug. 2, 1813
Dufour, John James, *et al.*	Extension of credit on last payment for lands.	15	2	Petition	122	Public Lands	Dec. 23, 1818	Favorable; bill	247	Rejected; laid on table.		
Dufour, Parfait	Confirmation of title to land in Missouri.	15	1	Petition	52	Priv. Land Claims.	....	....	......	Discharged; laid on table.		
Dufour, Parfait	Confirmation of title to land in Missouri.	16	1	Petition	72	Priv. Land Claims.	....	....	......	Discharged; laid on table.		
Dufour, Parfait	Confirmation of title to land in Missouri.	17	1	Petition	53	Public Lands	....	....	......	Discharged; laid on table.		
Dufour, Parfait	Confirmation of title to land in Missouri.	18	1	Petition	53	Public Lands	Jan. 26, 1824	General bill	65	Passed with amendm't.	Passed	App'd May 26, 1824
Dufresne, Pierre, heirs of.	Confirmation of title to land	18	2	Senate bill	255	Priv. Land Claims.	....	....	S. 61			
Dufresne, Pierre, heirs of.	Confirmation of title to land	23	2	Senate bill	442	Priv. Land Claims.	Feb. 28, 1835	With't amend.	S. 142	Passed	Passed	App'd March 3, 1835
Dufresne, Pierre, heirs of.	Confirmation of title to land	29	2	Senate bill	381	Priv. Land Claims.	Mar. 1, 1847	With't amend.	S. 144	Passed	Passed	App'd March 2, 1847
Dugan, Charles	Compensation as fireman on board steamship Alleghany.	31	1	Petition	255	Claims	410	Adverse	......	Laid on table.		
Dugan, Cumberland	Indemnity for French spoliations prior to 1800.	26	1	Memorial	182	Foreign Affairs	343	Favorable; bill	319	Referred to Committee Whole House.		
Dugan, George	Invalid pension	13	2	House bill	344	Whole House	Mar. 31, 1814	With't amend.	166	Passed	Passed	App'd April 18, 1814
Dugan, Joseph	(See Savage & Dugan)	26	1	....	182	....	343	....	319			
Duggan, Daniel	Invalid pension	27	2	Petition	246	Invalid Pensions	434	Adverse	......	Laid on table.		
Duggan, Daniel	Invalid pension	28	1	Petition	247	Invalid Pensions	....	....	......	Discharged; referred to Com. on Claims.		
Duggan, Daniel	Invalid pension	28	2	Petition	46	Claims.						
Duggan, Daniel	Invalid pension	29	1	Petition	116	Claims.						
Duggan, Jeremiah, widow and heirs of.	Compensation for services as a Canadian refugee.	2	2	Petition	656	....	....	....	......	Laid on table.		
Duggan, Jeremiah, widow and heirs of.	Grant of land	6	2	Resolution	733	Select	Jan. 19, 1801	Favorable; bill	280	Passed	Passed	App'd Feb. 18, 1801
Duggan, Jeremiah, widow and heirs of.	To cancel certificate, and another to issue to locate land.	11	2	Petition	200	Public Lands	....	....	......	Leave to withdraw.		
Duggan, William	Arrears of pension	21	2	Petition	159	Military Affairs	....	....	......	Discharged; laid on table.		
Duggan, William	Arrears of pension	23	2	Petition	76	Invalid Pensions	Dec. 22, 1834	Adverse	......	Laid on table.		
Duke, David	Compensation for services as mail contractor.	31	1	Petition	826	P. Of. and P. Roads.						
Duke, David	Compensation for services as mail contractor.	31	2	Petition	445	P. Of. and P. Roads.	96	Adverse	......	Laid on table.		

List of private claims presented to the House of Representatives of the United States from the 1*st to the* 31*st Congress, inclusive*—Continued.

Names of claimants.	Nature or object of the claim.	Congress.	Session.	How brought before the House of Reps.	Page of journal.	To what committee of the House referred.	No. or date of the report.	Nature of the report.	No. of the bill.	How disposed of by the House of Reps.	How disposed of by the Senate.	Date of the act of Congress, and remarks.
Duke, Joseph	Grant of land	22	1	Petition	189	Public Lands	246	Favorable; bill	334	Referred to Committee Whole House.		
Duke, Joseph	Grant of land	25	2	Petition	486	Indian Affairs	719	Favorable; bill	688	Referred to Committee Whole House.		
Duke, Joseph	Grant of land	25	3	Rep't Committee Whole House.	381	Whole House	Jan. 25, 1839	With amend.	688	Passed	Adverse.	
Duke, Joseph	Grant of land	26	1	Petition	180	Indian Affairs	....	....	....	Discharged; referred to Com. on Claims.		
Dulany, Sharp, surety of.	Release from payment of interest.	17	1	Petition	118	Ways and Means.						
Dulany, Sharp, surety of.	Release from payment of interest.	18	1	Senate bill	573	Judiciary	May 26, 1824	With't amend.	S. 110	Passed.	....	App'd May 26, 1824
Dulany, William H.	Compensation for carrying United States mail.	19	1	Petition	129	P. Of. and P. Roads.	Feb. 8, 1826	Adverse.	....	Laid on table.		
Dumal, John	Pension	10	1	House bill	232	Whole House	Mar. 17, 1808	General bill	78	Passed	Passed	App'd April 25, 1808
Dumartrait, Adrian	Additional pay as marshal of western district of Louisiana.	19	1	Petition	443	Judiciary	....	....	....	Discharged, laid on table.		
Dumas, Andre, representatives of.	Confirmation of land title	27	2	Senate bill	359	Whole House	Feb. 11, 1842	With't amend.	S. 76	Passed	Passed	App'd July 6, 1842
Dumas, Amelia L. and Louisa F.	Relief: claim formerly against Spanish government.	31	2	Petition	180	Claims.						
Dumas, or Durnass, Francis.	(See Francis Dunross)	19	1	....	58	....	164					
Dumas, John F.	Indemnity for French spoliations in 1807.	18	2	Petition	30	Foreign Affairs.						
Dumas, John F.	Indemnity for French spoliations in 1807.	19	1	Petition	132	Foreign Affairs	202	Adverse	....	Laid on table.		
Dumas, John F., by Abigail, widow of.	Indemnity for Spanish spoliations in 1803.	25	3	Memorial	115	Foreign Affairs.						
Dumas, John F., by Abigail, widow of.	Indemnity for Spanish spoliations in 1803.	26	1	Petition	182, 349	Foreign Affairs	421	Adverse	....	Laid on table.		
Dumas, John F., by Abigail, widow of.	Indemnity for Spanish spoliations in 1803.	27	2	Petition	152	Foreign Affairs	April 12, 1842	Adverse	....	Laid on table.		
Dummett, D.	Compensation for Indian depredations in Florida.	25	3	Petition	121	Claims	162	Adverse.	....	Laid on table.		
Dummett, F. H.	Compensation for Indian depredations in Florida.	25	3	Petition	121	Claims	162	Adverse	....	Laid on table.		
Dummer, Nathaniel	Revolutionary pension	3	1	Memorial	86	....	....	....	....	Referred to Secretary War.		
Dummer, Nathaniel	Revolutionary pension	3	2	Rep. of Secretary War.	278	Claims	Mar. 2, 1795	Adverse	....	Laid on table.		
Dummer, Nathaniel	Revolutionary pension	4	1	Petition	598	Claims	May 30, 1796	Adverse	....	Laid on table.		
Dummer, George, & Co.	Permission to import merchandize from Great Britain ordered previous to the non-importation act of March 2, 1811.	12	1	Petition	21	Com. and Manuf.						
Dumesti, John, heirs of	Indemnity for French spoliations prior to 1800.	29	2	Memorial	70	Foreign Affairs.						
Dumesti, John, heirs of	Indemnity for French spoliations prior to 1800.	31	1	Petition	647	Foreign Affairs	355	Favorable; bill	318	Referred to Committee Whole House.		
Dumison, Pierre	Invalid pension	4	1	Res. and docs.	445	Claims	Feb. 18, 1796	Favorable; bill ordered.	156	Passed	Passed	App'd April 20, 1796
Dumon, Jean Baptiste	Reimbursem't for money advanced, losses sustained, and compensation for services rendered in revolutionary war.	2	1	Petition	479	....	....	....	....	Refered to Secretary of Treasury.		

List of private claims presented to the House of Representatives of the United States from the 1st to the 31st Congress, inclusive—Continued.

Names of claimants.	Nature or object of the claim.	Congress.	Session.	How brought before the House of Reps.	Page of journal.	To what committee of the House referred.	No. or date of the report.	Nature of the report.	No. of the bill.	How disposed of by the House of Reps.	How disposed of by the Senate.	Date of the act of Congress, and remarks.
Dumon, Jean Baptiste....	Reimbursem't for money advanced, losses sustained, and compensation for services rendered in revolutionary war.	3	2	Petition and rep. Sec. Treasury.	284	Claims.						
Dumon, Jean Baptiste....	Reimbursem't for money advanced, losses sustained, and compensation for services rendered in revolutionary war.	4	1	Res. and docs...	373	Claims	Jan. 4, 1796	Adverse	......	Leave to withdraw.		
Dumon, Jean Baptiste....	Reimbursem't for money advanced, losses sustained, and compensation for services rendered in revolutionary war.	4	2	Memorial	620	Claims..........	Jan. 11, 1797	Adverse.				
Dumon, Jean Baptiste....	Reimbursem't for money advanced, losses sustained, and compensation for services rendered in revolutionary war.	5	2	Petition	157	....	....	....	......	Laid on table.		
Dumont, Ebenezer.......	Compensation for horse and equipments lost in war with Mexico.	31	1	Senate bill	1595	Whole House	....	....	S. 294			
Dumont, Ebenezer.......	Compensation for horse and equipments lost in war with Mexico.	31	2	Senate bill	170	Claims..........	....	....	S. 294			
Dumont, John..........	Pension	21	1	Petition	120	Military Pensions..	....	....	......	Discharged; laid on table.		
Dumont, John..........	Pension	21	2	Petition	53	Military Pensions.						
Dumont, John..........	Pension	22	1	Petition	174	Rev. Pensions....	....	....	......	Discharged; laid on table.		
Dumont, John, *et al.*....	Pre-emption right to purchase public lands on a credit of twelve years.	14	1	Petition	36	Public Lands.....	Feb. 8, 1816	Adverse	......	Laid on table.		
Dumouchel, Eugene C....	Confirmation of title to land.....	22	1	Petition	64	Priv. Land Claims.	62	Favorable; bill	125	Passed	Passed	App'd June 25, 1832
Dunant, Edward.........	Indemnity for French spoliations prior to 1800.	26	1	Memorial	182	Foreign Affairs ...	343	Favorable; bill	319	Referred to Committee Whole House.		
Dunbar, Amasa	(See Relief Dunbar, heirs of)....	25	3	....	564							
Dunbar, Captain Jacob...	Remuneration for property taken by pirates, recaptured, condemned and sold by United States.	28	1	Petition	297	Claims.						
Dunbar, Joseph.........	Invalid pension...............	2	2	Rep. of Secretary War.	649	Whole House.						
Dunbar, Joseph.........	Invalid pension	3	1	Rep. of Secretary War.	131	Select	May 26, 1794	Res. to refer to Sec. War.	J. R. 12	Passed	Passed	App'd June 9, 1794
Dunbar, Joseph.........	Invalid pension...............	3	2	Rep. of Secretary War.	337	Claims..........	Feb. 28, 1795	Favorable; bill	130	Passed	Postponed.	
Dunbar, Joseph.........	Invalid pension	4	1	Rep. of Secretary War.	447	Claims..........	Feb. 18, 1796	Favorable; bill	156	Passed	Passed	App'd April 20, 1796
Dunbar, Joseph.........	Compensation for extra services as receiver of public money.	19	2	Senate bill	351	Public Lands	Mar. 2, 1827	With amend..	S. 100	Passed	Concurred in .	App'd March 2, 1827
Dunbar, Peter, heirs of...	Revolutionary pension..........	26	1	Petition	171	Rev. Pensions	....	....	......	Discharged; laid on table.		
Dunbar, Peter, heirs of...	Revolutionary pension..........	29	1	Petition	118	Rev. Pensions	520	Adverse	......	Laid on table.		
Dunbar, Relief, heirs of...	Compensation for services of ancestor in revolutionary war.	25	3	Petition	564	Rev. Claims......	....	....	......	Discharged.		
Dunbar, Relief, heirs of...	Compensation for services of ancestor in revolutionary war.	27	2	Petition	484	Rev. Pensions	784	Adverse	......	Laid on table.		

List of private claims presented to the House of Representatives of the United States from the 1st to the 31st Congress, inclusive—Continued.

Names of claimants.	Nature or object of the claim.	Congress.	Session.	How brought before the House of Reps.	Page of journal.	To what committee of the House referred.	No. or date of the report.	Nature of the report.	No. of the bill.	How disposed of by the House of Reps.	How disposed of by the Senate.	Date of the act of Congress, and remarks.
Dunbar, Relief, heirs of	Compensation for services of ancestor in revolutionary war.	28	1	Petition	144	Rev. Pensions				Discharged; laid on table.		
Dunbar, Robert	Confirmation of title to land	10	1	Petition	126	Whole House.						
Dunbar, Simeon	Compensation for certificate of public debt not presented in time.	5	2	Petition	98	Claims				Discharged; referred to Com. Whole House.		
Dunbar, Thomas	(See Henry Dickins, *et al.*)	20	2		203							
Dunbar, William	(See George Galphin, executor of.)	2	2		619							
Dunbar, William	Relief from action of certain laws respecting grants of land south of Tennessee.	8	1	Petition	553, 635	Select				Leave to withdraw.		
Dunbar, William	Relief from action of certain laws respecting grants of land south of Tennessee.	8	2	Memorial & pet.	7, 13	Select.						
Dunbar, William	Relief from action of certain laws respecting grants of land south of Tennessee.	9	1	Petition	251	Public Lands	Feb. 9, 1806	Adverse.				
Duncan, Abner L., attorney of.	Compensation for supplies furnished militia in 1803.	9	2	Petition	563	Claims.						
Duncan, Abner L., attorney of.	Compensation for supplies furnished militia in 1803.	10	1	Petition	54	Claims.						
Duncan, Abner L., attorney of.	Compensation for supplies furnished militia in 1803.	17	1	Petition	273	Claims	April 3, 1822	Favorable; bill	169	Laid on table.		
Duncan, Abner L., attorney of.	Compensation for supplies furnished militia in 1803.	18	1	Petition	255	Claims	Mar. 26, 1824	Adverse		Laid on table.		
Duncan, Abner L., executors of.	Release from liability of certain bond.	23	1	Petition	338	Judiciary.						
Duncan, B. M	Pre-emption right to land	26	1	Petition	609	Public Lands.				Discharged; laid on table.		
Duncan, David	Grant of land	21	2	Pet. of citizens of Missouri.	272	Public Lands.						
Duncan, Dudley and Frederick F.	Authority to correct error in entry of land.	26	2	Petition	81	Public Lands.						
Duncan, Captain James, (Mo.)	Invalid pension	24	1	Petition	426	Invalid Pensions	April 15, 1836	Adverse		Laid on table.		
Duncan, Captain James, (Mo.)	Invalid pension	24	2	Petition	147	Invalid Pensions	Jan. 13, 1837	Adverse		Laid on table.		
Duncan, Captain James, (Mo.)	Invalid pension	25	2	Petition	401	Invalid Pensions				Discharged; laid on table.		
Duncan, Captain James, (Mo.)	Invalid pension	25	3	Petition	129	Invalid Pensions				Discharged; laid on table.		
Duncan, James, (Ga.)	Revolutionary pension	21	2	Petition	38	Military Pensions.						
Duncan, Jared	Invalid pension	11	2	Petition	228	Select	Mar. 7, 1810	Favorable		Laid on table.		
Duncan, Jared	Invalid pension	11	2	General bill	283	Whole House	Mar. 24, 1810	With't amend.	107	Passed	Passed	App'd April 27, 1810
Duncan, John	Increase of pension	16	1	Resolution	189	Rev. Pensions				Discharged; laid on table.		
Duncan, John	Revolutionary pension	28	1	Petition	857	Rev. Pensions.						
Duncan, J. B., & J. L. Allen.	Allowance as sub-Indian agent, and compensation for exposing fraud against Government.	21	1	Petition	264	Claims				Discharged; laid on table.		
Duncan, Jonas	Pay for use of house by U. States officers in 1812.	18	1	Petition	159	Naval Affairs	65	Favorable; bill	124	Passed	Passed	App'd May 19, 1824
Duncan, L. C.	Compensation for services as assistant surgeon in war with Mexico.	31	1	Petition	215	Military Affairs	209	Adverse		Laid on table.		

List of private claims presented to the House of Representatives of the United States from the 1st to the 31st Congress, inclusive—Continued.

Names of claimants.	Nature or object of the claim.	Congress.	Session.	How brought before the House of Reps.	Page of journal.	To what committee of the House referred.	No. or date of the report.	Nature of the report.	No. of the bill.	How disposed of by the House of Reps.	How disposed of by the Senate.	Date of the act of Congress, and remarks.
70 Duncan, Larby	(See Aquilla Bishop)	24	1		264							
Duncan, Matthew, (Mo.)	Confirmation of land title	18	1	Petition	287	Public Lands.						
Duncan, Matthew, (Mo.)	Permission to change location of land.	18	1	Resolution	317	Public Lands.						
Duncan, Matthew, (Ill.)	Release from deficiency on Treasury books.	25	2	Petition	274	Claims	804	Adverse		Laid on table.		
Duncan, Peggy	Revolutionary pension	26	1	Documents	885	Rev. Pensions.						
Duncan, Peggy	Revolutionary pension	26	2	Petition	78	Rev. Pensions				Discharged; laid on table.		
Duncan, Samuel	(See William H. Bedford)	28	1		262							
Duncan, Samuel C.	Compensation for additional work on National road in Indiana.	23	1	Petition	384	Claims	480	Adverse		Laid on table.		
Duncan, Samuel C.	Compensation for additional work on National road in Indiana.	23	2	Resolution	349	Claims.						
Duncan, Silas	Arrears of pension	23	1	Petition	241	Invalid Pensions	503	Favorable; bill	508	Referred to Committee Whole House.		
Duncan, Silas	Arrears of pension	24	1	Petition	214	Naval Affairs.						
Duncan, Silas, administratrix of.	Arrears of pension	25	2	Petition	722	Naval Affairs.						
Duncan, Silas, administratrix of.	Arrears of pension	26	1	Petition	180	Naval Affairs.						
Duncan, Silas, administratrix of.	Arrears of pension	29	1	Memorial	74	Naval Affairs	600	Favorable; bill	422	Referred to Committee Whole House.		
Duncan, Silas, administratrix of.	Arrears of pension	29	2	Rep't Committee Whole House.	382	Whole House	Jan. 24, 1847	With't amend.	423	Passed	Laid on table.	
Duncan, Silas, administratrix of.	Arrears of pension	30	1	Petition	115	Naval Affairs	190	Favorable; bill	200	Referred to Committee Whole House.		
Duncan, Silas, administratrix of.	Arrears of pension	30	2	Rep't Committee Whole House.	368	Whole House	Feb. 3, 1849	With't amend.	200	Passed	Ref. to Com. on Naval Affairs.	
Duncan, Silas, administratrix of.	Arrears of pension	31	1	Petition	500	Naval Affairs	118	Favorable; bill	138	Referred to Committee Whole House.		
Duncan, Silas, administratrix of.	Arrears of pension	31	2	Rep't Committee Whole House.	103	Whole House	Jan. 3, 1851	With't amend.	138	Passed	Ref. to Com. on Naval Affairs.	
Duncan, William B.	Compensation as agent of Chickasaw Indians.	21	1	Petition	294	Claims	249	Favorable; bill	308	Referred to Committee Whole House.		
Duncan, William C.	Remuneration for money expended, and release from certain liabilities, war with Mexico.	31	1	Petition	956	Military Affairs.						
Duncan, William H.	Remuneration for damages sustained by the illegal seizure of goods.	24	1	Petition	670	Claims.						
Duncan, William H.	Remuneration for damages sustained by the illegal seizure of goods.	24	2	Petition	217	Claims	217	Adverse		Laid on table.		
Duncan, William H.	Remuneration for damages sustained by the illegal seizure of goods.	25	2	Petition	275	Claims	Jan. 30, 1838	Adverse		Laid on table.		
Duncan, William L.	Compensation for professional services in certain cases.	17	1	Resolution	417	Judiciary				Discharged; laid on table.		
Duncan, William, trustees of.	Indemnity for French spoliations prior to 1800.	26	1	Memorial	182	Foreign Affairs	343	Favorable; bill	319	Referred to Committee Whole House.		
Dunscomb, Edward	Restoration of pension	17	2	Petition	69	Rev. Pensions				Discharged; leave to withdraw.		
Dundas, Agnes, heirs of	That the right which the United States may have acquired to certain property by escheat be vested in them.	25	3	Senate bill	547	Whole House			S. 145			

List of private claims presented to the House of Representatives of the United States from the 1st to the 31st Congress, inclusive—Continued.

Names of claimants.	Nature or object of the claim.	Congress.	Session.	How brought before the House of Reps.	Page of journal.	To what committee of the House referred.	No. or date of the report.	Nature of the report.	No. of the bill.	How disposed of by the House of Reps.	How disposed of by the Senate.	Date of the act of Congress, and remarks.
Dundas, Agnes, heirs of	That the right which the United States may have acquired to certain property by escheat be vested in them.	26	1	Senate bill	803	Judiciary	June 19, 1840	With't amend.	S. 140	Referred to Committee Whole House.		
Dundas, Agnes, heirs of	That the right which the United States may have acquired to certain property by escheat be vested in them.	26	2	Senate bill	203	Judiciary	March 3, 1841	With't amend.	S. 210	Passed	Passed	App'd March 3, 1841
Dunfee, Oliver, *et al*	(See David Moore, sureties of)	21	1		173							
Dunham, Ann, assignees of	Correction of erroneous numbers of certain sections of land, and issue of patents for same.	24	1	Senate bill	1078	Public Lands	July 1, 1836	With't amend.	227	Passed	Passed	App'd July 2, 1836
Dunham, Azariah, by James	Liquidation of certain bills of credit.	4	1	Rep. of Secretary Treasury.	388	Claims	74	Adverse		Laid on table.		
Dunham, Daniel, heirs of.	Invalid pension	22	2	Petition	260	Invalid Pensions.						
Dunham, Daniel, heirs of.	Invalid pension	23	1	Petition	353	Invalid Pensions				Discharged; laid on table.		
Dunham, Daniel, heirs of.	Invalid pension	23	2	Petition	47	Invalid Pensions	33	Adverse		Laid on table.		
Dunham, Daniel, heirs of.	Invalid pension	24	1	Petition	140	Invalid Pensions	June 15, 1836	Adverse		Laid on table.		
Dunham, Daniel, heirs of.	Invalid pension	26	1	Petition	287	Invalid Pensions.						
Dunham, Daniel, heirs of.	Invalid pension	26	2	Petition	212	Invalid Pensions	Feb. 12, 1841	Favorable; bill	654	Referred to Committee Whole House.		
Dunham, Daniel, heirs of.	Invalid pension	27	2	Petition	97	Invalid Pensions	Feb. 9, 1842	Adverse, (verbal.)		Laid on table.		
Dunham, Daniel, heirs of.	Invalid pension	27	3	Petition	72	Invalid Pensions	8	Favorable; bill	629	Passed	Ref. to Com. on Pensions.	
Dunham, Daniel, heirs of.	Invalid pension	28	1	Petition	189	Invalid Pensions	157	Favorable; bill	146	Passed	Adverse.	
Dunham, Daniel, heir of, (Conn.)	Indemnity for French spoliations prior to 1800.	26	1	Memorial	182	Foreign Affairs	343	Favorable; bill	319	Referred to Committee Whole House.		
Dunham, Daniel, heirs of, (Conn.)	Indemnity for French spoliations prior to 1800.	29	2	Memorial	87	Foreign Affairs.						
Dunham, David	Exemption from provision of revenue laws as to register of tonnage duties, and drawback on coal.	17	1	Petition	133	Commerce				Discharged; laid on table.		
Dunham, David R., *et al.*	Benefit of pre-emption law of 1824.	25	2	Petition	281	Priv. Land Claims.				Discharged; laid on table.		
Dunham, Elisha, & George Boardman.	Indemnity for French spoliations prior to 1800.	24	2	Petition	75	Foreign Affairs.						
Dunham, Elisha, & George Boardman.	Indemnity for French spoliations prior to 1800.	25	2	Memorial	232	Foreign Affairs.						
Dunham, Elisha, & George Boardman.	Indemnity for French spoliations prior to 1800.	26	1	Memorial	182	Foreign Affairs	343	Favorable; bill	319	Referred to Committee Whole House.		
Dunham, Enoch	Restoration of pension	17	2	Petition	61	Rev. Pensions				Discharged; laid on table.		
Dunham, Ezra	Credit for money lost as collector of district tax.	15	1	Petition	386	Ways and Means				Discharged; laid on table.		
Dunham, Ezra	Credit for money lost as collector of district tax.	15	2	Petition	90	Ways and Means	Dec. 14, 1818	Adverse		Leave to withdraw.		
Dunham, Ezra	Credit for money lost as collector of district tax.	16	1	Petition	332	Ways and Means				Leave to withdraw.		
Dunham, Captain Jacob, (N. Y.)	Remuneration for property taken by pirates, and recaptured by United States and sold.	27	2	Documents	740	Claims	702	Adverse		Laid on table.		

List of private claims presented to the House of Representatives of the United States from the 1st to the 31st Congress, inclusive—Continued.

Names of claimants.	Nature or object of the claim.	Congress.	Session.	How brought before the House of Reps.	Page of journal.	To what committee of the House referred.	No. or date of the report.	Nature of the report.	No. of the bill.	How disposed of by the House of Reps.	How disposed of by the Senate.	Date of the act of Congress, and remarks.
Dunham, Jacob, widow of.	Pension and half-pay	30	1	Petition	253	Rev. Pensions				Leave to withdraw.		
Dunham, Jeremiah	Compensation for services as blacksmith for Indians.	28	2	Petition	372	Indian Affairs.						
Dunham, John	(See Daniel Dunham, heir of.)	29	2		87							
Dunham, Joseph	(See John E. Metcalf, *et al.*)	25	2		1052				S. 213			
Dunham, Joseph, *et al*	Pre-emption right to purchase land.	24	2	Petition	324	Priv. Land Claims.						
Dunham, Joseph E	Authority to purchase land at minimum price.	28	1	Petition	77	Priv. Land Claims.	9	Favorable; bill.	35	Passed	Passed	App'd June 17, 1844
Dunham and Read	(See Minis and Henry, *et al.*	15	2		144							
Dunham, Sarah	(See Jacob Dunham, widow of.)	30	1		253							
Dunham, Stephen	Invalid pension	3	1	Rep. of Secretary War.	131	Select	May 26, 1794	Res. to refer to Sec. War.	J. R. 12	Passed	Passed	App'd June 9, 1794
Dunham, Stephen	Invalid pension	18	2	Petition	230	Rev. Claims.						
Dunham, Stephen	Invalid pension	19	1	Petition	150	Military Pensions	164	Adverse		Laid on table.		
Dunham, Stephen	Invalid pension	21	1	Petition	248	Military Pensions	May 25, 1830	Favorable; bill	490	Referred to Committee Whole House.		
Dunham, Stephen	Invalid pension	21	2	Rep't Committee Whole House.	319	Whole House	Feb. 16, 1831	By bill	490	Passed	With't amend.	
Dunham, Stephen	Invalid pension	22	1	Petition	34	Rev. Pensions	41	Favorable; bill	83	Passed	Indef. postp'd.	
Dunlap, Capt. A	(See William H. Bedford.)	28	1		262							
Dunlap, Elizabeth	Indemnity for losses sustained by self, and ancestors in 1794.	23	1	Petition	438	Claims.						
Dunlap, Hugh W	Compensation for mustering militia into service in 1836.	29	1	Resolution	238	Militia.						
Dunlap, James	(See Henry Ashton, *et al.*)	23	1		337							
Dunlap, John, heirs of	Indemnity for French spoliations prior to 1800.	29	2	Memorial	171	Foreign Affairs.						
Dunlap, John, heirs of	Indemnity for French spoliations prior to 1800.	30	1	Memorial	118	Foreign Affairs.						
Dunlap, John, heirs of	Indemnity for French spoliations prior to 1800.	31	1	Petition	285	Foreign Affairs	335	Favorable; bill	318	Referred to Committee Whole House.		
Dunlap, Joseph	Remuneration for provisions furnished United States troops.	16	1	Petition	271	Claims	April 5, 1820	Adverse		Laid on table.		
Dunlap, Joseph	Remuneration for provisions furnished United States troops.	20	1	Resolution	514	Claims				Discharged; laid on table.		
Dunlap, Joseph	Remuneration for provisions furnished United States troops.	27	2	Petition	613	Claims	1042	Adverse.		Laid on table.		
Dunlap, Joseph	Compensation for damages to property by United States troops.	16	1	Petition	303	Claims	Mar. 21, 1820	Adverse		Laid on table.		
Dunlap, Ringlang, and Anderson, *et al.*	(See Thomas Ringlang, *et al.*)	31	2		155							
Dunlap, R. G	Confirmation of title to land in Louisiana.	26	1	Petition	603	Priv. Land Claims.						
Dunlap, Richard T. and Robert P.	(See Jacob Pennell, *et al.*)	26	1		836							
Dunlap, Robert	(See John Dunlap, heirs of.)	29	2		171							
Dunlap, Samuel	(See John Dunlap, heirs of.)	29	2		171							
Dunlap, William	Indemnity for French spoliations prior to 1800.	7	1	Petition	108	Select.						
Dunlap, William, & Co.	Indemnity for French spoliations prior to 1800.	26	1	Memorial	182	Foreign Affairs	343	Favorable; bill	319	Referred to Committee Whole House.		
Dunlap, William, heirs of.	Indemnity for French spoliations prior to 1800.	31	1	Petition	233	Foreign Affairs	355	Favorable; bill	318	Referred to Committee Whole House.		

List of private claims presented to the House of Representatives of the United States from the 1st to the 31st Congress, inclusive—Continued.

Names of claimants.	Nature or object of the claim.	Congress.	Session.	How brought before the House of Reps.	Page of journal.	To what committee of the House referred.	No. or date of the report.	Nature of the report.	No. of the bill.	How disposed of by the House of Reps.	How disposed of by the Senate.	Date of the act of Congress, and remarks.
Dunlap, William	(See John Dunlap, heirs of)	29	2		171							
Dunn, Alexander	Revolutionary pension	22	1	Resolution	823	Rev. Pensions				Discharged; laid on table.		
Dunn, Benjamin, (Maine)	Release from judgment at suit of United States.	17	2	Petition	208	Military Affairs				Discharged: laid on table.		
Dunn, Capt. Benjamin	Credit for items disallowed on settlement.	20	2	Petition	58	Claims	Jan. 9, 1829	Adverse		Laid on table.		
Dunn, Cary, jr., *et al.*	Compensation for services in revolutionary war.	21	2	Petition	74	Rev. Claims	4	Favorable; bill.	567	Referred to Committee Whole House.		
Dunn, George W., & Co.	Reimbursement of certain duties imposed on carpet yarn.	22	1	Petition	62	Ways and Means.						
Dunn, George, *et al.*	Relief from arrest and imprisonment on ship-board.	26	1	Memorial	932	Commerce.						
Dunn, John	Pension	21	1	Petition	120	Military Pensions				Discharged; laid on table.		
Dunn, John L.	Compensation for property lost in expedition against Indians.	24	1	Petition	430	Claims.						
Dunn, Jonathan	Relief for wounds received in revolutionary war.	9	1	Petition	243	Claims	Mar. 28, 1796			Leave to withdraw.		
Dunn, Matilda B.	(See Thomas B. Dunn, widow of.)	21	1		295		216					
Dunn, Moses	Increase of pension	25	2	Petition	1029	Rev. Pensions				Discharged.		
Dunn, Moses	Increase of pension	26	1	Petition	173	Rev. Pensions.						
Dunn, Oswald	Compensation for ascertaining longitude of Capitol of U. States.	17	1	House bill	239	Whole House	Feb. 6, 1822	Favorable; bill	79	Passed	Passed	App'd April 30, 1822
Dunn, Robert	Pension as an express rider	16	2	Petition	85	Rev. Pensions	Feb. 15, 1821	Adverse		Leave to withdraw.		
Dunn, Robert	Pension as an express rider	17	1	Petition	272	Rev. Pensions				Dis.; referred to Com. Whole House.		
Dunn, Robert	Pension as an express rider	20	1	Petition	30	Claims				Discharged; laid on table.		
Dunn, Robert	Pension as an express rider	21	1	Petition	147	Military Pensions	May 29, 1830	Favorable; bill.	499	Referred to Committee Whole House.		
Dunn, Robert	Pension as an express rider	21	2	Rep't Committee Whole House.	319	Whole House	Feb. 16, 1831	By bill	499	Passed	With amend.	
Dunn, Robert	Pension as an express rider	22	1	Petition	56	Rev. Pensions	16	Favorable; bill.	65	Passed	Indef. postp'd.	
Dunn, Thomas B., widow of.	Relief for self and children	21	1	Petition	295	Military Affairs	216	Adverse		Referred to Committee Whole House.		
Dunn, Thomas	Compensation as assistant doorkeeper of House of Representatives.	5	2	Resolution	391	Select	July 15, 1798	By bill	133	Passed	Passed	App'd July 16, 1798
Dunn, Thomas	Permission to occupy house free of rent.	6	2	Resolution	834	Whole House	Feb. 28, 1801	Report	J. R.—	Passed	Passed	App'd March 2, 1801
Dunn, William, assignee of.	Confirmation of title to land in Missouri.	15	1	Petition	133	Priv. Land Claims.						
Dunn, William, assignee of.	Confirmation of title to land in Missouri.	16	1	Petition	72	Priv. Land Claims.						
Dunn, William, assignee of.	Confirmation of title to land in Missouri.	17	1	Petition	55	Public Lands.						
Dunn, William, assignee of.	Confirmation of title to land in Missouri.	18	1	Petition	55	Public Lands.						
Dunn, William, assignee of.	Confirmation of title to land in Missouri.	21	1	Petition	41	Priv. Land Claims.	22	Favorable; bill	31	Passed	Passed	App'd April 23, 1830
Dunning, Elisha B.	Invalid pension	17	1	Petition	298	Pens. & Rev. Cl'ms.				Discharged; referred to Secretary War.		

List of private claims presented to the House of Representatives of the United States from the 1st to the 31st Congress, inclusive—Continued.

Names of claimants.	Nature or object of the claim.	Congress.	Session.	How brought before the House of Reps.	Page of journal.	To what committee of the House referred.	No. or date of the report.	Nature of the report.	No. of the bill.	How disposed of by the House of Reps.	How disposed of by the Senate.	Date of the act of Congress, and remarks.
Dunross, Francis	Permission to change location of land.	19	1	Petition	58	Public Lands	54	Favorable; bill.	77	Passed	Passed	App'd May 22, 1826
Dunscomb, Andrew	Payment for services as commissioner of accounts.	1	2	Petition	160	....	....	....	......	Referred to Secretary Treasury.		
Dunscomb, Andrew	Payment for services as commissioner of accounts.	3	2	Petition and rep't Sec. Treasury.	284	....	....	....	......	Laid on table.		
Dunscomb, Andrew	Balance due for services as commissioner of accounts.	4	1	Petition	402	Claims	May 7, 1796	Adverse	......	Leave to withdraw.		
Dunscomb, Andrew	Balance due for services as commissioner of accounts.	4	2	Memorial	615	Claims	Jan. 16, 1797	Adverse.				
Dunscomb, Edward, by Mary, widow of.	Revolutionary pension	24	2	Memorial	44	Rev. Pensions	....	....	......	Discharged; laid on table.		
Dunscomb, Edward, by Mary, widow of.	Revolutionary pension	25	2	Petition	55	Rev. Pensions	....	....	......	Discharged; laid on table.		
Dunsmore, Robert	Invalid pension	23	2	Resolution	144	Invalid Pensions.						
Dunsmore, Robert	Invalid pension	28	2	Resolution	129, 216	Invalid Pensions.						
Dunton, William	Pension	2	1	Petition	477	....	....	....	......	Referred to Secretary War.		
Dunton, William	Pension	3	1	Report Secretary of War.	131	Select	May 26, 1794	Res. to refer to Sec. War.	J. R. 12	Passed	Passed	App'd June 9, 1794
Du Pasquier, Charles H., *et al.*	Grant of public lands	16	1	Petition	190	Public Lands	Mar. 3, 1820	Adverse.				
Dupee, Thomas	Compensation for services in revolutionary war.	2	1	Petition	500	....	....	....	......	Referred to Secretary War.		
Du Peron, Jean	Pension	14	1	House bill	622	Pens. & Rev. Cl'ms	April 11, 1816	Favorable; bill	171	Passed	Passed	App'd April 30, 1816
Dupey, Benjamin	(See Benjamin Depuy)	26	1	....	307							
Duplesses, Daniel F.	Confirmation of title to land	20	1	Petition	245	Priv. Land Claims.	....	....	......	Disch'd; laid on table.		
Dupont, Abraham	Payment for horse furnished for United States service.	25	2	Petition	397	Claims	833	Adverse	......	Laid on table.		
Dupont, Charles J.	(See M. A. Marquis and John B. Felicete, attorney of.)	20	1	....	728							
Dupont, Marie Jean	Confirmation of title to land in Alabama.	15	1	Petition	212	Priv. Land Claims.	....	....	......	Discharged; laid on table.		
Dupertail, Major General, heirs of, *et al.*	Bounty land for services in revolutionary war.	26	2	Petition	119	Priv. Land Claims.	....	....	......	Discharged; referred to Rev. Claims.		
Dupe tail, Major General, heirs of, *et al.*	Bounty land for services in revolutionary war.	27	2	Petition	62	Rev. Claims	14	Favorable; bill	55	Passed	Indef. postp'd.	Provided for in bill No. 26; approved July 27, 1842.
Dupre, Antoine	(See Baptiste Jeansonne, *et al.*)	22	2	....	42	....	60	....	701			
Dupre, Antoine	Confirmation of title to land in Louisiana.	29	1	Petition	487	Priv. Land Claims.						
Dupre, Antoine	Confirmation of title to land in Louisiana.	29	2	Petition	131	Priv. Land Claims.						
Dupre, Antoine	Confirmation of title to land in Louisiana.	30	1	Petition	239	Priv. Land Claims.						
Dupre, widow, heirs, and representatives of.	Compensation for damages to property in war of 1812.	21	1	Petition	75	Claims	73	Favorable; bill	105	Passed	Passed, with amendment.	App'd May 29, 1830
Duprey, John	Restoration of pension	27	3	Petition	499	Rev. Pensions.						
Dupuis, John B., assignee of.	Confirmation of title to land	19	2	Petition	49	Priv. Land Claims.	Jan. 12, 1827	Favorable; bill	375	Referred to Committee Whole House.		
Dupuis, John B., assignee of.	Confirmation of title to land	20	1	Petition	59	Priv. Land Claims.	55	Favorable; bill	56	Passed	Passed, with amendment.	App'd May 19, 1828

List of private claims presented to the House of Representatives of the United States from the 1st to the 31st Congress, inclusive—Continued.

Names of claimants.	Nature or object of the claim.	Congress.	Session.	How brought before the House of Reps.	Page of journal.	To what committee of the House referred.	No. or date of the report.	Nature of the report.	No. of the bill.	How disposed of by the House of Reps.	How disposed of by the Senate.	Date of the act of Congress, and remarks.
Dupuy, Daniel	(See Daniel Depuy.)	20	1		98							
Dupuy, Ebenezer	Extension of time to locate land	19	1	Petition	110	Public Lands				Discharged; laid on table.		
Dupuy, Peter	Amount and value of indent warrants, stock of United States.	9	2	Petition	480	Claims				Discharged; referred to Com. Whole House.		
Duran, Lewis	Confirmation of title to land	19	2	Letter and report	50	Public Lands	49	Favorable; bill.	378	Referred to Committee Whole House.		
Duran, Lewis	Confirmation of title to land	24	1	Docs. and report.	155	Priv. Land Claims.	93	Report		Ordered to be printed.		
Durand, Isaac	Pension	12	1	House bill	361	Whole House	June 8, 1812	With't amend.	138	Passed	Passed	App'd July 5, 1812
Durand, Isaac	Increase of pension	14	2	Letter from Sec. of War.	452	Pens. & Rev. Cl'ms.						
Durand, James R.	Arrears of pay as a seaman in U. S. service.	19	1	Petition	176	Naval Affairs	May 6, 1826	Adverse		Laid on table.		
Durand, James R.	Arrears of pay as a seaman in U. S. service.	19	2	Petition	133	Naval Affairs				Discharged.		
Durand, Marinus Francis.	Compensation for services as barrack master in U. S. army.	15	1	Petition	389					Referred to Secretary of War.		
Durand, Marinus Francis.	Settlement of claim for provisions, &c., furnished United States in war of 1812.	24	1	Petition	91	Claims.						
Durant, Elizabeth	(See Thomas Durant, widow of.)											
Durant, Lachlan	Confirmation of title to land in Alabama.	15	1	Petition	56	Priv. Land Claims.				Discharged; laid on table.		
Durant, Lachlan	Confirmation of title to land in Alabama.	21	2	Petition	211	Public Lands				Discharged; laid on table.		
Durant, Lachlan	Permission to sell lands in fee simple which he now holds for life, and which descends to his children.	20	2	Petition	206	Public Lands				Discharged; laid on table.		
Durant, Lachlan	Permission to sell lands in fee simple which he now holds for life, and which descends to his children.	21	1	Petition	100	Public Lands				Discharged; laid on table.		
Durant, Lachlan	Permission to sell lands in fee simple which he now holds for life, and which descends to his children.	21	2	Petition	47	Public Lands.						
Durant, Lachlan	Relinquishment of land by United States.	24	1	Resolution	440	Indian Affairs.						
Durant, Reuben	Arrears of pension	16	2	Petition	95	Pens. & Rev. Cl'ms.	Mar. 2, 1821	Adverse		Laid on table.		
Durant, Thomas, widow of	Revolutionary pension	25	2	Resolution	535	Rev. Pensions	881	Favorable; bill	787	Passed	Ref'd, & com. discharged.	
Durant, Thomas, widow of	Revolutionary pension	25	3	Documents	87	Rev. Pensions	32	Favorable; bill	932	Passed	Rejected.	
Durbanne, P. S. & W. A. Strong.	Permission to enter certain lands in Louisiana.	28	1	Petition	107	Priv. Land Claims.	148	Favorable	136	Passed	Passed	App'd June 17, 1844
Dure, Thomas, administrator of.	Arrears of pay for services in revolutionary war.	18	1	Petition	130	Claims				Discharged; referred to Pen. & Rev. Claims.		
Durell, John	Arrears of pension	14	1	House bill	622	Pens. & Rev. Cl'ms.	April 11, 1816	Favorable; bill ordered.	171	Passed	Passed	App'd April 30, 1816
Durell, William	To refund fine imposed under alien and sedition law.	28	1	Petition	754	Judiciary.						
Duret, Lewis, heirs of	Confirmation of title to land in Alabama.	15	1	Petition	212	Priv. Land Claims.	Feb. 18, 1818	Favorable; bill	92	Passed	Passed	App'd April 9, 1818

List of private claims presented to the House of Representatives of the United States from the 1st to the 31st Congress, inclusive—Continued.

Names of claimants.	Nature or object of the claim.	Congress.	Session.	How brought before the House of Reps.	Page of journal.	To what committee of the House referred.	No. or date of the report.	Nature of the report.	No. of the bill.	How disposed of by the House of Reps.	How disposed of by the Senate.	Date of the act of Congress, and remarks.
Duret, Lewis, heirs of....	United States to relinquish title, and that same be confirmed.	23	2	Petition	393	Priv. Land Claims.						
Duret, Lewis, heirs of....	United States to relinquish title, and that same be confirmed.	24	1	Petition	112	Priv. Land Claims.	Jan. 30, 1836	Favorable; bill	270	Referred to Committee Whole House.		
Duret, Lewis, heirs of....	United States to relinquish title, and that same be confirmed.	24	2	Rep't. Committee Whole House.	157	Priv. Land Claims.	Jan. 19, 1837	With amend..	270	Ref. to Com. Whole House on bill 576.		
Duret, Lewis, heirs of....	United States to relinquish title, and that same be confirmed.	26	1	Petition	369	Priv. Land Claims.	601	Favorable; bill	460	Referred to Committee Whole House.		
Duret, Lewis, heirs of....	United States to relinquish title, and that same be confirmed.	27	2	Petition	99	Public Lands.						
Durey, Francis, or Samuel	Remuneration for property taken by United States troops in 1816.	23	2	Petition	309	Claims.						
Durey, Francis, or Samuel	Remuneration for property taken by United States troops in 1816.	24	1	Petition	121	Claims	755	Adverse	......	Laid on table.		
Durfee, Benjamin	Restoration of pension..........	25	2	Resolution	465	Rev. Pensions	879	Favorable; bill	785	Passed	Passed	App'd July 7, 1839
Durfee, Earl............	Revolutionary pension	25	2	Petition	54	Rev. Pensions	....	....	......	Discharged; laid on table.		
Durfee, John	Compensation for services in revolutionary war.	22	1	Petition	29	Rev. Claims......	Jan. 3, 1832	Adverse	......	Laid on table.		
Durfee, Lieut. Col. Joseph.	Revolutionary pension..........	16	1	Petition	284	Rev. Pensions	April 22, 1820	Adverse	......	Laid on table.		
Durfee, Lieut. Col. Joseph.	Revolutionary pension..........	19	2	Petition	72	Military Pensions..	....	....	......	Discharged.		
Durfee, Lieut. Col. Joseph.	Revolutionary pension..........	20	1	Resolution	185	Military Pensions..	Mar. 11, 1828	Adverse	......	Laid on table.		
Durfee, Lieut. Col. Joseph.	Revolutionary pension..........	20	2	Petition	104	Military Pensions..	....	....	......	Discharged; laid on table.		
Durfee, Lieut. Col. Joseph.	Revolutionary pension..........	21	1	Petition	144	Military Pensions..	....	....	......	Discharged; laid on table.		
Durfee, Lieut. Col. Joseph.	Revolutionary pension..........	21	2	Petition	43	Military Pensions.						
Durfee, Lieut. Col. Joseph.	Revolutionary pension..........	22	1	Petition	51	Rev. Pensions	370	Favorable; bill	465	Referred to Committee Whole House.		
Durham, Hannibal.......	Compensation for horse lost in service of United States.	25	2	Documents.....	541	Claims.						
Durham, Hannibal.......	Compensation for horse lost in service of United States.	25	3	Documents.....	207	Claims.						
Durham, Isaac B........	Invalid pension................	30	1	Petition	423	Invalid Pensions.						
Durham, Martin.........	Revolutionary pension..........	21	2	Petition	300	Military Pensions.						
Durham, Martin.........	Revolutionary pension..........	24	2	Memorial	75	Rev. Pensions	....	....	......	Discharged; laid on table.		
Durham, Thomas, and J. Blackstone.	Relinquishment of interest of United States in certain Indian reservations.	26	2	Senate bill	229	Indian Affairs.....	Feb. 12, 1841	With't amend.	S. 157	Passed	Concurred in..	App'd Feb. 18, 1841
Durkee, Benjamin.......	Commutation pay for services in revolutionary war.	24	1	Resolution	285	Rev. Claims.						
Durkee, Benjamin.......	Commutation pay for services in revolutionary war.	24	2	Resolution	73	Rev. Claims......	Dec. 30, 1837	Adverse	......	Laid on table.		
Durkee, Chauncey.......	Pre-emption right to land	26	1	Petition	363	Public Lands.						
Durkee, Daniel	Revolutionary pension..........	22	1	Petition	441	Rev. Pensions	....	....	......	Discharged; laid on table.		
Durkee, Henry..........	Remuneration for losses sustained in supplying United States army with beef.	27	2	Petition	246	Claims	181	Adverse	......	Laid on table.		
Durkee, Henry..........	Remuneration for losses sustained in supplying United States army with beef.	28	1	Petition	645	Claims.						

List of private claims presented to the House of Representatives of the United States from the 1st to the 31st Congress, inclusive—Continued.

Names of claimants.	Nature or object of the claim.	Congress.	Session.	How brought before the House of Reps.	Page of journal.	To what committee of the House referred.	No. or date of the report.	Nature of the report.	No. of the bill.	How disposed of by the House of Reps.	How disposed of by the Senate.	Date of the act of Congress, and remarks.
Durkee, Col. John, representatives of.	Seven years' half-pay, with interest	12	1	Petition	183	Claims	Mar. 30, 1812	Favorable; bill	94	Passed	Passed	App'd July 1, 1812
Durkee, Nathan	Revolutionary pension	20	2	Petition	319	Military Pensions				Discharged; laid on table.		
Durkee, Nathan	Revolutionary pension	21	1	Petition	37	Military Pensions				Discharged; laid on table.		
Durkee, Nathan	Revolutionary pension	21	2	Petition	106	Military Pensions.						
Durkee, Nathan	Revolutionary pension	22	1	Petition	90	Rev. Pensions	168	Favorable; bill	244	Referred to Committee Whole House.		
Durkee, Nathan	Revolutionary pension	22	2	House bill	123					Laid on table.		
Durkee, Robert, heirs of	Commutation of half-pay	11	1	Memorial	60	Claims.						
Durkee, Robert, heirs of	Commutation of half-pay	11	2	Memorial	266	Claims	Mar. 14, 1810	Adverse.				
Durnell, John	Pension	5	2	Petition	240	Claims	April 17, 1798	Adverse		Laid on table.		
Durnell, John	Pension	5	3	Petition	432	Whole House.						
Durnell, John	Pension	8	1	Petition	482	Claims	Mar. 13, 1804	Report		Postponed.		
Durnell, John	Pension	10	1	House bill	232	Whole House	May 19, 1808	General bill	78	Passed	Passed	App'd Feb. 25, 1808
Durnell, John, representative of.	Pension	27	3	Petition	260	Rev. Pensions				Discharged; leave to withdraw.		
Durnell, John, representative of.	Pension	29	1	Petition	766	Rev. Pensions	826	Adverse		Laid on table.		
Durnell, John, representative of.	Pension	29	2	Petition	93	Rev. Pensions.						
Durnell, John, representative of.	Pension	30	1	Petition	406	Rev. Claims				Discharged; laid on table.		
Durrive, Frederick	Confirmation of title to lands in Louisiana.	29	1	Petition	913	Priv. Land Claims.						
Durrive, Frederick	Confirmation of title to land in Louisiana.	29	2	Report of Com. on Priv. Land Claims.	193	Whole House	Jan. 20, 1847	By bill	616	Referred to Committee Whole House.		
Durrive, Frederick	Confirmation of title to land in Louisiana.	30	1	Petition	103	Priv. Land Claims.	178	Favorable; bill	188	Passed	Passed	App'd Aug. 14, 1848
Durrive, Frederick	Relief from effect of proviso in act August 14, 1848.	31	1	Report and bill	727	Whole House	196	By bill	202	Referred to Committee Whole House.		
Durrive, Frederick	Relief from effect of provison in act August 14, 1848.	31	2	Rep't Committee Whole House.	181	Whole House	Jan. 24, 1851	By bill	202	Passed	Passed	App'd Feb. 14, 1851
Duryea, Ann	Pension	28	2	Petition	113	Rev. Pensions				Discharged; laid on table.		
Duryee, Charles H	Pay and rations during suspension from navy.	24	1	Memorial	61	Naval Affairs	177	Adverse		Laid on table.		
Duryee, Richard, *et al.*	Increase of salary as clerks in office of the Commissioner of Loans, New York.	4	1	Petition	441	Select.						
Dusenbury, L. B	Certain credits be passed to his account.	27	2	Petition	699	Ways and Means.						
Dusenbury, L. B	Certain credits be passed to his account.	27	3	Petition	258	Ways and Means.						
Dusenbury, Moses	Revolutionary pension	24	1	Petition	56	Rev. Pensions				Discharged; laid on table.		
Dusenbury, Moses	Revolutionary pension	25	3	Petition	127	Rev. Pensions				Discharged.		
Dusenbury, Moses	Revolutionary pension	26	1	Petition	173	Rev. Pensions.						
Dusenbury, Nancy	(See John Paulding, daughter of.)	28	1		272							
Dusseau, Joseph	Invalid pension for services in war of 1812.	29	1	Petition	373	Invalid Pensions	470	Favorable; bill	348	Passed	Passed	App'd Aug. 8, 1846

List of private claims presented to the House of Representatives of the United States from the 1st to the 31st Congress, inclusive—Continued.

71

Names of claimants.	Nature or object of the claim.	Congress.	Session.	How brought before the House of Reps.	Page of journal.	To what committee of the House referred.	No. or date of the report.	Nature of the report.	No. of the bill.	How disposed of by the House of Reps.	How disposed of by the Senate.	Date of the act of Congress, and remarks.
Dustin, Caleb	Indemnity for depreciation of money received by an ancestor for revolutionary services.	31	1	Petition	361	Rev. Pensions				Discharged; laid on table.		
Dustin, Cynthia	(See Oliver Parish, heirs of.)	24	2		161							
Dutaillis, Joseph, representatives of.	To confirm location of New Madrid certificates.	30	1	Senate bill	957	Public Lands	July 12, 1848	With't amend.	S. 157	Passed		App'd July 17, 1848
Dutill, John	Pension for services in revolutionary war.	10	2	Petition	358	Claims				Discharged; referred to Select Committee.		
Dutill, John	Pension for service in revolutionary war.	11	1	Petition	42	Claims.						
Dutill, John	Pension for services in revolutionary war.	11	2	Petition	147	Claims	Jan. 26, 1810	Adverse.				
Dutton, Ephraim	Revolutionary pension	22	1	Resolution	160	Rev. Pensions.				Discharged; laid on table.		
Dutton, James, heirs of	Permission to correct error in entry of land.	24	2	Senate bill	579	Whole House			S. 159			
Dutton, James, heirs of	Permission to correct error in entry of land.	25	2	Senate bill	745	Public Lands	May 11, 1838	With't amend.	S. 80	Referred to Committee Whole House.		
Dutton, James, heirs of	Permission to correct error in entry of land.	26	1	Senate bill	799	Priv. Land Claims.			S. 81			
Dutton, Jonas	Pension for services in war of 1812.	27	2	Petition	670	Invalid Pensions.						
Dutton, Jonas	Pension for services in war of 1812.	28	1	Petition	633	Invalid Pensions.						
Dutton, Jonas	Pension for services in war of 1812.	28	2	Petition	221	Invalid Pensions.						
Dutton, Jonas	Pension for services in war of 1812.	29	1	Petition	101	Invalid Pensions.				Discharged; laid on table.		
Dutton, Jonas	Pension for services in war of 1812.	30	1	Petition	394	Invalid Pensions	578	Adverse		Laid on table.		
Dutton, Joseph L.	Indemnity for property destroyed by United States troops.	15	2	Petition	117	Claims				Discharged; laid on table.		
Dutton, Joseph L.	Indemnity for property destroyed by United States troops.	16	1	Petition	136	Claims	Jan. 14, 1820	Adverse		Laid on table.		
Dutton, Joseph L.	Indemnity for property destroyed by United States troops.	16	2	Petition	119	Claims				Discharged; laid on table.		
Dutton, Joseph L.	Indemnity for property destroyed by United States troops.	17	1	Petition	201	Claims	April 5, 1822	Favorable; bill	154	Passed	Indef. postp'd.	
Dutton, Joseph L.	Indemnity for property destroyed by United States troops.	17	2	Senate bill	174	Claims	Jan. 31, 1823	With't amend.	S. 27	Passed		App'd March 3, 1823
Du Val, Ann F.	(See John Tebbs, heirs of)	22	2		88							
Duvall, Benjamin, (of Elisha.)	Pension	20	2	Petition	262	Military Pensions				Discharged; laid on table.		
Du Val, Captain Daniel, widow and heirs of.	Commutation pay for services in revolutionary war.	22	1	Petition	190	Rev. Claims				Discharged; laid on table.		
Du Val, Captain Daniel, widow and heirs of.	Commutation pay for services in revolutionary war.	22	2	Petition	54	Rev. Claims.						
Du Val, Captain Daniel, widow and heirs of.	Commutation pay for services in revolutionary war.	23	1	Petition	70, 110	Rev. Claims.						
Du Val, Captain Daniel, widow and heirs of.	Commutation pay for services in revolutionary war.	23	2	Petition	48	Rev. Claims.						
Du Val, Captain Daniel, widow and heirs of.	Commutation pay for services in revolutionary war.	24	1	Petition	275	Rev. Claims.						
Du Val, Captain Daniel, widow and heirs of.	Commutation pay for services in revolutionary war.	24	2	Petition	216	Rev. Claims.						
Du Val, Captain Daniel, widow and heirs of.	Commutation pay for services in revolutionary war.	25	2	Senate bill	610	Rev. Claims	April 6, 1838	With't amend.	S. 143	Passed		App'd June 13, 1838

List of private claims presented to the House of Representatives of the United States from the 1*st to the* 31*st Congress, inclusive*—Continued.

Names of claimants.	Nature or object of the claim.	Congress.	Session.	How brought before the House of Reps.	Page of journal.	To what committee of the House referred.	No. or date of the report.	Nature of the report.	No. of the bill.	How disposed of by the House of Reps.	How disposed of by the Senate.	Date of the act of Congress, and remarks.
Duval, Edward W., administrator of.	Settlement of accounts as Indian agent.	24	1	Petition	206	Claims	685	Favorable; bill	646	Referred to Committee Whole House.		
Duval, Edward W., administrator of.	Settlement of accounts as Indian agent.	25	2	Petition	36	Claims	47	Favorable; bill	59	Passed	Passed	App'd Feb. 15, 1838
Duval, Edward W., heirs of	Confirmation of title to land	27	2	Petition	106	Priv. Land Claims.	1034	Adverse	......	Laid on table.		
Duval, Edward W., heirs of	Confirmation of title to land	27	3	Petition	71	Priv. Land Claims.	281	Adverse	......	Laid on table.		
Duval, Edward W., heirs of	Confirmation of title to land	28	1	Petition	107	Priv. Land Claims.	....	....	......	Discharged; laid on table.		
Duval, Ellen	(See Edward W. Duval, heirs of)	27	2	....	106	....	1034					
Duval, Etienne	Confirmation of title to land	20	1	Resolution	28	Public Lands	42	Favorable; bill	34	Passed	Passed	App'd April 22, 1828
Duval, George, representatives of, *et al.*	Indemnity for depredations committed on property.	25	2	Senate bill	65	Indian Affairs	824	Adverse	S. 207	Referred to Committee Whole House on S. bill No. 85.		
Duval, George, representatives of, *et al.*	Indemnity for depredations committed on property.	26	1	Senate bill	837	Indian Affairs	....	....	S. 297			
Duval, George, representatives of, *et al.*	Indemnity for depredations committed on property.	28	1	Senate bill	868	Indian Affairs	....	....	S. 93			
Duval, George, representatives of, *et al.*	Indemnity for depredations committed on property.	28	2	Senate bill	430	Indian Affairs	....	....	S. 93			
Duval, George, representatives of, *et al.*	Indemnity for depredations committed on property.	29	1	Senate bill	401	Indian Affairs	March 5, 1846	With't amend.	S. 40	Passed	....	App'd June 6, 1846
Duval, George, representatives of, *et al.*	To correct clerical error in act of June 6, 1846.	29	1	S. joint resolut'n.	936	Whole House	Jan. 10, 1846	With't amend.	J. R. 27	Passed	....	App'd June 19, 1846
Du Val, John P., *et al.*	(See Thomas Tebbs, heirs of)	23	1	....	110							
Duval, Mareen, (Ohio)	Reimbursement for expenses for camp equipage, &c	18	1	Petition	130	Claims	49	Favorable; bill	97	Passed	Passed	App'd May 18, 1824
Duvall, William, representatives of.	Permission to locate certain lands.	27	2	Petition	253	Priv. Land Claims.						
Duvall, William, representatives of.	Permission to locate certain lands.	28	1	Petition	891	Priv. Land Claims.						
Duval, William, P.	Amount of judgment against United States, in Florida.	28	1	Petition	261	Judiciary	Mar. 27, 1844	Favorable; bill	266	Passed	Passed	App'd June 17, 1844
Duval, William, and Peter A. Carnes.	Indemnity for unlawful seizure of goods.	21	2	Senate bill	217	Claims	74	With't amend.	S. 93	Passed	Passed	App'd March 3, 1831
Duvant, Edward, heirs of.	Indemnity for French spoliations prior to 1800.	31	1	Petition	270	Foreign Affairs	355	Favorable; bill	318	Referred to Committee Whole House.		
Duverge, Berthelemy	Compensation for property used by United States troops at New Orleans.	14	2	Petition	299	Claims	Feb. 12, 1817	Favorable; bill	129	Passed	Indef. postp'd.	
Duverge, Berthelemy	Compensation for property used by United States troops at New Orleans.	15	1	Petition	72	Claims.						
Duverge, Berthelemy	Compensation for property used by United States troops at New Orleans.	15	2	Senate bill	325	Claims	141	Joint report	S. 70	Referred to Committee Whole House.		
Duverge, Berthelemy	Compensation for property used by United States troops at New Orleans.	16	1	Senate bill	269	Claims	....	....	S. 45			
Duverge, Berthelemy	Compensation for property used by United States troops at New Orleans,	16	2	Petition	102	Claims	Jan. 17, 1821	Favorable; bill	206	Passed	Passed	App'd March 2, 1821
Dwiggins, John, assignee of.	Compensation for land purchased of Tennessee Land Company.	25	2	Petition	543	Priv. Land Claims.						

List of private claims presented to the House of Representatives of the United States from the 1st to the 31st Congress, inclusive—Continued.

Names of claimants.	Nature or object of the claim.	Congress.	Session.	How brought before the House of Reps.	Page of journal.	To what committee of the House referred.	No. or date of the report.	Nature of the report.	No. of the bill.	How disposed of by the House of Reps.	How disposed of by the Senate.	Date of the act of Congress, and remarks.
Dwiggins, John, assignee of.	Compensation for land purchased of Tennessee Land Company.	25	3	Petition	223	Priv. Land Claims.						
Dwiggins, John, assignee of.	Compensation for land purchased of Tennessee Land Company.	28	2	Petition	308	Priv. Land Claims.						
Dwight, Edmund and Jonathan.	Remission of duties paid on steel in 1814.	14	2	Resolution	126	Ways and Means.	....	....	......	Discharged; laid on table.		
Dwight, Henry	Compensation for damages done to carriage.	14	1	Petition	58	Claims	Feb. 24, 1816	Adverse.				
Dwight, John and Sullivan	Renewal of patent to saw and polish stone.	22	2	Petition	215	Judiciary.						
Dwight, John and Sullivan	Renewal of patent to saw and polish stone.	23	1	Petition	58	Patents..........	....	....	......	Discharged; laid on table.		
Dwight, Theodore, *et al.* .	Remission of duties on printing machine.	19	1	Petition	221	Ways and Means..	May 10, 1826	Favorable; bill	264	Referred to Committee Whole House.		
Dwight, William........	Confirmation of title to certain lands.	27	3	Petition	77	Public Lands.....	6	Favorable; bill	625	Passed	Passed with amendment.	App'd March 3, 1843
Dwinnell, Benjamin, *et al.*	(See Clark Wilson, assignees of)	28	2	....	135							
Dye, Jonathan, heirs of ..	Commutation pay for services in Virginia line.	24	1	Documents.....	739	Rev. Claims.						
Dye, Jonathan, heirs of ..	Commutation pay for services in Virginia line.	25	2	Petition	546	Rev. Claims.......	758	Favorable; bill.	717	Passed	Rejected.	
Dye, Jonathan, heirs of ..	Commutation pay for services in Virginia line.	25	3	Petition	84	Rev. Claims......	52	Favorable; bill.	941	Referred to Committee Whole House.		
Dye, Jonathan, heirs of ..	Commutation pay for services in Virginia line.	26	1	Petition	164	Rev. Claims......	91	Favorable; bill	86	Engrossed.		
Dye, Jonathan, heirs of ..	Commutation pay for services in Virginia line.	26	2	Petition	35	Rev. Claims......	2	Favorable; bill	538	Referred to Committee Whole House.		
Dye, Jonathan, heirs of ..	Commutation pay for services in Virginia line.	27	2	Petition	61	Rev. Claims......	82	Favorable, bill	122	Referred to Committee Whole House.	....	See report of Judiciary, page 859 journal.
Dye, Jonathan, heirs of ..	Commutation pay for services in Virginia line.	29	1	Petition	179	Rev. Claims......	91	Favorable; bill	110	Rejected.		
Dye, Jonathan, heirs of ..	Commutation pay for services in Virginia line.	30	1	Petition	110	Rev. Claims......	674	Favorable; bill	538	Referred to Committee Whole House.		
Dye, Jonathan, heirs of ..	Commutation pay for services in Virginia line.	30	2	Rep't Committee Whole House.	319	Whole House.....	Jan. 26, 1849	By bill	538	Passed	Ref. to Com. Rev. Claims.	
Dye, Jonathan, heirs of ..	Commutation pay for services in Virginia line.	31	1	Petition	270	Rev. Claims.						
Dyer, Atkins............	To refund certain tonnage duties .	30	1	Petition	459	Commerce	378	Adverse	......	Laid on table.		
Dyer, Atkins	To refund certain tonnage duties .	30	2	Petition	281	Commerce	....	....	......	Disch'd; laid on table.		
Dyer, Atkins	To refund certain tonnage duties .	31	1	Petition	408	Commerce.						
Dyer & Blake	Reimbursement of excise duties ..	24	1	Memorial	382	Ways and Means..	Mar. 3, 1836	Favorable; bill	399	Referred to Committee Whole House.		
Dyer, Ebenezer, daughter of.	Compensation for services rendered and advances made in revolutionary war.	30	1	Petition	236	Rev. Pensions.						
Dyer, Capt. Edward, representative of.	Revolutionary pension..........	28	2	Petition	104	Rev. Pensions	Feb. 15, 1845	Adverse	......	Laid on table.		
Dyer, Capt. Edward, representative of.	Revolutionary pension..........	29	1	Petition	524	Rev. Pensions	....	....	......	Discharged; laid on table.		
Dyer, George, jr., *et al.* ..	Fishing bounty on schooner Three Brothers.	24	2	Petition	125	Commerce	136	Favorable; bill	865	Referred to Committee Whole House.		
Dyer, George, jr., *et al.* ...	Fishing bounty on schooner Three Brothers.	25	2	Petition	41	Commerce	84	Favorable; bill.	100	Passed	Indef. postp'd.	

List of private claims presented to the House of Representatives of the United States from the 1st to the 31st Congress, inclusive—Continued.

Names of claimants.	Nature or object of the claim.	Congress.	Session.	How brought before the House of Reps.	Page of journal.	To what committee of the House referred.	No. or date of the report.	Nature of the report.	No. of the bill.	How disposed of by the House of Reps.	How disposed of by the Senate.	Date of the act of Congress, and remarks.
Dyer, George, jr., *et al*....	Fishing bounty on schooner Three Brothers.	26	1	Petition	176	Commerce	73	Favorable; bill.	60	Passed	Indef. postp'd.	
Dyer, George, jr., *et al*....	Fishing bounty on schooner Three Brothers.	27	2	Petition	471	Commerce........	April 12, 1842	Favorable; bill	391	Referred to Committee Whole House.		
Dyer, George, jr., *et al*....	Fishing bounty on schooner Three Brothers.	27	3	Rep't Committee Whole House.	88	Whole House.....	....	By bill......	391	Passed	Indef. postp'd.	
Dyer, Horatio...........	(See Capt. Charles Smith, representative of.)	30	1	....	263							
Dyer, Joel Henry........	Compensation for services as judge advocate in Florida war.	25	3	Memorial	122	Military Affairs....	230	Adverse	......	Laid on table.		
Dyer, Joel Henry........	Compensation for services as judge advocate in Florida war.	31	1	Petition	224	Military Affairs ...	381	Favorable; bill	329	Referred to Committee Whole House.		
Dyer, Joel Henry........	Compensation for services as judge advocate in Florida war.	31	2	Rep. Committee Whole House.	194	Whole House.....	....	By bill......	329			
Dyer, Jonathan	Invalid pension	3	2	Rep. of Secretary War.	350	Claims	Mar. 3, 1795	Res. to refer to Sec. War.	......	Adopted.		
Dyer, Jonathan	Invalid pension	4	1	Res. and docs...	373	Claims..........	Mar. 4, 1796	Res. to refer to Sec. War.	J. R. 16	Passed	Passed	App'd April 20, 1796
Dyer, Jonathan	Invalid pension	4	2	Res. and docs...	614	Claims...........	Feb. 6, 1797	Favorable; bill	224	Passed	Indef. postp'd.	
Dyer, Jonathan	Invalid pension................	5	2	House bill......	127	Whole House	Jan. 11, 1798	With't amend.	38	Passed	Passed	App'd Feb. 2, 1798
Dyer, Miriam...........	(See Robert Dyer, widow of)....	27	1	....	101							
Dyer, Patsey, *et al*	Confirmation of title to land in Mississippi.	14	1	Petition	114	Public Lands.						
Dyer, Patsey, *et al*	Confirmation of title to land in Mississippi.	14	2	Petition	81	Public Lands.						
Dyer, Patsey, *et al*	Confirmation of title to land in Mississippi.	15	1	Petition	56	Priv. Land Claims.						
Dyer, Robert H., *et al*....	Compensation for horses and other property lost in Seminole war.	16	2	Petition	165	Whole House.						
Dyer, Robert Henry, heirs of.	Invalid pension................	31	1	Petition	223	Invalid Pensions.						
Dyer, Robert, widow of...	Revolutionary pension..........	27	1	Petition	101	Rev. Pensions.						
Dyer, Robert, widow of...	Revolutionary pension..........	27	2	Petition	58	Rev. Pensions....	....	....	......	Discharged; laid on table.		
Dyer, Thomas..........	Payment for property lost by destruction of United States ship John Adams.	25	2	Petition	326	Naval Affairs.						
Dyer, Thomas..........	Payment for property lost by destruction of United States ship John Adams.	25	3	Petition	91	Naval Affairs.						
Dyer, Thomas..........	Payment for property lost by destruction of United States ship John Adams.	26	1	Petition	180	Naval Affairs.						
Dyer, Walter...........	Invalid pension................	23	2	Petition	376	Invalid Pensions.						
Dyer, Walter...........	Invalid pension................	24	1	Petition	98	Invalid Pensions ..	408	Favorable; bill	419	Passed	Passed	App'd June 28, 1836
Dyer, William B........	Relief and confirmation of title to lot in Washington city.	17	2	Petition	65	....	....	....	......	Leave to withdraw.		
Dygert, Dennis	Invalid pension................	26	1	Petition and docs.	287	Invalid Pensions...	361	Favorable; bill	340	Referred to Committee Whole House.		
Dygert, Dennis	Invalid pension................	27	2	Petition	60	Invalid Pensions ..	254	Favorable; bill	220	Passed	Passed with amendment.	App'd Aug. 27, 1842
Dygert, Dennis	Arrears of pension.............	28	1	Petition	287	Invalid Pensions ..	110	Adverse	......	Laid on table.		
Dygert, Dennis	Arrears of pension.............	29	1	Petition	59	Invalid Pensions ..	77	Adverse	......	Laid on table.		

List of private claims presented to the House of Representatives of the United States from the 1st to the 31st Congress, inclusive—Continued.

Names of claimants.	Nature or object of the claim.	Congress.	Session.	How brought before the House of Reps.	Page of journal.	To what committee of the House referred.	No. or date of the report.	Nature of the report.	No. of the bill.	How disposed of by the House of Reps.	How disposed of by the Senate.	Date of the act of Congress, and remarks.
Dygert, Dennis	Arrears of pension	31	1	Petition	417	Invalid Pensions.						
Dygert, Honjost, *et al.*	Pension for services of their father.	3	1	Petition and rep't Sec. of War.	89	Select				Laid on table.		
Dygert, Peter, heirs of	Payment of evidences of public debt, revolutionary war.	20	1	Petition	440	Rev. Claims.						
Dygert, Peter, heirs of	Payment of evidences of public debt, revolutionary war.	22	1	Petition	442	Rev. Claims.						
Dygert, Peter, heirs of	Payment of evidences of public debt, revolutionary war.	23	1	Petition	242	Rev. Claims.						
Dygert, Peter, heirs of	Payment of evidences of public debt, revolutionary war.	24	1	Petition	137	Rev. Claims.						
Dygert, Peter, heirs of	Payment of evidences of public debt, revolutionary war.	29	1	Petition	209	Rev. Claims	405	Adverse		Laid on table.		
Dygert, Peter, heirs of	Payment of evidences of public debt, revolutionary war.	31	1	Rep't Committee.	834	Rev. Claims	274	Adverse		Laid on table.		
Dygert, Peter, heirs of	Payment of evidences of public debt, revolutionary war.	31	2	Petition	174	Rev. Claims	9	Adverse		Laid on table.		
Dykes, James	(See John Patton & James Dykes)	26	1		182		343		319			
Dysart, James	Pension	9	2	House bill	608	Whole House	Feb. 28, 1807	Favorable; bill	216	Passed	Passed	App'd March 3, 1807
Dysart, Col. James, heirs of	Revolutionary pension	22	1	Petition	52	Rev. Pensions				Discharged; laid on table.		
Dysart, Col. James, heirs of	Revolutionary pension	31	1	Petition	1245	Rev. Pensions.						
Dysart, Col. James, heirs of	Revolutionary pension	31	2	Petition	431	Rev. Pensions	55	Adverse		Laid on table.		Leave to withdraw.
Dyson, Lucinda, *et al.*	(See Hatch Dent, heirs of)	23	2		165							
Dyson, Leonard, & others.	Confirmation of title to land	19	1	Report of register and receiver of land office.	64	Public Lands	33	Adverse		Recommitted.		
Dyson, Leonard, & others.	Confirmation of title to land	19	1	Rep't Committee.	516	Public Lands	May 5, 1826	By bill	254	Referred to Committee Whole House.		
Eadus, William	Indemnity for property destroyed by the enemy.	15	1	Document	34	Claims	Feb. 17, 1818	Adverse		Laid on table.		
Eadus, William	Indemnity for property destroyed by the enemy.	16	1	Petition	160	Claims	Jan. 28, 1820	Adverse		Laid on table.		
Eadus, William	Indemnity for property destroyed by the enemy.	22	1	Petition	188	Claims	414	Adverse		Referred to Committee Whole House.		
Eadus, William	Indemnity for property destroyed by the enemy.	22	2	Petition	82	Claims	45	Adverse		Referred to Committee Whole House.		
Eadus, William	Indemnity for property destroyed by the enemy.	23	1	Petition	33	Claims	343	Adverse		Referred to Committee Whole House.		
Eadus, William	Indemnity for property destroyed by the enemy.	23	2	Rept. of last sess.	142	Claims.						
Eadus, William	Indemnity for property destroyed by the enemy.	24	1	Petition and doc.	284	Claims	673	Favorable	632	Referred to Committee Whole House.		
Eadus, William	Indemnity for property destroyed by the enemy.	25	2	Petition	36	Claims	44	Favorable	56	Passed	Passed	App'd April 6, 1838
Eagan, Thomas	Pension	4	1	Petition	445	Claims	Feb. 18, 1796	Pension bill	156	Passed	Passed	App'd April 20, 1[illegible]

List of private claims presented to the House of Representatives of the United States from the 1st to the 31st Congress, inclusive—Continued.

Names of claimants.	Nature or object of the claim.	Congress.	Session.	How brought before the House of Reps.	Page of journal.	To what committee of the House referred.	No. or date of the report.	Nature of the report.	No. of the bill.	How disposed of by the House of Reps.	How disposed of by the Senate.	Date of the act of Congress, and remarks.
Eagle, Henry	(See John Grant, jr., and others)	22	1		97							
Eaker, Joseph, attorney of	Compensation for services as hospital surgeon.	2	1	Petition	458					Referred to Secretary Treasury.		
Eaker, Joseph, attorney of	Compensation for services as hospital surgeon.	3	1	Rep. of Secretary Treasury.	78					Laid on table.		
Eaker, Joseph, attorney of	Compensation for services as hos pital surgeon.	7	1	Petition	12	Claims	Dec. 14, 1801	Adverse		Rejected.		
Eames, Charles	Extra compensation as commissioner to Sandwich islands.	31	1	Appropriation bill								See Statutes at Large, vol. 9, p. 536.
Eames, Josiah	(See William Baker, &c.)	22	1		288		480					
Eames, Thomas	Indemnity for seizure of cattle by revenue officers.	16	2	Petition	77	Ways and Means				Discharged; leave to withdraw.		
Eames, Thomas	Indemnity for seizure of cattle by revenue officers.	17	1	Petition	293	Judiciary	99	Adverse		Referred to Committee Whole House.		
Eames, Thomas	Indemnity for seizure of cattle by revenue officers.	17	2	Rept. of last sess.	168	Judiciary	18	Adverse		Laid on table.		
Eames, Thomas	Indemnity for seizure of cattle by revenue officers.	19	1	Petition	443	Judiciary						
				Documents	467	Judiciary				Discharged; laid on table.		
Eames, Thomas	Indemnity for seizure of cattle by revenue officers.	19	2	Petition	63	Judiciary				Discharged.		
Eames, Thomas	Indemnity for seizure of cattle by revenue officers.	20	2	Petitions	99	Ways and Means				Discharged.		
Earll, Aaron	Pension	21	2	Petition	68	Military Pensions.						
Earle, Abigail	(See Charles Howard, and others)	2	1		492							
Earle, Caleb, & J. Keen	Indemnity for vessel, &c., captured by enemy.	14	1	Petition	40	Claims	Dec. 21, 1815	Adverse		Rejected.		
Earle, Caleb, widow of	Indemnity for vessel, &c., captured by enemy.	22	1	Petition	512	Ways and Means				Discharged; laid on table.		
				Documents	672	Naval Affairs.						
Earl, Daniel, jr.	(See Canadian refugees)	4	2		614							
Earle, Col. Elias	Reimbursement of outlay in arming Cherokees.	14	2	Rep. of committee	496		101	To refer to Attorney Gen.		Laid on table.		
Earle, Col. Elias	Reimbursement of outlay in arming Cherokees.	15	1	Rept. and docs.	52	Exp. of War Dep't	43	Stat'nt of facts		Laid on table.		
Earle, Elias	(See sureties of Adam Carruth)	17	2		225							
Earle, James	Confirmation of title to land	15	1	Petition	56	Priv. Land Claims.						
Earles, James	(See heirs of William Tarvin)	18	1		105							
Earl, John, jr., and others.	Bounty on fishing schooner Abigail	9	1	Petition	195	Com. and Manuf.	Feb. 17, 1806	Adverse		Leave to withdraw.		
Earl, John, jr., and others.	Bounty on fishing schooner Abigail	10	1	Petition	212	Com. and Manuf.						
Ea le, Jonathan, and others	Permission to import card wire	12	1	Petition	137	Whole House		General bill	46	Referred to Committee Whole House.		
Earles, Joseph	Pension for revolutionary services.	25	2	Petition	180	Rev. Pensions				Discharged; laid on table.		
Earle, Samuel	Indemnity for depreciation in Continental money.	25	3	Resolution	175	Rev. Claims				Discharged.		
Earle, Samuel	Indemnity for depreciation in Continental money.	26	1	Petition	166	Rev. Claims.						
Earle, Samuel	Indemnity for depreciation in Continental money.	27	2	Petition	61	Rev. Claims	942	Adverse		Laid on table.		
Earle, Samuel	Indemnity for depreciation in Continental money.	28	1	Petition	432	Rev. Claims.						

List of private claims presented to the House of Representatives of the United States from the 1st to the 31st Congress, inclusive—Continued.

Names of claimants.	Nature or object of the claim.	Congress.	Session.	How brought before the House of Reps.	Page of journal.	To what committee of the House referred.	No. or date of the report.	Nature of the report.	No. of the bill.	How disposed of by the House of Reps.	How disposed of by the Senate.	Date of the act of Congress, and remarks.
Earle, William, or Willard	Renewal of a patent for shingle mill.	24	2	Petition	121	Judiciary.						
Earl, William	Prize-money for captures on board frigate Alliance.	15	1	Petition	286	Naval Affairs.						
Earl, William	Increase of pension	15	1	Petition	187	Select				Discharged.		
Earl, William Nichols	Release from a certain judgment	17	1	Petition	152	Judiciary	Jan. 28, 1822	Favorable	58	Passed	Indef. postp'd.	
Earl, William Nichols	Release from a certain judgment	17	2	Petition	150	Judiciary	Jan. 28, 1823	Favorable	255	Referred to Committee Whole House.		
Earl, William Nichols	Release from a certain judgment	18	1	Petition	132	Judiciary	Jan. 16, 1824	Favorable	61	Passed	Passed	App'd May 17, 1824
Early, Eleazer	Indemnity for abrogation of mail contract.	24	2	Memorial	80	Claims				Discharged.		
Early, Eleazer	Indemnity for abrogation of mail contract.	25	2	Petition	176	Claims				Discharged.		
Early, Eleazer, administrator of.	Indemnity for abrogation of mail contract.	27	2	Petition	246	Claims.						
Early, Peter	Additional allowance for work on national road.	20	2	Petition	320	Claims.						
Early, Peter	Additional allowance for work on national road.	23	1	Resolution	589	Claims	455	Adverse				See Report No. 449.
Early, Samuel	Pension	20	2	Petition	204	Military Pensions				Discharged; laid on table.		
Early, Simeon	Pension	25	2	Petition	54	Rev. Pensions				Discharged; laid on table.		
Earnest, Charles, widow of	Pension to a mute son	15	1	Petition	156	Rev. Claims.						
Earnest, Charles, widow of	Pension to a mute son	15	2	Pension bill	41	Whole House	Feb. 27, 1819	With't amend.	203	Passed	Passed	App'd March 3, 1819
Earnest, Frederick	(See Frederick Ernest)	15	1		107							
Earnest, Peter	(See Wm. H. Bedford, agent)	28	1		262							
Earnest, William	(See widow of Charles Earnest)	15	1		156							
Earp, Leonard	Pension	24	1	Resolution	951	Invalid Pensions				Discharged; laid on table.		
Earwood, Joel	Exchange of location of land	15	1	Resolution	30	Public Lands	Dec. 17, 1817	Favorable	12	Passed	Passed, with amendment.	App'd Jan. 22, 1818
Easby, William	Compensation for launching frigate Potomac.	24	1	Petition	433	Naval Affairs.	Mar. 21, 1836	Favorable	433	Referred to Committee Whole House.		
Easby, William	Compensation for launching frigate Potomac.	25	2	Petition	....	Naval Affairs	Dec. 22, 1837	Favorable	175	Referred to Committee Whole House.		
Easby, William	Compensation for launching frigate Potomac.	25	3	Rep't Committee Whole House.	375			With't amend.	175	Passed	Adverse report.	
Easby, William	Compensation for launching frigate Potomac.	27	2	Petition	63	Claims	169	Adverse		Laid on table.		
Easby, William	Compensation for launching frigate Potomac.	27	3	Petition	43	Claims.						
Easby, William	Compensation for launching frigate Potomac.	28	1	Petition	105	Naval Affairs	162	Adverse		Laid on table.		
Easby, William, surviving partner of Easby and Hanly.	Compensation for lime furnished on public acconnt.	28	1	Petition	297	Claims.						
Easby, William, surviving partner of Easby and Hanly.	Compensation for lime furnished on public account.	28	2	Petition	176	Claims.						

List of private claims presented to the House of Representatives of the United States from the 1st to the 31st Congress, inclusive—Continued.

Names of claimants.	Nature or object of the claim.	Congress.	Session.	How brought before the House of Reps.	Page of journal.	To what committee of the House referred.	No. or date of the report.	Nature of the report.	No. of the bill.	How disposed of by the House of Reps.	How disposed of by the Senate.	Date of the act of Congress, and remarks.
Easby, William, surviving partner of Easby and Hanly.	Compensation for lime furnished on public account.	29	1	Petition	194	Claims.						
Eason, Calvin W.	(See William Bedford, agent.)	28	1		262							
Eason, Joseph B.	Reimbursement of travelling expenses.	17	2	Petition	187	Claims				Discharged; leave to withdraw.		
Eason, Joseph B.	Reimbursement of travelling expenses.	18	1	Petition	32	Claims	Dec. 15, 1823	Adverse		Laid on table.		
East, Samuel G., representatives of.	Arrears of pay for naval services.	11	2	Petition	164							
				Rep. of Secretary Navy.	175	Claims	May 26, 1810	Favorable	75	Referred again to Secretary Navy.		
East, William	Compensation for horse shoes on public account.	24	1	Senate bill	1158	Claims	July 2, 1836	With't amend.	S. 267	Referred to Committee Whole House.		
East, William	Compensation for horse shoes on public account.	24	2	Senate bill	202	Claims	Jan. 17, 1837	With't amend.	S. 10	Referred to Committee Whole House.		
East, William	Compensation for horse shoes on public account.	25	2	Senate bill	309	Claims	Jan. 30, 1838	With't amend.	S. 34	Referred to Committee Whole House.		
East, William	Compensation for horse shoes on public account.	25	3	Senate bill	107	Claims	Jan. 2, 1839	With't amend.	S. 7	Passed	Passed	App'd Feb. 6, 1839
Eastabrook, Nathan	Compensation for revolutionary services.	25	2	Petition	915	Rev. Claims				Discharged; laid on table.		
Eastabrook, Nathan	Compensation for revolutionary services.	25	3	Petition	568	Rev. Pensions.						
Eastabrook, Nathan	Compensation for revolutionary services.	26	1	Petition	173	Rev. Pensions	551	Adverse		Laid on table.		
Eastburn, Thomas	Compensation for horse shoes	17	2	Petition	208	Claims.						
Easter, George	Pension	28	1	Petition	69	Invalid Pensions.						
Easterbrook, Benjamin	Pension	22	1	Petition	287	Rev. Pensions	551	Adverse		Laid on table.		
Eastforth, Samuel	(See Samuel Eathforth.)	21	2		165							
Eastham,	(See McAtee and Eastham.)	31	2		94							
Eastin, Ransom	(See Robert D. Richardson, representatives of.)	25	2		88							
Eastin, Sarah A.	(See Robert D. Richardson, representatives of.)	25	2		88							
Eastin, Thomas	Compensation for publishing laws of United States.	18	2	Documents	160	Claims.						
Eastman, Daniel	Pension	21	1	Petition	120	Military Pensions.						
Eastman, Ebenezer	To be restored to pension roll	17	1	Petition	30	Rev. Pensions.						
Eastman, Ebenezer	Indemnity for failure of title to United States property.	26	2	Petition	54	Judiciary.						
Eastman, Ebenezer	Indemnity for failure of title to United States property.	27	2	Petition	53	Judiciary	855	Adverse		Laid on table.		
Eastman, Eli, guardian of.	Pension	24	1	Petition	1062	Invalid Pensions.						
Eastman, Eli, guardian of.	Pension	24	2	Petition	73	Rev. Claims	70	Favorable	817	Referred to Committee Whole House.		
						Rev. Pensions	138	Favorable	867	Referred to Committee Whole House.		
Eastman, Eli, guardian of.	Pension	25	2	Petition	37	Rev. Pensions	382	Favorable	405	Passed	Passed	App'd June 28, 1838
Eastman, John P.	Pension	25	2	Resolution	1011	Invalid Pensions				Discharged; laid on table.		
Eastman, John P.	Pension	26	1	Petition	162	Invalid Pensions				Discharged; laid on table.		

List of private claims presented to the House of Representatives of the United States from the 1st to the 31st Congress, inclusive—Continued.

72

Names of claimants.	Nature or object of the claim.	Congress.	Session.	How brought before the House of Reps.	Page of journal.	To what committee of the House referred.	No. or date of the report.	Nature of the report.	No. of the bill.	How disposed of by the House of Reps.	How disposed of by the Senate.	Date of the act of Congress, and remarks.
Eastman, Jonathan B.	Settlement of accounts as paymaster United States army.	13	3	Petition	588	Claims.						
Eastman, Jonathan B.	Settlement of accounts as paymaster United States army.	14	1	Petition	32	Claims	Dec. 19, 1815	Favorable	......	Passed	Passed	App'd Jan. 17, 1816
Eastman, Jonathan, heirs of	Relative to the case of deceased	20	1	Petition	46	Ways and Means	Dec. 18, 1827	Adverse	......	Laid on table.		
Eastman, Robert	Renewal of a patent	23	1	Petition	221	Patents and Patent Laws.						
Eastman, Robert	Renewal of a patent	23	2	Petition	307	Judiciary	Feb. 24, 1835	Favorable	761	Passed	Passed	App'd March 3, 1835
Eastman, Thomas	(See agent of James Byers)	18	1	Petition	295	Claims.						
Eastman, Thomas	Pension for revolutionary services.	3	1	Rep. of Secretary War.	131	Select	May 26, 1794	Res. to refer to Sec. of War.	R. 12	Passed	Passed	App'd June 9, 1794
Eastman, Thomas	Pension for revolutionary services.	4	1	Rep. of Secretary War.	445	Claims	Feb. 18, 1796	Favorable	156	Passed	Passed	App'd April 20, 1796
Easton, David	(See Wm. Wilson and others)	7	2	....	291							
Easton, Eliphalet	Compensation for revolutionary services.	2	1	Petition	....	....	....	....	......	Referred to Secretary of War.		
Easton, Eliphalet	Pension	3	1	Rep. of Secretary War.	131	Select	May 26, 1794	Res. to refer to Sec. War.	R. 12	Passed	Passed	App'd June 9, 1794
Easton, Eliphalet	Pension	4	1	Rep. of Secretary War.	445	Claims	Mar. 4, 1796	Res. to refer to Sec. War.	R. 16	Passed	Passed	App'd April 16, 1796
Easton, Eliphalet	Pension	9	2	Pension bill	608	Whole House	Feb. 28, 1807	With amend.	216	Passed	Passed	App'd March 3, 1807
Easton, James	Compensation for revolutionary services and supplies.	1	3	Petition	352							
				Rep. of Secretary War.	....	....	....	....	......	Laid on table.		
Easton, James	Compensation for revolutionary services and supplies.	3	1	Rep. of Secretary War.	131	Select	May 26, 1794	Res. to refer to Sec. War.	R. 12	Passed	Passed	App'd June 9, 1794
Easton, James	Compensation for revolutionary services and supplies.	4	1	Rep. of Secretary War.	445	Claims	Mar. 4, 1796	Res. to refer to Sec. War.	R. 16	Passed	Passed	App'd April 18, 1796
Easton, Richard	Pension	22	1	Petition	412	Rev. Pensions.						
Easton, Rufus	Confirmation of title to land in Missouri.	15	2	Petition	110	Priv. Land Claims.						
Easton, Rufus	Exchange of an entry of land	23	1	Petition	220	Priv. Land Claims.						
Easton, Samuel	Pension	3	1	Rep. of Secretary War.	131	Select	May 26, 1794	Res. to refer to Sec. War.	R. 12	Passed	Passed	App'd June 9, 1794
Easton, Samuel	Pension	4	1	Rep. of Secretary War.	445	Claims	Mar. 4, 1796	Res. to refer to Sec. War.	R. 16	Passed	Passed	App'd April 18, 1796
Easton, Sarah	(See heirs of Robert H. Harrison)	13	3	....	560							
Easton, William C.	Increase of compensation as clerk Commissary Department.	23	2	Petition	....	Claims	Feb. 16, 1835	Adverse	......	Laid on table.		
Easton, William C.	Increase of compensation as clerk Commissary Department.	28	2	Senate bill	243	Military Affairs	Feb. 15, 1845	With't amend.	S. 57	Referred to Committee Whole House.		
Eathforth, Samuel	Pension for revolutionary services.	19	2	Petition	26	Military Pensions	....	....	......	Discharged.		
Eathforth, Samuel	Pension for revolutionary services.	20	1	Resolution	265	Military Pensions	April 29, 1828	Favorable	283	Passed.		
Eathforth, Samuel	Pension for revolutionary services.	20	2	Pension bill	55	Whole House	Jan. 15, 1829	With amend.	311	Passed	Laid on table.	
Eathforth, Samuel	Pension for revolutionary services.	21	1	Petition	48	Military Pensions.						
Eathforth, Samuel	Pension for revolutionary services.	21	2	Resolution	165	Military Pensions.						
Eathforth, Samuel	Pension for revolutionary services.	22	1	Petition	80	Rev. Pensions	376	Favorable	470	Referred to Committee Whole House.		
Eaton, Benjamin, (N. Y.)	Pension for revolutionary services.	23	1	Resolution	654	Rev. Pensions.						
Eaton, Benjamin, (N. Y.)	Increase of pension	25	3	Petition	125	Rev. Pensions	....	....	......	Disch'd; laid on table.		
Eaton, Benjamin, (Mass.,) heirs of.	Pension for revolutionary services.	26	1	Petition	706	Rev. Pensions	490	Adverse	......	Laid on table.		

List of private claims presented to the House of Representatives of the United States from the 1st to the 31st Congress, inclusive—Continued.

Names of claimants.	Nature or object of the claim.	Congress.	Session.	How brought before the House of Reps.	Page of journal.	To what committee of the House referred.	No. or date of the report.	Nature of the report.	No. of the bill.	How disposed of by the House of Reps.	How disposed of by the Senate.	Date of the act of Congress, and remarks.
Eaton, Christopher	To be restored to pension roll	25	2	Resolution	189	Rev. Pensions				Discharged; laid on table.		
Eaton, Christopher	To be restored to pension roll	25	3	Resolution	168	Rev. Pensions				Discharged; laid on table.		
Eaton, Christopher	To be restored to pension roll	26	1	Petition	173	Rev. Pensions.						
Eaton, Clemmons	Arrears of pension	31	1	Petition	449	Invalid Pensions.						
Eaton, Ebenezer	Pension for revolutionary services.	23	2	Petition	271	Rev. Pensions				Discharged; laid on table.		
Eaton, Ebenezer	Pension for revolutionary services.	24	1	Petition	1049	Rev. Pensions				Discharged; laid on table.		
Eaton, Ebenezer	Pension for revolutionary services.	25	3	Petition	217	Rev. Pensions.						
Eaton, Ebenezer, widow of	Pension for revolutionary services.	26	1	Petition	175	Rev. Pensions				Discharged.		
Eaton, Esther	Pension from 1841 to 1843	28	1	Petition	849	Rev. Pensions.						
Eaton, Ithamar	Remission of a certain penalty	13	2	Petition	309	Ways and Means	80	Favorable	163	Rejected.		
Eaton, Joseph	Reimbursement of amount paid for quarters.	21	1	Petition	497	Military Affairs	370	Favorable	430	Referred to Committee Whole House.		
Eaton, Joseph	Reimbursement of amount paid for quarters.	22	1	Petition	89	Military Affairs	92	Favorable	181	Referred to Committee Whole House.		
Eaton, Joseph	Reimbursement of amount paid for quarters.	22	2	Rep't Committee Whole House.	66			With't amend.	181	Passed	Passed	App'd Jan. 14, 1833
Eaton, Luther, widow of	Pension for revolutionary services.	25	2	Petition	775	Rev. Pensions				Discharged; laid on table.		
Eaton, Origen	Increase of pension	18	1	Petition	234	Pens. & Rev. Cl'ms.	Mar. 12, 1824	Adverse		Laid on table.		
Eaton, Origen	Increase of pension	23	1	Petition	436	Invalid Pensions	512	Favorable	517	Referred to Committee Whole House.		
Eaton, Origen	Increase of pension	23	2	Rep't Committee Whole House.	336			With't amend.	517	Passed	Passed, with amendment.	Senate amendment not acted on.
Eaton, Origen	Increase of pension	24	1	Petition	53	Invalid Pensions	46	Favorable	58	Passed	Passed	App'd May 14, 1836
Eaton, Robert S.	(See Henry A. Wise and others.)	31	1		1184							
Eaton, Robert	Reimbursement of duty on salt	21	1	Resolution	281	Ways and Means	309	Favorable	364	Referred to Committee Whole House.		
Eaton, Robert	Reimbursement of duty on salt	22	1	Petition	107	Ways and Means	136	Favorable	205	Referred to Committee Whole House.		
Eaton, Robert	Reimbursement of duty on salt	22	2	Rep't Committee Whole House.	66		Dec. 15, 1832	With't amend.	205	Passed	Passed	App'd March 2, 1833
Eaton, Uriah	Compensation for revolutionary services.	23	1	Petition	220	Rev. Claims.						
Eaton, Uriah	Compensation for revolutionary services.	24	1	Petition	138	Rev. Claims.						
Eaton, William	Pension	3	1	Rep. of Secretary of War.	131	Select	May 26, 1794	Res. to refer to Sec'y War.	R. 12	Passed	Passed	App'd June 9, 1794
Eaton, William, (Me.)	Pension	21	1	Petition	231	Military Pensions	April 27, 1830	Adverse		Laid on table.		
Eaton, William, (Me.)	Pension	21	2	Petition	114	Military Pensions.						
Eaton, William, (Me.)	Pension	22	1	Petition	68	Rev. Pensions				Discharged; laid on table.		
Eaton, William, (Conn.)	Reimbursement of expenses while consul at Tunis.	8	1	Memorial	587	Claims	Feb. 29, 1804	Adverse		Leave to withdraw.		
Eaton, William, (Conn.)	Reimbursement of expenses while consul at Tunis.	9	1	Documents	321	Claims	April 9, 1806	Favorable; bill ordered.	138	Laid on table.		
Eaton, William, (Conn.)	Reimbursement of expenses while consul at Tunis.	9	2	Documents	549	Claims	Feb. 18, 1807	Favorable; bill ordered.	208	Passed	Passed	App'd March 3, 1807
Eaton, William, widow of, (Conn.)	Remuneration for services of husband.	15	1	Petition	183	Military Affairs				Discharged; leave to withdraw.		

List of private claims presented to the House of Representatives of the United States from the 1st to the 31st Congress, inclusive—Continued.

Names of claimants.	Nature or object of the claim.	Congress.	Session.	How brought before the House of Reps.	Page of journal.	To what committee of the House referred.	No. or date of the report.	Nature of the report.	No. of the bill.	How disposed of by the House of Reps.	How disposed of by the Senate.	Date of the act of Congress, and remarks.
Eaton, William, widow of, (Conn.)	Equitable settlement of accounts as consul.	21	2	Petition	161	Foreign Affairs	Feb. 23, 1831	Adverse		Laid on table.		
Eaton, William, heirs of, (Conn.)	Compensation for military services at Tripoli.	24	1	Senate bill	390	Military Affairs	June 9, 1836	With't amend.	70	Report'd in Committee Whole House.		
Eaton, William, heirs of, (Conn.)	Compensation for military services at Tripoli.	24	2	Petition	89	Military Affairs.						
				Senate bill	250	Military Affairs	Feb. 14, 1837	With't amend.	6	Referred to Committee Whole House.		
Eaton, William, heirs of, (Conn.)	Compensation for military services at Tripoli.	25	2	Senate bill	519	Military Affairs	June 13, 1838	With amend.	124	Referred to Committee Whole House.		
Eaton, William, heirs of, (Conn.)	Compensation for military services at Tripoli.	28	1	Petition	109	Military Affairs	211	Favorable	166	Referred to Committee Whole House.		
Eaton, William, (N. Y.)	Provisions for his claim against Farrow & Harris.	18	1	Petition	236	Military Affairs				Discharged; leave to withdraw.		
Eaton, William, (N. Y.)	Indemnity for losses, war of 1812.	20	2	Petition	118	Claims				Discharged; laid on table.		
Eaton, William, (N. Y.)	Indemnity for breach of contract with Farrow & Harris.	20	2	Petition	118	Claims				Discharged; laid on table.		
Eaton, William, (N. Y.)	Compensation for work on fortification at Mobile.	20	2	Petition	118	Claims				Discharged; laid on table.		
Eaton, William, (N. Y.)	Indemnity for property destroyed by the British.	21	2	Petition	271	Claims	Feb. 15, 1831	Adverse		Laid on table.		
Eaton, William, (N. Y.)	Equitable settlement of his claims.	22	2	Petition	28	Claims.						
Eaton, William, (N. Y.)	Indemnity for losses under a contract, &c.	23	1	Petition	34	Claims.						
Eaton, William, (N. Y.)	Indemnity for property destroyed by the British.	23	1	Petition	35	Claims.						
Eaton, William, (N. Y.)	Indemnity for loss on contract to furnish bread.	23	2	Petition	60	Claims.						
Eaton, William, (N. Y.)	Indemnity for loss on contract to build fortification.	23	2	Petition	60	Claims.						
				Petition, (2)	114	Claims.						
Eaton, William, (N. Y.)	Indemnity for loss on bread contract.	24	1	Memorial	49	Claims	471	Adverse		Laid on table.		
Eaton, William, (N. Y.)	Indemnity for loss on contract to build fortification.	24	1	Memorial	49	Claims	542, 543	Adverse		Laid on table.		
Eaves, William, & others	Compensation for mail service	26	1	Petition	343	P. Of. and P. Roads.						
Eaves, William	Remission of fines as mail contractor.	29	1	Petition	465	P. Of. and P. Roads.	733	Adverse		Laid on table.		
Ebbs, Emanuel	Compensation for revolutionary services.	2	1	Petition	484					Referred to Secretary of War.		
Ebbs, Emanuel	Pension	14	1	Petition	99	Pens. & Rev. Cl'ms.	April 11, 1816	Pension bill	171	Laid on table.		
Eberly, Henry	Pension for revolutionary services.	26	1	Petition	937	Rev. Pensions				Discharged; laid on table.		
Eberly, John, attorney of.	Compensation for revolutionary services.	3	2	Memorial	305	Claims.						
Eberly, John, attorney of.	Compensation for revolutionary services.	4	1	Rep't Committee.	389			Adverse		Rejected		Leave to withdraw.
Eccles, Ann	(See heirs of J. & A. Pettigrew)	18	2		46							
Eccleston, Charles, representatives of.	(See sureties of James Frazier)	12	1		61							
Eccleston, Thomas, widow of.	(See surety of James Frazier)	12	1		61				178			

List of private claims presented to the House of Representatives of the United States from the 1st to the 31st Congress, inclusive—**Continued.**

Names of claimants.	Nature or object of the claim.	Congress.	Session.	How brought before the House of Reps.	Page of journal.	To what committee of the House referred.	No. or date of the report.	Nature of the report.	No. of the bill.	How disposed of by the House of Reps.	How disposed of by the Senate.	Date of the act of Congress, and remarks.
Eck, Samuel	Pension	18	2	Petition	117	Pens. & Rev. Cl'ms.				Discharged; referred to Com. Whole House.		
Eck, Samuel	Pension	19	1	Petition	73	Military Pensions	194	Favorable		Referred to Committee Whole House.		
Eck, Samuel	Pension	19	2	Pension bill	85	Whole House	Feb. 2, 1827	With amend.	314			Name not in the act.
Eckert, John, jr., administrator of.	Indemnity for French spoliations prior to 1800.	26	1	Memorial	182	Foreign Affairs	343	Favorable; bill	319	Referred to Committee Whole House.		
Eckert, John, jr., administrator of.	Indemnity for French spoliations prior to 1800.	29	2	Memorial	90	Foreign Affairs.						
Eckert, John, jr., administrator of.	Indemnity for French spoliations prior to 1800.	31	1	Petition	412	Foreign Affairs	355	General bill	318	Referred to Committee Whole House.		
Eckfeldt, Adam	Compensation for medals ordered by Congress.	25	2	Amend't to appropriation bill.					224			App'd April 6, 1838
Eckford, Henry	Compensation for use of land by government of United States.	20	1	Resolution	248	Claims				Discharged; referred to Secretary of Navy.		
Eckford, Henry	Compensation for use of land by government of United States.	20	2	Rep. of Secretary Navy.	48	Naval Affairs	84	Favorable	444	Referred to Committee Whole House.		
Eckford, Henry	Compensation for use of land by government of United States.	21	1	Rep. of Secretary Navy.	495	Naval Affairs.						
Eckford, Henry	Compensation for use of land by government of United States.	21	2	Documents	104	Naval Affairs	41	Favorable	570	Referred to Committee Whole House.		
Eckford, Henry	Compensation for use of land by government of United States.	23	1	Documents	80	Naval Affairs				Discharged; referred to Secretary of Navy.		
				Rep. of Secretary Navy.	424	Naval Affairs.						
				Senate bill	845	Naval Affairs	June 28, 1834	With't amend.	S. 132	Postponed.		
Eckford, Henry	Compensation for use of land by government of United States.	24	1	Senate bill	390	Claims			S. 76	Discharged; referred to Com. Nav. Affairs.		
Eckford, Henry	Compensation for use of lands by government of United States.	26	1	Senate bill	1132	Naval Affairs			S. 239			
Eckford, Henry	Compensation for use of lands by government of United States.	26	2	Senate bill	327	Whole House			S. 190			
Eckford, Henry	Compensation for use of lands by government of United States.	27	2	Senate bill	1126	Naval Affairs	Aug. 10, 1842	With amend.	S. 272	Passed with amendm't	Passed as am'd.	App'd Aug. 29, 1842
Eckhart, John, widow of.	Pension	27	2	Petition	329	Invalid Pensions.				Laid on table.		
Eckman, Jacob, heirs of	Redemption of land sold for taxes.	16	1	Petition	140	Select.						
Eckright, Isaac	Pension	20	2	Petition	288	Military Pensions				Discharged; laid on table.		
Eckright, Isaac	Pension	21	1	Petition	99	Military Pensions				Discharged; laid on table.		
Eckright, Isaac	Pension	23	2	Petition	166	Invalid Pensions	70	Favorable	691	Passed	Passed	App'd March 3, 1835
Eckright, Isaac	Arrears of pension	24	1	Petition	201	Invalid Pensions	753	Favorable	691	Passed	Passed and reconsidered.	
Eckright, Isaac	Increase of pension	28	1	Petition	441	Invalid Pensions.						
E-con-chat-ta-mico	Indemnity for slaves carried off	26	1	Petition	605	Indian Affairs.						
E-con-chat-ta-mico	Indemnity for slaves carried off	26	2	Petition	139	Claims.						
E-con-chat-ta-mico	Indemnity for slaves carried off	27	2	Petition	99	Indian Affairs.						
E-con-chat-ta-mico	Indemnity for slaves carried off	28	2	Petition	70	Indian Affairs	33	Adverse		Laid on table.		
Eddleman, Leonard	Pension for revolutionary services.	20	1	Resolution	318	Military Pensions	Mar. 28, 1828	Adverse		Laid on table.		
Eddleman, Leonard	Pension for revolutionary services.	20	2	Petition	26	Military Pensions				Discharged; laid on table.		
Eddleman, Leonard	Pension for revolutionary services.	21	1	Pension bill	130	Whole House	Feb. 12, 1830	With amend.	72	Passed	Passed with amendment.	App'd May 20, [20,] 1830.

List of private claims presented to the House of Representatives of the United States from the 1st to the 31st Congress, inclusive—Continued.

Names of claimants.	Nature or object of the claim.	Congress.	Session.	How brought before the House of Reps.	Page of journal.	To what committee of the House referred.	No. or date of the report.	Nature of the report.	No. of the bill.	How disposed of by the House of Reps.	How disposed of by the Senate.	Date of the act of Congress, and remarks.
Eddowes, Ralph	Indemnity for detention of a cargo of merchandise.	11	3	Memorial	59					Laid on table.		
Eddy, Benjamin, administrato of.	Indemnity for French spoliations prior to 1800.	26	1	Memorial	182	Foreign Affairs	343	Favorable; bill	319	Referred to Committee Whole House.		
Eddy, Caleb	(See Benjamin Eddy, administrator of.)											
Eddy, Caleb	Relief as a Canadian refugee	7	1	Petition	16	Claims	Jan. 12, 1802	Adverse		Laid on table.		
Eddy, Caleb	Relief as a Canadian refugee	7	2	Petition	272	Claims	Feb. 26, 1803	Adverse		Postponed.		
Eddy, Caleb	(See Canadian refugees)	4	2		614							
Eddy, Caleb	Drawback on coffee exported	17	1	Petition	25	Commerce.						
Eddy, Caleb	Drawback on coffee exported	27	2	Senate bill	215	Commerce	Feb. 18, 1842	With't amend.	103	Passed	Passed	App'd June 4, 1842
Eddy, Elias	(See Canadian refugees)	4	2		614							
Eddy, Ethan	Pension	25	2	Petition	588	Invalid Pensions				Discharged.		
Eddy, George	Liquidation of certain State bills of credit.	4	1	Rep. of Secretary Treasury.	388	Claims	74	Adverse		Laid on table.		
Eddy, John, jr	(See Canadian refugees)	4	2		614							
Eddy, Jonathan	(See Canadian refugees)	4	2		614							
Eddy, Joshua	Commutation pay for revolutionary services.	15	1	Petition	265	Pens. & Rev. Cl'ms.						
Eddy, Joshua	Commutation pay for revolutionary services.	15	2	Petition	....	Pens. & Rev. Cl'ms.	Dec. 9, 1818	Adverse		Rejected.		
Eddy, Joshua	Pension	19	1	Petition	250	Military Pensions	164	Adverse		Discharged.		
Eddy, Joshua	Pension	21	1	Petition	143	Military Pensions.						
Eddy, Joshua	Pension	22	1	Petition	187	Rev. Pensions				Discharged; laid on table.		
Eddy, Joshua, heirs of	Commutation pay for revolutionary services.	30	1	Petition	112	Rev. Claims.						
Eddy, Joshua, heirs of	Extra pay for revolutionary services.	30	1	Petition	117	Rev. Claims	369	Favorable	336	Referred to Committee Whole House.		
Eddy, Joshua, heirs of	Commutation pay for revolutionary services.	30	2	Rep't Committee Whole House.	143			With amend.	336	Passed	Postponed.	
Eddy, Joshua, heirs of	Commutation pay for revolutionary services.	31	1	Petition	270	Rev. Claims	112	Favorable	125	Referred to Committee Whole House.		
Eddy, Samuel	Pay for services during revolutionary war.	11	2	Petition	150	Claims	June 26, 1810	Adverse		Leave to withdraw.		
Eddy, Seth	To be restored to pension roll	17	1	Petition	37	Rev. Pensions				Leave to withdraw.		
Eddy, Thomas	Indemnity for French spoliations prior to 1800.	26	1	Memorial	182	Foreign Affairs	343	Favorable; bill	319	Referred to Committee Whole House.		
Eddy, William	(See Canadian refugees)	4	2		614							
Eddy, William, widow of.	Pension for revolutionary services.	30	1	Petition	644	Rev. Pensions	638	Adverse		Laid on table.		
Edegh, Jacob	Pension for revolutionary services.	3	1	Report Secretary of War.	131	Select	May 26, 1794	Res. to refer to Sec. War.	R. 12	Passed	Passed	App'd June 9, 1794
Edegh, Jacob	Pension for revolutionary services.	4	1	Rep. of Secretary War.	445	Claims	Mar. 4, 1796	Res. to refer to Sec. War.	R. 16	Passed	Passed	App'd April 18, 1796
Edgar, John	Adjustment of claim against United States.	1	3	Petition	368					Referred to Secretary Treasury.		
Edgar, John	Adjustment of claim against United States.	3	1	Rep't of Secretary Treasury.	77					Laid on table.		
Edgar, John	(See Canadian refugees)	4	2		614							
Edgar, John	Compensation for supplies on public account.	7	2	Petition	326	Claims	Feb. 26, 1803	Adverse		Postponed.		
Edgar, John	Compensation for supplies on public account.	8	1	Petition	442	Claims				Discharged, referred to Com. Whole House.		

List of private claims presented to the House of Representatives of the United States from the 1st to the 31st Congress, inclusive—Continued.

Names of claimants.	Nature or object of the claim.	Congress.	Session.	How brought before the House of Reps.	Page of journal.	To what committee of the House referred.	No. or date of the report.	Nature of the report.	No. of the bill.	How disposed of by the House of Reps.	How disposed of by the Senate.	Date of the act of Congress, and remarks.
Edgar, John	Compensation for supplies on public account.	9	1	Petition	343	Claims				Indef. postponed.		
Edgar, John	Compensation for supplies on public account.	19	2	Resolution	62	Indian Affairs	Jan. 30, 1827	Adverse		Laid on table.		
Edgar, John	Compensation for supplies on public account.	21	2	Petition	121	Claims	Jan. 10, 1831	Adverse		Laid on table.		
Edgar, John	Confirmation of title to land	16	1	Petition	118	Public Lands.						
Edgar, John	Confirmation of title to land	16	2	Petition	22	Priv. Land Claims.						
Edgar, John	Confirmation of title to land	17	1	Petition	41	Whole House.						
Edgar, John	Confirmation of title to land	20	1	Memorial	367	Priv. Land Claims.						
Edgar, John	Confirmation of title to land	20	2	Petition	96	Priv. Land Claims.						
Edgar, John	Confirmation of title to land	21	1	Senate bill	151	Priv. Land Claims.	Feb. 9, 1830	With't amend.	S. 36	Rejected.		
Edgar, John	Pension for revolutionary services.	21	1	Senate bill	517	Rev. Claims	April 16, 1830	With't amend.	S. 98	Passed	Passed	App'd May 26, 1830
Edgar, Nathaniel T.	Increase of pension	21	1	Resolution	432	Military Pensions.						
Edgar, William	(See Alexander Macomb, and W. Edgar.)	1	2		290							
Edgecomb, Gilbert	Pension	21	1	Petition	143	Military Pensions.						
Edgecomb, Gilbert	Pension	22	1	Petition	187	Rev. Pensions.						
Edgecomb, John	Bounty land under act of September, 1850.	31	2	Petition	179	Public Lands.						
Edgecomb, John	Indemnity for loss by destruction of United States ship Adams.	31	2	Petition	180	Claims.						
Edgecomb, Samuel, jr.	Pension for revolutionaay services.	3	2	Rep. of Secretary War.	278	Claims.						
Edgecomb, Samuel, jr.	Pension for revolutionary services.	4	1	Resolution	373	Claims.						
Edgecomb, Samuel, jr.	Pension for revolutionary services.	4	2	Resolution	614	Claims.						
Edgecomb, Samuel	Pension for revolutionary services.	24	2	Petition	120	Rev. Pensions	177	Favorable	898	Referred to Committee Whole House.		
Edgecomb, Samuel	Pension for revolutionary services.	25	2	Petition	37	Rev. Pensions	152	Favorable	177	Passed	Reported with amendments.	
Edgecomb, Samuel	Pension for revolutionary services.	25	3	Petition	127	Rev. Pensions	54	Favorable	943	Passed	Adverse.	
Edgecomb, Samuel	Pension for revolutionary services.	26	1	Petition	172	Rev. Pensions.						
Edgecomb, Samuel	Pension for revolutionary services.	26	2	Petition	134	Rev. Pensions	Feb. 12, 1841	Adverse		Laid on table.		
Edgecomb, Samuel	Pension for revolutionary services.	27	2	Petition	59	Rev. Pensions	127	Favorable	173	Passed	Indef. postp'd.	
Edgecomb, Samuel	Pension for revolutionary services.	27	3	Petition	74	Rev. Pensions	65	Favorable	702	Passed	Indef. postp'd.	
Edgerly, Richard, widow of	Arrears of pension	30	1	Petition	698	Rev. Pensions	783	Adverse		Laid on table.		
Edie, John, heirs of	Pay and interest for revolutionary services.	29	2	Memorial	86	Rev. Claims.						
Edie, John, heirs of	Pay and interest for revolutionary services.	30	1	Petition	575	Rev. Claims.						
Edie, John, heirs of	Pay and interest for revolutionary services.	31	1	Petition	472	Rev. Claims.						
Edinfield, David	Indemnity for losses in Creek war.	14	1	Petition	71	Ways and Means.						
Edington, H. S., sureties of.	Release from the balance of a judgment.	30	1	Senate bill	683	P. Of. and P. Roads.	May 16, 1848	With't amend.	S. 69	Referred to Committee Whole House.		
Edington, H. S., sureties of.	Release from the balance of a judgment.	30	2	Rep't Committee Whole House.	319			Report	S. 69	Passed	Passed	App'd Feb. 1, 1849
Edington, James	Compensation for mail service	24	1	Petition	59	P. Of. and P. Roads.						
Edmanson, John	Pension	23	1	Petition	493	Rev. Pensions.						
Edmonds, Daniel	Pension	19	1	Rep't Committee.	398		164	Adverse		Laid on table.		
Edmonds, Daniel	Pension	19	2	Petition	36	Military Pensions.						
Edmonds, Daniel	Pension	21	1	Resolution	405	Military Pensions.	April 7, 1830	Adverse		Laid on table.		

List of private claims presented to the House of Representatives of the United States from the 1st to the 31st Congress, inclusive—Continued.

Names of claimants.	Nature or object of the claim.	Congress.	Session.	How brought before the House of Reps.	Page of journal.	To what committee of the House referred.	No. or date of the report.	Nature of the report.	No. of the bill.	How disposed of by the House of Reps.	How disposed of by the Senate.	Date of the act of Congress, and remarks.
Edmonds, Daniel	Pension	21	2	Resolution	167	Military Pensions.						
Edmonds, Samuel, sureties of.	Release from liability	24	2	Petition	400	Judiciary.						
Edmonds, Samuel, sureties of.	Release from liability	25	2	Petition	402	Judiciary.						
Edmonds, Samuel, sureties of.	Release from liability	26	1	Petition	175	Judiciary.						
				Petition, (2)	298	Judiciary	326	Favorable	292	Referred to Committee Whole House.		
Edmonds, Samuel, sureties of.	Release from liability	27	2	Petition	63	Judiciary		Favorable	395	Ordered to 3d reading.		
Edmonds, Samuel, sureties of.	Release from liability	27	3	House bill					395	Passed	Passed	App'd March 3, 1843
Edmonds, Thomas, executor of.	Indemnity for French spoliations prior to 1800.	25	2	Memorial	509	Whole House				Discharged.		
Edmondson, John	(See Dr. William Rickman, heirs of.)	26	1		706							
Edmonson, John	Pension for revolutionary services.	25	2	Memorial	579	Rev. Pensions.						
Edmonson, John	Pension for revolutionary services.	26	1	Petition	173	Rev. Pensions				Discharged; laid on table.		
Edmonson John	Pension for revolutionary services.	28	1	Petition	335	Rev. Pensions	327	Favorable	235	Passed	Passed	App'd June 15, 1844
Edmondson, Samuel A.	Bounty land for military services.	21	2	Petition	100	Public Lands.						
Edmondson, Samuel A.	Bounty land for military services.	23	1	Petition	57	Claims	132	Favorable	142	Passed	Passed	App'd June 30, 1834
Edmonson, Samuel	(See Joseph Stewart and others)	14	1		249				65			App'd Feb. 8, 1817
Edmonson, Thomas	Pension	14	1	Resolution	181	Pens. & Rev. Cl'ms.	April 11, 1816	Favorable	171	Passed	Passed	App'd April 30, 1816
Edmonston, James	Compensation for lost lime on Treasury building.	25	3	Petition	110	Public Buildings				Discharged.		
Edmonston, James	Confirmation of land title	25	3	Petition	133	Priv. Land Claims.						
Edmonston, John, widow of.	Increase of pension	15	1	Petition	287	Pens. & Rev. Cl'ms.						
Edmonston, John, widow of.	Increase of pension	15	2	Petition	40	Pens. & Rev. Cl'ms.				Discharged; laid on table.		
Edmonston, Robert, heirs of.	Compensation for revolutionary services.	24	1	Documents	665	Select.						
Edmonston, Robert, heirs of.	Compensation for revolutionary services.	24	2	Documents	110	Select.						
Edmonston, Robert, heirs of.	Compensation for revolutionary services.	25	2	Resolution	171	Select.						
Edmunds, Nicholas	(See Thomas Edmunds, executors of.)	26	1		714							
Edmunds, Thomas, executor of.	Indemnity for French spoliations prior to 1800.	26	1	Petition	714	Foreign Affairs	343	Favorable; bill	319	Referred to Committee Whole House.		
Edmunds, Thomas, executor of.	Indemnity for French spoliations prior to 1800.	29	2	Memorial	228	Foreign Affairs.						
Edmunds, Thomas, executor of.	Indemnity for French spoliations prior to 1800.	31	1	Petition	196	Foreign Affairs	353	General bill	318	Referred to Committee Whole House.		
Edney, Edmund	Pension	27	2	Petition	218	Invalid Pensions.						
Edrington, Benjamin and Joseph.	Indemnity for property lost while in public service.	15	1	Petition	106	Claims	Feb. 24, 1818	Adverse		Laid on table.		
Edsall, Samuel	Indemnity for property destroyed by the enemy.	18	1	Petition	77	Claims.						
Edsall, Samuel	Indemnity for property destroyed by the enemy.	22	1	Petition	559	Claims	April 13, 1832	Adverse		Laid on table.		

List of private claims presented to the House of Representatives of the United States from the 1st to the 31st Congress, inclusive—Continued.

Names of claimants.	Nature or object of the claim.	Congress.	Session.	How brought before the House of Reps.	Page of journal.	To what committee of the House referred.	No. or date of the report.	Nature of the report.	No. of the bill.	How disposed of by the House of Reps.	How disposed of by the Senate.	Date of the act of Congress, and remarks.
Edson, Joseph, administrator of.	Payment of a balance due	24	2	Petition	37	Claims.						
Edson, Joseph, administrator of.	Allowance of a claim suspended at the treasury.	25	2	Resolution	1025	Claims	1004	Adverse		Laid on table.		
Edson, Joseph, administrator of.	Allowance of a claim suspended at the treasury.	27	3	Resolution	68	Judiciary	162	Adverse		Laid on table.		
Edson, Joseph, administrator of.	Allowance of a claim suspended at the treasury.	28	1	Petition	351	Judiciary	693	Adverse		Laid on table.		
Edson, Joseph, administrator of.	Poundage on execution as United States marshal.	28	2	Petition	88	Judiciary	162	Favorable	630	Referred to Committee Whole House.		
Edson, Joseph, administrator of.	Poundage on execution as United States marshal.	29	1	Petition	69	Judiciary	693	Favorable	466	Referred to Committee Whole House.		
Edson, Joseph, administrator of.	Poundage on execution as United States marshal.	29	2	House bill	211				466	Passed	Passed	App'd March 3, 1847
Edson, Royal	(See Joseph Edson, administrator of.)	24	2		37							
Edster, William, widow of.	Pension	27	2	Petition	720	Invalid Pensions				Discharged; laid on table.		
Edwards, Abraham	Pension as a revolutionary mariner.	15	2	Sen. amendment to House bill.					249			Statutes at Large, vol. 6, p. 231.
Edwards, Abraham	Right of pre emption to land in Michigan.	20	2	Petition	263	Public Lands				Discharged; laid on table.		
Edwards, Abraham	Settlement of accounts as register in land office.	30	2	Senate bill	518	Whole House	Feb. 28, 1849	With't amend.	227	Passed	Passed	App'd March 2, 1849
Edwards, Amos, sureties of	Equitable settlement of his accounts.	18	2	Petition	69	Ways and Means.						
Edwards, Amos, sureties of	Equitable settlement of his accounts.	19	1	Resolution	91	Ways and Means.						
Edwards, Amos, sureties of	Equitable settlement of his accounts.	19	2	Petition	31	Ways and Means	March 3, 1827	Favorable	447	Laid on table.		
Edwards, Amos, sureties of	Equitable settlement of his accounts.	20	1	Resolution	44	Ways and Means	Feb. 29, 1828	Adverse.				
Edwards, Amos, sureties of	Equitable settlement of his accounts.	21	2	Petition	55	Judiciary	Dec. 30, 1830	Favorable	522	Passed.		
Edwards, Amos, sureties of	Equitable settlement of his accounts.	22	1	Petition	43	Judiciary	Dec. 27, 1831	Favorable	127	Passed in Committee Whole House.		
				Senate bill	502	Whole House	Mar. 23, 1832	With't amend.	S. 37	Passed	Passed	App'd April 5, 1832
Edwards, Benjamin	Compensation for horse lost in public service.	10	1	Petition	188	Claims.						
Edwards, Benjamin	Compensation for horse lost in public service.	10	2	Petition	395	Claims.						
Edwards, Benjamin	Compensation for horse lost in public service.	11	2	Petition	119	Claims	Mar. 24, 1810	Adverse		Laid on table.		
Edwards, Brown	Compensation for property taken for public use.	23	1	Petition	42	Rev. Claims.						
Edwards, Brown	Indemnity for losses while a revolutionary soldier.	24	1	Petition	508	Rev. Claims.						
Edwards, Brown	Indemnity for losses while a revolutionary soldier.	24	2	Petition	91	Rev. Claims.						
Edwards, Cesar	Pension	1	2	Petition	174							
				Rep. of Secretary War.	231					Laid on table.		
Edwards, Daniel	Pension for revolutionary services.	19	1	Resolution	163	Military Pensions.						
Edwards, Dr. David S	Allowance for servants, forage, &c.	31	1	Petition	919	Naval Affairs.						
Edwards, Edward, widow of.	Compensation for property taken by Indians.	15	2	Petition	258	Claims				Discharged; laid on table.		
Edwards, Edward, widow of.	Compensation for property taken by Indians.	18	1	Petition	197	Claims	Mar. 19, 1824	Adverse		Laid on table.		

List of private claims presented to the House of Representatives of the United States from the 1st to the 31st Congress, inclusive—Continued.

Names of claimants.	Nature or object of the claim.	Congress.	Session.	How brought before the House of Reps.	Page of journal.	To what committee of the House referred.	No. or date of the report.	Nature of the report.	No. of the bill.	How disposed of by the House of Reps.	How disposed of by the Senate.	Date of the act of Congress, and remarks.
73 Edwards, Evan, heirs of..	Renewal of lost land warrant	23	1	Resolution	222	Priv. Land Claims.	209	Favorable....	229	Referred to Committee Whole House.		
Edwards, Evan, heirs of..	Renewal of lost land warrant	23	2	Rep't Committee Whole House.	82	....	Dec. 15, 1834	With't amend.	229	Passed	Passed	App'd Jan. 27, 1835
Edwards, Elizabeth......	Pension for naval services of husband.	26	1	Petition	303	Naval Affairs.						
Edwards, Elizabeth......	Pension for naval services of husband.	27	2	Resolution	523	Rev. Pensions	784	Adverse	......	Laid on table.		
Edwards, Gideon........	Pension	10	1	Memorial	30	Select...........	Mar. 28, 1808	Favorable.				
Edwards, Gideon........	Pension	10	2	Pension bill	499	Whole House.....	Feb. 20, 1809	With amend..	158	Passed	Passed, with amendment	App'd Mar. 3, 1809
Edwards, Isaiah.........	Right of pre emption	23	2	Petition	278	....	....	....	......	....	....	Not referred.
Edwards, James.........	(See administrator of Edward M. Wanton.)	28	1	....	802							
Edwards, James	Indemnity for property destroyed by United States troops.	28	1	Petition	571	Claims.						
Edwards, James	Indemnity for property destroyed by United States troops.	28	2	Petition	82	Claims.						
Edwards, James M.......	Pension	24	2	Petition	86	Invalid Pensions...	129	Favorable....	857	Referred to Committee Whole House.		
Edwards, James M.......	Pension	25	2	Petition	38	Invalid Pensions ..	216	Favorable....	254	Passed	Passed	App'd July 9, 1838
Edwards, John..........	(See representative of Joseph Slatton.)	24	1	....	776							
Edwards, John..........	(See administrator of Joseph Slatton.)	24	2	....	89							
Edwards, John, sen......	Release from demands on books of War Department.	11	3	Petition	540	Claims.						
Edwards, John, sen......	Release from demands on books of War Department.	13	2	Petition	175	Claims...........	March 7, 1814	Adverse	......	Rejected.		
Edwards, John..........	Continuation of naval pension....	27	2	Petition	254	Naval Affairs	603	Adverse	......	Laid on table.		
Edwards, John C., and others.	Renewal of a patent	22	1	Petition	538	Patent laws	May 1, 1832	Adverse	......	Laid on table.		
Edwards, John C. P.....	Authority to bring suit against the United States.	30	1	Memorial	1087	Judiciary.						
Edwards, John C. P.....	Authority to bring suit against the United States.	30	2	Petition	76	Judiciary.						
Edwards, John C. P.....	Authority to bring suit against the United States.	31	1	Petition	732	Judiciary.						
Edwards, Jonathan......	Pension	20	1	Resolution	264	Military Pensions..	April 29, 1828	Favorable....	283	Passed.		
Edwards, Jonathan......	Pension	20	2	Pension bill	55	Whole House.....	Jan. 11, 1829	With amend..	311	Passed............	Laid on table.	
Edwards, Jonathan......	Pension	21	1	Petition	48	Military Pensions..	Jan. 5, 1830	Pension bill ..	72	Passed	Passed, with amendment.	App'd May 20, 1830
Edwards, Leroy, heirs of..	Balance due for revolut'y services..	19	1	Resolution	238	Rev. Claims......	102	Favorable....	72	Passed............	Passed	App'd May 20, 1826
Edwards, Nathaniel......	Pension	16	1	Petition	58	Rev. Pensions	Jan. 14, 1820	Adverse	......	Laid on table.		
Edwards, Nathan........	Right of pre-emption...........	23	2	Petition	278	....	....	....	......	....	....	Not referred.
Edwards, Nervit	To be restored to pension roll	19	1	Resolution	186	Military Pensions..	164	Adverse	......	Laid on table.		
Edwards, Peter, assignee of	Confirmation of title to land in Arkansas.	22	1	....	....	....	....	....	......	....	....	Statutes at Large, vol. 6, p. 498.
Edwards, Robert	(See William Forbes, heirs of.)...	15	1	....	316							
Edwards, R. G., and others	Indemnity for damage to property at Savannah.	15	2	Petition	209	Claims	....	....	......	Discharged; laid on table.		
Edwards, Samuel.......	Increase of pension	25	2	Petition	586	Rev. Pensions....	....	....	......	Discharged; laid on table.		

List of private claims presented to the House of Representatives of the United States from the **1st** *to the* **31st** *Congress, inclusive*—**Continued.**

Names of claimants.	Nature or object of the claim.	Congress.	Session.	How brought before the House of Reps.	Page of journal.	To what committee of the House referred.	No. or date of the report.	Nature of the report.	No. of the bill.	How disposed of by the House of Reps.	How disposed of by the Senate.	Date of the act of Congress, and remarks.
Edwards, Seth	Indemnity for French spoliations prior to 1800.	26	1	Memorial	182	Foreign Affairs	343	Favorable; bill	319	Referred to Committee Whole House.		
Edwards, Timothy	(See Comfort Sands and others.)	1	3		358							
Edwards, Thomas	Pension	14	2	Resolution	209	Pens. & Rev. Cl'ms.	Jan. 29, 1817	Adverse		Laid on table.		
Edwards, Thomas, heirs of	Indemnity for French spoliations prior to 1800.	31	1	Petition	285	Foreign Affairs	355	General bill	318	Referred to Committee Whole House.		
Edwards, Thomas O.	Compensation for services as a public agent.	31	1	Appropriat'n bill					334			App'd Sept. 30, 1850
Edwards, William	Compensation for revolutionary services.	2	1	Petition	493					Referred to Secretary War.		
Edwards, William	Compensation for revolutionary services.	3	2	Rep. of Secretary War.	278					Laid on table.		
Edwards, William	Compensation for services as surveyor.	14	2	Senate bill	214	Public Lands	Jan. 25, 1817	With't amend.	S. 14			
Edwards, William	Compensation for services as surveyor.	15	1	Senate bill	104	Whole House	Mar. 21, 1818	With't amend.	S. 5	Passed	Passed	App'd April 3, 1818
Edwards, William B.	Right of pre-emption	23	2	Petition	278							Not referred
Edwards, William B.	Pension	29	2	Petition	147	Invalid Pensions.						
Edwards, William B.	Pension	30	1	Petition	117	Invalid Pensions	115	Adverse		Laid on table.		
Edwards, William B.	Pension	31	1	Petition	324	Invalid Pensions	306	Favorable	276	Referred to Committee Whole House.		
Edwards, William B.	Pension	31	2	Rep't Committee Whole House.	180		Jan. 24, 1851	With't amend.	276	Passed.		
Edwards, William L. D.	(See George Collier, and others)	26	1		623							
Edy, Samuel	Payment of revolutionary certificate.	4	1	Petition	518	Claims.						
Edy, Samuel	Payment of revolutionary certificate.	4	2	Resolution	614	Claims	Feb. 21, 1797	(Report not of record.)		Referred to Committee Whole House.		
Edy, Samuel	Payment of revolutionary certificate.	5	2	Resolution	89	Whole House	Mar. 19, 1798	Res. favorable.		Resolution rejected.		
Eells, John	Pension	22	1	Petition	164	Rev. Pensions				Discharged; laid on table.		
Eells, Marcellus, & others	Witness fees in contested election.	30	2	Petition	77	Accounts.						
Effinger, John J.	Payment of a promised revolutionary bounty.	22	2	Petition	175	Rev. Claims.						
Effinger, John J.	Payment of a promised revolutionary bounty.	23	1	Petition	307	Rev. Claims.						
Effinger, John J.	Payment of a promised revolutionary bounty.	23	2	Petition	239	Rev. Claims.						
Egan, Thomas	Pension	4	1	Rep. of Comm'r of Claims.	447	Claims	Feb. 18, 1796	Favorable	156	Passed	Passed	App'd April 20, 1796
Egabroudt, Joseph	(See Casper B. Cook, and others)	30	1		272							
Egbert, Maria	Renewal of a pension	22	2	Petition	266	Naval Affairs.						
Egbert, William	Compensation for horse lost in the public service.	23	1	Petition	439	Rev. Claims.						
Egberson, Cornelius, widow of.	Pension to revolutionary widows married after 1800.	31	2	Petition	269	Rev. Pensions.						
Egerton, Giles, representatives of.	Location of a land warrant	19	2	Senate bill	266	Public Lands	81	With't amend.	64	Passed	Passed	App'd March 3, 1827
Eggleston, Benjamin	Indemnity for losses, &c., war of 1812.	27	2	Petition	455	Claims	709	Adverse		Laid on table.		
Eggleston, Elijah, widow of.	Pension	28	2	Petition	146	Rev. Pensions.						

List of private claims presented to the House of Representatives of the United States from the 1st to the 31st Congress, inclusive—Continued.

Names of claimants.	Nature or object of the claim.	Congress.	Session.	How brought before the House of Reps.	Page of journal.	To what committee of the House referred.	No. or date of the report.	Nature of the report.	No. of the bill.	How disposed of by the House of Reps.	How disposed of by the Senate.	Date of the act of Congress, and remarks.
Eggleston, Joseph	Pension for revolutionary services.	29	1	Petition	463	Rev. Pensions	....	....	.....	Discharged; laid on table.	....	Leave to withdraw, 2d sess., 30th Cong.
Eggleston, Moses, heirs of.	Indemnity for property lost on board the California.	19	1	Resolution	297	Claims.						
Eglize, Dominique L.....	Increase of pension	1	2	Memorial	218	....	....	....	.....	Refered to Secretary of Treasury.		
Egnew, George, widow of.	Indemnity for property destroyed by Indians.	24	2	Petition	132	Claims.						
Egnew, George, widow of.	Indemnity for property destroyed by Indians.	25	3	Petition	462	Claims.						
Egnew, George, widow of.	Indemnity for property destroyed by Indians.	26	1	Petition	167	Claims.						
Egnew, George, widow of.	Indemnity for property destroyed by Indians.	28	1	Petition	204	Claims...........	345	Adverse	.....	Laid on table.		
Egnew, George, widow of.	Indemnity for property destroyed by Indians.	30	2	Memorial	91	Indian Affairs.....	59	Adverse	.....	Laid on table.		
Egnew, George M.......	Land in lieu of North Carolina grants.	20	1	Petition	457	Whole House.						
Egnew, Jesse W........	Land in lieu of North Carolina grants.	20	1	Petition	457	Whole House.						
Egnew, Nancy	(See George Egnew, widow of.)											
Egron, Pierre...........	Exemption from postage	3	2	Petition	231	Select	Dec. 5, 1794	Adverse.				
Eichelberger, Barnet, executor of.	Compensation for revolutionary services.	3	1	Memorial	107	....	....	....	.....	Referred to Secretary Treasury.		
Eichelberger, Barnet, executor of.	Compensation for revolutionary services.	3	2	Rep. of Secretary Treasury.	284	....	....	....	.....	Laid on table.		
Eichelberger, Barnet, executor of.	Compensation for revolutionary services.	29	2	Memorial	86	Rev. Claims.						
Eichelberger, Barnet, executor of.	Compensation for revolutionary services.	30	1	Petition	575	Rev. Claims.						
Eichelberger, Barnet, executor of.	Compensation for revolutionary services.	31	1	Petition	472	Rev. Claims.						
Eichelberger, Frederick and George.	Reimbursement of duties paid on stills.	18	1	Petition	213	Ways and Means..	Feb. 18, 1824	General bill ..	126	Passed	Passed	App'd May 26, 1834
Eights, James	Reimbursement of expenses, &c., on Exploring Expedition.	27	2	Memorial	227	Claims.						
				Senate bill	782	Claims...........	832	With amend..	141	Laid on table.		
Eiler, Laurentius M......	Compensation for services as deputy surveyor, Missouri.	23	1	Petition	35	Claims...........	67	Favorable	77	Passed	Reported with't amendment.	
Eiler, Laurentius M......	Compensation for services as deputy surveyor, Missouri.	23	2	Petition	109	Claims	16	Favorable	592	Referred to Committee Whole House.		
Eiler, Laurentius M......	Compensation for services as deputy surveyor, Missouri.	24	1	Petition	51	Claims...........	28	Favorable....	28	Passed	Passed	App'd Feb. 17, 1836
Eimbeck, George........	Compensation for revolutionary services.	4	1	Petition	426	Claims	May 31, 1796	Adverse	.....	Laid on table.		
Eiselen, Conrad, administrator of.	Indemnity for French spoliations prior to 1800.	26	1	Memorial	182	Foreign Affairs....	343	Favorable; bill	319	Referred to Committee Whole House.		
Eisell, or Eisler, John....	Pension for revolutionary services.	22	1	Petition	412	Rev. Pensions	Mar. 26, 1832	Favorable	513	Referred to Committee Whole House.		
Elam, James	Grant of land for wounds, &c....	17	2	Petition	144	Priv. Land Claims.	Jan. 29, 1823	Adverse	.....	Laid on table.		
Elbert, Lieut., widow of ..	Continuation of pension	17	2	Resolution	223	Naval Affairs	Mar. 1, 1823	Adverse, with resolution.	.....	Resolution adopted.		
Elbert, Lieut	Compensation for horse lost in public service.	22	1	Resolution	597	Claims.						

List of private claims presented to the House of Representatives of the United States from the 1st to the 31st Congress, inclusive—Continued.

Names of claimants.	Nature or object of the claim.	Congress.	Session.	How brought before the House of Reps.	Page of journal.	To what committee of the House referred.	No. or date of the report.	Nature of the report.	No. of the bill.	How disposed of by the House of Reps.	How disposed of by the Senate.	Date of the act of Congress, and remarks.
Eld, Henry	(See Exploring Expedition)	27	3		149		270		818			
Eld, Henry A	(See Louis F. Beeler and others)	30	1		115		482					
Elden, Silas C., widow of	Pension	31	1	Petition	623	Invalid Pensions.						
Elder, James	Compensation for horses lost in public service.	23	1	Petition	438	Claims	441	Adverse		Laid on table.		
Elder, John, widow of	Pension for revolutionary services.	27	2	Documents	614	Rev. Pensions	795	Favorable	449	Ordered to 3d reading.		
Elder, John, widow of	Pension for revolutionary services.	27	3	House bill	88				449	Passed	Indef. postp'd.	
Elder, Joseph, widow of	Pension for revolutionary services.	27	3	Petition	53	Military Pensions	295	Adverse		Laid on table.		
Elder, Robert	Pension	12	1	Pension bill	361	Whole House	June 15, 1812	With amend.	138	Passed	Passed with amendment.	App'd July 5, 1812
Eldred, Elisha	(See Julius Eldred and others)	28	2		167							
Eldred, Francis E	(See Julius Eldred and others)	28	2		167							
Eldred, John, widow of	Continuation of pension	18	2	Petition	91	Rev. Pensions	June 17, 1825	Adverse		Laid on table.		
Eldred, Julius, and others	Indemnity for seizure of copper rock.	28	2	Petition	167	Claims.						
Eldred, Julius, and others	Reimbursement of expenses for removing copper rock.	29	1	Petition	486	Public Lands	584	Favorable	404	Rep'd by Committee Whole House.		
Eldred, Julius, and others	Reimbursement of expenses for removing copper rock.	29	2	House bill	73				404	Passed	Passed	App'd Jan. 26, 1847
Eldred, Moses	Pension	14	2	Resolution	424	Pens. & Rev. Cl'ms.						
Eldred, Moses	Pension	25	2	Resolution	85	Invalid Pensions	650	Favorable	626	Passed	Passed	App'd July 7, 1838
Eldred, Robert, and others	Remission of duty on a cargo of salt.	24	2	Petition	124	Ways and Means.	Jan. 10, 1837	Adverse		Laid on table.		
Eldred, Robert, and others	Remission of duty on a cargo of salt.	28	1	Petition	89	Ways and Means.						
Eldred, Ward	Confirmation of title to land in Illinois.	23	2	Petition	214	Public Lands.						
Eldred, Ward	Confirmation of title to land in Illinois.	25	2	Petition	1010	Public Lands.						
Eldred, Ward	Confirmation of title to land in Illinois.	26	1	Petition	365	Priv. Land Claims				Discharged; laid on table.		
Eldridge, Alfred	Pension for military services	13	2	Petition	250	Pensions.						
Eldridge, Alfred	Bounty land for military services	13	2	Petition	250	Public Lands				Discharged.		
Eldridge, Daniel, (Ind.)	Pension for revolutionary services.	3	1	Rep. of Secretary of War.	131	Select	May 26, 1794	Res. to refer to Sec. War.	R. 12	Passed	Passed	App'd June 9, 1794
Eldridge, Daniel	Pension for revolutionary services.	8	2	Petition	24	Whole House.						
Eldridge, Daniel	Pension for revolutionary services.	9	1	Petition	222	Claims	Mar. 28, 1806			Indefinitely postponed.		Leave to withdraw.
Eldridge, Elisha	(See executor, &c., of Thomas H. Meredith.)	19	1		226							
Eldridge, Elisha	Remission of fine for breach of revenue laws.	25	3	Senate bill	546	Commerce	Feb. 25, 1839	With't amend.	S. 130	Referred to Committee Whole House.		
Eldridge, Ephraim	Pre emption to land as New Orleans branch pilot.	28	1	Petition	77	Priv. Land Claims.	9	Favorable	35	Passed	Passed	App'd June 17, 1844
Eldridge, Frederick W	(See heir of Levy Eldridge)	5	2		191							
Eldridge, Hannah	(See widow of Daniel Littlefield)	24	2		38		124		854			
Eldridge, Heber, widow of	Revolutionary pension	31	1	Petition	406	Rev. Pensions	137	Adverse		Laid on table.		
Eldridge, James, son of	Compensation for property taken for public use.	17	1	Petition	165	Pens. & Rev. Cl'ms.	Feb. 12, 1822	Adverse		Laid on table.		
Eldridge, James, son of	Compensation for property taken for public use.	20	1	Petition	69	Rev. Claims	Jan. 18, 1828	Adverse		Laid on table.		
Eldridge, James B	(See son of James Eldridge)	17	1		165							
Eldridge, Jeremiah	Pension for revolutionary services.	15	2	Petition	215	Pens. & Rev. Cl'ms.				Discharged; laid on table.		

List of private claims presented to the House of Representatives of the United States from the 1st to the 31st Congress, inclusive—Continued.

Names of claimants.	Nature or object of the claim.	Congress.	Session.	How brought before the House of Reps.	Page of journal.	To what committee of the House referred.	No. or date of the report.	Nature of the report.	No. of the bill.	How disposed of by the House of Reps.	How disposed of by the Senate.	Date of the act of Congress, and remarks.
Eldridge, Jeremiah	Pension for revolutionary services.	16	1	Petition	59	Pens. & Rev. Cl'ms.						
Eldridge, Joshua	(See William Gray, and others.)	14	2		310							
Eldridge, John J.	Pension	29	1	Petition	175	Invalid Pensions				Discharged; leave to withdraw.		
Eldridge, Levi, and others.	Bounty on fishing schooner Harriet.	25	3	Petition	214	Commerce	235	Adverse		Laid on table.		
Eldridge, Levi, and others.	Bounty on fishing schooner Harriet.	26	1	Petition	290	Commerce	387	Adverse		Laid on table.		
Eldridge, Levi, and others.	Bounty on fishing schooner Harriet.	26	2	Petition	90	Commerce.						
Eldridge, Levi, and others.	Bounty on fishing schooner Harriet.	27	2	Petition	96	Commerce	476	Favorable	326	Ordered to 3d reading.		
Eldridge, Levi, and others.	Bounty on fishing schooner Harriet.	27	3	House bill	87				326	Passed	Indef. postp'd.	
Eldridge, Levi, and others.	Bounty on fishing schooner Harriet.	28	1	Petition	122	Commerce	139	Favorable	128	Passed.		
Eldridge, Levi, and others.	Bounty on fishing schooner Harriet.	28	2	Petition	73	Commerce.						
Eldridge, Levi, and others.	Bounty on fishing schooner Harriet.	29	1	Petition	105	Commerce	264	Favorable	226	Referred to Committee Whole House.		
Eldridge, Levi, and others.	Bounty on fishing schooner Harriet.	30	1	Petition	288	Commerce.						
Eldridge, Levi, heir of	Pay and emoluments due for revolutionary services.	5	2	Petition	191	Claims	Mar. 8, 1798	Adverse.				
Eldridge, Mary	(See Heber Eldridge, widow of.)	31	1		406		137					
Eldridge, Samuel	Reimbursement of advances on public account.	13	2	Petition	287	Claims	Feb. 12, 1814	Adverse		Laid on table.		
Eldridge, Thomas	Remission of duties unjustly exacted.	26	2	Petition	52	Commerce	97	Favorable	603	Referred to Committee Whole House.		
Eldridge, William, by attorney.	Pension	18	2	Petition	183	Pens. & Rev. Cl'ms.						
Eldridge, Zoeth	(See Augustus G. Elliot, sureties of.)	19	1	Petition	221	Ways and Means	Feb. 24, 1826	Adverse		Laid on table.		
Elford, James, administrator of.	Extension of patent for marine telegraph.	23	2	Petition	274	Judiciary.						
Elholm, Christian G.	Compensation for capture of British prisoners.	2	1	Petition	544					Referred to Secretary War.		
Elholm, Christian G.	Compensation for capture of British prisoners.	3	2	Rep. of Secretary War.	278					Laid on table.		
Eliza, brig, owners of	Compensation for vessel sunk in Baltimore harbor.	21	1	Memorial	82	Commerce	Feb. 2, 1830	Favorable	191	Passed	Passed	App'd May 29, 1830
Elkins, Jonathan	Pension for revolutionary services.	23	1	Resolution	90	Rev. Pensions.						
Elkins, Jonathan	Pension for revolutionary services.	24	1	Senate bill	811	Rev. Pensions	May 17, 1836	With't amend.	236	Passed	Passed	App'd June 15, 1836
Elkins, Reuben H.	(See Goodman Oldham, sureties of.)	20	1		365							
Elkins, Samuel, administrator of.	Adjustment of claim under convention with Mexico.	29	1	Memorial	353	Foreign Affairs.						
Ella, John, jr.	(See Scholfield and Taylor, agent of.)	16	1	Petition	212	Ways and Means.						
Ellbright, Philip	Pension for revolutionary services.	21	1	Resolution	213	Military Pensions.						
Ellege, Tarleton, and others	Exchange of an entry of land	25	2	Petition	1209	Public Lands.						
Ellege, Tarleton, and others	Exchange of an entry of land	25	3	Petition	92	Public Lands.						
Ellege, Tarleton, and others	Exchange of an entry of land	26	1	Petition	436	Public Lands				Discharged; laid on table.		

List of private claims presented to the House of Representatives of the United States from the 1*st to the* 31*st Congress, inclusive*—**Continued.**

Names of claimants.	Nature or object of the claim.	Congress.	Session.	How brought before the House of Reps.	Page of journal.	To what committee of the House referred.	No. or date of the report.	Nature of the report.	No. of the bill.	How disposed of by the House of Reps.	How disposed of by the Senate.	Date of the act of Congress, and remarks.
Ellen, John W., and others	Right of pre emption	24	2	Petition	389	Public Lands.						
Ellenwood, Jedediah	Pension	16	1	Petition	26	Pens. & Rev. Cl'ms.				Discharged; referred to Secretary of War.		
Ellery, Christopher	Increase of compensation as collector of customs, Rhode Island.	21	2	Resolution	77	Commerce				Discharged; referred to Sec. Treasury.		
Ellery, Joseph	Pension	26	1	Petition	937	Invalid Pensions				Discharged; laid on table.		
Ellery, Joseph	Pension	27	2	Petition	154	Invalid Pensions.						
				Documents	746	Invalid Pensions	1005	Favorable	583	Referred to Committee Whole House.		
Ellery, Joseph	Pension	27	3	Rep. Committee Whole House.	91			With't amend.	583	Passed	Passed	App'd March 3, 1843
Ellery, William	Increase of compensation as collector at Newport.	2	2	Petition	655					Referred to Secretary Treasury.		
Ellery, William	Increase of compensation as collector at Newport.	3	2	Rep. of Secretary Treasury.	284	Select	Jan. 26, 1795	General bill	75	Passed	Passed	App'd Feb. 14, 1795
Ellery, William, executor of.	(Does not appear)	19	2	Memorial	31	Ways and Means				Discharged; leave to withdraw.		
Ellery, William, and others	Bounty on fishing schooners Sevo and Ida.	26	2	Petition	121	Claims.						
Ellery, William, and others	Bounty on fishing schooners Sevo and Ida.	27	2	Petition	95	Commerce	1018	Favorable	591	Referred to Committee Whole House.		
Ellery, William, and others	Bounty on fishing schooners Sevo and Ida.	27	3	Rep't Committee Whole House.	91			With't amend.	591	Passed	Indef. postp'd.	
Ellery, William, and others	Bounty on fishing schooners Sevo and Ida.	28	1	Petition	100	Commerce	62	Favorable	86	Passed	Adverse.	
Ellery, William, and others	Bounty on fishing schooners Sevo and Ida.	28	2	Petition	72	Commerce	56	Favorable	535			
Ellery, William, and others	Bounty on fishing schooners Sevo and Ida.	29	1	Petition	234	Commerce	541	Favorable	363			
Ellery, William, and others	Bounty on fishing schooners Sevo and Ida.	30	1	Petition	157	Commerce.						
Ellery, William, and others	Bounty on fishing schooners Sevo and Ida.	30	2	Petition	203	Commerce.						
Ellicott, Andrew	Compensation as boundary commissioner.	1	1	Petition	58	Select	July 8, 1789	Indefinite		Laid on table.		
				Report of Select Committee.	65		July 23, 1789	Favorable		Laid on table.		
Ellicott, Elias	(See David Stewart & Sons, trustees of.)											
Ellingwood, Joseph	Compensation for revolutionary services.	21	1	Petition	57	Rev. Claims	Dec. 21, 1829	Adverse		Laid on table.		
Ellingwood, William	To be restored to pension roll	23	1	Petition	466	Rev. Pensions				Discharged; leave to withdraw.		
Elliott, Adam	Compensation for horse lost in the Seminole war.	23	1	Documents	154	Claims.						
Elliott, Andrew	(See Wm. H. Bedford, agent)	28	1		262							
Elliott, Andrew	Permission to import merchandise.	12	1	Petition	19	Com. and Manuf.						
Elliott, Augustus G., sureties of.	Release from liability on a bond	19	1	Petition	221	Ways and Means	Feb. 24, 1826	Adverse		Laid on table.		
Elliott, Benjamin	Exchange of a land location	25	2	Petition	178	Priv. Land Claims.						
Elliott, Benjamin	Exchange of a land location	26	1	Petition	178	Public Lands				Discharged; laid on table.		
Elliott, Benjamin	Exchange of a land location	27	2	Petition	530	Public Lands	787	Adverse		Laid on table.		

List of private claims presented to the House of Representatives of the United States from the 1st to the 31st Congress, inclusive—Continued.

Names of claimants.	Nature or object of the claim.	Congress.	Session.	How brought before the House of Reps.	Page of journal.	To what committee of the House referred.	No. or date of the report.	Nature of the report.	No. of the bill.	How disposed of by the House of Reps.	How disposed of by the Senate.	Date of the act of Congress, and remarks.
Elliott, Bernard, executor of	Commutation pay for revolutionary services.	2	1	Petition .... Rep. of Secretary War.	439 459	Select	Nov. 25, 1791	Favorable	152	Passed	Passed	App'd March 27, 1792
Elliott, Charles	Confirmation of title to land	15	1	Petition	56	Priv. Land Claims.						
Elliott, David	Pension for revolutionary services.	8	2	Petition	80	Claims.						
Elliott, George	Payment of money unjustly withheld.	22	2	Resolution	322	Indian Affairs.						
Elliott, George	Payment of money unjustly withheld.	23	1	Resolution	57	Indian Affairs	88	Favorable	93	Passed	Passed	App'd June 28, 1834
Elliott, George	Indemnity for the loss of his improvements.	24	1	Petition	66	Indian Affairs.						
Elliott, George	Pension	24	1	Petition	52	Invalid Pensions...	Jan. 28, 1836	Favorable	252	Passed	Passed	App'd June 28, 1836
Elliott, Henry, widow of..	Pension for revolutionary services.	29	1	Petition	326	Rev. Pensions	....	....	.....	Discharged; laid on table.		
Elliott, Henry, widow of..	Pension for revolutionary services.	29	2	Petition	214	Rev. Pensions.						
Elliott, James	Confirmation of title to land in Mississippi Territory.	13	3	Petition	711	Public Lands	....	....	.....	Discharged.		
Elliott, James	Pension for services in Indian wars.	24	1	Petition	946	....	....	....	.....	Laid on table.		
Elliott, Jesse D	(See John Dickson and others)...	19	2	....	105							
Elliott, Jesse D., executor of.	Reimbursement of expenses in entertaining King of Greece.	30	1	Petition	807	Naval Affairs.						
Elliott, Jesse D., widow of	Reimbursement of expenses in entertaining King of Greece.	31	1	Petition	350	Naval Affairs.						
Elliott, John C., and others	(See Jonathan Hampton, *et al.*)..	17	1	....	129							
Elliott, John, and others..	Further compensation as revolutionary surgeon's mates.	2	1	Petition	463	....	....	....	.....	Referred to Secretary War.		
Elliott, John, and others..	Further compensation as revolutionary surgeon's mates.	2	2	Rep. of Secretary War.	696	....	....	....	.....	Laid on table.		
Elliott, John	Compensation for services as surgeon's mate.	9	2	Petition	598	....	....	....	.....	Laid on table.		
Elliott, John	Indemnity for injuries during revolutionary war.	10	1	Petition	44	Claims.						
Elliott, John	Indemnity for injuries during revolutionary war.	10	2	Resolution	380	Select.						
Elliott, John	Indemnity for injuries during revolutionary war.	11	2	Petition	280	Claims	Mar. 20, 1810	Adverse.				
Elliott, John	Pension for revolutionary services.	12	1	Petition	99	Claims	June 8, 1812	Pension bill ..	138	Passed	Passed with amendment.	App'd July 5, 1812
Elliott, John	Arrears of pension	13	2	Petition	250	Pensions	Mar. 28, 1814	....	.....	Referred to Committee Whole House.		
Elliott, John	Pension	21	1	Petition	447	Military Pensions..	April 13, 1830	Adverse	.....	Laid on table.		
Elliott, John	Pension	22	1	Petition	36	Rev. Pensions	7	Favorable	55	Passed	Indef. postp'd.	
Elliott, John	Bounty land to children of deceased son.	18	1	Petition	196	Rev. Pensions.						
Elliott, Jonathan	Extension of time to complete a payment.	16	1	Petition	182	Dist. of Columbia.	57	Favorable	66	Passed	Passed	App'd May 4, 1820
Elliott, Jonathan	Remission of interest on purchase of a lot of ground.	25	2	Memorial	279	Dist. of Columbia.	Jan. 25, 1838	Adverse	.....	Laid on table.		
Elliott, Jonathan	Compensation for use of his property by United States troops.	24	1	Petition	91	Claims	May 31, 1836	Favorable	655			
Elliott, Jonathan	Compensation for use of his property by United States troops.	25	2	Petition	36	Claims	57	Favorable	63	Passed	Passed	App'd April 20, 1838

List of private claims presented to the House of Representatives of the United States from the 1st to the 31st Congress, inclusive—Continued.

Names of claimants.	Nature or object of the claim.	Congress.	Session.	How brought before the House of Reps.	Page of journal.	To what committee of the House referred.	No. or date of the report.	Nature of the report.	No. of the bill.	How disposed of by the House of Reps.	How disposed of by the Senate.	Date of the act of Congress, and remarks.
Elliott, Joseph	Permission to sell land granted to him.	17	1	Petition	39	Public Lands.						
Elliott, Joseph	Fee simple title to his reservation	17	1	Resolution	321	Public Lands.						
Elliott, Joseph	Permission to sell his reservation	17	2	Petition	121	Public Lands	....	....	......	Discharged; leave to withdraw.	....	See report No. 72.
Elliott, Joseph	Confirmation of title to his children of reservation.	21	2	Petition	100	Public Lands.						
Elliott, Joseph	Relinquishment to him of his reversionary interest in U. States.	22	1	Senate bill	540	Public lands	April 10, 1832	With amend	76	Passed with amendm't.	Passed as am'd.	App'd July 13, 1832
Elliott, Joseph	Pension	10	2	Pension bill	499	Whole House	Feb. 20, 1809	With amend	158	Passed	Passed with amendment.	App'd March 3, 1809
Elliott, Jared L	(See Exploring Expedition)	27	3	....	149	....	270	....	818			
Elliott, Joseph, and others.	Fee-simple title to their reservations	20	2	Petition	64	Public Lands	42	Favorable	363	Referred to Committee Whole House.		
Elliott, Lucy	Continuation of pension	28	1	Petition	849	Rev. Pensions.						
Elliott, Luke, widow of	Renewal of pension	25	2	Petition	118	Naval Affairs	....	....	......	Discharged; laid on table.		
Elliott, Luke, widow of	Renewal of pension	27	2	Petition	48	Naval Affairs	603	Adverse	......	Laid on table.		
Elliott, Mary, and others	That their pensions may be continued.	22	2	Petition	40	Naval Affairs.						
Elliott, Mary, and others	That their pensions may be continued.	23	1	Memorial	73	Naval Affairs	Dec. 19, 1833	Favorable	49	Passed	Passed	App'd June 18, 1834
Elliott, Mary	Continuation of pension	28	1	Petition	950	Whole House.						
Elliott, Nathaniel	Pension	19	2	Petition	26	Military Pensions	....	....	......	Discharged.		
Elliott, Nathaniel	Pension	20	1	Resolution	303	Military Pensions	April 29, 1828	Favorable	283	Passed.		
Elliott, Nathaniel	Pension	20	2	Pension bill	55	Whole House	Jan. 15, 1829	With amend	311	Passed	Laid on table.	
Elliott, Nathaniel	Pension	21	1	Resolution	4[illegible]	Military Pensions	Jan. 5, 1830	Favorable	72	Passed	Passed, with amendment	App'd May 20, 1830
Elliott & Purviance	Remission of duty on coffee	3	1	Senate bill	137	....	....	....	9	Passed	Passed	App'd May 9, 1794
Elliott, Richard	Pension for revolutionary services.	24	1	Petition	944	Rev. Pensions	June 21, 1836	Favorable	715	Referred to Committee Whole House.		
Elliott, Richard	Pension for revolutionary services.	25	2	Petition	37	Rev. Pensions	265	Favorable	308	Passed	Adverse report.	
Elliott, Richard	Pension for revolutionary services.	27	3	Resolution	69	Rev. Pensions	295	Adverse	......	Laid on table.		
Elliott, Richard	Pension for revolutionary services.	28	1	Petition	109	Rev. Pensions	160	Favorable	149	Passed	Indef. postp'd.	
Elliott, Richard	Pension for revolutionary services.	28	2	Petition	58	Rev. Pensions.	8	Favorable	458	Passed	Indef. postp'd.	
Elliott, Richard	Pension for revolutionary services.	29	1	Senate bill	808	Rev. Pensions	July 13, 1846	With amend	S. 49	Passed	Passed	App'd Aug. 8, 1846
Elliott, Robert	Compensation for revolutionary services.	3	2	Petition	316	Claims	....	....	......	Discharged; laid on table.	....	Leave to withdraw.
Elliott, Robert	Half-pay for revolutionary services.	4	1	Resolution	373	Claims	Jan. 6, 1796	Adverse	......	Laid on table.		
Elliott, Robert	Pension	14	1	Petition	41	Pens. & Rev. Cl'ms.	....	....	......	....	....	Name not found in pension act.
Elliott, Robert	Commutation pay for revolutionary services.	23	2	Petition	138	Rev. Claims	Jan. 20, 1835	Adverse	......	Laid on table.		
Elliott, Robert, administrator of.	Commutation pay for revolutionary services.	23	2	Petition	47	Rev. Claims	Dec. 23, 1834	Adverse	......	Laid on table.		
Elliott, Robert, widow of	Indemnity for losses in Indian wars	6	1	Petition	608	Claims	April 26, 1800	Adverse	......	Postponed.		
Elliott, Robert, widow of	Indemnity for losses in Indian wars	7	2	Petition	303	Claims	Feb. 8, 1803	....	......	Discharged; referred to Com. Whole House.		
Elliott, Robert, widow of	Indemnity for losses in Indian wars	8	1	Petition	409	Claims	Feb. 14, 1804	....	......	Discharged; referred to Com. Whole House.		
Elliott, Robert, widow of	Indemnity for losses in Indian wars	8	2	Petition	17	Claims	Dec. 14, 1804	Favorable	27	Passed	Passed	App'd March 3, 1805
Elliott, Robert M	Reimbursement of advances on public account.	17	1	Petition	77	Claims	Jan. 30, 1822	Adverse	......	Rejected.		

List of private claims presented to the House of Representatives of the United States from the 1st to the 31st Congress, inclusive—Continued.

Names of claimants.	Nature or object of the claim.	Congress.	Session.	How brought before the House of Reps.	Page of journal.	To what committee of the House referred.	No. or date of the report.	Nature of the report.	No. of the bill.	How disposed of by the House of Reps.	How disposed of by the Senate.	Date of the act of Congress, and remarks.
Elliott, R. M. D. J.	Right of pre-emption	14	1	Petition	401	Public Lands.						
Elliott, Russell, and others.	Compensation for bringing prisoners from Nova Scotia.	31	1	Petition	624	Commerce.						
Elliott, Silence, heirs of	Compensation for land in Boston occupied by United States.	24	1	Senate bill	907	Judiciary	June 15, 1836	With't amend.	224	Referred to Committee Whole House.		
Elliott, S. B.	(See Exploring Expedition)	27	3		149		270		818			
Elliott, S. B.	Compensation for services as acting purser.	30	1	Petition	535	Naval Affairs	595	Favorable	475	Referred to Committee Whole House.		
Elliott, S. B.	Compensation for services as acting purser.	31	1	Petition	325	Naval Affairs.						
Elliott, Temple	(See Thomas Elliott, heir of)	5	2		186							
Elliott, Thomas O.	(See executor of Bernard Elliott)	2	1		439							
Elliott, Thomas	Pension for revolutionary services	12	1	Petition	334	Claims	June 12, 1812	Adverse		Laid on table		Leave to withdraw.
Elliott, Thomas, heirs of	Pension for revolutionary services	29	2	Petition	169	Rev. Pensions.						
Elliott, Thomas, heir of	Grant of land for revolutionary services.	5	2	Petition	186	Claims	April 2, 1798	Adverse		Referred to Committee Whole House.		
Elliott, Thomas, heir of	Grant of land for revolutionary services.	6	1	Petition	545	Claims	Feb. 25, 1800	Adverse		Referred to Committee Whole House.		
Elliott, Theodore E.	Compensation for a boat delivered to public agent.	31	1	Senate bill	1283	Indian Affairs			S. 317			
Elliott, Theodore E.	Compensation for a boat delivered to public agent.	31	2	Rep'rt Committee Whole House.	207	Whole House			S. 317			
Elliott, William	Increase of compensation as clerk in Patent office.	14	2	Petition	129	Ways and Means	Jan. 25, 1817	Favorable.				
Elliott, William	Indemnity for loss of a contract to which he was entitled by his bid.	14	1	Petition	71	Pub. Expenditures				Discharged; laid on table.		
Elliott, William	Indemnity for loss of a copy-right	21	2	Petition	207	Judiciary.						
Elliott, William	Compensation for assertaining longitude of Capitol.	17	1	Appropriat'n bill					177			App'd April 30, 1822
Elliott, William P.	Compensation for drawings for Patent office.	24	2	Appropriat'n bill					776			App'd March 3, 1837
Elliott, William P.	Compensation for designs for Treasury, &c.	24	2	Petition	218	Public Buildings.						
Elliott, William	Pension for revolutionary services	15	1	Petition	203	Pens. & Rev. Cl'ms.				Referred to Secretary of War.		
Elliott, William	Pension for revolutionary services	16	1	Petition	267	Pens. & Rev. Cl'ms.				Referred to Secretary of War.		
Elliott, William	Pension for revolutionary services	21	1	Resolution	536	Military Pensions.						
Elliott, William	Pension for revolutionary services	22	1	Petition	45	Rev. Pensions.						
Elliott, William, jr.	Right of pre-emption	28	1	Senate bill	1005	Public Lands			S. 176			
Elliott, William, jr.	Right of pre-emption	28	2	Senate bill	220	Public Lands			S. 17			
Elliott, William, jr.	Right of pre-emption	29	1	Senate bill	191	Public Lands	118	With't amend.	S. 8	Passed	Passed	App'd Mar. 11, 1846
Ellis, Abram	Confirmation of title to land in Mississippi.	10	2	Petition	347	Public Lands	Feb. 10, 1809	Favorable	161	Passed	Passed, with amendment.	App'd Feb. 28, 1809
Ellis, Amarylis	(See George Ellis, administrator of)											
Ellis, Charles, sen., administrator of.	Reimbursement of duties improperly exacted.	31	2	Petition	37	Commerce.						
Ellis, Daniel	(See executors of Samuel How)	1	3		355							
Ellis, David	Debenture on Madeira wine	20	1	Senate bill	444	Ways and Means	Mar. 31, 1828	With't amend.	93	Passed	Passed	App'd May 26, 1828
Ellis, Edward	Increase of pension	31	1	Petition	582	Invalid Pensions.						
Ellis, Elizabeth	(See daughter of Rachel Brown)	29	1		59							
Ellis, George, administrator of.	Indemnity for French spoliations prior to 1800.	26	1	Memorial	182	Foreign Affairs	334	Favorable; bill	319	Referred to Committee Whole House.		

List of private claims presented to the House of Representatives of the United States from the 1st to the 31st Congress, inclusive—Continued.

Names of claimants.	Nature or object of the claim.	Congress.	Session.	How brought before the House of Reps.	Page of journal.	To what committee of the House referred.	No. or date of the report.	Nature of the report.	No. of the bill.	How disposed of by the House of Reps.	How disposed of by the Senate.	Date of the act of Congress, and remarks.
Ellis, Giles, widow of	Half-pay commutation for bounty land.	16	1	Petition	267	Pens. & Rev. Cl'ms.				Referred to Secretary of War.		
Ellis, Giles U. and D. C. C.	Adjustment of claims for services in Florida.	30	1	Petition	407	Military Affairs.						
Ellis, Giles U. and D. C. C.	Adjustment of claims for services in Florida.	30	2	Petition	253	Military Affairs	57	Favorable	762	Referred to Committee Whole House.		
Ellis, Giles U. and D. C. C.	Adjustment of claims for services in Florida.	31	1	Petition	325	Military Affairs.						
Ellis, Giles U	Compensation for services in Florida war.	31	2	Rep't, Committee	241		Feb. 7, 1851	Favorable	457	Referred to Committee Whole House.		
Ellis, Jesse	Arrears of pension	29	1	Petition	93	Invalid Pensions	49	Adverse		Laid on table.		
Ellis, Jesse	Arrears of pension	29	2	Petition	141	Invalid Pensions						
Ellis, John, heirs of	Confirmation of title to land in Mississippi.	19	1	Petition	134	Priv. Land Claims.						
Ellis, John, heirs of	Confirmation of title to land in Mississippi.	19	2	Petition	37	Priv. Land Claims.				Discharged; laid on table.		
Ellis, John, heirs of	Confirmation of title to land in Mississippi.	20	1	Petition	224	Priv. Land Claims.				Discharged; laid on table.		
Ellis, John, heirs of	Confirmation of title to land in Mississippi.	20	2	Petition	60	Priv. Land Claims.	20	Favorable	336	Referred to Committee Whole House.		
Ellis, John, heirs of	Confirmation of title to land in Mississippi.	21	1	Petition	121	Priv. Land Claims.	62	Favorable	85	Passed	Passed, with amendment.	App'd May 29, 1830
Ellis, John, heirs of	Permission to locate a confirmed land claim.	22	1	Petition	47	Public Lands				Discharged; laid on table.		
Ellis, John, heirs of	Permission to locate a confirmed land claim.	22	2	Petition	55	Public Lands				Discharged; laid on table.		
Ellis, John, heirs of	Permission to locate a confirmed land claim.	23	1	Petition	138	Priv. Land Claims.						
Ellis, John, heirs of	Permission to locate a confirmed land claim.	23	2	Petition	142	Priv. Land Claims.						
Ellis, John	Arrears of pension	24	2	Resolution	76	Invalid Pensions				Discharged; laid on table.		
Ellis, John	Indemnity for loss in furnishing boats for removal of the Cherokees.	31	1	Petition	582	Claims.						
Ellis, John, widow of	Revolutionary pension	24	2	Petition	154	Rev. Pensions				Discharged; laid on table.		
Ellis, John L	Confirmation of title to land in Louisiana.	25	2	Petition	543	Priv. Land Claims.	785	Adverse		Laid on table.		
Ellis, John L	Confirmation of title to land in Louisiana.	26	1	Memorial	610	Priv. Land Claims.						
Ellis, Joseph	Pension	22	1	Petition	329	Rev. Pensions.						
Ellis, Leonard	Pension	22	1	Petition	330	Rev. Pensions				Disch'd; laid on table.		
Ellis, Phœnix Carp., administrator of.	Balance due on pension of deceased.	29	2	Petition	82	Invalid Pensions	Feb. 27, 1847	Favorable	692	Passed	Passed	App'd March 3, 1847
Ellis, Richard	(See William H. Bedford, agent)	28	1		262							
Ellis, Robert	(See children of William Ellis)	13	2		301							
Ellis, Robert, (Ind)	Increase of pension	29	1	Petition	358	Invalid Pensions	835	Favorable	552	Referred to Committee Whole House.		
Ellis, Robert, (Ind)	Increase of pension	29	2	Petition	327	Rev. Pensions.						
Ellis, Robert, (Ind)	Increase of pension	30	1	Petition	611	Rev. Pensions.						
Ellis, Robert, (Tenn)	Pension for revolutionary services.	30	1	Petition	164	Rev. Pensions	134	Favorable	123	Passed	Passed	App'd August 5, 1848
Ellis, Samuel	Indemnity against a suit, &c	12	1	Petition	264	Com. and Manuf.						

List of private claims presented to the House of Representatives of the United States from the 1st to the 31st Congress, inclusive—Continued.

Names of claimants.	Nature or object of the claim.	Congress.	Session.	How brought before the House of Reps.	Page of journal.	To what committee of the House referred.	No. or date of the report.	Nature of the report.	No. of the bill.	How disposed of by the House of Reps.	How disposed of by the Senate.	Date of the act of Congress, and remarks.
Ellis, Samuel	Indemnity against a suit, &c	12	2	Petition	566	Com. and Manuf.	June 20, 1813	Favorable	233	Passed	Postponed.	
Ellis, Samuel	Indemnity against a suit, &c	13	2	Petition	256	Com. and Manuf.	Feb. 4, 1814	Favorable	110	Passed	Passed	App'd Mar. 31, 1814
Ellis, Thomas	(See administrators of Chas. Ellis, sureties.)	31	2	Petition	37	Commerce.						
Ellis, William	Commutation pay, &c., for revolutionary services.	2	1	Petition	537					Referred to Secretary War.		
Ellis, William	Commutation pay, &c., for revolutionary services.	2	2	Rep. of Secretary War.	696					Laid on table.		
Ellis, William	Commutation pay, &c., for revolutionary services.	7	1	Petition	21	Claims	Dec. 31, 1801	Adverse.				
Ellis, William, children of.	Relief; father died in public service.	13	2	Petition	301	Military Affairs.						
Ellis, William	Pension	30	2	Petition	322	Invalid Pensions	82	Favorable	778	Referred to Committee Whole House.		
Ellis, William	Pre emption as New Orleans branch pilot.	28	1	Petition	77	Priv. Land Claims.	9	Favorable	35	Passed	Passed	App'd June 17, 1844
Ellis, William H.	Increase of compensation as surveyor of customs.	19	2	Petition	26	Commerce.						
Ellis, William H.	Increase of compensation as surveyor of customs.	20	1	Petition	51	Commerce	35	Indefinite		Referred to Secretary Treasury.		
Ellis, William, heirs of	To locate a Spanish claim	30	2	Memorial	457	Priv. Land Claims.						
Ellison, Jacob	(See Joseph Brown)	24	2		78							
Ellison, Thomas, executor of.	Prize money	2	2	Petition	699					Laid on table.		
Ellison, Thomas, executor of.	Pay and emoluments	5	2	Memorial	478	Claims	March 2, 1799	Adverse		Leave to withdraw.		
Ellison, William	Remission of penalty for breach of revenue laws.	4	2	Petition	696	Com. and Manuf.	March 3, 1797	Adverse		Laid on table		Leave to withdraw, 5th Cong., 2d sess.
Ellison, Price	(See William H. Bedford, agent.)	28	1		262							
Ellsworth, John, representative of.	Balance of pension	27	2	Petition	1041	Rev. Pensions.						
Ellsworth, John, representative of.	Balance of pension	28	1	Resolution Petition	313 318	Rev. Pensions. Rev. Pensions.						
Ellsworth, Henry L	Compensation for services as commissioner to Indians.	25	2	Appropr'n bill.					269			App'd July 7, 1838
Ellsworth, Ismel	Indemnity for property confiscated in Canada.	23	1	Petition	217	Claims	267	Adverse		Laid on table.		
Ellsworth, Verdine	(See Thaddeus Phelps & Co.,)	22	1		186							
Elmendorf, Edmund	Indemnity for French spoliations prior to 1800.	26	1	Memorial	182	Foreign Affairs	343	Favorable; bill.	319	Referred to Committee Whole House.		
Elmendorf, Peter	Pension for revolutionary services.	21	1	Resolution	248	Military Pensions.	May 3, 1830	Adverse		Laid on table.		
Elmendorf, Peter	Pension for revolutionary services.	21	2	Petition	48	Select.						
Elmer, Eli	Compensation for revolutionary services.	2	2	Petition	713					Referred to Secretary of War.		
Elmer, Eli	Compensation for revolutionary services.	3	1	Rep. of Secretary War.	93	Select.						
Elmer, Eli	Compensation for revolutionary services.	8	1	Petition	539	Claims				Referred to Committee Whole House.		
Elmer, Eli	Compensation for revolutionary services.	8	2	Petition	78	Claims.						
Elmer, Eli	Compensation for revolutionary services.	9	1	Memorial	212	Select.						

List of private claims presented to the House of Representatives of the United States from the 1st to the 31st Congress, inclusive—Continued.

Names of claimants.	Nature or object of the claim.	Congress.	Session.	How brought before the House of Reps.	Page of journal.	To what committee of the House referred.	No. or date of the report.	Nature of the report.	No. of the bill.	How disposed of by the House of Reps.	How disposed of by the Senate.	Date of the act of Congress, and remarks.
Elmer, Moses, heirs of	Commutation pay for revolutionary services.	24	2	Senate bill	250	Rev. Claims	259	Adverse	S. 53	Referred to Committee Whole House.		
Elmer, Moses, heirs of	Commutation pay for revolutionary services.	25	2	Senate bill	197	Rev. Claims	May 11, 1838	With amend.	S. 57	Referred to Committee Whole House.		
Elmore, Elizabeth	Continuation of pension	28	1	Petition	72	Rev. Pensions.						
Elmore, Robert	Pension for revolutionary services.	19	1	Resolution	115	Military Pensions.	164	Adverse.				
Elmslie, Alexander	Reimbursement of duties paid on copper bottom.	16	2	Petition	19	Commerce	Jan. 23, 1821	Favorable	217	Referred to Committee Whole House.		
Elmslie, Alexander	Reimbursement of duties paid on copper bottom.	17	1	Petition	23	Commerce	Dec. 18, 1821	Favorable	6	Passed	Passed	App'd Jan. 11, 1822
Elston, Isaac C	Release of reversionary interest of United States in Indian reservations.	30	1	Petition	316	Indian Affairs.						
Elton, Nathan N., widow of.	Pension	26	1	Petition	288	Invalid Pensions	252	Adverse	......	Laid on table.		
Elwell, Jonathan	Indemnity for illegal seizure of a vessel.	12	1	Petition	331	Com. and Manuf.						
Elwell, Payne	(See Joseph Cross, heirs of.)	22	1	....	435							
Elwell, Payne	Indemnity for French spoliations prior to 1800.	26	1	Memorial	182	Foreign Affairs	343	Favorable; bill	319	Referred to Committee Whole House.		
Elwell, Payne, executor of	Indemnity for French spoliations prior to 1800.	31	1	Petition	215	Foreign Affairs	355	General bill	318	Referred to Committee Whole House.		
Elwell, Robert	Indemnity for detention of ship Huntress.	10	1	Petition	185							
				Rep. of Secretary of Navy.	253	Claims.						
Elwell, Robert	Indemnity for detention of ship Huntress.	10	2	Petition	498	Claims.						
Elwell, Robert	Indemnity for detention of ship Huntress.	11	1	Petition	30	Claims.						
Elwell, Robert	Indemnity for detention of ship Huntress.	11	2	Petition	130	Claims	Jan. 31, 1810	Adverse	......	Referred to Committee Whole House.		
Elwell, William, jr	Pension	31	1	Petition	501	Invalid Pensions.						
Elwood, Abijah, widow of	Pension	26	1	Resolution	778	Rev. Pensions.						
Elwood, Abijah, widow of	Pension	26	2	Petition	78	Rev. Pensions	....	....	......	Leave to withdraw.		
Elwyn, John	Indemnity for losses in the public service.	27	2	Petition	76	Claims.						
Elwyn, John	Indemnity for losses in the public service.	28	1	Petition	297	Claims	292	Adverse	......	Laid on table.		
Ely, David A., and others.	Pre emption to land in Missouri	30	2	Memorial	91	Public Lands	115	Favorable	793	Referred to Committee Whole House.		
Ely, Elisha, heirs of	Commutation pay and interest for revolutionary services.	24	1	Petition	536	Rev. Claims.						
Ely, Elisha, heirs of	Commutation pay and interest for revolutionary services.	24	2	Resolution	135	Rev. Claims	166	Adverse	......	Laid on table.		
Ely, Elisha	(See Leonard Dennison and E Ely.)	20	2	....	119							
Ely, Henry	Pension	5	2	Petition	184	Claims	Mar. 12, 1798	Adverse.				
Ely, Hervey	Drawback on flour from Canada	26	1	Petition	291	Commerce.						
Ely, Hervey	Drawback on flour from Canada	27	2	Memorial	225	Commerce.						
Ely, Hervey	Drawback on flour from Canada	27	3	Petition	108	Commerce.						
Ely, Hervey	Drawback on flour from Canada	28	1	Petition	105	Ways and Means.						
Ely, Hervey, and others	Drawback on flour from Canada	31	1	Petition	212	Commerce.						

List of private claims presented to the House of Representatives of the United States from the 1st to the 31st Congress, inclusive—Continued.

Names of claimants.	Nature or object of the claim.	Congress.	Session.	How brought before the House of Reps.	Page of journal.	To what committee of the House referred.	No. or date of the report.	Nature of the report.	No. of the bill.	How disposed of by the House of Reps.	How disposed of by the Senate.	Date of the act of Congress, and remarks.
Ely, John	Compensation for revolutionary services and losses.	1	2	Petition	162							
				Rep. of Secretary War.	169	Select	Mar. 11, 1790	Favorable; bill ordered.	49	Rejected.		
				House bill	198	Whole House	April 30, 1790	With't amend.	56	Passed.		
Ely, Col. John, heirs of	Compensation for revolutionary services as surgeon.	22	2	Resolution	33	Rev. Claims	66	Favorable	709	Passed	Passed	App'd March 2, 1833
Ely, John C	Compensation for raising a sunken vessel.	25	2	Memorial	577	Commerce	690	Adverse		Laid on table.		
Elzande, Joseph	(See administrator of Antonia Pacheco.)	26	2		135							
Emanuel, David, executor of.	Release from judgment	12	1	Petition	....	Commerce.						
Emeline, Schooner, heirs of owners, &c.	Fishing bounty	23	1	Senate bill	175	Commerce	Mar. 26, 1834	With amend.	S. 24	Passed, with amend't.	Passed, with amendment.	App'd June 30, 1834
Emerick, Joseph	Reimbursement of excessive duty	30	1	Petition	157	Commerce	246	Adverse		Laid on table.		
Emerick, William	Pension	21	2	Petition	48	Military Pensions.						
Emerson, Edward	Indemnity for French spoliations prior to 1800.	31	1	Petition	196	Foreign Affairs	355	General bill	318	Referred to Committee Whole House.		
Emerson & Green	(See Peter H. Green, *et al.*)	16	2		230							
Emerson, John	Commutation pay for revolutionary services.	23	1	Petition	41	Rev. Claims	134	Favorable	144	Passed	Passed, with't amendment.	App'd June 30, 1834
Emerson, John	Interest on commutation pay	24	1	Resolution	269	Rev. Claims.						
Emerson, John	Interest on commutation pay	25	2	Resolution	77	Rev. Claims	671	Favorable	649	Postponed.		
Emerson, John	Interest on commutation pay	26	1	Petition	165	Rev. Claims						See report No. 436.
Emerson, John, representatives of.	Interest on commutation pay	27	2	Petition	61	Rev. Claims	373	Adverse		Laid on table.		
Emerson, John, representatives of.	Interest on commutation pay	31	1	Petition	500	Rev. Claims.						
Emmerson, John, heir of	Arrears of pay for revolutionary services.	28	2	Petition	54	Rev. Claims.						
Emerson, John B	Compensation for use of improved steam engine.	30	2	Memorial	92	Patents	126	Adverse		Laid on table.		
Emerson, John B	Compensation for use of improved steam engine.	31	1	Petition	1492	Patents.						
Emerson, Jonathan, executor of widow.	Half-pay for revolutionary services	29	1	Petition	704	Rev. Claims.						
Emerson, Jonathan, executor of widow.	Half pay for revolutionary services	29	2	Petition	69	Rev. Claims.						
Emerson, Joseph	(See executors of J. Libby)	17	1		83							
Emerson, Joseph	Indemnity for French spoliations prior to 1800.	26	1	Memorial	182	Foreign Affairs	343	Favorable; bill	319	Referred to Committee Whole House.		
Emerson, Keziah	Continuation of pension	28	1	Petition	849	Rev. Pensions.						
Emmerson, Oliver, widow of.	Pension	1	3	Petition	368					Referred to Secretary War.		
Emerson, Solomon	Pension	26	2	Petition	161	Invalid Pensions.						
Emerson, Solomon	Pension	27	2	Petition	377	Invalid Pensions	804	Favorable	458	Report'd by Committee Whole House.		
Emerson, Solomon	Pension	27	3	House bill	90				458	Passed	Passed	App'd March 3, 1843
Emerson, Thomas, sureties of.	Release from a judgment	27	2	Petition	100	Judiciary	992	Favorable	575	Referred to Committee Whole House.		
Emerson, Thomas, sureties of.	Release from a judgment	27	3	Rep't Committee Whole House.	91			With't amend.	575	Passed	Passed, with amendment.	App'd Feb. 4, 1843

List of private claims presented to the House of Representatives of the United States from the 1st to the 31st Congress, inclusive—Continued.

Names of claimants.	Nature or object of the claim.	Congress.	Session.	How brought before the House of Reps.	Page of journal.	To what committee of the House referred.	No. or date of the report.	Nature of the report.	No. of the bill.	How disposed of by the House of Reps.	How disposed of by the Senate.	Date of the act of Congress, and remarks.
Emerson, Thomas, sureties of.	Reimbursement of money paid on a judgment.	28	2	Senate bill	483	Judiciary	March 3, 1845	With't amend.	S. 110	Referred to Committee Whole House.		
Emerson, Thomas, sureties of.	Reimbursement of money paid on a judgment.	29	1	Senate bill	755	Judiciary	June 17, 1846	With't amend.	S. 131	Referred to Committee Whole House.		
Emerson, Thomas, sureties of.	Reimbursement of money paid on a judgment.	29	2	Petition	49	Judiciary	31	Favorable	614	Referred to Committee Whole House.		
Emerson, Thomas, sureties of.	Reimbursement of money paid on a judgment.	30	1	Petition	81	Judiciary	170	Favorable	181	Referred to Committee Whole House.		
Emerson, Thomas, sureties of.	Reimbursement of money paid on a judgment.	30	2	Rep't Committee Whole House	149	Judiciary		With't amend.	181	Passed	Passed	App'd March 3, 1849
Emerson, William	(See Beverly Chew, and others)	19	1		336							
Emerson, William	(See Peter H. Green, and others)	16	2		230							
Emery, Ephraim, widow of	Pension for revolutionary services	24	1	Petition	382	Rev. Pensions				Discharged; laid on table.		
Emery, Moses	Indemnity for French spoliations prior to 1800.	26	1	Memorial	182	Foreign Affairs	343	Favorable; bill	319	Referred to Committee Whole House.		
Emery, Samuel	Liquidation of certain revolutionary certificates.	4	1	Rep. of Secretary Treasury.	388	Claims	74	Adverse		Laid on table.		
Emison, John	Compensation for horse stolen by Indians.	19	1	Resolution	387	Claims	April 10, 1826	Adverse		Laid on table.		
Emlen, George	(See Archibald McCall and others)	2	1		520							
Emmett, James, heirs of	Compensation for team furnished, and advances.	25	2	Petition	177	Rev. Claims	913	Adverse		Laid on table.		
Ennett, James, heirs of	Compensation for team furnished, and advances.	26	1	Petition	359	Rev. Claims.						
Emmett, Joseph, representatives of.	Confirmation of title to land	25	2	Petition	905	Public Lands				Discharged.		
Emmett, John	Pension	21	2	Petition	120	Military Pensions.						
Emmett, John	Pension	22	1	Petition	113	Rev. Pensions.						
Emmons, Calvin	(See Uri Emmons, executor of)	29	2		49							
Emmons, George F	(See Exploring Expedition)	27	3		149		270		818			
Emmons, John	Pension	22	1	Petition	362	Rev. Pensions.						
Emmons, Solomon	Pension	21	2	Petition	143	Military Pensions.						
Emmons, Uri, executor of.	Extension of a patent	29	2	Petition	49	Patents	Jan. 20, 1847	Favorable	628	Referred to Committee Whole House.		
Emmons, Uri, executor of.	Extension of a patent	30	1	Petition	119	Patents	313	Favorable	28	Indefinitely postponed.		
Emmons, Uri, representatives of.	Extension of a patent	30	2	House bill	305	Patents			735			
Emory, Joseph	Indemnity for house burnt while in public use.	17	1	Petition	129	Claims.						
Emory, Joseph	Indemnity for house burnt while in public use.	17	2	Petition	64	Claims.						
Emory, Joseph	Indemnity for house burnt while in public use.	18	2	Petition	37	Claims	Dec. 22, 1824	Adverse		Laid on table.		
Emory, Joseph	Indemnity for house burnt while in public use.	19	1	Petition	249	Claims	Mar. 30, 1826	Adverse		Laid on table.		
Emory, Joseph	Indemnity for house burnt while in public use.	22	2	Petition	42	Claims	70	Adverse		Laid on table.		
Empie, John F	To be restored to pension roll	25	3	Petition	459	Rev. Pensions				Discharged; laid on table.		
Empie, John F	To be restored to pension roll	26	1	Petition	173	Rev. Pensions	490	Adverse.				

List of private claims presented to the House of Representatives of the United States from the 1st to the 31st Congress, inclusive—Continued.

Names of claimants.	Nature or object of the claim.	Congress.	Session.	How brought before the House of Reps.	Page of journal.	To what committee of the House referred.	No. or date of the report.	Nature of the report.	No. of the bill.	How disposed of by the House of Reps.	How disposed of by the Senate.	Date of the act of Congress, and remarks.
Endicott, John, and others.	Five years full pay for services of ancestors in revolutionary war.	29	1	Petition	947	Rev. Pensions.						
Endicott, Samuel	Prize money, Ketch and Intrepid.	19	2	House bill	98	Naval Affairs	74	With amend.	70	Referred to Committee Whole House.		
Endicott, Samuel	(See widow of Stephen Decatur, and others.)	20	1		295		201		S. 50			
Engels, Peter, sen	Pension	29	2	Senate bill	375	Invalid Pensions	Mar. 3, 1847	With't amend.	109			
Engels, Peter, sen	Pension	30	1	Senate bill	455	Invalid Pensions	Mar. 9, 1848	With't amend.	77	Passed	Passed	App'd April 12, 1848
England, John	Pension for revolutionary services.	25	2	Petition	70	Rev. Pensions	675	Favorable	653	Passed	Adverse.	
England, John	Pension for revolutionary services.	25	3	Petition	87	Rev. Pensions	27	Favorable	926	Passed	Adverse.	
England, John	Pension for revolutionary services.	26	1	Petition	171	Rev. Pensions	119	Favorable	129	Passed	Indef. postp'd.	
England, John	Pension for revolutionary services.	26	2	Petition	34	Rev. Pensions	3	Favorable	540	Referred to Committee Whole House.		
England, John	Pension for revolutionary services.	27	2	Petition	58	Rev. Pensions	20	Favorable	61	Passed	Indef. postp'd.	
England, John	Pension for revolutionary services.	30	1	Petition	785	Rev. Pensions	791	Adverse		Laid on table.		
Engles, Andrew, heirs of	Compensation for forage furnished revolutionary army.	28	1	Petition	572	Rev. Claims.						
Engles, Andrew, heirs of	Compensation for forage furnished revolutionary army.	29	1	Petition	501	Rev. Claims.						
Engleton, Henry A. F	Pension	23	1	Petition	45	Invalid Pensions	Dec. 24, 1833	Adverse		Laid on table.		
English, Andrew	Pay for subsistence furnished revolutionary army, &c.	11	3	Petition	496	Claims	Feb. 9, 1811	Adverse.				
English, Francis	Correction of erroneous land entry	20	1	Senate bill	604	Public Lands	April 28, 1828	With't amend.	105	Passed	Passed	App'd May 23, 1828
English, John	(See George Johnson and others.)	17	1		386							
English, John	Pension	30	2	Petition	174	Invalid Pensions				Discharged; laid on table.		
English, John	Pension	31	1	Petition	348	Invalid Pensions	397	Adverse		Laid on table.		
English, Joseph	Right of pre-emption	16	1	Petition	355	Priv. Land Claims.						
English, Joseph	Compensation for horses stolen by Indians.	20	1	Resolution	133	Indian Affairs	Jan. 22, 1828	Adverse		Laid on table.		
English, Joseph	Compensation for horses stolen by Indians.	21	1	Senate bill	87	Indian Affairs	Dec. 29, 1829	With't amend.	S. 8	Passed	Passed	App'd Mar. 25, 1830
English, Thomas	Indemnity for French spoliations prior to 1800.	26	1	Memorial	182	Foreign Affairs	343	Favorable; bill	319	Referred to Committee Whole House.		
English, William	Pension	14	2	Resolution	209	Pens. & Rev. Cl'ms.	Jan. 29, 1817	Favorable	91	Passed	Passed, with amendment.	App'd March 3, 1817
Ennis, Gregory	Compensation for improving public grounds.	18	2	Senate bill	123	Dist. of Columbia.	Jan. 18, 1825	With't amend.	S. 14	Passed	Passed	App'd March 3, 1825
Ennis, Peter	Compensation for lost time at Patent Office.	26	2	Petition	53	Claims.						
Ennis, Richard, widow of.	Pension for revolutionary services.	2	1	Petition	477					Referred to Secretary of War.		
Ennis, Richard, widow of.	Pension for revolutionary services.	2	2	Rep. of Secretary of War.	696					Laid on table.		
Enochs, Samuel D	Compensation for a horse lost in Black Hawk war.	26	1	Petition	1009	Claims	697	Adverse		Laid on table.		
Enochs, Samuel D	Compensation for a horse lost in Black Hawk war.	27	3	Petition	132	Claims	118	Adverse		Laid on table.		
Enochs, Samuel D	Compensation for a horse lost in Black Hawk war.	28	1	Petition	73	Claims.						
Enochs, Samuel D	Compensation for a horse lost in Black Hawk war.	28	2	Petition	198	Claims	125	Favorable	610	Referred to Committee Whole House.		

List of private claims presented to the House of Representatives of the United States from the 1st to the 31st Congress, inclusive—Continued.

Names of claimants.	Nature or object of the claim.	Congress.	Session.	How brought before the House of Reps.	Page of journal.	To what committee of the House referred.	No. or date of the report.	Nature of the report.	No. of the bill.	How disposed of by the House of Reps.	How disposed of by the Senate.	Date of the act of Congress, and remarks.
Enochs, Samuel D.	Compensation for a horse lost in Black Hawk war.	29	1	Petition	234	Claims	165	Favorable	165	Passed	Passed	App'd Aug. 8, 1846
Enochs, Stokeby	(See William H. Bedford.)	28	1		262							
Enos, Roger	Pay and emoluments for revolutionary services.	2	2	Petition	703							
Enos, Roger	Commutation pay for revolutionary services.	3	2	Petition	318	Claims.						
Enos, Roger	Commutation pay for revolutionary services.	4	1	Resolution	373	Claims	Jan. 6, 1796	Adverse		Leave to withdraw.		
Enos, Roger	Compensation for military services.	9	1	Petition	271	Public Lands	Feb. 24, 1806			Discharged; leave to withdraw.		
Enos, Roger	Moiety of a fine for breach of revenue laws.	21	1	Petition	142	Ways and Means	345	Favorable	406	Passed	Passed	App'd May 29, 1830
Enos, William	Exchange of bounty land	22	1	Petition	34	Public Lands				Discharged; laid on table.		
Enos, William	Exchange of bounty land	23	1	Petition	70	Rev. Pensions	158	Favorable	173	Passed	Passed	App'd June 30, 1834
Ensign, Elisha	Indemnity for property destroyed by the enemy.	15	2	Petition	288	Claims.						
Ensign, Elisha	Indemnity for property destroyed by the enemy.	17	1	Petition	46	Claims				Discharged; laid on table.		
Ensign, Ariel	Compensation for improvement on lands leased United States.	21	1	Petition	318	Claims	386	Favorable	447	Referred to Committee Whole House.		
Ensign, Ariel	Compensation for improvement on lands leased United States.	22	1	Petition	25	Claims	Dec. 19, 1831	Favorable	25	Passed	Passed	App'd Feb. 18, 1832
Ent, Daniel, sen.	Pension	19	2	Petition	215	Military Pensions.						
Ent, Daniel, sen.	Pension	20	1	Resolution	55	Military Pensions.						
Ent, Daniel, sen.	Pension	21	1	Petition	67	Military Pensions	May 4, 1830	Adverse		Laid on table.		
Enterprise, schooner, owners of.	Compensation for vessel sunk in Baltimore harbor.	21	1	Memorial	82	Commerce	Feb. 2, 1830	Favorable	191	Passed	Passed	App'd May 29, 1830
Enterprise, U. States brig.	(See Lawrence Kearney)	17	2		52							
Eoff, Isaac, widow of	Pension for revolutionary services.	29	1	Petition	86	Rev. Pensions.						
Epervier, U. States ship	Settlement of accounts of officers and crew.	14	2	Resolution	83	Naval Affairs.						
Epervier, U. States ship	Pensions to widows of officers and crew.	14	2	House bill	256	Whole House	Jan. 22, 1817	With amends.	68	Passed	Passed	App'd March 3, 1817
Epervier, U. States ship	Continuation of pension to widows of those lost in said vessel.	27	3	Resolution	133	Naval Affairs.						
Epervier, captors of	(See Lewis Warrington and others)	30	1		513							
Epler, George	Pension	21	1	Petition	46	Military Pensions.						
Epley, John and Sarah	Compensation for supplies, &c, to wounded soldiers.	23	1	Petition	637	Claims.						
Epperson, Jesse	Compensation for horse stolen by Cherokees.	25	3	Petition	368	Indian Affairs.						
Epperson, Richard, heirs of	(See heirs of Richard Apperson.)											
Eppes, Francis, heirs of	Commutation pay for revolutionary services.	24	1	Petition	105	Rev. Claims.						
Eppes, Francis, heirs of	Commutation pay for revolutionary services.	24	2	Petition	216	Rev. Pensions.						
Eppes, Francis, heirs of	Commutation pay for revolutionary services.	25	2	Petition	49	Rev. Claims	251	Favorable	292	Passed	Adverse.	
Eppes, Francis, heirs of	Commutation pay for revolutionary services.	25	3	Petition	84	Rev. Claims				Discharged; laid on table.		

List of private claims presented to the House of Representatives of the United States from the 1st to the 31st Congress, inclusive—Continued.

Names of claimants.	Nature or object of the claim.	Congress.	Session.	How brought before the House of Reps.	Page of journal.	To what committee of the House referred.	No. or date of the report.	Nature of the report.	No. of the bill.	How disposed of by the House of Reps.	How disposed of by the Senate.	Date of the act of Congress, and remarks.
75 Eppes, Francis, heirs of	Commutation pay for revolutionary services.	26	1	Petition	164	Rev. Claims	513	Favorable	414	Referred to Committee Whole House.		
Eppes, Francis, heirs of	Commutation pay for revolutionary services.	27	2	Petition	61	Rev. Claims	38	Favorable	69	Rejected.		
Eppes, Francis, heirs of	Compensation for revolutionary services.	24	1	Petition	204	Rev. Claims.						
Eppes, Francis, heirs of	Compensation for revolutionary services.	24	2	Petition	308	Rev. Claims.						
Eppes, Francis, heirs of	Compensation for revolutionary services.	25	2	Petition	393	Rev. Claims				Discharged; laid on table.		
Eppes, John S.	(See heirs of William Eppes)	22	2		143							
Eppes, Richard	Reimbursement of an overpayment	19	2	Petition	333	Claims.						
Eppes, Richard	Reimbursement of an overpayment	20	1	Petition	164	Claims	187	Favorable	215	Referred to Committee Whole House.		
Eppes, Richard	Reimbursement of an overpayment	20	2	Rep't Committee Whole House.	202		Jan. 24, 1829	With't amend	215	Passed	Reported without amend't.	
Eppes, Richard	Reimbursement of an overpayment	21	1	Petition	101	Claims	25	Favorable	33	Passed	Passed	App'd May 10, 1830
Eppes, William, heirs of	Scrip in lieu of land warrants	22	2	Petition	143	Rev. Claims	55	Favorable	698	Referred to Committee Whole House.		
Eppes, Wyatt	Payment of a certain bill of costs, Mississippi.	30	1	Petition	958	Judiciary				Discharged; laid on table.		
Eppes, Wyatt	Payment of a certain bill of costs, Mississippi.	30	2	Petition	164	Judiciary				Discharged; laid on table.		
Epplee, Andrew	(See administrator of Mary Hassanclever.)	16	1		39							
Erasmo, Miguel	Confirmation of title to land	19	2	Documents	50	Public Lands	49	Favorable	378	Referred to Committee Whole House.		
Erasmo, Miguel	Confirmation of title to land	24	1	Documents	150	Priv. Land Claims.	93					
Erb, Jacob	Pension for revolutionary services.	25	2	Petition	272	Rev. Pensions	453	Favorable	455	Passed	Adverse.	
Erb, Laurence	Release from imprisonment	6	1	Petition	544	Select	April 28, 1800	Favorable.				
Erb, Laurence	Release from imprisonment	6	2	Petition	780	Select	Feb. 4, 1801	Favorable	296	Passed.		
Erb, Laurence	Release from imprisonment	7	1	Petition	64	Whole House	Jan. 28, 1802	With't amend	1	Passed	Passed	App'd Feb. 3, 1802
Ercoffier, Quinil	(See Cornelius Innis.)	23	1		586							
Ericsson, John	Compensation for services as engineer of the Princeton.	28	1	Petition	941	Naval Affairs.						
Ericsson, John	Compensation for services as engineer of the Princeton.	28	2	Petition	283	Naval Affairs.						
Ericsson, John	Compensation for services as engineer of the Princeton.	29	1	Petition	70	Naval Affairs	144	Favorable	148	Referred to Committee Whole House.		
Ericsson, John	Compensation for services as engineer of the Princeton.	29	2	Rep't Committee Whole House.	381		Feb. 10, 1847	With amend.	148			
Ericsson, John	Compensation for services as engineer of the Princeton.	30	1	Petition	111	Naval Affairs.						
Erkelens, Gosuinus	Compensation for revolutionary services.	1	3	Petition	368					Referred to Secretary Treasury.		
Erkelens, Gosuinus	Compensation for revolutionary services.	2	1	Petition	447					Referred to Secretary Treasury.		
Erkelens, Gosuinus	Compensation for revolutionary services.	3	1	Rep. of Secretary Treasury.	77					Laid on table.		
Ermatinger, George	Compensation for horse lost in war of 1812.	19	2	Petition	217	Claims.						
Ermatinger, George	Compensation for horse lost in war of 1812.	21	1	Petition	83	Claims	Jan. 29, 1830	Favorable	178	Passed	Passed	App'd May 29, 1830

List of private claims presented to the House of Representatives of the United States from the 1st to the 31st Congress, inclusive—Continued.

Names of claimants.	Nature or object of the claim.	Congress.	Session.	How brought before the House of Reps.	Page of journal.	To what committee of the House referred.	No. or date of the report.	Nature of the report.	No. of the bill.	How disposed of by the House of Reps.	How disposed of by the Senate.	Date of the act of Congress, and remarks.
Ernest, Frederick	Pension for naval services	14	1	Petition	59	Naval Affairs				Discharged.		
Ernest, Frederick	Increase of pension	15	1	Petition	107	Naval Affairs				Discharged.		
				Rep. of Secretary Navy.	332					Laid on table.		
Ernest, William H.	(See executors of James Morrison)	21	1		122							
Erskine, Robert		17	2	Petition	167	Whole House				Discharged; leave to withdraw.		
Ervine, John, and others	Compensation for services as United States assessors, So. Carolina.	11	1	Petition	27	Claims				Discharged; laid on table.		
Erving, George W.	Indemnity for damage by erection of light-house.	6	2	Petition	786	Com. and Manuf.				Discharged; leave to withdraw.		
Erving, George W.	Compensation for services as public agent.	11	3	Appropriat'n bill.					177			App'd Feb. 20, 1811
Erving, Samuel	Right of pre-emption to land in Missouri.	15	1	Petition	279	Public Lands.						
Erwin, James	(See Jonathan Hampton, *et al*)	17	1		129							
Erwin, James	Payment of a lost revolutionary certificate.	22	2	Petition	64	Rev. Claims.						
Erwin, James, and others.	Indemnity for loss on contract to remove Indians.	29	1	Senate bill	1075	Indian Affairs	Aug. 1, 1846	With amend.	S. 102	Passed	Passed	App'd Aug. 10, 1846
Erwin, Joseph, heirs of	Renewal of land warrant	26	1	Resolution	671	Priv. Land Claims.	599	Favorable	458	Referred to Committee Whole House.		
Erwin, William	Pension for revolutionary services.	4	2	Petition	707	Claims.						
Erwin, William	Pension for revolutionary services.	5	2	Petition	103	Claims	Dec. 13, 1797	Adverse.				
Erwin, William	Balance of pay and emolument for revolutionary services.	10	2	Petition	500	Public Lands	Feb. 27, 1809	Adverse		Leave to withdraw.		
Erwin, William	Settlement of his accounts	13	3	Appropriat'n bill								App'd Feb. 13, 1813
Esenbeck, Wm., or Wm N., and others.	Bounty land as British deserters	11	3	Petition	570	Public Lands.						
Esenbeck, Wm., or Wm. N., and others.	Bounty land as British deserters	16	1	Resolution	249	Pens. & Rev. Cl'ms.				Discharged.		
				Rep. of Secretary War.	320					Laid on table.		
Esenbeck, William	Indemnity for property destroyed by the enemy.	13	3	Petition	511	Claims	Nov. 11, 1814	Adverse		Rejected.		
Esenbeck, William	Indemnity for property destroyed by the enemy.	14	2	Petition	212	Claims.						
Esenbeck, William	Indemnity for property destroyed by the enemy.	15	1	Petition	237	Claims	Feb. 18, 1818	Adverse		Leave to withdraw.		
Eskridge, Austin	Correction of an error in land entry.	23	1	Petition	637	Public Lands.						
Eskridge, Jeremiah	Pension	31	1	Petition	1044	Invalid Pensions.						
Eskridge, Malachi	Pension for revolutionary services.	23	1	Petition	569	Rev. Pensions				Discharged; laid on table.		
Eskridge, Samuel	Reimbursement of advances on public account.	23	2	Resolution	282	Claims	100	Adverse		Laid on table.		
Eskridge, Thomas P.	Reimbursement of land payment and interest.	24	1	Petition	58	Public Lands	67	Favorable	82	Passed	Passed, with amendment.	
Eskridge, Thomas P.	Reimbursement of land payment and interest.	25	2	Senate bill	1166	Public Lands	July 6, 1838	With amend.	S. 277			
Eskridge, Thomas P.	Reimbursement of land payment and interest.	25	3	Senate bill	492	Claims			S. 159			
Eskridge, Thomas P.	Reimbursement of land payment and interest.	26	1	Senate bill	420	Public Lands	Mar. 3, 1840	With't amend.	S. 56	Passed	Passed	App'd April 10, 1840

List of private claims presented to the House of Representatives of the United States from the 1st to the 31st Congress, inclusive—Continued.

Names of claimants.	Nature or object of the claim.	Congress.	Session.	How brought before the House of Reps.	Page of journal.	To what committee of the House referred.	No. or date of the report.	Nature of the report.	No. of the bill.	How disposed of by the House of Reps.	How disposed of by the Senate.	Date of the act of Congress, and remarks.
Eskridge, William, assignee of.	Renewal of a land warrant	6	2	Petition	765	Select	Feb. 18, 1801	Adverse	......	Rejected.		
Eskridge, William, assignee of.	Renewal of a land warrant	7	2	Petition	314	....	....	....	......	Leave to withdraw.		
Eskridge, William	Indemnity for spoliations under treaty of Ghent.	20	2	Petition	23	Foreign Affairs	79	Adverse	......	Laid on table.		
Eslava, Don Miguel, heirs of.	Confirmation of title to land in Louisiana.	18	1	Petition	86	Priv. Land Claims.	June 21, 1824	Favorable	76	Passed	Passed	App'd May 21, 1824
Eslava, Don Miguel, heirs of.	Confirmation of title to land in Louisiana.	18	2	Petition	47	Priv. Land Claims.						
Eslava, Don Miguel, heirs of.	Confirmation of title to land in Louisiana.	19	1	Petition	45	Priv. Land Claims.						
Eslava, Don Miguel, heirs of.	Confirmation of title to land in Louisiana.	19	2	Petition	157	Priv. Land Claims.						
Elsava, Don Miguel, heirs of.	Confirmation of title to land in Louisiana.	22	1	Documents	813	Public Lands.						
Eslava, Don Miguel, heirs of.	Confirmation of title to land in Louisiana.	24	1	Petition	436	Priv. Land Claims.	April 20, 1836	Favorable	576	Referred to Committee Whole House.		
Eslava, Don Miguel, heirs of.	Confirmation of title to land in Louisiana.	24	2	Documents	392	Whole House.						
Eslava, Don Miguel, heirs of.	Confirmation of title to land in Louisiana.	25	2	Documents	43	Priv. Land Claims.	575	Adverse	......	Recommitted.		
Eslava, Don Miguel, heirs of.	Confirmation of title to land in Louisiana.	25	3	Documents	251	Priv. Land Claims.						
				Senate bill	478	Priv. Land Claims.	Mar. 2, 1839	With't amend.	S. 266	Referred to Committee Whole House.		
Eslava, Don Miguel, heirs of.	Confirmation of title to land in Louisiana.	26	1	Senate bill	1236	....	....	....	S. 189			
Eslava, Don Miguel, heirs of.	Confirmation of title to land in Louisiana.	26	2	Senate bill	229	Priv. Land Claims.	....	....	S. 81	Passed	Passed	App'd March 3, 1841
Eslava, Miguel D.	(See Thomas F. Townley, guardian of the heirs of.)	23	1	....	111	....	287	....	324			
Espich, Christian	Compensation for service in war of 1812.	15	1	Petition	294	Claims.						
Espich, Christian	Compensation for services in war of 1812.	15	2	Petition	52	Claims.						
Espich, Jacob	Compensation for services in war of 1812.	15	1	Petition	294	Claims.						
Espich, Jacob	Compensation for services in war of 1812.	15	2	Petition	52	Claims.						
Espy, Andrew	(See Stephen Decatur, widow of, and others.)	20	1	....	295	....	201	....	S. 50			
Espy, Samuel	Pension	19	2	Petition	333	Military Pensions.						
Espy, Samuel	Pension	20	1	Petition	125	Military Pensions.	....	....	......	Discharged; laid on table.		
Espy, Samuel	Pension	20	2	Pension bill	55	Whole House	Jan. 15, 1829	With amend.	311	Passed	Laid on table.	
Espy, Samuel	Pension	21	1	Petition	48	Military Pensions.						
Espy, Samuel	Pension	21	2	Petition	189	Military Pensions.						
Espy, Samuel	Pension	22	1	Petition	193	Invalid Pensions.	Jan. 19, 1832	Favorable	288	Passed	Passed, with amendment.	App'd July 14, 1834
Essary, Jonathan D.	Exchange of a location of land	15	1	Petition	324	Public Lands.						
Esselstyn, R. M. and J. B.	Indemnity for store-house destroyed by the enemy.	14	1	Petition	185	Claims.						

List of private claims presented to the House of Representatives of the United States from the 1st to the 31st Congress, inclusive—Continued.

Names of claimants.	Nature or object of the claim.	Congress.	Session.	How brought before the House of Reps.	Page of journal.	To what committee of the House referred.	No. or date of the report.	Nature of the report.	No. of the bill.	How disposed of by the House of Reps.	How disposed of by the Senate.	Date of the act of Congress, and remarks.
Esselstyn, Richard M.	Compensation for property taken for public use.	14	1	Petition	186	Claims.						
Esselstyn, Richard M.	Compensation for property taken for public use.	15	1	Petition	294	Claims.						
Esselstyn, Richard M.	Compensation for property taken for public use.	16	1	Petition	65	Claims	Jan. 14, 1820	Adverse		Laid on table.		
Esselstyn, Richard M.	Compensati'n for property destroyed by United States troops.	22	1	Petition	442	Claims	Mar. 21, 1832	Adverse		Laid on table		Leave to withdraw, 2d sess. 23d Congress, page 410.
Essex, Isaac B.	Compensation for horse lost in public service.	24	1	Petition	92	Claims.						
Essick, John	Pension	16	1	Petition	91	Pens. & Rev. Cl'ms.				Discharged.		
				Report of Secretary of War.	350					Laid on table.		
Estabrook, Nathan	Pension for revolutionary services.	20	1	Petition	484	Military Pensions.				Discharged; laid on table.		
Estabrook, Nathan	Compensation for revolutionary services.	25	2	Petition	915	Rev. Claims.						
Estabrook, Nathan	Compensation for revolutionary services.	26	1	Petition	173	Rev. Pensions	557	Adverse		Laid on table.		
Estes, Aaron, widow of	Payment of balance for public services.	25	2	Petition	921	Claims	944	Ref rred to 3d Auditor.		Discharged; referred to 3d Auditor.		
Estes, Abraham	Pension	13	3	Pension bill	740	Whole House	Mar. 1, 1815	With't amend.	303	Passed	Passed	App'd March 3, 1815
Estes, Abraham, administratrix of.	Arrears of pension	19	1	Resolution	254	Military Pensions.	Feb. 21, 1826	Favorable	112	Passed	Passed, with amendment.	
Estes, Abraham, administratrix of.	Arrears of pension	20	1	Senate bill	379	Military Pensions.	May 29, 1828	With amend.	S. 8	Referred to Committee Whole House.		
Estes, Abraham, (Ky.)	Increase of pension	24	1	Petition	964	Rev. Pensions.						
Estes, Abraham, (Ky.)	Increase of pension	24	2	Petition	42	Rev. Pensions	Dec. 26, 1836	Adverse		Laid on table.		
Estes, Clement	Pension	14	2	Resolution	209	Pens. & Rev. Cl'ms.	Jan. 29, 1817	Favorable	91	Name strick'n from bill		
Estes, James P.	Compensation for property destroyed in Indian war.	28	1	Petition	189	Claims	500	Adverse		Laid on table.		
Estes, Lyddal	Pension for revolutionary services.	28	1	Petition	533	Rev. Pensions.						
Estes, Lyddal	Pension for revolutionary services.	28	2	Petition	56	Rev. Pensions.						
Estes, Lyddal	Pension for revolutionary services.	29	1	Petition	86	Rev. Pensions.						
Estes, Lyddal	Pension for revolutionary services.	29	2	Petition	....	Rev. Pensions	8	Adverse		Laid on table.		
Estes, William	Release from a government claim.	22	1	Petition	191	Judiciary	237	Favorable	367	Referred to Committee Whole House.		
Estes, Wm., sureties of	Release from liability on a judgment.	21	1	Petition	70	Judiciary	71	Favorable	100	Passed	Passed	App'd May 28, 1830
Estes, Wm., sureties of	Release from liability on a judgment.	22	1	Petition	164	Judiciary	237	Favorable	367	Referred to Committee Whole House.		
Estes, Wm., sureties of	Release from liability on a judgment.	23	1	Petition	38	Judiciary	Dec. 20, 1833	Adverse		Laid on table.		
Estes, Wm., sureties of	Release from liability on a judgment.	23	2	Petition	95	Judiciary.						
Estes, Wm., sureties of	Release from liability on a judgment.	24	1	Petition	106	Judiciary	434	Favorable	449	Referred to Committee Whole House.		
Estes, Wm., sureties of	Release from liability on a judgment.	25	2	Petition	41	Judiciary	Jan. 10, 1838	Favorable	375	Referred to Committee Whole House.		
Estes, Wm., sureties of	Release from liability on a judgment.	25	3	Rep't Committee Whole House.	378	Judiciary	Jan. 25, 1839	With't amend.	375	Passed	Amendm't and Adv. report.	
Estes, Wm., sureties of	Release from liability on a judgment.	26	1	Petition	175	Judiciary	89	Favorable	84	Passed	Indef. postp'd.	

List of private claims presented to the House of Representatives of the United States from the 1st to the 31st Congress, inclusive—Continued.

Names of claimants.	Nature or object of the claim.	Congress.	Session.	How brought before the House of Reps.	Page of journal.	To what committee of the House referred.	No. or date of the report.	Nature of the report.	No. of the bill.	How disposed of by the House of Reps.	How disposed of by the Senate.	Date of the act of Congress, and remarks.
Estes, Wm., sureties of	Release from liability on a judgment.	27	2	Petition	75	Judiciary.						
Estes, Wm., sureties of	Release from liability on a judgment.	28	2	Petition	64	Judiciary	34	Favorable	508	Referred to Committee Whole House.		
Estes, Wm., sureties of	Release from liability on a judgment.	29	1	Petition	83	Judiciary	Jan. 9, 1846	Favorable	61	Rejected.		
Estep, Alexander	Pension	23	2	Petition	105	Invalid Pensions.						
Estep, Alexander	Pension	24	1	Petition	507	Invalid Pensions	June 9, 1834	Favorable	694	Passed	Indef. postp'd.	
Esterly, George, and wife.	Compensation for board of revolutionary officer.	5	3	Petition	425	Claims	Feb. 26, 1799	Adverse		Leave to withdraw.		
Estevan, Louis, and others	Confirmation of title to land in Louisiana.	20	1	Petition	343	Priv. Land Claims.						
Estevan, Louis, and others	Confirmation of title to land in Louisiana.	21	1	Petition	51	Priv. Land Claims.	Mar. 23, 1830	Adverse		Laid on table.		
Estill, James	Confirmation of title to land in Louisiana.	22	2	Petition	165	Priv. Land Claims.						
Etchberger, Wm., widow of	Pension	25	1	Petition	102					Laid on table.		
Etchberger, Wm., widow of	Pension	25	2	Petition	115	Rev. Pensions				Discharged; laid on table.		
Etheridge, James	Right of pre-emption	18	2	Petition	137	Public Lands				Discharged; laid on table.		
Etheridge, John, widow of.	Continuation of pension	27	2	Petition	1049	Rev. Pensions				Discharged; laid on table.		
Ethell, Henry	Pension for revolutionary services.	25	2	Documents	914	Rev. Pensions.						
Ethell, Henry	Pension for revolutionary services.	25	3	Documents	88	Rev. Pensions.						
Ethell, Henry	Pension for revolutionary services.	26	1	Petition	173	Rev. Pensions.						
Ethell, Henry	Pension for revolutionary services.	26	2	Petition	78	Rev. Pensions.						
Etter, Joseph	Compensation for regulating clocks at President's House.	17	2	Petition	40	Public Buildings	Jan. 24, 1823	Adverse		Leave to withdraw.		
Etting, Henry	Indemnity for expenses in prosecuting bank at New Orleans.	29	1	Petition	152	Naval Affairs.						
				Senate bill	1041	Naval Affairs	July 24, 1846	With't amend.	74	Passed	Passed	App'd Aug. 10, 1846
Etting, Reuben	(See Rutter & Etting)	26	1		182				21			
Etting, Solomon	(See Robert G. Harper and others)	11	3		458							
Eubank, Joseph, jr	Renewal of a patent	24	1	Documents	735	Patent Laws.						
Euler, Jacob	Pension	25	3	Petition	129	Invalid Pensions	256	Favorable	1127	Referred to Committee Whole House.		
Euler, Jacob	Pension	26	1	Petition	161	Invalid Pensions	211	Favorable	223	Passed.		
Euler, Jacob	Pension	26	2	Petition	36	Invalid Pensions	91	Favorable	596	Referred to Committee Whole House.		
Euler, Jacob	Pension	27	2	Petition	97	Invalid Pensions	134	Favorable	180	Passed.		
Eulon, James	(See William H. Bedford, agent)	28	1		262							
Eustace, John, heirs of	Payment of specie allowance for 1783 and 1784.	19	1	Resolution	420	Rev. Claims	168	Favorable	219	Passed	Passed	App'd May 20, 1826
Eustace, John S	Commutation pay for revolutionary services.	5	2	Memorial	347	Claims	July 10, 1798	Adverse		Leave to withdraw.		
Eustis, Caroline L	(See A. Poor and others)	20	2		289							
Eustis, Joseph	Reimbursement of duties unjustly exacted.	24	1	Memorial	796	Ways and Means.						
Evans, A. H	Re-location of land certificate of R. Hazel.	27	2	Petition	140	Public Lands.						
Evans, A. H	Re-location of land certificate of R. Hazel.	27	3	Petition	71	Public Lands	41	Adverse		Laid on table.		

List of private claims presented to the House of Representatives of the United States from the 1st to the 31st Congress, inclusive—Continued.

Names of claimants.	Nature or object of the claim.	Congress.	Session.	How brought before the House of Reps.	Page of journal.	To what committee of the House referred.	No. or date of the report.	Nature of the report.	No. of the bill.	How disposed of by the House of Reps.	How disposed of by the Senate.	Date of the act of Congress, and remarks.
Evans, Anna de Neufville.	(See heir of John De Neufville)	31	1		1035							
Evans, Benjamin	Reimbursement of discriminating duties on schooner Ariel.	27	2	Memorial	685	Commerce	883	Favorable	508	Ordered to 3d reading.		
Evans, Benjamin	Reimbursement of discriminating duties on schooner Ariel.	27	3	House bill	89				508	Passed	Indef. postp'd.	
Evans, Benjamin	Reimbursement of discriminating duties on schooner Ariel.	28	1	Petition	333	Commerce	387	Adverse		Laid on table.		
Evans, Britton	Indemnity for property lost on a wreck.	25	2	Petition	577	Military Affairs	Mar. 24, 1838	Adverse		Laid on table.		
Evans, Britton	Indemnity for property lost on a wreck.	26	1	Petition	622	Claims	430	Adverse		Laid on table.		
Evans, Britton	Compensation for administering oaths to volunteers.	27	2	Petition	382	Claims	708	Adverse		Laid on table.		
Evans, Cotton	Arrears of pension	25	2	Petition	54	Rev. Pensions	500	Favorable	503	Passed	Adverse.	
Evans, Cotton	Arrears of pension	26	1	Petition	171	Rev. Pensions	460	Favorable	374			
Evans, Daniel	Pension	12	1	Petition	288	Claims	June 12, 1812	Favorable	138	Passed	Passed	App'd July 5, 1812
Evans, Daniel	Increase of pension	14	1	House bill	622	Whole House	April 23, 1816	With amend.	171	Passed	Passed	App'd April 29, 1816
Evans, Daniel	Payment of a loan office certificate.	14	1	Petition	409	Pens. & Rev. Cl'ms.						
Evans, Daniel	Payment of a loan office certificate.	15	1	Petition	21	Pens. & Rev. Cl'ms.	Dec. 15, 1817	Adverse		Laid on table		Leave to withdraw.
Evans, Daniel, sureties of	Reimbursement of money illegally exacted.	21	2	Senate bill	382	Ways and Means	March 2, 1831	With't amend.	S. 116	Passed	Passed	App'd March 2, 1831
Evans, David	Pension for revolutionary services.	18	1	Petition	210	Rev. Pensions				Discharged; leave to withdraw.		
Evans, Ebenezer	Pension	14	1	Petition	59	Naval Affairs.						
Evans, Ebenezer	Pension	15	1	Petition	107	Naval Affairs				Discharged.		
				Rep. of Secretary Navy.	332					Laid on table.		
Evans, Edward	Increase of pension	9	2	Pension bill	608	Whole House	Feb. 28, 1807	With't amend.	216	Passed	Passed	App'd March 3, 1807
Evans, Edward	(See surviving partner of O. & E. Evans.)	17	2		143							
Evans, Edward	Pension for revolutionary services.	23	1	Petition	242	Rev. Pensions.						
Evans, Edward	Pension for revolutionary services.	24	2	Resolution	384	Rev. Pensions.						
Evans, Edward	Pension for revolutionary services.	30	2	Petition	282	Rev. Pensions				Discharged; laid on table.		
Evans, Enoch	Right of pre-emption	26	1	Senate bill	837	Priv. Land Claims			S. 274			
Evans, Evan	(See administrator of James Evans)	2	1		540							
Evans, Eusebia	Continuation of pension	28	1	Petition	849	Rev. Pensions.						
Evans, George	Indemnity for disability incurred in public service.	23	2	Petition	344	Invalid Pensions.						
Evans, George, executor of	Commutation pay for revolutionary services.	31	1	Petition	234	Rev. Claims	Mar. 28, 1850	Adverse		Laid on table.		
Evans, George, widow of.	Relief for loss of husband in public service.	24	1	Petition	260	Invalid Pensions	462	Favorable	468	Passed	Passed	App'd June 28, 1836
Evans, George W., administrator of.	Settlement of accounts as quartermaster general of Georgia militia.	19	1	Petition	109	Claims	Jan. 23, 1826	Adverse		Recommitted.		
Evans, George W., administrator of.	Settlement of accounts as quartermaster general of Georgia militia.	19	2	Petition	50	Claims				Discharged; leave to withdraw.		
				Senate bill	266	Military Affairs	March 2, 1827	With't amend.	65	Laid on table.		
Evans, Henry F.	Indemnity for losses in the war of 1812.	24	1	Petition	943	Claims	June 18, 1836	Adverse		Laid on table.		
Evens, Capt. Henry F.	Increase of pension	31	1	Petition		Invalid Pensions	46	Favorable	76	Passed.		
Evans, Hooper, widow of.	Pension for revolutionary services.	27	2	Petition	80	Rev. Pensions	784	Adverse		Laid on table.		

List of private claims presented to the House of Representatives of the United States from the 1*st to the* 31*st Congress, inclusive*—Continued.

Names of claimants.	Nature or object of the claim.	Congress.	Session.	How brought before the House of Reps.	Page of journal.	To what committee of the House referred.	No. or date of the report.	Nature of the report.	No. of the bill.	How disposed of by the House of Reps.	How disposed of by the Senate.	Date of the act of Congress, and remarks.
Evans, Israel, widow of	Compensation for services as revolutionary chaplain.	20	2	Petition	141	Rev. Claims	Jan. 22, 1829	Adverse	......	Laid on table.		
Evans, Israel, widow of	Continuation of pension	28	1	Petition	950	Whole House.						
Evans, James, administrator of.	Renewal of lost revolutionary certificates.	2	1	Petition	540	....	....	....	......	Referred to Secretary Treasury.		
Evans, James	Indemnity for Indian depredations.	26	1	Petition	436	Indian Affairs.						
Evans, James S., & Co	Indemnity for loss on a certain contract.	26	1	Petition	620	Claims.						
Evans, John	Pension	15	1	Petition	195	Pens. & Rev. Cl'ms.						
Evans, John	Compensation for horse lost in public service.	17	1	Petition	100	Claims.						
Evans, John, mother of	Provision for her support on account of loss of son.	21	1	Petition	200	Naval Affairs.						
Evans, John, mother of	Provision for her support on account of loss of son.	23	1	Petition	440	Naval Affairs.						
Evans, John, mother of	Pension	23	2	Petition	121	Naval Affairs	Feb. 25, 1835	Adverse	......	Laid on table.		
Evans, Joseph	Right of pre-emption	25	2	Petition	86	Public Lands.						
Evans, Joseph	Right of pre-emption	25	3	Petition	98	Public Lands.						
Evans, Josiah	Compensation for revolutionary services.	15	2	Petition	18	Pens. & Rev. Cl'ms.	....	....	......	Discharged; laid on table.		
Evans, Lewis	Indemnity for salt taken for public use.	14	2	Petition	348	Claims	....	....	......	Referred to Secretary War.		
Evans, Lewis	Indemnity for salt taken for public use.	24	1	Documents	634	Indian Affairs.						
Evans, Lewis	Indemnity for salt taken for public use.	24	2	Petition	209	Indian Affairs.						
Evans, Lewis	Indemnity for salt taken for public use.	25	2	Documents	95	Indian Affairs	519	Adverse	......	Laid on table.		
Evans, Lewis	Compensation for provisions furnished.	26	1	Petition	1009	Claims.						
Evans, Lewis	Compensation for provisions furnished.	27	2	Petition	455	Indian Affairs	760	Adverse	......	Laid on table.		
Evans, Mark	Balance due from Ottawa Indians.	29	1	Memorial	160	Indian Affairs	287	Adverse	......	Laid on table.		
Evans, Moses	Pension	3	1	Rep. of Secretary War.	131	Select	May 26, 1794	Res. to refer to Sec. War.	R. 12	Passed	Passed	App'd June 9, 1794
Evans, Moses	Pension	4	1	Rep. of Secretary War.	445	Claims	Mar. 4, 1796	Res. to refer to Sec. War.	R. 16	Passed	Passed	App'd April 13, 1796
Evans & McLean	Compensation for use of scows	14	1	Petition	284							
				Rep. of Secretary War.	364	Claims	April 1, 1816	Favorable	......	Passed	Passed	App'd April 27, 1816
Evans, Nathan, widow of.	Pension	28	1	Petition	646	Invalid Pensions	....	....	......	Discharged; laid on table.		
Evans, Nathaniel	Compensation for raising volunteers, &c.	19	1	Petition	492	Claims.						
Evans, Nathaniel	Compensation for raising volunteers, &c.	19	2	Petition	112	Claims.						
Evans, Nathaniel	Pension	26	1	Documents	602	Invalid Pensions.						
Evans, Oliver	Extension of a patent for manufacturing flour.	8	2	Petition	63	Com. and Manuf.	Jan. 22, 1805	....	......	Referred to Committee Whole House.		
Evans, Oliver	Extension of a patent for manufacturing flour.	9	1	Petition	224	Select.						

List of private claims presented to the House of Representatives of the United States from the 1st to the 31st Congress, inclusive—Continued.

Names of claimants.	Nature or object of the claim.	Congress.	Session.	How brought before the House of Reps.	Page of journal.	To what committee of the House referred.	No. or date of the report.	Nature of the report.	No. of the bill.	How disposed of by the House of Reps.	How disposed of by the Senate.	Date of the act of Congress, and remarks.
Evans, Oliver	Extension of a patent for manufacturing flour.	9	2	Petition	490	Select.						
Evans, Oliver	Extension of a patent for manufacturing flour.	10	1	Petition	26	Select	Dec. 7, 1807	Favorable	15	Passed	Passed	App'd Jan. 21, 1808
Evans, Oliver	Extension of a patent for steam engines.	11	2	Resolution	235	Select.						
Evans, Oliver	Extension of a patent for steam engines.	13	3	Petition	185	Select	Feb. 17, 1814	Favorable	126	Referred to Committee Whole House.		
				Senate bill	560	Whole House	Jan. 24, 1815	With amend.	64	Passed with amendm'	Passed as am'd.	App'd Feb. 7, 1815
Evans, Owen and Edward, surviving partner of.	Increase of allowance on contract to furnish arms.	17	2	Petition	143	Claims.						
Evans, Owen and Edward, surviving partner of.	Increase of allowance on contract to furnish arms.	18	1	Petition	253	Claims	April 29, 1824	Favorable	220	Passed	Passed	App'd May 21, 1824
Evans, Pierce	Reimbursement of money paid for land.	27	3	Petition	205	Claims.						
Evans, Robert	Compensation for a slave who died in public service.	15	1	Petition	258	Claims	Mar. 9, 1818	Adverse		Rejected.		
Evans, Roxana	Indemnity for property destroyed by the enemy.	27	3	Petition	336	Claims.						
Evans, Roxana	Indemnity for property destroyed by the enemy.	28	1	Petition	189	Claims	293	Adverse		Laid on table.		
Evans, Samuel, heir of	Bounty land for revolutionary services.	23	1	Petition	242	Rev. Claims.						
Evans, Scioto	Compensation for horse lost in Indian wars.	23	2	Petition	59	Claims.						
Evans, Scioto	Compensation for horse lost in Indian wars.	24	1	Petition	50	Claims.						
Evans, Susannah	(See representatives of Abraham Nanna.)	14	1		339							
Evans, Thomas	Pension	16	1	Petition	218	Whole House.						
Evans, Thomas	Pension	21	2	Petition	158	Military Pensions.						
Evans, Thomas	Compensation for vessel taken into public service.	23	1	Petition	498	Claims	538	Adverse		Laid on table.		
Evans, Thomas	Compensation for vessel taken into public service.	23	2	Petition	120	Claims	Jan. 26, 1835	Adverse		Laid on table.		
Evans, Walter	Compensation for revolutionary services.	19	2	Petition	287	Rev. Claims.						
Evans, Walter	Pension for revolutionary services.	25	2	Petition	405	Rev. Pensions.				Recommitted.		
Evans, William	Compensation for revolutionary services.	2	1	Petition	494					Referred to Secretary War.		
Evans, William	Compensation for revolutionary services.	10	2	Pension bill	499	Whole House	Feb. 28, 1809	With amend.	158	Passed	Passed, with amendment.	App'd March 3, 1809
Evans, William, heirs of.	Arrears of pension	28	1	Petition	76	Invalid Pensions.						
Evans, William, heirs of.	Arrears of pension	28	2	Petition	87	Invalid Pensions	175	Favorable	645			
Evans, William, heirs of.	Arrears of pension	29	1	Memorial	124	Invalid Pensions	85	Favorable	96			
Evans, William, heirs of.	Arrears of pension	29	2	Petition	128	Invalid Pensions						
Evans, William, heirs of.	Arrears of pension	30	1	Petition	156	Invalid Pensions	193	Favorable	208	Passed	Passed second session.	App'd Jan. 8, 1849
Evans, William	Pension for revolutionary services.	28	1	Petition	296	Rev. Claims.						
Evat, Edward	Indemnity for house burnt while in public use.	14	1	Petition	295	Claims.						
Evat, Edward	Indemnity for house burnt while in public use.	17	2	Senate bill	278	Claims	Mar. 1, 1823	With amend.	S. 56	Passed with amendm't	Passed as am'd.	App'd March 1, 1823

List of private claims presented to the House of Representatives of the United States from the 1st to the 31st Congress, inclusive—Continued.

Names of claimants.	Nature or object of the claim.	Congress.	Session.	How brought before the House of Reps.	Page of journal.	To what committee of the House referred.	No. or date of the report.	Nature of the report.	No. of the bill.	How disposed of by the House of Reps.	How disposed of by the Senate.	Date of the act of Congress, and remarks.
76 Eve, Joseph, widow of	Reimbursement of expenses as chargé to Texas.	31	2	Petition	142	Claims.						
Eveland, Peter	Pension for revolutionary services.	22	1	Petition	265	Rev. Pensions.						
Eveleth, S.	(See John Crowninshield and others.)	23	1		32							
Eveleth, Wm. S., mother of	Balance due as U. S. Engineer	27	2	Petition	622	Claims.						
Eveleth, Wm. S., mother of	Balance due as U. S. Engineer	27	3	Petition	43	Claims	51	Favorable	683	Passed	Passed	App'd March 3, 1843
Everett, Alexander H.	Compensation for diplomatic services.	21	1	House bill	326	Whole House	May 5, 1830	With't amend.	275	Passed	Passed	App'd May 29, 1830
Everett, Alexander H.	Settlement of accounts as minister to Spain.	24	1	Petition	537	Foreign Affairs	562	Favorable	554	Referred to Committee Whole House.		
Everett, Alexander H.	Settlement of accounts as minister to Spain.	25	2	Petition	50	Foreign Affairs	565	Favorable	555	Referred to Committee Whole House.		
Everett, Alexander H.	Settlement of accounts as minister to Spain.	25	3	House bill	380				555	Referred to Committee Whole House.		
Everett, Alexander H.	Settlement of accounts as minister to Spain.	26	1	Petition	182	Foreign Affairs	107	Favorable	111	Passed	Laid on table.	
Everett, Alexander H.	Settlement of accounts as minister to Spain.	27	2	Petition	152	Foreign Affairs	July 21, 1842	Favorable	526	Referred to Committee Whole House.		
Everett, Alexander H.	Settlement of accounts as minister to Spain.	27	3	House bill	89				526	Passed	Adverse report.	
Everett, Alexander H.	Settlement of accounts as minister to Spain.	28	2	Petition	84	Foreign Affairs	50	Favorable	529	Referred to Committee Whole House.		
Everett, Alexander H.	Settlement of accounts as minister to Spain.	29	1	Petition	68	Foreign Affairs	256	Adverse		Laid on table.		
Everett, Alexander H., widow of.	Final settlement of accounts	30	2	Petition	75	Foreign Affairs.						
Everett, Alexander H., widow of.	Final settlement of accounts	31	1	Petition	276	Foreign Affairs.						
Everett, Alfred T.	Legalize transfer of a land warrant	31	1	Petition	1003	Public Lands.						
Everett & Battelle	Reimbursement of certain moneys.	30	1	Memorial	1057	Commerce.						
Everett & Battelle	Reimbursement of certain moneys.	31	1	Petition	715	Commerce.						
Everett, Edward	Compensation for services as clerk in quartermaster's department.	31	1	Petition	258	Military Affairs	86	Favorable	107	Passed.		
Everett, Hannah	Appropriation to pay her pension.	28	2	Petition	149	Naval Affairs				Discharged; laid on table.		
Everett, Isaac	(See executor of widow of Com. J. Barney.)	31	1		215							
Everett, Jeremiah	Pension for revolutionary services.	3	2	Rep. of Secretary War.	337	Claims	Feb. 28, 1795	Pension bill	130	Passed	Postponed.	
Everett, Jeremiah	Pension for revolutionary services.	4	1	Rep. of Secretary War.	445	Claims	Feb. 18, 1796	Pension bill	156	Passed	Passed	App'd April 20, 1796
Everett, Jeremiah	Pension for services as a revolutionary marine.	4	1	Petition	482	Claims	May 31, 1796	Adverse		Laid on table.		
Everett, Jeremiah, widow of.	Continuation of pension	25	2	Petition	587	Invalid Pensions	April 10, 1838	Adverse		Laid on table.		
Everett, Thomas	Compensation for horse lost in Seminole war.	23	1	Documents	154	Claims.						
Everett, Thomas	(See William H. Bedford, agent.)	28	1		262							
Everhard, Charles	Confirmation of title to land	20	1	Petition	398	Priv. Land Claims.				Discharged; laid on table.		
Everhard, Charles	Confirmation of title to land	20	2	Petition	75	Priv. Land Claims.						
Everhard, Charles	Confirmation of title to land	21	1	Petition	51	Priv. Land Claims.	Feb. 23, 1830	Adverse		Laid on table.		

List of private claims presented to the House of Representatives of the United States from the 1st to the 31st Congress, inclusive—Continued.

Names of claimants.	Nature or object of the claim.	Congress.	Session.	How brought before the House of Reps.	Page of journal.	To what committee of the House referred.	No. or date of the report.	Nature of the report.	No. of the bill.	How disposed of by the House of Reps.	How disposed of by the Senate.	Date of the act of Congress, and remarks.
Everhard, Charles	Confirmation of title to land	21	2	Petition	83	Priv. Land Claims				Discharged; laid on table.		
Everhart, Lawrence	Pension	5	2	Petition	258	Claims	April 17, 1798	Adverse		Laid on table.		
Everhart, Lawrence	Pension	5	3	Petition	432	Whole House.						
Everhart, Titus	Pension	26	1	Petition	602	Invalid Pensions				Discharged; laid on table.		Leave to withdraw.
Everitt, James A.	Compensation for services in Seminole war.	19	1	Resolution	274	Claims.						
Everly, John	Pension for revolutionary services.	26	2	Resolution	97	Rev. Pensions						
Everly, John	Pension for revolutionary services.	27	2	Petition	410	Rev. Pensions	784	Adverse		Laid on table.		
Everly, John	Pension for revolutionary services.	27	3	Petition	188	Rev. Pensions	215	Favorable	811	Passed.		
Everly, John	Pension for revolutionary services.	28	1	Petition	79	Rev. Pensions.						
Everly, John	Pension for revolutionary services.	28	2	Petition	119	Rev. Pensions.						
Everson, Adam, widow of.	Pension for revolutionary services.	25	2	Petition	272	Rev. Pensions.						
Everson, Levi, widow of.	Pension for revolutionary services.	26	1	Petition	283	Rev. Pensions	490	Adverse.				
Everson, Levi, widow of.	Pension for revolutionary services.	27	2	Petition	97	Rev. Pensions.	784	Adverse		Laid on table.		
Everson, Levi, widow of.	Pension for revolutionary services.	27	3	Petition	74	Rev. Pensions				Discharged; laid on table.		
Everts, Reuben	Arrears of pension	24	2	Petition	44	Rev. Pensions	Dec. 30, 1836			Discharged; laid on table.		
Everts, Stephen	Increase of pension	13	1	Pension bill	56	Whole House	July 20, 1813	With amend.	31	Passed	Passed with amendment.	App'd Aug. 2, 1813
Evrit, Maria	Pension for revolutionary services of husband.	27	3	Petition	401					Laid on table.		
Lwell, Charles	Pension for revolutionary services.	3	1	Petition	59							
				Rep. of Secretary War.	93	Select	April 22, 1794	Does not appear.		Laid on table.		
Ewell, Jesse	(See heirs of Thomas Ewell)	22	2		53							
Ewell, Joseph	(See heirs of Thomas Church)	24	1		56							
Ewell, Thomas, heirs of	Commutation pay for revolutionary services.	22	2	Petition	53	Rev. Claims.						
Ewell, Thomas	(See District of Columbia, Anacostia Bridge Company.)	13	3	Petition	513	Claims	Jan. 26, 1815	Favorable	273	Passed	Passed	App'd March 3, 1815
Ewell, Thomas	Equitable settlement of account for powder.	13	2	Petition	469	Naval Affairs				Discharged; referred to Secretary of Navy.		
Ewell, Thomas	Enforcement of a contract with a government agent.	14	2	Petition	233	Naval Affairs.						
Ewers, John	Pension for revolutionary services.	17	1	Petition	98	Rev. Pensions.						
Ewing, Charles	Pension	25	2	Petition	541	Invalid Pensions.						
Ewing, Charles	Pension	26	1	Petition	162	Invalid Pensions	275	Adverse		Laid on table		Leave to withdraw, 30th Cong., 1st sess.
Ewing, Eleazer	(See Joseph F. Rake, heirs of)	26	1		332							
Ewing, James	Increase of salary as commissioner of loans.	4	1	Memorial	390	Select.						
Ewing, James	Increase of salary as commissioner of loans.	4	2	Memorial	623	Select	Feb. 3, 1797	General bill	221	Passed	Passed	App'd March 3, 1797
Ewing, R. A.	(See W. Y. C. Ewing and others)	26	1		338							
Ewing, Reuben	(See sureties of Wm. Whitsett)	17	2		228							
Ewings, Samuel	Patent for tract of land under confirmed title.	17	1	Petition	249	Priv. Land Claims.	Mar. 28, 1822	Favorable	138	Passed	Passed	App'd May 7, 1822
Ewing, Thomas	Compensation for work on Cumberland road.	23	1	Documents	589	Claims	455	Adverse		Laid on table		See Report No. 449.
Ewing, William	(See Benjamin Wells and others)	13	3		521							

List of private claims presented to the House of Representatives of the United States from the 1*st to the* 31*st Congress, inclusive*—Continued.

Names of claimants.	Nature or object of the claim.	Congress.	Session.	How brought before the House of Reps.	Page of journal.	To what committee of the House referred.	No. or date of the report.	Nature of the report.	No. of the bill.	How disposed of by the House of Reps.	How disposed of by the Senate.	Date of the act of Congress, and remarks.
Ewing, William, widow of	Compensation for property destroyed by Indians.	15	2	Petition	209	Public Lands.						
Ewing, William, widow of	Compensation for use of property by United States troops.	23	1	Petition	111	Claims	207	Adverse	......	Laid on table.		
Ewing, William, widow of	Compensation for use of property by United States troops.	24	1	Petition	405	Claims.						
Ewing, William, widow of	Compensation for use of property by United States troops.	25	2	Petition	630	Claims	....	....	......	Discharged.		
Ewing, William, widow of	Compensation for use of property by United States troops.	27	2	Petition	829	Claims	1045	Adverse	......	Laid on table.		
Ewing, William L. D.	Release from liability to account for deposite in bank of Vandalia.	18	1	Resol'n and docs.	58	Public Lands	66	Adverse	......	Laid on table.		
Ewing, William L. D.	Release from liability to account for deposite in bank of Vandalia.	18	2	Petition	60	Public Lands.						
				Res. of Leg. of Illinois.	137	Public Lands	....	....	......	Discharged; referred to Com. Whole House.		
Ewing, William L. D.	Release from liability to account for deposite in bank of Vandalia.	19	1	Resolution	166	Ways and Means	117	Favorable	154	Passed	Passed	App'd May 20, 1826
Ewing, W. Y. C., & others	Compensation for horse lost in public service.	26	1	Petition	338	Claims	685	Adverse	......	Laid on table.		
Ewing, W. Y. C., & others	Compensation for horses lost in public service.	26	2	Petition	248	Claims.						
Exploring Expedition	Extra pay to the officers	27	3	Res. and report of Sec. Navy.	149, 341	Naval Affairs	270	Favorable; bill	818	Referred to Committee Whole House.		
Exploring Expedition	Extra pay to the officers	27	3	Civil and dip. appropriat'n bill.	394	Whole House	Feb. 27, 1843	With amend's.	804	Passed	Passed	App'd March 3, 1843
Exploring Expedition, forward officers of.	Extra compensation	29	1	Memorial	238	Naval Affairs	599	Favorable; bill	422	Referred to Committee Whole House.		
Exploring Expedition, for ward officers of.	Extra compensation	30	1	Senate bill	683	Naval Affairs	May 18, 1848	With't amend.	S. 81	Referred to Committee Whole House.		
Exploring Expedition, forward officers of.	Extra compensation	30	2	Rep't Committee Whole House.	319	....	....	....	S. 81	Passed	....	App'd Feb. 1, 1849
Eyerly, Jacob, administrator of.	Remission of balance due U. States as collector of direct tax.	22	2	Petition	321	Claims.						
Eyerly, Jacob, administrator of.	Remission of balance due U. States as collector of direct tax.	23	1	Petition	97	Claims	522	Favorable; bill	523	Referred to Committee Whole House.		
Eyerly, Jacob, administrator of.	Remission of balance due U. States as collector of direct tax.	24	1	Petition	51	Claims	23	Favorable; bill	23	Passed	Passed	App'd Feb. 17, 1836
Eyers, Samuel	Revolutionary pension	3	1	Rep. of Secretary War.	131	Select	May 26, 1794	Refer to Sec'y War.	R. 12	Passed	Passed	App'd June 9, 1794
Eyers, Samuel	Revolutionary pension	3	2	Rep. of Secretary War.	262	Claims	Feb. 28, 1795	Favorable; bill	136	Passed	Postponed.	
Eyers, Samuel	Revolutionary pension	4	1	Rep. of Secretary War.	447	Claims	Feb. 18, 1796	Favorable; bill	156	Passed	Passed	App'd April 20, 1796
Eyers, Samuel	Increase of pension	12	1	Pension bill	361	Whole House	June 15, 1812	With amend's.	138	Passed	Passed	App'd July 5, 1812
Eyma, L.	(See Charles Woodruff, assignees of.)	27	2	....	859							
Eyre & Massey	Refunding excess of duty on sugar	26	1	Petition	605	Ways and Means.						
Eyre & Massey	Refunding excess of duty on sugar	27	2	Petition	56	Commerce	62	Favorable; bill	97	Passed	Indef. postp'd.	
Ezzell, Thomas R.	Compensation for horse lost in public service.	23	2	Petition	37	....	....	....	......	Referred to 3d Auditor		

List of private claims presented to the House of Representatives of the United States from the 1st to the 31st Congress, inclusive—Continued.

Names of claimants.	Nature or object of the claim.	Congress.	Session.	How brought before the House of Reps.	Page of journal.	To what committee of the House referred.	No. or date of the report.	Nature of the report.	No. of the bill.	How disposed of by the House of Reps.	How disposed of by the Senate.	Date of the act of Congress, and remarks.
Faber, Conrad W., *et al.*	Release as sureties of German Empire.	31	1	Memorial	256	Foreign Affairs.						
Faber, Conrad W., *et al.*	Release as sureties of German Empire.	31	1	Senate bill	591	Whole House			S. 46	Passed		App'd March 6, 1850
Fabius, William	Fishing bounty on schooner Garland.	28	2	Petition	300	Commerce.						
Fabius, William	Fishing bounty on schooner Garland.	29	1	Petition	234	Commerce	544	Favorable	366	Referred to Committee Whole House.		
Fabius, William	Fishing bounty on schooner Garland.	30	1	Petition	157	Commerce	260	Favorable	252	Referred to Committee Whole House.		
Fabius, William	Fishing bounty on schooner Garland.	31	1	Petition	451	Commerce.						
Fabler, or Fablo, Maria	Bounty land for services in war of 1812.	24	1	Petition	853	Military Affairs				Discharged; laid on table.		
Fabre, William	Prize money for services in battle on Lake Champlain.	25	3	Resolution	163	Naval Affairs.						
Fabre, William	Prize money for services in battle on Lake Champlain.	26	1	Petition	179	Naval Affairs	341	Favorable	316	Referred to Committee Whole House.		
Fabre, William	Prize money for services in battle on Lake Champlain.	27	3	Petition	71	Naval Affairs	Jan. 6, 1843	Favorable	654	Passed	Passed	App'd March 1, 1843
Faddon, George W.	Pension	26	1	Petition	513	Invalid Pensions	Mar. 5, 1840	Adverse		Laid on table.		
Fagan, Levi, (N. C.)	Increase of compensation as collector.	12	1	Petition	98	Ways and Means	April 3, 1812	Favorable	100	Rep'd by Committee Whole House.		
Fagan, Levi, (N. C.)	Increase of compensation as collector.	12	2	Petition	583	Ways and Means	Jan. 5, 1813	Favorable	220	Referred to Committee Whole House.		
Fagan, Levi, (N. C.)	Increase of compensation as collector.	13	2	Petition	287	Ways and Means.						
Fagan, Levi, (N. C.)	Increase of compensation as collector.	14	2	Petition	106	Ways and Means	Feb. 7, 1817	Favorable	112	Passed	Passed	App'd March 3, 1817
Fagan, Levi	Reimbursement of money lost in United States mail.	25	2	Memorial	736	P. O. & P. Roads				Discharged, laid on table.		
Fagot, Charles, *et al.*	Confirmation of title to land	22	1	Petition	64	Priv. Land Claims.	Dec. 27, 1831	Favorable	125	Passed	Passed	App'd June 27, 1832
Fain, John	Pension	13	2	Pension bill	344	Whole House	May 31, 1814	With amend.	166	Passed	Passed	App'd April 18, 1814
Fair, Jonathan	Pension for revolutionary services.	23	1	Petition	493	Rev. Pensions				Discharged; laid on table.		
Fair, Jonathan	Pension for revolutionary services.	25	2	Petition	404	Rev. Pensions				Discharged; laid on table.		
Fair, Jonathan	Pension for revolutionary services.	26	2	Petition	82	Rev. Pensions.						
Fair, Jonathan	Pension for revolutionary services.	27	2	Petition	97	Rev. Pensions	784	Adverse		Laid on table.		
Fair, Jonathan, heirs of	Pension for revolutionary services.	30	1	Petition	785	Rev. Pensions	691	Adverse		Laid on table.		
Fairbank, Calvin	Compensation for military services of son.	22	1	Petition	440	Military Affairs.						
Fairbanks, Erastus and Thaddeus.	Reimbursement of money over-paid for patent.	24	2	Senate bill	375	Claims	252	Favorable	203	Referred to Committee Whole House.		
Fairbanks, Erastus and Thaddeus.	Reimbursement of money over paid for patent.	25	2	Senate bill	101	Claims	Dec. 22, 1837	Favorable	7	Referred to Committee Whole House.		
Fairbanks, Erastus and Thaddeus.	Reimbursement of money over paid for patent.	25	3	Senate bill	51	Patents	Jan. 2, 1839	Favorable	14	Passed	Passed	App'd Feb. 6, 1839
Fairbanks, Jason	(See Purley Keys, *et al.*)	15	1		47							
Fairbanks, Jonathan	Pension for revolutionary services.	19	1	Petition	43	Rev. Pensions	164	Adverse		Laid on table.		
Fairbanks, Jonathan	Pension for revolutionary services.	22	1	Petition	105	Rev. Pensions.						

List of private claims presented to the House of Representatives of the United States from the 1st to the 31st Congress, inclusive—Continued.

Names of claimants.	Nature or object of the claim.	Congress.	Session.	How brought before the House of Reps.	Page of journal.	To what committee of the House referred.	No. or date of the report.	Nature of the report.	No. of the bill.	How disposed of by the House of Reps.	How disposed of by the Senate.	Date of the act of Congress, and remarks.
Fairbanks, Joshua, *et al.*	Indemnity for property destroyed by the public enemy.	15	2	Petition	148	Claims.						
Fairbanks, Joshua, *et al.*	Indemnity for property destroyed by the public enemy.	19	2	Petition	240	Claims.						
Fairbanks, Joshua, *et al.*	(See Jonas Harrison, sureties of.)	16	2	....	170							
Fairbault, Jean B	Recognition as the legal owner of Pike Island.	31	1	Petition	936	Priv. Land Claims.						
Fairbrother, Richard	Increase of pension	9	2	On leave	608	Claims	Feb. 26, 1807	Favorable	216	Passed	Passed	App'd March 3, 1807
Fairbrother, Richard	Increase of pension	13	2	House bill	344	Whole House	....	....	166	Passed	Passed	App'd April 18, 1814
Fairchild, Aaron	Compensation as clerk to the clothing department, revolutionary war.	22	1	Petition	73	Rev. Claims.						
Fairchild, Aaron	Compensation as clerk to the clothing department, revolutionary war.	22	2	Petition	118	Rev. Claims.						
Fairchild, Stephen	Pension for revolutionary services.	22	1	Petition	381	Rev. Pensions.	....	....	......	Discharged; laid on table.		
Fairchild, Mary	(See Mary F. Russell	26	1	....	713							
Fairfield, John	Bounty land for services of his son Jack in war of 1812.	14	1	Petition	193	Claims.						
Fairfield, John	Bounty land for services of his son Jack in war of 1812.	15	1	Petition	89	Select	Feb. 24, 1818	Favorable	99	Referred to Committee Whole House.		
Fairfield, John, mother of	Bounty land for services of his son Jack in war of 1812.	15	2	Petition	43	Whole House	Nov. 26, 1818	Favorable	100	Passed	Passed	App'd Dec. 28, 1818
Fairfield, Joseph	(See widow of Stephen Decatur and others.)	20	1	....	295	....	201	....	S. 50			
Fairfield, William	Reimbursement for losses sustained in the war of 1812.	26	2	Petition	130	Claims.						
Fairman, Amasa	Indemnity for property destroyed by British in the war of 1812.	17	1	Petition	118	Claims.						
Fairman, Amasa	Indemnity for property destroyed by British in the war of 1812.	17	1	Petition (2)	180	Claims	Mar. 29, 1822	Adverse	......	Laid on table.		
Fairman, Amasa	Indemnity for property destroyed by British in the war of 1812.	19	1	Petition	312	Claims	April 12, 1826	Adverse	......	Laid on table.		
Fairman, Charles G	Additional compensation as assistant marshal of Chemung county, New York.	31	2	Petition	280	Judiciary.						
Fairweather, Abigail, widow of John.	Pension for revolutionary services.	3	1	Petition	106	....	....	....	......	Referred to Secretary of War.		
Fairweather, Abigail, widow of John.	Pension for revolutionary services.	3	2	Rep. of Secretary of War.	278	....	....	....	......	Laid on table.		
Falconer, Abraham	Indemnity for French spoliations prior to 1800.	26	1	Memorial	182	Foreign Affairs	343	Favorable; bill	319	Referred to Committee Whole House.		
Falconer, John	Compensation for property destroyed in revolutionary war.	1	2	Petition	274	....	....	....	......	Referred to Secretary of War.		
Falconer, John	Compensation for property destroyed in revolutionary war.	1	3	Rep. of Secretary War.	385	....	....	....	......	Laid on table.		
Falconer, Joseph	Payment of lost loan office certificates.	16	1	Petition	374	Rev. Claims	....	....	......	Discharged; laid on table.		
Falconer, Joseph	Payment of lost loan office certificates.	19	1	Petition	270	Rev. Claims	....	....	......	Discharged; laid on table.		
Falconer, Joseph, executors of.	Payment of lost loan office certificates.	20	2	Petition	43	Rev. Claims	Jan. 24, 1829	Favorable	393	Referred to Committee Whole House.		

List of private claims presented to the House of Representatives of the United States from the 1st to the 31st Congress, inclusive—Continued.

Names of claimants.	Nature or object of the claim.	Congress.	Session.	How brought before the House of Reps.	Page of journal.	To what committee of the House referred.	No. or date of the report.	Nature of the report.	No. of the bill.	How disposed of by the House of Reps.	How disposed of by the Senate.	Date of the act of Congress, and remarks.
Falconer, Joseph, executors of.	Payment of lost loan office certificates.	21	1	Petition	50	Rev. Claims	92	Favorable	126	Passed	Passed	App'd May 28, 1830
Falconer, Joseph, heirs of.	Payment of interest on loan office certificates.	21	2	Petition	54	Rev. Claims	....	....	.....	Discharged; laid on table.		
Falconer, Joseph, heirs of.	Payment of interest on loan office certificates.	22	1	Petition	51	Rev. Claims.						
Falconer, Joseph, heirs of.	Payment of interest on loan office certificates.	22	2	Petition	119	Rev. Claims	65	Favorable	707	Referred to Committee Whole House.		
Falconer, Joseph, heirs of.	Payment of interest on loan office certificates.	23	1	Petition	97	Rev. Claims	157	Favorable	172	Passed	Passed	App'd June 28, 1834
Falconer, Jonathan, and sisters.	Indemnity for French spoliations prior to 1800.	29	2	Memorial	83	Foreign Affairs.						
Falconer, Jonathan, *et al.*	Indemnity for French spoliations prior to 1800.	31	1	Petition	533	Foreign Affairs	355	Favorable	318	Referred to Committee Whole House.		
Falconer and Stewart	(See Isaac Lawrence, *et al.*)	14	1	....	386							
Fales, Atwood and Samuel	Compensation in land as Canadian and Nova Scotia refugees.	4	1	Petition	448							
Fales, Atwood	(See Canadian refugees)	6	2	....	748							
Fales, Elizabeth	Continuation of pension	27	2	Petition	256	Rev. Pensions.						
Fales, Samuel	(See Canadian refugees)	6	2	....	748							
Falkner, Hackless	(See Captain William Falkner, widow of.)	3	2	....	340							
Falkner, William, widow of.	Compensation for revolutionary services.	3	2	Petition	340	....	....	....	.....	Laid on table.		
Falkner, William, widow of.	Compensation for revolutionary services.	4	1	Petition	430	Claims	May 21, 1796	Adverse	.....	Laid on table.		
Fall, Joseph	Compensation for revolutionary services.	18	2	Petition	278							
Fallen, John H.	Pension for revolutionary services.	24	1	Petition	433	Rev. Pensions	....	....	.....	Discharged; laid on table.		
Fallen, John H.	Pension for revolutionary services.	25	2	Petition	181	Rev. Pensions	....	....	.....	Discharged; laid on table.		
Fallen, John H.	Pension for revolutionary services.	25	3	Petition	87	Rev. Pensions	....	....	.....	Discharged.		
Fallen, John H.	Pension for revolutionary services.	26	1	Petition	174	Rev. Pensions	....	....	.....	Discharged; laid on table.		
Fallen, John H.	Pension for revolutionary services.	31	1	Resolution	1298	....	....	....	.....	Leave to withdraw.		
Falley, Frederick	Compensation for his schooner and cargo impressed into the service.	15	1	Petition	161	Claims	Feb. 5, 1818	Adverse	.....	Laid on table.		
Falley, Frederick	Compensation for his schooner and cargo impressed into the service.	16	1	Petition	70	Claims	Jan. 17, 1820	Adverse	.....	Laid on table.		
Falley, Frederick	Compensation for his schooner and cargo impressed into the service.	17	1	Petition	119	Claims.						
Falls & Brown	Indemnity for French spoliations prior to 1800.	26	1	Memorial	182	Foreign Affairs	343	Favorable; bill	319	Referred to Committee Whole House.		
Falls, Stockton, & Co.	(See Stockton, Falls, & Co.)	27	2	....	870							
Fanche, Jonas, *et al.*	Arrears of pay due for services in an Indian expedition in 1793-'96.	4	2	Petition	625	....	....	....	.....	Referred to Secretary War.		
Fancher, Ira	Pension	26	1	Petition	602	Invalid Pensions	560	Adverse	.....	Laid on table.		
Fancher, John	Pension for revolutionary services.	20	2	Resolution	152	Military Pensions	....	....	.....	Discharged, referred to Com. Whole House.		
Fancher, John	Pension for revolutionary services.	22	1	Petition	67	Rev. Pensions	50	Favorable	104	Passed.		

List of private claims presented to the House of Representatives of the United States from the 1st to the 31st Congress, inclusive—Continued.

Names of claimants.	Nature or object of the claim.	Congress.	Session.	How brought before the House of Reps.	Page of journal.	To what committee of the House referred.	No. or date of the report.	Nature of the report.	No. of the bill.	How disposed of by the House of Reps.	How disposed of by the Senate.	Date of the act of Congress, and remarks.
Fancher, Thomas	Pension for revolutionary services	15	2	Petition	177	Rev. Pensions	Feb. 11, 1819	Adverse	.....	Laid on table.		
Fannell, John C.	Increase of pension	27	2	Petition	757	Invalid Pensions.						
Fannin, Abraham P.	Settlement of his accounts	29	1	Senate bill	1013	Judiciary	July 24, 1846	Favorable	152	Passed	Passed	App'd July 29, 1846
Fanning, Abigail	(See John Fanning, widow of)	31	1	....	284							
Fanning, Edmund, & Benjamin Pendleton.	Compensation for benefits opened up to American trade with the Auricanian nation, as commanders of vessels.	22	1	Petition	78	Commerce	....	....	.....	Discharged; laid on table.		
Fanning, Edmund, & Benjamin Pendleton.	Compensation for benefits opened up to American trade with the Auricanian nation, as commanders of vessels.	22	2	Memorial	30	Commerce.						
Fanning, Edmund, & Benjamin Pendleton.	Compensation for benefits opened up to American trade with the Auricanian nation, as commanders of vessels.	23	1	Memorial	37	Naval Affairs	....	....	.....	Discharged; laid on table.		
Fanning, Edmund, & Benjamin Pendleton.	Compensation for benefits opened up to American trade with the Auricanian nation, as commanders of vessels.	24	1	Memorial	61	Commerce.						
Fanning, Edmund, & Benjamin Morrell.	Compensation for benefits opened up to American trade with the Auricanian nation, as commanders of vessels.	23	1	Memorial	418	Naval Affairs.						
Fanning, Elisha	Pension	12	1	House bill	361	Whole House	June 15, 1812	Favorable	138	Passed	Passed	App'd July 5, 1812
Fanning, Henry	Release from imprisonment upon judgment of the United States.	13	2	Petition	193	Ways and Means	42	Favorable	89	Passed	Passed	App'd March 19, 1814
Fanning, Henry	Release from imprisonment upon judgment of the United States.	14	1	Petition	70	Select	Dec. 29, 1815	Favorable	14	Passed	Passed	App'd Jan. 17, 1816
Fanning, John	Compensation for revolutionary services.	14	1	Petition	592	Rev. Claims	....	....	.....	Discharged; laid on table.		
Fanning, John	Commutation pay	14	2	Petition	111	Rev. Claims	....	....	.....	Discharged; laid on table.		
Fanning, John	Commutation pay	15	1	Petition	90	Rev. Claims	....	....	.....	Discharged; leave to withdraw.		
Fanning, John	Pension for revolutionary services	20	1	Petition	98	Military Pensions	....	....	.....	Discharged; laid on table.		
Fanning, John	Pension for revolutionary services	21	1	Petition	36	Military Pensions	....	....	.....	Discharged; laid on table.		
Fanning, John, widow of.	Pension for revolutionary services	31	1	Petition	284	Rev. Pensions	23	Adverse	.....	Laid on table.		
Fanning, John B., executor of.	Settlement of his accounts as purser in the navy.	18	1	Petition	175	Naval Affairs	April 30, 1824	Favorable	211	Passed	Passed	App'd May 19, 1824
Fanning, John B., sureties of.	Release from liability	26	1	Memorial	297	Judiciary.						
Fanning, John B., sureties of.	Release from liability	26	2	Petition	78	Judiciary	115	Favorable	620	Referred to Committee Whole House.		
Fanning, John B., sureties of.	Release from liability	27	2	Petition	63	Judiciary	250	Favorable	216	Passed	Passed	App'd July 27, 1842
Fanning, Joshua	(See Joshua Fanning, heirs of.)											
Fanning, Joshua, heirs of.	Half pay for revolutionary services	4	1	Petition	427	Claims	May 31, 1796	Adverse	.....	Laid on table.		
Fanning, Joshua, heirs of.	Bounty land, prize money, &c	9	2	Petition	600	....	....	....	.....	Laid on table.		
Fanning, Joshua, heirs of.	Bounty land, prize money, &c	10	1	Petition	16	Public Lands.						

List of private claims presented to the House of Representatives of the United States from the 1st to the 31st Congress, inclusive—Continued.

Names of claimants.	Nature or object of the claim.	Congress.	Session.	How brought before the House of Reps.	Page of journal.	To what committee of the House referred.	No. or date of the report.	Nature of the report.	No. of the bill.	How disposed of by the House of Reps.	How disposed of by the Senate.	Date of the act of Congress, and remarks.
Fanning, Joshua, heirs of.	Half-pay for revolutionary services.	17	1	Petition	289	Rev. Claims				Discharged; leave to withdraw.		
Fanning, Joshua, heirs of.	Half-pay for revolutionary services.	23	1	Petition	157	Rev. Claims.						
Fanning, Joshua, heirs of.	Half-pay for revolutionary services.	23	2	Petition	105	Rev. Claims.						
Fanning, Joshua, heirs of.	Half-pay for revolutionary services.	24	1	Petition	103	Rev. Claims	463	Favorable	470	Referred to Committee Whole House.		
Fanning, Joshua, heirs of.	Half-pay for revolutionary services.	24	2	House bill	62	Whole House			470	Referred to Committee Whole House.		
Fanning, Joshua, heirs of.	Half-pay for revolutionary services.	25	2	Petition	40	Rev. Claims	110	Favorable	128	Passed	Passed	App'd July 7, 1838
Fanning, Patrick	(See John Thurston, heirs of)	29	2		87							
Fanning, Nathaniel, heirs of.	Prize-money for captures under John Paul Jones.	25	3	Memorial	130	Naval Affairs.						
Fanning, Nathaniel, heirs of.	Prize-money for captures under John Paul Jones.	26	2	Memorial	135	Naval Affairs.						
Fanny, schooner	(See Nathaniel Gunnison)	24	1		54							
Fanshee, Joseph	Pension	21	2	Petition	188	Military Pensions.						
Fanshee, Joseph	Pension	22	1	Petition	67	Rev. Pensions				Discharged; laid on table.		
Fansher, Sylvanus	Compensation for vaccinating United States soldiers in 1808.	19	1	Petition	102	Select				Discharged; laid on table.		
Fant, H. G., *et al.*	Arrears of mileage as volunters in the Mexican war.	31	1	Petition	643	Military Affairs				Discharged; laid on table.		
Fargo, William C	Extra compensation for mail service.	26	1	Petition	302	P. Of. & P. Roads.	400	Adverse		Laid on table.		
Faris, James	(See Leonard Dyson and others.)	19	1		64							
Faris, John	(See William Baker, agent, &c.)	22	1		288							
Faris, Nathaniel, heirs of	Compensation for revolutionary services.	24	1	Resolution	484	Rev. Claims	825	Adverse		Laid on table.		
Faris, Nathaniel, heirs of	Compensation for revolutionary services.	24	2	Petition	42	Rev. Claims	Jan. 19, 1837	Adverse		Laid on table.		
Faris, Nathaniel, heirs of	Compensation for revolutionary services.	25	2	Resolution	81	Rev. Claims				Discharged; laid on table.		
Faris, Nathaniel, heirs of	Compensation for revolutionary services.	25	3	Petition	84	Rev. Claims				Discharged.		
Faris, Nathaniel, heirs of	Compensation for revolutionary services.	28	1	Petition	371	Rev. Claims.						
Faris, William	(See Farris.)											
Farish, Thomas B	Compensation for property taken for public use.	13	3	Petition	591	Claims	Feb. 25, 1815	Favorable	309	Referred to Committee Whole House.		
Farish, Thomas B	Compensation for property taken for public use.	14	1	Petition	243	Claims	Feb. 8, 1816	Favorable		Passed	Postponed.	
Farish, Thomas B	Compensation for property taken for public use.	15	1	Petition	90	Claims	Mar. 9, 1818	Favorable	121	Referred to Committee Whole House.		
Farish, Thomas B	Compensation for property taken for public use.	15	2	House bill	102	Whole House			121	Passed	Passed, with amendment.	App'd Feb. 4, 1819
Farley, Charles, *et al.*	Compensation as weighers and gaugers.	28	1	Petition	352	Commerce.						
Farley, Jabez	Pension	21	2	Petition	299	Military Pensions.						
Farley, Joseph	Increase of compensation as collector.	9	1	Petition	261	Ways and Means.						
Farley, Joseph	Increase of compensation as collector.	9	2	Resolution	482	Ways and Means				Laid on table.		
Farley, Robert, administrator of.	Compensation as collector	18	1	Petition	47	Claims	Dec. 16, 1823	Adverse		Laid on table.		

List of private claims presented to the House of Representatives of the United States from the 1st to the 31st Congress, inclusive—Continued.

Names of claimants.	Nature or object of the claim.	Congress.	Session.	How brought before the House of Reps.	Page of journal.	To what committee of the House referred.	No. or date of the report.	Nature of the report.	No. of the bill.	How disposed of by the House of Reps.	How disposed of by the Senate.	Date of the act of Congress, and remarks.
77 Farley, Robert, administrator of.	Compensation as collector	20	1	Resolution	163	Claims	Jan. 28, 1828	Adverse	......	Laid on table.		
Farlow, Huldah	(See Joseph Moger, widow of.)	25	3	....	127							
Farman, Robert, devisees of	Indemnity for loss of certain lands.	11	2	Petition	149	Public Lands.						
Farmborough, John, heir of	Amount due for revolutionary services.	15	1	Petition	257	Rev. Claims	April 6, 1818	Adverse	......	Laid on table.		
Farmborough, John, heir of	Amount due for revolutionary services.	22	1	Petition	62	Rev. Claims	....	....	......	Discharged; laid on table.		
Farmborough, Robert	(See John Farmborough, heir of.)	15	1	....	257							
Farmer, George W	Compensation for labor on road in Tennessee.	26	1	Petition	336	Claims.						
Farmer, George W	Compensation for labor on road in Tennessee.	30	2	Petition	8	Claims	9	Adverse	......	Laid on table.		
Farmer, John	Compensation for surveying the point where Gen. T. J. Sutherland was arrested.	27	2	Petition	613	Claims.						
Farmer, John	Compensation for surveying the point where Gen. T. J. Sutherland was arrested.	27	3	Petition	73	Claims	289	Adverse	......	Laid on table.		
Farmer, Oliver	Pension for revolutionary services.	26	1	Petition	1001	Rev. Claims.						
Farmer, Oliver	Pension for revolutionary services.	26	2	Petition	297	Rev. Claims.						
Farmer, Robert, heirs of	Confirmation of title to land	23	2	Petition	220	Priv. Land Claims.						
Farmer, Robert, heirs of	Confirmation of title to land	24	1	Petition	112	Priv. Land Claims.	352	Favorable	358	Referred to Committee Whole House.		
Farmer, Robert, heirs of	Confirmation of title to land	25	2	Petition	42	Priv. Land Claims.	139	Favorable	157	Referred to Committee Whole House.		
Farmer, Robert, heirs of	Confirmation of title to land	25	3	House bill	375	Whole House	Jan. 25, 1839	With amend's.	157	Passed	Passed	App'd March 3, 1839
Farmer, Thomas	Remission of forfeiture of vessel and cargo.	13	2	Petition	188	Com. and Manuf.						
Farmers and Mechanics' bank of Indiana.	For an adjustment of the claims of said bank *vs.* the U. States.	22	1	Senate bill	701	Ways and Means	June 8, 1832	Favorable	194	Passed	Passed	App'd July 9, 1832
Farmsby, Nathan	Pension	14	2	Petition and rep't Sec. of War.	218	Rev. Claims	Jan. 17, 1817	Adverse	......	Rejected	....	Leave to withdraw.
Farnam, Benjamin, widow of.	Pension	29	1	Petition	168	Rev. Pensions	602	Favorable	425	Referred to Committee Whole House.		
Farnam, Benjamin, widow of.	Pension	29	2	Petition	211	Whole House	227	Favorable	425	Laid on table.		
Farnham and Davenport	Payment for goods per treaty stipu-	22	2	Senate bill	441	Ways and Means	Mar. 1, 1833	With't amend.	S. 128	Passed	Passed	App'd March 2, 1833
Farnham, John	Pension	26	2	Petition	55	Invalid Pensions.						
Farnham, John	Pension	27	2	Petition	321	Invalid Pensions	321	Favorable	290	Ordered to 3d reading.		
Farnham, John	Pension	27	3	House bill	87		....	....	290	Passed	Indef. postp'd.	
Farnham, John	Pension	28	1	Petition	131	Invalid Pensions	94	Favorable	110	Passed	Indef. postp'd.	
Farnham, John	Pension	28	2	Petition	58	Invalid Pensions	....	....	......	Discharged; laid on table.		
Farnham, John	Pension	29	1	Petition	107	Invalid Pensions	101	Adverse	......	Laid on table.		
Farnham, John	Pension	30	1	Petition	506	Invalid Pensions	562	Favorable	462	Passed	Passed	App'd Aug. 11, 1848
Farnham, P. J., & Co	Indemnity for vessel seized by British at St. Helena.	30	2	Petition	116	Foreign Affairs	142	Favorable	......	Referred to Committee Whole House.		
Farnham, P. J., & Co	Indemnity for vessel seized by British at St. Helena.	31	1	Petition	215	Foreign Affairs.						

List of private claims presented to the House of Representatives of the United States from the 1*st to the* 31*st Congress, inclusive*—Continued.

Names of claimants.	Nature or object of the claim.	Congress.	Session.	How brought before the House of Reps.	Page of journal.	To what committee of the House referred.	No. or date of the report.	Nature of the report.	No. of the bill.	How disposed of by the House of Reps.	How disposed of by the Senate.	Date of the act of Congress, and remarks.
Farnham, P. J., & Co.	Indemnity for vessel seized by British at St. Helena.	31	2	Petition	445	Foreign Affairs	103	Favorable	......	Laid on table.		
Farnham, Ralph	Pension	21	2	Resolution	124	Military Pensions.						
Farnham, Ralph	Pension	22	1	Resolution	70	Rev. Pensions	....	....	......	Disch'd; laid on table.		
Farnham, Peter	Indemnity for wounds received in public service.	24	1	Petition	533	Invalid Pensions	April 20, 1836	Adverse	......	Laid on table.		
Farnsworth, Henry	Money in lieu of land for service in war of 1812.	27	2	Petition	795	Claims.						
Farnsworth, Jonas	Pension	9	2	House bill	608	Whole House	Feb. 28, 1807	Favorable	216	Passed	Passed	App'd March 3, 1807
Farnsworth, Jonas	Pension	10	1	Memorial	117	Select.						
Farnsworth, Levi	Compensation for revolutionary services.	2	1	Petition	445	....	....	....	......	Referred to Secretary of War.		
Farnsworth, Levi	Compensation for revolutionary services.	3	1	Rep. of Secretary War.	131	Select	May 26, 1794	Ref. Secretary War.	J. R. 12	Passed	Passed	App'd June 9, 1794
Farnsworth, Levi	Compensation for revolutionary services.	3	2	Rep. of Secretary War.	278	Claims	Feb. 28, 1795	Favorable	130	Passed	Postponed.	
Farnsworth, Levi	Compensation for revolutionary services.	4	1	Rep. of Secretary War.	445	Claims	Feb. 18, 1796	Favorable	156	Passed	Passed	App'd April 20, 1796
Farnsworth, Nathan	Compensation for saving crew and stores of ship Charles Wharton.	25	2	Petition	408	Commerce	....	....	......	Discharged.		
Farnsworth, Nathan	Compensation for saving crew and stores of ship Charles Wharton.	25	3	Petition	118	Commerce	239	Favorable	1101	Referred to Committee Whole House.		
Farnsworth, Nathan	Compensation for saving crew and stores of ship Charles Wharton.	26	1	Petition	176	Commerce	35	Favorable	55	Passed	Indef. postp'd.	
Farnsworth, Nathan	Compensation for saving crew and stores of ship Charles Wharton.	26	2	Petition	38	Claims.						
Farnsworth, Nathan	Compensation for saving crew and stores of ship Charles Wharton.	27	2	Petition	57	Commerce	474	Favorable	324	Passed.		
Farnsworth, Nathan	Compensation for saving crew and stores of ship Charles Wharton.	27	3	Petition	45	Commerce.						
Farnsworth, Nathan	Compensation for saving crew and stores of ship Charles Wharton.	28	1	Petition	117	Commerce	195	Favorable	152	Referred to Committee Whole House.		
Farnsworth, Nathan	Compensation for saving crew and stores of ship Charles Wharton.	28	2	House bill	343	Whole House	....	....	152	Passed	Indef. postp'd.	
Farnsworth, Nathan	Compensation for saving crew and stores of ship Charles Wharton.	30	1	Petition	1025	Commerce	811	Favorable	632	Referred to Committee Whole House.		
Farnsworth, Nathan	Compensation for saving crew and stores of ship Charles Wharton.	31	1	Petition	500	Claims	268	Adverse	......	Laid on table.		
Farnsworth, Robert	Compensation for horse lost in 1832.	24	1	Petition	430	Claims.						
Farnum, Benjamin	Pension	3	1	Rep. of Secretary War.	131	Select	May 26, 1794	Res. to refer to Sec. War.	J. R. 12	Passed	Passed	App'd June 9, 1794
Farnum, Benjamin	Pension	3	2	Rep. of Secretary War.	337	Claims	Feb. 28, 1795	Favorable	130	Passed	Postponed.	
Farnum, Benjamin	Pension	4	1	Rep. of Secretary War.	445	Claims	Feb. 18, 1796	Favorable	156	Passed	Passed	App'd April 20, 1796
Farnum, Sarah	(See John Peters, heir of)	27	3	....	168							
Farquhar, Robert, heir of.	Compensation for supplies furnished United States during revolutionary war.	3	1	Petition	78	....	....	....	......	Laid on table.		
Farquhar, Robert, heir of.	Compensation for supplies furnished United States during revolutionary war.	3	2	Petition	330	Claims.						

List of private claims presented to the House of Representatives of the United States from the 1st to the 31st Congress, inclusive—Continued.

Names of claimants.	Nature or object of the claim.	Congress.	Session.	How brought before the House of Reps.	Page of journal.	To what committee of the House referred.	No. or date of the report.	Nature of the report.	No. of the bill.	How disposed of by the House of Reps.	How disposed of by the Senate.	Date of the act of Congress, and remarks.
Farquhar, Robert, heir of	Compensation for supplies furnished United States during revolutionary war.	5	2	Rep't Committee Whole House.	272	Claims	April 25, 1798	Adverse	......	Laid on table.		
Farr, William, and John Maxwell.	Compensation as musicians in marine corps.	14	2	Petition and rep't Sec. of Navy.	176, 287	Naval Affairs	Feb. 18, 1817	Adverse	......	Discharged; referred to Sec. of Navy.		
Farr, Childs, & Co	Remission of duties on goods destroyed by fire.	31	1	Petition	641	Commerce	329	Favorable	286	Referred to Committee Whole House.		
Farr, Samuel, heirs of	Compensation for revolutionary services.	18	1	Petition	134	Rev. Claims.						
Farr, Elsey, *et al.*	(See William Thompson, Va.)	19	1	....	312							
Farragut, Lieut. A. C	Pay as a captain from 1835	29	2	Petition	184	Naval Affairs.						
Farragut, Lieut. A. C	Pay as a captain from 1835	31	1	Petition	362	Naval Affairs	....	....	......	Discharged; laid on table.		
Farragut, David G	Compensation for extra naval services.	23	2	Petition	39	Naval Affairs.						
Farragut, David G	Compensation for extra naval services.	24	1	Petition	61	Naval Affairs.						
Farragut, David G	Compensation for extra naval services.	24	2	Memorial	46	Naval Affairs	279	Adverse	......	Laid on table.		
Farragut, David G	Compensation for extra naval services.	25	2	Petition	399	Naval Affairs	....	....	......	Discharged.		
Farragut, George	Balance of pay for military service.	5	3	Petition	487	Referred to Sec. of War.	Feb. 25, 1799	Report	......	Laid on table.		
Farragut, George	Balance of pay for military service.	6	1	Petition and rep't Sec. of War.	544	Claims	Jan. 13, 1800	Adverse	......	Laid on table.		
Farrall, Samuel	Pension for revolutionary services.	15	2	Petition	182	Rev. Pensions	....	....	......	Discharged; laid on table.		
Farrall, Samuel	Pension for revolutionary services.	17	1	Petition	73	Rev. Pensions	....	....	......	Discharged	....	Leave to withdraw.
Farran, Joseph	Invalid pension	24	2	Petition	395	Invalid Pensions.						
Farrand, Ebenezer	Payment of expenses in protecting live oak.	23	2	Petition	199	Naval Affairs	Feb. 10, 1835	Adverse	......	Laid on table.		
Farrar, Benjamin, *et al.*	Compensation for horses lost in public service.	11	1	Petition	41	Claims.						
Farrar, Benjamin, *et al.*	Compensation for horses lost in public service.	13	2	Petition	202	Claims	Jan. 19, 1814	Adverse	......	Laid on table.		
Farrar, Joseph	Pension	25	1	Petition	72	....	....	....	......	Laid on table.		
Farrar, Joseph	Pension	25	2	Petition	52	Claims	....	....	......	Discharged; referred to Invalid Pensions.		
Farrar, Joseph	Pension	26	1	Petition	161	Invalid Pensions	264	Adverse	......	Laid on table.		
Farrar, Joseph	Pension	30	2	Petition	191	Invalid Pensions	....	....	......	Discharged; laid on table.		
Farrar, Samuel	Compensation for revolutionary services.	2	1	Petition	442	....	....	....	......	Referred to Secretary War.		
Farrar, Samuel	Compensation for revolutionary services.	2	2	Report Secretary of War.	696	....	....	....	......	Laid on table.		
Farrer, Deevin	Pay for work done under contract with Indian agent in New York.	27	3	Petition	285	Claims.						
Farrer, Deevin	Pay for work done under contract with Indian agent in New York.	28	1	Petition	335	Claims.						
Farrer, Deevin	Pay for work done under contract with Indian agent in New York.	28	2	Petition	117	Claims	66	Adverse	......	Laid on table.		
Farrer, Deevin	Pay for work done under contract with Indian agent in New York.	29	1	Petition	75	Claims	99	Adverse	......	Laid on table.		

List of private claims presented to the House of Representatives of the United States from the 1st to the 31st Congress, inclusive—**Continued.**

Names of claimants.	Nature or object of the claim.	Congress.	Session.	How brought before the House of Reps.	Page of journal.	To what committee of the House referred.	No. or date of the report.	Nature of the report.	No. of the bill.	How disposed of by the House of Reps.	How disposed of by the Senate.	Date of the act of Congress, and remarks.
Farrer, Thomas, and William Young.	Compensation for taking an account of manufactures in the United States.	13	3	Petition and rep't Sec. of War.	497	Claims.						
Farrer, Thomas, and William Young.	Compensation for taking an account of manufactures in the United States.	14	1	Petition	275	Claims	Mar. 1, 1816	Favorable	103	Passed	Passed	App'd April 27, 1816
Farrell, James, (Pa.)	Invalid pension	20	1	Resolution	116	Military Pensions	April 29, 1828	Favorable	283	Passed.		
Farrell, James, (Pa.)	Invalid pension	20	2	House bill	5	Military Pensions	Dec. 12, 1828	Favorable	311	Passed		
Farrell, James, (Pa.)	Invalid pension	21	1	Resolution	43	Military Pensions	Jan. 5, 1830	Favorable	72	Passed	Passed	App'd May 14, 1830
Farrell, James, sister of	Prize money due for destruction of the frigate Philadelphia.	27	2	Petition	221	Naval Affairs.						
Farrell, James, sister of	Prize money due for destruction of the frigate Philadelphia.	27	3	Petition	107	Naval Affairs.						
Farrell, John C.	Arrears of pension	26	1	Petition	938	Invalid Pensions				Discharged; laid on table.		
Farrell, Michael	Remission of certain duties	26	1	Petition	297	Ways and Means	493	Adverse		Laid on table.		
Farrelly, Terrence, and Mary his wife.	(See John Lavergne, assignees of.)	22	1		62				425			
Farrington, Daniel	Arrears of pension	23	1	Petition	159	Invalid Pensions	Jan. 31, 1834	Adverse		Laid on table.		
Farrington, Jerusha	(See Thomas Farrington, widow of.	29	2	Petition	54							
Farrington, March	Pension	25	2	Petition	198	Invalid Pensions				Discharged; laid on table.		
Farrington, March	Pension	26	1	Petition	160	Invalid Pensions.						
Farrington, March	Pension	27	2	Petition	347	Invalid Pensions	627	Adverse		Laid on table.		
Farrington, March	Pension	27	3	Petition	44	Invalid Pensions	81	Adverse		Laid on table.		
Farrington, March	Pension	28	1	Petition	326	Invalid Pensions	179	Adverse		Laid on table.		
Farrington, March	Pension	28	2	Petition	56	Invalid Pensions	38	Favorable; bill	512	Passed	Passed	App'd March 3, 1845
Farrington, March	Pension	29	1	Petition	319	Invalid Pensions	502	Adverse		Laid on table.		
Farrington, March	Pension	30	1	Petition	274	Invalid Pensions	722	Adverse		Laid on table.		
Farrington, March	Pension	31	1	Petition	257	Invalid Pensions	69	Adverse		Laid on table.		
Farrington, Putnam	Pension	26	1	Petition	288	Invalid Pensions				Discharged; laid on table.		
Farrington, Thomas, widow of.	Pension for revolutionary services.	29	2	Petition	54	Rev. Pensions.						
Farrington, Thomas, heirs of.	Indemnity for losses on continental money.	30	2	Petition	32	Rev. Claims	143	Adverse		Laid on table.		
Farrington, William	Pension	22	1	Petition	218	Rev. Pensions				Discharged; laid on table.		
Farris, Elijah	Bounty land	31	2	Memorial	53	Priv. Land Claims.						
Farris, Francis	(See William Farris, widow of)	25	2		37							
Farris, James	Pension for revolutionary services.	28	1	Petition	946	Rev. Pensions.						
Farris, James	Pension for revolutionary services.	28	2	Petition	187	Rev. Pensions.						
Farris, John T.	Bounty land for services in the Mexican war.	30	2	Memorial	315	Priv. Land Claims.	62	Adverse		Leave to withdraw.		
Farris, William	Pension for revolutionary services.	23	2	Petition	197	Rev. Pensions				Discharged; laid on table.		
Farris, William	Pension for revolutionary services.	24	1	Petition	213	Rev. Pensions	389	Favorable; bill	394	Passed	Indef. postp'd.	
Farris, William	Pension for revolutionary services.	25	2	Petition	37	Rev. Pensions	215	Favorable; bill	252	Passed.		
Farris, William, widow of.	Pension for revolutionary services.	25	2	Petition	273	Rev. Pensions				Discharged; laid on table.		
Farris, William, widow of.	Pension for revolutionary services.	26	1	Petition	171	Rev. Pensions	490	Adverse		Laid on table.		

List of private claims presented to the House of Representatives of the United States from the 1st to the 31st Congress, inclusive—Continued.

Names of claimants.	Nature or object of the claim.	Congress.	Session.	How brought before the House of Reps.	Page of journal.	To what committee of the House referred.	No. or date of the report.	Nature of the report.	No. of the bill.	How disposed of by the House of Reps.	How disposed of by the Senate.	Date of the act of Congress, and remarks.
Farris, William	Indemnity for French spoliations prior to 1800.	26	1	Memorial	182	Foreign Affairs	343	Favorable; bill	319	Referred to Committee Whole House.		
Farrish, Thomas B.	Indemnity for tobacco burnt at Washington.	13	3	Petition	591	Claims	Feb. 25, 1815	Favorable	309	Referred to Committee Whole House.		
Farrish, Thomas B.	Indemnity for tobacco burnt at Washington.	15	1	Petition	90	Claims	Mar. 9, 1818	Favorable	121	Referred to Committee Whole House.		
Farrow, Abraham, heirs of	Compensation for revolutionary services.	28	1	Petition	868	Rev. Claims.						
Farrow, Ezekiel, widow of	Arrears of pension	27	2	Petition	320	Rev. Pensions.						
Farrow, Ezekiel, widow of	Arrears of pension	28	1	Petition	238	Rev. Pensions.						
Farrow, John	Restoration of pension	20	2	Petition	59	Military Pensions	Jan. 21, 1829	Adverse	......	Laid on table.		
Farrow, John	Restoration of pension	21	1	Petition	91	Military Pensions	May 3, 1830	Favorable	454			
Farrow, John	Restoration of pension	21	2	House bill	318	Whole House	....	....	454	Passed.		
Farrow, John	Restoration of pension	22	1	Petition	51	Rev. Pensions	Dec. 23, 1831	Favorable	111	Passed.		
Farrow, Miriam	(See Ezekiel Farrow, widow of).	27	2	....	320							
Farrow, Nimrod, and Richard Harris.	Indemnity for loss on contract to erect certain fortifications.	17	2	Petition	136	Military Affairs	Feb. 25, 1823	Favorable; bill	314	Passed.		
Farrow, Nimrod, and Richard Harris.	Indemnity for loss on contract to erect certain fortifications.	17	2	Senate bill	278	....	....	....	S. 64	Passed with amendm't.	Concurred in.	App'd March 3, 1823
Farrow, Nimrod, and Richard Harris.	For further relief	18	1	Resolution	403	Military Affairs.						
Farrow, Nimrod, and Richard Harris.	For further relief	18	1	Senate bill	573	Military Affairs	May 25, 1824	With amend's.	S. 95	Laid on table.		
Farrow, Nimrod, and Richard Harris.	For further relief	18	2	Bill and report of last session, & Rep. of Secretary War.	61 218	Claims	69	Favorable; bill	335	Passed	Passed	App'd March 3, 1825
Farrow, Nimrod, and Richard Harris.	For further relief to them as contractors of the United States.	19	2	Resolution	115	Claims	80	Favorable	435			
Farrow, Nimrod, and Richard Harris.	For further relief to them as contractors of the United States.	20	1	Resolution	132	Claims	181	Favorable	210	Referred to Committee Whole House.		
Farrow, Nimrod, and Richard Harris.	For further relief to them as contractors of the United States.	20	2	Rep. Committee Whole House.	202	....	....	....	210	Passed.		
Farrow, Nimrod, and Richard Harris.	For further relief to them as contractors of the United States.	21	1	Petition	98	Claims	315	Adverse	......	Laid on table.		
Farrow, Nimrod, and Richard Harris.	For further relief to them as contractors of the United States.	21	2	Rep. of last sess.	66	Claims	Feb. 15, 1831	Favorable	626	Passed.		
Farrow, Nimrod, and Richard Harris.	For further relief to them as contractors of the United States.	22	1	Resolution	146	Claims	Jan. 17, 1832	Favorable	277	Passed	Passed	App'd July 14, 1832
Farrow, Nimrod, and Richard Harris.	For further relief to them as contractors of the United States.	23	2	Report of Second Comptroller.	175	Claims.						
Farrow, Nimrod, and Richard Harris.	For further relief to them as contractors of the United States.	24	1	Petition	141	Claims.						
Farrow, Nimrod, and Richard Harris.	For further relief to them as contractors of the United States.	24	2	Petition	81	Claims	245	Favorable	944			
Farrow, Nimrod, and Richard Harris.	For further relief to them as contractors of the United States.	25	2	Petition	36	Claims	66	Favorable	78	Passed	Laid on table.	
Farrow, Nimrod, and Richard Harris.	For further relief to them as contractors of the United States.	25	3	Petition	86	Claims	39	Favorable	936	Passed.		
Farrow, Nimrod, and Richard Harris.	For further relief to them as contractors of the United States	26	1	Petition	167	Claims.						
Farrow, Nimrod, and Richard Harris.	For further relief to them as contractors of the United States.	26	2	Petition	80	Claims.						

List of private claims presented to the House of Representatives of the United States from the 1st to the 31st Congress, inclusive—Continued.

Names of claimants.	Nature or object of the claim.	Congress.	Session.	How brought before the House of Reps.	Page of journal.	To what committee of the House referred.	No. or date of the report.	Nature of the report.	No. of the bill.	How disposed of by the House of Reps.	How disposed of by the Senate.	Date of the act of Congress, and remarks.
Farrow, Nimrod, and Richard Harris.	For further relief to them as contractors of the United States.	27	2	Petition	55	Claims	50	Favorable	85	Rejected.		
Farrow, Nimrod, and Richard Harris, representatives of.	For further relief to them as contractors of the United States.	28	1	Petition	294	Claims.						
Farrow, Nimrod, and Richard Harris, representatives of.	For further relief to them as contractors of the United States.	29	1	Petition	....	Claims	190	Favorable	187			
Farrow, Nimrod, and Richard Harris, representatives of.	For further relief to them as contractors of the United States.	29	2	House bill	381	Whole House	....	....	187			
Farrow, Nimrod, and Richard Harris, representatives of.	For further relief to them as contractors of the United States.	30	1	Petition	145	Claims	167	Favorable	167			
Farrow, Nimrod, and Richard Harris, representatives of.	For further relief to them as contractors of the United States.	30	2	House bill	102	Whole House	....	....	167	Laid on table.		
Farrow, Nimrod, and Richard Harris, representatives of.	For further relief to them as contractors of the United States.	31	1	Petition	214	Claims	166	Adverse	....	Laid on table.		
Farrow, Pharaoh, & others.	Proceeds of sale of boats of the enemy captured in the late war.	14	1	Petition	221	Naval Affairs	Jan. 30, 1816	Favorable; bill	64	Passed	Passed	App'd April 27, 1816
Farrow, Thomas	Reimbursement of interest paid on judgment as surety for a postmaster.	20	2	Petition	75	Ways and Means	....	....	....	Discharged; leave to withdraw.		
Fartle, Foster	Confirmation of title to land	15	1	Petition	180	Priv. Land Claims	....	....	....	Discharged; laid on table.		
Fartle, Foster	Confirmation of title to land	17	1	Petition	53	Public Lands	....	....	....	Discharged; laid on table.		
Fartle, Foster	Confirmation of title to land	18	1	Petition	54	Public Lands.						
Farwell, David	(See David Beard and others)	17	2	....	121							
Fass, Elijah	Restoration of pension	17	2	Petition	25	Rev. Pensions	....	....	....	Discharged; leave to withdraw.		
Fassett, Hetty	(See John D. Avery, widow of)	26	1	....	285							
Fast, Christian	Compensation for revolutionary services.	19	2	Resolution	69	Rev. Claims.						
Fast, Chistopher	(See Lieut. M. Baker and others)	19	1	....	267							
Fatio, Francis J	Salary as secretary to Florida Land Convention.	19	1	Appropriation bill	....	....	....	....	42	....	....	App'd Mar. 14, 1826
Fatio, F. P.	Indemnity for destruction of property in Florida.	19	1	Memorial	252	Foreign Affairs	112	Adverse	....	Laid on table.		
Fatio, F. P.	Indemnity for destruction of property in Florida.	20	2	Petition	339	Foreign Affairs	99	Favorable	385	Referred to Committee Whole House.		
Fatio, F. P.	Indemnity for destruction of property in Florida.	23	1	Petition	67	Foreign Affairs	368	Favorable; bill	395	Passed	Passed	App'd June 26, 1834
Fauche, Jonas, *et al.*	Balance due for military services against the Indians in 1793-'96.	6	1	Rep. of Secretary War.	587	Whole House.						
Fauche, Jonas, *et al.*	Balance due for military services against the Indians in 1793-'96.	14	2	Petition	112	Select.						
Fauche, Jonas, *et al*	Balance due for military services against the Indians in 1793-'96.	19	2	Petition	159	Whole House.						
Fauche, Jonas, *et al*	Balance due for military services against the Indians in 1793-'96.	21	2	Petition	75	Indian Affairs	Dec. 29, 1830	Favorable	....	Referred to Committee Whole House.		

List of private claims presented to the House of Representatives of the United States from the 1st to the 31st Congress, inclusive—Continued.

Names of claimants.	Nature or object of the claim.	Congress.	Session.	How brought before the House of Reps.	Page of journal.	To what committee of the House referred.	No. or date of the report.	Nature of the report.	No. of the bill.	How disposed of by the House of Reps.	How disposed of by the Senate.	Date of the act of Congress, and remarks.
Fauche, Jonas, *et al*	Balance due for military services against the Indians in 1793-'96.	22	1	Petition	31	Indian Affairs.						
Fauche, Jonas, *et al*	Balance due for military services against the Indians in 1793-'96.	23	1	Petition	50	Indian Affairs	40	Favorable	153	Passed	Passed, with amendment.	
Faucher, James	Pension	23	2	Petition	183	Invalid Pensions.						
Faulac, Antony	Pay for transportation of provisions to Valparaiso in 1833.	24	1	Memorial	99	Naval Affairs.						
Faulk, Sarah	Indemnity for property destroyed in Florida.	19	1	Memorial	252	Foreign Affairs	112	Adverse	......	Laid on table.		
Faulk, Sarah	Indemnity for property destroyed in Florida.	20	2	Petition	339	Foreign Affairs	99	Favorable	385	Referred to Committee Whole House.		
Faulk, Sarah	Indemnity for property destroyed in Florida.	23	1	Petition	67	Foreign Affairs	368	Favorable	395	Passed	Passed	App'd June 26, 1834
Faulkner, Catharine	(See James Faulkner, widow of).	31	1	....	334							
Faulkner, Edward	Bounty land as refugees from Nova Scotia.	2	2	Petition and rep't Sec. of War.	623	....	....	....	......	Laid on table.		
Faulkner, Edward	Bounty land as refugees from Nova Scotia.	3	1	Petition	29	Select	April 1, 1794	Favorable; res.				
Faulkner, Edward	(See Canadian refugees)	6	2	....	766							
Faulkner, Eunice	Continuation of pension	28	1	Petition	849	Rev. Pensions.						
Faulkner, James, widow of.	Pension for revolutionary services.	31	2	Petition	334	Rev. Pensions.						
Faulkner, Ralph	Compensation for revolutionary services.	29	1	Memorial	873	Rev. Claims.						
Faulkner, Thomas	(See Canadian refugees)	6	2									
Faulkner, William	Reimbursement for expenses during war in 1790.	18	1	Petition	176	Claims	Feb. 26, 1824	Adverse	......	Laid on table.		
Faunce, John W	(See Oliver Perrin and others)	25	3	....	116							
Fauntleroy, Dangerfield	Services in purchasing horses for United States service.	30	2	Memorial	120	Naval Affairs.						
Fauntleroy, Robert, devisee of.	Commutation pay	24	1	Petition	274	Rev. Claims	780	Adverse	......	Laid on table.		
Fauntleroy, Robert, devisee of.	Commutation pay	24	2	Petition	92	Rev. Claims	Jan. 19, 1837	Adverse	......	Laid on table.		
Fauntleroy, Robert, devisee of.	Commutation pay	25	2	Petition	74	Rev. Claims	....	....	......	Discharged; laid on table.		
Fauntleroy, Robert, devisee of.	Commutation pay	25	3	Petition	85	Rev. Claims	....	....	......	Discharged.		
Faust, John	Pension for revolutionary services.	17	1	Petition	388	Whole House.						
Fauver, Frederick	Pension for revolutionary services.	22	1	Petition	66	Rev. Pensions	....	....	......	Discharged; laid on table.		
Favorite, John	Compensation for property taken in war of 1812.	15	1	Petition	198	Claims	....	....	......	Discharged; laid on table.		
Fawcet, Joseph, (Va.)	Exoneration from claim due United States government.	26	2	Petition	128	Judiciary.						
Fawcett, Joseph	Increase of compensation as postmaster at St. Charles, Missouri.	25	2	Petition	591	P. Of. and P. Roads.	Mar. 22, 1838	Adverse	......	Laid on table.		
Fawns, James A., *et al.*	Compensation for extra naval services.	30	1	Senate bill	328	Naval Affairs	Feb. 29, 1848	Favorable	S. 118	Referred to Committee Whole House.		
Fawns, James A., *et al.*	Compensation for extra naval services.	31	1	Petition	258	Naval Affairs.						
Fawns, James A., *et al.*	Compensation for extra naval services.	31	2	Rep't Committee	444	Naval Affairs	93	Favorable	490	Referred to Committee Whole House.		
Faxon, Caleb, widow of	Pension for revolutionary services.	25	3	Petition	110	Rev. Pensions	....	....	......	Discharged.		

List of private claims presented to the House of Representatives of the United States from the 1st to the 31st Congress, inclusive—Continued.

Names of claimants.	Nature or object of the claim.	Congress.	Session.	How brought before the House of Reps.	Page of journal.	To what committee of the House referred.	No. or date of the report.	Nature of the report.	No. of the bill.	How disposed of by the House of Reps.	How disposed of by the Senate.	Date of the act of Congress, and remarks.
Faxon, Caleb, widow of	Pension for revolutionary services	26	1	Petition	173	Rev. Pensions				Discharged; laid on table.		
Faxon, Caleb, widow of	Pension for revolutionary services	27	2	Petition	97	Rev. Pensions	784	Adverse		Laid on table.		
Faxon, Caleb, widow of	Pension for revolutionary services	27	3	Petition	74	Rev. Pensions.						
Faxon, Caleb, widow of	Pension for revolutionary services	28	1	Petition	238	Rev. Pensions				Discharged; laid on table.		
Faxon, Elisha	(See Isaac Champlin, *et al.*)	23	2		220							
Faxon, Lydia	(See Caleb Faxon, widow of.)	25	3		110							
Fay, Barnabas	Pension	20	2	Petition	39	Military Pensions	Jan. 15, 1829	Adverse		Laid on table.		
Fay, Barnabas	Pension	21	1	Petition	144	Military Pensions	May 4, 1830	Adverse		Laid on table.		
Fay, James, heirs of	Half-pay for revolutionary services	24	2	Petition	119	Rev. Claims	103	Adverse		Laid on table.		
Fay, James, heirs of	Bounty lands	25	2	Petition	232	Rev. Claims	577	Adverse		Laid on table.		
Fay, Levi	Pension	21	2	Petition	158	Military Pensions.						
Fay, Levi	Pension	22	1	Petition	123	Military Pensions	365	Favorable	460	Indefinitely postponed.		
Fay, Nathan, or Nahum	Compensation for military services in war of 1812.	23	1	Petition	111	Claims	483	Adverse		Laid on table.		
Fay, Theodore S.	Compensation as chargé d'affaires at Berlin.	31	1	Petition	992	Foreign Affairs						See appropriation bill, March 3, 1851.
Fayette, James, (colored)	Pension for revolutionary services	18	2	Petition	65	Rev. Pensions				Discharged; referred to Secretary War.		
Fayon, Lewis	Confirmation of title to land	15	1	Petition	280	Priv. Land Claims				Discharged; laid on table.		
Fayon, Lewis	Confirmation of title to land	16	1	Petition	36	Priv. Land Claims				Discharged; laid on table.		
Fead, George, heirs of	Confirmation of title to land	24	1	Petition	155	Priv. Land Claims	Jan. 19, 1836	Adverse		Laid on table.		
Fead, George, heirs of	Confirmation of title to land	24	2	Petition	107	Priv. Land Claims				Discharged; laid on table.		
Fealy, Thomas	Additional allowance for work on Cumberland road.	25	2	Petition	172	Claims.						
Feaman, Jacob	(See Pierre Menard, *et al.*)	28	1		948							
Fearing, Benjamin, *et al.*	Fishing bounty on schooner Joseph	26	2	Petition	192	Commerce	99	Favorable	605	Referred to Committee Whole House.		
Fearing, Benjamin, *et al.*	Fishing bounty on schooner Joseph	27	3	Petition	175	Commerce	135	Favorable	759	Referred to Committee Whole House.		
Fearns, Jacob	Pay for a rifle impressed into United States service.	20	1	Resolution	382	Claims	Mar. 31, 1828	Adverse		Laid on table.		
Fearns, Jacob	Pay for a rifle impressed into United States service.	21	1	Petition	201	Claims	Feb. 2, 1830	Adverse		Laid on table.		
Feathers, Jacob, widow of	Pension for revolutionary services	29	1	Memorial	533	Rev. Pensions				Discharged; laid on table.		
Feathers, Mary	(See Jacob Feathers, widow of)	29	1		533							
Fechem, George	Compensation for revolutionary services.	2	2	Petition	688					Referred to Secretary Treasury.		
Fechem, George	Compensation for revolutionary services.	3	1	Report of Secretary Treasury.	77					Laid on table.		
Fechon, A., *et al.*	(See Stephen Monot, *et al.*)	5	2		225							
Fee, John	Pension	14	1	Documents	193	Rev. Pensions.						
Feely, Timothy, heirs of	Compensation for revolutionary services.	24	1	Resolution	635	Rev. Claims	May 6, 1836	Favorable	612	Referred to Committee Whole House.		
Feely, Timothy, heirs of	Compensation for revolutionary services.	25	2	Petition	39	Rev. Claims	116	Favorable	134	Passed	Passed	App'd July 7, 1838
Fegan, Garrett	Increase of pension	2	1	Petition	498					Referred to Secretary War.		

List of private claims presented to the House of Representatives of the United States from the 1st to the 31st Congress, inclusive—Continued.

78

Names of claimants.	Nature or object of the claim.	Congress.	Session.	How brought before the House of Reps.	Page of journal.	To what committee of the House referred.	No. or date of the report.	Nature of the report.	No. of the bill.	How disposed of by the House of Reps.	How disposed of by the Senate.	Date of the act of Congress, and remarks.
Fegan, Garrett	Increase of pension	2	2	Rep. of Secretary War.	696	....	....	....	....	Laid on table.		
Feith, Frederick	For prize mo ey as cook of the U. States schooner Spitfire.	18	2	Petition	161	Naval Affairs.						
Feland, James	Pay for horse lost in war of 1812.	19	1	Resolution	362	Claims	211	Adverse	....	Laid on table.		
Feland, James	Pay for horse lost in war of 1812.	19	2	Rept. of last sess.	73	Claims	Jan. 3, 1827	Adverse	....	Laid on table.		
Felch, Jacob, and Henry Little.	R munerat'n for damages susta'ned in the erection of a breakwa'er in Merrimac river.	30	1	Petition	723	Commerce	648	Favorable	515	Referred to Committee Whole House.		
Felch, Jacob, and Henry Little.	Remunerat'n for damages sustained in the erection of a breakwater in Merrimac river.	31	1	Petition	235	Commerce.						
Felch, William, *et al.*	Extra compensation as clerks in the Treasury Department.	3	1	Petition	88	Select	April 17, 1794	Adverse.				
Felicite, John B	(See M. A. Marquis, *et al.*)	20	1	....	728							
Felix, Francois	(See Louis Boure, widow of)	20	1	....	152							
Felix, Francois, heirs of.	Permission to test title to land	30	1	Senate bill	678	Claims	April 26, 1848	With't amend.	S. 215	Passed	Passed	App'd July 20, 1848
Felix, Martin	(See William Zoll and others)	15	2	....	190							
Felker, David	Pension	27	2	Petition	836	Invalid Pensions.	1066	Adverse	....	Laid on table.		
Felker, David	Arrears of pension	29	2	Petition	128	Invalid Pensions.						
Fellany, Fernando	Invalid pension	29	2	Senate bill	374	Invalid Pensions	Mar. 3, 1847	Favorable	S. 40			
Fellany, Fernando	Invalid pension	30	1	Senate bill	455	Invalid Pensions.	Mar. 9, 1848	Favorable	S. 76	Passed	....	App'd June 13, 1848
Fellows, Caleb	Permission to bring property to U. States from the East Indies.	12	1	Petition	21	Com. and Manuf.						
Fellows Daniel, *et al.*	Indemnity due from the government of Portugal.	23	1	Petition	523	Ways and Means.						
Fellows, Isaac	Pension	22	1	Petition	287	Rev. Pensions	381	Favorable	472	Passed	Indef. postp'd.	
Fellows, Molly	Pension	28	1	Petition	950	Whole House.						
Fellows, Nathan	Pension	18	1	Petition	388	....	....	....	....	Laid on table.		
Fellows, Nathaniel	Indemnity for French spoliations prior to 1800.	26	1	Memorial	182	Foreign Affairs	343	Favorable	319	Referred to Committee Whole House.		
Fellows, Stephen	Increase of pension	12	1	Petition	201	Claims	June 12, 1812	Adverse	....	Laid on table.		
Fellows, Willis	Reconveyance of certain lands	20	1	Petition	310	Public Lands	....	....	....	Discharged; laid on table.		
Fellows, Willis	Donation for steam mill	26	1	Petition	596	....	....	....	....	Leave to withdraw.		
Felt, John	Compensation for aiding in destroying the frigate Philadelphia.	26	1	Petition	627	Naval Affairs.						
Felt, John, (N. Y.)	Release from payment of judgment in favor of the United States.	29	1	Petition	292	Claims	354	Adverse	....	Laid on table.		
Felt, Jonathan P., administrator of.	Remission of duties on goods destroyed by fire.	26	2	Petition	86	Commerce	71	Favorable	584	Referred to Committee Whole House.		
Felt, Naomi	Continuation of pension	28	1	Petition	849	Rev. Pensions.						
Felter, Peter	Invalid pension	3	1	Rep. of Secretary War.	175	Select	May 26, 1794	Res. to refer to Sec. War.	J. R. 12	Passed	Passed	App'd June 9, 1794
Felter, Tunis	Pension	19	2	Petition	285	Military Pensions.						
Felter, Tunis	Pension	20	2	Petition	59	Military Pensions.	....	....	....	Discharged; laid on table.		
Felton, Daniel	Pension for revolutionary services.	21	2	Petition	113	Military Pensions.						
Felton, Daniel	Pension for revolutionary services.	22	1	Petition	67	Rev. Pensions	98	Favorable	188	Referred to Committee Whole House.		
Felton, Daniel	Pension for revolutionary services.	22	2	House bill	66	Whole House	....	....	188	Laid on table.		

List of private claims presented to the House of Representatives of the United States from the 1st to the 31st Congress, inclusive—Continued.

Names of claimants.	Nature or object of the claim.	Congress.	Session.	How brought before the House of Reps.	Page of journal.	To what committee of the House referred.	No. or date of the report.	Nature of the report.	No. of the bill.	How disposed of by the House of Reps.	How disposed of by the Senate.	Date of the act of Congress, and remarks.
Felton, Sarah	(See Stephen Felton, widow of)	29	1		380							
Felton, Skelton	Equitable settlement of accounts for military services, &c.	16	2	Petition	170	Claims	Feb. 19, 1821	Adverse		Leave to withdraw.		
Felton, Skelton	Equitable settlement of accounts for military services, &c.	28	1	Petition	875	Claims	559	Adverse		Laid on table.		
Felton, Skelton	Compensation for extra services in war of 1812.	28	1	Petition	526	Claims.						
Felton, Skelton	Invalid pension	28	1	Petition	876	Invalid Pensions.						
Felton, Skelton	Invalid pension	30	1	Petition	208	Invalid Pensions	292	Favorable	288	Passed.		
Felton, Skelton	Invalid pension	31	1	Petition	214	Invalid Pensions	56	Favorable	86	Passed	Passed	App'd Sept. 16, 1850
Felton, Stephen, widow of	Arrears of pension	29	1	Petition	380	Rev. Claims.						
Felts, Archibald	Compensation for revolutionary services.	15	2	Petition	118	Rev. Claims	Dec. 23, 1818	Adverse		Leave to withdraw.		
Felts, Archibald	Pension for revolutionary services	16	1	Petition	153	Rev. Claims.						
Felts, Archibald	Pension for revolutionary services	17	1	Petition	60, 277	Referred to Secretary of War.	May 3, 1822	Report		Laid on table.		
Felts, Archibald	Pension for revolutionary services	18	2	Petition	54	Rev. Claims				Discharged; laid on table.		
Felts, Archibald	Pension for revolutionary services	19	1	Resolution	76	Military Pensions	164	Adverse		Laid on table.		
Fenasye, James	Prize money for aid in capturing Algerine vessels in 1815.	26	1	Resolution	672	Naval Affairs.						
Fencher, ——	(See Fancher.)											
Fenil, John	(See Seybert Scott, *et al*)	19	2		134							
Fenimore, Samuel	Pension	21	1	Report	149	Military Pensions	May 4, 1830	Adverse		Laid on table.		
Fenner, Jerah	Compensation for services in war of 1812.	22	2	Petition	143	Claims.						
Fenner, Jerah	Compensation for services in war of 1812.	23	1	Petition	59	Claims.						
Fenner, Jerah	Compensation for services in war of 1812.	24	1	Petition	284	Claims	295	Favorable	306	Referred to Committee Whole House.		
Fenner, Jerah	Compensation for services in war of 1812.	24	2	House bill	200	Whole House			306	Passed	Passed	App'd March 3, 1837
Fenney, Jonathan	Pension for revolutionary services.	15	2	Petition	192	Rev. Pensions	Feb. 11, 1819	Adverse		Laid on table.		
Fenno, Elizabeth H.	Permission to locate certain lands in Florida.	30	2	Petition	477	Priv. Land Claims.						
Fenter, Christian	Confirmation of title to land	15	1	Petition	39	Priv. Land Claims.						
Fenter, Christian	Confirmation of title to land	16	1	Petition	71	Priv. Land Claims.						
Fenter, Christian	Confirmation of title to land	17	1	Petition	53	Public Lands.						
Fenter, Christian	Confirmation of title to land	18	1	Petition	54	Public Lands.						
Fenton, Andrew	Indemnity for damages sustained by being stopped by government agents from cutting timber in Florida.	30	1	Petition	424	Claims	521	Adverse		Laid on table.		
Fenton, Francis	(See Thomas Fenton, widow of)	31	1		809							
Fenton, John	Pension	8	2	Petition	47	Claims				Dis.; referred to Com. Whole House.		
Fenton, John	Pension	14	1	House bill	622	Whole House	April 28, 1816	Favorable	171	Passed	Passed	App'd April 30, 1816
Fenton, Joseph, widow of	Half-pay due for revolutionary services.	4	2	Petition	648	Claims	Feb. 22, 1797	Adverse		Referred to Committee Whole House.		
Fenton, Sarah	(See Joseph Fenton, widow of)	4	2		648							
Fenton, Thomas, widow of	Pension for revolutionary services.	31	1	Petition	809	Rev. Pensions.						
Fentress, Lovett	Additional payment for repairs to Marine Hospital at Norfolk, Va.	14	2	Petition	384	Claims.						

List of private claims presented to the House of Representatives of the United States from the 1st to the 31st Congress, inclusive—Continued.

Names of claimants.	Nature or object of the claim.	Congress.	Session.	How brought before the House of Reps.	Page of journal.	To what committee of the House referred.	No. or date of the report.	Nature of the report.	No. of the bill.	How disposed of by the House of Reps.	How disposed of by the Senate.	Date of the act of Congress, and remarks.
Fenwick, Caroline, guardian of.	Indemnity for property destroyed while in public use.	15	1	Document	37	Claims	Dec. 18, 1817	Adverse	......	Referred to Committee Whole House.		
Fenwick, Caroline, guardian of.	Indemnity for property destroyed while in public use.	16	1	Document	197	Claims	Feb. 11, 1820	Adverse	......	Laid on table.		
Fenwick, Cornelius	Pension for revolutionary services.	23	1	Petition	493	Rev. Pensions	....	....	......	Discharged; laid on table.		
Fenwick, Cornelius	Pension for revolutionary services.	24	1	Petition	431	Rev. Claims	....	....	......	Discharged; laid on table.		
Fenwick, General J. R.	Pension	25	3	Petition	129	Invalid Pensions.						
Fenwick, James, jr.	Confirmation of title to land	22	1	Petition	337	Priv. Land Claims.	May 1, 1832	Adverse	......	Laid on table..		
Fenwick, Joseph, representatives of.	Confirmation of title to land	15	1	Petition	45	Priv. Land Claims.						
Fenwick, Joseph, representatives of.	Confirmation of title to land	16	1	Petition	71	Priv. Land Claims.						
Fenwick, Joseph, representatives of.	Confirmation of title to land	17	1	Petition	53	Public Lands.						
Fenwick, Joseph, representatives of.	Confirmation of title to land	18	1	Petition	54	Public Lands.						
Fenwick, Michael, heirs of	Indemnity for property destroyed by the enemy.	16	1	Petition	197	Claims	Feb. 11, 1820	Adverse	......	Laid on table.		
Fenwick, Michael, heirs of	Indemnity for property destroyed by the enemy.	19	1	Petition	131	Claims	81	Adverse	......	Laid on table.		
Fenwick, Michael, heirs of	Indemnity for property destroyed by the enemy.	20	1	Petition	99	Claims	April 16, 1828	Adverse	......	Laid on table.		
Fenwick, Michael, heirs of	Indemnity for property destroyed by the enemy.	21	1	Petition	35	Claims	Dec. 31, 1829	Adverse	......	Laid on table.		
Fenwick, Michael, heirs of	Indemnity for property destroyed by the enemy.	23	2	Petition	59	Claims	11	Favorable	586	Referred to Committee Whole House.		
Fenwick, Michael, heirs of	Indemnity for property destroyed by the enemy.	24	1	Petition	49	Claims	Jan. 12, 1836	Favorable	122	Passed	Passed	App'd July 1, 1836
Fenwick, Michael, heirs of	Indemnity for property destroyed by the enemy.	24	2	Memorial	37	Claims	Jan. 18, 1837	Favorable	J. R. 21	Passed.		
Fenwick, Michael, heirs of	Indemnity for property destroyed by the enemy.	25	2	Petition	73	Claims	529	Favorable	520	Referred to Committee Whole House.		
Fenwick, Michael, heirs of	Indemnity for property destroyed by the enemy.	25	3	House bill	379	Whole House	....	....	520	Passed	Passed	App'd March 3, 1839
Fenwick, Richard	Pension for revolutionary services.	16	2	Petition	88	Rev. Pensions	Feb. 15, 1821	Adverse	......	Withdrawn.		
Fenwick, Richard	Pension for revolutionary services.	17	1	Petition	82	Rev. Pensions.						
Fenwick, Richard	Pension for revolutionary services.	20	1	Petition	365	Military Pensions.	Mar. 28, 1828	Adverse	......	Laid on table.		
Fenwick, Thomas, assignee of.	Confirmation of title to land	15	1	Petition	45	Priv. Land Claims.						
Fenwick, Thomas	(See Joseph Fenwick, representatives of.)	15	1	....	45							
Fenwick, Thomas, assignee of.	Confirmation of title to land	15	1	Petition	45	Priv. Land Claims.						
Fenwick, Thomas, assignee of.	Confirmation of title to land	16	1	Petition	71	Priv. Land Claims.						
Fenwick, Thomas, assignee of.	Confirmation of title to land	17	1	Petition	54	Public Lands.						
Fenwick, Thomas, assignee of.	Confirmation of title to land	18	1	Petition	54	Public Lands.						
Fenwick, Thomas, assignee of.	Confirmation of title to land	20	2	Senate bill	149	Priv. Land Claims.	Jan. 23, 1829	Favorable	49	Referred to Committee Whole House.		

List of private claims presented to the House of Representatives of the United States from the 1st to the 31st Congress, inclusive—Continued.

Names of claimants.	Nature or object of the claim.	Congress.	Session.	How brought before the House of Reps.	Page of journal.	To what committee of the House referred.	No. or date of the report.	Nature of the report.	No. of the bill.	How disposed of by the House of Reps.	How disposed of by the Senate.	Date of the act of Congress, and remarks.
Fenwick, Thomas, assignee of.	Confirmation of title to land	21	1	Senate bill	151	Priv. Land Claims.	Feb. 9, 1830	Favorable	35	Passed	Passed	App'd May 26, 1830
Feran, Ann	(See John Feran, mother of.)	14	2		256							
Feran, John, mother of	Compensation for naval services	14	2	Petition	256	Naval Affairs	Jan. 26, 1819			Discharged.		
Fergus, John	Pension	10	2	House bill	499	Claims	Jan. 30, 1809	Favorable	158	Passed	Passed	App'd March 3, 1809
Ferguson, ———	(See Furguson.)											
Ferguson, Allen	Invalid pension	27	2	Petition	518	Invalid Pensions	823	Adverse		Laid on table.		
Ferguson, Andrew	Increase of pension	29	1	Petition	74	Invalid Pensions	39	Adverse		Laid on table.		
Ferguson, Benjamin B.	Invalid pension	28	1	Senate bill	951	Invalid Pensions	May 29, 1844	With't amend.	S. 141	Passed		App'd June 4, 1844
Ferguson, Catharine	(See John Ferguson, Ky., widow of.)	24	1		260							
Ferguson, David	Pension for revolutionary services.	21	1	Petition	399	Military Pensions	May 3, 1830	Adverse		Laid on table.		
Ferguson, David	Pension for revolutionary services.	21	2	Resolution	77	Military Pensions.						
Ferguson, David	Pension for revolutionary services.	22	1	Petition	45	Military Pensions				Discharged; laid on table.		
Ferguson, Edmund, widow of.	Pension for revolutionary services.	29	1	Memorial	647	Rev. Pensions	Aug. 8, 1846	Adverse		Laid on table.		
Ferguson, Edward	Bounty land for services in war of 1812.	23	2	Resolution	276	Military Affairs.						
Ferguson, Edward	Bounty land for services in war of 1812.	24	1	Resolution	438	Military Affairs.						
Ferguson, Elizabeth	(See Edmund Ferguson, widow of)	29	1		647							
Ferguson & Gibson	Indemnity for French spoliations prior to 1800.	26	1	Memorial	182	Foreign Affairs	343	Favorable	319	Referred to Committee Whole House.		
Ferguson, Hugh	Reimbursement of moneys expended for clothing and provisions in revolutionary war.	2	1	Petition	501					Referred to Secretary Treasury.		
Ferguson, Hugh	Reimbursement of moneys expended for clothing and provisions in revolutionary war.	3	1	Rep. of Secretary Treasury.	77					Laid on table.		
Ferguson, Hugh	Reimbursement of moneys expended for clothing and provisions in revolutionary war.	13	2	Petition	189	Rev. Claims	Jan. 14, 1814	Adverse		Laid on table.		
Ferguson, James	(See John Robb, executors of.)	26	1		182							
Ferguson, James, (Ky.)	Remuneration for securing certain offenders against the U. States.	15	1	Petition	254	Judiciary.						
Ferguson, James, (Miss.)	(See Joshua W. Prout, administrators of.)	18	2		66							
Ferguson, J	Settlement of accounts for naval service.	30	1	Senate bill	328	Naval Affairs	Feb. 29, 1848	With't amend.	S. 118	Referred to Committee Whole House.		
Ferguson, John, (Pa.)	Pension for revolutionary services.	20	1	Petition	484	Military Pensions	April 29, 1828	Favorable	283	Passed.		
Ferguson, John, (Pa.)	Pension for revolutionary services.	20	2	Petition	55	Military Pensions	Dec. 12, 1828	Favorable	311	Passed	Laid on table.	
Ferguson, John, (Pa.)	Pension for revolutionary services.	21	1	Petition	48	Military Pensions.						
Ferguson, John, (Pa.)	Pension for revolutionary services.	21	2	Resolution	77	Military Pensions.						
Ferguson, John, (Pa.)	Pension for revolutionary services.	22	1	Petition	35	Rev. Pensions	24	Favorable	70	Passed	Indef. postp'd.	
Ferguson, John, (Pa.)	Pension for revolutionary services.	28	2	Petition	207	Invalid Pensions.						
Ferguson, John, (Pa.)	Pension for revolutionary services.	29	2	Papers	314	Invalid Pensions.						
Ferguson, John, (Ky.,) widow of.	Compensation for revolutionary services.	24	1	Petition	260	Invalid Pensions				Discharged; laid on table.		
Ferguson, John, (Ohio,) heir of.	Bounty land and pay due for revolutionary services.	29	1	Petition	1203	Rev. Pensions.						
Ferguson, John, (Ohio,) heir of.	Bounty land and pay due for revolutionary services.	29	2	Petition	86	Rev. Pensions	43	Adverse		Laid on table.		

List of private claims presented to the House of Representatives of the United States from the 1st to the 31st Congress, inclusive—Continued.

Names of claimants.	Nature or object of the claim.	Congress.	Session.	How brought before the House of Reps.	Page of journal.	To what committee of the House referred.	No. or date of the report.	Nature of the report.	No. of the bill.	How disposed of by the House of Reps.	How disposed of by the Senate.	Date of the act of Congress, and remarks.
Ferguson, John, (Ohio,) heir of.	Bounty land and pay due for revolutionary services.	30	1	Petition	628	Rev. Pensions	540	Adverse		Laid on table.		
Ferguson, John	(See Robert Ferguson, executors of)	26	1		182		343		319			
Ferguson, John, jr., and William Reid.	Return of duties, and discharge from certain bonds.	27	3	Memorial	421	Commerce	273	Favorable	819	Referred to Committee Whole House.		
Ferguson, John, jr., and William Reid.	Return of duties, and discharge from certain bonds.	28	1	Memorial	60	Commerce	352	Favorable	255	Passed	Passed, with amendment.	App'd June 17, 1844
Ferguson and Milhado	To cancel certain duty bonds	30	2	Petition	254	Commerce	Jan. 25, 1849	Favorable	48	Passed.		
Ferguson and Milhado	To cancel certain duty bonds	31	1	Petition	201	Commerce	36	Favorable	64	Passed.		
Ferguson, Nancy	Confirmation of title to land	15	1	Petition	367	Priv. Land Claims.				Discharged; laid on table.		
Ferguson, Nancy	Confirmation of title to land	16	1	Petition	71	Priv. Land Claims.				Discharged; laid on table.		
Ferguson, Nancy	Confirmation of title to land	18	1	Petition	54	Public Lands.						
Ferguson, Robert, executors of.	Indemnity for French spoliations prior to 1800.	26	1	Memorial	182	Foreign Affairs	343	Favorable	319	Referred to Committee Whole House.		
Ferguson, Robert, executors of.	Indemnity for French spoliations prior to 1800.	31	1	Petition	533	Foreign Affairs	355	Favorable	318	Referred to Committee Whole House.		
Ferguson, Samuel	Pay for horse lost in public service	25	2	Senate bill	301	Claims	800	With amend.	S. 40	Referred to Committee Whole House.		
Ferguson, Samuel H.	(See John Ferguson, heir of, Ohio.)	29	1		1203							
Ferguson, Susanna	(See William Ferguson, widow of.)	2	1		537							
Ferguson, William, (Me.)	Invalid pension	20	1	Resolution	90	Military Pensions.						
Ferguson, William, (Me.)	Invalid pension	20	2	Petition	55	Military Pensions.	Dec. 12, 1828	Favorable	311	Passed	Laid on table.	
Ferguson, William, (Me.)	Invalid pension	21	1	Petition	46	Military Pensions.	Jan. 5, 1830	Favorable	72	Passed	Passed	App'd May 20, 1830
Ferguson, William, (Me.)	Arrears of pension	31	1	Petition	655	Invalid Pensions.	383	Adverse		Laid on table.		
Ferguson, William, (N. Y.)	Pension for revolutionary services.	25	2	Petition	404	Rev. Pensions	720	Favorable	689	Passed.		
Ferguson, William, administrator of, (Mass.)	Arrears of pension	20	2	Petition	262	Military Pensions.	100	Favorable	460	Referred to Committee Whole House.		
Ferguson, William, administrator of, (Mass.)	Arrears of pension	21	1	Petition	197	Military Pensions.				Discharged; laid on table.		
Ferguson, William, widow of.	Compensation for services against the Indians.	2	1	Petition	537	Whole House.						
Ferguson, William B., sureties of.	Release from payment of judgment	25	2	Petition	921	Claims	953	Favorable	830	Passed	With amend.	
Ferguson, William B., sureties of.	Release from payment of judgment	25	3	Senate bill	372	Claims	Feb. 6, 1839	Favorable	S. 186	Passed		App'd Feb. 13, 1839
Fern, Henry	(See Seybert Scott, *et al.*)	19	2		134							
Fernauld, Abigail	(See William Fernauld, widow of.)	15	2		143							
Fernauld, William, widow of.	Naval pension	15	2	Petition	143	Naval Affairs.						
Fernauld, William, widow of.	Naval pension	16	1	Petition	246	Naval Affairs	Feb. 24, 1820	Adverse		Laid on table.		
Ferney, John S.	(See Louis F. Beeler and others.)	30	1		115		482					
Ferr, Constant	Pre-emption right to land	18	2	Petition	137	Public Lands.						
Ferrall, Patrick	Increase of compensation as clerk to board of commissioners.	2	1	Petition	481					Laid on table.		
Ferrall, Thomas C	Land in lieu of land sold for taxes.	23	1	Petition	300	Public Lands				Discharged; laid on table.		
Ferralls, Michael D.	Indemnity for damages to property at Point Isabel.	30	2	Petition	216	Military Affairs				Discharged; laid on table.		

List of private claims presented to the House of Representatives of the United States from the 1st to the 31st Congress, inclusive—Continued.

Names of claimants.	Nature or object of the claim.	Congress.	Session.	How brought before the House of Reps.	Page of journal.	To what committee of the House referred.	No. or date of the report.	Nature of the report.	No. of the bill.	How disposed of by the House of Reps.	How disposed of by the Senate.	Date of the act of Congress, and remarks.
Ferrell, Enoch	Invalid pension	24	2	Documents	311	Invalid Pensions.						
Ferrell, James	Invalid pension	21	1	House bill	130	Whole House	Feb. 13, 1830	Favorable	72	Passed	Passed	App'd May 20, 1830
Ferrell, John, heirs of	Correction of error in relinquishment of land.	18	2	Senate bill	284	Priv. Land Claims.	March 1, 1825	Favorable	S. 48	Passed		App'd March 3, 1825
Ferrell, Samuel	Revolutionary pension	17	1	Documents	73	Rev. Pensions				Disch'd; laid on table.		
Ferriar, Thomas, jr.	(See John D. Needham, *et al.*)	15	1		136							
Ferrierra, Francis P.	(See Francis Pass, administrator of.)	30	1		1008		766		S. 48			
Ferriole, Alexander, heirs of	Compensation for losses and for services in revolutionary war.	22	1	Petition	332	Rev. Claims.						
Ferriole, Alexander, heirs of.	Compensation for losses and for services in revolutionary war.	22	2	Petition	118	Rev. Claims.						
Ferriole, Alexander, heirs of.	Compensation for losses and for services in revolutionary war.	23	1	Petition	144	Rev. Claims.						
Ferriole, Alexander, heirs of.	Compensation for losses and for services in revolutionary war.	26	1	Petition	946	Rev. Claims.						
Ferris, Barney	Pension for services in war of 1812.	15	2	Petition	78	Pens. & Rev. Cl'ms.				Discharged; referred to Secretary War.		
Ferris, Caleb	Invalid pension	1	3	Petition	392					Referred to Secretary of War.		
Ferris, Gould	Pension for revolutionary services.	21	2	Petition	188	Military Pensions.						
Ferris, Gould	Pension for revolutionary services.	22	1	Petition	67	Rev. Pensions.						
Ferris, Isaac	Benefit of acts for the relief of Canadian volunteers.	22	1	Petition	173	Priv. Land Claims.						
Ferris, John A.	Revolutionary pension	21	2	Petition	143	Military Pensions.						
Ferris, John A.	Revolutionary pension	22	1	Petition	255	Rev. Pensions.						
Ferris, John A.	Revolutionary pension	22	2	Petition	151	Rev. Pensions.						
Ferris, John A.	Arrears of pension	23	1	Petition	46	Rev. Pensions				Discharged; laid on table.		
Ferris, John A.	Arrears of pension	24	1	Petition	213	Rev. Pensions				Discharged; laid on table.		
Ferris, John A.	Arrears of pension	25	2	Petition	55	Rev. Pensions				Discharged; laid on table.		
Ferris, John A.	Arrears of pension	31	1	Petition	510	Rev. Pensions.	464	Adverse		Laid on table.		
Ferris, Jonathan D.	Extra pay for services as lieutenant in United States navy.	21	1	Petition	471	Naval Affairs				Discharged; laid on table.		
Ferris, Jonathan D.	Extra pay for services as lieutenant in United States navy.	21	2	Petition	88	Naval Affairs.						
Ferris, Jonathan D.	Extra pay for services as lieutenant in United States navy.	23	1	Petition	247	Naval Affairs	359	Adverse		Laid on table.		
Ferris, Ransford Avery	Increase of pension	12	1	House bill	361	Claims	June 8, 1812	Favorable	138	Passed	Passed	App'd July 5, 1812
Ferris, Squire	Compensation while prisoner of war.	20	2	Petition	262	Military Pensions.						
Ferris, Squire	Compensation while prisoner of war.	21	1	Petition	169	Military Pensions.	May 3, 1830	Adverse		Laid on table.		
Ferris, Squire	Pension for revolutionary services.	23	1	Petition	46	Rev. Pensions.						
Ferris, Squire	Pension for revolutionary services.	24	1	Petition	213	Rev. Pensions	Feb. 5, 1836	Adverse		Laid on table.		
Ferris, Squire	Pension for revolutionary services.	24	2	Petition	217	Rev. Pensions				Discharged; laid on table.		
Ferris, Squire	Pension for revolutionary services.	25	2	Petition	55	Rev. Pensions	370	Adverse		Laid on table.		
Ferris, Squire	Pension for revolutionary services.	26	1	Petition	937	Rev. Pensions.						
Ferris, Squire	Pension for revolutionary services.	26	2	Petition	148	Rev. Pensions				Discharged; laid on table.		

List of private claims presented to the House of Representatives of the United States from the 1st to the 31st Congress, inclusive—Continued.

Names of claimants.	Nature or object of the claim.	Congress.	Session.	How brought before the House of Reps.	Page of journal.	To what committee of the House referred.	No. or date of the report.	Nature of the report.	No. of the bill.	How disposed of by the House of Reps.	How disposed of by the Senate.	Date of the act of Congress, and remarks.
Ferris, Squire	Pension for revolutionary services	28	1	Petition	584	Rev. Pensions	....	....	......	Discharged; laid on table.		
Ferris, Squire	Pension for revolutionary services	28	2	Petition	240	Rev. Pensions.						
Ferris, Squire	Pension for revolutionary services	29	1	Petition	75	Rev. Pensions	....	....	......	Discharged: laid on table.		
Ferris, Squire	Pension for revolutionary services	29	2	Petition	164	Rev. Pensions	....	....	......	Discharged; laid on table.		
Ferris, Squire	Pension for revolutionary services	30	1	Petition	625	Rev. Pensions.						
Ferris, Squire	Pension for revolutionary services	30	2	Petition	175	Rev. Pensions.						
Ferroll, Robert, heirs of	Compensation for revolutionary services.	24	1	Petition	633	Rev. Claims.						
Ferry, Charity	Redress for enlistment of minor son.	18	2	Petition	229	Military Affairs	....	....	......	Discharged; leave to withdraw.		
Fertenburg, Jane	(See heirs of Hawkins Boone)	26	1	....	339	....	596	....	454			
Fessenden, Isaac	Remission of fine	26	2	Petition	161	Claims.						
Fessenden, Isaac	Remission of fine	27	2	Petition	154	Claims	54	Favorable	89	Passed	Passed	App'd July 27, 1842
Fessenden, Isaac	Remission of fine	28	1	Petition	216	Claims	83	Favorable	100	Passed	Passed	App'd June 15, 1844
Fette, M. M. & H. G.	(See Edward J. Davenport)	24	2	....	315							
Fette, M. M. & H. G.	Indemnity for French spoliations prior to 1800.	26	1	Memorial	182	Foreign Affairs	343	Favorable	319	Referred to Committee Whole House.		
Fettyplace, William	Compensation for loss of schooner Reward, and cargo.	24	1	Petition	661	Foreign Affairs	....	....	......	Discharged; laid on table.		
Fettyplace, William, *et al.*	Full indemnity for cargo of schooner Reward.	24	1	Memorial	753	Foreign Affairs	....	....	......	Discharged; laid on table.		
Fettyplace, William, *et al.*	Reimbursement of duties paid on merchandise.	23	2	Senate bill	259	Commerce	Feb. 3, 1835	With't amend.	S. 74	Referred to Committee Whole House.		
Fettyplace, William, *et al.*	Reimbursement of duties paid on merchandise.	24	1	Petition	725	Commerce	April 20, 1836	Favorable	580	Referred to Committee Whole House.		
Fettyplace, William, *et al.*	Reimbursement of duties paid on merchandise.	25	2	Petition	40	Commerce	....	....	......	Discharged.		
Fettyplace, William, *et al.*	Reimbursement of duties paid on merchandise.	25	3	Petition	349	Commerce	263	Adverse	......	Laid on table.		
Fetzer, Joachim	Restoration of pension	17	1	Petition	86	Rev. Pensions.						
Fetzer, Joachim	Restoration of pension	17	2	Petition	56	Rev. Pensions.						
Few, Henry	(See Henry Tew)	21	2	....	43							
Fichon, L. P. A.	(See Stephen Monot, *et al*)	5	2	....	225							
Ficklin, George, and Daniel Ward.	Relief on account of land purchased, upon which the United States has a lien.	21	2	Petition	255	Judiciary.						
Ficklin, George, and Daniel Ward.	Relief on account of land purchased, upon which the United States has a lien.	22	1	House bill	132	Judiciary	July 14, 1832	Favorable	616			
Ficklin, George, and Daniel Ward.	Relief on account of land purchased, upon which the United States has a lien.	22	2	Petition	425	Whole House	....	....	616	Laid on table.		
Ficklin, George, and Daniel Ward.	Relief on account of land purchased, upon which the United States has a lien.	23	1	Petition	38	Judiciary	May 31, 1834	Favorable	505	Referred to Committee Whole House.		
Ficklin, George, and Daniel Ward.	Relief on account of land purchased, upon which the United States has a lien.	24	1	Petition	53	Judiciary	765	Favorable	701	Referred to Committee Whole House.		
Ficklin, George, and Daniel Ward.	Relief on account of land purchased, upon which the United States has a lien.	25	2	Petition	41	Judiciary	404	Favorable	414	Referred to Committee Whole House.		

List of private claims presented to the House of Representatives of the United States from the 1*st to the* 31*st Congress, inclusive*—Continued.

Names of claimants.	Nature or object of the claim.	Congress.	Session.	How brought before the House of Reps.	Page of journal.	To what committee of the House referred.	No. or date of the report.	Nature of the report.	No. of the bill.	How disposed of by the House of Reps.	How disposed of by the Senate.	Date of the act of Congress, and remarks.
Ficklin, George, and Daniel Ward.	Relief on account of land purchased, upon which the United States has a lien.	25	3	House bill	38	Whole House	Jan. 25, 1839	With't amend.	414	Passed	Passed	App'd March 3, 1839
Ficklin, John	Pension	28	1	Petition	103	Invalid Pensions.						
Ficklin, John	Pension	28	2	Petition	58	Invalid Pensions	17	Favorable	184	Passed.		
Ficklin, John	Pension	29	1	Petition	83	Invalid Pensions	53	Favorable	42	Passed	Passed	App'd July 15, 1846
Ficklin, Thompson H.	Compensation for bringing the vote for President, of Missouri, to Washington city.	16	2	Petition	112	Ways and Means	Jan. 19, 1821	Adverse	......	Laid on table.		
Field, Benjamin	Half-pay for revolutionary services	23	1	Petition	221	Rev. Claims.						
Field, Benjamin	Half-pay for revolutionary services.	23	2	Petition	196	Rev. Claims.						
Field, Benjamin	Half-pay for revolutionary services.	24	1	Petition	152	Rev. Claims	856	Adverse	......	Laid on table.		
Field, Edmund J	Compensation for horse lost in the Mexican war.	31	2	Petition	145	Claims.						
Field, Edward, *et al.*	(See Nathan Leavenworth, heirs of.)	25	3	....	125							
Field, Henry, representatives of.	Pay and other emoluments due for services in Virginia line.	8	1	Petition	514	Claims	....	....	......	Discharged; referred to Com. Whole House.		
Field, Henry, representatives of.	Pay and other emoluments due for services in Virginia line.	10	2	Petition	465	Public Lands	....	....	......	Discharged.		
Field, Henry, representatives of.	Pay for services in Virginia line.	11	2	Petition	226	Claims	Mar. 2, 1810	Adverse.				
Field, Henry, representatives of.	Bounty land for services in Virginia line.	12	2	Petition	226	Public Lands	Mar. 12, 1810	Adverse	......	Leave to withdraw.		
Field, Henry, representatives of.	Half-pay as an officer in revolutionary army.	21	2	Petition	115	Rev. Claims.						
Field, Henry, representatives of.	Half-pay as an officer in revolutionary army.	22	1	Petition	190	Rev. Claims	Mar. 10, 1830	Favorable	458	Referred to Committee Whole House.		
Field, Henry, representatives of.	Half-pay as an officer in revolutionary army.	23	1	Petition	43	Rev. Claims	Dec. 17, 1833	Favorable	37	Passed	Passed	App'd June 30, 1834
Field, James	Compensation for property destroyed in war of 1812.	15	2	Petition	148	Claims.						
Field, James	Compensation for property destroyed in war of 1812.	17	2	Petition	74	Claims	....	....	......	Discharged	....	Leave to withdraw.
Field, Jeremiah, widow of	Pension	31	1	Petition	970	Rev. Pensions	373	Adverse	......	Laid on table.		
Field, Joseph	Bounty land for services in Lewis & Clarke's expedition.	9	2	Presid'ts message	284	Select	Jan. 23, 1807	Favorable	183	Passed	Passed	App'd March 3, 1807
Field, Joseph W	Permission to purchase land heretofore relinquished.	19	2	Petition	135	Public Lands	....	....	......	Discharged.		
Field, Joseph W	Permission to purchase land heretofore relinquished.	20	1	Petition	47	Public Lands.						
Field, Joseph W	Permission to purchase land heretofore relinquished.	20	2	Petition	75	Public Lands.						
Field, Margaret	(See Jeremiah Field, widow of)	31	1	....	970							
Field, Reuben	Bounty land for services in Lewis & Clarke's expedition.	9	2	Presid'ts message	284	Select	Jan. 23, 1807	Favorable	183	Passed	Passed	App'd March 3, 1807
Field, Spencer	Compensation for property destroyed in war of 1812.	15	2	Petition	148	Claims.						
Field, William	Compensation for services as clerk of supreme court of Arkansas	24	1	Petition	476	Judiciary	....	....	......	Discharged; laid on table.		
Field, William	Compensation for making statements as clerk of court in cases of bankruptcy.	30	1	Memorial	493	Ways and Means	....	....	......	Discharged; laid on table.		

List of private claims presented to the House of Representatives of the United States from the 1st to the 31st Congress, inclusive—Continued.

79

Names of claimants.	Nature or object of the claim.	Congress.	Session.	How brought before the House of Reps.	Page of journal.	To what committee of the House referred.	No. or date of the report.	Nature of the report.	No. of the bill.	How disposed of by the House of Reps.	How disposed of by the Senate.	Date of the act of Congress, and remarks.
Field, William	Compensation for making statements as clerk of court in cases of bankruptcy.	30	2	Memorial	194	Ways and Means.						
Field	(See Fields.)											
Filder, Sarah T., *et al.*	(See Dr. George Yates, heirs of.)	22	2		57							
Fielding, Daniel	Invalid pension	11	3	House bill	604	Claims	March 1, 1811	Favorable	218	Passed	Passed	App'd March 3, 1811
Fielding, Daniel, (Ohio)	Pay for a wagon and team lost in war of 1812.	17	2	Resolution	193	Claims				Discharged.		
Fielding, Daniel, (Ohio)	Pay for a wagon and team lost in war of 1812.	18	1	Petition	109	Claims	Jan. 23, 1824	Adverse.				
Fielding, Daniel, (Ohio)	Pay for a wagon and team lost in war of 1812.	18	2	Resolution	289	Claims				Leave to withdraw.		
Fielding, Daniel, (Ohio)	Pay for a wagon and team lost in war of 1812.	19	1	Resolution	55	Claims	98	Favorable	132	Passed.		
Fielding, Daniel, (Ohio)	Pay for a wagon and team lost in war of 1812.	19	2	Petition	31	Claims	Dec. 12, 1826	Favorable	285	Passed	Passed	App'd March 2, 1827
Fielding, Daniel, (Ohio)	Arrears of pension	25	3	Petition	461	Invalid Pensions				Discharged; laid on table.		
Fielding, Daniel, (Ohio)	Arrears of pension	26	1	Petition	161	Invalid Pensions	559	Adverse		Laid on table.		
Fielding, Daniel, (Ohio)	Arrears of pension	27	2	Petition	154	Invalid Pensions	441	Adverse		Laid on table.		
Fielding, Daniel, (Ohio)	Arrears of pension	27	3	Petition	72	Invalid Pensions.						
Fielding, Ebenezer	Invalid pension	1	3	Petition and rep't of Sec. War.	375					Laid on table.		
Fielding, Ebenezer	Invalid pension	3	1	Rep. of Secretary War.	131	Select	May 26, 1794	Res. to refer to Sec. War.	J. R. 12	Passed	Passed	App'd June 9, 1794
Fielding, James	(See Thomas Talbott, *et al.*)	20	1		312							
Fields, Abraham and Alexander.	(See Reuben Fields, heirs of.)	28	1		122							
Fields, Ann	(See Oliver Fields, widow of.)	15	2		87							
Fields, Elizabeth	(See William Fields, mother of.)	25	2		275							
Fields, George, (half-breed)	Pension	21	1	Petition	411	Military Pensions	April 23, 1830	Favorable	439	Referred to Committee Whole House.		
Fields, George, (half breed)	Pension	21	2	House bill	298	Whole House			439	Passed.		
Fields, George, (half-breed)	Pension	22	1	Petition	260	Invalid Pensions	346	Favorable	444	Passed.		
Fields, George, (half-breed)	Pension	22	2	Petition	53	Invalid Pensions	Dec. 19, 1832	Favorable	626	Passed	Pass'd, amend.	App'd March 2, 1833
Fields, George, (half-breed)	Arrears of pension	23	1	Petition	388	Invalid Pensions	Mar. 31, 1834	Favorable	388	Referred to Committee Whole House.		
Fields, George, (half-breed)	Arrears of pension	23	2	House bill	336	Whole House			388	Passed	With amend.	
Fields, George, (half breed)	Arrears of pension	24	1	Petition	202	Invalid Pensions	April 12, 1836	Favorable	519	Passed	Pass'd, amend.	App'd June 28, 1836
Fields, James	Compensation for services in war of 1812.	18	2	Petition	148	Pens. & Rev. Cl'ms.				Discharged; referred to Com. Public Lands.		
Fields, Jeremiah	To correct error in land entry	26	1	Petition	954	Public Lands.						
Fields, Jeremiah	To correct error in land entry	26	2	Petition	49	Public Lands	7	Favorable	545	Referred to Committee Whole House.		
Fields, John, jr.	Release from payment of United States funds stolen.	15	1	Petition	158	Ways and Means	Jan. 26, 1818	Adverse		Rejected.		
Fields, Joseph B.	Confirmation of title to land	27	2	Petition	1251	Public Lands.						
Fields, Oliver, widow of	Pension for revolutionary services.	15	2	Petition	87	Rev. Pensions	Jan. 5, 1819	Adverse		Laid on table.		
Fields, Reuben, heirs of	Commutation pay	27	2	Petition	132	Rev. Claims	533	Adverse		Laid on table.		
Fields, Reuben, heirs of	Commutation pay	27	3	Petition	239	Rev. Claims	235	Adverse		Laid on table.		
Fields, Reuben, heirs of	Commutation pay	28	1	Petition	122	Rev. Claims.						
Fields, Reuben, heirs of	Commutation pay	28	2	Petition	216	Rev. Claims.						
Fields, Richard	(See Wm. H. Bedford, agent, &c.)	28	1		262							

List of private claims presented to the House of Representatives of the United States from the 1st to the 31st Congress, inclusive—Continued.

Names of claimants.	Nature or object of the claim.	Congress.	Session.	How brought before the House of Reps.	Page of journal.	To what committee of the House referred.	No. or date of the report.	Nature of the report.	No. of the bill.	How disposed of by the House of Reps.	How disposed of by the Senate.	Date of the act of Congress, and remarks.
Fields, Richard	Reimbursement of expenses attending seat of government.	24	1	Appropriat'n bill					70			App'd June 14, 1836
Fields, Richard	Payment of award under treaty of 1836.	30	1	Senate resolution.	974	Claims	July 12, 1848	With't amend.	J. R. 28	Passed		See act Aug. 12, 1848
Fields, Samuel	Pension	19	2	Petition	95	Military Pensions				Discharged; laid on table.		
Fields, Simon	Pension	20	1	Petition	458	Military Pensions				Discharged; laid on table.		
Fields, Turtle, (an Indian)	Pension	23	2	Petition	274	Invalid Pensions.						
Fields, William, mother of	Naval pension	25	2	Petition	275	Naval Affairs				Discharged; leave to withdraw.		
Fields, William	Increase of pension	17	1	Petition	115	Rev. Pensions				Discharged; referred to Secretary of War.		Leave to withdraw.
Fieras, Conrad	Pension	21	2	Petition	48	Military Pensions.						
Fierer, Charles	Commutation pay	3	1	Petition and report Sec. War.	58, 93	Select	April 22, 1794	Favorable		Laid on table.		
Fierer, Charles	Pension	3	2	Resolution	250	Claims	Feb. 25, 1795	Favorable.				
Fierer, Charles	Compensation for revolutionary services.	4	2	Resolution	625	Claims.						
Fife, James, (an Indian)	Payment for horse stolen by whites	23	1	Senate bill	754	Indian Affairs	June 17, 1834	With amend.	S. 105	Passed	Passed	App'd June 30, 1834
Fifer, John	Correction of land entry	24	1	Petition	113	Public Lands	April 7, 1836	Favorable	540	Passed	Passed	App'd May 14, 1836
Files, Joseph	Increase of pension	31	2	Petition	112	Invalid Pensions.						
Filhiol, Grammont	Confirmation of title to land	19	2	Petition	49	Priv. Land Claims.	Jan. 16, 1827	Adverse		Laid on table.		
Filhiol, Lucy	(See Lewis White, representative of.)	20	1		485							
Filhiol, John	Confirmation of title to land	17	1	Petition	70	Priv. Land Claims.						
Filhiol, John	Confirmation of title to land	17	2	Petition	167	Priv. Land Claims.				Discharged; leave to withdraw.		
Filhiol, John	Confirmation of title to land	17	2	Resolution	289					Referred to Secretary Treasury.		
Filhiol, John	Confirmation of title to land	18	2	Rep. of Secretary Treasury.	264	Public Lands.						
Fillebrown, Catharine	Revolutionary pension	24	2	Petition	153	Rev. Pensions.						
Fillebrown, Thomas, jr.	Commissions on disbursements of the navy pension fund.	23	1	Senate bill	501	Claims	April 30, 1834	With't amend.	S. 47	Rejected.		
Fillebrown, Thomas, jr.	Commissions on disbursements of the navy pension fund.	24	1	Petition	48	Claims.						
Fillebrown, Thomas, jr.	Commissions on disbursements of the navy pension fund.	24	2	Petition	38	Claims	307	Favorable	968			
Fillebrown, Thomas, jr.	Commissions on disbursements of the navy pension fund.	25	2	Petition	36	Claims	69	Favorable	81	Referred to Committee Whole House.		
Fillebrown, Thomas, jr.	Commissions on disbursements of the navy pension fund.	25	3	Petition	51	Claims	2	Favorable	900	Referred to Committee Whole House.		
Fillebrown, Thomas, jr.	Commissions on disbursements of the navy pension fund.	26	1	Petition	168	Claims	25	Favorable	44	Passed	Indef. postp'd.	
Fillett, Isaac	(See Wm. H. Bedford, agent, &c.)	2[illegible]	1		262							
Fillmore, Cyrus, widow of	Continuation of pension	30	1	Petition	264	Rev. Pensions.						
Fillmore, Eunice	(See Septa Fillmore, widow of)	21	1		92							
Fillmore, Henry	Invalid pension	4	1	Petition	445	Claims	Feb. 18, 1796	Favorable	156	Passed	Passed	App'd April 20, 1796
Fillmore, Henry	Arrears of pension	23	2	Petition	343	Invalid Pensions.						
Fillmore, Jemima	(See Cyrus Fillmore, widow of)	30	1		264							
Fillmore, Septa	Payment for property destroyed at Plattsburg.	14	1	Petition	260	Claims	Feb. 26, 1816	Adverse		Rejected.		

List of private claims presented to the House of Representatives of the United States from the 1st to the 31st Congress, inclusive—Continued.

Names of claimants.	Nature or object of the claim.	Congress.	Session.	How brought before the House of Reps.	Page of journal.	To what committee of the House referred.	No. or date of the report.	Nature of the report.	No. of the bill.	How disposed of by the House of Reps.	How disposed of by the Senate.	Date of the act of Congress, and remarks.
Fillmore, Septa	Payment for property destroyed at Plattsburg.	15	1	Petition	243	Claims	Mar. 9, 1818	Adverse	......	Leave to withdraw.		
Fillmore, Septa	Payment for property destroyed at Plattsburg.	16	2	Petition	84	Claims	Dec. 20, 1820	Adverse	......	Referred to Committee Whole House.		
Fillmore, Septa	Payment for property destroyed at Plattsburg.	17	1	Petition	82	Claims	Mar. 4, 1822	Adverse	......	Referred to Committee Whole House.		
Fillmore, Septa	Payment for property destroyed at Plattsburg.	21	1	Petition	69	Claims.						
Fillmore, Septa, heirs of	Payment for property destroyed at Plattsburg.	22	2	Petition	151	Claims	Jan. 31, 1833	Adverse	......	Laid on table.		
Fillmore, Septa, heirs of	Payment for property destroyed at Plattsburg.	25	2	Petition	398	Claims	Mar. 20, 1838	Adverse	......	Laid on table.		
Fillmore, Septa, heirs of	Payment for property destroyed at Plattsburg.	26	1	Petition	294	Claims	65	Adverse	......	Laid on table.		
Fillmore, Septa, widow of	Compensation for revolutionary services.	21	1	Petition	92	Claims	Dec. 28, 1829	Adverse	......	Laid on table.		
Fillmore, Spiller	(See Anthony Burk, heirs of)	12	1	....	242							
Fils, Jean Mouton	Confirmation of title to land	22	1	Petition	514	Public Lands.						
Finch, Ceasar	(See Israel Pearce, heirs of)	27	2									
Finch, Charles B	Increase of pension	31	1	Petition	432	Invalid Pensions.						
Finch, Daniel	Payment for services as clerk in adjutant general's office in St Louis.	25	2	Memorial	921	Claims	....	....	......	Discharged.		
Finch, David	Additional compensation for painting the Capitol.	30	2	Memorial	87	Public Buildings.						
Finch, Elnathan	Pension	21	2	Petition	110	Military Pensions	....	....	......	Discharged; laid on table.		
Finch, Ephraim	(See Thomas Duer, or Dewar)	30	1	....	369							
Finch, Isaac	Invalid pension	11	2	House bill	283	Claims	Mar. 15, 1810	Favorable	107	Passed	Passed	App'd April 27, 1810
Finch, Isaac	Relief in settlement of his accounts as major in United States army.	17	1	Petition	31	Claims	Dec. 21, 1821	Favorable	8	Passed	Passed	App'd Feb. 4, 1822
Finch, James, jr	Benefit of certain acts relating to settlers on public lands.	17	1	Petition	39	Public Lands	....	....	......	Leave to withdraw.		
Finch, Jemima	(See Jeremiah Finch, widow of)	25	2	....	729							
Finch, Jeremiah, widow of.	Pension for revolutionary services.	25	2	Petition	729	Rev. Pensions.						
Finch, Jeremiah, widow of.	Pension for revolutionary services.	25	3	Petition	348	Rev. Pensions	....	....	......	Discharged; laid on table.		
Finch, Jeremiah, widow of.	Pension for revolutionary services.	26	1	Resolution	374	....	....	....	......	Leave to withdraw.		
Finch, Jeremiah, widow of.	Pension for revolutionary services.	27	2	Petition	220	Rev. Pensions	784	Adverse	......	Laid on table.		
Finch, Jeremiah, widow of.	Pension for revolutionary services.	28	1	Petition	257	Rev. Pensions	....	....	......	Discharged; laid on table.		
Finch, John	Pension for revolutionary services.	21	2	Petition	43	Military Pensions.						
Finch, John	Pension for revolutionary services.	22	1	Petition	382	Rev. Pensions.						
Finch, John J	Compensation for horse lost in Mexican war.	30	1	Petition	147	Claims	409	Favorable	359	Passed	Passed, 2d sess	App'd March 2, 1849
Finch, Lemuel S	(See Archibald Bull and L. S. Finch.)	29	1	....	524	....	583	....	401			
Finch, Philip	Compensation for revolutionary services.	4	1	Petition	425	Claims	May 7, 1796	Adverse	......	Leave to withdraw.		
Finch, Reuben	Pension for revolutionary services.	21	1	Petition	143	Military Pensions.						
Finch, Reuben	Pension for revolutionary services.	21	2	Petition	138	Military Pensions.						
Finch, Reuben	Pension for revolutionary services.	22	1	Petition	255	Military Pensions	Mar. 13, 1832	Favorable	467	Passed.		
Finch, William B	Compensation for naval service	21	2	Appropriat'n bill.	129	Ways and Means	....	With amends.	531	Passed	Passed	App'd March 2, 1831

List of private claims presented to the House of Representatives of the United States from the 1st to the 31st Congress, inclusive—Continued.

Names of claimants.	Nature or object of the claim.	Congress.	Session.	How brought before the House of Reps.	Page of journal.	To what committee of the House referred.	No. or date of the report.	Nature of the report.	No. of the bill.	How disposed of by the House of Reps.	How disposed of by the Senate.	Date of the act of Congress, and remarks.
Findlay, Charles	Payment of a draft on Indian department for money due from Shawnee Indians.	30	1	Petition	589	Indian Affairs	507	Favorable	R. 24			
Findlay, Hugh, postmaster, Alabama.	Release from payment of money destroyed by fire.	22	1	Petition	672	P. Of. and P. Roads.				Discharged; laid on table.		
Findlay, Samuel	Renewal of lost loan office certificates.	2	1	Petition	519					Refered to Secretary of Treasury.		
Findlay, Samuel	(See John Carlisle, *et al*)	20	1		368							
Findlay, Samuel	(See John Carlisle, *et al*)	21	1		264							
Findlay, Samuel, (Ala.)	For a grant of land	26	1	Petition	356	Public Lands.						
Findlay, Thomas	Reimbursement of money illegally exacted.	18	1	Petition	89	Ways and Means	Dec. 30, 1823	Adverse		Rejected.		
Findley, John	(See Dr. Robert Johnston, executors of.)	19	1		44							
Findley, John, administrator of.	(See William Amberson, deceased.)	29	1		510							
Findley, John, administrator of.	(See William Amberson, deceased.)	29	2		85							
Findley, J	(See executors of Wm. Findley)	17	1		388							
Findley, J. E. B	Payment for medical services rendered to United States troops.	23	2	Resolution	178	Military Affairs	Jan. 22, 1835	Favorable	665			
Findley, J. E. B	Payment for medical services rendered to United States troops.	24	1	Petition	97	Military Affairs	270	Favorable	194	Passed	Passed	App'd July 1, 1836
Findley, Polly	(See Nehemiah Stokely, heirs of.)	30	1									
Findley, William, executors of.	Balance of pay as late member of Congress.	17	1	Petition	388	Accounts	April 17, 1822	Adverse		Laid on table.		
Findley, William, executors of.	Balance of pay as late member of Congress.	23	1	Petition	246	Claims	335	Favorable	363			
Findley, William, executors of.	Balance of pay as late member of Congress.	24	1	Petition	50	Claims	6	Favorable	6	Passed	Passed	App'd Feb. 17, 1836
Fink, John L	That his pension may be applied to to the liquidation of $800 due the United States.	17	2	Petition	91	Military Affairs				Discharged; referred to Secretary of War.		
Finley, Andrew	Compensation for property destroyed during the insurrection in Pennsylvania.	4	2	Petition	648	Claims.						
Finley, Andrew, (Pa.)	Half-pay for revolutionary services.	16	2	Petition	21	Rev. Claims	Nov. 28, 1820	Adverse		Rejected.		
Finley, Andrew, (Pa.)	Half-pay for revolutionary services	19	2	Petition	333	Rev. Claims				Discharged.		
Finley, Andrew, (Pa.)	Half-pay for revolutionary services	20	1	Petition	110	Rev. Claims	Mar. 26, 1828	Adverse		Laid on table.		
Finley, Andrew, widow of.	Half-pay for revolutionary services.	21	2	Petition	74	Rev. Claims				Discharged; laid on table.		
Finley, Jane	(See Andrew Finley, widow of.)	21	2		74							
Finley, Capt. John, (Ohio)	Confirmation of title to land	3	2	Petition	289	Whole House.						
Finley, John, (Ind.)	Compensation for mail service in 1837.	26	1	Petition	347	P. Of. & P. Roads.	547	Adverse		Laid on table.		
Finley, John B	(See Joseph Finley, son of.)	29	1		232							
Finley, Joseph L., son of.	Arrears of pension	29	1	Petition	232	Rev. Pensions.						
Finley, Joseph L., son of.	Arrears of pension	29	2	Petition	85	Rev. Pensions	17	Adverse		Laid on table.		
Finley, Robert W., and Richard C. Tilton and others.	For a grant of land on the Sciota river.	4	1	Petition	456	Whole House.						
Finley, Samuel, (Ohio.)	For five years full pay	16	2	Petition	78	Rev. Claims.						
Finley, Samuel, (Ohio.)	For five years full pay	18	1	Petition	52	Rev. Claims	Dec. 19, 1823	Adverse		Laid on table.		

List of private claims presented to the House of Representatives of the United States from the 1st to the 31st Congress, inclusive—Continued.

Names of claimants.	Nature or object of the claim.	Congress.	Session.	How brought before the House of Reps.	Page of journal.	To what committee of the House referred.	No. or date of the report.	Nature of the report.	No. of the bill.	How disposed of by the House of Reps.	How disposed of by the Senate.	Date of the act of Congress, and remarks.
Finley, Samuel, (Ohio.)	For five years full pay	19	1	Petition	105	Rev. Claims.						
Finley, Samuel, (Pa.,) heirs of	Commutation pay	30	1	Petition	874	Rev. Claims.						
Finley, Samuel, (Pa.,) heirs of.	Commutation pay	31	1	Petition	472	Rev. Claims.						
Finley, William	Pension	4	1	Petition	370	Claims	Jan. 11, 1796	Adverse	......	Leave to withdraw.		
Finn, Dennis	Right of pre-emption as New Orleans branch pilot.	28	1	Petition	77	Priv. Land Claims.	9	Favorable	35	Passed	Passed	App'd June 17, 1844
Finnall and Graham	Indemnity for damages in the annulment of a mail contract.	30	1	Petition	254	P. Of. & P. Roads.	38	Favorable	66	Passed.		
Finney, Elkanah, *et al.*	Fishing bounty on schooner Juno	16	1	Petition	205	Commerce	Mar. 24, 1820	Favorable	117	Passed	Passed	App'd May 8, 1820
Finney, Jonathan	(See Jonathan Fenney)	15	2	....	192							
Finney, Lewis H	Pension	28	1	Petition	103	Invalid Pensions	19	Adverse	......	Laid on table.		
Finney, Philip	Fishing bounty on schooner William.	4	1	Petition	492	Com. and Manuf.	96	Adverse	......	Leave to withdraw.		
Finney, Walter	Reimbursement of expenses in curring a wound received in United States service.	2	1	Petition	509	....	....	....	......	Laid on table.		
Finney, Walter	For payment of certain certificates of public debt.	13	2	Petition	325	Ways and Means	April 9, 1814	Adverse	......	Laid on table.		
Finney, William	Compensation for two slaves lost during the war of 1812.	20	1	Petition	51	Claims.						
Finnie, William	Reimbursement of money expended in the public service.	1	1	Petition	55	Select	....	....	......	Discharged; referred to Secretary of War.		
Finnie, William, administrator of.	Payment of amount due on lost certificate of stock.	30	1	Petition	740	Ways and Means.						
Firhman & Leibert	Reimbursement of penalty on debenture bond.	27	2	Petition	1041	Ways and Means	949	Favorable	552	Referred to Committee Whole House.		
Firhman & Leibert	Reimbursement of penalty on debenture bond.	27	3	House bill	89	....	....	....	552	Passed	Passed	App'd Jan. 20, 1843
Firman, Joseph, *et al.*	Confirmation of title to land	18	1	Petition	75	Priv. Land Claims.	April 27, 1824	Favorable	206	Passed	Passed	App'd May 19, 1824
Firman, John	(See Lucius Storrs, *et al.*)	23	1	....	156							
Fischli, John, executor of.	(See Andrew P. Hay, surety of)	28	1	....	583							
Fish, Elizabeth	(See George Derrance, former widow of.)	2	2	....	712							
Fish, Ephraim	Pension for revolutionary services.	22	1	Petition	287	Rev. Pensions.						
Fish, Esther	(See John Ladd, former widow of)	30	1	....	66							
Fish, Gilbert S	Pension	21	2	Petition	159	Military Pensions.						
Fish, Gilbert S	Pension	22	1	Petition	510	Invalid Pensions.						
Fish, Gilbert S	Pension	24	2	Petition	72	Invalid Pensions	126	Favorable	856			
Fish, Gilbert S	Pension	25	2	Petition	38	Invalid Pensions	221	Favorable	259	Passed.		
Fish, Gilbert S	Pension	25	3	Petition	128	Invalid Pensions	136	Favorable	1003	Passed.		
Fish, Harriet	(See Crocker Sampson, heirs of.)	23	1	....	156							
Fish, Samuel	Payment for provisions furnished United States agent in Africa.	25	2	Petition	827	Claims	....	....	......	Discharged.		
Fish, Samuel	Payment for provisions furnished United States agent in Africa.	26	1	Petition	169	Claims.						
Fishback, Frederick, *et al.*	(See William Yates, heirs of.)	30	1	....	1013							
Fishel, Michael	Invalid pension	20	1	Petition	57	Military Pensions	Feb. 13, 1828	Favorable	166	Passed.		
Fishel, Michael	Invalid pension	20	2	Petition	55	Military Pensions	Dec. 12, 1828	Favorable	311	Passed	Laid on table.	
Fishel, Michael	Invalid pension	21	1	Petition	59	Military Pensions	June 5, 1830	Favorable	72	Passed	Passed	App'd May 20, 1830
Fisher, Andrew	Compensation for repairs to light-house.	27	2	Documents	382	Claims.						

List of private claims presented to the House of Representatives of the United States from the 1st to the 31st Congress, inclusive—Continued.

Names of claimants.	Nature or object of the claim.	Congress.	Session.	How brought before the House of Reps.	Page of journal.	To what committee of the House referred.	No. or date of the report.	Nature of the report.	No. of the bill.	How disposed of by the House of Reps.	How disposed of by the Senate.	Date of the act of Congress, and remarks.
Fisher, Andrew	Compensation for repairs to light-house.	27	3	Petition	73	Claims	76	Favorable	705	Passed	Passed	App'd March 3, 1843
Fisher, Benjamin	Confirmation of title to land	15	1	Petition	56	Priv. Land Claims.						
Fisher, Christina, *et al.*	Naval pensions	24	2	Petition	214	Naval Affairs.						
Fisher, Christina, *et al.*	Naval pensions	25	2	Petition	171	Naval Affairs				Discharged; laid on table.		
Fisher, Christina, *et al.*	Naval pensions	26	1	Petition	304	Naval Affairs.						
Fisher, Christina, *et al.*	Naval pensions	27	2	Petition	330	Naval Affairs	603	Adverse		Laid on table.		
Fisher, Christina, *et al.*	Naval pensions	28	1	Petition	177	Naval Affairs.						
Fisher, Coleman	Confirmation of title to land	21	1	Petition	236	Priv. Land Claims.	296	Favorable	355	Referred to Committee Whole House.		
Fisher, Coleman	Confirmation of title to land	22	1	Petition	263	Priv. Land Claims.	250	Favorable	336	Referred to Committee Whole House.		
Fisher, Coleman	Confirmation of title to land	23	1	Petition	75	Priv. Land Claims.	47	Favorable	52	Passed	Passed	App'd May 14, 1834
Fisher, Daniel	Pension	15	1	Petition	49	Rev. Pensions				Discharged; referred to Secretary of War.		
Fisher, Ebenezer	Pension	19	1	Petition	127	Military Pensions.	164	Adverse		Laid on table.		
Fisher, Elisha, & Co.	(See Thomas and John Clifford, *et al.*)	11	3		509							
Fisher, George, (Miss.)	Pre-emption right to land	13	2	Petition	146	Priv. Land Claims.	Mar. 22, 1814	Adverse.				
Fisher, George, (Miss.)	Pre-emption right to land	14	1	Petition	355	Whole House.						
Fisher, George, (Miss.)	Pre emption right to land	14	2	Petition	235	Priv. Land Claims.						
Fisher, George, (Miss.)	Extra compensation for mail service.	13	3	Petition	766					Referred to Postmaster General.		
Fisher, George, (Miss.)	Reimbursement for losses in the war with Creek Indians.	14	2	Petition	378	Claims.						
Fisher, George, (Miss.)	Reimbursement for losses in the war with Creek Indians.	22	1	Petition	337	Indian Affairs.						
Fisher, George, (Miss.)	Reimbursement for losses in the war with Creek Indians.	23	1	Petition	450	Indian Affairs				Discharged; laid on table.		
Fisher, George, (Miss.)	Reimbursement for losses in the war with Creek Indians.	25	2	Petition	173	Indian Affairs	484	Favorable	480	Referred to Committee Whole House.		
Fisher, George, (Miss.)	Reimbursement for losses in the war with Creek Indians.	25	3	House bill	378	Whole House			480	Laid on table.		
Fisher, George, (Miss.,) heirs of.	Reimbursement for losses in the war with Creek Indians.	26	1	Petition	180	Indian Affairs				Discharged; laid on table.		
Fisher, George, (Miss.,) heirs of.	Reimbursement for losses in the war with Creek Indians.	26	2	Petition	80	Claims	102	Adverse		Laid on table.		
Fisher, George, (Miss.,) heirs of.	Reimbursement for losses in the war with Creek Indians.	27	3	Petition	73	Claims	228	Adverse		Laid on table.		
Fisher, George, (Miss.,) heirs of.	Reimbursement for losses in the war with Creek Indians.	30	1	Senate bill	389	Claims	240	With't amend.	S. 25	Passed		App'd April 12, 1848
Fisher, George, (Ala.)	Reimbursement of money improperly paid to United States.	18	1	Resolution	294	Ways and Means.	March 8, 1824	Favorable	148	Passed	Passed, with amendment.	App'd May 26, 1824
Fisher, George	(See Col. T. H. Boyles, administrator of.)	23	1		195							
Fisher, George, representatives of.	Indemnity for property destroyed by United States troops.	29	2	Senate bill	374	Indian Affairs	Feb. 24, 1847	With't amend.	S. 78	Referred to Committee Whole House.		
Fisher, H. F., *et al.*	(See Richard M. Bouton)	30	1		338							
Fisher, Henry, heirs of	Compensation for revolutionary services.	24	1	Senate bill	940	Rev. Claims			S. 147			
Fisher, Henry, heirs of	Compensation for revolutionary services.	25	2	Senate bill	708	Rev. Claims	Jan. 2, 1838	Favorable	S. 108	Passed		App'd July 7, 1838

List of private claims presented to the House of Representatives of the United States from the 1st to the 31st Congress, inclusive—Continued.

Names of claimants.	Nature or object of the claim.	Congress.	Session.	How brought before the House of Reps.	Page of journal.	To what committee of the House referred.	No. or date of the report.	Nature of the report.	No. of the bill.	How disposed of by the House of Reps.	How disposed of by the Senate.	Date of the act of Congress, and remarks.
Fisher, Henry, widow of	Liquidation and settlement of claim against the United States.	1	3	Petition	357					Referred to Secretary Treasury.		
Fisher, Henry, widow of	Liquidation and settlement of claim against the United States.	2	2	Rep. of Secretary Treasury.	625					Laid on table.		
Fisher, Henry, widow of	Pension for revolutionary services.	27	2	Petition	799	Rev. Pensions				Discharged; laid on table.		
Fisher, Henry, widow of	Pension for revolutionary services.	27	3	Petition	342					Leave to withdraw.		
Fisher, Herman	Increase of pension	18	1	Petition	315	Rev. Pensions	May 13, 1824	Favorable	229			
Fisher, Herman	Increase of pension	18	2	House bill	259	Whole House			229	Passed	Indef. postp'd.	
Fisher, Herman	Increase of pension	19	1	Petition	73	Military Pensions	164	Adverse		Laid on table.		
Fisher, Herman	Increase of pension	19	2	Petition	132	Military Pensions				Discharged.		
Fisher, Herman	Increase of pension	21	1	Petition	231	Military Pensions	May 31, 1830	Favorable	499			
Fisher, Herman	Increase of pension	21	2	House bill	318	Whole House			499	Passed.		
Fisher, Herman	Increase of pension	22	1	Petition	98	Invalid Pensions	Feb. 1, 1832	Adverse		Referred to Committee Whole House.		
Fisher, Herman, widow of	Invalid pension	26	1	Petition	288	Invalid Pensions	354	Favorable	333	Referred to Committee Whole House.		
Fisher, Herman, widow of	Invalid pension	27	2	Petition	60	Invalid Pensions	216	Adverse		Laid on table.		
Fisher, Israel	Restoration of pension	17	1	Petition	124	Rev. Pensions				Discharged; laid on table.		
Fisher, James C.	Indemnity for French spoliations prior to 1800.	26	1	Memorial	182	Foreign Affairs	343	Favorable; bill	319	Referred to Committee Whole House.		
Fisher, James C. & S. W.	For payment of a lost loan office certificate.	4	1	Rep. of Secretary Treasury.	388	Claims	74	Adverse		Laid on table.		
Fisher, James C.	(See assignee of Peter Blight.)											
Fisher, James	Pension for revolutionary services.	26	1	Petition	1021	Rev. Pensions	551	Adverse		Laid on table.		
Fisher, Johannes	Compensation for wood furnished during the revolutionary war to United States.	4	1	Rep. of Secretary Treasury.	388	Claims	74	Adverse		Laid on table.		
Fisher, John	Increase of compensation as judge.	14	2	Petition	275	Judiciary	Feb. 5, 1817	Adverse		Laid on table.		
Fisher, John, *et al*	Payment of certain bills of credit.	3	1	Memorial	67					Referred to Secretary Treasury.		
Fisher, John, *et al*	Payment of certain bills of credit.	4	1	Rep. of Secretary Treasury.	388	Claims	74	Adverse		Laid on table.		
Fisher, John, (N. Y.)	Pension for revolutionary services.	25	2	Petition	404	Rev. Pensions				Discharged; laid on table.		
Fisher, John, (N. Y.)	Pension for revolutionary services.	26	1	Petition	285	Rev. Pensions	714	Adverse		Laid on table.		
Fisher, John	(See Lewis Ratcliffe, *et al*)	26	1		606							
Fisher, Lois	(See Herman Fisher, widow of)	26	1		288							
Fisher, Margaret	(See Henry Fisher, widow of)	1	3		357							
Fisher, Martin H.	Permission to enter certain lands.	30	2	Petition	294	Priv. Land Claims.						
Fisher, Mary Ann	(See Theresa Schindler)	20	1		485							
Fisher, Marvin W.	Compensation for patent for charging percussion caps.	30	2	Petition	216	Military Affairs	58	Favorable	763	Referred to Committee Whole House.		
Fisher, Marvin W.	Compensation for patent for charging percussion caps.	31	1	Petition	215	Military Affairs	197	Favorable	204	Referred to Committee Whole House.		
Fisher, Newton G.	Pre-emption right to land	30	2	Petition	298	Priv. Land Claims.						
Fisher, Samuel	(See John George, heir of.)	5	2		321							
Fisher, Samuel and Benjamin.	Confirmation of title to land	15	1	Petition	56	Priv. Land Claims.						
Fisher, Samuel, *et al.*	(See Vincent Fisher, heirs of.)	23	1		332							
Fisher, Silas D. (a Choctaw Indian.)	Authority to locate certain lands under treaty stipulations.	22	2	Petition	55	Public Lands	37	Favorable	680	Referred to Committee Whole House.		

List of private claims presented to the House of Representatives of the United States from the 1st to the 31st Congress, inclusive—Continued.

Names of claimants.	Nature or object of the claim.	Congress.	Session.	How brought before the House of Reps.	Page of journal.	To what committee of the House referred.	No. or date of the report.	Nature of the report.	No. of the bill.	How disposed of by the House of Reps.	How disposed of by the Senate.	Date of the act of Congress, and remarks.
Fisher, Silas D. (a Choctaw Indian)	Authority to locate certain lands under treaty stipulations.	23	1	Petition	50	Indian Affairs	191	Favorable	211	Referred to Committee Whole House.		
Fisher, Silas D. (a Choctaw Indian.)	Authority to locate certain lands under treaty stipulations.	23	2	House bill	82	Whole House			211	Passed	Passed	App'd Feb. 13, 1835
Fisher, Silas, D. (a Choctaw Indian.)	Confirmation of title to land	24	1	Petition	766	Indian Affairs	May 11, 1836	Favorable	624	Passed	Passed	App'd May 28, 1836
Fisher, Simahod	(See Nancy Baily, *et al.*)	14	2		72							
Fisher, Thomas	(See Abijah Downes, attorney of.)	26	1		182		343		319			
Fisher, Timothy	Arrears of pension	23	1	Petition	215	Rev. Pensions	Feb. 18, 1834	Adverse		Laid on table.		
Fisher, Timothy	Invalid pension	25	2	Petition	58	Invalid Pensions				Disch'd; laid on table.		
Fisher, Vincent, heirs of	Permission to locate bounty land warrants in Illinois.	23	1	Petition	332	Public Lands	291	Favorable	327	Referred to Committee Whole House.		
Fisher, William, (La.)	Permission to file a claim to land at Baton Rouge.	14	2	Petition	72	Public lands				Discharged; laid on table.		
Fisher, William, (La.)	Permission to file a claim to land at Baton Rouge.	15	1	Petition	76	Priv. Land Claims.						
Fisher, William, *et al.*, (Miss.)	Payment for cattle, &c., lost in war of 1812.	15	1	Petition	243	Claims	Feb. 25, 1818	Adverse		Rejected.		
Fisher, William, (N. C.)	Payment for timber taken by United States.	15	1	Petition	280	Claims.						
Fisher, William, (N. C.)	Payment for timber taken by United States.	15	2	Petition	36	Claims	Dec. 10, 1818	Adverse		Leave to withdraw.		
Fisher, William, (Ala.)	Confirmation of title to land	23	1	Petition	568	Public Lands.						
Fisher, Wm., (Ala.) heirs of.	Confirmation of title to land	25	2	Senate bill	785	Priv. Land Claims			S. 214			
Fisher, Wm., (Ala.) heirs of.	Confirmation of title to land	26	1	Petition	962	Priv. Land Claims.						
Fisher, Wm., (Ala.) heirs of.	Confirmation of title to land	27	2	Petition	1078	Priv. Land Claims.						
Fisher, Wm., (Ala.) heirs of.	Confirmation of title to land	27	3	Senate bill	346	Priv. Land Claims.	Feb. 22, 1843	Favorable	S. 109	Referred to Committee Whole House.		
Fisher, Wm., (Ala.) heirs of.	Confirmation of title to land	28	1	Senate bill	951	Whole House			S. 126	Referred to Committee Whole House.		
Fisher, Wm., (Ala.) heirs of.	Confirmation of title to land	28	2	Senate bill	220	Priv. Land Claims.	132	Adverse	S. 49			
Fishing Vessels, owners of.	Fishing bounty	3	2	Petition	313	Select	Feb. 11, 1795	Favorable.				
Fisk, Abijah	Pension for revolutionary services.	15	2	Petition	87	Rev. Pensions	Jan. 5, 1819	Adverse		Laid on table.		
Fisk, Abijah	Pension	22	1	Petition	161	Invalid Pensions	200	Favorable	287	Passed.		
Fisk, Abijah	Pension	22	2	Rep't Committee.	79	Invalid Pensions	Dec. 19, 1832	Favorable	626	Passed	Pass'd, amend.	App'd March 2, 1833
Fisk, Alvarez	Reimbursement of money paid for lands.	24	1	Petition	58	Public Lands.	67	Favorable	82	Passed	Pass'd, amend.	
Fisk, Alvarez	Reimbursement of money paid for lands.	25	2	Senate bill	1166	Claims	July 6, 1838	Favorable	277	Referred to Committee Whole House.		
Fisk, Alvarez	Reimbursement of money paid for lands.	25	3	Senate bill	492	Claims			S. 159			
Fisk, Alvarez	Reimbursement of money paid for lands.	26	1	Senate bill	420	Public Lands	Mar. 30, 1840	Favorable	S. 56	Passed		App'd April 10, 1840
Fisk, Bateman, sureties of.	Release from liability	14	2	Petition	69	Ways and Means.						
Fisk, Bateman, sureties of.	Release from liability	15	1	Petition	130	Ways and Means.	Jan. 22, 1818	Adverse		Rejected.		
Fisk, Jabez	Pension for revolutionary services.	14	1	Resolution	158	Rev. Pensions				Discharged; leave to withdraw.		
Fisk, James, (Vt.)	Reimbursement of money of which he was robbed.	20	1	Petition	104	Claims	Jan. 14, 1828	Adverse		Laid on table.		

List of private claims presented to the House of Representatives of the United States from the 1st to the 31st Congress, inclusive—Continued.

Names of claimants.	Nature or object of the claim.	Congress.	Session.	How brought before the House of Reps.	Page of journal.	To what committee of the House referred.	No. or date of the report.	Nature of the report.	No. of the bill.	How disposed of by the House of Reps	How disposed of by the Senate.	Date of the act of Congress, and remarks.
Fisk, James, (Vt.)	Reimbursement of money of which he was robbed.	20	2	Petition	39	Claims	Jan. 30, 1829	Adverse		Laid on table.		
Fisk, James, (Vt.)	Reimbursement of money of which he was robbed.	21	1	Petition	35	Claims	157	Favorable	199	Passed	Passed	App'd May 29, 1830
Fisk, John	(See John Pearson, executors of.)	28	1		245							
Fisk, Samuel	Pension for revolutionary services.	26	1	Petition	626	Rev. Pensions.						
Fiske, James B	(See John Drummond, and others.)	13	1		18							
Fitch, Benjamin	Increase of pension	22	1	Petition	288	Invalid Pensions	349	Favorable	444	Passed.		
Fitch, Benjamin, representatives of.	Increase of pension	22	2	Resolution	83	Invalid Pensions				Discharged; laid on table.		
Fitch, Benjamin, widow of.	Arrears of pension	23	1	Petition	60	Invalid Pensions	Jan. 28, 1834	Adverse		Laid on table.		
Fitch, Benjamin, widow of.	Arrears of pension	24	1	Petition	98	Invalid Pensions.						
Fitch, Charles B	Compensation as an express rider during war of 1812.	18	1	Petition	32	Claims.						
Fitch, Content	(See Benjamin Fitch, widow of).	23	1		60							
Fitch, Elijah, heirs of	Settlement of accounts, and for services in the French war.	30	1	Petition	170	Claims	43	Adverse		Laid on table.		
Fitch, Elizabeth	(See William Fitch, widow of)	25	3		161							
Fitch, Horatio	Renewal of pension	30	1	Memorial	958	Invalid Pensions	827	Favorable	645	Referred to Committee Whole House.		
Fitch, Horatio	Renewal of pension	30	2	House bill	363	Whole House			645	Passed.		
Fitch, Horatio	Renewal of pension	31	1	Petition	762	Invalid Pensions.						
Fitch, Horatio S., *et al.*	(See William Lyle, legal representatives of.)	27	3		140							
Fitch, Horatio S.	(See Louis F. Beeler and others.)	30	1		115		482					
Fitch, James	Pension for revolutionary services.	23	1	Petition	307	Rev. Pensions.				Discharged; laid on table.		
Fitch, James	Pension for revolutionary services.	23	2	Petition	197	Rev. Pensions				Discharged; laid on table.		
Fitch, James	Pension for revolutionary services.	24	1	Petition	57	Rev. Pensions	Jan. 27, 1836	Adverse		Laid on table.		
Fitch, John, representatives of.	Compensation in money or land for propelling boats by steam power.	28	2	Petition	317	Claims.						
Fitch, John, representatives of.	Compensation in money or land for propelling boats by steam power.	29	1	Petition	89	Claims	124	Adverse		Laid on table.		
Fitch, John, (Illinois)	Reimbursement of money improperly paid United States.	28	1	Petition	433	Public Lands.						
Fitch, John, master of ship Mars.	Reimbursement of money exacted of himself and crew at Norfolk.	13	2	Petition	224	Ways and Means	Mar. 3, 1814	Adverse		Leave to withdraw.		
Fitch, Lemuel	(See Ivory Holland, surety of)	17	1		31							
Fitch, Moses	Compensation for revolutionary services.	2	1	Petition	500					Referred to Secretary War.		
Fitch, Moses	Compensation for revolutionary services.	3	1	Rep. of Secretary War.	131	Select	May 26, 1794	Favorable	R. 12	Passed	Passed	App'd June 9, 1794
Fitch, Moses	Invalid pension	3	2	Rep. of Secretary War.	350	Claims	Feb. 28, 1795	Favorable	130	Passed	Postponed.	
Fitch, Moses	Invalid pension	4	1	Res. and docs	445	Claims	Mar. 4, 1796	Favorable	156	Passed	Passed	App'd April 20, 1796
Fitch, Pelatiah	Indemnity for French spoliations prior to 1800.	17	1	Petition	72	Claims				Discharged; referred to Secretary of State.		
Fitch, Pelatiah	Indemnity for French spoliations prior to 1800.	18	1	Resolution	578					Referred to Secretary of State.		
Fitch, Pelatiah	Indemnity for French spoliations prior to 1800.	18	2	Rep. of Secretary State.	71	Ways and Means	Dec. 27, 1824	Adverse		Laid on table.		

List of private claims presented to the House of Representatives of the United States from the 1st to the 31st Congress, inclusive—Continued.

Names of claimants.	Nature or object of the claim.	Congress.	Session.	How brought before the House of Reps.	Page of journal.	To what committee of the House referred.	No. or date of the report.	Nature of the report.	No. of the bill.	How disposed of by the House of Reps.	How disposed of by the Senate.	Date of the act of Congress, and remarks.
Fitch, Rufus	Compensation for revolutionary services.	4	1	Petition	384	Claims	Jan. 20, 1796	Adverse		Leave to withdraw.		
Fitch, Solomon, *et al.*	Indemnity for losses on certain contracts.	27	3	Petition	141	Claims.						
Fitch, Solomon, *et al.*	Indemnity for losses on certain contracts.	28	1	Petition	70	Claims	416	Adverse		Laid on table.		
Fitch, William, of N. Y., widow of.	Pension for revolutionary services.	25	3	Resolution	161	Rev. Pensions.						
Fitch, William, of N. Y., widow of.	Pension for revolutionary services.	26	1	Petition	945	Rev. Claims.						
Fitch, William, of N. Y., widow of.	Pension for revolutionary services.	26	2	Petition	77	Rev. Claims.						
Fitch, William, of N. Y., widow of.	Pension for revolutionary services.	27	2	Petition	58	Rev. Pensions	124	Favorable	170	Passed	Indef. postp'd.	
Fitch, William, of N. Y., widow of.	Pension for revolutionary services.	28	1	Resolution	227	Rev. Claims	212	Favorable	167	Passed	Adverse.	
Fitch, William, of N. Y., widow of.	Pension for revolutionary services.	28	2	Petition	45	Rev. Pensions	9	Favorable	459	Passed	Indef. postp'd.	
Fitch, William, of N. Y., widow of.	Pension for revolutionary services.	29	1	Petition	280	Rev. Pensions.	768	Favorable	507	Referred to Committee Whole House.		
Fitch, William, of N. Y., widow of.	Pension for revolutionary services	29	2	House bill	212	Whole House			507	Passed	Passed	App'd March 3, 1847
Fitz, Gideon	(See William Garrard *et al.*)	13	1		37							
Fitz, Gideon, *et al.*	Extra compensation for locating bounty land warrants.	31	1	Petition	225	Public Lands.						
Fitz, Phœbe	Pension in right of her father	30	2	Petition	101	Rev. Pensions.						
Fitzgerald, Aaron	Arrears and increase of pension	21	2	Senate bill	79	Military Pensions.	Dec. 24, 1830	Favorable	S. 16	Passed		App'd Jan. 13, 1831
Fitzgerald, Aaron	Increase of pension	23	1	Senate bill	754	Invalid Pensions	June 23, 1834	Favorable	S. 104	Passed		App'd June 30, 1834
Fitzgerald, Charles, heirs of	Arrears of pension	25	2	Resolution	755	Rev. Pensions.	821	Favorable	761	Passed.		
Fitzgerald, Charles, heirs of	Arrears of pension	25	3	Resolution	186	Rev. Pensions.	90	Favorable	969	Passed.		
Fitzgerald, Charles, heirs of	Arrears of pension	26	1	Resolution	171	Rev. Pensions	455	Favorable	369	Referred to Committee Whole House.		
Fitzgerald, Edward	Compensation for naval services.	29	1	Petition	124	Claims	632	Adverse		Laid on table.		
Fitzgerald, Edward H.	Reimbursement of money improperly paid into the treasury.	30	2	Petition	76	Claims	44	Favorable	733	Referred to Committee Whole House.		
Fitzgerald, Edward H.	Reimbursement of money improperly paid into the treasury.	31	1	Petition	624	Claims	241	Favorable	238	Referred to Committee Whole House.		
Fitzgerald, Edward H.	Reimbursement of money improperly paid into the treasury.	31	2	House bill	181	Whole House			238	Passed.		
Fitzgerald, John	(See Mary Sears)	13	3		652							
Fitzgerald, John, (Ireland)	Pay for rations while prisoner of war in England.	15	2	Petition	160	Military Affairs.						
Fitzgerald, John, (Maine).	Restoration of pension	17	1	Petition	114	Rev. Pensions.						
Fitzgerald, John, (Maine).	Restoration of pension	17	2	Petition	163	Whole House.						
Fitzgerald, John, (Maine).	Restoration of pension	19	2	Petition	36	Military Pensions.						
Fitzgerald, John, (Maine).	Restoration of pension	22	1	Resolution	88	Rev. Pensions.						
Fitzgerald, John, (Tenn.).	(See William H. Bedford, agent, &c.)	28	1		262							
Fitzgerald, John, (Wis.)	Privilege to drain lands in Wisconsin.	31	1	Petition	656	Public Lands.						
Fitzgerald, Joseph, (Ky.).	Pension for revolutionary services.	18	1	Petition	108	Rev. Pensions.	Jan. 7, 1824	Adverse		Leave to withdraw.		
Fitzgerald, Joseph, (Ky.).	Pension for revolutionary services.	22	1	Petition	330	Rev. Pensions.						
Fitzgerald, Joseph, (Ky.).	Pension for revolutionary services.	31	1	Petition	214	Rev. Pensions.						

List of private claims presented to the House of Representatives of the United States from the 1st to the 31st Congress, inclusive—Continued.

Names of claimants.	Nature or object of the claim.	Congress.	Session.	How brought before the House of Reps.	Page of journal.	To what committee of the House referred.	No. or date of the report.	Nature of the report.	No. of the bill.	How disposed of by the House of Reps.	How disposed of by the Senate.	Date of the act of Congress, and remarks.
Fitzgerald, Joseph, (Ky.)	Pension for revolutionary services	31	2	Resolution	183					Leave to withdraw.		
Fitzgerald, Philip, heirs of	Pre emption right to land	22	2	Petition	41	Priv. Land Claims	Jan. 29, 1833	Favorable	718	Referred to Committee Whole House.		
Fitzgerald, Philip, heirs of	Pre-emp ion right to land	23	1	Petition	93	Priv. Land Claims.	77	Favorable	84	Passed	Passed	App'd June 26, 1834
Fitzgerald, Thomas	Increase of pension	21	1	Senate bill	465	Military Pensions	May 21, 1830	Adverse	S. 78	Laid on table.		
Fitzgerald, Thomas	Increase of pension	21	2	Senate bill	90	Military Pensions	Dec. 29, 1830	Favorable	S. 18	Passed		App'd Jan. 19, 1831
Fitzgerald, Thomas	(See Louis F. Beeler, and others)	30	1		115		482					
Fitzgerald, William	Pension for revolutionary services	24	2	Petition	90	Rev. Pensions	123	Favorable	853	Referred to Committee Whole House.		
Fitzgerald, William	Pension for revolutionary services	25	2	Petition	37	Rev. Pensions	164	Favorable	189	Passed.		
Fitzgerald, William	Pension for revolutionary services	25	3	Petition	186	Rev. Pensions	88	Favorable	967	Passed.		
Fitzgerald, William	Pension for revolutionary services	26	1	Petition	171	Rev. Pensions	463	Favorable	377			
Fitzgerald, William	Pension for revolutionary services	27	2	Petition	97	Rev. Pensions	90	Favorable	137	Passed	Indef. postp'd.	
Fitzgerald, William B	Compensation for naval services	29	1	Petition	310	Naval Affairs.						
Fitzgerald, William B	Compensation for naval services	30	1	Petition	116	Naval Affairs.						
Fitzhugh, Alexander	(See John W. Bronaugh)	24	1		202							
Fitzhugh, Dennis	(See Worden Pope, *et al.*)	20	1		168							
Fitzhugh, Elizabeth	(See Peregrine Fitzhugh, widow of)	11	2		143							
Fitzhugh, Nicholas	(See William Cranch, *et al.*)	11	3		496							
Fitzhugh, Peregrine	Pension for revolutionary services	11	2	Petition	143	Claims	Feb. 23, 1810	Adverse		Laid on table.		
Fitzhugh, Peregrine, widow of	Arrears and increase of pension	30	1	Petition	886	Rev. Pensions				Discharged; leave to withdraw.		
Fitzpatrick, Edward	Compensation for losses, &c., while a prisoner at Tripoli	9	1	Petition	222	Claims	Mar. 28, 1806	Adverse		Indef. postponed		Leave to withdraw.
Fitzpatrick, John C	Compensation for work done at the penitentiary in District of Columbia.	23	1	Petition	418	Claims.						
Fitzpatrick, John C	Compensation for work done at the penitentiary in District of Columbia.	24	1	Petition	662	Claims	June 7, 1836	Adverse		Laid on table.		
Fitzpatrick, John C	Compensation for work done at the penitentiary in District of Columbia.	28	1	Petition	267	Dist. of Columbia				Discharged; laid on table.		
Fitzpatrick, Owen	(See Louis F. Beeler, and others)	30	1		115		482					
Fitzpatrick, Richard	Remuneration for Indian depredations.	26	2	Petition	124	Claims.						
Fitzpatrick, Richard	Remuneration for Indian depredations.	27	3	Documents	101	Claims.						
Fitzpatrick, Richard	Remuneration for Indian depredations.	28	1	Petition	526	Claims.						
Fitzpatrick, Richard	Remuneration for Indian depredations.	29	1	Petition	474	Military Affairs	479	Adverse		Laid on table.		
Fitzpatrick, Richard	Remuneration for Indian depredations.	30	1	Petition	594	Claims.						
Fitzpatrick, William	Compensation for horse lost in the Mexican war.	30	1	Petition	146	Claims	430	Adverse		Laid on table.		
Fitzsimmons, C	(See H. Silliman, *et al.*)	12	1		98							
Fitzsimmons, Charles	Indemnity for French spoliations prior to 1800.	26	1	Memorial	182	Foreign Affairs	343	Favorable; bill	319	Referred to Committee Whole House.		
Fitzimmons, George	Invalid pension	14	1	Resolution	488	Pens. & Rev. Cl'ms.	April 11, 1816	Favorable	171	Passed	Passed, with amendment.	App'd April 30, 1816
Fitzsimmons, James	Pension	17	2	Petition	186	Rev. Pensions				Discharged; laid on table.		

List of private claims presented to the House of Representatives of the United States from the 1st to the 31st Congress, inclusive—Continued.

Names of claimants.	Nature or object of the claim.	Congress.	Session.	How brought before the House of Reps.	Page of journal.	To what committee of the House referred.	No. or date of the report.	Nature of the report.	No. of the bill.	How disposed of by the House of Reps.	How disposed of by the Senate.	Date of the act of Congress, and remarks.
Fitzsimmons, Thomas	Pension for revolutionary services.	22	1	Petition	556	Rev. Pensions.						
Fitzsimmons, Thomas	Payment for revolutionary services.	23	1	Petition	128	Rev. Claims.						
Fitzsimmons, Thomas	Payment for revolutionary services.	24	1	Petition	205	Rev. Claims	828	Adverse		Laid on table.		
Fitzwater, Jonathan	Pension	30	1	Petition	208	Invalid Pensions	193	Favorable	203	Passed	Passed	App'd July 1, 1848
Fixaco, Ta'assee, and wife (Indians.)	Confirmation of title to land	23	1	Petition	158	Public Lands	Feb. 26, 1834	Favorable	316	Referred to Committee Whole House.		
Fixaco, Ta'assee, and wife (Indians.)	Confirmation of title to land	24	1	Petition	258	Public Lands				Discharged; laid on table.		
Flaget, Benedict J.	Remission of duties on church furniture.	18	2	Petition	91	Ways and Means.						
Flaget, Benedict J.	Remission of duties on church furniture.	19	1	Petition	99	Ways and Means	206	Favorable	263	Passed	Passed	App'd May 20, 1826
Flaget, Benedict J.	Remission of duties on other church furniture.	20	1	Resolution	403	Ways and Means	Mar. 14, 1828	Favorable	221	Referred to Committee Whole House.		
Flaget, Benedict J.	Remission of duties on other church furniture.	20	2	House bill	226	Whole House			221	Passed.		
Flaget, Benedict J.	Remission of duties on other church furniture.	21	1	House bill	476	Ways and Means	Mar. 29, 1830	Favorable	396	Referred to Committee Whole House.		
Flaget, Benedict J.	Remission of duties on other church furniture.	21	2	House bill	340	Whole House			396	Passed.		
Flaget, Benedict J.	Remission of duties on other church furniture.	22	1	Petition	31	Ways and Means	Dec. 23, 1831	Favorable	117	Passed	Passed	App'd March 31, 1832
Flagg, Elizabeth	(See Josiah Flagg, widow of.)	4	2		720							
Flagg, Henry C., widow of.	Pension for revolutionary services.	25	2	Petition	547	Rev. Pensions				Discharged; laid on table.		
Flagg, Jonathan	Pension	3	1	Report Secretary of War.	131	Select	Feb. 26, 1794	Favorable	R. 12	Passed	Passed	App'd June 9, 1794
Flagg, Josiah, *et al.*	Pay for revolutionary services	3	2	Memorial	276	Claims.						
Flagg, Josiah, *et al.*	Pay for revolutionary services	4	1	Res. and docs.	373	Claims.						
Flagg, Josiah, *et al.*	Pay for revolutionary services	5	2	Report	258	Claims	April 11, 1798	Adverse.				
Flagg, Josiah, widow of	Pay for revolutionary services of husband.	4	2	Petition	720					Laid on table.		
Flagg, Josiah, widow of	Pay for revolutionary services of husband.	5	2	Petition	237					Laid on table.		
Flagg, William	Pension	24	1	Petition	107	Naval Affairs				Discharged; laid on table.		
Flagg, Rachel	(See Henry C. Flagg, widow of.)	25	2		547							
Flagg, Samuel A.	Increase of pension	22	2	Petition	345	Rev. Pensions.						
Flamend, Pierre Joseph	(See Louis Le Guen.)	5	2		99							
Flanagan, Andrew	Invalid pension	24	1	Resolution	276	Invalid Pensions				Discharged; laid on table.		
Flanagan, Andrew	Invalid pension	29	1	Petition	511	Invalid Pensions.						
Flanagan, Andrew	Invalid pension	30	1	Resolution	124	Invalid Pensions	563	Favorable	463	Passed.		
Flanagan, Andrew	Invalid pension	30	2	H. bill from Sen.	648				463		Passed	App'd Mar. 3, 1849
Flanagan, John	Invalid pension	27	2	Petition	70	Invalid Pensions	239	Adverse		Laid on table.		
Flanagan, Thomas	Pension	25	3	Petition	129	Invalid Pensions				Discharged; laid on table.		
Flanagan, Thomas	Pension	28	1	Petition	551	Invalid Pensions.						
Flanagan, Thomas	Pension	29	1	Petition	250	Invalid Pensions				Leave to withdraw.		
Flanagan, Thomas	Pension	29	2	Petition	49	Invalid Pensions.						
Flanagan, Thomas	Pension	30	1	Petition	82	Invalid Pensions	392	Favorable	343	Passed.		
Flanagan, Thomas	Pension	31	1	Petition	233	Invalid Pensions	227	Favorable	222	Referred to Committee Whole House.		

List of private claims presented to the House of Representatives of the United States from the 1st to the 31st Congress, inclusive—Continued.

Names of claimants.	Nature or object of the claim.	Congress.	Session.	How brought before the House of Reps.	Page of journal.	To what committee of the House referred.	No. or date of the report.	Nature of the report.	No. of the bill.	How disposed of by the House of Reps.	How disposed of by the Senate.	Date of the act of Congress, and remarks.
Flanagan, Thomas	Pension	31	2	House bill	181	Whole House	....	....	222	Passed.		
Flanikin, James W	Compensation for horse lost in public service.	24	1	Petition	670	Claims.						
Flannagan, William, and William Parsons.	Additional pay for building the frigate Java.	14	2	Petition	176	Naval Affairs	....	....	......	Discharged; leave to withdraw.		
Flannagan, William, and William Parsons.	Additional pay for building the frigate Java.	15	1	Petition	184	Naval Affairs	March 2, 1818	Adverse	......	Laid on table.		
Flannagan, William, heirs of.	Additional pay for building the frigate Java.	23	1	Petition	335	Claims	479	Adverse	......	Laid on table.		
Flannegan, Daniel	Pension	3	1	Rep. of Secretary War.	131	Select	May 26, 1794	Favorable	R. 12	Passed	Passed	App'd June 9, 1794
Flatford, Thomas	Pension for revolutionary services.	16	1	Petition	235	Rev. Pensions	April 6, 1820	Adverse	......	Laid on table.		
Flatford, Thomas	Pension for revolutionary services.	21	1	Resolution	343	Military Pensions	....	....	......	Discharged; laid on table.		
Flaujac, Garrigues	Confirmation of title to land	14	2	Petition	200	Priv. Land Claims	....	....	......	Discharged; laid on table.		
Flaujac, Garrigues	Confirmation of title to land	15	1	Petition	238	Public Lands	....	....	......	Discharged; laid on table.		
Flaujac, Garrigues	Confirmation of title to land	19	1	Petition	83	Public Lands	Jan. 26, 1823	Favorable	66	Passed	Passed	App'd May 20, 1826
Flaujac, Garrigues	Authority to locate land	20	1	Petition	245	Priv. Land Claims.						
Flaujac, Garrigues	Authority to locate land	20	2	Petition	34	Priv. Land Claims.	Dec. 22, 1828	Adverse	......	Laid on table.		
Flaujac, Garrigues	Authority to locate land	21	1	Petition	51	Priv. Land Claims.	....	....	......	Discharged; laid on table.		
Flaujac, Garrigues	Authority to locate land	22	1	Petition	65	Priv. Land Claims.	270	Favorable	348	Referred to Committee Whole House.		
Flaujac, Garrigues	Authority to locate land	23	1	Petition	76	Priv. Land Claims.	48	Favorable	53	Passed	Passed	App'd May 1, 1834
Flaujac, Garrigues, assignee of.	Authority to locate land	26	1	Senate bill	836	Priv. Land Claims.	July 21, 1840	Adverse	S. 253			
Flaujac, Garrigues, assignee of.	Authority to locate land	26	2	Senate bill	225	Priv. Land Claims.	....	....	120			
Flaujac, Garrigues, assignee of.	Authority to locate land	27	2	Senate bill	1125	Priv. Land Claims.	Aug. 6, 1842	Favorable	S. 82	Passed	....	App'd Aug. 29, 1842
Flax, Michael	Pension for revolutionary services.	22	1	Petition	190	Rev. Pensions.						
Fleanor, Nicholas	Compensation for horse lost in public service.	28	1	Petition	289	Claims	135	Adverse	......	Laid on table.		
Fleck, Jacob	Pension for revolutionary services.	27	3	Petition	259	Rev. Pensions	....	....	......	Discharged; leave to withdraw.		
Fleece, John	Pension for revolutionary services.	16	2	Petition	21	Rev. Pensions	Dec. 20, 1820	Adverse	......	Leave to withdraw.		
Fleece, John	Pension for revolutionary services.	17	1	Petition	27	Rev. Pensions.						
Fleischman, Charles L	For a patent	26	1	Senate bill	1121	Patents	....	....	S. 243			
Fleisher, Jacob	Pension for revolutionary services.	15	2	Petition	190	Rev. Pensions	Jan. 21, 1819	Adverse	......	Rejected.		
Fleisher, Jacob	Pension for revolutionary services.	21	1	Petition	46	Military Pensions	....	General bill	248			
Fleisher, Jacob	Restoration of pension	22	1	Resolution	561	Rev. Pensions	472	Favorable	574			
Flemend, John B	Compensation for military services	17	1	Petition	151	Military Affairs.						
Flemend, John B	Compensation for military services	19	1	Petition	443	Claims.						
Fleming, Alexander	(See Bronaugh and Fleming)	27	2	....	747							
Fleming, George	Indemnity for property destroyed in Florida.	19	1	Memorial	252	Foreign Affairs	112	Adverse	......	Laid on table.		
Fleming, George	Indemnity for property destroyed in Florida.	20	2	Petition	339	Foreign Affairs	99	Favorable	385	Referred to Committee Whole House.		
Fleming, George	Indemnity for property destroyed in Florida.	23	1	Petition	67	Foreign Affairs	368	Favorable	395	Passed	Passed	App'd June 26, 1834
Fleming, James	Invalid pension	25	2	Petition	56	Invalid Pensions	277	Favorable	320	Passed.		

List of private claims presented to the House of Representatives of the United States from the 1st to the 31st Congress, inclusive—Continued.

Names of claimants.	Nature or object of the claim.	Congress.	Session.	How brought before the House of Reps.	Page of journal.	To what committee of the House referred.	No. or date of the report.	Nature of the report.	No. of the bill.	How disposed of by the House of Reps.	How disposed of by the Senate.	Date of the act of Congress, and remarks.
Fleming, James	Invalid pension	25	3	Petition	88	Invalid Pensions	77	Favorable	955	Passed.		
Fleming, James	Invalid pension	26	1	Petition	160	Invalid Pensions	175	Favorable	186	Passed	Indef. postp'd.	
Fleming, John, collector of taxes.	Reimbursement of money paid U. States through mistake.	21	2	Petition	160	Claims	Feb. 4, 1831	Adverse		Laid on table.		
Fleming, John, collector of taxes.	Reimbursement of money paid U. States through mistake.	22	1	Petition	143	Claims	Jan. 18, 1832	Adverse		Laid on table.		
Fleming, John, administrator of.	Compensation for Indian depredations.	26	1	Petition	621	Claims.						
Fleming, J. A	For the issue of a patent for land	25	2	Resolution	765	Priv. Land Claims.	April 20, 1838	Favorable	755	Passed	Passed	App'd June 28, 1838
Fleming, John C	Compensation for military services.	31	1	Petition	611	Claims.						
Fleming, John V	(See John Syme, administrator of)	22	1		143							
Fleming, John W. C., (Ala.)	Confirmation of title to land	18	1	Petition	97	Priv. Land Claims.						
Fleming, John W. C., representatives of.	(See John W. Simonton, *et al.*)	26	1		304							
Fleming, L	Indemnity for destruction of property in Florida.	19	1	Memorial	252	Foreign Affairs	112	Adverse		Laid on table.		
Fleming, L	Indemnity for destruction of property in Florida.	20	2	Petition	339	Foreign Affairs	99	Favorable	385	Referred to Committee Whole House.		
Fleming, L	Indemnity for destruction of property in Florida.	23	1	Petition	67	Foreign Affairs	368	Favorable	395	Passed	Passed	App'd June 26, 1834
Fleming, Robert	Pension	21	1	Petition	48	Military Pensions.						
Fleming, Robert, (Pa.)	Compensation for military services in 1790.	23	2	Petition	389	Rev. Claims.						
Fleming, Samuel	(See Thomas Fleming, *et al.*)	20	1		50							
Fleming, Thomas, *et al.*	Pension	19	2	Resolution	69	Military Pensions	Feb. 14, 1827	Favorable	436	Referred to Committee Whole House.		
Fleming, Thomas, *et al.*	Pension	20	1	Petition	50	Military Pensions	Feb. 13, 1828	Favorable	166	Passed.		
Fleming, Thomas, *et al.*	Pension	20	2	Rep't Committee	55	Military Pensions	Dec. 12, 1838	Favorable	311	Passed.		
Fleming, Thomas, *et al.*	Pension	21	1	Petition	46	Military Pensions	Jan. 5, 1830	Favorable	72	Passed	Passed	App'd May 20, 1830
Fleming, William, (Pa.)	Pay and bounty land for services in war of 1812.	18	1	Petition	130	Military Affairs	Feb. 13, 1821	Adverse		Laid on table.		
Fleming, William, (Pa.)	Pay and bounty land for services in war of 1812.	19	1	Resolution	157	Military Affairs				Discharged; leave to withdraw.		
Fleming, William, (Pa.)	Pay and bounty land for services in war of 1812.	22	1	Petition	534	Claims.						
Fleming, William, (Ala.)	Compensation for horses taken by Cherokee Indians in 1792.	25	3	Petition	462	Claims.						
Fleming, William, (Ala.)	Compensation for horses taken by Cherokee Indians in 1792.	26	1	Petition	168	Claims	690	Adverse		Laid on table.		
Fleming, William, (Ala.)	Compensation for horses taken by Cherokee Indians in 1792.	26	2	Petition	38	Claims.						
Fleming, William A	To correct error in entry of land	21	1	Petition	319	Public Lands.						
Fleming, William A	To correct error in entry of land	21	2	Petition	338	Public Lands.						
Fleming, William A	To correct error in entry of land	22	1	Petition	455	Public Lands	March 9, 1832	Favorable	45	Passed	Passed	App'd Mar. 15, 1832
Flesher, Adam, (Va.)	Pension	22	2	Petition	26	Invalid Pensions				Discharged; laid on table.		
Flesher, Adam, (Va.)	Release from payment of a certain judgment.	26	1	Petition	352	Judiciary	392	Adverse		Laid on table.		
Flesher, Adam, (Va.)	Release from payment of a certain judgment.	26	2	Petition	54	Judiciary.						
Flesher, Mary, *et al.*	Five years full pay and bounty land for services of their late husbands	23	1	Petition	45	Military Affairs	Jan. 21, 1834	Adverse		Laid on table.		

List of private claims presented to the House of Representatives of the United States from the 1st to the 31st Congress, inclusive—Continued.

Names of claimants.	Nature or object of the claim.	Congress.	Session.	How brought before the House of Reps.	Page of journal.	To what committee of the House referred.	No. or date of the report.	Nature of the report.	No. of the bill.	How disposed of by the House of Reps.	How disposed of by the Senate.	Date of the act of Congress, and remarks.
Fletchall, John	To correct error in land entry	24	1	Petition	113	Public Lands.						
Fletcher, Archelaus	Restoration of pension	17	1	Petition	92	Rev. Pensions.						
Fletcher, Charles	(See Fletcher & Ottway.)	26	1		182							
Fletcher, David	Pay for horse lost in war of 1812	22	2	Petition	74	Claims	26	Adverse		Laid on table.		
Fletcher, Ebenezer	Invalid pension	3	2	Rep. of Secretary War.	278	Claims	Feb. 28, 1795	Favorable	130	Passed	Postponed.	
Fletcher, Ebenezer	Invalid pension	4	1	Rep't. Committee	445	Claims	Feb. 18, 1796	Favorable	156	Passed	Passed	App'd April 20, 1796
Fletcher, Ebenezer	Increase of pension	15	2	Petition	46	Rev. Pensions.						
Fletcher, Ebenezer	Increase of pension	16	1	Petition	313	Rev. Pensions				Discharged; laid on table.		
Fletcher, James	(See Archibald Beard and others.)	30	1		239		597		478			
Fletcher, Joseph	Compensation for property destroyed in war of 1812.	28	1	Petition	684	Claims.						
Fletcher, Joseph	Compensation for property destroyed in war of 1812.	28	2	Petition	214	Claims.						
Fletcher, John W., representatives of.	Indemnity for French spoliations prior to 1800.	26	2	Petition	131	Whole House		Favorable	319			
Fletcher, Josiah, (Ala.)	Confirmation of title to land	18	2	Petition	42	Public Lands	Jan. 20, 1825	Favorable	301	Passed	Passed	App'd March 3, 1825
Fletcher, Josiah, of Alabama, representatives of.	Compensation for Indian depredations.	21	2	Petition	143	Claims	Jan. 21, 1831	Adverse		Laid on table.		
Fletcher, Josiah, of Alabama, representatives of.	Compensation for Indian depredations.	22	1	Petition	25	Claims.						
Fletcher, Josiah, of Alabama, representatives of.	Compensation for Indian depredations.	22	2	Petition	69	Indian Affairs.						
Fletcher, Josiah, of Alabama, representatives of.	Compensation for Indian depredations.	23	1	Petition	310	Indian Affairs.						
Fletcher, Josiah, of Alabama, representatives of.	Compensation for Indian depredations.	25	2	Petition	95	Indian Affairs	Feb. 20, 1838	Adverse		Laid on table.		
Fletcher, Lewis	Payment for horses lost in public service.	23	1	Documents	154	Claims.						
Fletcher, Lewis	(See Wm. H. Bedford, agent, &c.)	28	1		262							
Fletcher, Mary	Pension for husband who died in service of United States.	13	2	Petition	169	Claims	Mar. 23, 1814	Adverse		Rejected.		
Fletcher, Noah	Compensation as assistant Clerk of the House of Representatives.	27	3	Memorial	500	Whole House		Favorable; res.				
Fletcher & Ottway	Indemnity for French spoliations prior to 1800.	26	1	Memorial	182	Foreign Affairs	343	Favorable; bill	319	Referred to Committee Whole House.		
Fletcher, Patrick, widow of.	For an annuity for revolutionary services.	7	1	Petition	13	Select	Jan. 22, 1802	Favorable	60	Passed	Passed	App'd April 29, 1802
Fletcher, Richard	Renewal of a land warrant	13	2	Petition	280	Public Lands	April 14, 1814	Adverse		Leave to withdraw.		
Fletcher, Sarah	(See Patrick Fletcher, widow of.)	7	1		13							
Fletcher, Stoughton A	Reissue of lost land certificates	30	2	Petition	136	Judiciary	Feb. 1, 1849	Favorable	752	Passed.		
Fletcher, Stoughton A	Reissue of lost land certificates	31	1	Petition	439	Judiciary.						
Fletcher, Stoughton A	Reissue of lost land certificates	31	2	Resolution	226					Leave to withdraw.		
Fletcher, Thomas, (Va.)	Pension for revolutionary services.	22	1	Resolution	171	Rev. Pensions				Discharged; laid on table.		
Fletcher, Thomas, of Va., heirs of.	(See Cary Nicholas, sureties of)	30	2		204		27		718			
Fletcher, William	Payment for a horse lost in public service.	22	2	Petition	74	Claims	25	Adverse		Laid on table.		
Fleur, Augustus C	(See Stephen Decatur, widow of.)	20	1		295		201		S. 50			
Fleury, Henry M	Authority to locate land claim	25	2	Petition	373	Priv. Land Claims.	Feb. 17, 1838	Adverse		Laid on table.		
Fleury, Henry M	Authority to locate land claim	25	3	Petition	133	Priv. Land Claims.	149	Adverse		Laid on table.		

List of private claims presented to the House of Representatives of the United States from the 1st to the 31st Congress, inclusive—Continued.

Names of claimants.	Nature or object of the claim.	Congress.	Session.	How brought before the House of Reps.	Page of journal.	To what committee of the House referred.	No. or date of the report.	Nature of the report.	No. of the bill.	How disposed of by the House of Reps.	How disposed of by the Senate.	Date of the act of Congress, and remarks.
Fleury, Henry M., *et al.*	Confirmation of titles to land	31	1	Petition	277	Priv. Land Claims.						
Fleury, Lieut. Col. Lewis, and Lieut. Col. Gimot, heirs of.	Permission to enter lands in lieu of other lands.	19	2	Petition	202	Public Lands.						
Fleury, Lieut. Col. Lewis, and Lieut. Col. Gimot, heirs of.	Permission to enter lands in lieu of other lands.	20	1	Petition	75	Public Lands.						
Flick, Daniel	Pension for revolutionary services.	29	1	Petition	104	Rev. Pensions				Discharged; leave to withdraw.		
Flicker, Elizabeth	(See Henry Richardson, former widow of.)	24	1		408							
Flin, Daniel	Compensation for revolutionary services.	3	1	Petition	60					Laid on table.		
Fling, Erastus	Compensation for military services.	20	2	Petition	229	Priv. Land Claims.						
Fling, James	Pension for revolutionary services.	19	2	Resolution	118	Military Pensions.						
Fling, James	Pension for revolutionary services.	20	2	Resolution	213	Military Pensions.				Discharged; referred to Com. Whole House.		
Fling, James	Pension for revolutionary services.	21	1	Petition	231	Military Pensions.						
Fling, James	Pension for revolutionary services.	24	1	Petition	273	Rev. Pensions	493	Adverse		Laid on table.		
Flinn, Benjamin	Pension	21	2	Petition	43	Military Pensions.				Discharged.		
Flinn, Benjamin	Pension	22	1	Petition	104	Rev. Pensions	Mar. 13, 1832	Favorable	467	Passed	Indef. postp'd.	
Flinn, Hugh, widow of	Pension for revolutionary services.	13	2	Petition	331	Rev. Pensions				Discharged; referred to Secretary of War.		
Flinn, James, executrix of.	Pay for a horse lost in public service.	24	1	Petition	474	Claims	768	Adverse		Laid on table.		
Flinn, James, executrix of.	Pay for a horse lost in public service.	25	3	Petition	462	Claims.						
Flinn, James, executrix of.	Pay for a horse lost in public service.	26	1	Petition	168	Claims	40	Adverse		Laid on table.		
Flinn, Nancy	(See Thomas Flinn, widow of)	8	2		47							
Flinn, Nancy	(See Hugh Flinn, widow of)	13	2		331							
Flinn, Thomas, widow of.	Compensation for services against Indians in 1792.	8	2	Memorial	47	Claims	Mar. 1, 1805	Favorable		Referred to Committee Whole House.		
Flinn, Thomas, widow of.	Compensation for services against Indians in 1792.	8	2	Senate bill	165	Whole House			S. 15	Passed		App'd March 3, 1805
Flinn, Thomas	Pay for tools burnt at Capitol, and compensation for services at penitentiary.	22	1	Petition	267	Claims	Feb. 8, 1832	Favorable		Ref. to Commissioner Public Buildings.		
Flinn, Thomas	Invalid pension	23	2	Petition	105	Invalid Pensions				Discharged; laid on table.		
Flinn, William	Compensation for a horse lost in war of 1812.	24	1	Petition	474	Claims	768	Adverse		Laid on table.		
Flinn, William	Compensation for a horse lost in war of 1812.	25	3	Petition	462	Claims.						
Flinn, William	Compensation for a horse lost in war of 1812.	26	1	Petition	168	Claims	40	Adverse		Laid on table.		
Flint, Adolphus W.	Increase of pay as postmaster at New York.	22	1	Petition	512	P. Of. & P. Roads.				Discharged; laid on table.		
Flint, James, widow of	Compensation for revolutionary services.	25	2	Petition	576	Rev. Claims	865	Adverse		Laid on table.		
Flint, Jerusha	(See James Flint, widow of)	25	2		576							
Flint, Jonathan	Restoration of pension	24	1	Petition	840	Rev. Pensions	741	Favorable	686	Passed	Passed	App'd June 28, 1836

List of private claims presented to the House of Representatives of the United States from the 1st to the 31st Congress, inclusive—Continued.

Names of claimants.	Nature or object of the claim.	Congress.	Session.	How brought before the House of Reps.	Page of journal.	To what committee of the House referred.	No. or date of the report.	Nature of the report.	No. of the bill.	How disposed of by the House of Reps.	How disposed of by the Senate.	Date of the act of Congress, and remarks.
Flint, Thomas	Pension for revolutionary services	3	1	Petition	138					Referred to Secretary War.		
Flint, Thomas	Pension for revolutionary services	3	2	Rep. of Secretary War.	278					Laid on table.		
Flint, Thomas	Pension for revolutionary services	4	1	Petition	428	Claims	May 7, 1796	Adverse		Laid on table.		
Flint, Thomas	Increase of pension	16	1	Petition	39	Military Affairs	April 5, 1820	Adverse		Leave to withdraw.		
Flint, Timothy, executors of.	Confirmation of title to land	27	2	Memorial	615	Priv. Land Claims.						
Flint, Timothy, executors of.	Confirmation of title to land	27	3	Petition	45	Priv. Land Claims.						
Flippo, William, assignee of.	Compensation for a horse lost in the Black Hawk war.	27	3	Petition	305	Claims.						
Flippo, William, assignee of.	Compensation for a horse lost in the Black Hawk war.	28	1	Petition	713	Claims	498	Adverse		Laid on table.		
Flomerfelt, A.	Settlement of accounts, and allowances for extra services in navy.	30	1	Senate bill	328	Naval Affairs	Feb. 29, 1848	Favorable	S. 118	Referred to Committee Whole House.		
Flood, John	Invalid pension	26	1	Resolution	1011	Invalid Pensions	647	Favorable	480	Referred to Committee Whole House.		
Flood, John	Invalid pension	27	2	Petition	60	Invalid Pensions	17	Favorable	58	Passed	Passed	App'd Aug. 26, 1842
Flood, Martha	(See William Flood, of Virginia, widow of.)	15	2		205							
Flood, William, of Virginia, widow of.	Reimbursement of duties on distillery illegally exacted.	15	2	Petition	205	Ways and Means.						
Flood, William, of Virginia, widow of.	Reimbursement of duties on distillery illegally exacted.	16	1	Petition	146	Ways and Means	Jan. 18, 1820	Favorable	48	Passed	Passed	App'd May 12, 1820
Flood, William, widow of.	Invalid pension	30	1	Petition	594	Invalid Pensions	721	Adverse		Laid on table.		
Flood, William, widow of.	Invalid pension	30	2	Petition	115	Invalid Pensions.						
Flood, William, (La.)	Indemnity for property destroyed at New Orleans in 1812.	14	1	Petition	260	Claims	Feb. 16, 1816	Favorable	83	Passed	Passed	App'd April 24, 1816
Flores, Badio	Confirmation of title to land	26	1	Petition	365	Priv. Land Claims.						
Flores, Badio	Confirmation of title to land	28	1	Petition	132	Priv. Land Claims.						
Florida, inhabitants of	Confirmation of land titles	14	1	Petition	43	Public Lands				Discharged; laid on table.		
Florida, inhabitants of	Confirmation of land titles	14	2	Petition	51	Priv. Land Claims.				Discharged.		
Florida, inhabitants of	Confirmation of land titles	17	1	Petition	181	Public Lands				Discharged; laid on table.		
Florida, inhabitants of	Confirmation of land titles	17	1	Petition	289	Judiciary; disch'd, and referred to Public Lands.				Discharged; laid on table.		
Florida, inhabitants of Jackson county.	Confirmation of land titles	18	2	Petition	31	Public Lands.						
Florida, inhabitants of the Cape.	Confirmation of land titles	18	2	Petition	211	Public Lands.						
Florida, inhabitants of Jackson county.	Confirmation of land titles	19	1	Petition	37	Public Lands				Discharged; laid on table.		
Florida, inhabitants of the Cape.	Confirmation of land titles	19	1	Petition	45	Public Lands				Discharged; laid on table.		
Florida, inhabitants of	Confirmation of land titles	19	1	House bill	90	Public Lands	Dec. 23, 1825	Favorable	19	Passed	Indef. postp'd.	
Florida, inhabitants of	Confirmation of land titles	19	1	Petition	94	Public Lands				Discharged; laid on table.		
Florida, inhabitants of	Confirmation of land titles	19	1	Petition	110	Public Lands				Discharged; laid on table.		
Florida, inhabitants of	Confirmation of land titles	19	2	Petition	27	Public Lands				Discharged.		

List of private claims presented to the House of Representatives of the United States from the 1st to the 31st Congress, inclusive—Continued.

Names of claimants.	Nature or object of the claim.	Congress.	Session.	How brought before the House of Reps.	Page of journal.	To what committee of the House referred.	No. or date of the report.	Nature of the report.	No. of the bill.	How disposed of by the House of Reps.	How disposed of by the Senate.	Date of the act of Congress, and remarks.
Florida, inhabitants of	Confirmation of land titles	21	2	Petition	235	Public Lands	....	....	......	Discharged.		
Florida, inhabitants of	Confirmation of land titles	23	1	Petition	144	Priv. Land Claims.						
Florida, inhabitants of Escambia county.	Confirmation of land titles	28	1	Petition	257	Priv. Land Claims.						
Florida, inhabitants of	Pre-emption rights to lands	17	1	Petition	27	Public Lands	....	....	......	Discharged; laid on table.		
Florida, inhabitants of	Pre-emption rights to lands	18	2	Petition	43	Priv. Land Claims.						
Florida, inhabitants of	Pre-emption rights to lands	20	1	Petition	281	Public Lands	....	....	......	Discharged.		
Florida, inhabitants of	Pre-emption rights to lands	20	2	Petition	44	Public Lands	....	....	......	Discharged; laid on table.		
Florida, inhabitants of	Pre-emption rights to lands	20	2	Resolution	52	Public Lands	9	Favorable	320	Referred to Committee Whole House.		
Florida, inhabitants of	Pre-emption rights to lands	26	1	Petition	1004	....	....	....	......	Laid on table.		
Florida, inhabitants of	Pre-emption rights to lands	27	2	Petition	98	Public Lands.						
Florida Legislature, resolutions of.	Pre-emption rights to settlers	26	1	....	954	Public Lands.						
Florida Legislature, resolutions of.	Pre-emption rights to settlers	26	1	....	1004	....	....	....	......	Laid on table.		
Florida Legislature, resolutions of.	Pre-emption rights to settlers	27	3	....	107	Public Lands	....	....	......	Discharged; laid on table.		
Florida Legislature, resolutions of.	Pre-emption right to land in the county of Walton, for a court-house.	23	2	....	437	Public Lands.						
Florida Legislature, resolutions of.	Pre-emption right to land in the county of Walton, for a court-house.	24	1	....	58	Public Lands.						
Florida Legislature, resolutions of.	Pre-emption right to land in the county of Walton, for a court-house.	24	2	....	88	Public Lands.						
Florida Legislature, resolutions of.	For a grant of land for a court-house in Duval county.	24	1	....	66	Territories.						
Florida Legislature, resolutions of.	That other lands be granted for the seat of government in lieu of those now covered by grant to Lafayette.	19	2	....	308	Public Lands	....	....	......	Discharged.		
Florida Legislature, resolutions of.	That other lands be granted for the seat of government in lieu of those now covered by grant to Lafayette.	20	1	....	158	Public Lands	Jan. 11, 1828	Favorable	65	Referred to Committee Whole House.		
Florida Legislature, resolutions of.	Bounty land to officers and soldiers of the Florida war.	30	2	....	140	Military Affairs.						
Florida Legislature, resolutions of.	Indemnity for damages to the property of certain persons during the war of 1812.	23	1	....	294	Foreign Affairs	368	Favorable	395	Passed	Passed	App'd June 27, 1834
Florida Legislature, resolutions of.	Indemnity for damages to the property of certain persons during the Florida war.	30	1	....	160	Judiciary.						
Florida Legislature, resolutions of.	For payment to the militia who served in the Florida war.	25	2	....	544	Military Affairs	....	....	......	Discharged.		
Florida Legislature, resolutions of.	For payment to the militia who served in the Florida war.	26	1	....	306	Military Affairs.						
Florida Legislature, resolutions of.	Reimbursement of moneys expended in defence against the Indians	26	1	....	598	Territories.						

List of private claims presented to the House of Representatives of the United States from the 1st to the 31st Congress, inclusive—Continued.

Names of claimants.	Nature or object of the claim.	Congress.	Session.	How brought before the House of Reps.	Page of journal.	To what committee of the House referred.	No. or date of the report.	Nature of the report.	No. of the bill.	How disposed of by the House of Reps.	How disposed of by the Senate.	Date of the act of Congress, and remarks.
Florida Legislature, resolutions of.	Reimbursement of expenses of volunteers previous to being mustered into service.	30	1	....	320, 508	Military Affairs.						
Florida Legislature, resolutions of.	Compensation for horses lost in the Florida war.	26	1	....	963	Military Affairs.						
Florida Legislature, resolutions of.	Compensation for horses lost in the Florida war.	27	2	....	99	Military Affairs.						
Florida Legislature, resolutions of.	Provision for the widows and orphans of soldiers of the Mexican war.	30	1	....	495	Select.						
Florida, State of.........	Reimbursement of moneys expended during the Seminole war.	31	1	Senate bill	435	Military Affairs ..	Feb. 13, 1850	Favorable	1			
Florida, Corporation of Pensacola.	For a grant of land	17	1	Petition	188	Whole House.						
Florida, inhabitants of Pensacola.	For a grant of land	17	1	Petition	289	Public Lands	....	....	......	Discharged; laid on table.		
Florida, cities of Pensacola and St. Augustine.	For a grant of certain lots.......	18	1	Petition	288	Public Lands	Mar. 3, 1824	Favorable	141	Referred to Committee Whole House.		
Florida, city of Pensacola .	For a grant of certain lots.......	18	2	Pet. and House bill.	211	Public Lands	Feb. 7, 1825	Favorable	141	Indefinitely postponed.		
Florida, cities of Pensacola and St. Augustine.	For a grant of certain lots.......	19	1	Resolution	53	Public Lands.						
Florida, academy of Pensacola.	For a grant of certain lots.......	23	1	Memorial	382	Public Lands.						
Florida, academy of Pensacola.	For a grant of certain lots.......	24	1	Petition	58	Public Lands.....	....	....	......	Discharged; laid on table.		
Florida, academy of Quincy	For a grant of certain lots.......	27	2	Memorial	83	Territories.						
Florida, academy of Quincy	For a grant of certain lots.......	27	3	Petition	237	Territories	87	Adverse	......	Laid on table.		
Florida, Dade Institute of. .	For a grant of certain lots.......	26	1	Petition	177	Public Lands.	93	Favorable	89			
Florida, Collegiate Institute of.	For a grant of certain lots.......	28	1	Petition	840	Public Lands.						
Florida, city of St. Augustine.	For a grant of certain lots.......	17	2	Memorial	123	Judiciary dis.; ref. to Public Lands.	....	....	......	Discharged; leave to withdraw.		
Florida, Corporation of St. Augustine.	For a grant of certain lots.......	23	1	Petition	500	Territories.						
Florida, city of St. Augustine.	For a grant of certain lots.......	27	2	Memorial	370	Territories.						
Florida, city of St. Augustine.	For a grant of certain lots	28	1	Petition	133	Territories.						
Florida, Catholic congregation of St. Augustine.	For arbitration of contested claims to certain property.	30	1	Senate resolution	1012	Priv. Land Claims.	Aug. 8, 1848	Favorable	S.R. 32	Passed	....	App'd Aug. 11, 1848
Florida, inhabitants of St. Augustine.	Reimbursement of money expended for repairing fortifications.	24	2	Petition	81	Claims	218	Adverse	......	Laid on table.		
Florida, inhabitants of St. Augustine.	Reimbursement of money expended for repairing fortifications.	24	2	Petition	119	Claims.						
Florida, inhabitants of St. Augustine.	Reimbursement of money expended for repairing fortifications.	25	2	Petition	407	Military Affairs ...	724	Adverse	......	Laid on table.		
Florida, inhabitants of St. Augustine.	Reimbursement of money expended for repairing fortifications.	25	3	Petition	188	Claims	216	Adverse	......	Laid on table.		
Florida, inhabitants of....	(See Alabama)................	25	2	....	323							
Florida, city of Fernandina.	For a grant of certain lots.......	18	1	Petition	160	Public Lands.....	Feb. 2, 1824	Favorable.				
Florida, city of Fernandina.	For a grant of certain lots.......	19	1	Petition	83	Public Lands.....	....	....	......	Discharged; laid on table.		

List of private claims presented to the House of Representatives of the United States from the 1*st to the* 31*st Congress, inclusive*—Continued.

Names of claimants.	Nature or object of the claim.	Congress.	Session.	How brought before the House of Reps.	Page of journal.	To what committee of the House referred.	No. or date of the report.	Nature of the report.	No. of the bill.	How disposed of by the House of Reps.	How disposed of by the Senate.	Date of the act of Congress, and remarks.
Florida, city of Tallahassee.	For a grant of certain lots	19	1	Memorial	293	Public Lands				Disch'd; laid on table.		
Florida, inhabitants of, (late part of Mississippi.)	For further time to procure evidence of their claims to lands.	17	1	Petition	22	Public Lands				Discharged; laid on table.		
Florida, inhabitants of, (late Mississippi & Louisiana.	For payment of their claims under act of April, 1814.	19	2	Resolution	40	Ways and Means				Discharged; referred to Com. Whole House.		
Florida, inhabitants of, (late Mississippi & Louisiana.	For payment of their claims under act of April, 1814.	20	1	Resolution	153	Ways and Means	Feb. 20, 1828	Favorable	176	Referred to Committee Whole House.		
Florida, inhabitants of, (late Mississippi & Louisiana	For payment of their claims under act of April, 1814.	20	2	Resolution	56	Ways and Means	99	Favorable	329	Referred to Committee Whole House.		
Florida, Spanish officers & inhabitants of.	Indemnity for property destroyed by enemy.	18	2	Petition	55	Claims.						
Florida, Spanish officers & inhabitants of.	Indemnity for property destroyed by enemy.	19	1	Petition	52	Claims	Dec. 19, 1825	Adverse		Laid on table.		
Florida, Spanish officers & inhabitants of.	Indemnity for property destroyed by enemy.	19	1	Petition	252	Foreign Affairs	Mar. 10, 1826	Adverse		Laid on table.		
Florida, inhabitants of	Indemnity for property destroyed by enemy.	22	1	Resolution	39	Foreign Affairs	223	Favorable	297	Referred to Committee Whole House.		
Florida, inhabitants of	Indemnity for property destroyed by enemy.	22	2	House bill	323	Whole House			297	Recommitted.		
Florida, inhabitants of	Indemnity for property destroyed by enemy.	27	2	Petition	100	Territories.						
Florida, inhabitants of	Indemnity for property destroyed by enemy.	28	1	Petition	137	Territories.						
Florida, claimants under treaty of.	Against the deduction of the am'nt awarded.	19	1	Memorial	221	Ways and Means				Discharged; laid on table.		
Florida, judges and clerks of.	Compensation as ex-officio commissioners to adjust claims under treaty with Spain.	19	1	Resolution	186	Territories				Discharged; laid on table.		
Florida, judges of	For increase of compensation	23	1	Petition	354	Judiciary		Favorable	441	Passed	Passed	App'd June 30, 1834
Florida, inhabit's of Washington.	For increase of compensation to the judges of the supreme court.	23	1	Petition	139	Territories		Favorable	441	Passed	Passed	App'd June 30, 1834
Florida, grand jury of Jackson county.	For increase of salaries to the judges of the supreme court.	23	1	Petition	139	Territories.						
Florida, bar and citizens of.	Provision for the relief of the judges of the supreme court.	27	2	Memorial	85	Judiciary; disch'd, and to Claims.						
Florida, surveyors of	Increase of compensation	24	1	Petition	58	Public Lands.						
Florida, widows of officers and soldiers of.	Pensions	24	1	Petition	260	Invalid Pensions	Mar. 3, 1836	Favorable	426	Passed	Passed, with amendment.	App'd July 4, 1836
Florida, militia officers of	Payment for services against the Indians.	25	3	Documents	121	Claims	209	Favorable	1064	Passed	Passed	App'd March 3, 1839
Florida, register and receiver of Tallahassee.	Compensation for extra services in locating bounty land warrants.	20	1	Resolution	49	Public Lands				Discharged; laid on table.		
Florida, register, &c., of Tallahassee and St. Augustine.	Compensation for extra services in locating military bounty land warrants.	31	1	Memorial	448, 503	Public Lands.						
Florida, register, &c., of Newnansville.	Compensation for extra services in locating military bounty land warrants.	31	2	Petition	132	Public Lands.						
Florida, Union Bank of	Reimbursement of moneys advanced for the defence of the Territory against the Indians.	30	1	Petition	485	Claims	728	Favorable	569	Referred to Committee Whole House.		

List of private claims presented to the House of Representatives of the United States from the 1st to the 31st Congress, inclusive—Continued.

Names of claimants.	Nature or object of the claim.	Congress.	Session.	How brought before the House of Reps.	Page of journal.	To what committee of the House referred.	No. or date of the report.	Nature of the report.	No. of the bill.	How disposed of by the House of Reps.	How disposed of by the Senate.	Date of the act of Congress, and remarks.
Florida, Union Bank of...	Reimbursement of moneys advanced for the defence of the Territory against the Indians.	30	2	House bill	319	Whole House.....	....	....	569	Passed	Passed	App'd March 3, 1849
Florida, inhabitants of....	Compensation for losses by the invasion and occupancy of United States troops.	24	2	Documents.....	87	Public Lands.						
Florida, inhabitants of....	Compensation for losses by the invasion and occupancy of United States troops.	26	1	Petition	598	Territories.						
Florida, inhabitants of....	Compensation for losses by the invasion and occupancy of United States troops.	26	2	Petition	76	Territories........	131	Favorable	639	Referred to Committee Whole House.		
Florida, inhabitants of....	Compensation for losses by the invasion and occupancy of United States troops.	29	1	Memorial	146	Foreign Affairs.						
Florida, inhabitants of....	Indemnity for losses by Indian depredations.	22	1	Memorial	538	Indian Affairs.						
Florida, inhabitants of....	Indemnity for losses by Indian depredations.	25	3	Petition	121	Claims	162	Adverse	......	Laid on table.		
Florida, inhabitants of....	Indemnity for losses by Indian depredations.	26	1	Petition	306	Military Affairs.						
Florida, inhabitants of....	Indemnity for losses by Indian depredations.	29	1	Memorial	90	Claims.						
Florida, inhabitants of....	Indemnity for losses by Indian depredations.	29	2	Resolution	315	Judiciary.						
Florida, inhabitants of Fort Gatlin.	Indemnity for losses by Indian depredations.	31	1	Petition	325	Military Affairs.						
Florida, Alabama, and Georgia, citizens of.	Indemnity for losses by Indian depredations.	25	2	Pres. message...	323	Claims	1028	Favorable	865	Referred to Committee Whole House.		
Florida, settlers on the Arredondo grant.	Indemnity for loss of land and improvements by decision of the Supreme Court.	22	1	Memorial	788	Public Lands.						
Florida, magistrates of Duval county.	Payment for the use of the court-house by the militia.	25	2	Petition	918	Military Affairs....	....	....	......	Discharged.		
Florida, Spring Grove Guards of.	Compensation for military services in 1839.	27	2	Petition	94	Claims.						
Florida, Spring Grove Guards of.	Compensation for military services in 1839.	27	3	Documents.....	106	Military Affairs....	Jan. 19, 1843	Favorable....	693	Passed	Passed	App'd March 3, 1843
Florida, militia of, (under General Hernandez.)	Compensation for military services.	25	3	Documents.....	121	Claims	209	Favorable....	1064	Passed	Passed	App'd March 3, 1839
Florida, militia of........	Compensation for military services in 1839.	27	3	Documents.....	106	Military Affairs....	Jan. 19, 1843	Favorable....	693	Passed	Passed	App'd March 3, 1843
Florida, citizens of.......	Compensation for military services in 1839.	29	1	Petition	567	Military Affairs.						
Florida, citizens of Benton county.	Compensation for military services in 1839.	31	1	Petition	1084	Military Affairs.						
Florida, volunteers of	Compensation for services in Seminole war.	29	2	Resolution	147	Military Affairs.						
Florida, volunteers of	Compensation for services in Seminole war.	30	1	Petition	239	Claims.						
Florida, volunteers of	Compensation for services in Seminole war.	30	1	Petition	867	Military Affairs.						

List of private claims presented to the House of Representatives of the United States from the 1st to the 31st Congress, inclusive—Continued.

Names of claimants.	Nature or object of the claim.	Congress.	Session.	How brought before the House of Reps.	Page of journal.	To what committee of the House referred.	No. or date of the report.	Nature of the report.	No. of the bill.	How disposed of by the House of Reps.	How disposed of by the Senate.	Date of the act of Congress, and remarks.
Florida, commissioners of Hillsboro' county.	For a grant of land for a court-house.	30	1	Memorial	655	Public Lands.						
Florida, commissioners of Hillsboro' county.	For a grant of land for a court-house.	30	1	Senate bil	719	Public Lands	July 19, 1848	Favorable	S. 210	Passed	....	App'd July 25, 1848
Florida, Jillet A.	Pension	19	2	Petition	111	Military Pensions	....	....	......	Discharged.		
Floriddi, Francisco	Compensation for revolutionary services.	2	2	Petition	615	Select	Mar. 2, 1793	Adverse	......	Leave to withdraw.		
Florilla, schooner	(See Zaccheus Knowles)	27	2	....	822							
Flotilla, Barney's	(See officers, &c., of)	14	1	....	146							
Flour, Margaret	Compensation for services, &c., of her husband in the revolution.	2	1	Petition	444	....	....	....	......	Referred to Secretary of War.		
Flour, Margaret	Compensation for services, &c., of her husband in the revolution.	2	2	Rep. of Secretary War.	696	....	....	....	......	Laid on table.		
Flourjac, Garrigues	(See Garrigues Flaujac)	14	2	....	200							
Flournoy, Alfred	Commutation of his pension for land.	17	2	Senate bill	277	Priv. Land Claims.	Mar. 1, 1823	Favorable	S. 54	Indefinitely postponed.		
Flournoy, Alfred	Commutation of his pension for land.	19	1	Petition	66	Public Lands	....	....	......	Discharged; laid on table.		
Flournoy, Alfred	Commutation of his pension for land.	19	1	Senate bill	529	Priv. Land Claims.	May 10, 1826	Favorable	S. 63	Passed	Passed	App'd May 22, 1826
Flournoy, Alfred	Grant of patent for certain lands	19	2	Senate bill	276	Priv. Land Claims.	Feb. 14, 1827	Favorable	S. 60	Passed	Passed	App'd Feb. 22, 1827
Flournoy, Thomas	Indemnifying him against a judgment.	19	2	Resolution	136	Judiciary	62	Favorable	407	Referred to Committee Whole House.		
Flournoy, Thomas	Indemnifying him against a judgment.	20	1	Resolution	35	Judiciary	5	Favorable	7	Passed	Passed	App'd Feb. 12, 1828
Flournoy, Matthew, and Robert J. Ward.	Authorizing them to exchange for certain other lands.	21	1	Report	333	Priv. Land Claims.	225	Favorable	284	Referred to Committee Whole House.		
Flournoy & Ward	Authorizing them to exchange for certain other lands.	21	2	House bill	339	Whole House	....	....	284	Passed	Passed.	
Flournoy & Ward	Authorizing them to exchange for certain other lands.	22	1	Petition	106	Public Lands	151	Favorable	230	Referred to Committee Whole House.		
Flournoy & Ward	Authorizing them to exchange for certain other lands.	22	2	House bill	92	Whole House	....	....	230	Passed	Passed	App'd Jan. 28, 1833
Flower, Thomas	Confirmation of title to land	9	1	Petition	250	Public Lands	....	....	......	Indefinitely postponed.		
Flower, Thomas	Confirmation of title to land	16	2	Petition	244	Priv. Land Claims.						
Flowers Benjamin, heir of the widow.	Seven years' half-pay	29	1	Petition	233	Rev. Claims.						
Flowers, George	Pension	16	1	Petition	110	Rev. Claims	April 6, 1820	Adverse	......	Laid on table.		
Flowers, George	Pension	19	1	Petition	108	Military Pensions	168	Adverse	......	Laid on table.		
Flowers, John W., *et al.*	Indemnity for property lost under Indian treaties.	22	1	Resolution	596	Indian Affairs	May 10, 1832	Favorable	570	Referred to Committee Whole House.		
Flowers, John W., *et al.*	Indemnity for property lost under Indian treaties.	22	1	House bill	734	Whole House	....	Favorable	375	Passed	Passed	App'd July 13, 1832
Flowers, Mary	Pre-emption right to land	30	1	Petition	977	Public Lands.						
Flowers, Sidney	Pre-emption right to land	30	2	Petition	78	Priv. Land Claims.	25	Favorable; bill	677	Passed	Passed	App'd March 3, 1849
Flowers, Thomas, *et al.*	Renewal of bounty land warrant.	20	1	Resolution	175	Public Lands	Feb. 29, 1828	Report and bill.	194	Passed	Passed, with amendment.	App'd April 17, 1828
Floyd, Charles, heirs of	Land for services with Lewis and Clark.	9	2	Pres. Message	284	Select	Jan. 23, 1807	Favorable	183	Passed	Passed	App'd March 3, 1807
Floyd, Charles, heirs of	To locate land as compensation to Lewis and Clark.	14	1	Petition	43	Public Lands	Dec. 22, 1815	Adverse.				
Floyd, Davis, & H. Allen.	Compensation as commissioner under the Florida treaty.	22	1	Resolution	159	Public Lands	Mar. 29, 1832	Adverse	......	Leave to withdraw.		

List of private claims presented to the House of Representatives of the United States from the 1st to the 31st Congress, inclusive—Continued.

Names of claimants.	Nature or object of the claim.	Congress.	Session.	How brought before the House of Reps.	Page of journal.	To what committee of the House referred.	No. or date of the report.	Nature of the report.	No. of the bill.	How disposed of by the House of Reps.	How disposed of by the Senate.	Date of the act of Congress, and remarks.
Floyd, Davis, (Ind.) *et al.*	Permission to work salt springs	14	1	Petition of Leg. of Indiana.	153	Public Lands	Jan. 30, 1816	Adverse.				
Floyd, Davis, (Fla.)	Compensation for bringing to Washington the report of Commissioners of Florida.	19	1	Resolution	185	Public Lands	Feb. 6, 1826	Favorable	91	Passed	Passed	App'd May 16, 1826
Floyd, Davis, (Fla.)	Settlement of disbursement in 1812	19	1	Senate bill	466	Claims	May 1, 1826	Favorable	S. 59	Passed	....	App'd May 20, 1826
Floyd, Davis, (Fla.) *et al.*	Compensation as commissioner under Florida treaty.	22	1	Resolution	159	Public Lands	Mar. 29, 1832	Adverse	......	Leave to withdraw.		
Floyd, James	Remission of forfeiture on goods imported in 1814.	15	1	Petition	312	Ways and Means.						
Floyd, Jane	Pension	27	3	Petition	250	Rev. Pensions.						
Floyd, John	Indemnity for property destroyed by the enemy.	15	2	Petition	148	Claims	....	....	......	Discharged; laid on table.		
Floyd, John J.	(See James Watson, admin'r of.)	25	2	....	544							
Floyd, Jonathan	Arrears of pension	28	1	Petition	417	Invalid Pensions.						
Floyd, Perry	Pension	12	1	House bill	361	Whole House	June 8, 1812	Favorable	138	Passed	Passed	App'd July 5, 1812
Flye, William, professor in the navy.	Indemnity for lost time in waiting upon the Secretary of the Navy by orders.	31	1	Petition	711	Naval Affairs	437	Adverse	......	Laid on table.		
Fobb, Stephen, heirs of	To refund money paid on certain bond.	24	1	Petition	211	Judiciary	....	....	......	Discharged; leave to withdraw.		
Fobes, Eliab	Authority to convey certain land	18	1	Petition	316	Priv. Land Claims.						
Fobes, Simon	Pension for revolutionary services.	20	2	Petition	229	Military Pensions.						
Fobes, Simon	Pension for revolutionary services.	21	1	Petition	49	Military Pensions	Jan. 5, 1830	Favorable	72	Passed	Passed	App'd May 20, 1830
Fogg, J. A., *et al*	Additional remuneration in land for services in war with Mexico.	31	1	Petition	1009	Rev. Pensions	394	Adverse	......	Laid on table.		
Fogg, Jonathan	Revolutionary pension	21	2	Resolution	108	Military Pensions	49	Favorable	582	Passed.		
Fogg, Jonathan	Revolutionary pension	22	1	Petition	90	Rev. Pensions	109	Favorable	192	Referred to Committee Whole House.		
Fogg, Jonathan	Revolutionary pension	22	2	House bill	66	Whole House	....	....	192	Laid on table.		
Fogg, Lydia	(See A. Poor, and other widows)	20	2	....	289							
Fogg, William Brown	Compensation for revolutionary services.	3	1	Petition	43	....	....	....	......	Referred to Secretary Treasury.		
Fogg, William Brown	Compensation for revolutionary services.	3	2	Rep. of Secretary Treasury.	296	Claims	March 2, 1795	Adverse	......	Laid on table.		
Fogg, William Brown	Compensation for revolutionary services.	4	1	Report	598	Whole House	May 31, 1796	Adverse	......	Laid on table.		
Fogler, Simon	Increase of pension	5	2	Petition	107	Claims	Feb. 1, 1798	Adverse.				
Fogy, John H., (an Indian)	Grant of land on Mississippi river.	21	2	Petition	82	Indian Affairs.						
Fohly, Thomas, executor of.	Indemnity for French spoliations prior to 1800.	26	1	Memorial	182	Foreign Affairs	343	Favorable	319	Referred to Committee Whole House.		
Foley, Alice	(See John Foley, widow of.)	26	1	....	365							
Foley, Barrett	(See Kiser & Foley.)	27	2	....	411							
Foley, Elizabeth	(See Patrick Foley, widow of.)	25	2	....	233							
Foley, John, widow of	Confirmation of title to land	26	1	Petition	365	Priv. Land Claims.	96	Favorable	92	Passed	Passed	App'd July 20, 1840
Foley, Patrick, widow of	Confirmation of title to land	25	2	Petition	233	Public Lands	689	Adverse	......	Laid on table.		
Foley, Patrick, widow of	Confirmation of title to land	27	1	Petition	99	Priv. Land Claims.						
Foley, Patrick, widow of	Confirmation of title to land	27	2	Petition	140	Priv. Land Claims.	....	....	......	Leave to withdraw.		
Folger, Reuben M., *et al.*	Release from payment of a certain bond.	14	2	Petition	121	Ways and Means.						
Folger, Samuel B	Payment for work done at dredging machine at Nantucket, Massachusetts.	27	3	Petition	226	Claims.						

List of private claims presented to the House of Representatives of the United States from the 1st to the 31st Congress, inclusive—Continued.

Names of claimants.	Nature or object of the claim.	Congress.	Session.	How brought before the House of Reps.	Page of journal.	To what committee of the House referred.	No. or date of the report.	Nature of the report.	No. of the bill.	How disposed of by the House of Reps.	How disposed of by the Senate.	Date of the act of Congress, and remarks.
Folger, Samuel B	Payment for work done at dredging machine at Nantucket, Massachusetts.	28	1	Petition	122	Claims	70	Favorable	92	Passed	Passed	App'd June 15, 1844
Folger, Simon	Pension	3	1	Rep. of Secretary War.	131	Select	May 26, 1794	Favorable	62	Passed	Passed	App'd June 7, 1794
Follansbee, Jacob M	Arrears of pension	24	2	Petition	147	Invalid Pensions				Discharged; laid on table.		
Follansbee, Jacob M	Arrears of pension	25	2	Petition	118	Invalid Pensions				Discharged; laid on table.		
Follansbee, Joshua	Compensation as chief engineer United States navy.	31	1	Petition	385	Naval Affairs	13	Favorable	16	Referred to Committee Whole House.		
Follawell, John	Compensation for military services.	6	2	Petition	768	Claims				Discharged.		
Follawell, John	Compensation for military services.	7	1	Petition	19	Claims	April 3, 1802	Favorable	86	Postponed.		
Follawell, John	Compensation for military services.	7	2	Petition	248	Claims	Jan. 26, 1803	Favorable	86	Passed	Amended.	
Follett, Eliphalet	(See John Church, *et al.*)	25	2		391							
Follett, Frederick	Pension	4	1	Report	445	Claims	Feb. 18, 1796	Favorable	156	Passed	Passed	App'd April 20, 1796
Follett, Martin D	Indemnity for property destroyed in 1812.	21	2	Petition	145	Military Pensions	Jan. 12, 1831	Adverse		Laid on table.		
Follingsby, James, former widow of.	Pension for revolutionary services.	31	1	Petition	688	Rev. Pensions	462	Adverse		Laid on table.		
Follis, Arbina, widow of	Confirmation of title to land	22	2	Petition	264	Priv. Land Claims.						
Follis, Arbina, widow of	Confirmation of title to land	23	1	Petition	294	Priv. Land Claims.						
Follis, Susan	(See Arbina Follis, widow of)	22	2		264							
Folsom, Allen, (an Indian)	For a grant of land	22	1	Petition	710	Indian Affairs.						
Folsom, Gilman and Ezekiel.	Indemnity for property destroyed by the public enemy.	17	1	Petition	46	Claims.						
Folsom, Gilman and Ezekiel.	Indemnity for property destroyed by the public enemy.	17	2	Petition	74	Claims.						
Folsom, James B	Pension	23	1	Petition	96	Invalid Pensions	81	Favorable	88	Passed.		
Folsom, James B	Pension	24	1	Petition	52	Invalid Pensions	46	Favorable	58	Passed	Passed	App'd May 14, 1836
Folsom, Jeremiah	Pension for revolutionary services.	19	1	Petition	127	Military Pensions	164	Adverse		Laid on table.		
Folsom, Jeremiah	Pension for revolutionary services.	21	1	Petition	83	Military Pensions.						
Folsom, Jeremiah	Pension for revolutionary services.	22	1	Petition	104	Rev. Pensions				Discharged; laid on table.		
Folsom, Joseph R., *et al.*	Fishing bounty on schooner Galaxy.	23	1	Petition	440	Ways and Means	376	Favorable	398	Referred to Committee Whole House.		
Folsom, Joseph R., *et al.*	Fishing bounty on schooner Galaxy.	24	1	Petition	188	Commerce	Jan. 20, 1836	Favorable	197	Passed.		
Folsom, Joseph R., *et al.*	Fishing bounty on schooner Galaxy.	25	2	Petition	113	Commerce	Feb. 21, 1838	Favorable	582	Referred to Committee Whole House.		
Folsom, Joseph R., *et al.*	Fishing bounty on schooner Galaxy.	25	3	Hous ebill	380	Whole House	Jan. 26, 1839	With't amend.	582	Passed	Passed	App'd March 3, 1839
Folton, Christiana	Pension	25	2	Petition	167	Naval Affairs				Discharged; laid on table.		
Folwell & Adams	Relief on account of the purchase of a fraudulent land warrant.	31	1	Petition	640	Public Lands.						
Folwell & Adams	Relief on account of the purchase of a fraudulent land warrant.	31	2	Petition	132	Priv. Land Claims.						
Foltz, Frantz Jacob	Drawback on coffee and brandy	3	1	Memorial	123	Select	April 30, 1794	Favorable		Laid on table.		
Foltz, Frantz Jacob	Drawback on coffee and brandy	3	2	Memorial	330	Select	Feb. 20, 1795	Favorable	118	Passed	Passed	App'd March 2, 1795
Foltz, Frederick	For pay as a soldier while in captivity.	4	1	Petition	385	Claims	Jan. 20, 1796	Adverse		Leave to withdraw.		
Foltz, Dr. J. M	Payment for services in the United States navy.	25	3	Petition	285	Naval Affairs	192	Favorable	1050	Passed	Passed	App'd March 3, 1839

List of private claims presented to the House of Representatives of the United States from the 1st to the 31st Congress, inclusive—Continued.

82

Names of claimants.	Nature or object of the claim.	Congress.	Session.	How brought before the House of Reps.	Page of journal.	To what committee of the House referred.	No. or date of the report.	Nature of the report.	No. of the bill.	How disposed of by the House of Reps.	How disposed of by the Senate.	Date of the act of Congress, and remarks.
Foltz, Joshua	Compensation for revolutionary services.	20	1	Rep't Committee Whole House.	332	Rev. Claims	Feb. 22, 1828	Favorable	182	Referred to Committee Whole House.		
Foltz, Joshua	Compensation for revolutionary services.	20	2	House bill	174	Whole House			182	Passed	Passed	App'd March 3, 1829
Foltz & Mann	(See Mann & Foltz)	26	1		182							
Fonda, Douro	Pension for revolutionary services.	23	1	Petition	112	Rev. Pensions.						
Fonda, Jellis A., (or Tellis A.)	Pension for revolutionary services.	16	1	Petition	137	Rev. Pensions	Jan. 14, 1820	Adverse		Laid on table.		
Fonda, Jellis A., (or Tellis A.)	Pension for revolutionary services.	20	2	Resolution	223	Military Pensions.						
Fonda, Jellis A., (or Tellis A.)	Pension for revolutionary services.	20	2	Petition	262	Military Pensions.						
Fonda, Jellis A., (or Tellis A.)	Pension for revolutionary services.	21	1	Petition	99	Military Pensions	Feb. 15, 1830	General bill	248	Passed	Indef. postp'd.	
Fonda, Jellis A., (or Tellis A.)	Pension for revolutionary services.	21	2	Petition	53	Military Pensions.						
Fonda, Jellis A., (or Tellis A.)	Pension for revolutionary services.	22	1	Resolution	46	Rev. Pensions	33	Favorable; bill	80	Passed	Indef. postp'd.	
Fonda, Jellis A., (or Tellis A.)	Pension for revolutionary services.	22	1	Resolution	337	Rev. Pensions.						
Fonda, Jellis A., (or Tellis A.)	Pension for revolutionary services.	22	1	Petition	470	Rev. Pensions.						
Fonda, Jellis A., (or Tellis A.,) heirs of.	Compensation for property destroyed in revolution.	26	1	Petition	281	Rev. Claims.						
Fonda, Jellis A., (or Tellis A.,) heirs of.	Compensation for property destroyed in revolution.	26	2	Petition	77	Rev. Claims.						
Fonda, Jellis A., (or Tellis A.,) heirs of.	Compensation for property destroyed in revolution.	27	2	Petition	62	Rev. Claims	206	Adverse		Laid on table.		
Fonda, Lawrence	Compensation as assistant commissary in the revolution.	2	1	Petition	537					Referred to Secretary Treasury.		
Fonda, Lawrence	Compensation as assistant commissary in the revolution.	3	1	Rep. of Secretary Treasury.	11					Laid on table.		
Fonda, Lawrence	Compensation as assistant commissary in the revolution.	4	2	Petition	668	Claims	Feb. 9, 1797	Adverse		Laid on table.		
Fons, Joseph, widow of	Confirmation of title to land	22	1	Petition	64	Priv. Land Claims.	Dec. 27, 1831	Favorable	125	Passed	Passed	App'd June 25, 1832
Fontaine, James, heirs of	Compensation for horse taken by the Indians.	10	1	Petition	27	Claims.						
Fontaine, James, heirs of	Compensation for horse taken by the Indians.	10	2	Petition	417	Claims.						
Fontaine, Philip J	Remuneration for labor at Key West, Florida.	25	2	Petition	166	Commerce				Discharged; laid on table.		
Fontaine, Philip J	Remuneration for labor at Key West, Florida.	28	1	Petition	132	Commerce	526	Favorable; bill	401	Referred to Committee Whole House.		
Fontaine, Philip J	Remuneration for labor at Key West, Florida.	29	1	Petition	466	Commerce.						
Fontaine, Philip J	Remuneration for labor at Key West, Florida.	30	1	Petition	138	Commerce	601	Favorable; bill	484	Passed.		
Fontaine, Philip J	Remuneration for labor at Key West, Florida.	30	2	House bill from Senate.	143				484		Passed	App'd Jan. 8, 1849
Fontaine, William	Commutation pay for revolutionary services.	23	1	Petition	158	Rev. Claims.						
Fontaine, William	Commutation pay for revolutionary services.	23	2	Petition	56	Rev. Claims.						

List of private claims presented to the House of Representatives of the United States from the 1st to the 31st Congress, inclusive—Continued.

Names of claimants.	Nature or object of the claim.	Congress.	Session.	How brought before the House of Reps.	Page of journal.	To what committee of the House referred.	No. or date of the report.	Nature of the report.	No. of the bill.	How disposed of by the House of Reps.	How disposed of by the Senate.	Date of the act of Congress, and remarks.
Fontaine, William	Commutation pay for revolutionary services.	24	1	Petition	62	Rev. Claims	May 17, 1836	Favorable; bill	635	Referred to Committee Whole House.		
Fontaine, William	Commutation pay for revolutionary services.	25	2	Petition	70	Rev. Claims	429	Favorable; bill	438	Passed.		
Fontaine, William	Commutation pay for revolutionary services.	25	3	Petition	84	Rev. Claims	14	Favorable; bill	912	Referred to Committee Whole House.		
Fontaine, William	Commutation pay for revolutionary services.	26	1	Petition	164	Rev. Claims	May 25, 1840	Adverse	......	Laid on table.		
Fontaine, William	Commutation pay for revolutionary services.	27	2	Petition	61	Rev. Claims	375	Adverse	......	Laid on table.		
Foochee, Elijah	Pension for revolutionary services.	25	2	Resolution	213	Rev. Pensions	880	Favorable	786	Passed.		
Foochee, Elijah	Pension for revolutionary services.	25	3	Resolution	88	Rev. Pensions	198	Favorable	1060	Passed		
Foochee, Elijah	Pension for revolutionary services.	26	1	Petition	171	Rev. Pensions	125	Favorable	135	Passed	Indef. postp'd.	
Foochee, Elijah	Pension for revolutionary services.	27	2	Petition	703	Rev. Pensions	784	Adverse	......	Laid on table.		
Foord, E. G., *et al.*	(See Edward Davenport)	24	2	....	315							
Foord, E. G.	Indemnity for French spoliations prior to 1800.	26	1	Memorial	182	Foreign Affairs	343	Favorable	319	Referred to Committee Whole House.		
Foot, Charles	Pension	20	1	Petition	484	Military Pensions.						
Foot, Jesse	Pension for revolutionary services.	16	1	Resolution	63	Rev. Pensions	Jan. 14, 1820	Adverse	......	Laid on table.		
Foot, Lyman, widow of	Aid in consideration of death of husband.	30	1	Petition	202	Rev. Pensions	301	Adverse	......	Laid on table.		
Foot, Mary	(See Lyman Foot, widow of)	30	1	....	202							
Foote, Erastus	(See H. Woodbury, attorney of)	31	1	....	407							
Foote, George, widow of	Pension for revolutionary services.	28	1	Petition	585	Rev. Pensions.						
Foote, George, widow of	Pension for revolutionary services.	28	2	Petition	206	Rev. Pensions.						
Foote, Gervis	Indemnity for losses on government contract.	27	3	Petition	152	Claims.						
Foote, Gervis	Indemnity for losses on government contract.	28	1	Petition	70	Claims	88	Favorable	103	Passed	Passed	App'd June 15, 1844
Foote, Lucretia	(See George Foote, widow of)	28	1	....	585							
Footman, *et al.*	Extra compensation for services in Treasury Department.	3	1	Petition	88	Select	47	Adverse.				
Fooy, John Henry	Confirmation of title to land	22	1	Memorial	62	Public Lands	Feb. 28, 1832	Favorable	425	Passed	Passed	App'd June 25, 1832
Fopless, John C	Invalid pension	8	2	Petition	56	Claims	....	....	......	Discharged; referred to Com. Whole House.		
Forbes, Abraham	Indemnity for property confiscated in Canada in war of 1812.	15	2	Petition	246	Claims.						
Forbes, Abraham	Indemnity for property confiscated in Canada in war of 1812.	16	1	Petition	153	Claims	Jan. 26, 1820	Adverse	......	Leave to withdraw.		
Forbes, Abraham	Indemnity for property confiscated in Canada in war of 1812.	17	1	Petition	141	Claims.						
Forbes, Abraham	Indemnity for property confiscated in Canada in war of 1812.	18	2	Petition	46	Claims.						
Forbes, Abraham	Indemnity for property confiscated in Canada in war of 1812.	19	2	Petition	64	Claims	Jan. 4, 1827	Adverse	......	Laid on table.		
Forbes, Abraham	Indemnity for property confiscated in Canada in war of 1812.	20	1	Petition	224	Priv. Land Claims	....	....	......	Discharged; laid on table.		
Forbes, Abraham	Indemnity for property confiscated in Canada in war of 1812.	21	1	Petition	51	Claims	Mar. 2, 1830	Adverse	......	Laid on table.		
Forbes, Abraham	Indemnity for property confiscated in Canada in war of 1812.	21	2	Petition	62	Priv. Land Claims.	Feb. 10, 1831	Favorable; bill	616	Passed.		
Forbes, Abraham	Indemnity for property confiscated in Canada in war of 1812.	22	1	Petition	224	Priv. Land Claims.	239	Favorable; bill	321	Referred to Committee Whole House.		

List of private claims presented to the House of Representatives of the United States from the 1st to the 31st Congress, inclusive—Continued.

Names of claimants.	Nature or object of the claim.	Congress.	Session.	How brought before the House of Reps.	Page of journal.	To what committee of the House referred.	No. or date of the report.	Nature of the report.	No. of the bill.	How disposed of by the House of Reps.	How disposed of by the Senate.	Date of the act of Congress, and remarks.
Forbes, Abraham	Indemnity for property confiscated in Canada in war of 1812.	23	1	Petition	48	Priv. Land Claims.	22	Favorable; bill	22	Passed.		
Forbes, Abraham	Indemnity for property confiscated in Canada in war of 1812.	23	1	Petition (2)	122	Claims	Jan. 23, 1834	Adverse		Laid on table.		
Forbes, Abraham	Indemnity for property confiscated in Canada in war of 1812.	24	1	Petition	112	Priv. Land Claims.	118	Favorable; bill	138	Passed	Passed, with amendment.	App'd June 28, 1836
Forbes, Abraham	Indemnity for property confiscated in Canada in war of 1812.	24	2	Petition	210	Priv. Land Claims.	170	Favorable; bill	888	Referred to Committee Whole House.		
Forbes, Abraham	Indemnity for property confiscated in Canada in war of 1812.	25	2	Petition	43	Priv. Land Claims.						
Forbes, Abraham	Indemnity for property confiscated in Canada in war of 1812.	25	3	Petition	119	Claims	208	Adverse		Laid on table.		
Forbes, Abraham	Indemnity for property confiscated in Canada in war of 1812.	29	1	Petition	103	Priv. Land Claims.	780	Adverse		Laid on table.		
Forbes, Abraham	Indemnity for property confiscated in Canada in war of 1812.	30	1	Petition	936	Priv. Land Claims.						
Forbes, Barbara	(See William Forbes, widow of)	25	2		116							
Forbes, Daniel	Compensation for revolutionary services.	2	1	Petition	452					Referred to Secretary of War.		
Forbes, Daniel	Pension	2	2	Rep. of Secretary of War.	636					Laid on table.		
Forbes, Daniel	Pension	3	1	Rep. of Sec. War.	131	Select	May 26, 1794	Favorable; bill	62	Passed	Passed	App'd June 7, 1794
Forbes, Elisha	Pension	9	2	House bill	608	Claims	Feb. 24, 1807	Favorable; bill	216	Passed	Passed	App'd March 3, 1807
Forbes, Gordon	Indemnity for property destroyed during war of 1812.	17	1	Petition	68	Claims	Mar. 25, 1822	Adverse		Laid on table.		
Forbes, Gordon	Indemnity for property destroyed during war of 1812.	17	2	Petition	44	Claims				Discharged; leave to withdraw.		
Forbes, Gordon	Indemnity for property destroyed during war of 1812.	18	1	Petition	93	Claims	41	Adverse		Referred to Committee Whole House.		
Forbes, Hugh	Pension	19	1	Petition	34	Rev. Pensions	164	Adverse		Laid on table.		
Forbes, James G. & Ralph B.	For drawback of duties on certain merchandise.	10	1	Petition	158	Com. and Manuf.						
Forbes, James G. & Ralph B.	For drawback of duties on certain merchandise.	10	2	Petition	360	Com. and Manuf.						
Forbes, James G. & Ralph B.	For drawback of duties on certain merchandise.	26	1	Petition	293	Commerce	30	Favorable; bill	49	Passed	Passed with amendment.	App'd July 20, 1840
Forbes, Jehiel	(See William Liffengacle, *et al*)	18	1		526							
Forbes, Jehiel, & Son	(See Russell Hotchkiss, *et al*)	22	1		30							
Forbes, Jehiel	Indemnity for French spoliations prior to 1800.	26	1	Memorial	182	Foreign Affairs	343	Favorable; bill	319	Referred to Committee Whole House.		
Forbes, John W	Settlement of his accounts as consul	14	1	Petition	400	Select	Feb. 26, 1816	Favorable		Passed	Passed	App'd March 19, 1816
Forbes, John, & Co.	Confirmation of title to land	15	1	Petition	226	Priv. Land Claims.				Leave to withdraw.		
Forbes, John, & Co.	Confirmation of title to land	19	1	Petition	74	Select.						
Forbes, John, & Co.	Confirmation of title to land	22	1	Letter of Secretary Treasury.	813	Public Lands.						
Forbes, John, & Co.	Confirmation of title to land	24	1	Petition	671	Priv. Land Claims.	July 2, 1836	Favorable	747	Referred to Committee Whole House.		
Forbes, John, representatives of.	Confirmation of title to land	18	1	Senate bill	339	Priv. Land Claims.	Mar. 26, 1824	Adverse	S. 55	Referred to Committee Whole House.		
Forbes, Justin, *et al.*	Indemnity for losses as mail contractors.	24	1	Petition	914	P. Of. and P. Roads.						
Forbes, Justin, *et al.*	Indemnity for losses as mail contractors.	24	2	Report	47	P. Of. & P. Roads.						

List of private claims presented to the House of Representatives of the United States from the 1st to the 31st Congress, inclusive—Continued.

Names of claimants.	Nature or object of the claim.	Congress.	Session.	How brought before the House of Reps.	Page of journal.	To what committee of the House referred.	No. or date of the report.	Nature of the report.	No. of the bill.	How disposed of by the House of Reps.	How disposed of by the Senate.	Date of the act of Congress, and remarks.
Forbes, Lucy	(See William Forbes, widow of)	22	2		40							
Forbes, Samuel	Pension	19	1		407	Military Pensions	April 20, 1826	Adverse		Discharged; laid on table.		
Forbes, Samuel	Pension	22	1		329	Military Pensions.						
Forbes, William, heirs of	Indemnity for houses destroyed by the British.	15	1	Report of Com. of Claims.	316	Claims.						
Forbes, William, heirs of	Indemnity for houses destroyed by the British.	17	2	Report of Com. of Claims.	197	Claims	Feb. 5, 1823	Adverse		Laid on table.		
Forbes, William, heirs of	Indemnity for houses destroyed by the British.	18	1	Petition	168	Claims.						
Forbes, William, heirs of	Indemnity for houses destroyed by the British.	20	1	Petition	195	Claims	Feb. 20, 1828	Adverse		Laid on table.		
Forbes, William, heirs of	Indemnity for houses destroyed by the British.	20	2	Rep't of last sess.	65	Whole House.						
Forbes, William, heirs of	Indemnity for houses destroyed by the British.	21	1	Petition	56	Claims	May 11, 1830	Adverse		Laid on table.		
Forbes, William, heirs of	Indemnity for houses destroyed by the British.	24	1	Petition	50	Claims	133	Favorable	145	Passed	Passed	App'd July 1, 1836
Forbes, William	Restoration of pension	17	1	Petition	196	Rev. Pensions.						
Forbes, William, widow of, (Barbara.)	Arrears of pension	25	1	Petition	116	Rev. Pensions		Favorable	456			
Forbes, William, widow of, (Barbara.)	Arrears of pension	25	2	Petition	87	Rev. Pensions				Discharged; laid on table.		
Forbes, William, widow of, (Barbara.)	Arrears of pension	26	1	Petition	171	Rev. Pensions				Discharged; laid on table.		
Forbes, William, widow of, (Barbara.)	Arrears of pension	26	2	Petition	134	Rev. Pensions				Discharged; laid on table.		
Forbes, William, widow of, (Lucy.)	Pension for revolutionary services	12	2	Petition	40	Rev. Pensions				Discharged; laid on table.		
Forbes, William, widow of, (Lucy)	Pension for revolutionary services	28	2	Petition	149	Rev. Pensions.						
Forbes, William, widow of, (Lucy.)	Pension for revolutionary services	29	1	Petition	149	Rev. Pensions				Discharged: laid on table.		
Forbes, William, and Alexander.	(See Eustace Barron, *et al*)	31	1		256		16					
Forbes, John, & Co	(See James Innerarity)	24	1		671							
Force, Joseph	Pension	21	1	Petition	471	Military Pensions.						
Force, Peter, (a seaman)	Case not stated	19	2	Petition	53	Ways and Means.						
Ford, Amaziah	Arrears of pension	31	1	Petition	193	Invalid Pensions	101	Adverse		Laid on table.		
Ford, Augustus, (N. Y)	Compensation for making chart of Lake Ontario.	27	2	Petition	246	Claims.						
Ford, Augustus, (N. Y)	Compensation for making chart of Lake Ontario.	28	1	Petition	245	Claims.						
Ford, Augustus, (N. Y)	Compensation for making chart of Lake Ontario.	28	2	Petition	46	Claims.						
Ford, Augustus, (N. Y)	Compensation for making chart of Lake Ontario.	29	1	Petition	116	Claims.						
Ford, Augustus, (N. Y)	Compensation for making chart of Lake Ontario.	29	2	Petition	149	Claims.						
Ford, Augustus, (N. Y)	Compensation for making chart of Lake Ontario.	31	1	Petition	891	Claims.						
Ford, Augustus, (N. Y)	Reimbursement of certain money erroneously paid.	30	1	Petition	664	Claims	669	Favorable; bill	528	Referred to Committee Whole House.		

List of private claims presented to the House of Representatives of the United States from the 1st to the 31st Congress, inclusive—Continued.

Names of claimants.	Nature or object of the claim.	Congress.	Session.	How brought before the House of Reps.	Page of journal.	To what committee of the House referred.	No. or date of the report.	Nature of the report.	No. of the bill.	How disposed of by the House of Reps.	How disposed of by the Senate.	Date of the act of Congress, and remarks.
Ford, Augustus, (N. Y.)	Reimbursement of certain money erroneously paid.	30	2	House bill	318	Whole House			528	Passed.		
Ford, David	Confirmation of title to land	17	1	Petition	248	Public Lands				Disch'd; laid on table.		
Ford, David	Confirmation of title to land	17	2	Petition	74	Public Lands.						
Ford, David	Confirmation of title to land	20	2	Petition	205	Priv. Land Claims.						
Ford, Eli, and Joseph M.	Pre-emption right to land	20	1	Petition	33	Public Lands.						
Ford, Henry	To correct an error in entry of land	23	1	Petition	499	Public Lands.						
Ford, Hezekiah	Additional compensation as a revolutionary officer.	18	2	Petition	134	Rev. Claims	Feb. 16, 1825	Adverse		Laid on table.		
Ford, Jacob	Pension for revolutionary services.	26	1	Petition	324	Rev. Pensions				Disch'd; laid on table.		
Ford, James	Pension	3	2	Rep. of Sec. War	278	Claims	Feb. 28, 1795	Favorable	130	Passed	Postponed.	
Ford, James	Pension	4	1	Rep. of Sec. War	445	Claims	Mar. 4, 1796	Favorable	156	Passed	Passed	App'd April 20, 1796
Ford, James, *et al.*	(See James McFarland, *et al*)	15	2		200							
Ford, James, sen.	Pension for revolutionary services.	28	1	Petition	550	Rev. Pensions.						
Ford, James, sen.	Pension for revolutionary services.	28	2	Petition	58	Rev. Pensions.						
Ford, Jesse	Leave to locate a land warrant	17	1	Petition	27	Priv. Land Claims.						
Ford, Jesse	Leave to locate a land warrant	17	2	Petition	75	Priv. Land Claims.	Jan. 3, 1823	Adverse		Laid on table.		
Ford, Jesse	Leave to locate a land warrant	18	1	Petition	360	Priv. Land Claims.						
Ford, Jonathan W.	(See George Johnson, *et al.*)	17	1		386							
Ford, John G.	Pension for revolutionary services.	24	2	Petition	399	Rev. Pensions.						
Ford, John Gerard	Compensation for services as clerk in surveyor's office, Philadelphia, in 1835.	26	1	Petition	358	Ways and Means	708	Adverse		Laid on table.		
Ford, John Gerard	Compensation for services as clerk in surveyor's office, Philadelphia, in 1835.	27	2	Petition	948	Ways and Means	987	Favorable	568	Referred to Committee Whole House.		
Ford, John Gerard	Compensation for services as clerk in surveyor's office, Philadelphia, in 1835.	27	3	House bill	90	Whole House			568	Passed.		
Ford, John N., and John Scrivener.	Extra compensation for services in the General Land Office.	29	1	Memorial	588	Claims	631	Adverse		Laid on table.		
Ford, John	Prize-money, Ketch Intrepid	19	2	House bill	98	Naval Affairs	74	With amend.	70	Referred to Committee Whole House.		
Ford, John	(See widow of Stephen Decatur and others.)	20	1		295		201		S. 50	Referred to Committee Whole House.		
Ford, Joseph	Pension for revolutionary services.	22	1	Resolution	436	Rev. Pensions.						
Ford, Mahlon	Pension	12	1	Rep't Committee.	361	Claims	June 8, 1812	Favorable	138	Passed	Passed	App'd July 5, 1812
Ford, Mahlon, widow of.	Arrears of pension	17	2	Petition	81	Rev. Pensions	Feb. 7, 1823	Favorable	283	Passed	Passed	App'd March 3, 1823
Ford, Nathan	Pension	12	1	Rep't Committee.	361	Claims	June 8, 1812	Favorable	138	Passed	Passed	App'd July 5, 1812
Ford, Nathan	Indemnity for property destroyed in war of 1812.	15	1	Petition	332	Claims.						
Ford, Nathan	Indemnity for property destroyed in war of 1812.	15	2	Senate bill	280	Claims	Feb. 26, 1819	Favorable	S. 52	Referred to Committee Whole House.		
Ford, Nathan	Indemnity for property destroyed in war of 1812.	16	2	Senate bill	176	Claims	Feb. 5, 1821	Adverse	S. 27	Laid on table.		
Ford, Nathan	Indemnity for property destroyed in war of 1812.	17	1	Petition	133	Claims	77	Adverse		Referred to Committee Whole House.		
Ford, Nathan	Indemnity for property destroyed in war of 1812.	17	2	Rep't of last sess.	102	Claims.						
Ford, Nathan	Indemnity for property destroyed in war of 1812.	18	1	Petition	81	Claims.						
Ford, Nathaniel	Confirmation of title to land	21	1	Petition	41	Priv. Land Claims.	409	Favorable	482	Referred to Committee Whole House.		

List of private claims presented to the House of Representatives of the United States from the 1st to the 31st Congress, inclusive—Continued.

Names of claimants.	Nature or object of the claim.	Congress.	Session.	How brought before the House of Reps.	Page of journal.	To what committee of the House referred.	No. or date of the report.	Nature of the report.	No. of the bill.	How disposed of by the House of Reps.	How disposed of by the Senate.	Date of the act of Congress, and remarks.
Ford, Nathaniel	Confirmation of title to land	22	1	Petition	446	Priv. Land Claims.	Mar. 6, 1832	Adverse		Laid on table.		
Ford, Peter	Compensat'n for property destroyed in the war of 1812.	20	1	Petition	438	Claims	262	Favorable	289	Referred to Committee Whole House.		
Ford, Peter	Compensat'n for property destroyed in the war of 1812.	21	1	Petition	35	Claims	5	Favorable	5	Passed	Passed	App'd Feb. 11, 1830
Ford, Robert	Pension	1	3	Petition and rep't Sec. of War.	340					Laid on table.		
Ford, Robert G., *et al.*	Payment for forage, &c., furnished United States.	27	2	Petition	515	Claims.						
Ford, Robert G., *et al.*	Payment for forage, &c., furnished United States.	27	3	Petition	58	Claims	15	Favorable	638	Passed	Passed	App'd March 1, 1843
Ford, Sophia B.	(See Mahlon Ford, widow of)	17	2	Petition	81							
Ford, Stephen C.	Indemnity for losses on goods furnished United States.	28	2	Petition	113	Claims	32	Adverse		Laid on table.		
Ford, Stephen C.	Payment of amount due by United States troops.	29	1	Petition	567	Claims	630	Adverse		Laid on table.		
Ford, Theodosius	Pension for revolutionary services.	3	1	Petition	103					Referred to Secretary War.		
Ford, Theodosius	Pension for revolutionary services.	3	2	Rep. of Secretary War.	278					Laid on table.		
Ford, Thomas	For liquidation of certain evidences of public debt.	15	2	Petition	196	Rev. Claims	Jan. 28, 1819	Adverse		Laid on table.		
Ford, William	Restoration of pension	25	2	Petition	405	Rev. Pensions	708	Favorable	682	Passed.		
Ford, William	Restoration of pension	25	3	Petition	87	Rev. Pensions	70	Favorable	948	Passed	Passed	App'd March 3, 1839
Ford, William D.	Additional pay for services in war of 1812	21	1	Documents	321	Military Affairs				Discharged; laid on table.		
Ford, William P.	Payment for horse, &c., turned over to government in 1836.	26	1	Resolution	1023	Military Affairs.						
Ford, Willtam P.	Payment for horse, &c., turned over to government in 1836.	26	2	Resolution	79	Military Affairs	93	Favorable	599	Referred to Committee Whole House.		
Fordney, John	Pension	19	1	Petition	175	Military Pensions	164	Adverse		Laid on table.		
Fore, Right	Pension	22	1	Petition	88	Invalid Pensions.						
Fore, Right	Pension	22	2	Resolution	60	Invalid Pensions.						
Fore, Right	Pension	23	1	Resolution	137	Invalid Pensions.						
Foreman, ———, *et al.*	Extra compensation as clerks of Treasury Department.	3	1	Petition	88	Select	47	Adverse.				
Foreman, Alexander	Increase of pension	15	1	Petition	130	Rev. Pensions.						
Foreman, Alexander	Increase of pension	15	2	Petition	121	Rev. Pensions	Jan. 4, 1819	Adverse		Rejected.		
Foreman, Anthony, (an Indian.)	Payment for slaves stolen	21	1	Petition	524	Claims	367	Favorable	425	Referred to Committee Whole House.		
Foreman, Anthony, (an Indian.)	Payment for slaves stolen	21	2	House bill	339	Whole House			425	Passed.		
Foreman, Anthony, (an Indian.)	Payment for slaves stolen	22	1	Petition	43	Claims	Dec. 19, 1831	Favorable	22	Passed	Passed	App'd March 15, 1832
Foreman, Charles	Compensati'n for property destroyed by the enemy.	29	1	Petition	101	Claims	65	Adverse		Laid on table.		
Foreman, Charles	Compensati'n for property destroyed by the enemy.	29	2	Petition	110	Claims.						
Foreman, Charles	Compensati'n for property destroyed by the enemy.	30	1	Petition	68	Claims	54	Adverse		Laid on table.		
Foreman, Charles	Compensati'n for property destroyed by the enemy.	31	1	Petition	510	Claims.						

List of private claims presented to the House of Representatives of the United States from the 1st to the 31st Congress, inclusive—Continued.

Names of claimants.	Nature or object of the claim.	Congress.	Session.	How brought before the House of Reps.	Page of journal.	To what committee of the House referred.	No. or date of the report.	Nature of the report.	No. of the bill.	How disposed of by the House of Reps.	How disposed of by the Senate.	Date of the act of Congress, and remarks.
Foreman, James	Compensation for recapture of an American ship.	19	2	Petition	317	Naval Affairs.						
Foreman, James	Compensation for recapture of an American ship.	20	1	Petition	89	Naval Affairs	Jan. 25, 1828	Adverse	......	Laid on table.		
Foreman, John	Arrears of pay, &c., for military services.	22	1	Resolution	247	Claims.						
Foreman, Robert S.	Bounty land	18	1	Petition	97	Priv. Land Claims.	36	Favorable	75	Passed	Passed	App'd May 19, 1824
Forester, Arthur	Payment for work done on Cumberland road.	23	1	Res. and docs.	589	Claims	455	Adverse.				
Forman, F.	(See Levi Davis, *et al.*)	25	2	....	541							
Forman, Nathan and Obediah.	Compensation for revolutionary services.	17	2	Petition	47	Rev. Claims	Dec. 20, 1822	Adverse	......	Rejected.		
Forman, William G., administrator of.	Confirmation of title to land	14	2	Petition	143	Priv. Land Claims.						
Forman, William G., administrator of.	Confirmation of title to land	16	1	Petition	47	Priv. Land Claims.	75	Favorable	101	Passed	Passed, with amendment.	App'd May 8, 1820
Formby, Nathan	Pension for revolutionary services.	15	1	Petition	156	Rev. Pensions.						
Forrest, Andrew	Reimbursement of money advanced to marines at Washington city.	24	1	Petition	429	Claims.						
Forrest, Andrew	Reimbursement of money advanced to marines at Washington city.	27	2	Senate bill	1126	Naval Affairs	Aug. 10, 1842	Favorable	S. 243	Passed	....	App'd Aug. 29, 1842
Forrest, Daniel D.	Indemnity for French spoliations prior to 1800.	26	1	Memorial	182	Foreign Affairs.	343	Favorable; bill	319	Referred to Committee Whole House.		
Forrest, Dudley, widow of	Pension	21	1	Petition	413	Naval Affairs.						
Forrest, Ebenezer	Pension for revolutionary services.	16	1	Petition	237	Rev. Pensions	April 6, 1820	Adverse	......	Laid on table.		
Forrest, Ebenezer	Pension for revolutionary services.	19	1	Petition	250	Military Pensions.	164	Adverse	......	Laid on table.		
Forrest, Capt. F.	For amount due him as arrearages of pay.	31	1	Petition	1039	Naval Affairs.						
Forrest, Capt. F.	For amount due him as arrearages of pay.	31	2	Petition	446	Naval Affairs	March 3, 1851	Favorable	494	Referred to Committee Whole House.		
Forrest, James	Restoration of vessel seized under non-importation act.	12	1	Petition	25	Com. and Manuf.						
Forrest, John	Pension	29	1	Petition	856	Invalid Pensions.						
Forrest, John	Pension	29	2	Petition	86	Invalid Pensions.						
Forrest, John	Pension	30	1	Petition	457	Invalid Pensions	836	Adverse	......	Laid on table.		
Forrest, John	Pension	30	2	Memorial	116	Invalid Pensions	....	....	......	Discharged; laid on table.		
Forrest, John	Pension	31	1	Petition	298	Invalid Pensions	73	Adverse	......	Laid on table.		
Forrest, Joseph	Compensation for use of vessel by government.	12	2	Petition	654	Claims	....	....	......	Discharged; leave to withdraw.		
Forrest, Joseph	Compensation for use of vessel by government.	13	1	Petition	20	Claims	....	....	......	Discharged.		
Forrest, Joseph	Compensation for use of vessel by government.	13	2	Petition	203	Claims	Feb. 7, 1814	Adverse	......	Laid on table.		
Forrest, Joseph	Compensation for use of vessel by government.	13	3	Petition	474	Claims	11	Adverse.				
Forrest, Joseph	Compensation for use of vessel by government.	14	1	Petition	54	Claims.						
Forrest, Joseph	Compensation for use of vessel by government.	14	2	Petition	47	Claims	....	....	......	Discharged; referred to Secretary State.		
Forrest, Joseph	Compensation for use of vessel by government.	15	1	Rep. of Secretary State.	37	Claims	Dec. 16, 1817	Adverse	......	Leave to withdraw.		

List of private claims presented to the House of Representatives of the United States from the 1st to the 31st Congress, inclusive—Continued.

Names of claimants.	Nature or object of the claim.	Congress.	Session.	How brought before the House of Reps.	Page of journal.	To what committee of the House referred.	No. or date of the report.	Nature of the report.	No. of the bill.	How disposed of by the House of Reps.	How disposed of by the Senate.	Date of the act of Congress, and remarks.
Forrest, Joseph	Compensation for use of vessel by government.	18	1	Senate bill	568	Claims	May 26, 1824	With't amend.	28	Laid on table.		
Forrest, Joseph	Compensation for use of vessel by government.	18	2	Senate bill	76	Claims	Jan. 19, 1825	With't amend.	6	Passed	....	App'd March 3, 1825
Forrest, Mary T.	(See Dudley Forrest, widow of)	21	1		413							
Forrest, Richard	Increase of compensation as postmaster.	4	2	Petition	667	Whole House		By bill	205			
Forrest, Uriah, heirs of	Half-pay and arrears for revolutionary services.	23	1	Petition	585	Invalid Pensions.						
Forrest, Uriah, heirs of	Half-pay and arrears for revolutionary services.	24	1	Petition	62	Rev. Claims				Discharged; laid on table.		
Forrest, Uriah, heirs of	Half-pay and arrears for revolutionary services.	25	2	Petition	69	Rev. Claims.						
Forrest, Uriah, heirs of	Half-pay and arrears for revolutionary services.	25	3	Petition	84	Rev. Claims.						
Forrest, Uriah, heirs of	Half-pay and arrears for revolutionary services.	26	1	Petition	164	Rev. Claims	444	Adverse		Laid on table.		
Forrest, Uriah, heirs of	Half-pay and arrears for revolutionary services.	27	2	Petition	61	Rev. Claims	374	Adverse		Laid on table.		
Forrest, Uriah, heirs of	Half-pay and arrears for revolutionary services.	28	1	Petition	367	Rev. Claims.						
Forrest, Uriah, heirs of	Half-pay and arrears for revolutionary services.	28	2	Petition	59	Rev. Claims.						
Forrest, William	(See Joshua W. Prout, administrator of.)	18	2		66							
Forrester, Arthur	Compensation for work done on Cumberland road.	23	1	Resolution	589	Claims	455	Adverse		Laid on table.		
Forrester, Robert, administrator of.	For the issue of scrip for forfeited land.	21	1	Petition	319	Public Lands				Discharged; laid on table.		
Forrester, Robert, (Ohio)	Pension	22	1	Petition	575	Invalid Pensions.						
Forrester, Simon	Remission of duties on hemp	5	2	Petition	105	Com. and Manuf.	Jan. 2, 1798	Adverse		Laid on table.		
Forrester, Simon	Release of ship Resolution and cargo, seized for violation of non-importation act.	12	2	Petition	552	Ways and Means.						
Forstall, Edmund J., and others.	(See Hope & Co., of Amsterdam)	27	2		1062							
Forster, Robert	(See Canadian refugees)	4	2		614							
Forsyth, A. R.	Payment due from Ottowa Indians	29	1	Memorial	160	Indian Affairs	287	Adverse		Laid on table.		
Forsyth, A. R., and others	Payment due from Ottowa Indians	29	1	Memorial	160	Indian Affairs	287	Adverse		Laid on table.		
Forsyth, Fanny	(See Robert Forsyth, widow of)	4	2		627							
Forsyth & Hull	(See John E. Hunt, and others)	27	2		334							
Forsyth, James H.	(See John E. Hunt, and others)	27	2		334							
Forsyth, Jesse	For a grant of land	30	1	Petition	1013	Public Lands.						
Forsyth, John R.	(See Miguel Eslava, heirs of)	24	1		436							
Forsyth, John, heirs of	Compensation for cotton destroyed in Georgia.	28	1	Petition	480	Claims	260	Favorable; bill	190	Referred to Committee Whole House.		
Forsyth, John, heirs of	Compensation for cotton destroyed in Georgia.	30	1	Petition	69	Claims	8	Adverse		Laid on table.		
Forsyth, Joseph	Pension	21	1	Petition	231	Military Pensions	Feb. 15, 1830	General bill	248	Passed	Indef. postp'd.	
Forsyth, Jos., and T. Twitchell.	For a grant of land	20	1	Petition	581	Public Lands				Discharged; laid on table.		
Forsyth, Jos., and T. Twitchell.	For a grant of land	20	2	Petition	75	Public Lands	Dec. 31, 1828	Adverse		Laid on table.		

List of private claims presented to the House of Representatives of the United States from the 1st to the 31st Congress, inclusive—Continued.

83

Names of claimants.	Nature or object of the claim.	Congress.	Session.	How brought before the House of Reps.	Page of journal.	To what committee of the House referred.	No. or date of the report.	Nature of the report.	No. of the bill.	How disposed of by the House of Reps.	How disposed of by the Senate.	Date of the act of Congress, and remarks.
Forsyth & Kinzie	(See Kenzie & Forsyth)	12	2		671							
Forsyth, R. A.	(See John E. Hunt, and others)	27	2		334							
Forsyth, Robert, heirs of	Pension for revolutionary services	3	1	Senate bill	108	Whole House			S. 8	Rejected.		
Forsyth, Robert, heirs of	Pension for revolutionary services	4	1	Petition	528	Claims.						
Forsyth, Robert, heirs of	Pension for revolutionary services	4	2	Resol'n and docs.	614	Claims.						
Forsyth, Robert, (Ga.)	Compensation for services as marshal of Georgia.	3	1	Resolution	176	Select	May 24, 1794	Favorable; bill	54	Passed	Passed, with amendment.	App'd June 7, 1794
Forsyth, Robert, widow of	Release of title to certain lands	4	2	Petition and rep't of Att'y Gen.	529	Whole House	Jan. 12, 1797	Adverse		Leave to withdraw.		
Forsyth, Robert, heirs of	For relief under the acts in reference to Virginia land claims.	22	2	Resolution	65	Rev. Claims.						
Forsyth, Robert A.	Compensation for collecting Indians in Greenville, Ohio, in 1815.	21	1	Petition	262	Claims	285	Favorable; bill	337	Referred to Committee Whole House.		
Forsyth, Robert A.	Compensation for collecting Indians in Greenville, Ohio, in 1815.	21	2	House bill	340	Whole House			337	Passed.		
Forsyth, Robert A.	Compensation for collecting Indians in Greenville, Ohio, in 1815.	22	1	Petition	43	Claims	Dec. 19, 1831	Favorable; bill	11	Passed	Passed	App'd Jan. 23, 1832
Forsyth, William	Compensation for property taken for public use.	21	1	Petition	376	Claims	321	Favorable; bill	377	Referred to Committee Whole House.		
Forsyth, William	Compensation for property taken for public use.	22	1	Petition	43	Claims	Dec. 19, 1831	Favorable; bill	15	Passed	Passed	App'd Jan. 19, 1832
Fort, Abraham & Jacob, jr.	Compensation for property taken for use of the government.	2	2	Petition	682					Laid on table.		
Fort, Alston	Pension for revolutionary services	13	3	Petition	543	Rev. Pensions.						
Fort, Alston	Pension for revolutionary services	14	1	Petition	100	Rev. Pensions	April 23, 1816	Favorable; bill	171	Passed	Passed	App'd April 30, 1816
Fort, Benjamin	Pension for revolutionary services	20	1	Resolution	348	Military Pensions.						
Fort, Christopher	(See Melchior Baker, and others)	19	1		416							
Fortin, Eliza M.	Pension	28	1	Petition	256	Naval Affairs.						
Fortin, Eliza M.	Pension	28	2	Petition	70					Referred to Committee Whole House.		
Fortin, Eliza M.	Pension	29	1	Petition	70	Naval Affairs.						
Fortner, Thomas	Confirmation of title to land	14	2	Petition	372	Priv. Land Claims.						
Fortune, C. C.	Compensation for mail service	31	1	Petition	809	P. Of. and P. Roads.						
Fortune, Richard, heirs of	Bounty land for revolutionary services.	25	2	Petition	771	Rev. Claims	975	Adverse		Laid on table.		
Fortune, schooner, owners of, by agent.	Fishing bounty	25	2	Petition	40	Commerce	85	Favorable; bill	101	Passed	Passed, with amendment.	App'd June 12, 1838
Fosdick, Abigail	Compensation for her dower in land taken by United States for debt.	16	2	Petition	212	Claims.						
Fosdick, James	(See Stephen Waite and others.)	12	2		643							
Fosdick, Nathaniel F.	Release from excessive judgment obtained against him by United States.	10	1	Petition	195	Ways and Means.						
Fosdick, Nathaniel F.	Release from excessive judgment obtained against him by United States.	10	2	Petition	381	Ways and Means.						
Fosdick, Nathaniel F.	Release from excessive judgment obtained against him by United States.	11	1	Petition	17	Ways and Means	June 14, 1809	Rep. not found		Laid on table.		
Fosdick, Nathaniel F.	Release from excessive judgment obtained against him by United States.	11	3	Senate bill	499	Select	Feb. 8, 1811	Favorable; bill	S. 53	Passed	Passed	App'd Feb. 13, 1811
Foss, Elias	Pension for revolutionary services	18	2	Petition	54	Rev. Pensions	52	Adverse		Laid on table.		

List of private claims presented to the House of Representatives of the United States from the 1st to the 31st Congress, inclusive—Continued.

Names of claimants.	Nature or object of the claim.	Congress.	Session.	How brought before the House of Reps.	Page of journal.	To what committee of the House referred.	No. or date of the report.	Nature of the report.	No. of the bill.	How disposed of by the House of Reps.	How disposed of by the Senate.	Date of the act of Congress, and remarks.
Foss, Isaiah	Pension	21	2	Petition	336	Military Pensions.						
Foss, John, heirs of	Arrears of pension	30	1	Petition	460	Rev. Pensions.						
Foss, Joshua	Pension for revolutionary services.	15	1	Petition	31	Rev. Pensions				Referred to Secretary War.		
Foss, Nahum, and others	(See John Foss, heirs of.)	30	1		460							
Foss, Ruth	Continuation of pension	28	1	Petition	950	Whole House.						
Fossett, John	For allowance of certain expenses for mail service.	28	1	Petition	61	P. Of. and P. Roads.	66	Adverse		Laid on table.		
Fossett, John	For allowance of certain expenses for mail service.	28	2	Rep't Committee	230	P. Of. & P. Roads.						
Fossett, John	For allowance of certain expenses for mail service.	29	1	Petition	105	P. Of. and P. Roads.						
Fossett, John	For allowance of certain expenses for mail service.	29	2	Petition	309	P. Of. and P. Roads.						
Foster, Aaron D.	Pension	24	1	Petition	52	Invalid Pensions.	Feb. 18, 1836	Adverse		Laid on table.		
Foster, Abijah	Pension	27	2	Documents	329	Invalid Pensions.						
Foster, Allen	Compensation for improvement in machinery for making fire-arms.	24	2	Petition	72	Claims.						
Foster, Allen	Compensation for improvement in machinery for making fire-arms.	25	2	Petition	333	Military Affairs				Discharged; laid on table.		
Foster, Allen	Compensation for improvement in machinery for making fire-arms.	27	3	Petition	239	Claims.						
Foster, Andrew	(See Foster & Giraud.)	11	1		37							
Foster, Anthony	(See John Pitchlynn, attorney of.)	5	3		434							
Foster, Augustus G.	(See Walley & Foster.)	18	1		74							
Foster, Betsey	Continuation of pension	28	1	Petition	849	Rev. Pensions.						
Foster, Benjamin	Increase of pension	27	2	Petition	69	Rev. Pensions	784	Adverse		Laid on table.		
Foster, Cosby, widow of	Pension for revolutionary services.	26	1	Petition and docs.	857, 950	Rev. Pensions.						
Foster, Cosby, widow of	Pension for revolutionary services.	26	2	Documents	272	Rev. Pensions.						
Foster, David	(See Shapendoshia, *et al.*)	29	1		309							
Foster, Ebenezer	Compensation for revolutionary services.	2	2	Petition	668					Referred to Secretary Treasury.		
Foster, Ebenezer	Compensation for revolutionary services.	3	2	Rep. of Secretary Treasury.	284	Claims	March 2, 1795	Adverse		Laid on table.		
Foster, Ebenezer	Compensation for revolutionary services.	4	1	Petition	598	Claims	May 31, 1796	Adverse		Laid on table.		
Foster, Edmund	Pension	15	1	Petition	83	Rev. Pensions				Discharged; referred to Secretary of War.		
Foster, Edmund	Increase of pension	15	2	Petition	192	Rev. Pensions.						
Foster, Edmund	Increase of pension	20	2	Petition	39	Military Pensions.	Jan. 20, 1829	Adverse		Laid on table.		
Foster, Edmund	Arrears of pension	21	1	Petition	104	Military Pensions.						
Foster, Edmund	Arrears of pension	21	2	Petition	54	Military Pensions.						
Foster, Edmund	Arrears of pension	22	1	Petition	97	Invalid Pensions.						
Foster, Edmund, widow of	Arrears of pension	23	1	Petition	525	Invalid Pensions.						
Foster, Elijah	Pension for revolutionary services.	27	1	Petition	108	Invalid Pensions.						
Foster, Elisha, (N. Y.)	Compensat'n for property destroyed in war of 1812.	19	2	Petition	132	Claims	Jan. 19, 1827	Adverse		Laid on table.		
Foster, Elisha, (N. Y.)	Compensat'n for property destroyed in war of 1812.	22	1	Petition	188	Claims	Feb. 6, 1832	Adverse		Laid on table.		
Foster, Elisha, (N. Y.)	Compensat'n for property destroyed in war of 1812.	24	1	Petition	507	Claims	473	Adverse		Laid on table.		
Foster, Elisha, (N. Y.)	Compensat'n for property destroyed in war of 1812.	25	2	Petition	275	Claims.						

List of private claims presented to the House of Representatives of the United States from the 1st to the 31st Congress, inclusive—Continued.

Names of claimants.	Nature or object of the claim.	Congress.	Session.	How brought before the House of Reps.	Page of journal.	To what committee of the House referred.	No. or date of the report.	Nature of the report.	No. of the bill.	How disposed of by the House of Reps.	How disposed of by the Senate.	Date of the act of Congress, and remarks.
Foster, Elisha, (N. Y.)	Pension	29	1	Petition	59	Invalid Pensions	38	Adverse	......	Laid on table.		
Foster, Elisha, (N. Y.)	Pension	31	1	Petition	852	Invalid Pensions.						
Foster, Ezekiel, *et al.*	Release from judgment as surety of Jonas Harrison.	18	1	Petition	154	Ways and Means	Feb. 20, 1824	Adverse	......	Laid on table.		
Foster, Ezekiel, *et al.*	Release from judgment as surety of Jonas Harrison.	19	1	Petition	56	Ways and Means	Dec. 28, 1825	Adverse	......	Leave to withdraw.		
Foster, Ezekiel, *et al.*	Reimbursement of duties improperly paid.	20	1	Senate bill	379	Ways and Means	Mar. 7, 1828	Adverse	S. 62	Rejected.		
Foster, Ezekiel, *et al.*	Reimbursement of duties improperly paid.	21	1	Petition	231	Ways and Means	....	....	......	Discharged; laid on table.		
Foster, Ezekiel, *et al.*	Reimbursement of duties improperly paid.	22	1	Petition	186	Commerce	302	Favorable	379	Referred to Committee Whole House.		
Foster, Ezekiel, *et al.*	Reimbursement of duties improperly paid.	23	1	Petition	32	Commerce	Dec. 16, 1833	Favorable	29	Passed	Passed	App'd June 30, 1834
Foster, Ezekiel, *et al.*	Reimbursement of duties improperly paid.	23	2	Petition	36	Commerce	12	Adverse.				
Foster, Ezekiel, *et al.*	Reimbursement of duties improperly paid.	24	1	Petition	188	Commerce	....	....	......	Discharged; laid on table.		
Fostor, Flavel	Reimbursement of money paid for government lands.	28	1	Petition	551	Claims.						
Foster & Giraud	Restitution of a vessel condemned for importing slaves.	11	1	Petition	37	Com. and Manuf.	June 14, 1809	Favorable	26	Referred to Committee Whole House.		
Foster, Hackaliah	Pension	3	1	Rep. of Secretary War.	131	Select	May 26, 1794	Favorable	62	Passed	Passed	App'd June 7, 1794
Foster, Hannah	(See William C. Foster, widow of)	11	1	....	29							
Foster, Henry G	(See Walley and Foster)	17	1	....	374							
Foster, James and Robert, heirs of.	Commutation pay and bounty land for revolutionary services.	17	2	Petition	35	Pens. & Rev. Cl'ms.	Dec. 20, 1822	Adverse	......	Laid on table.		
Foster, James and Robert, heirs of.	Commutation pay and bounty land for revolutionary services.	18	1	Petition	65	Pens. & Rev. Cl'ms.	Jan. 9, 1824	Adverse	......	Laid on table.		
Foster, James, (Ohio.)	Indemnity for losses by seizure of vessel and cargo.	30	1	Documents	154	Commerce	266	Adverse	......	Laid on table.		
Foster, James, (Ohio.)	Indemnity for losses by seizure of vessel and cargo.	30	2	Resolution	408	....	....	....	......	Leave to withdraw.		
Foster, J.	(See Peter T. Vose)	26	1	....	712							
Foster, Joseph	Pension	14	1	Petition	41	Invalid Pensions	April 23, 1816	Favorable	171	Passed	Passed	App'd April 30, 1816
Foster, John	Relief for losses, &c., in revolutionary war.	1	2	Petition	244	....	....	....	......	Laid on table.		
Foster, John, (Mass.)	Restoration of pension	17	2	Petition	30	Rev. Pensions.						
Foster, John, (Va.)	Bounty land and arrears of pay	25	2	Petition	75	Military Affairs	Jan. 20, 1838	Adverse	......	Laid on table.		
Foster, Jonathan, widow of	Pension for revolutionary services.	28	1	Petition	685	Rev. Pensions	....	....	......	Discharged; laid on table.		
Foster, Lathrop	Pension	27	3	Petition	285	Invalid Pensions	216	Favorable	812	Referred to Committee Whole House.		
Foster, Lathrop	Pension	28	1	Petition	78	Invalid Pensions	265	Favorable	197	Passed	Passed	App'd June 17, 1844
Foster, Levi	Pension for revolutionary services.	31	1	Petition	582	Rev. Pensions	317	Adverse	......	Laid on table.		
Foster, Moses, jr	Confirmation of title to land	17	2	Petition	209	Public Lands.						
Foster, Moses, jr	Confirmation of title to land	18	1	Petition	316	Priv. Land Claims.						
Foster, Peter	Commutation pay	22	1	Petition	73	Rev. Claims	130	Favorable	200	Referred to Committee Whole House.		
Foster, Peter	Commutation pay	22	2	House bill	66	Whole House	....	....	200	Passed	Passed	App'd March 2, 1833
Foster, Pethuel	Pension	25	3	Petition	673	....	....	....	......	Laid on table.		

List of private claims presented to the House of Representatives of the United States from the 1*st to the* 31*st Congress, inclusive*—Continued.

Names of claimants.	Nature or object of the claim.	Congress.	Session.	How brought before the House of Reps.	Page of journal.	To what committee of the House referred.	No. or date of the report.	Nature of the report.	No. of the bill.	How disposed of by the House of Reps.	How disposed of by the Senate.	Date of the act of Congress, and remarks.
Foster, Pethuel	Pension	27	2	Petition	390	Invalid Pensions	824	Adverse		Laid on table.		
Foster, Pethuel	Pension	28	1	Petition	172	Invalid Pensions.						
Foster, Pethuel	Arrears of pension	29	1	Petition	532	Invalid Pensions				Discharged; laid on table.		
Foster, Robert, W	Redress for sequstration of his property, &c., by Brazil.	22	1	Memorial	334	Foreign Affairs				Discharged; referred to President of United States.		
Foster, Sarah	(See James Follingsby, former widow of.)	31	1		688							
Foster, Samuel	Pension for revolutionary services.	22	1	Petition	219	Rev. Pensions				Discharged; laid on table.		
Foster, Sarah	(See Edmund Foster, widow of.)	23	1		525							
Foster, Sarah	(See Jonathan Foster, widow of.)	28	1		685							
Foster, Susan	(See Crosby Foster, widow of.)	26	1		857, 950							
Foster, Thomas	Payment for horse lost in war of 1812.	19	1	Resolution	338	Claims	Mar. 22, 1826	Adverse		Laid on table.		
Foster, Thomas	Payment for horse lost in war of 1812.	20	1	Petition	311	Claims	Feb. 29, 1828	Adverse		Laid on table.		
Foster, Thomas, jr	Payment of a balance due for work at Dunkirk, N. Y.	24	1	Petition	283	Claims	419	Adverse.				
Foster and Walley	(See Walley and Foster.)	15	2		26							
Foster, William	Pension	3	1	Report of Secretary of War.	131	Select	May 26, 1794	Favorable	62	Passed	Passed	App'd June 7, 1794
Foster, William	Increase of pension	10	1	Petition	38	Select.						
Foster, William	Increase of pension	11	2	Rep't Committee Whole House.	283	Claims	May 15, 1810	Favorable	107	Passed	Passed	App'd April 27, 1810
Foster, William, (Mass.)	Pension for revolutionary services.	15	2	Petition	229	Rev. Pensions.						
Foster, William, administratrix of.	Indemnity for French spoliations prior to 1800.	26	1	Memorial	182	Foreign Affairs	343	Favorable; bill	319	Referred to Committee Whole House.		
Foster, William, (Maine) heirs of.	Indemnity for French spoliations prior to 1800.	31	1	Petition	406	Commerce	355	Favorable	318	Referred to Committee Whole House.		
Foster, William B	Payment of interest on money borrowed for use of army in war of 1812.	17	1	Petition	184	Military Affairs	April 3, 1822	Adverse		Laid on table.		
Foster, William B	Payment of interest on money borrowed for use of army in war of 1812.	17	2	Petition	71	Claims	Feb. 26, 1823	Adverse		Laid on table.		
Foster, William B	Payment of interest on money borrowed for use of army in war of 1812.	18	1	Petition	135	Claims.						
Foster, William B	Payment of interest on money borrowed for use of army in war of 1812.	19	1	Petition	67	Claims	Jan. 6, 1826	Adverse		Laid on table.		
Foster, William B	Compensation as deputy commissary in war of 1812.	17	1	Petition	184	Claims				Discharged; laid on table.		
Foster, William B	Compensation as deputy commissary in war of 1812.	31	1	Petition	542	Claims.						
Foster, William B	Compensation as deputy commissary in war of 1812.	31	2	Resolution	38					Leave to withdraw.		
Foster, William C. widow of.	Compensation for revolutionary services.	11	1	Petition	29	Claims	June 9, 1809	Adverse		Laid on table.		
Foster, William S	Settlement of his accounts as a major in war of 1812.	15	1	Petition	25	Military Affairs	Jan. 27, 1818	Favorable	59	Passed	Passed	App'd April 20, 1818

List of private claims presented to the House of Representatives of the United States from the 1st to the 31st Congress, inclusive—Continued.

Names of claimants.	Nature or object of the claim.	Congress.	Session.	How brought before the House of Reps.	Page of journal.	To what committee of the House referred.	No. or date of the report.	Nature of the report.	No. of the bill.	How disposed of by the House of Reps.	How disposed of by the Senate.	Date of the act of Congress, and remarks.
Foster, Winslow	Reimbursement of money expended for benefit of revenue service.	24	1	Petition	663	Commerce				Discharged; leave to withdraw.		
Foucher, Anthony, *et al.*	(See Joseph Baden, *et al*)	20	1		168							
Fougeres, Marquis de	(See Marquis de Fougeres)	30	1		678							
Fought, John M.	Commutation of half-pay	21	1	Petition	161	Rev. Claims				Discharged; leave to withdraw.		
Foulkner, Peter	Extension of time to locate Virginia land warrant.	17	2	Petition	40	Public Lands	Dec. 17, 1822	Favorable	196	Laid on table.		
Foulke, David	Pension for revolutionary services.	17	2	Petition	78					Laid on table.		
Foulk, Thomas D.	(See administ'r of Nathan Smith.)	17	2		215							
Foulke, Gen. Willis	Invalid pension	31	1	Petition	449	Invalid Pensions	470	Adverse		Laid on table.		
Foulks, William, attorney of.	Extension of benefit of certain acts relating to public lands.	17	1	Petition	221	Whole House.						
Fountaine, Garrett	Compensation for use of store-house on Long Island.	16	2	Petition	248	Claims.						
Fountaine, Garrett	Compensation for use of store-house on Long Island.	17	1	Petition	184	Claims.						
Fountaine, Garrett	Compensation for use of store-house on Long Island.	18	1	Petition	27	Claims	12	Favorable	36	Passed	Passed	App'd Jan. 31, 1824
Fountaine, Garrett	Compensation for use of store-house on Long Island.	21	1	Petition	147	Claims	212	Adverse		Referred to Committee Whole House.		
Fountaine, Garrett	Compensation for use of store-house on Long Island.	22	1	Petition	188	Claims	Jan. 2, 1832	Report		Referred to Secretary of War.		
				Rep. of Secretary War.	401	Claims	Feb. 27, 1832	Adverse		Laid on table.		
Fournoy, Matthews	(See Matt'w Flournoy, & J. Ward.)	21	1		333							
Fouquet, John L.	Indemnity for property destroyed at Plattsburg.	13	3	Petition	723	Claims	Feb. 15, 1815	Favorable	297	Passed	Passed	App'd March 3, 1815
Fournier, N. H. S.	Compensation for supplies furnished on public account.	5	3	Petition	405	Claims	Feb. 28, 1799	Adverse		Laid on table.		
Fowke, Chandler D.	Compensation for revolutionary services.	3	2	Petition	311	Claims.						
Fowke, Chandler D.	Compensation for revolutionary services.	4	1	Resol'n and docs.	373	Claims	Jan. 6, 1796	Adverse		Leave to withdraw.		
Fowke, Mary	(See Jane Stobo, heirs of)	4	1		518							
Fowle, Ebenezer, widow of.	Compensation for revolutionary services.	2	1	Petition	441	Select	Nov. 2, 1791	Adverse		Referred to Committee Whole House.		
Fowle, Ebenezer, widow of.	Compensation for revolutionary services.	6	1	Petition	535	Claims	Feb. 11, 1800	Adverse		Leave to withdraw.		
Fowle, Ebenezer, widow of.	Compensation for revolutionary services.	11	2	Petition	117	Claims.						
Fowle, George M.	Remuneration for services as deputy collector.	25	2	Petition	51	Claims.						
Fowle, George M.	Remuneration for services as deputy collector.	26	1	Petition	168	Claims.						
Fowle, George M.	Remuneration for services as deputy collector.	29	1	Petition	171	Claims	64	Adverse		Laid on table.		
Fowle, Susannah	(See Ebenezer Fowle, widow of)	2	1		441							
Fowler, Abraham, widow of.	Pension for revolutionary services.	25	2	Petition	116	Military Affairs	April 17, 1838	Favorable	745	Referred to Committee Whole House.		
Fowler, Abraham, widow of.	Pension for revolutionary services.	25	3	House bill	381	Whole House			745	Passed	Adverse.	

List of private claims presented to the House of Representatives of the United States from the 1st to the 31st Congress, inclusive—Continued.

Names of claimants.	Nature or object of the claim.	Congress.	Session.	How brought before the House of Reps.	Page of journal.	To what committee of the House referred.	No. or date of the report.	Nature of the report.	No. of the bill.	How disposed of by the House of Reps.	How disposed of by the Senate.	Date of the act of Congress, and remarks.
Fowler, Abraham, widow of.	Pension for revolutionary services.	26	1	Petition	182	Military Affairs.						
Fowler, Abraham, widow of.	Pension for revolutionary services.	27	2	Petition	506	Military Affairs	353	Adverse		Laid on table.		
Fowler, Abraham, widow of.	Pension for revolutionary services.	29	1	Petition	750	Invalid Pensions.				Discharged; laid on table.		
Fowler, Abraham, widow of.	Pension for revolutionary services.	30	1	Petition	187	Rev. Pensions.				Discharged; laid on table.		
Fowler, Alexander	Liquidation and settlement of claim.	1	3	Petition	330					Referred to Secretary Treasury.		
Fowler, Alexander	Liquidation and settlement of claim.	3	2	Rep. of Secretary Treasury.	284					Laid on table.		
Fowler, Alexander	Confirmation of land granted by the King in 1763.	4	1	Petition	430	Claims	May 17, 1796	Adverse.				
Fowler, Alexander	Confirmation of title to land	4	2	Petition	667	Claims	Feb. 13, 1797	Adverse.				
Fowler, Alexander	Confirmation of title to land	5	2	Petition	207	Whole House.						
Fowler, Alexander	Confirmation of title to land	7	1	Petition	184					Laid on table.		
Fowler, Alexander	Confirmation of title to land	7	2	Petition	248	Claims	Jan. 31, 1803	Adverse.				
Fowler, Alexander	Confirmation of title to land	8	1	Petition	491					Laid on table.		
Fowler, Alexander, widow of.	Confirmation of title to land	12	1	Petition	107	Claims.						
Fowler, Amy	(See John Fowler, widow of)	23	2		307							
Fowler, Benjamin	Invalid pension	3	1	Rep. of Secretary of War.	131	Select	May 26, 1794	Ref'd to Secretary War.	J. R. 12	Passed	Passed	App'd June 9, 1794
Fowler, Bernard	Compensation for horse lost in war of 1812.	23	1	Resolution	386	Claims	477	Adverse		Laid on table.		
Fowler, Bernard	Compensation for horse lost in war of 1812.	23	2	Resolution	299	Claims	Feb. 27, 1835	Adverse		Laid on table.		
Fowler, Bernard	Compensation for horse lost in war of 1812.	24	1	Resolution	512	Claims.	June 21, 1836	Adverse		Laid on table.		
Fowler, Christopher	(See Samuel Fowler, administrators of.)	4	1		423							
Fowler, Frances	(See Abraham Fowler, widow of.)	25	2		116							
Fowler, George	Pension for revolutionary services.	16	1	Petition	110	Rev. Pensions.	April 6, 1820	Adverse		Laid on table.		
Fowler, Capt. H. W	Additional rations for each five years' service.	27	2	Memorial	328	Claims.						
Fowler, Isaac	Pension for revolutionary services.	25	2	Petition	116	Rev. Pensions.				Discharged; laid on table.		
Fowler, Isaac	Pension for revolutionary services.	26	1	Petition	173	Rev. Pensions.						
Fowler, John	Renewal of patent	14	2	Petition	206	Com. and Manuf.						
Fowler, John	Renewal of patent	15	1	Petition	133	Select.				Discharged; referred to Secretary of War.		
Fowler, John	Renewal of patent	15	1	Petition, (2)	161	Com. and Manuf.				Discharged; laid on table.		
Fowler, John, (La.)	Right of pre-emption as New Orleans branch pilot.	28	1	Petition	77	Priv. Land Claims.	9	Favorable	35	Passed	Passed	App'd June 17, 1844
Fowler, Dr. John	Bounty land for services in Black Hawk war.	22	1	Rep't Committee.	128	Public Lands.	Dec. 30, 1831	Adverse		Laid on table.		
Fowler, Dr. John, widow of.	Bounty land for services in Black Hawk war.	23	2	Petition	307	Public Lands.						
Fowler, Maria	(See Theodosius Fowler, widow of)	27	2		220							
Fowler, Milo	Compensation for mail service	29	2	Petition	134	P. Of. & P. Roads.						
Fowler, Moses	Pension for revolutionary services.	29	1	Petition	353	Rev. Pensions.						

List of private claims presented to the House of Representatives of the United States from the 1st to the 31st Congress, inclusive—Continued.

Names of claimants.	Nature or object of the claim.	Congress.	Session.	How brought before the House of Reps.	Page of journal.	To what committee of the House referred.	No. or date of the report.	Nature of the report.	No. of the bill.	How disposed of by the House of Reps.	How disposed of by the Senate.	Date of the act of Congress, and remarks.
Fowler, Robert B	Increase of compensation as clerk in War Department.	31	2	Petition	53	Ways and Means.						
Fowler, Samuel	Reissue of a defaced certificate	2	1	Petition	519					Referred to Secretary Treasury.		
Fowler, Samuel	Reissue of a defaced certificate	3	2	Rep. of Secretary Treasury.	284	Claims.						
Fowler, Samuel	Reissue of a defaced certificate	4	1	Res. and docs	373	Claims.						
Fowler, Samuel, administrators of.	Indemnity for two certificates of public debt.	4	1	Memorial	423	Claims	May 7, 1796	Adverse.				
Fowler, Samuel, administrators of.	Indemnity for two certificates of public debt.	4	2	Res. and docs	614	Claims.						
Fowler, Samuel, administrators of.	Indemnity for two certificates of public debt.	5	2	Memorial	97	Claims	Dec. 5, 1797	Adverse.				
Fowler, Samuel, administrators of.	Indemnity for two certificates of public debt.	15	2	Senate bill	325	Rev. Claims			S. 74	Referred to Committee Whole House.		
Fowler, Samuel G	(See Samuel Fowler, administrators of.)	4	1		423							
Fowler, Sarah	(See Alexander Fowler, widow of.)	12	1		107							
Fowler, Theodosius, *et al.*	Permission to locate certain land warrants.	4	1	Petition	387	Select				Discharged, referred to Com. Whole House.		
Fowler, Theodosius	Relief from suit as contractor to supply rations for United States army.	6	2	Petition	783	Select	Feb. 26, 1801	Favorable	J.R.—	Passed	Postponed.	
Fowler, Theodosius	Relief from suit as contractor to supply rations for United States army.	7	1	Petition	93	Select	April 5, 1802	Favorable	49	Passed	Passed	App'd April 29, 1802
Fowler, Theodosius, widow of.	Continuation of pension	27	2	Petition	220	Invalid Pensions	97	Favorable	143	Passed	Indef. postp'd.	
Fowler, Theodosius, widow of.	Continuation of pension	27	3	Petition	239	Rev. Pensions	94	Favorable	718	Passed	Indef. postp'd.	
Fowler, Theodosius, representatives of.	Continuation of pension	27	3	Documents	423	Rev. Claims.						
Fowler, Thomas	Arrears of pension	28	1	Petition	324	Invalid Pensions.						
Fowler, William	Compensation for military service	13	2	Petition	315	Military Affairs.						
Fowler, William M	Invalid pension	20	1	Petition	637	Military Pensions.						
Fowler, William M	Invalid pension	20	2	Rep't Committee.	55	Military Pensions	Dec. 12, 1828	Favorable	311	Passed.		
Fowler, William M	Invalid pension	21	1	Petition	48	Military Pensions	Jan. 5, 1830	Favorable	72	Passed	Passed	App'd May 20, 1830
Fowler, William M	Increase of pension	28	1	Petition	98	Rev. Pensions				Discharged; laid on table.		
Fowler, William, & Co	Pay due from Ottowa Indians	29	1	Memorial	160	Indian Affairs	287	Adverse		Laid on table.		
Fox, Augustus C	Arrears of pension	22	1	Petition	224	Invalid Pensions.						
Fox, Benjamin F., & John Mitchell.	Balance due on contract for building mint at New Orleans.	26	1	Senate bill	1226	Claims	July 10, 1840	Favorable	S. 379	Referred to Committee Whole House.		
Fox, Benjamin F., & John Mitchell.	Balance due on contract for building mint at New Orleans.	26	1	See amendm't to House bill.	1343	Whole House	July 21, 1840	Favorable	27	Passed	Passed	App'd July 21, 1840
Fox, Champion	Invalid pension	17	1	Petition	263	Rev. Pensions	Feb. 22, 1822	Adverse		Leave to withdraw.		
Fox, Daniel	Relief for disabilities incurred in 1793.	9	2	Petition	519	Claims.						
Fox, David	Restoration of pension	17	1	Petition	314	Rev. Pensions.						
Fox, Edward, agent of	Pay for muskets impressed in war of 1812.	16	1	Senate bill	134	Claims	Mar. 30, 1820	Bill amended.	S. 16	Passed	Concurred in.	App'd April 7, 1820
Fox, Elijah	(See Nathaniel Fox, heirs of)	22	1		94							

List of private claims presented to the House of Representatives of the United States from the 1st to the 31st Congress, inclusive—Continued.

Names of claimants.	Nature or object of the claim.	Congress.	Session.	How brought before the House of Reps.	Page of journal.	To what committee of the House referred.	No. or date of the report.	Nature of the report.	No. of the bill.	How disposed of by the House of Reps.	How disposed of by the Senate.	Date of the act of Congress, and remarks.
Fox, George, *et al*	Pro-rata portion of Indian annuities.	30	2	Memorial	270	Indian Affairs.						
Fox, George Winthrop	Compensation for horse lost in war of 1812.	16	2	Petition	181	Claims	Feb. 19, 1821	Adverse		Laid on table.		
Fox, George Winthrop	Compensation for horse lost in war of 1812.	17	1	Petition	39	Claims	Dec. 26, 1821	Adverse		Referred to Committee Whole House.		
Fox, George W., widow & heirs of.	Indemnity for property destroyed by the enemy.	29	1	Petition	275	Claims.						
Fox, George W., widow & heirs of.	Indemnity for property destroyed by the enemy.	29	2	Petition	427	Claims.						
Fox, Jacob	Invalid pension	3	1	Rep. of Secretary War.	131	Select	May 26, 1794	Res. to refer to Sec. War.	J. R. 12	Passed	Passed	App'd June 9, 1794
Fox, Jacob	Invalid pension	3	2	Rep. of Secretary War.	350	Claims	Feb. 28, 1795	Favorable	130	Passed	Postponed.	
Fox, Jacob	Invalid pension	4	1	Rep. of Secretary War.	445	Claims	Mar. 4, 1796	Favorable	156	Passed	Passed	App'd April 20, 1796
Fox, Jacob C.	Relief for stolen land warrant	31	1	Petition	1095	Public Lands.						
Fox, James	Naval pension	26	1	Petition	713	Naval Affairs.						
Fox, James	Naval pension	26	2	Petition	79	Naval Affairs.						
Fox, Joel	Invalid pension	3	1	Rep. of Secretary War.	131	Select	May 26, 1794	Refer'd to Sec. War.	J. R. 12	Passed	Passed	App'd June 9, 1794
Fox, Joel	Invalid pension	3	2	Rep. of Secretary War.	350	Claims	Feb. 28, 1795	Favorable	130	Passed	Postponed.	
Fox, Joel	Invalid pension	12	1	House bill	361	Whole House	June 15, 1812	Favorable	138	Passed	Passed	App'd July 5, 1812
Fox, John	Compensation for revolutionary services.	2	1	Petition	444					Referred to Secretary War.		
Fox, John	Compensation for revolutionary services.	2	2	Rep. of Secretary War.	696					Laid on table.		
Fox, John	Pension for revolutionary services.	15	2	Petition	190	Rev. Pensions	Jan. 21, 1819	Adverse.				
Fox, John	Pension for revolutionary services.	19	1	Petition	128	Military Pensions	164	Adverse		Laid on table.		
Fox, John	Pension for revolutionary services.	20	2	Petition	203	Military Pensions				Discharged; laid on table.		
Fox, John	Pension for revolutionary services.	21	1	Petition	46	Military Pensions	Mar. 30, 1830	Favorable	248	Passed	Indef. postp'd.	
Fox, John	Restoration of pension	22	1	Resolution	561	Rev. Pensions	472	Favorable	574	Referred to Committee Whole House.		
Fox, John L.	(See Exploring Expedition)	27	3		149		270		818			
Fox, Joseph, (Pa.)	Pension for revolutionary services.	18	2	Petition	183	Rev. Pensions				Discharged; laid on table.		
Fox, Joseph, (Pa.)	Pension for revolutionary services.	19	1	Petition	81	Military Pensions	April 1, 1826	Adverse.				
Fox, Joseph, (Pa.)	Pension for revolutionary services.	22	1	Petition	287	Rev. Pensions	410	Favorable	510	Referred to Committee Whole House.		
Fox, Joseph, (Pa.)	Arrears of pension	24	1	Petition	140	Naval Affairs.						
Fox, Joseph, (Ala.)	Compensation for invention of boring the earth for water.	21	2	Petition	100	Public Lands				Discharged; laid on table.		
Fox, J. R., *et al.*, United States navy.	Settlement of accounts, and allowance for extra services.	30	1	Senate bill	328	Naval Affairs	Feb. 29, 1848	Favorable	S. 118	Referred to Committee Whole House.		
Fox, Maria E	Continuation of pension	26	2	Petition	122	Rev. Pensions.						
Fox, Nathaniel	Compensation for revolutionary services.	1	2	Rep. of Secretary War.	221					Laid on table.		
Fox, Nathaniel, heirs of.	Compensation for revolutionary services.	22	1	Petition	94	Rev. Claims.						
Fox, Nathaniel, heirs of.	Compensation for revolutionary services.	23	1	Petition	307	Rev. Claims.						

84

List of private claims presented to the House of Representatives of the United States from the 1st to the 31st Congress, inclusive—Continued.

Names of claimants.	Nature or object of the claim.	Congress.	Session.	How brought before the House of Reps.	Page of journal.	To what committee of the House referred.	No. or date of the report.	Nature of the report.	No. of the bill.	How disposed of by the House of Reps.	How disposed of by the Senate.	Date of the act of Congress, and remarks.
Fox, Nathaniel, heirs of..	Commutation pay	23	1	Petition	41	Rev. Claims.						
Fox, Nathaniel, heirs of..	Commutation pay	23	2	Petition	106	Rev. Claims.						
Fox, Nathaniel, heirs of..	Commutation pay	26	1	Petition	164	Rev. Claims.						
Fox, Peter C.	Compensation for services rendered sick soldiers in war of 1812.	25	3	Petition	120	Claims.						
Fox, Peter C.	Compensation for services rendered sick soldiers in war of 1812.	26	1	Petition	168	Claims	375	Adverse	......	Laid on table.		
Fox and Neptune, owners of.	Bounty for capturing certain prisoners.	23	1	Senate bill	811	Claims	May 18, 1830	Favorable	S. 148	Passed	....	App'd July 2, 1836
Fox, Rachel	(See William Fox, widow of)	25	3	....	285							
Fox, Samuel	Pension	17	2	Petition	64	Rev. Pensions	....	....	......	Leave to withdraw.		
Fox, Samuel	Pension	19	2	Petition	242	Military Pensions.	Feb. 14, 1827	Favorable	436	Referred to Committee Whole House.		
Fox, Samuel	Pension	20	1	Petition	38	Military Pensions.	Feb. 13, 1828	Favorable	166	Passed.		
Fox, Samuel	Pension	20	2	Rep't Committee Whole House.	55	Military Pensions.	Dec. 12, 1828	Favorable	311	Passed.	Laid on table.	
Fox, Samuel	Pension	21	1	Petition	48	Military Pensions.	Jan. 5, 1830	Favorable	72	Passed	Passed	App'd May 20, 1830
Fox, Stephen	Pre-emption right to land	26	1	Petition	610	Public Lands	....	....	......	Discharged; laid on table.		
Fox, Vause	(See William Vause, administrator of.)	24	1	....	138	....	429	....	435			
Fox, William	Pension for revolutionary services.	23	1	Petition	53	Rev. Pensions	Jan. 3, 1834	Adverse	......	Laid on table.		
Fox, William	Pension for revolutionary services.	25	2	Petition	55	Rev. Pensions.	369	Adverse	......	Laid on table.		
Fox, William	Pension for revolutionary services.	28	1	Petition	83	Rev. Pensions.	....	....	......	Discharged; laid on table.		
Fox, William, widow of..	Pension for revolutionary services.	25	3	Petition	285	Rev. Pensions.	....	....	......	Discharged; referred to Com. Whole House.		
Fox, William P	Pension	3	2	Rep. of Secretary War.	337	Claims	Mar. 2, 1795	Report	......	Postponed.		
Fox, William P	Pension	4	1	Res. and docs	373	Claims.	Mar. 4, 1796	Favorable	12	Passed	Passed	App'd April 17, 1796
Fox, William W	(See Leggett Fox & Co.)	21	2	....	81							
Foxwell, Henry	(See William Harris, *et al.*)	20	1									
Foxworthy, William	Pension for revolutionary services.	24	1	Petition	260	Rev. Pensions.	332	Favorable	347	Passed	Passed	App'd June 28, 1836
Foy, John	Compensation for extra work as public gardiner.	22	1	Memorial	802	Public Buildings.						
Foy, Louisa	(See Peter Foy, daughter of.)	29	2	....	49							
Foy, Moses	Pension	21	2	Resolution	124	Military Pensions.						
Foy, Moses	Pension	22	1	Resolution	70	Rev. Pensions	Dec. 29, 1831	Adverse	......	Laid on table.		
Foy, Peter, daughter of	Pension for revolutionary services.	29	2	Petition	49	Rev. Pensions.						
Frame, James	Pension	29	1	Petition	503	Invalid Pensions.						
Frame, James	Pension	30	1	Petition	100	Invalid Pensions.						
Frame, James	Pension	30	2	Petition	116	Invalid Pensions	17	Favorable; bill	712	Passed.		
Frame, James	Pension	31	1	Petition	251	Invalid Pensions.						
Frame, James	Pension	31	2	Petition	335	Invalid Pensions.	....	....	......	Leave to withdraw.		
Frame, P. P.	Indemnity for property destroyed by volunteers in Mexican war.	30	2	Petition	226	Military Affairs	....	....	......	Discharged; laid on table.		
France, emigrants from	Extension of act for their relief	16	1	Senate bill	369	Public Lands	....	....	......	Discharged; laid on table.		
France, ship Pactole, of	For the remission of certain duties	22	2	Pres. message	122	Foreign Affairs.						
France, citizens of	Pension to the widows and children of certain French seamen.	23	1	Senate bill	798	Whole House	Jan. 24, 1834	Favorable; bill	216	Passed	Passed	App'd June 30, 1834
France, Nathaniel J.	Pre-emption right as New Orleans branch pilot.	28	1	Petition	77	Priv. Land Claims.	9	Favorable; bill	35	Passed	Passed	App'd June 17, 1844

List of private claims presented to the House of Representatives of the United States from the 1st to the 31st Congress, inclusive—**Continued.**

Names of claimants.	Nature or object of the claim.	Congress.	Session.	How brought before the House of Reps.	Page of journal.	To what committee of the House referred.	No. or date of the report.	Nature of the report.	No. of the bill.	How disposed of by the House of Reps.	How disposed of by the Senate.	Date of the act of Congress, and remarks.
Francis & Eliza, ship	(See Herring & Richardson)	23	1		255							
Francher, James	Pension for revolutionary services.	24	1	Resolution	267	Rev. Pensions				Discharged; laid on table.		
Francher, James	Pension for revolutionary services.	24	2	Resolution	154	Rev. Pensions	111	Favorable; bill	843	Referred to Committee Whole House.		
Francher, James	Pension for revolutionary services.	25	2	Resolution	37	Rev. Pensions	271	Favorable; bill	314	Passed.		
Francher, James	Pension for revolutionary services.	26	1	Petition	17	Rev. Pensions	149	Favorable; bill	159	Passed	Passed	App'd July 20, 1840
Francia, Joseph de la	(See de la Francia)	28	2		89							
Francia & Thompson, attorneys of.	Payment of excess of duties due.	25	2	Petition	772	Judiciary				Discharged.		
Francia & Thompson, attorneys of.	Payment of excess of duties due.	26	1	Petition	175	Judiciary.						
Francis, Daniel, of Hartford, Connecticut.	Indemnity for French spoliations prior to 1800.	26	1	Memorial	182	Foreign Affairs	343	Favorable; bill	319	Referred to Committee Whole House.		
Francis, Daniel, of Hartford, Ct., heirs of.	Indemnity for French spoliations prior to 1800.	31	1	Petition	543	Commerce	355	Favorable; bill	318	Referred to Committee Whole House.		
Francis, Daniel, Wethersfield, Connecticut.	Indemnity for French spoliations prior to 1800.	26	1	Memorial	182	Foreign Affairs	343	Favorable; bill	319	Referred to Committee Whole House.		
Francis, Ebenezer, heirs of.	Arrearages of half-pay	28	2	Petition	216	Rev. Claims.						
Francis, Henry W	Payment for property stolen by the Cherokee Indians in 1798.	23	2	Petition	423	Indian Affairs.						
Francis, Henry W	Payment for property stolen by the Cherokee Indians in 1798.	25	2	Petition	88	Claims.						
Francis, James, widow of.	Pension for revolutionary services.	22	1	Petition	944	Rev. Pensions.						
Francis, James, widow of.	Pension for revolutionary services.	26	1	Petition	706	Rev. Pensions.						
Francis, James, widow of.	Pension for revolutionary services.	27	2	Petition	153	Rev. Pensions	102	Favorable; bill	148	Passed	Indef. postp'd.	
Francis, John, and others.	Release from prison at a suit of the United States.	14	1	Resolution	293	Ways and Means	Mar. 6, 1816	Favorable; bill	108	Passed	Passed	App'd April 27, 1816
Francis, John, heirs of.	Compensation for Indian depredations in Florida.	24	1	Petition	96	Indian Affairs				Discharged; laid on table.		
Francis, John, heirs of.	Compensation for Indian depredations in Florida.	28	2	Petition	221	Claims	150	Adverse		Laid on table.		
Francis, Mary	(See James Francis, widow of.)	26	1		706							
Francis, Miller	Pension	24	2	Memorial	267	Invalid Pensions.						
Francis, Miller	Pension	25	2	Petition	269	Invalid Pensions	677	Favorable; bill	656	Passed	Passed	App'd July 7, 1838
Francis, Tench	(See Comfort Sands and others)	1	3		358							
Francis, Tench, executors of.	For settlement of accounts as purveyor of supplies during the revolutionary war.	16	1	Petition	197	Select.						
Francis, Tench, executors of.	For settlement of accounts as purveyor of supplies during the revolutionary war.	16	1	Senate bill	389	Select	April 10, 1820	Favorable; bill	S. 85	Passed	Passed	App'd May 15, 1820
Francis, William	That merchandize imported in 1828 may be made subject to the previous tariff.	23	1	Petition	162	Whole House.						
Francis, William	That merchandize imported in 1828 may be made subject to the previous tariff.	26	1	Petition	340	Claims.						
Francis & Willing	(See Willing & Francis)	26	1		182							
Francisco, Colonel, (Ky.)	(See Kentucky militia, Francisco's regiment.)	14	2		268							
Francisco, John	(See sureties of Joseph Kinkaid)	19	1		181							
Francisco, John, (Mich.)	Arrears of pension	23	1	Petition	388	Invalid Pensions				Disch'd; laid on table.		

List of private claims presented to the House of Representatives of the United States from the 1st to the 31st Congress, inclusive—Continued.

Names of claimants.	Nature or object of the claim.	Congress.	Session.	How brought before the House of Reps.	Page of journal.	To what committee of the House referred.	No. or date of the report.	Nature of the report.	No. of the bill.	How disposed of by the House of Reps.	How disposed of by the Senate.	Date of the act of Congress, and remarks.
Francisco, Mary B	(See Peter Francisco, widow of.)	28	1		946							
Francisco, Peter, (Va.)	Pension	15	2	Resolution	38	Rev. Claims	Nov. 26, 1818	Favorable; bill	203	Passed	Passed	App'd March 3, 1819
Francisco, Peter, (Va.)	Continuation of pension	17	1	Petition	326	Rev. Pensions				Discharged; laid on table.		
Francisco, Peter, (Va.)	Continuation of pension	20	2	Petition	100	Rev. Pensions	Jan. 8, 1829	Adverse		Laid on table.		
Francisco, Peter, (Va.)	Continuation of pension	21	1	Petition	169	Military Pensions.						
Francisco, Peter, widow of.	Continuation of pension	28	1	Petition	946	Rev. Pensions.						
Francisco, Peter, widow of.	Continuation of pension	29	1	Petition	386	Rev. Pensions	612	Adverse		Laid on table.		
Francisco, Peter, widow of.	Continuation of pension	31	1	Petition	733	Rev. Pensions	253	Adverse		Laid on table.		
Francisco, Peter, (Va.)	Compensation for horse shot in revolutionary war.	19	2	Resolution	160	Rev. Claims.						
Francisco, Peter, (Va.)	Compensation for revolutionary services.	25	2	Petition and docs.	391	Rev. Claims				Discharged; laid on table.		
Frank, George	Pension	21	2	Petition	114	Military Pensions.						
Frank, John	Compensation for services in Indian wars.	5	2	Petition	94	Claims	Jan. 8, 1798	Favorable	39	Passed	Passed	App'd Jan. 20, 1798
Frank, John, (D. C.)	Compensation for property burned in Treasury Department in 1814.	13	3	Petition	511	Claims	Nov. 11, 1814	Adverse		Rejected.		
Frank, John, (D. C.,) widow of.	Compensation for property burned in Treasury Department in 1814.	22	1	Petition	226	Claims	Feb. 1, 1832	Adverse		Laid on table.		
Frank, John, (D. C.,) widow of.	Compensation for property burned in Treasury Department in 1814.	23	1	Petition	305	Claims	Mar. 4, 1834	Adverse		Laid on table.		
Frank, Mary	(See John Frank, widow of)	22	1		226							
Frankenburg, Lewis	Restoration of pension	17	2	Petition	99	Whole House.						
Frankford, John	(See George Watts, executor of)	7	2		321							
Franklin, Abraham	(See Samuel Franklin, *et al.*)	3	1		134							
Franklin, Benjamin	Invalid pension	26	1	Petition	326	Invalid Pensions	July 21, 1840			Laid on table.		
Franklin, Benjamin	Invalid pension	27	2	Petition	60	Invalid Pensions	132	Favorable	178	Passed	Passed	App'd June 1, 1842
Franklin, Benjamin	Arrears of pension	28	1	Resolution	212	Invalid Pensions.						
Franklin, David	Pension	16	1	Petition	88	Rev. Pensions	Jan. 14, 1820	Adverse		Laid on table.		
Franklin, David	Pension	20	2	Petition	203	Military Pensions				Discharged; laid on table.		
Franklin, Hannah	(See William Franklin, widow of)	23	1		53							
Franklin, James, executor of	Commutation pay	22	2	Petition	88	Rev. Claims	Feb. 6, 1833	Adverse		Laid on table.		
Franklin, John	Compensation for property furnished for use of government.	2	1	Petition	456	Referred to Secretary Treasury.	April 17, 1792	Report		Laid on table.		
Franklin, John	Compensation for property furnished for use of government.	5	2	Rep. of Secretary Treasury.	145	Claims	Feb. 28, 1798	Adverse		Laid on table.		
Franklin, Samuel, *et al.*	Exemption from embargo act on ship Ontario and cargo.	3	1	Petition	134	Select	May 1, 1794	Favorable	4	Passed	Passed	App'd May 8, 1794
Franklin, schooner	(See sister of James Mugford)	28	1		516							
Franklin, Stephen P	Compensation for removing carpets from hall of House of Representatives.	30	2	Petition	282	Accounts.						
Franklin, Thomas	Liquidation of certificates of revolutionary debts.	4	1	Rep. of Secretary Treasury.	388	Claims	74	Adverse		Laid on table.		
Franklin, Thomas G	Correction of error in entry of land	20	1	Petition	557	Public Lands.						
Franklin, Thomas P	Increase of pension	28	2	Resolution	290	Invalid Pensions.						
Franklin, Thomas P	Increase of pension	29	1	Petition	124	Rev. Pensions	238	Adverse		Laid on table.		
Franklin, Thomas P	Increase of pension	29	2	Petition	128	Rev. Pensions.						
Franklin, Thomas P	Increase of pension	30	1	Petition	747	Rev. Pensions.						
Franklin, William T., widow of.	Pension for revolutionary services.	23	1	Petition	53	Rev. Pensions.						

List of private claims presented to the House of Representatives of the United States from the 1st to the 31st Congress, inclusive—Continued.

Names of claimants.	Nature or object of the claim.	Congress.	Session.	How brought before the House of Reps.	Page of journal.	To what committee of the House referred.	No. or date of the report.	Nature of the report.	No. of the bill.	How disposed of by the House of Reps.	How disposed of by the Senate.	Date of the act of Congress, and remarks.
Franklin, Zephaniah	Compensation for revolutionary services.	19	1	Petition	94	Rev. Claims	Feb. 1, 1826	Adverse		Laid on table.		
Franklin, Zephaniah	Compensation for revolutionary services.	20	1	Petition	440	Rev. Claims				Discharged; laid on table.		
Franklin, Zephaniah	Compensation for revolutionary services.	21	1	Petition	261	Military Pensions	April 2, 1830	Adverse		Laid on table.		
Franks, David S.	Compensation for revolutionary services.	1	2	Petition	162	Select	Mar. 11, 1790	Adverse		Laid on table.		
Franks, David S.	Compensation for revolutionary services.	4	2	Petition	625	Claims				Discharged.		
Franks, George	(See Michael and George Franks.)	17	2		75							
Franks, Henry, *et al.*	Pension for revolutionary services.	3	1	Petition and report Sec. War.	59	Select	April 22, 1794	Adverse		Laid on table.		
Franks, Henry	Compensation for revolutionary services.	19	1	Petition	267	Rev. Claims.						
Franks, Henry	Compensation for revolutionary services.	19	2	Resolution	69	Rev. Claims				Discharged.		
Franks, Isaac	Compensation for revolutionary services.	13	1	Petition	143	Claims				Discharged; laid on table.		
Franks, Isaac	Compensation for revolutionary services.	13	2	Petition	172	Pens. & Rev. Cl'ms.	Mar. 17, 1814	Adverse		Laid on table.		
Franks, Michael & George	To locate lands in lieu of other lands.	17	2	Petition	75	Priv. Land Claims.	Jan. 3, 1823	Adverse		Laid on table.		
Franks, Thomas L.	(See Gregnon & Lawe, administrators of.)	26	1		1004							
Franzoni, Virginia	(See Guiseppe Franzoni)	23	1		60							
Franzoni, Guiseppe	(See Francis Iardella, heirs of.)											
Fraunces, Andrew G.	Payment of certain treasury warrants.	3	1	Memorial	18	Select	Dec. 30, 1798	Adverse.				
Fraser, Daniel	Patent for a weaver's loom	23	1	Petition	307	Patents.						
Fraser, John	Pension for revolutionary services.	10	1	Petition	130	Select.						
Fraser, John	Pension for revolutionary services.	13	2	Petition	246	Rev. Pensions	Mar. 28, 1814	Favorable	166	Referred to Committee Whole House.		
Fraser, John	Pension for revolutionary services.	13	3	Petition	468	Rev. Pensions	Dec. 9, 1814	Favorable; bill	303	Passed	Passed	App'd March 3, 1815
Fraser, John, and Geo. A. Trenholm.	Reimbursement of money paid on forfeited goods.	28	1	Petition	76	Claims	290	Favorable; bill	202	Passed	Passed, with amendment.	App'd June 17, 1844
Fraser, Thomas, by attorney	Indemnity for French spoliations prior to 1800.	26	1	Memorial	182	Foreign Affairs	343	Favorable; bill	319	Referred to Committee Whole House.		
Fraser, Thomas, heirs of	Indemnity for French spoliations prior to 1800.	31	1	Petition	391	Foreign Affairs	355	Favorable; bill	318	Referred to Committee Whole House.		
Frasier, Robert	Bounty land	9	2	Presid'ts message	284	Select	Jan. 23, 1807	Favorable; bill	183	Passed	Passed	App'd March 3, 1807
Frayer, David	Pension for revolutionary services.	24	1	Petition	107	Rev. Pensions.						
Frazar, Samuel A	Indemnity for French spoliations prior to 1800.	26	1	Memorial	182	Foreign Affairs	343	Favorable; bill	319	Referred to Committee Whole House.		
Frazee, John	Balance due as architect to custom-house, New York.	30	1	Petition	973	Claims.						
Frazer, Angus O., & others	For the portion of cargo of British ship Ardent.	15	2	Petition	89	Ways and Means.						
Frazer, Angus O., & others	For the portion of cargo of British ship Ardent.	16	1	Petition	34	Ways and Means.	Feb. 10, 1820	Favorable; bill	72	Passed	Passed, with amendment.	App'd May 11, 1820
Frazer, Angus O., executor of.	For the payment of money due under act of May 11, 1820.	20	1	Resolution	408	Naval Affairs				Discharged; laid on table.		

List of private claims presented to the House of Representatives of the United States from the 1st to the 31st Congress, inclusive—Continued.

Names of claimants.	Nature or object of the claim.	Congress.	Session.	How brought before the House of Reps.	Page of journal.	To what committee of the House referred.	No. or date of the report.	Nature of the report.	No. of the bill.	How disposed of by the House of Reps.	How disposed of by the Senate.	Date of the act of Congress, and remarks.
Frazer, Angus O., executor of.	For the payment of money due under act of May 11, 1820.	20	2	Resolution	125	Naval Affairs	Jan. 16, 1829	Adverse	......	Laid on table.		
Frazer, George, and others.	Fishing bounty on lost vessel	24	2	Senate bill	552	Commerce	May 2, 1837	Favorable; bill	S. 248	Passed	Passed	App'd March 3, 1837
Frazer, John	Pension	13	3	House bill	740	Whole House	Mar. 1, 1815	Favorable; bill	303	Passed	Passed	App'd March 3, 1815
Frazer, John, & Co	Reimbursement of duty paid on planes.	23	1	Petition	334	Ways and Means	April 25, 1834	Favorable	447	Referred to Committee Whole House.		
Frazer, John, & Co	Reimbursement of duty paid on planes.	23	2	House bill	299	Whole House	....	....	447	Passed	Laid on table.	
Frazer, John, & Co	Reimbursement of duty paid on planes.	24	1	Petition	95	Ways and Means	Jan. 12, 1836	Favorable; bill	109	Passed	Passed	App'd June 23, 1836
Frazer, Samuel, (Md.)	Pension and bounty land	7	2	Petition	260	Claims	Jan. 12, 1803	Adverse.				
Frazer, Samuel, (Md.)	Pension and bounty land	12	1	Petition	317	Public Lands.						
Frazer, Samuel, (Md.)	Pension and bounty land	13	2	Petition	201	Rev. Claims	Jan. 31, 1814	Adverse	......	Leave to withdraw.		
Frazer, Samuel A., & others	Indemnity for French spoliations prior to 1800.	26	1	Memorial	182	Foreign Affairs	343	Favorable; bill	319	Referred to Committee Whole House.		
Frazier, Charles M	Compensation for property destroyed during war of 1812.	23	2	Petition	119	Claims	125	Favorable; bill	764	Referred to Committee Whole House.		
Frazier, Charles M	Compensation for property destroyed during war of 1812.	24	1	Petition	51	Claims	45	Favorable; bill	50	Passed	Passed	App'd June 23, 1836
Frazier, Daniel	(See Stephen Decatur, widow of, &c.)	20	1	....	295							
Frazier, James	(See John Henry and John Anderson, administrators of.)	26	2	....	81							
Frazier, James	Increase of compensation as collector of customs.	4	2	Petition	704	....	....	....	......	Laid on table.		
Frazier, James	For services as a cooper	20	1	Senate bill	420	Claims	April 21, 1828	Favorable; bill	S. 84	Passed	Passed	App'd May 26, 1828
Frazier, James	Pension	25	2	Petition	117	Invalid Pensions.						
Frazier, James	Pension	25	3	Petition	89	Naval Affairs.						
Frazier, James	Pension	26	1	Petition	180	Naval Affairs.						
Frazier, James	Refunding certain fines in case of schooner Hazard.	27	3	Petition	58	Commerce	....	....	......	Discharged; laid on table.		
Frazier, James	Refunding certain fines in case of schooner Hazard.	29	1	Petition	472	Commerce	513	Adverse	......	Laid on table.		
Frazier, James, surety of.	Release from liability	12	1	Petition	61	Select	July 2, 1812	Favorable; bill	178	Referred to Committee Whole House.		
Frazier, James, surety of.	Release from liability	12	2	Petition	609	Ways and Means	March 1, 1813	....	......	Referred to Committee Whole House.		
Frazier, James, surety of.	Release from liability	13	1	Petition	12	Ways and Means.						
Frazier, James, surety of.	Release from liability	13	2	Petition	257	Ways and Means.						
Frazier, James, surety of.	Release from liability	13	3	Petition	462	Ways and Means	55	Favorable; bill	300	Passed	Passed	App'd Mar. 1, 1815
Frazier, James	Compensation for military services	31	1	Petition	1467	Rev. Pensions.						
Frazier, James	Pension for revolutionary services.	31	2	Petition	431	Rev. Pensions	57	Adverse	......	Laid on table.		
Frazier, Jemimah	(See William Pinckney, daughter of.)	28	1	....	946							
Frazier, Jeremiah	Pension	22	1	Resolution	194	Rev. Pensions.						
Frazier, John, and John Read.	(See Joseph Boyd, sureties of.)	31	1	....	1095							
Frazier, Mary	Indemnity for house destroyed in 1812.	15	1	Report Commissioners.	37	Claims	Feb. 19, 1818	Adverse	.....	Laid on table.		
Frazier, Mahlon	(See John E. Metcalf, and others.)	25	2	....	1052							
Frazier, Paul	(See Stephen Decatur, widow of.)	19	2	....	98							
Frazier, Preston	Compensation for a horse lost in Florida war.	25	3	Resolution	171	Claims.						

List of private claims presented to the House of Representatives of the United States from the 1st to the 31st Congress, inclusive—Continued.

Names of claimants.	Nature or object of the claim.	Congress.	Session.	How brought before the House of Reps.	Page of journal.	To what committee of the House referred.	No. or date of the report.	Nature of the report.	No. of the bill.	How disposed of by the House of Reps.	How disposed of by the Senate.	Date of the act of Congress, and remarks.
Frazier, Preston	Compensation for a horse lost in Florida war.	26	1	Petition	169	Claims	61	Adverse	......	Laid on table.		
Frazier, Rezin, assignee of	Permission to change entry of land.	24	1	Petition	215	Public Lands	441	Favorable; bill	455	Referred to Committee Whole House.		
Frazier, Rezin, assignee of	Permission to change entry of land	25	2	Petition	456	Public Lands	558	Favorable; bill	547	Referred to Committee Whole House.		
Frazier, Rezin, assignee of	Permission to change entry of land.	25	3	Bill of last sess.	380	Whole House	Jan. 25, 1839	With't amend.	547	Passed	Passed	App'd March 3, 1839
Frazier, Robert	Compensation for revolutionary services.	1	1	Petition	49	Select	Jan. 11, 1790	Favorable	......	Laid on table.		
Frazier, Robert	Pension	23	1	Petition	570	Invalid Pensions.						
Frazier, Robert	Pension	24	1	Petition	426	Invalid Pensions	840	Favorable; bill	742			
Frazier, Robert	Pension	25	2	Petition	38	Invalid Pensions	320	Favorable; bill	362	Passed.		
Frazier, Robert	Pension	26	1	Petition	161	Invalid Pensions	196	Favorable; bill	208	Passed	Indef. postp'd.	
Frazier, Solomon	Release from judgment on surety bond.	11	3	Petition	454	Ways and Means.						
Frazier, Solomon	Release from judgment on surety bond.	12	1	Petition	89	Select	July 2, 1812	Favorable; bill	178	Referred to Committee Whole House.		
Frazier, Solomon	Release from judgment on surety bond.	12	2	Petition	609	Ways and Means.	Mar. 1, 1813	Rep. not found				
Frazier, Solomon	Release from judgment on surety bond.	13	1	Petition	12	Ways and Means.						
Frazier, Solomon	Release from judgment on surety bond.	13	2	Petition	259	Ways and Means.						
Frazier, Solomon	Release from judgment on surety bond.	13	3	Petition	463	Ways and Means.	55	Favorable; bill	300	Passed	Passed	App'd Mar. 1, 1815
Frazier, Solomon	Release from judgment on surety bond.	16	1	Petition	295	Claims	April 3, 1820	Adverse	......	Laid on table.		
Frazier, Thomas, assignee of.	Confirmation of title to land	24	2	Petition	83	Priv. Land Claims.						
Frazier, Thomas, assignee of.	Confirmation of title to land	25	2	Petition	180	Priv. Land Claims.	Jan. 25, 1838	Adverse	......	Laid on table.		
Frazier, Thomas	Pension	24	1	Petition	73	Invalid Pensions	June 2, 1836	Adverse	......	Laid on table.		
Frazier, Thomas	Pension	24	2	Petition	72	Invalid Pensions	Jan. 19, 1837	Adverse	......	Laid on table.		
Frazier, Thomas	Pension	25	2	Petition	118	Invalid Pensions	423	Favorable; bill	430	Passed	Passed	App'd July 7, 1838
Frazier, William	Pension for revolutionary services.	24	2	Resolution	318	Rev. Pensions.						
Fream, Thomas	Pre emption right to land	14	1	Petition	368	Public Lands	....	....	......	Discharged; laid on table.		
Frederick, Andrew, Philip	To locate pre-emption right	23	1	Petition	567	Public Lands.						
Frederick, George	For other lands in lieu of those heretofore granted.	19	1	Petition	179	Public Lands	54	Favorable; bill	77	Passed	Passed	May 22, 1826, leave to withdraw papers.
Frederick, Joseph, heirs of	For prize money on board the brig Alliance.	30	1	Petition	635	Rev. Claims	....	....	......	Discharged; laid on table.		
Frederick, Philip	Confirmation of title to land	19	1	Resolution	64	Public Lands	33	Favorable; bill	254	Referred to Committee Whole House.		
Frederick, Widow Manly.	Compensation for wood furnished United States.	4	1	Rep. of Secretary Treasury.	388	Claims	May 31, 1796	Adverse	......	Laid on table.		
Fredien, Henry, and others	Pre-emption right to land	30	1	Senate bill	976	Priv. Land Claims.	....	....	S. 189			
Fredien, Honore, & others	Pre-emption right to land	27	2	Petition	1437	Priv. Land Claims.						
Fredien, Honore, & others	Pre-emption right to land	28	1	Petition	122	Priv. Land Claims.						
Free, John	Compensation for saving property from the fire of 1814 in Washington city.	14	1	Petition	376	Claims	Mar. 27, 1816	Adverse	......	Rejected.		

List of private claims presented to the House of Representatives of the United States from the 1st to the 31st Congress, inclusive—Continued.

Names of claimants.	Nature or object of the claim.	Congress.	Session.	How brought before the House of Reps.	Page of journal.	To what committee of the House referred.	No. or date of the report.	Nature of the report.	No. of the bill.	How disposed of by the House of Reps.	How disposed of by the Senate.	Date of the act of Congress, and remarks.
Free, John	Compensation for saving property from the fire of 1814 in Washington city.	15	1	Petition	202	Claims	Feb. 6, 1818	Adverse		Rejected.		
Freeborn, Peter	Pension for revolutionary services.	18	1	Petition	28	Rev. Pensions	Jan. 2, 1824	Adverse		Laid on table.		
Freeberger, George	(See Louis F. Beeler, and others)	30	1		115							
Freeland, Benjamin	To change entry of land	16	2	Petition	93	Public Lands	37	Favorable; bill	208			
Freeland, Benjamin	To change entry of land	17	1	Petition	52	Public Lands	Dec. 31, 1821	Favorable; bill	14	Rejected.		
Freeland, Benjamin	To change entry of land	18	2	Petition	119	Public Lands.						
Freeland, Benjamin	To change entry of land	20	1	Petition	40	Public Lands	73	Favorable; bill	71	Passed	Passed, with amendment.	App'd May 24, 1828
Freeland, George, sr.	Confirmation of title to land	13	2	Petition	168	Public Lands.						
Freelove, David	Pension for revolutionary services.	25	2	Petition	913	Rev. Pensions.						
Freelove, David	Pension for revolutionary services.	25	3	Petition	87	Rev. Pensions.						
Freelove, David	Pension for revolutionary services.	26	1	Petition	284	Rev. Pensions	538	Favorable; bill	437	Referred to Committee Whole House.		
Freelove, David	Pension for revolutionary services.	27	2	Petition	60	Rev. Pensions	92	Favorable; bill	138	Passed	Passed	App'd Aug. 27, 1842
Freeman, Catharine	(See John Freeman, widow of)	30	1		245							
Freeman, Constant	Compensation as Canadian refugee and indemnity for damages to property.	4	2	Petition	615	Whole House		By bill	209			
Freeman, Constant	Compensation as Canadian refugee and indemnity for damages to property.	7	1	Petition	29	Claims	April 1, 1802	Adverse		Referred to Committee Whole House.		
Freeman, Constant, widow of.	For benefit of act of 1810, in relation to Canadian refugees.	24	1	Petition	64	Priv. Land Claims.				Discharged; laid on table.		
Freeman, Constant, widow of.	For benefit of act of 1810, in relation to Canadian refugees.	27	3	Petition	120	Rev. Claims	236	Adverse		Laid on table.		
Freeman, Edgar	Pension	21	2	Petition	55	Naval Affairs				Discharged; leave to withdraw.		
Freeman, Edgar	Pension	22	1	Petition	36	Invalid Pensions	207	Favorable	288	Passed	Passed, with amendment	App'd July 14, 1832
Freeman, Elijah, (a lunatic,) by Steph'n Freeman.	Arrears of pension	22	1	Resolution	576	Rev. Pensions.						
Freeman, Elijah, (a lunatic,) by Steph'n Freeman.	Arrears of pension	22	2	Petition	90	Rev. Pensions.						
Freeman, Elijah, (a lunatic,) by Steph'n Freeman.	Arrears of pension	23	1	Petition	142	Rev. Pensions				Discharged; laid on table.		
Freeman, Elijah, (a lunatic,) by Steph'n Freeman.	Arrears of pension	24	2	Petition	110	Rev. Pensions				Discharged; laid on table.		
Freeman, Elijah, (a lunatic,) by Steph'n Freeman.	Arrears of pension	25	2	Petition	55	Rev. Pensions	703	Adverse		Referred to Committee Whole House.		
Freeman, Elijah, (a lunatic,) by Steph'n Freeman.	Arrears of pension	25	3	Petition	216	Rev. Pensions.						
Freeman, Elijah, (a lunatic,) by Steph'n Freeman.	Arrears of pension	26	1	Petition	173	Rev. Pensions	Mar. 5, 1840	Adverse		Laid on table.		
Freeman, Franklin	Confirmation of title to land	30	2	Memorial	91	Public Lands	115	Favorable	793	Referred to Committee Whole House.		
Freeman, Frederick	Indemnity for property taken for the public service.	14	1	Petition	621	Claims.						
Freeman, Henry, postmaster at Georgia.	Release from payment of money stolen from his post office.	18	2	Resolution	50	P. O. & P. Roads.	Jan. 13, 1825	Adverse		Laid on table.		
Freeman, Henry, postmaster at Georgia.	Release from payment of money stolen from his post office.	19	1	Resolution	55	P. Of. and P. Roads.	47	Adverse		Laid on table.		

List of private claims presented to the House of Representatives of the United States from the 1st to the 31st Congress, inclusive—Continued.

Names of claimants.	Nature or object of the claim.	Congress.	Session.	How brought before the House of Reps.	Page of journal.	To what committee of the House referred.	No. or date of the report.	Nature of the report.	No. of the bill.	How disposed of by the House of Reps.	How disposed of by the Senate.	Date of the act of Congress, and remarks.
Freeman, Henry, (N. J.)	Pension for revolutionary services	21	2	Petition	67	Military Pensions.						
Freeman, Henry, (N. J.)	Pension for revolutionary services	27	2	Petition	374	Rev. Pensions	570	Favorable	366	Referred to Committee Whole House.		
Freeman, Henry, (N. J.)	Pension for revolutionary services	27	3	House bill	87	Whole House			366			
Freeman, Henry, (N. J.)	Pension for revolutionary services	28	1	Petition	238	Rev. Pensions	153	Favorable	141	Passed	Indef. postp'd.	
Freeman, Henry, (N. J.)	Pension for revolutionary services	30	1	Petition	397	Rev. Pensions	534	Adverse		Laid on table.		
Freeman, Israel	Pension	21	2	Petition	103	Military Pensions.						
Freeman, J. D	(See Exploring Expedition)	27	3		149		270		818			
Freeman, James, (Ct.)	Bounty land for revolutionary services	22	1	Petition	470	Rev. Claims.						
Freeman, James, (Ct.)	Bounty land for revolutionary services.	22	2	Petition	67	Rev. Claims.						
Freeman, James, (Ct.)	Bounty land for revolutionary services.	23	1	Petition	54	Rev. Claims	Jan. 14, 1834	Adverse		Laid on table.		
Freeman, James, of Vermont, widow of.	Pension	17	1	Petition	567					Laid on table.		
Freeman, James, of Vermont, widow of.	Pension	17	2	Petition	165	Rev. Pensions				Discharged; referred to Secretary of War.		
Freeman, John, widow of.	Pension for revolutionary services	30	1	Res. and docs	245	Rev. Pensions				Discharged; laid on table.		
Freeman, Joshua	Remuneration for Indian depredations.	24	1	Petition	426	Indian Affairs.						
Freeman, Joshua	Remuneration for Indian depredations.	24	2	Petition	93	Indian Affairs.						
Freeman, Joshua	(See Reuben E. Gentry & others)	25	2		97							
Freeman, Pearson	Pension	21	2	Petition	159	Military Pensions.						
Freeman, Pearson	Pension	23	1	Petition	46	Rev. Pensions	40	Favorable; bill	46	Passed	Passed	App'd June 26, 1834
Freeman, Pearson	Increase of pension	29	1	Petition	91	Rev. Pensions				Discharged; laid on table.		
Freeman, Pearson, widow of.	Increase of pension	30	1	Petition	886	Rev. Pensions	829	Favorable; bill	648			
Freeman, Pearson, widow of.	Increase of pension	30	2	House bill	363	Whole House			648	Passed.		
Freeman, Pearson, widow of.	Increase of pension	31	1	Petition	496	Rev. Pensions	226	Favorable; bill	221	Referred to Committee Whole House.		
Freeman, Pearson, widow of.	Increase of pension	31	2	House bill	182	Whole House			221	Passed.		
Freeman, Peyton R	Payment of claim as late clerk of the district court of New Hampshire.	22	2	Resolution	250	Judiciary.						
Freeman, Rebecca	(See Pearson Freeman)	30	1		886							
Freeman, Richard, widow of	Pension for revolutionary services	28	2	Petition	333	Rev. Pensions.						
Freeman, Rogers	Pension	15	1	Resolution	372	Rev. Pensions.						
Freeman, Ruth	(See James Freeman, widow of.)	17	1		567							
Freeman, Ruth	(See Thomas Freeman, widow of.)	29	1		440							
Freeman, Samuel	Increase of compensation as postmaster at Portland.	4	2	Petition	625					Laid on table.		
Freeman, Samuel, (N. C.)	Pension and balance of pay for revolutionary services.	11	2	Petition	363					Laid on table.		
Freeman, Samuel, (N. C.)	Pension and balance of pay for revolutionary services.	11	3	Petition	474	Claims.						
Freeman, Samuel, (N. C.)	Pension and balance of pay for revolutionary services.	12	2	Petition	664	Claims.						

List of private claims presented to the House of Representatives of the United States from the 1st to the 31st Congress, inclusive—Continued.

Names of claimants.	Nature or object of the claim.	Congress.	Session.	How brought before the House of Reps.	Page of journal.	To what committee of the House referred.	No. or date of the report.	Nature of the report.	No. of the bill.	How disposed of by the House of Reps.	How disposed of by the Senate.	Date of the act of Congress, and remarks.
Freeman, Samuel, (Ga.)	Bounty land	24	1	Petition	476	Priv. Land Claims.						
Freeman, Susan	(See William H. Freeman, widow of.)	29	1		65							
Freeman, Thomas	(See Colonel William Anderson).	12	1		188							
Freeman, Thomas	Remuneration for services and money advanced to the U. S.	28	1	Petition	769	Claims.						
Freeman, Thomas, widow of.	Remuneration for services and money advanced to the U. S.	29	1	Petition	440	Claims	800	Adverse		Laid on table.		
Freeman, Thomas, widow of.	Remuneration for services and money advanced to the U. S.	29	2	Petition	56	Militia.						
Freeman, Thomas, widow of.	Remuneration for services and money advanced to the U. S.	30	1	Petition	380	Militia.						
Freeman, Thomas, widow of.	Remuneration for services and money advanced to the U. S.	31	1	Petition	234	Military Affairs	212	Adverse		Laid on table.		
Freeman, William H., lieut. U. S. M. C.	Relief from sentence of court martial.	28	1	Petition	345	Naval Affairs.						
Freeman, William H., widow of.	Relief from sentence of court martial.	29	1	Memorial	65	Naval Affairs.						
Freeman, William H., Col. U. S. M. Corps.	Relief from payment of amount lost by failure of a bank at Boston.	26	1	Petition	293	Claims.						
Freeman, William H., Col. U. S. M. Corps, representatives of.	Relief from payment of amount lost by failure of a bank at Boston.	29	1	Petition	1261	Claims	821	Favorable; bill	546	Referred to Committee Whole House.		
Freeman, William H., Col. U. S. M. Corps, representatives of.	Relief from payment of amount lost by failure of a bank at Boston.	30	1	Petition	166, 835	Claims	476	Adverse		Laid on table.		
Freeman, William H, Col. U. S. M. Corps, representatives of.	Relief from payment of amount lost by failure of a bank at Boston.	31	1	Petition	324	Claims.						
Freeman, William R., administrator of.	Compensation for a horse lost in United States service.	27	2	Memorial	750	Claims						See act Aug. 23, 1842. General Law.
Feer, Daniel	Renewal of lost loan office certificate.	2	1	Petition and rep't Sec. Treasury.	487	Select.						
Freligh, George	Indemnity for property destroyed at Plattsburg.	13	3	Petition	723	Claims	Feb. 15, 1815	Favorable; bill	297	Passed	Passed	App'd March 3, 1815
Fremont, Lieutenant S. L.	Relief on account of having lost his rank as a staff officer.	31	1	Petition	692	Military Affairs.						
Fremont, Lieutenant S. L.	Relief on account of having lost his rank as a staff officer.	31	2	Petition	293	Military Affairs	31	Adverse		Laid on table.		
French, Commel, widow of	Pension for revolutionary services.	24	2	Petition	271	Rev. Pensions				Discharged; laid on table.		
French, Commel, widow of	Pension for revolutionary services.	25	2	Petition	180	Rev. Pensions	388	Favorable; bill	406	Passed	Postponed.	
French, Commel, widow of	Pension for revolutionary services.	25	3	Petition	88	Rev. Pensions	69	Favorable; bill	947	Passed.		
French, Commel, widow of	Pension for revolutionary services.	26	1	Petition	171	Rev. Pensions	126	Favorable; bill	136	Passed	Indef. postp'd.	
French, Elizabeth	(See Commel French, widow of).	21	2		271							
French, Elkanah	Pension	21	2	Petition	126	Military Pensions.						
French, Frederick L.	Payment for services as master's mate of ship North Carolina.	26	1	Petition	713	Naval Affairs	July 21, 1840	Favorable; bill	524	Referred to Committee Whole House.		
French, Frederick L.	Payment for services as master's mate of ship North Carolina.	27	2	Petition	99	Naval Affairs.						
French, Frederick L.	Payment for services as master's mate of ship North Carolina.	27	3	Petition	134	Naval Affairs	175	Adverse		Laid on table.		

List of private claims presented to the House of Representatives of the United States from the 1st to the 31st Congress, inclusive—**Continued.**

Names of claimants.	Nature or object of the claim.	Congress.	Session.	How brought before the House of Reps.	Page of journal.	To what committee of the House referred.	No. or date of the report.	Nature of the report.	No. of the bill.	How disposed of by the House of Reps.	How disposed of by the Senate.	Date of the act of Congress, and remarks.
French, Hains	Relief from payment of arrears of taxes.	9	1	Petition	188	Claims	Dec. 10, 1805	Adverse.				
French, Gidion	Pension for revolutionary services.	22	2	Petition	310	Rev. Pensions	....	....	......	Discharged; laid on table.		
French, James, representatives of.	Arrears of pension	28	1	Petition	79	Rev. Pensions	....	....	......	Discharged; laid on table.		
French, James M.	Pension	30	1	Petition	641	Invalid Pensions	835	Adverse	......	Laid on table.		
French, James M.	Pension	31	1	Petition	863	Invalid Pensions.						
French, Joanna	(See Nathaniel French, widow of)	28	2	....	111							
French, John	(See Harry Richardson)	26	1	....	885							
French, Jonathan, (N. H.)	Bounty land for services in the late war.	15	2	Petition	121	Military Affairs.						
French, Jonathan, (Ohio.)	Pension for revolutionary services.	21	1	Petition	478	Military Pensions.						
French, Jonathan, (Ohio.)	Pension for revolutionary services.	22	1	Petition	188	Rev. Pensions.						
French, Judah	Pension for revolutionary services of husband.	28	1	Resolution	557	Rev. Pensions.						
French, Mary	Pension for revolutionary services of husband.	28	1	Petition	950	Whole House.						
French, Nathaniel	Restoration of pension	17	1	Petition	150	Rev. Pensions.						
French, Nathaniel	Arrears of pension	25	2	Petition	230	Rev. Pensions	....	....	......	Discharged; laid on table.		
French, Nathaniel, widow of.	Pension for revolutionary services of husband.	28	2	Petition	111	Rev. Pensions	....	....	......	Discharged; laid on table.		
French, Nathaniel, widow of.	Pension for revolutionary services of husband.	29	1	Petition	118	Rev. Pensions	528	Adverse	......	Laid on table.		
French, Raphael	Pension for revolutionary services.	29	1	Petition	198	Rev. Pensions.						
French, Samuel	Pension	4	1	Rep't Committee	445	Claims	Feb. 18, 1796	Favorable	156	Passed	Passed	App'd April 20, 1796
French, Samuel, (Ct.)	Pension for revolutionary services.	19	2	Petition	131	Military Pensions	....	....	......	Discharged.		
French, Samuel, (Ct.)	Pension for revolutionary services.	20	1	House bill	645	Military Pensions	April 29, 1828	Favorable	283	Passed.		
French, Samuel, (Ct.)	Pension for revolutionary services.	20	2	Rep't Committee	55	Military Pensions	Dec. 12, 1829	Favorable	311	Passed.		
French, Samuel, (Ct.)	Pension for revolutionary services.	21	1	Petition	48	Military Pensions	Jan. 5, 1830	Favorable	72	Passed	Passed	App'd May 20, 1830
French, Samuel	Commutation pay	10	1	Petition and rep't Sec. of War.	180	....	....	....	......	Laid on table.		
French, Samuel	Pension	11	2	House bill	283	Claims	Mar. 15, 1810	Favorable	107	Passed	Passed	App'd April 27, 1810
French, Tamson	Pension for revolutionary services.	28	1	Petition	950	Whole House.						
French, Thomas	(See A. Kinsley, *et al.*)	14	2	....	58							
French vessels, owners of.	Remission of foreign tonnage duty	3	1	Petition	18	Select	Jan. 24, 1794	Favorable	11	Passed	Passed	App'd March 7, 1794
French, Volney, *et al.*	(Case not on Journal.)	25	3	Resolution	519	Public Lands.						
French, William	Increase of pension	27	2	Petition	219	Invalid Pensions	784	Adverse	......	Laid on table.		
French, William	Increase of pension	29	1	Petition	947	Invalid Pensions.						
French war, officers who served in.	Confirmation of title to land granted by the King of Great Britain.	9	1	Petition	357	Public Lands	April 9, 1806	Resol'n to postpone indef.	......	Resolution adopted.		
French war, officers who served in.	Confirmation of title to land granted by the King of Great Britain.	9	2	Petition	485	Public Lands.	Feb. 3, 1807	Not of record.	......	Referred to Committee Whole House.		
French war, officers who served in.	Confirmation of title to land granted by the King of Great Britain.	10	1	Petition	185	Public Lands.						
French war, heirs of officers who served in.	Bounty land	12	1	Petition	32	Claims.						
Frenier, John	Pre-emption right to land	18	2	Petition	137	Public Lands.						
Freres, Nathan	(See Denton, Hall, & Nathan)	10	1	....	173							
Freshour, Adam, heirs of.	Pension for revolutionary services.	27	3	Petition	421	Rev. Pensions.						

List of private claims presented to the House of Representatives of the United States from the 1st to the 31st Congress, inclusive—Continued.

Names of claimants.	Nature or object of the claim.	Congress.	Session.	How brought before the House of Reps.	Page of journal.	To what committee of the House referred.	No. or date of the report.	Nature of the report.	No. of the bill.	How disposed of by the House of Reps.	How disposed of by the Senate.	Date of the act of Congress, and remarks.
Frethy, Edward	Exoneration from judgment of United States.	16	2	Petition	149	Claims.						
Frew, Archibald	Commission on collections of the direct tax.	16	1	Resolution	104	Ways and Means	Jan. 19, 1820	Adverse	......	Rejected.		
Frey, Frederick, & Co.	Drawback of duties on cards	24	2	Petition	205	Commerce	157	Favorable	884	Referred to Committee Whole House.		
Frey, Frederick, & Co.	Drawback of duties on cards	25	2	Petition	40	Commerce	235	Favorable	275	Referred to Committee Whole House.		
Frey, Frederick, & Co.	Drawback of duties on cards	25	3	House bill	376	Whole House	....	....	275	Passed	Passed, with amendment.	App'd March 2, 1839
Frey, Frederick, & Co.	Drawback of duties on sheep's wool.	26	1	Petition	358	Ways and Means.						
Frey, Frederick, & Co.	Drawback of duties on sheep's wool.	26	2	Petition	248	Ways and Means.						
Freyer, James	Pension	25	2	Petition	587	Invalid Pensions	....	....	......	Discharged; laid on table.		
Freyer, James	Pension	25	3	Petition	89	Invalid Pensions	....	....	......	Discharged; laid on table.		
Frias, Antonio de	(See Antonio De Frias)	24	1	....	115							
Fricker, Peter	Pension for revolutionary services.	17	2	Petition	165	Rev. Pensions	....	....	......	Discharged; laid on table.		
Friday, Robert	Confirmation of title to land	28	1	Petition	802	Public Lands.						
Fridge, Alexander	Confirmation of title to land	20	2	Petition	41	Priv. Land Claims.						
Fridge, Alexander	Confirmation of title to land	21	1	Petition	51	Priv. Land Claims.	76	Favorable	108	Passed	Passed	App'd May 28, 1830
Friebeau, Jean Baptiste	Payment of certain bills of credit.	14	1	Petition	40	Rev. Claims	....	....	......	Disch'd; laid on table.		
Fried, Henry	Payment of certain bills of credit.	21	1	Petition	295	Rev. Claims.						
Fried, Henry	Payment of certain bills of credit.	21	2	Petition	55	Rev. Claims	62	Adverse	......	Laid on table.		
Fried, Henry	Payment of certain bills of credit.	29	1	Petition	424	Ways and Means.						
Friend, Gabriel	Release from payment as surety	23	1	Petition	234	P. Of. & P. Roads.						
Friend, Gabriel	Release from payment as surety	29	1	Petition	576	P. Of. & P. Roads.						
Frierson, William J.	Compensation for a negro lost in United States service.	25	1	Petition	166	....	....	....	......	Laid on table.		
Frierson, William J.	Compensation for a negro lost in United States service.	25	2	Petition	176	Claims.						
Frigate Constitution, officers, &c., of.	(See Charles Stewart, *et al.*)	14	1	....	116							
Friley, Martin	Payment for a horse lost in public service.	21	1	Petition	303	Claims.						
Frink, David	Compensation for boarding prisoners.	21	2	Resolution	165	Claims	Jan. 28, 1831	Adverse	......	Laid on table.		
Frink, David	Compensation for boarding prisoners.	23	1	Petition	355	Claims	Mar. 11, 1834	Adverse	......	Laid on table.		
Frink & Haddock	Compensation for mail service	30	1	Petition	722	P. Of. & P. Roads.						
Frink, John	Pension for revolutionary services.	15	2	Petition	113	Rev. Pensions	57	Favorable	249	Passed	Passed, with amendment.	App'd March 3, 1819
Frink, Peter	Compensation for revolutionary services.	11	3	Petition	559	Claims	....	....	......	Discharged; laid on table.		
Frisbee, Levi	Pension	14	1	Petition	63	Rev. Pensions	April 23, 1816	Favorable; bill	......	Passed	Passed	App'd April 30, 1816
Frisbee, Levi, widow of	Pension	27	2	Petition	1112	Invalid Pensions.						
Frisbee, Sally	(See Levi Frisbee, widow of)	27	2	....	1112							
Frisbie, Edward, heirs of	Pension for revolutionary services.	26	2	Petition	131	Rev. Claims	....	....	......	Discharged; laid on table.		
Frisbie, George	(See Edward Frisbie, heir of)	26	2	....	131							
Frisbie, Gideon, *et al.*	Indemnity for property confiscated by Canada.	14	1	Petition	98	Select	Jan. 24, 1816	Favorable	51	Passed	Passed	App'd March 5, 1816

List of private claims presented to the House of Representatives of the United States from the 1st to the 31st Congress, inclusive—Continued.

Names of claimants.	Nature or object of the claim.	Congress.	Session.	How brought before the House of Reps.	Page of journal.	To what committee of the House referred.	No. or date of the report.	Nature of the report.	No. of the bill.	How disposed of by the House of Reps.	How disposed of by the Senate.	Date of the act of Congress, and remarks.
Frisbie, Jacob	Pension	3	1	Rep. of Sec. War	131	Select	May 26, 1794	Favorable	62	Passed	Passed	App'd June 7, 1794
Frisby, Elizabeth	(See Elizabeth Edwards, heir of; also see Jas. Biays, creditors of.)	29	2		437							
Frisby, Richard	Compensat'n for property destroyed in the war of 1812.	15	2	Petition	36	Claims	Dec. 16, 1818	Adverse		Leave to withdraw.		
Frisby, Richard	Compensat'n for property destroyed in the war of 1812.	18	1	Petition	236	Claims	Mar. 10, 1824	Adverse		Laid on table.		
Frisby, Richard	Compensat'n for property destroyed in the war of 1812.	22	2	Petition	42	Claims.						
Frisby, Richard	Compensat'n for property destroyed in the war of 1812.	23	1	Petition	154	Claims.						
Frisby, Richard	Compensat'n for property destroyed in the war of 1812.	23	2	Petition	128	Claims.						
Frisby, Richard	Compensat'n for property destroyed in the war of 1812.	24	1	Petition	93	Claims	693	Favorable	651	Referred to Committee Whole House.		
Frisby, Richard	Compensat'n for property destroyed in the war of 1812.	25	2	Petition	36	Claims	48	Favorable	60	Passed	Passed	App'd July 7, 1838
Fritters, Travers	Pension	23	2	Petition	105	Invalid Pensions				Discharged; laid on table.		
Fritters, Travers	Pension	24	1	Petition	201	Invalid Pensions	603	Favorable; bill	584	Passed	Passed	App'd June 28, 1836
Fritters, Travers	Arrears of pension	24	2	Resolution	92	Invalid Pensions				Discharged; laid on table.		
Frizzell, (or Frizzle,) Elisha.	Pension	3	1	Rep. of Secretary War.	131	Select	May 26, 1794	Favorable; bill	62	Passed	Passed	App'd June 7, 1794
Frizzell, (or Frizzle,) Elisha.	Arrears of pension	3	2	Petition	237	Claims	Feb. 25, 1795	Adverse		Referred to Committee Whole House.		
Frizzell, (or Frizzle,) Elisha.	Arrears of pension	4	2	Petition	649	Claims	Jan. 18, 1797	Adverse		Rejected		Leave to withdraw.
Frizzell, (or Frizzle,) Elisha.	Arrears of pension	7	2	Petition	246	Claims	Feb. 4, 1803	Adverse		Laid on table.		
Frizzell, (or Frizzle,) Elisha.	Arrears of pension	8	2	Petition	89	Claims.						
Frizzell, (or Frizzle,) Elisha.	Increase of pension	9	2	House bill	608	Whole House	Feb. 28, 1807	With amends.	216	Passed	Passed	App'd March 3, 1807
Frizzell, (or Frizzle,) Elisha.	Further increase of pension	10	2	House bill	499	Whole House	Feb. 20, 1809	With amends.	158	Passed	Passed	App'd March 3, 1809
Frizell, William	(See James McFarland and others)	15	2		200							
Frizzell, William W	Confirmation of title to land	25	2	Petition	373	Priv. Land Claims.						
Frizzell, William W	Confirmation of title to land	25	3	Petition	134	Priv. Land Claims.						
Frizzell, William W	Confirmation of title to land	26	1	Petition	179	Priv. Land Claims.						
Frizini, Louis	Confirmation of title to land in Louisiana.	27	2	House bill	342	Whole House			124			
Frogge, Arthur R	Pension	28	1	Petition	273	Invalid Pensions	95	Favorable; bill	111	Passed	Indef. postp'd.	
Frogge, Arthur R	Pension	28	2	Petition	72	Invalid Pensions	18	Favorable; bill	485	Passed.		
Frogge, Arthur R	Pension	29	1	Petition	101	Invalid Pensions	55	Favorable; bill	44	Passed	Passed	App'd July 15, 1846
Frost, Dorcas, by attorney.	Compensation for losses in revolutionary war.	1	3	Petition and rep't Sec. of War.	337					Laid on table.		
Frost, George P	Reissue of a lost bounty land warrant.	5	2	Petition	82	Claims	May 19, 1798	Adverse		Laid on table.		
Frost, George P	Grant of land for services in revolutionary war.	20	2	Petition	60	Priv. Land Claims.	32	Favorable; bill	348	Passed.		
Frost. George P	Grant of land for services in revolutionary war.	21	1	Petition	146	Priv. Land Claims.				Discharged; laid on table.		
Frost, Isaiah	Compensation for work on Cumberland road.	23	2	Appropriat'n bill.	209	Whole House	Feb. 24, 1835	With amends.	632	Passed	Passed	App'd March 3, 1835
Frost, Isaiah	Compensation for work on Cumberland road.	24	1	Petition	206	Claims	774	Adverse		Laid on table.		
Frost, J. A	(See Exploring Expedition)	27	3		149							

List of private claims presented to the House of Representatives of the United States from the 1st to the 31st Congress, inclusive—Continued.

Names of claimants.	Nature or object of the claim.	Congress.	Session.	How brought before the House of Reps.	Page of journal.	To what committee of the House referred.	No. or date of the report.	Nature of the report.	No. of the bill.	How disposed of by the House of Reps.	How disposed of by the Senate.	Date of the act of Congress, and remarks.
Frost, John, heirs of	Indemnity for French spoliations prior to 1800.	26	1	Memorial	182	Foreign Affairs	343	Favorable; bill	319	Referred to Committee Whole House.		
Frost, John T., (Dist. Col.)	Compensation for making an index to Executive documents.	29	1	Petition	90	Claims	Jan. 15, 1846	Res. to pay out of the contingent fund of the House.		Resolution adopted.		
Frost, John T., (Dist. Col.)	Compensation for a house burnt by the British in 1814, and for his services in preserving the public archives.	31	1	Petition	1227	Claims.						
Frost, Johnson	Payment for two horses impressed into United States service.	29	1	Documents	269	Military Affairs				Discharged; leave to withdraw.		
Frost, Joseph	Pension	3	2	Rep. of Secretary War.	350	Claims	Feb. 28, 1795	Favorable; bill	130	Passed	Postponed.	
Frost, Joseph	Pension	4	1	Rep. of Secretary War.	445	Claims	Feb. 18, 1796	Favorable; bill	156	Passed	Passed	App'd April 20, 1796
Frost, Josiah	Compensation for work on Cumberland road.	23	1	Petition	838	Claims.						
Frost, Josiah	Compensation for work on Cumberland road.	23	2	Petition	110	Ways and Means.						
Frost, Oliver	Remuneration for certain duties paid at St. John's, New Brunswick.	28	2	Petition	310	Foreign Affairs.						
Frost, Peter	Invalid pension	29	2	Senate bill	307	Invalid Pensions	Feb. 24, 1847	With't amend.	S. 68	Passed		App'd Feb. 25, 1847
Frost, Peter	Arrears of pension	30	2	Petition	271	Invalid Pensions				Discharged; laid on table.		
Frost, Peter	Arrears of pension	31	1	Petition	417	Invalid Pensions	229	Favorable; bill	224	Referred to Committee Whole House.		
Frost, Peter	Bounty land for services in war of 1812.	30	2	Petition	270	Priv. Land Claims.						
Frost, William, (Mass.)	Compensation for various service in revolutionary war.	4	1	Petition	414	Claims	May 7, 1796	Adverse		Laid on table		Leave to withdraw.
Frost, William, (Mass.)	Commutation pay and bounty land for revolutionary services.	10	2	Petition	501					Resolution to refer to Whole House on bill No. 129.		
Frost, William, (Mass.)	Commutation pay and bounty land for revolutionary services.	15	1	Petition	250	Pens. & Rev. Cl'ms.	Feb. 24, 1818	Adverse		Laid on table.		
Frost, William, (Mass.)	Commutation pay and bounty land for revolutionary services.	15	2	Petition	217	Pens. & Rev. Cl'ms.						
Frothingham, Abigail, heirs of.	Compensation for a dwelling-house destroyed by American troops in revolutionary war.	3	1	Petition	20					Refered to Secretary of Treasury.		
Frothingham, Abigail, heirs of.	Compensation for a dwelling-house destroyed by American troops in revolutionary war.	3	2	Petition	285	Claims	Mar. 2, 1795	Adverse		Laid on table.		
Frothingham, Abigail, heirs of.	Compensation for a dwelling-house destroyed by American troops in revolutionary war.	4	2	Petition	700	Claims	Feb. 5, 1797	Adverse		Laid on table.		
Frothingham, Abigail, heirs of.	Compensation for a dwelling-house destroyed by American troops in revolutionary war.	6	1	Petition	594	Select	Mar. 11, 1800	Adverse		Referred to Committee Whole House.		
Frothingham, Andrew, for self and others.	Indemnity for French spoliations prior to 1800.	26	1	Memorial	182	Foreign Affairs	343	Favorable; bill	319	Referred to Committee Whole House.		
Frothingham, Benjamin	(See Andrew Frothingham.)											
Frothingham, Henry	Indemnity for French spoliations prior to 1800.	26	1	Memorial	182	Foreign Affairs	343	Favorable; bill	319	Referred to Committee Whole House.		

List of private claims presented to the House of Representatives of the United States from the 1st to the 31st Congress, inclusive—Continued.

Names of claimants.	Nature or object of the claim.	Congress.	Session.	How brought before the House of Reps.	Page of journal.	To what committee of the House referred.	No. or date of the report.	Nature of the report.	No. of the bill.	How disposed of by the House of Reps.	How disposed of by the Senate.	Date of the act of Congress, and remarks.
Frothingham, John	Release from penalty for violation of non importation act.	13	1	Petition	46	Ways and Means.						
Frothingham, Joshua P	(See Thos. Frothingham, heirs of.)	21	2		128							
Frothingham, Richard	Pay and bounty land for revolutionary services.	15	1	Petition	126	Pens. & Rev. Cl'ms.	Feb. 18, 1818	Adverse		Laid on table.		
Frothingham, Rich'd, heir of.	Payment of balance due as appears by the books of the Treasury Department.	29	1	Petition	120	Claims.						
Frothingham, Samuel	Pension	19	1	Petition	203	Military Pensions	April 1, 1826	Adverse		Laid on table.		
Frothingham, Samuel	Pension	21	1	Petition	120	Military Pensions	Feb. 15, 1830	General bill	248	Passed	Indef. postp'd.	
Frothingham, Samuel	Pension	21	2	Petition	95	Military Pensions.						
Frothingham, Samuel	Pension	22	1	Petition	35	Rev. Pensions	99	Favorable; bill	188	Referred to Committee Whole House.		
Frothingham, Samuel	Pension	22	2	Bill of last sess.	66	Whole House			188	Laid on table.		
Frothingham, Samuel	Pension	27	2	Petition	239	Rev. Pensions	784	Adverse		Laid on table.		
Frothingham, Samuel	Pension	28	2	Petition	163	Rev. Pensions.						
Frothingham, Samuel	Pension	29	1	Petition	273	Rev. Pensions	122	Adverse		Laid on table.		
Frothingham, Stephen	Indemnity for French spoliations prior to 1800.	26	1	Memorial	182	Foreign Affairs	343	Favorable; bill	319	Referred to Committee Whole House.		
Frothingham, Thomas, and others.	(See Abigail Frothingham, heirs of.)	3	1		20							
Frothingham, Thos., heirs of.	Compensation for a house burnt by American troops in revolutionary war.	21	2	Petition	128	Rev. Claims	68	Favorable; bill	605	Referred to Committee Whole House.		
Frothingham, Thos., heirs of.	Compensation for a house burnt by American troops in revolutionary war.	22	1	Petition	29	Rev. Claims	171	Favorable; bill	171	Passed.		
Frothingham, Thos., heirs of.	Compensation for a house burnt by American troops in revolutionary war.	22	2	Petition	28	Rev. Claims	11	Favorable; bill	632	Passed	Passed	App'd March 2, 1833
Frothingham, Thos., heirs of.	For interest on amount allowed by act of March 2, 1833.	23	1	Petition	110	Rev. Claims.						
Frothingham, Thos., heirs of.	For interest on amount allowed by act of March 2, 1833.	23	2	Petition	164	Rev. Claims.						
Frothingham, Thos., heirs of.	For interest on amount allowed by act of March 2, 1833.	24	1	Petition	102	Rev. Claims.						
Frougot, Reynhart	Revolutionary pension	22	1	Resolution	250	Rev. Pensions.						
Frougot, Reynhart	Revolutionary pension	23	1	Resolution	82	Rev. Pensions.						
Fruge, Jean	Confirmation of title to land	21	1	Petition	173	Priv. Land Claims.	258	Favorable	316	Referred to Committee Whole House.		
Fruge, Jean	Confirmation of title to land	21	2	House bill	340	Whole House			316	Passed.		
Fruge, Jean	Confirmation of title to land	23	1	Petition	586	Priv. Land Claims.	459	Favorable	477	Referred to Committee Whole House.		
Frull, John	(See Ephraim Jones, *et al*)	14	2		121							
Frumento, or Trumento, Augustino.	Drawback of duty on puncheon of spirits.	18	2	Petition	186	Ways and Means				Discharged; referred to Sec. Treasury.		
Fry, Benjamin	Pension	4	1	Petition	422	Claims	May 7, 1796	Adverse		Leave to withdraw.		
Fry, Benjamin	Pension	12	1	Rep't Committee	361	Claims	June 8, 1812	Favorable	138	Passed	Passed	App'd July 5, 1812
Fry, Benjamin, (R. I.)	For payment of amount found due by suit against the United States.	19	2	Petition	31	Claims	Jan. 4, 1827	Adverse		Leave to withdraw.		
Fry, Benjamin, (R. I.)	Indemnity for French spoliations prior to 1800.	19	2	Petition	157	Foreign Affairs.						

List of private claims presented to the House of Representatives of the United States from the 1st to the 31st Congress, inclusive—Continued.

Names of claimants.	Nature or object of the claim.	Congress.	Session.	How brought before the House of Reps.	Page of journal.	To what committee of the House referred.	No. or date of the report.	Nature of the report.	No. of the bill.	How disposed of by the House of Reps.	How disposed of by the Senate.	Date of the act of Congress, and remarks.
Fry, Benjamin, (R. I.)	Indemnity for French spoliations prior to 1800.	26	1	Memorial	182	Foreign Affairs	343	Favorable; bill	319	Referred to Committee Whole House.		
Fry, Benjamin	Settlement of claim as agent for erecting fortifications.	24	1	Petition	715	Judiciary	June 15, 1836	Favorable	702	Referred to Committee Whole House.		
Fry, Benjamin	Settlement of claim as agent fo erecting fortifications.	25	2	Petition	41	Judiciary	342	Favorable	372	Referred to Committee Whole House.		
Fry, Benjamin	Settlement of claim as agent for erecting fortifications.	25	3	House bill	378	Judiciary	....	....	372	Passed.		
Fry, Benjamin	Settlement of claim as agent for erecting fortifications.	26	1	Petition	175	Judiciary	87	Favorable	82	Passed	Indef. postp'd.	
Fry, Benjamin, administrator of.	Settlement of claim as agent for erecting fortifications.	26	2	Petition	38	Judiciary.						
Fry, Benjamin, administrator of.	Settlement of claim as agent for erecting fortifications.	27	2	Petition	153	Judiciary	778	Adverse	......	Referred to Committee Whole House.		
Fry, Benjamin, administrator of.	Settlement of claim as agent for erecting fortifications.	28	1	Petition	368	Judiciary	368	Adverse	......	Laid on table.		
Fry, Benjamin, administrator of.	Settlement of claim as agent for erecting fortifications.	28	2	Petition	340	Judiciary.						
Fry, Benjamin, administrator of.	Settlement of claim as agent for erecting fortifications.	29	1	Petition	91	Judiciary.						
Fry, Benjamin, administrator of.	Settlement of claim as agent for erecting fortifications.	29	2	Petition	110	Judiciary.						
Fry, Benjamin, administrator of.	Settlement of claim as agent for erecting fortifications.	30	1	Petition	587	Judiciary.						
Fry, Benjamin, administrator of.	Settlement of claim as agent for erecting fortifications.	31	1	Petition	502	Judiciary	161	Favorable	181	Referred to Committee Whole House.		
Fry, Carey H.	Compensation for horse lost in United States service.	30	1	Petition	682	Claims	....	....	......	Discharged; laid on table.		
Fry, Carey H.	Compensation for horse lost in United States service.	31	1	Petition	308	....	....	....	......	Leave to withdraw.		
Fry, Christopher	Indemnity for French spoliations prior to 1800.	26	1	Memorial	182	Foreign Affairs	343	Favorable; bill	319	Referred to Committee Whole House.		
Fry, Henry	Pension	27	2	Senate bill	1126	Naval Affairs	Aug. 10, 1842	Favorable	S. 260	Passed	....	App'd Aug. 29, 1842
Fry, Henry	(See assignees of Thomas Tupper.)	22	2	....	142							
Fry, J.	(See Clayton & Mitchell)	26	1	....	323							
Fry, John B.	Extra compensation as clerk to the sergeant-at-arms.	30	2	Resolution	93	....	....	....	......	Rejected.		
Fry, Philip	Pension for revolutionary services.	21	2	Resolution	71	Military Pensions.						
Fry, Robert	(See John D. Needham, *et al*)	15	1	....	136							
Fry & Spalding, attorney of.	Settlement of claim to land	17	1	Petition	124	Priv. Land Claims.						
Fry & Spalding, attorney of.	Settlement of claim to land	17	2	Petition	88	Ways and Means.						
Fry & Spalding, attorney of.	Settlement of claim to land	18	1	Resolution	217	Ways and Means	April 5, 1824	Favorable	184	Passed	Passed	App'd May 19, 1824
Fry, William W., (Ala.)	Permission to import iron free of duty.	25	2	Petition	1177	Agriculture.						
Fry, William W., (Ala.)	Permission to import iron free of duty.	25	2	Senate bill	1276	Whole House	July 7, 1838	With amend.	S. 147	Passed	Passed	App'd July 7, 1838
Frye, J.	(See P. J. Farnham & Co.)	30	2	....	116							
Frye, Nathaniel, jr.	Compensation for services as paymaster general.	19	1	Petition	364	Ways and Means	....	....	......	Discharged; laid on table.		

List of private claims presented to the House of Representatives of the United States from the 1st to the 31st Congress, inclusive—Continued.

Names of claimants.	Nature or object of the claim.	Congress.	Session.	How brought before the House of Reps.	Page of journal.	To what committee of the House referred.	No. or date of the report.	Nature of the report.	No. of the bill.	How disposed of by the House of Reps.	How disposed of by the Senate.	Date of the act of Congress, and remarks.
Frye, Nathaniel, jr.	Compensation for services as paymaster general.	23	1	Petition	186	Ways and Means	256	Adverse		Laid on table.		
Fryer, Leonard	Relief as a disabled soldier	19	1	Petition	268	Military Pensions	164	Adverse		Laid on table.		
Fudge, George	(See Stephen Decatur, widow of)	20	1		295		201		S. 50			
Fugate, James	Pension	29	1	Petition	168	Invalid Pensions.						
Fugate, James	Pension	29	2	Petition	33	Invalid Pensions.						
Fugate, James	Pension	30	1	Petition	115	Invalid Pensions	284	Favorable	280	Referred to Committee Whole House.		
Fugate, James	Pension	30	2	House bill	652	Whole House			280	Passed	Passed	App'd March 3, 1849
Fugate, Thomas	Pension for revolutionary services	14	1	Petition	257	Rev. Pensions	April 11, 1816	Favorable	171	Passed	Passed	App'd April 30, 1816
Fulford, John	Pension	3	1	Rep. of Sec. War	131	Select	May 26, 1794	Favorable	62	Passed	Passed	App'd June 7, 1794
Fulford, John, heirs of	Compensation for revolutionary services.	25	2	Senate bill	763	Rev. Claims	May 23, 1838	Adverse	S. 187	Laid on table.		
Fulham, George	Pension	3	1	Rep. of Secretary War.	186	Select	May 26, 1794	Favorable	R. 12	Referred to Secretary War.		
Fulham, George	Pension	3	2	Rep. of Secretary War.	262	Claims.						
Fulham, George	Pension	4	1	Res. and docs	373	Claims.						
Fulham, George	Pension	4	2	Res. and docs	614	Claims.						
Fulks, John B., heirs of	Pension for revolutionary services	26	2	Petition	82	Rev. Pensions	206	Adverse		Laid on table.		
Fullam, Sewall	(See Samuel Rist, guardian of)	18	1		31							
Fuller, Abigail, (N. Y.)	Continuation of pension	28	1	Petition	72	Rev. Pensions.						
Fuller, Abigail	(See Timothy Newman, widow of)	24	2	Petition	45							
Fuller, Abijah	For an exchange of land	23	1	Petition	382	Public Lands.						
Fuller, Anna	Continuation of pension	27	2	Petition	256	Rev. Pensions.						
Fuller, Asa	Indemnity for property destroyed by enemy.	15	1	Rep't of Committee.	393	Claims.						
Fuller, Asa	Indemnity for property destroyed by enemy.	15	2	Petition	196	Claims.						
Fuller, Asa	Indemnity for property destroyed by enemy.	16	1	Petition	28	Claims	Dec. 20, 1819	Adverse		Laid on table.		
Fuller, Asa	Indemnity for property destroyed by enemy.	18	1	Petition	295	Claims.						
Fuller, Asa	Indemnity for property destroyed by enemy.	21	2	Petition	165	Claims	Jan. 18, 1831	Adverse		Laid on table.		
Fuller, Azariah	Increase of pension	28	1	Petition	210	Rev. Pensions.						
Fuller, A. G.	(See Henry Williams, and others)	30	2		237							
Fuller, Belcher, executor of	Indemnity for French spoliations prior to 1800.	26	1	Memorial	182	Foreign Affairs	343	Favorable; bill	319	Referred to Committee Whole House.		
Fuller, Benjamin	Indemnity for property destroyed in revolutionary war.	1	3	Petition	383					Referred to Secretary Treasury.		
Fuller, Benjamin	Indemnity for property destroyed in revolutionary war.	2	2	Rep. of Secretary Treasury.	626	Whole House.						
Fuller, Benjamin	Arrears of pay and clothing	1	3	Petition	392					Referred to Secretary War.		
Fuller, Benjamin	Pension for revolutionary services	22	1	Petition	255	Rev. Pensions				Discharged; laid on table.		
Fuller, Benjamin A. G., et al.	Compensation for loss of schooner Ticonia.	30	2	Senate bill	237	Claims	Feb. 21, 1849	Favorable	211	Passed	Passed	App'd March 3, 1849
Fuller, Catharine	(See Charles Fuller, widow of.)	27	2		182							
Fuller, Charles, widow of	Remuneration for loss of property, and for imprisonment.	27	2	Petition	182	Claims	710	Adverse		Laid on table.		
Fuller, Daniel	Pension	19	1	Petition	407	Military Pensions	April 20, 1826	Adverse		Rejected.		

List of private claims presented to the House of Representatives of the United States from the 1st to the 31st Congress, inclusive—Continued.

Names of claimants.	Nature or object of the claim.	Congress.	Session.	How brought before the House of Reps.	Page of journal.	To what committee of the House referred.	No. or date of the report.	Nature of the report.	No. of the bill.	How disposed of by the House of Reps.	How disposed of by the Senate.	Date of the act of Congress, and remarks.
Fuller, Daniel	Pension	19	2	Petition	132	Military Pensions.						
Fuller, Daniel	Pension	20	1	Petition	155	Military Pensions.						
Fuller, Daniel	Pension	21	2	Petition	158	Military Pensions.						
Fuller, Daniel	Pension	22	1	Petition	295	Invalid Pensions	347	Favorable	444	Passed.		
Fuller, Daniel	Pension	22	2	Petition	27	Invalid Pensions	Dec. 19, 1832	Favorable	626	Passed	With amend.	
Fuller, Daniel	Pension	23	1	Petition	44	Invalid Pensions	1	Favorable	1	Passed	Passed, with amendment.	App'd June 25, 1834
Fuller, Elisha, *et al.*	Pension for revolutionary services.	3	1	Petition	60					Referred to Secretary War.		
Fuller, Elisha, *et al.*	Pension for revolutionary services.	3	2	Rep. of Secretary War.	278					Laid on table.		
Fuller, Farley	(See John Post and F. Fuller)	17	1		160							
Fuller & Grace	(See Grace & Fuller)	20	1		465							
Fuller, James	Arrears of pension	22	1	Resolution	327	Invalid Pensions	July 11, 1832	Adverse		Laid on table.		
Fuller, James	Arrears of pension	22	2	Resolution	27	Invalid Pensions	Feb. 15, 1833	Favorable	738	Referred to Committee Whole House.		
Fuller, James	Arrears of pension	23	1	Petition	44	Invalid Pensions	1	Favorable	1	Passed	Rejected.	
Fuller, James	Arrears of pension	23	2	Resolution	206	Invalid Pensions.						
Fuller, James	Arrears of pension	24	1	Petition	98	Invalid Pensions				Discharged; referred to Com. Whole House.		
Fuller, James	Arrears of pension	25	2	Petition	85	Invalid Pensions				Discharged; laid on table.		
Fuller, James	Arrears of pension	27	2	Petition	68	Invalid Pensions.	435	Adverse		Laid on table.		
Fuller, Jesse	(See William H. Bedford, agent, &c.)	28	2		262							
Fuller, John B.	Pension for revolutionary services.	14	1	Petition	266	Rev. Pensions.	April 11, 1816	Favorable	171	Passed	Passed, with amendment.	App'd April 30, 1816
Fuller, Joseph	(See Caleb Thornley, *et al.*)	4	1		388							
Fuller, Nathaniel, *et al*	Compensation for revolutionary services.	2	2	Petition and rep't Sec. of War.	142					Laid on table.		
Fuller, Nathaniel, *et al*	Balance of moneys due for subsistence.	2	2	Petition and rep. Sec. of War.	665					Laid on table.		
Fuller, Nathan & Belcher, heirs of.	Indemnity for French spoliations prior to 1800.	29	2	Memorial	292	Foreign Affairs.						
Fuller, Nathaniel	Pension for revolutionary services.	20	2	Petition	112	Military Pensions.	Feb. 13, 1829	Favorable	440	Referred to Committee Whole House.		
Fuller, Nathaniel	Pension for revolutionary services.	21	1	Petition	49	Military Pensions.	Jan. 5, 1830	Favorable	72	Passed	Passed	App'd May 20, 1830
Fuller, Samuel	Indemnity for property destroyed at Ogdensburg.	23	1	Petition	120	Claims	17	Adverse		Laid on table.		
Fuller, Silas	Arrears of pension	26	1	Petition	287	Invalid Pensions.						
Fuller, Silas	Arrears of pension	26	2	Petition	36	Invalid Pensions.						
Fuller, Silas	Arrears of pension	27	2	Petition	60	Invalid Pensions.	827	Adverse		Laid on table.		
Fuller, Stephen	Invalid pension	3	2	Rep. of Secretary War.	278	Claims	Mar. 2, 1795			Referred to Secretary of War.		
Fuller, Stephen	Invalid pension	4	1	Res. and docs.	373	Claims	Mar. 4, 1796	Favorable	156	Passed	Passed	App'd April 20, 1796
Fuller, Stephen, (S. C.)	Invalid pension	20	1	Resolution	176	Military Pensions.	April 29, 1828	Favorable	288	Passed.		
Fuller, Stephen, (S. C.)	Invalid pension	20	2	Rep't Committee	55	Military Pensions.	Dec. 12, 1828	Favorable	311	Passed.		
Fuller, Stephen, (S. C.)	Invalid pension	21	1	Petition	48	Military Pensions.	Jan. 5, 1830	Favorable	72	Passed	Passed	App'd May 20, 1830
Fuller, Thomas	(See James Averill, jr., *et al.*)	12	1		85							
Fuller, William, (Ala.)	Grant of land in lieu of other land	19	2	Resolution	127	Public Lands.						
Fuller, William, (Ga.)	Compensation for mail service	27	2	Petition	699	P. Of. & P. Roads.						
Fuller, William, (Ga.)	Compensation for mail service	27	3	Petition	58	P. Of. & P. Roads.						

List of private claims presented to the House of Representatives of the United States from the 1st to the 31st Congress, inclusive—Continued.

Names of claimants.	Nature or object of the claim.	Congress.	Session.	How brought before the House of Reps.	Page of journal.	To what committee of the House referred.	No. or date of the report.	Nature of the report.	No. of the bill.	How disposed of by the House of Reps.	How disposed of by the Senate.	Date of the act of Congress, and remarks.
Fuller, William, (Ga.)	Compensation for mail service	28	1	Petition	183	Claims	202	Favorable	R. 11	Passed.		
Fuller, William, (Ga.)	Compensation for mail service	29	1	Petition	75	P. Of. & P. Roads.	512	Adverse	......	Leave to withdraw.		
Fuller, William, (Ga.)	Compensation for mail service	30	1	Petition	346	Judiciary	268	Favorable	261	Referred to Committee Whole House.		
Fuller, William, & Charles Savage.	Compensation for mail service	30	2	House bill	142	Whole House	....	....	261	Passed	Passed, with amendment.	App'd Feb. 10, 1849
Fuller, William, & Charles Savage.	Damages under contract with Post-office department.	30	1	Petition	271	Judiciary	614	Adverse	......	Laid on table.		
Fuller, William, & Charles Savage.	Damages under contract with Post-office department.	30	2	Petition	240	....	....	....	......	Leave to withdraw.		
Fuller, William, & Orlando Saltmarsh.	Compensation for mail service in United States.	27	2	Petition	757	P. Of. & P. Roads.						
Fuller, William, & Orlando Saltmarsh.	Compensation for mail service in United States.	27	3	Petition	59	P. Of. & P. Roads.						
Fuller, William, & Orlando Saltmarsh.	Compensation for mail service in United States.	28	1	Petition	183	Claims	201	Favorable	R. 10	Passed.		
Fuller, William, & Orlando Saltmarsh.	Compensation for mail service in United States.	29	2	Senate resolution.	307	P. Of. and P. Roads.	Feb. 16, 1847	Favorable	R. 6	Referred to Committee Whole House.		
Fuller, William, & Orlando Saltmarsh.	Compensation for mail service in United States.	30	1	Petition	80	P. Of. & P. Roads.	102	Favorable	92	Referred to Committee Whole House.		
Fuller, William, & Orlando Saltmarsh.	Compensation for mail service in United States.	30	2	House bill	92	Whole House	....	....	92	Passed	Passed	App'd Feb. 10, 1849
Fullerton, Anna	(See Dr. Humphrey Fullerton, late widow of.)	10	1	....	180							
Fullerton, Catharine	(See James Fullerton, widow of.)	18	1	....	134							
Fullerton, Dr. Humphrey, late widow of.	Compensati'n for services and losses in revolutionary war.	9	1	Petition	321	Claims	April 11, 1806	Res'n. to postpone.	......	Resolution adopted.		
Fullerton, Dr. Humphrey, late widow of.	Compensati'n for services and losses in revolutionary war.	10	1	Petition	180	....	....	....	......	Referred to Committee Whole House, on bill No. 20.		
Fullerton, Humphrey	(See Joseph Kerr, surety of.)	20	1	....	368							
Fullerton, Humphrey, widow of.	Compensation for revolutionary services.	9	1	Petition	321	Claims	April 11, 1806	Resol'n to postpone.	......	Resolution adopted.		
Fullerton, Humphrey, widow of.	Compensation for revolutionary services.	10	1	Petition	180	....	....	....	......	Referred to Committee Whole House on bill No. 20.		
Fullerton, James, widow of	Naval pension	18	1	Petition	134	Naval Affairs	Jan. 27, 1824	Adverse	......	Laid on table.		
Fullerton, T. W., & A. G. Sloo.	Permission to import iron for steamboats free of duty.	27	2	Petition	686	Ways and Means.						
Fullerton, William, *et al.*	Fishing bounty on schooner Joanna	26	1	Petition	710	Commerce.						
Fullerton, William, *et al.*	Fishing bounty on schooner Joanna	27	2	Petition	57	Commerce	477	Favorable	327	Referred to Committee Whole House.		
Fullerton, William, *et al.*	Fishing bounty on schooner Joanna	27	3	House bill	87	Whole House	....	....	327	Passed	Indef. postp'd.	
Fulmer, Jacob	Pension	19	2	Petition	307	Military Pensions.						
Fulmer, Jacob	Pension	20	1	Petition	223	Military Pensions	Mar. 11, 1828	Adverse	......	Laid on table.		
Fulmer, Jacob	Pension	20	2	Petition	204	Military Pensions.						
Fulmer, Jacob	Pension	21	1	Petition	47	Military Pensions	....	....	......	Discharged; laid on table.		
Fulmer, Jacob	Pension	21	2	Petition	53	Military Pensions.						
Fulmer, Jacob	Pension	22	1	Petition	67	Rev. Pensions.						
Fulmer, John	Compensation for revolutionary services.	2	1	Petition	474	....	....	....	......	Referred to Secretary of War.		
Fullmore, Speller	(See Canadian refugees)	4	2	....	614							

List of private claims presented to the House of Representatives of the United States from the 1st to the 31st Congress, inclusive—Continued.

Names of claimants.	Nature or object of the claim.	Congress.	Session.	How brought before the House of Reps.	Page of journal.	To what committee of the House referred.	No. or date of the report.	Nature of the report.	No. of the bill.	How disposed of by the House of Reps.	How disposed of by the Senate.	Date of the act of Congress, and remarks.
Fulsom, Gilman, Jr., & Ezekiel.	Indemnity for buildings destroyed by enemy.	15	2	Petition	32	Claims	Dec. 16, 1818	Adverse	......	Laid on table.		
Fulton, Alexander, heirs of	Permission to locate certain lands	26	1	Petition	798	Priv. Land Claims.						
Fulton, Catharine	(See Samuel Fulton, widow of)	29	1	....	198							
Fulton, James	Pension for revolutionary services.	22	1	Petition	131	Rev. Pensions.						
Fulton, John	Grant of land as a Nova Scotia refugee.	11	2	Petition	112	Public Lands	Dec. 7, 1809	Favorable	35	Passed	Passed	App'd Feb. 26, 1810
Fulton, John	Compensation for losses in removing from Nova Scotia.	12	1	Petition	214	Public Lands	....	....	......	....	....	Provided for in act of April 23, 1812.
Fulton, John	(See Canadian refugees)	4	2	....	614							
Fulton, Robert, (Ohio)	Pay for work on Cumberland road.	23	1	Res. and docs.	589	Claims	455	Adverse.				
Fulton, Robert, (Ohio)	Pay for work on Cumberland road.	24	1	Petition	429	Claims	744	Adverse	......	Laid on table.		
Fulton, Robert, heirs of, (Ohio.)	Pay for work on Cumberland road.	30	1	Petition	405	Claims	256	Favorable	249	Passed.		
Fulton, Robert	Extension of patent	12	1	Senate bill	100	Whole House	....	....	S. 8			
Fulton, Robert	(See Henry Devlin and others)	23	1	....	589							
Fulton, Robert, heirs of	Pay for use of steamboat Vesuvius	14	1	Senate bill	597	Select	....	Favorable	......	Indefinitely postponed.		
Fulton, Robert, heirs of	Pay for use of steamboat Vesuvius	18	1	Petition	298	Select.						
Fulton, Robert, heirs of	Pay for use of steamboat Vesuvius	20	2	Petition	120	Select	64	Favorable	409	Referred to Committee Whole House.		
Fulton, Robert, heirs of	Pay for use of steamboat Vesuvius	21	1	Resolution	133	Select	267	Favorable	320	Referred to Committee Whole House.		
Fulton, Robert, heirs of	Pay for use of steamboat Vesuvius	22	1	Memorial	257	Select.						
Fulton, Robert, heirs of	Pay for use of steamboat Vesuvius	23	1	Petition	59	Claims.						
Fulton, Robert, heirs of	Pay for use of steamboat Vesuvius	23	2	Petition	101	Select.						
Fulton, Robert, heirs of	Pay for use of steamboat Vesuvius	24	1	Petition	121	Claims	551	Joint resolut'n to refer.	11	Referred to Secretary of the Navy.		
Fulton, Robert, heirs of	Pay for use of steamboat Vesuvius	24	2	Rep. of Secretary Navy.	176	Claims	300	Favorable	965	Referred to Committee Whole House.		
Fulton, Robert, heirs of	Pay for use of steamboat Vesuvius	25	1	Petition	49	....	....	....	......	Laid on table.		
Fulton, Robert, heirs of	Pay for use of steamboat Vesuvius	25	2	Memorial	36	Claims	68	Favorable	80	Passed	Laid on table.	
Fulton, Robert, heirs of	Pay for use of steamboat Vesuvius	25	3	Memorial	86	Claims.						
Fulton, Robert, heirs of	Pay for use of steamboat Vesuvius	26	1	Petition	168	Claims.						
Fulton, Robert, heirs of	Pay for use of steamboat Vesuvius	26	2	Petition	125	Claims.						
Fulton, Robert, heirs of	Pay for use of steamboat Vesuvius	27	2	Petition	94	Claims	588	Favorable	387	Referred to Committee Whole House.		
Fulton, Robert, heirs of	Pay for use of steamboat Vesuvius	27	3	House bill	90	Whole House	....	....	387	Passed.		
Fulton, Robert, heirs of	Pay for use of steamboat Vesuvius	28	1	Petition	191	Claims	127	Favorable	120	Referred to Committee Whole House.		
Fulton, Robert, heirs of	Pay for use of steamboat Vesuvius	28	1	Senate bill	985	Whole House	....	....	S. 143			
Fulton, Robert, heirs of	Pay for use of steamboat Vesuvius	28	2	Senate bill	100	Claims	3	Favorable	S. 6	Referred to Committee Whole House.		
Fulton, Robert, heirs of	Pay for use of steamboat Vesuvius	29	1	Memorial	201	Naval Affairs	145	Favorable	149	Passed	Passed	App'd Aug. 7, 1846
Fulton, Samuel, (Indiana)	Pension for revolutionary services.	29	1	Petition	487	Rev. Pensions.	604	Adverse	......	Laid on table.		
Fulton, Samuel, (Indiana)	Pension for revolutionary services.	29	2	Petition	184	Rev. Pensions						
Fulton, Samuel, widow of	Pension for revolutionary services.	29	1	Petition	198	Rev. Pensions	461	Favorable	338	Passed	Indef. postp'd.	
Fulton, Samuel, widow of	Pension for revolutionary services.	30	1	Petition	78	Rev. Pensions	135	Favorable	124	Passed	Passed	App'd August 5, 1848
Fulton, Thomas	Pension for revolutionary services.	26	1	Petition	394	Rev. Pensions	490, 664	Adverse	......	Laid on table.		
Fulton, William	(See Canadian refugees)	11	2	....	115							
Fulton, William S.	Compensation for services as superintendent of Indian affairs.	25	2	Resolution	213	Indian Affairs.						
Fulwiler, J. B., *et al.*	(See Louis Drouillard)	30	1	....	104							

List of private claims presented to the House of Representatives of the United States from the 1st to the 31st Congress, inclusive—Continued.

Names of claimants.	Nature or object of the claim.	Congress.	Session.	How brought before the House of Reps.	Page of journal.	To what committee of the House referred.	No. or date of the report.	Nature of the report.	No. of the bill.	How disposed of by the House of Reps.	How disposed of by the Senate.	Date of the act of Congress, and remarks.
Fulwood, James	Compensation as assistant quartermaster.	23	1	Resolution	601	Indian Affairs.						
Fulwood, James	Compensation as assistant quartermaster.	27	2	Papers	1377					Laid on table.		
Fultz, Joshua	Compensation for revolutionary services.	17	2	Petition	81	Rev. Claims	Jan. 8, 1823	Adverse		Laid on table.		
Fultz, Joshua	Compensation for revolutionary services.	19	2	Petition	96	Rev. Claims	41	Adverse		Referred to Committee Whole House.		
Fultz, Joshua	Compensation for revolutionary services.	20	1	Petition	39	Rev. Claims	Feb. 22, 1828	Favorable	182	Referred to Committee Whole House.		
Funchiss, Daniel	Payment for transporting baggage for United States militia.	14	1	Petition	83	Claims				Discharged; leave to withdraw.		
Funk, Henry	Compensation for revolutionary services.	2	1	Petition	474					Referred to Secretary of War.		
Fuqua, Joseph	Release from judgment on surety bond.	20	1	Petition	128	Judiciary				Discharged; laid on table.		
Fur Company, American	Lot No. 14, in Prarie du Chien	18	2	Documents	188	Priv. Land Claims.						
Fur Company, American	Compensation for fire-arms furnished the United States.	20	1	Resolution	185	Ways and Means				Discharged; laid on table.		
Furbeck, John	Pension for revolutionary services.	24	1	Petition	107	Rev. Pensions				Discharged; laid on table.		
Furgus, Francis	Pension for revolutionary services.	24	1	Resolution	216	Rev. Pensions				Discharged; laid on table.		
Furguson, John	Pension for revolutionary services.	29	2	Petition	195	Rev. Pensions	Jan. 28, 1847	Adverse		Laid on table.		
Furguson, Robert	Pension for revolutionary services.	21	1	Resolution	431	Military Pensions.						
Furlong, John, son of	Pension for revolutionary services.	28	1	Petition	788	Rev. Pensions.						
Furlong, Lawrence	Settlement of claim for pilotage	2	1	Petition	479					Referred to Secretary Treasury.		
Furlong, Lawrence	Settlement of claim for pilotage	3	2	Rep. of Secretary Treasury.	284	Claims.						
Furlong, Lawrence	Settlement of claim for pilotage	4	1	Petition	439	Claims	May 31, 1796	Adverse		Laid on table.		
Furlong, Lawrence	Settlement of claim for pilotage	4	2	Res. and docs.	614	Claims.						
Furlong, Robert	(See John Furlong, son of)	28	1		788							
Furman, Benjamin	Compensation for wood furnished United States.	4	1	Rep. of Secretary Treasury.	388	Claims	74	Adverse		Laid on table.		
Furness, John, (N. H.)	(See Joshua Green, *et al.*)	4	1		385							
Furney, Abel	Increase of pension	9	2	House bill	608	Claims	Feb. 24, 1807	Favorable	216	Passed	Passed	App'd March 3, 1807
Furnival, Alexander	Increase of compensation as P. M., Baltimore.	4	2	Memorial	603	Select.						
Furst, Moritz	Damages for violation of contract by American consul at Leghorn.	18	2	Petition	30	Claims	June 13, 1825	Adverse		Laid on table.		
Furst, Moritz	Damages for violation of contract by American consul at Leghorn.	19	1	Petition	67	Claims	Dec. 28, 1825	Adverse		Laid on table.		
Furst, Moritz	Damages for violation of contract by American consul at Leghorn.	19	2	Petition	84	Claims				Leave to withdraw.		
Furst, Moritz	Damages for violation of contract by American consul at Leghorn.	20	1	Petition	195	Claims	133	Adverse		Laid on table.		
Furst, Moritz	Damages for violation of contract by American consul at Leghorn.	20	2	Petition	176	Claims.						
Furst, Moritz	Damages for violation of contract by American consul at Leghorn.	21	1	Petition	128	Claims	84	Adverse		Referred to Committee Whole House.		
Furst, Moritz	Damages for violation of contract by American consul at Leghorn.	23	1	Petition	33	Claims	192	Adverse		Laid on table.		

List of private claims presented to the House of Representatives of the United States from the 1st to the 31st Congress, inclusive—Continued.

Names of claimants.	Nature or object of the claim.	Congress.	Session.	How brought before the House of Reps.	Page of journal.	To what committee of the House referred.	No. or date of the report.	Nature of the report.	No. of the bill.	How disposed of by the House of Reps.	How disposed of by the Senate.	Date of the act of Congress, and remarks.
Furst, Moritz	Damages for violation of contract by American consul at Leghorn.	24	1	Petition	93	Claims	Jan. 25, 1836	Adverse	......	Laid on table.		
Furst, Moritz	Damages for violation of contract by American consul at Leghorn.	24	2	Petition	73	Claims	Dec. 23, 1836	Adverse	......	Laid on table.		
Furst, Moritz	Damages for violation of contract by American consul at Leghorn.	25	2	Petition	121	Claims	Jan. 9, 1838	Adverse	......	Recommitted.		
Fussell, John	(See Colonel Joseph Brown)	24	2	....	78							
Fustian, Thomas, and wife	(See Joseph Blake, heirs of)	11	3	....	495							
Futch, William, administrator of.	Pay for land in public certificates.	22	1	Petition	417	Public Lands.						
Futton, Alexander	(See William Miller, *et al*)	14	2	....	148	....	60					
Gaar, Staunton W	Payment for forage and damage to property in late war.	30	1	Petition	305	Claims	646	Favorable	513	Referred to Committee Whole House.		
Gaar, Staunton W	Payment for forage and damage to property in late war.	30	2	House bill	318	Whole House	Jan. 26, 1849	Favorable	513	Passed.		
Gaar, Staunton W	Payment for forage and damage to property in late war.	31	1	Petition	298	Claims.						
Gabriel, William, & others	Confirmation of title to land	14	2	Petition	285	Priv. Land Claims.						
Gad, Thomas	Pension	14	1	Letter of Secretary of War.	703	Pens. & Rev. Cl'ms.	April 11, 1816	General bill	171	Passed	Passed, with amendment.	App'd April 30, 1816
Gad, Thomas	Increase of pension	14	2	Resolution	148	Pens. & Rev. Cl'ms.	Jan. 29, 1817	General bill	91	Passed	Passed	Bill 91 became a law, omitting petitioner's name.
Gad, William	Pension	20	2	Resolution	186	Military Pensions.						
Gad, William	Pension	21	1	Resolution	217	Military Pensions.	....	....	......	....	....	See bill No. 248.
Gaffney, Daniel	For fishing bounty on schooner Henrietta.	28	1	Petition	100	Commerce.						
Gaffney, Daniel	For fishing bounty on schooner Henrietta.	28	2	Petition	82	Commerce.						
Gaffney, Daniel	For fishing bounty on schooner Henrietta.	29	1	Petition	106	Commerce	96	Favorable	115	Rejected.		
Gaffney, Daniel	For fishing bounty on schooner Henrietta.	30	1	Petition	157	Commerce.						
Gaffney, Daniel	For fishing bounty on schooner Henrietta.	30	2	Petition	205	Commerce.						
Gafford, Mary	Pension	27	3	Petition	422	Rev. Pensions.						
Gafford, Mary	Pension	28	1	Petition	62	....	....	....	......	Leave to withdraw.		
Gage, Aaron	Pension	20	1	Petition	338	Military Pensions.	April 29, 1828	General bill	283	Passed.		
Gage, Aaron	Pension	20	2	House bill	55	Military Pensions.	Dec. 12, 1828	General bill	311	Passed	Laid on table.	
Gage, Aaron	Pension	21	1	Resolution	48	Military Pensions.	Feb. 13, 1830	General bill	72	Passed	Passed	App'd May 20, 1830 Petitioner's name omitted in act.
Gage, Abner	Pension	3	1	Petition	49							
				Rep. of Secretary State.	93	Select	....	....	......	Laid on table.		
Gage, Abner	Pension	10	1	House bill	232	Claims	April 21, 1808	General bill	78	Passed	Passed	App'd April 25, 1808
Gage, Abner	Increase of pension	10	1	Petition	168	Claims.						
Gage, Abner	Increase of pension	10	2	Petition	352	Claims.						
Gage, Abner	Increase of pension	13	1	Petition	56	Claims.						

List of private claims presented to the House of Representatives of the United States from the 1st to the 31st Congress, inclusive—Continued.

Names of claimants.	Nature or object of the claim.	Congress.	Session.	How brought before the House of Reps.	Page of journal.	To what committee of the House referred.	No. or date of the report.	Nature of the report.	No. of the bill.	How disposed of by the House of Reps.	How disposed of by the Senate.	Date of the act of Congress, and remarks.
Gage, Abner	Increase of pension	13	2	Petition	351	Rev. Pensions	....	....	......	Discharged; referred to Secretary War.		
Gage, Asa	Pension	17	1	Petition	59	Rev. Pensions	....	....	......	Discharged; leave to withdraw.		
Gage and Davenport	Confirmation of title to land	20	1	Resolution	28	Public Lands	42	Favorable	34	Passed	....	See Statutes at Large, vol. 4, p. 260.
Gage, Captain Edmond	Relief from imprisonment and penalty incurred by carrying slaves.	18	1	Memorial	450	Judiciary.						
Gage, George	Pension	26	1	Petition	962	Rev. Pensions.						
Gage, Isaac	To be allowed to import iron duty free.	25	3	Petition	191	Manufactures	Jan. 17, 1839	Favorable	1048	Referred to Committee Whole House.		
Gage, Isaac	To be allowed to import iron duty free.	26	1	Petition	182	Manufactures	April 25, 1840	Favorable	365	Referred to Committee Whole House.		
Gage, Isaac, *et al.*	Extension of credit on certain duties.	12	2	Petition	604	Ways and Means	Jan. 9, 1813	Adverse	......	Rejected.		
Gage, Jonathan	Indemnity for French spoliations prior to 1800.	26	1	Memorial	182	Foreign Affairs	243	Favorable; bill	310	Referred to Committee Whole House.		
Gage, Samuel	Pension	16	1	Resolution	63	Rev. Pensions	Jan. 14, 1820	Adverse	......	Laid on table.		
Gagnon, P. A.	(See H. Frederic, *et al.*)	30	1	....	976							
Gaiennie, Francois	(See Benjamin Metoyer, *et al.*)	29	1	....	1069							
Gailey, Ezekiel	Indemnity for damages to property by United States troops.	26	1	Petition	335	Claims.						
Gaillard, Theodore	Confirmation of title to land	16	1	Petition	182	Select.						
Gaillard, Theodore	Reimbursement of money erroneously paid into the United States treasury.	27	2	Petition	226	Claims.						
Gaillard, Theodore *et al*	(See Elisha Hall Bay, *et al.*)	17	1	....	389							
Gain, John	(See John Cain)	27	2	....	76							
Gaines, Barnard	Pension	14	2	Petition	164	Pens. & Rev. Cl'ms.	Jan. 31, 1817	Adverse	......	Laid on table.		
Gaines, Barnard	Pension	15	1	Petition	130	Pens. & Rev. Cl'ms.	....	....	......	Discharged; laid on table.		
Gaines, George S	(See Allen Glover, *et al.*)	20	2	....	119							
Gaines, George S	Compensation as pension agent	28	1	Petition	159	Claims	....	....	......	Discharged; laid on table.		
Gaines, George S	Compensation for removing Choctaw Indians.	28	1	Petition	123	Indian Affairs	....	....	......	Discharged; laid on table.		
Gaines, George S	Compensation for removing Choctaw Indians.	28	2	Petition	235	Claims.						
Gaines, John P	Payment for horse lost in United States service.	30	1	House bill	622	Claims	413	Favorable	364			
Gaines, Myra Clark	Pension	31	2	Petition	264	Invalid Pensions.						
Gaines, Richard	Confirmation of title to land	18	2	Petition	55	Public Lands.						
Gaines, Sarah	Pension, bounty land, and extra pay.	31	1	Petition	542	Claims.						
Gaines, Thomas	Pension	19	1	Petition	36	Rev. Pensions	164	Adverse	......	Laid on table.		
Gaines, William D	Confirmation of title to land	22	1	House bill	127	Public Lands	Dec. 30, 1831	Favorable	168	Passed	Passed	App'd July 14, 1832
Gaines, Young	For land in lieu of Spanish grant.	9	1	Petition	259	Public Lands.						
Gaines, Young	For land in lieu of Spanish grant.	9	2	Petition	479	Public Lands.						
Gaines, Young	For land in lieu of Spanish grant.	10	1	Petition	18	Public Lands.						
Gainey, Abram	Confirmation of title to land	27	2	Petition	338	Priv. Land Claims.						
Gainey, Abram	Confirmation of title to land	27	3	Petition	406	Priv. Land Claims.						
Gaither, Edward B	Payment for horse lost in United States service.	18	1	Petition	214	Claims	Mar. 8, 1824	Adverse	......	Laid on table.		

List of private claims presented to the House of Representatives of the United States from the 1st to the 31st Congress, inclusive—Continued.

Names of claimants.	Nature or object of the claim.	Congress.	Session.	How brought before the House of Reps.	Page of journal.	To what committee of the House referred.	No. or date of the report.	Nature of the report.	No. of the bill.	How disposed of by the House of Reps.	How disposed of by the Senate.	Date of the act of Congress, and remarks.
Gaither, Edward B	Payment for horse lost in United States service.	19	1	Resolution	54	Claims	Jan. 18, 1826	Adverse		Laid on table.		
Gaither, Henry B	Compensation for keeping book for Cherokee Indian agent.	30	1	Senate joint resolution.	958	Indian Affairs	June 26, 1848	Favorable	13	Passed		App'd Aug. 14, 1848
Gaither, James	Payment for work done on Navy Department.	27	3	Petition	448	Expend's of Navy Department.				Discharged; laid on table.		
Gale, Abraham	Renewal of certificate of public debt.	10	1	Petition	24	Select.						
Gale, Abraham	Renewal of certificate of public debt.	10	2	Petition	421	Select.						
Gale, Anthony	Compensation for extra services as military agent.	16	1	Petition	375	Military Affairs	April 10, 1820	Adverse		Leave to withdraw.		
Gale, Anthony	Compensation for extra duties as quartermaster.	17	1	Petition	40	Naval Affairs				Discharged; leave to withdraw.		
Gale, Anthony	Compensation for extra duties as quartermaster.	27	2	Petition	93	Claims.	340	Adverse		Laid on table.		
Gale, Anthony	Compensation for services in the staff, while a subaltern officer.	18	2	Petition	116	Naval Affairs	Feb. 15, 1825	Adverse		Laid on table.		
Gale, Anthony	Compensation for services as an officer of marines.	20	1	Petition	311	Claims	Mar. 19, 1828	Adverse		Laid on table.		
Gale, Anthony	Compensation for services as an officer of marines.	22	1	Petition	809	Naval Affairs.						
Gale, Anthony	Compensation for services as an officer of marines.	22	2	Petition	96	Naval Affairs.						
Gale, Anthony	Compensation for services as an officer of marines.	23	1	Petition	247	Naval Affairs	375	Adverse		Laid on table.		
Gale, Anthony	Compensation for services as an officer of marines.	23	2	Petition	39	Naval Affairs	62	Adverse		Laid on table.		
Gale, Anthony	Pension	18	1	Petition	114	Claims	Mar. 24, 1824	Adverse		Laid on table.		
Gale, Anthony	Pension	21	2	Petition	271	Naval Affairs.						
Gale, Anthony	For pay to the present time	20	2	Petition	176	Military Affairs	Jan. 27, 1829	Adverse		Laid on table.		
Gale, Anthony, wife of	Pension from the navy fund	16	2	Petition	236	Naval Affairs				Discharged; laid on table.		
Gale, Anthony, widow of.	For arrears of pay	28	1	Petition	787	Naval Affairs.						
Gale, Anthony, widow of.	For arrears of pay	29	1	Petition	298	Rev. Pensions.						
Gale, Daniel, widow of	Pension	25	2	Petition	349	Invalid Pensions.						
Gale, Daniel, widow of	Pension	26	1	Petition	162	Invalid Pensions	Mar. 5, 1840	Adverse		Laid on table.		
Gale, George	Payment for wagon and team lost in United States service.	14	1	Petition	40	Claims.						
Gale, George	Payment for wagon and team lost in United States service.	23	1	Petition	217	Claims	225	Adverse		Laid on table		
Gale, George	Payment for wagon and team lost in United States service.	25	2	Petition	176	Claims.						
Gale, George	Payment for wagon and team lost in United States service.	25	3	Petition	86	Claims.						
Gale, George	Payment for wagon and team lost in United States service.	26	1	Petition	168	Claims	46	Adverse		Laid on table.		
Gale, George	Payment for wagon and team lost in United States service.	26	2	Petition	81	Claims	65	Adverse		Laid on table.		
Gale, George W	(See A. J. Pickett and G. W. Gale)	25	2		894							
Gale, Henry	For confirmation of title to Pea Patch island.	24	1	Petition	97	Military Affairs	92	Favorable	87	Laid on table.		

List of private claims presented to the House of Representatives of the United States from the 1st to the 31st Congress, inclusive—Continued.

Names of claimants.	Nature or object of the claim.	Congress.	Session.	How brought before the House of Reps.	Page of journal.	To what committee of the House referred.	No. or date of the report.	Nature of the report.	No. of the bill.	How disposed of by the House of Reps.	How disposed of by the Senate.	Date of the act of Congress, and remarks.
Gale, Isaac	Pension	25	2	Petition	58	Military Affairs	588	Favorable	575	Passed	Passed	App'd July 7, 1838
Gale, Levin, assignee of	Payment to him of balance due said Gale.	23	1	Petition	449	Military Affairs				Discharged; leave to withdraw.		
Gale, Levin, assignee of	Payment to him of balance due said Gale.	24	2	Petition	107	Military Affairs.						
Gale, William	Renewal of patent	26	2	Petition	50	Patents.						
Gule, William	Renewal of patent	27	2	Petition	100	Patents	671	Favorable	401	Ref'd to Com. W. H.		
Gale, William	Renewal of pa'ent	27	3	House bill	88	Whole House	Dec. 23, 1842	Favorable	401	Passed	Passed	App'd March 3, 1843
Gale, William, assignee of	Pay and rations due for services in 1812.	17	1	Petition	220	Claims				Discharged; laid on table.		
Galucia, Jacob	Payment for erecting monument at Swampscot Beach.	25	2	Petition	113	Commerce	1048	Favorable	882	Referred to Committee Whole House.		
Galucia, Jacob	Payment for erecting monument at Swampscot Beach.	25	3	House bill	432	Whole House	Feb. 1, 1839	Favorable	882	Passed	Rejected.	
Galucia, Jacob	Payment for erecting monument at Swampscot Beach.	26	1	Petition	176	Commerce.						
Galivey, ———	(See Aquirre & Galway.)											
Gallagher, Jacintha, assignee of.	Confirmation of title to land	16	2	Petition	48	Priv. Land Claims.						
Gallagher, Adam, *et al.*	(See Shakers, Society of)	14	1		433							
Gallagher, Ebenezer	Pension	19	1	Resolution	523	Military Affairs.						
Gallagher, John	Increase of pension	31	1	Petition	193	Invalid Pensions.						
Gallagher, John, of Baltimore.	Pension	31	2	Petition	112	Invalid Pensions.						
Gallagher, John, widow of.	Pension	29	1	Petition	904	Invalid Pensions.						
Gallaway, William, widow of.	Pension	14	1	Petition	221	Whole House.						
Gallespie, James	Pension	10	2	House bill	499	Claims	Jan. 30, 1809	General bill	158	Passed	Passed	App'd March 3, 1809
Galligo, George	Pension	14	1	Petition	59	Naval Affairs				Disch'd; laid on table.		
Galligo, George	Pension	15	2	Petition	107	Naval Affairs				Discharged; referred to Secretary War.		
Gallier, ———	(See Calvin Pollard, *et al.*)	23	1		523							
Gallion, George	(See William H. Bedford)	28	1		262							
Gallison, James	(See Charles Whitmarsh, *et al.*)	25	3		103							
Gallop, Andrew	Increase of pension	10	2	House bill	499	Whole House	Jan. 30, 1809	Favorable	158	Passed	Passed	App'd March 3, 1809
Gallop, William	Pension	19	2	Petition	36	Military Pensions	Feb. 14, 1827	General bill	437	Referred to Committee Whole House.		
Gallop, William	Pension	20	2	Petition	78	Military Pensions.						
Gallop, William	Pension	21	1	Petition	47	Military Pensions	307	Favorable	362	Referred to Committee Whole House.		
Gallop, William	Pension	21	2	House bill	318	Whole House	Feb. 17, 1831	Favorable	362	Passed.		
Gallop, William	Pension	22	1	Petition	35	Invalid Pensions	206	General bill	288	Passed	Passed, with amendment.	App'd July 14, 1832
Galloway, James	(See Eli Baldridge, sureties of)	14	2		76							
Galloway, James, *et al.*	Pa'ent for certain lands	24	2	Petition	268	Public Lands.						
Galloway, Jane	(See Samuel Galloway, heir of)	22	1		221							
Galloway, John	Compensation for services in revolutionary war.	11	2	Petition	146	Claims				Discharged; leave to withdraw.		
Galloway, John, heirs of	Commutation pay for revolutionary services.	25	2	Resolution	524	Rev. Claims	933	Adverse		Laid on table.		
Galloway, Samuel, heir of	Indemnity for losses in United States service.	22	1	Petition	221	Claims	Feb. 6, 1832	Adverse		Laid on table.		
Galloway, Samnel, heir of	Indemnity for losses in United States service.	24	1	Petition	207	Claims	Feb. 4, 1836	Adverse		Laid on table.		

List of private claims presented to the House of Representatives of the United States from the 1st to the 31st Congress, inclusive—Continued.

87

Names of claimants.	Nature or object of the claim.	Congress.	Session.	How brought before the House of Reps.	Page of journal.	To what committee of the House referred.	No. or date of the report.	Nature of the report.	No. of the bill.	How disposed of by the House of Reps.	How disposed of by the Senate.	Date of the act of Congress, and remarks.
Gallup, Andrew	Pension	10	2	House bill	499	Whole House	Feb. 20, 1809	With amends.	158	Passed	Passed	App'd March 3, 1809
Gallup, Benjamin	Pension	26	2	Petition	200	Rev. Pensions				Discharged; laid on table.		
Galphin, George, executors of.	Compensation due as commissioner of Indian affairs.	2	2	Petition	619	Select	Nov. 30, 1792	Favorable		Rejected.		
Galphin, George, heirs of.	Payment of a debt due from Cherokees at the breaking out of the revolutionary war.	26	1	Petition	605	Claims.						
Galphin, George, executors of.	Settlement of claim under treaty with Creek and Cherokee Indians in 1773.	29	2	Senate bill	374	Judiciary	77	Adverse	S. 88	Laid on table.		
Galphin, George, executors of.	Settlement of claim under treaty with Creek and Cherokee Indians in 1773.	30	1	Senate bill	269	Judiciary	Feb. 29, 1848	With't amend.	S. 40	Passed		App'd Aug. 14, 1848
Galphin, Milledge, *et al.*	(See George Galphin, heirs of)	26	1		605							
Galphin, Milledge	(See John Galphin, executors of)	29	2		374							
Galphin, Milledge	(See Thos. Galphin, executors of)	19	1		134							
Galphin, Thomas, executors of.	Interest on amount allowed by Indian treaty for slaves surrendered to the Creeks.	19	1	Petition	134	Indian Affairs	Mar. 18, 1826	By bill	163	Referred to Committee Whole House.		Leave to withdraw, 2d session.
Galphin, Thomas, executors of.	Interest on amount allowed by Indian treaty for slaves surrendered to the Creeks.	20	1	Petition	47	Indian Affairs				Leave to withdraw.		
Galphin, Thomas, executors of.	Interest on amount allowed by Indian treaty for slaves surrendered to the Creeks.	21	2	Petition	82	Indian Affairs	Dec. 29, 1830	By bill	155	Referred to Committee Whole House.		
Galphin, Thomas, executors of.	Interest on amount allowed by Indian treaty for slaves surrendered to the Creeks.	22	1	Petition	31	Indian Affairs.						
Galphin, Thomas, executors of.	Interest on amount allowed by Indian treaty for slaves surrendered to the Creeks.	23	1	Petition	168	Indian Affairs	Jan. 7, 1834	General bill	153	Passed	Passed	App'd April 30, 1834
Galphin, Thomas, executors of.	Payment of a debt due from Cherokee Indians, and confirmed by treaty stipulations.	28	1	Petition	194	Claims.						
Galpin, Amos	Pension	21	1	Petition	66	Military Pensions	April 7, 1830	Adverse		Laid on table.		
Galpin, Daniel	Arrears of pension	21	1	Petition	318	Military Pensions	April 6, 1830	Adverse		Laid on table.		
Galt, Alex., and Wm. H.	Indemnity for French spoliations prior to 1800.	31	1	Petition	312	Foreign Affairs	355	Favorable; bill	318	Referred to Committee Whole House.		
Galway & Aquirrie	To be released from custom-house bond.	31	1	Petition	1084	Commerce	Sept. 16, 1850	Favorable; bill	396	Passed		
Gamble, Abraham	Pension	10	2	House bill	499	Whole House	Feb. 20, 1809	With amends.	158	Passed	Passed	App'd March 3, 1809
Gamble, Abraham	Arrears of pension	11	2	Petition	442	Claims	Jan. 22, 1811	Favorable	218	Passed	Passed	App'd March 3, 1811
Gamble, Archibald	(See John B. Thibault, representatives of.)	22	1		125							
Gamble, Edmond, heirs of	Commutation pay	25	3	Petition	175	Rev. Claims.						
Gamble, Edmond, heirs of	Commutation pay	26	1	Petition	166	Rev. Claims.						
Gamble, Edmond, heirs of	Commutation pay	27	2	Petition	62	Rev. Claims	1085	Adverse		Leave to withdraw.		
Gamble, Edmond, heirs of.	Commutation pay	28	1	Petition	272	Rev. Claims.						
Gamble, Francis, B. widow of.	Pension	18	2	Petition	116	Naval Affairs	Jan. 28, 1825	Adverse		Leave to withdraw.		
Gamble, Francis B., widow of.	Pension	19	1	Petition	271	Naval Affairs	April 15, 1826	Adverse		Laid on table.		

List of private claims presented to the House of Representatives of the United States from the 1st to the 31st Congress, inclusive—Continued.

Names of claimants.	Nature or object of the claim.	Congress.	Session.	How brought before the House of Reps.	Page of journal.	To what committee of the House referred.	No. or date of the report.	Nature of the report.	No. of the bill.	How disposed of by the House of Reps.	How disposed of by the Senate.	Date of the act of Congress, and remarks.
Gamble, Francis B., widow of.	Pension	23	2	Petition	96	Naval Affairs	Feb. 25, 1835	Adverse		Laid on table.		
Gamble, Francis B., administrator of late widow.	Arrears of pension	31	2	Petition	38	Naval Affairs.						
Gamble, H. L.	(See John M. Gamble, widow of.)	25	2		400							
Gamble, James	To be credited with money stolen.	3	1	Petition and rep't Sec. Treasury.	39, 77					Laid on table.		
Gamble, James, *et al.*	Reimbursement of money paid for provisions.	28	1	Petition	98	Claims.						
Gamble, John G.	Payment for two mules lost in U. S. service.	29	1	Petition	738	Claims.						
Gamble, John G.	Payment for two mules lost in U S. service.	30	1	Petition	598	Claims.						
Gamble, John G.	Payment for two mules lost in U. S. service.	30	2	Petition	664	Claims				Leave to withdraw.		
Gamble, John G.	Payment for two mules lost in U. S. service.	31	1	Petition	255	Claims	95	Adverse		Laid on table.		
Gamble, John M., *et al.*	Payment of prize money for a vessel captured by them.	18	1	Petition	344	Naval Affairs.						
Gamble, John M., *et al.*	Payment of prize money for a vessel captured by them.	18	2	Petition	294	Naval Affairs	89	Adverse		Laid on table.		
Gamble, John M., *et al.*	Payment of prize money for a vessel captured by them.	20	2	Petition	176					Laid on table.		
Gamble, John M., *et al.*	Payment of prize money for a vessel captured by them.	21	1	Petition	175	Naval Affairs.						
Gamble, John M., *et al.*	(See R. D. Wainwright, *et al.*)	22	1		443							
Gamble, John M., *et al.*	Compensation for taking care of prisoners of war, and for performing staff duty.	24	1	Senate bill	899	Claims	763	Favorable	120	Passed	Passed	App'd July 2, 1836
Gamble, John M., widow of.	Pension	25	2	Petition	400	Naval Affairs				Discharged; laid on table.		
Gamble, John M., widow of.	Pension	25	3	Petition	91	Naval Affairs.						
Gamble, John M., widow of.	Pension	26	1	Petition	179	Naval Affairs.						
Gamble, John M., widow of.	Pension	28	1	Petition	211	Naval Affairs.						
Gamble, Robert	Payment for a slave who died of hurt received in United States service.	25	2	Petition	397	Claims.						
Gamble, Robert	Payment for a slave who died of hurt received in United States service.	26	1	Petition	169	Claims.						
Gamble, Robert	Payment for a slave who died of hurt received in United States service.	26	2	Petition	135	Claims.						
Gamble, Robert	Payment for a slave who died of hurt received in United States service.	28	1	Petition	133	Claims.						
Gamble, Robert	Payment for a slave who died of hurt received in United States service.	30	1	Petition	493	Military Affairs				Discharged; laid on table.		
Gamble, Thomas, heir of.	Confirmation of title to land	10	1	Petition	210	Public Lands.						

List of private claims presented to the House of Representatives of the United States from the 1st to the 31st Congress, inclusive—Continued.

Names of claimants.	Nature or object of the claim.	Congress.	Session.	How brought before the House of Reps.	Page of journal.	To what committee of the House referred.	No. or date of the report.	Nature of the report.	No. of the bill.	How disposed of by the House of Reps.	How disposed of by the Senate.	Date of the act of Congress, and remarks.
Gamble, William	Additional compensation as inspector of customs.	11	2	Petition	137	Com. and Manuf.				Recommitted.		
Gamble, William	Additional compensation as inspector of customs.	12	1	Petition	151	Ways and Means	May 12, 1812	Adverse		Rejected.		
Gamble, William	Additional compensation as inspector of customs.	13	1	Petition	37	Claims				Referred to Committee Whole House.		
Gamble, William	Additional compensation as inspector of customs.	13	2	Petition	181	Claims	21	Adverse		Referred to Committee Whole House.		
Gamble, William	Additional compensation as inspector of customs.	13	3	Senate bill	651	Claims	Feb. 1, 1815	Adverse		Laid on table.		
Gamble, William	Additional compensation as inspector of customs.	14	2	Petition	46	Claims.						
Gamble, William	Additional compensation as inspector of customs.	15	1	Petition	31	Claims	Feb. 16, 1818	Adverse		Rejected.		
Gamble, William	Additional compensation as inspector of customs.	22	1	Petition	472	Claims	Mar. 28, 1832	Adverse		Laid on table.		
Gamble, William	Indemnity for house destroyed by the British.	21	1	Petition	448	Claims	Mar. 24, 1830	Adverse		Laid on table.		
Gamblin, Peirre	Payment for horse lost in United States service.	23	1	Petition	305	Claims	300	Adverse		Laid on table.		
Gamblin, Peirre	Payment for horse lost in United States service.	23	2	Petition	106	Claims.						
Gamblin, Noel	Confirmation of title to land	15	1	Petition	102	Priv. Land Claims.						
Gammage, Sarah E.	(See Benjamin Eaton, heirs of.)	26	1	...	706							
Gammage, Thomas T.	Payment for property taken for use of United States.	30	1	Petition	954	Claims	750	Favorable	589	Referred to Committee Whole House.		
Gammage, Thomas T.	Payment for property taken for use of United States.	30	2	House bill	362	Whole House	Feb. 2, 1849	Favorable	589	Passed	Passed	App'd Feb. 22, 1849
Gammage, William	Pension	20	1	Petition	417	Military Pensions	April 29, 1828	General bill	283	Passed.		
Gammage, William	Pension	21	1	Petition	48	Military Pensions	Feb. 13, 1830	General bill	72	Passed	Passed	App'd May 20, 1830
Gammell, Joseph	Payment for a horse lost in United States service.	23	1	Documents	164	Claims.						
Gammell, Joseph	Payment for a horse lost in United States service.	28	1	Petition	262	Claims.						
Gammons, James	(See Archibald Jackson)	17	1		200							
Gandy, Alford	Payment for a horse lost in United States service.	25	2	Petition	922	Claims.						
Gandy, Alford	Payment for a horse lost in United States service.	26	1	Petition	306	Claims	699	Adverse		Laid on table.		
Gandy, Enoch	Pension	21	1	Petition	168	Military Pensions	April 2, 1830	Adverse		Laid on table.		
Gandy, James, and son	Remission of duties	21	1	Petition	39	Ways and Means				Discharged; leave to withdraw.		
Gandy, James, and son	Remission of duties	21	2	Petition	164	Ways and Means				Discharged; laid on table.		
Gandy, James, and son	Remission of duties	22	1	Petition	121	Ways and Means.						
Gandy, Willis	Pension	15	1	House bill	405	Rev. Pensions	April 16, 1818	Favorable	172	Passed	Postponed.	
Ganley, Charles M. D.	Compensation as express rider in late war.	22	1	Petition	293	Claims	March 7, 1832	Adverse		Laid on table.		
Gann, William	For land in lieu of pension	23	2	Petition	67	Public Lands.						
Gann, William	For land in lieu of pension	24	1	Petition	114	Public Lands	242	Adverse		Referred to Committee Whole House.		
Gannett, Benjamin	(See Deborah Gannett, widower of)	24	2		180							

List of private claims presented to the House of Representatives of the United States from the 1st to the 31st Congress, inclusive—Continued.

Names of claimants.	Nature or object of the claim.	Congress.	Session.	How brought before the House of Reps.	Page of journal.	To what committee of the House referred.	No. or date of the report.	Nature of the report.	No. of the bill.	How disposed of by the House of Reps.	How disposed of by the Senate.	Date of the act of Congress, and remarks.
Gannett, Deborah, *alias* Robert Shurtliff.	Pension	5	2	Petition	90	Claims	March 9, 1798	Adverse	......	Rejected.		
Gannett, Deborah, *alias* Robert Shurtliff.	Pension	11	2	Petition	228	Select	Mar. 27, 1810	Adverse	......	Rejected.		
Gannett, Deborah, *alias* Robert Shurtliff.	Increase of pension	16	1	Petition	343	Pens. & Rev. Cl'ms.						
Gannett, Deborah, widower of.	Pension for military services of his late wife.	24	2	Petition	180	Rev. Pensions	172	Favorable	890	Referred to Committee Whole House.		
Gannett, Deborah, widower of.	Pension for military services of his late wife.	25	2	Petition	38	Rev. Pensions	159	Favorable	184	Passed	Passed	App'd July 9, 1839
Gano, Daniel	Pension	17	1	Petition	220	Pens. & Rev. Cl'ms.	....	....	......	Discharged, referred to Com. Whole House.		
Gano, Daniel	Pension	17	2	Petition	43	Rev. Pensions.						
Gano, Daniel	For bounty land	19	1	Petition	336	Rev. Claims.						
Gano, Daniel	For bounty land	19	2	Petition	243	Rev. Claims.						
Gano, Daniel	For bounty land	20	1	Petition	159	Rev. Claims	Jan. 25, 1828	Adverse	......	Laid on table.		
Ganesvoort, H.	(See Exploring Expedition)	27	3	....	149							
Ganesvoort, Peter, jr.	Increase of salary	10	1	Memorial	67							
				Rep. of Secretary of War.	71	Ways and Means.						
Gant, James	(See James Lamar and Jas. Gant.)	25	3	Memorial	567							
Gantt, Benj. Rush	Credit for a sum of money	31	1	....	....	....	....	....	......	....	....	App'd Sept. 16, 1850
Gantt, Thomas	Pension	14	1	Petition	682	Pens. & Rev. Cl'ms.						
Garanger, Lewis & Charles	Pensions	2	1	Petition	495	Select	April 26, 1792	Adverse	......	Laid on table.		
Garanger, Lewis & Charles	Pensions	2	2	Petition	628	Select	Dec. 6, 1792	Favorable	203	Passed	Rejected.	
Garanger, Lewis & Charles	Pensions	11	2	Petition	316	Claims	April 9, 1810	Favorable	131	Leave to withdraw.		
Garanger, Lewis & Charles	Pensions	11	3	Petition	578	Claims.						
Garanger, Lewis & Charles	Pensions	12	2	Petition	609	Claims	Jan. 22, 1813	Adverse	......	Rejected.		
Garanger, Lewis & Charles	Payment of certificates of public debt.	2	2	Petition and rep't Sec. Treasury.	700	....	....	....	......	Laid on table.		
Gard, Job, *et al*	Payment for services rendered United States.	19	2	Petition	217	Claims.						
Garde, John, child of	Arrears of pension	26	1	Resolution	662	Naval Affairs.						
Garden, Alexander	Compensation for services in revolutionary war.	20	1	Petition	31	Rev. Claims	65	Favorable	64	Passed	Passed	App'd May 23, 1828
Garden, Alexander, heirs of	Compensation for services in revolutionary war.	23	1	Resolution	129	Rev. Claims	118	Favorable	123	Referred to Committee Whole House.		
Garden, Alexander, heirs of	Compensation for services in revolutionary war.	24	1	Petition	672	Rev. Claims.						
Garden, Alexander, executors of.	Interest on commutation pay	22	1	Petition	538	Rev. Claims	425	Favorable	530	Referred to Committee Whole House.		
Garden, Alexander, executors of.	Interest on commutation pay	24	2	Petition	91	Rev. Claims.						
Garden, Alexander, executors of.	To locate land warrant	22	2	Petition	207	Public Lands.						
Garden, Alexander, executors of.	To locate land warrant	23	1	Petition	148	Rev. Claims	118	Favorable	123	Passed.		
Gardere, Francis	Payment for land taken by United States.	31	1	Petition	308	Priv. Land Claims.	433	Favorable	361	Referred to Committee Whole House.		
Gardiner, Elizabeth	Pension	28	1	Petition	72	Rev. Pensions	....	....	......	Discharged; laid on table.		
Gardiner, Geo. W., widow of.	Indemnity for property destroyed at Fort Brooks.	24	1	Petition	708	Claims	611	Favorable	600	Referred to Committee Whole House.		

List of private claims presented to the House of Representatives of the United States from the 1st to the 31st Congress, inclusive—Continued.

Names of claimants.	Nature or object of the claim.	Congress.	Session.	How brought before the House of Reps.	Page of journal.	To what committee of the House referred.	No. or date of the report.	Nature of the report.	No. of the bill.	How disposed of by the House of Reps.	How disposed of by the Senate.	Date of the act of Congress, and remarks.
Gardiner, Geo. W., widow of.	Indemnity for property destroyed at Fort Brooks.	25	2	Petition	36	Claims	35	Favorable	47	Passed	Passed	App'd March 7, 1838
Gardiner, Geo. W., widow of.	For half-pay	24	1	Petition	457	Claims	March 3, 1836 415	General bill	426	Passed	Passed	App'd July 4, 1836
Gardiner, Geo. W., widow of.	Pension	26	2	Petition	119	Military Affairs	194	Adverse		Laid on table.		
Gardiner, Geo. W., widow of.	Pension	29	1	Petition	81	Invalid Pensions				Discharged; laid on table.		
Gardiner, Geo. W., widow of.	Pension	30	1	Petition	187	Rev. Pensions				Discharged; laid on table.		
Gardiner, Geo. W., widow of.	Pension	31	1	Senate bill	1531				234			
Gardiner, Geo. W., widow of.	Pension	31	2	Senate bill	169	Rev. Pensions			234			
Gardiner, Henry, administratrix of.	Payment for property destroyed in the late war.	24	2	Petition	79	Claims	63	Adverse		Laid on table.		
Gardiner, Henry, administratrix of.	Payment for property destroyed in the late war.	25	2	Petition	275	Claims	515	Adverse		Laid on table.		
Gardiner, James	(See William Baker, &c.)	22	1		288		480					
Gardiner, John	For a patent	7	1	Petition	107	Select.						
Gardiner, John	Renewal of patent	20	1	Petition	398	Naval Affairs	April 25, 1828	Adverse		Laid on table.		
Gardiner, John, *et al*	Compensation for extra services in land office.	19	2	Petition	72	Public Lands.						
Gardiner, John, *et al*	Compensation for extra services in land office.	25	2	Petition	652	Claims.						
Gardiner, John, widow of.	For bounty land	15	2	Petition	71	Military Affairs.						
Gardiner, William	For drawback duties on indigo	7	2	Petition	298	Com. and Manuf.	Jan. 26, 1803	Adverse		Leave to withdraw.		
Gardiner, William	For drawback duties on indigo	8	1	Petition	428	Com. and Manuf.	Nov. 28, 1803	Adverse		Recommitted.		
							Jan. 20, 1804	Adverse		Discharged; referred to Comptroller Treas'y.		
Gardipier, Alexander	Confirmation of title to land	20	2	Petition	64	Public Lands	40	Favorable	357	Referred to Committee Whole House.		
Gardipier, Alexander	Confirmation of title to land	21	1	Petition	93	Priv. Land Claims.						
Gardipier, Alexander	(See Jacques Porlier and others)	22	1		125							
Gardner, Abraham J	(See John Shaver, executor of widow of.)	26	2		49							
Gardner, Alexander	Pension	14	2	Petition	336	Pens. & Rev. Cl'ms.						
Gardner, Alexander	Increase of pension	16	1	Petition	45	Pens. & Rev. Cl'ms.				Leave to withdraw.		
Gardner, Caleb, executors of.	Liquidation of loan office certificat	9	2	Petition and rep't Sec. Treasury.	554, 580					Referred to Committee Whole House.		Leave to withdraw, page 646.
Gardner, Caleb, executors of.	Liquidation of loan office certificate	10	1	Petition	100	Whole House.						
Gardner, Caleb, executors of.	Indemnity for French spoliations prior to 1800.	26	1	Memorial	182	Foreign Affairs	343	Favorable; bill	319	Referred to Committee Whole House.		
Gardner, Calvin, widow of.	Pension	25	2	Petition	268	Invalid Pensions				Discharged; laid on table.		
Gardner, Charles	Compensation for services and supplies in revolutionary war.	2	1	Petition	440					Referred to Secretary of War.		
Gardner, David, widow of.	To have her claim included in bill for relief of J. Paul Jones.	30	1	Petition	144	Claims	152	Favorable	131	Passed.		
Gardner, David A	Indemnity for losses by fire	27	2	Joint resolution	820	Claims			J.R. 11			
Gardner, Ebenezer	(See Canadian refugees)	6	2		733							
Gardner, Edwin, widow of	Pension	25	2	Petition	57	Invalid Pensions.						

List of private claims presented to the House of Representatives of the United States from the 1st to the 31st Congress, inclusive—Continued.

Names of claimants.	Nature or object of the claim.	Congress.	Session.	How brought before the House of Reps.	Page of journal.	To what committee of the House referred.	No. or date of the report.	Nature of the report.	No. of the bill.	How disposed of by the House of Reps.	How disposed of by the Senate.	Date of the act of Congress, and remarks.
Gardner, Elisha	Payment of certificate of public debt.	6	2			Claims		Adverse.				
Gardner, Elisha, *et al.*	Reimbursement of foreign tonnage duties.	5	2	Petition	157	Com. and Manuf.	Feb. 26, 1798	Adverse		Leave to withdraw.		
Gardner, Ezekiel	Payment for shoes furnished United States army.	13	2	Petition	209	Pens. & Rev. Cl'ms	Mar. 28, 1814	Adverse		Laid on table.		
Gardner, F.	Pay as naval storekeeper	29	1	Petition	206	Whole House			50	Passed	Passed	App'd Aug. 10, 1846
Gardner, Fergus	(See Clark Woodruff, assignees of)	27	2		622					Leave to withdraw.		
Gardner, Francis, widow of	Pension	28	1	Petition	332	Naval Affairs.						
Gardner, Francis, widow of	Pension	28	2	Petition	206	Naval Affairs				Referred to Committee Whole House.		
Gardner, Francis R., widow of.	Pension	31	1	Petition	475	Invalid Pensions.						
Gardner, Henry	Pension	15	1	Petition	279	Pens. & Rev. Cl'ms						
Gardner, Henry, *et al.*	Indemnity for land released to United States.	30	1	Petition	110	Judiciary	765	Favorable	601	Referred to Committee Whole House.		
Gardner, Henry, *et al.*	Indemnity for land released to United States.	28	1	Senate bill	941	Judiciary	June 6, 1844	Favorable	66	Referred to Committee Whole House.		
Gardner, Henry, *et al.*	Indemnity for land released to United States.	28	1	Petition	1087	Judiciary.						
Gardner, Henry, *et al.*	Indemnity for land released to United States.	28	2	Petition	88	Judiciary	164	Favorable	631	Referred to Committee Whole House.		
Gardner, James	Indemnity for French spoliations prior to 1800.	26	1	Memorial	182	Foreign Affairs	343	Favorable; bill	819	Referred to Committee Whole House.		
Gardner, James, administrator of.	Indemnity for French spoliations prior to 1800.	31	1	Petition	285	Foreign Affairs	355	Favorable	318	Referred to Committee Whole House.		
Gardner, Jared	(See Joseph Chase, *et al*)	10	1		176							
Gardner, J. M.	Increase of salary	31	1	Petition	619	P. Of. & P. Roads.				Discharged; laid on table.		
Gardner, Job W., & John.	To be released from judgment at suit of United States	15	1	Petition	258	Ways and Means.						
Gardner, John	Payment of bills of credit	4	1	Rep. of Secretary War.	388	Claims	Mar. 31, 1796	Adverse		Laid on table.		
Gardner, John	Payment of bills of credit	4	2	Rep. of Secretary War.	614	Claims.						
Gardner, John M, widow o	Pension	14	2	Petition	213	Naval Affairs				Referred to Committee Whole House.		
Gardner, Jonathan	Pension	31	1	Petition	285	Naval Affairs	215	Adverse		Laid on table.		
Gardner, Paul, & Sons	Indemnity for French spoliations prior to 1800.	26	1	Memorial	182	Foreign Affairs	343	Favorable; bill	319	Referred to Committee Whole House.		
Gardner, Peregrine	Payment for horse lost in United States service.	18	2	Petition	36	Claims				Leave to withdraw.		
Gardner, Peregrine	Indemnity for property destroyed on Niagara frontier.	20	2	Petition	143	Claims.						
Gardner, Peregrine	Indemnity for property destroyed on Niagara frontier.	21	1	Petition	358	Claims	Mar. 15, 1830	Adverse		Laid on table.		
Gardner, Peregrine	Indemnity for property destroyed on Niagara frontier.	22	1	Petition	54	Claims	127	Adverse		Laid on table.		
Gardner, Peregrine	Indemnity for property destroyed on Niagara frontier.	22	2	Petition	66	Claims	15	Favorable	644	Referred to Committee Whole House.		
Gardner, Peregrine	Indemnity for property destroyed on Niagara frontier.	23	1	Petition	34	Claims	15	Favorable	15	Passed	Passed	App'd June 25, 1834
Gardner, Rowland	(See Bartholomew Calvin, *et al*)	21	1		68							

List of private claims presented to the House of Representatives of the United States from the 1st to the 31st Congress, inclusive—Continued.

Names of claimants.	Nature or object of the claim.	Congress.	Session.	How brought before the House of Reps.	Page of journal.	To what committee of the House referred.	No. or date of the report.	Nature of the report.	No. of the bill.	How disposed of by the House of Reps.	How disposed of by the Senate.	Date of the act of Congress, and remarks.
Gardner, Samuel	Increase of salary	14	2	Petition	142	P. Of. and P. Roads.						
Gardner, Sophia	Pension	21	2	Senate bill	387	Naval Affairs	Mar. 2, 1831	Adverse	109	Laid on table.		
Gardner, Sophia	Pension	22	1	Petition	124	Naval Affairs.						
Gardner, Thomas, widow of.	Pension	1	2	Petition	336	....	....	....	......	Referred to Secretary War.		
Gardner, Thomas, widow of.	Pension	2	2	Rep. of Secretary War.	711	....	....	....	......	Laid on table.		
Gardner, William	Additional compensation as commissioner of loans.	2	1	Petition	500	Select	March 7, 1792	Favorable	194	Passed	Passed	App'd May 8, 1792
Gardner, William	Additional compensation as commissioner of loans.	3	2	Memorial, and report of Secretary of War.	262, 312	Select	Feb. 6, 1795	Favorable	......	Referred to Committee Whole House.		
Gardner, William, widow of.	Indemnity for property destroyed by the enemy.	15	2	Petition	148	Claims.						
Garein, Hyacinth	To be allowed drawback of duties.	9	2	Petition	574	Com. and Manuf.	....	....	......	Discharged; leave to withdraw.		
Gareschе, Paul	Reimbursement of duties	21	2	Petition	210	Ways and Means.						
Garey, George	Increase and arrears of pension	30	2	Petition	87	Invalid Pensions.						
Garey, James	Bounty land	15	1	Petition	217	Public Lands	Mar. 21, 1818	Adverse	......	Leave to withdraw.		
Garie, Madam	Confirmation of title to land	22	1	House bill	107	Priv. Land Claims.	Dec. 27, 1831	General bill	125	Passed	Passed	App'd June 25, 1832
Garland, Lieut. A	Compensation for acting purser	28	2	Petition	199	Naval Affairs.						
Garland, Lieut. A	Compensation for acting purser	29	2	Petition	161	Naval Affairs.						
Garland, Lieut. A	Compensation for acting purser	30	1	Petition	240	Naval Affairs	....	....	......	Discharged; laid on table.		
Garland, Benjamin	(See Richard Thurston, *et al*)	18	2	....	69							
Garland, George, administrator of.	Reimbursement of money paid into United States treasury illegally.	19	2	Memorial	293	Ways and Means.						
Garland, George, administrator of.	Reimbursement of money paid into United States treasury illegally.	20	1	Petition	226	Ways and Means.						
Garland, Jacob, widow of	Pension	29	2	Senate bill	381	Rev. Pensions	Feb. 26, 1847	Favorable	146	Referred to Committee Whole House.		
Garland, Jacob, widow of.	Pension	30	1	Senate bill	683	Rev. Pensions	Aug. 12, 1848	Favorable	87	Passed		
Garland, Peter, heir of	Commutation pay	23	2	Petition	182	Rev. Claims.					Passed	App'd Aug. 14, 1848
Garland, Peter, heir of	Commutation pay	24	1	Petition	62	Rev. Claims	124	Adverse	......	Laid on table.		
Garlick, Adam	Compensation for services as artificer.	9	2	Petition	524	Claims.						
Garlock, Adam	Pension	29	1	Petition	648	Rev. Pensions.						
Garlock, Adam	Pension	30	1	Petition	576	Rev. Pensions	530	Adverse	......	Laid on table.		
Garlock, Adam	Pension	31	1	Petition	396	Rev. Pensions	225	Favorable	220	Referred to Committee Whole House.		
Garlock, Adam	Pension	31	2	House bill	181	Whole House	Jan. 24, 1851	Favorable	220	Passed.		
Garner, Andrew	Pension	18	1	Petition	60	Pens. & Rev. Cl'ms.	Dec. 23, 1823	Adverse	......	Laid on table.		
Garner, James R	(See William H. Bedford, agent.)	28	1	....	262							
Garner, Capt. G., widow of.	Pension	27	2	Petition	128	Military Affairs	353	Adverse	......	Laid on table.		
Garner, John	Pension	12	1	House bill	361	Whole House	June 17, 1812	Favorable	138	Passed	Passed	App'd July 5, 1812
Garner, Thomas	Pension	27	2	Petition	239	Invalid Pensions	418	Adverse	......	Laid on table	....	Leave to withdraw, 2d sess., 30th Cong.
Garner, William	Payment for a horse lost in United States service.	25	2	Documents	396	Claims.						
Garner, William	Payment for a horse lost in United States service.	25	3	Documents	207	Claims.						
Garnett, Frances	Pension	22	1	House bill	479	Whole House	Mar. 13, 1832	Favorable	467	Passed	Postponed.	
Garnett, James	(See Alexander Dick, devisee of).	4	1	....	437							
Garnett, James M., *et al.*	(See Alexander Dick, heirs of)	22	1	....	44							

List of private claims presented to the House of Representatives of the United States from the 1*st to the* 31*st Congress, inclusive*—Continued.

Names of claimants.	Nature or object of the claim.	Congress.	Session.	How brought before the House of Reps.	Page of journal.	To what committee of the House referred.	No. or date of the report.	Nature of the report.	No. of the bill.	How disposed of by the House of Reps.	How disposed of by the Senate.	Date of the act of Congress, and remarks.
Garnett, James M., Muscoe, and Maria H.	Redress for illegal taxation	23	1	Memorial	67	Territories	258	Favorable	295	Referred to Committee Whole House.		
Garnett, John	Pension	1	2	Petition and rep't of Sec. War.	188	....	....	....	.....	Laid on table.		
Garnett, John	Pension	3	1	Petition and rep't of Sec. War.	131	Select	May 26, 1794	Ref'd to Secretary War.	J. R. 12	Passed	Passed	App'd June 9, 1794
Garnett, John	Pension	4	1	Petition and rep't of Sec. War.	445	Claims.						
Garnett, Robert S	Credit for amount of Joshua Yeaton's bond.	25	3	Petition	206	Claims.						
Garnett, Robert S	Credit for amount of Joshua Yeaton's bond.	26	1	Petition	169	Claims.						
Garnier, John	For leave to correct error in entry of land.	24	2	Petition	208	Priv. Land Claims.						
Garnier, John	For leave to correct error in entry of land.	25	2	Petition	719	Public Lands.						
Garnier, John	For leave to correct error in entry of land.	25	3	Petition	93	Public Lands.						
Garnier, John	For leave to correct error in entry of land.	29	1	Petition	462	Public Lands.						
Garnier, Joseph V	Compensation as clerk of United States court, and to land commissioners.	15	1	Petition	302	Claims.						
Garnier, Joseph V	Compensation as clerk of United States court, and to land commissioners.	17	1	Petition	89	Judiciary.						
Garnier, Joseph V	Compensation as clerk of United States court, and to land commissioners.	21	2	Petition	192	Judiciary.						
Garnier, Joseph V	Compensation as clerk of United States court, and to land commissioners.	22	1	Petition	225	Judiciary	344	Favorable	443	Referred to Committee Whole House.		
Garnier, Joseph V	Compensation as clerk of United States court, and to land commissioners.	23	1	Petition	73	Judiciary	333	Favorable	361	Referred to Committee Whole House.		
Garnier, Joseph V	Compensation as clerk of United States court, and to land commissioners.	24	1	Petition	53	Judiciary.						
Garnier, Joseph V	Compensation as clerk of United States court, and to land commissioners.	24	2	Petition	93	Rev. Pensions.						
Garnier, Joseph V	Compensation as clerk of United States court, and to land commissioners.	25	2	Petition	96	Judiciary	....	....	.....	Discharged; laid on table.		
Garnsey, Daniel G	Reimbursement of money advanced, and compensation for services in removing New York Indians.	30	1	Petition	507	Claims	759	Adverse	.....	Laid on table.		
Garnsey, Daniel G	Compensation for services as interpreter.	30	1	Petition	522	Claims	480	Adverse	.....	Leave to withdraw.		
Garrard, Martha, *et al.*	(See William Christian, heirs of.)	31	1	....	891							
Garrard, William	Compensation as land commissioner.	12	1	Petition	49	Claims	Mar. 17, 1812	Favorable	125	Passed	Passed	App'd June 10, 1812

List of private claims presented to the House of Representatives of the United States from the 1st to the 31st Congress, inclusive—Continued.

Names of claimants.	Nature or object of the claim.	Congress.	Session.	How brought before the House of Reps.	Page of journal.	To what committee of the House referred.	No. or date of the report.	Nature of the report.	No. of the bill.	How disposed of by the House of Reps.	How disposed of by the Senate.	Date of the act of Congress, and remarks.
88 Garrard, William, *et al*...	Compensation as land commissioner.	13	1	Petition	37	Claims.						
Garrard, William, *et al*...	Compensation as land commissioner.	13	2	Petition	181	Public Lands.						
Garrard, William, *et al*...	(See William Crawford, *et al.*) ..	14	1	....	635							
Garrard, William W	Reimbursement of money expended in buying horses for U. States.	25	2	Petition	724	Claims.						
Garrard, William W	Reimbursement of money expended in buying horses for U. States.	27	2	Petition	75	Claims	180	Adverse	......	Laid on table.		
Garresche, Gabriel.......	Reimbursement of duties........	21	2	Petition	301	Ways and Means.						
Garretson, Isaac, administrator of.	Reimbursement of money paid for house rent.	24	1	Petition	751	Claims	662	Adverse	......	Laid on table.		
Garretson, Isaac, administrator of.	Reimbursement of money paid for house rent.	28	1	Petition	335	Claims.						
Garretson, Isaac, administrator of.	Reimbursement of money paid for house rent.	28	2	Senate bill	473	Naval Affairs.....	....	....	S. 132			
Garretson, Samuel.......	Pension	1	2	House bill	271	Whole House.....	July 19, 1790	With amend..	88	Passed	Passed	App'd Aug. 11, 1790
Garrett, Alexander	Pension	3	2	Rep't Committee	352	Claims	Feb. 28, 1795	Favorable....	130	Passed	Postponed.	
Garrett, Alexander	Pension	4	1	Rep. of Secretary War.	445	Claims	Mar. 14, 1796	Favorable	156	Passed	Passed	App'd April 20, 1796
Garrett, Ashton, sureties of	Release from liability	22	1	Petition	104	Claims	505	Favorable; bill	612	Referred to Committee Whole House.		
Garrett, Ashton, sureties of	Release from liability	23	1	Petition	34	Claims	11	Favorable: bill	11	Passed	Passed	App'd May 1, 1834
Garrett, Andrew	Pension	17	1	Petition	78	Pens. & Rev. Cl'ms.						
Garrett, Andrew	Pension	17	2	Petition	31	Pens. & Rev. Cl'ms.						
Garrett, Charles B. and Joel W.	To be allowed to exchange land ..	27	3	House bill	339	Public Lands	160	Favorable	776			
Garrett, Edward	Pension	23	1	Petition	569	Rev. Pensions.....	....	....	......	Laid on table.		
Garrett, Francis.........	Pension	22	1	Petition	56	Rev. Pensions.....	Mar. 13, 1832	Favorable	467	Passed	Indef. postp'd.	
Garrett, Hezekiah	Payment for a horse lost in United States service.	24	1	Petition	670	Claims.						
Garrett, Joab	Relief from error in entering land.	11	2	Petition	128	Public Lands.....	Jan. 5, 1810	Favorable	59	Passed	Passed, with amendment	App'd Feb. 24, 1810
Garrett, Joel W.........	(See Charles B. and Joel W. Garrett.)											
Garrett, John Low, *et al*..	Confirmation of title to land.....	28	1	Petition	449	Public Lands.						
Garrett, John D.........	(See William H. Bedford, agent).	28	1	....	262							
Garrett, Nathan.........	Pension	3	1	Petition	132	Select.						
Garrett, Obadiah	Compensation for property destroyed by Indians.	26	1	Petition	621	Claims.						
Garrette, Richard........	Pension	9	1	Petition	330	Claims	Mar. 28, 1806	Adverse	......	Indef. postponed, and leave to withdraw.		
Garrett, Samuel.........	Reimbursement of money paid for land.	28	1	Petition	433	Public Lands.						
Garrett, Samuel.........	Reimbursement of money paid for land.	28	2	Petition	65	Public Lands.						
Garrett, Stephen, widow of	Pension	27	2	Resolution	398	Rev. Pensions	784	Adverse	......	Laid on table.		
Garrett, Stephen, widow of	Pension	28	1	Petition	238	Rev. Pensions	....	....	......	Discharged; laid on table.		
Garrett, William	Payment for beef and pork for United States army, lost in the Mississippi river.	23	2	Petition	131	Claims	Jan. 16, 1835	Adverse	......	Laid on table.		

List of private claims presented to the House of Representatives of the United States from the 1st to the 31st Congress, inclusive—Continued.

Names of claimants.	Nature or object of the claim.	Congress.	Session.	How brought before the House of Reps.	Page of journal.	To what committee of the House referred.	No. or date of the report.	Nature of the report.	No. of the bill.	How disposed of by the House of Reps.	How disposed of by the Senate.	Date of the act of Congress, and remarks.
Garrett, William W.	Payment for a horse lost in United States service.	23	1	Documents	154	Claims.						
Garrett, William W.	Payment for a horse lost in United States service.	28	1	Petition	262	Claims.						
Garrido, John and Joseph.	Confirmation of title to land	20	1	Petition	312	Priv. Land Claims.						
Garrido, John and Joseph.	Confirmation of title to land	20	2	Petition	34	Priv. Land Claims.						
Garrido, John and Joseph.	Confirmation of title to land	21	1	Petition	40	Priv. Land Claims.						
Garrido, John and Joseph.	Confirmation of title to land	22	1	Petition	75	Priv. Land Claims.	Dec. 28, 1831	Adverse		Laid on table.		
Garrigues, Jacob	For settlement of claim	1	3	Petition	380					Referred to Secretary Treasury.		
Garrigues, Jacob	For settlement of claim	2	2	Report of Secretary Treasury.	626					Laid on table.		
Garrison, Abraham, administrator of.	Payment of two loan office certificates.	18	1	Petition	315	Pens. & Rev. Cl'ms.						
Garrison, Abraham	Pension	21	2	Petition	299	Military Pensions.						
Garrison, Bennett, & wife.	Pension	2	1	Petition	500					Referred to Secretary War.		
Garrison, Bennett, & wife.	Pension	2	2	Rep. of Secretary War.	696					Laid on table.		
Garrison, Darius, administrator of.	Payment for supplies to United States troops.	30	1	Petition	780	Claims	645	Favorable	512	Referred to Committee Whole House.		
Garrison, Darius, representatives of.	Payment for supplies to United States troops.	30	2	House bill	318	Whole House	Jan. 26, 1849	Favorable	512	Passed.		
Garrison, Henry D.	Payment of money under treaty with Chippewa Indians.	30	2	Senate bill	181	Indian Affairs	Feb. 8, 1849	Favorable	198	Passed	Passed	App'd March 3, 1849
Garrison, James	(See Shadrack Bond, heirs of.)	26	1		359							
Garrison, Jonah	Pension	21	1	Petition	91	Military Pensions	April 23, 1830	General bill	439	Laid on table.		
Garrison, Jonah	Pension	21	2	Resolution	65	Military Pensions	75	Favorable	611	Passed.		
Garrison, Jonah	Pension	22	1	Petition	188	Rev. Pensions				Laid on table.		
Garrison, Jonah	Pension	22	2	Petition	41	Rev. Pensions				Laid on table.		
Garrot, (or Govort) Etienne	Confirmation of title to land	18	1	Petition	55	Public Lands.						
Garrow, Samuel H	(See Robert Williamson, *et al.*)	14	2		398							
Garrow, Samuel H	Compensation for vessel taken for United States.	15	1	Petition	286	Claims	Mar. 18, 1818	Adverse				Leave to withdraw, 1st sess., 17th Cong.
Garrow, Samuel H	Pre-emption right to land	18	1	Petition	97	Priv. Land Claims.						
Garrow, Samuel H., *et al.*	To be released from interest on judgment in favor of the United States.	24	1	Senate bill	1157	Claims	July 2, 1836	Adverse	263	Referred to Committee Whole House.		
Garrow, Samuel H., *et al.*	To be released from interest on judgment in favor of the United States.	24	2	Senate bill	250	Judiciary	Feb. 28, 1837	Favorable	50	Referred to Committee Whole House.		
Garrow, Samuel H., *et al.*	To be released from interest on judgment in favor of the United States.	25	2	Senate bill	483	Judiciary	Feb. 20, 1838	Favorable	101	Referred to Committee Whole House.		
Garrow, Samuel H., *et al.*	To be released from interest on judgment in favor of the United States.	25	3	Senate bill	372	Judiciary	Jan. 25, 1839	Favorable	241	Referred to Committee Whole House.		
Garrow, Samuel H., *et al.*	To be released from interest on judgment in favor of the United States.	26	1	Senate bill	189	Whole House			1			
Garrow, Samuel H., *et al.*	To be released from interest on judgment in favor of the United States.	27	2	Senate bill	1169	Judiciary	Aug. 4, 1842	Favorable	271	Passed		App'd Aug. 30, 1842

List of private claims presented to the House of Representatives of the United States from the 1st to the 31st Congress, inclusive—Continued.

Names of claimants.	Nature or object of the claim.	Congress.	Session.	How brought before the House of Reps.	Page of journal.	To what committee of the House referred.	No. or date of the report.	Nature of the report.	No. of the bill.	How disposed of by the House of Reps.	How disposed of by the Senate.	Date of the act of Congress, and remarks.
Garsed, Joshua	Patent	17	1	Petition	416	Judiciary	April 8, 1822	Favorable	160	Passed	Passed	App'd May 7, 1822
Garth, Jesse W.	Patent for land	27	3	Memorial	112	Priv. Land Claims.						
Garton, Thomas	Pension	30	2	Petition	174	Invalid Pensions.						
Garvaies, Benjamin, and Julian, *et al.*	Indemnity for land set apart for military use.	30	2	Petition	313	Claims.						
Garvey, (or Gawry,) Lawrence	Indemnity for damage to light-house by storm, while building.	29	2	Petition	56	Claims.						
Garvin, Thomas	Pension	22	1	Petition	36	Rev. Pensions.						
Gary, David	Pension	15	2	Petition	160	Rev. Pensions.						
Gary, Peter	Pension	17	1	Petition	124	Rev. Pensions.						
Gaskin, Job	Pension	5	1	Petition	64	....	....	....	......	Laid on table.		
Gaskin, Job	Pension	5	2	Petition	128	Claims	April 17, 1798	Adverse	......	Laid on table.		
Gaskin, Job	Pension	5	3	Petition	432	....	....	....	......	Referred to Committee Whole House.		
Gaskins, H. L., *et al.*, representatives of.	For further time to settle the accounts of Le Roy Opie.	16	2	Petition	137	Claims.						
Gasney, Peter	Payment for a horse lost in the United States service.	21	1	Petition	110	Claims	65	Favorable	89	Passed	Passed	App'd May 28, 1830
Gassaway, Elizabeth	(See John Gassaway, widow of)	22	2	....	245							
Gassaway, Henry	Pension	11	3	Petition	506	Claims.						
Gassaway, Henry	Pension	12	2	Petition	631	Select	Feb. 4, 1813	Adverse	......	Leave to withdraw.		
Gassaway, Henry	Pension	14	1	Petition	340	Pens. & Rev. Cl'ms.	Feb. 14, 1816	Adverse	......	Rejected.		
Gassaway, Henry, widow of.	Compensation for revolutionary services.	15	1	Petition	465	Pens. & Rev. Cl'ms.						
Gassaway, John, widow of.	Pension	22	2	Petition	245	Rev. Pensions	....	....	......	Discharged; laid on table.		
Gassaway, John, widow of.	Pension	24	1	Petition	204	Rev. Pensions	....	....	......	Laid on table.		
Gassaway, John, widow of.	Pension	25	2	Petition	181	Rev. Pensions	....	....	......	Discharged; laid on table.		
Gassaway, John, widow of.	Pension	25	3	Petition	88	Rev. Pensions	....	....	......	Discharged; laid on table.		
Gassaway, John	Arrears of pension	25	3	Petition	460	Invalid Pensions.						
Gassaway, John	Arrears of pension	26	1	Petition	162	Invalid Pensions	265	Adverse	......	Laid on table.		
Gassaway, Lavinia	(See Henry Gassaway, widow of.)	15	1	Petition	465							
Gassett, David	Arrears of pay for military services	19	1	Petition	407	Claims	165	Favorable	217	Passed	Passed, with amendment.	
Gassett, David	Arrears of pay for military services	19	2	Petition	82	Claims	Dec. 22, 1826	Favorable	313	Passed	Passed	App'd Feb. 22, 1827
Gassett, Lindsey	To be released as surety of Isaac Puitzman, P. M.	31	2	Petition	192	P. Of. and P. Roads.						
Gaston, John, widow of	Compensation for losses in revolutionary war.	23	2	Petition	94	Rev. Claims	....	....	......	Discharged; laid on table.		
Gaston, Joseph	Pension	22	2	Petition	216	Invalid Pensions	Feb. 15, 1833	General bill	738	Referred to Committee Whole House.		
Gaston, Joseph	Pension	22	2	Senate bill	441	Invalid Pensions	Mar. 1, 1833	With amend.	90	Passed with amendm't	Concurred in.	App'd March 2, 1833
Gaston, William	To be released from bond	11	1	Petition	52	Com. and Manuf.						
Gaston, William	To be released from bond	11	2	Petition, & letter of Sec. Treas.	169	Com. and Manuf.	April 7, 1810	Favorable	......	Referred to Committee Whole House.		
Gass, Charles	Pay for services in United States army.	27	2	Petition	382	Claims.						
Gass, Henry	(See John McElroy, *et al.*)	3	2	....	267							
Gass, Patrick	Grant of land for services in Lewis & Clark's expedition.	9	2	Resolution	507	Select	Jan. 23, 1807	General bill	183	Passed	Passed	App'd March 3, 1807

List of private claims presented to the House of Representatives of the United States from the 1st to the 31st Congress, inclusive—Continued.

Names of claimants.	Nature or object of the claim.	Congress.	Session.	How brought before the House of Reps.	Page of journal.	To what committee of the House referred.	No. or date of the report.	Nature of the report.	No. of the bill.	How disposed of by the House of Reps.	How disposed of by the Senate.	Date of the act of Congress, and remarks.
Gass, Patrick	Invalid pension	29	1	Petition	193	Invalid Pensions				Discharged; laid on table.		
Gatchell, James	Arrears of pension	24	2	Petition	267	Invalid Pensions				Discharged; laid on table.		
Gatcheli, James	Arrears of pension	25	2	Petition	269	Invalid Pensions				Discharged; laid on table.		
Gatchell, James	Arrears of pension	26	1	Petition	708	Invalid Pensions.						
Gateran, Cæsar	For drawback of duties	18	2	Petition	41	Ways and Means				Referred to Secretary of Treasury		
Gates, Asa, widow of	Pension	25	2	Petition	52	Rev. Pensions				Discharged; laid on table.		
Gates, Benjamin	Pension	20	1	Petition	192	Military Pensions		General bill	283	Passed.		
Gates, Benjamin	Pension	20	2	House bill	55	Whole House	Dec. 12, 1828	Favorable	311	Passed.		
Gates, Benjamin	Pension	21	1	Petition	48	Rev. Claims	Feb. 13, 1830	General bill	72	Passed	Passed	App'd May 20, 1830
Gates, Cornelius	Compensation for extra services and expenses in late war.	17	1	Petition	89	Claims	Feb. 1, 1822	Adverse		Rejected.		
Gates, Darius	Reimbursement of cost in defending land title.	10	1	Petition	145	Claims	Feb. 5, 1808	Favorable	53	Passed	Passed	App'd April 21, 1808
Gates, Darius, *et al*	Reimbursement of money paid for land afterwards sold by United States.	10	1	Petition	145	Claims	Feb. 5, 1808	Favorable	53	Passed	Passed	App'd April 21, 1808
Gates, Henry	Pension	2	2	Rep. of Secretary War.	649	Whole House.						
Gates, Henry	Pension	3	1	Rep. of Secretary War.	131	Select	May 26, 1794	Refer'd to Sec. War.	J. R. 12	Passed	Passed	App'd June 9, 1794
Gates, Henry	Pension	4	1	Rep. of Secretary War.	445	Claims.						
Gates, Henry	Pension	4	2	Rep. of Secretary War.	614	Claims.						
Gates, Henry	Pension	10	1	House bill	232	Claims	April 18, 1808	Favorable	78	Passed	Passed	App'd April 25, 1808
Gates, Henry	Increase of pension	18	2	Petition	59	Pens. & Rev. Cl'ms.	Jan. 26, 1825	Adverse		Laid on table.		
Gates, Henry	Increase of pension	19	1	Petition	43	Rev. Pensions	164	Adverse		Discharged; laid on table.		
Gates, Henry	Increase of pension	20	1	Petition	110	Military Pensions				Discharged; laid on table.		
Gates, John	For depreciation of pay and other emoluments for revolutionary services.	3	1	Petition	88	Claims	Mar. 31, 1794	Adverse		Leave to withdraw.		
Gates, John	For depreciation of pay and other emoluments for revolutionary services.	3	2	Petition	313	Claims	Jan. 6, 1795	Adverse		Laid on table.		
Gates, John	For depreciation of pay and other emoluments for revolutionary services.	4	1	Petition	403	Claims	Jan. 6, 1796	Adverse		Laid on table.		
Gates, John, jr	Payment of balance due as paymaster United States army.	19	1	Petition	110	Claims				Discharged; laid on table.		
Gates, John, jr	Payment of balance due as paymaster United States army.	19	2	Petition	92	Claims.						
Gates, John, jr	Payment of balance due as paymaster United States army.	20	1	Petition	52	Claims	217	Favorable	248	Referred to Committee Whole House.		Leave to withdraw.
Gates, John, jr	Payment of balance due as paymaster United States army.	20	2	House bill	284	Whole House	Feb. 13, 1829	Favorable	248	Passed.		
Gates, John, widow of	Payment for revolutionary services.	22	1	Petition	260	Rev. Claims.						

List of private claims presented to the House of Representatives of the United States from the 1st to the 31st Congress, inclusive—Continued.

Names of claimants.	Nature or object of the claim.	Congress.	Session.	How brought before the House of Reps.	Page of journal.	To what committee of the House referred.	No. or date of the report.	Nature of the report.	No. of the bill.	How disposed of by the House of Reps.	How disposed of by the Senate.	Date of the act of Congress, and remarks.
Gates, John, widow of	Payment for revolutionary services.	22	1	Senate bill	858	Rev. Claims	June 26, 1832	Favorable	162	Passed	Passed	App'd July 14, 1832
Gates, Lemuel, widow of	Pension	25	2	Petition	75	Military Affairs.						
Gates, Lemuel, widow of	Pension	25	3	Petition	91	Naval Affairs				Discharged; leave to withdraw.		
Gates, Nathan	Pension	22	1	Petition	130	Rev. Claims				Discharged; laid on table.		
Gates, Nathaniel, *et al.*	Payment for board of John Nelson	13	2	Petition	185	Claims.						
Gates, Nathaniel, *et al.*	Payment for board of John Nelson	13	3	Petition	618	Claims				Discharged; referred to Secretary of War.		
Gates, Oliver	Pension	19	2	Petition	307	Military Pensions.						
Gates, Oliver	Pension	21	2	Petition	120	Military Pensions.						
Gates, Oliver	Pension	22	1	Petition	90	Rev. Pensions.						
Gates, Reuben	Pension	15	2	Petition	160	Rev. Pensions.						
Gates, Stephen	Pension	2	2	Rep. of Secretary War.	649	Whole House.						
Gates, Stephen	Pension	3	1	Rep. of Secretary War.	131	Select	May 26, 1794	Resolution	J. R. 12	Passed	Passed	App'd June 9, 1794
Gates, Stephen	Pension	4	1	Rep. of Secretary War.	445	Claims.						
Gates, Stephen	Pension	4	2	Rep. of Secretary War.	614	Claims.						
Gates, Stephen	Reimbursement of money paid P. Napier for land.	22	1	Petition	33	Public Lands				Discharged; laid on table.		
Gates, William	Indemnity for expense of court martial.	25	3	Petition	211	Military Affairs	323	Adverse		Laid on table.		
Gates, William, *et al.*	Payment for horses lost in United States service.	13	3	Petition	493	Claims	Nov. 14, 1814	Favorable	228	Passed	Indef. postp'd.	
Gatewood, F.	Indemnity for French spoliations prior to 1800.	26	1	Memorial	182	Foreign Affairs	343	Favorable; bill	319	Referred to Committee Whole House.		
Gatewood, John S.	Payment for horse lost in United States service.	25	2	Petition	1028	Claims.						
Gatewood, John S.	Payment for horse lost in United States service.	27	3	Petition	239	Claims	207	Adverse		Laid on table.		
Gatewood, John S.	Payment for horse lost in United States service.	31	2	Petition	53	Claims.						
Gatewood, Philemon	Increase of salary as naval officer at Norfolk.	14	2	Petition	206	Com. and Manuf.				Discharged; laid on table.		
Gatewood, Philemon	Increase of salary as naval officer at Norfolk.	26	1	Resolution	671	Naval Affairs.						
Gatewood, Richard	Indemnity for French spoliations prior to 1800.	26	1	Memorial	182	Foreign Affairs	343	Favorable; bill	319	Referred to Committee Whole House.		
Gatlin, Stephen	Pension	23	1	Resolution	130	Invalid Pensions	241	Favorable	268	Referred to Committee Whole House.		
Gatlin, Stephen	Pension	23	2	House bill	300	Whole House	Jan. 31, 1835	Favorable	268	Passed	Passed	App'd March 3, 1835
Gaton, Churchill, widow of.	Pension	14	1	Petition	367	Pens. & Rev. Cl'ms.	Jan. 4, 1816	General bill		Indef. postponed.		
Gauban, Augustine	Pension	24	2	Petition	215	Invalid Pensions				Discharged; laid on table.		
Gauban, Augustine	Pension	28	2	Petition	72	Invalid Pensions.						
Gaudry & Dufour	Remission of duties on wine	16	1	Petition	224	Ways and Means				Discharged; laid on table.		

List of private claims presented to the House of Representatives of the United States from the 1st to the 31st Congress, inclusive—Continued.

Names of claimants.	Nature or object of the claim.	Congress.	Session.	How brought before the House of Reps.	Page of journal.	To what committee of the House referred.	No. or date of the report.	Nature of the report.	No. of the bill.	How disposed of by the House of Reps.	How disposed of by the Senate.	Date of the act of Congress, and remarks.
Gavett, Joseph, widow of.	Relief for husband killed in public service.	25	2	Petition	117	Invalid Pensions	....	....	....	Discharged; laid on table.		
Gavett, Joseph, widow of.	Relief for husband killed in public service.	26	1	Petition	306	Invalid Pensions	404	Adverse	....	Laid on table.		
Gavett, William	Pension	28	2	Petition	142	Rev. Pensions.						
Gavett, William	Pension	29	1	Petition	103	Rev. Pensions	....	....	....	Discharged; laid on table.		
Gaw, Chambers	Pension	25	2	Petition	404, 585	Rev. Pensions.						
Gaw, Chambers	Pension	25	3	Petition	226	Rev. Pensions.						
Gaw, Chambers	Pension	26	1	Petition	173	Rev. Pensions.						
Gawney, John	Pension	29	1	Petition	425	Invalid Pensions	Aug. 10, 1846	Adverse	....	Laid on table.		
Gawney, John	Pension	30	1	Petition	261	Invalid Pensions	810	Favorable	629	Referred to Committee Whole House.		
Gawney, John	Pension	30	2	House bill	363	Whole House	Feb. 2, 1849	Favorable	629	Passed.		
Gawney, John	Pension	31	2	Petition	71	Invalid Pensions.						
Gay, Abel	(See Walter Loomis, *et al*)	21	2	....	45							
Gay, Abel, *et al*	Payment for work on Cumberland road.	23	2	Senate bill	428	Claims	March 2, 1835	Favorable	73			
Gay, Abel, *et al*	Payment for work on Cumberland road.	24	1	Senate bill	320	Claims	Feb. 12, 1836	Favorable	27	Passed	Passed	App'd July 2, 1836
Gay, Abel, *et al*	Additional pay for work on Cumberland road.	24	2	Senate bill	552	Claims	308	Adverse	134			
Gay, Abel, *et al*	Additional pay for work on Cumberland road.	26	1	Senate bill	189	Claims	April 4, 1839	Adverse	18	Referred to Committee Whole House.		
Gay, Abel, *et al*	Additional pay for work on Cumberland road.	26	2	Senate bill	151	Claims	190	Adverse	127			
Gay, Asahel	Pension	22	1	Petition	595	Rev. Pensions	....	....	....	Discharged; laid on table.		
Gay, David	Grant of land	4	1	Petition	448	Whole House.						
Gay, David	Grant of land	6	2	Rep't Committee.	766	Whole House	Jan. 19, 1801	Favorable	280	Passed	Passed	App'd Feb. 18, 1801
Gay, Harriet	Pension to her father, E. Stevens.	30	1	Petition	780	Rev. Pensions.						
Gay, James	Pension and compensation for revolutionary services.	22	1	Petition	381	Rev. Pensions.						
Gay, James	Payment of a certificate of debt	22	1	Petition	381	Rev. Claims.						
Gay, James	Payment of a certificate of debt	22	2	Petition	82	Rev. Claims.						
Gay, Orris	Increase of pension	24	1	Senate bill	811	Invalid Pensions	June 1, 1836	Favorable	180	Passed	....	App'd June 15, 1836
Gay, Peyton	(See Jona. Davis, *et al*)	13	2	....	270							
Gay, Dr. Samuel, heir of.	Commutation pay	24	1	Petition	204	Rev. Claims.						
Gay, Dr. Samuel, heir of.	Commutation pay	25	3	Petition	125	Rev. Claims.						
Gay, Dr. Samuel, heir of.	Commutation pay	26	1	Petition	360	Rev. Claims.						
Gay, Dr. Samuel, hoir of.	Commutation pay	29	1	Petition	460	Rev. Claims.						
Gay, Dr. Samuel, heir of.	Commutation pay	30	1	Petition	1225	....	....	....	....	Leave to withdraw.		
Gay, Dr. Samuel, heir of.	Commutation pay	31	1	Petition	233	Rev. Claims.						
Gayle, George W	(See A. J. Pickett & G. W. Gayle.)	25	2	....	894							
Gaylord, Aaron, administrator of.	Indemnity for French spoliations prior to 1800.	26	1	Memorial	182	Foreign Affairs	343	Favorable; bill	319	Referred to Committee Whole House.		
Gaylord, Ambrose	Pension	17	1	Petition	45	Rev. Claims	....	....	....	Disch'd; laid on table.		
Gaylord, Jonathan	Compensation for revolutionary services.	4	1	Petition	425	Claims	May 7, 1796	Adverse	....	Leave to withdraw.		
Gaylord, Levi	Compensation for serviees in war of 1812.	25	3	Petition	121	Claims.						
Gaylord, Lucinda	Indemnity for French spoliations prior to 1800.	31	1	Petition	255	Foreign Affairs	355	Favorable	318	Referred to Committee Whole House.		

List of private claims presented to the House of Representatives of the United States from the 1st to the 31st Congress, inclusive—Continued.

Names of claimants.	Nature or object of the claim.	Congress.	Session.	How brought before the House of Reps.	Page of journal.	To what committee of the House referred.	No. or date of the report.	Nature of the report.	No. of the bill.	How disposed of by the House of Reps.	How disposed of by the Senate.	Date of the act of Congress, and remarks.
Gaylord, Wm	(See Aaron Gaylord, administrator of.)	26	1	....	182							
Gaynor, John B	Pension and other relief	22	2	Petition	216	Claims.						
Gaynor, John B	Pension and other relief	23	1	Petition	583	Claims	548	Adverse	......	Laid on table.		
Gazzam, Audley H	(See Miguel Eslava, heirs of)	24	1	....	436							
Gazzam, Taylor, and Jones.	Payment of certificates of debenture for goods exported.	5	2	Petition	112	Com. and Manuf	Mar. 29, 1798	Favorable	72			
Gazzam, Taylor, and Jones.	Payment of certificates of debenture for goods exported.	5	3	Petition	441	Com. and Manuf	Jan. 28, 1799	Favorable	148½	Passed	Passed	App'd Feb. 19, 1799
Gear, George	Pension	19	1	Petition	203	Military Pensions	April 1, 1826	Adverse.				
Gebhart, Frederick	Reimbursement of duties	20	1	Petition	68	Ways and Means	Jan. 29, 1830	Adverse	......	Laid on table.		
Gebhart, Peter	Pension	15	2	Petition	182	Pens. & Rev. Cl'ms.	Jan. 20, 1819	Adverse	......	Rejected.		
Gebhart, Peter	Pension	24	2	Petition	399	Rev. Pensions.						
Gedney, Thomas R	Compensation for services on coast survey.	31	1	Petition	1095	Judiciary.						
Geddings Edward	(See William White, *et al*)	9	2	....	555							
Gee, Henry	To exchange land	27	2	Memorial	142	Public Lands	478	Favorable	330	Passed	Passed	App'd Aug. 11, 1842
Gee, Howell, heirs of	Compensation for revolutionary services.	24	1	Documents	475	Rev. Claims.						
Gee, James	Arrears of pension	26	1	Petition	288	Invalid Pensions	403	Adverse	......	Laid on table.		
Gee, James	Pension	28	1	Petition	371	Invalid Pensions	376	Adverse	......	Laid on table.		
Cee, James	Pension	29	1	Petition	101	Invalid Pensions	331	Favorable	266	Passed	Passed	App'd Aug. 8, 1846
Gee, N., & Co	For amount due out of moneys coming to Ottawa Indians.	29	1	Memorial	160	Indian Affairs	287	Adverse.				
Geensut, Agrenis	Indemnity for property destroyed by the enemy.	15	2	Petition	148	Claims	....	....	......	Discharged; laid on table.		
Geer, Roger, heir of	Pension	31	1	Petition	712	Rev. Claims	342	Adverse	......	Laid on table.		
Geese, Thomas	Reimbursement of duties on teas	2	1	Petition	469	....	....	....	......	Referred to Secretary Treasury.		
Geese, Thomas	Reimbursement of duties on teas	3	2	Rep. of Secretary Treasury.	284	....	....	....	......	Laid on table.		
Geesey, (or Giesey,) Valentine.	Payment of two years' salary as superintendent of Cumberland road.	22	2	Amendm't to appropriation bill.	471	Whole House.						
Geesey, or (Giesey,) Valentine.	Payment of two years' salary as superintendent of Cumberland road.	23	1	Resolution	129	Ways and Means	Jan. 21, 1834	Favorable	221			
Geesey, (or Giesey,) Valentine.	Payment of two years' salary as superintendent of Cumberland road.	23	2	Resolution	230	Ways and Means	....	See bill	616	Passed	Passed	App'd March 3, 1835
Geesey, (or Giesey,) Valentine, widow of.	Indemnity for losses as superintendent of Cumberland road.	27	3	Petition	140	Claims.						
Geesey, (or Giesey,) Valentine,) widow of.	Indemnity for losses as superintendent of Cumberland road.	28	1	Petition	132	Claims	381	Favorable	279	Passed	Passed, with amendment.	App'd June 15, 1844
Gehnet, Christiana	Pension	28	2	Petition	59	Rev. Pensions	....	....	......	Discharged; laid on table.		
Gehon, Francis	Settlement of accounts as United States marshal.	26	1	Senate bill	1138	Claims	....	....	238			
Gehon, Francis	Settlement of accounts as United States marshal.	26	2	Senate bill	178	Claims	189	Adverse	139	Laid on table.		
Geiofer, John	(See F. M. Arredondo, *et al.*)	19	1	....	252							

List of private claims presented to the House of Representatives of the United States from the 1st to the 31st Congress, inclusive—Continued.

Names of claimants.	Nature or object of the claim.	Congress.	Session.	How brought before the House of Reps.	Page of journal.	To what committee of the House referred.	No. or date of the report.	Nature of the report.	No. of the bill.	How disposed of by the House of Reps.	How disposed of by the Senate.	Date of the act of Congress, and remarks.
Geiser, Henry	Compensation for services in revolutionary war.	3	1	Petition	103					Referred to Secretary War.		
Gelston, David	Indemnity for costs of suits against him while in discharge of duty.	9	2	Petition	506	Com. and Manuf.	Feb. 4, 1807	Favorable	194	Passed	Passed	App'd Feb. 5, 1807
Gelston, David, *et al.*	To be released from judgment at suit of G. Hoyt.	14	1	House bill	538	Ways and Means	Mar. 27, 1816	Favorable	151	Laid on table.		
Gelston, David, *et al.*	To be released from judgment at suit of G. Hoyt.	15	1	Petition	331	Ways and Means	Mar. 21, 1818	Adverse		Laid on table.		
Gelston, David, executor of	Settlement of accounts	22	2	Petition	28	Claims.						
Gelston, David, executor of	Settlement of accounts	23	1	Petition	33	Claims	276	Favorable	314			
Gelston, David, executor of	Settlement of accounts	24	1	Petition	613	Claims	614	Favorable	603			
Gelston, David, executor of	Settlement of accounts	25	2	Petition	36	Claims	38	Favorable	50	Passed	Passed	App'd July 9, 1838
Gelston, David, executor of	To be credited in settlement of accounts, with certain duties.	27	2	Senate bill	469	Claims	April 12, 1842	Favorable	111	Passed		App'd Aug. 11, 1842
Gendio, Jean Baptiste	Land and money for revolutionary services.	26	1	Resolution	359							
Gendry, (or Gentry,) N.	Confirmation of title to land	27	3	Petition	274	Public Lands.						
Gendry, (or Gentry,) N.	Confirmation of title to land	28	1	Petition	76	Priv. Land Claims.						
General Armstrong, brig	(See Samuel C. Reed, *et al*)	15	1		63							
Genks, George W.	(See assignee of Thomas Tupper)	22	2		142							
Gennell, Peter	To be released from judgment as Postmaster.	26	1	Petition		P. Of. and P. Roads.	396	Adverse.				
Genther, John H.	Pension	20	1	Petition	223	Military Affairs	Feb. 13, 1828	General bill	166	Passed.		
Genther, John H.	Pension	20	2	House bill	142	Whole House	Dec. 12, 1828	General bill	311	Passed	Laid on table.	
Genther, John H.	Pension	21	1	Petition	130	Military Pensions	Jan. 5, 1830	General bill	72	Passed	Passed	App'd May 14, 1830
Genther, John H.	Pension	22	1	Petition	67	Rev. Pensions	54	Favorable	105	Passed	Indef. postp'd.	
Genther, John H.	Pension	22	2	Petition	34	Rev. Pensions	Jan. 7, 1833	Favorable	664			
Genther, John H.	Pension	23	1	Petition	97	Rev. Pensions.						
Genther, John H.	Pension	24	1	Petition	102	Rev. Pensions.						
Genther, John H.	Pension	25	2	Petition	55	Rev. Pensions				Discharged; laid on table.		
Genther, John H.	Pension	26	1	Petition	173	Rev. Pensions	108	Favorable	118	Passed	Indef. postp'd.	
Gentry, Allen	Indemnity for depredations on property by Tennessee volunteers.	25	2	Petition	541	Claims	1036	Adverse		Laid on table.		
Gentry, Allen	Indemnity for depredations on property by Tennessee volunteers.	26	1	Petition	339	Claims	376	Adverse		Laid on table.		
Gentry, James H., assignee of.	Confirmation of title to land	28	1	Petition	632	Public Lands.						
Gentry, James H., assignee of.	Confirmation of title to land	28	2	Petition	164	Public Lands.						
Gentry, Meshal	Pension	30	1	Petition	217	Rev. Pensions	141	Adverse		Laid on table.		
Gentry, Reuben E., *et al.*	Indemnity for Indian depredations	23	1	Petition	138, 600	Indian Affairs				Discharged; laid on table.		
Gentry, Reuben E., *et al.*	Indemnity for Indian depredations	24	1	Petition	96, 212	Indian Affairs	266	Favorable	273	Referred to Committee Whole House.		
Gentry, Reuben E., *et al.*	Indemnity for Indian depredations	24	2	House bill	200	Whole House	Jan. 13, 1837	With't amend.	273			
Gentry, Reuben E., *et al.*	Indemnity for Indian depredations	25	2	Petition	43	Indian Affairs	212	Favorable	248	Referred to Committee Whole House.		
Gentry, Reuben E., *et al.*	Indemnity for Indian depredations	25	3	House bill	376	Whole House	Jan. 25, 1839	With't amend.	248			
Gentry, Reuben E., *et al.*	Indemnity for Indian depredations	26	1	Resolution	396	Claims.						
Gentry, Reuben E., *et al.*	Indemnity for Indian depredations	28	2	Senate bill	515	Indian Affairs	Mar. 1, 1845	With amend.	S. 92	Referred to Committee Whole House.		
Gentry, Reuben E., *et al.*	Indemnity for Indian depredations	29	1	House bill	442	Indian Affairs	Jan. 17, 1846	Adverse	252	Laid on table.		

List of private claims presented to the House of Representatives of the United States from the 1st to the 31st Congress, inclusive—Continued.

89

Names of claimants.	Nature or object of the claim.	Congress.	Session.	How brought before the House of Reps.	Page of journal.	To what committee of the House referred.	No. or date of the report.	Nature of the report.	No. of the bill.	How disposed of by the House of Reps.	How disposed of by the Senate.	Date of the act of Congress, and remarks.
Gentry, Reuben E., *et al.*	Indemnity for Indian depredations	30	1	Petition	110	Indian Affairs				Discharged; laid on table.		
Gentry, Reuben E., *et al.*	Indemnity for Indian depredations	30	2	Petition	124	Indian Affairs.						
Gentry, William	Permission to correct error in land entry.	20	1	Senate bill	69	Priv. Land Claims.	Jan. 9, 1828	With't amend.	S. 20	Passed		App'd May 9, 1828
Geiofer, John	Indemnity for property destroyed by United States troops.	19	1	Memorial	252	Foreign Affairs	112	Adverse.				
Geiofer, John	Indemnity for property destroyed by United States troops.	20	2	Petition	339	Foreign Affairs	99	Favorable	385	Referred to Committee Whole House.		
Geiofer, John	Indemnity for property destroyed by United States troops.	23	1	Petition	67	Foreign Affairs	368	Favorable	395	Passed	Passed	App'd June 26, 1834
Geoghegan, John	Bounty land for revolutionary services.	16	2	Petition	153	Pens. & Rev. Cl'ms.	Jan. 29, 1821	Adverse		Rejected.		
Geoghegan, Moses	(See Joseph Stewart, *et al*)	13	3		751							
Geoghegan, William	(See Joseph Stewart, *et al*)	13	3		751							
George, Alfred	Compensation for a horse lost in public service.	24	1	Petition	264	Claims	April 15, 1836	Adverse		Laid on table.		
George, Alfred	Compensation for a horse lost in public service.	25	2	Petition	724	Claims.						
George, Alfred	Compensation for a horse lost in public service.	26	1	House bill	645	Claims			255			
George, Brig, owners of	Indemnity for vessel sunk in defence of Baltimore.	21	1	House bill	248	Whole House	April 30, 1830	With't amend.	191	Passed	Passed	App'd May 29, 1830
George, James	Bounty land	31	1	Petition	976	Public Lands.						
George, James K.	Compensation for services, and for injuries received, in war of 1812.	26	1	Documents	339	Invalid Pensions.						
George, James K.	Compensation for services, and for injuries received, in war of 1812.	26	2	Petition	77	Invalid Pensions	81	Adverse		Laid on table.		
George, John, heirs of	Compensation for military services	5	2	Petition	321	Claims				Discharged; leave to withdraw.		
George, John	Pension	15	1	Petition	106	Pens. & Rev. Cl'ms.				Discharged; laid on table.		
George, John D., *et al.*	Compensation as extra clerks in custom-house, Philadelphia.	24	2	Petition	206	Commerce	257	Favorable	946	Referred to Committee Whole House.		
George, John D., *et al.*	Compensation as extra clerks in custom-house, Philadelphia.	25	2	Rep't and House bill.	224	Commerce	292	Favorable	332	Referred to Committee Whole House.		
George, John D., *et al.*	Compensation as extra clerks in custom-house, Philadelphia.	25	3	House bill	377	Whole House			332	Passed.		
George, Moses Sweat	Pension	3	2	Rep. of Secretary War.	350	Claims				Discharged; laid on table.		
George, Moses Sweat	Pension	4	1	Rep. of Secretary War.	445	Claims	Mar. 14, 1796	General bill	156	Passed	Passed	App'd April 20, 1796
George, Phineas	Increase of compensation as keeper of light-house.	24	2	Petition	207	Commerce.						
George, Phineas	Increase of compensation as keeper of light-house.	25	2	Petition	46	Commerce.						
George, Phineas	Pension	26	1	Petition	962	Invalid Pensions.						
George Samuel K.	Reimbursement of certain duties	28	2	Petition	69	Ways and Means	154	Favorable	626	Referred to Committee Whole House.		
George, Schooner, owners of.	Indemnity for French spoliations prior to 1800.	26	1	Memorial	182	Foreign Affairs	343	Favorable	319	Referred to Committee Whole House.		
George, Sidney	(See Joshua Louttit, representative of.)	4	2		630							

List of private claims presented to the House of Representatives of the United States from the 1st to the 31st Congress, inclusive—Continued.

Names of claimants.	Nature or object of the claim.	Congress.	Session.	How brought before the House of Reps.	Page of journal.	To what committee of the House referred.	No. or date of the report.	Nature of the report.	No. of the bill.	How disposed of by the House of Reps.	How disposed of by the Senate.	Date of the act of Congress, and remarks.
George, William, widow of.	Half-pay due late husband	3	1	Petition and rep't Sec. of War.	16, 93	Select	April 23, 1794	Favorable	......	Laid on table.		
Georgia, sufferers by fire at Savannah.	For relief	16	1	Senate bill	353	Ways and Means	April 6, 1820	With't amend.	57	Passed	....	App'd April 11, 1820
Georgia, inhabitants of	Payment of claims against Indians prior to 1802.	20	1	Resolution	66	Indian Affairs	Feb. 5, 1828	Adverse	......	Laid on table.		
Georgia, inhabitants of	Payment of claims against Indians prior to 1802.	20	2	Rep. of last sess.	115	Whole House	....	....	......	Discharged; laid on table.		
Georgia, inhabitants of	Payment of claims against Indians prior to 1802.	21	1	Resolution	44	Indian Affairs	115	Favorable	155			
Georgia, inhabitants of	Payment of claims against Indians prior to 1802.	22	1	Resolution	38	Indian Affairs	65	Favorable	128			
Georgia, inhabitants of	Payment of claims against Indians prior to 1802.	23	1	House bill	50	Indian Affairs	140	Favorable	153	Passed	Passed	App'd June 30, 1834
Georgia, inhabitants of	Indemnity for Creek Indian depredations.	21	2	Rep. of Secretary War.	78	Indian Affairs.						
Georgia, inhabitants of	Indemnity for Creek Indian depredations.	22	1	Resolution	147	Indian Affairs	Feb. 20, 1832	Favorable	378			
Georgia, inhabitants of	Indemnity for Creek Indian depredations.	23	1	Resolution	601	Indian Affairs.						
Georgia, steamboat company.	Permission to import two iron steamboats free of duty.	24	1	Petition	53	Ways and Means	....	....	......	Discharged; laid on table.		
Georgian Native, (steamboat) owners of.	Compensation for transporting Tennessee volunteers.	25	3	Documents	121	Claims.						
Georgia, purchasers of land in.	Reference of claim to Supreme Court.	9	2	Petition	536	....	....	....	......	Laid on table.		
Georgia, State of	Reimbursement of judgment obtained by R. Farquhar.	3	2	Resolution	304	Claims.						
Georgia, State of	Reimbursement of judgment obtained by R. Farquhar.	5	2	Rep't Committee	272	Claims	April 25, 1798	Adverse	......	Laid on table.		
Georgia, revolutionary officers of.	Payment of depreciation of certificates.	2	2	Petition	697	....	....	....	......	Laid on table.		
Georgia, State of	To be allowed 15 per cent. discount on its quota of direct tax paid.	14	2	Documents	190	Ways and Means	46	Favorable	62	Passed	Passed	App'd March 3, 1817
Georgia, State of	Reimbursement of amount of costs of suit instituted by the executors of R. Farquahar to recover payment for goods sold to said State, use of United States troops, revolutionary war.	3	2	Resolution	304	Claims.						
Georgia, State of	Reimbursement of amount of costs of suit instituted by the executors of R. Farquahar to recover payment for goods sold to said State, use of United States troops, revolutionary war.	4	1	Res. of last sess.	373	Claims.						
Georgia, State of	Reimbursement of amount of costs of suit instituted by the executors of R. Farqushar to recover payment for goods sold to said State, use of United States troops, revolutionary war.	4	2	Res. former sess.	614	Claims.						

List of private claims presented to the House of Representatives of the United States from the 1st to the 31st Congress, inclusive—Continued.

Names of claimants.	Nature or object of the claim.	Congress.	Session.	How brought before the House of Reps.	Page of journal.	To what committee of the House referred.	No. or date of the report.	Nature of the report.	No. of the bill.	How disposed of by the House of Reps.	How disposed of by the Senate.	Date of the act of Congress, and remarks.
Georgia, State of	Reimbursement of amount of costs of suit instituted by the executors of R. Farquahar to recover payment for goods sold to said State, use of United States troops, revolutionary war.	5	2	Res. former sess.	272	Claims	April 25, 1798	Adverse	......	Rejected.		
Georgia, State of	Indemnification against act of Congress, adjusting land claims in Mississippi Territory.	14	2	Pres. Message	359	Select	76	Favorable	124	Passed	Passed, with amendment.	App'd March 3, 1817
Georgia, State of	Payment for services of militia in 1841-'42.	28	1	House bill	842	Claims	549	With't amend.	349	Referred to Committee Whole House.		
Georgia, State of	Reimbursement of moneys expended on volunteers in Creek and Seminole wars.	24	2	Amendm't to appropriati'n bill.	524	Whole House	Feb. 25, 1837	Adverse	755			
Georgia, State of	Reimbursement of moneys expended on volunteers in Creek and Seminole wars.	27	3	Resolution	188	Claims.						
Georgia, State of	Payment for services of militia in Florida war, 1836.	27	2	Documents	592	Military Affairs.						
Georgia, State of	Payment of expense incurred in repelling invasion of Indians.	25	3	Resolution	276	Claims.						
Georgia, State of	Payment of expense incurred in repelling invasion of Indians.	26	1	Resolution	773	Claims	July 10, 1840	Favorable	491			
Georgia, State of	Payment of expense incurred in repelling invasion of Indians.	27	2	Resolution	107	Military Affairs.						
Georgia, State of	Payment of expense incurred in repelling invasion of Indians.	27	2	Senate bill	409	Military Affairs	684	With amends.	17	Passed	Passed with amendment.	App'd Aug. 12, 1842
Georgia, State of	Interest on money expended in suppressing Indian hostilities in 1836-'37-'38.	31	1	Senate bill	1118	Judiciary	....	....	210	Referred to Committee Whole House.		
Georgia, State of	Interest on money expended in suppressing Indian hostilities in 1836-'37-'38.	31	2	Senate bill	49	Judiciary	Dec. 12, 1850	Favorable	210	Passed	....	App'd March 3, 1851
Georgia, United States marshal in.	Increase of compensation	26	1	Resolution	548	Judiciary.						
Georgia, merchants of Savannah.	To be released from penalty for importing British manufactures in 1812.	12	1	Petition	360	Ways and Means.						
Georgia militia, detachment of.	Payment for services in defending the frontiers.	14	2	Resolution	180	Select	55	Favorable	78	Laid on table.		
Georgia militia, detachment of.	Payment for services in defending the frontiers.	14	2	Senate bill	345	Whole House	Feb. 5, 1817	Favorable	78	Laid on table.		
Georgia militia, detachment of.	Payment for services in defending the frontiers.	15	1	Resolution	41	Select	16	Favorable	16	Rejected.		
Georgia militia, detachment of.	Payment for services in defending the frontiers.	17	1	Resolution	322	Military Affairs	Mar. 26, 1822	Adverse	......	Laid on table.		
Georgia militia, detachment of.	Payment for services in defending the frontiers.	17	2	Resolution	61	Whole House.						
Georgia militia, detachment of.	Payment for services in defending the frontiers.	17	2	Senate bill	214	Military Affairs	52	Adverse	44			
Georgia militia, detachment of.	Payment for services in defending the frontiers.	18	1	Memorial	29	Military Affairs	45	Adverse	......	Referred to Committee Whole House.		

List of private claims presented to the House of Representatives of the United States from the 1st to the 31st Congress, inclusive—Continued.

Names of claimants.	Nature or object of the claim.	Congress.	Session.	How brought before the House of Reps.	Page of journal.	To what committee of the House referred.	No. or date of the report.	Nature of the report.	No. of the bill.	How disposed of by the House of Reps.	How disposed of by the Senate.	Date of the act of Congress, and remarks.
Georgia militia, detachment of.	Payment for services in defending the frontiers.	18	2	Memorial	242	Whole House	Feb. 16, 1825	Adverse.				
Georgia militia, detachment of.	Payment for services in defending the frontiers.	19	1	Resolution	72	Military Affairs				Discharged; laid on table.		
Georgia militia, detachment of.	Payment for services in defending the frontiers.	19	2	Memorial	50	Military Affairs	Feb. 10, 1827	Report		Referred to Committee Whole House.		
Georgia militia, detachment of, resolution of State of.	Payment for services in defending the frontiers.	19	2	Resolution	134	Military Affairs	Feb. 19, 1827	General bill	372	Passed	Passed	App'd March 2, 1827
Georgia militia, detachment of.	For balance due for military service under act of March 2, 1827.	21	1	Resolution	78	Military Affairs	Jan. 4, 1830	Favorable	64			
Georgia militia, detachment of.	For balance due for military service under act of March 2, 1827.	22	1	Resolution	263	Military Affairs	Feb. 15, 1832	Favorable	373			
Georgia militia, detachment of.	For balance due for military service under act of March 2, 1827.	23	1	Resolution	571	Ways and Means	May 20, 1834	Favorable	486	Passed	Passed, with amendment.	App'd June 18, 1834
Georgia, inspectors of revenue for Savannah.	Increase of compensation	15	2	Petition	21	Ways and Means	Dec. 2, 1818	Adverse		Leave to withdraw.		
Georgia, inhabitants of Washington, in Wilks county.	Repayment of money advanced to volunteers in the Florida war.	24	2	Documents	209	Claims	322	Adverse		Laid on table.		
Georgia, citizens of Camden county.	Repayment of money advanced to volunteers in 1836	26	1	Resolution	773	Claims.						
Georgia, corporation of Savannah.	That the site of old Fort Wayne, heretofore granted to the city, be given in *fee simple*.	28	1	Petition	116	Military Affairs	Mar. 27, 1844	Favorable	J. R. 19	Referred to Committee Whole House.		
Georgia, Society of United Brethren of the South.	Indemnity for building erected, and improvements made in the Cherokee country.	23	1	Memorial	248	Indian Affairs.						
Georgia, Railroad and Banking Company.	Reimbursement of duties paid on railroad iron.	25	2	Senate bill	763	Manufactures	May 7, 1838	Favorable	175	Passed		App'd July 7, 1838
Georgia, Central Railroad and Banking Company.	That bonds given for duties on railroad iron be cancelled.	30	1	Memorial	342	Judiciary.						
Georgia, Central Railroad and Banking Company.	That bonds given for duties on railroad iron be cancelled.	30	1	Senate bill	892	Judiciary	July 19, 1848	Favorable	218	Passed		App'd July 25, 1848
Georgia, Monroe Railroad and Banking Company.	To be released from their bonds given as the sureties of said county for duties on railroad iron.	31	1	Papers	520	Judiciary	337	Favorable	302			
Georgia, State of, by agent.	Reimbursement of amount of a final settlement certificate, paid by the State to her officers in revolutionary war.	23	2	Memorial	308	Rev. Claims.						
Georgia, State of, by agent.	Reimbursement of amount of a final settlement certificate, paid by the State to her officers in revolutionary war.	24	1	Petition	259	Rev. Claims.						
Georgia, State of, by agent.	Reimbursement of amount of a final settlement certificate, paid by the State to her officers in revolutionary war.	24	2	Petition	91	Rev. Claims.						
Georgia, State of, by agent.	Reimbursement of amount of a final settlement certificate, paid by the State to her officers in revolutionary war.	25	2	Petition	81	Rev. Claims				Discharged; laid on table.		

List of private claims presented to the House of Representatives of the United States from the 1st to the 31st Congress, inclusive—Continued.

Names of claimants.	Nature or object of the claim.	Congress.	Session.	How brought before the House of Reps.	Page of journal.	To what committee of the House referred.	No. or date of the report.	Nature of the report.	No. of the bill.	How disposed of by the House of Reps.	How disposed of by the Senate.	Date of the act of Congress, and remarks.
Georgia, State of, by agent.	Reimbursement of amount of a final settlement certificate, paid by the State to her officers in revolutionary war.	25	3	Petition	117	Select	311	Favorable	1174	Referred to Committee Whole House.		
Georgia, State of, by agent.	Reimbursement of amount of a final settlement certificate, paid by the State to her officers in revolutionary war.	26	1	Papers	596	Select.						
Georgia, State of, by agent.	Reimbursement of amount of a final settlement certificate, paid by the State to her officers in revolutionary war.	27	2	Pet. and papers .	73	Rev. Claims......	1090	Adverse	......	Laid on table.		
Georgia, Legislature of ...	Payment for supplies furnished friendly Indians, by citizens of said State.	19	2	Resolution	156	Indian Affairs.....	....	....	......	Discharged; referred to Secretary of War.		
Georgia, Battalion of officers and soldiers of.	Payment for horses lost during the Mexican war.	31	1	Petition	1053	Military Affairs.						
Georgia, Battalion of officers and soldiers of.	Payment for horses lost during the Mexican war.	31	2	Petition	291	Military Affairs....	28	Adverse	......	Laid on table.		
Georgia, Legislature......	Payment for horses lost by soldiers in Nelson's brigade, Florida war.	25	3	Resolution	276	Military Affairs.						
Georgia, Legislature......	Payment for property of her citizens destroyed by United States troops in Florida war.	25	3	Resolution	276	Claims.						
Georgia, 7th company of militia of.	Compensation for military services rendered in 1840 and 1841.	27	2	Letter of Secret'y of War.	275	Military Affairs....	April 12, 1842	Favorable	380	Referred to Committee Whole House.		
Georgia, 7th company of militia of.	Compensation for military services rendered in 1840 and 1841.	27	3	House bill	88	Whole House.....	....	Favorable....	380	Passed.............	Passed, with amendment.	App'd Feb. 4, 1843
Georgia, city of Augusta .	Repayment of money advanced to volunteers in Florida war.	24	2	Suggestion	584	Claims	319	Adverse	......	Laid on table.		
Georgia & Alabama	Indemnity for Indian depredation in 1836.	29	1	Petition	176	Indian Affairs.						
Georgia, Alabama, and Florida, citizens of.	Indemnity for depredations committed on their property by Creek and Seminole Indians.	25	2	Presid'ts message	323	Claims	1028	Favorable	865			
Georgia, Republican Blues, company of.	Reimbursement of duties paid on materials imported for a standard.	28	2	Petition	250	Ways and Means.						
Geortner, *alias* Gordiner, Peter, heir of.	Compensation for revolutionary services.	24	2	Petition	38	Rev. Claims......	174	Adverse	......	Laid on table.		
Gerard, Francis, & wife ..	Confirmation of title to land.....	15	1	Petition	212	Priv. Land Claims.						
Gerard, Joseph, heirs of ..	Compensation as guide and Indian interpreter.	28	1	Petition	724	Claims.						
Gerard, Joseph, heirs of ..	Compensation as guide and Indian interpreter.	28	2	Petition	221	Claims	174	Favorable	644			
Gerard, Joseph, heirs of ..	Compensation as guide and Indian interpreter.	29	1	Petition	67	Claims.						
Gerard, Joseph, heirs of ..	Compensation as guide and Indian interpreter.	29	2	Petition	74	Claims.						
Gerard, Joseph, heirs of ..	For bounty land for military services in 1792.	30	1	Petition	204	Claims	121	Favorable	111	Passed.		
Gerard, Joseph, heirs of ..	For bounty land for military services in 1792.	30	1	Petition	432	Claims.						

List of private claims presented to the House of Representatives of the United States from the 1st to the 31st Congress, inclusive—Continued.

Names of claimants.	Nature or object of the claim.	Congress.	Session.	How brought before the House of Reps.	Page of journal.	To what committee of the House referred.	No. or date of the report.	Nature of the report.	No. of the bill.	How disposed of by the House of Reps.	How disposed of by the Senate.	Date of the act of Congress, and remarks.
Gere, Rezin, heirs of	Remuneration for losses in revolutionary war.	24	2	Petition	155	Rev. Pensions				Discharged; laid on table.		
Gere, William, heirs of	Pension	30	1	Petition	576	Rev. Pensions.						
Geren, Simon, (Ala.)	For a grant of land to erect mills on.	18	1	Petition	136	Public Lands.						
Gerin, Nathan	To be exonerated from penalty for selling spirituous liquors.	14	1	Petition	284	Ways and Means				Discharged; referred to Sec. of Treasury.		
Germain, Martial St.	Confirmation of title to land	22	1	Petition	107	Military Affairs	Dec. 27, 1831	General bill	125	Passed	Passed	App'd June 25, 1832
Germans, Committee of	To be allowed to purchase a township of land in Illinois.	24	1	Memorial	277	Public Lands				Discharged; laid on table.		
Germond, Jacob	Compensation for revolutionary services.	14	2	Petition	79	Pens. & Rev. Cl'ms.	Dec. 30, 1816	Adverse		Rejected.		
Germon, Richard	Indemnity for losses by the act suspending commercial intercourse with France.	5	3	Petition	432	Whole House.						
Gerock, Samuel	Pension	19	1	Resolution	185	Military Pensions	April 1, 1826	Adverse		Laid on table.		
Gerock, Samuel	Pension	20	2	Petition	99	Military Pensions	Feb. 13, 1829	General bill	440	Passed.		
Gerock, Samuel	Pension	21	1	Petition	49	Military Pensions	Jan. 5, 1830	General bill	72	Passed	Passed	App'd May 20, 1830
Gerodelle, John	Pension	23	1	Petition	54	Invalid Pensions	448	Favorable	466	Ref'd to Com. W. H.		
Gerodelle, John	Pension	23	2	House bill	336	Whole House	Feb. 6, 1835	Favorable	466	Passed	Passed	App'd March 3, 1835
Gerould, Azubah	Pension	28	1	Petition	850	Rev. Pensions.						
Gerrald, George	(See Thomas Owens, *et al.*)	12	1		66							
Gerrish, Jacob	Indemnity for French spoliations prior to 1800.	26	1	Memorial	182	Foreign Affairs	343	Favorable	319	Referred to Committee Whole House.		
Gerrish, William	Remission of penalty for breach of revenue laws.	4	1	Petition	456	Com. and Manuf.						
Gerry, Elbridge, widow of.	That salary be continued to widow and children.	14	1	Petition	185	Select	Feb. 22, 1816	Favorable	92	Indefinitely postponed.		
Gervais, Benjamin	Indemnity for damages by sale of land by government.	30	2	Petition	313	Claims.						
Gervais, John G	Grant of land	3	2	Senate bill	352	Claims	March 2, 1795	Favorable	34	Passed		App'd May 3, 1795
Gervais, Juliana	Indemnity for damages by sale of land by government.	30	2	Petition	313	Claims.						
Gervais, Raymond	Remission of duties on earthen ware.	16	2	Petition	83	Commerce				Laid on table.		
Gervais, Sinclair D	Permission to relinquish land bought of United States.	22	1	Petition	134	Public Lands	387	Favorable	479	Referred to Committee Whole House.		
Gervais, Sinclair D	Permission to relinquish land bought of United States.	22	2	House bill	93	Whole House	Jan. 2, 1833	With't amend.	479	Passed.		
Gest, J	(See George Troutman, *et al.*)	17	1		100							
Gevelot, Nicholas	Payment of balance due for sculpture work.	19	2	Petition	297	Public Buildings.						
Gevelot, Nicholas	Payment of balance due for sculpture work.	20	2	Petition	204	Public Buildings				Discharged; laid on table.		
Gevelot, Nicholas	Payment of balance due for sculpture work.	20	2	Appropriat'n bill.	241	Whole House	Feb. 24, 1829	With amend.	413	Passed	Passed	App'd March 3, 1829
Geyer, Andrew	(See sureties of George and Jacob Gilbert.)	7	1		29							
Geyer, F. W., *et al.*	Indemnity for French spoliations prior to 1800.	31	1	Memorial	409	Foreign Affairs	355	Favorable	318	Referred to Committee Whole House.		
Geyer, John	Pension for wounds received in Dartmouth prison.	14	1	Petition	294	Naval Affairs				Discharged; laid on table.		
Geyer, John, (S. C.)	Indemnity for French spoliations prior to 1800.	26	1	Memorial	182	Foreign Affairs	343	Favorable	319	Referred to Committee Whole House.		

List of private claims presented to the House of Representatives of the United States from the 1st to the 31st Congress, inclusive—Continued.

Names of claimants.	Nature or object of the claim.	Congress.	Session.	How brought before the House of Reps.	Page of journal.	To what committee of the House referred.	No. or date of the report.	Nature of the report.	No. of the bill.	How disposed of by the House of Reps.	How disposed of by the Senate.	Date of the act of Congress, and remarks.
Ghent, claimants under treaty of.	For distribution of amount of indemnity paid, to be paid by Great Britain under 1st article.	19	2	Senate bill	345	Whole House	Mar. 1, 1827	With amend.	S. 68	Passed	Concurred in.	App'd March 2, 1827
Ghent, claimants under treaty of.	For an act in addition to act March 2, 1827.	20	1	Senate bill	384	Judiciary	Mar. 22, 1828	With amend.	S. 96	Passed	Concurred in.	App'd May 9, 1828
Ghent, claimants under treaty of.	Interest on claims awarded	20	2	Petition	231	Foreign Affairs.	79	Adverse	......	Laid on table.		
Ghequire, Charles, trustee of.	Indemnity for French spoliations prior to 1800.	26	1	Memorial	182	Foreign Affairs	343	Favorable	319	Referred to Committee Whole House.		
Gianoply, Juan	(See F. M. Arredondo, *et al.*)	19	1	....	252							
Gibault, P	Confirmation of title to land	1	3	Senate bill	352	Select	....	....	S. 15	Passed	....	App'd March 3, 1791
Gibbert, George	Indemnity for French spoliations prior to 1800.	26	1	Memorial	182	Foreign Affairs	343	Favorable	319	Referred to Committee Whole House.		
Gibbon, Edward R	Compensation for services under resolution of Congress, May 24, 1824.	19	1	Resolution	170	Ways and Means.	Feb. 20, 1826	Favorable	107	Passed.		
Gibbon, Edward R	Compensation for services under resolution of Congress, May 24, 1824.	19	2	Papers	31	Ways and Means.	Dec. 29, 1826	Favorable	322	Passed.	Passed	App'd March 2, 1827
Gibbon, Edward R	Pre-emption right to land	19	2	Petition	217	Public Lands.						
Gibbon, F. A	Indemnity for losses in building light-house.	30	1	Petition	794	Claims.						
Gibbon, James	Compensation for revolutionary services.	1	1	Petition	96	Select	....	....	......	Discharged; referred to Secretary of War.		
Gibbon, James	Compensation for revolutionary services.	1	2	Rep. of Secretary War.	141	....	....	....	......	Leave to withdraw.		
Gibbon, James	Commutation pay for revolutionary services.	10	2	Petition	427	Whole House.						
Gibbon, James	Commutation pay for revolutionary services.	11	2	Petition	251	Claims.						
Gibbon, Captain James	Commutation pay	21	1	Petition	111	Rev. Claims	251	Favorable	312	Referred to Committee Whole House.		
Gibbon, Captain James	Commutation pay	21	2	House bill	340	Whole House	Feb. 22, 1831	With't amend.	312	Passed.		
Gibbon, James, *et al.*	Commutation pay	22	2	Senate bill	466	Rev. Claims	Mar. 2, 1833	Favorable	105	Passed	Passed, with amendment.	App'd March 2, 1833
Gibbons, John H	Payment for writing for the Attorney General.	27	2	Petition	349	Claims	....	....	......	Discharged; leave to withdraw.		
Gibbon, Lawrence, administrator of.	Release from judgment at suit of United States.	20	2	Senate bill	108	Judiciary	Jan. 12, 1829	Favorable	33	Passed	....	App'd March 2, 1829
Gibbons, William	Compensation for fitting up court-house at Jackson, Missi sippi.	31	1	Petition	311	Claims	111	Adverse	......	Laid on table.		
Gibbs, Benjamin, executors of.	Payment of a final settlement certificate, No. 21,227.	21	1	Resolution	95	Rev. Claims	168	Favorable	214	Referred to Committee Whole House.		
Gibbs, Benjamin, executors of.	Payment of a final settlement certificate, No. 21,227.	21	2	House bill	264	Whole House	Feb. 4, 1831	Favorable	214	Passed.		
Gibbs, Benjamin, executors of.	Payment of a final settlement certificate, No. 21,227.	22	1	Petition	31	Rev. Claims	108	Favorable	191	Passed.	Passed	App'd July 4, 1832
Gibbs & Channing	(See Walter Channing)	10	1	....	82							
Gibbs, Churchill	Commutation pay	21	2	Petition	67	Rev. Claims.						
Gibbs, Churchill	Commutation pay	25	2	Petition	392	Rev. Claims	....	....	......	Discharged; laid on table.		
Gibbs, Churchill	Commutation pay	25	3	Petition	85	Rev. Claims.						
Gibbs, Churchill	Commutation pay	26	1	Petition	163	Rev. Claims.						
Gibbs, Churchill	Commutation pay	26	2	Petition	134	Rev. Claims.						

List of private claims presented to the House of Representatives of the United States from the 1st to the 31st Congress, inclusive—Continued.

Names of claimants.	Nature or object of the claim.	Congress.	Session.	How brought before the House of Reps.	Page of journal.	To what committee of the House referred.	No. or date of the report.	Nature of the report.	No. of the bill.	How disposed of by the House of Reps.	How disposed of by the Senate.	Date of the act of Congress, and remarks.
Gibbs, Churchill	Commutation pay	27	2	Petition	96	Rev. Claims.						
Gibbs, Churchill	Commutation pay	28	1	Petition	321	Rev. Claims.						
Gibbs, Churchill	Commutation pay	29	2	Petition	372	Rev. Claims	88	Adverse		Leave to withdraw.		
Gibbs, Churchill, administrator of.	Payment of half-pay	30	1	Petition	165	Rev. Claims	Jan. 12, 1848	Report		Referred to Secretary War.		
Gibbs, Churchill, administrator of.	Payment of half-pay	30	2	Memorial	344	Rev. Claims	138	Adverse		Discharged; leave to withdraw.		
Gibbs, Elizabeth	Pension	26	1	Resolution	1012	Rev. Pensions.						
Gibbs, Elizabeth	(See Abraham Smith, widow of)	26	2		82							
Gibbs, Ellen M.	(See Crowell Hatch)	27	2		272							
Gibbs, Frederick	Arrears of pension	27	2	Petition	351	Rev. Pensions	784	Adverse		Laid on table.		
Gibbs, Frederick	Arrears of pension	29	1	Petition	74	Rev. Pensions	57	Adverse		Laid on table.		
Gibbs, George	To be allowed drawback duties	3	2	Petition	263	Claims	Feb. 9, 1795	Favorable	108	Passed	Passed	App'd Feb. 25, 1795
Gibbs, Harvey	Pension	14	2	Petition	59	Pens. & Rev. Cl'ms.				Discharged; laid on table.		
Gibbs, Laman	Pension	31	2	Petition	224	Invalid Pensions.						
Gibbs, Reuben M.	Arrears of pension	26	2	Petition	84	Invalid Pensions	221	Adverse		Laid on table.		
Gibbs, Rufus	Pension	21	2	Petition	40	Military Pensions.						
Gibbs, Rufus	Pension	22	1	Petition	34	Rev. Pensions	104	Favorable	190	Referred to Committee Whole House.		
Gibbs, Rufus	Pension	22	2	House bill	66				190	Laid on table.		
Gibbs, Samuel	Increase of pension	2	1	Petition	468					Referred to Secretary War.		
Gibbs, Samuel	Increase of pension	10	2	House bill	499	Whole House	Feb. 20, 1809	Favorable	158	Passed	Passed	App'd April 27, 1809
Gibbs, Samuel	Renewal of two loan office certificates.	6	2	Petition	788	Whole House	Feb. 20, 1801	Adverse		Rejected.		
Gibbs, Samuel	Payment of two loan office certificates.	14	2	Petition	147	Pens. & Rev. Cl'ms.				Discharged; laid on table.		
Gibbs, Samuel	Payment of two loan office certificates.	15	1	Petition	63	Pens. & Rev. Cl'ms.						
Gibbs, Samuel	Payment of two loan office certificates.	15	2	Petition	31	Pens. & Rev. Cl'ms.	Dec. 14, 1818	Favorable	223	Referred to Committee Whole House.		
Gibbs, Samuel	Payment of two loan office certificates.	16	1	Petition	211	Pens. & Rev. Cl'ms.	67	Adverse		Laid on table.		
Gibbs, Samuel, heirs of	Payment of two loan office certificates.	22	2	Resolution	91	Rev. Claims.						
Gibbs, Samuel, heirs of	Payment of two loan office certificates.	23	1	Petition	42	Rev. Claims	166	Favorable	177	Passed	Passed	App'd June 28, 1834
Gibbs, Samuel, widow of	Arrears of pension	24	1	Senate bill	811	Invalid Pensions	June 2, 1836	Favorable	198	Passed		App'd June 15, 1836
Gibbs, Samuel, widow of	Pension	24	2	Senate bill	579				212	Referred to Committee Whole House.		
Gibbs, Samuel, widow of	Pension	25	2	Petition	167	Invalid Pensions				Disch'd; laid on table.		
Gibbs, Samuel, widow of	Pension	26	1	Petition	936	Invalid Pensions.						
Gibbs, Samuel, widow of	Pension	28	1	Petition	99	Invalid Pensions				Discharged; laid on table.		
Gibbs, Samuel, widow of	Pension	30	1	Petition	676	Invalid Pensions.						
Gibbs, Simon	Pension	11	2	House bill	283	Whole House	Mar. 24, 1810	Favorable	107	Passed	Passed	App'd April 27, 1810
Gibbs, William	(See William Thompson, of Va.)	19	1		312							
Gibbs, William, sureties of.	To be released from liability	21	1	Senate bill	603	Claims	May 7, 1830	Adverse	171	Referred to Committee Whole House.		
Gibbs, William R.	(See Mann & Foltz)	26	1		182							
Gibbs, William, *et al.*	Indemnity for French spoliations prior to 1800.	31	1	Petition	307	Foreign Affairs	355	General bill	318			
Gibbs, Zeno	Pension	21	2	Resolution	125	Military Affairs.						

List of private claims presented to the House of Representatives of the United States from the 1st to the 31st Congress, inclusive—Continued.

Names of claimants.	Nature or object of the claim.	Congress.	Session.	How brought before the House of Reps.	Page of journal.	To what committee of the House referred.	No. or date of the report.	Nature of the report.	No. of the bill.	How disposed of by the House of Reps.	How disposed of by the Senate.	Date of the act of Congress, and remarks.
Gibson, Abigail	(See George Gibson, widow of)	1	2		537							
Gibson, Abraham, *et al.*	Confirmation of title to land	15	1	Petition	157	Priv. Land Claims.				Disch'd; laid on table.		
Gibson, Alexander	Arrears of pension	24	1	Resolution	347	Rev. Pensions	725	Favorable	672	Ref'd to Com. W. H.		
Gibson, Alexander	Arrears of pension	24	2	House bill	198	Whole House	Jan. 14, 1837	Favorable	672	Passed	Passed	App'd March 3, 1837
Gibson, A. P	Compensation for acting chargé d'affaires at St. Petersburg.	28	1	Petition	102	Foreign Affairs.						
Gibson, A. P	Compensation for acting chargé d'affaires at St. Petersburg.	29	1	Petition	150	Foreign Affairs.						
Gibson, Charles M	Payment for a wagon and six horses lost in United States service.	28	1	Petition	60	Claims	133	Favorable	123			
Gibson, Charles M	Payment for a wagon and six horses lost in United States service.	29	1	Petition	93	Claims	28	Favorable	34	Laid on table.		
Gibson, Charles M	Payment for a wagon and six horses lost in United States service.	30	1	Senate bill	975	Claims	April 12, 1848	Favorable	171	Passed		App'd Aug. 14, 1848
Gibson, Charles M	Indemnity for Indian depredations.	29	2	Senate bill	375	Claims	Feb. 26, 1847	Favorable	93	Referred to Committee Whole House.		
Gibson, David	Compensation for services, and for sufferings while prisoner.	24	1	Petition	266	Rev. Pensions	652	Adverse		Laid on table.		
Gibson, Edward	Pre-emption right to land	21	2	Petition	34	Public Lands.						
Gibson, George	Compensation for revolutionary services.	1	3	Petition	360	Select	Jan. 28, 1791	Favorable	138	Referred to Committee Whole House.		
Gibson, George, (Ark)	Grant of land as indemnity for loss by a change of the boundary of Arkansas.	22	1	Petition	34	Public Lands.						
Gibson, George, *et al.*	Grant of land	9	2	Resolution	507	Select	Jan. 23, 1807	General bill	183	Passed	Passed	App'd March 3, 1807
Gibson, George, heirs of	Commutation pay	23	1	Petition	40	Rev. Claims	194	Favorable	214	Referred to Committee Whole House.		
Gibson, George, heirs of	Commutation pay	23	2	House bill	82	Whole House			214			
Gibson, George, heirs of	Commutation pay	24	1	Petition	102	Rev. Claims	345	Favorable	356			
Gibson, George, heirs of	Commutation pay	25	2	Petition	39	Rev. Claims	113	Favorable	131	Postponed.		
Gibson, George, heirs of	Commutation pay	25	3	House bill	155	Whole House	Dec. 27, 1838	Favorable	131	Laid on table.		
Gibson, George, representatives of.	Compensation for extra revolutionary service.	2	1	Senate bill	585	Whole House	May 8, 1792	Favorable	36	Passed	Passed	App'd May 8, 1792
Gibson, George, widow of.	For the benefit of the act for the relief of widows and orphans.	1	2	Petition	537	Whole House.						
Gibson, George, widow of.	Compensation for revolutionary services.	4	1	Memorial	406	Claims	May 11, 1796	Adverse		Laid on table.		
Gibson, George, widow of.	Pension	28	1	Petition	366	Rev. Pensions	217	Favorable	171	Passed	Passed, with amendment.	App'd May 31, 1844
Gibson, Henry, and John Peters.	Compensation as clerks United States court.	24	1	Petition	53	Judiciary	Jan. 1, 1836	General bill	184			
Gibson, Henry, and John Peters.	Compensation as clerks United States court.	25	2	Petition	41	Judiciary	356	General bill	385			
Gibson, Henry, and John Peters.	Compensation as clerks United States court.	26	1	Petition	175	Judiciary.						
Gibson, Jacob	Pension	22	1	Resolution	171	Rev. Pensions				Discharged; laid on table.		
Gibson, James, (Pa)	Correction of error in boundaries of land.	14	2	Petition	32	Priv. Land Claims.	Jan. 14, 1817	Adverse		Leave to withdraw.		
Gibson, James, (Pa)	Correction of error in boundaries of land.	15	1	Petition	85	Priv. Land Claims.				Discharged; laid on table.		
Gibson, James, (Pa)	Correction of error in boundaries of land.	23	2	Petition	210	Claims.						

List of private claims presented to the House of Representatives of the United States from the 1st to the 31st Congress, inclusive—Continued.

Names of claimants.	Nature or object of the claim.	Congress.	Session.	How brought before the House of Reps.	Page of journal.	To what committee of the House referred.	No. or date of the report.	Nature of the report.	No. of the bill.	How disposed of by the House of Reps.	How disposed of by the Senate.	Date of the act of Congress, and remarks.
Gibson, James, (Pa)	Correction of error in boundaries of land.	26	2	Petition	162	Claims.						
Gibson, James	Pension	15	2	Petition	31	Rev. Pensions	Jan. 5, 1819	Adverse		Laid on table.		
Gibson, James	Pension	16	1	Petition	376	Rev. Pensions	April 5, 1820	Adverse		Laid on table.		
Gibson, James, (Ia)	Pension	19	1	Senate bill	488	Military Pensions.	Mar. 3, 1826	Favorable	115	Passed		App'd May 16, 1826
Gibson, James	(See Peter McCall, administrator of)	26	1		182							
Gibson, John	For half-pay in lieu of commutation.	10	2	Petition	380	Select.						
Gibson, John	Indemnity for French spoliations prior to 1800.	26	1	Memorial	182	Foreign Affairs	343	Favorable; bill	319	Referred to Committee Whole House.		
Gibson, John, (Maine)	Pension	21	2	Petition	87	Military Pensions.				Discharged; laid on table.		
Gibson, John, (Indiana)	Compensation as secretary of Louisiana.	7	2	Petition	509	Claims.						
Gibson, John, (Indiana)	Compensation for acting governor.	13	1	Petition	45	Claims.						
Gibson, John, (Indiana)	Compensation for acting governor.	13	2	Petition	176	Claims	Mar. 7, 1814	Favorable		Referred to Committee Whole House.		
Gibson, John, administrator of.	Payment for a horse lost in United States service.	25	2	Documents	396	Claims.						
Gibson, John, administrator of.	Payment for a horse lost in United States service.	25	3	Documents	207	Claims.						
Gibson, John, *et al.*, administrator of.	Indemnity for French spoliations prior to 1800.	29	2	Memorial	50	Foreign Affairs.						
Gibson, John D	Compensation for acting purser in United States navy.	30	1	Petition	380	Naval Affairs				Discharged; laid on table.		
Gibson, John H	Payment for a horse lost in United States service.	23	1	Documents	155	Claims.						
Gibson, Johnson	For a donation of certain lands	26	1	Petition	356	Public Lands.						
Gibson, Jonathan	Settlement of accounts as major	2	2	Petition	705					Referred to Secretary of War.		
Gibson, J. Y	(See Henry White, heirs of)	27	2		330							
Gibson, Martha Ann, *et al.*	(See Henry White, heirs of)	27	2		330							
Gibson, Samuel	Permission to locate lands in lieu of others.	15	1	Petition	65	Priv. Land Claims.						
Gibson, Samuel	Permission to locate lands in lieu of others.	15	2	Petition	91	Priv. Land Claims.	Dec. 14, 1818	Adverse		Rejected.		
Gibson, Samuel	Confirmation of title to land	21	2	Petition	46	Priv. Land Claims.	Dec. 30, 1830	Adverse		Laid on table.		
Gibson, Samuel	Confirmation of title to land	22	1	Petition	79	Priv. Land Claims.	Jan. 6, 1832	Adverse		Laid on table.		
Gibson, Thomas, widow of.	Increase of pension	29	1	Petition	380	Rev. Claims	785	Adverse		Laid on table.		
Gibson, William	Reimbursement of money paid for oxen for United States service.	30	1	Petition	522	Claims	421	Adverse		Laid on table.		
Gibson, William, *et al.*	Compensation as members of court martial.	17	1	Petition	361	Ways and Means.				Discharged; laid on table.		
Giddens, Ishmael	(See Ismey and Custis Giddens, brothers of.)	8	2		138							
Giddens, Ismey and Custis, brothers of.	Arrears of pay and other emoluments for revolutionary services.	8	2	Petition	138	Claims.						
Giddens, Ismey and Custis, brothers of.	Arrears of pay and other emoluments for revolutionary services.	9	1	Petition	193					Referred to Committee Whole House, on bill No. 11.		
Giddon, Edward	(See William Robinson, *et al.*)	9	2		555							
Gideon, Jacob, sen	Payment of one moiety of the forfeiture of Priestman & Austin.	7	2	Petition	296	Claims	Feb. 15, 1803	Adverse		Rejected.		

List of private claims presented to the House of Representatives of the United States from the 1st to the 31st Congress, inclusive—Continued.

Names of claimants.	Nature or object of the claim.	Congress.	Session.	How brought before the House of Reps.	Page of journal.	To what committee of the House referred.	No. or date of the report.	Nature of the report.	No. of the bill.	How disposed of by the House of Reps.	How disposed of by the Senate.	Date of the act of Congress, and remarks.
Gideon, Jacob, jr	Indemnity for loss of contract to furnish blank books.	27	3	Petition	255	Claims	577	Favorable	395			
Gideon, Jacob, jr	Indemnity for loss of contract to furnish blank books.	29	1	Petition	334	Claims.						
Gideon, Jacob, jr	Indemnity for loss of contract to furnish blank books.	30	1	Petition	69	Claims	36	Favorable	33	Passed.		
Gideon, Jacob, jr	Indemnity for loss on contract to furnish blank books.	31	1	Petition	395	Claims.						
Gideon, Joseph	Compensation as purser to brig Porpoise.	29	1	Petition	330	Naval Affairs	701	Favorable	476	Referred to Committee Whole House.		
Gideon, Joseph	Compensation as purser to brig Porpoise.	29	2	House bill	382	Whole House	Feb. 19, 1847	Favorable	476	Passed	Passed	App'd March 3, 1847
Gideon, Pierre	For bounty land	27	2	Petition	251	Military Affairs.						
Gideon, Pierre	For bounty land	29	1	Petition	69	Military Affairs	25	Adverse	......	Laid on table.		
Gideon, Richard, widow of	Pension	29	2	Petition	100	Rev. Pensions.						
Giesey, Valentine	(See Valentine Geesey, or Giesey)											
Giffin, Anna	(See Benjamin Farnham)	29	1	....	168							
Giffin, Anna	Pension	30	1	Petition	69	Rev. Pensions	277	Favorable	273	Passed.		
Giffin, David, *et al*	Indemnity for destruction of fences by United States army.	18	1	Petition	32	Claims	19	Favorable	45	Passed	Passed	App'd May 18, 1824
Gifford, Eseek	Remission of penalty of bond	28	1	Petition	795	Commerce	....	....	......	Discharged; laid on table.		
Gifford, Isaac H.	Pension	25	2	Petition	84	Invalid Pensions	....	....	......	Discharged; laid on table.		
Gifford, Isaac H.	Pension	27	2	Petition	219	Invalid Pensions	416	Adverse	......	Laid on table.		
Gigo, Francis, heirs and representatives of.	Bounty land	31	2	Petition	365	Rev. Claims.						
Gilbeault, Charles	Confirmation of title to land	15	1	Petition	102	Priv. Land Claims	....	....	......	Discharged; laid on table.		
Gilbert, Allen	Pension	3	1	Rep. of Secretary War.	131	Select	May 26, 1794	Favorable	J. R. 12	Passed	Passed	App'd June 9, 1794
Gilbert, Allen	Pension	4	1	Rep. of Secretary War.	445	Claims.						
Gilbert, Allen	Pension	4	2	Rep. of Secretary War.	614	Claims.						
Gilbert, Allen	Arrears of pension	3	2	Petition	289	Whole House.						
Gilbert, Angelica	(See Joseph Olney, heir of)	24	2	....	271							
Gilbert & Aspinwall	Indemnity for French spoliations prior to 1800.	26	1	Memorial	182	Foreign Affairs	343	Favorable; bill	319	Referred to Committee Whole House.		
Gilbert, Benjamin	Pension	19	1	Petition	203	Military Pensions	April 1, 1826	Adverse.				
Gilbert, Burr	Pension	2	1	Petition	467	....	....	....	......	Referred to Secretary of War.		
Gilbert, Burr	Pension	2	2	Rep. of Secretary War.	649	Whole House.						
Gilbert, Burr	Pension	3	1	Rep. of Secretary War.	131	Select	May 26, 1794	Favorable	J. R. 12	Passed	Passed	App'd June 9, 1794
Gilbert, Burr	Pension	4	1	Rep. of Secretary War.	445	Claims	Feb. 18, 1796	Favorable	156	Passed	Passed	App'd April 20, 1796
Gilbert, Burr	Increase of pension	10	2	House bill	499	Whole House	Feb. 20, 1809	Favorable	158	Passed	Passed	App'd March 3, 1809
Gilbert, Burr, widow of	Pension for services of former husband.	26	1	Petition	281	Rev. Pensions.						

List of private claims presented to the House of Representatives of the United States from the 1*st to the* 31*st Congress, inclusive*—Continued.

Names of claimants.	Nature or object of the claim.	Congress.	Session.	How brought before the House of Reps.	Page of journal.	To what committee of the House referred.	No. or date of the report.	Nature of the report.	No. of the bill.	How disposed of by the House of Reps.	How disposed of by the Senate.	Date of the act of Congress, and remarks.
Gilbert, Burr, widow of	Pension for services of former husband.	27	2	Petition	59	Rev. Pensions	98	Favorable	144	Passed	Passed	App'd July 9, 1842
Gilbert, Ebenezer	Pension	2	2	Rep of Secretary War.	649	Whole House.						
Gilbert, Ebenezer	Pension	3	1	Rep. of Secretary War.	131	Select	Mar. 26, 1794	Favorable	J. R. 12	Passed	Passed	App'd June 9, 1794
Gilbert, Ebenezer	Pension	4	1	Rep. of Secretary War.	445	Claims.						
Gilbert, Ebenezer	Pension	4	2	Rep. of Secretary War.	614	Claims.						
Gilbert, Ebenezer	Compensation as surgeon in navy	15	1	Petition	309	Pens. & Rev. Cl'ms.						
Gilbert, Ebenezer	Compensation as surgeon in navy	15	2	Petition	84	Pens. & Rev. Cl'ms.	Dec. 11, 1818	Adverse		Rejected.		
Gilbert, Ebenezer	Compensation as surgeon in navy	20	2	Petition	26	Rev. Claims	Jan. 29, 1829	Adverse		Laid on table.		
Gilbert, Ebenezer	Compensation as surgeon in navy	21	2	Petition	64	Rev. Claims	Jan. 13, 1831	Adverse		Laid on table.		
Gilbert, Ebenezer	Compensation as surgeon in navy	22	1	Petition	72	Rev. Claims	Jan. 18, 1832	Adverse		Laid on table.		
Gilbert, Capt. Ephraim F.	Pension	22	2	Resolution	216	Invalid Pensions.						
Gilbert, Capt. Ephraim F.	Pension	23	1	Petition	44	Invalid Pensions	444	Favorable	462	Referred to Committee Whole House.		
Gilbert, Capt. Ephraim F.	Pension	23	2	House bill	336	Whole House	Feb. 13, 1835	Favorable	462	Passed	Passed, with amendment.	
Gilbert, Capt. Ephraim F.	Pension	24	1	Res. and docs	202	Invalid Pensions	253	Favorable	359	Passed	Passed	App'd June 28, 1836
Gilbert, Ephraim F.	Indemnity for losses on cont act	16	1	Petition	225	Claims	April 7, 1820	Adverse		Laid on table.		
Gilbert, Ephraim F.	Indemnity for losses on contract	17	1	Petition	145	Claims	Feb. 15, 1822	Adverse		Laid on table.		
Gilbert, Ephraim F.	Indemnity for losses on contract	18	1	Petition	176	Claims	Mar. 3, 1824	Adverse		Laid on table.		
Gilbert, Ephraim F.	Indemnity for losses on contract	19	1	Petition	442	Claims				Discharged; laid on table.		
Gilbert, Ephraim F.	Indemnity for losses on contract	21	1	Petition	128	Claims	226	Favorable	282	Passed	Passed	App'd May 29, 1830
Gilbert, Ephraim F.	Relief in settling accounts under act of last session.	22	1	Memorial	62	Claims	June 18, 1832	Adverse		Laid on table.		
Gilbert, Ephraim F.	Relief in settling accounts under act of last session.	25	2	Petition	51	Claims.						
Gilbert, Ephraim F.	Relief in settling accounts under act of last session.	26	1	Petition	169	Claims	715	Adverse		Laid on table.		
Gilbert, Ephraim F.	Relief in settling accounts under act of last session.	26	2	Petition	38	Claims	Feb. 4, 1841	Adverse		Laid on table		Leave to withdraw.
Gilbert, Ephraim F.	Relief in settling accounts under act of last session.	27	2	Petition	410	Claims	April 1, 1842	Adverse		Laid on table.		
Gilbert, Ephraim F.	Relief in settling accounts under act of last session.	27	3	Petition	175	Claims	204	Adverse.		Laid on table.		
Gilbert, Ephraim F.	Relief in settling accounts under act of last session.	29	1	Petition	106	Judiciary	19	Adverse.		Laid on table.		
Gilbert, Ephraim F.	Relief in settling accounts under act of last session.	30	1	Petition	102	Claims.						
Gilbert, Ephraim F.	Relief in settling accounts under act of last session.	30	2	Petition	112	Claims				Leave to withdraw.		
Gilbert, George, executors of.	Indemnity for French spoliations prior to 1800.	29	1	Memorial	87	Foreign Affairs.						
Gilbert, George and Jacob.	Indemnity for losses on contract	3	1	Petition	136					Referred to Secretary Treasury.		
Gilbert, George and Jacob.	Indemnity for losses on contract	6	1	Petition and rep. Sec. Treasury.	608					Laid on table.		
Gilbert, George and Jacob, sureties of.	Reimbursement of money paid	7	1	Rep't Committee	29					Rejected.		

List of private claims presented to the House of Representatives of the United States from the 1st to the 31st Congress, inclusive—Continued.

Names of claimants.	Nature or object of the claim.	Congress.	Session.	How brought before the House of Reps.	Page of journal.	To what committee of the House referred.	No. or date of the report.	Nature of the report.	No. of the bill.	How disposed of by the House of Reps.	How disposed of by the Senate.	Date of the act of Congress, and remarks.
Gilbert, Jacob B.	Indemnity for property lost and destroyed in late war.	15	1	Report of Com. Claims.	393	Claims.						
Gilbert, Jacob B.	Indemnity for a house destroyed by the enemy.	22	1	Petition	84	Claims.						
Gilbert, Jacob B.	Indemnity for a house destroyed by the enemy.	22	2	Petition	124	Claims.						
Gilbert, Jacob B.	Indemnity for a house destroyed by the enemy.	23	1	Petition	154	Claims.						
Gibert, Jacob B.	Indemnity for a house destroyed by the enemy.	23	2	Petition	119	Claims	123	Favorable	763			
Gilbert, Jacob B.	Indemnity for a house destroyed by the enemy.	24	1	Petition	51	Claims	35	Favorable	35	Passed	Passed	App'd Feb. 17, 1836
Gilbert, John	Pension	11	2	House bill	283	Whole House	Mar. 24, 1810	Favorable	107	Passed	Passed	App'd April 27, 1810
Gilbert, John (Pa.)	Pension	13	2	Petition	322	Pens. & Rev. Cl'ms.	April 4, 1814	General bill	166	Passed	Passed	App'd April 18, 1814
Gilbert, John, (Pa.)	Compensation for services and disabilities in late war.	23	2	Petition	436	Invalid Pensions.						
Gilbert, John, (Pa.)	Compensation for services and disabilities in late war.	25	2	Petition	920	Invalid Pensions	.....	.....	.....	Discharged; laid on table.		
Gilbert, John, (Pa.)	Increase of pension	30	1	Petition	82	Invalid Pensions	460	Adverse	.....	Laid on table.		
Gilbert, John, widow of	Indemnity for property destroyed by the enemy.	21	1	Petition	56	Claims	Dec. 28, 1829	Adverse	.....	Laid on table.		
Gilbert, Joseph	Arrears of pension	23	1	Petition	493	Rev. Pensions	453	Favorable	472	Ref'd to Com. W. H.		
Glibert, Joseph	Arrears of pension	23	2	House bill	337	Whole House	Feb. 6, 1835	Favorable	472	Passed	Passed	App'd March 3, 1835
Gilbert, Lewis	Pension	21	1	Resolution	243	Military Pensions	Feb. 15, 1830	General bill	248	Passed	Indef. postp'd.	
Gilbert, Lewis	Pension	21	2	Petition	68	Military Pensions.						
Gilbert, Lewis	Pension	22	1	Resolution	71	Rev. Pensions	28	Favorable	72	Passed	Indef. postp'd.	
Gilbert, Marinus W.	Indemnity for goods, &c., destroyed by British.	16	1	Petition	158	Claims	.....	.....	.....	Discharged; laid on table.		
Gilbert, Marinus W.	Indemnity for goods, &c., destroyed by British.	16	2	Petition	50	Claims	Jan. 8, 1821	Adverse	.....	Laid on table.		
Gilbert, Marinus W.	Indemnity for goods, &c., destroyed by British.	17	1	Petition	52	Claims	38	Adverse	.....	Referred to Committee Whole House.		
Gilbert, Marinus W.	Indemnity for goods, &c., destroyed by British.	18	1	Petition	32	Claims.						
Gilbert, Marinus W.	Indemnity for goods, &c., destroyed by British.	18	2	Petition	32	Claims	Jan. 21, 1825	Adverse	.....	Laid on table.		
Gilbert, Marinus W.	Indemnity for goods, &c., destroyed by British.	19	1	Petition	312	Claims	.....	.....	.....	Discharged; laid on table.		
Gilbert, Marinus W.	Indemnity for goods, &c., destroyed by British.	19	2	Petition	37	Claims	38	Favorable	353			
Gilbert, Marinus W.	Indemnity for goods, &c., destroyed by British.	20	1	Petition	52	Claims	28	Favorable	20	Passed	Passed	App'd May 23, 1828
Gilbert, Marinus W.	Interest on money advanced to pay United States troops.	23	1	Petition	217	Claims	339	Favorable	366			
Gilbert, Marinus W.	Interest on money advanced to pay United States troops.	24	1	Petition	50	Claims	7	Favorable	7	Passed	Passed	App'd Feb. 17, 1836
Gilbert, Marinus W.	For additional bounty on prisoners	24	2	Petition	72	Claims	31	Adverse	.....	Laid on table.		
Gilbert, Marinus W.	(See Thomas Gilbert, surety of.)	23	1	.....	191							
Gilbert, Nathan, administrator of.	For land warrant.	23	1	Petition	156	Priv. Land Claims.						
Gilbert, Samuel	Indemnity for Indian depredations.	19	2	Senate bill	352	Claims	March 3, 1827	Adverse	63	Laid on table.		
Gilbert, Samuel	To be allowed bounty on a fishing vessel.	21	2	Petition	206	Commerce.						

List of private claims presented to the House of Representatives of the United States from the 1st to the 31st Congress, inclusive—Continued.

Names of claimants.	Nature or object of the claim.	Congress.	Session.	How brought before the House of Reps.	Page of journal.	To what committee of the House referred.	No. or date of the report.	Nature of the report.	No. of the bill.	How disposed of by the House of Reps.	How disposed of by the Senate.	Date of the act of Congress, and remarks.
Gilbert, Samuel	To be allowed bounty on a fishing vessel.	24	1	Petition	200	Commerce	Jan. 28, 1836	Favorable	248	Passed.		
Gilbert, Samuel, administrator of.	For one year's pay as revolutionary officer.	4	1	Memorial	451	Claims	May 31, 1796	Adverse		Laid on table.		
Gilbert, Shadrack, *et al.*	Reimbursement of duties paid on fish taken in Lake Erie.	22	1	Petition	225	Judiciary				Discharged: laid on table.		
Gilbert, Thaddeus	Pension	17	1	Petition	299	Rev. Pensions				Discharged; laid on table.		
Gilbert, Thaddeus	Pension	18	1	Petition	285	Rev. Pensions				Discharged; laid on table.		
Gilbert, Thomas	Pension	18	2	Petition	95	Pens. & Rev. Cl'ms.						
Gilbert, Thomas	Pension	19	1	Petition	442	Military Pensions				Discharged; leave to withdraw.		
Gilbert, Thomas	Pension	19	2	Petition	187	Military Pensions	Feb. 14, 1827	General bill	437	Referred to Committee Whole House.		
Gilbert, Thomas	Pension	20	1	Petition	243	Military Pensions	Mar. 19, 1828	General bill	283	Passed.		
Gilbert, Thomas	Pension	20	2	House bill	55	Whole House	Aug. 12, 1828	Favorable	311	Passed	Laid on table.	
Gilbert, Thomas	Pension	21	1	Petition	48	Military Pensions	Jan. 5, 1830	General bill	72	Passed	Passed	App'd May 20, 1830
Gilbert, Thomas	Arrears of pension	22	1	Petition	142	Invalid Pensions				Discharged; laid on table.		
Gilbert, Thomas	Arrears of pension	22	2	Petition	216	Invalid Pensions.						
Gilbert, Thomas	Arrears of pension	23	1	Petition	44	Invalid Pensions				Discharged; laid on table.		
Gilbert, Thomas	Arrears of pension	23	2	Petition	101	Invalid Pensions	Jan. 5, 1835	Adverse		Laid on table.		
Gilbert, Thomas, surety of.	Payment of sums due from officers and soldiers.	23	1	Petition	191	Claims	350	Favorable	378			
Gilbert, Thomas, surety of.	Payment of sums due from officers and soldiers.	24	1	Petition	50	Claims	9	Favorable	9	Passed	Passed	App'd Feb. 17, 1836
Gilchrist, Adam	(See Robert Hazlehurst, assignee of.)	12	1		180							
Gilchrist, Edward	(See Exploring Expedition)	27	3		149							
Gilchrist, William, *et al.*	Confirmation of title to land	14	1	Petition	422	Public Lands				Discharged; laid on table.		
Gilchrist, William, *et al.*	Confirmation of title to land	14	2	Petition	124	Public Lands.						
Gilchrist, William, *et al.*	Confirmation of title to land	15	1	Petition	173	Priv. Land Claims.						
Gilden, Guilford P	Indemnity for property destroyed by United States troops.	25	2	Petition	541	Claims.						
Gilden, Guilford P	Indemnity for property destroyed by United States troops.	26	1	Petition	169	Claims.						
Gilder, Daniel	Compensation for revolutionary services.	9	2	Petition	501	Claims	Jan. 6, 1807	Adverse		Leave to withdraw.		
Gilder, John, *et al.*	For a grant of land in Florida	17	1	Petition	155	Public Lands	Feb. 20, 1822	Adverse		Leave to withdraw.		
Gilder, John, *et al.*	For a grant of land in Florida	17	2	Petition	78	Public Lands				Discharged; laid on table.		
Gildersleeve, Asa	Pension	21	1	Petition	46	Military Pensions	April 3, 1830	Adverse.				
Gile, Samuel	(See Samuel Gill)	24	1		127							
Giles, Aquilla	Settlement of claim against United States.	1	2	Petition	267					Referred to Secretary of Treasury.		
Giles, Aquilla	Settlement of claim against United States.	2	2	Rep. of Secretary Treasury.	626					Laid on table.		
Giles, Aquilla	Settlement of claim against United States.	3	2	Rep. of Secretary Treasury.	284					Laid on table.		

List of private claims presented to the House of Representatives of the United States from the 1st to the 31st Congress, inclusive—Continued.

Names of claimants.	Nature or object of the claim.	Congress.	Session.	How brought before the House of Reps.	Page of journal.	To what committee of the House referred.	No. or date of the report.	Nature of the report.	No. of the bill.	How disposed of by the House of Reps.	How disposed of by the Senate.	Date of the act of Congress, and remarks.
Giles, Aquilla	Settlement of claim against United States.	5	2	Petition & report Sec. Treasury.	208	Claims	Jan. 13, 1798	Adverse	......	Postponed.		
Giles, Aquilla	Payment of warrant for pay as major.	15	1	Senate bill	439	Whole House	....	....	67			
Giles, Aquilla	Payment of warrant for pay as major.	15	2	Senate bill	130	Pens. & Rev. Clm's.	Jan. 12, 1819	Favorable	17	Passed	....	App'd March 3, 1819
Giles, Benjamin, *et al*	(See Henry Thorndike, administrator of.)	12	1	....	263							
Giles, Samuel	Pension	21	2	Resolution	108	Military Pensions.						
Gilham, Ann	Confirmation of title to land	13	3	Rep't Committee	686	Whole House	Jan. 25, 1815	General bill	272	Passed	Passed	App'd Feb. 27, 1815
Gilham, James	Indemnity for expense of redeeming his family from Indian captivity.	9	1	Petition	262	Claims	Feb. 11, 1806	Adverse	......	Rejected.		
Gilkey, Charles	(See Elijah Browning, *et al*.	13	3	....	455							
Gill, Harrison	Compensation for services as Indian sub agent.	31	2	Senate bill	207	Indian Affairs	Jan. 29, 1851	Favorable	171	Passed	....	App'd March 3, 1851
Gill, Moses	Payment of loan office certificates.	4	1	Rep. of Secretary Treasury.	388	Claims	Mar. 31, 1796	Adverse.				
Gill, Moses	Payment of loan office certificates.	5	2	Petition	179	Whole House.						
Gill, Moses	Payment of loan office certificates.	6	1	Petition	590	Claims	Feb. 20, 1801	Adverse	......	Rejected.		
Gill, Robert	Pension	29	1	Petition	168	Rev. Pensions	....	....	......	....	....	2d session, 31st Congress, referred to department.
Gill, R. W.	(See J Biays, trustee of)	31	1	....	1076							
Gill, Samuel	Pension	24	1	Petition	127	Claims	123	Adverse	......	Laid on table.		
Gill, Samuel, heirs of	Compensation for revolutionary services.	28	2	Petition	57	Rev. Claims	....	....	......	Discharged; laid on table.		
Gill, Samuel, heirs of	Payment of one year's full pay	29	1	Petition	266	Rev. Pensions	....	....	......	Discharged; laid on table.		
Gill, Whitford	Indemnity for boat captured by British.	21	1	Petition	499	Claims	364	Favorable	422			
Gill, Whitford	Indemnity for boat captured by British.	22	1	Petition	25	Claims	Dec. 19, 1831	Favorable	20	Passed.		
Gill, Whitford	Indemnity for boat captured by British.	22	2	Petition	29	Claims	4	Favorable	620			
Gill, Whitford	Indemnity for boat captured by British.	23	1	Petition	34	Claims	14	Favorable	14	Passed	Passed	App'd May 1, 1834
Gill, Whitford, *et al*	Indemnity for two boats captured by British.	16	1	Petition	162	Claims	Jan. 28, 1820	Adverse	......	Laid on table.		
Gillard, Joseph	Confirmation of title to land	14	2	Petition	163	Public Lands	74	Favorable	117			
Gillard, Joseph	Confirmation of title to land	15	1	Petition	76	Priv. Land Claims	....	....	......	Discharged; laid on table.		
Gillchrist, Peter, and wife	Confirmation of title to land	15	1	Petition	212	Priv. Land Claims.						
Gillchrist, Samuel	Pension	15	1	Petition	167	Pens. & Rev. Cl'ms	....	....	......	Discharged; laid on table.		
Giller, George	Pension	20	1	Petition	30	Military Pensions	Feb. 13, 1827	General bill	166	Passed.		
Giller, George	Pension	20	2	Petition	55	Military Pensions	Dec. 12, 1828	General bill	311	Passed	Laid on table.	
Giller, George	Pension	21	1	Petition	48	Military Pensions	Jan. 5, 1830	General bill	72	Passed	Passed	App'd May 20, 1830
Gilleylen, John	Reimbursement of money paid for land not subject to entry.	28	1	Petition	903	Public Lands.						
Gilleylen, John	Reimbursement of money paid for land not subject to entry.	28	2	Petition	228	Public Lands.						
Gilleylen, John	Reimbursement of money paid for land not subject to entry.	29	1	Petition	303	Public Lands	....	....	......	Discharged; laid on table.		

List of private claims presented to the House of Representatives of the United States from the 1st to the 31st Congress, inclusive—Continued.

Names of claimants.	Nature or object of the claim.	Congress.	Session.	How brought before the House of Reps.	Page of journal.	To what committee of the House referred.
Gillespie, David H.	Bounty land	30	1	Petition	263	Public Lands.
Gillespie, James, (N. C.)	Compensation for carrying United States mail.	7	2	Memorial	337	Claims
Gillespie, James, (N. C.)	Compensation for carrying United States mail.	8	1	Memorial	444	Claims
Gillespie, James, *et al.*	To be released as sureties of John Smith Punch.	24	1	Petition	672	Judiciary
Gillespie, John F	To be allowed to enter certain tract of land.	29	1	Petition	498	Priv. Land Claims.
Gillespie, Menzies	To locate land in Illinois	25	2	Petition	631	Public Lands.
Gillespie, Menzies	For reissue of land warrant	25	3	Petition	93	Public Lands
Gillespie, Peake, Vernon *et al.*	Compensation for military services in 1836.	30	1	Resolution	448	Military Affairs.
Gillespie, Robert, *et al.*	To be released from paying duties on wine destroyed by fire.	18	1	Petition	286	Ways and Means
Gillespie, William	Payment for a horse lost in United States service.	19	1	Resolution	544	Claims
Gillespie, William	Pension	21	2	Resolution	147	Military Pensions
Gillet, Elijah	Pension	21	1	Petition	399	Military Pensions
Gillet, Elijah	Pension	21	2	Petition	63	Military Pensions.
Gillet, Elijah	Pension	22	1	Petition	35	Military Pensions
Gillet, Joel	Pension	2	2	Rep. of Secretary War.	649	Whole House.
Gillet, Joel	Pension	3	1	Rep. of Secretary War.	131	Select
Gillet, Joel	Pension	4	1	Rep. of Secretary War.	445	Claims.
Gillet, Joel	Pension	4	2	Rep. of Secretary War.	614	Claims.
Gillet, John	To be allowed to locate land warrant.	27	2	Petition	530	Public Lands.
Gillet, Joseph	Pension	14	1	Petition	41	Pens. & Rev. Cl'ms.
Gillet, Othniel	Arrears of pension	19	1	Petition	381	Military Pensions
Gillet, Othniel	Arrears of pension	28	1	Petition	144	Rev. Pensions.
Gillet, Shadrach, *et al.*	Pre-emption right to land	29	2	Senate bill	306	Priv. Land Claims.
Gillet, Shadrach, *et al.*	Pre-emption right to land	30	1	House bill	320	Public Lands
Gillet, Shadrach, *et al.*	Pre-emption right to land	30	1	Senate bill	1174	Priv. Land Claims.
Gillet, Shadrach, *et al.*	Pre-emption right to land	30	2	Senate bill	112	Priv. Land Claims.
Gillet, Solomon, *et al.*	(See Rufus Spalding, *et al.*)	15	2		148	
Gillham, Isaac and David	Pre-emption right to land	15	1	Petition	386	Public Lands.
Gilliam, William, representative of.	Pay for bounty land	22	2	Resolution	124	Rev. Claims
Gillilan, William	Pension	26	1	Petition	624	Rev. Pensions
Gillis, Alexander	Pension	24	1	Resolution	541	Rev. Pensions
Gillis, Alexander	Pension	25	2	Petition	38	Rev. Pensions
Gillis, Alexander	Pension	25	3	Petition	88	Rev. Pensions

Names of claimants.	No. or date of the report.	Nature of the report.	No. of the bill.	How disposed of by the House of Reps.	How disposed of by the Senate.	Date of the act of Congress, and remarks.
Gillespie, David H.						
Gillespie, James, (N. C.)	Feb. 26, 1803	Adverse		Postponed.		
Gillespie, James, (N. C.)	Feb. 9, 1804	Adverse		Leave to withdraw.		
Gillespie, James, *et al.*				Laid on table.		
Gillespie, John F						
Gillespie, Menzies						
Gillespie, Menzies	220	Favorable	1075	Passed	Passed	App'd March 3, 1839
Gillespie, Peake, Vernon *et al.*						
Gillespie, Robert, *et al.*				Discharged; laid on table.		
Gillespie, William				Discharged; laid on table.		
Gillespie, William				Discharged; laid on table.		
Gillet, Elijah				Discharged; laid on table.		
Gillet, Elijah						
Gillet, Elijah				Discharged; laid on table.		
Gillet, Joel						
Gillet, Joel	May 26, 1794	Favorable	J.R. 12	Passed	Passed	App'd June 9, 1794
Gillet, Joel						
Gillet, Joel						
Gillet, John						
Gillet, Joseph	April 11, 1816	General bill	171	Passed	Passed	App'd April 30, 1816
Gillet, Othniel	April 1, 1826	Adverse		Laid on table.		
Gillet, Othniel						
Gillet, Shadrach, *et al.*			11			
Gillet, Shadrach, *et al.*	496	Favorable	140, 408			
Gillet, Shadrach, *et al.*			344			
Gillet, Shadrach, *et al.*	64	Favorable	344	Laid on table.		
Gillet, Solomon, *et al.*						
Gillham, Isaac and David						
Gilliam, William, representative of.	Jan. 10, 1833	Adverse		Laid on table.		
Gillilan, William	714	Adverse		Laid on table.		
Gillis, Alexander	803	Favorable	719	Referred to Committee Whole House.		
Gillis, Alexander	175	Favorable	200	Passed	Rejected.	
Gillis, Alexander	249	Favorable	1120	Referred to Committee Whole House.		Leave to withdraw papers, 2d sess. 31st Cong.

List of private claims presented to the House of Representatives of the United States from the 1st to the 31st Congress, inclusive—Continued.

91

Names of claimants.	Nature or object of the claim.	Congress.	Session.	How brought before the House of Reps.	Page of journal.	To what committee of the House referred.	No. or date of the report.	Nature of the report.	No. of the bill.	How disposed of by the House of Reps.	How disposed of by the Senate.	Date of the act of Congress, and remarks.
Gillis, Alexander	Pension	26	1	Petition	172	Rev. Pensions.						
Gillis, J. Melville	Compensation for duties connected with Exploring Expedition.	28	1	Petition	319	Claims.						
Gillis, J. Melville	Compensation for duties connected with Exploring Expedition.	29	2	Petition	56	Naval Affairs	64	Favorable	J. R. 56			
Gillis, J. Melville	Compensation for duties connected with Exploring Expedition.	30	1	Joint resolution	223	Naval Affairs	86	Favorable	J. R. 6	Passed.		
Gillis, J. Melville	Compensation for duties connected with Exploring Expedition.	30	2	Joint resolution	466	Whole House			J. R. 6	Passed	Passed	App'd Feb. 26, 1849
Gillis, William, *et al.*	Pre-emption right in the purchase of land.	25	2	Petition	192	Public Lands.						
Gillis, William, *et al.*	Pre-emption right in the purchase of land.	25	3	Petition	98	Public Lands.						
Gillispy, Alexander, heir of	To be allowed to locate bounty land.	6	2	Petition	756	Claims	Jan. 19, 1801	Adverse		Leave to withdraw.		
Gillock, John, guardian of son of.	Compensation for revolutionary services.	4	1	Petition	385	Claims	Jan. 26, 1796	Adverse		Leave to withdraw.		
Gillock, John, guardian of son of.	Compensation for revolutionary services.	8	1	Petition	453	Claims				Discharged; referred to Com. Whole House.		
Gillon, William	Pension	16	2	Petition	155	Naval Affairs				Discharged; referred to Secretary Navy.		
Gillon, (or Gillin,) Wm.	Pension	20	2	Petition	144	Naval Affairs	Jan. 16, 1829	Adverse		Laid on table.		
Gillpatrick, Joshua, or Joseph.	Compensation for revolutionary services.	15	2	Petition	88	Pens. & Rev. Cl'ms.	Dec. 16, 1818	Adverse		Rejected.		
Gilman, Charles	Pension	16	1	Petition	237	Rev. Pensions	April 22, 1820	Adverse		Laid on table.		
Gillman, Charles	Pension	22	1	Petition	767	Rev. Pensions				Discharged; laid on table.		
Gilman, Ephraim	Indemnity for goods destroyed by British.	23	2	Petition	163	Claims.						
Gilman, Ephraim, *et al.*	Indemnity for goods destroyed by British.	16	1	Petition	194	Claims	Feb. 20, 1820	Adverse		Laid on table		Leave to withdraw, 1st session, 18th Cong.
Gilman, John Taylor	Compensation for endorsing new emission bills of New Hampshire, under act of March 18, 1780.	4	1	Rep. of Secretary of Treasury.	388	Claims	May 31, 1796	Favorable		Laid on table.		
Gilman, Joseph	Compensation for revolutionary services.	17	1	Petition	511	Pens. & Rev. Cl'ms.				Discharged, laid on table.		
Gilman, Joseph	Compensation for revolutionary services.	17	2	Petition	287					Leave to withdraw.		
Gilman, Joseph H	Pension	28	1	Petition	428	Invalid Pensions				Discharged; laid on table.		
Gilman, Joseph H	Pension	29	1	Petition	425	Invalid Pensions.						
Gilman, Joshua	Pension	2	2	Rep. of Secretary of War.	649	Whole House.						
Gilman, Joshua	Pension	3	1	Report Secretary of War.	131	Select	May 26, 1794	Res. to refer to Sec. War.	J. R. 12	Passed	Passed	App'd June 9, 1794
Gilman, Joshua	Pension	3	2	Rep. of Secretary of War.	262	Claims	Feb. 28, 1795	Favorable	130	Passed.	Postponed.	
Gilman, Joshua	Pension	4	1	Rep. of Secretary of War.	445	Claims	Feb. 18, 1796	Favorable	156	Passed	Passed	App'd April 20, 1796
Gilman, Mehitable	Pension	28	1	Petition	839	Whole House.						
Gilman, Nicholas	Indemnity for French spoliations prior to 1800.	26	1	Memorial	182	Foreign Affairs	343	Favorable; bill	319	Referred to Committee Whole House.		

List of private claims presented to the House of Representatives of the United States from the 1st to the 31st Congress, inclusive—Continued.

Names of claimants.	Nature or object of the claim.	Congress.	Session.	How brought before the House of Reps.	Page of journal.	To what committee of the House referred.	No. or date of the report.	Nature of the report.	No. of the bill.	How disposed of by the House of Reps.	How disposed of by the Senate.	Date of the act of Congress, and remarks.
Gilman, Peter	Pension	22	1	Petition	412	Rev. Pensions	410	Favorable	510			
Gilman, (or Gilmore,) Samuel.	Pension	3	2	Rep't Committee	352	Claims	Feb. 28, 1795	Favorable	130	Passed	Postponed.	
Gilman, (or Gilmore,) Samuel.	Pension	4	1	Rep. of Secretary of War.	445	Claims	Mar. 14, 1796	General bill	156	Passed	Passed	App'd April 20, 1796
Gilman, Samuel	Compensation for revolutionary services.	25	2	Petition	270	Rev. Claims				Discharged; laid on table.		
Gilman, Samuel	Compensation for revolutionary services.	25	3	Petition	221	Rev. Claims.						
Gilman, Samuel	Compensation for revolutionary services.	26	1	Petition	166	Claims.						
Gilman, Samuel, (N. Y.)	Pension	29	1	Petition	399	Invalid Pensions.						
Gilman, Samuel, (N. Y.)	Pension	31	1	Petition	269	Rev. Pensions	363	Adverse		Laid on table.		
Gilman, Samuel, *et al.*	Pension	27	2	Petition	244	Select	361	General bill	295			
Gilmer, Mary	(See Adam Shapley, representatives of.)	25	3		220							
Gilmer, R. H.	(See Thomas Malone, *et al.*)	14	2		379							
Gilmer, Robert, and son	Indemnity for French spoliations prior to 1800.	26	1	Memorial	182	Foreign Affairs	343	Favorable; bill	319	Referred to Committee Whole House.		
Gilmore, David	Pension	24	2	Senate bill	579				214			
Gilmore, David	Pension	25	2	Senate bill	785	Rev. Pensions	April 20, 1838	Favorable	79	Passed		App'd May 31, 1838
Gilmore, David	Indemnity for costs of suits against him by hands employed to collect the remains of frigate John Adams.	18	2	Petition	116	Naval Affairs	43	Favorable	303	Passed	Passed	App'd March 3, 1825
Gilmore, John	Reimbursement of money advanced for public lands.	18	2	Petition	254	Public Lands.						
Gilmore, John	Reimbursement of money advanced for public lands.	19	1	Petition	337	Public Lands				Discharged; laid on table.		
Gilmore, John	Reimbursement of money advanced for public lands.	19	2	Petition	38	Public Lands				Discharged; laid on table.		
Gilmore, Joseph	Pension	12	1	House bill	361	Whole House	June 15, 1812	Favorable	138	Passed	Passed	App'd July 5, 1812
Gilmore, Robert, surety of.	Release from liability	15	1	Petition	48	Claims	Jan. 2, 1818	Favorable	25	Passed	Passed	App'd April 3, 1818
Gilmore, Robert, executors of.	Indemnity for French spoliations prior to 1800.	29	2	Memorial	70	Foreign Affairs.						
Gilmore, Robert, *et al.*	Indemnity for the ship Aurora and cargo, captured by the French.	24	2	Petition	75	Foreign Affairs	299	Adverse		Laid on table.		
Gilmore, Thomas, widow of.	Pension	27	2	Petition	1001	Rev. Pensions				Discharged; laid on table.		
Gilpatrick, Richard	Indemnity for French spoliations prior to 1800.	26	1	Memorial	182	Foreign Affairs	343	Favorable; bill	319	Referred to Committee Whole House.		
Gilpin, Joshua	Indemnity for French spoliations prior to 1800.	26	1	Memorial	182	Foreign Affairs	343	Favorable; bill	319	Referred to Committee Whole House.		
Gilpin, George, *et al.*	Increase of compensation as judge of orphans' court.	8	1	Petition	520	Select.						
Gilpin, Dr. John	Payment of loan office certificate	29	1	Res. and docs	404	Rev. Claims.						
Gilson, David	To be exonerated from duties on spirits destroyed by fire.	5	3	Petition	491	Com. and Manuf.	Mar. 2, 1799	Adverse		Postponed.		
Gilson, Jacob	Compensation for revolutionary services.	4	1	Petition	425	Claims	May 7, 1796	Adverse		Rejected.		
Gilson & Jones	(See Stephen Van Scyoe)	13	1		36							
Gilson, Thomas D.	Compensation as marshal for enforcing neutrality law.	27	2	Petition	246	Claims	327	Favorable	298	Passed.		

List of private claims presented to the House of Representatives of the United States from the 1st to the 31st Congress, inclusive—Continued.

Names of claimants.	Nature or object of the claim.	Congress.	Session.	How brought before the House of Reps.	Page of journal.	To what committee of the House referred.	No. or date of the report.	Nature of the report.	No. of the bill.	How disposed of by the House of Reps.	How disposed of by the Senate.	Date of the act of Congress, and remarks.
Gilson, Thomas D.	Compensation as marshal for enforcing neutrality law.	27	3	Petition	43	Claims	4	Favorable	622	Passed	Passed	App'd March 1, 1843
Gimblet, Michael, assignee of.	Confirmation of title to land	22	1	House bill	421	Whole House	Feb. 28, 1832	With't amend.	425	Passed	Passed	App'd June 25, 1832
Gimot, Lieutenant Colonel, heirs of.	To be allowed to locate land warrant.	19	2	Petition	202	Public Lands.						
Gimot, Lieutenant Colonel, heirs of.	(See Louis Fleury, *et al.*)	20	1		75							
Ginnaty, Thomas	For right to hold and transmit real estate.	31	1	Senate bill	1520	Whole House	Sept. 24, 1850	Favorable	358	Passed		App'd Sept. 26, 1850
Girardeau, John B.	Compensation for services of his company of dragoons.	5	2	Petition	145					Referred to Secretary of War.		
Girardeau, John B.	Compensation for services of his company of dragoons.	6	1	Petition and rep't Sec. of War.	626	Whole House.						
Girard, David, (Ia.)	For right to purchase land next to his.	21	1	Petition	107	Public Lands.				Discharged; laid on table.		
Girard, Gabriel, widow and child of.	Pension	30	1	Petition	606	Rev. Pensions				Discharged; laid on table.		
Girard, Stephen	To be released from obligation to pay 20 per cent., and exchange on bills of exchange, sold by Secretary of Treasury.	8	1	Memorial	676	Claims	Mar. 24, 1804	Adverse		Postponed.		
Girard, Stephen	To be permitted to enter a cargo of goods now at Amelia island, at some United States custom-house.	12	1	Petition	252	Whole House	April 9, 1812	General bill	46	Referred to Committee Whole House.		
Girard, Stephen	Reimbursement of duties paid on cargo of ship Montesquieu.	13	2	Petition	351	Com. and Manuf.	April 5, 1814	Adverse		Rejected.		
Girard, Stephen	For the benefit of the act laying duties on bank notes.	13	2	Petition	239	Ways and Means.	Feb. 1, 1814	Favorable	101	Passed	Postponed.	
Girard, Stephen	For the benefit of the act laying duties on bank notes.	13	3	Petition	493	Ways and Means.						
Girard, Stephen, *et al.*	Remission of forfeiture for importing certain British manufactures.	13	1	Petition and rep't Sec. Treasury.	22	Ways and Means.						
Girard, Stephen, representatives of.	Confirmation of title to land	25	2	Memorial	580					Referred to Committee Whole House, on bill No. 84.		
Girard, Stephen, representatives of.	Confirmation of title to land	27	2	Memorial	916	Priv. Land Claims.						
Girard, Stephen	Indemnity for French spoliations prior to 1800.	26	1	Memorial	182	Foreign Affairs	343	Favorable; bill	319	Referred to Committee Whole House.		
Girault, John, representatives.	Confirmation of title to land	16	2	Petition	155	Priv. Land Claims.	62	Favorable	256	Referred to Committee Whole House.		
Girault, John, representatives.	Confirmation of title to land	17	1	Petition	34	Priv. Land Claims.	Jan. 22, 1822	Favorable	54	Passed	Passed	App'd May 7, 1822
Giraud, Jacob P.	(See Foster & Giraud.)	11	1		37							
Giraud, John James	Renewal of patent	23	1	Petition	38	Judiciary				Discharged; laid on table.		
Giraud, John James	Renewal of patent	23	2	Petition	198	Judiciary.						
Giraud, Joseph, and wife	Payment for lost loan office certificate.	29	1	Petition	806	Ways and Means.						

List of private claims presented to the House of Representatives of the United States from the 1st to the 31st Congress, inclusive—**Continued.**

Names of claimants.	Nature or object of the claim.	Congress.	Session.	How brought before the House of Reps.	Page of journal.	To what committee of the House referred.	No. or date of the report.	Nature of the report.	No. of the bill.	How disposed of by the House of Reps.	How disposed of by the Senate.	Date of the act of Congress, and remarks.
Girod, Jean Francis	Payment for a boat and other articles taken for United States service.	18	1	Petition	109	Military Affairs	Feb. 20, 1824	Adverse	......	Laid on table.		
Girod, John F	Confirmation of title to land	21	1	Petition	51	Priv. Land Claims.	252	Favorable	314	Ref'd to Com. W. H.		
Girod, John F	Confirmation of title to land	21	2	House bill	340	Whole House	Feb. 22, 1831	Favorable	314	Passed.		
Girod, John F	Confirmation of title to land	22	1	Senate bill	844	Priv. Land Claims.	June 6, 1832	Favorable	132	Passed	....	App'd July 14, 1832
Girod, Nicholas	Confirmation of title to land	21	1	Petition	110	Priv. Land Claims.	Mar. 6, 1830	Adverse	......	Laid on table.		
Girod, Nicholas	Confirmation of title to land	21	1	Petition	321	Priv. Land Claims.	....	....	......	Discharged; laid on table.		
Girod, Nicholas	Confirmation of title to land	21	2	Petition	55	Priv. Land Claims.						
Girod, Nicholas	Confirmation of title to land	22	1	Petition	66	Priv. Land Claims.	Dec. 29, 1831	Adverse	......	Laid on table.		
Gist, Captain Henry	Credit at department for amount of vouchers lost.	15	1	Documents	223	Military Affairs	Feb. 10, 1818	Favorable	80	Passed	Passed with amendment.	App'd April 20, 1818
Gist, Nathaniel	Compensation for revolutionary services.	2	1	Petition	510	....	....	....	......	Referred to Secretary War.		
Gist, Nathaniel	Compensation for revolutionary services.	3	2	Petition & letter Sec. War.	278	....	....	....	......	Laid on table.		
Gist, Nathaniel	Compensation for revolutionary services.	4	1	Rep. of Secretary War.	445	Claims.						
Gist, Nathaniel	Compensation for revolutionary services.	4	2	Rep. of Secretary War.	614	Claims.						
Gist, Spencer C., United States Navy.	To be paid difference between pay of midshipman and lieutenant, and sailing-master and lieutenant.	23	1	Petition	440	Naval Affairs	....	....	......	Discharged; leave to withdraw.		
Gist, Spencer C., United States Navy.	To be paid difference between pay of midshipman and lieutenant, and sailing-master and lieutenant.	24	1	Petition	440	Naval Affairs	360	Favorable	366	Referred to Committee Whole House.		
Gist, Spencer C., United States Navy.	To be paid difference between pay of midshipman and lieutenant, and sailing-master and lieutenant.	25	2	Petition	41	Naval Affairs	150	Favorable	172	Referred to Committee Whole House.		
Gist, Spencer C., United States Navy.	To be paid difference between pay of midshipman and lieutenant, and sailing-master and lieutenant.	25	3	House bill	375	Whole House	Jan. 25, 1839	Favorable	172	Passed	Passed	App'd Mar. 3, 1839
Gitt, William W	Extension of act of 1815, for the benefit of sufferers by earthquake at New Madrid.	30	1	Petition	336	Public Lands	173	Adverse	......	Laid on table.		
Gitts, Michael	Addititional compensation for service in Treasury Department at Philadelphia, 1793.	4	2	Petition	486	Claims.						
Gitzelman, J., heir of	Bounty land	29	1	Petition	1189	Rev. Pensions.						
Gladding, Nathaniel, *et al.*	Indemnity for French spoliations prior to 1800.	23	1	Memorial	37	Foreign Affairs.						
Gladding, Nathaniel	Indemnity for French spoliations prior to 1800.	26	1	Memorial	182	Foreign Affairs	343	Favorable; bill	319	Referred to Committee Whole House.		
Gladding, Samuel	Drawback of duties on sugar	28	1	Petition	100	Commerce.						
Gladding, Samuel	Drawback of duties on sugar	28	2	Petition	45	Commerce.						
Gladding, Samuel	Drawback of duties on sugar	29	2	Petition	100	Commerce.						
Gladhill, Ely	Pension	1	2	Petition and rep't Sec. of War.	244	....	....	....	......	Laid on table.		
Gladhill, Ely	Pension	3	1	Rep. of Secretary War.	131	Select	May 26, 1794	Favorable	62	Passed	Passed	App'd June 7, 1794
Gladney, Samuel	Payment for land taken by pre-emption.	25	2	Petition	281	Priv. Land Claims.	....	....	......	Discharged; laid on table.		

List of private claims presented to the House of Representatives of the United States from the 1st to the 31st Congress, inclusive—Continued.

Names of claimants.	Nature or object of the claim.	Congress.	Session.	How brought before the House of Reps.	Page of journal.	To what committee of the House referred.	No. or date of the report.	Nature of the report.	No. of the bill.	How disposed of by the House of Reps.	How disposed of by the Senate.	Date of the act of Congress, and remarks.
Gladney, Samuel	Pre-emption right to land	25	3	Petition	451	Public Lands.						
Gladney, Samuel	Pre-emption right to land	26	1	Petition	436	Claims.						
Gladney, Samuel	Pre-emption right to land	27	2	Petition	155	Priv. Land Claims.	779	Adverse	......	Laid on table.		
Gladney, Samuel	For a grant of land	26	1	Petition	611	Priv. Land Claims.	July 20, 1840	Favorable	514			
Gladney, Samuel	Confirmation of title to land	30	2	Petition	534	Public Lands.						
Gladney, Samuel	Confirmation of title to land	31	1	Petition	272	Public Lands.						
Gladwin, Clark & Hall	(See Thomas Tupper, assignees of)	22	2	....	142							
Gladwin, William	(See Thomas Tupper, assignees of)	22	2	....	142							
Glanding, James A	Pension	31	2	Petition	308	Invalid Pensions.						
Glanville, John, widow of.	Arrears of pension	24	2	Petition	398	Invalid Pensions.						
Glanville, John, widow of.	Arrears of pension	25	2	Petition	588	Invalid Pensions.						
Glascock, Spencer	Compensation for horses and wagon lost in United States service.	13	3	Petition	593	Claims	....	....	......	Referred to Committee Whole House, on bill No. 228.		
Glascock, General Thomas,	Payment for horses lost in United States service.	17	1	Petition	164	Claims	Mar. 29, 1822	Adverse	......	Laid on table.		
Glascock, General Thomas,	Payment for horses lost in United States service.	17	2	Petition	61	Whole House.						
Glascock, Lieut. Thomas, heirs of.	Payment of balance due for revolutionary services.	24	1	Petition	740	Rev. Claims	778	Favorable	703	Referred to Committee Whole House.		
Glascock, Lieut. Thomas, heirs of.	Payment of balance due for revolutionary services.	25	2	Petition	70	Rev. Claims	432	Favorable	440	Referred to Committee Whole House.		
Glascock, Lieut. Thomas, heirs of.	Payment of balance due for revolutionary services.	25	3	House bill	264	Whole House	June 2, 1839	Favorable	440	Passed	Passed	App'd Feb. 26, 1839
Glascock, Lieut. Thomas, heirs of.	Payment of balance due for revolutionary services.	26	1	Petition	164	Rev. Claims	330	Favorable	302			
Glascock, Lieut. Thomas, heirs of.	Interest on amount paid under act of February 26, 1839.	27	2	Petition	61	Rev. Claims	1057	Adverse	......	Laid on table.		
Glascock, William B., heirs of.	Bounty land	28	1	Petition	84	Priv. Land Claims.						
Glasgow, Edward J., *et al.*	To be placed on a footing with those of the Mexican army.	31	1	Petition	960							
Glasgow, John	Confirmation of title to land	21	2	Petition	114	Public Lands.						
Glasier, Benjamin	Indemnity for French spoliations prior to 1800.	26	1	Memorial	182	Foreign Affairs	343	Favorable	319	Referred to Committee Whole House.		
Glass, John	To be allowed to complete payment for land.	21	1	Petition	70	Public Lands	87	Favorable	120	Passed	Passed	App'd May 20, 1830
Glass, Joseph	(See Abiel Roads, *et al.*)	22	2	....	137							
Glass, Michael	Correction of error in land entry	25	2	Petition	547	Public Lands.						
Glass, Michael	Correction of error in land entry	25	3	Petition	98	Public Lands.						
Glass, Michael	Correction of error in land entry	26	1	Petition	178	Public Lands	319	Favorable	284			
Glass, William, and wife	(See Joseph Holt, heirs of)	23	2	....	47							
Glassburn, G., *et al*	Payment for military services	14	1	Petition	33	Claims	....	....	......	Discharged; laid on table.		
Glasssell, Andrew, heirs of	Indemnity for French spoliations prior to 1800.	30	2	Memorial	77	Foreign Affairs.						
Glassell, Andrew, heirs of	Indemnity for French spoliations prior to 1800.	31	1	Petition	232	Foreign Affairs	355	General bill	318			
Glavary, Francis R	Indemnity for French spoliations prior to 1800.	26	1	Memorial	182	Foreign Affairs	343	Favorable; bill	319	Referred to Committee Whole House.		

List of private claims presented to the House of Representatives of the United States from the 1st to the 31st Congress, inclusive—Continued.

Names of claimants.	Nature or object of the claim.	Congress.	Session.	How brought before the House of Reps.	Page of journal.	To what committee of the House referred.	No. or date of the report.	Nature of the report.	No. of the bill.	How disposed of by the House of Reps.	How disposed of by the Senate.	Date of the act of Congress, and remarks.
Glavary, Francis R., heir of.	Indemnity for French spoliations prior to 1800.	31	1	Petition	692	Foreign Affairs	355	General bill	318	Referred to Committee Whole House.		
Glaze, Adam	Confirmation of title to land	12	1	Petition	22	Public Lands.						
Glaze, Adam	Confirmation of title to land	12	2	Petition	549	Public Lands.						
Glaze, Adam	Confirmation of title to land	13	2	Petition	170	Public Lands	Mar. 26, 1814	Resolution		Leave to withdraw.		
Glazier, Asa	Pension	14	1	Petition	266	Pens. & Rev. Cl'ms	April 11, 1816	General bill	171	Passed	Passed, with amendment.	App'd April 30, 1816
Glazier, Asa	Increase of pension	28	1	Petition	113	Invalid Pensions	46	Adverse		Laid on table.		
Gleason, Eleanor	Pension	28	1	Petition	950	Whole House.						
Gleason, Luther	For the issue of a land patent	25	2	Resolution	1176	Priv. Land Claims				Discharged; laid on table.		
Gleason, Thomas	Pension	2	2	Rep. of Secretary War.	649	Whole House.						
Gleason, Thomas	Pension	3	1	Rep. of Secretary War.	131	Select	May 26, 1794	Res. for add'l evidence.	J.R. 12	Passed	Passed	App'd June 9, 1794
Gleason, Thomas	Pension	4	1	Rep. of Secretary War.	445	Claims.						
Gleason, Thomas	Pension	4	2	Rep. of Secretary War.	614	Claims.						
Gleason, Windsor	Pension	3	2	Rep. of Secretary War.	350					Laid on table.		
Gleason, Windsor	Pension	4	1	Rep. of Secretary War.	445	Claims	Feb. 18, 1796	General bill	156	Passed	Passed	App'd April 20, 1796
Glen, Henry, (N. Y.)	Compensation for revolutionary services.	3	2	Memorial	313	Claims.						
Glen, Henry, (N. Y.)	Compensation for revolutionary services.	4	1	Petition	444	Claims				Leave to withdraw.		
Glen, Henry, (N. Y.)	Compensation for revolutionary services.	5	2	Petition	260	Claims	April 13, 1798	Adverse		Laid on table.		
Glen, Henry, (N. Y.)	Compensation for revolutionary services.	8	1	Petition	454	Claims	Mar. 13, 1804	Adverse		Postponed.		
Glen, Hugh, assignee of	Balance due for rations furnished Indian department at Fort Harrison.	18	1	Petition	335	Claims				Discharged; leave to withdraw.		
Glencer, Ann Margaretta	Continuation of pension	26	2	Petition	122	Rev. Pensions	Feb. 12, 1841	Adverse		Laid on table.		
Glenn, Anthony	Pension	21	2	Petition	52	Select.						
Glenn, Anthony	Pension	22	1	Petition	164	Rev. Pensions.						
Glenn, Bernard	Permission to locate bounty land in Ohio.	7	2	Petition	256	Claims	Feb. 11, 1803	Favorable		Referred to Committee Whole House.		
Glenn, Bernard	Permission to locate bounty land in Ohio.	11	2	Petition	307	Public Lands.						
Glenn, Bernard	Permission to locate bounty land in Ohio.	11	3	Petition	491	Public Lands.						
Glenn, Elias, (Md.)	Compensation for examining witnesses.	18	2	Petition	185	Naval Affairs	Feb. 8, 1825	Favorable	326	Passed	Passed	App'd March 3, 1825
Glenn, James M.	That a patent be issued to him for a quarter section of land.	24	1	Petition	425	Priv. Land Claims.						
Glenn, James M.	Confirmation of title to land	24	2	Petition	107	Priv. Land Claims.						
Glenn, John	(See Robt. Barry, administrator of.)	31	1		193		32		60			
Glenny, William, representatives of.	Commutation pay	9	1	Petition	262	Claims				Discharged; referred to Com. Whole House.		
Glentworth, George	Compensation for acting surgeon general.	1	3	Memorial & rep't Sec. of War.	355					Laid on table.		

List of private claims presented to the House of Representatives of the United States from the 1*st to the* 31*st Congress, inclusive*—Continued.

Names of claimants.	Nature or object of the claim.	Congress.	Session.	How brought before the House of Reps.	Page of journal.	To what committee of the House referred.	No. or date of the report.	Nature of the report.	No. of the bill.	How disposed of by the House of Reps.	How disposed of by the Senate.	Date of the act of Congress, and remarks.
Glentworth, James	That provision be made for defining his fees and emoluments, and that the amount claimed by United States be relinquished.	18	2	Petition	95	Ways and Means	Feb. 28, 1825	Favorable	371	Laid on table.		
Glentworth, Thos., *et al.*	Increase of compensation as bargeman.	4	2	Petition	715	....	....	....	....	Laid on table.		
Glickner, Jacob	Payment for work and materials on Cumberland road.	23	1	Resolution	589	Claims	455	Adverse	....	....	....	See Report No. 449.
Gliddon, John	Reimbursement of certain expenses in discharging his consular duties at Alexandria, Egypt.	27	2	Petition	794	Foreign Affairs.						
Gliddon, John	Reimbursement of certain expenses in discharging his consular duties at Alexandria, Egypt.	28	1	Petition	876	Foreign Affairs.						
Gliddon, John	Reimbursement of certain expenses in discharging his consular duties at Alexandria, Egypt.	29	1	Petition	124	Foreign Affairs.						
Glinn, Thomas	(See Exploring Expedition)	27	3	....	149							
Gloss, Daniel	Payment for cattle taken by Canadians in late war.	14	2	Petition	212	Claims	....	....	....	Discharged; laid on table.		
Glossbrenner, A. J.	Payment for work in State Department.	30	2	Civil and diplomatic bill.	....	....	....	....	....	....	....	Statutes at Large, vol. 9, p. 365.
Glover, Allen, *et al.*	Redress on account of land purchased.	21	2	Petition	119	Public Lands	Jan. 27, 1829	Adverse	....	Laid on table.		
Glover, Benjamin	Pension	21	2	Resolution	108	Military Pensions.						
Glover, Cread	Payment for a horse lost in United States service.	20	2	Resolution	152	Claims	80	Favorable	381	Referred to Committee Whole House.		
Glover, Cread	Payment for a horse lost in United States service.	21	1	Petition	83	Claims	28	Favorable	36	Passed	Passed	App'd March 25, 1830
Glover, Elijah	Payment for provisions and forage furnished the Ohio militia.	16	1	Petition	258	Claims	April 19, 1820	Adverse	....	Laid on table	....	Leave to withdraw.
Glover, Ezekiel	Relief in consideration of revolutionary services.	19	1	Petition	224	Rev. Claims	April 1, 1826	Adverse	....	Laid on table.		
Glover, Ezekiel	Relief in consideration of revolutionary services.	23	2	Petition	342	Rev. Pensions	....	....	....	Discharged; laid on table.		
Glover, Ezekiel	Relief in consideration of revolutionary services.	25	2	Petition	403	Rev. Pensions	1017	Adverse	....	Laid on table.		
Glover, Ezekiel	Relief in consideration of revolutionary services.	26	1	Resolution	851	Rev. Pensions.						
Glover, William	Pension	24	2	Petition	41	Rev. Pensions	6	Favorable	763	Referred to Committee Whole House.		
Glover, William	Pension	25	2	Petition	38	Invalid Pensions	355	Favorable	384	Passed.		
Glover, William	Pension	25	3	Petition	460	Invalid Pensions.						
Glover, William	Pension	26	1	Petition	161	Invalid Pensions	231	Favorable	243	Passed	Indef. postp'd.	
Glover, William	Pension	26	2	Petition	107	Military Affairs	....	....	....	Laid on table.		
Glover, William	Pension	27	2	Petition	268	Invalid Pensions	315	Favorable	284	Passed	Indef. postp'd.	
Glover, William	Pension	27	3	Petition	61	Invalid Pensions.						
Glover, William	Pension	28	1	Petition	115	Invalid Pensions	15	Favorable	42	Passed	Passed, with amendment.	App'd May 31, 1844
Glover, William	Naval pension	26	1	Petition	1007	Naval Affairs	182	....	....	Discharged; laid on table.		
Glover, Sanders	Compensation as assessor of direct tax.	13	2	Petition	294	Claims	Mar. 17, 1814	Adverse	....	Leave to withdraw.		

List of private claims presented to the House of Representatives of the United States from the 1st to the 31st Congress, inclusive—Continued.

Names of claimants.	Nature or object of the claim.	Congress.	Session.	How brought before the House of Reps.	Page of journal.	To what committee of the House referred.	No. or date of the report.	Nature of the report.	No. of the bill.	How disposed of by the House of Reps.	How disposed of by the Senate.	Date of the act of Congress, and remarks.
Glum, Philip	Pension	11	2	Petition	127	Claims	April 9, 1810	Adverse	......	Rejected.		
Glynn, Lieut. James, *et al.*	For an appropriation to defray expense of coast surveys.	26	2	Petition	52	Naval Affairs	128	Favorable	635			
Glynn, Lieut. James, *et al.*	For an appropriation to defray expense of coast surveys.	27	2	Petition	390	Naval Affairs.						
Glynn, Lieut. James, *et al.*	For an appropriation to defray expense of coast surveys.	28	1	Petition	515	Naval Affairs.						
Glynn, Lieut. James, *et al.*	For an appropriation to defray expense of coast surveys.	29	2	Petition	83	Naval Affairs	1	Favorable	578			
Glynn, Lieut. James, *et al.*	For an appropriation to defray expense of coast surveys.	30	1	Petition	115	Naval Affairs	77	Favorable	62	Referred to Committee Whole House.		
Glynn, Lieut. James, *et al.*	For an appropriation to defray expense of coast surveys.	30	2	House bill	466	Whole House	Feb. 19, 1849	Favorable	62	Passed	Passed	App'd Feb. 2, 1849
Glynn, Samuel	For pay and emoluments due his father for revolutionary services.	10	1	Petition	23	Select.						
Goad, Caleb	(See William H. Bedford, agent).	28	1	....	262							
Goben, William	Pension	17	1	Petition	361	Rev. Pensions	....	....	......	Discharged; laid on table.		
Gobert, Charles	Drawback on duties	5	3	Petition	432	Com. and Manuf.						
Goddard, Rene, heirs of	Land and money due by Virginia for revolutionary services.	26	1	Resolution	359	Rev. Claims.						
Godbold, John W. W	Pension	25	2	Petition	53	Rev. Pensions	....	....	......	Discharged; laid on table.		
Godbold, John W. W	Pension	25	3	Petition	334	Rev. Pensions	....	....	......	Discharged; laid on table.		
Godbold, John W. W	Pension	26	1	Petition	199	Rev. Claims.						
Goddard, Edward	Pension	3	2	Petition	259	Claims	Feb. 25, 1795	Adverse	......	Leave to withdraw.		
Goddard, Edward	Pension	4	2	Rep't Committee.	649	Claims	Jan. 18, 1797	Adverse	......	Rejected; leave to withdraw.		
Goddard, Eli	(See Joseph M. Robertson, *et al.*)	28	1	....	189							
Goddard, James	Indemnity for property destroyed by the British.	14	2	Petition	46	Claims	Dec. 20, 1816	Adverse	......	Rejected.		
Goddard, James	Indemnity for property destroyed by the British.	17	1	Petition	200	Claims	Mar. 15, 1822	Adverse	......	Rejected.		
Goddard, James	Reimbursement of duties paid on iron.	25	2	Petition	768	Com. and Manuf.	May 24, 1838	Favorable	809	Referred to Committee Whole House.		
Goddard John B	Increase of compensation	14	2	Petition	378	Judiciary	Feb. 18, 1817	Adverse	......	Rejected; leave to withdraw.		
Goddard, Mary C	Payment of claims against United States.	1	2	Petition	218	....	....	....	......	Referred to Secretary War.		
Goddard, Mary C	Payment of claims against United States.	3	2	Rep. of Secretary War.	248	....	....	....	......	Laid on table.		
Goddard, Nathaniel	(See Ezekiel Hubbell)	12	1	....	11							
Goddard, Nathaniel	Reimbursement of certain duties	24	1	Memorial	94	Ways and Means	Jan. 27, 1836	General bill	233			
Goddard, Nathaniel	Indemnity for French spoliations prior to 1800.	26	1	Memorial	182	Foreign Affairs	343	Favorable; bill	319	Referred to Committee Whole House.		
Goddard, Nathaniel, *et al.*	Reimbursement of half the value of the ship Ariadne and cargo.	15	1	Petition	143	Ways and Means	83	Favorable	76	Rejected.		
Goddard, Nathaniel, *et al.*	Reimbursement of half the value of the ship Ariadne and cargo.	16	1	Petition	27	Ways and Means.						
Goddard, Nathaniel, *et al.*	Reimbursement of half the value of the ship Ariadne and cargo.	18	2	Petition	79	Ways and Means.						
Goddard, Nathaniel, *et al.*	Reimbursement of half the value of the ship Ariadne and cargo.	19	1	Petition	221	Ways and Means	Mar. 1, 1826	Adverse	......	Laid on table.		

List of private claims presented to the House of Representatives of the United States from the 1st to the 31st Congress, inclusive—Continued.

Names of claimants.	Nature or object of the claim.	Congress.	Session.	How brought before the House of Reps.	Page of journal.	To what committee of the House referred.	No. or date of the report.	Nature of the report.	No. of the bill.	How disposed of by the House of Reps.	How disposed of by the Senate.	Date of the act of Congress, and remarks.
92 Goddard, Nathaniel, *et al.*	Reimbursement of half the value of the ship Ariadne and cargo.	24	1	Petition	95	Claims.						
Goddard, Nathaniel, *et al.*	Reimbursement of half the value of the ship Ariadne and cargo.	24	2	Petition	72	Claims.						
Goddard, Nathaniel, *et al.*	Reimbursement of half the value of the ship Ariadne and cargo.	25	2	Petition	52	Claims	199	Favorable	91	Referred to Committee Whole House.		
Goddard, Nathaniel, *et al.*	Reimbursement of half the value of the ship Ariadne and cargo.	25	3	House bill	375	Whole House	Jan. 25, 1839	Favorable	91			
Goddard, Nathaniel, *et al.*	Reimbursement of half the value of the ship Ariadne and cargo.	26	1	Petition	167	Claims	20	Favorable	39	Referred to Committee Whole House.		
Goddard, Nathaniel, *et al.*	Reimbursement of half the value of the ship Ariadne and cargo.	26	2	House bill	165	Whole House	Jan. 16, 1841	Favorable	39			
Goddard, Nathaniel, *et al.*	Reimbursement of half the value of the ship Ariadne and cargo.	29	1	Senate bill	732	Claims	808	Adverse	38	Referred to Committee Whole House.		
Goddard, Nicholas	(See William Storer, *et al.*)	16	2		112							
Goddard, Samuel	Pension	20	2	Petition	203	Military Pensions				Referred to Committee Whole House.		
Goddard, Thatcher, administrator of.	Indemnity for French spoliations prior to 1800.	26	1	Memorial	182	Foreign Affairs	343	Favorable; bill	319	Referred to Committee Whole House.		
Goden, Victor L., *et al.*	Difference of pay between assistant and passed assistant surgeon in United States navy.	27	2	Petition	343	Claims	768	Adverse		Laid on table.		
Goden, Victor L., *et al.*	Difference of pay between assistant and passed assistant surgeon in United States navy.	27	2	Petition	869	Naval Affairs.						
Godenberger, Adam	Pension	3	2	Rep't Committee.	352	Claims	Feb. 28, 1795	Favorable	130	Passed	Postponed.	
Godenberger, Adam	Pension	4	1	Rep. of Secretary of War.	445	Claims	Mar. 14, 1796	General bill	156	Passed	Passed	App'd April 20, 1796
Godet, Theodore	(See Thomas Nelmes, admin'r of.)	2	1		539							
Godfrey, Jane	Indemnity for losses and damage to property in revolutionary war.	3	2	Petition	306	Claims.						
Godfrey, Jane	Indemnity for losses and damage to property in revolutionary war.	4	1	Petition	389	Claims	Dec. 28, 1795	Adverse		Leave to withdraw.		
Godfrey, John	Arrears of pension	26	1	Petition	287	Invalid Pensions	644	Favorable	477			
Godfrey, John	Arrears of pension	26	2	House bill	91	Invalid Pensions				Discharged; laid on table.		
Godfrey, John Wm	Payment of certificate No. 29, signed Cornelius Cox, deputy quartermaster general.	4	1	Letter of Secretary Treasury.	388	Claims.						
Godfrey, John Wm	Payment of certificate No. 29, signed Cornelius Cox, deputy quartermaster general.	14	2	Petition	40	Pens. & Rev. Cl'ms.				Discharged; laid on table.		
Godfrey, John Wm	Payment of certificate No. 29, signed Cornelius Cox, deputy quartermaster general.	15	1	Petition	27	Pens. & Rev. Cl'ms.	Feb. 3, 1818	Adverse		Laid on table.		
Godfrey, John Wm	Payment of certificate No. 29, signed Cornelius Cox, deputy quartermaster general.	23	1	Petition	459	Rev. Claims.						
Godfrey, John Wm	Payment of certificate No. 29, signed Cornelius Cox, deputy quartermaster general.	23	2	Petition	53	Rev. Claims.						
Godfrey, John W	Payment for supplies furnished U. States army.	12	2	Petition	631	Claims.						

List of private claims presented to the House of Representatives of the United States from the 1st to the 31st Congress, inclusive—Continued.

Names of claimants.	Nature or object of the claim.	Congress.	Session.	How brought before the House of Reps.	Page of journal.	To what committee of the House referred.	No. or date of the report.	Nature of the report.	No. of the bill.	How disposed of by the House of Reps.	How disposed of by the Senate.	Date of the act of Congress, and remarks.
Godfrey, Louis, *et al.*	To ascertain quantity of land in his grant.	25	2	Petition	456	Public Lands	Feb. 7, 1838	Favorable	548	Passed	Passed	App'd July 4, 1838
Godfrey, William E., heir of.	Bounty land	27	2	Petition	1298	Rev. Claims.						
Godfrey, William E., heir of.	Bounty land	28	1	Petition	109	Rev. Claims	18	Adverse	......	Laid on table.		
Godfroy, Gabriel	Indemnity for property destroyed by order of American officer.	15	1	Report of Com. of Claims.	195	Claims	......	......	......	Discharged; laid on table.		
Godfroy, Gabriel	Indemnity for property destroyed by order of American officer.	15	2	Senate bill	280	Claims	Feb. 26, 1819	Adverse	50	Laid on table.		
Godfroy, Gabriel	Indemnity for property destroyed by order of American officer.	16	1	Petition	106	Claims.						
Godfroy, Gabriel	Indemnity for property destroyed by order of American officer.	16	1	Senate bill	300	Claims	Mar. 17, 1820	Adverse	53	Laid on table.		
Godfroy, Gabriel	Indemnity for property destroyed by order of American officer.	16	2	Petition	120	Claims	33	Adverse	......	Referred to Committee Whole House.		
Godfroy, Gabriel	Indemnity for property destroyed by order of American officer.	20	2	Petition	79	Claims	81	Favorable	438			
Godfroy, Gabriel	Indemnity for property destroyed by order of American officer.	21	1	Petition	93	Claims	35	Favorable	47	Passed	Passed	App'd May 31, 1830
Godfroy, Gabriel, *et al.*	Indemnity for a house destroyed by the enemy.	17	1	Petition	47	Claims	34	Adverse	......	Referred to Committee Whole House.		
Godfroy, Gabriel, *et al.*	Indemnity for a house destroyed by the enemy.	21	2	Petition	62	Claims	35	Favorable	556			
Godfroy, Gabriel, *et al.*	Indemnity for a house destroyed by the enemy.	22	1	Petition	26	Claims	128	Favorable	199	Referred to Committee Whole House.		
Godfroy, Gabriel, *et al.*	Indemnity for a house destroyed by the enemy.	22	2	House bill	66	Whole House	Dec. 15, 1832	Favorable	199	Passed	Passed	App'd Feb. 9, 1833
Godfroy, Gabriel, *et al.*	To be allowed to pay arrearages on land.	20	2	Resolution	66	Public Lands	Jan. 9, 1829	Favorable	358	Passed.		
Godfroy, Gabriel, *et al.*	To be allowed to pay arrearages on land.	21	1	Resolution	62	Public Lands	Dec. 23, 1829	Favorable	29	Passed	Passed	App'd April 23, 1830
Godfroy, Peter	Compensation for extra duties as keeper of a light-house.	19	1	Petition	34	Commerce.						
Godsey, William, widow of	Pension	24	2	Petition	418	Rev. Pensions.						
Godsey, William, widow of	Pension	26	1	Petition	323	Rev. Pensions	......	......	......	Discharged; laid on table.		
Godwin, William	(See Banister Howe)	25	2	......	579							
Goelet, Peter, executors of.	Indemnity for French spoliations prior to 1800.	26	1	Memorial	182	Foreign Affairs	343	Favorable; bill	319	Referred to Committee Whole House.		
Goell, Alvin C	Compensation for improvement in rocket machine.	27	3	Petition	284	Military Affairs	......	......	......	Discharged; leave to withdraw.		
Goell, Alvin C	Compensation for improvement in rocket machine.	28	1	Petition	346	Select.						
Goell, Alvin C	Compensation for improvement in rocket machine.	28	2	Petition	157	Select	138	Favorable	621			
Goell, Alvin C	Compensation for improvement in rocket machine.	29	1	Petition	321	Select	273	Favorable	240	Referred to Committee Whole House.		
Goell, Alvin C	Compensation for improvement in rocket machine.	29	2	House bill	76	Whole House	Feb. 24, 1846	Favorable	240	Passed.		
Goell, Alvin C	Compensation for improvement in rocket machine.	30	1	Petition and docs.	112	Naval Affairs.						

List of private claims presented to the House of Representatives of the United States from the 1st *to the* 31st *Congress, inclusive*—Continued.

Names of claimants.	Nature or object of the claim.	Congress.	Session.	How brought before the House of Reps.	Page of journal.	To what committee of the House referred.	No. or date of the report.	Nature of the report.	No. of the bill.	How disposed of by the House of Reps.	How disposed of by the Senate.	Date of the act of Congress, and remarks.
Goetschin, J Mauritius	For a grant of land as indemnity for property destroyed by the British.	16	1	Petition	45	Pens. & Rev. Cl'ms.	Dec. 21, 1819	Adverse	......	Rejected.		
Goetz, Frederick, *et al.*	Additional compensation for arms furnished United States.	16	1	Senate bill	274	Claims	Mar. 17, 1820	Adverse	47	Referred to Committee Whole House.		
Goetz, Frederick, administrator of.	Additional compensation for arms furnished United States.	18	2	Petition	59	Claims	Feb. 18, 1825	Favorable	346	Passed	Passed	App'd March 3, 1825
Goff, Adam	Pension	18	1	Petition	134	Pens. & Rev. Cl'ms.						
Goff, Comfort	Pension	18	1	Petition	482	Pens. & Rev. Cl'ms.						
Goff, David	Compensation for extra services in revolutionary war.	11	2	Petition	111	Claims	Mar. 14, 1810	Adverse	......	Rejected.		
Goff, Gideon	Pension	25	2	Petition	53	Rev. Pensions	......	......	......	Discharged; laid on table.		
Goff, John K.	For pre-emption right to certain lands.	22	2	Petition	55	Public Lands	......	......	......	Laid on table.		
Goff, John K.	For pre-emption right to certain lands.	23	1	Petition	138	Priv. Land Claims	......	......	......	Laid on table.		
Goff, John K.	For pre-emption right to certain lands.	23	2	Petition	242	Priv. Land Claims	......	......	......	Discharged; laid on table.		
Goff, Joseph	Compensation for revolutionary services.	2	1	Petition	528	......	......	......	......	Referred to Secretary of War.		
Goff, Thomas	For bounty land	18	2	Petition	31	Priv. Land Claims.	Jan. 4, 1825	Adverse	......	Rejected.		
Goffney, Daniel	(See Daniel Gaffney.)	28	1	......	100							
Goforth, William, widow of.	Pension	24	2	Petition	45	Rev. Pensions	......	......	......	Discharged; laid on table.		
Goggin, John, heirs of	For seven years' half-pay	24	1	Resolution	1082	Rev. Claims.						
Goggin, John, heirs of	For seven years' half-pay	25	2	Petition	546	Rev. Claims	......	......	......	Discharged; laid on table.		
Goguet, Margueritta	Confirmation of title to land	19	1	Petition	381	Public Lands	......	......	......	Discharged; laid on table.		
Goin, Thomas	Compensation for establishing naval schools on board receiving ships.	26	1	Memorial	713	Naval Affairs.						
Goin, Thomas	Compensation for establishing naval schools on board receiving ships.	26	2	Petition	181	Naval Affairs.						
Goin, Thomas	Compensation for establishing naval schools on board receiving ships.	27	2	Petition	382	Claims	497	Adverse	......	Laid on table	......	Leave to withdraw.
Goin, Thomas, administrator of.	Pension to children	30	1	Petition	440	Naval Affairs.						
Going, Jesse	Pension	31	2	Petition	50	Invalid Pensions.						
Going, Preston	(See James H. Grant, *et al.*)	25	3	......	380							
Goings, Daniel W	Pension	24	2	Petition	302	Invalid Pensions	262	Favorable	950	Referred to Committee Whole House.		
Goings, Daniel W	Pension	25	2	Petition	38	Invalid Pensions	426	Favorable	433	Passed		
Goings, Daniel W	Pension	26	1	Petition	161	Invalid Pensions	182	Favorable	194	Passed	Passed	App'd July 20, 1840
Gold, Peter	(See Joseph White, heir of.)	29	2	......	228							
Golden Fleece	(See H. Silliman, *et al.*)	12	1	......	98							
Golder, John	To be released from bond and judgment.	25	1	Memorial	103	......	......	......	......	Laid on table.		
Golding, John	Compensation for extra services in land office.	19	2	Petition	72	Public Lands.						

List of private claims presented to the House of Representatives of the United States from the 1st to the 31st Congress, inclusive—**Continued.**

Names of claimants.	Nature or object of the claim.	Congress.	Session.	How brought before the House of Reps.	Page of journal.	To what committee of the House referred.	No. or date of the report.	Nature of the report.	No. of the bill.	How disposed of by the House of Reps.	How disposed of by the Senate.	Date of the act of Congress, and remarks.
Goldman, George W	(See Charles Lee, *et al.*)	28	1		372							
Goldman, George W	Confirmation of title to land	31	1	Petition	672	Priv. Land Claims.						
Gold Mining Company, (Union.)	Remission of duties	24	1	Petition	94	Ways and Means	Jan. 27, 1836	Favorable	223	Referred to Committee Whole House.		
Gold Mining Company, (Union.)	Remission of duties	24	2	House bill	62	Whole House			223			
Goldsborrough, Charles, widow of.	Pension	25	3	Petition	460	Rev. Pensions.						
Goldsborrough, Charles, widow of.	Pension	26	1	Petition	174	Rev. Pensions				Discharged; laid on table.		
Goldsborrough, Howes	Redress for damages to property by Chesapeake and Ohio canal.	21	2	Memorial	174	Internal Imp'ments.						
Goldsborrough, Howes	Redress for damage to property by Chesapeake and Ohio canal.	22	1	Memorial	193	Dist. of Columbia.						
Goldsborrough, Robert, heirs of.	Commutation pay	27	2	Petition	226	Rev. Claims	658	Adverse		Laid on table.		
Goldsbury, Samuel	Indemnity for property taken by the Neapolitan Government.	25	2	Petition	327	Foreign Affairs	799	Adverse		Laid on table.		
Goldsby, John H	(See John H. Goolsby)	28	1		218							
Goldsmith, Jeremiah, guardian of.	Pension	24	1	Petition	382	Rev. Claims	Mar. 3, 1836	Favorable	420	Passed	Passed	App'd June 28, 1836
Goldsmith, Morris, *et al.*	Compensation for taking pirates	17	1	Petition	77	Claims				Discharged; laid on table.		
Goldsmith, Morris, *et al.*	Compensation for taking pirates	18	1	Petition	98	Claims	91	Favorable	173	Passed	Passed	App'd May 19, 1824
Golliher, John	Payment for horse lost in United States service.	18	1	Resolution	220	Claims	May 3, 1824	Adverse		Laid on table.		
Gomber, John	Pension	15	2	Petition	182	Pens. & Rev. Cl'ms.				Discharged; laid on table.		
Gomber, John	Pension	19	2	Petition	64	Military Pensions.						
Gonet, Marcellino	Further time to discharge a judgment against him.	14	2	Petition	136	Ways and Means				Discharged; laid on table.		
Gonmer, Mathias, heirs of.	Compensation for revolutionary services.	19	2	Petition	105	Rev. Claims	Feb. 13, 1827	Adverse		Laid on table		Leave to withdraw, 1st session, 20th Congress.
Gonon, E	Payment for exhibiting telegraphs.	27	2	Petition	396	Select	325	Favorable	296			
Gonoro, Antoine	For patent of certain lands	22	1	Petition	263	Priv. Land Claims.	Feb. 17, 1832	Favorable	380	Referred to Committee Whole House.		
Gonsoulin, Francois, heirs of.	Confirmation of title to land	23	1	Petition	309	Priv. Land Claims.						
Gonsoulin, Francois, heirs of.	Confirmation of title to land	23	2	Petition	48	Priv. Land Claims.						
Gonsoulin, Francois, heirs of.	Confirmation of title to land	27	2	Petition	75	Priv. Land Claims.				Title papers withd'wn.		
Gonzalez, Andria	Confirmation of title to land	22	1	Rep't Committee.	108	Whole House		Favorable	125	Passed	Passed	App'd June 25, 1832
Gonzales, Bastien	Confirmation of title to land	22	1	Rep't Committee.	108	Whole House		Favorable	125	Passed	Passed	App'd June 25, 1832
Gonzales, Juan, heirs of	Confirmation of title to land	20	1	Petition	51	Priv. Land Claims.	Jan. 17, 1828	Adverse		Laid on table.		
Gonzales, Manuel	(Journal does not show nature of claim.)	19	2	Petition	105	Claims	Feb. 5, 1827	Adverse		Laid on table.		
Gooch, Cornelius, son of	Remuneration for losses by Indian depredations.	27	2	Petition	699	Claims	713	Adverse		Laid on table.		
Gooch, James, widow of	Arrears of pension	23	2	Petition	66	Rev. Claims.						
Good, E	(See Reuben E. Gentry, *et al.*)											
Good, Jacob	Pension	27	3	Resolution	144	Rev. Pensions	295	Adverse		Laid on table.		

List of private claims presented to the House of Representatives of the United States from the 1st to the 31st Congress, inclusive—Continued.

Names of claimants.	Nature or object of the claim.	Congress.	Session.	How brought before the House of Reps.	Page of journal.	To what committee of the House referred.	No. or date of the report.	Nature of the report.	No. of the bill.	How disposed of by the House of Reps.	How disposed of by the Senate.	Date of the act of Congress, and remarks.
Good, John	Indemnity for damage by location of Cumberland road.	16	1	Petition	30	Roads and Canals	Jan. 17, 1820	Adverse	......	Referred to Committee Whole House.		
Good, John	Indemnity for damage by location of Cumberland road.	16	2	Rep't Committee.	47	Roads and Canals	Jan. 9, 1821	Adverse	......	Referred to Secretary Treasury.		
Good, John	Indemnity for damage by location of Cumberland road.	17	1	Rep. of Secretary Treasury.	301	Roads and Canals	April 24, 1822	Adverse	......	Leave to withdraw.		
Good, John	Indemnity for damage by location of Cumberland road.	19	1	Petition	365	Roads and Canals	140	Adverse	......	Laid on table.		
Good, John	Indemnity for damage by location of Cumberland road.	20	1	Petition	127	Claims	75	Adverse	......	Laid on table.		
Good, John	Indemnity for damage by location of Cumberland road.	20	2	Rep't Committee.	65	Whole House.						
Good, John	Indemnity for damage by location of Cumberland road.	21	1	Petition	99	Claims	334	Adverse	......	Referred to Committee Whole House.		
Good, John	Indemnity for damage by location of Cumberland road.	22	1	Petition	34	Claims	251	Adverse	......	Referred to Committee Whole House.		
Good, John	Indemnity for damage by location of Cumberland road.	23	1	Petition	194	Roads and Canals.						
Good, John	Indemnity for damage by location of Cumberland road.	23	2	Petition	85	Roads and Canals.						
Good, John	Indemnity for damage by location of Cumberland road.	24	1	Petition	107	Claims	....	....	......	Leave to withdraw.		
Good, Thomas	Revolutionary pension	19	1	Petition	149	Military Pensions	....	....	......	Discharged; leave to withdraw.		
Goodall, Eli	Pension	22	1	Petition	131	Rev. Claims.						
Goodall, Chester	Pension	23	2	Petition	110	Invalid Pensions	Dec. 29, 1834	Adverse	......	Laid on table.		
Goodall, Jeremiah, heirs of	Exchange location of land	25	2	Petition	178	Priv. Land Claims.						
Goodall, John	Relief in settlement of accounts	17	2	Petition	75	Military Affairs	Jan. 7, 1823	Favorable	218			
Goodall, John, widow and children of.	Pension	25	2	Petition	72	Rev. Claims	....	....	......	Discharged; laid on table.		
Goodall, John, widow and children of.	Pension	25	3	Petition	85	Rev. Claims.						
Goodall, John, widow and children of.	Pension	26	2	Petition	60	Rev. Claims	180	Adverse	......	Laid on table.		
Goodall, John, widow and children of.	Pension	27	2	Petition	61	Rev. Claims	376	Adverse	......	Laid on table.		
Goodall, John, widow and children of.	Pension	28	1	Petition	300	Rev. Claims.						
Goode, Samuel	Payment for transporting a sick soldier.	22	2	Senate bill	325	Claims	Feb. 22, 1833	Favorable	72	Passed	....	App'd March 2, 1833
Goodell, Jabez	Indemnity for property destroyed by the enemy.	15	2	Petition	148	Claims	....	....	......	Discharged; laid on table.		
Goodell, James, widow of.	Pension	30	1	Petition	69	Rev. Pensions.						
Goodenough, Adino, heirs of.	Bounty land	28	1	Petition	514	Priv. Land Claims.	528	Favorable	406	Referred to Committee Whole House.		
Goodenough, Adino, heirs of.	Bounty land	28	2	House bill	344	Whole House	Feb. 7, 1845	Favorable	406	Passed.		
Goodenough, Adino, heirs of.	Bounty land	29	1	Petition	68	Priv. Land Claims.	485	Adverse	......	Laid on table.		
Goodenough, Adino, heirs of.	Bounty land	29	2	Petition	70	Priv. Land Claims.						
Goodenough, Adino, heirs of.	Bounty land	30	1	Petition	103	Priv. Land Claims.	Feb. 8, 1848	Adverse	......	Laid on table.		

List of private claims presented to the House of Representatives of the United States from the 1st to the 31st Congress, inclusive—Continued.

Names of claimants.	Nature or object of the claim.	Congress.	Session.	How brought before the House of Reps.	Page of journal.	To what committee of the House referred.	No. or date of the report.	Nature of the report.	No. of the bill.	How disposed of by the House of Reps.	How disposed of by the Senate.	Date of the act of Congress, and remarks.
Goodenough, Adino, heirs of.	Compensation for revolutionary services.	31	2	Petition	157	Rev. Pensions.						
Goodenow, Nahum	Pension	21	1	Petition	498	Military Pensions.				Discharged; laid on table.		
Goodenow, Nahum	Pension	21	2	Petition	81	Military Pensions.						
Goodenow, Nathan	Compensation for revolutionary services.	19	1	Petition	381	Military Pensions	Mar. 3, 1826	Adverse		Rejected.		
Good Friends, owners of ship.	Release of forfeiture	13	1	Senate bill	82	Ways and Means	July 20, 1813	With't amend.	S. 20	Passed	Passed	App'd July 29, 1813
Goodhard, David	Pension	23	1	Petition	46	Rev. Claims.						
Goodhue, Benjamin, executors of.	Indemnity for French spoliations prior to 1800.	26	1	Memorial	182	Foreign Affairs	343	Favorable; bill	319	Referred to Committee Whole House.		
Goodhue, Benjamin, executors of.	Indemnity for French spoliations prior to 1800.	31	1	Petition	216	Foreign Affairs	355	General bill	318			
Goodhue & Co	For amount due out of moneys coming to Ottawa Indians.	29	1	Memorial	160	Indian Affairs	287	Adverse.				
Goodhue & Co., *et al.*	Remission of duties on certain goods destroyed by fire.	26	1	Memorial	291	Commerce	Feb. 29, 1840	Favorable	53	Rejected.		
Gooding, George, administratrix of.	Payment of pension money	18	1	Petition	176	Claims	Mar. 3, 1824	Adverse		Leave to withdraw.		
Gooding, George, widow of.	Pre-emption right to land	25	2	Petition	1030	Public Lands.						
Gooding, George, widow of.	Pre-emption right to land	25	3	Petition	92	Public Lands.						
Gooding, John, of Baltimore	Payment of interest on bill of exchange.	14	1	Petition	291	Claims	Mar. 11, 1816	Adverse		Laid on table.		
Gooding, John, of Baltimore	Payment of interest on bill of exchange.	15	1	Petition	141	Ways and Means				Discharged; leave to withdraw.		
Gooding, John, *et al.*	Indemnity for losses by chartering a ship to United States.	13	1	Petition	35	Com. and Manuf.				Leave to withdraw.		
Gooding, John, *et al.*	Bounty on prisoners of war	15	1	Petition	480					Laid on table.		
Gooding, John, *et al.*	Bounty on prisoners of war	15	2	Petition	21	Ways and Means	74	Favorable	261	Referred to Committee Whole House.		
Gooding, John, *et al.*	Bounty on prisoners of war	16	1	Petition	24	Ways and Means	1	Favorable	4	Rejected.		
Gooding, John, *et al.*	Bounty on prisoners of war	16	2	Senate bill	287	Ways and Means	Mar. 1, 1821	Favorable	23	Referred to Committee Whole House.		
Gooding, John, *et al.*	Bounty on prisoners of war	17	1	Senate bill	374	Ways and Means	Mar. 21, 1822	Favorable	37	Passed		App'd May 7, 1822
Goodlett, Adam G	Relief from certain land purchase	15	1	Petition	184	Public Lands				Discharged; laid on table.		
Goodloe, Daniel S	For land in lieu of land patented to University of Alabama.	19	1	Petition	58	Public Lands				Discharged; laid on table.		
Goodman, Aquilla	Pension	29	1	Appropriat'n bill								App'd Aug. 8, 1846
Goodman, Christiana	(See J. Gitzelman, heir of)	29	1		1189							
Goodman, John	Payment for horse lost in United States service.	3	1	Petition	96					Referred to Secretary War.		
Goodman, John	Payment for horse lost in United States service.	3	2	Rep. of Secretary War.	278					Laid on table.		
Goodman, John	Payment for horse lost in United States service.	4	1	Petition	403	Claims	Jan. 6, 1796	Favorable		Laid on table.		
Goodman, John	Payment for horse lost in United States service.	23	1	Documents	154	Claims.						
Goodman, John	Payment for horse lost in United States service.	28	1	Petition	262	Claims.						
Goodman, John	Pension	26	1	Petition	513	Rev. Pensions				Discharged; laid on table.		

List of private claims presented to the House of Representatives of the United States from the 1st to the 31st Congress, inclusive—Continued.

Names of claimants.	Nature or object of the claim.	Congress.	Session.	How brought before the House of Reps.	Page of journal.	To what committee of the House referred.	No. or date of the report.	Nature of the report.	No. of the bill.	How disposed of by the House of Reps.	How disposed of by the Senate.	Date of the act of Congress, and remarks.
Goodno, Calvin	Arrears of pension	25	2	Petition	116	Rev. Pensions	....	....	......	Discharged; laid on table.		
Goodno, Calvin	Arrears of pension	25	3	Petition	87	Rev. Pensions	....	....	......	Discharged; laid on table.		
Goodno, Calvin	Arrears of pension	26	1	Petition	174	Rev. Pensions	....	....	......	Discharged; laid on table.		
Goodrich, Aaron	(See George Walker, *et al.*)	16	1	....	28							
Goodrich, Aaron	Compensation for military services	26	1	Papers	702	Claims.						
Goodrich, Benjamin	Pension	22	1	Petition	161	Invalid Pensions	426	General bill	528	Passed	Passed, with amendment.	App'd July 14, 1832. Petitioner's name omitted in act.
Goodrich, Benjamin	Pension	22	2	Petition	39	Invalid Pensions	Dec. 19, 1832	General bill	626			
Goodrich, Benjamin	Pension	23	1	Petition	86	Invalid Pensions	Dec. 17, 1833	General bill	42	Passed	Passed, with amendment.	App'd June 30, 1834
Goodrich, Bethuel	Pension	14	1	Petition	41	Pens. & Rev. Cl'ms.	April 11, 1816	General bill	171	Passed	Passed	App'd April 30, 1816
Goodrich, David, heir of	Pension	25	3	Petition	216	Rev. Pensions	Jan. 16, 1839	Adverse	......	Laid on table.		
Goodrich, Ebenezer	Indemnity for damage to property by Pennsylvania militia.	13	2	Petition	258	Claims	Feb. 28, 1814	Adverse	......	Laid on table.		
Goodrich, Elizabeth	Payment for a horse lost in United States service.	15	2	Petition	24	Claims	Nov. 30, 1818	Adverse	......	Laid on table.		
Goodrich, Elizabeth	Payment for a horse lost in United States service.	16	1	Petition	142	Claims	Jan. 17, 1820	Adverse	......	Laid on table.		
Goodrich, Elizabeth	(See Samuel Q. Richardson, *et al.*)	19	1	....	337							
Goodrich, George	Interest on claim for transporting United States mail.	24	2	Petition	397	P. Of. & P. Roads.						
Goodrich, Gilbert	Pension	10	1	Petition	93	Claims.						
Goodrich, Gilbert	Pension	12	1	Petition	42	Claims	April 6, 1812	Adverse	......	Leave to withdraw.		
Goodrich, Gilbert	Pension	22	1	Petition	219	Rev. Claims	....	....	......	Discharged; laid on table.		
Goodrich, James	(See Wm. Liffingacle and others.)	18	1	....	526							
Goodrich, James	Pension	21	2	Petition	40	Military Pensions.						
Goodrich, James	Indemnity for French spoliations prior to 1800.	26	1	Memorial	182	Foreign Affairs	343	Favorable; bill	319	Referred to Committee Whole House.		
Goodrich, James	Indemnity for French spoliations prior to 1800.	29	2	Memorial	171	Foreign Affairs.						
Goodrich, John	Compensation for extra services, and to be released from judgment of United States.	17	1	Petition	52	P. Of. & P. Roads.	Feb. 8, 1822	Adverse	......	Laid on table.		
Goodrich, Levi, widow of	Pension	19	2	Petition	43	Military Pensions.						
Goodrich, Silas	Grant of land	9	2	Resolution	507	Select	Jan. 23, 1807	General bill	183	Passed	Passed	App'd March 3, 1807
Goodridge, Israel, *et al.*	For fishing bounty on the schooner Blooming Youth.	26	2	Petition	99	Commerce.						
Goodridge, Israel, *et al.*	For fishing bounty on the schooner Blooming Youth.	27	3	Petition	223	Commerce	172	Favorable	784			
Goodridge, Israel, *et al.*	For fishing bounty on the schooner Blooming Youth.	28	1	Petition	102	Commerce.						
Goodridge, Israel, *et al.*	For fishing bounty on the schooner Blooming Youth.	28	1	Petition	528	Commerce.						
Goodridge, Israal, *et al.*	For fishing bounty on the schooner Blooming Youth.	28	2	Petition	82	Commerce.						
Goodridge, Israel, *et al.*	For fishing bounty on the schooner Blooming Youth.	29	1	Petition	266	Commerce.						
Goodridge, Israel, *et al.*	For fishing bounty on the schooner Blooming Youth.	30	1	Petition	157	Commerce.						

List of private claims presented to the House of Representatives of the United States from the 1st to the 31st Congress, inclusive—Continued.

Names of claimants.	Nature or object of the claim.	Congress.	Session.	How brought before the House of Reps.	Page of journal.	To what committee of the House referred.	No. or date of the report.	Nature of the report.	No. of the bill.	How disposed of by the House of Reps.	How disposed of by the Senate.	Date of the act of Congress, and remarks.
Goodridge, Israel, *et al.*	For fishing bounty on the schooner Blooming Youth.	30	2	Petition	203	Commerce.						
Goodridge, John	Pension	15	2	Petition	160	Rev. Pensions				Discharged; laid on table.		
Goodridge, Joseph	Pension	2	2	Report of Secretary of War.	649	Whole House.						
Goodridge, Joseph	Pension	3	1	Rep. of Secretary War.	131	Select	May 26, 1794	To refer to Secretary War.	J. R. 12	Passed	Passed	App'd June 9, 1794
Goodridge, Joseph	Pension	4	1	Rep. of Secretary War.	445	Claims.						
Goodridge, Joseph	Pension	4	2	Rep. of Secretary War.	614	Claims	Feb. 6, 1797	Favorable	224	Passed	Postponed.	
Goodridge, Joseph	Pension	5	2	House bill	127	Whole House	Jan. 11, 1798	Favorable	38	Passed	Passed	App'd Feb. 2, 1798
Goodrum, John	Pay for emoluments for revolutionary services.	10	2	Petition	390	Select.						
Goodrum, John	Pay for emoluments for revolutionary services.	19	2	Petition	63	Rev. Claims	Jan. 2, 1827	Adverse		Laid on table.		
Goodrum, John	Pay for emoluments for revolutionary services.	20	1	Petition	58	Rev. Claims	April 11, 1828	Adverse		Laid on table.		
Goodrum, John	Pay for emoluments for revolutionary services.	22	1	Petition	339	Rev. Claims.						
Goodrum, Thomas	Pension	4	1	Petition	455	Claims	Mar. 31, 1796	Adverse		Laid on table.		
Goodrum, Thomas	Pension	11	2	House bill	283	Whole House	Mar. 24, 1810	Favorable	107	Passed	Passed	App'd April 27, 1810
Goodrum, Thomas	Increase of pension	11	3	Petition	567	Claims.						
Goodrum, Thomas	Increase of pension	13	2	Petition	172	Pensions				Referred to Secretary of War.		
Goodrum, Thomas	Increase of pension	13	3	Petition	469	Pens. & Rev. Cl'ms.						
Goodrum, Thomas	Pension	14	1	Petition	41	Pens. & Rev. Cl'ms.	Mar. 19, 1816	Adverse		Leave to withdraw.		
Goodsell, Lewis	Pension	19	2	Petition	215	Military Pensions.						
Goodsell, Lewis	Pension	20	1	Petition	243	Military Pensions				Discharged; laid on table.		
Goodsell, Norman	Compensation as witness before a committee of Congress.	21	1	Petition	572	Claims				Discharged; laid on table.		
Goodsell, Norman	Compensation as witness before a committee of Congress.	22	1	Petition	442	Claims.						
Goodsell, Norman	Compensation as witness before a committee of Congress.	23	1	Resolution	143	Claims.						
Goodsell, Norman	Compensation as witness before a committee of Congress.	27	2	Petition	381	Claims	711	Adverse		Laid on table.		
Goodsell, Norman	Compensation as witness before a committee of Congress.	30	1	Petition	679	Claims.						
Goodsell, Samuel P., heirs of.	Pension	23	1	Petition	45	Invalid Pensions	Jan. 27, 1834	Adverse.				
Goodsell, Samuel P., heirs of.	Pension	23	2	Petition	101	Invalid Pensions	Feb. 5, 1835	Adverse		Laid on table.		
Goodsell, Samuel P., heirs of.	Pension	24	1	Petition	507	Invalid Pensions	April 15, 1836	Adverse		Laid on table.		
Goodsell. Samuel P., heirs of.	Arrears of pension	28	2	Petition	69	Invalid Pensions.						
Goodson, Benjamin	Increase of pension	30	2	Memorial	140	Rev. Pensions				Discharged; laid on table.		
Goodshead, Charles	Payment of balance for stabling and hay furnished U. S. troops.	24	1	Petition	91	Claims	484	Adverse		Referred to 3d Auditor.		

List of private claims presented to the House of Representatives of the United States from the 1st to the 31st Congress, inclusive—Continued.

Names of claimants.	Nature or object of the claim.	Congress.	Session.	How brought before the House of Reps.	Page of journal.	To what committee of the House referred.	No. or date of the report.	Nature of the report.	No. of the bill.	How disposed of by the House of Reps.	How disposed of by the Senate.	Date of the act of Congress, and remarks.
Goodwill, Johnson	Payment of reward for apprehension of H. Bainbridge Coxe.	20	2	Resolution	66	P. Of. and P. Roads.	59	Favorable	396			
Goodwin, Aaron, heirs of	Payment of prize money	30	1	Petition	344	Rev. Claims				Laid on table.		
Goodwin, Abigail	(See Thomas Hammitt, heirs of).	30	1		344							
Goodwin, Amaziah	Pension	24	2	Petition	117	Naval Affairs	Dec. 28, 1836	Adverse		Laid on table.		
Goodwin, Amaziah	Pension	26	1	Petition	198	Invalid Pensions	355	Favorable	334			
Goodwin, Amaziah	Pension	27	2	Petition	60	Invalid Pensions	150	Favorable	197	Passed	Passed, with amendment.	App'd Aug. 29, 1842
Goodwin, Amaziah	Increase of pension	28	1	Resolution	315	Rev. Pensions	325	Favorable	233	Referred to Committee Whole House.		
Goodwin, Amaziah	Increase of pension	31	1	Petition	417	Invalid Pensions.						
Goodwin, Aquilla	Pension	27	2	Petition	255	Invalid Pensions	316	Favorable	285	Ref'd to Com. W. H.		
Goodwin, Aquilla	Pension	27	3	House bill	95	Whole House	Dec. 23, 1842	Favorable	285	Passed.		
Goodwin, Aquilla	Pension	28	1	Petition	284	Invalid Pensions.						
Goodwin, Aquilla	Pension	28	2	Petition	83	Invalid Pensions.						
Goodwin, Aquilla	Pension	29	1	Petition	107	Invalid Pensions	474	Favorable	352	Passed	Passed	App'd Aug. 8, 1846
Goodwin, Aquilla	Pension	30	1	Petition	156	Invalid Pensions	304	Adverse		Laid on table.		
Goodwin, Benjamin, executors of.	Indemnity for damage to property, and payment of rent for wharf house taken for public use.	3	2	Petition	294	Claims	Dec. 23, 1795	Adverse		Leave to withdraw.		
Goodwin, Benjamin, executors of.	Indemnity for damage to property, and payment of rent for wharf house taken for public use.	4	1	Petition	373	Claims	Feb. 22, 1795	Favorable		Referred to Committee Whole House.		
Goodwin, Benjamin, executors of.	Indemnity for damage to property, and payment of rent for wharf house taken for public use.	13	2	Petition	196	Pens. & Rev. Cl'ms.	Jan. 31, 1814	Favorable		Referred to Committee Whole House.		
Goodwin, Benjamin, executors of.	Indemnity for damage to property, and payment of rent for wharf house taken for public use.	16	1	Petition	210	Pens. & Rev. Cl'ms.	Feb. 21, 1820	Adverse		Rejected.		
Goodwin, Benjamin, executors of.	Indemnity for damage to property, and payment of rent for wharf house taken for public use.	20	1	Petition	167	Rev. Claims	154	Favorable	178	Referred to Committee Whole House.		
Goodwin, Benjamin, executors of.	Indemnity for damage to property, and payment of rent for wharf house taken for public use.	20	2	House bill	58	Whole House	Dec. 15, 1828	Favorable	178	Passed	Passed, with amendment.	App'd Feb. 5, 1829
Goodwin, Benjamin, executors of.	Additional compensation	21	1	Petition	54	Rev. Claims	314	Favorable	371	Referred to Committee Whole House.		
Goodwin, Benjamin, executors of.	Additional compensation	22	1	Petition	73	Rev. Claims	149	Favorable	228	Referred to Committee Whole House.		
Goodwin, Benjamin, executors of.	Additional compensation	22	2	House bill	92	Whole House	Dec. 22, 1832	Favorable	228	Passed	Passed	App'd March 2, 1833
Goodwin, Benjamin, administrator of.	Interest on amount allowed by acts of 5th February, 1829, and 2d March, 1833.	23	1	Petition	188	Rev. Claims.						
Goodwin, Benjamin, administrator of.	Interest on account allowed by acts of 5th February, 1829, and 2d March, 1833.	24	1	Petition	404	Rev. Claims	June 15, 1836	Adverse		Laid on table.		
Goodwin, Daniel	(See executor of Benjamin Goodwin.)	3	2		294							
Goodwin, Francis L. B., heirs of.	Commutation pay	25	2	Senate bill	763	Rev. Claims	May 11, 1838	Favorable	180	Referred to Committee Whole House.		
Goodwin, Francis L. B., heirs of.	Commutation pay	30	1	Memorial	1052	Rev. Claims.						

List of private claims presented to the House of Representatives of the United States from the 1*st to the* 31*st Congress, inclusive*—Continued.

Names of claimants.	Nature or object of the claim.	Congress.	Session.	How brought before the House of Reps.	Page of journal.	To what committee of the House referred.	No. or date of the report.	Nature of the report.	No. of the bill.	How disposed of by the House of Reps.	How disposed of by the Senate.	Date of the act of Congress, and remarks.
Goodwin, Francis L. B., heirs of.	Commutation pay	30	2	Petition	192	Rev. Claims.						
Goodwin, Francis L. B., heirs of.	Commutation pay	31	1	Petition	1072	Rev. Claims	455	Adverse		Laid on table.		
Goodwin, Isaac	Pension	26	1	Petition	175	Rev. Pensions.						
Goodwin, John	Pension	24	2	Petition	84	Rev. Pensions				Discharged; laid on table.		
Goodwin, John	Pension	25	2	Petition	984	Rev. Pensions				Discharged; laid on table.		
Goodwin, John	Pension	26	1	Petition	175	Rev. Pensions.						
Goodwin, Joseph	(See widow of Stephen Decatur, *et al.*)	20	1		295							
Goodwin, Lewis	Pension	31	1	Petition	1156	Invalid Pensions.						
Goodwin, Nathaniel, heirs of.	Pay and emoluments for revolutionary services.	11	2	Petition	179	Claims.						
Goodwin, Capt. Nathaniel, heirs of.	For seven years' half-pay	23	1	Resolution	42	Rev. Claims	Jan. 7, 1834	General bill	149	Passed	Passed, with amendment.	App'd June 30, 1834
Goodwin, Samuel	(See Absalom Tatom, executors of.)	13	3		700							
Goodwin, Samuel, *et al*	Payment for services on board private armed vessels.	27	2	Petition	96	Rev. Claims	531	Adverse		Laid on table.		
Goodwin, Samuel, *et al*	Payment for services on board private armed vessels.	28	1	Petition	517	Rev. Claims.						
Goodwin, Samuel, *et al*	Payment for services on board private armed vessels.	28	2	Petition	72	Rev. Claims.						
Goodwin, Samuel, *et al*	Payment for services on board private armed vessels.	29	1	Petition	904	Rev. Claims.						
Goodwin, Seth	Pension	21	2	Petition	80	Military Pensions.						
Goodwin, Simon	Pension	22	1	Petition	122	Rev. Pensions	Dec. 29, 1831	Adverse		Laid on table.		
Goodwin, Uriah	Pension	2	2	Petition	649	Whole House.						
Goodwin, Uriah	Pension	3	1	Rep. of Secretary War.	131	Select	May 26, 1794	Res. to refer to Sec. War.	J. R. 12	Passed	Passed	App'd June 9, 1794
Goodwin, Uriah	Pension	4	1	Rep. of Secretary War.	445	Claims	Feb. 18, 1796	General bill	156	Passed	Passed	App'd April 20, 1796
Goodwin, William	(See Banister Howe)	25	3		86							
Goodwyn, Samuel, *et al*	(See Samuel Goodwin)	13	3		700							
Goodwyn, William	Compensation for services in revolutionary war.	11	3	Petition	491	Claims.						
Goodwin, William B.	(See Thomas L. B. Goodwin, heir of.)	25	2		763							
Goodyear, Theophilus	Pension	3	1	Report Secretary War.	131	Select	May 26, 1794	Favorable	62	Passed	Passed	App'd June 7, 1794
Gooesbeck, Walter, P., widow of.	Pension	2	1	Petition	197	Claims	Mar. 2, 1830	Adverse		Laid on table.		
Gookin, Daniel, *et al*	That their claims for revolutionary services be allowed.	19	1	Petition	34	Select.						
Goolsby, John H.	Pension	28	1	Petition	218	Rev. Pensions	Jan. 31, 1844	Adverse		Laid on table.		
Goolsby, John H.	Pension	29	1	Petition	1072	Rev. Pensions				Discharged; laid on table.		
Goolsby, John H.	Pension	30	1	Petition	261	Rev. Pensions				Discharged; laid on table.		
Goolsby, John H.	Pension	30	2	Memorial	73	Rev. Pensions	4	Adverse		Laid on table.		
Goolsby, Reuben	Pension	14	1	House bill	622	Pens. & Rev. Cl'ms.	April 11, 1816	General bill	171	Passed	Passed	App'd April 30, 1816
Goorley, David	Payment of passage from Leghorn	21	2	Resolution	123	Claims.						

List of private claims presented to the House of Representatives of the United States from the 1st to the 31st Congress, inclusive—Continued.

Names of claimants.	Nature or object of the claim.	Congress.	Session.	How brought before the House of Reps.	Page of journal.	To what committee of the House referred.	No. or date of the report.	Nature of the report.	No. of the bill.	How disposed of by the House of Reps.	How disposed of by the Senate.	Date of the act of Congress, and remarks.
Goorley, David	Payment of passage from Leghorn	21	2	Petition	160	Claims.						
Goorley, David	Payment of passage from Leghorn	22	1	Petition	43	Naval Affairs.						
Goorley, David	Payment of passage from Leghorn	22	2	Resolution	71	Naval Affairs	Feb. 25, 1833	Adverse	......	Laid on table.		
Goorley, David	Payment of passage from Leghorn	23	1	Petition	160	Naval Affairs.						
Goorley, David	Payment of passage from Leghorn	23	2	Petition	110	Naval Affairs.						
Goorley, David	Payment of passage from Leghorn	24	1	Petition	100	Naval Affairs.						
Goorley, David	Payment of passage from Leghorn	24	2	Petition	325	Naval Affairs	289	Adverse	......	Laid on table.		
Gordon, Albin	Increase of pension	7	2	Petition	255	Claims	Jan. 11, 1803	Adverse	......	Rejected.		
Gordon, Anna	(See William Herrick, widow of)	29	2	....	74							
Gordon, Archibald	(See Joseph Gordon, heir of)	9	1	....	253							
Gordon, Charles	Compensation for services under Senate resolution, July, 1836.	24	2	Petition	...	....	....	Appropr'n bill.	......	....	....	Stat. at Large, vol. 5, p. 165.
Gordon, Charles	For services in making maps	26	1	Appropr'n bill	178	Ways and Means	....	....	27	Passed	Passed	App'd July 21, 1840
Gordon, Charles, (Me.)	For fishing bounty on the schooner Two Sons.	23	1	Petition	184	Commerce	186	Favorable	205	Referred to Committee Whole House.		
Gordon, Charles, *et al*	For fishing bounty on the schooner Two Sons.	23	2	House bill	82	Whole House	Dec. 15, 1834	Favorable	205	Passed	Passed	App'd Jan. 27, 1835
Gordon, Charles, *et al*	For fishing bounty on the schooner Two Sons.	27	2	Petition	319	Commerce	736	Favorable	413	Ordered to be engros'd		
Gordon, Charles, *et al*	For fishing bounty on the schooner Two Sons.	27	3	House bill	88	Whole House	....	Favorable	413	Passed	Passed	App'd March 3, 1843
Gordon, Christopher	Pension	28	2	Petition	251	Invalid Pensions.						
Gordon, Daniel, heirs of	Bounty land	27	2	Petition	533	Priv. Land Claims.						
Gordon, Elisha	Renewal of a lost loan office certificate.	4	1	Petition	457	Claims.						
Gordon, Elisha	Renewal of a lost loan office certificate.	4	2	Petition	668	Claims	Jan. 31, 1797	Adverse	......	Rejected.		
Gordon, Elisha	Renewal of a lost loan office certificate.	10	1	Petition	104	Whole House.						
Gordon, Elisha	Renewal of a lost loan office certificate.	12	2	Petition	678	Claims.						
Gordon, Elisha	Payment of loan office certificate	15	1	Petition	72	Pens. & Rev. Cl'ms.	Feb. 24, 1818	Adverse	......	Rejected.		
Gordon, Elisha	Payment of loan office certificate	15	2	Petition	102	Claims	....	....	......	Discharged; laid on table.		
Gordon, Elisha	Payment of loan office certificate	16	2	Senate bill	183	Pens. & Rev. Cl'ms.	Feb. 10, 1821	Adverse	S. 25	Laid on table.		
Gordon, Elisha	Payment of loan office certificate	17	1	Petition	100	Pens. & Rev. Cl'ms.	....	....	......	Discharged; laid on table.	....	Leave to withdraw, 1st sess., 19th Cong.
Gordon, Elisha, widow of.	Payment of loan office certificate	19	1	Senate bill	478	Whole House	May 12, 1826	Adverse	S. 107	Laid on table.		
Gordon, Elisha, widow of.	Payment of loan office certificate	19	2	Senate bill	305	Rev. Claims	Feb. 22, 1827	Adverse	S. 72	Referred to Committee Whole House.		
Gordon, Elisha, widow of.	Payment of loan office certificate	20	1	Senate bill	186	Rev. Claims	Feb. 4, 1828	Adverse	S. 42	Passed	Passed	App'd May 19, 1828
Gordon, George	Compensation for services as collector of revenue, and credit for half the proceeds of forfeited whiskey.	9	1	Petition and rep't Sec. Treasury.	297	....	....	....	......	Laid on table..		
Gordon, George	Confirmation of title to land	29	1	Senate bill	1075	Public Lands	....	....	87			
Gordon, George	Confirmation of title to land	29	2	Senate bill	307	Public Lands	Feb. 16, 1847	Favorable	56	Passed	....	App'd Feb. 25, 1847
Gordon, George	(See heirs of Matthew Ramey)	22	1	....	514							
Gordon, James	Pension	14	1	Res. and docs	440	Pens. & Rev. Cl'ms.	April 11, 1816	General bill	171	Passed	Passed, with amendment.	App'd April 30, 1816; petitioner's name left out.
Gordon, Jesse	Increase of pension	30	1	Petition	359	Rev. Pensions.						
Gordon, John, (Ky.)	(See William Robinson, *et al.*)	9	2	....	555							

List of private claims presented to the House of Representatives of the United States from the 1st to the 31st Congress, inclusive—Continued.

Names of claimants.	Nature or object of the claim.	Congress.	Session.	How brought before the House of Reps.	Page of journal.	To what committee of the House referred.	No. or date of the report.	Nature of the report.	No. of the bill.	How disposed of by the House of Reps.	How disposed of by the Senate.	Date of the act of Congress, and remarks.
Gordon, John, (Ohio)	Pension	30	1	Petition	739	Invalid Pensions	....	....	......	Discharged; laid on table.		
Gordon, John, (Ohio)	Pension	30	2	Petition	241	Invalid Pensions	80	Favorable	776			
Gordon, John, (Ohio)	Pension	31	1	Petition	425	Invalid Pensions.						
Gordon, John, *et al.*	Compensation for locating land warrants.	31	1	Petition	337	Public Lands.						
Gordon, John, *et al.*	(See William Rogers, heirs of)	23	1	....	376							
Gordon, John, heirs of	Compensation for revolutionary services.	23	1	Resolution	160	Rev. Claims.						
Gordon, John, heirs of	Compensation for revolutionary services.	24	1	Petition	104	Rev. Claims	....	....	......	Discharged; laid on table.		
Gordon, John, heirs of	Compensation for revolutionary services.	25	2	Petition	232	Rev. Claims.						
Gordon, Jonathan	Pension	27	2	Petition	784	Rev. Pensions	May 24, 1842	Adverse	......	Laid on table.		
Gordon, Joseph, heir of	Indemnity for losses in the commissary department.	9	1	Petition	258	Select.						
Gordon, Lewis	Pension	27	2	Petition	377	Invalid Pensions	622	Adverse	......	Laid on table.		
Gordon, Lewis	Pension	27	3	Petition	193	Invalid Pensions	140	Adverse	......	Laid on table.		
Gordon, Lewis	Pension	28	1	Petition	117	Invalid Pensions	Mar. 7, 1844	Adverse	......	Laid on table.		
Gordon, Martin, jr	Compensation as clerk in custom-house.	27	2	Petition	319	Commerce.						
Gordon, Martin, *et al.*	Compensation as clerk in custom-house.	27	3	Petition	44	Ways and Means.						
Gordon, Moses	(See William Robinson, *et al.*)	9	2	....	555							
Gordon, Morgan S	Payment of amount received of Brazilian government as indemnity for capture of schooner Sarah George.	23	1	Resolution	84	Ways and Means	148	Favorable	158	Passed	Passed, with amendment.	App'd June 30, 1834
Gordon, Nathaniel, *et al.*	Confirmation of title to land	1	1	Petition	66	Select	July 31, 1789	Adverse	......	Laid on table.		
Gordon, Patience	(See widow of Elijah Gordon)	19	1	....	478	....	....	....	S. 107			
Gordon, Powhatan	Payment for horses lost in United States service.	24	1	Documents	80	Claims.						
Gordon, R. H.	Increase of compensation	29	2	Memorial	67	P. O. & P. Roads.						
Gordon, Samuel	Pension for injuries in carrying mail.	11	2	Petition	144	....	....	....	......	Referred to Postmaster General.		
Gordon, Samuel	Pension for injuries in carrying mail.	15	1	Petition	35	Pens. & Rev. Cl'ms.	Jan. 5, 1818	Adverse	......	Rejected	....	Leave to withdraw, 1st session, 19th Cong.
Gordon, Samuel	Pension for injuries in carrying mail.	20	1	Petition	92	Rev. Claims	....	....	......	Discharged; leave to withdraw.		
Gordon, Samuel	Compensation for revolutionary services.	21	1	Petition	37	Military Pensions	....	....	......	Discharged; laid on table.		
Gordon, Samuel, *et al.*	Remission of tonnage duties	8	2	Petition	127	Com. and Manuf	Feb. 15, 1805	Favorable	62	Passed	Passed	App'd March 3, 1805
Gordon & Stoddard	Reimbursement of excess of duties	23	2	Petition	182	Commerce.						
Gordon & Stoddard	(See Benjamin Adams & Co.)											
Gordon, Susan E.	(See George Fisher)	29	2	....	374							
Gordon, Thomas, representative of.	Payment of certificate of paymaster general.	19	1	Resolution	391	Rev. Claims	....	....	......	Discharged; laid on table.		
Gordon, Thomas, representative of.	Payment of certificate of paymaster general.	19	2	Resolution	136	Rev. Claims.						
Gordon, Thomas, representative of.	Payment of certificate of paymaster general.	21	1	Petition	199	Rev. Claims	Feb. 10, 1830	Favorable	227	Referred to Committee Whole House.		
Gordon, Thomas, representative of.	Payment of certificate of paymaster general.	21	2	House bill	264	Whole House	July 4, 1831	Favorable	227	Passed.		

List of private claims presented to the House of Representatives of the United States from the 1st to the 31st Congress, inclusive—Continued.

Names of claimants.	Nature or object of the claim.	Congress.	Session.	How brought before the House of Reps.	Page of journal.	To what committee of the House referred.	No. or date of the report.	Nature of the report.	No. of the bill.	How disposed of by the House of Reps.	How disposed of by the Senate.	Date of the act of Congress, and remarks.
Gordon, Thomas, representative of.	Payment of certificate of paymaster general.	22	1	Petition	143	Rev. Claims	310	Favorable	390			
Gordon, Thomas, representative of.	Payment of certificate of paymaster general.	23	1	Petition	157	Rev. Claims.						
Gordon, Thomas, representative of.	Payment of certificate of paymaster general.	23	2	Petition	239	Rev. Claims.						
Gordon, Thomas, representative of.	Payment of certificate of paymaster general.	24	1	Petition	102	Rev. Claims	799	Favorable	716			
Gordon, Thomas, representative of.	Payment of certificate of paymaster general.	25	2	Resolution	39	Rev. Claims	120	Favorable	138	Postponed.		
Gordon, Thomas, representative of.	Payment of certificate of paymaster general.	26	1	Petition	166	Rev. Claims	330	Favorable	302			
Gordon, Thomas, representative of.	Payment of certificate of paymaster general.	27	3	Petition	188	Rev. Claims	237	Adverse	......	Laid on table.		
Gordon, Thomas	(See Nathaniel Tracy, representatives of.)											
Gordon, Thomas F	Settlement of accounts on principle of equity.	19	1	Petition	73	Claims	Mar. 10, 1826	Adverse	......	Referred to Secretary War.		
Gordon, Thomas F	Settlement of accounts on principle of equity.	21	1	Petition	294	Claims	....	....	......	Discharged; laid on table.		
Gordon, Thomas F	Settlement for index to documents, and digest of laws.	26	1	Petition	182	Library.						
Gordon, Thomas F	For aid in publishing several indexes to proceedings of both Houses of Congress.	28	1	Memorial	317	Ways and Means	April 10, 1844	Favorable	320	Referred to Committee Whole House.		
Gordon, Thomas F	For an appropriation to pay for his digest of United States laws.	30	1	Memorial	493	Ways and Means	....	General bill	298	Passed	Passed	App'd Aug. 12, 1848
Gordon, Thomasin	(See Col. John White, widow of)	1	1	....	88							
Gordon, William	(See Z. M. Pike, *et al.*)	10	1	....	189							
Gordon, William	Payment for tobacco burnt in warehouse by the British.	15	1	Petition	27	Claims	116	Adverse	......	Discharged; leave to withdraw.		
Gordon, William, widow of	Pension	24	2	Petition	74	Rev. Pensions	106	Adverse	......	Laid on table.		
Gordon, William, *et al*	For further time to settle accounts of LeRoy Opie.	16	2	Petition	137	Claims	Jan. 19, 1821	Favorable	212	Passed	Passed	App'd March 3, 1821
Gordon, William A	Compensation for services in quartermaster's department.	24	1	Senate bill	899	Claims	....	....	119			
Gordon, W. R., *et al.*	(See William Rogers, heirs of)	26	1	....	630							
Gore, Daniel	Pension	11	1	Petition	57	Claims.						
Gore, Obadiah	(See Timothy Pierce, administrators of.)	2	1	....	471							
Gore, Samuel	Pension	22	1	Petition	120	Rev. Pensions	....	....	......	Discharged; laid on table.		
Gore, William, Governor of Upper Canada.	Remission of duties on books	14	1	House bill	235, 628	Ways and Means	March 6, 1816	Favorable	......	Passed	Passed	App'd April 9, 1816
Gorey, George	Pension	30	2	Petition	181	Invalid Pensions	....	....	......	Disch'd; laid on table.		
Gorham, Allen	Compensation for services as ship carpenter.	27	2	Petition	247	Claims	644	Adverse	......	Laid on table.		
Gorham, Allen	Compensation for services as ship carpenter.	27	3	Petition	43	Claims	117	Adverse	......	Laid on table.		
Gorham, Allen	Compensation for services as ship carpenter.	28	1	Petition	98	Claims.						
Gorham, Allen	Compensation for services as ship carpenter.	28	2	Petition	47	Claims.						

List of private claims presented to the House of Representatives of the United States from the 1st to the 31st Congress, inclusive—**Continued.**

Names of claimants.	Nature or object of the claim.	Congress.	Session.	How brought before the House of Reps.	Page of journal.	To what committee of the House referred.	No. or date of the report.	Nature of the report.	No. of the bill.	How disposed of by the House of Reps.	How disposed of by the Senate.	Date of the act of Congress, and remarks.
Gorham, Allen	Compensation for services as ship carpenter.	29	2	Petition	49	Claims				Discharged; laid on table.		
Gorham, Allen	Compensation for services as ship carpenter.	30	1	Petition	145	Claims	242	Adverse		Laid on table.		
Gorham, James, wife of	Pension	17	2	Petition	165	Pens. & Rev. Cl'ms.				Discharged; laid on table.		
Gorham, Nathaniel	(See Nathaniel Gordon, *et al.*)	1	1		66							
Gorham, William	(See Marquis Quincy, *et al.*)	22	2		73							
Gorham, William	(See Marquis Quincy, *et al.*)	23	1		58							
Gorham, William	(See Marquis Quincy, *et al.*)	23	2		82							
Gorham, William	(See Marquis Quincy, *et al.*)	25	2		199							
Gorham, William	(See Marquis Quincy, *et al.*)	26	1		176							
Gorman, A. G.	(See A. Glassell, executors of)	31	1		232							
Gorman, John	Pension	30	1	Petition	208	Rev. Pensions	300	Adverse		Laid on table.		
Gorman, John B.	To be employed as painter to the Capitol.	18	2	Petition	287	Whole House.						
Gorman, Peter	Payment of balance due on contract.	29	1	Senate Joint resolution.	531	Claims	Mar. 10, 1846	Favorable	J. R. 17	Passed.		App'd May 29, 1846
Gorman, Peter	Payment for stone for Pennsylvania avenue.	31	1	Civil and diplomatic bill.	1034	Whole House		With amends.	334			App'd Sept. 30, 1850
Gorrill, Andrew	Pension	17	1	Rep't Committee	277	Whole House	Feb. 19, 1822	Favorable	91	Passed	Postponed.	
Gorrill, Andrew	Pension	17	2	Rep't Committee	48	Whole House	Dec. 16, 1822	Favorable	195	Passed	Postponed.	
Gorrill, Andrew	Pension	18	1	Petition	74	Pens. & Rev. Cl'ms.	Dec. 31, 1823	Favorable	35	Passed	Passed	App'd May 19, 1824
Gorrill, Andrew	Pension	20	1	Petition	124	Military Pensions	Mar. 10, 1828	Adverse		Laid on table.		
Gorrill, Andrew	Pension	22	1	Petition	414	Invalid Pensions				Discharged; laid on table.		
Gorsline, Richard, *et al.*	To be released from judgment for duties on a distillery.	15	1	Petition	418	Ways and Means				Discharged; laid on table.		
Gorton, Benjamin	Compensation for revolutionary services.	19	2	Petition	188	Rev. Claims.						
Gorton, Benjamin	Compensation for revolutionary services.	20	1	Petition	196	Rev. Claims	Jan. 30, 1828	Adverse		Laid on table.		Leave to withdraw.
Gorton, Benjamin	Compensation for revolutionary services.	22	1	Petition	106	Rev. Pensions.						
Gorton, Samuel, widow of	Payment for a horse taken for United States service.	24	1	Petition	203	Rev. Claims	June 21, 1836	Adverse		Laid on table.		
Goshel, Peter	Increase of pension	22	1	Petition	46	Naval Affairs.						
Goshel, Peter	Increase of pension	22	1	Petition	415	Naval Affairs.						
Goslee, Henry	Pension	12	2	Petition	617	Claims	Feb. 26, 1813	Adverse		Laid on table.		
Gosney, Peter	Payment for a horse lost in United States service.	20	2	Resolution	160	Claims				Discharged; laid on table.		
Goss, Comfort	Pension	22	1	Petition	255	Rev. Pensions	Mar. 13, 1832	Favorable	467	Passed	Indef. postp'd.	
Goss, Jonathan	Bounty land	18	1	Petition	238	Priv. Land Claims.						
Goss, Jonathan	Bounty land	19	1	Petition	224	Rev. Claims				Discharged; laid on table.		
Goss, Joseph	Compensation for revolutionary services.	4	2	Petition	701	Claims.						
Goss, Joseph	Compensation for revolutionary services.	5	2	Petition	102	Claims	Dec. 12, 1797	Adverse		Rejected.		
Goss, Joseph	Compensation for revolutionary services.	7	1	Petition	12	Claims	Dec. 16, 1801	Adverse		Rejected.		
Goss, Leonard, *et al*	Indemnity for property destroyed by Indians.	24	1	Petition	50	Claims	580	Adverse		Laid on table.		

List of private claims presented to the House of Representatives of the United States from the 1st to the 31st Congress, inclusive—Continued.

Names of claimants.	Nature or object of the claim.	Congress.	Session.	How brought before the House of Reps.	Page of journal.	To what committee of the House referred.	No. or date of the report.	Nature of the report.	No. of the bill.	How disposed of by the House of Reps.	How disposed of by the Senate.	Date of the act of Congress, and remarks.
Goss, Russell	Pension	29	1	Petition	573	Invalid Pensions.						
Goss, Russell	Pension	29	2	Petition	110	Invalid Pensions.						
Goss, Russell	Pension	30	1	Petition	117	Invalid Pensions	29	Favorable	26	Passed	Passed	App'd June 27, 1848
Gossage, Jared	Arrears of pension	23	1	Petition	72	Invalid Pensions	399	Favorable	418	Ref'd to Com. W. H.		
Gossage, Jared	Arrears of pension	23	2	House bill	336	Invalid Pensions	Feb. 6, 1835	Favorable	418	Passed	With amend.	
Gossage, Jared	Arrears of pension	24	1	Petition	202	Invalid Pensions.						
Gossage, Jared	Arrears of pension	24	2	Petition	86	Invalid Pensions.						
Gossage, Jared	Arrears of pension	25	2	Petition	486	Invalid Pensions				Discharged; laid on table.		
Gossage, Jared	Arrears of pension	26	1	Petition	327	Invalid Pensions				Discharged; laid on table.		
Gossage, Jared	Arrears of pension	26	2	Petition	77	Invalid Pensions	79	Adverse		Laid on table.		
Gossage, Jared	Arrears of pension	27	2	Petition	60	Invalid Pensions	130	Favorable	176	Passed	Indef. postp'd.	
Gossage, Jared	Arrears of pension	29	1	Petition	501	Invalid Pensions	495	Adverse		Laid on table.		
Gossline, Louis, heirs of	Indemnity for property confiscated in Canada.	23	1	Petition	491	Rev. Claims.						
Gott, Benjamin, and son	Reimbursement of additional duties.	16	1	Petition	284	Ways and Means	April 20, 1820	Adverse		Rejected.		Leave to withdraw.
Gott, George, *et al.*	For fishing bounty on the schooner May Flower.	23	1	Petition	239	Commerce						
Gott, George, *et al.*	For fishing bounty on the schooner May Flower.	23	2	Petition	196	Commerce	47	Favorable	637			
Gott, George, *et al.*	For fishing bounty on the schooner May Flower.	24	1	Petition	54	Commerce	51	Favorable	63	Passed	Passed	App'd June 23, 1836
Gott, William	Pension	30	1	Petition	698	Invalid Pensions	564	Favorable	464	Passed.		
Gott, William	Pension	30	2	House bill	605				464		Passed	App'd Mar. 3, 1849
Goudram, Nicholas	(See Antonio Segura, *et al.*)	24	1		907							
Gough, John, *et al*	For correction of error in land entry.	21	2	Senate bill	245	Priv. Land Claims.	Feb. 15, 1831	Favorable	104	Passed		App'd March 3, 1831
Gould, Asa	Pension	4	1	Rep. of Secretary War.	445	Claims	Mar. 14, 1796	General bill	156	Passed	Passed	App'd April 20, 1796
Gould, Asa	Increase of pension	12	1	House bill	361	Whole House	June 15, 1812	Favorable	138	Passed	Passed	App'd July 5, 1812
Gould, Asa, (N. Y.)	Pension	19	1	Petition	310	Military Pensions	164	Adverse.				
Gould, Asa, (N. Y.)	Pension	20	1	Petition	124	Military Pensions	Mar. 11, 1828	Adverse		Laid on table.		
Gould, Benjamin B	Pension	3	1	Rep. of Secretary War.	175					Laid on table.		
Gould, Benjamin B	Pension	3	2	Rep. of Secretary War.	262	Claims	Feb. 28, 1796	Favorable	130	Passed	Postponed.	
Gould, Benjamin B	Pension	4	1	Rep. of Secretary War.	445	Claims	Mar. 14, 1796	General bill	156	Passed.	Passed	App'd April 20, 1796
Gould, Betsey	Pension	29	1	Petition	292	Rev. Pensions.						
Gould, Daniel, *et al.*	Payment for military services late war.	14	1	Petition	83	Claims	Jan. 29, 1816	Favorable		Passed	Passed	App'd April 26, 1816
Gould, David, heirs of	Payment of claim for revolutionary services.	1	2	Petition and rep't of Sec. War.	231	Select	June 23, 1790	Favorable	79	Passed	Rejected.	
Gould, David, heirs of	Payment of claim for revolutionary services.	3	2	Petition	262	Claims	Feb. 27, 1795	Adverse		Laid on table.		
Gould, David, heirs of	Payment of claim for revolutionary services.	16	1	Petition	81	Whole House.						
Gould, David, heirs of	Payment of claim for revolutionary services.	25	2	Petition	81	Rev. Claims	952	Favorable	827	Passed.		
Gould, David, heirs of	Payment of claim for revolutionary services.	25	3	Petition	86	Rev. Claims	53	Favorable	942	Referred to Committee Whole House.		

List of private claims presented to the House of Representatives of the United States from the 1st to the 31st Congress, inclusive—Continued.

Names of claimants.	Nature or object of the claim.	Congress.	Session.	How brought before the House of Reps.	Page of journal.	To what committee of the House referred.	No. or date of the report.	Nature of the report.	No. of the bill.	How disposed of by the House of Reps.	How disposed of by the Senate.	Date of the act of Congress, and remarks.
Gould, David, heirs of	Payment of claim for revolutionary services.	26	1	Petition	165	Rev. Claims.						
Gould, Elias B	(See John B. Strong, attorney for heirs of.)	22	2		185							
Gould, John	Compensation for revolutionary services.	2	1	Petition	507					Referred to Secretary War.		
Gould, John, (N. Y.)	Pension	22	1	Petition	632	Rev. Pensions.						
Gould, John, widow of	For an amendment to the act of 23d August last.	27	3	Petition	70	Rev. Pensions.						
Gould, Josiah	(See John Soyer, heirs of.)	24	1		751							
Gould, Reuben	Compensation for revolutionary services.	1	3	Petition and rep Sec. of War.	337					Laid on table.		
Gould, Samuel H	Reimbursement of money paid for land.	28	1	Petition	840	Public Lands.						
Gould, Samuel H	Reimbursement of money paid for land.	28	2	Petition	112	Public Lands.						
Gould, Samuel H	Reimbursement of money paid for land.	29	1	Petition	125	Public Lands.						
Gould, Theodore	Pension	27	3	Petition	224	Invalid Pensions.						
Gould, Theodore	Pension	28	1	Petition	116	Invalid Pensions	59	Adverse		Laid on table.		
Gould, William	Arrears of pension	22	1	Petition	188	Rev. Pensions.						
Gould, William	Arrears of pension	22	2	Petition	151	Rev. Pensions				Disch'd; laid on table.		
Gould, William, *et al.*	Confirmation of a copy right to law reports.	22	1	Petition	54	Judiciary	Dec. 27, 1831	Favorable	131	Recom'd to Judiciary.		
Gould, William & George, sureties of.	Release from a judgment against them as bail.	29	1	Petition	411	Judiciary.						
Gould, William P	Compensation for services as register of land office at Tuscaloosa.	18	2	Petition	160	Claims				Discharged; leave to withdraw.		
Gould, William P	Compensation for services as register of land office at Tuscaloosa.	19	1	Senate bill	458	Public Lands	April 25, 1826	Favorable	61	Passed		App'd May 20, 1826
Goulding, John	Extension of patent	30	1	Petition	593	Patents	556	Favorable	466			
Goulding, John	Extension of patent	31	1	Petition	384	Patents.						
Goulding, Joshua	Extension of patent	13	2	Petition	230	Judiciary.						
Goumer, Mathias	Compensation for revolutionary services.	25	2	Petition	111	Rev. Claims				Discharged; laid on table.		
Goundie, G. H	To be allowed office rent at Basle, Switzerland.	30	2	Petition	235	Ways and Means.						
Gourjon, J	Drawback of duties on goods exported.	5	3	Petition	452	Com. and Manuf				Discharged; leave to withdraw.		
Gourley, Charles McD	Compensation for riding express in late war.	22	2	Resolution	273	Claims	Mar. 7, 1832	Adverse.				
Gourrege, Pierre	(See Benjamin Bird)	23	1									
Gouveneur, Joseph, executor of.	Indemnity for French spoliations prior to 1800.	26	1	Memorial	182	Foreign Affairs	343	Favorable; bill	319	Referred to Committee Whole House.		
Gouveneur, S	(See Jos. Goveneur, executors of.)	26	1		182							
Gove, Geo. B. R., (N. Y.)	That half of the forfeiture (of his goods from Canada) belonging to United States service, be paid to him, with expense of seizure.	16	1	Petition	267	Ways and Means				Discharged; laid on table.		
Gove, Geo. B. R., (N. Y.)	That half of the forfeiture (of his goods from Canada) belonging to United States service, be paid to him, with expense of seizure.	17	1	Petition	325	Ways and Means				Discharged; laid on table.		

List of private claims presented to the House of Representatives of the United States from the 1st to the 31st Congress, inclusive—Continued.

Names of claimants.	Nature or object of the claim.	Congress.	Session.	How brought before the House of Reps.	Page of journal.	To what committee of the House referred.	No. or date of the report.	Nature of the report.	No. of the bill.	How disposed of by the House of Reps.	How disposed of by the Senate.	Date of the act of Congress, and remarks.
Gove, Geo. B. R., (N. Y.)	That half of the forfeiture (of his goods from Canada) belonging to United States service, be paid to him, with expense of seizure.	17	2	Petition	60	Ways and Means	60	Favorable	209			
Gove, Geo. B. R., (N. Y.)	That half of the forfeiture (of his goods from Canada) belonging to United States service, be paid to him, with expense of seizure.	18	1	Petition	115	Ways and Means	Jan. 12, 1824	Favorable	50	Passed	Passed	App'd May 17, 1824
Gove, Jesse	To have money paid United States in error refunded.	20	2	Petition	176	Ways and Means				Discharged; laid on table.		
Gove, Jesse	To have money paid United States in error refunded.	21	1	Petition	58	Ways and Means	Feb. 15, 1830	Adverse		Laid on table.		
Gove, Jesse	To have money paid United States in error refunded.	21	2	Petition	160	Ways and Means.						
Gove, Jesse	To have money paid United States in error refunded.	23	1	Resolution	117	Ways and Means	204	Adverse		Laid on table.		
Gove, Nathaniel	Compensation for injuries in United States service.	1	2	Petition and rep't Sec. War.	162, 197	Whole House	April 26, 1796	General bill		Passed	Passed	App'd Aug. 11, 1790
Gove, Nathaniel	Increase of pension	11	2	Petition	195	Select				Discharged; referred to Secretary War.		
Gove, Nathaniel	Increase of pension	12	1	Petition	177	Select				Discharged.		
Gove, William	Pension	24	2	Petition	117	Naval Affairs	Dec. 28, 1836	Adverse		Laid on table.		
Gove, William	Pension	28	1	Petition	711	Naval Affairs	530	Favorable	408	Referred to Committee Whole House.		
Gove, William	Pension	28	2	House bill	344	Whole House	Feb. 7, 1845	Favorable	408	Passed.		
Gove, William	Pension	29	2	Petition	233	Naval Affairs.						
Gove, William	Pension	30	1	Petition	637	Naval Affairs	514	Favorable	441	Referred to Committee Whole House.		
Gove, William	Pension	30	2	House bill	318	Whole House	Jan. 26, 1849	Favorable	441	Passed.		
Gove, William	Pension	31	1	Petition	236	Naval Affairs	230	Favorable	225	Referred to Committee Whole House.		
Gove, William	Pension	31	2	House bill	182	Whole House	Jan. 24, 1851	With amend	225	Passed.		
Goven, Peter Marcus	(See Zachariah Schoonmaker)	17	1		38							
Gover, Daniel	Pension	19	1	Petition	268	Military Pensions	164	Adverse.				
Gover, ——	(See Van Gover)	26	1		182							
Governeur & Kemble	(See Isaac Lawrence, *et al.*)											
Govrot, Etienne	(See Etienne Parent, heirs of)	15	2		28							
Gowan, Charles	Pension	9	2	House bill	608	Whole House	Feb. 28, 1807	Favorable	216	Passed	Passed	App'd March 3, 1807
Gowan, David G.	Settlement of accounts; vouchers lost.	17	1	Petition	511	Claims				Discharged; laid on table.		
Gowell, Richard	Pension	24	2	Petition	267	Invalid Pensions				Discharged; laid on table.		
Gower, Robert	(See Wm. Kingsbury, assignee of)	30	1		525		837					
Graaf, John	Pension	3	1	Rep. of Secretary War.	131	Select	May 26, 1794	Favorable	62	Passed	Passed	App'd June 7, 1794
Grabill, Daniel, late widow of.	For benefit of act for widows and orphans.	19	1	Petition	366	Claims				Referred to 3d Auditor.		
Grace & Fuller	For bounty land	20	1	Resolution	465	Public Lands				Discharged; laid on table.		
Grace & Fuller	For bounty land	20	2	Resolution	52	Public Lands.						
Grace, John	Pension	2	1	Petition	528					Referred to Secretary War.		

List of private claims presented to the House of Representatives of the United States from the 1st to the 31st Congress, inclusive—Continued.

Names of claimants.	Nature or object of the claim.	Congress.	Session.	How brought before the House of Reps.	Page of journal.	To what committee of the House referred.	No. or date of the report.	Nature of the report.	No. of the bill.	How disposed of by the House of Reps.	How disposed of by the Senate.	Date of the act of Congress, and remarks.
Grace, John	Pension	2	2	Rep. of Secretary War.	649	Whole House.						
Grace, John	Pension	3	1	Rep. of Secretary War.	131	Select	May 26, 1794	Refer to Sec'ry War.	J. R. 12	Passed	Passed	App'd June 9, 1794
Grace, John	Pension	4	1	Rep. of Secretary War.	445	Claims.						
Grace, John	Pension	4	2	Rep. of Secretary War.	614	Claims.						
Grace, Samuel	For land in lieu of land sold for taxes.	19	2	Resolution	127	Public Lands.						
Grace, William	Payment for a horse stolen in United States service.	18	1	Resolution	220	Claims	May 3, 1824	Adverse	......	Laid on table.		
Gracia, John P.	Remission of duties on chain cables.	21	1	Petition	224	Ways and Means	Feb. 26, 1830	Adverse	......	Laid on table.		
Gracia, John P.	Remission of duties on chain cables.	21	2	Petition	128	Ways and Means	Jan. 11, 1831	Adverse	......	Laid on table.		
Gracia, John P.	Remission of duties on chain cables.	22	1	Petition	174	Ways and Means.						
Gracias, Joseph, widow of	Payment of horses and fire-arms taken by the Indians.	26	1	Petition	602	P. Of. and P. Roads.						
Gracias, Joseph, widow of	Relief in consideration of the murder of her husband.	27	2	Petition	382	Claims	712	Adverse	......	Laid on table.		
Gracie, Archibald	Relief from the operation of the French Berlin decrees.	18	1	Petition	60	Foreign Affairs.						
Gracie, Archibald	Redress for the capture of ship and cargo by the French government.	19	1	Petition	132	Foreign Affairs	202	Adverse	......	Laid on table.		
Gracie, W.	Indemnity for French spoliations prior to 1800.	26	1	Memorial	182	Foreign Affairs	343	Favorable; bill	391	Referred to Committee Whole House.		
Gracey, Robert	Pension	22	2	Resolution	169	Rev. Pensions	....	....	......	Discharged; laid on table.		
Gracy, William	Pension	30	1	Petition	208	Invalid Pensions	463	Adverse	......	Laid on table.		
Gracy, William	Pension	31	1	Petition	865	Invalid Pensions.						
Grady, Henry	To be released from contract	25	2	Petition	88	Claims.						
Grady, Henry	To be released from contract	25	3	Petition	87	Claims	141	Favorable	1008	Passed	Passed	App'd March 3, 1839
Grady, William	Increase of pension	18	2	Petition	32	Rev. Pensions	Feb. 14, 1825	Adverse	......	Laid on table.		
Grady, Younger	Increase of pension	13	1	House bill	56	Whole House	July 20, 1813	Favorable	31	Passed	Passed	App'd Aug. 2, 1813
Graeff, Jacob, widow of	To be released from interest on money due United States.	15	1	Petition	28	Ways and Means	51	Adverse	......	Recommitted.		
								Favorable	183	Passed	Passed	App'd April 20, 1818
Graff, Frederick C.	Relief from certain duties	24	1	Memorial	95	Ways and Means.						
Graff, Frederick C.	Relief from certain duties	25	2	Petition	72	Ways and Means.						
Graffam, Anna	(See Joshua Patfield, former widow of.)	28	2	....	212							
Graffam, Thomas	Pension	24	1	Petition	473	Invalid Pensions	June 22, 1836	Adverse	......	Laid on table.		
Grafford, Mary	Pension	27	3	Petition	422	Rev. Pensions.						
Graffton, James, widow of	Pension	27	3	Petition	317	Rev. Pensions.						
Gragg, Henry	Pension	23	1	Petition	113	Rev. Pensions	....	....	......	Discharged; leave to withdraw.		
Graham, Daniel	For compensation for services in land office.	24	2	Appropriat'n bill	......	....	....	....	......	....	....	App'd March 3, 1837
Graham, Daniel, *et al*	Compensation for revolutionary services.	3	1	Petition	49	....	....	....	......	Referred to Secretary Treasury.		

List of private claims presented to the House of Representatives of the United States from the 1st to the 31st Congress, inclusive—Continued.

Names of claimants.	Nature or object of the claim.	Congress.	Session.	How brought before the House of Reps.	Page of journal.	To what committee of the House referred.	No. or date of the report.	Nature of the report.	No. of the bill.	How disposed of by the House of Reps.	How disposed of by the Senate.	Date of the act of Congress, and remarks.
Graham, Daniel, *et al*	Compensation for revolutionary services.	3	2	Report of Secretary Treasury.	284	....	....	....	.....	Laid on table.		
Graham, Edward	Payment for services as teacher of Indians.	23	1	Petition	167	Indian Affairs	....	....	.....	Discharged; laid on table.		
Graham, Edward	Relief as late unsuccessful candidate for teacher of Indians.	24	1	Petition	66	Indian Affairs	....	....	.....	Discharged; laid on table.		
Graham & Fennel	Indemnity for damages by mail contract.	31	1	Petition	254	P. Of. & P. Roads.	38	Favorable	66	Passed.		
Graham, G., administrator of.	Indemnity for French spoliations prior to 1800.	26	1	Memorial	182	Foreign Affairs	343	Favorable; bill	319	Referred to Committee Whole House.		
Graham, George	(See George Greaham, widow of.)											
Graham, Hiram	Payment for horses and other property lost in public service.	24	1	Petition	430	Claims.						
Graham, Isaac	Pension	31	1	Petition	870	Invalid Pensions	392	Adverse	.....	Laid on table.		
Graham, James	(See William Whitehead, *et al*).	16	2	....	300							
Graham, James	Pension	21	1	Petition	447	Military Pensions	....	....	.....	Discharged; laid on table.		
Graham, James	Pension	21	2	Petition	68	Military Pensions.						
Graham, James, *et al.*	Payment for advertising land sales in New Orleans papers.	29	1	Petition	1162	Claims.						
Graham, James, *et al.*	Payment for advertising land sales in New Orleans papers.	30	1	Petition	108	Claims	Feb. 3, 1848	Adverse	.....	Laid on table.		
Graham, John	(See Robert Peebles & J. Graham.)	24	1	....	662							
Graham, John, widow of.	Pension	23	1	Petition	436	Rev. Pensions	....	....	.....	Discharged; laid on table.		
Graham, John, administrator of.	Indemnity for property taken for public use.	24	1	Petition	152	Claims	Feb. 5, 1836	Adverse	.....	Laid on table.		
Graham, John Lorimer	For credit in settlement of accounts for moneys overpaid.	30	1	Senate bill	719	P. Of. & P. Roads.	April 25, 1848	Favorable	194	Passed	....	App'd Aug. 14, 1848
Graham, Joseph	Pension	30	1	Resolution	329	Rev. Pensions.						
Graham, Joseph	Compensation as special agent to Paraguay.	30	1	House bill	523	Whole House	Jan. 22, 1848	Favorable	298	Passed	Passed	App'd Aug. 12, 1848
Graham, Richard, *et al.*	(See Elias T. Langham, sureties of.)	25	3	....	176							
Graham, Rignald, widow of.	Payment of money advanced United States revolutionary war.	23	2	Resolution	90	Rev. Claims	90	Adverse	91	Laid on table.		
Graham, Robert	(See A. St. Clair, heir of)	29	1	....	256							
Graham, Robert	Confirmation of title to land	26	1	Petition	364	Priv. Land Claims.						
Graham, Robert	Confirmation of title to land	26	2	Petition	106	Priv. Land Claims.	....	....	.....	Discharged; leave to withdraw.		
Graham, Robert	Confirmation of title to land	31	1	Petition	537	Priv. Land Claims.						
Graham, Robert	Reimbursement of money paid for land sold by United States.	28	1	Petition	83	Priv. Land Claims.						
Graham, Robert	Reimbursement of money paid for land sold by United States.	28	2	Petition	84	Priv. Land Claims.	180	Adverse	.....	Laid on table.		
Graham, Robert	Reimbursement of money paid for land sold by United States.	29	1	Petition	89	Priv. Land Claims.						
Graham, Robert	Reimbursement of money paid for land sold by United States.	30	1	Petition	493	Judiciary	....	....	.....	Laid on table.		
Graham, Stephen, heirs of.	Commutation pay	25	3	Petition	124	Rev. Claims.						
Graham, Stephen, heirs of.	Commutation pay	26	1	Petition	164	Rev. Claims	621	Adverse	.....	Laid on table.		
Graham, Stephen, heirs of.	Commutation pay	27	2	Petition	61	Rev. Claims	377	Adverse	.....	Laid on table.		
Graham, T., (Va.)	Indemnity for French spoliations prior to 1800.	26	1	Memorial	182	Foreign Affairs	343	Favorable; bill.	319	Referred to Committee Whole House.		

List of private claims presented to the House of Representatives of the United States from the 1st to the 31st Congress, inclusive—Continued.

Names of claimants.	Nature or object of the claim.	Congress.	Session.	How brought before the House of Reps.	Page of journal.	To what committee of the House referred.	No. or date of the report.	Nature of the report.	No. of the bill.	How disposed of by the House of Reps.	How disposed of by the Senate.	Date of the act of Congress, and remarks.
Graham, Thomas	Pension	11	2	Petition	277	Claims				Discharged; leave to withdraw.		
Graham, Thomas	Pension	12	1	Petition	24	Claims	Mar. 6, 1812	Adverse		Leave to withdraw.		
Graham, Thomas B	Indemnity for damage to flat boats by collision with United States ship Alleghany.	30	1	Petition	102	Claims	341	Favorable	321	Passed.		
Graham, Thomas B	Indemnity for damage to flat boats by collision with United States ship Alleghany.	31	1	Petition	1052	Claims.						
Graham, T., heirs of	Indemnity for French spoliations prior to 1800.	26	1	Memorial	182	Foreign Affairs	343	Favorable	319	Referred to Committee Whole House.		
Graham, Tidsley	Payment for bread baked for United States navy.	22	1	Petition	144	Claims.						
Graham, William	(See assignee of Thomas Dowler)	24	2		37							
Graham, William	(See widow of Stephen Decatur, *et al.*)	20	1		295							
Graham, William, (N. Y.)	Pension	19	1	Petition	203	Military Pensions	164	Adverse		Discharged; leave to withdraw.		
Graham, William, (N. Y.)	Pension	21	2	Petition	113	Military Pensions.						
Graham, William, (N. Y.)	Pension	22	1	Petition	35	Military Pensions				Discharged; laid on table.		
Graham, William, (Ct.)	For lots of land in Washington city in lieu of a house.	25	2	Petition	581	Dist. of Columbia				Discharged; laid on table.		
Graham, Wm., heirs of	Confirmation of title to land	22	2	Petition	246	Priv. Land Claims.						
Graham, Wm., heirs of	Confirmation of title to land	23	1	Petition	76	Priv. Land Claims.	210	Favorable	230	Ref'd to Com. W. H.		
Graham, Wm., heirs of	Confirmation of title to land	23	2	House bill	82	Whole House	Dec. 15, 1834	Favorable	230	Passed	Indef. postp'd.	
Graham, Wm., heirs of	Confirmation of title to land	24	1	Petition	121	Priv. Land Claims.	Jan. 19, 1830	Favorable	176	Passed.		
Graham, Wm., heirs of	Confirmation of title to land	25	2	Petition	374	Priv. Land Claims.	704	Favorable	677	Ref'd to Com. W. H.		
Graham, Wm., heirs of	Confirmation of title to land	25	3	House bill	380	Whole House	Jan. 26, 1839	Favorable	677	Passed	Passed, with amendment.	App'd March 3, 1839
Graham, Wm. C	(See Jos. R. Chandler, *et al*)	23	3		43							
Graham, Wm. C., *et al.*	To be allowed sundry credits on judgment.	27	3	Appropriation bill								App'd March 3, 1843
Graham, Wm., jr	Renewal of lost final settlement on loan office certificate.	2	1	Petition and rep. Sec. Treasury.	500	Select.						
Graham, Wm. M	Payment for services as acting Indian agent.	25	2	Letter of Secretary of War.	899	Indian Affairs.						
Graham, Wm. M	Payment for services as acting Indian agent.	26	1	Petition	180	Claims.						
Graham, Wm. M	Payment for services as acting Indian agent.	26	2	Petition	135	Claims.						
Graham, Wm. M	Payment for services as acting Indian agent.	27	2	Petition	99	Claims	347	Adverse		Laid on table.		
Graham & Williams	Payment for advertising land sales.	29	1	Petition	1162	Claims.						
Graham & Williams	Payment for advertising land sales.	29	2	Petition	372	Claims.						
Graham & Williams	Payment for advertising land sales.	30	1	Petition	108	Claims	168	Adverse		Laid on table.		
Gramillion, Francois, widow and heirs of.	Confirmation of title to land	29	2	Petition	92	Priv. Land Claims.	38	Favorable	626	Referred to Committee Whole House.		
Gramillion, Francois, widow and heirs of.	Confirmation of title to land	30	1	Petition	109	Priv. Land Claims.	182	Favorable	192	Passed	Passed	App'd Aug. 11, 1848
Gramling, Adam	Pension	22	1	Resolution	561	Rev. Pensions	472	Favorable	574	Referred to Committee Whole House.		
Grampus, schooner, widows, &c.	Compensation for naval service of officers, &c.	28	1	Petition	205	Naval Affairs	Aug. 11, 1844	By bill	36	Passed	Passed, with amendment.	App'd June 15, 1844

List of private claims presented to the House of Representatives of the United States from the 1st to the 31st Congress, inclusive—Continued.

Names of claimants.	Nature or object of the claim.	Congress.	Session.	How brought before the House of Reps.	Page of journal.	To what committee of the House referred.	No. or date of the report.	Nature of the report.	No. of the bill.	How disposed of by the House of Reps.	How disposed of by the Senate.	Date of the act of Congress, and remarks.
Granberry, John, administrator of.	Indemnity for French spoliations prior to 1800.	26	1	Memorial	182	Foreign Affairs	343	Favorable; bil	319	Referred to Committee Whole House.		
Granberry, Mary	Indemnity for French spoliations prior to 1800.	26	1	Memorial	182	Foreign Affairs	343	Favorable; bill	319	Referred to Committee Whole House.		
Grange, Gerritt, (La.)	(See Gerrit L. Dix)	21	1		66							
Granger, Charlotte	(See Frederick Granger, widow of)	31	1		1388							
Granger, Daniel	Increase of compensation as collector of customs.	15	1	Petition	190	Ways and Means				Discharged; laid on table.		
Granger, Daniel	Pension	24	1	Resolution	750	Rev. Pensions	Jan. 7, 1836	Favorable	687	Passed	Passed	App'd June 28, 1836
Granger, Daniel R.	Pension	29	1	Petition	766	Invalid Pensions				Discharged; laid on table.		
Granger, Enoch M.	(See Thomas W. Phelps, *et al*)	15	1		211							
Granger, Epaphras K.	Reimbursement of money paid J. Carver for land.	17	1	Petition	187	Public Lands				Discharged; laid on table.		
Granger, Erastus	To be exonerated from loss of public money.	14	1	Petition	339	Claims				Discharged; laid on table.		
Granger, Erastus	To be exonerated from loss of public money.	14	2	Petition	255	Claims				Discharged; laid on table.		
Granger, Erastus	To be exonerated from loss of public money.	15	1	Petition	199	Claims				Discharged; laid on table.		
Granger, Erastus	To be exonerated from loss of public money.	16	1	Petition	65	P. Of. & P. Roads.	Jan. 22, 1820	Adverse		Laid on table.		
Granger, Erastus	To be exonerated from loss of public money.	16	2	Petition	27	P. Of. & P. Roads.	Jan. 5, 1821	Adverse		Laid on table.		
Granger, Erastus	To be exonerated from loss of public money.	17	1	Petition	41	P. Of. and P. Roads.	Jan. 24, 1822	Adverse		Laid on table.		
Granger, Erastus	To be exonerated from loss of public money.	19	2	Petition	82	P. Of. and P. Roads.						
Granger, Erastus	To be exonerated from loss of public money.	20	1	Petition	485	Judiciary				Discharged; laid on table.		
Granger, Erastus	To be exonerated from loss of public money.	20	2	Petition	243	Judiciary	Feb. 29, 1829	Favorable		Referred to Committee Whole House.		
Granger, Erastus	To be exonerated from loss of public money.	21	1	Petition	84	Judiciary	29	Favorable	41	Passed	Passed	App'd April 2, 1830
Granger, Erastus, executor of.	Indemnity for property destroyed by British.	22	1	Petition	442	Claims	April 16, 1832	Adverse		Laid on table.		
Granger, Frederick, widow of.	Pension	31	1	Petition	1388	Rev. Pensions.						
Granger, Frederick, widow of.	Pension	31	2	Petition	431	Rev. Pensions	61	Adverse		Laid on table.		
Granger, Gideon, *et al*.	For compromise of their claims to land.	8	2	Memorial	28	Claims	Feb. 5, 1805	Favorable	49			
Granger, Jeremiah	Compensation for revolutionary services.	20	1	Petition	557	Rev. Claims.						
Granger, John Baptiste	Permission to locate land in Opelousas, Louisiana.	23	1	Petition	338	Priv. Land Claims.	305	Favorable	340			
Granger, John Baptiste	Permission to locate land in Opelousas, Louisiana.	24	1	Petition	121	Priv. Land Claims.	166	Favorable	173	Passed.		
Granger, John Baptiste	Permission to locate land in Opelousas, Louisiana.	24	2	Petition	49	Priv. Land Claims.	1	Favorable	759	Referred to Committee Whole House.		
Granger, John Baptiste	Permission to locate land in Opelousas, Louisiana.	25	2	Petition	43	Priv. Land Claims.						

List of private claims presented to the House of Representatives of the United States from the 1*st to the* 31*st Congress, inclusive*—Continued.

Names of claimants.	Nature or object of the claim.	Congress.	Session.	How brought before the House of Reps.	Page of journal.	To what committee of the House referred.	No. or date of the report.	Nature of the report.	No. of the bill.	How disposed of by the House of Reps.	How disposed of by the Senate.	Date of the act of Congress, and remarks.
Granger, John Baptiste...	Permission to locate land in Opelousas, Louisiana.	27	2	Petition	328	Priv. Land Claims.						
Granger, John Baptiste...	Permission to locate land in Opelousas, Louisiana.	28	1	Petition	904	Priv. Land Claims.						
Granger, John Baptiste...	Permission to locate land in Opelousas, Louisiana.	29	1	Petition	657	Priv. Land Claims.						
Granger, John Baptiste...	Permission to locate land in Opelousas, Louisiana.	30	1	Petition	305	Priv. Land Claims.						
Granger, John Baptiste...	Permission to locate land in Opelousas, Louisiana.	31	1	Petition	432	Priv. Land Claims.						
Granger, Justin	Pension	19	1	Petition	88	Military Pensions..	164	Adverse	......	Laid on table.		
Granger, Justin	Pension	20	2	Resolution	104	Military Pensions..	....	....	......	Discharged; laid on table.		
Granger, Justin	Pension	21	1	Petition	49	Military Pensions..	Jan. 5, 1830	General bill ..	72	....	....	Bill became a law, omitting petitioner's name.
Granger, Justin	Pension	21	2	Resolution	165	Military Pensions.						
Granger, Justin	Pension	22	1	Petition	329	Invalid Pensions ..	....	....	......	Discharged; laid on table.		
Granger, Dr. J	Indemnity for French spoliations prior to 1800.	26	1	Memorial	182	Foreign Affairs....	343	Favorable; bill	319	Referred to Committee Whole House.		
Granniss, Enos..........	Compensation for revolutionary services, and for bounty land.	15	1	Petition	199	Pens. & Rev. Cl'ms.	Feb. 18, 1818	Adverse	......	Rejected..........	....	Leave to withdraw.
Granniss, Enos, heirs of ..	For commutation pay	22	2	Resolution	273	Rev. Claims......	118	Favorable....	757			
Granniss, Enos, heirs of ..	For commutation pay	23	1	Petition	43	Rev. Claims......	117	Favorable	122	Passed	Passed	App'd June 30, 1834
Grant, Alexander........	Payment for a horse lost in United States service.	17	1	Petition	220	Claims	....	....	......	Discharged; laid on table.		
Grant, Alexander........	Payment for a horse lost in United States service.	20	1	Petition	127	Claims	Feb. 11, 1828	Adverse	......	Laid on table.		
Grant, Alexander.......	Payment for a horse lost in United States service.	25	2	Petition	921	Claims..........	May 25, 1838	Adverse	......	Laid on table.		
Grant, Alexander........	Reimbursement of money overpaid on land.	26	1	Petition	333	Public Lands.....	....	....	......	Discharged; laid on table.		
Grant, Alexander........	Reimbursement of money overpaid on land.	27	2	Petition	98	Public Lands.						
Grant, Benjamin, heir of..	For seven years' half-pay........	29	1	Petition	397	Rev. Claims......	....	....	......	Discharged; laid on table.		
Grant, Daniel, *et al*......	For bounty on the fishing schooner James Henry.	28	1	Petition	130	Commerce	138	Favorable	127	Passed.		
Grant, Daniel, *et al*......	For bounty on the fishing schooner James Henry.	28	2	Petition	110	Commerce	58	Favorable	537			
Grant, Daniel, *et al*......	For bounty on the fishing schooner James Henry.	29	1	House bill	392	Commerce	260	Favorable....	222			
Grant, Daniel, *et al*......	For bounty on the fishing schooner James Henry.	30	1	Petition	288	Commerce.						
Grant, David, attorney of..	Pension	4	1	Petition	383	Claims..........	Jan. 20, 1796	Adverse	......	Leave to withdraw.		
Grant, Edward	Pension	11	2	House bill	283	Whole House.....	Mar. 24, 1810	Favorable....	107	Passed	Passed	App'd April 27, 1810
Grant, Elisha...........	Pension	21	2	Petition	336	Military Pensions.						
Grant, Forbes, & Co	(See James G. Forbes, *et al*.)....	10	1	....	159							
Grant, James	Compensation for losses and expenses as witness in the case of Senator W. Blount.	5	2	Petition	96	Claims..........	May 24, 1798	Adverse	......	Laid on table.		
Grant, Jas. H., *et al*.....	Payment for military services	25	2	Petition	279	Military Affairs ...	746	Favorable	708	Ref'd to Com. W. H.		
Grant, Jas. H., *et al*.....	Payment for military services	25	3	House bill	380	Whole House.....	Jan. 26, 1839	Favorable	708	Passed	Passed	App'd March 3, 1839

List of private claims presented to the House of Representatives of the United States from the 1st to the 31st Congress, inclusive—**Continued.**

Names of claimants.	Nature or object of the claim.	Congress.	Session.	How brought before the House of Reps.	Page of journal.	To what committee of the House referred.	No. or date of the report.	Nature of the report.	No. of the bill.	How disposed of by the House of Reps.	How disposed of by the Senate.	Date of the act of Congress, and remarks.
Grant, Jesse	Pension	3	2	Rep. of Secretary War.	278	Claims.						
Grant, Jesse	Pension	4	1	Rep. of Secretary War.	445	Claims.						
Grant, Jesse	Pension	4	2	Rep. of Secretary War.	614	Claims.						
Grant, John M., administrator of.	Indemnity for damages to property by United States troops.	15	1	Petition	371	Claims.						
Grant, John M., administrator of.	Indemnity for damages to property by United States troops.	17	1	Petition	92	Claims.						
Grant, John M., administrator of.	Indemnity for damages to property by United States troops.	17	2	Petition	77	Claims	Jan. 6, 1823	Adverse		Referred to Committee Whole House.		
Grant, John, jr., *et al.*	Compensation as commissioners to erect piers in Oswego harbor, on Lake Ontario.	22	1	Petition	97	Claims	Jan. 23, 1832	Adverse		Laid on table.		
Grant, Joseph	Renewal of patent	23	1	Petition	37	Judiciary				Discharged; laid on table.		
Grant, Joseph	Renewal of patent	23	2	Senate bill	456	Judiciary	Mar. 2, 1835	Favorable	113			
Grant, Joseph	Renewal of patent	24	1	Senate bill	1152	Patents			103			
Grant, J. P., *et al.*	Bounty land	31	1	Petition	412	Public Lands.						
Grant, Peter M.	(See Jacob Philips, executor of.)	30	2		224							
Grant, Robert	To have interest on money refunded.	23	1	Petition	138	Public Lands.						
Grant, Robert	To have interest on money refunded.	23	2	Petition	238	Claims.						
Grant, Robert	To have interest on money refunded.	24	1	Petition	508	Claims	539	Favorable		Referred to Commissioner General Land office.		
Grant, Robert	For an appropriation to try experiments with his gas in light-houses.	27	2	Petition	916	Commerce.						
Grant, Sever, & Co.	Reimbursement of excessive duties	23	2	Petition	182	Commerce.						
Grant, Seth	(See Daniel Grant, *et al.*)	28	1		130							
Grant, Thomas, surviving partner of Grant & Fine	Payment for mahogany taken by United States government.	2	1	Petition	560					Referred to Secretary Treasury.		
Grant, Thomas, surviving partner of Grant & Fine.	Payment for mahogany taken by United States government.	2	2	Rep. of Secretary Treasury.	626					Referred to Committee Whole House.		
Grant, Lieutenant, U. S. A.	To be released from paying money to government which was stolen in Mexico.	30	2	Memorial	345	Military Affairs.						
Grant, Lieutenant, U. S. A.	To be released from paying money to government which was stolen in Mexico.	31	1	Petition	1073	Military Affairs.						
Grant, Vincent	Indemnity for property destroyed by enemy.	15	2	Senate bill	334	Claims			84			
Grant, Vincent	Indemnity for property destroyed by enemy.	17	1	Petition	164	Claims				Discharged; laid on table.		
Grant, Vincent	Indemnity for property destroyed by enemy.	18	1	Petition	130	Claims	Jan. 28, 1824	Adverse		Laid on table.		
Grantland, Seaton	(See Charles Williamson, administrator of.)	23	1		211							
Grantland, Seaton	(See Farrish Carter, *et al.*)	24	1		65							
Grapps, James	(See Jacques Toutant.)	22	1		64							

List of private claims presented to the House of Representatives of the United States from the 1st to the 31st Congress, inclusive—Continued.

Names of claimants.	Nature or object of the claim.	Congress.	Session.	How brought before the House of Reps.	Page of journal.	To what committee of the House referred.	No. or date of the report.	Nature of the report.	No. of the bill.	How disposed of by the House of Reps.	How disposed of by the Senate.	Date of the act of Congress, and remarks.
Grass, Antoine	Confirmation of Spanish grant of land.	19	1	Senate bill	529	Priv. Land Claims.	Mar. 29, 1826	Favorable	138	Laid on table.		
Grass, A., heirs of	Confirmation of Spanish grant of land.	20	1	Petition	52	Priv. Land Claims.						
Grass, A., heirs of	Confirmation of Spanish grant of land.	21	1	Petition	202	Priv. Land Claims.						
Grass, Daniel	Pension	19	1	Petition	73	Military Pensions	164	Adverse		Laid on table		Leave to withdraw papers.
Grass, J. L., *et al.*	(See A. Grass, heirs of.)	20	1		52							
Grasse, Charles P.	Grant of land	17	2	Petition	87	Public Lands				Discharged; laid on table.		
Gratiot, Lieutenant Colonel Charles.	Compensation for extra services	18	1	Petition	93	Military Affairs				Discharged; laid on table.		
Gratiot, Charles, administrator of.	Confirmation of title to land	15	1	Petition	312	Priv. Land Claims.				Discharged; laid on table.		
Gratiot, Charles, administrator of.	Confirmation of title to land	15	2	Petition	44	Priv. Land Claims.						
Gratiot, Charles, administrator of.	Confirmation of title to land	16	1	Petition	71	Priv. Land Claims.						
Gratiot, Charles, administrator of.	Confirmation of title to land	17	1	Petition	54	Public Lands.						
Gratiot, Charles, administrator of.	Confirmation of title to land	18	1	Petition	54	Public Lands	Jan. 16, 1824	General bill	65	Passed	Passed	App'd May 26, 1824
Gratiot, Charles, heir of	Confirmation of title to land	20	2	Petition	79	Priv. Land Claims.				Leave to withdraw.		
Gratiot, Henry	Compensation for negotiating Indian treaties.	21	1	Petition				Approp'n bill.				Statutes at Large, vol. 4, p. 394.
Gratiot, Henry, administrator of.	Compensation for services and for property lost in Indian war.	24	2	Petition	266	Indian Affairs.						
Gratiot, Henry, administrator of.	Compensation for services and for property lost in Indian war.	25	2	Petition	120	Indian Affairs	1053	Favorable	889	Referred to Committee Whole House.		
Gratiot, Henry, administrator of.	Compensation for services and for property lost in Indian war.	25	3	House bill	432	Whole House	441	Favorable	889	Passed	Passed	App'd March 3, 1839
Gratiot, Susan, & J. P. B.	Indemnity for rents of lead mines.	27	2	Petition	455	Claims.						
Gratiot, Susan, & J. P. B.	Indemnity for rents of lead mines.	28	2	Petition	164	Claims.						
Gratiot, Susan, & J. P. B.	Indemnity for rents of lead mines.	29	1	Petition	92	Claims.						
Gratiot, Susan, & J. P. B.	Indemnity for rents of lead mines.	30	1	Petition	219	Claims	591	Favorable	470	Passed	Passed	App'd Aug. 14, 1848
Graton, James	Pension	18	2	Documents	52	Rev. Pensions		Adverse		Laid on table.		
Graton, James	Pension	19	1	Petition	43	Rev. Pensions	164	Adverse		Laid on table.		
Gratz, Michael, administrator of.	Payment of loan office certificates.	16	2	Petition	112	Pens. & Rev. Cl'ms.	Jan. 17, 1821	Adverse		Rejected.		
Gratz, Michael, administrator of.	Payment of loan office certificates.	22	2	Petition	74	Rev. Claims.						
Gratz, Michael, heir of	Payment of loan office certificates.	23	1	Petition	42	Rev. Claims	71	Favorable	81	Passed	Passed	App'd June 27, 1834
Grauberry, John, (Va.) administrator of.	Indemnity for French spoliations prior to 1800.	26	1	Memorial	182	Foreign Affairs	343	Favorable; bill	319	Referred to Committee Whole House.		
Graves, Abraham	Pension	17	2	Petition	74	Pens. & Rev. Cl'ms.	Jan. 8, 1823	Adverse		Rejected.		
Graves, Asa, widow of	Pension	21	1	Petition	104	Military Pensions	April 2, 1830	Adverse		Laid on table.		
Graves, Balcus	Compensation for discovery of a cure for the milk disease.	23	1	Petition	196	Agriculture.						
Graves, Ebenezer	Increase of pension	23	1	Petition	308	Rev. Pensions				Discharged; laid on table.		
Graves, George E.	Indemnity for losses by carrying mail.	29	1	Petition	285	Claims	275	Adverse		Laid on table.		

List of private claims presented to the House of Representatives of the United States from the 1st to the 31st Congress, inclusive—Continued.

Names of claimants.	Nature or object of the claim.	Congress.	Session.	How brought before the House of Reps.	Page of journal.	To what committee of the House referred.	No. or date of the report.	Nature of the report.	No. of the bill.	How disposed of by the House of Reps.	How disposed of by the Senate.	Date of the act of Congress, and remarks.
Graves, James, (N. Y.)	Pension	22	1	Petition	416	Rev. Pensions	410	Favorable	510			
Graves, John	Compensation for revolutionary services and supplies.	3	1	Petition	29	Select.						
Graves, John, *et al.*	Pre-emption right to land	27	2	Petition	620	Public Lands.						
Graves, Joseph	Compensation for revolutionary services.	4	1	Petition	425	Claims	May 7, 1796	Adverse	......	Rejected.		
Graves, Lewis, widow of	Increase of pension	28	1	Petition	357	Rev. Pensions	......	......	......	Discharged; laid on table.		
Graves, Richard	Payment for a horse and equipments lost in United States service.	23	1	Documents	154	Claims.						
Graves, Richard	Payment for a horse and equipments lost in United States service.	28	1	Petition	262	Claims.						
Graves, Samuel	Pension	28	2	Petition	355	Naval Affairs.						
Graves, Samuel	Pension	29	1	Petition	739	Naval Affairs.						
Graves, Samuel	Pension	29	2	Petition	132	Naval Affairs	33	Favorable	617			
Graves, Samuel	Pension	30	1	Petition	758	Naval Affairs	718	Favorable	563	Referred to Committee Whole House.		
Graves, Samuel	Pension	30	2	House bill	319	Whole House	Jan. 26, 1849	Favorable	563	Passed.		
Graves, Samuel	Pension	31	1	Petition	434	Naval Affairs	88	Favorable	109			
Graves, Samuel, sister of	Compensation for naval services	24	2	Petition	397	Invalid Pensions.						
Graves, Samuel, widow of	Pension	25	2	Petition	1209	Rev. Pensions.						
Graves, Samuel, widow of	Pension	25	3	Petition	217	Rev. Pensions.						
Graves, Samuel, widow of	Pension	26	1	Petition	283	Rev. Pensions.						
Graves, Samuel, widow of	Pension	26	2	Petition	35	Rev. Pensions	54	Adverse	......	Laid on table.		
Graves, Samuel, widow of	Pension	27	2	Petition	97	Rev. Pensions	784	Adverse	......	Laid on table.		
Graves, Thomas	Indian spoliations	20	1	Appropriation bill	......	......	......	......	......	......	......	Statutes at Large, vol. 4, p. 301.
Graves, Thomas, (Ky.)	Payment for services as express rider in revolutionary war.	23	1	Petition	655	Rev. Claims.						
Graves, Thomas, (Ky.)	Payment for services as express rider in revolutionary war.	24	1	Petition	105	Rev. Claims	564	Adverse	......	Laid on table.		
Graves, Thomas, (Ky.)	Payment for services as express rider in revolutionary war.	24	2	Petition	42	Rev. Claims	81	Adverse	......	Laid on table.		
Graves, Thomas, (Ky.)	Payment for services as express rider in revolutionary war.	25	2	Petition	393	Rev. Claims	765	Adverse	......	Laid on table.		
Graves, Thomas, (Ky.)	Payment for services as express rider in revolutionary war.	27	2	Petition	73	Rev. Claims	199	Adverse	......	Laid on table.		
Graves, Thomas, (Ky.)	Pension	28	1	Petition	623	Rev. Claims.						
Graves, Thomas, heirs of, (Va.)	Payment for property taken for use of United States army.	24	2	Petition	215	Rev. Claims.						
Graves, William	Payment for beef furnished United States army.	24	1	Petition	775	Rev. Claims	June 21, 1836	Adverse	......	Laid on table.		
Graves, William	Payment for beef furnished United States army.	24	2	Petition	40	Rev. Claims.						
Gray, Alexander	Compensation for revolutionary services.	13	1	Petition	31	Claims.						
Gray, Alexander	Compensation for revolutionary services.	14	1	House bill	622	Pens. & Rev. Cl'ms.	April 11, 1816	General bill	171	Passed	Passed	App'd April 30, 1816
Gray, Alexander	Pension	19	2	Petition	242	Military Pensions.						
Gray, Alexander M.	Increase of pension	21	1	Petition	294	Military Pensions	Mar. 26, 1830	Adverse	......	Laid on table.		

List of private claims presented to the House of Representatives of the United States from the 1st to the 31st Congress, inclusive—Continued.

Names of claimants.	Nature or object of the claim.	Congress.	Session.	How brought before the House of Reps.	Page of journal.	To what committee of the House referred.	No. or date of the report.	Nature of the report.	No. of the bill.	How disposed of by the House of Reps.	How disposed of by the Senate.	Date of the act of Congress, and remarks.
Gray, Amos	Pension	2	2	Rep. of Secretary War.	649	Whole House.						
Gray, Amos	Pension	3	1	Rep. of Secretary War.	131	Select	May 26, 1794	To refer to Sec. War.	J. R. 12	Passed	Passed	App'd June 9, 1794
Gray, Amos	Pension	4	1	Rep. of Secretary War.	445	Claims.						
Gray, Amos	Pension	4	2	Rep. of Secretary War.	614	Claims.						
Gray, Andrew	Pension	24	1	Petition	475	Rev. Pensions	April 12, 1836	Favorable	547	Passed	Passed	App'd June 28, 1836
Gray, Ann	Commutation pay due her deceased son.	5	2	Petition	89	Claims	Nov. 30, 1797	Adverse		Rejected.		
Gray, Brevity	For money in lieu of bounty land.	19	2	Resolution	299	Rev. Claims.						
Gray, Daniel	Payment for supplies furnished United States army.	2	1	Petition	491					Referred to Secretary War.		
Gray, Daniel	Payment for supplies furnished United States army.	3	2	Rep. of Secretary Treasury.	284					Laid on table.		
Gray, Daniel	Payment for supplies furnished United States army.	21	2	Resolution	283	Military Pensions.						
Gray, Daniel	Payment for supplies furnished United States army.	22	1	Petition	124	Rev. Pensions	365	Favorable	460	Passed	Indef. postp'd.	
Gray, David	Pension	23	1	Petition	53	Rev. Pensions.						
Gray, David	Pension	24	1	Petition	213	Rev. Pensions.						
Gray, Ebenezer, widow of.	Compensation for revolutionary services.	19	1	Petition	205	Rev. Claims	April 12, 1826	Adverse		Laid on table.		
Gray, Ebenezer, widow of.	Pension	20	2	Petition	118	Military Pensions.				Discharged; laid on table.		
Gray, Ebenezer, widow of.	Pension	21	1	Petition	128	Rev. Claims				Discharged; laid on table.		
Gray, Ebenezer, widow of.	Pension	21	2	Petition	43	Select.						
Gray, Ebenezer, widow of.	Pension	22	1	Petition	518	Rev. Claims				Discharged; laid on table.		
Gray, Ebenezer, widow of.	Pension	22	2	Petition	40	Rev. Claims				Discharged; laid on table.		
Gray, Ebenezer, widow of.	Pension	23	1	Petition	54	Rev. Claims.						
Gray, Ebenezer, widow of.	Pension	23	2	Petition	128	Rev. Pensions.						
Gray, Ebenezer, heir of	Pension	28	1	Petition	99	Rev. Claims.						
Gray, Ebenezer, heir of	Commutation pay	31	1	Senate bill	1430	Whole House			322			Postponed to 2d Dec. next.
Gray, Ebenezer, heir of	Commutation pay	31	2	Petition	269	Rev. Pensions	40	Favorable	J. R. 40	Referred to Committee Whole House.		
Gray, Edward	Indemnity for French spoliations prior to 1800.	26	1	Memorial	182	Foreign Affairs	343	Favorable; bill	319	Referred to Committee Whole House.		
Gray, Elliot	(See F. & William Brewster, *et al.*)	21	1		151							
Gray, Francis C	Indemnity for French spoliations prior to 1800.	26	1	Memorial	182	Foreign Affairs	343	Favorable; bill	319	Referred to Committee Whole House.		
Gray, Francis	Pension	9	1	Petition	234	Claims	Mar. 28, 1806	Adverse		Indefinitely postponed.		**Leave to withdraw.**
Gray, George	Extension of patent	22	1	Petition	114	Select	April 20, 1832	Favorable		Referred to Committee Whole House.		
Gray, George	Extension of patent	24	1	Petition	926	Patents.						
Gray, George	Extension of patent	25	2	Petition	731	Patents.						
Gray, George	Extension of patent	25	3	Petition	209	Patents				Discharged; laid on table.		

List of private claims presented to the House of Representatives of the United States from the 1st to the 31st Congress, inclusive—Continued.

Names of claimants.	Nature or object of the claim.	Congress.	Session.	How brought before the House of Reps.	Page of journal.	To what committee of the House referred.	No. or date of the report	Nature of the report.	No. of the bill.	How disposed of by the House of Reps.	How disposed of by the Senate.	Date of the act of Congress, and remarks.
Gray, Capt. George, heirs of.	Commutation pay	23	1	Petition	110	Rev. Claims.						
Gray, Capt. George, heirs of.	Commutation pay	24	1	Petition	213	Rev. Claims	326	Adverse		Laid on table.		
Gray, Lieut George R.	Indemnity for losses by the burning of the United States frigate Missouri.	28	1	Petition	352	Naval Affairs.						
Gray, Gideon	Pension	22	1	Petition	219	Rev. Pensions	March 1, 1832	Adverse		Laid on table.		
Gray, Henry W.	Compensation for military services, and pay for arms and equipments lost.	23	1	Petition	141	Claims	182	Adverse		Laid on table.		
Gray, Hilliard & Co.	Compensation for printing infantry tactics.	22	3	Appropriation bill								Stat. at Large, vol. 4, page 627.
Gray, Isaac	(See James Heath, heirs of)	28	1		724							
Gray, Isaac	Pension	13	3	House bill	740	Whole House	Mar. 1, 1815	Favorable	303	Passed	Passed	App'd March 3, 181
Gray, Jacob	Pension	21	1	Petition	231	Military Pensions	April 7, 1830	Adverse		Laid on table.		
Gray, James	Commutation pay	2	1	Petition	537					Referred to Secretary War.		
Gray, James	Commutation pay	2	2	Rep. of Secretary War.	696					Laid on table.		
Gray, James, (Pa.)	Pension	27	2	Petition	218	Invalid Pensions	Mar. 8, 1842	Adverse		Laid on table.		
Gray, James, (Pa.)	Pension	27	3	Petition	58	Invalid Pensions	33	Favorable	• 656	Passed	Passed	App'd March 3, 1843
Gray, James, mother of	Commutation pay due her deceased son.	5	2	Petition	89	Claims	Nov. 30, 1797	Adverse		Rejected.		
Gray, James, representat's of.	Commutation pay	22	2	Resolution	116	Rev. Claims.						
Gray, James W.	(See Dr. John Gray, heirs of)	25	2		120							
Gray, Jedediah	Pension	31	1	Petition	788	Invalid Pensions.						
Gray, Jeremiah	Pension	30	1	Petition	138	Invalid Pensions.						
Gray, John	(See Wm. Gray, and others)	18	1		238							
Gray, John	Pension	22	1	Petition	574	Rev. Pensions	Jan. 10, 1832	Adverse		Laid on table.		
Gray, John	Payment for horses taken for United States service.	22	1	Resolution	140	Claims	Jan. 10, 1832	Adverse		Laid on table.		
Gray, Dr. John, heirs of.	Indemnity for property destroyed by military forces of the United States.	25	2	Petition	120	Claims.						
Gray, Dr. John, heirs of.	Indemnity for property destroyed by military forces of the United States.	25	3	Petition	86	Claims	165	Adverse		Laid on table.		
Gray, Dr. John, heirs of.	Indemnity for property destroyed by military forces of the United States.	26	1	Petition	335	Claims	306	Favorable	268	Referred to Committee Whole House.		
Gray, Dr. John, heirs of.	Indemnity for property destroyed by military forces of the United States.	28	1	Petition	511	Claims.						
Gray, Dr. John, heirs of.	Indemnity for property destroyed by military forces of the United States.	28	2	Petition	56	Claims	197	Adverse		Laid on table.		
Gray, Dr. John, heirs of.	Indemnity for property destroyed by military forces of the United States.	29	1	Petition	90	Claims	131	Favorable	136	Passed	Passed	App'd August 8, 1846
Gray, John C.	(See William Gray)	26	1		182							
Gray, John V.	Confirmation of title to land	28	1	Petition	527	Priv. Land Claims.						

List of private claims presented to the House of Representatives of the United States from the 1st to the 31st Congress, inclusive—Continued.

Names of claimants.	Nature or object of the claim.	Congress.	Session.	How brought before the House of Reps.	Page of journal.	To what committee of the House referred.	No. or date of the report.	Nature of the report.	No. of the bill.	How disposed of by the House of Reps.	How disposed of by the Senate.	Date of the act of Congress, and remarks.
Gray, Joseph	Pension	22	1	Petition	556	Rev. Pensions				Discharged; laid on table.		
Gray, Joseph, *et al*	Payment for horses lost in United States service.	25	3	Petition	205	Claims.						
Gray, Mary	(See Philipina Beckley, heirs of)	11	2		227							
Gray & Morrel	(See Charles Josslyn)	21	1		270							
Gray, Presley	Payment for transporting forage	22	2	Resolution	155	Military Affairs	90	Adverse		Laid on table.		
Gray, Presley	Pension	24	2	Petition	49	Rev. Pensions	54	Favorable	803	Referred to Committee Whole House.		
Grey, Presley	Pension	25	2	Petition	38	Rev. Pensions	269	Favorable	312	Passed	Adverse.	
Gray, Presley	Pension	26	1	Petition	172	Rev. Pensions	461	Favorable	375	Referred to Committee Whole House.		
Gray, Presley	Pension	27	2	Petition	390	Rev. Pensions	290	Favorable	258	Passed	Indef. postp'd.	
Gray, Presley	Pension	27	3	Petition	74	Rev. Pensions				Discharged; laid on table.		
Gray, Robert	Pension	22	2	Petition	442	Rev. Pensions				Discharged; laid on table.		
Gray, Robert, widow of	Compensation for revolutionary services and the discovery of Columbia river.	29	1	Petition	600	Rev. Pensions	456	Favorable	333			
Gray, Robert, widow of	Compensation for revolutionary services and the discovery of Columbia river.	30	1	Petition	543	Public Lands	502	Favorable	420			
Gray, Sampson, heirs of	To be allowed to correct error in land entry.	23	2	Documents	201	Priv. Land Claims.						
Gray, Samuel	Payment for two masts for the United States ship Constitution, in 1799.	25	2	Petition	351	Rev. Claims				Discharged; laid on table.		
Gray, Samuel	Pension	26	1	Petition	174	Rev. Pensions				Discharged; laid on table.		
Gray, Samuel, (Ohio)	Pension	29	2	Petition	69	Invalid Pensions.						
Gray, Samuel, (Ohio)	Pension	30	1	Petition	111	Invalid Pensions	285	Favorable	281	Passed.		
Gray, Samuel, widow of	Pension	29	1	Petition	107	Rev. Pensions	423	Favorable	298	Passed	Passed	App'd Aug. 8, 1846
Gray & Taylor, *et al*	Drawback of duties on certain teas	26	1	Petition	327	Commerce	Feb. 29, 1840	Favorable; bill	49	Passed	Passed	App'd July 20, 1840
Gray, William	(See P. C. Tupper)	14	2		154							
Gray, William, (Ky.)	Pension	26	1	Petition	624	Rev. Pensions.						
Gray, William, (Ky.)	Pension	28	1	Petition	84	Rev. Pensions.						
Gray, William, (Ohio)	Pension	28	1	Petition	452	Rev. Pensions.						
Gray, William, Lieut. Col.	Compensation as lieutenant colonel of Arkansas volunteers.	31	1	Petition	810	Military Affairs.						
Gray, William, Lieut. Col.	Compensation as lieutenant colonel of Arkansas volunteers.	31	2	Petition	288	Military Affairs	Feb. 18, 1851	Favorable	466	Passed	Passed	App'd Feb. 27, 1851
Gray, William, widow of	Pension	26	1	Petition	322	Rev. Pensions.						
Gray, William, widow of	Pension	26	2	Petition	148	Rev. Claims.						
Gray, William, executors and legatees of.	Indemnity for French spoliations prior to 1800.	26	1	Petition	1115	Foreign Affairs	343	Favorable	319	Referred to Committee Whole House.		
Gray, William, *et al*	Fishing bounty	14	2	Petition	310	Com. and Manuf.				Disch'd; laid on table.		
Gray, William F	Increase of compensation	17	2	Memorial & res.	54	P. Of. & P. Roads.				Discharged; leave to withdraw.		
Gray, William F	Increase of compensation	18	1	Resolution	207	P. Of. and P. Roads.	Mar. 24, 1824	Adverse		Referred to Committee Whole House.		
Gray, William, *et al.*	Indemnity for French spoliations prior to 1800.	18	1	Memorial	238	Foreign Affairs.						

List of private claims presented to the House of Representatives of the United States from the 1st to the 31st Congress, inclusive—Continued.

Names of claimants.	Nature or object of the claim.	Congress.	Session.	How brought before the House of Reps.	Page of journal.	To what committee of the House referred.	No. or date of the report.	Nature of the report.	No. of the bill.	How disposed of by the House of Reps.	How disposed of by the Senate.	Date of the act of Congress, and remarks.
Gray, William, (Mass)	Indemnity for French spoliations prior to 1800.	26	1	Memorial	182	Foreign Affairs	343	Favorable; bill.	319	Referred to Committee Whole House.		
Gray, William W	Renewal of patent	30	2	Memorial	234	Patents.						
Graydon, Andrew	Increase of salary as clerk in Treasury Department.	2	1	Petition	501					Laid on table.		
Graydon, Andrew	Increase of salary as clerk in Treasury Department.	3	1	Petition	28	Select	Mar. 11, 1794	Favorable		Passed.		
Grayson, John, heirs of	Grant of land	22	2	House bill	101				232	Passed	Passed	App'd Feb. 9, 1833
Grayson, Thos., heirs of	Commutation pay	28	1	Petition	669	Rev. Claims	527	Favorable	405	Referred to Committee Whole House.		
Grayson, Thos., heirs of	Commutation pay	29	1	Petition	91	Rev. Claims	11	Favorable	24	Rejected.		
Grazon, John B	(See Reuben E. Gentry, *et al.*)											
Greaham, Geo., widow of	Pension	27	3	Appropriation bill								App'd Mar. 3, 1843
Great Britain, subjects of	Indemnity for losses in property by the acts of civil and military officers in late war.	15	2	Presid'ts message	233	Claims				Discharged; laid on table.		
Great Britain, subjects of	Indemnity for losses in property by the acts of civil and military officers in late war.	16	1	Presid'ts message	103	Foreign Affairs				Discharged; laid on table.		
Greathouse, Daniel, *et al*	(See James Erwin, *et al.*)	29	1		1075							
Greaton, John, widow of	Payment of his subsistance account.	2	2	Petition	697					Referred to Secretary Treasury.		
Greaton, John, widow of	Payment of his subsistance account.	3	1	Rep. of Secretary Treasury.	77					Laid on table.		
Greaves, Jacob	Pension	26	1	Senate bill	738	Invalid Pensions	May 20, 1840	Favorable	280	Referred to Committee Whole House.		
Greaves, Jacob	Pension	27	2	Senate bill	1126	Naval Affairs	Aug. 10, 1842	Favorable	206	Passed		App'd Aug. 29, 1842
Greely, Aaron	Additional compensation as district surveyor in Michigan.	12	1	Petition	245	Claims	Mar. 31, 1812	Favorable	96	Passed	Passed	App'd April 24, 1812
Greely, Aaron	Confirmation of title to land	12	1	Petition	237	Public Lands.						
Greely, Aaron	To carry into effect the act of 24th April, 1812.	12	1	Appropriation bill								Stat. at Large, vol. 2, p. 734.
Greely, Ebenezer S	Indemnity for losses sustained by being arrested by the British in Madawaska.	25	2	Appropriation bill								Stat. at Large, vol. 5, p. 265.
Greely, Ebenezer S	Indemnity for losses sustained by being arrested by the British in Madawaska.	25	3	Petition	223	Foreign Affairs.						
Greely, Ebenezer S	Indemnity for losses sustained by being arrested by the British in Madawaska.	26	1	Petition	182	Foreign Affairs.						
Greely, Ebenezer S	Indemnity for losses sustained by being arrested by the British in Madawaska.	31	1	Petition	620	Claims.						
Greely, Joseph	Pension	3	2	Rep. of Secretary War.	278	Claims	Mar. 2, 1795	Favorable	130	Passed	Postponed.	
Greely, Joseph	Pension	4	1	Rep. of Secretary War.	447	Claims	Mar. 14, 1796	Favorable	156	Passed	Passed	App'd April 20, 1796
Greely, Joseph	Increase of pension	16	1	Petition	26	Pens. & Rev. Cl'ms.				Discharged; laid on table.		

List of private claims presented to the House of Representatives of the United States from the 1st to the 31st Congress, inclusive—Continued.

Names of claimants.	Nature or object of the claim.	Congress.	Session.	How brought before the House of Reps.	Page of journal.	To what committee of the House referred.	No. or date of the report.	Nature of the report.	No. of the bill.	How disposed of by the House of Reps.	How disposed of by the Senate.	Date of the act of Congress, and remarks.
Greely, Philip and Eliphalet	Remission of duties on salt destroyed by fire.	21	1	Petition	497	Ways and Means	382	Favorable	444			
Greely, Philip and Eliphalet	Remission of duties on salt destroyed by fire.	22	1	Petition	24	Ways and Means	327	Favorable	410			
Greely, Philip and Eliphalet	Remission of duties on salt destroyed by fire.	23	1	Petition	58	Ways and Means				Discharged; laid on table.		
Greely, Philip and Eliphalet	Remission of duties on salt destroyed by fire.	24	1	Petition	95	Ways and Means	100	Favorable	115	Referred to Committee Whole House.		
Greely, Philip and Eliphalet	Remission of duties on salt destroyed by fire.	24	2	House bill	255	Whole House	Jan. 21, 1837	Favorable	115	Rejected.		
Greely, Philip, and others	Remission of duties	28	1	Memorial	325	Commerce.						
Greely, Philip, and others	Remission of duties	29	1	Memorial	266	Commerce	421	Favorable	168	Passed	Postponed.	
Green, A	(See George Schnabel, *et al.*)	26	1		332							
Green, Abbott, *et al.*	Permission to apply money deposited in United States treasury to pay for land at private entry, to public sales.	26	2	Resolution	61	Public Lands.						
Green, Abner	Pension	24	1	Resolution	511	Rev. Pensions.						
Green Academy, Mississippi Territory.	For a vested right in certain lands	13	1	Petition	37	Public Lands.						
Green Academy, Mississippi Territory.	For a vested right in certain lands	13	2	Petition	176	Public Lands.						
Green, Anderson	Pension	19	2	Petition	84	Military Pensions.						
Green, Anderson	Pension	20	1	Petition	167	Military Pensions	Feb. 26, 1828	Adverse		Laid on table.		
Green, Andrew	Pension	13	2	House bill	344	Whole House	Mar. 30, 1814	Favorable	166	Passed	Passed	App'd April 18, 1814
Green, Andrew	Increase of pension	14	2	Petition	32	Pens. & Rev. Cl'ms.				Discharged; laid on table.		
Green, Andrew	Increase of pension	16	1	Petition	53	Pens. & Rev. Cl'ms.				Discharged, laid on table.		
Green, Ann Temple, heir of Samuel Nicholson.	Arrears of pay as captain in United States navy, and for pay while under arrest.	24	2	Petition	214	Naval Affairs.						
Green, Ann Temple, heir of Samuel Nicholson.	Arrears of pay as captain in United States navy, and for pay while under arrest.	25	3	Petition	120	Rev. Claims				Discharged; referred to Fourth Auditor of Treasury.		
Green, Ann Temple, heir of Samuel Nicholson.	Arrears of pay as captain in United States navy, and for pay while under arrest.	26	1	Petition	632	Naval Affairs.						
Green, Ann Temple, heir of Samuel Nicholson.	Arrears of pay as captain in United States navy, and for pay while under arrest.	28	1	Petition	687	Rev. Pensions.						
Green, Ann Temple, heir of Samuel Nicholson.	Arrears of pay as captain in United States navy, and for pay while under arrest.	31	1	Petition	1043	Rev. Pensions	460	Adverse		Laid on table.		
Green, Archer	Pension	23	2	Petition	40	Invalid Pensions	Feb. 24, 1835	Adverse		Laid on table.		
Green, Arthur	Patent	1	1	Petition	29	Select.						
Green, Ann, widow of	Arrears of pension	25	3	Petition	51	Invalid Pensions				Discharged; laid on table.		
Greene, Benjamin	Pension	14	2	Petition	283	Pens. & Rev. Cl'ms.						
Greene, Benjamin	Pension	22	2	Petition	216	Rev. Pensions				Laid on table.		
Greene, Benjamin	Pension	23	2	Petition	67	Select	Feb. 25, 1835	Favorable	749	Referred to Committee Whole House.		

List of private claims presented to the House of Representatives of the United States from the 1st to the 31st Congress, inclusive—Continued.

Names of claimants.	Nature or object of the claim.	Congress.	Session.	How brought before the House of Reps.	Page of journal.	To what committee of the House referred.	No. or date of the report.	Nature of the report.	No. of the bill.	How disposed of by the House of Reps.	How disposed of by the Senate.	Date of the act of Congress, and remarks.
Greene, Benjamin	Pension	24	1	Documents	136	Select	337	Favorable	352	Referred to Committee Whole House.		
Green, Benjamin E	Compensation as chargé d'affaires at Mexico.	28	2	Petition	166	Foreign Affairs	90	Favorable	606			
Green, Benjamin E	Compensation as chargé d'affaires at Mexico.	28	2	Appropriat'n bill.	177				498	Passed	Passed	App'd March 3, 1845
Green, Benjamin E	Balance due	29	1	Petition	107	Foreign Affairs.						
Green, Benjamin E	Balance due	29	1	Appropriat'n bill.	206				50	Passed	Passed	App'd Aug. 10, 1846
Green, Berryman	Satisfaction of a Virginia land warrant.	15	1	Petition	98	Priv. Land Claims.				Discharged; laid on table.		
Green, Berryman	(See Lieutenant S. Kerby)	16	1		199							
Green, Charles W., administrator of.	Indemnity for French spoliations prior to 1800.	26	1	Memorial	182	Foreign Affairs	343	Favorable; bill	319	Referred to Committee Whole House.		
Greene, Charles	(See Absalom Packard, *et al.*)	22	1		514							
Green, Charles W	(See David Green, admin'tor of)	22	1		286							
Greene, Christopher	Interest on indemnity allowed by Congress.	2	2	Appropriat'n bill.								Statutes at large, vol 1, p. 299.
Green, Christopher A	Confirmation of title to land	22	2	Petition	120	Priv. Land Claims.	61	Existing laws sufficient.				
Green, Daniel	Compensation for work on Cumberland road.	23	1	Resolution	589	Claims	456	Statem't of facts		Referred to Secretary War.		See report No. 449.
Green, David	To be allowed to correct error in land entry.	18	2	Petition	231	Priv. Land Claims.						
Green, David, administrator of.	Indemnity for losses by insuring property captured by the French prior to 1800.	22	1	Petition	286	Foreign Affairs.						
Green, Dexter, widow of	Pension	28	1	Petition	114	Rev. Pensions				Discharged; laid on table.		
Green, Duff	(See Seybut Scott, *et al.*)	19	2		131							
Green, Duff	For printing abstract of pension laws.	22	1	Appropriat'n bill.								App'd May 5, 1832
Green & Emerson	(See Peter H. Green, *et al.*)	16	2		230							
Green, Edward	Compensation for services as collector of customs.	31	1	Petition	1055	Ways and Means.						
Green, Elijah	Arrears of pension	22	2	Petition	74	Rev. Pensions				Laid on table.		
Green, Elijah, heirs of	Payment of pension	24	1	Petition	433	Rev. Pensions	May 17, 1836	Favorable	645	Passed	Passed	App'd June 28, 1836
Green, Elizabeth	Pension	28	1	Petition	850	Rev. Pensions.						
Green, Forrest	Pension	8	2	Petition	66	Claims.						
Green, Forrest	Pension	12	2	Petition	652	Claims	Feb. 26, 1812	Adverse		Laid on table.		
Green, Frances	(See Robert Green, widow of)	26	1		546							
Green, Francis	Pension	27	2	Petition	869	Invalid Pensions	1006	Adverse		Laid on table.		
Green, Francis	Pension	27	3	Petition	193	Invalid Pensions.						
Green, Francis	Payment for cattle taken by United States troops.	31	1	Petition	366	Military Affairs.						
Green, Franklin	(See John Earle, jr., *et al.*)	10	1		212							
Green, Gabriel, heirs of	Commutation pay	22	2	Petition	313	Rev. Claims.						
Green, Gabriel, heirs of, (Ky.)	Compensation for revolutionary services.	28	2	Petition	45	Rev. Pensions				Discharged; laid on table.		
Green, George, (N. Y.)	Pension	25	2	Petition	117	Invalid Pensions.						
Green, George, (Geo.)	Pension	25	2	Petition	525	Rev. Pensions.						
Green, George, (Penn.)	For purchase of land on credit	29	1	Memorial	939	Claims.						
Green, George, (Penn.)	For purchase of land on credit	29	2	Petition	89	Claims.						

List of private claims presented to the House of Representatives of the United States from the 1*st to the* 31*st Congress, inclusive*—Continued.

Names of claimants.	Nature or object of the claim.	Congress.	Session.	How brought before the House of Reps.	Page of journal.	To what committee of the House referred.	No. or date of the report.	Nature of the report.	No. of the bill.	How disposed of by the House of Reps.	How disposed of by the Senate.	Date of the act of Congress, and remarks.
Green, George, (Penn.)	For purchase of land on credit	30	1	Petition	457	Priv. Land Claims				Discharged; laid on table.		
Green, George, *et al*	Pension	22	1	Resl'n Gen. Assembly Illinois.	97	Rev. Pensions				Laid on table.		
Green, George J., (Va.)	Pension	28	2	Petition	88	Rev. Pensions.						
Green, Gideon	Pension	27	2	Petition	525	Rev. Pensions	784	Adverse		Laid on table.		
Green, Griffin	(See Ohio Company of Associates)	2	1		525							
Green, Henry, attorney of	Remission of forfeiture of merchandise for breach of revenue laws.	4	1	Memorial & rep't Sec. Treasury.	451, 482					Laid on table.		
Green, H. H., (Ia.)	Compensation for services in Mexican war.	31	1	Petition	852	Claims.						
Green, Isaac, *et al*	To be released as surety of Thomas Emerson.	27	2	Petition	100	Judiciary	992	Favorable	575	Referred to Committee Whole House.		
Green, Isaac, *et al*	(See Thomas Emerson, sureties of)											
Green, Isaac, heirs of, *et al*	Reimbursement of money paid on bond.	27	3	House bill	91	Whole House	Dec. 23, 1842	Favorable	575	Passed	Passed	App'd Feb. 4, 1843
Green, Isaac, heirs of, *et al*	Reimbursement of money paid on bond.	28	2	Senate bill	483	Judiciary	March 3, 1845	Favorable	110			
Green, Isaac, heirs of, *et al*	Reimbursement of money paid on bond.	29	2	Petition	49	Judiciary	31	Favorable	614			
Green, Isaac, heirs of, *et al*	Reimbursement of money paid on bond.	30	1	Petition	81	Judiciary	170	Favorable	181	Referred to Committee Whole House.		
Green, Isaac, heirs of, *et al*	Reimbursement of money paid on bond.	30	2	House bill	149	Whole House	Dec. 23, 1848	Favorable	181	Passed	Passed	App'd March 3, 1849
Green, Jacob, *et al*	Payment for supplies furnished in revolutionary war.	2	1	Petition and rep't Sec. Treasury.						Laid on table.		
Green, Lieut. James	To be released from judgment and confinement.	17	1	Petition	101	Judiciary				Discharged; referred to Sec'ry Treasury.		
Green, James, (Ky.)	Payment for horse lost in United States service.	23	1	Petition	386	Claims	477	Adverse		Laid on table.		
Green, James, (Ky.)	Payment for horse lost in United States service.	23	2	Resolution	299	Claims	131	Adverse		Laid on table.		
Green, James, (Ky.)	Payment for horse lost in United States service.	24	1	Resolution	512	Claims	Jan. 21, 1836	Adverse		Laid on table.		
Green, James	Pension	29	2	Petition	150	Rev. Pensions	Jan. 9, 1847	Adverse		Laid on table.		
Green, James, (Va.)	Pension	29	1	Memorial	151	Rev. Pensions	715	Favorable	257	Referred to Committee Whole House.		
Green, James, (Va.)	Pension	29	2	House bill	212	Whole House	Jan. 22, 1847	Favorable	257	Passed	Passed	App'd March 3, 1847
Green, Major James	Pension	30	2	Petition	462	Rev. Pensions				Leave to withdraw.		
Green, James, *et al*	(See William Green, representatives of.	31	1		880							
Green, James, representatives of.	Payment of a certificate for revolutionary services.	30	1	Petition	270	Rev. Claims.						
Green, James F., (Pa)	Pension	31	1	Petition	439	Invalid Pensions	299	Favorable	268	Ref'd to Com. W. H.		
Green, James F., (Pa)	Pension	31	2	House bill	181	Whole House	Jan. 24, 1851	Favorable	268	Passed.		
Green, Jeremiah N.	Bounty land	24	1	Documents	664	Military Affairs.						
Green, John	Compensation for revolutionary services.	2	2	Petition	696					Referred to Secretary of War.		
Green, John	Compensation for revolutionary services.	3	1	Rep. of Secretary War.	93	Select.						
Green, John	Bounty land	25	2	Resolution	535	Rev. Claims				Discharged; laid on table.		
Green, John, heirs of	Pension	26	1	Petition	705	Rev. Pensions.						

List of private claims presented to the House of Representatives of the United States from the 1st to the 31st Congress, inclusive—Continued.

Names of claimants.	Nature or object of the claim.	Congress.	Session.	How brought before the House of Reps.	Page of journal.	To what committee of the House referred.	No. or date of the report.	Nature of the report.	No. of the bill.	How disposed of by the House of Reps.	How disposed of by the Senate.	Date of the act of Congress, and remarks.
Green, John, widow of	Pension	26	1	Petition	282	Rev. Pensions.						
Green, John, widow of	Pension	26	2	Petition	35	Rev. Pensions	Feb. 12, 1841	Favorable	650	Referred to Committee Whole House.		
Green, John, widow of	Pension	27	3	Petition	74	Rev. Pensions	....	....	......	Discharged; leave to withdraw.		
Green, John R., widow of	Pension	16	2	Petition	54	Claims	....	....	......	Discharged; laid on table.		
Green, Jonas	Pension	2	2	Report Secretary of War.	649	Whole House.						
Green, Jonas	Pension	3	1	Rep. of Secretary of War.	131	Select	May 26, 1794	Favorable	J.R. 12	Passed	Passed	App'd June 9, 1794
Green, Jonas	Pension	4	1	Rep. of Secretary of War.	445	Claims.						
Green, Jonas	Pension	10	1	House bill	232	Whole House	April 18, 1808	Favorable	78	Passed	Passed	App'd April 25, 1808
Green, Jonathan	Arrears of pension	21	2	Petition	103	Military Pensions	....	....	......	Discharged; laid on table.		
Green, Joseph	(See Canadian refugees.)											
Green, Joseph, and others	Compensation for revolutionary services.	2	1	Petition	581	....	....	....	......	Referred to Secretary of War.		
Green, Joseph, and others	Compensation for revolutionary services.	2	2	Rep. of Secretary of War.	733	....	....	....	......	Laid on table.		
Green, Joseph, and others	Compensation for revolutionary services.	3	2	Rep. of Secretary War.	350	Claims.						
Green, Joseph, and others	Compensation for revolutionary services.	4	1	Resolution	470	Claims	Mar. 14, 1796	General bill	156	Passed	Passed	App'd April 20, 1796
Green, Joseph, (Ohio.)	Pension	28	2	Petition	299	Rev. Pensions.						
Green, Joseph, (Ohio.)	Pension	29	1	Petition	218	Rev. Pensions	611	Adverse	......	Laid on table.		
Green, Joseph, *et al.*	Bounty land as refugees from Canada and Nova Scotia.	3	1	Rep. of Secretary War.	29	Select	April 1, 1794	Adverse	......	Referred to Committee Whole House.		
Green, Joseph, *et al.*	Bounty land as refugees from Canada and Nova Scotia.	4	2	Rep't Committee.	632	Whole House	Dec. 29, 1796	Adverse	......	Rejected.		
Green, Joseph, *et al.*	Bounty land as refugees from Canada and Nova Scotia.	11	2	Petition	322	Public Lands.						
Green, Joseph J.	(See James Savage, *et al.*	13	3	....	723							
Green, Joseph J.	Indemnity for damages to property in Plattsburg by firing cannon.	14	1	Petition	220	Claims	....	....	......	Discharged: laid on table.		
Green, Joseph J.	Indemnity for damages to property in Plattsburg by firing cannon.	14	2	Petition	123	Claims	Jan. 27, 1817	Favorable	80	Passed	Passed	App'd March 3, 1817
Green, Joseph W.	Bounty on the fishing schooner Two Brothers.	23	1	Petition	617	Commerce	461	Favorable	478			
Green, Joseph W.	Bounty on the fishing schooner Two Brothers.	24	1	Petition	54	Commerce	50	Favorable	62	Passed	Passed	App'd July 1, 1836
Green, Joshua	Payment of certificate of public debt.	16	1	Petition	26	Pens. & Rev. Cl'ms.	....	....	......	Discharged; laid on table.		
Green, Joshua, *et al.*	Increase of compensation as clerk in loan office, Massachusetts.	4	2	Petition	385	Select	....	....	......	....	....	See act May 30, 1796
Green, Josiah	Pension	5	2	Petition	245	Claims	April 14, 1798	Adverse	......	Laid on table.	....	Leave to withdraw.
Green, Josiah L.	Increase of compensation as collector of customs.	19	1	Petition	363	Commerce	....	....	......	Discharged; laid on table.		
Green, Josiah L.	Increase of compensation as collector of customs.	20	2	Petition	192	Commerce.						
Green, Lucy P. (Va.)	(See Cadwalader Jones, heir of.)	26	1	....	361							
Green, Mary	(See Jas. McKinney, representatives of.)	29	1	....	592							

List of private claims presented to the House of Representatives of the United States from the 1st to the 31st Congress, inclusive—Continued.

Names of claimants.	Nature or object of the claim.	Congress.	Session.	How brought before the House of Reps.	Page of journal.	To what committee of the House referred.	No. or date of the report.	Nature of the report.	No. of the bill.	How disposed of by the House of Reps.	How disposed of by the Senate.	Date of the act of Congress, and remarks.
Green, McKeen	Compensation for revolutionary services.	23	2	Petition	240	Rev. Claims.						
Green, McKeen	Compensation for revolutionary services.	24	1	Petition	104	Rev. Claims	....	....	......	Discharged; laid on table.		
Green, McKeen, widow of.	Compensation for revolutionary services.	29	1	Petition	495	Rev. Pensions	....	....	......	Discharged; laid on table.		
Green, McKeen, widow of.	Compensation for revolutionary services.	30	1	Petition	571	Rev. Pensions.						
Green, General Nathaniel, widow of	That inqniry be made into claims due her late husband.	1	2	Petition	168	Select.	Jan. 29, 1790	Favorable	......	Referred to Secretary Treasury.		
Green, General Nathaniel, widow of.	Indemnity as surety on the bond of John Banks & Co.	2	1	Rep. of Secretary Treasury.	481	Whole House.						
Green, General Nathaniel. widow of.	For further indemnity on account of being surety on the bond of John Banks, & Co.	2	1	Resolution	517	Whole House	April 5, 1792	Favorable	177	Passed	Passed	App'd April 27, 1792
Green, General Nathaniel, widow of.	For payment of balance due from treasury.	3	1	Appropriat'n bill	....	....	....	....	......	....	....	Statutes at Large, vol. 1, page 344.
Green, General Nathaniel, widow of.	To be released from judgment as surety for Hunter, Banks & Co.	4	1	Memorial	470	Claims	May 23, 1796	Favorable	199	Passed	Passed	App'd June 1, 1796
Green, General Nathaniel, *et al.*, representatives of.	Relief against decisions of the Treasury Department, in settlement of claims of respective decedent's estates.	4	2	Petition	651	Claims	Feb. 16, 1797	Adverse	......	Referred to Committee Whole House.	....	Leave to withdraw.
Green, Nathaniel, & Co., surviving partners of.	Payment for supplies furnished United States army, revolutionary war.	2	1	Petition and rep't Sec. Treasury.	....	....	....	....	......	Laid on table.		
Green, Nehemiah	Pension	29	2	Petition	146	Rev. Pensions.						
Green, Patrick	Relief for wounds received while guarding the United States mail.	21	1	Petition	498	P. Of. and P. Roads.	392	Favorable	432			
Green, Patrick	Relief for wounds received while guarding the United States mail.	22	1	Petition	165	P. Of. and P. Roads.	179	Favorable	255	Referred to Committee Whole House.		
Green, Patrick	Relief for wounds received while guarding the United States mail.	22	2	House bill	92	Whole House	Dec. 28, 1832	Favorable	255	Passed.		
Green, Patrick	Relief for wounds received while guarding the United States mail.	23	1	Petition	304	P. Of. & P. Roads.	346	Favorable	373			
Green, Patrick	Relief for wounds received while guarding the United States mail.	24	1	Petition	111	P. Of. & P. Roads.	155	Favorable	164	Passed	Passed, with amendment.	
Green, Patrick	Relief for wounds received while guarding the United States mail.	24	2	Petition	85	P. Of. and P. Roads.	60	Favorable	810	Referred to Committee Whole House.		
Green, Patrick	Relief for wounds received while guarding the United States mail.	25	2	Petition	40	P. Of. & P. Roads.	102	Favorable	120	Passed.		
Green, Patrick	Relief for wounds received while guarding the United States mail.	25	3	Petition	90	P. Of. & P. Roads.	95	Favorable	971	Passed	Passed, with amendment.	App'd March 3, 1839
Green, Peleg	Compensation for revolutionary services and property.	21	1	Petition	161	Rev. Claims.						
Green, Peter H., *et al.*	Payment for supplies furnished United States army.	16	2	Petition	230	Claims	....	....	......	Discharged; laid on table.		
Green, Peter H., *et al.*	Payment for supplies furnished United States army.	23	1	Senate bill	845	Claims	Jan. 30, 1834	Favorable	116	Laid on table.		
Green, Peter H., *et al.*	Payment for supplies furnished United States army.	23	2	Senate bill	214	Claims	March 2, 1835	Favorable	52			
Green, Peter H., *et al.*	Paymant for supplies furnished United States army.	24	1	Senate bill	287	Claims	596	With amend.	51	Referred to Committee Whole House.		

List of private claims presented to the House of Representatives of the United States from the 1st to the 31st Congress, inclusive—Continued.

Names of claimants.	Nature or object of the claim.	Congress.	Session.	How brought before the House of Reps.	Page of journal.	To what committee of the House referred.	No. or date of the report.	Nature of the report.	No. of the bill.	How disposed of by the House of Reps.	How disposed of by the Senate.	Date of the act of Congress, and remarks.
Green, Peter H., *et al.*	That the amount due on contracts to P. H. Green, and Green & Emerson be applied to the credit of Wm. King & P. H. Green.	26	2	Senate bill	221	Claims	....	....	221			
Green, Purdon C., heirs of.	Indemnity for damage by United States government taking possession of Key West island.	26	1	Memorial	304	Naval Affairs.						
Green, Purdon C., heirs of.	Indemnity for damage by United State government taking possession of Key West island.	28	1	Petition	105	Naval Affairs.						
Green, Richard	Payment for a boat burnt by order of General Putnam.	2	1	Petition	510	....	....	....	....	Referred to Secretary of War.		
Green, Richard	Pension	15	1	Petition	330	Pens. & Rev. Cl'ms.	....	....	....	Discharged; laid on table.		
Green, Richard	Confirmation of title to land	27	2	Papers	75	Priv. Land Claims.						
Green, Robert	Pension	26	1	Resolution	516	Rev. Pensions	467	Favorable	381	Referred to Committee Whole House.		
Green, Robert, heirs of	Payment of two certificates of public debt.	23	1	Petition	243	Rev. Claims.						
Green, Robert, heirs of	Payment of two certificates of public debt.	26	1	Petition	263	Rev. Claims.						
Green, Robert, heirs of	Payment of two certificates of public debt.	26	2	Petition	182	Rev. Claims.						
Green, Robert, heirs of	Payment of two certificates of public debt.	27	2	Petition	96	Rev. Claims	545	Adverse	....	Laid on table.		
Green, Salmon	Compensation for military services.	27	2	Petition	247	Claims	490	Adverse	....	Laid on table.		
Green, Samuel	Increase of compensation as postmaster.	4	2	Memorial	648	Whole House	....	....	....	....	....	See House bill No. 205
Green, Samuel	Payment for work and materials on the Cumberland road.	23	1	Resolution	589	Claims	455	Adverse	....	....	....	See Report No. 449.
Green, Samuel	Increase of pension	23	2	Petition	114	Rev. Pensions	....	....	....	Discharged; laid on table.		
Green, Samuel C.	Arrears of pension	31	2	Petition	50	Invalid Pensions.						
Green, Samuel H.	Compensation for revolutionary services of ancestor.	24	2	Petition	132	Rev. Claims.						
Green, Samuel, attorney of.	Indemnity for French spoliations prior to 1800.	26	1	Memorial	182	Foreign Affairs	343	Favorable; bill	319	Referred to Committee Whole House.		
Greene, Simon	Payment for corn and fodder for United States troops.	25	2	Documents	396	Claims.						
Greene, Simon	Payment for corn and fodder for United States troops.	26	1	Petition	169	Claims	39	Adverse	....	Laid on table.		
Greene, Thomas, commissioner of Virginia.	For an amendment to the act of July, 1832, authorizing the payment of certain claims of the State of Virginia.	28	1	Memorial	914	Ways and Means	475	Favorable	365			
Greene, Thomas, commissioner of Virginia.	For an amendment to the act of July, 1832, authorizing the payment of certain claims of the State of Virginia.	29	1	House bill	221	Whole House	71	Favorable	91			
Greene, Thomas, commissioner of Virginia.	For an amendment to the act of July, 1832, authorizing the payment of certain claims of the State of Virginia.	30	1	House bill	277	Ways and Means	Mar. 9, 1848	Favorable	248	Passed	Passed, with amendment.	App'd Aug. 12, 1848

List of private claims presented to the House of Representatives of the United States from the 1st to the 31st Congress, inclusive—Continued.

Names of claimants.	Nature or object of the claim.	Congress.	Session.	How brought before the House of Reps.	Page of journal.	To what committee of the House referred.	No. or date of the report.	Nature of the report.	No. of the bill.	How disposed of by the House of Reps.	How disposed of by the Senate.	Date of the act of Congress, and remarks.
Green, T. E.	For amount due out of moneys coming to Ottawa Indians.	29	1	Memorial	160	Indian Affairs	287	Adverse.				
Green, Thomas C.	Indemnity for an error of United States land officers.	29	2	Petition	180	Priv. Land Claims.						
Green, Thomas C.	Indemnity for an error of United States land officers.	30	1	Petition	773	Priv. Land Claims.						
Green, Thomas C.	Indemnity for an error of United States land officers.	31	1	Petition	197	Priv. Land Claims.						
Green, Thomas F., sureties of.	Release from liability	23	1	Memorial	226	P. Of. & P. Roads.	451	Favorable	468	Referred to Committee Whole House.		
Green, Thomas F., sureties of.	Release from liability	24	1	Petition	111	P. Of. & P. Roads.						
Green, Thomas F., sureties of.	Release from liability	24	1	Senate bill	990	Judiciary	June 17, 1836	With't amend.	S. 188	Passed		App'd July 2, 1836
Green, Timothy	Payment for hogs taken for use of United States army.	21	2	Petition	233	Claims	Feb. 7, 1831	Adverse		Laid on table.		
Green, Timothy	Payment for hogs taken for use of United States army.	27	2	Petition	76	Claims	714	Adverse		Laid on table.		
Greene, Wardwell	Compensation for revolutionary services.	1	3	Petition and rep't Sec. of War.	352					Laid on table.		
Greene, Wardwell	Pension	2	2	Rep. of Secretary War.	649	Whole House.						
Greene, Wardwell	Pension	3	1	Rep. of Secretary War.	131	Select	May 26, 1794	J. Res. to refer to Sec. War.	J. R. 12	Passed	Passed	App'd June 9, 1794
Greene, Wardwell	Pension	4	1	Rep. of Secretary War.	445	Claims.						
Greene, Wardwell	Pension	4	2	Rep. of Secretary War.	614	Claims.						
Greene, Wardwell	Pension	15	1	Rep. of Secretary War.	405	Pens. & Rev. Cl'ms.	April 1, 1818	Favorable	172	Passed	Indef. postp'd.	
Greene, Wardwell	Pension	16	1	Petition	145	Pens. & Rev. Cl'ms.				Discharged; laid on table.		
Greene, Wardwell	Pension	16	2	Petition	24					Referred to Secretary of War.		
Greene, Wardwell	Increase of pension	17	1	Resolution	181	Pens. & Rev. Cl'ms.				Discharged; referred to Secretary of War.		
Greene, Wardwell	Increase of pension	17	2	Petition	31	Pens. & Rev. Cl'ms.	Dec. 16, 1822	Favorable	195	Passed		
Green, William	Pension	10	1	House bill	232	Whole House	April 19, 1808	Favorable	78	Passed	Passed	App'd April 25, 1808
Green, William	Pension	25	2	Petition	117	Invalid Pensions.						
Green, William	Pension	25	3	Petition	460	Invalid Pensions.						
Green, William	Pension	28	1	Petition	527	Invalid Pensions.						
Green, William, widow of.	Pension	28	2	Petition	354	Rev. Pensions.						
Green, William, representatives of.	Compensation in lieu of bounty land for revolutionary services.	31	1	Petition	880	Rev. Claims.						
Greenelch, Edward	Pension	21	1	Petition	144	Military Pensions	April 7, 1830	Adverse		Laid on table.		
Greenelch, Edward	Pension	22	1	Resolution	86	Rev. Pensions.						
Greenfield, Jane H. T.	(See S. Dorset, heir of)	31	1		391							
Greenleaf, Jacob	Indemnity for French spoliations prior to 1800.	26	1	Memorial	182	Foreign Affairs	343	Favorable; bill	319	Referred to Committee Whole House.		
Greenlief, David	Patent and exclusive right to construct mills in United States.	1	1	Petition	74	Select				Laid on table.		
Greenlief, James	Relief as debtor in prison, Philadelphia.	5	2	Petition	255	Select	April 25, 1798	Favorable		Referred to Committee Whole House.		

List of private claims presented to the House of Representatives of the United States from the 1st to the 31st Congress, inclusive—**Continued.**

Names of claimants.	Nature or object of the claim.	Congress.	Session.	How brought before the House of Reps.	Page of journal.	To what committee of the House referred.	No. or date of the report.	Nature of the report.	No. of the bill.	How disposed of by the House of Reps.	How disposed of by the Senate.	Date of the act of Congress, and remarks.
Greenlief, Mary	Pension	28	1	Petition	950	Whole House.						
Greenlief, Simon	Extension of copy right	31	1	Senate bill	970	Judiciary			247			
Greenlief, Simon	Extension of copy right	31	2	Senate bill	48	Judiciary	Dec. 12, 1850	Adverse	247			
Greenleaf, Simon, attorney of.	(See Joseph Cross, heirs of, by attorney of.)	26	1		182							
Greenman, Ann	Pension	28	2	Petition	169	Rev. Pensions.						
Greeman, Jeremiah	(See George House, *et al.*)	4	1		371							
Greenough, Horatio	Payment for statuary for capitol	26	1	Appropriation bill	230	Whole House		With amends.	8	Passed	Passed	App'd May 8, 1840
Greenough, Horatio	Payment for statuary for capitol	26	2	Appropriation bill	173	Whole House		With amends.	601	Passed	Passed	App'd March 3, 1841
Greenough, Horatio	Payment for statuary for capitol	27	1	Appropriation bill	358	Whole House		With amends.	29	Passed	Passed	App'd Sept. 9, 1841
Greenough, Horatio	Payment for statuary for capit l	28	1	Appropriation bill	196	Whole House		With amends.	32	Passed	Passed	App'd June 17, 1844
Greenough, Horatio	Payment for statuary for capitol	29	1	Appropriation bill	206	Whole House		With amends.	50	Passed	Passed	App'd Aug. 10, 1846
Greenup, C. C	Compensation for printing laws of Florida.	22	1	Appropriation bill								Statutes at large, vol. 4, p. 581.
Greenwald, Abraham	Pension	18	2	Petition	117	Rev. Pensions	Jan. 17, 1825	Adverse		Laid on table.		
Greenwalt, Philip	Compensation for revolutionary services and supplies.	2	1	Petition	455					Referred to Secretary War.		
Greenwalt, Philip	Compensation for revolutionary services and supplies.	2	2	Rep. of Secretary War.	735					Laid on table.		
Geenway, George	Pay and bounty land for revolutionary services.	15	1	Petition	242	Pens. & Rev. Clm's.	Feb. 24, 1818	Adverse		Rejected.		
Greenwood, John	Confirmation of title to land	18	1	Petition	177	Priv. Land Claims.						
Greenwood, William M	Payment for a horse lost in United States service.	23	1	Petition	49	Claims.						
Greer, Green B	(See William H. Bedford, agent.)	28	1		262							
Greer, Hugh, former widow of.	Bounty land for revolutionary services.	29	2	Petition	323	Priv. Land Claims.						
Greer, Hugh, former widow of.	Bounty land for revolutionary services.	30	1	Petition	344	Public Lands	265	Adverse		Laid on table.		
Greer, Jacob	Compensation for collecting direct tax.	8	2	Petition	112	Ways and Means.						
Greer, Jacob	Compensation for collecting direct tax.	9	1	Petition	192	Ways and Means.						
Greer, Jacob	Compensation for collecting direct tax.	12	1	Petition	72	Ways and Means	Feb. 4, 1812	Adverse		Rejected.		
Greer, Jacob	Compensation for collecting direct tax.	14	1	Petition	53	Claims				Discharged; laid on table.		
Greer, Jacob	Compensation for collecting direct tax.	14	2	Petition	33	Claims				Laid on table.		
Greer, Jacob	To be released from paym't of direct tax left uncollected by Js. Greer.	13	2	Petition	183	Claims	Feb. 28, 1814	Adverse		Leave to withdraw.		
Greer, Jacob	Reimbursement of expenses, and to be allowed further time to collect direct tax.	15	1	Petition	31	Claims	Dec. 29, 1817	Adverse		Laid on table.		Leave to withdraw.
Greer, Jacob	Reimbursement of expenses, and to be allowed further time to collect direct tax.	15	2	Petition	109	Ways and Means				Discharged; laid on table.		
Greer, Jacob	Reimbursement of expenses, and to be allowed further time to collect direct tax.	16	1	Petition	114	Ways and Means.	Jan. 12, 1820	Adverse		Rejected.		
Greer, Jacob	Reimbursement of expenses, and to be allowed further time to collect direct tax.	17	1	Petition	32	Ways and Means	Feb. 14, 1822	Adverse		Rejected.		

List of private claims presented to the House of Representatives of the United States from the 1st to the 31st Congress, inclusive—Continued.

Names of claimants.	Nature or object of the claim.	Congress.	Session.	How brought before the House of Reps.	Page of journal.	To what committee of the House referred.	No. or date of the report.	Nature of the report.	No. of the bill.	How disposed of by the House of Reps.	How disposed of by the Senate.	Date of the act of Congress, and remarks.
Greer, Jacob	Compensation for collecting tax in North Carolina.	18	1	Petition	28	Ways and Means	Dec. 19, 1823	Adverse		Rejected.		
Greer, Jacob	Compensation for collecting tax in North Carolina.	19	1	Petition	67	Claims	Feb. 13, 1826	Adverse		Laid on table.		
Greer, Jacob	(See J. Steele, representative of.)	21	2		397							
Greer, James	For the purchase of his invention for boring gun barrels.	16	1	Petition	221							
Greer, James	For the purchase of his invention for boring gun barrels.	17	1	Petition	238	Military Affairs	Mar. 2, 1822	Adverse		Leave to withdraw.		
Greer, James, heirs of	For the purchase of his invention for boring gun barrels.	27	3	Petition	168	Military Affairs.						
Greer, James, heirs of	For the purchase of his invention for boring gun barrels.	28	1	Petition	132	Military Affairs	104	Adverse		Laid on table.		
Greer, James, heirs of	For the purchase of his invention for boring gun barrels.	31	1	Petition	370	Military Affairs				Discharged; laid on table.		
Greer, Jefferson	(See John Wiley, *et al*)	24	1		114							
Greer, Jefferson	(See John Wiley, *et al*)	24	2		200							
Greer, Jefferson	(See John Wiley, *et al*)	25	2		42							
Greer, Priscilla	(See John McClellan, heirs of)	25	2		269							
Greer, Robert, heirs of	Payment of two certificates of public debt.	23	1	Petition	243	Rev. Claims.						
Greer, Robert, heirs of	Payment of two certificates of public debt.	26	2	Petition	182	Rev. Claims.						
Greer, Robert, heirs of	Payment of two certificates of public debt.	27	2	Petition	96	Rev. Claims	April 1, 1842	Adverse		Laid on table.		
Greer, Seth	(See Calvin Pollard, *et al*)	23	1		523							
Greer, Thomas	Pension	5	2	House bill	127	Whole House	Jan. 11, 1798	Favorable	38	Passed	Passed	App'd Feb. 2, 1798
Greer, William	Reimbursem't of postage on vouchers for post office blanks sent from Georgia.	29	1	Petition	921	Claims.						
Greer, William	Reimbursem't of postage on vouchers for post office blanks sent from Georgia.	29	2	Petition	82	Claims	87	Favorable	693			
Greer, William	Reimbursem't of postage on vouchers for post office blanks sent from Georgia.	30	1	Petition	154	Claims	55	Adverse		Laid on table.		
Greer, William	Reimbursem't of postage on vouchers for post office blanks sent from Georgia.	30	2	Senate bill	518	P. Of. & P. Roads			231			
Greer, William	Reimbursem't of postage on vouchers for post office blanks sent from Georgia.	31	1	Petition	698	Claims.						
Greer, William	Payment of balance due for printing.	31	1	Petition	231	Claims.						
Greese, Ernest	Compensation for revolutionary services and losses.	3	2	Petition	308	Claims.						
Greese, Ernest	Compensation for revolutionary services and losses.	4	1	Petition	373	Claims	Dec. 28, 1795	Adverse		Leave to withdraw.		
Greese, Ernest	Compensation for revolutionary services and losses.	10	1	Petition	54	Select.						
Greese, Ernest	Compensation for revolutionary services and losses.	13	2	Petition	168	Pens. & Rev. Cl'ms.	Mar. 3, 1814	Adverse		Leave to withdraw.		

List of private claims presented to the House of Representatives of the United States from the 1st to the 31st Congress, inclusive—Continued.

Names of claimants.	Nature or object of the claim.	Congress.	Session.	How brought before the House of Reps.	Page of journal.	To what committee of the House referred.	No. or date of the report.	Nature of the report.	No. of the bill.	How disposed of by the House of Reps.	How disposed of by the Senate.	Date of the act of Congress, and remarks.
Gregg, David	Pension	24	1	Resolution	822	Rev. Pensions				Laid on table.		
Gregg, James, widow of	Pension	15	2	Petition	138	Pens. & Rev. Cl'ms.				Discharged; laid on table.		
Gregg, John, (Ohio)	Pay and bounty land for revolutionary services.	15	2	Petition	163	Pens. & Rev. Cl'ms.	Jan. 13, 1819	Adverse		Rejected.		
Gregg, John, (Ohio)	Pay and bounty land for revolutionary services.	18	1	Petition	196	Pens. & Rev. Cl'ms.				Discharged; laid on table.		
Gregg, John, (Ohio)	Pension	21	2	Petition	375					Laid on table.		
Gregg, John, (Ohio)	Commutation pay	22	1	Petition	416	Rev. Claims.						
Gregg, John, heir of, (Ohio)	Commutation pay	24	1	Petition	62	Rev. Claims.						
Gregg, John, heir of, (Ohio)	Commutation pay	30	1	Petition	480	Rev. Claims.						
Gregg, John, heir of, (Ohio)	Commutation pay	30	2	Petition	239	Rev. Claims				Leave to withdraw.		
Gregg, Thomas	Extension of patent	20	1	Petition	225	Judiciary				Discharged; leave to withdraw.		
Gregg, Thomas	Extension of patent	28	1	Petition	352	Naval Affairs				Discharged; laid on table.		
Gregg, Thomas	Extension of patent	29	1	Petition	255	Naval Affairs.						
Gregg, Thomas	Extension of patent	30	1	Memorial	316, 641	Patents	468	Adverse		Laid on table.		
Gregg, Thomas	That his improvements for propelling vessels by steam be adopted by government.	30	1	Petition	422	Naval Affairs	348	Adverse		Laid on table.		
Gregnon & Lawe, administrator of.	Compensation for property used by United States troops.	26	1	Documents	1004	Public Lands.						
Gregnon & Lawe, administrator of.	Compensation for property used by United States troops.	29	1	Petition	106	Claims						
Gregnon & Lawe, administrator of.	Compensation for property used by United States troops.	29	2	Petition	74	Claims						
Gregorie, J. B. and P.	Confirmation of sale of school lands.	31	1	Senate bill	1206	Priv. Land Claims.			63			
Gregorie, J. B. and P.	Confirmation of sale of school lands.	31	2	Senate bill	175	Priv. Land Claims.	Jan. 22, 1851	Favorable	63			
Gregory, Asahel	Pension	16	1	Petition	174	Pens. & Rev. Cl'ms.	April 6, 1820	Adverse		Laid on table.		
Gregory, Asahel	Pension	20	1	Petition	223	Military Pensions.	May 13, 1828	Adverse		Laid on table.		
Gregory, Asahel	Pension	21	1	Resolution	275	Military Pensions.				Discharged; laid on table.		
Gregory, Asahel	Pension	21	2	Resolution	91	Military Pensions.						
Gregory, Asahel	Pension	22	1	Petition	120	Rev. Pensions	369	Favorable	464	Referred to Committee Whole House.		
Gregory, David, *et al*	(See Abraham Freeman)	6	2		619							
Gregory, Lieut. Francis H., and others.	Prize money for capturing British gun-boats.	18	1	Senate bill	179	Naval Affairs	Feb. 3, 1824	With't amend.	S. 20	Passed	Passed	App'd May 24, 1824
Gregory, Lieut. Francis H., and others.	Reimbursement of expense in prosecuting Spanish brig Palmira, captured by the Grampus.	20	1	Senate bill	466	Naval Affairs	April 15, 1828	Favorable	104	Passed.	Passed	App'd May 26, 1828
Gregory, George, heirs of.	Indemnity for French spoliations prior to 1800.	26	1	Memorial	182	Foreign Affairs	343	Favorable; bill	319	Referred to Committee Whole House.		
Gregory, John, heir of.	Commutation pay	23	2	Petition	390	Rev. Claims.						
Gregory, John, heir of.	Commutation pay	24	1	Petition	130	Rev. Claims.						
Gregory, John	(See George Gregory, heirs of.	26	1		182							
Gregory, John M.	(See John and William Gregory, heir of.)											
Gregory, John and William, heir of.	Commutation pay and bounty land.	13	1	Petition	28	Public Lands.						

List of private claims presented to the House of Representatives of the United States from the 1st to the 31st Congress, inclusive—Continued.

Names of claimants.	Nature or object of the claim.	Congress.	Session.	How brought before the House of Reps.	Page of journal.	To what committee of the House referred.	No. or date of the report.	Nature of the report.	No. of the bill.	How disposed of by the House of Reps.	How disposed of by the Senate.	Date of the act of Congress, and remarks.
Gregory, John and William, heir of.	Commutation pay and bounty land.	13	2	Petition	384	Public Lands.						
Gregory, John and William, heir of.	Commutation pay and bounty land.	18	1	Petition	215	Pens. & Rev. Cl'ms.						
Gregory, John and William, heir of.	Payment of seven years' half-pay.	22	1	Petition	470	Rev. Pensions	421	Favorable	521			
Gregory, John and William, heir of.	Payment of seven years' half-pay.	23	1	Petition	70	Rev. Claims	124	Favorable	130	Passed	Passed, with amendment.	App'd June 30, 1834
Gregory, Jonathan	(See Nathan Brougham, surety of)	15	1		264							
Gregory, Joseph	(See Napthelam Gregory, heir of)	12	1		152							
Gregory, Lucy, *et al.*	(See John M. Grant, admins'tr of.)	15	1		371							
Gregory, Luther	Pension	14	1	Petition	63	Pens. & Rev. Cl'ms.	April 11, 1816	General bill	171	Passed	Passed	App'd April 30, 1816
Gregory, Luther	Increase of pension	15	2	Petition	43	Pens. & Rev. Cl'ms.				Referred to Secretary War.		
Gregory, Luther	Increase of pension	16	1	Petition	65	Pens. & Rev. Cl'ms.				Discharged; referred to Secretary War.		
Gregory, Luther, (Maine)	Pension	27	2	Petition	745	Invalid Pensions	828	Adverse		Laid on table.		
Gregory, Naphthelam, heirs of.	Compensation for revolutionary services.	12	1	Petition	152	Claims.						
Gregory, Nehemiah, widow of.	Pension	29	2	Petition	82	Rev. Pensions.						
Gregory, Samuel	Pension	29	1	Petition	274	Rev. Pensions.						
Gregory, Samuel	Pension	30	1	Petition	306	Rev. Pensions	222	Adverse		Laid on table		Leave to withdraw; 1st sess. 31st Cong.
Gregory, Spittsby	Pension	22	1	House bill	478	Rev. Pensions	367	Favorable	462	Passed	Indef. postp'd.	
Gregory, William, heirs of.	Payment of seven years' half-pay.	25	2	Petition	48	Rev. Claims	294	Favorable	334	Passed.		
Gregory, William, heirs of	Payment of seven years' half-pay.	25	3	Petition	84	Rev. Claims	8	Favorable	905			
Gregory, William, heirs of.	Payment of seven years' half-pay.	26	1	Petition	164	Rev. Claims	90	Favorable	85	Ref'd to Com. W. H.		
Gregory, William, heirs of.	Payment of seven years' half pay.	26	2	Petition	148	Rev. Claims						
Gregory, William, heirs of.	Payment of seven years' half-pay.	27	2	Petition	62	Rev. Claims	275	Favorable	241			
Greiner, John	(See Jacob Ritter, *et al*)	13	3		693							
Greiner, John, *et al.*	Remission of duties	14	1	Petition	43	Ways and Means	Feb. 14, 1816	Adverse		Rejected.		
Greiner, John, *et al.*	Remission of duties	14	2	Petition	48	Ways and Means.						
Gremellion, Francois, widow and heirs of.	Confirmation of title to land	29	1	Petition	630	Priv. Land Claims.						
Gremellion, Francois, widow and heirs of.	Confirmation of title to land	29	2	Petition	92	Priv. Land Claims.	38	Favorable	626			
Gremellion, Francois, widow of.	Confirmation of title to land	30	1	Petition	109	Priv. Land Claims.	182	Favorable	192	Passed	Passed	App'd Aug. 11, 1848
Grinall, Owen	Pension	14	2	Petition	283	Pens. & Rev. Cl'ms.						
Grinall, Owen	Pension	23	2	Memorial	67	Select	Feb. 25, 1835	Favorable	769	Referred to Committe Whole House.		
Grinall, Owen	Pension	24	1	Documents	136	Select	337	Favorable	352	Referred to Committee Whole House.		
Greneaux, Charles E., *et al*	Pre-emption right to land	23	2	Petition	138	Priv. Land Claims.						
Greneaux, Charles E., *et al*	Compensation for taking testimony by order of the House of Representatives	27	2	Petition	131	Accounts.						
Griner, John	(See Jacob Ritter, jr., and others.)	13	3		693							
Grenier, Colonel	Pension	20	2	Petition	203	Military Pensions				Discharged; laid on table.		
Grennell, William	Pension	19	2	Petition	156	Military Pensions.						
Grennell, William	Pension	20	1	Resolution	159	Military Pensions				Disch'd; laid on table.		

List of private claims presented to the House of Representatives of the United States from the 1st to the 31st Congress, inclusive—Continued.

Names of claimants.	Nature or object of the claim.	Congress.	Session.	How brought before the House of Reps.	Page of journal.	To what committee of the House referred.	No. or date of the report.	Nature of the report.	No. of the bill.	How disposed of by the House of Reps.	How disposed of by the Senate.	Date of the act of Congress, and remarks.
Grennell, William	Pension	21	1	Petition	46	Military Pensions				Discharged; laid on table.		
Grennell, William	Pension	21	2	Petition	68	Military Pensions.						
Grennell, William	Pension	22	1	Petition	51	Rev. Pensions	18	Favorable	69	Passed.		
Gresham, Elizabeth	(See George Gresham, widow of.)	26	1		625							
Gresham, George, widow of.	Pension	26	1	Petition	625	Rev. Pensions	459	Favorable	373			
Gresham, George, widow of.	Pension	27	2	Petition	268	Rev. Pensions	99	Favorable	145	Passed.		
Gresham, George, widow of.	Pension	27	3	Petition	131	Rev. Pensions	38	Favorable	665	Passed	Passed	App'd March 3, 1843
Gresham, George, widow of.	For an act explanatory of the act 3d March, 1843.	28	1	Petition	272	Rev. Pensions	261	Favorable	193	Passed	Passed	App'd May 23, 1844
Gresham, George, widow of.	Commutation pay	29	2	Petition	50	Rev. Pensions						Leave to withdraw, 2d session, 30th Cong.
Gresham, Joseph	Payment of balance due on contract.	24	1	Petition	49	Claims	52	Favorable	65	Passed	Passed	App'd June 14, 1836
Gresham, Joseph, widow of.	Settlement of claim for revolutionary services.	8	1	Petition	552	Claims				Referred to Committee Whole House.		
Gresham, Joseph, widow of.	Settlement of claim for revolutionary services.	8	2	Petition	29	Claims.						
Gresham, Joseph, widow of.	To be placed on a footing with those who received known wounds in revolutionary war.	9	1	Petition	289	Claims				Referred to Committee Whole House.		Leave to withdraw.
Gresham, Joseph, widow of.	To be placed on a footing with those who received known wounds in revolutionary war.	9	2	Petition	492	Claims	Jan. 6, 1807	Adverse		Leave to withdraw.		
Gresham, Joseph, widow of.	To be placed on a footing with those who received known wounds in revolutionary war.	11	2	Petition	197	Claims.						
Gresham, Thomas	Pension	31	1	Petition	983	Invalid Pensions.						
Gressum, Richard	Increase of pension	13	3	House bill	740	Whole House	Mar. 1, 1815	Favorable	303	Passed	Passed	App'd March 3, 1815
Gretton, George G.	Pension	14	2	Rep't Committee.	307	Whole House	Mar. 2, 1817	Favorable	91	Passed	Passed	App'd March 3, 1817
Grey, Rawden T.	To locate land in lieu of land taken by a pre-emption claimant.	24	1	Petition	258	Public Lands.						
Grice, Charles	Remission of forfeiture under embargo act of 1807.	16	2	Petition	34	Commerce				Discharged; laid on table.		
Grice, Charles	Remission of forfeiture under embargo act of 1807.	17	1	Petition	32	Commerce				Discharged; referred to Sec. Treasury.		
Grice, Charles	Remission of forfeiture under embargo act of 1807.	18	1	Petition	101	Commerce.						
Grice, Charles	Remission of forfeiture under embargo act of 1807.	19	1	Petition	35	Commerce				Discharged; laid on table.		
Grice, Charles	Remission of forfeiture under embargo act of 1807.	19	2	Petition	27	Commerce				Discharged; laid on table.		Leave to withdraw papers.
Grice, Francis	Compensation for his improvement of securing ships in dry dock.	30	2	Petition	337	Naval Affairs.						
Grice, Samuel	Payment for ship timber	22	1	Petition	63	Claims	61	Favorable	121	Laid on table.		
Grice, Samuel	Indemnity for damage by seizure of boats by United States officers in Florida, 1836.	30	1	Senate bill	957	Claims	April 12, 1848	With amend.	161	Passed	Passed, with amendment.	App'd Aug. 14, 1848
Gridley, Richard, heirs of.	Commutation pay	24	1	Resolution	854	Rev. Pensions.						

List of private claims presented to the House of Representatives of the United States from the 1st to the 31st Congress, inclusive—Continued.

Names of claimants.	Nature or object of the claim.	Congress.	Session.	How brought before the House of Reps.	Page of journal.	To what committee of the House referred.	No. or date of the report.	Nature of the report.	No. of the bill.	How disposed of by the House of Reps.	How disposed of by the Senate.	Date of the act of Congress, and remarks.
Grier, David, heirs of	Commutation pay	30	1	Petition	229	Rev. Claims	522	Favorable	308	Ref'd to Com. W. H.		
Grier, David, heirs of	Commutation pay	30	2	House bill	142	Whole House	Dec. 22, 1848	Favorable	308	Passed.		
Grier, David, heirs of	Commutation pay	31	1	Petition	391	Rev. Claims.						
Grier, James, widow of	Pension	19	1	Petition	334	Rev. Pensions	164	Adverse		Laid on table.		
Grier, James, widow of	Pension	29	1	Petition	424	Rev. Pensions.						
Grier, John	For extension of the act of September 28, 1850.	31	2	Petition	95	Public Lands.						
Grier, Samuel A	Reimbursement of money paid as surety of T. M. Dennis.	30	1	Petition	435	Claims	485	Favorable	403	Passed.		
Grier, Samuel A	Reimbursement of money paid as surety of T. M. Dennis.	30	2	House bill	619				403		Passed	App'd March 3, 1849
Griffin, Anna	Pension	31	1	Petition	526	Rev. Pensions	90	Favorable	111	Passed.		
Griffin, Benjamin	Pension	17	1	Petition	77	Rev. Pensions				Discharged; laid on table.		
Griffin, Benjamin	Pension	21	1	Petition	471	Military Pensions				Discharged; laid on table.		
Griffin, Benjamin	Pension	21	2	Petition	300	Military Pensions.						
Griffin, Corbin	(See Thomas Griffin, executors of.)	23			49							
Griffin, Cyrus	(See Benjamin Lincoln, *et al*)	2	1		484							
Griffin, ——	(See Giffin.)											
Griffin, Daniel	(See assignees of Thomas Tupper.)	22	2		142							
Griffin, Ezekiel, late widow of.	To refund money paid on forfeited land.	11	2	Petition	197	Public Lands	Feb. 21, 1810	Adverse		Rejected.		
Griffin, Greenbury	Payment for a vessel captured by the British.	14	2	Petition	58	Claims				Discharged; laid on table.		
Griffin, Greenbury	Payment for a vessel captured by the British.	15	1	Petition	183	Claims	Mar. 14, 1818	Adverse		Leave to withdraw.		
Griffin, Greenbury	Payment for a vessel captured by the British.	16	1	Petition	252	Claims	April 12, 1820	Adverse		Laid on table.		
Griffin, Greenbury	Payment for a vessel captured by the British.	17	1	Petition	276	Claims	Mar. 29, 1822	Adverse		Laid on table.		
Griffin, Greenbury	Payment for a vessel captured by the British.	21	1	Petition	547	Claims	April 29, 1830	Adverse		Laid on table.		
Griffin, Greenbury	Payment for a vessel captured by the British.	23	2	Petition	344	Claims.						
Griffin, Israel	Pension	29	1	Petition	303	Invalid Pensions.						
Griffin, Israel	Pension	30	2	Petition	237	Invalid Pensions	98	Adverse		Laid on table.		
Griffin, J. B. sureties of	Refunding money paid by them	22	1	Senate bill	892	Claims			S. 39			
Griffin, J. B. sureties of	Refunding money paid by them	23	1	Senate bill	692	P. Of. & P. Roads	June 20, 1834	With't amend.	S. 13	Passed	Passed	App'd June 30, 1834
Griffin, Joab	(See Willis Clemons, *et al.*)	24	1		476							
Griffin, John, (Pa.)	Pension	4	1	Petition	385	Claims	Jan. 26, 1796	General bill		Passed	Passed	App'd March 23, 1796
Griffin, John	Pension	14	2	Resolution	366	Pens. & Rev. Cl'ms.				Discharged; laid on table.		
Griffin, John, widow of	Pension	29	1	Memorial	362	Rev. Pensions.						
Griffin, John Talve, heir of	Indemnity for losses and payment of money advanced for public use.	25	2	Petition	269	Rev. Claims.						
Griffin, Jonathan	(See James Savage, *et al.*)	13	3		723							
Griffin, Joshua	Pension	17	1	Petition	45	Rev. Pensions				Discharged; laid on table.		
Griffin, Roberts	Pension	24	1	Petition	260	Invalid Pensions				Discharged; laid on table.		
Griffin, Samuel	(See John Hook, heirs of.)	21	1		360							
Griffin, Sianna	(See Thomas Kibby, widow of.)	31	1		628							

List of private claims presented to the House of Representatives of the United States from the 1st to the 31st Congress, inclusive—Continued.

Names of claimants.	Nature or object of the claim.	Congress.	Session.	How brought before the House of Reps.	Page of journal.	To what committee of the House referred.	No. or date of the report.	Nature of the report.	No. of the bill.	How disposed of by the House of Reps.	How disposed of by the Senate.	Date of the act of Congress, and remarks.
Griffin, Stephen	Pension	22	1	Petition	66	Rev. Pensions.						
Griffin, Stephen	Pension	25	2	Petition	547	Rev. Pensions				Discharged; laid on table.		
Griffin, Thomas	(See L. Gibbon, administrator of.)	20	2		108							
Griffin, Thomas	(See Wm. Morgan, administr'r of.)	15	1		135							
Griffin, Thomas, executor of.	Bounty land	23	1	Petition	49	Rev. Claims.						
Griffin, Thomas, executor of.	Bounty land	25	2	Petition	391	Rev. Claims				Discharged; laid on table.		
Griffin, Thomas, executor of.	Bounty land	26	1	Petition	167	Rev. Claims	446	Adverse		Laid on table.		
Griffin, Thomas, executor of.	Boun y land	28	1	Petition	193	Rev. Claims.						
Griffing, David	Payment for a sloop destroyed by the British.	25	3	Petition	118	Commerce	202	Adverse		Laid on table.		
Griffith, Abraham	Compensation for revolutionary services.	13	1	Petition	20	Claims.						
Griffith, Abraham	Compensation for discovering flour secreted by the British.	18	2	Petition	252	Pens. & Rev. Cl'ms.						
Griffith, Cornelius	For additional price as contractor for rations furnished U. State troops	14	2	Petition	355	Claims				Discharged; laid on table.		
Griffith, Cornelius	For additional price as contractor for rations furnished U. States troops.	15	1	Petition	192	Military Affairs				Discharged; laid on table.		
Griffith, Daniel	Confirmation of title to land	15	2	Petition	21	Priv. Land Claims				Discharged; laid on table.		
Griffith, Daniel	Confirmation of title to land	17	1	Petition	53	Public Lands				Discharged; laid on table.		
Griffith, Daniel	Confirmation of title to land	18	1	Petition	54	Public Lands				Discharged; laid on table.		
Griffith, F. L.	Reimbursement of expense of suits for acts done by order of his commanding officer.	21	2	Petition	163	Military Affairs.						
Griffith, Francis, (Ia.)	Pension	25	2	Petition	588	Invalid Pensions.						
Griffith, Francis, (Ia.)	Pension	25	3	Petition	416	Invalid Pensions	Feb. 16, 1839	Adverse		Laid on table.		
Griffith, Francis, (Ia.)	Pension	26	2	Petition	55	Invalid Pensions	64	Adverse		Laid on table.		
Griffith, Francis, (Ia.)	Pension	27	2	Petition	772	Invalid Pensions	826	Adverse		Laid on table.		
Griffith, Francis R.	Indemnity for French spoliations prior to 1800.	31	1	Petition	647	Foreign Affairs	355	General bill	318	Referred to Committee Whole House.		
Griffith, Griffin	Pension	4	2	Petition	648	Claims	May 3, 1797	Adverse				Provided for by act of 23d March, 1792.
Griffith, Isaac W.	Increase of pension	30	2	Memorial & joint resl'n of Legislature of Iowa.	241, 281, 296	Invalid Pensions.						
Griffith, Isaac W.	Increase of pension	31	1	Senate bill	1430	Invalid Pensions			48			
Griffith, Isaac W.	Increase of pension	31	2	Senate amendm't to House bill.	154	Whole House	Feb. 9, 1851	Favorable	85	Passed	Passed	App'd March 3, 1851
Griffith, John	Settlement of claim against United States	1	2	Petition	285					Referred to Secretary Treasury.		
Griffith, John	Settlement of claim against United States.	2	2	Rep. of Secretary Treasury.	626					Laid on table.		
Griffith, John	Pension	23	2	Petition	182	Rev. Pensions				Discharged; laid on table.		

List of private claims presented to the House of Representatives of the United States from the 1*st to the* 31*st Congress, inclusive*—Continued.

Names of claimants.	Nature or object of the claim.	Congress.	Session.	How brought before the House of Reps.	Page of journal.	To what committee of the House referred.	No. or date of the report.	Nature of the report.	No. of the bill.	How disposed of by the House of Reps.	How disposed of by the Senate.	Date of the act of Congress, and remarks.
Griffith, John	Pension	24	1	Petition	57	Rev. Pensions				Discharged; laid on table.		
Griffith, Levi	Compensation for revolutionary services.	12	1	Petition	142					Ref. to Com. Whole House on bill 15.		
Griffith, Philomen	Pension	15	2	Petition	27	Rev. Pensions	Jan. 21, 1819	Adverse		Laid on table.		
Griffith, Robert	(See D. Moore)	21	1		173							
Griffith, Robert E.	(See Nicklin & Griffith)	8	2		122							
Griffith, Robert E.	(See Nicklin & Griffith)	9	1		281							
Griffith, Robert E.	(See Nicklin & Griffith, surviving partners of.)	19	1		312							
Griffith, Robert E.	(See Thomas Phillips, administrator of.	26	1		182							
Griffith, Robert E.	Indemnity for French spoliations prior to 1800.	26	1	Memorial	182	Foreign Affairs	343	Favorable; bill	319	Referred to Committee Whole House.		
Griffith, Sally	(See Mrs. George Thompson, executrix of.)	15	1		34							
Griffith, Samuel	Arrears of pension	19	2	Petition	91	Military Pensions.						
Griffith, Samuel	Arrears of pension	23	1	Petition	525	Invalid Pensions				Discharged; laid on table.		
Griffith, Samuel	Arrears of pension	24	1	Memorial	201	Invalid Pensions	June 28, 1836	Adverse		Laid on table.		
Griffith, Samuel	Arrears of pension	25	2	Petition	197	Invalid Pensions				Discharged; laid on table.		
Griffith, Samuel	Increase of pension	26	1	Petition	326	Invalid Pensions				Discharged; laid on table.		
Griffith, Samuel	Increase of pension	27	2	Petition	460	Invalid Pensions	612	Adverse		Laid on table.		
Griffith, Stephen, agent of the owners of the Atalanta.	Indemnity for French spoliations prior to 1800.	26	1	Memorial	182	Foreign Affairs	343	Favorable	319	Referred to Committee Whole House.		
Griffith, Stephen, heirs of.	Indemnity for French spoliations prior to 1800.	31	1	Petition	408	Foreign Affairs	355	General bill	318	Referred to Committee Whole House.		
Griffith, William	(See William Tilghman, *et al*)	7	2		307							
Griffith, William B.	(See heirs of Thomas Tyler)	19	1		134							
Griggs, Abel	Compensation as messenger to officers of marine corps.	21	2	Petition	83	Claims	Dec. 27, 1830	Adverse		Laid on table.		
Griggs, Abel	Compensation as messenger to officers of marine corps.	23	1	Petition	92	Naval Affairs	485	Adverse		Laid on table.		
Griggs, Abel	Compensation as messenger to officers of marine corps.	26	1	Petition	330	Naval Affairs.						
Griggs, Abel	Compensation as messenger to officers of marine corps.	26	2	Petition	79	Naval Affairs.						
Griggs, Gideon	Pension	11	2	House bill	283	Whole House	Mar. 24, 1810	Favorable	107	Passed	Passed	App'd April 27, 1810
Griggs, John	Pension	11	3	House bill	604	Whole House	March 2, 1811	Favorable	218	Passed	Passed	App'd March 3, 1811
Grignon, Augustine, and Lewis.	(See Daniel Whitney, *et al.*)	23	1		450							
Grignon, Charles A.	Confirmation of title to land	24	1	Petition	538	Priv. Land Claims.	Mar. 31, 1836	Favorable	520			
Grignon, Charles A.	Confirmation of title to land	25	2	Petition	43	Priv. Land Claims.	Jan. 10, 1838	Adverse		Laid on table		
Grignon, John B., heirs of	Resurvey of land on Fox river	23	1	Petition	450	Priv. Land Claims.				Discharged; laid on table.		
Grignon, Pierre, *et al.*	Patent of certain lands	25	2	Senate bill	508	Public Lands	782	Adverse	17	Ref'd to Com. W. H.		
Grignon, Robert	Patent of certain lands	25	2	Resolution	1176	Priv. Land Claims.				Discharged; laid on table.		
Grignon, Robert	Pension	27	2	Petition	611	Invalid Pensions	968	Adverse		Laid on table.		
Grigsby, John	Pension	26	2	Petition	61	Rev. Pensions	Dec. 22, 1840	Adverse		Laid on table.		

List of private claims presented to the House of Representatives of the United States from the 1st to the 31st Congress, inclusive—Continued.

Names of claimants.	Nature or object of the claim.	Congress.	Session.	How brought before the House of Reps.	Page of journal.	To what committee of the House referred.	No. or date of the report.	Nature of the report.	No. of the bill.	How disposed of by the House of Reps.	How disposed of by the Senate.	Date of the act of Congress, and remarks.
Grigsby, John	Pension	28	1	Petition	435	Rev. Pensions.						
Grigsby, Spitsby	Pension	22	1	Resolution	71	Rev. Pensions.						
Grim, Henry	Payment for horse lost in United States service.	24	2	Petition	80	Claims	Feb. 14, 1837	Ref. to Third Auditor.		Report adopted.		
Grimball, John, heirs of	Reimbursement of money paid for land.	24	2	Petition	210	Priv. Land Claims.						
Grimball, John, heirs of	Reimbursement of money paid for land.	25	2	Petition	374	Public Lands	802	Adverse		Laid on table.		
Grimball, John, heirs of	Reimbursement of money paid for land.	25	3	Petition	134	Priv. Land Claims.	47	Favorable	938	Passed		Recommitted to Com. Whole House.
Grimball, John, heirs of	Reimbursement of money paid for land.	26	1	Petition	177	Public Lands	83	Favorable	75	Passed	Passed	App'd May 2, 1840
Grimball, Thomas	(See Abraham M. Scott, *et al.*)	14	1		113							
Grimes, Cunningham	Correction of error in land entry	25	2	Petition	418	Priv. Land Claims.						
Grimes, Hiram	Payment for supplies furnished United States troops.	31	2	Petition	280	Naval Affairs.						
Grimes, James, widow of.	Pension	27	3	Petition	260	Rev. Pensions				Discharged; laid on table.		
Grimes, Jesse	Not stated	19	2	Petition	54	P. Of. and P. Roads.	Jan. 17, 1818	Favorable	380			
Grimes, John	Payment for a horse and other property lost in United States service.	15	2	Petition	24	Claims	Dec. 2, 1818	Adverse		Leave to withdraw.		
Grimes, John	Payment for a horse and other property lost in United States service.	16	1	Petition	142	Claims				Discharged; leave to withdraw.		
Grimes, John	(See Samuel Q. Richardson, *et al.*)	19	1		337							
Grimes, John (Tenn.)	Pension	20	1	Petition	278	Military Pensions				Discharged; laid on table.		
Grimes, William	To be allowed to exchange land	15	1	Petition	178	Public Lands	Jan. 15, 1819	Adverse		Rejected.		
Grimes, William, (Pa.)	Pension	22	1	Petition	41	Invalid Pensions.						
Grimm, John	Increase of pension	26	1	Resolution	552	Rev. Pensions	April 4, 1840	Adverse		Laid on table.		
Grinal, Owen	Pension	14	2	Petition	283	Pens. & Rev. Cl'ms.						
Grinal, Owen	Pension	23	2	Memorial	67	Select	Feb. 25, 1835	Favorable	769	Referred to Committee Whole House.		
Grinal, Owen	Pension	24	1	Documents	136	Select	337	Favorable	352	Referred to Committee Whole House.		
Grinnell, Elizabeth	(See Archclaus Batchelder)	29	1		284							
Grinnell, Mentune, & Co.	Reimbursement of duties on lace goods.	28	1	Petition	525	Commerce				Laid on table.		
Grinnell, Peter	To be released from judgment	26	1	Petition	619	P. Of. and P. Roads.	April 4, 1840	Adverse		Laid on table.		
Grist, Allen, *et al.*	(See Jacob A., Blackwell)	17	2		118							
Grist, Jacob	Pension	25	2	Petition	272	Rev. Pensions	608	Favorable	588	Passed.		
Grist, Jacob	Pension	25	3	Petition	87	Rev. Pensions.						
Grist, Jacob	Pension	26	1	Petition	174	Rev. Pensions				Discharged; laid on table.		
Griswold, Andrew	Pension	2	1	Petition	486					Referred to Secretary War.		
Griswold, Andrew	Pension	15	1	Petition	150	Pens. & Rev. Cl'ms.				Discharged; laid on table.		
Griswold, Chester	Pension	22	2	Resolution	121	Invalid Pensions				Discharged; laid on table.		
Griswold, Chester	Pension	23	1	Petition	44	Invalid Pensions	Dec. 13, 1833	Adverse		Laid on table.		
Griswold, Chester	Pension	23	2	Petition	41	Invalid Pensions	Dec. 23, 1834	Adverse		Laid on table.		

List of private claims presented to the House of Representatives of the United States from the 1st to the 31st Congress, inclusive—Continued.

Names of claimants.	Nature or object of the claim.	Congress.	Session.	How brought before the House of Reps.	Page of journal.	To what committee of the House referred.	No. or date of the report.	Nature of the report.	No. of the bill.	How disposed of by the House of Reps.	How disposed of by the Senate.	Date of the act of Congress, and remarks.
Griswold, Chester	Pension	25	2	Petition	269	Invalid Pensions				Discharged; laid on table.		
Griswold, Chester	Pension	26	1	Petition	863	Invalid Pensions	564	Adverse		Laid on table.		
Griswold, Daniel, *et al.*	(See Louis Drouillard)	31	2		102							
Griswold, Daniel, heirs of.	Pension	30	1	Petition	471	Invalid Pensions.						
Griswold, George	Indemnity for French spoliations prior to 1800.	26	1	Memorial	182	Foreign Affairs	313	Favorable; bill	319	Referred to Committee Whole House.		
Griswold, George, *et al.*	Indemnity for French spoliations prior to 1800.	27	2	Petition	237	Foreign Affairs.						
Griswold, Nathan	Pension	25	2	Petition	54	Rev. Pensions				Discharged; laid on table.		
Griswold, Simon	Pension	21	2	Petition	174	Military Pensions				Discharged; laid on table.		
Griswold, Simon	Pension	22	1	Petition	163	Rev. Pensions.						
Griswold, Solomon	Pension	16	1	Petition	51	Rev. Pensions	Jan. 14, 1820	Adverse		Laid on table.		
Griswold, Solomon	Pension	19	2	Resolution	193	Military Pensions.						
Griswold, Stanley	Increase of salary, Secretary Michigan.	9	1	Petition	229	Select				Discharged; referred to Com. Whole House.		
Groat, John	Pension	25	2	Petition	117	Invalid Pensions.						
Grobe, Peter	Compensation for revolutionary services.	3	1	Petition	106					Referred to Secretary of War.		
Grobe, Peter	Compensation for revolutionary services.	3	2	Rep. of Secretary War.	278					Laid on table.		
Groce, Jared E	Correction of error in land payment.	20	1	House bill	513	Public Lands	230	Favorable	216	Referred to Committee Whole House.		
Groce, Jared E	Correction of error in land payment.	20	2	House bill	284	Whole House	Feb. 13, 1829	Favorable	261	Passed.		
Groce, Jared E	Correction of error in land payment.	21	1	Petition	413	Public Lands	328	Favorable	385			
Groce, Jared E	Correction of error in land payment.	22	1	Petition	173	Public Lands	Jan. 20, 1832	Favorable	298	R f'd to Com. W. H.		
Groce, Jared E	Correction of error in land payment.	22	2	House bill	171	Whole House	Jan. 12, 1833	Favorable	298	Passed	Passed	App'd March 2, 1833
Groesbeck, Gerrit, jr	Payment for losses and expenses by fracture of his leg while in United States service.	22	2	Petition	218	Claims	Feb. 5, 1833	Adverse		Laid on table.		
Grogan, Nelson	(See David A. Ely, *et al.*)	30	2		91							
Gronia, Valentine	Pension	22	1	Petition	288	Rev. Pensions	Feb. 15, 1832	Adverse		Laid on table.		
Groning, Lewis, *et al*	Indemnity for French spoliations prior to 1800.	20	1	Petition	32	Foreign Affairs	263	Adverse		Referred to President United States.		
Groom, Abraham	(See Joseph Boggs, *et al.*)	22	2		122							
Groom, Abraham	(See Reuben E. Gentry, *et al.*)	24	1		96							
Groom, Jacob	Indemnity for Indian depredations.	26	1	Petition	436	Indian Affairs.						
Groom, Jacob, *et al.*	Indemnity for Indian depredations.	24	1	Documents	426	Indian Affairs.						
Groom, Jacob, *et al.*	Indemnity for Indian depredations.	25	3	Petition	124	Indian Affairs.						
Groom, Wright	Payment for pack saddles	24	2	Petition	208	Claims	237	Favorable		Referred to Quartermaster General.		
Groom, Wright	Payment for pack saddles	25	2	Petition	398	Claims.						
Groscrost, Jacob	Indemnity for damage to wagon and team, and for a horse lost in United States service.	16	1	Petition	258	Claims	April 12, 1820	Adverse		Laid on table.		
Groscrost, Jacob	Indemnity for damage to wagon and team, and for a horse lost in United States service.	19	2	Petition	112	Claims	Jan. 5, 1827	Adverse		Laid on table.		
Grose, Samuel	Pension	3	1	Rep. of Secretary War.	131	Select	May 26, 1794	Joint res. to refer to Sec. of War.	J. R. 12	Passed	Passed	App'd June 9, 1794

List of private claims presented to the House of Representatives of the United States from the 1st to the 31st Congress, inclusive—Continued.

Names of claimants.	Nature or object of the claim.	Congress.	Session.	How brought before the House of Reps.	Page of journal.	To what committee of the House referred.	No. or date of the report.	Nature of the report.	No. of the bill.	How disposed of by the House of Reps.	How disposed of by the Senate.	Date of the act of Congress, and remarks.
Grose, Samuel	Pension	4	1	Rep. of Secretary War.	445	Claims.						
Grose, Samuel	Pension	4	2	Rep. of Secretary War.	614	Claims.						
Gross, Frederick	Payment for wagon and team lost in United States service.	14	1	Petition	48	Claims				Discharged; laid on table.		
Gross, Jacob and George	(See Casper B. Cook, *et al.*)	30	1		272							
Gross, George	(See Archibald Beard, *et al.*)	30	1		239							
Gross, Henry	Pension	16	1	Petition	174	Rev. Pensions				Discharged; laid on table.		
Grosvenor, Abel M., heir of.	Indemnity for property destroyed by the enemy.	29	1	Petition	567	Claims.						
Grosvenor, Samuel	Pension	21	2	Petition	43	Military Pensions.						
Grosvenor, Samuel	Pension	22	1	Petition	105	Rev. Pensions				Discharged; laid on table.		
Grote, John D.	Compensation for revolutionary services of his father.	30	1	Petition	288	Claims.						
Grouard, George, *et al.*	To be allowed one dollar per day as volunteers, Florida war.	26	1	Petition	702	Claims.						
Grouard, George, *et al.*	To be allowed one dollar per day as volunteers, Florida war.	27	2	Petition	443	Claims.						
Grouard, George, *et al.*	To be allowed one dollar per day as volunteers, Florida war.	31	1	Petition	632	Claims.						
Groning, Lewis and R.	Indemnity for French spoliations prior to 1800.	26	1	Memorial	182	Foreign Affairs	343	Favorable; bil	319	Referred to Committee Whole House.		
Groun, Benjamin	Pension	22	1	Petition	206	Invalid Pensions	July 13, 1832	General bill	288	Passed	Passed	App'd July 14, 1832
Grout, Philip	Pension	29	2	Petition	100	Invalid Pensions.						
Grout, Theophilus	Indemnity for expenses of his son who was wounded while assisting to enforce revenue laws.	23	1	Petition	245	Claims	489	Adverse		Laid on table.		
Grout, William	Pension	16	1	Petition	147	Pens. & Rev. Cl'ms.				Discharged; referred to Secretary of War.		
Grove, Federick, *et al.*	(See William McGhee, heirs of.)	30	1		398							
Grove, Peter, Adam, and administrator of Michael.	Payment for supplies furnished United States army, revolutionary war.	4	2	Petition	678	Claims	Feb. 10, 1797	Adverse		Rejected.		
Groveman, A.	Indemnity for French spoliations prior to 1800.	29	2	Memorial	87	Foreign Affairs.						
Groveman A., administrator of.	Indemnity for French spoliations prior to 1800.	31	1	Memorial	271	Foreign Affairs	355	General bill	318	Referred to Committee Whole House.		
Grover, Amasa	Pension	4	1	Rep. of Secretary War.	445	Claims	Mar. 14, 1796	Favorable	156	Passed	Passed	App'd April 20, 1796
Grover, Amasa	Increase of pension	12	1	House bill	361	Whole House	June 15, 1812	Favorable	138	Passed	Passed	App'd July 5, 1812
Grover, Benjamin	Pension	20	2	Petition	99	Military Pensions.		General bill.	440			
Grover, Benjamin	Pension	21	2	Petition	336	Military Pensions.						
Grover, Benjamin	Pension	24	1	Petition	72	Invalid Pensions	214	General bill	288	Passed	Passed, with amendment.	App'd July 14, 1832 omitting petitioner's name.
Grover, Benjamin	To correct an error in act 14th July, 1832.	22	2	Resolution	44	Invalid Pensions	Feb. 15, 1833	Favorable	738	Referred to Committee Whole House.		
Grover, Benjamin	To correct an error in act 14th July, 1832.	23	1	Petition	72	Invalid Pensions	37	Favorable	42	Passed	Passed, with amendment.	App'd June 30, 1834

List of private claims presented to the House of Representatives of the United States from the 1st to the 31st Congress, inclusive—Continued.

Names of claimants.	Nature or object of the claim.	Congress.	Session.	How brought before the House of Reps.	Page of journal.	To what committee of the House referred.	No. or date of the report.	Nature of the report.	No. of the bill.	How disposed of by the House of Reps.	How disposed of by the Senate.	Date of the act of Congress, and remarks.
Grover, William, widow of	Pension	24	2	Petition	45	Naval Affairs	8	Favorable	765	Referred to Committee Whole House.		
Groves, James	Compensation for services of an apprentice in revolutionary war.	2	1	Petition	456					Referred to Secretary of War.		
Groves, James	Compensation for services of an apprentice in revolutionary war.	2	2	Rep. of Secretary of War.	735					Laid on table.		
Groves, John	Pension	25	3	Petition	460	Rev. Pensions.						
Groves, John	Pension	26	1	Petition	174	Rev. Pensions	490	Adverse		Laid on table.		
Grozer, William	Remission of forfeiture for violation of revenue laws.	25	2	Petition	199	Commerce	817	Favorable	758	Referred to Committee Whole House.		
Grozer, William	Remission of forfeiture for violation of revenue laws.	25	3	House bill	381	Whole House	Jan. 26, 1839	Favorable	758	Passed	Passed	App'd March 3, 1839
Grubb, Adam, wife of	Relief for wounds received in naval service.	2	1	Petition	489					Referred to Secretary War.		
Grubb, Catherine	(See James Fullerton, widow of.)	18	1		134							
Grubb, Curtis	Indemnity for damage done to his farm by United States troops.	23	1	Petition	437	Claims.						
Grubb, Curtis	Indemnity for damage done to his farm by United States troops.	24	1	Petition	141	Claims	630	Favorable	613			
Grubb, Curtis	Indemnity for damage done to his farm by United States troops.	25	2	Petition	36	Claims	42	Favorable	54	Passed	Passed	App'd April 20, 1838
Grubb, Curtis and Peter, heirs of.	Payment of a treasury certificate	28	2	Petition	83	Rev. Claims.						
Grubb, Curtis and Peter, heirs of.	Payment of a treasury certificate	29	1	Petition	310	Claims.						
Grubb, Curtis and Peter, heirs of.	Payment of a treasury certificate	30	1	Petition	298	Ways and Means.						
Grubb, Daniel	To exchange bounty land	22	1	Resolution	561	Public Lands.						
Grubb, James, executrix of	Indemnity for French spoliations prior to 1800.	26	1	Memorial	182	Foreign Affairs	343	Favorable; bill	319	Referred to Committee Whole House.		
Grubb, John	To be paid amount due for rations while in the military service of United States.	21	1	Petition	83	Claims	Jan. 5, 1830	Adverse		Laid on table.		
Grubb, John, widow of	Pension	27	2	Resolution	241	Rev. Pensions	784	Adverse		Laid on table.		
Gruber, Valentine	Arrears of pension	24	2	Petition	216	Rev. Pensions				Discharged; laid on table.		
Gruber, Valentine	Arrears of pension	25	2	Petition	182	Rev. Pensions				Discharged; laid on table.		
Grundy, George, trustee of	Indemnity for French spoliations prior to 1800.	26	1	Memorial	182	Foreign Affairs	343	Favorable: bill	319	Referred to Committee Whole House.		
Grunner, Martin	(See Martin Brunner.)	24	1		913							
Grymes, Benjamin, heirs and representatives of.	Confirmation of title to land	9	1	Petition	253	Public Lands	April 14, 1806	Adverse		Laid on table.		
Grymes, Benjamin, heirs and representatives of.	Confirmation of title to land	9	2	Petition	586	Whole House.						
Grymes, William, heirs of.	Payment of seven years' half-pay	23	1	Petition	55, 157	Rev. Claims.						
Grymes, William, heirs of.	Payment of seven years' half-pay	23	2	Petition	120	Rev. Claims	112	Favorable	739			
Grymes, William, heirs of.	Payment of seven years' half-pay	24	1	Petition	104	Rev. Claims	Jan. 12, 1836	Favorable	125	Passed	Passed	App'd July 2, 1836
Grymes, William, heirs of.	Interest on amount allowed by act of July 2, 1836.	24	2	Petition	40	Rev. Claims.						

List of private claims presented to the House of Representatives of the United States from the 1st to the 31st Congress, inclusive—Continued.

Names of claimants.	Nature or object of the claim.	Congress.	Session.	How brought before the House of Reps.	Page of journal.	To what committee of the House referred.	No. or date of the report.	Nature of the report.	No. of the bill.	How disposed of by the House of Reps.	How disposed of by the Senate.	Date of the act of Congress, and remarks.
98 Grymes, William, heirs of.	Interest on amount allowed by act of July 2, 1836.	25	2	Petition	81	Rev. Claims	250	Favorable	291			
Grymes, William, heirs of.	Interest on amount allowed by act of July 2, 1836.	26	1	Petition	163	Rev. Claims.						
Grymes, William, heirs of.	Interest on amount allowed by act of July 2, 1836.	27	2	Petition	62	Rev. Claims	April 1, 1842	Adverse	......	Laid on table.		
Grymes, William, heirs of.	Interest on amount allowed by act of July 2, 1836.	28	1	Petition	319	Rev. Claims.						
Grymes, William, heirs of.	Interest on amount allowed by act of July 2, 1836.	29	1	Petition	435	Rev. Claims.						
Grymes, William, heirs of.	Interest on amount allowed by act of July 2, 1836.	29	2	Petition	131	Rev. Claims	32	Favorable	615	Referred to Committee Whole House.		
Grymes, William, heirs of.	Interest on amount allowed by act of July 2, 1836.	31	1	Petition	511	Rev. Claims	428	Adverse	......	Laid on table.		
Grymes, William, heirs of.	Interest on amount allowed by act of July 2, 1836.	31	2	Petition	118	Invalid Pensions.						
Grymes, William F., *et al.*	(See Benjamin Grymes, heirs and representatives of.)	9	1	....	253							
Guard, Daniel	Pension	9	2	House bill	608	Whole House	Feb. 28, 1807	Favorable	216	Passed	Passed	App'd March 3, 1807
Guard, David	(See David Girard)	21	1	....	289, 107							
Gue, Francis, (Florida)	Compensation for materials taken from his property, called the Burnt Barrack, and used by United States.	19	1	Petition	365	Claims	April 25, 1826	Adverse	......	Laid on table.		
Gue, Francis, (Florida)	Compensation for materials taken from his property, called the Burnt Barrack, and used by United States.	19	2	Petition	132	Claims	Jan. 18, 1827	Adverse	......	Laid on table.		
Guedry, David	Confirmation of title to land in Louisiana.	27	2	Senate bill	359	Priv. Land Claims.	Feb. 26, 1842	Favorable	S. 76	Passed	Passed	App'd July 6, 1842
Guedry, Joseph	Confirmation of title to land	22	2	Petition	89	Priv. Land Claims.	18	Favorable	648			
Guedry, Joseph	Confirmation of title to land	23	1	Petition	93	Priv. Land Claims.	72	Favorable	82	Passed	Passed	App'd June 27, 1834
Guedry, Onezime	Confirmation of title to land	27	2	Senate bill	359	Priv. Land Claims.	Feb. 26, 1842	Favorable	76	Passed	Passed	App'd July 6, 1842
Guedry, Pierre, widow of	Confirmation of title to land	21	2	Petition	46	Priv. Land Claims.						
Guedry, Pierre, representative of.	Confirmation of title to land	22	1	Petition	75	Priv. Land Claims.	82	Favorable	162	Passed	Passed	App'd July 14, 1832
Guen, Lewis L.	For an extension of time to export indigo.	5	2	Rep't Committee	99	Whole House	Dec. 22, 1797	Favorable	......	Rejected.		
Guenet, Charles	Reimbursement of duties on silks	26	1	Petition	358	Ways and Means.						
Guenet, Charles	Reimbursement of duties on silks	27	3	Petition	257	Ways and Means.						
Guera, Antonio	Confirmation of title to land	22	1	Petition	64	Priv. Land Claims.	Dec. 27, 1831	Favorable	125	Passed	Passed	App'd June 25, 1832
Guerlain, Lewis H.	(See Bethman & Son)	4	2	....	633							
Guerlain, Lewis H.	Indemnity for damage to plantation by United States army.	15	1	Petition	294	Claims	....	....	......	Discharged; laid on table.		
Guerlain, Lewis H.	Indemnity for damage to plantation by United States army.	15	2	Senate bill	316	Claims	....	....	58			
Guerlain, Lewis H.	Indemnity for damage to plantation by United States army.	16	1	Senate bill	498	Claims	....	....	116			
Guerlain, Lewis H.	Indemnity for damage to plantation by United States army.	16	2	Petition	20	Claims	Dec. 20, 1820	Favorable	176	Passed	Passed	App'd March 2, 1821
Guerrant, Daniel	Pension	26	1	Petition	797	Invalid Pensions.						
Guerrant, Daniel	Pension	27	2	Petition	97	Invalid Pensions.						

List of private claims presented to the House of Representatives of the United States from the 1st *to the* 31st *Congress, inclusive*—Continued.

Names of claimants.	Nature or object of the claim.	Congress.	Session.	How brought before the House of Reps.	Page of journal.	To what committee of the House referred.	No. or date of the report.	Nature of the report.	No. of the bill.	How disposed of by the House of Reps.	How disposed of by the Senate.	Date of the act of Congress, and remarks.
Guerrant, Daniel	Pension	27	3	Petition	44	Invalid Pensions.						
Guerrant, Daniel	Pension	28	2	Petition	170	Invalid Pensions.						
Guerrant, Daniel	Pension	30	2	Petition	366	Invalid Pensions	Feb. 13, 1849	Adverse	......	Laid on table.		
Guerrant, Daniel	Pension	31	1	Petition	898	Invalid Pensions.						
Guess, George	Indian spoliations	20	1	Appropriation bill	....	....	....	....	......	....	....	Statutes at Large, vol. 4, p. 301.
Guess, Isaac	Confirmation of title to land	29	1	Petition	502	Priv. Land Claims.	655	Favorable	437	Ref'd to Com. W. H.		
Guess, Isaac	Confirmation of title to land	29	2	House bill	211	Whole House	Jan. 22, 1847	Favorable	437	Passed	Passed	App'd March 3, 1847
Guess, William	Compensation as agent to collect property under treaty with Cherokee Indians.	27	2	Petition	886	Claims.						
Guess, William	Compensation as agent to collect property under treaty with Cherokee Indians.	27	3	Petition	237	Claims.						
Guest, John, widow of	Indemnity for damage to property by the British.	20	1	Petition	195	Claims	186	Favorable	214	Referred to Committee Whole House.		
Guest, John, widow of	Indemnity for damage to property by the British.	20	2	House bill	202	Whole House	Jan. 24, 1829	Favorable	214	Passed	Passed	App'd March 3, 1829
Guest, John, widow of	For drawback of duties on goods exported.	25	2	Memorial	984	Ways and Means.						
Guest, John, widow of	For drawback of duties on goods exported.	25	3	Petition	226	Ways and Means.						
Guest, John, widow of	For drawback of duties on goods exported.	26	1	Petition	328	Commerce.						
Guest, John, widow of	For drawback of duties on goods exported.	26	2	Petition	78	Commerce	164	Favorable	680			
Guest, John, widow of	For drawback of duties on goods exported.	27	2	Petition	152	Commerce.						
Guest, John, widow of	For drawback of duties on goods exported.	27	3	Petition	45	Commerce	Jan. 28, 1843	Favorable	734	Passed	Indef. postp'd.	
Guest, John, widow of	For drawback of duties on goods exported.	28	1	Petition	141	Commerce.						
Guest, John, widow of	For drawback of duties on goods exported.	28	2	Petition	112	Commerce.						
Guest, Russel	(See William H. Bedford, agent.)	28	1	....	262							
Guestier, Peter A., and others.	Reimbursement of duties paid by former owners of ship Blairrau.	8	2	Petition	104	Claims.						
Guestier, Peter A., and others.	Reimbursement of duties paid by former owners of ship Blairrau.	9	1	Petition	191	Claims.	Mar. 10, 1806	Adverse	......	Referred to Committee Whole House.		
Guestier, Peter A., and others.	Reimbursement of duties paid by former owners of ship Blairrau.	17	1	Petition	263	Ways and Means.						
Guestier, Peter A., and others.	Reimbursement of duties paid by former owners of ship Blairrau.	17	2	Petition	48	Ways and Means	Jan. 6, 1823	Adverse	......	Laid on table.		
Guestier, Peter A., and others.	Reimbursement of duties paid by former owners of ship Blairrau.	18	1	Petition	366	Ways and Means.						
Guestier, Peter A., and others.	Reimbursement of duties paid by former owners of ship Blairrau.	18	2	Petition	46	Ways and Means	Dec. 22, 1824	Adverse	......	Rejected.		
Guestier, Peter A., and others.	Reimbursement of duties paid by former owners of ship Blairrau.	19	1	Petition	291	Ways and Means	....	....	......	Discharged; leave to withdraw.		
Guffy, Alexander	Bounty land	19	1	Petition	224	Rev. Claims	April 5, 1826	Adverse	......	Laid on table.		
Guibourd, Jaquez	Confirmation of title to land	22	1	Petition	372	Priv. Land Claims.	Feb. 17, 1832	Favorable	380	Referred to Committee Whole House.		
Guichot, Maturin	Confirmation of title to land	18	1	Petition	75	Priv. Land Claims.	April 27, 1824	Favorable	205	Passed	Passed	App'd May 19, 1824

List of private claims presented to the House of Representatives of the United States from the 1st to the 31st Congress, inclusive—Continued.

Names of claimants.	Nature or object of the claim.	Congress.	Session.	How brought before the House of Reps.	Page of journal.	To what committee of the House referred.	No. or date of the report.	Nature of the report.	No. of the bill.	How disposed of by the House of Reps.	How disposed of by the Senate.	Date of the act of Congress, and remarks.
Guier, E. P., *et al*	For pay as mail contractors	29	2	Petition	183	P. Of. & P. Roads.						
Guier, E. P., *et al*	For pay as mail contractors	30	2	Petition	262	P. Of. & P. Roads.	49	Adverse.				
Guier, George	(See John S. Ardis, heirs of)	29	1		511							
Guild, Ann, *et al*	Pension	27	2	Petition	256	Rev. Pensions.						
Guild, ———,	Pension	21	1	Resolution	207	Military Pensions				Discharged; laid on table.		
Guild, Holly	Pension	27	1	Petition	107	Invalid Pensions.						
Guild, Holly	Pension	27	2	Petition	154	Invalid Pensions	630	Adverse		Laid on table.		
Guild, Holly	Pension	28	1	Petition	337	Invalid Pensions	177	Adverse		Laid on table.		
Guild, Jesse, *et al*	Pension	22	1	Petition	105	Rev. Pensions	158	Favorable	237	Referred to Committee Whole House.		
Guild, Jesse, *et al*	Pension	22	2	House bill	123	Whole House	Jan. 2, 1833	Favorable	237	Laid on table.		
Guild, Moses, jr	(Not stated.)	19	2	Petition	26	Ways and Means				Discharged; leave to withdraw.		
Guild, Richard	Pension	17	1	Petition	51	Rev. Pensions				Discharged; laid on table.		
Guilhon, Jules	(Not stated.)	19	2	Petition	37	Commerce				Discharged; laid on table.		
Guillemard, Arnauld	(See Marcos DeVilliers, *et al.*)	17	1		281							
Guillemard, Arnauld	For rent of store-house in Florida	19	1	Petition	99	Claims	Jan. 4, 1826	Adverse		Laid on table.		
Guillet, Urbain, *et al.*, of the Society of La Trappe.	Confirmation of title to land, and permission to buy on credit, and to locate land warrants adjoining.	11	2	Petition	307	Public Lands.						
Guillet, Urbain, *et al.*, of the Society of La Trapp.	Confirmation of title to land, and permission to buy on credit, and to locate land warrants adjoining.	11	2	Senate bill	364	Whole House			31			
Guillet, Urbain, *et al.*, of the Society of La Trapp.	Confirmation of title to land, and permission to buy on credit, and to locate land warrants adjoining.	11	3	Petition	479	Public Lands.						
Guilliam, William	For bounty land	15	1	Petition	35	Pens. & Rev. Cl'ms.				Discharged; laid on table.		
Guillon, Charles F	Indemnity for losses by the wreck of the U. S. ship Peacock.	28	2	Petition	391	Naval Affairs				Discharged; laid on table.		
Guillon, C. T. B.	(See Exploring Expedition)	27	3		149							
Guillow, Francis	Compensation for revolutionary services.	4	1	Petition	439	Claims				Referred to Committee Whole House.		
Guillow, Francis	Compensation for revolutionary services.	4	2	Petition	709	Claims.						
Guillow, Francis	Compensation for revolutionary services.	5	2	Petition	89	Claims	Mar. 19, 1798	Adverse.		Rejected.		
Guinard, William	Increase of pension	31	1	Petition	863	Naval Affairs	Aug. 1, 1850	Favorable	369	Referred to Committee Whole House.		
Guion, Frederick	Payment of certificate of public debt.	4	1	Letter of Secret'y Treasury.	388	Claims	Mar. 31, 1796	Adverse.				
Guion, Isaac	Compensation for services rendered under the direction of the President.	1	2	Appropriat'n bill.								Stat. at Large, vol. 1, p. 185.
Guion & McLaughlin	Compensation for carrying the mail.	30	2	Petition	262	P. Of. and P. Roads.	49	Adverse.				
Guiteau, Calvin	Renewal of patent	30	1	Petition	682	Patents.						
Gulion, Jeremiah, widow of	Pension	26	1	Resolution	546	Rev. Pensions.						
Gullion, Robert	To be allowed to buy land on credit	17	1	Petition	294	Public Lands				Discharged; laid on table.		
Gullodge, Thomas	To correct error in land entry	19	2	Senate bill	227	Priv. Land Claims.	Feb. 9, 1827	Favorable	55			App'd March 3, 18[illegible]

List of private claims presented to the House of Representatives of the United States from the 1st to the 31st Congress, inclusive—Continued.

Names of claimants.	Nature or object of the claim.	Congress.	Session.	How brought before the House of Reps.	Page of journal.	To what committee of the House referred.	No. or date of the report.	Nature of the report.	No. of the bill.	How disposed of by the House of Reps.	How disposed of by the Senate.	Date of the act of Congress, and remarks.
Gumbleton, Robert	Pension	20	1	Petition	278	Military Pensions	Mar. 19, 1828	General bill	283	Passed.		
Gumbleton, Robert	Pension	21	1	Petition	3[illegible]	Military Pensions	Jan. 5, 1830	General bill	72	Passed	Passed	App'd May 20, 1830
Gump, William	Pension	28	1	Petition	724	Invalid Pensions.						
Gump, William	Pension	28	2	Petition	88	Invalid Pensions	16	Favorable	483	Passed.		
Gump, William	Pension	29	1	Petition	118	Invalid Pensions	426	Favorable	301	Passed	Passed	App'd Aug. 8, 1846
Gundy, Jacob	Pension	20	2	Petition	118	Military Pensions				Discharged; laid on table.		
Gunn, James	(See Jonathan White, assignee of)	14	1		35							
Gunn, John	Payment of claim against Wyandott Indians.	22	1	Petition	295	Indian Affairs.						
Gunn, William	Confirmation of title to land	23	1	Petition	382	Public Lands.						
Gunning, Bedford	Increase of salary of judge United States court.	3	2	Memorial	332	Select.						
Gunning, Bedford	Increase of salary of judge United States court.	3	2	Senate bill	338	Whole House	Feb. 24, 1795	Favorable	29	Passed	Passed	App'd Feb. 27, 1795
Gunnison, John, heir of	Prize money for capture of Bon Homme Richard.	25	2	Petition	49	Naval Affairs.						
Gunnison, John, heir of	Prize money withheld by the government of Denmark.	25	2	Petition	49	Foreign Affairs	389	Favorable, res. reported.		Adopted.		
Gunnison, Nathaniel	Bounty on a fishing voyage	19	1	Petition	31	Commerce.						
Gunnison, Nathaniel	Bounty on fishing schooner Fanny	24	1	Petition	54	Commerce	248	Favorable	255	Passed.		
Gunnison, Nathaniel	Bounty on fishing schooner Fanny	25	2	Petition	40	Commerce	Dec. 28, 1837	Adverse		Laid on table.		
Gunckard, John, administrator of.	(See Samuel Page, administrator of.)	26	1		182							
Gunter, Charles	Confirmation of title to land	26	1	Senate bill	738	Public Lands	Jan. 19, 1840	Favorable	90			
Gunter, Charles G.	Confirmation of title to land	31	1	Senate bill	613	Public Lands	May 22, 1850	Favorable	75	Referred to Committee Whole House.		
Gunter, Edward	Pension	23	2	Petition	182	Invalid Pensions.						
Gunton, Thomas	Compensation for extra services in General Land Office.	19	2	Petition	72	Public Lands				Discharged.		
Gunton, William	Relief in relation to the purchase of a certain bridge by the United States.	31	2	Memorial	133	Dist. of Columbia.						
Gunton, William	Relief in relation to the purchase of a certain bridge by the United States.	31	2	Memorial	217	Public Buildings & Grounds.						
Gunyon, John, representative of.	Compensation for revolutionary services.	13	3	Petition	510	Rev. Pensions	Nov. 4, 1814	Adverse		Leave to withdraw.		
Gurard, Timothy	Remission of interest on debt due United States.	25	2	Petition	95	Judiciary.						
Gurnee, Samuel	Pension	14	1	Petition	622	Pens. & Rev. Cl'ms.	April 11, 1816	General bill	171	Passed	Passed, with amendment.	App'd April 30, 1816
Gurney, John	Pension	25	3	Petition	220	Invalid Pensions.						
Gurney, John	Pension	26	1	Petition	162	Invalid Pensions.						
Gurney, Levi	Arrears of pension	21	1	Petition	411	Military Pensions	May 7, 1830	Adverse		Laid on table.		
Gurney, Levi	Arrears of pension	25	2	Petition	180	Rev. Pensions				Discharged; laid on table.		
Gurney & Smith	Indemnity for French spoliations prior to 1800.	26	1	Memorial	182	Foreign Affairs	343	Favorable; bill	319	Referred to Committee Whole House.		
Gurriet, Joseph	Bounty land	24	1	Petition	664	Public Lands				Discharged; laid on table.		
Gurriet, Joseph	Bounty land	25	2	Petition	233	Public Lands	595	Adverse		Laid on table.		
Gustee, Edward	(See John Ross, *et al.*)	20	2		292							

List of private claims presented to the House of Representatives of the United States from the 1*st to the* 31*st Congress, inclusive*—Continued.

Names of claimants.	Nature or object of the claim.	Congress.	Session.	How brought before the House of Reps.	Page of journal.	To what committee of the House referred.	No. or date of the report.	Nature of the report.	No. of the bill.	How disposed of by the House of Reps.	How disposed of by the Senate.	Date of the act of Congress, and remarks.
Gustin, John A., *et al.*	Release from suretyship for Wm. F. Rogers.	28	1	Petition	417	Claims.						
Guthrey, John	Payment of sundry loan office certificates.	15	2	Petition	297	Rev. Pensions.						
Guthrey, John	Payment of sundry loan office certificates.	16	1	Petition	88	Pens. & Rev. Cl'ms.						
Guthrey, John	Payment of sundry loan office certificates.	16	2	Rep't Committee	185		Jan. 31, 1821	Favorable	235	Referred to Committee Whole House.		
Guthrey, John	Payment of sundry loan office certificates.	17	1	Petition	30	Pens. & Rev. Cl'ms.	31	Favorable	67	Passed	Passed	App'd May 7, 1822
Guthridge, Alexander	Pension	28	2	Petition	58	Invalid Pensions.						
Guthridge, William	Pension	27	3	Petition	284	Invalid Pensions.						
Guthridge, William, widow of.	Pension	28	2	Petition	170	Invalid Pensions.						
Guthrie, Abel, *et al*	Arrears of pay due a deceased brother for revolutionary service.	23	1	Petition	40	Rev. Claims.						
Guthrie, Abel, *et al*	Arrears of pay due a deceased brother for revolutionary service.	23	2	Petition	101	Rev. Claims.						
Guthrie, Abel, *et al*	Arrears of pay due a deceased brother for revolutionary service.	24	1	Petition	63	Rev. Claims.						
Guthrie, Abelard	(See Joseph Hover, *et al.*)	27	2	Petition	618							
Guthrie, Abelard	Patent for land entered by him	27	3	Appropriation bill								App'd March 1, 1843
Guthrie, Abelard	Patent for land entered by him	28	1	Petition	80	Priv. Land Claims.	418	Favorable	322	Passed	Passed	App'd June 17, 1844
Guthrie, Benjamin	Pension	28	1	Petition	515	Rev. Pensions.						
Guthrie, Benjamin	Pension	28	2	Petition	58	Rev. Pensions	Feb. 15, 1845	Adverse		Laid on table.		
Guthrie, Benjamin	Pension	29	1	Petition	337	Rev. Pensions	611	Adverse		Laid on table.		
Guthrie, George, heir of	Commutation pay	23	1	Petition	98	Rev. Claims.						
Guthrie, Henry	Pension	24	1	Petition	506	Rev. Pensions.						
Guthrie, James	Pension	14	1	House bill	622	Whole House	April 11, 1816	Favorable	171	Passed	Passed, with amendment.	App'd April 30, 1816
Guthrie, John	Pension	5	2	House bill	127	Whole House			38	Passed	Passed	App'd Feb. 2, 1798
Guthrie, Joseph	Pension	18	1	Petition	250	Rev. Pensions	Mar. 8, 1824	Adverse		Laid on table.		
Guthrie, Nathaniel	Pension	20	1	Petition	440	Military Pensions.						
Guthrie, Peter	Correction of error in land enntry	24	1	Petition	113	Public Lands	April 7, 1836	Favorable	540	Passed	Passed	App'd May 14, 1836
Guthrie, Robert, widow of.	Pension	22	1	Petition	219	Invalid Pensions.						
Guthrie, Robert, widow of.	Pension	24	1	Petition	275	Invalid Pensions	June 28, 1836	Adverse		Laid on table.		
Guthrie, William	Indemnity for property lost in revolutionary war.	19	1	Petition	130	Claims	Feb. 22, 1826	Adverse		Laid on table.		
Guthrie, William	Indemnity for property lost in revolutionary war.	19	2	Petition	132	Claims	Jan. 12, 1827	Adverse		Leave to withdraw.		
Guthry, John, sen.	Pay for certain loan office certificate.	15	2	Petition	297	Rev. Pensions.						
Guthry, John, sen.	Pay for certain loan office certificate.	17	1	Petition	30	Rev. Pensions	Jan. 31, 1822	Favorable	67	Passed	Passed	App'd May 7, 1822
Gutierres, Antonio, Bernard, Francisco & Juan.	Confirmation of title to land	22	1	Petition	64	Priv. Land Claims.	Dec. 27, 1831	Favorable	125	Passed	Passed	App'd June 25, 1832
Gutler, George G.	Pension	14	2	Petition	275	Pens. & Rev. Cl'ms.						
Guvine, Joseph	Bounty land	24	2	Documents	390	Public Lands.						
Guy, Henry	Pension	28	1	Petition	368	Rev. Pensions.						
Guy, James	(See John McCafferty, exec's of.)	3	1		48							
Guy, John	Pension	22	1	Petition	164	Rev. Pensions.						
Guy, Jonathan	Compensation for revolutionary services and losses.	2	1	Petition	452					Referred to Secretary War.		

List of private claims presented to the House of Representatives of the United States from the 1st to the 31st Congress, inclusive—Continued.

Names of claimants.	Nature or object of the claim.	Congress.	Session.	How brought before the House of Reps.	Page of journal.	To what committee of the House referred.	No. or date of the report.	Nature of the report.	No. of the bill.	How disposed of by the House of Reps.	How disposed of by the Senate.	Date of the act of Congress, and remarks.
Guy, Matthew	Bounty for capture of five English prisoners.	13	3	Resolution	616	Naval Affairs	Jan. 13, 1815	Favorable	259	Passed.		
Guy, Matthew	(See Joseph Stewart, *et al.*)	14	1		249							
Guy, Matthew	Compensation for military services	29	1	Petition	752	Claims.						
Guy, Matthew	Compensation for military services	29	2	Petition	89	Claims.						
Guyant, Luke	Pension	12	1	Petition	155	Claims	June 8, 1812	General bill	138	Passed	Passed	App'd July 5, 1812
Guyant, Luke	Pension	20	1	Petition	337	Military Pensions	Mar. 18, 1828	Adverse		Laid on table.		
Guyer, Stephen	Reimbursement of judgment and cost in a certain suit.	1	2	Petition	174					Referred to Secretary of War.		
Guyer, Stephen	Reimbursement of judgment and cost in a certain suit.	1	2	Rep. of Secretary War.	251					Laid on table.		
Gwathmey, George C.	Payment for a lot of land	27	2	Memorial	415	Commerce.						
Gwathmey, Humphrey B.	Drawback of duties on Carthagena cotton.	23	1	Petition	156	Ways and Means	203	Favorable	226	Referred to Committee Whole House.		
Gwathmey, Humphrey B.	Drawback of duties on Carthagenia cotton.	23	2	House bill	82				226	Passed	Passed	App'd Jan. 27, 1831
Gwathmey, Samuel	(See Sureties of Chas. M. Taylor)	20	1		168							
Gwin, Eliza P.	(See Presley Thornton.)	22	1		672							
Gwinnup, George, widow of.	Pension	28	1	Petition	975	Rev. Pensions.						
Gwinnup, George, widow of.	Pension	29	1	Petition	59	Rev. Pensions	393	Favorable	292	Passed	Passed	App'd Aug. 8, 1846
Gwyne, Joseph	Compensation for revolutionary services.	15	1	Petition	80	Pens. & Rev. Cl'ms.	Feb. 16, 1818	Adverse		Rejected.		
Gwynn, John, heirs of	Bounty land	20	2	Senate bill	338	Rev. Claims	Feb. 27, 1829	Favorable	55	Passed.	Passed	App'd March 2, 1829
Gwynn, William	Compensation for a horse killed in battle.	17	1	Petition	106	Claims	Mar. 8, 1822	Favorable	109	Passed	Passed	App'd May 7, 1822
Gwynne, Charles	Reimbursement of money erroneously paid into U. S. treasury.	18	1	Senate bill	349	Claims	April 2, 1824	Favorable	69	Passed	Passed	App'd May 5, 1824
Gwynne, John, widow of.	Compensation for revolutionary services.	20	1	Petition	45	Rev. Claims	87	Favorable	93	Passed.		
Gyzelaar, Caroline	(See Robert McNeill, heirs of)	30	1		723							

DIGESTED SUMMARY

AND

ALPHABETICAL LIST OF PRIVATE CLAIMS

WHICH HAVE BEEN

PRESENTED TO THE HOUSE OF REPRESENTATIVES

FROM THE FIRST TO THE THIRTY-FIRST CONGRESS,

EXHIBITING

THE ACTION OF CONGRESS ON EACH CLAIM,

WITH

REFERENCES TO THE JOURNALS, REPORTS, BILLS, &c.,

ELUCIDATING ITS PROGRESS.

COMPILED BY ORDER OF THE HOUSE OF REPRESENTATIVES.

VOL. II.

From H to O inclusive.

GENEALOGICAL PUBLISHING CO., INC.
Baltimore 1970

Originally Printed for the
House of Representatives of the United States
32d Congress, 1st Session
as House Miscellaneous Documents, unnumbered, Series 653-655
Washington, D. C., 1853

Reprinted with added Publisher's Preface
Genealogical Publishing Company
Baltimore, 1970

Library of Congress Catalog Card Number 79-135476
International Standard Book Number 0-8063-0447-2

The publisher gratefully acknowledges
the loan of the original of this book
by the
George Peabody Branch
Enoch Pratt Free Library
Baltimore, Maryland

NOTICE

This work was reproduced by the photo-offset process from the original edition. A characteristic of this copy, from which the offset printer worked, was that the image was uneven. Every effort has been made by our photo-offset printer to produce as fine a reprint of the original edition as possible.

Genealogical Publishing Company

Made in the United States of America

In the House of Representatives U. S.,
January 27, 1848.

Resolved, That the Clerk of the House be directed to cause to be prepared an Alphabetical List of Private Claims which have been before the House of Representatives from the commencement of the First Congress to the close of the Twenty-ninth Congress, with the proceedings of the House of Representatives and Senate thereon: showing the names of the claimants; the nature or object of each claim; at what session, and in what manner, it was brought before the House; to what committee it was referred; the nature of the report, and the number of the report if printed, and, if not, the date of the report; the number of the bills, distinguishing between the Senate and House bills; the manner in which the claim was disposed of in the House, and, in cases where it passed both Houses, the date of the act of Congress:—the whole to be compiled from the Journals of the House of Representatives, and by reference, when necessary, to the Journals of the Senate, the reports of committees, the bills of the two Houses, and the laws of the United States. And that the Clerk be authorized to employ James Young, of the city of Washington, with a compensation not exceeding the sum now paid the engrossing clerks of this House, to be paid out of the contingent fund of the House; and that the Clerk of the House furnish such aid, by the clerks of his office, as may not be inconsistent with the discharge of their ordinary duties.

In the House of Representatives U. S.,
September 2, 1850.

Resolved, That the more effectually to carry out the intention of the House, as expressed in a resolution passed on the 27th day of January, 1848, the Clerk of this House be, and he is hereby, directed to employ such number of experienced clerks (in addition to his own clerks, whose duty it shall be to assist thereat, without additional compensation when not otherwise officially employed) as will insure the completion, within twelve months, of an alphabetical list of all claims submitted to this House from the day of its organization to the end of the present Congress, according to the plan indicated in the above resolution. Their compensation shall be the same as that allowed the engrossing clerks of the House. The clerk shall cause the work to be printed as a public document, and, to insure *accuracy,* shall take care, to have the clerks carefully compare the proofsheets with their manuscript copy.

In the House of Representatives U. S.,
December 22, 1851.

Resolved, That the Clerk of this House be, and he is hereby, directed to have completed, in the shortest possible time consistent with accuracy, the digest of claims authorized by the resolutions of the House of the 27th of January, 1848, and the 2d of September, 1850, in the manner and at the rate of compensation therein authorized to the extra clerks employed upon the same; and that he pay the compensation due for services already performed on the work, which has been withheld in consequence of the restriction as to time in the resolution of 1850.

Resolved, further, That the Clerk be, and he is hereby, required to withhold the work from the press until the whole of it shall have been completed and subjected to a re-examination with the journals, reports, laws, &c.; and to have reprinted so much of that now printed as shall, by the discovery of errors in it, connected with that now incomplete or otherwise, be deemed necessary; and that the work, when ready for the press, be printed by the printer now engaged upon it.

An Alphabetical list of Private Claims presented to the House of Representatives of the United States from the commencement of the 1st to the close of the 31st Congress.

Names of claimants.	Nature or object of the claim.	Congress.	Session.	How brought before the House of Reps.	Page of journal.	To what committee of the House referred.	No. or date of the report.	Nature of the report.	No. of the bill.	How disposed of by the House of Reps.	How disposed of by the Senate.	Date of the act of Congress, and remarks.
Hagg, Benjamin	Reimbursement of duties on imported grass seed.	18	1	Petition	187	Ways and Means	Feb. 28, 1825	Adverse		Laid on table.		
Hagg, Benjamin	Reimbursement of duties on imported grass seed.	22	1	Petition	25	Ways and Means	Jan. 26, 1832	Adverse		Laid on table.		
Haas & Co	(See Denghausen, Haas & Co.)	31	2		142							
Haas, Jacob	For a land patent	26	1	Petition	179	Priv. Land Claims.						
Haas, Jacob	Confirmation of title to land	26	1	Petition	603	Priv. Land Claims.	335	Favorable	307	Referred to Committee Whole House.		
Haas, Jacob	Confirmation of title to land	27	2	Petition	58	Priv. Land Claims.	407	Adverse		Laid on table.		
				Petition (2)	559	Priv. Land Claims.						
Haas, Jacob	Confirmation of title to land	27	3	Petition	71	Priv. Land Claims.	69	Adverse		Laid on table.		
Haas, Peter, widow of	Pension for revolutionary services.	25	2	Petition	460	Rev. Pensions				Discharged.		
Haas, Peter, widow of	Pension for revolutionary services.	26	1	Petition	174	Rev. Pensions	May 5, 1840			Discharged; laid on table.		
Haas, Valentine	Additional compensation as artificer.	4	1	Petition	447	Claims	May 11, 1796	Adverse		Laid on table.		
Habersham, John, representatives of.	Payment for naval materials	7	2	Appropriat'n bill.								App'd March 2, 1803
Habersham, John, representatives of.	Release from liability as revenue officer, Savannah.	8	1	Petition	538	Com. and Manuf	Jan. 27, 1804	Favorable; bill ordered.	213	Passed	Passed, with amendment.	App'd March 26, 1804
Habersham, John, executor of.	Credits for drafts transmitted to Treasury Department.	8	1	Petition	581	Com. and Manuf.	Mar. 9, 1804	Favorable; bill ordered.	213			
Habersham, John, representatives of.	Compensation for military supplies.	8	1	Appropriat'n bill.	548	Whole House	Feb. 21, 1804	With amends.	165	Passed	Passed	App'd March 14, 1804
Habersham, John, representatives of.	Nature of claim not on journal	29	1	Joint resolution.	406	Claims			R. 20			
Habersham, John, representatives of.	Balance due on treasury books	30	1	Appropriat'n bill.	523	Whole House		With amends.	298	Passed	Passed	App'd Aug. 12, 1848
Habersham, Joseph	(See representatives of John Habersham.)	8	1		538							
Habersham, Hon. Richard W., widow of.	Allowance of mileage	27	3	Resolution	134	Accounts.						
Haberson, John, surety of.	Release from a judgment	8	1	Petition	502	Select.						
Haburn, William	Compensation for revolutionary services and disability.	2	1	Petition	444					Referred to Secretary War.		
Haburn, William	Compensation for revolutionary services and disability.	2	1	Petition	578	Select	April 18, 1792	Adverse		Laid on table.		
Haburn, William	Compensation for revolutionary services and disability.	2	2	Petition	621	Select.						
Hackelbander, Joseph	Pension for revolutionary services.	24	2	Petition	93	Rev. Pensions.				Discharged; laid on table.		
Hackelbander, Joseph	Pension for revolutionary services.	26	1	Documents	624	Rev. Pensions	April 4, 1840	Adverse		Laid on table.		

List of private claims presented to the House of Representatives of the United States from the 1st to the 31st Congress, inclusive—Continued.

Names of claimants.	Nature or object of the claim.	Congress.	Session.	How brought before the House of Reps.	Page of journal.	To what committee of the House referred.	No. or date of the report.	Nature of the report.	No. of the bill.	How disposed of by the House of Reps.	How disposed of by the Senate.	Date of the act of Congress, and remarks.
Hackenbury, Samuel	Permission to make an entry of land.	23	2	Petition	243	Public Lands.						
Hacker, George	Confirmation of title to land in Missouri.	15	1	Petition	367	Priv. Land Claims				Discharged; laid on table.		
Hacker, George	Confirmation of title to land in Missouri.	16	1	Petition	72	Priv. Land Claims				Discharged; laid on table.		
Hacker, George	Confirmation of title to land in Missouri.	17	1	Petition	54	Public Lands				Discharged; laid on table.		
Hacker, George	Confirmation of title to land in Missouri.	18	1	Petition	54	Public Lands.						
Hacker, Hoystead	Pension for disabilities in revolutionary naval service.	12	2	Petition	604	Claims.						
Hacker, Jonathan	Pension	22	2	Petition	26	Invalid Pensions	Dec. 29, 1832			Discharged; laid on table.		
Hackett, Ann	(See heirs of Thomas Kelly)	27	2		73		1076					
Hackett, John W	(See John W. Hockett)	29	1		90							
Hackett, Joseph	Increase of pension	16	1	Petition	38	Pens. & Rev. Cl'ms.				Discharged; laid on table.		
Hackett, Joseph	Increase of pension	16	2	Petition	96	Pens. & Rev. Cl'ms.	Feb. 2, 1821			Discharged; laid on table.		
Hackett, Joseph	Increase of pension	25	3	Petition	128	Invalid Pensions.						
Hacketer, James	Indemnity for French spoliations prior to 1800.	26	1	Memorial	182	Foreign Affairs	343	Favorable; bill	319	Referred to Committee Whole House.		
Hackley, Elliott	(See S. Henderson & E. H.)	14	1		323							
Hackley, James, heirs of	Commutation pay for revolutionary services as a lieutenant.	25	2	Petition	391	Rev. Claims	905	Report and bill.	799	Passed	Adverse report.	
Hackley, James, heirs of	Commutation pay for revolutionary services as a lieutenant.	26	1	Petition	164	Rev. Claims	436	Adverse		Laid on table.		
Hackley, James, heirs of	Commutation pay for revolutionary services as a lieutenant.	27	2	Petition	61	Rev. Claims	378	Adverse		Laid on table.		
Hackley, James, heirs of	Commutation pay for revolutionary services as a lieutenant.	28	1	Petition	275	Rev. Claims.						
Hackley, James, heirs of	Commutation pay for revolutionary services as a lieutenant.	31	1	Petition	1003	Rev. Claims.						
Hackley, Richard	Pension	20	2	Petition	82	Military Pensions	Feb. 23, 1829				Disch'd; laid on table.	
Hackley, Richard S., by Jos. E. Bloomfield, agent.	Reimbursement of expenses in detaining an American ship by order of the chargé d'affaires.	15	2	Petition	177	Select.						
Hackley, Richard S., by Jos. E. Bloomfield, agent.	Reimbursement of expenses in detaining an American ship by order of the chargé d'affaires.	16	1	Petition	164	Select	April 11, 1820	Report and bill.	137	Passed	Passed	App'd May 15, 1820
Hackley, Richard S., by Jos. E. Bloomfield, agent.	Reimbursement of money expended, and an equitable settlement of his accounts as consul in Spain.	21	1	Memorial	40	Foreign Affairs	298	Report and bill	357			
Hackley, Richard S., by Jos. E. Bloomfield, agent.	Reimbursement of money expended, and an equitable settlement of his accounts as consul in Spain.	22	1	Memorial	54	Foreign Affairs	Dec. 19, 1831	Report and bill.	43	Passed	Passed	App'd March 15, 1832
Hackley, Richard S., by Jos. E. Bloomfield, agent.	For a speedy settlement of his claim to lands in Florida.	27	3	Petition	259	Priv. Land Claims.						
Hackney, John, widow of.	Pension for revolutionary services.	28	1	Petition	1096	Rev. Pensions.						
Hackney, Joseph, widow of.	Pension for revolutionary services.	23	1	Petition	242	Rev. Pensions	Feb. 28, 1834			Discharged; laid on table.		

List of private claims presented to the House of Representatives of the United States from the 1st to the 31st Congress, inclusive—Continued.

Names of claimants.	Nature or object of the claim.	Congress.	Session.	How brought before the House of Reps.	Page of journal.	To what committee of the House referred.	No. or date of the report.	Nature of the report.	No. of the bill.	How disposed of by the House of Reps.	How disposed of by the Senate.	Date of the act of Congress, and remarks.
Hackney, Robert	Pension for revolutionary services.	26	1	Petition	962	Rev. Pensions.						
Hackworth, William	Pension for his services as a revolutionary soldier.	17	1	Petition	37	Rev. Pensions	....	....	......	Discharged; laid on table.		
Hackworth, William	Pension for his services as a revolutionary soldier.	19	1	Petition	407	Military Pensions	April 20, 1826	Adverse	......	Rejected.		
Hackworth, William, heirs of.	Bounty land for revolutionary services.	28	1	Petition	452	Rev. Claims.						
Hadden, Joseph	Reimbursement of duty on a still, which was burnt.	13	3	Petition	459	Ways and Means	Jan. 14, 1815	Report by bill.	262	Passed	Passed	App'd Feb. 4, 1815
Hadden, Elisha	Pension	15	1	Petition	35	Pens. & Rev. Cl'ms.	....	....	......	Discharged; laid on table.		
Haddock, John, heir of	Indemnity for house destroyed by the enemy in the war of 1812.	24	1	Petition	92	Claims.						
Haddock, William W., and Thomas W. Jenkins.	Remission of foreign duty and ligh money on a cargo of slate.	15	1	Petition	114	Ways and Means	....	....	......	Discharged; laid on table.		
Haddock, William W., and Thomas W. Jenkins.	Remission of foreign duty and light money on a cargo of slate.	16	1	Petition	101	Commerce	....	....	......	Discharged; laid on table.		
Haddock, William W., and Thomas W. Jenkins.	Remission of foreign duty and light money on a cargo of slate.	17	2	Petition	165	Ways and Means	....	....	......	Discharged; laid on table.		
Haden, Josiah, heirs of	Half-pay for revolutionary services.	24	2	Petition	91	Rev. Claims	119	Adverse	......	Laid on table.		
Hadfield, George	Compensation for a plan of the public offices.	15	2	Petition	270	Claims.						
Hadfield, George	Compensation for a plan of the public offices.	16	1	Petition	66	Public Buildings.						
Hadfield, George	Compensation for a plan of the public offices.	16	2	Petition	150	Public Buildings	Jan. 19, 1821	Adverse	......	Rejected	....	Leave to withdraw.
Hadgo, Poas, (an Indian)	For a fee simple title to a tract of land.	24	1	Petition	476	Indian Affairs	488	Report and bill.	490	Referred to Committee Whole House.		
Hadgo, Poas, (an Indian)	For a fee simple title to a tract of land.	25	2	Petition	43	Indian Affairs	Jan. 19, 1838	Report by bill.	358	Referred to Committee Whole House.		
Hadgo, Poas, (an Indian)	For a fee simple title to a tract of land.	25	3	House bill	377	Whole House	....	....	358	Passed	Adverse report.	
Hadgo, Poas, (an Indian)	Compensation for improvement on his land.	26	1	Petition	180	Indian Affairs.						
Hadley, George	Pension for revolutionary services.	22	1	Petition	55	Rev. Pensions.						
Hadley, John	Pension	15	1	Petition	26	Pens. & Rev. Cl'ms.	Dec. 15, 1817	....	......	Discharged; referred to Secretary War.		
Hadley, Josiah	Pension for revolutionary services.	24	1	Petition	433	Rev. Pensions	....	....	......	Discharged; laid on table.		
Hadley, Stephen	Pension for revolutionary services.	22	1	Petition	56	Rev. Pensions.						
Hadman, Simon	Pension	28	1	Petition	976	Invalid Pensions.						
Hadon, Isaiah, heirs of	Seven years' half-pay for revolutionary services.	25	2	Petition	1119	Rev. Claims	....	....	......	Discharged; laid on table.		
Hadon, Isaiah, heirs of	Seven years' half-pay for revolutionary services.	25	3	Petition	84	Rev. Claims	....	....	......	Discharged.		
Hadon, Isaiah, heirs of	Seven years' half-pay for revolutionary services.	26	1	Petition	163	Rev. Claims.						
Hadon, Isaiah, heirs of	Seven years' half-pay for revolutionary services.	26	2	Petition	167	Rev. Claims.						
Hadon, Isaiah, heirs of	Seven years' half-pay for revolutionary services.	28	1	Petition	601	Rev. Claims.						
Hadon, Isaiah, heirs of	Seven years' half-pay for revolutionary services.	28	2	Petition	208	Rev. Claims.						

List of private claims presented to the House of Representatives of the United States from the 1st to the 31st Congress, inclusive—Continued.

Names of claimants.	Nature or object of the claim.	Congress.	Session.	How brought before the House of Reps.	Page of journal.	To what committee of the House referred.	No. or date of the report.	Nature of the report.	No. of the bill.	How disposed of by the House of Reps.	How disposed of by the Senate.	Date of the act of Congress, and remarks.
Haga, Godfrey, *et al.*	Drawback on a return cargo from East Indies, ordered prior to act of May 13, 1800.	7	1	Memorial	12	Com. and Manuf.						
Haga, Godfrey, *et al.*	Indemnity for French spoliations prior to 1800.	31	1	Petition	233	Foreign Affairs	355	Rep't and general bill.	318			
Hagadorn, John	Pension for revolutionary services.	16	1	Resolution	351	Rev. Pensions				Discharged; laid on table.		
Hagan, Daniel	Release of a judgment for excise duties.	16	1	Petition	335	Ways and Means				Discharged; laid on table.		
Hagan, Hannah	Pension in consideration of debility contracted while a nurse in United States army.	18	1	Petition	85	Pens. & Rev. Cl'ms.	Jan. 14, 1824	Adverse		Laid on table.		
Hagan, Malachi	Compensation for property destroyed by United States troops in Florida war.	28	2	Petition	144	Claims.						
Hagan, Malachi	Compensation for property destroyed by United States troops in Florida war.	29	1	Petition	474	Military Affairs.						
Hagan, Malachi	Compensation for property destroyed by United States troops in Florida war.	30	1	Petition	228	Claims	160	Adverse		Laid on table.		
Hagan, Peter, *et al*	Confirmation of military title to land south of the Ohio river for his revolutionary services.	3	2	Petition	267	Select	Jan. 6, 1795	Adverse.				
Hagan, Welford, or Wilfred.	Confirmation of title to land in Missouri.	15	1	Petition	312	Priv. Land Claims.				Discharged; laid on table.		
Hagan, Welford, or Wilfred.	Confirmation of title to land in Missouri.	16	1	Petition	72	Priv. Land Claims.				Discharged; laid on table.		
Hagan, Welford, or Wilfred.	Confirmation of title to land in Missouri.	17	1	Petition	54	Public Lands				Discharged; laid on table.		
Hagan, Welford, or Wilfred.	Confirmation of title to land in Missouri.	18	1	Petition	54	Public Lands.						
Hagar, Daniel, jr	Pension wounds and disability in war of 1812.	31	1	Petition	324	Invalid Pensions.						
Hagedorn & Cramer	Drawback on three bales of prints.	26	1	Petition	956	Ways and Means.						
Hageman, Barnet	Pension for revolutionary services.	24	2	Petition	93	Rev. Pensions	Jan. 3, 1837			Discharged; laid on table.		
Hager, or Huger, Jona., heirs of.	Compensation for revolutionary services.	25	3	Petition	220	Rev. Claims				Discharged.		
Hager, Capt. Jona., heirs of.	Compensation for revolutionary services.	26	1	Petition	164	Rev. Claims.						
Hager, Capt. Jona., heirs of.	Compensation for revolutionary services.	26	2	Petition	77	Rev. Claims.						
Hager, Capt. Jona., heirs of.	Compensation for revolutionary services.	27	2	Petition	62	Rev. Claims	519	Adverse		Laid on table.		
Hager, Joseph	Invalid pension	3	1	Rep. of Secretary War.	131	Select	May 26, 1794	Favorable; bill ordered.	62	Passed	Passed	App'd June 7, 1794
Hager, Levi	(See administrator of James Anderson.)	29	1		117							
Hagerman, Barnet	Pension for revolutionary services.	24	2	Resolution	319	Rev. Pensions	Feb. 14, 1837			Discharged; laid on table.		
Hagerman, Samuel	Pension for services in the war of 1812.	20	1	Resolution	382	Military Pensions.	April 29, 1828	Report by bill.	283	Passed.		

List of private claims presented to the House of Representatives of the United States from the 1st to the 31st Congress, inclusive—Continued.

Names of claimants.	Nature or object of the claim.	Congress.	Session.	How brought before the House of Reps.	Page of journal.	To what committee of the House referred.	No. or date of the report.	Nature of the report.	No. of the bill.	How disposed of by the House of Reps.	How disposed of by the Senate.	Date of the act of Congress, and remarks.
Hagerman, Samuel	Pension for services in the war of 1812.	20	2	House bill	55	Military Pensions	Dec. 12, 1828	General bill	311	Passed.		
Hagerman, Samuel	Pension for services in the war of 1812.	21	1	Resolution	48	Military Pensions	Jan. 5, 1830	General bill	72	Passed	Passed	App'd May 20, 1830
Hagey, —— (Indian)	Pension for revolutionary services.	19	1	Resolution	144	Military Pensions	April 1, 1826			Discharged; laid on table.		
Haggard, Nancy	(See heir of William Grymes)	23	1		55							
Haggerty & Austin	Indemnity for damages sustained in sundry suits brought by the United States.	21	2	Petition	128	Ways and Means	Jan. 18, 1831	Adverse		Referred to Committee Whole House.		
Haggerty & Austin	Indemnity for losses in consequence of the seizure of a quantity of teas in 1825.	22	2	Senate bill	405	Ways and Means	Feb. 27, 1833	Reported with't amendment.	S. 76			
Haggerty & Austin	Indemnity for losses in consequence of the seizure of a quantity of teas in 1825.	23	1	Senate bill	175	Ways and Means	Jan. 14, 1834	Rep. amended.	S. 39	Passed	Passed as am'd.	App'd April 15, 1834
Haggerty, Murty, widow of.	Relief in consideration of the death of her husband in battle, revolutionary war.	4	1	Petition	422	Claims	May 7, 1796	Adverse		Leave to withdraw.		
Haggerty, Eleanor	Compensation for services as a witness, and indemnity for imprisonment while awaiting trial.	7	1	Petition	164	Claims	Mar. 31, 1802	Adverse		Leave to withdraw.		
Haggett, Benjamin	Pension	19	1	Petition	423	Military Pensions	193	Favorable		Referred to Committee Whole House, on general bill.		
Haggett, Benjamin	Pension	19	2	Petition	67	Military Pensions	Dec. 11, 1826	Rep't and general bill.	315	Passed.		
Haggin, John, *et al.*	(See Northwestern Territory, inhabitants of.)	6	1		591							
Hagie, John	Pension for revolutionary services.	25	2	Petition	181	Rev. Pensions	436	Adverse		Referred to Committee Whole House.		
Hagie, John	Pension for revolutionary services.	26	1	Petition	325	Rev. Pensions	640	Report and bill.	473			
Hagin, Charles	Pension	14	1	Documents	105	Pens. & Rev. Cl'ms.	April 11, 1816	Report by bill	171	Passed	Passed	App'd April 30, 1816
Hagin, James	Arrears of pay for services as a revolutionary soldier.	20	2	Resolution	126	Military Pensions				Discharged; laid on table.		
Hagner, Peter	Compensation for services under acts of 1816 and 1817.	14	2	Senate bill	534	Whole House				Passed	Passed	App'd March 3, 1817
Hagner, Peter	Compensation for services under act of March 3, 1825.	19	1	Resolution	523	Ways and Means.						
Hagner, Peter	Compensation for services in settling claims for lost property in war of 1812.	19	2	Senate bill	351	Claims	March 1, 1827	Rep'd amended	S. 103	Passed amended.	Passed as am'd.	App'd March 3, 1827
Hahn, Paul	Pension for revolutionary services.	25	2	Petition	546	Rev. Pensions	Mar. 13, 1838			Discharged; laid on table.		
Haight, Benjamin	(See Benjamin Hoyt or Haight)	27	3		260							
Haight, Daniel	Right of pre-emption to certain lands.	27	3	Petition	271	Public Lands.						
Haight, John	Compensation for property of which he was robbed while a prisoner in the war of 1812.	23	1	Petition	59	Claims	96	Adverse		Laid on table.		
Haight, John	Compensation for clothing destroyed by Indians in war of 1812.	31	1	Petition	988	Invalid Pensions.						

List of private claims presented to the House of Representatives of the United States from the 1st to the 31st Congress, inclusive—Continued.

Names of claimants.	Nature or object of the claim.	Congress.	Session.	How brought before the House of Reps.	Page of journal.	To what committee of the House referred.	No. or date of the report.	Nature of the report.	No. of the bill.	How disposed of by the House of Reps.	How disposed of by the Senate.	Date of the act of Congress, and remarks.
Haight, John and Nicholas.	An act to secure the benefit of an improvement in machinery for carpet weaving.	16	2	Memorial	152	Judiciary				Discharged; laid on table.		
Haight, Stephen	Reimbursement of advances made during revolutionary war.	2	1	Petition	519					Referred to Secretary Treasury.		
Haight, Stephen	Reimbursement of advances made during revolutionary war.	3	2	Rep. of Secretary Treasury.	284					Laid on table.		
Haight, Thomas J.	Pension	23	1	Petition	190	Invalid Pensions	Feb. 21, 1834	Adverse		Laid on table.		
Hailandiere, C. de la	Remission of duty on a church bell.	26	1	Petition	358	Ways and Means.						
Hailandiere, C. de la	Remission of duty on a church bell.	26	2	Petition	51	Ways and Means	216	Adverse		Laid on table.		
Hail, John	Pension	23	1	Petition	92	Rev. Pensions.						
Hail, John	(See William H. Bedford, agent).	28	1		262							
Hail, Dr. William P. A.	Compensation for medical services to a company of Tennessee volunteers.	31	1	Documents	193	Claims	493	Report and bill.	394			
Haile, Benjamin	Pension	14	2	Petition	45	Pens. & Rev. Cl'ms.	Jan. 29, 1817	Favorable, and general bill.	91	Passed	Passed	App'd March 3, 1817
Haile, John	Compensation for a house occupied by government and destroyed by the enemy.	14	1	Petition	126	Not referred.						
Haile, John	Compensation for a house occupied by government, and destroyed by the enemy.	15	1	Petition	48	Claims	Feb. 24, 1818	Adverse		Referred to Committee Whole House.		
Haile, John	Compensation for a house occupied by government, and destroyed by the enemy.	15	2	Rept. of last sess.	69	Whole House	Dec. 7, 1818			Rejected.		
Haile, Robert	Renewal of a lost land warrant	23	1	Petition	49	Priv. Land Claims.	Jan. 23, 1834	Report by bill.	228	Ref'd to Com. W. H.		
Haile, Robert	Renewal of a lost land warrant	23	2	House bill	82	Whole House			228	Passed	Passed	App'd June 27, 1835
Haile, William	Invalid pension	12	1	House bill	361	Whole House	June 15, 1812	With amend.	138	Passed	Passed	App'd July 5, 1812
Hailey, John	Compensation for revolutionary services.	2	1	Petition	489					Referred to Secretary War.		
Hain, John, surety of	Release from liability	15	1	Petition	307	Ways and Means.						
Hain, John	Pension for services as a revolutionary soldier.	19	1	Resolution	182	Military Pensions.	164	Adverse		Laid on table.		
Haines, Eunice	Continuation of pension	28	1	Petition	849	Rev. Pensions.						
Haines, Henry	Pension for revolutionary services.	30	1	Petition	339	Rev. Pensions	Aug. 8, 1848			Discharged; laid on table.		
Haines, Henry	Pension for revolutionary services.	30	2	Petition	137	Rev. Pensions.						
Haines, Henry	Pension for revolutionary services.	31	1	Petition	194	Rev. Pensions	June 22, 1850			Disch'd; laid on table.		
Haines, John	Reimbursement of duties on goods ordered prior to act of 1828.	21	2	Petition	74	Ways and Means.						
Haines, John	Reimbursement of duties on goods ordered prior to act of 1828.	22	2	Petition	141	Ways and Means.						
Haines, Samuel	Grant of land on which he settled prior to the surrender of Mobile.	14	2	Petition	86	Public Lands				Discharged; laid on table.		
Haines, Thomas	Increase of pension	10	2	House bill	499	Whole House	Feb. 20, 1809	Favorable	158	Passed	Passed	App'd March 3, 1809
Hainesworth, Jas. P., widow of.	Right of pre-emption	23	1	Senate bill	754	Public Lands	June 20, 1834	With't amend.	S. 108	Passed		App'd June 30, 1834
Hair, Thomas	Right of pre-emption to improved land.	9	2	Petition	574	Public Lands				Discharged.		
Hait, Thomas	For land in Wisconsin, in consideration of money paid during war of 1812.	24	2	Petition	89	Military Affairs.						

List of private claims presented to the House of Representatives of the United States from the 1st to the 31st Congress, inclusive—Continued.

Names of claimants.	Nature or object of the claim.	Congress.	Session.	How brought before the House of Reps.	Page of journal.	To what committee of the House referred.	No. or date of the report.	Nature of the report.	No. of the bill.	How disposed of by the House of Reps.	How disposed of by the Senate.	Date of the act of Congress, and remarks.
Hairfield, James, heirs of..	Land due for revolutionary services	18	1	Petition	234	Pens. & Rev. Cl'ms.						
Ha-la-ta-emathla, and other Seminole warriors.	Compensation for three months' service in the Florida war, 1836.	29	2	Petition	228	Military Affairs.						
Halbert, William........	(See William H. Bedford, agent.)	28	1	Petition	262							
Halbert, William........	Reimbursement of money paid into land office.	31	1	Petition	1076	Priv. Land Claims.						
Halberstodt, Anthony	Pension for revolutionary services.	22	1	Resolution	262	Rev. Pensions.						
Halcyon, Schooner	(See Samuel Bragdon, *et al*)....	23	2	....	82							
Haldeman, John, *et al*....	Compensation for loss of a boat in the public service.	23	2	Petition	275	Claims.						
Haldeman, John, *et al*....	Compensation for loss of a boat in the public service.	24	1	Petition	93	Claims	90	Adverse	......	Laid on table.		
Haldeman, Peter........	(See John Haldeman, *et al*).....	23	2	....	275							
Hale, Capt. Benjamin, and Lieut. A. Levy.	Compensation for services in Florida war.	31	1	Petition	1499	Military Affairs.						
Hale, David M.........	Not found on journal..........	20	1	Petition	111	Ways and Means..	Feb. 18, 1828	Adverse	......	Recommitted.		
Hale, David and Samuel..	Confirmation of title to the lands on which they reside.	14	2	Petition	72	Public Lands	....	....	......	Discharged; laid on table.	....	Leave to withdraw, 1st sess., 19th Cong.
Hale, David and Samuel..	Confirmation of title to the lands on which they reside.	19	2	Petition	37	Public Lands	24	Report and bill	320			
Hale, David and Samuel..	Confirmation of title to the lands on which they reside.	20	1	Petition	40	Public Lands.....	May 13, 1828	Report by bill.	299			
Hale, E................	(See John Burton)	21	1	....	39							
Hale, George...........	Compensation for horse lost in the public service.	23	2	Petition	391	Claims.						
Hale, Hannah, guardian of the heirs of.	Indemnity for losses in Creek war	14	2	Petition	71	Ways and Means..	Jan. 29, 1817	Report by bill.	93	Passed	Passed	App'd March 3, 1817
Hale, Hannah, guardian of the heirs of.	Indemnity for losses in Creek war	15	1	Rep't Committee.	188	Claims	Jan. 28, 1818	Adverse	......	Rejected.		
Hale, Hannah, guardian of the heirs of.	Confirmation of title to land in Alabama.	15	1	Petition	44	Public Lands.						
Hale, Israel	Pension for revolutionary services.	22	1	Resolution	89	Rev. Pensions.						
Hale, Israel	Renewal of pension...........	22	1	Senate bill	205	Rev. Pensions	Jan. 21, 1832	With amend..	S. 48	Rejected.		
Hale, James C..........	(See heirs of Dr. Mordecai Hale).	24	1	....	814							
Hale, Joseph	Invalid pension...............	3	2	Rep. of Secretary War.	337	Claims	Feb. 28, 1795	Favorable; bill ordered.	130	Passed	Postp'd to next session.	
Hale, Joseph	Invalid pension...............	4	1	Rep. of Secretary War.	445	Claims	Mar. 4, 1796	Favorable; bill ordered.	156	Passed	Passed	App'd April 17, 1796
Hale, Joseph, of Florida..	Compensation for forage furnished army in Florida.	30	1	Petition	435	Claims	400	Adverse	......	Laid on table.		
Hale, Meshack..........	Compensation for horse lost in the public service.	24	2	Petition	213	Invalid Pensions ..	Feb. 24, 1837	Adverse	......	Laid on table.		
Hale, Mordecai, heirs of..	Commutation pay due as revolutionary surgeon.	24	1	Petition	814	Rev. Claims.						
Hale, Mordecai, heirs of..	Commutation pay due as revolutionary surgeon.	26	1	Petition	281	Rev. Claims.						
Hale, Mordecai, heirs of..	Commutation pay due as revolutionary surgeon.	29	1	Petition	102	Rev. Pensions.						
Hale, Gen. Nathan, widow of.	Pay and emoluments due for revolutionary services.	2	1	Petition	490	....	....	....	.....	Referred to Secretary War.		
Hale, Roswell	Increase of pension............	28	2	Petition	166	Invalid Pensions.						
Hale, Roswell	Increase of pension............	29	1	Petition	124	Invalid Pensions ..	209	Report and bill.	203	Ref'd to Com. W. H.		
Hale, Roswell	Increase of pension............	29	2	House bill	71	Whole House.....	Dec. 18, 1846	With't amend.	203	Passed	Passed	App'd March 3, 1847

List of private claims presented to the House of Representatives of the United States from the 1st to the 31st Congress, inclusive—Continued.

Names of claimants.	Nature or object of the claim.	Congress.	Session.	How brought before the House of Reps.	Page of journal.	To what committee of the House referred.	No. or date of the report.	Nature of the report.	No. of the bill.	How disposed of by the House of Reps.	How disposed of by the Senate.	Date of the act of Congress, and remarks.
Hale, Sally	Continuation of pension	24	1	Petition	433	Rev. Pensions				Discharged; laid on table.		
Hale, Silas	Additional compensation for transportation of the mail.	25	2	Petition	822	P. Of. & P. Roads.	1057	Adverse		Laid on table.		
Hale, Thomas	Indemnity for French spoliations prior to 1800.	26	1	Memorial	182	Foreign Affairs	343	Favorable; bill	319	Referred to Committee Whole House.		
Hale, William, widow of.	Bounty land for services in Indian wars.	23	2	Petition	307	Public Lands.						
Haley, Barbas	Increase of revolutionary pension.	29	1	Petition	162	Rev. Pensions	359	Adverse		Laid on table.		
Haley, Barnaby	Pension for revolutionary services.	24	1	Declaration	268	Rev. Pensions	324	Adverse		Referred to Committee Whole House.		
Haley, Barnaby	Pension for revolutionary services.	24	2	Petition	42	Rev. Pensions				Discharged, laid on table.		
Haley, D. W.	Compensation for two slaves who escaped from prison while confined on a charge of robbing the mail.	24	2	Petition	308	Claims	210	Report and bill.	926			
Haley, D. W.	Compens'n for apprehending mail robbers.	25	2	Petition	36	Claims	72	Report and bill.	84	Passed	Passed	App'd April 20, 1838
Haley, D. W., *et al.*	Release of interest on a debt as sureties of Alfred W. McDaniel.	26	1	Petition	605	Ways and Means	710	Adverse		Laid on table.		
Haley, D. W., *et al.*	Release of interest on a debt as sureties of Alfred W. McDoniel.	26	2	Petition	76	Select.	50	Report and bill.	579			
Haley, D. W., *et al.*	Release of interest on a debt as sureties of Alfred W. McDaniel.	27	2	Petition	131	Select	585	Report and bill.	381	Referred to Committee Whole House.		
Haley, D. W., *et al.*	Release of interest on a debt as sureties of Alfred W. McDaniel.	27	3	House bill	88	Whole House			381	Passed	Indef. postp'd.	
Haley & Harris	Compensation for extra services as mail contractors.	19	2	Senate bill	305	P. Of. and P. Roads.	Feb. 22, 1827	With't amend.	75	Passed	Passed	App'd March 3, 1827
Haley, John	Invalid pension	3	2	Report of Com. of Claims.	252		Feb. 28, 1795	Favorable; bill ordered.	130	Passed	Postp'd to next session.	
Haley, John	Invalid pension	4	1	Rep. of Secretary War.	445	Claims	Feb. 18, 1796	Favorable; bill ordered.	156	Passed	Passed	App'd April 20, 1796
Haley, John	Compensation for a horse lost in public service.	15	2	Petition	24	Claims	Jan. 28, 1818	Adverse		Laid on table.		
Haley, John	(See Sam'l Q. Richardson & J. H.)	16	1		142							
Haley, John	Compensation for property lost during war of 1812.	15	2	Petition	24	Claims	13	Adverse		Laid on table.		
Haley, Samuel	For aid in maintaining a harbor in Massachusetts.	6	1	Petition	596					Referred to Secretary of Treasury.		
Halfpenny, John	Pension	14	2	Petition	147	Pens. & Rev. Cl'ms.	Jan. 18, 1817			Discharged; leave to withdraw.		
Halfpenny, John	Pension	15	1	Petition	74	Pens. & Rev. Cl'ms.				Discharged; laid on table.		
Hall, Adam	Compensation for two horses lost in the public service.	21	2	Petition	160	Claims	Jan. 18, 1831	Adverse		Laid on table.		
Hall, Adam	Compensation for two horses lost in the public service.	24	2	Petition	394	Claims	269			Referred to 3d Auditor.		
Hall, Adam	Compensation for two horses lost in the public service.	26	1	Petition	1009	Claims	704	Adverse		Laid on table.		
Hall, Anna	(See heirs of Ebenezer Francis)	28	2		216							
Hall, Arthur E.	Increase of compensation as postmaster.	30	2	Petition	275	P. Of. and P. Roads.				Laid on table.		

List of private claims presented to the House of Representatives of the United States from the 1st to the 31st Congress, inclusive—Continued.

Names of claimants.	Nature or object of the claim.	Congress.	Session.	How brought before the House of Reps.	Page of journal.	To what committee of the House referred.	No. or date of the report.	Nature of the report.	No. of the bill.	How disposed of by the House of Reps.	How disposed of by the Senate.	Date of the act of Congress, and remarks.
Hall, Asa	Pension	22	1	Petition	329	Rev. Pensions				Discharged; laid on table.		
Hall, Asa	Back pension for services in war of 1812.	29	1	Petition	476	Invalid Pensions	667	Adverse		Laid on table.		
Hall, Asa	Back pension for services in war of 1812.	29	2	Petition	177	Invalid Pensions	Feb. 24, 1847			Discharged; laid on table.		
Hall, Barrett	Compensation for horse lost in war of 1812.	26	1	Petition	336	Claims.						
Hall, Benjamin	To be restored to pension roll	23	1	Petition	242	Rev. Pensions				Discharged; laid on table.		
Hall, Benjamin	Back pension for revolutionary services.	29	1	Petition	673	Rev. Pensions	785	Adverse		Laid on table.		
Hall, Bolling	Reimbursement of an overpayment for land.	22	1	Petition	417	Public Lands.						
Hall, Caleb	(See Louis F. Beeler)	30	1		115							
Hall, Caleb B., *et al.*	Remission of duty on goods imported into Castine, while in possession of the enemy.	15	1	Petition	165	Ways and Means.						
Hall, Caleb B., *et al.*	Remission of duty on goods imported into Castine, while in possession of the enemy.	15	2	Petition	54	Ways and Means				Discharged; laid on table.		
Hall, Caleb B, *et al.*	Remission of duty on goods imported into Castine, while in possession of the enemy.	16	1	Senate bill	108	Ways and Means	April 4, 1820	With amend.	S. 13	Passed with amendmt'.	Passed as am'd	App'd April 11, 1820
Hall, Catharine	(See heirs of Robert McNiel)	30	1		723							
Hall, Dr. Charles	Compensation for medical service attending two wounded dragoons.	26	2	Petition	53	Claims.						
Hall, Dr. Charles	Compensation for medical service, attending a wounded officer.	28	1	Petition	718	Claims	564	Adverse		Laid on table.		
Hall, Charles B.	Indemnity for illegal seizure of his goods.	27	2	Petition	72	Commerce	245	Report and bill	205	Referred to Committee Whole House.		
Hall, Charles B.	Indemnity for illegal seizure of his goods.	27	3	House bill	90	Whole House			205	Passed	Passed	App'd March 3, 1843
Hall, Charles Henry	Reimbursement of a part of the proceeds of certain wines sold for an alleged violation of the revenue laws.	21	1	Petition	363	Ways and Means	May 9, 1830	Report by bill.	335	Passed	Passed	App'd April 15, 1830
Hall, Cyrenius, (an alien)	Indemnity for the seizure of his schooner by the collector at Sandusky bay in 1821.	22	1	Presid'ts message	232	Foreign Affairs	453	Report and bill	553			
Hall, Cyrenius, (an alien)	Indemnity for the seizure of his schooner by the collector at Sandusky bay in 1821.	22	2	Appropriation bill	145	Whole House		With amend.	669	Passed	Passed	App'd March 2, 1833
Hall, Clark & Gladwin	(See assignees of Thomas Tupper)	22	2		142							
Hall, Dan, *et al.*	(See Seth Hawes, *et al.*)	3	1		48							
Hall, Daniel	Settlement of a revolutionary claim	3	1	Petition	215					Referred to Sec. War.		
Hall, Daniel	Settlement of a revolutionary claim	3	2	Rep. of Secretary War.	278	Claims				Laid on table.		
Hall, Daniel, widow of	Pension for revolutionary services.	26	1	Petition	937	Rev. Pensions.						
Hall, Daniel, widow of	Pension for revolutionary services.	26	2	Petition	214	Rev. Pensions.						
Hall, David	Invalid pension	3	1	Rep. of Secretary War.	131	Select	May 26, 1794	Joint Resl'n to refer to Sec. War.	12	Passed	Passed	App'd June 19, 1794

2—2

List of private claims presented to the House of Representatives of the United States from the 1st to the 31st Congress, inclusive—Continued.

Names of claimants.	Nature or object of the claim.	Congress.	Session.	How brought before the House of Reps.	Page of journal.	To what committee of the House referred.	No. or date of the report.	Nature of the report.	No. of the bill.	How disposed of by the House of Reps.	How disposed of by the Senate.	Date of the act of Congress, and remarks.
Hall, David	Invalid pension	4	1	Rep. of Secretary War.	445	Claims	Mar. 4, 1796	Favorable; bill ordered.	156	Passed	Passed	App'd April 20, 1796
Hall, David	Increase of pension	10	1	House bill	232	Whole House	April 19, 1808	Favorable	78	Passed	Passed	App'd April 25, 1808
Hall, Dudley	(See executor of John Brooks)	31	1		680							
Hall, Elias	Pension	21	2	Petition	336	Military Pensions.						
Hall, Elijah, heirs of	Indemnity for the capture of his vessel, Aurora, by a French privateer.	28	2	Petition	72	Claims.						
Hall, Elijah	Pension for services, war of 1812.	24	1	Petition	97	Invalid Pensions	June 2, 1836	Adverse		Laid on table.		
Hall, Elijah, (N. H.)	Indemnity for French spoliations prior to 1800.	26	1	Memorial	182	Foreign Affairs	343	Favorable; bill	319	Referred to Committee Whole House.		
Hall, Elisha F.	Credit for $641, of which he was robbed while paymaster.	14	1	Petition	135	Ways and Means.				Discharged; laid on table.		
Hall, Elisha F.	Credit for $641, of which he was robbed while paymaster.	14	2	Petition	406	Ways and Means.				Discharged; laid on table.		
Hall, Elisha F.	Credit for $641, of which he was robbed while paymaster.	18	2	Petition	136	Claims.						
Hall, Elisha F.	Credit for $641, of which he was robbed while paymaster.	18	2	Petition	253	Claims.						
Hall, Elizabeth	Pension in consideration of the revolutionary services of her husband.	28	1	Petition	839	Whole House.						
Hall, Enoch	Pension	22	1	Petition	287	Rev. Pensions.						
Hall, Gardner, *et al.*	(See railroad, Fitchburg extension)	28	1		358		113					
Hall, George	Pension	21	1	Resolution	484	Military Pensions.				Discharged; laid on table.		
Hall, George	Pension	28	1	Petition	128	Invalid Pensions.						
Hall, George	Pension	28	2	Petition	64	Invalid Pensions.						
Hall, Gervas, *et al.*	Extra pay as clerks in Treasury Department, Philadelphia.	3	1	Petition	88	Select	47	Adverse.				
Hall, Hannah	(See child of James Hubbard, deceased.)	24	2		73							
Hall, Henry	Pension	21	2	Petition	143	Military Pensions.						
Hall, Henry H.	Reimbursement of moneys paid for land.	24	1	Senate bill	993	Public Lands	Jan. 2, 1836	With't amend.	S. 156	Passed		App'd July 2, 1836
Hall, Hudson	Pension for revolutionary services.	22	1	Petition	124	Rev. Pensions.						
Hall, Hugh	(See Lewis & Clark and companions.)	9	1		284							See Statutes at Large, vol. 6, p. 65.
Hall, Israel	Confirmation of title to land in Missouri.	16	1	Petition	71	Priv. Land Claims.				Discharged; laid on table.		
Hall, Jabez	Renewal of revolutionary certificate destroyed by fire.	5	2	Petition	82	Claims	Mar. 19, 1798			Referred to Committee Whole House.		
Hall, Jacob	Compensation for revolutionary services.	2	1	Petition	442					Referred to Secretary of War.		
Hall, Jacob	Compensation for revolutionary services.	2	2	Report Secretary of War.	696					Laid on table.		
Hall, Jacob, heirs of	Commutation pay for his services as revolutionary surgeon.	24	1	Memorial	474	Rev. Claims.						
Hall, James	(See Matthews, Wood, & Hall)	24	2		119		117					
Hall, James	Pension for revolutionary services.	3	1	Petition	103					Referred to Secretary of War.		
Hall, James	Pension for revolutionary services.	3	2	Rep. of Secretary of War.	278	Claims				Laid on table.		

List of private claims presented to the House of Representatives of the United States from the 1st to the 31st Congress, inclusive—Continued.

Names of claimants.	Nature or object of the claim.	Congress.	Session.	How brought before the House of Reps.	Page of journal.	To what committee of the House referred.	No. or date of the report.	Nature of the report.	No. of the bill.	How disposed of by the House of Reps.	How disposed of by the Senate.	Date of the act of Congress, and remarks.
Hall, James	Pension for revolutionary services.	19	1	Resolution	239	Military Pensions	164	Adverse	......	Laid on table.		
Hall, James	(See F. M. Arredondo and others.)	19	1		252							
Hall, James	Confirmation of title to land in Indiana Territory.	24	1	Memorial	212	Indian Affairs.						
Hall, James, widow of	To be restored to pension roll	27	2	Petition	320	Rev. Pensions.						
Hall, James, widow of	To be restored to pension roll	27	3	Petition	365	Rev. Pensions.						
Hall, James S	Invalid pension	26	1	Resolution	1023	Invalid Pensions.						
Hall, James S	Invalid pension	26	2	Petition	36	Invalid Pensions	58	Adverse	......	Laid on table.		
Hall, James S	Invalid pension	28	1	Petition	337	Invalid Pensions.						
Hall, James S	Invalid pension	28	2	Petition	87	Invalid Pensions.						
Hall, James S	Invalid pension	29	1	Petition	358	Invalid Pensions.						
Hall, John	Credit for certain disbursements by order of court.	6	2	Petition	784	Claims	....	....	......	Postponed to next session.		
Hall, John	Credit for certain disbursements by order of court.	7	1	Petition	19	Claims	April 3, 1802	....	......	Postponed.		
Hall, John	Credit for certain disbursements by order of court.	8	1	Petition	526	Claims	Jan. 18, 1804	Adverse	......	Leave to withdraw.		
Hall, John	Bounty land and other compensation for revolutionary services.	16	1	Petition	174	Pens. & Rev. Cl'ms.	....	....	......	Discharged; laid on table.		
Hall, John	Grant of land for services during whiskey insurrection.	20	1	Petition	441	Public Lands	....	....	......	Discharged: laid on table.		
Hall, John	Relief in settlement of his accounts with United States	15	1	Senate bill	450	Claims	April 14, 1818	With't amend.	S. 72	Passed	....	App'd April 20, 1818
Hall, John	Compensation for a slave drowned in service of United States.	23	2	Petition	132	Claims	Jan. 19, 1835	Adverse	......	Laid on table.		
Hall, John	Pension for revolutionary services.	24	2	Petition	399	Rev. Pensions.						
Hall, John	Indemnity for property lost in revolutionary war.	25	2	Petition	47	Rev. Claims	633	Adverse	......	Laid on table.		
Hall, John, heir of	Indemnity for property lost in revolutionary war.	29	1	Petition	666	Rev. Claims.						
Hall, John H	Compensation for the invention of certain fire-arms.	24	1	Petition	142	Military Affairs	375	Report and bill.	377	Referred to Committee Whole House.		
Hall, John H	Compensation for the invention of certain fire-arms.	25	2	Petition	41	Military Affairs	257	Report and bill.	300	Referred to Committee Whole House.		
Hall, John H	Compensation for the invention of certain fire-arms.	25	3	House bill	376	Whole House	....	....	300			
Hall, John H	Compensation for the invention of certain fire-arms.	26	1	Petition	182	Military Affairs	453	Report and bill.	367	Referred to Committee Whole House.		
Hall, John H., representatives of.	Compensation for the invention of certain fire-arms.	27	2	Petition	771	Military Affairs.						
Hall, John Y	Pension	19	1	Petition	290	Military Pensions	May 5, 1826	Favorable	......	Referred to Committee Whole House.		
Hall, John Y	Pension	19	2	House bill	85	Whole House	Feb. 2, 1827	Favorable	314	Passed	Passed	App'd March 3, 1827
Hall, John Y	Arrears of pension	23	1	Petition	103	Invalid Pensions	Jan. 27, 1834	Adverse	......	Laid on table.		
Hall, John Y	Arrears of pension	23	2	Petition	198	Invalid Pensions	....	....	......	Discharged; laid on table.		
Hall, John Y	Arrears of pension	24	1	Petition	507	Invalid Pensions	April 15, 1836	Adverse	......	Laid on table.		
Hall, Joseph	Reimbursement of certain moneys paid into the treasury	24	1	Petition	473	Claims	460	Report and bill.	466			
Hall, Joseph	Reimbursement of certain moneys paid into the treasury.	25	2	Petition	36	Claims	20	Report and bill.	32	Passed	Passed	App'd March 2, 1838
Hall, Joseph	Invalid pension	26	1	Petition	288	Invalid Pensions	408	Adverse	......	Laid on table.		
Hall, Joseph	Invalid pension	28	2	Petition	69	Invalid Pensions.						

List of private claims presented to the House of Representatives of the United States from the 1st to the 31st Congress, inclusive—Continued.

Names of claimants.	Nature or object of the claim.	Congress.	Session.	How brought before the House of Reps.	Page of journal.	To what committee of the House referred.	No. or date of the report.	Nature of the report.	No. of the bill.	How disposed of by the House of Reps.	How disposed of by the Senate.	Date of the act of Congress, and remarks.
Hall, Joshua M.	Compensation for services as purser's clerk.	31	1	Petition	629	Naval Affairs.						
Hall, Josiah R.	Compensation for a horse lost in the public service.	25	2	Petition	724	Claims				Discharged		
Hall, Jonathan	Compensation for property seized by the enemy, war of 1812.	23	1	Petition	335	Claims	Mar. 11, 1834	Adverse		Laid on table.		
Hall, Jonathan	Compensation for property seized by the enemy, war of 1812.	29	1	Petition	347	Claims	339	Adverse		Laid on table.		
Hall, Laban	To be restored to pension roll	17	1	Petition	186	Whole House				Discharged; laid on table.		
Hall, Laban	Back pension	25	2	Petition	52	Rev. Pensions				Discharged; laid on table.		
Hall, Laban	Back pension	26	2	Petition	121	Rev. Pensions.						
Hall, Lebbeus, widow of.	Pension for revolutionary services.	23	1	Petition	584	Rev. Pensions.						
Hall, Lot	Compensation for revolutionary services.	10	1	Petition	154					Referred to Committee Whole House.		
Hall, Lot, widow and heirs of.	Back pay and prize-money	26	1	Petition	288	Rev. Claims	511	Report and bill.	412			
Hall, Lot, widow and heirs of.	Back pay and prize-money	27	2	Petition	61	Rev. Claims	517	Adverse		Laid on table.		
Hall, Lot, widow and heirs of.	Back pay and prize-money	29	1	Petition	257	Rev. Claims	443	Report and bill.	316			
Hall, Lyman	Pension	15	2	Petition	88	Pens. & Rev. Cl'ms.	Jan. 5, 1819	Adverse		Laid on table.		
Hall, Lyman	Pension	20	2	Petition	147	Military Pensions				Discharged; laid on table.		
Hall, Lyman	Pension	21	1	Petition	197	Military Pensions				Discharged; laid on table.		
Hall, Lyman	Pension	21	2	Petition	127	Military Pensions				Discharged; laid on table.		
Hall, Lyman	Pension	22	1	Petition	35	Rev. Pensions.						
Hall, Margaret, (late McKenzie.)	Confirmation of title to land granted her by Indians.	16	1	Petition	153	Public Lands	Feb. 8, 1820	Report by bill.	70	Passed	Indef. postp'd.	
Hall, Margaret, (late McKenzie.)	Confirmation of title to land granted her by Indians.	17	1	Petition	278	Public Lands				Discharged; laid on table.		
Hall, Meshack	Compensation for a horse lost in service of United States.	24	1	Documents	206	Claims.						
Hall, Moses	Right to purchase certain lands at a fixed price.	9	2	Petition	560	Public Lands				Discharged.		
Hall, Moses	Remission of tax on a distillery	15	1	Petition	126	Ways and Means	Jan. 23, 1818	Adverse		Rejected.		
Hall, Nathaniel	Pension	25	2	Petition	587	Invalid Pensions				Discharged; laid on table.		
Hall, Nathan'l, administrator of.	Indemnity for depredations by United States troops in Florida.	28	1	Petition	452	Claims.						
Hall, Major N. Nye	Half-pay and back pay as assistant inspector general.	29	1	Memorial	1000	Invalid Pensions				Leave to withdraw.		
Hall, Phebe	(See widow of Alexan'r Torrence)	28	1		72							
Hall, Primus, *alias* Trask.	Pension for revolutionary services.	24	2	Petition	153	Rev. Pensions	74	Report and bill	820			
Hall, Primus, *alias* Trask.	Pension for revolutionary services.	25	2	Petition	38	Rev. Pensions	275	Report and bill	318	Passed	Passed	App'd June 28, 1838
Hall, Reuben	Pension	21	1	Petition	319	Military Pensions				Discharged; laid on table.		
Hall, Richard	Pension	23	1	Petition	112	Invalid Pensions.						
Hall, Richard	Pension	24	1	Petition	140	Invalid Pensions	837	Report and bill	737			
Hall, Richard	Pension	25	2	Petition	39	Invalid Pensions	279	Report and bill	322	Passed	Indef. postp'd.	

List of private claims presented to the House of Representatives of the United States from the 1st to the 31st Congress, inclusive—Continued.

Names of claimants.	Nature or object of the claim.	Congress.	Session.	How brought before the House of Reps.	Page of journal.	To what committee of the House referred.	No. or date of the report.	Nature of the report.	No. of the bill.	How disposed of by the House of Reps.	How disposed of by the Senate.	Date of the act of Congress, and remarks.
Hall, Richard	Pension	25	3	Petition	90	Invalid Pensions.						
Hall, Richard	Pension	26	1	Petition	162	Invalid Pensions	295	Adverse		Laid on table.		
Hall, Richard, representatives of.	Compensati'n for property destroyed by the enemy, war of 1812.	27	2	Petition	382	Claims	717	Adverse		Laid on table.		
Hall, Richard, representatives of.	Compensati'n for property destroyed by the enemy, war of 1812.	29	1	Petition	310	Claims	344	Adverse		Laid on table.		
Hall, Samuel	Pension	14	1	Petition	35	Pens. & Rev. Cl'ms.	Jan. 30, 1816			Referred to Secretary of War.		
Hall, Samuel	Pension	24	2	Resolution	318	Invalid Pensions				Discharged; laid on table.		
Hall, Samuel	Pension	25	2	Documents	400	Invalid Pensions.						
Hall, Samuel, (an alien)	Patent for saving fuel in working steam engines.	20	2	Petition	204	Judiciary				Discharged; laid on table.		
Hall, Samuel, (an alien)	Patent for saving fuel in working steam engines.	21	1	Petition	129	Judiciary.						
Hall, Samuel, (an alien)	Patent for saving fuel in working steam engines.	22	1	Petition	447	Patent Laws.						
Hall, Samuel, (an alien)	Patent for saving fuel in working steam engines.	22	2	Petition	137	Judiciary	Jan. 22, 1833	Report by bill.	702	Passed	Passed	App'd March 2, 1833
Hall, Samuel	(See George Janverin, executor of)	26	1		182							
Hall, Sarah	Indemnity for property destroyed in war of 1812.	15	1	Rep't Commiss'r of Claims.	316	Claims				Discharged; laid on table.		
Hall & Sellers, surviving partner of.	Liquidation and payment of a claim for printing under the former constitution of government.	10	2	Memorial	495					Referred to Committee Whole House.		
Hall & Sellers, surviving partner of.	Liquidation and payment of a claim for printing under the former constitution of government.	11	2	Memorial	305	Claims.						
Hall, Stephen	(See Minis & Henry, and others)	15	2		144							
Hall, Stephen	Payment of a soldier's certificate war of 1812.	15	2	Petition	144	Military Affairs	Jan. 16, 1819	Adverse		Laid on table.		
Hall, Stephen	Payment of a soldier's certificate, war of 1812.	16	2	Petition	89	Claims	Feb. 6, 1821			Discharged; leave to withdraw.		
Hall, Thomas	Reimburs'nt of the value of goods seized for the breach of revenue laws.	4	2	Petition	668	Com. and Manuf.	Feb. 6, 1797	Adverse		Leave to withdraw.		
Hall, Thomas	Compensation for revolutionary services.	23	2	Petition	389	Rev. Pensions.						
Hall, Thomas	Compensation for revolutionary services.	25	2	Petition	55	Rev. Pensions	371	Adverse		Referred to Committee Whole House.		
Hall, Thomas	Compensation for revolutionary services.	26	1	Petition	324	Rev. Pensions				Discharged; laid on table.		
Hall, Thomas	Pension for revolutionary services.	26	2	Petition	51	Rev. Pensions	Jan. 8, 1841			Discharged; laid on table.		
Hall, Thomas B.	(See H. C. Schneb'y)	24	1		514							
Hall, Thomas B.	(See John Harry)	21	1		102							
Hall, Thomas S.	(See assignees of Thomas Tupper)	22	2		142							
Hall, Washington	(See administrator of Robt. Barry)	31	1		193							
Hall, William	Payment of a certain certificate of public debt.	4	1	Rep. of Secretary Treasury.	388	Claims	74	Adverse		Laid on table.		
Hall, William	Indemnity for depreciated revolutionary money.	22	2	Petition	244	Rev. Claims.						

List of private claims presented to the House of Representatives of the United States from the 1st to the 31st Congress, inclusive—Continued.

Names of claimants.	Nature or object of the claim.	Congress.	Session.	How brought before the House of Reps.	Page of journal.	To what committee of the House referred.	No. or date of the report.	Nature of the report.	No. of the bill.	How disposed of by the House of Reps.	How disposed of by the Senate.	Date of the act of Congress, and remarks.
Hall, William	Pension for military services in 1792.	24	2	Memorial	216	Rev. Pensions				Discharged; laid on table.		
Hall, William	Pension for his services as a revolutionary soldier.	20	2	Petition	224	Military Pensions				Discharged; referred to Com. Whole House.		
Hall, William	Pension for his services as a revolutionary soldier.	21	1	Resolution	255	Military Pensions.						
Hall, William	Pension for his services as a revolutionary soldier.	23	1	Petition	600	Rev. Pensions.						
Hall, William	Pension for his services as a revolutionary soldier.	23	2	Petition	66	Rev. Pensions	Feb. 10, 1835	Adverse		Laid on table.		
Hall, William	Pension for his services as a revolutionary soldier.	24	1	Petition	613	Rev. Pensions				Discharged; laid on table.		
Hall, William, widow of.	Pension for revolutionary services.	25	3	Petition	97	Rev. Pensions				Discharged; laid on table.		
Hall, William, widow of.	Pension for revolutionary services.	27	3	Petition	61	Rev. Pensions.						
Hall, Capt. William	Increase of pension	18	1	Petition	180	Pens. & Rev. Cl'ms.	Mar. 4, 1824	Report by bill.	143	Passed	Passed	App'd May 19, 1824
Hall, William W.	Pension and restoration to rank as surgeon.	16	2	Petition	63	Military Affairs	46	Adverse		Referred to Pens. and Rev. Claims.		
						Pens. & Rev. Cl'ms.	Jan. 5, 1821	Adverse		Leave to withdraw.		
Hall, William W.	Revision of settlement of accounts, and further credit.	17	1	Petition	142	Military Affairs	Jan. 18, 1822	Adverse		Laid on table.		
Hall, William W.	Arrears of pension	18	1	Petition	196	Pens. & Rev. Cl'ms.	Feb. 18, 1824	Adverse		Laid on table.		
Hall, William W.	Arrears of pension	18	2	Rep't of last sess.	138	Pens. & Rev. Cl'ms.						
Hall, William W.	Arrears of pension	19	1	Petition	129	Military Pensions	164	Adverse		Laid on table.		
Hall, William W.	Arrears of pension	20	1	Petition	50	Military Pensions	Jan. 29, 1828	Adverse		Laid on table.		
Hall, William W.	Arrears of pension	23	1	Petition	188	Invalid Pensions.						
Hall, William W.	Compensation for services and injuries, war of 1812.	24	1	Petition	473	Invalid Pensions	April 15, 1836	Adverse		Laid on table.		
Hall, Zachariah, widow of.	Pension for naval services in revolutionary war.	25	3	Petition	217	Rev. Pensions.						
Hallack, Joshua, widow of	Bounty land for services in war of 1812.	31	1	Petition	654	Priv. Land Claims.						
Hallam, George	Indemnity for French spoliations prior to 1800.	26	1	Memorial	182	Foreign Affairs	343	Favorable; bill	319	Referred to Committee Whole House.		
Hallam, Robert	Pension	20	2	Resolution	214	Whole House.						
Hallam, Robert	Pension	21	1	Resolution	59	Military Pensions				Discharged; laid on table.		
Hallam, Robert	Pension	22	1	Petition	45	Rev. Pensions				Discharged; laid on table.		
Hallock, Fitz Green	(See Jacob Barker, assignees of.)	18	2		223							
Hallenback, Ruth	(See widow of William Scutt)	30	1		122							
Hallet, Abraham S.	(See Henry Cotheal and others)	18	1		77							
Hallett, Benj., and others.	Drawback of duty on salt for a fish voyage.	18	1	Petition	235	Commerce						Leave to withdraw, 2d session.
Hallett, Jonathan, widow of.	Relief in consideration of revolutionary services.	21	1	Petition	147	Rev. Claims.						
Hallett	(See Wilson & Hallett)	20	1		557							
Hallett, Richard	Indemnity for French spoliations prior to 1800.	26	1	Memorial	182	Foreign Affairs	343	Favorable; bill	319	Referred to Committee Whole House.		
Hallert, Solomon	To be restored to pension roll	17	1	Petition	72	Rev. Pensions				Discharged; laid on table.		
Halley, Creed P.	(See James Hunter & C. P. H.)	22	2		398							

List of private claims presented to the House of Representatives of the United States from the 1st to the 31st Congress, inclusive—Continued.

Names of claimants.	Nature or object of the claim.	Congress.	Session.	How brought before the House of Reps.	Page of journal.	To what committee of the House referred.	No. or date of the report.	Nature of the report.	No. of the bill.	How disposed of by the House of Reps.	How disposed of by the Senate.	Date of the act of Congress, and remarks.
Halley, Henry S	Pension for revolutionary services.	24	2	Petition	313	Rev. Pensions				Discharged; laid on table.		
Halley, Thomas	(See William H. Bedford, agent).	28	1		262							
Halliday, Nehemiah	Arrears of pension, war of 1812	27	2	Petition	47	Invalid Pensions.						
Halliday, Nehemiah	Arrears of pension, war of 1812	29	2	Petition	237	Invalid Pensions				Discharged; laid on table.		
Halliday, Nehemiah	Arrears of pension, war of 1812	30	1	Petition	575	Invalid Pensions				Discharged; laid on table.		
Halliday, Thomas, widow of.	Reimbursement of moneys expended as armorer.	22	1	Petition	54	Claims	Feb. 8, 1832	Adverse		Recommitted.		
Halliday, Thomas, widow of.	Reimbursement of moneys expended as armorer.	23	1	Petition	154	Claims	411	Report and bill.	429			
Halliday, Thomas, representatives of.	Reimbursement of moneys expended as armorer.	24	1	Petition	93	Claims	74	Report and bill.	74	Passed	Passed	App'd June 14, 1836
Halliday, Thomas, administrator of.	Compensation for services in war of 1812.	25	2	Petition	192	Claims				Discharged.		
Halliday, Thomas, administrator of.	Compensation for services in war of 1812.	25	3	Petition	87	Claims.						
Halliday, Thomas, administrator of.	Compensation for services in war of 1812.	26	1	Petition	339	Claims.						
Halliday, Thomas, administrator of.	Compensation for services in war of 1812.	26	2	Petition	167	Claims.						
Halliday, Thomas, administrator of.	Reimbursement of moneys expended on government account.	27	2	Petition	335	Claims	242	Adverse		Laid on table.		
Hallock, James C	Pension for disabilities, war of 1812.	24	1	Petition	97	Invalid Pensions	Jan. 14, 1836	Adverse		Laid on table.		
Hallock, James C	Pension for disabilities, war of 1812.	26	1	Petition	289	Invalid Pensions	529	Report and bill.	425			
Hallock, James C	Pension for disabilities, war of 1812.	27	2	Petition	98	Invalid Pensions	137	Report and bill.	183	Laid on table.		
Hallock, James C	Pension for disabilities, war of 1812.	28	1	Petition	84	Invalid Pensions	38	Report and bill.	69	Passed	Passed	App'd May 23, 1844
Hallock, Joshua, widow of.	Interest on claim for half-pay due.	26	1	Petition	296	Military Affairs.						
Hallock, Joshua, widow of.	Interest on claim for half-pay due.	27	2	Petition	509	Military Affairs				Discharged; laid on table.		
Hallock, Sarah	Continuation of revolutionary pension.	27	2	Petition	238	Rev. Pensions.						
Hallowell, Edward	Release from penalty for violation of non-importation act.	13	2	Petition	317	Ways and Means	April 5, 1814	Report by bill.	183	Referred to Committee Whole House.		
Hallowell, Edward	Release from penalty for violation of non-importation act.	13	3	Petition	679	Ways and Means	Feb. 2, 1815	Report by bill.	281	Passed	Passed	App'd Feb. 27, 1815
Hallowell, Edward	Amendment of the act of last session.	14	1	Petition	99	Ways and Means	Jan. 13, 1816	Report by bill.	33	Passed	Passed	App'd April 24, 1816
Hallowell, Henry	To be restored to pension roll	17	1	Petition	91	Whole House.						
Hallowell, Henry	Pension for revolutionary services.	18	1	Petition	81	Rev. Claims	Jan. 16, 1824	Adverse		Laid on table.		
Hallowell, Henry	Arrears of pension	22	1	Petition	115	Rev. Pensions				Discharged; laid on table.		
Hallowell, Henry	Arrears of pension	22	2	Petition	44	Rev. Pensions.						
Hallowell, Henry	Arrears of pension	23	1	Petition	158	Rev. Pensions				Discharged; laid on table.		
Hallowell, Henry	Increase of pension	24	1	Petition	382	Rev. Pensions				Discharged; laid on table.		
Hallowell, Henry	Arrears of pension	24	2	Petition	44	Rev. Pensions				Discharged; laid on table.		
Hallowell, Henry	Arrears of pension	25	2	Petition	117	Rev. Pensions				Discharged; laid on table.		

List of private claims presented to the House of Representatives of the United States from the 1st to the 31st Congress, inclusive—Continued.

Names of claimants.	Nature or object of the claim.	Congress.	Session.	How brought before the House of Reps.	Page of journal.	To what committee of the House referred.	No. or date of the report.	Nature of the report.	No. of the bill.	How disposed of by the House of Reps.	How disposed of by the Senate.	Date of the act of Congress, and remarks.
Hallowes, Miller	Indemnity for Indian depredations in Florida.	25	2	Petition	541	Claims	790	Adverse		Laid on table.		
Hallowes, Miller	Indemnity for Indian depredations in Florida.	27	2	Petition	94	Claims	762	Adverse		Laid on table.		
Halman, Mary	Pension	20	1	Petition	365	Military Pensions	Mar. 18, 1828	Adverse		Laid on table.		
Halsey, Frederick	Reimbursement of money paid to Gen. Macomb, war of 1812.	15	1	Petition	213	Claims	Mar. 24, 1818	Adverse		Rejected		Leave to withdraw.
Halsey, Frederick	Reimbursement of money paid to Gen. Macomb, war of 1812.	17	1	Petition	82	Claims	Mar. 4, 1822	Adverse		Referred to Committee Whole House.		
Halsey, Frederick	Reimbursement of money paid to Gen. Macomb, war of 1812.	23	1	Petition	716	Claims	534	Adverse		Laid on table.		
Halsey, Job	Pension for revolutionary services.	25	2	Petition	529	Rev. Pensions	669	Report and bill.	673	Passed	Adverse report.	
Halsey, Job	Pension for revolutionary services.	25	3	Resolution	226	Rev. Pensions	288	Report and bill.	1152			
Halsey, Job	Pension for revolutionary services.	26	1	Petition	172	Rev. Pensions	134	Report and bill.	144	Ref'd to Com. W. H.		
Halsey, Job	Pension for revolutionary services.	26	2	House bill	149	Whole House			144			
Halsey, John	Pension for revolutionary services.	24	2	Petition	399	Rev. Pensions.						
Halsey, Kelly	Lands in lieu of bounty land in Arkansas.	19	1	Petition	199	Public Lands	Jan. 27, 1826	General bill	77	Passed	Passed	App'd May 22, 1826
Halsey, Luther	Compensation for a hospital site near Pittsburg.	27	2	Memorial	526	Claims	788	Adverse		Laid on table.		
Halsey, Thomas Lloyd	Remission of duties on teas	6	2	Rep't Committee.	825	Whole House		With't amend.	320	Passed	Passed	App'd March 3, 1801
Halsey, Thomas Loyd, jr.	Indemnity for French spoliations prior to 1800.	26	1	Memorial	182	Foreign Affairs	343	Favorable; bill.	319	Referred to Committee Whole House.		
Halsey, Thomas Lloyd	Indemnity for French spoliations prior to 1800.	29	2	Memorial	337	Foreign Affairs.						
Halsey, Zephaniah	Pension	22	1	Petition	131	Rev. Pensions	390	Report and bill.	485			
Halsey, Zephaniah, heirs of.	Pension	30	1	Petition	896	Rev. Pensions				Discharged; laid on table.		Leave to withdraw, 1st sess. 31st Cong.
Halstead, Christopher N.	Compensation for services in Indian wars.	23	2	Petition	276	Military Affairs				Discharged; laid on table.		
Halstead, Christopher N.	Compensation for services in Indian wars.	24	1	Petition	157	Military Affairs	Feb. 4, 1836			Discharged; laid on table.		
Halstead, Haines & Co.	To refund excess of duties on merchandise.	29	1	Amend't to House bill.	206	Whole House	Feb. 27, 1846	Favorable	54	Passed	Passed	App'd Aug. 8, 1846
Halstead, Henry N	Pension for disability, war of 1812.	28	1	Petition	744	Invalid Pensions.						
Halstead, Henry N	Pension for disability, war of 1812.	28	2	Petition	140	Military Pensions	39	Report and bill.	513	Passed.		
Halstead, Henry N	Pension for disability, war of 1812.	29	1	Petition	658	Invalid Pensions.						
Halstead, Henry N	Pension for disability, war of 1812	30	1	Petition	575	Invalid Pensions	560	Report and bill.	460	Passed.		
Halstead, Henry N	Pension for disability, war of 1812.	31	1	Res. and doc.	493	Invalid Pensions.						
Halstead, John	(See Canadian refugees.)	4	2		614							
Halstead, John	Interest due him by resolution of Congress.	2	2	Petition	697					Referred to Secretary of Treasury.		
Halstead, John	Interest due him by resolution of Congress.	3	2	Rep. of Secretary Treasury.	284	Claims				Laid on table.		
Halstead, John	For an allowance by the accounting officers.	7	1	Petition	27	Claims	Jan. 5, 1802	Adverse		Rejected.		
Halstead, Joseph	Compensation for losses and services in revolutionary war.	1	2	Petition	160					Laid on table.		
Halstead, Samuel	Pension for revolutionary services.	27	2	Petition	1024	Rev. Pensions.						
Halt, Joshua	(See John Rogers)	14	1		416							
Halton, Sally	Bounty land and pension	20	2	Memorial	312	Military Pensions.						
Haly, David M.	(See David M. Hale)	20	1		111							

List of private claims presented to the House of Representatives of the United States from the 1st to the 31st Congress, inclusive—Continued.

2—3

Names of claimants.	Nature or object of the claim.	Congress.	Session.	How brought before the House of Reps.	Page of journal.	To what committee of the House referred.	No. or date of the report.	Nature of the report.	No. of the bill.	How disposed of by the House of Reps.	How disposed of by the Senate.	Date of the act of Congress, and remarks.
Ham, Richard	Compensation for services and supplies furnished U. S. States navy.	1	1	Petition	125					Laid on table.		
Ham, Thomas	Indemnity for French spoliations prior to 1800.	26	1	Memorial	182	Foreign Affairs	343	Favorable; bill	319	Referred to Committee Whole House.		
Ham, William	Increase of compensation as the officer of a revenue cutter.	14	2	Petition	184	Com. and Manuf.						
Ham, William	Indemnity for French spoliations prior to 1800.	26	1	Memorial	182	Foreign Affairs	343	Favorable; bill	319	Referred to Committee Whole House.		
Ham, William, administrator of.	Indemnity for French spoliations prior to 1800.	31	1	Petition	196	Foreign Affairs	355	General bill	318			
Hambleton, Samuel	Credit on settlement for money expended in public service.	22	2	Petition	137	Naval Affairs	82	Report and bill	725			
Hambleton, Samuel	Credit on settlement for money expended in public service.	23	1	Petition	190	Naval Affairs	554	Report and bill	552			
Hambleton, Samuel	Office rent and clerk hire as purser United States navy.	25	2	Petition	41	Naval Affairs	260	Report and bill	303	Referred to Committee Whole House.		
Hambleton, Samuel	Office rent and clerk hire as purser United States navy.	25	3	House bill	377	Whole House			303	Passed	Laid on table.	
Hambleton, Samuel	Credit for $374 77 in settlement of account.	26	1	Petition	180	Naval Affairs	533	Report and bill	432			
Hambleton, Samuel	Relief as a purser in United States navy.	27	2	Petition	63	Claims	469	Report and bill	319	Referred to Committee Whole House.		
Hambleton, Samuel	Relief as a purser in United States navy.	27	3	House bill	87	Whole House			319	Passed	Passed	App'd Jan. 28, 1843
Hambleton, Samuel	Arrears of pension	24	1	Petition	99	Naval Affairs	331	Report and bill	346	Referred to Committee Whole House.		
Hambleton, Samuel	Arrears of pension	24	2	Petition	90	Naval Affairs.						
Hamblin, Levi	Interest on balance due for services as a soldier, war of 1812.	22	1	Resolution	511	Claims	April 12, 1832	Adverse		Laid on table.		
Hambly, William	Exchange of a grant of land	18	2	Petition	31	Priv. Land Claims.	7	Report and bill	248	Passed.		
Hambly, William	Exchange of a grant of land	19	1	Petition	37	Priv. Land Claims.	27	Report and bill	4	Passed	Passed, with amendment.	App'd May 16, 1826
Hambright, John, widow of	Pension for revolutionary services.	27	2	Petition	255	Rev. Pensions	579	Report and bill	375	Referred to Committee Whole House.		
Hambright, John, widow of	Pension for revolutionary services.	27	3	House bill	88	Whole House			375	Passed	Passed	App'd Feb. 24, 1843
Hamburgh, citizens of	(See C. N. Buck)	19	1		152							
Hamburgh, P. G.	Compensation for property destroyed by Indians in Florida, 1839.	26	1	Petition	621	Claims.						
Hambaugh, P. G., assignee of.	Compensation for property destroyed by Indians in Florida, 1839.	29	1	Petition	415	Claims	278	Adverse.				
Hamburgh, ——	(See Dallum & Hamburgh)	26	2		135							
Hamelin, Augustin, jr.	Payment of money to extinguish land title.	24	1	Appropriation bill	1012	Whole House	June 30, 1836	With amend'ts	695	Passed	Passed	App'd July 2, 1836
Hamer, Christian	Indemnity for damage to property during revolutionary war.	1	3	Petition	391					Referred to Secretary Treasury.		
Hamil, John and Abner R. Moore, representatives of.	Compensation for team taken for northwestern army, war of 1812.	15	2	Petition	168	Claims	Dec. 31, 1819	Adverse.		Laid on table.		
Hamilton, Alexander, widow of.	Half-pay for revolutionary services	11	1	Petition	27	Claims.						
Hamilton, Alexander, widow of.	Half-pay for revolutionary services	11	2	Petition	117	Claims	Jan. 11, 1810	Adverse	97	Passed	Rejected.	
Hamilton, Alexander, widow of.	Commutation pay for revolutionary services.	14	1	Petition	165	Pens. & Rev. Cl'ms.	Feb. 24, 1816	Report by bill.	93	Passed	Passed	App'd Aug. 29, 1816

List of private claims presented to the House of Representatives of the United States from the 1st to the 31st Congress, inclusive—Continued.

Names of claimants.	Nature or object of the claim.	Congress.	Session.	How brought before the House of Reps.	Page of journal.	To what committee of the House referred.	No. or date of the report.	Nature of the report.	No. of the bill.	How disposed of by the House of Reps.	How disposed of by the Senate.	Date of the act of Congress, and remarks.
Hamilton, Alexander, widow of.	Renewal of a lost land warrant...	25	2	Resolution	981	Priv. Land Claims.	June 2, 1838	Rep't by Joint Resolution.	J. R. 15	Passed	With't amend.	
Hamilton, Alexander, widow of.	Renewal of a lost land warrant...	25	3	Senate bill	657	....	....	....	S. 174	Passed	Passed	App'd March 3, 1839
Hamilton, General Alexander.	(See New York Merchants' Exchange Company.)	19	1	....	73							
Hamilton, Allen.........	Compensation for services as secretary of Indian commissioner.	25	2	Appropriation bill	....	....	....	....	.....	....	....	App'd July 7, 1838
Hamilton, Archibald W...	Indemnity for loss of pay and commission in British army.	15	1	Petition	272	Claims	Mar. 2, 1818	Adverse	.....	Referred to Committee Whole House.		
Hamilton, Archibald W...	Indemnity for loss of pay and commission in British army.	15	2	Rep. of last sess.	87	Whole House.....	....	....	.....	Discharged; leave to withdraw.		
Hamilton, Archibald W...	Settlement of accounts as assistant deputy quartermaster general U. States army.	19	2	Memorial	65	Claims	66	Report and bill	418	Passed	....	Leave to withd'w, page 363.
Hamilton, Archibald W...	Compensation for services, and reimbursement of advances on public account.	20	1	Petition	342	Claims	190	Report and bill	218	Referred to Committee Whole House.		
Hamilton, Archibald W...	Compensation for services, and reimbursement of advances on public account.	20	2	House bill	202	Whole House.....	Jan. 24, 1829	With't amend.	218	Passed.		
Hamilton, Archibald W...	Compensation for services, and reimbursement of advances on public account.	22	1	Petition	536	Claims	442	Report and bill	544	Referred to Committee Whole House.		
Hamilton, Archibald W...	Compensation for services, and reimbursement of advances on public account.	22	2	House bill	456	Whole House.....	Feb. 28, 1833	With't amend.	544	Passed	Passed	App'd March 2, 1833
Hamilton, Archibald W...	Increase of compensation for services as collector in Florida.	23	1	Petition	567	Claims	June 20, 1830	Adverse	.....	Laid on table.		
Hamilton, Archibald W...	Indemnity for losses resulting from his refusal to bear arms against the United States.	24	1	Memorial	944	Military Affairs.						
Hamilton, Lieut. Charles, widow of.	Pension for revolutionary services.	26	1	Resolution	385	Rev. Pensions	664	Adverse	.....	Laid on table.		
Hamilton, Christiana and Samuel S.	Indemnity for property destroyed by the enemy at Washington.	14	2	Petition	279	Claims	....	....	.....	Discharged; laid on table.		
Hamilton, Christiana and Samuel S.	Indemnity for property destroyed by the enemy at Washington.	15	1	Petition	102	Claims	....	....	.....	Discharged; laid on table.		
Hamilton, Christiana and Samuel S.	Indemnity for property destroyed by the enemy at Washington.	16	1	Petition	39	Claims	Dec. 27, 1819	Adverse	.....	Rejected.		
Hamilton, Christiana and Samuel S.	Indemnity for property destroyed by the enemy at Washington.	17	1	Petition	52	Claims..........	Jan. 16, 1822	Adverse	.....	Rejected...........	....	Leave to withdraw.
Hamilton, Christiana and Samuel S.	Indemnity for property destroyed by the enemy at Washington.	22	1	Petition	172	Claims.						
Hamilton, Christiana and Samuel S.	Indemnity for property destroyed by the enemy at Washington.	22	2	Petition	86	Claims.						
Hamilton county, Ohio, court house of.	(See Ohio, Hamilton county court-house.)	14	1	....	234							
Hamilton, David	Pension	11	2	House bill......	283	Whole House	Mar. 24, 1810	Favorable	107	Passed	Passed	App'd April 27, 1810
Hamilton, David	Right of pre-emption to land in Missouri.	24	2	Petition	312	Public Lands.						
Hamilton, Eliakim.......	To be restored to pension roll	17	2	Petition	142	Whole House.....	....	General bill ..	207	Passed	Passed	App'd March 1, 1823
Hamilton, Eliphalet......	Invalid pension...............	4	1	Petition	439	Claims	May 7, 1796	Adverse	.....	Leave to withdraw.		

List of private claims presented to the House of Representatives of the United States from the 1st to the 31st Congress, inclusive—Continued.

Names of claimants.	Nature or object of the claim.	Congress.	Session.	How brought before the House of Reps.	Page of journal.	To what committee of the House referred.	No. or date of the report.	Nature of the report.	No. of the bill.	How disposed of by the House of Reps.	How disposed of by the Senate.	Date of the act of Congress, and remarks.
Hamilton, Empson	Increase of pension	21	2	Petition	62	Military Pensions.						
Hamilton, Empson	Increase of pension	24	2	Memorial	42	Invalid Pensions	149	Report and bill.	873	Passed	Passed	App'd March 3, 1837
Hamilton, Empson	Increase of pension	25	2	Petition	41	Naval Affairs	418	Report and bill.	424	Passed	Indef. postp'd.	
Hamilton, Empson	Increase of pension	26	1	Petition	179	Naval Affairs.						
Hamilton, Empson	Pension for wounds received in service of United States.	26	1	Memorial	713	Naval Affairs.						
Hamilton, Empson	Pension for wounds received in service of United States.	27	2	Memorial	64	Naval Affairs	597	Adverse	......	Laid on table.		
Hamilton, Empson	Pension for wounds received in service of United States.	27	2	Petition	883	Invalid Pensions	966	Adverse	......	Laid on table.		
Hamilton, Empson	Pension for wounds received in service of United States.	27	3	Petition	239	Invalid Pensions	192	Adverse	......	Laid on table.		
Hamilton, Empson	Pension for wounds received in service of United States.	28	1	Petition	103	Invalid Pensions	18	Adverse	......	Laid on table.		
Hamilton, Empson	(See heir of W. E. Godfrey)	27	2	....	1298							
Hamilton, Francis	To be placed on pension roll	19	1	Petition	128	Military Pensions	....	....	......	Discharged; laid on table.		
Hamilton, Frederick	Confirmation of title to land in Alabama.	23	2	Petition	67	Public Lands	....	....	......	Discharged; laid on table.		
Hamilton, Frederick, widow of.	Pension in consideration of the death of her husband in public service.	30	1	Petition	274	Rev. Pensions	207	Adverse	......	Laid on table.		
Hamilton, George	Release from liability incurred as sheriff in Pennsylvania.	13	2	Petition	205	Ways and Means	April 9, 1814	Report by bill.	190	Passed	Passed	App'd April 18, 1814
Hamilton, Hannah	(See John Hamilton, widow of.)	28	1	....	103							
Hamilton, Hosea, widow of.	Pension for revolutionary services.	30	1	Petition	886	Rev. Pensions	....	....	......	Discharged; laid on table.		
Hamilton, James, by attorney.	Indemnity for French spoliations prior to 1800.	26	1	Memorial	182	Foreign Affairs	343	Favorable; bill	319	Referred to Committee Whole House.		
Hamilton, James	(See Wm. S. Wetmore & J. H.).	31	1	....	520							
Hamilton, John	Pension	14	1	Documents	206	Pens. & Rev. Cl'ms.	April 11, 1816	Report by bill.	171	Passed	Passed, with amendment.	App'd April 30, 1816
Hamilton, John	Relief for disability incurred in public service.	15	1	Petition	286	Claims	....	....	......	Discharged; laid on table.		
Hamilton, John	Reimbursement of advances of bounty to soldiers in war of 1812.	30	1	Petition	369	Claims	376	Adverse	......	Laid on table.		
Hamilton, John, executor of.	Compensation for a team taken by the enemy at Detroit.	14	1	Petition	300	Claims.						
Hamilton, John, executor of.	Remission of interest on land purchase.	15	1	Petition	207	Public Lands	Feb. 16, 1818	Adverse	......	Rejected	....	Leave to withdraw.
Hamilton, John, widow of.	Pension for services in war of 1812.	28	1	Petition	103	Invalid Pensions	26	Adverse	......	Laid on table.		
Hamilton, Joseph D.	(See Amos Edwards, sureties of).	18	2	....	69							
Hamilton, Joseph, widow of.	Pension for revolutionary services.	25	2	Memorial	351	Rev. Pensions	Jan. 2, 1838	....	......	Discharged; laid on table.		
Hamilton, Mehitabel	(See daughter of Ebenezer Dyer).	30	1	....	236							
Hamilton, Nathan, legal representative of Abigail Hamilton, widow of.	Arrears of pension due said widow.	30	1	Petition	606	Rev. Pensions	Aug. 8, 1838	....	......	Discharged; laid on table.		
Hamilton, N. G.	Compensation for a horse taken for public use.	26	1	Senate bill	837	Claims	518	Adverse	S. 296	Referred to Committee Whole House.		
Hamilton, Richard J.	(See Gurdon S. Hubbard & others.)	26	2	....	271							

List of private claims presented to the House of Representatives of the United States from the 1st to the 31st Congress, inclusive—Continued.

Names of claimants.	Nature or object of the claim.	Congress.	Session.	How brought before the House of Reps.	Page of journal.	To what committee of the House referred.	No. or date of the report.	Nature of the report.	No. of the bill.	How disposed of by the House of Reps.	How disposed of by the Senate.	Date of the act of Congress, and remarks.
Hamilton, Richard, widow of.	Continuation of revolutionary pension.	26	1	Petition	198	Rev. Pensions	424	That com. be discharged.				
				Docs. recommit'd	651	Rev. Pensions	424	Adverse	......	Laid on table.		
Hamilton, Rufus	Compensation for property taken for public use.	1	2	Petition and rep't Sec. War.	177	....	....	....	......	Laid on table.		
Hamilton, Rufus	Compensation for property taken for public use.	2	1	Rep. of Secretary of War.	454	Whole House	Nov. 14, 1791	Res.; adverse.				
Hamilton, Thomas	To be restored to pension roll	17	2	Petition	40	Rev. Pensions	Feb. 25, 1823	....	......	Leave to withdraw.		
Hamilton, Tilley	Pension for revolutionary services.	30	1	Resolution	567	Rev. Pensions.						
Hamilton, William	Confirmation of title to land in Indiana Territory.	12	1	Petition	22	Public Lands.						
Hamilton, William	Pension	14	2	Petition	132	Pens. & Rev. Cl'ms.	....	....	......	Discharged; laid on table.		
Hamilton, William, by Wm. Wood, attorney.	Land due Thos. Hamilton for revolutionary services.	12	2	Petition	579	Public Lands.						
Hamlin, Africa	Release from the payment of certain certificates.	2	2	Petition	652	Select.						
Hamlin, Africa	Release from the payment of certain certificates.	4	1	Petition	406	Claims	Jan. 26, 1796	Adverse	......	Leave to withdraw.		
Hamlin, America, & others.	Pension for services as a revolutionary soldiers.	22	1	Resolution	89	Rev. Pensions.						
Hamlin, America, & others.	Pension for services as a revolutionary soldiers.	22	1	Senate bill	205	Rev. Pensions	July 7, 1832	....	S. 48	Rejected.		
Hamlin, Asa	To be restored to pension roll	21	2	Petition	137	Military Pensions.						
Hamlin, Cornelius	Invalid pension	2	2	Rep. of Secretary of War.	649	Whole House	....	....	214	Passed	Passed	App'd Feb. 28, 1793
Hamlin, Cornelius	Invalid pension	3	1	Rep. of Secretary of War.	131	Select	May 26, 1796	Jt. res. to refer to Sec. War.	12	Passed	Passed	App'd June 9, 1794
Hamlin, Cornelius	To be restored to pension roll	17	1	Petition	150	Whole House, on bill No. 37.	Mar. 25, 1823	With amend.	37	Passed	Indef. postp'd.	
Hamlin, Cornelius	To be restored to pension roll	17	2	Petition	52	Rev. Pensions	....	....	......	Discharged; leave to withdraw.		
Hamlin, J. & N.	Compensation for wood furnished United States troops in Florida.	26	1	Petition	169	Claims.						
Hamlin, J. & N.	Compensation for wood furnished United States steamer Muscogee.	27	2	Petition	857	Claims	766	Adverse	......	Laid on table.		
Hamlin, J. G. & N.	Confirmation of title to land in Florida.	24	2	Memorial	210	Priv. Land Claims.						
Hamlin, J. G. & N.	Confirmation of title to land in Florida.	25	2	Memorial	59	Priv. Land Claims.	....	....	......	Discharged.		
Hamlin, J. G. & N.	Confirmation of title to land in Florida.	25	3	Memorial	87	Priv. Land Claims.						
Hamlin, J. G. & N.	Confirmation of title to land in Florida.	25	3	Memorial	207	Priv. Land Claims.						
Hamlin, J. G. & N.	Confirmation of title to land in Florida.	26	1	Memorial	472	Priv. Land Claims.	53	Adverse	......	Laid on table.		
Hamlin, J. G. & N.	Confirmation of title to land in Florida.	26	2	Petition	125	Priv. Land Claims.						
Hammell, George	Pension	22	2	Petition	39	Invalid Pensions.						
Hammell, George	Pension	25	2	Documents	85	Invalid Pensions	....	....	......	Disch'd; laid on table.		
Hammell, George	Pension	25	2	Petition	629	Invalid Pensions	955	Report and bill	833			
Hammell, John, administrator of.	Compensation for a team lost in the public service.	18	2	Documents	188	Whole House.						

List of private claims presented to the House of Representatives of the United States from the 1st to the 31st Congress, inclusive—Continued.

Names of claimants.	Nature or object of the claim.	Congress.	Session.	How brought before the House of Reps.	Page of journal.	To what committee of the House referred.	No. or date of the report.	Nature of the report.	No. of the bill.	How disposed of by the House of Reps.	How disposed of by the Senate.	Date of the act of Congress, and remarks.
Hammill, Hugh	Invalid pension	26	1	Petition	602	Invalid Pensions	May 25, 1840			Discharged; laid on table.		
Hammer, John P.	Pension	19	2	Petition	31	Military Pensions				Discharged.		
Hammer, Philip	Additional compensation for revolutionary services.	22	1	Petition	29	Rev. Claims	Jan. 3, 1832	Adverse		Laid on table.		
Hammersly, George W.	Continuation of naval pension for five years.	21	1	Petition	233	Naval Affairs				Discharged; laid on table.		
Hammersly, George W.	(See Exploring Expedition)	27	3		149		270		818	Ref'd to Com. W. H.		
Hammett, Alexander	Compensation for serving as acting consul at Naples.	21	1	Petition	477	Foreign Affairs	829	Report and bill	730	Referred to Committee Whole House.		
Hammett, Alexander	Compensation for serving as acting consul at Naples.	25	2	Petition	39	Foreign Affairs	566	Report and bil	556	Referred to Committee Whole House.		
Hammett, Alexander	Compensation for serving as acting consul at Naples.	25	3	House bill	380	Whole House			556			
Hammett, Alexander	Compensation for serving as acting consul at Naples.	26	1	Petition	182	Foreign Affairs	342	Report and bill	318	Referred to Committee Whole House.		
Hammett, Alexander	Compensation for serving as acting consul at Naples.	27	2	Petition	63	Foreign Affairs.						
Hammett, Alexander	Compensation for serving as acting consul at Naples.	27	2	Senate bill	1042	Foreign Affairs	July 9, 1842	With't amend.	159	Passed		App'd Aug. 11, 1842
Hammett, Alexander	Compensation for serving as acting consul at Naples.	31	1	Petition	955	Foreign Affairs.						
Hammett, Potter, administrator of.	Compensation for revolutionary services.	4	1	Petition	406	Claims	Jan. 26, 1796	Adverse		Leave to withdraw.		
Hammitt, Thomas, heir of	Prize money as a seaman with J. P. Jones.	30	1	Petition	344	Rev. Claims				Discharged; laid on table.		
Hammon, John	Increase of pension	24	1	Resolution	854	Rev. Pensions.						
Hammon, John	Increase of pension	24	2	Resolution	217	Rev. Pensions	Jan. 16, 1837			Discharged; laid on table.		
Hammons, Philip	Compensation for services as a revolutionary soldier.	21	1	Petition	320	Rev. Claims				Discharged; laid on table.		
Hammons, Philip	Compensation for services as a revolutionary soldier.	21	2	Petition	82	Rev. Claims.						
Hammons, Philip	Compensation for services as a revolutionary soldier.	22	1	Petition	51	Rev. Claims	Dec. 23, 1831	Adverse		Laid on table.		
Hammond, Alonzo G.	(See Charles M. Davis)	21	2		192							
Hammond, Charles D.	(See sureties of Solomon D. Betton.)	27	2		1126				S. 266			
Hammond, Elisha	Pension for revolutionary services.	22	1	Petition	329	Rev. Pensions	368	Report and bill	463	Passed	Indef. postp'd.	
Hammond, George	Pension	15	1	Petition	63	Pens. & Rev. Clm's.				Discharged; laid on table.		
Hammond, Henry, heirs of	Indemnity for French spoliations prior to 1800.	18	1	Petition	80	Foreign Affairs.						
Hammond, John	Arrears of pay and bounty land for revolutionary services.	11	1	Petition	28	Claims.						
Hammond, John, widow of	Pension for revolutionary services.	28	1	Petition	481	Rev. Pensions	Mar. 12, 1844			Discharged; laid on table.		
Hammond, John, widow of	Pension for revolutionary services.	29	1	Petition	168	Rev. Pensions	528	Adverse		Laid on table.		
Hammond, John, widow of	Pension for revolutionary services.	30	1	Petition	685	Rev. Pensions	June 20, 1848			Discharged; laid on table.		
Hammond, Jonathan	For the lease of a quarter section of land.	17	1	Petition	294	Public Lands				Discharged; laid on table.		

List of private claims presented to the House of Representatives of the United States from the 1st to the 31st Congress, inclusive—Continued.

Names of claimants.	Nature or object of the claim.	Congress.	Session.	How brought before the House of Reps.	Page of journal.	To what committee of the House referred.	No. or date of the report.	Nature of the report.	No. of the bill.	How disposed of by the House of Reps.	How disposed of by the Senate.	Date of the act of Congress, and remarks.
Hammond, Leonard	Fishing bounty refused by collector for informality.	17	2	Petition	163	Commerce.						
Hammond, Leonard, & Allen Dexter.	Payment of money due for services rendered and damages sustained.	26	2	Petition	123	Claims.						
Hammond, Leonard, & Allen Dexter.	Additional allowance for work and material over contract to build light-houses.	27	2	Petition	1189	Claims	983	Adverse		Laid on table.		
Hammond, Leonard, & Allen Dexter.	Additional allowance for work and materials over contract to build light-houses.	28	1	Petition	753	Claims	496	Adverse		Laid on table.		
Hammond, Philip	Grant of land for revolutionary services.	17	1	Petition	228	Priv. Land Claims.				Discharged; laid on table.		
Hammond, Philip, heirs of	Indemnity for French spoliations prior to 1800.	29	2	Memorial	150	Foreign Affairs.						
Hammond, Philip, heirs of	Indemnity for French spoliations prior to 1800.	31	1	Petition	616	Foreign Affairs.	355	General bill	318			
Hammond, Col. Samuel	Release from imprisonment on a judgment in favor of U. States.	19	1	Memorial	382	Ways and Means.						
Hammond, Seneca	(See William Baker, agent, New York.)	22	1		288		480					
Hammond, Staats	Pension	11	2	House bill	283	Whole House	Mar. 24, 1810	Favorable	107	Passed	Passed	App'd April 27, 1810
Hammond, William	Compensation for a horse lost in war of 1812.	21	1	Petition	262	Claims	Feb. 11, 1830	Adverse		Laid on table.		
Hamon, William	Drawback on sugar exported	10	1	Senate bill	277	Whole House			20	Indefinitely postponed.		
Hamon, William	Drawback on sugar exported in 1805.	14	1	Petition	35	Com. and Manuf.	Jan. 16, 1816	Report by bill.		Passed	Passed	App'd April 27, 1816
Hampson, James	(See Henry Develin, *et al*)	23	1		589		456					
Hampson, James	Compensation for services as superintendent, &c., on Cumberland road.	27	2	Memorial	1204	Claims.						
Hampson, James	Compensation for services as superintendent, &c., on Cumberland road.	27	3	Memorial	132	Claims.						
Hampson, James	Compensation for services as superintendent, &c., on Cumberland road.	28	1	Memorial	601	Claims.						
Hampson, James	Compensation for services as superintendent, &c., on Cumberland road.	28	2	Memorial	110	Claims.						
Hampson, James	Compensation for services as superintendent, &c., on Cumberland road.	29	1	Petition	92	Claims	227	Adverse		Laid on table		
Hampson, Edward	(See Canadian refugees.)	4	2		614							
Hampstead, Nathaniel	Pension for services as a revolutionary officer.	23	1	Petition	523	Rev. Pensions	April 30, 1834			Discharged; laid on table.		
Hampton, Andrew, heir of	Indemnity for land sold by United States.	15	2	Petition	267	Priv. Land Claims.						
Hampton, Andrew, heir of	Indemnity for land sold by United States	16	1	Petition	184	Priv. Land Claims.	Jan. 31, 1820	Adverse		Leave to withdraw.		
Hampton, Andrew, heir of	Indemnity for land sold by United States.	18	2	Petition	118	Priv. Land Claims.						
Hampton, Ann	(See James Miller & James Love, heirs of.)	10	2		431							

List of private claims presented to the House of Representatives of the United States from the 1st to the 31st Congress, inclusive—Continued

Names of claimants.	Nature or object of the claim.	Congress.	Session.	How brought before the House of Reps.	Page of journal.	To what committee of the House referred.	No. or date of the report.	Nature of the report.	No. of the bill.	How disposed of by the House of Reps.	How disposed of by the Senate.	Date of the act of Congress, and remarks.
Hampton, Elisha	Reimbursement of money deposited at the land office of Fairfield, Iowa.	30	1	House bill	1225	Public Lands	838	Favorable	651	Referred to Committee Whole House.		
Hampton, Elisha	Reimbursement of money deposited at the land office of Fairfield, Iowa.	30	1	Petition	307	Public Lands.						
Hampton, Jacob	Patent for a tract of land purchased and paid for.	19	1	Petition	179	Priv. Land Claims.	Mar. 24, 1825	Report and bill.	155	Passed	Passed	App'd May 20, 1826
Hampton, Joel, widow of	Pension and arrears of pension for revolutionary services.	30	1	Petition	339	Rev. Pensions	382	Adverse	......	Laid on table.		
Hampton, John	Pension	10	1	House bill	232	Whole House	April 19, 1800	Favorable	78	Passed	Passed	App'd April 25, 1808
Hampton, John	Increase of pension	16	2	Petition	236	Pens. & Rev. Cl'ms.	Feb. 16, 1831	....	......	Referred to Secretary of War.		
Hampton, Jonathan	Release of property seized to pay a judgment in favor of United States.	1	2	Petition	195	Select.						
Hampton, Jonathan, and others.	Release as surety of John H. Alley.	17	1	Petition	128	Ways and Means	Mar. 12, 1822	Report by bill.	118	Passed	Passed	App'd May 7, 1822
Hampton, Noah	(See Jonathan Hampton, *et al*)	17	1	....	128							
Hampton, Preston, widow of.	Pension for revolutionary services.	26	1	Resolution Add'l testimony.	385 624	Rev. Pensions.						
Hampton, Preston, widow of.	Pension for revolutionary services.	27	2	Petition	509	Rev. Pensions	915	Adverse	......	Laid on table.		
Hampton, Presley, widow of.	Pension for revolutionary services.	27	2	Petition	509	Rev. Pensions.						
Hampton, Gen. Wade	Indemnity from a judgment for the arrest of a British spy.	14	2	Petition	391	Claims	....	....	......	Discharged; laid on table		
Hamrick, Benjamin	Pension for revolutionary services.	22	1	Petition	173	Rev. Pensions.						
Hamson, Jonas	(See Samuel Tupper and J. H.)	22	1	....	43							
Hamson, Jonas, widow of.	Compensation for property destroyed by the enemy in war of 1812.	22	1	Petition	49	Claims.						
Hamtramck, Major	(See Arthur St. Clair.)											
Hancock, Ann	(See Jacob Moore, heirs of)	29	1	....	425							
Hancock, Bennett	Pension for his services as a revolutionary soldier.	20	1	Resolution	386	Military Pensions.	....	....	......	Discharged; laid on table.		
Hancock, Bennett	Pension for his services as a revolutionary soldier.	21	1	Petition	67	Military Pensions.	April 6, 1830	Adverse	......	Laid on table.		
Hancock, John	(See Charles J. Scott, executor of.)	26	1	....	182							
Hancock, Jubal B	Reservation of land under Choctaw treaty.	24	1	Resolution	352	Indian Affairs	430	Report and bill.	441	Referred to Committee Whole House.		
Hancock, Jubal B	Indemnity for the loss of a reservation of land.	26	1	Senate bill	837	Indian Affairs	June 23, 1840	With't amend.	S. 298	Referred to Committee Whole House.		
Hancock, Jubal B	Indemnity for the loss of a reservation of land.	26	2	Senate bill	178	Whole House	....	....	S. 33			
Hancock, Jubal B	Permission to exchange an entry of land.	27	2	Senate bill	782	Indian Affairs	May 25, 1842	With amend.	S. 3	Passed	Passed as am'd	App'd Aug. 11, 1842
Hancock, Jubal B	Confirmation of title to land	28	1	Petition	754	Public Lands.						
Hancock, Lot W., *et al.*	Compensation for losses in Black Hawk war.	23	2	Petition	436	Claims.						
Hancock, Robert, by Duff Green, attorney	Indemnity for losses by depredations of Indians.	19	2	Petition	134	Indian Affairs	....	....	......	Referred to Committee Whole House.		

List of private claims presented to the House of Representatives of the United States from the 1st to the 31st Congress, inclusive—Continued.

Names of claimants.	Nature or object of the claim.	Congress.	Session.	How brought before the House of Reps.	Page of journal.	To what committee of the House referred.	No. or date of the report.	Nature of the report.	No. of the bill.	How disposed of by the House of Reps.	How disposed of by the Senate.	Date of the act of Congress, and remarks.
Hancock, Robert	(See John McGilbry, *et al*)	22	1		264							
Hancock, Sophia, (Choctaw Indian.)	(See Samuel Mitchell, daughters of)	17	1		354							
Hancock, William	Pension for revolutionary services.	23	2	Petition	303	Rev. Pensions	Feb. 17, 1835			Discharged; laid on table.		
Hancock, William	Pension for revolutionary services.	24	1	Petition	108	Rev. Pensions	April 12, 1836	Adverse		Laid on table.		
Hancock, William	Pension for revolutionary services.	24	2	Petition	48	Invalid Pensions	Feb. 28, 1837	Adverse		Laid on table.		
Hancox, Edward, jr.	Relief in consideration of injuries sustained while assisting custom-house officer at Stonington, Connecticut.	12	1	Petition	214	Select	April 7, 1812	Adverse		Leave to withdraw.		
Hand, Charles J	Compensation for recovering lost horses.	23	1	Senate bill	654	Claims	May 31, 1834	Adverse	S. 74	Passed		App'd June 30, 1834
Hand, Elizabeth	(See widow of Amos Hunt)	25	2		273							
Hand, Jacob	Pension for revolutionary services.	24	1	Petition	260	Rev. Pensions	June 7, 1836			Discharged; laid on table.		
Hand, John B	Reimbursement of money paid to a public agent.	31	1	Petition	467	Indian Affairs.						
Hand, Thomas, widow of.	Pension in consideration of the death of her husband from disease contracted in war of 1812.	17	1	Petition	119	Pens. & Rev. Cl'ms.	Jan. 22, 1822	Adverse		Rejected.		
Handerson, Abigail	Pension for revolutionary services of her husband.	28	1	Petition	839	Whole House.						
Handsley, John M	Pension for disability incurred at Serro Gordo.	31	1	Petition	1226	Rev. Pensions.						
Handsley, John M	Pension for disability incurred at Serro Gordo.	31	2	Rep. of committee	431	Rev. Pensions	59	Adverse		Laid on table.		
Handy, Charles, jr., daughter of.	Revolutionary pension	25	3	Petition	126	Rev. Pensions.						
Handy, Gamaliel	Invalid pension	3	2	Rep. of Secretary War.	337	Claims	March 3, 1795			Discharged; laid on table.		
Handy, Gamaliel	Invalid pension	4	1	Rep. of Secretary War.	445	Claims	Mar. 4, 1796	Favorable: bill ordered.	156	Passed	Passed	App'd April 20, 1796
Handy, George	(See William Harris, *et al*)	20	1		51							
Handy, Joseph	To be restored to pension roll, and payment of arrears.	25	2	Petition	116	Invalid Pensions	Feb. 20, 1838			Discharged; laid on table.		
Handy, Peter, heirs of	Relief from the effects of an error in the sale of land by a government officer.	23	1	Petition	49	Priv. Land Claims.	340	Adverse		Laid on table.		
Handy, William	For the removal of his property from the custody of the southern to that of the northern district of New York.	17	1	Petition	246	Judiciary	Mar. 13, 1818	Adverse		Leave to withdraw.		
Handy, William	Indemnity for French spoliations prior to 1800.	29	2	Petition	57	Foreign Affairs.						
Handy, William	Indemnity for French spoliations prior to 1800.	31	1	Petition	196	Foreign Affairs	355	General bill	318			
Hanes, John	Examination and payment of his claim against the United States.	19	2	Petition	240	Claims				Discharged.		
Hanes, John	Examination and payment of his claim against the United States.	20	1	Petition	119	Claims	Jan. 4, 1828	Adverse		Laid on table.		
Hanes, John, by his attorney, Robert Carr Lane.	Examination and payment of his claim against the United States.	21	1	Petition	69	Claims	Mar. 10, 1830	Adverse		Laid on table.		

List of private claims presented to the House of Representatives of the United States from the 1st to the 31st Congress, inclusive—Continued.

Names of claimants.	Nature or object of the claim.	Congress.	Session.	How brought before the House of Reps.	Page of journal.	To what committee of the House referred.	No. or date of the report.	Nature of the report.	No. of the bill.	How disposed of by the House of Reps.	How disposed of by the Senate.	Date of the act of Congress, and remarks.
Haney, John	Pension for revolutionary services.	14	2	Res. and docs	73	Pens. & Rev. Cl'ms.	Jan. 29, 1817	Report by bill.	91	Passed	Passed, with amendment.	App'd March 3, 1817
Haney, William, widow of	Compensation for revolutionary services.	25	2	Petition	181	Rev. Pensions				Discharged; laid on table.		
Hangendobler, Nicholas, by his attorney, Anthony Musgenug.	Compensation for revolutionary services.	1	3	Petition and rep't Sec. of War.	351					Laid on table.		
Hanger, George	Pension for revolutionary services.	26	1	Documents	871	Rev. Pensions.						
Hanger, George	Pension for revolutionary services.	26	2	Petition	78	Rev. Pensions.						
Hankart, John	Reimbursement of excise duties illegally collected.	7	2	Memorial	264	Com. and Manuf.	Feb. 12, 1803	Adverse		Leave to withdraw.		
Hankins, William	Compensation for services and for loss on contract for wood at fort John on.	26	1	Memorial	613	Military Affairs.						
Hanks, Jacob	Compensation for horse lost in Indian war.	25	2	Senate bill	1249	Claims	1061	With't amend.	S. 202			
Hanks, John	Invalid pension	12	2	Petition	629	Claims	Feb. 26, 1813	Adverse		Laid on table.		
Hanlin, Patrick	To be restored to pension roll	17	1	Petition	142	Referred to Secretary of War.	Feb. 19, 1822	Rep't of Sec'ry War.		Referred to Committee Whole House.		
Hanlin, Patrick	To be restored to pension roll	17	1	House bill	394				37	Passed	Rejected.	
Hanly, Jonathan, widow of	Pension for revolutionary services.	27	2	Resolution	1048	Rev. Pensions	Aug. 20, 1842			Discharged; laid on table.		
Hanna, Israel	(See William H. Bedford, agent).	28	1		262		480					
Hanna, Capt. Josiah	Compensation for horse and equipmen's lost in Seminole war.	23	1	Documents	154	Claims.						
Hanna, Robert	Compensation for property lost in public service.	24	1	Petition	430	Claims.						
Hanna, Samuel	(See Francis Lafontaine and son).	22	2		124							
Hannah, Daniel	Pension	14	1	House bill	622	Pens. & Rev. Cl'ms.	April 11, 1816	Report by bill.	171	Passed	Passed, with amendment.	App'd April 30, 1816
Hannah, Enos	Confirmation of title to half section of land.	24	1	Memorial	58	Public Lands.						
Hannah, John	Pension for his services, war of 1812.	26	1	Petition	602	Invalid Pensions.						
Hannah, John	Pension for his services, war of 1812.	26	2	Petition	212	Invalid Pensions.						
Hannah, John	Pension for his services, war of 1812.	27	2	Petition	60	Invalid Pensions.						
Hannah, Owners of brig.	(See widow of William B. Dolliber, and others.)	23	1		140							
Hannigan, Thomas	Pension	28	1	Petition	777	Invalid Pensions				Discharged; laid on table.		
Hannigan, Thomas	Pension	29	1	Petition	83	Invalid Pensions.						
Hannigan or Hanagan, Ths.	Pension for wounds received in the public service.	29	1	Memorial	1017	Invalid Pensions.						
Hanning, John	Indemnity for property lost in the war of 1812.	24	1	Petition	662	Claims	June 7, 1836	Adverse		Laid on table.		
Hannis, David P.	Compensation for horse and equipments lost in Seminole war.	23	1	Documents	154	Claims.						
Hansburg, Edward	Right of pre-emption as New Orleans branch pilot.	28	1	Petition	77	Priv. Land Claims.	9	Favorable	35	Passed	Passed	App'd June 17, 1844

List of private claims presented to the House of Representatives of the United States from the 1st to the 31st Congress, inclusive—Continued.

Names of claimants.	Nature or object of the claim.	Congress.	Session.	How brought before the House of Reps.	Page of journal.	To what committee of the House referred.	No. or date of the report.	Nature of the report.	No. of the bill.	How disposed of by the House of Reps.	How disposed of by the Senate.	Date of the act of Congress, and remarks.
Hansborough, John, heirs of.	Compensation for a schooner destroyed by enemy, war of 1812.	26	1	Petition	340	Claims.						
				Documents	808	Claims.						
				Documents	918	Claims.						
Hansborough, John, heirs of.	Compensation for a schooner destroyed by enemy, war of 1812.	26	2	Petition	38	Claims.						
Hansborough, John, heirs of.	Compensation for a schooner destroyed by enemy, war of 1812.	27	2	Petition	56	Claims	637	Adverse		Laid on table.		
Hansborough, John, heirs of.	Compensation for a schooner destroyed by enemy, war of 1812.	27	2	Documents	694	Whole House.						
Hansborough, John, heirs of.	Compensation for a schooner destroyed by enemy, war of 1812.	29	1	Petition	578	Claims.						
Hanscom, Uriah	Increase of pension	26	1	Petition	199	Naval Affairs.						
Hanscom, Uriah	Increase of pension	26	2	Petition	37	Naval Affairs.						
Hanscom, Uriah	Increase of pension	27	2	Petition	55	Naval Affairs	April 12, 1842	Adverse		Laid on table.		
Hanse, Michael	Pension for wounds and disability, revolutionary war.	6	1	Petition	564	Claims	Jan. 28, 1800	Adverse.				
Hansell, William Y.	(See Samuel Rockwell, representatives of.)	26	1		623							
Hansford, Benjamin	Pension for revolutionary services.	28	1	Petition	129	Rev. Pensions	May 2, 1844			Disch'd; laid on table.		
Hansford, Benjamin	Pension for revolutionary services.	28	2	Petition	208	Rev. Pensions.						
Hansford, Benjamin	Pension for revolutionary services.	29	1	Petition	326	Rev. Pensions.	Mar. 27, 1846			Disch'd; laid on table.		
Hanson, Alexander Contee.	Remuneration for expenses under an appointment by Congress.	1	3	Petition	362					Referred to Secretary Treasury.		
Hanson, Alexander Contee.	Remuneration for expenses under an appointment by Congress.	2	1	Rep. of Secretary Treasury.	592					Laid on table.		
Hanson, Alexander Contee.	Remuneration for expenses under an appointment by Congress.	2	2	Resolution	689	Select	Feb. 5, 1793	By bill	225	Rejected.		
Hanson, Charles W.	(See Richard Ridgely)	13	3		679							
Hanson, Charles	(See Richard Ridgely)	14	1		179							
Hanson, John M.	Compensation for work on sea-wall at St. Augustine.	30	1	Petition	962	Claims.						
Hanson, Martin, daughter of.	Naval pension	25	2	Petition	723	Naval Affairs				Discharged; laid on table.		
Hanson, Samuel	Compensation for extra services as purser in United States navy.	11	3	Petition	462	Claims.						
Hanson, Samuel	Compensation for extra services as purser in United States navy.	12	1	Petition	13	Claims.						
Hanson, Thomas	Compensation for a team in war of 1812.	21	2	Petition	114	Claims	Jan. 24, 1831	Adverse		Laid on table.		
Hanson, Thomas	Compensation for a team in war of 1812.	23	2	Petition	345	Claims.						
Hanson, Thomas	Compensation for a team in war of 1812.	24	1	Petition	93	Claims	Jan. 5, 1836	Adverse		Laid on table.		
Hanson, Weightman K., widow of.	Pension for military services	29	1	Petition	209	Invalid Pensions	April 6, 1846			Discharged; laid on table.		
Haradon, Nathaniel, heir of.	Pension for naval services	25	2	Petition	1209	Naval Affairs.						
Haradon, Nathaniel, heir of.	Pension for naval services	26	2	Petition	168	Naval Affairs	197	Adverse.		Laid on table.		
Haraden, Susan	Renewal of her pension for five years.	21	1	Resolution	213	Naval Affairs				Discharged; laid on table.		
Harbach, Abraham	Payment of a draft of James Reeside.	29	1	Documents	145	P. Of. and P. Roads.						
Harbaugh, John R.	(See Robert Coltman, *et al*)	23	1		418							

List of private claims presented to the House of Representatives of the United States from the 1st to the 31st Congress, inclusive—Continued.

Names of claimants.	Nature or object of the claim.	Congress.	Session.	How brought before the House of Reps.	Page of journal.	To what committee of the House referred.	No. or date of the report.	Nature of the report.	No. of the bill.	How disposed of by the House of Reps.	How disposed of by the Senate.	Date of the act of Congress, and remarks.
Harbaugh, Leonard	For a patent	1	1	Petition	62					Laid on table.		
Harbeson, John	Invalid pension	2	1	House bill	361	Whole House		General bill	138	Passed	Passed	App'd July 5, 1842
Harbeson, John Massey, widow of.	Continuation of pension	21	1	Petition	516	Military Affairs.						
Harbeson, John Massey, widow of.	Continuation of pension	21	2	Resolution	91	Military Affairs.						
Harbeson, John Massey, widow of.	Continuation of pension	22	1	Resolution	541	Rev. Pensions.						
Harbeson, John Massey, widow of.	Continuation of pension	22	2	Resolution	349	Military Affairs	Feb. 22, 1843			Discharged; laid on table.		
Harbeson, John Massey, widow of.	Continuation of pension	24	2	Petition	217	Rev. Pensions				Discharged; laid on table.		
Harbison, John	Pension	14	2	Petition	361	Pens. & Rev. Cl'ms.						
Harbison, William	Pension	21	1	Resolution	536	Military Pensions				Discharged; laid on table.		
Harbison, William	Pension	21	2	Resolution	48	Military Pensions.						
Harbison, William	Pension	22	1	Petition	45	Rev. Pensions.						
Harbin, Wiley	Compensation for provisions, and for a horse killed in public service.	21	2	Resolution	68	Claims	116	Adverse		Laid on table.		
Harbo, F.	(See H. Fredien, *et al*)	30	1		976				S. 189			
Harbour, L. B.	Compensation for a horse taken for public use in Florida war.	30	1	Petition	962	Claims.						
Harbour, L. B.	Compensation for a horse taken for public use in Florida war.	30	2	Petition	120	Claims.						
Harbour, L. B.	Compensation for a horse taken for public use in Florida war.	31	1	Petition	324	Claims.						
Hard, Benjamin F.	Additional compensation for transportation of the mail.	25	3	Petition	458	P. Of. and P. Roads.				Discharged.		
Hard, Benjamin F.	Additional compensation for transportation of the mail.	26	1	Petition	623	P. Of. and P. Roads.	July 21, 1840	Report by bill.	505			
Hard, Benjamin F.	Additional compensation for transportation of the mail.	27	2	Petition	268	Claims	153	Report and bill	200	Passed	Passed	App'd Aug. 1, 1842
Hard, Benjamin F., & Gilbert Longstreet.	Compensation for services and losses under a mail contract.	23	2	Petition	263	P. Of. & P. Roads.						
Hard, Benjamin F., & Gilbert Longstreet.	Compensation for transportation of the United States mail.	24	1	Petition	109	P. Of. & P. Roads.	670	Report & Joint Resolution.	J. R. 14			
Hard, Benjamin F., & Gilbert Longstreet.	Compensation for transportation of the United States mail.	25	2	Senate bill	877	P. Of. & P. Roads.	May 17, 1838	With amend.	326	Passed with amendm't	Passed as am'd	App'd May 21, 1838
Hardage, Wm. and Joseph, (Creek Indian chiefs.)	Titles in fee for certain reservations of land.	22	1	Petition	121	Priv. Land Claims.	192	Report and bill	275	Referred to Committee Whole House.		
Hardage, Wm. and Joseph, (Creek Indian chiefs.)	Titles in fee for certain reservations of land.	22	2	House bill	93	Whole House	Dec. 28, 1832	With't amend.	275	Passed	Passed	App'd Feb. 5, 1833
Hardar, William	Pension	21	1	Petition	149	Military Pensions				Discharged; laid on table.		
Hardar, William	Increase of pension	28	1	Petition	904	Rev. Pensions.						
Hardaway, Joel, heirs of.	Commutation pay and payment of a revolutionary warrant.	25	2	Petition	69	Rev. Claims	290	Adverse		Laid on table.		
Hardaway, Joel, heirs of.	Commutation pay and payment of a revolutionary warrant.	25	3	Petition	84	Rev. Claims				Discharged.		
Hardaway, Joel, heirs of.	Commutation pay and payment of a revolutionary warrant.	26	1	Petition	164	Rev. Claims.						
Hardaway, Joel, heirs of.	Commutation pay and payment of a revolutionary warrant.	26	2	Petition	134	Rev. Claims.						

List of private claims presented to the House of Representatives of the United States from the 1st to the 31st Congress, inclusive—Continued.

Names of claimants.	Nature or object of the claim.	Congress.	Session.	How brought before the House of Reps.	Page of journal.	To what committee of the House referred.	No. or date of the report.	Nature of the report.	No. of the bill.	How disposed of by the House of Reps.	How disposed of by the Senate.	Date of the act of Congress, and remarks.
Hardaway, Joel, heirs of	Commutation pay and payment of a revolutionary warrant.	27	2	Petition	61	Rev. Claims	379	Adverse		Laid on table.		
Hardaway, Joel, heirs of	Commutation pay and payment of a revolutionary warrant.	27	3	Petition	70	Rev. Claims	239	Adverse		Laid on table.		
Hardaway, Joseph, representatives of.	Arrears of pay due for revolutionary services.	30	1	Petition	405	Rev. Claims.						
Hardaway, Joseph, representatives of.	Arrears of pay due for revolutionary services.	30	2	Petition	86	Rev. Claims.						
Hardcastle, Robert	Grant of land for public services	21	1	Petition	378	Public Lands				Discharged; laid on table.		
Hardcastle, William, widow of.	Pension for revolutionary services.	28	1	Petition	912	Rev. Pensions.						
Hardell, Nancy	Pension for the revolutionary services of her husband.	28	1	Resolution	668	Rev. Pensions.						
Hardesty, R. C.	Compensation for extra services as postmaster.	25	2	Petition	425	P. Of. & P. Roads.	743	Adverse		Laid on table.		
Hardesty, Richard	Compensation for damage by construction of the Cumberland road.	21	1	Petition	262	Claims	403	Adverse		Referred to Committee Whole House.		
Hardesty, Richard	Compensation for damage by construction of the Cumberland road.	22	1	Petition	34	Claims	457	Report and bill.	558			
Hardesty, Richard	Compensation for damage by construction of the Cumberland road.	23	1	Petition	97	Claims	357	Report and bill.	387			
Hardesty, Richard	Compensation for damage by construction of the Cumberland road.	24	1	Petition	50	Claims	10	Report and bill.	10	Passed	Passed	App'd Feb. 17, 1836
Hardesty, Samuel	Compensation for slaves carried off by the enemy in war of 1812.	24	1	Petition	741	Judiciary.						
Harden, Minard		30	2	Petition	112					Leave to withdraw.		
Harden, Richard	Invalid pension	3	1	Rep. of Secretary War.	131	Select	May 26, 1794	Favorable; bill ordered.	62	Passed	Passed	App'd June 7, 1794
Harden, Richard	Increase of pension	9	2	House bill	608	Whole House	Feb. 28, 1807	Favorable	216	Passed	Passed	App'd March 3, 1807
Hardin, Colden W	Confirmation of a pre-emption right	30	2	Memorial	91	Public Lands	Feb. 27, 1849	Report by bill.	793	Ref'd to Com. W. H.		
Hardin, George W	Pension	21	1	Petition	120	Military Pensions.	April 24, 1830	Adverse		Laid on table.		
Hardin, Isam	Pension	26	1	Documents	1285	Invalid Pensions.						
Hardin, John, widow of	Compensation for maintenance of two Indian girls.	5	2	Petition	185	Claims	Mar. 16, 1798	Recomm'd reference to Sec. of War.		Laid on table.		
Hardin, Richard	Pension for services, war of 1812.	23	2	Resolution	89	Invalid Pensions				Discharged; laid on table.		
Hardin, Rowan B	Bounty land for services and expenses in Mexican war.	30	1	Petition	109	Priv. Land Claims.						
Hardin, Rowan B	Bounty land for services and expenses in Mexican war.	30	2	Petition	92	Military Affairs.						
Hardin, Thomas	Pension	22	1	Petition	72	Rev. Pensions				Discharged; laid on table.		
Hardin, William	Compensation for services and expenses as agent among Cherokee Indians.	30	1	Memorial	274	Claims.						
Hardin, William	Compensation for services and expenses as agent among Cherokee Indians.	30	2	Memorial	120	Claims.						

List of private claims presented to the House of Representatives of the United States from the 1st to the 31st Congress, inclusive—Continued.

Names of claimants.	Nature or object of the claim.	Congress.	Session.	How brought before the House of Reps.	Page of journal.	To what committee of the House referred.	No. or date of the report.	Nature of the report.	No. of the bill.	How disposed of by the House of Reps.	How disposed of by the Senate.	Date of the act of Congress, and remarks.
Hardin, William	Compensation for services and expenses as agent among Cherokee Indians.	31	1	Senate bill	1414	Whole House	...	...	S. 179			
Hardin, William	Compensation for services and expenses as agent among Cherokee Indians.	31	2	Senate bill	420	Whole House	Mar. 3, 1851	With't amend.	S. 179	Passed	Passed	App'd March 3, 1851
Hardin, William and Benjamin.	(See Robert Tobin)	24	2	...	318							
Harding, James D.	Indemnity for losses under contract to furnish provisions to emigrating Indians.	23	1	Petition	387	Claims	390	Adverse	...	Laid on table.		
Harding, James D.	Indemnity for losses under contract to furnish provisions to emigrating Indians.	24	1	Petition	634	Claims	June 8, 1836	Adverse.				
Harding, John	Pension for revolutionary services.	15	1	Petition	184	Select	...	...	...	Discharged; laid on table.		
Harding, John	Compensation for horses and equipments lost in Seminole war.	23	1	Documents	154	Claims.						
Harding, John	(See William H. Bedford, agent).	28	1	...	262							
Harding, John, *et al*	Indemnity for destruction of boats at Baton Rouge, 1815.	16	1	Senate bill	300	Claims	Mar. 24, 1820	With't amend.	32	Passed	Passed	App'd April 5, 1820
Harding, John, heirs of	Compensation for revolutionary services.	2	2	House bill	628	Whole House	Jan. 3, 1793	With amend.	199	Passed	Passed	App'd Feb. 27, 1793
Harding, John, widow and children of.	Annual allowance per act of February 27, 1793	3	1	House bill	36	Whole House	...	...	5	Passed	Passed	App'd Mar. 14, 1794
Harding, John, widow and children of.	Annual allowance per act of February 27, 1793.	3	2	Resolution	258	Select	Dec. 8, 1794	Report by bill.	81	Passed	Passed	App'd Jan. 2, 1795
Harding, John, widow and children of.	Annual allowance per act of February 27, 1793.	4	1	Resolution	420	Ways and Means.	Jan. 18, 1796	Report by bill.	142	Passed	Passed	App'd Feb. 5, 1796
Harding, John, widow and children of.	Annual allowance per act of February 27, 1793.	4	2	Resolution	676	Ways and Means.	Feb. 3, 1797	Report by bill.	223	Passed	Passed	App'd March 3, 1797
Harding, John, widow and children of.	Further provision by law for their relief.	6	1	Resolution	650	Select	April 9, 1800	Report and bill	244	Passed	Passed	App'd May 13, 1800
Harding, John	Annuity	6	2	Senate bill	752	Ways and Means.	Jan. 5, 1801	General bill	277	Passed	Passed	App'd March 3, 1801
Harding, Nathan	Pension	21	1	Petition	411	Military Pensions.	Mar. 30, 1830	General bill	248	Passed	Indef. postp'd.	
Harding, Samuel	Revolutionary pension	17	1	Petition	45	Rev. Pensions	...	...	...	Discharged; laid on table.		
Harding, Samuel	Revolutionary pension	20	1	Res. and petition.	189, 192	Military Pensions.	April 29, 1828	Report and bill	283	Passed.		
Harding, Samuel	Revolutionary pension	20	2	House bill	55	Military Pensions.	Dec. 12, 1828	General bill	311	Passed.		
Harding, Samuel	Revolutionary pension	21	1	House bill	48	Military Pensions.	Jan. 5, 1830	General bill	72	Passed	Passed, with amendment.	App'd May 20, 1830; name of petitioner omitted in law.
Harding, Samuel	Revolutionary pension	21	2	Resolution	78	Military Pensions.						
Harding, Samuel	Revolutionary pension	22	1	Petition	90	Rev. Pensions	164	Report and bill	237	Ref'd to Com. W. H.		
Harding, Samuel	Revolutionary pension	22	2	House bill	123	Rev. Pensions	Jan. 10, 1832	Report and bill	237	Laid on table.		
Harding, Seth	Compensation for services in United States navy, revolutionary war.	1	2	Petition	268	Select	Jan. 27, 1790	Favorable, in part.	88	Passed	Passed	App'd Aug. 11, 1790
Harding, Seth	Compensation for services in United States navy, revolutionary war.	1	3	Petition	346	Select	Jan. 22, 1791	Favorable	...	Rejected.		

List of private claims presented to the House of Representatives of the United States from the 1st to the 31st Congress, inclusive—Continued.

Names of claimants.	Nature or object of the claim.	Congress.	Session.	How brought before the House of Reps.	Page of journal.	To what committee of the House referred.	No. or date of the report.	Nature of the report.	No. of the bill.	How disposed of by the House of Reps.	How disposed of by the Senate.	Date of the act of Congress, and remarks.
Harding, Seth	Compensation for services in United States navy, revolutionary war.	5	3	Petition	432	Claims	Feb. 8, 1799			Leave to withdraw.		
Harding, Seth	Relief for disability incurred during revolutionary war.	9	1	Senate bill	268	Whole House			S. 20	Indefinitely postponed.		
Harding, Seth	Relief for disability incurred during revolutionary war.	9	2	Senate bill	550	Whole House			S. 38	Passed		App'd Feb. 6, 1807
Harding, Captain S.	Increase of naval pension	21	2	Rep't Committee N. P. Fund.	225	Naval Affairs	86	Report and bill	639	Passed.		
Harding, Seth	Permission to locate certain lands in Northwestern territory.	6	1	Senate bill	661	Select			S. 60			
Harding, Seth	Permission to locate certain lands in Northwestern territory.	6	2	House bill	703				265	Passed	Passed	App'd Feb. 18, 1801
Harding, Captain Seth	(See Thomas Park)	26	1		281							
Harding, Seth	(See Canadian refugees)	4	2		614							
Harding, William	Remission of penalty for violation of revenue laws.	30	1	Petition	270	Commerce	318	Report and bill.	295	Passed.		
Harding, William	Remission of penalty for violation of revenue laws.	30	2	House bill	279				295	Passed	Passed	App'd Jan. 26, 1849
Harding, Winthrop S	Release from interest on judgment against him as surety.	31	1	Petition	324	Claims	170	Report and bill.	93	Passed	Passed	App'd Sept. 16, 1850
Hardie, Allen W	Permission to complete payment for land.	22	1	Petition	46	Priv. Land Claims.	31	Report end bill.	76	Passed	Passed	App'd May 19, 1832
Hardie, Allen W	Indemnity for loss on land through the fault of land offices.	22	2	Petition	32	Priv. Land Claims.	Dec. 30, 1832	Adverse		Laid on table.		
Hardie, Allen W	Indemnity for loss on land through the fault of land offices.	23	1	Petition	48	Claims	86	Adverse		Laid on table.		
Hardie, James	Bounty land for services in war of 1812.	15	1	Petition	59	Military Affairs				Discharged; leave to withdraw.		
Hardie, Thomas	Pension	19	2	Petition	285	Military Pensions.				Discharged.		
Hardy, Benjamin	Relief from the effects of a sale of his property for direct tax.	16	1	Petition	101	Judiciary	Jan. 17, 1820	Adverse		Leave to withdraw.		
Hardy, David G	Additional compensation for transporting United States mail.	25	3	Petition	641	P. Of. & P. Roads.				Discharged.		
Hardy, David G	Additional compensation for transporting United States mail.	26	1	Petition	183	P. Of. and P. Roads.						
Hardy, Edward	(See Smith, Thurger, & Co.)	29	1		151							
Hardy, Elisha	Compensation for taking census in a district in Kentucky.	27	2	Petition	77	Claims				Discharged; laid on table.		
Hardy, James, and others.	Bounty land, &c., to mariners serving in Mexican war.	31	1	Memorial	1007	Military Affairs				Discharged; laid on table.		
Hardy, Joseph	Release from an unjust tax on mineral lands.	27	1	Petition	449	Claims.						
Hardy, Lucy	Continuation of revolutionary pension.	28	1	Petition	850	Rev. Pensions.						
Hardy, Robert M., heirs of.	Compensation for losses in Florida, as provided per treaty.	28	1	Petition	862	Claims.						
Hardy, William	Compensation for revolutionary services.	1	2	Petition	221					Referred to Secretary Treasury.		
Hardy, William	Compensation for revolutionary services.	3	1	Rep. of Secretary Treasury.	77					Laid on table.		
Hardy, William	Compensation for revolutionary services.	10	2	Petition	795	Select.						

List of private claims presented to the House of Representatives of the United States from the 1st to the 31st Congress, inclusive—Continued.

Names of claimants.	Nature or object of the claim.	Congress.	Session.	How brought before the House of Reps.	Page of journal.	To what committee of the House referred.	No. or date of the report.	Nature of the report.	No. of the bill.	How disposed of by the House of Reps.	How disposed of by the Senate.	Date of the act of Congress, and remarks.
Hardyman, John	Pension for wounds received in St. Clair's army.	8	2	Petition	142	Claims.						
Hardyman, John	Pension for wounds received in St. Clair's army.	9	1	Petition	193	Claims	Mar. 28, 1806			Leave to withdraw.		
Hardyman, John	Pension for wounds received in St. Clair's army.	9	2	Petition	519	Select				Reference not in order.		
Hardyman, John	Pension for wounds received in St. Clair's army.	10	2	Petition	481	Claims.						
Hardyman, John	Pension for wounds received in St. Clair's army.	11	2	Petition	277	Claims	Mar. 20, 1810			Rejected.		
Hardison, Benjamin	Compensation for services rendered and injuries received in the revolutionary war.	1	2	Petition and rep't Sec. of War.	206, 250	Claims	July 16, 1790	Favorable	88	Passed	Passed, with amendment.	App'd Aug. 11, 1790
Hardorp, John	Remission of penalty for violation of revenue laws.	30	1	Petition	370	Commerce	524	Report and bill	414	Passed	Passed	App'd Aug. 7, 1848
Hardridge, William	For the relinquishment of certain Indian reservations.	20	1	Petition	101	Public Lands	May 13, 1828	Report by bill.	299			
Hardridge, Wm. & Joseph	For a land patent	22	2	House bill	93	Whole House			275	Passed	Passed	App'd Feb. 5, 1833
Hare, Charles W.	(See William Bingham)	7	1		90							
Harford, Charles	(See widow of William Ewing)	23	1		111							
Harford, Sarah	(See widow of William Ewing)	15	2		209							
Harford, Peter	Pension	11	2	House bill	283	Whole House	Mar. 24, 1810	Favorable	107	Passed	Passed	App'd April 27, 1810
Hargiss, Abraham, son of.	Compensation for revolutionary services.	29	1	Petition	533	Rev. Claims	785	Adverse		Laid on table.		
Hargisheimer, John	Relief in consideration of revolutionary services.	9	2	Petition	480	Select.						
Hargous, Louis Eugene	Compensation for services at Vera Cruz in absence of consul.	27	2	Petition	527	Commerce	988	Adverse		Laid on table.		
Hargous, Louis Eugene	Compensation for services at Vera Cruz in absence of consul.	30	1	Petition	644	Foreign Affairs.						
Hargrave, William	Confirmation of title to land in Mississippi.	14	2	Petition	364	Priv. Land Claims.						
Hargrave, William	Commutation pay for services and recompensation for suffering in revolutionary war.	14	2	Petition	297	Pens. & Rev. Cl'ms.						
Hargraw, Lewis	Indemnity for expenses incurred in curing a wound in 1832.	24	1	Petition	426	Invalid Pensions	April 12, 1836	Adverse		Laid on table.		
Hargrove, Joshua	Benefit of the act for relief of purchasers of public land.	17	2	Petition	40	Public Lands	Feb. 5, 1823	Report by bill.	271	Passed	Passed	App'd March 1, 1823
Hargroves, William H.	Right of pre-emption to the land on which he resides.	12	1	Petition	20	Public Lands.						
Hargroves, William H.	Right of pre-emption to the land on which he resides.	12	2	Petition	663	Public Lands.						
Hargus, or Hargis, John.	Commutation pay for revolutionary services.	24	1	Petition	259	Rev. Claims	560	Adverse		Laid on table.		
Harker, Isaiah	(See John Bagley)	5	2		113							
Harkness, Thomas F.	Compensation for services as clerk in Pension office.	28	2	Petition	104	Claims.						
Harkness, Thomas F.	Compensation for services as clerk in Pension office.	29	1	Petition	75	Claims	125	Adverse		Laid on table.		
Harkness, Thomas F.	Compensation for services as clerk in Pension office.	30	1	Petition	148	Claims.						

List of private claims presented to the House of Representatives of the United States from the 1st to the 31st Congress, inclusive—Continued.

Names of claimants.	Nature or object of the claim.	Congress.	Session.	How brought before the House of Reps.	Page of journal.	To what committee of the House referred.	No. or date of the report.	Nature of the report.	No. of the bill.	How disposed of by the House of Reps.	How disposed of by the Senate.	Date of the act of Congress, and remarks.
Harkness, Thomas F.	Compensation for services as clerk in Pension office.	30	2	Petition	116	Claims.						
Haring, Samuel, widow of	Continuation of pension	25	2	Petition	56	Invalid Pensions	Jan. 18, 1838	Adverse		Laid on table.		
Haring, Samuel, widow of	Continuation of pension	26	1	Petition	288	Invalid Pensions	254	Adverse		Laid on table, and recommitted.		
				Add'l testimony.	988	Invalid Pensions.						
Harlan, John T., (Choctaw Indian.)	For the rights granted by treaty of Dancing Rabbit creek.	23	1	Petition	227	Public Lands	328	Report and bill	411			
Harlan, John T., (Choctaw Indian.)	For the rights granted by treaty of Dancing Rabbit creek.	23	1	Petition	523	Indian Affairs.						
Harlan, Margaret Amelia.	(See heirs of Stephen Porter)	24	1		205							
Harlan, Roger R.	Pension for revolutionary services.	23	1	Petition	569	Rev. Pensions	May 6, 1834			Disch'd; laid on table.		
Harlan, Roger R.	Pension for revolutionary services.	23	2	Petition	59	Rev. Pensions	Jan. 6, 1835			Disch'd; laid on table.		
Harlin, Ezekiel, widow of.	Compensation for improvements in Cherokee Nation.	23	1	Petition	79	Indian Affairs.						
Harlin, Ezekiel, widow of.	Compensation for improvements in Cherokee Nation.	23	2	Petition	94	Indian Affairs.						
Harlin, George, (Cherokee Indian.)	That government may purchase his reservation erroneously located.	18	1	Petition	136	Priv. Land Claims.	70	Report and bill.	118	Indef. postponed.		
Harley, James	Renewal of a patent	30	1	Petition	748	Patents.						
Harley, James	Renewal of a patent	30	2	Petition	131	Patents.	6	Report and bill.	687			
Harley, John	Compensation for a house occupied as a hospital and burnt.	2	1	Petition and rep. Sec. of War.	478					Laid on table.		
Harlowe, Charity	Extension of widow's pension act.	30	1	Petition	230	Rev. Pensions.	Jan. 25, 1848	Adverse		Laid on table.		
Harman, George	Pension for revolutionary services.	25	2	Petition	271	Rev. Pensions.	Feb. 20, 1838	Favorable		Referred to Committee Whole House on bill No. 369.		
Harman, George	Pension for revolutionary services.	25	3	Petition	88	Rev. Pensions	Jan. 11, 1839			Referred to Committee Whole House.		
Harman, George	Pension for revolutionary services.	26	1	Petition	173	Rev. Pensions.	Mar. 5, 1840			Discharged; laid on table.		
Harman, George	Pension for revolutionary services.	26	2	Petition	78	Rev. Pensions.						
Harman, John	Bounty land for services in war of 1812.	31	1	Petition	511	Public Lands	246	Report and bill.	244	Passed	Passed	App'd Sept. 28, 1850
Harman, John, heirs of.	Pension or other relief in consideration of his death from wounds received in the public service.	15	1	Resolution	319	Military Affairs	Mar. 13, 1818			Discharged; laid on table.		
Harman, Priscilla B.	(See heirs of William Rogers)	23	1		40							
Harmanson, John	(See heirs of John Robbins)	23	1		40							
Harmer, William R	Correction of an erroneous entry of land.	23	1	Petition	499	Priv. Land Claims.	423	Report and bill.	448			
Harmick, Benjamin	Pension for revolutionary services.	21	2	Resolution	102	Military Pensions.						
Harmon, John and William.	Compensation for a horse lost in war of 1812.	25	3	Petition	86	Claims				Discharged; referred to Third Auditor.		
Harmon, William	Compensation for a horse lost in war of 1812.	23	2	Resolution	397	Claims.						
Harmon, William	Compensation for a horse lost in war of 1812.	25	2	Petition	921	Claims				Discharged.		
Harmony, Manuel X.	Indemnity for seizure and detention of property in New Mexico.	30	1	Petition	145							
				Add'l evidence.	276							
				Add'l evidence.	299	Claims	458	Report and bill.	388			

List of *private claims presented to the House of Representatives of the United States from the* 1*st to the* 31*st Congress, inclusive*—Continued.

Names of claimants.	Nature or object of the claim.	Congress.	Session.	How brought before the House of Reps.	Page of journal.	To what committee of the House referred.	No. or date of the report.	Nature of the report.	No. of the bill.	How disposed of by the House of Reps.	How disposed of by the Senate.	Date of the act of Congress, and remarks.
Harmony, Manuel X.	Indemnity for seizure and detention of property in New Mexico.	30	2	Senate bill	518	Whole House			270			
Harmony, Manuel X.	Indemnity for seizure and detention of property in New Mexico.	31	1	Memorial	272	Military Affairs	Feb. 13, 1850	Rebort by bill.	106			
Harmony, Nicholas, widow of.	Pension for revolutionary services.	25	2	Petition	586	Rev. Pensions	April 18, 1838			Referred to Committee Whole House.		
Harmony, Peter	(See J. Balastier, *et al*)	19	2		81							
Harmony, Peter	Drawback on exportation of playing cards.	19	1	Petition	36	Ways and Means	April 28, 1826	Report by bill.	240	Passed.		
Harmony, Peter	Drawback on exportation of playing cards.	21	1	House bill	560	Commerce	April 23, 1830	Report by bill.	436	Passed.		
Harmony, Peter	Drawback on exportation of playing cards.	24	1	Petition	280	Ways and Means	Feb. 10, 1836	Report by bill.	310	Referred to Committee Whole House.		
Harmony, Peter	Drawback on exportation of playing cards.	24	2	House bill	200	Whole House			310	Passed	Passed	App'd March 3, 1837
Harmony, Schooner	(See William Barlett, *et al*)	18	1		30							
Harner, Christian	Compensation for damage to property in revolutionary war.	1	3	Petition	391					Referred to Secretary Treasury.		
Harner, Christian	Compensation for damage to property in revolutionary war.	2	1	Rep. of Secretary Treasury.	580					Laid on table.		
Harney, Col. Selby, heirs of.	Bounty land for services as lieut. colonel in revolutionary war.	21	1	Petition	202	Priv. Land Claims				Discharged; laid on table.		
Harney, Col. Selby, heirs of.	Bounty land for services as lieut. colonel in revolutionary war.	21	2	Petition	63	Priv. Land Claims	Jan. 7, 1831	Adverse		Laid on table.		
Harney, Col. Selby, heirs of.	Bounty land for services as lieut colonel in revolutionary war.	22	1	Petition	227	Priv. Land Claims	Feb. 7, 1832	Adverse		Laid on table.		
Harold, Ann	Compensation for services rendered during revolutionary war.	1	3	Petition	378					Referred to Secretary War.		
Harold, Ann	Compensation for services rendered during revolutionary war.	2	2	Rep. of Secretary War.	696					Laid on table.		
Harper, Adam	Pension for revolutionary services.	28	1	Petition	550	Rev. Pensions.						
Harper, Adam	Pension for revolutionary services.	28	2	Petition	58	Rev. Pensions.						
Harper, Adam	Pension for revolutionary services.	30	1	Petition	798	Rev. Pensions	Aug. 8, 1848			Disch'd; laid on table.		
Harper, Andrew	Indemnity for loss on contract with Commissioner of Public Buildings.	23	1	Petition	353	Dist. of Columbia.	April 18, 1834	Adverse		Laid on table.		
Harper, Daniel	Compensation for services in United States navy, revolutionary war.	21	2	Petition	337	Rev. Claims.						
Harper, Daniel	Compensation for services in United States navy, revolutionary war.	22	1	Petition	224	Rev. Claims				Discharged; laid on table.		
Harper, Daniel E., & Geo. W. Harper.	Right of pre-emption to a tract of land on which to erect a mill.	23	1	Petition	113	Public Lands				Discharged; laid on table.		
Harper, James A., representatives of.	Payment of an amount due from United States.	20	1	Resolution	355	Claims	178	Report and bill	206	Referred to Committee Whole House.		
Harper, James A., representatives of.	Payment of an amount due from United States.	20	2	House bill	202	Whole House	Jan. 24, 1829	With't amend.	206	Passed	Passed	App'd March 3, 1829
Harper, John	Authority to institute a suit against the United States.	25	2	Petition	278	Judiciary				Discharged.		
Harper, John	Authority to institute a suit against the United States.	26	1	Petition	175	Judiciary				Leave to withdraw.		

List of private claims presented to the House of Representatives of the United States from the 1st to the 31st Congress, inclusive—Continued.

Names of claimants.	Nature or object of the claim.	Congress.	Session.	How brought before the House of Reps.	Page of journal.	To what committee of the House referred.	No. or date of the report.	Nature of the report.	No. of the bill.	How disposed of by the House of Reps.	How disposed of by the Senate.	Date of the act of Congress, and remarks.
Harper, John	Authority to institute a suit against the United States.	27	2	Petition	308	Judiciary.						
Harper, John	Act restraining government agents from occupying his land.	31	1	Petition	617	Judiciary	Mar. 13, 1850			Discharged; laid on table.		
Harper, John	Authority to institute a suit against the United States.	31	2	Petition	51	Judiciary.						
Harper, John	Purchase of certain lands belonging to him.	26	2	Petition	173	Judiciary	243	Adverse		Discharged.		
Harper, John	Purchase of certain lands belonging to him.	28	1	Petition	78	Judiciary	367	Adverse		Laid on table.		
Harper, John	Compensation for services and materials furnished the Mint, Philadelphia.	4	1	Memorial & rep of Director.	434					Referred to Committee Whole House.		
Harper, John	Pension for revolutionary services.	24	1	Petition	433	Rev. Pensions.						
Harper, John	Pension for revolutionary services.	30	1	Petition	798	Rev. Pensions.						
Harper, John	(See James Sanderson, *et al*)	14	1		292							
Harper, John, widow of	Land and other compensation for revolutionary services.	9	1	Petition	262	Public Lands	April 8, 1806			Indefinitely postponed.		
Harper, John, widow of	Land and other compensation for revolutionary services.	9	2	Petition	510	Public Lands				Leave to withdraw.		
Harper, Joseph M.	Reimbursement of expenses on sick soldiers, war of 1812.	22	1	Petition	49	Claims	267	Report and bill.	345			
Harper, Joseph M.	Reimbursement of expenses on sick soldiers, war of 1812.	23	1	Petition	33	Claims	26	Report and bill.	26	Passed	Passed	App'd Feb. 26, 1834
Harper, Leonard, sen.	Payment of a claim against Creek Indians.	22	2	Documents	138	Indian Affairs.						
Harper, Lucien	Payment of a loan office certificate.	21	1	Senate bill	699	Rev. Claims	May 29, 1830	With't amend.	142			
Harper, Lucien	Payment of a loan office certificate.	21	2	Senate bill	78	Rev. Claims	Dec. 31, 1830	With't amend	S. 8	Passed	Passed	App'd March 2, 1831
Harper, Robert	Compensation for transportation of the mail.	15	2	Petition	176	Claims				Discharged.		
Harper, Robert	Compensation for transportation of the mail.	26	1	Petition	169	Claims.						
Harper, Robert G., and others.	Compromise of Illinois land claim.	11	3	Memorial	458	Public Lands.						
Harper, Samuel H.	Compensation for public services.	14	2	Petition	268	Priv. Land Claims.	Feb. 1, 1817	Report by bill.	96			
Harper, Samuel H.	Compensation for public services.	15	1	Petition	172	Claims				Discharged; laid on table.		
Harper, Samuel H.	Increase of compensation as a land officer.	15	1	Petition	151	Claims	April 14, 1818	Report by bill.	193	Referred to Committee Whole House.		
Harper, Samuel H.	Increase of compensation as a land officer.	15	2	House bill	102	Whole House			193	Passed	Passed	App'd Feb. 4, 1819
Harper, Samuel H.	(See Beverly Chew, *et al*)	19	1		326							
Harper, Thomas, executrix of.	Compensation for clothing furnished revolutionary army.	2	1	Petition	526					Referred to Secretary Treasury.		
Harper, Thomas, executrix of.	Compensation for clothing furnished revolutionary army.	3	2	Rep. of Secretary Treasury.	284	Claims.						
Harper, Thomas, representatives of.	Pension due under act of May 1, 1820.	18	2	Resolution	129	Rev. Pensions	Feb. 25, 1825	Adverse		Laid on table.		
Harper, William	Pension for revolutionary services.	24	1	Petition	751	Rev. Pensions.						
Harper, William	Pension for revolutionary services.	24	2	Petition	91	Rev. Pensions	94	Report and bill.	839			
Harper, William	Pension for revolutionary services.	25	2	Petition	38	Rev. Pensions	268	Report and bill.	311	Passed.		

List of private claims presented to the House of Representatives of the United States from the 1st to the 31st Congress, inclusive—Continued.

Names of claimants.	Nature or object of the claim.	Congress.	Session.	How brought before the House of Reps.	Page of journal.	To what committee of the House referred.	No. or date of the report.	Nature of the report.	No. of the bill.	How disposed of by the House of Reps.	How disposed of by the Senate.	Date of the act of Congress, and remarks.
Harper, William	Pension for revolutionary services	25	3	Petition	218	Rev. Pensions	177	Report and bill.	1040	Passed	Adverse report.	
Harper, William	Pension for revolutionary services	26	1	Petition	172	Rev. Pensions	536	Report and bill.	435			
Harper, William	Pension for revolutionary services	27	2	Petition	50	Rev. Pensions	90	Report and bill.	136	Passed	Passed	App'd July 27, 1842
Harper's Ferry Armory	(See Superintendent of Armories.)	14	1		692							
Harpham, Jeremiah	Arrears of pension for disability in war of 1812.	30	1	Petition	581	Invalid Pensions	572	Adverse		Laid on table.		
Harpole, George	Indemnity for horses lost in war of 1812.	15	2	Petition	139	Claims				Discharged; laid on table.		
Harralson, Paul	To be exonerated from the payment of moneys due United States.	7	2	Petition	366	Claims	Feb. 26, 1803			Postponed.		
Harralson, Paul	To be exonerated from the payment of moneys due United States.	8	1	Petition	586	Claims	Feb. 27, 1804	Adverse		Leave to withdraw.		
Harregal, Daniel	Confirmation of title to land	10	2	House bill	518	Whole House	Feb. 13, 1809	With't amend.	161	Passed	Passed	App'd Feb. 28, 1809
Harriden, Nathaniel, daughter of.	(Nature of claim not on Journal.)	2	26	Petition	168	Naval Affairs	Feb. 11, 1841	Adverse		Laid on table.		
Harrie, Daniel	Right of pre-emption	26	1	Petition	608	Public Lands.						
Harriet, schooner	(See Levi Eldridge, *et al*)	27	2		96		476		326			
Harriott, Samuel	Compensation for a horse lost in public service, 1832.	24	1	Petition	430	Claims.						
Harrigan, John	Pension for services in war of 1812.	29	1	Petition	315	Invalid Pensions	May 27, 1846			Disch'd; laid on table.		
Harrigan, John	Pension for services in war of 1812.	29	2	Petition	309	Invalid Pensions.						
Harrigan, John	Pension for services in war of 1812.	30	1	Petition	457	Invalid Pensions	841	Adverse		Laid on table.		
Harrigan, John	Pension for services in war of 1812.	31	1	Petition	788	Invalid Pensions.						
Harriman, Leonard	Pension for wounds received in revolutionary war.	17	1	Petition	194	Rev. Pensions				Discharged; laid on table.		
Harrington, Ahab, (Phebe,) widow of.	Pension	25	2	Resolution	780	Rev. Pensions				Discharged; laid on table.		
Harrington, Ahab, (Phebe,) widow of.	Pension	25	3	Resolution	125	Rev. Pensions				Discharged.		
Harrington, Ahab, (Phebe,) widow of.	Pension	26	2	Petition	50	Rev. Pensions.						
Harrington, Azubah	(See widow of Thomas Bryant)	25	3		564							
Harrington, Azubah	(See widow of Sardius Stone)	25	3		564							
Harrington, Azubah	(See widow of John Harrington)	25	3		564							
Harrington, Ebenezer, widow of.	Bounty land for revolutionary services.	25	2	Petition	594	Public Lands				Discharged.		
Harrington, Ebenezer, heirs of.	Compensation for revolutionary services.	31	1	Petition	468	Rev. Claims.						
Harrington, Estes H	Pension	15	2	Petition	70	Pens. & Rev. Cl'ms.				Referred to Sec. War.		
Harrington, Giles	(See Vermont, town of Aburgh)	26	1		711							
Harrington, James	Pension	23	1	Resolution	509	Invalid Pensions	439	Report and bill.	459	Ref'd to Com. W. H.		
Harrington, James	Pension	23	2	House bill	336	Whole House			459	Passed	Passed	App'd March 3, 1835
Harrington, John, widow of.	Pension for revolutionary services.	25	3	Petition	564	Rev. Pensions.						
Harrington, John, widow of.	Pension for revolutionary services.	26	1	Petition	171	Rev. Pensions				Discharged; laid on table.		
Harris, Ann	(See heirs of John Neiler)	19	2		134							
Harris, Abijah	Pension	22	1	Petition	36	Rev. Pensions				Discharged; laid on table.		
Harris, Abraham	Pension for revolutionary services.	25	2	Petition	272	Rev. Pensions	Feb. 17, 1838	Favorable		Referred to Committee Whole House.		
Harris, Benjamin	Permission to enter land at minimum price.	29	1	Senate bill	1041				S. 61	Passed		App'd July 15, 1846

List of private claims presented to the House of Representatives of the United States from the 1st to the 31st Congress, inclusive—Continued.

Names of claimants.	Nature or object of the claim.	Congress.	Session.	How brought before the House of Reps.	Page of journal.	To what committee of the House referred.	No. or date of the report.	Nature of the report.	No. of the bill.	How disposed of by the House of Reps.	How disposed of by the Senate.	Date of the act of Congress, and remarks.
Harris & Blatchford, attorney of.	Payment of money due from U. States to J. Banks.	2	2	Petition	615	Select	Feb. 1, 1793	Favorable	235	Passed	Postponed.	
Harris & Blatchford, attorney of.	Payment of money due from U. States to J. Banks.	4	2	Petition	651	Claims.						
Harris, C. A	(See George Collier, *et al.*)	26	1		623					Leave to withdraw.		
Harris, Daniel, child of, by Elley Brown, agent of.	Increase of pension for revolutionary services.	26	1	Petition	282	Rev. Pensions	April 25, 1840	Adverse		Rejected.		
Harris, Dennis	Reimbursement of duties on sugar destroyed by fire.	30	1	Petition	859	Commerce.						
Harris, Egbert	(See Fleming Wood & E. Harris)	28	2		117							
Harris, Elisha B	Confirmation of title to a certain lot of land.	24	1	Petition	258	Public Lands.						
Harris, Ezekiel	Compensation for revolutionary services as a mariner.	8	2	Petition	12	Claims.						
Harris, Ezekiel, widow of.	Pension for revolutionary services.	27	2	Petition	556	Rev. Pensions	793	Report and bill.	447	Ref'd to Com. W. H.		
Harris, Ezekiel, widow of.	Pension for revolutionary services.	27	3	House bill	88	Whole House			447	Passed.		
Harris, Ezekiel, widow of.	Pension for revolutionary services.	29	1	Petition	502	Rev. Pensions						
Harris, George	Compensation for cattle taken for public use.	22	2	Petition	32	Military Affairs	Dec. 18, 1832	Adverse		Discharged.		
Harris, George E.	Compensation for horses and equipage lost in Seminole war.	20	1	Petition	38	Claims	Dec. 17, 1827	Adverse		Laid on table.		
Harris, George E.	Compensation for horses and equipage lost in Seminole war.	22	1	Petition	288	Claims	480	Adverse		Laid on table.		
Harris, George E.	Compensation for horses and equipage lost in Seminole war.	23	1	Documents	154	Claims.						
Harris, George E., assignee of.	Compensation for horses and equipage lost in Seminole war.	29	1	Petition	807	Claims.						
Harris, Henry	Pension for wounds received in revolutionary war.	13	1	Petition	15					Referred to Secretary War.		
				Rep. of Secretary War.	24	Claims				Leave to withdraw.		
Harris, Herman	Reimbursement of a fine for an alleged violation of the revenue laws.	25	2	Petition	409	Commerce	783	Report and bill.	735	Referred to Committee Whole House.		
Harris, Herman	Reimbursement of a fine for an alleged violation of the revenue laws.	25	3	House bill	381	Whole House			735	Passed	Passed, with amendment.	App'd March 3, 1839
Harris, Ira, *et al*	Right of pre-emption to land on which they reside.	17	2	Petition	209	Public Lands				Discharged; leave to withdraw.		
Harris, Isaac	(See George Brown, sureties of.)	21	1		132							
Harris, James M.	(See Benjamin T. Whitner, *et al.*)	24	1		751							
Harris, James	Additional compensation for transportation of the mail.	25	3	Petition	205	P. Of. & P. Roads				Discharged; leave to withdraw.		
Harris, James	Additional compensation for transportation of the mail.	26	1	Petition	965	P. Of. & P. Roads.						
Harris, John	Pension for revolutionary services.	23	1	Petition	333	Rev. Pensions	Feb. 24, 1834	Adverse		Laid on table.		
Harris, John	(See Alexander McCorkle)	24	2		312							
Harris, John, heirs of	Compensation for land enclosed in navy-yard, Charlestown.	22	1	Petition	163	Naval Affairs	July 5, 1832	Adverse		Laid on table.		
Harris, John, heirs of	Compensation for land enclosed in navy-yard, Charlestown.	25	2	Petition	56	Naval Affairs	258	Report and bill.	301	Referred to Committee Whole House.		
Harris, John, heirs of	Compensation for land enclosed in navy-yard, Charlestown.	25	3	House bill	377	Whole House			301	Passed	Passed, with amendment.	App'd March 3, 1839

List of private claims presented to the House of Representatives of the United States from the 1st to the 31st Congress, inclusive—Continued.

Names of claimants.	Nature or object of the claim.	Congress.	Session.	How brought before the House of Reps.	Page of journal.	To what committee of the House referred.	No. or date of the report.	Nature of the report.	No. of the bill.	How disposed of by the House of Reps.	How disposed of by the Senate.	Date of the act of Congress, and remarks.
Harris, Captain John, heirs of.	Commutation pay for revolutionary services.	23	1	Petition	41	Rev. Claims				Discharged; laid on table.		
Harris, John, son of	Compensation for revolutionary services.	29	1	Petition	1203	Claims.						
Harris, John, son of	Compensation for revolutionary services.	29	2	Petition	87	Claims.						
Harris, John, son of	Compensation for revolutionary services.	30	1	Petition	457	Claims	350	Adverse.		Laid on table.		
Harris, John, widow of	Extension of the widow's pension act.	30	1	Petition	406	Rev. Pensions	Mar. 14, 1848	Adverse		Laid on table.		
Harris, John, devisee of	Proportion of land for revolutionary services.	10	1	Petition	121	Public Lands				Discharged; leave to withdraw.		
Harris, John, representatives of.	Indemnity for loss and injuries sustained in service of United States, revolutionary war.	1	2	Petition & report of Sec. War.	186					Laid on table.		
Harris, John, representatives of.	Indemnity for loss and injuries sustained in service of United States, revolutionary war.	1	3	Rep. of Secretary War.	394					Bill ordered.		
Harris, John, representatives of.	Indemnity for loss and injuries sustained in service of United States, revolutionary war.	2	1	Petition	486					Referred to Secretary War.		
Harris, John, representatives of.	Indemnity for loss and injuries sustained in service of United States, revolutionary war.	2	2	Rep. of Secretary War.	711					Laid on table.		
Harris, John L.	Permission to enter a lot in Madison parish, Louisiana.	28	2	Petition	112	Public Lands.						
Harris, John L.	Permission to enter a lot in Madison parish, Louisiana.	29	1	Memorial	435	Priv. Land Claims.						
Harris, John M	Compensation for horses lost in the Creek war.	22	1	Resolution	149	Claims	Feb. 6, 1832	Adverse		Laid on table.		
Harris, Jonathan	Payment of certain State bills of credit.	4	1	Rep. of Secretary Treasury.	388	Claims	74	Adverse		Laid on table.		
Harris, Joseph	Invalid pension	1	2	Petition and rep't of Sec. War.	177					Laid on table.		
Harris, Joseph	(See John Christopher Kempff, *et al.*)	7	1		59							
Harris, Joseph	Right of pre-emptiom to land on which he resides.	15	1	Petition	217	Public Lands	March 4, 1818	Adverse		Rejected.		
Harris, Joseph, (Alex'dria.)	Proportion of the proceeds of a vessel and cargo condemned for violation of non-intercourse act.	16	1	Petition	424	Ways and Means				Discharged; laid on table.		
Harris, Joseph, (Alex'dria.)	Proportion of the proceeds of a vessel and cargo condemned for violation of non-intercourse act.	16	2	Petition	48	Judiciary				Discharged; laid on table.		
Harris, Joseph, (Alex'dria.)	Proportion of a forfeiture remitted by the President	17	1	Petition	264	Ways and Means	Feb. 28, 1822	Adverse.		Rejected.		
Harris, Joseph, (Alex'dria.)	Proportion of a forfeiture remitted by the President.	27	2	Petition	390	Commerce.						
Harris, Joseph	Compensat'n for services as weigher and measurer, Alexandria.	26	1	Petition	179	Commerce.						
Harris & Lamphier	Compensat'n for services as weigher and measurer, Alexandria.	25	2	Petition	657	Ways and Means				Discharged; laid on table.		

List of private claims presented to the House of Representatives of the United States from the 1st to the 31st Congress, inclusive—**Continued.**

Names of claimants.	Nature or object of the claim.	Congress.	Session.	How brought before the House of Reps.	Page of journal.	To what committee of the House referred.	No. or date of the report.	Nature of the report.	No. of the bill.	How disposed of by the House of Reps.	How disposed of by the Senate.	Date of the act of Congress, and remarks.
Narris, Joseph & W. L.	Compensa'n for services as weigher and measurer, Alexandria.	25	3	Petition	90	Ways and Means.						
Harris, Joseph & W. L.	Compensat'n for services as weigher and measurer, Alexandria.	26	1	Petition	179	Ways and Means.						
Harris, Joseph & W. L.	Compensat'n for services as weigher and measurer, Alexandria.	29	1	Petition	234	Judiciary	Jan. 27, 1846	Adverse	......	Rejected.		
Harris, Joseph, heirs of	Land at the Navy-yard, Charleston	26	1	Letter of Secret'y Navy.	402	Ways and Means.						
Harris, Joseph	(See Captain Charles Richardson, of Brig Leontine.)	27	2	......	321							
Harris, Levi	Pension	14	1	Resolution	497	Pens. & Rev. Cl'ms.	April 11, 1816	By bill	171	......	......	Bill passed, but petitioner's name omitted in the law.
Harris, Levi	Pension	14	2	Resolution	166	Pens. & Rev. Cl'ms	Jan. 29, 1817	By bill	91	......	......	Bill passed, but petitioner's name omitted in the law.
Harris, Luther	(See James Williams)	26	1	......	293							
Harris, Mathew	Remuneration for p oper'y confiscated in Nova Scotia.	12	1	Petition	26	......	......	......	......	Referred to Commissioners act of April 7, 1798.		
arris, McNary	Settlement of account as quartermaster and acting commissary.	25	3	Resolution	413	Claims.						
Harris, McNary	Settlement of account as quartermaster and acting commissary.	26	1	Petition	339	Claims.						
Harris, Moses	Pension for revolutionary services.	17	1	Petition	60	Pens. & Rev. Cl'ms.	Dec. 21, 1821	Adverse	......	Laid on table.		
Harris, Moses	Compensation for revolutionary services.	19	1	Petition	44	Pens. & Rev. Cl'ms.	Dec. 29, 1825	Adverse.	......	Laid on table.		
Harris, Nathaniel	Invalid pension	4	1	Petition	458	Claims.						
Harris, Nathaniel	Invalid pension	5	2	Rep't Committee.	264	......	April 17, 1798	Adverse	......	Laid on table.		
Harris, Nathaniel	Invalid pension	5	3	Rep't Committee.	432	......	......	......	......	Referred to Committee Whole House.		
Harris, Newsom, widow of.	Pension for revolutionary services.	28	1	Petition	481	Rev. Pensions	Jan. 7, 1844	......	......	Discharged; laid on table.		
Harris, Oliver	Indemnity for advances and attendance on sick marines.	28	1	Petition	274	Claims.						
Harris, Oliver, widow of.	Arrears of pension due husband.	22	2	Petition	29	Rev. Claims	Feb. 28, 1832	......	......	Discharged; referred to Rev. Pensions.		
Harris, Oliver, widow of.	Arrears of pension due husband.	22	1	Petition	446	Rev. Pensions	May 20, 1832	......	......	Discharged; laid on table.		
Harris, Oliver, widow of.	Arrears of pension due husband.	24	1	Petition	137	Rev. Pensions	Jan. 19, 1836	Report by bill	181	Passed	Passed	App'd June 28, 1836
Harris, Oliver C	Renewal of letters patent	30	1	Petition	656	Patents	567	Report and bill.	467			
Harris, Oliver C	Renewal of letters patent	30	1	Senate bill	681	Patents	Aug. 8, 1848	With't amend.	S. 101	Passed	Passed	App'd Aug. 11, 1848
Harris, Oliver C	Renewal of letters patent	30	2	Petition	657	......	......	......	......	Leave to withdraw.		
Harris, Overton	Compensation for military services in war of 1812.	22	2	Petition	152	Military Affairs	......	......	......	Discharged; laid on table.		
Harris, Richard	(See Farrow & Harris	17	2	......	136							
Harris, Richard	Additional compensation for loss on a contract with United States.	19	1	Petition	223	Claims.						
Harris, Richard	Additional compensation for loss on a contract with United States.	19	2	Memorial	115	Claims	Feb. 14, 1827	......	415			
Harris, Riehard	Additional compensation for loss on a contract with United States.	20	1	Memorial	75	Claims	Mar. 7, 1828	......	210			

List of private claims presented to the House of Representatives of the United States from the 1st to the 31st Congress, inclusive—Continued.

Names of claimants.	Nature or object of the claim.	Congress.	Session.	How brought before the House of Reps.	Page of journal.	To what committee of the House referred.	No. or date of the report.	Nature of the report.	No. of the bill.	How disposed of by the House of Reps.	How disposed of by the Senate.	Date of the act of Congress, and remarks.
Harris, Robert	Commutation pay for revolutionary services.	3	2	Memorial	247	Claims	Feb. 25, 1795	Adverse	......	Referred to Committee Whole House.		
Harris, Robert	Invalid pension	4	1	Rep. of Secretary War.	445	Claims	Mar. 4, 1796	Favorable; bill ordered.	156	Passed	Passed	App'd April 20, 1796
Harris, Robert	Invalid pension	4	2	Rep't Committee.	628	Claims	Dec. 26, 1796	Adverse	......	Laid on table.		
Harris, Lieut. Robert, widow of.	Half-pay of a lieutenant in the revolutionary navy.	16	1	Petition	114	Claims	April 22, 1820	Adverse	......	Laid on able		
Harris, Salathiel	Pension	20	2	Petition	203	Military Pensions.						
Harris, Salathiel	Pension	23	1	Resolution	295	Invalid Pensions	Feb. 21, 1834	Adverse	......	Laid on table.		
Harris, Samuel D.	Sundry allowances as marshal of Massachusetts.	17	1	Petition	213	Judiciary	....	....	......	Discharged; laid on table.		
Harris, Stephen	Compensation for a vessel taken for public use.	23	2	Memorial	37	Claims	107	Adverse	......	Laid on table.		
Harris, Thomas	Compensation for revolutionary services.	6	2	Petition	779	Claims	Feb. 9, 1801	Adverse	......	Rejected.		
Harris, Thomas	Pension	9	2	House bill	608	Whole House	Feb. 28, 1807	Favorable	216	Passed	Passed	App'd March 3, 1807
Harris, Capt. Thomas, heirs of.	Commutation pay for revolutionary services.	24	1	Petition	508	Rev. Claims	638	Adverse	......	Referred to Committee Whole House.		
Harris, Capt. Thomas, heirs of.	Commutation pay for revolutionary services.	25	2	Petition	194	Rev. Claims	393	Adverse	......	Laid on table.		
Harris, Thomas J.	Share of appropriation for the capture of a private vessel.	24	2	Documents	314	Naval Affairs	....	Appro. bill	754	Passed	Passed	App'd March 3, 1837
Harris, Waterman	Bounty land and increase of pension.	14	2	Petition	297	Pens. & Rev. Cl'ms.	....	....	......	Discharged; laid on table.		
Harris, Waterman	Increase of pension	22	1	Resolution	597	Invalid Pensions	....	....	......	Discharged; laid on table.		
Harris, William	Compensation for property destroyed in revolutionary war.	1	2	Petition	278	....	....	....	......	Referred to Secretary War.		
Harris, William	Compensation for property destroyed in revolutionary war.	2	1	Rep. of Secretary War.	580	....	....	....	......	Laid on table.		
Harris, William	Pension	19	2	Petition	53	Rev. Claims	Dec. 19, 1826	Adverse	......	Discharged; laid on table.		
Harris, William	Pension	20	1	Petition	557	Military Pensions.						
Harris, William	Pension	20	2	Petition	55	Military Pensions	Dec. 12, 1828	General bill	311	Passed	Laid on table.	
Harris, William	Pension	21	1	Petition	36	Military Pensions	....	....	......	Laid on table.		
Harris, William	Pension	21	1	House bill	130	Whole House	Feb. 13, 1830	Favorable	72	Passed	Passed	App'd May 20, 1830
Harris, William	Reimbursement of expenses incurred in Seminole war.	16	1	Petition	346	Claims	April 10, 1820	Adverse	......	Laid on table.		
Harris, William	Compensation for horees and equipments lost in Seminole war.	23	1	Documents	154	Claims.						
Harris, William	(See sureties of Wm. and George Gould.)	29	1	....	411							
Harris, William	Compensation for losses by depredation of Indians.	30	1	Petition	77	Claims	51	Adverse	......	Laid on table.		
Harris, William, & others.	Compensation for slaves carried off by the British.	20	1	Petition	51	Judiciary	77	Adverse	......	Laid on table.		
Harris, Major William	Compensation for certain services, war of 1812.	18	2	Resolution	198	Military Affairs	....	....	......	Discharged; leave to withdraw.		
Harris, Wynans	Revolutionary pension	22	1	Resolution	194	Rev. Pensions	Mar. 13, 1832	Repor and bill	464	Referred to Committee Whole House.		
Harrison, Audley	(See William H. Bedford, agent).	28	1	....	262							
Harrison, Auderley	Compensation for horses and equipments lost in Seminole war.	23	1	Documents	154	Claims.						

List of private claims presented to the House of Representatives of the United States from the 1st to the 31st Congress, inclusive—Continued.

Names of claimants.	Nature or object of the claim.	Congress.	Session.	How brought before the House of Reps.	Page of journal.	To what committee of the House referred.	No. or date of the report.	Nature of the report.	No. of the bill.	How disposed of by the House of Reps.	How disposed of by the Senate.	Date of the act of Congress, and remarks.
Harrison, Benj., heirs of	Compensation for revolutionary services.	24	1	Petition	431	Rev. Claims.						
Harrison, Benj., heirs of	Compensation for revolutionary services.	25	3	Petition	84	Rev. Claims				Discharged.		
Harrison, Benj., widow of	Compensation for revolutionary services.	29	1	Petition	90	Claims	5	Adverse		Laid on table.		
Harrison, Benj., heirs of	Settlement of accounts as revolutionary paymaster general.	24	1	Petition	431	Rev. Claims.						
Harrison, Benj., heirs of	Settlement of accounts as revolutionary paymaster general.	24	2	Petition	92	Rev. Claims.						
Harrison, Benj., heirs of	Settlement of accounts as revolutionary paymaster general.	25	2	Petition	270	Rev. Claims				Discharged; laid on table.		
Harrison, Benj., heirs of	Settlement of accounts as revolutionary paymaster general.	27	3	Petition	426	Rev. Claims	238	Adverse		Laid on table.		
Harrison, Benj., heirs of	Settlement of accounts as revolutionary paymaster general.	29	1	Petition	310	Rev. Claims.						
Harrison, Benj. J., sureties of.	Release from judgment	27	2	Petition	77	Judiciary.						
Harrison, Benj. J., sureties of.	Release from judgment	27	3	Petition	107	Judiciary.						
Harrison, Benj. J., sureties of.	Release from judgment	28	1	Petition	141	Judiciary.						
Harrison, Benj. J., sureties of.	Release from judgment	28	2	Petition	82	Judiciary				Discharged; laid on table.		
Harrison, Benj. J., sureties of.	Release from judgment	29	1	Petition	226	Judiciary.						
Harrison, Benj. J., sureties of.	Release from judgment	29	2	Petition	69	Judiciary.						
Harrison, Benj. J., sureties of.	Release from judgment	30	1	Petition	81	Judiciary	107	Adverse		Laid on table.		
Harrison, Burr	(See George Harrison)	28	1		435							
Harrison, Charles L.	Compensation for baggage lost, war of 1812.	23	1	Petition	305	Claims	April 9, 1834	Adverse		Laid on table.		
Harrison, Cuthbert, heir of	Commutation pay as a captain in Virginia line, revolutionary army.	29	1	Petition	689	Rev. Claims.						
Harrison, Francis A.	Compensation for losses by the burning of post office.	26	1	Senate bill	836	P. Of. & P. Roads			S. 262			
Harrison, Francis A.	Compensation for losses by the burning of post office.	26	2	Senate bill	230	P. Of. & P. Roads.	Feb. 12, 1841	With't amend.	S. 158	Laid on table.		
Harrison, Francis A.	Compensation for losses by the burning of post office.	27	2	Senate bill	822	P. Of. & P. Roads.			S. 144	Laid on table.		
Harrison, Francis L.	Compensation for property seized by the British.	13	3	Petition	588	Claims	Jan. 9, 1815	Adverse		Rejected.		
Harrison, Francis L.	Compensation for property seized by the British.	14	1	Petition	586	Claims				Discharged; laid on table.		
Harrison, Francis L.	Compensation for property seized by the British.	14	2	Petition	223	Claims				Discharged; laid on table.		
Harrison, Francis L.	Compensation for property seized by the British.	15	1	Petition	133	Claims	Jan. 26, 1818	Adverse		Rejected.		
Harrison, Francis L.	Compensation for property seized by the British.	17	2	Petition	24	Claims	Dec. 10, 1822	Adverse		Rejected.		
Harrison, G., *et al.*, (midshipmen.)	Back pay, &c.	31	1	Petition	881	Naval Affairs.						

List of private claims presented to the House of Representatives of the United States from the 1st to the 31st Congress, inclusive—Continued.

Names of claimants.	Nature or object of the claim.	Congress.	Session.	How brought before the House of Reps.	Page of journal.	To what committee of the House referred.	No. or date of the report.	Nature of the report.	No. of the bill.	How disposed of by the House of Reps.	How disposed of by the Senate.	Date of the act of Congress, and remarks.
Harrison, George	Reimbursement of overpayments and release of judgment.	27	3	Petition	139	Claims	148	Report and bill.	765	Passed.		
Harrison, George	Reimbursement of certain overpayments as paymaster in 1812.	28	1	Documents	435	Claims						
Harrison, George	Reimbursement of certain overpayments as paymaster in 1812.	28	1	Senate bill	884	Claims	May 15, 1844	With't amend.	S. 163	Passed		App'd June 15, 1820
Harrison, George	Remission of a fine	27	2	Petition	534	Claims.						
Harrison, George	Remission of a fine	27	3	Petition	43	Claims.						
Harrison, George	Remission of a fine	28	1	Petition	110	Claims.						
Harrison, Jabez	Permission to import merchandise from St. Johns, N. B.	12	1	Petition	63	Com. and Manuf.						
Harrison, James	(See Jaques Da Costa, sureties of)	10	1		150							
Harrison, James	Indulgence as surety for Collector at Louisville.	26	2	Petition	346	Commerce.						
Harrison, James	Release as surety on a bond	27	2	Memorial	534	Claims	689	Adverse		Laid on table.		
Harrison, James	(See Overstreet & Didlake)	28	1		141							
Harrison, James P.	Indemnity for loss on a government contract.	24	1	Petition and docs.	914	Claims	745	Adverse		Laid on table.		
Harrison, John H.	(See surety for Francis Adams)	20	2		26							
Harrison, Captain John, heirs of.	Commutation pay due as a revolutionary officer.	23	1	Petition	110	Rev. Claims.						
Harrison, John Peyton, heirs of.	Commutation pay for revolutionary services.	25	2	Petition	915	Rev. Claims	935	Report and bill.	815	Rejected.		
Harrison, John Peyton, heirs of.	Commutation pay for revolutionary services.	25	3	House bill	155	Whole House			815	Refused to reconsider vote to reject.		
Harrison, John Peyton, heirs of.	Commutation pay for revolutionary services.	26	1	Petition	164	Rev. Claims.						
Harrison, John Peyton, heirs of.	Commutation pay for revolutionary services.	26	2	Petition	37	Rev. Claims.						
Harrison, John Peyton, heirs of.	Commutation pay for revolutionary services.	27	2	Petition	61	Rev. Claims.	380	Adverse		Laid on table.		
Harrison, John S. & William H. McCullough.	Additional compensation for transportation of the mail.	31	1	Petition	57	P. O. & P. Roads.						
Harrison, John S. & William H. McCullough.	Additional compensation for transportation of the mail.	31	1	Petition	916	P. Of. and P. Roads.						
Harrison, Jonas	Release from liability for taxes not collectable.	15	1	Petition	165	Ways and Means	Feb. 10, 1818	Report by bill.	77	Passed	Passed	App'd April 20, 1818
Harrison, Jonas	Settlement of accounts as collector of direct tax.	21	1	Resolution	133	Claims.						
Harrison, Jonas, sureties of	Release from liability	16	2	Petition	170	Ways and Means.						
Harrison, Jonas, sureties of	Release from liability	18	1	Petition	154	Ways and Means	Feb. 20, 1824	Adverse		Laid on table		Leave to withdraw.
Harrison, Joseph	Compensation for a team lost in the public service.	14	1	Petition	48	Claims				Discharged; leave to withdraw.		
Harrison, Joseph	Pension for services as a revolutionary soldier.	21	1	Resolution	806	Military Pensions				Discharged; laid on table.		
Harrison, Joseph, widow of	Compensation for revolutionary services.	25	2	Petition	181	Rev. Claims						
Harrison, Joseph, widow of	Compensation for revolutionary services.	26	1	Resolution	385	Rev. Pensions	664	Adverse		Laid on table.		
Harrison, Joseph, (Sarah) widow of.	Patent for a tract of land bid off	12	1	Petition	22	Public Lands.	Dec. 5, 1811	Favorable; bill	89	Passed	Passed	App'd April 23, 1812
Harrison, J. C. S.	Increase of compensation as land officer.	18	2	Petition	96	Public Lands.						

List of private claims presented to the House of Representatives of the United States from the 1st to the 31st Congress, inclusive—Continued.

Names of claimants.	Nature or object of the claim.	Congress.	Session.	How brought before the House of Reps.	Page of journal.	To what committee of the House referred.	No. or date of the report.	Nature of the report.	No. of the bill.	How disposed of by the House of Reps.	How disposed of by the Senate.	Date of the act of Congress, and remarks.
Harrison, J. C. S., widow of.	Equitable settlement of accounts..	21	2	Petition	103	Public Lands.....	65	Report and bill.	602	Passed	Passed, with amendment.	App'd March 2, 1831
Harrison & Lewis.......	Permission to import goods without duty.	12	1	Petition	56	Com. and Manuf...	Jan. 7, 1812	General bill ..	46	Referred to Committee Whole House.		
Harrison, Maria	(See child of John Garde)	26	1	....	662							
Harrison, Nathaniel	Pension for disability, war of 1812.	30	1	Petition	173	Invalid Pensions.						
Harrison, N............	Bounty land for services in war of 1812.	25	2	Petition	577	Military Affairs...	....	....	......	Discharged.		
Harrison, Richard	Pension for revolutionary services.	22	1	Petition	574	Rev. Pensions.						
Harrison, Captain Richard, heirs of.	Half-pay for revolutionary services.	24	1	Resolution	951	Rev. Claims.						
Harrison, Richard	Compensation for services as acting consul at Cadiz.	24	2	Memorial	87	Foreign Affairs....	265	Report and bill.	952			
Harrison, Richard	Compensation for services as acting consul at Cadiz.	25	1	Petition	102	....	....	....	......	Laid on table.		
Harrison, Richard	Compensation for services as acting consul at Cadiz.	25	2	Memorial	260	Foreign Affairs....	381	Report and bill.	404	Passed	Passed	App'd July 7, 1838
Harrison, Robert Hanson, representatives of.	Commutation pay and bounty land for revolutionary services.	13	3	Petition	560	Pens. & Rev. Cl'ms.	52	Adverse	......	Laid on table.		
Harrison, Robert Hanson, representatives of.	Commutation pay and bounty land for revolutionary services.	14	1	Petition	170	Pens. & Rev. Cl'ms.	Mar. 13, 1816	Report and bill	......	Laid on table.		
Harrison, Robert Hanson, representatives of.	Commutation pay and bounty land for revolutionary services.	14	2	Petition	70	Pens. & Rev. Cl'ms.						
Harrison, Robert Hanson, representatives of.	Commutation pay and bounty land for revolutionary services.	15	2	Petition	103	Select	Feb. 5, 1819	....	......	Leave to withdraw.		
Harrison, Robert Hanson, representatives of.	Commutation pay and bounty land for revolutionary services.	17	1	Petition	294	Pens. & Rev. Cl'ms.	75	Adverse	......	Referred to Committee Whole House.		
Harrison, Robert Hanson, representatives of.	Commutation pay and bounty land for revolutionary services.	17	2	Petition	204	Whole House.....	....	....	.....	Leave to withdraw.		
Harrison, Robert Hanson, representatives of.	Commutation pay and bounty land for revolutionary services.	18	2	Petition	75	Pens. & Rev. Cl'ms.	....	....		Leave to withdraw.		
Harrison, Robert Hanson, representatives of.	Commutation pay and bounty land for revolutionary services.	19	1	Petition	154	Rev. Pensions	164	Adverse	......	Laid on table.		
Harrison, Robert Hanson, representatives of.	Commutation pay and bounty land for revolutionary services.	21	1	Petition	57	Rev. Claims......	130	Report and bill	174	Passed	Passed	App'd May 29, 1830
Harrison, Robert Hanson, representatives of.	Commutation pay and bounty land for revolutionary services.	21	2	Petition	44	Rev. Claims......	116	Report and bill	646			
Harrison, Robert Hanson, representatives of.	Commutation pay and bounty land for revolutionary services.	22	1	Petition	44	Rev. Claims.......	79	Report and bill.	155	Passed	Passed	App'd July 14, 1832
Harrison, Robert Hanson, representatives of.	Commutation pay and bounty land for revolutionary services.	22	2	Petition	29	Rev. Claims.						
Harrison, Robert Hanson, representatives of.	Commutation pay and bounty land for revolutionary services.	23	1	Petition	70	Rev. Claims.						
Harrison, Robert M	Indemnity for damage as surety ..	29	2	Senate bill	380	Judiciary.........	....	....	S. 133			
Harrison, Samuel	(See J. T. Courtney)...........	13	3	....	263							
Harrison, Samuel	(See heirs of Lt. William Harrison)	31	1	....	1043							
Harrison, Samuel C	To correction of land entry).....	27	2	Petition	794	Public Lands.						
Harrison, Stephen.......	Pension	19	1	Petition	290	Military Pensions..	164	Favorable	......	Referred to Committee Whole House.		
Harrison & Sterrett......	(See assignees of James Swan) ..	4	1	....	546							
Harrison, Thomas.......	Increase of pension.	24	1	Senate bill	811	Invalid Pensions ..	Jan. 1, 1836	With't amend.	S. 168	Passed	....	App'd June 15, 1836
Harrison, Major Thomas .	Invalid pension...............	24	2	Petition	398	Invalid Pensions ..	Jan. 23, 1797	....	......	Discharged; laid on table.		

List of private claims presented to the House of Representatives of the United States from the 1st to the 31st Congress, inclusive—Continued.

Names of claimants.	Nature or object of the claim.	Congress.	Session.	How brought before the House of Reps.	Page of journal.	To what committee of the House referred.	No. or date of the report.	Nature of the report.	No. of the bill.	How disposed of by the House of Reps.	How disposed of by the Senate.	Date of the act of Congress, and remarks.
Harrison, Major Thomas	Invalid pension	25	2	Petition	167	Invalid Pensions	796	Report and bill	746	Rejected.		
Harrison, Major Thomas	Invalid pension	25	3	Petition	220	Invalid Pensions	Feb. 16, 1839	....	......	Discharged; leave to withdraw.		
Harrison, Major Thomas	Invalid pension	27	2	Petition	255	Invalid Pensions	319	Report and bill	288	Referred to Committee Whole House.		
Harrison, Major Thomas	Invalid pension	27	3	Rep't Committee.	87	Whole House	....	....	288	Passed	Indef. postp'd.	
Harrison, Major Thomas	Invalid pension	28	1	Petition	130	Invalid Pensions	52	Report and bill	75	Passed	Passed	App'd June 17, 1844
Harrison, Thomas	To refer his accounts to Solicitor of the Treasury.	24	2	Memorial	313	Military Affairs.						
Harrison, Thomas	Compensation for extra services as an officer.	25	2	Petition	176	Claims	1006	Adverse	......	Laid on table.		
Harrison, Thomas	Compensation for extra services as an officer.	26	1	Petition	169	Claims	68	Adverse	......	Laid on table.		
Harrison, Valentine, heirs of	Commutation pay due as a revolution officer.	23	1	Petition	525	Rev. Claims.						
Harrison, William B	For time to collect testimony to lessen the amount for which he is liable as surety for R. B. Harrison.	19	1	Petition	424	Claims.						
Harrison, William Henry.	Compensation for services as Superintendent of Indian Affairs, &c.	9	2	Petition	509	Claims.						
Harrison, William Henry.	Compensation for the time he was detained on his return as minister to Columbia.	21	1	Mem'l & petition	479	Foreign Affairs	378	Report and bill.	437			
Harrison, William Henry, widow of.	Gratuity	27	1	House bill	62	Whole House	....	....	1	Passed	Passed	App'd June 30, 1841
Harrison, William, deceased brother of.	Arrears of pension	25	2	Petition	722	Invalid Pensions	....	Favorable; bill	749			
Harrison, William, deceased brother of.	Arrears of pension	26	1	Resolution	1023	Invalid Pensions.						
Harrison, Lieut. William, heirs of.	Commutation pay due as revolutionary officer.	31	1	Petition	1043	Rev. Pensions	453	Adverse	......	Laid on table.		
Harrison, Zephaniah	Pension for revolutionary services.	24	2	Memorial	122	Rev. Pensions	313	....	......	Discharged; laid on table.		
Harrison, Zephaniah	Pension for revolutionary services.	25	2	Memorial	93	Rev. Pensions	....	....	......	Discharged; laid on table.		
Harrold or Harrad, James, heirs of.	Pension for revolutionary services.	24	2	Resolution	71	Rev. Pensions	....	....	......	Discharged; laid on table.		
Harrup, Joseph	Increase of pension	10	1	House bill	232	Whole House	April 19, 1808	General bill	78	Passed	Passed	App'd April 25, 1808
Harry, Charles, widow of.	Pension for revolutionary services.	28	1	Petition	891	Rev. Pensions.						
Harry, John	Credit for the proceeds of the property of T. B. Hall.	24	1	Petition	102	Judiciary	192	Adverse	......	Laid on table.		
Harry, John	Credit for the proceeds of the property of T. B. Hall.	25	2	Petition	274	Claims	517	Adverse	......	Laid on table.		
Harshfield, Henry	Pension for services as a revolutionary soldier.	21	2	Petition	38	Military Pensions.						
Harshman, Jacob	Exchange of a Virginia military land warrant.	29	2	Petition	169	Public Lands.						
Harsom, David	To be restored to pension roll	22	1	House bill	580	Rev. Pensions	439	....	543	Referred to Committee Whole House.		
Harsom, Samuel	Revolutionary pension	22	1	Rep't Committee	539	....	Mar. 24, 1832	....	......	Disch'd; laid on table.		
Hart, Adam, deceased, legatee of.	Duplicate of revolutionary land warrant No. 1469.	30	1	Petition	171	Rev. Claims	March 9, 1849	Report by bill.	309	Passed.		

List of private claims presented to the House of Representatives of the United States from the 1st to the 31st Congress, inclusive—**Continued.**

Names of claimants.	Nature or object of the claim.	Congress.	Session.	How brought before the House of Reps.	Page of journal.	To what committee of the House referred.	No. or date of the report.	Nature of the report.	No. of the bill.	How disposed of by the House of Reps.	How disposed of by the Senate.	Date of the act of Congress, and remarks.
Hart, Adam, deceased, legatee of.	Duplicate of revolutionary land warrant No. 1469.	31	1	Petition	899	Public Lands.						
Hart, Albert	(See Louis F. Beeler, *et al.*)	30	1		115							
Hart, Benjamin F., executors of, *et al.*	Release from a bond as purser United States navy.	31	1	Petition	285	Naval Affairs	119	Report and bill.	139	Referred to Committee Whole House.		
Hart, Benjamin F., executors of, *et al.*	Release from a bond as purser United States navy.	31	2	House bill	103	Whole House	Jan. 3, 1851	With't amend.	139	Passed.		
Hart & Bosworth	Compensation for arms and ammunition taken for public use.	26	1	Appropriat'n bill.								App'd July 21, 1840
Hart, Daniel	(See legatee of Adam Hart)	30	1		171							
Hart, Daniel	Pension for revolutionary services.	22	2	Petition	142	Rev. Pensions	Jan. 24, 1833			Discharged; referred to Rev. Claims.		
Hart, Daniel	Pension for revolutionary services.	24	2	Petition	216	Rev. Pensions	Jan. 24, 1837			Discharged; laid on table.		
Hart, Derville, heirs of	Commutation pay for revolutionary services.	31	1	Petition	215	Rev. Claims	420	Adverse		Laid on table.		
Hart, Eli	Indemnity for property destroyed by the enemy, war of 1812.	15	1	Petition	247	Claims				Referred to Commissioner of Claims.		
Hart, Eli	Indemnity for property destroyed by the enemy, war of 1812.	15	2	Senate bill	316	Claims	Feb. 27, 1819	Adverse	61			
Hart, Eli	Indemnity for property destroyed by the enemy, war of 1812.	16	1	Senate bill	74	Claims	Jan. 3, 1820	Adverse	9			
Hart, Eli	Indemnity for property destroyed by the enemy, war of 1812.	16	2	Petition	45	Claims	Jan. 15, 1821	Adverse		Referred to Committee Whole House.		
Hart, Eli	Indemnity for property destroyed by the enemy, war of 1812.	17	1	Petition	39	Claims	19	Adverse		Referred to Committee Whole House.		
Hart, Eli	Indemnity for property destroyed by the enemy, war of 1812.	18	1	Petition	131	Claims	Jan. 26, 1824	Adverse.		Referred to Committee Whole House.		
Hart, Eli	Payment of a balance due on a draft on War Department.	15	1	Petition	248	Claims.						
Hart, Eli	Payment of a balance due on a draft on War Department.	16	2	Petition	75	Claims	Dec. 29, 1820	Adverse		Discharged; leave to withdraw.		
Hart, Eli	Payment of a balance due on a draft on War Department.	17	1	Petition	39	Claims	Jan. 21, 1822	Adverse		Referred to Committee Whole House.		
Hart, Eli	Payment of a balance due on a draft on War Department.	18	1	Petition	131	Claims.						
Hart, Ephraim	Payment of a mislaid revolutionary certificate.	13	2	Petition	354	Pens. & Rev. Cl'ms.	92	Adverse		Referred to Committee Whole House.		
Hart, Frederick A., widow of.	Pension for revolutionary services.	28	1	Petition	840	Rev. Pensions.						
Hart, Frederick A., widow of.	Pension for revolutionary services.	29	1	Petition	396	Rev. Pensions	729	Adverse.		Laid on table.		
Hart, Frederick A., widow of.	Pension for revolutionary services.	30	1	Petition	780	Rev. Pensions	June 20, 1848			Discharged; laid on table.		
Hart, George H	(See Jos. R. Chandler, *et al*)	27	3		43							
Hart, Henry	Bounty land due him for services in United States army.	22	1	Petition	672	Priv. Land Claims.						
Hart, Henry	Pension for revolutionary services.	23	1	Petition	273	Rev. Pensions.						
Hart, Ithuel	Pension for revolutionary services.	21	2	Petition	40	Military Pensions.						
Hart, Ithuel	Pension for revolutionary services.	22	1	Petition	34	Invalid Pensions.	Jan. 10, 1832	Adverse		Laid on table.		
Hart, Jacob	Remission of tax upon a distillery.	15	3	Petition	133	Ways and Means				Disch'd; laid on table.		

List of private claims presented to the House of Representatives of the United States from the 1st to the 31st Congress, inclusive—Continued.

Names of claimants.	Nature or object of the claim.	Congress.	Session.	How brought before the House of Reps.	Page of journal.	To what committee of the House referred.	No. or date of the report	Nature of the report.	No. of the bill.	How disposed of by the House of Reps.	How disposed of by the Senate.	Date of the act of Congress, and remarks.
Hart, John	Compensation for arms and ammunition taken for public use.	26	1	Appropriat'n bill								App'd July 21, 1840
Hart, John, executor of	Renewal of a land warrant	28	1	Petition	516	Priv. Land Claims.	419	Report and bill	323	Passed.		
Hart, John, executor of	Renewal of a land warrant	28	2	Petition	176	Priv. Land Claims.	Jan. 28, 1845	Report by bill.	352	Passed.		
Hart, John, executor of	Renewal of a land warrant	29	1	Petition	515	Priv. Land Claims.						
Hart, John, executor of	Renewal of a land warrant	29	2	Petition	151	Priv. Land Claims.						
Hart, John, executor of	Renewal of a land warrant	30	1	Petition	312	Priv. Land Claims.						
Hart, John, widow of	Pension	28	2	Petition	140	Rev. Pensions.						
Hart, John, widow of	Pension	30	1	Petition	306	Rev. Pensions	297	Adverse		Laid on table.		
Hart, Major Jonathan, widow of.	Pay due officers of same rank in revolutionary army, in consideration of the death of her husband killed in battle with the Indians in 1791.	2	2	Petition	628	Select				Laid on table.		
Hart, Josiah	(See Richard Wells, *et al*)	1	2		165							
Hart, Monmouth B	(See Benjamin F. Hart, executor of.)	31	2		103							
Hart, Nicholas	Duplicate of land warrant No. 443.	19	1	Resolution	255	Priv. Land Claims.	103	Report and bill.	139	Passed.		
Hart, Nicholas	Duplicate of land warrant No. 443.	21	1	Petition	296	Public Lands	Feb. 25, 1830	Report by bill.	291	Referred to Committee Whole House.		
Hart, Nicholas, heirs of	Duplicate of land warrant No. 443.	21	2	House bill	240	Whole House	Feb. 21, 1831	With't amend.	291	Passed.		
Hart, Nicholas, heirs of	Duplicate of land warrant No. 443.	22	1	Petition	106	Public Lands	153	Report and bill.	232	Referred to Committee Whole House.		
Hart, Nicholas, heirs of	Duplicate of land warrant No 433.	22	2	House bill	92	Whole House	Dec. 22, 1832	With amend.	232	Passed	Passed, with amendment.	App'd Feb. 9, 1833
Hart & Nazro	Permission to import merchandise ordered prior to President's proclamation of November 2, 1810.	12	1	Petition	232	Whole House		General bill	46			
Hart, Nazro	Release from penalty incurerd by the importation of British merchandise.	12	2	Petition	577	Whole House						See Statutes at Large, vol. 2, p. 789, (general law.)
Hart, Patrick	Pension	11	3	House bill	604	Whole House	Mar. 2, 1811	Favorable	218	Passed	Passed	App'd March 3, 1811
Hart, Patrick	Increase of pension	14	1	Petition	71	Pens. & Rev. Cl'ms.				Discharged; laid on table.		
Hart, Patrick H	Compensation for a horse stolen by Indians.	22	1	Resolution	561	Claims.						
Hart, Richard	Compensation for a horse lost in war of 1812.	24	1	Petition	92	Claims	Jan. 29, 1836	Adverse		Laid on table.		
Hart, Richard	Compensation for a horse lost in war of 1812.	24	2	Petition	103	Claims.						
Hart, Richard W	Indemnity for French spoliations prior to 1800.	26	1	Memorial	182	Foreign Affairs	343	Favorable; bill	319	Referred to Committee Whole House.		
Hart, Richard G	Balance due him as paymaster of a Kentucky regiment.	23	2	Petition	200	Claims	Feb. 24, 1835	Adverse		Laid on table.		
Hart, Richard G	Balance due him as paymaster of a Kentucky regiment.	24	1	Petition	153	Claims.						
Hart, Robert	Invalid pension	3	1	Rep. of Secretary War.	131	Select	May 26, 1794	Favorable; bill ordered.	62	Passed	Passed	App'd June 7, 1794
Hart, Samuel	Invalid pension	3	1	Rep. of Secretary War.	131	Select	May 26, 1794	Favorable; bill ordered.	62	Passed	Passed	App'd June 7, 1794

List of private claims presented to the House of Representatives of the United States from the 1st to the 31st Congress, inclusive—Continued.

Names of claimants.	Nature or object of the claim.	Congress.	Session.	How brought before the House of Reps.	Page of journal.	To what committee of the House referred.	No. or date of the report.	Nature of the report.	No. of the bill.	How disposed of by the House of Reps.	How disposed of by the Senate.	Date of the act of Congress, and remarks.
Hart, Samuel	(See Railroad company, Norristown and Valley.)	28	1		357							
Hart, Thomas	Liquidation of his claim against United States.	1	2	Petition	267					Referred to Secretary Treasury.		
Hart, Thomas	Liquidation of his claim against United States.	2	1	Rep. of Secretary Treasury.	580					Laid on table.		
Hart, William	(See John Bush.)	2	1		447							
Hart, William B	(See Alexander Anderson, *et al.*)	30	1		288							
Hartfield, Asa	(See Thomas Dennis.)	22	1		455							
Hartfield, Asa	Exchange of a tract of land in Arkansas.	23	1	House bill	226	Public Lands	Jan. 21, 1834	With't amend.	225	Passed	Passed	App'd June 18, 1834
Hartfield, Benjamin H. G.	Lease of Little river, Salt Lick, Arkansas.	22	1	Petition	809	Public Lands.						
Hartford, Eunice	Continuation of the pension of her deceased husband.	28	1	Petition	72	Rev. Pensions.						
Hartford, Solomon	Pension for disability incurred in war of 1812.	29	1	Petition	834	Invalid Pensions	July 25, 1846			Discharged; laid on table.		
Hartle or Fartle, Peter	Confirmation of title to land in Missouri.	16	1	Petition	71	Priv. Land Claims.				Discharged; laid on table.		
Hartlett, Jane	Compensation for revolutionary services, and supplies furnished.	3	1	Petition	185					Laid on table.		
Hartley, Henry	(See F. M. Arredondo, and others.)	19	1		252							
Hartley, John	Pension for disability incurred war of 1812.	30	2	Petition	322	Invalid Pensions	93	Adverse		Laid on table.		
Hartley, William, assignee of.	Confirmation of title to land	24	2	Petition	84	Priv. Land Claims.						
Hartley, William, assignee of.	Confirmation of title to land	25	2	Petition	180	Priv. Land Claims.	416	Adverse		Laid on table.		
Hartman, Dietrick	(See John Snyder, attorney of.)	2	1		477							
Hartman, Philip	Arrears of pension, and to be restored to pension roll.	24	1	Res. and docs	707	Rev. Pensions	809	Report and bill	726	Referred to Committee Whole House.		
Hartman, Philip	Arrears of pension, and to be restored to pension roll.	25	2	Resolution	38	Rev. Pensions	457	Report and bill	460	Passed	Adverse report.	
Hartman, Philip	Arrears of pension, and to be restored to pension roll.	25	3	Resolution	446	Rev. Pensions	252	Peport and bill	1123	Referred to Committee Whole House.		
Hartman, Philip	Arrears of pension, and to be restored to pension roll.	26	1	Resolution	172	Rev. Pensions	156	Report and bill	166	Passed	Passed	App'd July 20, 1840
Hartman, Peter	Grant of land for public service during revolutionary period.	9	1	Petition	291	Public Lands	April 9, 1806			Indefinitely postponed.		
Hartman, Peter	Grant of land for public service during revolutionary period.	9	2	Petition	496	Public Lands.						
Hartshorne, Rineleader, & Co.	Indemnity for French spoliations prior to 1800.	26	1	Memorial	182	Foreign Affairs	343	Favorable; bill	319	Referred to Committee Whole House.		
Hartshorne, Richard, heir of.	Indemnity for French spoliations prior to 1800.	31	1	Memorial	411	Claims	355	Report and bill	318	Referred to Committee Whole House.		
Hartshorne Richard	(See Hartshorne, Rhineleader, & Co.)	26	1		182							
Hartshorne,	(See Robinson & Hartshorne, assignee of.)	12	1		295							
Hartstene, H. J	(See Exploring Expedition)	27	3		149		270		818			
Hartwell, Betsey H	(See William Snow, heirs of.)	25	2		406							
Hartwell, Thomas	Pension for loss of an eye in revolutionary war.	12	2	Petition	552	Claims	Feb. 26, 1813	Adverse		Laid on table.		Leave to withdraw, July 14, 1813.

List of private claims presented to the House of Representatives of the United States from the 1st to the 31st Congress, inclusive—Continued.

Names of claimants.	Nature or object of the claim.	Congress.	Session.	How brought before the House of Reps.	Page of journal.	To what committee of the House referred.	No. or date of the report.	Nature of the report.	No. of the bill.	How disposed of by the House of Reps.	How disposed of by the Senate.	Date of the act of Congress, and remarks.
Hartwell, Thomas	Pension for injuries received in revolutionary war.	13	2	Petition	177	Pens. & RevCl'ms.						
Hartwick, George	Indemnity for damage to his vessel in public service.	31	1	Petition	232	Claims	28	Adverse	......	Laid on table.		
Harvard College, President and Fellows of.	Remission of duties on imported books.	14	1	Petition	235	Ways and Means.	Mar. 6, 1816	Report by bill.	110	Passed	Passed	App'd April 9, 1816
Harvard College, President and Fellows of.	Remission of duties on books and telescope.	30	1	Petition	170	Ways and Means.						
Harvey, Benjamin, heirs of	Compensation for revolutionary services.	23	1	Resolution	94	Rev. Claims.						
Harvey, Benjamin, heirs of	Compensation for revolutionary services.	24	1	Resolution	404	Rev. Claims.						
Harvey, David	Patent for land reserved to his wife by treaty.	24	2	Petition	273	Indian Affairs.						
Harvey, Erastus C	Bounty land for services war of 1812.	29	1	Petition	209	Public Lands.						
Harvey, George	Reimbursement of costs unjustly exacted.	31	1	Petition	783	Naval Affairs.						
Harvey, Isaac, jr.	(See Paul Beck, jr., & I. H. jr.)	15	2	....	94							
Harvey James, and Robert L. Porter.	Indemnity for loss by destruction of Chesapeake flotilla.	28	2	Petition	316	Naval Affairs.						
Harvey, James & R. L. P.	Indemnity for loss by destruction of Chesapeake flotilla.	29	1	Memorial	398	Naval Affairs.						
Harvey, John heir of	Indemnity for French spoliations prior to 1800.	26	1	Memorial	182	Foreign Affairs	343	Favorable; bill	319	Referred to Committee Whole House.		
Harvey, John	(See Isaac Taylor & John Harvey)	3	1	....	267							
Harvey, John	Remission of duty on salt destroyed in a storm.	8	1	Petition	410	Com. and Manuf.	Oct. 26, 1803	Adverse	......	Rejected.		
Harvie, John	Liquidation and settlement of accounts of George Webb.	4	1	Memorial	433	Claims	May 31, 1796	Adverse	......	Laid on table.		
Harvey, Jonathan	Pension	21	1	Petition	66	Military Pensions.	....	....	......	Discharged; laid on table.		
Harvey, Joshua, *et al.*	Release from liabilities on certain custom house bonds.	7	2	Petition & Mem'l	343	Select	Feb. 18, 1803	Report by bill.	117, 129	Passed	Passed	App'd March 3, 1803
Harvey, Joshua B	Pension for services in the war of 1812.	26	1	Petition	708	Invalid Pensions.						
Harvie, J. B	(See Nathaniel Denby, sureties of.)	30	2	....	350							
Harvey, Peter	Arrears of pay and clothing as a revolutionary war.	7	1	Petition	12	Claims	Dec. 15, 1801	Adverse	......	Rejected.		
Harvey & Stagg	Drawback on ten cases of muslin.	26	1	Petition	708	Commerce	310	Report and bill	272			
Harvey & Stagg	Drawback on ten cases of muslin.	27	3	Petition	108	Commerce.						
Harvey & Stagg	Drawback on ten cases of muslin.	28	1	Petition	514	Commerce	503	Report and bill	379	Ref'd to Com. W. H.		
Harvey & Stagg	Drawback on ten cases of muslin.	28	2	House bill	343	Whole House	....	....	379	Passed	Passed	App'd March 3, 1845
Harvey, Thomas	Pension under act of June 7, 1832	25	2	Petition	857	Rev. Pensions	....	....	......	Discharged; laid on table.		
Harvey, Thomas	Pension under act of June 7, 1832	25	3	Petition	87	Rev. Pensions.	....	....	......	Discharged.		
Harvey, Thomas	Pension under act of June 7, 1832	26	1	Petition	174	Rev. Pensions	Jan. 5, 1840	....	......	Discharged; laid on table.		
Harvey, Thomas	Pension under act of June 7, 1832	26	2	Petition	106	Rev. Pensions.	Feb. 12, 1841	....	......	Discharged; laid on table.		
Harvey, Thomas	Pension under act of June 7, 1832	27	2	Petition	97	Rev. Pensions	784	Adverse	......	Laid on table.		
Harvey, Thomas	Pension under act of June 7, 1832	27	3	Petition	43	Rev. Pensions.	295	Adverse	......	Laid on table.		
Harvey, Thomas	Pension under act of June 7, 1832	28	1	Petition	190	Rev. Claims.						

List of private claims presented to the House of Representatives of the United States from the 1st to the 31st Congress, inclusive—Continued.

Names of claimants.	Nature or object of the claim.	Congress.	Session.	How brought before the House of Reps.	Page of journal.	To what committee of the House referred.	No. or date of the report.	Nature of the report.	No. of the bill.	How disposed of by the House of Reps.	How disposed of by the Senate.	Date of the act of Congress, and remarks.
Harvey, Thomas	Pension under act of June 7, 1832	29	1	Petition	149	Rev. Pensions	257	Adverse		Laid on table.		
Harvey, Thomas B	Pension for disability, war of 1812	31	1	Petition	755	Invalid Pensions.						
Harvey, William	Indemnity for the seizure and condemnation of vessel by officers of the Spanish government.	9	1	Petition	312					Referred to Secretary State.		
Harvey, William	Pension for revolutionary services.	21	2	Petition	80	Military Pensions.						
Harvey, William	Pension for revolutionary services.	22	1	Petition	45	Rev. Pensions	Jan. 4, 1832			Discharged; laid on table.		
Harvey, William	(See F. M. Arredondo and others.)	19	1	Petition	252							
Harwood, Andrew	Pension for wounds and disabilities in war of 1812.	31	1	Petition	1039	Invalid Pensions.						
Harwood, Benjamin	Pension for revolutionary services.	1	2	Petition	199	Ref'd to Sec. Treas.						
Harwood, Benjamin	Pension for revolutionary services.	3	2	Rep. of Secretary of Treasury.	284	Claims.						
Harwood, Benjamin	Pension for revolutionary services.	4	1	Rep. of Secretary Treasury.	373	Claims.						
Harwood, Benjamin	Pension for revolutionary services.	4	2	Rep. of Secretary Treasury.	614	Claims.						
Harwood, Benjamin	(See Robert Coltman, *et al.*)	23	1		418							
Harwood, John	Increase of pension	21	1	Petition	168	Military Pensions	Mar. 26, 1830	Adverse		Laid on table.		
Harwood, John	(See William H. Bedford, agent).	28	1		262							
Harwood, Zachariah	Compensation for expense and attendance on a sick son, a volunteer in the war of 1812.	15	1	Petition	94	Claims	Feb. 20, 1818	Adverse		Rejected.		
Hasbrouck, Jacob, jr	Permission to fund certain loan office certificates.	5	2	Petition	82	Claims	Dec. 27, 1797			Referred to Committee Whole House.		
Hascall, John, and Hiram Moore.	Extension of a patent for a reaping machine.	31	1	Petition	212	Patents	9	Report and bill	11	Passed.		
Haselton, William	(See William Hazeltine)	3	2		337							
Haselton, Daniel	Compensation for extra work	22	1	Resolution	378	Claims	Mar. 2, 1832	Report and bill	411	Referred to Committee Whole House.		
Hasey, John	Pension for revolutionary services.	25	3	Petition	218	Rev. Pensions				Discharged.		
Hasey, John	Pension for revolutionary services.	26	1	Petition	174	Rev. Pensions	Mar. 5, 1840			Discharged; laid on table.		
Haskell, Andrew, (Lois,) widow of.	Pension for revolutionary services.	15	2	Petition	160	Rev. Pensions	Feb. 6, 1819	Adverse		Rejected.		
Haskell, Ignatius and Solomon.	Indemnity for capture of schooner Gideon by the French.	19	2	Petition	213	Foreign Affairs				Discharged; laid on table.		
Haskell, Ignatius and Solomon.	Indemnity for French spoliations prior to 1800.	26	1	Memorial	182	Foreign Affairs	343	Favorable; bill	319	Referred to Committee Whole House.		
Haskell, Ignatius, attorney of.	Indemnity for French spoliations prior to 1800.	26	1	Memorial	182	Foreign Affairs	343	Favorable; bill	319	Referred to Committee Whole House.		
Haskall, James	Grant of land for services in United States army.	27	2	Petition	131	Public Lands				Discharged; laid on table.		
Haskell, John	Reimbursement of money expended in recruiting service.	2	1	Petition	456					Referred to Secretary War.		
Haskell, John	Pension	14	1	House bill	622	Pens. & Rev. Cl'ms.	April 11, 1816	General bill	171	Passed	Passed	App'd April 30, 1816
Haskell, John C.	(See George Reed, *et al.*)	26	1		702							
Haskill, John C	(See George Randall, *et al.*)	27	3		43							
Haskill, Jonathan	Release from liability for a sum of money advanced government.	2	2	Rep. of Secretary War.	704					Laid on table.		
Haskill, Jonathan	Release from liability for a sum of money advanced government.	4	1	Resolution	389	Claims	May 31, 1796	Adverse		Laid on table.		

List of private claims presented to the House of Representatives of the United States from the 1st to the 31st Congress, inclusive—Continued.

2—7

Names of claimants.	Nature or object of the claim.	Congress.	Session.	How brought before the House of Reps.	Page of journal.	To what committee of the House referred.	No. or date of the report.	Nature of the report.	No. of the bill.	How disposed of by the House of Reps.	How disposed of by the Senate.	Date of the act of Congress, and remarks.
Haskill, Jonathan	Release from liability for a sum of money advanced government.	5	2	Resolution	248	Claims	April 16, 1798	Favorable; res.	......	Referred to Committee Whole House.		
Haskill, Jonathan	Release from liability for a sum of money advanced government.	5	3	Res. and rep. of Committee.	418	Whole House	Jan. 28, 1799	Bill ordered	148	Passed	Passed	App'd Feb. 19, 1799
Haskell, Josiah	Compensation for services as superintendent agent, Sandy bay breakwater.	29	1	Petition	67	Claims	254	Report and bill	218	Referred to Committee Whole House.		
Haskell, Josiah	Compensation for services as superintendent agent, Sandy bay breakwater.	29	2	House bill	71	Whole House	Dec. 18, 1846	With't amend.	218	Passed	Passed	App'd March 3, 1847
Haskell, Moses	To be restored to revolutionary pension roll.	20	1	Resolution	413	Military Pensions	....	....	......	Discharged; laid on table.		
Haskell, Moses	To be restored to revolutionary pension roll.	20	2	Petition	123	Military Pensions.						
Haskell, S., heir of	Indemnity for French spoliations prior to 1800.	26	1	Memorial	182	Foreign Affairs	343	Favorable; bill	319	Referred to Committee Whole House.		
Haskell, Samuel	Further compensation for service as a revolutionary soldier.	22	2	Petition	46	Rev. Claims.						
Haskell, Solomon	(See Solomon Hewton, administrator of.)	26	1	....	182							
Haskell, Solomon	Indemnity for French spoliations prior to 1800.	26	1	Memorial	182	Foreign Affairs	343	Favorable; bill	319	Referred to Committee Whole House.		
Haskell, Thaddeus P., sureties of.	Reimbursement of payment on forfeited recognizance.	29	2	Senate bill	375	Judiciary	Feb. 24, 1847	With't amend	S. 97	Referred to Committee Whole House.		
Haskell, Thaddeus P., sureties of.	Reimbursement of payment on forfeited recognizance.	30	1	Senate bill	314	Judiciary	429	With't amend.	S. 75	Passed	....	App'd June 13, 1848
Haskell, William, agent of the owners of schooner Friendship.	For fishing bounty on a wrecked vessel.	22	1	Petition	131	Commerce.						
Haskell, William, agent of the owners of schooner Friendship.	For fishing bounty on a wrecked vessel.	22	2	Petition	46	Commerce.						
Haskell, William, agent of the owners of schooner Friendship.	For fishing bounty on a wrecked vessel.	23	1	Petition	243	Commerce	254	Report and bill	291	Referred to Committee Whole House.		
Haskell, William, agent of the owners of schooner Friendship.	For fishing bounty on a wrecked vessel.	23	2	House bill	300	Whole House	....	....	291	Passed	Passed	App'd March 3, 1835
Haskin, Adam	Pension	16	2	Petition	78	Pens. & Rev. Cl'ms.	Feb. 9, 1821	Adverse	......	Laid on table.		
Haskin, Adam	Pension	17	1	Petition	39	Pens. & Rev. Cl'ms.	....	....	......	Referred to Secretary of War.	....	Leave to withdraw.
Haskins, Benj., jr., widow of.	Pension for revolutionary services.	31	1	Petition	1310	Rev. Pensions.						
Haskins & Co., and Haskins G.	(See Nicols Haskins & Co.)	26	1	....	182							
Haskins, Jeremiah	Compensation for losses and services, war of 1812.	31	2	Petition	44	Claims.						
Haskins, Samuel	Pension	20	2	Petition	49	Military Pensions	Jan. 20, 1829	Adverse	......	Laid on table.		
Haskins, Thomas & Ralph.	Settlement of claim and reconveyance of two lots of land.	24	1	Petition	477	Ways and Means.						
Haskins, Thomas & Ralph.	Reconveyance of land, &c	24	2	Memorial	102	Judiciary.						
Haskins, Thomas & Ralph.	Reconveyance of land, &c	25	2	Memorial	50	Judiciary	....	....	......	Discharged.		
Haskins, Thomas & Ralph.	Reconveyance of land, &c	26	1	Senate bill	837	Judiciary	....	....	S. 302			

List of private claims presented to the House of Representatives of the United States from the 1*st to the* 31*st Congress, inclusive*—Continued.

Names of claimants.	Nature or object of the claim.	Congress.	Session.	How brought before the House of Reps.	Page of journal.	To what committee of the House referred.	No. or date of the report.	Nature of the report.	No. of the bill.	How disposed of by the House of Reps.	How disposed of by the Senate.	Date of the act of Congress, and remarks.
Haskins, Thomas & Ralph.	Reconveyance of land, &c	26	2	Senate bill	178	Judiciary	....	....	S. 146			
Haskins, Thomas & Ralph.	Reconveyance of land, &c	27	2	Senate bill	782	Judiciary	May 25, 1842	With't amend.	S. 143	Passed	Passed	App'd Aug. 11, 1842
Haslett, John	Remission of forfeiture of Spanish rum imported in 1812.	14	2	Petition	207	Ways and Means.	....	....	......	Discharged; laid on table.		
Haslett, John	Remission of forfeiture of Spanish rum imported in 1812.	14	2	Senate bill	330	Ways and Means.	Feb. 21, 1817	With't amend.	......	Referred to Committee Whole House.		
Haslett, John	For the proceeds of the sale of his ship and cargo illegally condemned in the district Court of S. C.	21	2	Petition	163	Judiciary	....	....	......	Discharged; laid on table.		
Haslett, John	Indemnity for French spoliations prior to 1800.	26	1	Memorial	182	Foreign Affairs	343	Favorable; bill	319	Referred to Committee Whole House.		
Haslet, Colonel John, heirs of.	Compensation for revolutionary services.	24	1	Senate bill	811	Rev. Claims	May 31, 1836	With't amend.	S. 179	Passed	....	App'd July 2, 1836
Haslet, Samuel	Compensation for a horse lost in public service.	25	2	Documents	397	Claims	....	....	......	Discharged.		
Haslett, William	Indemnity for a ship seized by the Bey of Tunis.	14	1	Petition	558	....	....	....	......	Referred to Secretary of State.		
				Rep. of Secretary State.	644	Claims	....	....	......	Discharged; laid on table.		
Haslett, William	Indemnity for a ship seized by the Bey of Tunis.	14	2	Rep. of Secretary State.	29	Claims	18	Report and bill	11	Passed	Passed	App'd Jan. 20, 1817
Haslett, William	Reimbursement of money paid for land not received.	23	1	Petition	93	Public Lands	Jan. 10, 1834	Report by bill.	179	Passed	Passed	App'd Jan. 30, 1834
Haslett, William	Compensation for revolutionary services.	24	2	Documents	269	Rev. Claims.						
Haslet, Colonel William, heirs of.	Emoluments of a colonel for a limited period of the revolutionary war.	24	2	Petition	38	Rev. Claims	Feb. 28, 1837	Adverse	......	Laid on table.		
Hass, Haas, Peter	Arrears of pay for revolutionary service.	3	1	Petition and rep't Sec. of War.	27	....	....	....	......	Laid on table.		
Hass, Haas, Valentine	(See Nicholas Reid.)	3	1	....	26							
Hassal, William	Commutation pay for revolutionary services.	1	2	Petition and rep't of Sec. War.	151	....	....	....	......	Laid on table.		
Hassal, William	Compensation for revolutionary services.	2	1	Petition	484	....	....	....	......	Referred to Secretary of War.		
Hassal, William	Compensation for revolutionary services.	2	2	Rep. of Secretary War.	696	....	....	....	......	Laid on table.		
Hasancleyer, Mary, heirs of.	That a certain bond may be cancelled.	16	1	Petition	39	Ways and Means.	Jan. 22, 1820	Report by bill.	57	Passed	Passed	App'd May 4, 1820
Hassler, Charles J., widow of.	Pension for service as surgeon in United States navy.	30	1	Senate bill	826	Naval Affairs	....	With't amend.	S. 126	Passed	Passed	App'd Aug. 14, 1848
Hassler, F. R., *et al.*	Arrears and increase of pay as coast surveyor.	24	2	Rep. of Secretary Treasury.	35	Commerce.						
Hastings, Asa	Pension for disability, war of 1812	29	1	Petition	520	Invalid Pensions.						
Hastings, Daniel	Permission to import merchandise ordered prior to non-import act.	12	1	Petition	12	Com. and Manuf.	....	General bill	46			
Hastings, John	To be placed on pension roll	19	1	Petition	127	Military Pensions.	164	Adverse	.....	Laid on table.		
Hastings, Jonathan	Increase of salary as postmaster at Boston.	4	1	Memorial	412	Select	May 3, 1796	Report by bill.	183	Passed	Rejected.	
Hastings, Jonathan	Indemnity for charges in defending himself in a suit.	7	2	Petition	316	Claims	Feb. 12, 1803	Adverse	......	Leave to withdraw.		
Hastings, Jonas, administrator of.	(See John Granberry, administrator of.)	26	1	Petition	182							

List of private claims presented to the House of Representatives of the United States from the 1st to the 31st Congress, inclusive—Continued.

Names of claimants.	Nature or object of the claim.	Congress.	Session.	How brought before the House of Reps.	Page of journal.	To what committee of the House referred.	No. or date of the report.	Nature of the report.	No. of the bill.	How disposed of by the House of Reps.	How disposed of by the Senate.	Date of the act of Congress, and remarks.
Hastings, Lewis	Pension for disability, war of 1812	29	1	Petition	233	Invalid Pensions	332	Report and bill.	266			
Hastings, Lewis	Pension for disability, war of 1812	30	1	Petition	156	Invalid Pensions	291	Report and bill	287	Passed.		
Hastings, Lewis	Pension for disability, war of 1812	31	1	Petition	348	Invalid Pensions	50	Report and bill.	80	Passed	....	Leave to withdraw, 2d session.
Hastings, Theophilus	To be restored to pension roll	17	1	Petition	45	Rev. Pensions	....	....	......	Discharged; laid on table.		
Hastings, William	Increase of revolutionary pension	8	2	House bill	141	Claims.						
Hastings, William	Increase of revolutionary pension	10	1	Petition	232	Whole House	April 19, 1818	Favorable	78	Passed	Passed	App'd April 25, 1808
Hastings, William	Indemnity for expense of amputating a limb.	10	2	Petition	361	Claims	Mar. 2, 1809	Report by bill.	173	Passed	Rejected.	
Hastings, William	Indemnity for expense of amputating a limb.	11	2	Petition	197	Claims	Feb. 7, 1810	Report by bill.	78			
Hastings, William	Indemnity for expense of amputating a limb.	11	3	Petition	454	Claims.						
Hastings, Zenas	Pension for wounds received in 1812.	12	2	Petition	678	Claims	Feb. 26, 1813	Adverse	......	Laid on table.		
Hastings, Zenas	Pension for wounds received in 1812.	13	1	Petition	18	Claims	....	....	......	Discharged.		
Hastings, Zenas	Pension for wounds received in 1812.	14	1	Resolution	59	Pens. & Rev. Clm's.	April 11, 1816	Report by bill.	171	Passed	Passed, with amendment.	App'd April 30, 1816
Hasty, Robert	(See J. Libbey, executors of.)	17	1	Petition	83							
Hasty, William	Release from part of a judgment against him as surety for John Morrill.	18	1	Petition	131	Judiciary	....	....	......	Discharged; leave to withdraw.		
Hasty, William, executor of.	Indemnity for French spoliations prior to 1800.	26	1	Memorial	182	Foreign Affairs	343	Favorable; bill	319	Referred to Committee Whole House.		
Hatch, Amos	Indemnity for French spoliations prior to 1800.	26	1	Memorial	182	Foreign Affairs	343	Favorable; bill	319	Referred to Committee Whole House.		
Haswell, Anthony, heirs of.	Indemnity for costs of prosecution under sedition act.	26	2	Petition	54	Judiciary.						
Haswell, Anthony, heirs of.	Indemnity for costs of prosecution under sedition act.	28	1	Petition	104	Judiciary	49	Report and bill.	72	Passed	Passed	App'd June 17, 1844
Haswell, Nathan B.	(See John H. Peaslee)	13	3	....	484							
Haswell, Nathan B.	(See heirs of Anthony Haswell)	26	2	....	54							
Hatch, Crowell, administrator of.	Indemnity for French spoliations prior to 1800.	21	2	Petition	53	Foreign Affairs.						
Hatch, Crowell, administrator of.	Indemnity for French spoliations prior to 1800.	22	1	Petition	49	Foreign Affairs.						
Hatch, Crowell, administrator of.	Indemnity for French spoliations prior to 1800.	22	2	Petition	54	Foreign Affairs.						
Hatch, Crowell, administrator of.	Indemnity for French spoliations prior to 1800.	23	1	Petition	55	Foreign Affairs.						
Hatch, Crowell, administrator of.	Indemnity for French spoliations prior to 1800.	24	1	Petition	59	Foreign Affairs.						
Hatch, Crowell, administrator of.	Indemnity for French spoliations prior to 1800.	24	2	Memorial	46	Foreign Affairs.						
Hatch, Crowell, administrator of.	Indemnity for French spoliations prior to 1800.	25	1	Petition	131	Foreign Affairs	....	....	......	Laid on table.		
Hatch, Crowell, administrator of.	Indemnity for French spoliations prior to 1800.	25	2	Petition	172	Foreign Affairs	....	....	......	Discharged.		
Hatch, Crowell, administrator of.	Indemnity for French spoliations prior to 1800.	25	3	Petition	97	Foreign Affairs.						

List of private claims presented to the House of Representatives of the United States from the 1st to the 31st Congress, inclusive—Continued.

Names of claimants.	Nature or object of the claim.	Congress.	Session.	How brought before the House of Reps.	Page of journal.	To what committee of the House referred.	No. or date of the report.	Nature of the report.	No. of the bill.	How disposed of by the House of Reps.	How disposed of by the Senate.	Date of the act of Congress, and remarks.
Hatch, Crowell, administrator of	Indemnity for French spoliations prior to 1800.	26	1	Petition	201	Foreign Affairs	343	Favorable	319	Referred to Committee Whole House.		
Hatch, Crowell, administrator of.	Indemnity for French spoliations prior to 1800.	26	2	Petition	56	Whole House.						
Hatch, Crowell, administrator of.	Indemnity for French spoliations prior to 1800.	27	2	Petition	46	Foreign Affairs.						
Hatch, Crowell, administrator of.	Indemnity for French spoliations prior to 1800.	27	2	Petition	272	Whole House.						
Hatch, Crowell, administrator of.	Indemnity for French spoliations prior to 1800.	28	2	Petition	55	Foreign Affairs.						
Hatch, Hannah	(See widow of Daniel Littlefield.)	28	2		239							
Hatch, Henry	(see admin'tor of Crowell Hatch.)	21	2		53							
Hatch, Henry	(See Charles Bulfinch, *et al*)	26	1		202							
Hatch, Henry	Indemnity for French spoliations prior to 1800.	27	3	Petition	61	Foreign Affairs.						
Hatch, Jabez	(See heirs of Gilbert Dench)	24	2		302							
Hatch, James	(See Gates Hoit and J. Hatch)	17	1		248							
Hatch, Joshua, *et al*	Fishing bounty on vessel lost at sea.	24	1	Senate bill	811	Commerce	June 7, 1836	With't amend.	S. 153	Passed		App'd July 2, 1836
Hatch, Lewis	Pension for revolutionary services.	24	2	Petition	125	Rev. Pensions	104	Adverse		Laid on table.		
Hatch, Lewis	Pension for revolutionary services.	25	2	Petition	55	Rev. Pensions	455	Report and bill.	458	Passed	Passed	App'd July 7, 1838
Hatch, Mark	Indemnity for French spoliations prior to 1800.	26	1	Memorial	182	Foreign Affairs	343	Favorable; bil	319	Referred to Committee Whole House.		
Hatch, Martin	Arrears of pension	31	1	Petition	311	Invalid Pensions	Feb. 5, 1850			Discharged; laid on table.		
Hatch, M., heirs of	Indemnity for French spoliations prior to 1800.	31	1	Petition	225	Foreign Affairs	355	General bill	318	Referred to Committee Whole House.		
Hatch, Obed S	Pension	20	1	Petition	98	Military Pensions	Jan. 28, 1828	Adverse		Laid on table.		
Hatch, Obed S	Increase of pension	21	1	Petition	318	Military Pensions	May 14, 1830	Adverse		Laid on table.		
Hatch, Robert, widow of	To be restored to navy pension roll.	28	1	Petition	75	Naval Affairs.						
Hatch, Robert, widow of	To be restored to navy pension roll.	28	2	Petition	250	Invalid Pensions.						
Hatcher, John		20	1	Petition	57	Military Affairs				Discharged; laid on table.		
Hatfield, Peter, widow of	Pension for revolutionary services.	26	1	Petition	285	Rev. Pensions.						
Hathaway, Amzi	Redemption of a cancelled treasury note.	28	1	Petition	333	Claims.						
Hathaway, Amzi	Redemption of a cancelled treasury note.	29	1	Petition	151	Claims				Referred to Committee Whole House.		
Hathaway, Benoni	Pension	9	2	House bill	608	Whole House	Feb. 28, 1807	Favorable	216	Passed	Passed	App'd March 3, 1807
Hathaway, Elijah	Indemnity for property destroyed by the enemy in war of 1812.	15	2	Petition	148	Claims	Jan. 16, 1819			Discharged; laid on table.		
Hathaway, Ephraim	Pension	21	2	Petition	300	Military Pensions.						
Hathaway, Ephraim	Pension	22	1	Petition	509	Invalid Pensions.						
Hathaway, James, administrator of.	Indemnity for French spoliations in 1799.	21	1	Petition	171	Foreign Affairs				Discharged; laid on table.		
Hathaway, James, administrator of.	Indemnity for French spoliations prior to 1800.	26	1	Memorial	182	Foreign Affairs	343	Favorable; bill	319	Referred to Committee Whole House.		
Hathaway, Joseph	Compensation for services in war of 1812.	17	2	Petition	208	Claims				Leave to withdraw.		
Hathaway, Joseph	Compensation for services in war of 1812.	18	1	Petition	296	Claims						Leave to withdraw, 2d session.
Hathaway, Levi	Pension for revolutionary services.	17	1	Petition	60	Pens. & Rev. Cl'ms.	Dec. 21, 1821	Adverse		Recommitted.		
Hathaway, Levi	Pension for revolutionary services.	17	2	Petition	31	Pens. & Rev. Cl'ms.	Dec. 16, 1822	General bill	195	Passed.		

List of private claims presented to the House of Representatives of the United States from the 1st to the 31st Congress, inclusive—Continued.

Names of claimants.	Nature or object of the claim.	Congress.	Session.	How brought before the House of Reps.	Page of journal.	To what committee of the House referred.	No. or date of the report.	Nature of the report.	No. of the bill.	How disposed of by the House of Reps.	How disposed of by the Senate.	Date of the act of Congress, and remarks.
Hathaway, Levi	Pension for revolutionary services.	18	1	Petition	65	Pens. & Rev. Cl'ms.	Dec. 31, 1823	General bill	135	Passed	Passed, with amendment.	House refuse to concur to Senate insist.
Hathaway, Levi	Pension for revolutionary services.	18	2	Petition	59	Pens. & Rev. Cl'ms	Jan. 18, 1825	General bill	279	Passed with amend't.		
Hathaway, Levi	Pension for revolutionary services.	19	1	Petition	53	Military Pensions				Discharged; laid on table.		
Hathaway, Levi	Pension for revolutionary services.	19	1	Petition	224	Claims	May 25, 1826	Favorable		Referred to Committee Whole House.		
Hathaway, Levi	Pension for revolutionary services.	19	2	Petition	53	Military Pensions	Feb. 2, 1827	Favorable	314	Passed	Passed	App'd March 3, 1827
Hathaway, Levi	Pension for revolutionary services.	20	1	Petition	337	Military Pensions	April 29, 1828	Report and bill.	283	Passed.		
Hathaway, Levi	Increase of pension	21	1	Petition	130	Whole House	Feb. 13, 1830	Favorable	72	Passed	Passed with amendment.	App'd May 20, 1830
Hathaway, Levi	Arrears of pension	21	1	Petition	197	Military Pensions	April 6, 1830	Adverse		Laid on table.		
Hathaway, Levi	Arrears of pension	22	1	Petition	330	Rev. Pensions				Discharged; laid on table.		
Hathaway, Richard	Compensation for a horse taken by Indians in 1812.	24	1	Petition	474	Claims	768	Adverse		Laid on table.		
Hathaway, Richard	Compensation for a horse taken by Indians in 1812.	25	2	Petition	921	Claims				Discharged.		
Hathaway, Richard	Compensation for a horse taken by Indians in 1812.	25	3	Petition	462	Claims.						
Hathaway, Richard	Compensation for a horse taken by Indians in 1812.	26	1	Petition	168	Claims	40	Adverse		Laid on table.		
Hathaway, T. N., administrator of.	Indemnity for French spoliations prior to 1800.	31	1	Memorial	413	Foreign Affairs	355	General bill	318			
Hatton, Nathaniel, *et al.*	Compensation for damage to property by United States troops in 1813.	21	1	Petition	235	Claims				Discharged; laid on table.		
Hatton, Nathaniel, *et al.*	Compensation for damage to property by United States troops in 1813.	22	1	Petition	222	Claims	Feb. 6, 1832	Adverse		Recommitted.		
Hatton, Nathaniel, *et al.*	Compensation for damage to property by United States troops in 1813.	22	2	Petition	82	Claims.						
Hatton, Nathaniel, *et al.*	Compensation for damage to property by United States troops in 1813.	23	1	Petition	81	Military Affairs	Dec. 31, 1833	Adverse		Laid on table.		
Hatton, Samuel, sen	Pension for revolutionary services.	25	2	Petition	405	Rev. Pensions	777	Report and bill	728	Passed	Adverse report.	
Hatton, Samuel, sen	Pension for revolutionary services.	25	3	Petition	88	Rev. Pensions	71	Report and bill.	949	Passed	Adverse report.	
Hatton, Samuel, sen	Pension for revolutionary services.	26	1	Petition	172	Rev. Pensions.						
Hatton, Samuel	Pension for disability, war of 1812.	28	1	Petition	583	Invalid Pensions.						
Haucelman, Michael	Right of pre-emption to a certain tract of land.	26	2	Petition	50	Public Lands.						
Haughery, Elizabeth	Pension	30	2	Petition	434	Invalid Pensions				Discharged; laid on table.		
Haughey, Robert, heir of.	Compensation for services and for loss on Continental money.	25	2	Petition	392	Rev. Claims				Discharged; laid on table.		
Haumall, William	Pension for wounds received in Mexico.	31	2	Petition	225	Invalid Pensions.						
Haup, John	Increase of pension in consideration of wounds received at Chepultepec.	30	1	Petition	771	Invalid Pensions	631	Report and bill.	506	Passed.		

List of private claims presented to the House of Representatives of the United States from the 1st to the 31st Congress, inclusive—Continued.

Names of claimants.	Nature or object of the claim.	Congress.	Session.	How brought before the House of Reps.	Page of journal.	To what committee of the House referred.	No. or date of the report.	Nature of the report.	No. of the bill.	How disposed of by the House of Reps.	How disposed of by the Senate.	Date of the act of Congress, and remarks.
Haupt, John M	Bounty land for services as a revolutionary soldier.	12	1	Petition	315	Claims.						
Haupt, John M	Bounty land for services as a revolutionary soldier.	12	2	Petition	568	Claims.						
Hauser, Henry	Pension	20	1	House bill	645	Military Pensions	April 29, 1828	Report by bill.	283	Passed.		
Hauser, Henry	Pension	20	2	Petition	55	Military Pensions	Dec. 12, 1828	General bill	311	Passed.		
Havens, Daniel	Pension for revolutionary services.	24	1	Resolution	285	Rev. Pensions	498	Report and bil.	498	Passed	Passed	App'd June 28, 1836
Havens, Gabriel	(See Philetus Havens & Co.)	26	1		182							
Havens, Gabriel, and Philetus.	Remission of duty on whale oil and bone.	10	1	Memorial	43	Com. and Manuf.						
Haven, Jesse	(See guardian of Artemas Conant)	30	1		143							
Havens, John	Indemnity for French spoliations prior to 1800.	26	1	Memorial	182	Foreign Affairs	343	Favorable; bill.	319	Referred to Committee Whole House.		
Harris, John	Pension for revolutionary services.	20	1	Petition	337	Military Pensions				Discharged; laid on table.		
Haven, Nathaniel A., executor of.	Indemnity for French spoliations prior to 1800.	26	1	Memorial	182	Foreign Affairs	343	Favorable; bill	319	Referred to Committee Whole House.		
Havens, Philetus, administrator of.	Indemnity for French spoliations prior to 1800.	26	1	Memorial	182	Foreign Affairs	343	Favorable; bill	319	Referred to Committee Whole House.		
Havens, Rensselaer	(See Noah Brown, *et al.*)	15	1		183							
Havens, ——	(See Brown & Havens)	23	1		111							
Havens, Sylvester	Compensation for improvement on a lot leased to government.	21	1	Petition	318	Claims	Mar. 12, 1830	Report by bill.	342			
Havens, Sylvester	Compensation for improvement on a lot leased to government.	22	1	Petition	25	Claims	Dec. 19, 1831	Report by bill.	13	Passed	Passed	App'd Mar. 22, 1832
Havens, Sylvester	To correct an error in a law of present session.	22	1	Resolution	594	Claims	452	Report by bill.	552	Referred to Committee Whole House.		
Havens, Sylvester	To correct an error in a law of last session.	22	2	House bill	66	Whole House	Dec. 15, 1832	With't amend.	552	Passed	Passed	App'd Feb. 5, 1833
Haven, Thomas	Compensation for services and injuries in revolutionary war.	1	3	Petition	378					Referred to Secretary of Treasury.		
Haven, William, assignee of.	(See Reuben Shapley, assignee of)	26	1	Petition	182							
Haverd, John, and others.	Compensation for losses and injuries in revolutionary war.	1	3	Petition	352					Referred to Secretary Treasury.		
Haverd, John, and others.	Compensation for losses and injuries in revolutionary war.	2	2	Rep. of Secretary Treasury.	626	Whole House.						
Haviland, Isaac	Pension for services as teamster in revolutionary war.	25	3	Petition	459	Rev. Pensions				Discharged.		
Haviland, Isaac	Pension for services as teamster in revolutionary war.	26	1	Petition	174	Rev. Pensions				Discharged; laid on table.		
Havis, James, widow of	Compensation for services under Bouquet in 1760 and 1761.	8	2	Petition	57	Claims	Dec. 28, 1804	Adverse		Leave to withdraw.		
Hawes, Jabez	Pension	21	2	Petition	67	Military Pensions				Discharged; laid on table.		
Hawes, Jabez	Pension	22	1	Petition	66	Rev. Pensions	106	Report and bill.	190	Ref'd to Com W. H.		
Hawes, Jabez	Pension	22	2	House bill	66	Whole House			190	Laid on table.		
Hawes, Seth and others	Compensation for property taken for public use, revolutionary war.	3	1	Petition	48					Laid on table.		
Hawes, Silas	Renewal of patent for improvement in carpenters tools.	23	1	Petition	247	Patents and patent laws.						

List of private claims presented to the House of Representatives of the United States from the 1st to the 31st Congress, inclusive—Continued.

Names of claimants.	Nature or object of the claim.	Congress.	Session.	How brought before the House of Reps.	Page of journal.	To what committee of the House referred.	No. or date of the report.	Nature of the report.	No. of the bill.	How disposed of by the House of Reps.	How disposed of by the Senate.	Date of the act of Congress, and remarks.
Hawes, Silas	Renewal of patent for improvement in carpenters tools.	23	2	Petition	102	Judiciary.						
Hawes, Silas	Renewal of patent for improvement in carpenters tools.	24	1	Petition	106	Judiciary.						
Hawes, William	Pension for revolutionary services.	23	1	Petition	333	Rev. Pensions				Discharged; laid on table.		
Hawgerdon, John	Invalid pension	3	1	Rep. of Secretary War.	131	Select	May 26, 1794	To refer to Sec. War.	R. 12	Passed	Passed	App'd June 9, 1794
Hawkes, Benjamin	Increase of salery as clerk navy-yard Boston.	24	2	Petition	158	Naval Affairs.						
Hawkes, Benjamin	Increase of salary as clerk navy-yard Boston.	25	3	Petition	225	Naval Affairs.						
Hawke, Benjamin	Increase of salary as clerk navy-yard Boston.	26	1	Petition	302	Naval Affairs.						
Hawke, Corporal Charles.	Amount found due him by the Fourth Auditor.	31	1	Appropriat'n bill					334			App'd Sept. 30, 1850
Hawk, Jacob	Pension	19	2	Petition	31	Military Pensions				Discharged.		
Hawks, Henry	Invalid pension	3	1	Rep. of Secretary War.	131	Select	May 26, 1794	To refer to Secretary War.	R 12	Passed	Passed	App'd June 9, 1794
Hawks, Henry	Invalid pension	4	1	Rep. of Secretary War.	373	Claims.						
Hawks, Ruth	(See Millington Lockwood, heirs of.)	25	2		658							
Hawkesworth, Mark	Compensation for services on board schooner Dolphin.	25	3	Resolution	285	Naval Affairs.						
Hawkesworth, Mark	Compensation for services on board schooner Dolphin.	26	1	Resolution	378	Naval Affairs.						
Hawkins, Augustus	(See Lieutenant Francis Ware, representatives of.)	29	1		120							
Hawkins, Bartlett	Increase of pension and bounty land for revolutionary services.	11	2	Petition	266	Claims	Mar. 24, 1810	General bill	107	Passed	Passed	App'd April 27, 1810
Hawkins, Benjamin, widow of.	Confirmation of title to land granted by the Creeks.	14	2	Petition	296	Priv. Land Claims.						
Hawkins, Benjamin, widow of.	Confirmation of title to land granted by the Creeks.	15	1	Petition	267	Priv. Land Claims				Discharged: laid on table.		
Hawkins, Benjamin, widow of.	Confirmation of title to land granted by the Creeks.	22	1	Petition	943	Priv. Land Claims				Discharged; laid on table.		
Hawkins, Benjamin	(See General A. Jackson.)	14	2		134							
Hawkins, Christian	(See George Sheaf, widow of.)	26	1		937							
Hawkins, Darius	Arrears of pension for services in war of 1812.	25	3	Petition	219	Invalid Pensions.						
Hawkins, Darius	Arrears of pension for services in war of 1812.	26	1	Petition	162	Invalid Pensions	267	Adverse		Laid on table.		
Hawkins, Darius	Arrears of pension for services in war of 1812.	27	2	Petition	60	Invalid Pensions	438	Adverse		Laid on table.		
Hawkins, Darius	Arrears of pension for services in war of 1812.	27	3	Petition	44	Invalid Pensions	30	Adverse		Laid on table.		
Hawkins, Darius	Arrears of pension for services in war of 1812.	28	1	Petition	76	Invalid Pensions	112	Adverse		Laid on table.		
Hawkins, Darius	Arrears of pension for services in war of 1812.	28	2	Petition	207							
Hawkins, Darius	Arrears of pension for services in war of 1812.	29	1	Petition	482	Invalid Pensions				Discharged; laid on table.		

List of private claims presented to the House of Representatives of the United States from the 1st to the 31st Congress, inclusive—Continued.

Names of claimants.	Nature or object of the claim.	Congress.	Session.	How brought before the House of Reps.	Page of journal.	To what committee of the House referred.	No. or date of the report.	Nature of the report	No. of the bill.	How disposed of by the House of Reps.	How disposed of by the Senate.	Date of the act of Congress, and remarks.
Hawkins, Darius	Arrears of pension for services in war of 1812.	30	1	Petition	104	Invalid Pensions				Discharged; laid on table.		
Hawkins, David	Pension	14	1	Petition	28	Pens. & Rev. Cl'ms.	April 11, 1816	Report by bill		Passed	Passed, with amendment.	App'd April 30, 1816
Hawkins, George S	(See Thomas Meriwether)	25	2		393							
Hawkins, James	Pension for services as a revolutionary soldier.	21	1	Resolution	217	Military Pensions	May 4, 1830	Adverse		Laid on table.		
Hawkins, James	Pension for services as a revolutionary soldier.	22	1	Petition	803	Rev. Pensions.						
Hawkins, Job	To be restored to revolutionary pension roll.	25	3	Resolution	288	Rev. Pensions				Discharged.		
Hawkins, Job	To be restored to revolutionary pension roll.	26	1	Petition	166	Rev. Pensions	458	Report and bill.	372			
Hawkins, Job	To be restored to revolutionary pension roll.	27	2	Petition	58	Rev. Pensions.						
Hawkins, Job	To be restored to revolutionary pension roll.	27	2	Petition	344	Rev. Pensions	89	Report and bill	135	Passed	Indef. postp'd.	
Hawkins, Job	To be restored to revolutionary pension roll.	27	3	Petition	43	Rev. Pensions				Discharged; laid on table.		
Hawkins, Job	To be restored to revolutionary pension roll.	28	2	Petition	228	Rev. Pensions.						
Hawkins, Job	To be restored to revolutionary pension roll.	29	1	Petition	120	Rev. Pensions	309	Report and bill	247	Referred to Committee Whole House.		
Hawkins, Job	To be restored to revolutionary pension roll.	29	2	House bill	71	Whole House	Dec. 18, 1846	With't amend.	247	Passed	Passed	App'd March 3, 1847
Hawkins, Capt. John, heirs of.	Commutation pay and bounty land for revolutionary services.	24	1	Petition	204	Rev. Claims.						
Hawkins, Capt. John, heirs of.	Commutation pay and bounty land for revolutionary services.	25	2	Senate bill	496	Rev. Claims	Mar. 13, 1838	Adverse	S. 117			
Hawkins, Joseph	(See Beverly Winslow, *et al*)	2	1		461							
Hawkins, Joseph	Services as commissary	4	1	Letter of Secretary Treasury.	383	Claims	Jan. 26, 1796	Adverse		Leave to withdraw.		
Hawkins, Joseph	(See A. Plantou)	20	2		33							
Hawkins, Joshua	Pension	10	2	House bill	499	Whole House		Favorable	158	Passed	Passed	App'd March 3, 1809
Hawkins, Moses, heirs of.	Half-pay to which they are entitled by law.	23	1	Petition	42	Rev. Claims.						
Hawkins, Moses, heirs of.	Half-pay to which they are entitled by law.	23	2	Petition	132	Rev. Claims	Feb. 7, 1835	Adverse		Laid on table.		
Hawkins, Rich'd F., (alien.)	Patent for an improvement in anchors.	17	2	Petition	224	Judiciary				Discharged; leave to withdraw.		
awkins, Samuel	Relief in consideration of wounds received in public service.	12	2	Petition	641	Claims	Feb. 26, 1813	Adverse		Leave to withdraw.		
Hawkins, Samuel	Invalid pension	13	2	House bill	344	Whole House	Mar. 30, 1814	Favorable	166	Passed	Passed	App'd April 18, 1814
Hawkins, Stephen	Pension for revolutionary services.	22	1	Resolution	82	Rev. Pensions	171	Report and bill.	244	Passed.		
Hawkins, Stephen	Pension for revolutionary services.	22	2	House bill	123	Rev. Pensions	Jan. 10, 1832	Report by bill	244	Laid on table.		
Hawkins, S. V	(See Exploring Expedition)	27	3		149		270		818			
Hawkins, Uriah	To be placed on pension roll	19	1	Petition	221	Military Pensions	164	Adverse		Laid on table.		
Hawkins, Whitehurst J	Compensation for horses lost in Florida war.	28	1	Petition	443	Claims.						
Hawkins, William	Released from a judgment rendered for violation of embargo law.	10	2	Petition and rep't of Sec. War.	532, 574					Laid on table.		
Hawkins, William	Released from a judgment rendered for violation of embargo law.	11	1	Petition	60	Com. and Manuf.						

List of private claims presented to the House of Representatives of the United States from the 1st to the 31st Congress, inclusive—Continued.

Names of claimants.	Nature or object of the claim.	Congress.	Session.	How brought before the House of Reps.	Page of journal.	To what committee of the House referred.	No. or date of the report.	Nature of the report.	No. of the bill.	How disposed of by the House of Reps.	How disposed of by the Senate.	Date of the act of Congress, and remarks.
Hawkins, William	Released from a judgment rendered for violation of embargo law.	11	2	Petition	141	Com. and Manuf.	Dec. 27, 1809	Report and bill	54	Passed	Passed	App'd Feb. 20, 1810
Hawkins, William	Compensation as assistant superintendent on Cumberland road.	19	1	Appropriation bill	....	....	....	....	....	....	....	App'd March 14, 1826
Hawkins, William	Pension for services as a revolutionary soldier.	19	1	Resolution	348	Military Pensions	April 1, 1826	Adverse	......	Discharged.		
Hawkins, William, widow of	Compensation for improvem't upon property sold under a judgment in favor of United States.	18	1	Petition	253	Ways and Means	Mar. 15, 1824	Report and bill	161	Passed	Passed	See act May 19, 1824
Hawkins, William, widow of	Further time to pay a debt due to government.	21	1	Petition	85	Ways and Means	Feb. 10, 1830	Report by bill.	223			
Hawkins, William	Further time to pay a debt due to government.	21	2	House bill	264	Whole House	Feb. 4, 1831	With't amend.	223	Passed.		
Hawkins, William	Compensation for wood delivered on contract.	25	2	Petition	396	Claims	....	....	......	Discharged.		
Hawkins, William	Compensation for wood delivered on contract.	25	3	Petition	348	Claims	279	Adverse	......	Laid on table.		
Hawkins, William	Compensation for wood delivered on contract.	26	2	Petition	376	Military Affairs	Mar. 3, 1841	Adverse	......	Laid on table.		
Hawkins, William	Compensation for wood delivered on contract.	27	2	Petition	154	Military Affairs	208	Adverse	......	Laid on table.		
Hawkins, William	Compensation for wood delivered on contract.	31	1	Petition	349	Military Affairs	199	Report and bill	206			
Hawkins, William	Compensation for wood delivered on contract.	31	2	House bill	181	Whole House	Jan. 24, 1851	With't amend.	206	Passed.		
Hawkley, James	Pension	10	1	House bill	232	Whole House	April 19, 1808	With amend's.	78	Passed	Passed	App'd April 25, 1808
Hawley, David	Pension	9	2	House bill	608	Whole House	Feb. 28, 1807	Favorable	216	Passed	Passed	App'd March 3, 1807
Hawley, David W	Arrears of pension	23	1	Petition	132	Invalid Pensions	....	....	......	Discharged; laid on table.		
Hawley, David W	Arrears of pension	25	2	Petition	638	Invalid Pensions	....	....	......	Discharged; laid on table.		
Hawley, David W., (Ohio)	Patent for Grassy Point at minimum price.	24	2	Petition	211	Public Lands	....	....	......	Discharged; laid on table.		
Hawley, David W., (Ohio)	Patent for Grassy Point at minimum price.	25	2	Petition	548	Public Lands	....	....	......	Discharged.		
Hawley, David W., (New York.)	Compensation for a house destroyed in the war of 1812.	24	2	Documents.								
Hawley, David W., (New York.)	Compensation for a house destroyed in the war of 1812.	25	2	Petition	398	Claims	....	....	......	Discharged; laid on table.		
Hawley, Ebenezer R	Pension for revolutionary services.	18	2	Petition	251	Pens. & Rev. Cl'ms.						
Hawley, Ebenezer R	Pension for revolutionary services.	21	2	Petition	300	Military Pensions.						
Hawley, Isaac P., sister of.	Prize money due from the republic of South America.	26	1	Petition	291	Commerce	....	....	......	Discharged; laid on table.		
Hawley, Isaac P., sister of.	Prize money due from the republic of South America.	30	1	Petition	587	Foreign Affairs.						
Hawley, Isaac P., sister of.	Search in State Department for documents relating to settlement of the estate of deceased at Porto Bello.	30	1	Petition	638	Foreign Affairs.						
Hawley, James	Pension	20	2	Petition	26	Military Pensions	....	....	......	Discharged; laid on table.		
Hawley, Nathan	Invalid pension	4	1	Rep. of Secretary War.	445	Claims	Mar. 4, 1796	Favorable; bill ordered.	156	Passed	Passed	App'd April 20, 1796

List of private claims presented to the House of Representatives of the United States from the 1st to the 31st Congress, inclusive—Continued.

Names of claimants.	Nature or object of the claim.	Congress.	Session.	How brought before the House of Reps.	Page of journal.	To what committee of the House referred.	No. or date of the report.	Nature of the report.	No. of the bill.	How disposed of by the House of Reps.	How disposed of by the Senate.	Date of the act of Congress, and remarks.
Hawley, Nathan	Increase of pension	11	2	House bill	283	Whole House	Mar. 24, 1810	Favorable	107	Passed	Passed	App'd April 27, 1810
Hawley, Nathan	Increase of pension	12	1	House bill	361	Whole House			138	Passed	Passed	App'd July 5, 1812
Hawley, Nathan	Increase of pension	14	1	House bill	622	Pens. & Rev. Cl'ms.	April 11, 1816	With't amend.	171	Passed	Passed	App'd April 30, 1816
Hawley, Nero	Increase of pension	11	2	House bill	283	Whole House	Mar. 24, 1810	With amend's.	107	Passed	Passed	App'd April 27, 1810
Hawley, Nero	Increase of pension	14	1	House bill	755	Whole House	April 23, 1816	Favorable	171	Passed	Passed	App'd April 30, 1816
Hawley, Samuel	Pension for revolutionary services	18	2	Petition	209	Rev. Pensions				Discharged; laid on table.		
Hawschurst, George	(See Henry Cahoone)	14	2		225							
Hawtyn, Christiana	(See executor of Thomas Ellison)	2	2		699							
Hawtyn, Christiana	(See executor of Thomas Ellison)	5	3		478							
Haxman, Henrich	Confirmation of title to certain lands	30	2	Petition	240	Public Lands.						
Hay, Andrew P., sureties of.	Release from payment of interest on judgment.	22	1	Petition	558	Judiciary				Discharged; laid on table.		
Hay, Andrew. P., sureties of.	Release from payment of interest on judgment.	22	2	Petition	31	Judiciary				Discharged; laid on table.		
Hay, Andrew P., sureties of.	Release from payment of interest on judgment.	23	1	Petition	38	Judiciary	101	Adverse		Laid on table.		
Hay, Andrew P., sureties of.	Release from payment of interest on judgment.	24	1	Petition	425	Judiciary.						
Hay, Andrew P., sureties of.	Release from payment of interest on judgment.	24	2	Petition	89	Judiciary.						
Hay, Andrew P., sureties of.	Release from payment of interest on judgment.	28	1	Petition	583	Ways and Means.						
Hay, Archibald	(See Edwin Safford and A. Hay.)	14	1		84							
Hay, Charles, heirs of	For grant of land as a Canadian refugee.	6	2	Petition	779	Claims				Postponed to next session.		
Hay, Charles, heirs of	For grant of land as a Canadian refugee.	7	1	Petition	19	Claims	April 3, 1802			Postponed.		
Hay, Daniel	Compensation for services as pension agent, Illinois.	27	2	Petition	375	Rev. Pensions	409	Adverse		Laid on table.		
Hay, David	Compensation for hats furnished revolutionary army.	18	1	Petition	214	Pens. & Rev. Cl'ms.	Feb. 25, 1824	Adverse		Laid on table.		
Hay, David	Compensation for hats furnished revolutionary army.	19	2	Petition	158	Rev. Claims	Feb. 6, 1827	Adverse		Laid on table.		
Hay, Isaac	Pension for revolutionary services.	22	1	Petition	509	Rev. Pensions.						
Hay, James	Compensation for a horse lost in the public service.	23	1	Petition	438	Claims.						
Hay, James	Compensation for a horse lost in the public service.	25	2	Documents	396	Claims				Discharged.		
Hay, James	Compensation for a horse lost in the public service.	25	3	Documents	207	Claims.						
Hay, John D	Release from payment of public moneys destroyed by fire.	13	2	Petition	374	Ways and Means	April 7, 1814	Report by bill.	187	Passed	Passed	App'd April 18, 1814
Hay, John D	Release from payment of certain costs.	17	1	Petition	360	P. Of. & P. Roads.	Mar. 19, 1822	Adverse		Rejected.		
Hay, John D	For the amendment of an act passed for his relief.	17	2	Resolution	62	P. Of. & P. Roads				Discharged; leave to withdraw.		
Hay, John D	Release from payment of certain costs.	18	1	Resolution	38	P. Of. & P. Roads.	Jan. 8, 1824	Adverse		Rejected.		
Hay, John, widow of	Pension for revolutionary services.	23	1	Petition	436	Rev. Pensions				Discharged; leave to withdraw.		
Hay, Martha	Compensation for 600 cords of wood, revolutionary war.	4	1	Report of Secretary Treasury.	388	Claims	74	Adverse		Laid on table.		

List of private claims presented to the House of Representatives of the United States from the 1st to the 31st Congress, inclusive—Continued.

Names of claimants.	Nature or object of the claim.	Congress.	Session.	How brought before the House of Reps.	Page of journal.	To what committee of the House referred.	No. or date of the report.	Nature of the report.	No. of the bill.	How disposed of by the House of Reps.	How disposed of by the Senate.	Date of the act of Congress, and remarks.
Hay, Udney	Reimbursement of advances to American prisoners in Canada.	2	1	Petition	501					Referred to Secretary Treasury.		
Hay, Udney	Reimbursement of damage and costs in a certain suit.	2	1	Petition	510					Referred to Secretary Treasury.		
Hay, Udney	Reimbursement of advances to American prisoners in Quebec.	2	1	Rep. of Secretary Treasury.	626	Whole House	Dec. 26, 1792	Report and bill	208	Passed	Passed	App'd Jan. 14, 1793
Hay, Udney	Reimbursement of damage and costs in a certain suit.	3	2	Rep. of Secretary Treasury.	284					Laid on table.		
Hay, Udney, heir of	Compensation for services and losses in revolutionary war.	19	1	Petition	251	Rev. Claims	April 28, 1826	Adverse		Laid on table.		
Hay, Udney, heir of	Benefit of act for relief of Canadian refugees.	19	1	Petition	270	Whole House				Discharged; laid on table.		
Hay, Udney, representative of.	Payment of a loan office certificate.	29	1	Petition	120	Rev. Claims	181	Adverse		Laid on table.		
Hay, Udney, representative of.	Payment of a loan office certificate.	29	2	Petition	135	Claims.						
Hay, Udney, representative of.	Payment of a loan office certificate.	30	1	Petition	145	Rev. Claims.						
Hay, Udney, representative of.	Payment of a loan office certificate.	31	1	Petition	610	Rev. Claims.						
Hay, William	Pension	21	1	Petition	377	Military Pensions				Discharged; laid on table.		
Hayatt, Frederick, by his attorney, Duff Green.	Indemnity for losses sustained by the depredations of Indians.	19	2	Petition	134	Indian Affairs	Jan. 23, 1827			Referred to Committee Whole House.		
Haycraft, Samuel	Compensation for his services as a revolutionary soldier.	16	1	Petition	139	Pens. & Rev. Cl'ms.	Jan. 21, 1820	Adverse.		Laid on table.		
Hayes, Ahaz	Payment of two lost treasury notes	21	1	Petition	110	Claims	Jan. 8, 1830			Referred to Secretary of Treasury.		
Hayes, Ahaz	Payment of two lost treasury notes	22	1	Petition	221	Claims	Feb. 3, 1832	Adverse		Laid on table.		
Hayes, Ahaz	Payment of two lost treasury notes	23	1	Petition	355	Claims	387	Adverse		Laid on table.		
Hays, Dr. B. M.	Compensation for hospital stores, &c., Indian wars.	23	2	Petition	139	Claims	Jan. 22, 1835	Adverse		Laid on table.		
Hays, Benjamin F.	Authority to locate a certain land warrant.	31	2	Petition	87	Public Lands.						
Hayes, Bradstreet M.	Right of pre-emption to land on which he resides.	23	1	Petition	447	Whole House.						
Hays, Dudley	Pension and arrears of pension	18	2	Petition	251	Pens. & Rev. Cl'ms.						
Hays, Hugh	Pension	14	1	House bill	622	Pens. & Rev. Cl'ms.	April 11, 1816	With't amend.	171	Passed	Passed	App'd April 30, 1816
Hays, H. H. B.	Release of part of judgment against his sureties.	25	2	Resolution	481	Claims	652	Report and bill.	628			
Hays, H. H. B.	Release of part of judgment against his sureties.	25	3	House bill	380	Whole House			628	Passed	Adverse report.	
Hays, H. H. B.	Release of part of judgment against his sureties.	26	1	Petition	306	Claims.						
Hays, H. H. B.	Release of part of judgment against his sureties.	26	1	Petition	748	P. Of. and P. Roads.	302	Report and bill.	264			
Hays, James	Pension for services, war of 1812.	15	2	Petition	74	Pens. & Rev. Cl'ms.	Feb. 5, 1819	General bill	308	Passed	Postponed.	
Hays, James	Pension for services, war of 1812.	16	2	Petition	137	Pens. & Rev. Cl'ms.						
Hays, James	Pension for services, war of 1812.	17	2	Petition	31	Pens. & Rev. Cl'ms.	Dec. 15, 1822	General bill	195	Passed.		
Hays, John	Renewal of a loan office certificate.	2	1	Petition	474							
				Rep. of Secretary War.	583	Select.						

List of private claims presented to the House of Representatives of the United States from the 1st to the 31st Congress, inclusive—Continued.

Names of claimants.	Nature or object of the claim.	Congress.	Session.	How brought before the House of Reps.	Page of journal.	To what committee of the House referred.	No. or date of the report.	Nature of the report.	No. of the bill.	How disposed of by the House of Reps.	How disposed of by the Senate.	Date of the act of Congress, and remarks.
Hays, John	Compensation for certain public services.	25	3	Resolution	511	Claims.						
Hays, John	Additional compensation as collector of Internal duties.	14	1	Petition	604	Ways and Means				Discharged; laid on table.		
Hayes, John Hawkins	Pension for revolutionary services.	24	1	Petition	751	Rev. Pensions				Discharged; laid on table.		
Hayes, Joseph	Compensation for a rifle taken for public use.	20	1	Resolution	382	Claims	Mar. 18, 1828	Adverse		Laid on table.		
Hays, Joseph	(See Clement Reynolds, *et al.*)	21	1		201							
Hays, Judah	Indemnity for French spoliations prior to 1800.	26	1	Memorial	182	Foreign Affairs	343	Favorable; bill	319	Referred to Committee Whole House.		
Hays, Leonard	Release from the payment of public money of which he was robbed.	20	2	Petition	289	P. Of. and P. Roads.						
Hayes, Loys	(See heir of William Young)	27	3		260							
Hayes, Patrick, attorney of	Bounty land for services in war of 1812.	24	1	Petition	409	Public Lands.						
Hayes, Patrick, attorney of	Bounty land for services in war of 1812.	25	2	Petition	233	Public Lands	595	Adverse		Laid on table.		
Hays, Pliny	Pension for revolutionary services.	26	1	Petition	322	Rev. Pensions.						
Hays, Robert	Compensation for property taken by Indians in 1789.	14	1	Petition	120	Claims	Jan. 24, 1816	Adverse		Rejected.		
Hays, Robert	Compensation for property taken by Indians in 1787.	15	1	Petition	222	Claims	Feb. 16, 1818	Adverse		Leave to withdraw.		
Hayes, Samuel	Indemnity for property seized at Antwerp by the French government.	19	1	Memorial	153	Foreign Affairs	202	Negotiat'ns are progressing.		Discharged; laid on table.		
Hays, Sheldon B.	Compensation for transporting mail in four horse coaches.	29	1	Memorial	279	P. Of. and P. Roads.	219	Rep. and joint resolution.	J.R. 14	Passed	Passed	App'd Aug. 8, 1846
Hays, Thomas	Compensation for property taken for public use.	1	2	Petition	160					Referred to Secretary Treasury.		
Hays, Thomas	Pension for his services as a revolutionary soldier.	19	1	Petition	282	Military Pensions	Feb. 23, 1826	General bill	119	Passed.		
Hays, Thomas	Pension for his services as a revolutionary soldier.	19	2	Petition	66	Military Pensions	Dec. 11, 1826	General bill	315	Passed.		
Hays, Thomas	(See James Perry & Thomas Hays, attorney of.)	2	2		227							
Hays, Thomas, son and heir of.	Pension for revolutionary services.	27	3	Petition	260	Rev. Pensions				Discharged; leave to withdraw.		
Hays, William, by J. Hays and J. Boyland.	Balance due on iron furnished revolutionary army.	4	1	Rep. of Secretary Treasury.	388	Claims	74	Adverse		Laid on table.		
Hays, William, representatives of.	Compensation for horse and equipments lost in the public service.	20	1	Petition	366	Claims	Mar. 18, 1828	Adverse		Laid on table.		
Hays, William	Pension for services in 1782 and 1791–'92.	28	2	Petition	64	Invalid Pensions.						
Hays, William	(See Laurent Bazadone, administrator of.)	24	1		942							
Hayden, Aaron	(See Jabez Mowry, *et al.*)	14	1		242							
Hayden, Charles	Pension	15	1	Petition	265	Pens. & Rev. Cl'ms.				Discharged; laid on table.		Leave to withdraw, 2d session.
Hayden, Clement, administrator of.	Confirmation of title to land in Missouri Territory.	15	1	Petition	312	Priv. Land Claims.						
Hayden & Coale	To change the name of barque John Potter.	30	2	Memorial	239	Commerce.						

List of private claims presented to the House of Representatives of the United States from the 1st to the 31st Congress, inclusive—Continued.

Names of claimants.	Nature or object of the claim.	Congress.	Session.	How brought before the House of Reps.	Page of journal.	To what committee of the House referred.	No. and date of the report.	Nature of the report.	No. of the bill.	How disposed of by the House of Reps.	How disposed of by the Senate.	Date of the act of Congress, and remarks.
Hayden, Dennis E.	Indemnity for loss on contract with Engineer department.	22	2	Petition	184	Military Affairs.						
Hayden, Dennis E.	Indemnity for loss on contract with Engineer department.	23	1	Petition	224	Military Affairs	Jan. 21, 1834	Adverse		Laid on table.		
Hayden, Edward	(See Joseph Atwell & E. H.)	23	1		246							
Hayden, Jane	(See John Watson, heirs of.)	15	2		40							
Hayden, Jerem'h, D. widow of.	Release from payment of a balance claimed by United States.	21	1	Petition	572	Claims	May 3, 1830	Adverse		Laid on table.		
Hayden, Jeremiah, D. sureties of.	Release from liability	22	1	Petition	943	Claims.						
Hayden, Jeremiah, D. sureties of.	Release from liability	22	2	Petition	54	Claims	Jan. 9, 1833	Adverse		Laid on table.		
Hayden, Jeremiah, D. sureties of.	Release from liability	25	2	Memorial	75	Judiciary	Jan. 18, 1838	Favorable	436	Referred to Committee Whole House.		
Hayden, Jeremiah, D. sureties of.	Release from liability	26	1	Petition	175	Judiciary	Mar. 5, 1840	Favorable	81	Referred to Committee Whole House.		
Hayden, Jeremiah, D. sureties of.	Release from liability	27	2	Petition	63	Judiciary.						
Hayden, Jeremiah, D. sureties of.	Release from liability	31	1	Petition	486	Judiciary.						
Hayden, John	Renewal of a final settlement certificate.	2	1	Petition and rep't Sec. Treasury.	518, 583	Select.						
Hayden, Mariah	(See Jeremiah D. Hayden, sureties of.)	21	1									
Hayden, William	Pension for revolutionary services.	23	1	Petition	121	Rev. Pensions				Discharged; laid on table.		
Hayden, Ziba	Pension	21	1	Petition	43	Military Pensions	Feb. 11, 1832			Discharged; laid on table.		
Hayden, Ziba	To be restored to pension roll	22	1	Resolution	93	Rev. Pensions	365	Report by bill.	460	Passed	Indef. postp'd.	
Haydock & Jenkins	(See Haddoc & Jenkins.)	16	1		101							
Hayland, John, widow of.	Compensation for services as seamnn	19	2	Petition	53	Ways and Means				Discharged.		
Hayle, Philip C	Pension for revolutionary services.	23	1	Resolution	236	Rev. Pensions				Discharged; leave to withdraw.		
Hayley, John	Increase of pension	14	1	Petition	318	Pens. & Rev. Cl'ms.	Mar. 23, 1816	Adverse		Rejected.		
Hayman, Casper, representatives of.	Indemnity for French spoliations prior to 1800.	26	1	Petition	714	Foreign Affairs	343	General bill	319	Referred to Committee Whole House.		
Hayman, William	(See executor of Catharine Redmon.)	20	2	Petition	61	Dist. of Columbia.	Feb. 24, 1829	Report by bill.	457	Passed.		
Haymaker, Lucretia	(See heirs of John Bowen, of Pennsylvania.)	22	1		733							
Hayne, Francis	Relief, in consideration of injuries received in the naval service.	19	1	Petition	205	Naval Affairs	April 14, 1828			Laid on table.		
Haynes, Henry	Pension for revolutionary services.	30	1	Resolution	253	Rev. Pensions.						
Haynes, H. M.	Confirmation of title to land	27	2	Memorial	614	Priv. Land Claims.				Discharged; laid on table.		
Hane, Colonel Isaac, representatives of.	Compensation for destruction of iron works by the enemy in revolutionary war.	21	1	Petition	98	Rev. Claims				Discharged; laid on table.		
Haynes, John, attorney of.	Adjustment of accounts for keeping Africans imported into the United States.	19	2	Petition	202	Claims.						
Haynes, Jonathan	Invalid pension	2	2	Petition	465					Referred to Secretary of War.		

List of private claims presented to the House of Representatives of the United States from the 1st to the 31st Congress, inclusive—Continued.

Names of claimants.	Nature or object of the claim.	Congress.	Session.	How brought before the House of Reps.	Page of journal.	To what committee of the House referred.	No. or date of the report.	Nature of the report.	No. of the bill.	How disposed of by the House of Reps.	How disposed of by the Senate.	Date of the act of Congress, and remarks.
Haynes, Jonathan	Invalid pension	3	1	Rep. of Secretary War.	131	Select	May 24, 1794	Jt. res. to refer to Sec. War.	12	Passed	Passed	App'd June 9, 1794
Haynes, Jonathan	Invalid pension	3	2	Rep. of Secretary of War.	278	Claims	Feb. 28, 1795	Favorable: bill ordered.	130	Passed	Postp'd to next session.	
Haynes, Jonathan	Invalid pension	4	1	Rep. of Secretary War.	445	Claims	Feb. 18, 1796	Favorable; bill ordered.	156	Passed	Passed	App'd April 20, 1796
Haynes, Jonathan	Arrears of pension	4	1	Petition	546	Claims.						
Haynes, Jonathan	Arrears of pension	4	2	Resolution	614	Claims	Jan. 25, 1797	Adverse.				
Haynes, Joseph	Invalid pension	4	1	Petition	391	Claims	May 31, 1796	Adverse		Laid on table.		
Hayne, Joseph	Arrears of pension	29	2	Petition	149	Invalid Pensions.						
Haynes, Joshua	Invalid pension	3	2	Report Secretary of War.	278	Claims.						
Haynes, Joshua	Invalid pension	4	1	Rep. of Secretary War.	455	Claims	Mar. 11, 1796	Favorable; bill ordered.	156	Passed	Passed	App'd April 20, 1796
Haynes, Joshua	Invalid pension	12	1	House bill	361	Whole House	June 8, 1812	With amend.	138	Passed	Passed	App'd July 5, 1812
Haynes, Richard	Pension for revolutionary services.	22	1	Resolution	262	Rev. Pensions.						
Haynes, Thomas	Arrears of pension	19	1	Petition	220	Military Pensions.						
Hayne, ——	(See McDowall, Hayne & Co.)	27	2		89		264					
Haynor, John	Compensation for a horse lost in war of 1812.	21	1	Petition	145	Claims	135	Report and bill.	179	Passed	Passed	App'd May 29, 1830
Hayward, Caleb, widow of.	Arrears of pension	24	2	Petition	311	Invalid Pensions	Feb. 22, 1837	Adverse		Laid on table.		
Hayward, Caleb, widow of.	Arrears of pension	25	2	Petition	168	Invalid Pensions	Jan. 25, 1838	Adverse		Recommitted.		
Hayward, Caleb, widow of.	Arrears of pension	25	3	Petition	187	Invalid Pensions	Feb. 14, 1839			Disch'd; laid on table.		
Hayward, Caleb, widow of.	Arrears of pension	26	1	Petition	325	Rev. Pensions	714	Adverse		Laid on table.		
Hayward, P. A	Balance on stationary furnished legislature of Florida.	28	2	Petition	85	Claims.						
Hayward, Richard & Thos.	Compensation for supplies furnished, Florida war.	31	1	Petition	250	Military Affairs				Discharged; laid on table.		
Hazard, Cord	Pension	21	1	Senate bill	352	Military Pensions	Mar. 11, 1830	With't amend.	S. 76	Passed		App'd May 29, 1830
Hazard, Ebenezer	(See J. Conklin and J. Frost)	4	1		437							
Hazard, James	To be restored to revolutionary pension roll.	22	1	Resolution	389	Rev. Pensions	365	Report and bill	460	Passed	Indef. postp'd.	
Hazard, Jason	Pension	22	1	House bill	476	Rev. Pensions	Mar. 12, 1832	Report by bill.	460	Passed	Indef. postp'd.	
Hazard, Rodman	(See John Reynolds, representatives of.)	21	1		37							
Hazard, schooner	(See James Frazier)	27	3		58							
Hazard, Thomas H	(See John Earle, jr., and others)	9	1		195							
Hazzard, Betty	Pension for revolutionary services of husband.	28	1	Petition	839	Whole House.						
Hazzard, Ebenezer	(See Jacobus Van Buskirk)	4	1		388							
Hazzard, Ebenezer, executor of.	Balance due as postmaster, Philadelphia.	30	1	Petition	299	Claims	477	Adverse		Laid on table.		
Hazzard, Ezekiel, son of	Commutation pay and bounty land.	23	1	Petition	385	Priv. Land Claims.				Discharged; laid on table.		
Hazzard, Ezekiel, widow of	Benefit of the act of April 16, 1816.	24	1	Petition	406	Invalid Pensions	April 15, 1836	Report by bill.	560			
Hazzard, Ezekiel, widow of	Benefit of the act of April 16, 1816.	24	2	House bill	198	Whole House			560	Passed.		
Hazzard, Ezekiel, widow of	Benefit of the act of April 16, 1816.	25	2	Petition	269	Invalid Pensions				Discharged; laid on table.		
Hazzard, Ezekiel, widow of	Benefit of the act of April 16, 1816.	25	3	Petition	219	Invalid Pensions.						
Hazzard, Ezekiel, widow of	Benefit of the act of April 16, 1816.	26	1	Petition	161	Invalid Pensions	293	Adverse		Laid on table.		
Hazzard, Hannah	Pension in consideration of the death of her husband while a soldier in the U. S. army.	23	1	Petition	386	Invalid Pensions	April 11, 1834			Discharged; leave to withdraw.		

List of private claims presented to the House of Representatives of the United States from the 1st to the 31st Congress, inclusive—Continued.

Names of claimants.	Nature or object of the claim.	Congress.	Session.	How brought before the House of Reps.	Page of journal.	To what committee of the House referred.	No. or date of the report.	Nature of the report.	No. of the bill.	How disposed of by the House of Reps.	How disposed of by the Senate.	Date of the act of Congress, and remarks.
Hazzard, William C	Bounty land for services of his father in 1814.	24	1	Petition	112	Priv. Land Claims.	385	Report and bill.	391			
Hazzard, William C	Exchange of bounty land for half-pay.	25	2	Petition	43	Priv. Land Claims.	256	Report and bill.	299			
Hazzard, William C	Exchange of bounty land for half-pay.	25	3	House bill	375	Whole House			299	Passed	Passed	App'd March 3, 1839
Hazzard, William, widow of.	Pension for revolutionary services.	26	1	Petition	285	Rev. Pensions	424	Adverse		Laid on table.		
Hazelhurst, Robert	(See Henry Sayward, sureties of.)	11	3		505							
Hazelhurst, Robert	(See Henry Ingraham, *et al.*)	16	1		35							
Hazelhurst, Robert, assignees of.	Release of interest on a debt due United States from deceased as surety for T. Morris.	11	3	Petition	559	Com. and Manuf.						
Hazelhurst, Robert, assignees of.	Release of interest on a debt due United States from deceased as surety for T. Morris.	12	1	Report	180	Com. and Manuf.						
Hazeltine, Benjamin	Reimbursement of duty paid on merchandise, imported into Castine while in possession of the enemy.	17	1	Petition	99	Ways and Means				Discharged; laid on table.		
Hazeltine, Benjamin	Reimbursement of duty paid on merchandise, imported into Castine while in possession of the enemy.	18	1	Petition	27	Ways and Means	Jan. 15, 1824	General bill	60	Passed	Passed	App'd May 19, 1824
Hazeltine, William	Invalid pension	3	2	Rep. of Secretary War.	337	Claims	Feb. 28, 1795	Favorable; bill ordered.	130	Passed	Postp'd to next session.	
Hazeltine, William	Invalid pension	4	1	Rep. of Secretary War.	445	Claims	Mar. 11, 1796	General bill	156	Passed	Passed	App'd April 20, 1796
Hazeltine, William	Increase of pension	12	1	House bill	361	Whole House	June 15, 1812	With amend.	138	Passed	Passed	App'd July 5, 1812
Hazleton, Daniel, and William Palmer.	Compensation for extra work on the foundation of Whale's back light-house.	22	1	Resolution	378	Claims	343	Report and bill.	441			
Hazleton, Daniel, and William Palmer.	Compensation for copper bolts used in constructing Whale's back light-house.	22	2	Resolution	111	Claims	74	Favorable; bill reintroduced.	441			
Hazleton, Daniel, and William Palmer.	Compensation for copper bolts used in constructing Whale's back light-house.	23	1	Resolution	33	Claims	24	Report and bill.	24	Passed	Passed	App'd April 15, 1834
Hazleton, Jacob, widow of	Compensation for property destroyed in Indian wars.	24	1	Petition	153	Claims	Jan. 27, 1836	Adverse		Laid on table.		
Hazlewood, John	For supplies furnished on public account.	2	2	Petition	615					Laid on table.		
Hazen, Cornelius	Pension	20	2	House bill	55	Military Pensions	Dec. 12, 1828	With amend.	311	Passed	Laid on table.	
Hazen, F	(See Giles Harrington)	26	1		711							
Hazen, John	Invalid pension	31	1	Petition	407	Invalid Pensions	375	Report and bill.	323			
Hazen, Moses	Settlement of claims as revolutionary officer.	1	2	Petition	184	Sec. of Treasury	Aug. 9, 1790	Report		Laid on table.		
Hazen, Moses	Settlement of claims as revolutionary officer.	2	1	Petition	452					Referred to Secretary Treasury.		
Hazen, Moses	Settlement of claims as revolutionary officer.	3	2	Rep. of Secretary War.	284					Laid on table.		
Hazen, Moses	Settlement of claims as revolutionary officer.	7	2	Memorial	324	Claims	Feb. 22, 1803	Adverse		Leave to withdraw.		

List of private claims presented to the House of Representatives of the United States from the 1st to the 31st Congress, inclusive—Continued.

Names of claimants.	Nature or object of the claim.	Congress.	Session.	How brought before the House of Reps.	Page of journal.	To what committee of the House referred.	No. or date of the report.	Nature of the report.	No. of the bill.	How disposed of by the House of Reps.	How disposed of by the Senate.	Date of the act of Congress, and remarks.
Hazen, Moses, executor of.	Indemnity for losses and sacrifices, revolutionary war.	8	1	Petition	582	Claims	Feb. 27, 1804	Favorable; bill ordered.	210	Passed	Postponed.	
Hazen, Moses, executor of.	Indemnity for losses and sacrifices, revolutionary war.	8	2	Petition	6	Ways and Means	Dec. 12, 1804	Favorable; bill ordered.	19	Passed	Passed	App'd June 23, 1805
Hazen, Moses, executor of.	Indemnity for losses and sacrifices, revolutionary war.	9	1	Petition	235	Ways and Means	Mar. 5, 1806	Adverse	......	Rejected.		
Hazen, Moses, executor of.	Indemnity for losses and sacrifices, revolutionary war.	16	1	Petition	109	Ways and Means	Feb. 28, 1820	Adverse	......	Rejected.		
Hazen, Moses, executor of.	Equitable adjustment of the revolutionary claims of deceased.	16	2	Petition	136	Pens. & Rev. Cl'ms.						
Hazen, Moses, executor of.	Settlement as per acts of January, 1776, and April, 1781.	17	1	Petition	269	Pens. & Rev. Cl'ms.	....	....	......	....	....	Leave to withdraw, Jan. 21, 1825.
Hazen, Moses, executor of.	Settlement of claims	18	2	Petition	159	Pens. & Rev. Cl'ms.	....	....	......	Discharged; leave to withdraw.		
Hazen, Moses, representatives of.	Compensation for revolutionary services, &c.	19	1	Senate bill	496	Rev. Claims	May 4, 1826	Adverse	S. 106	Laid on table.		
Hazen, Moses, representatives of.	Compensation for revolutionary services, &c.	20	1	Senate bill	388	Rev. Claims	216	With amend.	S. 66	Passed with amendm't.	Passed as am'd	App'd May 26, 1828
Hazen, Moses, representatives of.	Compensation for revolutionary services, &c.	21	2	Senate bill	326	Rev. Claims	Feb. 25, 1831	With amend.	S. 7	Passed with amendm't.	Passed as am'd	App'd March 3, 1831
Hazen, Moses, widow of.	Relief as the widow of a Canadian refugee.	8	1	Memorial	592	Whole House.						
Hazen, Moses, widow of.	Bounty land as the widow of a Canadian refugee.	11	2	Petition	112	Public Lands	Dec. 7, 1809	General bill	35	Passed	Passed	App'd Feb. 24, 1810
Hazen, Moses, widow of.	(See Canadian refugees.)											
Heacock, Reuben B.	Compensat'n for property destroyed by the enemy, war of 1812.	17	2	Petition	74	Claims	....	....	......	Discharged; leave to withdraw.		
Heacock, Reuben B.	Compensat'n for property destroyed by the enemy, war of 1812.	18	1	Petition	131	Claims	Jan. 28, 1824	Adverse	......	Laid on table.		
Heacock, Reuben B.	Compensat'n for property destroyed by the enemy, war of 1812.	21	1	Petition	262	Claims	Feb. 17, 1830	Adverse	......	Laid on table.		
Heacock, Reuben B.	(See A. M. Grovenor, heirs of.)	29	1	....	567							
Head, James, heirs of.	Land and money for revolutionary services.	26	1	Resolution	359	Rev. Claims.						
Head, Joseph	Permission to enter merchandise arrived since the date of non-importation act.	12	1	Petition	297	Com. and Manuf.						
Head, Moses	Arrears of pension	21	1	Petition	260	Military Pensions	May 4, 1830	Adverse	......	Laid on table.		
Head, Moses	Relief on account of the loss of a land warrant.	31	1	Petition	764	Priv. Land Claims.						
Head, Moses	Relief on account of the loss of a land warrant.	31	2	Rep't Committee	....	....	12	Adverse	......	Laid on table.		
Head, Richard M., widow of.	Continuation of pension	23	1	Petition	525	Rev. Pensions	May 1, 1834	....	......	Discharged; laid on table.		
Head, Richard M., widow of.	Continuation of pension	27	2	Petition	685	Rev. Pensions	784	Adverse	......	Laid on table.		
Head, William	(See Reuben E. Gentry, *et al.*)	28	2	....	515							
Head, William	Indemnity for Indian depredations.	24	1	Petition	265	Indian Affairs.						
Head, William, administrator of.	Indemnity for Indian depredations.	24	2	Petition	93	Indian Affairs.						
Head, William, administrator of.	Indemnity for Indian depredations.	25	2	Petition	97	Indian Affairs	....	....	......	Discharged.		

List of private claims presented to the House of Representatives of the United States from the 1st to the 31st Congress, inclusive—Continued.

2—9

Names of claimants.	Nature or object of the claim.	Congress.	Session.	How brought before the House of Reps.	Page of journal.	To what committee of the House referred.	No. or date of the report.	Nature of the report.	No. of the bill.	How disposed of by the House of Reps.	How disposed of by the Senate.	Date of the act of Congress, and remarks.
Head or Heard, William B.	Pension for revolutionary services.	23	1	Petition	128	Rev. Pensions	Jan. 9, 1834			Discharged; laid on table.		
Headerick, Jacob	Pension for services in the war of 1812.	24	1	Resolution	437	Invalid Pensions	June 4, 1836			Discharged; laid on table.		
Headerick, Jacob	Pension for services in the war of 1812.	24	2	Resolution	147	Invalid Pensions	Mar. 2, 1837			Discharged; laid on table.		
Headerick, Jacob	Pension for services in the war of 1812.	25	2	Resolution	722	Invalid Pensions	May 11, 1838			Discharged; laid on table.		
Headerick, Jacob	Pension for services in the war of 1812.	25	3	Resolution	129	Invalid Pensions	Jan. 22, 1839			Discharged; laid on table.		
Headerick, Jacob	Pension for services in the war of 1812.	26	1	Petition	327	Invalid Pensions	552	Adverse		Laid on table.		
Headington & Co.	(See J. Riddle, *et al.*)	19	1		86							
Headly, William	Pension for revolutionary services.	22	1	Resolution	70	Rev. Pensions	25	Report and bill.	70	Passed	Indef. postp'd.	
Heady, William J	Indemnity for loss on saddles purchased for army.	30	1	Petition	379	Claims	351	Adverse		Laid on table.		
Heald, Arba	Indemnity for Indian depredations 1831.	29	2	Petition	127	Indian Affairs.						
Heald, Arba	Indemnity for Indian depredations 1831.	30	1	Memorial	571	Indian Affairs.						
Heald, Arba	Indemnity for Indian depredations 1831.	30	2	Petition	547	Indian Affairs	Feb. 28, 1849	Adverse		Laid on table.		
Heald, Nathan	For the equitable settlement of his accounts.	13	2	Petition	246					Referred to Secretary of War.		
Heald, Nathan	Credit for the amount of a draft on War department.	13	3	Petition	668	Claims				Discharged.		
Heald, Major Nathan	For admission to invalid corps when established.	14	1	Petition	347					Laid on table.		
Healy, Bethia	(See George Healy, widow of.)	28	1		435							
Healey, Eleanor	Compensation for revolutionary services of her husband.	2	1	Petition	455					Referred to Secretary of War.		
Healey, Eleanor	Compensation for revolutionary services of her husband.	2	2	Rep. of Secretary War.	696					Laid on table		Leave to withdraw, 1st sess., 3d Cong.
Healey, Eliphaz	Pension for revolutionary services.	22	1	Petition	44	Rev. Claims	Dec. 20, 1831	Report by bill.	52	Passed	Indef. postp'd.	
Healey, George, widow of.	Pension for revolutionary services.	28	1	Petition	435	Rev. Pensions	214	Report and bill	168	Passed	Passed	App'd June 17, 1844
Healey, George, widow of.	Pension for revolutionary services.	29	2	Senate bill	380	Rev. Pensions	Feb. 24, 1847	With't amend.	S. 122			
Healey, George, widow of.	Pension for revolutionary services.	30	1	Senate bill	957	Rev. Pensions			S. 155			
Healey, George, widow of.	Pension for revolutionary services.	30	2	Senate bill	119	Whole House	Feb. 2, 1849	With't amend.	S. 155	Passed with amendm't.	Passed as am'd.	App'd Feb. 19, 1849
Heap, John	Compensation for services as clerk in quartermaster's department, revolutionary war.	10	1	Petition	264	Claims.						
Heap, John	Compensation for services as clerk in quartermaster's department, revolutionary war.	10	2	Resolution	354	Claims.						
Heap, John	Compensation for services as clerk in quartermaster's department, revolutionary war.	11	2	Petition	147	Claims	Mar. 2, 1810	Adverse		Rejected.		
Heap, John	Compensation for services in revolutionary war.	20	1	Petition	311	Rev. Claims				Discharged; laid on table.		
Heaps, John, heirs of	Relief, in consideration of the death of said Heaps at the hands of a mail robber.	16	1	Resolution	345	P. Of. and P. Roads.	April 7, 1820	Report by bill.	128	Passed	Passed	App'd May 8, 1820

List of private claims presented to the House of Representatives of the United States from the 1st to the 31st Congress, inclusive—Continued.

Names of claimants.	Nature or object of the claim.	Congress.	Session.	How brought before the House of Reps.	Page of journal.	To what committee of the House referred.	No. or date of the report.	Nature of the report.	No. of the bill.	How disposed of by the House of Reps.	How disposed of by the Senate.	Date of the act of Congress, and remarks.
Heard, Benedict J.	Remuneration for property destroyed by the enemy, war of 1812	24	1	Petition	507	Claims	632	Adverse		Laid on table.		
Heard, Benedict J.	Remuneration for property destroyed by the enemy, war of 1812.	24	2	Petition	81	Claims	325	Adverse		Laid on table.		
Heard, Benedict J.	Remuneration for property destroyed by the enemy, war of 1812.	25	2	Petition	234	Claims				Discharged.		
Heard, Benedict J.	Remuneration for property destroyed by the enemy, war of 1812.	25	3	Petition	121	Claims	65	Adverse		Laid on table.		
Heard, Benedict J.	Remuneration for property destroyed by the enemy, war of 1812.	30	1	Petition	724	Claims	753	Adverse		Laid on table.		
Heard, Benedict J.	Remuneration for property destroyed by the enemy, war of 1812.	30	2	Petition	114	Claims.						
Heard, Edward J.	Authority to purchase a tract of land in Louisiana.	28	2	Petition	112	Priv. Land Claims.				Discharged; laid on table.		
Heard, James	Arrears of pension for services as a revolutionary officer.	12	1	Petition	99	Claims				Leave to withdraw.		
Heard, James	Pension for services as lieutenant of dragoons, revolutionary war.	14	2	Resolution	149	Pens. & Rev. Cl'ms.	Jan. 29, 1817	Report by bill.	91	Passed	Passed, with amendment.	App'd March 3, 1817
Heard, James	Reimbursement of money deposited with paymaster general.	15	2	Petition	20	Pens. & Rev. Cl'ms.	Nov. 23, 1818	Adverse		Rejected.		
Heard, John, sureties of	Release from liability	9	2	Petition	542	Ways and Means.						
Heard, John	Release from imprisonment on a debt due United States.	10	2	Petition	366	Select	Dec. 30, 1808	Report and bill.	130			
Heard, John	Release from imprisonment on a debt due United States.	11	1	Petition	27	Select	June 6, 1809	Report and bill.	9	Passed	Passed	App'd June 26, 1809
Heard, John	Remission of a part of a tax on a still.	14	2	Petition	280	Ways and Means.	Jan. 25, 1817	Report by bill.	72			
Heard, John, jr.	(See Amasa Davis, assignee of)	19	2		44							
Heard, Richard, heir of	Pension for revolutionary services.	29	1	Memorial	319	Rev. Pensions.						
Heard, Richard, heir of	Pension for revolutionary services.	29	2	Memorial	146	Rev. Pensions.						
Heard, Simon	Pension	22	1	Petition	329	Rev. Pensions.						
Heard, Stephen, *et al.*	(See John Donaldson, representatives of, *et al.*)	15	1		184							
Hearn, William	Release from imprisonment as bail for J. Perry.	9	2	Petition	473	Select	Dec. 23, 1806	Report by bill.	154	Passed	Passed, with amendment.	App'd Feb. 10, 1807
Hearst, Thomas and John.	Right of pre-emption to lands on which they have made improvements.	24	1	Petition	435	Public Lands.						
Heartt, Benjamin	Release from imprisonment on a judgment in favor of United States.	16	1	Petition	393	Ways and Means.				Discharged; leave to withdraw.		
Heartt, Benjamin	Indemnity for imprisonment on an unjust judgment.	25	3	Petition	122	Judiciary				Discharged; laid on table.		
Heartt, Benjamin	Indemnity for imprisonment on an unjust judgment.	28	1	Petition	223	Judiciary	250	Adverse		Laid on table.		
Heath, Asahel	Land in lieu of a Virginia military warrant.	17	2	Petition	100	Priv. Land Claims.	Jan. 7, 1823	Adverse		Rejected.		
Heath, Elizabeth	Continuation of the pension of her deceased husband.	28	1	Petition	839	Whole House.						
Heath, Henry	Compensation for a team impressed into public service.	16	2	Petition	145	Claims				Discharged; laid on table.		
Heath, James, heir of	Compensation for depredations of Cherokee Indians.	28	1	Petition	724	Indian Affairs.						

List of private claims presented to the House of Representatives of the United States from the 1st to the 31st Congress, inclusive—Continued.

Names of claimants.	Nature or object of the claim.	Congress.	Session.	How brought before the House of Reps.	Page of journal.	To what committee of the House referred.	No. or date of the report.	Nature of the report.	No. of the bill.	How disposed of by the House of Reps.	How disposed of by the Senate.	Date of the act of Congress, and remarks.
Heath, James, heir of	Compensation for depredations of Cherokee Indians.	29	1	Petition	269	Indian Affairs.						
Heath, James	Pension	17	1	Petition	31	Rev. Pensions				Discharged; laid on table.		
Heath, John	Invalid pension	3	1	Rep. of Secretary War.	131	Select	May 26, 1794	Res. to refer to Sec. War.	12	Passed	Passed	App'd June 9, 1794
Heath, John G. & Robert A.	(See Reuben E. Gentry, & others)	25	2									
Heath, Nathaniel H	(See Daniel Renner)	13	3		480							
Heath, Phineas	Pension for revolutionary services.	11	3	Petition	490					Referred to Secretary War.		
Heath & Renner	(See Daniel Renner)	18	1		345							
Heath, Robert A. & John G.	Right of pre-emption to lands confirmed to P. Choteau.	20	1	Petition	59	Indian Affairs.						
Heath, Robert A. & John G.	Right of pre-emption to lands confirmed to P. Choteau.	24	1	Petition	796	Whole House		General bill	S. 61			
Heath, Robert A. & John G.	Right of pre-emption to lands confirmed to P. Choteau.	24	2	Petition	160	Indian Affairs.						
Heath, Robert A. & John G.	Right of pre-emption to lands confirmed to P. Choteau.	25	2	Petition	97	Indian Affairs				Discharged.		
Heath, Robert A. & John G.	Right of pre-emption to lands confirmed to P. Choteau.	25	2	Petition	193	Priv. Land Claims.				Discharged.		
Heath, Sarah	(See widow of Calvin Gardner)	25	2	Petition	268	Invalid Pensions				Discharged; laid on table.		
Heathcote, John	Permission to import merchandise ordered prior to non importation act.	12	1	Petition	88	Com. and Manuf.		General bill	46			
Heatherly, Benjamin	Compensation for revolutionary services.	31	1	Petition	1003	Claims.						
Heaton, James, widow of.	Relief in consideration of the revolutionary services of husband.	19	1	Petition	565	Military Pensions.				Discharged; laid on table.		
Heaton, James	Pension	19	2	Petition	111	Military Pensions.						
Heaton, Orange, & J. Hubbard.	Reimbursement of duty paid on cattle from Canada.	18	1	Petition	30	Ways and Means.	Dec. 17, 1823	Adverse.		Rejected.		
Heaton, Robert	Exemption from duty on imported horses and cattle.	2	2	Petition	668	Select	Jan. 29, 1793	Favorable with resolution.		Laid on table.		
Heaton, Robert	Compensation for revolutionary services.	21	1	Petition	618	Rev. Claims.				Discharged; laid on table.		
Heaton, William	(See William H. Bedford, agent.)	28	1		262							
Hebb, John, widow of	Compensation for duty performed by husband in revolutionary war.	26	1	Petition	335	Claims.						
Hebb, John, widow of	Compensation for duty performed by husband in revolutionary war.	26	2	Petition	79	Claims	246	Adverse		Laid on table.		
Hebert, Hildebrand Oakes, (alien.)	Patent for improved vapor bath	7	2	Petition	285	Select.						
Hebert, Ursin	Confirmation of title and reimbursement of money erroneously paid for land.	24	1	Petition	121	Priv. Land Claims.				Discharged; laid on table.		
Hebert, Ursin	Confirmation of title and reimbursement of money erroneously paid for land.	24	2	Resolution	111	Claims	Dec. 23, 1836	Report by bill.	767			

List of private claims presented to the House of Representatives of the United States from the 1st to the 31st Congress, inclusive—Continued.

Names of claimants.	Nature or object of the claim.	Congress.	Session.	How brought before the House of Reps.	Page of journal.	To what committee of the House referred.	No. or date of the report.	Nature of the report.	No. of the bill.	How disposed of by the House of Reps.	How disposed of by the Senate.	Date of the act of Congress, and remarks.
Hebert, Ursin	Confirmation of title and reimbursement of money erroneously paid for land.	25	2	Petition	374	Priv. Land Claims.	870	Adverse	......	Laid on table.		
Hebert, Valentine	Permission to purchase a certain tract of land in Louisiana.	26	1	Petition	935	Public Lands.						
Hebit, William	(See Henry Duchuquette, *et al.*)	24	1	....	739							
Hebner, Frederick	Compensation for powder furnished revolutionary army.	4	2	Petition	631	Claims	Jan. 16, 1797	Adverse.	......	Laid on table.		
Hebron, William	Invalid pension	3	1	Rep. of Secretary War.	131	Select	May 26, 1794	Joint resoluton to refer Sec. War.	J. R. 12	Passed	Passed	App'd June 9, 1794
Heck, John	(See Nicholas Kran, sureties of.)	18	1	....	153							
Heckelbander, Joseph	(See Joseph Hackelbarder.)	24	2	....	93							
Hedden, Amos, assignees of.	Change of location of bounty land	23	2	Petition	352	Priv. Land Claims.	97	Report and bill.	722	Referred to Committee Whole House.		
Hedden, Amos, assignees of.	Change of location of bounty land	29	2	Petition	316	Priv. Land Claims.						
Hedden, Amos, assignees of.	Change of location of bounty land	30	1	Petition	279	Public Lands	324	Report and bill.	300	Passed.		
Hedden, James	(See Albert Pawling, *et al.*)	22	1	....	72							
Hedden, Zadock	(See Cary Dunn, jr., *et al.*)	21	2	....	74							
Heddinger, John	Payment of a loan office certificate.	15	1	Petition	172	Pens. & Rev. Cl'ms.	....	....	......	Discharged; leave to withdraw.		
Hedgcock, Thomas	Pension for revolutionary services.	25	2	Petition	271	Rev. Pensions						
Hedge, B	Indemnity for French spoliations prior to 1800.	26	1	Memorial	182	Foreign Affairs	343	Favorable; bill	319	Referred to Committee Whole House.		
Hedge, B., administrator of	Indemnity for French spoliations prior to 1800.	29	1	Memorial	75	Foreign Affairs.						
Hedge, Isaac L., & T	Fishing bounty withheld for informality.	19	1	Petition	222	Commerce.	....	....	......	Discharged; laid on table.		
Hedge, James	Indemnity for time lost at Quarantine, North Carolina.	19	1	Petition	248	Commerce.	82	Adverse.	......	Rejected.		
Hedger, Stephen	Pension for revolutionary services.	28	1	Petition	527	Rev. Pensions.						
Hedger, William	Pension	22	1	Petition	72	Invalid Pensions.						
Hedges, Elijah	Pension for wounds received in Indian expedition in 1791.	3	1	Petition	111	Select	May 17, 1794	Favorable	......	Laid on table.		
Hedges, Elijah	Pension for wounds received in Indian expedition in 1791.	4	1	Rep't Committee	384	Claims.						
Hedges, Elijah	Pension for wounds received in Indian expedition in 1791.	4	2	Report and res.	614	Claims	Jan. 24, 1797	Adverse	......	Rejected.		
Hedges, E. W	Payment due from Ottaway Indians	29	1	Memorial	160	Indian Affairs	287	Adverse.	......	Laid on table.		
Hedges, Josiah	Confirmation of claim to land in Ohio.	22	1	Documents	263	Public Lands	304	Report and bill.	381			
Hedges, Nicholas	Compensation for services as crier of circuit court, Dist. of Columbia.	24	1	Petition	534	Claims	576	Report and bill	561			
Hedges, Nicholas	Compensation for services as crier of circuit court, Dist. of Columbia.	25	2	Petition	36	Claims	33	Report and bill.	45	Passed	Rejected.	
Hedges, Nicholas	Compensation for services as crier of circuit court, Dist. of Columbia.	26	1	Petition	176	Claims	10	Report and bill.	29	Passed	Indef. postp'd.	
Hedges, Nicholas	Compensation for services as crier of circuit court, Dist. of Columbia.	26	2	House bill	191	Claims	11	Favorable	549	Referred to Committee Whole House.		

List of private claims presented to the House of Representatives of the United States from the 1st to the 31st Congress, inclusive—Continued.

Names of claimants.	Nature or object of the claim.	Congress.	Session.	How brought before the House of Reps.	Page of journal.	To what committee of the House referred.	No. or date of the report.	Nature of the report.	No. of the bill.	How disposed of by the House of Reps.	How disposed of by the Senate.	Date of the act of Congress, and remarks.
Hedges, W. B	(See trustees of school lands, Mercer county, Ohio.	28	1		516							
Hedrick, Peter	Pension for revolutionary services.	25	2	Resolution	213	Rev. Pensions	706	Report and bill.	680	Passed		
Hedrick, Peter	Pension for revolutionary services.	25	3	Resolution	88	Rev. Pensions	250	Report and bill.	1121			
Hedrick, Peter	Pension for revolutionary services.	26	1	Petition	172	Rev. Pensions	165	Report and bill.	175	Passed	Indef. postp'd.	
Heems, Charles	New register for brig Solitaire	3	2	Petition	288	Select	Jan. 17, 1794	Favorable		Rejected.		
Heerman, Lewis	(See widow of Stephen Decatur, and others.)	20	1		295		201		S. 50			
Heffernan, Ann	(See widow of John Davidson)	26	1		624							
Hefferman, Hugh	Pension	14	1	Petition	179	Pens. & Rev. Cl'ms.				Discharged; laid on table.		
Hefferman, Stephen, *et al.*	Bounty on fishing sloop Lydia	5	2	Petition	324	Com. and Manuf.						
Hege, Peter, or Hegy	Pension for revolutionary services.	24	2	Petition	216	Rev. Pensions				Discharged; laid on table.		
Hegeman, Joseph W	Right of pre emption to a certain tract of land.	23	1	Petition	138	Priv. Land Claims.				Discharged; laid no table.		
Hegeman, Joseph W	Right of pre-emption to a certain tract of land.	23	2	Petition	212	Priv. Land Claims.	Feb. 3, 1835	Adverse		Laid on table.		
Hegins, Charles	Credit for $2,000 paid by Secretary of War to J. Irwin.	16	1	Petition	205	Claims				Discharged; leave to withdraw.		
Hegins, Charles, widow of.	Credit for $2,000 paid by Secretary of War to J. Irwin.	18	1	Petition	236	Claims.						
Hegins, Pentland & Steele	Remission of duty on Canada flour imported for United States army.	14	2	Petition and rep. of Secretary of War.	32 and 67	Claims.				Discharged; laid on table.		
Hegins, Pentland & Steele	Remission of duty on Canada flour imported for United States army.	15	1	Petition	90	Ways and Means.	Jan. 23, 1818	Adverse		Rejected.		
Heidel, Leonard	Additional compensation as employee in Treasury Department.	4	1	Petition	486	Claims.						
Heidel, Leonard	Additional compensation as employee in Treasury Department.	4	2	Petition	614	Claims.						
Heidelbach, John H	Indemnity for goods destroyed by the enemy, war of 1812.	31	2	Petition	335	Claims.						
Heilbronn, Adolph, and Samuel B. Barrell.	For a patent	20	2	House bill	291	Judiciary	Feb. 16, 1829	With't amend.	442	Passed.		
Heilbronn, Adolph	Reimbursement of extra duties paid on wool.	21	1	Petition	297	Ways and Means.				Discharged; laid on table.		
Heilbronn, Adolph	Reimbursement of extra duties paid on wool.	22	1	Petition	41	Ways and Means.						
Heileman, Col. Julius, widow of.	Relief, in consideration of services in Florida war.	24	2	Memorial	110	Military Affairs	225	Report and bill.	931	Referred to Committee Whole House.		
Heileman, Col. Julius, widow of.	Relief, in consideration of services in Florida war.	25	2	Memorial	41	Military Affairs	501	Report and bill.	504	Referred to Committee Whole House.		
Heileman, Col. Julius, widow of.	Relief, in consideration of services in Florida war.	25	2	Senate bill	652	Military Affairs	April 13, 1838	With't amend.	S. 149	Passed		App'd June 22, 1838
Heileman, Col. Julius, widow of.	Relief in consideration of services in Florida war.	27	2	Memorial	107	Military Affairs	353	Adverse		Laid on table.		
Heim, David	Release from a judgment for tax on distillery.	16	2	Petition	200	Ways and Means.				Discharged; laid on table.		
Heim, David	Release from a judgment for tax on distillery.	18	1	Petition	197	Ways and Means.	Feb. 18, 1834	Adverse		Rejected.		

List of private claims presented to the House of Representatives of the United States from the 1st to the 31st Congress, inclusive—Continued.

Names of claimants.	Nature or object of the claim.	Congress.	Session.	How brought before the House of Reps.	Page of journal.	To what committee of the House referred.	No. or date of the report.	Nature of the report.	No. of the bill.	How disposed of by the House of Reps.	How disposed of by the Senate.	Date of the act of Congress, and remarks.
Heim, David	Reimbursement of money paid on a judgment in favor of United States.	19	1	Petition	93	Ways and Means	Jan. 23, 1826	Adverse		Laid on table.		
Heiman, William	Pension for wounds, &c., war with Mexico.	31	1	Petition	383	Invalid Pensions.						
Heineman, F. W	(See administrator of John Jackson.)	28	1		645							
Heiskell, H. L	Indemnity for loss of a servant and horse, Seminole war.	24	1	Petition	840	Claims	746	Adverse		Laid on table.		
Heiskell, John	(See Cyrus W. Murray, surety of.)	17	2		231							
Heisler, Peter	(See Ezekiel Malthus, sureties of.)	2	1		466							
Heisley, Fred'k Augustus	Pension for wounds received in war of 1812.	27	1	Petition	107	Invalid Pensions.						
Heisley, Fred'k Augustus	Arrears of pension	31	2	Petition	36	Invalid Pensions.						
Heller, Jacob	Pension for revolutionary services.	22	1	Petition	44	Rev. Claims.						
Heller, Jacob	Compensation for revolutionary services.	2	1	Petition	442					Referred to Secretary War.		
Helm, John D	Pension	24	2	Petition	109	Invalid Pensions	Dec. 23, 1836	Adverse		Laid on table.		
Holm, John D	Pension	25	2	Petition	74	Select				Discharged; laid on table.		Leave to withdraw, 1st sess. 31st Cong.
Helm, Lina T	Equitable adjustment of his accounts.	12	2	Petition	591	Claims	Feb. 12, 1813	Report by bill.	257			
Helm, Lina T	Pension	19	1	Petition	203	Military Pensions	164	Adverse		Recommitted.		
Helm, Lina T	Pension	19	2	Petition	31	Military Pensions	Dec. 22, 1826	General bill	314	Passed	Passed	App'd March 3, 1827
Helm, Samuel, agent of	Increase of pension	27	2	Deposition	374	Rev. Pensions	784	Adverse		Laid on table.		
Helm, Thomas, heirs of	Commutation pay for revolutionary services.	23	1	Petition	494	Rev. Claims.						
Helm, Thomas, heirs of	Commutation pay for revolutionary services.	23	2	Petition	84	Rev. Claims.						
Helm, Thomas, heirs of	Commutation pay for revolutionary services.	24	1	Petition	63	Rev. Claims	842	Adverse		Laid on table.		
Helm, Thomas, heirs of	Commutation pay for revolutionary services.	25	3	Petition	457	Rev. Claims				Discharged.		
Helm, Thomas, heirs of	Commutation pay for revolutionary services.	26	1	Petition	164	Rev. Claims.						
Helm, Thomas, heirs of	Commutation pay for revolutionary services.	27	2	Petition	61	Rev. Claims	381	Adverse		Laid on table.		
Helm, William and Samuel	Remission of duty on rum	1	2	Petition	151					Laid on table.		
Helmbold, George	Land bounty due him as a soldier in United States army.	14	1	Petition	366					Laid on table.		
Helme, Simon	Pension	21	2	Petition	336	Military Pensions.						
Helme, Simon	Pension	22	1	Petition	415	Invalid Pensions				Discharged; laid on table.		
Helmer, John G	Invalid pension	3	1	Rep. of Secretary War.	131	Select	May 26, 1794	Res. to refer to Sec. War.	12	Passed	Passed	App'd June 9, 1794
Helmer, John G	Invalid pension	3	2	Rep. of Secretary War.	350	Claims				Discharged; laid on table.		
Helmer, John G	Invalid pension	4	1	Rep of Secretary War.	445	Claims	Mar. 4, 1796	Res. to refer to Sec. War.	16	Passed	Passed	App'd April 17, 1796
Helmes, Michael	Indemnity for property destroyed by the enemy, war of 1812.	1	2	Petition	148	Claims				Discharged; laid on table.		
Helmes, Michael	(See John Waterhouse and M. Helmes.)	15	2		148							

List of private claims presented to the House of Representatives of the United States from the 1st to the 31st Congress, inclusive—Continued.

Names of claimants.	Nature or object of the claim.	Congress.	Session.	How brought before the House of Reps.	Page of journal.	To what committee of the House referred.	No. or date of the report.	Nature of the report.	No. of the bill.	How disposed of by the House of Reps.	How disposed of by the Senate.	Date of the act of Congress, and remarks.
Helphinstine, Peter	Compensation for provisions furnished revolutionary army.	4	1	Petition	426	Claims	May 7, 1796	Adverse	......	Laid on table.		
Helphinstine, Peter	Compensation for provisions furnished revolutionary army.	4	2	Petition	615	Claims	......	......	......	Leave to withdraw.		
Helphinstine, Major Peter, heirs of.	Pay and bounty land for revolutionary services.	15	1	Petition	271	Pens. & Rev. Cl'ms	Mar. 14, 1818	Adverse	......	Rejected.		
Helphinstine, Major Peter, heirs of.	Commutation pay for revolutionary services.	22	1	Petition	175	Rev. Claims.						
Helphinstine, Major Peter, heirs of.	Half-pay for revolutionary services.	23	1	Petition	243	Rev. Claims.						
Helphinstine, Major Peter, heirs of.	Half-pay for revolutionary services.	23	2	Petition	84	Rev. Claims.						
Helphinstine, Major Peter, heirs of.	Half pay for revolutionary services.	24	1	Petition	103	Rev. Claims	707	Report by bill.	660			
Helphinstine, Major Peter, heirs of.	Half-pay for revolutionary services.	25	2	Petition	40	Rev. Claims	193	Report and bill.	219			
Helphinstine, Major Peter, heirs of.	Half-pay for revolutionary services.	25	2	Senate bill	197	Rev. Claims	Jan. 11, 1838	With amend.	S. 59	Passed without amend.	......	App'd June 12, 1838
Helton, Peter	(See Peter Hilton, or Helton)	31	1	......	840							
Hembaugh, Jonas	Reimbursement of certain moneys	28	1	Petition	433	Public Lands.						
Hemburn, John M	Increase of salary as clerk in War Department.	24	1	Petition	200	Military Affairs	......	......	......	Discharged; laid on table.		
Hemburn, John M	Increase of salary as clerk in War Department.	21	1	Senate bill	639	Ways and Means	June 28, 1836	With't amend.	S. 101	Referred to Committee Whole House.		
Hemenway, Stephen P	Arrears and increase of pension	28	1	Petition	143	Invalid Pensions	173	Adverse	......	Laid on table.		
Hemmenway, Peter	Invalid pension	3	1	Rep. of Secretary War.	131	elect	May 26, 1794	Jt. res to refer to Sec. War.	12	Passed	Passed	App'd June 9, 1794
Hemmenway, Peter	Invalid pension	4	1	Report Secretary War.	455	Claims	Mar. 4, 1796	Favorable; bill ordered.	156	Passed	Passed	App'd April 20, 1796
Hemmenway, Peter	Increase of pension	1	3	House bill	601	Whole House	March 2, 1811	Favorable	218	Passed	Passed	App'd March 3, 1811
Hemmenway, Ruth	Continuation of the pension of her husband.	28	1	Petition	850	Rev. Pensions.						
Heminway, Truman	(See William Wilcox, *et al.*)	26	1	......	297							
Hemkin, Bernard	Confirmation of title to land in Red River district, Louisiana.	28	1	Petition	76	Priv. Land Claims.	78	Report and bill.	98			
Hemphill, Samuel, executor of.	Compensation or services in Georgia militia, 1794.	25	3	Documents	125	Rev. Claims	......	......	......	Discharged.		
Hemphill, Samuel, executor of.	Compensation for services in Georgia militia, 1794.	26	1	Petition	166	Rev. Claims.						
Hempstead, Edward, heirs of.	Confirmation of title to land in Missouri Territory.	15	1	Petition	284	Priv. Land Claims.	......	......	......	Discharged; laid on table.		
Hempstead, Edward, heirs of.	Confirmation of title to land in Missouri Territory.	16	1	Petition	71	Priv. Land Claims.	......	......	......	Discharged; laid on table.		
Hempstead, Edward, heirs of.	Confirmation of title to land in Missouri Territory.	17	1	Petition	54	Public Lands.						
Hempstead, Edward, heirs of.	Confirmation of title to land in Missouri Territory.	18	1	Petition	54	Public Lands.						
Hempstead, Josiah	Indemnity for French spoliations prior to 1800.	26	1	Memorial	182	Foreign Affairs	343	Favorable; bill	319	Referred to Committee Whole House.		
Hempstead, Josiah, executors of.	Indemnity for French spoliations prior to 1800.	29	2	Memorial	53	Foreign Affairs.						
Hempstead, Nathaniel	Pension for revolutionary services.	23	1	Petition	523	Rev. Pensions	April 30, 1834	......	......	Disch'd; laid on table.		

List of private claims presented to the House of Representatives of the United States from the 1st to the 31st Congress, inclusive—Continued.

Names of claimants.	Nature or object of the claim.	Congress.	Session.	How brought before the House of Reps.	Page of journal.	To what committee of the House referred.	No. or date of the report	Nature of the report.	No. of the bill.	How disposed of by the House of Reps.	How disposed of by the Senate.	Date of the act of Congress, and remarks.
Hempstead, Samuel B	Invalid pension	3	2	Report of Secretary of War.	27	Claims	Mar. 3, 1795			Discharged; laid on table.		
Hempstead, Samuel B	Invalid pension	4	1	Rep. of Secretary War.	445	Claims	Mar. 4, 1796	Jt. res. to refer to Sec. War.	16	Passed	Passed	App'd April 20, 1796
Hempstead, Stephen	Increase of pension	11	2	House bill	283	Whole House	Mar. 24, 1810	Favorable	107	Passed	Passed	App'd April 27, 1810
Henderson, Archibald	Pension	21	2	Resolution	86	Military Pensions	Jan. 26, 1831			Discharged; laid on table.		
Henderson, Bennett	Compensation for services as commissary of issues, revolutionary war.	4	1	Rep. of Secretary Treasury.	388	Claims	74	Adverse		Laid on table.		
Henderson, David	Compensation for services and wounds revolutionary war.	2	1	Petition	462					Referred to Secretary of War.		
Henderson, David	Compensation for services and wounds revolutionary war.	2	2	Rep. of Secretary War.	725					Laid on table.		
Henderson, David, jr., and William, Cairns.	Reimbursement of a deposite embezzled by a clerk of the district court.	17	1	Petition	416	Judiciary				Discharged; laid on table.		
Henderson, Dubar	(See John Burton.)	21	1		39							
Henderson, Ferguson, and Gibson, executors and attorney of.	Indemnity for French spoliations prior to 1800.	26	1	Memorial	182	Foreign Affairs	319	Favorable; bill	319	Referred to Committee Whole House.		
Henderson, Francis	(See John Laurens, heirs of.)	14	2		347							
Henderson, George	Confirmation of title to land in Missouri.	15	2	Petition	193	Priv. Land Claims				Discharged; laid on table.		
Henderson, George	Confirmation of title to land in Missouri.	17	1	Petition	54	Public Lands				Discharged; laid on table.		
Henderson, George	Confirmation of title to land in Missouri.	18	1	Petition	54	Public Lands.						
Henderson, Gustavus, representative of.	Compensation for revolutionary services as surgeon's mate.	2	1	Petition	554					Referred to Secretary War.		
Henderson, Gustavus, representative of.	Compensation for revolutionary services as surgeon's mate.	2	2	Rep. of Secretary War.	696					Laid on table.		
Henderson, Hendrick	(See James Crawford.)											
Henderson, John	(See David M. Hughes)	26			351							
Henderson, John	Compensation for revolutionary services.	1	3	Petition	375					Referred to Secretary War.		
Henderson, Joseph	Compensation for services as paymaster United States navy.	1	2	Petition	189					Referred to Secretary Treasury.		
Henderson, Joseph	Compensation for services as paymaster United States navy.	2	1	Rep. of Secretary Treasury.	592					Laid on table.		
Henderson, Joseph	Compensation for services as paymaster United States navy.	2	2	Petition and rep't Sec. Treasury.	622	Select	Jan. 2, 1793	Report and bill	222	Passed	Passed	App'd Feb. 22, 1793
Henderson, Joseph	Pension for wounds received in war of 1812.	13	3	Petition	700	Pens. & Rev. Cl'ms.						
Henderson, Joseph	Pension for wounds received in war of 1812.	14	1	Petition	284	Pens. & Rev. Cl'ms.	April 11, 1816	Report and bill	171	Passed	Passed, with amendment.	App'd April 3, 1816
Henderson, Joseph	Pension	16	1	Petition	381	Pens. & Rev. Cl'ms.				Disch'd; laid on table.		
Henderson, Joseph	Pension	14	1	Petition	516	Pens. & Rev. Cl'ms.				Discharged; laid on table.		
Henderson, Joseph	Bounty land for the military service of an apprentice	15	2	Petition	223	Military Affairs				Discharged; laid on table.		
Henderson, Joseph	Relief in relation to certain lost papers.	24	1	Petition	58	Public Lands	202	Favorable; bill	205	Referred to Committee Whole House.		

List of private claims presented to the House of Representatives of the United States from the 1st to the 31st Congress, inclusive—Continued.

Names of claimants.	Nature or object of the claim.	Congress.	Session.	How brought before the House of Reps.	Page of journal.	To what committee of the House referred.	No. or date of the report.	Nature of the report.	No. of the bill.	How disposed of by the House of Reps.	How disposed of by the Senate.	Date of the act of Congress, and remarks.
Henderson, Joseph	Relief in relation to certain lost papers.	24	2	House bill	62	Whole House			205			
Henderson, Joseph	Relief in relation to certain lost papers.	25	2	House bill	153	Public Lands	301	Report and bill	237			
Henderson, Joseph	Exchange of an entry of land	25	3	House bill	377	Whole House			237	Passed	Passed	App'd March 2, 1839
Henderson, Magor or Major	Compensation for horses lost in Seminole war.	17	1	Petition	96	Claims				Discharged; laid on table.		
Henderson, Magor or Major	Compensation for horses lost Seminole war.		1	Petition	60	Pens. & Rev. Cl'ms.						
Henderson, Margaret, heirs of.	(See widow of Ja[illegible] Armstrong Wilson.)	29	2		162							
Henderson, Pleasant, *et al.*	Compensation for certain lands conveyed to Indians.	6	2	Memorial	747	Select	Feb. 24, 1801	Rep. and res.: adverse.				
Henderson, Pleasant, *et al.*	Confirmation of title to certain lands in North Carolina.	7	1	Petition	55	Select.						
Henderson, Pleasant, *et al.*	Confirmation of title to certain lands in North Carolina.	8	1	Petition	459	Select.						
Henderson, Raymond A.	Compensation for orange trees destroyed by Indians.	25	2	Petition	575	Claims				Discharged.		
Henderson, Raymond A.	Compensation for orange trees destroyed by Indians.	26	1	Petition	169	Claims	45	Adverse		Laid on table.		
Henderson, Raymond A.	Compensation for orange trees destroyed by Indians.	26	2	Petition	80	Claims	66	Adverse		Laid on table.		
Henderson, Richard & Co.	Indemnity for land purchased from the Cherokees.	3	2	Memorial	285	Select.						
Henderson, Robert	Increase of compensation for transportation of the mail.	8	2	Memorial	74							
				Rep't of Postmaster General.	79	Whole House	Jan. 14, 1805	Favorable; bill ordered.	33	Passed	Passed	App'd Feb. 14, 1805
Henderson, Sampson	Compensation for wounds received in revolutionary war.	7	2	Petition	262	Claims	Feb. 17, 1803	Adverse		Leave to withdraw.		
Henderson, Stephen	(See William Nott, *et al.*)	17	1		374							
Henderson, Stephen, and Elliot Hackley.	Confirmation of title, or right of pre-emption, to land in Missouri.	14	1	Petition	361	Public Lands				Discharged; laid on table.		
Henderson, Stephen, and Elliot Hackley.	Confirmation of title, or right of pre-emption, to land in Missouri.	14	2	Petition	50	Priv. Land Claims.	Jan. 16, 1817			Discharged; leave to withdraw.		
Henderson, Stephen, and Elliot Hackley.	Confirmation of title, or right of pre-emption, to land in Missouri.	15	2	Petition	55	Priv. Land Claims.				Laid on table.		
Henderson, Stephen	Right of pre-emption to a tract of land in Missouri.	17	1	Petition	40	Priv. Land Claims.	80	Adverse		Referred to Committee Whole House.		
Henderson, Stephen	Right of pre-emption to a tract of land in Missouri.	17	2	Petition	264					Leave to withdraw.		
Henderson, Thomas	(See Turk and Henderson)	16	1		52							
Henderson, William	Payment of certain State bills of credit.	4	1	Rep. of Secretary Treasury.	388		Feb. 26, 1798			Referred to Committee Whole House.		
Henderson, William	Payment of certain State bills of credit.	5	2	Memorial	202	Claims.						
Henderson, William	Indemnity for property destroyed by the enemy, war of 1812.	15	1	Petition	27	Claims	Mar. 6, 1818	Adverse		Referred to Committee Whole House.		
Hendereon, William	Indemnity for property destroyed by the enemy, war of 1812.	15	2	Rep't Committee	76	Claims	Jan. 6, 1819	Adverse		Referred to Committee Whole House.		

List of private claims presented to the House of Representatives of the United States from the 1st to the 31st Congress, *inclusive*—Continued.

Names of claimants.	Nature or object of the claim.	Congress.	Session.	How brought before the House of Reps.	Page of journal.	To what committee of the House referred.	No. or date of the report.	Nature of the report.	No. of the bill.	How disposed of by the House of Reps.	How disposed of by the Senate.	Date of the act of Congress, and remarks.
Henderson, William	Indemnity for property destroyed by the enemy, war of 1812.	16	1	Petition	28	Claims	19	Adverse		Rejected.		
Henderson, William	Indemnity for property destroyed by the enemy, war of 1812.	17	1	Petition	47,	Claims	5	Adverse		Recommitted.		
					163	Claims under instructions.	Jan. 23, 1822	Report by bill.	56	Passed	Passed	App'd May 7, 1822
Henderson, William	Right of pre-emption to a section of land.	24	1	Petition	634	Public Lands.						
Henderson, William	Pension for services in the war of 1812.	28	1	Petition	276	Invalid Pensions	275	Adverse		Laid on table.		
Hendley, Elkanah	Arrears and increase of pension	23	1	Petition	155	Invalid Pensions				Laid on table.		
Hendley, Richard	Compensation for keeping guard at Post Office.	25	2	Petition	731	P. Of. & P. Roads.	May 11, 1838	Report by bill.	769	Referred to Committee Whole House.		
Hendley, Richard	Compensation for keeping guard at Post Office.	25	3	House bill	431	Whole House			769	Passed	Passed	App'd March 3, 1839
Hendrey, Samuel	Pension	15	1	Petition	23	Pens. & Rev. Cl'ms.						
Hendrey, Samuel	Compensation for services rendered Gen. Perkins in 1812.	25	3	Petition	121	Claims.						
Hendrick, (Stockbridge Indian)	Remuneration for expenses of visit to the capital.	24	2	Appropriat'n bill.	127	Whole House		With amend's.	776	Passed	Passed	App'd March 3, 1837
Hendrick, Harmon	Reimbursement of duties paid on copper.	11	3	Petition	565	Com. and Manuf.						
Hendrick, Harmon	Reimbursement of duties paid on copper.	12	1	Petition	22	Com. and Manuf.				Discharged; leave to withdraw.		
Hendrick, Harmon	Reimbursement of duties paid on copper.	15	2	Petition	37	Ways and Means	Nov. 30, 1818	Report by bill.	207			
Hendrick, Harmon	Reimbursement of duties paid on copper.	16	1	Petition	36	Ways and Means	Dec. 13, 1819	Report by bill.	3	Passed	Passed	App'd Feb. 18, 1820
Hendricks, Benjamin	Invalid pension	4	1	Rep. of Secretary War.	479	Claims.						
Hendricks, David	Bounty on fishing vessel "Packet"	15	1	Petition	156	Com. and Manuf.				Discharged; laid on table.		
Hendricks, David	Pension for services as a revolutionary soldier.	20	1	Resolution	413	Military Pensions	April 29, 1828	Report by bill.	283	Passed.		
Hendricks, David	Pension for services as a revolutionary soldier.	20	2	Petition	55	Whole House	Dec. 12, 1828	General bill	311	Passed	Laid on table.	
Hendricks, David	Pension for services as a revolutionary.	21	1	Petition	47	Military Pensions	Jan. 5, 1830	General bill	72	Passed	Passed, with amendment.	App'd May 20, 1830
Hendricks, George	Pension	14	2	Resolution	209	Pens. & Rev. Cl'ms.	Jan. 29, 1817	Report by bill.	91	Passed	Passed, with amendment.	App'd March 3, 1817
Hendricks, John M.	Remission of part of the tax on a still.	14	2	Petition	141	Ways and Means	Jan. 25, 1817	Report by bill.	72			
Hendricks, William	Invalid pension	13	2	Petition	291	Pens. & Rev. Cl'ms.	Mar. 18, 1814	Report not extant.		Referred to Committee Whole House.		
Hendricks, William	Invalid pension	13	3	Petition	470	Pens. & Rev. Cl'ms.						
Hendricks, Wm., heirs of.	Pension for revolutionary services.	24	1	Petition	203	Rev. Claims	334	Report and bill	349			
Hendricks, Wm., heirs of.	Pension for revolutionary services.	25	2	Petition	39	Rev. Claims	194	Report and bill.	220	Passed	Adverse report.	
Hendricks, Wm., heirs of.	Pension for revolutionary services.	26	1	Petition	165	Rev. Claims.						
Hendricks, William	(See represent's of Robert Leckie.)	26	1		175							
Hendrickson, Henderson, consignee of.	Permission for vessel to sail which had cleared before embargo act was known.	3	1	Petition	131	Com. and Manuf.						
Hendrickson, Margaret	Extension of the pension laws	26	1	Petition	830	Rev. Pensions				Disch'd; laid on table.		

List of private claims presented to the House of Representatives of the United States from the 1st to the 31st Congress, inclusive—Continued.

Names of claimants.	Nature or object of the claim.	Congress.	Session.	How brought before the House of Reps.	Page of journal.	To what committee of the House referred.	No. or date of the report.	Nature of the report.	No. of the bill.	How disposed of by the House of Reps.	How disposed of by the Senate.	Date of the act of Congress, and remarks.
Hendrickson, Peter	Revolutionary pension	17	1	Petition	118	Rev. Pensions	....	....	......	Discharged; laid on table.		
Hendry, Samuel	Compensation for services in war of 1812.	25	3	Petition	121	Claims.						
Hendschey, Henry H.	Indemnity for loss on lands purchased of United States.	21	1	Petition	60	Internal Imp'ments.	....	....	......	Discharged; laid on table.		
Hendschey, Henry H.	Indemnity for loss on lands purchased of United States.	21	2	Petition	233	Internal Imp'ments.						
Hendschey, Henry H.	Indemnity for loss on lands purchased of United States.	23	1	Petition	145	Roads and Canals.						
Hendy, John	Pension	16	1	Petition	26	Pens. & Rev. Cl'ms.	Dec. 15, 1819	Adverse	......	Rejected.		
Hendy, Col. John	Pension	21	1	Petition	143	Military Pensions.	....	....	......	Discharged; laid on table.		
Hengst, Michael	(See John Keuffett & M. H.)	14	1	....	392							
Henkle, Anthony	Compensation for supplies furnished revolutionary army.	2	2	Petition	615	....	....	....	......	Laid on table.		
Henkle, Joseph	(See trustees of school lands, Mercer county, Ohio.	28	1	....	516							
Henley, David	Release from payment of balance against him at War Department	12	1	Petition	167	Claims	....	....	......	Discharged.		
				Rep. of Secretary War.	394	Whole House	June 12, 1812	Favorable; bill ordered.	168	Rejected.		
Henley, David	Release from payment of balance against him at War Department.	12	2	Petition	576	Claims.						
Henley, David	Release from payment of balance against him at War Department.	13	1	Petition	13	Claims	Jan. 7, 1813	Rebort by bill.	1	Passed	Passed	App'd Aug. 2, 1813
Henley, David, (Tenn.)	Compensation for arms taken for public use, war of 1812.	15	2	Senate bill	280	Claims	Feb. 19, 1819	With't amend.	S. 53			
Henley, Col. David, heirs of.	Release of the estate from liability for his acts as a public agent.	18	1	Petition	70	Claims	Jan. 20, 1824	Report by bill	70	Passed	Passed	App'd May 26, 1824
Henley, David	(See agent of Edward Fox)	16	1	....	134							
Henley, Hezekiah	Pension for revolutionary services.	24	1	Petition	532	Rev. Pensions	May 10, 1836	....	......	Discharged; laid on table.		
Henley, John D.	Compensation for property lost by self and crew of schooner Caroline, at the defence of New Orleans.	14	1	Petition	136	Naval Affairs	Jan. 30, 1816	Adverse	......	Rejected.		
Henley, More, or Moore	Confirmation of title to land in Missouri.	15	1	Petition	367	Priv. Land Claims.	....	....	......	Discharged; laid on table.		
Henley, More, or Moore	Confirmation of title to land in Missouri.	16	1	Petition	72	Priv. Land Claims.	....	....	......	Discharged; laid on table.		
Henley, More, or Moore	Confirmation of title to land in Missouri.	17	1	Petition	54	Public Lands	....	....	......	Discharged; laid on table.		
Henley, More, or Moore	Confirmation of title to land in Missouri.	18	1	Petition	54	Public Lands.						
Henley, Samuel	Indemnity for losses during revolutionary war.	3	2	Petition	324	Claims	....	....	......	Discharged; laid on table.		
Henley, Samuel	Indemnity for losses during revolutionary war.	4	1	....	373	Claims	Jan. 6, 1796	Adverse	......	Laid on table.		
Henlon, Marmaduke	Compensation for revolutionary services.	2	1	Petition	539	....	....	....	......	Referred to Secretary War.		
Henner, Matthew	Commutation pay for services as a revolutionary officer.	13	1	Petition	284	Pens. & Rev. Cl'ms.						

List of private claims presented to the House of Representatives of the United States from the 1st to the 31st Congress, inclusive—Continued.

Names of claimants.	Nature or object of the claim.	Congress.	Session.	How brought before the House of Reps.	Page of journal.	To what committee of the House referred.	No. or date of the report.	Nature of the report.	No. of the bill.	How disposed of by the House of Reps.	How disposed of by the Senate.	Date of the act of Congress, and remarks.
Henninger, Henry	Confirmation of title to land in Michigan Territory.	14	1	Petition	127	Public Lands				Laid on table.		
Henninger, Henry	Confirmation of title to land in Michigan Territory.	14	2		57	Public Lands				Laid on table.		
Henop, Fred'k and Catharine S.	(See heirs of Colonel Ludowick Wiltner.)	23	1		40							
Henrick, Brigantine	(See Danish Brigantine)	7	2		363							
Henry, Andrew	Confirmation of title to land in Missouri.	15	2	Petition	67	Priv. Land Claims				Discharged; laid on table.		
Henry, Andrew	Confirmation of title to land in Missouri.	16	1	Petition	71	Priv. Land Claims				Discharged; laid on table.		
Henry, Andrew	Confirmation of title to land in Missouri.	17	1	Petition	54	Public Lands				Discharged; laid on table.		
Henry, A. G	Compensation for supplies furnished volunteers.	30	1	Petition	115	Claims	253	Report and bill	246	Passed.		
Henry, Andrew	(See heirs of Francois Valle)	15	2		47							
Henry, Bernard	Balance due him as naval storekeeper, Gibraltar.	29	1	Memorial	339	Naval Affairs.						
Henry, Bernard	Balance due him as naval storekeeper, Gibraltar.	30	1	Petition	81	Naval Affairs.						
Henry, Bernard	Balance due him as naval storekeeper, Gibraltar.	31	1	Memorial	258	Naval Affairs.						
Henry, Dan Drake	Indemnity for losses and compensation for services in Mexico.	30	1	Petition	480	Claims	413	Peport and bill	363	Referred to Committee Whole House.		
Henry, Dan Drake	Indemnity for losses and compensation for services in Mexico.	30	2	House bill	290	Whole House			363	Passed	Passed	App'd Jan. 26, 1849
Henry, George G	(See heirs of William Henry)	22	1		104							
Henry, John	Pension, or other relief for services, war of 1812.	19	2	Petition	136	Claims				Discharged.		
Henry, John	Pension, or other relief for services, war of 1812.	21	1	Petition	511	Military Pensions				Discharged; laid on table.		
Henry, John, (William,) son of.	Compensation for revolutionary services, and for arms furnished.	23	1	Petition	569	Rev. Claims.						
Henry, John, (William,) son of.	Compensation for revolutionary services, and for arms furnished.	23	2	Petition	120	Rev. Claims.						
Henry, John, (William,) son of.	Compensation for revolutionary services, and for arms furnished.	24	1	Petition	475	Rev. Claims.						
Henry, John, (William,) son of.	Compensation for revolutionary services, and for arms furnished.	26	2	Documents	61	Rev. Claims	Jan. 4, 1841	Adverse		Laid on table.		
Henry, John, administrator of.	Balance due withheld by 2d Auditor.	26	2	Memorial	81	Claims	31	Adverse		Laid on table.		
Henry, John, administrator of.	Balance due withheld by 2d Auditor.	27	2	Memorial	155	Claims	167	Adverse		Laid on table.		
Henry, John, widow and heir of.	Compensation for services and expenditures in revolutionary war.	27	2	Petition	61	Rev. Claims	1061	Adverse		Laid on table.		
Henry, John, heirs of	Compensation for revolutionary services.	29	1	Documents	571	Rev. Claims.						
Henry, John, N	Pension for wounds and compensation for property destroyed by Creek Indians, war of 1812.	17	1	Petition	176	Pens. & Rev. Cl'ms.	Jan. 25, 1822	Adverse in part		Leave to withdraw.		
Henry, Joseph	(See Matthias Bush, assignee of.)	1	3		396							
Henry, Moses	Pension	20	1	Resolution	415	Military Pensions				Discharged; laid on table.		

List of private claims presented to the House of Representatives of the United States from the 1st to the 31st Congress, inclusive—Continued.

Names of claimants.	Nature or object of the claim.	Congress.	Session.	How brought before the House of Reps.	Page of journal.	To what committee of the House referred.	No. or date of the report.	Nature of the report.	No. of the bill.	How disposed of by the House of Reps.	How disposed of by the Senate.	Date of the act of Congress, and remarks.
Henry, Moses	Arrears of pension	21	1	Petition	405	Military Pensions	April 7, 1830	Adverse	......	Laid on table.		
Henry,	(See Minis & Henry.)	15	2	....	144							
Henry, Nathaniel	Invalid pension	12	2	Petition	647	Claims.						
Henry, Nathaniel	Invalid pension	13	1	House bill	56	Whole House	July 20, 1813	Favorable; bill	31	Passed	Passed	App'd Aug. 2, 1813
Henry, Nathaniel	Arrears of pension	15	1	Petition	49	Pens. & Rev. Cl'ms.	....	....	......	Discharged; laid on table.		
Henry, Nathaniel, widow of.	Arrears of pension	22	2	Petition	216 223	Rev. Pensions discharged, and to Inv lid Pensions.	....	....	......	Discharged; laid on table.		
Henry, Nathaniel, widow of.	Arrears of pension	23	1	Petition	306	Rev. Claims	....	....	......	Discharged; laid on table.		
Henry, Robert	Compensation for wood furnished revolutionary army.	4	1	Rep. of Secretary Treasury.	388	Claims	74	Adverse	......	Laid on table.		
Henry, Robert, (Alabama.)	Permission to change and entry of land.	18	1	Petition	34	Public Lands.	Dec. 15, 1823	General bill	7	Passed	Passed	App'd May 26, 1824
Henry, Rufus	To be placed on the pension roll	26	2	Petition	54	Invalid Pensions	83	Adverse	......	Laid on table.		
Henry, Thomas, executors of.	Indemnity for French spoliations prior to 1800.	26	1	Memorial	182	Foreign Affairs	343	Favorable; bill	319	Referred to Committee Whole House.		
Henry, Williams	Compensation for protection afforded Galena miners against hostile Indians.	27	2	Memorial	807	Claims	1030	Adverse	......	Laid on table.		
Henry, William	(See John D. Mathey, and others, attorney of.)	18	2	....	60							
Henry, William	Equitable settlement of accounts as paymaster U. S. army.	18	2	Petition	60	Claims.						
Henry, William	Exchange of a location of land	21	1	Petition	149	Public Lands	259	Adverse	......	Laid on table.		
Henry, William, administrator of.	Compensation for services as midshipman in 1799.	26	1	Petition	956	Naval Affairs.						
Henry, Capt. William	(See Mississippi, cavalry of.)	15	1	....	287							
Henry, William	(See John D. Matthey, and others, a torney of.)	22	1	....	633							
Henry, William, heir of	Compensation for services in war of 1812.	22	1	Petition	104	Claims.						
Henry, William, heir of	Compensation for services in war of 1812.	23	2	Petition	309	Claims.						
Henry, William & John J.	Additional compensation for muskets made on contract.	16	1	Petition	34	Claims	....	....	......	Referred to Secretary War.		
Henry, William, & Thos. Jenkins.	For a new location of land	25	2	Petition	90	Public Lands	....	....	......	Referred to Committee Whole House, on bill No. 601.		
Henry, William, agent for a troop of volunteer cavalry.	Compensation for services in war of 1812.	18	2	Petition	80	Military Affairs.						
Henry, Capt. William, and Capt. Wells.	Compensation for the services of two companies of cavalry in the war of 1812.	15	1	Petition	287	Military Affairs	....	....	......	Discharged; laid on table.		
Henshaw, Andrew	Compensation for services as deputy surveyor.	18	2	Petition	42	Public Lands	Jan. 21, 1825	Adverse	......	Laid on table.		
Henshaw, Andrew	Compensation for surveying public lands.	23	1	Petition	382	Public Lands	....	....	......	Discharged; laid on table.		
Henshaw, David	Indemnity for French spoliations prior to 1800.	18	1	Petition	196	Foreign Affairs.						

List of private claims presented to the House of Representatives of the United States from the 1st to the 31st Congress, inclusive—**Continued.**

Names of claimants.	Nature or object of the claim.	Congress.	Session.	How brought before the House of Reps.	Page of journal.	To what committee of the House referred.	No. or date of the report.	Nature of the report.	No. of the bill.	How disposed of by the House of Reps.	How disposed of by the Senate.	Date of the act of Congress, and remarks.
Henshaw, David, heirs of.	Indemnity for French spoliations prior to 1800.	24	1	Petition	852	Foreign Affairs.						
Henshaw, David, heirs of.	Indemnity for French spoliations prior to 1800.	29	2	Memorial	129	Foreign Affairs.						
Henshaw, David, heirs of.	Indemnity for French spoliations prior to 1800.	31	1	Petition	311	Foreign Affairs....	355	General bill ..	318			
Henshaw, David, (Vt.)...	Indemnity for French spoliations prior to 1800.	26	1	Memorial	182	Foreign Affairs....	343	Favorable; bill	319	Referred to Committee Whole House.		
Henshaw, Foster, and W. A. Sheppard.	Compensation for military services in revolutionary war.	28	1	Petition	375	Rev. Pensions.						
Henshaw, J. Sidney, and D. Bradford.	Four months extra pay, &c......	30	2	Memorial	389	Claims.						
Henshaw, J. Sidney, and D. Bradford.	Four months extra pay, &c	31	1	Petition	349	Naval Affairs.....	437	Adverse......	.....	Ordered to be printed.		
Hens n, John, widow of..	Pension for revolutionary services.	27	3	Petition	168	Rev. Pensions.						
Hension, William.......	Compensation for enrolling and subsisting Cherokee Indians.	28	1	Senate bill	697	Indian Affairs	May 25, 1844	With amend..	S. 69	Passed without amendment.	....	App'd June 17, 1844
Hension, William.......	Compensation for enrolling and subsisting Cherokee Indians.	28	2	Senate bill	115	Indian Affairs.....	Mar. 3, 1845	Adverse	S. 135	Laid on table.		
Hepburn, John M.......	To be restored to his former salary	23	2	Petition	391	Ways and Means.						
Hepburn, John M.......	Increase of compensation as clerk in adjutant general's office.	24	1	Petition	200	Military Affairs...	....	....	.....	Discharged; laid on table.		
Hepburn, John M.......	Increase of compensation as clerk in adjutant general's office.	24	2	Petition	40	Military Affairs.						
Hepburn, John M.......	Increase of compensation as clerk in adjutant general's office.	25	2	Petition	279	Military Affairs ...	....	....	.....	Discharged.		
Hepner, John	Compensation for revolutionary services.	2	1	Petition	451	....	....	....	.....	Referred to Secretary War.		
Herald, ship...........	(See John H. Hodges)	28	2	....	235							
Herback, Yost..........	Pension	20	1	Petition	242	Military Pensions..	Feb. 15, 1828	....	.....	Discharged; laid on table.		
Herbert, Hilairc.........	Confirmation of claim to land in Louisiana.	21	2	Petition	189	Priv. Land Claims.						
Herbert, Joseph.........	Confirmation of claim to land in Louisiana.	21	2	Petition	189	Priv. Land Claims.						
Herbert, Nathaniel	Increase of compensation as assistant messenger in Post Office Department.	29	2	Memorial	67	P. Of. & P. Roads.						
Herbert, Nathaniel	Increase of compensation as assistant messenger in Post Office Department.	31	2	Petition	184	P. Of. and P. Roads.						
Hereford, John	Pension for services as a revolutionary soldier.	21	1	Resolution	609	Military Pensions..	....	....	.....	Discharged; laid on table.		
Hereford, John	Pension for services as a revolutionary soldier.	22	1	Resolution	126	Rev. Pensions.						
Heriot, B. D............	(See David R. Denham, *et al.*) ..	25	3	....	121	....	162					
Heriot, Benjamin D......	Indemnity for losses in Seminole War.	29	1	Petition	75	Claims.						
Herkimer, Gen. Nicholas, widow of.	Half-pay for revolutionary services	3	1	Petition and rep't Sec. of War.	21	Select	....	....	.....	Laid on table.		
Hermingen, Jeptha L....	Pension	31	1	Petition	542	Invalid Pensions.						
Herman, Jacob..........	Compensation for services as a revolutionary soldier.	6	1	Petition	561	Claims	Feb. 11, 1801	Adverse	.....	Rejected.		

List of private claims presented to the House of Representatives of the United States from the 1st to the 31st Congress, inclusive—Continued.

Names of claimants.	Nature or object of the claim.	Congress.	Session.	How brought before the House of Reps.	Page of journal.	To what committee of the House referred.	No. or date of the report.	Nature of the report.	No. of the bill.	How disposed of by the House of Reps.	How disposed of by the Senate.	Date of the act of Congress, and remarks.
Hermans, Andrew, widow of.	Pension for revolutionary services.	25	2	Petition	116	Rev. Pensions.						
Hern, Reddick	(Claim not stated.)	26	1	Petition	169	Claims.						
Hern, Samuel	Compensation for a horse lost in revolutionary war.	24	2	Documents	215	Rev. Claims.						
Hern, Samuel, heirs of	Compensation for a horse lost in revolutionary war.	25	2	Documents	81	Rev. Pensions	413	Adverse		Laid on table.		
Hernandez, Joseph	Confirmation of Spanish title to land in Florida.	24	1	Petition	425	Priv. Land Claims.						
Hernandez, Joseph	Confirmation of Spanish title to land in Florida.	24	2	Petition	49	Priv. Land Claims.	19	Adverse		Laid on table.		
Hernandez, Joseph M.	(See David R. Denham, *et al.*)	25	3		121							
Hernandez, Joseph M.	(See agent for the estate of Francis Pellicer.)	26	1		339							
Hernandez, Joseph M.	(See assignee of Saml. H. Williams)	29	2		146							
Hernandez, Joseph M.	Compensation for supplies furnish'd United States troops.	25	2	Petition	647	Claims	1043	Report and bill	877			
Hernandez, Joseph M.	Compensation for supplies furnish'd United States troops.	25	3	House bill	432	Whole House			877	Passed	Passed, with amendment.	App'd March 3, 1839
Hernandez, Joseph M., widow of.	Confirmation of title to land	22	1	Petition	64	Priv. Land Claims.	Dec. 27, 1831	General bill	125	Passed	Passed	App'd June 25, 1832
Hernandez, Joseph M	Indemnity for losses sustained in Seminole war.	26	1	Senate bill	1277				S. 107			
Hernandez, Joseph M	Indemnity for losses sustained in Seminole war.	26	2	Senate bill	329	Whole House			S. 93			
Hernandez, Joseph M	Indemnity for losses sustained in Seminole war.	27	2	Resolution	1205					Referred to Sec. War.		
Hernandez, Joseph M.	Indemnity for losses sustained in Seminole war.	27	3	Petition	61	Claims	104	Adverse		Referred to Committee Whole House.		
Hernandez, Joseph M.	Indemnity for losses sustained in Seminole war.	28	1	Petition	71	Claims	58	Report and bill.	90	Laid on table		Majority and minority report.
Hernandez, Joseph M., representatives of.	(See Samuel H. Williams, assignee of.)	29	2		146							
Hernandez, Pedro	Confirmation of title to land	22	1	Petition	64	Priv. Land Claims.	Dec. 27, 1831	General bill	125	Passed	Passed	App'd June 25, 1832
Herndon, Edward	Pension	19	1	Petition	36	Rev. Pensions	164	Adverse		Laid on table.		
Herndon, Edward	Pension	19	2	Petition	84	Military Pensions.						
Herndon, Edward	Pension	22	1	Petition	66	Rev. Pensions	396	Report and bill	495			
Herndon, Edward, and James A. McHatton.	Indemnity for losses on mail contracts.	29	1	Petition	387	P. Of. & P. Roads.	374	Adverse		Laid on table.		
Herndon, Joseph	Additional compensation for revolutionary services.	21	2	Petition	82	Rev. Claims.						
Herndon, Joseph	Increase of pension	31	1	Petition	533	Rev. Pensions	449	Adverse		Laid on table.		
Hernken, Bernard	Confirmation of sale of a tract of land.	29	1	Petition	337	P. Of. & P. Roads.	374	Adverse		Laid on table.		
Herrick, Abel	Pension for revolutionary services.	26	1	Resolution	407	Rev. Pensions	663	Adverse		Laid on table.		
Herrick, Andrew	Pension for services as a revolutionary soldier.	19	2	Petition	160	Military Pensions.		General bill	431			
Herrick, Andrew	Pension for services as a revolutionary soldier.	20	1	Petition	243	Military Pensions.	April 28, 1828	General bill	283	Passed	Discharged.	
Herrick, Andrew	Pension for services as a revolutionary soldier.	20	2	House bill	55	Whole House	Dec. 12, 1828	Amended.	311	Passed	Laid on table.	
Herrick, Andrew	Pension for services as a revolutionary soldier.	21	1	House bill	130	Whole House	Feb. 13, 1830	Favorable	72	Passed	Passed	App'd May 20, 1830

List of private claims presented to the House of Representatives of the United States from the 1st to the 31st Congress, inclusive—Continued.

Names of claimants.	Nature or object of the claim.	Congress.	Session.	How brought before the House of Reps.	Page of journal.	To what committee of the House referred.	No. or date of the report.	Nature of the report.	No. of the bill.	How disposed of by the House of Reps.	How disposed of by the Senate.	Date of the act of Congress, and remarks.
Herrick, George R.	For the compensation prescribed by law for his services as a clerk in Indian Office.	31	1	Petition	578	Claims.						
Herrick, John	(See William Baker, New York).	22	1		288		480					
Herrick, John	Arrears of pension	23	1	Petition	45	Invalid Pensions.	231	Report and bill.	257			
Herrick, John	Arrears of pension	23	2	House bill	299	Whole House			257	Passed	Indef. postp'd.	
Herrick, John	Arrears of pension	24	1	Petition	201	Invalid Pensions	461	Report and bill.	467	Passed	Passed	App'd June 28, 1836
Herrick, Jonathan	Pension for disability incurred in war of 1812.	24	2	Petition	132	Invalid Pensions	Jan. 26, 1837	Adverse		Laid on table.		
Herrick, Oliver	Compensation for a team sold to government, war of 1812.	15	1	Petition	367	Claims				Discharged; laid on table.		
Herrick, Oliver	Pension	22	1	Petition	383	Invalid Pensions	426	Report and bill.	528	Passed	With amend.	App'd July 16, 1382; name of petitioner omitted in act.
Herrick, Oliver	Pension	22	2	House bill	79	Whole House	Dec. 22, 1832	With amend.	626	Passed	With amend.	App'd March 3, 1833
Herrick, Oliver	Pension for disability incurred in war of 1812.	28	1	Petition	357	Invalid Pensions	377	Adverse		Laid on table.		
Herrick, Oliver	Pension for disability incurred in war of 1812.	29	1	Petition	337	Invalid Pensions	507	Adverse		Laid on table.		Leave to withdraw.
Herrick, Oliver	Increase of pension	31	2	Petition	236	Invalid Pensions.						
Herrick, Samuel, heirs of.	Renewal of a patent right	21	2	Petition	167	Judiciary				Disch'd; laid on table.		
Herrick, William	Pension	15	2	Petition	46	Pens. & Rev. Cl'ms.	Jan. 5, 1819	Adverse		Discharged; leave to withdraw.		
Herrick, William, former widow of.	Revolutionary pension	29	2	Petition	74	Rev. Pensions.						
Herring, Asa	Release from liability as surety for William Myers.	19	1	Petition	203	P. Of. and P. Roads.	115	Adverse		Laid on table.		
Herring, Asa	Release from liability as surety for William Myers.	20	1	Petition	32	P. O & P. Roads.	50	Report and bill	48	Passed	Passed	App'd April 28, 1828
Herring, Elbert	Release from imprisonment on a judgment in favor of U. S.	15	1	Petition	166	Judiciary	Feb. 6, 1818	Report and bill	69			
Herring, Elbert	Relative to the purchase of paintings taken from him by the Treasury Department.	28	1	Petition	301	Joint Library.						
Herring, Gardner	Pension for disability incurred in war of 1812.	27	2	Petition	106	Invalid Pensions	818	Adverse		Laid on table.		
Herring, Gardner	Pension for disability incurred in war of 1812.	28	1	Petition	176	Invalid Pensions						
Herring, Gardner	Pension for disability incurred in war of 1812.	28	2	Petition	250	Invalid Pensions.						
Herring, Gardner	Pension for disability incurred in war of 1812.	29	1	Petition	194	Invalid Pensions.						
Herring, Gardner	Pension for disability incurred in war of 1812.	29	2	Petition	162	Invalid Pensions.						
Herring, Gardner	Pension for disability incurred in war of 1812.	30	1	Petition	166	Invalid Pensions.	715	Report and bill	560	Referred to Committee Whole House.		
Herring, Gardner	Pension for disability incurred in war of 1812.	30	2	House bill	319	Whole House	Jan. 26, 1829	With't amend.	560	Passed.		
Herring, Gardner	Pension for disability incurred in war of 1812.	31	1	Petition	472	Invalid Pensions.	303	Report and bil	273			
Herring, Gardner	Pension for disability incurred in war of 1812.	31	2	House bill	182	Whole House			273	Passed.		

List of private claims presented to the House of Representatives of the United States from the 1st to the 31st Congress, inclusive—Continued.

Names of claimants.	Nature or object of the claim.	Congress.	Session.	How brought before the House of Reps.	Page of journal.	To what committee of the House referred.	No. or date of the report.	Nature of the report.	No. of the bill.	How disposed of by the House of Reps.	How disposed of by the Senate.	Date of the act of Congress, and remarks.
Herring, James, secretary of the American Academy of Fine Arts.	Remission of duty on steel plates for the National Portrait Gallery.	22	2	Petition	86	Ways and Means.						
Herring, James, secretary of the American Academy of Fine Arts.	Remission of duty on steel plates for the National Portrait Gallery.	22	2	Petition	206	Ways and Means.						
Herring & Richardson, of England.	Indemnity for the seizure of ship Frances and Eliza.	23	1	Presid'ts message	525	Judiciary.						
Herring & Richardson, of England.	Indemnity for the seizure of ship Frances and Eliza.	23	2	Presid'ts message	237	Judiciary	140	Adverse		Laid on table.		
Herring & Richardson, of England.	Indemnity for the seizure of ship Frances and Elisa.	24	1	Resolution	174	Judiciary	Mar. 25, 1836	Adverse		Referred to Committee Whole House.		
Herrington, Charity	Authority to enter a tract of land at minimum price.	30	1	Senate bill	1143				S. 276	Passed with amendm't	Passed as am'd	App'd Aug. 12, 1848
Herrington, James	Pension	19	1	Petition	203	Military Pensions	164	Adverse		Laid on table.		
Herrington, James	Grant of land in consideration of valuable public services.	22	2	Petition	266	Public Lands.						
Herron, Alanson	(See William A. Bryan)	27	2		682							
Herron, Gardner	(See Gardner Herring)	28	2		250							
Herron, James	Reimbursement of money paid into the treasury.	23	2	Resolution	296	Claims.						
Herron, James	Reimbursement of money paid into the treasury.	24	1	Resolution	207	Claims	249	Report and bill	256	Passed	Passed, with amendment.	
Herron, James	Reimbursement of money paid into the treasury.	24	2	House bill	111	Claims	Dec. 23, 1836	With't amend.	767			
Herron, James	Reimbursement of money paid into the treasury.	25	2	Petition	36	Claims	60	Report and bill	72	Passed.		
Herron, James	Reimbursement of money paid into the treasury.	26	1	Senate bill	1226	Patents			S. 289			
Herron, James	Extra compensation as engineer in charge at Pensacola navy-yard.	31	1	Appropriation bill								App'd Sept. 28, 1850
Herron, John	Pension	10	1	House bill	232	Whole House	April 19, 1808	General bill	78	Passed	Passed	App'd April 23, 1808
Hersey, ——	(See Smith & Hersey)	31	1		406							
Hersey, Eliza	Indemnity for French spoliations prior to 1800.	26	1	Memorial	182	Foreign Affairs	343	Favorable; bill	319	Referred to Committee Whole House.		
Hersey, Solomon	Compensation for property furnished troops, war of 1812.	22	2	Resolution	115	Claims.						
Hersey, Solomon	Compensation for property furnished troops, war of 1812.	24	2	Petition	124	Claims	Jan. 11, 1837	Adverse		Laid on table.		
Hersey, Solomon	Indemnity for damage to property by United States troops.	25	2	Petition	175	Claims	831	Adverse		Laid on table.		
Hersey, Solomon	Indemnity for damage to property by United States troops.	29	1	Petition	969	Claims.						
Hersey, Solomon	Indemnity for damage to property by United States troops.	30	1	Petition	219	Claims.						
Hersey, S., and P. Chudwick.	Release of schooner Horizon, seized for a violation of non-importation act.	12	1	Petition	137	Whole House			46			
Hertick, Joseph	Compensation for a boat lost in the public service.	13	3	Petition	735	Claims				Discharged.		
Hertick, Joseph	Compensation for a boat lost in the public service.	14	1	Petition	65	Claims				Discharged; laid on table.		

List of private claims presented to the House of Representatives of the United States from the 1st to the 31st Congress, inclusive—Continued.

Names of claimants.	Nature or object of the claim.	Congress.	Session.	How brought before the House of Reps.	Page of journal.	To what committee of the House referred.	No. or date of the report.	Nature of the report.	No. of the bill.	How disposed of by the House of Reps.	How disposed of by the Senate.	Date of the act of Congress, and remarks.
Hertick, Joseph	Compensation for a boat lost in the public service.	14	2	Petition	115	Claims				Discharged; laid on table.		
Hertick, Joseph	Compensation for a boat lost in the public service.	15	1	Petition	198	Claims	Feb. 25, 1818	Adverse		Rejected.		
Hertick, Joseph	Compensation for a boat lost in the public service.	24	1	Senate bill	899	Claims	June 2, 1836	With't amend.	S. 25	Passed		App'd July 2, 1836
Hertick, Joseph	Confirmation of title to land in Missouri.	15	1	Petition	76	Priv. Land Claims				Discharged; laid on table.		
Hertick, Joseph	Confirmation of title to land in Missouri.	16	1	Petition	71	Priv. Land Claims				Discharged; laid on table.		
Hertick, Joseph	Confirmation of title to land in Missouri.	17	1	Petition	54	Public Lands				Discharged; laid on table.		
Hertick, Joseph	Confirmation of title to land in Missouri.	18	1	Petition	54	Public Lands.						
Hertz, Conrad	Increase of pension	26	2	Petition	60	Invalid Pensions	Feb. 12, 1841			Discharged; laid on table.		
Hertzog, Jean Francois	Confirmation of title to land in Louisiana.	22	2	Petition	41	Priv. Land Claims.	13	Report and bill	638			
Hervey, George, attorney for owners of ship James Mitchell and cargo.	For certain taxable costs	23	1	Petition	189	Naval Affairs	197	Report and bill.	219	Referred to Committee Whole House.		See act of January 24, 1834, bill 110.
Hervey, George, attorney for owners of ship James Mitchell and cargo.	For certain taxable costs	30	1	Petition	111	Naval Affairs	509	Report and bill.	436	Referred to Committee Whole House.		
Hervey, George, attorney for owners of ship James Mitchell and cargo.	Foi certain taxable costs	31	1	Petition	611	Claims	April 11, 1850	Adverse		Laid on table.		
Heslop, Thomas	Compensati'n for supplies furnished revolutionary army.	3	2	Petition	288					Laid on table.		
Heess, Felix	Indemnity for loss of a vessel by neglect of a light house keeper.	23	2	Petition	344	Claims.						
Hess, Jeremiah	Pension	31	1	Petition	1222	Invalid Pensions	Aug. 2, 1850			Discharged; laid on table.		
Hess, Oliver	Pension for services, war of 1812.	31	1	Petition	256	Invalid Pensions.						
Hess, Peter	Increase of pension	24	1	Petition	944	Invalid Pensions.						
Hesser, Peter	Pre-emption right to a tract of land in Ohio.	8	2	Memorial	110	Select.						
Hetfield, Moses	Pension and arrears of revolutionary pension.	4	1	Petition	444	Claims	May 31, 1796	Adverse		Laid on table.		
Heth, Andrew, administrator of.	Commutation pay for revolutionary services.	24	1	Petition	508	Rev. Claims				Discharged; laid on table.		
Heth, Harvey	Indemnity for Indian depredations.	28	1	Documents	508	Indian Affairs	388	Report and bill	181	Passed	Passed	App'd June 17, 1744
Heth, Col. William, heirs of.	Compensation for revolutionary services.	24	1	Petition	344	Rev. Claims	717	Adverse		Laid on table.		
Hethner, Nicholas	Pension	22	1	Petition	114	Invalid Pensions	Jan. 13, 1832	Adverse		Laid on table.		
Hetsey, Famide or Bigskin	(See To-hon-do-che, Sen. Indian.)	15	2		123							
Hetzell, A. R., administratrix of.	Commissions on moneys disbursed by deceased.	31	1	Senate bill	1035	Military Affairs			S. 130			
Hetzell, A. R., administratrix of.	Commissions on moneys disbursed by deceased.	31	2	Senate bill	239	Military Affairs	Feb. 6, 1851	With't amend.	S. 130	Referred to Committee Whole House.		
Henstler, Thomas	Compensat'n for property destroyed by the enemy.	17	2	Petition	74	Claims				Discharged; leave to withdraw.		

List of private claims presented to the House of Representatives of the United States from the 1st to the 31st Congress, inclusive—Continued.

Names of claimants.	Nature or object of the claim.	Congress.	Session.	How brought before the House of Reps.	Page of journal.	To what committee of the House referred.	No. or date of the report.	Nature of the report.	No. of the bill.	How disposed of by the House of Reps.	How disposed of by the Senate.	Date of the act of Congress, and remarks.
Hevron, Gadner	(See Gardner Herring.)	27	2		106							
Hewes, Adeline	(See William Watts, widow and heirs of.)	29	3		210		255					
Hewes, Alpheus	To be restored to pension roll	18	2	Petition	117	Rev. Pensions	Jan. 21, 1825			Discharged; leave to withdraw.		
Hewes, Alpheus	To be restored to pension roll	19	2	Petition	116	Military Pensions				Discharged.		
Hewes, Alpheus	To be restored to pension roll	21	1	Petition	144	Military Pensions				Discharged; laid on table.		
Hewes, Alpheus	To be restored to pension roll	22	1	Petition	534	Rev. Pensions				Discharged; laid on table.		
Hews, Daniel	Pension for revolutionary services	30	1	Petition	394	Rev. Pensions.						
Hewes, Daniel, jr	Release from imprisonment on judgment in favor of United States.	13	3	Petition	677	Ways and Means				Discharged.		
Hewes, George R. T.	Increase of pension	26	1	Petition	287	Invalid Pensions	245	Adverse		Laid on table.		
Hewes, Joseph	Pension	21	2	Petition	208	Military Pensions.						
Hewes, Joseph	Pension	22	1	Petition	131	Rev. Pensions	395	Report and bill.	494	Referred to Committee Whole House.		
Hewes, Thomas	Reimbursement of money unjustly collected on an execution.	18	1	Senate bill	422	Ways and Means	April 19, 1824	With't amend.	S. 83	Referred to Committee Whole House.		
Hewes, Thomas	Reimbursement of money unjustly collected on an execution.	18	2	Senate bill	76	Ways and Means	Dec. 27, 1824	With't amend.	S. 5	Passed		App'd March 3, 1825
Hewes, William	Pension for revolutionary services.	23	1	Petition	333	Rev. Pensions				Disch'd; laid on table.		
Hewes, William	Pension for revolutionary services.	24	1	Petition	107	Rev. Pensions	144	Report and bill.	151	Passed	Passed	App'd June 28, 1836
Hewey, Richard	(See William H. Bedford, agent.)	28	1		262							
Hewins, Joseph	Pension for revolutionary services.	24	1	Petition	56	Rev. Pensions	Mar. 21, 1836			Discharged; laid on table.		
Hewins, Joseph	Arrears of pension	26	1	Petition	706	Rev. Pensions	643	Report and bill	476	Referred to Committee Whole House.		
Hewins, Joseph	Arrears of pension	27	2	Petition	749	Rev. Pensions.						
Hewit, A., and H. Steffey, assignee of.	Bounty land for services in Mexican war.	30	2	Petition	361	Priv. Land Claims.						
Hewitt, Benjamin	Compensation for a slave taken by the British.	22	2	Resolution	273	Claims.						
Hewitt, Benjamin	Compensation for a slave taken by the British.	23	1	Petition	370	Foreign Affairs	415	Report and bill.	426	Referred to Committee Whole House.		
Hewitt, Benjamin	Compensation for a slave taken by the British.	24	1	Petition	408	Foreign Affairs	500	Report and bill.	500	Referred to Committee Whole House.		
Hewitt, Benjamin	Compensation for a slave takan by the British.	25	2	Petition	39	Foreign Affairs	261	Report and bill	304	Referred to Committee Whole House.		
Hewitt, Benjamin	Compensation for a slave taken by the British.	25	3	House bill	377	Whole House			304	Passed	Passed, with amendment.	App'd March 3, 1839
Hewitt, Benjamin	Extension of time to complete a contract.	23	1	Petition	369	Naval Affairs	April 24, 1834	Report by bill.	444	Referred to Committee Whole House.		
Hewitt, Benjamin	Extension of time to complete a contract.	24	1	Petition	945	Naval Affairs	June 15, 1836	Report by bill.	698	Referred to Committee Whole House.		
Hewitt, Benjamin	Equitable settlement of his accounts with United States.	25	2	Petition	41	Naval Affairs	Dec. 22, 1837	Report by bill.	173	Referred to Committee Whole House.		
Hewitt, Benjamin	Equitable settlement of his accounts with United States.	25	3	House bill	375	Whole House		With't amend.	173	Passed	Passed	App'd March 3, 1839
Hewitt, Benjamin	Equitable settlement of his claim under a timber contract.	25	3	Resolution	449	Claims			J R.446			
Hewitt, Daniel	Invalid pension	3	1	Rep. of Secretary of War.	131	Select	May 26, 1794	Jt. res. to refer to Sec. War.	J. R. 12	Passed	Passed	App'd June 9, 1794

List of private claims presented to the House of Representatives of the United States from the 1st to the 31st Congress, inclusive—Continued.

Names of claimants.	Nature or object of the claim.	Congress.	Session.	How brought before the House of Reps.	Page of journal.	To what committee of the House referred.	No. or date of the report.	Nature of the report.	No. of the bill.	How disposed of by the House of Reps.	How disposed of by the Senate.	Date of the act of Congress, and remarks.
Hewitt, Daniel	Invalid pension	4	1	Rep. of Secretary of War.	445	Claims	Mar. 4, 1796	Favorable; bill	156	Passed	Passed	App'd April 20, 1796
Hewitt, Captain Dothick, daughter of.	Pay and bounty land for revolutionary services.	26	1	Documents	961	Rev. Claims.						
Hewit, Job	Bounty land for services in the war of 1812.	16	1	Petition	218	Priv. Land Claims.	Mar. 6, 1820	Adverse	......	Leave to withdraw.		
Hewitt, John W	Compensation for services rendered as express rider.	27	2	Petition	1298	Claims.						
Hewitt, Joseph	(See Rufus Spalding, *et al.*)	15	2	....	148							
Hewitt, Nathaniel	Pension	10	2	House bill	449	Whole House	Feb. 20, 1809	Favorable	158	Passed	Passed	App'd March 3, 1809
Hewitt, Randall	Compensation for revolutionary services and losses.	25	2	Petition	270	Rev. Claims	....	....	......	Discharged; laid on table.		
Hewitt, Randall	Pay and emoluments while a prisoner of war.	26	1	Petition	281	Claims.						
Hewlett, Lemuel	Pension	14	1	Petition	309	Pens. & Rev. Cl'ms.	April 11, 1816	Report by bill.	171	Passed	Passed, with amendment.	App'd April 30, 1816
Hewson, Tewill	Further compensation for services in the Florida war.	27	3	Petition	345	Military Affairs.						
Hewton, Solomon, administrator of.	Indemnity for French spoliations prior to 1800.	26	1	Memorial	182	Foreign Affairs	343	Favorable; bill	319	Referred to Committee Whole House.		
Heyberger, Jacob	(See Weaver & Heyberger)	27	3	....	207	....	....	....	725			
Heym, Henry	(See Louis F. Beeler, *et al.*)	30	1	....	115							
Heyer, Walter, *et al.*	Increase of salary as clerks in loan office, New York.	3	1	Petition	67	Select	May 16, 1794	Favorable; bill ordered.	69	Passed	Rejected.	
Heysham, Robert	Arrears of pay as clerk in naval office, Philadelphia.	26	1	Memorial	358	Ways and Means	....	....	......	Discharged; laid on table.		
Heysham, Robert	Arrears of pay as clerk in custom-house, Philadelphia.	27	2	Memorial	95	Ways and Means.						
Heysham, Robert	Arrears of pay as clerk in custom-house, Philadelphia.	27	3	Memorial	44	Ways and Means.						
Hibbard, Shubael P.	Pension	14	2	Petition	70	Pens. & Rev. Cl'ms.	Dec. 23, 1816	Adverse	......	Rejected.		
Hibbard, Shubael P.	Increase of pension	15	2	Petition	20	Pens. & Rev. Cl'ms.	Feb. 5, 1819	General bill	308	Passed	Postponed.	
Hibbard, Shubael P.	Increase of pension	17	1	Petition	60	Pens. & Rev. Cl'ms.						
Hibbert, James, widow of.	Pension, war of 1812	25	2	Petition	1120	Invalid Pensions.						
Hibbert, John	Pension for services and disability, war of 1812.	25	2	Petition	57	Invalid Pensions.						
Hibbert, John	Pension for services and disability, war of 1812.	25	3	Petition	89	Invalid Pensions	Jan. 22, 1839	....	......	Discharged; laid on table.		
Hibbert, John	Pension for services and disability, war of 1812.	26	1	Petition	198	Invalid Pensions	279	Adverse	......	Laid on table.		
Hibbert, John	Pension for services and disability, war of 1812.	29	1	Petition	638	Invalid Pensions	July 25, 1846	....	......	Discharged; laid on table.		
Hibbert, John	Pension for services and disability, war of 1812.	30	1	Petition	203	Invalid Pensions	287	Report and bill.	283	Passed	Passed second session.	App'd Feb. 19, 1849
Hibbits, David C.	Pension for wounds received in war of 1812.	25	3	Petition	368	Invalid Pensions.						
Hibbits, David C.	Pension for wounds received in war of 1812.	26	1	Petition	163	Invalid Pensions	April 4, 1840	Adverse	......	Laid on table.		
Hibbs, Mary Fanning	(See heir of Joshua Fanning)	9	2	....	600							
Hibbs, Charles	Increase of salary as messenger at Pension office.	31	1	Petition	1153	Ways and Means.						
Hibden, Peter	(See William H. Bedford, agent)	28	1	....	262							

List of private claims presented to the House of Representatives of the United States from the 1st to the 31st Congress, inclusive—Continued.

Names of claimants.	Nature or object of the claim.	Congress.	Session.	How brought before the House of Reps.	Page of journal.	To what committee of the House referred.	No. or date of the report.	Nature of the report.	No. of the bill.	How disposed of by the House of Reps.	How disposed of by the Senate.	Date of the act of Congress, and remarks.
Hibert, Jean Baptiste	Authority to locate a certain tract of land.	24	1	Petition	207	Public Lands				Discharged; laid on table.		
Hibert, William	(See Henry Duchuquette, *et al*)	23	2		353							
Hick, John	(See John Heck)	18	2									
Hickack, Samuel	Bounty land	28	2	Petition	184	Priv. Land Claims.						
Hickey, Daniel	Pension	9	2	House bill	608	Whole House	Feb. 28, 1807	Favorable	216	Passed	Passed	App'd March 3, 1807
Hickey, David	Invalid pension	3	1	Rep. of Secretary War.	131	Select	May 26, 1794	Joint res. to refer to Sec. of War.	12	Passed	Passed	App'd June 9, 1794
Hickey, David	Invalid pension	3	2	Rep. of Secretary War.	262	Claims	Mar. 3, 1795			Discharged; laid on table.		
Hickey, David	Invalid pension	4	1	Rep. of Secretary War.	445	Claims	Mar. 4, 1796	Favorable; bill ordered.	156	Passed	Passed	App'd April 20, 1796
Hickey, James, and James Gamb'e.	Compensation for provisions and expenses while removing Cherokee Indians.	28	1	Petition	98	Claims.						
Hickey, Philip	Compensation for timber cut by United States troops.	22	1	Petition	26	Claims	338	Report and bill	430	Referred to Committee Whole House.		
Hickey, Philip	Compensation for timber cut by United States troops.	23	1	Petition	33	Claims	21	Report and bill.	21	Passed	Passed	App'd Mar. 24, 1834
Hickman, Edna	(See Alexander D. Peck, wife of)	30	1		240							
Hickman, George	Bounty land for services of two minor sons, war of 1812.	17	1	Petition	165	Military Affairs	Feb. 1, 1822	Report by bill.	72	Passed	Passed, with amendment.	App'd May 8, 1822
Hickman, George	Invalid pension	29	1	Petition	82	Invalid Pensions.	July 25, 1846	Adverse		Laid on table.		
Hickman, Harris Hampden	Compensation for property destroyed on board brig Detroit.	13	2	Petition	190	Claims	Feb. 7, 1815			Leave to withdraw.		
Hickman, James L.	Exchange of a location of land	29	2	Petition	56	Priv. Land Claims.						
Hickman, James L.	Exchange of a location of land	30	1	Petition	305	Priv. Land Claims.						
Hickman, John H.	Special pre-emption act for his relief.	26	1	Petition	356	Public Lands	377	Adverse		Laid on table.		
Hickman, John P., administrator of	Adjustment of his accounts as quartermaster general in Florida war.	27	2	Petition	228	Claims	265	Report and bill	223	Passed	Passed	App'd Aug. 1, 1842
Hickman, Nancy	(See General William Hull, heirs of.)	21	2		95							
Hickman, N. & J., assignee of.	Confirmation of title to land	22	1	Petition	65	Priv. Land Claims.	73	Report and bill.	141	Passed	Passed	App'd July 14, 1832
Hickman, Captain Paschal, administrator of.	Compensation for rifles captured by the enemy in 1813.	22	1	Senate bill	892	Claims	July 2, 1832	With't amend.	170	Laid on table.		
Hickman, Captain Paschal, widow of.	Compensation for rifles captured by the enemy in 1813.	22	2	Petition	290	Claims	92	Report and bill	734	Referred to Committee Whole House.		
Hickman, Captain Paschal, representatives of.	Compensation for rifles captured by the enemy in 1813.	23	1	Petition & Docs.	249	Military Affairs	260	Report and bill.	298			
Hickman, Captain Paschal, administrator of.	Compensation for rifles captured by the enemy in 1813.	23	1	Senate bill	550	Claims	260	Adverse	69	Rejected.		
Hickman, Captain Paschal, widow of.	Compensation for rifles captured by the enemy in 1813.	24	1	Petition	93	Claims.						
Hickman, Captain Paschal, representatives of.	Compensation for rifles captured by the enemy in 1813.	24	2	Memorial	275	Claims.						
Hickman, Reuben & Fielding.	(See George Hickman.)	17	1		165							
Hickman, Thomas	Invalid pension	12	1	House bill	361	Whole House	June 20, 1812	Amended	138	Passed	Passed	App'd July 5, 1812
Hickman, Thomas	Invalid pension	23	2	Petition	105	Invalid Pensions	Feb. 17, 1854			Discharged; laid on table.		

List of private claims presented to the House of Representatives of the United States from the 1st to the 31st Congress, inclusive—**Continued.**

Names of claimants.	Nature or object of the claim.	Congress.	Session.	How brought before the House of Reps.	Page of journal.	To what committee of the House referred.	No. or date of the report.	Nature of the report.	No. of the bill.	How disposed of by the House of Reps.	How disposed of by the Senate.	Date of the act of Congress, and remarks.
Hickock, Ebenezer	Invalid pension	24	1	Petition	151	Invalid Pensions	300	Report and bill	313	Passed	Indef. postp'd.	
Hickock, Nathaniel	Pension for revolutionary services	18	2	Petition	36	Pens. & Rev. Cl'ms.	Dec. 17, 1821	Adverse		Laid on table.		
Hickock, Nathaniel	Pension for revolutionary services	19	1	Petition	464	Military Pensions	May 3, 1826	Adverse		Rejected.		
Hickock, Samuel	To be restored to pension roll	17	1	Petition	45	Rev. Pensions				Discharged; laid on table.		
Hickock, Samuel	Bounty land for services in the war of 1812.	24	1	Petition	94	Claims	126	Adverse		Laid on table.		
Hickox & brother	Compensation for transportation of Illinois volunteers.	30	1	Petition	507	Claims.						
Hicks, Abraham	Prize money for captures by United States ship Confederacy, revolutionary war.	23	1	Petition	39	Rev. Claims.						
Hicks, Abraham, widow of	Pension for revolutionary services	25	3	Petition	562	Rev. Pensions.						
Hicks, Abraham, widow of	Pension for revolutionary services	26	1	Petition	172	Rev. Pensions	Mar. 5, 1840			Discharged; laid on table.		
Hicks, Demsey	Pension for revolutionary services	23	1	Resolution	442	Rev. Pensions				Discharged; laid on table.		
Hicks, Demsey	Pension for revolutionary services	23	2	Resolution	164	Rev. Pensions.						
Hicks, Elijah	(See John Ross and others, Cherokees.)	19	1		155							
Hicks, Francis A	(See Indians, Wyandots)	27	3		294		160		776			
Hicks, Gabrial	Pension for his services in rev. war.	24	2	Petition	217	Rev. Pensions				Discharged; laid on table.		
Hicks, Gabrial	Pension for his services in rev. war.	25	3	Petition	562	Rev. Pensions.						
Hicks, Gabrial	Pension for his services in rev. war.	26	1	Petition	172	Rev. Pensions				Discharged; laid on table.		
Hicks, George	(See Benjamin C. Lockwood, and G. H.)	23	1		369							
Hicks, James	Compensation for rations furnished during war of 1812.	15	1	Petition	265	Claims	Mar. 13, 1818	Adverse		Laid on table.		
Hicks, Jesse T., and others	(See Ebenezer Nickerson)	12	1		315							
Hicks, Jenkins & Co	(See Samuel Rodman)	14	1		82							
Hicks, John	To be placed on invalid pension roll.	26	2	Petition	84	Invalid Pensions	146	Report and bill	657	Referred to Committee Whole House.		
Hicks, John	To be placed on invalid pension roll.	27	2	Petition	604	Invalid Pensions	808	Report and bill	462	Ordered to 3d reading.		
Hicks, John	To be placed on invalid pension roll.	27	3	House bill	89				462	Passed	Passed	App'd March 3, 1843
Hicks, Joseph	Reimbursement of expenses of sickness occasioned by a tour of military duty.	15	1	Petition	198	Claims				Discharged; laid on table.		
Hicks, Mary	(See William Hicks, widow of)	28	1		716							
Hicks, Moses	Invalid pension	3	1	Petition	82					Laid on table.		
Hicks, Nathan	To be restored to pension roll	17	1	Petition	37	Rev. Pensions				Discharged; laid on table.		
Hicks, N. H	Compensation for transporting a detachment of Georgia militia.	27	2	Documents	1377					Laid on table.		
Hicks, Oliver H., and L. De Forrest.	Permission to enter damaged wines as vinegar.	14	1	Petition	491	Com. and Manuf.				Discharged; laid on table.		
Hicks, Oliver, and L. De Forrest.	Abatement of duty on coffee	14	2	Petition	197	Com. and Manuf.				Discharged; laid on table.		
Hicks, Oliver, and L. De Forrest.	Abatement of duty on coffee	15	1	Petition	207	Com. and Manuf.	Mar. 24, 1818			Rejected.		

List of private claims presented to the House of Representatives of the United States from the 1st to the 31st Congress, inclusive—Continued.

Names of claimants.	Nature or object of the claim.	Congress.	Session.	How brought before the House of Reps.	Page of journal.	To what committee of the House referred.	No. or date of the report.	Nature of the report.	No. of the bill.	How disposed of by the House of Reps.	How disposed of by the Senate.	Date of the act of Congress, and remarks.
Hicks, Samuel & Sons	Compensation for loss on goods bought prior to June 30, 1848.	25	2	Memorial	42	Ways and Means	1013	Adverse	......	Laid on table.		
Hicks, Sarah	(See heirs of John Davis)	30	1	....	799							
Hicks, William, widow of.	Pension for revolutionary services.	28	1	Petition	716	Rev. Pensions.						
Hicks, William, widow of.	Continuation of revolutionary pension.	29	1	Petition	147	Rev. Pensions.						
Hicks, William, widow of.	Continuation of revolutionary pension.	29	2	Rep't Committee.	....	....	14	Adverse	......	Rejected	....	Case does not appear on Journal.
Hicks, Zachariah	Pension for revolutionary services.	24	1	Petition	532	Rev. Pensions	April 20, 1836	Adverse	......	Laid on table.		
Hickson, John	Invalid pension	14	2	House bill	307	Whole House	Feb. 21, 1817	With amend's.	91	Passed	Passed	App'd March 3, 1717
Hidden, Enoch	Employment in making gun locks, pursuant to an agreement with Com. Decatur.	18	1	Petition	236	Naval Affairs	April 21, 1824	Adverse	......	Laid on table.		
Hidden, Enoch	Compensation for use of patent for elevating carronades.	27	2	Senate bill	673	Naval Affairs	Aug. 10, 1842	With amend.	S. 135	Passed with amend't.	Passed as am.	App'd Aug. 29, 1842
Hidden, Enoch	Compensation for use of patent for elevating carronades.	27	3	Petition	125	Naval Affairs.						
Hidden, Enoch	Compensation for use of patent for elevating carronades.	28	1	Petition	364	Naval Affairs	294	Report and bill	205	Passed.		
Hidden, Joseph	Bounty on fishing schooner Mary Frances.	28	1	Petition	100	Commerce	224	Report and bill.	178	Passed	Passed	App'd June 15, 1844
Hidden, Zadock	(See Cary Dunn, jr., *et al.*)	21	2	....	74							
Higbee, Elnathan	Compensation for revolutionary services.	19	2	Petition	59	Rev. Claims	Dec. 26, 1826	Adverse	......	Laid on table.		
Higbee, Elnathan, widow of.	Increase of revolutionary pension.	30	1	Petition	711	Rev. Pensions	688	Adverse	......	Laid on table.		
Higby, John	Renewal of a loan office certificate.	2	1	Petition and rep. Sec. Treasury.	459, 583	Select.						
Higby, John	Renewal of a loan office certificate.	4	1	Petition	384	Claims	Jan. 20, 1796	Adverse	......	Leave to withdraw.		
Higby, Seth	Pension for revolutionary services.	19	2	Resolution	203	Rev. Pensions	Feb. 14, 1827	By bill	436	Referred to Committee Whole House.		
Higden, Samuel, by attorney.	Compensation for services in revolutionary war.	12	1	Petition	292	Claims.						
Higden, Samuel, by C. C.	Compensation for services in revolutionary war.	13	3	Petition	475	Pens. & Rev. Cl'ms.						
Higgason, Samuel	Pension	21	1	Resolution	255	Military Pensions	....	....	......	Discharged; laid on table.		
Higgason, Samuel	Pension	21	2	Resolution	110	Military Pensions.						
Higginbotham, Arthur	(See Thomas B. Scott, *et al.*)	29	1	....	440							
Higginbotham, Eleanor	(See heir of Capt. James Wilson)	29	1	....	524							
Higginbotham, Thomas	Indemnity for French spoliations prior to 1800.	26	1	Memorial	182	Foreign Affairs	343	Favorable; bill	319	Referred to Committee Whole House.		
Higginbotham, Thos., heirs of.	Indemnity for French spoliations prior to 1800.	31	1	Petition	348	Foreign Affairs	355	General bill	318	Referred to Committee Whole House.		
Higginbotham, William	Pension	20	1	Petition	68	Military Pensions.						
Higginbotham, William	Pension	21	1	Petition	48	Military Pensions.						
Higginbotham, William	Pension	21	1	House bill	130	Whole House	Feb. 13, 1830	Favorable	72	Passed	Passed	App'd May 20, 1830
Higgins, A. G., *et al.*	Bounty on fishing schooner Madison.	28	2	Petition	228	Commerce.						
Higgins, A. G., *et al.*	Bounty on fishing schooner Madison.	29	1	Petition	152	Commerce	Aug. 16, 1846	Report by bill.	391	Referred to Committee Whole House.		
Higgins, A. G., *et al.*	Bounty on fishing schooner Madison.	30	1	Petition	70	Commerce	259	Report and bill.	252	Referred to Committee Whole House.		

List of private claims presented to the House of Representatives of the United States from the 1st to the 31st Congress, inclusive—Continued.

Names of claimants.	Nature or object of the claim.	Congress.	Session.	How brought before the House of Reps.	Page of journal.	To what committee of the House referred.	No. or date of the report.	Nature of the report.	No. of the bill.	How disposed of by the House of Reps.	How disposed of by the Senate.	Date of the act of Congress, and remarks.
Higgins, A. G., *et al.*	Bounty on fishing schooner Madison.	31	1	Petition	299	Commerce.						
Higgins, Cecilia	(See heir of Richard Davis)	29	1	....	395							
Higgins, Cornelius	Compensation for services as a revolutionary soldier.	21	1	Petition	143	Military Pensions	April 27, 1850	General bill	348	Referred to Committee Whole House.		
Higgins, Cornelius	Compensation for services as a revolutionary soldier	21	2	Resolution	42	Military Pensions.						
Higgins, Cornelius	Compensation for services as a revolutionary soldier.	22	1	Petition	194	Rev. Pensions.						
Higgins, Isaac	Invalid pension	3	1	Rep. of Secretary War.	131	Select	May 26, 1794	Jt. res. to refer to Sec. War.	22	Passed	Passed	App'd June 9, 1794
Higgins, Isaac	Invalid pension	4	1	Rep. of Secretary War.	445	Claims	Mar. 4, 1796	Favorable; bill ordered.	156	Passed	Passed	App'd April 20, 1796
Higgins, Isaac	Invalid pension	10	1	House bill	232	Whole House	April 19, 1808	With amends.	78	Passed	Passed	App'd April 25, 1808
Higgins, Isaac, (Hannah,) widow of.	Pension for revolutionary services.	25	2	Petition	586	Rev. Pensions	....	....	....	Discharged; laid on table.		
Higgins, James R. or K.	Pension	20	2	Petition	118	Military Pensions	....	....	....	Laid on table.		
Higgins, James R. or K.	Pension	23	1	Petition	137	Invalid Pensions	Mar. 21, 1834	Adverse	....	Laid on table.		
Higgins, John, heirs of	Confirmation of title to land in Missouri.	15	2	Petition	28	Priv. Land Claims.						
Higgins, John, heirs of	Confirmation of title to land in Missouri	17	1	Petition	54	Public Lands	....	....	....	Laid on table.		
Higgins, John, heirs of	Confirmation of title to land in Missouri	18	1	Petition	54	Public Lands.						
Higgins, Lucius M.	(See Daniel Jackson & L. M. H.)	21	2	....	62							
Higgins, Mathew, widow of.	Pension	22	1	Petition	36	Invalid Pensions	Jan. 11, 1832	Adverse	....	Laid on table.		
Higgins, Moses	Pension for revolutionary services.	22	1	Petition	36	Rev. Pensions	113	Report and bill.	193	Referred to Committee Whole House.		
Higgins, Moses	Pension for revolutionary services.	22	2	House bill	193	....	....	....	....	Laid on table.		
Higgins, Nathan	Increase of compensation as postmaster at Pembroke, Maine.	29	2	Petition	316	P. Of. & P. Roads.						
Higgins, Richard	Right of pre-emption	27	2	Senate bill	782	Public Lands	Aug. 5, 1842	With't amend.	S. 140	Passed	....	App'd Aug. 11, 1842
Higginson, Stephen	Indemnity for French spoliations prior to 1800.	26	1	Memorial	182	Foreign Affairs	343	Favorable; bill	319	Referred to Committee Whole House.		
High, Ezekiel	(See Louis F. Beeler, *et al*)	30	1	....	115							
Highland, or Hyland, William.	To be restored to revolutionary pension roll.	22	1	Petition	171	Rev. Pensions	365	Report and bill.	460	Passed	Indef. postp'd.	
Hightower, Capt. Richard.	Indemnity from suits resulting from loss of vouchers in battle.	17	2	Petition and docs.	36	Claims	Jan. 26, 1823	Report and bill.	232	Passed	Passed, with amendment.	App'd March 3, 1823
Hightower, Capt. Richard	Revision of a settlement under the act for his relief.	18	1	Documents	296	Claims.						
Hightower, Capt. Richard.	Revision of a settlement under the act for his relief.	18	2	House bill	243	Claims	72	With't amend.	341	Passed	Passed	App'd March 3, 1825
Hightower, Thomas	Indemnity for an injury to a slave, war of 1812.	16	1	Petition	35	Claims	Dec. 31, 1819	Adverse	....	Rejected.		
Higle, Jacob	Arrears of pension	25	2	Petition	663	Invalid Pensions.						
Higle, Jacob	Arrears of pension	26	1	Petition	163	Invalid Pensions	261	Adverse	....	Laid on table.		
Higley, Elam	Pension for disability incurred in the war of 1812.	24	1	Petition	398	Invalid Pensions	....	....	....	Discharged; laid on table.		
Higley, Elam	Pension for disability incurred in the war of 1812.	25	2	Petition	722	Invalid Pensions	877	Report and bill.	782			
Higley, Elam	Pension for disability incurred in the war of 1812.	26	1	Petition	16	Invalid Pensions.						

List of private claims presented to the House of Representatives of the United States from the 1st to the 31st Congress, inclusive—Continued.

Names of claimants.	Nature or object of the claim.	Congress.	Session.	How brought before the House of Reps.	Page of journal.	To what committee of the House referred.	No. or date of the report.	Nature of the report.	No. of the bill.	How disposed of by the House of Reps.	How disposed of by the Senate.	Date of the act of Congress, and remarks.
Higley, Seth	Pension for revolutionary services.	20	1	Resolution	153	Military Pensions	April 29, 1828	Report by bill.	283	Passed.		
Higley, Seth	Pension for revolutionary services.	20	2	Petition	55	Military Pensions	Dec. 2, 1828	General bill	311	Passed.		
Higley, Seth	Pension for revolutionary services.	21	1	Petition	48	Military Pensions.	Feb. 13, 1830	By bill	72	Passed	Passed	App'd May 20, 1830
Hildebrand, Daniel	Confirmation of title to land in Missouri.	15	1	Petition	226	Priv. Land Claims.	....	....	......	Discharged; laid on table.		
Hildebrand, Daniel	Confirmation of title to land in Missouri.	16	1	Petition	71	Priv. Land Claims.						
Hildebrand, Daniel	Confirmation of title to land in Missouri.	17	1	Petition	54	Public Lands.						
Hildebrand, Daniel	Confirmation of title to land in Missouri.	18	1	Petition	54	Public Lands	....	....	......	....	....	See act May 26, 1824
Hildreth, John, widow of.	Pension for services, war of 1812.	25	3	Petition	128	Invalid Pensions.						
Hildreth, John, widow of.	Pension for services, war of 1812.	26	1	Petition	162	Invalid Pensions	528	Report and bill	424	Referred to Committee Whole House.		
Hildreth, John, widow of.	Pension for services, war of 1812.	27	3	Petition	70	Invalid Pensions	10	Adverse	......	Laid on table.		
Hildreth, John, widow of.	Pension for services, war of 1812.	28	1	Petition	83	Invalid Pensions	....	....	......	Discharged; laid on table.		
Hildreth, John, widow of.	Pension for services, war of 1812.	29	1	Petition	82	Invalid Pensions	....	....	......	Discharged; laid on table.		
Hildreth, John, widow of.	Pension for services, war of 1812.	29	2	Petition and add'l evidence.	57	Invalid Pensions	....	....	......	Discharged; laid on table.		
Hildreth, John, widow of.	Pension for services, war of 1812.	30	1	Petition	82	Invalid Pensions	194	Report and bill	204	Passed.		
Hildreth, John, widow of.	Pension for services, war of 1812.	31	1	Petition	827	Invalid Pensions.						
Hildreth, Reuben	Arrears of revolutionary pension	28	1	Petition	130	Rev. Pensions	....	....	......	Disch'd; laid on table.		
Hildreth, William H.	Payment of certain drafts drawn by officers of the government for goods furnished Indians.	28	2	Petition	347	Indian Affairs.						
Hildrup, William, administrator of.	Relief from payment of a bond for duties.	8	1	Petition	544	Com. and Manuf.						
Hiley, Abraham	(See Melchier Baker, *et al.*)	19	1	....	267							
Hill, Adam	Compensation for revolutionary services.	2	1	Petition	521	....	....	....	......	Referred to Secretary Treasury.		
Hill, Adam	Compensation for supplies furnished revolutionary army.	3	3	Rep. of Secretary Treasury.	284	Claims	....	....	......	Laid on table.		
Hill, Alexander	Bounty land for revolutionary services, Pennsylvania line.	7	1	Petition	12	Claims	Dec. 21, 1801	Adverse	......	Rejected.		
Hill, Alexander, attorney of.	Pension for revolutionary services.	25	2	Documents	585	Rev. Pensions.						
Hill, Alexander Johnston.	Pension	26	1	Petition	602	Invalid Pensions.						
Hill, Alpheus	Pension	14	2	Petition	39	Pens. & Rev. Cl'ms.	Jan. 29, 1817	Report by bill.	91	Passed	Passed, with amendment.	App'd March 3, 1817
Hill, Amos, assignee of widow of.	Scrip certificate in lieu of Virginia military land warrant.	23	1	Petition	368							
				Petition	385	Priv. Land Claims.	Jan. 4, 1834	Report by bill.	336	Passed	With amend.	
Hill, Amos, assignee of widow of.	Scrip certificate in lieu of Virginia military land warrant.	23	2	Petition	69	Priv. Land Claims.	Dec. 18, 1834	Report by bill.	575	Passed	Rejected.	
Hill, Baylor	Commutation pay for revolutionary services.	2	1	Petition	481	....	....	....	......	Referred to Secretary of War.		
Hill, Capt. B. F., & others	Settlement of accounts as Texas mounted rangers.	31	1	Indian appropriation bill.	1012	Whole House	June 14, 1850	With amend.	331	Passed	Passed, with amendment.	App'd Sept. 30, 1850
Hill, Dennis	Compensation for services as issuing commissary in the battalions of Nelson and Pain.	26	2	Resolution	198	Claims.						

2—12

List of private claims presented to the House of Representatives of the United States from the 1st to the 31st Congress, inclusive—Continued.

Names of claimants.	Nature or object of the claim.	Congress.	Session.	How brought before the House of Reps.	Page of journal.	To what committee of the House referred.	No. or date of the report.	Nature of the report.	No. of the bill.	How disposed of by the House of Reps.	How disposed of by the Senate.	Date of the act of Congress, and remarks.
Hill, Edward, *et al.*	Indemnity for French spoliations prior to 1800.	31	1	Petition	413	Foreign Affairs	355	General bill	318	Referred to Committee Whole House.		
Hill, Elijah	(See Elizabeth Mason, assignees of)	22	1	...	227				354			
Hill, Frederick	Pension for services as a revolutionary soldier.	21	1	Resolution	343	Military Pensions	May 3, 1830	General bill	454	Referred to Committee Whole House.		
Hill, Frederick	Pension for services as a revolutionary soldier.	24	2	Resolution	222	Rev. Pensions	223	Report and bill	930	Referred to Committee Whole House.		
Hill, Frederick	Pension for services as a revolutionary soldier.	25	2	Resolution	38	Rev. Pensions	168	Report and bill	193	Passed	Passed	App'd June 28, 1838
Hill, Frederick, widow of.	Continuation of pension	25	3	Resolution	126	Rev. Pensions				Discharged.		
Hill, George	Invalid pension	12	2	Petition	664	Claims.						
Hill, George	Invalid pension	13	1	House bill	56	Whole House	July 20, 1813	Favorable	31	Passed	Passed	App'd Aug. 2, 1813
Hill, Henry, *et al*	For a portion of the amount due J. Banks; they being creditors of said Banks.	3	1	Petition	17	Select	Jan. 7, 1794	Favorable		Referred to Committee Whole House.		
Hill, Henry, *et al*	For a portion of the amount due J. Banks; they being creditors of said Banks.	3	2	Report of Select Committee.	299	Claims.						
Hill, Henry, *et al*	For a portion of the amount due J. Banks; they being creditors of said Banks.	4	1	Petition and docs.	373	Claims	May 26, 1796	Favorable		Referred to Committee Whole House.		
Hill, Henry, *et al*	For a portion of the amount due J. Banks; they being creditors of said Banks.	4	2	Petition and docs.	612	Claims	Jan. 13, 1797	Favorable		Referred to Committee Whole House.		
Hill, Henry, *et al*	For a portion of the amount due J. Banks; they being creditors of said Banks.	5	2	Petition and doc.	83	Whole House	Feb. 14, 1798	Res.; favorable		Passed.		
Hill, Henry, (consul at Brazil.)	Reimbursement of foreign tonnage duties on brig Rivid.	12	1	Petition	354	Com. and Manuf.						
Hill, Henry	Indemnity for losses on bills drawn by Captain Biddle for supplies furnished U. S. ship Hornet.	23	1	Memorial	114	Claims	435	Adverse		Laid on table.		
Hill, Henry	Indemnity for losses on bills drawn by Captain Biddle for supplies furnished U. S. ship Hornet.	23	2	Petition	163	Claims	Jan. 26, 1835	Adverse		Laid on table.		
Hill, Henry	Indemnity for losses on bills drawn by Captain Biddle for supplies furnished U. S. ship Hornet.	24	1	Petition	93	Claims	292	Adverse		Laid on table.		
Hill, Henry	Indemnity for losses on bills drawn by Captain Biddle for supplies furnished U. S. ship Hornet.	24	2	Memorial	73	Claims	Dec. 28, 1836	Adverse		Laid on table.		
Hill, Henry	Indemnity for losses on bills drawn by Captain Biddle for supplies furnished U. S. ship Hornet.	25	2	Memorial	51, 396	Claims	Dec. 22, 1837	Adverse		Laid on table.		
Hill, Henry	Indemnity for losses on bills drawn by Captain Biddle for supplies furnished U. S. ship Hornet.	25	3	Memorial	86	Claims	36	Adverse		Laid on table.		
Hill, Henry, heirs of	Indemnity for losses on bills drawn by Captain Biddle for supplies furnished U. S. ship Hornet.	31	2	Memorial	244	Naval Affairs.						
Hill, Isaac & Sons	Indemnity for non-fulfilment of contract by Post Office Department.	30	1	Petition	647	Claims.						

List of private claims presented to the House of Representatives of the United States from the 1st to the 31st Congress, inclusive—Continued.

Names of claimants.	Nature or object of the claim.	Congress.	Session.	How brought before the House of Reps.	Page of journal.	To what committee of the House referred.	No. or date of the report.	Nature of the report.	No. of the bill.	How disposed of by the House of Reps.	How disposed of by the Senate.	Date of the act of Congress, and remarks.
Hill, Isaac & Sons	Indemnity for non-fulfilment of contract by Post Office Department.	31	1	Petition	369	P. Of. & P. Roads.						
Hill, Isaac & Sons	Indemnity for non-fulfilment of contract by Post Office Department.	31	2	Bill on leave	39	Judiciary			407			
Hill, Isaac	Relief on account of certain libel suits.	31	1	Memorial	609	P. Of. & P. Roads.				Discharged; laid on table.		
Hill, Israel	Confirmation of title to land in Missouri.	15	1	Petition	133	Priv. Land Claims.				Discharged; laid on table.		
Hill, Israel	Confirmation of title to land in Missouri.	17	1	Petition	54	Public Lands.				Discharged; laid on table.		
Hill, Israel	Confirmation of title to land in Missouri.	18	1	Petition	54	Public Lands.						
Hill, Israel	(See Israel Hall)	16	1		71							
Hill, J. R	(See T. K. Hill)	31	1		224							
Hill, Jabez	Compensation for losses and services in revolutionary war.	1	3	Petition	352					Referred to Secretary of War.		
Hill, Jeremiah	For his share of a judgment recovered in behalf of United States.	13	1	Petition	120	Ways and Means.						
Hill, Jeremiah	Reimbursement of expenses in attending a certain suit.	13	3	Petition	566	Ways and Means.	64	Adverse		Laid on table.		
Hill, James W	(See Elizabeth Mason, assignees of.)	22	1		227				354			
Hill, James	(See Henry Develin, *et al.*)	23	1		589		449					
Hill, Joel, heirs and representatives of.	Further compensation for services on public works at East Baton Rouge.	21	1	Petition	472	Claims	April 28, 1830	Adverse		Laid on table.		
Hill, John	Permission to change location of land.	19	1	Petition	58	Public Lands	54	Favorable; bill	77	Passed	Passed	App'd May 22, 1826
Hill, John	Compensation for revolutionary services.	30	2	Petition	458	Rev. Pensions.						
Hill, John, heirs of	Compensation for revolutionary services.	31	1	Petition	671	Rev. Pensions	314	Adverse		Laid on table.		
Hill, John	Pension for revolutionary services.	24	2	Petition	399	Rev. Pensions.						
Hill, John	Pension for revolutionary services.	26	2	Petition	320	Rev. Pensions	Jan. 27, 1838	Adverse		Laid on table.		
Hill, John	Compensation for trunk, &c., lost in revolutionary service.	25	2	Petition	312	Rev. Claims	612	Adverse		Laid on table.		
Hill, John, (Tenn.)	Pension for revolutionary services.	30	2	Memorial	462	Rev. Pensions.						
Hill, John, heir of	Extension of time for locating Virginia military land warrant.	17	2	Petition	26	Public Lands	Dec. 17, 1822	General bill	196	Laid on table.		
Hill, John, (Huldah,) widow of.	Pension for revolutionary services.	27	2	Petition	219	Rev. Pensions	784	Adverse		Laid on table.		
Hill, John, widow & children of.	Reimbursement of money paid for certain lands.	26	1	Senate bill	802	Priv. Land Claims.	April 25, 1840	With amend.	S. 80	Referred to Committee Whole House.		
Hill, John, widow & children of.	Reimbursement of money paid for certain lands.	26	2	Senate bill	329	Whole House			S. 170			
Hill, John, and others	Bounty land and pension	31	1	House bill	638	Rev. Pensions	138	Favorable	152	Referred to Committee Whole House.		
Hill, John B.	To be restored to revolutionary pension roll.	25	2	Petition	349	Rev. Claims.						
Hill, Joseph D.	Release from suretyship for P. Houston.	24	1	Petition	740	Judiciary.						
Hill, Joseph D.	Release from suretyship for P. Houston.	24	2	Petition	218	Judiciary				Leave to withdraw.		

List of private claims presented to the House of Representatives of the United States from the 1st to the 31st Congress, inclusive—Continued.

Names of claimants	Nature or object of the claim.	Congress.	Session.	How brought before the House of Reps.	Page of journal.	To what committee of the House referred.	No. or date of the report.	Nature of the report.	No. of the bill.	How disposed of by the House of Reps.	How disposed of by the Senate.	Date of the act of Congress, and remarks.
Hill, Joseph D.	Release from suretyship for P. Houston.	29	1	Petition	284	Claims						Leave to withdraw, 2d session.
Hill, Josiah	Pension	21	1	Petition	448	Military Pensions				Discharged; laid on table.		
Hill, Josiah	Pension	21	2	Petition	127	Military Pensions.						
Hill, Josiah	(See Wm. H. Bedford, agent)	28	1		262							
Hill, Levi	Pension for revolutionary services.	22	1	Petition	412	Rev. Pensions				Disch'd; laid on table.		
Hill, Mark L., and others.	Indemnity for French spoliations prior to 1800.	26	1	Memorial	182	Foreign Affairs	343	Favorable; bill	319	Referred to Committee Whole House.		
Hill, Mark Langdon, and Thos. McCobbs.	Remission of duties on goods	13	2	Petition	195	Ways and Means	Jan. 28, 1814	Adverse		Rejected.		
Hill, Marvell	Pension for services, war of 1812.	30	2	Memorial	492	Invalid Pensions.						
Hill, Marvell	Pension for services, war of 1812.	31	1	Memorial	214	Invalid Pensions				Discharged; leave to withdraw.		
Hill, N. B.	(See Stalker, Gilbert & Hill	27	2		1126				S. 248			
Hill, Parker, widow of	Pension for revolutionary services.	26	1	Petition	283	Rev. Pensions.						
Hill, Parker, widow of	Pension for revolutionary services.	26	2	Petition	35	Rev. Pensions.						
Hill, Parker, widow of	Pension for revolutionary services.	27	2	Petition	59	Rev. Pensions	784	Adverse		Laid on table.		
Hill, Philip, heirs of	Commutation pay for revolutionary services.	22	1	Petition	288	Rev. Claims	Feb. 18, 1832	Adverse		Laid on table.		
Hill, Rees	Settlement of his accounts	15	2	Senate bill	280	Claims	Feb. 20, 1819	With't amend.	S. 46	Passed		App'd March 3, 1819
Hill, Col. Rees	Compensat'n for supplies furnished militia, war of 1812.	18	1	Petition	271	Claims.						
Hill, Col. Rees	Compensat'n for supplies furnished militia, war of 1812.	23	2	Petition	238	Claims.						
Hill, Col. Rees	Compensat'n for supplies furnished militia, war of 1812.	24	1	Petition	905	Claims	715	Adverse		Laid on table.		
Hill, Col. Rees	Compensat'n for supplies furnished militia, war of 1812.	24	2	Petition	222					Leave to withdraw.		
Hill, Samuel	To be restored to pension roll	17	2	Petition	119	Whole House				Discharged; leave to withdraw.		
Hill, Samuel, widow of	Indemnity for loss of land purchased of the United States.	24	1	Petition	600	Public Lands.						
Hill, Samuel, representatives of.	Indemnity for loss of land purchased of the United States.	25	2	Senate bill	1166	Public Lands	July 6, 1838	With't amend.	S. 246	Referred to Committee Whole House.		
Hill, Samuel, representatives of.	Indemnity for loss of land purchased of the United States.	25	3	Senate bill	477	Public Lands	Feb. 13, 1839	With't amend.	S. 73	Referred to Committee Whole House.		
Hill, Samuel, widow of	Indemnity for loss of land purchased of the United States.	27	2	Senate bill	1042	Public Lands	July 21, 1842	With't amend.	S. 128	Passed		App'd Aug. 11, 1842
Hill, Samuel, heirs of	Indemnity for French spoliations prior to 1800.	31	1	Petition	348	Foreign Affairs	355	General bill	318	Referred to Committee Whole House.		
Hill, & Sears	Remission of duty on books imported for gratuitous distribution.	31	1	Appropriat'n bill.	1034				334			App'd Sept. 30, 1850
Hill, Thomas	Invalid pension	3	1	Rep. of Secretary War.	131	Select.	May 26, 1794	Favorable; bill ordered.	62	Passed	Passed	App'd June 7, 1794
Hill, Thomas	Invalid pension	22	1	Petition	51	Rev. Pensions				Discharged, laid on table.		
Hill, Thomas	(See William H. Bedford, agent.)	28	1		262							
Hill, F. K.	Compensation for services as surgeon in Mexican war.	31	1	Petition	224	Military Affairs				Discharged; laid on table.		
Hill, William, and others.	Compensation for their lands conveyed by treaty to Chickasaw and Cherokee Indians.	6	1	Petition	617	Select	April 4, 1800	Favorable		Referred to Committee Whole House.		

List of private claims presented to the House of Representatives of the United States from the 1st to the 31st Congress, inclusive—Continued.

Names of claimants.	Nature or object of the claim.	Congress.	Session.	How brought before the House of Reps.	Page of journal.	To what committee of the House referred.	No. or date of the report.	Nature of the report.	No. of the bill.	How disposed of by the House of Reps.	How disposed of by the Senate.	Date of the act of Congress, and remarks.
Hill, William, and Martin Hoffman.	Drawback on goods exported....	14	1	Petition	386	Com. and Manuf..	April 12, 1816	Report by bill.	......	Indef. postponed.		
Hill, William, and Martin Hoffman.	Drawback on goods exported.....	14	2	Petition	101	Com. and Manuf..	Dec. 31, 1816	Report by bill.	36	Passed............	Passed	App'd March 3, 1817
Hill, William...........	(See Isaac Lawrence and others.)	14	2	....	101							
Hill, Col. William, executors of.	Indemnity for the destruction of the iron works of deceased by the enemy, revolutionory war.	21	1	Petition	98	Rev. Claims.						
Hill, William, heirs of ...	Compensation for property taken for public use, war of 1812.	23	1	Petition	131	Claims	Jan. 3, 1834	....	......	Laid on table.		
Hills, Frederick.........	Invalid pension................	3	1	Rep. of Secretary War.	131	Select...........	May 26, 1794	J't. res. to refer to Sec. War.	J. R. 12	Passed	Passed	App'd June 9, 1794
Hills, Frederick.........	Invalid pension................	3	2	Rep. of Secretary War.	262	Claims	Mar. 3, 1794	....	......	Discharged; laid on table.		
Hills, H. W. & S.......	(See Gabriel W. Denton.)......	24	1	....	153							
Hills, J., and forty others .	Compensation for a horses lost in the public service.	27	2	Petition	612	Claims.						
Hills, Maria............	(See Isaac Ostertrout, widow of.)	31	1	....	519							
Hills, Thomas..........	Indemnity for property lost in the retreat from New York in 1776.	24	2	Resolution	73	Rev. Claims.						
, Zimri.............	Invalid pension	3	1	Rep. of Secretary War.	131	Select...........	May 26, 1794	J't. res. to refer to Sec. War.	12	Passed	Passed	App'd June 9, 1794
Hill, Zimri.............	Invalid pension	3	2	Rep. of Secretary War.	337	Claims	Feb. 28, 1795	Favorable; bill ordered.	130	Passed	Postp'd to next session.	
Hill, Zimri.............	Invalid pension................	4	1	Rep. of Secretary War.	445	Claims	Mar. 4, 1796	Favorable; bill ordered.	156	Passed	Passed	App'd April 20, 1796
Hilliard, Gray, & Co.....	Balance due for printing	22	2	Appropriat'n bill.	....	....	....	....	......	....	....	App'd March 2, 1833
Hilliard, Thurston.......	Compensation for revolutionary services.	2	1	Petition	447	....	....	....	......	Referred to Secretary War.		
Hillary, Christopher, heir of.	Commutation pay due for his services as a lieutenant in revolutionary army.	23	1	Petition	335	Rev. Claims.						
Hillary, Rignal, heirs of...	Commutation pay due at the time of his death.	21	2	Resolution	101	Rev. Claims......	101	Favorable; bill	560	Referred to Committee Whole House.		
Hillary, Rignal, heirs of...	Commutation pay due at the time of his death.	22	1	Resolution	30	Rev. Claims......	Jan. 3, 1832	Report by bill.	187	Passed	Passed	App'd May 25, 1832
Hillary, Rignal, heirs of...	Commutation pay due at the time of his death.	25	2	Resolution	882	Rev. Claims......	891	Report and bill.	790	Rejected.		
Hillary, Rignal, heirs of...	Commutation pay due at the time of his death.	25	3	Resolution	85	Rev. Claims......	104	Report and bill	979	Referred to Committee Whole House.		
Hillary, Rignal, heirs of...	Commutation pay due at the time of his death.	26	1	Petition	166	Rev. Claims.						
Hillary, Rignal, heirs of...	Commutation pay due at the time of his death.	26	2	Petition	77	Rev. Claims	116	Report and bill	621	Referred to Committee Whole House.		
Hillary, Rignal, heirs of...	Commutation pay erroneously paid Mary Magruder.	27	2	Petition	62	Rev. Claims	382	Adverse	......	Laid on table.		
Hillary, Rignal, heirs of...	Indemnity for bounty land of which they were defrauded.	28	2	Petition	145	Rev. Pensions.						
Hillary, Rignal, heirs of...	Indemnity for bounty land of which they were defrauded.	29	1	Petition	262	Rev. Claims......	511	Adverse	......	Laid on table.		
Hillary, Rignal, heirs of...	Pension for revolutionary services.	29	2	Petition	164	Rev. Claims.						
Hillary, Rignal, heirs of...	Remuneration for bounty land and commutation pay.	30	1	Petition	77	Claims	63	Report and bill	45	Passed.		

List of private claims presented to the House of Representatives of the United States from the 1st to the 31st Congress, inclusive—Continued.

Names of claimants.	Nature or object of the claim.	Congress.	Session.	How brought before the House of Reps.	Page of journal.	To what committee of the House referred.	No. or date of the report.	Nature of the report.	No. of the bill.	How disposed of by the House of Reps.	How disposed of by the Senate.	Date of the act of Congress, and remarks.
Hillary, Rignal, heirs of...	Remuneration for bounty land and commutation pay.	30	2	House bill.....	518	....	....	....	45	....	Indef. postp'd.	
Hillary, Rignal, heirs of...	Indemnity for bounty land of which they were defrauded.	31	1	Petition.......	449	Rev. Claims......	186	Adverse.....	......	Laid on table.		
Hillegas, Michael........	Payment of claim as treasurer under old confederation.	4	1	Petition.......	457	Claims.						
Hillegas, Michael........	Payment of claim as treasurer under old confederation.	4	2	Petition.......	614	Claims..........	Jan. 11, 1797	Adverse.				
Hillegas, S.............	(See Thomas Stiner)...........	15	2	....	150							
Hillen, or Helen, Mary...	(See mother of James A. Dudley.)	26	1	....	169							
Hillen, John...........	Indemnity for French spoliations prior to 1800.	26	1	....	182	Foreign Affairs...	343	Favorable; bill	319	Referred to Committee Whole House.		
Hillen, Nathaniel, heirs of.	Confirmation of title to land.....	22	1	Petition.......	32	Priv. Land Claims.	Dec. 23, 1831	Report by bill.	149	Passed............	Passed......	App'd July 14, 1832
Hiller, Jacob..........	Pension for revolutionary services.	23	1	House bill.....	580	Rev. Pensions.....	438	Report and bill	542	Referred to Committee Whole House.		
Hilliard, Thurston.......	(See Thurston Hillard).........	2	1	....	447							
Hilliard, Thurston.......	Invalid pension................	3	1	Rep. of Secretary War.	131	Select..........	May 26, 1794	Jt. res. to refer to Sec. War.	J.R. 12	Passed............	Passed......	App'd June 9, 1794
Hilliard, Thurston.......	Invalid pension................	3	2	Rep. of Secretary of War.	337	Claims..........	....	....	......	Discharged; laid on table.		
Hilliard, Thurston.......	Invalid pension................	4	1	Rep. of Secretary War.	445	Claims..........	Mar. 4, 1796	Favorable; bill ordered.	156	Passed............	Passed......	App'd April 20, 1796
Hilliard, Jonathan, widow of.	Half-pay due for disability incurred in United States navy.	26	1	Resolution.....	561	Naval Affairs.						
Hilliard, Jonathan, (Polly C.,) widow of.	Half-pay due for disability incurred in United States navy.	28	1	Petition.......	615	Naval Affairs.						
Hilliard, Jonathan, (Polly C.,) widow of.	Half-pay due for disability incurred in United States navy.	29	1	Petition.......	255	Naval Affairs.....	....	....	......	Discharged; laid on table.		
Hilliard, Nancy.........	(See heirs of William Gregory)...	26	1	....	164	....	90					
Hilliburton, A..........	Indemnity for French spoliations prior to 1800.	26	1	Memorial......	182	Foreign Affairs....	343	Favorable; bill	319	Referred to Committee Whole House.		
Hillyard, Charles M......	Compensation for supplies furnished United States troops in 1814.	26	1	Documents.....	408	Claims.						
Hillyard, Charles M......	Compensation for supplies furnished United States troops in 1814.	26	2	Petition.......	80	Claims..........	22	Adverse.....	......	Laid on table.		
Hillyard, Jonathan, widow of	Arrears of revolutionary pension..	27	1	Petition.......	101	Rev. Pensions.						
Hillyard, Jonathan, widow of	Arrears of revolutionary pension..	27	2	Petition.......	48	Rev. Pensions....	784	Adverse.....	......	Laid on table.		
Hillyard, Joshua........	Compensation for forage furnished, war of 1812.	24	1	Petition.......	91	Claims..........	May 31, 1836	Adverse.....	......	Laid on table.		
Hillyard, Joshua........	Compensation for forage furnished, war of 1812.	26	2	Petition.......	80	Claims..........	28	Adverse.....	......	Laid on table.		
Hillyard, Joshua........	Compensation for forage furnished, war of 1812.	30	1	Petition.......	480	Claims.						
Hillyard, Joshua........	Compensation for forage furnished, war of 1812.	31	1	Petition.......	533	Claims..........	260	Adverse.....	......	Laid on table.		
Hillyard, Thomas........	Pension for services as a revolutionary soldier.	13	3	Petition.......	732	Pens. & Rev. Cl'ms.						
Hillman, Benjamin......	Pension......................	10	1	House bill.....	232	Whole House.....	April 19, 1808	Favorable....	78	Passed............	Passed......	App'd April 25, 1808
Hillman, Benjamin, mother of.	Exchange of an entry of land....	25	3	Petition.......	463	Priv. Land Claims.						
Hillman, Benjamin, mother of.	Exchange of an entry of land....	26	1	Petition.......	179	Priv. Land Claims.						

List of private claims presented to the House of Representatives of the United States from the 1st to the 31st Congress, inclusive—Continued.

Names of claimants.	Nature or object of the claim.	Congress.	Session.	How brought before the House of Reps.	Page of journal.	To what committee of the House referred.	No. or date of the report.	Nature of the report.	No. of the bill.	How disposed of by the House of Reps.	How disposed of by the Senate.	Date of the act of Congress, and remarks.
Hillman, James	Pension for revolutionary services	29	1	Petition	86	Rev. Pensions	75	Favorable; bill	94	Passed.		
Hillman, James	Pension for revolutionary services	30	1	Petition	69	Rev. Pensions	90	Adverse.				
Hillman, James	Pension for services in the war of 1812.	30	1	Petition	253	Rev. Pensions.						
Hillman, Mary	Pension for services of husband in preventing the use of a liberty pole by the enemy.	24	2	Petition	302	Rev. Claims.						
Hillman, Mary	Pension for services of husband in preventing the use of a liberty pole by the enemy.	25	3	Petition	220	Rev. Claims	....	....	......	Discharged.		
Hillen, Robert	Confirmation of title to land in Louisiana.	20	2	Petition	41	Priv. Land Claims	....	....	......	Discharged; laid on table.		
Hillen, Robert	Confirmation of title to land in Louisiana.	21	1	Petition	51	Priv. Land Claims	....	....	......	Discharged; laid on table.		
Hillen, Robert	Confirmation of title to land in Louisiana.	21	2	Petition	83	Priv. Land Claims	Jan. 6, 1831	Adverse	......	Laid on table.		
Hillen, Robert	Confirmation of title to land in Louisiana.	22	1	Petition	32	Priv. Land Claims	76	Report and bill	149	Passed	Passed	App'd July 14, 1832
Hillsman, Jose, widow of	Compensation for revolutionary services.	27	2	Petition	703	Rev. Pensions	913	Report and bill.	529	Referred to Committee Whole House.		
Hillsman, Jose, widow of	Compensation for revolutionary services.	27	3	House bill	89	Whole House	....	....	529	Passed.		
Hillyer, Andrew	Pension for revolutionary services	16	1	Petition	245	Rev. Pensions	April 20, 1820	Adverse	......	Laid on table.		
Hilton, Hale	Indemnity for French spoliations prior to 1800.	26	1	Memorial	182	Foreign Affairs	343	Favorable; bill	319	Referred to Committee Whole House.		
Hilton, Isaac	Pension for revolutionary services	24	2	Petition	117	Rev. Pensions	143	Report and bill	871	Referred to Committee Whole House.		
Hilton, Isaac	Pension for revolutionary services	25	2	Petition	38	Rev. Pensions	153	Report and bill.	178	Passed	Adverse report.	
Hilton, Joseph	Invalid pension	4	1	Rep. of Secretary War.	445	Claims	March 4, 1796	Favorable; bill ordered.	156	Passed	Passed	App'd April 20, 1796
Hilton, Joseph	Compensation for revolutionary services.	12	1	Petition	262	Claims.						
Hilton, Joshua	Release of penalty incurred by violation of non-importation act.	13	1	Petition	43	Ways and Means.						
Hilton, Joshua	Release of penalty incurred by violation of non-importation act.	13	2	Petition	234	Ways and Means	April 5, 1814	Adverse	......	Leave to withdraw.		
Hilton, Luke	Indemnity for injuries received in locating lines between Canada and the United States.	29	1	Petition	220	Claims	338	Adverse	......	Laid on table.		
Hilton or Helton, Peter	Pension for revolutionary services	30	1	Petition	840	Rev. Pensions	367	Adverse	......	Laid on table.		
Hilton, Samuel	Compensation for horses lost in war of 1812.	31	2	Petition	72	Claims.						
Hilton, William	Compensation for services as a revolutionary soldier.	16	2	Petition	212	Pens. & Rev. Cl'ms.	....	....	......	Referred to Secretary of War.		
Hilton, William	Increase of revolutionary pension	29	1	Petition	568	Rev. Pensions	785	Adverse	......	Rejected.		
Hilton, William	Increase of revolutionary pension	29	2	Petition	67	Rev. Pensions.						
Hime or Himes, David	Reimbursement of payment on a judgment for distillery license.	25	2	Petition	574	Claims	811	Adverse	......	Laid on table.		
Hime or Himes, David	Reimbursement of payment on a judgment for distillery license.	25	3	Petition	122	Claims	42	Adverse	......	Rejected.		
Himell, Marie Francoise	Confirmation of title to land in Louisiana.	22	2	Petition	41	Priv. Land Claims.						
Hinant, Gary or Garry	Indemnity for Indian depredations	26	2	Senate bill	329	Whole House	....	....	S. 195			

List of private claims presented to the House of Representatives of the United States from the 1st to the 31st Congress, inclusive—Continued.

Names of claimants.	Nature or object of the claim.	Congress.	Session.	How brought before the House of Reps.	Page of journal.	To what committee of the House referred.	No. or date of the report.	Nature of the report.	No. of the bill.	How disposed of by the House of Reps.	How disposed of by the Senate.	Date of the act of Congress, and remarks.
Hinant, Gary or Garry	Indemnity for Indian depredations	27	3	Resolution	249	Indian Affairs	286	Res. to disch'e.	......	Leave to withdraw.		
Hinckley, Captain Elijah	Compensation for freight of arms in 1813.	23	2	Petition	277	Claims.						
Hinckley, John	Pension for revolutionary services.	28	1	Petition	318	Rev. Pensions.						
Hinckley, Nymphas, widow of.	Pension for revolutionary services.	27	2	Petition	823	Rev. Pensions	784	Adverse	......	Laid on table.		
Hinckley, Samuel	Pension for revolutionary services.	24	1	Resolution	666	Rev. Pensions	....	....	......	Discharged; laid on table.		
Hincks, Jesse Y	(See Ebenezer Nickerson and J. Y. H.)	12	1	....	315							
Hindman, James	(See Archibald Campbell, executor of.)	26	1	....	182							
Hindman, John	(See Leighton Wood, *et al.*)											
Hindron, Madame	(See Madame Hindson, assignee of)	20	2	....	119							
Hinds, Abijah	Invalid pension	3	2	Rep. of Secretary War.	278	Claims	....	....	......	Discharged; laid on table.		
Hinds, Abijah	Invalid pension	4	1	Rep. of Secretary War.	445	Claims	Mar. 4, 1796	Jt. res. to refer to Sec. War.	J. R. 16	Passed	Passed	App'd April 17, 1796
Hinds, Bartlett, for self & others.	Relief for injuries sustained under act of late Congress.	1	1	Petition	35	....	....	....	......	Laid on table.		
Hinds, Bartlett	Increase of pension	15	2	Petition	32	Pens. & Rev. Cl'ms.	Jan. 14, 1819	Report by bill.	274			
Hinds, Bartlett	Increase of pension	16	1	Petition	445	Pens. & Rev. Clm's.	....	....	......	Discharged: laid on table.		
Hinds, Bartlett	Increase of pension	16	2	Petition	84	....	....	....	......	Referred to Secretary War.		
Hinds, Bartlett, heirs of	Commutation pay for revolutionary services.	29	2	Petition	85	Rev. Claims.						
Hinds, Bartlett, heirs of	Commutation pay for revolutionary services.	30	1	Petition	117	Rev. Claims	616	Report and bill	495	Referred to Committee Whole House.		
Hinds, Bartlett, heirs of	Commutation pay for revolutionary services.	30	2	House bill	318	Whole House	Jan. 26, 1849	With't amend.	495	Passed.		
Hinds, Bartlett, heirs of	Commutation pay for revolutionary services.	31	1	Petition	383	Rev. Claims	114	Report and bill.	127	Referred to Committee Whole House.		
Hinds, Charles W	Compensation for property lost in the public service.	27	2	Documents	618	Claims	715	Adverse	......	Laid on table.		
Hinds or Hines, Daniel	Pension for services as a revolutionary soldier.	19	1	Resolution	304	Military Pensions	164	Adverse	......	Laid on table.		
Hinds or Hines, Daniel	Pension for services as a revolutionary soldier.	20	1	Resolution	350	Military Pensions	April 29, 1828	Report and bill.	283	Passed.		
Hinds or Hines, Daniel	Pension for services as a revolutionary soldier.	20	2	Resolution	55	Military Pensions	Dec. 12, 1828	General bill	311	Passed	Laid on table.	
Hinds or Hines, Daniel	Pension for services as a revolutionary soldier.	21	1	Resolution	48	Military Pensions	....	....	......	Discharged; laid on table.		
Hinds or Hines, Daniel	Pension for services as a revolutionary soldier.	21	1	House bill	130	Whole House	Feb. 13, 1830	Favorable	72	Passed	Passed	App'd May 20, 1830
Hinde, Thomas	Compension for medical services in revolutionary army.	12	1	Petition	59	Claims	May 7, 1812	Adverse	......	Laid on table.		
Hindson, Madame, assignee of.	Confirmation of title to land	20	2	Petition	119	Public Lands	86	Favorable	447	Referred to Committee Whole House.		
Hindson, Madame, assignee of.	Confirmation of title to land	21	1	Petition	41	Public Lands.						
Hindson, Madame, assignee of.	Confirmation of title to land	21	2	Petition	83	Priv. Land Claims.	Feb. 24, 1831	Favorable	651	Passed.		

List of private claims presented to the House of Representatives of the United States from the 1st to the 31st Congress, inclusive—Continued.

Names of claimants.	Nature or object of the claim.	Congress.	Session.	How brought before the House of Reps.	Page of journal.	To what committee of the House referred.	No. or date of the report.	Nature of the report.	No. of the bill.	How disposed of by the House of Reps.	How disposed of by the Senate.	Date of the act of Congress, and remarks.
Hindson, Madame, assignee of.	Confirmation of title to land	22	1	Petition	32	Priv. Land Claims.	187	Favorable	265	Referred to Committee Whole House.		
Hindson, Madame, assignee of.	Confirmation of title to land	22	2	House bill	93	Whole House			265	Passed	Passed	App'd Feb. 9, 1833
Hines, Abraham F.	Payment of certain claims against United States.	31	2	Petition	131	Claims.						
Hines, Henry	To be restored to pension roll	18	1	Resolution	105	Rev. Pensions.						
Hines, Hezekiah	Pension for revolutionary services.	21	1	Petition	384	Military Pensions.	May 4, 1830	Adverse; May 26, bill rep'd	491	Referred to Committee Whole House.		
Hines, Hezekiah	Pension for revolutionary services.	21	2	House bill	318	Whole House	Feb. 16, 1831	With't amend.	491	Passed.		
Hine, John	Compensation for arms manufactured for the government of the United States.	24	1	Petition	534	Claims	773	Adverse		Laid on table.		
Hines, Paine	Pension for revolutionary services.	17	2	Petition	24	Rev. Pensions				Discharged; leave to withdraw.		
Hines, William H., sureties of.	Release from a judgment in favor of the United States.	29	1	Memorial	460	Judiciary				Discharged; laid on table.		
Hinkle, Charles	Invalid pension	31	1	House bill	988	Invalid Pensions	382	With't amend.	312	Referred to Committee Whole House.		
Hinkley, Benjamin	Pension for services in the war of 1812.	25	3	Petition	219	Invalid Pensions.						
Hinkley, Benjamin	Pension for services in the war of 1812.	26	1	Petition	163	Invalid Pensions	281	Adverse		Laid on table.		
Hinkley, Jared, jr.	Pension	10	1	House bill	232	Whole House	April 19, 1808	Favorable	78	Passed	Passed	App'd April 25, 1808
Hinkley, Nathaniel	Compensation for transportation of provisions and army stores, 1813.	24	1	Documents	904	Claims	712	Adverse		Laid on table.		
Hinkley, Wiatt	Increase of pension	9	2	House bill	608	Whole House	Feb. 28, 1807	Favorable	216	Passed	Passed	App'd March 3, 1807
Hinkson, John	Pension	14	2	Resolution	209	Pens. & Rev. Cl'ms.	Jan. 29, 1817	Report by bill.	91	Passed	Passed, with amendment.	App'd March 3, 1817
Hinkstone, Humphrey	(See administrator of Thomas Ravenscroft.)	23	1		189							
Hinman, Joel	Pension	10	2	House bill	499	Whole House	Feb. 20, 1809	Favorable	158	Passed	Passed	App'd March 3, 1809
Hinman, Michael	Compensation for revolutionary services.	20	2	Petition	40	Rev. Claims	Jan. 5, 1829	Adverse		Laid on table.		
Hinman, Samuel	Interest on certain army pay rolls.	20	2	Petition	320	Claims				Discharged; laid on table.		
Hinman, Samuel	Interest on certain army pay rolls.	21	1	Petition	376	Claims	April 9, 1830	Adverse		Laid on table.		
Hinton, Joseph B.	(See heir of Covington Simpkins)	24	2		87							
Hinton, Joseph	(See Carrington Simkins, administrator of.)	26	1		182							
Hiorns, Caleb	Permission to import merchandize ordered prior to President's proclamation of Nov. 2, 1810.	12	1	Petition	171	Whole House		General bill	46			
Hipkins, Batram G.	Settlement of his accounts as commander gun-boats.	11	2	Petition	239					Referred to Secretary of the Navy.		
Hipolit, Robert	For patent for land under Spanish grant.	22	1	Petition	263	Priv. Land Claims.	Feb. 17, 1832	Report by bill.	380	Referred to Committee Whole House.		
Hipple, Lawrence	Invalid pension	3	1	Rep. of Secretary War.	131	Select	May 26, 1794	Jt. res. to refer to Sec. War.	J. R. 12	Passed	Passed	App'd June 9, 1794
Hipple, Lawrence	Invalid pension	3	2	Rep. of Secretary of War.	262	Claims	Feb. 28, 1795	Favorable; bill ordered.	130	Passed	Postp'd to next session.	
Hipple, Lawrence	Invalid pension	4	1	Rep. of Secretary War.	445	Claims	Mar. 4, 1796	Favorable: bill ordered.	156	Passed	Passed	App'd April 20, 1796
Hisle, Benjamin	Pension for revolutionary services.	22	1	Petition	868	Rev. Pensions.						

List of private claims presented to the House of Representatives of the United States from the 1st to the 31st Congress, inclusive—Continued.

Names of claimants.	Nature or object of the claim.	Congress.	Session.	How brought before the House of Reps.	Page of journal.	To what committee of the House referred.	No. or date of the report.	Nature of the report.	No. of the bill.	How disposed of by the House of Reps.	How disposed of by the Senate.	Date of the act of Congress, and remarks.
Hiscock, William	Pension for revolutionary services.	27	2	Petition	69	Rev. Pensions	784	Adverse		Laid on table.		
Hiske, Homa, alias Capt Red Pepper.	Confirmation of reservation of land	23	1	Senate bill	501	Public Lands	May 20, 1834	With't amend.	S. 110	Passed		App'd June 30, 1834
Hitchcock, Abel, widow of.	Benefit of the act of July 4, 1836.	25	2	Petition	116	Rev. Pensions	Jan. 25, 1838	General bill	426	Referred to Committee Whole House.		
Hitchcock, Abijah	Increase of pension	25	3	Petition	126	Rev. Pensions	Jan. 26, 1839	Adverse		Laid on table.		
Hitchcock, Abijah	Increase of pension	26	1	Petition	286	Rev. Pensions	424	Adverse		Laid on table.		
Hitchcock, Abraham	Pension for revolutionary services.	19	2	Resolution	143	Military Pensions				Discharged.		
Hitchcock, Abraham	Pension for revolutionary services.	22	1	Petition	36	Rev. Pensions	111	Report and bill.	193			
Hitchcock, Abraham	Pension for revolutionary services.	22	2	House bill	66	Whole House			193	Laid on table.		
Hitchcock, Ebenezer	Pension for disability incurred in the war of 1812.	28	2	Petition	396	Invalid Pensions.						
Hitchcock, Gaius	Pension	24	1	Senate bill	811	Rev. Pensions	May 17, 1836	With't amend.	S. 250	Passed		App'd June 15, 1836
Hitchcock, Henry	Credit of $270 in his account as paymaster of militia.	18	2	Petition	223	Claims.						
Hitchcock, Henry	Credit of $270 in his account as paymaster of militia.	19	1	Petition	44	Claims	20	Report and bill	34	Passed	Passed	App'd May 18, 1826
Hitchcock, Levi	Pension	21	2	Petition	159	Military Pensions.						
Hitchcock, Luke	To be restored to pension roll	17	1	Petition	199	Rev. Pensions				Discharged; laid on table.		
Hitchcock, Mary	Continuation of her pension	26	2	Petition	122	Rev. Pensions	205	Adverse		Laid on table.		
Hitchcock, Samuel	(See William Tilghman, *et al.*)	7	2		307							
Hitchcock, Samuel B	(See John Bement, and S. B. H.)	16	1		101							
Hite, George	Compensation for negroes stolen by the Cherokee Indians.	13	3	Petition	645	Pens. & Rev. Cl'ms	Jan. 26, 1815	Adverse		Rejected.		
Hite, James	To be placed on revolutionary pension roll.	27	3	Resolution	410	Rev. Pensions.						
Hite, James	To be placed on revolutionary pension roll.	28	1	Resolution	449	Rev. Pensions.						
Hittles, Jacob	Remission of tax on distillery	15	1	Petition	445	Ways and Means				Discharged; laid on table.		
Hittles, Jacob	Remission of tax on distillery	15	2	Petition	55	Claims	Jan. 4, 1819	Adverse		Laid on table.		
Hix, George	Compensation for property taken by United States troops.	29	1	Memorial	472	Claims	788	Adverse		Laid on table.		
Hix, George	Compensation for property taken by United States troops.	30	1	Petition	70	Claims	46	Adverse		Laid on table.		
Hix, George	Compensation for property taken by United States troops.	30	2	Petition	369	Indian Affairs.						
Hix, George	Compensation for property taken by United States troops.	31	1	Petition	542	Claims.						
Hixon, James	Pension	19	2	Petition	26	Military Pensions				Discharged.		
Hixt, William, heirs of	Commutation pay for revolutionary services.	31	1	Petition	310	Rev. Claims	183	Adverse		Laid on table.		
Hoadley, Samuel	Invalid pension	19	2	Petition	187	Military Pensions				Discharged.		
Hoadley, Samuel	Invalid pension	20	2	Resolution	92	Military Pensions	Feb. 15, 1829	General bill	440	Passed.		
Hoadley, Samuel	Invalid pension	21	1	Resolution	47	Military Pensions				Discharged; laid on table.		
Hoadley, Samuel	Invalid pension	21	1	House bill	130	Whole House	Feb. 13, 1830	Favorable	72	Passed	Passed	App'd May 20, 1830
Hoag, Samuel	(See Daniel Griffin and S. Hoag)	18	1		32							
Hoag, William H., *et al*	Balance due on contract for La Plaisance bay road.	27	3	Petition	153	Claims.						
Hoag, William H., *et al*	Balance due on contract for La Plaisance bay road.	28	1	Petition	239	Claims	131	Report and bill.	121	Passed	Passed	App'd June 15, 1844

List of private claims presented to the House of Representatives of the United States from the 1st to the 31st Congress, inclusive—Continued.

Names of claimants.	Nature or object of the claim.	Congress.	Session.	How brought before the House of Reps.	Page of journal.	To what committee of the House referred.	No. or date of the report.	Nature of the report.	No. of the bill.	How disposed of by the House of Reps.	How disposed of by the Senate.	Date of the act of Congress, and remarks.
Hoagland, James	(See James Hogland)	21	2	......	244							
Hoagland, John, widow of.	Revolutionary pension	25	2	Petition	404	Rev. Pensions	769	Favorable; bill	723	Passed	Adverse report	
Hoagland, John, widow of.	Revolutionary pension	25	3	Petition	88	Rev. Pensions	124	Favorable; bill	991	Passed	Adverse report.	
Hoagland, John, widow of	Revolutionary pension	26	1	Petition	172	Rev. Pensions.						
Hoar, Mercy	Pension	28	2	Resolution	90	Rev. Pensions.						
Hoard, David, (Lydia,) widow of.	Increase of revolutionary pension	26	1	Resolution	556	Invalid Pensions.						
Hoard, David, (Lydia,) widow of.	Increase of revolutionary pension	26	2	Resolution	88	Invalid Pensions	139	Report and bill.	646	Referred to Committee Whole House.		
Hoard, David, (Lydia,) widow of.	Increase of revolutionary pension	27	2	Resolution	59	Invalid Pensions	784	Adverse	......	Laid on table.		
Hoard, Robert C	Payment of the reward offered by the territorial government of Michigan for apprehending a fugitive.	25	2	Petition	770	Claims	......	......	......	Discharged; laid on table.		
Hobart, Daniel, widow of.	Pension for revolutionary services.	28	1	Petition	240	Rev. Pensions	......	......	......	Discharged; laid on table.		
Hobart, Daniel, widow of.	Pension for revolutionary services.	28	2	Petition	68	Rev. Pensions.						
Hobert, Daniel, widow of.	Pension for revolutionary services.	29	1	Petition	118	Rev. Pensions	518	Adverse	......	Laid on table.		
Hobart, Jonas	Invalid pension	12	1	House bill	361	Whole House	......	......	138	Passed	Passed	App'd July 5, 1812
Hobart, Rebecca	Two years pension for revolutionary services of husband.	28	1	Petition	950	Whole House.						
Hobards, Jesse	Pension	27	2	Petition	1189	Claims	983	Adverse	......	Laid on table.		
Hobbs, H	Indemnity for office rent, &c., while postmaster.	31	1	Petition	616	P. Of. & P. Roads	......	......	......	Discharged; laid on table.		
Hobbs, Joseph	Bounty land for service prior to February 11, 1847.	30	1	Petition	624	Military Affairs.						
Hobbs, Josiah	Back pension for revolutionary services.	25	2	Petition	52	Rev. Pensions	......	......	......	Discharged; laid on table.		
Hobbs, Josiah	Back pension for revolutionary services.	30	1	Petition	954	Rev. Pensions	......	......	......	Discharged; laid on table.		
Hobby, John	Payment of a revolutionary certificate.	2	1	Petition	579	......	......	......	......	Referred to Secretary Treasury.		
Hobby, John	Payment of a revolutionary certificate.	3	1	Rep. of Secretary of Treasury.	77	......	......	......	......	Laid on table.		
Hobby, John	Payment of a revolutionary certificate.	4	1	Rep. of Secretary Treasury.	388	Claims	74	Adverse	......	Laid on table.		
Hobby, John	Increase of compensation as marshal of the district of Maine.	4	2	Memorial & rep't Attorney Gen.	713	......	......	......	......	Referred to Committee Whole House.		
Hobby, John	Release from imprisonment on a judgment in favor United States.	7	1	Memorial	16							
				Rep. of Secretary Treasury.	31	Select	Jan. 4, 1802	Favorable; bill ordered.	8	Passed	Rejected.	
Hobby, John, (Hannah) widow of.	Release from a judgment existing against deceased.	8	2	Petition	49	Claims	Jan. 22, 1805	Adverse	......	Leave to withdraw.		
Hobby, Thomas	Invalid pension	1	3	Petition and rep't Sec. of War.	367	......	......	......	......	Laid on table.		
Hobby, Thomas	Invalid pension	3	1	Rep. of Secretary War.	131	Select	May 26, 1794	J't. res. to refer to Sec. War.	J. R. 12	Passed	Passed	App'd June 9, 1794
Hobby, Thomas	Invalid pension	3	2	Rep. of Secretary War.	268	Claims	Feb. 28, 1795	Favorable; bill ordered.	130	Passed	Postp'd to next session.	
Hobby, Thomas	Invalid pension	4	1	Rep. of Secretary War.	445	Claims	Feb. 18, 1796	Favorable; bill ordered.	156	Passed	Passed	App'd April 20, 1796

List of private claims presented to the House of Representatives of the United States from the 1st to the 31st Congress, inclusive—Continued.

Names of claimants.	Nature or object of the claim.	Congress.	Session.	How brought before the House of Reps.	Page of journal.	To what committee of the House referred.	No. or date of the report.	Nature of the report.	No. of the bill.	How disposed of by the House of Reps.	How disposed of by the Senate.	Date of the act of Congress, and remarks.
Hobby, William	Additional compensation for services as clerk in pay department.	20	2	Petition	141	Military Affairs	Feb. 13, 1829	Adverse	......	Leave to withdraw.		
Hobby, William	Additional compensation for services as clerk in pay department.	21	1	Petition	69, 110	Military Affairs	Jan. 7, 1831	Adverse	......	Laid on table.		
Hobby, William	Compensation for detecting and exposing the frauds of a paymaster.	21	1	Petition	69	Military Affairs	Jan. 18, 1830	Adverse	......	Discharged.		
Hobert, Peter H., & Lewis Judson.	Confirmation of title to a certain tract of land in Alabama.	18	1	Senate bill	233	Priv. Land Claims.	Mar. 26, 1824	Adverse	S. 32	Laid on table.		
Hobert, Peter H., & Lewis Judson.	Confirmation of title to a certain tract of land in Alabama.	18	2	Petition	47	Priv. Land Claims.						
Hobert, Peter H., & Lewis Judson.	Confirmation of title to a certain tract of land in Alabama.	19	1	Petition	45	Priv. Land Claims.	....	....	......	Discharged; laid on table.		
Hobert, Peter H., & Lewis Judson.	Confirmation of title to a certain tract of land in Alabama.	19	2	Petition	157	Priv. Land Claims.						
Hobkirk, John B., assignee of.	Payment of account for attendance as a witness before a court-martial.	22	1	Petition	809	Claims.						
Hobkirk, John B., assignee of.	Payment of account for attendance as a witness before a court-martial.	23	1	Petition	60	Claims.						
Hobson, Isaac N.	Pension	21	2	Petition	300	Military Pensions.						
Hobson, Joseph, lagatee of	Bounty land due deceased as an officer, Virginia line.	26	1	Petition	946	Rev. Claims.						
Hobson, Joseph, lagatee of	Bounty land due deceased as an officer, Virginia line.	26	2	Petition	214	Claims	178	Adverse	......	Laid on table.		
Hockaday, Capt. John, heirs of.	Commutation pay for revolutionary services.	26	1	Documents	946	Rev. Claims.						
Hockett, John W.	Compensation for labor on Cumberland road.	28	1	Petition	430	Claims.						
Hockett, John W.	Compensation for labor on Cumberland road.	28	2	Petition	60	Claims	101	Report and bill.	583	Referred to Committee Whole House.		
Hockett, John W.	Compensation for labor on Cumberland road.	30	1	Petition	108	Claims	71	Report and bill.	53	Passed	Passed 2d sess. page 647.	App'd March 3, 1849
Hodgson, Charlotte	Indemnity for French spoliations prior to 1800.	26	1	Memorial	182	Foreign Affairs	343	Favorable; bill	319	Referred to Committee Whole House.		
Hodgson, Joseph, representatives of.	Value of house destroyed by fire occupied by United States.	17	1	Senate bill	426	Public Lands and to Judiciary.	....	Senate bill	73	Passed	Passed	App'd May 7, 1822
Hodgdon, Samuel	(See surety of John Smith.)	17	2	....	174							
Hodge, Andrew	(See Laurent Millandan, *et al.*)	28	1	....	76							
Hodge, David	Pension for military services, war of 1812.	24	1	Petition	98	Invalid Pensions	Feb. 4, 1836	Adverse	......	Laid on table.		
Hodge, David	Pension for military services, war of 1812.	24	2	Petition	42	Invalid Pensions.						
Hodge, David	Pension for military services, war of 1812.	25	3	Documents	220	Invalid Pensions.						
Hodge, David	Pension for military services, war of 1812.	26	1	Petition	1001	Invalid Pensions.	....	....	......	Discharged; laid on table.		
Hodge, Francis	Grant of land for services in defence of Tennessee frontier.	16	1	Petition	110	Public Lands	Jan. 13, 1820	Adverse	......	Rejected.		
Hodge, George	Indemnity for loss by the burning of Washington.	14	1	Senate bill	252	Claims	Feb. 19, 1816	With't amend.	......	Laid on table.		

List of private claims presented to the House of Representatives of the United States from the 1st to the 31st Congress, inclusive—Continued.

Names of claimants.	Nature or object of the claim.	Congress.	Session.	How brought before the House of Reps.	Page of journal.	To what committee of the House referred.	No. or date of the report.	Nature of the report.	No. of the bill.	How disposed of by the House of Reps.	How disposed of by the Senate.	Date of the act of Congress, and remarks.
Hodge, George	Indemnity for loss by the burning of Washington.	14	2	Petition	38	Claims	Dec. 20, 1816	Adverse.				
Hodge, George	Indemnity for loss by the burning of Washington.	15	1	Petition	22	Claims	Jan. 5, 1818	Adverse	......	Laid on table.		
Hodge, George, widow of.	Indemnity for loss by the burning of Washington.	16	2	Petition	159	Claims.						
Hodge, George, widow of.	Indemnity for loss by the burning of Washington.	17	1	Petition	145	Claims.						
Hodge, George, widow of.	Indemnity for loss by the burning of Washington.	17	2	Petition	95	Claims	Jan. 24, 1823	Adverse	......	Leave to withdraw.		
Hodge, George, widow of.	Pension from the navy pension fund.	17	2	Petition	232	Naval Affairs	Feb. 24, 1823	Adverse	......	Leave to withdraw.		
Hodge, George, widow of.	Provision for her support	18	2	Petition	116	Naval Affairs	Jan. 17, 1825	Adverse.	......	Laid on table.		
Hodge, George, widow of.	Indemnity for property destroyed at burning of navy-yard.	20	2	Petition	49	Claims	Dec. 22, 1830	Adverse	......	Laid on table.		
Hodge, George, widow of.	Indemnity for property destroyed at burning of navy-yard.	21	1	Petition	145	Claims	Jan. 18, 1830	Adverse	......	Laid on table.		
Hodge, George, widow of.	Indemnity for property destroyed at burning of navy-yard.	22	2	Senate bill	277	Naval Affairs	Feb. 14, 1833	With't amend.	S. 66	Passed	Passed	App'd March 2, 1833
Hodge, John	(See Edward Barry and J. Hodge)	14	2	....	38							
Hodge, John	Compensation for services and injuries, revolutionary war.	1	3	Petition and rep't Sec. of War.	346	....	Feb. 21, 1791	....	......	Laid on table.		
Hodge, John	Compensation for services and injuries, revolutionary war.	2	1	Petition	446	....	....	....	......	Referred to Secretary War.		
Hodges, Asa	Additional compensation for taking 4th census in Alabama.	22	1	Petition	266	Claims	Feb. 8, 1832	Adverse.	......	Laid on table.		
Hodges, Benjamin	Indemnity for French spoliations prior to 1800.	26	1	Memorial	182	Foreign Affairs	343	Favorable; bill	319	Referred to Committee Whole House.		
Hodges, Benjamin, widow of.	Compensation for negro taken by the enemy, war of 1812.	23	2	Petition	390	Foreign Affairs.						
Hodges, Benjamin, widow of.	Compensation for negro taken by the enemy, war of 1812.	24	1	Petition	662	Foreign Affairs.						
Hodges, Benjamin, widow of.	Compensation for negro taken by the enemy, war of 1812.	24	2	Petition	87	Foreign Affairs	241	Report and bill.	941	Referred to Committee Whole House.		
Hodges, Benjamin, widow of.	Compensation for negro taken by the enemy, war of 1812.	25	2	Petition	39	Foreign Affairs	262	Report and bill	305	Referred to Committee Whole House.		
Hodges, Benjamin, widow of.	Compensation for negro taken by the enemy, war of 1812.	25	3	House bill	377	Whole House	....	....	305	Passed	Adverse report.	
Hodges, Benjamin, widow of.	Compensation for negro taken by the enemy, war of 1812.	26	1	Petition	182	Foreign Affairs.						
Hodges, Benjamin, widow of.	Compensation for negro taken by the enemy, war of 1812.	27	2	Petition	307	Claims	1043	Adverse	......	Laid on table.		
Hodges, Benjamin, widow of.	Compensation for negro taken by the enemy, war of 1812.	29	1	Memorial	464	Foreign Affairs	767	Report and bill.	506	Referred to Committee Whole House.		
Hodges, Benjamin, widow of.	Compensation for negro taken by the enemy, war of 1812.	30	1	Petition	79	Foreign Affairs	81	Report and bill.	68	Passed.		
Hodges, Benjamin, widow of.	Compensation for negro taken by the enemy, war of 1812.	31	2	Petition	143	Foreign Affairs.						
Hodges, Curtis	Lands in lieu of those of which he has been deprived by the State of Missouri.	29	2	Petition	316	Public Lands.						
Hodges, Gilbert, heirs of.	Confirmation of title to land in Missouri.	23	1	Senate bill	844	Priv. Land Claims.	Jan. 27, 1834	With't amend.	S. 86	Passed	....	App'd June 30, 1834

List of private claims presented to the House of Representatives of the United States from the 1st to the 31st Congress, inclusive—Continued.

Names of claimants.	Nature or object of the claim.	Congress.	Session.	How brought before the House of Reps.	Page of journal.	To what committee of the House referred.	No. or date of the report.	Nature of the report.	No. of the bill.	How disposed of by the House of Reps.	How disposed of by the Senate.	Date of the act of Congress, and remarks.
Hodges, John	Compensation for revolutionary services.	20	2	Petition	61	Rev. Claims	Jan. 8, 1829	Adverse.	......	Laid on table.		
Hodges, John	Compensation for revolutionary services.	21	1	Petition	148	Rev. Claims	Feb. 2, 1830	Adverse	......	Laid on table.		
Hodges, John	Compensation for revolutionary services.	22	1	Petition	190	Rev. Claims.						
Hodges, John H	Reimbursement of money paid American consul at Plymouth, England.	27	2	Petition	1251	Claims.						
Hodges, John H	Reimbursement of money paid American consul at Plymouth, England.	27	3	Petition	223	Commerce.	280	Report and bill.	832			
Hodges, John H	Reimbursement of money paid American consul at Plymouth, England.	28	1	Petition	570	Commerce.						
Hodges, John H., administrator of.	Reimbursement of money paid American consul at Plymouth, England.	29	1	Petition	436	Commerce.	575	Adverse	......	Laid on table.		
Hodges, John H., administrator of.	Reimbursement of tonnage duty paid on brig Herald.	28	2	Petition	235	Commerce	94	Report and bill.	580	Referred to Committee Whole House.		
Hodges, John H., administrator of.	Reimbursement of tonnage duty paid on brig Herald.	29	1	Petition	678	Commerce	572	Report and bill	390	Passed	Passed	App'd Aug. 8, 1846
Hodges, John P.	(See Joseph H. McMaken)	27	3	....	103					table.		
Hodges, Josiah	(See Josiah Hedges)	22	1	....	372							
Hodges, Mary	Pension for revolutionary services of her husband.	24	2	Petition	153	Naval Affairs.						
Hodges, Thomas Harris	(See adm'r of John H. Hodges.)	28	2	....	235							
Hodges, William	Compensation for damage by United States troops at Norfolk, war of 1812.	20	2	Resolution	267	Claims.						
Hodges, William, heirs of	Compensation for damage by United States troops at Norfolk, war of 1812.	21	1	Resolution	134	Claims	May 19, 1830	Adverse	......	Laid on table.		
Hodges, William, heirs of	Compensation for damage by United States troops at Norfolk, war of 1812.	31	1	Petition	1044	Claims.						
Hodgkin, John	Compensation for work on New York custom-house.	27	3	Petition	60	Claims	102	Report and bill	729	Passed	Passed	App'd March 3, 1843
Hodgkins, Stickney	Pension for disability incurred in war of 1812.	27	2	Petition	836	Invalid Pensions.						
Hodgkins, William	Compensation for repairing boats in 1815.	22	2	Petition	94	Claims.						
Hodgkins, William	Compensation for repairing boats in 1815.	23	1	Petition	55	Claims	93	Adverse	......	Laid on table.		
Hodgkinson, Ann	Pension; husband killed while acting as prize master of a privateer.	13	3	Petition	633	Naval Affairs	Jan. 14, 1815	Adverse	......	Rejected.		
Hodgson, Isaac	Indemnity for prosecution on account of acts as a public officer.	15	1	Petition	182	Claims	....	....	......	Discharged; leave to withdraw.		
Hodgson, Isaac	Indemnity for prosecution on account of acts as a public officer.	15	2	Petition	227	Claims	....	....	......	Discharged; laid on table.		
Hodgson, Isaac	Indemnity for prosecution on account of acts as a public officer.	16	1	Petition	101	Judiciary	Jan. 17, 1820	Adverse	......	Leave to withdraw.		

List of private claims presented to the House of Representatives of the United States from the 1st to the 31st Congress, inclusive—Continued.

Names of claimants.	Nature or object of the claim.	Congress.	Session.	How brought before the House of Reps.	Page of journal.	To what committee of the House referred.	No. or date of the report.	Nature of the report.	No. of the bill.	How disposed of by the House of Reps.	How disposed of by the Senate.	Date of the act of Congress, and remarks.
Hodgson, Isaac	Indemnity for prosecution on account of acts as a public officer.	17	1	Petition	276	Military Affairs.						
Hodgson, Isaac	Indemnity for prosecution on account of acts as a public officer.	17	2	Petition	50	Military Affairs	Jan. 24, 1823	Report by bill.	253	Referred to Committee Whole House.		
Hodgson, Isaac	Indemnity for prosecution on account of acts as a public officer.	18	1	Petition	47	Military Affairs.						
Hodgson, Isaac	Indemnity for prosecution on account of acts as a public officer.	19	1	Petition	57	Claims	8	Report and bill.	20	Passed	Passed	App'd May 16, 1826
Hodgson, Joseph	Indemnity for loss of a house by fire while occupied by government.	6	2	Petition	771	Claims	....	....	......	Leave to withdraw.		
Hodgson, Joseph	Indemnity for loss of a house by fire while occupied by government.	8	2	Petition	50	Claims.						
Hodgson, Joseph, widow of	Indemnity for loss of a house by fire while occupied by government.	9	1	Petition	268	Claims	April 1, 1806	Adverse	......	Laid on table.		
Hodgson, Joseph, heirs of.	Indemnity for loss of a house by fire while occupied by government.	11	2	Petition	187	Claims.						
Hodgson, Joseph, heirs of.	Indemnity for loss of a house by fire while occupied by government.	12	1	Petition	30	Claims.						
Hodgson, Joseph, heirs of.	Indemnity for loss of a house by fire while occupied by government.	12	2	Petition	552	Claims	244	Adverse	......	Recommitted.		
Hodgson, Joseph, heirs of.	Indemnity for loss of a house by fire while occupied by government.	13	1	Petition	18	Claims	....	....	......	Discharged.		
Hodgson, Joseph, heirs of.	Indemnity for loss of a house by fire while occupied by government.	13	2	Petition	181	Claims	25	Adverse	......	Referred to Committee Whole House.		
Hodgson, Joseph, heirs of.	Indemnity for loss of a house by fire while occupied by govern ment.	13	3	Petition	464	Claims	14	Adverse	......	Laid on table.		
Hodgson, Joseph, heirs of.	Indemnity for loss of a house by fire while occupied by government.	14	1	Petition	70	Claims	....	....	......	Discharged; laid on table.		
Hodgson, Joseph, heirs of.	Indemnity for loss of a house by fire while occupied by government.	15	2	Petition	54	Claims	....	....	......	Discharged; leave to withdraw.		
Hodgson, Joseph, heirs of.	Indemnity for loss of a house by fire while occupied by government.	17	1	Senate bill	426	Judiciary	April 9, 1822	With't amend	S. 73	Passed	....	App'd May 7, 1822
Hodgson, William B.	For certain credits in settling his account as consul at Algiers.	24	1	Petition	1077	Foreign Affairs.						
Hodgson, William B.	For certain credits in settling his account as consul at Algiers.	24	2	Petition	87	Foreign Affairs.						
Hodgson, William, trustee of.	Indemnity for French spoliations prior to 1800.	30	1	Petition	118	Foreign Affairs	Jan. 4, 1848	General bill	21	Referred to Committee Whole House.		
Hodgson, William, trustee of.	Indemnity for French spoliations prior to 1800.	31	1	Petition	256	Foreign Affairs	355	General bill	318	Referred to Committee Whole House.		
Hodsdon, Ebenezer	(See James Crawford, *et al*)	16	2	....	101							

List of private claims presented to the House of Representatives of the United States from the 1st to the 31st Congress, inclusive—Continued.

Names of claimants.	Nature or object of the claim.	Congress.	Session.	How brought before the House of Reps.	Page of journal.	To what committee of the House referred.	No. or date of the report.	Nature of the report.	No. of the bill.	How disposed of by the House of Reps.	How disposed of by the Senate.	Date of the act of Congress, and remarks.
Hodsden, Isaac	(See Isaac Hodgson)	15	1		182							
Hodson, Thomas J	(See John W. Argyle)	30	2		192							
Hodson, William, administrator of.	Indemnity for property destroyed by the enemy, war of 1812.	24	1	Petition	751	Claims.						
Hodson, William, administrator of.	Indemnity for property destroyed by the enemy, war of 1812.	25	2	Petition	1255	Claims	1046	Report and bill.	880	Referred to Committee Whole House.		
Hodson, William, administrator of.	Indemnity for property destroyed by the enemy, war of 1812.	25	3	House bill	432	Whole House			880	Passed	Adverse report.	
Hodson, William, administrator of.	Indemnity for property destroyed by the enemy, war of 1812.	27	2	Petition	106	Claims	55	Report and bill.	90	Passed	Passed	App'd Aug. 26, 1842
Hoel, Philip Coonrod	Pension for services as a revolutionary soldier.	20	1	Resolution	267	Military Pensions				Discharged; leave to withdraw.		
Hoey, William H., *et al.*	(See William H. Hoag, *et al*)	27	3		153							
Hoff, ——	(See Cotheal & Hoff)	14	1		538							
Hoff, Jacob	To be restored to pension roll	17	1	Petition	299	Whole House.						
Hoff, John	Pension for services as a revolutionary officer.	14	2	Petition	40	Pens. & Rev. Cl'ms.	Dec. 30, 1816	Adverse		Rejected.		
Hoff, John	Pension for services as a revolutionary officer.	18	1	Petition	78	Pens. & Rev. Cl'ms.	Jan. 6, 1824	Adverse		Laid on table.		
Hoff, John	Pension for services as a revolutionary officer.	20	2	Petition	175	Military Pensions	Feb. 19, 1829	Adverse		Laid on table.		
Hoff, Luke	Remission of tax on a distillery	15	1	Petition	36	Ways and Means	Dec. 15, 1817	Adverse		Discharged; laid on table.		
Hoff, Michael	Reimbursement of tax paid on a distillery.	17	2	Petition	96	Ways and Means.						
Hoff, Michael	Reimbursement of tax paid on a distillery.	18	1	Petition	254	Ways and Means.						
Hoff, Michael	Reimbursement of tax paid on a distillery.	19	1	Petition	152	Ways and Means.	Jan. 18, 1826	Report by bill.	57	Passed	Passed	App'd May 20, 1826
Hoff, Michael	Reimbursement of an overpayment on a judgment.	21	1	Petition	497	Ways and Means.						
Hoff, Michael	Reimbursement of an overpayment on a judgment.	21	2	Petition	210	Ways and Means.						
Hoff, Nicholas	Pension	10	1	House bill	232	Whole House	April 19, 1808	Favorable	78	Passed	Passed	App'd April 25, 1808
Hoffman, Anthony N., *et al.*	Indemnity for breach of contract by Postmaster General.	17	1	Petition	164	P. Of. & P. Roads				Discharged; leave to withdraw.		
Hoffman, Henrietta	(See heir of Philip Rogers)	31	1		384							
Hoffman, Henry	Compensation for revolutionary services.	23	2	Resolution	434	Rev. Claims.						
Hoffman, Henry	Compensation for revolutionary services.	25	2	Resolution	105	Rev. Claims	Feb. 6, 1838	Report by bill.	522	Passed	With amend.	
Heffman, Henry	Compensation for revolutionary services.	25	3	Resolution	84	Rev. Claims	242	Report and bill.	1106	Referred to Committee Whole House.		
Hoffman, Henry	Compensation for revolutionary services.	26	1	Resolution	165	Rev. Claims.						
Hoffman, Henry, representatives of.	Compensation for revolutionary services.	27	2	Resolution	1030	Rev. Claims	1024	Report and bill.	597	Referred to Committee Whole House.		
Hoffman, Henry, representatives of.	Compensation for revolutionary services.	27	3	House bill	91	Whole House			597	Passed	Indef. postp'd.	
Hoffman, Henry, representatives of.	Compensation for revolutionary services.	28	2	Petition	150	Rev. Claims.						
Hoffman, Henry, representatives of.	Compensation for revolutionary services.	29	1	Resolution	105	Rev. Claims.						

List of private claims presented to the House of Representatives of the United States from the 1st to the 31st Congress, inclusive—Continued.

Names of claimants.	Nature or object of the claim.	Congress.	Session.	How brought before the House of Reps.	Page of journal.	To what committee of the House referred.	No. or date of the report.	Nature of the report.	No. of the bill.	How disposed of by the House of Reps.	How disposed of by the Senate.	Date of the act of Congress, and remarks.
Hoffman, Henry, representatives of.	Compensation for revolutionary services.	29	2	Petition	214	Rev. Claims.						
Hoffman, Henry, representatives of.	Compensation for revolutionary services.	30	1	Petition	480	Rev. Claims.						
Hoffman, Henry, representatives of.	Compensation for revolutionary services.	31	1	Petition	496	Rev. Claims.						
Hoffman, John	Pension for services in Wayne's army, 1794.	18	2	Petition	41	Pens. & Rev. Cl'ms.	Dec. 22, 1824	Adverse		Laid on table.		
Hoffman, Martin	(See William Hill)	14	1		386							
Hoffman, Martin	(See Robinson & Hartshorne)	26	1		182							
Hoffman, Martin	(See Robinson & Hartshorne, assignee of.)	12	1		295							
Hoffman, Martin	(See Isaac Lawrence and others.)	14	2		101							See Statutes at Large vol. 6, p. 187.
Hoffman, Nicholas	Invalid pension	3	1	Petition and rep't Sec. War.	78		April 22, 1794			Laid on table		
Hoffman, Peter, jr., *et al.*	Release for a ship seized for a breach of embargo law.	12	1	Petition	307	Select	April 28 1812	Report by bill.	120	Rejected.		
Hoffman, Peter, and son, heirs of.	Indemnity for French spoliations prior to 1800.	26	1	Memorial	182	Foreign Affairs	343	Favorable; bill	319	Referred to Committee Whole House.		
Hoffman, Samuel	Drawback on merchandise exported to East Indies.	14	2	Petition	76	Com. and Manuf.						
Hoffman, Samuel	Drawback on exported merchandise	25	3	Petition	118	Commerce	210	Report and bill.	1065	Passed	Passed, with amendment.	
Hoffman, Samuel	Drawback on exported merchandise	26	1	Petition	176	Commerce.						
Hoffman, Samuel	Drawback on exported merchandise	27	3	Petition	108	Commerce	79	Report and bill.	708	Passed	Indef. postp'd.	
Hoffman and Seton	Indemnity for French spoliations prior to 1800.	26	1	Memorial	182	Foreign Affairs	343	Favorable; bill	319	Referred to Committee Whole House.		
Hoffman, William	Bounty land for services as a Canadian volunteer, war of 1812.	21	1	Petition	356	Priv. Land Claims.						
Hoffman, William	Bounty land for services as a Canadian volunteer, war of 1812.	21	2	Petition	189	Priv. Land Claims.	Feb. 8, 1831	Report by bill.	606	Referred to Committee Whole House.		
Hoffman, William	Bounty land for services as a Canadian volunteer, war of 1812.	22	1	Petition	91	Priv. Land Claims.	84	Report and bill.	167	Passed	Passed	App'd July 14, 1832
Hoffman, Lieutenant Col. William, widow of.	Pension, in consideration of long and faithful services and death while in service.	30	1	Petition	207	Invalid Pensions	565	Report and bill.	465	Passed	Passed	App'd Aug. 7, 1848
Hoga, Godfrey & Co.	Indemnity for French spoliations prior to 1800.	26	1	Memorial	182	Foreign Affairs	343	Favorable; bill	319	Referred to Committee Whole House.		
Hoga, Godfrey	Indemnity for French spoliations prior to 1800.	26	1	Memorial	182	Foreign Affairs	343	Favorable; bill	319	Referred to Committee Whole House.		
Hogaboom, Peter	Invalid pension	3	1	Rep. of Secretary War.	131	Select	May 26, 1794	Favorable; bill ordered.	62	Passed	Passed	App'd June 7, 1794
Hogadorn, John	Additional compensation for revolutionary services.	19	2	Petition	333	Rev. Claims.						
Hogan, Daniel	(Claim not stated)	19	2	Petition	83	Ways and Means				Discharged; leave to withdraw.		
Hogan, James	For proceeds of the sale of his property.	24	1	Memorial & docs.	408	Ways and Means	Mar. 15, 1836	Adverse		Laid on table.		
Hogan, Gen. James, heirs of.	Bounty land for revolutionary services.	24	1	Petition	432	Rev. Claims	June 15, 1836	Adverse		Laid on table.		

2—14

List of private claims presented to the House of Representatives of the United States from the 1st to the 31st Congress, inclusive—Continued.

Names of claimants.	Nature or object of the claim.	Congress.	Session.	How brought before the House of Reps.	Page of journal.	To what committee of the House referred.	No. or date of the report.	Nature of the report.	No. of the bill.	How disposed of by the House of Reps.	How disposed of by the Senate.	Date of the act of Congress, and remarks.
Hogan, Gen. James, heirs of.	Bounty land for revolutionary services.	24	2	Petition	40	Rev. Claims.						
Hogan, Gen. James, heirs of.	Bounty land for revolutionary services.	25	2	Petition	270	Rev. Claims	531	Adverse		Laid on table.		
Hogan, John B	Credit for advances to Tennessee volunteers.	17	2	Petition	164	Military Affairs	Feb. 21, 1823	Report by bill.	308	Passed	Passed	App'd March 3, 1823
Hogan, John B	For the amendment or repeal of an act for his relief.	18	1	Resolution	323	Military Affairs	Mar. 19, 1824	Report by bill.	169	Recommitted.		
					341	Military Affairs	Mar. 26, 1824	With amend.	169	Passed.	Passed	App'd April 22, 1824
Hogan, John	Compensation for services as special agent of government.	29	1	Memorial	517	Foreign Affairs.						
Hogan, John	Compensation for services as special agent of government.	30	1	Petition	408							See Civil and Dip. bill, August 12, 1848.
Hogan, John	Settlement of accounts as confidential agent at St. Domingo.	31	1	Jt. res., Senate.	580	Foreign Affairs	May 2, 1850	With't amend.	S.J.R 8	Referred to Committee Whole House.		
Hogan, Malachi	(See Malachi Hagan)	30	1		228							
Hogan, Michael	Indemnity for damage to his house by United States troops.	13	2	Petition	188	Claims	Dec. 13, 1813	Report by bill.	68	Passed	Rejected.	
Hogan, Michael	Indemnity for damage to his house by United States troops.	15	1	Senate bill	393	Claims	140	With amend.	S. 46	Referred to Committee Whole House.		
Hogan, Michael	Indemnity for damage to his house by United States troops.	15	2	Senate bill	270	Claims.	Feb. 22, 1819	With amend.	S. 38	Passed with amend't.	Passed as am'd	App'd March 3, 1819
Hogan, Michael	Compensation for diplomatic services while consul at Chili.	22	1	Memorial	286	Foreign Affairs	Mar. 2, 1832	Report and bill.	438	Referred to Committee Whole House.		
Hogan, Michael	Compensation for diplomatic services while consul at Chili.	22	2	Memorial	69	Foreign Affairs	105	Report and bill.	747	Passed	Passed	App'd March 2, 1833
Hogan, Michael, administrator of.	Indemnity for neglect of Navy Department to settle his accounts.	23	2	Senate bill	194	Naval Affairs	Feb. 10, 1835	With't amend.	S. 27	Referred to Committee Whole House.		
Hogan, Michael, administrator of.	Indemnity for neglect of Navy Department to settle his accounts.	24	1	Senate bill	394	Claims	518	With amend.	S. 31	Referred to Committee Whole House.		
Hogan, Michael, administrator of.	Indemnity for neglect of Navy Department to settle his accounts.	24	2	Senate bill	251	Naval Affairs.	273	With't amend.	S. 55	Referred to Committee Whole House.		
Hogan, Michael, administrator of.	Payment of a certified debt due from government.	29	1	Memorial	358	Claims.						
Hogan, Michael, administrator of.	Reimbursement of advances while navy agent, Valparaiso.	29	2	Memorial	69	Claims.						
				Supplement'l memorial.	613	Claims	89	Report and bill.	695	Referred to Committee Whole House.		
Hogan, Michael, administrator of.	Immediate payment of a debt due him.	29	2	Petition	151	Judiciary.						
Hogan, Michael, administrator of.	Reimbursement of advances while navy agent, Valparaiso.	30	1	Petition	77	Claims	47	Report and bill.	40	Passed	Passed	App'd Aug. 14, 184
Hogan, Michael, administrator of.	Interest on his claim	30	2	Memorial	567	Claims.						
Hogan, Michael, administrator of.	Interest on his claim	31	2	Petition	247	Claims.						
Hogan, Stephen C	Pension for disability incurred in public service.	30	1	Petition	280	Invalid Pensions				Discharged; laid on table.		
Hogan, William	Remission of duties on spirits destroyed by fire.	14	1	Petition	587	Ways and Means.				Discharged; laid on table.		
Hogeboom, Abraham, representatives of.	Commissions on disbursements while agent for removing Indians.	30	1	House bill	453	Indian Affairs	523	With't amend.	232	Referred to Committee Whole House.		

List of private claims presented to the House of Representatives of the United States from the 1st to the 31st Congress, inclusive—Continued.

Names of claimants.	Nature or object of the claim.	Congress.	Session.	How brought before the House of Reps.	Page of journal.	To what committee of the House referred.	No. or date of the report.	Nature of the report.	No. of the bill.	How disposed of by the House of Reps.	How disposed of by the Senate.	Date of the act of Congress, and remarks.
Hogeboom, Abraham, representatives of.	Commissions on disbursements while agent for removing Indians.	30	2	House bill	319	Whole House			232	Passed.		
Hoge, James, and John Davis.	Reimbursement of an over-payment for land.	21	1	Petition	70	Public Lands				Discharged; laid on table.		
Hoge, John, (Pa.)	Compensation for revolutionary services.	2	2	Petition	686					Referred to Secretary of War.		
Hoge, Lieut. John, son of	Pension for revolutionary services.	29	1	Petition	199	Rev. Pensions.						
Hoge, Lieut. John, son of	Pension for revolutionary services.	31	1	Petition	471	Rev. Claims	180	Adverse		Laid on table.		
Hoge, Jonathan, executor of.	One years' pay and interest for revolutionary services.	29	1	Memorial	199	Invalid Pensions				Discharged; laid on table.		
Hoge, Jonathan, executor of.	One years' pay and interest for revolutionary services.	30	1	Petition	575	Rev. Claims	July 19, 1848	Adverse		Laid on table.		
Hoge, Jonathan	(See Lieut. John Hoge, son of.)											
Hogencamp, Gyrbert	Compensation for wood and rails furnished revolutionary army.	4	1	Report of Secretary Treasury.	388	Claims	Dec. 24, 1795	Adverse		Laid on table.		
Hogg, Catharine, and Thomas Burnside.	Indemnity for property destroyed by the enemy, war of 1812.	24	1	Memorial	662	Claims.						
Hogg, Catharine and T. B.	Indemnity for property destroyed by the enemy, war of 1812.	25	2	Memorial	73	Claims	918	Adverse		Laid on table.		
Hogg, Catharine and T. B.	Indemnity for property destroyed by the enemy, war of 1812.	31	2	Petition	226	Military Affairs.						
Hogg, John	Compensation for services as a juror.	17	2	Petition	27	Judiciary	Feb. 3, 1823	Adverse.		Rejected.		
Hogg, John	Pension	26	2	Petition	82	Rev. Pensions	Feb. 12, 1841	Report and bill.	649	Referred to Committee Whole House.		
Hogg, John, trustees of	Indemnity for French spoliations prior to 1800.	26	1	Memorial	182	Foreign Affairs	343	Favorable; bill	319	Referred to Committee Whole House.		
Hogg, John, heir of	Indemnity for French spoliations prior to 1800.	29	2	Memorial	151	Foreign Affairs.						
Hogg, John, of Fayetteville, N. C.	Indemnity for French spoliations prior to 1800.	26	1	Memorial	182	Foreign Affairs	343	Favorable; bill	319	Referred to Committee Whole House.		
Hogg, Samuel	Pension for his services in the war of 1812.	27	2	Memorial	90	Invalid Pensions	582	Report and bill	378	Referred to Committee Whole House.		
Hogg, Samuel	Pension for his services in the war of 1812.	27	3	House bill	311	Whole House			378			
Hoggatt, Nathaniel	Confirmation of title to land in Louisiana.	30	1	Senate bill	361	Priv. Land Claims			S. 61			
Hoghland, William, *et al.*, by John Tizdale, attorney.	Compensation for services rendered and supplies furnished, war of 1812.	14	1	Petition	156	Claims.						
Hogland, James	Correction of an erroneous entry of land.	21	2	Senate bill	244	Priv. Land Claims	Feb. 11, 1831	With amend.	103	Passed	Passed as am'd.	App'd March 3, 1831
Hogue, Mildred	Exchange of a land entry	28	1	Petition	718	Priv. Land Claims.						
Hogue, Sam'l S., widow of.	Release from a judgment	28	1	Petition	406	P. Of. and P. Roads.						
Hogue, William G., widow of.	Pension, in consideration of the services and death of her husband, in Mexico.	30	1	Petition	581	Invalid Pensions	573	Adverse		Laid on table.		
Hoisington, Abishai	Compensation for use of a stage and horses taken for public service, war of 1812.	24	1	Petition	430	Claims	754	Adverse		Laid on table.		
Hoit, Asa	Pension for disability incurred in war of 1812.	22	1	Resolution	136	Invalid Pensions	208	Report and bill	288	Passed	Passed, with amendment.	App'd July 14, 1832

List of private claims presented to the House of Representatives of the United States from the 1st to the 31st Congress, inclusive—**Continued.**

Names of claimants.	Nature or object of the claim.	Congress.	Session.	How brought before the House of Reps.	Page of journal.	To what committee of the House referred.	No. or date of the report.	Nature of the report.	No. of the bill.	How disposed of by the House of Reps.	How disposed of by the Senate.	Date of the act of Congress, and remarks.
Hoit, Elisha	Pension	25	3	Resolution	156	Rev. Pensions.						
Hoit, Gates, and James Hatch.	Compensation for secret services in Canada, war of 1812.	17	1	Petition	248	Claims	Mar. 15, 1822	Adverse		Laid on table		Leave to withdraw.
Hoit, Gates	Compensation for secret service in Canada, war of 1812.	18	1	Petition	129	Claims	Feb. 24, 1824	Adverse		Laid on table		Leave to withdraw.
Hoit, Gates	Compensation for secret service in Canada, war of 1812.	19	1	Petition	130	Claims	April 17, 1826	Adverse		Laid on table.		
Hoit, Gates	Compensation for secret service in Canada, war of 1812.	20	1	Petition	243	Claims	Mar. 14, 1828	Adverse		Laid on table.		
Hoit, Gates	Compensation for secret service in Canada, war of 1812.	21	1	Petition	147	Military Affairs	214	Report and bill	268	Referred to Committee Whole House.		
Hoit, Gates	Compensation for secret service in Canada, war of 1812.	21	2	House bill	339	Whole House	Feb. 21, 1831	With't amend.	268	Passed.		
Hoit, Gates	Compensation for secret service in Canada, war of 1812.	22	1	Petition	54	Military Affairs	75	Report and bill	146	Passed	Passed	App'd July 14, 1832
Hoit, Gates	Compensation for secret service in Canada, war of 1812.	23	1	Petition	192	Claims	385	Adverse		Laid on table.		
Hoit, Gates	Compensation for secret service in Canada, war of 1812.	23	2	Resolution	115	Claims.						
Hoit, Gates	Compensation for secret service in Canada, war of 1812.	24	1	Resolution	141	Claims	771	Adverse		Laid on table.		
Hoit, Gates	Compensation for secret service in Canada, war of 1812.	25	2	Petition	241	Claims	Jan. 9, 1838	Adverse		Laid on table.		
Hoit, Gates	Compensation for secret service in Canada, war of 1812.	25	3	Petition	303	Claims	280	Adverse		Laid on table.		
Hoit or Hoyt, Moses	Reimbursement of expenses incurred in recruiting service.	15	2	Petition	102	Claims.						
Hoit or Hoyt, Moses	Reimbursement of expenses incurred in recruiting service.	16	1	Petition	115	Claims	Jan. 7, 1820			Discharged; laid on table.		
Holben, Frederick	Confirmation of title to land in Ohio.	28	1	Petition	277	Priv. Land Claims.						
Holberd, Robert	Pension	13	3	House bill	740	Whole House	Mar. 1, 1815	With't amend.	303	Passed	Passed	App'd March 3, 1813
Holbrook, Amos	To be restored to pension roll	17	2	Petition	36	Rev. Pensions				Discharged; leave to withdraw.		
Holbrook & Brooks	Remission of duties on goods imported into Castine.	16	1	Senate bill	108	Ways and Means	Jan. 14, 1820	With amend.	S. 13	Passed	Concurred in	Statutes at Large, vol. 6, p. 24.
Holbrook, David	To be restored to pension roll	17	1	Petition	30	Rev. Pensions				Discharged; laid on table.		
Holbrook, David	To be restored to pension roll	17	2	Petition	30	Rev. Pensions				Discharged; leave to withdraw.		
Holbrook, Edward	Indemnity for French spoliations prior to 1800.	26	1	Memorial	182	Foreign Affairs	343	Favorable; bill	319	Referred to Committee Whole House.		
Holbrook, Hannah	(See widow of Alexander Boughen)	2	1		447							
Holbrook, Henry	Balance due on contract with Navy Department.	26	2	Petition	53	Claims	26	Adverse		Laid on table.		
Holbrook, Henry	Balance due on contract with Navy Department.	27	2	Documents	613	Claims	716	Adverse		Laid on table.		
Holbrook, Henry	Balance due on contract with Navy Department.	27	3	Petition	395	Claims.						
Holbrook, Henry	Balance due on contract with Navy Department.	28	2	Petition	216	Claims.						
Holbrook, Henry	Balance due on contract with Navy Department.	29	1	Petition	625	Claims.						

List of private claims presented to the House of Representatives of the United States from the 1st to the 31st Congress, inclusive—Continued.

Names of claimants.	Nature or object of the claim.	Congress.	Session.	How brought before the House of Reps.	Page of journal.	To what committee of the House referred.	No. or date of the report.	Nature of the report.	No. of the bill.	How disposed of by the House of Reps.	How disposed of by the Senate.	Date of the act of Congress, and remarks.
Holbrook, Henry	Balance due on contract with Navy Department.	31	2	Petition	205	Claims.						
Holbrook, John	Compensation for losses and injuries, revolutionary war.	1	2	Petition	142	......	......	......	......	Referred to Secretary of Treasury.		
Holbrook, John	Compensation for losses and injuries, revolutionary war.	2	1	Rep. of Secretary Treasury.	580	......	......	......	......	Laid on table.		
Holbrook, Oliver	(See Johnson Jorden, heirs of)	28	1	......	840							
Holcomb, Elijah	Compensation for revolutionary services.	4	2	Petition	677	Claims	Feb. 8, 1797	Adverse.				
Holcomb, James	Pension for revolutionary services.	24	1	Petition	670	Rev. Pensions	......	......	......	Discharged; laid on table.		
Holcomb, James	Pension for revolutionary services.	24	2	Petition	146	Rev. Pensions	......	......	......	Discharged; laid on table.		
Holcombe, John	Pension	10	1	House bill	232	Whole House.	April 19, 1808	Favorable	78	Passed	Passed	App'd April 25, 1808
Holcombe, John, heirs of	Commutation pay for revolutionary services.	23	2	Petition	106	Rev. Claims.						
Holcombe, John, heirs of	Commutation pay for revolutionary services.	24	1	Petition	672	Rev. Claims.						
Holcombe, John, heirs of	Commutation pay for revolutionary services.	24	2	Petition	270	Rev. Claims.						
Holcombe, John, heirs of	Commutation pay for revolutionary services.	25	2	Petition	112	Rev. Claims	477	Adverse	......	Laid on table.		
Holcomb, Joseph	Pension for revolutionary services.	22	2	Petition	44	Rev. Pensions	......	......	......	Discharged; laid on table.		
Holcomb, Roger	Pension for revolutionary services.	24	1	Petition	107	Rev. Pensions	Feb. 4, 1836	Adverse	......	Laid on table.		
Holcomb, Roger	Pension for revolutionary services.	25	2	Petition	586	Rev. Pensions	......	......	......	Discharged; laid on table.		
Holcum, Nathaniel, heirs of, by Titus Strickland, guardian.	Confirmation of title to a tract of land in Missouri.	15	1	Petition	65	Priv. Land Claims.						
Holcum, Nathaniel, heirs of, by Titus Strickland, guardian.	Confirmation of title to a tract of land in Missouri.	16	1	Petition	72	Priv. Land Claims.						
Holcum, Nathaniel, heirs of, by Titus Strickland, guardian.	Confirmation of title to a tract of land in Missouri.	17	1	Petition	55	Priv. Land Claims.						
Holcum, Nathaniel, heirs of, by Titus Strickland, guardian.	Confirmation of title to a tract of land in Missouri.	18	1	Petition	55	Priv. Land Claims.						
Holden, Asa	To be restored to revolutionary pension roll.	22	1	Resolution	389	Rev. Pensions	365	Report and bill.	460	Passed	Indef. postp'd.	
Holden, Asa	To be restored to revolutionary pension roll.	24	1	Petition	258	Rev. Claims	396	Adverse	......	Laid on table.		
Holden, Joshua	Right of pre-emption to a tract of land in Louisiana.	30	2	Petition	78	Priv. Land Claims.	14	Report and bill.	709	Passed	Passed	App'd Feb. 19, 1849
Holden, Joshua	(See James P. Sexton & J. Holden.)	30	0									
Holden, Moses	Arrears of pension	19	1	Petition	221	Military Pensions	164	Adverse	......	Laid on table.		
Holden, Moses	Pension	19	2	Petition	132	Military Pensions	......	......	......	Discharged.		
Holden, Moses	Pension	20	1	Petition	192	Military Pensions	May 13, 1828	Adverse	......	Laid on table.		
Holden, Moses	Pension	23	1	Petition	45	Invalid Pensions.						
Holden, Moses	Pension	23	2	Petition	140	Invalid Pensions.						
Holden, Moses	Pension	25	2	Petition	168	Invalid Pensions	Feb. 17, 1838	Adverse	......	Laid on table.		

List of private claims presented to the House of Representatives of the United States from the 1st to the 31st Congress, inclusive—Continued.

Names of claimants.	Nature or object of the claim.	Congress.	Session.	How brought before the House of Reps.	Page of journal.	To what committee of the House referred.	No. or date of the report.	Nature of the report.	No. of the bill.	How disposed of by the House of Reps.	How disposed of by the Senate.	Date of the act of Congress, and remarks.
Holden, Moses	Pension	26	1	Petition	289	Invalid Pensions	246	Adverse		Laid on table.		
Holden, Moses	Pension	29	1	Petition	101	Invalid Pensions				Discharged; laid on table.		
Holden, Nehemiah	Pension	23	1	Petition	466	Invalid Pensions.						
Holden, Nehemiah	Pension	23	2	Petition	303	Invalid Pensions.						
Holden, Nehemiah	Increase of pension	31	1	Petition	537	Invalid Pensions	350	Adverse		Laid on table.		
Holden, Thomas	Compensation for supplies furnished troops.	26	1	Petition	169	Claims	60	Adverse		Laid on table.		
Holden, Phineas H., and Jonathan Bailey.	Remission of foreign tonnage duty on schooner Astrea.	10	2	Petition	415	Com. and Manuf.						
Holding, Eber	Pension for disability incurred, war of 1812.	25	2	Petition	58	Invalid Pensions				Discharged; laid on table.		
Holdridge, John	To be restored to pension roll	17	1	Petition	51	Rev. Pensions				Discharged; laid on table.		
Holdridge, John	To be restored to pension roll	17	2	Petition	43	Rev. Pensions				Leave to withdraw.		
Hole, James	Invalid pension	5	2	Petition	81	Claims	April 17, 1798	Adverse		Laid on table.		
Hole, James	Invalid pension	5	3	Rep't Committee.	432					Referred to Committee Whole House.		
Holgate, Samuel	Indemnity for losses sustained in the war of 1812.	19	1	Petition	43	Claims	Dec. 21, 1825	Adverse		Laid on table.		
Holgate, Samuel	Indemnity for losses sustained in the war of 1812.	20	1	Petition	38	Claims	Jan. [illegible]2, 1828	Adverse		Laid on table.		
Holgate, Samuel	Indemnity for losses sustained in the war of 1812.	20	2	Petition	40	Claims	Dec. 12, 1828	Adverse		Laid on table.		
Holgate, Samuel	Indemnity for losses sustained in the war of 1812.	21	1	Petition	99	Claims	78	Adverse		Referred to Committee Whole House.		
Holgate, Samuel	Indemnity for losses sustained in the war of 1812.	23	1	Petition	55	Claims	398	Adverse		Laid on table.		
Holgate, Samuel	Indemnity for losses sustained in the war of 1812.	25	2	Petition	177	Claims				Discharged; laid on table.		
Holgate, Samuel	Indemnity for losses sustained in the war of 1812.	25	3	Petition	87	Claims.						
Holgate, Samuel	Indemnity for losses sustained in the war of 1812.	26	1	Petition	169	Claims.						
Holgate, Samuel	Indemnity for losses sustained in the war of 1812.	26	2	Petition	80	Claims	32	Adverse		Laid on table.		
Holgate, Samuel	Indemnity for losses sustained in the war of 1812.	28	1	Petition	429	Claims.						
Holgate, Samuel, administrator of.	Indemnity for losses sustained in the war of 1812.	29	1	Petition	354	Claims	419	Adverse		Laid on table.		
Holgate, Samuel, administrator of.	Indemnity for losses sustained in the war of 1812.	30	1	Petition	136	Claims	124	Adverse		Laid on table.		
Holgate, Samuel, administrator of.	Indemnity for losses sustained in the war of 1812.	31	1	Petition	283	Claims.						
Holgate, William	Pension for services as a revolutionary soldier.	20	1	Resolution	454	Military Pensions	April 29, 1828	Report by bill.	283	Passed.		
Holgate, William	Pension for services as a revolutionary soldier.	20	2	Resolution	55	Military Pensions	Dec. 12, 1828	General bill	311	Passed	Laid on table.	
Holgate, William	Pension for services as a revolutionary soldier.	21	1	Resolution	47	Military Pensions				Discharged; laid on table.		
Holgate, William	Pension for services as a revolutionary soldier.	21	1	House bill	130	Whole House	Feb. 13, 1830	Favorable	72	Passed	Passed	App'd May 20, 1830

List of private claims presented to the House of Representatives of the United States from the 1st to the 31st Congress, inclusive—Continued.

Names of claimants.	Nature or object of the claim.	Congress.	Session.	How brought before the House of Reps.	Page of journal.	To what committee of the House referred.	No. or date of the report.	Nature of the report.	No. of the bill.	How disposed of by the House of Reps.	How disposed of by the Senate.	Date of the act of Congress, and remarks.
Holker, John	Relief from prosecution as surety for Duer & Parker.	4	1	Memorial	522	Claims				Discharged; leave to withdraw.		
Holker, John	Relief from a prosecution as surety for Duer & Parker.	4	2	Memorial	614	Claims.						
Holker, John	Renewal of a loan office certificate	4	1	Petition	427					Referred to Secretary of Treasury.		
Holker, John	Renewal of a loan office certificate	5	2	Petition	251	Claims	April 3, 1798	Favorable		Laid on table.		
Holker, John	Renewal of a loan office certificate	10	1	Petition	112					Referred to Committee Whole House.		
Holker, John	Renewal of a loan office certificate	11	2	Petition	163	Claims.						
Holker, John	Renewal of a loan office certificate	11	3	Petition	503	Claims.						
Holker, John	Renewal of a loan office certificate	14	1	Senate bill	533	Ways and Means	April 8, 1816	With't amend.		Passed		App'd April 26, 1816
Holl, Edward, executor of	Indemnity for French spoliations prior to 1800.	26	1	Memorial	182	Foreign Affairs	343	Favorable; bill	319	Referred to Committee Whole House.		
Holl, Robert, *et al*	Indemnity for British ship Union burnt by U. S. ship Peacock.	20	1	Senate bill	465	Commerce	April 11, 1828	With't amend.	103	Passed		App'd May 26, 1828
Holland, Benjamin	Pension	23	2	Petition	176	Invalid Pensions	54	Report and bill.	653	Passed	Passed	App'd March 3, 1835
Holland, Benjamin	Arrears of pension for services in war of 1812.	29	1	Petition	397	Invalid Pensions	350	Adverse		Laid on table.		
Holland, Benjamin	Arrears of pension for services in war of 1812.	30	1	Petition	217	Invalid Pensions	632½	Adverse		Laid on table.		
Holland, Benjamin	Arrears of pension for services in war of 1812.	31	1	Petition	537	Invalid Pensions.						
Holland, Charles	Pension for revolutionary services.	22	1	Petition	570	Rev. Pensions.						
Holland, Drury, heirs of.	Arrears of the revolutionary pension of deceased.	28	1	Petition	452	Rev. Pensions.						
Holland, Edward	Compensation for a vessel destroyed while in the public service.	11	2	Petition	146	Claims	Mar. 31, 1810	Adverse		Laid on table.		
Holland, Ivory, surety of	Release from liability	17	1	Petition	31	P. Of. & P. Roads	Dec. 28, 1821	Adverse		Rejected.		
Holland, Jacob	Pension for revolutionary services.	20	2	Petition	228	Military Pensions.						
Holland, Jacob	Pension for revolutionary services.	21	1	Petition	49	Military Pensions		General bill	72			Bill became a law, omitting petitioner's name.
Holland, Jacob	Pension for revolutionary services.	22	1	Petition	34	Rev. Claims.						
Holland, James	Compensation for services as a revolutionary soldier.	21	2	Petition	190	Rev. Claims.						
Holland, John	Compensation for revolutionary services.	2	1	Petition	477					Referred to Secretary of War.		
Holland, John	Right of pre-emption as New Orleans branch pilot.	28	1	Petition	77	Priv. Land Claims.	9	Favorable	35	Passed	Passed	App'd June 17, 1844
Holland, John	Pension for wounds received in the public service.	30	1	Petition	482	Invalid Pensions	569	Adverse		Laid on table.		
Holland, John, jr.	Abatement of duties on the cargo of schooner Hazard.	7	1	Petition	13	Com. and Manuf.	Mar. 22, 1802			Referred to Committee Whole House.		
Holland, John, jr.	Abatement of duties on the cargo of schooner Hazard.	7	2	Petition & report.	255	Com and Manuf.	Dec. 22, 1802	Favorable; bill ordered.	94	Referred to Committee Whole House.		
Holland, John E.	Allowance of traveling expenses while captain's clerk in United States navy.	29	1	Memorial	87	Naval Affairs	68	Report and bill.	63	Passed	Passed	App'd July 15, 1846
Holland, John H.	Indemnity for charges incurred by the custody of a number of Africans.	24	1	Resolution	173	Claims	223	Report and bill.	232	Passed	Passed, with amendment.	App'd July 2, 1836
Holland, Joseph	(See John D. Needham, *et al.*)	15	1	Petition	136	Select.						

List of private claims presented to the House of Representatives of the United States from the 1st to the 31st Congress, inclusive—Continued.

Names of claimants.	Nature or object of the claim.	Congress.	Session.	How brought before the House of Reps.	Page of journal.	To what committee of the House referred.	No. or date of the report.	Nature of the report.	No. of the bill.	How disposed of by the House of Reps.	How disposed of by the Senate.	Date of the act of Congress, and remarks.
Holland Land Company, agent of.	Indemnity for loss by error in execution of stamps.	7	2	Petition	260	Claims	....	....	......	Leave to withdraw.		
Holland, Lavina	Pension	28	1	Resolution	557	Rev. Pensions.						
Holland, Park	Release from imprisonment at the suit of the United States.	14	2	Petition	314	Claims	Feb. 7, 1817	Report by bill.	108	Passed	Passed	App'd March 1, 1817
Holland, Park	Increase of revolutionary pension.	26	1	Petition	733	Rev. Pensions	....	....	......	Discharged; laid on table.		
Holland, Stephen	Indemnity for French spoliations prior to 1800.	26	1	Memorial	182	Foreign Affairs	343	Favorable; bill	319	Referred to Committee Whole House.		
Holland, William T.	Compensation for services in attending as a witness.	30	1	Petition	276	Claims	212	Report and bill.	212	Passed	Passed	App'd July 20, 1848
Holloway, William and W. Watson.	Indemnity for loss in erecting a light-house.	19	2	Petition	155	Commerce	54	Adverse	......	Laid on table.		
Holleman, Abner S., sureties of.	Release from liability	27	2	Petition	783	P. Of. & P. Roads.	....	....	......	Discharged; laid on table.		
Hollenback, George, *et al*	Indemnity for Indian depredations in Illinois.	25	2	Documents	87	Claims	351	Adverse	......	Laid on table.		
Hollenback, George, *et al.*	Indemnity for Indian depredations in Illinois.	29	1	Petition	179	Claims	3	Adverse	......	Laid on table.		
Hollenback, George, *et al.*	Indemnity for Indian depredations in Illinois.	30	1	Petition	169	Claims	53	Adverse	......	Laid on table.		
Hollenback, George B.	Indemnity for Indian depredations in Illinois.	30	1	Petition	169	Claims	12	Adverse	......	Laid on table.		
Holleville, Lewis M. S.	Permission to purchase the land on which he resides.	21	1	Petition	53	Public Lands	Dec. 22, 1829	Adverse	......	Laid on table.		
Holley, Benjamin	Pension for revolutionary services.	22	1	Resolution	535	Rev. Pensions	....	....	......	Disch'd; laid on table.		
Holley, James	Pension	18	2	Petition	207	Rev. Pensions	Feb. 5, 1825	Adverse	......	Laid on table.		
Holley, John M., wdo	Mileage and per diem due deceased as member of Congress.	30	1	Resolution	889							
Holley, Leonard	Pay and bounty land for services, war of 1812.	22	1	Resolution	535	Military Affairs	423	Report and bill	523			
Holley, Leonard	Pay and bounty land for services, war of 1812.	23	1	Petition	249	Priv. Land Claims.	238	Report and bill.	265	Passed	Passed	App'd June 30, 1834
Holley, Robert	Pension for revolutionary services.	22	1	Petition	219	Rev. Pensions	June 16, 1832	Adverse	......	Laid on table.		
Holly, Simon	Pension	14	2	Documents	90	Pens. & Rev. Cl'ms.	Jan. 29, 1817	Report by bill.	91	Passed	Passed	App'd March 3, 1817
Holliday, John	Compensation for team lost in the public service.	14	1	Petition	450	Claims.						
Holliday, John	Compensation for team lost in the public service.	15	2	Petition	182	Claims.						
Holliday, John	Compensation for team lost in the public service.	18	1	Petition	130	Claims	62	Report and bill.	117	Passed	Passed	App'd May 26, 1824
Holliday, John	Refunding money paid to extinguish land title.	24	1	Appropriation bill	......	....	....	....	......	....	....	App'd July 2, 1836
Holliday, John	Grant of land for revolutionary services.	22	1	Petition	388	Priv. Land Claims.	Feb. 29, 1832	Adverse	......	Laid on table.		
Holliday, John	Permission to enter land as New Orleans branch pilot.	28	1	Petition	77	Priv. Land Claims.	9	Favorable; bill	35	Passed	Passed	App'd June 17, 1844
Holliday, Lt. Joseph, heirs of.	Commutation pay for revolutionary services.	26	1	Petition	797	Rev. Claims.						
Holliday, Lt. Joseph, heirs of.	Commutation pay for revolutionary services.	26	2	Petition	35	Rev. Claims.						
Holliday, Lt. Joseph, heirs of.	Commutation pay for revolutionary services.	27	2	Petition	59	Rev. Claims	383	Adverse	......	Laid on table.		

List of private claims presented to the House of Representatives of the United States from the 1st to the 31st Congress, inclusive—Continued.

Names of claimants.	Nature or object of the claim.	Congress.	Session.	How brought before the House of Reps.	Page of journal.	To what committee of the House referred.	No. or date of the report.	Nature of the report.	No. of the bill.	How disposed of by the House of Reps.	How disposed of by the Senate.	Date of the act of Congress, and remarks.
Holliday, Mary	Repayment of money to extinguish land title.	24	1	Appropriation bill								App'd July 2, 1836
Holliday, Maria	Confirmation of title to land in Louisiana.	22	1	Senate bill	205	Priv. Land Claims.	Jan. 24, 1832	With't amend.	46	Passed		App'd July 13, 1832
Holliday, Robert	Right of pre-emption as New Orleans branch pilot.	28	1	Petition	77	Priv. Land Claims.	9	Favorable	35	Passed	Passed	App'd June 17, 1844
Hollidayoke, Daniel, heir of.	Grant of land for public services.	27	2	Petition	220	Rev. Claims	659	Adverse		Laid on table.		
Hollidayoke, John	Pension	23	1	Petition	368	Invalid Pensions	379	Adverse		Laid on table.		
Hollinger, William	Permission to sell land on Creek Indian reservation.	19	1	Petition	272	Public Lands	91	Report and bill	128	Passed	Passed	App'd May 16, 1826
Hollingshead, John	Compensation for revolutionary services.	3	2	Petition	306	Claims.						
Hollingshead, John	Compensation for revolutionary services.	4	1	Rep. of Secretary War.	373	Claims	Dec. 18, 1795	Adverse		Leave to withdraw.		
Hollingsworth, Henry	Compensation for a horse lost in the public service.	15	2	Petition	27	Claims	Dec. 1, 1818	Adverse		Rejected.		
Hollingsworth, Henry	Compensation for a horse lost in the public service.	19	2	Petition	240	Claims				Discharged.		
Hollingsworth, H.	Mileage and compensation for military services.	30	2	Petition	338	Military Affairs.						
Hollingsworth, Jacob	Payment or renewal of loan office certificate.	4	1	Memorial & rep. Sec. Treasury.	388, 488	Claims	74	Adverse		Laid on table.		
Hollingsworth, Jacob	Payment or renewal of loan office certificate.	4	2	Memorial	614	Claims	Feb. 1, 1797	Adverse		Rejected.		
Hollingsworth, Jehu	Correct error in land entry	24	2	Petition	47	Public Lands	15	Report and bill	772	Referred to Committee Whole House.		
Hollingsworth, Jehu	Correct error in land entry	25	2	Petition	87	Public Lands	93	Report and bill.	110	Passed	Passed	App'd June 28, 1838
Hollingsworth, Jehu, widow of.	Exchange entry of land	28	1	Supplemental bill	224	Public Lands	118	Favorable	57	Passed.		
Hollingsworth, Jehu, widow of.	Exchange entry of land	28	2	Supplemental bill	278	Whole House			544	Passed	Indef. postp'd.	
Hollingsworth, John, jr.	Permission to import merchandise from the West Indies to the amount of his claims there.	12	1	Petition	59					Referred to Committee Whole House, on bill No. 46.		
Hollingsworth, Joseph	Release from a judgment at the suit of the United States.	17	2	Petition	70	Ways and Means.				Discharged; leave to withdraw.		
Hollingsworth, Thomas & Samuel.	Indemnity for French spoliations prior to 1800.	26	1	Memorial	182	Foreign Affairs.	343	Favorable; bill	319	Referred to Committee Whole House.		
Hollingsworth, Samuel and Thomas.	Payment of sundry certificates of public debt.	8	2	Petition	85					Referred to Committee Whole House.		
Hollingsworth, William	(See F. M. Arredondo and others.)	19	1		252							
Hollingsworth, Zebulon	Examination of his accounts and abatement on a judgment.	14	1	Petition	659					Referred to Secretary Treasury.		
Hollingsworth, Zebulon	Release from imprisonment on a judgment in favor of U. States	14	2	Petition	308	Judiciary.						
Hollingsworth, Benj., *et al.*	Right of pre-emption lost by the location of Indian reservation.	28	2	Petition	65	Public Lands.						
Hollins, John	Indemnity for French spoliations prior to 1800.	26	1	Memorial	182	Foreign Affairs	343	Favorable; bill	319	Referred to Committee Whole House.		
Hollins, John	(See Maryland Insurance Comp'y.)	26	1		182					Leave to withdraw.		

List of private claims presented to the House of Representatives of the United States from the 1st to the 31st Congress, inclusive—Continued.

Names of claimants.	Nature or object of the claim.	Congress.	Session.	How brought before the House of Reps.	Page of journal.	To what committee of the House referred.	No. or date of the report.	Nature of the report.	No. of the bill.	How disposed of by the House of Reps.	How disposed of by the Senate.	Date of the act of Congress, and remarks.
Hollins, John	Abatement of duty on a cargo imported by him.	1	3	Petition	370					Leave to withdraw.		
Hollins & McBlair	(See John Gooding and others)	13	1		377							
Hollins, William	For certain real estate in the District of Columbia.	24	2	Petition	146	Dist. of Columbia				Discharged; laid on table.		
Hollins, W. S., *et al.*	Settlement and allowance of the accounts of certain acting officers.	30	1	Senate bill	328	Naval Affairs	Feb. 29, 1848	With't amend.	S. 118	Referred to Committee Whole House.		
Hollis, Barnabas, widow of.	Pension and half pay for revolutionary services.	24	2	Petition	346	Rev. Pensions	235	Report and bill for half-pay.	938	Referred to Committee Whole House.		
Hollis, Phebe	Benefit of the act of March 3, 1837.	29	1	Petition	476	Rev. Pensions.						
Hollister, B. F.	(See John E. Hunt and others)	27	2		334							
Hollister, Jesse W	Arrears of pension and reimbursement of money taken by the enemy, war of 1812.	30	2	Memorial	140	Invalid Pensions.						
Hollister, Jesse W	Arrears of pension and reimbursement of money taken by the enemy, war of 1812.	31	1	Memorial	257	Invalid Pensions				Discharged; laid on table.		
Hollister, John, *et al.*	(See John E. Hunt, *et al.*)	28	2		340							
Hollister, J. W. & Co., and G. Anderson.	Reimbursement of duty paid on merchandise shipped from Buffalo to Sandusky.	20	2	Petition	64	Ways and Means	Jan. 19, 1829	Report by bill.	378	Referred to Committee Whole House.		
Hellister, J. W. & Co., and G. Anderson.	Reimbursement of duty paid on merchandise shipped from Buffalo to Sandusky.	21	1	Petition	50	Ways and Means	Jan. 4, 1830	Report by bill.	67	Passed	Passed	App'd April 7, 1830
Hollister, Josiah	Pension	19	1	Petition	221	Military Pensions	164	Adverse		Laid on table.		
Hollister, Nathan & Jesse	Remuneration for losses by the depreciation of revolutionary certificates.	19	1	Petition	269	Whole House				Discharged; laid on table.		
Holloway, David	Release from imprisonment on a judgment against him as surety on custom-house bonds.	5	3	Petition	427	Com. and Manuf.						
Holloway, James	Arrears of pension	23	1	Petition	45	Invalid Pensions.						
Holloway, James	Arrears of pension	23	2	Petition	88	Invalid Pensions				Discharged; laid on table.		
Holloway, James	Arrears of pension	24	1	Petition	98	Invalid Pensions	Jan. 12, 1794			Discharged; laid on table.		
Holloway, John	Invalid pension	3	1	Rep. of Secretary of War.	131	Select	May 26, 1794	Jt. res. to refer to Sec. War.	J. R. 12	Passed	Passed	App'd June 9, 1794
Holloway, John	Pension for services in the war of 1812.	28	1	Petition	812	Invalid Pensions.						
Holloway, Peter	Reward for improvement in the manufacture of nails.	9	1	Petition	231	Select.						
Holloway, Peter	Reward for improvement in the manufacture of nails.	10	1	Resolution	97					Leave to withdraw.		
Hollowell, Henry	Arrears of pension	23	2	Petition	164	Rev. Pensions				Discharged; laid on table.		
Holman, George	Compensation for services and injuries, revolutionary war.	28	1	Petition	429	Claims.						
Holmenhouser, Charles	(See John Burton, *et al.*)	21	1		39							
Holmes, Abijah	Pension for revolutionary services.	22	1	Petition	36	Rev. Pensions	114	Report and bill	193	Referred to Committee Whole House.		
Holmes, Abijah	Pension for revolutionary services.	22	2	House bill	66				193	Laid on table.		
Holmes, Alexander, & B. Hough.	Reimbursement of expenses in preparing to survey public lands.	14	1	Petition	393	Claims.						

List of private claims presented to the House of Representatives of the United States from the 1st to the 31st Congress, inclusive—Continued.

Names of claimants.	Nature or object of the claim.	Congress.	Session.	How brought before the House of Reps.	Page of journal.	To what committee of the House referred.	No. or date of the report.	Nature of the report.	No. of the bill.	How disposed of by the House of Reps.	How disposed of by the Senate.	Date of the act of Congress, and remarks.
Holmes, Alexander, & B Hough.	Reimbursement of expenses in preparing to survey public lands.	14	2	Petition	72	Claims	Jan. 27, 1817	Report by bill.	82	Passed	Passed, with amendment.	App'd March 3, 1817
Holmes, Asher, *et al.*	Grant of three islands in Kankakee river.	25	2	Petition	85	Public Lands				Discharged.		
Holmes, B., heir of	(See Henry Bass & Co.)	27	2		253							
Holmes, B	(See B. Homes, heirs of.)	31	1		276							
Holmes, Bartlett	Pension for disability incurred in war of 1812.	23	2	Petition	303	Invalid Pensions.						
Holmes, Bartlett	Pension for disability incurred in war of 1812.	24	1	Petition	233	Invalid Pensions	Feb. 4, 1836	Adverse		Laid on table.		
Holmes, Bartlett	Pension for disability incurred in war of 1812.	25	2	Petition	167	Invalid Pensions				Discharged; laid on table.		
Holmes, Bartlett	Pension for disability incurred in war of 1812.	28	1	Petition	251	Invalid Pensions	236	Adverse		Laid on table.		
Holmes, Barzillai, of the firm of Henry Bass & Co.	Indemnity for French spoliations prior to 1800.	29	2	Memorial	101	Foreign Affairs.						
Holmes, Caleb	(See M. W. Bostwick, sureties and heirs of.)	26	1		509							
Holmes, Charles	Bounty land for military services.	26	1	Resolution	554	Public Lands.						
				Additional docs.	947	Public Lands	626	Adverse		Laid on table.		
Holmes, David	Pension for revolutionary services.	22	1	Petition	36	Rev. Pensions				Disch'd; laid on table.		
Holmes, (Temp.) widow of	For the allowance to widows of officers dying in the revolutionary service	2	1	Petition	500					Referred to Secretary War.		
Holmes, (Temp.) widow of	For the allowance to widows of officers dying in the revolutionary service.	23	1	Petition	42	Rev. Claims	Jan. 7, 1834	Report by bill.	149	Name stricken out.		
Holmes, Ebenezer	Pension for revolutionary services.	22	1	Petition	475	Rev. Pensions	381	Peport and bill	472	Passed	Indef. postp'd.	
Holmes, Elisha H	(See George Randall, *et al.*)	27	2		56							
Holmes, Elisha H	Extension of patent for a dredging machine.	28	2	Petition	167	Patents.						
Holmes, Elisha H	Extension of patent for a dredging machine.	29	1	Petition	120	Patents	160	Report and bill.	164	Passed.		
Holmes, Elisha H	Extension of patent for a dredging machine.	29	2	Petition	55	Patents	62	Report and bill	667	Referred to Committee Whole House.		
Holmes, Elisha H	Extension of patent for a dredging machine.	30	1	Petition	70	Patents	293	Report and bill.	289	Referred to Committee Whole House.		
Holmes, Elisha H	Extension of patent for a dredging machine.	31	1	Petition	434	Patents.						
Holmes Hastings, & Co.	Indemnity for French spoliations prior to 1800.	26	1	Memorial	182	Foreign Affairs	343	Favorable; bill	319	Referred to Committee Whol House.		
Holmes, Jesse	Indemnity for the confiscation of his property in Canada.	17	2	Petition	26	Claims	Dec. 13, 1822	Adverse		Rejected		**Leave to withdraw.**
Holmes, Jacob	Compensation for sufferings and sacrifices as a ranger.	20	2	Resolution	72	Military Pensions.						
Holmes, Jacob	Pension	22	2	Petition	264	Invalid Pensions.						
Holmes, Jacob	Pension for disability incurred in war of 1812.	24	2	Petition	397	Invalid Pensions	Feb. 22, 1837	Adverse		Laid on table.		
Holmes, James S.	(See agent of Ebenezer Lobdell)	24	1		477							
Holmes, James S.	(See Ebenezer Lobdell, attorney of)	26	1		182							
Holmes, John	Compensation for a horse lost in Seminole war.	16	2	Senate bill	67	Claims	Jan. 13, 1821	With't amend.	S. 9	Referred to Committee Whole House.		

List of private claims presented to the House of Representatives of the United States from the 1st to the 31st Congress, inclusive—Continued.

Names of claimants.	Nature or object of the claim.	Congress.	Session.	How brought before the House of Reps.	Page of journal.	To what committee of the House referred.	No. or date of the report.	Nature of the report.	No. of the bill.	How disposed of by the House of Reps.	How disposed of by the Senate.	Date of the act of Congress, and remarks.
Holmes, John	Compensation for a horse lost in Seminole war.	17	1	Senate bill	115	Claims	Feb. 22, 1822	With't amend.	S. 8	Passed		App'd May 7, 1822
Holmes, John	To be placed on pension roll	20	1	Resolution	208	Military Pensions.						
Holmes, John	To be restored to pension roll	20	2	Petition	59	Military Pensions	Jan. 16, 1829	Adverse		Laid on table.		
Holmes, John D.	Pecuniary relief for services rendered in 1792.	24	2	Petition	48	Invalid Pensions.						
Holmes, John, (Md.)	Indemnity for French spoliations prior to 1800.	26	1	Memorial	182	Foreign Affairs	343	Favorable; bill	319	Referred to Committee Whole House.		
Holmes, John W.	Compensation for a slave killed by a fall while sweeping a light-house.	21	2	Petition	45	Claims	Dec. 21, 1830	Adverse		Laid on table.		
Holmes, John, administrator of.	Indemnity for French spoliations prior to 1800.	26	1	Memorial	182	Foreign Affairs	343	Favorable; bill	319	Referred to Committee Whole House.		
Holmes, Jonathan, attorney of.	Revolutionary pension	18	2	Petition	183	Pens. & Rev. Cl'ms				Discharged; laid on table.		
Holmes, Joseph	Bounty on fishing schooner Industry.	25	3	Petition	214	Commerce.						
Holmes, Joseph	Bounty on fishing schooner Lydia.	26	1	Petition	177	Commerce	313	Report and bill.	276	Referred to Committee Whole House.		
Holmes, Joseph, *et al*	Bounty on fishing schooner Industry.	27	2	Petition	518	Commerce	739	Report and bill.	416	Referred to Committee Whole House.		
Holmes, Joseph, *et al*	Bounty on fishing schooner Industry.	27	3	House bill	88	Whole House			416	Passed	Indef. postp'd.	
Holmes, Joseph, *et al*	Bounty on fishing schooner Industry.	28	2	Petition	136	Commerce	Dec. 26, 1844	Report by bill.	473	Referred to Committee Whole House.		
Holmes, Joseph, *et al*	Bounty on fishing schooner Industry.	29	1	Petition	116	Commerce	261	Report and bill	223	Referred to Committee Whole House.		
Holmes, Joseph, *et al*	Bounty on fishing schooner Industry.	29	2	Memorial	205	Commerce.						
Holmes, Joseph, *et al*	Bounty on fishing schooner May Bee.	30	1	Petition	110	Commerce	259	Report and bill.	252	Referred to Committee Whole House.		
Holmes, Josiah	Fishing bounty withheld for informality.	26	1	Petition	290	Commerce	316	Report and bill.	276	Referred to Committee Whole House.		
Holmes, Josiah, as agent.	Bounty on fishing schooner Lydia.	27	2	Petition	96	Commerce	67	Report and bill	102	Passed	Passed	App'd July 27, 1842
Holmes, Micah	Arrears of pay and bounty land for services, war of 1812.	26	1	Petition	702	Claims.						
Holmes, Moses	Pension	20	2	Petition	26	Military Pensions	Jan. 15, 1829	Adverse		Laid on table.		
Holmes, Nathaniel	Reimbursement expenses in transporting troops to quell the whiskey insurrection in 1794.	6	2	Petition	715	Claims	Feb. 10, 1801	Favorable; bill ordered.	304	Passed	Passed	App'd Feb. 26, 1801
Holmes, Oliver	(See Benjamin Hallett, *et al.*)	18	1		235							
Holmes, Orsamus	Compensation for revolutionary services.	19	1	Resolution	208	Rev. Claims				Discharged; laid on table.		
Holmes, Orsamus	Compensation for revolutionary services.	19	1	Petition	312	Rev. Claims				Discharged; leave to withdraw.		
Holmes, Orsamus	Compensation for revolutionary services.	19	1	Petition	32	Rev. Claims	14	Adverse		Laid on table.		
Holmes, Orsamus	Compensation for revolutionary services.	19	1	Petition	108	Military Pensions	Feb. 14, 1827	Adverse		Referred to Committee Whole House.		
Holmes, Orsamus	Compensation for revolutionary services.	20	1	Petition	62	Military Pensions	136	Pension bill	283	Passed.		
Holmes, Orsamus	Compensation for revolutionary services.	20	2	Petition	55	Military Pensions	Dec. 12, 1838	General bill	311	Passed	Laid on table.	

List of private claims presented to the House of Representatives of the United States from the 1st to the 31st Congress, inclusive—Continued.

Names of claimants.	Nature or object of the claim.	Congress.	Session.	How brought before the House of Reps.	Page of journal.	To what committee of the House referred.	No. or date of the report.	Nature of the report.	No. of the bill.	How disposed of by the House of Reps.	How disposed of by the Senate.	Date of the act of Congress, and remarks.
Holmes, Orsamus	Compensation for revolutionary services.	21	1	Petition	48	Military Pensions.						
Holmes, Orsamus	Compensation for revolutionary services.	21	2	Petition	62	Military Pensions.						
Holmes, Orsamus	Compensation for revolutionary services.	22	1	Petition	44	Rev. Pensions	411	Report and bill	511	Referred to Committee Whole House.		
Holmes, Orsamus	Indemnity for losses, &c., while prisoner at Quebec.	20	1	Resolution	62	Rev. Claims	Jan. 14, 1828	Adverse		Laid on table.		
Holmes, Orsamus	Indemnity for losses, &c., while prisoner at Quebec.	20	1	Resolution	243	Military Pensions	April 29, 1828	Report by bill	283	Passed.		
Holmes, Orsamus	Pension	21	1	Petition	48	Military Pensions			72	Passed	Passed	App'd May 20, 1830
Holmes, Orsamus	Increase and arrears of pension	23	1	Petition	585	Rev. Pensions.						
Holmes, Orsamus	Increase and arrears of pension	23	2	Petition	120	Rev. Claims				Disch'd; laid on table.		
Holmes, Pelham	(See heirs of Ebenezer Lobdell)	29	2	Memorial	353							
Holmes, Philip B., and William Pedrick.	Compensation for the use of a patent for cutting raw hides for rope.	28	1	Petition	517	Naval Affairs	389	Report and bill	291	Referred to Committee Whole House.		
Holmes, Philip B., and William Pedrick.	Compensation for the use of a patent for cutting raw hides for rope	29	1	Petition	70	Naval Affairs	117	Report and bill.	125	Rejected.		
Holmes, Philip B., and William Pedrick.	Compensation for the use of a patent for cutting raw hides for rope.	30	1	Petition	280	Naval Affairs.						
Holmes, Nathaniel	Pension	19	2	Petition	215	Military Pensions				Dischardge.		
Holmes, Nathaniel	Pension and bounty land	24	1	Petition	1102	Rev. Pensions.						
Holmes, Nathaniel	Pension and bounty land	24	2	Petition	90	Rev. Pensions	107	Adverse		Laid on table.		
Holmes, Samuel	Pension for revolutionary services.	22	1	Petition	710	Rev. Pensions.						
Holmes, Silas, sureties of.	Release from liability	26	2	Petition	249	Judiciary.						
Holmes, Silas, sureties of.	Release from liability	27	2	Petition	63	Judiciary	271	Favorable; bill	236	Passed	Passed	App'd June 27, 1842
Holmes, Silas	(See Exploring Expedition)	27	3		149		270		818			
Holmes, Thomas	Relief in consideration of wounds, &c., in revolutionary war.	9	1	Petition	280	Claims	Mar. 28, 1806	Adverse		Leave to withdraw.		
Holmes, Thomas G.	Bounty land for services in war of 1812.	30	1	Petition	738	Public Lands	661	Adverse		Laid on table.		
Holmes, Valentine	Pension for services as a revolutionary soldier.	19	1	Resolution	139	Military Pensions				Discharged; laid on table.		
Holmes, Valentine	Pension for services as a revolutionary soldier.	19	1	Petition	149	Military Pensions	Feb. 23, 1826	General bill	119	Passed.		
Holmes, Valentine	Pension for services as a revolutionary soldier.	19	2	Petition	66	Military Pensions	Dec. 22, 1826	General bill	315	Passed.		
Holmes, William	(See John George, heir of.)	5	2		321							
Holmes, William	Pension	19	2	Petition	72	Military Pensions				Discharged.		
Holmes, William B.	(See William B. Storkes.)	15	1		87							
Holmes & Co.	(See J. Remsen, Holmes & Co.)	14	2		327							
Holridge, John	Invalid pension	3	1	Rep. of Secretary War.	131	Select	May 26, 1794	Favorable; bill	62	Passed	Passed	App'd June 7, 1794
Holridge, John	Pension and arrearages	4	1	Memorial	436	Claims	May 7, 1796	Adverse		Leave to withdraw.		
Holsey, Job	Pension for revolutionary services.	25	2	Resolution	529	Rev. Pensions	669	Report and bill.	673	Passed	Adverse report.	
Holstein, Peter	Pension	19	1	Petition	364	Military Pensions	164	Adverse		Laid on table.		
Holstein, Samuel	(See heirs of Wm. McMillan)	25	2		899							
Holt, Charles, (N. Y.)	Reimbursement of fine imposed under sedition law.	26	1	Petition	1284	Judiciary.						
Holt, Charles, (N. Y.)	Reimbursement of fine imposed under sedition law.	26	2	Petition	85	Judiciary	113	Report and bill.	618	Referred to Committee Whole House.		
Holt, Charles, (N. Y.)	Reimbursement of fine imposed under sedition law.	27	2	Petition	63	Judiciary	273	Report and bill.	239	Referred to Committee Whole House.		

List of private claims presented to the House of Representatives of the United States from the 1st to the 31st Congress, inclusive—Continued.

Names of claimants.	Nature or object of the claim.	Congress.	Session.	How brought before the House of Reps.	Page of journal.	To what committee of the House referred.	No. or date of the report.	Nature of the report.	No. of the bill.	How disposed of by the House of Reps.	How disposed of by the Senate.	Date of the act of Congress, and remarks.
Holt, Charles, (N. Y.)	Reimbursement of fine imposed under sedition law.	27	3	House bill	87	Whole House			239	Passed.		
Holt, Charles, (N. Y.)	Reimbursement of fine imposed under sedition law.	28	1	Petition	361	Judiciary	206	Report and bill.	161	Passed	Passed	App'd June 17, 1844
Holt, Drury	Compensation for a horse lost in the war of 1812.	23	1	Petition	656	Claims.						
Holt, Henry	(See William H. Bedford, agent).	28	1		262							
Holt, Jesse	Invalid pension	1	3	Petition	336					Referred to Secretary War.		
Holt, Jesse	Invalid pension	3	2	Rep. of Secretary War.	350	Claims				Discharged; laid on table.		
Holt, Jesse	Invalid pension	4	1	Rep. of Secretary War.	445	Claims	March 4, 1796	Favorable; bill ordered.	156	Passed	Passed	App'd April 20, 1796
Holt, Jacob H	Compensation for services as clerk in quartermaster's department.	25	2	Petition	58	Military Affairs				Laid on table.		
Holt, Jacob W	Pension	20	1	Petition	223	Military Pensions				Discharged; laid on table.		
Holt, John	Arrears of pay for revolutionary services.	3	2	Petition	274	Claims.						
Holt, John	Arrears of pay for revolutionary services.	4	1	Rep. of Secretary of War.	373	Claims	May 31, 1796	Adverse		Laid on table.		
Holt, John	Pension	23	1	Petition	308	Invalid Pensions				Discharged; laid on table.		
Holt, Joseph, heirs of	Commutation pay for revolutionary services.	23	2	Petition	47	Claims.						
Holt, Joseph, heirs of	Commutation pay for revolutionary services.	24	1	Petition	431	Rev. Claims						See Wm. Glass and wife.
Holt, Magor	Payment for services in Creek war.	24	2	Appropriation bill								App'd March 1, 1837
Holt, Nathan	Invalid pension	3	2	Rep of Secretary War.	278	Claims	Feb. 28, 1795	Favorable; bill ordered.	130	Passed	Postponed till next sess.	
Holt, Nathan	Invalid pension	4	1	Rep. of Secretary War.	445	Claims	Mar. 4, 1796	Favorable; bill ordered.	156	Passed	Passed	App'd April 20, 1796
Holt, Norman	Correction of an erroneous entry of land in Indiana.	24	2	Petition	49	Priv. Land Claims.	Dec. 21, 1836	Report by bill.	760	Passed	Passed	App'd Jan. 31, 1837
Holt, Patsy	Pension in consideration of the revolutionary services of her husband.	28	1	Petition	950	Whole House.						
Holt, Samuel	Grant of land for military services.	19	1	Petition	271	Priv. Land Claims.	Mar. 8, 1826	Adverse.		Laid on table.		
Holt, Uzziel or Uriel	Pension for services, war of 1812.	24	1	Petition	52	Invalid Pensions	193	Adverse		Laid on table.		
Holt, Uzziel or Uriel	Arrears of pension	25	2	Resolution	161	Invalid Pensions				Discharged; laid on table.		
Holt, William, widow of	Pension	22	1	Petition	187	Rev. Pensions.						
Holt, Zedidiah	(See heir of Ambrose Atkins.)											
Holting, David	(See William Baker, N. Y.)	22	1		288		480					
Holton, Amos	Remuneration for expenses as brigade quartermaster, war of 1812.	28	2	Petition	405	Claims.						
Holton, David	Pension	15	2	Rep of Secretary War.	48	Pens. & Rev. Cl'ms.	Feb. 5, 1819	By bill	308	Passed	Postponed.	
Holton, Francis	Pension	28	2	Petition	83	Naval Affairs				Discharged; laid on table.		
Holton, Francis S., or M	Pension for wounds and disability, war of 1812.	29	2	Petition	112	Invalid Pensions.						
Holton, Francis S., or M	Pension for wounds and disability, war of 1812.	30	1	Petition	245	Invalid Pensions	450	Report and bill	380	Passed	Passed	App'd Aug. 11, 1848

List of private claims presented to the House of Representatives of the United States from the 1st to the 31st Congress, inclusive—Continued.

Names of claimants.	Nature or object of the claim.	Congress.	Session.	How brought before the House of Reps.	Page of journal.	To what committee of the House referred.	No. or date of the report.	Nature of the report.	No. of the bill.	How disposed of by the House of Reps.	How disposed of by the Senate.	Date of the act of Congress, and remarks.
Holton, Jonathan	Invalid pension	3	2	Rep. of Secretary War.	350	Claims				Discharged; laid on table.		
Holton, Jonathan	Invalid pension	4	1	Rep. of Secretary War.	445	Claims	Mar. 4, 1796	Favorable; bill ordered.	156	Passed	Passed	App'd April 20, 1796
Holton, Jonathan	Invalid pension	9	2	House bill	608	Whole House	Feb. 28, 1807	Favorable	216	Passed	Passed	App'd March 3, 1807
Holton, Jonathan	Increase of pension	15	1	Petition	349	Pens. & Rev. Cl'ms.				Discharged; laid on table.		
Holtzbecher, F. H	Drawback on merchandise refused by officers of customs.	5	3	Petition	432	Com. and Manuf				Discharged; leave to withdraw.		
Homa Hishe, or Captain Red Pepper.	Confirmation of title to land	23	1	Senate bill	501	Public Lands	May 20, 1834	With amend.	S. 110	Passed with amendm't	Passed as am'd.	App'd June 30, 1834
Homan, Ambrose	Pension	10	1	House bill	238	Whole House			78	Passed	Passed	App'd April 25, 1808
Homan, William	(See Henry Thorndike, administratrix of, and others.)	12	1		263							
Homans, Benjamin	Compensation as clerk in Navy Department, 1823.	21	1	Petition	110	Claims	74	Report and bill	106	Passed	Passed	App'd May 29, 1830
Homans, Benjamin, and Alfred B. Claxton.	Release of forfeiture on account of the non-fulfilment of contract to print and bind Biennial Register.	26	1	Memorial	697	Judiciary.						
Homans, Benjamin, and Alfred B. Claxton.	Release of forfeiture on account of the non-fulfilment of contract to print and bind Biennial Register.	26	2	Memorial	222	Judiciary.						
Homans, Daniel	Indemnity for damage, and compensation for extra work on hospital.	23	1	Petition	448	Claims	518	Report and bill.	520	Referred to Committee Whole House.		
Homans, Daniel	Indemnity for damage, and compensation for extra work on hospital.	24	1	Petition	51	Claims	22	Report and bill	22	Passed	Passed	App'd Feb. 17, 1836
Homans, Daniel	Indemnity for damage, and compensation for extra work on hospital.	24	2	Documents	395	Claims.						
Homans, Daniel	Indemnity for damage, and compensation for extra work on hospital.	27	2	Petition	110	Claims	53	Report and bill	88	Passed	Passed	App'd July 27, 1842
Homans, Daniel	Indemnity for damage, and compensation for extra work on hospital.	27	3	House bill	256	Whole House			727			
Homans, Daniel	Indemnity for damage, and compensation for extra work on hospital.	28	1	Petition	216	Claims.						
Homans, Daniel	Indemnity for damage, and compensation for extra work on hospital.	28	2	Petition	72	Claims	14	Report and bill.	476	Passed	Passed	App'd March 3, 1845
Homes, Barzillai	Indemnity for French spoliations prior to 1800.	26	1	Memorial	182	Foreign Affairs	343	Favorable; bill	319	Referred to Committee Whole House.		
Homes, B., heir of	Indemnity for French spoliations prior to 1800.	31	1	Petition	276	Foreign Affairs	355	General bill	318	Referred to Committee Whole House.		
Homer, James, by attorney	Correction of an error in a judgment, and further credit for payments thereon.	16	2	Petition	177	Commerce				Discharged; laid on table.		
Homer, James, by attorney	Correction of an error in a judgment, and further credit for payments thereon.	17	1	Petition	72	Commerce	17	Adverse		Laid on table.		

List of private claims presented to the House of Representatives of the United States form the 1st to the 31st Congress, inclusive—Continued.

Names of claimants.	Nature or object of the claim.	Congress.	Session.	How brought before the House of Reps.	Page of journal.	To what committee of the House referred.	No. or date of the report.	Nature of the report.	No. of the bill.	How disposed of by the House of Reps.	How disposed of by the Senate.	Date of the act of Congress, and remarks.
Hommel, George	Pension	22	2	Petition	181	Invalid Pensions	Jan. 15, 1839	Adverse		Laid on table.		
Hommel, George	Pension	25	3	House bill	432	Whole House			833	Passed	Adverse report.	
Hommel, George	Pension	26	1	Petition	161	Invalid Pensions	210	Report and bil	222	Passed	Indef. postp'd.	
Hommel, George	Pension	26	2	Petition	36	Invalid Pensions	150	Report and bill	661	Referred to Committee Whole House.		
Hommel, George	Pensi n	27	2	Petition	97	Invalid Pensions	314	Report and bill	283	Referred to Committee Whole House.		
Hommel, George	Pension	27	3	House bill	87	Whole House			283	Passed.		
Hone, John, and sons	(See Haggerty & Austin.)	22	2		405							
Hone, John, and sons	Indemnity for costs in sundry abortive suits.	21	2	Memorial	137	Ways and Means	Jan. 18, 1831	Adverse		Referred to Committee Whole House.		
Hone, John, and sons	Indemnity for costs in sundry abortive suits.	23	1	Senate bill	175	Ways and Means	Jan. 4, 1834	With't amend.	S. 40	Passed		App'd March 24, 1834
Honeyman, Susanne	(See Charles Morgan.)											
Honeywell, Israel, representatives of.	Indemnity for losses sustained during revolutionary war.	24	2	Petition	397	Rev. Claims.						
Honeywell, Israel, representatives of.	Indemnity for losses sustained during revolutionary war.	25	2	Petition	112	Rev. Claims	469	Report and bill.	476	Referred to Committee Whole House.		
Honeywell, Israel, representatives of	Indemnity f r losses sustained during revolutionary war.	25	3	House bill	378	Whole House			476			
Honeywell, Israel, representatives of.	Indemnity for losses sustained during revolutionary war.	26	1	Petition	165	Rev. Claims.						
Honeywell, Matthias	Pension for revolutionary services.	22	1	Resolution	250	Rev. Pensions.						
Honeywell, Matthias, widow of.	Renewal of pension	26	1	Resolution	661	Rev. Pensions	663	Adverse		Laid on table.		
Honeywell, Matthias, widow of.	Renewal of pension	26	2	Resolution	121	Rev. Pensions.						
Honore, Madame, & L. T. H.	Confirmation of title to land in Missouri.	15	1	Petition	85	Priv. Land Claims.						
Honore, Madame, & L. T. H.	Confirmation of title to land in Missouri.	16	1	Petition	36	Priv. Land Claims.						
Honore, Madame, & L. T. H.	Confirmation of title to land in Missouri.	17	1	Petition	54	Public Lands.						
Honore, Madame, & L. T. H.	Confirmation of title to land in Missouri.	18	1	Petition	54	Public Lands.						
Honore, Louis Tesson	Confirmation of title to land in Missouri	22	2	Resolution	186	Priv. Land Claims.						
Honore, Louis Tesson	Confirmation of title to land in Missouri.	23	1	Petition	114	Priv. Land Claims.	Feb. 18, 1834	Adverse		Laid on table.		
Honore, Louis Tesson, assignee of.	Confirmation of title to land in Missouri.	23	2	Petition	49	Public Lands	31	Report and bill.	611	Referred to Committee Whole House.		
Honucus, William C.	Bounty land for services in United States army.	30	1	Petition	259	Military Affairs.						
Hoobler, John	Compensation for revolutionary services.	23	2	Petition	320	Rev. Pensions				Discharged; laid on table.		
Hood, George	Pension	20	1	Petition	365	Military Pensions				Discharged; laid on table.		
Hood, George	Pension	21	1	Petition	48	Rev. Pensions	Jan. 5, 1830	General bill	72	Passed	Passed	App'd May 20, 1830
Hood, George	Increase of pension	23	1	Petition	46	Rev. Pensions	Jan. 23, 1834	Adverse		Laid on table.		
Hood, George, widow of	Pension for revolutionary services.	27	2	Petition	941	Rev. Claims				Discharged; laid on table.		
Hood, George, representatives of.	Pension for revolutionary services.	28	1	Petition	176	Rev. Claims.						

List of private claims presented to the House of Representatives of the United States from the 1st to the 31st Congress, inclusive—Continued.

Names of claimants.	Nature or object of the claim.	Congress.	Session.	How brought before the House of Reps.	Page of journal.	To what committee of the House referred.	No. or date of the report.	Nature of the report.	No. of the bill.	How disposed of by the House of Reps.	How disposed of by the Senate.	Date of the act of Congress, and remarks.
Hood, Jacob, heir of	For arrears of pay due	26	2	Petition	122	Rev. Pensions.						
Hood, John	Compensation for provisions furnished Ensign Stockton 1814.	19	2	Petition	287	Claims.						
Hood, John	Right of pre-emption to lands in Wisconsin.	25	2	Memorial	179	Public Lands	625	Report and bill	601	Referred to Committee Whole House.		
Hood, John	Right of pre-emption to lands in Wisconsin.	27	2	Memorial	749	Public Lands.						
Hooe, John and wife	(See heirs of John Hansbrough)	26	1		340							
Hooe, Nathaniel H.	Right of pre-emption	25	2	Petition	178	Priv. Land Claims.	626	Report and bill.	602	Referred to Committee Whole House.		
Hooe, Nathaniel H.	Right of pre-emption	25	3	House bill	380	Whole House			602	Passed	Passed	App'd March 2, 1839
Hoogland, John, widow of	(See Hoagland)	25	2		404		769		723			
Hook, Major James H.	Pay and emolument for his brevet rank.	24	1	Memorial	508	Military Affairs	618	Report and bill.	605	Referred to Committee Whole House.		
Hook, Major James H.	Pay and emolument for his brevet rank.	25	2	Memorial	41	Military Affairs.						
Hook, John, heirs of	Confirmation of title to land on Tennessee river, or an equivalent.	21	1	Petition	360	Priv. Land Claims.						
Hook, John, heirs of	Confirmation of title to land on Tennessee river, or an equivalent.	23	1	Petition	161	Public Lands				Discharged; laid on table.		
Hook, Joseph, sen.	Arrears of revolutionary pension	25	1	Petition	205					Laid on table.		
Hook, Joseph, (Ann) widow of.	Arrears of pension	25	2	Petition	181	Rev. Pensions				Discharged; laid on table.		
Hook, Josiah, jr.	Indemnity for losses sustained while collector of customs.	17	1	Senate bill	171	Claims	Feb. 13, 1822	Adverse	S. 13	Laid on table.		
Hook, Josiah, jr.	Indemnity for losses sustained while collector of customs.	17	2	Resolution	75	Claims	Feb. 5, 1823	Adverse		Laid on table.		
Hook, Josiah, jr.	Indemnity for losses sustained while collector of customs.	18	1	Senate bill	138	Claims	Jan. 21, 1824	Adverse	S. 5		Passed	App'd May 18, 1824
Hook, Moses, son of	Reimbursement of advances during revolutionary war.	26	1	Petition	281	Rev. Claims.						
Hook, Stephen	Indemnity for losses and expenses in bringing murderers to trial.	20	1	Resolution	175	Judiciary.						
Hook, Stephen	Indemnity for losses and expenses in bringing murderers to trial	20	2	Resolution	26					Referred to Committee Whole House.		
Hook, Stephen	Indemnity for losses and expenses in bringing murderers to trial.	21	1	Resolution	83	Claims	219	Report and bill.	277	Referred to Committee Whole House.		
Hook, Stephen	Indemnity for losses and expenses in bringing murderers to trial.	21	2	House bill	339	Whole House	Feb. 21, 1831	With't amend.	277	Passed.		
Hook, Stephen	Indemnity for losses and expenses in bringing murderers to trial.	22	1	Resolution	43	Claims	Dec. 19, 1831	Report by bill.	8	Passed	Passed	App'd Jan. 23, 1832
Hook, Thomas	Pension	15	2	Petition	43					Referred to Secretary War.		
Hook, William	(See widow of Stephen Decatur, and others.)	20	1		295		201		S. 50			
Hooke, Moses	Right of pre-emption to land in Mississippi Territory.	12	2	Petition	614	Public Lands.						
Hooke, Moses	Confirmation of title to land in Mississippi Territory.	13	2	Petition	172	Public Lands	Dec. 28, 1814	By bill	63	Passed	Passed	App'd Jan. 25, 1814
Hooke, Robert, & others.	Compensation for repelling Creek and Cherokee Indians.	29	1	Petition	947	Rev. Claims.						

List of private claims presented to the House of Representatives of the United States from the 1st to the 31st Congress, inclusive—**Continued.**

Names of claimants.	Nature or object of the claim.	Congress.	Session.	How brought before the House of Reps.	Page of journal.	To what committee of the House referred.	No. or date of the report.	Nature of the report.	No. of the bill.	How disposed of by the House of Reps.	How disposed of by the Senate.	Date of the act of Congress, and remarks.
Hooker & Crane	(See assignees of Thomas Tupper)	22	2	....	142							
Hooker, Damon	Bounty land as heir of a soldier in war of 1812.	24	1	Petition	411							
Hooker, Damon	Bounty land as heir of a soldier in war of 1812.	24	2	Petition & Docs.	145	Priv. Land Claims.						
Hooker, Homer, heirs of	Indemnity for French spoliations prior to 1800.	31	1	Petition	384	Foreign Affairs	355	Favorable; bill	318	Referred to Committee Whole House.		
Hooker, Horace, heirs of	Indemnity for French spoliations prior to 1800.	31	1	Petition	276	Foreign Affairs	355	Favorable; bill	318	Referred to Committee Whole House.		
Hooker, John, deceased, assignee of.	Compensation for services in the war of 1812.	31	1	Petition	681	Claims.						
Hooker, Samuel F	Compensation for property taken for public use in 1814.	15	1	Petition	324	Claims	16	Report and bill	150	Referred to Committee Whole House.		
Hooker, Samuel F	Compensation for property taken for public use in 1814.	15	1	Senate bill	449	Claims	April 17, 1818	With't amend.	S. 66	Passed	....	App'd April 20, 1818
Hooker, Samuel F	Compensation for property taken for public use in 1814.	15	2	House bill	142	Whole House	Dec. 29, 1818	With't amend.	150	Passed	Passed	App'd Feb. 15, 1819
Hooker, Samuel F	(See assignees of Thomas Tupper.)	22	2	....	142							
Hooker, Samuel F	Compensation for naval stores and for property captured by the enemy.	17	2	Senate bill	174	Naval Affairs	Feb. 4, 1823	With amend.	S. 33	Passed with amendm't.	Passed as am'd.	App'd Dec. 28, 1823
Hooker, Samuel F	Indemnity for merchandise captured by the enemy on Lake Ontario.	22	2	Petition	28	Claims	62	Adverse	......	Laid on table.		
Hooper, A. M	(See John Hogg, trustee of)	26	1	....	182							
Hooper, Barton	Pension for services in the war of 1812.	24	1	Petition	426	Invalid Pensions	710	Adverse; recommitted.				
						Invalid Pensions	May 31, 1836	Report and bill.	663	Passed	Indef. postp'd.	
Hooper, Barton	Pension for services in the war of 1812.	25	2	Petition	38	Invalid Pensions	490	Report and bill.	487	Passed	Adverse report.	
Hooper, Barton	Pension for services in the war of 1812.	25	3	Petition	89	Invalid Pensions	181	Report and bill	1044	Passed	Adverse report.	
Hooper, Barton	Pension for services in the war of 1812.	26	1	Petition	161	Invalid Pensions	193	Report and bill	205	Passed	Indef. postp'd.	
Hooper, James	(See Joseph Stewart and others)	14	2	....	236							
Hooper, James	Compensation for team lost during the revolutionary war.	21	2	Petition	337	Rev. Claims.						
Hooper, James	Compensation for team lost during the revolutionary war.	22	1	Petition	44	Rev. Claims	....	....	......	Discharged; laid on table.		
Hooper, James	Compensation for team lost during the revolutionary war.	23	1	Petition	43	Rev. Claims.						
Hooper, James	Compensation for team lost during the revolutionary war.	23	2	Petition	239	Rev. Claims.						
Hooper, Joshua	Pension for disability incurred in the war of 1812.	31	1	Petition	1044	Invalid Pensions.						
Hooper, Robert	Drawback on exported wines	5	2	Petition	92	Com. and Manuf.	Dec. 29, 1797	Adverse	......	Referred to Committee Whole House.		
Hooper, Robert	Drawback on exported wines	5	3	Rep't Committee.	429	Com. and Manuf.						
Hooper, Robert	Drawback on exported wines	6	1	Petition	535	Com. and Manuf.	....	....	......	Discharged; postponed to next session.		
Hooper, Robert	Drawback on exported wines	6	2	Petition	734	Com. and Manuf.	Dec. 9, 1800	Favorable: bill ordered.	271	Passed	Rejected.	

List of private claims presented to the House of Representatives of the United States from the 1st to the 31st Congress, inclusive—Continued.

Names of claimants.	Nature or object of the claim.	Congress.	Session.	How brought before the House of Reps.	Page of journal.	To what committee of the House referred.	No. or date of the report.	Nature of the report.	No. of the bill.	How disposed of by the House of Reps.	How disposed of by the Senate.	Date of the act of Congress, and remarks.
Hooper, Robert and John.	Distribution among Danish claimants of amount due from the United States on account of the capture of the Henrick.	21	2	Memorial	207	Foreign Affairs....	100	Adverse	......	Laid on table.		
Hooper, William and Nathaniel.	Indemnity for French spoliations prior to 1800.	18	1	Memorial	238	Foreign Affairs.						
Hooper, William and Nathaniel.	Indemnity for French spoliations prior to 1800.	26	1	Memorial	182	Foreign Affairs....	343	Favorable; bill	319	Referred to Committee Whole House.		
Hooton, Elijah, executrix of	Indemnity for property taken by United States troops.	6	1	Petition	548	Claims	Jan. 7, 1800	Adverse	......	Laid on table.		
Hoover, Andrew, sen.....	Indemnity for a horse lost in war with hostile Indians.	23	1	Petition	498	Claims.						
Hoover, Andrew, sen.....	Indemnity for a horse lost in war with hostile Indians.	23	3	Petition	59	Claims.						
Hoover, Andrew, sen.....	Indemnity for a horse lost in war with hostile Indians.	24	1	Petition	50	Claims	111	Report and bill.	127	Passed	Passed	App'd July 1, 1836
Hoover, George.........	Compensation for property destroyed by United States troops, 1794.	12	2	Petition	551	Claims.						
Hoover, Jacob	To be restored to pension roll	17	2	Petition	82	Whole House.						
Hoover, John............	Pension for revolutionary services.	26	1	Resolution	554	Rev. Pensions.....	423	Adverse	......	Laid on table.		
Hoover, John, (Ky).....	Pension for services as teamster in revolutionary war.	26	1	Petition	625	Rev. Pensions.....	490	Adverse	......	Laid on table.		
Hoover, Voluntine.......	Compensation for a horse and equipments lost in Seminole war.	23	1	Documents.....	154	Claims.						
Hoovey, Thomas........	Indemnity for French spoliations prior to 1800.	26	1	Memorial	182	Foreign Affairs ...	343	Favorable; bill	319	Referred to Committee Whole House.		
Hooz, Jacob............	Confirmation of title to an Indian reservation.	25	3	Petition	463	Priv. Land Claims.						
Hope, Thomas..........	(See Louis F. Beeler and others).	30	1	....	115							
Hope, Thomas H., representatives of.	Compensation for services as a revolutionary officer.	23	1	Petition	439	Rev. Claims.						
Hope & Co., by their agent	Payment of principal and interest due them as bond holders of the Bank of Pensacola.	27	2	Memorial	1062	Foreign Affairs.						
Hope & Co., by their agent	Payment of principal and interest due them as bond holders of the Bank of Pensacola.	27	3	Memorial	319	Foreign Affairs.						
Hope & Co., by their agent	Payment of principal and interest due them as bond holders of the Bank of Pensacola.	28	1	Memorial	145	Foreign Affairs.						
Hope & Co., by their agent	Payment of principal and interest due them as bond holders of the Bank of Pensacola.	29	1	Memorial	146	Foreign Affairs.						
Hope & Co., by their agent	Payment of principal and interest due them as bond holders of the Bank of Pensacola.	29	2	Memorial	323	Judiciary.						
Hopewell, John.........	Compensation for revolutionary services.	9	2	Petition	555	Claims	....	....	......	Referred to Committee Whole House.		
Hopkins, Alexander......	Compensation for two horses lost in public service, 1804.	22	2	Petition	218	Claims.						
Hopkins, Benjamin W., representatives of.	Indemnity for breach of contract..	20	2	Senate bill	312	Claims	Feb. 23, 1829	With't amend.	S. 68	Referred to Committee Whole House.		

List of private claims presented to the House of Representatives of the United States from the 1st to the 31st Congress, inclusive—Continued.

Names of claimants.	Nature or object of the claim.	Congress.	Session.	How brought before the House of Reps.	Page of journal.	To what committee of the House referred.	No. or date of the report.	Nature of the report.	No. of the bill.	How disposed of by the House of Reps.	How disposed of by the Senate.	Date of the act of Congress, and remarks.
Hopkins, Benjamin W., representatives of.	Indemnity for breach of contract.	21	1	Senate bill	118	Claims	Jan. 4, 1830	With amend.	S. 14	Passed with amend'ts.	Passed as am'd	App'd Feb. 11, 1830
Hopkins, Benjamin W., representatives of.	Indemnity for breach of contract.	26	2	Petition	100	Claims.						
Hopkins, Benjamin W., representatives of.	Indemnity for breach of contract.	27	2	Petition	76	Claims	59	Report and bill.	94	Rejected.		
Hopkins, Benjamin W., representatives of.	Indemnity for breach of contract.	27	3	....	127	....	....	....	......	Leave to withdraw.		
Hopkins, Colonel Caleb, widow of.	Pension	15	2	Resolution	248	Pens. & Rev. Cl'ms.	....	....	......	Discharged; laid on table.		
Hopkins, David	Compensation for revolutionary services.	14	1	Resolution	514	Pens. & Rev. Cl'ms.						
Hopkins, David, heirs of.	Commutation pay for revolutionary services.	24	1	Senate bill	907	Rev. Claims	June 7, 1836	With't amend.	S. 130	Passed with amendm't.	Passed as am'd.	App'd July 2, 1836
Hopkins, David, heirs of.	Commutation pay for revolutionary services.	29	1	Petition	379	Rev. Claims.						
Hopkins, Maj. David, heirs of.	Commutation pay for revolutionary services.	29	1	Petition	430	Rev. Pensions.						
Hopkins, Col. David, heirs of.	Commutation pay for revolutionary services, and reimbursement of advances.	30	1	Petition	99	Rev. Claims	271	Report and bill	264	Referred to Committee Whole House.		
Hopkins, Col. David, heirs of.	Commutation pay for revolutionary services, and reimbursement of advances.	31	1	Petition	215	Rev. Claims	192	Report and bill.	198	Referred to Committee Whole House.		
Hopkins, Col. David, heirs of.	Commutation pay for revolutionary services, and reimbursement of advances.	31	2	House bill	181	Whole House	....	....	•198			
Hopkins, David Jefferson.	Additional pay and bounty land for military services.	14	1	Petition	64	Claims.						
Hopkins, Dennis	Pension for revolutionary services.	28	1	Resolution	557	Rev. Pensions.						
Hopkins, Ebenezer	Pension	16	1	Petition	23	Rev. Pensions	April 22, 1820	Adverse	......	Laid on table.		
Hopkins, Ebenezer	Pension	19	1	Petition	423	Military Pensions.	April 20, 1826	Adverse	......	Rejected.		
Hopkins, Ebenezer	Pension	22	1	Petition	66	Rev. Pensions.						
Hopkins, Eliza	(See Charles Brown, heirs of.)	25	3									
Hopkins, Ferdinand, heirs and representatives of.	Commutation pay for revolutionary services.	29	1	Petition	596	Rev. Claims	....	....	......	Discharged; laid on table.		
Hopkins, Ferdinand, heirs and representatives of.	Commutation pay for revolutionary services.	29	2	Petition	172	Rev. Claims.						
Hopkins, Frederick	Pension for revolutionary services.	23	1	Petition	120	Invalid Pensions.						
Hopkins, Frederick	Pension for revolutionary services.	23	2	Petition	87	Rev. Pensions	....	....	......	Discharged; laid on table.		
Hopkins, Frederick	Pension for revolutionary services.	25	2	Petition	180	Rev. Pensions	....	....	......	Discharged; laid on table.		
Hopkins, Frederick	Pension for revolutionary services.	25	3	Resolution	161	Rev. Pensions	....	....	......	Discharged.		
Hopkins, Frederick	Pension for revolutionary services.	26	1	Petition	174	Rev. Pensions.						
Hopkins, Frederick	Pension for revolutionary services.	26	2	Petition	34	Rev. Pensions.						
Hopkins, Frederick	Pension for revolutionary services.	27	2	Petition	58	Rev. Pensions	87	Report and bill.	133	Passed	Indef. postp'd.	
Hopkins, Frederick	Pension for revolutionary services.	27	3	Petition	132	Rev. Pensions	182	Report and bill	797	Referred to Committee Whole House.		
Hopkins, Frederick	Pension for revolutionary services.	28	1	Petition	101	Rev. Pensions	93	Report and bill.	109	Passed.		
Hopkins, Frederick	Pension for revolutionary services.	29	1	Petition	202	Rev. Pensions	217	Report and bill.	211	Referred to Committee Whole House.		
Hopkins, Frederick	Pension for revolutionary services.	29	2	House bill	71	....	Dec. 18, 1846	Favorable	211	Passed	Passed	App'd March 3, 1847

List of private claims presented to the House of Representatives of the United States from the 1st to the 31st Congress, inclusive—Continued.

Names of claimants.	Nature or object of the claim.	Congress.	Session.	How brought before the House of Reps.	Page of journal.	To what committee of the House referred.	No. or date of the report.	Nature of the report.	No. of the bill.	How disposed of by the House of Reps.	How disposed of by the Senate.	Date of the act of Congress, and remarks.
Hopkins, Gardner, widow of.	Pension for revolutionary services.	24	2	Petition	398	Rev. Claims.						
Hopkins, George W	Indemnity for losses in transporting United States mail.	30	1	Petition	859	Claims.						
Hopkins, George W	Indemnity for losses in transporting United States mail.	31	2	Petition	68	P. Of. and P. Roads.						
Hopkins, James E	(See Charles Burkham, *et al.*)	23	1		592							
Hopkins, John Burroughs	Invalid pension	4	1	Petition	449	Claims	May 7, 1796	Adverse		Laid on table.		
Hopkins, Joseph, *et al.*	Pecuniary aid for long service at Springfield, Massachusetts.	25	2	Petition	58	Military Affairs				Laid on table.		
Hopkins, Josiah, heirs of.	Pension for naval service, war of 1812.	23	2	Resolution	98	Invalid Pensions				Discharged; laid on table.		
Hopkins, Laurence	Pension for revolutionary services.	20	1	Resolution	49	Military Pensions				Discharged; laid on table.		
Hopkins, Perry G	Redemption of a sum of Continental money.	25	2	Petition	576	Rev. Claims	787	Adverse		Laid on table.		
Hopkins, Peter	Invalid pension	3	1	Rep. of Secretary War.	131	Select	May 26, 1794	Jt. res. to refer to Sec. War.	J. R. 12	Passed	Passed	App'd June 9, 1794
Hopkins, Robert	Pension	22	1	Petition	164	Rev. Pensions				Discharged; aid on table.		
Hopkins, Roswell	Pension	15	2	Petition	65	Rev. Pensions	Jan. 5, 1819	Adverse		Laid on table.		
Hopkins, Roswell	Pension	16	1	Petition	51	Rev. Pensions	April 22, 1820	Adverse		Laid on table.		
Hopkins, Samuel G	Equitable settl ment of his accounts	16	2	Resolution	103					Resolution rejected.		
Hopkins, Samuel G	Equitable settlement of his accounts	17	1	Petition	389	Military Affairs.						
Hopkins, Silas	Indemnity for property destroyed by the enemy.	23	1	Petition	136	Claims.						
Hopkins Stephen	(See R. S. Burroughs, & S. H.)	4	1		449							
Hopkins, Stephen, & Robert S. Burroughs.	Increase of compensation as weighers and measurers at Providence, Rhode Island.	4	2	Memorial	449	Whole House.						
Hopkins, Stephen, & Robert S. Burroughs.	Increase of compensation as weighers and measurers at Providence, Rhode Island.	6	2	Petition	786	Com. and Manuf.				Discharged; postponed to next session.		
Hopkins, Thankful D	Pension	27	2	Res. and docs	1209	Rev. Pensions				Discharged; laid on table.		
Hopkins, Watson	Increase of salary as light-house keeper, Maine.	27	2	Petition	319	Commerce				Discharged; leave to withdraw.		
Hoppas, George	(See Samuel Watson and G. Hoppas.)	21	1		202							
Hopper, John	Relief for disability and sufferings in revolutionary war.	9	1	Petition	277	Claims	Mar. 28, 1806			Leave to withdraw.		
Hopper, John, heirs of	Indemnity for property destroyed by the enemy, revolutionary war.	19	1	Resolution	64	Rev. Claims	May 17, 1826	Adverse		Laid on table.		
Hopper, John, heirs of	Indemnity for property destroyed by the enemy, revolutionary war.	25	2	Resolution	270	Rev. Claims	694	Report and bill.	667	Referred to Committee Whole House.		
Hopper, John, heirs of	Indemnity for property destroyed by the enemy, revolutionary war.	25	3	House bill	380	Whole House			667			
Hopper, John, heirs of	Indemnity for property destroyed by the enemy, revolutionary war.	26	1	Petition	165	Rev. Claims.						
Hopper, John, heirs of	Indemnity for property destroyed by the enemy, revolutionary war.	27	3	Petition	344	Rev. Claims	261	Adverse		Laid on table.		
Hopper, John A., (Mary,) widow of.	Compensation for losses in revolutionary war.	25	2	Petition	575	Rev. Claims	792	Report and bill.	739	Referred to Committee Whole House.		

List of private claims presented to the House of Representatives of the United States from the 1st to the 31st Congress, inclusive—Continued.

Names of claimants.	Nature or object of the claim.	Congress.	Session.	How brought before the House of Reps.	Page of journal.	To what committee of the House referred.	No. or date of the report.	Nature of the report.	No. of the bill.	How disposed of by the House of Reps.	How disposed of by the Senate.	Date of the act of Congress, and remarks.
Hopper, John A., (Mary,) widow of.	Compensation for losses in revolutionary war.	26	1	Petition	165	Rev. Claims.						
Hoppin, Benjamin	Pension; revolutionary Rhode Island brigade.	14	2	Petition	283	Pens. & Rev. Cl'ms.						
Hoppin, Benjamin	Pension; revolutionary Rhode Island brigade.	23	2	Memorial	67	Select	Feb. 25, 1835	Report by bill.	769	Referred to Committee Whole House.		
Hoppin, Benjamin	Pension; revolutionary Rhode Island brigade.	24	1	Documents	136	Select	337	Report and bill	352	Referred to Committee Whole House.		
Hopping, Thomas	(See heirs of Thomas Frothingham.)	21	2		128							
Hopseker, Powles	Invalid pension	3	1	Rep. of Secretary War.	131	Select	May 26, 1794	Favorable bill ordered.	62	Passed	Passed	App'd June 7, 1794
Hopson, Joseph	Bounty land for services as a revolutionary officer.	19	2	Petition	333	Rev. Claims.						
Hopson, Joseph	Bounty land for services as a revolutionary officer.	20	1	Petition	126	Rev. Claims	Jan. 15, 1828	Adverse		Laid on table.		
Hopwood, John	Release from a suit for arrears of excise duties.	4	1	Petition	448	Claims.						
Hopwood, John	Release from a suit for arrears of excise duties.	4	2	Petition	614	Claims.						
Horback, Abraham	Payment of a draft of James Reeside.	27	3	Petition	350	Judiciary.						
Horback, Abraham	Payment of a draft of James Reeside.	28	2	Petition	205	P. Of. and P. Roads.						
Horback, Abraham	Payment of a draft of James Reeside.	29	1	Petition	284	Judiciary	Feb. 10, 1846	Report by bill.	194	Passed	Passed	App'd Aug. 10, 1846
Hord, Edwin, *et al*	Pensions for services in Indian wars.	26	1	Petition	624	Rev. Pensions.						
Hord, Edwin	Indemnity for the litigation and difficulty he has sustained by reason of the vagueness of the land laws.	26	1	Memorial	940	Claims.						
Hord, Robert	Patent for certain Caddo Indian treaty land.	27	2	Memorial	223	Indian Affairs.						
Horine, Jacob	Pension for revolutionary services.	19	1	Resolution	425	Military Pensions.	April 20, 1826	Adverse		Rejected.		
Horine, Jacob, administrator of.	Compensation for revolutionary services.	25	2	Resolution	612	Rev. Claims				Discharged; laid on table.		
Horley, James	Compensation for improvements in cannon and shot.	27	3	Petition	155	Commerce.						
Horn, Daniel	Invalid pension	3	1	Rep. of Secretary War.	131	Select	May 26, 1794	Favorable; bill ordered.	62	Passed	Passed	App'd June 7, 1794
Horn, Ebenezer	Pension for services as a revolutionary soldier.	15	2	Petition	167	Rev. Pensions	Jan. 21, 1819	Adverse		Leave to withdraw.		
Horn, Philip	Pension for revolutionary services.	27	2	Petition	765	Rev. Pensions	784	Adverse		Laid on table.		
Horn, Patrick	Pension for revolutionary services.	25	3	Petition	126	Rev. Pensions				Discharged.		
Horn, Patrick	Pension for revolutionary services.	26	1	Petition	174	Rev. Pensions	714	Adverse		Laid on table.		
Horn, Ralph R., heirs of.	Compen'tion for services as a sailor in revolutionary war.	23	2	Petition	109	Rev. Pensions				Discharged; laid on table.		
Horn, Ralph R., heirs of.	Compen'tion for services as a sailor in revolutionary war.	24	1	Petition	536	Rev. Claims				Discharged; laid on table.		
Horn, Ralph R., heirs of.	Compen'tion for services as a sailor in revo utionary war.	24	2	Petition	92	Rev. Claims.						
Horn, Reddick	Compensation for services as chaplain in Black Hawk war.	25	2	Documents	87	Claims.						

List of private claims presented to the House of Representatives of the United States from the 1st to the 31st Congress, inclusive—Continued.

Names of claimants.	Nature or object of the claim.	Congress.	Session.	How brought before the House of Reps.	Page of journal.	To what committee of the House referred.	No. or date of the report.	Nature of the report.	No. of the bill.	How disposed of by the House of Reps.	How disposed of by the Senate.	Date of the act of Congress, and remarks.
Horne, Andrew	(See Rhoda Cook, administratrix of.)	21	2	....	99							
Horne, John, *et al*	Additional compensation as surveyors of the revenue, Philadelphia.	7	1	Memorial	51	Select	Mar. 11, 1802	Adverse	......	Rejected.		
Horne, John H.	Exchange of a location of Choctaw land.	23	1	Petition	161	Public Lands.						
Horne, John H.	Exchange of a location of Choctaw land.	23	2	Petition	242	Indian Affairs.						
Horne, John H.	Confirmation of title to certain Indian reservation.	31	1	Petition	654	Indian Affairs.						
Horne, John H.	Confirmation of title to certain Indian reservation.	31	2	Petition	207	Indian Affairs	Jan. 9, 1851	Rep. and joint resolution.	J. R. 33	Passed.		
Horne, John S., trustee of.	Indemnity for French spoliations prior to 1800.	26	1	Memorial	182	Foreign Affairs	343	Favorable; bill	319	Referred to Committee Whole House.		
Horne, Ralph	Pension for services as a revolutionary soldier.	18	1	Resolution	232	Rev. Pensions	....	....	......	Discharged; laid on table.		
Hornbeck, Jacob D., widow of.	Pension for revolutionary services.	25	2	Petition	403	Rev. Pensions	982	Report and bill.	842	Referred to Committee Whole House.		
Hornbeck, Jacob D., widow of.	Pension for revolutionary services.	25	3	House bill	432	Whole House	....	....	842	Passed	Adverse report.	
Hornbeck, Jacob D., widow of.	Pension for revolutionary services.	26	1	Petition	172	Rev. Pensions	....	....	......	Discharged; laid on table.		
Hornbeck, Hon. John W., widow of.	Balance of pay and mileage as a member of Congress.	30	1	Resolution	599	Accounts	Mar. 23, 1848	Favorable, res.	......	....	....	Paid out of contingent fund.
Hornbeck, Lodewyck, jr.	(See J. Quick and J. Sluyter, assignee of.)	17	2	....	91							
Horner, Benjamin P.	Indemnity for French spoliations prior to 1800.	26	1	Memorial	182	Foreign Affairs	343	Favorable; bill.	319	Referred to Committee Whole House.		
Horner, Eliza	(See Lucy P. Brent.)											
Horner, Gustavus B., heirs of.	Commutation pay as revolutionary surgeon.	23	2	Petition	165	Rev. Claims.						
Horner, Gustavus B., heirs of.	Commutation pay as revolutionary surgeon.	24	1	Petition	63	Rev. Claims.						
Horner, Gustavus B., heirs of.	Commutation pay as revolutionary surgeon.	24	1	Senate bill	744	Rev. Claims	798	Adverse	S. 110	Referred to Committee Whole House.		
Horner, Gustavus B., heirs of.	Commutation pay and bounty land for revolutionary services.	24	2	Senate bill	251	Rev. Claims	259	Adverse	S. 84	Referred to Committee Whole House.		
Horner, Gustavus B., heirs of.	Commutation pay and bounty land for revolutionary services.	25	2	Senate bill	496	Rev. Claims	May 11, 1838	With amend.	S. 109	Referred to Committee Whole House.		
Horner, Gustavus B., heirs of.	Compensation for services as surgeon's mate, revolutionary army.	28	1	Petition	319	Rev. Claims.						
Horner, Gustavus B., heirs of.	Compensation for services as surgeon's mate, revolutionary army.	28	2	Petition	114	Rev. Claims.						
Horner, Gustavus B., heirs of.	Compensation for services as surgeon's mate, revolutionary army.	29	1	Petition	306	Rev. Claims	140	Adverse	......	Laid on table.		
Horner, John S.	Compensation for extra services as acting Governor of Michigan.	24	1	Petition	670	Claims	665	Adverse	......	Laid on table.		
Horner, John S.	Compensation for extra services as acting Governor of Michigan.	24	2	Memorial	126	Claims	Jan. 5, 1837	Adverse	......	Laid on table.		
Horner, John S.	Compensation for extra services as acting Governor of Michigan.	25	2	Memorial	71	Claims	Jan. 4, 1838	Adverse	......	Laid on table.		
Horner, Robert	Compensation for use of a team, revolutionary war.	3	1	Petition	24	....	....	....	......	Laid on table.		

List of private claims presented to the House of Representatives of the United States from the 1st to the 31st Congress, inclusive—Continued.

Names of claimants.	Nature or object of the claim.	Congress.	Session.	How brought before the House of Reps.	Page of journal.	To what committee of the House referred.	No. or date of the report	Nature of the report.	No. of the bill.	How disposed of by the House of Reps.	How disposed of by the Senate.	Date of the act of Congress, and remarks.
Horner, Robert	Compensation for services and supplies, revolutionary war.	4	2	Petition	629	Claims.						
Horner, Robert	Compensation for services and supplies, revolutionary war.	5	2	Petition	98	Claims	Dec. 6, 1797	Adverse		Rejected.		
Hornet, United States ship, officers, &c., of.	Compensation for capturing the Penguin.	14	1	House bill	94	Whole House	Feb. 12, 1816	With amend't.		Passed	Passed	App'd Feb. 28, 1816
Hornet, United States ship, widows and children of officers, &c., of.	Six months' pay and arrears of pay.	21	1	Resolution	208	Naval Affairs	Feb. 9, 1830	Favorable; bill	218	Passed	Passed	App'd April 24, 1830
Hornet, United States ship.	Pension to widows of officers who perished in the Gulf of Mexico.	27	3	Resolution	309	Naval Affairs.						
Horrill, Joseph M.	(See John Mitchell and others)	31	2		74							
Horrow, John, *et al.*	Pension	31	1	Petition	730	Rev. Pensions	216	Adverse		Laid on table.		
Horsford, John	Invalid pension	3	1	Rep. of Secretary War.	131	Select	May 26, 1794	Jt. res. to refer to Sec. War.	J.R. 12	Passed	Passed	App'd June 9, 1794
Horsford, John	Invalid pension	3	2	Rep. of Secretary of War.	362	Claims	Feb. 8, 1798	Favorable; bill ordered.	130	Passed	Postp'd to next session.	
Horsford, John	Invalid pension	4	1	Rep. of Secretary War.	445	Claims	Mar. 4, 1796	Favorable; bill ordered.	156	Passed	Passed	App'd April 20, 1796
Horsley, David Y.	Confirmation of title to land in Missouri.	15	1	Petition	102	Priv. Land Claims				Discharged; laid on table.		
Horsley, Thomas Y.	Confirmation of title to land in Missouri.	15	1	Petition	102	Priv. Land Claims				Discharged; laid on table.		
Horton, Benjamin	Indemnity for an erroneous survey of land.	21	1	Petition	149	Public Lands				Discharged; laid on table.		
Horton, Eli	Reimbursement of money paid for a patent.	24	1	Resolution	709	Claims	613	Report and bill.	602	Referred to Committee Whole House.		
Horton, Eli	Reimbursement of money paid for a patent	25	2	Resolution	36	Claims	37	Report and bill.	49	Passed	Passed	App'd March 7, 1838
Horton, George	Pension	21	1	Petition	75	Military Pensions				Discharged; laid on table.		
Horton, Ira T.	Indemnity for expenses and time while attending as a witness.	30	1	Petition	725	Claims	668	Report and bill.	527	Referred to Committee Whole House.		
Horton, Ira T.	Indemnity for expenses and time while attending as a witness.	30	2	House bill	318	Whole House			527	Passed.		
Horton, Ira T.	Indemnity for expenses and time while attending as a witness.	31	1	Petition	579	Commerce	332	Report and bill	290	Referred to Committee Whole House.		
Horton, James	To be restored to pension list	17	1	Petition	118	Rev. Pensions				Disch'd; laid on table.		
Horton, John	Pension	21	1	Petition	59	Military Pensions	April 27, 1830	Adverse		Laid on table.		
Horton, John, (Mary,) widow of.	Pension for revolutionary services.	26	1	Petition	625	Rev. Pensions.						
Horton, John, *et al.*	Bounty on fishing schooner Cod hook.	26	1	Petition	710	Commerce.						
Horton, John, *et al.*	Bounty on fishing schooner Codhook.	27	2	Petition	57	Commerce	270	Report and bill	228	Referred to Committee Whole House.		
Horton, John, *et al.*	Bounty on fishing schooner Codhook.	27	3	House bill	87	Whole House			228	Passed	Indef. postp'd.	
Horton, John, *et al.*	Confirmation of title to land in Louisiana.	24	2	Petition	273	Priv. Land Claims				Discharged; laid on table.		
Horton, Jonathan P.	Pension for disability incurred in the war of 1812.	27	2	Petition	557	Invalid Pensions	810	Report and bill.	463	Referred to Committee Whole House.		
Horton, Jonathan P.	Pension for disability incurred in the war of 1812.	27	3	House bill	91	Whole House			463	Passed.		

List of private claims presented to the House of Representatives of the United States from the 1st to the 31st Congress, inclusive—Continued.

Names of claimants.	Nature or object of the claim.	Congress.	Session.	How brought before the House of Reps.	Page of journal.	To what committee of the House referred.	No. or date of the report.	Nature of the report.	No. of the bill.	How disposed of by the House of Reps.	How disposed of by the Senate.	Date of the act of Congress, and remarks.
Horton, Julia S.	(See Samuel, Sherburne, daughter of.)	25	2		273							
Horton, Rufus & John	Indemnity for French spoliations prior to 1800.	26	1	Memorial	182	Foreign Affairs	343	Favorable; bill	319	Referred to Committee Whole House.		
Hosanna, William	Pension	25	2	Petition	313	Invalid Pensions				Discharged; laid on table.		
Hosford, Daniel	Pension	15	2	Petition	50	Rev. Pensions	Jan. 5, 1819	Adverse		Laid on table.		
Hosford, Daniel	Pension	16	1	Petition	51	Rev. Pensions	April 22, 1820	Adverse		Laid on table.		
Hosier, John, (Phebe) widow of.	Pension for revolutionary services.	28	1	Petition	318	Rev. Pensions						
Hoskins, Benjamin, widow of.	Revolutionary pension	31	2	Petition	431	Rev. Pensions	47	Adverse		Laid on table.		
Hoskins, Jeremiah	Indemnity for losses in the war of 1812.	31	1	Petition	745	Claims.						
Hoskins, Mary	(See Benjamin Hoskins, widow of.)	31	2		431		47					
Hosley, Stephen H.	Pension	23	1	Petition	353	Invalid Pensions	April 8, 1834	Adverse		Laid on table.		
Hosmer, Ashbel	Invalid pension	3	1	Rep. of Secretary War.	131	Select	May 26, 1794	Favorable; bill ordered.	62	Passed	Passed	App'd June 7, 1794
Hosmer, Ashbel	Increase of pension	10	1	House bill	499	Whole House	Feb. 20, 1809	Favorable	158	Passed	Passed	App'd March 3, 1809
Hosmer, Reuben	Compensation for suffering during revolutionary war.	9	1	Petition	324	Claims	Mar. 28, 1806			Indefinitely postponed.		Leave to withdraw.
Hosmer, Simon or Simeon.	Pension for revolutionary services.	20	2	Petition	26	Military Pensions	Jan. 13, 1829	Favorable		Referred to Committee Whole House.		
Hosmer, Simon or Simeon.	Pension for revolutionary services.	21	1	Petition	37	Military Pensions				Discharged; laid on table.		
Hosmer, Timothy	Indemnity for depreciation pay as surgeon, U. S. army.	1	2	Petition and rep't Sec. of War.	218		June 25, 1790			Laid on table.		
Hosmer, Timothy	Compensation for service as surgeon revolutionary army.	13	2	Petition	294	Pens. & Rev. Cl'ms.	Feb. 23, 1814	Adverse		Rejected.		
Hospital, Pa., managers of	(See Pennsylvania Hospital.)	14	1		343							
Hospital, Baltimore, agent of.	Compensation for damage by United States troops.	14	1	Petition	421	Claims.						
Hotchkiss, James	Right of pre-emption to lands	30	2	Senate bill	573	Whole House	Mar. 1, 1849	With't amend.	S. 338	Passed		App'd March 3, 1849
Hotchkiss, Jeremiah	Pension for revolutionary services.	21	2	Resolution	65	Military Pensions.						
Hotchkiss, Russell, *et al.*	Remission of extra tonnage duty on brig Stranger.	22	1	Petition	30	Commerce	126	Report and bill	197	Referred to Committee Whole House.		
Hotchkiss, Russell, *et al.*	Remission of extra tonnage duty on brig Stranger.	22	2	House bill	66	Whole House	Dec. 15, 1832	With't amend.	197	Passed	Passed	App'd Feb. 9, 1833
Hotchkiss, William H., jr.,	(See David Tomlinson, attorney of.)	26	1		182							
Hotchkiss, William	Pre-emption in lieu of a confirmed claim.	23	2	Petition	201	Public Lands.						
Hotsenpiller, Amelia	(See Dr. Frederick Seigle, heir of.)	29	1		654							
Hottenstein, William	Pension for revolutionary services.	23	2	Petition	343	Invalid Pensions.						
Houck, Jacob	Protection to certain patent rights.	23	1	Petition	160	Select				Disch'd; laid on table.		
Houck, Peter	Pension for revolutionary services.	26	1	Petition	625	Rev. Pensions	714	Adverse		Laid on table.		
Houck, Solomon	(See Thomas Talbot, *et al.*)	20	1		312							
Houdin, Michael	Compensation for revolutionary services.	1	3	Petition and rep't of Sec. War.	357					Rejected.		
Hough, Benjamin	(See Alexander Holmes, & B. H.)	14	1		393							
Hough, Benjamin K.	Indemnity for French spoliations prior to 1800.	26	1	Memorial	182	Foreign Affairs	343	Favorable; bill	319	Referred to Committee Whole House.		

List of private claims presented to the House of Representatives of the United States from the 1st to the 31st Congress, inclusive—Continued.

Names of claimants.	Nature or object of the claim.	Congress.	Session.	How brought before the House of Reps.	Page of journal.	To what committee of the House referred.	No. or date of the report.	Nature of the report.	No. of the bill.	How disposed of by the House of Reps.	How disposed of by the Senate.	Date of the act of Congress, and remarks.
Hough, Ephraim	Compensation for losses in carrying the mail.	28	1	Resolution	228	Claims.						
Hough, Joseph, and James McBride.	Damages and interest on a protested draft.	13	2	Petition	304	Claims.						
Hough, Joseph, and James McBride.	Damages and interest on a protested draft.	13	3	Petition	497	Claims.						
Hough, Joseph, and James McBride.	Damages and interest on a protested draft.	14	1	Petition	49	Claims				Discharged; leave to withdraw.		
Hough, Joseph, and James McBride.	Damages and interest on a protested draft.	14	1	Petition	467	Claims.						
Hough, Joseph, and James McBride.	Damages and interest on a protested draft.	19	2	Petition	132	Claims.						
Hough, Dr. Walter, heirs of the widow of.	Arrears of revolutionary pension	29	1	Documents	947	Rev. Pensions.						
Hough, Dr. Walter, heirs of the widow of.	Arrears of revolutionary pension	29	2	Petition	58	Rev. Pensions.						
Hough, Dr. Walter, heirs of the widow of.	Arrears of revolutionary pension	30	1	Petition	156	Rev. Pensions.						
Hough, Dr. Walter, heirs of the widow of.	Arrears of revolutionary pension	30	2	Memorial	284	Rev. Pensions.						
Houghtaling, James	Pension for revolutionary services.	22	1	Petition	219	Rev. Pensions	411	Report and bill	511	Referred to Committee Whole House.		
Houghtaling, Tunis, heir of.	Revolutionary claim	3	1	Petition	215					Referred to Secretary War.		
Houghtaling, Tunis, heir of.	Revolutionary claim	3	2	Rep. of Secretary War.	278					Laid on table.		
Houghton, Jonathan	Compensation for revolutionary services.	2	1	Petition	467					Referred to Secretary War.		
Houghton, Jonathan	Compensation for revolutionary services.	3	2	Rep. of Secretary War.	337	Claims	Mar. 3, 1795			Discharged; laid on table.		
Houghton, Jonathan	Compensation for revolutionary services.	4	1	Rep. of Secretary War.	445	Claims	Mar. 4, 1796	J't. res. to refer to Sec. War.	J R. 16	Passed	Passed	App'd April 17, 1796
Houghton, Joseph, heirs of	Compensation for revolutionary services.	24	2	Petition	38	Rev. Claims	159	Adverse		Laid on table.		
Houghton, Joseph, heirs of	Compensation for revolutionary services.	25	2	Petition	201	Rev. Claims	Jan. 18, 1838	Adverse		Laid on table.		
Houghton, Silas	Compensation for revolutionary services.	19	1	Petition	312	Rev. Claims.						
Houlder, Thomas	Compensation for provision and forage furnished U. S. troops.	23	1	Petition	384	Claims	463	Adverse		Laid on table.		
Houlder, Thomas	Compensation for provision and forage furnished U. S. troops.	23	2	Petition	163	Claims.						
Houlder, Thomas	Compensation for provision and forage furnished U. S. troops.	24	1	Petition	93	Claims.						
Houlder, Thomas	Compensation for provision and forage furnished U. S. troops.	24	2	Petition	120	Claims.						
Houlder, Thomas	Compensation for provision and forage furnished U. S. troops.	25	2	Petition	121	Claims				Discharged.		
Houlder, Thomas	Compensation for provision and forage furnished U. S. troops.	26	1	Petition	168	Claims	60	Adverse		Laid on table.		
Houlder, Thomas	Compensation for provision and forage furnished U. S. troops.	26	1	Petition	169	Claims.						

List of private claims presented to the House of Representatives of the United States from the 1st to the 31st Congress, inclusive—Continued.

Names of claimants.	Nature or object of the claim.	Congress.	Session.	How brought before the House of Reps.	Page of journal.	To what committee of the House referred.	No. or date of the report.	Nature of the report.	No. of the bill.	How disposed of by the House of Reps.	How disposed of by the Senate.	Date of the act of Congress, and remarks.
Houlder, Thomas	Compensation for provision and forage furnished U. S. troops.	26	[illegible]	Petition	52	Claims.						
House, Benjamin H., surety of.	Release from judgment	22	2	Petition	265	Claims	110	Adverse	......	Laid on table.		
House, Conrad	Compensat'n for property destroyed by the enemy, war of 1812.	24	2	Petition	208	Claims	Feb. 24, 1837	Adverse	......	Laid on table.		
House, Conrad	Compensat'n for property destroyed by the enemy, war of 1812.	25	2	Petition	575	Claims	844	Adverse	......	Laid on table.		
House, Conrad	Compensat'n for property destroyed by the enemy, war of 1812.	26	1	Petition	168	Claims	507	Report and bill	404	Referred to Committee Whole House.		
House, Conrad	Compensat'n for property destroyed by the enemy, war of 1812.	27	2	Petition	56	Claims	12	Report and bill.	51	Passed	Indef. postp'd.	
House. Conrad	Compensat'n for property destroyed by the enemy, war of 1812.	27	3	Petition	73	Claims	13	Report and bill	631	Passed	Indef. postp'd.	
House, Conrad	Compensat'n for property destroyed by the enemy, war of 1812.	28	1	Petition	110	Claims	278	Adverse	......	Recommitted.		
House, Conrad	Compensat'n for property destroyed by the enemy, war of 1812.	29	1	Petition	270	Claims	320	Adverse	......	Laid on table.		
House, Cornelius	To be restored to pension roll	17	2	Petition	119	Whole House.	....	....	......	Discharged; leave to withdraw.		
House, George, *et al.*	Increase of salaries as mates of revenue cutter Argus.	4	1	Petition and rep't Sec. Treasury.	371	Select	Mar. 15, 1796	By bill	167	Passed	Passed, with amendment.	App'd May 6, 1796
House, Geo., daughter of.	Compensation for revolutionary services.	25	3	Petition	220	Rev. Claims.						
House, Geo., daughter of.	Compensation for revolutionary services.	26	1	Petition	167	Rev. Claims.						
House, Henry	Payment of note for revolutionary services destroyed by fire.	15	2	Petition	23	Pens. & Rev. Cl'ms.	Dec. 4, 1818	Adverse	......	Laid on table	....	Leave to withdraw.
House, James	Pension	21	1	Petition	498	Military Pensions.	May 4, 1830	Adverse	......	Laid on table.		
House, James	Pension	21	2	Petition	127	Military Pensions.						
House, John K.	Compensation for revolutionary services.	2	1	Petition	539	....	....	....	......	Referred to Secretary War.		
House, Joseph, widow of.	Pension for the services of deceased, and in consideration of her own sufferings while an Indian captive, revolutionary war.	17	1	Petition	96	Pens. & Rev. Cl'ms.	Jan. 15, 1822	Adverse	......	Rejected.		
House, Samuel	Invalid pension	30	1	Petition	927	Invalid Pensions	....	....	......	Discharged; laid on table.		
House, Samuel & William	(See James S. Douglass, *et al.*)	22	2	....	105	....	....	....	......	Laid on table.		
House, William	(See George B. Dameron)	20	1									
House, William	Right of pre-emption	24	1	Petition	426	Priv. Land Claims.	May 17, 1836	Report and bill	636	Referred to Committee Whole House.		
Houseman, Conrad, administrator of.	Compensation for services in revolutionary war.	3	2	Petition	330	Claims.						
Houseman, Conrad, administrator of.	Compensation for services in revolutionary war.	4	1	Petition	373	Claims	Jan. 6, 1796	Adverse	......	Laid on table.		
Houseman, Jacob	(See Thomas Rook, *et al.*)	21	1	....	558							
Houseman, Jacob, representative of.	Reimbursement of expense for defending Indian Key, Florida.	24	2	Petition	266	Claims	215	Adverse	......	Laid on table.		
Houseman, Jacob, representative of.	Reimbursement of expense for defending Indian Key, Florida.	25	2	Petition	176	Claims	Jan. 12, 1838	Adverse	......	Laid on table.		
Houseman, Jacob, representative of.	Reimbursement of advances to government troops in Florida.	26	1	Petition	331	Military Affairs.						

List of private claims presented to the House of Representatives of the United States from the 1st to the 31st Congress, inclusive—Continued.

Names of claimants.	Nature or object of the claim.	Congress.	Session.	How brought before the House of Reps.	Page of journal.	To what committee of the House referred.	No. or date of the report.	Nature of the report.	No. of the bill.	How disposed of by the House of Reps.	How disposed of by the Senate.	Date of the act of Congress, and remarks.
Houseman, Jacob, representative of.	Reimbursement of advances to government troops in Florida.	27	2	Petition	63	Military Affairs	207	Adverse		Laid on table.		
Houseman, Jacob, representative of.	Indemnity for loss of property occupied by United States troops.	30	1	Petition	214	Claims	798	Adverse		Laid on table.		
Houser, Henry	Pension	20	1	Petition	242	Military Pensions				Discharged; laid on table.		
Houser, Henry	Pension	21	1	Petition	49	Military Pensions				Discharged; laid on table.		
Houser, Henry	Pension	21	1	House bill	130	Whole House	Feb. 13, 1830	Favorable	72	Passed	Passed	App'd May 20, 1830
Housewright, John	Compensation for extra expenses in transporting United States mail.	25	3	Resolution	136	P. Of. & P. Roads.						
Housewright, John	Compensation for extra expenses in transporting United States mail.	26	1	Petition	183	P. Of. & P. Roads.	398	Adverse		Laid on table.		
Housewright, John	Compensation for extra expenses in transporting United States mail.	27	3	Petition	155	P. Of. & P. Roads.				Discharged; laid on table.		
Housler, David	Increase of pension	23	1	Petition	638	Rev. Pensions				Discharged; laid on table.		
Hou-saye, Le Paltier De La, *et al.*	Confirmation of title to land in Louisiana.	18	1	Petition	31	Priv. Land Claims.						See De la Houssaye.
Houstin & Blackburn	Equitable settlement of claim for property taken by Creek Indians.	19	1	Resolution	369	Indian Affairs.						
Houston, James	Pension	10	1	House bill	232	Whole House	April 19, 1808	Favorable	78	Passed	Passed	App'd April 25, 1808
Houston, Dr. James, heirs of.	Commutation pay as surgeon in revolutionary war.	24	1	Petition	205	Claims	820	Adverse		Laid on table.		
Houston, James A	Compensation for reporting proceedings and debates of Senate.	30	1	Appropriation bill								App'd Aug. 12, 1848
Houston, James E	(See Lieut. Col. Morsman Houston, brother of.)	14	1		422							
Houston, James F	Increase of compensation as postmaster, Frederick, Maryland.	15	1	Petition	98	P. Of. & P. Roads.						
Houston, James F	Increase of compensation as postmaster, Frederick, Maryland.	15	2	Petition	182	P. Of. & P. Roads.						
Houston, James F	Increase of compensation as postmaster, Frederick, Maryland.	16	2	Petition	141	P. Of. & P. Roads.						
Houston, James F	Increase of compensation as postmaster, Frederick, Maryland.	18	1	Petition	193	P. Of. & P. Roads.	Mar. 24, 1824	Adverse		Laid on table.		
Houston, John H	(See Commodore Truxton)	26	1		182							
Houston, John P	Settlement of accounts as brigade major, war of 1812.	21	1	Petition	472	Claims	April 9, 1830	Adverse		Laid on table.		
Houston, Leonard	Pension for revolutionary services.	22	1	Petition	45	Rev. Claims	101	Report and bill	189	Ref'd to Com. W. H.		
Houston, Leonard	Pension for revolutionary services.	22	2	House bill	66	Whole House			189	Laid on table.		
Houston, Lieut. Colonel Morsman, brother of.	Relief in consideration of mental derangement incurred in the public service.	14	1	Petition	422	Pens. & Rev. Cl'ms.						
Houston, Lieut. Colonel Morsman, brother of.	Relief in consideration of mental derangement incurred in the public service.	14	2	Resolution	183	Pens. & Rev. Cl'ms.	Jan. 29, 1817	Report and bill	91	Referred to Committee Whole House.		
Houston, Purnel, surety of.	Release from certain bond	24	1	Petition	740	Judiciary						Leave to withdraw, 2d session.
Houston, Purnel, surety of.	Release from certain bond	29	1	Petition	284	Claims.						

List of private claims presented to the House of Representatives of the United States from the 1st to the 31st Congress, inclusive—Continued.

Names of claimants.	Nature or object of the claim.	Congress.	Session.	How brought before the House of Reps.	Page of journal.	To what committee of the House referred.	No. or date of the report.	Nature of the report.	No. of the bill.	How disposed of by the House of Reps.	How disposed of by the Senate.	Date of the act of Congress, and remarks.
Houston, Peter	Pension	21	2	Resolut'n Indiana legislature.	209	Military Pensions.						
Houston, Peter	Bounty land for revolutionary services.	26	1	Resolut'n Indiana legislature.	680	Public Lands.						
Houston, Robert	Compensation for supplies furnished United States troops in 1812.	19	2	Petition	32	Claims	46	Favorable	379	Referred to Committee Whole House.		
Houston, Robert	Compensation for supplies furnished United States troops in 1812.	20	1	Resolution	205	Claims	137	Report and bill	157	Passed	Passed	App'd May 26, 1828
Houston, Lieut. William, widow of.	Arrears of pay and clothing due deceased for revolutionary services.	2	1	Petition	472	......	......	......	......	Referred to Secretary of War.		
Houston, Lieut. William, widow of.	Grant of land	13	1	Petition	18	Pens. & Rev. Cl'ms.	Jan. 31, 1814	Adverse	......	Leave to withdraw.		
Houston, William, (Penn.)	Credit for $225 transmitted by mail and lost.	15	2	Petition	78	Ways and Means	Dec. 16, 1818	Adverse	......	Rejected.		
Houston, William, (Penn.)	Credit for $225 transmitted by mail and lost.	16	1	Petition	145	Ways and Means.						
Houston, William, (Penn.)	Credit for $225 transmitted by mail and lost.	16	2	Petition	43	Ways and Means	Nov. 30, 1820	Adverse	......	Laid on table.		
Houston, William, (Penn.)	Credit for $225 transmitted by mail and lost.	19	1	Petition	115	Ways and Means	May 10, 1826	Adverse	......	Laid on table.		
Houston, William A.	Arrears of pension	26	1	Petition	288	Invalid Pensions	665	Adverse	......	Laid on table.		
Houston, William A.	Arrears of pension	26	2	Petition	84	Invalid Pensions	80	Adverse	......	Laid on table.		
Houzie, William	(See Dameron & Houzie)	21	2	......	217							
Houze, William, and Geo. B. Dameron.	Compensation for extra services as land officer.	22	1	Senate bill	806	Public Lands	July 3, 1832	Adverse	S. 107	Rejected.		
Houze, William and Sam'l.	(See James S. Douglass, *et al*)	22	2	......	105							
Hover, Emanuel or Manuel, heirs of.	Compensation for revolutionary services.	29	1	Petition	939	Claims.						
Hover, Emanuel or Nanuel. heirs of.	Compensation for revolutionary services.	29	2	Petition	87	Claims.						
Hover, Emanuel or Manuel, heirs of.	Compensation for revolutionary services.	30	1	Petition	398	Claims	425	Adverse	......	Laid on table.		
Hover, Emanuel or Manuel, heirs of.	Compensation for revolutionary services.	31	1	Petition	361	Claims	......	......	......	Discharged; laid on table.		
Hover, Joseph, and Abelard Guthrie.	Confirmation of title to land	27	2	Petition	618	Public Lands	926	Report and bill.	543	Referred to Committee Whole House.		
Hover, Joseph, and Abelard Guthrie.	Confirmation of title to land	27	3	House bill	89	......	......	......	543	Passed	Passed, with amendment.	App'd March 3, 1843
Hovey, Nathaniel	(See William Baker, N. Y.)	22	1	......	288	......	480					
Howard, Aaron	Pension for revolutionary services.	22	1	Petition	470	Rev. Pensions.						
Howard, Andrew	To be restored to pension roll	17	2	Petition	86	Whole House	......	......	......	Leave to withdraw.		
Howard, Blackstone	Right of pre emption to the land on which he resides.	15	1	Petition	386	Public Lands	......	......	......	Discharged, laid on table.		
Howard, Benjamin C.	(See James Jaffrey, administrator of.)	26	1	......	182							
Howard, Benjamin, widow of.	Pension for revolutionary services.	29	1	Petition	577	Rev. Pensions	603	Adverse	......	Laid on table.		
Howard, Caleb, executors of.	Indemnity for the illegal sale of a vessel.	22	1	Petition	259	Commerce	April 11, 1832	Adverse	......	Laid on table.		
Howard, Caleb, executors of.	Indemnity for the illegal sale of a vessel.	22	2	Petition	27	Commerce	Dec. 20, 1832	Adverse	......	Laid on table.		

List of private claims presented to the House of Representatives of the United States from the 1st to the 31st Congress, inclusive—Continued.

Names of claimants.	Nature or object of the claim.	Congress.	Session.	How brought before the House of Reps.	Page of journal.	To what committee of the House referred.	No. or date of the report.	Nature of the report.	No. of the bill.	How disposed of by the House of Reps.	How disposed of by the Senate.	Date of the act of Congress, and remarks.
Howard, Charles, and J. McKinty, by Abigail Earle, attorney.	Payment of prize-money as mariners in the United States navy.	2	1	Petition	492					Referred to Secretary Treasury.		
Howard, Charles	(See George Rust, *et al*)	22	2		138							
Howard, Charles	Increase of compensation as military storekeeper at Springfield, Massachusetts.	24	1	Petition	200	Military Affairs.						
Howard, David G., assignee of.	Value of horse and equipments lost in public service.	22	1	Resolution	126	Claims	188	Favorable; bill	269	Referred to Committee Whole House.		
Howard, David G., assignee of.	Value of horse and equipments lost in public service.	22	2	House bill	93	Whole House	Dec. 28, 1832	With't amend.	269	Passed	Passed	App'd Feb. 27, 1833
Howard, D. S.	(See L. R. Lyon & D. S. Howard.)	26	1		293							
Howard, G. W	Increase of pension	21	1	Senate bill	352	Military Pensions	Mar. 11, 1830	With't amend.	S. 76	Passed	Passed	App'd May 29, 1830
Howard, G. W	Arrears of pension	22	1	Senate bill	883	Invalid Pensions	June 22, 1832	With't amend.	S. 146	Passed		App'd July 9, 1832
Howard, G. W	Pension for wounds received in the war of 1812, &c.	14	1	Petition	659					Referred to Secretary of War.		
Howard, G. W	Pension for wounds received in the war of 1812, &c.	20	1	Petition	278	Military Pensions	April 23, 1828	Adverse		Laid on table.		
Howard, George W	Increase of pension	21	1	Senate bill	352	Military Pensions	Mar. 11, 1830	With't amend.	S. 76	Passed	Passed	App'd May 29, 1830
Howard, George W	Arrears of pension	23	1	Petition	92	Invalid Pensions	Mar. 25, 1834	Adverse		Laid on table.		
Howard, Geo. W., (Eliza,) widow of.	Arrears of pension	25	3	Documents	218	Invalid Pensions.						
Howard, Geo. W., (Eliza,) widow of.	Arrears of pension	26	1	Petition	163	Invalid Pensions	286	Adverse		Laid on table.		
Howard, Geo. W., (Eliza,) widow of.	Arrears of pension	26	2	Petition	161	Invalid Pensions.						
Howard, Ichabod	(See heirs of Israel Pearce)	27	2									
Howard, Isaac, representatives of.	Compensation for revolutionary services.	25	3	Petition	103	Rev. Claims.						
Howard, Isaac, representatives of.	Compensation for revolutionary services.	26	1	Petition	166	Rev. Claims				Discharged; laid on table.		
Howard, James	Pension for revolutionary services.	10	2	Petition	365	Claims				Discharged; leave to withdraw.		
Howard, James	Pension	11	2	House bill	283	Whole House	Mar. 24, 1810	Favorable	110	Passed	Passed	App'd April 27, 1810
Howard, James	(See Thomas Sparrow, *et al.*)	21	1		169							
Howard, James, (Sarah) widow of.	Pension for revolutionary services.	28	1	Petition	683	Rev. Pensions.						
Howard, James, (Sarah) widow of.	Pension for revolutionary services.	28	2	Petition	59	Rev. Pensions.						
Howard, John	Arrears and increase of pension	28	1	Petition	323	Invalid Pensions				Discharged; laid on table.		
Howard, John D	Pension for revolutionary services.	22	1	Petition	66	Rev. Pensions	100	Report and bill	189	Referred to Committee Whole House.		
Howard, John D	Pension for revolutionary services.	22	2	House bill	66	Whole House			189			
Howard, John, widow of	Indemnity for lands of deceased sold by United States.	18	2	Petition	60	Priv. Land Claims.						
Howard, John H	(See John H. Holland.)	24	1									
Howard, John H	Confirmation of title to land	27	3	House bill	138	Priv. Land Claims.	113	Adverse	652	Laid on table.		
Howard, John and Jane	(See William Marshall, heirs of.)	30	1		287							
Howard, Jonathan, heir of.	Grant of land for revolutionary services.	31	1	Petition	857	Rev. Pensions	395	Adverse		Laid on table.		

List of private claims presented to the House of Representatives of the United States from the 1st to the 31st Congress, inclusive—Continued.

Names of claimants.	Nature or object of the claim.	Congress.	Session.	How brought before the House of Reps.	Page of journal.	To what committee of the House referred.	No. or date of the report.	Nature of the report.	No. of the bill.	How disposed of by the House of Reps.	How disposed of by the Senate.	Date of the act of Congress, and remarks.
Howard, Capt. Joshua	Compensation for extra services superintending erection of an arsenal.	23	2	Memorial	304	Military Affairs	....	....	......	Discharged; laid on table.		
Howard, Capt. Joshua	Compensation for extra services superintending erection of an arsenal.	24	1	Memorial	97	Military Affairs	....	....	......	Discharged; laid on table.		
Howard, Lewis	Pension for services in the war of 1812.	25	3	Petition	461	Invalid Pensions.						
Howard, Lewis	Pension for services in the war of 1812.	26	1	Petition	514	Invalid Pensions	274	Adverse	......	Laid on table.		
Howard, Mary	Extension of the act of June 17, 1844.	30	1	Petition	230	Rev. Pensions	Jan. 25, 1848	Adverse	......	Laid on table.		
Howard, Peter	Invalid pension	3	1	Rep. of Secretary War.	131	Select	May 26, 1794	Favorable; bill ordered.	62	Passed	Passed	App'd June 7, 1794
Howard, Prince Edward	Exchange of an entry of land	18	2	Petition	60	Priv. Land Claims.						
Howard, Samuel Harvey	Authority to collect fees as register in chancery Maryland within the District of Columbia.	7	1	Memorial	44	Select	Jan. 28, 1802	General bill	21	Passed	Rejected.	
Howard, Stephen, jr.	Pay and bounty land for services, war of 1812.	17	1	Petition	26	Military Affairs	71	Report and bill	127	Passed	Indef. postp'd.	
Howard, Stephen, jr.	Pay and bounty land for services, war of 1812.	17	2	Petition	145	Military Affairs	Jan. 23, 1823	Report by bill.	246	Referred to Committee Whole House.		
Howard, Stephen	Bounty land for revolutionary services.	26	1	Petition	947	Rev. Claims.						
Howard, Stephen	Bounty land for revolutionary services.	26	2	Petition	77	Rev. Claims.						
Howard, Stephen	Pay and bounty land for services, war of 1812.	30	1	Petition	831	Priv. Land Claims.						
Howard, Stephen H.	Bounty lrnd for services, war of 1812.	31	1	Petition	693	Priv. Land Claims.	395	Adverse	......	Laid on table.		
Howard, Thomas, representatives of.	Bounty land for revolutionary services.	14	2	Petition	268	Military Affairs	Feb. 14, 1817	Adverse	......	Rejected.		
Howard, Thomas	Pension for revolutionary services.	28	1	Petition	723	Rev. Pensions	....	....	......	Discharged; laid on table.		
Howard, Thomas	Pension for loss of sight while a naval apprentice.	31	1	Petition	396	Invalid Pensions	377	Report and bill	325	Referred to Committee Whole House.		
Howard, Thomas P.	(See Lewis & Clarke, and companions.)	9	1	....	*284							
Howard, Thomas P.	(See Robert Haile)	23	1	....	49							
Howard, William, (Maine)	Indemnity for French spoliations prior to 1800.	26	1	Memorial	182	Foreign Affairs	343	Favorable; bil	319	Referred to Committee Whole House.		
Howard, William A.	Increase of pay as captain in revenue service.	26	1	Petition	303	Naval Affairs.						
Howard, William A.	Increase of pay as captain in revenue service.	29	1	Memorial	718	Naval Affairs.						
Howan, Lewis	Invalid pension	26	1	Petition	162	Invalid Pensions.						
Howd, Benjamin	Invalid pension	3	1	Rep. of Secretary War.	131	Select	May 26, 1794	J't. res. to refer to Sec. War.	J. R. 12	Passed	Passed	App'd June 9, 1794
Howd, Benjamin	Invalid pension	4	1	Rep. of Secretary War.	445	Claims	Mar. 4, 1796	Favorable; bill	156	Passed	Passed	App'd April 20, 179[illegible]
How, Joseph	Compensation for revolutionary services.	2	1	Petition	547	....	....	....	......	Referred to Secretary of War.		

List of private claims presented to the House of Representatives of the United States from the 1st to the 31st Congress, inclusive—Continued.

Names of claimants.	Nature or object of the claim.	Congress.	Session.	How brought before the House of Reps.	Page of journal.	To what committee of the House referred.	No. or date of the report.	Nature of the report.	No. of the bill.	How disposed of by the House of Reps.	How disposed of by the Senate.	Date of the act of Congress, and remarks.
How, Joseph	Compensation for revolutionary services.	2	2	Rep. of Secretary of War.	735					Laid on table.		
How, Joseph	Pay and emolument of an ensign, revolutionary war.	3	1	Petition	32					Laid on table.		
How, Joseph	Commutation pay for revolutionary services.	4	1	Petition	409	Claims	Jan. 29, 1796	Adverse		Referred to Committee Whole House.		
How, Micah	Pension	21	2	Petition	158	Military Pensions.						
How, Nathan	Pension	21	2	Petition	208	Military Pensions.						
How, Nathan	Pension	22	1	Petition	255	Rev. Pensions				Discharged; laid on table.		
How, Thomas Yardley, jr.	Patent for a certain tract of land, &c.	26	2	Petition	122	Public Lands.						
How, Thomas Yardley, jr.	Damage for refusal of land office to issue a patent.	29	1	Petition	261	Judiciary.						
Howes, Abner, heir of	Payment of wages due for revolutionary services.	27	2	Petition	376	Rev. Claims	660	Adverse		Laid on table.		
Howe, Asa	Pension	15	1	Petition	177	Pens. & Rev. Cl'ms.				Referred to Secretary War.		
Howe, Asahel	(See Minis & Henry, *et al.*)	16	2		89							
Howe, Amos	Abatement in the price of his land.	20	1	Petition	40	Public Lands				Discharged; laid on table.		
Howe, Amos	Abatement in the price of his land.	20	2	Petition	44	Public Lands	45	Report and bill	366	Referred to Committee Whole House.		
Howe, Amos	Abatement in the price of his land.	23	1	Petition	638	Public Lands.						
Howe, Azor	To be restored to pension roll	17	1	Petition	67	Rev. Pensions				Discharged; laid on table.		
Howe, Banister, administrator of.	Half-pay for revolutionary services.	25	2	Petition	579	Rev. Claims.						
Howe, Banester, representative of.	Half pay for revolutionary services.	25	3	Petition	86	Rev. Claims.						
Howe, Banester, representative of.	Half-pay for revolutionary services.	26	1	Petition	166	Rev. Claims.						
Howe, Bezaleel (U. S. A.)	Indemnity for loss sustained by change of position under an act of last Congress.	4	2	Petition and rep't Sec. of War.	666					Referred to Committee Whole House.		
Howe, Charles	Indemnity for Indian depredations	26	2	Petition	100	Claims	Jan. 4, 1841	Adverse		Laid on table.		
Howe, Charles	Indemnity for Indian depredations	27	2	Petition	94	Claims	671	Adverse		Laid on table.		
Howe, Charles	Indemnity for Indian depredations	27	2	Petition	534	Claims	638	Adverse		Laid on table.		
Howe, David	(See James Crawford, *et al.*)	16	2		101							
Howe, David	Pension	21	1	Petition	168	Military Pensions.						
Howe, David	Pension	22	1	Petition	116	Rev. Pensions	Dec. 28, 1831	Adverse		Laid on table.		
Howe, Door, & Co.	(See W. & S. Lawrence, *et al.*)	21	2		67							
Howe, Ebenezer	Pension for revolutionary services.	21	1	Resolution	302	Military Pensions	April 13, 1830	Adverse		Laid on table.		
Howe, Ebenezer	Pension for revolutionary services.	23	1	Resolution	107	Rev. Pensions				Disch'd; laid on table.		
Howe, George, & Co.	(See Benj. Adams & Co., *et al.*)	23	2		182							
Howe, John	Compensation for team, work, &c., war of 1812.	25	2	Petition	51	Claims.						
Howe, John	Compensation for team, work, &c., war of 1812.	25	3	Petition	86	Claims	188	Favorable; bill	1047	Passed.		
Howe, John	Compensation for team, work, &c., war of 1812.	26	2	Petition	101	Claims	14	Favorable; bill	552	Referred to Committee Whole House.		
Howe, John	Compensation for team, work, &c., war of 1812.	30	1	Petition	559	Claims	743	Favorable; bill	584	Referred to Committee, Whole House.		

List of private claims presented to the House of Representatives of the United States from the 1st to the 31st Congress, inclusive—Continued.

Names of claimants.	Nature or object of the claim.	Congress.	Session.	How brought before the House of Reps.	Page of journal.	To what committee of the House referred.	No. or date of the report.	Nature of the report.	No. of the bill.	How disposed of by the House of Reps.	How disposed of by the Senate.	Date of the act of Congress, and remarks.
Howe, John	Compensation for team, work, &c., war of 1812.	30	2	House bill	319	Whole House			584	Passed.		
Howe, John	Compensation for supplies furnish'd army in 1816, 1817.	26	1	Petition	168	Claims	13	Report and bill	32	Passed	Indef. postp'd.	
Howe, John	Invalid pension	15	1	Petition	405	Pens. & Rev. Cl'ms.	April 1, 1818	Report & general bill.	172	Postp'd to July next.		
Howe, John, widow of	Pension for revolutionary services.	22	1	Petition	412	Rev. Pensions				Discharged; laid on table.		
Howe, Joseph N.	Indemnity for loss on Treasury notes.	17	1	Petition	199	Naval Affairs.						
Howe, Lucy	To be restored to revolutionary pension roll.	27	2	Petition	320	Rev. Pensions.						
Howe, Lucy	To be restored to revolutionary pension roll.	28	1	Petition	849	Rev. Pensions.						
Howe, Peter, & Phineas Whitney, jr.	Payment for medical aid to a soldier.	13	3	Petition	677	Claims				Referred to Secretary War.		
Howe, Samuel, executor of	Compensation for pork taken for public use.	1	3	Petition	355					Referred to Secretary Treasury.		
Howe, Samuel, executor of	Compensation for pork taken for public use.	2	1	Rep. of Secretary of Treasury.	580					Laid on table.		
Howe, Samuel	Pension	19	1	Petition	442	Military Pensions.	May 23, 1826	Adverse		Rejected.		
Howe, Samuel	Pension	19	2	Petition	132	Military Pensions.				Discharged.		
Howe, Samuel	Compensation for revolutionary services.	20	1	Petition	278	Rev. Claims				Discharged; laid on table.		
Howe & Fitch, surety of.	Release from custom-house bond	27	2	Petition	224	Commerce	834	Favorable	467	Ordered to 3d reading		
Howe & Fitch, surety of.	Release from custom-house bond	27	3	House bill	89				467	Passed	Passed	App'd March 3, 1843
Howe, Selah	Bounty land for services as a revolutionary soldier.	26	1	Petition	701	Rev. Claims				Discharged; laid on table.		
Howe, Selah, widow of	Pension for revolutionary services.	27	2	Petition	107	Rev. Pensions	118	Report and bill.	164	Passed	Indef. postp'd.	
Howes, Solomon L.	Compensation for revolutionary services of his father.	31	2	Petition	155	Rev. Claims.						
				Add'l testimony.	204	Rev. Claims.						
Howe, Thomas M.	Settlement of his accounts as pension agent at Pittsburgh.	30	2	Letter of Second Comptroller.	296	Rev. Pensions	Feb. 13, 1849	Report by joint resolution.	J. R. 53	Passed	Passed	App'd Feb. 22, 1849
Howe, Timothy	Compensation for undrawn rations due him as an officer, rev. war.	4	1	Petition	384	Claims	Jan. 20, 1796	Adverse		Leave to withdraw.		
Howe, William	Relief from judicial proceedings in Nova Scotia.	2	1	Petition and rep't Sec. of State.	447, 453					Leave to withdraw.		
Howe, William	(See Canadian refugees)	4	2		614							
Howe, William	Indemnity for losses during revolutionary war.	4	1	Petition	507	Claims.						
Howe, William	Indemnity for losses during revolutionary war.	4	2	Petition	614	Select	Jan. 23, 1797	Report by bill.	209	Referred to Committee Whole House.		
Howe, William	Compensation for revolutionary services.	3	2	Petition	324	Claims.						
Howe, William	Compensation for revolutionary services.	4	1	Rep. of Secretary War.	373	Claims	Jan. 6, 1796	Adverse		Referred to Committee Whole House.		
Houze, William	(See George B. Dameron and W. H.)	21	2		217							
Howell & Coats	Compensation for the loss of a flat boat.	30	1	Petition	1157	Claims.						
Howell & Coats	Compensation for the loss of a flat boat.	31	1	Petition	347	Claims	261	Adverse		Laid on table.		

List of private claims presented to the House of Representatives of the United States from the 1st to the 31st Congress, inclusive—Continued.

Names of claimants.	Nature or object of the claim.	Congress.	Session.	How brought before the House of Reps.	Page of journal.	To what committee of the House referred.	No. or date of the report.	Nature of the report.	No. of the bill.	How disposed of by the House of Reps.	How disposed of by the Senate.	Date of the act of Congress, and remarks.
Howell, Gilbert	Indemnity for services, &c., in war of 1812.	25	3	Petition	120	Claims	205	Adverse	......	Laid on table.		
Howell, Hugh, and Isaac B. Tyler.	Compensation for provisions furnished United States troops in the war of 1812.	14	2	Petition	311	Claims	....	....	......	Referred to Secretary War.		
Howell, Hugh	Pension	21	2	Petition	299	Military Pensions.						
Howell, Hugh	Compensation for property taken for public use, war of 1812.	22	1	Resolution	301	Claims	Mar. 19, 1832	Adverse	......	Laid on table.		
Howell, Jacob	Confirmation of title to land	12	2	....	......	....	....	....	......	....	....	See Statutes at Large, vol. 2, p. 800.
Howell, John	Compensation for a negro, &c., taken for public use.	3	1	Petition and rep't Sec. of War.	52	Select	April 22, 1794	....	......	Laid on table.		
Howell, John	Confirmation of title to land in Missouri.	23	2	Petition	234	Public Lands	Dec. 25, 1834	Report by bill.	766	Referred to Committee Whole House.		
Howell, John	Confirmation of title to land in Missouri.	24	1	Petition	114	Public Lands	204	Report and bill	204	Passed	Passed	App'd July 2, 1836
Howell, John	(See Lewis Snapp and J. Howell.)	29	1	....	873							
Howell, John	Pension for services in the war of 1812.	30	2	Memorial	85	Invalid Pensions	20	Adverse	......	Laid on table.		
Howell, Jonathan D	(See William Baker, N. Y.)	22	1	....	288	....	480					
Howell, Joseph	Increase of compensation as accountant, War Department.	3	2	Petition	302	Select.						
Howell, Levi, *et al.*	Confirmation and guarantee of title to lots in Cincinnati.	18	1	Petition	286	Judiciary.						
Howell, Samuel	Relief in consideration of his revolutionary services and his poverty.	17	2	Petition	121	Rev. Pensions	Feb. 18, 1823	Report and bill	303	Rejected.		
Howell, Samuel	Relief in consideration of his revolutionary services and his poverty.	18	1	Petition	78	Rev. Pensions	Jan. 16, 1824	Adverse.	......	Recommitted.		
Howell, Samuel	Relief in consideration of his revolutionary services and his poverty.	18	1	Rep't Committee	165	Rev. Claims	Feb. 4, 1824	Adverse	......	Leave to withdraw.		
Howell, Samuel	Relief in consideration of his revolutionary services and his poverty.	19	1	Petition	66	Military Pensions	164	Adverse	......	Leave to withdraw.		
Howell, Samuel	Relief in consideration of his revolutionary services and his poverty.	19	2	Petition	26	Military Pensions	....	....	......	Discharged; leave to withdraw.		
Howell, Samuel	Additional compensation as express rider in revolutionary war.	18	2	Petition	117	Pens. & Rev. Cl'ms.	....	....	......	Discharged; leave to withdraw.		
Howell, Samuel	Pension for revolutionary services.	20	2	Petition	59	Pens. & Rev. Cl'ms.	Feb. 13, 1829	By bill	440	Passed.		
Howell, Samuel	Pension	21	1	Petition	49	Military Pensions	Jan. 5, 1830	General bill	72	....	....	Bill became a law, omitting petitioner's name
Howell, Squire	(See William Bedford, agent.)	28	1	....	262							
Howell, Vincent, agent of.	Bounty land for services in revolutionary war.	23	1	Petition	195	Rev. Claims.						
Howell, Vincent, agent of.	Bounty land for services in revolutionary war.	24	1	Petition	431	Rev. Claims	April 21, 1836	Adverse	......	Laid on table.		
Howell, William	Pension for revolutionary services.	22	1	Petition	36	Rev. Pensions	107	Report and bill	190	Ref'd to Com. W. H.		
Howell, William	Pension for revolutionary services.	22	2	Petition	27	Rev. Pensions	....	....	......	Disch'd; laid on table.		
				House bill	66	....	....	....	190	Laid on table.		
Howell, William, heirs of.	Pension for revolutionary services.	27	3	Resolution	138	Rev. Pensions	295	Adverse	......	Laid on table.		
Howell, William	Increase of invalid pension	29	1	Memorial	499	Invalid Pensions.						
Howell, William	Pension for services, war of 1812.	29	1	Memorial	1038	Invalid Pensions.						
Howell, William & Son, in behalf of owners of Spanish brig Restaurador.	Reimbursement of tonnage duties erroneously exacted.	27	3	Petition	285	Commerce.						

List of private claims presented to the House of Representatives of the United States from the 1st to the 31st Congress, inclusive—Continued.

Names of claimants.	Nature or object of the claim.	Congress.	Session.	How brought before the House of Reps.	Page of journal.	To what committee of the House referred.	No. or date of the report.	Nature of the report.	No. of the bill.	How disposed of by the House of Reps.	How disposed of by the Senate.	Date of the act of Congress, and remarks.
Howell, William, & Son, in behalf of owners of Spanish brig Restaurador.	Reimbursement of tonnage duties erroneously exacted.	28	2	Petition	88	Commerce.						
Howell, William, & Son, in behalf of owners of Spanish brig Restaurador.	Reimbursement of tonnage duties erroneously exacted.	29	1	Petition	678	Commerce	571	Report and bill	389	Referred to Committee Whole House.		
Howison, James R.	Compensation for services as disbursing agent.	31	1	Petition	672	Naval Affairs.						
Howison, William G.	Compensation for services as auxiliary guard.	31	1	Petition	892	Dist. of Columbia.						
Howland & Aspinwall	Payment of a draft of Jas. Reeside.	29	2	Appropriat'n bill.	.....	.....	.....	.....	.....	.....	.....	App'd March 2, 1847
Howland, Cornelius	Indemnity for French spoliations prior to 1800.	26	1	Memorial	182	Foreign Affairs	343	Favorable; bill	319	Report'd by Committee Whole House.		
Howland, Daniel	(See Marine Insurance Company, Baltimore.)	26	1	.....	182							
Howland, Gilbert, and Sands Wing.	Permission to import plaster from a British island.	12	1	Petition	196	Com. and Manuf.	.....	General bill	46	Referred to Committee Whole House.		
Howland, John	Revolutionary pension, Rhode Island brigade.	14	2	Petition	282	Pens. & Rev. Cl'ms.						
Howland, John	Revolutionary pension, Rhode Island brigade.	23	2	Memorial	67	Select	Feb. 25, 1835	Report by bill.	769	Referred to Committee Whole House.		
Howland, John	Revolutionary pension, Rhode Island brigade.	24	1	Documents	136	Select	337	Report and bill	352	Referred to Committee Whole House.*		
Howland, John H.	Drawback on sugar exported to Hamburgh.	18	1	Senate bill	518	Ways and Means	May 19, 1824	With't amend.	S. 98	Passed	.....	App'd May 26, 1824
Howland, ———	(See Coit, Woolsey & Howland.)	26	1	.....	182							
Howland, Joseph, assignees of.	Indemnity for French spoliations prior to 1800.	26	1	Memorial	182	Foreign Affairs	343	Favorable	319	Referred to Committee Whole House.		
Hoxie, Christopher	Renewal of patent for an auger for earth boring.	15	1	Petition	277	Judiciary	Mar. 13, 1818	Adverse	.....	Leave to withdraw.		
Hoxie, John	Cummutation of pension	7	1	Petition	16	Claims	Dec. 16, 1801	Adverse	.....	Rejected.		
Hoxie, John B.	Compensation for services as surgeon Georgia volunteers.	30	1	Petition	711	Claims	657	Adverse	.....	Laid on table.		
Hoxie, Peleg	To be restored to pension roll	17	2	Petition	163	Whole House	.....	.....	.....	Discharged; leave to withdraw.		
Hoxie, Peleg	To be restored to pension roll	17	2	Resolution	211	Pens. & Rev. Cl'ms.	.....	.....	.....	Discharged; leave to withdraw.		
Hoy, Barney	Bounty land for services, war of 1812.	21	1	Petition	319	Military Pensions.						
Hoy, Bernard	Bounty land for services, war of 1812	27	3	Petition	59	Invalid Pensions	29	Adverse	.....	Laid on table.		
Hoy, William	Compensation for the discovery of a cure for hydrophobia.	1	1	Petition	113	.....	.....	.....	.....	Laid on table.		
Hoyt, Adam H.	Pension for services, war of 1812.	29	1	Petition	1203	Rev. Pensions.						
Hoyt, Adam H.	Pension for services, war of 1812.	29	2	Petition	86	Invalid Pensions.						
Hoyt, Adam H.	Pension for services, war of 1812.	30	1	Petition	625	Invalid Pensions	.....	.....	.....	Discharged; laid on table.		
Hoyt, Adam H.	Pension for services, war of 1812.	30	2	Petition	116	Invalid Pensions.						
Hoyt, Adam H.	Pension for services, war of 1812.	31	1	Petition	298	Invalid Pensions	.....	.....	.....	Discharged: laid on table.		
Hoyt, Asa	(See Asa Hoit)	22	1	.....	136							

List of private claims presented to the House of Representatives of the United States from the 1st to the 31st Congress, inclusive—Continued.

Names of claimants.	Nature or object of the claim.	Congress.	Session.	How brought before the House of Reps.	Page of journal.	To what committee of the House referred.	No. or date of the report.	Nature of the report.	No. of the bill.	How disposed of by the House of Reps.	How disposed of by the Senate.	Date of the act of Congress, and remarks.
Hoyt, or Haight, Benjamin	Pension for revolutionary services.	27	3	Petition	260	Rev. Pensions				Discharged; leave to withdraw.		
Hoyt, Benjamin	Pension for revolutionary services.	28	1	Petition	901	Rev. Pensions.						
Hoyt, Elijah	Invalid pension	3	2	Rep. of Secretary War.	284					Laid on table.		
Hoyt, Elijah	Invalid pension	4	1	Rep. of Secretary War.	445	Claims	Mar. 4, 1796	Favorable; bill ordered.	156	Passed	Passed	App'd April 20, 1796
Hoyt, Emily	(See heirs of Samuel Hoyt)	28	1		944							
Hoyt, Enoch	Pension	21	1	Petition	143	Military Pensions	April 26, 1830	Report and bill.	445	Referred to Committee Whole House.		
Hoyt, Enoch	Pension	21	2	Petition	209	Military Pensions.						
Hoyt, Enoch	Pension	22	1	Petition	56	Rev. Pensions	Dec. 21, 1831	Report and bill.	67	Passed	Indef. postp'd.	
Hoyt, Gould	Payment of a judgment against Gilston & Schenck.	15	1	Appropriat'n bill								App'd April 9, 1818
Hoyt, Henry, jr.	Pay and emolument as a lieutenant, until notified that his name was stricken from the rolls.	16	1	Petition	214	Claims.						
Hoyt, Henry, jr.	Pay and emolument as a lieutenant, until notified that his name was stricken from the rolls.	16	2	Petition	165	Claims	Jan. 24, 1821	Adverse		Referred to Committee Whole House.		
Hoyt, James	(See James Brisban)	17	1		100							
Hoyt, Jesse	Release from balance claimed by the U.S., from him, &c., as collector	27	3	Memorial	342	Judiciary				Discharged; laid on table.		
Hoyt, Jonathan	Pension for disability incurred in war of 1812.	20	1	Resolution	303	Military Pensions.						
Hoyt, Jonathan	Pension for disability incurred in war of 1812.	20	2	Petition	55	Military Pensions	Dec. 28, 1828	General bill	311	Passed.		
Hoyt, Jonathan	Pension for disability incurred in war of 1812.	21	1	Petition	48	Military Pensions.						
Hoyt, Jonathan	Pension for disability incurred in war of 1812.	21	1	House bill	130	Whole House	Feb. 13, 1830	Favorable	72	Passed	Passed	App'd May 20, 1830
Hoyt, Jonathan	Increase of pension	28	1	Petition	803	Invalid Pensions.						
Hoyt, Jonathan	Increase of pension	29	1	Petition	162	Invalid Pensions	771	Report and bill.	511	Referred to Committee Whole House.		
Hoyt, Jonathan	Increase of pension	29	2	House bill	212	Whole House			511	Passed	Passed	App'd March 3, 1847
Hoyt, Joseph D.	Indemnity for property destroyed by the enemy, war of 1812.	15	2	Report of Com'r Claims.	210					Leave to withdraw.		
Hoyt, Joseph D.	Indemnity for property destroyed by the enemy, war of 1812.	16	1	Petition	28	Claims	Jan. 5, 1820	Adverse		Laid on table.		
Hoyt, Joseph	Indemnity for French spoliations prior to 1800.	26	1	Memorial	182	Foreign Affairs	343	Favorable; bill	319	Referred to Committee Whole House.		
Hoyt, Merriam	Pension for revolutionary services of her husband.	28	1	Petition	950	Whole House.						
Hoyt, Moses	(See Moses Hoit)	15	2		102							
Hoyt, Moses, (late Captain U. S. army.)	Pension in consideration of bodily infirmity.	16	2	Petition	205	Pens. & Rev. Cl'ms.				Discharged; laid on table.		
Hoyt, Moses, (late Captain U. S. army.)	Pension in consideration of bodily infirmity.	17	1	Petition	46	Pens. & Rev. Cl'ms.				Discharged; leave to withdraw.		
Hoyt, Moses	Arrears of pension	22	2	Resolution	172	Invalid Pensions				Discharged; laid on table.		
Hoyt, Nathan	Indemnity for French spoliations prior to 1800.	26	1	Memorial	182	Foreign Affairs	343	Favorable; bill	319	Referred to Committee Whole House.		

List of private claims presented to the House of Representatives of the United States from the 1st to the 31st Congress, inclusive—Continued.

Names of claimants.	Nature or object of the claim.	Congress.	Session.	How brought before the House of Reps.	Page of journal.	To what committee of the House referred.	No. or date of the report.	Nature of the report.	No. of the bill.	How disposed of by the House of Reps.	How disposed of by the Senate.	Date of the act of Congress, and remarks.
Hoyt, Samuel, widow of	For an amendment of the pension laws.	23	1	Petition	584	Rev. Claims.						
Hoyt, Samuel, widow of	For an amendment of the pension laws.	24	2	Petition	90	Rev. Pensions				Discharged; laid on table.		
Hoyt, Samuel, heirs of	Pension for revolutionary services.	28	1	Petition	944	Rev. Pensions.						
Hoyt, Samuel, heirs of	Pension for revolutionary services.	30	1	Petition	422	Rev. Pensions				Discharged; laid on table.		
Hoyt, Stephen, heirs of	Land in California for revolutionary services.	31	1	Petition	936	Rev. Claims	424	Adverse		Laid on table.		
Hoyt, Thomas	Pension for revolutionary services.	26	1	Petition	706	Rev. Pensions.						
Hoyt & Tom, heirs of	Indemnity for French spoliations prior to 1800.	26	1	Memorial	182	Foreign Affairs	343	Favorable; bill	319	Referred to Committee Whole House.		
Hubbard, Adolphus F	Additional compensation for bringing Presidential votes from Illinois.	16	2	Petition	206	Elections				Discharged.		
Hubbard, David	Pension	14	1	House bill	622	Pens. & Rev. Cl'ms.	April 11, 1816	With amend'ts	171	Passed	Passed	App'd April 30, 1816
Hubbard, David	Increase of pension	14	2	Petition	183	Pens. & Rev. Cl'ms				Discharged; laid on table.		
Hubbard, Ebenezer	Indemnity for a vessel captured by the enemy.	16	2	Petition	68	Claims	Dec. 22, 1820	Adverse		Rejected.		
Hubbard, Ebenezer	Indemnity for a vessel captured by the enemy.	19	2	Petition	216	Claims.						
Hubbard, Ebenezer	Indemnity for a vessel captured by the enemy.	21	1	Petition	69	Claims	Jan. 11, 1830	Adverse; recommitted.				
					403	Claims	288	Report and bill	341	Referred to Committee Whole House.		
Hubbard, Ebenezer	Indemnity for a vessel captured by the enemy.	22	1	Petition	42	Claims	Dec. 19, 1831	Report and bill	12	Passed	Passed	App'd March 7, 1832
Hubbard, E. K	(See Gurdon S. Hubbard)	26	2		229							
Hubbard, Elisha, administrator of.	Arrears of pension	29	1	Petition	189	Rev. Pensions	123	Adverse		Laid on table.		
Hubbard, Elizur	Release from payment of distillery bond.	13	3	Petition	715	Ways and Means	Feb. 18, 1815	Adverse		Laid on table.		
Hubbard, George, (Emily,) widow of.	Pension for revolutionary services.	30	1	Petition	747	Rev. Pensions	694	Adverse		Laid on table.		
Hubbard, Gurdon S	(See assignee of J. & L. Veaux).	25	2		1012							
Hubbard, Gurdon S., and H. G.	Relinquishment by U. S. of reversionary interest in certain Indian reservations.	26	2	Senate bill	229	Indian Affairs	Feb. 12, 1841	With amend's.	S. 157	Passed	Passed	App'd Feb. 18, 1841
Hubbard James	(See William H. Bedford, agent).	28	1		262							
Hubbard, James, heir of	Half-pay for revolutionary services.	24	2	Petition	73	Rev. Pensions.						
Hubbard, James, heir of	Half-pay for revolutionary services.	25	2	Petition	117	Rev. Claims				Discharged; laid on table.		
Hubbard, James, heir of	Half pay for revolutionary services.	29	1	Petition	202	Rev. Claims.						
Hubbard, John	Pension	9	2	House bill	608	Whole House			216	Passed	Passed	App'd May 3, 1807
Hubbard, John	Pension for revolutionary services.	14	2	Petition	255	Pens. & Rev. Cl'ms				Discharged; laid on table.		
Hubbard, John	Pension for revolutionary services.	15	1	Petition	63	Pens. & Rev. Cl'ms				Discharged; laid on table.		
Hubbard, John	Bounty land for services as a revolutionary soldier.	21	1	Petition	57	Rev. Claims	Jan. 15, 1830	Adverse		Laid on table.		
Hubbard, Jonathan, widow of.	(Claim not stated on Journal)	19	2	Petition	37	Claims	Jan. 15, 1827	Adverse		Laid on table.		

List of private claims presented to the House of Representatives of the United States form the 1st to the 31st Congress, inclusive—Continued.

Names of claimants.	Nature or object of the claim.	Congress.	Session.	How brought before the House of Reps.	Page of journal.	To what committee of the House referred.	No. or date of the report.	Nature of the report.	No. of the bill.	How disposed of by the House of Reps.	How disposed of by the Senate.	Date of the act of Congress, and remarks.
Hubbard, Jonathan, widow of.	(Claim not stated on Journal)	20	1	Petition	104	Claims	Jan. 15, 1828	Adverse		Laid on table.		
Hubbard, Josiah, jr.	(See Orange Heaton, & J. H. jr.)	18	1		30							
Hubbard, Justus	Release from a judgment in favor of the United States.	23	1	Petition	69	Judiciary				Discharged; laid on table.		
Hubbard, Laban A.	Pension	27	2	Petition	618	Invalid Pensions.						
Hubbard, Nehemiah, heirs of.	Payment of a lost certificate of public debt.	29	1	Memorial	352	Ways and Means.						
Hubbard, Nehemiah, heirs of.	Payment of a lost certificate of public debt.	30	1	Memorial	229	Ways and Means.						
Hubbard, Samuel	Arrears of pension	23	1	Petition	242	Rev. Pensions	Feb. 18, 1834	Adverse		Laid on table.		
Hubbard, Samuel	Pension for revolutionary services.	24	1	Petition	56	Rev. Pensions				Discharged; laid on table.		
Hubbard Silas	Invalid pension	3	1	Rep. of Secretary War.	131	Select	May 26, 1794	Jt. res. to refer to Sec. War.	J. R. 12	Passed	Passed	App'd June 9, 1794
Hubbard, Thaddeus	Indemnity for a vessel condemned under the British orders in council.	22	2	Petition	39	Foreign Affairs.						
Hubbard, Thaddeus	Pension for disability incurred in public service.	24	2	Petition	97	Invalid Pensions	Jan. 7, 1837	Adverse		Laid on table.		
Hubbard, Thaddeus	Pension for disabilty incurred in public service.	25	2	Petition	118	Invalid Pensions				Discharged.		
Hubbard, Thaddeus	Pension for disability incurred in public service.	25	3	Petition	219	Invalid Pensions.						
Hubbard, Thaddeus	Pension for disability incurred in public service.	26	1	Petition	197	Invalid Pensions.						
Hubbard, Thaddeus	Pension for disability incurred in public service.	27	2	Petition	329	Invalid Pensions	432	Adverse		Laid on table.		
Hubbard, Thaddeus	Pension for disability incurred in public service.	28	1	Petition	116	Invalid Pensions				Discharged; laid on table.		
Hubbard, Thomas	Compensation for a horse lost in the public service.	22	1	Documents	266	Claims	Feb. 8, 1832	Adverse		Laid on table.		
Hubbard, Thomas	Compensation for a horse lost in the public service.	23	1	Petition	132	Claims	Jan. 8, 1834	Adverse		Laid on table.		
Hubbard, William	Compensation for services in the revolutionary war.	27	3	Petition	77	Rev. Claims	295	Adverse		Laid on table.		
Hubbard, William H. & Co.	(See Virginia Woollen Manufacturing company.)	30	2		328							
Hubbell, Aaron	Bounty land for services as a Canadian volunteer, war of 1812.	23	1	Petition	274	Priv. Land Claims.	Mar. 14, 1834	Adverse		Laid on table.		
Hubbell, Aaron	Pay and bounty land due him as a Canadian volunteer.	28	1	Petition	482	Public Lands	423	Adverse		Laid on table.		
Hubbell, Abijah	Invalid pension	3	1	Rep. of Secretary War.	131	Select	May 26, 1794	Jt. res. to refer to Sec. War.	J. R. 12	Passed	Passed	App'd June 9, 1794
Hubbell, David	Invalid pension	4	1	Rep. of Secretary War.	445	Claims	Mar. 4, 1796	Favorable; bill ordered.	156	Passed	Passed	App'd April 20, 1796
Hubbell, David	Increase of pension	10	1	House bill	232	Whole House	April 19, 1808	Favorable	78	Passed	Passed	App'd April 25, 1808
Hubbell, Ezbon	Pension for revolutionary services.	15	1	Petition	418	Invalid Pensions.						
Hubbell, Ezekiel	Reimbursement of an excess of tonnage duties.	11	3	Petition	533	Com. and Manuf.						
Hubbell, Ezekiel	Reimbursement of an excess of tonnage duties.	12	1	Petition	11	Com. and Manuf.	Dec. 30, 1811	Report and bill	35	Passed	Passed, with amendment.	App'd Jan. 31, 1812

List of private claims presented to the House of Representatives of the United States from the 1st to the 31st Congress, inclusive—**Continued.**

Names of claimants.	Nature or object of the claim.	Congress.	Session.	How brought before the House of Reps.	Page of journal.	To what committee of the House referred.	No. or date of the report.	Nature of the report.	No. of the bill.	How disposed of by the House of Reps.	How disposed of by the Senate.	Date of the act of Congress, and remarks.
Hubbell, William	Equitable settlement of accounts as tax collector.	12	1	Petition	139	Claims	Mar. 13, 1812	Report by bill.	92	Passed	Passed	App'd April 23, 1812
Hubbell, William	Equitable settlement of accounts as tax collector.	12	2	Petition	548	Claims	Nov. 17, 1812	Adverse		Laid on table.		
Hubbell, William	Bounty land for services in revolutionary war.	19	1	Petition	336	Rev. Claims.						
Hubbell, William	Bounty land for services in revolutionary war.	19	2	Petition	243	Rev. Claims.						
Hubbell, William	Bounty land for services in revolutionary war.	20	1	Petition	159	Rev. Claims	Jan. 25, 1828	Adverse		Laid on table.		
Hubbell, William G.	Compensation for services as assistant commissary of forage in revolutionary war.	20	2	Resolution	52	Rev. Claims.						
Hubble, Daniel	(See heirs of Joseph Peirce)	17	2		232							
Hubble, Ebenezer	Confirmation of title to land in Missouri.	15	2	Petition	28	Priv. Land Claims.						
Hubble, Ebenezer	Confirmation of title to land in Missouri.	17	1	Petition	54	Public Lands.						
Hubble, Ebenezer	Confirmation of ti le to land in Missouri.	18	1	Petition	54	Public Lands.						
Hubble, Mary	(See executor of James Flinn)	24	1		474							
Hubble, Nathaniel	Invalid pension	4	1	Rep. of Secretary War.	445	Claims	May 4, 1796	Favorable; bill ordered.	156	Passed	Passed	App'd April 20, 1796
Hubbs, Alexander	Pension	15	2	Petition	62	Rev. Pensions				Discharged; laid on table.		
Hubbs, Alexander	Compensation for various revolutionary services.	17	1	Petition	30	Pens. & Rev. Cl'ms.	Dec. 21, 1821	Adverse		Laid on table.		
Hubbs, Alexander	Pension	21	1	Petition	36	Military Pensions.	April 2, 1830	Adverse		Laid on table.		
Hubbs, James	Dismissal of a suit in favor of United States.	1	2	Petition	142					Referred to Secretary of Treasury.		
Hubbs, James	Dismissal of a suit in favor of United States.	2	2	Rep. of Secretary Treasury.	626					Laid on table.		
Huber, Peter	Renewal of a lost Continental certificate.	2	1	Petition	459							
				Rep. of Secretary Treasury.	583	Select.						
Hubley, Bernard	Pension for revolutionary services.	11	2	Petition	305	Claims.						
Huchens, Hezekiah	(See Hezekiah Hutchins)	17	1		280							
Huckleberry, Alfred	Compensation for a horse lost in public service.	25	2	Documents	396	Claims.						
Huckleberry, Alfred	Compensation for a horse lost in public service.	25	3	Documents	207	Claims.						
Huddleston, Solomon	(See Zebulon Pike & Companions.)	10	1		189				78			
Huddy, Joshua, heir of	Pecuniary relief in consideration of revolutionary services.	24	2	Memorial	98	Select	227	Report and bill	935	Referred to Committee Whole House.		
Huddy, Joshua, heir of	Pecuniary relief in consideration of revolutionary services.	25	2	Memorial	393	Rev. Claims.						
Huddy, Joshua, heir of	Pecuniary relief in consideration of revolutionary services.	25	3	House bill	332	Whole House	Feb. 1, 1839	With't amend.	1051	Passed	Laid on table.	
Huddy, Joshua, heir of	Pecuniary relief in consideration of revolutionary services.	26	1	Petition	165	Rev. Claims.						
Huddy, Joshua, heir of	Pecuniary relief in consideration of revolutionary services.	27	2	Petition	256	Rev. Pensions	535	Adverse		Laid on table.		

List of private claims presented to the House of Representatives of the United States from the 1st to the 31st Congress, inclusive—Continued.

Names of claimants	Nature or object of the claim.	Congress.	Session.	How brought before the House of Reps.	Page of journal.	To what committee of the House referred.	No. or date of the report.	Nature of the report.	No. of the bill.	How disposed of by the House of Reps.	How disposed of by the Senate.	Date of the act of Congress, and remarks.
Hudgens, Ambrose, jr.	Bounty land for services in the war of 1812.	22	1	Petition	32	Priv. Land Claims.				Discharged; laid on table.		
Hudly, John, heirs of	Commutation pay for revolutionary services.	24	1	Resolution	676	Rev. Claims				Discharged; laid on table.		
Hudnut, Richard, (Grace,) widow of.	Pension for revolutionary services.	29	1	Petition	440	Rev. Pensions.						
Hudnut, Richard, (Grace,) widow of.	Pension for revolutionary services.	29	2	Petition	150	Rev. Pensions	16	Adverse		Laid on table.		
Hudnut, Richard, (Grace,) widow of.	Pension for revolutionary services.	30	1	Petition	1021	Rev. Pensions.						
Hudny, Jean	Compensation for equiping and maintaining French volunteers.	23	2	Senate bill	259	Military Affairs	Jan. 28, 1835	With't amend.	S. 117	Referred to Committee Whole House.		
Hudson, Chamberlain	Pension	19	1	Petition	290	Military Pensions	164	Adverse		Laid on table.		
Hudson, Chamberlain	Pension	20	1	Petition	167	Military Pensions	April 29, 1828	Report by bill.	283	Passed.		
Hudson, Chamberlain	Pension	20	2	Petition	55	Military Pensions	Dec. 12, 1828	General bill	311	Passed.	Laid on table.	
Hudson, Chamberlain	Pension	21	1	Petition	48	Military Pensions				Discharged; laid on table.		
Hudson, Chamberlain	Pension	21	1	House bill	130	Whole House	Feb. 13, 1830	Favorable	72	Passed	Passed	App'd May 20, 1830
Hudson, Eleazer	Increase of pension.	11	3	House bill	604	Whole House	Mar. 2, 1811	Favorable	218	Passed	Passed	App'd March 3, 1811
Hudson, Hall	Pension	19	1	Petition	88	Military Pensions	164	Adverse		Laid on table.		
Hudson, Hall	Pension	22	1	Petition	124	Rev. Pensions.						
Hudson, Henry	Reimbursement of advances to pay soldiers.	18	1	Petition	432	Claims.						
Hudson, James	Right of pre-emption	26	1	Resolution	397	Public Lands	May 25, 1840	Report by bill.	409	Referred to Committee Whole House.		
Hudson, John, (Va.)	Pension	20	1	Petition	110	Military Pensions	April 29, 1828	Report by bill.	283	Passed.		
Hudson, John, (Va.)	Pension	20	2	Petition	55	Military Pensions	Dec. 12, 1828	General bill	311	Passed	Laid on table.	
Hudson, John, (Va.)	Pension	21	1	House bill	130	Whole House	Feb. 13, 1830	Favorable	72	Passed	Passed	App'd May 20, 1830
Hudson & Co.	(See Holmes, Hudson, & Co.)	26	1		182							
Hudson, John, (Ohio)	Arrears of pension for revolutionary services.	28	1	Petition	1126	Rev. Pensions.						
Hudson, John, (Ohio)	Arrears of pension for revolutionary services.	29	1	Petition	748	Rev. Pensions	614	Adverse		Laid on table.		
Hudson, John, heirs of	Indemnity for French spoliations prior to 1800.	29	2	Memorial	224	Foreign Affairs.						
Hudson, Jonathan	Reimbursem't of tonnage duty paid on Spanish brig.	18	2	Senate bill	285	Ways and Means	Mar. 1, 1825	With't amend	S. 58	Passed		App'd March 3, 1825
Hudson, Jonathan	Interest on tonnage duties refunded	19	1	Petition	525	Ways and Means.						
Hudson, Jonathan	Interest on tonnage duties refunded	19	2	Petition	105	Ways and Means				Discharged; laid on table.		
Hudson, Jonathan, administrator of.	Indemnity for French spoliations prior to 1800.	23	2	Memorial	346	Foreign Affairs.						
Hudson, Jonathan, administrator of.	Indemnity for French spoliations prior to 1800.	26	1	Memorial	182	Foreign Affairs	343	Favorable; bill	319	Referred to Committee Whole House.		
Hudson, Joshua	Increase of revolutionary pension.	27	2	Petition	70	Rev. Pensions	784	Adverse		Laid on table.		
Hudson, Rush	Arrears of pay and emolument for revolutionary services.	7	1	Petition	200					Laid on table.		
Hudson, Samuel	Remission of duty on soured wine.	14	1	Petition	133	Com. and Manuf.						
Hudson, Samuel	Increase of pension and bounty land.	25	2	Petition	270	Rev. Claims				Discharged; laid on table.		
Hudson, Thomas	(Claim not stated on Journal)	20	1	Petition	92	Commerce				Discharged; referred to Sec'ry Treasury.		

List of private claims presented to the House of Representatives of the United States from the 1st to the 31st Congress, inclusive—Continued.

Names of claimants.	Nature or object of the claim.	Congress.	Session.	How brought before the House of Reps.	Page of journal.	To what committee of the House referred.	No. or date of the report.	Nature of the report.	No. of the bill.	How disposed of by the House of Reps.	How disposed of by the Senate.	Date of the act of Congress, and remarks.
Hudson, Timothy	Pension for services and injuries in revolutionary war.	17	1	Petition	118	Rev. Pensions				Discharged; laid on table.		
Hudson, William, heirs of	Relief in consideration of revolutionary services.	29	1	Petition	1203	Claims.						
Hudson, William, heirs of	Relief in consideration of, revolutionary services.	29	2	Petition	87	Claims.						
Hudson, William, heirs of	Relief in consideration of revolutionary services.	30	1	Petition	398	Claims	422	Adverse		Laid on table.		
Hudson, William, heirs of	Relief in consideration of revolutionary services.	31	1	Petition	361	Claims.						
Hudson, W. H.	(See Exploring Expedition)	27	3		149		270		818			
Hudson, William L., *et al.*	Relating to wreck of the United States ship Peacock.	28	1	Petition	763	Naval Affairs	427	Adverse		Laid on table.		
Hudson, William	(See Exploring Expedition)	27	3		149		270		818			
Hudspeth, Airs & A. W.	Right of pre-emption	25	2	Petition	595	Public Lands.						
Hudspeth, Airs & A. W.	Right of pre-emption	25	3	Petition	135	Public Lands.						
Hudspeth, Airs & A. W.	Right of pre-emption	26	1	Petition	178	Public Lands				Discharged; laid on table.		
Hudspeth, Airs & A. W.	Right of pre-emption	26	1	Petition	435	Public Lands				Discharged; laid on table.		
Hudspeth, Charles M.	Indemnity for property destroyed in Seminole war.	29	1	Petition	354	Claims	563	Adverse		Laid on table.		
Huff, Aaron, heirs of	Commutation of bounty land due for money.	18	1	Resolution	376					Rejected.		
Huff, John	Compensation for property destroyed by United States troops.	31	1	Petition	534	Military Affairs.						
Huff, Lavinia	(See heirs of Myndert Van Everen.)	17	1		68							
Huff, Lewis	(See Lewis Moore, *et al.*)	19	2		105							
Huffington, John	Indemnity for the loss of two vessels while in the service of the United States.	31	1	Petition	223	Claims.						
Huffman, Benjamin	Reimbursement of expenses in an attempt to reclaim his child from Indian captivity.	17	2	Petition	31	Select.						
Huffman, Benjamin	Reimbursement of expenses in an attempt to reclaim his child from Indian captivity.	18	1	Petition	34	Indian Affairs	Dec. 24, 1823	Report by bill.	28	Passed	Passed	App'd May 26, 1824
Huffnagle, Michael, widow of.	Pension for revolutionary services.	25	2	Petition	585	Rev. Pensions				Discharged; laid on table.		
Huffslider, George	To be placed on navy pension roll.	14	1	Petition	405	Naval Affairs				Disch'd; laid on table.		
Huger, Major Benjamin widow of, by attorney.	Half-pay for revolutionary services	2	1	Petition and rep't of Sec. War.	440, 459	Select.	Nov. 25, 1791	By bill	152	Passed	Passed	App'd Mar. 27, 1792
Huger, Jonathan, representatives of.	Bounty land and commutation pay for revolutionary services.	25	3	Petition	220	Rev. Claims.						
Huger,	(See Hagar.)											
Hugg, Joseph	Invalid pension	1	3	Petition & report of Sec. War.	347					Laid on table.		
Huggans, Robert	Pension	25	2	Petition	180	Rev. Pensions				Discharged; laid on table.		
Huggins, Robert	Compensation for services in the revolutionary war.	20	1	Petition	92	Military Pensions	April 29, 1828	Report by bill.	283	Passed.		
Huggins, Robert	Compensation for services in the revolutionary war.	20	2	Petition	55	Military Pensions	Dec. 12, 1828	General bill	311	Passed	Laid on table.	

List of private claims presented to the House of Representatives of the United States from the 1st to the 31st Congress, inclusive—Continued.

Names of claimants.	Nature or object of the claim.	Congress.	Session.	How brought before the House of Reps.	Page of journal.	To what committee of the House referred.	No. or date of the report.	Nature of the report.	No. of the bill.	How disposed of by the House of Reps.	How disposed of by the Senate.	Date of the act of Congress, and remarks.
Huggins, Robert	Compensation for services in the revolutionary war.	21	1	Petition	37	Military Pensions.						
Huggins, Robert	Compensation for services in the revolutionary war.	21	1	Petition	48	Military Pensions.						
Hughart, Thomas	Pension for revolutionary services.	26	1	Petition	326	Rev. Pensions	551	Adverse		Laid on table.		
Hughart, Thomas	Pension for revolutionary services.	27	2	Documents	559	Invalid Pensions	608	Adverse		Laid on table.		
Hughes, A. K.	Indemnity for expenses while sick at Port Praya.	30	1	Petition	102	Claims	113	Adverse		Laid on table.		
Hughes, A. K.	Indemnity for expenses while sick at Port Praya.	30	2	Petition	573	Claims				Leave to withdraw.		
Hughes, A. K.	Indemnity for expenses while sick at Port Praya.	31	1	Petition	584	Naval Affairs.						
Hughes, Andrew S.	(See Jonathan L. Bean, & A. S. H.)	24	2		160							Stat. at Large, vol. 5, p. 161.
Hughes, Charles	Confirmation of title to land in Missouri.	21	1	Petition	41	Priv. Land Claims.	409	Report and bill.	482	Referred to Committee Whole House.		
Hughes, Charles	Confirmation of title to land in Missouri.	22	1	Petition	446	Priv. Land Claims.	Mar. 6, 1832	Adverse		Laid on table.		
Hughes, Cornelius	Pension for services in the war of 1812.	25	2	Petition	400	Invalid Pensions	May 7, 1838	Adverse		Laid on table.		
Hughes, Cornelius	Pension for services in the war of 1812.	27	2	Petition	377	Invalid Pensions.						
Hughes, Cornelius	Pension for services in the war of 1812.	28	2	Petition	170	Invalid Pensions.						
Hughes, Cornelius	Pension for services in the war of 1812.	30	1	Petition	439	Invalid Pensions	571	Adverse		Laid on table.		
Hughes, Cornelius	Pension for services in the war of 1812.	30	2	Petition	174	Invalid Pensions	86	Report and bill.	782	Referred to Committee Whole House.		
Hughes, Cornelius	Pension for services in the war of 1812.	31	1	Petition	275	Invalid Pensions	481	Report and bill.	378	Referred to Committee Whole House.		
Hughes, David M., & others	Indemnity for Indian depredations in Mississippi.	26	1	Petition	351	Claims.						
Hughes, David M., & others	Indemnity for Indian depredations in Mississippi.	27	2	Petition	92	Claims	267	Report and bill.	225	Passed	Passed	App'd Aug. 9, 1842
Hughes, David M., & others	Indemnity for Indian depredations in Mississippi.	27	3	Letter of Secre'y Treasury.	154					Laid on table.		
Hughes, David M.	Confirmation of title to land	27	2	Petition	106	Priv. Land Claims.	282	Report and bill.	248	Passed	Passed	App'd Aug. 1, 1842:
Hughes, George, by attorney.	Compensation for revolutionary services.	10	1	Petition and rep't Sec. of War.	140					Ref. to Com. Whole House on House bill No. 20.		
Hughes, George W.	Increase of the compensation of the Maryland and District of Columbia volunteers.	31	2	Petition	199	Military Affairs.						
Hughes, Hugh	Compensation for revolutionary services.	2	2	Petition	712					Referred to Secretary Treasury.		
Hughes, Hugh	Compensation for revolutionary services.	3	2	Rep. of Secretary Treasury.	284					Laid on table.		
Hughes, Hugh	Compensation for revolutionary services.	7	1	Memorial	78	Claims	Feb. 17, 1802	Adverse		Leave to withdraw.		
Hughes, Hugh, (Charity,) widow of.	Compensation for revolutionary services.	9	1	Petition	313	Whole House.						

List of private claims presented to the House of Representatives of the United States from the 1st to the 31st Congress, inclusive—Continued.

Names of claimants.	Nature or object of the claim.	Congress.	Session.	How brought before the House of Reps.	Page of journal.	To what committee of the House referred.	No. or date of the report.	Nature of the report.	No. of the bill.	How disposed of by the House of Reps.	How disposed of by the Senate.	Date of the act of Congress, and remarks.
Hughes, Hugh, children of	Settlement of his accounts as revolutionary quartermaster general.	15	1	Petition	293	Pens. & Rev. Cl'ms.						
Hughes, Hugh, children of	Settlement of his accounts as revolutionary quartermaster general.	16	1	Petition	53	Pens. & Rev. Cl'ms.	Feb. 23, 1820	Adverse	......	Laid on table.		
Hughes, Hugh, representatives of.	Payment for certain loan office certificates.	29	1	Petition	190	Claims	222	Adverse	......	Laid on table.		
Hughes, James	Redress for the acts of an United States officer.	15	1	Petition	65	Public Lands.						
Hughes, James	Redress for the acts of an United States officer.	15	2	Petition	156	Priv. Land Claims.	Feb. 3, 1819	Report by bill.	306	Referred to Committee Whole House.		
Hughes, James	Redress for the acts of an United States officer.	16	1	House bill	47	Public Lands	....	....	11	Passed	Passed	App'd Jan. 28, 1820
Hughes, James	Pension for revolutionary services.	25	3	Resolution	275	Rev. Pensions	....	....	......	Discharged.		
Hughes, James	Compensation for clothing for volunteers in the Seminole war.	31	1	Petition	1240	Military Affairs.						
Hughes, John	Remission of duty on salmon destroyed by fire.	4	2	Petition	683	Com. and Manuf.	Jan. 3, 1797	Adverse	......	Laid on table.		
Hughes, John	Reimbursement of duty paid on church furniture.	22	1	Petition	196	Ways and Means.	Mar. 1, 1832	Report and bill	435	Passed	Passed	App'd May 25, 1832
Hughes, John	Commutation pay for services as a revolutionary officer.	23	1	Petition	110	Rev. Claims.						
Hughes, John, widow of.	Pension for revolutionary services.	23	1	Petition	46	Rev. Pensions.						
Hughes, Joseph S.	Compensation for services as chaplain to army under Gen. Hull.	13	2	Petition	183	Claims	April 14, 1814	Report by bill.	195	Referred to Committee Whole House.		
Hughes, Joseph S.	Compensation for services as chaplain to army under Gen. Hull.	13	3	Petition	519	Claims	....	....	......	Leave to withdraw.		
Hughes, Joseph B., sureties of.	Reimbursement of costs on a judgment.	25	2	Petition	203	P. Of. and P. Roads.	....	....	......	Laid on table.		
Hughes, Joseph B., sureties of.	Reimbursement of costs on a judgment.	26	1	Petition	183	P. Of. and P. Roads.						
Hughes, Levina	Arrearage of pay for board, &c., of sailors of brig Vixen.	18	1	Petition	214	Claims.						
Hughes, Levina	Arrearage of pay for board, &c., of sailors of brig Vixen.	19	1	Petition	57	Claims	....	....	......	Discharged; laid on table.		
Hughes, Levina	Arrearage of pay for board, &c., of sailors of brig Vixen.	20	1	Petition	311	Claims	Feb. 25, 1828	Adverse	......	Laid on table	....	Leave to withdraw.
Hughes, Margaret	(See heirs of Moses McCurdy.)	8	1	....	486							
Hughes, Rose	Confirmation of title to land in Louisiana.	22	2	Petition	42	Priv. Land Claims.	....	....	......	Discharged; laid on table.		
Hughes, Samuel	Indemnity for damage to his foundry by the enemy.	14	2	Petition	343	Claims.						
Hughes, Samuel	Indemnity for damage to his foundry by the enemy.	15	1	Report of Com. of Claims.	87	Claims	75	Adverse	......	Laid on table.		
Hughes, Samuel	Indemnity for damage to his foundry by the enemy.	16	1	Petition	24	Claims	6	Adverse.	......	Rejected.	....	Leave to withdraw, 2d session.
Hughes, Samuel M.	Arrears of pay as a volunteer in Seminole war.	29	1	Petition	297	Military Affairs	342	Adverse	......	Laid on table.		
Hughes, Thomas	Pension	23	2	Petition	164	Rev. Pensions	....	....	......	Discharged; laid on table.		
Hughes, William, (Ala.).	Pension	22	1	Petition	189	Invalid Pensions	....	....	......	Discharged; laid on table.		
Hughes, William, (Ala.).	Pension	25	2	Petition	401	Invalid Pensions	....	....	......	Discharged.		
Hughes, William, (Ala.).	Pension	25	3	Petition	220	Invalid Pensions.						

List of private claims presented to the House of Representatives of the United States from the 1st to the 31st Congress, inclusive—Continued.

Names of claimants.	Nature or object of the claim.	Congress.	Session.	How brought before the House of Reps.	Page of journal.	To what committee of the House referred.	No. or date of the report.	Nature of the report.	No. of the bill.	How disposed of by the House of Reps.	How disposed of by the Senate.	Date of the act of Congress, and remarks.
Hughes, William, (Ala.)	Pension	26	1	Petition	163	Invalid Pensions	187	Favorable; bill	199	Passed.		
Hughes, William, (Ala.)	Arrears of pension	27	2	Petition	525	Invalid Pensions	610	Adverse		Laid on table.		
Hughes, William, (Sarah,) widow of.	Pension for revolutionary services.	27	3	Petition	190	Rev. Pensions	295	Adverse		Laid on table.		
Hughes, Willis G	Extra compensation for transporting United States mail.	26	1	Petition	343	P. Of. and P. Roads.						
Hughes, Willis G	Extra compensation for transporting United States mail.	26	2	Petition	38	P. Of. and P. Roads.						
Hugo, Samuel B	Pension for services and compensation for a horse lost, war of 1812.	24	1	Petition	140	Invalid Pensions	752	Report and bill.	691	Passed.		
Hugo, Samuel B	Pension for services and compensation for a horse lost, war of 1812.	24	2	Petition	86	Invalid Pensions	183	Report and bill.	905	Referred to Committee Whole House.		
Hugo, Samuel B	Pension for services and compensation for a horse lost, war of 1812.	25	2	Petition	38	Invalid Pensions	217	Report and bill.	255	Passed	Adverse report.	
Hugo, Samuel B	Pension for services and compensation for a horse lost, war of 1812.	25	3	Petition	89	Invalid Pensions	103	Report and bill.	978	Passed	Adverse report.	
Hugo, Samuel B	Pension for services and compensation for a horse lost, war of 1812.	26	1	Petition	161	Invalid Pensions	191	Report and bill.	203	Passed	Indef. postp'd.	
Hugo, Samuel B	Pension for services and compensation for a horse lost, war of 1812.	26	2	Petition	133	Invalid Pensions	147	Report and bill.	658	Referred to Committee Whole House.		
Hugo, Samuel B	Pension for services and compensation for a horse lost, war of 1812.	27	2	Petition	68	Invalid Pensions	139	Report and bill.	185	Passed	Passed	App'd July 27, 1842
Hugunin, Robert	Cancellation of a contract to raise sundry war vessels at Sackett's Harbor.	19	1	Petition	251	Ways and Means.						
Hugunin, Robert	Compensation for a chart of Lake Erie.	28	1	Petition	338	Commerce.						
Hugunin, Robert	(See assignees of Thomas Tupper.)	22	2		142							
Huie, John, *et al.*	Pension for services in New York militia.	14	1	Resolution	158	Pens. & Rev. Cl'ms.	April 11, 1816	General bill	171	Passed	Passed	App'd April 30, 1816
Hulbert, Elijah	Compensation for board and expenses of sick soldiers.	16	1	Petition	140	Claims				Referred to Secretary of War.		
Hulet, Asa	Pension for his services	25	3	Petition	729	Rev. Pensions				Discharged; laid on table.		
Hulin, William	Right of pre-emption	27	3	Petition	305	Public Lands.						
Hull, David, *et al*	Payment of pension money lost in the mail.	20	2	Petition	147	Military Pensions				Discharged; laid on table.		
Hull, David	Indemnity for property destroyed by the enemy, war of 1812.	21	2	Resolution	60	Claims	37	Adverse		Laid on table.		
Hull, David	Indemnity for property destroyed by the enemy, war of 1812.	23	1	Resolution	305	Claims.						
Hull, David	Indemnity for property destroyed by the enemy, war of 1812.	23	2	Resolution	59	Claims.						
Hull, David	Indemnity for property destroyed by the enemy, war of 1812.	24	1	Resolution	93	Claims	770	Adverse		Laid on table.		
Hull, Dawson and John, representatives of.	Right of pre-emption to certain lands.	21	1	Petition	68	Priv. Land Claims.	Mar. 16, 1830	Adverse		Laid on table.		
Hull, Dawson and John, representatives of.	Right of pre-emption to certain lands.	21	2	Petition	55	Priv. Land Claims.	Feb. 8, 1831	Adverse		Laid on table.		
Hull, Dawson and John, representatives of.	Right of pre-emption to certain lands.	22	1	Petition	65	Priv. Land Claims.				Discharged; laid on table.		
Hull, Edwin, widow of	Commutation pay for revolutionary services.	24	1	Petition	274	Rev. Claims.						

List of private claims presented to the House of Representatives of the United States from the 1st to the 31st Congress, inclusive—Continued.

Names of claimants.	Nature or object of the claim.	Congress.	Session.	How brought before the House of Reps.	Page of journal.	To what committee of the House referred.	No. or date of the report.	Nature of the report.	No. of the bill.	How disposed of by the House of Reps.	How disposed of by the Senate.	Date of the act of Congress, and remarks.
Hull, Edwin, widow of	Commutation pay for revolutionary services.	24	2	Petition	126	Rev. Claims.						
Hull, Edwin, widow of	Commutation pay for revolutionary services.	25	2	Petition	70	Rev. Claims.						
Hull, Edwin, widow of	Commutation pay for revolutionary services.	25	3	Petition	85	Rev. Claims.						
Hull, Edwin, widow of	Commutation pay for revolutionary services.	26	1	Petition	166	Rev. Claims.						
Hull, Edwin, widow of	Commutation pay for revolutionary services.	26	2	Petition	181	Rev. Pensions.						
Hull, Edwin, widow of	Commutation pay for revolutionary services.	27	2	Petition	59	Rev. Pensions	784	Adverse		Laid on table.		
Hull, Edwin, heirs of	Commutation pay for revolutionary services.	29	1	Petition	430	Rev. Pensions	606	Adverse		Laid on table.		
Hull, Emmerson	(See Charles M. Davis)	21	2		192							
Hull & Forsyth	(See John E. Hunt, *et al*)	27	2		334							
Hull, Hannah	(See heir of James Hubbard)	24	2		73							
Hull, Isaac, Captain	Prize money	12	2	Joint resolution	544	Select	Nov. 12, 1812	Favorable		Passed	Passed	App'd March 3, 1813
Hull, Isaac	Compensation for extra services as navy agent at Washington.	22	2	Petition	123	Naval Affairs	81	Report and bill.	724	Referred to Committee Whole House.		
Hull, Isaac	Compensation for services and reimbursement of advances.	22	2	Senate bill	441	Naval Affairs	Mar. 2, 1833	With't amend.	S. 86	Laid on table.		
Hull, Isaac	Compensation for extra services as navy agent at Washington.	23	1	Memorial	36	Naval Affairs	201	Report and bill.	224	Referred to Committee Whole House.		
Hull, Isaac	Compensation for extra services as navy agent at Washington.	23	2	House bill	82	Whole House			224	Passed.		
Hull, Isaac	Compensation for extra services as navy agent at Washington.	24	1	Petition	139	Naval Affairs.						
Hull, Isaac	Compensation for extra services as navy agent at Washington.	24	2	Petition	46	Naval Affairs.						
Hull, Isaac	Compensation for extra services as navy agent at Washington.	25	2	Petition	56	Naval Affairs	147	Report and bill.	169	Referred to Committee Whole House.		
Hull, Isaac	Compensation for extra services as navy agent at Washington.	25	3	House bill	375	Whole House			169			
Hull, Isaac	Compensation for extra services as navy agent at Washington.	26	1	Petition	179	Naval Affairs	340	Report and bill.	315	Referred to Committee Whole House.		
Hull, Isaac	Compensation for extra services as navy agent at Washington.	27	2	Petition	105	Claims	52	Report and bill.	87	Passed.		
Hull, Isaac	Reimbursement of money paid for live-oak timber.	27	2	Senate bill	716	Naval Affairs	May 17, 1842	With't amend.	S. 137	Passed		App'd Aug. 30, 1842
Hull, Isaac	(See John E. Hunt, *et al.*)	27	2		334							
Hull, Jabez	Compensation for property taken for public use.	14	1	Petition	33	Claims	Dec. 19, 1815	Report by bill.		Passed.		
Hull, Joseph	Commutation pay for revolutionary services.	3	1	Memorial	98	Select.	April 22, 1794	Adverse.		Laid on table.		
Hull, Joseph	Commutation pay for revolutionary services.	3	2	Rep. & memorial	250	Claims	Feb. 25, 1795	Adverse		Referred to Committee Whole House.		
Hull, Joseph	Commutation pay for revolutionary services.	4	2	Petition	628	Claims	Dec. 26, 1796	Adverse.		Rejected; leave to withdraw.		
Hull, Samuel	Invalid pension	3	1	Rep. of Secretary War.	131	Select	May 26, 1794	J't. res. to refer to Sec. War.	12	Passed	Passed	App'd June 9, 1794
Hull, Samuel	Invalid pension	5	2	House bill	127	Whole House			38	Passed	Passed	App'd Feb. 2, 1798

List of private claims presented to the House of Representatives of the United States from the 1st to the 31st Congress, inclusive—Continued.

Names of claimants.	Nature or object of the claim.	Congress.	Session.	How brought before the House of Reps.	Page of journal.	To what committee of the House referred.	No. or date of the report.	Nature of the report.	No. of the bill.	How disposed of by the House of Reps.	How disposed of by the Senate.	Date of the act of Congress, and remarks.
Hull, Sarah	(See General William Hull, representatives of)											
Hull, Gen. William, representatives of.	Equitable settlement of accounts	19	1	Petition	223	Claims				Discharged; leave to withdraw.		
Hull, Gen. William, representatives of.	Equitable settlement of accounts	19	1	Petition	522	Claims				Discharged; laid on table.		
Hull, Gen. William, representatives of.	Equitable settlement of accounts	19	2	Petition	31	Claims	63	Report and bill.	415	Referred to Committee Whole House.		
Hull, Gen. William, representatives of.	Equitable settlement of accounts	20	1	Petition	38	Claims	18	Report and bill.	15	Passed	Passed	App'd Mar. 10, 1828
Hull, Gen. William, representatives of.	Equitable settlement of accounts	20	2	Petition	75	Claims				Leave to withdraw.		
Hull, Gen. William, heir of.	Balance of salary due as governor of Michigan.	21	2	Petition	95	Claims	84	Report and bill.	632	Referred to Committee Whole House.		
Hull, Gen. William, heir of.	Balance of salary due as govenor of Michigan.	22	1	Petition	25	Claims	Dec. 19, 1831	Report and bill.	41	Referred to Committee Whole House.		
Hull, William L.	Release from a judgment as surety for J. Draper.	15	2	Petition	190	Judiciary				Referred to Secretary of Treasury.		
Hull, Zephaniah	To be restored to pension roll	17	2	Petition	119	Whole House				Leave to withdraw.		
Hullam, Robert	Pension	20	2	Petition	64	Military Pensions				Discharged; laid on table.		
Hulse, Joseph, widow and heirs of.	Relief in consideration of the loss of their improved land by decision of the Supreme Court.	21	1	Petition	202	Priv. Land Claims.	232	Report and bill.	289	Referred to Committee Whole House.		
Hulse, Joseph, widow and heirs of.	Relief in consideration of the loss of their improved land by decision of the Supreme Court.	21	2	House bill	240	Whole House	Feb. 21, 1831	With't amend.	289	Passed.		
Hume, Henry (R. I.)	Indemnity for French spoliations prior to 1800.	26	1	Memorial	182	Foreign Affairs	343	Favorable; bill	319	Referred to Committee Whole House.		
Humes, James	Commissions on taxes collected in Pennsylvania in 1814.	14	2	Petition	38	Ways and Means	16	Adverse		Laid on table.		
Humfries, William A.	Bounty land for military services in Mexico.	30	1	Petition	457	Public Lands.						
Humphry, Asa	Pension for revolutionary services.	16	2	Petition	34	Rev. Pensions	Feb. 15, 1821	Adverse		Leave to withdraw.		
Humphrey, Charles	Reimbursement of expenses in a suit with the United States.	18	1	Petition	60	Claims	Jan. 23, 1824	Report and bill	81	Passed	Passed	App'd May 17, 1824
Humphrey, Daniel, representatives of.	Amount due as judge of the district court of New Hampshire.	22	2	Resolution	250	Judiciary.						
Humphrey, Captain Jacob.	Renewal of certain military land warrant.	6	1	Petition	622	Select.						
Humphrey, James	Compensation for services, &c., revolutionary war.	21	1	Petition	356	Rev. Claims				Discharged; laid on table.		
Humphrey, John	(See heirs of John Hamilton)	15	1		207							
Humphrey, Joshua	(See Daniel Richards & J. H.)	14	2		278							
Humphreys, Alexander & Sylvester.	Indemnity for damage to wharf by a storm, built for government by contract, before completed.	17	1	Senate bill	445	Commerce	May 26, 1822	Adverse	S. 70	Laid on table.		
Humphreys, Alexander & Sylvester.	Indemnity for damage to wharf by a storm, built for government by contract, before completed.	17	2	Senate bill	93	Commerce	Feb. 4, 1823	Adverse	S. 18	Laid on table.		
Humphreys, Alexander & Sylvester.	Indemnity for damage to wharf by a storm, built for government by contract, before completed.	18	1	Petition	251	Commerce.						

List of private claims presented to the House of Representatives of the United States from the 1st to the 31st Congress, inclusive—Continued.

Names of claimants.	Nature or object of the claim.	Congress.	Session.	How brought before the House of Reps.	Page of journal.	To what committee of the House referred.	No. or date of the report.	Nature of the report.	No. of the bill.	How disposed of by the House of Reps.	How disposed of by the Senate.	Date of the act of Congress, and remarks.
Humphreys, Alexander & Sylvester.	Indemnity for damage to wharf by a storm, built for government by contract, before completed.	18	2	Petition	32	Commerce.						
Humphreys, Alexander & Sylvester.	Indemnity for damage to wharf by a storm, built for government by contract, before completed.	19	1	Petition	222	Commerce.						
Humphreys, Alexander & Sylvester.	Indemnity for damage to wharf by a storm, built for government by contract, before completed.	19	2	Petition	63	Commerce.						
Humphreys, Alexander & Sylvester.	Indemnity for damage to wharf by a storm, built for government by contract, before completed.	21	2	Petition	111	Commerce.	Jan. 31, 1831	Adverse	......	Laid on table.		
Humphreys, Alexander & Sylvester.	Indemnity for damage to wharf by a storm, built for government by contract, before completed.	22	1	Petition	512	Claims	Mar. 28, 1832	Adverse	......	Laid on table.		
Humphreys, Alexander & Sylvester.	Indemnity for damage to wharf by a storm, built for government by contract, before completed.	23	1	Petition	80	Claims	94	Adverse	......	Laid on table.		
Humphreys, Alexander & Sylvester.	Indemnity for damage to wharf by a storm, built for government by contract, before completed.	24	1	Petition	48	Claims	Jan. 6, 1836	Adverse	......	Laid on table.		
Humphreys, Alexander & Sylvester.	Indemnity for damage to wharf by a storm, built for government by contract, before completed.	25	2	Petition	121	Claims.						
Humphreys, Alexander & Sylvester.	Indemnity for damage to wharf by a storm, built for government by contract, before completed.	25	3	Petition	87	Claims	63	Adverse	......	Laid on table.		
Humphreys, Ailsey	Pension under act of March 4, 1836.	27	2	Petition	132	Rev. Claims	....	....	......	Discharged; laid on table.		
Humphreys, Curtis	(See John B. Denton and Curtis Humphreys.)	28	2	....	331							
Humphreys, David	(See Benjamin Lincoln, *et al.*)	2	1	....	484							
Humphreys, Gad	Indemnity for land relinquished to Seminole Indians.	22	1	Petition	33	Priv. Land Claims.	May 10, 1832	Adverse	......	Laid on table.		
Humphreys, Gad	Indemnity for Indian depredations, &c.	25	3	Senate bill	355	Claims	Feb. 25, 1839	With't amend.	S. 185	Referred to Committee Whole House.		
Humphreys, Gad	Indemnity for Indian depredations, &c.	28	1	Petition	483	Claims.						
Humphreys, Gad	Indemnity for Indian depredations, &c.	29	1	Petition	74	Military Affairs.	203	Report and bill	198	Rejected.		
Humphrey, G. and H.	(See John E. Hunt, *et al.*)	29	1	....	160	....	287					
Humphreys, Hiram	Indemnity for timber swept off by a flood.	25	3	Memorial	182	Claims	45	Adverse	......	Laid on table.		
Humphreys, Hiram	Indemnity for timber swept off by a flood.	28	2	Memorial	193	Claims.						
Humphreys, Hiram	Indemnity for timber swept off by a flood.	29	1	Petition	175	Claims	341	Adverse	......	Laid on table.		
Humphries, Robert, widow of.	Pension for revolutionary services.	29	1	Petition	86	Rev. Pensions.	527	Adverse	......	Laid on table.		
Humphreys, Timothy	To be restored to pension roll	17	1	Petition	98	Rev. Pensions	....	....	......	Discharged; laid on table.		

List of private claims presented to the House of Representatives of the United States from the 1st to the 31st Congress, inclusive—Continued.

Names of claimants.	Nature or object of the claim.	Congress.	Session.	How brought before the House of Reps.	Page of journal.	To what committee of the House referred.	No. or date of the report.	Nature of the report.	No. of the bill.	How disposed of by the House of Reps.	How disposed of by the Senate.	Date of the act of Congress, and remarks.
Humphreys, William, jr.	Bounty on fishing schooner "Good Exchange."	29	1	Petition	461	Commerce	543	Report and bill.	365	Referred to Committee Whole House.		
Humphreys, William, jr.	Bounty on fishing schooner "Good Exchange."	30	1	Petition	157	Commerce.						
Humphreys, William, jr.	Bounty on fishing schooner "Good Exchange."	30	2	Petition	203	Commerce.						
Humphreys, William, jr.	Bounty on fishing schooner "Good Exchange."	31	1	Petition	451	Commerce.						
Hundson, Hans	Arrears of wages due him for services, United States navy.	27	3	Petition	205	Naval Affairs.						
Hungerford, Dexter	Discharge from liability as surety for Solomon White.	27	2	Petition	381	Claims	925	Report and bill	541	Referred to Committee Whole House.		
Hungerford, Dexter	Discharge from liability as surety for Solomon White.	27	3	House bill	89	Whole House	....	....	541	Passed	Adverse.	
Hungerford, Dexter	(See assignees of Thomas Tapper)	22	2	....	142							
Hungerford, Elbert V	Reimbursement of money paid for a fraudulent entry of land.	28	2	Petition	46	Claims.						
Hungerford, Elbert V	Reimbursement of money paid for a fraudulent entry of land.	29	1	Petition	67	Claims	70	Adverse	......	Laid on table.		
Hungerford, Mary	Continuation of revolutionary pension four years.	28	1	Petition	72	Rev. Pensions.						
Hungerf rd, John P	Compensation for property destroyed at St. Marks, Florida.	28	1	Petition	999	Claims.						
Hungerford, Orvile	(See assignees of Thomas Tupper)	22	2	....	142							
Hunn, Peter F	Equitable settlement of accounts as paymaster of militia.	17	1	Petition	305	Claims.						
Hunn, Peter F	Equitable settlement of accounts as paymaster of militia.	18	1	Petition	358	Claims.						
Hunn, Peter F	Equitable settlement of accounts as paymaster of militia.	18	2	Petition	157	Claims	Jan. 27, 1825	Adverse	......	Laid on table.		
Hunnel, Robert	(See William H. Bedford, agent).	28	1	....	262							
Hunneman, F. W	(See administrator of John Jackson)	27	2	....	382							
Hunnewell, Jonathan	Pension for revolutionary services.	27	2	Petition	613	Rev. Pensions	784	Adverse	......	Laid on table.		
Hunsaker, J. J	Indemnity for losses in Black Hawk war.	23	2	Documents	436	Claims.						
Hunsdon, John	Pension and indemnity for property destroyed by U. S. troops.	16	1	Petition	293	Claims	....	....	......	Discharged; laid on table.		
Hunsinger, Jacob	Permission to pay for land at land office, Shawneetown, Illinois.	16	2	Petition	21	Priv. Land Claims.	5	Report and bill	156	Passed	Indef. postp'd.	
Hunt, Abel, widow of	Pension for revolutionary services.	25	2	Petition	273	Rev. Pensions	Feb. 17, 1838	Adverse	......	Laid on table.		
Hunt, Abijah, executor of.	Confirmation of title to land	14	1	Petition	143	Priv. Land Claims.						
Hunt, Abjah, executor of.	Confirmation of title to land	15	1	Petition	192	Priv. Land Claims.						
Hunt, Abijah, executor of.	Confirmation of title to land	16	1	Petition	47	Priv. Land Claims.	75	Report and bill	101	Passed	With amend.	App'd May 8, 1820
Hunt, Abraham	Commutation pay for revolutionary services.	1	2	Petition	272	....	....	....	......	Referred to Secretary War.		
Hunt, Abraham	Commutation pay for revolutionary services.	1	3	Rep. of Secretary War.	378	....	....	....	......	Laid on table.		
Hunt, Abraham	Commutation pay for revolutionary services.	2	1	Petition	448	Select.						
Hunt, Anna	Continuation of revolutionary pension.	28	1	Petition	850	Rev. Pensions.						

List of private claims presented to the House of Representatives of the United States from the 1st to the 31st Congress, inclusive—Continued.

Names of claimants.	Nature or object of the claim.	Congress.	Session.	How brought before the House of Reps.	Page of journal.	To what committee of the House referred.	No. or date of the report.	Nature of the report.	No. of the bill.	How disposed of by the House of Reps.	How disposed of by the Senate.	Date of the act of Congress, and remarks.
Hunt, Benjamin F.	To dispense with the clearance of his vessel while transporting slaves in South Carolina.	20	2	Petition	58	Commerce	Jan. 28, 1829	Report and bill	399	Referred to Committee Whole House.		
Hunt, Benjamin	Pension for services in the war of 1812.	26	1	Petition	937	Invalid Pensions.						
Hunt, Benjamin	Pension for services in the war of 1812.	26	2	Petition	84	Invalid Pensions	Feb. 12, 1840	Report and bill	666	Referred to Committee Whole House.		
Hunt, Benjamin	Pension for services in the war of 1812.	27	2	Petition	60	Invalid Pensions	136	Report and bill.	182	Laid on table.		
Hunt, Benjamin	Pension for services in the war of 1812.	28	1	Petition	513	Invalid Pensions.						
Hunt, Benjamin	Pension for services in the war of 1812.	28	2	Petition	240	Invalid Pensions.						
Hunt, Benjamin	Pension for services in the war of 1812.	29	1	Petition	70	Invalid Pensions	100	Adverse	......	Laid on table.		
Hunt, Betty, executrix of.	Indemnity for French spoliations prior to 1800.	26	1	Memorial	182	Foreign Affairs	343	Favorable; bill	319	Referred to Committee Whole House.		
Hunt, Caleb	Invalid pension	3	2	Rep. of Secretary War.	262	Claims	....	....	......	Discharged; laid on table.		
Hunt, Caleb	Invalid pension	4	1	Rep. of Secretary War.	445	Claims	March 4, 1796	Favorable; bill ordered.	156	Passed	Passed	App'd April 20, 1796
Hunt, Caleb	Increase of pension	10	1	House bill	235	Whole House	April 19, 1808	Favorable	78	Passed	Passed	App'd April 25, 1808
Hunt, Charles	Additional compensation as clerk in late Census Bureau.	28	1	Petition	828	Claims.						
Hunt, Charles C. P.	Increase of salary as collector of customs, Ohio.	25	3	Petition	561	Commerce.						
Hunt, C. S.	(See A. G. Blanchard, *et al.*)	30	2	....	285							
Hunt, Daniel	(See William H. Bedford, agent.)	28	1	....	262							
Hunt, David	(See heirs of Elisha Winter & Son.)	19	2	....	159							
Hunt, David	(See executor of Abijah Hunt.)	14	2	....	143							
Hunt, David, Anna, and Russell.	(See Stephen Decatur, widow of.)	23	1	Petition	...							
Hunt, Davis	Pension for revolutionary services.	24	1	....	106	Rev. Pensions	Jan. 19, 1836	Report by bill.	179	Passed	Passed	App'd June 28, 1836
Hunt, Eli	(See William H. Bedford, agent.)	28	1	....	262							
Hunt, Elizabeth	(See heir of William Hendricks.)	24	1	....	203							
Hunt, Elizabeth	(See widow of Isaac Seely.)	9	1	....	246							
Hunt, Ephraim	Pension for revolutionary services.	21	2	Petition	43	Military Pensions	....	....	......	Discharged; laid on table.		
Hunt, Ephraim	Pension for revolutionary services.	22	1	Resolution	93	Rev. Pensions	438	Report and bill.	542	Referred to Committee Whole House.		
Hunt, Gilbert	Compensation for wood furnished revolutionary army.	4	1	Rep. of Secretary Treasury.	388	Claims	74	Adverse	......	Laid on table.		
Hunt, Hardy	(See William H. Bedford, agent.)	28	1	....	262							
Hunt, Humphrey	Invalid pension	3	2	Report Secretary of War.	278	Claims	Feb. 28, 1795	Favorable; bill ordered.	130	Passed	Postponed till next sess.	
Hunt, Humphrey	Invalid pension	4	1	Petition	445	Claims	Feb. 18, 1796	Favorable; bill ordered.	156	Passed	Passed	App'd April 20, 1796
Hunt, James	Confirmation of title to land in Mississippi.	14	1	Petition	121	Public Lands.						
Hunt, James	Confirmation of title to land in Mississippi.	14	2	Petition	51	Public Lands.						

List of private claims presented to the House of Representatives of the United States from the 1st to the 31st Congress, inclusive—Continued.

Names of claimants.	Nature or object of the claim.	Congress.	Session.	How brought before the House of Reps.	Page of journal.	To what committee of the House referred.	No. or date of the report.	Nature of the report.	No. of the bill.	How disposed of by the House of Reps.	How disposed of by the Senate.	Date of the act of Congress, and remarks.
Hunt, James	Pension	21	1	Petition	36	Military Pensions				Discharged; laid on table.		
Hunt, James and John	Arrest of proceedings for an alleged violation of the non-importation act.	12	1	Petition	66	Com. and Manuf.						
Hunt, Jedediah	Arrears of pension	23	1	Petition	333	Invalid Pensions				Discharged; laid on table.		
Hunt, Jeremiah	(See execu'or of Abijah Hunt)	14	2		143							
Hunt, Jeremiah	(See heirs and representatives of Elisha Winter & Son.)	19	2		159							
Hunt, Jesse, *et al*	Extension of time on certain custom-house bonds.	14	2	Petition	69	Ways and Means.						
Hunt, Jesse	Remission of duty on merchandise destroyed by fire.	14	2	Petition	76	Ways and Means	Jan. 28, 1817	Adverse		Rejected.		
Hunt, Jesse	(See heirs and representatives of Elisha Winter & Son.)	19	2		159							
Hunt, John	Remission of duty on a still, &c.	7	1	Petition	63	Claims	Jan. 29, 1802	Adverse		Rejected.		
Hunt, John	Pension	21	2	Petition	158	Military Pensions.						
Hunt, John, (Conn.)	Pension	21	2	Petition	208	Military Pensions.						
Hunt, John, *et al.*	Grant of land for opening a canal.	23	2	Petition	157	Public Lands				Discharged; laid on table.		
Hunt, John E., *et al.*	Payment of a claim against Ottawa Indians.	27	2	Petition	56	Claims	51	Report by bill.	86	Passed	Adverse report.	
Hunt, John E., *et al.*	Payment of a claim against Ottawa Indians.	27	3	Petition	112	Claims	12	Report and bill.	633	Passed	Passed	App'd March 1, 1843
Hunt, John E., *et al.*	Payment of a claim against Ottawa Indians.	29	1	Memorial	160	Indian Affairs	287	Adverse		Laid on table.		
Hunt, John C.	Bounty land for services in Mexican war.	31	1	Petition	596	Public Lands.						
Hunt, Jonathan	Confirmation of title to land in Alabama.	24	1	Petition	436	Public Lands				Discharged; referred to Priv. Land Claims.		
Hunt, Jonathan	Confirmation of title to land in Alabama.	26	2		229							See act for the relief of Miguel Eslava; Approved Mar. 3, 1841.
Hunt, Josiah	Arrears of pension	26	1	Petition	287	Invalid Pensions.						
Hunt, Josiah	Arrears of pension	26	2	Petition	77	Invalid Pensions	88	Adverse		Laid on table.		
Hunt, Memucan	Confirmation of State title to lands in North Carolina.	7	1	Petition	55	Select	Mar. 24, 1802	Report not recorded.		Postponed.		
Hunt, Memucan	Confirmation of State title to lands in North Carolina.	7	2	Pet. and report of Select Com.	252	Whole House.						
Hunt, Memucan	Confirmation of State title to lands in North Carolina.	8	1	Petition	459	Select	Jan. 10, 1804	Favorable, with resolution.		Rejected.		
Hunt, Moses N.	Increase of pension	31	1	Petition	616	Ways and Means	471	Adverse		Laid on table.		
Hunt, Nathaniel, *et al*	Examination and payment of their claims.	19	2	Petition	242	Ways and Means.						
Hunt, Nathaniel, *et al*	Examination and payment of their claims.	20	1	Petition	39	Invalid Pensions	13	Adverse		Laid on table.		
Hunt, Peter	Remission of duty on stills inundated.	7	1	Petition	48	Com. and Manuf.	Jan. 14, 1802	Adverse		Rejected.		
Hunt, Peter	Pension	22	1	Petition	130	Rev. Pensions				Discharged; laid on table.		
Hunt, Riddle, & Platt	(See Jesse Hunt, *et al*)	14	2		69							
Hunt, Roswell	Pension	21	2	Petition	159	Military Pensions.						

List of private claims presented to the House of Representatives of the United States from the 1*st to the* 31*st Congress, inclusive*—Continued.

Names of claimants.	Nature or object of the claim.	Congress.	Session.	How brought before the House of Reps.	Page of journal.	To what committee of the House referred.	No. or date of the report.	Nature of the report.	No. of the bill.	How disposed of by the House of Reps.	How disposed of by the Senate.	Date of the act of Congress, and remarks.
Hunt, Roswell	Pension	22	1	Petition	68	Invalid Pensions	238	Report and bill.	344	Passed	....	See H. B. 157, and S. B. 1.
Hunt, Roswell	Pension	22	2	Petition	45	Invalid Pensions	7	Report and bill.	626	Passed	Passed	App'd March 2, 1833
Hunt, Russell, David, and Amos.	Balance due for anchors furnished U. States navy.	22	1	Petition	333	Claims.						
Hunt, Russell, David, and Amos.	Balance due for anchors furnished U. States navy.	22	2	Petition	28	Claims	120	Report and bill.	758	Referred to Committee Whole House.		
Hunt, Russell, David, and Amos.	Balance due for anchors furnished U. States navy.	23	1	Petition	34	Claims	20	Peport and bill	20	Passed	Passed	App'd Feb. 5, 1834
Hunt, Samuel	Increase of pension	23	1	Petition	88	Invalid Pensions	215	Report and bill	233	Referred to Committee Whole House.		
Hunt, Samuel	Increase of pension	23	2	House bill	82	Whole House	....	....	233			
Hunt, Samuel	Pension for loss of a leg in revolutionary war.	24	1	Petition	140	Invalid Pensions	203	Report and bill.	206	Passed	Passed	App'd June 28, 1836
Hunt, Samuel	Pension	25	2	Petition	775							
Hunt, Samuel	Pension	26	1	Petition	285	Rev. Pensions	490	Adverse	......	Rejected.		
Hunt, Seth, for self and others.	Confirmation of title to land in West Florida.	14	1	Petition	121	Public Lands	Feb. 12, 1816	General bill.				
Hunt, Stephen W	(See Williams & Hunt)	25	2	....	922							
Hunt, Thomas	Compensation for revolutionary services.	2	1	Petition	440	....	....	....	......	Referred to Secretary War.		
Hunt, Thomas	Compensation for revolutionary services.	2	2	Rep. of Secretary War.	696	....	....	....	......	Laid on table.		
Hunt, Thomas, (Eunice,) widow of.	Compensation for services of deceased as a revolutionary officer.	10	2	Petition	498	....	....	....	......	Laid on table.		
Hunt, Thomas	Compensation for services as an officer, war of 1812.	20	1	Petition	279	Claims	139	Report and bill	207	Referred to Committee Whole House.		
Hunt, Thomas	Compensation for services as an officer, war of 1812.	20	2	House bill	202	Whole House	Jan. 24, 1829	With't amend.	207	Passed	Passed	App'd March 3, 1829
Hunt, Thomas F	Amount found due him on trial of a suit with United States.	20	2	Petition	33	Claims.						
Hunt, Thomas F	Amount found due him on trial of a suit with United States.	21	1	Petition	110	Claims	419	Adverse	......	Discharged; laid on table.		
Hunt, Tirzah	(See widow of Joshua Bates)	26	1	....	283	....	714					
Hunt, William	Invalid pension	3	2	Rep. of Secretary War.	337	Claims	Feb. 28, 1795	Favorable; bill ordered.	130	Passed	Postp'd to next session.	
Hunt, William	Invalid pension	4	1	Rep. of Secretary War.	445	Claims	Mar. 4, 1796	Favorable; bill ordered.	156	Passed	Passed	App'd April 20, 1796
Hunt, William	(See administrator of General Ira Allen.)	18	1	....	525							
Hunt, William	Pension	22	2	Petition	169	Invalid Pensions	Feb. 15, 1833	General bill	738	Referred to Committee Whole House.		
Hunt, William	Pension	23	1	Petition	131	Invalid Pensions	122	Report and bill	128	Passed	Passed	App'd June 30, 1834
Hunt, W. G	Indemnity for French spoliations prior to 1800.	26	1	Memorial	182	Foreign Affairs	343	Favorable; bill	319	Referred to Committee Whole House.		
Hunt, William Hasell	Compensation for services as clerk in U. S. court, West Flordia.	20	1	Petition	419	Territories.						
Hunt, William Hasell	Compensation for services as clerk in U. S. court, West Florida.	20	2	Petition	321	Territories.						
Hunt, William Hasell	Compensation for services as clerk in U. S. court, West Florida.	21	1	Petition	236	Territories.						

List of private claims presented to the House of Representatives of the United States from the 1st to the 31st Congress, inclusive—**Continued.**

Names of claimants.	Nature or object of the claim.	Congress.	Session.	How brought before the House of Reps.	Page of journal.	To what committee of the House referred.	No. or date of the report.	Nature of the report.	No. of the bill.	How disposed of by the House of Reps.	How disposed of by the Senate.	Date of the act of Congress, and remarks.
Hunt, William Hasell	Compensation for services as clerk in U. S. court, West Florida.	23	1	Petition	354	Judiciary.						
Hunt, William Hasell	Compensation for services as clerk in U. S. court, West Florida.	23	2	Petition	86	Territories	Dec. 29, 1839	Report by bill.	593	Referred to Committee Whole House.		
Hunt, William Hasell	(See administrator of John Miller)	20	2		322							
Hunt, William P	(See sureties of Alpha Kingsley)	19	1		488							
Hunt, Wilson	Pension	25	2	Resolution	525	Rev. Pensions				Discharged; laid on table.		
Hunt, Wilson P	(See Alpha Kingsley, sureties of.)	19	1		488							
Hunt, Wilson P	Patent for land to which he is entitled.	23	1	Senate bill	501	Claims			S. 58			
Hunt, Wilson P	Confirmation of title to land	26	1	Petition	611	Priv. Land Claims.						
Hunt, Wilson P	Patent for 1 square league of land	27	2	Petition	75	Priv. Land Claims.						
Hunter, Alexander	(See Archibald S. Bullock, *et al.*)	17	1		151							
Hunter, Alexander	Settlement of accounts as marshal of the District of Columbia.	30	1	Petition	274	Judiciary	331	Report & Joint Resolution.	J. R. 19	Referred to Committee Whole House.		
Hunter, Alexander	Settlement of accounts as marshal of the District of Columbia.	30	2	Joint resolution.	179	Judiciary	122	Adverse	J. R. 19	Laid on table.		
Hunter, Andrew, widow of, and others.	Provision for support of widows of revolutionary officers.	20	2	Memorial	290	Whole House.						
Hunter, Andrew, widow of, and others.	Provision for support of widows of revolutionary officers.	21	1	Memorial	37	Military Pensions.						
Hunter, Andrew, widow of, and others.	Provision for support of widows of revolutionary officers.	21	2	Memorial	76	Select	4	Favorable; bill	567	Passed.		
Hunter, Andrew, widow of, and others.	Provision for support of widows of revolutionary officers.	22	1	Memorial	97	Rev. Pensions				Discharged.		
Hunter, Andrew, widow of, and others.	Provision for support of widows of revolutionary officers.	22	2	Petition	41	Rev. Claims.						
Hunter, Ann	(See Robert Hunter, widow of)	27	2		70							
Hunter, Archibald R. S.	Indemnity for damage to his crops by Tennessee volunteers.	25	1	Memorial	181					Laid on table.		
Hunter, Archibald R. S.	Indemnity for damage to his crops by Tennessee volunteers.	25	2	Memorial	88	Claims	341	Report and bill	371	Referred to Committee Whole House.		
Hunter, Archibald R. S.	Indemnity for damage to his crops by Tennessee volunteers.	25	3	House bill	378	Whole House			371	Passed	Passed	App'd March 2, 1839
Hunter, Archibald R. S.	Indemnity for damage to his crops by Tennessee volunteers.	28	1	Petition	132	Claims	569	Report and bill	422	Referred to Committee Whole House.		
Hunter, Archibald R. S.	Indemnity for damage to his crops by Tennessee volunteers.	30	1	Petition	136	Claims	61	Adverse		Laid on table.		
Hunter & Banks	(See Henry Hill, *et al.*)	2	1		562							
Hunter, Charles W	Confirmation of title to land in Missouri.	15	1	Petition	81	Priv. Land Claims.						
Hunter, Charles W	Confirmation of title to land in Missouri.	16	1	Petition	72	Priv. Land Claims.						
Hunter, Charles G., (U. S. N.)	Pay and emoluments while suspended from duty.	24	2	Senate bill	251	Naval Affairs	295	Adverse	S. 103	Referred to Committee Whole House.		
Hunter, George	Compensation for saltpetre destroyed by fire.	10	1	Petition Rep. of Secretary War.	205 208	Ways and Means.	Mar. 10, 1808	Report and bill	73	Referred to Committee Whole House.		
Hunter, George	Compensation for saltpetre destroyed by fire.	10	1	Senate bill	291	Whole House			S. 26	Passed		App'd April 20, 1808
Hunter, George	(See Joseph Eaker, attorney of.)	2	1		458							
Hunter, George	(See William W. Smith, *et al.*)	3	1		78							

List of private claims presented to the House of Representatives of the United States from the 1st to the 31st Congress, inclusive—Continued.

Names of claimants.	Nature or object of the claim.	Congress.	Session.	How brought before the House of Reps.	Page of journal.	To what committee of the House referred.	No. or date of the report.	Nature of the report.	No. of the bill.	How disposed of by the House of Reps.	How disposed of by the Senate.	Date of the act of Congress, and remarks.
Hunter, Dr. George, widow of.	Confirmation of title to land in Louisiana.	27	2	Petition	459	Priv. Land Claims.						
Hunter, George and Jonathan.	Compensation for property taken for public use in revolutionary war.	2	1	Petition	547	...	...	...	...	Referred to Secretary Treasury.		
Hunter, George and Jonathan.	Compensation for property taken for public use in revolutionary war.	2	2	Rep. of Secretary Treasury.	626	...	...	...	...	Referred to Committee Whole House.		
Hunter, Henry D., *et al.*	Increase of pay as officers of revenue cutters.	22	2	Petition	53	Commerce.						
Hunter, Hiram A.	Compensation for a horse lost in Seminole war.	21	1	Petition	524	Claims	April 20, 1830	Adverse	...	Laid on table.		
Hunter, Hiram A.	Compensation for a horse lost in Seminole war.	23	1	Senate bill	501	Claims	...	...	S. 58			
Hunter, Hiram A.	Compensation for a horse lost in Seminole war.	23	2	Senate bill	244	Claims	Jan. 23, 1835	With't amend.	S. 12	Referred to Committee Whole House.		
Hunter, Hiram A.	Compensation for a horse lost in Seminole war.	24	1	Senate bill	320	Claims	Feb. 12, 1836	With't amend.	S. 15	Passed	...	App'd July 2, 1836
Hunter, James	(See Elias De Butts)	9	2	...	616							
Hunter, Capt. James	Arrears of pension	24	2	Resolution	221	Invalid Pensions	178	Report and bill	899	Referred to Committee Whole House.		
Hunter, Capt. James	Arrears of pension	25	2	Resolution	38	Invalid Pensions	611	Report and bill	591	Passed	Rejected.	
Hunter, Capt. James	Pension for services as an officer in the war of 1812.	25	3	Petition	128	Invalid Pensions	33	Report and bill.	933	Passed.		
Hunter, James, and C. P. Halley.	Permission to locate two military land warrants in Tennessee.	22	2	Petition	398	Priv. Land Claims.						
Hunter, James, and C. P. Halley.	Permission to locate two military land warrants in Tennessee.	23	1	Petition	75	Priv. Land Claims.	Jan. 7, 1834	Adverse	...	Laid on table.		
Hunter, James, (Mary,) widow of.	Invalid pension	26	1	Petition	161	Invalid Pensions	172	Report and bill	183	Passed	Indef. postp'd.	
Hunter, James, (Mary,) widow of.	Arrears of pension	26	1	Ho. bill, on leave.	126	Whole House	...	...	557			
Hunter, John	Invalid pension	3	2	Rep. of Secretary of War.	337	Claims	...	...	...	Discharged; laid on table.		
Hunter, John	Invalid pension	4	1	Rep. of Secretary War.	445	Claims	Mar. 4, 1796	Jt. res. to refer to Sec. War.	J. R. 16	Passed	Passed	App'd April 17, 1796
Hunter, John	Rent of naval office, Alexandria, Virginia.	8	1	Petition	440	Claims	Nov. 10, 1803	Adverse	...	Leave to withdraw.		
Hunter, John	Balance due for services on Cumberland road.	19	2	Petition	188	Roads and Canals.						
Hunter, John	Balance due for services on Cumberland road.	20	1	Petition	32	Roads and Canals.	Jan. 4, 1828	Report and bill.	54	Laid on table.		
Hunter, John	Balance due for services on Cumberland road.	20	2	Resolution	212	Claims	Feb. 4, 1829	Adverse	...	Laid on table.		
Hunter, John	Pension for services, revolutionary navy.	23	2	Petition	39	Rev. Pensions	...	...	...	Discharged; laid on table.		
Hunter, John, 2d	Pension	16	1	Petition	312	Rev. Pensions	April 22, 1820	Adverse	...	Laid on table.		
Hunter, Lewis	(See James Miller and James Love, heirs of.)	10	2	...	431							
Hunter, Robert	(See Thomas Burbridge)	3	1	...	131							
Hunter, Robert	(See Cary Dunn, jr., *et al*)	21	2	...	74							
Hunter, Robert	(See Albert Pawling, *et al*)	22	1	...	72							

List of private claims presented to the House of Representatives of the United States from the 1st to the 31st Congress, inclusive—Continued.

Names of claimants.	Nature or object of the claim.	Congress.	Session.	How brought before the House of Reps.	Page of journal.	To what committee of the House referred.	No. or date of the report.	Nature of the report.	No. of the bill.	How disposed of by the House of Reps.	How disposed of by the Senate.	Date of the act of Congress, and remarks.
Hunter, Robert	Bounty land for services in the war of 1812.	31	1	Petition	596	Priv. Land Claims.						
Hunter, Robert, (Ann,) widow of.	Pension for revolutionary services.	27	2	Petition	70	Rev. Pensions	784	Adverse		Laid on table.		
Hunter, Robert, (Ann,) widow of.	Pension for revolutionary services.	28	1	Petition	717	Rev. Pensions	448	Report and bill	346	Passed	Passed	App'd June 17, 1844
Hunter, R. A., (Sarah,) mother of.	Relief in consideration of being a naval apprentice.	28	1	Petition	75	Naval Affairs.						
Hunter, Thomas	Sundry claims as a soldier in the war of 1812.	16	1	Senate bill	429	Military Affairs	April 22, 1820	With't amend.	82	Passed	Passed	App'd May 15, 1820
Hunter, Thomas	(See Alexander Caldwell.)	28	1		325							
Hunter, William	Bounty land for services as sergean of artillery.	24	1	Petition	664	Public Lands				Discharged; aid on table.		
Hunter, William	Bounty land for services as sergeant of artillery.	24	2	Documents	390	Public Lands.						
Hunter, William	Compensation for extra services as clerk to the Fourth Auditor.	25	3	Petition	120	Claims.						
Hunter, William	Compensation for extra services as clerk to the Fourth Auditor.	26	1	Petition	169	Claims	62	Adverse		Laid on table		Leave to withdraw, 2d session.
Hunter, William H	(See Alexander Caldwell and Thomas Hunter.)	28	1		325							
Hunting, Amos	Pension for revolutionary services.	26	1	Petition	936	Rev. Pensions	July 21, 1840	Report by bill	500	Referred to Committee Whole House.		
Hunting, Amos	Pension for revolutionary services.	27	2	Petition	59	Rev. Pensions	122	Report by bill.	168	Passed	Indef. postp'd.	
Hunting, Amos	Pension for revolutionary services.	28	1	Petition	99	Rev. Pensions.						
Hunting, Amos	Pension for revolutionary services.	28	2	Petition	59	Rev. Pensions.						
Hunting, Amos	Pension for revolutionary services.	29	1	Petition	175	Rev. Pensions	July 13, 1846	Report by bill.	510	Passed	Passed	App'd Aug. 8, 1846
Hunting, Samuel	Release from surety ship on bonds under embargo act.	11	2	Petition	169	Com. and Manuf.						
Huntington, Asher	Pension	22	1	Petition	36	Invalid Pensions	264	Report and bill.	344	Passed.		
Huntington, Asher	Pension	22	2	Petition	27	Invalid Pensions	7	Report and bill.	626	Passed	Passed, with amendment.	App'd March 2, 1833
Huntington, G. W	(See Gabriel W. Denton, & others)	24	1		153							
Huntington, Hezekiah	(See John Woodward.)	26	1		939							
Huntington, Hiram	Pension	21	2	Petition	375	Military Pensions.						
Huntington, Hiram	To be restored to pension roll	22	1	Petition	160	Rev. Pensions	439	Report and bill.	543	Referred to Committee Whole House.		
Huntington, Jabez	Indemnity for French spoliations prior to 1800.	26	1	Memorial	182	Foreign Affairs	343	Favorable; bill	319	Referred to Committee Whole House.		
Huntington, Jabez, heirs of	Indemnity for French spoliations prior to 1800.	31	1	Petition	284	Foreign Affairs	355	General bill	318			
Huntington, Jabez	(See Peabody & Huntington.)	26	1		182							
Huntington, Jeannette C.	(See W. D. Cheever, executor of.)	28	1		602							
Huntington, John	Pension	22	1	Petition	329	Rev. Pensions.						
Huntington, Nehemiah	Release as the surety of D. Petrie.	17	1	Petition	151	P. Of. and P. Roads.	Mar. 1, 1822	Adverse		Laid on table.		
Huntington, Roger	Compensation for revolutionary services as assistant commissary of purchases.	19	1	Petition	381	Rev. Claims	April 12, 1826	Adverse.				
Huntington, Samuel, administrator of.	Equitable settlement of accounts as paymaster.	19	2	Petition	159	Claims.						
Huntington, Samuel G.	(See W. D. Cheever, executors of.)	28	1		602							
Huntington, Theophilus	Compensation for revolutionary services.	10	1	Petition	174	Whole House.						

List of private claims presented to the House of Representatives of the United States from the 1st to the 31st Congress, inclusive—Continued.

Names of claimants.	Nature or object of the claim.	Congress.	Session.	How brought before the House of Reps.	Page of journal.	To what committee of the House referred.	No. or date of the report.	Nature of the report.	No. of the bill.	How disposed of by the House of Reps.	How disposed of by the Senate.	Date of the act of Congress, and remarks.
Huntington, Theophilus..	Compensation for revolutionary services.	12	1	Petition	188	Claims	June 12, 1812	Adverse	......	Laid on table.		
Huntington, William.....	Pension	22	1	Resolution	228	Rev. Pensions.....	377	Report and bill.	471	Referred to Committee Whole House.		
Huntley, Elihu, widow of	Continuation of pension	25	2	Petition	273	Rev. Pensions	....	....	......	Discharged; laid on table.		
Hunton, Charles	Increase of pension............	13	3	House bill......	740	Whole House	Mar. 1, 1815	With't amend.	303	Passed	Passed	App'd March 3, 1815
Huntoon, Charles, jr.	Invalid pension...............	3	2	Rep. of Secretary War.	350	Claims.						
Huntoon, Charles, jr.....	Invalid pension...............	4	1	Rep. of Secretary War.	445	Claims	Feb. 18, 1796	Favorable; bill ordered.	156	Passed	Passed, with amendment	App'd April 20, 1796
Huntoon, Joseph........	Balance of pay, &c., as lieutenant in revolutionary army.	8	1	Petition	507	Claims	....	....	......	Referred to Committee Whole House.		
Huntoon, Joseph........	Balance of pay, &c., as lieutenant in revolutionary army.	8	2	Petition	77	Claims.						
Huntoon, Joseph........	Balance of pay, &c., as lieutenant in revolutionary army.	9	1	Petition	308	Claims	Mar. 28, 1806	....	......	Indef. postponed.....	....	Leave to withdraw.
Huntoon, Joseph........	Increase of revolutionary pension..	11	1	Petition	32	Claims	....	....	......	Leave to withdraw.		
Huntoon, Joseph........	Increase of revolutionary pension..	12	1	House bill	361	Whole House	....	....	138	Passed	Passed	App'd July 5, 1812
H ntoon, Moses..	Pension	21	2	Petition	103	Military Pensions.						
Huntress, Daniel, executors of.	Indemnity for French spoliations prior to 1800.	26	1	Memorial	182	Foreign Affairs ...	343	Favorable; bill	319	Referred to Committee Whole House.		
Huntress, Daniel, administrator of.	Indemnity for French spoliations prior to 1800.	31	1	Petition	197	Foreign Affairs ...	355	General bill ..	318	Referred to Committee Whole House.		
Huntriss, Pearson	Compensation for revolutionary services.	2	1	Petition	511	....	....	....	......	Referred to Secretary of War.		
Huntsman, Elizabeth	(See John Huntsman, widow of).	31	1	....	768							
Huntsman, John, widow of	Pension for revolutionary services.	31	1	Petition	768	Rev. Pensions	361	Adverse	......	Laid on table.		
Huntt, William H.......	Increase of compensation as postmaster, (Georgia.)	16	2	Petition	97	P. Of. & P. Roads.						
Hupper, William L., *et al.*	Bounty on a fishing vessel.......	14	2	Petition	39	Ways and Means.						
Hurd, Daniel, children of.	Indemnity for losses during revolutionary war.	30	1	Petition	264	Rev. Pensions	....	....	......	Discharged; laid on table.		
Hurd, David	Pension	11	2	House bill	283	Whole House	Mar. 24, 1810	Favorable....	107	Passed	Passed	App'd April 27, 1810
Hurd, David	Increase of pension............	12	1	House bill	361	Whole House	June 5, 1812	....	133	Passed	Passed	App'd July 5, 1812
Hurd, Jesse, heirs of.....	Indemnity for French spoliations prior to 1800.	26	1	Memorial	182	Foreign Affairs....	343	Favorable; bill	319	Referred to Committee Whole House.		
Hurd, Joseph, sureties of..	To be allowed certain offsets in a suit against them as sureties of said J. Hurd.	23	1	Petition	79	Judiciary	486	Favorable	495	Referred to Committee Whole House.		
Hurd, Joseph, sureties of..	To be allowed certain offsets in a suit against them as sureties of said J. Hurd.	24	1	Petition	53	Judiciary	311	Adverse	......	Laid on table.		
Hurd, Joseph, sureties of..	To be allowed certain offsets in a suit against them as sureties of said J. Hurd.	25	2	Petition	172	Judiciary	Feb. 2, 1838	Favorable....	516	Referred to Committee Whole House.		
Hurd, Joseph, sureties of..	To be allowed certain offsets in a suit against them as sureties of said J. Hurd.	25	2	House bill......	1208	Whole House.....	July 2, 1838	Favorable....	875	Referred to Committee Whole House.		
Hurd, Joseph, sureties of..	To be allowed certain offsets in a suit against them as sureties of said J. Hurd.	25	3	House bill......	379	Whole House.....	Jan. 25, 1839	Favorable	516	Passed.		

List of private claims presented to the House of Representatives of the United States from the 1st to the 31st Congress, inclusive—Continued.

Names of claimants.	Nature or object of the claim.	Congress.	Session.	How brought before the House of Reps.	Page of journal.	To what committee of the House referred.	No. or date of the report.	Nature of the report.	No. of the bill.	How disposed of by the House of Reps.	How disposed of by the Senate.	Date of the act of Congress, and remarks.
Hurd, Joseph, sureties of	To be allowed certain offsets in a suit against them as sureties of said J. Hurd.	26	1	Senate bill	415	Whole House	Feb. 18, 1840	Favorable	212	Passed		App'd May 27, 1840
Hurd, Simon	Pension	22	1	Petition	466	Rev. Pensions				Discharged; laid on table.		
Hurd, Zadock	Invalid pension	3	2	Rep. of Secretary War.	278	Claims	Feb. 28, 1795	Favorable; bill ordered.	130	Passed	Postp'd to next session.	
Hurd, Zadock	Invalid pension	4	1	Report Secretary War.	445	Claims	Feb. 18, 1796	Favorable; bill ordered.	156	Passed	Passed	App'd April 20, 1796
Hurlburt, Collins, heirs of	Pension—killed in the war of 1812	19	1	Resolution	386	Military Pensions				Discharged; leave to withdraw.		
Hurlburt, Collins, heirs of	Pension—killed in the war of 1812	19	2	Resolution	70	Military Pensions.						
Hurlburt, Collins, heirs of	Pension—killed in the war of 1812	20	1	Resolution	50	Military Pensions	April 29, 1818	Report by bill.	283			
Hurlburt, Collins, heirs of	Pension—killed in the war of 1812	20	2	Resolution	55	Military Pensions	Dec. 12, 1828	General bill	311	Passed.		
Hurlburt, Collins, heirs of	Pension—killed in the war of 1812	21	1	Resolution	48	Military Pensions				Disch'd; laid on table.		
Hurlburt, Collins, minor children of	Pension—killed in the war of 1812	21	1	Resolution	130	Whole House	Feb. 13, 1830	Favorable	72	Passed	Passed	App'd April 20, 1830
Hurlburt, Captain George, executors of.	Commutation pay and bounty land for revolutionary services.	4	2	Petition	683	Claims	Feb. 7, 1797	Adverse		Referred to Committee Whole House.		
Hurlburt, Captain George, executors of.	Commutation pay and bounty land for revolutionary services.	5	2	Petition and rep't of Committee.	109	Claims	Dec. 19, 1797	Report and bill.	27	Recommitted.		
Hurlburt, Captain George, executors of.	Commutation pay and bounty land for revolutionary services.	9	2	Petition	511	Claims.						
Hurlburt, Captain George, executors of.	Commutation pay and bounty land for revolutionary services.	12	1	Petition	151	Claims.						
Hurlburt, Captain George, executors of.	Commutation pay and bounty land for revolutionary services.	14	1	Docs. and petition	261	Pens. & Rev. Clm's.				Discharged; laid on table.		
Hurlburt, Captain George, executors of.	Commutation pay and bounty land for revolutionary services.	14	2	Petition	58	Pens. & Rev. Cl'ms.	Dec. 23, 1816	Report		Laid on table.		
Hurlburt, Captain George, executors of.	Commutation pay and bounty land for revolutionary services.	18	1	Petition	197	Pens. & Rev. Cl'ms.	April 3, 1824	Adverse		Laid on table.		
Hurlburt, Captain George, heirs of.	Commutation pay and bounty land for revolutionary services.	23	1	Petition	39	Rev. Claims	60	Report and bill.	70	Passed	Passed, with amendment.	App'd June 30, 1834
Hurlburt, Captain George, heirs of.	Interest on commutation pay allowed last session.	23	2	Petition	108	Rev. Claims.						
Hurlburt, Captain George, heirs of.	Interest on commutation pay allowed by act June 30, 1834.	23	2	Senate bill	354	Rev. Claims	Feb. 19, 1835	With't amend.	S. 97	Referred to Committee Whole House.		
Hurlburt, Captain George, heirs of.	Interest on commutation pay allowed by act June 30, 1834.	24	1	Senate bill	744	Rev. Claims	May 10, 1836	With't amend.	S. 109	Passed		App'd July 2, 1836
Hulbert, John C	Release from imprisonment for an alleged violation of embargo act.	13	3	Senate bill	572	Ways and Means	Dec. 12, 1814	With't amend.	S. 66	Passed		App'd Jan. 2, 1815
Hulbert, Wright	Pension for disability incurred in the war of 1812.	25	2	Petition	268	Invalid Pensions	591	Report and bill.	578	Passed	With amend.	
Hulbert, Wright	Pension for disability incurred in the war of 1812.	25	3	Petition	90	Invalid Pensions	137	Report and bill	1004	Passed	Passed	App'd March 3, 1839
Hurley, Martin, heir of	Bounty land for revolutionary services.	9	1	Petition	330	Public Lands				Leave to withdraw.		
Hurlick, Thomas C	For a per diem compensation	26	2	Petition	124	Claims.						
Hurst, Henry	Reimbursement of advances made on public account.	17	1	Petition	26	Claims	Jan. 25, 1822	Adverse		Laid on table.		
Hurst, Henry	(See John Fischli.)	28	1		583							

List of private claims presented to the House of Representatives of the United States from the 1st to the 31st Congress, inclusive—Continued.

Names of claimants.	Nature or object of the claim.	Congress.	Session.	How brought before the House of Reps.	Page of journal.	To what committee of the House referred.	No. or date of the report.	Nature of the report.	No. of the bill.	How disposed of by the House of Reps.	How disposed of by the Senate.	Date of the act of Congress, and remarks.
Hurst, John	Compensation for services as revolutionary chaplain.	1	1	Petition	35					Referred to Secretary of War.		
Hurst, John	Compensation for services as revolutionary chaplain.	1	2	Rep. of Secretary War.	141					Laid on table.		
Hurtell, John	Patent for a certain tract of land	23	1	Senate bill	175	Public Lands	Jan. 16, 1834	With't amend.	S. 44	Passed		App'd Feb. 5, 1834
Huson, Cornelius	Pension and compensation for horse lost, war of 1812.	16	1	Petition	312	Pens. & Rev. Cl'ms.				Discharged; laid on table.		
Huson, Cornelius	Pension and compensation for horse lost, war of 1812.	16	2	Petition	58	Claims	Dec. 7, 1820	Adverse		Laid on table.		
Huson, Cornelius	Compensntion for horses and sleigh lost, war of 1812.	17	1	Petition	82	Claims.						
Huson, Cornelius	Pension for wounds, &c., in war of 1812.	17	1	Petition	82	Pens. & Rev. Cl'ms.	Mar. 5, 1822	Favorable	125	Passed	Passed	App'd April 26, 1832
Huson, Cornelius	Pension for wounds, &c., in war of 1812.	17	2	Petition	31	Pens. & Rev. Cl'ms.	Dec. 16, 1822	General bill	195	Passed.		
Huson, Cornelius	Pension for wounds, &c., in war of 1812.	18	2	Petition	36	Claims.						
Huson, Cornelius	Pension for wounds, &c., in war of 1812.	20	1	Resolution	159	Military Pensions				Discharged; laid on table.		
Huson, Cornelius	Increase of pension	21	1	House bill	130	Whole House	Feb. 13, 1830	Favorable	72	Passed	Passed	App'd May 20, 1830
Huson, Cornelius, widow of.	Bounty land for services in war of 1812.	30	2	Petition	385	Invalid Pensions	Feb. 13, 1849	Adverse		Laid on table.		
Hussey, Anthony	(See administrator of Joseph Roe.)	22	1		222							
Hussey, Isaac	Pension	14	1	Petition	64	Pens. & Rev. Cl'ms.	April 11, 1816	Report by bill.	171	Laid on table.		
Hussey, Samuel F.	(See John Bagley, *et al.*)	5	2		113							
Hussey, Tristram	Remission of duty on oil imported from Cape de Verds.	8	1	Petition	567	Com. and Manuf.	Mar. 1, 1804			Postponed to December 1, 1804.		
Hussey, Tristram	Remission of duty on oil imported from Cape de Verds.	9	1	Petition	272	Com. and Manuf.	Feb. 26, 1806			Referred to Committee Whole House.		
Hussey, Tristram	Remission of duty on oil imported from Cape de Verds.	11	1	Petition	20	Com. and Manuf.						
Hussey, Tristram	Remission of duty on oil imported from Cape de Verds.	11	2	Petition	116	Com. and Manuf.	Feb. 6, 1810	Report by bill.	104	Passed	Passed	App'd April 11, 1810
Hustler, Catharine	Pension for services as a nurse for twenty years in the United States army.	17	1	Petition	272	Pens. & Rev. Cl'ms.	Feb. 22, 1822	Adverse		Rejected.		
Huston, James	Pension	20	2	Petition	228	Military Pensions				Discharged; laid on table.		
Huston, James	Pension	21	1	Petition	59	Military Pensions				Discharged; laid on table.		
Huston, John	Pension for wounds, in revolutionary war.	13	2	Petition	175	Pensions	Mar. 14, 1814	Report not extant.		Referred to Committee Whole House.		
Huston, John	Pension for services as a revolutionary soldier.	17	1	Petition	220	Pens. & Rev. Cl'ms.				Referred to Secretary War.		
Huston, Nathan	Compensation for services as pay master, 1794.	6	1	Petition	551	Claims	Feb. 7, 1800	Adverse		Rejected.		
Huston, Peter	Pension for services as an officer, war of 1812.	25	3	Petition	129	Invalid Pensions				Discharged; laid on table.		
Huston, Peter	Pension for services as an officer, war of 1812.	26	1	Petition	938	Invalid Pensions.						
Huston, Peter	Pension for services as an officer, war of 1812.	26	2	Petition	77	Invalid Pensions	212	Adverse		Laid on table.		

List of private claims presented to the House of Representatives of the United States from the 1st to the 31st Congress, inclusive—Continued.

Names of claimants.	Nature or object of the claim.	Congress.	Session.	How brought before the House of Reps.	Page of journal.	To what committee of the House referred.	No. or date of the report.	Nature of the report.	No. of the bill.	How disposed of by the House of Reps.	How disposed of by the Senate.	Date of the act of Congress, and remarks.
Huston, Peter	Pension for services as an officer, war of 1812.	29	1	Petition	1102	Invalid Pensions.						
Hus'on, Peter	Pension for services as an officer, war of 1812.	29	2	Petition	100	Invalid Pensions.						
Huston or Houston, Robert	Compensation for supplies furnished, war of 1812.	18	2	Petition	55	Claims.						
Huston or Houston, Robert	Compensation for supplies furnished, war of 1812.	19	1	Petition	57	Claims.						
Huston or Houston, Robert	Compensation for supp ies furnished, war of 1812.	19	2	Petition	32	Claims	46	Report and bill.	379	Referred to Committee Whole House.		
Huston or Houston, Robert	Compensation for supplies furnished, war of 1812.	20	1	Resolution	205	Claims	137	Report and bill.	157	Passed	Passed	App'd May 26, 1828
Huston, William, representatives of.	Renewal of a lost land warrant	8	2	Petition	13	Claims.						
Huston, William, representatives of.	Bounty land for revolutionary services.	21	1	Petition	295	Rev. Claims.						
Huston, William, widow of.	Bounty land for revolutionary services.	13	1	Petition	18	Claims				Discharged.		
Huston, William, widow of.	Bounty land for revolutionary services.	13	2	Petition	205	Pens. & Rev. Cl'ms.	Jan. 13, 1814	Rep. and res.; leave to withdraw.		Adopted.		
Huston, William, widow of.	Bounty land for revolutionary services.	16	1	Petition	248	Public Lands				Laid on table.		
Hutchins, Alpheus	Bounty land for services, war of 1812.	15	2	Petition	128	Military Affairs.						
Hutchins, Alpheus	Bounty land and indemnity for money lost while a prisoner.	21	1	Petition	83	Claims	Jan. 6, 1830	Adverse		Laid on table.		
Hutchins, Alpheus	To be placed on the pension roll	24	1	Petition	201	Invalid Pensions	Feb. 18, 1836	Report by bill.	362	Passed	Passed	App'd June 28, 1836
Hutchins, Anthony, and others.	Confirmation of title to land in Louisiana.	25	3	Petition	133	Priv. Land Claims.						
Hutchins, Bennett, widow of.	Release from suretyship on a distillery bond.	14	2	Petition	128	Ways and Means	Feb. 4, 1817	Adverse		Rejected.		
Hutchins, Buckley	Arrears of pension	21	1	Petition	260	Military Pensions	May 4, 1830	Adverse		Laid on table.		
Hutchins, Buckley	Arrears and increase of pension	31	1	Petition	653	Rev. Pensions	368	Adverse		Laid on table.		
Hutchings, Eliakim W	Pension for disability incurred in war of 1812.	27	2	Petition	799	Invalid Pensions	816	Adverse		Laid on table.		
Hutchings, Eliakim W	Pension for disability incurred in war of 1812.	27	3	Petition	346	Invalid Pensions.						
Hutchins, Hezekiah	Pension	15	2	Petition	153	Rev. Pensions	Jan. 14, 1819	Adverse		Rejected.		
Hutchins, Hezekiah	Pension	16	1	Petition	271	Rev. Pensions	April 22, 1820	Adverse		Laid on table.		
Hutchins or Huchens, Hezekiah.	Increase of pension	17	1	Petition	280	Pens. & Rev. Cl'ms.				Referred to Committee Whole House.		
Hutchins, James	Invalid pension	3	2	Rep. of Secretary War.	278	Claims	March 3, 1795			Discharged; laid on table.		
Hu'chins, James	Invalid pension	4	1	Rep. of Secretary War.	445	Claims	March 4, 1796	Joint resoluton to refer Sec. War.	J. R. 16	Passed	Passed	App'd April 17, 1796
Hutchins, John	Right of pre-emption	27	3	Senate bill	413	Public Lands	Feb. 28, 1843	With't amend.	S. 100	Laid on table.		
Hutchins, John	Right of pre-emption	29	1	Memorial	147	Public Lands.						
Hutchins, Jonathan	Pension and bounty land for revolutionary services.	31	1	Petition	595	Rev. Pensions	256	Adverse		Laid on table.		
Hutchins, Levi	Pension	20	1	Petition	192	Military Pensions	April 29, 1828	Report by bill.	283	Passed.		
Hutchins, Levi	Pension	20	2	Petition	55	Military Pensions	Dec. 12, 1828	General bill	311	Passed	Laid on table.	

List of private claims presented to the House of Representatives of the United States from the 1st to the 31st Congress, inclusive—Continued.

Names of claimants.	Nature or object of the claim.	Congress.	Session.	How brought before the House of Reps.	Page of journal.	To what committee of the House referred.	No. or date of the report.	Nature of the report.	No. of the bill.	How disposed of by the House of Reps.	How disposed of by the Senate.	Date of the act of Congress, and remarks.
Hutchins, Levi	Pension	21	1	Petition	48	Military Pensions	....	....	......	Discharged; laid on table.		
Hutchins, Levi	Pension	21	1	House bill	130	Whole House	Feb. 13, 1830	With't amend.	72	Passed	Passed	App'd May 20, 1830
Hutchins, Moses	Pensions	21	1	Petition	120	Military Pensions	....	....	......	Discharged; laid on table.		
Hutchins, Moses	Pensions	21	2	Petition	375	Military Pensions.						
Hutchins, Moses	Pensions	30	1	Petition	204	Rev. Pensions.						
Hutchins, Thatcher	Bounty on fishing schr. Calypso	27	1	Petition	95	Commerce.						
Hutchins, Thomas, heir of.	Compensation for losses sustained and services rendered as Geographer during revolutionary war.	5	2	Memorial	153	Claims	....	....	......	Discharged; leave to withdraw.		
Hutchinson, Henry, representatives of.	For benefit of bounty land warrant.	31	1	Petition	277	Priv. Land Claims.	83	Report and bill.	103	Passed.		
Hutchinson, Israel	Pension	22	1	Resolution	136	Rev. Pensions	367	General bill	462	Passed	Indef. postp'd.	
Hutchinson, Israel P.	Compensation for services and expenses as consul at Lisbon.	24	2	Memorial	75	Foreign Affairs	115	Report and bill.	849	Referred to Committee Whole House.		
Hutchinson, Israel P.	Compensation for services and expenses as consul at Lisbon.	25	2	Memorial	39	Foreign Affairs	749	Adverse	......	Laid on table.		
Hutchinson, Israel P.	Compensation for services and expenses as consul at Lisbon.	27	2	Memorial	373	Foreign Affairs.						
Hutchinson, Israel P.	Compensation for services and expenses as consul at Lisbon.	28	1	Memorial	337	Foreign Affairs.						
Hutchinson, Israel P.	Compensation for services and expenses as consul at Lisbon.	28	1	Senate bill	980	Foreign Affairs	....	....	106			
Hutchinson, Israel P.	Compensation for services and expenses as consul at Lisbon.	28	2	Appropriat'n bill.	....	....	....	....	......	....	....	App'd March 3, 1845
Hutchinson, James A.	(See representatives of Lewis Clarke *et al.*)	18	2	....	253							
Hutchinson, J. Pemberton.	Payment for diplomatic services	28	2	....	....	....	....	....	......	....	....	Statutes at Large, vol. 5, page 763.
Hutchinson, John	Additional compensation as postmaster, Tennessee.	16	1	Petition	213	P. O. & P. Roads.	Mar. 3, 1820	Adverse	......	Laid on table.		
Hutchinson, John	To be restored to pension roll	17	1	Petition	361	Whole House.						
Hutchinson, John	Increase of pension	29	1	Petition	984	Rev. Pensions.						
Hutchinson, John	Increase of pension	29	2	Petition	68	Rev. Pensions.						
Hutchinson, Luther	Compensation for a horse lost in the war of 1812.	17	1	Petition	320	Claims	April 3, 1822	Adverse	......	Laid on table.		
Hutchinson, Robert and Thomas.	Drawback, denied on account of informality.	14	1	Petition	491	Com. and Manuf.						
Hutchinson, Robert and Thomas.	Drawback, denied on account of informality.	14	2	Petition	185	Com. and Manuf.						
Hutchinson, Robert and Thomas.	Drawback, denied on account of informality.	15	1	Petition	179	Com. and Manuf.	Mar. 27, 1818	Adverse	......	Rejected.		
Hutchinson, Robert and Thomas.	Drawback, denied on account of informality.	26	1	Petition	292	Commerce	30	Report and bill	49	Passed	Passed	App'd July 20, 1840
Hutchinson, Samuel	Pension for revolutionary services.	25	2	Resolution	688	Rev. Pensions.						
Hutchinson, Samuel	Pension for revolutionary services.	25	3	Resolution	88	Rev. Pensions.						
Hutchinson, Samuel	Pension for revolutionary services.	26	1	Resolution	286	Rev. Pensions	349	Report and bill.	328	Ref'd to Com. W. H.		
Hutchinson, Samuel	Pension for revolutionary services.	27	2	Resolution	239	Rev. Pensions	291	Report and bill.	259	Passed	Indef. postp'd.	
Hutchinson, Samuel	Pension for revolutionary services.	30	1	Petition	116	Rev. Pensions	296	Adverse	......	Laid on table.		
Hutchinson, Thos., heir of.	Pension for revolutionary services.	25	2	Petition	547	Rev. Pensions	983	Report and bill	843	Referred to Committee Whole House.		
Hutchinson, Thos., heir of.	Pension for revolutionary services.	25	3	House bill	432	Whole House	....	....	843	Passed	Adverse report.	

List of private claims presented to the House of Representatives of the United States from the 1st to the 31st Congress, inclusive—**Continued.**

Names of claimants.	Nature or object of the claim.	Congress.	Session.	How brought before the House of Reps.	Page of journal.	To what committee of the House referred.	No. or date of the report.	Nature of the report.	No. of the bill.	How disposed of by the House of Reps.	How disposed of by the Senate.	Date of the act of Congress, and remarks.
Hutchinson, Thos., heir of.	Pension for revolutionary services.	26	1	Petition	171	Rev. Pensions	117	Report and bill	127	Referred to Committee Whole House.		
Hutchinson, Thos., heir of.	Pension for revolutionary services.	26	2	House bill	194	Whole House			127			
Hutchinson, Thos., heir of.	Pension for revolutionary services.	27	2	Petition	58	Rev. Pensions	19	Report and bill.	60	Passed.		
Hutchinson, Thos., heir of.	Pension for revolutionary services.	27	3	Petition	43	Rev. Pensions.				Laid on table.		
Hutchinson, Thos., heir of.	Pension for revolutionary services.	28	1	Petition	109	Rev. Pensions.	50	Report and bill.	73	Passed	Indef. postp'd.	
Hutchinson, Thos., heir of.	Pension for revolutionary services.	28	2	Petition	59	Rev. Pensions.						
Hutchinson, Thos., heir of.	Pension for revolutionary services.	29	1	Petition	91	Claims	15	Report and bill	29	Ref'd to Com W. H		
Hutchinson, Thos., heir of.	Pension for revolutionary services.	30	1	Senate bill	683	Rev. Pensions	July 19, 1848	With't amend.	S. 92	Laid on table.		
Hutchinson, Thos., heir of.	Pension for revolutionary services.	31	2	Senate bill	191				S. 95			
Hutchinson, Thompson	(See Thomas Hutchinson, heir of.)	25	2		547							
Hutchinson, Titus	Consul fees in the case of Holgate & McDonough.	19	1	Resolution	461	Ways and Means	April 26, 1826	Report by bill.	227	Passed.		
Hutchinson, Titus	Consul fees in the case of Holgate & McDonough.	19	2	Resolution	128	Ways and Means.						
Hutchinson, William	Payment of a certificate of public debt.	19	1	Petition	291	Rev. Claims	Mar. 30, 1826	Adverse		Laid on table.		
Hutchinson, William	Payment of a certificate of public debt.	22	1	Petition	557	Rev. Claims	April 11, 1832	Adverse		Laid on table.		
Hutchinson, William	Compensation for services as a spy, war of 1812.	31	1	Petition	870	Military Affairs				Discharged; laid on table.		
Hutinack, Francis	Arrears of revolutionary pension	28	1	Petition	124	Rev. Pensions				Disch'd; laid on table.		
Hutinack, Francis	Arrears of revolutionary pension	28	2	Petition	103	Rev. Pensions.						
Hutinack, Francis	Arrears of revolutionary pension	29	1	Petition	337	Rev. Pensions	464	Report and bill.	341	Referred to Committee Whole House.		
Hutinack, Francis	Arrears of revolutionary pension	30	1	Petition	69	Rev. Pensions	337	Report and bill.	315	Passed.		
Hutinack, Francis	Arrears of revolutionary pension	31	1	Petition	533	Rev. Pensions	Aug. 1, 1850	Adverse		Laid on table.		
Huttleston, Henry	Indemnity for property confiscated at Naples.	20	1	Memorial	341	Foreign Affairs	265	Adverse		Discharged; laid on table.		
Hutton, James	Pension	14	1	Petition	41	Pens. & Rev. Cl'ms.	Mar. 13, 1816	Adverse		Rejected.		
Hutton, James	Relief in consideration of the erroneous sale of his bounty land.	17	2	Petition	118	Pens. & Rev. Cl'ms.						
Huyck, James	Pension	20	2	Petition	175	Military Pensions				Discharged; laid on table.		
Hyams, Henry M.	(See Richard King, *et al*)	27	2		459							
Hyatt, Lewis	(See Samuel Fisk)	26	1		626							
Hyde, Charles	Compensation for services as judge advocate.	6	2	Petition	782	Claims				Discharged; postponed to next session.		
Hyde, Charles	Compensation for services as judge advocate.	7	1	Petition	19	Claims	April 3, 1802			Postponed.		
Hyde, Charles	Compensation for services as judge advocate.	7	2	Petition	248	Claims	Dec. 29, 1802	Favorable: bill ordered.	73	Passed	Passed with amendment.	App'd Jan. 14, 1803
Hyde, Charles	Compensation for services and expenses as an officer in United States army.	7	2	Petition	336	Claims	Feb. 15, 1803	Adverse		Laid on table.		
Hyde, Charles	Compensation for services and expenses as an officer in United States army.	8	1	Petition	660	Claims.						
Hyde, Charles	Compensation for services and expenses as an officer in United States army.	8	2	Petition	12	Claims.						
Hyde, Edward	Right of pre-emption and confirmation of a survey of lands.	24	2	Petition	107	Priv. Land Claims.						

List of private claims presented to the House of Representatives of the United States from the 1st to the 31st Congress, inclusive—Continued.

Names of claimants.	Nature or object of the claim.	Congress.	Session.	How brought before the House of Reps.	Page of journal.	To what committee of the House referred.	No. or date of the report	Nature of the report.	No. of the bill.	How disposed of by the House of Reps.	How disposed of by the Senate.	Date of the act of Congress, and remarks.
Hyde, Elias, widow of....	Indemnity for loss of husband, war of 1812.	24	1	Petition	474	Claims	May 17, 1836	Favorable	639	Referred to Committee Whole House.		
Hyde, Elias, widow of....	Pension for services	25	2	Petition	36	Claims	45	Favorable	57	Passed	Passed	App'd March 28, 1838
Hyde, Jedediah	Pension for revolutionary services.	10	1	House bill	232	Whole House.....	April 19, 1808	Favorable	78	Passed	Passed	App'd April 25, 1808
Hyde, James	Release from imprisonm'nt as surety for D. Waterman.	17	2	Petition	185	P. Of. & P. Roads.	Feb. 6, 1823	Report by bill.	276	Passed.		
Hyde, Jane Ann.........	(See Udney Hay, heirs and representatives of.)	19	1	....	251							
Hyde, John E..........	Remission of penalty for importing British goods, war of 1812.	14	1	Petition	540	Ways and Means.						
Hyde, Russell B........	Pension for military services U. S. army.	27	2	Resolution	453	Invalid Pensions.						
Hyde, Russell B........	Pension for military services U. S. army.	27	3	Resolution	72	Invalid Pensions.						
Hyde, Russell B........	Pension for military services U. S. army.	28	1	Resolution	109	Invalid Pensions.						
Hyden, Daniel..........	Pension for revolutionary services as a soldier.	15	1	Resolution	229	Pens. & Rev. Cl'ms						
Hyland, Mary...........	(See William T. Abbot.)........	15	2	....	172							
Hyland, William........	(See William Highland.)	22	1	....	171							
Hyler, William.........	Pension for injuries received on board U. S. ship Constitution while repairing, 1803.	11	3	Petition	454	Claims.						
Hynum, James, heirs of..	Confirmation of title to land under a Spanish grant.	12	1	Petition	14	Public Lands.						
Hynum, James, heirs of..	Confirmation of title to land under a Spanish grant.	12	2	Petition	663	Public Lands.						
Hynum, James, heirs of..	Confirmation of title to land under a Spanish grant.	13	3	Petition	561	Public Lands	Dec. 3, 1814	Report and bill.	234	Passed	Passed	App'd March 1, 1815
Hynum, James, (Margaret) widow of.	Confirmation of title to land in Mississippi Territory.	13	2	Petition	414	....	....	....	......	Laid on table.		
Hynum, James, (Margaret) widow of.	Confirmation of title to land in Mississippi Territory.	13	3	Petition	454	Public Lands.						
Hyslop, Robert..........	(See John Paul Jones, attorney for the heirs of.)	5	2	....	81							
Iardella, Francis.......	(See Francis Jardella)..........	20	1	....	342							
Icard, Joseph, administrator of.	Payment of award in case of ship Cardoz.	28	1	Memorial	853	Judiciary.........	Jan. 7, 1844	Favorable	404	Referred to Committee Whole House.		
Icard, Joseph, administrator of.	Payment of award in case of ship Cardez.	28	2	House bill	344	Whole House.....	Feb. 7, 1845	With't amend.	404	Passed	Passed	App'd March 3, 1845
Iddings, William........	Pension for revolutionary services.	21	1	Petition	319	Military Pensions.						
Iddings, William........	Pension for revolutionary services.	21	2	Resolution	48	Military Pensions.						
Iddings, William........	Pension for revolutionary services.	22	1	Petition	45	Rev. Pensions	....	....	......	Discharged; laid on table.		

List of private claims presented to the House of Representatives of the United States from the 1st to the 31st Congress, inclusive—Continued.

Names of claimants.	Nature or object of the claim.	Congress.	Session.	How brought before the House of Reps.	Page of journal.	To what committee of the House referred.	No. or date of the report.	Nature of the report.	No. of the bill.	How disposed of by the House of Reps.	How disposed of by the Senate.	Date of the act of Congress, and remarks.
Ide, Cort, & Co.	Reimbursement of duties on damaged merchandise.	31	1	Petition	788	Commerce.						
Idler, Jacob	(See Jacob Ritter, jr., *et al*.)	13	3		693							
Idler, Jacob	Enforcement of a claim against Venezuela.	29	2	Memorial	142	Foreign Affairs				Discharged; referred to Sec. of State.		
Idler, Jacob	Enforcement of a claim against Venezuela.	30	1	Memorial	461	Foreign Affairs.						
Ilgenfritz, Christain	Confirmation of title to land	9	2	Petition	489	Public Lands.						
Illinois, Chicago, clerks in post office.	Increase of salaries	31	2	Petition	344	P. Of. and P. Roads.						
Illinois, mayor and common council of Chicago.	Arrears due for harbor improvements.	31	1	Memorial	961	Commerce.						
Illinois, churches, Methodist, at Shiloe.	Pre emption to land on which a church has been erected.	13	2	Petition	313	Public Lands	Mar. 22, 1814	Adverse		Rejected.		
Illinois, inhabitants of Bond county.	Pre-emption to lands they reside upon.	22	1	Petition	440	Public Lands.						
Illinois, inhabitants of Clark county.	Pre-emption to lands they reside upon.	21	1	Petition	173	Whole House						See act Mar. 31, 1830
Illinois, inhabitants of Cook county.	Pre emption to lands they reside upon.	23	1	Petition	387	Public Lands.						
Illinois, inhabitants of Crawford county.	Pre-emption to lands they reside upon.	15	2	Petition	226	Public Lands				Discharged; laid on table.		
Illinois, inhabitants of Crawford county.	Pre emption to lands they reside upon.	16	1	Petition	126	Public Lands				Discharged; laid on table.		See act Mar. 30, 1820
Illinois, inhabitants of Edgar county.	Relinquishment of certain lands and to apply the payments made on them to other lands.	20	1	Petition	246	Public Lands				Discharged; laid on table.		
Illinois, inhabitants of Gallatin county.	Indemnity for sixteenth section withheld.	29	1	Petition	100	Public Lands.						
Illinois, inhabitants of Kendall county.	Indemnity for losses in Black Hawk war.	28	1	Petition	417	Claims.						
Illinois, inhabitants of Kendall county.	Indemnity for losses in Black Hawk war.	28	2	Petition	89	Claims.						
Illinois, inhabitants of Kendall county.	Indemnity for losses in Black Hawk war.	29	1	Petition	68	Claims	3	Adverse		Laid on table.		
Illinois, inhabitants of La Salle county.	Pre emption to lands they reside upon.	23	1	Petition	387	Public Lands.						
Illinois, inhabitants of La Salle county.	Indemnity for Indian depredations.	24	1	Petition	705	Claims	579	Adverse		Laid on table.		
Illinois, inhabitants of Madison county.	Confirmation of their titles to land.	14	2	Petition	137	Public Lands.						
Illinois, inhabitants of Ogle county.	Indemnity for losses in Black Hawk war.	28	1	Petition	571	Indian Affairs.						
Illinois, inhabitants of Putnam county.	Pre-emption to lands they reside upon.	22	1	Petition	106	Public Lands.						
Illinois, inhabitants of Putnam county.	Pre emption to lands they reside upon.	22	2	Petition	266	Public Lands.						
Illinois, inhabitants of Putnam county.	Pre-emption to lands they reside upon.	23	1	Petition	387	Public Lands.						
Illinois, inhabitants of Tazewell county.	Pre-emption to lands they reside upon.	23	1	Petition	67	Public Lands	Dec. 31, 1833	Favorable	104	Referred to Committee Whole House.		See act June 9, 1834
Illinois, inhabitants of White county.	Relief in completing land payments.	20	1	Petition	168	Public Lands.						See act May 23, 1828

List of private claims presented to the House of Representatives of the United States from the 1st to the 31st Congress, inclusive—Continued.

Names of claimants.	Nature or object of the claim.	Congress.	Session.	How brought before the House of Reps.	Page of journal.	To what committee of the House referred.	No. or date of the report.	Nature of the report.	No. of the bill.	How disposed of by the House of Reps.	How disposed of by the Senate.	Date of the act of Congress, and remarks.
Illinois, inhabitants of the State of.	Pre-emption to lands they reside upon.	14	1	Petition	60	Public Lands.						
Illinois, inhabitants of the State of.	Extension of time for making land payments.	16	1	Petition	221	Public Lands	....	....	......	....	....	See act Mar. 30, 1820
Illinois, inhabitants of the State of.	Relinquishment of lands not paid for.	16	2	Petition	66	Public Lands.						
Illinois, inhabitants of the frontier settlements	Indemnity for property destroyed by Indians.	23	2	Petition	200	Claims.						
Illinois, inhabitants of the frontier settlements.	Indemnity for property destroyed by Indians.	24	1	Petition	50	Claims	580	Adverse	......	Laid on table.		
Illinois, inhabitants of Peoria	Indemnity for property destroyed by United States troops.	13	2	Petition	280	Claims	Feb. 12, 1814	Not found	......	Laid on table.		
Illinois, inhabitants of Peoria	Indemnity for property destroyed by United States troops.	15	1	Petition	261	Claims	....	....	......	Discharged; laid on table.		
Illinois, inhabitants of Peoria	Indemnity for property destroyed by United States troops.	16	1	Senate bill	505	Priv. Land Claims.	May 4, 1820	With't amend.	S. 117	Passed	Passed	App'd May 18, 1820
Illinois, inhabitants of Peoria	Confirmation of title to their village lots.	17	1	Petition	101	Public Lands	April 12, 1822	Favorable	167	Referred to Committee Whole House.		
Illinois, inhabitants of Peoria	Confirmation of title to their village lots.	17	2	House bill	77	....	....	....	167	Passed	Passed	App'd March 3, 1823
Illinois, inhabitants of Prairie du Chien.	Confirmation of title to their lands	14	2	Petition	276	Public Lands	....	....	......	Discharged; laid on table.		
Illinois, inhabitants of Prairie du Chien.	Confirmation of title to their lands	15	1	Petition	36	Public Lands	Feb. 25, 1818	Favorable	107	Referred to Committee Whole House.		
Illinois, inhabitants of Prairie du Chien.	Confirmation of title to their lands	16	1	Petition	36	Public Lands.						
Illinois, inhab'ants of Shawneetown.	Remission of payment of purchase money of town lots.	14	2	Petition	102	Public Lands	Dec. 31, 1816	Adverse	......	Rejected.		
Illinois, inhab'ants of Shawneetown.	Remission of payment of purchase money of town lots.	15	2	Petition	271	Public Lands	....	....	......	Discharged; laid on table.		
Illinois, inhab'ants of Shawneetown.	Remission of payment of purchase money of town lots.	16	1	Petition	73	Public Lands	Dec. 23, 1819	Favorable	18	Rejected.		
Illinois, inhab'ants of Shawneetown.	Remission of payment of purchase money of town lots.	17	1	Senate bill	199	Public Lands	Feb. 7, 1822	With't amend.	S. 24	Referred to Committee Whole House.		
Illinois, inhab'ants of Shawneetown.	Remission of payment of purchase money of town lots.	17	2	Petition	122	Public Lands	Jan. 14, 1823	Favorable	229	Passed	Passed, with amendment.	App'd March 3, 1823
Illinois, legislature of	Confirmation of title to seat of government.	16	2	Memorial	120	Public Lands	Jan. 24, 1821	Favorable	220	Passed	Passed	App'd March 2, 1821
Illinois, legislature of	Compensation to inhabitants on Fever river for military services.	20	2	Petition	320	Public Lands.						
Illinois, legislature of	Compensation to inhabitants on Fever river for military services.	21	1	Petition	76	Claims.						
Illinois, staff of the governor of.	For pay of majors of infantry for services in the war of 1812.	14	2	Resolution	340	Military Affairs	Feb. 7, 1817	Favorable; bill	113	Passed	Passed	App'd March 3, 1817
Illinois & Michigan militia.	Compensation for military services on frontier.	20	1	Resolution	89	Ways and Means	Feb. 18, 1828	As amendm't to military approp'tion bill	142	Passed	Passed	App'd Mar. 21, 1828
Illinois & Michigan militia.	Compensation for horses lost on frontier.	22	2	Senate bill	262	Claims	83	With amends.	S. 20	Passed	Passed	App'd Feb. 19, 1833
Illinois volunteers, (Captain Morgan's company.)	Compensation for military services at Fort Dearborn.	20	2	Resolution	201	Ways and Means	Feb. 20, 1829	As amendm't to military approp'tion bill	388	Passed	Passed	App'd March 2, 1829

List of private claims presented to the House of Representatives of the United States from the 1st to the 31st Congress, inclusive—Continued.

Names of claimants.	Nature or object of the claim.	Congress.	Session.	How brought before the House of Reps.	Page of journal.	To what committee of the House referred.	No. or date of the report.	Nature of the report.	No. of the bill.	How disposed of by the House of Reps.	How disposed of by the Senate.	Date of the act of Congress, and remarks.
Illinois volunteers, (Captain Morgan's company.	Compensation for military services on frontier.	22	1	Resolution	735	Ways and Means						Provided for in act of April 5, 1832.
Illinois volunteers, (Pierce's company.)	Compensation for military services on frontier.	24	1	Resolution	267	Claims.						
Illinois volunteers, (Siglor's company.)	Compensation for military services on frontier.	24	1	Senate bill	810	Claims	May 17, 1836	With't amend.	S. 131	Passed	Passed	App'd July 2, 1836
Illinois and Ouabache Land Companies.	Confirmation of Indian titles to land.	7	1	Memorial	132	Select				Discharged.		
Illinois and Ouabache Land Companies.	Confirmation of Indian titles to land.	8	1	Memorial	421	Select	Feb. 14, 1804	Adverse		Rejected.		
Illinois and Wabash Land Companies.	(See Robert G. Harper, *et al.*)	11	3		458							
Ilsley, Henry	(See Robert and Henry Ilsley)	8	1		561							
Ilsley, Henry	(See Caleb S. Carter, *et al.*)	26	1		710							
Ilsley, Isaac	Reimbursement of money erroneously paid as collector of customs.	26	1	Petition	201	Judiciary				Discharged; laid on table.		
Ilsley, Isaac	Reimbursement of money erroneously paid as collector of customs.	27	1	Petition	102	Judiciary.						
Ilsley, Isaac	Reimbursement of money erroneously paid as collector of customs.	27	2	Petition	63	Judiciary.						
Ilsley, Robert and Henry	Remission of duty on rum	8	1	Petition	561	Ways and Means	Feb. 3, 1804	Adverse		Leave to withdraw.		
Imbeau, Baptiste	Confirmation of land title under Quapaw treaty.	19	2	Petition	137	Public Lands	60	Favorable	401	Laid on table.		
Imbeau, Francois	Confirmation of land title under Quapaw treaty.	19	2	Petition	137	Public Lands	66	Favorable	401	Laid on table.		
Imboden, Frederick	To refund money paid for distillery license.	19	1	Petition	152	Ways and Means	Jan. 18, 1826	Adverse		Laid on table.		
Imlay, Robert	(See Joseph Clark)	13	2		305							
Imlay, William	Increase of salary as loan commissioner.	4	2	Petition	630	Select.						
Imlay, William	Increase of salary as loan commissioner.	5	2	Senate bill	114	Claims	Dec. 26, 1797	With't amend.	9	Passed	Passed	App'd May 14, 1798
Immel, John	Pension	20	2	Petition	175	Military Pensions				Discharged; laid on table.		
Imponah & Cunneubba	Reservation of land under Choctaw treaty.	21	1	Documents	426	Indian Affairs.						
Imponah & Cunneubba	Reservation of land under Choctaw treaty.	26	1	Documents	586	Indian Affairs.						
Incox, Jacob	Pension for revolutionary services.	16	1	Petition	137	Rev. Pensions	Jan. 14, 1820	Adverse		Laid on table.		
Indiana, Clark county, inhabitants of.	Indemnity for property lost at Tippecanoe.	12	2	Petition	609	Claims.						
Indiana, Clark county, inhabitants of.	Compensation for military services.	13	3	Petition	616	Claims				Discharged.		
Indiana, Clark county, inhabitants of.	Bounty land for military services.	16	1	Petition	183	Public Lands.				Discharged; laid on table.		
Indiana, Clark county, inhabitants of.	Bounty land for military services.	17	1	Petition	83	Public Lands				Discharged; laid on table.		
Indiana, Harrison county, inhabitants of.	Additional indemnity for losses in Indian wars.	12	2	Petition	579	Claims.						
Indiana, Harrison county, inhabitants of.	Compensation for military services.	12	2	Petition	598	Claims.						
Indiana, Knox county, inhabitants of.	Indemnity for property destroyed by United States troops.	12	2	Petition	609	Select				Discharged; laid on table.		

List of private claims presented to the House of Representatives of the United States from the 1st to the 31st Congress, inclusive—Continued.

Names of claimants.	Nature or object of the claim.	Congress.	Session.	How brought before the House of Reps.	Page of journal.	To what committee of the House referred.	No. or date of the report.	Nature of the report.	No. of the bill.	How disposed of by the House of Reps.	How disposed of by the Senate.	Date of the act of Congress, and remarks.
2—22 Indiana, Knox county, inhabitants of.	Indemnity for property destroyed by United States troops.	13	2	Petition	172	Claims	9	Adverse	......	Referred to Committee Whole House.		
Indiana, Knox county, inhabitants of.	Indemnity for property destroyed by United States troops.	14	2	Petition	276	Select	....	....	......	Discharged; laid on table.		
Indiana, Knox, Randolph, and St. Clair counties, inhabitants of.	Confirmation of title to land	8	1	Petition	512	Select	....	....	......	Discharged.		
Indiana, Randolph county, inhabitants of.	Right of pre-emption	10	2	Petition	463	Public Lands.						
Indiana, Randolph and St. Clair counties, inhabitants of.	Right of pre-emption	8	2	Memorial	51	Select.						
Indiana, Randolph and St. Clair counties, inhabitants of.	Right of pre-emption	9	1	Memorial	275	Public Lands.						
Indiana, Randolph and St. Clair counties, inhabitants of.	Right of pre-emption	10	2	Petition	458	Public Lands.						
Indiana, Switzerland county, inhabitants of.	Extension of time for completing land payments.	16	2	Petition	22	Public Lands	....	....	......	Discharged; laid on table.		
Indiana, Switzerland county, inhabitants of.	Remission of interest on land payments.	16	2	Petition	91	Public Lands	....	....	......	Discharged; laid on table.		
Indiana, Warren and Tippecanoe counties, inhabitants of.	Right of pre-emption	22	1	Petition	227	Public Lands.						
Indiana, governor, judges, &c., of.	Compensation for extra services	9	1	Petition	209	Claims	Feb. 11, 1806	Favorable	101	Passed.	Passed, with amendment.	
Indiana, governor, judges, &c., of.	Compensation for extra services	9	2	House bill	556	Whole House	Mar. 3, 1807	With amend.	189	Passed	Passed	App'd March 3, 1807
Indiana, governor, judges, &c., of.	Compensation for extra services	19	1	Resolution	200	Judiciary.						
Indiana, inhabitants of the State of.	Pre-emption to lands they reside upon.	22	1	Petition	47	Public Lands	....	....	......	....	....	See act Jan. 3, 1832
Indiana, inhabitants of the State of.	Extension of time to complete land payments.	12	2	Petition	575	Whole House.						
Indiana, inhabitants of the State of.	Confirmation of title to their land	13	3	Petition	461	Public Lands	....	....	......	Discharged.		
Indiana, inhabitants of the State of.	Pre-emption to lands they reside upon.	13	2	Petition	294	Public Lands	Feb. 19, 1814	Favorable	130	Referred to Committee Whole House.		
Indiana, inhabitants of the State of.	Pre-emption to lands they reside upon.	14	1	Petition	114	Public Lands.						
Indiana, inhabitants of the State of.	Pre-emption to lands they reside upon.	26	1	Petition	697	Public Lands.						
Indiana, inhabitants of congressional district No. 11.	Pre-emption to lands they reside upon.	23	1	Petition	196	Public Lands.						
Indiana, inhabit's of Driftwood Settlement.	Extension of time to complete land payments.	12	2	Petition	672	Public Lands.						
Indiana, inhabitants of Fort Massac.	Confirmation of land titles	9	1	Petition	264	Public Lands.						
Indiana, inhabitants of Miama reservation.	Pre-emption to lands they reside upon.	26	1	Petition	363	Public Lands.						
Indiana, inhabitants of Miama reservation.	Pre-emption to lands they reside upon.	27	2	Petition	1239	Public Lands.						

List of private claims presented to the House of Representatives of the United States from the 1st to the 31st Congress, inclusive—Continued.

Names of claimants.	Nature or object of the claim.	Congress.	Session.	How brought before the House of Reps.	Page of journal.	To what committee of the House referred.	No. or date of the report.	Nature of the report.	No. of the bill.	How disposed of by the House of Reps.	How disposed of by the Senate.	Date of the act of Congress, and remarks.
Indiana, inhabitants of Vincennes.	Extension of time to prove land title.	9	1	Petition	303	Public Lands.						
Indiana, inhabitants of Vincennes.	Indemnity for property destroyed by Kentucky militia.	13	1	Petition	33	Claims				Discharged.		
Indiana, inhabitants of Vincennes.	Indemnity for property destroyed by Kentucky militia.	13	2	Petition	170	Claims	9	Adverse		Referred to Committee Whole House.		
Indiana, legislature of	Compensation to militia	13	2	Petition	189	Select	70	Legislation unnecessary.		Leave to withdraw.		
Indiana, legislature of	Compensation to militia	13	3	Petition	463					Referred to Sec. War.		
Indiana, legislature of	Compensation to rangers for a horse lost.	23	1	Memorial	383	Claims.						
Indiana, legislature of	Compensation to rangers for a horse lost.	24	1	Resolution	430	Claims						Sec act Mar. 9, 1836
Indiana, legislature of	Compensation to adjutant general raising volnnteers.	30	1	Resolution	458	Military Affairs				Discharged; laid on table.		
Indiana, legislature of	Payment of 3 per cent on land sales.	15	1	Senate bill	124	Public Lands	Jan. 16, 1818	With't amend.	S. 7	Passed	Passed	App'd April 11, 1818
Indiana militia, (3 companies of.)	Compensation for services	25	2	Petition	274	Claims	465	Favorable	469	Referred to Committee Whole House.		
Indiana militia, (3 companies of.)	Compensation for services	25	3	Rep't Committee Whole House.	431				469	Passed	Passed, with amendment.	App'd March 3, 1839
Indiana rangers, Biggar's company of.	Compensation for military services.	14	1	Petition	368	Claims.						
Indiana rangers, Biggar's company of.	Compensation for military services.	15	1	Petition	72	Military Affairs	Feb. 10, 1818	General bill	79	Passed	Postponed.	
Indiana, rangers, Biggar's company of.	Compensation for military services.	16	1	Memorial	183	Military Affairs.						
Indianna rangers, Biggar's company of.	Compensation for military services.	17	2	Petition	120	Military Affairs	Jan. 23, 1823	Adverse		Rejected.		
Indiana rangers, Biggar's company of.	Compensation for military services.	18	1	Petition	33	Military Affairs	Jan. 23, 1824	Adverse		Laid on table.		
Indiana rangers, Biggar's company of.	Compensation for military services.	19	1	Senate bill	383	Military Affairs	Mar. 31, 1826	With't amend.	S. 46	Passed	Concurred in.	App'd May 20, 1826
Indiana rangers, Biggar's company of.	Compensation for horses lost in public service.	22	1	Resolution	338	Claims.						
Indiana rangers, Biggar's company of.	Compensation for horses lost in public service.	23	1	Petition	253	Claims.						
Indiana, registers and receivers of Indianopolis.	Compensation for locating land warrants.	31	2	Petition	58, 266	Public Lands.						
Indiana, registers and receivers of Jeffersonville.	Compensation for locating land warrants.	31	2	Petition	122	Public Lands.						
Indiana, registers and receivers of Kaskaskia.	Compensation for locating land warrants.	31	1	Petition	448	Public Lands.						
Indiana, registers and receivers of Quincy.	Compensation for locating land warrants.	31	1	Petition	95	Public Lands.						
Indiana, registers and receivers of Springfield.	Compensation for locating land warrants.	31	1	Petition	448	Public Lands.						
Indiana, registers and receivers of Springfield.	Compensation for locating land warrants.	31	2	Petition	115	Public Lands.						
Indiana, registers and receivers of Vandalia.	Release from liability for money stolen.	18	1	Resolution	58					Laid on table.		
				Rep. of Secretary Treasury.	170	Public Lands	66	Adverse		Laid on table.		

List of private claims presented to the House of Representatives of the United States from the 1st to the 31st Congress, inclusive—Continued.

Names of claimants.	Nature or object of the claim.	Congress.	Session.	How brought before the House of Reps.	Page of journal.	To what committee of the House referred.	No. or date of the report.	Nature of the report.	No. of the bill.	How disposed of by the House of Reps.	How disposed of by the Senate.	Date of the act of Congress, and remarks.
Indiana, registers and receivers of Vandalia.	Compensation for locating land warrants.	31	1	Petition	30	Public Lands.						
Indiana, registers and receivers of Vandalia.	Compensation for locating land warrants.	31	2	Petition	44	Public Lands.						
Indiana, registers and receivers of Winamac.	Compensation for locating land warrants.	31	2	Petition	53	Public Lands.						
Indiana Shakers, trustees of.	(See Shakers society of.)	16	1	....	33							
Indiana, Creek Indians, (friendly.)	Indemnity for property destroyed by hostile Indians.	14	2	Resolution	130	Ways and Means..	62	Favorable	93	Passed	Passed.......	App'd March 3, 1817
Indiana, Creek Indians, (friendly.)	Indemnity for property destroyed in Creek war.	18	1	Resolution	280	Ways and Means..	101	Adverse	......	Laid on table.		
Indiana, Creek Indians, (nation.)	Indemnity for property destroyed by citizens of Georgia.	21	2	Memorial	303	Indian Affairs.....	109	Adverse	......	Laid on table.		
Indiana, Creek Indians, (nation.)	Payment of a balance due them...	21	2	Memorial	303	Indian Affairs.....	....	....	......	....	....	See act Mar. 2, 1831
Indiana, Creek Indians, (nation.)	Balance due from citizens of Georgia.	30	1	Petition	809	Indian Affairs.....	826	Favorable; bill	643	Passed	Passed.......	App'd Aug. 12, 1848
Indiana, Creek Indians, (half breed.)	Indemnity for losses in Indian wars.	23	1	Petition of Alab'a legislature.	310	Indian Affairs.						
Indiana, Creek Indians, (half breed.)	Indemnity for losses in Indian wars.	25	2	Memorial	255	Indian Affairs.....	....	....	......	Discharged.		
Indiana, Cherokee Indians, (warriors.)	Pension	26	1	Senate bill	1267	....	....	....	S. 387			
Indiana, Cherokee Indians, (warriors.)	Pension	27	2	Senate bill	115	Indian Affairs	Feb. 8, 1842	With't amend.	S. 11	Passed	Passed	App'd April 14, 1842
Indiana, Cherokee Indians, (nation.)	Interest on money due, &c......	21	1	Memorial	448	Indian Affairs.....	....	....	......	Discharged; laid on table.		
Indiana, Cherokee Indians, (nation.)	Adjustment of claims under treaty.	30	1	Senate resolution.	1126	Indian Affairs.....	....	....	S.R. 33	Passed	Passed	App'd Aug. 7, 1848
Indiana, Cherokee Indians, (nation.)	Allowance for subsistence.......	30	1	Resolution	326	Indian Affairs.....	738	Favorable....	508	Referred to Committee Whole House.	....	See act July 29, 1848
Indiana, Cherokee Indians, (nation.)	Fulfillment of treaty stipulation...	30	2	Petition	416	Indian Affairs.....	....	....	......	Discharged; laid on table.		
Indiana, Cherokee Indians, (agent of three.)	Indemnity for loss of certain lands.	21	2	Petition	233	Claims.						
Indiana, Cherokee Indians, (in North Carolina.)	Adjustment of certain claims.....	27	3	Memorial	327	Indian Affairs....	Feb. 9, 1843	Favorable	R. 37	Passed	Passed	Retained by the President.
Indiana, Cherokee Indians, (in North Carolina.)	Indemnity for property destroyed by government agents.	27	3	Resolution	387	Indian Affairs.						
Indiana, Cherokee Indians, (in North Carolina.)	Payment of money due by treaty..	30	2	Petition	163	Indian Affairs.						
Indiana, Cherokee Indians, (heirs of family.)	Indemnity for spoliations........	30	1	Memorial	188	Indian Affairs.						
				Senate resolution.	1127	Indian Affairs.....	....	....	S.R. 33	Passed	Passed	App'd Aug. 7, 1848
Indiana, Chippewa Indians.	(See Wyandot and others.)......	10	1	....	98							
Indiana, Choctaw Indians, (agent of.)	Confirmation of title—indemnity, &c.	24	1	Petition	265	Indian Affairs.....	479	Favorable	622	Passed.		
Indiana, Choctaw Indians.	Reimbursement of money paid Joseph Boggy.	25	2	Resolution	759	Indian Affairs.						
Indiana, Oneida Indians..	Reimbursement of expenses at Washington.	23	2	Petition	128	Indian Affairs.....	Jan. 19, 1835	Adverse	......	Laid on table.		
Indiana, Oneida Indians..	Payment of money due by treaty.	31	1	Petition	385	Indian Affairs.						

List of private claims presented to the House of Representatives of the United States from the 1st to the 31st Congress, inclusive—**Continued.**

Names of claimants.	Nature or object of the claim.	Congress.	Session.	How brought before the House of Reps.	Page of journal.	To what committee of the House referred.	No. or date of the report.	Nature of the report.	No. of the bill.	How disposed of by the House of Reps.	How disposed of by the Senate.	Date of the act of Congress, and remarks.
Indiana, Oneida Indians..	Payment of money due by treaty.	31	2	Petition	118	Indian Affairs.....	18	Favorable....	450	Referred to Committee Whole House.		
Indiana, Oneida Indians..	Bounty land for services in the war of 1812.	31	1	Petition	983	Public Lands.						
Indiana, Ottawa Indians..	(See Wyandot and others.)......	10	1	....	98							
Indiana, Pottawattamie Indians.	(See Wyandot and others.)......	10	1	....	98							
Indiana, Sac and Fox Indians.	Survey and grant of reservation..	23	1	Petition	248	Public Lands.....	April 8, 1834	Favorable....	409	Passed	Passed	App'd June 30, 1834
Indiana, Seminole Indians, (friendly.)	Compensation for military services.	27	2	Petition of W. G. S.	369	Indian Affairs.						
Indiana, Seneca Indians..	Payment of arrears of annuity....	22	1	Resolution	82	Indian Affairs	Dec. 28, 1831	Favorable ...	163	Passed	Passed	App'd July 13, 1832
Indiana, Seneca Indians..	Payment of annuities withheld...	27	1	Memorial	169	Indian Affairs.						
Indiana, Seneca Indians..	Payment of money embezzled by agent.	27	2	Petition	1025	Indian Affairs.						
Indiana, Seneca Indians..	Allowance of certain claims......	30	2	Petition	476	Indian Affairs.						
Indiana, Seneca Indians, (agents of.)	Indemnity for acts of sub-Indian agents.	26	1	Petition	295	Claims.						
Indiana, Shawnee Indians.	Additional compensation for certain reservation.	22	1	Resolution	795	Ways and Means.						
Indiana, Shawnee Indians.	Balance due for services in Florida war.	28	1	Joint resolution..	902	Indian Affairs.....	541	Favorable....	J.R. 40	Referred to Committee Whole House.		
Indiana, Shawnee Indians.	Balance due under treaty stipulations.	31	1	Petition	544	Indian Affairs.						
Indiana, Stockbridge Indians, (nation.)	Confirmation of land titles.......	16	1	Petition	140	Select...........	70	Favorable....	88	Rejected	....	Leave to withdraw, 2d session.
Indiana, Stockbridge Indians, (nation.)	Compensation for military services.	16	1	Petition	145	Claims	Feb. 18, 1820	Favorable....	82	Passed	Passed	App'd May 4, 1820
Indiana, Stockbridge Indians, (nation.)	Reimbursement of expenses of removal.	26	1	Petition	351	Indian Affairs.						
Indiana, Stockbridge Indians, (nation.)	Grant of land in fee simple and for individual partition.	27	2	Petition	1188	Indian Affairs.....	July 30, 1842	Favorable....	559	Laid on table.		
Indiana, Stockbridge Indians, (nation.)	Grant of land in fee simple and for individual partition.	27	3	House bill......	96	....	....	....	559	Passed	Passed	App'd March 3, 1843
Indiana, Stockbridge Indians, (nation.)	Arrears of annuities	29	1	Memorial	888	Whole House.						
Indiana, Stockbridge Indians, (nation.)	Patents for land in payment of money withheld.	31	1	Petition	520	Judiciary.						
Indiana, Stockbridge and Munsee Indians.	Change in direction of the payments under treaty stipulation.	27	2	Petition	765	Indian Affairs.						
Indiana, Talungowon Indians.	Payment of balance due them and annuity.	26	1	Petition	604	Indian Affairs.						
Indiana, Tuscarora Indians.	Indemnity for the destruction of a church.	15	1	Petition	35	Select...........	Jan. 8, 1818	Adverse	......	Rejected.		
Indiana, Indian volunteers, company of.	Compensation for services in war of 1846.	30	1	Rep. of Secretary War.	734	Select...........	April 26, 1848	By bill	431	Referred to Committee Whole House.		
Indiana, Wyandot Indians.	Reservation of a tract of land in Michigan.	12	1	Petition	211	Public Lands.						
Indiana, Wyandot Indians.	Interest on annuities	25	2	Petition	776	Indian Affairs.....	....	....	.....	Discharged.		
Indiana, Wyandot Indians.	Exchange of a location of land ...	27	3	Petition	259	Public Lands.....	160	Favorable....	776	Ref'd to Com. W. H.		
Indiana, Wyandot Indians and others.	Confirmation of title to land in Michigan.	10	1	Petition	98	Public Lands.....	Mar. 7, 1808	Favorable....	70	Passed	Passed	App'd April 25, 1808
Indian, Robin...........	(See Robin Loyd)............	26	1	....	324							

List of private claims presented to the House of Representatives of the United States from the 1st to the 31st Congress, inclusive—Continued.

Names of claimants.	Nature or object of the claim.	Congress.	Session.	How brought before the House of Reps.	Page of journal.	To what committee of the House referred.	No. or date of the report.	Nature of the report.	No. of the bill.	How disposed of by the House of Reps.	How disposed of by the Senate.	Date of the act of Congress, and remarks.
Indian wars, soldiers of	Compensation for military services.	24	1	Petition	197	Select	Dec. 16, 1836	Favorable	353	Referred to Committee Whole House.		
Inez, George	(See Nathaniel Hand and others.)											
Ingalls, Daniel	Pension for revolutionary services.	26	1	Petition	198	Rev. Pensions	714	Adverse		Laid on table.		
Ingalls, Daniel	Pension for revolutionary services.	26	2	Petition	134	Rev. Pensions				Discharged; laid on table.		
Ingalls, Daniel	Pension for revolutionary services.	27	2	Petition	1069	Rev. Pensions				Discharged; laid on table.		
Ingalls, Daniel	Pension for revolutionary services.	28	1	Petition	73	Rev. Pensions	216	Favorable	170	Passed	Indef. postp'd.	
Ingalls, Daniel	Pension for revolutionary services.	29	1	Petition	151	Rev. Pensions	76	Favorable	95	Passed	Passed	App'd Mar. 15, 1846
Ingalls, Israel, widow of	Pension for revolutionary services.	26	1	Petition	624	Rev. Pensions	465	Favorable	379	Referred to Committee Whole House.		
Ingalls, Israel	Pension for revolutionary services.	24	1	Petition	157	Rev. Pensions	Jan. 13, 1826	Favorable	144	Passed	Passed	App'd May 14, 1836
Ingalls, Joseph, widow of	Pension for revolutionary services.	26	1	Petition	282	Rev. Pensions	490	Adverse		Laid on table.		
Ingell, Zadock	Pension for revolutionary services.	21	2	Petition	159	Military Pensions.						
Ingell, Zadock	Pension for revolutionary services.	22	1	Petition	330	Rev. Pensions	365	Favorable	460	Passed	Indef. postp'd.	
Ingersoll, Briggs	Pension	19	1	Petition	98	Military Pensions	164	Adverse		Laid on table.		
Ingersoll, Charles J.	(See David Caldwell and C. J. Ingersoll.)	23	1		636							
Ingersoll, Charles J.	Settlement of accounts as district attorney, Philadelphia.	26	1	Rep. of Secretary Treasury.	147	Claims.						
Ingersoll, Charles J.	Pay and mileage while contesting seat in Congress.	29	1	Memorial	531	Elections	June 17, 1846	Favorable		Referred to Committee Whole House.		
Ingersoll, Charles J.	Reimbursement of expenses contesting seat, &c.	31	1	Petition	646	Elections	249	Favorable		Referred to Committee Whole House.		
Ingersoll, George, widow of	Pension for revolutionary services.	25	3	Petition	127	Rev. Pensions				Leave to withdraw.		
Ingersoll, Huldah	(See widow of Col. John Brown).	3	1		70							
Ingersoll, Jonathan, *et al.*	Indemnity for spoliations by Italian government.	12	1	Petition	94	Com. and Manuf.						
Ingersoll, Justus	Pension	14	2	Petition	255	Pens. & Rev. Cl'ms.				Discharged; laid on table.		
Ingersoll, Stephen M.	(Journal does not show nature of claim.)	20	1	Petition	168	Indian Affairs.						
Ingoldsby, John H.	(See John H. Gooldsby)	28	1		218							
Ingham, David	Pension	19	1	Petition	398	Military Pensions	164	Adverse		Laid on table.		
Ingham, John	Compensation for property lost in public service.	23	1	Petition	305	Claims	297	Adverse		Laid on table.		
Ingles, John	Compensation for revolutionary services.	2	1	Petition	542					Referred to Secretary War.		
Ingles, John	Indemnity for damage to property, revolutionary war.	4	1	Rep. of Secretary Treasury.	388	Claims.						
Ingles, John	Indemnity for damage to property, revolutionary war.	14	1	Petition	42	Pens. & Rev. Cl'ms.				Discharged; laid on table.		
Ingles, John	Indemnity for damage to property, revolutionary war.	14	2	Petition	70	Pens. & Rev. Cl'ms.	Jan. 13, 1817	Adverse		Rejected.		
Inglis, Minet	(See assignees of Thomas Tupper)	22	2		142							
Ingle, John P.	(See Daniel Carroll, and others)	20	1		309							
Ingle, Joseph	Arrears of salary as clerk to paymaster marine corps.	30	1	Petition	204	Claims	475	Adverse		Laid on table.		
Ingraham, Amos	Pension for revolutionary services.	20	1	Resolution	542	Military Pensions.						
Ingraham, Amos	Pension for revolutionary services.	21	1	Petition	48	Military Pensions	Jan. 5, 1830	Favorable	72	Passed	Passed, with amendment.	App'd May 20, 1830

List of private claims presented to the House of Representatives of the United States form the 1st to the 31st Congress, inclusive—Continued.

Names of claimants.	Nature or object of the claim.	Congress.	Session.	How brought before the House of Reps.	Page of journal.	To what committee of the House referred.	No. or date of the report.	Nature of the report.	No. of the bill.	How disposed of by the House of Reps.	How disposed of by the Senate.	Date of the act of Congress, and remarks.
Ingraham, D. G.	Additional compensation for manuscript journal of Joseph Ingraham, deceased.	30	1	Petition	882	Library.						
Ingraham, Edward	Indemnity for illegal seizure of schooner Eliza by schooner Victory, of Nova Scotia.	26	1	Petition	201	Foreign Affairs.						
Ingraham, Francis	Pension for revolutionary services.	27	3	Resolution	193	Rev. Pensions.						
Ingraham, Francis	Pension for revolutionary services.	28	2	Petition	206	Rev. Pensions.						
Ingraham, Francis	Pension for revolutionary services.	29	2	Petition	68	Rev. Pensions.						
Ingraham, Francis	Pension for revolutionary services.	30	1	Petition	771	Rev. Pensions	692	Adverse		Laid on table.		
Ingraham, Henry, surviving partner of N. Ingraham & Son.	Release of interest on a balance due the U. S. as navy agents.	16	1	Petition	35	Select				Discharged; laid on table.		
Ingraham, Henry, surviving partner of N. Ingraham & Son.	Release of interest on a balance due the U. S. as navy agents.	18	1	Memorial	337	Naval Affairs.						
Ingraham, Holt	Compensation for services as purser's steward.	28	2	Memorial	119	Naval Affairs.						
Ingraham, Holt	Compensation for services as purser's steward.	29	1	Petition	87	Naval Affairs				Discharged; laid on table.		
Ingraham, John	Release of vessel for violation of revenue laws.	1	2	Petition	160					Laid on table.		
Ingraham, John	Arrears of pension	29	1	Petition	209	Invalid Pensions	501	Adverse		Laid on table.		
Ingraham, Joseph, widow of.	Annuity for naval service of husband.	7	1	Petition	13	Select	Jan. 22, 1802	Favorable	60	Passed	Passed	App'd April 29, 1802
Ingraham, Joseph	(See D. G. Ingraham)	30	1		882							
Ingraham, Nath'iel G., *et al*	Release from imprisonment	12	2	Senate bill	711	Ways and Means	Mar. 3, 1813	With amends.	S. 65	Passed	Passed	App'd March 3, 1813
Ingram, Edwin	Pension for revolutionary services.	24	1	Petition	944	Rev. Pensions				Discharged; laid on table.		
Ingram, John	Interest on claims under treaty of Ghent.	20	2	Petition	231	Foreign Affairs	79	Adverse		Laid on table.		
Ingram, Josias	Interest on claims under treaty of Ghent.	20	2	Petition	231	Foreign Affairs	79	Adverse		Laid on table.		
Ingram, Morgan	Payment of an award against an officer of the United States for trespass.	29	1	Documents	262	Claims.						
Ingram, Sally	Interest on claim under treaty of Ghent.	20	2	Petition	231	Foreign Affairs	79	Adverse		Laid on table.		
Ingram, Sarah	(See Lemuel Thorowgood, widow of.)	15	2		61							
Inman, Henry	Compensation for a painting in Rotunda of Capitol.	24	2	Appropriation bill	127	Whole House	Feb. 28, 1837	With amends.	776	Passed	Passed	App'd March 3, 1837
Innerarity, James & wife	(See Peter Trouillet, heirs of)	12	1		60							
Inskeep, John, President, &c.	(See Pennsylvania North American Insurance Company.)	26	1		182		343		319			
Innis, Cornelius, *alias* Quinil Ercoffier.	Confirmation of title to land	23	1	Petition	586	Priv. Land Claims.						
Innis, Cornelius, *alias* Quinil Ercoffier.	Confirmation of title to land	23	2	Petition	48	Priv. Land Claims.	Jan. 8, 1835	Adverse		Laid on table.		
Innis, George	Extra services as custom house officer, New York.	21	1	Petition	67	Commerce	200	Favorable	247	Referred to Committee Whole House.		
Innis, George	Extra services as custom house officer, New York.	21	1	Rep't Committee.	265			With't amend.	247	Passed	With amend.	

List of private claims presented to the House of Representatives of the United States from the 1st to the 31st Congress, inclusive—Continued.

Names of claimants.	Nature or object of the claim.	Congress.	Session.	How brought before the House of Reps.	Page of journal.	To what committee of the House referred.	No. or date of the report.	Nature of the report.	No. of the bill.	How disposed of by the House of Reps.	How disposed of by the Senate.	Date of the act of Congress, and remarks.
Innis, George	Extra services as custom house officer, New York.	22	1	Petition	53	Commerce	11	Favorable	60	Rejected.		
Innis, George	Extra services as custom house officer, New York.	22	2	Petition	53	Commerce				Referred to Secretary Treasury.		
Innis, George	Extra services as custom house officer, New York.	23	1	Petition	239	Commerce	279	Adverse		Laid on table.		
Innis, George	Extra services as custom house officer, New York.	24	1	Petition	479	Commerce	485	Adverse		Recommitted.		
Innis, George	Extra services as custom house officer, New York.	24	2	Petition	75	Commerce	261	Favorable	949	Referred to Committee Whole House.		
Innis, George	Extra services as custom house officer, New York.	25	2	Petition	40	Commerce	307	Favorable	344	Referred to Committee Whole House.		
Innis, George	Extra services as custom house officer, New York.	25	3	Rep. Committee Whole House.	377			With't amend.	344	Passed	Passed	App'd March 3, 1839
Iowa, Amisy association	Right of pre emption	27	3	Petition	349	Public Lands.						
Iowa, Johnson county, commissioners of.	Pre-emption to land for county seat	26	1	Memorial	607	Public Lands.						
Iowa, Johnson county, commissioners of.	Pre-emption to land for county seat	26	2	Senate bill	306				S. 179			
Iowa, Johnson county, commissioners of.	Pre-emption to land for county seat	27	2	House bill	500	Whole House	July 19, 1842	With't amend.	230	Passed	Passed	App'd Aug. 1, 1842
Iowa, Johnson county, commissioners of.	Pre emption to land for county seat	27	2	Senate bill	1126	Public Lands	Aug. 2, 1842	With't amend.	S. 171	Laid on table.		
Iowa, Linn county	Pre-emption to land for county seat	27	2	Memorial of legislature.	84	Public Lands	Feb. 9, 1842	Favorable	108	Referred to Committee Whole House.		
Iowa, Dubuque county, mayor, &c., of.	Right of pre-emption	30	1	Petition	344	Public Lands.						
Iowa, inhabitants of the State of.	Confirmation of their titles to land	26	1	Petition	608	Public Lands.						
Iowa, inhabitants of the State of.	Pre emption to the lands they occupy.	27	3	Memorial	125	Public Lands.						
Iowa, legislature of	Payment of territorial debts	28	1	Memorial	540	Ways and Means.						
Iowa, legislature of	Compensation to inhabitants for defence of the frontier.	28	1	Resolution	540	Militia	371	Favorable	275	Passed.		
Iowa, legislature of	Compensation to inhabitants for defence of the frontier.	28	2	House bill	304	Whole House			576	Laid on table.		
Iowa, legislature of	Reimbursement of expenses incurred in the boundary difficulties.	27	2	Memorial	369	Military Affairs.						
Iowa, registers and receivers of Fairfield.	Extra compensation for locating land warrant.	31	1	Petition	595	Public Lands.						
Iowa, registers and receivers of Fairfield.	Extra compensation for locating land warrant.	31	2	Petition	308	Public Lands.						
Iowa city	Extra compensation for locating land warrant.	31	2	Petition	122	Public Lands.						
Ira, Schooner	(See Wm. Ellery, and others.)	27	2		95							
Ireland, Jeremiah	Pension for services in the war of 1812.	22	2	Petition	109	Invalid Pensions.						
Ireland, Jeremiah	Pension for services in the war of 1812.	23	1	Petition	44	Invalid Pensions	Jan. 31, 1834	Adverse		Laid on table.		
Ireland, Jeremiah	Pension for services in the war of 1812.	31	1	Petition	589	Invalid Pensions.						
Ireland, Jeremiah	Pension for services in the war of 1812.	31	2	Petition		Invalid Pensions	86	Adverse		Laid on table.		

List of private claims presented to the House of Representatives of the United States from the 1st to the 31st Congress, inclusive—Continued.

Names of claimants.	Nature or object of the claim.	Congress.	Session.	How brought before the House of Reps.	Page of journal.	To what committee of the House referred.	No. or date of the report.	Nature of the report.	No. of the bill.	How disposed of by the House of Reps.	How disposed of by the Senate.	Date of the act of Congress, and remarks.
Ireland, John, (Md.)	Indemnity for property destroyed by the enemy.	15	1	Rep't Commiss'r of Claims.	37	Claims	Feb. 16, 1818	Adverse	......	Laid on table.		
Ireland, John, (Penn.)	Pension	23	1	Petition	369	Rev. Pensions	....	....	......	Discharged; laid on table.		
Ireson, John, jr., widow of	Continuation of pension	28	1	Petition	541	Rev. Pensions.						
Irish, F. M.	Refunding amount of public money entrusted to his care, lost accidentally, and paid by him.	28	2	House bill	295	Claims	152	Adverse	574	Laid on table.		
Irish, Nathaniel	Commutation pay for revolutionary services.	9	1	Petition	197	Claims	....	....	......	Referred to Committee Whole House.		
Irish, Nathaniel	Commutation pay for revolutionary services.	9	2	Petition	490	Claims.						
Irish, Nathaniel	Commutation pay for revolutionary services.	10	1	Petition	59	Claims.						
Irish, Nathaniel	Commutation pay for revolutionary services.	10	2	Petition	354	Claims.						
Irish, Nathaniel	Commutation pay for revolutionary services.	11	1	Petition	31	Claims.						
Irish, Nathaniel	Commutation pay for revolutionary services.	11	2	Petition	116	Claims	....	....	......	Discharged.		
Irish, Nathaniel	Commutation pay for revolutionary services.	12	1	Petition	131	Claims.						
Irish, Nathaniel, exec'r of.	Commutation pay for revolutionary services.	16	1	Petition	221	Pens. & Rev. Cl'ms.						
Irish, Nathaniel, exec'r of.	Commutation pay for revolutionary services.	24	2	Petition and docs.	91	Rev. Claims.						
Irish, Nathaniel, exec'r of.	Commutation pay for revolutionary services.	25	2	Petition	111	Rev. Claims	718	Favorable	687	Recommitted.		
Irish, Nathaniel, exec'r of.	Commutation pay for revolutionary services.	26	1	Petition	165	Rev. Claims.						
Irish, Nathaniel, exec'r of.	Commutation pay for revolutionary services.	26	2	Petition	134	Rev. Claims	117	Favorable	622	Referred to Committee Whole House.		
Irish, Nathaniel, exec'r of.	Commutation pay for revolutionary services.	27	2	Petition	62	Rev. Claims	384	Adverse	......	Laid on table.		
Irish, Nathaniel, exec'r of.	Commutation pay for revolutionary services.	29	1	Memorial	193	Rev. Claims.						
Irish, Nathaniel, exec'r of.	Commutation pay for revolutionary services.	29	2	Petition	99	Rev. Claims.						
Irish, Nathaniel, heirs of.	Commutation pay for revolutionary services.	30	1	Petition	273	Rev. Claims.						
Irish, Stephen	(See administr'n of Jonathan Stark)	29	2	....	162							
Irland, Capt. William	Payment for arms and accoutrements of his company lost by being taken prisoners.	13	3	Petition	673	Claims	Nov. 14, 1814	Favorable	288	Passed	Indef. postp'd.	
Ironson, John	Pension	19	1	Petition	102	Military Pensions	164	Adverse	......	Laid on table.		
Irvine, Alexander	Pension for revolutionary services.	5	2	Pension bill	127	Whole House	....	....	38	Passed	Passed	App'd Feb. 7, 1798
Irvine, Alexander, administrator of.	Payment of his share of a forfeiture for violation of the law in relation to the importation of slaves.	17	1	Petition	151	Claims	Feb. 28, 1822	Adverse	......	Laid on table.		
Irvine, Callender	Increase of salary as superintendent of military stores.	11	2	Petition	170	....	....	....	......	Referred to Secretary of War.		
Irvine, Callender	Extra services as commissary general.	27	2	Petition	227	Claims	187	Adverse	......	Laid on table.		

List of private claims presented to the House of Representatives of the United States from the 1st to the 31st Congress, inclusive—Continued.

Names of claimants.	Nature or object of the claim.	Congress.	Session.	How brought before the House of Reps.	Page of journal.	To what committee of the House referred.	No. or date of the report.	Nature of the report.	No. of the bill.	How disposed of by the House of Reps.	How disposed of by the Senate.	Date of the act of Congress, and remarks.
Irvine, Callender, administrator of.	Extra services as commissary general.	31	1	Petition	471	Military Affairs.						
Irvine, George	(See heirs of James Sharp.)	17	2		26							
Irvine, Joseph	Reimbursment of the amount of a judgment.	18	1	Petition	526	Claims.						
Irvine, Joseph	Reimbursment of the amount of a judgment.	20	1	Petition	438	Claims	April 4, 1828	Adverse		Laid on table.		
Irvine, James, widow of	Pension for revolutionary services.	25	2	Petition	914	Rev. Pensions				Discharged, laid on table.		
Irvine, Maria C.	(See Dr. Mordecai Hall, heirs of.)	24	1		814							
Irwin, Archibald, heir of.	Compensation for revolutionary services.	24	1	Petition	137	Rev. Claims.						
Irwin, Archibald, heir of.	Compensation for revolutionary services.	24	2	Petition	270	Rev. Claims.						
Irwin, Alexander J.	Confirmation of title to land in Wisconsin.	25	3	Memorial	416	Public Lands.						
Irwin, David, and others.	Confirmation of title to land	27	3	Petition	296	Public Lands				Leave to withdraw.		
Irwin, Henry, heirs of	Commutation pay for revolutionary services.	24	1	Petition	404	Rev. Claims	838	Favorable	738	Referred to Committee Whole House.		
Irwin, Henry, heirs of	Commutation pay for revolutionary services.	25	2	Petition	81	Rev. Claims	107	Favorable	125	Passed	Passed	App'd July 9, 1838
Irwin, James	Payment of a revolutionary certificate.	22	1	Petition	416	Rev. Claims				Discharged; laid on table.		
Irwin, James	Payment of a revolutionary certificate.	23	1	Petition	111	Rev. Claims.						
Irwin, James	(See Archibald Irwin, heir of.)	24	1		137							
Irwin, James, widow of	Release of estate of deceased from liability as postmaster.	25	2	Petition	1029	P. Of. and P. Roads.				Discharged; laid on table.		
Irwin, Joseph, representatives of.	Confirmation of title to land	25	2	Petition	373	Priv. Land Claims.						
Irwin Robert.	Compensation for supplies on public account.	20	1	Petition	100	Claims	144	Adverse		Referred to Committee Whole House.		
Irwin, Robert	Compensation for supplies on public account.	21	2	Petition	161	Claims	Feb. 4, 1831	Adverse		Laid on table.		
Irwin, Robert	Compensation for supplies on public account.	22	1	Petition	133	Claims	Jan. 18, 1832	Adverse		Laid on table.		
Irwin, Robert	Compensation for supplies on public account.	23	1	Petition	309	Indian Affairs.						
Irwin, Robert	Indemnity in land for non-fulfilment of contract.	24	2	Petition	94	Indian Affairs.						
Irwin, Robert, (Penn.)	Pension	27	2	Resolution	216	Invalid Pensions.	420	Adverse		Laid on table.		
Irwin, Robert, jr	Confirmation of title to land	21	1	Petition	85	Priv. Land Claims.	Jan. 28, 1830	Adverse		Laid on table.		
Irwin,	(See Spaulding & Irwin.)	24	1		534							
Irwin, Thomas, sen., executor of.	Indemnity for French spoliations prior to 1800.	26	2	Petition	131	Whole House.						
Irwin, William	Right of pre-emption	27	2	Documents	75	Public Lands	503	Adverse		Laid on table.		
Irwin, William	Pension for revolutionary services.	28	1	Petition	103	Invalid Pensions				Discharged; laid on table.		
Isaacs, John S.	Compensation for services as acting collector.	31	1	Petition	582	Claims.						
Isaacs, Robert	(See Andrew Low & Co.)	16	1		194							
Isaacs, William	(See Henry Cahoone and others).	15	1		225							

List of private claims presented to the House of Representatives of the United States from the 1st to the 31st Congress, inclusive—**Continued.**

Names of claimants.	Nature or object of the claim.	Congress.	Session.	How brought before the House of Reps.	Page of journal.	To what committee of the House referred.	No. or date of the report.	Nature of the report.	No. of the bill.	How disposed of by the House of Reps.	How disposed of by the Senate.	Date of the act of Congress, and remarks.
Isacks, Jacob	Compensation for a discovery in the method of distilling salt water.	1	3	Petition	*390					Referred to Secretary of State.		
Isacks, Jacob	Compensation for a discovery in the method of distilling salt water.	2	1	Rep. of Secretary State.	459					Laid on table.		
Isahart, Jacob	Compensation for disability, war of 1812.	17	2	Petition	143	Pens. & Rev. Cl'ms.				Discharged; laid on table.		
Isenangle, David	Pension	19	2	Resolution	69	Military Pensions				Discharged; laid on table.		
Isett, Thomas M.	Exchange of an entry of land	27	2	Senate bill	581	Public Lands	April 12, 1842	With't amend.	S. 120	Passed	Passed	App'd Aug. 14, 1842
Ish, Christian, representatives of.	Payment of a revolutionary certificate.	21	1	Petition	298	Rev. Claims.						
Ish, Christian, representatives of.	Payment of a revolutionary certificate.	21	2	Petition	67	Rev. Claims	Feb. 2, 1831	Favorable	594	Referred to Committee Whole House.		
Ish, Christian, representatives of.	Payment of a revolutionary certificate.	22	1	Petition	300	Rev. Claims.						
Ish, Christian, representatives of.	Payment of a revolutionary certificate.	23	1	Petition	111	Rev. Claims	Dec. 33, 1830	Favorable	100	Passed	Passed	App'd June 27, 1834
Isherwood, B. F.	Additional compensation as chief engineer.	31	1	Petition	385	Naval Affairs	13	Favorable	16	Referred to Committee Whole House.		
Isom, John	(William H. Bedford, agent)	28	1		262							
Israel, Isaac, (Pa.)	Compensation for services as revolutionary officer.	10	1	Petition	56	Select.						
Israel, Isaac, (Va.)	Liquidation of a revolutionary claim.	10	1	Petition	59	Claims				Referred to Committee Whole House.		
Israel, Isaac	Commutation pay for revolutionary services.	23	1	Petition	157	Rev. Claims.						
Israel, Isaac	Commutation pay for revolutionary services.	23	2	Petition	94	Rev. Claims	Jan. 9, 1835	Adverse		Laid on table.		
Israel, John	Pension for revolutionary services.	20	1	Resolution	393	Military Pensions.						
Israel, John	Pension for revolutionary services.	21	1	Pension bill	130	Whole House	Feb. 13, 1830	With't amend.	72	Passed	Passed, with amendment.	App'd May 20, 1830
Israel, J. M.	(See J. A. Fogg, *et al*)	31	1				394					
Israel, Joseph	(See Isaac Israel)	23	1		157							
Israel, Samuel, assignee and attorney of.	Indemnity for French spoliations prior to 1800.	26	1	Memorial	182	Foreign Affairs	343	Favorable	319	Referred to Committee Whole House.		
Ives, Elisha	Compensation for a boat captured by the enemy.	16	1	Petition	163	Claims.						
Ives, Elisha	Compensation for a boat captured by the enemy.	18	2	Petition	36	Claims.						
Ives, Elisha	Compensation for a boat captured by the enemy.	19	1	Petition	312	Claims				Discharged; laid on table.		
Ives, Elisha	Compensation for a boat captured by the enemy.	20	2	Petition	176	Claims				Discharged; laid on table.		
Ives, Elisha	Compensation for a boat captured by the enemy.	21	1	Petition	69	Claims	142	Favorable	186	Passed	Passed	App'd May 19, 1830
Ives, Elisha	Compensation for a boat captured by the enemy.	31	1	Petition	752	Claims.						
Ives, Joseph, [Elisha]	Indemnity for property destroyed, war of 1812.	24	2	Petition	125	Claims	Jan. 5, 1837	Adverse		Laid on table.		
Ives, Orin	(See assignees of Thomas Tupper.)	22	2		142							
Ives, Thomas P.	(See Nicholas Brown and others.)	23	1		273							
Ives, Thomas P.	Indemnity for French spoliations prior to 1800.	26	1	Memorial	182	Foreign Affairs	343	Favorable	319	Referred to Committee Whole House.		

List of private claims presented to the House of Representatives of the United States from the 1st to the 31st Congress, inclusive—Continued.

Names of claimants.	Nature or object of the claim.	Congress.	Session.	How brought before the House of Reps.	Page of journal.	To what committee of the House referred.	No. or date of the report.	Nature of the report.	No. of the bill.	How disposed of by the House of Reps.	How disposed of by the Senate.	Date of the act of Congress, and remarks.
Ivey, John	Extension of a timber contract	28	1	Petition	84	Naval Affairs.						
Ivins, Mary	Compensation for revolutionary services of husband.	5	2	Petition	103	Claims	Dec. 18, 1797	Adverse		Rejected.		
Ivory, James	To be restored to a pension roll	25	2	Petition	588	Invalid Pensions				Discharged; laid on table.		
Ivory, James	To be restored to a pension roll	25	3	Petition	89	Invalid Pensions		Adverse		Discharged; laid on table.		
Ivory, James	To be restored to a pension roll	27	2	Petition	720	Invalid Pensions	815	Adverse		Laid on table.		
Ivory, Thomas	Compensation for work on Cumberland road.	23	1	Res. and docs	589	Claims	456	Adverse		Referred to Secretary War.		
Ivy, or Joy, William N.	Balance due on a timber contract.	23	2	Petition	423	Claims.						
Ivy, or Joy, William N.	Balance due on a timber contract.	24	1	Petition	94	Claims	125	Adverse		Laid on table.		
Izard, Ralph	(See widow of Stephen Decatur and others.)	20	1		295		201		S. 50			
Jaccard, Peter S	Leave to locate land in lieu of that entered by mistake.	25	2	Memorial	547	Public Lands.						
Jaccard, Peter S	Leave to locate land in lieu of that entered by mistake.	25	3	Petition	93	Public Lands	157	Favorable	1024	Passed	Passed	App'd March 3, 1839
Jack, James	Pension	24	2	Resolution	78	Rev. Pensions				Laid on table.		
Jack, Captain Matthew	Compensation for revolutionary services.	20	1	Petition	311	Rev. Claims	Mar. 4, 1828	Adverse		Laid on table.		
Jack, Captain Matthew, heirs of.	Arrears of pension	29	1	Memorial	199	Invalid Pensions.						
Jack, Captain Matthew, heirs of.	Commutation pay for revolutionary services.	30	1	Petition	981	Rev. Claims.						
Jack, Captain Matthew, heirs of.	Commutation pay for revolutionary services.	31	1	Petition	610	Rev. Claims.						
Jack, Captain Matthew, heirs of.	Commutation pay for revolutionary services.	31	2	Petition	174	Rev. Claims	8	Adverse		Laid on table.		
Jack, Patrick, (Pa.)	Indemnity for land ceded to Indians.	2	2	Petition	712					Laid on table.		
Jack, Patrick, (Pa.)	Indemnity for land ceded to Indians.	3	1	Petition	57	Select.						
Jack, Samuel	(See Matthew Jack, heirs of)	30	1		981							
Jackaway, Samuel	Pension	14	1	Documents	63	Pens. & Rev. Cl'ms.	April 23, 1816	Favorable	171	Passed	Passed	App'd April 30, 1816
Jackson, Abigail	(See Ebenezer Jackson, widow of)	27	2		525							
Jackson, A. C	Pay for overtaking vessel under order of Navy Department.	31	1	Petition	654	Naval Affairs.						
Jackson, Abraham, heirs of	Indemnity for French spoliations prior to 1800.	26	1	Memorial	182	Foreign Affairs	343	Favorable	319	Referred to Committee Whole House.		
Jackson, Agnes	Compensation for house destroyed by fire.	13	2	Petition	190	Claims				Leave to withdraw.		
Jackson, Alexander S.	Pension	28	1	Petition	240	Invalid Pensions	270	Adverse		Laid on table.		
Jackson, Alfred E.	(See Samuel Jackson, heirs of)	29	1		718							
Jackson, Amasa	(See Harry Caldwell and Amasa Jackson.)	11	2		122							

List of private claims presented to the House of Representatives of the United States from the 1st to the 31st Congress, inclusive—Continued.

Names of claimants.	Nature or object of the claim.	Congress.	Session.	How brought before the House of Reps.	Page of journal.	To what committee of the House referred.	No. or date of the report.	Nature of the report.	No. of the bill.	How disposed of by the House of Reps.	How disposed of by the Senate.	Date of the act of Congress, and remarks.
Jackson, Andrew	Remission of duties on stills	7	2	Petition	337	Claims	Feb. 19, 1803	Adverse		Laid on table.		
Jackson, Andrew	Compensation as district attorney	2	1	Petition and rep't Att'y General.	528	Select.	Mar. 29, 1792	Adverse		Laid on table.		
Jackson, Andrew	Compensation as district attorney	3	2	Petition	309	Claims.						
Jackson, Andrew	Compensation as district attorney	4	1	Res. and docs	373	Claims	Jan. 6, 1796	Adverse		Leave to withdraw.		
Jackson, General Andrew	Indemnity for damages sustained in discharge of duty.	27	3	Senate bill	419	Whole House.			S. 12			
Jackson, General Andrew	To refund certain fines	27	2	Petition	534	Judiciary	878	Favorable	503	Referred to Committee Whole House.		
Jackson, General Andrew	To refund certain fines	27	2	Res. of legislature of Ohio.	541	Judiciary				Laid on table.		
Jackson, General Andrew	To refund certain fines	27	2	Res. of legislature of Michigan.	458					Laid on table.		
Jackson, General Andrew	To refund certain fines	27	3	Res. of legislature of Virginia.	98	Whole House on bill No. 503.						
Jackson, General Andrew	To refund certain fines	27	3	Res. of legislature of S. Carolina.	111	Judiciary.						
Jackson, General Andrew	To refund certain fines	37	3	Res. of legislature of Illinois.	166					Laid on table.		
Jackson, General Andrew	To refund certain fines	27	3	Res. of legislature of New Hamp.	170					Laid on table.		
Jackson, General Andrew	To refund certain fines	27	3	Res. of legislature of R. Island.	251					Laid on table.		
Jackson, General Andrew	To refund certain fines	27	3	Res. of legislature of Maine.	290					Laid on table.		
Jackson, General Andrew	To refund certain fines	27	3	Res. of legislature of Penn.	572	Whole House.						
Jackson, General Andrew	To refund certain fines	27	3	Res. of legislature Missouri.	435	Whole House.						
Jackson, General Andrew	To refund certain fines	27	3	Res. of legislature of Georgia.	499	Whole House.						
Jackson, General Andrew	To refund certain fines	27	3	Presid't's message	28	Judiciary	122	Favorable	503			
Jackson, General Andrew	To refund certain fines	28	1	House bill	29	Whole House			1	Passed	Passed	App'd Feb. 16, 1844
Jackson, General Andrew	Confirmation of land titles granted by Creek Indians.	14	2	Pres. message	134	Priv. Land Claims.						
Jackson, General Andrew	Confirmation of land titles granted by Creek Indians.	15	2	Pres. Message	25	Priv. Land Claims.						
Jackson, Andrew	(See heirs of Col. John Donaldson)	15	1		184							
Jackson, Andrew, (Indian.)	Grant of land	22	1	Memorial	388	Public Lands.						
Jackson, Andrew, (N. Y.)	Grant of land	18	1		145					Leave to withdraw.		
Jackson, Andrew McDonell, widow of.	Pension	27	3	Petition	320	Naval Affairs						
Jackson, Andrew McDonell, widow of.	Pension	28	1	Petition	85	Invalid Pensions	40	Adverse		Laid on table.		
Jackson, Archibald	Bounty land and pay for services of his slave James Gammons.	17	1	Petition	200	Military Affairs	Feb. 5, 1822	Adverse		Rejected.		
Jackson, Archibald	Bounty land and pay for services of his slave James Gammons.	18	1	Petition	37	Military Affairs	Jan. 20, 1824	Adverse		Laid on table.		
Jackson, Archibald	Bounty land and pay for services of his slave James Gammons.	18	2	Report	39					Referred to Committee Whole House.		
Jackson, Archibald	Bounty land and pay for services of his slave James Gammons.	19	1	Petition	57	Claims.						

List of private claims presented to the House of Representatives of the United States from the 1st to the 31st Congress, inclusive—Continued.

Names of claimants.	Nature or object of the claim.	Congress.	Session.	How brought before the House of Reps.	Page of journal.	To what committee of the House referred.	No. or date of the report.	Nature of the report.	No. of the bill.	How disposed of by the House of Reps.	How disposed of by the Senate.	Date of the act of Congress, and remarks.
Jackson, Archibald	Bounty land and pay for services of his slave James Gammons.	19	2	Petition	32	Claims	Jan. 5, 1827	Adverse		Laid on table.		
Jackson, Archibald	Bounty land and pay for services of his slave James Gammons.	20	1	Petition	31	Military Affairs.						
Jackson, Archibald	Bounty land and pay for services of his slave James Gammons.	20	2	Petition	83	Priv. Land Claims.						
Jackson, Archibald	Bounty land and pay for services of his slave James Gammons.	21	1	Petition	128	Priv. Land Claims.				Referred to 3d Auditor.		
Jackson, Archibald	Bounty land and pay for services of his slave James Gammons.	21	2	Petition	193	Claims	Jan. 18, 1831	Adverse		Laid on table.		
Jackson, Archibald	Bounty land and pay for services of his slave James Gammons.	21	2	Petition	299	Priv. Land Claims.	78	Favorable	623	Referred to Committee Whole House.		
Jackson, Archibald	Bounty land and pay for services of his slave James Gammons.	22	1	Resolution	82	Priv. Land Claims.	184	Favorable	261	Referred to Committee Whole House.		
Jackson, Archibald	Bounty land and pay for services of his slave James Gammons.	22	2	House bill	93	Whole House			261	Passed	Rejected.	
Jackson, Archibald	Restoration of pension	18	1	Resolution	99	Rev. Pensions				Laid on table.		
Jackson, Archibald	Restoration of pension	20	2	Resolution	50	Military Pensions	Feb. 13, 1829	Favorable	440	Passed.		
Jackson, Archibald	Restoration of pension	21	1	Petition	49	Military Pensions	Jan. 5, 1830	Favorable	72	Passed	Passed, with amendment.	App'd May 20, 1830
Jackson, Archibald	Arrears of pension	21	2	Resolution	124	Military Pensions				Laid on table.		
Jackson, Archibald	Arrears of pension	22	1	Resolution	94	Rev. Pensions				Laid on table.		
Jackson, Archibald	Arrears of pension	22	2	Resolution	273	Rev. Pensions.				Laid on table.		
Jackson, Benjamin, *et al.*	Compensation as teamsters in revolutionary war.	3	1	Petition	60					Referred to Secretary War.		
Jackson, Catharine	(See John Jackson, widow of.)	28	1		890							
Jackson, Charles	Renewal of land warrant	4	2	Petition	683	Claims.						
Jackson, Charles	Renewal of land warrant	5	2	Petition	229	Claims	Mar. 19, 1798			Referred to Committee Whole House.		
Jackson, Charles, (Mich.)	Indemnity for losses on building contract.	22	1	Petition	471	Commerce.						
Jackson, Charles, (Mich.)	Indemnity for losses on building contract.	23	1	Petition	240	Claims	288	Adverse		Laid on table.		
Jackson, Charles, heirs of.	Commutation pay	28	2	Petition	386	Rev. Claims.						
Jackson, Charles, administrator of.	Compensation as assistant commissary.	2	1	Petition	498					Referred to Secretary War.		
Jackson, Charles A.	(See heirs of Michael Jackson.)	28	2		386							
Jackson, Charles S., (Ill.)	Pay for deficiency of compensation as inspector.	26	1	Memorial	933	Commerce.						
Jackson, Charles S., (Ill.)	Pay for deficiency of compensation as inspector.	26	2	Memorial	78	Commerce.						
Jackson, Charles S., (Ill.)	Pay for deficiency of compensation as inspector.	27	2	Memorial	604	Commerce.						
Jackson, Charles S., (Ill.)	Pay for deficiency of compensation as inspector.	30	1	Memorial	115	Claims.						
Jackson, Charles S., (Ill.)	Pay for deficiency of compensation as inspector.	30	2	Memorial	115	Claims.						
Jackson, Major Daniel	Additional rations	6	2	Petition	738	Claims	Jan. 26, 1801			Referred to Committee Whole House.		
Jackson, Daniel, and S. M. Higgins.	Register to a British vessel rebuilt in United States.	21	2	Petition	62	Commerce.	Dec. 31, 1830	Favorable	529	Passed	Passed	App'd March 2, 1831
Jackson, David B., and Nathaniel Brown.	Compensation for bringing Perry Anthony from Honduras.	18	2	Petition	228	Claims.						
Jackson, Durant K	(See William H. Bedford, agent.)	28	1		262							

List of private claims presented to the House of Representatives of the United States from the 1st to the 31st Congress, inclusive—Continued.

Names of claimants.	Nature or object of the claim.	Congress.	Session.	How brought before the House of Reps.	Page of journal.	To what committee of the House referred.	No. or date of the report.	Nature of the report.	No. of the bill.	How disposed of by the House of Reps.	How disposed of by the Senate.	Date of the act of Congress, and remarks.
Jackson, Ebenezer, widow of.	Pension	27	2	Petition	525	Rev. Pensions	784	Adverse	......	Laid on table.		
Jackson, Lieutenant Ebenezer, heirs of.	Commutation pay	28	2	Petition	171	Rev. Pensions.						
Jackson, Lieutenant Ebenezer, heirs of.	Commutation pay	30	2	Petition	664	....	....	....	......	Leave to withdraw.		
Jackson, Elisha, (Va.)	Payment of drafts on Post Office department by Wm. Smith.	24	2	Resolution	77	P. Of. & P. Roads.						
Jackson, Elisha, (Va.)	Payment of drafts on Post Office department by Wm. Smith.	25	2	Resolution	101	P. Of. & P. Roads.	560	Favorable	549	Referred to Committee Whole House.		
Jackson, Ephriam, (Ga.)	Compensation for military service under Wayne.	31	1	Petition	198	Public Lands.						
Jackson, George, (Ohio)	Pay for horse and wagon lost in war of 1812.	21	1	Petition	694	Claims.						
Jackson, George, (Mo.)	Pay for horses stolen by Indians	24	1	Documents	265	Indian Affairs.						
Jackson, George, (Mo.)	Pay for horses stolen by Indians	24	2	Petition	92	Indian Affairs.						
Jackson, George, (Mo.)	Pay for horses stolen by Indians	25	2	Petition	97	Indian Affairs.						
Jackson, George, (Mo.)	(See Reuben E. Gentry, *et al.*)	29	1	....	442							
Jackson, George R.	Reimbursement of duties paid on furniture.	4	1	Petition	446	Com. and Manuf.	Mar. 7, 1796	Favorable	160	Passed	Rejected.	
Jackson, George R., (Ind.)	Correction of land entry	22	1	Petition	227	Public Lands.						
Jackson, George R., (Ind.)	Correction of land entry	23	1	Petition	145	Priv. Land Claims.	136	Favorable	148	Passed	Passed	App'd June 18, 1834
Jackson, George W.	Settlement of accounts as paymaster, vouchers lost.	14	2	Petition	411	Claims.						
Jackson, George W.	Settlement of accounts as paymaster, vouchers lost.	15	1	Petition	140	Claims.						
Jackson, George W.	Payment for work on Cumberland road.	23	1	Res. and papers.	589	Claims	455	Adverse	......	Laid on table	....	See report No. 449.
Jackson, George W.	Payment for work on Cumberland road.	28	2	Petition	435	Claims.						
Jackson, George W.	Payment for work on Cumberland road.	29	1	Petition	572	Claims	736	Adverse	......	Laid on table.		
Jackson, George W.	Payment for work on Cumberland road.	31	1	Petition	486	Claims.						
Jackson, Jacob J., executors of.	Release from judgment in favor of United States.	22	1	Memorial	144	Judiciary.						
Jackson, Jacob, (N. Y.)	Increase of pension	26	1	Resolution	556	Rev. Pensions.						
Jackson, Jacob, (N. Y.)	Pension	26	1	Resolution	654	Invalid Pensions.						
Jackson, Jacob, (N. Y.)	Pension	26	1	Petition	707	Invalid Pensions.						
Jackson, Jacob, (N. Y.)	Increase of pension	26	2	Petition	36	Invalid Pensions	45	Favorable	574	Referred to Committee Whole House.		
Jackson, Jacob, (N. Y.)	Increase of pension	27	2	Petition	60	Invalid Pensions	255	Favorable	221	Passed	Passed	App'd Aug. 26, 1842
Jackson, James	Pension	14	1	House bill	622	Whole House	April 11, 1816	Favorable	171	Passed	Passed	App'd April 30, 1816
Jackson, General James, executors of.	(See sureties of Thomas D. M. Johnson.)	12	1	....	180							
Jackson, James, (England)	Pension and amount promised by Paul Jones.	23	2	Memorial	308	Rev. Claims.						
Jackson, James, (England)	Pension and amount promised by Paul Jones.	24	1	Petition	138	Rev. Claims	566	Adverse	......	Laid on table.		
Jackson, James, (England)	Pension and amount promised by Paul Jones.	25	2	Petition	111	Rev. Claims.						
Jackson, James, (England)	Pension and amount promised by Paul Jones.	25	3	Petition	188	Rev. Claims.						

List of private claims presented to the House of Representatives of the United States from the 1st to the 31st Congress, inclusive—Continued.

Names of claimants.	Nature or object of the claim.	Congress.	Session.	How brought before the House of Reps.	Page of journal.	To what committee of the House referred.	No. or date of the report.	Nature of the report.	No. of the bill.	How disposed of by the House of Reps.	How disposed of by the Senate.	Date of the act of Congress, and remarks.
Jackson, James, (England)	Pension and amount promised by Paul Jones.	26	1	Petition	166	Rev. Claims	April 24, 1840	Adverse	......	Laid on table.		
Jackson, James, (England)	Pension and amount promised by Paul Jones.	26	2	Petition	135	Naval Affairs	200	Adverse	......	Laid on table.		
Jackson, James, (England)	Pension and amount promised by Paul Jones.	27	2	Petition	155	Rev. Claims	1059	Adverse	......	Laid on table.		
Jackson, Jarvis	Compensation as deputy postmaster in Kentucky.	18	2	Documents	70	P. Of. and P. Roads	36	Favorable	292	Passed	Rejected.	
Jackson, Jarvis	Compensation as deputy postmaster in Kentucky.	19	1	Senate bill	529	P. Of. and P. Roads.	May 15, 1826	Favorable	60	Passed	Passed	App'd May 20, 1826
Jackson, Jarvis, and Wm. B. Moore.	(See Calvin Carter, sureties of.)	27	2	Senate bill	792							
Jackson, Jeremiah	(See Zebulon Pike & companions)	10	1	....	189							
Jackson, Jesse R.	....	31	1	Resolution	980	....	....	....	......	Leave to withdraw.		
Jackson, Jesse W., (Ky.)	Pension	29	2	Petition	53	Invalid Pensions.						
Jackson, Jesse W., (Ky.)	Pension	30	1	Petition	207	Invalid Pensions	283	Favorable	279	Passed.		
Jackson, Jesse W., (Ky.)	Pension	30	2	House bill	648	....	....	....	279	....	Passed	App'd May 3, 1849
Jackson, John, (Ohio.)	Pay for services in war of 1812	20	1	Petition	47	Claims	22	Adverse	......	Laid on table.		
Jackson, John, widow of (Va.)	Pension	28	1	Petition	890	Rev. Pensions.						
Jackson, John, widow of (Va.)	Pension	28	2	Petition	144	Rev. Pensions.						
Jackson, John, widow of (Va.)	Pension	29	1	Petition	260	Rev. Pensions	526	Adverse	......	Laid on table.		
Jackson, Capt. John, representatives of.	Pension	25	3	Petition	454	Military Affairs.						
Jackson, John, heirs of	Pension	26	1	Petition	179	Naval Affairs.						
Jackson, John, heirs of	Pension	30	1	Petition	575	Rev. Claims	819	Favorable	637	Referred to Committee Whole House.		
Jackson, John, heirs of	Pension	31	1	Petition	433	Rev. Pensions	356	Favorable	320	Referred to Committee Whole House.		
Jackson, Capt. John, representatives of.	Asking credit of $750 on books, Treasury Department.	26	1	Resolution	1011	Claims.						
Jackson, Capt. John, administrator of.	Pay, services on revenue cutter, and release from a debt due United States.	27	2	Petition	382	Claims	749	Favorable	427	Referred to Committee Whole House.		
Jackson, Capt. John, administrator of.	Pay, services on revenue cutter, and release from a debt due United States.	27	3	House bill	88	....	....	....	427	Passed	Passed	App'd Jan. 28, 1843
Jackson, Capt. John, administrator of.	Pay, services on revenue cutter, and release from a debt due United States.	28	1	Petition	645	Claims.						
Jackson, Capt. John, administrator of.	Pay, services on revenue cutter, and release from a debt due United States.	28	2	Petition	113	Claims.						
Jackson, Jonathan	Increase of pay as supervisor, eastern district, Massachusetts.	5	2	Petition & report Sec. Treasury.	90	Ways and Means	....	....	......	Laid on table	....	Recommitted with instructions.
Jackson, Jonathan	(See Jacob J. Jackson, executors of.)	22	1	....	144							
Jackson, Joseph	(See William Carter, executors of.)	8	1	....	489							
Jackson, Joseph, (Tenn.)	Pay for horses lost in Florida war.	25	3	Petition	120	Claims	196	Favorable	1053	Passed	Passed	App'd March 3, 1839
Jackson, Lemuel	Pension	27	2	Petition	320	Invalid Pensions	606	Adverse	......	Laid on table.		
Jackson Lyman	Pension	21	1	Petition	82	Military Pensions.						

List of private claims presented to the House of Representatives of the United States from the 1st to the 31st Congress, inclusive—Continued.

Names of claimants.	Nature or object of the claim.	Congress.	Session.	How brought before the House of Reps.	Page of journal.	To what committee of the House referred.	No. or date of the report.	Nature of the report.	No. of the bill.	How disposed of by the House of Reps.	How disposed of by the Senate.	Date of the act of Congress, and remarks.
Jackson, Lyman	Pension	21	2	Petition	73	Military Pensions.						
Jackson, Mary	(See Charles Jackson, administratrix of.)	2	1		498							
Jackson, Mary	(See Thomas H. Jackson, widow of.)	28	2		199							
Jackson, McDowell	Pension	24	2	Petition	398	Invalid Pensions				Laid on table.		
Jackson, Michael	Pension	1	3	Petition	374					Referred to Secretary of War.		
Jackson, Michael	Pension	3	1	Rep. of Secretary War.	131	Select	May 26, 1794	Favorable	62	Passed	Passed	App'd June 28, 1794
Jackson, Michael	Arrears of pension	4	1	Petition and rep't Sec. of War.	480	Whole House.						
Jackson, Michael	Arrears of pension	5	2	Petition	264	Claims	April 17, 1798	Adverse		Laid on table.		
Jackson, Michael	Arrears of pension	5	3	Petition	432	Whole House.						
Jackson, Michael, heirs of	Commutation pay	28	2	Petition	386	Rev. Claims.						
Jackson, Nathaniel, (Me.)	Restoration of pension	18	1	Petition	250	Rev. Pensions	Mar. 11, 1824	Adverse		Laid on table.		
Jackson, Nathaniel, *et al.*	Additional compensation as custom house officers.	26	1	Resolution	289	Commerce.						
Jackson, Nathaniel	(See Abraham Jackson, heirs of)	26	1		182							
Jackson, Pattin	Commutation pay	1	2	Petition and rep't Sec. of War.	196					Laid on table.		
Jackson, Pattin	Commutation pay	10	1	Petition	196	Whole House.						
Jackson, Pattin	Commutation pay	10	2	Petition	360	Select.						
Jackson, Pattin	Commutation pay	11	2	Petition	171	Claims	Jan. 26, 1810	Adverse		Referred to Committee Whole House.		
Jackson, Richard	Indemnity for French spoliations prior to 1800.	26	1	Memorial	182	Foreign Affairs	343	Favorable	319	Referred to Committee Whole House.		
Jackson, Richard	(See Nicholas Brown, *et al.*)	23	1		273							
Jackson, Samuel	Pay for secret services under Gen. Dearborn.	15	1	Petition	267	Public Lands	Mar. 12, 1818	Adverse		Leave to withdraw.		
Jackson, Samuel	Pay for secret services under Gen. Dearborn.	18	1	Petition	135	Military Affairs.						
Jackson, Samuel, (Conn.)	(See Elisha Sanford, *et al.*)	19	1		82							
Jackson, Samuel	(See Stephen Decatur, widow of)	20	1		295		201		S. 50			
Jackson, Samuel, (Tenn.)	Pension	20	2	Petition	59	Military Pensions				Laid on table.		
Jackson, Samuel, heirs of	Arrears of pension	29	1	Petition	718	Rev. Pensions				Leave to withdraw.		
Jackson, Samuel, (Tenn.)	Bounty land	22	2	Petition	124	Rev. Claims	Feb. 6, 1833	Adverse		Laid on table.		
Jackson, Samuel, (Tenn.)	Bounty land	24	1	Petition	104	Rev. Claims	524	Adverse		Recommitted.		
Jackson, Simeon, *et al.*	For interest on new emission of money.	6	2	Memorial	762	Whole House	Jan. 15, 1801	Adverse		Rejected.		
Jackson, Stephen, assignees of.	Grant of bounty land	18	1	Petition	69	Public Lands	Jan. 20, 1824	Adverse		Laid on table.		
Jackson, Stephen, (Va.)	Pension	22	2	Petition	26	Invalid Pensions				Laid on table.		
Jackson, Stephen, (Va.)	Reimbursement of money for redeeming captives from Indians.	23	2	Petition	115	Indian Affairs	Jan. 9, 1835	Adverse		Laid on table.		
Jackson, Stephen, (Va.)	Reimbursement of money for redeeming captives from Indians.	24	1	Petition	672	Indian Affairs.						
Jackson, Stephen, (Va.)	Reimbursement of money for redeeming captives from Indians.	25	2	Petition	95	Indian Affairs	Jan. 9, 1838	Adverse		Laid on table.		
Jackson, Susan J.	(See Andrew McD. Jackson, widow of.)	27	3		320							
Jackson, Thomas	(See Joshua Green, *et al.*)	4	2		385							
Jackson, Thomas	(See William H. Bedford, agent)	28	1		262							

List of private claims presented to the House of Representatives of the United States from the 1st to the 31st Congress, inclusive—Continued.

2—24

Names of claimants.	Nature or object of the claim.	Congress.	Session.	How brought before the House of Reps.	Page of journal.	To what committee of the House referred.	No. or date of the report.	Nature of the report.	No. of the bill.	How disposed of by the House of Reps.	How disposed of by the Senate.	Date of the act of Congress, and remarks.
Jackson, Thomas and William, (Mass.)	Indemnity for French spoliations prior to 1800.	26	1	Memorial	182	Foreign Affairs	342	Favorable	319	Referred to Committee Whole House.		
Jackson, Thomas H., widow of.	Pension	28	2	Petition	199	Naval Affairs.						
Jackson, Thomas H., widow of.	Pension	29	1	Petition	202	Naval Affairs	742	Adverse	......	Laid on table.		
Jackson, W., (Md.)	Increase of compensation as surveyor of customs.	10	2	Petition	472	Com. and Manuf.						
Jackson, William	Additional pay due aids de-camp of the line.	2	1	Petition	509	....	....	....	.....	Laid on table.		
Jackson, William	Relief from improper construction of revenue laws.	6	1	Petition	693	Com. and Manuf.	....	....	.....	Discharged.		
Jackson, William, (N. Y.)	Services and supplies, revolutionary war.	15	1	Petition	150	Pens. & Rev. Cl'ms.	....	....	.....	....	....	Leave to withdraw
Jackson, William, (N. Y.)	Services and supplies, revolutionary war.	16	1	Petition	217	Pens. & Rev. Cl'ms.	Feb. 20, 1820	Adverse	.....	Rejected.		
Jackson, William, heirs of.	Services and supplies, revolutionary war.	19	1	Petition	61	Rev. Claims	Jan. 18, 1826	Adverse	.....	Laid on table.		
Jackson, William, heirs of.	Services and supplies, revolutionary war.	22	1	Petition	190	Rev. Claims.						
Jackson, William, heirs of.	Services and supplies, revolutionary war.	22	2	Petition	40	Rev. Claims.						
Jackson, William, heirs of.	Services and supplies, revolutionary war.	25	2	Petition	178	Rev. Claims	620	Adverse	.....	Laid on table.		
Jackson, William, heirs of.	Services and supplies, rev. war	31	1	Petition	1039	Rev. Claims.						
Jackson, William	Pension	22	1	House bill	135	Whole House	....	....	193			
Jackson, William	Pension	22	2	House bill	66	....	....	....	193			
Jackson, William	Confirmation of title to land	21	2	Amendm't to Ho. bill.	240	....	....	....	526	Passed	Amended and passed.	App'd Feb. 3, 1831
Jackson, William, (Ohio)	Arrears of pension	27	2	Petition	68	Invalid Pensions	259	Adverse	.....	Laid on table.		
Jackway, Robert	Pension	3	2	Rep. of Secretary War.	278	Claims	....	....	.....	Laid on table.		
Jacobs, Benjamin	(See Colonel John Bayard, executor of.)											
Jacobs, Benjamin	Payment of loan office certificates.	12	1	Petition	131	Claims.						
Jacobs, Benjamin	Payment of loan office certificates.	22	2	Petition	29	Rev. Claims.						
Jacobs, Benjamin	Payment of loan office certificates.	23	1	Resolution	42	Rev. Claims	157	Favorable	172	Passed	Passed	App'd June 28, 1834
Jacobs, Enoch	Pension	4	1	Petition	445	Claims	Mar. 4, 1796	Favorable	156	Passed	Passed	App'd April 20, 1796
Jacobs, Francis, (N. Y.)	Pension	22	1	Petition	260	Invalid Pensions	293	Favorable	377	Passed.		
Jacobs, Francis, (N. Y.)	Pension	23	1	Petition	114	Invalid Pensions	122	Favorable	128	Passed	Passed	App'd June 30, 1834
Jacobs, George W., widow of.	Pension	22	1	Petition	36	Invalid Pensions.						
Jacobs, Hannah	(See George W. Jacobs, widow of.)	22	1	....	36							
Jacobs, Hetty	Indemnity for French spoliations prior to 1800.	31	1	....	256	Foreign Affairs	355	Favorable	318	Referred to Committee Whole House.		
Jacobs, Jacob	Confirmation of title to land	15	1	Petition	312	Priv. Land Claims.						
Jacobs, Jacob	Confirmation of title to land	16	1	Petition	72	Priv. Land Claims.						
Jacobs, Jacob	Confirmation of title to land	17	1	Petition	54	Priv. Land Claims.						
Jacobs, Jacob	Confirmation of title to land	[illegible]	1	Petition	[illegible]	Public Lands	July 16, 1824	Favorable	65	Passed	Passed	App'd May 26, 1824
Jacobs, James	Restoration of pension	17	2	Petition	119	Whole House.						
Jacobs, John	Pension	12	1	House bill	361	Whole House	June 15, 1812	Favorable	138	Passed	Passed	App'd July 5, 1812
Jacobs, John	Pension	15	1	Petition	226	Pens. & Rev. Cl'ms.						
Jacobs, John, (Mass.)	Pension	19	2	Petition	156	Military Pensions.						

List of private claims presented to the House of Representatives of the United States from the 1st to the 31st Congress, inclusive—Continued.

Names of claimants.	Nature or object of the claim.	Congress.	Session.	How brought before the House of Reps.	Page of journal.	To what committee of the House referred.	No. or date of the report.	Nature of the report.	No. of the bill.	How disposed of by the House of Reps.	How disposed of by the Senate.	Date of the act of Congress, and remarks.
Jacobs, John, sen., (Ky.)	Increase of pension	20	1	Resolution	47	Military Pensions.						
Jacobs, John, sen., (Ky.)	Increase of pension	27	2	Resolution	401	Rev. Pensions	784	Adverse		Laid on table.		
Jacobs, John, (N. York,) widow of.	Pension	25	3	Petition	460	Rev. Pensions				Discharged.		
Jacobs, John C., (Indiana)	Pay for horses lost in public service.	24	1	Petition	430	Claims.						
Jacobs, John J., (Virginia)	Pension	21	1	Senate amendm't to House bill.	766	Whole House		Favorable	157	Passed, with Senate amendment.	Passed	App'd May 29, 1830
Jacobs, John J.	Half pay or commutation	19	1	Petition	336	Rev. Claims.						
Jacobs, John J.	Half-pay or commutation	19	2	Petition	53	Rev. Claims	Dec. 19, 1826	Adverse		Laid on table.		
Jacobs, John J.	Half-pay or commutation	20	1	Petition	243	Rev. Claims				Laid on table.		
Jacobs, John J.	Half-pay or commutation	20	2	Petition	231	Rev. Claims	Feb. 12, 1829	Adverse		Laid on table.		
Jacobs, John J.	Half-pay or commutation	22	1	Senate bill	302	Rev. Claims	Feb. 20, 1832	Favorable	S. 28	Passed	Passed	App'd July 14, 1832
Jacobs, Julius, (Pa.)	Payment of money lost by mail	25	3	Petition	494	P. Of. & P. Roads.						
Jacobs, Julius, (Pa.)	Payment of money lost by mail	26	1	Petition	183	P. Of. & P. Roads.						
Jacobs, Justin	Pension	28	2	Petition	112	Invalid Pensions	41	Favorable	515	Passed	Indef. postp'd.	
Jacobs, Justin	Pension	29	1	Petition	101	Invalid Pensions	467	Favorable	345	Passed	Passed	App'd Aug. 8, 1846
Jacobs, Ruby	(See John Jacobs, (N. Y.,) widow of.)	25	3		460							
Jacobs, Samuel, (Indiana)	Permission to locate land warrants.	24	1	Petition	741	Priv. Land Claims				Laid on table.		
Jacobs, Thomas	Bounty land	25	2	Petition	631	Priv. Land Claims.	734	Adverse		Laid on table.		
Jacobs, Whitcomb	Pension	3	2	Rep. of Secretary War.	350	Claims				Laid on table.		
Jacobs, William, (Virginia)	Pension	17	1	Petition	266	Pens. & Rev. Cl'ms.	Feb. 22, 1822	Adverse		Laid on table.		
Jacobs, William, (Indiana)	Pay for horse lost in Indian war	24	1	Petition	430	Claims.						
Jacocks, John H	Pay as inspector of revenue	25	2	Senate bill	675	Commerce	755	Favorable	S. 282	Referred to Committee Whole House.		
Jacocks, John H	Pay as inspector of revenue	25	3	Senate bill	636				S 301			
Jacocks, John H	Pay as inspector of revenue	26	1	Senate bill	185	Commerce	Feb. 29, 1840	Favorable	S. 125	Passed	Passed	App'd April 10, 1840
Jacocks, William	Bounty land	20	2	Petition	229	Military Affairs	74	Favorable	429	Passed.		
Jacocks, William	Bounty land	21	1	Petition	52	Military Affairs	17	Favorable	24	Passed	Passed	App'd Feb. 11, 1830
Jacquelin, John M., (N. Y.)	Reimbursement of duties on merchandise.	25	3	Petition	213	Commerce				Discharged.		
Jacquelin, John M., (N. Y.)	Reimbursement of duties on merchandise.	26	1	Petition	473	Commerce	33	Favorable	52	Ordered to 3d reading.		
Jacquelin, John M., (N. Y.)	Reimbursement of duties on merchandise.	27	2	Petition	152	Commerce	1044	Adverse		Laid on table.		
Jacques, Nathan	Pension	3	1	Rep. of Secretary War.	131	Select	May 29, 1794	Favorable	J. R. 12	Passed	Passed	App'd June 9, 1794
Jacques, Nathan	Pension	3	2	Rep. of Secretary War.	337	Claims	Feb. 28, 1795	Favorable	130	Passed	Postponed.	
Jacques, Nathan	Pension	4	1	Resolution	445	Claims	Mar. 4, 1796	Favorable	156	Passed	Passed	App'd April 20, 1796
Jacquette, Peter	Balance due for services in revolutionary war.	22	2	Petition	68	Rev. Claims	80	Favorable	722	Referred to Committee Whole House.		
Jacquette, Peter	Balance due for services in revolutionary war.	23	1	Petition	70	Rev. Claims	262	Favorable	302	Referred to Committee Whole House.		
Jaffrey, James, administrator of.	Indemnity for French spoliations prior to 1800.	26	1	Memorial	182	Foreign Affairs	343	Favorable	319	Referred to Committee Whole House.		
Jagers, Nathan	Pension	20	1	Petition	356	Military Pensions	May 13, 1828	Adverse		Laid on table.		
Jahucke, Trapman & Co.	(See Trapman, Jahucke & Co.)	17	1		253							
Jakins, Frederick	Pension	15	2	Petition	153	Rev. Pensions	Feb. 11, 1819	Adverse		Laid on table.		
Jakins, Frederick	Pension	16	1	Petition	32	Pens. & Rev. Cl'ms.						
Jakins, Frederick	Pension	16	2	Documents	212	Rev. Pensions.						

List of private claims presented to the House of Representatives of the United States from the 1st to the 31st Congress, inclusive—Continued.

Names of claimants.	Nature or object of the claim.	Congress.	Session.	How brought before the House of Reps.	Page of journal.	To what committee of the House referred.	No. or date of the report.	Nature of the report.	No. of the bill.	How disposed of by the House of Reps.	How disposed of by the Senate.	Date of the act of Congress, and remarks.
James, Amanda M.	Right of pre-emption	27	2	Senate bill	716	Public Lands.		Senate bill	190			
James, Ebenezer	Pension	24	2	Petition	245	Invalid Pensions	Jan. 19, 1837	Adverse		Laid on table.		
James, Elisha	Restoration of pension	20	1	Resolution	715	Military Pensions.						
James, Elisha	Restoration of pension	20	2	Resolution	57	Military Pensions	Feb. 13, 1829	Favorable	440	Passed	Laid on table.	
James, Elisha	Restoration of pension	21	1	Resolution	63	Military Pensions	414	Favorable	489	Ref'd to Com. W. H.		
James, Elisha	Restoration of pension	21	2	House bill	318	Whole House		Favorable	489	Passed.		
James, Elisha	Restoration of pension	22	1	Petition	45	Rev. Pensions	Dec. 20, 1831	Favorable	52	Passed	Postponed.	
James, Elizabeth	(See William James, widow of.)	27	2		375							
James & Flack	Relief from penalties for importing, &c.	12	2	Petition	641	Ways and Means.						
James, George	(See William H. Bedford.)	28	1		262							
James, Henry	Pension	27	2	Petition	526	Invalid Pensions	618	Adverse		Laid on table.		
James and Henry, schooner, owners of.	(See Daniel Grant, *et al.*)	29	1		125							
James, James, heirs of	Confirmation of title to land	22	2	Petition	42	Priv. Land Claims.						
James, John, (N. J.)	Pension	21	1	Petition and docs.	36, 318	Military Pensions.						
James, John, (N. J.)	Pension	21	2	Petition	159	Military Pensions				Laid on table.		
James, John, (N. J.)	Pension	22	1	Petition	165	Rev. Pensions	369	Favorable	464	Referred to Committee Whole House.		
James, Johnson, widow of, (Va.)	Pension	17	2	Petition	87	Pens. & Rev. Cl'ms.				Laid on table.		
James, Johnson, widow of, (Va.)	Pension	18	1	Petition	89	Pens. & Rev. Cl'ms	Jan. 5, 1824	Favorable	37	Passed.	Postponed.	
James, Johnson, widow of, (Va.)	Pension	19	1	Petition	98	Military Pensions.						
James, Johnson, widow of, (Va.)	Pension	20	1	Petition	30	Military Pensions	80	Favorable	84	Passed	Passed	App'd May 24, 1828
James, Mary	(See Johnson, James, widow of.)	17	2		87							
James, Morris, representatives of.	Compensation for wood taken by United States troops.	23	1	Resolution	116	Claims.						
James, Morris, representatives of.	Compensation for wood taken by United States troops.	24	1	Petition	94	Claims.						
James Munroe, schooner	(See Nathan Smith, *et al.*, owners of.)	24	1		198							
James, Nicholas, (Pa.)	Pension	29	1	Petition	573	Rev. Pensions.						
James, Nicholas, (Pa.)	Pension	29	2	Petition	54	Rev. Pensions.						
James, Noble	(See widow of Stephen Decatur, *et al.*)	20	1		295		201		S. 50			
James, Paul, (N. Y.)	Pension	24	2	Memorial	125	Rev. Pensions				Laid on table.		
James, Reuben	(See widow of Stephen Decatur, and others.)	20	1		295		201		S. 50			
James, Reuben	Pension	24	2	Petition	398	Invalid Pensions				Laid on table.		
James, Richard	For leave to import pimento	12	1	Petition	139	Com. and Manuf.						
James, Robert, (Tenn.)	For leave to import certain machinery free of duty.	31	1	Petition	224	Commerce				Laid on table.		
James & Shoemaker	Drawback on goods imported	3	1	Petition	167	Select	May 29, 1794	Favorable.		Ref'd to Com. W. H.		
James, Thomas	(See widow of Stephen Decatur, and others.)	20	1		295		201		S. 50			
James, Thomas, (Ky.)	Pension	22	1	Petition	45	Invalid Pensions				Laid on table.		
James, Thomas, (Ky.)	Pension	23	2	Petition	237	Rev. Pensions				Laid on table.		
James, Thomas, (Mo.)	Pre-emption right	19	2	Memorial	243	Public Lands.						

List of private claims presented to the House of Representatives of the United States from the 1st to the 31st Congress, inclusive—**Continued.**

Names of claimants.	Nature or object of the claim.	Congress.	Session.	How brought before the House of Reps.	Page of journal.	To what committee of the House referred.	No. or date of the report.	Nature of the report.	No. of the bill.	How disposed of by the House of Reps.	How disposed of by the Senate.	Date of the act of Congress, and remarks.
James, Thomas, (Mo.)	Permission to buy land at minimum price.	25	2	Petition	417	Public Lands	May 15, 1838	Favorable	789	Referred to Committee Whole House.		
James, Thomas, (Mo.)	Permission to buy land at minimum price.	25	3	House bill	431	Whole House	Jan. 39, 1831	Favorable	789	Passed	Passed	App'd March 3, 1839
James, William, (Ind.)	Pay for horses lost in war of 1832.	24	1	Petition	430	Claims.						
James, William, widow of, (Ill.)	Pension	27	2	Petition	375	Rev. Pensions	784	Adverse	......	Laid on table.		
James, William, widow of, (Ill.)	Pension	28	1	Petition	527	Rev. Pensions	....	....	......	Laid on table.		
Jameson, Col. David, (Va.)	Pay for revolutionary services	22	1	Petition	289	Rev. Claims	....	....	......	Laid on table.		
Jameson, Dr. David, widow of.	Pay for medicine and medical service.	6	1	Petition	642	Claims	April 7, 1800	Adverse	......	Leave to withdraw.		
Jameson, Elizabeth	(See Dr. David Jameson, widow of.)	6	1	....	642							
Jameson, Dr. Horatio G.	For medical services	23	1	Petition	437	....	490	Adverse	......	Laid on table.		
Jameson, Robert	(See William Wilson, administrator of.)	27	2	....	72							
Jamieson, George	Donation of land	24	1	Petition	57	Public Lands	208	Favorable	208	Referred to Committee Whole House.		
Jameson, John, (Va.)	Commutation pay for fathers' services.	21	2	Petition	190	Rev. Claims.						
Jameson, John, (Va.)	Commutation pay for father's services.	22	1	Petition	124	Rev. Pensions.						
Jamison, Benjamin	Pension	25	3	Petition	218	Invalid Pensions.						
Jamison, Henry M., (Md.)	Land for lost land script	26	1	Petition	1009	Priv. Land Claims.	July 21, 1840	Adverse	......	Laid on table.		
Jamison, Henry M.	To admit church bell free of duty.	24	1	Petition	852	Ways and Means.						
Jamison, John (Indian.)	Pay for horses stolen Indian war 1832.	24	1	Petition	430	Claims.						
Jamison, Margaret	(See Samuel Jamison, widow of.)	26	1	....	1277							
Jamison, Samuel, widow of.	Pension	26	1	Senate bill	1277	....	....	Favorable	S. 363	Referred to Committee Whole House.		
Jamison, Samuel, widow of.	Pension	26	2	Senate bill	329	....	....	Favorable	S. 200	Referred to Committee Whole House.		
Jamison, Samuel, widow of.	Pension	27	2	Senate bill	101	Rev. Pensions	Feb. 9, 1842	Favorable	S. 40	Passed	Passed	App'd Mar. 19, 1842
Jamison & Williamson	Pay for extra services in carrying mail and for losses.	25	2	Resolution	480	P. Of. and P. Roads.	991	Favorable	851	Referred to Committee Whole House.		
Jamison & Williamson	Pay for extra services in carrying mail and for losses.	25	3	House bill	432	....	Feb. 1, 1839	Favorable	851	Passed	Passed	App'd March 3, 1839
Jamison & Williamson	Pay for extra services in carrying mail and for losses.	26	2	Explanatory bill.	282	P. Of. and P. Roads.	....	....	681			
Janes, Elijah	Pension	2	1	Petition	474	Whole House.	....	....	......	Referred to Secretary of War.		
Janes, Elijah	Pension	3	1	Rep. of Secretary War.	131	Select	May 26, 1794	Favorable	62	Passed	Passed	App'd June 7, 1794
Janes, James	Pension	21	1	Petition	91	Military Pensions.						
Janes, Joseph	Pay as inspector at Salem, Massachusetts.	26	1	Petition	290	Commerce	384	Adverse	......	Laid on table.		
Janin, Louis	Confirmation of title to land	28	1	Petition	76	Priv. Land Claims.						
Janis, Jean Baptiste, (Mo.)	Confirmation of title to land	22	2	Petition	347	Priv. Land Claims.						
Janis, Jean Baptiste	Pension	24	1	Senate bill	811	Rev. Pensions	Jan. 3, 1836	Favorable	S. 237	Passed	Passed	App'd July 2, 1836
Janney, Joseph	Indemnity for property destroyed 1814.	15	1	Letter of Com. on Claims.	37	Claims.						

List of private claims presented to the House of Representatives of the United States from the 1st to the 31st Congress, inclusive—Continued.

Names of claimants.	Nature or object of the claim.	Congress.	Session.	How brought before the House of Reps.	Page of journal.	To what committee of the House referred.	No. or date of the report.	Nature of the report.	No. of the bill.	How disposed of by the House of Reps.	How disposed of by the Senate.	Date of the act of Congress, and remarks.
Janney, Joseph	Indemnity for property destroyed 1814.	15	2	Petition	33	Claims	24	Adverse		Referred to Committee Whole House.		
Janney, Joseph	Indemnity for property destroyed 1814.	16	1	Rep't Committee.	149	Claims	45	Adverse		Referred to Committee Whole House.		
Janney, Joseph	Indemnity for property destroyed 1814.	16	2	Rep't Committee	36	Whole House				Rejected.		
Janney, Joseph	Indemnity for property destroyed 1814.	18	1	Petition	105	Claims	17	Adverse		Referred to Committee Whole House.		
Janney, Joseph, heirs of	Indemnity for tobacco destroyed in 1812.	31	2	Petition	58	Claims	64	Favorable	479	Referred to Committee Whole House.		
Janney, Stephen	(See John B. Fanning, sureties of)	26	1		297							
Janson, Cornelius T., widow of.	Pension	26	1	Petition	286	Rev. Pensions.						
Janson, Cornelius T., widow of.	Pension	26	2	Petition	34	Rev. Pensions.						
Janson, Cornelius T., widow of.	Pension	27	2	Petition	329	Rev. Pensions	300	Favorable	268	Passed	Passed	App'd Aug. 23, 1842
January, Thomas T., (Mo.)	Confirmation of title to land	29	1	Petition	226	Public Lands	586	Favorable	403	Referred to Committee Whole House.		
Janverin, George, executor of.	Indemnity for French spoliations prior to 1800.	26	1	Memorial	182	Foreign Affairs	343	Favorable	319	Referred to Committee Whole House.		
Janverin Joseph	Indemnity for French spoliations prior to 1800.	26	1	Memorial	182	Foreign Affairs	343	Favorable	319	Referred to Committee Whole House.		
Janvier, Isaac	Pension	23	1	Memorial	45	Invalid Pensions	306	Favorable	341	Referred to Committee Whole House.		
Janvier, Isaac	Pension	23	2	House bill	336	Whole House			341	Passed	Passed	App'd March 3, 1835
Jaquays, Joseph	Pension	15	2	Petition	32	Rev. Pensions	Dec. 24, 1818	Adverse		Leave to withdraw.		
Jaques, David	Indemnity for French spoliations prior to 1800.	26	1	Memorial	182	Foreign Affairs	343	Favorable	319	Referred to Committee Whole House.		
Jardella, Francis	Arrears of salary and expenses to Italy.	20	1	Petition	342, 725	Public Buildings	Mar. 4, 1828	Adverse		Laid on table.		
Jardella, Francis, heirs of.	Compensation for sculpture on the Capitol.	22	1	Petition	98	Claims.						
Jardella, Francis, heirs of.	Compensation for sculpture on the Capitol.	23	1	Petition	60	Claims	296	Favorable	333	Referred to Committee Whole House.		
Jardella, Francis, heirs of.	Compensation for sculpture on the Capitol.	24	1	Petition	50	Claims	5	Favorable	5	Passed	Passed	App'd Feb. 9, 1836
Jardine, John, sen.	(See William Jardine, heir of.)	31	1		415							
Jardine, William, heir of.	Balance due for service in United States navy.	31	1	Memorial	415	Claims	162	Adverse		Laid on table.		
Jarott, Joseph, alias Rock.	(See Rock)	24	1		95							
Jarrard, Benjamin	Pension	28	1	Petition	338	Rev. Pensions				Laid on table.		
Jarrett, Thomas, (Md.)	Pay for vessel purchased by United States.	28	2	Petition	272	Claims.						
Jarrett, Thomas, (Md.)	Pay for vessel purchased by United States.	29	1	Petition	175	Claims	281	Adverse		Laid on table.		
Jarrett, Thomas, (Md.)	Pay for vessel purchased by United States.	31	1	Petition	324	Claims	29	Adverse		Laid on table.		
Jarrott, John, rep's of	Confirmation of title to land	30	1	Petition	236	Priv. Land Claims.						
Jarrott, Nicholas	To locate land claim	15	2	Petition	118	Priv. Land Claims.	Jan. 13, 1819	Favorable	270	Referred to Committee Whole House.		
Jarrott, Nicholas	To locate land claim	16	1	Petition	24	Priv. Land Claims.				Laid on table.		

List of private claims presented to the House of Representatives of the United States from the 1st to the 31st Congress, inclusive—Continued.

Names of claimants.	Nature or object of the claim.	Congress.	Session.	How brought before the House of Reps.	Page of journal.	To what committee of the House referred.	No. or date of the report.	Nature of the report.	No. of the bill.	How disposed of by the House of Reps.	How disposed of by the Senate.	Date of the act of Congress, and remarks.
Jarrott, Nicholas	To locate land claim	16	2	Petition	20	Public Lands	2	Favorable	151	Passed	Passed, with amendment.	App'd March 2, 1821
Jarrott, Nicholas, heirs of	Confirmation of title to land	30	1	Senate bill	913	Priv. Land Claims.			S. 147			
Jarrott, Nicholas, heirs of	Confirmation of title to land	30	2	Senate bill	119	Priv. Land Claims.	Dec. 19, 1848	Favorable	S. 147	Passed	Passed	App'd Dec. 21, 1848
Jarvis, Francis, heirs of	Scrip for land warrants	23	1	Petition	309	Priv. Land Claims.						
Jarvis, Francis, heirs of	Scrip for land warrants	23	2	Petition	85	Priv. Land Claims.				Laid on table.		
Jarvis, Francis, heirs of	Scrip for land warrants	24	1	Petition	112	Priv. Land Claims.				Laid on table.		
Jarvis, Francis, heirs of	Scrip for land warrants	24	2	Petition	84	Priv. Land Claims.	35	Favorable	782	Referred to Committee Whole House.		
Jarvis, Francis, heirs of	Scrip for land warrants	25	2	Petition	43	Priv. Land Claims.	145	Favorable	166			
Jarvis, Francis, heirs of	Scrip for land warrants	25	3	House bill	375	Whole House		Favorable	166	Passed	Passed	App'd March 3, 1839
Jarvis, James J.	Right of pre-emption as New Orleans branch pilot.	28	1	Petition	77	Priv. Land Claims.	9	Favorable	35	Passed	Passed	App'd June 17, 1844
Jarvis, John	Remission of duties on goods	16	1	Senate bill	108	Ways and Means	Jan. 14, 1820	Favorable	13	Passed with amendm't.	Passed	App'd April 11, 1820
Jarvis, Leonard, (Mass.)	Reimbursement of money advanced to United States in 1798.	6	2	Memorial	773	Claims				Discharged.		
Jarvis, Leonard, (Mass.)	Reimbursement of money advanced to United States in 1798.	7	1	Petition	19	Claims	Dec. 31, 1801	Adverse		Rejected.		
Jarvis, Leonard, (Mass.)	Reimbursement of money advanced to United States in 1798.	12	2	Petition	578	Claims.						
Jarvis, Leonard, (Mass.)	Refund balance due as inspector of revenue.	7	2	Petition	291	Claims	Feb. 4, 1803			Laid on table.		
Jarvis, Louisa A.	(See Jotham Wright, heirs of.)	31	1		1184							
Jarvis, Solomon	Pension	26	1	Resolution	385	Rev. Pensions	664	Adverse		Laid on table.		
Jarvis, Solomon	Pension	30	2	Resolution	289	Rev. Pensions				Leave to withdraw.		
Jarvis, ——	(See Brown & Jarvis)	24	1		143							
Jasper, Sergeant, daughter of.	Pension	25	2	Resolution	525, 707	Rev. Pensions.				Leave to withdraw.		
Javens, John	Pension	27	1	Petition	107	Invalid Pensions.						
Javens, John	Pension	27	2	Petition	218	Invalid Pensions	320	Favorable	289	Referred to Committee Whole House.		
Javens, John	Pension	27	3	House bill	87	Whole House		Favorable	289	Passed	Passed	App'd March 3, 1843
Jay, James, (N. Y.)	Pay for services and reimbursement of money advanced to United States.	9	2	Petition and rep't Sec. of State.	525	Select	Feb. 17, 1807	Indefinite		Referred to Committee Whole House.		
Jay, James, (N. Y.)	Compensation for invention of secret correspondence.	10	1	Memorial	17	Select	Nov. 13, 1807	Favorable	12	Referred to Committee Whole House.		
Jay, James, (N. Y.)	Compensation for invention of secret correspondence.	10	1	Memorial	203	Select	April 20, 1808	Favorable		Postponed.		
Jayne, Ebenezer	Increase of pension	31	1	Petition	865	Invalid Pensions.						
Jeans, Joseph, representatives of.	Pay for horses lost in war of 1812.	17	1	Petition	100	Claims	Feb. 20, 1822	Adverse		Leave to withdraw.		
Jeans, Joseph, representatives of.	Pay for horses lost in war of 1812.	17	2	Petition	120	Claims.						
Jeans, Joseph, representatives of.	Pay for horses lost in war of 1812.	18	1	Petition	159	Claims	Mar. 10, 1824	Adverse		Laid on table.		
Jeans, Joseph, representatives of.	Pay for horses lost in war of 1812.	19	1	Petition	52	Claims	Mar. 8, 1826	Favorable	141	Passed.		
Jeans, Joseph, representatives of.	Pay for horses lost in war of 1812.	19	2	Petition	44	Claims	29	Favorable	339	Passed	Passed	App'd March 3, 1827
Jeans, Joseph, representatives of.	Further compensation	20	1	Documents	386	Claims	203	Favorable	235	Referred to Committee Whole House.		

List of private claims presented to the House of Representatives of the United States from the 1st to the 31st Congress, inclusive—Continued.

Names of claimants.	Nature or object of the claim.	Congress.	Session.	How brought before the House of Reps.	Page of journal.	To what committee of the House referred.	No. or date of the report.	Nature of the report.	No. of the bill.	How disposed of by the House of Reps.	How disposed of by the Senate.	Date of the act of Congress, and remarks.
Jeans, Joseph, representatives of.	Further compensation	20	2	House bill	227	Whole House	....	Favorable	235	Passed.		
Jeans, Joseph, representatives of.	Further compensation	21	1	Resolution	510	Claims	360	Favorable	419	Passed	Passed	App'd May 29, 1830
Jeansome, Baptiste, and others, (La.)	Confirmation of title to land	22	2	Petition	42	Priv. Land Claims.	60	Favorable	701	Referred to Committee Whole House.		
Jeansome, Baptiste, and others, (La.)	Confirmation of title to land	23	1	Petition	93	Priv. Land Claims.	83	Favorable	89	Passed	Passed, with amendment.	App'd June 27, 1834
Jeffers, John, (Conn.)	Pension	7	2	Petition	321	Claims	....	....	......	Leave to withdraw.		
Jeffers, John	Scrip for lands forfeited to government.	24	1	Petition	113	Public Lands	228	Favorable	240	Passed.		
Jeffers, John	Scrip for lands forfeited to government.	24	2	Petition	88	Public Lands	Jan. 10, 1837	Favorable	827	Passed	Passed	App'd March 3, 1837
Jefferson, Cicero	(See heirs of James Pepper, *et al.*)	27	3	....	136							
Jefferson College, trustees of.	Confirmation of title to land	8	2	Petition	7	Select	Feb. 7, 1805	Adverse	......	Referred to Committee Whole House.		
Jefferson College, trustees of.	Confirmation of title to land	9	1	Petition	151	Public Lands	Mar. 4, 1806	Adverse	......	Referred to Committee Whole House.		
Jefferson County Bank	(See assignees of Thomas Tupper.)											
Jefferson, John R., *et al.*	Pay for extra service as mail carriers.	27	3	Petition	61	P. Of. & P. Roads.						
Jefferson, John R., *et al.*	Pay for extra service as mail carriers.	28	1	Petition	508	P. Of. & P. Roads.	Feb. 28, 1844	Favorable	J.R. 13	Passed	Passed	App'd May 31, 1844
Jefferson, Russell	Arrears of pension	23	1	Resolution	81	Invalid Pensions	June 24, 1834	Adverse	......	Laid on table.		
Jefferson, Russell	Arrears of pension	30	1	Petition	927	Invalid Pensions	June 20, 1848	Adverse	......	Laid on table.		
Jeffrey, A., *et al*	Indemnity for French spoliations prior to 1800.	31	1	Petition	311	Foreign Affairs	355	Favorable	318	Referred to Committee Whole House.		
Jeffries, Richard, clerk United States court, Virginia.	Allowance for office rent	15	1	Petition	36	Judiciary	Dec. 16, 1817	Adverse	......	Laid on table.		
Jellison, Zachariah	Refund duties paid on tobacco	23	2	Petition	250	Commerce.						
Jellison, Zachariah	Refund duties paid on tobacco	24	1	Memorial	852	Ways and Means	June 7, 1836	Favorable	681	Referred to Committee Whole House.		
Jellison, Zachariah	Refund duties paid on tobacco	25	2	Memorial	42	Ways and Means	440	Favorable	445	Referred to Committee Whole House.		
Jellison, Zachariah	Refund duties paid on tobacco	25	3	House bill	378	Whole House	....	Favorable	445	Passed.		
Jellison, Zachariah	Refund duties paid on tobacco	26	1	Petition	178	Ways and Means	7	Favorable	25	Passed	Indef. postp'd.	
Jellison, Zachariah	Refund duties paid on tobacco	26	2	Petition	80	Ways and Means.						
Jellison, Zachariah	Refund duties paid on tobacco	27	2	Senate bill	1056	Ways and Means	July 27, 1842	....	S. 174	Passed	Passed	App'd Aug. 11, 1842
Jells, John, sureties of	Release from liability	8	1	Petition	428	Com. and Manuf.	Nov. 30, 1803	Favorable	......	Referred to Comptroller of the Treasury.		
Jencks, Benjamin, agent	(See Springfield Manufacturing Company, Massachusetts.)	23	1	....	191							
Jencks, John, *et al.*	(See Nathaniel Sawyier, *et al.*)	14	1	....	153							
Jenison, Joseph B	Pension	19	1	Resolution	445	Military Pensions.						
Jenison, Joseph B	Pension	19	2	Resolution	100	Military Pensions.						
Jenison, Joseph B	Pension	20	1	Resolution	338	Military Pensions	April 29, 1828	General bill	283	Passed.		
Jenison, Joseph B	Pension	20	2	Resolution	55	Military Pensions	Dec. 12, 1828	Favorable	311	Passed	Laid on table.	
Jenison, Joseph B	Pension	21	1	Petition	48	Military Pensions	Jan. 5, 1830	Favorable	72	Passed	Passed, with amendment.	App'd May 20, 1830
Jenison, Silas H	(See Vermont, governor of.)	26	1	....	711							
Jenkins, Benjamin	Pension	10	1	House bill	232	Whole House	April 19, 1808	Favorable	81 or 78	Passed	Passed	App'd April 25, 1808
Jenkins, Benjamin	Increase of pension	13	2	House bill	344	Whole House	Mar. 31, 1814	Favorable	166	Passed	Passed	App'd April 18, 1814

List of private claims presented to the House of Representatives of the United States from the 1st to the 31st Congress, inclusive—Continued.

Names of claimants.	Nature or object of the claim.	Congress.	Session.	How brought before the House of Reps.	Page of journal.	To what committee of the House referred.	No. or date of the report.	Nature of the report.	No. of the bill.	How disposed of by the House of Reps.	How disposed of by the Senate.	Date of the act of Congress, and remarks.
Jenkins, Benjamin, (R. I.)	Pension	21	2	Petition	126	Military Pensions.						
Jenkins, Benjamin, (R. I.)	Pension	22	1	Petition	80	Rev. Pensions.						
Jenkins, B. W	(See Langtry & Jenkins)	27	2		605							
Jenkins, Elisha, executor of.	Indemnity for French spoliations prior to 1800.	31	1	Petition	233	Foreign Affairs	355	Favorable	318	Referred to Committee Whole House.		
Jenkins, Ezekiel	Pension	22	1	Petition	56	Rev. Pensions				Laid on table.		
Jenkins, Frederick	(See Noah Brown, *et al.*)	15	1		83							
Jenkins, George	(See Edward Toppan, *et al.*)	8	1		96							
Jenkins, George	Relief from duties on merchandise.	10	1	Petition	162	Com. and Manuf.						
Jenkins, Hannah	(See James Jenkins, widow of.)	27	2		105							
Jenkins & Haven	(See Noah Brown, *et al.*)	22	1		286							
Jenkins, James, (Ark.)	Pension	20	2	Petition	31	Military Pensions	Jan. 20, 1829	Adverse		Laid on table.		
Jenkins, James, (La.)	For land in lieu of that sold for taxes.	22	1	Petition	336	Pens. & Rev. Cl'ms.	Feb. 21, 1832	Adverse		Laid on table.		
Jenkins, James, widow of.	Pension	27	2	Petition	105	Rev. Pensions	784	Adverse		Laid on table.		
Jenkins, James, widow of.	Pension	27	3	Petition	107	Rev. Pensions	132	Favorable	754	Passed	Passed	App'd March 3, 1843
Jenkins, James H	Indemnity for violation of contract by Post Office Department.	27	2	Memorial	808	P. Of. and P. Roads.						
Jenkins, James H	Indemnity for violation of contract by Post Office Department.	27	3	Petition	155	P. Of. & P. Roads.	179	Favorable	790	Referred to Committee Whole House.		
Jenkins, James H	Indemnity for violation of contract by Post Office Department.	28	1	Petition	434	P. Of. & P. Roads.	552	Adverse		Laid on table.		
Jenkins, James H	Indemnity for violation of contract by Post Office Department.	29	1	Memorial	261	P. Of. & P. Roads.						
Jenkins, James H	Indemnity for violation of contract by Post Office Department.	30	1	Memorial	879	P. Of. & P. Roads.						
Jenkins, James H	Indemnity for violation of contract by Post Office Department.	31	1	Petition	609	P. Of. & P. Roads.						
Jenkins, James H	Indemnity for violation of contract by Post Office Department.	31	2	Memorial	445	P. Of. & P. Roads.	97	Adverse		Laid on table.		
Jenkins, John, (La.)	Pre-emption right to land	17	1	Petition	228	Priv. Land Claims.						
Jenkins, John, (La.)	Pre-emption right to land	17	2	Petition	27	Priv. Land Claims.	11	Favorable	198	Passed.		
Jenkins, John, (La.)	Pre-emption right to land	18	1	Petition	28	Priv. Land Claims.	Dec. 23, 1823	Favorable	23	Postponed.		
Jenkins, John, (Ala.)	Pension	20	2	Resolution	97	Military Pensions	Feb. 13, 1829	Favorable	440	Passed.		
Jenkins, John, (Ala.)	Pension	21	1	Petition	49	Military Pensions.						
Jenkins, John, (Ala.)	Pension	22	1	Petition	134	Invalid Pensions.						
Jenkins, John	Indemnity for injuries from government vessels.	24	2	Petition	346	Naval Affairs				Referred to Secretary of the Navy.		
Jenkins, John	Indemnity for injuries from government vessels.	25	2	Petition	594	Naval Affairs				Laid on table.		
Jenkins, John	Indemnity for injuries from government vessels.	26	1	Petition and docs.	199, 674	Naval Affairs.						
Jenkins, John M	(See Benjamin Freeland, *et al.*)	17	1		102							
Jenkins & Langtry	(See Langtry & Jenkins.)	27	2		605							
Jenkins, Martha, (Ky.)	For land as widow of revolutionary soldier.	22	1	Petition	293	Priv. Land Claims.				Laid on table.		
Jenkins, Thomas, (D. C.)	Pension	17	1	Petition	201	Whole House.						
Jenkins, Thomas	(See David G. Bates, *et al.*)	30	2		124							
Jenkins, Thomas and Alonzo T.	(See Jerkins)	22	1		557							
Jenkins, Thomas & Co	Remission of duties on merchandise	1	2	Petition	213	Select	May 14, 1790	Favorable	67	Passed	Passed	App'd June 14, 1790
Jenkins, Thomas & Sons.	To be exonerated from duties required on foreign vessels.	3	1	Rep. of Secretary Treasury.	21	Select	Feb. 5, 1794	Favorable	8	Passed	Passed	App'd Feb. 19, 1794

List of private claims presented to the House of Representatives of the United States from the 1st to the 31st Congress, inclusive—Continued.

2—25

Names of claimants.	Nature or object of the claim.	Congress.	Session.	How brought before the House of Reps.	Page of journal.	To what committee of the House referred.	No. or date of the report.	Nature of the report.	No. of the bill.	How disposed of by the House of Reps.	How disposed of by the Senate.	Date of the act of Congress, and remarks.
Jenkins, Thomas & Sons	Register to vessel rebuilt	6	2	Petition	734	Com. and Manuf.	Dec. 8, 1800	Adverse	......	Laid on table.		
Jenkins, Thomas W	(See W. W. Haddock, *et al.*)	15	1		114							
Jenkins, Thomas C	(See R. and George McCandless.)	26	1		182							
Jenkins, Thomas C	(See Bedford & Morton, trustees of.)	26	1		182							
Jenkins, Weston, *et al*	For proceeds of a prize capture	13	3	Petition	626	Naval Affairs	41	Favorable	260	Passed	Passed	App'd Feb. 17, 1815
Jenkins, William, (Ky.)	Refund amount of judgment recovered against his securities.	29	1	Memorial	354	Claims	415	Adverse	......	Laid on table.		
Jenkins, William B	For a credit of $195 in his account.	26	1	Resolution	542	P. Of. and P. Roads.	395	Adverse	......	Laid on table.		
Jenkinson, William	Pension	24	1	Petition	406	Rev. Pensions	559	Favorable	551	Passed	Indef. postp'd.	
Jenkinson, William	Pension	24	2	Petition	217	Rev. Pensions	151	Favorable	880	Referred to Committee Whole House.		
Jenkinson, William	Pension	25	2	Petition	38	Rev. Pensions	165	Favorable	190	Passed.		
Jenkinson, William	Pension	26	1	Petition	174, 513	Rev. Pensions	....	....	......	Laid on table.		
Jenks, Arnold	(See Stephen Jenks & Sons)	14	2		241							
Jenks, Charles	Confirmation of title to land	15	1	Petition	249	Public Lands	Feb. 16, 1818	Adverse	......	Leave to withdraw.		
Jenks, David	(See Stephen Jenks & Sons)	14	2		241							
Jenks, David	(See Canadian refugees)	4	2		614							
Jenks, George	(See Stephen Jenks & Sons)	14	2		241							
Jenks, John	Pay for revolutionary services	23	1	Petition	54	Rev. Claims	Jan. 21, 1834	Adverse	......	Laid on table.		
Jenks, Stephen & Sons	Additional pay for muskets	14	2	Petition	241	Claims.						
Jenks, Stephen & Sons	Additional pay for muskets	15	1	Petition	157	Military Affairs.						
Jenks, Stephen & Sons	Additional pay for muskets	15	2	Petition	196	Claims.						
Jenks, Stephen & Sons	Additional pay for muskets	16	1	Petition	111	Claims	34	Adverse	......	Laid on table.		
Jenks, Stephen & Sons	Additional pay for muskets	17	1	Petition	164	Claims	....	....	......	Leave to withdraw.		
Jenks, Stephen & Sons	Additional pay for muskets	17	1	Petition (2)	432	Claims.						
Jenks, Stephen & Sons	Additional pay for muskets	17	2	Petition	69	Claims.						
Jenks, Stephen & Sons	Additional pay for muskets	18	1	Petition	481	Claims	May 10, 1824	Favorable	225	Ref'd to Com. W. H.		
Jenks, Stephen & Sons	Additional pay for muskets	18	2	Bill	259	Whole House	....	Favorable	225	Passed	Passed	App'd March 3, 1825
Jenks, Stephen & Sons	For further additional pay	19	1	Petition	442	Claims.						
Jenks, Stephen & Sons	For further additional pay	20	1	Petition	78	Claims	168	Favorable	197	Passed	Passed	App'd May 24, 1828
Jenks, Stephen & Sons	For further additional pay	21	1	Petition	376							
Jenne, Thomas, (N. Y.)	Land and extra pay for services, war of 1812.	28	1	Petition	941	Claims.						
Jenne, Thomas, (N. Y.)	Land and extra pay for services, war of 1812.	30	1	Petition	103	Priv. Land Claims.	92	Adverse	......	Laid on table.		
Jenne, Thomas, (N. Y.)	Land and extra pay for services, war of 1812.	31	1	Petition	647	Priv. Land Claims.						
Jennet, Jesse	Pay as chaplain, war of 1812	12	2	Petition	686	Claims.						
Jennet, Jesse	Pay as chaplain, war of 1812	13	2	Petition	176	Claims	Feb. 7, 1814	Favorable	113	Referred to Committee Whole House.		
Jenney, Thomas	Pay for services, revolutionary war	2	1	Petition	451	....	....	....	......	Referred to Secretary of War.		
Jenney, Thomas	Pay for services, revolutionary war	3	2	Rep. of Secretary War.	278	....	....	....	......	Laid on table.		
Jennings, Daniel, (Ohio.)	Relief from expenses incurred in discharge of official duty as collector.	10	1	Petition	268	....	....	....	......	Referred to Secretary Treasury.		
Jennings, Daniel, (Ohio.)	Relief from expenses incurred in discharge of official duty as collector.	10	2	Rep. of Secretary Treasury.	564	....	....	....	......	Laid on table.		

List of private claims presented to the House of Representatives of the United States from the 1st to the 31st Congress, inclusive—**Continued.**

Names of claimants.	Nature or object of the claim.	Congress.	Session.	How brought before the House of Reps.	Page of journal.	To what committee of the House referred.	No. or date of the report.	Nature of the report.	No. of the bill.	How disposed of by the House of Reps.	How disposed of by the Senate.	Date of the act of Congress, and remarks.
Jennings, Ebenezer	Pension	3	2	Rep. of Secretary War.	350	Claims	Feb. 28, 1795	Favorable	130	Passed	Postponed.	
Jennings, Ebenezer	Pension	4	1	Petition	445	Claims	Mar. 4, 1796	Favorable	156	Passed	Passed	App'd April 20, 1796
Jennings, Eliphalet	Pension	19	1	Petition	108	Military Pensions.						
Jennings, George, (Fla.)	Indemnity for Indian depredations.	28	2	Memorial	84	Claims.						
Jennings, George H	Pay for bringing to justice two of crew of brig Orbit.	22	1	Petition	43	Claims	408	Favorable	508	Referred to Committee Whole House.		
Jennings, George H	Pay for bringing to justice two of crew of brig Orbit.	23	1	Petition	34	Claims	8	Favorable	8	Passed	Passed	App'd Feb. 5, 1834
Jennings, Isaiah	Extension of patent	16	1	Petition	65	Judiciary				Leave to withdraw.		
Jennings, Isaiah	Extension of patent	17	1	Petition	288	Judiciary	May 7, 1822	Adverse		Laid on table.		
Jennings, James, (Ohio.)	(See Joseph Reynolds, surety of.)	17	2		185							
Jennings, John, heirs of	Half-pay for revolutionary services.	24	1	Petition	138	Rev. Claims.						
Jennings, John, heirs of	Half-pay for revolutionary services	27	3	Petition	320	Rev. Claims	242	Adverse		Laid on table.		
Jennings, John, heirs of	Half pay for revolutionary services.	28	1	Petition	216	Rev. Claims.						
Jennings, John, heirs of	Half-pay for revolutionary services	28	2	Petition	221	Rev. Claims.						
Jennings, John S., (Penn.)	Pension	29	1	Memorial	474	Claims.						
Jennings, Joseph, (N. Y.)	Pension	20	2	Petition	26	Military Pensions.	Feb. 12, 1829	Favorable	440	Passed.		
Jennings, Joseph, (N. Y.)	Pension	21	1	Petition	49	Military Pensions.						
Jennings, Robert C	Equitable settlement of accounts of Jennings & Roddy.	22	1	Senate bill	745	Claims	487	With amend.	S. 96	Passed with amendm't.	Passed as am'd	App'd July 14, 1832
				Petition	815	Claims.						
Jennings, Robert C	Extension of the act of July 1832	22	2	Resolution	70	Claims	10	Favorable	629	Passed	Passed*	App'd Feb. 5, 1833
Jennings, Robert C	Further extension of the act of 1832.	23	1	Petition	55	Claims	206	Favorable	227	Referred to Committee Whole House.		
Jennings, Robert C	Further extension of the act of 1832.	23	2	House bill	93				227	Recommitted.		
Jennings, Robert C	Further extension of the act of 1832.	24	1	Petition	507	Claims.						
Jennings, Robert C	Further extension of the act of 1832.	27	2	Petition	56	Claims.						
Jennings, Robert C	Further extension of the act of 1832.	27	3	Petition	73	Claims	128	Favorable	750	Referred to Committee Whole House.		See Journal, p. 476.
Jennings, Robert C	Further extension of the act of 1832.	28	1	Report of Secre'y Treasury.	408	Claims.						
Jennings, Robert C	(See James Roddy, executors of.)	18	1		287							
Jennings, Robert C	(See See Robert B. Carter, administrator of.)	23	2		275							
Jennings, Runeford, widow of.	Pension	31	1	Petition	996	Invalid Pensions.						
Jennings, Samuel K	Renewal of patent	27	3	Petition	137	Patents	Jan. 28, 1843	Favorable	732	Passed	Passed	App'd March 3, 1843
Jennings, William	(See John S. Westwood, executors of.)	26	1		622							
Jennings, William, (Va.)	Pension	31	1	Petition	449	Invalid Pensions.						
Jemison, Timothy L	(See Nathan Gilbert, administrator of.)	23	1		156							
Jemison, William	(See J. B. Hobkirk, assignee of.)	22	1		809							
Jephson & Reade	(See Reade & Jephson.)	10	2		463							
Jerkins, Thomas and Alonzo T.	Remission of duties on sugar	22	1	Petition	557	Ways and Means.						
Jerkins, Thomas and Alonzo T.	Remission of duties on sugar	22	2	Petition	41	Ways and Means.						
Jernigan, H. W. & Co	Pay for house burnt by Indians	27	2	Documents	1377					Laid on table.		

List of private claims presented to the House of Representatives of the United States from the 1st to the 31st Congress, inclusive—Continued.

Names of claimants.	Nature or object of the claim.	Congress.	Session.	How brought before the House of Reps.	Page of journal.	To what committee of the House referred.	No. or date of the report.	Nature of the report.	No. of the bill.	How disposed of by the House of Reps.	How disposed of by the Senate.	Date of the act of Congress, and remarks.
Jernigan, H. W. & Co.	Pay for house burnt by Indians	27	3	Documents	345	Claims.						
Jernigan, H. W. & Co.	Pay for house burnt by Indians	30	2	Resolution	381	....	....	....	......	Leave to withdraw.		
Jernigan, H. W. & Co.	Pay for house burnt by Indians	31	1	Indian appropriation bill.	1012	Whole House	Aug. 3, 1850	With amends.	331	Passed	Passed	App'd Sept. 30, 1850
Jerome, Charles, (Ohio)	Release as surety of Robert Harper.	28	2	Petition	71	Judiciary.						
Jerome, Jean Baptiste, *et al.*	Indemnity for property destroyed in the war of 1812.	15	1	Letter of Com'r of Claims.	195	Claims.						
Jerome, Jean Baptiste, *et al.*	Indemnity for property destroyed in the war of 1812.	16	1	Petition	106	Claims.						
Jerome, Jean Baptiste, *et al.*	Indemnity for property destroyed in the war of 1812.	16	2	Petition	120	Claims	33	Adverse	......	Leave to withdraw.		
Jerome, Jean Baptiste, *et al.*	Indemnity for property destroyed in the war of 1812.	17	1	Petition	47	Claims	34	Adverse	......	Referred to Committee Whole House.		
Jerome, Jean Baptiste, *et al.*	Indemnity for property destroyed in the war of 1812.	17	2	Documents	70	Whole House	....	....	......	....	....	See report No. 26.
Jerome, Jean Baptiste, *et al.*	Indemnity for property destroyed in the war of 1812.	18	1	Petition	106	Claims.						
Jerome, Jean Baptiste, *et al.*	Indemnity for property destroyed in the war of 1812.	20	2	Resolution	73	Claims	80	Favorable	439	Referred to Committee Whole House.		
Jerome, Jean Baptiste, *et al.*	Indemnity for property destroyed in the war of 1812.	21	1	Petition	93	Claims	34	Favorable	46	Passed	Passed with amendment.	App'd May 31, 1830
Jerome, John Baptiste, by John Anderson, assignee of.	For authority to locate land claims.	22	1	Petition	294	Public Lands	April 10, 1832	Favorable	540	Passed	Passed	App'd July 10, 1832
Jerom, Robert	Pension	3	1	Rep. of Secretary of War.	131	Select.	May 26, 1794	Favorable	J.R.12	Passed	Passed	App'd June 9, 1794
Jerom, Robert	Pension	3	2	Rep. of Secretary War.	278	Claims	Feb. 28, 1795	Favorable	130	Passed	Postponed.	
Jerom, Robert	Pension	4	1	Petition	445	Claims	Feb. 18, 1796	Favorable	156	Passed	Passed	App'd April 20, 1796
Jervey, Thomas H.	Half of two vessels condemned for violating slave act.	15	1	Petition	202	Ways and Means	Feb. 28, 1818	Favorable	111	Referred to Committee Whole House.		
Jervey, Thomas H.	Half of two vessels condemned for violating slave act.	15	2	House bill	83	Whole House	....	....	111	Passed.	Passed	App'd Feb. 24, 1819
Jervis, John	Losses and injuries sustained in revolutionary war.	5	2	Petition	147	Claims	Feb. 13, 1798	Adverse	......	Laid on table.		
Jessup, A.	Payment of claims against Ottawa Indians.	29	1	Memorial	160	Indian Affairs	287	Adverse	......	Laid on table.		
Jessup, William, *et al.*	Increase of pay as inspector, (N. Y.)	20	1	Memorial	191	Commerce.						
Jester, Joseph, *et al.*	Full pay while in captivity in Mexico.	30	1	Petition	521	Military Affairs.						
Jeter, Fielding, widow of.	Pension	28	1	Petition	510	Rev. Claims.						
Jett, Benjamin P., *et al.*	Additional pay for locating military land warrants.	31	1	Petition	392	Public Lands.						
Jett, Charles C	(See Thomas Jett, representatives of.)	30	1	....	587							
Jett, James, (Va.)	Pay for property destroyed in 1812.	22	2	Petition	177	Claims.						
Jett, Thomas, representatives of.	Payment of lost loan office certificates.	25	2	Petition	69	Rev. Claims	360	Favorable	389	Postponed.		
Jett, Thomas, representatives of.	Payment of lost loan office certificates.	26	1	Petition	164	Rev. Claims	330	Favorable	302	Referred to Committee Whole House.		
Jett, Thomas, representatives of.	Payment of lost loan office certificates.	27	2	Petition	61	Rev. Claims	1082	Adverse	......	Laid on table.		

List of private claims presented to the House of Representatives of the United States form the 1st to the 31st Congress, inclusive—**Continued.**

Names of claimants.	Nature or object of the claim.	Congress.	Session.	How brought before the House of Reps.	Page of journal.	To what committee of the House referred.	No. or date of the report.	Nature of the report.	No. of the bill.	How disposed of by the House of Reps.	How disposed of by the Senate.	Date of the act of Congress, and remarks.
Jett, Thomas, representatives of.	Payment of lost loan office certificates.	30	1	Petition	587	Rev. Claims......	503	Favorable....	424	Referred to Committee Whole House.		
Jett, Thomas, representatives of.	Payment of lost loan office certificates.	31	1	Petition	270	Rev. Claims......	7	Favorable....	9	Laid on table.		
Jett, Wm. S., administrator and heir of Thomas.	Payment of loan office certificate..	27	3	Petition	45	Rev. Claims......	241	Adverse	.....	Laid on table.		
Jett, jr., William S......	Settlement of accounts as officer in late war.	18	1	Petition	388	Claims	....	....	.....	Leave to withdraw.		
Jett, William, (Va.)	Compensation for property lost in war of 1812.	23	1	Petition	438	Claims	406	Adverse	.....	Laid on table.		
Jewell, Dorcas T........	(See Kinchen Jewell, widow of)..	30	1	....	405							
Jewell, Kinchen, widow of.	Pay for Indian depredations in Florida.	30	1	....	405	Claims	396	Adverse	.....	Laid on table.		
Jewell, John, (Mass.)....	Pension	23	1	Petition	352	Invalid Pensions.						
Jewell, John, (Mass.)....	Pension	25	2	Petition	198	Invalid Pensions ..	....	....	.....	Laid on table.		
Jewell, John M., (Vt.)...	Pension	24	1	Res. and petition	635, 661	Invalid Pensions...	....	....	.....	Discharged; laid on table.		
Jewell, John M., (Vt.)...	Pension	24	2	Memorial	73	Invalid Pensions...	131	Favorable....	860	Referred to Committee Whole House.		
Jewell, John M., (Vt.)...	Pension	25	2	Resolution	38	Invalid Pensions...	425	Favorable....	432	Passed	Passed	App'd July 7, 1838
Jewett, Abraham	(See assignees Thomas Tupper)..	23	2	....	142							
Jewett, David	Pension	19	1	Petition	127	Military Pensions..	April 1, 1826	Adverse	.....	Laid on table.		
Jewett, David, heirs of....	Pay for revolutionary services	30	1	Petition	435	Rev. Pensions.....	383	Adverse	.....	Laid on table.		
Jewett, Isaac............	Payment for lost loan certificates..	17	2	Petition	118	Rev. Claims......	Jan. 24, 1823	Adverse	.....	Laid on table.		
Jewett, James, of Maine..	Release from judgment of United States.	14	1	Petition	82	Select	Jan. 2, 1815	Favorable; bill	.....	Passed	Rejected.	
Jewett, Joshua R........	Half-pay for revolutionary services.	31	1	Petition	862	Rev. Claims.						
Jewett, Othniel..........	Pay for service in war of 1812...	25	2	Petition	58	Military Affairs ...	Dec. 28, 1837	Adverse	.....	Laid on table.		
Jewett, Solomon, *et al*....	(See David Jewett, heirs of.)....	30	1	....	435							
Jewit, Ezekiel	Arrears of pension............	23	2	Resolution	355	Invalid Pensions.						
Jilson, Henry...........	Pension	15	2	Petition	20	Pens. & Rev. Cl'ms.	....	....	.....	Referred to Secretary of War.		
Jinkins, Josiah..........	Indemnity for Indian depredations.	21	2	Documents.....	89	Indian Affairs.....	....	....	.....	Laid on table.		
Jipson, Bradley True.....	Pension	24	1	Petition	98	Invalid Pensions ..	839	Favorable....	741	Referred to Committee Whole House.		
Jipson, Bradley True.. ..	Pension	25	2	Petition	38	Invalid Pensions ..	185	Favorable....	211	Passed	Passed	App'd June 28, 1838
Jipson, Bradbury True....	Correction of error in name......	25	3	Resolution	156	Invalid Pensions ..	Jan. 2, 1839	Favorable....	961	Passed	Passed	App'd Jan. 25, 1839
Joanna, schooner........	(See Henry Bowers, *et al*)......	25	2	....	923							
Joanna, schooner........	(See Wm. Fullerston, *et al*).....	26	1	....	710							
John George, schooner ...	(See John B. Pierce, *et al*)......	27	2	....	45							
Johns, Elias, of Tenn....	Pay for lost horse in war of 1812.	23	1	Petition	136	Claims.						
Johns, Elias, of Tenn....	Pay for lost horse in war of 1812.	23	2	Petition	250	Claims	Feb. 2, 1835	Adverse	.....	Laid on table.		
Johns, Elias, of Tenn....	Pay for lost horse in war of 1812.	24	1	Petition	627	Claims	535	Favorable....	530	Referred to Committee Whole House.		
Johns, Elias, of Tenn....	Pay for lost horse in war of 1812.	25	2	Petition	36	Claims	27	Favorable....	39	Passed	Passed	App'd April 20, 1838
Johns, Henry V. D	Remit duty on books..........	31	1	Petition	881	Commerce.						
Johns, Hobson..........	Indemnity for loss on tobacco contract.	29	2	Senate bill	374	Claims..........	Feb. 24, 1847	Favorable....	82	Passed...........	Passed	App'd March 2, 1847
Johns, John and Thomas	Pay for military services in 1812..	31	1	Petition	225	Public Lands.						
Johnson, Abraham	Pension	14	1	Resolution	514	Rev. Claims......	April 11, 1816	Favorable....	171	Passed	Passed, with amendment.	App'd April 30, 1816
Johnson, Abraham, administrator of.	Pension	27	3	Petition	260	Rev. Pensions	....	....	.....	Leave to withdraw.		

List of private claims presented to the House of Representatives of the United States from the 1st to the 31st Congress, inclusive—Continued.

Names of claimants.	Nature or object of the claim.	Congress.	Session.	How brought before the House of Reps.	Page of journal.	To what committee of the House referred.	No. or date of the report.	Nature of the report.	No. of the bill.	How disposed of by the House of Reps.	How disposed of by the Senate.	Date of the act of Congress, and remarks.
Johnson, Absalom	Confirmation of title to land	14	2	Petition	378	Public Lands.						
Johnson, Adam	Grant of land	6	2	Bill	766	Whole House	....	Favorable	280	Passed	Passed	App'd April 18, 1801
Johnson, Alexander	Pension	27	2	Memorial	720	Invalid Pensions.						
Johnson, Allen	Pension	27	3	Petition	102	Invalid Pensions.						
Johnson, Allen G	Pay for services in Florida war	30	1	Memorial	321	Military Affairs.						
Johnson, Allen G	Leave to reclaim land in Florida	29	1	Petition	634	Public Lands	558	Adverse	......	Laid on table.		
Johnson, Allen G	Balance due on his account	31	2	Senate bill	46	....	....	....	S. 77			
Johnson, Amos, widow of	Permission to make the last payment on forfeited land.	2[illegible]	1	Petition	413	Public Lands	....	....	......	Laid on table.		
Johnson, Andrew	Pay for medicine and services, revolutionary war.	3	1	Petition	29	Select.						
Johnson, Andrew	Pay for medicine and services, revolutionary war.	3	2	Petition	305	Claims.						
Johnson, Andrew	Pay for medicine and services, revolutionary war.	4	1	Petition	373	Claims	Dec. 28, 1795	Adverse	......	Leave to withdraw.		
Johnson, Andrew	Pension	12	1	House bill	361	Whole House	June 15, 1812	Favorable	138	Passed	Passed	App'd July 5, 1812
Johnson, Andrew, (Ky.)	(See John Johnson, representatives of.)	26	1	....	547							
Johnson, Andrew, (Va.)	Pension	25	2	Petition	271	Rev. Pensions	....	....	......	Discharged: laid on table.		
Johnson, Andrew, widow of, (Pa.)	Pension	19	1	Petition	492	Military Pensions	May 3, 1836	Adverse	......	Laid on table.		
Johnson, Andrew, widow of, (Pa.)	Pension	20	1	Petition	396	Military Pensions	Mar. 28, 1828	Adverse	......	Laid on table.		
Johnson, Ann W	(See William Johnson, widow of, N. Y.)	25	2	....	36	....	73	....	85			
Johnson, Archibald	Relief for lost certificates of public debt.	4	1	Petition	492	Claims.						
Johnson, Archibald	Relief for lost certificates of public debt.	4	2	Petition	614	Claims	Feb. 1, 1797	Adverse	......	Rejected.		
Johnson, Archibald	Bounty land	26	1	Petition	325	Rev. Pensions	551	Adverse	......	Laid on table.		
Johnson, Archibald	Bounty land	26	1	Petition	357	Public Lands.						
Johnson, Barbara	(See Andrew Johnson, widow of)	19	1	....	492							
Johnson, Benjamin	Settlement of accounts as captain United States army.	15	1	Documents	223	Military Affairs	Feb. 10, 1818	Favorable	80	Passed	Passed, with amendment.	App'd April 20, 1818
Johnson, Benjamin, (Ky.)	Pension	28	2	Petition	53	Rev. Pensions.						
Johnson, Benjamin, (Ky.)	Pension	29	1	Petition	132	Rev. Pensions	615	Adverse	......	Laid on table.		
Johnson, Benjamin, (Ky.)	Pension	29	2	Petition	59	Rev. Pensions	....	....	......	Disch'd; laid on table.		
Johnson, Benjamin, (Ky.)	Pension	30	1	Petition	78	Rev. Pensions	87	Adverse	......	Laid on table.		
Johnson, Benjamin, (Va.)	Pension	21	2	Resolution	91	Military Pensions.						
Johnson, Caleb	Pension for revolutionary services	16	1	Resolution	63	Rev. Pensions	Jan. 14, 1820	Adverse	......	Laid on table.		
Johnson, Calvin, (N. Y.)	Confirmation of title to land	18	2	Petition	135	Judiciary.						
Johnson, Catharine	(See William Johnson, widow of, (N. Y.)	28	1	....	61							
Johnson, Catharine H. F.	(See Captain Hezekiah Johnson, widow of.	27	3	....	95							
Johnson, Charles	Pension	30	1	Petition	317	Naval Affairs.						
Johnson, Charles	Pension	30	2	Memorial	216	Naval Affairs.						
Johnson, Charles G.	(See Benjamin Collins and C. G. Johnson.)	23	1	....	307							
Johnson, Christopher, executor of.	Indemnity for French spoliations prior to 1800.	26	1	Memorial	182	Foreign Affairs	343	Favorable	319	Referred to Committee Whole House.		

List of private claims presented to the House of Representatives of the United States from the 1st to the 31st Congress, inclusive—Continued.

Names of claimants.	Nature or object of the claim.	Congress.	Session.	How brought before the House of Reps.	Page of journal.	To what committee of the House referred.	No. or date of the report.	Nature of the report.	No. of the bill.	How disposed of by the House of Reps.	How disposed of by the Senate.	Date of the act of Congress, and remarks.
Johnson, Crawford	Reissue of lost warrant	22	2	Resolution	425	Public Lands.						
Johnson, Crawford	Reissue of lost warrant	24	1	Resolution	675	Rev. Claims	June 28, 1836	Favorable	732	Referred to Committee Whole House.		
Johnson, Crawford	Reissue of lost warrant	24	2	Resolution	276	Rev. Claims.						
Johnson, Crawford	Reissue of lost warrant	25	2	Resolution	40, 103	Rev. Claims	114	Favorable	132	Passed	Passed	App'd July 7, 1838
Johnson, Daniel	Remit penalties for illegal importing.	12	2	Petition	713	Ways and Means				Discharged.		
Johnson, Daniel	Remit penalties for illegal importing.	13	2	Petition	366	Ways and Means				Discharged.		
Johnson, Daniel	Remit penalties for illegal importing.	16	2	Petition	101	Ways and Means	Feb. 13, 1821	Favorable	251	Referred to Committee Whole House.		
Johnson, Daniel	Remit penalties for illegal importing.	17	1	Petition	114	Ways and Means	Feb. 1, 1822	Favorable	69	Laid on table.		
Johnson, Daniel	Remit penalties for illegal importing.	17	2	Petition	76	Ways and Means.						
Johnson, Daniel	Remit penalties for illegal importing.	18	1	House bill	148	Whole House		Favorable	60	Passed	Passed	App'd May 19, 1824
Johnson, Daniel, (Va.)	Compensation for work at arsenal, Harper's Ferry.	20	1	Petition	127	Military Affairs				Leave to withdraw.		
Johnson, Daniel, (Va.)	Compensation for work at arsenal, Harper's Ferry.	21	1	Documents	378	Military Affairs	330	Favorable	388	Referred to Committee Whole House.		
Johnson, Daniel, (Va.)	Compensation for work at arsenal, Harper's Ferry.	22	1	Petition	74	Military Affairs	83	Favorable	180	Referred to Committee Whole House.		
Johnson, Daniel, (Va.)	Compensation for work at arsenal, Harper's Ferry.	22	2	House bill	66	Whole House		Favorable	180	Passed	Passed	App'd Feb. 5, 1833
Johnson, David, widow of, (N. Y.)	Pension	26	1	Petition	705	Rev. Pensions	499	Favorable	401	Referred to Committee Whole House.		
Johnson, David, widow of, (N. Y.)	Pension	27	2	Petition and affidavit.	59, 69	Rev. Pensions	115	Favorable	161	Passed	Passed	App'd Aug. 16, 1842
Johnson, David, (Ohio)	Pension	28	1	Petition	879	Rev. Pensions.						
Johnson, David, son of	Settlement of claim for revolutionary services.	8	2	Memorial	66	Claims.						
Johnson, David	Pre-emption as New Orleans branch pilot.	28	1	Petition	77	Priv. Land Claims.	9	Favorable	35	Passed	Passed	App'd June 17, 1844
Johnson, Delilah	Pension	28	1	Resolution	557	Rev. Pensions.						
Johnson, Ebenezer, (N. Y.)	Pension	24	1	Petition	107	Rev. Pensions				Laid on table.		
Johnson, Ebenezer, (N. Y.)	Pension	26	2	Resolution	87	Rev. Pensions	Feb. 12, 1841	Adverse		Laid on table.		
Johnson, Ebenezer	(See Pierre A. Barker, surety of).	27	2		972							
Johnson, Eleazer, (Mass.)	(See Geo. Williamson, *et al.*)	2	2		626							
Johnson, Eleazer	Payment of certain bills of credit	3	1	Memorial	67					Referred to Secretary Treasury.		
Johnson, Eleazer	Payment of certain bills of credit	4	1	Rep. of Secretary Sec. Treasury.	388	Claims	74	Adverse		Laid on table.		
Johnson, Eleazer	Indemnity for French spoliations prior to 1800.	26	1	Memorial	182	Foreign Affairs	343	Favorable	319	Referred to Committee Whole House.		
Johnson, Elijah, (N. H.)	Pension	19	2	Petition	156	Military Pensions	Feb. 14, 1827	Favorable	436	Ref'd to Com. W. H.		
Johnson, Elijah, (N. H.)	Pension	20	1	Petition	193	Military Pensions	April 29, 1828	Favorable	283	Passed.		
Johnson, Elijah, (N. H.)	Pension	20	2	Petition	55	Military Pensions	Dec. 12, 1828	Favorable	311	Passed	Laid on table.	
Johnson, Elijah, (N. H.)	Pension	21	1	Petition	48	Military Pensions	Jan. 5, 1830	Favorable	72	Passed	Passed, with amendment.	App'd May 20, 1830
Johnson, Esther	Pay for supplies furnished government.	2	2	Petition	634					Referred to Secretary of Treasury.		

List of private claims presented to the House of Representatives of the United States from the 1st to the 31st Congress, inclusive—Continued.

Names of claimants.	Nature or object of the claim.	Congress.	Session.	How brought before the House of Reps.	Page of journal.	To what committee of the House referred.	No. or date of the report.	Nature of the report.	No. of the bill.	How disposed of by the House of Reps.	How disposed of by the Senate.	Date of the act of Congress, and remarks.
Johnson, Esther	Pay for supplies furnished government.	3	1	Rep. of Secretary Treasury.	78					Laid on table.		
Johnson, Euphemia	(See Amos Johnson, widow of)	21	1		413							
Johnson, Eliza	(See Francis Johnson, widow of)	30	2		333							
Johnson, Ezekiel	Pension	1	3	Petition	364	Referred to Secretary of War.	Feb. 26, 1791	Indefinite		Laid on table.		
Johnson, Francis, widow of	Treasury scrip for services in Mexican war.	30	2	House bill	365				753			
Johnson, Francis, (Va.)	(See Drury Holland, heirs of)	28	1		452							
Johnson, Francis, (Tenn.)	Pay for horse lost in war of 1812.	28	1	Petition	685	Claims	561	Adverse		Laid on table.		
Johnson, Francis, (Tenn.)	Pay for horse lost in war of 1812.	28	2	Petition	84	Claims.						
Johnson, Frederick, (N. C.)	Bounty land for revolutionary services.	20	2	Petition	61	Rev. Claims	Jan. 5, 1829	Adverse		Laid on table.		
Johnson, George, (La.)	Release as surety of B. F. Bourne	21	1	Petition	75	Judiciary				Discharged; laid on table.		
Johnson, George, (La.)	Release as surety of B. F. Bourne	21	1	Senate bill	430	Claims	356	Adverse	S. 73	Referred to Committee Whole House.		
Johnson, George, (La.)	Release as surety of B. F. Bourne	21	2	Senate bill	196	Claims	90	Favorable	S. 11	Passed	Passed	App'd March 2, 1831
Johnson, George, (La.)	For amount of act 2d March, 1831	22	1	Senate bill	119	Claims	Dec. 30, 1831	Amended	S. 18	Passed	Passed	App'd July 14, 1832
Johnson, George, *et al*	Relief as inspector of customs	17	1	Petition	386	Commerce.						
Johnson, George, *et al*	Relief as inspector of customs	18	2	Petition	116	Ways and Means.						
Johnson, George, *et al*	Relief as inspector of customs	19	1	Petition	150	Claims	159	Favorable	213	Passed.		
Johnson, George, *et al*	Relief as inspector of customs	19	2	Petition	26	Claims	Feb. 5, 1827	Favorable	422	Passed.		
Johnson, George, *et al*	Relief as inspector of customs	20	1	Petition	78	Claims	44	Favorable	30	Passed	Passed	App'd April 3, 1828
Johnson, George C.	Payment of debt due by Shawnee Indians.	24	2	Senate bill	579				S. 180			
Johnson, George C.	Payment of debt due by Shawnee Indians.	25	2	Petition	173	Indian Affairs	744	Favorable	493	Referred to Committee Whole House.		
Johnson, George C.	Payment of debt due by Shawnee Indians.	25	3	House bill	379	Whole House		Favorable	493	Passed.		
Johnson, George C.	Payment of debt due by Shawnee Indians.	27	3	Petition	100	Indian Affairs	24	Favorable	653	Passed	Passed	App'd March 3, 1843
Johnson, George C.	Payment of debt due by Shawnee Indians.	31	1	Memorial	450	Indian Affairs.						
Johnson, Henry, (Ind.)	Pension	20	1	Resolution	448	Military Pensions.	April 2, 1828	Favorable	283	Passed	Postponed.	
Johnson, Henry, (Ind.)	Pension	20	2	General bill	55	Whole House	Jan. 15, 1829	Favorable	311	Passed	Laid on table.	
Johnson, Henry, (Ind.)	Pension	21	1	General bill	48	Whole House	Feb. 13, 1830	With amends.	72	Passed	Passed	App'd May 20, 1830
Johnson, Henry	Pre-emption as N. Orleans branch pilot.	28	1	Petition	77	Priv. Land Claims.	9	Favorable	35	Passed	Passed	App'd June 17, 1844
Johnson, Henry, (Ohio)	Grant of portion of public lands.	19	1	Petition	206	Indian Affairs				Discharged; laid on table.		This case was previously presented, but does not appear on Journal.
Johnson, Henry, (Ohio)	Pension	30	1	Resolution	188, 274	Rev. Pensions	539	Adverse		Discharged; laid on table.		
Johnson, Henry, (Ohio)	Pension	31	1	Memorial	391	Rev. Pensions	20	Adverse		Discharged; laid on table.		
Johnson, H. D., (Mass.)	Pay as judge advocate on Mediterranean.	29	1	Petition	70	Naval Affairs	208	Favorable	202	Referred to Committee Whole House.		
Johnson, H. D., (Mass.)	Pay as judge advocate on Mediterranean.	30	1	Petition	81	Naval Affairs	109	Favorable	98	Passed.		

List of private claims presented to the House of Representatives of the United States from the 1st to the 31st Congress, inclusive—Continued.

Names of claimants.	Nature or object of the claim.	Congress.	Session.	How brought before the House of Reps.	Page of journal.	To what committee of the House referred.	No. or date of the report.	Nature of the report.	No. of the bill.	How disposed of by the House of Reps.	How disposed of by the Senate.	Date of the act of Congress, and remarks.
Johnson, H. D., (Mass.)	Pay as judge advocate on Mediterranean.	31	1	Petition	269	Claims	94	Adverse		Laid on table.		
Johnson, Capt. Hezekiah, widow of.	Pension	27	3	Petition	95	Invalid Pensions	153	Adverse		Laid on table.		
Johnson, Capt. Hezekiah, widow of.	Pension	28	1	Petition	130	Invalid Pensions	106	Adverse		Laid on table.		
Johnson, Capt. Hezekiah, widow of.	Pension	29	1	Petition	446	Invalid Pensions.						
Johnson, Capt. Hezekiah, widow of.	Pension	30	1	Petition	78	Invalid Pensions				Laid on table.		
Johnson, Capt. Hezekiah, widow of.	Pension	30	2	Petition	217	Invalid Pensions				Laid on table.		
Johnson, Capt. Hezekiah, widow of.	Pension	31	2	Petition	77	Invalid Pensions.						
Johnson, Hickman	(See Juliet Eliza Sellers, guardian of.)	15	1		256							
Johnson, Homer, widow of	Pay for superintendence on Cumberland road.	29	1	Documents	265	Claims.						
Johnson, Homer, widow of	Pay for superintendence on Cumberland road.	29	2	Documents	74	Claims.						
Johnson, Hugh	Pension	27	2	Documents	219	Invalid Pensions	442	Adverse		Laid on table.		
Johnson, Ichabod, *et al.*	Pay as United States seamen	1	2	Petition	182					Referred to Secretary Treasury.		
Johnson, Isaac	Pension	23	1	Petition	353	Rev. Pensions				Laid on table.		
Johnson, Israel	Pay for revolutionary services	16	2	Petition	101	Rev. Pensions	Feb. 15, 1821	Adverse		Rejected.		
Johnson, Israel, (Indiana)	Pay as Indian agent	28	2	Petition	141	Indian Affairs	183	Adverse		Laid on table.		
Johnson, Israel, (Indiana)	Pay as Indian agent	29	1	Petition	167	Indian Affairs.						
Johnson, Israel, (Indiana)	Pay as Indian agent	30	1	Petition	271	Indian Affairs	505	Favorable	426	Referred to Committee Whole House.		
Johnson, Israel, (Indiana)	Pay as Indian agent	30	2	House bill	318	Whole House		Favorable	426	Passed.		
Johnson, Israel, (Indiana)	Pay as Indian agent	31	1	Petition	276	Indian Affairs	97	Adverse		Laid on table.		
Johnson, Jabez	Pay for canon for government use.	3	1	Petition	53	Select	April 4, 1794			Laid on table.		
Johnson, Jabez	Pay for canon for government use.	3	2	Petition	313	Claims.						
Johnson, Jabez	Pay for canon for government use.	4	1	Res. and docs	373	Claims	Jan. 6, 1796	Adverse		Recommitted.		
					410	Claims	Jan. 15, 1796	Adverse				Leave to withdraw.
Johnson, Jacob	Pension	3	1	Rep. of Secretary War.	131	Select	May 26, 1794	Favorable	62	Passed	Passed	App'd June 7, 1794
Johnson, Jacob, (Penn.)	Pension	20	1	Petition	56	Military Affairs				Laid on table.		
Johnson, Jacob, (N. J.)	Pension	23	1	Documents	617	Rev. Pensions.						
Johnson, Jacob, (N. J.)	Pension	24	2	Resolution	139	Rev. Pensions.						
Johnson, Jacob, (N. Y.)	Pension	26	1	Petition and docs.	286	Rev. Pensions.						
Johnson, Jacob, (N. Y.)	Pension	26	2	Petition	134	Rev. Pensions.						
Johnson, Jacob, (N. Y.)	Pension	27	2	Petition	153	Rev. Pensions	784	Adverse		Laid on table.		
Johnson, James, (Ga.)	Permission to file evidence of title to lands.	13	3	Petition	640	Select.						
Johnson, James (Ind.)	For new certificate for land which has been fraudulently taken by J. Dougherty.	15	2	Petition	200	Public Lands.				Discharged.		Leave to withdraw.
Johnson, James, (N. J.)	Restoration of pension	17	1	Petition	51	Rev. Pensions.						
Johnson, James, (N. J.)	Restoration of pension	17	2	Petition	25	Rev. Pensions.						
Johnson, James, (Vt.)	Restoration of pension	17	1	Petition	155	Whole House.						
Johnson, James, (Vt.)	Restoration of pension	17	2	Petition	119	Whole House.						
Johnson, James, (N. Y.)	Pension	18	1	Petition	178	Rev. Pensions	May 17, 1824	Adverse		Leave to withdraw.		

List of private claims presented to the House of Representatives of the United States from the 1st to the 31st Congress, inclusive—Continued.

Names of claimants.	Nature or object of the claim.	Congress.	Session.	How brought before the House of Reps.	Page of journal.	To what committee of the House referred.	No. or date of the report.	Nature of the report.	No. of the bill.	How disposed of by the House of Reps.	How disposed of by the Senate.	Date of the act of Congress, and remarks.
Johnson, James, (Va.)	Pension	20	1	Petition	38	Military Pensions				Leave to withdraw.		
Johnson, James, (Va.)	Pension	21	1	Petition	48	Military Pensions	Jan. 5, 1830	Favorable	72	Passed	Passed, with amendment.	See act May 20, 1830
Johnson, James, widow of	Remuneration for loss of husband who deserted to the Mexicans.	30	2	Petition	338	Military Affairs.						
Johnson, James, U. S. A.	Equitable settlement of account as paymaster.	18	1	Senate bill	259	Claims	Feb. 25, 1824	Favorable	19	Passed	Passed	App'd May 4, 1824
Johnson, James, (S. C.)	Pension	19	2	Petition	215	Military Pensions.						
Johnson, James, (S. C.)	Pension	20	1	Petition	193	Military Pensions	April 29, 1828	Favorable	283	Passed.		
Johnson, James, (S. C.)	Pension	20	2	Petition	319	Military Pensions		General bill	311	Passed.		
Johnson, James, (Md.)	Pay for services of father, and for munitions during revolutionary war.	28	1	Petition	783	Rev. Pensions.						
Johnson, James, (Md.)	Pay for services of father, and for munitions during revolutionary war.	29	1	Petition	623	Rev. Pensions	826	Adverse		Laid on table.		
Johnson, James, (Md.)	Pay for services of father, and for munitions during revolutionary war.	30	1	Petition	559	Rev. Claims.						
Johnson, James	(See George C. Branham.)	29	1		270							
Johnson, James, (Ill.)	Payment of Treasury notes destroyed by fire.	29	1	Petition	510	Claims.						
Johnson, James, (Penn.)	Pay as assistant commissary in Mexican war.	31	1	Petition	612	Military Affairs.						
Johnson, James	(See William Baker, New York.)	22	1		288		480					
Johnson, Jared	Pension	22	1	Memorial	899	Rev. Pensions.						
Johnson, Jesse	Refund money deposited in land office, Indiana.	29	1	Petition	125	Public Lands	31	Adverse		Laid on table.		
Johnson, John	Pay for wood furnished in revolutionary war.	4	1	Rep. of Secretary Treasury.	388	Claims	Jan. 19, 1795	Adverse		Laid on table.		
Johnson, John	Confirmation of title to land	12	1	Petition	13	Public Lands.						
Johnson, John	Confirmation of title to land	12	2	Petition	663	Public Lands.						
Johnson, John	Confirmation of title to land	14	2	Petition	372	Priv. Land Claims.	Feb. 11, 1817	Favorable	123	Ref'd to Com. W. H.		
Johnson, John	Confirmation of title to land	15	1	Petition	39	Priv. Land Claims.	Mar. 26, 1818	Favorable	160	Ref'd to Com. W. H.		
Johnson, John	Pension	12	1	House bill	361	Whole House	June 15, 1812	Favorable	138	Passed	Passed	App'd July 5, 1812
Johnson, John, (Maine.)	Pension	20	2	Petition	288	Military Pensions.						
Johnson, John, (N. Y.)	Pension	21	1	Petition	260	Military Pensions				Discharged.		
Johnson, John, (N. Y.)	Pension	21	2	Petition	68	Military Pensions.						
Johnson, John, (Indiana)	To cut mill-race through United States land.	14	2	Petition	399	Public Lands				Discharged; laid on table.		
Johnson, John, (Indiana)	Correct land entry	18	2	Senate bill	285	Public Lands	March 1, 1825	Favorable	S. 60	Passed with amendm't	Passed	App'd March 3, 1825
Johnson, John, (Indiana)	Pension	26	1	Petition	628	Invalid Pensions	672	Adverse		Laid on table.		
Johnson, John, (Indiana.)	Pension	26	2	Petition	55	Invalid Pensions	226	Adverse		Laid on table.		
Johnson, John, *et al.*, (N. Y.)	Indemnity for property destroyed in war of 1812.	15	1	Petition	247	Claims.						
Johnson, John, *et al.*, (N. Y.)	Indemnity for property destroyed in war of 1812.	15	2	Petition	40	Claims	71	Adverse		Laid on table.		
Johnson, John, *et al.*, (N. Y.)	Indemnity for property destroyed in war of 1812.	18	2	Petition	160	Claims.						
Johnson, John, *et al.*, (N. Y.)	Indemnity for property destroyed in war of 1812.	19	1	Petition	62	Claims	Jan. 10, 1826	Adverse		Laid on table.		
John on, John, heirs of, (Ky.)	Commutation pay	25	2	Petition	392	Rev. Claims				Laid on table.		

List of private claims presented to the House of Representatives of the United States from the 1st to the 31st Congress, inclusive—Continued.

Names of claimants.	Nature or object of the claim.	Congress.	Session.	How brought before the House of Reps.	Page of journal.	To what committee of the House referred.	No. or date of the report.	Nature of the report.	No. of the bill.	How disposed of by the House of Reps.	How disposed of by the Senate.	Date of the act of Congress, and remarks.
Johnson, John, representatives of, (Va.)	Bounty land	26	1	Resolution	547	Priv. Land Claims.	502	Adverse	......	Laid on table.		
Johnson, John, (Ohio)	Lands to Wyandot Indians for others erroneously sold.	18	1	Petition	238	Public Lands	Mar. 16, 1824	Favorable	162	Passed	Passed	App'd May 26, 1824
Johnson, John, (Ohio)	Reimburse money paid on judgment.	26	2	Petition	54	Judiciary	114	Favorable	619	Referred to Committee Whole House.		
Johnson, John, (Ohio.)	Reimburse money paid on judgment.	27	2	Petition	63	Judiciary	252	Favorable	218	Passed	Passed	App'd Aug. 11, 1842
Johnson, John, (Ohio)	Payment for services as Indian agent, and for losses as disbursing agent, &c.	31	1	Petition	306	Claims.						
Johnson, John, (Ohio)	Payment for services as Indian agent, and for losses as disbursing agent, &c.	31	2	Documents	58	Claims.						
Johnson, John J.	Pension	15	2	Petition	40	Claims	Jan. 5, 1819	Adverse	......	Laid on table.		
Johnson, John T.	Pay as captain and aid to General Harrison.	18	1	Senate bill	472	Whole House	April 29, 1842	Favorable	S. 191	Passed	Passed	App'd May 18, 1824
Johnson, Jonathan	(See William Baker, N. Y.)	22	1	....	288	....	480					
Johnson, Jonathan, *et al.*	Bounty land for military services.	31	1	Petition	869	Public Lands.						
Johnson, Jonathan, (Ga.)	Pay for corn destroyed by Cherokee Indians.	23	1	Petition	50	Indian Affairs	....	....	......	Laid on table.		
Johnson, Joseph	(See Jane Rodman, assignee of)	2	1	....	477							
Johnson, Joseph	Pension	11	2	House bill	283	Whole House	Mar. 24, 1810	Favorable	107	Passed	Passed	App'd April 27, 1810
Johnson, Joseph, former widow of.	Pension	30	1	Petition	334, 358	Rev. Pensions	517	Favorable	445	Referred to Committee Whole House.		
Johnson, Joseph, former widow of.	Pension	30	2	House bill	318	Whole House	Jan. 26, 1849	Favorable	445	Passed.		
Johnson, Joseph, (Vt.)	Pension	28	2	Petition	229	Invalid Pensions.						
Johnson, Joseph, (Vt.)	Pension	29	1	Petition	70	Invalid Pensions	182	Adverse	......	Laid on table.		
Johnson, Joseph, (Vt.)	Pension	29	2	Petition	75	Invalid Pensions.						
Johnson, Joseph, (Vt.)	Pension	31	1	Petition	194	Invalid Pensions	142	Favorable	158	Referred to Committee Whole House.		
Johnson, Joseph, (Vt.)	Pension	31	2	House bill	103	Whole House	Jan. 3, 1851	Favorable	150	Passed.		
Johnson, Joseph S	(See William Miller, *et al.*, agent of.)	14	2	....	148, 164							
Johnson, Joshua	Refund tonnage duties	4	1	Petition	469	Com. and Manuf.	April 5, 1796	Adverse	......	Leave to withdraw.		
Johnson, Joshua, (Consul)	Reimbursement of expenses incurred in discharge of duties.	6	1	Petition	571	Claims	April 2, 1800	Adverse	......	Laid on table.		
Johnson, Joshua, heirs of	Settlement of account as consul at London.	30	1	Petition	1093	Claims.						
Johnson, Levi, (Ohio)	Pension	22	2	Resolution	155	Invalid Pensions.						
Johnson, Levi, (Ohio)	Pension	24	1	Resolution	951	Invalid Pensions	....	....	......	Laid on table.		
Johnson, Levi, (Ohio)	Pension	24	2	Petition	66	Invalid Pensions	....	....	......	Laid on table.		
Johnson, Levi, (Ohio)	Pension	25	2	Petition	83	Invalid Pensions	592	Favorable	579	Passed	Adverse.	
Johnson, Levi, (Ohio)	Pension	26	1	Petition	161	Invalid Pensions	192	Favorable	204	Passed	Indef. postp'd.	
Johnson, Levi, (Ind.)	Pension	28	1	Petition	509	Invalid Pensions.						
Johnson, Lewis	(See Eleazer Early, administrator of.)	27	2	....	246							
Johnson, Lucy, (Va.)	(See Sarah Victor, heirs of.)	29	1	....	104							
Johnson, Lucy	(See widow of George Gooding)	25	2	....	1030							
Johnson, Lucy	Pension	28	1	Petition	218	Invalid Pensions.						
Johnson, Luke	Pension	16	1	Petition	76	Rev. Pensions	Jan. 14, 1820	Adverse	......	Laid on table.		
Johnson, Luke	Pension	16	2	Petition	151	Rev. Pensions	Feb. 15, 1821	Adverse	......	Rejected.		

List of private claims presented to the House of Representatives of the United States from the 1st to the 31st Congress, inclusive—Continued.

Names of claimants.	Nature or object of the claim.	Congress.	Session.	How brought before the House of Reps.	Page of journal.	To what committee of the House referred.	No. or date of the report.	Nature of the report.	No. of the bill.	How disposed of by the House of Reps.	How disposed of by the Senate.	Date of the act of Congress, and remarks.
Johnson, Luke	Pension	17	1	Petition	247	Rev. Claims				Referred to Committee Whole House.		
Johnson, Luticha	Pay for Indian depredations	28	2	Memorial	84	Claims.						
Johnson, Marcus F	Pre-emption right to land	29	1	Petition	624	Public Lands.						
Johnson, Marcus F	Pre-emption right to land	29	2	Petition	92	Priv. Land Claims.						
Johnson, Marcus F	Pre-emption right to land	30	1	Petition	109	Priv. Land Claims.	Feb. 8, 1848	Favorable	195	Passed.		
Johnson, Marcus F	Pre-emption right to land	30	2	House bill	239				195		Passed	App'd Jan. 19, 1849
Johnson, Maria S	(See Christopher Johnson, executor of.)	26	1		182							
Johnson, Mary	(See Michael and Jane Rodman, assignee of.)	2	2		712							
Johnson, Mary	(See James Johnson, widow of.)	30	2		338							
Johnson, Mary	(See David Johnson, widow of.)	26	1		705							
Johnson, Michael, (N. Y.)	Pay for provisions, late war	25	3	Petition	120	Claims.						
Johnson, Michael, (N. Y.)	Pay for provisions, late war	26	1	Petition	168, 295	Claims.						
Johnson, Michael, (N. Y.)	Pay for provisions, late war	27	2	Petition	56	Claims	341	Adverse		Laid on table.		
Johnson, Michael, (N. Y.)	Pay for provisions, late war	28	2	Petition	258	Claims.						
Johnson, Michael, (N. Y.)	Pay for provisions, late war	31	1	Petition	830	Claims.						
Johnson, Moses, (Vt.)	Pension	17	1	Petition	92	Rev. Claims	Jan. 2, 1822	Adverse		Leave to withdraw.		
Johnson, Moses, (Vt.)	Pension	18	2	Petition	69	Rev. Pensions	Jan. 17, 1825	Adverse		Laid on table.		
Johnson, Nancy, (late Killy)	Land for that lost by virtue of Choctaw treaty.	24	1	Petition	57	Public Lands		Favorable	208	Referred to Committee Whole House.		
Johnson, Patsy	(See Samuel Johnson, widow of.)	21	2		99							
Johnson, Peter	Pension	1	3	Petition	360					Referred to Secretary War.		
Johnson, Peter	Pension	3	2	Rep. of Secretary War.	278	Claims	Feb. 28, 1795	Favorable	130	Passed	Postponed.	
Johnson, Peter	Pension	4	1	Petition	445	Claims	Feb. 18, 1796	Favorable	156	Passed	Passed	App'd April 20, 1796
Johnson, Peter, wife of	Title to land to be vested in her; the husband supposed to be dead.	21	2	Petition	100	Public Lands	Feb. 8, 1831	Adverse		Laid on table.		
Johnson, Rachel	Pension	27	2	Petition	238	Rev. Pensions.						
Johnson, Ralph	(See William Tee, *et al.*)	22	1		61							
Johnson, Ransom	Pension	25	2	Petition	117	Invalid Pensions				Discharged.		
Johnson, Ransom	Pension	25	3	Petition and docs.	460	Invalid Pensions.						
Johnson, Ransom, wife of.	Pension	30	2	Petition	92	Invalid Pensions	36	Adverse		Laid on table.		
Johnson, Richard M	Settlement for rations, war of 1812.	15	1	Senate bill	245	Claims	Feb. 16, 1818		19	Passed	Passed	App'd April 20, 1818
Johnson, Richard M	Pay for building used as Choctaw academy.	30	1	Senate bill	1157	Indian Affairs	Aug. 8, 1848		291	Passed	Passed	App'd Aug. 14, 1848
Johnson, Rich'd and Martin	Correct land entry	25	2	Documents.	719	Public Lands				Discharged.		
Johnson, R. M., (La.)	Indemnity for losses, &c., Mexican war.	31	1	Petition	1477	Claims.						
Johnson, Rinaldo	Remission duties on stills	8	2	Petition	76	Claims	Jan. 22, 1805			Leave to withdraw.		
Johnson, Rinaldo	Relief from judgment	9	1	Petition	328	Select	Mar. 27, 1806	Favorable	122	Ref'd to Com. W. H.		
Johnson, Rinaldo	Relief from judgment	9	2	Petition	596	Select		Favorable	211	Referred to Committee Whole House.		
Johnson, Rinaldo	Relief from judgment	10	1	Petition	60	Select.						
Johnson, Rinaldo	Relief from judgment	10	2	Petition	364	Claims.						
Johnson, Rinaldo	Relief from judgment	11	2	Petition	282	Ways and Means.						
Johnson, Rinaldo, administrator of.	Relief from judgment	12	2	Petition	591	Ways and Means.				Discharged		Leave to withdraw.
Johnson, Rinaldo, administrator of.	Relief from judgment	13	1	Petition	20	Ways and Means.						

List of private claims presented to the House of Representatives of the United States from the 1st to the 31st Congress, inclusive—Continued.

Names of claimants.	Nature or object of the claim.	Congress.	Session.	How brought before the House of Reps.	Page of journal.	To what committee of the House referred.	No. or date of the report.	Nature of the report.	No. of the bill.	How disposed of by the House of Reps.	How disposed of by the Senate.	Date of the act of Congress, and remarks.
Johnson, Robert, (Conn.,) attorney of.	Indemnity for French spoliations prior to 1800.	26	1	Memorial	182	Foreign Affairs	343	Favorable	319	Referred to Committee Whole House.		
Johnson, Robert	Pension	3	1	Report Secretary War.	131	Select	May 26, 1794	Favorable	J R.12	Passed	Passed	App'd Jan. 9, 1794
Johnson, Robert, (Wis.)	Pension	27	2	Petition	935	Invalid Pensions.						
Johnson, Robert	(See Abraham Johnson, administrator of.)	27	3		260							
Johnson, Dr. Robert, executors of	Payment for three lost loan office certificates.	19	1	Petition	44	Pens. & Rev. Cl'ms.						
Johnson, Dr. Robert, executors of.	Payment for three lost loan office certificates.	19	2	Petition	84	Ways and Means	Jan. 5, 1827	By bill	343	Referred to Committee Whole House.		
Johnson, Dr. Robert, executors of.	Payment for three lost loan office certificates.	20	1	Petition	30	Rev. Claims	63	Favorable; bill	62	Passed	Passed, with amendment.	App'd May 26, 1828
Johnson, Dr. Robert, executors of.	Interest on loan office certificate	21	1	Petition	37	Claims	Dec. 31, 1829	Adverse, (verbal.)		Laid on table.		
Johnson, Robert	(See Louis Roy, administrator of.)	25	3		124							
Johnson, R. E.	(See Exploring Expedition)	27	3		149		270		818			
Johnson, Sally	(See Peter Johnson, wife of)	21	2		100							
Johnson, Samuel	(See Shakers' Society, trustees of.)	14	1		433							
Johnson, Samuel	Pension	11	2	House bill	283	Whole House	Mar. 24, 1810	Favorable	107	Passed	Passed	App'd April 27, 1810
Johnson, Samuel, (N. Y.)	Pension	27	2	Petition	69, 747	Invalid Pensions	784	Adverse		Laid on table.		
Johnson, Samuel, (N. Y.)	For passage of a law which shall give him the benefit of Wm. McKenzie's will.	30	1	Petition	145	Judiciary	174	Favorable	183	Passed	Passed	App'd Aug. 5, 1848
Johnson, Samuel, widow of.	Arrears of pension	21	2	Petition	99	Military Pensions				Discharged; laid on table.		
Johnson, Samuel, widow of.	Arrears of pension	25	2	Petition	70	Rev. Pensions				Discharged; laid on table.		
Johnson, Sheperd	Pension	3	1	Rep. of Secretary War.	175					Laid on table.		
Johnson, Stephen, late widow of.	Praying government support for children.	17	2	Petition	208	Rev. Claims				Discharged; laid on table.		
Johnson, Sterling	Remuneration for injury to property by construction of Cumberland road.	21	2	Resolution	182	Claims	81	Adverse		Referred to Committee Whole House.		
Johnson, Sterling	Remuneration for injury to property by construction of Cumberland road.	22	1	Petition	188	Claims	240	Adverse		Referred to Committee Whole House.		
Johnson, Sylvester	Pension	21	1	Resolution	384	Military Pensions	May 3, 1830	Adverse		Laid on table.		
Johnson, Sylvester	Pension	21	2	Petition	126	Military Pensions.						
Johnson, Sylvester	Pension	22	1	Petition	80	Rev. Pensions.						
Johnson, Thomas	Pension	2	2	Petition	616	Select	Dec. 14, 1792			Referred to Secretary War.		
Johnson, Thomas	Pension	3	1	Rep. of Secretary War.	131	Select	May 26, 1794	Favorable	J.R. 12	Passed	Passed	App'd June 9, 1794
Johnson, Major Thomas, of Tennessee, *et al.*	Pay for military services in revolutionary war.	6	1	Petition	593	Claims	April 16, 1800	Favorable	254	Passed	Passed	App'd May 13, 1800
Johnson, Thomas, *et al.*	Pay for capture of vessel by French government.	12	1	Petition	368					Referred to Secretary of State.		
Johnson, Thomas	Increase of pension	10	1	House bill	232	Whole House	April 19, 1808	Favorable	158	Passed	Passed	App'd April 25, 1808
Johnson, Thomas, (N. Y.)	Pay for wagon and team in war of 1812.	14	1	Petition	53	Claims.						

List of private claims presented to the House of Representatives of the United States from the 1st to the 31st Congress, inclusive—Continued.

Names of claimants.	Nature or object of the claim.	Congress.	Session.	How brought before the House of Reps.	Page of journal.	To what committee of the House referred.	No. or date of the report.	Nature of the report.	No. of the bill.	How disposed of by the House of Reps.	How disposed of by the Senate.	Date of the act of Congress, and remarks.
Johnson, Thomas, (N. Y.)	Pay for wagon and team in war of 1812.	15	1	Petition	143	Claims.						
Johnson, Thomas, (N. Y.)	Pay for wagon and team in war of 1812.	19	1	Petition	78	Claims	Jan. 23, 1826	Adverse	......	Laid on table.		
Johnson, Thomas, (N. Y.)	Pay for wagon and team in war of 1812.	19	2	Petition	190	Claims.						
Johnson, Thomas, (N. Y.)	Pay for wagon and team in war of 1812.	20	1	Petition	58	Claims	Feb. 13, 1828	Adverse	......	Laid on table.		
Johnson, Thomas, (N. Y.)	Pay for wagon and team in war of 1812.	21	1	Petition	201	Claims	Jan. 29, 1830	Adverse	......	Laid on table.		
Johnson, Thomas, (N. Y.)	Pay for wagon and team in war of 1812.	22	1	Petition	25	Claims	Dec. 28, 1831	Adverse	......	Laid on table.		
Johnson, Thomas, and Michael Dickson, commissioners of road.	Pay for their chain carrier.......	15	1	Petition	310	Claims	Mar. 30, 1818	Adverse	......	Rejected.		
Johnson, Thomas, and Michael Dickson, commissioners of road.	Pay for their chain carrier.......	15	2	Petition	205	Roads and Canals.						
Johnson, Thomas, (Va.)..	Commutation pay..............	23	2	Petition	165	Rev. Claims.						
Johnson, Thomas, (Va.)..	Commutation pay..............	24	1	Petition	138	Rev. Claims......	656	Adverse	......	Laid on table.		
Johnson, Thomas, (Va.)..	Commutation pay..............	24	2	Petition	133	Rev. Claims......	....	....	......	Discharged; laid on table.		
Johnson, Thomas, (Va.)..	Commutation pay..............	25	2	Petition	72	Rev. Claims......	381	Adverse	......	Laid on table.		
Johnson, Thomas B......	Compensation for services as marshal of Iowa.	31	1	Petition	971	Claims.						
Johnson, Thos. D. M., sureties of.	Release from liability...........	12	1	Petition	180	Com. and Manuf.						
Johnson, Thomas E......	(See John C. Edwards, *et al.*)....	22	1	....	538							
Johnson, Vance, administrator of.	Payment of amount of certain Post Office drafts.	29	1	Petition	423	P. O. & P. Roads.	....	....	......	Leave to withdraw.		
Johnson, Vincent	Pay for horse lost in war of 1812.	15	2	Petition	24	Claims	Nov. 23, 1818	Adverse	......	Laid on table.		
Johnson, Vincent	Pay for horse lost in war of 1812.	16	1	Petition	142	Claims	Jan. 17, 1820	Adverse	......	Laid on table.		
Johnson, Walter R., (Pa.)	Reimbursement of money expended in Exploring Expedition.	25	3	Memorial	563	Naval Affairs.						
Johnson, Walter R., (Pa.)	Reimbursement of money expended in Exploring Expedition.	26	1	Petition	330	Naval Affairs.						
Johnson, Walter R., (Pa.)	Reimbursement of money expended in Exploring Expedition.	26	2	Senate bill	231	Naval Affairs.	....	....	S. 164			
Johnson, Walter R., (Pa.)	Reimbursement of money expended in Exploring Expedition.	27	1	Petition	107	Claims.						
Johnson, Walter R., (Pa.)	Reimbursement of money expended in Exploring Expedition.	27	2	Petition & Senate bill.	56 782	Claims	May 25, 1842	Favorable	S. 141	Laid on table.		
Johnson, Walter R., (Pa.)	Reimbursement of money expended in Exploring Expedition.	28	1	Senate bill	942	Naval Affairs	Jan. 7, 1844	Favorable	S. 96	Referred to Committee Whole House.		
Johnson, Walter R., (N. Y.)	Payment of balance due for testing plans to prevent explosion of steam boilers.	29	1	Petition	511	Naval Affairs.						
Johnson, Walter R., (N. Y.)	Payment of balance due for testing plans to prevent explosion of steam boilers.	29	2	Senate bill	374	Naval Affairs	Feb. 24, 1847	Favorable....	S. 86	Referred to Committee Whole House.		
Johnson, Walter R., (N. Y.)	Payment of balance due for testing plans to prevent explosion of steam boilers.	30	1	Senate bill	203	Naval Affairs	Jan. 19, 1848	Favorable....	S. 24	Passed	Passed	App'd March 20, 1848

List of private claims presented to the House of Representatives of the United States from the 1st to the 31st Congress, inclusive—Continued.

Names of claimants.	Nature or object of the claim.	Congress.	Session.	How brought before the House of Reps.	Page of journal.	To what committee of the House referred.	No. or date of the report.	Nature of the report.	No. of the bill.	How disposed of by the House of Reps.	How disposed of by the Senate.	Date of the act of Congress, and remarks.
Johnson, Walter R., (N. Y.)	Payment of balance due for testing plans to prevent explosion of steam boilers.	30	1	House bill	224	Whole House	April 8, 1848	Favorable	65	Passed.		
Johnson, Walter R., (N. Y.)	Payment of balance due for testing plans to prevent explosion of steam boilers.	31	1	Senate bill	1438	Claims			S. 7			
Johnson, Wiley B.	(See William H. Bedford, agent.)	28	1		262							
Johnson, Wiley B.	Pay for horses, &c., lost in Seminole war.	23	1	Documents	154	Claims.						
Johnson, William	(See William H. Bedford, agent.)	28	1		262							
Johnson, William	Pension	10	1	House bill	232	Whole House	April 19, 1808	Favorable	78	Passed	Passed	App'd April 25, 1808
Johnson, William	Increase of pension	10	2	House bill	499	Whole House	Feb. 20, 1809	Favorable	158	Passed	Passed	App'd March 3, 1809
Johnson, William, (Pa.)	Pension	19	1	Petition	334	Military Pensions	164	Adverse		Laid on table.		
Johnson, William, (Pa.)	Pension	20	1	Petition	440	Military Pensions	April 29, 1828	Favorable	283	Passed	Postponed.	
Johnson, William, (Pa.)	Pension	20	2	Petition	55	Military Pensions	Dec. 12, 1828	Favorable	311	Passed	Laid on table.	
Jonhson, William, (S. C.)	Pay for extra duties as judge U. S. court.	15	1	Resolution	105	Judiciary.						
Johnson, William, (Vt.)	Pay for revolutionary services	15	1	Petition	172	Select	Mar. 21, 1818			Discharged.		
Johnson, William, (Me.)	Pay for revolutionary services	21	1	Petition	37	Rev. Claims	Jan. 14, 1830	Adverse		Laid on table.		
Johnson, William, (R. I.)	Pension	21	2	Resolution	165	Military Pensions.						
Johnson, William, (R. I.)	Pension	22	1	Petition	66	Rev. Pensions	115	Favorable	193	Referred to Committee Whole House.		
Johnson, William, (R. I.)	Pension	22	2	House bill	66	Whole House			193	Laid on table.		
Johnson, William, (Ind.)	(See William Caldwell, *et al.*)	24	1		851							
Johnson, William, (Ky.)	Pension	26	1	Resolution	950	Rev. Pensions.						
Johnson, William, (Ky.)	Pension	27	2	Documents	509, 883	Rev. Pensions	July 21, 1842	Adverse		Laid on table.		
Johnson, Capt. Wm., heirs of, (Va.)	Commutation pay	23	2	Petition	239	Rev. Claims.						
Johnson, Capt. Wm., heirs of. (Va.)	Commutation pay	24	1	Petition	138	Rev. Claims.						
Johnson, Capt. Wm., heirs of, (Va.)	Commutation pay	24	2	Petition	126	Rev. Claims				Discharged; laid on table.		
Johnson, Capt. Wm., heirs of, (Va.)	Commutation pay	25	2	Petition	70	Rev. Claims	410	Adverse		Laid on table.		
Johnson, Capt. Wm., heirs of, (Va.)	Pay for naval services revolutionary war.	25	2	Petition	275	Naval Affairs				Discharged; laid on table.		
Johnson, William, (N. Y.)	Additional pay as assistant marshal	31	2	Petition	283	Judiciary.						
Johnson, William, widow of. (N. Y.)	Pay for horses lost in war 1812	24	1	Petition	406	Claims	610	Favorable	599	Recommitted.		
Johnson, William, widow of, (N. Y.)	Pay for horses lost in war 1812	30	1	Petition	36	Claims	73	Favorable	85	Passed	Passed	App'd April 20, 1838
Johnson, William, widow of, (Va.)	Pension	28	1	Petition	61	Rev. Pensions.						
Johnson, William, *et al.*	(See Archibald Beard, *et al.*)	30	1		800							
Johnston, Alexander	(See John and Alex'r Johnston.)	19	2		189							
Johnston & Boorman	(See Boorman & Johnston.)	18	2		80							
Johnston & Boorman	(See Kantzow & Biel, agents of.)	18	2		136							
Johnston, Chas. H., (N. Y.)	Pension	28	1	Petition	999	Naval Affairs.						
Johnston, Chas. H., (N. Y.)	Pension	28	2	Petition	240	Naval Affairs.						
Johnston, David	(See Captain Jas. Johnston, son of)	24	1		144							
Johnston, David	Pre-emption as New Orleans branch pilot.	28	1	Petition	77	Priv. Land Claims.	9	Favorable	35	Passed	Passed	App'd June 17, 1844

List of private claims presented to the House of Representatives of the United States from the 1st to the 31st Congress, inclusive—Continued.

Names of claimants.	Nature or object of the claim.	Congress.	Session.	How brought before the House of Reps.	Page of journal.	To what committee of the House referred.	No. or date of the report.	Nature of the report.	No. of the bill.	How disposed of by the House of Reps.	How disposed of by the Senate.	Date of the act of Congress, and remarks.
Johnston, George W.	(See Joseph and Geo. W. Johnston.)	25	3	....	462							
Johnston, Gideon, (Va)	Indemnity for property destroyed in revolutionary war.	16	2	Petition	209	Rev. Claims	Feb. 16, 1821	Adverse	......	Laid on table.		
Johnston, Gideon, (Va.)	Indemnity for property destroyed in revolutionary war.	17	1	Petition	69	Rev. Claims	Jan. 2, 1822	Adverse	......	Rejected.		
Johnston, Dr. Jacob	Pay for damages to property by Indians in revolutionary war.	3	1	Petition	47	Select	April 1, 1794	Adverse	......	Laid on table.		
Johnston, James, (Va)	Pay for revolutionary services	19	1	Petition	35	Rev. Pensions	164	Adverse	......	Laid on table.		
Johnston, James, (Va)	Pay for revolutionary services	19	2	Petition	37	Military Pensions	....	....	......	Discharged.		
Johnston, Captain James, of Virginia, son of.	Seven years' half pay	24	1	Resolution	144	Rev. Claims	Jan. 20, 1836	Adverse	......	Laid on table.		
Johnston, Captain James, of Virginia, son of.	Seven years' half-pay	24	2	Resolution	270	Rev. Claims.						
Johnston, John	Amount of judgment in favor of United States and interest.	27	2	Petition	63	Judiciary	252	Favorable	218	Passed	Passed	App'd Aug. 11, 1842
Johnston, John and Alexander.	Redress for captured vessels and cargo by a Danish vessel in the Baltic.	19	2	Petition	189	Foreign Affairs	....	....	......	Discharged.		
Johnston, John, administratrix of.	Pay for loss of property in war of 1812.	24	1	Petition	153	Claims	515	Adverse	......	Laid on table.		
Johnston, John, administratrix of.	Pay for loss of property in war of 1812.	30	1	Petition	685	Claims	677	Adverse	......	Laid on table.		
Johnston, Joseph P. and George W.	Pay for horse lost in 1836	25	3	Documents	462	Claims	....	....	......	....	....	Previously presented, but does not appear on Journal.
Johnston, Joseph P. and George W.	Pay for horse lost in 1836	26	1	Petition	168	Claims	431	Adverse	......	Laid on table.		
Johnston, Joseph P. and George W.	Pay for horse lost in 1836	26	2	Petition	38	Claims.						
Johnston, Josiah S.	(See William Miller, *et at.*, agent of.	14	2	....	148	....	60					
Johnston, R., (Pa)	Relief touching certain lands	31	1	Petition	1477	Priv. Land Claims.						
Johnston, Dr. Robert, executors of.	Payment for lost loan office certificates.	19	1	Petition	44	Rev. Claims.						
Johnston, Dr. Robert, executors of.	Payment for lost loan office certificates.	19	2	Petition	84	Ways and Means	Jan. 5, 1827	Favorable	343	Referred to Committee Whole House.		
Johnston, Dr. Robert, executors of.	Payment for lost loan office certificetes.	20	1	Petition	30	Rev. Claims.	Jan. 11, 1828	Favorable	62	Passed	Passed, with amendment.	App'd May 24, 1828
Johnston, Dr. Robert, executors of.	Payment of interest on certificates.	21	1	Petition	37	Rev. Claims.	Dec. 31, 1829	Adverse	......	Laid on table.		
Johnston, Samuel	To locate two land warrants issued by Georgia.	20	2	Petition	101	Public Lands	....	....	......	Discharged; laid on table.		
Johnston, Samuel	To locate two land warrants issued by Georgia.	21	1	Petition	413	Public Lands	....	....	......	Discharged; laid on table.		
Johnston, Sarah	Pension	27	2	Petition	1111	Rev. Pensions	....	....	......	Discharged; laid on table.		
Johnston, Stephen, heirs of	To change land location	26	1	Petition	504	Priv. Land Claims.	103	Favorable	99	Passed	Passed	App'd July 20, 1840
Johnston, Stephen, heirs of	That land certificate be taken for half section of land.	29	1	Memorial	446	Public Lands	716	Favorable	J. R. 38			
Johnston, Stephen, heirs of	That land certificate be taken for half section of land.	29	2	Joint resolution.	211	Whole House	....	Favorable	38	Passed	Passed	App'd March 3, 1847
Johnston, Stephen, heirs of	That land certificate be taken for half section of land.	31	1	Petition	695	Priv. Land Claims.	....	....	......	Discharged; laid on table.		

List of private claims presented to the House of Representatives of the United States from the 1st to the 31st Congress, inclusive—Continued.

Names of claimants.	Nature or object of the claim.	Congress.	Session.	How brought before the House of Reps.	Page of journal.	To what committee of the House referred.	No. or date of the report.	Nature of the report.	No. of the bill.	How disposed of by the House of Reps.	How disposed of by the Senate.	Date of the act of Congress, and remarks.
Johnston, Susan	(See John Johnston, administratrix of.)	24	1	Petition	153							
Johnston, Thomas, *et al.*	(See Joseph Moore)	29	2		223							
Johnston, William	Pay for revolutionary services	2	1	Petition	475					Referred to Secretary of War.		
Johnston, William, (N. H.)	Pay for revolutionary services	17	1	Petition	179	Rev. Claims	Jan. 29, 1822	Adverse		Referred to Committee Whole House.		
Johnston, William, (N. H.)	Pay for revolutionary services	18	1	Petition	88	Rev. Claims.						
Johnston, William, (N. H.)	Pay for revolutionary services	19	1	Petition	105	Rev. Claims	164	Adverse		Laid on table.		
Johnston, William, (N. H.)	Pension	20	1	Petition	440	Military Pensions	April 29, 1828	Favorable	283	Passed	Discharged.	
Johnston, William, (N. H.)	Pension	20	2	Petition	55	Military Pensions	Dec. 12, 1828	Favorable	311	Passed	Laid on table.	
Johnston, William, (N. H.)	Pension	21	1	Petition	48	Military Pensions	Jan. 14, 1830	Adverse		Laid on table.		
Johnston, William	(See John Chandler and W. Johnston.)	22	1		892							
Johnston, William, (Mich.)	Remission of fine and costs	26	2	Petition	54	Judiciary.						
Johnston, William, (Mich.)	Remission of fine and costs	29	2	Petition	164	Judiciary.						
Johnston, William R.	(See George Evans, executor of.)	31	1		234							
Johnston, Wilter	Pension	20	2	Petition	142	Whole House.						
Johnston, Peter, (Va.)	Pension	20	1	Petition	56	Military Affairs.						
Johnston, Susan, (Mich.)	Pay for merchandise taken by British in 1814.	21	1	Petition	69	Claims	Mar. 2, 1830	Adverse.		Laid on table.		
Johonnot, Francis	(See Richard Caton, sureties of.)	8	2		132							
Johonnot, Dr. William, heirs of.	Commutation pay	23	1	Petition	80	Rev. Claims	214	Favorable	232	Passed.		
Johonnot, Dr. William, heirs of.	Commutation pay	23	2	Petition	94	Rev. Claims.						
Johonnot, Dr. William, heirs of.	Commutation pay	24	1	Petition	104	Rev. Claims	239	Favorable	244	Referred to Committee Whole House.		
Johonnot, Dr. William, heirs of.	Commutation pay	24	2	House bill	62	Whole House			244	Referred to Committee Whole House.		
Johonnot, Dr. William, heirs of.	Commutation pay	25	2	Petition	40	Rev. Claims	117	Favorable	135	Passed	Passed	App'd July 7, 1838
Joines, John	(See Exploring Expedition)	27	3		149		270		818			
Joines, Leonard	Pension	24	2	Petition	312	Invalid Pensions	206	Adverse		Laid on table.		
Joines, Leonard	Pension	25	1	Petition	102					Laid on table.		
Joines, Leonard	Pension	25	2	Petition	74	Invalid Pensions	Jan. 18, 1838	Adverse		Laid on table.		
Joines, Leonard	Pension	25	3	Petition	89	Invalid Pensions				Discharged; laid on table.		
Joines, Leonard	Pension	27	2	Petition	510	Invalid Pensions	28	Adverse		Laid on table.		
Joines, Leonard	Pension	27	3	Petition	72	Invalid Pensions	28	Adverse		Laid on table.		
Jollieff, James	Pay for rifle lost in war 1812	20	1	Resolution	200	Claims	Jan. 30, 1828	Adverse		Laid on table.		
Jolly, Desire	(See William Jolly, widow of.)	26	1		285							
Jolly, John A., sureties of.	Remission of interest on bond	8	2	Rep. of Secretary Treasury.	132	Com. and Manuf.						
Jolly, John A., sureties of.	Remission of interest on bond	9	1	Petition	191	Com. and Manuf	Feb. 11, 1806	Favorable in part; bill.	104	Referred to Committee Whole House.		
Jolly, William, widow of.	Increase of pension	26	1	Petition	285	Rev. Pensions	424	Adverse		Laid on table.		
Jonas, John	Pension	3	1	Rep. of Secretary War.	131	Select	May 26, 1794	Favorable	62	Passed	Passed	App'd June 7, 1794
Joncaise, Francis C.	Confirmation of title to land	12	1	Petition	22	Public Lands.						
Jones, Abel, widow of	Pension	1	3	Petition	382					Referred to Secretary of War.		

List of private claims presented to the House of Representatives of the United States from the 1st to the 31st Congress, inclusive—Continued.

Names of claimants.	Nature or object of the claim.	Congress.	Session.	How brought before the House of Reps.	Page of journal.	To what committee of the House referred.	No. or date of the report.	Nature of the report.	No. of the bill.	How disposed of by the House of Reps.	How disposed of by the Senate.	Date of the act of Congress, and remarks.
2—27 Jones, Abel, widow of	Pension	2	2	Rep. of Secretary War.	735					Laid on table.		
Jones, Abraham	Pay for revolutionary service	5	2	Petition	95	Claims	Feb. 9, 1798	Adverse		Laid on table.		
Jones, Alexander	Pension	10	1	House bill	232	Whole House	April 19, 1808	Favorable	78	Passed	Passed	App'd April 25, 1808
Jones, Alonzo, widow of	Renew and continue pension	30	1	Memorial	315	Naval Affairs	444	Favorable	375	Referred to Committee Whole House.		
Jones, Amos, *et al.*	Bounty land	24	1	Petition	411					Laid on table.		
Jones, Amos, *et al.*	Bounty land	24	2	Petition	145	Priv. Land Claims.						
Jones, Andrew A	Pay for services as clerk customs, New York.	29	1	Memorial	257	Claims	192	Favorable	183	Referred to Committee Whole House.		
Jones, Andrew A	Pay for services as clerk customs, New York.	29	2	House bill	383	Whole House			183	Laid on table.		
Jones, Andrew A	Pay for services as clerk customs, New York.	30	1	Petition	116	Claims	241	Favorable	240	Referred to Committee Whole House.		
Jones, Andrew A	Pay for services as clerk customs, New York.	31	1	Petition	371	Claims.						
Jones, Andrew B	Remit duty on "stills"	13	3	Petition	528	Ways and Means	Jan. 14, 1815	Favorable	262	Passed	Passed	App'd Feb. 2, 1815
Jones, Anna	(See Nehemiah Jones, widow of)	26	1		626							
Jones, Arthur	For patent for bertainlands	19	1	Resolution	236	Priv. Land Claims.	80	Favorable	111	Passed	Passed	App'd May 18, 1826
Jones, Asa	Pension	20	2	Petition	89	Military Pensions.						
Jones, Asa	Pension	21	2	Resolution	65	Military Pensions.						
Jones, Baraman	Pension	22	1	Petition	381	Rev. Pensions				Discharged; laid on table.		
Jones, Benjamin, (N. Y.)	Pension	18	2	Petition	251	Rev. Claims				Discharged; laid on table.		
Jones, Benjamin, (N. Y.)	Pension	20	1	Petition	396	Military Pensions.						
Jones, Benjamin, (N. Y.)	Pension	20	2	Petition	55	Military Pensions	Dec. 12, 1828	Favorable	311	Passed	Laid on table.	
Jones, Benjamin, (N. Y.)	Pension	21	1	Petition	48	Military Pensions				Discharged; laid on table.		
Jones, Benjamin, (N. Y.)	Pension	21	1	House bill	130	Whole House	Feb. 12, 1830	Favorable	72	Passed	Passed	App'd May 20, 1830
Jones, Benjamin, (Pa.)	Pension	27	2	Petition	351	Rev. Pensions	784	Adverse		Laid on table.		
Jones, Benjamin	Pay for services, revolutionary war	19	1	Petition	34	Rev. Claims				Discharged; laid on table.		
Jones, Benjamin A	(See A. W. Mitchell, *et al.*)	19	1		53							
Jones & Borer	Indemnity for treasury notes stolen	29	1	Petition	515	Ways and Means.						
Jones & Borer	Indemnity for treasury notes stolen	30	1	Senate bill	389	Judiciary	Mar. 9, 1848	Favorable	J R. 73	Passed	Passed	App'd June 13, 1848
Jones, Cadwallader, daughter of.	Commutation pay	26	1	Petition	361	Rev. Claims.						
Jones, Charles A	(See Joshua T. Jones, *et al.*)	30	1		66							
Jones, Charles F	Indemnity for French spoliations prior to 1800.	29	2	Memorial	317	Foreign Affairs.						
Jones, Charles Lee	Redress for grievances connected with raising volunteer corps.	30	1	Memorial	624	Military Affairs.						
Jones, Charles Lee	Redress for grievances connected with raising volunteer corps.	30	1	Memorial	1155	Military Pensions.						
Jones, Charles Lee	Redress for grievances connected with raising volunteer corps.	31	1	Petition	370	Military Pensions	285, 292	Favorable	134	Referred to Committee Whole House.		
Jones, Chas. S., and Richard Buckeny.	(See William Jones, administrators of.)	15	2		160							
Jones, Connelesky, (an Indian.)	(See Wm. Wilson, *et al.*)	17	2		96							
Jones & Clark	Indemnity for French spoliations prior to 1800.	26	1	Memorial	182	Foreign Affairs	343	Favorable; bill	319	Referred to Committee Whole House.		

List of private claims presented to the House of Representatives of the United States from the 1*st to the* 31*st Congress, inclusive*—Continued.

Names of claimants.	Nature or object of the claim.	Congress.	Session.	How brought before the House of Reps.	Page of journal.	To what committee of the House referred.	No. or date of the report	Nature of the report.	No. of the bill.	How disposed of by the House of Reps.	How disposed of by the Senate.	Date of the act of Congress, and remarks.
Jones, Cornelius	Indemnity for depreciated Continental certificates.	2	1	Petition	517	Whole House.						
Jones, Capt. Daniel	Pay for services and money advanced in revolutionary war.	11	2	Petition	268	Claims	Mar. 24, 1810			Laid on table.		
Jones, Capt. Daniel	Pay for services and money advanced in revolutionary war.	13	3	Petition	677	Rev. Claims	Jan. 27, 1815	Adverse		Rejected.		
Jones, Capt. Daniel	Pay for services and money advanced in revolutionary war.	14	2	Petition	75	Rev. Claims	Dec. 30, 1816			Rejected.		
Jones, Capt. Daniel	Pay for services and money advanced in revolutionary war.	15	1	Petition	94	Rev. Claims	Feb. 18, 1818	Adverse		Laid on table.		
Jones, Daniel, *et al.*	Release from payment of duties on tea.	9	1	Petition	324	Com. and Manuf.						
Jones, David, (N. C.)	(See Timothy Bloodworth, sureties of.)	11	2		226							
Jones, Rev. David	Pay for revolutionary services and supplies.	3	1	Petition	185					Laid on table.		
Jones, Rev. David	Pay for revolutionary services and supplies.	4	2	Memor'l and rep't of Sec. War.	677	Whole House.						
Jones, Rev. David	Land for services in revolutionary war.	6	1	Petition	555	Claims	Mar. 10, 1800	Favorable		Referred to Committee Whole House.		
Jones, Rev. David	Renew lost loan office certificate.	6	1	Petition	614	Claims	April 22, 1800			Referred to Committee Whole House.		
Jones, Rev. David	Renew lost loan office certificate.	6	2	Petition	731	Claims	Jan. 26, 1801			Rejected.		
Jones, David, of Missouri, by Duff Green, attorney.	Indemnity for Indian depredations.	19	2	Petition	134	Indian Affairs.						
Jones, David, (Ala.)	Indemnity for loss of vessel	26	1	Petition	328	Commerce.						
Jones, David, (Ala.)	Indemnity for loss of vessel	26	2	Petition	132	Commerce.						
Jones, David, (Ala.)	Indemnity for loss of vessel	27	3	Petition	77	Judiciary				Discharged; laid on table.		
Jones, David	(See heirs of William Jones)	30	1		723							
Jones, David, (Pa.)	To exchange military land warrants for vacant lands.	8	1	Petition	592	Whole House.						
Jones, David C	Pay for horse lost in Mexican war.	30	1	Petition	147	Claims	409	General bill	659	Passed	Passed	App'd March 2, 1849
Jones, D. G.	(See F., and W. Brewster, *et al.*)	21	1		151							
Jones, De Garmo	Pay for supplies in late war	21	1	Petition	472	Claims				Discharged.		
Jones, De Garmo	Pay for supplies in late war	21	2	Petition	107	Claims	76	Favorable	612	Referred to Committee Whole House.		
Jones, De Garmo	Pay for supplies in late war	22	1	Petition	26	Claims	Dec. 19, 1831	Favorable	40	Passed	Passed with amendment.	App'd May 22, 1832
Jones, Degar M	Payment of receipts given by General C. McArthur during war of 1812.	14	1	Resolution	243	Claims.						
Jones, Dennis	Pension	20	2	Resolution	250	Military Pensions.				Discharged; laid on table.		
Jones, Dennis	Pension	21	1	Petition	49	Military Pensions	Jan. 5, 1830	Favorable	72	Passed	Passed, with amendment.	App'd May 20, 1830
Jones, Edmund, heir of	Indemnity for French spoliations prior to 1800.	31	1	Petition	598	Foreign Affairs	355	Favorable	318	Referred to Committee Whole House.		
Jones, Edward, representatives of, (Miss.)	To make land title valid	22	2	Resolution	59	Public Lands.						

List of private claims presented to the House of Representatives of the United States from the 1st to the 31st Congress, inclusive—Continued.

Names of claimants.	Nature or object of the claim.	Congress.	Session.	How brought before the House of Reps.	Page of journal.	To what committee of the House referred.	No. or date of the report.	Nature of the report.	No. of the bill.	How disposed of by the House of Reps.	How disposed of by the Senate.	Date of the act of Congress, and remarks.
Jones, Edward, representatives of, (Miss.)	To make land title valid	23	1	Resolution	237	Public Lands.						
Jones, Edward, (Pa.)	Increase of pay as inspector and surveyor at Pittsburg.	23	1	Petition	155	Commerce.						
Jones, Edward, (Pa.)	Increase of pay as inspector and surveyor at Pittsburg.	23	2	Petition	196							
Jones, Elizabeth	(See Richard Jones, widow of.)	2	1		490							
Jones, Elizabeth	(See John Carr, deceased, daughter of.)	25	2		70							
Jones, Elizabeth	(See Jason Jones, widow of.)	25	3		88							
Jones, Elizabeth	(See Thomas Jones, widow of, D. C.)	26	1		625							
Jones, Epaphras, *et al.*	Remission of tonnage duties on brigatine Peru.	3	2	Petition	261	Select	Dec. 18, 1794	Favorable	92	Passed	Passed, with amendment.	App'd Jan. 28, 1795
Jones, Ephraim, *et al*	Permission to surrender license by paying for time used.	14	2	Petition	121	Ways and Means	Jan. 25, 1817	Favorable	72	Passed	Passed	App'd March 3, 1817
Jones, Ephraim	Pension	23	1	Petition	493	Rev. Pensions				Disch'd; laid on table.		
Jones, Esther M.	Confirmation of title to land	27	2	Petition	681	Priv. Land Claims.						
Jones, Esther M.	Confirmation of title to land	27	3	Petition	45	Priv. Land Claims.						
Jones, Evan and James, representatives of.	For other lands in lieu of grants from British governmen .	21	2	Memorial	104	Public Lands				Discharged; laid on table.		
Jones, Evan and James, representatives of.	For other lands in lieu of grants from British government.	22	1	Petition	945	Judiciary.						
Jones, Evan and James, representatives of.	For other lands in lieu of grants from British government.	22	2	Petition	178	Priv. Land Claims.						
Jones, Ezekiel	Pay for revolutionary services	31	2	Petition	372					Laid on table.		
Jones, Capt. Ezekiel	For further allowances while in Florida.	24	2	Resolution	71	Naval Affairs.						
Jones, Capt. Ezekiel	For further allowances while in Florida.	25	2	Petition	56	Naval Affairs	487	Favorable	483	Referred to Committee Whole House.		
Jones, Capt. Ezekiel	For further allowances while in Florida.	25	3	House bill	379	Whole House	Jan. 25, 1839		483	Passed	Passed	App'd March 3, 1839
Jones, Capt. Ezekiel	Pension	25	2	Petition	118	Invalid Pensions	288	Adverse		Laid on table.		
Jones, Fielding	Pay for horse lost in military service.	16	1	Petition	28	Claims	Dec. 31, 1819	Favorable	31	Passed	Passed	App'd May 2, 1820
Jones, Frances	(See John Jones, widow of)	25	3		225							
Jones, Gabriel, child of	Seven years' half pay	26	1	Petition	323	Rev. Pensions	714	Adverse		Laid on table.		
Jones, George, (Me.)	(See Paul Pearson, *et al*)	23	1		328							
Jones, George M.	Balance for excavating bar, Nantucket harbor.	28	1	Petition	204	Claims	73	Favorable	95	Passed	Passed	App'd June 15, 1844
Jones, George W.	Drawback of duties paid	16	1	Petition	186	Commerce.						
Jones, Gilson	(See Stephen Van Scyoe, *et al*)	13	1		36							
Jones, Gory	To withdraw entry of land	15	1	Senate bill	245	Whole House		Favorable	S. 23	Passed	Passed	App'd March 9, 1818
Jones, Griffith	Pay for leather furnished government.	2	1	Rep. of Secretary Treasury.	494					Laid on table.		
Jones, Griffith	Pay for leather furnished government.	2	2	Rep. of Secretary Treasury.	619	Select.						
Jones, Griffith	Pay for leather furnished government.	3	1	Petition	86	Select	June 6, 1794	Favorable	67	Passed	Postponed.	
Jones, Griffith	Pay for leather furnished government.	4	1	Petition	384	Claims	Feb. 2, 1796	Adverse		Leave to withdraw.		
Jones, Griffith	Pay for leather furnished government.	10	1	Petition	70	Select.						

List of private claims presented to the House of Representatives of the United States from the 1st to the 31st Congress, inclusive—Continued.

Names of claimants.	Nature or object of the claim.	Congress.	Session.	How brought before the House of Reps.	Page of journal.	To what committee of the House referred.	No. or date of the report.	Nature of the report.	No. of the bill.	How disposed of by the House of Reps.	How disposed of by the Senate.	Date of the act of Congress, and remarks.
Jones, Griffith	Pay for leather furnished government.	14	1	Petition	77	Rev. Claims	Feb. 15, 1816	Adverse		Rejected.		
Jones, Griffith, executor of	Renewal of lost loan office certificate.	6	1	Petition	614	Claims	April 22, 1800	Adverse		Referred to Committee Whole House.		
Jones, Griffith, executor of	Renewal of lost loan office certificate.	6	2	Petition	731	Claims	Jan. 26, 1801	Adverse		Rejected.		
Jones, Harvey, (N. Y.)	Pension	30	1	Petition	289	Invalid Pensions	200	Favorable	210	Passed.		
Jones, Harvey, (N. Y.)	Pension	30	2	House bill	647	Invalid Pensions			210	Passed	Passed	App'd March 3, 1849
Jones, Henry J., (S. C.)	(See surety of John McMichan)	17	1		166							
Jones, Herbert	For drawback on cargo of ship Enterprise.	3	2	Bill	305	Whole House	Feb. 4, 1795	Favorable	102	Passed	Passed	App'd Feb. 13, 1795
Jones, Horatio	Pay for revolutionary service	3	1	Petition	55	Select.						
Jones, Isaac	Allowance and abatement of duties on tobacco destroyed.	4	1	Memorial	434	Com. and Manuf.						
Jones, Israel, agent of	(See Joshua Ashbridge.)	1	3		355							
Jones, Jacob	Distribution of prize money	12	2	Senate bill	710	Whole House	Mar. 3, 1813	With't amend.	S. 62	Passed	Passed	App'd March 3, 1813
Jones, James	Release from penalty as surety to prevent violation of embargo act.	11	2	Letter of Secret'y Treasury.	169	Com. and Manuf.	April 7, 1810			Referred to Committee Whole House.		
Jones, James	Release from penalty as surety to prevent violation of embargo act.	12	1	Petition and docs	72					Refered to Secretary of Treasury.		
Jones, James	(See William H. Bedford, agent.)	28	1		262							
Jones, James, (Ind.)	Indemnity for purchase of property fraudulently sold by agent of government.	31	1	Petition	448	Claims	333	Adverse		Laid on table.		
Jones, James, (Conn.)	Pension	19	1	Petition	203	Military Pensions	April 1, 1826	Adverse		Laid on table.		
Jones, James, (N. Y.)	Pension	29	1	House bill	601	Naval Affairs			342			
Jones, James, (N. Y.)	Pension	29	2	House bill	193	Naval Affairs	Jan. 20, 1847	Favorable	619	Passed	Passed	App'd March 3, 1847
Jones, James, (Ky.)	Pension	20	2	Resolution	126	Military Pensions.						
Jones, James, (Ky.)	Pension	21	1	Petition	36	Military Pensions				Discharged.		
Jones, James, (Ky.)	Pay for a horse lost in public service.	30	1	Petition	146	Claims	238	Favorable	238	Referred to Committee Whole House.		
Jones, James, (England)	For a patent	23	1	Petition	444	Patents	Jan. 18, 1834	Favorable	533	Postponed.		
Jones, James, (England)	For a patent	23	2	House bill	162				533	Passed	Passed	App'd March 3, 1835
Jones, James	(See J. D. Hayden, sureties of.)	22	1		943							
Jones, Jason, widow of	Pension	25	3	Petition	88	Rev. Pensions				Discharged; laid on table.		
Jones, Jesse	Pension	22	1	Petition	72	Rev. Pensions.						
Jones, Joanna	(See Solomon, Jones, widow of.)	25	2		546							
Jones, John	Payment of claim against United States.	1	3	Petition	369					Referred to Secretary War.		
Jones, John	Payment of claim against United States.	2	2	Rep. of Secretary of War.	626					Laid on table.		
Jones, John, (Ky.)	Pension	30	1	Petition	744	Rev. Pensions	548	Adverse		Laid on table.		
Jones, John, (Ky.)	Pension	30	2	Petition	123	Rev. Pensions.						
Jones, John, (Ky.)	Pension	31	1	Petition	232	Rev. Pensions	April 11, 1850	Adverse		Laid on table.		
Jones, John, (Pa.)	Pay for property damaged by United States troops.	1	3	Petition	396					Referred to Secretary Treasury.		
Jones, John, (Penn.)	Pay for property damaged by United States troops.	2	1	Report of Secretary Treasury.	580					Laid on table.		
Jones, John, (S. C.)	Pension	21	1	Resolution	343	Military Pensions	May 29, 1830	Favorable	499	Referred to Committee Whole House.		
Jones, John, (S. C.)	Pension	21	2	House bill	319	Whole House	Feb. 16, 1831	Favorable	499	Passed.		

List of private claims presented to the House of Representatives of the United States from the 1st to the 31st Congress, inclusive—Continued.

Names of claimants.	Nature or object of the claim.	Congress.	Session.	How brought before the House of Reps.	Page of journal.	To what committee of the House referred.	No. or date of the report.	Nature of the report.	No. of the bill.	How disposed of by the House of Reps.	How disposed of by the Senate.	Date of the act of Congress, and remarks.
Jones, John, (Penn.)	Pension	23	2	Petition	198	Rev. Pensions	....	....	....	Discharged; laid on table.		
Jones, John	Pay for wood furnished government in revolutionary war.	4	1	Rep. of Secretary Treasury.	388	Claims	Jan. 19, 1795	Adverse	....	Laid on table.		
Jones, John, (Va.)	Remit duties on stills destroyed by fire.	7	2	Petition	339	Claims	Feb. 19, 1803	Adverse	....	Laid on table.		
Jones, John, (Mo.)	Payment of draft for carrying mail.	18	1	Petition	360	P. Of. & P. Roads.						
Jones, John, (Va.)	Pay for revolutionary services	12	1	Petition	126	Claims.						
Jones, John, (Va.)	Pension	25	2	Petition	729	Rev. Pensions	893	Favorable	792	Passed	Discharged.	
Jones, John, widow of.	Pension	25	3	Petition	225	Rev. Pensions	123	Favorable	990	Passed	Passed	App'd April 3, 1839
Jones, John, (Ohio.)	To change land entry	15	1	Petition	28	Public Lands	Jan. 16, 1818	Favorable	41	Referred to Committee Whole House.		
Jones, John, (Del.)	Pay for repairs done on Pea Patch Island.	23	1	Petition	192	Claims.						
Jones, John, *et al.*	Pay for repairs done on Pea Patch Island.	24	1	Petition	50	Claims	July 2, 1836	....	....	Referred to Secretary War.		
Jones, John, *et al.*	Pay for repairs done on Pea Patch Island.	27	2	Petition	470	Claims	747	Favorable	425	Rejected.		
Jones, John, *et al.*	Pay for repairs done on Pea Patch Island.	27	3	Papers	145	Claims.						
Jones, John, *et al.*	Pay for repairs done on Pea Patch Island.	29	1	Senate bill	1016	Claims	799	....	S. 112	Passed with amend't.	Passed	App'd Aug. 10, 1846
Jones, John, *et al.*	Compensation for expenses incurred in unloading stone at Pea Patch Island.	25	2	House bill	952	Claims	922	Favorable	807	Referred to Committee Whole House.		
Jones, John, *et al.*	Compensation for expenses incurred in unloading stone at Pea Patch Island.	25	3	House bill	431	....	....	....	807	Passed	Passed	App'd March 3, 1839
Jones, John	(See Joshua Jones)	29	1	....	309							
Jones, John C.	Release from liability	15	2	Petition	246	Ways and Means	....	....	....	Discharged; laid on table.		
Jones, John C.	Release from liability	16	1	Petition	225	Ways and Means	....	....	....	Discharged	....	Leave to withdraw.
Jones, John C., (Mo.)	Renew certificates of debt	3	1	Petition	62		....	....	....	Laid on table	....	See act April 21, 1794
Jones, John C., executors of.	Indemnity for French spoliations prior to 1800.	26	1	Memorial	182	Foreign Affairs	343	Favorable	319	Referred to Committee Whole House.		
Jones, John H.	Indemnity for contract to supply United States army with corn.	16	1	Petition	295	Claims.						
Jones, John M.	Pay for invention to destroy rats on shipboard.	16	1	Petition	170	....	....	....	....	Laid on table.		
Jones, John Paul, heir of, by attorney.	For payment of certificates of public debt.	5	2	Petition	81	Claims	....	....	....	Referred to Committee Whole House.		
Jones, John Paul, heir and other representatives of.	For prize money for capturing British vessels, restored by authorities of Denmark to the British.	22	1	Petition	78	Naval Affairs.						
Jones, John Paul, heir and other representatives of.	For prize money for capturing British vessels, restored by authorities of Denmark to the British.	22	2	Resolution	181	Rev. Claims.						
Jones, John Paul, heir and other representatives of.	For prize money for capturing British vessels, restored by authorities of Denmark to the British.	23	1	Memorial	79	Naval Affairs.						
Jones, John Paul, heir and other representatives of.	For prize money for capturing British vessels, restored by authorities of Denmark to the British.	24	1	Documents	119	Rev. Claims.						

List of private claims presented to the House of Representatives of the United States from the 1st to the 31st Congress, inclusive—Continued.

Names of claimants.	Nature or object of the claim.	Congress.	Session.	How brought before the House of Reps.	Page of journal.	To what committee of the House referred.	No. or date of the report.	Nature of the report.	No. of the bill.	How disposed of by the House of Reps.	How disposed of by the Senate.	Date of the act of Congress, and remarks.
Jones, John Paul, heir and other representatives of.	For prize money for capturing British vessels, restored by authorities of Denmark to the British.	24	2	Petition and docs.	269, 308	Rev. Claims.						
Jones, John Paul, heir and other representatives of.	For prize money for capturing British vessels, restored by authorities of Denmark to the British.	27	2	Petition	61	Rev. Claims......	1058	Adverse	......	Laid on table.		
Jones, John Paul, heir and other representatives of.	For prize money for capturing British vessels, restored by authorities of Denmark to the British.	27	3	Petition	381	Foreign Affairs.						
Jones, John Paul, heir and other representatives of.	For prize money for capturing British vessels, restored by authorities of Denmark to the British.	29	1	Memorial......	91	Naval Affairs.....	206	Favorable	200	Referred to Committee Whole House.		
Jones, John Paul, heir and other representatives of.	For prize money for capturing British vessels, restored by authorities of Denmark to the British.	29	2	House bill......	382	Whole House.....	....	Favorable	200	Passed	Passed	Failed to reach the President in time for his signature.
Jones, John Paul, heir and other representatives of.	For prize money for capturing British vessels, restored by authorities of Denmark to the British.	30	1	Senate bill	54	Claims	9	Favorable	S. 1	Passed with amendm't.	Passed	See act Mar. 21, 1848
Jones, John Paul, heir and other representatives of.	For prize money for capturing British vessels, restored by authorities of Denmark to the British.	30	1	Petition	77	Claims.						
Jones, John Paul, heir and other representatives of.	For payment of balance advanced government in revolutionary war.	24	2	Petition	38	Rev. Claims.						
Jones, John Paul, heir and other representatives of.	For payment of balance advanced government in revolutionary war.	25	2	Petition	48	Rev. Claims.						
Jones, John Paul, heir and other representatives of.	For payment of balance advanced government in revolutionary war.	25	3	Petition	85	Rev. Claims.						
Jones, John Paul, heir and other representatives of.	For payment of balance advanced government in revolutionary war.	26	1	Petition	164	Rev. Claims.						
Jones, John Paul, heir and other representatives of.	For payment of balance advanced government in revolutionary war.	26	2	Petition	35	Rev. Claims.						
Jones, John Paul, heir and other representatives of.	For payment of balance advanced government in revolutionary war.	27	3	Petition	168	Rev. Claims.						
Jones, John Paul, heir and other representatives of.	For payment of balance advanced government in revolutionary war.	28	1	Petition	216	Rev. Claims.						
Jones, John Paul, heir and other representatives of.	For payment of balance advanced government in revolutionary war.	28	2	Pet. and papers.	135	Pens. & Rev. Cl'ms.						
Jones, John Paul, heir and other representatives of.	For other lands in lieu of those purchased from Indiana Land Company.	28	1	Memorial	211	Public Lands	115	Adverse	......	Laid on table.		
Jones, John Rice, attorney of.	Pay as interpreter to land commissioners in Indiana.	13	1	Petition	20	Claims	June 29, 1813	Discharged.				
Jones, John Rice, attorney of.	Pay as interpreter to land commissioners in Indiana.	13	2	Petition	172	Claims	Jan. 25, 1814					
Jones, John Rice, attorney of.	Pay as interpreter to land commissioners in Indiana.	14	1	Petition	231	Claims.						
Jones, John Rice, attorney of.	Pay as interpreter to land commissioners in Indiana.	14	2	Petition	102	Public Lands.						
Jones, John Rice, attorney of.	Pay as interpreter to land commissioners in Indiana.	15	1	Petition	94	Priv. Land Claims.						
Jones, John Rice, attorney of.	Pay as interpreter to land commissioners in Indiana.	15	2	Petition	25	Priv. Land Claims	30	Favorable	224	Referred to Committee Whole House.		

List of private claims presented to the House of Representatives of the United States from the 1st to the 31st Congress, inclusive—Continued.

Names of claimants.	Nature or object of the claim.	Congress.	Session.	How brought before the House of Reps.	Page of journal.	To what committee of the House referred.	No. or date of the report.	Nature of the report.	No. of the bill.	How disposed of by the House of Reps.	How disposed of by the Senate.	Date of the act of Congress, and remarks.
Jones, John Rice, attorney of.	Pay as interpreter to land commissioners in Indiana.	15	2	Senate bill	140	Public Lands	Jan. 5, 1819	Favorable	S. 18	Passed	Passed	App'd March 3, 1819
Jones, John Rice, representatives of.	Pay as interpreter to land commissioners in Indiana.	29	2	Senate bill	143	Priv. Land Claims.			S. 43			
Jones, John Rice, representatives of.	Pay as interpreter to land commissioners in Indiana.	31	2	Senate bill	46				S. 79			
Jones, John W	(See William H. Bedford, agent).	28	1		262							
Jones, John W	(See H. Steffey and A. Hewitt, assignees of.)	30	2		36							
Jones, John, executor and attorney of.	Indemnity for French spoliations prior to 1800.	26	1	Memorial	182	Foreign Affairs	343	Favorable	319	Referred to Committee Whole House.		
Jones, Jonathan	Indemnity for property lost in war of 1812.	15	2	Petition	148	Claims	Jan. 16, 1819	Adverse		Laid on table.		
Jones, Joshua, heirs of	Arrears of pension	29	1	Petition	309	Rev. Pensions	613	Adverse		Laid on table.		
Jones, Joshua T., *et al.*	Register for barque Sarah & Eliza	30	1	Memorial	66	Commerce	Dec. 30, 1847	By bill	14	Passed	Passed	App'd Jan. 24, 1848
Jones, Joshua	To cancel duty bonds or extend time of payment.	8	2	Petition	89	Com. and Manuf.	Jan. 18, 1805	Favorable	35	Laid on table.		
Jones, Josiah	Pension	6	1	Petition	583	Claims	April 8, 1800	Adverse		Leave to withdraw.		
Jones, Josiah	Pension	9	2	House bill	608	Whole House	Feb. 28, 1807	Favorable	216	Passed.	Passed	App'd March 3, 1807
Jones, Josiah	Increase of pension	13	1	House bill	56	Whole House	July 20, 1813	Favorable	31	Passed	Passed	App'd Aug. 2, 1813
Jones, Leroy	Pension	14	2	Resolution	209	Rev. Claims	Jan. 29, 1817	Favorable	91	Passed	Passed, with amendment.	App'd March 3, 1817
Jones, Levin	Release vessel for violating Slave Importing act.	11	2	Petition	136	Com. and Manuf.	Jan. 11, 1810	Favorable	50	Passed	Passed	App'd Feb. 5, 1810
Jones, Lewis, (Ky.)	To locate land warrant in Illinois	22	1	Petition	576	Public Lands.						
Jones, Lewis, widow of	Arrears of pension	30	1	Petition	918	Rev. Pensions.						
Jones, Mary	(See Zebular Jones, widow of.)	25	2		664							
Jones, Mary S	Pay for certificate of public debt	4	2	House bill	341	Whole House			122			
Jones, Martha, and others.	(See heirs of William Langbourne.)	22	2		29							
Jones, M. L., and others	(See Samuel J. Axson, heirs of.)	25	2		1118							
Jones, Michael	Additional pay as land commissioner in Illinois.	15	1	Petition	331	Claims.						
Jones, Michael	Additional pay as land commissioner in Illinois.	15	1	Senate bill	420	Public Lands	April 10, 1818	Favorable	S. 62	Passed	Passed	App'd April 16, 1818
Jones, Michael, representatives of.	Additional pay as register land office, Illinois.	18	1	Resolution	139	Public Lands.						
Jones, Mildred	(See Lewis Jones, widow of.)	30	1		918							
Jones, Moses, widow of	Pension	25	3	Petition	127	Rev. Pensions				Discharged.		Leave to withdraw.
Jones, Moses, widow of	Pension	26	1	Petition	284	Rev. Pensions.				Discharged; laid on table.		
Jones, Moses, widow of	Pension	27	2	Petition	59	Rev. Pensions	784	Adverse		Laid on table.		
Jones, Nathaniel	Indemnity for a boat captured in late war.	16	2	Petition	240	Claims.						
Jones, Nathaniel	Indemnity for a boat captured in late war.	17	1	Petition	100	Claims	Feb. 14, 1822	Adverse		Laid on table.		
Jones, Nathaniel	Indemnity for a boat captured in late war.	18	1	Petition	158	Claims	61	Favorable	116	Passed	Passed	App'd May 17, 1824
Jones, Nehemiah, (N. Y.)	Restoration of pension	17	1	Petition	51	Rev. Pensions.						
Jones, Nehemiah, (N. Y.)	Restoration of pension	26	1	Petition	626	Rev. Pensions.						
Jones, Nehemiah, (N. Y.)	Restoration of pension	27	2	Petition	509	Rev. Pensions	798	Favorable	452	Referred to Committee Whole House.		
Jones, Nehemiah. (N. Y.)	Restoration of pension	27	3	House bill	88	Whole House	Dec. 23, 1842	Favorable	452	Passed	Indef. postp'd.	

List of private claims presented to the House of Representatives of the United States from the 1st to the 31st Congress, inclusive—Continued.

Names of claimants.	Nature or object of the claim.	Congress.	Session.	How brought before the House of Reps.	Page of journal.	To what committee of the House referred.	No. or date of the report.	Nature of the report.	No. of the bill.	How disposed of by the House of Reps.	How disposed of by the Senate.	Date of the act of Congress, and remarks.
Jones, Nelce	Pension	3	2	Rep. of Secretary War.	350	Claims	Feb. 28, 1795	Favorable	130	Passed	Postponed.	
Jones, Nelce	Pension	4	1	Res. and docs	373	Claims.						
Jones, Nelce	Pension	4	2	Res. and docs	720	Claims.						
Jones, Nelce	Pension	5	2	House bill	127	Whole House	Jan. 11, 1798	Favorable	38	Passed	Passed	App'd Feb. 2, 1798
Jones, Obadiah	(See Benjamin S. Pope)	19	1		179							
Jones, Peter	Restoration of pension	17	2	Petition	47	Rev. Pensions.						
Jones, Philip F	Pay for clothing and rifle lost in late war.	25	1	Petition	49					Laid on table.		
Jones, Philip F	Pay for clothing and rifle lost in late war.	25	2	Petition	89	Claims	897	Adverse		Laid on table.		
Jones, Polly	Indemnity for Indian depredations.	14	2	Petition	71	Claims.						
Jones, Polly	Indemnity for Indian depredations.	15	1	Petition	44	Claims	Jan. 28, 1818	Adverse		Rejected.		
Jones, Polly	Confirmation for title to land	14	2	Petition	72	Public Lands.						
Jones, Polly	(See Joshua Jones, heirs of.)	29	1		309							
Jones, Reuben	Pension	23	1	Petition	69	Rev. Pensions				Discharged; laid on table.		
Jones, Richard, (Ohio.)	Pay for work on Cumberland road	20	1	Petition	280	Claims	April 17, 1828	Adverse		Laid on table.		
Jones, Richard, (Ohio.)	Pay for work on Cumberland road	23	1	Res. and docs	589	Claims	455	Adverse				See Report No. 449.
Jones, Richard D., (N. C.)	Pension	30	2	Petition	284	Invalid Pensions	79	Favorable	775	Referred to Committee Whole House.		
Jones, Richard J., (Md.)	Indemnity for vessels destroyed in late war.	22	1	Petition	124	Claims	Feb. 27, 1832	Adverse		Recommitted.		
Jones, Richard J., (Md.)	Indemnity for vessels destroyed in late war.	25	2	Petition	234	Claims				Discharged.		
Jones, Richard J., (Md.)	Indemnity for vessels destroyed in late war.	26	1	Petition	169	Claims	64	Adverse		Laid on table.		
Jones, Richard L	Arrears of pension	31	1	Petition	917	Rev. Claims.						
Jones, Richard L	Arrears of pension	31	2	Petition	175	Rev. Pensions.						
Jones, Richard, widow of.	Pay for revolutionary services of husband.	2	1	Petition	490					Referred to Secretary War.		
Jones, Richard, widow of.	Pay for revolutionary services of husband.	2	2	Rep. of Secretary War.	696					Laid on table.		
Jones, Robert	Relief for wounds received in revolutionary war.	2	1	Petition	509					Laid on table.		
Jones, Robert, (Ala.)	Correct entry of land	22	1	Petition	33	Public Lands	Dec. 19, 1831	Favorable	45	Passed	Passed	Sec act Mar. 15, 1832
Jones, General Roger	For pay and emoluments of his brevet rank.	24	2	Petition	395	Military Affairs.						
Jones, General Roger	For pay and emoluments of his brevet rank.	25	2	Petition	73	Military Affairs	485	Favorable	481	Referred to Committee Whole House.		
Jones, General Roger	For pay and emoluments of his brevet rank.	25	3	House bill	379	Whole House		Favorable	481	Passed	Passed	App'd March 3, 1839
Jones, General Roger	For pay and emluments from 1821 to 1825.	31	1	Senate bill	923	Military Affairs.	June 14, 8250	Favorable	52	Referred to Committee Whole House.		
Jones, Rosina	(See Abel Jones, widow of.)	1	3		382							
Jones, Russell	(See John H. Peaslee.)	13	3		484							
Jones, Salmon	Confirmation of title to land	24	1	Petition	1165	Priv. Land Claims.				Discharged; laid on table.		
Jones, Salmon	Confirmation of title to land	24	2	Petition	578	Priv. Land Claims.				Discharged; laid on table.		
Jones, Samuel	Balance of pension	5	2	Petition	246	Claims	April 12, 1798			Referred to Committee Whole House.		

List of private claims presented to the House of Representatives of the United States from the 1st to the 31st Congress, inclusive—Continued.

2—28

Names of claimants.	Nature or object of the claim.	Congress.	Session.	How brought before the House of Reps.	Page of journal.	To what committee of the House referred.	No. or date of the report.	Nature of the report.	No. of the bill.	How disposed of by the House of Reps.	How disposed of by the Senate.	Date of the act of Congress, and remarks.
Jones, Samuel, *et al*	Payment of claims against government.	1	2	Petition	193					Referred to Secretary War.		
Jones, Samuel, (N. Y.)	Increase of pension	21	1	Petition	46	Military Pensions	May 4, 1830	Adverse		Laid on table.		
Jones, Capt. Samuel, heirs of.	Commutation pay	23	1	Petition	837	Rev. Claims.						
Jones, Capt. Samuel, heirs of.	Commutation pay	24	1	Petition	103	Rev. Claims	796	Favorable	714	Referred to Committee Whole House.		
Jones, Capt. Samuel, heirs of.	Commutation pay	25	2	Petition	40	Rev. Claims	125	Favorable	143	Passed.		
Jones, Capt. Samuel, heirs of.	Commutation pay	25	3	Petition	85	Rev. Claims	15	Favorable	913			
Jones, Capt. Samuel, heirs of.	Commutation pay	26	1	Petition	165	Rev. Claims	618	Adverse		Laid on table.		
Jones, Capt. Samuel, heirs of.	Commutation pay	26	2	Petition	38	Rev. Claims				Discharged; laid on table.		
Jones, Capt. Samuel, heirs of.	Commutation pay	27	2	Petition	62	Rev. Claims	1092	Adverse		Laid on table.		
Jones, Capt. Samuel, heirs of.	Commutation pay	27	3	Petition	44	Rev. Claims	240	Adverse		Laid on table.		
Jones, Capt. Samuel, heirs of.	Commutation pay	28	1	Petition	514	Rev. Claims.						
Jones, Capt. Samuel, heirs of.	Commutation pay	30	1	Petition	202	Rev. Claims	329	Favorable	306	Referred to Committee Whole House.		
Jones, Capt. Samuel, heirs of.	Commutation pay	30	2	House bill	142	Whole House			306	Passed.		
Jones, Capt. Samuel, heirs of.	Commutation pay	31	1	Petition	270	Rev. Claims.						
Jones, Samuel, heirs of, (Penn.)	Renewal of patent	28	2	Petition	435	Patents.						
Jones, Samuel, (Maine.)	Pension	21	1	Petition	99	Military Pensions	May 30, 1831	Favor'ble, general bill.	248	Passed	Postponed.	
Jones, samuel, (Maine.)	Pension	22	1	Petition	34	Rev. Pensions.						
Jones, Sarah	(See Alonzo Jones, widow of.)	30	1		313							
Jones, Sarah	(See William Jones, widow of.)	20	1		48							
Jones, Seaborn	(See Thomas F. Green, sureties of.)	23	1		226							
Jones, Solomon, widow of.	Pension	25	2	Petition	546	Rev. Pensions						See House bill, No. 456
Jones, Stephen and Phereley, assignees of.	Confirmation of title to land	15	1	Petition	102	Priv. Land Claims.						
Jones, Stephen and Phereley, assignees of.	Confirmation of title to land	16	1	Petition	72	Priv. Land Claims.						
Jones, Stephen and Phereley, assignees of.	Confirmation of title to land	17	1	Petition	54	Public Lands.						
Jones, Stephen and Phereley, assignees of.	Confirmation of title to land	18	1	Petition	54	Public Lands.						
Jones, Stephen and Wm Delesdernier.	Refund duties paid on cargo of brig Commerce.	18	1	Petition	154	Ways and Means	Feb. 17, 1824	Adverse		Laid on table.		
Jones, Stephen and Wm. Delesdernier.	Refund duties paid on cargo of brig Commerce.	23	2	Petition	105	Commerce.						
Jones, Strother, heirs of	Commutation pay	23	2	Petition	106	Rev. Claims.						
Jones, Strother, heirs of	Commutation pay	26	1	Petition	164	Rev. Claims.						
Jones, Strother, heirs of	Commutation pay	27	2	Petition	61	Rev. Claims	385	Adverse		Laid on table.		
Jones, Strother, heirs of	Commutation pay	28	1	Petition	132	Rev. Claims.						

List of *private claims presented to the House of Representatives of the United States from the 1st to the 31st Congress, inclusive*—**Continued.**

Names of claimants.	Nature or object of the claim.	Congress.	Session.	How brought before the House of Reps.	Page of journal.	To what committee of the House referred.	No. or date of the report.	Nature of the report.	No. of the bill.	How disposed of by the House of Reps.	How disposed of by the Senate.	Date of the act of Congress, and remarks.
Jones, Thomas	Pay for revolutionary services	2	1	Petition	483					Referred to Secretary War.		
Jones, Thomas, (Indiana)	Pay for merchandise seized by United States.	13	3	Petition	674	Select.						
Jones, Thomas, (Indiana)	Pay for merchandise seized by United States.	14	1	Petition	146	Claims	Feb. 4, 1816	Adverse		Rejected.		
Jones, Thomas, (Indiana)	Pay for merchandise seized by United States.	14	2	Petition	85	Claims.						
Jones, Thomas, (Indiana)	Pay for merchandise seized by United States.	15	1	Petition	232	Claims.						
Jones, Thomas, (Indiana)	Pay for merchandise seized by United States.	17	1	Petition	314	Claims.						
Jones, Thomas, (Indiana)	Pay for merchandise seized by United States.	18	1	Petition	159	Claims	Feb. 27, 1824	Adverse		Laid on table.		
Jones, Thomas, (Ky.)	Pension	19	1	Petition	398	Military Pensions	164	Adverse		Laid on table.		
Jones, Thomas	(See representatives of Wm. Jones, deceased.)	23	2		197							
Jones, Thomas, (Maine)	Pension	19	1	Petition	381	Military Pensions	May 5, 1826	Favorable		Ref'd to Com W. H		
Jones, Thomas, (Maine)	Pension	19	2	Petition	36	Military Pensions	Dec. 22, 1826	Favorable	314	Passed	Passed, with amendment.	App'd March 3, 1827
Jones, Thomas, (Mass.)	Pay for revolutionary services	19	2	Petition	25	Rev. Claims.						
Jones, Thomas, (Mass.)	Pay for revolutionary services	20	1	Petition	45	Rev. Claims	Dec. 24, 1827	Adverse		Laid on table.		
Jones, Thomas, of District of Columbia, widow of.	Pension	26	1	Petition	625	Rev. Pensions.						
Jones, Thomas, of District of Columbia, widow of.	Pension	27	2	Petition	509	Rev. Pensions				Discharged; laid on table.		
Jones, Thomas Ap Catesby	Settlement of accounts, vouchers taken by enemy in late war.	14	1	Petition	180	Claims	Feb. 26, 1816	Favorable	H. B.	Passed	Passed	App'd April 27, 1816
Jones, Thomas Ap Catesby	Increase of pension	21	2	Memorial	271	Naval Affairs	104	Adverse		Laid on table.		
Jones, Thomas Ap Catesby	Increase of pension	22	2	Memorial	120	Naval Affairs	108	Favorable	752	Referred to Committee Whole House.		
Jones, Thomas Ap Catesby	Increase of pension	23	1	Memorial	68	Naval Affairs	35	Favorable	41	Passed	Passed	App'd May 10, 1834
Jones, Thomas Ap Catesby	Pay for diplomatic services	25	2	Memorial	407	Foreign Affairs	920	Favorable	806	Referred to Committee Whole House.		
Jones, Thomas Ap Catesby	Pay for diplomatic services	25	3	Bill	431	Whole House	Feb. 1, 1839	Favorable	806			
Jones, Thomas Ap Catesby	Pay for diplomatic services	26	1	Memorial	182	Foreign Affairs.						
Jones, Thomas Ap Catesby	Pay for diplomatic services	27	2	Petition	1005	Foreign Affairs.						
Jones, Thomas Ap Catesby	Pay for diplomatic services	27	3	Memorial	134	Foreign Affairs.						
Jones, Thomas Ap Catesby	Pay for diplomatic services	28	1	Memorial	60	Foreign Affairs.						
Jones, Thomas Ap Catesby	Pay for diplomatic services	28	2	Memorial	57	Foreign Affairs	92	Favorable	577	Laid on table.		
Jones, Thomas Ap Catesby	Reimbursement and arrears of pension.	29	1	Memorial	103	Naval Affairs.						
Jones, Thomas Ap Catesby	Reimbursement and arrears of pension.	29	2	Petition	365	Naval Affairs	60	Favorable	665	Referred to Committee Whole House.		
Jones, Thomas Ap Catesby	Reimbursement and arrears of pension.	30	1	Petition	105	Naval Affairs	273	Favorable	268	Referred to Committee Whole House.		
Jones, Thomas Ap Catesby	Pay of expenses for fitting out expedition to South Sea islands.	25	2	Memorial	542	Naval Affairs	May 23, 1838	Favorable; bill	806	Referred to Committee Whole House.		
Jones, Thomas Ap Catesby	Pay of expenses for fitting out expedition to South Sea islands.	26	1	Memorial	179	Naval Affairs.						
Jones, Thomas Ap Catesby	Pay of expenses for fitting out expedition to South Sea islands.	29	1	Petition	147	Foreign Affairs	108	Favorable	122	Passed	Passed	App'd Aug. 8, 1846
Jones, Thomas K.	Debenture on wines exported to Havana.	7	1	Memorial	31	Com. and Manuf.	Jan. 15, 1802	Favorable	34	Passed	Passed	App'd April 14, 1802

List of private claims presented to the House of Representatives of the United States from the 1st to the 31st Congress, inclusive—Continued.

Names of claimants.	Nature or object of the claim.	Congress.	Session.	How brought before the House of Reps.	Page of journal.	To what committee of the House referred.	No. or date of the report.	Nature of the report.	No. of the bill.	How disposed of by the House of Reps.	How disposed of by the Senate.	Date of the act of Congress, and remarks.
Jones, Thomas K., *et al.*	Relief from paying duties on tea	9	1	Petition	324	Com. and Manuf.						
Jones, Thomas P.	Pay for examining subject of steamboat explosions.	29	1	Memorial	276	Ways and Means	....	....	......	Leave to withdraw.		
Jones, Thomas P.	Pay for examining subject of steamboat explosions.	30	1	House bill	224	Whole House	April 8, 1848	Favorable	65	Passed.		
Jones, Thomas P., representatives of.	Pay for examining subject of steamboat explosions.	30	1	Senate bill	1438	Claims	....	....	S. 7			
Jones, Walter	Increased pay as postmaster	15	2	Petition	144	P. Of. and P. Roads.						
Jones, Walter, U. S. attorney.	Increase of compensation	25	2	Petition	75	Judiciary	Jan. 18, 1838	Favorable	437	Referred to Committee Whole House.		
Jones, Walter, U. S. attorney.	Increase of compensation	25	3	House bill	378	Whole House	....	....	437	Passed	Passed	App'd March 3, 1839
Jones, Wiley, executor of.	Pay for property destroyed by Indians.	27	2	Memorial	617	Claims	731	Adverse	......	Laid on table.		
Jones, William, (negro)	Release from imprisonment in District of Columbia.	28	1	Petition	133	Judiciary	29	Favorable	56	Referred to Committee Whole House.		
Jones, William	Renewal of lost loan office certificates.	2	1	Petition and rep't Sec. Treasury.	530	Select.						
Jones, William, widow of.	Renewal of lost loan office certificates.	3	2	Memorial	265	Select	Dec. 22, 1794	Favorable	122	Referred to Committee Whole House.		
Jones, William, widow of.	Renewal of lost loan office certificates.	4	1	Memorial	388	Claims.						
Jones, William, widow of	Renewal of lost loan office certificates.	4	2	Memorial	614	Claims.						
Jones, William, widow of.	Renewal of lost loan office certificates.	5	2	Memorial	232	Whole House.						
Jones, William, (Ind.)	Pension	3	2	Rep. of Secretary War.	278	Claims	....	....	......	Discharged; laid on table.		
Jones, William, (Ky.)	Pension	19	2	Petition	285	Military Pensions.						
Jones, William, administrator of.	Release from government claim	15	2	Petition	160	Ways and Means	....	....	......	Discharged; laid on table.		
Jones, William, administrator of.	Release from government claim	16	1	House bill	154	Ways and Means	Jan. 20, 1820	Favorable	55	Passed	Passed	App'd May 8, 1820
Jones, William, (Ind.)	Lease or donation of land	16	2	Petition	260	Public Lands.						
Jones, William, widow of.	Land and pay for services done in late war.	20	1	Resolution	48	Military Pensions	255	Favorable	298	Referred to Committee Whole House.		
Jones, William, (Geo.)	Pension	21	2	Resolution	172	Military Pensions.						
Jones, Wm., heir of, (Mo.)	Pay for revolutionary services	30	1	Petition	723	Rev. Pensions.						
Jones, William	Pay for horses lost in war of 1812	22	2	Resolution	286	Claims	111	Adverse	......	Laid on table.		
Jones, William	Pay for horses lost in war of 1812	23	2	Resolution	348	Claims.						
Jones, William	Pay for horses lost in war of 1812	24	2	Resolution	395	Claims	270	To refer to 3d Auditor.	......	Report adopted.		
Jones, William, representatives of.	Pay of lost loan office certificates.	23	2	Petition	197	Rev. Claims.						
Jones, William, representatives of.	Pay of lost loan office certificates.	24	1	Petition	205	Rev. Claims.						
Jones, William, representatives of.	Pay of lost loan office certificates.	25	2	Senate bill	605	Rev. Claims	May 11, 1838	With't amend.	S. 135	Referred to Committee Whole House.		
Jones, William, (Mass.)	Pension and pay for losses in revolutionary war.	24	2	Petition	301	Rev. Pensions	....	....	......	Discharged; laid on table.		
Jones, William, (Ala.)	For certificate for money paid for land granted to Alabama.	25	2	Senate bill	1241	Public Lands	July 6, 1838	Favorable	S. 275	Referred to Committee Whole House.		

List of private claims presented to the House of Representatives of the United States from the 1st to the 31st Congress, inclusive—**Continued.**

Names of claimants.	Nature or object of the claim.	Congress.	Session.	How brought before the House of Reps.	Page of journal.	To what committee of the House referred.	No. or date of the report.	Nature of the report.	No. of the bill.	How disposed of by the House of Reps.	How disposed of by the Senate.	Date of the act of Congress, and remarks.
Jones, William, (Ala.)	For certificate for money paid for land granted to Alabama.	25	3	Senate bill	98	Priv. Land Claims.	Feb. 6, 1839	Favorable	S. 6	Referred to Committee Whole House.		
Jones, William, (Ala.)	For certificate for money paid for land granted to Alabama.	25	3	Documents	488	Priv. Land Claims.						
Jones, William, (Ala.)	For certificate for money paid for land granted to Alabama.	26	1	Senate bill	802	Public Lands	April 24, 1840	Favorable	S. 31	Referred to Committee Whole House.		
Jones, William, (Ala.)	For certificate for money paid for land granted to Alabama.	26	2	Senate bill	99	Priv. Land Claims.	Jan. 4, 1841	Favorable	S. 16	Passed	Passed	App'd March 2, 1841
Jones, Dr. William	Pay for extra services as postmaster	26	1	Petition	622	Claims.						
Jones, Dr. William	Pay for extra services as postmaster	26	2	Petition	38	Claims	242	Adverse		Laid on table.		
Jones, William C., (Iowa.)	For grant of land in Iowa	30	2	Petition	164	Public Lands	Feb. 27, 1849	Adverse		Laid on table.		
Jones, William D.	Pay as consul at Mexico	25	3	Resolution	289	Foreign Affairs.						
Jones, William D.	Pay as consul at Mexico	26	1	Resol'n and letter	441	Foreign Affairs	633	Favorable	464	Referred to Committee Whole House.		
Jones, William D.	Pay as consul at Mexico	26	1	Senate bill	1156	Foreign Affairs			S. 366			
Jones, William D.	Pay as consul at Mexico	26	1	Petition	178	Ways and Means.	Feb. 29, 1840	Favorable	27	Passed	Passed	App'd July 21, 1840
Jones, William G.	Release from prison	15	1	Petition	355	Judiciary.						
Jones, Wm. S.	(See heir of Strother Jones)	23	2		106							
Jones, William	(See Jones & Clark)	26	1		182							
Jones, Wood, representatives of.	Commutation pay	25	2	Petition	816	Rev. Claims				Discharged; laid on table.		
Jones, Wood, representatives of.	Commutation pay	25	3	Petition	85	Rev. Claims				Discharged.		
Jones, Wood, representatives of.	Commutation pay	26	1	Petition	166	Rev. Claims.						
Jones, Wood, representatives of.	Commutation pay	26	2	Petition	106	Rev. Claims	Feb. 12, 1841	Adverse		Laid on table.		
Jones, Wood, representatives of.	Commutation pay	27	2	Petition	96	Rev. Claims	386	Adverse		Laid on table.		
Jones, Wood, representatives of.	Commutation pay	29	1	Petition	532	Rev. Claims.						
Jones, Zebulon, widow of	Pension	25	2	Petition	664	Rev. Pensions.						
Jones, Zebulon, agent	(See Daniel Miller, representatives of.)	2	1		500							
Jones, Zenas, (Conn.)	Arrears and increase of pension	26	1	Petition	287	Rev. Pensions				Discharged; laid on table.		
Jorda, Pierré	Confirmation of title to land	22	1	Resolution	86	Public Lands	Dec. 27, 1831	Favorable	125	Passed	Passed	App'd June 25, 1832
Jordan, Benjamin	Pension	22	1	Petition	494	Rev. Pensions	381	Favorable	472	Passed	Indef. postp'd.	
Jordan, Charles, (Mo.)	Pension	14	2	Resolution	166	Rev. Claims	Jan. 29, 1817	Favorable	91	Passed	Passed	App'd March 3, 1817, name of petitioner omitted in act.
Jordan, Jacob C	Correction of land entry	22	1	Senate bill	1029	Public Lands	July 3, 1832	Favorable	S. 175	Passed	Passed	App'd July 13, 1832
Jordan, Capt. John, (Pa.)	Arrears of pension	26	1	Petition	325	Invalid Pensions	521	Favorable	418	Referred to Committee Whole House.		
Jordan, John, and other	Prize money for services on Bon Homme Richare.	3	1	Rep. of Secretary War.	83	Select	April 22, 1794			Laid on table.		
Jordan, John, (Va.)	Pension	12	1	Petition	139	Claims	June 8, 1812	General bill	138	Passed	Passed	App'd July 5, 1812
Jordan, John, (Ky.)	Pension	14	1	Documents	232	Rev. Claims.						
Jordan, John, (Ill.)	Exchange location of bounty land warrant.	23	1	Petition	215	Public Lands	291	Favorable	327	Referred to Committee Whole House.		
Jordan, John, (Ill.)	Exchange location of bounty land warrant.	26	1	Petition	609	Public Lands.						

List of private claims presented to the House of Representatives of the United States from the 1st to the 31st Congress, inclusive—**Continued.**

Names of claimants.	Nature or object of the claim.	Congress.	Session.	How brought before the House of Reps.	Page of journal.	To what committee of the House referred.	No. or date of the report.	Nature of the report.	No. of the bill.	How disposed of by the House of Reps.	How disposed of by the Senate.	Date of the act of Congress, and remarks.
Jordan, John, (N. Y.)	Pension	26	1	Petition	937	Invalid Pensions.						
Jordan, John, (N. Y.)	Pension	27	2	Petition	348	Invalid Pensions	148	Favorable	195	Passed	Passed	App'd Aug. 16, 1846
Jordan, Captan John, *et al.*	Commutation pay for revolutionary services.	6	1	Petition	640					Laid on table.		
Jordan, Captain John, executor of.	Commutation pay for revolutionary services.	24	1	Petition	138	Rev. Claims	536	Favorable	531	Referred to Committee Whole House.		
Jordan, Captain John, executor of.	Commutation pay for revolutionary services.	25	2	Petition	40	Rev. Claims	123	Favorable	141	Referred to Committee Whole House.		
Jordan, Captain John, executor of.	Commutation pay for revolutionary services.	25	2	Senate bill	197	Rev. Claims	Jan. 25, 1838	Favorable	S. 58	Rejected.		
Jordan, Captain John, executor of.	Commutation pay for revolutionary services.	25	3	House bill	375				141			
Jordan, Captain John, executor of.	Commutation pay for revolutionary services.	26	1	Petition	165	Rev. Claims	April 25, 1840	Favorable				
Jordan, Johnson	Pension	22	1	Resolution	93, 261	Rev. Pensions	159	Favorable	237	Referred to Committee Whole House.		
Jordan, Johnson	Pension	22	2	House bill	123	Whole House			237	Laid on table.		
Jordan, Johnson, heirs of	Arrears of pension	28	1	Petition	840	Rev. Pensions.						
Jordan, Johnson, heirs of	Arrears of pension	28	2	Petition	55	Rev. Pensions.						
Jordan, Josiah, (Vt.)	Pension	15	2	Petition	36	Rev. Pensions	Dec. 24, 1818	Adverse		Leave to withdraw.		
Jordan, Josiah, (Vt.)	Pension	19	1	Petition	268	Military Pensions	164	Adverse		Laid on table.		
Jordan, Josiah, (Vt.)	Pension	21	1	Petition	59	Military Pensions	April 7, 1830	Adverse		Laid on table.		
Jordan, Josiah, (N. C.)	Indemnity for capture of vessel by Spanish cruiser.	18	1	Petition	296	Foreign Affairs	90	Adverse		Laid on table.		
Jordan, Lydia	Pension	29	1	Petition	280	Rev. Claims.						
Jordan, Lydia	Extension of pension	30	1	Petition	406	Rev. Pensions	537	Adverse		Laid on table.		
Jordan, Samuel	Increase of pension	16	1	Petition	203	Rev. Claims.						
Jordan, Samuel	Increase of pension	25	2	Resolution	975	Rev. Pensions				Discharged; laid on table.		
Jordan, Samuel	Increase of pension	25	3	Resolution	457	Rev. Pensions				Discharged; laid on table.		
Jordan, Samuel	Increase of pension	26	1	Petition	174	Rev. Pensions				Discharged; laid on table.		
Jordan, Samuel, (Penn.)	Pension	29	1	Petition	104	Rev. Pensions	109	Favorable	123	Passed	Passed	App'd Aug. 8, 1846
Jordan, Thomas	Pension	28	1	Petition	877	Rev. Pensions.						
Jordan, Thomas W.	Pay as purser on ship On-ka-hye.	28	1	Petition	774	Naval Affairs	462	Adverse		Laid on table.		
Jordan, Timothy	Pension	23	1	Petition	436	Rev. Pensions	500	Favorable	506	Referred to Committee Whole House.		
Jordan, Timothy	Pension	23	2	House bill	337	Whole House		Favorable	506	Passed	Passed	App'd March 3, 1835
Jordan, Timothy	Pay for revolutionary services	24	1	Petition	73	Rev. Claims	Jan. 12, 1836	Adverse		Laid on table.		
Joseph, John	(See widow of Stephen Decatur, *et al.*)	20	1		295		201		S. 50			
Joseph, schooner, owners of	Fishing bounty	25	3	Documents	569	Commerce				Discharged.		
Josiah, Capt., revenue navy, widow of.	Pension	23	1	Petition	369	Rev. Pensions				Discharged; aid on table.		
Josiah, Capt., revenue navy, widow of.	Pension	27	2	Petition	611	Rev. Pensions	784	Adverse		Laid on table.		
Joslin, James	(See William H. Bedford)	28	1		262							
Joslin, Rebecca	Continuation of pension	28	1	Petition	850	Rev. Pensions.						
Joslin, William	Pay for horses, &c., lost in Seminole war.	23	1	Documents	154	Claims.						
Josselyn, Francis	Restoration of pension	17	2	Petition	99	Whole House.						

List of private claims presented to the House of Representatives of the United States form the 1st to the 31st Congress, inclusive—Continued.

Names of claimants.	Nature or object of the claim.	Congress.	Session.	How brought before the House of Reps.	Page of journal.	To what committee of the House referred.	No. or date of the report.	Nature of the report.	No. of the bill.	How disposed of by the House of Reps.	How disposed of by the Senate.	Date of the act of Congress, and remarks.
Jossylyn, Charles, sureties of.	Reimbursement of money paid for him as defaulter.	21	1	Resolution	133	P. Of. and P. Roads.	167	Favorable	213	Passed.		
Jouet, Robert, representatives of.	Commutation pay	23	2	Senate bill	403	Rev. Claims	Feb. 24, 1835	Favorable	S. 102	Referred to Committee Whole House.		
Jouet, Robert, representatives of.	Commutation pay	24	1	Senate bill	175	Rev. Claims	Jan. 19, 1836	Favorable	S. 29	Passed		App'd May 20, 1836
Jouet, Captain Wm. R.	Refund expenses paid in suit against him.	23	2	Senate amendm't to House bill.	494	Whole House		Favorable	664	Passed	Passed	App'd Nov. 3, 1835
Jourdan, B. and P	Indemnity for property destroyed in war of 1812.	15	1	Petition	166	Claims	100	Favorable	89	Passed.		
Jourdan, B. and P	Indemnity for property destroyed in war of 1812.	15	2	Senate bill	270	Whole House	Feb. 27, 1819	Favorable	S. 35	Passed		App'd March 3, 1819
Jourdan, John	Pension	13	1	House bill	56	Whole House	July 20, 1813	Favorable	31	Passed	Passed	App'd Aug. 2, 1813
Jourdin, Joseph	Confirmation of title to land	20	2	Petition	64	Public Lands	40	Favorable	357	Referred to Committee Whole House.		
Jourdin, Joseph	Confirmation of title to land	21	1	Petition	93	Public Lands	81	Favorable	114	Rejected.		
Journey, James	Confirmation of Spanish grant	25	2	Petition	418	Priv. Land Claims.				Discharged.		
Journey, James	Confirmation of Spanish grant	26	1	Petition	179	Priv. Land Claims.	July 21, 1840	Favorable	513	Referred to Committee Whole House.		
Journey, James	Confirmation of Spnnish grant	27	2	Petition	155	Priv. Land Claims.	554	Favorable	346	Passed.		
Journey, James	Confirmation of Spanish grant	28	1	Petition	351	Priv. Land Claims.	210	Favorable	165	Passed.		
Journey, James	Confirmation of Spanish grant	29	1	Petition	208	Priv. Land Claims.	444	Favorable	317	Passed	Passed	App'd Aug. 8, 1846
Joy, Richard, (Va.)	Increase of pension	17	1	Petition	45	Referred to Secretary of War.	Feb. 19, 1822	Report		Leave to withdraw.		
Joy, Samuel	Pension	3	1	Rep. of Secretary War.	131	Select	May 26, 1794	Favorable	J. R. 12	Passed	Passed	App'd June 9, 1794
Joyal, John B.	Payment of bridge toll for United States troops of Vermont.	14	1	Petition	595	Claims.						
Joyal, John B.	Payment of bridge toll for United States troops of Vermont.	14	2	Petition	75	Claims.						
Joyal, John B.	Payment of bridge toll for United States troops of Vermont.	15	1	Petition	31	Claims	Jan. 12, 1818	Adverse		Rejected.		
Joyce, Daniel	Increase of pension	31	2	Petition	44	Invalid Pensions.						
Joyce, Thomas F.	(See William Shannon, administrators of.)	19	1		269							
Joyner, Benjamin	Pension	23	1	Resolution	161	Rev. Pensions.						
Joynes, William R.	Pension	24	1	Petition	1057	Invalid Pensions.						
Joynes, William R.	Pension	24	2	Petition	86	Invalid Pensions	Mar. 2, 1837	Adverse		Laid on table.		
Joynes, William R.	Pension	25	2	Petition	193	Invalid Pensions	651	Favorable	627	Passed	Adverse.	
Joynes, William R.	Pension	26	1	Petition	161	Invalid Pensions.						
Joynes, William R.	Pension	26	2	Petition	182	Invalid Pensions	143	Favorable	653	Referred to Committee Whole House.		
Joynes, William R.	Pension	27	2	Petition	471	Invalid Pensions	619	Adverse		Laid on table.		
Joynes, William R.	Pension	28	1	Petition	236	Invalid Pensions	296	Favorable	206	Passed	Adverse.	
Joynes, William R.	Pension	28	2	Petition	207	Invalid Pensions.						
Judah, Benjamin S., (N.Y.)	Payment of certificates of public debt.	12	1	Petition	180	Claims.						
Judah, Benjamin S., (N.Y.)	Payment of certificates of public debt.	12	2	Petition	660	Claims.						
Judah, Benjamin S., (N.Y.)	Payment of certificates of public debt.	15	1	Petition	59	Rev. Claims	Feb. 11, 1818	Adverse		Laid on table.		
Judah, Benjamin S., (N.Y.)	Payment of certificates of public debt.	16	1	Petition	91	Rev. Claims	Jan. 31, 1820	Adverse		Laid on table.		

List of private claims presented to the House of Representatives of the United States from the 1st to the 31st Congress, inclusive—Continued.

Names of claimants.	Nature or object of the claim.	Congress.	Session.	How brought before the House of Reps.	Page of journal.	To what committee of the House referred.	No. or date of the report.	Nature of the report.	No. of the bill.	How disposed of by the House of Reps.	How disposed of by the Senate.	Date of the act of Congress, and remarks.
Judah, Benjamin S., (N.Y.)	Payment of certificates of public debt.	19	2	Petition	63	Rev. Claims	Jan. 16, 1827	Adverse	......	Laid on table.		
Judah, Benjamin S., (N.Y.)	Payment of certificates of public debt.	20	1	Petition	166	Rev. Claims	Mar. 4, 1828	Adverse	......	Leave to withdraw.		
Judah, Benjamin S., heirs of	Payment of certificates of public debt.	22	2	Resolution	53	Rev. Claims.						
Judah, Manuel	(See Chancellor H. Saunders and Manuel Judah.)	14	1	....	180							
Judd, Amzy	Bounty land and money for services in war of 1812.	30	1	Petition	81	Public Lands	67	Favorable	49	Passed	Passed	App'd Aug. 5, 1848
Judd, Demas	Pension	21	2	Petition	103	Military Pensions.						
Judd, Eben W., (Vt.)	Renewal of patent	21	1	Petition	147	Judiciary	Jan. 21, 1830	Adverse	......	Laid on table.		
Judd, Freeman	Pension	20	1	Resolution	715	Military Pensions.						
Judd, Freeman	Pension	20	2	Petition	55	Military Pensions	Dec. 12, 1828	Favorable	311	Passed	Laid on table.	
Judd, Freeman	Pension	21	1	Documents	171	Rev. Claims	Feb. 22, 1830	Adverse	......	Laid on table.		
Judd, Jehiel	Increase of pension	10	2	House bill	499	Whole House	Feb. 20, 1809	Favorable	158	Passed	Passed	App'd March 3, 1809
Judd, Jehiel	Increase of pension	15	2	Rep. of Secretary War.	48	Rev. Claims.						
Judd, Margaret	Pension	25	2	Resolution	982	Rev. Pensions	....	....	......	Discharged; laid on table.		
Judd, Mary, heir of	(See William Brown, deceased)	26	1	....	337							
Judd, Ozias	Pension	3	1	Rep. of Secretary War.	131	Select	May 26, 1794	Favorable	J. R. 12	Passed	Passed	App'd June 9, 1794
Judd, Ozias	Pension	4	1	Petition	473	Claims	May 31, 1796	Adverse	......	Laid on table.		
Judge, John, (D. C.)	(See James Tucker & John Judge)	22	2	....	313							
Judge, Thomas L.	Refund money advanced to Seminoles.	30	1	Petition	370	Claims	726	Favorable	567	Referred to Committee Whole House.		
Judge, Thomas L.	Refund money advanced to Seminoles.	30	2	House bill	319	Whole House	....	Favorable	567	Passed.		
Judge, Thomas L.	Refund money advanced to Seminoles.	31	1	Petition	956	Claims.						
Judkins, Sarah, (N. H.)	Pension	28	1	Petition	839	Whole House.						
Judkins, Dr. William	Renewal of patent	20	1	Petition	728	Judiciary	....	....	......	Discharged; laid on table.		
Judkins, Dr. William	Renewal of patent	20	2	Petition	79	Judiciary	....	....	......	Discharged; laid on table.		
Judkins, Dr. William	Renewal of patent	21	1	Petition	361	Judiciary	March 9, 1830	Adverse	......	Laid on table.		
Judson, Alfred	To import machinery for iron steam-boat duty free.	24	2	Memorial	316	Whole House.						
Judson Lewis & P. H. Hobart.	Confirmation of title to land	18	1	Senate bill	233	Priv. Land Claims.	Mar. 26, 1824	Adverse	S. 32	Laid on table.		
Judson Lewis & P. H. Hobart.	Confirmation of title to land	18	2	Petition	47	Priv. Land Claims.						
Judson, Lewis	Confirmation of title to land	19	2	Petition	157	Priv. Land Claims.						
Judson, William	Indem'ty for building custom-house at New London.	24	1	Petition	100	Commerce.						
Judy, Jacob, *et al*	Pay for locating land warrants	31	1	Petition	216	Public Lands.						
Juhel John	Remit duties on goods burnt	4	2	Petition	627	Com. and Manuf.	Jan. 3, 1797	Adverse	......	Laid on table.		
Julian, Dr. John, representatives of.	Commutation pay	23	1	Petition	494	Rev. Claims.						
Julian, Dr. John, representatives of.	Commutation pay	23	2	Petition	164	Rev. Claims.						

List of private claims presented to the House of Representatives of the United States from the 1st to the 31st Congress, inclusive—Continued.

Names of claimants.	Nature or object of the claim.	Congress.	Session.	How brought before the House of Reps.	Page of journal.	To what committee of the House referred.	No. or date of the report.	Nature of the report.	No. of the bill.	How disposed of by the House of Reps.	How disposed of by the Senate.	Date of the act of Congress, and remarks.
Julian, Dr. John, representatives of.	Commutation pay	24	1	Petition	62	Rev. Claims.						
Julian, Dr. John, representatives of.	Commutation pay	24	2	Petition	40	Rev. Claims.						
Julian, Dr. John, representatives of.	Commutation pay	25	2	Petition	70	Rev. Pensions				Discharged; laid on table.		
Julian, Dr. John, representatives of.	Commutation pay	25	3	Petition	84	Rev. Claims				Discharged.		
Julian, Dr. John, representatives of.	Commutation pay	26	1	Petition	164	Rev. Claims.						
Julian, Dr. John, representatives of.	Commutation pay	27	2	Petition	61	Rev. Claims	537	Adverse		Laid on table.		
Julian, Dr. John, representatives of.	Commutation pay	31	1	Petition	1298	Rev. Claims				Leave to withdraw.		
Julian, Dr. John, administrator of.	Commutation pay	31	2	Petition	36	Rev. Claims.						
Julian, Dennis	Indemnity for Indian spoliations	16	1	Petition	140	Claims	Jan. 19, 1820	Adverse		Laid on table.		
Julineau, Francis	Pay for goods furnished United States troops, 1818-'19.	16	1	Res. and docs	394	Ways and Means.						
Julineau, Francis	Pay for goods furnished United States troops, 1818-'19.	16	2	Resolution	225	Claims				Discharged.		Leave to withdraw
Julineau, Francis	Pay for goods furnished United States troops, 1818-'19.	17	1	Petition	151	Claims.						
Julineau, Francis	Pay for goods furnished United States troops, 1818-'19.	17	2	Petition	64	Claims	Jan. 22, 1823	Adverse		Laid on table.		
June, Araham	Pension	22	1	Resolution	337	Rev. Pensions	381	Favorable	472	Passed	Postponed.	
Jungmsan, Guttlob	Pension	22	1	Petition	330	Rev. Pensions.						
Junkin, Joseph	(See Benjamin Wells, *et al.*)	13	3		521							
Justis, Lieut. Isaac	Pension	25	2	Petition	245	Invalid Pensions	322	Favorable	364	Referred to Committee Whole House.		
Justis, Lieut. Isaac	Pension	25	3	Petition	89	Invalid Pensions	82	Favorable	960	Passed	Adverse.	
Justis, Lieut. Isaac	Pension	26	1	Petition	162	Invalid Pensions	194	Favorable	206	Passed	Postponed indefinitely.	
Justis, Lieut. Isaac	Pension	26	2	Petition	36	Invalid Pensions	90	Favorable	595	Referred to Committee Whole House.		
Justis, Lieut. Isaac	Pension	27	2	Petition	130	Invalid Pensions	151	Favorable	198	Rejected.		
Justis, Lieut. Isaac	Pension	27	3	House bill	126	Whole House			198	Passed	Refer'd to Pensions.	
Justis, Lieut. Isaac	Pension	28	1	Petition	137	Invalid Pensions	99	Favorable	115	Passed	Passed	App'd May 23, 1844
Juzon, Pelagie Lorriens	Confirmation of title to land	23	1	Petition	220	Priv. Land Claims	Mar. 4, 1834	Adverse		Laid on table.		

List of private claims presented to the House of Representatives of the United States from the 1st to the 31st Congress, inclusive—Continued.

Names of claimants.	Nature or object of the claim.	Congress.	Session.	How brought before the House of Reps.	Page of journal.	To what committee of the House referred.	No. or date of the report.	Nature of the report.	No. of the bill.	How disposed of by the House of Reps.	How disposed of by the Senate.	Date of the act of Congress, and remarks.
Kabeno-yuah, daughter of.	Restoration of annuity	23	2	Petition	393	Indian Affairs.						
Kager, Joseph	Indemnity for non-payment of a treasury note.	29	1	Petition	616	Claims	673	Adverse	......	Laid on table.		
Kaime, John	Pension	21	1	Petition	46	Military Pensions	Mar. 26, 1830	Favorable	390	Referred to Committee Whole House.		
Kaime, John	Pension	2	2	House bill	318	Whole House	Feb. 16, 1831	With't amend.	390	Passed.		
Kaime, John	Pension	22	1	Petition	104	Invalid Pensions	Feb. 2, 1832	Favorable	344	Passed.		
Kaime, John	Pension	22	2	Resolution	250	Invalid Pensions						
Kaime, John	Pension	23	2	Resolution	126	Invalid Pensions	Feb. 3, 1835	Adverse	......	Laid on table.		
Kaime, John	Pension	25	2	Petition	269	Invalid Pensions	Jan. 30, 1838	Adverse	......	Laid on table.		
Kain, Edward	Payment of bounty money	15	1	Petition	160	Pens. & Rev. Cl'ms	Feb. 16, 1818	Adverse	......	Rejected.		
Kain, Edward	Payment of bounty money	15	2	Petition	342	....	....	....	......	Leave to withdraw.		
Kain, Edward	Payment of bounty money	16	1	Petition	33	Pens. & Rev. Cl'ms.	Dec. 30, 1819	Adverse	......	Rejected.		
Kain, Edward	Payment of bounty money	17	1	Petition	176	Claims.						
Kaine, Robert, (N. Y.)	Compensation for military services.	19	1	Petition	335	Claims	April 20, 1826	Adverse	......	Laid on table.		
Kaine, Robert, (N. Y.)	Compensation for military services.	20		Petition	196	Claims	Feb. 22, 1828	Adverse	......	Laid on table.		
Kaine, Robert, (N. Y.)	Compensation for military services.	21	1	Petition	52	Claims	Dec. 29, 1829	Adverse	......	Recommitted.		
Kaine, Robert, (N. Y.)	Compensation for military services.	21	1	Resolution	206	Claims	Mar. 31, 1830	Favorable	400	Referred to Committee Whole House.		
Kaine, Robert, (N. Y.)	Compensation for military services.	21	2	Petition	62	Claims.						
Kaine, Robert, (N. Y.)	Pay for services and for horse and equipments lost, and also for property taken for public use.	22	1	Petition	63	Claims	Dec. 19, 1831	Favorable	19	Passed	Passed	App'd May 31, 1831, for property only.
Kaine, Robert, (N. Y.)	Arrears and increase of pension	22	1	Petition	67	Invalid Pensions	Jan. 19, 1832	Favorable	288	Passed	Passed, with amendment.	App'd July 14, 1832
Kaine, Robert, (N. Y.)	Compensation for equipments, &c., lost in public service.	22	2	House bill	93	Whole House	Jan. 2, 1833	With't amend.	278	Passed	Passed	App'd March 2, 1833
Kaine, Robert, (N. Y.)	Compensation for military services.	22	2	Petition	136	Claims	Jan. 14, 1834	Adverse	......	Laid on table.		
Kaine, Robert, (N. Y.)	Compensation for military services	23	2	Petition	37	Claims	13	Adverse.	......	Laid on table.		
Kalkman, Charles F.	Extension of time for payment of duties and exemption from imprisonment.	15	1	Petition	48	Ways and Means.						
Kamber, Joseph	Correction of land entry	22	1	Petition	63	Priv. Land Claims.	70	Favorable	138	Passed	Passed	App'd July 13, 1832
Kanary, James	Reissue of military land warrant	14	1	Resolution	658	Military Affairs	....	....	......	....	....	Statutes at Large, vol. 3, page 317.
Kane, Elijah K.	Compensation for services as physician and for expenses.	29	2	Memorial	176	Foreign Affairs.						
Kane, Peter W.	Revolutionary pension	22	1	Resolution	597	Rev. Pensions.						
Kane, Robert	Pension	20	2	Petition	64	Military Pensions.						
Kane, Robert	Pension	21	1	House bill	340	Military Pensions	Mar. 6, 1830	With amend.	60	Passed	Passed	App'd May 20, 1830
Kannons, John	Revolutionary pension	19	1	Petition	35	Rev. Pensions	164	Adverse	......	Laid on table.		
Kanores, John	Revolutionary pension and bounty land.	16	1	Petition	145	Pens. & Rev. Cl'ms.	Feb. 3, 1820	Adverse	......	Rejected.		
Kantzow & Biel	Release from payment of duties	18	2	Petition	136	Ways and Means	Jan. 31, 1825	Adverse		Rejected.		
Kantz, Philip	(See Conrad Houseman, administrator of)	4	1	....	373							
Karr, Henry	Revolutionary pension	4	1	Rep. of Secretary War.	445	Claims	Mar. 4, 1796	Joint resolut'n.	16	Passed	Passed	App'd April 18, 1796
Karthans, Peter A.	Indemnity for French spoliations prior to 1800.	24	1	Petition	723	Foreign Affairs	July 4, 1836	Adverse	......	Laid on table.		
Karthans, Peter A.	Indemnity for French spoliations prior to 1800.	25	2	Memorial	233	Judiciary	437	Adverse	......	Laid on table.		

List of private claims presented to the House of Representatives of the United States from the 1st to the 31st Congress, inclusive—Continued.

Names of claimants.	Nature or object of the claim.	Congress.	Session.	How brought before the House of Reps.	Page of journal.	To what committee of the House referred.	No. or date of the report.	Nature of the report.	No. of the bill.	How disposed of by the House of Reps.	How disposed of by the Senate.	Date of the act of Congress, and remarks.
Karuthers, Wilson C	(See John Kinkle, *et al.*)	26	1		227							
Kasselman, Johannes	Relief for his company	4	1	Petition	545							Leave to withdraw.
Kast, Frederick	(See Joshua Harvey, *et al.*)	7	2		343							
Kauffett, John, and others.	(See Henry Wittly, administrators of.)	14	1		392							
Kauffman, Christian H.	Drawback on wines exported	14	2	Petition	342	Com. and Manuf.						
Kaul, John, and Conrad Opp.	Indemnity for their land granted to others.	20	1	Petition	398	Priv. Land Claims.				Leave to withdraw.		Provided for in act of Mar. 23, 1828.
Kaull, Johan A.	Revolutionary pension	25	2	Petition	180	Rev. Pensions				Discharged; laid on table.		See pension act of Mar. 10, 1838.
Kaw-che-chaw-wa-qui	(See Cecilia Boyer)	20	1		197							
Kay, James	Pension	19	1	Senate bill	488	Military Pensions.	May 3, 1826	With amend's.	115	Passed	Passed	App'd May 16, 1826
Kaysir, Jacob	Restoration of pension	17	2	Petition	96	Whole House on bill No. 207.				Leave to withdraw.		
Kean, Edward	Arrears of revolutionary pay	11	2	Petition	354	Claims.						
Kena, Edward	Arrears of revolutionary pay	11	3	Petition	438	Claims.						
Kean, Edward	Arrears of revolutionary pay	12	1	Petition	11	Claims.						
Kean, Edward	Arrears of revolutionary pay	12	2	Petition	568	Claims	Jan. 30, 1813	Favorable	242	Referred to Committee Whole House.		
Kean, Edward	Arrears of revolutionary pay	13	2	Petition	169	Pens. & Rev. Cl'ms.	Jan. 31, 1814	Adverse		Leave to withdraw.		
Kean, Edward	Arrears of revolutionary pay	13	3	Petition	571	Pens. & Rev. Cl'ms.	July 21, 1815	Adverse		Laid on table.		
Kean, Edward	Arrears of revolutionary pay	14	1	Petition	117	Pens. & Rev. Cl'ms.	Jan. 11, 1816	Adverse		Laid on table.		
Kean, Edward	Arrears of revolutionary pay	15	1	Petition	160	Pens. & Rev. Cl'ms.	Feb. 16, 1818	Adverse		Rejected.		
Kean, Edward	Arrears of revolutionary pay	15	2	Petition	342					Leave to withdraw.		
Kean, Edward	Arrears of revolutionary pay	16	1	Petition	33	Pens. & Rev. Cl'ms.	Dec. 20, 1819	Adverse		Rejected.		
Kean, Edward	Arrears of revolutionary pay	17	1	Petition	176	Claims.						
Kean, Edward	Arrears of revolutionary pay	18	1	Petition	343	Pens. & Rev. Cl'ms.						
Kean, Edward	Arrears of revolutionary pay	18	2	Petition	184	Pens. & Rev. Cl'ms.						
Kean, Manus	Revolutionary pension	3	1	Petition and rep't of Sec. War.	60					Laid on table.		
Kean, Manus	Revolutionary pension	3	2	Petition	276	Claims	Mar. 2, 1795	Adverse		Laid on table.		
Kean, Manus	Revolutionary pension	4	1	Petition and doc.	381	Whole House	Dec. 17, 1795			Leave to withdraw.		
Keane, Robert	Compensation for property destroyed.	15	1	Petition	265	Claims	Mar. 16, 1818	Adverse		Rejected.		
Kearney, Edward	Restoration of revolutionary pension	24	2	Petition	272	Rev. Pensions	284	Adverse		Laid on table.		
Kearney, James, widow of.	Indemnity for French spoliations prior to 1800.	31	1	Petition	196	Foreign Affairs	353	Favorable	318	Referred to Committee Whole House.		
Kearney, James, widow of.	Indemnity for French spoliations prior to 1800.	31	2	Senate bill	183				S. 101	Laid on table.		
Kearney, John A., *et al.*	Increase of salaries of surgeons in navy.	20	1	Mem'l & papers.	171	Naval Affairs	Feb. 12, 1828	Favorable	162	Referred to Committee Whole House.		Provided for by act 24th May, 1828.
Kearney, John W.	(See Augustus Van Horn, and others.)	18	1		387							
Kearney, Lawrence, and others.	Indemnity for expenses in prosecuting prize cases.	17	2	Memorial	52	Naval Affairs.						
Kearney, Lawrence, and others.	Indemnity for expenses in prosecuting prize cases.	18	2	Memorial	149					Leave to withdraw.		
Kearney, Lawrence, and others.	Payment of prize money	23	1	Petition	440	Naval Affairs.						
Kearney, Lawrence, and others.	Payment of prize money	23	2	Petition	121	Naval Affairs.						
Kearney, Lawrence, and others.	Payment of prize money	24	1	Petition	99	Naval Affairs	June 7, 1836	Adverse		Laid on table.		

List of private claims presented to the House of Representatives of the United States from the 1st to the 31st Congress, inclusive—Continued.

Names of claimants.	Nature or object of the claim.	Congress.	Session.	How brought before the House of Reps.	Page of journal.	To what committee of the House referred.	No. or date of the report.	Nature of the report.	No. of the bill.	How disposed of by the House of Reps.	How disposed of by the Senate.	Date of the act of Congress, and remarks.
Kearney, Philip	(See Augustus Van Horn, *et al.*)	18	1	....	387							
Kearns, William	Pension	15	1	Documents	140	Pens. & Rev. Clm's.	....	....	....	Discharged; referred to Secretary of War.		
Kearns, William	Pension	23	1	Petition	189	Naval Affairs	June 3, 1834	Rep. not found	....	Laid on table.		
Kearns, William	Pension	24	1	Petition	140	Invalid Pensions	June 28, 1836	Adverse	....	Laid on table.		
Kearny, Stephen W., and others.	Payment of judgment against them.	22	1	Senate bill	540	Claims	April 9, 1832	With amend.	160	Passed	Passed	App'd July 14, 1832
Kearny, Stephen W	Payment of attorney's fees	23	1	Appropriat'n bill.	253	Whole House	June 26, 1834	With amends.	238	Passed	Passed	App'd June 28, 1834
Kearsley, Jonathan	Compensation as clerk in United States court.	20	1	Petition	197	Territories.						
Kearsley, Jonathan	Compensation as clerk in United States court.	21	1	Petition	263	Judiciary	Mar. 13, 1830	Adverse	....	Laid on table.		
Kearsley, Jonathan	Compensation as receiver of public moneys.	23	1	Petition	499	Public Lands.						
Kearsley, Samuel	Compensation for revolutionary services.	1	3	Petition and rep't Sec. of War.	357	....	Feb. 16, 1790	....	....	Laid on table.		
Keary, William V., widow of.	Confirmation of title to land	19	1	Petition	134	Priv. Land Claims.	50	Favorable	68	Passed	Passed	App'd May 20, 1826
Keates, Thomas	Bounty land for revolutionary services.	22	1	Petition	107	Public Lands	....	....	....	Discharged; laid on table.		
Keates, Thomas	Arrears and increase of pension	25	3	Petition	125	Rev. Claims.						
Keates, Thomas	Arrears and increase of pension	26	1	Petition	166	Rev. Claims.						
Keates, Thomas	Arrears and increase of pension	26	2	Petition	36	Rev. Pensions.						
Keating, John	(See John Bowers, heirs of, by attorney of.	26	1	....	182							
Keating, Oliver	Indemnity for seizure of vessel	19	1	Memorial	204	Foreign Affairs	202	Fovorable, in part.	....	Laid on table.		
Keating, Oliver, heirs and representatives of.	Indemnity for seizure of vessel	29	2	Petition	353	Foreign Affairs	....	....	....	See Ho. bill No. 561.		
Keaton, Thomas P	Increase of compensation as postmaster.	22	1	Petition	162	P. Of. & P. Roads.	....	....	....	Discharged; laid on table.		
Keaton, Thomas P	Increase of compensation as postmaster.	22	2	Petition	75	P. Of. & P. Roads.						
Keaver, Henry M., and others.	(See Johnson Shrum, *et al.*)	31	1	....	730	....	216					
Keefe, Benjamin	Compensation for revolutionary services.	2	1	Petition	468	....	....	....	....	Referred to Secretary of War.		
Keefe, Benjamin	Pension	2	2	Petition	652	....	....	....	....	Laid on table.		
Keefe, Benjamin	Compensation for revolutionary services.	3	1	Petition	117	....	....	....	....	Leave to withdraw.		
Keefer, Henry	Pension	24	1	Petition	97	Invalid Pensions	147	Favorable	155	Passed	Passed	App'd June 29, 1836
Keel Elizabeth	Change of entry of land	19	2	Petition	308	Public Lands.						
Keeler, Aaron	Revolutionary pension	31	1	Petition	323	Rev. Pensions	61	Adverse	....	Laid on table.		
Keeler, Ebenezer, and John Francis.	Release from imprisonment	14	1	Resolution	293	Ways and Means	Mar. 6, 1816	Favorable		Passed	Passed	App'd April 29, 1816
Keeler, Ebenezer, widow of	Revolutionary pension	23	1	Petition	436	Rev. Pensions	....	....	....	Laid on table.		
Keele, John	Pension	25	2	Petition	198	Invalid Pensions	876	Favorable	781	Passed	Discharged.	
Keeler, John	Pension	25	3	Petition	188	Invalid Pensions	183	Favorable	1046	Passed	Adverse report.	
Keeler, John	Pension	26	1	Petition	161	Invalid Pensions	173	Favorable	184	Passed	Indef. postp'd.	
Keeler, John	Pension	27	2	Petition	830	Invalid Pensions.						
Keemle, John	Revolutionary pension	1	3	Rep. of Secretary War.	380	....	....	....	....	Laid on table.		

st of private claims presented to the *House of Representatives of the United States from the 1st to the 31st Congress, inclusive*—Continued.

of claimants.	Nature or object of the claim.	Congress.	Session.	How brought before the House of Reps.	Page of journal.	To what committee of the House referred.	No. or date of the report.	Nature of the report.	No. of the bill.	How disposed of by the House of Reps.	How disposed of by the Senate.	Date of the act of Congress, and remarks.
mle, John	Arrears and depreciation of revolutionary pay.	9	1	Petition	212	Select.						
eemle, John	Compens'n for supplies furnished in revolutionary war.	9	2	Petition	542	Claims.				Discharged.		
Keemle, John	Compensati'n for supplies furnished in revolutionary war.	10	1	Petition	54	Select.						
Keemle, John	Arrears and depreciation of pay.	10	2	Memorial	495					Re 'd to Com. W. H. on bill No. 129.		
Keemle, John	Compensa i'n for supplies furnished in revolutio ary war.	11	1	Petition	42	Claims.						
Keemle, John	Pension and commutation of half-pay.	15	1	Peti ion	156	Pens. & Rev. Cl'ms.	Feb. 24, 1818	Adverse		Rejected.		
Keemle, John	Revolutionary pension	17	1	Petition	30	Rev. Pensions.						
Keen, Elisha L., widow of	Reimbursement of money advanced Un ted S ates.	30	1	Petition	102	Claims.						
Kenn, Elisha L., widow of	Reimbursement of money advanced United States.	30	1	Senate bill	203	Claims	Jan. 14, 1848	With't amend.	23	Passed		App'd Mar. 14, 1848
Keen, John, and Caleb Earl.	Indemnity for capture of vessel, &c.	14	1	Petition	40	Claims	Dec. 21, 1816	Adverse		Rejected.		
Keen, John, and T. Earl.	Indemnity for capture of vessel &c.	22	1	Petition	512	Ways and Means.				Referred to Commitee on Naval Affairs.		
Keen, Jonas W., and J. Snowden.	(See George Watts, administrators of.)	9	2		554							
Keen, Abram	Revolutionary Pension	27	3	Petition	317	Rev. Pensions.						See act Mar. 3, 1843
Keene, Benjamin	(See Joseph Stewart, and others)	14	2		56							
Keene, John	Indemnity for loss of vessel and cargo.	14	1	Petition	40	Claims	Dec. 21, 1815	Adverse		Rejected.		
Keene, Pollard, administrator of.	Compensation for property lost in public service.	15	2	Petition	24, 27	Claims	Nov. 30, 1818	Adverse		Laid on table.		
Keene, Richard Raynal	Compensation for information respecting Algiers.	18	2	Petition	136	Naval Affairs.						
Keene, Richard Raynal	Indemnity for losses in Spain	20	2	Memorial	289	Foreign Affairs.						
Keene, Dr. Samuel Y., representatives of.	Compensation for medical service.	23	1	Papers	42							Not referred.
Keene, Dr. Samuel Y., representatives of.	Compensation for medical service.	24	1	Senate bill	956	Rev. Claims	798	Adverse	167	Referred to Committee Whole House.		
Keene, Dr. Samuel Y., representatives of.	Commutation of revolutionary pay.	24	2	Senate bill	250	Rev. Claims	259	Adverse	25	Referred to Committee Whole House.		
Keene, Dr. Samuel Y., representatives of.	Commutation of revolutionary pay.	25	2	Senate bill	159	Rev. Claims	887	With amend'ts	44	Referred to Committee Whole House.		
Keene, William B	Confirmation of title to land	22	1	Petition	115	Priv. Land Claims.	166	Favorable	243	Referred to Committee Whole House.		
Keene, William B	Confirmation of title to land	22	2	House bill	92	Whole House	Dec. 22, 1823	With't amend.	243	Passed	Passed	App'd Jan. 18, 1833
Keene, William B	Confirmation of title to land	29	1	Senate bill	1108	Priv. Land Claims			169			
Keene, William B	Confirmation of title to land	29	2	Senate bill	199	Priv. Land Claims.	Mar. 1, 1847	With't amend	44	Passed	Passed	App'd March 3, 1847
Keener, Francis, or Kurner.	Confirmation of title to land	15	1	Petition	232	Priv. Land Claims.						
Keener, Francis, or Kurner.	Confirmation of title to land	16	1	Petition	70	Priv. Land Claims.						
Keener, Francis, or Kurner	Confirmation of title to land	17	1	Petition	54	Public Lands.						
Keener, Francis, or Kurner.	Confirmation of title to land	18	1	Petition	54	Public Lands.						
Keener, Hugh	(See Lewis Evans.)	26	1		1009							
Keep, Samuel	Indemnity for breach of contract.	21	1	Memorial	128	Claims	365	Favorable	423	Referred to Committee Whole House.		

List of private claims presented to the House of Representatives of the United States from the 1st to the 31st Congress, inclusive—Continued.

Names of claimants.	Nature or object of the claim.	Congress.	Session.	How brought before the House of Reps.	Page of journal.	To what committee of the House referred.	No. or date of the report.	Nature of the report.	No. of the bill.	How disposed of by the House of Reps.	How disposed of by the Senate.	Date of the act of Congress, and remarks.
Keep, Samuel, representatives of.	Indemnity for breach of contract	21	2	House bill	264	Whole House	Feb. 4, 1831	With amend's.	423	Passed with amend't.		
Keep, Samuel, representatives of.	Indemnity for breach of contract	22	1	House bill	68	Whole House	Dec. 22, 1831	With amend	21	Passed with amendm't.	Passed	App'd Mar. 15, 1832
Keepharte, Martin	Depreciation of revolutionary pay	3	1	Petition	301	Claims.						
Keepharte, Martin	Depreciation of revolutionary pay	4	1	Petition	373	Claims	Dec. 28, 1795	Adverse		Leave to withdraw.		
Keepharte, Martin	Revolutionary pension	9	1	Petition	224	Claims.						See act April 10, 1806 chapter 25.
Keer, John	Release from imprisonment	11	1	Petition	33	Select	June 13, 1809	Favorable	24	Referred to Committee Whole House.		
Keer, John	Release from imprisonment	11	2	Petition	282	Select.	Mar. 20, 1810	Favorable	110	Passed	Passed, with amendment.	App'd April 20, 1810
Keese, George	Compensation for military services	16	2	Petition	47	Claims	Dec. 14, 1820	Adverse		Laid on table.		
Keese, John M., and others	(See Emmanuel Berri, *et al.*)	30	1		436							
Keeser, Daniel	Pension	25	2	Petition	197	Invalid Pensions	Jan. 25, 1838	Adverse		Laid on table.		
Keeser, Daniel	Pension	25	3	Petition	219	Invalid Pensions				Discharged; laid on table.		
Keeton, Henry	Pre-emption right to land	30	1	Petition	236	Public Lands	328	Adverse		Ordered to be printed.		
Keith, Adam	Grant of land	20	1	Petition	85	Priv. Land Claims.						
Keith, Calvin C.	(See Samuel Elkins, administrator.)	29	1		353							
Keith, Ichabod	Revolutionary pension	17	1	Petition	50	Pens. & Rev. Cl'ms.	565	Adverse		Leave to withdraw.		
Keith, Isham, heirs of	Commutation of half-pay	23	1	Petition	57	Rev. Claims	Jan. 9, 1834	Adverse		Laid on table.		
Keith, John	Revolutionary pension	25	3	Resolution	160	Rev. Pensions.						
Keith, John	Revolutionary pension	26	1	Petition	171	Rev. Pensions	466	Favorable	380	Referred to Committee Whole House.		
Keith, John	Revolutionary pension	27	2	Petition	268	Rev. Pensions	286	Favorable	254	Passed	Laid on table.	
Keith, John	Revolutionary pension	29	1	Resolution	129	Rev. Pensions.						
Keith, John	Revolutionary pension	29	1	Senate bill	826	Rev Pensions	Jan. 17, 1846	With amend	155	Passed	Passed	App'd Aug. 5, 1846
Keith, Matthew J.	Relief in case of sale of plantation	26	1	Petition	338	Claims	427	Adverse		Laid on table.		
Keith, Oliver	Pension	27	2	Petition	130	Invalid Pensions	970	Adverse		Laid on table.		
Keith, Simeon	Revolutionary pension	2	2	Petition	618	Select.						
Keith, Thomas, widow of.	Revolutionary pension	29	1	Petition	118	Rev. Pensions	Jan. 16, 1846	Res. to refer to Sec. War.		Resolution adopted.		
Keith, Thomas, widow of.	Commutation of pay	29	1	Petition	370	Rev. Pensions				Discharged; laid on table.		
Keith, William	Payment of prize money	3	1	Petition	57					Laid on table		Adj. under act March 27, 1792.
Keith'y, Henry	(See William H. Bedford, agent.)	28	1		262							
Keizer, David	Indemnity for loss of patent	21	1	Petition	129	Judiciary				Discharged; laid on table.		
Kelcey, Joel	Revolutionary pension	22	1	Petition	251	Rev. Pensions				Discharged; laid on table.		
Kelgon, Wilson	(See Archibald Beard, and others)	30	1		239		597		478			
Kellam, Jesse S.	Remission of forfeiture by breach of revenue laws.	22	2	Petition and rep't Sec. Treasury.	89	Commerce.						
Kellam, Jesse S.	Remission of forfeiture by breach of revenue laws.	23	1	Petition	69	Commerce				Discharged.		
Kellam, Jesse S.	Remission of forfeiture by breach of revenue laws.	23	1	Petition	301	Ways and Means.						
Kellam, Jesse S.	Remission of forfeiture by breach of revenue laws.	23	2	Petition	84	Ways and Means	Jan. 28, 1835	Adverse		Laid on table.		
Kellam, Jesse S.	Remission of forfeiture by breach of revenue laws.	24	1	Petition	95	Ways and Means						See House bill, 129.

List of *private claims presented to the House of Representatives of the United States from the* 1st *to the* 31st *Congress, inclusive*—Continued

Names of claimants.	Nature or object of the claim.	Congress.	Session.	How brought before the House of Reps.	Page of journal.	To what committee of the House referred.	No. or date of the report.	Nature of the report.	No. of the bill.	How disposed of by the House of Reps.	How disposed of by the Senate.	Date of the act of Congress, and remarks.
Kellar, Charles M.	Increase of compensation as machinist of Patent office.	23	1	Petition	386	Patents.						
Kellar, C. M., & H. Stone	Compensat'n for property destroyed	25	2	Senate bill	763	Claims	866	Rep. & amendments.	170	Referred to Committee Whole House.		
Kellar, C. M., & H. Stone	Compensat'n for property destroyed	26	1	Senate bill	811	Claims	April 24, 1840	With't amend.	170	Referred to Committee Whole House.		
Kellar, C. M., & H. Stone	Compensat'n for property destroyed	26	2	Senate bill	178	Claims	Jan. 16, 1841	With't amend.	62	Passed	Passed	App'd March 3, 1841
Kellar, Charles M.	Relief from disability to receive a patent.	27	2	Senate bill	782	Patents	July 21, 1842	With't amend.	147	Referred to Committee Whole House.		
Kellar, Charles M.	Relief from disability to receive a patent.	27	3	Senate bill	477	Patents			80			
Kellar, Francis	Pre-emption right to land	2	2	Petition	668	Select	Feb. 18, 1793	Adverse		Laid on table.		
Kellar, George	Grant of military land warrant	18	1	Petition	253	Military Affairs				Laid on table.		
Kellar, Margaret, & others.	Continuation of pension	27	2	Petition	614	Rev. Pensions	784	Adverse		Rejected.		
Kellar, Matthew	Extra compensation for ringing fog bell on Libby island.	31	2	Petition	142	Commerce.						
Kellar, Philip	Release from payment of money	30	1	Petition	708	P. Of. and P. Roads.						
Kellar, William	Increase of pension	22	1	Resolution	846	Invalid Pensions.						
Kellar, William	Increase of pension	23	1	Resolution	259	Invalid Pensions				Discharged; laid on table.		
Kellar, William	Increase of pension	23	2	Resolution	71	Invalid Pensions	Jan. 26, 1835	Favorable	679	Passed.		
Kellar, William	Increase of pension	24	1	Resolution	275	Invalid Pensions.	315	Favorable	328	Passed	Indef. postp'd.	
Kellar, William	Increase of pension	24	2	Petition	267	Invalid Pensions.	Feb. 2, 1837	Adverse		Laid on table.		
Kellar, William	Increase of pension	25	2	Petition	181	Invalid Pensions.				Discharged.		
Kellar, William	Increase of pension	26	1	Petition	324	Rev. Pensions	414	Adverse		Laid on table.		
Kellar, William	Increase of pension	27	2	Petition	611	Rev. Pensions	969	Adverse		Laid on table.		
Kellar, William	Increase of pension	28	1	Resolution	227	Invalid Pensions.	184	Adverse		Referred to Committee Whole House.		
Keller, Catherine	Continuation of pension	29	1	Petition	85	Rev. Pensions.	110	Adverse		Laid on table		
Keller, Catherine	Continuation of pension	30	1	Petition	576	Rev. Pensions.	525	Adverse.		Laid on table.		
Keller, Catherine	Revolutionary pension	31	1	Petition	543	Rev. Pensions.						
Keller, Edward	(See Stephen Decatur, widow of)	19	2		98		74		70			
Keller, George	Pension	31	1	Petition	214	Invalid Pensions.	144	Favorable	160	Referred to Committee Whole House.		
Kellett, Charles A	Refund tonnage duty	30	1	Petition	571	Commerce.	416	Favorable	368	Referred to Committee Whole House.		
Kelley, Bernard	Relief as postmaster	20	2	Petition	31	P. Of. and P. Roads.						
Kelley, Bernard	Relief as postmaster	21	2	Petition	39	P. Of. & P. Roads.	2	Favorable	501	Rejected.		
Kelley, Bernard	Relief as postmaster	22	1	Petition	42	P. Of. & P. Roads.	67	Favorable	135	Rejected.		
Kelley, Hanson	Compensation for provisions furnished.	18	1	Senate bill	187	Claims	April 30, 1824	With't amend.	22	Passed		App'd May 5, 1824
Kelley, James	Pension	18	1	Petition	454	Pens. & Rev. Cl'ms.						
Kelley, James	Increase of naval pension	22	1	Petition	559	Invalid Pensions				Discharged; laid on table.		
Kelley, James	Pre-emption right to land as a New Orleans branch pilot.	28	1	Petition	77	Priv. Land Claims.	9	Favorable; bill	35	Passed	Passed	App'd June 17, 1844
Kellock, Findley	Revolutionary pension	24	1	Resolution	544	Rev. Pensions.	577	Favorable	565	Referred to Committee Whole House.		
Kellock, Findley	Revolutionary pension	24	2	Doc. and H. bill	73, 198	Whole House			565	Passed.	Passed	App'd March 3, 1837
Kellogg, Eldad, widow of.	Revolutionary pension	26	1	Petition	324	Rev. Pensions.						
Kellogg, Eldad, widow of.	Revolutionary pension	28	1	Petition	160	Rev. Pensions				Discharged; laid on table.		See act June 17, 1844

List of private claims presented to the House of Representatives of the United States from the 1st to the 31st Congress, inclusive—Continued.

Names of claimants.	Nature or object of the claim.	Congress.	Session.	How brought before the House of Reps.	Page of journal.	To what committee of the House referred.	No. or date of the report.	Nature of the report.	No. of the bill.	How disposed of by the House of Reps.	How disposed of by the Senate.	Date of the act of Congress, and remarks.
Kellogg, Elijah	Increase of pension	25	2	Petition	664	Rev. Pensions	....	....	......	Discharged; laid on table.		
Kellogg, Elisha	Pension	26	1	Petition	1001	Invalid Pensions.						
Kellog, Enos	To receive his father's pension	19	1	Petition	334	Military Pensions	164	Adverse	......	Laid on table.		
Kellogg, Giles, Capt., and others.	Remuneration for losses at capture of Ogdensburg.	15	1	Petition	172	Claims	Mar. 3, 1818	Adverse	......	Referred to Committee Whole House.		
Kellogg, Giles, Capt., and others.	Remuneration for losses at capture of Ogdensburg.	15	2	Report and pet.	102	Whole House	Dec. 17, 1818	Adverse	......	Rejected.		
Kellogg, Giles, Capt., and others.	Remuneration for losses at capture of Ogdensburg,	28	1	Petition	595	Claims.						
Kellogg, Shirley	Pension	22	1	Documents	768	Invalid Pensions.						
Kellogg, Shirley	Pension	22	2	Petition	93	Invalid Pensions	Feb. 5, 1833	Favorable	738	Referred to Committee Whole House.		
Kellogg, Shirley	Arrears of pension	26	1	Petition	327	Invalid Pensions	....	....	......	Discharged: laid on table.		
Kellogg, Stephen	Pension	3	2	Rep. of Secretary War.	337	Claims	Mar. 2, 1895	To postpone	......	Adopted.		
Kellogg, Stephen	Pension	4	1	Rep. of Secretary War.	445	Claims	Mar. 4, 1796	Joint resolut'n.	16	Passed	Passed	App'd April 18, 1796 pet'rs name omitted.
Kellogg, Stephen	Pension	4	2	Rep. of Secretary War.	680	Claims	Feb. 17, 1797	Favorable	224	Passed	Postponed.	
Kellogg, Stephen	Pension	5	2	House bill	127	Whole House	Jan. 11, 1798	With amends.	38	Passed	Passed, with amendment.	App'd Feb. 2, 1798
Kellogg, Thomas H.	(See Richard Gorsline, *et al.*)	15	1	....	418							
Kellogg, Trueman	Pension	25	2	Petition	118	Invalid Pensions	808	Favorable	753	Passed.		
Kellogg, Trueman	Pension	26	1	Petition	161	Invalid Pensions.						
Kellogg, William	To refund foreign duties, &c	18	1	Petition	154	Commerce	May 3, 1824	Favorable	218	Passed.		
Kellogg, William	To refund foreign duties, &c	18	2	Petition	80	Commerce	Feb. 26, 1825	Favorable	366	Passed	Indef. postp'd.	
Kellogg, William	To refund foreign duties, &c	19	1	Petition	132	Commerce	Mar. 6, 1826	Favorable	136	Passed	Passed	App'd May 22, 1826
Kelly, Allen P.	(See William H. Bedford, agent)	28	1	....	262							
Kelly, Ann	Revolutionary pension	15	2	Petition	61	Rev. Pensions	Dec. 9, 1818	Adverse.	......	Leave to withdraw.		
Kelly, Charles	Confirmation of title to land	16	2	Petition	79	Priv. Land Claims	....	....	......	....	....	See act Mar. 2, 1821
Kelly, David	Pension	21	1	Petition	377	Military Pensions	April 2, 1830	Adverse	......	Laid on table.		
Kelly, David	Pension	22	1	Petition	287	Rev. Pensions	....	....	......	....	....	See act June 4, 1832
Kelly, Ebenezer O.	Indemnity for confiscation of property in Canada.	22	1	Petition	224	Claims	Mar. 6, 1832	Adverse.	......	Laid on table.		
Kelly, Edward J	To refund money lost in mail	28	1	Petition	352	Claims	130	Adverse	......	Laid on table.		
Kelly, Granville J., and others.	(See Maj. James Wright, heirs of)	29	1	....	638							
Kelly, Griffin	Pension	28	1	Petition	141	Invalid Pensions	189	Adverse	......	Laid on table.		
Kelly, Griffin	Pension	28	2	Petition	236	Invalid Pensions.						
Kelly, Griffin	Pension	29	1	Petition	381	Invalid Pensions	472	Favorable	350	Passed	Passed	App'd Aug. 8, 1846
Kelly, G. W	(See James Kelley, heir of.)	26	2	....	82							
Kelly, Hall T	(See Charles Bullfinch, *et al.*)	27	3	....	350							
Kelly, Hall J	Grant of land	28	1	Petition	237	Foreign Affairs.						
Kelly, Hall J	Grant of land	30	1	Petition	81	Public Lands	....	....	......	Laid on table.		
Kelly, Henry	(See Henry O'Kelly, assignee of)	2	2	....	697							
Kelly, Henry	Pension	20	2	Petition	229	Military Pensions	....	....	......	Discharged; laid on table.		
Kelly, Henry	Pension	21	1	Petition	67	Military Pensions	April 2, 1830	Adverse	......	Laid on table.		
Kelly, Irad, & Datus	Additional compensation for stones furnished under contract.	25	2	Resolution	522	Claims	917	Favorable	803	Referred to Committee Whole House.		

List of private claims presented to the House of Representatives of the United States from the 1st to the 31st Congress, inclusive—Continued.

Names of claimants.	Nature or object of the claim.	Congress.	Session.	How brought before the House of Reps.	Page of journal.	To what committee of the House referred.	No. or date of the report.	Nature of the report.	No. of the bill.	How disposed of by the House of Reps.	How disposed of by the Senate.	Date of the act of Congress, and remarks.
Kelly, Irad & Datus	Additional compensation for stones furnished under contract.	25	3	House bill	431	Whole House	Feb. 1, 1839	With't amend.	803	Passed	Passed	App'd March 3, 1839
Kelly, James, heir of	Commutation of revolutionary pay.	26	2	Petition	82	Rev. Pensions				Discharged; laid on table.		
Kelly, James, administrator of.	Compensation for revolutionary services.	27	2	Petition	70	Rev. Pensions	784	Adverse		Laid on table.		
Kelly, James	Payment of award	27	3	House bill	120, 394	Whole House			644, 804	Passed	Passed	App'd March 3, 1843
Kelly, James, (La.)	Confirmation of title to land	28	1	House bill	205	Whole House	Feb. 23, 1844	With amends.	35	Passed	Passed	App'd June 17, 1844
Kelly, Joel	(See Benjamin F. Hart, executor of.)	31	1		285							
Kelly, John	Compensation for arresting incendiaries.	24	2	Memorial	395	Claims	293	Adverse		Laid on table.		
Kelly, John	Compensation for arresting incendiaries.	25	2	Memorial	275	Claims.						
Kelly, John	Compensation for arresting incendiaries.	25	3	Petition	462	Claims.						
Kelly, John	Compensation for arresting incendiaries.	26	1	Petition	169	Claims	48	Res.; adverse		Laid on table.		
Kelly, John H	(See Wm. Kelly, heir of)	25	3		220							
Kelly, Joseph	Pension	29	2	Memorial	439	Invalid Pensions.						
Kelly, Joseph	Pension	30	1	Petition	625	Invalid Pensions	581	Adverse		Laid on table.		
Kelly, Joseph H	Remuneration for false arrest	27	1	Petition	102	Judiciary.						
Kelly, Joseph H	Remuneration for false arrest	27	2	Petition	53	Judiciary				Discharged; laid on table.		
Kelly, Joshua	Pension	23	1	Resolution	501	Rev. Pensions				Discharged; laid on table.		
Kelly, Michael, *et al*	Indemnity for French spoliations prior to 1800.	20	1	Memorial	32	Foreign Affairs				Laid on table.		
Kelly, Michael	Indemnity for Spanish spoliations.	22	1	Petition	911	Foreign Affairs.						
Kelly Michael	Indemnity for French spoliations prior to 1800.	23	1	Petition	75	Foreign Affairs				Leave to withdraw.		
Kelly, Michael	Indemnity for French spoliations prior to 1800.	24	1	Petition	152	Claims.						
Kelly, Michael, widow of	Pension	21	2	Petition	230	Rev. Pensions.						
Kelly, Patrick, sen	Revolutionary pension	29	1	Petition	85	Rev. Pensions	Feb. 10, 1846		210	Passed	Passed	App'd Aug. 8, 1846
Kelly, Patrick, sen	Increase of pension	29	2	Petition	177	Rev. Pensions.						
Kelly, Richard, *alias* Patrick	Pension	29	1	Petition	1166	Invalid Pensions	July 28, 1846	Favorable	528	Referred to Committee Whole House.		
Kelly, Richard, *alias* Patrick	Pension	29	2	House bill	79			Favorable	528	Passed	Passed	App'd Feb. 20, 1847
Kelly, Robert A., representatives of.	Compensation for services reporting on claims.	27	3	Petition	136	Claims	49	Favorable	681	Passed	Passed	App'd March 3, 1843
Kelly, Robert E	Pension	27	2	Petition	1189	Invalid Pensions				Discharged; laid on table.		
Kelly, Robert E	Arrears of pension	28	1	Petition	73	Invalid Pensions	22	Adverse		Laid on table.		
Kelly, Samuel	Pension	19	1	Petition	565	Military Pensions.						
Kelly, Thomas	Revolutionary pension	3	1	Petition and rep't Sec. of War.	31	Select	April 22, 1794			Laid on table.		
Kelly, Thomas, (Miss.)	Confirmation of title to land	14	2	Petition	399	Priv. Land Claims.						See act Mar. 3, 1817
Kelly, Thomas, heirs of	Reissue of land warrants	27	2	Petition	73	Rev Claims	Aug. 20, 1842	Adverse		Laid on table.		
Kelly, Thomas, heirs of	Reissue of land warrants	29	1	Petition	1111	Priv. Land Claims.	273	Favorable	229	Passed	Passed	App'd Aug. 8, 1846

List of private claims presented to the House of Representatives of the United States from the 1st to the 31st Congress, inclusive—Continued.

2—30

Names of claimants.	Nature or object of the claim.	Congress.	Session.	How brought before the House of Reps.	Page of journal.	To what committee of the House referred.	No. or date of the report.	Nature of the report.	No. of the bill.	How disposed of by the House of Reps.	How disposed of by the Senate.	Date of the act of Congress, and remarks.
Kelly, Thomas F	Compensation for a horse lost in public service	25	2	Documents	396	Claims.						
Kelly, Thomas F	Compensation for a horse lost in public service.	25	3	Documents	207	Claims	226	Adverse	......	Laid on table.		
Kelly, William, heir of	Seven years' half-pay	25	3	Petition	220	Rev. Claims	....	....	......	Discharged.		
Kelly, William, heir of	Seven years' half-pay	26	1	Petition	166	Rev. Claims	595	Favorable	453	Referred to Committee Whole House.		
Kelly, William, heir of	Seven years' half-pay	27	2	Petition	62	Rev. Claims	39	Favorable	69	Passed	Indef. postp'd.	
Kelly, William, heir of	Seven years' half-pay	29	1	Petition	284	Rev. Claims.						
Kelsey, Aaron	Pension	4	1	Rep. of Secretary War.	445	Claims	Mar. 4, 1796	Favorable	156	Passed	Passed	App'd April 20, 1796
Kelsey, Giles	Pension	3	2	Rep. of Secretary War.	350	Claims	Mar. 4, 1796	Postponed	......	Adopted.		
Kelsey, Giles	Pension	4	1	Rep. of Secretary War.	445	Claims	Mar. 4, 1796	Jt. res. to refer to Sec. War.	16	Passed	Passed	App'd April 20, 1796, omitting petitioner's name.
Kelsey, Mary	(See Captain John Pearson, representatives of.)	26	1	....	360							
Kelsey, Porter	Amount due out of moneys to Ottawa Indians.	29	1	Memorial	160	Indian Affairs	287	Adverse	......	Laid on table.		
Kelso, Charles W	Increase of salary, and change of the name of Presque' Isle to that of Erie.	27	2	Petition	225	Commerce	....	....	......	Discharged.		
Kelton, Edward	Pension	19	2	Petition	215	Military Pensions.						
Kemble, Peter	(See Isaac Lawrence and others)	14	1	....	386							
Kemble, Robert	Further time for payment of duties.	2	1	Petition	520	Select.						
Kemble, William, executor of.	Indemnity for French spoliations prior to 1800.	26	1	Memorial	182	Foreign Affairs	343	Favorable; bill	319	Referred to Committee Whole House.		
Kemmena, Englebert	Compensation as surgeon and for medicines.	1	1	Petition	77	....	....	....	......	Referred to Secretary Treasury.		
Kemmena, Englebert	Compensation as surgeon and for medicines.	1	2	Petition	137	....	....	....	......	Referred to Secretary of Treasury.		
Kemmena, Englebert	Compensation as surgeon and for medicines.	3	1	Rep. of Secretary Treasury.	78	....	....	....	......	Laid on table.		
Kemp, Thomas	Additional compensation for building the Erie, &c.	14	1	Petition	284	Claims	Mar. 11, 1816	Adverse	......	Laid on table.		
Kemp, Thomas	Additional compensation for building the Erie, &c.	17	1	Petition	165	Naval Affairs	44	Adverse	......	Referred to Committee Whole House.		
Kemp, Thomas	Additional compensation for building the Erie, &c.	17	2	Documents	132	Naval Affairs	27	Adverse	......	Laid on table.		
Kempee, John	Compensation for use of horse, &c.	13	3	Petition	593	Claims	....	....	......		....	See act April 9, 1816
Kemper, Daniel	Revolutionary pension	20	1	Petition	126	Rev. Claims	Jan. 25, 1828	Adverse	......	Laid on table.		
Kemper, Daniel	Revolutionary pension	22	1	Petition	574	Rev. Pensions	....	....	......	....	....	See act June 4, 1832
Kemper, Henry, and others	(See Andrew O'Bannon, heirs of.)	31	1	....	714							
Kemper, Presley	Release from certain judgments	21	1	Petition	547	Claims	May 5, 1830	Adverse	......	Laid on table.		
Kemper, Presley	Compensation as wagon master	24	1	Petition	49	Claims	Jan. 6, 1836	Adverse	......	Recommitted.		
Kemper, Presley	Release from certain judgments	26	1	Petition	630	Judiciary.						
Kemper, Presley	Release from certain judgments	26	1	Petition	762	Judiciary.						
Kempff, J. C., and others.	Increase of compensation	7	1	Petition	59	Com. and Manuf.	Jan. 25, 1802	Adverse	......	Leave to withdraw.		
Kemphall, Eliza, and others	(See Martin Patterson, heirs of)	30	1	....	77							
Kampton, Thomas	(See Andrew Knox and B. S. Pope.)	12	1	....	137							
Kenan, Augustus H	(See sureties of Solomon D. Betton.)	27	2	....	1126	....	....	....	S. 266			

List of private claims presented to the House of Representatives of the United States from the 1st *to the* 31st *Congress, inclusive*—Continued.

Names of claimants.	Nature or object of the claim.	Congress.	Session.	How brought before the House of Reps.	Page of journal.	To what committee of the House referred.	No. or date of the report	Nature of the report.	No. of the bill.	How disposed of by the House of Reps.	How disposed of by the Senate.	Date of the act of Congress, and remarks.
Kendall, Amos	Release from a judgment	27	2	Memorial	929	Judiciary	Jan. 21, 1842	Adverse	.....	Laid on table.		
Kendall, Amos	Restoration to personal liberty and reimbursement of expenses, &c.	27	3	Petition	274	Claims.						
Kendall, Amos	Restoration to personal liberty and reimbursement of expenses, &c.	27	3	Petition	275	Claims.						
Kendall, Amos	Restoration to personal liberty and reimbursement of expenses, &c.	27	3	Petition	296	Claims.						
Kendall, Amos	Restoration to personal liberty and reimbursement of expenses, &c.	27	3	Petition	306	Claims.						
Kendall, Amos	Restoration to personal liberty and reimbursement of expenses, &c.	27	3	Petition	317	Whole House.						
Kendall, Amos	Restoration to personal liberty and reimbursement of expenses, &c.	27	3	Petition	319	Claims	147	Favorable	764	Referred to Committee Whole House.		
Kendall, Amos	Restoration to personal liberty and reimbursement of expenses, &c.	27	3	Memorial	424	Whole House.						
Kendall, Amos	Restoration to personal liberty and reimbursement of expenses, &c.	27	3	Memorial	424	.....	.....	.....	.....	Referred to Committee Whole House.		
Kendall, Amos	Restoration to personal liberty and reimbursement of expenses, &c.	27	3	Petition	475	Whole House on bill No. 764.						
Kendall, Amos	Restoration to personal liberty and reimbursement of expenses, &c.	27	3	Resolution	492	.....	.....	.....	.....	Laid on table.		
Kendall, Amos	Restoration to personal liberty and reimbursement of expenses, &c.	27	3	Resolution	497	.....	.....	.....	.....	Laid on table.		
Kendall, Amos	Indemnity for losses and expenses	28	2	Petition	353	Judiciary.						
Kendall, Amos	Indemnity for losses and expenses	29	1	Memorial	95	Claims.						
Kendall, Amos	Indemnity for losses and expenses	29	1	Senate bill	826	Claims	May 29, 1846	With't amend.	S. 89	Passed	.....	App'd July 29, 1846
Kendall, Amos and J. E.	Compensation for services as Indian agents.	29	2	Memorial	439	Indian Affairs.						
Kendall, Amos and J. E.	Compensation for services as Indian agents.	30	1	Memorial	1111	Indian Affairs.						
Kendall, Amos and J. E.	Compensation for services as Indian agents.	31	1	Petition	835	Indian Affairs.						
Kendall, Amos and J. E.	Compensation for services as Indian agents.	31	2	Petition	283	Military Affairs.						
Kendall & Butterfield, assignees of.	Settlement of accounts as sutlers	19	2	Senate bill	348	Military Affairs	Mar. 1, 1827	With't amend.	80	Passed	.....	App'd March 3, 1827
Kendall, Peter	Indemnity for goods destroyed by enemy.	14	2	Petition	176	Claims	Feb. 12, 1817	Favorable	133	Passed	Passed	App'd March 3, 1817
Kendall, Robert R.	Allowance of money advanced to government.	16	1	Petition	64	Claims	Feb. 9, 1820	Adverse	.....	Laid on table.		
Kendall, William	Exchange of location of land	14	2	Petition	117	Priv. Land Claims.						
Kendall, William	Exchange of location of land	15	2	Petition	220	Public Lands	.....	.....	.....	Leave to withdraw.		
Kendall, William	Exchange of location of land	17	1	Petition	176	Public Lands.						
Kendall, William	Exchange of location of land	17	2	Petition	122	Priv. Land Claims.	84	Favorable	278	Referred to Committee Whole House.		
Kendall, William	Exchange of location of land	18	1	Petition	71	Priv. Land Claims.	10	Favorable	24	Passed	Passed	App'd Jan. 19, 1824
Kender, George, and others.	To refund money paid for land	25	2	Documents	547	Public Lands.						
Kender, George, and others.	To refund money paid for land	25	3	Petition	93	Public Lands	.....	.....	.....	Discharged.		
Kender, George, and others.	To refund money paid for land	26	1	Petition	803	Public Lands	.....	.....	.....	Discharged; laid on table.		
Kender, George, and others.	To refund money paid for land	28	1	Petition	550	Public Lands	.....	.....	.....	Discharged; laid on table.		
Kender, George, and others	To refund money paid for land	28	2	Petition	70	Public Lands.						

List of private claims presented to the House of Representatives of the United States from the 1st to the 31st Congress, inclusive—Continued.

Names of claimants.	Nature or object of the claim.	Congress.	Session.	How brought before the House of Reps.	Page of journal.	To what committee of the House referred.	No. or date of the report.	Nature of the report.	No. of the bill.	How disposed of by the House of Reps.	How disposed of by the Senate.	Date of the act of Congress, and remarks.
Kendle, Mary A.	(See Joseph Lake, daughter of.)	31	1		1436							
Kendle, Mary A	Pens on and bounty land	31	2	Petition	431	Rev. Pensions	43	Adverse		Laid on table.		
Kendlesperyer, Jacob	Pension	13	3	Petition	618	Pens. & Rev. Cl'ms.	Jan. 27, 1815	Adverse		Leave to withdraw.		
Kendlesperyer, Jacob	Pension	14	1	Petition	42	Pens. & Rev. Cl'ms.	April 11, 1816	By bill		Passed	Passed	App'd April 30, 1816
Kendoll, Samuel K.	Increase of pension	15	2	House bill	41				203	Passed	Passed as am'd.	App'd March 3, 1819
Kendrick, Alfred	(See Charles Bulfinch, and others)	26	1		202							
Kendrick, Austin	Revolutionary bounty land	17	1	Petition	129	Military Affairs	Jan. 28, 1822	Adverse		Rejected.		
Kendrick, Benjamin	Pension	3	1	Rep. of Secretary War.	131	Select	May 26, 1794	J't. res. to refer to Sec. War.	J.R. 12	Passed	Passed	App'd June 9, 1794
Kendrick, Benjamin	Pension	6	1	Petition	580	Claims	April 17, 1800	Adverse		Laid on table		
Kendrick, Benjamin	Pension	6	2	Petition and rep't	777	Claims	Feb. 21, 1801	Res. adverse		Adopted.		
Kendrick, Benjamin	Pension	10	1	House bill	232	Whole House	Mar. 17, 1808	With amends.	78	Passed	Passed	App'd April 25, 1808
Kendrick, Benjamin, heirs of widow of.	Revolutionary pension	26	1	Resolution	950	Rev. Pensions.						
Kendrick, Franky	(See Benjamin Kendrick, heirs of widow of.)	26	1		950							
Kendrick, H. L.	Indemnity for money stolen in Mexico.	30	2	Petition	236	Military Affairs.						
Kendrick, Jacob	Pension	24	2	Resolution	504	Rev. Pensions				Discharged; laid on table.		
Kendrick, Jacob	Pension	25	3	Petition	89	Invalid Pensions				Discharged; laid on table.		
Kendrick, John, heirs of.	Confirmation of title to land	30	1	Petition	457	Public Lands				Discharged; laid on table.		
Kenedy, Dr. Samuel, heirs of.	Compensation for medical services revolutionary war.	21	1	Petition	37	Rev. Claims	351	Favorable	413	Referred to Committee Whole House.		
Kenedy, Dr. Samuel, heirs of.	Compensation for medical services revolutionary war.	22	1	Petition	29	Rev. Claims	48	Favorable	100	Passed	Passed	App'd May 25, 1832
Kenedy, Dr. Samuel, heirs of.	Grant of bounty land	22	2	Petition	40	Rev. Claims	58	Adverse		Referred to Committee Whole House.		
Kenedy, Dr. Samuel, heirs of.	Grant of bounty land	23	1	Petition	144	Rev. Claims	Jan. 16, 1834	Adverse		Laid on table.		
Kenedy, Dr. Samuel, heirs of.	Grant of bounty land	24	1	Petition	152	Rev. Claims	507	Adverse		Laid on table.		
Kenedy, Dr. Samuel, heirs of.	Grant of bounty land	25	2	Petition	82	Rev. Claims.						
Kenedy, Dr. Samuel, heirs of.	Grant of bounty land	26	1	Petition	165	Rev. Claims.						
Kenedy, Dr. Samuel, heirs of.	Interest on seven years half-pay	25	2	Petition	269	Rev. Claims	Jan. 27, 1839	Favorable	489	Postponed.		
Kenedy, Dr. Samuel, heirs of.	Interest on seven years half pay	26	1	Petition	670	Rev. Claims.						
Kenedy, Dr. Samuel, heirs of.	Interest on seven yerrs half-pay	27	2	Petition	268	Rev. Claims	387	Adverse		Laid on table.		
Kennaird, David, (Va.)	Revolutionary pension	21	1	Petition	523	Military Pensions	April 23, 1830	Favorable	468	Referred to Committee Whole House.		
Kennaird, David, (Va.)	Revolutionary pension	21	2	House bill	381	Whole House	Feb. 16, 1831	With't amend.	468	Passed.		
Kennaird, David, (Va.)	Revolutionary pension	22	1	Petition	29	Rev. Pensions	Dec. 20, 1831	Favorable	53	Passed	Postponed.	
Kennard, Edward	To refund certain fine	28	1	Senate bill	225	Judiciary	May 25, 1844	With't amend.	S. 29	Passed		App'd June 10, 1844
Kennard, James	Indemnity for French spoliations prior to 1800.	26	1	Petition	182	Foreign Affairs	343	Favorable	319	Referred to Committee Whole House.		

List of private claims presented to the House of Representatives of the United States from the 1st to the 31st Congress, inclusive—Continued.

Names of claimants.	Nature or object of the claim.	Congress.	Session.	How brought before the House of Reps.	Page of journal.	To what committee of the House referred.	No. or date of the report.	Nature of the report.	No. of the bill.	How disposed of by the House of Reps.	How disposed of by the Senate.	Date of the act of Congress, and remarks.
Kennard, John S., & wife	Indemnity for French spoliations prior to 1800.	26	1	Memorial	182	Foreign Affairs	343	Favorable	319	Referred to Committee Whole House.		
Kennard, Joshua	Renewal of certificate of debt	5	2	Petition	87	Claims	Mar. 6, 1798	Adverse		Leave to withdraw.		
Kennard, Samuel, & wife.	Indemnity for French spoliations prior to 1800.	26	1	Memorial	182	Foreign Affairs	343	Favorable	319	Referred to Committee Whole House.		
Kennedy, Andrew	Release from forfeiture for breach of the revenue laws.	5	2	Petition	316	Com. and Manuf.						
Kennedy, Andrew	Release from forfeiture for breach of the revenue laws.	5	3	Petition	457	Com. and Manuf.				Discharged; leave to withdraw.		
Kennedy, Andrew	Pension	15	1	House bill	405	Whole House			172	Postponed.		
Kennedy, Andrew	Arrears of pension	20	2	Petition	288	Military Pensions				Discharged; laid on table.		
Kennedy, Anthony	To refund surplus money paid on land.	16	1	Petition	293	Ways and Means				Discharged; leave to withdraw.		
Kennedy, Anthony	To refund surplus money paid on land.	16	2	Petition	17	Judiciary	Nov. 24, 1820	Favorable	153	Referred to Committee Whole House.		
Kennedy, Anthony	To refund surplus money paid on land.	17	1	Petition	26	Judiciary	Jan. 8, 1822	Favorable	28	Passed	Passed	App'd May 7, 1822
Kennedy & Darling	Indemnity for store burned by Seminole Indians.	31	1	Petition	1528	Military Affairs.						
Kennedy & Darling	Indemnity for store burned by Seminole Indians.	31	2	Resolution	424					Laid on table.		
Kennedy, D. S., *et al.*	Payment of certain certificates	15	2	Petition	209	Com. and Manuf.						
Kennedy, Edmund P.	Settlement of accounts	15	2	Petition	250	Claims	Feb. 23, 1819	Favorable	328	Passed	Passed	App'd March 3, 1819
Kennedy, James B.	Remission of forfeiture	13	2	Petition	172	Ways and Means.						
Kennedy, James, heirs of.	Bounty land	22	1	Petition	79	Public Lands	Dec. 30, 1831	Adverse		Laid on table.		
Kennedy, James, heirs of.	Bounty land	23	1	Petition	48	Priv. Land Claims.						
Kennedy, James, administratrix of.	Indemnity for French spoliations prior to 1800.	26	1	Memorial	182	Foreign Affairs	343	Favorable	319	Referred to Committee Whole House.		
Kennedy, James, widow of	Indemnity for French spoliations prior to 1800.	29	2	Memorial	136	Foreign Affairs						See House bill 561.
Kennedy, John	Arrears of pension	20	2	Petition	288	Military Pensions				Discharged; laid on table.		
Kennedy, John	Revolutionary pension	21	1	Petition	59	Military Pensions	April 2, 1830	Adverse		Laid on table.		
Kennedy, John	Revolutionary pension	21	2	Resolution	48	Rev. Pensions.						
Kennedy, John	Revolutionary pension	22	1	Petition	45	Rev. Pensions				Discharged; laid on table.		See act June 4, 1832
Kennedy, John	Compensation for horse lost in public service.	24	1	Petition	943	Claims	783	Adverse		Laid on table.		
Kennedy, John	Compensation for horse lost in public service.	24	2	Petition	309	Claims	Feb. 2, 1837			Discharged; referred to Third Auditor.		
Kennedy, John, and others	(See heirs of Samuel Kennedy)	24	1		152							
Kennedy, John, representatives of.	To authorize receiver to take evidence, &c.	12	1	Petition	20	Public Lands.						
Kennedy, John, representatives of.	To authorize receiver to take evidence, &c.	12	2	Petition	663	Public Lands.						
Kennedy, John, representatives of.	To authorize receiver to take evidence, &c.	15	1	Petition	133	Priv. Land Claims				Discharged.		
Kennedy, John, representatives of.	Donation right to land	14	2	Petition	311	Priv. Land Claims.						
Kennedy, John, & H. Nail, or representatives of.	Donation right to land	15	1	House bill	218	Whole House			70			

List of private claims presented to the House of Representatives of the United States from the 1st to the 31st Congress, inclusive—Continued.

Names of claimants.	Nature or object of the claim.	Congress.	Session.	How brought before the House of Reps.	Page of journal.	To what committee of the House referred.	No. or date of the report.	Nature of the report.	No. of the bill.	How disposed of by the House of Reps.	How disposed of by the Senate.	Date of the act of Congress, and remarks.
Kennedy, Joshua........	Confirmation of title to land.....	21	1	Petition	360	Priv. Land Claims.	327	Favorable....	384	Referred to Committee Whole House.		
Kennedy, Joshua........	Confirmation of title to land.....	22	1	Senate bill	102	Priv. Land Claims.	Dec. 28, 1831	With't amend.	10	Passed	....	App'd May 5, 1832
Kennedy, Joshua........	Confirmation of title to land	23	2	Petition	393	Priv. Land Claims.						
Kennedy, Joshua........	Confirmation of title to land.....	24	1	Petition	112	Priv. Land Claims.						
Kennedy, Joshua........	(See Cornelius McCurtin, assignee of.)	26	2	....	282	....	....	....	82			
Kennedy, Joshua........	Indemnity for property destroyed by Creek Indians in 1813.	21	2	Senate bill	181	Claims	March 3, 1831	Adverse	60	Laid on table.		
Kennedy, Joshua, heirs of.	Indemnity for property destroyed by Creek Indians in 1813.	22	1	Senate bill	425	Claims	357	Adverse	57	Referred to Committee Whole House.		
Kennedy, Joshua, heirs of.	Indemnity for property destroyed by Creek Indians in 1813.	28	2	Senate bill	92	Claims	61	With't amend.	5	Referred to Committee Whole House.		
Kennedy, Joshua, executors of.	Indemnity for property destroyed by Creek Indians in 1813.	29	1	Petition	123	Claims	June 17, 1846	Favorable....	461	Referred to Committee Whole House.		
Kennedy, Joshua, representatives of.	Indemnity for property destroyed by Creek Indians in 1813.	30	1	Petition	69	Claims	155	Favorable....	159	Passed.		
Kennedy, Joshua, representatives of.	Indemnity for property destroyed by Creek Indians in 1813.	31	1	Petition	202	Claims	....	....	......	Leave to withdraw.		
Kennedy, J. P..........	(See Francis Stringer, and others)	12	1	....	13							
Kennedy, Letitia........	(See James Kennedy, administrator of.)	26	1	....	182							
Kennedy, Lampas, & Co., executors of.	Remission of duties	14	2	Petition	59	Ways and Means..	Jan. 25, 1817	General bill ..	72	Passed	Passed	App'd March 3, 1817
Kennedy, Martin........	Payment for provisions furnished in war of 1812.	16	1	Petition	312	Claims	April 7, 1830	Adverse	......	Laid on table.		
Kennedy, Martin........	Payment for provisions furnished in war of 1812.	22	1	Petition	732	Claims.						
Kennedy, Martin........	Payment for provisions furnished in war of 1812.	23	1	Petition	246	Claims	507	Adverse	......	Laid on table.		
Kennedy, Robert J	(See Elisha Moreland, *et al.*)	26	1	....	179							
Kennedy, Thomas.......	Payment for a horse lost, &c.....	19	2	Resolution	56	Claims	Dec. 15, 1826	Adverse	......	Laid on table.		
Kennedy, William	Pension	30	1	Petition	240	Invalid Pensions ..	805	Favorable....	626	Ref'd to Com. W. H.		
Kennedy, William, jr....	Revolutionary pension..........	15	2	Petition	177	Pens. & Rev. Cl'ms.	....	....	......	Discharged; referred to Secretary War.		
Kennedy, William representatives of.	Commutation of half-pay........	22	2	Petition	142	Rev. Claims.						
Kennedy, William, widow of.	Compensation for revolutionary services.	2	1	Petition	491	....	....	....	......	Referred to Secretary of War.		
Kennedy, William, widow of.	Compensation for revolutionary services.	2	2	Rep. of Secretary War.	690	....	....	....	......	Laid on table.		
Kennedy, William, widow of.	Revolutionary pension..........	24	2	Petition	102	Rev. Pensions	....	....	......	Laid on table.		
Kennedy, William E	Time to complete title to land....	18	2	Petition	188	Public Lands.						
Kennedy, William E	Confirmation of title to land.....	22	1	Letter of Secretary Treasury.	813	Public Lands.						
Kennedy, William E	Confirmation of title to land.....	22	2	Senate bill	405	Claims	....	....	74			
Kennedy, William E	Confirmation of title to land	26	1	Senate bill	240	Priv. Land Claims.	Mar. 5, 1840	With't amend.	40	Passed	Passed	App'd May 27, 1840
Kennedy, William L	(See James Kennedy, administrator of.)	26	1		182							
Kennedy, William M., and others.	(See Elisha Moreland, *et at.*)....	24	2	....	88							

List of private claims presented to the House of Representatives of the United States from the 1st to the 31st Congress, inclusive—Continued.

Names of claimants.	Nature or object of the claim.	Congress.	Session.	How brought before the House of Reps.	Page of journal.	To what committee of the House referred.	No. or date of the report.	Nature of the report.	No. of the bill.	How disposed of by the House of Reps.	How disposed of by the Senate.	Date of the act of Congress, and remarks.
Kenner, Francis	(See Francis Keener)	15	1		232							
Kenner, Howson	Revolutionary pension	18	1	Petition	78	Pens. & Rev. Cl'ms.				Discharged; leave to withdraw.		
Kenner, Howson, heirs of.	Revolutionary pension	31	2	Petition	100	Rev. Claims.						
Kenner, James L.	Payment for a horse lost in public service.	24	2	Petition	37	Claims	3	Favorable	762	Referred to Committee Whole House.		
Kenner, James L.	Payment for a horse lost in public service.	25	2	Resolution	36	Claims	32	Favorable	71	Passed	Passed	App'd April 20, 1838
Kenney, David, heir of	Permission to purchase land at minimum price.	25	3	Petition	564	Public Lands.						
Kenney, David, heir of	Pre-emption to certain land	26	1	Petition	603	Priv. Land Claims.						
Kenney, Henry, widow and heirs of.	Pre-emption right to land	26	1	House bill	755	Whole House			309			
Kenney, Kyman	Revolutionary pension	3	1	Rep. of Secretary War.	131	Select	Mar. 26, 1794	Favorable	62	Passed	Passed	App'd June 7, 1794
Kenney, Moses	To exchange certain lands	19	1	Senate bill	541	Public Lands.	Mar. 12, 1826	With't amend.	124	Passed	Passed	App'd May 15, 1826
Kenney, Nancy	(See David Kenney, heirs of.)	25	3		564							
Kenney, William	Compensation for a horse lost in public service.	20	2	Petition	43	Claims	Dec. 16, 1816	Adverse		Laid on table.		
Kenney, William	Compensation for a horse lost in public service.	21	1	Petition	104	Claims	Jan. 14, 1830	Adverse		Laid on table.		
Kenney, William	Compensation for a horse lost in public service.	21	2	Petition	191	Claims	Feb. 15, 1831	Adverse		Laid on table.		
Kenney, William	Compensation for a horse lost in public service.	22	2	Petition	86	Claims.						
Kenniston, (or Kermison) Job, late widow of.	Compensation for revolutionary services.	23	1	Petition	127	Rev. Claims.						
Kenniston, (or Kermison) Job, late widow of.	Compensation for revolutionary services.	24	1	Petition	63	Rev. Claims:						
Kenniston, (or Kermison) Job, late widow of.	Compensation for revolutionary services.	29	1	Petition	532	Rev. Claims.						
Kenniston, (or Kermison) Job, late widow of.	Compensation for revolutionary services.	30	1	Petition	925	Rev. Claims.						
Kennon & Nishwagner	(See Michael L. Sullivant.)	27	2		66							
Kennon, Patrick	Pension	26	1	Petition	602	Invalid Pensions				Disch'd; laid on table.		
Kennon, Richard, heirs of	Commutation pay	23	1	Petition	157	Rev. Claims.						
Kennon, Richard, heirs of.	Commutation pay	23	2	Petition	38	Rev. Claims.						
Kennon, Robert L.	To refund excess of money paid for land.	20	1	Petition	93	Public Lands	160	Favorable	189	Referred to Committee Whole House.		
Kennon, Robert L.	To refund excess of money paid for land.	20	2	House bill	174	Whole House	Jan. 17, 1829	With't amend.	189	Passed	Passed	App'd Feb. 24, 1829
Kennon, William, j., and others.	Grant of patent for land	28	1	Petition	107	Public Lands				Discharged; laid on table.		
Kenny, Samuel, late widow of.	Compensation for revolutionary services.	2	1	Petition	463					Referred to Secretary of War.		
Kenny, William	Pension	21	1	House bill	722				491	Referred to Committee Whole House.		
Kent, Abner	Increase of pension	11	2	House bill	604	Whole House	Mar. 2, 1811	With amends.	218	Passed	Passed	App'd April 27, 1810
Kent, Catharine	(See Ludwick Kent, widow of.)	22	1		556							
Kent, Ebenezer	Commutation of half-pay	1	3	Petition	392					Referred to Secretary War.		
Kent, Ebenezer	Commutation of half-pay	2	2	Rep. of Secretary War.	696					Laid on table.		

List of private claims presented to the House of Representatives of the United States from the 1st to the 31st Congress, inclusive—Continued.

Names of claimants.	Nature or object of the claim.	Congress.	Session.	How brought before the House of Reps.	Page of journal.	To what committee of the House referred.	No. or date of the report.	Nature of the report.	No. of the bill.	How disposed of by the House of Reps.	How disposed of by the Senate.	Date of the act of Congress, and remarks.
Kent, Ebenezer	Revolutionary pension	3	1	Rep. of Secretary War.	131	Select	May 31, 1794	Jt. res. to refer to Sec. War.	J.R. 12	Passed	Passed	App'd June 9, 1794
Kent, Ebenezer	Revolutionary pension	3	2	Petition	260	Claims	Feb. 25, 1795	Adverse		Referred to Committee Whole House.		
Kent, Ebenezer	Revolutionary pension	4	1	Petition	409	Claims.						
Kent, Ebenezer	Revolutionary pension	4	2	Petition	649	Claims	Jan. 18, 1797	Adverse		Leave to withdraw.		
Kent, Ebenezer	Pension	26	1	Petition	937	Invalid Pensions.						
Kent, Ebenezer	Pension	27	2	Petition	154	Invalid Pensions	214	Adverse		Laid on table.		
Kent, Emanuel	Pension	13	3	House bill	740	Whole House	Mar. 1, 1815	With't amend.	303	Passed	Passed	App'd March 3, 1815
Kent, Jesse, late widow of.	Pension	22	1	Petition	556	Invalid Pensions.						
Kent, John	Pension	21	2	Petition	53	Military Pensions.						
Kent, Ludwick, widow of.	Pension	22	1	Petition	556	Invalid Pensions.						
Kenton, Elizabeth	(See Simon Kenton, widow of.)	25	2		478							
Kenton, Simon, (Ohio.)	Compensation for military services	14	1	Petition	339	Claims				Discharged; leave to withdraw.		
Kenton, Simon	Land for military services	18	2	Petition	75	Public Lands.						
Kenton, Simon	Land for military services	18	2	Petition	254	Public Lands.						
Kenton, Simon	Pension	20	2	Petition	109	Military Pensions	Feb. 18, 1829	Adv.; bill ord'd	453	Ref'd to Com. W. H.		
Kenton, Simon	Pension	22	1	Petition and bill.	58	Military Pensions	April 6, 1830	Favorable	408	Passed	Passed	App'd May 28, 1830
Kenton, Simon, widow of.	Continuation of pension	25	2	Resolution	478	Rev. Pensions.						
Kenton, Simon, (Ind.)	Land for military services	27	3	Petition	258	Invalid Pensions	187	Adverse		Laid on table.		
Kenton, Simon, (Ind.)	Land for military serviees	29	1	Petition	88	Public Lands.						
Kentucky, Catholic bishop of Bardstown.	(See Benedict J. Flaget)	20	1		403							
Kentucky, Catholic college at Bardstown.	Exemption of duties on certain articles.	16	2	Resolution	212	Ways and Means.						
Kentucky, postmaster at Danville.	Increase of compensation	16	2	Resolution	66	P. Of. and P. Roads.						
Kentucky, deaf and dumb asylum.	Aid for education	18	1	Memorial	359	Select	122	Favorable	219	Referred to Committee Whole House.		
Kentucky, deaf and dumb asylum.	Aid for education	18	2	House bill	146	Whole House			283			
Kentucky, deaf and dumb asylum.	Aid for education	19	1	Memorial	37	Select	7	Favorable	17	Passed	Passed	App'd April 5, 1826
Kentucky, deaf and dumb asylum.	Extension of time for selling lands	27	2	House bill	339	Whole House			114	Passed	Passed, with amendment.	App'd April 14, 1842
Kentucky, postmaster at Frankfort.	Increase of compensation	17	2	Resolution	110	P. Of. & P. Roads.						
Kentucky, postmaster at Frankfort.	Increase of compensation	18	1	Resolution	303	P. Of. & P. Roads.						
Kentucky, governor of	Compensation for expenses in Indian expeditions.	2	2	Papers	678					Laid on table.		
Kentucky, governor of	Compensation for expenses in Indian expeditions.	3	1	Resolution	48					Referred to Secretary Treasury.		
Kentucky, governor and legislature of.	Compensation for military services of militia.	13	2	Petition	240	Military Affairs	55	Favorable in part.	107	Passed	Postponed.	
Kentucky, postmaster near Hazelhatch.	Increase of compensation	17	2	Resolution	89	P. Of. & P. Roads.						
Kentucky, inhabitants of	Compromise of land purchase	16	2	Petition	45	Public Lands					Passed	Provided in act March 2, 1821.
Kentucky, judges and bar of United States district court.	Increase of judges salaries	18	2	Petition	231	Whole House.						

List of private claims presented to the House of Representatives of the United States from the 1st to the 31st Congress, inclusive—Continued.

Names of claimants.	Nature or object of the claim.	Congress.	Session.	How brought before the House of Reps.	Page of journal.	To what committee of the House referred.	No. or date of the report.	Nature of the report.	No. of the bill.	How disposed of by the House of Reps.	How disposed of by the Senate.	Date of the act of Congress, and remarks.
Kentucky, inhabitants of Knox county.	Indemnity for damages by U. States troops.	9	2	Petition	555	Claims.						
Kentucky, inhabitants of Knox county.	Indemnity for damages by U. States troops.	10	1	Petition	177	Claims	Feb. 25, 1808	Favorable; res.		Referred to Committee Whole House.		
Kentucky, inhabitants of Knox county.	Indemnity for damages by U. States troops.	10	2	Petition	350	Claims	Nov. 18, 1808	Favorable; bill	106	Passed.		
Kentucky, inhabitants of Knox county.	Indemnity for damages by U. States troops.	11	2	Memorial	127	Claims	Dec. 19, 1809	Favorable; bill	51	Referred to Committee Whole House.		
Kentucky, inhabitants of Knox county.	Indemnity for damages by U. States troops.	13	3	Petition	455	Claims	15	Adverse	242	Passed.	Passed	App'd Jan. 28, 1815
Kentucky, citizens of Laurel county.	Increase compensation for postmaster at London.	31	1	Petition	698	P. Of. & P. Roads.						
Kentucky, Simrall's regiment of light dragoons.	Compensation for horses lost in war of 1812.	12	2	Petition	691	Claims.						
Kentucky, citizens of	Compensation for horses lost in war of 1812.	14	1	Memorial	139					Laid on table.		
Kentucky, legislature of	Compensation for military services under Gaines.	24	2	Resolution	159	Claims.						
Kentucky, legislature of	Increase of compensation to Mexican volunteers.	29	2	Resolution	231					Laid on table.		
Kentucky, legislature of	Bounty land to soldiers of 1812	31	1	Joint resolution	898	Rev. Pensions						See act Sept. 28, 1850
Kentucky militia, Francisco's regiment.	For six months' pay for military services.	14	2	Petition	268	Military Affairs.						
Kentucky, Lexington and Ohio railroad company.	(See Lexington and Ohio railroad company.)	24	1		95		152		160			
Kentucky, Louisville and Portland canal company.	Permission to retain dividends on United States stock.	24	1	Petition.	108	Roads and Canals.						
Kentucky, Louisville Savings Institute.	Reimbursement of money improperly paid government.	25	2	Documents	176	Claims	466	Favorable	470	Referred to Committee Whole House.		
Kentucky, Louisville Savings Institute.	Reimbursement of money improperly paid government.	25	3	Rep. Committee Whole House.	378				470	Passed	Passed	App'd March 2, 1839
Kentucky, assistant marshals of.	Additional compensation for taking sixth census.	27	2	Documents	89	Claims	Feb. 9, 1842	Favorable	202	Passed	Passed, with amendment.	App'd Aug. 30, 1842
Kentucky, clerks in Maysville's post office.	Increase of compensation	31	2	Memorial	198	P. Of. & P. Roads.						
Kentucky, citizens of Mason county.	Bounty land to soldiers of 1812	31	1	Memorial, &c.	503	Public Lands						See act Sept. 28, 1850
Kentucky, officers and soldiers of 1st regiment.	Compensation for horses lost in public service.	31	2	Petition	251	Military Affairs						See H. bill No. 73.
Kentucky, officer of 2d regiment.	Bounty land	31	2	Petition	415	Military Affairs.						
Kentucky, pension agent at Louisville.	(See Newton Lane)	31	1		436							
Kentucky, senators and representatives of the legislature of.	Additional compensation to assistant marshal.	27	2	Memorial	77	Judiciary.						
Kentucky, citizens of Scott county.	Bounty land to soldiers of 1812	31	1	Petition	520	Public Lands						See act Sept. 28, 1850
Kentucky, Shelby & Henry counties.	Bounty land to soldiers of 1812	31	1	Memorial	414	Public Lands						See act Sept. 28, 1850
Kentucky, soldiers of	Bounty land to soldiers of 1812	31	1	Petition, &c.	436	Public Lands						See act Sept. 28, 1850
Kentucky, soldiers of	Bounty land to soldiers of 1812	31	1	Petition, &c.	436	Public Lands						See act Sept. 28, 1850
Kentucky, soldiers of	Bounty land to soldiers of 1812	31	1	Memorial	503	Public Lands.						

List of private claims presented to the House of Representatives of the United States from the 1st to the 31st Congress, inclusive—Continued.

Names of claimants.	Nature or object of the claim.	Congress.	Session.	How brought before the House of Reps.	Page of journal.	To what committee of the House referred.	No. or date of the report.	Nature of the report.	No. of the bill.	How disposed of by the House of Reps.	How disposed of by the Senate.	Date of the act of Congress, and remarks.
Kentucky, State of	Compensation to mounted riflemen and militia of 1812.	13	1	Resolution	20	Military Affairs	245	Favorable				See H. bill No. 230.
Kentucky, State of	Compensation for keeping criminals in penitentiary.	28	1	Documents	509	Judiciary	443	Am'd to appropriation bill.	32	Passed	Passed	App'd June 17, 1844
Kentucky, troops of	Compensation for services under Gaines.	24	2	Resolution	57	Claims.						
Kentucky, troops of	Compensation for services under Gaines.	24	2	Senate bill	420	Claims	Feb. 22, 1837	With't amend.	171	Referred to Committee Whole House.		
Kenyon, Hezekiah	(See Joseph Kenyon, widow of.)	29	1		701							
Kenyon, Jacob	(See Stephen Decatur, widow of, and others.)	20	1		295		201		850			
Kenyon, Jacob	(See Stephen Decatur, widow of, and others.)	23	1		36		45		50			
Kenyon, Joseph, widow of	Revolutionary pension	29	1	Petition	701	Rev. Pensions.						
Kenyon, Samuel	Confirmation of title to land	15	1	Petition	312	Priv. Land Claims.						
Kenyon, Samuel	Confirmation of title to land	16	1	Petition	70	Priv. Land Claims.						
Kenyon, Samuel	Confirmation of title to land	17	1	Petition	54	Public Lands.						
Kenyon, Samuel	Confirmation of title to land	18	1	Petition	54	Public Lands.						See acts May 26, 1824
Kenzie & Forsythe	Indemnity for property destroyed at Fort Chicago.	12	2	Petition	671	Claims.						
Kenzie & Forsythe	Indemnity for property destroyed at Fort Chicago.	13	2	Petition	168	Claims	243	Adverse		Referred to Committee Whole House.		
Kenzie & Forsythe	Indemnity for property destroyed at Fort Chicago.	13	3	Petition	643	Claims				Referred to Committee Whole House.		
Kenzie & Forsythe	Indemnity for property destroyed at Fort Chicago.	14	1	Petition	65	Claims.						
Kenzie & Forsythe	Indemnity for property destroyed at Fort Chicago.	15	1	Petition	261	Claims	171	Favorable	164	Referred to Committee Whole House.		
Kenzie & Forsythe	Indemnity for property destroyed at Fort Chicago.	15	2	House bill	181	Whole House	Jan. 13, 1819	With't amend.	164	Passed	Passed	App'd Feb. 24, 1819, leave to withdraw petition and papers.
Kenzie, John	Confirmation of title to lot in Detroit.	19	2	Petition	217	Priv. Land Claims.						See act April 17, 1828
Kenzie, John H., and others	Compensation for services in negotiating Indian treaties.	21	1	House bill	326	Whole House	Mar. 16, 1830	With't amend.	278	Passed	Passed	App'd April 7, 1830
Kenzie, John H.	Cession of reversionary interest in land.	27	2	Resolution	399	Indian Affairs.						
Keough, William	Pension	10	1	Petition	262					Referred to Secretary of War.		
Keough, William	Pension	10	2	House bill	400	Whole House	Jan. —, 1809	Favorable	158	Passed	Passed	App'd March 3, 1809
Kepler, Leonard, heirs of	Confirmation of title to land	25	2	Documents	281	Priv. Land Claims.				Discharged; laid on table.		
Kerbaugh, John	Pension	30	2	Petition	122	Invalid Pensions	77	Favorable	771	Referred to Committee Whole House.		
Kerbaugh, John	Pension	31	1	Petition	510	Invalid Pensions.						
Kerber, Peter	Exchange of tract of land	22	2	Petition	266	Public Lands.						
Kerby, Lieut. Samuel	Settlement of account	16	1	Petition	199	Military Affairs	Feb. 18, 1820	Favorable	83	Laid on table.		
Kercheval, Jane	(See John Kercheval, widow of.)	27	3		61							
Kercheval, John	Payment of balance due him as assistant quartermaster in United States army in 1813.	23	2	Petition	275	Claims						See act Jan. 27, 1835
Kercheval, John, widow of	Revolutionary pension	27	3	Petition	61	Rev. Pensions						See act Mar. 3, 1843
Kerchsletter, George	Restoration of pension	17	1	Petition	175	Rev. Pensions						See act Feb. 4, 1822

List of private claims presented to the House of Representatives of the United States from the 1st to the 31st Congress, inclusive—Continued.

Names of claimants.	Nature or object of the claim.	Congress.	Session.	How brought before the House of Reps.	Page of journal.	To what committee of the House referred.	No. or date of the report.	Nature of the report.	No. of the bill.	How disposed of by the House of Reps.	How disposed of by the Senate.	Date of the act of Congress, and remarks.
Kerford & Jenkins	Indemnity for illegal detention of good.	30	1	Memorial	899	Claims.						
Kerkendale, Robert	Indemnity for trespass by Indians.	21	1	Senate bill	87	Indian Affairs	Dec. 29, 1829	With't amend.	8	Passed	Passed	App'd Mar. 25, 1830
Kerlin, Benjamin	Pension	28	2	Petition	420	Invalid Pensions.						
Kerlin, Benjamin	Pension	29	1	Resolution	260	Invalid Pensions	306	Adverse		Laid on table.		
Kerlin, Jacob	(See John Kerlin, executors of.)	18	2		228							
Kerlin, John, executors of.	Additional allowance for arms manufactured for United States.	18	2	Petition	229	Claims.						
Kerlin, John, executors of.	Additional allowance for arms manufactured for United States.	19	1	Petition	131	Claims	March 8, 1826	Favorable	142	Passed.		
Kerlin, John, executors of.	Additional allowance for arms manufactured for United States.	19	2	Petition	64	Claims	Dec. 18, 1826	Favorable	309	Passed	Passed	App'd March 2, 1827
Kermer, John	Revolutionary pension	3	1	Rep. of Secretary War.	131	Select	May 22, 1794	J't. res. to refer to Sec. War.	12	Passed	Passed	App'd June 9, 1794
Kern, John, and others	Compensation for services in custom house.	24	2	Petition	206	Commerce	257	Favorable	946	Referred to Committee Whole House.		
Kern, John, and others	Compensation for services in custom house.	25	2	H. bill and rep't.	224	Commerce	292	Favorable	332	Referred to Committee Whole House.		
Kern, John, and others	Compensation for services in custom house.	25	3	House bill	377	Whole House.			332	Passed	Adverse.	
Kern, John F., representatives of.	Indemnity for French spoliations prior to 1800.	26	1	Memorial	182	Foreign Affairs	343	Favorable; bil	319	Referred to Committee Whole House.		
Kern, Nicholas	Release from imprisonment	19	2	Petition	307	Judiciary.						
Kern, Nicholas	Release from imprisonment	20	1	Petition	39	Judiciary				Referred to President of United States.		
Kern, Nicholas, sureties of	Discharged from liability, &c.	23	2	Petition	238	Claims	137	Favorable	772	Ref'd to Com W. H		
Kern, Nicholas, sureties of	Discharged from liability, &c.	24	1	Petition	51	Claims	187	Favorable.	193	Passed	Passed	App'd July 2, 1836
Kerns, John	Compensation for revolutionary services.	27	2	Petition	226	Rev. Pensions	784	Adverse		Laid on table.		
Kerns, William	Pension	26	1	Petition	325	Invalid Pensions	356	Favorable	335	Referred to Committee Whole House.		
Kerns, William	Pension	27	2	Petition	60	Invalid Pensions				Leave to withdraw.		
Ker, Mary, heirs of	Compensation for property lost	28	2	Resolution	130	Claims	98	Adverse		Laid on table.		
Ker, Robert B	Compensation for services as deputy surveyor.	26	2	Petition	124	Claims.						
Ker, Robert R	Compensation for a horse lost in United States service.	27	2	Petition	142	Claims	342	Adverse		Laid on table.		
Kerr, David	Pension	23	1	Petition	308	Rev. Pensions				Laid on table.		
Kerr, David	Pension	23	2	Petition	403	Rev. Pensions				Laid on table.		
Kerr, F. A	Reimburse expenses incurred with Osage Indians.	28	1	Senate bill	582	Indian Affairs	May 2, 1844	With amends.	62	Passed	Passed	App'd June 17, 1844
Kerr, Gabriel	Extension of time for payment on land.	16	2	Petition	97	Whole House on bill No. 94.						See act Mar. 2, 1820
Kerr, Hugh	Pension	22	1	Resolution	250	Invalid Pensions.						
Kerr, Hugh H	Pension	5	2	House bill	127	Whole House	Jan. 11, 1798	With amend.	38	Passed	Passed	App'd Feb. 2, 1798
Kerr, Jacob, (N. Y.)	Indemnity for land warrants never located.	26	2	Petition	82	Priv. Land Claims.						
Kerr, Jacob, (N. Y.)	Indemnity for land warrants never located.	26	2	Petition	279	Priv. Land Claims.						
Kerr, Jacob, (N. Y.)	Indemnity for land warrants never located.	27	2	Petition	58	Priv. Land Claims.						
Kerr, Jacob, (N. Y.)	Indemnity for land warrants never located.	28	1	Petition	73	Priv. Land Claims.	362	Adverse		Referred to Committee Whole House.		

List of private claims presented to the House of Representatives of the United States from the 1st to the 31st Congress, inclusive—Continued.

Names of claimants.	Nature or object of the claim.	Congress.	Session.	How brought before the House of Reps.	Page of journal.	To what committee of the House referred.	No. or date of the report.	Nature of the report.	No. of the bill.	How disposed of by the House of Reps.	How disposed of by the Senate.	Date of the act of Congress, and remarks.
Kerr, Jacob, (N. Y.)	Indemnity for land warrants never located.	29	1	Petition	73	Priv. Land Claims.	486	Adverse		Laid on table.		
Kerr, Jacob, (N. Y.)	Indemnity for land warrants never located.	29	2	Petition	151	Priv. Land Claims.						
Kerr, Jacob, (N. Y.)	Indemnity for land warrants never located.	30	1	Petition	166	Priv. Land Claims.				Discharged; laid on table.		
Kerr, Jacob, (N. Y.)	Indemnity for land warrants never located.	31	1	Petition	276	Priv. Land Claims.						
Kerr, Jacob, (N. Y.)	Indemnity for land warrants never located.	31	2	Petition		Priv. Land Claims.	13	Adverse		Laid on table.		
Kerr, Jacob	Remuneration for land conveyed to others.	29	2	Petition	236	Priv. Land Claims.						
Kerr, James	Pension	19	1	Petition	88	Military Pensions.	164	Adverse		Laid on table.		
Kerr, James	Pension	22	1	Petition	35	Rev. Pensions				Discharged; laid on table.		See act June 4, 1832
Kerr, John	Release from imprisonment	11	1	Petition	33	Select	June 13, 1809	Favorable	24	Referred to Committee Whole House.		
Kerr, John	Release from imprisonment	11	2	Petition	282	Select	Mar. 20, 1810	Favorable	110	Passed	Passed	App'd April 20, 1810
Kerr, Joseph, sureties of	Release from liability	20	1	Petition	368	Judiciary				Discharged; laid on table.		
Kerr, Joseph, sureties of	Release from liability	21	1	Petition	264	Judiciary				Discharged.		Leave to withdraw.
Kerr, Joseph	Pension	14	1	Resolution	395	Pens. & Rev. Cl'ms.	April 11, 1816	Pension bill		Passed	Passed	App'd April 30, 1816
Kerr, Nathaniel, widow of	Revolutionary pension	30	2	Resolution	123	Claims	98	Adverse		Laid on table.		
Kerr, Samuel	Indemnity for horse lost	25	2	Petition	723	Claims.						
Kerr, Samuel	Indemnity for horse lost	25	3	Petition	226	Claims	174	Adverse		Laid on table.		
Kerr, Samuel	Indemnity for horse lost	27	2	Petition	154	Claims	342	Adverse		Laid on table.		
Kerr, Stephen	(See Andrew Mitchell, administrator of.)	19	1		151							
Kerr, William	Revolutionary pension	23	2	Resolution	74	Rev. Pensions.						
Kerr, William	Revolutionary pension	25	2	Petition	629	Rev. Pensions.						
Kerr, William	Revolutionary pension	25	3	Petition	226	Rev. Pensions				Discharged; laid on table.		
Kerr, William	Revolutionary pension	28	1	Petition	337	Rev. Pensions.				Discharged; laid on table.		
Kerr, William	Revolutionary pension	28	2	Petition	82	Rev. Pensions.						
Kerr, William	Revolutionary pension	28	2	Additional papers	164	Rev. Pensions.						
Kerr, William H	Compensation for supplies furnished, &c.	31	1	Petition	534	Military Affairs	283	Adverse		Laid on table.		
Kerrigan, Daniel, brother of.	Balance due for services in navy paid to a stranger.	16	1	Petition	91	Claims	Jan. 12, 1820	Adverse		Rejected.		
Kerrigan, Edward	(See Daniel Kerrigan, brother of.)	16	1		91							
Kerschmer, Michael	Restoration of pension	17	1	Petition	184	Rev. Pensions						
Kersenar, John	Pension	13	2	House bill	344	Whole House						See act Feb. 4, 1822
Kersey, William	Revolutionary pension	15	2	Petition	23	Pens. & Rev. Cl'ms.	Nov. 25, 1818	Adverse	166	Passed Laid on table.	Passed	App'd April 18, 1814
Kershaw, Henry	Extra compensation as a clerk	31	2	Petition	78	Ways and Means.						
Kershaw, Jeremiah	Release as surety	26	1	Petition	348	Judiciary.						
Kershaw, Miria L	Compensation for property destroyed by Indians.	24	2	Petition	308	Claims				Discharged; laid on table.		
Kershaw, Miria L	Compensation for property destroyed by Indians.	25	2	Petition	398	Claims.						
Kershaw, Miria L	Compensation for property destroyed by Indians.	25	3	Petition	188	Claims	127	Adverse		Laid on table.		
Kershaw, Miria L	Compensation for property destroyed by Indians.	26	1	Petition	341	Claims.						

List of private claims presented to the House of Representatives of the United States from the 1st to the 31st Congress, inclusive—Continued.

Names of claimants.	Nature or object of the claim.	Congress.	Session.	How brought before the House of Reps.	Page of journal.	To what committee of the House referred.	No. or date of the report.	Nature of the report.	No. of the bill.	How disposed of by the House of Reps.	How disposed of by the Senate.	Date of the act of Congress, and remarks.
Kerslick, Abraham	Pension	17	2	Petition	186	Pens. & Rev. Cl'ms.						
Kerslick, Abraham	Pension	19	2	Petition	242	Military Pensions.						
Kesler, John	Revolutionary pension	3	1	Rep. of Secretary War.	131	Select	May 26, 1794	Jt. res. to refer to Sec. War.	J. R. 12	Passed	Passed	App'd June 9, 1794
Kesley, Mary	(See John Pearson, representatives of.)	26	1		360							
Kesselbaugh, Oswold	Compensation for revolutionary services.	2	1	Petition	446					Referred to Secretary War.		
Kesselbaugh, Oswold	Commutation pay for revolutionary services.	3	1	Rep. of Secretary War.	131	Select	May 26, 1794	Favorable	62	Passed	Passed	App'd June 7, 1794
Ketchum, Daniel, Major	Indemnity for depreciation of pay	18	2	Petition	191	Claims.						
Ketchum, Isaac S	Payment of money advanced Indians.	28	1	Petition	368	Indian Affairs	421	Favorable	324	Passed	Passed	App'd June 17, 1844
Ketchum, Isaac S	Indemnity for bringing Indians to Washington.	28	1	House bill	763	Whole House	422	With't amend.	325	Passed	Passed	App'd June 17, 1844
Ketchum, Israel	Pay as sub contractor	20	2	Petition	58	Claims	19	Adverse		Laid on table.		
Ketchum, Israel	Pay as sub contractor	23	1	Petition	120	Claims	496	Adverse		Laid on table.		
Ketchum, Israel	(See Thomas and Platt Ketchum)	24	2		218							
Ketchum, John J., widow of.	Indemnity for French spoliations prior to 1800.	18	1	Petition	134	Pens. & Rev. Cl'ms.				Discharged; laid on table.		
Ketchum, John J., widow of.	Indemnity for French spoliations prior to 1800.	26	1	Memorial	182	Foreign Affairs	343	Favorable	319	Referred to Committee Whole House.		
Ketchum, Joseph, widow of.	Revolutionary pension	29	1	Petition	520	Rev. Pensions	826	Adverse		Laid on table.		
Ketchum, Joseph, widow of.	Revolutionary pension	30	1	Petition	279	Rev. Pensions				Discharged; laid on table.		
Ketchum, Mary	(See Major Thomas Ketchum, widow of.)	25	2		116							
Ketchum, Sally	(See Joseph Ketchum, widow of.)	29	1		520							
Ketchum, Singleton	Pension	13	3	Petition	639	Pens. & Rev. Cl'ms.				Discharged.		
Ketchum, Singleton	Pension	24	1	Petition	716	Invalid Pensions	667	Favorable	626	Passed	Passed	App'd June 28, 1836
Ketchum, Solomon	Compensation for revolutionary services.	23	2	Petition	272	Rev. Pensions				Discharged; laid on table.		
Ketchum, Solomon	Restoration of pension	24	1	Petition	532	Rev. Pensions	737	Favorable	680	Passed	Indef. postp'd.	
Ketchum, Solomon	Restoration of pension	24	2	Petition	158	Rev. Pensions	80	Favorable	826	Referred to Committee Whole House.		
Ketchum, Solomon	Restoration of pension	25	2	Petition	55	Rev. Pensions	162	Favorable	187	Passed	Passed	App'd June 28, 1838
Ketchum, Stephen, assignee of.	Payment of loan office certificates	21	2	Petition	67	Rev. Claims	Feb. 4, 1831	Favorable	598	Referred to Committee Whole House.		
Ketchum, Stephen, assignee of.	Payment of loan office certificates	22	1	Senate bill	152	Rev. Claims	Feb. 20, 1832	With't amend.	S. 32	Passed		App'd July 13, 1832
Ketchum, Susannah	(See John J. Ketchum, widow of)	18	1		134							
Ketchum, Thomas	Payment of money due as inspector in New York.	24	1	Petition	272	Commerce	349	Adverse		Laid on table.		
Ketchum, Thomas & Platt	Half pay to their orphans	24	2	Petition	218	Invalid Pensions				Discharged; laid on table.		
Ketchum, Major Thomas, widow of.	Compensation for military services	25	2	Documents	116	Military Affairs	Mar. 1, 1838	Adverse		Laid on table.		
Ketchum & White	(See White and Ketchum)	27	3		153							
Ketchum, William S.	Allowance of money robbed whilst acting as commissary.	25	2	Petition	396	Claims	723	Adverse		Laid on table.		
Ketchum, William S.	Allowance of money robbed whilst acting as commissary.	26	1	Petition	334	Claims.						

List of private claims presented to the House of Representatives of the United States from the 1st to the 31st Congress, inclusive—Continued.

Names of claimants.	Nature or object of the claim.	Congress.	Session.	How brought before the House of Reps.	Page of journal.	To what committee of the House referred.	No. or date of the report.	Nature of the report.	No. of the bill.	How disposed of by the House of Reps.	How disposed of by the Senate.	Date of the act of Congress, and remarks.
Ketchum, William S.	Allowance of money robbed whilst acting as commissary.	27	2	Petition	382	Claims	719	Adverse	......	Laid on table.		
Ketchum, William S.	Allowance of money robbed whilst acting as commissary.	27	2	Petition	999	Claims.						
Ketchum, William S.	Allowance of money robbed whilst acting as commissary.	27	3	Petition	101	Claims.						
Ketchum, Zebulon	Indemnity for damage to his land by troops.	20	1	Petition	243	Claims	Feb. 13, 1828	Adverse	......	Laid on table.		
Ketchum, Zebulon	Indemnity for damage to his land by troops.	23	1	Petition	355	Claims	May 29, 1834	Adverse	......	Laid on table.		
Ketland, Thomas, assignee of.	Indemnity for French spoliations prior to 1800.	26	1	Memorial	182	Foreign Affairs	343	Favorable; bill	319	Referred to Committee Whole House.		
Ketland, Thomas	Drawback of duties, &c.	7	2	Memorial	339	Com. and Manuf.	Feb. 23, 1803	Indefinite	......	Leave to withdraw.		
Ketland, Thomas	Drawback of duties, &c.	8	1	Memorial	441	Com. and Manuf.	Nov. 14, 1803	Adverse	......	Rejected.		
Ketland, Thomas	Drawback of duties, &c.	8	2	Memorial	51	Com. and Manuf.	Jan. 11, 1805	Adverse	......	Ref'd to Com. W. H.		
Ketland, Thomas	Drawback of duties, &c.	9	1	Memorial	196	Com. and Manuf.	Jan. 8, 1806	Adverse	......	Rejected.		
Ketlett, Charles A.	To refund tonnage duties paid	30	1	Petition	571	Commerce	416	Favorable	638	Referred to Committee Whole House.		
Ketlett, Charles A.	To refund tonnage duties paid	30	2	House bill	144	Whole House	Dec. 22, 1848	With't amend.	368	Passed.		
Ketlett, Charles A.	To refund tonnage duties paid	31	1	Petition	371	Commerce.						
Kettell, Charles A.	To refund tonnage duties paid	31	1	Senate bill	1438	Commerce	....	....	313			
Kettell, James	(See Richard Skimmer, and others)	19	1	....	222							
Kettle, Thomas	Indemnity for French spoliations prior to 1800.	26	1	Memorial	182	Foreign Affairs	343	Favorable; bill	319	Referred to Committee Whole House.		
Kettlewell, Charles	(See John Kettlewell, representative of.)	16	1	....	215							
Kettlewell, John, representative of.	Refund money paid for land	16	1	Petition	215	Public Lands	Feb. 25, 1820	Adverse	......	Leave to withdraw.		
Kettlewell, John, representative of.	Refund money paid for land	20	1	Petition	343	Priv. Land Claims.						
Kettlewell, John, representative of.	Refund money paid for land	20	2	Petition	258	....	....	....	......	Leave to withdraw.		
Keweda, Alva, and others.	Refund money paid at land office.	28	1	Petition	75	Public Lands	144	General bill	132	Passed	Passed	Not approved.
Key, Andrew	Increase of pension	27	2	Petition	869	Invalid Pensions	....	....	......	....	....	See act Aug. 23, 1842
Key, Francis S., & others.	(See United States and Mexican claimants.)	27	1	....	350							
Key, George	Land for revolutionary services	21	2	Petition	211	Public Lands.						
Key, John	Pay of claim for military service	21	1	Documents	448	Claims	April 20, 1830	Adverse	......	Laid on table.		
Key, John	Revolutionary pension	22	1	Petition	265	Rev. Pensions	....	....	......	....	....	See act June 4, 1832
Key, Peyton A.	Refund money advanced for troops	30	1	Petition	379	Claims	....	....	......	Discharged; laid on table.		
Key, Peyton A.	Refund money advanced for troops	31	1	Petition	1344	Claims.						
Key, Peyton R.	Reduction of price of lots	20	1	Petition	399	Public Lands.						
Key, Phillip B., & others.	Compensation for judicial services.	7	2	Petition	307	Whole House	June 27, 1803	Adverse resl'n.	......	Rejected	....	Leave to withdraw.
Key, Phillip B., sr.	Compensation for judicial services.	28	1	Petition	319	Judiciary.						
Keyes, Amasa	(See Stephen Keyes, executors of)	2	2	....	656							
Keyes, Elnathan	(See Stephen Keyes, executors of)	2	2	....	656							
Keyes, Jeremiah	Pension	22	1	Petition	46	Invalid Pensions.						
Keyes, Jeremiah	Pension	23	1	Petition	44	Invalid Pensions	1	Favorable	1	Passed	Passed	App'd June 25, 1834
Keyes, J. M.	(See Johnson Vance, administrator of.)	29	1	....	423							
Keyes, Purdy, and J. Fairbanks	(See Sam'l Whittlesey, sureties of)	15	1	....	47							

List of private claims presented to the House of Representatives of the United States from the 1st to the 31st Congress, inclusive—Continued.

Names of claimants.	Nature or object of the claim.	Congress.	Session.	How brought before the House of Reps.	Page of journal.	To what committee of the House referred.	No. or date of the report.	Nature of the report.	No. of the bill.	How disposed of by the House of Reps.	How disposed of by the Senate.	Date of the act of Congress, and remarks.
Keyes, Stephen, executors of.	Renewal of a lost certificate	2	2	Petition	656	Whole House.						
Keys, Malcolm	Pension	12	1	House bill	361	Whole House	June 15, 1812	With amends.	138	Passed	Passed	App'd July 5, 1812
Keys, Margaret	(See Jas. M. Devenny, *et al*)	10	2		382							
Keys, Richard	Compensation for services as wagon master, and for supplies, &c.	3	2	Petition	296	Claims	Mar. 2, 1795	Adverse		Laid on table.		
Keys, Richard	Compensation for services as wagon master, and for supplies, &c.	4	2	Petition and rep't	629	Claims	Dec. 27, 1796	Adverse resl'n.		Rejected		Leave to withdraw.
Keys, Richard	Indemnity for Spanish spoliations	18	2	Petition	41	Ways and Means.						
Keys, Richard	Indemnity for Spanish spoliations	19	1	Petition	271	Foreign Affairs	201	Adverse		Laid on table.		
Keys, Samuel	Vestment of title in land to children	21	2	Petition	100	Public Lands				Discharged; laid on table.		
Keyser, Charles C.	(See Sam'l Shannon, executor of)	28	1		502							
Keyser, Lee De	(See Lee De Keyser)	5	2		144							
Keyser, Michael J.	Revolutionary pension	22	2	Resolution	285	Rev. Pensions.						
Keyser, Michael J.	Revolutionary pension	22	2	Petition	312	Rev. Pensions				Discharged; laid on table.		
Keytes, James	Land in lieu of other land	23	1	Petition	385	Priv. Land Claims.	347	Favorable	374	Referred to Committee Whole House.		
Keytes, James	Land in lieu of other land	24	1	Petition	258	Priv. Land Claims.	316	Favorable	326	Referred to Committee Whole House.		
Keytes, James	Land in lieu of other land	24	2	House bill	200	Whole House	Jan. 13, 1837	With't amend	326	Passed	Passed	App'd March 3, 1837
Keyworth, Robert	Additional compensation for swords manufactured.	24	2	Rep. of Secretary War.	188	Claims	188	Favorable	910	Referred to Committee Whole House.		
Keyworth, Robert	Additional compensation for swords manufactured.	25	2	House bill	99	Claims	74	With't amend.	86	Passed	Passed	App'd June 7, 1838
Kibben, James M.	Release of reversionary interest in Indian reservation.	30	1	Petition	316	Indian Affairs				Discharged; laid on table.		
Kibbey, Phillip W	Restoration of pension	17	1	Petition	128	Rev. Pensions						See act Feb. 4, 1822
Kibby, Sidnah	(See Thomas Kibby, widow of.)	25	2		923							
Kibby, Thomas, widow of.	Pension	25	2	Petition	923	Naval Affairs	997	Favorable	859	Referred to Committee Whole House.		
Kibby, Thomas, widow of.	Pension	25	3	House bill	432	Whole House	Feb. 1, 1839	With't amend.	859	Passed	Passed	App'd March 3, 1839
Kibby, Thomas, late widow of.	Pension	31	1	Pet. and papers	628, 647	Rev. Pensions	259	Favorable	111	Passed.		
Kicks, William	Pension	31	2	Petition	52	Invalid Pensions.						
Kid, Robert	Reimbursement of duties, &c.	12	1	Petition	61	Com. and Manuf.						
Kid, Robert, and others	Reimbursement of duties, &c.	15	2	Petition	168	Com. and Manuf	Feb. 2, 1819	Favorable	302	Passed	Passed	App'd March 3, 1819
Kid, Robert	Cancel of bond, &c.	13	2	Petition	654	Ways and Means.						
Kid, Robert	Cancel of bond, &c.	14	1	Petition	152	Ways and Means	Mar. 6, 1816	Favorable	111	Passed	Rejected.	
Kidd, Benjamin	(See Richard and Benjamin Kidd.)	29	1		1075							
Kidd, John	Revolutionary pension	29	1	Resolution	434	Military Pensions.						
Kidd, John	Revolutionary pension	22	1	Petition	193	Invalid Pensions	391	Favorable	486	Referred to Committee Whole House.		See act June 4, 1832
Kidd, George W.	Compensation for loss of property in Mexico.	30	1	House bill	389	Claims			222	Laid on table.		
Kidd, George W.	Compensation for loss of property in Mexico.	30	2	Petition	193	Claims	134	Adverse		Laid on table.		
Kidd, Richard and Benjamin.	Reimbursement of certain duties	29	1	Senate bill	1075	Ways and Means	July 24, 1846	With't amend.	96	Passed	Passed	App'd Aug. 10, 1846
Kiddall, Eliza M.	(See Claudius Besse, heirs of.)	29	2		163							
Kidder, Daniel, former widow of.	Relief for revolutionary service	25	2	Petition	53	Rev. Pensions				Ref'd to Com. W. H. on bill No. 456.		

List of private claims presented to the House of Representatives of the United States from the 1st to the 31st Congress, inclusive—Continued.

Names of claimants.	Nature or object of the claim.	Congress.	Session.	How brought before the House of Reps.	Page of journal.	To what committee of the House referred.	No. or date of the report.	Nature of the report.	No. of the bill.	How disposed of by the House of Reps.	How disposed of by the Senate.	Date of the act of Congress, and remarks.
Kidney, Jonathan	Increase of pension	23	2	Petition	120	Rev. Pensions	....	....	......	Disch'd; laid on table.		
Kiersted, Christopher N.	Release from imprisonment	13	2	Petition	198	Ways and Means	Feb. 1, 1844	Adverse	......	Leave to withdraw.		
Kierzkowski, Alexander	Return money paid for patent	27	2	Petition	240	Patents.						
Kiff, Daniel	Fishing bounty	22	1	Petition	253	Commerce	268	Favorable	346	Referred to Committee Whole House.		
Kiff, Daniel	Fishing bounty	23	1	Petition	32	Commerce	367	Favorable	......	Referred to Committee Whole House.	....	Provided in act June 30, 1834.
Kilbourn, Asahel	Pension	2	2	Rep. of Secretary of War.	649	Whole House.						
Kilbourn, Asahel	Pension	3	1	Rep. of Secretary War.	131	Select	Mar. 26, 1794	Joint resoluton	12	Passed	Passed	App'd June 7, 1794
Kilbourn, Byron	Compelling Wisconsin Territory to pay certain bonds.	28	1	Memorial	432	Territories.						
Kilbourn, Charles	Land for revolutionary services	23	2	Petition	76	Rev. Claims.						
Kilbourn, David	Compensation for military services and as secret agent.	19	2	Petition	216	Claims.						
Kilbourn, David	Compensation for military services and as secret agent.	20	1	Petition	342	Claims.						
Kilbourn, David	Compensation for military services and as secret agent.	21	1	Petition	200	Military Affairs	189	Favorable	238	Referred to Committee Whole House.		
Kilbourn, David	Compensation for military services and as secret agent.	21	2	House bill	265	Whole House	Feb. 4, 1831	With't amend.	238	Passed.		
Kilbourn, David	Compensation for military services and as secret agent.	22	1	Petition	31	Military Affairs	Dec. 27, 1831	Favorable	143	Passed	Passed	App'd July 14, 1832; provides for services only.
Kilbourn, David	Further indemnity for losses sustained in war of 1812.	22	2	Petition	31	Military Affairs.						
Kilbourn, David	Further indemnity for losses sustained in war of 1812.	22	2	Petition	68	Military Affairs.						
Kilbourn, David	Further indemnity for losses sustained in war of 1812.	23	1	Petition	35	Military Affairs	174	Favorable	190	Postponed.		
Kilbourn, David	Further indemnity for losses sustained in war of 1812.	23	2	House bill	113	Whole House	....	....	190	Rejected.		
Kilbourn, David	Further indemnity for losses sustained in war of 1812.	24	1	Petition	64	Military Affairs	107	Favorable	123	Postponed.		
Kilbourn, David	Further indemnity for losses sustained in war of 1812.	24	2	House bill	338	Whole House	....	....	123	Passed	Passed	App'd March 3, 1837
Kilbourn, Henry	Compensation for improvement on a lot.	21	1	Petition	376	Claims	331	Favorable	389	Referred to Committee Whole House.		
Kilbourn, Henry	Compensation for improvement on a lot.	22	1	Petition	25	Claims	Dec. 19, 1831	Favorable	18	Passed	Passed	App'd Jan. 23, 1832
Kilbourn, Henry	Compensation for improvement on a lot.	22	2	Petition	67	Claims.						
Kilbourn, Jacob, widow of.	Revolutionary pension	26	1	Petition	283	Rev. Pensions	714	Adverse	......	Laid on table.		
Kilbourn, Mary	(See Jacob Kilbourn, widow of.)	26	1	....	283							
Kilby, John	Payment of prize-money	17	1	Petition	125	Naval Affairs.						
Kilby, John	Payment of prize-money	17	2	Petition	31	Naval Affairs.	Feb. 12, 1823	Adverse	......	Laid on table.		
Kilby, Turpin	Renewal of a register	6	2	Petition	786	Com. and Manuf.	Feb. 9, 1801	Adverse	......	Rejected.	....	Leave to withdraw.
Kilgore, Charles	Pension	11	2	House bill	283	Whole House	April 10, 1801	Favorable	107	Passed	Passed	App'd April 27, 1810
Kilgore, James E.	Compensat'n for property destroyed	24	2	Documents	209	Claims	162	Adverse	......	Laid on table.		
Kilgore, James E.	Compensat'n for property destroyed	25	3	Documents	207	Claims.						
Kilgore, John	Compensation for plank furnished United States.	15	1	Petition	267	....	....	....	......	Referred to Secretary of the Navy.		
Kilgore, William	Indemnity for property destroyed	24	1	Documents	753	Foreign Affairs.						

List of private claims presented to the House of Representatives of the United States form the 1st to the 31st Congress, inclusive—Continued.

Names of claimants.	Nature or object of the claim.	Congress.	Session.	How brought before the House of Reps.	Page of journal.	To what committee of the House referred.	No. or date of the report.	Nature of the report.	No. of the bill.	How disposed of by the House of Reps.	How disposed of by the Senate.	Date of the act of Congress, and remarks.
Kilgore, William	Indemnity for property destroyed	25	3	Documents	305	Claims	190	Adverse		Laid on table.		
Kilgore, William, executor of.	Indemnity for property destroyed	31	1	Petition	449	Claims	243	Favorable	240	Referred to Committee Whole House.		
Killan, James	(See Canadian refugees.)	4	2		614							
Kilen, James	Pension	30	1	Petition	104	Invalid Pensions.						
Kilman, Ezekiel, widow of	Compensation for military services	24	1	Petition	429	Rev. Claims	593	Adverse		Laid on table.		
Kilman, Ezekiel, widow of	Compensation for military services	25	2	Petition	194	Rev. Pensions				Discharged; laid on table.		
Kilman, Polly	(See Ezekiel Kilman.)	24	1		429							
Kimore, George	Indemnity for property destroyed	3	1	Petition	124					Laid on table.		
Kiltenger, John	Pension	26	1	Petition	325	Invalid Pensions				Laid on table.		
Kimball, Abraham	Pension	2	2	Rep. of Secretary War.	649	Whole House.						
Kimball, Abraham	Pension	3	1	Rep. of Secretary War.	131	Select	May 26, 1794	Joint resolut'n.	12	Passed	Passed	App'd June 8, 1794
Kimball, Abraham	Pension	4	1	Documents	445	Claims	Mar. 4, 1796	Favorable	156	Passed	Passed	App'd April 20, 1796
Kimball, Benjamin	Compensation for revolutionary services.	24	1	Petition	259	Rev. Claims	397	Adverse		Laid on table.		
Kimball, Benjamin, widow of.	Compensation for revolutionary services.	28	1	Petition	584	Rev. Pensions				Discharged; laid on table.		
Kimball, Benjamin, widow of.	Compensation for revolutionary services.	28	2	Petition	414	Rev. Pensions.						
Kimball, Benjamin, widow of.	Compensation for revolutionary services.	30	1	Petition	786	Rev. Pensions	787	Adverse		Discharged; laid on table.		
Kimball, Edmund	Indemnity for French spoliation prior to 1800.	26	1	Memorial	182	Foreign Affairs	343	Favorable; bill	319	Referred to Committee Whole House.		
Kimball, Gordon, widow of.	Renewal of pension	22	2	Petition	346	Naval Affairs.						
Kimball, Gordon, widow of.	Renewal of pension	28	1	Petition	850	Rev. Pensions.						
Kimball, Jeremiah	Restoration of pension	27	2	Petition	68	Invalid Pensions	318	Favorable	287	Passed	Indef. postp'd.	
Kimball, Jeremiah	Restoration of pension	27	3	Petition	44	Invalid Pensions	46	Favorable	674	Passed	Passed	App'd March 3, 1843
Kimball, Jeremiah	Arrears of pension	28	1	Petition	103	Invalid Pensions	105	Adverse		Laid on table.		
Kimball, John	Compensation for revolutionary services, and depreciation of money.	19	1	Petition	205	Rev. Claims				Discharged; laid on table.		
Kimball, Joseph	(See Thomas Tupper, assignee of.)	22	2		142							
Kimball, Joseph	Payment of balance on due bill	28	1	Petition	206	Claims	11	Favorable	38	Laid on table.		
Kimball, Joseph	Payment of balance on due bill	28	2	Petition	46	Claims.						
Kimball, Joseph	Payment of balance on due bill	29	1	Petition	67	Claims	1	Favorable	16	Passed	Passed	App'd July 15, 1846
Kimball, Judith	(See Joshua O. Alley, children of.)	26	1		199							
Kimball, Lovell, and others	Patents for lands	24	2	Petition	268	Public Lands.						
Kimball, Lucia	(See Gordon Kimball, widow of)	22	2		346							
Kimball, Lydia	(See Nathan Kimball, widow of)	25	2		984							
Kimball, Nathan, widow of	Revolutionary pension	25	2	Petition	984	Rev. Pensions.						
Kimball, Samuel	Revolutionary pension	19	1	Petition	26	Military Pensions.						
Kimball, Samuel	Revolutionary pension	20	1	Resolution	303	Military Pensions.						
Kimball, Samuel	Revolutionary pension	22	1	Petition	66	Military Pensions.						
Kimball, Samuel	Revolutionary pension	21	2	Resolution	165	Military Pensions						See act June 14, 1832
Kimball, Susannah	(See Benj. Kimball, widow of)	28	1		584							
Kimball, Thomas	Pension	2	2	Rep. of Secretary War.	649	Whole House.						
Kimball, Thomas	Pension	3	1	Rep. of Secretary War.	131	Select	May 26, 1794	Res. to refer to Sec. of War.	J.R.12	Passed	Passed	App'd June 9, 1794

List of private claims presented to the House of Representatives of the United States from the 1st to the 31st Congress, inclusive—Continued.

Names of claimants.	Nature or object of the claim.	Congress.	Session.	How brought before the House of Reps.	Page of journal.	To what committee of the House referred.	No. or date of the report.	Nature of the report.	No. of the bill.	How disposed of by the House of Reps.	How disposed of by the Senate.	Date of the act of Congress, and remarks.
Kimball, Thomas	Pension	3	2	Rep. of Secretary of War.			Feb. 28, 1795			Laid on table.		
Kimball, Thomas	Pension	4	1	Rep. of Secretary of War.	445	Claims	March 4, 1796	Favorable	156	Passed	Passed	App'd April 20, 1796
Kimber, Isaac	Indemnity for liquors destroyed by the enemy.	18	2	Petition	229	Claims						See act Mar. 3, 1825
Kimberlin, John	Compensation for supplies taken by troops.	21	2	Mem'l of Indiana legislature.	376					Laid on table.		
Kimberlin, John	Compensation for supplies taken by troops.	22	1	Petition	226	Claims	Feb. 3, 1832	Adverse		Laid on table.		
Kimberlin, John	Compensation for supplies taken by troops.	23	1	Senate bill	170	Claims	Jan. 14, 1834	With amend.	38	Passed	Passed	App'd Mar. 24, 1834
Kimberly, Eli	Increase of compensation as light-house keeper.	25	2	Petition	199	Commerce	338	Adverse		Laid on table.		
Kimberly, Ephraim	Permission to locate land, &c.	2	1	Petition	574	Select.						
Kimberly, Ephraim	Permission to locate land, &c.	2	2	Petition	668	Select	Feb. 18, 1793	By bill	244	Ref'd to Com. W. H.		
Kimberly, Ephraim	Permission to locate land, &c.	3	1	Rep. and petition.	40	Select.	March 5, 1794	By bill	6	Passed	Passed	App'd April 18, 1794
Kimble, Titan, assignee of.	Deficiency of land patent	25	2	Papers	281	Priv. Land Claims.				Laid on table.		
Kimble, Titan, assignee of.	Deficiency of land patent	25	3	Papers	136	Public Lands.						
Kimble, Walter	Compensation for revolutionary services.	25	2	Petition	392	Rev. Pensions.						
Kimmerly, Jacob	(See Conrad Houseman, administrator of)	3	2		330							
Kimplin, William	Revolutionary pension	12	1	Petition	19	Claims	June 12, 1812	Adverse		Laid on table.		
Kimplin, William	Revolutionary pension	12	2	Petition	577	Claims	Feb. 26, 1813	Adverse		Laid on table.		
Kims, Elizabeth	(See George Kims, widow of)	31	1		537							
Kims, George, widow of.	Indemnity for French spoliations prior to 1800.	31	1	Petition	537	Commerce	355	Favorable	318	Referred to Committee Whole House.		
Kincade, John	Pension	22	1	Petition	631	Invalid Pensions.				Discharged; laid on table.		
Kincade, John	Pension	22	2	Petition	27	Invalid Pensions	Feb. 15, 1833	Favorable	738	Referred to Committee Whole House.		
Kincade, John	Pension	23	1	Petition	44	Invalid Pensions	1	Favorable	1	Passed	Passed, with amendment.	App'd June 25, 1834
Kincade, Thomas	(See assignee of Samuel Young)	3	1		31							
Kincaid, Andrew	Confirmation of title to land	27	2	Petition	681	Priv. Land Claims.						See act Mar. 31, 1843
Kincaid, Andrew	Confirmation of title to land	27	3	Petition	45	Priv. Land Claims.						
Kincaid, Daniel, and others	Remuneration for losses by Indian depredations.	19	2	Petition	134	Indian Affairs	51	Favorable		Referred to Committee Whole House.		
Kincaid, David	Land patent	23	1	Resolution	252	Priv. Land Claims.	234	Favorable	260	Referred to Committee Whole House.		
Kincaid, David	Land patent	23	2	House bill	299	Whole House	Jan. 31, 1835	With't amend.	260	Passed	Passed	App'd March 3, 1835
Kincaid, G. W	Permission to change location of land.	30	1	Petition	594	Priv. Land Claims.	792	Adverse		Laid on table.		
Kincaid, Samuel	Pension	24	1	Petition	97	Invalid Pensions.	222	Favorable	231	Passed	Passed	App'd June 28, 1836
Kincaid, Samuel	Increase of pension	25	3	Petition	219	Invalid Pensions.						
Kincaid, Samuel	Increase of pension	26	1	Petition	514	Invalid Pensions	244	Adverse		Laid on table.		
Kincaid, William	Land and compensation for revolutionary services.	9	2	Petition	474	Select.						
Kincaid, William	Land and compensation for revolutionary services.	10	1	Petition	15	Claims.						
Kincart, John, and others.	Land and pay for military services.	30	2	Senate bill	358	Military Affairs			407			
Kincart, John, and others.	Land and pay for military services.	31	1	Petition	215	Military Affairs.						

List of private claims presented to the House of Representatives of the United States from the 1st to the 31st Congress, inclusive—Continued.

Names of claimants.	Nature or object of the claim.	Congress.	Session.	How brought before the House of Reps.	Page of journal.	To what committee of the House referred.	No. or date of the report.	Nature of the report.	No. of the bill.	How disposed of by the House of Reps.	How disposed of by the Senate.	Date of the act of Congress, and remarks.
Kincheloe, Thomas	Revolutionary pension	25	2	Petition	587	Rev. Pensions				Discharged; laid on table.		Provided in act March 10, 1838.
Kincheloe, Thomas	Increase of pension	25	3	Resolution	170	Rev. Pensions				Discharged.		
Kinder, George, and others	(See George Kender, *et al.*)	25	2		547							
Kinder, George, and others	(See Joel Whitesides, *et al.*)	28	1		850							
Kindelsperger, Jacob	Pension	13	3	Petition	618	Pens. & Rev. Cl'ms.	Jan. 27, 1815	Adverse		Leave to withdraw.		
Kindelsperger, Jacob	Pension	14	1	Petition	42	Pens. & Rev. Cl'ms.	April 11, 1816	Favorable	171	Passed	Passed	App'd April 30, 1816
Kindred, Josiah	Pension	29	1	Petition	616	Invalid Pensions.						
Kindren, William	Pension	15	1	Petition	401	Pens. & Rev. Cl'ms.				Discharged; referred to Secretary War.		
King, A	Land script in lieu of land patent.	27	2	Petition	794	Public Lands.						
King, Abraham H	Revolutionary pension	25	3	Petition	215	Rev. Pensions.						
King, Abraham H	Revolutionary pension	26	1	Petition	322	Rev. Pensions.						
King, Adam, on behalf of militia of District of Columbia.	Compensation for damage to clothing.	13	2	Petition	226	Select				Leave to withdraw.		
King, Alexander	(See Henry King, heirs of.)	28	2		192							
King, Alfred P	Compensation for horses and wagon, impressed.	26	1	Senate bill	837	Claims	May 16, 1846	With amend.	291	Referred to Committee Whole House.		See act July 21, 1840
King, Amanda	(See George W. Fox)	29	1		275							
King, A. P., and H. Lucas	Indemnity for teams and wagons taken, &c.	25	2	Petition	397	Claims.						
King, A. P., and H. Lucas	Indemnity for teams and wagons taken, &c.	25	3	Petition	189	Claims				Discharged; leave to withdraw.		
King, Barbara	(See Peter King, heirs of)	18	1		59							
King, Benjamin	Release from payment of interest on judgment.	17	2	Petition	164	Naval Affairs	Feb. 26, 1823	Favorable	317	Laid on table.		
King, Benjamin	Release from payment of interest on judgment.	18	1	Petition	101	Naval Affairs	April 22, 1824	Favorable	201	Passed	Passed	App'd May 19, 1824
King, Benjamin, Dr	Compensation for medical services to Indians.	24	1	Petition	924	Indian Affairs.						
King, Benjamin, and others	(See Elias Bates, and others)	15	2		109							
King, Benjamin, heirs of.	Renewal of land warrant	24	1	Senate bill	1055	Priv. Land Claims.	July 2, 1836	With't amend.	190	Referred to Committee Whole House.		
King, Benjamin, heirs of.	Renewal of land warrant	24	2	Senate bill	250	Rev. Claims	Jan. 31, 1837	With't amend.	2	Referred to Committee Whole House.		
King, Benjamin, heirs of.	Renewal of land warrant	25	2	Senate bill	1166	Claims	July 2, 1838	With amend.	273	Referred to Committee Whole House.		
King, Benjamin, heirs of.	Renewal of land warrant	25	3	Senate bill	263	Rev. Claims	Jan. 16, 1839	With't amend.	16	Passed	Passed	App'd Feb. 6, 1839
King, Charles	Revolutionary pension	2	2	Petition	661					Laid on table.		
King, Charles	Revolutionary pension	14	2	Petition	347	Pens. & Rev. Cl'ms.						
King, Charles	Revolutionary pension	18	1	Petition	358	Pens. & Rev. Cl'ms.	April 7, 1824	Adverse		Laid on table.		
King, Charles	(See Theodore Dwight, & others)	19	1		221							
King, Daniel P., attorney of.	Balance due on mileage and per diem.	31	1	Resolution	1251							Paid out of contingent fund.
King, David	Pension	22	1	Resolution	561	Invalid Pensions	474	Favorable	576	Passed.		
King, David	Pension	25	2	Resolution	105	Rev. Pensions				Discharged; laid on table.		
King, David	Pension	25	2	Petition	722	Invalid Pensions	April 18, 1838	Adverse		Laid on table.		
King, Elizabeth	(See John King, widow of)	16	1		33							
King, Ezekiel	(See John Coyle, and others)	18	2		158							
King, Felty, and others	(See Peter King)—	18	1		59							
King, Francis	(See Wm. King, assignees of)	19	2		100							

List of private claims presented to the House of Representatives of the United States from the 1st to the 31st Congress, inclusive—Continued.

Names of claimants.	Nature or object of the claim.	Congress.	Session.	How brought before the House of Reps.	Page of journal.	To what committee of the House referred.	No. or date of the report.	Nature of the report.	No. of the bill.	How disposed of by the House of Reps.	How disposed of by the Senate.	Date of the act of Congress, and remarks.
King, George	Indemnity for horses lost in public service.	16	1	Petition	140	Claims	Jan. 22, 1820	Adverse	......	Laid on table.		
King, George	Revolutionary pension	21	1	Resolution	433	Military Pensions	Feb. 15, 1830	Favorable	248	Passed	Indef. postp'd.	
King, George	Revolutionary pension	22	1	Resolution	120	Rev. Pensions.						
King, George, jr.	Additional compensation as postmaster.	21	2	Petition	45	P. Of. & P. Roads.	Jan. 7, 1830	Adverse	......	Laid on table.		
King, Gideon, representatives of.	(See King & Thurber)	20	1	....	360							
King, Henry	Reimbursement of money advanced and compensation for revolutionary services.	3	1	Petition	92	Select.	April 4, 1794	Favorable in part; adverse	......	Laid on table.		
King, Henry	Reimbursement of money advanced and compensation for revolutionary services.	15	1	Petition	80	Pens. & Rev. Cl'ms.	121	Favorable	134	Passed	Postponed.	
King, Henry	Reimbursement of money advanced and compensation for revolutionary services.	18	2	Resolution	139	Pens. & Rev. Cl'ms.						
King, Henry	Reimbursement of money advanced and compensation for revolutionary services.	21	1	Petition	74	Rev. Claims	Mar. 8, 1830	Adverse	......	Laid on table.		
King, Henry, heirs of	Reimbursement of money advanced and compensation for revolutionary services.	22	1	Resolution	475	Rev. Claims	Mar. 21, 1832	Adverse	......	Laid on table.		
King, Henry, heirs of	Reimbursement of money advanced and compensation for revolutionary services.	22	2	Resolution	60	Rev. Claims	Jan. 30, 1833	Adverse	......	Laid on table.		
King, Henry, heirs of	Reimbursement of money advanced and compensation for revolutionary services.	23	1	Petition	189	Rev. Claims	May 29, 1834	Adverse	......	Laid on table.		
King, Henry, heirs of	Reimbursement of money advanced and compensation for revolutionary services.	24	1	Petition	152	Rev. Claims.						
King, Henry, heirs of	Reimbursement of money advanced and compensation for revolutionary services.	24	2	Petition	40	Rev. Claims.						
King, Henry, heirs of	Reimbursement of money advanced and compensation for revolutionary services.	25	2	Petition	82	Rev. Claims	1023	Adverse	......	Laid on table.		
King, Henry, heirs of	Reimbursement of money advanced and compensation for revolutionary services.	26	1	Petition	631	Rev. Claims.						
King, Henry, heirs of	Reimbursement of money advanced and compensation for revolutionary services.	27	2	Petition	62	Rev. Claims	198	Adverse	......	Laid on table.		
King, Henry, heirs of	Reimbursement of money advanced and compensation for revolutionary services.	28	1	Petition	321	Rev. Claims	319	Favorable	227	Referred to Committee Whole House.		
King, Henry, heirs of	Reimbursement of money advanced and compensation for revolutionary services.	28	2	Pet. and House bill.	192	....	....	....	227	Leave to withdraw.		
King, Henry, heirs of	Reimbursement of money advanced and compensation for revolutionary services.	29	1	Petition and docs.	592	Claims	Mar. 27, 1846	Adverse	......	Laid on table.		

List of private claims presented to the House of Representatives of the United States from the 1st to the 31st Congress, inclusive—Continued

Names of claimants.	Nature or object of the claim.	Congress.	Session.	How brought before the House of Reps.	Page of journal.	To what committee of the House referred.	No. or date of the report.	Nature of the report.	No. of the bill.	How disposed of by the House of Reps.	How disposed of by the Senate.	Date of the act of Congress, and remarks.
King, Henry	Relief from bonds for duties	17	2	Petition	77	Ways and Means	Dec. 31, 1822	Adverse		Rejected.		
King, Henry, and others, by Peout, &c.	Compensation for military services	18	2	Senate bill	284	Military Affairs	March 1, 1825	With't amend.	S. 41	Passed		App'd March 3, 1825
King, Henry W.	Increase of salary	31	1	Petition	668	Ways and Means.						
King, Hosea	Pension	21	1	Petition	490	Military Pensions	April 2, 1830	Adverse		Laid on table.		
King, Hosea	Bounty land	23	2	Petition	48	Priv. Land Claims	Dec. 18, 1834	Adverse		Laid on table.		
King, Ichabod	Restoration of pension	17	1	Petition	51	Rev. Pensions						See act Feb. 4, 1822
King, Isaac	Compensation for forage furnished	30	1	Petition	435	Claims	424	Adverse		Laid on table.		
King, James	Pension	21	1	Petition	479	Military Pensions	Mar. 30, 1830	Favorable	248	Passed	Indef. postp'd.	
King, James	Increase of salary as light-house keeper.	25	1	Petition	72					Laid on table.		
King, James	Indemnity for French spoliations prior to 1800.	26	1	Memorial	182	Foreign Affairs	343	Favorable; bill	319	Referred to Committee Whole House.		
King, James, and others	Relief in relation to the purchase of certain lands.	27	2	Petition	368	Public Lands.						
King, James H.	Indemnity for injuries received on board of steamboat Carolina.	25	2	Petition	920	Invalid Pensions.						
King, Job	Renewal of letters patent	22	1	Petition	444	Patent laws	May 14, 1832	Adverse		Laid on table.		
King, John	Pension	6	1	Petition	555	Claims	May 5, 1800	Adverse		Rejected.		
King, John	Pension	9	2	House bill	608	Whole House	Mar. 2, 1807	With amend.	216	Passed	Passed	App'd March 3, 1807
King, John	Extension of pension	10	2	Petition	347	Claims.						
King, John, (Va.)	Rebuilding of a house destroyed by enemy.	14	1	Petition	53	Claims	Dec. 21, 1815	Adverse		Rejected.		
King, John, (Va.)	Rebuilding of a house destroyed by enemy.	15	1	Rep. of Comm'r of Claims.	316	Claims.						
King, John, (Va.)	Indemnity for house destroyed by enemy.	22	1	Petition	413	Claims	Mar. 6, 1832	Adverse		Laid on table.		
King, John, (Va.)	Indemnity for house destroyed by enemy.	22	2	Petition	32	Claims	Dec. 21, 1832	Adverse		Laid on table.		
King, John, (Va.)	Indemnity for house destroyed by enemy.	23	1	Petition	141	Claims	Feb. 10, 1834	Adverse		Laid on table.		
King, John, (Va.)	Indemnity for house destroyed by enemy.	26	1	Petition	622	Claims.						
King, John, (Va.)	Indemnity for house destroyed by enemy.	26	2	Petition	35	Rev. Claims.						
King, John, (Va.)	Indemnity for house destroyed by enemy.	27	2	Petition	55	Claims	268	Favorable	226	Passed	Passed	App'd Aug. 26, 1842
King, John, and Joseph Shankland.	Compensation for supplies furnished crew of United States brig Vixen.	15	1	Petition	130	Claims	Mar. 1, 1818	Adverse		Rejected.		
King, John, (Phila.)	Balance of pay for supplies furnished United States in 1813.	17	2	Petition	208	Claims.						
King, John, (Phila.)	Balance of pay for supplies furnished United States in 1813.	18	1	Petition	52	Claims	Jan. 7, 1824	Adverse		Laid on table		Leave to withdraw.
King, John, (Phila.)	Balance of pay for supplies furnished United States in 1813.	18	2	Petition	119	Claims	Feb. 14, 1825	Adverse		Rejected.		
King, John	Pension	17	1	Petition	78	Pens. & Rev. Cl'ms.	Mar. 1, 1822	Adverse		Leave to withdraw.		
King, John	Revolutionary pension	21	1	Resolution	342	Military Pensions	May 3, 1830	Favorable	454	Ref'd to Com. W. H.		
King, John	Revolutionary pension	21	2	House bill	318	Whole House	Feb. 17, 1831	With amend.	454	Passed.		
King, John	Revolutionary pension	22	1	Petition	35	Rev. Pensions	Dec. 21, 1831	Favorable	67	Passed	Indef. postp'd.	See act June 7, 1832
King, John, (Tenn.)	Compensation for a horse lost in war of 1812.	23	1	Petition	217	Claims.						
King, John, (Ky.)	Revolutionary pension	24	2	Petition	85	Invalid Pensions.						
King, John, (Mo.)	(See William Gillis, *et al.*)	25	2		192							

List of private claims presented to the House of Representatives of the United States from the 1st to the 31st Congress, inclusive—Continued.

Names of claimants.	Nature or object of the claim.	Congress.	Session.	How brought before the House of Reps.	Page of journal.	To what committee of the House referred.	No. or date of the report.	Nature of the report.	No. of the bill.	How disposed of by the House of Reps.	How disposed of by the Senate.	Date of the act of Congress, and remarks.
King, John Glen	(See James King, administrator of)	26	1		182							
King, John Glen	(See John Norris, administrator of)	26	1		182							
King, John, widow of	Pension	16	1	Petition	33	Rev. Pensions				Leave to withdraw		See act May 15, 1820
King, John A	Compensation for expenses incurred as captain's clerk in U. S. navy	27	2	Petition	382	Claims	718	Adverse		Laid on table.		
King, John G	Restoration of pension	17	1	Petition	30	Rev. Pensions						See act Feb. 4, 1822
King, John H	(See Williams & King)	25	2		668							
King, John H	Compensation for use of invention	31	1	Petition	307	Military Affairs.						
King, John H	Compensation for services as inspector of rifle factory at Harper's ferry.	31	1	Petition & papers	370, 668	Military Affairs.						
King, John L	Increase of salary as clerk of navy yard, Gosport, Virginia.	24	2	Memorial	46	Naval Affairs.						
King, John L	Increase of salary as clerk of navy yard, Gosport, Virginia.	26	1	Petition	956	Naval Affairs.						
King, John L	Increase of salary as clerk of navy yard, Gosport, Virginia.	26	2	Petition	181	Naval Affairs.						
King, John L	Increase of salary as clerk of navy yard, Gosport, Virginia.	27	2	Petition	224	Commerce.						
King, John M	Land for military services	25	3	Petition	287	Rev. Claims.						
King, John M	Land for military services	28	1	Memorial	83	Priv. Land Claims.						
King, Joseph	Pension	13	2	House bill	344	Whole House	Mar. 30, 1814	With amend.	166	Passed	Passed	App'd April 18, 1814
King, Joseph	Restoration of pension	17	1	Petition	155				37	Ref'd to Com. W. H. on bill No. 37.		
King Joshua, (Conn.)	Indemnity for French spoliations prior to 1800.	26	1	Memorial	183	Foreign Affairs	343	Favorable; bill	319	Referred to Committee Whole House.		
King, Josiah, jr	Indemnity, loss of land in N. Scotia	25	3	Petition	221	Rev. Claims.						
King, Josiah, jr	Indemnity, loss of land in N. Scotia	26	1	Petition	282	Rev. Claims.						
King, Josiah, jr	Indemnity, loss of land in N. Scotia	26	2	Petition	77	Rev. Claims.						
King, Josiah, jr	Indemnity, loss of land in N. Scotia	27	2	Petition	154	Rev. Claims	862	Adverse		Laid on table.		
King, Josiah, jr	Indemnity, loss of land in N. Scotia	28	1	Petition	216	Rev. Claims.						
King, Josiah, jr	Indemnity loss of land in N. Scotia	28	2	Petition	57	Rev. Claims.						
King, Josias W	Compensation for services as assistant clerk in the House of Representatives and interest.	9	1	Memorial	280	Accounts	Mar. 5, 1806	Rept. not found		Referred to Committee Whole House.		
King, Lemuel	Pension	10	1	House bill	232	Whole House	April 19, 1808	With't amend.	78	Passed	Passed	App'd April 25, 1808
King, Lyman	Compensation for timber taken and used by U. S. troops.	25	3	Petition	119	Claims	55	Adverse		Laid on table.		
King, Lyman	Compensation for timber taken and used by U. S. troops.	26	1	Petition	293, 707	Claims	43	Adverse		Laid on table.		
King, Lyman	Compensation for timber taken and used by U. S. troops.	28	1	Petition	513	Claims.						
King, Lyman	Compensation for timber taken and used by U. S. troops.	28	2	Petition	239	Claims.						
King, Lyman	Compensation for timber taken and used by U. S. troops.	29	1	Petition	75	Claims	4	Adverse		Laid on table.		
King, Mary	Pre-emption right to land	30	1	Petition	236	Public Lands	328	Adverse		Laid on table.		
King, Martin	Revolutionary pension	21	1	Petition	149	Military Pensions	May 3, 1830	Adverse		Laid on table.		
King, Miles	Leave to institute suit *vs.* U. States for settlement of claim.	21	2	Petition	232	Judiciary				Discharged; laid on table.		
King, Miles, and others	Payment of claims	28	1	Petition	333	Claims.						
King Miles, assignee of	Payment of debt due	28	2	Senate bill	209	Judiciary	Feb. 7, 1845	With't amend	S. 27	Referred to Committee Whole House.		

List of private claims presented to the House of Representatives of the United States from the 1st to the 31st Congress, inclusive—Continued.

Names of claimants.	Nature or object of the claim.	Congress.	Session.	How brought before the House of Reps.	Page of journal.	To what committee of the House referred.	No. or date of the report.	Nature of the report.	No. of the bill.	How disposed of by the House of Reps.	How disposed of by the Senate.	Date of the act of Congress, and remarks.
King, Miles, Dr., heirs of.	Five years' pay	23	1	Petition	306	Rev. Claims.						
King, Miles, Dr., heirs of.	Five years' pay	23	2	Petition	84	Rev. Claims.						
King, Miles, Dr., heirs of.	Five years' pay	24	1	Petition	103	Rev. Claims	826	Adverse	......	Laid on table.		
King, Miles, Dr., heirs of.	Five years' pay	24	2	Petition	94	Rev. Claims	98	Adverse	......	Laid on table.		
King, Nancy	(See Jesse Tucker, widow of)	29	1		86							
King, Nathaniel	Pension	21	2	Petition	103	Military Pensions.						
King, Nathaniel	Pension	22	1	Petition	68	Rev. Pensions.						
King, Olive	(See William Eddy, widow of.)	30	1		644							
King, Peter	(See Mary Whitesides, executrix of.)	29	2		128							
King, Peter, heirs of	Revolutionary pension	18	1	Petition	59	Pens. & Rev. Cl'ms.	....	....	......	Discharged; laid on table.		
King, Lieut. Philip	Relief in consideration of disease contracted in U. S. army.	14	2	Petition	207	Claims.						
King, Lieut. Philip	Pension	20	2	Petition	118	Military Pensions	....	....	......	Discharged.		
King, Prosper	Confirmation of title to land in Mississippi.	12	1	Petition	334	Public Lands.						
King, Reuben	Arrears of pension	3	2	Petition	311	Claims.						
King, Reuben	Arrears of pension	4	1	Petition	403	Claims	Jan. 6, 1796	Adverse	......	Rejected.	....	Leave to withdraw
King, Richard	Confirmation of title to land in Mississippi.	12	1	Petition	334	Public Lands.						
King, Richard, *et al.*	Confirmation for title to land	27	2	Petition	459	Priv. Land Claims.						
King, Richard, *et al.*	Confirmation of title to land	27	3	Petition	45	Priv. Land Claims.						
King, Richard	(See James McCoy, representatives of.)	27	2		459							
King, Robert	Pension	1	3	Petition and rep't Sec. of War.	368	Select	Feb. 29, 1791	Favorable	139	Passed	Postponed.	
King, Robert	Pension	2	1	House bill	462	Whole House	Nov. 29, 1791	With't amend.	152	Passed	Passed, see bill No. 159.	App'd March 29, 1827
King, Robert, assignee of.	Arrears of pay for military services	19	1	Petition	407	Claims	165	Favorable	217	Passed.		
King, Robert, assignee of.	Arrears of pay for military services	19	2	Petition	82	Claims	Dec. 22, 1826	Favorable	313	Passed	Passed	App'd Feb. 22, 1827
King, Sackville	Compensation for revolutionary services.	23	1	Petition	439	Rev. Claims.						
King, Sampson S.	Equitable settlement of accounts	14	1	Petition	93	Claims.						
King, Sampson S.	Equitable settlement of accounts	15	1	Petition	132	Claims	Mar. 20, 1818	Favorable; bill	152	Referred to Committee Whole House.		
King, Sampson S.	Equitable settlement of accounts	15	2	House bill	142	Whole House	Dec. 29, 1818	With amends.	152	Passed	Passed with amendment.	App'd Feb. 4, 1819
King, Sampson S.	Compensation for time in settling accounts	23	1	Petition	637	Claims.						
King, Sampson S.	Compensation for time in settling accounts.	23	2	Petition	37	Claims.						
King, Thomas, (Md.)	Pension	11	2	Petition	251	Claims	Mar. 20, 1810	Adverse	......	Laid on table.		
King, Thomas, (Tenn.)	Pension	21	1	Petition	619	Military Pensions.						
King, Thomas, (Tenn.)	Pension	24	2	Petition	86	Invalid Pensions	47	Favorable: bill	794	Referred to Committee Whole House.		
King, Thomas, (Tenn.)	Pension	25	2	Petition and docs.	245	Invalid Pensions	332	Adverse	......	Laid on table.		
King, Thomas, (Tenn.)	Pension	26	1	Petition	602	Invalid Pensions.						
King, Thomas, (Tenn.)	Pension	27	2	Petition	611	Invalid Pensions	1032	Favorable; bill	601			
King, Thomas, (Tenn.)	Pension	27	3	House bill	91	Whole House	....	....	601	Passed	Passed	App'd Feb. 24, 1843
King, Thomas, (Tenn.)	Explanatory of the act of February 24, 1843.	27	3	Joint resolution.	518	....	....	....	J.R. 47	Passed	Passed	App'd March 3, 1843
King & Thurber	Indemnity for vessel captured	16	2	Petition	285	....	....	....	......	Laid on table.		

List of private claims presented to the House of Representatives of the United States from the 1st to the 31st Congress, inclusive—Continued.

Names of claimants.	Nature or object of the claim.	Congress.	Session.	How brought before the House of Reps.	Page of journal.	To what committee of the House referred.	No. or date of the report.	Nature of the report.	No. of the bill.	How disposed of by the House of Reps.	How disposed of by the Senate.	Date of the act of Congress, and remarks.
King & Thurber	Indemnity for vessel captured	17	1	Petition	23	Claims	Dec. 27, 1821	Adverse		Recommitted.		
King & Thurber	Indemnity for vessel captured	17	2	Petition	30	Claims	Jan. 29, 1823	Adverse		Laid on table.		
King & Thurber	Indemnity for vessel captured	18	1	Petition	296	Claims.						
King & Thurber	Indemnity for vessel captured	19	1	Petition	62	Claims	34	Adverse		Referred to Committee Whole House.		
King & Thurber	Indemnity for vessel captured	20	1	Petition and res.	360	Claims.						
King & Thurber	Indemnity for vessel captured	20	2	Petition	28	Claims	19	Favorable; bill	338	Referred to Committee Whole House.		
King & Thurber	Indemnity for vessel captured	21	1	Petition	50	Claims	Dec. 23, 1829	Favorable; bill	22	Passed	Passed	App'd Feb. 27, 1830
King, William	Equitable settlement of accounts	15	1	Petition	302	Military Affairs	Mar. 10, 1818	Favorable; bill	130	Referred to Committee Whole House.		
King, William	Equitable settlement of accounts	15	2	House bill	70	Whole House	Dec. 7, 1818	With't amend.	130	Passed	Postponed.	
King, William	Equitable settlement of accounts	16	1	Petition	165	Military Affairs	Jan. 24, 1820	Favorable; bill	58	Laid on table.		
King, William	Equitable settlement of accounts	18	1	Petition	135	Military Affairs	52	Favorable; bill	95	Referred to Committee Whole House.		
King, William, (N. Y.)	For benefit of act for relief of surviving officers of the revolution.	21	1	Resolution	345	Rev. Claims.						
King, William, (Tenn.)	Pension	21	2	Petition	114	Military Pensions.						
King, William, (Tenn.)	Pension	22	1	Petition	89	Invalid Pensions	Jan. 11, 1832	Adverse		Laid on table.		
King, William, (Tenn.)	Pension	23	1	Petition	131	Invalid Pensions	Feb. 21, 1834	Adverse		Laid on table.		
King, William, (Tenn.)	Pension	25	2	Petition	400	Invalid Pensions	Mar. 7, 1838	Adverse		Laid on table.		
King, William, (Tenn.)	Pension	26	1	Petition	327	Invalid Pensions	270	Adverse		Laid on table.		
King, William, assignee of	Compensation for furniture furnished President's house.	19	1	Resolution	307	Claims	157	Favorable; bill	209	Passed.		
King, William, assignee of	Compensation for furniture furnished President's house.	19	2	Resolution	55					Leave to withdraw.		
King, William, assignee of	Compensation for furniture furnished President's house.	19	2	Senate bill	100	Claims	Jan. 10, 1827	With't amend.	S. 31	Passed	Passed	App'd Feb. 8, 1827
King, William D.	Compensation as Indian agent	21	1	Petition	294	Claims	Mar. 2, 1830	Favorable; bill	308	Referred to Committee Whole House.		
King, William D.	Compensation as Indian agent	21	2	House bill	333	Whole House	Feb. 19, 1831	With't amend.	308	Passed.		
King, William D.	Compensation as Indian agent	22	1	Petition	43	Claims	Dec. 19, 1831	Favorable; bill	9	Passed	Passed	App'd Jan. 23, 1832
King, William M	(See William H. Bedford, agent)	28	1		262							
King, William M	Confirmation of title to land	21	2	Petition	163	Public Lands				Discharged; laid on table.		
King, William M	Confirmation of title to land	22	1	Petition	79	Public Lands	85	Favorable; bill	168	Passed	Passed	App'd July 14, 1832
King, William, and Thomas Rowland.	Additional compensation for military services.	27	2	Petition	1298	Claims.						
King, William, and Thomas Rowland.	Additional compensation for military services.	28	1	Petition	371	Claims.						
King, William, and Thomas Rowland.	Additional compensation for military services.	28	2	Petition	84	Claims.						
King, William, and Thomas Rowland.	Additional compensation for military services.	29	1	Petition	326	Invalid Pensions				Discharged; laid on table.		
King & Williams, (D. C.).	Indemnity for losses on post office contract.	25	2	Memorial	668	P. Of. and P. Roads.						
King & Williams, (D. C.).	Indemnity for losses on post office contract.	25	3	Memorial	132	P. Of. and P. Roads.						
King, Wright	Compensation for military services.	14	1	Petition	70	Claims.						
King, Young	Pension	14	1	Resolution	240	Pens. & Rev. Cl'ms.	Feb. 15, 1816	Favorable; bill		Passed	Passed	App'd April 27, 1816
King, Zenas	Compensation for services in custom house.	29	1	Petition	89	Claims.						

List of private claims presented to the House of Representatives of the United States from the 1st to the 31st Congress, inclusive—Continued.

Names of claimants.	Nature or object of the claim.	Congress.	Session.	How brought before the House of Reps.	Page of journal.	To what committee of the House referred.	No. or date of the report.	Nature of the report.	No. of the bill.	How disposed of by the House of Reps.	How disposed of by the Senate.	Date of the act of Congress, and remarks.
King, Zenas	Compensation for services in custom house.	29	1	Memorial	461	Claims	559	Adverse		Laid on table.		
King, Zenas	Compensation for services in custom house.	29	2	Petition	110	Claims.						
King, Zenas	Compensation for services in custom house.	30	1	Petition	685	Claims.						
King, Zenas	Compensation for services in custom house.	31	1	Petition	214	Claims	26	Adverse		Laid on table.		
Kingman, Alexander	Restoration of pension	17	1	Petition	259	Whole House				Leave to withdraw.		
Kingman, Alexander	Restoration of pension	17	2	Petition	36	Rev. Pensions						See act March 1, 1823
Kingman, Eliab	Compensation for services as clerk in House of Representatives.	27	3	House order	501							Paid out of contingent fund of House.
Kingry, John	Restoration of pension	18	1	Resolution	420	Pens. & Rev. Cl'ms.						See act of April 9, 1824
Kingsbury, Byron	(See Simon Spaulding, administrator of.)	28	2		227							
Kingsbury, Isaac	Pension	24	2	Petition	398	Invalid Pensions.						
Kingsbury, Jacob, widow of.	Indemnity for a horse lost in revolutionary war.	25	2	Petition	200	Claims	847	Adverse		Laid on table.		
Kingsbury, John	(See Thomas Flowers, and others)	20	1		175							
Kingsbury, Joseph	Indemnity for French spoliations prior to 1800.	31	1	Petition	191	Foreign Affairs	355	Favorable; bill	318	Referred to Committee Whole House.		
Kingsbury, Margaret	(See Oliver Kingsbury, widow of)	22	2		224							
Kingsbury, Oliver	Pension	22	1	Resolution	436	Rev. Pensions.						
Kingsbury, Oliver, widow of.	Grant of land for military services	22	2	Resolution	224	Priv. Land Claims.						
Kingsbury, Oliver, widow of.	Grant of land for military services.	23	2	Resolution	398	Priv. Land Claims.						
Kingsbury, Oliver, widow of.	Grant of land for military services.	24	2	Petition	273	Priv. Land Claims.	March 3, 1837	Favorable; bill	974	Referred to Committee Whole House.		
Kingsbury, Oilver, widow of.	Grant of land for military services.	25	2	Petition	43	Priv. Land Claims.	Dec. 22, 1837	Favorable; bill	161	Referred to Committee Whole House.		
Kingsbury, Oliver, widow of.	Grant of land for military services.	25	3	House bill	375	Whole House	Jan. 25, 1839	With't amend	161	Passed	Passed	App'd March 3, 1839
Kingsbury, Solomon	Release from payment of bond	18	1	Petition	213	Ways and Means.	Feb. 19, 1824	Adverse		Laid on table.		
Kingsbury, William	Permission to exchange location of land.	27	2	Petition	535	Priv. Land Claims.						
Kingsbury, Wm., assignee of.	Permission to exchange location of land.	30	1	Petition	525	Public Lands	837	Favorable; bil	650	Referred to Committee Whole House.		
Kingsbury, Wm., assignee of.	Permission to exchange location of land.	30	2	House bill	363	Whole House	Feb. 3, 1849	With't amend.	650	Passed.		
Kingsland, Daniel, assignee of.	Arrears of pay	19	2	Petition	82	Claims	Dec. 22, 1826	Favorable; bill	313	Passed	Passed	App'd Feb. 22, 1827
Kingsley, Alpha, sureties of.	Release from liability	19	1	Senate bill	488	Judiciary	May 5, 1826	Adverse	S. 121	Laid on table.		
Kingsley, Alpha, sureties of.	Release from liability	20	2	Senate bill	353	Claims	Mar. 2, 1829	With't amend.	S. 8	Passed		App'd March 2, 1829
Kingsley, Asahel	Revolutionary pension	25	2	Petition	53	Rev. Pensions	537	Favorable; bill	530	Passed.		
Kingsley, Asahel	Revolutionary pension	26	1	Petition	172	Rev. Pensions	454	Favorable; bill	368	Referred to Committee Whole House.		
Kingsley, Asahel	Revolutionary pension	27	2	Petition	59	Rev. Pensions	109	Favorable; bill	155	Passed	Indef. postp'd.	
Kingsley, Asahel	Revolutionary pension	27	3	Petition	139	Rev. Pensions	295	Adverse		Laid on table.		
Kingsley, Ebenezer C	Settlement of his accounts	15	2	Petition	225	Claims	Feb. 15, 1819	Adverse		Leave to withdraw.		

List of private claims presented to the House of Representatives of the United States from the 1st to the 31st Congress, inclusive—Continued.

Names of claimants.	Nature or object of the claim.	Congress.	Session.	How brought before the House of Reps.	Page of journal.	To what committee of the House referred.	No. or date of the report.	Nature of the report.	No. of the bill.	How disposed of by the House of Reps.	How disposed of by the Senate.	Date of the act of Congress, and remarks.
Kingsley, Hezekiah	(See Elisha Phinney, executors of.)	22	1		559							
Kingsley, Jedediah	Pension	21	2	Petition	188	Military Pensions.						
Kingsley, Rufus	Pension	21	2	Petition	53	Military Pensions.						
Kingsley, Rufus	Pension	22	1	Petition	120	Rev. Pensions.						See act June 4, 1832
Kingsley, Uriah	Arrears of pension	23	2	Petition	95	Rev. Pensions				Discharged; laid on table.		
Kingsley, Uriah	Arrears of pension	25	2	Petition	180	Rev. Pensions				Discharged; laid on table.		
Kingsley, Uriah	Arrears of pension	30	1	Petition	675	Rev. Pensions.						
Kingsley, Uriah	Arrears of pension	30	2	Petition	116	Rev. Pensions.						
Kingsley, Wareham	Revolutionary pension	27	2	Senate bill	1126	Rev. Pensions.	Aug. 27, 1842	With't amend.	249	Referred to Committee Whole House.		
Kingsley, Wareham	Revolutionary pension	27	3	Senate bill	171	Invalid Pensions.	Feb. 3, 1843	With't amend.	53	Referred to Committee Whole House.		
Kingston, Stephen	Drawback of duties on certain merchandise.	7	2	Memorial	335	Com. and Manuf.	Feb. 21, 1803	Res. to postpone.		Adopted.		
Kingston, Stephen	Drawback of duties on certain merchandise.	8	1	Memorial	410	Com. and Manuf.	Oct. 31, 1803	Favorable		Referred to Committee Whole House.		
Kingston, Stephen	Drawback of duties on certain merchandise.	8	2	Memorial	45	Com. and Manuf.						
Kingston, Stephen	Drawback of duties on certain merchandise.	9	1	Memorial	190	Com. and Manuf.	Feb. 12, 1806	Favorable		Referred to Committee Whole House.		
Kingston, Stephen	Drawback of duties on certain merchandise.	9	2	Memorial	471	Com. and Manuf.	Dec. 30, 1806	Favorable		Referred to Committee Whole House.		
Kingston, Stephen	Drawback of duties on certain merchandise.	10	1	Memorial	28	Com. and Manuf.						
Kingston, Stephen	Drawback of duties on certain merchandise.	12	1	Petition	29	Com. and Manuf.	Nov. 26, 1811	Favorable		Referred to Committee Whole House.		
Kingston, Stephen	Delivery of goods captured by his privateer.	12	2	Petition	584	Ways and Means.	Jan. 5, 1813	Adverse		Referred to Committee Whole House.		
Kingston, Stephen	Drawback of duties on certain merchandise.	23	1	Petition	32	Commerce	198	Favorable; bill	215	Passed	Passed	App'd June 30, 1834
Kingston, Stephen	Indemnity for seizure of his ship.	23	1	Memorial	37	Foreign Affairs				Referred to Secretary of State.		
Kinkade, John	Pension	22	1	Petition	631	Invalid Pensions				Disch'd; laid on table.		
Kinkade, John	Pension	22	2	Petition	27	Invalid Pensions	Feb. 15, 1833	Favorable; bill	738B.	Referred to Committee Whole House.		
Kinkade, J hn	Pension	23	1	Petition	44	Invalid Pensions	Dec. 12, 1833	Favorable; bill	1	Passed	Passed	App'd June 25, 1834
Kinkaid, Joseph, sureties of.	Release from liability	19	1	Resolution	181	Judiciary	Jan. 31, 1826	Adverse		Laid on table.		
Kinkaid, Joseph, sureties of.	Release from liability	24	1	Petition	264	Claims	340	Adverse		Laid on table.		
Kinkead, James	Additional compensation for transporting United States mail.	22	2	Petition	207	P. Of. & P. Roads.				Discharged; laid on table.		
Kinkead, James	Payment for work done and material furnished, on Cumberland road.	23	1	Res. and papers.	589	Claims				Referred to Secretary War.		
Kinkead, Robert	Increase of pension	25	3	House bill	275	Rev. Pensions.				Discharged; laid on table.		
Kinkle, John, and others.	Compensation for opening a post road.	24	2	Senate bill	579				S. 200	Referred to Committee Whole House.		
Kinkle, John, and others.	Compensation for opening a post road.	26	1	Senate bill	227	P. Of. & P. Roads.	July 21, 1840	Adverse	S. 29	Referred to Committee Whole House.		

List of private claims presented to the House of Representatives of the United States from the 1st to the 31st Congress, inclusive—Continued.

Names of claimants.	Nature or object of the claim.	Congress.	Session.	How brought before the House of Reps.	Page of journal.	To what committee of the House referred.	No. or date of the report.	Nature of the report.	No. of the bill.	How disposed of by the House of Reps.	How disposed of by the Senate.	Date of the act of Congress, and remarks.
Kinkle, John, and others	(See James Walker and John Kinkle and others.)	28	1	....	76							
Kinlock, Cleland	(See Major Benjamin Huger)	2	1	....	440							
Kinlock, Francis	Confirmation of title to land	19	1	Petition	44	Priv. Land Claims.						
Kinlock, Francis, heirs of.	Confirmation of title to land	19	2	Petition	189	Priv. Land Claims.	....	....	....	....	....	See act Feb. 8, 1827
Kinnard, Edward	(See Edward Kennary.)	28	1	....	225							
Kinnard, Nathaniel	Pension	15	1	Petition	97	Pens. & Rev. Cl'ms.						
Kinnard, Samuel G., and John Anderson.	(See Anderson & Moody, representatives of.)	24	2	....	273							
Kinnard, William, heirs of	Compensation for revolutionary services.	16	2	Petition	216	Pens. & Rev. Cl'ms.	Feb. 16, 1821	Adverse	....	Laid on table.		
Kinne, Lyman	Invalid pension	2	2	Rep. of Secretary War.	649	Whole House.						
Kinne, Lyman	Invalid pension	3	1	Rep. of Secretary War.	131	Select	May 26, 1794	Joint resolut'n	12	Passed	Passed	App'd June 9, 1794
Kinnersley, Thomas	Reimbursement of duties overpaid.	16	1	Petition	140	Ways and Means	Feb. 3, 1820	Adverse	....	Laid on table	....	Leave to withdraw.
Kinney, Allen, & Co.	(See Thomas Tupper, assistant of)	22	2	....	142							
Kinney, Amos, widow of	Revolutionary pension	30	1	Petition	717	Rev. Pensions	July 19, 1848	Favorable	610	Referred to Committee Whole House.		
Kinney, Amos, widow of	Revolutionary pension	30	2	Petition	121	Rev. Pensions.						
Kinney, Amos, widow of	Revolutionary pension	30	2	House bill	362	Whole House	Feb. 2, 1849	With't amend.	610	Passed.		
Kinney, Daniel	Arrears of pension	23	1	Petition	353	Rev. Pensions	....	....	....	Discharged; laid on table.		
Kinney, Daniel	Arrears of pension	23	2	Petition	256	Rev. Pensions.						
Kinney, Daniel	Arrears of pension	25	2	Petition	38	Rev. Pensions	Jan. 9, 1838	Favorable; bill	365	Passed.		
Kinney, David, widow of	Pension	30	1	Petition	682	Rev. Pensions	684	Favorable	546	Referred to Committee Whole House.		
Kinney, David, widow of	Pension	30	2	House bill	319	Whole House	Jan. 26, 1849	With't amend.	546	Passed.		
Kinney, Elizabeth	(See David Kinney, widow of)	30	1	....	682							
Kinney, Hannah	(See Amos Kinney, widow of)	30	1	....	717							
Kinney, James	Amount due from money due Indians.	29	1	Petition	160	Indian Affairs	287	Adverse	....	Laid on table.		
Kinney, James	Grant of land patent on payment of minimum price.	24	2	Petition	211	Public Lands	....	....	....	Discharged; laid on table.		
Kinney, John	Pension	21	1	Petition	36	Military Pensions	Mar. 30, 1830	....	....	Discharged; laid on table.		
Kinney, John, surety of	Release from liability	16	1	Petition	288	Ways and Means	....	....	....	Discharged	....	Leave to withdraw.
Kinney, Peter	Indemnity for money lost in United States mail.	31	1	Petition	310	P. Of. & P. Roads.	5	Adverse	....	Laid on table.		
Kinney, William, (Va.)	Revolutionary pension	17	1	Petition	45	Rev. Pensions.						
Kinney, William, (Va.)	Revolutionary pension	21	1	Resolution	244	Military Pensions	May 26, 1830	Favorable	491	Referred to Committee Whole House.		
Kinney, William, (Va.)	Revolutionary pension	21	2	House bill	318	Whole House	Feb. 4, 1831	With't amend.	491	Passed.		
Kinney, William, (Va.)	Revolutionary pension	22	1	Resolution	250	Rev. Pensions	....	....	....	....	....	See act June 4, 1832
Kinney, William, (Va.)	Indemnity for horse lost in United States service.	17	2	Petition	82	Claims.						
Kinnie, John W., (Ga.)	(See John McKinne)	24	2	....	80							
Kinnie, J. F., (judge)	Payment for official services	31	2	Resolution	428	Whole House	....	....	....	....	....	Paid out of contingent fund.
Kensey, Edmund, and William Smiley.	Release from payment of judgment	17	1	Petition	221	Judiciary	Feb. 12, 1822	Favorable; bill	84	Passed	Rejected.	
Kensey, Edmund, and William Smiley.	Release from payment of judgment	17	2	Petition	167	Judiciary	Feb. 13, 1823	Favorable; bill	292	Referred to Committee Whole House.		

List of private claims presented to the House of Representatives of the United States from the 1st to the 31st Congress, inclusive—Continued.

Names of claimants.	Nature or object of the claim.	Congress.	Session.	How brought before the House of Reps.	Page of journal.	To what committee of the House referred.	No. or date of the report.	Nature of the report.	No. of the bill.	How disposed of by the House of Reps.	How disposed of by the Senate.	Date of the act of Congress, and remarks.
Kinsey, H. L.	Indemnity for property stolen and destroyed.	31	1	Petition	810	Indian Affairs.						
Kinsley, Abraham H.	Pension	24	1	Petition	532	Invalid Pensions	...	...	...	Discharged; laid on table.		
Kinsley, Abraham H.	Pension	25	2	Petition	168	Invalid Pensions	329	Adverse	...	Laid on table.		
Kinsley, Adam, & Thomas French.	Additional compensation for arms furnished.	14	2	Petition	58	Claims.						
Kinsley, Adam, & Thomas French.	Additional compensation for arms furnished.	15	1	Petition	106	Claims	Mar. 24, 1818	Favorable	155	Referred to Committee Whole House.		
Kinsley, Adam, & Thomas French.	Additional compensation for arms furnished.	15	2	House bill	176	Whole House	Jan. 12, 1819	With amends.	155	Passed	Passed	App'd Feb. 20, 1819
Kinsman, Israel	(See Jonathan Davis and others)	13	2	...	177							
Kinsolving, P	Compensation for revolutionary services.	26	2	Petition	77	Rev. Claims	...	...	...	Discharged; laid on table.		
Kintzing, Abraham	Indemnity for French spoliations prior to 1800.	26	1	Memorial	182	Foreign Affairs	343	Favorable; bill	319	Referred to Committee Whole House.		
Kintzing & Pratt	(See Pratt & Kintzing)	5	3	...	431							
Kinzie & Forsythe	(See Kenzie & Forsyth)	12	2	...	671							
Kinzie, Robert, and others.	Confirmation of title to land	26	2	Senate bill	229	Indian Affairs	Feb. 12, 1841	With't amend.	157	Passed	Passed	App'd Feb. 18, 1841
Kipp, Peter, widow of	Pension	20	1	Petition	278	Military Pensions	...	...	...	Discharged; laid on table.		
Kipple, Lawrence	Pension	2	1	Petition	478	...	...	...	...	Referred to Secretary War.		
Kirby, Andrew J	Invalid pension	25	2	Resolution	533	Invalid Pensions.						
Kirby, Edmund, and others	Compensation as paymester	25	2	Memorial	327	Military Affairs.						
Cirby, Edmund, and others	Compensation as paymaster	26	1	Memorial	331	Military Affairs.						
Kirby, Colonel Edmund widow of.	Pension	31	1	Petition	768	Rev. Pensions	447	Adverse	...	Laid on table.		
Kirby, Eliza	(See Colonel Edmund Kirby, widow of.)	31	1	...	768							
Kirby, Joshua	Remission of duties, &c	3	1	Petition	75	...	...	...	...	Laid on table.		
Kirby, Robert B., widow of.	Pension	31	1	Petition	1014	Invalid Pensions.						
Kirk, Abraham	Claim not stated	14	2	Petition	485	...	...	...	...	Leave to withdraw.		
Kirk & Casper	(See Major John Campbell, heirs of.)	27	2	...	62							
Kirk, George	Revolutionary pension	30	1	Resolution	329	Rev. Pensions.						
Kirk, George J	Invalid pension	30	1	Petition	313	Rev. Pensions.						
Kirk, Job, guardian of the heirs of.	Half pay pension	15	2	Petition	154	Military Affairs.						
Kirk, John	Revolutionary pension	11	3	Documents	465	...	...	...	...	Referred to Secretary War.		
Kirk, John	Revolutionary pension	12	1	House bill	361	Whole House	June 15, 1812	With amends.	138	Passed	Passed	App'd July 5, 1812
Kirk, John	(See Kirk & Larkins, attorney of.)	26	1	...	182							
Kirk & Larkin, attorney of.	Indemnity for French spoliations prior to 1800.	26	1	Memorial	182	Foreign Affairs	342	Favorable; bill	319	Referred to Committee Whole House.		
Kirk, Nathan	Compensation for a horse and other property lost.	24	1	Petition	430	Claims.						
Kirk, Robert, heirs of	Commutation pay	31	1	Petition	225	Rev. Claims	...	...	...	Discharged; laid on table.		
Kirk, Ruth	(See Job Kirk, guardian of the heirs of.)	15	2	...	154							

List of private claims presented to the House of Representatives of the United States from the 1st to the 31st Congress, inclusive—Continued.

Names of claimants.	Nature or object of the claim.	Congress.	Session.	How brought before the House of Reps.	Page of journal.	To what committee of the House referred.	No. or date of the report.	Nature of the report.	No. of the bill.	How disposed of by the House of Reps.	How disposed of by the Senate.	Date of the act of Congress, and remarks.
Kirk, Sarah, and others	(See John Campbell, heirs of.)	21	1		295							
Kirkham, Robert	Indemnity for damages by troops.	30	2	Memorial	140	Claims				Disch'd; laid on table.		
Kirkpatrick, John, and others.	(See James Roddy and others, executors of.)	18	1		287							
Kirkpatrick, John (Ind.)	Scrip for money paid on land which has been forfeited.	23	1	Senate bill	395	Public Lands	Mar. 11, 1834	With amends.	55	Passed	Passed	App'd June 30, 1834
Kirkpatrick, Kesiah, and others.	Extension of act granting 5 years pension.	27	2	Petition	69	Rev. Pensions	784	Adverse		Laid on table.		See act Aug. 23, 1842
Kiskum, Philomon	Pension	21	2	Petition	53	Military Pensions.						
Kirkwood, Capt., Robert administrator of.	Relief to his orphan children	2	2	Petition	634					Laid on table.		
Kirlin, Jacob	(See John Kirlin, executors of.)	18	2		229							
Kirlin, John, executor of	Additional compensation for arms furnished U. S. in 1808.	18	2	Petition	229	Claims.						
Kirlin, John, executor of	Additional compensation for arms furnished U. S. in 1808.	19	1	Petition	131	Claims	108	Favorable; bill	142	Passed.		
Kirlin, John, executor of	Additional compensation for arms furnished U. S. in 1808.	19	2	Petition	64	Claims	Dec. 20, 1826	By bill	309	Passed	Passed	App'd March 2, 1827
Kirper, Julius	Compensation for occupation of house and property destroyed by troops.	2	2	Petition	680					Laid on table.		
Kirshner, Michael	Pension	19	1	Petition	82	Military Pensions	164	Adverse		Laid on table.		
Kirtland, Elizur	Revolutionary pension	23	2	Petition	120	Rev. Pensions.						
Kirtland, Elizur	Revolutionary pension	25	2	Petition	729	Rev. Pensions	884	Adverse		Laid on table.		
Kisby, Richard	Pension	10	1	House bill	232	Whole House	April 19, 1808	With amend.	78	Passed	Passed	App'd April 25, 1808
Kiser James, and Barnett Foley.	Pre-emption right to land	27	2	Senate bill	411	Public Lands	May 8, 1842	With't amend.	117	Passed	Passed	App'd June 4, 1842
Kissam, Benjamin, widow of.	Pension	20	2	Memorial	345	Naval Affairs	103	Adverse		Laid on table.		
Kissam, Benjamin, widow of.	Pension	21	1	Memorial	84	Naval Affairs.						
Kissam, Harriet J.	(See Benjamin Kissam, widow of.)	20	2		315							
Kitchell, Asa	(See Samuel Dick and others.)	9	1		236							
Kitchen, Abraham	Pension	22	1	Resolution	203	Invalid Pensions						See act June 4, 1832
Kitchen, Benjamin	Revolutionary pension	27	2	Resolution	328	Rev. Pensions	July 21, 1842	Adverse		Laid on table.		
Kitchen, Benjamin	Revolutionary pension	28	1	Petition	874	Rev. Pensions.						
Kitchens, James	Correction of land entry	23	1	Petition	332	Public Lands	Mar. 5, 1834	Favorable; bill	347	Passed	Laid on table.	
Kitchie, James	Compensation, work and materials furnished on Cumberland road.	23	1	Res. and papers.	589	Claims	455	Adverse		Laid on table.		
Kitterland, John	Pre-emption right to land.	26	1	Petition	610	Priv. Land Claims						See act June 1, 1840
Kittle, Simeon D.	(See Alphonso Wetmore, surety of.)	26	1		297							
Kittredge, Joseph, & others	(See William Kittredge, heirs of.)	2	1		521							
Kittredge, William, heirs of	Renewal of certain certificates of settlement, destroyed by fire.	2	1	Petition and rep't Sec. Treasury.	521	Select.						
Kettridge, Joseph W.	Remission of duties on salt	21	1	Petition	260	Ways and Means				Disch'd; laid on table.		
Kitzmiller, A. M	Increase of salary as clerk	28	1	Petition	78	Military Affairs	Jan. 31, 1844	Adverse		Laid on table.		
Kitzmiller, A. M	Increase of salary as clerk	29	1	Petition	93	Military Affairs				Discharged; laid on table.		
Klacner, D.	Remission of certain duties	29	1	Memorial	1031	Commerce.						
Klaus, Catharine	Confirmation of title to land	30	2	Memorial	241	Public Lands.						
Kleiss, Daniel	Compensat'n for services as armorer.	27	2	Senate bill	680	Claims	Jan. 11, 1842	Favorable; bill	138	Passed		App'd Aug. 11, 1842
Kline, Abraham, representatives of.	Permission to locate land	25	2	Petition	596	Priv. Land Claims.						

List of private claims presented to the House of Representatives of the United States from the 1st to the 31st Congress, inclusive—Continued.

Names of claimants.	Nature or object of the claim.	Congress.	Session.	How brought before the House of Reps.	Page of journal.	To what committee of the House referred.	No. or date of the report.	Nature of the report.	No. of the bill.	How disposed of by the House of Reps.	How disposed of by the Senate.	Date of the act of Congress, and remarks.
Kline, Christian	Payment of balance due on contract.	17	1	Petition	361	Claims.						
Kline, Conrad	Pension	20	2	Petition	143	Military Pensions				Discharged; laid on table.		
Kline, Francis and John, representatives of.	Revolutionary pension	29	2	Petition	169	Rev. Pensions.						
Kline, George S	Pension	31	1	Petition	1040	Invalid Pensions.						
Kline, Jacob, and others	Separation of interest in the case of brig "Bayard."	25	3	Petition	119	Foreign Affairs.						
Kline, John	(See Francis and John Kline, representatives of.)	29	2		169							
Kline, John	Pension	20	1	Petition	310	Military Pensions				Discharged; laid on table.		
Kline, John	Pension	20	2	Petition	74	Military Pensions				Discharged; laid on table.		
Kline, John	Arrears of pension	29	1	Petition	265	Invalid Pensions	505	Adverse		Laid on table.		
Kline, John L., Lieutenant	To refund money paid on judgment.	27	2	Petition	55	Claims	Dec. 29, 1841	Favorable; bill	40	Passed	Passed	App'd July 9, 1842
Kline, Nicholas	Pension	20	2	Petition	26	Military Pensions.						
Kline, Nicholas	Pension	21	1	Petition	197	Military Pensions.						
Klockgethe, W	(See Louis F. Beeler and others)	30	1		115		482					
Klump, Jeremiah	Pension	23	1	Petition	436	Rev. Pensions				Discharged; laid on table.		
Knaggs, George	(See Whitmore Knaggs, heirs of)	23	2		200							
Knaggs, John	Pre-emption right to land	23	1	Petition	309	Priv. Land Claims.	301	Favorable; bill	337	Referred to Committee Whole House.		
Knaggs, John	Pre-emption right to land	24	1	Petition	156	Priv. Land Claims.	Jan. 14, 1836	Adverse		Laid on table.		
Knaggs, Whitmore	Confirmation of title to land	10	1	Petition	98	Public Lands.						
Knaggs, Whitmore	Confirmation of title to land	10	2	Petition	510	Public Lands.						
Knaggs, Whitmore	Confirmation of title to land	12	1	Petition	183	Public Lands.						
Knaggs, Whitmore	Confirmation of title to land	15	1	Report of Com'r of Claims.	256	Claims						See act May 11, 1820
Knaggs, Whitmore, heirs of	Indemnity for property destroyed	21	1	Petition	235	Claims.						
Knaggs, Whitmore, heirs of	Indemnity for property destroyed	23	2	Petition	200	Claims.						
Knaggs, Whitmore, heirs of	Indemnity for property destroyed	24	1	Petition	153	Claims.						
Knaggs, Whitmore, heirs of	Indemnity for property destroyed	31	2	Petition	37	Claims.						
Knapp, Abiel	Pension	11	2	House bill	283	Whole House	April 10, 1810	Favorable	107	Passed	Passed	App'd April 28, 1810
Knapp, Amos	Pension	30	1	Petition	647	Invalid Pensions.						
Knapp, Amos	Pension	30	2	Petition	366	Invalid Pensions				Discharged; laid on table.		
Knapp, Amos	Pension	31	1	Petition	337	Invalid Pensions	477	Favorable; bill	374	Referred to Committee Whole House.		
Knapp, Anthony	Indemnity for French spoliations prior to 1800.	26	1	Petition	182	Foreign Affairs	343	Favorable	319	Referred to Committee Whole House.		
Knapp, Anthony, administrator of.	Indemnity for French spoliations prior to 1800.	31	1	Petition	337	Foreign Affairs	355	Favorable; bill	318	Referred to Committee Whole House.		
Knapp, Charity	(See Joshua Knapps, (N. Y.,) widow of.)	27	3		252							
Knapp, Elijah	Revolutionary pension	2	1	Petition	451					Referred to Secretary War.		
Knapp, Elijah	Revolutionary pension	3	1	Rep. of Secretary War.	131	Select	May 26, 1794	Favorable; bill	62	Passed	Passed	App'd June 7, 1794
Knapp, Isaac	Pension	19	2	Petition	131	Military Pensions.						
Knapp, Isaac	Pension	21	1	Petition	377	Military Pensions				Discharged; laid on table.		

List of private claims presented to the House of Representatives of the United States from the 1st to the 31st Congress, inclusive—Continued.

Names of claimants.	Nature or object of the claim.	Congress.	Session.	How brought before the House of Reps.	Page of journal.	To what committee of the House referred.	No. or date of the report.	Nature of the report.	No. of the bill.	How disposed of by the House of Reps.	How disposed of by the Senate.	Date of the act of Congress, and remarks.
Knapp, Jabez	Compensation for revolutionary services.	4	1	Petition	425	Claims	May 7, 1797	Adverse		Rejected		Leave to withdraw.
Knapp, Jared	Pension	3	1	Rep. of Secretary War.	131	Select	May 26, 1794	Favorable; bill	62	Passed	Passed	App'd June 7, 1794
Knapp, Jared	Increase of pension	11	3	House bill	604	Whole House		Favorable; bill	218	Passed	Passed	App'd March 3, 1811
Knapp, Joel	Pension	1	2	Petition and rept' Sec. of War.	207	Select.						
Knapp, John H. and Nathaniel.	Confirmation of title to land	24	1	Petition	612	Public Lands						See act July 2, 1836
Knapp, Joshua, of N. Y., widow of.	Revolutionary pension	27	3	Petition	252	Rev. Pensions.						
Knapp, Joshua, widow of, (Ohio.)	Revolutionary pension	28	1	Petition	685	Rev. Pensions.						
Knapp, Josiah	Indemnity for French spoliations prior to 1800.	26	1	Memorial	182	Foreign Affairs	343	Favorable; bill	319	Referred to Committee Whole House.		
Knapp, Lodema	(See Joshua Knapp, widow of, Ohio)	28	1		685							
Knapp, Mary	Pension	26	1	Resolution	555	Rev. Pensions	423	Adverse		Laid on table.		
Knapp, Shadrach	Pension	21	1	Petition	294	Military Pensions	May 4, 1830	Adverse		Laid on table.		
Knapp, T. S.	Arrears due on a claim	21	2	House bill	223	Whole House	Feb. 17, 1831	With amend	584	Passed	Passed	App'd March 2, 1831
Knapp, Uzal	Compensation for revolutionary services.	4	1	Petition	425	Claims	May 7, 1796	Adverse		Rejected.		Leave to withdraw.
Knause, John	(See Richard Brannin and others.)	25	3		205		207					
Knecht, Jacob	Revolutionary pension	25	2	Petition	585	Rev. Pensions				Discharged; laid on table.		
Kneedigh, John	Pension	18	2	Petition	41	Pens. & Rev. Cl'ms.	Dec. 22, 1824	Adverse		Laid on table.		
Kneffenberger, Henry, and others.	(See Johnson Shrum, *et al.*)	31	1		730							
Knepley, Ann	(See James Butler, heirs of.)	26	1		173							
Knies, Michael, heirs of	Revolutionary pension	23	1	Petition	110	Rev. Claims.						
Knies, Michael, heirs of	Revolutionary pension	24	1	Petition	63	Rev. Claims.						
Knies, Michael, heirs of	Revolutionary pension	24	2	Petition	270	Rev. Claims.						
Knight, Amos	Indemnity for French spoliations prior to 1800.	26	1	Memorial	182	Foreign Affairs	343	Favorable; bill	319	Referred to Committee Whole House.		
Knight, Benjamin	Pension	3	2	Rep. of Secretary War.	350	Claims.						
Knight, Benjamin	Pension	4	1	Rep. of Secretary War.	445	Claims	Mar. 4, 1796	Favorable; bill	156	Passed	Passed	App'd April 20, 1796
Knight, Elijah	Pension	4	1	Rep. of Secretary War.	445	Claims	Mar. 4, 1796	Favorable; bill	156	Passed	Passed	App'd April 20, 1796
Knight, Elijah	Increase of pension	12	1	House bill	361	Whole House	June 15, 1812	With amend't.	138	Passed	Passed	App'd July 5, 1812
Knight, Elizabeth	(See James Knight, widow of)	28	1		707							
Knight, George J.	Indemnity for a vessel captured and destroyed.	21	1	Petition	446	Commerce.						
Knight, George J.	Indemnity for a vessel captured and destroyed.	21	2	Petition	158	Naval Affairs	89	Favorable; bill	640	Referred to Committee Whole House.		
Knight, George J.	Indemnity for a vessel captured and destroyed.	22	1	Petition	63	Naval Affairs	47	Favorable; bil	99	Passed	Passed	App'd May 25, 1832
Knight, George J.	Additional indemnity for a vessel captured and destroyed.	22	2	Petition	105	Naval Affairs.						
Knight, George J.	Additional indemnity for a vessel captured and destroyed.	23	1	Petition	128	Naval Affairs	Mar. 4, 1834	Adverse		Laid on table.		
Knight, George J.	Additional indemnity for a vessel captured and destroyed.	24	2	Senate bill	552	Claims			S. 120			

List of private claims presented to the House of Representatives of the United States from the 1st to the 31st Congress, inclusive—Continued.

Names of claimants.	Nature or object of the claim.	Congress.	Session.	How brought before the House of Reps.	Page of journal.	To what committee of the House referred.	No. or date of the report.	Nature of the report.	No. of the bill.	How disposed of by the House of Reps.	How disposed of by the Senate.	Date of the act of Congress, and remarks.
Knight, George J.	Additional indemnity for a vessel captured and destroyed.	25	2	Senate bill	994	Claims	1055	Adverse	195	Referred to Committee Whole House.		
Knight, George J.	Additional indemnity for a vessel captured and destroyed.	25	3	Resolution	399	Claims.						
Knight, George J.	Additional indemnity for a vessel captured and destroyed.	29	1	Petition	327	Claims	226	Adverse		Laid on table.		
Knight, George J.	Additional indemnity for a vessel captured and destroyed.	30	1	Petition	398	Claims				Discharged; laid on table.		
Knight, George J.	Additional indemnity for a vessel captured and destroyed.	30	2	Petition	664					Leave to withdraw.		
Knight, James, widow of.	Revolutionary pension	28	1	Memorial	707	Rev. Pensions						See act June 17, 1844
Knight, James D.	Payment of freight on Mexican indemnity.	28	2	Petition	145	Naval Affairs	Jan. 28, 1845	Adverse		Laid on table.		
Knight, J. B., and others.	Fishing bounty on schooner Martha.	26	1	Petition	199	Commerce.						
Knight, J. B., and others.	Fishing bounty on schooner Martha.	27	2	Petition	95	Commerce	296	Favorable; bill	227	Referred to Committee Whole House.		
Knight, J. B., and others.	Fishing bounty on schooner Martha.	27	3	House bill	87	Whole House			227	Passed	Indef. postp'd.	
Knight, John, (N. H.)	Pension	2	2	Rep. of Secretary War.	735					Laid on table.		
Knight, John, (N. H.)	Pension	3	2	Rep. of Secretary War.	278	Claims	Mar. 2, 1795	Refer'd to Sec. War.		Apopted.		
Knight, John, (N. H.)	Pension	4	1	Rep. of Secretary War.	445	Claims	Mar. 4, 1796	Favorable; bill	156	Passed	Passed	App'd April 20, 1796
Knight, John, (Ky.)	Compensation for services as surgeon's mate, revolutionary war.	1	3	Petition	376					Referred to Secretary of War.		
Knight, John, (Ky.)	Commutation of half-pay, revolutionary war.	11	2	Petition	238	Claims				Discharged; laid on table.		
Knight, John, (Ky.)	Commutation of half-pay, revolutionary war.	19	2	Petition	59	Rev. Claims	Jan. 29, 1827	Adverse		Laid on table.		
Knight, John, (Ky.)	Commutation of half pay, revolutionary war.	21	1	Petition	359	Rev. Claims	Mar. 9, 1830	Favorable; bill	333	Referred to Committee Whole House.		
Knight, John, (Ky.)	Commutation of half-pay, revolutionary war.	21	2	House bill	340	Whole House	Feb. 22, 1831	With't amend.	333	Passed.		
Knight, John, (Ky.)	Commutation of half-pay, revolutionary war.	22	1	Petition	29	Rev. Claims	Dec. 27, 1831	Favorable; bill	130	Passed	Passed	App'd June 15, 1832
Knight, John, widow of, (N. C.)	Revolutionary pension	29	1	Petition	435	Rev. Pensions.						
Knight, John, widow of, (N. C.)	Revolutionary pension	29	2	Petition	150	Rev. Pensions	27	Adverse		Laid on table.		
Knight, John, widow of, (N. C.)	Revolutionary pension	30	1	Petition	230	Rev. Pensions	441	Adverse		Laid on table.		
Knight, John, widow of, (N. C.)	Revolutionary pension	31	1	Petition	415	Rev. Pensions	129	Adverse		Laid on table.		
Knight, John, (Md.)	Pension	29	1	Memorial	888	Invalid Pensions.						
Knight, John, (Md.)	Pension	30	1	Petition and docs.	124	Claims	391	Favorable; bill	342	Passed.		
Knight, Jonathan. (Conn.)	Restoration of pension	17	1	Petition	159	Whole House	Mar. 25, 1822	With't amends	37	Passed	Indef. postp'd.	
Knight, Dr. Jonathan, heirs of.	Commutation of half pay	23	1	Petition	306	Rev. Claims.						
Knight, Dr. Jonathan, heirs of.	Commutation of half-pay	24	1	Petition	763	Rev. Claims	617	Adverse		Laid on table.		

List of private claims presented to the House of Representatives of the United States from the 1st to the 31st Congress, inclusive—Continued.

Names of claimants.	Nature or object of the claim.	Congress.	Session.	How brought before the House of Reps.	Page of journal.	To what committee of the House referred.	No. or date of the report.	Nature of the report.	No. of the bill.	How disposed of by the House of Reps.	How disposed of by the Senate.	Date of the act of Congress, and remarks.
Knight, Dr. Jonathan, heirs of.	Commutation of half pay	25	2	Petition	49	Rev. Claims.						
Knight, Dr. Jonathan, heirs of.	Commutation of half-pay	25	3	Petition	84	Rev. Claims.						
Knight, Joseph, administrator of.	Indemnity for French spoliations prior to 1800.	26	1	Memorial	182	Foreign Affairs	343	Favorable; bill	319	Referred to Committee Whole House.		
Knight, Joseph	Compensation for revolutionary services.	21	1	Resolution	136	Invalid Pensions	173	Favorable; bill	246	Referred to Committee Whole House.		
Knight, Joseph	Compensation for revolutionary services.	22	2	Resolution	27	Invalid Pensions	8	Favorable; bill	627	Passed	Passed	App'd Feb. 20, 1833
Knight, Josiah, heirs of	Arrears of pension	31	1	Petition	501	Rev. Pensions	463	Adverse	......	Laid on table.		
Knight, Riley	Compensation for losses and injuries	28	2	Petition	84	Claims.						
Knight, Sarah	(See John Knight, widow of.)	29	1	....	435							
Knight, Simeon	Credit for money paid for subsistence.	11	3	Petition	446	Claims	Feb. 14, 1811	Favorable; bill	207	Indefinitely postponed.		
Knight, Simeon	Credit for money paid for subsistence.	12	1	Petition	146	Claims	229	Favorable; bill	68	Referred to Committee Whole House.		
Knight, Simeon	Credit for money paid for subsistence.	25	2	Petition	176	Indian Affairs	1025	Adverse	......	Laid on table.		
Knight, Simeon, widow of.	Credit for money paid for subsistence.	27	3	Petition	175	Military Affairs.						
Knight, Simeon, widow of.	Credit for money paid for subsistence.	28	1	Petition	862	Claims.						
Knight, Simeon, (N. Y.).	Pension	25	2	Petition	401	Invalid Pensions	646	Favorable; bill	622	Passed	Adverse.	
Knight, Simeon, (N. Y.).	Pension	26	1	Petition	162	Invalid Pensions	227	Favorable; bill	239	Passed	Indef. postp'd.	
Knight, Susannah	(See John Knight, widow of.)	30	1	....	230							
Knight, Thomas	(See John Jordan, and others)	3	1	....	83							
Knights, Thomas, & others	(See Thomas Knight, heirs of)	25	2	....	181							
Knights, Thomas, heirs of.	Compensation for revolutionary services.	25	2	Petition	181	Rev. Pensions.						
Knipe, Christian	Payment for a wagon impressed	1	3	Rep. of Secretary Treasury.	391	....	....	....	......	Refered to Secretary of Treasury.		
Knipe, Christian	Payment for a wagon impressed	2	1	Rep. of Secretary Treasury.	580	....	....	....	......	Laid on table.		
Knipe, Henry	Revolutionary pension	19	1	Petition	149	Military Pensions	164	Adverse	......	Laid on table.		
Knipe, Henry	Revolutionary pension	20	1	Petition	311	Military Pensions	....	....	......	....	....	See act May 15 & 24, 1828.
Knipe, Joseph W.	Pension	25	2	Petition	57	Invalid Pensions	459	Favorable; bill	462	Passed	Adverse report.	
Knipe, Joseph W.	Pension	26	1	Petition	161	Invalid Pensions	206	Favorable; bill	218	Passed	Indef postp'd.	
Knipe, Joseph W.	Pension	27	2	Petition	154	Invalid Pensions	Feb. 9, 1842	Adverse	......	Laid on table.		
Knipe, Joseph W.	Pension	29	2	Petition	181	Invalid Pensions	....	....	......	Discharged; laid on table.		
Knipe, Joseph W.	Pension	30	1	Petition	759	Invalid Pensions	807	Adverse	......	Laid on table.		
Knobb, Jehu	Pension	25	2	Memorial	984	Rev. Pensions.						
Knoechel, Elizabeth Margaret.	(See Victor Christian Chas. Knoechel.)	4	1	....	446							
Knoechel, Victor Christian Charles.	Revolutionary pension	4	1	Petition	446	Claims	May 31, 1796	Adverse	......	Laid on table.		
Knoggs, Thomas, widow of	Indemnity for Indian depredations	28	1	Petition	517	Claims.						
Knolton, Anna	Seven years' half-pay	3	2	Petition	316	Claims.						
Knolton, Anna	Seven years' half-pay	4	1	Report of Com. of Claims.	428	....	....	Adverse	......	Leave to withdraw.		
Knott, John	Pension	30	1	Papers	124	Claims.						

List of private claims presented to the House of Representatives of the United States from the 1st to the 31st Congress, inclusive—Continued.

Names of claimants.	Nature or object of the claim.	Congress.	Session.	How brought before the House of Reps.	Page of journal.	To what committee of the House referred.	No. or date of the report.	Nature of the report.	No. of the bill.	How disposed of by the House of Reps.	How disposed of by the Senate.	Date of the act of Congress, and remarks.
Knott, Wilford	Pension	24	1	Petition	691	Invalid Pensions	649	Adverse		Laid on table.		
Knott, Wilford	Pension	25	2	Petition	406	Invalid Pensions	649	Favorable; bill	625	Passed	Adverse.	
Knott, Wilford	Pension	26	1	Petition	289	Invalid Pensions	230	Favorable; bill	242	Passed	Indef. postp'd.	
Knott, Wilford	Pension	26	2	Petition	276	Invalid Pensions	144	Favorable; bill	655	Referred to Committee Whole House.		
Knott, Wilford, heirs of	Pension	27	3	Petition	140	Invalid Pensions	156	Adverse		Laid on table.		
Knott, Wilford, heirs of	Pension	28	1	Petition	142	Invalid Pensions	Jan. 31, 1844	Adverse		Laid on table.		
Knott, Wilford, heirs of	Pension	28	2	Petition	250	Invalid Pensions.						
Knott, Wilford, heirs of	Pension	29	1	Petition	70	Invalid Pensions	658	Favorable; bill	441	Referred to Committee Whole House.		
Knott, Wilford, heirs of	Pension	29	2	House bill	211	Whole House	Jan. 22, 1847	With't amend.	441	Passed	Passed	App'd March 3, 1847
Knott, Wilford, heirs of	Pension	30	1	Petition	299	Invalid Pensions	464	Adverse		Laid on table.		
Knower & Bronson	(See Thos. Tupper, assignees of)	22	2		142							
Knowles, Benjamin B.	Pension	19	2	Petition	104	Military Pensions.						
Knowles, Charles, heirs of	Compensat'n for services, and commutation pay, &c.	9	2	Petition	471	Claims	Dec. 11, 1806	Adverse		Leave to withdraw.		
Knowles, Charles & James	Revolutionary pension	18	1	Petition	113	Pens. & Rev. Cl'ms.	Mar. 10, 1824	Adverse		Leave to withdraw.		
Knowles, Daniel	Indemnity for defect in title to land	23	2	Petition	164	Judiciary.						
Knowles, Daniel	Indemnity for defect in title to land	24	1	Petition	106	Judiciary						See act July 2, 1836
Knowles, Ezekiel	Pension	16	1	Petition	42	Pens. & Rev. Cl'ms.						
Knowles, Ezekiel	Pension	17	1	Petition	37	Rev. Pensions.						
Knowles, Ezekiel	Pension	18	1	Petition	36	Pens. & Rev. Cl'ms.				Leave to withdraw.		
Knowles, Ezekiel	Pension	19	1	Petition	290	Military Pensions	164	Adverse		Laid on table.		
Knowles, Ezekiel	Pension	20	1	Petition	365	Military Pensions.						
Knowles, Ezekiel	Pension	21	1	Petition	48	Military Pensions	Jan. 5, 1830	Favorable; bil	72	Passed		App'd May 20, 1830
Knowles, Ezekiel	Pension	22	2	Petition	114	Invalid Pensions.						
Knowles, Ezekiel	Pension	23	1	Petition	119	Invalid Pensions	Jan. 31, 1834	Adverse		Laid on table.		
Knowles, Hazard	Grant of a patent	25	2	Petition	595	Patents	April 12, 1838	Favorable; bill	736	Referred to Committee Whole House.		
Knowles, Hazard	Grant of a patent	25	3	House bill	381	Whole House			736			
Knowles, Hazard	Grant of a patent	26	1	Petition	181	Patents.						
Knowles, Hazard	Relief from disability to receive a patent.	26	1	Senate bill	811	Patents	April 25, 1840	With't amend.	160	Referred to Committee Whole House.		
Knowles, Hazard	Grant of a patent.	26	2	Petition	135	Patents.						
Knowles, Hazard	Grant of a patent	27	2	Petition	240	Patents	670	Favorable; bill	400	Referred to Committee Whole House.		
Knowles, Henry	Indemnity for horse impressed	22	2	Petition	218	Claims.						
Knowles, Henry	Indemnity for horse impressed	23	1	Petition	305	Claims	504	Favorable; bill	509	Referred to Committee Whole House.		
Knowles, Henry	Indemnity for horse impressed	24	1	Petition	51	Claims	20	Favorable; bill	20	Passed	Passed	App'd Feb. 17, 1836
Knowles, John, of Maine	Pension	3	2	Rep. of Secretary War.	278	Claims	Feb. 28, 1795	Favorable; bill	130	Passed	Postponed.	
Knowles, John, of Maine	Pension	4	1	Rep. of Secretary War.	445	Claims	Feb. 18, 1796	Favorable; bill	156	Passed	Passed	App'd April 20, 1796
Knowles, John, (N. C.)	Invalid pension	4	1	Report and docs.	447	Claims	Mar. 7, 1796	Favorable; bil	156	Passed	Passed	App'd April 20, 1796
Knowles, John, (England.)	Grant of a patent.	22	1	Petition	557	Patents	May 2, 1832			Laid on table.		
Knowles, Joshua, jr.	Fishing bounty on schooner Garnet.	27	2	Petition	829	Commerce	1091	Favorable; bill	605	Referred to Committee Whole House.		
Knowles, Joshua, jr.	Fishing bounty on schooner Garnet.	27	3	House bill	91	Whole House			605	Passed	Indef. postp'd.	
Knowles, Joshua, jr.	Fishing bounty on schooner Garnet.	28	1	Petition	289	Commerce	225	Favorable; bill	179	Passed	Adverse.	

2—34

List of private claims presented to the House of Representatives of the United States from the 1st to the 31st Congress, inclusive—Continued.

Names of claimants.	Nature or object of the claim.	Congress.	Session.	How brought before the House of Reps.	Page of journal.	To what committee of the House referred.	No. or date of the report.	Nature of the report.	No. of the bill.	How disposed of by the House of Reps.	How disposed of by the Senate.	Date of the act of Congress, and remarks.
Knowles, Joshua, jr	Fishing bounty on schooner Garnet.	28	2	Petition	73	Commerce.						
Knowles, Joshua. jr	Fishing bounty on schooner Garnet.	29	1	Petition	106	Commerce	262	Favorable; bill	224	Referred to Committee Whole House.		
Knowles, Joshua, jr	Fishing bounty on schooner Garnet.	30	1	Petition	289	Commerce.						
Knowles, Lucy, and Margaret Williams.	(See Richard Fortune.)	25	2		771							
Knowles, Seth	Allowance of debenture on rum exported.	19	2	Petition	78	Ways and Means	Jan. 2, 1827	Favorable; bill	333	Referred to Committee Whole House.		
Knowles, Seth	Allowance of debenture on rum exported.	20	1	Petition	45	Ways and Means	131	Favorable; bill	152	Passed	Passed	App'd May 26, 1828
Knowles, Thomas, & others	(See Elish Abil and others.)	22	1		260							
Knowles, Zacheus	Fishing bounty on schooner Flo rilla.	27	2	Petition	822	Commerce.						
Knowles, Zacheus	Fishing bounty on schooner Florilla.	27	3	Petition	45	Commerce	174	Favorable; bill	786	Referred to Committee Whole House.		
Knowles, Zacheus	Fishing bounty on schooner Florilla.	28	1	Petition	289	Commerce	226	Favorable	180	Passed	Adverse.	
Knowles, Zacheus	Fishing bounty on schooner Florilla.	28	2	Petition	73	Commerce	62	Favorable	540	Referred to Committee Whole House.		
Knowles, Zacheus	Fishing bounty on schooner Florilla.	29	1	Petition	105	Commerce	95	Favorable; bill	114	Rejected.		
Knowles, Zacheus	Fishing bounty on schooner Florilla.	30	1	Petition	289	Commerce.						
Knowlton, Frederick	(See Col. Thomas Knowlton, heirs of.)	29	1		172							
Knowlton, Sally	(See Elijah Bragdon, widow of.)	29	1		102							
Knowlton, Col. Thomas, heirs of.	Compensation and emoluments for revolutionary services.	15	1	Petition	140	Pens. & Rev. Cl'ms.						
Knowlton, Col. Thomas, heirs of.	Compensation and emoluments for revolutionary serv ces.	15	2	Petition	85	Pens. & Rev. Cl'ms	Dec. 11, 1818	Adverse		Rejected.		
Knowlton, Col. Thomas, heirs of.	Compensation and emoluments for revolutionary s rvices.	23	1	Petition	54	Rev. Cla'ms.						
Knowlton, Col. Thomas, heirs of.	Commutation of seven years' half-pay.	23	1	Petition	70	Rev. Claims.						
Knowlton, Col. Thomas, heirs of.	Commutation of seven years' half-pay.	23	2	Petition	113	Rev. Claims.						
Knowlton, Col. Thomas, heirs of.	Commutation of seven years' half-pay.	24	1	Petition	63	Rev. Claims	238	Favorable; bill	243	Referred to Committee Whole House.		
Knowlton, Col. Thomas, heirs of.	Commutation of seven years' half-pay.	24	2	House bill	62	Whole House			243			
Knowlton, Col. Thomas, heirs of.	Commutation of seven years' half-pay.	25	2	Petition	40	Rev. Claims	130	Favorable; bill	148	Passed.		
Knowlton, Col. Thomas, heirs of.	Commutation of seven years' half-pay.	25	3	House bill	183	Whole House			940			
Knowlton, Col. Thomas, heirs of.	Commutation of seven years' half-pay.	26	1	Petition	165	Rev. Claims.						
Knowlton, Col. Thomas, heirs of.	Commutation of seven years' half-pay.	26	2	Petition	35	Rev. Claims	118	Favorable; bill	623	Referred to Committee Whole House.		
Knowlton, Col. Thomas, heirs of.	Commutation of seven years' half-pay.	27	2	Petition	1372	Rev. Claims	1078	Adverse		Laid on table.		

List of private claims presented to the House of Representatives of the United States from the 1st to the 31st Congress, inclusive—Continued.

Names of claimants.	Nature or object of the claim.	Congress.	Session.	How brought before the House of Reps.	Page of journal.	To what committee of the House referred.	No. or date of the report.	Nature of the report.	No. of the bill.	How disposed of by the House of Reps.	How disposed of by the Senate.	Date of the act of Congress, and remarks.
Knowlton, Col. Thomas, heirs of.	Commutation of seven years' half pay.	28	2	Petition	208	Rev. Claims.						
Knowlton, Col. Thomas, heirs of.	Commutation of seven years' half pay.	29	1	Petition	172	Rev. Claims	365	Favorable; bill	276	Referred to Committee Whole House.		
Knox, Andrew, and B. S. Pope.	Indemnity for ship captured by the British.	12	1	Petition	137					Referred to Secretary State.		
Knox, Andrew, (Ala.)	Pre-emption right to land	23	1	Senate bill	170	Public Lands			S. 36			
Knox, Andrew, (Ala.)	Pre-emption right to land	23	2	Senate bill	244	Priv. Land Claims.	Jan. 26, 1835	With't amend.	49	Referred to Committee Whole House.		
Knox, Andrew, (Ala.)	Pre-emption right to land	24	2	Petition	107	Priv. Land Claims.						
Knox, Andrew, (Ala.)	Pre emption right to land	24	2	Senate bill	280	Public Lands	Feb. 2, 1831	With't amend.	105	Passed	Passed	App'd Feb. 3, 1837
Knox, Benjamin, and Geo. Lgier.	(See United Society of Shakers.)	17	2		22							
Knox, Catharine	(See Saul Knox, widow of.)	29	1		86							
Knox, David	Restoration of pension	17	2	Petition	223	Rev. Pensions				Discharged; laid on table.		
Knox, Ebenezer	Pay and emoluments during suspension.	15	1	Petition	222	Claims	Feb. 26, 1818	Adverse		Rejected.		
Knox, George	Indemnity for French spoliations prior to 1800.	26	1	Memorial	182	Foreign Affairs	343	Favorable; bill	319	Referred to Committee Whole House.		
Knox, George, administrator o	Indemnity for French spoliations prior to 1800.	29	2	Memorial	292	Foreign Affairs	Feb. 9, 1847	By bill	561	Referred to Committee Whole House.		
Knox, Isaac	Pension	23	1	Petition	418	Invalid Pensions				Discharged; laid on table.		
Knox, Isaac	Pension	24	1	Petition	753	Rev. Pensions				Discharged; laid on table.		
Knox, James, devisee of	Compensation for revolutionary services and interest.	29	1	Petition	199	Invalid Pensions.						
Knox, James, devisee of	Compensation for revolutionary services and interest.	31	1	Petition	542	Claims.						
Knox, Jonathan	Pension	22	1	Petition	122	Rev. Pensions	Dec. 29, 1831	Adverse		Laid on table.		
Knox, Joseph, (N. Y.)	Payment of money advanced United States, and for transportation of military stores.	10	1	Petition	15	Select.						
Knox, Patrick	Renewal of lost certificate	2	2	Petition	618	Whole House.						
Knox, Robert, heirs of	Confirmation of title to land	12		Petition	316	Public Lands.						
Knox, Robert, heirs of	Confirmation of title to land	12	2	Petition	663	Public Lands.						
Knox, Robert, heirs, of	Confirmation of title to land	17	1	Petition	474	Priv. Land Claims.						
Knox, Robert, heirs of	Confirmation of title to land	26	1	Petition	798	Priv. Land Claims.						
Knox, Robert, (England)	Remission of tonnage duty	18	1	Petition	48	Ways and Means.						
Knox, Robert, (Ky.)	Increase of pension	24	1	Petition	670	Rev. Pensions				Disch'd; laid on table		
Knox, Saul, widow of	Revolutionary pension	29	1	Petition	86	Rev. Pensions.						
Knox, Thomas, (Pa.)	Pension	20	1	Petition	338	Military Pensions.						
Knox, William, widow of	Revolutionary pension	3	1	Petition	86	Select	Mar. 31, 1794	Adverse		Leave to withdraw.		
Knox, William, and John Brownlee	(See Thomas Knox)	20	1		338							
Knox, William, John Halderman, and others.	Indemnity for loss of a boat in service of the United States.	23	2	Petition	275	Claims.						
Knox, William, John Halderman, and others.	Indemnity for loss of a boat in services of the United States.	24	1	Petition	93	Claims	90	Adverse		Laid on table		
Knush, Philip	Pension	15	1	House bill	405	Whole House	April 16, 1818	With amends.	172	Passed	Postponed.	
Koat, Elizabeth	Continuation of revolutionary pension.	28	1	Petition	72	Rev. Pensions						Provided in act June 17, 1844.

List of private claims presented to the House of Representatives of the United States from the 1st to the 31st Congress, inclusive—Continued.

Names of claimants.	Nature or object of the claim.	Congress.	Session.	How brought before the House of Reps.	Page of journal.	To what committee of the House referred.	No. or date of the report.	Nature of the report.	No. of the bill.	How disposed of by the House of Reps.	How disposed of by the Senate.	Date of the act of Congress, and remarks.
Koch, Adam	Compensation for revolutionary services.	2	1	Petition	452					Referred to Secretary of War.		
Koch, Adam	Pension	3	1	Rep. of Secretary War.	131	Select	May 26, 1794	Joint resolut'n.	12	Passed	Passed	App'd June 30, 1834
Koch, Adam	Pension	5	2	Petition	130	Claims	April 17, 1798			Laid on table.		
Koch, Adam	Pension	5	3	Petition & docs.	43	Whole House.						
Koch, Adam	Bounty land for revolutionary services.	7	2	Petition & docs.	259	Claims	Jan. 24, 1805	Adverse		Rejected.		
Koch, Severinus	Revolutionary pension	1	2	House bill	271	Whole House	July 19, 1790	With amend.	88	Passed	Passed	App'd Aug. 11, 1790
Koch, Severinus	Increase of pension	3	1	Petition	62					Referred to Secretary War.		
Koch, Severinus	Increase of pension	3	2	Rep. of Secretary War.	278					Laid on table.		
Koch, Severinus	Increase of pension	4	1	Petition	457	Claims.						
Koch, Severinus	Increase of pension	5	2	Petition	157	Claims	Feb. 1, 1798	Adverse		Rejected.		
Koch, Christian	Revolutionary pension	21	1	Resolution	432	Military Pensions.						
Kohler, Charles	Compensation for services as pilot.	25	3	Petition	213	Commerce.	Feb. 13, 1839	Adverse		Laid on table.		
Kohler, Charles	Compensation for services as pilot.	26	1	Petition	272	Commerce.						
Kohn, Doran, & Co.	Remission of duties	27	1	Petition	97	Ways and Means.						
Kolb, Jehu	Revolutionary pension	25	3	Resolution	168	Rev. Pensions.						
Kone, William W.	Grant of land for naval services.	31	1	Petition	983	Public Lands.						
Koning, Frederick	Indemnity for French spoliations prior to 1800.	26	1	Memorial	182	Foreign Affairs	343	Favorable; bill	319	Referred to Committee Whole House.		
Koning, F. and H.	Indemnity for French spoliations prior to 1800.	26	1	Memorial	182	Foreign Affairs	343	Favorable; bill	319	Referred to Committee Whole House.		
Konig, Frederick, & others	Indemnity for French spoliations prior to 1800.	31	1	Petition	471	Foreign Affairs	355	Favorable; bill	318	Referred to Committee Whole House.		
Konkapot, Abraham	(See John Konkapot, *et al.*)	4	1		494							
Konkapot, John, *et al.*	Compensation for revolutionary services.	4	1	Petition	494	Claims	May 10, 1896	Adverse		Leave to withdraw.		
Konkin, John	Increase of pension	26	2	Petition	60	Invalid Pensions				Discharged; laid on table.		
Konkin, John	Increase of pension	27	2	Petition	507	Invalid Pensions.						
Konkin, John	Increase of pension	28	1	Petition	803	Invalid Pensions.						
Konkopot, Jacob	(See Jacob Kunkopot, and others)	16	1		226							
Koon, Frederick, and W. A. Dean.	(See W. A. Dean and F. Koons.)	30	1		470							
Koontz, Francis, heirs of	Compensation for revolutionary services.	5	2	Petition	210	Claims	Mar. 9, 1798	Adverse		Rejected.		
Korn, John Jacob, heirs of	Indemnity for French spoliations prior to 1800.	29	2	Memorial	92	Foreign Affairs.						
Kortright, N. G.	(See John E. Seaman)	29	1		984							
Kortz, James, by attorney.	Grant of military bounty land	24	1	Petition	664	Public Lands				Discharged; laid on table.		
Kortz, James, by attorney.	Grant of military bounty land	25	2	Petition	233	Public Lands	595	Adverse		Laid on table.		
Kosciusko, General	Interest on revolutionary certificate	5	2	Resol'n and letter Sec. Treasury.	114	Select	Jan. 2, 1898	Favorable; bil	33	Passed	Passed	App'd Jan. 3, 1798
Kosnaloski, Napoleon	Compensation for military services.	30	2	Petition	274	Military Affairs.						
Kounston, F. A., and others	Indemnity for French spoliations prior to 1800.	31	1	Memorial	215	Foreign Affairs	355	General bill	318	Referred to Committee Whole House.		
Kouwrnhoven, William	Pay for boarding officers while prisoners.	7	1	Memorial	59	Claims	Mar. 8, 1802	Adverse		Leave to withdraw.		

List of private claims presented to the House of Representatives of the United States from the 1st to the 31st Congress, inclusive—Continued.

Names of claimants.	Nature or object of the claim.	Congress.	Session.	How brought before the House of Reps.	Page of journal.	To what committee of the House referred.	No. or date of the report.	Nature of the report.	No. of the bill.	How disposed of by the House of Reps.	How disposed of by the Senate.	Date of the act of Congress, and remarks.
Krail, Nicholas, surety of.	Release from liability	18	1	Petition	96	P. Of. & P. Roads.	26	Adverse.		Referred to Committee Whole House.		
Krail, Nicholas, surety of.	Release from liability	18	2	Petition and docs.	153	P. Of. & P. Roads.	60	Favorable.	323	Passed	Passed	App'd March 3, 1825
Kramer, Balthazar, widow of.	Arrears of pension	19	1	Petition	34	Claims	158	Favorable; bill	210	Passed.		
Kramer, Balthazar, representatives of.	Arrears of pension	19	2	Senate bill	348	Military Pensions.	Mar. 1, 1827	With't amend.	79	Passed	Passed	App'd March 2, 1827
Kramer, Balthazar, widow of.	Arrears of pension	21	1	Petition	57	Claims.						
Kramer, Elizabeth	(See Balthazar Kramer, widow of)	19	1		34							
Kramer, Elizabeth	(See Thomas Craig, representatives of.)	23	2		84							
Kramer, Johannes	Pension	5	2	Petition	251	Claims	April 17, 1798	Adverse		Laid on table.		
Kramer, Johannes	Pension	5	3	Petition and docs.	432	Claims.						
Krebs, Hugo, heirs of	Confirmation of title to land	27	2	Senate bill	1169	Priv. Land Claims.	Aug. 9, 1842	With't amend.	276	Passed	Passed	App'd Aug. 29, 1842
Krebs, Joseph, and wife	Confirmation of title to land	15	1	Petition	212	Priv. Land Claims.						
Kremer, Conrad	Arrears of pension	21	2	Petition	159	Military Pensions.						
Kremer, Conrad	Arrears of pension	22	1	Petition	56	Rev. Pensions.	Dec. 28, 1831	Adverse		Laid on table.		
Kremer, Conrad	Arrears of pension	22	2	Petition	176	Rev. Pensions				Laid on table.		
Kremer, Conrad	Arrears of pension	23	2	Petition	105	Rev. Pensions.	Jan. 12, 1835	Adverse		Laid on table.		
Kremer, Conrad	Arrears of pension	24	1	Petition	213	Rev. Pensions	263	Adverse.		Laid on table.		
Krepps, John	Adjustment of account	24	1	Resolution	512	Claims.						
Krepps, John	Adjustment of account	24	2	Resolution	38	Claims	148	Favorable; bill	906	Referred to Committee Whole House.		
Krepps, John	Adjustment of account	25	2	Resolution	36	Claims	32	Favorable; bill	44	Passed	Passed	App'd March 7, 1838
Krewson, Simon	Increase of pension	25	3	Petition	217	Rev. Pensions				Discharged: laid on table.		
Krieg, Peter, widow of	Pension	31	1	Petition	542	Invalid Pensions.						
Kriel, Andrew J	Bounty land for military services	30	1	Petition	80	Military Affairs.						
Krittman, Joseph	Indemnity for damage to person and property.	20	2	Petition	83	Foreign Affairs	39	Favorable		Laid on table.		
Krittman, Joseph	Indemnity for damage to person and property.	21	1	Petition	69	Foreign Affairs	Dec. 23, 1829	Adverse		Laid on table.		
Kroft, Abraham	Reimbursement of excess money paid for lands.	16	2	Petition	58	Public Lands.						
Kroft, Abraham	Reimbursement of excess money paid for lands.	17	1	Petition	249	Public Lands	43	Adverse		Laid on table.		
Kroft, Abraham	Reimbursement of excess money paid for lands.	20	2	Petition	263	Public Lands.						
Kronkhite, David	Revolutionary pension	25	2	Petition	586	Rev. Pensions				Discharged; laid on table.		
Krugh, Philip	Invalid pension	12	1	House bill	361	Whole House	Jan. 15, 1812	With amends.	138	Passed	Passed	App'd July 5, 1812
Krugh, Philip	Invalid pension	15	2	House bill	108	Military Affairs	Jan. 26, 1819	With amends.	129	Passed	Passed	App'd March 3, 1819
Krumholt, Jacob	Compensation for revolutionary services.	25	1	Petition	180					Laid on table.		
Krumholt, Jacob	Compensation for revolutionary services.	25	2	Petition	282	Priv. Land Claims.				Discharged; laid on table.		
Krumholt, Lewis	Compensation for military services.	25	1	Petition	180					Laid on table.		
Krumholt, Lewis	Compensation for military services.	25	2	Petition	282	Priv. Land Claims.				Discharged; laid on table.		
Kryster, John	Compensation for revolutionary services.	2	1	Petition	483					Referred to Secretary of War.		

List of private claims presented to the House of Representatives of the United States from the 1st to the 31st Congress, inclusive—Continued.

Names of claimants.	Nature or object of the claim.	Congress.	Session.	How brought before the House of Reps.	Page of journal.	To what committee of the House referred.	No. or date of the report.	Nature of the report.	No. of the bill.	How disposed of by the House of Reps.	How disposed of by the Senate.	Date of the act of Congress, and remarks.
Kuffee, Benjamin	Revolutionary pension	1	2	Petition and rep't of Sec. War.	209					Laid on table.		
Kuhl, Casper	Revolutionary pension	2	2	Petition	632	Select.						
Kuhl, Casper	Revolutionary pension	3	1	Rep. of Secretary War.	131	Select	May 26, 1794		J. R. 12	Passed	Passed	App'd June 9, 1794
Kuhl, Casper	Revolutionary pension	4	2	Rep. of Secretary War.	651	Claims	Feb. 6, 1797	Favorable; bill.	224	Passed	Postponed.	
Kuhn, Christian	Pension	1	1	House bill	113	Whole House	Sept. 24, 1789	With't amend.	29	Passed	Passed	App'd Sept. 29, 1789
Kuhn, Christian	Pension	1	2	Petition and rep't Sec. of War.	181	Select	July 16, 1790	Favorable; bill.	88	Passed	Passed	App'd Aug. 11, 1790
Kuhn, Elizabeth	Compensation for revolutionary services.	1	3	Petition	378					Referred to Secretary War.		
Kuhn, Ludwig	Payment for supplies furnished	1	3	Petition	381					Referred to Secretary of Treasury.		
Kuhn, Ludwig	Payment for supplies furnished	2	1	Rep. of Secretary Treasury.	476					Laid on table.		
Kuhn, Ludwig	Payment for supplies furnished	2	2	Petition and rep't Sec. Treasury.	628					Laid on table.		
Kuhn, Ludwig	Payment for supplies furnished	4	2	Petition	661	Claims	Feb. 11, 1779	Adverse		Rejected.		
Kuhn, Ludwig	Payment for supplies furnished	6	1	Petition	560	Claims	Feb. 20, 1800	Adverse		Rejected.		
Kuhn, Ludwig	Payment for supplies furnished	7	1	Petition	97	Claims	Mar. 8, 1802	Adverse		Rejected.		
Kuhn, Ludwig	Payment for supplies furnished	8	1	Petition	595					Leave to withdraw.		
Kuhn, Ludwig	Payment for supplies furnished	8	1	Petition	630					Laid on table.		
Kuhn, Ludwig	Payment for supplies furnished	9	1	Petition	212	Whole House				Leave to withdraw.		
Kuhn, Ludwig	Bayment for supplies furnished	9	2	Petition	471	Select.						
Kuhn, Ludwig	Payment for supplies furnished	10	1	Petition	23	Select.						
Kuhn, Ludwig	Payment for supplies furnished	10	2	Petition	374	Select.						
Kuhn, Ludwig	Payment for supplies furnished	11	1	Petition	34	Claims	June 9, 1809	Adverse		Laid on table.		
Kuhn, Ludwig	Payment for supplies furnished	11	2	Petition	124	Claims.						
Kuhn, Ludwig	Payment for supplies furnished	11	3	Petition	438	Claims	Jan. 9, 1811	Adverse		Rejected.		
Kuhn, Ludwig, heirs of	Payment for supplies furnished	19	2	Petition	63	Rev. Claims	Jan. 17, 1827	Adverse		Laid on table.		
Kunkopet, Jacob, & others	Compensation for military services.	16	1	Docs. and bill	226	Whole House	April 7, 1820	With't amend.	82	Passed	Passed, with amendment.	App'd May 4, 1820
Kurtz, Andrew	Issue of a patent	14	1	Petition	432	Select	March 6, 1816	Favorable; bill.		Passed		App'd April 2, 1816
Kurtz, John	(See Bowie & Kurtz and others.)	13	2		176							
Kutrz, John, surviving partner of Bowie & Kurtz.	Indemnity for loss of ship	24	1	Memorial	534	Claims.						
Kurtz, John, surviving partner of Bowie & Kurtz.	Indemnity for loss of ship	24	2	Memorial	81	Claims.						
Kurtz, John, surviving partner of Bowie & Kurtz.	Indemnity for loss of ship	25	2	Memorial	51	Claims.						
Kurtz, John, surviving partner of Bowie & Kurtz.	Indemnity for loss of ship	25	1	Memorial	168	Claims	May 20, 1840	Adverse		Laid on table.		
Kutts, John	Compensation for plan of custom-house.	23	1	Petition	466	Claims	405	Adverse		Laid on table.		
Kuykendall, Nathaniel	Compensation for extra services for carrying mail.	28	1	Petition	316	P. Of. & P. Roads.	547	Adverse		Laid on table.		
Kuykendall, Nathaniel	Compensation for extra services for carrying mail.	29	1	Senate bill	1075	P. Of. & P. Roads.			S. 78			
Kuykendall, Nathaniel	Compensation for extra services for carrying mail.	29	2	Senate bill	307	P. Of. & P. Roads.	Feb. 24, 1847	With't amend.	57	Referred to Committee Whole House.		
Kuykendall, Nathaniel	Compensation for extra services for carrying mail.	30	1	Senate bill	683	P. Of. & P. Roads.	609	Favorable	86	Referred to Committee Whole House.		

List of private claims presented to the House of Representatives of the United States form the 1st to the 31st Congress, inclusive—Continued.

Names of claimants.	Nature or object of the claim.	Congress.	Session.	How brought before the House of Reps.	Page of journal.	To what committee of the House referred.	No. or date of the report.	Nature of the report.	No. of the bill.	How disposed of by the House of Reps.	How disposed of by the Senate.	Date of the act of Congress, and remarks.
Kuykendall, Nathaniel	Compensation for extra services for carrying mail.	31	1	Senate bill	440	P. Of. and P. Roads	....	....	91			
Kyan, John Howard	Grant of a patent	23	2	Petition	237	Judiciary	Feb. 20, 1835	Favorable; bill.	756			
Kyan, John Howard	Grant of a patent	24	1	Senate bill	773	Patent Laws	....	....	104			
Kyan, John Howard	Grant of a patent	25	2	Petition	59	Patent Laws	662	Favorable; bill.	635	Referred to Committee Whole House.		
Kyan, John Howard	Grant of a patent	25	2	Senate bill	784	Patent Laws	May 11, 1838	With't amend.	210	Passed	Passed	App'd May 31, 1838
Labadie, Sylvester, heirs of.	Confirmation of title to land in Missouri.	15	5	Petition	118	Priv. Land Claims.						
Labadie, Sylvester, heirs of.	Confirmation of title to land in Missouri.	16	1	Petition	36	Priv. Land Claims.						
Labadie, Sylvester, heirs of.	Confirmation of title to land in Missouri.	17	1	Petition	54	Priv. Land Claims.						
Labadie, Sylvester, heirs of.	Confirmation of title to land in Missouri.	18	1	Petition	54	Priv. Land Claims.						
Labarr, John	Pension	5	2	Petition	104	Claims	April 17, 1798	Adverse	......	Referred to Committee Whole House.		
Labarr, John	Pension	5	3	Resolution	432	Whole House.						
Labeaume, Louis, representatives of.	Confirmation of title to land in Missouri.	24	1	Petition	257	Public Lands.						
Labeaume, Louis, representatives of.	Confirmation of title to land in Missouri.	24	2	Petition	98	Priv. Land Claims.						
Labeaume, Louis, representatives of.	Confirmation of title to land in Missouri.	25	2	Petition	97	Priv. Land Claims.	....	....	......	Discharged; laid on table.		
Labeaume, Susan.	(See Louis Labeaume, representatives of.)	24	1	....	257							
Labigarre, Magaret	(See De Labigarre.)	10	1	....	268							
Laborde, representatives of.	Confirmation of title to land in Michigan.	20	1	Resolution	28	Public Lands	42	Favorable	34	Passed	Passed	App'd April 22, 1828
Labriche, Francis	(See Lewis & Clarke, and companions.)	9	1	....	284							
Lacasse, Etienne	Confirmation of title to land in Louisiana.	22	2	Petition	41	Priv. Land Claims.	53	Favorable	696	Referred to Committee Whole House.		
Lacasse, Etienne	Confirmation of title to land in Louisiana.	23	1	Petition	93	Priv. Land Claims.	Jan. 8, 1834	Indefinite	......	Laid on table.		
Lacey, Edward	Compensation for services as forage master.	4	2	Petition	668	Claims	Feb. 9, 1797	Adverse	......	Rejected.		
Lacey, Josiah	Pension	3	1	Rep. of Secretary War.	131	Select	May 26, 1794	Res. to refer to Sec. War.	J. R. 12	Passed	Passed	App'd June 9, 1794
Lacey, Obed P.	Permission to relocate land	25	2	Senate bill	672	Priv. Land Claims.	Mar. 28, 1838	With amend.	S. 38	Referred to Committee Whole House.		
Lacey, Obed P.	Permission to relocate land	25	3	Senate bill	477	Priv. Land Claims.	Feb. 16, 1839	With amend.	S. 20	Referred to Committee Whole House.		

List of private claims presented to the House of Representatives of the United States from the 1st to the 31st Congress, inclusive—**Continued.**

Names of claimants.	Nature or object of the claim.	Congress.	Session.	How brought before the House of Reps.	Page of journal.	To what committee of the House referred.	No. or date of the report.	Nature of the report.	No. of the bill.	How disposed of by the House of Reps.	How disposed of by the Senate.	Date of the act of Congress, and remarks.
Lacey, Obed P., assignee of.	Permission to relocate land	26	1	Senate bill	270	Priv. Land Claims.	April 4, 1840	Favorable	S. 49	Referred to Committee Whole House.		
Lacey, Obed P., assignee of.	Permission to relocate land	26	2	Petition	132	Priv. Land Claims.	120	Favorable	625	Referred to Committee Whole House.		
Lacey, Obed P., assignee of.	Permission to relocate land	27	2	Petition	67	Priv. Land Claims.	Dec. 29, 1841	Favorable	54	Passed	Passed	App'd July 9, 1842
Lacey, Walter	(See administrators of Benjamin Clarke.)	19	2		190							
Lacey, ——	(See Lacy.)											
La Chance, Nicholas, heirs of.	Compensation for supplies during Illinois campaign.	24	2	Senate bill	250	Rev. Claims			S. 22			
La Chance, Nicholas, heirs of.	Compensation for supplies during Illinois campaign.	30	1	House bill	533	Claims	343	Favorable	324	Referred to Committee Whole House.		
La Chance, Nicholas, heirs of.	Compensation for supplies during Illinois campaign.	31	1	House bill	474	Rev. Claims	179	With't amend.	45	Referred to Committee Whole House.		
La Chapelle, Antoine	Confirmation of title to land in Michigan.	17	1	Petition	184	Public Lands.						
Lackin, William	Pension	15	2	Pension bill	41				203	Passed	Passed, with amendment.	App'd March 3, 1819
Lackwood, Joseph, widow of.	Pension for revolutionary services.	28	2	Petition	208	Rev. Pensions.						
Lackwood, Lydia	(See Joseph Lackwood, widow of.)	28	2		208							
Lacon, William	(See L. H. Bates & Co)	23	1		48							
Lacoste, ——	(See William Lane, *et al.*)	18	2		161							
Lacoste, Augustin	Confirmation of title to land in Alabama.	25	2	Petition	690	Priv. Land Claims.						
Lacoste, Augustin	Confirmation of title to land in Alabama.	25	3	Petition	133	Priv. Land Claims.						
Lacoste, Augustin	Confirmation of title to land in Alabama.	26	1	Petition	179	Priv. Land Claims.	95	Favorable	91	Passed	Passed	App'd July 20, 1840
Lacoste, Peter	Indemnity for slaves captured by British.	14	2	Petition	306					Referred to Secretary of State.		
Lacoste, Peter	Indemnity for slaves captured by British.	15	1	Rep. of Secretary War.	46	Claims	Dec. 23, 1817	Adverse		Leave to withdraw.		
Lacoste, Stephen	(See Joseph Avela)	11	3		574							
Lacount, Samuel	Increase of pension	21	2	Petition	143	Military Pensions.						
Lacount, Samuel	Increase of pension	22	1	Petition	66	Rev. Pensions.	Jan. 13, 1832	Adverse		Laid on table.		
La Cource, assignee of	Confirmation of title to land in Arkansas.	22	1	House bill	421	Whole House	Mar. 23, 1832	With't amend.	425	Passed	Passed	App'd June 25, 1832
La Croix, Archange	(See Hubert La Croix, widow of.)	25	2		1048							
La Croix, Bernard	Confirmation of title to land in Louisiana.	27	2	Senate bill	359	Priv. Land Claims.	Feb. 26, 1842	With amend.	S. 76	Passed	Passed	App'd July 6, 1842
La Croix, Hubert	Indemnity for property destroyed in Michigan.	15	1	Rep't of Comm'r of Claims.	195	Claims.						
La Croix, Hubert	Indemnity for property destroyed in Michigan.	16	1	Petition	106	Claims.						
La Croix, Hubert	Indemnity for property destroyed in Michigan.	16	2	Petition	120	Claims	33	Adverse		Laid on table.		
La Croix, Hubert	Indemnity for property destroyed in Michigan.	17	1	Petition	47	Claims	34	Adverse		Referred to Committee Whole House.		
La Croix, Hubert	Indemnity for property destroyed in Michigan.	19	2	Petition	159	Claims.						
La Croix, Hubert	Indemnity for property destroyed in Michigan.	20	1	Petition	47	Claims.						

List of private claims presented to the House of Representatives of the United States from the 1st to the 31st Congress, inclusive—Continued.

Names of claimants.	Nature or object of the claim.	Congress.	Session.	How brought before the House of Reps.	Page of journal.	To what committee of the House referred.	No. or date of the report.	Nature of the report.	No. of the bill.	How disposed of by the House of Reps.	How disposed of by the Senate.	Date of the act of Congress, and remarks.
La Croix, Hubert	Indemnity for property destroyed in Michigan.	20	2	Petition	40	Claims	46	Favorable	367	Referred to Committee Whole House.		
La Croix, Hubert	Indemnity for property destroyed in Michigan	21	1	Petition	93	Claims	36	Favorable	48	Passed	Passed	App'd April 7, 1830
La Croix, Hubert, widow of.	Indemnity for property destroyed in Michigan.	25	2	Petition	1048	Claims.						
La Croix, Hubert, widow of.	Indemnity for property destroyed in Michigan.	25	3	Petition	86	Claims	37	Adverse	......	Laid on table.		
La Croix, Hubert, widow of.	Indemnity for property destroyed in Michigan.	26	1	Petition	949	Claims.						
La Croix, Hubert, widow of.	Indemnity for property destroyed in Michigan.	26	2	Petition	13[illegible]	Claims	Jan. 8, 1841	Adverse	......	Laid on table.		
La Croix, Hubert, widow of.	Indemnity for property destroyed in Michigan.	28	1	Petition	802	Claims.						
La Croix, Hubert, widow of.	Indemnity for property destroyed in Michigan.	31	1	Petition	39[illegible]	Claims	....	....	......	Discharged; laid on table.		
La Croix, Isidore, representatives of	Confirmation of title to land in Missouri.	15	1	Petition	133	Priv. Land Claims.						
La Croix, John	Pension	16	1	Petition	448	Rev. Pensions.						
Lacy, Andrew, (an Indian)	Permission to sell treaty land	17	2	Petition	9	Public Lands	72	Adverse	......	Laid on table.		
Lacy, Ellen	(See Isaac Lacy, widow of.)	25	2	....	272							
Lacy, Isaac, widow of	Continuation of pension	25	2	Petition	272	Rev. Pensions.						
Lacy, John	Indemnity for loss on contract with United States.	21	1	Petition	572	Naval Affairs	May 24, 1830	Favorable	485	Referred to Committee Whole House.		
Lacy, John	Indemnity for loss on contract with United States.	22	1	Petition	63	Naval Affairs	139	Favorable	213	Passed	Passed	App'd July 3, 1832
Ladd, Alexander	(See Nathaniel A. Haven, executor of.)	26	1	....	182	....	343	....	319			
Ladd, Alexander	Indemnity for French spoliations prior to 1800.	30	1	Petition	264	Foreign Affairs	Jan. 4, 1848	General bill	21	Referred to Committee Whole House.		
Ladd, Benjamin W	Correction of error in land entry	19	1	Petition	36[illegible]	Public Lands.						
Ladd, Benjamin W	Reimbursement of expenses, defending certain suit.	26	1	Petition	935	Public Lands.						
Ladd, Benjamin W	Reimbursement of expenses, defending certain suit.	26	2	Petition	134	Public Lands.						
Ladd, Benjamin W	Reimbursement of expenses, defending certain suit.	27	2	Petition	98	Public Lands	Feb. 9, 1842	Adverse	......	Recommitted.		
Ladd, Caroline	(See Otis F. Ladd, widow of)	27	3	....	258							
Ladd, David	Pension	29	1	Petition	10[illegible]	Invalid Pensions	243	Adverse	......	Recommitted.		
Ladd, David	Pension	30	1	Petition	572	Invalid Pensions	....	....	......	Discharged; laid on table.		
Ladd, Eliphalet	Remission of duties on wrecked merchandise.	2	1	Petition and rep't Sec. of War.	583	Select.						
Ladd, Eliphalet	Remission of duties on wrecked merchandise.	3	1	Petition	22	Select	Feb. 5, 1794	Favorable	10	Rejected.		
Ladd, Eliphalet	Remission of duties on wrecked merchandise.	7	2	Petition	310	Com. and Manuf.	....	....	......	Discharged; leave to withdraw.		
Ladd, Eliphalet, executor of	Indemnity for French spoliations prior to 1800.	26	1	Memorial	182	Foreign Affairs	343	Favorable	319	Referred to Committee Whole House.		
Ladd, Ezekiel	Revolutionary pension	17	1	Petition	3	Rev. Pensions.						
Ladd, Henry	See Eliphalet Ladd, executor of)	26	1	....	182	....	343	....	319			
Ladd, Ira	Right of pre emption to land in Illinois.	23	1	Petition	447	Public Lands.						

List of private claims presented to the House of Representatives of the United States from the 1st to the 31st Congress, inclusive—Continued

Names of claimants.	Nature or object of the claim.	Congress.	Session.	How brought before the House of Reps.	Page of journal.	To what committee of the House referred.	No. or date of the report.	Nature of the report.	No. of the bill.	How disposed of by the House of Reps.	How disposed of by the Senate.	Date of the act of Congress, and remarks.
Ladd, James	Pension for revolutionary services	17	1	Petition	131	Rev. Pensions.						
Ladd, James	Pension for revolutionary services	22	1	Petition	130	Rev. Pensions.						
Ladd, John, former widow of.	Pension for revolutionary services	30	1	Petition	66	Rev. Pensions				Discharged; laid on table.		
Ladd, John G	(See William and John G. Ladd)	12	1		157							
Ladd, Joseph	Pension for revolutionary services	17	1	Petition	31	Rev. Pensions.						
Ladd, Joseph	Correction of error in land entry	19	1	Petition	366	Public Lands.						
Ladd, Nathaniel	Pension for revolutionary services	10	2	Petition and rep't Sec. of War.	521, 525					Laid on table.		
Ladd, Nathaniel	Pension for revolutionary services	11	2	Pension bill	283	Whole House	Mar. 16, 1810	With amend.	107	Passed	Passed	App'd April 27, 1810
Ladd, Nathaniel	Increase of pension	15	1	Petition	132	Pens. & Rev. Cl'ms.						
Ladd, Nathaniel	Increase of pension	20	1	Petition	63	Military Pensions.						
Ladd, Nathaniel	Increase of pension	24	2	Petition	41	Invalid Pensions	Dec. 12, 1836	Adverse		Laid on table.		
Ladd, Otis F., widow of.	Pension for services in war of 1812	27	3	Petition	258	Invalid Pensions.						
Ladd, Otis F., widow of.	Pension for services in war of 1812	28	1	Petition	116	Invalid Pensions.						
Ladd, Otis F., widow of.	Pension for services in war of 1812	28	2	Petition	308	Invalid Pensions.						
Ladd, Otis F., widow of.	Pension for services in war of 1812	29	1	Petition	315	Invalid Pensions				Discharged; laid on table.		
Ladd, Samuel	Pension	23	1	Petition	474	Rev. Pensions				Discharged; leave to withdraw.		
Ladd, William and John G.	Remission of penalty	12	1	Petition	157	Select	April 22, 1812	Bill ordered.				
Ladd, William	Pension for revolutionary services	22	1	Petition	77	Rev. Pensions.				Discharged; laid on table.		
Ladieu, James	Pension	22	1	Petition	142	Invalid Pensions				Discharged; laid on table.		
Ladieu, James	Pension	23	1	Petition	44	Invalid Pensions	Dec. 20, 1833	Adverse		Laid on table.		
Ladieu, James	Pension	23	2	Petition	113	Invalid Pensions	Jan. 5, 1835	Adverse		Laid on table.		
Ladner, Dominique	Confirmation of title to land in Mississippi.	21	2	Petition	211	Public Lands				Discharged; laid on table.		
Laduc, M. P.	Confirmation of title to land in Missouri.	15	1	Petition	102	Priv. Land Claims.						
Laduc, M. P.	Confirmation of title to land in Missouri.	17	1	Petition	53	Public Lands.						
Laduc, M. P.	Confirmation of title to land in Missouri.	18	1	Petition	53	Public Lands	Jan. 16, 1824	General bill	65	Passed	Passed	App'd May 26, 1824
Laducier, Jean Baptiste	Confirmation of title to land in Illinois.	18	1	Petition	177	Public Lands	Mar. 12, 1834	Favorable	155	Indefinitely postponed.		
Laducier, Jean Baptiste	Confirmation of title to land in Illinois.	19	1	Resolution	331	Priv. Land Claims.	April 28, 1826	Favorable	241	Passed.		
Laerlaw, Seth	Payment of office rent	28	1	House bill	648	Public Lands	350	Favorable	250	Referred to Committee Whole House.		
Laeur, Philip	(See Philip Laeur)	2	1		494							
La Fayette, Major General	Pay and emoluments for revolutionary services.	3	1	Senate bill	92	Whole House	Mar. 22, 1794	With't amend.	5	Passed	Passed	App'd Mar. 27, 1794
La Fayette, Major General	Compensation for revolutionary services and sacrifices.	18	2	House bill	66	Select	Dec. 21, 1824	Favorable	243	Passed	Passed	App'd Dec. 28, 1824
La Fayette, Major General	Grant of 11,520 acres of land	7	2	House bill	344	Select	Feb. 16, 1803	Favorable	111	Passed	Passed	App'd March 3, 1803
Lafever & Gallier	(See Calvin Pollard, *et al.*)	23	1		523							
Lafevre, Joseph	Indemnity for losses sustained from enemy.	16	1	Senate bill	300	Claims			S. 56			
Lafite & Co., trustees of.	Indemnity for property confiscated by French government.	27	2	Presid'ts message	1128	Foreign Affairs	918	Adverse		Laid on table.		

List of private claims presented to the House of Representatives of the United States from the 1st to the 31st Congress, inclusive—Continued.

Names of claimants.	Nature or object of the claim.	Congress.	Session.	How brought before the House of Reps.	Page of journal.	To what committee of the House referred.	No. or date of the report.	Nature of the report.	No. of the bill.	How disposed of by the House of Reps.	How disposed of by the Senate.	Date of the act of Congress, and remarks.
Lafitte, Pierre	Confirmation of title to land in Louisiana.	22	2	Petition	246	Priv. Land Claims.						
Lafitte, Pierre	Confirmation of title to land in Louisiana.	23	1	Petition	93	Priv. Land Claims.	304	Favorable	339	Referred to Committee Whole House.		
Lafontaine, Francis & Son	Confirmation of title to land	22	2	Petition	125	Priv. Land Claims.						
Lafontaine, Francis & Son	Confirmation of title to land	23	1	Senate bill	395	Priv. Land Claims.	Mar. 11, 1824	Favorable	54	Passed	....	App'd June 30, 1834
Laforge, Pierre A.	Authority to locate land certificate	24	1	Petition	537	Priv. Land Claims.	....	....	.....	Discharged; laid on table.		
Laforge, Pierre A.	Authority to locate land certificates	24	2	Petition	93	Priv. Land Claims.	....	....	.....	Discharged; laid on table.		
Laforge, Pierre A.	Authority to locate land certificates	25	2	Petition	97	Priv. Land Claims.	349	Adverse	.....	Laid on table.		
Laforge, Pierre A.	Authority to locate land certificates	25	3	Petition	463	Priv. Land Claims.						
La Forrest, Francis	(See Francis Valle, heirs of)	15	2	....	67							
Lafoy, James	Pension for revolutionary services	23	1	Petition	379	Rev. Pensions	....	....	.....	Disch'd; laid on table.		
La Grange, Gerrit	(See Gerrit L. Dox)	21	1	....	66							
Laidley, James G., *et al.*	Compensation as jurors	1[illegible]	1	Petition	304	....	....	....	.....	Laid on table.		
Laidlow, Peter	Allowance for office rent	28	1	Petition	405	Public Lands.						
Laight, Wm. & Charles	Indemnity for French spoliations prior to 1800.	26	1	Memorial	182	Foreign Affairs	343	Favorable	319	Referred to Committee Whole House.		
Laighton, Hannah	(See Isaac Davis, former widow of)	26	1	....	937							
Laighton, Wm. M., *et al.*	Compensation for extra service on Exploring Expedition.	30	1	Petition	167	Naval Affairs.						
Laighton, William A.	(See Exploring Expedition)	27	3	....	149							
Laing, Lewis	Pension	29	1	Petition	86	Priv. Land Claims.	420	Favorable	300	Passed	Passed	App'd Aug. 8, 1846
Laird, Nathaniel	Pension	18	1	Petition	285	Rev. Claims	Mar. 9, 1824	Adverse	.....	Laid on table.		
Laird, Nathaniel	Pension	19	1	Petition	36	Rev. Claims	164	Adverse	.....	Laid on table.		
Laird, Robert	(See Robert Laird, representatives of.)	24	1	....	345							
Laiten, Richard	Pension	24	1	Resolution	951	Rev. Pensions.						
La Jeunesse, Prudent	Compensation for military services.	1	1	Petition	90	....	....	....	.....	Referred to Secretary Treasury.		
La Jeunesse, Prudent	Compensation for military services.	2	2	Report of Secretary Treasury	626	....	....	....	.....	Laid on table.		
La Jeunesse, Prudent	Compensation for military services.	21	2	Resolution	85	Military Pensions.						
La Jeunesse, Prudent, heirs of.	Arrears of pension	29	2	Petition	92	Rev. Pensions.						
La Jeunesse, Prudent, heirs of.	Arrears of pension	30	1	Petition	205	Rev. Pensions	228	Adverse	.....	Laid on table.		
Lakanal, Joseph	Pre-emption right to certain land.	18	2	Petition	137	Public Lands.						
Lakanal, Joseph	Pre-emption right to certain land.	19	1	Petition	45	Priv. Land Claims.	Dec. 20, 1825	Adverse	.....	Laid on table.		
Lakanal, Joseph	Pre-emption right to certain land.	19	2	Petition	157	Priv. Land Claims.						
Lake, Jonathan	Pension	3	2	Rep. of Secretary War.	278	Claims	Feb. 28, 1795	Pension bill	130	Passed	Postponed.	
Lake, Jonathan	Pension	4	1	Rep. of Sec. War.	445	Claims	Feb. 18, 1796	Pension bill	156	Passed	Passed	App'd April 20, 1796
Lake, Jonathan, daughter of.	Arrears of pension	31	1	Petition	1436	Rev. Pensions.						
Lake, William	Pension	20	1	Petition	417	Military Pensions	....	....	.....	Discharged; laid on table.		
Laken, William	Pension	3	2	Petition	332	Claims.						
Laken, William, attorney of.	Pension	4	1	Petition	383	Claims	Jan. 6, 1796	Adverse				
Laken, William, attorney of.	Pension	4	2	Petition	721	Claims	Feb. 25, 1797	Adverse	.....	Rejected.		

List of private claims presented to the House of Representatives of the United States from the 1st to the 31st Congress, inclusive—Continued.

Names of claimants.	Nature or object of the claim.	Congress.	Session.	How brought before the House of Reps.	Page of journal.	To what committee of the House referred.	No. or date of the report.	Nature of the report.	No. of the bill.	How disposed of by the House of Reps.	How disposed of by the Senate.	Date of the act of Congress, and remarks.
Lakens, ——	(See Kirk & Lakens.)	26	1	....	182	....	343	....	319			
Lakin, Loes	Continuation of pension	28	1	Petition	850	Rev. Pensions.						
Lalande, Etienne Stephen	Confirmation of title to land in Alabama.	23	2	Petition	393	Priv. Land Claims.						
Lalande, Etienne Stephen	Confirmation of title to land in Alabama.	24	1	Petition	112	Priv. Land Claims.	512	Favorable	509	Referred to Committee Whole House.		
Lalande, Etienne Stephen	Confirmation of title to land in Alabama.	25	2	Petition	42	Priv. Land Claims.	141	Favorable	160	Referred to Committee Whole House.		
Lalande, Etienne Stephen	Confirmation of title to land in Alabama.	25	3	House bill	375	....	....	....	160	Passed	Passed	App'd March 3, 1839
Lalonet, Antoinette, assignee of.	Confirmation of title to land in Michigan.	20	1	Resolution	28	Public Lands	42	General bill	34	Passed	Passed	App'd April 17, 1828
Lamar, Gassaway B	Permission to import S. B. iron free of duty.	23	1	Senate bill	278	Ways and Means	Feb. 7, 1824	With't amend.	S. 73	Passed	Passed	App'd Feb. 26, 1824
		25	2	Resolution	1025	Manufactures	June 27, 1883	Favorable	854	Referred to Committee Whole House.		
				Amend't to Sen bill.	1276	....	....	....	S. 147	Passed	Passed	App'd July 7, 1838
Lamar, James, and J. Gant	Reimbursement of expenses subsisting their companies of volunteers.	25	3	Memorial	567	Claims.						
Lamar, John T	Permission to import iron free of duty.	23	2	Petition	241	Ways and Means.						
Lamar, Marcelina	Confirmation of title to land in Terre aux Bœuf.	22	1	House bill	107	Whole House	Mar. 23, 1822	With't amend.	125	Passed	Passed	App'd June 25, 1836
Lamarche, Charles	(See Pelardie and C. Lamarche.)	24	2	....	49							
Lamarlere, Anthony	(See F. Mulen'eim.)	9	1	....	338							
Lamarque, Etienne, and others.	(See Louis, Bolduc, heirs of)	15	2	Petition	28	Priv. Land Claims.	....	....	......	Discharged; laid on table.		
Lamb, Benjamin, administrator of.	Balance of pension	20	1	Petition	440	Military Pensions.	....	....	......	Discharged; laid on table.		
Lamb, Benjamin, administrator of.	Balance of pension	20	2	Petition	237	Military Pensions.	....	....	......	Discharged; laid on table.		
Lamb, David	Remission of penalty for importing British goods.	12	2	Petition	563	Ways and Means.						
Lamb, Henry F	(See John Lamb, heirs of.)	24	1	....	474							
Lamb, Larned	Release from liability for public money lost.	11	1	Petition	46	Claims.						
Lamb, James	Restoration of a condemned vessel.	13	3	Petition	740	Ways and Means.						
Lamb, James	Restoration of a condemned vessel.	14	1	Petition	222	Ways and Means.	Mar. 12, 1816	Adverse	......	Rejected.		
Lamb, John	Pension	14	1	House bill	622	Whole House	April 22, 1816	With amend.	171	Passed	Passed	App'd April 30, 1816
Lamb, John, widow of	Compensation for diplomatic services.	17	1	Memorial	195							
				Rep. of Secretary State.	569	....	....	....	......	Laid on table.		
Lamb, John, widow of	Compensation for diplomatic services.	17	2	Resolution	41	Claims	Dec. 16, 1822	Adverse	......	Laid on table.		
Lamb, John, widow of	Compensation for diplomatic services.	21	1	Petition	318	Claims	May 19, 1830	....	......	Referred to Secretary State.		
Lamb, John, widow of	Compensation for diplomatic services.	22	1	Petition	144	Foreign Affairs	Feb. 3, 1832	Adverse	......	Laid on table.		
Lamb, John, heirs of	Compensation for diplomatic services.	24	1	Documents	474	Claims	622	Adverse	......	Laid on table.		

List of private claims presented to the House of Representatives of the United States from the 1st to the 31st Congress, inclusive—Continued

Names of claimants.	Nature or object of the claim.	Congress.	Session.	How brought before the House of Reps.	Page of journal.	To what committee of the House referred.	No. or date of the report.	Nature of the report.	No. of the bill.	How disposed of by the House of Reps.	How disposed of by the Senate.	Date of the act of Congress, and remarks.
Lamb, John, heirs of	Compensation for diplomatic services.	24	2	Memorial	568	Claims	305	Adverse	......	Laid on table.		
Lamb, John, heirs of	Compensation for diplomatic services.	25	2	Petition	398	Claims	Mar. 20, 1838	Adverse	......	Laid on table.	....	Leave to withdraw, 1st sess 27th Congress, page 228.
Lamb, John, administrator of.	(See John Laub, administrator of.)	31	1	....	390							
Lamb, Joshua	(See Canadian Refugees.)											
Lamb, Joshua, widow of..	Pension for revolutionary services.	25	2	Petition	1029	Rev. Pensions	July 2, 1838	Favorable....	870	Referred to Committee Whole House.		
Lamb, Joshua, widow of..	Pension for revolutionary services.	25	3	Rep't Committee Whole House	432	....	....	With't amend.	870	Passed	Passed	App'd Mar. 3, 1839
Lamb, Lucy	(See John Lamb, widow of.)	1	1	....	159							
Lamb, Richard	Pension	11	2	Pension bill	283	Whole House.....	Mar. 16, 1816	With't amend.	107	Passed	Passed	App'd April 27, 1810
Lamb, Richard, son of....	Balance due as revolutionary commissary.	22	1	Petition	383	Rev. Claims.						
Lamb, Washington, and others.	Increase of pension	30	1	Petition	290	Rev. Pensions	....	....	......	Discharged; laid on table.		
Lamb, William.........	(See son of Richard Lamb)	22	1	....	383							
Lamb, William	Compensation for revolutionary services.	15	1	Petition	184	Select..........	....	....	......	Discharged; leave to withdraw.		
Lamb, W. B..........	(See represent. of Wm. Camack.)	25	2	....	1209							
Lamb, Wm. B., President of Bank of Virginia.	Indemnity for French spoliations prior to 1800.	26	1	Memorial	182	Foreign Affairs....	343	Favorable....	319	Referred to Committee Whole House.		
Lambert, Benjamin	(See Hugh Alexander and others.)	7	2	....	286							
Lambert, Christopher	To be restored to pension roll....	26	1	Petition	728	Rev. Pensions.						
Lambert, Christopher	To be restored to pension roll	26	2	Petition	106	Invalid Pensions...	....	....	......	Discharged; laid on table.		
Lambert, Christopher	To be restored to pension roll	27	2	Petition	97	Invalid Pensions ..	419	Adverse	......	Laid on table.		
Lambert, Christopher	To be restored to pension roll	27	3	Petition	72	Invalid Pensions ..	90	Adverse	......	Laid on table.		
Lambert, Christopher	To be restored to pension roll	28	1	Petition	509	Rev. Pensions	....	....	......	Discharged; laid on table.		
Lambert, Christopher, heirs of.	Pension for revolutionary services.	31	1	Petition	954	Rev. Pensions.						
Lambert, Christopher, heirs of.	Pension for revolutionary services.	31	2	Petition	431	Rev. Pensions.....	56	Adverse	......	Laid on table.		
Lambert, Cornelius	Pension for revolutionary services.	19	2	Resolution	143	Military Pensions.						
Lambert, Cornelius......	Pension for revolutionary services.	22	1	Petition	36	Rev. Pensions	110	Favorable....	193	Referred to Committee Whole House.		
Lambert, Cornelius	Pension for revolutionary services.	22	2	House bill......	66	....	....	....	193	Laid on table.		
Lambert, Edward........	Confirmation of title to land in Louisiana.	22	2	Petition	89	Priv. Land Claims.	18	Favorable....	648	Referred to Committee Whole House.		
Lambert, Edward........	Confirmation of title to land in Louisiana.	23	1	Petition	93	Priv. Land Claims.	72	Favorable....	82	Passed	Passed	App'd June 27, 1834
Lambert, Edward A......	Extra compensation for blank books	28	1	Petition	853	Claims	568	Favorable....	421	Ref'd to Com. W. H.		
Lambert, Edward A......	Extra compensation for blank books	28	2	Rep't Committee Whole House.	344	....	....	With't amend.	421	Passed	Passed	App'd March 3, 1845
Lambert, Dr. Francis	Compensation for medical attendance on volunteers.	24	2	Petition	394	Claims.						
Lambert, Dr. Francis	Compensation for medical attendance on volunteers.	25	2	Petition	351	Claims	623	Favorable....	598	Referred to Committee Whole House.		
Lambert, Dr. Francis	Compensation for medical attendance on volunteers.	25	3	Rep't Committee Whole House.	380	....	....	With't amend	598	Passed	Adverse report.	

List of private claims presented to the House of Representatives of the United States from the 1st to the 31st Congress, inclusive—Continued.

Names of claimants.	Nature or object of the claim.	Congress.	Session.	How brought before the House of Reps.	Page of journal.	To what committee of the House referred.	No. or date of the report.	Nature of the report.	No. of the bill.	How disposed of by the House of Reps.	How disposed of by the Senate.	Date of the act of Congress, and remarks.
Lambert, Isaac, and others.	Right of pre-emption to a mill site.	13	3	Petition	525	....	....	....	....	Referred to Committee Whole House.		
Lambert, Isaac, and others.	Right of pre-emption to a mill site.	14	1	Petition	56	Public Lands.						
Lambert, William	Salary as clerk in House of Representatives.	9	1	Document	257	Claims	Feb. 14, 1806	Adverse.				
Lambert, William	Compensation for ascertain'g longitude of Washington.	17	1	Appropriat'n bill.	....	....	....	....	....	....	....	Statutes at Large, vol. 3, p. 373.
Lambert, William, executor of.	Indemnity for French spoliations prior to 1800.	26	1	Memorial	182	Foreign Affairs	343	Favorable	319	Referred to Committee Whole House.		
Lambert, William, representatives of.	Compensation for revolutionary services and supplies.	3	1	Petition	133	Select.						
Lambert, William, representatives of.	Compensation for revolutionary services and supplies.	4	1	Petition	450	Claims.						
Lambert, William, representatives of.	Compensation for revolutionary services and supplies.	4	2	Resolution	614	Claims.						
Lambkin, John, widow of	Arrears of pension	24	1	Petition	273	Rev. Pensions	743	Favorable	688	Passed	Passed	App'd June 28, 1836
Lampkin, Mary	(See John Lampkin, widow of.)	24	1	....	273							
La Meineur, Rene	Confirmation of title to land in Missouri.	15	1	Petition	52	Priv. Land Claims.						
La Meineur, Kene	Confirmation of title to land in Missouri.	16	1	Petition	72	Priv. Land Claims.						
La Meineur, Rene	Confirmation of title to land in Missouri.	17	1	Petition	53	Public Lands.						
La Meineur, Rene	Confirmation of title to land in Missouri.	18	1	Petition	53	Public Lands.						
Lamkin, Matthew	(See Le Roy Opie, sureties of.)	16	2	....	137							
Lamme, Nathan	Commutation pay for revolutionary services.	22	1	Petition	416	Rev. Claims.						
Lamme, Nathan	Commutation pay for revolutionary services.	24	1	Petition	431	Rev. Claims	552	Favorable	543	Referred to Committee Whole House.		
Lamme, Nathan, representatives of.	Commutation pay for revolutionary services.	25	2	Petition	40	Rev. Claims	313	Favorable	354	Passed	Adverse.	
Lamme, Nathan, representatives of.	Commutation pay for revolutionary services.	25	3	Petition	85	Rev. Claims	4	Favorable	902	Referred to Committee Whole House.		
Lamme, Nathan, representatives of.	Commutation pay for revolutionary services.	26	1	Petition	165	Rev. Claims	389	Adverse	....	Laid on table.		
Lamme, Nathan, representatives of.	Commutation pay for revolutionary services.	31	1	Petition	194	Rev. Claims.						
Lamme, William T	Confirmation of title to land in Missouri.	15	1	Petition	232	Priv. Land Claims.						
Lamme, William T	Confirmation of title to land in Missouri.	16	1	Petition	72	Priv. Land Claims.						
Lamme, William T	Confirmation of title to land in Missouri.	17	1	Petition	54	Priv. Land Claims.						
Lamme, William T	Confirmation of title to land in Missouri.	18	1	Petition	54	Priv. Land Claims.						
Lamont, Hannah	(See Robert Lamont, widow of.)	13	3	....	674							
Lamont, Robert, widow of.	Indemnity for loss of husband in public service.	13	3	Petition	674	Claims	Jan. 21, 1815	Adverse	....	Rejected.		
Lamontt, Cyrus	Right of pre-emption as New Orleans branch pilot.	28	1	Petition	77	Priv. Land Claims.	9	Favorable	35	Passed	Passed	App'd June 17, 1844
Lamore, Martha	(See John Smith, daughter of.)	25	2	....	585							
Lamothe, W. P	Compensation for mail service	30	1	Petition	882	P. Of. and P. Roads.						

List of private claims presented to the House of Representatives of the United States from the 1st to the 31st Congress, inclusive—Continued.

Names of claimants.	Nature or object of the claim.	Congress.	Session.	How brought before the House of Reps.	Page of journal.	To what committee of the House referred.	No. or date of the report.	Nature of the report.	No. of the bill.	How disposed of by the House of Reps.	How disposed of by the Senate.	Date of the act of Congress, and remarks.
Lamothe, W. P.	Compensation for mail service	30	2	Petition	125	P. Of. and P. Roads.						
Lampade, Joseph	Right of pre-emption as New Orleans branch pilot.	28	1	Petition	77	Priv. Land Claims.	9	Favorable	35	Passed	Passed	App'd June 17, 1844
Lamphere, Stacy	(See Stacy Lanpher)	29	1		59							
Lamphier, William, *et al.*	Increase of compensation as inspectors.	7	1	Petition	59	Com. and Manuf.	Jan. 25, 1802	Adverse		Leave to withdraw.		
Lampkin, ——	(See Lambkin.)											
Lamson, Gideon	Drawback of duties on sugar.	9	2	Petition	478	Com. and Manuf.	Jan. 21, 1807	Adverse		Rejected.		
Lamson, Thomas	Pension for revolutionary services.	22	2	Petition	40	Rev. Pensions.						
Lamson, William K., sureties of.	Release from liability	21	1	Petition	234	Judiciary	Feb. 12, 1830	Adverse		Laid on table.		
Lanahan, J. J. W.	(See Robert and John Montgomery, assignee of.)	26	1		182		343		319			
Lanaux, Arnaud	Confirmation of title to land in Louisiana.	22	1	Petition	63	Priv. Land Claims.	80	Favorable	75	Passed	Passed	App'd May 10, 1832
Lancaster, Barbara	(See widow of Hugh Greer)	29	2		323							
Lancaster, Joseph B.	Compensation for horses lost in public service	21	1	Resolution	303	Claims.						
Lancaster, Samuel	Pension for revolutionary services.	21	2	Resolution	283	Military Pensions.						
Lancaster, Thomas, surety of.	Release from liability	12	1	Petition	214	Com. and Manuf.						
Lancaster, William, jr.	Relief on account of lost vouchers.	17	1	Petition	335	Judiciary	May 7, 1822	Adverse		Leave to withdraw.		
Lance, William	(See Thomas Fraser, attorney of)	26	1		182		343		319			
Lancelot, Alexander	(See Louis Estevan, and others)	20	1		343							
Lancer, Robert	(See heir of Francis Eppes)	27	2		61							
Lancero, Spanish vessel	(See Spanish vessels Maria and Lancero.	27	2		555		1099					
Landais, Peter	Prize money as commander frigate Alliance.	8	1	Memorial	419	Whole House.						
Landais, Peter	Prize money as commander frigate Alliance.	8	2	Memorial	31	Claims	Dec. 28, 1804	Adverse		Rejected.		
Landais, Peter	Prize money as commander frigate Alliance.	9	1	Memorial	198							
				Rep. of Secretary State.	225	Claims	Feb. 11, 1806	Favorable	113	Passed	Passed	App'd Mar. 28, 1806
Landais, Peter	Examination and settlement of prize account.	9	2	Memorial	511	Claims	Jan. 28, 1807	Adverse		Leave to withdraw.		
Landais, Peter	Prize money as commander frigate Alliance.	10	1	Memorial	40	Claims	Dec. 23, 1807	Adverse		Laid on table		Leave to withdraw.
				Letter from clm't.	238	Claims				Laid on table.		
Landais, Peter	Prize money as commander frigate Alliance.	11	2	Petition	144	Claims	Feb. 5, 1810	Adverse		Rejected.		
Landais, Peter	Prize money as commander frigate Alliance	11	3	Memorial	461					Laid on table.		
				Letter from clm't.	502					Laid on table.		
Landais, Peter	Prize money as commander frigate Alliance.	12	1	Petition	85	Select	Mar. 18, 1812	Adverse		Rejected		Leave to withdraw.
Landais, Peter	Prize money as commander frigate Alliance.	13	3	Petition	471					Laid on table.		
Landais, Peter	Compensation as captain United States navy.	5	2	Petition	116	Claims	Jan. 3, 1798	Adverse		Rejected.		
Land commissioners, Mississippi.	Additional compensation for services.	10	1	Resolution	28	Public Lands	Jan. 11, 1808	Adverse		Laid on table.		

List of private claims presented to the House of Representatives of the United States from the 1st to the 31st Congress, inclusive—Continued.

Names of claimants.	Nature or object of the claim.	Congress.	Session.	How brought before the House of Reps.	Page of journal.	To what committee of the House referred.	No. or date of the report.	Nature of the report.	No. of the bill.	How disposed of by the House of Reps.	How disposed of by the Senate.	Date of the act of Congress, and remarks.
Land commissioners, Mississippi.	Additional compensation for services.	11	3	Resolution	466	....	....	....	......	Referred to Secretary Treasury.		
				Rep. of Secretary Treasury.	476	Claims.						
Land commissioners, Mississippi.	Additional compensation for services.	12	1	Resolution	25	Claims	Jan. 7, 1812	Favorable....	44	Passed	Passed	App'd Mar. 10, 1812
Land commissioners, Louisiana.)	Additional compensation for services.	16	2	Resolution	510	Public Lands.						
Lander, George A........	Redemption of Continental money.	24	1	Petition	599	Rev. Claims.						
Landereau, John P., heirs of.	Confirmation of title to land in Louisiana.	19	1	Petition	493	Priv. Land Claims.	....	....	......	Discharged; laid on table.		
Landerreau, John P., heirs of.	Confirmation of title to land in Louisiana.	19	2	Petition	37	Priv. Land Claims.	Dec. 23, 1826	Adverse	......	Discharged; laid on table.		
Landerreau, John P., heirs of.	Confirmation of title to land in Louisiana.	20	1	Petition	33	Priv. Land Claims.	34	Favorable....	......	Referred to Committee Whole House.		
Landerreau, John P., heirs of.	Confirmation of title to land in Louisiana.	20	2	Petition	55	Priv. Land Claims.	33	Favorable	349	Referred to Committee Whole House.		
Landerreau, John P., heirs of.	Confirmation of title to land in Louisiana.	2	1	Petition	40	Priv. Land Claims.	21	Favorable	30	Passed.............	Passed	App'd Mar. 23, 1830
Landerreau, John P., heirs of.	Confirmation of title to land in Louisiana.	28	1	Documents.....	366	Priv. Land Claims.	248	Adverse	......	Laid on table.		
Landes, Daniel	Exchange of a grant of land	27	2	Petition	379	Priv. Land Claims.						
Landier, Antoine........	Confirmation of title to land, (Terre aux Bœuf.)	2.	1	House bill......	107	Whole House.....	Mar. 23, 1832	With't amend.	125	Passed	Passed	App'd June 25, 1832
Landon, Charles........	(See Sylvester Phelps and C. Landon.)	14	1	....	76							
Landon, Charles.......	(See surviving partner of S. Phelps & Co.)	23	1	....	35							
Landon, Charles, heirs of.	Indemnity for property destroyed by United States troops.	27	2	Petition	55	Claims	13	Favorable....	52	Passed	Passed	App'd Aug. 1, 1842
Landon, Daniel.........	Pre-emption right to land in Indiana.	12	1	Petition	165	Public Lands.						
Landon, Daniel.........	Pre-emption right to land in Indiana.	13	2	Petition	170	Public Lands.						
Landon, Daniel.........	Compensation for property destroyed at Fort Wayne.	13	2	Petition	414	Claims.						
Landon, Giles	(See Giles Loudon)............	30		....	104							
Landon, Laban	Restoration of pension	17	1	Petition	45	Rev. Pensions.						
Landon, Laban	Restoration of pension	20	1	Resolution	715	Military Pensions.						
Landon, Joseph.........	(See sureties of Bateman Fisk)...	14	2	....	69							
Landon, Joseph.........	Compensa'n for property destroyed by British.	17	2	Petition	74	Claims.						
Landon, Joseph.........	Compensat'n for property destroyed by British.	22	1	Petition	188	Claims	Feb. 6, 1832	Adverse	......	Laid on table.		
Landry, Manuel	Confirmation of title to land in Louisiana.	20	2	Resolution	52	Priv. Land Claims.						
Landry, Manuel	Confirmation of title to land in Louisiana.	21	1	Petition	173	Priv. Land Claims.	Feb. 5, 1830	Favorable	205	Passed	Passed	App'd May 29, 1830
Landry, Marie..........	(See Pierre Gundry, widow of) ..	21	2	....	46	....	52	....	587			
Lane, Benjamin.........	Not found....................	28	2	Petition	72	Claims.						
Lane, Charles	(See Rufus & Charles Lane)	27	3	....	276							
Lane, Daniel (Me.)	Annual salary as collector	16	1	Petition	64	Commerce.						
Lane, Daniel, (Me.)	Annual salary as collector	22	1	Petition	53	Ways and Means.						

List of private claims presented to the House of Representatives of the United States from the 1st to the 31st Congress, inclusive—Continued.

Names of claimants.	Nature or object of the claim.	Congress.	Session.	How brought before the House of Reps.	Page of journal.	To what committee of the House referred.	No. or date of the report.	Nature of the report.	No. of the bill.	How disposed of by the House of Reps.	How disposed of by the Senate.	Date of the act of Congress, and remarks.
Lane, Job	Compensation for revolutionary services.	2	1	Petition	500					Referred to Secretary War.		
Lane, Job	Pension	3	1	Rep. of Secretary War.	131	Select	May 26, 1794	Res. to refer to Sec. War.	J. R. 12	Passed	Passed	App'd June 9, 1794
Lane, Job	Pension	3	2	Rep. of Secretary War.	350	Claims.						
Lane, Job	Pension	4	1	Resolution	445	Claims	Mar. 4, 1796	Pension bill	156	Passed	Passed	App'd April 20, 1796
Lane, Joseph	Pension	21	2	Petition	188	Military Pensions.						
Lane, Joseph, *et al*	Reimbursement of expenses, going to Oregon.	31	1	Notice of bill	204							
Lane, Mordicai	Pension	8	2	Petition	27	Whole House.						
Lane, Newton	Credit for payments as pension agent.	31	1	Senate resolution.	435	Whole House	Feb. 6, 1850	With't amend.	S. 4	Passed	Passed	App'd Feb. 12, 1850
Lane, Robert Carr	Compensation for horse lost in Seminole war.	16	1	Petition	91	Claims	Jan. 13, 1820	Adverse		Laid on table.		
Lane, Robert Carr	Compensation for horse lost in Seminole war.	18	2	Petition	134	Claims.						
Lane, Robert Carr	Compensation for horse lost in Seminole war.	19	1	Petition	44	Claims	Jan. 11, 1836	Adverse		Laid on table.		
Lane, Robert Carr	Compensation for horse lost in Seminole war.	19	2	Petition	45	Claims.						
Lane, Robert Carr	(See John Haynes, attorney of)	19	2		202							
Lane, Rufus & Charles	Fishing bounty on schooner Twin.	27	3	Senate bill	276	Commerce	Feb. 14, 1843	Favorable	S. 75	Referred to Committee Whole House.		
Lane, Ruth	Pension for revolutionary services of husband.	28	1	Petition	839	Whole House.						
Lane, Sally H.	(See James Woodbury, heirs of)	25	2		1120							
Lane, Samuel	Reimbursement of overpayment for land.	27	3	Petition	475	Public Lands.						
Lane, Timothy	Invalid pension	1	3	Petition and rep't Sec. of War.	364, 393					Laid on table.		
Lane, William	Indemnity for destruction of property by revolutionary army.	1	3	Petition	360					Referred to Secretary Treasury.		
Lane, William	Indemnity for destruction of property by revolutionary army.	2	1	Rep. of Secretary Treasury.	580					Laid on table.		
Lane, William	Pension for revolutionary services.	14	1	Resolution	614	Pens. & Rev. Cl'ms.						
Lane, William	Pension for revolutionary services.	16	1	Petition	33	Pens. & Rev. Cl'ms.				Discharged; referred to Secretary of War.		
Lane, William, *et al.*	Credit for certain land payments.	18	2	Petition	161	Priv. Land Claims.						
Lane, William, *et al.*	Credit for certain land payments.	19	1	Petition	86	Priv. Land Claims.						
Lang, John, widow of	Arrears of pension	29	1	Petition	533	Naval Affairs.						
Lang, John S. B.	Invalid pension	12	2	Petition	548	Claims				Laid on table.		
Lang, Robert	Invalid pension	27	2	Petition	218	Invalid Pensions	421	Adverse		Laid on table.		
Lang, William B.	Reimbursement of duties paid by mistake.	29	1	Petition	276	Commerce	April 6, 1846	Favorable	392	Passed	Passed	App'd Aug. 10, 1846
Langbourne, William, heirs of.	Commutation pay for revolutionary services.	22	2	Petition	29	Rev. Claims.						
Langbourne, William, heirs of.	Commutation pay for revolutionary services.	23	1	Petition	65	Rev. Claims.						
Langbourne, William, heirs of.	Commutation pay for revolutionary services.	23	2	Petition	84	Rev. Claims.						
Langbourne, William, heirs of.	Commutation pay for revolutionary services.	24	1	Petition	104	Rev. Claims	400	Favorable	405	Referred to Committee Whole House.		

List of private claims presented to the House of Representatives of the United States from the 1st to the 31st Congress, inclusive—Continued.

Names of claimants.	Nature or object of the claim.	Congress.	Session.	How brought before the House of Reps.	Page of journal.	To what committee of the House referred.	No. or date of the report.	Nature of the report.	No. of the bill.	How disposed of by the House of Reps.	How disposed of by the Senate.	Date of the act of Congress, and remarks.
Langbourne, William, heirs of.	Commutation pay for revolutionary services.	25	2	Petition	70	Rev. Claims	430	Favorable	439	Passed	Adverse.	
Langbourne, William, heirs of.	Commutation pay for revolutionary services.	25	3	Petition	84	Rev. Claims	17	Favorable	915	Laid on table.		
Langbourne, William, heirs of.	Commutation pay for revolutionary services.	26	1	Petition	164	Rev. Claims	241	Adverse		Laid on table.		
Langbourne, William, heirs of.	Commutation pay for revolutionary services.	27	2	Petition	61	Rev. Claims	388	Adverse		Laid on table.		
Langbourne, William, heirs of.	Commutation pay for revolutionary services.	28	1	Petition	375	Rev. Claims.						
Langdon, Edmond	(See Samuel Langdon, *et al.*)	12	1		138							
Langdon, John	Compensation for services and advances in war of 1812.	31	1	Petition	269	Claims.						
Langdon, Richard C	Payment of balance due two soldiers assigned to petitioner.	23	1	Petition	362	Claims	325	Adverse		Laid on table.		
Langdon, Richard C	Payment of balance due two soldiers assigned to petitioner.	24	1	Petition	429	Claims	695	Adverse		Laid on table.		
Langdon, Richard C	Payment of balance due two soldiers assigned to petitioner.	26	2	Petition	81	Claims	67	Adverse		Laid on table.		
Langdon, Richard C	Payment of balance due two soldiers assigned to petitioner.	27	2	Petition	1049					Leave to withdraw.		
Langdon, Samuel, *et al.*	Release of brig Frances, seized for violation of non-importation act.	12	1	Petition	138					Ref'd to Com. W. H. on bill No. 46.		
Langdon, Thomas	(See John V. Delano, *et al.*)	21	1		388							
Lange, Heinrich	Confirmation of title to land in Missouri.	30	2	Petition	240	Public Lands.						
Langford, Thomas, *et al.*	Compensation for services in Seminole war.	30	2	Resolution	346	Military Affairs.						
Langham, Elias T., sureties of.	Release from liability	25	3	Petition	176	Claims				Discharged; leave to withdraw.		
Langham, Elias T., sureties of.	Release from liability	25	3	Senate bill	478	Claims	Feb. 13, 1839	With amend.	S 206	Passed	Passed	App'd Feb. 16, 1839
Langham, John S., sureties of.	Release from liability	22	1	Petition	473	Judiciary.						
Langlee, Thomas	Pension for revolutionary services.	21	1	Resolution	465	Military Pensions				Discharged; laid on table.		
Langley, Hezekiah, and Benjamin M. Belt.	Compensation for labor on City Hall, D. C.	18	1	Senate bill	422	Claims	May 3, 1824	Adverse	S. 80	Recommitted.		
					489	Claims	May 7, 1824	With't amend.	S. 80	Passed	Passed	App'd May 25, 1824
Langley, Miles	Revolutionary pension	27	2	Petition	607	Rev. Pensions	784	Adverse		Laid on table.		
Langley, Philip	Claim under treaty of Ghent	20	2	Petition	231	Foreign Affairs	79	Adverse		Laid on table.		
Langley, William	Revolutionary pension	2	1	Petition	482					Referred to Secretary of War.		
Langley, William S	Naval pension	31	1	Petition	338	Naval Affairs.						
Langley, Wm. T., mother of.	Pension	30	2	Petition	440	Invalid Pensions				Discharged; laid on table.		
Langlois, Hilary, sureties of.	Release from liability	9	2	Petition	497	Com. and Manuf.				Discharged; laid on table.		
Langlois, Hilary, sureties of.	Release from liability	10	1	Petition	58	Com. and Manuf.						
Langlois, Hilary, sureties of.	Release from liability	10	2	Petition	395	Com. and Manuf.						

List of private claims presented to the House of Representatives of the United States from the 1st to the 31st Congress, inclusive—Continued.

Names of claimants.	Nature or object of the claim.	Congress.	Session.	How brought before the House of Reps.	Page of journal.	To what committee of the House referred.	No. or date of the report.	Nature of the report.	No. of the bill.	How disposed of by the House of Reps.	How disposed of by the Senate.	Date of the act of Congress, and remarks.
Langlois, Peter, wife of	Purchase of section of land granted by treaty of St. Joseph's.	22	2	Senate bill	441	Ways and Means	Mar. 1, 1833	With't amend.	S. 128	Passed with amendm't.	Passed	App'd March 2, 1833
Langlois, Peter, (Ind.)	Patent for certain tract of land	28	1	Petition	741	Public Lands.						
Langlois, Peter, (Ind.)	Payment of money and goods	20	1	Appropriat'n bill	698	Whole House	May 20, 1828	With amends.	293	Passed	Passed	App'd May 24, 1828
Langreen, Peter, widow of.	Pension	28	1	Petition	223	Invalid Pensions	191	Adverse		Laid on table.		
Langreen, Peter, widow of.	Pension	29	1	Res. and docs	70, 274	Naval Affairs	303	Adverse		Laid on table.		
Langreen, Peter, widow of	Pension	30	1	Petition	79	Naval Affairs.						
Langtry & Jenkins	Indemnity for loss on violated contract.	27	2	Petition	605	Judiciary.						
Langtry & Jenkins	Indemnity for loss on violated contract.	27	3	House bill	426	Judiciary	210	Favorable	807	Referred to Committee Whole House.		
Langtry & Jenkins	Indemnity for loss on violated contract.	28	1	Petition	251	Judiciary	291	Favorable	204	Passed	Adverse.	
Langtry & Jenkins	Indemnity for loss on violated contract.	28	2	Petition	56	Claims	1	Favorable	450	Referred to Committee Whole House.		
Langtry & Jenkins	Indemnity for loss on violated contract.	29	1	Petition	102	Claims	190	Favorable	181	Passed	Passed	App'd Aug. 8, 1846
Languille, Francis B	Indemnity for damage to property by U. S. army.	15	1	Petition	294	Claims.						
Languille, Francis B	Indemnity for damage to property by U. S. army.	15	2	Senate bill	316	Claims	Mar. 2, 1819	With amend	S. 57	Referred to Committee Whole House.		
Languille, Francis B	Indemnity for damage to property by U. S. army.	16	1	Senate bill	290	Claims	80	Adverse	S. 49	Referred to Committee Whole House.		
Languille, Francis B	Indemnity for damage to property by U. S. army.	16	2	Petition	102	Claims	29	Favorable	197	Passed	Passed	App'd March 2, 1821
Lanier, Alexander	Pension	15	1	Petition	378	Pens. & Rev. Cl'ms.				Discharged; referred to Secretary War.		
Lanier, J. F. D	Increase of compensation as pension agent.	27	2	Petition	383	Rev. Pensions	786	Adverse		Laid on table.		
Lanier, Robert	(See Francis Eppes, heirs of)	24	1		105							
Lankford, James	Pension	20	2	Petition	204	Military Pensions				Discharged; laid on table.		
Lanpher, Jerusha	(See Fitch Lanpher, widow of)	27	2		238							
Lanpher, Fitch, widow of.	Continuation of pension	27	2	Petition	238	Rev. Pensions	748	Adverse		Laid on table.		
Lanpher, Stacy	Pension	22	1	Petition	189	Invalid Pensions	Feb. 15, 1832	Adverse		Laid on table.		
Lanpher, Stacy	Arrears of pension	29	1	Petition	59	Invalid Pensions	185	Adverse		Laid on table.		
Lanpher, Stacy	Arrears of pension	29	2	Petition	50	Invalid Pensions	Feb. 14, 1847	Adverse		Laid on table.		
Lanphier, William	(See Harris & Lamphier.)	25	3		90							
Lansdale, Issac	(See John Haberson, surety of.)	8	1		502							
Lansdale, Oliver G	(See Louis F. Beeler, *et al.*)	30	1		115		482					
Lansdown, Nathaniel	Invalid pension	30	1	Petition	603	Invalid Pensions	574	Adverse		Laid on table.		
Lansing, Abraham	Compensation for naval services	24	1	Petition	205	Claims	573	Favorable	557	Referred to Committee Whole House.		
Lansing, Abraham	Compensation for naval services	25	2	Petition	36	Claims	30	Favorable	42	Passed	Passed	App'd Mar. 7, 1838
Lansing, S	Increase of pay to military store keepers.	30	1	Petition	589	Military Affairs.						
Lantz, Frederick	Invalid pension	25	2	Petition	629	Invalid Pensions.						
Lantz, Frederick	Invalid pension	25	3	Petition	446	Invalid Pensions				Discharged; laid on table.		
Lantz, Frederick	Invalid pension	27	2	Petition	107	Invalid Pensions	215	Adverse		Laid on table.		
Lanusse, Paul, widow of	Confirmation of title to land in Louisiana.	23	1	Petition	76	Priv. Land Claims.						
Lapham, Anna	(See Ezekiel Bennett, daughter of.)	23	1		499							

List of private claims presented to the House of Representatives of the United States from the 1st to the 31st Congress, inclusive—Continued.

Names of claimants.	Nature or object of the claim.	Congress.	Session.	How brought before the House of Reps.	Page of journal.	To what committee of the House referred.	No. or date of the report.	Nature of the report.	No. of the bill.	How disposed of by the House of Reps.	How disposed of by the Senate.	Date of the act of Congress, and remarks.
Lapham, Hamilton	Extension of patent	30	1	Petition	160	Patents	340	Favorable	319	Referred to Committee Whole House.		
Lapham, Molly	(See Charles Tuel, widow of.)	27	2		69							
Lapish,, John	Pension	3	2	Rep. of Secretary War.	350	Claims.						
Lapish, John	Pension	4	1	Rep. of Secretary War.	445	Claims	Feb. 18, 1796	Pension bill	156	Passed	Passed	App'd April 20, 1796
Laplant, Lewis	(See Reuben E. Gentry, *et al.*)	23	1		138							
Laplante, John B	Compensation for a horse lost in public service	20	1	Resolution	54	Claims	Feb. 1, 1828	Adverse		Laid on table.		
Laptante, John B	Compensation for a horse lost in public service.	23	1	Petition	92	Claims	Jan. 26, 1834	Adverse		Laid on table.		
Laplante, John B	Compensation for a horse lost in public service.	23	2	Petition	106	Claims.						
Laplante, John B	Compensation for a horse lost in public service.	25	2	Petition	275	Claims.						
Laplante, Pierre	Compensation for a horse lost in public service.	23	2	Petition	106	Claims.						
Laplante, Pierre	Compensation for a horse lost in public service.	26	1	Petition	169	Claims.						
Laprade, W	Credit for public money stolen	16	1	Petition	221	Claims	Mar. 15, 1820	Adverse		Rejected.		
Lapsey, Samuel, representatives of.	Renewal of certificates	5	2	Senate bill	238	Claims	July 5, 1798	Adverse	S. 15	Rejected.		
Lapsey, Samuel, representatives of.	Renewal of certificates	6	1	Senate bill	563	Claims	April 22, 1800	Adverse	S. 57	Referred to Committee Whole House.		
Lapsey, Samuel, representatives of.	Renewal of certificates	6	2	Petition & report.	731	Claims	Jan. 26, 1801	Adverse.		Report dsagreed to.		
Lapsey, Samuel, representatives of.	Renewal of certificates	7	1	Petition and rep't	49	Claims.						
Lapsey, Samuel, representatives of.	Renewal of certificates	10	2	Petition	357	Claims.						
Lapsley, Samuel, representatives of.	Renewal of certificates	11	2	Petition	167	Claims	Jan. 17, 1810	Adverse.				
Lapsley, Samuel, representatives of.	Renewal of certificates	11	2	House bill	283	Whole House	April 6, 1810	With amend	108	Passed	Rejected.	
Lapsley, Samuel, representatives of.	Renewal of certificates	12	2	Senate bill	711	Whole House	Mar. 3, 1813	With't amend.	S. 67	Passed	Passed	App'd March 3, 1813
Lapuce, P. N	(See Thomas Tyler, heirs of)	19	1		134							
Larabee, Charles	Compensation for baggage lost in United States service.	15	1	Petition	106	Claims				Discharged; laid on table.		Leave to withdraw.
Larabee, Charles	Pension	19	2	Petition	216	Military Pensions				Leave towithdraw.		
Larabee, Charles	Pension	20	1	Petition	124	Military Pensions	May 6, 1828	Adverse		Laid on table.		
Larabee, Charles	Increase of pension	21	1	Senate bill	139	Military Pensions	Jan. 21, 1830	Favorable	S. 32	Passed	Passed	App'd April 2, 1830
Larabee, Charles	Pension for wounds received in war of 1812.	24	2	Petition	86	Invalid Pensions	Dec. 30, 1836	Adverse		Laid on table.		
Larabee, Charles	Pension for wounds received in war of 1812.	25	2	Petition	58	Invalid Pensions	656	Adverse		Laid on table.		
Larabee, Charles	Pension for wounds received in war of 1812.	25	3	Petition	128	Invalid Pensions				Discharged; leave to withdraw.		
Larabee, Charles	Arrears of pension and losses sustained.	26	1	Res. and petition	287 559	Invalid Pensions	253	Adverse		Laid on table.		
Larabee, Charles	Arrears of pension	26	2	Petition	84	Invalid Pensions.						
Larabee, Charles	Arrears of pension	27	3	Petition	243	Invalid Pensions	428	Adverse		Laid on table.		

List of private claims presented to the House of Representatives of the United States from the 1st to the 31st Congress, inclusive—Continued.

Names of claimants.	Nature or object of the claim.	Congress.	Session.	How brought before the House of Reps.	Page of journal.	To what committee of the House referred.	No. or date of the report.	Nature of the report.	No. of the bill.	How disposed of by the House of Reps.	How disposed of by the Senate.	Date of the act of Congress, and remarks.
Larabee, Charles	Arrears of pension	27	3	Petition	386	Invalid Pensions				Leave to withdraw.		
Larabee, Charles	Increase of pension	28	2	Petition	57	Invalid Pensions	22	Adverse		Laid on table.		
Larabee, Charles	Increase of pension	30	2	Petition	224	Invalid Pensions	Feb. 13, 1849	Favorable	773	Passed	Passed	App'd March 3, 1849
Larabee, Joseph	Invalid pension	25	2	Petition	117	Invalid Pensions	Mar. 7, 1838	Adverse		Laid on table.		
Larabee, Samuel	Revolutionary pension	28	1	Petition	552	Rev. Pensions.						
Larabee, Samuel	Revolutionary pension	28	2	Petition	119	Rev. Pensions.						
Larche, Francis	Compensation for slave killed in United States service.	19	1	Senate bill	387	Claims	April 20, 1826	Adverse	S. 36	Recommitted.		
				Senate bill	477	Claims	May 5, 1826	With evidence	S. 36	Referred to Committee Whole House.		
Larche, Francis	Compensation for slave killed in United States service.	19	2	Senate bill	86	Claims			S. 21			
Larche, Francis	Compensation for slave killed in United States service.	20	1	Senate bill	137	Claims	236	Adverse	S. 37	Laid on table.		
Larche, Francis	Compensation for slave killed in United States service.	21	1	Senate bill	118	Claims	401	Adverse	S. 24	Referred to Committee Whole House.		
Larche, Francis	Compensation for slave killed in United States service.	21	2	Senate bill	164	Claims	Jan. 19, 1831	Adverse	S. 53	Laid on table.		
Lard, Robert, representatives of.	Arrears of pension	24	1	Resolution	345	Rev. Pensions				Discharged; laid on table.		
Lard, Robert, representatives of.	Arrears of pension	25	2	Documents	93	Rev. Pensions	615	Favorable	593	Passed	Passed	App'd July 7, 1838
Lardis, Jacob	Compensation for horse lost in public service.	24	1	Petition	430	Claims.						
La Reintree, Henry	Compensation for services as interpreter, translator.	29	1	Petition	362	Naval Affairs	June 17, 1846	Favorable	482	Ordered to 3d reading.		
La Reintree, Henry	Compensation for services as interpreter, translator.	29	2	House bill	212				482	Passed	Passed	App'd March 3, 1847
La Reintree, Henry	Compensation for services as secretary of legation, &c., at Chili.	31	1	Petition	195	Foreign Affairs	123	Favorable	147	Referred to Committee Whole House.		
Larkin, John	To correct error in land entry	24	1	Petition	538	Public Lands				Discharged; laid on table.		
Larkin, Lorin	Indemnity for seizure of vessel by British.	29	1	Petition	1163	Foreign Affairs.						
Larkin, Peter	Pension	14	2	Rep. of Secretary War.	131	Pens. & Rev. Cl'ms.	Jan. 18, 1817	Indefinite		Leave to withdraw.		
Larkins, Bradford	Bounty land for services in war of 1812.	30	1	Petition	172	Public Lands.						
Larkins, James	Compensation for making clothing for revolutionary army.	10	2	Petition	495	Whole House.						
Larkins, Presley	Revolutionary pension	24	1	Petition	753	Rev. Pensions.						
Larkins, Presley	Revolutionary pension	24	1	Petition	50	Rev. Pensions				Discharged; laid on table.		
Larned, Thomas	(See Wm. Baker, New York)	22	1		288		480					
Larochelle, Joseph	(See Joseph Sorin)	24	1		928							
Larue, Antonio	Confirmation of title to land in Louisiana.	26	1	Petition	365	Priv. Land Claims.						
Larue, Antonio	Confirmation of title to land in Louisiana.	28	1	Petition	132	Priv. Land Claims				Discharged; laid on table.		
Larue, Isaac, heir of	Compensation for revolutionary services.	23	1	Petition	494	Rev. Claims.						
Lasala, John B.	Reimbursement of duties paid on segars	25	2	Petition	119	Ways and Means	Dec. 28, 1837	Favorable	228	Referred to Committee Whole House.		

List of private claims presented to the House of Representatives of the United States from the 1st to the 31st Congress, inclusive—Continued.

Names of claimants.	Nature or object of the claim.	Congress.	Session.	How brought before the House of Reps.	Page of journal.	To what committee of the House referred.	No. or date of the report.	Nature of the report.	No. of the bill.	How disposed of by the House of Reps.	How disposed of by the Senate.	Date of the act of Congress, and remarks.
Lasala, John B	Reimbursement of duties paid on segars.	25	3	House bill	376	Whole House	Jan. 25, 1839	With't amend.	228	Passed	Adverse report.	
Lasala, John B	Reimbursement of duties paid on segars.	26	1	Petition	178	Ways and Means	299	Favorable	259	Referred to Committee Whole House.		
Lashels, John, widow of	Pension	26	1	Petition	325	Invalid Pensions	272	Adverse		Laid on table.		
Lashels, Mary	(See John Lashels, widow of)	26	1		325							
Lasley, George	Remission of a fine	26	2	Petition	54	Judiciary.						
Lasley, Samuel C	Indemnity for property destroyed by enemy.	21	1	Petition	104	Claims	Jan. 4, 1830	Adverse		Laid on table.		
Lasselle, Francis, *et al*	Compensation for military services in 1812.	22	2	Petition	32	Claims.						
Lasselle, Francis, *et al*	Compensation for military services in 1812.	23	1	Petition	93	Claims	219	Favorable	236	Referred to Committee Whole House.		
Lasselle, Francis, *et al*	Compensation for military services in 1812.	23	2	House bill	82	Whole House	Dec. 15, 1834	With't amend.	236	Passed	Passed	App'd March 3, 1835
Lasselle, Hyacinth	Permission to relocate land	26	1	Petition	365	Priv. Land Claims.	101	Favorable	97	Passed	Passed	App'd July 21, 1840
Lasselle, Hyacinth	Permission to relocate land	28	1	Petition	508	Public Lands	June 7, 1844	Favorable	182	Passed	Passed	App'd June 17, 1844
Lasselle, Hyacinth	Extension of time for relocation	29	1	Petition	713	Indian Affairs	June 17, 1846	Favorable	474	Referred to Committee Whole House.		
Lasselle, Hyacinth	Extension of time for relocation	29	2	House bill	211	Whole House	Jan. 22, 1847	With't amend.	474	Passed	Passed	App'd March 3, 1847
Lassita, Reuben	Indemnity for slave killed in Florida war.	24	2	Petition	144	Claims.						
Lassita, Reuben	Indemnity for slave killed in Florida war.	25	2	Petition	120	Claims				Discharged.		
Lassita, Reuben	Indemnity for slave killed in Florida war.	27	2	Documents	142	Claims	491	Adverse		Laid on table.		
Lastrope, Andre, administrator of.	Confirmation of title to land in Louisiana.	26	1	Memorial	610	Priv. Land Claims.						
Laswell, Ezekiel	Revolutionary pension	24	1	Petition	602	Rev. Pensions				Discharged; laid on table.		
Latel, Louis A	Confirmation of title to land in Louisiana.	27	2	Petition	406	Priv. Land Claims.	1093	Adverse		Laid on table.		
Latel, Louis A	Confirmation of title to land in Louisiana.	29	2	Petition	109	Priv. Land Claims.						
Latel, Louis A	Confirmation of title to land in Louisiana.	30	1	Petition	109	Priv. Land Claims.						
Latel, Louis A	(See Pierre Clermont, heirs of)	30	2		379							
Latham, Benjamin	Pension	18	1	Petition	343	Pens. & Rev. Cl'ms.	April 20, 1824	Adverse		Laid on table.		
Latham, Christopher	Pension	10	2	House bill	499	Whole House	Feb. 20, 1809	With amend.	158	Passed	Passed	App'd March 3, 1809
Latham, James, heir of	Indemnity for damages resulting from an act of Congress.	23	1	Documents	447	Public Lands	Mar. 17, 1834	Favorable	481	Passed	Passed	App'd June 30, 1834
Latham, James	Invalid pension	1	3	Petition	357					Laid on table.		
Latham, James, heirs of	To exchange location of land	23	2	Petition	103	Priv. Land Claims.	23	Favorable	595	Passed.		
Latham, James, heirs of	To exchange location of land	24	1	Petition	65	Priv. Land Claims.	42	Favorable	42	Referred to Committee Whole House.		
Latham, James, heirs of	To exchange location of land	24	2	House bill	176				42	Laid on table.		
Latham, James, heirs of	To exchange location of land	25	2	Senate bill	1169	Priv. Land Claims.			S. 289			
Latham, P. C	(See James Latham, heir of.)	23	1		447							
Latham, Thomas	(See Lewis Leroy, surety of.)	20	2		215							
Lathram, John	Restoration of pension	25	2	Resolution	240	Rev. Pensions	606	Favorable	586	Passed.		
Lathram, John	Restoration of pension	25	3	Resolution	88	Rev. Pensions	72	Favorable	950	Passed	Adverse.	
Lathram, John	Restoration of pension	26	1	Petition	171	Rev. Pensions	129	Favorable	139	Passed	Indef. postp'd.	
Lathram, John	Restoration of pension	26	2	Petition	35	Rev. Pensions	Feb. 12, 1841	Adverse		Laid on table.		

List of private claims presented to the House of Representatives of the United States from the 1st to the 31st Congress, inclusive—Continued.

Names of claimants.	Nature or object of the claim.	Congress.	Session.	How brought before the House of Reps.	Page of journal.	To what committee of the House referred.	No. or date of the report.	Nature of the report.	No. of the bill.	How disposed of by the House of Reps.	How disposed of by the Senate.	Date of the act of Congress, and remarks.
Lathrop, Daniel	Release from liability on account of defalcation, person left in charge of post office.	16	1	Petition	228	Ways and Means.						
Lathrop, Daniel	Release from liability on account of defalcation, person left in charge of post office.	16	2	Petition	32	Ways and Means	Nov. 24, 1820	Adverse	......	Concurred in.		
Lathrop, J. H	(See Thomas Tupper, assignees of.)	22	2	....	142							
Lathrop, Samuel	Pension	10	1	House bill	232	Select	Mar. 17, 1808	Favorable	78	Passed	Passed	App'd April 25, 1808
La'il, Louis A	(See Louis A. Latel.)	27	2	....	406							
Latil, Lazarus	Confirmation of title to land	19	2	Petition	32	Priv. Land Claims.						
Latil, Lazarus	Confirmation of title to land	20	1	Petition	128	Priv. Land Claims.						
Latil, Lazarus	Confirmation of title to land	21	1	Petition	499	Priv. Land Claims.						
Latimer, George	Increase of compensation as collector at Philadelphia.	5	3	Petition	454	Com. and Manuf.						
Latimer, George, *et al.*	Drawback of duties on sugar and coffee.	3	2	Petition	292	Select	Jan. 20, 1795	Favorable	102	Passed	Passed	App'd Feb. 13, 1795
Latimer, James	Revolutionary pension	25	2	Petition	55	Rev. Pensions	Jan. 25, 1838	Adverse	......	Laid on table.		
Latimer, James	Indemnity for French spoliations prior to 1800.	26	1	Memorial	182	Foreign Affairs	343	Favorable	319	Referred to Committee Whole House.		
Latimer, John K., representatives of.	Indemnity for pilot boat burnt by enemy.	20	1	Resolution	381	Claims	Mar. 26, 1828	Adverse	......	Laid on table.		
Latimer, John K., representatives of.	Indemnity for pilot boat burnt by enemy.	24	2	Resolution	78	Claims.						
Latimer, John K., representatives of.	Indemnity for pilot boat burnt by enemy.	24	2	Petition	308	Claims.						
Latimer, John K., representatives of.	Indemnity for pilot boat burnt by enemy.	25	2	Petition	275	Claims	736	Adverse	......	Laid on table.		
Latimer, Roe and Mosely	Increase of pay as officer of revenue cutter.	14	2	Petition	184	Com. and Manuf.						
Latiolais, Lenfroi	Confirmation of title to land in Louisiana.	23	1	Petition	309	Priv. Land Claims.	Feb. 25, 1834	Favorable	321	Referred to Committee Whole House.		
Latour, Anthony	Revolutionary pension	14	2	Petition	40	Pens. & Rev. Cl'ms.	Dec. 31, 1816	Adverse	......	Laid on table.		
Latour, Anthony	Revolutionary pension	23	1	Petition	71	Rev. Claims.						
Latour, John C	Invalid pension	4	2	Petition	620	Claims	Jan. 9, 1797	Adverse	......	Rejected.		
La Tourrettee, Daniel	Compensation for revolutionary services.	12	1	Petition	99	Claims.						
La Tourrettee, Daniel	Compensation for revolutionary services.	12	2	Petition	570	Claims	....	....	......	Laid on table.		
La Tourrettee, Daniel	Compensation for revolutionary services.	13	1	Petition	20	Claims.						
La Tourrettee, John	Refunding of money overpaid for land.	24	1	Senate bill	496	Public Lands	Mar. 21, 1836	Favorable	S. 72	Passed	Passed	App'd July 2, 1836
La Trappe, monks of the order of.	(See Guillet.)											
Latta, Anna and James	(See Robert Latta, widow and administrator of.)	3	1	....	32							
Latta, Robert, widow and administrator of.	Compensation for use of a wagon and team in revolutionary war.	3	1	Petition & report Sec. Treasury.	32	....	....	....	......	Laid on table.		
Latta, Thomas, administrator of.	Compensation for services of servant on public works.	14	1	Petition	495	Claims.						
Latting, Jacob	Permission to raise locust trees in Florida as indemnity for spoliations committed, &c.	25	3	Petition	672	....	....	....	......	Laid on table.		

List of private claims presented to the House of Representatives of the United States from the 1st to the 31st Congress, inclusive—Continued.

Names of claimants.	Nature or object of the claim.	Congress.	Session.	How brought before the House of Reps.	Page of journal.	To what committee of the House referred.	No. or date of the report.	Nature of the report.	No. of the bill.	How disposed of by the House of Reps.	How disposed of by the Senate.	Date of the act of Congress, and remarks.
Latting, Jacob, heirs of	Indemnity for French spoliations prior to 1800.	31	1	Petition	197	Foreign Affairs	355	Favorable	318	Referred to Committee Whole House.		
Laub, Conrad	Compensation for revolutionary services.	2	2	Petition	674					Referred to Secretary Treasury.		
Laub, Conrad	Compensation for revolutionary services.	3	2	Rep. of Secretary Treasury.	284					Laid on table.		
Laub, Conrad, administrator of.	Compensation for extra services	15	1	Petition	114	Claims.						
Laub, Conrad, administrator of.	Compensation for extra services	16	1	Petition	452	Ways and Means	April 29, 1820	Favorable	144	Passed	Passed	App'd May 15, 1820
Laub, John	Compensation for services as acting comptroller.	24	2	Petition	37	Claims.						
Laub, John	Compensation for services as acting comptroller.	25	2	Petition	52	Claims.						
Laub, John	Compensation for services as acting comptroller.	25	3	Petition	86	Claims.						
Laub, John	Compensation for services as acting comptroller.	26	1	Petition	169	Claims.						
Laub, John, administrator of.	Compensation for services as acting comptroller.	27	2	Petition	154	Claims	645	Adverse		Laid on table.		
Laub, John, administrator of.	Compensation for services as acting comptroller.	29	1	Petition	347	Claims	843	Adverse		Laid on table.		
Laub, John, administrator of.	Compensation for services as acting comptroller.	31	1	Petition	390	Claims	163	Adverse		Laid on table.		
Lauck, Peter	Pension	22	1	Petition	534	Claims				Discharged; laid on table.		
Lauderdale's battalion	Payment for horses turned over to United States.	25	3	Petition	121	Rev. Claims.						
Lauderman	(See Louderman.)											
Lauderman, Newman	Pension	11	2	Pension bill	283	Whole House	Mar. 16, 1810	With amend.	107	Passed	Passed	App'd April 27, 1810
Lauer, Philip	Compensation for revolutionary services	2	1	Petition	494					Referred to Secretary War.		
Lauer, Philip	Compensation for revolutionary services.	3	1	Rep. of Secretary War.	131	Select	May 26, 1794	Res. to refer to Sec. War.	J. R. 12	Passed	Passed	App'd June 9, 1794
Lauer, Philip	Compensation for revolutionary services.	4	1	Rep. of Secretary War.	445	Claims	May 4, 1796	Favorable	156	Passed	Passed	App'd April 20, 1796
Laughlin, Charles	Compensation for property lost in United States service.	24	1	Petition	477	Indian Affairs.						
Laughlin, Charles	Compensation for property lost in United States service.	24	2	Petition	93	Indian Affairs.						
Laughlin, Dennis	Pension	12	1	House bill	361	Whole House	June 15, 1812	Favorable	138	Passed	Passed	App'd July 5, 1812
Laughlin, Robert, heirs of.	Indemnity for property lost in revolutionary war.	10	1	Petition	270	Rev. Claims	467	Adverse		Laid on table.		
Laughlin, Thaddeus	Release from judgment at suit of United States.	19	1	Petition	491	Ways and Means	May 5, 1826	Res. to refer to Sec. Treas'y.				
Laughlin, Thaddeus	Release from judgment at suit of United States.	19	2	Rep. of Secretary Treasury.	153	Ways and Means				Discharged; referred to Sec'ry Treasury.		
Laughlin, Thaddeus	Release from judgment at suit of United States.	20	1	Rep. of Secretary Treasury.	53	Judiciary.						
Laughlin, Thaddeus	Release from judgment at suit of United States.	20	2	Petition	83	Judiciary	97	Adverse		Laid on table.		
Laughrey, Col. Archibald, heirs of.	Bounty land for revolutionary services.	29	2	Petition	192	Public Lands	30	Favorable	611	Referred to Committee Whole House.		

List of private claims presented to the House of Representatives of the United States from the 1st to the 31st Congress, inclusive—Continued.

2—37

Names of claimants.	Nature or object of the claim.	Congress.	Session.	How brought before the House of Reps.	Page of journal.	To what committee of the House referred.	No. or date of the report.	Nature of the report.	No. of the bill.	How disposed of by the House of Reps.	How disposed of by the Senate.	Date of the act of Congress, and remarks.
Laughrey, Col. Archibald, heirs of.	Bounty land for revolutionary services.	30	1	Petition	182	Public Lands	605	Adverse	......	Laid on table.		
Laughrey, William	Repayment of land found deficient in quantity.	18	2	Petition	115	Priv. Land Claims.	Jan. 21, 1825	Adverse	......	Referred to Committee Whole House.		
Lauligne, Joseph, assignee of.	Confirmation of title to land in Louisiana.	26	1	Petition	1346	Priv. Land Claims.	July 21, 1840	Adverse	......	Laid on table.		
Lauligne, Joseph, assignee of.	Confirmation of title to land in Louisiana.	27	2	Petition	58	Priv. Land Claims.						
Laurens, Edward R......	(See Thomas Rutledge, administrator of.)	25	2	....	699							
Laurens, Francis E......	(See Col. John Laurens, child of)	1	3	....	346							
Laurens, Henry, (guardian)	(See Col. John Laurens, child of)	1	3									
Laurens, Col. John, child of.	Interest on allowance, as per resolution of Congress, March 1, 1785.	1	3	Petition	346	Select	Jan. 28, 1791	Adverse	......	Laid on table.		
Laurens, Col. John, child of.	Interest on allowance, as per resolution of Congress, March 1, 1785.	2	1	Petition	530	Select	Mar. 22, 1792	Adverse	......	Laid on table.		
Laurens, Col. John, representatives of.	Compensation for services and advances to government for public service.	14	2	Petition	347	Pens. & Rev. Cl'ms.						
Laurens, Col. John, representatives of.	Compensation for services and advances to government for public services.	15	1	Petition	324	Pens. & Rev. Cl'ms.						
Laurens, Col. John, representatives of.	Compensation for services and advances to government for public service.	20	1	Petition	69	Foreign Affairs....	May 7, 1828	Adverse.				
Laurens, Col. John, representatives of.	Compensation for services and advances to government for public service.	21	1	Petition	121	Rev. Claims......	March 2, 1830	Favorable....	310	Referred to Committee Whole House.		
Laurens, Col. John, representatives of.	Compensation for services and advances to government for public service.	21	2	House bill......	333	Whole House	Feb. 19, 1831	With't amend.	310	Passed.		
Laurens, Col. John, representatives of.	Compensation for services and advances to government for public service.	22	1	Petition	143	Rev. Claims......	Feb. 17, 1832	Favorable....	386	Referred to Committee Whole House.		
Laurens, Col. John, representatives of.	Compensation for services and advances to government for public service.	22	1	Senate bill	783	Rev. Claims......	May 24, 1832	With't amend.	S. 40	Passed	Passed	App'd July 14, 1832
Laurens, Col. John, representatives of.	Compensat'n as minister to France.	23	2	Senate bill	400	Rev. Claims......	134	Adverse	S. 100	Referred to Committee Whole House.		
Laurents, Benoit, sureties of.	Release from liability...........	29	1	House bill......	1069	Whole House	July 25, 1846	With't amend.	497	Referred to Committee Whole House.		
Laurents, Benoit, sureties of.	Release from liability...........	29	2	House bill......	212	....	....	....	497	Passed.............	Passed	App'd March 3, 1847
Laurie, Ann Eliza.......	(See Joseph Tarbell, child of) ...	25	3	....	360							
Lauries & Tucker	(See Tucker & Lauries)	15	1	....	84							
Lauriston, M., *et al*......	Confirmation of title to land	26	1	Petition	948	Priv. Land Claims.						
Laval, Jacint	Relief in settlement of accounts, vouchers destroyed by fire.	14	2	Senate bill	374	Military Affairs....	Feb. 15, 1817	With't amend.	......	Passed	Passed	App'd Feb. 22, 1817
Laval, John............	Allowance of drawback on jewelry.	26	1	Petition	292	Commerce	30	Favorable....	49	Passed	Passed	App'd July 20, 1840
Lavellet, Eugenio........	Confirmation of title to land	19	[illegible]	Petition	135	Priv. Land Claims.						
Lavellet, Eugenio........	Confirmation of title to land	24	1	Petition	425	Priv. Land Claims.						
Lavellett, E. A., U. S. N..	To refund moneys paid interpreter.	31	1	Petition	1269	Foreign Affairs.						

List of private claims presented to the House of Representatives of the United States from the 1st to the 31st Congress, inclusive—Continued.

Names of claimants.	Nature or object of the claim.	Congress.	Session.	How brought before the House of Reps.	Page of journal.	To what committee of the House referred.	No. or date of the report.	Nature of the report.	No. of the bill.	How disposed of by the House of Reps.	How disposed of by the Senate.	Date of the act of Congress, and remarks.
Lavender, George M., administrator of.	Compensation for property destroyed by enemy.	28	1	Petition	345	Claims	May 24, 1844	Adverse	......	Laid on table.		
Lavender, George M., administrator of.	Compensation for procuring Cherokee treaty.	28	2	Petition	102	Claims.						
Laventure, Francis, *et al.*	Confirmation of title to land	25	2	Resolution	1176	Priv. Land Claims.						
Laventure, Francis, *et al.*	Confirmation of title to land	26	1	Senate bill	1105	Public Lands	July 21, 1840	With't amend.	S. 57	Laid on table.		
Laventure, Francis, *et al.*	Confirmation of title to land	26	2	Senate bill	178	Public Lands	....	....	S. 90			
Lavergne, Celestine	Confirmation of title to land	19	2	Petition	50	Priv. Land Claims.						
Lavergne, Celestine	Confirmation of title to land	22	1	Petition	538	Priv. Land Claims.						
Lavergne, Celestine	Confirmation of title to land	23	1	Petition	76	Priv. Land Claims.						
Lavergne, Celestine	Confirmation of title to land	23	2	Petition	48	Priv. Land Claims.						
Lavergne, Celestine	Confirmation of title to land	24	1	Petition	155	Priv. Land Claims.	93	Favorable	......	Ordered to be printed.		
Lavergne, John, assignees of.	Confirmation of title to land	22	1	Memorial	62	Public Lands	Feb. 28, 183[illegible]	Favorable	425	Passed	Passed	App'd June 25, 1832
Laviolet, Marguritte	(See Charles Combs and wife.)											
Lavonture, Francis	Confirmation of title to land	24	1	House bill	219	Whole House	May 13, 1836	With't amend	172			
Law, Alexander	(See Stephen Decatur, widow of, *et al.*)	23	1	....	36							
Law, Andrew	Extension of patent for printing music.	14	1	Petition	257	Select	Mar. 20, 1816	Favorable	139	Indefinitely postponed.		
Law, Andrew	Extension of patent for printing music.	14	2	Petition	127	Select	Jan. 28, 1817	Favorable	87	Referred to Committee Whole House.		
Law, Andrew	Extension of patent for printing music.	15	1	Petition	122	Select	Feb. 24, 1818	Favorable	100	Referred to Committee Whole House.		
Law, Andrew	Extension of patent for printing music.	16	1	Petition	284	Judiciary.						
Law, Andrew	Extension of patent for printing music.	16	2	Petition	172	Judiciary.						
Law, Benjamin, *alias* William.	Invalid pension	6	2	Petition	740	Claims	Dec. 18, 1800	Adverse	......	Rejected.		
Law, Christiana	(See Cornelius T. Janson, widow of.)	26	1	....	286							
Law, George	(See George Smith, administrator of.)	24	2	....	399							
Law, George, President of Marine Insurance Co.	Indemnity for French spoliations prior to 1800.	29	2	Petition	161	Foreign Affairs.						
Law, John	Pension	21	1	Resolution	484	Military Pensions	April 2, 1830	Adverse	......	Laid on table.		
Law, John	Further time to make payment for lot.	16	1	Petition	182	Dist. of Columbia.	57	Favorable	66	Passed	Passed	App'd May 4, 1820
Law, John, *et al.*	(See Maria and Lancero, Spanish vessels.)	27	2	....	1456							
Law, John, heirs of	Confirmation of title to land in Louisiana.	20	1	Petition	728	Priv. Land Claims.						
Law, John, heirs of	Confirmation of title to land in Louisiana.	21	1	Petition	236	Priv. Land Claims.						
Law, Joseph F., by Matthias B aver.	Bounty land and extra pay for services in war with Mexico.	30	2	Petition	296	Judiciary.						
Law, Nathan	Arrears of revolutionary pension	24	2	Petition	313	Rev. Pensions	....	....	......	Discharged; laid on table.		
Law, Nathan	Arrears of revolutionary pension	25	2	Petition	55	Rev. Pensions	Jan. 25, 1838	Adverse	......	Laid on table.		
Law, Peter W., *et al*	Benefit of act concerning armed occupation in Florida.	30	1	Petition	678	Public Lands.						

List of private claims presented to the House of Representatives of the United States form the 1st to the 31st Congress, inclusive—Continued.

Names of claimants.	Nature or object of the claim.	Congress.	Session.	How brought before the House of Reps.	Page of journal.	To what committee of the House referred.	No. or date of the report.	Nature of the report.	No. of the bill.	How disposed of by the House of Reps.	How disposed of by the Senate.	Date of the act of Congress, and remarks.
Law, jr., Richard	Relief as late master commandant of sloop of war Richmond.	8	1	Petition	409	Claims				Postponed.		
Law, jr., Richard	Relief as late master commandant of sloop of war Richmond.	8	2	Petition	6	Claims.						
Law, jr., Richard	Relief as late master commandant of sloop of war Richmond.	9	2	Petition	481	Claims.						
Law, jr., Richard	Relief as late master commandant of sloop of war Richmond.	12	1	Petition	92	Claims.						
Law, jr., Richard	Relief as late master commandant of sloop of war Richmond.	14	2	Petition	141					Referred to Secretary of the Navy.		
Law, William	Compensation for revolutionary services.	9	2	Petition	490	Claims.						
Law, William	Invalid pension	11	2	Petition and rep't Sec. of War.	138					Laid on table.		
Law, William	Invalid pension	12		Petition	346	Claims	June 12, 1812	Adverse		Laid on table.		
Law, William	Invalid pension	12	2	Petition	624					Leave to withdraw.		
Law, W. C., (Ind.)	Increase of pension	31	1	Petition	840	Invalid Pensions.						
Lawder, George, heirs of	Continuation of their father's pension.	25	3	Petition	130	Naval Affairs.						
Lawe, or Lowe, John	(See Gregnon & Lawe, administrator of.)	29	1		166							
Lawe, John	To change boundary of certain lot	23	1	Petition	450	Priv. Land Claims.				Discharged; leave to withdraw.		
Lawe, John	Compensation for use of and damage to land.	21	1	Petition	264	Claims				Discharged; laid on table.		
Lawe, John	Compensation for use of and damage to land.	21	2	Petition	62	Claims	Dec. 27, 1830	Adverse		Laid on table.		
Lawe, John	Compensation for use of and damage to land.	22	1	Petition	226	Claims.						
Lawe, John	Compensation for use of and damage to land.	22	2	Petition	219	Claims.						
Lawes, Alexander	(See Stephen Decatur, widow of, *et al.*)											
Lawler, Joab	Additional salary as receiver of public moneys.	23	1	Petition	75	Public Lands				Discharged; laid on table.		
Lawler, Thomas J., & S. M. Miles.	Compensation for custody of negroes brought into United States in contravention of law.	24	1	Resolution	635	Claims	574	Favorable	558	Referred to Committee Whole House.		
Lawler, Thomas J., & S. M. Miles.	Compensation for custody of negroes brought into United States in contravention of law.	25	2	Resolution	36	Claims	31	Favorable	43	Passed	Passed	**App'd March 7, 1838**
Lawman, or Lawrence, Jacob.	Revolutionary pension	23	2	Petition	87	Rev. Pensions				Discharged; laid on table.		
Lawman, or Lawrence, Jacob.	Revolutionary pension	24	1	Petition	137	Rev. Pensions				Discharged; laid on table.		
Lawrence, Aaron	(See Leighton Wood, *et al.*)	3	1		88							
Lawrence, Abraham	Pension	16	1	Petition	33	Rev. Pensions	Jan. 14, 1820	Adverse		Laid on table.		
Lawrence, Abraham	Pension	21	1	Petition	104	Military Pensions				Discharged; laid on table.		
Lawrence, Abraham	Pension	21	2	Petition	95	Military Pensions.						
Lawrence, Abraham	Pension	22	1	Petition	412	Rev. Pensions	411	Favorable	511	Referred to Committee Whole House.		
Lawrence, Abraham	Pension	22	2	Petition	74	Rev. Pensions				Disch'd; laid on table.		

List of private claims presented to the House of Representatives of the United States from the 1st to the 31st Congress, inclusive—Continued.

Names of claimants.	Nature or object of the claim.	Congress.	Session.	How brought before the House of Reps.	Page of journal.	To what committee of the House referred.	No. or date of the report.	Nature of the report.	No. of the bill.	How disposed of by the House of Reps.	How disposed of by the Senate.	Date of the act of Congress, and remarks.
Lawrence, Abraham	Pension	23	1	Petition	46	Rev. Pensions.						
Lawrence, Amos	Pension for revolutionary services.	18	2	Petition	222	Rev. Pensions				Discharged; laid on table.		
Lawrence, A. H.	Indemnity for French spoliations prior to 1800.	26	1	Memorial	182	Foreign Affairs	343	Favorable	319	Referred to Committee Whole House.		
Lawrence, Clark	Pension for revolutionary services.	25	2	Petition	729	Rev. Pensions.						
Lawrence, Clark	Pension for revolutionary services.	25	3	Petition	88	Rev. Pensions.						
Lawrence, Clark	Pension for revolutionary services.	26	1	Petition	174	Rev. Pensions.						
Lawrence, Clark	Pension for revolutionary services.	27	2	Petition	792	Rev. Pensions				Disch'd; laid on table.		
Lawrence, Daniel, widow of	Pension for revolutionary services.	24	1	Petition	56	Rev. Pensions				Discharged; laid on table.		
Lawrence, Daniel, widow of	Pension for revolutionary services.	25	2	Petition	914	Rev. Pensions.						
Lawrence, Daniel, widow of	Pension for revolutionary services.	26	1	Petition	174	Rev. Pensions				Disch'd; laid on table.		
Lawrence, Edward	Balance due on settlement	19	1	Petition	83	Claims	Jan. 13, 1826	Adverse		Laid on table.		
Lawrence, Eleanor	Compensat'n for damages from erection of military works on farm.	17	2	Senate bill	217	Claims	Feb. 14, 1823	Favorable	51	Passed	Passed	App'd March 1, 1823
Lawrence, Elizabeth	(See Jonathan Hager)	25	3		220							
Lawrence, Ho l.	(See Thomas Tupper, assignee.)	22	2		142							
Lawrence, Isaac, *et al.*	Drawback on merchandise exported	14	1	Petition	386	Com. and Manuf	April 12, 1826	Favorable		Ref'd to Com. W. H.		
Lawrence, Isaac, *et al.*	Drawback on merchandise exported	14	2	Petition	101	Com. and Manuf	Dec. 31, 1816	Favorable	36	Passed	Passed	App'd March 3, 1817
Lawrence, Jacob and Valentine.	Compensation for revolutionary services.	19	1	Resolution	134	Rev. Claims	April 5, 1826	Adverse		Laid on table.		
Lawrence, Jacob and Valentine.	Compensation for revolutionary services.	19	2	Resolution	69	Rev. Claims	Jan. 9, 1827	Adverse		Laid on table.		
Lawrence, James	Pension	20	2	Petition	118	Military Pensions	Jan. 20, 1829	Adverse		Laid on table.		
Lawrence, James	(See S. Decatur, widow of, *et al*).	19	2		98							
Lawrence, James, representatives of.	Continuance of pension	15	1	Resolution	96	Naval Affairs.						
Lawrence, James, representatives of.	Continuance of pension	17	2	Resolution	61	Naval Affairs.						
Lawrence, James, representatives of.	Continuance of pension	17	2	Petition	74	Naval Affairs	66	Adverse		Referred to Committee Whole House.		
Lawrence, James, representatives of.	Continuance of pension	18	1	Petition	32	Naval Affairs	[illegible]5	Favorable	15	Passed	Passed	App'd Jan. 22, 1824
Lawrence, James, heirs of.	(See S. Decatur, widow of, *et al.*)	19	2		98							
Lawrence, John C., parents of.	Pension	30	1	Petition	380	Naval Affairs				Discharged; laid on table.		
Lawrence, Jonathan	Remission of forfeiture	14	2	Petition	310	Ways and Means.						
Lawrence, Jonathan, widow of.	Continuance of pension	19	1	Petition	82	Military Pensions	164	Adverse		Laid on table.		
Lawrence, Jonathan, widow of.	Continuance of pension	19	2	Petition	156	Military Pensions.						
Lawrence, Jonathan, widow of.	Continuance of pension	20	1	Petition	30	Military Pensions	122	Favorable	141	Passed.		
Lawrence, Jonathan, widow of.	Continuance of pension	20	2	Petition	175	Military Pensions.						
Lawrence, Jonathan, widow of.	Continuance of pension	21	1	Petition	36	Military Pensions	May 21, 1830	Favorable	478	Referred to Committee Whole House.		
Lawrence, Jonathan, widow of.	Continuance of pension	22	1	Petition	46	Invalid Pensions	216	Favorable	288	Passed	Passed	App'd July 14, 1832
Lawrence, Joseph	Compensation for revolutionary services.	2	2	Petition and rep. Sec. War.	676					Laid on table.		
Lawrence, Joseph	Remission of duty on guano	28	2	Petition	120	Ways and Means.						

List of private claims presented to the House of Representatives of the United States from the 1st to the 31st Congress, inclusive—Continued.

Names of claimants.	Nature or object of the claim.	Congress.	Session.	How brought before the House of Reps.	Page of journal.	To what committee of the House referred.	No. or date of the report.	Nature of the report.	No. of the bill.	How disposed of by the House of Reps.	How disposed of by the Senate.	Date of the act of Congress, and remarks.
Lawrence, Joshua	Pension for revolutionary services.	22	1	Petition	219	Rev. Pensions.						
Lawrence, Joshua	(See John Cox, representatives of)	29	1		275							
Lawrence, J. A. D., administrator of.	Compensat'n for supplies furnished army.	31	1	Petition	433	Military Affairs				Discharged; laid on table.		
Lawrence, Margaret	(See Daniel Lawrence, widow of.)	24	1		56							
Lawrence, Lt. N. S., parents of.	Pension on account of services	30	1	Petition	380	Naval Affairs				Discharged; laid on table.		
Lawrence, Nathaniel and Catharine.	(See Lieut. N. S. Lawrence, parents of.)	30	1		380							
Lawrence, Richard	For benefit of lunatic asylum	25	2	Resolution	734	Dist. of Columbia.	923	Favorable	808	Passed	With amend's.	
Lawrence, Richard	For benefit of lunatic asylum	26	1	Petition	181	Dist. of Columbia.						
Lawrence, Samuel	(See John De Trevelle)	31	1									
Lawrence, Submit	Continuance of pension	28	1	Petition	850	Rev. Pensions.						
Lawrence, Valentine	(See Jacob & Valentine Lawrence)	19	1		134							
Laurence, William	Indemnity for losses as a Canadian refugee.	3	1	Petition	29	Select	April 1, 1794	Favorable		Referred to Committee Whole House.		
Laurence, William	Indemnity for losses as a Canadian refugee.	11	3	Petition	459					Referred to Secretary of War.		
Laurence, William	Indemnity for losses as a Canadian refugee.	15	1	Petition	21	Rev. Claims	Dec. 18, 1817	Adverse		Laid on table.		
Laurence, William	Indemnity for losses as a Canadian refugee.	15	2	Rep't of last sess.	57					Referred to Secretary War.		
Laurence, William	Indemnity for losses as a Canadian refugee.	16	1	Petition	252					Referred to Secretary War.		
Laurence, William	Indemnity for losses as a Canadian refugee.	19	1	Petition	36	Claims	Dec. 19, 1825	Adverse		Laid on table.		
Laurence, William	Indemnity for losses as a Canadian refugee.	20	1	Petition	396	Rev. Claims	May 16, 1828	Favorable	283	Passed.		
Laurence, William	Indemnity for losses as a Canadian refugee.	20	2	House bill	55	Whole House	Dec. 12, 1828	With amends.	311	Passed	Laid on table.	
Laurence, William	(See Canadian refugees.)	6	2									
Laurence, William	Pension for revolutionary services.	21	1	Pension bill	130	Whole House	Feb. 12, 1830	With amend.	72	Passed	Passed	App'd May 20, 1830
Laurence, William	Arrears of pension	25	2	Petition	198	Rev. Pensions				Disch'd; laid on table.		
Laurence, William	Arrears of pension	25	3	Petition	88	Rev. Pensions	Jan. 16, 1839	Adverse		Laid on table.		
Laurence, Col. William	Pension	23	1	Petition	112, 190	Invalid Pensions	343	Favorable	275	Referred to Committee Whole House.		
Laurence, Col. William	Pension	23	2	House bill	300	Whole House	Jan. 31, 1835	With amend.	275	Passed.		
Laurence, Col. William	Pension	24	1	Petition	98	Invalid Pensions	196	Favorable	198	Passed	Passed	App'd June 28, 1836
Laurence, Col. Wm., *et al*	Payment for vessel and cargo captured.	14	1	Senate bill	375	Military Affairs		With't amend.		Passed	Passed	App'd March 5, 1816
Laurence, Col. Wm., *et al.*	Payment for vessel and cargo captured.	24	1	Appropriat'n bill.	239				216	Passed	Passed	App'd May 9, 1836
Laurence, Col. Wm., *et al.*	Payment for vessel and cargo captured.	28	2	Appropriat'n bill.	177				498	Passed	Passed	App'd Mar. 3, 1845
Laurence, William B., *et al*	Settlement of accounts	21	1	House bill	326	Whole House	May 5, 1830	With't amend.	275	Passed	Passed	App'd May 29, 1830
Laurence, William P.	Payment for a negro who died of disease contracted in attending sick soldiers.	14	1	Petition	244	Claims	Feb. 24, 1816	Adverse		Concurred in.		
Laurence, William P.	Payment for a negro who died of disease contracted in attending sick soldiers.	18	2	Petition	160	Claims.						

List of private claims presented to the House of Representatives of the United States from the 1st to the 31st Congress, inclusive—Continued.

Names of claimants.	Nature or object of the claim.	Congress.	Session.	How brought before the House of Reps.	Page of journal.	To what committee of the House referred.	No. or date of the report.	Nature of the report.	No. of the bill.	How disposed of by the House of Reps.	How disposed of by the Senate.	Date of the act of Congress, and remarks.
Laurence, W. & S., *et al*	Repayment of excess of duties...	21	2	Petition	67	Ways and Means.						
Laurence, W. & S., *et al.*	Repayment of excess of duties...	22	1	Petition	333	Ways and Means.						
Lawrence, Zachariah.....	Compensation for capture of British sloop Venture.	28	1	Petition	875	Claims	567	Favorable....	420	Referred to Committee Whole House.		
Lawrence, Zachariah.....	Compensation for capture of British sloop Venture.	29	1	Petition	146	Claims	319	Adverse	......	Laid on table.		
Lawrence, Zachariah.....	Compensation for capture of British sloop Venture.	30	1	Petition	370	Claims	249	Favorable....	242	Referred to Committee Whole House.		
Lawrence, Zachariah.....	Compensation for capture of British sloop Venture.	30	2	House bill	142	Whole House.....	Dec. 22, 1848	With't amend.	242	Passed.		
Lawrence, Zachariah.....	Compensation for capture of British sloop Venture.	31	1	Petition	192	Claims	404	Adverse	......	Laid on table.		
Laws, Bolitha, administrator of.	Payment of balance due on contract.	22	2	Petition	124	Claims.						
Laws, Bolitha, administrator of.	Payment of balance due on contract.	23	1	Petition	59	Claims.						
Laws, Bolitha, administrator of.	Payment of balance due on contract.	23	1	Senate bill	654	Claims	May 31, 1834	With't amend.	81	Passed	Passed	App'd June 30, 1834
Laws, Bolitha, administrator of.	Interest on amount received under former act.	23	2	Petition	59	Claims.						
Laws, Bolitha, administrator of.	Interest on amount received under former act.	24	1	Petition	272	Claims	Mar. 21, 1836	Favorable....	460	Referred to Committee Whole House.		
Laws, Bolitha, administrator of.	Interest on amount received under former act.	25	2	Petition	37	Claims	19	Favorable....	31	Passed	Indef. postp'd.	
Laws, Bolitha, administrator of.	Interest on amount received under former act.	25	3	Petition	87	Claims	152	Favorable....	1019	Referred to Committee Whole House.		
Laws, Bolitha, administrator of.	Interest on amount received under former act.	26	1	Petition	168	Claims.						
Laws, Bolitha, administrator of.	Interest on amount received under former act.	27	2	Petition	346	Claims	688	Favorable....	412	Referred to Committee Whole House.		
Laws, Bolitha, administrator of.	Interest on amount received under former act.	28	1	Petition	194	Claims..........	495	Adverse	......	Laid on table.		
Laws, Bolitha, administrator of.	Interest on amount received under former act.	28	2	Petition	141	Claims	147	Adverse	......	Laid on table.		
Laws, Bolitha, administrator of.	Interest on amount received under former act.	29	1	Petition	146	Claims..........	173	Adverse	......	Laid on table.		
Lawshe or Loshe, Andrew	Pension for revolutionary services.	23	2	Res. and petition	53, 58	Rev. Pensions	....	....	......	Discharged; laid on table.		
Lawson, Benjamin, former widow of	Arrears of pension	23	2	Petition	49	Rev. Pensions	Feb. 10, 1835	Adverse	......	Laid on table.		
Lawson, Benjamin, former widow of.	Arrears of pension	24	2	Petition	84	Rev. Pensions	....	....	......	Discharged; laid on table.		
Lawson, Columbus......	Compensation as clerk to board of land commissioners.	12	1	Petition	370	Claims.						
Lawson, Columbus	Compensation as clerk to board of land commissioners.	12	2	Petition	671	Claims.						
Lawson, Hugh	Pension for revolutionary services.	5	2	House bill......	127	Claims	Jan. 9, 1798	Favorable....	38	Passed	Passed	App'd Feb. 2, 1798
Lawson, Jacob.........	Military bounty land...........	27	2	Petition	721	Rev. Pensions	784	Adverse	......	Laid on table.		
Lawson, John, executors of, by attorney.	Indemnity for vessel and cargo taken for use of revolutionary army.	4	1	Petition	526	Claims.						

List of private claims presented to the House of Representatives of the United States from the 1st to the 31st Congress, inclusive—Continued.

Names of claimants.	Nature or object of the claim.	Congress.	Session.	How brought before the House of Reps.	Page of journal.	To what committee of the House referred.	No. or date of the report.	Nature of the report.	No. of the bill.	How disposed of by the House of Reps.	How disposed of by the Senate.	Date of the act of Congress, and remarks.
Lawson, John, executors of, by attorney.	Indemnity for vessel and cargo taken for use of revolutionary army.	4	2	Petition	637	Claims	Jan. 5, 1797	Adverse	......	Rejected.		
Lawson, John, administrator of.	Arrears of pay	29	1	Petition	824	Claims	757	Favorable	495	Referred to Committee Whole House.		
Lawson, John, administrator of.	Arrears of pay	29	2	House bill	212	Whole House	Jan. 22, 1847	With't amend.	495	Passed	Passed	App'd March 3, 1847
Lawson, Randolph	Pension for revolutionary services.	28	1	Petition	567	Rev. Pensions.						
Lawson, Robert, *et al.*	Confirmation of title to land	22	2	Petition	120	Priv. Land Claims.	Jan. 22, 1833	Adverse	......	Laid on table.		
Lawyer, Isaac	(See Isaac Sawyer.)											
Lawyer, Lawrence	Revolutionary pension	30	1	Petition	849	Rev. Pensions.						
Lawyer, Lawrence	Revolutionary pension	31	1	Petition	1298	......	......	......	......	Leave to withdraw.		
Lay, John O	Release from liability for non-performance of contract.	21	1	Petition	300	Claims	278	Adverse	......	Laid on table	......	Leave to withdraw
Lay, John O	Release from liability for non-performance of contract.	22	1	Petition	632	Claims	Jan. 18, 1832	Adverse	......	Referred to Committee Whole House.		
Lay, Lee	Invalid pension	3	2	Rep. of Secretary War.	278	Claims	Feb. 28, 1795	Favorable	130	Passed	Indef. postp'd.	
Lay, Lee	Invalid pension	4	1	Rep. of Secretary War.	445	Claims	Feb. 18, 1796	Favorable	156	Passed	Passed	App'd April 30, 1796
Lay, Lee	Increase of pension	11	2	Pension bill	283	Whole House	Mar. 16, 1810	With amends.	107	Passed	Passed	App'd April 27, 1810
Lay, Old	Confirmation of title to land	18	2	Report of land officers.	182, 287	Public Lands.						
Lay, Old	Confirmation of title to land	19	1	Report of land officers.	64	Public Lands	3	Favorable	254	Referred to Committee Whole House.		
Layhue, David	Revolutionary pension	20	2	Resolution	250	Military Pensions	......	......	......	Discharged; laid on table.		
Layman, Jacob	Payment for work on Cumberland road.	23	1	Res. and papers.	589	Claims	455	Adverse	......	......	......	See report No. 449.
Layman or Lyman, Justin.	Exoneration from penalty for violation of non-intercourse act.	14	2	Petition	190	Ways and Means	......	......	......	Discharged; laid on table.		
Layman, William	Pension	19	1	Petition	57	Military Pensions	164	Adverse	......	Laid on table.		
Layssard, Boin	Confirmation of title to land in Louisiana.	15	2	Petition	89	Priv. Land Claims.	Jan. 12, 1819	Adverse	......	Laid on table.		
Layton, Charles G.	Compensation for vessel captured in 1814.	29	1	Petition	208	Claims	648	Adverse	......	Discharged; laid on table.		
Layton, Charles G.	Compensation for vessel captured in 1814.	31	1	Petition	299	Military Affairs	......	......	......	Discharged; laid on table.		
Layton, John	Confirmation of title to land in Missouri.	15	1	Petition	312	Priv. Land Claims.						
Layton, John	Confirmation of title to land in Missouri.	16	1	Petition	72	Priv. Land Claims.						
Layton, John	Confirmation of title to land in Missouri.	17	1	Petition	54	Priv. Land Claims.						
Layton, John	Confirmation of title to land in Missouri.	18	1	Petition	54	Priv. Land Claims.						
Layton, John, heirs of	Commutation pay	23	1	Petition	221	Rev. Claims.						
Layton, John, heirs of	Commutation pay	23	2	Petition	106	Rev. Claims.						
Layton, John, heirs of	Commutation pay	24	1	Petition	63	Rev. Claims.						
Layton, John, heirs of	Commutation pay	24	2	Documents	91	Rev. Claims.						
Layton, Robert	Confirmation of title to land in Louisiana.	20	2	Petition	74	Public Lands.						

List of private claims presented to the House of Representatives of the United States from the 1st to the 31st Congress, inclusive—Continued.

Names of claimants.	Nature or object of the claim.	Congress.	Session.	How brought before the House of Reps.	Page of journal.	To what committee of the House referred.	No. or date of the report.	Nature of the report.	No. of the bill.	How disposed of by the House of Reps.	How disposed of by the Senate.	Date of the act of Congress, and remarks.
Layton, Robert	Confirmation of title to land in Louisiana.	21	1	Petition	40	Public Lands.						
Layton, Robert	Confirmation of title to land in Louisiana.	22	1	Petition	75	Priv. Land Claims.	Dec. 28, 1831	Adverse		Laid on table.		
Layton, Robert	Commutation pay	23	1	Petition	220	Rev. Claims.						
Layton, Robert	Commutation pay	24	1	Petition	63	Rev. Claims				Discharged; laid on table.		
Layton, Robert, heirs of	Arrears of pension	27	2	Petition	524	Rev. Pensions	794	Favorable	448	Referred to Committee Whole House.		
Layton, Robert, heirs of	Arrears of pension	27	3	House bill	88				448	Passed	Passed	App'd March 3, 1843
Lazarus, Frederick	(See Anthony Selin, orphan children of.)	6	1		636							
Lazenby, Alexander	(See William H. Bedford, agent.)	28	1		262							
Lea, ——	(See Carey, Lea & Blanchard.)	23	1		128							
Leach, Amelia	Confirmation of title to land	24	1	Petition	113	Priv. Land Claims.	116	Favorable	133	Passed	Rejected.	
Leach, Amelia	Confirmation of title to land	24	2	Petition	89	Priv. Land Claims.	Dec. 26, 1836	Favorable	775	Referred to Committee Whole House.		
Leach, Amelia	Confirmation of title to land	25	2	Petition	43	Priv. Land Claims.	143	Favorable	164	Referred to Committee Whole House.		
Leach, Amelia	Confirmation of title to land	25	3	Petition	375	Whole House	Jan. 25, 1839	With't amend.	164	Passed	Adverse.	
Leach, Andrew, *et al*	Bounty on fish	9	2	Petition	639					Laid on table.		
Leach, Andrew, representatives of.	Half-pay for revolutionary services.	23	1	Petition	189	Rev. Claims.						
Leach, Andrew, widow of.	Half-pay for revolutionary services.	25	2	Petition	729	Rev. Pensions.						
Leach, Andrew, widow of.	Half pay for revolutionary services.	26	1	Petition	173	Rev. Pensions.						
Leach, Anna	Pensions to widows of revolutionary soldiers who married prior to 1848.	30	1	Petition	606	Rev. Pensions				Discharged; laid on table.		
Leach, Asa	Pension	31	1	Petition	835					Laid on table.		
Leach, George	Arrears of pension	25	2	Petition	664	Rev. Pensions.						
Leach, George	(See Charles Burzette, widow of.)	26	1		701		629					
Leach, Levin	Pension	30	2	Petition	345	Invalid Pensions.				Discharged; laid on table.		
Leach, Samuel	Pension	20	2	Petition	203	Military Pensions.				Discharged; laid on table.		
Leach, Thomas, and others.	Bounty on salted fish exported	8	2	Petition	639					Laid on table.		
Leach, William	Pension	10	2	House bill	499	Whole House	Feb. 20, 1809	With amend.	158	Passed	Passed	App'd March 3, 1809
Leach, William	Additional compensation as draw-keeper.	28	2	Petition	367	Dist. of Columbia.	79	Adverse		Laid on table.		
Leach, William	Additional compensation as draw-keeper.	29	1	Petition	331	Public Buildings & Grounds.						
Leach, William	Additional compensation as draw keeper.	31	1	Petition	589	Dist. of Columbia.	272	Favorable	253	Laid on table.		
Leach, ——	(See Leach.)											
Leadbetter, Richard	Indemnity for losses as contractor.	31	1	Petition	815	P. Of. & P. Roads.						
Leadon, Amos	(See William H. Bedford, agent)	28	1		262							
Leake, Wesley	Compensation for horse taken for public use.	30	1	Petition	406	Claims				Discharged; laid on table.		
Leake, Wesley	Compensation for horse taken for public use.	30	2	Petition	445					Leave to withdraw.		

List of private claims presented to the House of Representatives of the United States from the 1st to the 31st Congress, inclusive—Continued.

Names of claimants.	Nature or object of the claim.	Congress.	Session.	How brought before the House of Reps.	Page of journal.	To what committee of the House referred.	No. or date of the report.	Nature of the report.	No. of the bill.	How disposed of by the House of Reps.	How disposed of by the Senate.	Date of the act of Congress, and remarks.
Leable, Squire	(See James Whitaker, *et al*)	21	1		173							
Leaky, Levi	Indemnity for losses as contractor	30	1	Petition	228	Claims	402	Adverse		Laid on table.		
Leaman, John	Compensation for revolutionary services.	9	1	Petition	222	Whole House.						
Leaman, John	Compensation for revolutionary services.	11	2	Petition	334	Claims.						
Leamaster, James, widow of.	Compensation for corn destroyed by United States troops.	24	1	Senate bill	955	Claims	June 8, 1836	With't amend.	S. 158	Passed		App'd July 2, 1836
Leamaster, Nancy	(See James Leamaster, widow of)	24	1		955							
Leamy, John, *et al.*	Relief from partial operation of duties on stamped vellum, parchment and paper.	5	1	Memorial	70					Laid on table.		
Lear, Joshua	Pension for revolutionary services.	24	1	Petition	433	Rev. Pensions.						
Lear, Tobias	Compensation for services and loss of property as commercial agent at S. Domingo.	7	2	Memor'l and rep't Sec. of State.	283	Claims	Feb. 18, 1803	Adverse		Referred to Committee Whole House.		
Learned, Ebenezer	Compensation for services, &c., in revolutionary war.	2	1	Petition	442					Referred to Secretary War.		
Learned, Ebenezer	Compensation for services, &c., in revolutionary war.	3	1	Rep. of Secretary War.	75	Select	May 26, 1794	Res. to refer to Sec. War.	J. R. 12	Passed	Passed	App'd June 9, 1794
Learned, Ebenezer	Invalid pension	3	2	Rep. of Secretary War.	278	Claims	Feb. 28, 1795	Favorable	130	Passed	Postponed.	
Learned, Ebenezer	Invalid pension	4	1	Rep. of Secretary War.	445	Claims	Feb. 18, 1796	Favorable	156	Passed	Passed	App'd April 20, 1796
Learned, John	Payment of sundry bills of credit.	3	2	Petition	259	Claims	Feb. 25, 1795	Adverse		Referred to Committee Whole House.		
Learned, John	Commutation pay for revolutionary services.	4	2	Petition	628	Claims	Dec. 26, 1797	Adverse		Rejected.		
Learny, John	Indemnity for French spoliations prior to 1800.	26	1	Memorial	182	Foreign Affairs	343	Favorable	319	Referred to Committee Whole House.		
Leary, Edward	Invalid pension	12	1	House bill	361	Whole House	June 8, 1812	With amend'ts	138	Passed	Passed	App'd July 5, 1812
Leath, William, widow of.	Pension for services as purser's steward.	28	2	Petition	309	Naval Affairs.						
Leath, William, widow of.	Pension for services as purser's steward.	29	1	Memorial	353	Naval Affairs.						
Leath, William, widow of.	Pension for services as purser's stewart.	31	1		1552					Leave to withdraw.		
Leatherman, Daniel	Pre emption right to land	22	2	Petition	353	Public Lands.						
Leatherman, Francis	Pension for revolutionary services.	22	2	Petition	30	Rev. Pensions				Discharged; laid on table.		
Leavenworth, Abigail	(See John Mather, widow of)	2	1		521							
Leavenworth, Edmund	Pension for revolutionary services.	25	3	Petition	127	Rev. Pensions				Discharged; laid on table.		
Leavenworth, Edmund	Pension for revolutionary services.	28	2	Petition	89	Rev. Pensions				Discharged; laid on table.		
Leavenworth, Edmund	Indemnity for French spoliations prior to 1800.	26	1	Memorial	182	Foreign Affairs	343	Favorable	319	Referred to Committee Whole House.		
Leavenworth, Harriet	(See Gen. Henry Leavenworth, widow of.)	23	2		143							
Leavenworth, Gen. Henry, widow of.	Pay and emoluments from time of death to December 31, 1834.	23	2	Resolution	143	Military Affairs.						
Leavenworth, Gen. Henry, widow of.	Pay and emoluments from time of death to December 31, 1834.	26	2	Petition	50	Military Affairs.						

List of private claims presented to the House of Representatives of the United States from the 1st to the 31st Congress, inclusive—Continued.

Names of claimants.	Nature or object of the claim.	Congress.	Session.	How brought before the House of Reps.	Page of journal.	To what committee of the House referred.	No. or date of the report.	Nature of the report.	No. of the bill.	How disposed of by the House of Reps.	How disposed of by the Senate.	Date of the act of Congress, and remarks.
Leavenworth, Gen. Henry, widow of.	Pay and emoluments from time of death to December 31, 1834.	27	2	Petition	506	Military Affairs	353	Adverse	......	Laid on table.		
Leavenworth, Mark, heirs of.	Commutation pay	26	1	Petition	164	Rev. Claims.						
Leavenworth, Mark, heirs of.	Commutation pay	27	2	Petition	61	Rev. Claims	389	Adverse	......	Laid on table.		
Leavenworth, M. C.	Compensation for horse lost in Seminole war.	24	2	Petition	209	Claims	......	......	......	Referred to 3d Auditor.		
Leavenworth, Nathan, heirs of.	Commutation pay	25	3	Petition	125	Rev. Claims.						
Leavenworth, Seth M.	Indemnity for annulling mail contract.	28	2	Joint resolution	357	P. Of. and P. Roads.	......	......	S. R. 15			
Leavenworth, Seth M.	Indemnity for annulling mail contract.	29	1	Petition	167	P. Of. & P. Roads.	130	Favorable	J. R. 10	Passed	Passed	App'd Aug. 6, 1846
Leaver, or Leavear, William.	Pension	12	1	Pension bill	361	Whole House	June 15, 1812	With amends.	138	Passed	Passed	App'd July 5, 1812
Leavett, Nehemiah	Pension	12	1	Pension bill	361	Whole House	June 15, 1812	With amends.	138	Passed	Passed	App'd July 5, 1812
Leavitt, John	(See Benjamin Bailey, *et al*)	19	1	......	98							
Leavitt, Nathaniel	Pension	3	2	Rep. of Secretary War.	278	Claims	Mar. 3, 1795	Res. to refer to Sec. War.	......	Resolution adopted.		
Leavitt, Nathaniel	Pension	4	1	Rep. of Secretary War.	445	Claims	Feb. 18, 1796	Favorable	156	Passed	Passed	App'd April 20, 1796
Leavitt, Nathaniel	Increase of pension	12	1	Pension bill	361	Whole House	June 15, 1812	With amends.	138	Passed	Passed	App'd July 5, 1812
Leaward, Swain	Arrears of pension	23	1	Petition	45	Invalid Pensions.						
Leaycraft, George	(See Viner Leaycraft, executors of.)	5	2	......	159							
Leaycraft, Viner, executors of.	Compensation for cannon taken by American army.	5	2	Petition	159	Claims	Feb. 16, 1798	Adverse	......	Rejected.		
Le Barron, Francis	Leave to work copper mines	14	2	Petition	84	Select	Jan. 28, 1817	Favorable	......	Referred to Committee Whole House.		
Le Barron, Francis	Indemnity for property taken for use of United States troops.	16	2	Petition	177	Claims.						
Le Basques, Jean	Confirmation of title to land	15	1	Petition	371	Priv. Land Claims.						
Le Basques, Jean	Confirmation of title to land	16	1	Petition	72	Priv. Land Claims.						
Le Basques, Jean	Confirmation of title to land	17	1	Petition	54	Public Lands.						
Le Blanc, ———	(See Francis Charpenkie)	18	1	......	177							
Le Blanc, Joseph	Confirmation of title to land	18	1	Petition	101	Priv. Land Claims.						
Le Blanc, Joseph	Confirmation of title to land	18	2	Petition	52	Priv. Land Claims.						
Le Blanc, Pierre, assignee of.	Indemnity for property taken for public use.	23	1	Petition	111	Claims	494	Favorable	499	Referred to Committee Whole House.		
Le Blanc, Pierre, assignee of.	Indemnity for property taken for public use.	24	1	Petition	50	Claims	19	Favorable	19	Passed	Passed	App'd Feb. 17, 1836
Le Blance, Terence	Reimbursement of moneys paid for land.	23	1	Petition	132	Priv. Land Claims.	115	Favorable	120	Passed	Passed	App'd June 28, 1834
Le Blanc, Villeneuve	Compensation for reclaiming land.	26	1	Petition	337	Public Lands	433	Favorable	347	Referred to Committee Whole House.		
Le Blanc, Villeneuve	Compensation for reclaiming land.	27	2	Petition	155	Public Lands.	515	Adverse	......	Laid on table.		
Le Breton, Peter, executor of.	Indemnity for French spoliations prior to 1800.	26	1	Memorial	182	Foreign Affairs	343	Favorable	319	Referred to Committee Whole House.		
Lebo, Henry	Compensation for revolutionary services.	2	1	Petition	447	......	......	......	......	Referred to Secretary War.		
Leboeuf, Michael	Confirmation of title to land	22	2	Petition	89	Priv. Land Claims.	18	Favorable	648	Referred to Committee Whole House.		
Leboeuf, Michael	Confirmation of title to land	23	1	Petition	93	Priv. Land Claims.	72	Favorable	82	Passed	Passed	App'd June 27, 1834

List of private claims presented to the House of Representatives of the United States from the 1st to the 31st Congress, inclusive—Continued.

Names of claimants.	Nature or object of the claim.	Congress.	Session.	How brought before the House of Reps.	Page of journal.	To what committee of the House referred.	No. or date of the report.	Nature of the report.	No. of the bill.	How disposed of by the House of Reps.	How disposed of by the Senate.	Date of the act of Congress, and remarks.
Le Brun, Jerom, heirs of	Compensation for revolutionary services.	2	2	Document	687					Referred to Secretary Treasury.		
Le Carpenter, Joseph	Drawback on goods	18	2	Petition	37	Commerce				Discharged; referred to Sec. Treasury.		
Le Carpenter, Joseph	Drawback on goods	19	1	Resolution	39	Ways and Means	May 3, 1826	Favorable	247	Passed.		
Le Carpenter, Joseph	Drawback on goods	19	2	Petition	45	Ways and Means	23	Favorable	323	Passed	Passed	pp'd March 3, 1827
Leckie, Robert	(See Jeremiah D. Hayden, sureties of.)	22	1		943							
Le Cleer, Peter	Pension	17	1	Petition	145	Rev. Pensions.						
Le Cleer, Peter	Pension	17	2	Resolution	176	Rev. Pensions				Discharged; leave to withdraw.		
Le Cleer, Peter	Pension	18	2	Petition	59	Rev. Pensions	Jan. 21, 1825	Adverse		Laid on table.		
Le Clerc, Francis	(See Francis Valle, heirs of)	15	2		47							
Le Clere, Pierre	Indian annuity	22	2	Senate bill	441	Ways and Means	Mar. 1, 1833	With't amend.	128	Passed	Passed	App'd March 2, 1833
Lecompte, Fountain	(See Joseph Stewart, *et al.*)	14	2		56							
Lecompte, James	(See Joseph Stewart, *et al.*)	14	2		56							
Lecompte, John B	Confirmation of title to land	26	1	Senate bill	837	Priv. Land Claims	July 21, 1840	With amends.	S. 279	Referred to Committee Whole House.		
Lecompte, John B	Confirmation of title to land	26	2	Senate bill	225	Priv. Land Claims			S. 122			
Lecompte, John B	Confirmation of title to land	27	2	Senate bill	782	Priv. Land Claims			S. 77			
Le Compte, Samuel W	Remuneration for losses by wreck	21	1	Petition	233	Naval Affairs.						
Le Conte, Hyacinth	(See Cecile Compare)	23	1		300							
Lecount, Samuel	Increase of pension	13	1	House bill	56	Claims	July 20, 1813	With amends.	31	Passed	Passed	App'd Aug. 2, 1813
Lecourtois, Anthony	Relief for vessel and cargo captured	18	1	Memorial	344	Foreign Affairs.						
Lecourtois, Anthony	Relief for vessel and cargo captured	18	2	Memorial	102	Foreign Affairs.						
Lecraft, Benjamin	(See James Manney, sureties of)	25	3		149							
Ledbetter, Rowland	Revolutionary pension	26	2	Resolution	117	Rev. Pensions	Feb. 12, 1841	Adverse		Laid on table.		
Ledford, William	Revolutionary pension	30	1	Petition	471	Rev. Pensions				Disch'd; laid on table.		
Ledman, William	Pension	20	2	Petition	59	Military Pensions.						
Ledman, William	Pension	21	1	Petition	47	Military Pensions	May 25, 1830	Favorable	490	Referred to Committee Whole House.		
Ledman, William	Pension	22	1	Petition	36	Invalid Pensions	232	Favorable	344	Passed.		
Ledman, William	Pension	22	2	House bill	79	Invalid Pensions	Dec. 19, 1832	Favorable	626	Passed	Passed	App'd March 2, 1833
Ledoux, John Pierre, widow of.	Confirmation of title to land	23	1	Petition	49	Priv. Land Claims	143	Favorable	145	Passed	Passed	App'd June 28, 1834
Leduc, M. P., (Mo.)	Confirmation of title to land	25	2	Petition	596	Priv. Land Claims				Leave to withdraw.		
Leduc, Mary Philipe	Compensation as translator to land commissioners in Missouri Territory.	12	2	Petition	608	Claims.						
Leduc, Mary Philipe	Compensation as translator to land commissioners in Missouri Territory.	13	1	Petition	28	Claims				Discharged.		
Leduc, Mary Philipe	Compensation as traslator to land commissioners in Missouri Territory.	13	2	Petition	168	Claims	16	Favorable	72	Passed	Passed	App'd Mar. 28, 1814
Ledurney, Lewis	(See Canadian refugees.)	6	2		766							
Ledwith, Michael	Not stated	30	2	Resolution	346	Claims.						
Ledwith, Thomas	Indemnity for property destroyed by Indians in Florida.	25	2	Documents	192	Claims	506	Adverse		Laid on table.		
Ledyard, Ann	(See Isaac Ledyard, widow and administratrix of.)	8	1		547							
Ledyard, Henry	Compensation for services as chargé to France.	28	2	House bill	154	Foreign Affairs	26	Favorable	489	Referred to Committee Whole House.		

List of private claims presented to the House of Representatives of the United States from the 1st to the 31st Congress, inclusive—Continued

Names of claimants.	Nature or object of the claim.	Congress.	Session.	How brought before the House of Reps.	Page of journal.	To what committee of the House referred.	No. or date of the report.	Nature of the report.	No. of the bill.	How disposed of by the House of Reps.	How disposed of by the Senate.	Date of the act of Congress, and remarks.
Ledyard, Henry	Compensation for services as chargé to France.	28	2	Amend'nt to Ho. bill.	177				498	Passed	Passed	App'd March 3, 1845
Ledyard, Isaac	Settlement of claim against United States.	1	3	Petition	380					Referred to Secretary Treasury.		
Ledyard, Isaac	Compensation for revolutionary services.	2	1	Petition	532					Referred to Secretary Treasury.		
Ledyard, Isaac	Compensation for revolutionary services.	2	2	Rep. of Secretary Treasury.	625					Leave to withdraw.		
Ledyard, Isaac	Compensation for revolutionary services.	2	2	Rep. of Secretary Treasury.	696					Laid on table.		
Ledyard, Isaac	Commutation pay	3	1	Memorial	86	Select.						
Ledyard, Isaac	Commutation pay	3	2	Memorial	296	Claims	Mar. 2, 1795	Adverse		Laid on table.		
Ledyard, Isaac	Commutation pay	4	1	Petition	598	Claims	May 31, 1796	Adverse		Laid on table.		
Ledyard, Isaac, widow and administratrix of.	Commutation of half pay	8	1	Memorial	547	Claims.				Discharged; referred to Com. Whole House.		
Ledyard, Isaac, widow and administratrix of.	Commutation of half pay	8	2	Memorial	59	Claims.						
Ledyard, Isaac, widow and administratrix of.	Commutation of half-pay	9	1	Memorial	199	Claims				Discharged, referred to Com. Whole House.		
Ledyard, Isaac, widow and administratrix of.	Commutation of half-pay	9	2	Memorial	491	Select.						
Ledyard, Isaac, heirs of	Commutation of half-pay	22	2	Resolution	49	Rev. Claims	52	Favorable	694	Passed	Passed	App'd Mar. 2, 1833
Ledyard, John	Invalid pension	4	1	Rep. of Secretary War.	445	Claims	Feb. 18, 1796	Favorable	156	Passed	Passed	App'd April 20, 1796
Lee, Andrew	For settlement of claim	1	2	Petition	184					Referred to Secretary Treasury.		
Lee, Andrew	Compensation for revolutionary services.	3	2	Petition	290	Claims	March 2, 1795	Adverse		Laid on table.		
Lee, Andrew	Compensation for revolutionary services.	4	1	Petition	598	Claims	May 31, 1796	Adverse		Laid on table.		
Lee, Andrew, sen	Pension for revolutionary services.	27	2	Petition	1042	Rev. Pensions.						
Lee, Andrew, sen	Pension for revolutionary services.	27	3	Petition	107	Rev. Pensions	295	Adverse		Laid on table.		
Lee, Asahel	Compensation for work on Cumberland road.	27	2	Memorial	140	Claims	49	Favorable	84	Passed.		
Lee, Asahel	Compensation for work on Cumberland road.	27	3	Memorial	43	Claims	1	Favorable	619	Passed	Passed	App'd March 3, 1843
Lee, Cassius F	(See trustee of William Hodgson)	30	1		118							
Lee, Charles, *et al.*	Confirmation of title to land	28	1	Petition	372	Priv. Land Claims.				Discharged; laid on table.		
Lee, Charles, *et al.*	Confirmation of title to land	31	1	Petition	672	Priv. Land Claims.						
Lee, Charles and Eliza	(See Oliver Lee, administrator of)	30	1		624							
Lee, Edmund	Change of land entry	28	2	Petition	484	Public Lands.						
Lee, Edmund J	For amendment of law relative to fees of office.	17	2	Petition	143	Dist. of Columbia.						
Lee, Edward	Payment for bread furnished United States troops.	19	1	Petition	131	Claims	107	Favorable	143	Passed.		
Lee, Edward	Payment for bread furnished United States troops.	19	2	Petition	28	Claims	Dec. 13, 1826	Favorable	287	Passed	Passed	App'd Dec. 27, 1826
Lee, Edward	Payment for bread furnished United States troops.	20	2	Petition	109	Claims.						
Lee, Edward	Payment for bread furnished United States troops.	21	1	Petition	69	Claims	217	Favorable	269	Referred to Committee Whole House.		

List of private claims presented to the House of Representatives of the United States from the 1st to the 31st Congress, inclusive—Continued.

Names of claimants.	Nature or object of the claim.	Congress.	Session.	How brought before the House of Reps.	Page of journal.	To what committee of the House referred.	No. or date of the report.	Nature of the report.	No. of the bill.	How disposed of by the House of Reps.	How disposed of by the Senate.	Date of the act of Congress, and remarks.
Lee, Edward	Payment for bread furnished United States troops.	21	2	House bill	332	Whole House	Feb. 19, 1831	With amends.	269	Passed.		
Lee, Edward	Payment for bread furnished United States troops.	22	1	Petition	43	Claims	Dec. 19, 1831	Favorable	7	Passed	Passed	App'd March 7, 1832
Lee, Edward	Revival of act for his relief.	27	2	Resolution	81	Ways and Means.						
Lee, Edward, legal representatives of.	Revival of act for his relief	27	2	Amemd. to H. B.	274	....	....	....	74	Passed	Passed	App'd May 18, 1842
Lee, Edward, son of	Re-appropriation of money not drawn.	30	1	Petition	718	Claims	655	Adverse	......	Laid on table.		
Lee, Edward S.	(See son of Edward Lee)	30	1	....	718	Whole House	Feb. 20, 1809	With amend.	158	Passed	Passed	App'd March 3, 1809
Lee, Elisha	Pension	10	2	Pension bill	499							
Lee, Ezra	Grant of land for military services.	15	1	Petition	184	Public Lands.						
Lee, Francis	(See heirs of Reuben Fields)	28	1	....	122							
Lee, George W	Proceeds of the wreck of brig Plats	29	1	Petition	198	Claims.						
Lee, George W	Increase of salary	24	2	Petition	214	Naval Affairs.						
Lee, George W	Increase of salary	28	2	Petition	188	Naval Affairs	....	....	......	Disch'd; laid on table.		
Lee, Harvey	Compensation for work on Cumberland road.	27	2	Memorial	140	Claims	49	Favorable	84	Passed.		
Lee, Harvey	Compensation for work on Cumberland road.	37	3	Memorial	43	Claims	1	Favorable	619	Passed	Passed	App'd March 3, 1843
Lee, Henry	Reduction of duties on goods	14	2	Petition	295	Com. and Manuf.	17	Favorable	116	Passed	Passed	App'd March 3, 1817
Lee, Henry	Refunding of amount of bonds for goods lost at sea.	16	2	Petition	41	Commerce.						
Lee, Henry	Refunding of amount of bonds for goods lost at sea.	17	1	Petition	51	Commerce	April 23, 1822	Favorable	179	Passed	Passed	App'd May 7, 1822
Lee, Henry	(See John Ricaud, surety of)	17	2	....	184							
Lee, Henry	Indemnity for French spoliations prior to 1800.	26	1	Memorial	182	Foreign Affairs	343	Favorable	319	Referred to Committee Whole House.		
Lee, Isaac	Additional pay as agent of land commissioners.	17	1	Petition	172	Public Lands.						
Lee, James	Remission of duties on certain goods destroyed by fire.	26	1	Memorial	291	Commerce.	Feb. 29, 1840	Favorable	53	Rejected.		
Lee, James, sen	Grant of land for revolutionary services.	17	2	Petition	21	Rev. Pensions.						
Lee, Jeremiah	For amount paid for redemption of an American citizen.	15	1	Petition	418	Claims.						
Lee, Jeremiah	For amount paid for redemption of an American citizen.	15	2	Petition	55	Claims.						
Lee, John	(See James Crawford, *et al*)	16	2	....	101							
Lee, John	(See William Whitehead, *et al*)	18	1	....	27							
Lee, John	Compensation for horse lost in service.	25	2	Documents	397	Claims.						
Lee, John	Compensation for horse lost in service.	26	1	Petition	167	Claims.						
Lee, John	Compensation for use, &c., of horses for House of Representatives.	29	1	Petition	190, 1163	Claims.						
Lee, John	Compensation for use, &c., of horses for House of Representatives.	29	2	Petition	172	Claims.						
Lee, John	Compensation for use, &c., of horses for House of Representatives.	30	1	Petition	154	Accounts.						

List of private claims presented to the House of Representatives of the United States from the 1st to the 31st Congress, inclusive—Continued.

Names of claimants.	Nature or object of the claim.	Congress.	Session.	How brought before the House of Reps.	Page of journal.	To what committee of the House referred.	No. or date of the report.	Nature of the report.	No. of the bill.	How disposed of by the House of Reps.	How disposed of by the Senate.	Date of the act of Congress, and remarks.
Lee, John	Compensation for use, &c., of horses for House of Representatives.	30	2	Petition	227	Claims.						
Lee, John	Compensation for services in House of Representatives.	29	1	Resolution	420					Laid on table.		
Lee, John	Compensation for services in House of Representatives.	29	2	Resolution	517							Paid out of contingent fund.
Lee, John	Compensation for services in House of Representatives.	30	1	Resolution	333	Accounts	Mar. 1, 1848	Adverse		Laid on table.		
Lee, John	Compensation for services in House of Representatives.	31	1	Petition	283	Accounts.						
Lee, John	Compensation for services in House of Representatives.	31	2	Petition	74	Claims.						
Lee, John W	Pension	18	1	Petition	134	Rev. Claims	Jan. 29, 1824	Adverse		Laid on table.		
Lee, Joseph, jr., *et al*)	Indemnity for French spoliations prior to 1800.	7	1	Petition	134	Select				Discharged; referred to Secretary State.		
Lee, Josiah	For repayment of overpayment on land.	23	1	Petition	439	Public Lands				Discharged; laid on table.		
Lee, Lemuel	Compensation for work on Cumberland road.	27	2	Memorial	140	Claims	49	Favorable	84	Passed.		
Lee, Lemuel	Compensation for work on Cumberland road.	27	3	Memorial	43	Claims	1	Favorable	619	Passed	Passed	App'd March J, 1843
Lee, Levi	Pension for revolutionary services.	14	2	Petition	283	Pens. & Rev. Cl'ms.						
Lee, Levi	Pension for revolutionary services.	23	2	Memorial	67	Select	Feb. 25, 1835	Favorable	769	Referred to Committee Whole House.		
Lee, Levi	Pension for revolutionary services.	24	1	Documents	136	Select	337	Favorable	352	Referred to Committee Whole House.		
Lee, Mary Jane	(See heirs of Thomas Pearson)	28	1		687							
Lee, Nathan, (La.)	Compensation for mail service	31	1	Petition	742	P. Of. and P. Roads				Discharged; laid on table.		
Lee, Nathan, *et al.*, (La.)	Indemnity for expenses as witness.	31	1	Petition	743	Judiciary.						
Lee, Oliver	Payment of a judgment	29	1	Petition	269	Claims.						
Lee, Oliver	Payment of a judgment	29	2	Memorial	164	Claims.						
Lee, Oliver, administrator of.	Payment of a judgment	30	1	Petition	624	Claims	478	Favorable	399	Referred to Committee Whole House.		
Lee, Oliver, administrator of.	Payment of a judgment	30	2	House bill	321			With't amend.	399	Passed		
Lee, Oliver, administrator of.	Indemnity for illegal seizure of vessel.	31	1	Petition	432	Commerce	326	Favorable	283	Referred to Committee Whole House.		
Lee, Oliver, administrator of.	Indemnity for illegal seizure of vessel.	31	2	House bill	182			With amend.	283	Passed		
Lee, Peter	Pension	4	2	Petition	615	Claims	Jan. 9, 1797	Adverse		Rejected.		
Lee, Peter, (free negro)	Compensation for injuries in revolutionary war.	7	1	Petition	23					Rejected.		
Lee, Polly and Stephen	(See John Harris, representatives of.)	2	1		486							
Lee, Richard Bland	Indemnity for waste committed on his property by U. S. troops.	9	2	Petition and rept' Sec. of War.	581					Laid on table.		
Lee, Richard Bland	Indemnity for waste committed on his property by U. S. troops.	10	1	Petition	174	Select	Mar. 11, 1808	Favorable	75	Referred to Committee Whole House.		
Lee, Richard Bland	Indemnity for waste committed on his property by U. S. troops.	10	2	Petition	458	Select.						

List of private claims presented to the House of Representatives of the United States from the 1st to the 31st Congress, inclusive—Continued.

Names of claimants.	Nature or object of the claim.	Congress.	Session.	How brought before the House of Reps.	Page of journal.	To what committee of the House referred.	No. or date of the report.	Nature of the report.	No. of the bill.	How disposed of by the House of Reps.	How disposed of by the Senate.	Date of the act of Congress, and remarks.
Lee, Richard Bland	Indemnity for waste committed on his property by U. S. troops.	12	1	Petition	60	Claims.						
Lee, Richard Bland	Indemnity for waste committed on his property by U. S. troops.	13	1	Petition	35	Claims				Leave to withdraw.		
Lee, Richard Bland	Additional compensation for services as commissioner of claims.	15	1	Petition	485					Laid on table.		
Lee, Richard Bland	Additional compensation for services as commissioner of claims.	15	2	Petition	174	Claims	Jan. 21, 1819	Adverse		Laid on table.		
Lee, Richard H	Reimbursement of fine for breach of revenue laws.	22	1	Petition	512	Ways and Means	Mar. 28, 1832	Favorable	515	Referred to Committee Whole House.		
Lee, Richard H	Reimbursement of fine for breach of revenue laws.	23	1	Petition	155	Ways and Means	Feb. 7, 1834	Favorable	288	Referred to Committee Whole House.		
Lee, Richard H	Reimbursement of fine for breach of revenue laws.	28	2	House bill	301				288	Passed.		
Lee, Richard H	Reimbursement of fine for breach of revenue laws.	29	1	Petition	58	Ways and Means	378	Favorable	285	Passed	Passed	App'd Aug. 8, 1846
Lee, Robert	Compensat'n for property destroyed by British.	17	2	Petition	74	Claims.						
Lee, Robert	Reimbursement excess of duties on goods imported.	20	2	Petition	230	Ways and Means.						
Lee, Roswell	Compensation for inspecting arms.	22	2	Petition	109	Military Affairs				Referred to Secretary War.		
Lee, Roswell	Compensation for inspecting arms.	23	1	Resolution	239	Military Affairs	327	Favorable	354	Referred to Committee Whole House.		
Lee, Roswell	Compensation for inspecting arms.	24	1	Petition	51	Claims	426	Favorable	428	Referred to Committee Whole House.		
Lee, Roswell	Compensation for inspecting arms.	25	2	Petition	36	Claims	17	Favorable	29	Passed	Indef. postp'd.	
Lee, Roswell	Compensation for inspecting arms.	26	1	Petition	168	Claims.						
Lee, Roswell	Compensation for inspecting arms.	27	2	Petition	56	Claims	349	Adverse		Laid on table.		
Lee, R. R. G	Compensation for services as assistant surgeon.	26	1	Petition	602	Invalid Pensions	485	Adverse		Laid on table.		
Lee, R. R. G	Compensation for services as assistant surgeon.	28	1	Petition	297	Claims.						
Lee, Samuel	Compensation for making known improvements in manufacturing woolen cloth.	16	2	Petition	91	Manufactories				Discharged; laid on table.		
Lee, Samuel	Compensation for revolutionary services.	19	2	Petition	91	Rev. Claims	Jan. 16, 1827	Adverse		Laid on table.		
Lee, Samuel	Compensation for revolutionary services.	20	1	Petition	341	Rev. Claims	Mar. 11, 1828	Adverse		Laid on table.		
Lee, Solomon J	Compensation for revolutionary services.	25	2	Petition	48	Rev. Claims	766	Adverse		Laid on table.		
Lee, Solomon J	Compensation for revolutionary services.	25	3	Petition	457	Rev. Claims.						
Lee, Soloman J	Compensation for revolutionary services.	26	1	Petition	165	Rev. Claims.						
Lee, Soloman J	Compensation for revolutionary services.	27	2	Petition	62	Rev. Claims	40	Adverse		Laid on table.		
Lee, S. P	(See Exploring Expedition.)	27	3	Petition	149		270		818			
Lee, Thomas	Pension	20	2	Petition	143	Military Pensions				Discharged; referred to Com. Whole House.		
Lee, Thomas	Pension	21	1	Petition	67	Military Pensions	April 6, 1830	Adverse		Laid on table.		
Lee, Thomas	Pension	21	2	Resolution	71	Military Pensions				Disch'd; laid on table.		

List of private claims presented to the House of Representatives of the United States from the 1st to the 31st Congress, inclusive—Continued.

Names of claimants.	Nature or object of the claim.	Congress.	Session.	How brought before the House of Reps.	Page of journal.	To what committee of the House referred.	No. or date of the report.	Nature of the report.	No. of the bill.	How disposed of by the House of Reps.	How disposed of by the Senate.	Date of the act of Congress, and remarks.
Lee, Thomas B., *et al.*	Compensation for removing obstructions on Red river.	27	2	Petition	694	Claims	648	Adverse	......	Laid on table.		
Lee, Washington	Compensation for services as Judge Advocate.	12	2	Senate bill	655	Claims	Feb. 3, 1813	With't amend.	55	Passed	Passed	App'd March 3 1813
Lee, William, representatives of.	Pay and prize-money	16	1	Resolution	351	Claims	April 24, 1820	Adverse	......	Laid on table.		
Lee, William, representatives of.	Pay and prize-money	16	2	Documents	43	Claims	Dec. 11, 1820	Adverse	......	Laid on table.		
Lee, William, representatives of.	Pay and prize money	17	1	Petition	176	Claims.						
Lee, William, representatives of.	Pay and prize-money	17	2	Petition	116	Claims	Feb. 5, 1823	Adverse	......	Laid on table.		
Lee, William	(See Louis F. Beeler, *et al.*)	30	1	....	115	....	482					
Lee, William R., *et al*	Confimation of certain payments made to owners of fishing vessels.	10	2	Petition	414	Com. and Manuf.	Feb. 10, 1809	Favorable	162	Referred to Committee Whole House.		
Lee, William, R., *et al*	Confirmation of certain payments made to owners of fishing vessels.	11	1	Petition	17	Com. and Manuf.						
Leech, Elijah	Indemnity for property destroyed by British.	15	2	Petition	66	Claims	Jan. 6, 1819	Adverse	......	Laid on table.		
Leech, Samuel	Compensation for services in investigating sales in Wisconsin.	30	1	Senate bill	308	Public Lands	Mar. 24, 1848	With amend.	S. 85	Passed	Passed	App'd April 11, 1848
Leech, William	Invalid pension	3	1	Rep. of Secretary War.	131	Select	May 26, 1794	Favorable	62	Passed	Passed	App'd June 9, 1794
Leech, William	Compensation for taking census in South Carolina.	14	1	Petition	284	Claims	....	....	......	Discharged; referred to Com. Whole House.		
Leech, William	Compensation for taking census in South Carolina.	14	1	Amend'nt to Ho. bill.	617	....	....	....	......	Passed	Passed	App'd April 27, 1816
Leech, William, executor of.	Indemnity for French spoliations prior to 1800.	29	2	Memorial	129	Foreign Affairs.						
Leeds, Gideon	Increase of compensation as collector of customs.	14	2	Petition	437	Ways and Means.						
Leeds, William	Pension for revolutionary services.	2	1	Petition	469	....	....	....	......	Referred to Secretary of War.		
Leeds, William	Pension for revolutionary services.	3	1	Rep. of Secretary War.	131	Select	May 26, 1794	Res. to refer to Sec. War.	J.R.12	Passed	Passed	App'd June 9, 1794
Leef, Henry	Indemnity for illegal seizure of vessel.	30	1	Petition	988	Commerce.						
Leef, Henry	Indemnity for illegal seizure of vessel.	30	2	Petition	91	Commerce	47	Favorable	740	Referred to Committee Whole House.		
Leef, Henry	Indemnity for illegal seizure of vessel.	31	1	Petition	392	Commerce	104	Favorable	121	Referred to Committee Whole House.		
Leet, Charles	Pre-emption right to lands in Wisconsin.	24	2	Memorial	83	Priv. Land Claims.	....	....	......	Discharged; laid on table.		
Leet, G. J	Indemnity for French spoliations prior to 1800.	26	1	Memorial	182	Foreign Affairs.	343	Favorable	319	Referred to Committee Whole House.		
Leet, C. B	Compensation for attendance as a witness.	30	2	Petition	77	Accounts.						
Lefavour, Philip, *et al.*	Fishing bounty	16	1	Petition	271	Ways and Means.						
Lefebre, Joseph	Indemnity for losses by invasion of British.	15	2	Senate bill	334	Whole House	....	....	S. 85			

List of private claims presented to the House of Representatives of the United States from the 1st to the 31st Congress, inclusive—Continued.

Names of claimants.	Nature or object of the claim.	Congress.	Session.	How brought before the House of Reps.	Page of journal.	To what committee of the House referred.	No. or date of the report.	Nature of the report.	No. of the bill.	How disposed of by the House of Reps.	How disposed of by the Senate.	Date of the act of Congress, and remarks.
Lefebre, Joseph	Indemnity for losses by invasion of British.	16	1	Senate bill	300	Claims	Mar. 24, 1820	Adverse	S. 56	Referred to Committee Whole House.		
Lefebvre, Pierre	Drawback on goods exported to Havanna.	16	1	Resolution	446	Ways and Means.						
Lefever, Joseph	Renewal of patent	18	1	Petition	177	Judiciary.						
Lefever, Menard	Pension	21	1	Petition	568	Military Pensions.						
Lefevre, Bernice, heirs of.	Confirmation of title to land	12	2	House bill	609	Whole House	Jan. 18, 1813	Favorable	222	Passed	Passed	App'd Feb. 13, 1813
Lefevre, Cyprian	Confirmation of title to land	22	1	Resolution	86	Public Lands	Dec. 27, 1831	Favorable	125	Passed	Passed	App'd June 25, 1832
Lefevre, Jacob	To refund money paid for land	23	1	Petition	381	Public Lands	June 6, 1831	Favorable	519	Referred to Committee Whole House.		
Lefferts, Daniel	(See Richard DeCantillon & Daniel Lefferts.)	4	2		613							
Lefferts, Esther	(See William S. Thorn, widow of.)	26	1		281							
Lefferts, Leffert, and Thos. Carpenter.	Remission of foreign tonnage duty on brigantine Susan and Polly	3	1	Petition	103	Select	April 2, 1794	Favorable	36	Passed	Passed	App'd April 18, 1794
Leffingwell & Pierpont	Indemnity for French spoliation prior to 1800.	26	1	Memorial	182	Foreign Affairs	343	Favorable	319	Referred to Committee Whole House.		
Leffingwell, William	Indemnity for French spoliations prior to 1800.	26	1	Memorial	182	Foreign Affairs	343	Favorable	319	Referred to Committee Whole House.		
Leflore, Greenwood, *et al.*	(See Jacob Thompson)	22	1		388							
Leflore, Greenwood	Permission to purchase land at government price.	23	1	Petition	450	Priv. Land Claims.						
Leflore, Greenwood	Permission to purchase land at government price.	23	2	Petition	78	Priv. Land Claims.	Jan. 12, 1835	Adverse	......	Laid on table.		
Leflore, Lewis, (Indian)	Permission to locate lands reserved to him	24	1	Petition	55	Public Lands	....	....	......	Discharged; laid on table.		
Leflore, Lewis, (Indian)	Permission to locate lands reserved to him.	22	2	Petition	55	Public Lands.						
Lefoe, John	Pension for revolutionary services.	20	1	Petition	319	Military Pensions.						
Le Foy, Abraham	Pension for revolutionary services.	15	2	Rep. of Secretary War.	48	Pens. & Rev. Cl'ms.						
Le Foy, Abraham	Pension for revolutionary services.	18	2	Petition	230	Rev. Pensions	Feb. 25, 1825	Adverse	......	Laid on table.		
Leframbose, Claude	(See John H. Kenzie)	27	2		400							
Leframbois, Joseph	Payment for land	24	1	Appropriation bill	1012	Whole House	June 30, 1836	With amends.	695	Passed	Passed	App'd July 2, 1836
Leftwish, Joel	Increase of pension	25	3	Petition	215	Rev. Pensions.						
Leftwish, Joel	Increase of pension	[illegible]	1	Petition	172	Rev. Pensions	480	Adverse	......	Laid on table.		
Leftwish, Joel	Increase of pension	27	2	Petition	108	Rev. Pensions	784	Adverse	......	Laid on table.		
Legare, Samuel, *et al.*	Remission of penalty for breach of revenue laws.	4	1	Petition	493	Com. and Manuf.						
Legare, Samuel, *et al.*	Remission of penalty for breach of revenue laws.	4	2	Petition	629	Com. and Manuf.	105	Adverse	......	Postponed.		
Le Gendre, Baptiste	Confirmation of title to land	[illegible]	2	Petition	41	Priv. Land Claims.						
Le Gendre, Baptiste, heirs of.	Confirmation of title to land	21	1	Petition	51	Priv. Land Claims.	75	Favorable	107	Passed	Passed	App'd May 28, 1830
Legg, Nathan	Restoration of pension	17	1	Petition	36	Rev. Pensions	....	....	......	Leave to withdraw.		
Legg, Nathan	Restoration of pension	17	2	Petition	36	Rev. Pensions.						
Legg, William	Compensation for horse lost in public service.	[illegible]	1	Resolution	363	Claims	211	Adverse	......	Laid on table.		
Legg, William	Compensation for horse lost in public service.	[illegible]	2	Petition	73	Claims	June 3, 1827	Adverse	......	Laid on table.		
Legg, William	Compensation for horse lost in public service	[illegible]	1	Petition	423	Claims	501	Adverse	......	Laid on table.		
Leggett, Fox, & Co.	Reimbursement of duties	21	2	Petition	81	Ways and Means.						

2—39

List of private claims presented to the House of Representatives of the United States from the 1st to the 31st Congress, inclusive—Continued.

Names of claimants.	Nature or object of the claim.	Congress.	Session.	How brought before the House of Reps.	Page of journal.	To what committee of the House referred.	No. or date of the report.	Nature of the report.	No. of the bill.	How disposed of by the House of Reps.	How disposed of by the Senate.	Date of the act of Congress, and remarks.
Leggett, Fox, & Co.	Reimbursement of duties	22	1	Petition	142	Ways and Means.						
Leggett, Aaron	Indemnity for Mexican spoliations.	27	2	Memorial	1121	Foreign Affairs.						
Leggett, Aaron	Indemnity for Mexican spoliations.	29	2	Memorial	231	Foreign Affairs.						
Leggett, Aaron	Indemnity for Mexican spoliations	30	1	Resolution	141							
Leggett, Aaron	Indemnity for Mexican spoliations.	30	1	Rep. of Secretary State.	1271	Foreign Affairs.						
Leggett, John	(See Nathaniel Hunt, *et al*)	19	2		242							
Leggett, John H	Compensation for services as revenue officer.	28	1	Petition	98	Claims.						
Leggett, John H	Compensation for services as revenue officer.	28	2	Petition	118	Claims.						
Leggett, Thomas H	Reimbursement of duties	29	1	Petition	69	Commerce	150	Adverse		Laid on table.		
Leggett, Thomas H	Reimbursement of duties	30	1	Petition	522	Commerce.	500	Favorable	415	Passed.		
Leggett, Thomas H	Reimbursement of duties	31	1	Petition	224	Commerce.						
Leggett, William, heirs of.	Pension for revolutionary services.	31	2	Petition	326	Rev. Claims.						
Legier, George	(See Shakers Society, trustees of)	17	2		22							
Leglize, Pierre	Confirmation of title to land	20	2	Senate bill	349	Public Lands	Feb. 28, 1829	With amend.	75	Referred to Committee Whole House.		
Leglize, Pierre	Confirmation of title to land	21	1	Senate bill	814	Public Lands	June 8, 1832	With amend.	115	Passed	Passed	App'd July 14, 1832
Le Grand, Paulina	(See Edmund Read, executor of, widow of)	29	1		1103							
Le Grange, Garrett	(See Gerret L. Dox, sureties of)	21	1		66							
Le Guen, Louis, by P. J. Flamend.	Extension of time for re-exporting indigo, &c.	4	2	Petition	708	Com. and Manuf.	Feb. 23, 1797	Favorable		Laid on table.		
Le Guen, Louis, by P. J. Flamend.	Extension of time for re-exporting indigo, &c.	5	2	Petition and docs.	99					Referred to Committee Whole House.		
Lehman, Anthony, widow of.	Pension for revolutionary services.	27	2	Petition	351	Rev. Pensions	309	Favorable	278	Passed	Passed, with amendment.	App'd Aug. 30, 1842
Lehman, Lyon	Remission of duties on fire-arms.	6	2	Petition	786	Com. and Manuf.	Feb. 10, 1801	Adverse		Laid on table		
Lehman, Lyon	Remission of duties on fire arms.	7	1	Memorial	54	Com. and Munuf.	Jan. 28, 1802	Favorable	20	Passed	Passed	App'd March 6, 1802
Lehman, Jacob	Arrears of pension	29	1	Petition	573	Invalid Pensions	830	Adverse		Laid on table.		
Lehman, Jacob	Arrears of pension	29	2	Petition	53	Invalid Pensions.						
Lehr, Philip	Pension	18	1	Petition	78	Pens. & Rev. Cl'ms.	Jan. 9, 1824	Adverse		Laid on table.		Leave to withdraw.
Lehr, Philip	Arrears of pension	23	1	Petition	333	Invalid Pensions	Mar. 25, 1834	Adverse		Laid on table.		
Lehr, Philip	Arrears of pension	27	2	Petition	377	Invalid Pensions	609	Adverse		Laid on table.		
Lehr, Philip	Arrears of pension	28	1	Petition	744	Invalid Pensions.						
Leibengood, Henry	Pension for revolutionary services.	28	2	Petition	171	Rev. Pensions.						
Leibengood, Jacob	Pension for revolutionary services.	28	1	Petition	359	Invalid Pensions	March 7, 1844	Adverse		Laid on table.		
Leibengood, Jacob	Pension for revolutionary services.	28	2	Petition	197	Invalid Pensions.						
Leibert, Ferdinand	(See Firhman & Leibert)	27	2		1041							
Leich, Andrew, representatives of.	(See Andrew Leitch, representatives of.)	23	1		189							
Leighton, Hannah	(See Isaac Davis, former widow of)	15	1		156							
Leighton, Hannah	Compensation for revolutionary services of former husband, (Isaac Davis.)	24	1	Petition	662	Rev. Pensions				Discharged; laid on table.		
Leighton, Hannah	Compensation for revolutionary services of former husband, (Isaac Davis.)	25	2	Senate bill	994	Rev. Pensions	July 7, 1838	With't amend.	231	Referred to Committee Whole House.		
Leighton, Hannah	Compensation for revolutionary services of former husband, (Isaac Davis.)	25	3	Senate bill	657				165	Referred to Committee Whole House.		

List of private claims presented to the House of Representatives of the United States from the 1st to the 31st Congress, inclusive—Continued.

Names of claimants.	Nature or object of the claim.	Congress.	Session.	How brought before the House of Reps.	Page of journal.	To what committee of the House referred.	No. or date of the report.	Nature of the report.	No. of the bill.	How disposed of by the House of Reps.	How disposed of by the Senate.	Date of the act of Congress, and remarks.
Leighton, Hannah	Compensation for revolutionary services of former husband, (Isaac Davis.)	26	1	Petition	937	Rev. Pensions	714	Adverse	.....	Laid on table.		
Leighton, Hannah	Compensation for revolutionary services of former husband, (Isaac Davis.)	26	1	Senate bill	882	Rev. Pensions	May 25, 1840	With't amend.	118	Referred to Committee Whole House.		
Leighton, Hannah	Compensation for revolutionary services of former husband, (Isaac Davis.)	26	2	Senate bill	106	Rev. Pensions	Jan. 4, 1841	With't amend.	69	Passed	Passed	App'd March 3, 1841
Leiper, Thomas	For duplicates of loan office certificates.	1	2	Petition	165	.....	.....	.....	.....	Referred to Secretary of Treasury.		
Leiper, Thomas	For duplicates of loan office certificates.	6	1	Petition	655	Claims	April 22, 1800	Adverse	.....	Referred to Committee Whole House.		
Leiper, Thomas	Payment of lost certificates	16	1	Petition	135	Pens. & Rev. Cl'ms.	.....	.....	.....	Leave to withdraw.		
Leiper, Thomas	Payment of lost certificates	16	1	Senate bill	444	Pens. & Rev. Clm's.	April 26, 1820	With amends.	93	Passed	Passed	App'd May 15, 1820
Leister, Allen, heir of	Pension for revolutionary services.	25	2	Petition	197	Rev. Pensions	Mar. 20, 1838	Adverse	.....	Laid on table.		
Leister, Daniel	(See heir of Allen Leister)	25	2	.....	197							
Leitch, Andrew, children of	Half pay for services	1	3	Petition and rep't Sec. of War.	362	Select	Feb. 28, 1791	Favorable	139	Passed	Postponed.	
Leitch, Andrew, representatives of.	Seven years' half-pay	23	1	Petition	189	Rev. Claims.						
		23	1	Amend't to House bill.	902	.....	.....	.....	149	Passed	Passed	App'd June 30, 1834
Leitch, Andrew, heirs of	Half-pay for services	26	1	Petition	946	Rev. Claims.						
Leitch, Andrew, heirs of	Half-pay for services	26	2	Petition	35	Rev. Claims.						
Leitch, Andrew, heirs of	Half-pay for services	27	2	Petition	61	Rev. Claims	532	Adverse	.....	Laid on table.		
Leitch, Margaret	(See Col. Wm. Bond, representatives of.)	23	1	.....	168							
Leitensdorfer, John E	Compensation for military services and sacrifices.	23	2	Senate bill	149	Military Affairs	Jan. 6, 1835	With't amend.	S. 41	Passed	Passed	App'd Feb. 6, 1835
Leith, George	Compensation for his gun	22	1	Resolution	422	Claims	Mar. 2, 1832	Adverse	.....	Laid on table.		
Leith, George	Correction of erroneous entry of land.	22	2	Petition	185	Priv. Land Claims.						
Leitheiser, Hartman	Restoration of pension	17	2	Petition	119	.....	.....	.....	.....	Referred to Committee Whole House.		
Leitheiser, Hartman, representatives of.	Commutation pay	29	1	Petition	435	Rev. Claims.						
Leitzendorfer, Eugene dé	Compensation for services in operation against Tripoli.	11	2	Petition	271	Select	April 6, 1810	Adverse	.....	Leave to withdraw.		
Leitzendorfer, Eugene dé	Compensation for services in operation against Tripoli.	11	3	Senate bill	517	Claims	Feb. 5, 1811	With amends.	S. 56	Passed	Passed	App'd Feb. 13, 1811
Lekie, Thomas	(See William Scott, heirs of)	24	1	.....	106							
Lelachaise, P. A	(See H. and R. Use, assignee of.)	26	1	.....	362							
Leland, Baldwin M	Indemnity for damages to property, war of 1812.	20	1	Petition	419	Claims	April 17, 1828	Adverse	.....	Laid on table.		
Leland, Baldwin M	Indemnity for damages to property, war of 1812.	20	2	Petition	28	Claims	Dec. 12, 1828	Adverse	.....	Laid on table.		
Leland, Baldwin M	Indemnity for damages to property, war of 1812.	21	1	Petition	56	Claims	203	Adverse	.....	Referred to Committee Whole House.		
Leland, Baldwin M	Indemnity for damages to property, war of 1821.	22	1	Petition	91	Claims	Dec. 30, 1831	Adverse	.....	Laid on table.		
Leland, Jeremiah	Pension	22	1	Resolution	261	Rev. Pensions.						

List of private claims presented to the House of Representatives of the United States from the 1st to the 31st Congress, inclusive—Continued.

Names of claimants.	Nature or object of the claim.	Congress.	Session.	How brought before the House of Reps.	Page of journal.	To what committee of the House referred.	No. or date of the report.	Nature of the report.	No. of the bill.	How disposed of by the House of Reps.	How disposed of by the Senate.	Date of the act of Congress, and remarks.
Le Maigre, Peter	Remission of duties on merchandise captured by British.	3	1	Petition	137	....	....	....	....	Referred to Secretary Treasury.		
Le Maigre, Peter	Remission of duties on merchandise captured by British.	3	2	Rep. of Secretary Treasury.	284	....	....	....	....	Laid on table.		
Le Maitre, John B.	Drawback on cards to be exported.	15	2	Petition	44	Ways and Means.	Dec. 2, 1818	Adverse	....	Rejected.		
Le Maitre, John B.	Drawback of duties on cotton exported.	16	2	Petition	268	Ways and Means.						
Le Maitre, John B.	Drawback of duties on cotton exported.	18	1	Petition	38	Ways and Means.						
Le Maitre, John B.	Allowance of debenture on cards exported.	19	2	Petition	78	Ways and Means.	Dec. 29, 1826	Favorable	325	Referred to Committee Whole House.		
Le Maitre, John B.	Allowance of debenture on cards exported.	20	1	Petition	39	Ways and Means.	24	Favorable	174	Passed.		
Le Maitre, John B.	Allowance of debenture on cards exported.	20	2	Petition	32	Ways and Means.	Dec. 10, 1828	Favorable	305	Passed	Passed	App'd June 6, 1829
Leman, Polly	Leave to locate land in Louisiana.	24	1	Petition	635	Priv. Land Claims.						
Leman, Polly	Leave to locate land in Louisiana.	24	2	Petition	49	Priv. Land Claims.	29	Favorable	777	Referred to Committee Whole House.		
Leman, Polly	Leave to locate land in Louisiana.	25	2	Petition	43	Priv. Land Claims.	253	Favorable	294	Referred to Committee Whole House.		
Leman, Polly	Leave to locate land in Louisiana.	25	3	House bill	376	Whole House	Jan. 25, 1839	With amend.	294	Passed	Passed	App'd March 3, 1839
Lemay, Lewis	Indemnity for losses occasioned by Indians.	8	1	Petition	525	Claims	Dec. 21, 1803	Adverse.				
Lemay, Lewis	Indemnity for losses occasioned by Indians.	20	1	Petition	127	Claims	Jan. 30, 1828	Adverse	....	Laid on table.		
Lemay, Lewis	Indemnity for losses occasioned by Indians.	21	1	Petition	294	Claims	Mar. 2, 1830	Adverse	....	Laid on table.		
Lemen, B. F.	Increase of compensation as postmaster.	29	1	Petition	688	P. Of. & P. Roads.						
Leming, Sergeant C., widow of.	Pension	26	1	Resolution	551	Invalid Pensions	556	Adverse	....	Laid on table.		
Lemman, Patrick	Compensation for revolutionary services.	2	1	Petition	447	....	....	....	....	Referred to Secretary of War.		
Lemmon, Robert	(See William Priestman, administrator of.)	26	1	....	182	....	343	....	319			
Lemoine, Jean Baptiste	Confirmation of title to land	23	1	Petition	76	Priv. Land Claims.	Jan. 8, 1834	Adverse	....	Laid on table.		
Lemon, John	Pension for revolutionary services.	19	1	Petition	88	Military Pensions.	164	Adverse	....	Laid on table.		
Lemon, John	Pension for revolutionary services.	19	2	Petition	109	Military Pensions.	....	....	....	Leave to withdraw.		
Lemon, John	Pension for revolutionary services.	20	1	Petition	310	Military Pensions.						
Lemon, John	Pension for revolutionary services.	20	1	House bill	645	Whole House	May 16, 1828	With amends.	283	Passed.		
Lemon, John	Pension for revolutionary services.	20	2	House bill	55	Whole House	Dec. 12, 1828	With amends.	311	Passed	Laid on table.	
Lemon, John	Pension for revolutionary services.	21	1	Petition	47	Military Pensions.						
Lemon, John	Pension for revolutionary services.	21	1	Pension bill	130	Whole House	Feb. 12, 1830	With't amend.	72	Passed	Passed	App'd May 20, 1830
Lemon, John, widow of.	Pension for revolutionary services.	26	1	Resolution	386	Rev. Pensions	664	Adverse	....	Laid on table.		
Lemon, Martha	(See John Lemon, widow of.)	26	1	....	386							
Lemon, Moses	Pension for revolutionary services.	18	2	Petition	251	Pens. & Rev. Cl'ms.						
Lemon, Polly	(See Polly Leman.)	24	1	....	635							
Lemsford, George, heirs of.	Compensation for military services.	26	1	Resolution	359	Rev. Claims.						
Lenake, Henry A.	Payment for land	24	1	Appropriat'n bill.	1012	Whole House	June 30, 1836	With amends.	695	Passed	Passed	App'd July 2, 1836
Lendon, Amos	Compensation for horse lost in public service.	23	1	Documents	154	Claims.						
Lendrum, George, (La.).	Confirmation of title to land, or pay for improvements on same.	28	1	Petition	945	Public Lands.						

List of private claims presented to the House of Representatives of the United States from the 1st to the 31st Congress, inclusive—Continued.

Names of claimants.	Nature or object of the claim.	Congress.	Session.	How brought before the House of Reps.	Page of journal.	To what committee of the House referred.	No. or date of the report.	Nature of the report.	No. of the bill.	How disposed of by the House of Reps.	How disposed of by the Senate.	Date of the act of Congress, and remarks.
Lendrum, George, (La.)	Compensation for beef furnished United States army.	30	2	Petition	384	Military Affairs				Discharged; laid on table.		
Lendrum, George, (La.)	Compensation for beef furnished United States army.	31	1	Petition	312	Military Affairs				Discharged; laid on table.		
L'Enfant, Peter Charles	Additional pay for planning and constructing public buildings at Washington.	6	2	Petition	738	Claims	Dec. 7, 1800	Adverse		Rejected.		
L'Enfant, Peter Charles	Additional pay for planning and constructing public buildings at Washington.	6	2	Petition	807	Claims				Discharged.		
L'Enfant, Peter Charles	Additional pay for planning and constructing public buildings at Washington.	7	1	Petition	19	Claims	April 15, 1802	Adverse		Postponed.		
L'Enfant, Peter Charles	Additional pay for planning and constructing public buildings at Washington.	7	2	Petition	259	Claims	Feb. 17, 1803	Favorable		Referred to Committee Whole House.		
L'Enfant, Peter Charles	Additional pay for planning and constructing public buildings at Washington.	8	1	Petition	440	Claims	Dec. 14, 1803	Favorable		Referred to Committee Whole House.		
L'Enfant, Peter Charles	Additional pay for planning and constructing public buildings at Washington.	9	2	Petition	563	Claims.						
L'Enfant, Peter Charles	Additional pay for planning and constructing public buildings at Washington.	11	2	Petition	120	Select	April 27, 1810	Favorable	143	Passed	Passed	App'd May 1, 1810
L'Enfant, Peter Charles	Additional pay for planning and constructing public buildings at Washington.	11	3	Petition	469	Claims				Discharged.		
L'Enfant, Peter Charles	Additional pay for planning and constructing public buildings at Washington.	12	2	Petition	660	Claims.						
Lenfent, Benjamin	Indemnity for property destroyed by enemy.	23	1	Petition	159	Claims	266	Adverse		Laid on table.		
Lenhart, Henry, sen	Release from judgment	8	1	Petition	582	Claims	Mar. 13, 1804	Adverse		Postponed.		
Lenhart, Henry, sen	Release from judgment	8	2	Petition	6	Claims	Dec. 14, 1804	Adverse		Laid on table.		
Le Normand, John	Remission of duties on wines destroyed by fire.	5	2	Petition	82	Com. and Manuf.	Dec. 4, 1797	Adverse		Rejected		Leave to withdraw.
Lenals, Joshua	(See William Baker, N. Y.)	22	1		288		480					
Lenox, Aaron	Pension	28	1	Petition	753	Invalid Pensions.						
Lenox, David	Reimbursement of money	4	1	Resolution	421	Ways and Means	Jan. 18, 1797	Favorable	142	Passed	Passed	App'd Feb. 5, 1796
Lenox, James	(See Thomas L. Ogden, *et al.*)	17	1		38							
Lenox, James, *et al.*	Payment of certain drawbacks	17	1	Petition	32	Commerce.						
Lenox, James, *et al.*	Payment of certificates of debenture	18	1	Petition	193	Commerce.	May 14, 1824	Favorable	232	Referred to Committee Whole House.		
Lenox, James, *et al.*	Payment of certificates of debenture	18	2	House bill	259	Whole House	Feb. 22, 1825	With amend.	232	Passed	Passed	App'd March 3, 1825
Lenox, Levi	(See Edah Vemeule, *et al.*)	9	1		192							
Lenox, Robert	(See Thomas L. Ogden, *et al.*)	17	1		38							
Lent, James W. jr., by his father.	For settlement of accounts	19	1	Petition	335	Military Affairs	April 17, 1826	Favorable	218	Passed.		
Lent, James W. jr., by his father.	For settlement of accounts	19	2	Senate bill	139	Military Affairs	Jan. 17, 1827	With amend.	44	Passed	Passed	App'd Feb. 8, 1827
Lent, John	Restoration of pension	24	1	Petition	273	Rev. Pensions	377	Favorable	380	Passed	Passed	App'd June 28, 1836

List of private claims presented to the House of Representatives of the United States from the 1st to the 31st Congress, inclusive—**Continued.**

Names of claimants.	Nature or object of the claim.	Congress.	Session.	How brought before the House of Reps.	Page of journal.	To what committee of the House referred.	No. or date of the report.	Nature of the report.	No. of the bill.	How disposed of by the House of Reps.	How disposed of by the Senate.	Date of the act of Congress, and remarks.
Lent, John, widow of	Pension for revolutionary pension	4	1	Petition	384	Claims	Jan. 20, 1796	Adverse		Rejected; leave to withdraw.		
Lent, Margaret	(See John Lent, widow of)	4	1		384							
Lentry, David	(See John Day and David Lentry)	25	2		931							
Leon, Spanish brig	Indemnity for loss in rescuing American citizen.	22	1	Presid'ts message	53	Commerce	34	General bill	79	Passed	Passed	App'd July 14, 1832
Leonard, Bernard	Confirmation of title to land	21	2	Petition	338	Priv. Land Claims.						
Leonard, Bernard	Confirmation of title to land	22	1	Petition	65	Priv. Land Claims.	73	Favorable	141	Passed	Passed	App'd July 14, 1832
Leonard, Charles S.	Additional allowance on contract	14	2	Petition	183	Claims.						
Leonard, Charles S.	Additional allowance on contract	15	1	Petition	106, 237	Claims.						
Leonard, Charles S.	Additional allowance on contract	15	2	Petition	115	Claims	Jan. 12, 1819	Favorable	144	Passed	Passed	App'd Feb. 20, 1819
Leonard, Daniel S.	(See William Robertson, widow of)	22	1		33							
Leonard, Enoch	Compensation for revolutionary services.	2	1	Petition	490					Referred to Secretary War.		
Leonard, Enoch	Compensation for revolutionary services.	3	2	Rep. of Secretary War.	278					Laid on table.		
Leonard, Gilbert	Right of pre-emption as New Orleans branch pilot.	28	1	Petition	77	Priv. Land Claims.	9	Favorable	35	Passed	Passed	App'd June 17, 1844
Leonard, Henry	Pension	15	1	Resolution	54	Pens. & Rev. Cl'ms.				Discharged; referred to Secretary War.		
Leonard, Isabella	(See John Leonard, widow of.)	27	3		207							
Leonard, James H.	(See Samuel Allen, *et al.*)	17	1		388							
Leonard, John, widow of.	Indemnity for French spoliations prior to 1800.	26	1	Memorial	182	Foreign Affairs	343	Favorable	319	Referred to Committee Whole House.		
Leonard, John, widow of.	Indemnity for French spoliations prior to 1800.	27	3	Petition	207					Laid on table.		
Leonard, John, heirs of	Indemnity for French spoliations prior to 1800.	31	1	Petition	681	Claims	355	General bill	318	Referred to Committee Whole House.		
Leonard, Josiah	Pension	21	2	Petition	270	Military Pensions.						
Leonard, Lot	Pension for revolutionary services.	24	1	Petition	406	Rev. Pensions	439	Favorable	452	Passed	Passed	App'd June 28, 1836
Leonard, Nathan	Pension	21	1	Petition	127	Military Pensions.						
Leonard, Nathan	Pension	22	1	Petition	80	Rev. Pensions.						
Leonard, Oliver	Permission to import property from Jamaica.	12	1	Petition	157	Whole House	Jan. 7, 1812	General bill	46	Postponed.		
Leonard, Patrick	Pension	14	2	Petition	438					Laid on table.		
Leonard, Robert	Increase of pension	5	2	Petition	115	Claims	Feb. 1, 1798	Adverse		Rejected.		
Leonard, Roger	Pension for revolutionary services.	15	2	Petition	124	Pens. & Rev. Cl'ms.				Discharged; referred to Secretary of War.		
Leonard, Rowland	Pension for revolutionary services.	22	1	Petition	254	Rev. Pensions	Jan. 16, 1812	Adverse		Laid on table.		
Leonard, Samuel	Pension	12	1	House bill	361	Whole House	June 8, 1812	Favorable	138	Passed	Passed	App'd July 5, 1812
Leonard, Samuel	Release from liability for money burnt.	27	2	Petition	1111	P. Of. & P. Roads.	1053	Adverse		Laid on table.		
Leonardy, Roque	Indemnity for Indian depredations.	25	2	Petition	575	Claims	May 15, 1838	Adverse		Laid on table.		
Le Page, John Baptiste	(See Lewis & Clarke, and companions.)	9	2		284							
Leprade, W.	Settlement of his accounts	16	1	Petition	221	Claims	Mar. 15, 1820	Adverse		Rejected.		
Lequeux, Apling, & Co.	Remission of forfeited military stores	16	1	Petition	70	Commerce.						
Lerillard, William	Bounty land for military services	30	1	Petition	259	Military Affairs.						
Lerillard, William	Bounty land for military services	30	2	Petition	181					Leave to withdraw.		
Le Roy, George, agents of.	Interest on certificates to be paid in Paris.	1	3	Petition	372					Laid on table.		

List of private claims presented to the House of Representatives of the United States from the 1st to the 31st Congress, inclusive—Continued.

Names of claimants.	Nature or object of the claim.	Congress.	Session.	How brought before the House of Reps.	Page of journal.	To what committee of the House referred.	No. or date of the report.	Nature of the report.	No. of the bill.	How disposed of by the House of Reps.	How disposed of by the Senate.	Date of the act of Congress, and remarks.
Leroy, Herman	(See Thomas L. Ogden, *et al.*)	17	1		38							
Leroy, Helen	(See Lewis Leroy, widow of.)	29	2		171							
Leroy, Isaac	Bounty land for military services	25	2	Petition	577	Military Affairs.						
Leroy, John	Pension	31	1	Senate bill	1444	Invalid Pensions			56			
Leroy, Lewis	Indemnity for French spoliations prior to 1800.	26	1	Memorial	182	Foreign Affairs	343	Favorable	319	Referred to Committee Whole House.		
Leroy, Lewis, widow of	Indemnity for French spoliations prior to 1800.	29	2	Petition	171	Foreign Affairs.						
Leroy, Lewis, widow of	Indemnity for French spoliations prior to 1800.	31	1	Petition	196	Foreign Affairs	355	General bill	318	Referred to Committee Whole House.		
Leroy, Lewis, *et al.*	(See Jacob Blackwell)	17	2		118							
Leroy, Lewis, surety of	Release from liability	20	2	Petition	215	Ways and Means				Discharged; laid on table.		
Leroy, Lewis, surety of	Release from liability	21	1	Petition	297	Ways and Means				Discharged; laid on table.		
Leroy, Lewis, surety of	Release from liability	25	3	Petition	119	Ways and Means	273	Favorable	1142	Referred to Committee Whole House.		
Leroy, Lewis, surety of	Release from liability	26	1	Petition	178	Ways and Means	300	Favorable	262	Passed	Passed	App'd July 20, 1840
Leroy, P. S., widow of	Compensation for property lost	17	1	Petition	78	Claims	Jan. 23, 1822	Adverse		Rejected.		
Leroy, P. S., widow of	Compensation for property lost	17	2	Petition and docs.	76							
Leroy, P. S., widow of	Compensation for property lost	18	1	Petition	432	Claims				Ref'd to Com. W. H. on bill No. 23.		
Lesassier, John C	Allowance of office rent	22	1	Petition	224	Judiciary				Disch'd; laid on table.		
Lescieur, J	Confirmation of title to land	26	1	Petition	365	Priv. Land Claims.						
Lesh, Peter	Pension	31	1	Petition	542	Invalid Pensions.						
Lesher, John	Compensation for revolutionary services.	2	1	Petition	528					Referred to Secretary of War.		
Lesher, John	Compensation for revolutionary services.	2	2	Rep. of Secretary War.	696					Laid on table.		
Le Sieur, Firman, representatives of.	Authority to relocate land	18	1	Senate bill	179	Public Lands	April 6, 1824	Favorable	S. 12	Passed	Passed	App'd May 5, 1824
Lesley, James	Pension	22	1	Petition	189	Invalid Pensions.						
Lesley, James	Pension	25	2	Petition	588	Invalid Pensions	May 18, 1838	Adverse		Laid on table.		
Lesley, John	Grant of land for revolutionary services.	20	2	Petition	119	Priv. Land Claims.						
Lesley, John	Grant of land for revolutionary services.	21	1	Petition	98	Rev. Claims	Feb. 8, 1830	Adverse		Laid on table.		
Leslie, Benjamin	Pension	22	2	Petition	315	Invalid Pensions.						
Leslie, Benjamin	Pension	23	1	Petition	454	Invalid Pensions	410	Favorable	428	Referred to Committee Whole House.		
Leslie, Benjamin	Pension	23	2	House bill	336	Whole House	Feb. 6, 1835	With amend't	428	Passed	Passed	App'd March 3, 1835
Leslie, David	To direct adjustment of his claim	23	1	Petition	585	Foreign Affairs	June 14, 1834	Favorable	527	Ref'd to Com. W. H.		
Leslie, Samuel, widow of	Pension for revolutionary services	26	1	Resolution	596	Rev. Pensions	490	Adverse		Laid on table.		
Leslie, Sarah	(See Samuel Leslie, widow of.)	26	1		596							
Lester, Benjamin L	(See sureties of S. D. Betton.)	27	2		70							
Lester, Champlin	Compensation for support of United States prisoners.	21	2	Petition	299	Judiciary.						
Lester, Christopher	(See Elijah Bailey, *et al.*)	17	2		56							
Lester, Christopher, *et al.*	Fishing bounty	10	1	Petition	263	Com. and Manuf.						
Lester, Ebenezer	Commutation pay for revolutionary services.	25	2	Petition	47	Rev. Claims	May 18, 1838	Adverse		Laid on table.		
Lester, Ebenezer A	Balance due on engine for United States.	23	1	Petition	245	Claims.						

List of private claims presented to the House of Representatives of the United States from the 1st to the 31st Congress, inclusive—Continued.

Names of claimants.	Nature or object of the claim.	Congress.	Session.	How brought before the House of Reps.	Page of journal.	To what committee of the House referred.	No. or date of the report.	Nature of the report.	No. of the bill.	How disposed of by the House of Reps.	How disposed of by the Senate.	Date of the act of Congress, and remarks.
Lester, Ebenezer A	Balance due on engine for United States.	23	2	Petition	114	Claims.						
Lester, Ebenezer A	Balance due on engine for United States.	24	1	Petition	93	Claims	318	Favorable	331	Referred to Committee Whole House.		
Lester, Ebenezer A	Balance due on engine for United States.	25	2	Petition	36	Claims	8	Favorable	17	Passed	Indef. postp'd.	
Lester, Ebenezer A	Balance due on engine for United States.	25	3	Petition	189	Claims	195	Favorable	1052	Passed	Adverse.	
Lester, Ebenezer A	Balance due on engine for United States.	26	1	Petition	168	Claims	9	Favorable	28	Passed	Indef. postp'd.	
Lester, Ebenezer A	Balance due on engine for United States.	26	2	Petition	101	Claims	13	Favorable	551	Referred to Committee Whole House.		
Lester, Ebenezer A	Balance due on engine for United States.	28	1	Petition	183	Naval Affairs.						
Lester, Ebenezer A	Balance due on engine for United States.	28	2	Petition	45	Naval Affairs.						
Lesser, Ebenezer A	Balance due on engine for United States.	29	1	Petition	70	Naval Affairs.						
Lester, Elihu	Pension for revolutionary services.	14	2	Petition	44	Pens. & Rev. Cl'ms.	Jan. 29, 1817	Favorable	91	Passed	Passed	App'd March 3, 1817
Lester, Elihu	Bounty land for revolutionary services.	19	1	Petition	82	Priv. Land Claims.	Dec. 28, 1825	Adverse		Laid on table.		
Lester, John	Arrears of pay	11	2	Petition and rep't Sec. of War.	201					Laid on table.		
Lester, John	(See Robert Courtney, attorney of)	26	1		182		343		319			
Lester, Noah	Compensation for rebuilding Fort Griswold.	14	1	Petition	415	Claims.						
Lester, William	Pension	25	2	Petition	271	Invalid Pensions				Discharged; laid on table.		
Lesure, Hannah	(See Samuel Lesure, widow of)	27	2		612							
Lesure, Samuel, widow of.	Continuation of pension	27	2	Petition	612	Rev. Pensions	784	Adverse		Laid on table.		
Lether, John	Compensation for revolutionary services.	2	1	Petition	447					Referred to Secretary War.		
Letil, Louis A	(See Pierre Clermont, attorney for heirs of.)	30	2		379							
Letson, William	Pension	21	2	Petition	188	Military Pensions.						
Letton, J. W	(See John Graves, *et al*)	27	2		620							
Letts, Daniel	Increase of pension	31		Petition	719	Rev. Claims	315	Adverse		Laid on table.		
Letts, James	Pension for revolutionary services.	22	1	Petition	466	Rev. Claims.						
Levacher, John, widow of.	(See John L. De Van Brun, widow of.)	24	2		94							
Levall, Henry D	Restoration of property seized	12	2	Petition	610	Ways and Means.						See act Feb. 27, 1813
Levan, Isaac	Pension for revolutionary services.	26	1	Petition	324	Rev. Pensions.						
Levan, Isaac	Pension for revolutionary services.	26	1	Resolution	549	Rev. Pensions	490	Adverse		Laid on table.		
Levan, Isaac	Pension for revolutionary services.	27	2	Resolution	428	Rev. Pensions	784	Adverse		Laid on table.		
Levan, Jacob	Compensation for revolutionary services.	2	1	Petition	458					Referred to Secretary War.		
Levan, Jocob	Compensation for revolutionary services.	2	2	Rep. of Secretary War.	696					Laid on table.		
Levanway, A. & F	Compensation for revolutionary services.	23	1	Petition	40	Rev. Claims.						
Levea, Charles, heirs of	Compensat'n for services in Clark's regiment.	26	1	Resolution	359	Rev. Claims.						

List of private claims presented to the House of Representatives of the United States from the 1st to the 31st Congress, inclusive—Continued.

Names of claimants.	Nature or object of the claim.	Congress.	Session.	How brought before the House of Reps.	Page of journal.	To what committee of the House referred.	No. or date of the report.	Nature of the report.	No. of the bill.	How disposed of by the House of Reps.	How disposed of by the Senate.	Date of the act of Congress, and remarks.
Levell, Jacob	Indemnity for French spoliations prior to 1800.	26	1	Memorial	182	Foreign Affairs	343	Favorable	319	Referred to Committee Whole House.		
Levely, Henry	Arrears of pension	24	1	Petition	407	Naval Affairs.						
Leverett, Mary G	(See Thomas Leverett, widow of.)	30	1		344							
Leverett, Thomas	Pension for revolutionary services.	23	1	Resolution	160	Rev. Pensions				Discharged; leave to withdraw.		
Leverett, Thomas, widow of.	Benefit of act of July 7, 1838	30	1	Petition	344	Rev. Pensions	685	Favorable	547	Referred to Committee Whole House.		
Leverett, Thomas, widow of.	Benefit of act July 7, 1838	30	2	Rep't Committee Whole House.	319			Favorable	547	Passed	Passed	App'd Mar. 3, 1849
Levi, Judas	Increase of pension	10	1	Petition	14					Referred to Secretary War.		
Levick, Robert	Compensation for revolutionary services.	23	1	Petition	617	Rev. Claims.						
Levins, James	Compensation for capture of midshipman and 4 seamen of British navy.	14	1	Petition	186	Naval Affairs	Jan. 27, 1816	Favorable	53	Passed	Passed	App'd April 26, 1816
Levinworth, Gen Henry	(See General Henry Leavinworth, widow of.)	23	2		143							
Levittre, Joseph	(See Canadian Refugees.)	6	2		766							
Levy, Abraham	Compensation for revolutionary services	2	1	Petition	446					Referred to Secretary War.		
Levy, Almond	(See Benjamin Hale, *et al.*)	31	1		1499							
Levy, Chapman	Right of pre-emption, &c.	27	2	Senate bill	550	Public Lands	May 12, 1842	Favorable	195	Passed	Passed	App'd Aug. 11, 1842
Levy, Judah	Pension	10	2	Pension bill	499	Whole House	Feb. 20, 1809	With amend.	158	Passed	Passed	App'd March 3, 1809
Levy, Louis P	(See Michael Boune, representatives of.)	16	1		177							
Levy, Moses Elias	For leave to hold real estate	16	1	Petition	313	Public Lands	Mar. 23, 1820	Adverse		Rejected.		
Levy, Moses Elias	Confirmation of title to land	18	1	Documents	499	Public Lands.						
Levy, Moses Elias	Confirmation of title to land	20	1	Petition	419	Public Lands				Discharged; laid on table.		
Levy, Moses Elias	Confirmation of title to land	21	1	Petition	40	Priv. Land Claims	Jan. 11, 1830	Adverse		Laid on table.		
Levy, Moses Elias	Payment for land ceded by United States.	22	1	Petition	133	Priv. Land Claims				Discharged; laid on table.		
Levy, Moses E	Indemnity for property destroyed by Indians.	25	2	Petition	120	Claims.						
Levy, Moses E	Indemnity for property destroyed by Indians.	25	3	Petition	86	Claims	236	Adverse		Laid on table.		
Levy, Moses E	Indemnity for property destroyed by Indians.	2[illegible]	2	Petition	136	Claims.						
Levy, Moses E	Indemnity for property destroyed by Indians.	30	1	Petition	116	Claims.						
Levy, Nathan	Reimbursement of moneys paid into treasury.	24	1	Petition	799	Commerce	705	Favorable	658	Referred to Committee Whole House.		
Levy, Nathan	Reimbursement of moneys paid into treasury.	25	2	Petition	40	Commerce	87	Favorable	103	Passed.		
Levy, Nathan	Reimbursement of moneys paid into treasury.	[illegible]5	3	Petition	416	Commerce	238	Favorable	1099	Referred to Committee Whole House.		
Levy, Nathan	Reimbursement of moneys paid into treasury.	26	1	Petition	176	Commerce	72	Favorable	59	Passed	Passed	App'd May 2, 1840
Levy, M. P	Compensation for prosecuting pirates.	14		Petition	438	Claims.						
Lewis, Aaron	Pension	19	2	Petition	111	Military Pensions.						

List of private claims presented to the House of Representatives of the United States from the 1st to the 31st Congress, inclusive—Continued.

Names of claimants.	Nature or object of the claim.	Congress.	Session.	How brought before the House of Reps.	Page of journal.	To what committee of the House referred.	No. or date of the report.	Nature of the report.	No. of the bill.	How disposed of by the House of Reps.	How disposed of by the Senate.	Date of the act of Congress, and remarks.
Lewis, Abigail	(See Ichebod Lewis, widow of)	3	2		239							
Lewis, Addin	Relinquishment of right of United States to lot of land.	20	2	Petition	145	Public Lands				Discharged; laid on table.		
Lewis, Ambrose	Compensation for revolutionary services.	10	2	Petition	374	Claims				Discharged; leave to withdraw.		
Lewis, Ambrose	Compensation for revolutionary services.	11	2	House bill	283	Whole House	Mar. 16, 1810	With amend.	107	Passed	Passed	App'd April 27, 1810
Lewis, Ambrose	Penion for revolutionary services	12	1	House bill	361	Claims	June 8, 1812	With amend.	138	Passed	Passed	App'd July 5, 1812
Lewis, Ambrose	Arrears of pension	12	2	Petition	574	Claims	Feb. 26, 1813	Adverse		Laid on table.		
Lewis, Ambrose	Arrears of pension	13	2	Petition	269	Pens. & Rev. Cl'ms.	Mar. 28, 1814	Adverse		Referred to Committee Whole House.		
Lewis, Ambrose	Arrears of pension	13	3	Petition	664	Pens. & Rev. Cl'ms.	Jan. 27, 1815	Adverse		Rejected.		
Lewis, Ambrose	Arrears of pension	14	1	Petition	134	Pens. & Rev. Cl'ms.	April 11, 1816	Favorable	171			Bill became a law, omitting petitioner's name.
Lewis, Ambrose	Increase of pension	14	2	House bill	307	Pens. & Rev. Cl'ms.	Jan. 29, 1817	Favorable	91			Became a law, omitting petitioner's name.
Lewis, Ambrose	Increase of pension	16	1	Resolution	236	Pens. & Rev. Cl'ms.						
Lewis, Amos	Pension	12	1	House bill	361	Whole House	June 15, 1812	With't amend.	138	Passed	Passed	App'd July 5, 1812
Lewis, Andrew	Pension	4	1	Petition	432	Whole House.						
Lewis, Andrew	Pension	23	1	Petition	493	Military Affairs.						
Lewis, Andrew, widow of.	Indemnity for loss of time and expenses incurred in defending certain suit.	28	1	Petition	159	Claims	339	Adverse		Laid on table.		
Lewis, A. J., and Lewis & Co.	Return of extra duties paid	21	2	Petition	53	Ways and Means.						
Lewis & Clarke, and companions.	Compensation for exploration of western waters.	9	1	Presid'ts message.	284					Laid on table.		
Lewis & Clarke, and companions.	Compensation for exploration of western waters.	9	2	Resolution	470, 507	Select	Jan. 23, 1807	Favorable	183	Passed	Passed	App'd Mar. 3, 180[illegible]
Lewis & Clarke, and companions.	Benefit of act of March 3, 1807	10	2	Petition	480	Public Lands.						
Lewis, Charles, representatives of.	Commutation pay	22	2	Petition	142	Rev. Claims.						
Lewis, Charles, representatives of.	Commutation pay	23	1	Petition	42	Rev. Claims.						
Lewis, Charles, representatives of.	Commutation pay	23	2	Petition	109	Rev. Claims.						
Lewis, Charles, representatives of.	Commutation pay	24	1	Petition	431	Rev. Claims.						
Lewis, Charles, representatives of.	Commutation pay	24	2	Petition	94	Rev. Claims.						
Lewis, Charles, representatives of.	Commutation pay	25	2	Petition	72	Rev. Claims.						
Lewis, Charles, representatives of.	Commutation pay	26	1	Petition	165, 361	Rev. Claims	603	Adverse		Laid on table.		
Lewis, Charles, representatives of.	Commutation pay	27	2	Petition	61	Rev. Claims	201	Adverse		Laid on table.		
Lewis, Charles, representatives of.	Commutation pay	30	1	Petition	165, 342	Rev. Claims.						
Lewis, Charles, representatives of.	Commutation pay	30	2	Petition	102	Rev. Claims.						

List of private claims presented to the House of Representatives of the United States from the 1st to the 31st Congress, inclusive—Continued.

Names of claimants.	Nature or object of the claim.	Congress.	Session.	How brought before the House of Reps.	Page of journal.	To what committee of the House referred.	No. or date of the report.	Nature of the report.	No. of the bill.	How disposed of by the House of Reps.	How disposed of by the Senate.	Date of the act of Congress, and remarks.
Lewis, Charles, representatives of.	Commutation pay	31	1	Petition	419	Rev. Claims				Leave to withdraw.		
Lewis, Charles, assignee of.	Fees as acting counsel of United States.	25	2	Petition	921	Claims	1045	Favorable	879	Referred to Committee Whole House.		
Lewis, Charles, assignee of.	Fees as acting counsel of United States.	25	3	House bill	432	Whole House	Feb. 1, 1839	With't amend.	879	Passed	Passed	App'd Mar. 3, 1839
Lewis, Christopher	Increase of pension	25	2	Petition	586	Rev. Pensions				Discharged; laid on table.		
Lewis, Curtis	Relief for illegal acts of judicial officers.	16	2	Petition	20	Judiciary	Nov. 24, 1820	Adverse		Leave to withdraw.		
Lewis, Curtis	Restitution of certain slaves captured by United States cutter.	18	1	Petition	98	Judiciary				Discharged; leave to withdraw.		
Lewis, Daniel	Compensation for discovery of medicine for cure of bite of mad dog.	7	2	Memorial	265	Select	Jan. 20, 1803	Adverse		Leave to withdraw.		
Lewis, Daniel	Indemnity for damages to house by United States troops.	19	1	Petition	177	Claims	Jan. 27, 1826	Adverse		Laid on table.		
Lewis, David	Pension	3	1	Rep. of Secretary War.	131	Select	May 26, 1794	Res. to refer to Sec. War.	J. R. 12	Passed	Passed	App'd June 9, 1794
Lewis, David	Pension	8	2	Petition	147	Claims.						
Lewis, David	Pension	9	1	Petition	190	Claims	Mar. 28, 1806	Indef. postp'd.		Leave to withdraw.		
Lewis, David	Compensation for losses in removing United States property on invasion of St. Mary's, Georgia.	14	1	Petition	111	Claims	Jan. 24, 1816	Adverse		Rejected.		
Lewis, David	Compensation for losses in removing United States property on invasion of St. Mary's, Georgia.	24	1	Resolution	341	Claims	346	Adverse		Laid on table.		
Lewis, David	(See Weston Allen, *et al.*)	22	1		132							
Lewis, David M	Compensation for flour destroyed by British.	18	1	Petition	357	Claims				Leave to withdraw.		
Lewis, David M	Compensation for flour destroyed by British.	19	2	Petition	132	Claims	Jan. 27, 1817	Adverse		Laid on table.		
Lewis, David M	Compensation for flour destroyed by British.	21	1	Petition	69	Claims	201	Adverse		Referred to Committee Whole House.		
Lewis, David M	Compensation for flour destroyed by British.	22	1	Petition	378	Claims	March 2, 1832	Adverse		Laid on table.		
Lewis, David M	Compensation for flour destroyed by British.	22	2	Petition	71	Claims				Referred to Committee Whole House.		
Lewis, Ebenezer	Pension for revolutionary services.	19	2	Petition	111	Military Pensions.						
Lewis, Edmund	Indemnity for French spoliations prior to 1800.	26	1	Memorial	182	Foreign Affairs	343	Favorable	319	Referred to Committee Whole House.		
Lewis, E. E	Indemnity for French spoliations prior to 1800.	26	1	Memorial	182	Foreign Affairs	343	Favorable	319	Referred to Committee Whole House.		
Lewis, E. E	Indemnity for loss of trunk at Vera Cruz.	30	2	Memorial	379	Military Affairs				Discharged; laid on table.		
Lewis, Edward W., father of.	Compensation for services as an extra clerk in War Department.	18	1	Petition	38					Referred to Secretary of War.		
Lewis, Edward W., father of.	Compensation for services as an extra clerk in War Department.	19	1	Petition	110	Claims	Jan. 25, 1826	Adverse		Laid on table.		
Lewis, Edward W., father of.	Compensation for services as an extra clerk in War Department.	19	2	Petition	240	Claims.						
Lewis, Edward W., father of.	Compensation for services as an extra clerk in War Department.	21	2	Petition	75	Claims	Dec. 24, 1830	Adverse		Laid on table.		

List of private claims presented to the House of Representatives of the United States from the 1st to the 31st Congress, inclusive—Continued.

Names of claimants.	Nature or object of the claim.	Congress.	Session.	How brought before the House of Reps.	Page of journal.	To what committee of the House referred.	No. or date of the report.	Nature of the report.	No. of the bill.	How disposed of by the House of Reps.	How disposed of by the Senate.	Date of the act of Congress, and remarks.
Lewis, Edward W., father of.	Compensation for services as an extra clerk in War Department.	22	1	Senate bill	814	Claims			S. 87			
Lewis, Edward W., father of.	Compensation for services as an extra clerk in War Department.	22	2	Petition	132	Claims.						
Lewis, Edward W., father of	Compensation for services as an extra clerk in War Department.	23	1	Petition	39	Claims	Dec. 30, 1833	Adverse		Laid on table.		
Lewis, Edwin	(See Henry Nail, representatives of.)	8	2		106							
Lewis, Edwin	(See William Burke, heirs of)	12	1		26							
Lewis, Edwin	(See John Doase, attorney of)	12	2		663							
Lewis, Edwin	(See J. B. Beaudreaux, *et al*)	1[illegible]	3		674							
Lewis, Edwin	(See John Kennedy, representatives of)	14	2		31[illegible]							
Lewis, Edwin	Pre-emption right to land in Mississippi Territory.	9	1	Petition	212	Public Lands	Mar. 11, 1806	Adverse		Referred to Committee Whole House.		
Lewis, Edwin	Pre-emption right to land in Mississippi Territory.	9	2	Petition	480	Public Lands.						
Lewis, Edwin	Pre-emption right to land in Mississippi Territory.	11	2	Petition	316	Public Lands	Mar. 27, 1810	Favorable	137	Laid on table.		
Lewis, Edwin	Pre-emption right to land in Mississippi Territory.	11	3	Petition	457	Public Lands	Jan. 7, 1811	Favorable	170	Passed	Passed	February 11, 1811—vetoed by President; House refuse to pass by two-thirds.
Lewis, Edwin	Pre-emption right to land in Mississippi Territory.	11	3	Senate bill	612	Whole House	Mar. 2, 1811	With amend.	S. 68	Passed	Passed	App'd March 3, 1811
Lewis, Edwin	Pre-emption right to land in Mississippi Territory.	15	1	Petition	133	Priv. Land Claims.						
Lewis, Edwin	Pre-emption right to land in Mississippi Territory.	18	1	Petition	225	Priv. Land Claims.						
Lewis, Edwin	Pre-emption right to land in Mississippi Territory.	20	1	Petition	225	Public Lands.						
Lewis, Edwin	Pre-emption right to land in Mississippi Territory.	21	1	Petition	123	Public Lands				Discharged; laid on table.		
Lewis, Edwin	Indemnity for timber cut by United States troops.	11	3	Petition	510	Claims.						
Lewis, Edwin	Indemnity for timber cut by United States troops	13	2	Petition	419					Laid on table.		
Lewis, Edwin	Indemnity for timber cut by United States troops.	13	3	Petition	454	Claims	Oct. 4, 1814	Adverse		Adopted.		
Lewis, Edwin	Indemnity for timber cut by United States troops.	15	1	Petition	243	Claims				Discharged.		
Lewis, Edwin	That land claimed by him be not included in grant of land to Mobile.	19	1	Petition	178	Public Lands				Discharged; laid on table.		
Lewis, Edwin	Confirmation of title to land, &c.	11	3	Petition	560	Public Lands.						
Lewis, Edwin	Confirmation of title to land, &c.	12	2	Petition	560	Public Lands.						
Lewis, Edwin	Grant of land	14	1	Petition	121	Public Lands.						
Lewis, Edwin	Grant of land	14	2	Petition	5[illegible]	Public Lands.						
Lewis, Edwin	Authority to have evidence taken.	12	1	Petition	20	Public Lands.						
Lewis, Edwin, and wife	Confirmation of title to land	13	3	Petition	711	Public Lands.						
Lewis, Edwin, and wife	Confirmation of title to land	14	1	Petition	55	Public Lands.						
Lewis, Ezra, administrator of.	Indemnity for French spoliations prior to 1800.	26	1	Memorial	182	Foreign Affairs	343	Favorable	319	Referred to Committee Whole House.		
Lewis, Frances	(See William Palmer, widow of)	27	3		190							

List of private claims presented to the House of Representatives of the United States from the 1st *to the* 31st *Congress, inclusive*—Continued.

Names of claimants.	Nature or object of the claim.	Congress.	Session.	How brought before the House of Reps.	Page of journal.	To what committee of the House referred.	No. or date of the report.	Nature of the report.	No. of the bill.	How disposed of by the House of Reps.	How disposed of by the Senate.	Date of the act of Congress, and remarks.
Lewis, Frances M	(See Capt. William Lewis, widow of.)	27	3		221							
Lewis, George	Amount of loan office certificate	15	2	Petition	268	Pens. & Rev. Cl'ms.						
Lewis, George	Amount of loan office certificate	18	1	Petition	130	Pens. & Rev. Cl'ms.				Leave to withdraw.		
Lewis, George	Amount of loan office certificate	18	2	Petition	65	Select	Jan. 20, 1825	Adverse		Discharged; leave to withdraw.		
Lewis, George	Amount of loan office certificate	19	1	Petition	224	Rev. Claims				Discharged.		
Lewis, George	Pay for services of father in revolutionary war.	22	1	Petition	55	Rev. Claims				Discharged; laid on table.		
Lewis, George	Revolutionary pension	22	1	Petition	56	Rev. Pensions	Dec. 28, 1831	Adverse		Laid on table.		
Lewis, G. K	Indemnity for Indian depredations.	31	1	Petition	199	Indian Affairs.						
Lewis, Henry	(See Henry Schnebly)	24	1		514							
Lewis, Henry	(See Winslow and Henry Lewis)	14	2		197							
Lewis, Hervey	Pension	3	1	Rep. of Secretary War.	131	Select	May 26, 1794	Favorable	62	Passed	Passed	App'd June 7, 1794
Lewis, Ichabod, widow of.	Indemnity for property destroyed by United States troops.	3	2	Petition	239	Claims	Feb. 25, 1795	Adverse		Referred to Committee Whole House.		
Lewis, Isaac	Increase of pension	16	1	Petition	284	Pens. & Rev. Cl'ms.				Discharged; referred to Secretary War.		
Lewis, Jabez	Pension for revolutionary services.	3	1	Rep. of Secretary War.	131	Select	May 26, 1794	Res. to refer to Sec. War.	J.R. 12	Passed	Passed	App'd June 9, 1794
Lewis, James	Indemnity for damages sustained by being forcibly brought from Sandwich islands as a witness for United States.	31	1	Petition	584	Judiciary	349	Favorable	300	Referred to Committee Whole House.		
Lewis, James	Pension for revolutionary services.	5	2	House bill	127	Whole House	Jan. 11, 1798	With amend.	38	Passed	Passed, with amendment.	App'd Feb. 2, 1798
Lewis, James, (Tenn.)	Compensation for revolutionary services.	22	1	Petition	442	Rev. Claims.						
Lewis, James B	(See Exploring Expedition)	27	3		149		270		818			
Lewis, James M	Pension	28	2	Petition	82	Invalid Pensions.						
Lewis, James M	Pension	29	2	Petition	86	Invalid Pensions.						
Lewis, James M	Pension	30	1	Petition	594	Invalid Pensions.						
Lewis, James M	Pension	30	2	Petition	656					Leave to withdraw.		
Lewis, Jane	(See Captain Thomas Lewis, widow of.)	20	1		356							
Lewis, John	Adjustment of claim against United States.	1	3	Petition	330					Referred to Secretary Treasury.		
Lewis, John	Adjustment of claim against United States.	2	2	Rep. of Secretary Treasury.	626					Laid on table.		
Lewis, John	Pension for revolutionary services.	21	2	Resolution	41	Military Pensions.						
Lewis, John	Pension for revolutionary services.	21	2	Petition	67	Military Pensions.						
Lewis, John	Pension for revolutionary services.	22	1	Petition	45	Rev. Pensions.						
Lewis, John	(See James Count, administrator of.)	26	1		182		343		319			
Lewis, John F	Remission of duties on Indian matting.	21	1	Petition	375	Ways and Means.				Discharged; laid on table.		
Lewis, John F	Remission of duties on Indian matting.	21	2	Petition	67	Ways and Means.						
Lewis, John F	Remission of duties on Indian matting.	22	1	Petition	25	Ways and Means.						
Lewis, John F	Remission of duties on Indian matting.	23	2	Petition	306	Ways and Means.	95	Favorable	720	Referred to Committee Whole House.		

List of private claims presented to the House of Representatives of the United States form the 1st to the 31st Congress, inclusive—Continued.

Names of claimants.	Nature or object of the claim.	Congress.	Session.	How brought before the House of Reps.	Page of journal.	To what committee of the House referred.	No. or date of the report.	Nature of the report.	No. of the bill.	How disposed of by the House of Reps.	How disposed of by the Senate.	Date of the act of Congress, and remarks.
Lewis, John F	Remission of duties on Indian matting.	24	1	Petition	53	Ways and Means	Jan. 12, 1836	Favorable	135	Passed	Passed	App'd June 28, 1836
Lewis, Jonah	Renewal of lost land warrant	17	1	Petition	291	Priv. Land Claims.						
Lewis, Jonah	Renewal of lost land warrant	17	1	Amend. to H. B.	593				89	Passed	Passed	App'd May 7, 1822
Lewis, Jonathan	Indemnity for Indian depredations.	30	1	Resolution	683	Indian Affairs	June 14, 1848	With amend.	J. R. 7	Referred to Committee Whole House.		
Lewis, Lawrence	(See Bushron Washington, *et al.*)	9	1		320							
Lewis, Mary Aurelia	(See Andrew Lewis, widow of)	28	1		159		339					
Lewis, Mason E	Confirmation of pre-emption right to land in Alabama.	24	2	Petition	88	Public Lands	137	Favorable	866	Referred to Committee Whole House.		
Lewis, Mason E	Confirmation of pre-emption right to land in Alabama.	25	2	Petition	87	Public Lands	Dec. 22, 1837	Favorable	109	Referred to Committee Whole House.		
Lewis, Mason E	Confirmation of pre emption right to land in Alabama.	26	1	Petition	179	Public Lands	June 19, 1840	Favorable	450	Referred to Committee Whole House.		
Lewis, Mason E	Confirmation of pre-emption right to land in Alabama.	27	2	Memorial	823	Public Lands	844	Favorable	487	Referred to Committee Whole House.		
Lewis, Mason E	Confirmation of pre-emption right to land in Alabama.	27	3	House bill	99	Whole House			487	Passed	Passed	App'd Jan. 20, 1843
Lewis, Meriwether, representatives of.	Permission to locate bounty land warrant.	20	1	Resolution	403	Public Lands	April 28, 1828	Favorable	282	Passed	Passed	App'd May 23, 1828
Lewis, Michael	Naval pension	20	1	Petition	484	Naval Affairs	248	Favorable	292	Referred to Committee Whole House.		
Lewis, Michael	Naval pension	21	1	Petition	175	Naval Affairs	116	Favorable	156	Passed	Passed	App'd May 28, 1830
Lewis, Moses	Release from imprisonment	14	1	Petition	399	Ways and Means	Mar. 6, 1816	Favorable		Passed	Passed	App'd April 26, 1816
Lewis, Naboth	Pension for revolutionary services.	4	1	Rep. of Secretary War.	445	Claims	Feb. 18, 1796	Favorable	156	Passed	Passed	App'd April 20, 1796
Lewis, Naboth	Increase of pension	19	2	Petition	186	Military Pensions.						
Lewis, Naboth	Increase of pension	21	1	Petition	82	Military Pensions	April 2, 1830	Adverse		Laid on table.		
Lewis, Nathaniel	Pension for revolutionary services.	3	1	Rep. of Secretary War.	131	Select.	May 26, 1794	Res. to refer to Sec. War.	J. R. 12	Passed	Passed	App'd June 9, 1794
Lewis, Nathaniel	Pension for revolutionary services.	4	1	Rep. of Secretary War.	445	Claims	Feb. 18, 1796	Favorable	156	Passed	Passed	App'd April 20, 1796
Lewis, Reuben	(See Roxanna Evans)	27	3		336							
Lewis, Robert, representatives of.	Compensation for losses and services in United States service.	1	2	Rep. of Secretary War.	245					Laid on table.		
Lewis, Robert, representatives of.	Compensation for losses and service in United States service.	1	3	Rep. of Secretary War.	393	Select	Feb. 36, 1791	Favorable	139	Passed	Postponed.	
Lewis, Robert	Prize money for capture of two Algerine vessels.	29	1	Petition	523	Claims.						
Lewis, Robert B	Reimbursement of payment for reissue of patent.	26	2	Petition	50	Patents.						
Lewis, Robert B	Reimbursement of payment for reissue of patent.	27	2	Senate bill	581	Patents			S. 125			
Lewis, Robert B	Reimbursement of payment for reissue of patent.	27	3	Senate bill	551	Whole House	Mar. 3, 1843	With't amend.	S. 6	Passed	Passed	App'd March 3, 1843
Lewis, Samuel, surety of	Authority to make payment in bank notes.	17	1	Petition	281	P. Of. & P. Roads.	Mar. 29, 1822	Adverse		Rejected.		
Lewis, Samuel, (Va.)	Compensation for house destroyed by British.	22	1	Petition	144	Claims	June 25, 1832	Adverse		Laid on table.		
Lewis, Samuel, (Va.)	Compensation for house destroyed by British.	22	2	Petition	74	Claims	Dec. 26, 1832	Adverse		Laid on table.		
Lewis, Samuel, (Va.)	Compensation for house destroyed by British.	23	1	Petition	218	Claims	Jan. 29, 1833	Adverse		Laid on table.		

List of private claims presented to the House of Representatives of the United States from the 1st to the 31st Congress, inclusive—Continued.

Names of claimants.	Nature or object of the claim.	Congress.	Session.	How brought before the House of Reps.	Page of journal.	To what committee of the House referred.	No. or date of the report.	Nature of the report.	No. of the bill.	How disposed of by the House of Reps.	How disposed of by the Senate.	Date of the act of Congress, and remarks.
Lewis, Samuel	Indemnity for loss in erecting an arsenal, Missouri.	29	1	Memorial	738	Claims	790	Adverse		Laid on table.		
Lewis, Samuel S.	(See Thomas Lewis, administrator of.)	26	1		182		343		319			
Lewis, Samuel, jr.	(See Edward W. Lewis, father of.)	18	1		38							
Lewis, Samuel, sen.	Discharge from prison as a defaulter.	6	1	Petition and rep't Sec. of War.	587	Select.						
Lewis, Samuel, sen.	Discharge from prison as a defaulter.	6	2	Petition	738	Select	Jan. 19, 1801	Favorable	279	Passed	Passed	App'd Feb. 25, 1801
Lewis, Theodore	Compensation for horse lost in Florida war.	24	1	Resolution	872	Claims.						
Lewis, Theodore	(See Albert G. Blanchard, *et al.*)	30	2		285							
Lewis, Thomas, survivor of T. Lewis & Son.	Indemnity for French spoliations prior to 1800.	15	1	Petition	237	Ways and Means.						
Lewis, Thomas, administrator of.	Indemnity for French spoliations prior to 1800.	26	1	Memorial	182	Foreign Affairs	343	Favorable	319	Referred to Committee Whole House.		
Lewis, Thomas	Compensation as aid-de-camp to General Wayne.	4	2	Petition	728	Claims.						
Lewis, Thomas	Compensation as aid-de camp to General Wayne.	5	1	Petition	71	Select	July 6, 1797	Favorable	18	Passed	Postponed.	
Lewis, Thomas	Compensation as aid-de-camp to General Wayne.	5	2	Petition	83	Claims	Feb. 15, 1798	Adverse; bill ordered.	88	Passed	Laid on table.	
Lewis, Thomas	Compensation as aid-de-camp to General Wayne.	5	3	Senate bill	457	Whole House	Feb. 7, 1799	With't amend.	37	Passed	Passed	App'd Feb. 15, 1799
Lewis, Thomas	Compensation for revolutionary services.	2	1	Petition	466					Referred to Secretary War.		
Lewis, Thomas, (Ky.)	Increase of pension	25	3	Resolution	275	Rev. Pensions.						
Lewis, Thomas	(See Exploring Expedition)	27	3		149							
Lewis, Thomas, widow & executor of.	(See Thomas L. Patterson, surety of.)	19	1		68		30		44			
Lewis, Captain Thomas, widow of.	Compensation for military services in war of 1812.	20	1	Resolution	356	Claims				Discharged; leave to withdraw.		
Lewis, Captain Thomas, heirs of.	Half-pay for revolutionary services	24	1	Resolution	157	Rev. Claims	July 2, 1836	Adverse		Laid on table.		
Lewis, Captain Thomas, heirs of.	Half-pay for revolutionary services	25	2	Resolution	270	Rev. Claims				Discharged; laid on table.		
Lewis, Thomas D.	(See Archibald Beard, *et al.*)	30	1		800							
Lewis, Captain William, widow of.	Continuation of pension	27	3	Jt. resoluton No. 31.	221	Naval Affairs	67	Changed into bill.	736	Passed	Adverse	Leave to withdraw, 2d sess. 28th Congress.
Lewis, William	(See John Deitz.)	13	2		302							
Lewis, William	(See Lewis F. Beeler, *et al.*)	30	1		115							
Lewis, William	Pension for revolutionary services.	18	1	Petition	41	Rev. Pensions	Jan. 21, 1825	Adverse.		Laid on table.		
Lewis, General William, family of.	Grant of land	19	1	Petition	313	Priv. Land Claims.						
Lewis, William, widow and heirs of.	Commutation pay	24	1	Petition	431	Rev. Claims.						
Lewis, William, widow and heirs of.	Commutation pay	24	2	Petition	40	Rev. Claims.						
Lewis, William, widow and heirs of.	Commutation pay	25	2	Petition	72	Rev. Claims	May 31, 1838	Favorable	821	Passed.		
Lewis, William, widow and heirs of.	Commutation pay	25	3	Petition	85	Rev. Claims.						

List of private claims presented to the House of Representatives of the United States from the 1st to the 31st Congress, inclusive—Continued.

Names of claimants.	Nature or object of the claim.	Congress.	Session.	How brought before the House of Reps.	Page of journal.	To what committee of the House referred.	No. or date of the report.	Nature of the report.	No. of the bill.	How disposed of by the House of Reps.	How disposed of by the Senate.	Date of the act of Congress, and remarks.
Lewis, William, widow and heirs of.	Commutation pay	26	1	Petition	165	Rev. Claims.						
Lewis, William, widow and heirs of.	Commutation pay	26	2	Petition	134	Rev. Claims.						
Lewis, William, widow and heirs of.	Commutation pay	27	2	Petition	62	Rev. Claims	775	Adverse		Laid on table.		
Lewis, William, widow and heirs of.	Commutation pay	27	3	Petition	70	Rev. Claims	243	Adverse		Laid on table.		
Lewis, William B	Allowance of credit in settlement of accounts.	15	1	Petition	203	Military Pensions	Feb. 24, 1818	Favorable	102	Referred to Committee Whole House.		
Lewis, William B	Allowance of credit in settlement of accounts.	15	2	House bill	73	Whole House	Dec. 8, 1818	With amend.	102	Passed	Passed	App'd Jan. 8, 1819
Lewis, William S	Pre-emption right to land in Louisiana.	21	1	Petition	913	Public Lands.						
Lewis, Winslow	Reimbursement of balance on land purchased for government.	16	1	Petition	91	Commerce.						
Lewis, Winslow	Reimbursement of balance on land purchased for government.	19	1	Petition	36					Referred to Secretary of Treasury.		
Lewis, Winslow	Extra expenses in building light-house.	25	2	Petition	50	Claims	373	Favorable	396	Referred to Committee Whole House.		
Lewis, Winslow	Extra expenses in building light house.	25	3	House bill	378	Whole House	Jan. 25, 1839	With't amend.	396	Passed	Passed	App'd March 3, 1839
Lewis, Winslow and Henry	Repayment of money advanced to ransom American citizens.	14	2	Petition	197					Referred to Secretary of State.		
Lewis, Winslow and Henry	Repayment of money advanced to ransom American citizens.	15	1	Rep. of Secretary State.	37	Claims	10	Favorable	9	Passed	Passed	App'd July 22, 1818
Lewright, Robert	Remission of duty on stills	7	1	Petition	123	Claims	Mar. 11, 1802	Adverse		Rejected.		
Lexington and Ohio Rail-road Company.	Reimbursement of duties paid on railroad iron.	24	1	Petition	95	Ways and Means	152	Favorable; bil	160	Passed	Passed	App'd July 2, 1836
Lexington, ship	(See F. C. Sanford)	26	2		121							
Ley, Henry	Renewal of certificate	2	1	Petition and rep't Sec. Treasury.	492	Select.						
Libbee, William	Pension for revolutionary services.	26	1	Petition	174	Rev. Pensions.						
Libbey, Benjamin	Pension	21	2	Petition	120	Military Pensions				Discharged: laid on table.		
Libbey, Ephraim, widow of	Pension	25	2	Petition	984	Rev. Pensions.						
Libbey, Harvey	Restoration of pension	17	2	Petition	25	Rev. Pensions.						
Libbey, Harvey	Restoration of pension	18	2	Petition	54	Rev. Pensions	54	Adverse		Laid on table.		
Libbey, Judiah	(See Ephraim Libbey, widow of)	25	2		984							
Libbey, Jeremiah	Increase of compensation as post-master.	4	2	Petition	647	Whole House.						
Libbey, Nathaniel	Compensation for revolutionary services.	6	1	Petition	533	Claims	Jan. 6, 1800	Adverse		Rejected.		
Libbey, Nathaniel	Compensation for revolutionary services.	21	2	Petition	103	Military Pensions.						
Libbey, Nathaniel	Compensation for revolutionary services.	22	1	Petition	68	Rev. Pensions.						
Libby, Daniel	Indemnity for French spoliations prior to 1800.	26	1	Memorial	182	Foreign Affairs	343	Favorable	319	Referred to Committee Whole House.		
Libby, Jonathan, executor of.	Indemnity for capture of brigantine.	17	1	Petition	83	Foreign Affairs	April 27, 1822	Adverse		Discharged.		
Libby, Luke, son of	Pension for revolutionary services.	25	2	Petition	117	Rev. Pensions.						
Libby, William	Pension for revolutionary services.	21	2	Petition	103	Military Pensions.						

List of private claims presented to the House of Representatives of the United States from the 1st to the 31st Congress, inclusive—Continued.

Names of claimants.	Nature or object of the claim.	Congress.	Session.	How brought before the House of Reps.	Page of journal.	To what committee of the House referred.	No. or date of the report.	Nature of the report.	No. of the bill.	How disposed of by the House of Reps.	How disposed of by the Senate.	Date of the act of Congress, and remarks.
Libby, William	Pension for revolutionary services	22	1	Petition	68	Rev. Pensions	Dec. 29, 1831	Adverse		Laid on table.		
Libengood, Jacob	Invalid pension	28	1	Petition	359	Invalid Pensions	277	Adverse.		Laid on table.		
Liblee, James, heir of	Bounty land and other emoluments for revolutionary services.	8	2	Petition	30	Claims.						
Liddle, Robert	Pension	21	2	Petition	73	Military Pensions.						
Liffingacle, William, *et al.*	Indemnity for French spoliations prior to 1800.	18	1	Petition	526					Laid on table.		
Ligg tt, William, heirs of	Pension for revolutionary services	31	2	Petition	326	Rev. Claims.						
Light, John	Pension	21	2	Petition	162	Military Pensions.						
Lightelle, W. E	Increase of compensation	29	2	Memorial	67	P. Of. and P. Roads.						
Lightfoot, Philip, (Ky.)	Compensation for a horse lost in public service.	25	2	Petition	192	Claims	507	Adverse		Laid on table.		
Lightfoot, Philip, (Ky.)	Compensation for a horse lost in public service.	26	2	Petition	125	Claims.						
Lightfoot, Philip; (Ky.)	Compensation for a horse lost in public service.	27	2	Petition	55	Claims	342	Adverse		Laid on table.		
Lightfoot, Philip	Compensation for extra services	6	2	Memorial	738	Claims				Discharged.		
Lightfoot, Philip	Compensation for extra services	7	1	Memorial	16	Claims	Mar. 17, 1802	Adverse		Leave to withdraw.		
Lightfoot, Philip	Compensation for extra services	7	2	Memorial	272	Claims	Feb. 26, 1803	Rep. not of record.		Postponed.		
Lightfoot, Philip, heir of	Compensation for revolutionary services.	24	1	Resolution	144	Rev. Claims	812	Adverse.				
Lightfoot, Philip, heir of	Compensation for revolutionary services.	24	2	Petition	39	Rev. Claims	274	Adverse		Laid on table.		
Lightfoot, Philip, heir of	Compensation for revolutionary services.	25	2	Resolution	72	Rev. Claims	759	Favorable	718	Postponed.		
Lightfoot, Philip, heir of	Compensation for revolutionary services.	26	1	Petition	165	Rev. Claims	Mar. 5, 1840	Adverse		Laid on table.		
Lightfoot, Philip, heir of	Compensation for revolutionary services.	27	2	Petition	61	Rev. Claims	390	Adverse		Laid on table.		
Lightfoot, Samuel L	Increase of compensation	25	2	Petition	410	Commerce.						
Lightfoot, William	Indemnity for property taken for public use.	3	1	Memorial	107	Select	April 22, 1794	Adverse		Laid on table.		
Lightfoot, William	Pension	25	2	Petition	400	Invalid Pensions.						
Lightfoot, William	Pension	26	1	Petition	163	Invalid Pensions	249	Adverse		Laid on table.		
Lightfoot, William A., heirs of.	Compensation for property taken for public use.	22	2	Resolution	285	Rev. Claims.						
Lighthall, Wm., heirs of	Commutation pay	29	1	Petition	233	Rev. Claims				Discharged; laid on table.		
Lightheiser, Hartman	Pension	9	2	Petition	544	Claims.						
Lightner, Henry	Release from judgments	18	1	Petition	173	P. Of. and P. Roads.	73	Favorable	134	Passed	Passed	App'd May 17, 1824
Light vessels, commanders of.	Increase of compensation	24	2	Petition	82	Commerce.						
Ligon, John P	(See Reuben Perry, *et al.*)	25	2		724							
Ligon, John T	Pension for revolutionary services of his father.	26	2	Petition	222	Rev. Pensions.						
Ligon, Joseph	Pension	4	1	Petition	444	Claims	May 7, 1796	Adverse		Laid on table.		
Ligon, Joseph	Pension	9	2	Pension bill	608	Whole House	Feb. 28, 1807	With amend.	216	Passed	Passed	App'd March 3, 1807
Ligon, Joseph	Increase of pension	15	2	Petition	31	Pens. & Rev. Cl'ms.						
Ligon, Joseph	Increase of pension	16	1	Petition	323	Pens. & Rev. Cl'ms.				Discharged; laid on table.		
Ligon, Joseph	Arrears of pension	18	1	Petition	42	Pens. & Rev. Cl'ms.	Dec. 19, 1823			Laid on table; leave to withdraw.		

List of private claims presented to the House of Representatives of the United States from the 1st to the 31st Congress, inclusive—Continued.

Names of claimants.	Nature or object of the claim.	Congress.	Session.	How brought before the House of Reps.	Page of journal.	To what committee of the House referred.	No. or date of the report.	Nature of the report.	No. of the bill.	How disposed of by the House of Reps.	How disposed of by the Senate.	Date of the act of Congress, and remarks.
Ligon, Thomas P.	(See Reuben Perry, *et al.*)	29	2	Petition	82							
Ligon, William B.	Compensation for vessel lost in United States service.	15	2	Petition	237	Claims				Laid on table.		
Ligon, William B.	Compensation for vessel lost in United States service.	16	1	Petition	66	Claims	Dec. 22, 1819	Adverse		Discharged; laid on table.		
Ligon, William B.	Compensation for vessel lost in United States service.	17	2	Petition	77	Claims	June 31, 1823	Adverse		Rejected.		
Ligon, William B.	Compensation for vessel lost in United States service.	18	1	Petition	158	Claims.						
Ligon, William B.	Compensation for vessel lost in United States service.	18	2	Petition	38	Naval Affairs	Feb. 21, 1825	Adverse		Leave to withdraw.		
Ligon, William B.	Compensation for vessel lost in United States service.	19	1	Petition	99	Claims	Mar. 11, 1828	Adverse		Discharged; laid on table.		
Ligon, William B.	Compensation for vessel lost in United States service.	20	1	Petition	341	Claims				Laid on table.		
Ligon, William B.	Compensation for transporting military stores.	29	1	Petition	226	Judiciary	258	Favorable	220	Passed.		
Lillard, Elizabeth, *et al.*	(See John Whitsett, heirs of)	29	1		353							
Lilley, Emmons, widow of.	Continuation of pension	25	3	Petition	126	Rev. Pensions	Jan. 16, 1839	Adverse		Laid on table.		
Lilley, Susannah	(See Emmons Lilley, widow of)	25	3		126							
Lillie, Anson	Increase of pension	17	1	Petition	567					Laid on table.		
Lillie, Anson	Increase of pension	17	2	Petition	165	Pens. & Rev. Cl'ms.				Discharged; laid on table.		
Lillings, Richard	(See Thomas Russell, *et al*)	3	1		67							
Lilly, Aaron, *et al.*	(See James James, heirs of)	22	2		42							
Lilly, Isaac	Indemnity for seizure of brig Planter	22	1	Petition	28[illegible]	Ways and Means.						
Lilly, Isaac	Indemnity for seizure of brig Planter	24	1	Petition	715	Claims.						
Lilly, Isaac	Indemnity for seizure of brig Planter	24	2	Petition	154	Claims.						
Lilly, Isaac	Indemnity for seizure of brig Planter	25	2	Petition	351	Claims	947	Favorable	825	Referred to Committee Whole House.		
Lilly, Isaac	Indemnity for seizure of brig Planter	25	3	House bill	432			With't amend.	825	Passed	Passed	App'd March 3, 1839
Lilly, Peter	Pension	27	2	Petition	347	Rev. Pensions.						
Lilly, schooner	(See Orren Prentice)	27	2		318							
Lilly, Silas	Pension	27	2	Petition	239	Rev. Pensions				Discharged; referred to Com. Whole House.		
Lilly, Thomas	Compensation for revolutionary services.	2	1	Petition	442					Referred to Secretary of War.		
Lillybridge, Clarke	Balance due as physician to emigrating Indians.	29	1	Memorial	292	Indian Affairs	Feb. 28, 1846	Favorable	739	Referred to Committee Whole House.		
Lillybridge, Clarke	Balance due as physician to emigrating Indians.	29	2	House bill	71				279	Passed	Passed	App'd March 3, 1847
Limber, Sarah	(See Wm. Huston, representatives of.)	21	1		295							
Limon, William	Pension	14	2	Resolution	209	Pens. & Rev. Cl'ms.						
Limpurg, Count F. R. de R.	Bounty land for revolutionary services.	25	3	Petition	220	Claims				Leave to withdraw.		
Lincecum, Garland R.	Reimbursement of purchase money of land.	29	1	Petition	234	Priv. Land Claims.	267	Adverse		Laid on table.		
Lincicum, Garland	Compensation as Indian agent	21	1	Petition	294	Claims	249	Favorable	308	Referred to Committee Whole House.		
Lincicum, Garland	Compensation as Indian agent	21	2	House bill	333	Whole House			308	Passed.		
Lincicum, Garland	Compensation as Indian agent	22	1	House bill	68	Whole House	Dec. 22, 1831	With't amend.	9	Passed	Passed	App'd Jan. 19, 1832

List of private claims presented to the House of Representatives of the United States from the 1st to the 31st Congress, inclusive—Continued.

Names of claimants.	Nature or object of the claim.	Congress.	Session.	How brought before the House of Reps.	Page of journal.	To what committee of the House referred.	No. or date of the report.	Nature of the report.	No. of the bill.	How disposed of by the House of Reps.	How disposed of by the Senate.	Date of the act of Congress, and remarks.
Lincoln, Benjamin, *et al.*	Expenses as Indian commissioner.	2	1	Memorial & rep't of Sec. War.	484	Select	Jan. 5, 1792	Favorable	160	Referred to Committee Whole House.		
Lincoln, Benjamin, *et al.*	Expenses as Indian commissioner.	4	2	Appropriation bill	675	Whole House			223	Passed	Passed	App'd March 3, 1797
Lincoln, Benjamin, *et al.*	For the settlement of their accounts.	18	1	Senate bill	349	Judiciary	April 13, 1824	With amend.	70	Passed	Passed	App'd May 5, 1824
Lincoln, Caleb, representatives of.	Renewal of land warrant	21	2	Resolution	85	Rev. Claims				Discharged; laid on table.		
Lincoln, Elijah	Renewal of land warrant	23	1	House bill	104	Priv. Land Claims.	Dec. 20, 1833	Favorable	65	Passed	Passed	App'd June 28, 1834
Lincoln, Ezekiel	Pension	27	2	Petition	550	Invalid Pensions.						
Lincoln, Ezekiel	Pension	28	1	Petition	317	Invalid Pensions	175	Adverse		Laid on table.		
Lincoln, Esther	(See Thos. Lincoln, heirs of the widow of.)	30	1		713							
Lincoln, Jesse	Compensation for work on Cumberland road.	15	1	Petition	27	Claims	Feb. 9, 1818	Adverse		Laid on table.		
Lincoln, Jesse	Compensation for work on Cumberland road.	16	2	Petition	97	Claims.						
Lincoln, Jesse	Compensation for work on Cumberland road.	17	1	Petition	151	Claims.						
Lincoln, Jesse	Compensation for work on Cumberland road.	20	1	Resolution	202	Roads and Canals.						
Lincoln, Jesse	Compensation for work on Cumberland road.	20	2	Resolution	63	Claims	Jan. 5, 1829	Adverse		Laid on table.		
Lincoln, Jesse	Compensation for work on Cumberland road.	22	2	Petition	79	Roads and Canals.						
Lincoln, Jesse	Compensation for work on Cumberland road.	23	2	Petition	85	Claims.						
Lincoln, John	Pension	3	2	Rep. of Secretary War.	278	Claims.	Feb. 28, 1795	Favorable	130	Passed	Postponed.	
Lincoln, John	Pension	4	1	Rep. of Secretary War.	445	Claims.	Feb. 18, 1796	Favorable	156	Passed	Passed	App'd April 20, 1796
Lincoln, John	Increase of pension	11	3	Pension bill	604	Whole House	Mar. 2, 1811	With amend.	218	Passed	Passed	App'd March 3, 1811
Lincoln, John H.	Pension	24	2	Petition	267	Invalid Pensions.						
Lincoln, John H.	Pension	25	2	Petition	118	Invalid Pensions	771	Favorable	725	Passed.		
Lincoln, John H.	Pension	25	3	Petition	89	Invalid Pensions.	255	Favorable	1126	Referred to Committee Whole House.		
Lincoln, John H.	Pension	26	1	Petition	161	Invalid Pensions	Mar. 5, 1840	Favorable	196	Passed	Postponed.	
Lincoln, John H.	Pension	27	2	Petition	60	Invalid Pensions.						
Lincoln, John H.	Pension	27	3	Petition	309	Invalid Pensions	138	Adverse		Laid on table.		
Lincoln, John H.	Pension	28	1	Petition	481	Invalid Pensions.						
Lincoln, John H.	Pension	28	2	Petition	229	Invalid Pensions.						
Lincoln, Jotham	(See Samuel B. Lincoln, administrator of.)	21	1		34							
Lincoln, Levi R.	(See John Crowninshield)	23	2		32							
Lincoln, Mark, and wife.	(See Major Willard Moore, heirs of.)	2	1		458							
Lincoln, Rufus	Compensation for revolutionary services.	1	2	Petition and rep't of Sec. War.	147					Laid on table.		
Lincoln, Rufus	Compensation for revolutionary services.	12	1	Petition	32	Claims.						
Lincoln, Rufus	Compensation for revolutionary services.	15	1	Petition	456					Laid on table.		
Lincoln, Rufus	Compensation for revolutionary services.	15	2	Petition	65	Pens. & Rev. Cl'ms.	Dec. 11, 1818	Adverse		Rejected.		
Lincoln, Rufus	Restoration of pension	17	1	Petition	67	Rev. Pensions.						

List of private claims presented to the House of Representatives of the United States from the 1st to the 31st Congress, inclusive—Continued.

Names of claimants.	Nature or object of the claim.	Congress.	Session.	How brought before the House of Reps.	Page of journal.	To what committee of the House referred.	No. or date of the report.	Nature of the report.	No. of the bill.	How disposed of by the House of Reps.	How disposed of by the Senate.	Date of the act of Congress, and remarks.
Lincoln, Rufus	Restoration of pension	17	2	Petition	99					Referred to Committee Whole House.		
Lincoln, Rufus	Restoration of pension	18	2	Petition	117	Rev. Pensions				Discharged; laid on table.		
Lincoln, Samuel B., administrator of.	Indemnity from failure of United States to fulfil contract.	21	1	Petition	34	Claims	139	Favorable	187	Passed.		
Lincoln, Samuel B., administrator of.	Indemnity from failure of United States to fulfil contract.	21	2	Petition	45	Claims	1	Favorable	500	Referred to Committee Whole House.		
Lincoln, Samuel B., administrator of.	Indemnity from failure of United States to fulfil contract.	22	1	Petition	42	Claims	Dec. 19, 1831	Favorable	30	Passed.		
Lincoln, Samuel B., administrator of.	Indemnity from failure of United States to fulfil contract.	22	2	Petition	148	Claims	29	Favorable	675	Referred to Committee Whole House.		
Lincoln, Samuel B., administrator of.	Indemnity from failure of United States to fulfil contract.	23	1	Petition	34	Claims	17	Favorable	17	Passed	Passed	App'd June 27, 1834
Lincoln, Thomas, heirs of the widow of.	Arrears of pension	30	1	Petition	713, 739	Rev. Pensions.						
Lindenbuger, Dorcas, *et al.*	Pension for revolutionary services	30	1	Petition	290	Rev. Pensions				Discharged; laid on table.		
Lindley, Abraham	(See Jonathan Budge, administrator of.)	18	1		196							
Lindley, Joseph, executors of.	Indemnity for French spoliations prior to 1800.	26	1	Memorial	182	Foreign Affairs	343	Favorable	319	Referred to Committee Whole House.		
Lindley, Lieut. Levi, widow of.	Pension for revolutionary services.	27	3	Petition	799	Rev. Pensions.						
Lindley, Lieut. Levi, widow of.	Pension for revolutionary services.	27	3	Petition	257	Rev. Pensions.						
Lindley, Lieut. Levi, widow of.	Pension for revolutionary services.	29	1	Petition	124	Rev. Pensions	528	Adverse		Laid on table.		
Lindsay, Cyrus	(See John Lindsay, administrator of.)	26	1		323							
Lindsay, John	Pension for revolutionary services.	5	2	House bill	127	Claims	Jan. 9, 1798	Favorable	38	Passed	Passed	App'd Feb. 2, 1798
Lindsay, John, administrator of.	Arrears of pension	26	1	Petition	323	Rev. Pensions	141	Favorable	151	Passed	Indef. postp'd.	
Lindsay, Robert, widow of	Compensation for a slave captured by British.	25	2	Petition	407	Foreign Affairs	Mar. 29, 1838	Adverse		Laid on table.		
Lindsay, Robert, widow of	Compensation for a slave captured by British.	28	2	Petition	53	Claims.						
Lindsay, Samuel	Compensation for revolutionary services.	2	2	Petition and rep't Sec. War.	658					Laid on table.		
Lindsay, Samuel	Pension	3	1	Rep. of Secretary War.	131	Select	May 26, 1794	Res. to refer to Sec. War.	12	Passed	Passed	App'd June 9, 1794
Lindsay, William	Pension for revolutionary services.	20	2	Resolution	92	Military Pensions.						
Lindsey, David	Pension	21	2	Petition	144	Military Pensions.						
Lindsey, J. J. M	(See William B. Ferguson, sureties of.)	25	2		921							
Lindsey, John	Payment for a horse lost in United States service.	20	2	Resolution	223	Claims	Feb. 4, 1829	Adverse		Laid on table.		
Lindsey, Morris, assignees of.	Compensation for blacksmith's work for Tennessee volunteers.	18	1	Senate bill	307	Military Pensions	April 9, 1824	With amend.	47	Passed	Passed	App'd May 5, 1824
Lindsey, Thomas	Restoration of forfeited vessel	11	1	Petition	64	Com. and Manuf.						
Lindsey, William	Pension	21	2	Resolution	209	Military Pensions.						
Lindsley, Ahiel, widow of.	Pension for revolutionary services.	29	1	Memorial	397	Rev. Pensions				Discharged; laid on table.		
Lindsley, Anne	(See Abiel Lindsley, widow of.)	29	1		397							

List of private claims presented to the House of Representatives of the United States from the 1st to the 31st Congress, inclusive—Continued.

Names of claimants.	Nature or object of the claim.	Congress.	Session.	How brought before the House of Reps.	Page of journal.	To what committee of the House referred.	No. or date of the report.	Nature of the report.	No. of the bill.	How disposed of by the House of Reps.	How disposed of by the Senate.	Date of the act of Congress, and remarks.
Lindsley, Samuel	Pension	10	2	Pension bill	499	Whole House	Feb. 20, 1809	With amend.	158	Passed	Passed	App'd March 3, 1809
Linen, William	(See David Witherspoon, assignee of.)	7	2		312							
Ling, William	Indemnity for French spoliations prior to 1800.	30	1	Petition	117	Foreign Affairs	Jan. 4, 1848	General bill	21	Referred to Committee Whole House.		
Lingan, James M.	Additional compensation	5	2	Resolution	331	Com. and Manuf.						
Lingenfelter, George	Pension	20	1	Petition	417	Military Pensions.						
Lingenfelter, George	Pension	20	2	House bill	645	Whole House	May 16, 1828	With amend.	283	Passed.		
Lingenfelter, George	Pension	21	1	Pension bill	130	Whole House	Feb. 12, 1830	With amend.	72	Passed	Passed	App'd May 20, 1830
Lingenfelter, John	Compensation for military services	27	2	Petition	383	Claims	720	Adverse		Laid on table.		
Linguist, Charles	Right of pre-emption	28	1	Petition	77	Priv. Land Claims.	9	Favorable	35	Passed	Passed	App'd June 17, 1844
Lining, Charles	(See Edward Blake, executor of.)	24	1		102							
Link, Absalom	(See William Ramey, *et al.*)	29	1		160							
Link, Allen	Right of pre-emption	30	1	Petition	236	Public Lands	328	Adverse		Laid on table.		
Linn, John	Compensation for revolutionary services.	1	3	Petition and rep't Sec. of War.	337					Laid on table.		
Linn, Joseph	Pension	22	1	Petition	435	Invalid Pensions	474	Favorable	576	Passed.		
Linn, Joseph	Pension	22	2	Petition	27	Invalid Pensions	Dec. 19, 1832	Favorable	626	Passed	Passed	App'd March 2, 1833
Linn, Joseph C.	Indemnity for damage to steamboat.	30	2	Petition	294	Military Affairs				Disch'd; laid on table.		
Linn, Joseph C.	Additional compensation for transporting Indiana volunteers.	31	2	Petition	36	Claims.						
Linnard, Thomas	Compensation for work on Cumberland road.	23	2	Petition	163	Claims.						
Linnard, William	Increase of pay as military agent.	11	1	Petition and rep't Sec. of War.	28					Laid on table.		
Linnard, William	Increase of pay as military agent.	11	2	Petition	131	Select	Dec. 26, 1809	Favorable	52	Referred to Committee Whole House.		
Linnell, Samuel	Pension	23	1	Petition	216	Invalid Pensions	Jan. 31, 1834	Adverse		Laid on table.		
Linnig, Nicholas	Drawback on coffee	17	1	Petition	32	Ways and Means.	Feb. 14, 1822	Adverse		Rejected.		
Linsey, James	Relief for defective title in land purchased of United States marshal.	12	2	Petition	24	Claims				Discharged; leave to withdraw.		
Linsey, James	Relief for defective title in land purchased of United States marshal.	13	3	Petition	543	Claims	Dec. 13, 1814	Adverse.		Report agreed to.		
Linsey, James	Relief for defective title in land purchased of United States marshal.	18	1	Petition	157	Priv. Land Claims.	Feb. 25, 1824	Adverse		Laid on table.		
Linsey, James	Relief for defective title in land purchased of United States marshal.	20	2	Petition	33	Judiciary	Dec. 16, 1828	Adverse		Laid on table.		
Linsey, James	Relief for defective title in land purchased of United States marshal.	21	1	Petition	83	Judiciary	48	Adverse		Laid on table.		
Linton, George	Right of pre emption	28	1	Petition	77	Priv. Land Claims.	9	Favorable	35	Passed	Passed	App'd June 17, 1844
Linton, Joseph	Pension	21	1	Petition	197	Military Pensions.						
Linton, Mary Ann	(See William S. Linton, widow of.)	20	1		50							
Linton, Samuel	Pension	21	2	Petition	188	Military Pensions.						
Linton, Thomas	Indemnity for property destroyed.	27	2	Petition	142	Claims	492	Adverse		Laid on table.		
Linton, William S., widow of.	Pension for military services, &c.	20	1	Petition	50	Military Pensions.	Jan. 25, 1828	Adverse		Laid on table.		

List of private claims presented to the House of Representatives of the United States from the 1st to the 31st Congress, inclusive—Continued

Names of claimants.	Nature or object of the claim.	Congress.	Session.	How brought before the House of Reps.	Page of journal.	To what committee of the House referred.	No. or date of the report.	Nature of the report.	No. of the bill.	How disposed of by the House of Reps.	How disposed of by the Senate.	Date of the act of Congress, and remarks.
Linton, William S., widow of.	Pension for military services, &c. .	27	3	Petition	337	Rev. Pensions	277	Favorable....	828	Referred to Committee Whole House.		
Linton, William S., widow of.	Pension for military services, &c. .	28	1	Petition	267	Rev. Pensions	328	Favorable....	236	Passed	Passed	App'd June 17, 1844
Linton, William S., widow of.	Explanatory of act June 17, 1844	29	2	Petition & Senate joint res.	352, 38	Rev. Pensions	Feb. 24, 1847	With't amend.	R. 3	Passed	Passed.......	App'd Feb. 25, 1847
Linville, William, *et al* ..	Modification of pension laws	30	1	Petition	723	Invalid Pensions ..	....	....	......	Discharged; laid on table.		
Lionberger, Peter........	Compensation for team lost in public service.	27	2	Petition	383	Claims	751	Favorable....	429	Ordered to 3d reading.		
Lionberger, Peter........	Compensation for team lost in public ssrvice.	27	3	House bill......	88	....	....	....	429	Passed	Passed	App'd Jan. 20, 1843
Lipe, John C...........	(See Caspar B. Cook, *et al.*)...	26	1	....	702							
Lipe, Johannes	Compensation for use of block-house.	4	1	Petition	370	Claims..........	Jan. 15, 1796	Adverse	......	Leave to withdraw.		
Liplong, Joseph	(See John Nailor, assignee of administrator of.)	2	1	....	475							
Lippincott, Caleb, widow of.	Naval pension	20	2	Petition	32	Naval Affairs	103	Adverse	......	Laid on table.		
Lippincott, Caleb, widow of.	Naval pension	21	2	Petition	160	Naval Affairs .						
Lippincott, J. and W., & Co.	Indemnity for damage sustained by illegal seizure of tea.	22	1	Petition	440	Judiciary	July 12, 1832	Favorable....	590	Passed	....	App'd July 14, 1832
Lippincott, J. and W., & Co.	Indemnity for damages srstained by illegal seizure of tea.	22	1	Senate bill	1029	Ways and Means..	July 9, 1832	With amends.	S. 172	Referred to Committee Whole House.		
Lippincott, Jonathan.....	Compensation for revolutionay services, &c.	4	1	Petition	389	Claims	Jan. 26, 1796	Adverse	......	Rejected; leave to withdraw.		
Lippincott, Susanna	(See Caleb Lippincott, widow of.)	2[illegible]	2	....	32							
Lipscomb, Bernard, heirs of.	(See Rueben Lipscomb, heirs of.)	23	2	....	109							
Lipscomb, David S.......	Relief for mistake in land entry ..	24	1	Petition	113	Priv. Land Claims.	....	....	......	Discharged; laid on table.		
Lipscomb, Lucy M......	Repayment of money erroneously deposited with the United States.	21	1	Senate bill	271	Ways and Means..	Feb. 22, 1830	With amend..	59	Passed	Passed	App'd May 26, 1830
Lipscomb, Rueben, heirs of.	Commutation pay	23	2	Petition	109	Rev. Claims......	Jan. 8, 1835	Adverse	......	Laid on table.		
Lipscomb, Rueben, heirs of.	Commutation pay	24	1	Petition	536	Rev. Claims......	....	....	......	Discharged; laid on table.		
Lipscomb, Rueben, heirs of.	Commutation pay	24	2	Petition	92	Rev. Claims......	Jan. 13, 1837	Adverse	......	Laid on table.		
Lipscomb, Thomas......	(See Nathaniel Fox, administrator of.)	23	2	....	106							
Lipscomb, William C....	(See Catharine Redmond, executors and trustees of.)	20	2	....	61							
Lisa, Joaquin...........	(See Joaquin De Lisa.).........	15	1	....	85							
Lisa, Manuel...........	(See Manual De Lisa.).........	15	1	....	85							
Lisle, Charles P.........	(See John Kinney, surety of.)...	16	1	....	288							
Liston, Dr. James T.....	Compensation for professional services, and Indian depredations.	24	1	Petition	741	Indian Affairs.						
Liswell, Jeremiah	Arrears of pension............	24	2	Petition	219	Invalid Pensions ..	....	....	......	Discharged; laid on table.		
Liswell, Jeremiah	Arrears of pension............	25	2	Petition	57	Invalid Pensions ..	Jan. 9, 1838	Adverse	......	Laid on table.		
Litchfield, Joseph	(See Joshua T. Chase, *et al.*)....	20	1	....	29							

List of private claims presented to the House of Representatives of the United States from the 1st to the 31st Congress, inclusive—Continued.

Names of claimants.	Nature or object of the claim.	Congress.	Session.	How brought before the House of Reps.	Page of journal.	To what committee of the House referred.	No. or date of the report.	Nature of the report.	No. of the bill.	How disposed of by the House of Reps.	How disposed of by the Senate.	Date of the act of Congress, and remarks.
Lithgow, Arthur	Pension for revolutionary services	22	1	Petition	631	Rev. Pensions.						
Litle, Alexander	Pension for revolutionary services	22	1	Petition	509	Rev. Pensions.						
Little, William	(See Elisha Winters & son, representatives of.)	19	2		159							
Litly, Thomas	Pension	3	1	Rep. of Secretary War.	131	Select	May 26, 1794	Res. to refer to Seç. War.	J. R. 12	Passed	Passed	App'd June 9, 1794
Little, Samuel	Pension	17	2	Petition	232	Pens. & Rev. Cl'ms.	Feb. 22, 1823	Adverse		Laid on table.		
Little, Samuel	Pension	18	1	Petition	36	Pens. & Rev Cl'ms.	Dec. 19, 1823	Adverse		Laid on table.		
Little, Samuel	Pension	18	2	Petition	54	Pens. & Rev. Cl'ms.						
Litteral, Frances	(See Rhodeham Letteral, widow of.)	26	1		950							
Litteral, Rhodeham, widow of.	Pension for revolutionary services	26	1	Petition	950	Rev. Pensions.						
Little, Anna	(See William Little, widow of)	23	2		41							
Little, Anson	Redress for malversation of New York district judge.	30	2	Petition	191	Judiciary	103	Adverse.				
Little, Charles, and others.	Fishing bounty on schooner Milo	21	1	Petition	169	Commerce				Discharged; laid on table.		
Little, Charles, and others	Fishing bounty on schooner Milo	21	2	Petition	189	Ways and Means.						
Little, Charles, and others.	Fishing bounty on schooner Milo	23	1	Petition	184	Commerce	187	Favorable	206	Referred to Committee Whole House.		
Little, David	Relief as purchaser of public lands	17	2	Petition	121	Public Lands	Feb. 5, 1823	Favorable	271	Passed	Passed	App'd March 3, 1823
Little, David	Compensation for extra services	29	1	Petition	519	Claims	789	Adverse		Laid on table.		
Little, David	Compensation for extra services	30	1	Petition	577	Claims	593	Adverse		Laid on table.		
Little, David	Compensation for extra services	31	1	Petition	276	Patents.						
Little, Doty	Remission of duties	16	1	Senate bill	108	Ways and Means	Jan. 4, 1820	With amend.	13	Passed	Passed	App'd April 11, 1820
Little, Doty	Indemnity for French spoliations prior to 1800.	26	1	Memorial	182	Foreign Affairs	343	Favorable	319	Referred to Committee Whole House.		
Little, George	Pension	19	1	Resolution	387	Military Pensions.						
Little, George	Reimbursement of judgment, costs, &c.	8	2	Memorial	11	Claims	Feb. 20, 1805	Adverse		Referred to Committee Whole House.		
Little, George	Reimbursement of judgment, costs, &c.	9	1	Memorial	188	Claims	Dec. 10, 1805	Favorable		Referred to Committee Whole House.		
Little, George	Reimbursement of judgment, costs, &c.	9	2	Memorial	478	Claims	Dec. 31, 1807	Favorable	160	Passed	Passed	App'd Jan. 17, 1807
Little, Henry, and J. Felch	Indemnity for damages in erection of breakwater.	30	1	Petition	723	Commerce	648	Favorable	515	Referred to Committee Whole House.		
Little, Henry, and J. Felch	Indemnity for damages in erection of breakwater.	31	1	Petition	235	Commerce.						
Little, James	Compensation for property destroyed in revolution.	3	1	Petition	124					Laid on table.		
Little, James	Pension for revolutionary services	16	1	Petition	353	Pens. & Rev. Cl'ms.	April 17, 1820	Adverse		Rejected.		
Little, James	Pension for revolutionary services	21	2	Petition	270	Military Pensions				Discharged; laid on table.		
Little, James	Pension for revolutionary services	22	1	Petition	114	Rev. Pensions	367	Favorable	462	Passed	Indef. postp'd.	
Little, James	Compensation for services as keeper of Congressional burial ground	28	2	Petition	435	Claims.						
Little, James	Compensation for services as keeper of Congressional burial ground.	29	1	Petition	618	Claims				Discharged; laid on table.		
Little, James	Compensation for services as keeper of Congressional burial ground.	30	1	Petition	354	Claims	159	Adverse		Laid on table.		
Little, James	Compensation for services as keeper of Congressional burial ground.	31	1	Petition	1044	Claims.						

List of private claims presented to the House of Representatives of the United States from the 1st to the 31st Congress, inclusive—Continued.

Names of claimants.	Nature or object of the claim.	Congress.	Session.	How brought before the House of Reps.	Page of journal.	To what committee of the House referred.	No. or date of the report.	Nature of the report.	No. of the bill.	How disposed of by the House of Reps.	How disposed of by the Senate.	Date of the act of Congress, and remarks.
Little, John	(See Leighton Wood, *et al*)	3	1		88							
Little, John	Pension	3	1	Rep. of Secretary War.	131	Select	May 26, 1794	Res. to refer to Sec. War.	J.R. 12	Passed	Passed	App'd June 9, 1794
Little, John	Pension	5	2	Petition	212	Claims	April 17, 1798	Adverse		Laid on table.		
Little, John	Pension	5	3	Petition	432	Whole House.						
Little, John	Pension	6	1	Petition	625	Claims.				Discharged.		
Little, John	Pension	8	2	Petition	100	Claims.				Discharged; referred to Com. Whole House.		
Little, John	Pension	9	1	Petition	296	Claims.	Mar. 28, 1806	Not of record		Postponed.		Leave to withdraw.
Little, John	Pension	9	2	Resolution	485			Res. to refer to Sec. War.		Disagreed to.		
Little, John	Pension	9	2	Pension bill	608	Whole House	Feb. 28, 1807	With amend.	216	Passed	Passed	App'd March 3, 1807
Little, Jonathan	Remission of duties	29	1	House bill	206	Whole House	Feb. 27, 1846	With't amend.	54	Passed	Passed	App'd Aug. 8, 1846
Little, Joseph	Grant of land for revolutionary services.	15	1	Petition	265	Pens. & Rev. Cl'ms.	Mar. 14, 1818	Adverse		Leave to withdraw.		
Little, Joseph	Restoration of pension	17	1	Petition	109	Rev. Pensions.						
Little, Leonard	Pension	26	1	Petition	325	Invalid Pensions.						
Little, Otis	(See James Crawford, *et al.*)	16	2		101							
Little, Otis	Indemnity for French spoliations prior to 1800.	26	1	Memorial	182	Foreign Affairs	343	Favorable	319	Referred to Committee Whole House.		
Little, Otis, administrator of.	Indemnity for French spoliations prior to 1800.	31	1	Petition	232	Foreign Affairs	355	General bill	318	Referred to Committee Whole House.		
Little, Robert	(See Elias Bates, *et al.*)	15	2		109							
Little, Robert	Bounty land for military services	23	2	Petition	39	Military Affairs.				Discharged; laid on table.		
Little, William	(See Minor Reeves, administrator of.)	18	2		131							
Little, William	Pension	11	2	Pension bill	283	Whole House	Mar. 16, 1810	With amend.	107	Passed	Passed	App'd April 27, 1810
Little, William	Remission of forfeiture	3	2	Petition	323	Claims.						
Little, William	Remission of forfeiture	4	1	Petition	373	Commerce				Discharged; referred to Sec'ry Treasury.		
Little, William, administrator of.	Balance of pension	20	1	Resolution	172	Military Pensions	April 29, 1828	Favorable	283	Passed.		
Little, William, administrator of.	Balance of pension	20	2	House bill	55	Whole House	Dec. 12, 1828	With amend.	311	Passed	Laid on table.	
Little, William, administrator of.	Balance of pension	21	1	Petition	47	Military Pensions.						
Little, William, administrator of.	Balance of pension	21	1	Pension bill	130	Whole House	Feb. 12, 1830	With amend't.	72	Passed	Passed	App'd May 20, 1830
Little, William, widow of.	Pension for revolutionary services.	23	2	Petition	41	Rev. Pensions				Discharged; laid on table.		
Littlefield, Daniel, widow of.	Compensation for revolutionary services.	24	2	Petition	38	Rev. Pensions	124	Favorable	854	Referred to Committee Whole House.		
Littlefield, Daniel, widow of.	Commutation pay	28	2	Petition	239	Rev. Claims.						
Littlefield, Daniel, widow of.	Commutation pay	29	1	Petition	202	Rev. Claims.						
Littlefield, John	Increase of pension	18	2	Petition	117	Pens. & Rev. Cl'ms.						
Littlefield, Noah, administrator of.	To be allowed military certificate	17	2	Petition	223	Pens. & Rev. Cl'ms.				Discharged; laid on table.		
Littlefield, Noah, administrator of.	To be allowed military certificate	18	1	Petition	108	Pens. & Rev. Cl'ms.	Jan. 7, 1824	Adverse		Referred to Committee Whole House.		

List of private claims presented to the House of Representatives of the United States from the 1st to the 31st Congress, inclusive—Continued.

Names of claimants.	Nature or object of the claim.	Congress.	Session.	How brought before the House of Reps.	Page of journal.	To what committee of the House referred.	No. or date of the report.	Nature of the report.	No. of the bill.	How disposed of by the House of Reps.	How disposed of by the Senate.	Date of the act of Congress, and remarks.
Littlefield, Noah, administrator of.	To be allowed military certificate	19	1	Petition	130	Pens. & Rev. Cl'ms.						
Littlefield, Pelatiah	(See Noah Littlefied, administrator of)	17	2		223							
Littlefield, Samuel	Remission of duties	16	1	Senate bill	108	Ways and Means	Jan. 14, 1820	With amend.	13	Passed	Passed	App'd April 11, 1820
Littlejohn, Leonard, surety of.	Release from liability	18	2	Petition	41	Military Affairs				Discharged; leave to withdraw.		
Littlejohn, John	Balance due on public contract	29	2	Petition	281	Claims.						
Livanda, B. E.	Confirmation of title to land	22	1	Resolution	86	Public Lands	Dec. 27, 1831	Favorable	125	Passed	Passed	App'd June 25, 1832
Liveley, Robert, *et al.*	(See Virginia, church wardens of Elizabeth city.)	20	1		68							
Lively, William	(See Virginia, church wardens of Elizabeth city.)	20	1		68							
Livermore, Edward St. L.	Compensation for judicial services.	4	1	Petition	384	Claims.						
Livermore, Edward S. L.	Compensation for judicial services.	4	2	Petition	614	Claims	Jan. 24, 1797	Favorable		Referred to Committee Whole House.		
Livermore, Edward St. L.	Compensation for judicial services.	5	2	Rep't Committee.	100	Whole House	Dec. 18, 1797			Disagreed to.		
Livermore, John C.	Indemnity for expenses in United States service.	22	2	Petition	313	Claims.						
Livesay, William B.	Correction of error in land entry	25	2	Petition	548	Public Lands.						
Livesay, William B.	Correction of error in land entry	25	3	Petition	93	Public Lands	154	Favorable	1021	Passed.		
Livesay, William B.	Correction of error in land entry	26	1	Petition	177	Public Lands.	July 21, 1840	Favorable	508	Referred to Committee Whole House.		
Livezey, Thomas	Payment for horses taken for public use.	4	2	Petition	627	Claims.						
Livezey, Thomas	Payment for horses taken for public use.	5	2	Petition	148	Claims	Jan. 25, 1798	Adverse		Rejected.		
Livingston, Abraham, heirs of.	Commutation pay	26	1	Petition	280	Rev. Claims	236	Adverse		Laid on table.		
Livingston, Abraham, heirs of.	Reimbursement of advances	29	1	Petition	178	Rev. Claims	249	Adverse		Recommitted.		
Livingston, Abraham, heirs of.	Reimbursement of advances	29	2	Petition	128	Rev. Claims.						
Livingston, Abraham, heirs of.	Reimbursement of advances	30	1	Petition	148	Rev. Claims.						
Livingston, Abraham, heirs of.	Reimbursement of advances	30	2	Petition	127	Rev. Claims.						
Livingston, Abraham, heirs of.	Reimbursement of advances	31	1	Petition	391	Rev. Claims.						
Livingston, Edward	Confirmation of title to land	10	2	Petition	374					Referred to Attorney General.		
Livingston, Edward	Confirmation of title to land	11	1	Report of Attorney General.	53	Select.						
Livingston, Edward	Confirmation of title to land	11	2	Petition	378					Leave to withdraw.		
Livingston, Edward, widow of.	Confirmation of title to land	27	2	Petition	106	Priv. Land Claims.	282	Favorable	248	Passed	Passed	App'd Aug. 1, 1842
Livingston, Edward	Compensation for fuel, &c., taken for public use.	18	2	Petition	89	Claims.						
Livingston, Edward	Compensation for fuel, &c., taken for public use.	19	1	Petition	292	Claims	April 14, 1826	Adverse		Laid on table.		
Livingston, Edward	Compensation for fuel, &c., taken for public use.	19	2	Petition	96	Claims.						

2—42

List of private claims presented to the House of Representatives of the United States from the 1st to the 31st Congress, inclusive—Continued.

Names of claimants.	Nature or object of the claim.	Congress.	Session.	How brought before the House of Reps.	Page of journal.	To what committee of the House referred.	No. or date of the report.	Nature of the report.	No. of the bill.	How disposed of by the House of Reps.	How disposed of by the Senate.	Date of the act of Congress, and remarks.
Livingston, Edward	Compensation for fuel, &c., taken for public use.	21	2	Petition	104	Claims	53	Favorable	589	Referred to Committee Whole House.		
Livingston, Edward	Compensation for fuel, &c., taken for public use.	22	1	Petition	20	Claims	Dec. 19, 1831	Favorable	38	Passed	Passed	App'd Mar. 15, 1832
Livingston, Edward	Provision for defence of suits	18	2	Petition	95	Judiciary.						
Livingston, Edward	Provision for defence of suits	22	1	Petition	473	Judiciary.						
Livingston, Gilbert J	Compensation for revolutionary services.	11	2	Petition	131	Claims	Dec. 28, 1809	Adverse		Referred to Committee Whole House.		
Livingston, Henry A	(See Abraham Livingston, heir of)	29	1		178							
Livingston, Henry B	Compensation for revolutionary services.	3	2	Rep. of Secretary of War.	278	Claims	Mar. 2, 1795	Adverse		Laid on table.		
Livingston, Henry B	Compensation for revolutionary services.	4	1	Memorial	425	Claims	Mar. 7, 1796	Adverse		Rejected		Leave to withdraw.
Livingston, Henry B	Compensation for advances, losses, services, &c., in revolution.	11	2	Petition	144	Claims	Mar. 31, 1810	Adverse		Referred to Committee Whole House.		
Livingston, Henry B	Compensation for advances, losses, services, &c., in revolution.	14	1	Petition	407	Pens. & Rev. Cl'ms.						
Livingston, Henry B	Compensation for advances, losses, services, &c., in revolution.	16	1	Petition	139	Pens. & Rev. Cl'ms	51	Adverse		Laid on table		Leave to withdraw.
Livingston, Henry B	Pension	21	1	Petition	498	Military Pensions.						
Livingston, James	(See Canadian refugees)	6	2		766							
Livingston, James, Colonel	Compensation for revolutionary services	16	1	Petition	162	Pens. & Rev. Cl'ms.						
Livingston, James, Colonel	Compensation for revolutionary services.	16	2	Petition	32	Pens. & Rev. Cl'ms.	Dec. 15, 1820	Adverse		Rejected.		
Livingston, James, Colonel, heir of.	Compensation for revolutionary services.	28	2	Petition	171	Rev. Claims	181	Adverse		Laid on table.		
Livingston, John	(See Canadian refugees)	6	2		766							
Livingston, John	Pension	21	2	Petition	302	Military Pensions.						
Livingston, John R	Compensation for powder furnished government.	1	2	Petition	269					Referred to Secretary of Treasury.		
Livingston, John R	Compensation for powder furnished government.	3	1	Rep. of Secretary Treasury.	78	Whole House	June 6, 1794	Favorable	67	Passed	Postponed.	
Livingston, John R	Compensation for powder furnished government.	3	2	Resolution	238	Select	Nov. 27, 1794	By bill	72	Referred to Committee of Claims.		
Livingston, John R	Compensation for powder furnished government.	4	1	Petition and docs.	380	Whole House.						
Livingston, Louisa	(See Edward Livingston, widow of)	27	2		106							
Livingston, Louisa, *et al.*	Relief on account of non-payment of Mexican indemnity.	29	1	Memorial	339	Foreign Affairs.						
Livingston, Madison C	Indemnity for non-fulfilment of contract by United States.	27	2	Petition	227	Claims	494	Adverse		Laid on table.		
Livingston, P. W	Indemnity for French spoliations prior to 1800.	26	1	Memorial	182	Foreign Affairs	343	Favorable	319	Referred to Committee Whole House.		
Livingston, Richard, heirs of.	Indemnity for losses, &c., as Canadian refugee.	19	2	Petition	82	Rev. Claims	83	Favorable	439	Referred to Committee Whole House.		
Livingston, Richard, heirs of.	Indemnity for losses, &c., as Canadian refugee.	20	1	Petition	69	Rev. Claims				Discharged; laid on table.		
Livingston, Richard, heirs of.	Indemnity for losses, &c., as Canadian refugee.	20	2	Petition	113	Rev. Claims.						
Livingston, Richard, heirs of.	Indemnity for losses, &c., as Canadian refugee.	21	1	Resolution	217	Rev. Claims	172	Favorable	220	Referred to Committee Whole House.		

List of private claims presented to the House of Representatives of the United States from the 1st to the 31st Congress, inclusive—Continued.

Names of claimants.	Nature or object of the claim.	Congress.	Session.	How brought before the House of Reps.	Page of journal.	To what committee of the House referred.	No. or date of the report.	Nature of the report.	No. of the bill.	How disposed of by the House of Reps.	How disposed of by the Senate.	Date of the act of Congress, and remarks.
Livingston, Richard, heirs of.	Indemnity for losses, &c., as Canadian refugee.	21	2	House bill	264	Whole House	Feb. 4, 1831	With amend.	220	Passed.		
Livingston, Richard, heirs of.	Indemnity for losses, &c., as Canadian refugee.	22	1	Petition	333	Rev. Claims	329	Favorable	412	Referred to Committee Whole House.		
Livingston, Richard, heirs of.	Indemnity for losses, &c., as Canadian refugee.	23	1	Petition	39	Rev. Claims	61	Favorable	71	Passed	Passed	App'd June 27, 1834
Livingston, Richard, heirs of.	Indemnity for losses, &c., as Canadian refugee.	25	2	Petition	48	Rev. Claims				Discharged; leave to withdraw.		
Livingston, Richard M	(See Col. Jas. Livingston, heir of.)	28	2		171		181					
Livingston, Col. Richard, heirs of.	Permission to locate a section of land.	25	2	Petition	179	Priv. Land Claims.	447	Adverse		Laid on table.		
Livingston, Col. Richard, heirs of.	Commutation pay	26	1	Petition	701	Rev. Claims				Discharged; laid on table.		
Livingston, Col. Richard, heirs of.	Commutation pay	26	2	Petition	77	Rev. Claims				Discharged; laid on table.		
Livingston, Robert S	(See Walter Livingston, heirs of.)	21	1		71							
Livingston, Stephen	(See Colonel Richard Livingston, heirs of.)	25	2		179							
Livingston, T	(See Benjamin T. Whitner, *et al.*)	24	1		751							
Livingston, Taliaferro, administrators of.	Compensation for maintenance of captured Africans.	20	1	House bill	345	Whole House	May 22, 1828	With amend.	190	Passed	Passed	App'd May 24, 1828
Livingston, T., and F. W. Armstrong.	Compensation for support of Africans illegally imported.	21	2	Senate bill	134	Ways and Means	Jan. 19, 1831	With amend.	50	Passed	Passed	App'd Feb. 25, 1831
Livingston, Thomas B	For expenses as consul at Halifax.	31	2	Petition	78	Ways and Means.						
Livingston, Walter, heirs of, *et al.*	Payment of award for supplies to revolutionary army.	14	2	Petition	147	Pens. & Rev. Cl'ms.						
Livingston, Walter, executor of.	Payment of award for supplies to revolutionary army.	18	2	Petition	91	Pens. & Rev. Cl'ms.						
Livingston, Walter, executor of.	Payment of award for supplies to revolutionary army.	19	1	Petition	34	Pens. & Rev. Cl'ms.	May 18, 1826	Favorable	277	Referred to Committee Whole House.		
Livingston, Walter, executor of.	Payment of award for supplies to revolutionary army.	19	2	Petition	390					Referred to Secretary Treasury.		
Livingston, Walter, executor of.	Payment of award for supplies to revolutionary army.	20	1	Rep. of Secretary Treasury.	361	Rev. Claims	227	Favorable	255	Referred to Committee Whole House.		
Livingston, Walter, executor of.	Payment of award for supplies to revolutionary army.	20	2	House bill	284	Whole House			255			
Livingston, Walter, executor of.	Payment of award for supplies to revolutionary army.	21	1	Petition	71	Rev. Claims	93	Favorable	127	Rejected.		
Livingston, Walter, executor of.	Payment of award for supplies to revolutionary army.	22	1	Petition	44	Rev. Claims	254	Favorable	341	Referred to Committee Whole House.		
Livingston, Walter, executor of.	Payment of award for supplies to revolutionary army.	23	1	Petition	39	Rev. Claims	56	Favorable	66	Passed	Passed	App'd June 28, 1834
Livingston, William	Remission of amount of cargo condemned.	18	1	Petition	388	Ways and Means.						
Livingston, William	Remission of amount of cargo condemned.	18	2	Petition	38	Ways and Means	Jan. 31, 1825	Adverse		Laid on table.		
Llewellen, J. M	(See Wm. B. Llewellen, son of.)	31	2		177							
Llewellen, Wm. B., son of.	Reimbursement of expenses as consul.	31	2	Petition	177	Claims.						
Lloyd, Edward	Pension	11	2	Pension bill	283	Whole House	Mar. 16, 1810	With amend.	107	Passed	Passed	App'd April 27, 1810
Lloyd, Edward, heirs of	Location of revolutionary land warrant.	23	1	Petition	381	Public Lands	April 18, 1834	Favorable	439	Passed	Passed	App'd June 30, 1834

List of private claims presented to the House of Representatives of the United States from the 1st to the 31st Congress, inclusive—Continued.

Names of claimants.	Nature or object of the claim.	Congress.	Session.	How brought before the House of Reps.	Page of journal.	To what committee of the House referred.	No. or date of the report.	Nature of the report.	No. of the bill.	How disposed of by the House of Reps.	How disposed of by the Senate.	Date of the act of Congress, and remarks.
Lloyd, Francis	(See Dr. John Roberts, administrator of.)	29	1	....	389							
Lloyd, James	Compensation for invention of combustible agent.	13	2	Senate bill	409	Whole House	April 16, 1816	With't amend.	54	Indefinitely postponed.		
Lloyd, James, & T. Tuttle, surety of.	Release from liability	15	1	Petition	320	Ways and Means.						
Lloyd, James, & T. Tuttle, surety of.	Release from liability	15	2	Petition and docs.	186	Ways and Means.						
Lloyd, James L	Increase of pension	28	1	Petition	622	Invalid Pensions.						
Lloyd, James L	Increase of pension	29	1	Petition	93	Invalid Pensions	352	Adverse	......	Laid on table.		
Lloyd, James L	Increase of pension	29	2	Petition	233	Invalid Pensions.						
Lloyd, John	(See John Loyd.)	29	1	....	461							
Lloyd, Owen	(See Owen Loyd.)	28	1	....	332							
Lloyd, Richard	Compensation for services as agent	1	2	Petition	286	....	....	....	......	Referred to Secretary War.		
Lloyd, Richard	Compensation for services as agent	1	3	Rep. of Secretary War.	385	....	....	....	......	Laid on table.		
Lloyd, Richard	Compensation for services as agent	2	1	Petition	476	Select	Jan. 13, 1792	Adverse	......	Laid on table.		
Lloyd, W. B. & A. M.	Compensation for use of land at Cleveland.	31	2	Petition	53	Claims.						
Loans, commissioners of.	Payment of certain expenses	3	1	Senate bill	180	Whole House	June 4, 1794	With amend.	16	Passed	Passed	App'd June 6, 1794
Lobdell, Ebenezer	Additional compensation for removing obstructions from Kennebec river.	21	2	Senate bill	214	Claims	March 2, 1831	Adverse	S. 86	Referred to Committee Whole House.		
Lobdell, Ebenezer	Additional compensation for removing obstructions from Kennebec river.	22	2	Senate bill	211	Claims	....	....	S. 17			
Lobdell, Ebenezer	Additional compensation for removing obstructions from Kennebec river.	23	1	Senate bill	175	Claims	....	....	S. 34			
Lobdell, Ebenezer	Additional compensation for removing obstructions from Kennebec river.	24	1	Petition	324	Claims	May 17, 1836	Adverse	......	Laid on table.		
Lobdell, Ebenezer	Additional compensation for removing obstructions from Kennebec river.	24	2	Petition	38	Claims.						
Lobdell, Ebenezer	Additional compensation for removing obstructions from Kennebec river.	25	2	Petition	52	Claims	324	Favorable	366	Referred to Committee Whole House.		
Lobdell, Ebenezer	Additional compensation for removing obstructions from Kennebec river.	25		House bill	377	....	....	....	366	Passed	Adverse.	
Lobdell, Ebenezer	Additional compensation for removing obstructions from Kennebec river.	26	1	Petition	169	Claims	11	Favorable	30	Passed	Passed	App'd April 20, 1840
Lobdell, Ebenezer	Indemnity for French spoliations prior to 1800.	26	1	Memorial	182	Foreign Affairs	343	Favorable; bill	319	Referred to Committee Whole House.		
Lobdell, Ebenezer	Indemnity for French spoliations prior to 1800.	29	2	Memorial	353	Foreign Affairs.						
Lobdell, Ebenezer, heirs of.	Indemnity for French spoliations prior to 1800.	31	1	Petition	699	Foreign Affairs	355	General bill	318	Referred to Committee Whole House.		
Lobdell, John L	Confirmation of title to land	22	1	Petition	32	Priv. Land Claims.	324	Favorable	407	Referred to Committee Whole House.		

List of private claims presented to the House of Representatives of the United States from the 1st to the 31st Congress, inclusive—Continued.

Names of claimants.	Nature or object of the claim.	Congress.	Session.	How brought before the House of Reps.	Page of journal.	To what committee of the House referred.	No. or date of the report.	Nature of the report.	No. of the bill.	How disposed of by the House of Reps.	How disposed of by the Senate.	Date of the act of Congress, and remarks.
Lobdell, John L.	Confirmation of title to land	23	1	Petition	48	Priv. Land Claims.	34	Favorable	40	Passed	Passed	App'd May 1, 1834
Loch, John	Pension for revolutionary services	24	1	Petition	738	Rev. Pensions.						
Locher, Henry	Compensation for introduction of clover seed into Maryland.	23	1	Petition	443	Agriculture.						
Locke, Dr.	Compensation for magnetic clock	30	2	Amend'nt to Ho. bill.	157	....	....	....	692	Passed.	Passed	App'd March 3, 1849
Lock, John, widow of	Pension for revolutionary services.	29	2	Petition	417	Rev. Pensions.						
Locker, Philip	Compensation for revolutionary services.	19	2	Petition	287	Rev. Claims.						
Lockhart, Philip, assignee of.	Compensation for services in United States army.	9	1	Petition	192	Claims.						
Lockhart, Philip, assignee of.	Compensation for services in United States army.	10	2	Petition	459	Claims.						
Lockhart, Philip, assignee of.	Compensation for services in United States army.	11	2	Petition	127	Claims.						
Lockhart, Philip, assignee of.	Compensation for services in United States army.	12	1	Petition	39	Claims.						
Lockhart, Philip, assignee of.	Compensation for services in United States army.	14	1	Petition	146	Pens. & Rev. Cl'ms.						
Lockhart, Philip, assignee of.	Compensation for services in United States army.	16	1	Petition	139	Pens. & Rev. Cl'ms.	Jan. 21, 1820	Adverse	......	Laid on table.		
Lockhart, Philip, assignee of.	Compensation for services in United States army.	19	2	Petition	158	Rev. Claims.						
Lockhart, Philip, assignee of	Compensation for services in United States army.	20	1	Petition	126	Rev. Claims	Feb. 8, 1828	Adverse	......	Laid on table.		
Lockhart, Philip, assignee of.	Compensation for services in United States army.	21	2	Petition	74	Rev. Claims.						
Lockhart, Philip, assignee of.	Compensation for services in United States army.	22	1	Petition	190	Rev. Claims	Jan. 25, 1832	Adverse	......	Laid on table.		
Lockhart, Philip, assignee of.	Compensation for services in United States army.	22	2	Petition	137	Rev. Claims	Jan. 11, 1833	Adverse	......	Laid on table.		
Lockman, Charles	Compensation as surgeon's mate in revolutionary war.	1	3	Petition	371	....	....	....	......	Referred to Secretary War.		
Lockman, Charles	Compensation as surgeon's mate in revolutionary war.	2	2	Rep. of Secretary War.	696	....	....	....	......	Laid on table.		
Lockwood, Benjamin C., and George Hicks.	Reimbursement of duties on wrecked goods.	23	1	Petition	369	Ways and Means	May 13, 1834	Adverse	......	Laid on table.		
Lockwood, Buckingham	Indemnity for French spoliations prior to 1800.	26	1	Memorial	182	Foreign Affairs	343	Favorable	319	Referred to Committee Whole House.		
Lockwood, Buckingham	Indemnity for French spoliations prior to 1800.	31	1	Petition	307	Foreign Affairs	355	Favorable	318	Referred to Committee Whole House.		
Lockwood, Ebenezer, representatives of.	Compensation for property destroyed by British.	23	1	Petition	584	Rev. Claims.						
Lockwood, Ebenezer, representatives of.	Compensation for property destroyed by British.	23	2	Petition	276	Rev. Claims.						
Lockwood, Eliphalet, administrator of.	Indemnity for French spoliations prior to 1800.	26	1	Memorial	182	Foreign Affairs	343	Favorable	310	Referred to Committee Whole House.		
Lockwood, Isaac	Relief on account of failure of land title.	31	2	Petition	88	Claims.						
Lockwood, Joseph, widow of.	Pension for revolutionary services.	26	1	Resolution	778	Rev. Pensions.						
Lockwood, Joseph, widow of.	Pension for revolutionary services.	29	1	Petition	353	Rev. Pensions.						

List of private claims presented to the House of Representatives of the United States from the 1st to the 31st Congress, inclusive—Continued.

Names of claimants.	Nature or object of the claim.	Congress.	Session.	How brought before the House of Reps.	Page of journal.	To what committee of the House referred.	No. or date of the report.	Nature of the report.	No. of the bill.	How disposed of by the House of Reps.	How disposed of by the Senate.	Date of the act of Congress, and remarks.
Lockwood, Joseph, widow of.	Pension for revolutionary services.	30	2	....	321	....	....	....	......	Leave to withdraw.		
Lockwood, Lydia	(See Joseph Lockwood, widow of)	26	1	....	778							
Lockwood, Millington, heir of.	Indemnity for property destroyed in revolutionary war.	25	2	Petition	658	Rev. Claims	971	Adverse	......	Laid on table.		
Lockwood, Nathan	Pension	14	1	House bill	622	Pens. & Rev. Cl'ms.	April 11, 1816	Favorable	171	Passed	Passed	App'd April 30, 1816
Lockwood, Nathan	Increase of pension	21	1	House bill	130	Whole House	Feb. 12, 1830	With amend.	72	Passed	Passed	App'd May 20, 1830
Lockwood, Nathaniel	Pension for revolutionary services.	20	2	Resolution	46	Military Pensions.						
Lockwood, Nathaniel	Pension for revolutionary services.	21	1	Petition	49	Military Pensions.						
Lockwood, Nathaniel	Pension for revolutionary services.	21	1	House bill	130	Whole House	Feb. 12, 1830	With amend.	72	Passed	Passed	App'd May 20, 1830
Lockwood, Ransom	Further time to execute contract.	21	1	Petition	597	Naval Affairs.						
Lockwood, William	Indemnity for French spoliations prior to 1800.	26	1	Memorial	182	Foreign Affairs	343	Favorable	319	Referred to Committee Whole House.		
Lœhman, Dr. John	Pension for revolutionary services.	2	1	Petition	502	....	....	....	......	Referred to Secretary War.		
Lœhman, Dr. John	Pension for revolutionary services.	2	2	Petition	618	Select.						
Lœhman, Dr. John	Pension for revolutionary services.	3	1	Rep. of Secretary War.	56	Select.						
Lœhman, Dr. John	Pension for revolutionary services.	3	2	Rep. of Secretary War.	250	Claims	Feb. 28, 1795	Adverse	......	Referred to Committee Whole House.		
Lœhman, Dr. John	Pension for revolutionary services.	4	2	Petition	649	Claims	Jan. 18, 1797	Adverse	......	Leave to withdraw.		
Lœhman, Dr. John	Pension for revolutionary services.	5	2	Petition	87	Claims	....	....	......	Discharged; leave to withdraw.		
Lœhman, Dr. John	Pension for revolutionary services.	9	2	Petition	471	Claims	Dec. 6, 1806	Adverse	......	Leave to withdraw.		
Lœhman, Dr. John	Pension for revolutionary services.	10	1	Petition	101	....	....	....	......	Referred to Committee Whole House.		
Lœhman, Dr. John	Pension for revolutionary services.	10	2	Petition	358	Select	....	....	......	Referred to Committee Whole House.		
Lœhman, Dr. John	Pension for revolutionary services.	11	1	Petition	42	Claims.						
Lœhman, Dr. John	Pension for revolutionary services.	11	2	Petition	135	Claims	Feb. 14, 1810	Adverse	......	Rejected.		
Lœhman, Dr. John	Pension for revolutionary services.	11	3	Petition	443	Claims.						
Lœhman, Dr. John	Pension for revolutionary services.	12	1	Petition	72	Claims	June 12, 1812	Adverse	......	Laid on table.		
Lœhman, Dr. John	Pension for revolutionary services.	12	2	Petition	568	Claims	Feb. 26, 1813	Adverse	......	Laid on table.		
Lofland, Benjamin H.	Compensation for horse, &c., lost in Seminole war.	19	1	Petition	136	Claims	Jan. 20, 1826	Adverse	......	Laid on table.		
Lofland, Benjamin H	Compensation for horse, &c., lost in Seminole war.	20	2	Petition	230	Claims.						
Lofland, Benjamin H	Compensation for horse, &c., lost in Seminole war.	21	1	Petition	506	Claims	April 6, 1830	Adverse	......	Laid on table.		
Logan, Benjamin	(See James Knox, devisee of)	29	1	....	199							
Logan, Henry	Pension	16	1	Petition and rep't Sec. of War.	208	Pens. & Rev. Cl'ms.	Mar. 29, 1820	Adverse	......	Laid on table.		
Logan, James E.	Bounty land for military service	31	1	Petition	415	Military Affairs.						
Logan, John, (Ohio)	Compensation for revolutionary services.	18	2	Petition	27	Pens. & Rev. Cl'ms.	Dec. 14, 1824	Adverse	......	Laid on table.		
Logan, John	Pension for revolutionary services.	19	2	Resolution	116	Military Pensions.						
Logan, John	Pension for revolutionary services.	20	1	Resolution	175	Military Pensions.	....	....	......	Discharged; laid on table.		
Logan, John	Pension for revolutionary services.	21	1	Petition	67	Military Pensions.	May 25, 1830	Favorable	490	Referred to Committee Whole House.		
Logan, John	Pension for revolutionary services.	22	1	Petition	104	Rev. Pensions	Mar. 13, 1832	Favorable	467	Passed	Indef. postp'd.	
Logan, John	Pension for revolutionary services.	24	1	Petition	260	Rev. Pensions	302	Favorable	316	Passed	Passed	App'd June 28,

List of private claims presented to the House of Representatives of the United States from the 1st to the 31st Congress, inclusive—Continued.

Names of claimants.	Nature or object of the claim.	Congress.	Session.	How brought before the House of Reps.	Page of journal.	To what committee of the House referred.	No. or date of the report.	Nature of the report.	No. of the bill.	How disposed of by the House of Reps.	How disposed of by the Senate.	Date of the act of Congress, and remarks.
Logan, John, and J. P. Losey.	Compensation for revolutionary services, &c.	4	1	Petition	466	Claims.						
Logan, John, and J. P. Losey.	Compensation for revolutionary services, &c.	4	2	Petition	614	Claims.						
Logan, John, and J. P. Losey.	Compensation for revolutionary services, &c.	5	2	Petition	265	Claims	April 18, 1798	Adverse	......	Rejected.		
Logan, John, and J. P. Losey.	Compensation for revolutionary services, &c.	7	1	Petition	127	Claims	Mar. 11, 1842	Adverse	......	Rejected.		
Logan, Joshua, *et al.*	Bounty land for military services.	31	2	Petition	110	Public Lands.						
Logan, Patrick	Pension	13	1	House bill	56	Claims	June 29, 1813	Favorable	31	Passed	Passed	App'd Aug. 2, 1813
Lognon, Louis	(See Richard Smith, *et al.*)	15	2	....	33							
Lohr, Joseph	Pension for revolutionary services.	20	2	Petition	262	Military Pensions.						
Lohr, Joseph	Pension for revolutionary services.	21	1	Resolution	350	Military Pensions.	....	....	......	Discharged; laid on table.		
Lollar, Daniel	Pension	1	3	Petition and rep't Sec. of War.	368	....	....	....	......	Laid on table.		
Lollar, Daniel	Pension	3	1	Rep. of Secretary of War.	131	Select	May 26, 1794	Res. to refer to Sec. War.	J. R. 12	Passed	Passed	App'd June 9, 1794
Lomax, Mann P., widow of.	Half pay	28	2	Resolution	93	Invalid Pensions.						
Lomax, Josiah	Compensation for horse, &c., lost in Seminole war.	23	1	Documents	154	Claims.						
Lomax, Jasiah	(See William H. Bedford, agent.)	28	1	....	262							
Lomax, Wm., representatives of.	Arrears of pension	25	2	Resolution	473	Rev. Pensions	....	....	......	Discharged; laid on table.		
Lomax, Wm., representatives of	Arrears of pension	25	3	Resolution	88	Rev. Pensions.						
Lomax, Wm., representatives of.	Arrears of pension	26	1	Petition	174	Rev. Pensions	114	Favorable	120	Passed	Indef. postp'd.	
Lomax, Wm., representatives of.	Arrears of pension	27	2	Petition	1227	Rev. Pensions	1097	Favorable	608	Referred to Committee Whole House.		
Lomax, Wm., representatives of.	Arrears of pension	27	3	Rep'rt Committee Whole House.	91	....	....	With't amend.	608	Passed	Indef. postp'd.	
Lombard, Daniel, *et al.*	Payment of certain bills of credit.	3	1	Petition	71	....	....	....	......	Referred to Secretary Treasury.		
Lombard, Daniel, *et al*	Payment of certain bills of credit.	3	2	Rep. of Secretary Treasury.	312	....	....	....	......	Laid on table.		
Lombard, Gabriel	Compensation for military services.	25	2	Petition	175	Claims	1002	Adverse	......	Laid on table.		
Lombard, Stephen	Pension for revolutionary services.	22	1	Petition	219	Rev. Pensions.						
Lombars, Manuel	Confirmation of title to land	22	1	Resolution	86	Public Lands	Dec. 27, 1831	Favorable	125	Passed	Passed	App'd June 25, 1832
Lond, Warren, heir of	Money in lieu of bounty land	24	2	Petition	346	Invalid Pensions.	....	....	......	Discharged; laid on table.		
London, John, and wife	(See representatives of Wm. Lambreth.)	3	1	....	133							
Long, Abner	Pension for revolutionary services.	27	3	Petition	251	Invalid Pensions.						
Long, Abner	Pension for revolutionary services.	30	1	Petition	406	Invalid Pensions	633	Adverse	......	Laid on table.		
Long, A. K.	(See Exploring Expedition)	27	3	....	149							
Long, Alton	To correct erroneous land entry.	28	2	Petition	213	Priv. Land Claims.	167	Favorable	635	Discharged; laid on table.		
Long, Alton	To correct erroneous land entry.	29	1	Petition	193	Priv. Land Claims.						
Long, Alton, *et al.*	(See Arabia Brown)	31	1	....	234	....	336	....	296			
Long, Anthony	Increase of pension	25	3	Petition	89	Invalid Pensions.						

List of private claims presented to the House of Representatives of the United States from the 1st *to the* 31*st Congress, inclusive*—Continued.

Names of claimants.	Nature or object of the claim.	Congress.	Session.	How brought before the House of Reps.	Page of journal.	To what committee of the House referred.	No. or date of the report.	Nature of the report.	No. of the bill.	How disposed of by the House of Reps.	How disposed of by the Senate.	Date of the act of Congress, and remarks.
Long, Anthony	Increase of pension	26	1	Petition	161	Invalid Pensions				Discharged; leave to withdraw.		
Long, Derrett, administrator of.	Bounty land for revolutionary services.	29	1	Petition	905	Rev. Claims.						
Long, Derrett, administrator of.	Bounty land for revolutionary services.	30	1	Petition	173	Rev. Claims.						
Long, Derrett, administrator of.	Bounty land for revolutionary services.	31	1	Petition	383	Rev. Claims.						
Long, Ethan A	Change of location of land	27	3	Petition	259	Public Lands	160	Favorable	776	Ref'd to Com. W. H		
Long, Gideon	Commutation pay	18	1	Petition	284	Pens. & Rev. Cl'ms.				Discharged; laid on table.		
Long, Hugh	(See Joseph Brown)	24	2		78							
Long, Irwin P	Change of land location	27	3	Petition	259	Public Lands	160	Favorable	776	Referred to Committee Whole House.		
Long, James	Pension for revolutionary services.	20	2	Resolution	126	Military Pensions.						
Long, James	Pension for revolutionary services.	21	1	Petition	49	Military Pensions.						
Long, James	Pension for revolutionary services.	21	1	Pension bill	130	Whole House	Feb. 12, 1830	With amend.	72	Passed	Passed	App'd May 20, 1830
Long, John	Compensation for a horse lost in United States service.	17	2	Petition	163	Claims	Feb. 7, 1823	Adverse		Laid on table.		
Long, John	Compensation for a horse lost in United States service.	20	2	Petition	49	Claims	17	Favorable	333	Referred to Committee Whole House.		
Long, John	Compensation for a horse lost in United States service.	21	1	Petition	51	Claims	Dec. 21, 1829	Favorable	11	Passed	Passed	App'd Feb. 11, 1830
Long, John	Pension	11	3	Pension bill	604	Whole House	Mar. 2, 1811	With amend.	218	Passed	Passed	App'd March 3 1811
Long, John	Increase of pension	15	2	Pension bill	41	Whole House	Feb. 17, 1819	With amend.	203	Passed	Passed, with amendment.	App'd March 3, 1819
Long, John P	Compensation for services of company of volunteers.	25	2	Petition	274	Claims.						
Long, John P	Compensation for services of company of volunteers.	26	1	Petition	169	Claims.						
Long, John	(See William H. Bedford, agent.)	28	1		262							
Long, Joseph, attorney of.	Compensation for revolutionary services.	3	2	Petition	335	Claims.						
Long, Joseph, attorney of.	Compensation for revolutionary services.	4	1	Petition	373	Claims				Discharged.		
Long, Joshua	(See Derret Long, administrator of.)	29	1		905							
Long, Mary	(See Matthias Long, widow of.)	27	2		845							
Long, Matthew	(See David R. Denham, *et al.*)	25	3		121							
Long, Capt. Matthew P.	(See Missouri militia.)	24	1		810							
Long, Matthias, widow of.	Pension for revolutionary services.	27	2	Petition	845	Rev. Pensions				Discharged; laid on table.		
Long, Michael	Grant of land	31	1	Petition	349	Priv. Land Claims.				Discharged; laid on table.		
Long, Nathan	Indemnity for French spoliations prior to 1800.	26	1	Memorial	343	Foreign Affairs	343	Favorable	319	Referred to Committee Whole House.		
Long, Nicholas	Pension for revolutionary services.	21	1	Petition	243	Military Pensions.						
Long, Richard	Compensation for revolutionary services.	10	2	Petition	500	Public Lands	Feb. 27, 1809	Adverse		Leave to withdraw.		
Long, Samuel	For leave to make land entry in a certain way.	22	1	Resolution	810	Public Lands.						
Long, Stephen H	Compensation for use of patent by United States.	23	2	Petition	129	Military Affairs.						

List of private claims presented to the House of Representatives of the United States from the 1st to the 31st Congress, inclusive—Continued.

Names of claimants.	Nature or object of the claim.	Congress.	Session.	How brought before the House of Reps.	Page of journal.	To what committee of the House referred.	No. or date of the report.	Nature of the report.	No. of the bill.	How disposed of by the House of Reps.	How disposed of by the Senate.	Date of the act of Congress, and remarks.
Long, Stephen H.	Compensation for use of patent by United States.	24	1	Petition	152	Military Affairs.						
Long, Thomas T	Compensation for services as secretary of senate in Florida.	28	1	Petition	319	Territories.	April 2, 1844	Favorable	296	Laid on table.		
Long, William	Compensation for a horse lost in public service.	24	2	Petition	42	Claims	Feb. 22, 1837	Adverse		Leave to withdraw.		
Long, William, executor of	Compensation for revolutionary services.	24	1	Petition	275	Rev. Claims	May 17, 1836	Adverse		Laid on table.		
Long, Zadock	Compensation for securing military stores.	3	1	Petition	136	Select	May 14, 1794	Adverse		Laid on table.		
Longaback, Michael	Compensation for revolutionary services.	18	1	Petition	214	Pens. & Rev. Cl'ms.	Feb. 25, 1824	Adverse		Laid on table.		
Longcammon, A. W.	Relief on account of loss of her husband in public service.	1	3	Petition and rep. Sec. War.	344					Laid on table.		
Longchamp, J. P.	Drawback on goods exported	14	1	Petition	386	Com. and Manuf.	April 12, 1816	Favorable		Indefinitely postponed.		
Longchamp, J. P.	Drawback on goods exported	14	2	Petition	101	Com. and Manuf.	Dec. 31, 1816	Favorable	36	Passed	Passed	App'd March 3, 1817
Longley, Mary	(See Wm. S. Longley, mother of.)	30	2		440							
Longley, Wm. S., mother of.	Naval pension	30	2	Petition	440	Invalid Pensions				Discharged; laid on table.		
Longstreet, Gilbert	(See Hard & Longstreet.)	23	2		263							
Longstreet, Gilbert	Payment of money withheld by Postmaster General.	24	2	Petition	214	P. Of. & P. Roads.						
Longstreet, Gilbert	Reimbursement of fine imposed by Postmaster General.	26	2	Petition	83	P. Of. & P. Roads.						
Longstreth, Joshua	(See Thomas Witherspoon, assignee of.)	26	1		152		343		319			
Longworth, Nicholas	(See John H. Piatt, administrators of.)	17	2		87							
Look, Noah	Pension	21	1	Petition	99	Military Pensions	Mar. 26, 1830	Adverse		Laid on table.		
Look, Thomas	Pension for revolutionary services.	24	1	Petition	944	Rev. Pensions.						
Look, Thomas	Pension for revolutionary services.	24	2	Petition	217	Rev. Pensions				Discharged; laid on table.		
Looker, Othriel	Pension for revolutionary srrvices.	28	1	Petition	99	Rev. Pensions.				Discharged; laid on table.		
Looker, William	Pension	4	1	Rep. of Secretary War.	373	Claims.	Jan. 6, 1796	Adverse		Referred to Committee Whole House.		
Loomis, Amasa, widow of.	Pension for revolutionary services.	30	1	Petition	165	Rev. Pensions	384	Adverse		Laid on table.		
Loomis, Andrew	Pension	21	1	Petition	573	Military Pensions.				Discharged; laid on table.		
Loomis, Andrew	Pension	21	2	Petition	126	Military Pensions.						
Loomis, Benjamin	Pension	29	1	Petition	647	Invalid Pensions.				Discharged; laid on table.		
Loomis, Benjamin	Pension	29	2	Petition	82	Invalid Pensions				Discharged; laid on table.		
Loomis, Benjamin	Pension	31	1	Petition	714	Invalid Pensions.						
Loomis, Daniel	Compensation for extra work on Cumberland road.	19	1	Petition	249	Claims	131	Favorable	171	Referred to Committee Whole House.		
Loomis, Daniel	Compensation for extra work on Cumberland road.	20	1	Petition	226	Claims.	Mar. 27, 1828	Res. to withdraw and refer to Treas. Departm't.		Adopted.		
Loomis, Daniel	Further compensation for extra work on Cumberland road.	22	1	Petition	383	Claims.						

2—43

List of private claims presented to the House of Representatives of the United States from the 1st to the 31st Congress, inclusive—Continued.

Names of claimants.	Nature or object of the claim.	Congress.	Session.	How brought before the House of Reps.	Page of journal.	To what committee of the House referred.	No. or date of the report.	Nature of the report.	No. of the bill.	How disposed of by the House of Reps.	How disposed of by the Senate.	Date of the act of Congress, and remarks.
Loomis, Daniel	Further compensation for extra work on Cumberland road.	23	1	Petition	245	Claims.						
Loomis, Daniel	Further compensation for extra work on Cumberland road.	23	2	Petition	109	Claims.						
Loomis, Daniel	Further compensation for extra work on Cumberland road.	24	1	Petition	143	Claims	776	Adverse.		Laid on table.		
Loomis, Daniel	Interest on his account as settled	22	1	Petition	114	Claims	Jan. 18, 183[illegible]	Adverse		Laid on table.		
Loomis, Erastus	Compensation, &c., as acting lieutenant marines on Lake Champlain.	14	1	Petition	283	Naval Affairs	Feb. 12, 1816	Favorable		Passed	Passed	App'd Mar. 25, 1816
Loomis, Erastus	Pension	15	2	Petition	288					Laid on table.		
Loomis, Erastus	Pension	19	1	Petition	342	Naval Affairs	Mar. 23, 1826	Adverse		Laid on table.		
Loomis, Erastus	Pension	19	2	Petition	155	Naval Affairs.						
Loomis, Gustavus	For settlement of accounts	14	1	Petition	291	Claims	Mar. 8, 1816	Favorable	116	Passed	Passed	App'd March 19, 1816
Loomis, Jacob	Pension	3	1	Rep. of Secretary War.	131	Select	May 26, 1794	Res. to refer to Sec. of War.	12	Passed	Passed	App'd June 9, 1794
Loomis, Jacob	Pension	6	1	Petition	578	Claims	Feb. 13, 1800	Adverse		Rejected.		
Loomis, Jacob	Pension	22	1	Petition	164	Rev. Pensions.						
Loomis, Jairus, and James Bassett.	Extra compensation for capture of post occupied by negroes and Indians.	15	1	Petition	127	Naval Affairs	Mar. 24, 1818	Favorable	158	Referred to Committee Whole House.		
Loomis, Jairus, and James Bassett.	Extra compensation for capture of post occupied by negroes and Indians.	15	2	House bill	181	Whole House	Jan. 13, 1819	With amend.	158	Passed	Rejected.	
Loomis, Jairus, and James Bassett.	Extra compensation for capture of post occupied by negroes and Indians	21	1	Petition	50	Naval Affairs	190	Favorable	239	Referred to Committee Whole House.		
Loomis, Jarius, and James Basset.	Extra compensation for capture of post occupied by negroes and Indians.	25	2	Petition	201	Naval Affairs	416	Favorable	422	Referred to Committee Whole House.		
Loomis, Jaius, and James Bassett.	Extra compensation for capture of post occupied by negroes and Indians.	25	3	House bill	378	Whole House	Feb. 8, 1839	With amend.	422	Passed	Passed	App'd March 3, 1839
Loomis, Jesse, widow of.	Commutation pay	22	2	Petition	119	Military Affairs	95	Favorable	737	Referred to Committee Whole House.		
Loomis, Jesse, widow of.	Commutation pay	23	1	Petition	35	Military Affairs	Dec. 20, 1833	Favorable	55	Passed	Passed	App'd June 19, 1834
Loomis, Leonard	Pension	24	2	Petition	212	Invalid Pensions	181	Favorable	903	Referred to Committee Whole House.		
Loomis, Leonard	Pension	25	2	Petition	38	Invalid Pensions	319	Favorable	361	Passed	Passed	App'd June 28, 1838
Loomis, Lucy	(See Jesse Loomis, widow of)	22	2		119							
Loomis, Ruth	(See Amasa Loomis, widow of)	30	1		165							
Loomis, Samuel	Pension	3	1	Rep. of Secretary War.	131	Select	May 26, 1794	Res. to refer to Sec. War.	12	Passed	Passed	App'd June 9, 1794
Loomis, Samuel	Pension	4	1	Rep. of Secretary War.	445	Claims	Feb. 18, 1796	Favorable	156	Passed	Passed	App'd April 20, 1796
Loomis, Samuel	Increase of pension	11	2	Pension bill	604	Whole House	Mar. 2, 1811	With amend.	218	Passed	Passed	App'd March 3, 1811
Loomis, Captain Thomas.	For the benefit of act May 15, 1828.	21	1	Resolution	207	Rev. Claims	Feb. 9, 1830	Adverse		Laid on table.		
Loomis, Uriah	Pension for revolutionary services.	27	3	Petition	240	Rev. Pensions.						
Loomis, Uriah	Pension for revolutionary services.	28	1	Petition	360	Rev. Pensions	324	Favorable	232	Passed.		
Loomis, Walter, and Abel Gay.	Payment of balance due for work on Cumberland road.	21	2	Petition	45	Claims	28	Adverse		Laid on table.		

List of private claims presented to the House of Representatives of the United States from the 1st to the 31st Congress, inclusive—Continued.

Names of claimants.	Nature or object of the claim.	Congress.	Session.	How brought before the House of Reps.	Page of journal.	To what committee of the House referred.	No. or date of the report.	Nature of the report.	No. of the bill.	How disposed of by the House of Reps.	How disposed of by the Senate.	Date of the act of Congress, and remarks.
Loomis, Walter, and Abel Gay.	Payment of balance due for work on Cumberland road.	23	2	Senate bill	428	Claims	Mar. 2, 1835	With amend.	73	Referred to Committee Whole House.		
Loomis, Walter, and Abel Gay.	Payment of balance due for work on Cumberland road.	24	1	Senate bill	320	Claims	Feb. 12, 1836	With amend.	27	Passed	Passed	App'd July 2, 1836
Loomis, Walter, and Abel Gay.	Addition to act of July 2, 1836	24	2	Senate bill	552	Claims	308	Adverse	134	Referred to Committee Whole House.		
Loomis, Walter, and Abel Gay.	Addition to act of July 2, 1836	25	2	Senate bill	605	Claims			146			
Loomis, Walter, and Abel Gay.	Addition to act of July 2, 1836	25	3	Senate bill	355	Claims			67			
Loomis, Walter, and Abel Gay.	Addition to act of July 2, 1836	26	1	Senate bill	189	Claims	363	Adverse	18	Referred to Committee Whole House.		
Loomis, Walter, and Abel Gay.	Addition to act of July 2, 1836	26	2	Senate bill	151	Claims	190	Adverse	127	Referred to Committee Whole House.		
Loomis, Walter, and Abel Gay.	Addition to act of July 2, 1836	29	1	Senate bill	1016	Claims	796	Favorable	69	Referred to Committee Whole House.		
Loomis, Walter, and Abel Gay.	Addition to act of July 2, 1836	30	1	Senate bill	366	Claims	Mar. 24, 1848	Favorable	63	Passed	Passed	App'd Mar. 29, 1848
Looney, John	Increase of pension	27	2	Petition	107	Invalid Pensions	141	Favorable	187	Passed	Passed	App'd Aug. 27, 1842
Looney, John	Arrears of pension	27	3	Petition	125	Invalid Pensions.						
Looney, John	Arrears of pension	28	1	Petition	717	Invalid Pensions.						
Lopez, Antonio	Confirmation of title to land	22	1	Resolution	86	Public Lands	Dec. 27, 1831	Favorable	125	Passed	Passed	App'd June 25, 1832
Lopez, Francisco	Confirmation of title to land	22	1	Resolution	86	Public Lands	Dec. 27, 1831	Favorable	125	Passed	Passed	App'd June 25, 1832
Lopez, Juan	Confirmation of title to land	19	2	Documents	50	Public Lands	49	Favorable	378	Referred to Committee Whole House.		
Lopez, Juan	Confirmation of title to land	24	1	Documents	155	Priv. Land Claims.	93	Favorable		Ordered to be printed.		
Lopez, Marie	Confirmation of title to land	22	1	Resolution	86	Public Lands	Dec. 27, 1831	Favorable	125	Passed	Passed	App'd June 25, 1832
Loranger, Joseph	Compensation for property destroyed by enemy.	23	1	Petition	489	Claims.						
Loranger, Joseph	Compensation for property destroyed by enemy.	23	2	Petition	59	Claims.						
Lord, Aaron	Pension	20	2	Petition	39	Military Pensions				Discharged.		
Lord, Aaron	Pension	22	1	Petition	124	Rev. Pensions.						
Lord, Archibald B., *et al.*	Additional portion of proceeds of brig condemned.	15	2	Petition	178	Naval Affairs.						
Lord, Asa, surety of	Release from liability	20	1	Petition	39	P. Of. & P. Roads.	Jan. 25, 1828	Adverse		Rejected.		
Lord, Daniel, widow of	Pension for revolutionary services.	25	2	Resolution	768	Rev. Pensions.						
Lord, Daniel, widow of	Pension for revolutionary services.	30	1	Petition	637	Rev. Pensions				Discharged; laid on table.		
Lord, Ebenezer and Sarah.	(See Nathaniel Byles, administratrix of.)	4	1		370							
Lord, Ebenezer	Pension for services in 1794	17	1	Petition	39	Pens. & Rev. Cl'ms.	Jan. 25, 1822	Adverse		Leave to withdraw.		
Lord, Ebenezer	Pension for services in 1794	18	1	Petition	69	Pens. & Rev. Cl'ms.	Dec. 31, 1823	Favorable	35	Passed	Passed	App'd May 19, 1824
Lord, Ebenezer	Pension for services in 1794	19	1	Petition	53	Military Pensions.						
Lord, Ebenezer	Pension for services in 1894	19	2	Petition	31	Military Pensions.						
Lord, Ebenezer	Pension for services in 1794	19	2	Pension bill	85	Whole House	Feb. 2, 1827	With amend.	314	Passed	Passed	App'd March 3, 1827
Lord, Ebenezer	Pension for services in 1794	21	1	Pension bill	130	Whole House	Feb. 12, 1830	With amend.	72	Passed	Passed	App'd May 20, 1830
Lord, Ebenezer	Pension for services in late war	18	2	Petition	58	Pens. & Rev. Cl'ms.						
Lord, Ebenezer	Pension for services in late war	20	1	Petition	30	Military Pensions	Feb. 13, 1828	Favorable	166	Passed.		
Lord, Ebenezer	Pension for services in late war	20	2	House bill	55	Whole House	Dec. 12, 1828	With amends.	311	Passed.		
Lord, Ebenezer	Increase of pension	21	1	Petition	48	Military Pensions.						
Lord, George	Pension	3	1	Rep. of Secretary War.	131	Select	May 26, 1794	Res. to refer to Sec. War.	12	Passed	Passed	App'd June 9, 1794

List of private claims presented to the House of Representatives of the United States from the 1st to the 31st Congress, inclusive—Continued.

Names of claimants.	Nature or object of the claim.	Congress.	Session.	How brought before the House of Reps.	Page of journal.	To what committee of the House referred.	No. or date of the report.	Nature of the report.	No. of the bill.	How disposed of by the House of Reps.	How disposed of by the Senate.	Date of the act of Congress, and remarks.
Lord, George	Pension	4	1	Rep. of Secretary War.	445	Claims	March 4, 1796	Favorable	156	Passed	Passed	App'd April 20, 1796
Lord, Hannah	(See Daniel Lord, widow of)	25	2		768							
Lord, John	Compensation as mariner on board the Ranger.	20	2	Petition	81	Rev. Claims.						
Lord, John	Compensation as mariner on board the Ranger.	21	1	Petition	98	Rev. Claims	178	Favorable	228	Referred to Committee Whole House.		
Lord, John	Compensation as mariner on board the Ranger.	21	2	House bill	264	Whole House	Feb. 4, 1831	With amend.	228	Passed.		
Lord, John	Compensation as mariner on board the Ranger.	23	1	Petition	43	Rev. Claims.						
Lord, John, representatives of.	Arrears of pay	22	1	Resolution	337	Rev. Claims.						
Lord, Mercy	(See Matthew Whaley, widow of)	26	1		706							
Lord, Nathan	Pension for revolutionary services.	21	2	Petition	42	Military Pensions.						
Lord, Nathan	Pension for revolutionary services.	22	1	Petition	45	Rev. Pensions				Discharged; laid on table.		
Lord, Samuel	Pension	23	2	Petition	237	Rev. Pensions				Discharged; laid on table.		
Lord, Samuel	Benefit of certain acts	26	1	Senate bill	836	Judiciary			254			
Lord, Samuel, executor of.	Indemnity for French spoliations prior to 1800.	26	1	Memorial	182	Foreign Affairs	346	Favorable	319	Referred to Committee Whole House.		
Lord, Samuel	(See Howe & Fitch, surety of)	27	2		224							
Lord, Samuel S.	Fishing bounty	23	1	Petition	212	Commerce	211	Favorable	231	Referred to Committee Whole House.		
Lord, Samuel S.	Fishing bounty	23	2	House bill	82	Whole House	Dec. 12, 1834	With amend.	231	Passed	Passed	App'd Jan. 27, 1835
Lord, Tobias, *et al.*	Compensation for erecting pier at Kennebunk river.	3	2	Petition	296	Select.						
Lord, Tobias, *et al.*	Compensation for erecting pier at Kennebunk river.	4	1	Petition and rep't Sec. of War.	402	Com. and Manuf.	Mar. 26, 1796	Favorable	165	Referred to Committee Whole House.		
Lorens, John	Confirmation of title to land	15	2	Petition	193	Priv. Land Claims.						
Lorens, John	Confirmation of title to land	17	1	Petition	54	Public Lands.						
Lorens, John	Confirmation of title to land	18	1	Petition	54	Public Lands.						
Loring, Caleb, *et al.*	Reimbursement of part of duties paid on iron.	22	1	Petition	257	Ways and Means.						
Loring, Charles G.	(See Israel Thorndike, executors of.)	29	2		129							
Loring, Charles G.	(See Abiel Winship.)	26	1		182		343		319			
Loring, Israel	Drawback on a quantity of indigo.	4	1	Petition	395	Com. and Manuf.	90	Favorable; bill ordered.	149	Passed	Passed	App'd Mar. 10, 1796
Loring, Jacob	Pension	22	1	Resolution	193	Rev. Pensions	367	Favorable	462	Passed	Indef. postp'd.	
Loring, Joseph	Pension as lieutenant in Colonel Knox's artillery.	3	1	Rep. of Secretary War.	131	Select	May 26, 1794	Res. to refer to Sec. War.	J. R. 12	Passed	Passed	App'd June 9, 1794
Loring, Joseph	Pension as artificer in Colonel Baldwin's regiment.	3	1	Rep. of Secretary War.	131	Select	May 26, 1794	Res. to refer to Sec. War.	J. R. 12	Passed	Passed	App'd June 9, 1794
Loring, Joseph.	Compensation for services in late war, and for losses by depreciation of Treasury notes	24	1	Petition	188	Claims	621	Adverse		Laid on table.		
Loring, Joseph, jr.	(See Seth Adams & J. Loring.)	9	1		226							
Loring, William	Compensation for revolutionary services.	2	1	Petition and rep't Sec. of War.	455					Laid on table.		
Lorkin, Josiah	(See Robert Smith, assignee of.)	30	1		262							

List of private claims presented to the House of Representatives of the United States from the 1st to the 31st Congress, inclusive—Continued.

Names of claimants.	Nature or object of the claim.	Congress.	Session.	How brought before the House of Reps.	Page of journal.	To what committee of the House referred.	No. or date of the report.	Nature of the report.	No. of the bill.	How disposed of by the House of Reps.	How disposed of by the Senate.	Date of the act of Congress, and remarks.
Lorman, William, (Md.)	Indemnity for French spoliations prior to 1800.	26	1	Memorial	182	Foreign Affairs	243	Favorable	319	Referred to Committee Whole House.		
Lorrain, Edwin, heirs of	(See Beverly Chew, *et al.*)	19	1		336							
Lorreins, Louis	(See Pelegie L. Juzon.)	23	1		220							
Losey, James Puff	(See John Logan, *et al.*)	4	1		466							
Loskey, Andrew	Pension for revolutionary services.	26	1	Petition	553	Rev. Pensions	423	Adverse		Laid on table.		
Losselle, Francois	Compensation for services of self and company, war of 1812.	22	2	Petition	32	Claims.						
Lott, Jesse	Pre-emption right to land in Alabama.	16	1	Petition	81	Public Lands	Jan. 4, 1820	Adverse		Laid on table.		
Lott, Johannes E., *et al.*	Compensation for board of American officers revolutionary war.	5	2	Memorial	144	Claims	Jan. 24, 1798	Adverse		Leave to withdraw.		
Lott, Johannes E., *et al.*	Compensation for board of American officers revolutionary war.	7	1	Memorial	60	Claims	Mar. 8, 1802	Adverse		Leave to withdraw.		
Lott, Johannes J	(See Johannes E. Lott, *et al.*)	5	2		144							
Lott, Nicholas	Pension	10	1	House bill	232	Select	Mar. 17, 1808	Favorable	78	Passed	Passed	App'd April 25, 1808
Lotz, Hervey	Pension for services as a marine in revolutionary war.	15	2	Petition	190	Rev. Pensions	Jan. 21, 1819	Adverse		Rejected.		
Lotz, Hervey	Arrears of pension	28	2	Petition	59	Rev. Pensions.				Discharged; laid on table.		
Loucks, Henry S	(See Caspor B. Cook, *et al.*)	30	1		272							
Loud, Eliphalet, & Samuel Bayley.	Redress for unlawful capture of vessel by officers of Russian government.	18	2	Petition	209	Commerce.						
Loud, Eliphalet, & Samuel Bayley.	Redress for unlawful capture of vessel by officers of Russian government.	19	1	Petition	66	Foreign Affairs	Jan. 6, 1826	Adverse		Leave to withdraw.		
Louderman, Catharine	(See John Londerman, mother of.)	16	2		88							
Louderman, John, mother of.	Pension	16	2	Petition	88	Pens. & Rev. Cl'ms.	Jan. 9, 1820	Adverse		Rejected.		
Louderman, John, mother of.	Pension	17	1	Petition	333					Leave to withdraw.		
Louderman, John, mother of.	Pension	18	1	Petition	196	Rev. Claims	58	Favorable	107	Passed	Passed	App'd May 19, 1824
Louderman,	(See Lauderman)											
Loudon, Giles	Pension	29	1	Petition	303	Invalid Pensions.						
Loudon, Giles	Pension	30	1	Petition	104	Invalid Pensions	714	Favorable	559	Referred to Committee Whole House.		
Loudon, Samuel	Compensation for supplies furnished during revolutionary war.	4	2	Petition	704	Claims.						
Loudon, Samuel	Compensation for supplies furnished during revolutionary war.	5	2	Petition	123	Claims	Jan. 4, 1798	Adverse		Rejected.		
Lough, George A	Pension for revolutionary services.	27	2	Petition	374	Rev. Pensions	784	Adverse		Laid on table.		
Loughrey, Archibald, heirs of.	Bounty land	29	2	Petition	67	Public Lands	30	Favorable	611	Referred to Committee Whole House.		
Loughrey, Archibald, heirs of.	Bounty land	30	1	Petition	182	Public Lands	May 26, 1848	Adverse		Laid on table.		
Loughrey, William	Reimbursement of overpayment for land.	18	1	Petition	78	Priv. Land Claims.	May 11, 1824	Favorable	227	Referred to Committee Whole House.		
Loughrey, William	Reimbursement of overpayment for land.	18	2	Petition	115	Priv. Land Claims.	Jan. 21, 1825	Adverse		Referred to Committee Whole House.		
Loughrey, William	Reimbursement of overpayment for land.	21	2	Petition	111	Public Lands				Discharged; laid on table.		

List of private claims presented to the House of Representatives of the United States form the 1st to the 31st Congress, inclusive—Continued.

Names of claimants.	Nature or object of the claim.	Congress.	Session.	How brought before the House of Reps.	Page of journal.	To what committee of the House referred.	No. or date of the report.	Nature of the report.	No. of the bill.	How disposed of by the House of Reps.	How disposed of by the Senate.	Date of the act of Congress, and remarks.
Louisiana, inhabitants of..	Confirmation of title to land held under requette of French and Spanish governors.	13	3	Petition	487	Public Lands.....	....	....	......	Discharged; laid on table.		
Louisiana, inhabitants of..	Confirmation of title to land held under requette of French and Spanish governors.	14	1	Petition	90	Public Lands	Mar. 23, 1816	Favorable; bill	......	Passed	Passed	App'd April 30, 1816
Louisiana, sundry inhabitants of, (formerly West Florida.)	Confirmation of Spanish grants and surveys in West Florida, issued prior to its being taken possession of by the United States.	14	1	Petition	360	Public Lands.						
Louisiana, sundry inhabitants of, (formerly West Florida.)	Confirmation of Spanish grants and surveys in West Florida, issued prior to its being taken possession of by the United States.	14	2	Petition	51	Public Lands.						
Louisiana, sundry inhabitants of, (formerly West Florida.)	Confirmation of Spanish grants and surveys in West Florida, issued prior to its being taken possession of by the United States.	15	1	Petition	108	Public Lands.						
Louisiana, sundry inhabitants of, (formerly West Florida.)	Confirmation of Spanish grants and surveys in West Florida, issued prior to its being taken possession of by the United States.	18	1	Petition	82	Public Lands.						
Louisiana, sundry inhabitants of, (formerly West Florida.)	Payment of claims adjudicated by Secretary of State, under act of April 18, 1814.	19	1	Resolution	450	Ways and Means.						
Louisiana, inhabitants of Bayon Bœuf.	Confirmation of their titles to land.	14	2	Petition	164	Public Lands.						
Louisiana, inhabitants of Bayon Bœuf.	Confirmation of their titles to land.	15	1	Petition	76	Public Lands.						
Louisiana, inhabitants of western land district.	For a revision of the decision of the board of land commissioners rejecting their claims.	14	2	Petition	438	Priv. Land Claims.						
Louisiana, inhabitants of western land district.	For a revision of the decision of the board of land commissioners rejecting their claims.	15	1	Petition	49	Priv. Land Claims.						
Louisiana, inhabitants of western land district.	Pre-emption right to land on which they reside.	15	1	Petition	102	Public Lands.						
Louisiana, New Orleans Navigation Company.	Confirmation of title to land.....	14	1	Senate bill	155	Public Lands	Jan. 23, 1816	With't amend.	......	Passed............	Passed	App'd April 16, 1816
Louisiana, inhabitants of Ouachita.	Confirmation of title to land used as a burying ground.	16	1	Resolution	209	Public Lands.						
Louisiana, inhabitants of Ouachita.	(See Baron de Bastrop.)											
Louisiana, inhabitants of East Baton Rouge.	Compensation for property taken by United States troops for public use in 1810.	17	1	Petition	26	Claims	Jan. 28, 1822	Adverse	......	Laid on table.		
Louisiana, inhabitants of East Baton Rouge.	Compensation for property taken by United States troops for public use in 1810.	18	1	Petition	77	Claims	Jan. 23, 1824	Adverse	......	Laid on table.		
Louisiana, inhabitants of East Baton Rouge.	Compensation for property taken by United States troops for public use in 1810.	19	1	Petition	83	Claims.						

List of private claims presented to the House of Representatives of the United States from the 1st to the 31st Congress, inclusive—Continued.

Names of claimants.	Nature or object of the claim.	Congress.	Session.	How brought before the House of Reps.	Page of journal.	To what committee of the House referred.	No. or date of the report.	Nature of the report.	No. of the bill.	How disposed of by the House of Reps.	How disposed of by the Senate.	Date of the act of Congress, and remarks.
Louisiana, inhabitants of East Baton Rouge.	Compensation for property taken by United States troops for public use in 1810.	19	2	Petition	54	Claims	Jan. 24, 1827	Adverse	......	Laid on table.		
Louisiana, inhabitants of East Baton Rouge.	Compensation for property taken by United States troops for public use in 1810.	20	1	Petition	127	Claims	Jan. 28, 1828	Adverse	......	Laid on table		
Louisiana, inhabitants of East Baton Rouge.	For an adjudication of their Spanish land claims.	24	1	Memorial	155	Priv. Land Claims.						
Louisiana, sundry inhabitants of.	Confirmation of land titles	17	1	Petition	201	Public Lands.						
Louisiana, sundry inhabitants of.	Confirmation of land titles	20	1	Petition	52	Public Lands	Jan. 25, 1828	By bill	109	Referred to Committee Whole House.		
Louisiana, inhabitants of New Orleans.	Land in lieu of college buildings, which have been converted into a court-house.	15	1	Petition	317	Com. and Manuf.						
Louisiana, Planters' Bank of New Orleans.	Refunding money advanced upon pay rolls of United States army.	16	2	Res. and docs.	245	Claims.						
Louisiana, Planters' Bank of New Orleans.	Refunding money advanced upon pay rolls of United States army.	17	1	Senate bill	316	Ways and Means.	March 6, 1822	With't amend.	S. 30	Passed	Passed	App'd May 8, 1822
Louisiana, Mayor, &c., of New Orleans.	Permission to sell, for building lots, a portion of the quays in said city.	20	1	Memorial	100	Priv. Land Claims.						
Louisiana, inhabitants of St. Helena.	Pre-emption right to certain lands.	20	1	Resolution	85	Public Lands	Dec. 24, 1827	Favorable; bill	21	Passed	Passed	App'd Mar. 19, 1828
Louisiana, inhabitants of Point Coupee.	Confirmation of title to land	11	2	Petition	142	Public Lands.						
Louisiana, inhabitants of Point Coupee.	Confirmation of title to land	11	3	Petition	456	Public Lands.						
Louisiana, inhabitants of Assumption.	Confirmation of title to land	12	1	Petition	269	Public Lands.						
Louisiana Board of Land Commissioners, clerk and translator of.	Increase of compensation	10	2	Resolution	510	Public Lands.						
Louisiana, city of New Orleans.	For a grant of all the lands made vacant by laying off said city into streets, squares, &c.	18	1	Resolution	305	Public Lands.						
Louisiana, city of New Orleans.	Confirmation of title to a square in said city.	26	1	Petition	353	Judiciary.						
Louisiana, city of New Orleans.	Confirmation of title to a square in said city.	27	2	Petition	771	Judiciary.						
Louisiana, legislature of	For a grant of land in the city of New Orleans for certain purposes.	19	1	Resolution	185	Public Lands	....	....	......	Discharged; laid on table.		
Louisiana, legislature of	Permission to exchange school lands which prove valueless, for other lands.	30	1	Memorial	458	Public Lands	794	Adverse	......	Laid on table.		
Louisiana, legislature of	Indemnity in land to the parish of Point Coupee, for erecting levee to protect government property.	23	1	Resolution	385	Priv. Land Claims.						
Louisiana, legislature of	Confirmation of title to the cypress swamps in said State.	18	1	Resolution	201	Public Lands.						
Louisiana, legislature of	Confirmation of title to the cypress swamps in said State.	19	1	Resolution	49	Public Lands	....	....	......	Discharged; laid on table.		

List of private claims presented to the House of Representatives of the United States from the 1st to the 31st Congress, inclusive—Continued.

Names of claimants.	Nature or object of the claim.	Congress.	Session.	How brought before the House of Reps.	Page of journal.	To what committee of the House referred.	No. or date of the report.	Nature of the report.	No. of the bill.	How disposed of by the House of Reps.	How disposed of by the Senate.	Date of the act of Congress, and remarks.
Louisiana, legislature of...	Confirmation of title to the cypress swamps in said State.	20	1	Resolution	201	Public Lands	....	....	......	Discharged; laid on table.		
Louisiana, legislature of...	Refunding amount expended in equiping Florida volunteers.	27	2	Senate bill	155	Military Affairs...	Mar. 8, 1842	With amend's.	S. 57	Passed	Passed	App'd Aug. 30, 1842
Louisiana, Catholic church of St. John the Baptist.	Refunding money paid to United States for land previously granted it by Spanish government.	21	2	Memorial	302	Public Lands.						
Louisiana, collector of the district of Teche.	For additional salary	22	1	Resolution	561	Commerce.						
Louisiana, merchants of N. Orleans.	Refunding excess of duties paid under tariff of 1828.	21	2	Memorial	301	Ways and Means.						
Louisiana, Commercial bank of New Orleans.	For leave to import iron water-pipes free of duty.	23	1	Petition	145	Ways and Means.						
Louisiana, corporation of New Orleans.	For the relinquishment of the right set up by the United States to the quay in said city.	23	1	Memorial	219	Judiciary	400	Favorable; bill	420	Referred to Committee Whole House.		App'd June 17, 1844
Louisiana, New Orleans Branch pilots.	Pre-emption right to land at Plaquamines.	28	1	Petition	77	Priv. Land Claims.	9	Favorable; bill	35	Passed	Passed	
Louisiana, inhabitants of La Fourche.	For a grant of land to aid in preserving the outlet to Lake du Boeuf.	23	1	Petition	442	Roads and Canals.						
Louisiana, surveyor of Port Pontchartrain.	To be allowed a salary and office rent.	23	1	Resolution	514	Commerce.						
Louisiana, sundry inhabitants of.	Land in lieu of land bought by them from the Spanish government, but since sold by the United States.	21	1	Memorial	150	Foreign Affairs.						
Louisiana, Mexican Gulf Railroad Company.	Remission of duty on railroad iron.	28	1	Petition	729	Commerce.						
Louisiana, clerks in the Custom-house at New Orleans.	For arrears due on their salaries ..	28	2	Petition	56	Commerce.	114	Favorable......	......	Referred to Committee Whole House.		
Louisiana, New Orleans and Carrollton Railroad Company.	Release of certain judgments against them.	26	2	Petition	132	Commerce.						
Louisiana, New Orleans and Carrollton Railroad Company.	Belease of certain judgments against them.	28	1	Petition	77	Commerce	90	Favorable; bill	105	Referred to Committee Whole House.		
Louisiana, inhabitants of Carroll parish.	Compensation for making a levee on the Mississippi river.	28	1	Petition	623	Claims.						
Louisiana, Red river Railroad Company.	Remission of duty on railroad iron.	28	1	Petition	552	Commerce.						
Louisiana, Red river Railroad Company.	Remission of duty on railroad iron.	28	2	Petition	112	Commerce.						
Louisiana, Red river Railroad Company.	To cancel bonds for duty on railroad iron.	29	1	Petition	593	Commerce	436	Favorable; bill	304	Referred to Committee Whole House.		
Louisiana, Red river Railroad Company.	To cancel bonds for duty on railroad iron.	30	1	Petition	99	Commerce.......	Jan. 25, 1848	Favorable; bill	106	Passed	Passed	App'd Aug. 11, 1848
Louisiana, surviv'g defenders of New Orleans.	Bounty land..................	28	1	Petition	370	Military Affairs.						
Louisiana, surviv'g defenders of New Orleans.	Bounty land..................	29	1	Petition	398	Military Affairs.						

List of private claims presented to the House of Representatives of the United States from the 1st to the 31st Congress, inclusive—Continued.

Names of claimants.	Nature or object of the claim.	Congress.	Session.	How brought before the House of Reps.	Page of journal.	To what committee of the House referred.	No. or date of the report.	Nature of the report.	No. of the bill.	How disposed of by the House of Reps.	How disposed of by the Senate.	Date of the act of Congress, and remarks.
Louisiana, registers and receiver of the land office at Greensburgh.	Compensation for locating military land warrants.	31	1	Petition	511	Public Lands.						
Louisiana, revenue officers at New Orleans.	Increased compensation	31	2	Petition	226	Ways and Means.						
Louisiana, West Feliciana Railroad Company.	Reimbursement of duties paid on railroad iron.	27	3	Senate bill	446	Ways and Means.	Feb. 28, 1843	With't amend.	S. 58	Laid on table.		
Louisiana, West Feliciana Railroad Company.	Remission of duty on railroad iron	28	1	Petition	85	Ways and Means.						
Louisiana, West Feliciana Railroad Company.	Remission of duty on railroad iron	28	2	Petition	120	Ways and Means.						
Louisiana, West Feliciana Railroad Company.	Release of judgment for duties on railroad iron.	30	1	Bill on leave	793	Ways and Means.			477			
Louisiana, West Feliciana Railroad Company.	Release of judgment for duties on railroad iron.	31	1	Senate bill	1315	Ways and Means.			S. 261			
Louisiana, clerks in the post office at New Orleans.	Increased compensation	31	2	Petition	280	P. Of. and P. Roads.						
Louisville and Portland Canal Company.	(See Kentucky, Louisville, and Portland Canal Company.	24	1		108							
Lounsberry, Nathan M.	Arrears of pension	29	1	Petition	54	Rev. Pensions.						
Lounsbury, Joshua	Compensation for revolutionary services and supplies furnished.	3	1	Petition	185					Laid on table.		
Louttit, Joshua, representatives of.	Payment for services as quartermaster's clerk in revolutionary war.	4	2	Petition	630	Claims	Jan. 13, 1797	Adverse		Rejected.		
Love, Alexander	Confirmation of title to land	20	2	Petition	205	Priv. Land Claims.						
Love, Alexander	Confirmation of title to land	21	1	Petition	52	Priv. Land Claims.	125	Favorable	165	Passed	Passed	App'd May 29, 1830
Love, Charles	Arrears of pension	25	3	Petition	461	Invalid Pensions.						
Love, David	Grant of land for revolutionary services.	20	1	Petition	33	Rev. Claims	Dec. 18, 1838	Adverse		Laid on table.		
Love, George	Payment of money due from United States.	18	2	Petition	186	Claims	65	Favorable	329	Passed	Passed	App'd March 3, 1825
Love, James	(See James Miller and James Love, heirs of.)	16	2		431							
Love, John, (Md.)	Confirmation of title to land	20	1	Petition	46	Priv. Land Claims.	Jan. 8, 1828	Adverse		Laid on table.		
Love, John, (Md.)	Confirmation of title to land	21	1	Petition	473	Priv. Land Claims.						
Love, John, (Tenn.)	Military bounty land	22	2	Resolution	286	Public Lands.						
Love, Robert	(See Stephen Decatur, widow of, *et al*.)	20	1		295							
Love, Rufus King	Compensation for horse lost in public service.	26	1	Petition	336	Claims	684	Adverse		Laid on table.		
Love, Samuel	(See James Drybread, assignee of)	15	2		21							
Love, Valentine	Confirmation of title to land	15	1	Petition	267	Priv. Land Claims.						
Love, Valentine	Confirmation of title to land	15	2	Petition	207	Priv. Land Claims.						
Love, Valentine	Confirmation of title to land	16	1	Petition	72	Priv. Land Claims.						
Love, Valentine	Confirmation of title to land	17	1	Petition	54	Public Lands.						
Love, Valentine	Confirmation of title to land	18	1	Petition	54	Public Lands.						
Love, William	Pension	3	1	Rep. of Secretary War.	131	Select	May 26, 1794	Res. to refer to Sec. War.	J.R. 12	Passed	Passed	App'd June 9, 1794
Love, William	Pension	8	2	Petition	21	Claims				Discharged: referred to Com. Whole House.		
Love, William	Pension	9	1	Petition	196	Claims.						
Love, William	Pension	9	2	Petition	575	Claims				Leave to withdraw.		

List of private claims presented to the House of Representatives of the United States from the 1st to the 31st Congress, inclusive—**Continued.**

Names of claimants.	Nature or object of the claim.	Congress.	Session.	How brought before the House of Reps.	Page of journal.	To what committee of the House referred.	No. or date of the report.	Nature of the report.	No. of the bill.	How disposed of by the House of Reps.	How disposed of by the Senate.	Date of the act of Congress, and remarks.
Loveain, Alfred, (La.)	Additional compensation as receiver.	15	1	Petition	151	Claims.						
Lovegrove, Hampton	Pension for revolutionary services.	24	2	Petition	271	Rev. Pensions	168	Adverse		Laid on table.		
Lovejoy, George H	Relief for blindness—afflicted while in service of United States.	9	1	Petition	222	Claims	Jan. 10, 1806	Adverse		Rejected.		
Lovejoy, Henry	Compensation for property destroyed by British.	21	1	Petition	98	Claims.						
Lovejoy, Jacob	Pension	29	1	Documents	806	Invalid Pensions.						
Lovejoy, John N	Indemnity for property destroyed by enemy.	13	3	Petition	511	Claims	Nov. 11, 1814	Adverse.		Rejected.		
Lovejoy, John N	Indemnity for property destroyed by enemy.	14	2	Petition	212	Claims.						
Lovejoy, John N	Indemnity for property destroyed by enemy.	15	1	Petition	237	Claims	Feb. 18, 1818	Adverse		Leave to withdraw.		
Lovejoy, Joshua	Pens on	3	2	Rep. of Secretary War.	278	Claims	Feb. 28, 1795	Favorable	130	Passed	Postponed.	
Lovejoy, Joshua	Pension	4	1	Rep. of Secretary War.	445	Claims	Feb. 18, 1796	Favorable	156	Passed	Passed	App'd April 20, 1796
Lovejoy, Joshua	Increase of pension	10	1	House bill	232	Whole House	Mar. 17, 1808	Favorable	78	Passed	Passed	App'd April 25, 1808
Lovejoy, Joshua	Increase of pension	10	2	Petition	540					Referred to Secretary War.		
Lovejoy, Joshua	Indemnity for property destroyed by British.	15	2	Petition	182	Claims.						
Lovejoy, Joshua	Indemnity for property destroyed by British.	17	1	Petition	46	Claims.						
Lovejoy, Samuel	Pension for revolutionary services.	18	2	Petition	185	Rev. Pensions	Feb. 19, 1825	Adverse		Laid on table.		
Loveland, Samuel W	Arrears of pension	27	2	Petition	47	Invalid Pensions	210	Adverse		Laid on table.		
Loveless, Mary	(See Hugh Smith, heirs of)	18	1		82							
Lovell, C. S., and others	Reimbursement of expenses at Old Point Comfort.	30	2	Petition	117	Military Affairs.						
Lovell, Elizabeth	(See Robert Lovell, widow of)	2	1		529							
Lovell, James	(See Benjamin Hallet, *et al*)	18	1		235							
Lovell, Robert, widow of	Depreciation pay for revolutianary services.	2	1	Petition	529					Referred to Secretary War.		
Lovell, Robert, widow of	Depreciation pay for revolutionary services.	3	2	Petition	309	Claims.						
Lovell, Robert, widow of	Depreciation pay for revolutionary services.	4	1	Rep. of Secretary War.	373	Claims	Jan. 6, 1796	Adverse		Leave to withdraw.		
Lovely, L. S., widow of	Relief in case of land illegally taken from her.	21	1	Petition	53	Public Lands.						
Lovely, L. S., widow of	Relief in case of land illegally taken from her.	21	2	Petition	112	Public Lands	Jan. 6, 1831	Favorable	541	Passed	Passed	App'd March , 1831
Lovely, Persis	(See L. S. Lovely, widow of)	21	1		53							
Lovely, Persis	Change of life estate in land to fee simple title.'	22	2	Petition	132	Public Lands				Discharged; laid on table.		
Lovett, Daniel	Pension for naval service in revolutionary war.	17	2	Petition	165	Pens. & Rev. Cl'ms.	Feb. 3, 1823	Adverse		Laid on table.		
Lovett, John J	Benefit of acts for purchasers of public land.	18	1	Petition	69	Public Lands.						
Lovred, Mary	(See William McGhee, heirs of)	30	1		398							
Low, Alche	(See Daniel Low, mother of)	15	1		277							
Low, Alexander	Compensation for revolutionary services.	2	1	Petition	452					Referred to Secretary War.		

List of private claims presented to the House of Representatives of the United States from the 1st to the 31st Congress, inclusive—Continued

Names of claimants.	Nature or object of the claim.	Congress.	Session.	How brought before the House of Reps.	Page of journal.	To what committee of the House referred.	No. or date of the report.	Nature of the report.	No. of the bill.	How disposed of by the House of Reps.	How disposed of by the Senate.	Date of the act of Congress, and remarks.
Low, Alexander	Compensation for revolutionary services.	2	2	Rep. of Secretary War.	735	....	....	....	......	Laid on table.		
Low, Andrew	(See Low, Taylor, & Co., assignee of.)	25	2	....	194							
Low, Andrew, & Co	Remission of duties on goods destroyed by fire.	16	1	Petition	194	Ways and Means	....	....	......	Discharged: laid on table.		
Low, Andrew, & Co	Remission of duties on goods de stroyed by fire.	18	1	Petition	237	Ways and Means.						
Low, Andrew, & Co	Remission of duties on goods destoyed by fire.	22	2	Petition	27	Commerce.						
Low, Andrew, & Co	Remission of duties on goods destroyed by fire.	23	2	Petition	196	Commerce.						
Low, Andrew, & Co	Remission of duties on goods destroyed by fire.	26	1	Petition	600	Commerce.						
Low, Catharine	Relief for loss of husband, two sons, and son-in-law in United States service.	15	1	Resolution	252	Military Affairs	....	....	......	Discharged; referred to Com. Whole House.		
Low, Christiana	(See Cornelius T. Janson, widow of.)	26	1	....	286							
Low, Daniel, mother of	Pension for services of son	15	1	Petition	277	Pens. & Rev. Cl'ms.						
Low, Henry	Bounty land for revolutionary services.	16	1	Petition	66	Rev. Pensions.						
Low, James	Pension	29	1	Senate bill	1075	Naval Affairs	July 24, 1846	Favorable	85	Passed	Passed	App'd Aug. 3, 1846
Low, James W., *et al.*	For part of proceeds of captured vessel.	15	1	Petition	366	Naval Affairs	....	....	......	Discharged; laid on table.		
Low, James W., *et al.*	For part of proceeds of captured vessel.	16	1	Petition	272	Judiciary.						
Low, James W., *et al.*	For part of proceeds of captured vessel.	30	1	Petition	807	Naval Affairs.						
Low, James W., *et al.*	For part of proceeds of captured vessel.	31	1	Petition	371	Commerce	330	Favorable	287	Referred to Committee Whole House.		
Low, James W., *et al.*	For part of proceeds of captured vessel.	31	2	Rep't Committee Whole House.	181	....	....	....	287	Passed.		
Low, John	Additional compensation as tax collector.	7	2	Petition	272	Claims	Feb. 1, 1803	Adverse	......	Rejected.		
Low, John	Indemnity for French spoliations prior to 1800.	26	1	Memorial	182	Foreign Affairs	343	Favorable	319	Referred to Committee Whole House.		
Low, John	Pension	15	2	House bill	41	....	....	....	203	Passed	Passed	App'd March 3, 1819
Low, John J	Pension for revolutionary services.	21	2	Petition	48	Military Pensions.						
Low, Jonathan, jr., *et al.*	For proceeds of vessel captured	13	3	Petition	633	Naval Affairs	Mar. 3, 1815	Adverse	......	Laid on table.		
Low, Rachael	(See Ebenezer Francis, heirs of.)	28	2	....	216							
Low, Taylor, & Co., assignee of.	Reimbursement of money	25	2	Memorial	194	Ways and Means	....	....	......	Discharged.		
Low, Taylor, & Co., assignee of.	Reimbursement of money	26	1	Petition	178	Ways and Means	5	Favorable	22	Passed	Indef. postp'd.	
Low, Taylor, & Co., assignee of.	Reimbursement of money	31	2	Petition	37	Commerce.						
Low, Willis F	Compensation for horse lost in Florida war.	26	1	Petition	623	Claims.						
Low, Willis F	Compensation for horse lost in Florida war.	26	2	Petition	38	Claims.						
Low, Willis F	Compensation for horse lost in Florida war.	27	2	Documents	792	Claims	....	....	......	....	....	See General bill, No. 309.

List of private claims presented to the House of Representatives of the United States from the 1st to the 31st Congress, inclusive—Continued.

Names of claimants.	Nature or object of the claim.	Congress.	Session.	How brought before the House of Reps.	Page of journal.	To what committee of the House referred.	No. or date of the report.	Nature of the report.	No. of the bill.	How disposed of by the House of Reps.	How disposed of by the Senate.	Date of the act of Congress, and remarks.
Low, Willis F.	Compensation for horse lost in Florida war.	27	3	Petition	43	Claims.						
Low,	(See Lowe.)											
Lowden, John	Drawback on goods exported	16	2	Petition	153	Commerce.				Discharged; laid on table.		
Lowdon, John	(See John Paul Jones, heirs of.)	24	2		269							
Lowe, Barton	Pension	21	2	Resolution	56	Military Pensions				Discharged; laid on table.		
Lowe, Barton	Pension	22	1	Petition	105	Military Pensions				Discharged; laid on table.		
Lowe, Catharine	(See Cornelius Lowe, widow of.)	24	2		212							
Lowe, Cornelius, widow of.	Pension	24	2	Resolution	212	Invalid Pensions				Discharged; laid on table.		
Lowe, Isaac	Compensation for horse lost in Seminole war.	23	1	Documents	154	Claims.						
Lowe, Isaac	(See William H. Bedford, agent.)	28	1		262							
Lowe, Captain James	Compensation in land for services to crew and cargo of brig Despatch.	24	1	Petition	140	Foreign Affairs.						
Lowe, Captain James	Compensation in land for services to crew and cargo of brig Despatch.	25	2	Petition	76	Naval Affairs	Jan. 18, 1838	Favorable	426	Referred to Committee Whole House.		
Lowe, Captain James	Compensation in land for services to crew and cargo of brig Despatch.	25	3	Rep't Committee Whole House.	378				426	Passed.		
Lowe, Captain James	Compensation in land for services to crew and cargo of brig Despatch.	26	1	Petition	179	Naval Affairs.						
Lowe, Captain James	Compensation in land for services to crew and cargo of brig Despatch.	26	2	Petition	37	Naval Affairs.						
Lowe, Captain James	Compensation in land for services to crew and cargo of brig Despatch.	27	2	Petition	63	Naval Affairs	565	Favorable	360	Ordered to 3d reading.		
Lowe, Captain James	Compensation in land for services to crew and cargo of brig Despatch.	27	3	House bill	87				360	Passed	Passed	App'd March 1, 1843
Lowe, Captain James	Permission to assign a section of land.	28	1	Joint resolution	989				J.R. 37	Passed	Passed	App'd June 17, 1844
Lowe, Joseph	Indemnity for French spoliations prior to 1800.	26	1	Memorial	182	Foreign Affairs	343	Favorable	319	Referred to Committee Whole House.		
Lowell, Abner, *et al.*	Bounty on fishing schooner William.	27	2	Petition	318	Commerce	1000	Favorable	580	Referred to Committee Whole House.		
Lowell, Abner, *et al.*	Bounty on fishing schooner William.	27	3	Rep't Committee Whole House.	91				580	Passed	Indef. postp'd.	
Lowell, Abner, *et al.*	Bounty on fishing schooner William.	30	1	Petition	203	Commerce.						
Lowell, Abner, *et al.*	Bounty on fishing schooner William.	31	1	Petition	583	Commerce.						
Lowell, James and R. Clay.	Remission of duty on goods burnt.	24	2	Petition	40	Ways and Means	208	Adverse		Laid on table.		
Lowell, James and R. Clay.	Remission of duty on goods burnt.	25	2	Petition	112	Ways and Means	522	Adverse		Laid on table.		
Lowell, John	Pension for revolutionary services.	22	1	House bill	580	Rev. Pensions	438	Favorable	542	Ref'd to Com. W. H.		

List of private claims presented to the House of Representatives of the United States from the 1st to the 31st Congress, inclusive—Continued.

Names of claimants.	Nature or object of the claim.	Congress.	Session.	How brought before the House of Reps.	Page of journal.	To what committee of the House referred.	No. or date of the report.	Nature of the report.	No. of the bill.	How disposed of by the House of Reps.	How disposed of by the Senate.	Date of the act of Congress, and remarks.
Lowell, John, widow of	(See Benjamin Bailey, *et al.*)	19	1		98							
Lowell, Mary Ann	(See Noah Wiseman, heirs of.)	26	1		296							
Lowell, Thomas	Compensation for information of fraudulent pensions.	21	1	Petition	98	Claims	Jan. 8, 1830	Adverse		Laid on table.		
Lowell, Thomas	Compensation for taking testimony relative to fraudulent pension cases.	21	1	Petition	318	Claims	March 2, 1830	Adverse		Laid on table.		
Lowell, William	Pension	3	2	Rep. of Secretary War.	278	Claims	Mar. 2, 1795	Res. to refer to Sec. War.		Resolution adopted.		
Lowell, William	Pension	4	1	Rep. of Secretary War.	445	Claims	Feb. 18, 1796	Favorable	156	Passed	Passed	App'd April 20, 1796
Lower, Hartman	Pension for revolutionary services.	20	1	Resolution	356	Military Pensions				Discharged; laid on table.		
Lower, Hartman	Pension for revolutionary services.	20	1	House bill	645	Whole House	May 16, 1828	With amend.	283	Passed	Postponed.	
Lower, Hartman	Pension for revolutionary services.	20	2	House bill	55	Whole House	Dec. 12, 1828	With amend.	311	Passed	Laid on table.	
Lower, Hartman	Pension for revolutionary services.	20	2	Petition	26	Military Pensions				Discharged; laid on table.		
Lower, Hartman	Pension for revolutionary services.	21	1	Pension bill	130	Whole House	Feb. 12, 1830	With amend.	72	Passed	Passed	App'd May 20, 1830
Lowery, Phineas	(See William Baker.)	22	1		288		480					
Lowman, Emory	Pension	14	1	House bill	622	Pens. & Rev. Cl'ms.	April 11, 1816	Favorable	171	Passed	Passed	App'd April 30, 1816
Lowman, John	Pension for services in Wayne's army.	18	2	Petition	41	Pens. & Rev. Cl'ms.	Dec. 22, 1824	Adverse		Laid on table.		
Lowry, Catharine	(See Wm. Stevenson, widow of.)	4	1		409							
Lowry, David	(See E. Baldridge, sureties of)	14	2		76							
Lowry, Heman	Compensation for services as pension agent.	28	2	Petition	235	Claims.						
Lowry, Heman	Compensation for services as pension agent.	29	1	Petition	67	Claims.						
Lowry, Heman	Compensation for services as pension agent.	29	2	Petition	164	Claims.						
Lowry, Heman	Compensation fer services as pension agent.	30	1	Petition	154	Claims	248	Adverse		Laid on table.		
Lowry, John	Relief for wounds received in blasting rocks for government.	6	1	Petition	577	Claims				Discharged.		
Lowry, John	Compensation as attorney for Cherokees.	25	2	Documents	426	Indian Affairs	916	Adverse		Laid on table.		
Lowry, John, (Md)	Increase of pension	8	2	Petition	100	Whole House.						
Lowry, John, (Md)	Increase of pension	9	1	Petition	198	Claims	Mar. 28, 1806	Adverse		Indefinitely postponed; leave to withdraw.		
Lowry, John, (Md)	Increase of pension	10	2	Pension bill	499	Whole House	Feb. 20, 1809	With't amend.	158	Passed	Passed	App'd March 3, 1809
Lowry, John, heirs of	Bounty land for revolutionary services.	25	2	Petition	270	Rev. Claims				Discharged; laid on table.		
Lowry, Robert J	Pension	14	1	Resolution	499	Pens. & Rev. Cl'ms.	April 11, 1816	Favorable	171			Became a law without petitioner's name.
Lowry, Robert J	Pension	14	2	Resolution	119	Pens. & Rev. Cl'ms.	Jan. 29, 1817	Favorable	91	Passed	Passed	App'd March 3, 1817
Lowry, Samuel	Compensation for horse and other property lost in public service.	14	2	Petition	33	Claims				Discharged; laid on table.		
Lowry, S. B	Compensation for services as interpreter.	31	1	Amend't to House bill.	1034				334	Passed	Passed	App'd Sept. 30, 1850
Lowry, Thomas J	Compensation for improvement on land claimed.	25	2	Petition	200	Priv. Land Claims.				Discharged; laid on table.		

List of private claims presented to the House of Representatives of the United States from the 1st to the 31st Congress, inclusive—Continued.

Names of claimants.	Nature or object of the claim.	Congress.	Session.	How brought before the House of Reps.	Page of journal.	To what committee of the House referred.	No. or date of the report.	Nature of the report.	No. of the bill.	How disposed of by the House of Reps.	How disposed of by the Senate.	Date of the act of Congress, and remarks.
Lowther, Jesse	Pension	22	2	Petition	26	Invalid Pensions				Discharged; laid on table.		
Lowzadar, Agnes	Renewal of privateer pension law	25	2	Memorial	171	Naval Affairs				Discharged; laid on table.		
Loyd, John	Compensation for military services	29	1	Petition	461	Claims.						
Loyd, Owen	Pension for revolutionary services	25	2	Resolution	162	Rev. Pensions				Disch'd; laid on table.		
Loyd, Owen	Pension for revolutionary services	28	1	Resolution	332	Rev. Pensions.						
Loyd, Robin, or Indian Robin.	Pension for revolutionary services	26	1	Documents	324	Rev. Pensions.						
Loyer, John, representatives of.	Leave to locate a section of land in Arkansas.	24	1	Petition	751	Priv. Land Claims.						
Loyer, John, representatives of.	Leave to locate a section of land in Arkansas.	24	2	Petition	49	Priv. Land Claims.						
Loyless, R. J.	(See Geo. B. Russell and others.)	29	2		210							
Lozier, Abraham	Pension	20	1	Petition	396	Military Pensions.						
Lozier, Arbaham	Pension	21	1	Petition	82	Military Pensions				Discharged; laid on table.		
Luc, Peter, wife of	Grant of land at Galliopolis	5	2	Senate bill	225	Select	June 13, 1798	Favorable	S. 13	Passed	Passed	App'd June 25, 1798
Lucas, Barnabas	Pension	1	3	Petition and rep't Sec. of War.	339					Laid on table.		
Lucas, Charles	(See S. and P. Jones, assignee of)	15	1		102							
Lucas, Elijah, heir of	Compensation for revolutionary services.	22	1	Petition	224	Rev. Claims	Feb. 8, 1832	Adverse		Laid on table.		
Lucas, Elisha	Pension for revolutionary services	23	1	Res. and petition.	106, 242	Rev. Pensions	261	Favorable	300	Referred to Committee Whole House.		
Lucas, Elisha	Pension for revolutionary services	24	1	Petition	107	Rev. Pensions	150	Favorable	158	Passed	Passed	App'd June 28, 1836
Lucas, George	Payment of claim barred by statute	4	1	Memorial	425	Claims	May 7, 1796	Adverse		Rejected.		
Lucas, George	Compensation for revolutionary services.	4	2	Petition	627	Claims	Jan. 10, 1797	Adverse		Rejected.		
Lucas, George	Restoration of pension	20	1	Resolution	465	Military Pensions				Discharged; laid on table.		
Lucas, George	Restoration of pension	20	1	House bill	645	Whole House	May 16, 1828	With amend.	283	Passed	Postponed.	
Lucas, George	Restoration of pension	20	2	House bill	55	Whole House	Dec. 12, 1828	With amend.	311	Passed	Laid on table.	
Lucas, George	Restoration of pension	21	1	Petition	48	Military Pensions				Discharged; laid on table.		
Lucas, George	Restoration of pension	21	1	Pension bill	130	Whole House	Feb. 12, 1830	With amend.	72	Passed	Passed	App'd May 20, 1830
Lucas, Henry, and A. P. King.	Compensation for wagon, &c., taken for public use.	25	2	Petition	397	Claims.						
Lucas, Henry, and A. P. King.	Compensation for wagon, &c., taken for public use.	26	1	Senate bill	837	Claims	May 16, 1840	With't amend.	292	Referred to Committee Whole House.		
Lucas, Henry, and A. P. King.	Compensation for wagon, &c., taken for public use.	26	1	Amend. to H. B.	1355				27	Passed	Passed	App'd July 21, 1840
Lucas, Ignatius	Increase of compensation as watchman.	25	2	Petition	923	Naval Affairs.						
Lucas, Ignatius	Increase of compensation as watchman.	26	1	Petition	180	Naval Affairs	544	Adverse		Laid on table.		
Lucas, Jesse	(See Samuel Lucas, children, &c., of.)	27	2		613							
Lucas, John	(See William H. Bedford, agent)	28	2		262							
Lucas, John B. C., and C. B. Pemose.	Additional compensation as land commissioners.	14	1	Petition	258	Public Lands.						
Lucas, John B. C., and C. B. Pemose.	Additional compensation as land commissioners.	15	2	Petition	52	Select	37	Favorable	228	Postponed.		

List of private claims presented to the House of Representatives of the United States from the 1st to the 31st Congress, inclusive—Continued.

Names of claimants.	Nature or object of the claim.	Congress.	Session.	How brought before the House of Reps.	Page of journal.	To what committee of the House referred.	No. or date of the report.	Nature of the report.	No. of the bill.	How disposed of by the House of Reps.	How disposed of by the Senate.	Date of the act of Congress, and remarks.
Lucas, John B. C., and C. B. Pemose.	Additional compensation as land commissioners.	16	1	Petition	49	Public Lands	13	Favorable	23	Rejected.		
Lucas, John B. C., and C. B. Pemose.	Additional compensation as land commissioners.	16	2	House bill	98	Public Lands	Jan. 2, 1821	Favorable	182	Referred to Committee Whole House.		
Lucas, Jonathan	Renewal of patent	19	1	Petition	424	Judiciary.						
Lucas, Jonathan, jr	Renewal of patent	19	1	Senate bill	520	Judiciary	May 8, 1826	With amend.	137	Laid on table.		
Lucas, Nathaniel	Commutation pay	2	1	Petition	464	....	....	....	.....	Referred to Secretary War.		
Lucas, Nathaniel	Commutation pay	2	2	Rep. of Secretary War.	696	....	....	....	.....	Laid on table.		
Lucas, Richard, heirs of	Commutation pay	23	2	Petition	106	Rev. Claims.						
Lucas, Richard, heirs of	Commutation pay	28	1	Petition	526	Rev. Claims.						
Lucas, Richard, heirs of	Commutation pay	29	1	Petition	399	Rev. Claims.						
Lucas, Richard, heirs of	Commutation pay	29	2	Petition	54	Rev. Claims.						
Lucas, Robert	(See James Parks & Robert Lucas)	8	1	....	488							
Lucas, Robert, (Md.)	Pension	22	1	Petition	89	Rev. Pensions.						
Lucas, Robert	Pension	23	1	Petition	309	Invalid Pensions	555	Favorable	553	Referred to Committee Whole House.		
Lucas, Robert	Pension	23	2	House bill	336	Whole House	Feb. 6, 1835	With amend.	553	Passed.		
Lucas, Robert	Pension	24	1	Petition	201	Invalid Pensions	405	Favorable	413	Passed	Indef. postp'd.	
Lucas, Robert	Pension	24	2	Petition	86	Invalid Pensions	75	Favorable	821	Referred to Committee Whole House.		
Lucas, Robert	Pension	25	2	Petition	39	Invalid Pensions	225	Favorable	263	Passed.		
Lucas, Robert	Pension	26	1	Petition	161	Invalid Pensions	228	Favorable	240	Passed	Indef. postp'd.	
Lucas, Samuel, heir of	Compensation for revolutionary services.	12	1	Petition	141	Claims.						
Lucas, Samuel, children of.	Pension for revolutionary services.	27	2	Petition	613	Rev. Pensions	784	Adverse	.....	Laid on table.		
Lucas, Samuel, children of	Pension for revolutionary services.	27	3	Petition	73	Rev. Pensions	295	Adverse	.....	Laid on table.		
Lucas, Samuel, children of.	Pension for revolutionary services.	29	1	Petition	666	Rev. Pensions	....	....	.....	Discharged; leave to withdraw.		
Lucas, Simon	Pension for revolutionary services.	24	1	Petition	944	Rev. Pensions	....	....	.....	Discharged; laid on table.		
Lucas, Thomas, wife of	Pension	15	2	House bill	128	Whole House	Jan. 26, 1819	With amend.	249	Passed	Passed	App'd March 3, 1819
Lucas, Thomas, heir of	Commutation pay	25	2	Petition	632	Rev. Claims.						
Luce, Elisha	Fishing bounty on schooner Dove.	27	3	Petition	252	Commerce	173	Favorable	785	Referred to Committee Whole House.		
Luce, Elisha	Fishing bounty on schooner Dove.	28	1	Petition	275	Commerce	386	Favorable	284	Passed	Adverse.	
Luce, Elisha	Fishing bounty on schooner Dove	28	2	Petition	73	Commerce	57	Favorable	536	Referred to Committee Whole House.		
Luce, Elisha	Fishing bounty on schooner Dove.	29	1	Petition	106	Commerce	259	Favorable	221	Referred to Committee Whole House.		
Luce, Elisha	Fishing bounty on schooner Dove.	30	1	Petition	288	Commerce.						
Luce, Rowland	Restoration of pension	17	1	Petition	67	Rev. Pensions.						
Lucket, Craven P.	Compensation for carrying report of land commissioners.	18	2	Resolution	180	Public Lands	Feb. 3, 1825	Favorable	313	Passed	Passed	App'd March 3, 1825
Lucroy, Louis	Patent for Spanish grant of land	22	1	Petition	263	Priv. Land Claims.	Feb. 17, 1832	Favorable	380	Referred to Committee Whole House.		
Lucy Ann, schooner	(See John H. Russell)	25	3	....	214							
Ludeman, W. J., heirs of.	Bounty land for revolutionary services.	30	1	Petition	627	Rev. Claims.						
Ludlow, Cornelius V. C.	Indemnity for vessel captured by British.	23	2	Petition	140	Claims.						

List of private claims presented to the House of Representatives of the United States from the 1st to the 31st Congress, inclusive—Continued.

Names of claimants.	Nature or object of the claim.	Congress.	Session.	How brought before the House of Reps.	Page of journal.	To what committee of the House referred.	No. or date of the report.	Nature of the report.	No. of the bill.	How disposed of by the House of Reps.	How disposed of by the Senate.	Date of the act of Congress, and remarks.
Ludlow, Cornelius V. C.	Indemnity for vessel captured by British.	28	1	Petition	365	Claims	244	Adverse	......	Laid on table.		
Ludlow, Daniel	Indemnity for French spoliation prior to 1800.	26	1	Memorial	182	Foreign Affairs	343	Favorable	319	Referred to Committee Whole House.		
Ludlow, Gulian	(See D. S. Kennedy, *et al*)	15	2	....	209							
Ludlow, Gulian	(See James Lenox, *et al*)	17	1	....	32							
Ludlow, Robert C., surety of.	Allowance of credit on settlement of accounts.	22	1	Petition	63	Claims	Feb. 1, 1832	Adverse	......	Laid on table.		
Ludlow, Thomas, executor of.	Indemnity for French spoliations prior to 1800.	26	1	Memorial	182	Foreign Affairs	343	Favorable	319	Referred to Committee Whole House.		
Ludlum, George, widow & children of.	Bounty land for revolutionary services.	22	2	Resolution	154	Military Affairs	56	Favorable	699	Referred to Committee Whole House.		
Ludlum, George, widow & children of.	Bounty land for revolutionary services.	23	1	Petition	89	Military Affairs	Dec. 19, 1833	Favorable	51	Passed	Passed	App'd June 19, 1834
Luffborough, Nathan	Compensation as acting comptroller.	14	1	Petition	518	Claims.						
Luffman, John	Compensation for revolutionary services.	19	2	Petition	158	Rev. Claims.						
Luffman, John	Compensation for revolutionary services.	20	1	Petition	58	Rev. Claims	Jan. 2, 1828	Adverse	......	Laid on table.		
Luggs, George	Restoration of pension	17	1	Petition	270	Whole House	....	....	......	....	....	See H. bill No. 37.
Luke, Paul D	Increase of salary as keeper of light house.	14	2	Petition & report Sec. Treasury.	111	Ways and Means.						
Lukins, Isaiah	Compensation for a bell and clock made for government.	27	3	Petition	205	Dist. of Columbia.	225	Adverse	......	Laid on table.		
Luman, Samuel	Compensation for preventing mail robbery.	31	1	Petition	995	Claims.						
Lumuraux, James	Pension for revolutionary services.	22	1	Petition	509	Rev. Pensions.						
Lumpkin, Dickinson	Pension for revolutionary services.	30	1	Petition	714	Rev. Pensions	782	Adverse	......	Laid on table.		
Lumpkin, Mary	Pension	27	3	Petition	394	Rev. Pensions.						
Lunceford, George, representatives of.	Amount paid for land sold by United States.	17	1	Petition	187	Public Lands	....	....	......	Discharged; referred to Com. Whole House.		
Lund, Jonathan	Restoration of condemned vessel.	12	1	Petition	328	Com. and Manuf.						
Lund, Stephen	Pension for revolutionary services.	17	1	Petition	31	Rev. Pensions.						
Lungenback, Frederick	(See Louis F. Beeler, *et al*)	30	1	....	115							
Lunsford, John	To refund certain duties	18	1	Petition	93	Ways and Means	Dec. 30, 1823	Adverse	......	Laid on table.	....	Leave to withdraw.
Lunt, Abel, heirs of	Indemnity for French spoliations prior to 1800.	26	1	Memorial	182	Foreign Affairs	343	Favorable	319	Referred to Committee Whole House.		
Lunt, Amos	Pension for revolutionary services.	22	1	Petition	381	Rev. Pensions.						
Lunt, jr., Benjamin	Indemnity for French spoliations prior to 1800.	26	1	Memorial	182	Foreign Affairs	343	Favorable	319	Referred to Committee Whole House.		
Lunt, sen., Benjamin	Indemnity for French spoliations prior to 1800.	26	1	Memorial	182	Foreign Affairs	343	Favorable	319	Referred to Committee Whole House.		
Lunt, George	(See Abel Lunt, heirs of)	26	1	....	182	....	343	....	319			
Lunt, J. C.	Indemnity for French spoliations prior to 1800.	26	1	Memorial	182	Foreign Affairs	343	Favorable	319	Referred to Committee Whole House.		
Lunt, Micajah	Indemnity for French spoliations prior to 1800.	26	1	Memorial	182	Foreign Affairs	343	Favorable	319	Referred to Committee Whole House.		
Lunt, Thomas	Indemnity for French spoliations prior to 1800.	26	1	Memorial	182	Foreign Affairs	343	Favorable	319	Referred to Committee Whole House.		
Lunt, William	Pension	3	1	Rep. of Secretary War.	131	Select	May 26, 1794	Res. to refer to Sec. War.	J.R. 12	Passed	Passed	App'd June 9, 1794
Lunt, William	Pension	3	2	Rep. of Secretary of War.	337	Claims	Feb. 28, 1795	Favorable	130	Passed	Postponed.	

List of private claims presented to the House of Representatives of the United States from the 1st to the 31st Congress, inclusive—Continued.

Names of claimants.	Nature or object of the claim.	Congress.	Session.	How brought before the House of Reps.	Page of journal.	To what committee of the House referred.	No. or date of the report.	Nature of the report.	No. of the bill.	How disposed of by the House of Reps.	How disposed of by the Senate.	Date of the act of Congress, and remarks.
Lunt, William	Pension	4	1	Rep. of Secretary War.	445	Claims	Mar. 4, 1796	Favorable	156	Passed	Passed	App'd April 20, 1796
Lusby, Thomas	Confirmation of title to land	16	1	Petition	24	Priv. Land Claims.	Dec. 17, 1819	Adverse		Leave to withdraw.		
Luscombe, Francis	Pension	16	1	Petition	32	Pens. & Rev. Cl'ms.	Dec. 20, 1819	Adverse		Leave to withdraw.		
Lush, James	(See Wm. H. Bedford, agent)	28	1		262							
Lusher, George	Restoration of forfeited vessel	11	1	Petition	85	Whole House.						
Lusk, Hugh, (Ky)	Pension	21	1	Petition	596	Military Pensions.						
Lusk, Hugh, (Ky)	Pension	23	1	Amendm't to Ho. bill.	325				128	Passed	Passed	App'd June 30, 1834
Lusk, James, widow of	Pre emption right to land in Indiana Territory.	8	2	Petition	55	Select.						
Lusk, James, widow of	Pre-emption right to land in Indiana Territory.	9	1	Petition	271	Public Lands.						
Lusk, John	Pension	31	1	Petition	680	Invalid Pensions	323	Adverse		Laid on table.		
Lusk, Sally	(See James Lusk, widow of)	8	2		55							
Lusk, Samuel	Pension for services in Indian wars.	28	1	Petition	527	Invalid Pensions	452	Adverse.		Laid on table.		
Lusk, William	Compensation for revolutionary services.	19	2	Petition	44	Rev. Claims	Jan. 18, 1827	Adverse.		Laid on table.		
Lusley, William	Payment for land	24	1	Appropriat'n bill.	1012	Whole House	June 30, 1836	With amends	695	Passed	Passed	App'd July 2, 1836
Luther, Cromwell	Restoration of pension	17	2	Petition	77	Rev. Pensions.						
Luther, Fanny H	(See Septa Fillmore, heirs of.)	22	2		151							
Luther, James	Pension	15	1	Petition	195	Select	Mar. 21, 1818	Adverse		Discharged.		
Luther, Mary	(See Jabez Chase, heirs of)	24	2		38							
Luther, Thomas	Pension	21	2	Petition	159	Military Pensions.						
Luther, Thomas	Pension	22	1	Petition	80	Rev. Pensions	Mar. 26, 1832	Favorable	513	Referred to Committee Whole House.		
Lutterloh, Henry E	Pay and emoluments for revolutionary services.	1	2	Petition and rep't Sec. of War.	193					Reprot disagreed to		Leave to withdraw.
Lutterloh, Henry E	Pay and emolumonts for revolutionary services.	1	3	Petition	337					Rejected.		
Lutterloh, Henry E	Pay and emoluments for revolutionary services.	2	1	Petition and rep't Sec. of War.	469, 470	Select	May 8, 1792	Adverse as to part, and favorable as to part.		Laid on table.		
Lutterloh, Henry E	Pay and emoluments for revolutionary services.	2	2	Petition and docs.	677	Select	Jan. 3, 1793	Favorable	223	Passed	Rejected.	
Lutz, John, and Jesse Lipscomb.	Reimbursement for money lost in mail.	25	2	Petition	176	P. Of. & P. Roads.	725	Adverse		Laid on table.		
Lybrook, John	Pension for revolutionary services.	25	2	Petition	181	Rev. Pensions	Mar. 20, 1838	Favorable	671	Passed.		
Lybrook, John	Pension for revolutionary services.	25	3	Petition	225	Rev. Pensions	Jan. 9, 1839	Favorable	988	Passed.		
Lybrook, John	Pension for revolutionary services.	26	1	Petition	172	Rev. Pensions	151	Favorable	161	Passed	Indef. postp'd.	
Lybrook, John	Pension for revolutionary services.	26	2	Petition	134	Rev. Pensions.	75	Favorable	590	Referred to Committee Whole House.		
Lyddal, Estes	Pension for revolutionary services.	29	1	Petition	86	Rev. Pensions.						
Lydia, (privateer)	(See David Robinson, *et al.*)	24	2		551							
Lyell, Robert	Pay and emoluments for revolutionary services.	3	1	Petition	61	Select	Mar. 24, 1794	Favorable	J. R. 13	Rejected.		
Lyford, Nathaniel	Pension for revolutionary services.	28	2	Petition	206	Rev. Pensions.						
Lyford, Nathaniel	Pension for revolutionary services.	29	1	Petition	588	Rev. Pensions	610	Adverse.		Laid on table.		
Lyle & Newman, *et al.*	Leave to import goods from Great Britain.	12	1	Petition	283	Whole House	Jan. 7, 1812	Favorable	46	Postponed.		
Lyle, Richard	Compensation for revolutionary services, &c.	4	1	Petition	466	Claims	May 31, 1796	Adverse		Laid on table.		

List of private claims presented to the House of Representatives of the United States from the 1st to the 31st Congress, inclusive—Continued.

Names of claimants.	Nature or object of the claim.	Congress.	Session.	How brought before the House of Reps.	Page of journal.	To what committee of the House referred.	No. or date of the report.	Nature of the report.	No. of the bill.	How disposed of by the House of Reps.	How disposed of by the Senate.	Date of the act of Congress, and remarks.
Lyle, Richard	Compensation for revolutionary services, &c.	10	1	Petition	86	Select.						
Lyle, Richard	Compensation for revolutionary services, &c.	13	2	Petition	311	Pens. & Rev. Cl'ms.	92	Adverse		Referred to Committee Whole House.		
Lyle, Richard	Compensation for revolutionary services, &c.	24	1	Petition	735	Rev. Pensions				Discharged; laid on table.		
Lyle, William, representatives of.	Pension for revolutionary services.	27	3	Memorial	140	Rev. Pensions				Discharged; laid on table.		
Lyle, William, representatives of.	Pension for revolutionary services.	28	1	Memorial	183	Invalid Pensions	177	Adverse		Laid on table.		
Lyle, William, representatives of.	Pension for revolutionary services.	29	2	Memorial	110	Invalid Pensions.						
Lyle, William, representatives of.	Pension for revolutionary services.	30	1	Memorial	217	Invalid Pensions				Discharged; laid on table.		See Report No. 482.
Lyles, John	Grant of land for revolutionary services.	19	1	Petition	128	Public Lands				Discharged; laid on table.		
Lyles, Thomas C.	(See William Lyles, heirs of)	24	1		204							
Lyles, Richard	(See Richard Lyle)	4	1		466							
Lyles, William, heirs of	Indemnity for revolutionary losses	24	1	Memorial	204	Rev. Claims.						
Lyles, William, heirs of	Indemnity for revolutionary losses.	25	2	Memorial	111	Rev. Claims				Discharged; laid on table.		
Lyles, William, heirs of	Indemnity for revolutionary losses.	26	1	Memorial	360	Rev. Claims.						
Lyles, William, heirs of	Indemnity for revolutionary losses.	26	2	Memorial	80	Claims.						
Lyles, William, heirs of	Indemnity for revolutionary losses	30	1	Memorial	217	Invalid Pensions				Discharged; laid on table.		
Lyman, Rev. Andrew	Pension for revolutionary services.	24	2	Documents	106	Rev. Pensions	73	Favorable	819	Referred to Committee Whole House.		
Lyman, Rev. Andrew	Pension for revolutionary services.	28	1	Petition	541	Rev. Pensions.						
Lyman, Charles	Pension	30	2	Petition	345	Invalid Pensions				Discharged; laid on table.		
Lyman, David, widow of	Pension	28	1	Petition	959	Military Affairs.						
Lyman, David, widow of	Pension	29	1	Petition	74	Invalid Pensions	668	Adverse		Laid on table.		
Lyman, E. D	Compensation for use of sloop Commodore Hull.	31	1	Petition	224	Claims.						
Lyman, Justin and Elias	Release from penalty for importing coffee.	13	3	Petition	470	Ways and Means	22	Adverse		Leave to withdraw.		
Lyman, Justin and Elias	Release from penalty for importing coffee.	14	2	Petition	190	Ways and Means.						
Lyman, Micah J.	Relief in case of property seized by revenue officers.	12	2	Petition	633	Ways and Means						See act Feb. 27, 1813
Lyman, Richard	Pension	3	2	Rep. of Secretary War.	350	Claims.						
Lyman, Richard	Pension	4	1	Rep. of Secretary War.	445	Claims	Mar. 4, 1796	Jt. res. to refer to Sec. War.	16	Passed	Passed	App'd April 18, 1796
Lyman, Theodore	Indemnity for French spoliations prior to 1800.	26	1	Memorial	182	Foreign Affairs	343	Favorable	319	Referred to Committee Whole House.		
Lynch, Anselm	Remuneration for deficiency in land.	23	2	Senate bill	231	Public Lands	Jan. 31, 1835	With amends.	46	Referred to Committee Whole House.		
Lynch, Charles	Remuneration for deficiency in land.	23	2	Senate bill	250	Public Lands	Feb. 5, 1835	With amends.	71	Referred to Committee Whole House.		
Lynch, Charlotte	(See Col. Ebenezer Gray, heirs of)	28	1		99							
Lynch, Dominick	Release from judgment of United States.	23	1	Petition	159	Ways and Means	394	Favorable	412	Referred to Committee Whole House.		

List of private claims presented to the House of Representatives of the United States from the 1st to the 31st Congress, inclusive—Continued.

Names of claimants.	Nature or object of the claim.	Congress.	Session.	How brought before the House of Reps.	Page of journal.	To what committee of the House referred.	No. or date of the report.	Nature of the report.	No. of the bill.	How disposed of by the House of Reps.	How disposed of by the Senate.	Date of the act of Congress, and remarks.
Lynch, Dominick	Release from judgment of United States.	23	2	Rep. Committee Whole House.	299			With amends.	412	Passed	Passed	App'd March 3, 1835
Lynch, Dominick, surety of	Restoration of patrimonial estate	24	2	Petition	313	Ways and Means.						
Lynch, Dominick, surety of	Restoration of patrimonial estate	25	2	Petition	112	Ways and Means	Jan. 3, 1838	Favorable	270	Referred to Committee Whole House.		
Lynch, Dominick, surety of	Restoration of patrimonial estate	25	3	Rep't Committee Whole House.	376			With't amend.	270	Passed	Passed	App'd March 3, 1839
Lynch, Elijah	(See William H. Bedford, agent).	28	1		262							
Lynch, George	Pension	23	1	Pension bill	86	Whole House	Dec. 17, 1833	With amend.	42	Passed	Passed	App'd June 30, 1834
Lynch, George	Increase of pension	25	2	Petition	167	Invalid Pensions	Mar. 29, 1838	Adverse		Laid on table.		
Lynch, George	Arrears of pension	28	1	Petition	123	Invalid Pensions	108	Adverse		Laid on table.		
Lynch, Henry	(See Dominick Lynch, surety of).	24	2		313							
Lynch, Jane	(See John B. Lynch, widow of).	6	1		640							
Lynch, John	Compensation for revolutionary services.	3	1	Petition	106					Referred to Secretary of War.		
Lynch, John	Compensation for revolutionary services.	3	2	Rep. of Secretary War.	278					Laid on table.		
Lynch, John	(See Peter Lynch)	20	1		74							
Lynch, John	Compensation for horses, &c., taken for public use.	26	1	Resolution	1023	Military Affairs.						
Lynch, John	Compensation for horses, &c., taken for public use.	26	2	Petition	79	Military Affairs	93	Favorable	599	Referred to Committee Whole House.		
Lynch, John R., widow of.	Compensation for revolutionary services.	6	1	Petition	640	Claims	April 26, 1800	Adverse		Referred to Committee Whole House.		
Lynch, Joseph M.	Indemnity for loss of claim by act of Indian agent.	23	1	Petition	517	Claims.						
Lynch, Peter	Appropriation for purchase of Indian reserve.	19	2	Resolution	68	Indian Affairs				Discharged.		
Lynch, Peter	Appropriation for purchase of Indian reserve.	20	1	Resolution	74	Indian Affairs	Jan. 16, 1828	Favorable	81	Passed	Passed	App'd May 23, 1828
Lynch, Samuel	(See William H. Bedford, agent.)	28	1		262							
Lynch, William	Pension	30	1	Petition	879	Invalid Pensions	828	Favorable	646	Referred to Committee Whole House.		
Lynch, William	Pension	30	2	Rep't Committee Whole House	363			With't amend	646	Adopted.		
Lynch, William	Pension	31	1	Petition	449	Invalid Pensions	298	Favorable	267	Referred to Committee Whole House.		
Lynch, William	Pension	31	2	Rep. Committee Whole House.	182			With amend.	267	Passed.		
Lynd, John, heirs of	Confirmation of title to land	28	1	Petition	261	Priv. Land Claims.				Discharged; laid on table.		
Lynde, Henrietta	(See John Lynde, administratrix of.)	18	1		136							
Lynde, John, administratrix of.)	Confirmation of title to land	18	1	Petition	136	Priv. Land Claims.	Feb. 23, 1824	Adverse		Laid on table.		
Lynn, David, widow of	Pension for revolutionary services.	28	1	Petition	705	Rev. Pensions.						
Lynn, Jane	(See John Lynn, widow of.)	30	1	Petition	342							
Lynn, John, widow of	Pension for revolutionary services.	30	1	Petition	342	Rev. Pensions	310	Adverse		Laid on table.		
Lynn, Joseph	(See Joseph Linn.)	22	1		435							
Lynn, Mary	(See David Lynn, widow of.)	28	1		705							
Lyon, Aaron	Compensation for boats taken for public use.	3	1	Petition	21					Referred to Secretary Treasury.		

List of private claims presented to the House of Representatives of the United States from the 1st to the 31st Congress, inclusive—Continued.

Names of claimants.	Nature or object of the claim.	Congress.	Session.	How brought before the House of Reps.	Page of journal.	To what committee of the House referred.	No. or date of the report.	Nature of the report.	No. of the bill.	How disposed of by the House of Reps.	How disposed of by the Senate.	Date of the act of Congress, and remarks.
Lyon, Aaron	Compensation for boats taken for public use.	3	2	Rep. of Secretary Treasury.	284					Laid on table.		
Lyon, Aaron	(See John Sparding, attorney of.)	13	1		12							
Lyon, Abraham	Increase of pension	27	2	Petition	91	Invalid Pensions	257	Adverse		Laid on table.		
Lyon, Asa	Payment of loan office certificates.	14	2	Resolution	328	Pens. & Rev. Cl'ms.	Feb. 3, 1817	Favorable	96	Ref'd to Com. W. H.		
Lyon, Asa	Payment of loan office certificates.	15	1	Petition	446	Pens. & Rev. Cl'ms.				Discharged; leave to withdraw.		
Lyon, Benjamin	Pension for revolutionary services.	26	1	Petition	739	Rev. Pensions	714	Adverse		Leave to withdraw.		
Lyon, David S., and M. S. Swartwout.	Increase of compensation as deputy collector.	21	2	Petition	230	Commerce				Discharged; referred to Sec. Treasury.		
Lyon, Elijah	Relief as land purchaser	17	1	Petition	166	Public Lands.						
Lyon, Elizabeth	Compensation for loss of son in Florida war.	28	2	Petition	266	Claims.						
Lyon, George	Compensation for clerical services in Patent Office.	12	1	Petition	284	Claims	April 29, 1812	Favorable	121	Passed	Postponed.	
Lyon, George	Compensation for clerical services in Patent Office.	12	2	Petition	551	Claims.						
Lyon, George	Compensation for clerical services in Patent Office.	13	1	Petition	21	Ways and Means	July 24, 1813	Favorable	50	Passed	Passed	App'd Aug. 2, 1813
Lyon, James G	Compensation for mail service	18	2	Petition	228	P. Of. and P. Roads.	Feb. 28, 1825	Adverse		Laid on table.		
Lyon, James G	Compensation for mail service	19	1	Petition	311	P. Of. & P. Roads.	April 12, 1826	Adverse		Laid on table.		
Lyon, J. G.	Reimbursement of advances to Alabama militia.	25	2	Documents	397	Claims	889	Adverse		Laid on table.		
Lyon, John, widow of	Pension for revolutionary services.	27	2	Petition	524	Rev. Pensions				Discharged; laid on table.		
Lyon, Joseph	Pension	22	1	Resolution	38	Rev. Pensions	17	Favorable	69	Passed.		
Lyon, Justus, representatives of.	Compensation for damages to property in revolution.	19	1	Resolution	275	Claims.						
Lyon, Lucius	Compensation or survey of northern boundary of Illinois.	23	1	Appropriat'n bill.	283				283	Passed	Passed	App'd June 27, 1834
Lyon, Lyman, and D. S. Howard.	Compensation for extra work on dredging machine.	26	1	Petition	293	Claims.						
Lyon, Lyman, and D. S. Howard.	Compensation for extra work on dredging machine.	26	1	Documents	702	Claims.						
Lyon, Lyman, and D. S. Howard.	Compensation for extra work on dredging machine.	26	2	Petition	38	Claims.						
Lyon, Lyman, and D. S. Howard.	Compensation for extra work on dredging machine.	26	2	Documents	177	Claims.						
Lyon, Lyman, and D. S. Howard.	Compensation for extra work on dredging machine.	27	2	Petition	56	Claims.						
Lyon, Lyman, and D. S. Howard.	Compensation for extra work on dredging machine.	29	1	Petition	120	Claims	30	Favorable	36	Referred to Committee Whole House.		
Lyon, Lyman, and D. S. Howard.	Compensation for extra work on dredging machine.	30	1	Petition	235	Claims	163	Favorable	163	Referred to Committee Whole House.		
Lyon, Lyman, and D. S. Howard.	Compensation for extra work on dredging machine.	30	2	Rep. Committee Whole House.	368			With't amend.	163	Laid on table.		
Lyon, Lyman, and D. S. Howard.	Compensation for extra work on dredging machine.	31	1	Petition	214	Claims.						
Lyon, Mary	(See John Lyon, widow of)	27	2		524							
Lyon, Matthew	Remission of fine imposed under alien and sedition law.	12	1	Memorial	19	Select.						
Lyon, Matthew	Remission of fine imposed under alien and sedition law.	15	2	Memorial	24	Judiciary	Nov. 24, 1818	Adverse		Referred to Committee Whole House.		

List of private claims presented to the House of Representatives of the United States from the 1st to the 31st Congress, inclusive—Continued.

Names of claimants.	Nature or object of the claim.	Congress.	Session.	How brought before the House of Reps.	Page of journal.	To what committee of the House referred.	No. or date of the report.	Nature of the report.	No. of the bill.	How disposed of by the House of Reps.	How disposed of by the Senate.	Date of the act of Congress, and remarks.
Lyon, Matthew	Remission of fine imposed under alien and sedition law.	16	1	Memorial	23	Judiciary.						
Lyon, Matthew	Remission of fine imposed under alien and sedition law.	16	2	Memorial	25	Select	8	Favorable	160	Referred to Committee Whole House.		
Lyon, Matthew, heirs of	Remission of fine imposed under alien and sedition law.	22	1	Memorial	174	Judiciary	218	Favorable	290	Referred to Committee Whole House.		
Lyon, Matthew, heirs of	Remission of fine imposed under alien and sedition law.	22	2	Ho. bill last sess.	171	Whole House	Jan. 11, 1833	With amend.	290	Passed.		
Lyon, Matthew, heirs of	Remission of fine imposed under alien and sedition law.	23	1	Petition	58	Judiciary	491	Favorable	498	Referred to Committee Whole House.		
Lyon, Matthew, heirs of	Remission of fine imposed under alien and sedition law.	24	1	Petition	211	Judiciary	304	Favorable	318	Referred to Committee Whole House.		
Lyon, Matthew, heirs of	Remission of fine imposed under alien and sedition law.	25	2	Petition	41	Judiciary	377	Favorable	401	Referred to Committee Whole House.		
Lyon, Matthew, heirs of	Remission of fine imposed under alien and sedition law.	26	1	Petition	499	Judiciary	86	Favorable	80	Passed	Passed	App'd July 4, 1840
Lyon, Robert	Compensation for services against Indians.	2	2	Petition	687	Whole House.						
Lyon, Robert	Pension for revolutionary services.	3	1	Petition	49	Select	Feb. 19, 1793	Favorable	......	Laid on table.		
Lyon, Robert	Pension for revolutionary services.	14	1	Petition	475	Pens. & Rev. Cl'ms.	April 11, 1817	Favorable	171	......	......	Name striken out before passage.
Lyon, Robert	Pension for revolutionary services.	14	2	Resolution	322	Pens. & Rev. Cl'ms.	Jan. 29, 1817	Favorable	91	Passed	Passed	App'd March 3, 1817
Lyon, Robert	Pension for revolutionary services.	15	1	Petition	113	Pens. & Rev. Cl'ms.						
Lyon, Thomas	Compensation as teamster in revolutionary war.	3	1	Petition	60	......	......	......	......	Referred to Secretary War.		
Lyon, Thomas	Compensation as teamster in revolutionary war.	3	2	Rep. of Secretary War.	278	......	......	......	......	Laid on table.		
Lyons, Peter, jr	Settlement of revolutionary certificate.	4	1	Rep. of Secretary Treasury.	388	Claims	74	Adverse	......	Laid on table.		
Lysle, John and Margaret	(See Samuel Lapsley)	12	2	......	711							
Lytle, Charles L	Reimbursement of money erroneously paid.	25	2	Memorial	267	Military Affairs	......	......	......	Discharged; laid on table.		
Lytle, David	For relief as land purchaser	17	1	Petition	267	......	......	......	......	Referred to Committee Whole House.		
Lytle, James W	Pension for revolutionary services.	26	1	Petition	285	Rev. Pensions	490	Adverse	......	Laid on table.		
Lytle, Robert T., sureties of.	Equitable settlement of his liability	30	2	Senate resolution	438	Public Lands	Feb. 28, 1849	With't amend.	59	Passed	Passed	App'd March 2, 1849
Lytle, William, executor of A. St. Clair.	(See Elisha Winter and sons.)	19	2	......	159							
Lytle, William, 3d	Reimbursement of money lost in public services.	23	1	Documents	384	Claims	484	Adverse	......	Laid on table.		
Lytle, William, administrator of.	Balance of pension	24	1	Petition	273	Rev. Pensions	Feb. 13, 1836	Adverse	......	Laid on table.		

List of private claims presented to the House of Representatives of the United States from the 1st *to the* 31st *Congress, inclusive*—Continued.

Names of claimants.	Nature or object of the claim.	Congress.	Session.	How brought before the House of Reps.	Page of journal.	To what committee of the House referred.	No. or date of the report.	Nature of the report.	No. of the bill.	How disposed of by the House of Reps.	How disposed of by the Senate.	Date of the act of Congress, and remarks.
Mabary, Benjamin	Increase of pension	21	1	Petition	231	Military Pensions	April 7, 1830	Adverse	......	Laid on table.		
Mabary, Benjamin	Increase of pension	21	2	Petition	110	Military Pensions.						
Maberry, Thomas, (S. C.)	Settlement of accounts for iron furnished United States army in revolutionary war.	11	3	Petition	505	Claims.						
Mabery, Thomas, (S. C.)	Settlement of accounts for iron furnished United States army in revolutionary war.	12	1	Petition	265	Claims.						
Mabry, David	Relief for having been deprived of pre-emption right to land.	23	2	Resolution	243	Priv. Land Claims.	79	Favorable; bill	696	Referred to Committee Whole House.		
Mabry, John	Pension and bounty land for revolutionary services.	15	2	Petition	118	Pens. & Rev. Cl'ms.	....	....	......	Discharged; referred to Sec. of war.		
Mabry, John	Pension and bounty land for revolutionary services.	16	2	Petition	155	Pens. & Rev. Cl'ms.	Jan. 29, 1821	Adverse	......	Laid on table.		
Mabry, John	Pension	21	2	Petition	80	Military Pensions.						
Mabry, John	Pension	22	1	Petition	130	Rev. Claims.						
Mabry, Robert, (Va.)	Compensation for services in revolutionary war.	9	1	Petition	205	Claims	....	....	......	Discharged, referred to Com. Whole House.		
Mabry, Robert, (Va.)	Compensation for services in revolutionary war.	10	1	Petition	91	Whole House.						
Mabson, Samuel E. (N. C.)	Invalid pension	31	1	Petition	762	Invalid Pensions	392	Adverse	......	Disch'd, laid on table.		
Mabson, Samuel, (S. C.)	Pension	21	2	Petition	300	Military Pensions.						
Macan, John G., and others	(See Louisiana Land company.)	9	1	....	267							
Macarty, Bartholomy, heirs of.	Confirmation of title to land in Louisiana.	23	1	Petition	76	Priv. Land Claims.						
Macarty, Celeste	(See Paul Lanusse, widow of)	23	1	....	76							
Macarty, Edmond, heirs of.	Confirmation of title to land in Louisiana.	23	1	Petition	76	Priv. Land Claims.						
Macarty, Jeane Baptiste, heirs of.	Confirmation of title to land in Louisiana.	23	1	Petition	76	Priv. Land Claims.						
Macarty, Jeane Baptiste, heirs of.	Confirmation of title to land in Louisiana.	23	2	Petition	138	Priv. Land Claims.						
Macarty, J. L. B	Indemnity for damage to property by British in war of 1812.	15	1	Petition	179	Claims	....	....	......	Discharged; laid on table.		
Macarty, J. L. B	Indemnity for damage to property by British in war of 1812.	16	2	Senate bill	287	Claims	Mar. 21, 1801	With't amend.	S. 43	Referred to Committee Whole House.		
Macauley, Alexander, administrator of.	Indemnity for French spoliations prior to 1800.	26	1	Memorial	182	Foreign Affairs	343	Favorable	319	Referred to Committee Whole House.		
Macauley, Alexander, heirs of.	Indemnity for French spoliations prior to 1800.	29	2	Petition	100	Foreign Affairs.						
Macauley, Alexander, administrator of.	Indemnity for French spoliations prior to 1800.	31	1	Petition	413	Foreign Affairs	355	Favorable; bill	318	Referred to Committee Whole House.		
Macauley, Daniel, (S. C.)	Relief from penalty for imported goods from Great Britain.	12	2	Petition	706	Ways and Means	....	....	......	Discharged.		
Macauley, Daniel, (S. C.)	Relief from penalty for imported goods from Great Britain.	13	1	Petition	24	Ways and Means.						
Macauley, Daniel, (S. C.)	Relief from penalty for imported goods from Great Britain.	13	2	Petition	182	Ways and Means	Feb. 1, 1814	Favorable; bill	102	Passed	Passed, with amendment.	App'd April 6, 1814
Macausland, John	Indemnity for French spoliations prior to 1800.	26	1	Memorial	182	Foreign Affairs	343	Favorable; bill	319	Referred to Committee Whole House.		
Macdonald, Alexander	(See John Holmes, administrator of.)	26	1	....	182							

List of private claims presented to the House of Representatives of the United States from the 1st to the 31st Congress, inclusive—Continued.

Names of claimants.	Nature or object of the claim.	Congress.	Session.	How brought before the House of Reps.	Page of journal.	To what committee of the House referred.	No. or date of the report.	Nature of the report.	No. of the bill.	How disposed of by the House of Reps.	How disposed of by the Senate.	Date of the act of Congress, and remarks.
Mace, Joseph	Increase of pension	29	1	Petition	385	Rev. Pensions	Mar. 5, 1846	Adverse	......	Laid on table.		
Machett, William	(See Andrew C. Dorr, *et al*)	7	1	....	31							
Machin, Susanna	(See Thomas Machin, widow of)	14	2	....	45							
Machin, Thomas	Invalid pension	10	1	Petition	232	Claims	Mar. 17, 1808	Favorable; bill	78	Passed	Passed, with amendment.	App'd April 25, 1808
Machin, Thomas	Increase of pension	13	3	Petition	740	Claims	Feb. 20, 1815	Favorable; bill	303	Passed	Passed, with amendment.	App'd March 3, 1815
Machin, Thomas, widow of.	Arrears of pension	14	2	Petition	45	Pens. & Rev. Cl'ms.	Dec. 31, 1816	Adverse	......	Rejected.		
Machin, Thomas, widow of.	Arrears of pension	15	2	Rep. of Secretary War.	48	Pens. & Rev. Cl'ms.	....	....	......	Discharged; laid on table.		
Mack, Elisha	(See John E. Hunt and others	27	2	....	334							
Mack, Robert	Compensation for revolutionary services.	26	1	Resolution	392	Rev. Claims	610	Adverse	......	Laid on table.		
Mack, Stephen, and S. Conant.	Payment of certain quartermasters' certificates.	17	1	Petition	253	Claims	Mar. 18, 1822	Adverse	......	Referred to Committee Whole House.		
Mack, Stephen, and S. Conant.	Payment of certain quartermasters' certificates.	19	1	Petition	151	Claims	Jan. 18, 1826	Adverse	......	Leave to withdraw.		
Mack, Stephen, and S. Conant.	Equitable settlement of accounts	19	1	Senate bill	496	Claims	May 12, 1826	With amend.	120	Passed	Passed	App'd May 22, 1826
Mackall, Benjamin H.	Indemnity for houses destroyed by British in the war of 1812.	15	1	Report of Commissioners.	37	Claims	....	....	......	Discharged; laid on table.		
Mackall, Benjamin H., heirs of.	Indemnity for houses destroyed by British in the war of 1812.	24	1	Resolution	158	Claims	398	Favorable; bill	403	Referred to Committee Whole House.		
Mackall, Benjamin H., heirs of.	Indemnity for houses destroyed by British in the war of 1812.	25	2	Resolution	37	Claims	13	Favorable; bill	25	Passed	Passed	App'd Mar. 19, 1838
Mackall, James	Indemnity for damages sustained by not having received title to a tract of land paid for.	30	1	Petition	954	Claims.						
Mackall, James	Indemnity for damages sustained by not having received title to a tract of land paid for.	31	1	Petition	510	Claims.						
Mackall, Jas. J., and others.	(See John G. Mackall, and others.)	27	2	....	227							
Mackall, John G.	Indemnity for houses destroyed by British in war of 1812.	15	1	Report of Commissioners.	37	Claims	Dec. 17, 1817	Adverse	......	Rejected.		
Mackall, John G.	Indemnity for houses destroyed by British in war of 1812.	23	2	Petition	119	Claims	Jan. 21, 1835	Adverse	......	Laid on table.		
Mackall, John G.	Indemnity for houses destroyed by British in war of 1812.	24	1	Petition	474	Claims	570	Adverse	......	Laid on table.		
Mackall, John G.	Indemnity for houses destroyed by British in war of 1812.	24	2	Petition	81	Claims	Feb. 22, 1837	Adverse	......	Laid on table.		
Mackall, John G., heirs of.	Indemnity for houses destroyed by British in war of 1812.	27	2	Petition	227	Claims.						
Mackall, John G., heirs of.	Indemnity for houses destroyed by British in war of 1812.	27	3	Petition	155	Claims.						
Mackall, John G., heirs of.	Indemnity for houses destroyed by British in war of 1812.	28	1	Petition	294	Claims.						
Mackall, John G., heirs of.	Indemnity for houses destroyed by British in war of 1812.	28	2	Petition	56	Claims.						
Mackall, John G., heirs of.	Indemnity for houses destroyed by British in war of 1812.	29	1	Petition	90	Claims	Mar. 27, 1846	....	......	Discharged; laid on table.		
Mackall, Leonard	(See John Mitchell, and others)	7	1	....	176							
Mackall, Richard	Compensation for property destroyed by British in late war.	24	1	Petition	474	Claims	578	Adverse	......	Laid on table.		

List of private claims presented to the House of Representatives of the United States from the 1st to the 31st Congress, inclusive—Continued.

Names of claimants.	Nature or object of the claim.	Congress.	Session.	How brought before the House of Reps.	Page of journal.	To what committee of the House referred.	No. or date of the report.	Nature of the report.	No. of the bill.	How disposed of by the House of Reps.	How disposed of by the Senate.	Date of the act of Congress, and remarks.
Mackall, Richard	Compensation for property destroyed in late war.	24	2	Petition	81	Claims	Feb. 22, 1837	Adverse	......	Laid on table.		
Mackall, Richard	Compensation for property destroyed in late war.	25	2	Petition	72	Claims	601	Adverse	......	Laid on table.		
Mackall, Richard	Compensation for property destroyed in late war.	25	3	Petition	121	Claims	214	Adverse	......	Laid on table.		
Mackall, Richard	Compensation for property destroyed in late war.	30	1	Petition	276	Claims.						
Mackay, Eliza	Payment for property lost in U. S. service.	25	3	Resolution	168	Claims	116	Adverse	......	Laid on table.		
Mackay, Eliza	Payment for property lost in U. S. service.	26	1	Resolution	169	Claims.						
Mackay, George	Compensation for goods furnished officers, &c., Seminole war.	30	1	Petition	1025	Claims.						
Mackay, James	(See Dr. John Watkins, heirs of.)	15	1	....	85							
Mackay, James	Confirmation of title to land in Missouri.	15	1	Petition	288, 297	Priv. Land Claims.	Mar. 26, 1818	By bill; to refer to record'r of land titles.	161	Passed	Passed	App'd April 20, 1818
Mackay, James	Confirmation of title to land in Missouri.	15	2	Rep't of recorder of land titles.	194	Priv. Land Claims.	95	Favorable; bill	285	Referred to Committee Whole House.		
Mackay, James	Confirmation of title to land in Missouri	22	1	Rep't of recorder of land office.	404	Public Lands.						
Mackay, James, and others	Confirmation of title to land	15	2	Petition	89	Priv. Land Claims.	Jan. 18, 1819	Adverse	......	Rejected.		
Mackay, James	Confirmation of title to four tracts of land.	16	1	Petition	35, 36	Priv. Land Claims.	41	Favorable; bill	43	Referred to Committee Whole House.		
Mackay, James	Confirmation of title to four tracts of land.	17	1	Petition	54	Public Lands.						
Mackay, James	Confirmation of title to four tracts of land.	18	1	Petition	54	Public Lands	Jan. 16, 1824	By bill; refer'd case to court of law.	65	Passed	Passed	App'd May 26, 1824
Mackay, James, representatives of.	Confirmation of title to land	24	1	Petition	671	Priv. Land Claims.	April 22, 1836	By bill	587	Referred to Committee Whole House.		
Mackay, James, representatives of.	Confirmation of title to land	25	2	Petition	513	Judiciary.						
Mackay, R. C., administrator of.	Indemnity for French spoliations prior to 1800.	26	1	Memorial	182	Foreign Affairs	343	Favorable; bill	319	Referred to Committee Whole House.		
Mackay, R. W., & others.	(See Robert Walker, heirs of)	30	1	Petition	118	Foreign Affairs	....	Senate bill	21			
Mackay, Samuel	Release from contract to subsist emigrating Indians.	25	3	Senate bill	661	....	....	....	S. 247			
Mackay, Samuel	Release from contract to subsist emigrating Indians.	26	1	Senate bill	837	Claims	659	Adverse	S. 265	Referred to Committee Whole House.		
Mackay, Samuel	Release from contract to subsist emigrating Indians.	26	2	Senate bill	205	Indian Affairs	....	....	S. 215			
Mackay, Sarah D.	Pension	31	2	Senate bill	146	Whole House	....	....	S. 365			
Mackenzie, Jane	Remission of duties on chemical apparatus.	20	2	Petition	116	Ways and Means	....	....	......	Discharged; laid on table.		
Mackey, James, (Pa.)	Release from imprisonment at suit of the United States.	4	1	Petition and rep't Att'y General.	402	....	....	....	......	Laid on table.		
Mackey, Thomas, (Md.)	Pension	16	2	Petition	37	Rev. Pensions	Feb. 15, 1821	Adverse	......	Leave to withdraw.		
Mackey, William	Compensation for revolutionary services.	2	2	Petition and rep't Sec. of War.	735	....	....	....	......	Laid on table.		
Mackie, Peter	(See Isaac Lawrence, and others).	14	1	....	386							
Mackie, Thomas & Peter.	Release from embargo laws	3	1	Memorial	139	....	....	....	......	Laid on table.		

List of private claims presented to the House of Representatives of the United States from the 1st to the 31st Congress, inclusive—Continued.

Names of claimants.	Nature or object of the claim.	Congress.	Session.	How brought before the House of Reps.	Page of journal.	To what committee of the House referred.	No. or date of the report.	Nature of the report.	No. of the bill.	How disposed of by the House of Reps.	How disposed of by the Senate.	Date of the act of Congress, and remarks.
Mackins, Samuel	Invalid pension	2	1	Petition	505					Referred to Secretary War.		
Mackins, Samuel	Invalid pension	3	1	Rep. of Secretary War.	131	Select	May 26, 1794	Rep. and res.	12	Referred to Secretary War.		
Mackins, Samuel	Invalid pension	4	1	Rep. of Secretary War.	445	Claims	Feb. 18, 1796	Rep. and res.	16	Referred to Secretary War.		
Mackirder, W. R.	Indemnity for French spoliations prior to 1800.	26	1	Memorial	182	Foreign Affairs	343	Favorable; bill	319	Referred to Committee Whole House.		
Macklin, Mathew	Pension	30	2	Petition	123	Invalid Pensions	19	Adverse		Laid on table.		Leave to withd'w, Dec. 30, 1850.
Maclay, John M., sureties of.	Release from liability	19	2	Petition	217	Ways and Means.						
Maclay, John M., sureties of.	Release from liability	20	1	Petition	31	Judiciary	Dec. 24, 1827	Adverse		Laid on table.		
Maclean, Andrew	(See Nathan Hall, administ'r of.)	28	1		452							
Maclot, John, (La.)	Pre-emption right to land	10	2	Petition	454	Public Lands.						
Macleur, Mathew	Invalid pension	30	1	Petition	280	Invalid Pensions	586	Adverse		Laid on table.		
Maclure, or McClure, William.	Compensation for services rendered under treaty with France in 1803.	20	1	Petition and res.	44, 163	Claims	94	Favorable; bill	104	Passed	Passed	App'd May 19, 1828
Macnamara, John	Release from penalty for bringing slaves into the United States in violation of law.	11	3	Petition	534	Com. and Manuf.	Feb. 18, 1811	Favorable; bill	211	Passed	Passed	App'd March 2, 1811
Macollan, John	Pension	21	1	Petition	36	Military Pensions.				Disch'd; laid on table.		
Macomb, Alexander and William Edgar.	Release from contract for the purchase of western lands.	1	2	Petition	290					Referred to Secretary Treasury.		
Macomb, Alexander and William Edgar.	Release from contract for the purchase of western lands.	3	2	Rep. of Secretary Treasury.	284					Laid on table.		
Macomb, Alexander and William Edgar.	Permission to complete the payment for certain lands, or restore money already paid.	4	1	Memorial	554	Claims.						
Macomb, Alexander and William Edgar.	Permission to complete the payment for certain lands, or restore money already paid.	4	2	Memorial	614	Claims.						
Macomb, Alexander and William Edgar.	Permission to complete the payment for certain lands, or restore money already paid.	5	2	Memorial	153	Claims	Jan. 30, 1798	Adverse		Rejected.		
Macomb, Alexander and William Edgar.	Permission to complete the payment for certain lands, or restore money already paid.	9	1	Petition	313	Ways and Means.						
Macomb, Alexander and William Edgar.	Permission to complete the payment for certain lands, or restore money already paid.	9	2	Petition	524	Ways and Means.						
Macomb, Alexander and William Edgar.	Permission to complete the payment for certain lands, or restore money already paid.	10	2	Petition	469	Public Lands.						
Macomb, Alexander and William Edgar.	Permission to complete the payment for certain lands, or restore money already paid.	11	2	Petition	225	Public Lands.						
Macomb, Alexander and William Edgar.	Permission to complete the payment for certain lands, or restore money already paid.	12	1	Petition	137	Claims.						
Macomb, Alexander and William Edgar.	Refunding payment on forfeited lands.	17	1	Petition	118	Public Lands				Discharged; laid on table.		

List of private claims presented to the House of Representatives of the United States from the 1st to the 31st Congress, inclusive—Continued.

Names of claimants.	Nature or object of the claim.	Congress.	Session.	How brought before the House of Reps.	Page of journal.	To what committee of the House referred.	No. or date of the report.	Nature of the report.	No. of the bill.	How disposed of by the House of Reps.	How disposed of by the Senate.	Date of the act of Congress, and remarks.
Macomb, Alexander and William Edgar.	Refunding payment on forfeited lands.	17	2	Petition	65	Public Lands	Jan. 28, 1823	Adverse	......	Laid on table.		
Macomb, Alexander and William Edgar.	Refunding payment on forfeited lands.	18	1	Petition	55	Public Lands	Jan. 20, 1824	Adverse	......	Laid on table.		
Macomb, Alexander	Confirmation of title to land in Michigan.	15	2	Senate bill	270	Priv. Land Claims	Feb. 17, 1819	With't amend.	36	Passed	Passed	App'd March 2, 1819
Macomb, Major General Alexander.	Full pay, &c, while acting as brevet major general.	22	2	Memorial	32	Military Affairs	6	Favorable; bill	624	Recommitted.		
							Feb. 25, 1833	Adverse	......	Laid on table.		
Macomb, Major General Alexander.	Full pay, &c., while acting as brevet major general.	23	1	Memorial	65	....	....	....	......	Referred to Secretary War.		
Macomb, Major General Alexander.	Full pay, &c., while acting as brevet major general.	23	2	Rep. of Secretary War.	213	Claims.						
Macomb, Major General Alexander.	Full pay, &c., while acting as brevet major general.	24	1	Petition and docs.	118	Claims	265	Favorable; bill	272	Referred to Committee Whole House.		
Macomb, Major General Alexander.	Full pay, &c., while acting as brevet major general.	24	2	Bill of last sess.	200	Whole House	....	....	272			
Macomb, Major General Alexander.	Full pay, &c, while acting as brevet major general.	25	2	Petition	37	Claims	3	Favorable; bill	15	Passed	Rejected.	
Macomb, Alexander, heirs of and others.	Release from certain bonds	26	1	Petition	168	Claims	July 21, 1840	Favorable; bill	519	Referred to Committee Whole House.		
Macomb, Alexander, heirs of and others.	Release from certain bonds	27	2	Petition	154	Judiciary	594	Favorable; bill	397	Referred to Committee Whole House.		
Macomb, Alexander, heirs of and others.	Release from certain bonds	27	3	Bill of last sess.	90	Whole House	Dec. 23, 1842	With't amend.	397	Passed	Passed	App'd Feb. 15, 1843
Macomb, James, (N. Y.).	Renewal of patent	10	2	Petition	379	Select	Feb. 28, 1809	Adverse	......	Leave to withdraw.		
Macomb, James, (N. Y.).	Renewal of patent	11	2	Petition	393	....	....	....	......	Laid on table.		
Macomb, James, (N. Y.).	Depreciation of pay as assistant commissary of prisoners during revolutionary war.	11	2	Petition	393	....	....	....	......	Laid on table.		
Macomb, John, William, and David, by attorney.	For a revision of their land claims, and for a confirmation of right.	12	1	Petition	22	Public Lands.						
Macomb, Sarah, and others.	(See William Macomb, representatives of.)	4	2	....	686							
Macomb, William, representatives of.	Confirmation of title to land	4	2	Memorial	686	Select.						
Macomb, William, representatives of.	Compensation for property destroyed in war of 1812.	16	2	Report of Commissioners.	165	Claims	44	Favorable; bill	218	Referred to Committee Whole House.		
Macomb, William, representatives of.	Compensation for property destroyed in war of 1812.	17	1	Report of Commissioners.	107	Claims	7	Favorable; bill	16	Passed	Passed	App'd May 1, 1822
Macomber, Charles H	Payment of certain bills of credit with interest.	26	1	Petition	297	Ways and Means.						
Macomber, Charles H	Payment of certain bills of credit with interest.	27	2	Petition	95	Rev. Pensions.						
Macomber, Charles H	Payment of certain bills of credit with interest.	27	3	Petition	74	Rev. Claims	247	Adverse	......	Laid on table.		
Macomber, Ebenezer	Revolutionary pension	24	1	Resolution	914	Rev. Pensions.						
Macpherson, William	For additional compensation as naval officer of Philadelphia.	12	1	Petition	36	Ways and Means	Dec. 30, 1811	Favorable; bill	34	Recommitted.		
							May 15, 1812	Adverse	......	Rejected.		
Macquillan, Joseph	(See Cynthia H. Prince)	24	1	....	258							
Mactier, Alexander, and others.	Indemnity for French spoliations prior to 1800.	17	1	Petition	40	Foreign Affairs	32	Adverse	......	Referred to Committee Whole House.		

List of private claims presented to the House of Representatives of the United States from the 1st to the 31st Congress, inclusive—Continued.

Names of claimants.	Nature or object of the claim.	Congress.	Session.	How brought before the House of Reps.	Page of journal.	To what committee of the House referred.	No. or date of the report.	Nature of the report.	No. of the bill.	How disposed of by the House of Reps.	How disposed of by the Senate.	Date of the act of Congress, and remarks.
Mactier, Alexander	Indemnity for French spoliations prior to 1800.	26	1	Memorial	182	Foreign Affairs	343	Favorable; bill	319	Referred to Committee Whole House.		
Mactier, Alexander	Indemnity for ship and cargo captured by British in war of 1812.	17	1	Petition	40	Commerce	Jan. 15, 1822	Adverse	......	Laid on table.		
Mactier, Alexander	Indemnity for ship and cargo captured by British in war of 1812.	17	2	Petition	141	Commerce	Mar. 3, 1823	Adverse	......	Leave to withdraw.		
Mactier, Alexander	Indemnity for ship and cargo captured by British in war of 1812.	18	1	Petition	38	Commerce	Dec. 16, 1823	Adverse	......	Leave to withdraw.		
Mactier, Alexander	Indemnity for ship and cargo captured by British in war of 1812.	19	1	Petition	57	Commerce	Feb. 6, 1826	Adverse	......	Leave to withdraw.		
Mactier, Alexander	Indemnity for ship and cargo captured by British in war of 1812.	21	2	Petition	45	Commerce	....	....	......	Discharged; laid on table.		
Macullaugh, Alexander	(See McCullough)	11	2	....	227							
Macy, Charles C	Permission to locate land, one quarter section, in lieu of one sold by mistake by land office.	29	1	Petition	147	Public Lands.						
Macy, Francis G., *et al*	Remission of foreign tonnage duty on ship General Jackson.	18	1	Petition	132	Ways and Means	32	Favorable; bill	62	Passed	Passed	App'd May 17, 1824
Macy, Francis G	Indemnity for French spoliations prior to 1800.	26	1	Memorial	182	Foreign Affairs	343	Favorable; bill	319	Referred to Committee Whole House.		
Macy, Thomas	Increase of compensation as postmaster at Nantucket, Mass.	16	1	Petition	28	P. Of. & P. Roads	Mar. 3, 1820	Adverse	......	Laid on table.		
Macy, Thomas	Increase of compensation as postmaster at Nantucket, Mass.	18	2	Petition	134	Claims	....	....	......	Discharged; laid on table.		
Macy, Thomas	Indemnity for French spoliations prior to 1800.	29	2	Memorial	70	Foreign Affairs.						
Maddan, Patrick H	Bounty land as Canadian refugee.	15	1	Petition	157	Military Affairs	Mar. 14, 1818	Adverse	......	Rejected.		
Maddin, William J	(See James H. Gentry, assignee of.)	28	1	....	632							
Maddin, Thomas	Confirmation of title to land in Michigan.	15	1	Petition	180	Priv. Land Claims	....	....	......	Discharged; laid on table.		
Maddin, Thomas	Confirmation of title to land in Michigan.	16	1	Petition	71	Priv. Land Claims.						
Maddin, Thomas	Confirmation of title to land in Michigan.	17	1	Petition	54	Priv. Land Claims	....	....	......	Discharged; laid on table.		
Maddin, Thomas	Confirmation of title to land in Michigan.	18	1	Petition	54	Priv. Land Claims	Jan. 16, 1824	Favorable; bill	65	Passed	Passed	App'd May 26, 1824
Madding, Daniel	Arrears of pension	24	2	Petition	311	Invalid Pensions	....	....	......	Discharged; laid on table.		
Maddis, Charles	Compensation for services in late war.	27	2	Petition	369	Military Affairs	....	....	......	Discharged; laid on table.		
Maddis, Charles	Compensation for services in late war.	27	3	Petition	71	Military Affairs	221	Adverse	......	Laid on table.		
Maddocks, Samuel	Revolutionary pension	23	1	Petition	174	Rev. Claims.						
Maddox, John	Increase of pension	26	2	Petition	122	Rev. Pensions.						
Maddox, Matthew	Invalid pension	5	3	Petition	422	Claims	....	....	......	Discharged; leave to withdraw.		
Maddox, William R., and Gregory Ennis.	Compensation for grading streets around the Capitol.	18	2	Senate bill	123	Dist. of Columbia	Jan. 18, 1825	With't amend.	14	Passed	Passed	App'd March 3, 1825
Maddox, William R	Payment for bricks used on United States Capitol.	16	2	Petition	181	Public Buildings.						
Maddox, William R	Payment for bricks used on United States Capitol.	17	1	Petition	474	Public Buildings	April 29, 1822	Favorable; bill	185	Passed	Passed	App'd May 7, 1822

List of private claims presented to the House of Representatives of the United States from the 1st to the 31st Congress, inclusive—Continued.

Names of claimants.	Nature or object of the claim.	Congress.	Session.	How brought before the House of Reps.	Page of journal.	To what committee of the House referred.	No. or date of the report.	Nature of the report.	No. of the bill.	How disposed of by the House of Reps.	How disposed of by the Senate.	Date of the act of Congress, and remarks.
Maddox, William R.	Additional payment for brick, &c.	17	2	Petition	122	Public Buildings				Discharged; leave to withdraw.		
Maddox, William R.	Additional payment for brick, &c.	18	1	Petition	198	Public Buildings	April 30, 1824	Adverse		Laid on table.		
Maddox, William R.	Additional payment for brick, &c.	19	1	Petition	151	Select	April 1, 1826	Favorable; bill	198	Passed.		
Maddox, William R.	Additional payment for brick, &c.	19	2	Petition	50	Public Buildings	16	Favorable; bill	311	Laid on table.		
Maddox, William R.	Additional payment for brick, &c.	20	1	Petition	166	Public Buildings	172	Favorable; bill	203	Referred to Committee Whole House.		
Maddox, William R.	Additional payment for brick, &c.	20	2	Bill of last sess.	202	Whole House			203	Passed	Passed	App'd March 3, 1829
Madeore, Benedict	For arbitration of conflicting claims to property of U. S. and Catholic church.	30	1	Joint resolution from Senate.	1012	Priv. Land Claims.	Aug. 8, 1848	With't amend.	32	Passed	Passed	App'd Aug. 11, 1848
Madera, Nicholas	Revolutionary pension	23	1	Petition	379	Rev. Pensions.						
Madison, Channing	Indemnity for loss on contract with government.	24	1	Petition	430	Claims	698	Adverse		Laid on table.		
Madison, George, daughter of.	Compensation for revolutionary services.	25	3	Senate bill	618				S. 267			
Madison, James, executor of.	Payment of a loan office certificate	25	2	Memorial	722	Rev. Claims	May 11, 1838	By bill	770	Postponed.		
Madison, James, executor of.	Payment of a loan office certificate	26	1	Memorial	165	Rev. Claims.						
Madison, William	Commutation pay for revolutionary services.	25	2	Petition	392	Rev. Claims	728	Favorable; bill	694	Referred to Committee Whole House.		
Madison, William	Commutation pay for revolutionary services.	25	3	House bill	266	Whole House			694	Rejected.		
Madison, William	(See James Madison, executor of.)	25	2		722							
Madrazo, Don Juan	For losses by illegal seizure of his property by officers of the United States.	23	1	Resolution	630	Claims	June 33, 1834	Adverse		Laid on table.		
Madrazo, Don Juan	For loss by illegal seizure of his property by officers of the United States.	23	2	Resolution	92	Claims.						
Madrazo, Don Juan	For loss by illegal seizure of his property by officers of the United States.	24	1	Petition	50	Claims	629	Referred to the President for opinion of Att'y General		Case returned by the President and recommitted to Com. on Claims.		
Madrazo, Don Juan	For losses by illegal seizure of his property by officers of the United States.	24	2	Petition	123	Claims	250	Adverse		Laid on table.		
Madry, Samuel	Revolutionary pension	23	1	Petition	113	Rev. Pensions				Discharged; laid on table.		
Mæstre, John	Confirmation of title to land in Florida.	21	1	Petition	524	Priv. Land Claims				Discharged; laid on table.		
Maffet, Eliza	(See William and John Welsh, heirs of.)	27	2		1030							
Maffit, John S	(See John S. Moffitt.)	17	2		225							
Maggart, Henry	Invalid pension	22	1	Resolution	455, 582	Invalid Pensions.						
Maggart, Henry	Invalid pension	22	2	Petition	40	Invalid Pensions	Mar. 2, 1833	Adverse		Laid on table.		
Maggart, Henry	Invalid pension	23	1	Petition	44	Invalid Pensions	Dec. 20, 1833	Adverse		Laid on table.		
Maggart, Henry	Invalid pension	24	1	Resolution	676	Invalid Pensions	711	Favorable; bill.	664	Passed	Passed	App'd June 28, 1836
Magee, Hugh	Pension	18	2	Petition	117	Pens. & Rev. Cl'ms						
Magee, W. F.	(See Megee)	6	2		825							

List of private claims presented to the House of Representatives of the United States from the 1st to the 31st Congress, inclusive—Continued.

Names of claimants.	Nature or object of the claim.	Congress.	Session.	How brought before the House of Reps.	Page of journal.	To what committee of the House referred.	No. or date of the report.	Nature of the report.	No. of the bill.	How disposed of by the House of Reps.	How disposed of by the Senate.	Date of the act of Congress, and remarks.
Maginn, Daniel	Invalid pension	29	2	Documents	136	Naval Affairs.						
Magill, David	Indemnity for Indian depredations.	22	2	Petition	122	Indian Affairs	91	Adverse		Laid on table.		
Magill, David	Indemnity for Indian depredations.	24	1	Petition	96	Indian Affairs	266	Favorable; bill.	273	Ref'd to Com. W. H.		
Magill, David	Indemnity for Indian depredations.	25	2	Petition	43	Indian Affairs	212	Favorable; bill.	248	Referred to Committee Whole House.		
Maglaughlin, Andrew	Increase of pension	29	1	Petition	85	Rev. Pensions.						
Maglenen, Elizabeth A	(See James Maglenen, heirs of.)	25	3		120							
Maglenen, James, heirs of.	Payment for property lost in war 1812.	25	3	Petition	120	Claims	172	Favorable; bill	1035	Passed	Adverse report.	
Maglenen, James, heirs of.	Payment for property lost in war 1812.	26	1	Petition	168	Claims.						
Maglenen, James, heirs of.	Payment for property lost in war 1812.	26	2	Petition	79	Claims	37	Favorable; bill	565	Referred to Committee Whole House.		
Maglenen, James, heirs of.	Payment for property lost in war 1812.	27	2	Petition	154	Claims	46	Favorable; bill	81	Passed	Indef. postp'd.	
Maglenen, Susan	(See James Maglenen, heirs of.)	25	3		120							
Magness, Morgan	Permission to enter lands in Arkansas.	18	1	Petition	238	Public Lands				Discharged; leave to withdraw.		
Magness, Morgan	Permission to enter lands in Arkansas.	19	2	Petition	50	Public Lands	18	Adverse		Laid on table.		
Magoon, John	Revolutionary pension	25	2	Petition	54	Rev. Pensions.						
Magoon, John	Revolutionary pension	26	1	Petition	284	Rev. Pensions	635	Favorable; bill	648	Referred to Committee Whole House.		
Magoon, John	Revolutionary pension	27	2	Petition	59	Rev. Pensions	784	Adverse		Laid on table.		
Magoun, Thatcher	Refunding a fine in case of ship Timoleon.	24	1	Petition	691					Referred to 1st Comptroller to adjust.		
Magraw, Samuel B., administrator of.	Compensation for whiskey destroyed by British in war of 1812.	17	1	Petition	248	Claims	Feb. 25, 1822	Adverse		Rejected.		
Magraw, William	(See Samuel B. Magraw, administrator of.)	17	1		248							
Magruder, Elizabeth	(See Rignall Hillary, heirs of.)	21	2		101							
Magruder, Elizabeth	(See Ann Brashears, by representatives of.)	22	1		502							
Magruder, George, and others.	(See Bowie & Kurtz, and others.)	13	2		176							
Magruder, George B	(See John Mitchell, and others.)	7	1		176							
Magruder, Nathan	Revolutionary pension	23	1	Petition	436	Rev. Pensions.						
Magruder, Thomas B	(See Ann Brashears)											
Magruder, William B. & Co., trustee of.	Indemnity for French spoliations prior to 1800.	26	1	Memorial	182	Foreign Affairs	343	Favorable; bill	319	Referred to Committee Whole House.		
Magrue, Andrew	Remission of duty on distilled spirits.	14	1	Petition	157	Ways and Means	Feb. 24, 1816	Adverse		Rejected.		
Maguet, Anthony	(See Stephen Monot, and others.)	5	2		225							
Maguire, Bartholomew	Arrears of pension	28	1	Petition	114	Invalid Pensions	264	Favorable; bill	196	Passed	Passed	App'd May 23, 1844
Maguire & Douglass	Compensation for property lost in an expedition against the Indians.	24	1	Petition	430	Claims.						
Maguire, James, (D. C.)	Compensation as surperintendent of lithographic press at War Department.	23	1	Petition	245	Claims	Feb. 5, 1834	Adverse		Laid on table.		
Maguire, James, (Mo.)	Compensation for extra services in subsistence department.	24	1	Petition	49	Claims	135	Adverse		Laid on table.		
Maguire, James, (Mo.)	Compensation for extra services in subsistence department.	26	1	Petition	338	Claims.						

List of private claims presented to the House of Representatives of the United States from the 1st to the 31st Congress, inclusive—Continued.

Names of claimants.	Nature or object of the claim.	Congress.	Session.	How brought before the House of Reps.	Page of journal.	To what committee of the House referred.	No. or date of the report.	Nature of the report.	No. of the bill.	How disposed of by the House of Reps.	How disposed of by the Senate.	Date of the act of Congress, and remarks.
Maguire, James, (Mo.)	Compensation for extra services in subsistence department.	26	2	Petition	80	Claims	68	Adverse		Laid on table.		
Maguire, John H.	Compensation for extra services as secretary to navy pension fund.	22	2	Petition	53	Claims	98	Favorable; bill	739	Referred to Committee Whole House.		
Maguire, John H.	Compensation for extra services as secretary to navy pension fund.	23	1	Petition	34	Claims	18	Favorable; bill	18	Passed	Passed	App'd May 10, 1834
Mahan, Alfred	Compensation for a horse lost in United States service.	24	2	Resolution	98					Referred to 3d Auditor.		
Mahan, Sarah, widow of, John.	Commutation pay for revolutionary services.	21	2	Petition	191	Rev. Claims				Laid on table.		
Maher, James and John	Indemnity for property destroyed in war of 1812.	15	2	Petition	44	Claims	Dec. 21, 1818	Adverse		Rejected.		
Maher, James	Payment for trees furnished public grounds.	31	2	Petition	178	Public Buildings & Grounds.						
Maher, John	(See William Gale, by assignees.)	17	1		220							
Maher, John, (N. Y.)	Indemnity for losses in advancing money to quartermaster's department in war of 1812.	17	1	Petition	289	Claims				Discharged; laid on table.		
Maher, John, (N. Y.)	Indemnity for losses in advancing money to quartermaster's department in war of 1812.	18	1	Petition	249	Claims	April 26, 1826	Adverse		Laid on table.		
Maher, Mathias	Confirmation of title to land in Mississippi.	8	2	Memorial	128					Ref'd to Com. W. H. on bill No. 49.		
Maher & McDermott	Remission of alien duty on rum	6	2	Petition	786	Com. and Manuf.	Feb. 9, 1801	Adverse		Leave to withdraw.		
Maher, Patrick	Revolutionary pension	21	1	Resolution	342	Military Pensions				Discharged; laid on table.		
Mahew, Thadeus	Indemnity for property destroyed in war of 1812.	15	1	Petition	34	Claims	Mar. 13, 1818	Favorable; bill	137	Referred to Committee Whole House.		
Mahew, Thadeus	Indimnity for property destroyed in war of 1812.	15	2	Bill of last sess.	116	Whole House	61	With amend.	137	Recommitted.		
Mable & Cable	Confirmation of title to land	27	2	Documents	75	Priv. Land Claims.						
Mahle, Frederick, widow of.	Pension	29	1	Memorial	260	Rev. Claims	527	Adverse		Laid on table.		
Mahle, John H.	Land in lieu of that which he has been deprived of by government.	26	1	Petition	947	Priv. Land Claims.						
Mahl, Polly	(See Frederick Mahl, widow of)	29	1		260							
Mahon, John	Bounty land for services in 1774	15	2	Petition	163	Public Lands				Discharged; leave to withdraw.		
Mahon, John, and Asa Munger.	Release from judgment as sureties of Daniel Holt.	24	1	Resolution	173	P. Of. & P. Roads.	626	Adverse		Laid on table.		
Mahon, John, and Asa Munger.	Release from judgment as sureties of Daniel Holt.	25	2	Resolution	425	P. Of. & P. Roads.	714	Adverse		Laid on table.		
Mahon, Patrick	Revolutionary pension	22	1	Resolution	535	Rev. Pensions				Disch'd; laid on table.		
Mahoney, James, (Pa)	Invalid pension	12	1	Petition	165					Ref'd to Com. W. H. on bill No. 15.		
Mahoney, James	Compensation for horse lost in Mexican war.	30	1	Petition	146	Claims	238	Favorable; bill	238	Referred to Committee Whole House.		
Mahey, William	Pension and bounty land for service in army and navy.	16	2	Rept's Secretaries War and Navy.	105					Laid on table.		
Main, John	(See John Wain)	27	3		259							
Maine, merchants of Portland.	Indemnity for French spoliations prior to 1800.	17	1	Memorial	173	Select	April 22, 1802	Adverse		Laid on table.		
Maine, merchants of Portland.	Indemnity for French spoliations prior to 1800.	18	1	Memorial	284	Foreign Affairs	94	Adverse		Laid on table.		

List of private claims presented to the House of Representatives of the United States form the 1st to the 31st Congress, inclusive—Continued.

Names of claimants.	Nature or object of the claim.	Congress.	Session.	How brought before the House of Reps.	Page of journal.	To what committee of the House referred.	No. or date of the report.	Nature of the report.	No. of the bill.	How disposed of by the House of Reps.	How disposed of by the Senate.	Date of the act of Congress, and remarks.
Maine, merchants of Portland.	Indemnity for French spoliations prior to 1800.	19	2	Memorial	30	Foreign Affairs.						
Maine, merchants of Kennebunk.	Indemnity for French spoliations prior to 1800.	18	1	Memorial	296	Foreign Affairs....	94	Adverse	......	Laid on table.		
Maine, sundry citizens of..	Indemnity for French spoliations prior to 1800.	27	3	Memorial	284	Whole House.						
Maine, sundry citizens of..	Indemnity for French spoliations prior to 1800.	28	1	Memorial	116	Foreign Affairs.						
Maine, sundry citizens of..	Compensation for services as militia under authority of United States.	13	1	Petition	78	....	....	....	......	Referred to Secretary War.		
Maine, State of..........	Compensation for services of militia.	26	1	Senate bill	853	Military Affairs....	566	Favorable, with amendments.	S. 325	Referred to Committee Whole House.		
Maine, State of..........	Compensation for services of militia.	26	2	H. bill, on leave .	58	Military Affairs. ..	78	Favorable, with amendments.	527	Referred to Committee Whole House.		
Maine, State of..........	Compensation for services of militia.	27	2	H. bill, on leave.	106	Military Affairs...	....	....	66			
Maine, State of..........	Compensation for services of militia.	27	2	Senate bill	411	Military Affairs....	363	Favorable, with amendments.	S. 4	Passed	Passed	App'd June 13, 1842
Maine, legislature of......	Refunding money paid her citizens for losses in settling Northeast boundary.	24	2	Presid'ts message	325	Foreign Affairs....	249	Adverse	......	Laid on table.		
Maine, legislature of......	Refunding money paid her citizens for losses in settling Northeast boundary.	25	2	Presid'ts message	949	Foreign Affairs.						
Maine, legislature of......	Refunding money, with interest, advanced for protection of North east frontier.	31	1	Bill on leave....	967	Ways and Means..	....	....	308			
Maine, legislature of......	Refunding money, with interest, advanced for protection of North-east frontier.	31	1	Senate bill	1118	Judiciary	....	....	S. 232			
Maine, legislature of......	Refunding money, with interest, advanced for protection of North-east frontier.	31	2	Senate bill of last session.	174	Judiciary.........	Jan. 22, 1851	With't amend.	S. 232	Passed	....	App'd March 3, 1851
Maine, sundry citizens of..	For an equitable adjustment of claims, on the Arostook, under treaty.	29	1	Petition	280	Judiciary.						
Maine, citizens of Penobscot.	Relief from forfeitures for violation of non-importation act.	13	2	Petition	266	Ways and Means..	April 5, 1814	Res. for leave to withdraw.	......	Resolution adopted.		
Maine, sundry citizens of..	Remission of duty on railroad iron.	28	1	Petition	355, 415	Commerce.						
Maine, merchants of Bangor.	Drawback of duties on domestic spirits distilled from foreign molasses.	28	1	Petition	297	Commerce	....	....	......	Discharged; laid on table.		
Maine, citizens of Eastport.	Remission of duties on goods found at Eastport.	15	2	Petition	109	Ways and Means.						
Maine, citizens of Hampden.	To be allowed the property recovered from wreck of United States ship Adams, as compensation for losses in late war.	13	3	Petition	484	....	....	....	......	Referred to Secretary Navy.		
Maine, citizens of Portland.	For a share of prize money of brig Herrick, captured in revolutionary war.	21	2	Petition	207	Foreign Affairs....	100	Adverse	......	Laid on table.		

List of private claims presented to the House of Representatives of the United States from the 1st to the 31st Congress, inclusive—Continued.

Names of claimants.	Nature or object of the claim.	Congress.	Session.	How brought before the House of Reps.	Page of journal.	To what committee of the House referred.	No. or date of the report.	Nature of the report.	No. of the bill.	How disposed of by the House of Reps.	How disposed of by the Senate.	Date of the act of Congress, and remarks.
Maine, soldiers of revolutionary war, residing in.	Pension	21	2	Petition	42, 113	Military Pensions.						
Maine, soldiers of revolutionary war, residing in.	Pension	22	1	Petition	45	Rev. Pensions.						
Maine, officers of Hancock barracks.	(See officers, &c.)	22	2		397							
Maine, Fire and Marine Insurance Co., agent of.	Indemnity for French spoliations prior to 1800.	26	1	Memorial	182	Foreign Affairs	343	Favorable; bill	319	Referred to Committee Whole House.		
Mainard, Daniel, (Ky.)	Compensation for losses and injuries at the battle of Tippecanoe.	12	2	Petition	578	Claims.						
Mains, or Moins, James	Invalid pension	26	•2	Petition	55	Invalid Pensions.						
Mains, or Moins, James	Invalid pension	27	2	Petition	321	Invalid Pensions	624	Adverse		Laid on table.		
Mains, or Moins, James	Invalid pension	27	3	Petition	132	Invalid Pensions	217	Favorable; bill	813	Referred to Committee Whole House.		
Mains, or Moins, James	Invalid pension	28	1	Petition	131	Invalid Pensions	283	Adverse		Laid on table.		
Mains, or Moins, James	Invalid pension	29	1	Petition	107	Invalid Pensions	44	Favorable; bill	39	Passed	Passed	App'd July 15, 1846
Mains, or Moins, James	Invalid pension	31	1	Petition	623	Invalid Pensions	300	Favorable; bill	269	Referred to Committee Whole House.		
Mains, or Moins, James	Invalid pension	31	2	Bill of last sess.	182	Whole House	Jan. 24, 1851	With amends.	269	Passed.		
Maitland, Phelps & Co.	Relief on account of burning merchandise in the public stores in the city of New York.	31	2	Petition	177	Commerce.						
Maitland, Robert	Remission of duties on coffee destroyed by fire.	8	1	Petition	646	Com. and Manuf.						
Maitland, William	(See J. Lenox, and others)	17	1		32							
Major, Alexander, & others	Confirmation of title to a tract of land.	31	1	Petition	1227	Priv. Land Claims.						
Major, Julie	(See Alexander Major, and others)	31	1		1227							
Major, Martin	(See Alexander Major, and others)	31	1		1227							
Majors, Thomas	(See David Shaver, and others)	21	2		75							
Makepeace, George, heirs of.	Indemnity for French spoliations prior to 1800.	23	2	Petition	307	Foreign Affairs.						
Makepeace, George, administrator of.	Indemnity for French spoliations prior to 1800.	26	1	Memorial	182	Foreign Affairs	343	Favorable; bill	319	Referred to Committee Whole House.		
Makins, Samuel, widow of	Revolutionary pension	27	3	Petition	151	Rev. Pensions.						
Makins, Sarah	(See Samuel Makins, widow of)	27	3		151							
Malachowsky, Marie Amede.	(See widow of Mauritz Von Malachowsky.)	31	1		640							
Malachowsky, Mauritz Von, widow of.	Pension and bounty land	31	1	Petition	640	Invalid Pensions.						
Malarin, Gregorie	Confirmation of title to land in Louisiana.	22	1	Petition	64	Priv. Land Claims.	Dec. 27, 1831	Favorable; bill	125	Passed	Passed	App'd June 25, 1832
Malary, James	(See John Phelps, in behalf of his minor son.)	31	2		78							
Malcolm, Henry	Compensation for revolutionary services.	1	1	Petition	112					Referred to Secretary of War.		
Malcolm, Henry	Compensation for revolutionary services.	1	2	Rep. of Secretary War.	141	Select.						
Malcolm, Henry, collector of New York.	For a credit of $1,000 lost in mail	11	2	Petition	239	Select	April 16, 1810	Adverse		Rejected.		
Malcolm, Henry, collector of New York.	For a credit of $1,000 lost in mail	12	1	Petition	60	Select.						

List of private claims presented to the House of Representatives of the United States from the 1st to the 31st Congress, inclusive—Continued

Names of claimants.	Nature or object of the claim.	Congress.	Session.	How brought before the House of Reps.	Page of journal.	To what committee of the House referred.	No. or date of the report.	Nature of the report.	No. of the bill.	How disposed of by the House of Reps.	How disposed of by the Senate.	Date of the act of Congress, and remarks.
Malcolm, Henry, collector of New York.	For a credit of $1,000 lost in mail	13	1	Petition	31	Select.						
Malcolm, Henry, collector of New York.	For a credit of $1,000 lost in mail	13	2	Petition	171	Select	Feb. 11, 1814	Favorable; bill	117	Passed	Postponed.	
Malcolm, Henry, collector of New York.	For a credit of $1,000 lost in mail	14	1	Petition and rep't Sec. Treasury.	256	Ways and Means	Feb. 14, 1816	Favorable; bill	79	Passed	Rejected.	
Malcolm, Henry, collector of New York.	For a credit of $1,000 lost in mail	14	2	Petition	59	Ways and Means	Dec. 18, 1816	Favorable; bill	16	Passed	Passed	App'd Feb. 8, 1817
Malcolm, Richard M.	Arrears of pension	17	1	Petition	474	Pens. & Rev. Cl'ms.				Discharged; laid on table.		
Malcolm, Richard M.	Arrears of pension	17	2	Petition	118	Pens. & Rev. Cl'ms.				Discharged; laid on table.		
Malcolm, Col. R. M.	Equitable settlement of accounts, and release from judgment as a defaulter.	17	2	Petition	208	Claims				Discharged; leave to withdraw.		
Malcolm, William	(See Comfort Sands, and others).	1	3		358							
Malcolm, Wm., and others	Payment of proceeds of two prizes which had reverted to the United States.	13	2	Petition	368	Ways and Means.						
Malette, Theresa	(See Gaspard Phiole, heirs of widow of.	26	2		225							
Maley, James	Refunding money erroneously paid for land in Ohio.	22	2	Resolution	35	Ways and Means.						
Maley, James	Refunding money erroneously paid for land in Ohio.	23	1	Resolution	116	Ways and Means				Discharged; laid on table.		
Maley, James	Refunding money erroneously paid for land in Ohio.	24	1	Resolution	429	Claims	700	Adverse		Laid on table.		
Malin, Jonathan	Compensation for services in war of 1812.	22	1	Petition	172	Claims	Jan. 20, 1832	Adverse		Leave to withdraw.		
Mallaby, Francis	Allowance for quarters as sailing master.	25	2	Petition	371	Claims	553	Favorable; bill	541	Referred to Committee Whole House.		
Mallaby, Francis	Allowance for quarters as sailing master.	25	3	Bill of last sess.	379	Whole House	Jan. 26, 1839	With't amend.	541	Passed	Passed	App'd March 3, 1839
Mallard, John, widow of.	Revolutionary pension	31	1	Petition	472	Rev. Pensions	132	Adverse		Laid on table.		
Mallard, Polly	(See John Mallard, widow of)	31	1		472							
Mallary, David, (Conn.)	Revolutionary pension	22	1	Petition	219	Rev. Pensions.						
Mallery, Henry S	Compensation for services as brevet captain in United States army.	23	2	Petition	347	Military Affairs.						
Mallery, Henry S	Compensation for services as brevet captain in United States army.	24	1	Petition	97	Military Affairs.						
Mallett, Francis	Revolutionary pension	23	1	Petition	46	Rev. Pensions.						
Mallett, Louis, and others.	Confirmation of title to land in Indiana.	12	2	Petition	609	Public Lands.						
Mallett, Louis, and others.	Confirmation of title to land in Indiana.	13	2	Petition	197	Public Lands	Mar. 23, 1814	Adverse; leave to withdraw.		Report adopted.		
Mallory, David	Revolutionary pension	25	2	Resolution	533	Rev. Pensions				Discharged; laid on table.		
Mallory, David	Revolutionary pension	26	1	Resolution	174	Rev. Pensions.						
Mallory, Enos	Revolutionary pension	31	1	Petition	628	Invalid Pensions.						
Mallory, George	Compensation for services as master armorer at Harper's Ferry.	27	2	Petition	833	Claims.						
Mallory, George	Compensation for services as master armorer at Harper's Ferry.	27	3	Petition	209	Claims.						

List of private claims presented to the House of Representatives of the United States from the 1st to the 31st Congress, inclusive—Continued.

Names of claimants.	Nature or object of the claim.	Congress.	Session.	How brought before the House of Reps.	Page of journal.	To what committee of the House referred.	No. or date of the report.	Nature of the report.	No. of the bill.	How disposed of by the House of Reps.	How disposed of by the Senate.	Date of the act of Congress, and remarks.
Mallory, John H	Release from judgment of United States.	18	1	Petition	331	Claims.						
Mallory, John H	Release from judgment of United States.	21	1	Petition	499	Judiciary				Discharged; laid on table.		
Mallory, Thomas, (Va.)	For allowance of pay and rations during sickness as lieutenant in Virginia militia.	13	3	Petition	463	Claims				Discharged.		
Mallory, Thomas, (Va.)	For allowance of pay and rations during sickness as lieutenant in Virginia militia.	14	1	Petition	400	Claims				Discharged; laid on table.		
Malone, Daniel	Correction of land entry	22	2	Senate bill	85	Priv. Land Claims.	Dec. 22, 1832	With't amend.	16	Referred to Committee Whole House.		
Malone, Daniel	Correction of land entry	23	2	Resolution	332	Public Lands.						
Malone, Daniel	Correction of land entry	24	1	Petition	478	Public Lands	489	Favorable; bill	491	Referred to Committee Whole House.		
Malone, Daniel	Correction of land entry	25	2	Petition	42	Public Lands	375	Favorable; bill.	398	Referred to Committee Whole House.		
Malone, Daniel	Correction of land entry	25	3	Bill of last sess.	378	Whole House	Jan. 25, 1839	With't amend.	398	Passed	Passed	App'd March 2 1839
Malone, Francis	Compensation for services in revolutionary war.	26	1	Resolution	392	Rev. Claims	615	Adverse		Laid on table.		
Malone, Isaac	Revolutionary pension	28	1	Petition	318	Rev. Pensions				Discharged; laid on table.		
Malone, John	Invalid pension	3	1	Rep. of Secretary War.	131	Select	May 26, 1794	Favorable	J. R. 12	Referred to Secretary War.		
Malone, John	Invalid pension	4	1	Rep. of Secretary War.	445	Claims	Feb. 18, 1796	Favorable	J. R. 16	Referred to Secretary War.		
Malone, John or Peter	Confirmation of title to land in Mississippi.	12	1	Petition	13	Public Lands.						
Malone, John or Peter	Confirmation of title to land in Mississippi.	12	2	Petition	663	Public Lands.						
Malone, John, and others	Confirmation of title to land in Mississippi.	15	1	Petition	158	Priv. Land Claims				Discharged; laid on table.		
Malone, John (Tenn.)	(See John Melone)	20	1		366							
Malone, John, heirs of	Compensation for wagon and team lost in revolutionary war.	23	1	Petition	639	Rev. Claims.						
Malone, John, heirs of	Compensation for wagon and team lost in revolutionary war.	23	2	Petition	77	Rev. Claims.						
Malone, John, heirs of	Compensation for wagon and team lost in revolutionary war.	24	1	Petition	431	Rev. Claims	653	Adverse		Laid on table.		
Malone, Leslie	Revolutionary pension	24	2	Memorial	153	Rev. Pensions	105	Adverse		Laid on table.		
Malone, Richard	(See heirs of John Malone)	23	1		639							
Malone, Thomas	(See Josias Bullock)	11	3		510							
Malone, Thomas, *et al.*	Confirmation of title to land in Mississippi.	14	1	Petition	153	Public Lands.						
Malone, Thomas, *et al.*	Confirmation of title to land in Mississippi.	14	2	Petition	50	Priv. Land Claims.	Feb. 11, 1817	Favorable; bill	123	Referred to Committee Whole House.		
Malone, Thomas, *et al.*	Confirmation of title to land in Mississippi.	15	1	Petition	39	Priv. Land Claims				Discharged; laid on table.		
Malone, William	(See William H. Bedford, agent.)	28	1		262							
Maloy, Bartholomew	Revolutionary pension	18	1	Resolution	64	Rev. Pensions	Jan. 12, 1824	Adverse		Laid on table.		
Maloy, Bartholomew	Revolutionary pension	19	1	Resolution	143	Military Pensions	164	Adverse		Laid on table.		
Maloy, James	Revolutionary pension	25	2	Petition	271	Rev. Pensions	Mar. 30, 1838	Adverse		Laid on table.		

List of private claims presented to the House of Representatives of the United States from the 1st to the 31st Congress, inclusive—Continued.

Names of claimants.	Nature or object of the claim.	Congress.	Session.	How brought before the House of Reps.	Page of journal.	To what committee of the House referred.	No. or date of the report.	Nature of the report.	No. of the bill.	How disposed of by the House of Reps.	How disposed of by the Senate.	Date of the act of Congress, and remarks.
Malphus, Ezekiel, assignee of.	That a certain military certificate may inure to the benefit of the assignee of.	2	1	Petition	466	....	....	....	......	Referred to Secretary of Treasury.		
Maltby, Jasper A	Bounty land for services in Mexican war.	31	1	Petition	596	Public Lands	248	Favorable; bill.	245	Referred to Committee Whole House.		
Maltby, Jasper, A	Bounty land for services in Mexican war.	31	2	Bill of last sess.	181	Whole House	Jan. 24, 1851	With't amend.	245	Passed.		
Maltier, Chilo A	Relief for unjust deprivation of his land in Arkansas.	19	1	Petition	179	Public Lands	....	....	......	Discharged; leave to withdraw.		
Malusky, Daniel	Pension	21		Resolution	432	Military Pensions	....	....	......	Disch'd; laid on table.		
Malusky, Daniel	Pension	21	2	Resolution	77	Military Pensions.						
Malusky, Daniel	Pension	22	1	Resolution	45	Rev. Pensions	....	....	......	Discharged; laid on table.		
Man & Foltz, agents of	Indemnity for French spoliations prior to 1800.	26	1	Memorial	182	Foreign Affairs	343	Favorable; bill	319	Referred to Committee Whole House.		
Man, Geo. F. and Samuel F.	Compensation for services in Rhode Island brigade in revolutionary war.	14	2	Petition	283	Pens & Rev. Clm's.						
Man, Geo. F. and Samuel F.	Compensation for services in Rhode Island brigade in revolutionary war.	23	2	Memorial	67	Select	Feb. 25, 1835	By bill	769	Referred to Committee Whole House.		
Man, Geo. F. and Samuel F.	Compensation for services in Rhode Island brigade in revolutionary war.	24	1	Petition and docs.	136	Select	337	Favorable; bill	352	Referred to Committee Whole House.		
Manac, Samuel	Compensation for property destroyed by Creek Indians.	14	1	Petition	438	Claims	April 16, 1816	Favorable; bill	......	Passed	Passed	App'd April 27, 1816
Manakin, Isaiah	(See Joshua Harvey and others.)	7	2	....	343							
Manayhan, John	(See John Stoop, administrator of.)	24	1	....	613							
Manchester, Gershom	Revolutionary pension	31	2	Petition	431	Rev. Pensions	46	Adverse	......	Laid on table.		
Manchester, Isaac	Indemnity for French spoliations prior to 1800.	26	1	Memorial	182	Foreign Affairs	343	Favorable	319	Referred to Committee Whole House.		
Manchester, Isaac	Indemnity for French spoliations prior to 1800.	31	1	Petition	197	Foreign Affairs	355	Favorable; bill	318	Referred to Commitee Whole House.		
Manchester, James	Compensation for services in Rhode Island brigade in revolutionary war.	14	2	Petition	283	Pens. & Rev. Cl'ms.						
Manchester, James	Compensation for services in Rhode Island brigade in revolutionary war.	23	2	Memorial	67	Select	Feb. 25, 1835	By bill	769	Referred to Committee Whole House.		
Manchester, James	Compensation for services in Rhode Island brigade in revolutionary war.	24	1	Petition and docs.	136	Select	337	Favorable; bill	352	Referred to Committee Whole House.		
Mancius, Jacob, and wife.	(See William Barber, heirs of.)	11	2	....	120							
Mandeville, John, widow of.	Compensation for property destroyed in revolutionary war.	25	2	Petition	111	Rev. Claims	470	Favorable; bill	477	Referred to Committee Whole House.		
Mandeville, John, widow of.	Compensation for property destroyed in revolutionary war.	25	3	Bill of last sess.	378	Whole House	....	....	477			
Mandeville, John, widow of.	Compensation for property destroyed in revolutionary war.	26	1	Petition	165	Rev. Claims.						
Mandeville, John, widow of.	Compensation for property destroyed in revolutionary war.	27	2	Petition	268	Rev. Claims	1070	Adverse	......	Laid on table.		
Mandeville, John, widow of.	Compensation for property destroyed in revolutionary war.	28	1	Petition	435	Rev. Claims.						

List of private claims presented to the House of Representatives of the United States from the 1st to the 31st Congress, inclusive—Continued.

Names of claimants.	Nature or object of the claim.	Congress.	Session.	How brought before the House of Reps.	Page of journal.	To what committee of the House referred.	No. or date of the report.	Nature of the report.	No. of the bill.	How disposed of by the House of Reps.	How disposed of by the Senate.	Date of the act of Congress, and remarks.
Mandeville, John, widow of.	Compensation for property destroyed in revolutionary war.	30	1	Petition	270	Rev. Claims	675	Favorable; bill	539	Referred to Committee Whole House.		
Mandeville, John, widow of.	Compensation for property destroyed in revolutionary war.	31	1	Petition	275	Rev. Claims.						
Mandeville, John, widow of.	Compensation for property destroyed in revolutionary war.	31	2	Petition	174	Rev. Claims				Discharged; laid on table.		
Mandeville, Sarah	(See John Mandeville, widow of.)	25	2		111							
Maney, Jno. H., and others.	Indemnity for Indian depredations.	21	2	Petition	163	Indian Affairs.						
Mangham, Thomas, and others.	Indemnity for Indian depredations.	31	2	Senate bill	352	Indian Affairs	37	With amends.	S. 293	Referred to Committee Whole House.		
Mangnall, John, representatives of.	Compensation for capture of British vessel in revolutionary war.	5	2	Petition	270	Claims	May 18, 1798	Adverse		Rejected.		
Manhart, John	Compensation and land for revolutionary services.	19	1	Petition	336	Rev. Pensions.						
Manice, Deforest	Refunding duties paid on goods	24	2	Petition	146	Ways and Means.						
Manice, Deforest	Refunding duties paid on goods	27	3	Memorial	108	Claims						Leave to withdraw; May 17, 1848.
Manice, Gold & Co. } Manice, Phelps & Co. }	(See Smith Thurger & Co.)	29	1		151							
Manin, Barnabas	Pension	19	1	Petition	66	Military Pensions	164	Adverse		Laid on table.		
Manish, Francis	Confirmation of title to land in Missouri.	22	1	Petition	263	Priv. Land Claims.	Feb. 17, 1832	Favorable; bill	380	Referred to Committee Whole House.		
Mankin, Henry	Further time to pay a judgment of the United States.	21	2	Petition	231	Ways and Means.						
Mankin, Isaiah	(See Joshua Harvey, and others.)	7	2		343							
Manley, Daniel	Remission of the forfeiture of his vessel Sarah, for supposed violation of act of 1811.	14	2	Petition	28	Ways and Means				Discharged; laid on table.		
Manley, Daniel	Remission of the forfeiture of his vessel Sarah, for supposed violation of act of 1811.	15	1	Resolution	256	Ways and Means	Mar. 3, 1818	Adverse		Referred to Committee Whole House.		
Manley, Daniel	Remission of the forfeiture of his vessel Sarah, for supposed violation of act of 1811.	15	2	Rept. of last sess.	35	Ways and Means	Nov. 24, 1818	Adverse		Rejected.		
Manley, James, or John	Pension for services as midshipman in revolutionary war.	29	1	Petition	541	Rev. Pensions	826	Adverse		Laid on table.		
Manley, Jesse	Compensation for property destroyed by Creek Indians.	23	1	Petition	438	Claims	402	Adverse		Laid on table.		
Manley, Jesse	Compensation for property destroyed by Creek Indians.	24	1	Petition	672	Indian Affairs.						
Manley, John	Revolutionary pension	30	1	Petition	104, 122	Rev. Pensions	110	Favorable; bill	99	Passed	Passed	App'd Aug. 5, 1848
Manley, John	Arrears of pay and prize-money for revolutionary services.	2	1	Petition	447					Referred to Secretary of War.		
Manley, John	Arrears of pay and prize-money for revolutionary services.	2	2	Petition and rep't of Sec. War.	627					Laid on table.		
Manley, John	Invalid pension	3	1	Rep. of Secretary War.	141	Select	May 26, 1794	Rep. and res.	12	Referred to Secretary of War.		
Manley, John	Invalid pension	4	1	Rep. of Secretary War.	445	Claims	Feb. 18, 1796	Rep. and res.	16	Referred to Secretary of War.		
Manlief, Benjamin H.	Pension	26	1	Petition	962	Naval Affairs	670	Adverse		Laid on table.		
Manlief, Benjamin H.	Pension	28	2	Petition	307	Invalid Pensions.						
Mann, Ariel	(See sureties of Daniel Evans)	21	2		382				S. 116			

List of private claims presented to the House of Representatives of the United States from the 1st to the 31st Congress, inclusive—Continued.

Names of claimants.	Nature or object of the claim.	Congress.	Session.	How brought before the House of Reps.	Page of journal.	To what committee of the House referred.	No. or date of the report.	Nature of the report.	No. of the bill.	How disposed of by the House of Reps.	How disposed of by the Senate.	Date of the act of Congress, and remarks.
Mann, Elijah, (Mass.)	Revolutionary pension	12	2	Petition	595	Claims.						
Mann, Elijah, (Mass.)	Revolutionary pension	16	1	Petition	33	Rev. Pensions	April 22, 1820	Adverse	.....	Rejected.		
Mann & Foltz	Indemnity for French Spoliations prior to 1800.	26	1	Memorial	182	Foreign Affairs	343	Favorable; bill	319	Referred to Committee Whole House.		
Mann, John	Indemnity for damages to his sleigh and horses pressed in late war.	17	1	Petition	206	Claims	....	....	.....	Discharged; laid on table.		
Mann, Justice	Invalid pension	4	1	Petition	447	Claims	Feb. 18, 1796	Favorable; bill	156	Passed	Passed	App'd April 20, 1796
Mann, Moody	Indemnity for depredations by Menominie Indians.	27	2	Petition	611	Indian Affairs.						
Mann, Robert	Increase of pension	26	1	Petition	708	Indian Affairs.						
Mann, Spencer, and Frantz Jacob Foltz.	Drawback of duty on coffee	3	1	Petition	123	Select	April 30, 1794	Favorable	.....	Laid on table.		
Mann, Spencer, and Frantz Jacob Foltz.	Drawback of duty on coffee	3	2	Resolution	330	Select	Feb. 20, 1795	Favorable; bill	118	Passed	Passed as am'd.	App'd March 2, 17
Mann, William, (Va.)	Settlement of accounts as United States marshal.	23	1	Senate bill	654	Claims	550	With amend.	164	Passed	Passed	App'd June 30, 18
Mann, William, (Mo.)	For benefit of act of March 2, 1821, relating to purchase of public lands.	17	1	Petition	33	Public Lands	....	....	.....	Discharged; laid on table.		
Mann, William	Compensation for extra services during the war of 1812.	31	2	Petition	193	Military Affairs.						
Manney, James	Indemnity for losses on contract with War Department.	22	1	Petition	333	Claims	Mar. 21, 1832	Adverse	.....	Laid on table.		
Manney, James, sureties of.	Release from judgment	25	3	Senate bill	149	Claims	Jan. 4, 1839	With't amend.	S. 76	Passed	....	App'd Feb. 6, 1839
Mannhardt, Bohn & Co.	Drawback of certain duties	7	2	Petition	264	Com. and Manuf.	Jan. 5, 1803	Adverse, leave to withdraw.	.....	Report adopted.		
Manning, Cornelius	Compensation for a servant taken away by the British in late war.	24	1	Resolution	541	Foreign Affairs.						
Manning, Cornelius	Compensation for a servant taken away by the British in late war	24	2	Petition	87	Foreign Affairs	291	Favorable; bill	962	Referred to Committee Whole House.		
Manning, Cornelius	Compensation for a servant taken away by the British in late war.	25	2	Petition	39	Foreign Affairs	263	Favorable; bill	306	Referred to Committee Whole House.		
Manning, Cornelius	Compensation for a servant taken away by the British in late war.	25	3	Bill of last sess.	377	Whole House	Jan. 25, 1839	With't amend.	306	Passed	Adverse.	
Manning, Cornelius	Compensation for a servant taken away by the British in late war.	26	1	Petition	182	Foreign Affairs.						
Manning, Cornelius, executors of.	Compensation for a servant taken away by the British in late war.	29	1	Memorial	519	Foreign Affairs	766	Favorable; bill	505	Referred to Committee Whole House.		
Manning, Cornelius, executors of.	Compensation for a servant taken away by the British in late war.	30	1	Petition	79	Foreign Affairs	82	Favorable; bill	69	Passed.		
Manning, Cornelius, executors of.	Compensation for a servant taken away by the British in late war.	31	1	Petition	486	Foreign Affairs.						
Manning, Ebenezer T.	Pension	16	1	Petition and rep't Sec. of War.	76, 350	....	....	....	.....	Laid on table.		
Manning, Enos	Pre emption right to land	17	1	Petition	119	Public Lands	Feb. 21, 1822	Adverse	.....	Laid on table.		
Manning, Enos	Pre-emption right to land	27	1	Petition	100	Public Lands.						
Manning, Enos	Pre-emption right to land	27	2	Petition	518	Public Lands.	956	Adverse	.....	Laid on table.		
Manning, Enos	Pre-emption right to land	28	1	Petition	812	Public Lands.						
Manning, Enos	Pre-emption right to land	29	1	Petition	340	Public Lands.						
Manning, Isaac, widow of.	Continuance of pension	29	1	Petition	1124	Rev. Pensions	824	Favorable; bill	549	Referred to Committee Whole House.		
Manning, Jeremiah	Compensation for forage furnished troops in 1813.	16	1	Resolution	414	Claims.						

List of private claims presented to the House of Representatives of the United States from the 1st to the 31st Congress, inclusive—Continued.

Names of claimants.	Nature or object of the claim.	Congress.	Session.	How brought before the House of Reps.	Page of journal.	To what committee of the House referred.	No. or date of the report.	Nature of the report.	No. of the bill.	How disposed of by the House of Reps.	How disposed of by the Senate.	Date of the act of Congress, and remarks.
Manning, Jeremiah	Compensation for forage furnished troops in 1813.	17	1	Petition	100	Claims	Mar. 20, 1822	Adverse	......	Laid on table.		
Manning, Jeremiah	Compensation for forage furnished troops in 1813.	17	2	Petition	56	Claims	Jan. 24, 1823	Favorable; bill	254	Referred to Committee Whole House.		
Manning, Jeremiah	Compensation for forage furnished troops in 1813.	18	1	Petition	37	Claims	Dec. 17, 1823	Favorable; bill	11	Passed	Passed	App'd Jan. 7, 1824
Manning, John	(See Caroline Fenwick, guardian of.)	15	1	....	37							
Manning, John	Restoration of pension	19	1	Resolution	172	Military Pensions	164	Adverse	......	Laid on table.		
Manning, John	Restoration of pension	22	1	Resolution	308	Rev. Pensions	....	....	......	Disch'd; laid on table.		
Manning, John	Invalid pension	24	1	Resolution	989	Invalid Pensions.						
Manning, John	Invalid pension	24	2	Resolution	217	Invalid Pensions.						
Manning, John	Invalid pension	25	2	Resolution	85	Invalid Pensions	....	....	......	Discharged; laid on table.		
Manning, John	Invalid pension	25	3	Resolution	225	Invalid Pensions.						
Manning, John	Invalid pension	26	1	Resolution	162	Invalid Pensions.						
Manning, Lawrence	Compensation for revolutionary services.	2	1	Petition	554	....	....	....	......	Laid on table.		
Manning, Lawrence	Relief; his commutation pay having been paid to a person authorized to reeive it.	5	2	Memorial	265	Claims	July 12, 1798	Adverse	......	Laid on table.		
Manning, Mark	(See William Reed, heirs of)	15	1	....	39							
Manning, Pierce	(See Edward Simpson, and others)	4	1	....	428							
Manning, Rosanna	(See Isaac Manning, widow of)	29	1	....	1124							
Manning, Simon	(See John W. Brown, and others)	23	1	....	93							
Manning, Thomas, administrator of.	Indemnity for French spoliations prior to 1800.	26	1	Memorial	182	Foreign Affairs	343	Favorable; bill	319	Referred to Committee Whole House.		
Manning, Thomas	Relief for breach of contract by the government of France.	3	1	Petition	22	....	....	....	......	Referred to Secretary of State.		
Manning or Mauning, William.	Pension	21	1	Resolution	294	Military Pensions.						
Mansell, George, administrator of.	Allowance of commissions as collector of direct taxes.	19	2	Senate bill	100	Ways and Means	Jan. 3, 1827	With't amend.	32	Passed	Passed	App'd March 3, 1827
Mansfield, Adolpheus, and others.	Bounty land for services in war of 1812.	30	1	Petition	617	Priv. Land Claims.						
Mansfield, Amos	Invalid pension	24	1	Petition	51	Invalid Pensions	....	....	......	Discharged; laid on table.		
Mansfield, Carter, & others	(See Harrison Gill, and others)	31	2	....	207							
Mansfield, Duncan	(See widow of Stephen Decatur, and others.)	20	1	....	295	....	201	....	50			
Mansfield, Isaac, (Mass.)	Compensation as chaplain in revolutionary war.	1	3	Petition	338	....	....	....	......	Referred to Secretary of War.		
Mansfield, Isaac. (Mass.)	For amount due for undrawn rations as chaplain, revolutionary war.	12	2	Petition	663	Claims.						
Mansfield, Isaac, (Mass.)	For amount due for undrawn rations as chaplain, revolutionary war.	13	1	Petition	11	Claims.						
Mansfield, Isaac, (Mass.)	For amount due for undrawn rations as chaplain, revolutionary war.	13	2	Petition	234	Rev. Claims.						
Mansfield, James C.	(See Mary M. Nowland, by her next friend.)	30	1	....	114							

List of private claims presented to the House of Representatives of the United States from the 1st to the 31st Congress, inclusive—Continued.

Names of claimants.	Nature or object of the claim.	Congress.	Session.	How brought before the House of Reps.	Page of journal.	To what committee of the House referred.	No. or date of the report.	Nature of the report.	No. of the bill.	How disposed of by the House of Reps.	How disposed of by the Senate.	Date of the act of Congress, and remarks.
Mansfield, Joseph, (Conn.)	Compensation for revolutionary services.	3	1	Petition and rep't of Sec. War.	58	Select.						
Mansfield, Joseph K. F.	Compensation for services as disbursing agent of the government.	31	2	Senate bill	124	Whole House.						
Mansfield, Mary	Continuation of pension	27	2	Petition	255	Rev. Pensions.						
Mansfield, Richard	Compensation for property destroyed, war of 1812.	15	1	Rep't of Comm'r of Claims.	87	Claims	Feb. 17, 1818	Adverse	......	Laid on table.		
Mansfield, Richard	Compensation for property destroyed, war of 1812.	16	1	Petition	77	Claims	Jan. 10, 1820	Adverse	......	Laid on table.		
Mansfield, Richard	Compensation for property destroyed, war of 1812.	18	1	Petition	236	Claims	Feb. 25, 1824	Adverse	......	Laid on table.		
Mansfield, Mary	Continuation of pension	27	2	Petition	255	Rev. Pensions.						
Manson, Nehemiah	Pension	21	1	Petition	35	Military Pensions	....	....	......	Disch'd; laid on table.		
Manson, Nehemiah	Pension	21	2	Petition	43	Military Pensions.						
Manson, Nehemiah	Pension	22	1	Petition	45	Rev. Pensions.						
Manns, Ambrose	Revolutionary pension	26	1	Petition	324	Rev. Pensions.						
Mannypeny, Bryan, & Co.	(See Bryan Mannypeny, & Co.)	27	3	....	156							
Mannypenny, George W.	(See Wilson Shannon, assignee of)	28	1	....	300							
Manuel, Peter	(See widow of Stephen Decatur, and others.)											
Manville, George	Compensation for mail service	31	2	Petition	307	P. Of. & P. Roads.						
Manzanal, Cuest, & Bros.	Cancellation of certain bond	20	1	Senate bill	123	Judiciary	April 26, 1828	With amends.	S. 35	Passed	Passed	App'd May 2, 1828
Mapel, David, (Ky.)	Payment for a wagon and team lost by his father in revolutionary war.	23	1	Petition	335	Rev. Claims.						
Mapel, David, (Ky.)	Payment for a wagon and team lost by his father in revolutionary war.	26	2	Petition	52	Rev. Claims.						
Mapel, David, (Ky.)	Payment for a wagon and team lost by his father in revolutionary war.	30	2	Petition	337	Rev. Claims.						
Maples, Marmaduke	Relief for injuries received in the revolutionary war.	6	1	Petition	655	Claims	April 11, 1800	Adverse	......	Leave to withdraw.		
Maples, Marmaduke	Bounty land for revolutionary services.	22	2	Resolution	182	Rev. Claims.						
Maquet, Anthony	(See Stephen Monot, *et al.*)	5	2	....	225							
Marantette, Patrick	Payment of an audited Indian claim	30	1	Petition	228	Indian Affairs	442	Favorable; bill	374	Referred to Committee Whole House.		
Marble, Mehetable	(See Samuel Marble, widow of.)	30	1	....	280							
Marble, Samuel, widow of	Revolutionary pension	30	1	Petition	280	Rev. Pensions	219	Adverse	......	Laid on table.		
Marbury, F. F.	Compensation for services as counsel.	30	1	Petition	422	Accounts	Mar. 13, 1848 Mar. 30, 1848	Res. to pay out of contingent fund of the House.	......	Resolution adopted.		
Marbury, William, (La.)	Pre emption right to land in Louisiana.	22	1	Petition	144	Priv. Land Claims.	174	Favorable; bill	247	Referred to Committee Whole House.		
Marbury, William, (La.)	Pre-emption right to land in Louisiana.	22	2	House bill of last session.	92	Whole House	Dec. 22, 1832	Witht amends	247	Passed.		
Marbury, William, (La.)	Permission to include his improvements in locating a confirmed land title.	23	1	Petition	49	Priv. Land Claims.						
Marbury, William, (La.)	Permission to include his improvements in locating a confirmed land title.	23	2	Petition	58	Priv. Land Claims.	Jan. 12, 1835	Adverse	......	Laid on table.		

List of private claims presented to the House of Representatives of the United States from the 1st to the 31st Congress, inclusive—Continued.

Names of claimants.	Nature or object of the claim.	Congress.	Session.	How brought before the House of Reps.	Page of journal.	To what committee of the House referred.	No. or date of the report.	Nature of the report.	No. of the bill.	How disposed of by the House of Reps.	How disposed of by the Senate.	Date of the act of Congress, and remarks.
Marbury, William, (La.)..	Permission to include his improvements in locating a confirmed land title.	24	1	Petition	208	Priv. Land Claims.	Jan. 28, 1836	Favorable; bill	250	Referred to Committee Whole House.		
Marbury, William, (La.)..	Permission to include his improvements in l cating a confirmed land title.	24	2	House bill of last session.	63	Whole House.....	....	....	250			
Marbury, William, (La.)..	Permission to include his improvements in locating a confirmed land title.	25	2	Petition	43	Priv. Land Claims.	209	Favorable; bill	244	Referred to Committee Whole House.		
Marbury, William, (La.)..	Permission to include his improvements in lo ating a confirmed land title.	25	3	Bill of last sess..	376	Whole House	Jan. 25, 1839	With't amend.	244	Passed	Adverse.	
Marbury, William, (La.)..	Permission to include his improvements in locating a confirmed land title.	26	1	Petition	179	Priv. Land Claims.	100	Favorable; bill	96	Passed	Passed	App'd July 20, 1840
Marcell, F ancis.........	Bounty land for services in war of 1812.	15	1	Petition	27	Pens. & Rev. Cl'ms.	....	....	......	Discharged; referred to Secretary War.		
Marceron, P. T.	Compensation for damage to his property by grading New Jersey avenue.	31	2	Petition	280	Dist. of Columbia.						
March, John	Pension	23	2	Petition	113	Naval Affairs.....	129	Adverse	......	Laid on table.		
March, John	Pension	24	1	Petition	61	Naval Affairs.....	706	Favorable; bill	659	Referred to Committee Whole House.		
March, John	Pension	25	2	Petition	41	Naval Affairs.....	Jan. 18, 1838	By bill	423	Passed.		
March, John, widow of...	Pension	25	2	Petition	275	Naval Affairs.						
March, John, widow of...	Pension	25	3	Petition	91	Naval Affairs.....	191	Favorable; bill	1049	Passed	Passed	App'd March 3, 1839
March, Lydia...........	(See John March, widow of.)....	25	2	....	275							
March, Nathaniel	Indemnity for French spoliations prior to 1800.	26	1	Memorial	·182	Foreign Affairs ...	343	Favorable; bill	319	Referred to Committee Whole House.		
March, Samu l	R volutionary pension	24	1	Petition	532	Rev. Pensions	....	....	......	Discharged; laid on table.		
March, Samuel, (Me.)....	Invalid pension, services in war of 1812.	24	1	Petition	942	Invalid Pensions ..	June 23, 1836	Adverse	......	Laid on table.		
Marchand, D., (A k.).....	Ind mnity for French spoliations prior to 1800.	26	1	Memorial	182	Foreign Affairs ...	343	Favorable: bill	319	Referred to Committee Whole House.		
Marchand, D.	Indemnity under the treaty with France in 1800.	26	1	Petition	599	Foreign Affairs.						
Marchand, Louis	(See Frederick de Laporte, administrator of.)	23	1	....	637							
Marchand, L...........	(See Frederick de Laporte, administrator of.)	26	1	....	182							
Marchand, L. D.........	Indemnity for French spoliations prior to 1800.	27	3	Petition	255	Whole House.						
Marchand, L. D........	Indemnity for French spoliations prior to 1800.	28	1	Petition	122	Foreign Affairs.						
Marchand, Louis	Release from liability as surety of Arthur G. Follingsby.	23	2	Petition	238	Claims.						
Ma chand, Louis	Release from liability as surety of Arthur G. Follingsby.	24	1	Petition	49	Claims..........	Jan. 27, 1836	Adverse	......	Laid on table.		
Marchand, Louis	Release from liability as surety of Arthur G. Follingsby.	24	2	Petition	266	Claims	Feb. 28, 1837	Adverse	......	Laid on table.		
Marchant, Cornelius	Revolutionary pension..........	25	2	Petition	586	Rev. Pensions.						

List of private claims presented to the House of Representatives of the United States from the 1st to the 31st Congress, inclusive—Continued.

Names of claimants.	Nature or object of the claim.	Congress.	Session.	How brought before the House of Reps.	Page of journal.	To what committee of the House referred.	No. or date of the report.	Nature of the report.	No. of the bill.	How disposed of by the House of Reps.	How disposed of by the Senate.	Date of the act of Congress, and remarks.
Marchant, Louis	Indemnity for French spoliations prior to 1800.	29	2	Memorial	386	Foreign Affairs.						
Marchant, Louis	Indemnity for French spoliations prior to 1800.	30	1	Petition	369	Foreign Affairs	Jan. 4, 1848	By bill	21	Referred to Committee Whole House.		
Marchant, Louis	Indemnity for French spoliations prior to 1800.	31	1	Petition	271	Foreign Affairs	355	Favorable; bill	318	Referred to Committee Whole House.		
Marchard, D. R.	Pension and bounty land for services in war of 1812.	31	1	Petition	311	Rev. Pensions	138	Favorable; bill	152	Referred to Committee Whole House.		
Marcus, William	Permission to enter certain lands in lieu of other lands to which he was entitled.	23	1	Petition	76	Public Lands	Feb. 11, 1834	By bill	297	Referred to Committee Whole House.		
Marcus, William	Permission to enter certain lands in lieu of other lands to which he was entitled.	23	2	House bill	300	Whole House	....	....	297			
Marcus, William	Permission to enter certain lands in lieu of other lands to which he was entitled.	24	1	Petition	58	Public Lands.						
Marcus, William	Permission to enter certain lands in lieu of other lands to which he was entitled.	25	2	Petition	543	Public Lands	664	Favorable; bill	637	Referred to Committee Whole House.		
Marcus, William	Permission to enter certain lands in lieu of other lands to which he was entitled.	25	3	Bill of last sess.	380	Whole House	Jan. 26, 1839	With amend.	637	Passed	Passed	App'd March 3, 1839
Marcy, Daniel, sureties of.	Relief in the case of certain bonds.	8	1	Petition	428	Com. and Manuf.	Nov. 30, 1803 Jan. 20, 1804	Adverse. Report to refer to Comptrol'r of Treasury.	....	Recommitted. Resolution adopted.		
Mare, Thomas	(See George Marks, assignee of)	6	1	....	580							
Marechal, Joseph	Release from judgment of United States.	17	2	Petition	144	Judiciary	Feb. 5, 1823	Favorable; bill	272	Referred to Committee Whole House.		
Marechal, Joseph	Release from judgment of United States.	18	1	Petition and rep't Sec. of War.	33, 62	Military Affairs	42	Favorable; bill	85	Passed	Passed	App'd May 18, 1824
Margery, Jonathan	Invalid pension	3	2	Rep. of Secretary of War.	278	Claims	Feb. 28, 1795	Favorable; bill	130	Passed	Postponed.	
Margery, Jonathan	Invalid pension	4	1	Petition	447	Claims	Feb. 18, 1796	Favorable; bill	156	Passed	....	App'd April 20, 1796
Maria and Lancero, (Spanish vessels) owners of.	Remission of duties on cargoes	27	2	President's mess.	1455	Ways and Means	1099	Adverse	......	Rejected	....	See Ex. Doc. No. 146
Marie, Antoine, heirs of	Confirmation of title to land in Indiana.	11	2	Petition	146	Public Lands	Mar. 27, 1810	Adverse	......	Rejected.		
Marie, Margaret	(See Antoine Marie, heirs of)	11	2	....	146							
Marigny, Bernard	(See Antoine Bonnabel, assignee of.)	21	2	....	111							
Marigny, Bernard	Confirmation of title to land in Louisiana.	22	1	Petition	70	Priv. Land Claims.	3	Favorable; bill	45	Passed	Passed	App'd Mar. 15, 1832
Marigny, Bernard, & others	Confirmation of lands lying between the Mississippi and Perdido rivers.	22	2	Memorial	153	Foreign Affairs.						
Marigny, Bernard, & others	Confirmation of lands lying between the Mississippi and Perdido rivers.	23	1	President's mess.	145	Public Lands.						
Marigny, Bernard, & others	Confirmation of lands lying between the Mississippi and Perdido rivers.	28	1	Petition	77	Priv. Land Claims.	4	Favorable; bill	23	Referred to Committee Whole House.		

List of private claims presented to the House of Representatives of the United States from the 1st to the 31st Congress, inclusive—Continued.

Names of claimants.	Nature or object of the claim.	Congress.	Session.	How brought before the House of Reps.	Page of journal.	To what committee of the House referred.	No. or date of the report	Nature of the report.	No. of the bill.	How disposed of by the House of Reps.	How disposed of by the Senate.	Date of the act of Congress, and remarks.
Marigny, Prosper	Confirmation of title to land in Louisiana.	22	1	Petition	46	Priv. Land Claims.	12	Favorable; bill	61	Passed	Passed	App'd May 19, 1832
Marin, E., and others	Confirmation of title to land in Louisiana.	22	1	Petition	64	Priv. Land Claims.	62	Favorable; bill	125	Passed	Passed	App'd June 23, 1832
Marine Corps, captains and subalterns.	Benefit of act of March 2, 1827, relative to officers of the army.	23	1	Petition	36	Naval Affairs	42	Favorable; bill	47	Passed	Passed	App'd June 30, 1834
Marine Insurance Company, of Baltimore.	Indemnity for French Spoliations prior to 1800.	26	1	Memorial	182	Foreign Affairs	343	Favorable; bill	319	Referred to Committee Whole House.		
Marine Insurance Company, of Massachusetts.	Indemnity for French Spoliations prior to 1800.	26	1	Memorial	182	Foreign Affairs	343	Favorable; bill	319	Referred to Committee Whole House.		
Marine guard of the Exploring Expedition.	Extra compensation for the time they were kept over the term of their enlistment.	27	2	Memorial	1001	Naval Affairs.						
Marine guard of the Exploring Expedition.	Extra compensation for the time they were kept over the term of their enlistment.	27	3	Memorial	150	Foreign Affairs	....	....	......	Discharged; laid on table.		
Maritaurus, Joseph	Confirmation of title to land in Louisiana.	27	2	Report of register and receiver.	125	Priv. Land Claims.	84	Favorable; blil	124	Referred to Committee Whole House.		
Maritaurus, Joseph	Confirmation of title to land in Louisiana.	27	2	Senate bill	359	Priv. Land Claims.	Feb. 26, 1842	With amend.	S. 76	Passed	Passed	App'd July 6, 1842
Mark, Elisha	(See John E. Hunt, and others)	27	2	....	334							
Mark, Jacob & Co.	Indemnity for French Spoliations prior to 1800.	26	1	Memorial	182	Foreign Affairs	343	Favorable; bill	319	Referred to Committee Whole House.		
Mark, Louis, agent of	Remission of duties on books	21	1	Petition	170	Commerce	160	Favorable; bill	204	Passed.		
Mark, Louis, agent of	Remission of duties on books	22	1	Petition	118	Commerce	80	Favorable; bill	159	Passed	Passed	App'd July 14, 1832
Marker, George and wife	(See Frederick Seagle, heirs of.)	4	1	....	524							
Markham, Jeremiah	Invalid pension	4	1	Petition	445	Claims	Feb. 18, 1796	Favorable; bill	156	Passed	Passed	App'd April 20, 1796
Markham, Jeremiah	Increase of pension	10	2	Rep. of Secretary War.	480	Claims	Jan. 30, 1809	Favorable; bill	158	Passed	Passed	App'd March 3, 1809
Markham, Jeremiah	Further increase of pension	11	2	Petition	283	Claims	Mar. 15, 1810	Favorable; bill	107	Passed	Passed	App'd April 27, 1810
Markham, William	Refunding amount paid as security of William Reed.	26	1	Petition	875	Judiciary.						
Markham, William	Refunding amount paid as security of William Reed.	27	2	Petition	100	Judiciary	Feb. 9, 1842	Favorable; bill	117	Passed	Passed	App'd July 27, 1842
Markin, Charles	Correction of error in land entry	14	1	Petition	66	Public Lands	Dec. 22, 1815	Favorable; bill	......	Passed	Passed	App'd Feb. 6, 1816
Markland, Alice	(See Edward Markland, widow of.)	30	2	....	430							
Markland, Edward, widow of.	Revolutionary pension	30	2	Petition	430	Rev. Pensions.						
Markland, Edward, widow of.	Revolutionary pension	31	1	Petition	542	Rev. Pensions	223	Favorable; bill	218	Referred to Committee Whole House.		
Markle, Abraham, and others.	Bounty land as Canadian refugees.	14	1	Petition	98	Select	Jan. 24, 1816	Favorable; bill	51	Passed	Passed	App'd March 5, 1816
Markley, Charles	Compensation for revolutionary services.	1	1	Petition	11	....	....	....	......	Referred to Secretary War.		
Markley, Charles	Compensation for revolutionary services.	1	2	Rep. of Secretary War.	141	Select	July 16, 1790	By bill	88	Passed	Passed	App'd Aug. 11, 1790
Marks, Andrew	Invalid pension	25	2	Petition	1119	Naval Affairs.						
Marks, Andrew	Invalid pension	25	3	Petition	131	Naval Affairs.						
Marks, Andrew	Invalid pension	26	1	Petition	330	Naval Affairs.						
Marks, George, assignee of.	Payment of a certain certificate	6	1	Petition	580	Claims	Feb. 11, 1800	Adverse	......	Rejected.		
Marks, Henry	Subsistence and quarters furnished volunteers, May, 1846.	30	1	Petition	576	Claims.						
Marks, Hastings	Invalid pension	25	2	Petition	722	Invalid Pensions	....	....	......	Disch'd; laid on table.		

List of private claims presented to the House of Representatives of the United States from the 1st to the 31st Congress, inclusive—Continued.

Names of claimants.	Nature or object of the claim.	Congress.	Session.	How brought before the House of Reps.	Page of journal.	To what committee of the House referred.	No. or date of the report.	Nature of the report.	No. of the bill.	How disposed of by the House of Reps.	How disposed of by the Senate.	Date of the act of Congress, and remarks.
Marks, Isaac D	Payment of claim against Mexico.	31	2	Petition	158	Ways and Means.						
Marks, Jacob	Increase of pension	25	3	Petition	130	Naval Affairs.						
Marks, Jacob	Increase of pension	26	1	Petition	330	Naval Affairs.						
Marks, John, widow and heirs of.	Commutation pay for revolutionary services.	23	2	Petition	240	Rev. Claims.						
Marks, John, widow and heirs of.	Commutation pay for revolutionary services.	24	1	Petition	104	Rev. Claims	475	Favorable; bill	476	Referred to Committee Whole House.		
Marks, John, widow and heirs of.	Commutation pay for revolutionary services.	25	2	Petition	40	Rev. Claims	132	Favorable; bill	150	Passed	Reported with amendm'nts.	
Marks, John, widow and heirs of.	Commutation pay for revolutionary services.	25	3	Petition	85	Rev. Claims.						
Marks, John, widow and heirs of.	Commutation pay for revolutionary services.	26	1	Petition	165	Rev. Claims.						
Marks, John, widow and heirs of.	Commutation pay for revolutionary services.	26	2	Petition	134	Rev. Claims.						
Marks, John, widow and heirs of.	Commutation pay for revolutionary services.	27	2	Petition	61	Rev. Claims	774	Adverse	......	Laid on table.		
Marks, John, widow and heirs of.	Commutation pay for revolutionary services.	28	1	Petition	685	Rev. Pensions.						
Marks, John, widow and heirs of.	Commutation pay for revolutionary services.	29	1	Petition	207	Rev. Claims.						
Marks, Lucy	(See John Marks, widow of.)	23	2	....	240							
Marks, Lucy	(See William Lewis, widow and heirs of)	24	1	....	431							
Marks, Soloman, jr	(See Warren Ashley, executors of.)	25	3	....	119							
Markward, William	Payment for property destroyed by fire in War Department.	6	2	Petition	762	Claims	Jan. 19, 1801	Adverse	......	Rejected.		
Marlow, Gabriel	(See Reuben E. Gentry, and others)	23	1	....	138							
Marlow, James, daughter of	Reservation of land under treaty of F. Jackson.	23	2	Senate bill	126	Public Lands	Jan. 20, 1835	With amend's.	S. 4	Referred to Committee Whole House.		
Marlow, James, daughter of	Reservation of land under treaty of F. Jackson.	24	1	Senate bill	552	Public Lands	April 22, 1836	With't amend.	S. 18	Passed	Passed	App'd July 2, 1836
Marlow, James, daughter of	An act amendatory for her relief.	24	2	Senate bill	551	....	....	....	S. 118	Passed	Passed	App'd March 3, 1837
Marlow, Marguerite	(See widow of ——— Nunez)	22	1	....	107							
Marlow, Susan	(See James Marlow, daughter of)	23	2	....	126							
Marlow, Susan	(See Samuel Smith, and others)	31	1	....	390							
Marnesia, Claudius L	Pre-emption right to land	2	1	Petition	579	Select.						
Marple, David	(See Exploring Expedition)	27	3	....	149							
Marple, Enoch, widow of.	Compensation for corn furnished revolutionary army.	10	1	Petition	69	Select.						
Marple, Mary	(See Enoch Marple, widow of)	10	1	....	69							
Marquand, Joseph, heirs of.	Share of certain forfeitures	29	1	Memorial	148	Commerce.						
Marquand, Joseph, administrator of.	Indemnity for French spoliations prior to 1800.	26	1	Memorial	182	Foreign Affairs	343	Favorable; bill	319	Referred to Committee Whole House.		
Marquis, M. A., and John B. Felicite.	Confirmation of title to land in Louisiana.	20	1	Memorial	728	Priv. Land Claims.	....	....	......	Discharged; laid on table.		
Marquis, M. A., and John B. Felicite.	Confirmation of title to land in Louisiana.	21	1	Memorial	236	Priv. Land Claims.	March 5, 1830	Adverse	......	Laid on table.		
Marran, John	Revolutionary pension	21	2	Resolution	203	Military Pensions						
Marrast, John, heirs of	Indemnity for French spoliations prior to 1800.	31	1	Petition	197	Foreign Affairs	355	Favorable; bill	318	Referred to Committee Whole House.		

List of private claims presented to the House of Representatives of the United States from the 1st to the 31st Congress, inclusive—Continued.

Names of claimants.	Nature or object of the claim.	Congress.	Session.	How brought before the House of Reps.	Page of journal.	To what committee of the House referred.	No. or date of the report.	Nature of the report.	No. of the bill.	How disposed of by the House of Reps.	How disposed of by the Senate.	Date of the act of Congress, and remarks.
Marrast, John	Indemnity fr French spoliatiors pr or to 1800.	26	1	Memorial	182	Foreign Affairs	343	Favorable; bill	319	Referred to Committee Whole House.		
Marrero, Felix and Bisente	C nfirmation of title to land in Louisiana.	22	1	Petition	64	Priv. Land Claims.	Dec. 27, 1831	Favorable; bill	125	Passed	Passed	App'd June 25, 1832
Marriner, Edward	(See Archibald B. Lord, and others)	15	2		178							
Marriott, William	Arrears of pensi n	25	2	Petition	268	Invalid Pensions				Discharged; laid on table.		
Marr, Samuel	Indemnity for French spoliations prior to 1800.	26	1	Memorial	182	Foreign Affairs	343	Favorable; bill	319	Referred to Committee Whole House.		
Mars, Darby	Naval pension	13	2	Petition	185	Pens. & Rev. Cl'ms.	Mar. 15, 1814	Favorable; bill	166	Passed	Passed	App'd April 18, 1814
Marsaque, Daniel	Confirmat on of ti le to land	25	2	Senate bill	1155	Priv. Land Claims.			S. 263			
Marseque, Daniel	Confirmation of title to land	25	3	Senate bill	478	Priv. Land Claims.	Feb. 25, 1839	With't amend.	253	Laid on table.		
Marsaque, Daniel	Confirmati n of ti le to land	26	1	Senate bill	443	Priv. Land Claims.	April 4, 1840	With't amend.	60	Ref'd to Com. W. H.		
Marschalk, Andrew	Land for military services	22	1	Memorial	473	Public Lands				Discharged; laid on table.		
Marsden, George, widow of.	Revolutionary pensi n	26	1	Resolution	556	Rev. Pensions	423	Adverse.		Laid on table		Leave to withdraw, June 22, 1841.
Marsden, George, widow of.	Revolutionary pension	27	2	Petition	239	Rev. Pensions	920	Favorable; bill	532	Ordered to 3d reading.		
Marsden, George, widow of.	Revolutionary pension	27	3	Bill of last sess.	89				532	Passed.		
Marsden, George, widow of.	Revolutionary pension	28	1	Petition	60	Rev. Pensions	236	Favorable; bill	234	Passed.		
Marsden, George, widow of.	Revolutionary pension	28	2	Petition	299	Rev. Pensions						
Marsden, Wilmot	(See George Marsden.)	26	1		556							
Marsh, Allyn	Invalid pension	4	1	Petition	447	Claims	Feb. 18, 1796	Favorable; bill	156	Passed	Passed	App'd April 20, 1796
Marsh, Charles, executors of.	Paym nt of amount due from government with interest.	25	2	Petition	121	Claims.						
Marsh, Charles, executors of.	Payme t of amount due from government with interest.	26	1	Petition	169	Claims.						
Marsh, Charles, executors of.	Paym nt of amount due from government wi h interest.	26	2	Petition	80	Claims.						
Marsh, Charles, executors of.	Payment of amount due from government with interest.	31	1	Petition	533	Claims.						
Marsh, George M., administrator of.	Ind mni y for French spoliations prior to 1800.	26	1	Memorial	182	Foreign Affairs	343	Favorable; bill	319	Referred to Committee Whole House.		
Marsh, Henry H	To have money refunded for land erroneously entered.	29	1	Senate bill	1108	Public Lands			S. 168			
Marsh, James, (Ohio.)	Payment of drawback of duties on certain goods.	21	1	Petition	210	Commerce.	99	Favorable; bil	648	Referred to Committee Whole House.		
Marsh, James, (Ohio.)	Payment of drawback of duties on certain goods.	22	1	Petition	332	Commerce.	July 7, 1832	Favorable; bill	611	Referred to Committee Whole House.		
Marsh, James, (Ohio.)	Payment of drawback of duties on certain goods.	23	1	Petition	156	Commerce	153	Favorable; bill	163	Passed	Passed	App'd June 30, 1834
Marsh, Richard	Revolutionary pension	27	2	Petition	415	Rev. Pensions	577	Favorable; bill	373	Ordered to 3d reading.		
Marsh, Richard	Revolutionary pension	27	3	Bill of last sess.	88				373	Passed	Indef. postp'd.	
Marsh, Samuel B	(See Edward Jones, representatives of.)	22	2		59							
Marsh, Samuel	(See Edward C. Delevan & others.)	27	2		886							
Marsh, Silas	(See Charles Marsh, executor of.)	25	2		121							
Marsh, Thomas, and sureties.	Release from penalty for violation of act 1812.	15	1	Petition	179	Ways and Means	Feb. 3, 1818	Adverse		Leave to withdraw.		

List of private claims presented to the House of Representatives of the United States from the 1st to the 31st Congress, inclusive—Continued.

Names of claimants.	Nature or object of the claim.	Congress.	Session.	How brought before the House of Reps.	Page of journal.	To what committee of the House referred.	No. or date of the report.	Nature of the report.	No. of the bill.	How disposed of by the House of Reps.	How disposed of by the Senate.	Date of the act of Congress, and remarks.
Marsh, Thomas, and Joseph, Yaw.	Refunding money paid for driving fat cattle into Canada in 1814.	18	1	Petition	115	Ways and Means.						
Marsh, Thomas, and Joseph Yaw.	Refunding money paid for driving fat cattle into Canada in 1814.	20	1	Petition	46	Ways and Means..	12	Adverse	......	Laid on table.		
Marsh, Thomas, and Joseph Yaw.	Refunding money paid for driving fat cattle into Canada in 1814.	20	2	Rep. of last sess.	154	Ways and Means..	....	....	......	Discharged; laid on table.		
Marsh, Thomas	Payment for a horse lost in Seminole war in 1818.	23	1	Documents.....	154	Claims.						
Marsh, Thomas.........	(See William H. Bedford, agent.)	28	1	....	262							
Marsh, William.........	Payment of a protested bill of exchange drawn on Secretary of war.	14	1	Petition	110	Claims	....	....	......	Discharged; laid on table.		
Marsh, William.........	Payment of a protested bill of exchange drawn on Sectetary of war.	14	2	Resolution	177	....	....	....	......	Leave to withdraw.		
Marshall, Amon.........	Revolutionary pension..........	22	1	Petition	36	Rev. Pensions.....	369	Favorable; bill	464	Referred to Committee Whole House.		
Marshall, Andres, sureties of.	Release from liability...........	20	2	Petition	106	P. Of. and P. Roads.	Jan. 12, 1829	Adverse	......	Laid on table.		
Marshall, B., and others ..	(See Creek Indians.)	30	1	....	809	....	826					
Marshall, Benjamin......	Revolutionary pension..........	18	1	Petition	454	Pens. & Rev. Cl'ms.	....	....	......	Discharged; laid on table.		
Marshall, Benjamin, late widow of.	Compensation for services in revolutionary war, and for property destroyed by the enemy.	24	1	Petition	138	Rev. Claims......	821	Adverse	......	Laid on table.		
Marshall, Benjamin, daughter of.	Pension for revolutionary services.	25	2	Petition	231	Rev. Claims......	....	....	......	Discharged; laid on table.		
Marshall, Daniel	Payment for horse, &c., lost in Seminole war.	23	1	Documents.....	154	Claims.						
Marshall, David, widow of.	Revolutionary pension	25	2	Resolution	529	Rev. Pensions	....	....	......	Discharged; laid on table.		
Marshall, David, widow of.	Revolutionary pension..........	25	3	Resolution	400	Rev. Pensions	....	....	......	Discharged; laid on table.		
Marshall, David, widow of.	Revolutionary pension..........	26	1	Resolution	174	Rev. Pensions.						
Marshall, Dixon, (N. C.).	Compensation for revolutionary services.	12	1	Petition	274	Claims...........	April 7, 1812	Adverse	......	Rejected.		
Marshall, Isaac..........	Pension	19	2	Petition	131	Military Pensions.						
Marshall, Isaac..........	Pension	20	1	Petition	57	Military Pensions.						
Marshall, Isaac, (N. C.)..	Compensation for revolutionary services.	31	2	Petition	157	Rev. Pensions	....	....	......	Leave to withdraw.		
Marshall, James, heirs of..	Commutation pay for revolutionary services.	24	1	Petition	274	Rev. Claims.						
Marshall, James, heirs of..	Further compensation for revolutionary services.	25	2	Petition	269	Rev. Claims......	....	....	......	Discharged; laid on table.		
Marshall, James, heirs of..	Further compensation for revolutionary services.	25	3	Petition	86	Rev. Claims.						
Marshall, James, heirs of..	Further compensation for revolutionay services.	26	1	Petition	166	Rev. Claims.						
Marshall, James, heirs of..	Further compensation for revolutionary services.	26	2	Petition	248	Rev. Claims.						
Marshall, James W......	Grant of land for having made the first discovery of gold in California.	31	1	Petition	1179	Public Lands.						

List of private claims presented to the House of Representatives of the United States from the 1st to the 31st Congress, inclusive—Continued.

Names of claimants.	Nature or object of the claim.	Congress.	Session.	How brought before the House of Reps.	Page of journal.	To what committee of the House referred.	No. or date of the report.	Nature of the report.	No. of the bill.	How disposed of by the House of Reps.	How disposed of by the Senate.	Date of the act of Congress, and remarks.
Marshall, Joel	Revolutionary pension	23	2	Resolution	184	Rev. Pensions.						
Marshall, John	Compensation for services as superintendent of War and Navy buildings.	21	2	Civil and diplomatic bill.	121				582			App'd March 2, 1831
Marshall, John, representatives of.	Additional compensation for services in revenue departments.	24	1	Petition	206	Claims	624	Favorable; bill	609	Referred to Committee Whole House.		
Marshall, John, representatives of.	Additional compensation for services in revenue department.	25	2	Petition	37	Claims	41	Favorable; bill	53	Passed	Passed	App'd April 20, 1838
Marshall, Josiah	Refunding certain duties paid by him.	26	2	Petition	51	Ways and Means.						
Marshall, Margaret	(See David Marshall, widow of).	25	2		529							
Marshall, Philip	Additional compensation for services in revenue service.	24	1	Petition	206	Claims	624	Favorable; bill	609	Referred to Committee Whole House.		
Marshall, Philip	Additional compensation for services in revenue service.	25	2	Petition	37	Claims	41	Favorable; bill	53	Passed	Passed	App'd April 20, 1838
Marshall, Philip	Compensation for services as lieutenant in revenue service.	25	3	Petition	86	Claims.						
Marshall, Robert	Compensation for a horse lost in service of United States.	32	2	Resolution	294	Claims	Feb. 6, 1835	Adverse		Laid on table.		
Marshall, Robert	Compensation for a horse lost in service of United States.	24	1	Resolution	429	Claims.						
Marshall, Robert	Compensation for a horse lost in service of United States.	25	2	Petition	87	Claims	March 9, 1838	Adverse		Laid on table.		
Marshall, Robert	Renewal of bounty land warrant.	25	2	Petition	177	Rev. Claims.	364	Adverse		Laid on table.		
Marshall, Robert	Invalid pension	26	1	Petition	794	Invalid Pensions	562	Adverse		Laid on table.		
Marshall, Robert	Invalid pension	26	2	Petition	119	Invalid Pensions	238	Adverse		Laid on table.		
Marshall, Robert	Invalid pension	27	2	Petition	130	Invalid Pensions	617,	Adverse		Recommitted.		
							1067	Adverse		Laid on table.		
Marshall, Samuel W	Pension	27	2	Petition	239	Invalid Pensions	439	Adverse		Laid on table.		
Marshall, Samuel W	Pension	28	1	Petition	60	Invalid Pensions	20	Adverse		Laid on table.		
Marshall, Thomas	Invalid pension	3	2	Petition	239	Claims	Feb. 25, 1795	Adverse		Referred to Committee Whole House.		
Marshall, Thomas	Invalid pension	5	2	Petition	188	Claims	Feb. 16, 1798	Adverse		Rejected.		
Marshall, William, (S. C.)	Release from judgment in favor of United States.	15	1	Petition	312	Ways and Means.						
Marshall, William, heirs of	Bounty land for revolutionary services.	22	1	Petition	165	Public Lands				Discharged; laid on table.		
Marshall, William, heirs of	Bounty land for revolutionary services.	26	1	Petition	334	Public Lands	592	Favorable; bill	452	Referred to Committee Whole House.		
Marshall, William, heirs of	Bounty land for revolutionary services.	27	2	Petition	62	Public Lands	509	Adverse		Laid on table.		
Marshall, William, heirs of	Bounty land for revolutionary services.	28	1	Resolution	312	Public Lands	401	Favorable; bill	311	Passed	Passed	App'd June 15, 1844
Marshall, William, heirs of	Bounty land for revolutionary services.	30	1	Petition	287	Public Lands	363	Adverse		Laid on table.		
Marshall, William	Refunding amount advanced Indian commissioner in 1832.	23	2	House bill	252	Whole House	Feb. 23, 1835	With't amend.	664	Passed	Passed	App'd March 3, 1835
Marshall, William	Refunding money advanced Indians on public account.	28	2	Petition	303	Indian Affairs.						
Marshall, William	Refunding money advanced Indians on public account.	29	1	Petition	89	Indian Affairs	400	Adverse		Laid on table.		

List of private claims presented to the House of Representatives of the United States from the 1st *to the* 31st *Congress, inclusive*—Continued.

Names of claimants.	Nature or object of the claim.	Congress.	Session.	How brought before the House of Reps.	Page of journal.	To what committee of the House referred.	No. or date of the report.	Nature of the report.	No. of the bill.	How disposed of by the House of Reps.	How disposed of by the Senate.	Date of the act of Congress, and remarks.
Marshall, W	Payment for services as Indian commissioner.	25	2	Appropriation bill for Indian department.	213				269	Passed	Passed	App'd July 7, 1838
Marsten, John.	Payment of certain bills of credit	5	2	Petition	202	Claims	Feb. 26, 1796	Adverse		Leave to withdraw.		
Marsters, James	Refunding amount erroneously paid for land.	24	1	Petition	1184	Priv. Land Claims.	July 2, 1836	Favorable; bill	746	Referred to Committee Whole House.		
Marsters, Stephen	Correction of error in entry of land.	24	1	Petition	1013	Priv. Land Claims.						
Marsters, Stephen	Correction of error in entry of land.	25	2	Petition	43	Priv. Land Claims.	Dec. 28, 1837	By bill	245	Referred to Committee Whole House.		
Marsters, Stephen	Correction of error in entry of land.	25	3	Bill of last sess.	376	Whole House	Jan. 25, 1839	With't amend.	245	Passed	Passed	App'd March 3, 1839
Marston, Asa, (N. C.)	Pension	21	2	Petition	270	Military Pensions.						
Marston, David	Pension	21	2	Petition	188	Military Pensions.						
Marston, David	Pension	22	1	Resolution	136	Military Pensions.	365	Favorable; bill	460	Passed	Postponed.	
Marston, William J.	Payment for a horse lost in service of United States.	25	2	Petition	922	Claims.						
Marston, William J.	Payment for a horse lost in service of United States.	26	1	Petition	169	Claims.						
Martha, schooner	(See S. C. Nickerson, administrator of.)	25	3		214							
Martha, schooner	(See J. B. Knight and others)	26	1		199							
Martin, Absalom	Confirmation of title to land	3	2	Petition	291	Select.						
Martin, Absalom	Confirmation of title to land	4	1	Petition	381	Whole House.						
Martin, Andrew	Confirmation of title to land in Louisiana.	23	1	Petition	638	Public Lands.						
Martin, Andrew	Confirmation of title to land in Louisiana.	23	2	Petition	49	Priv. Land Claims.				Discharged; laid on table.		
Martin, Andrew, *alias* Valerin, jr.	Confirmation of title to land	19	2	Petition	217	Priv. Land Claims.						
Martin, Anna	Renewal of lost loan office certificate.	2	2	Petition	712					Laid on table.		
Martin, Anthony, and others	Payment of $227 50 due under treaty with Great Britain in 1794.	17	1	Resolution	279	Ways and Means.				Discharged; laid on table.		
Martin, Armand	Compensation for clothing furnished by himself while a soldier in United States army.	29	1	Petition	510	Claims	747	Adverse		Laid on table.		
Martin, Arnold and Sarah, representatives of.	(See James Mugford, former widow of.)	4	2		645							
Martin, Bartholomew	Confirmation of title to land in Louisiana.	19	2	Petition	53	Priv. Land Claims.	Jan. 6, 1827	Adverse.		Laid on table.		
Martin, Bartholomew	Confirmation of title to land in Louisiana.	20	1	Petition	40	Priv. Land Claims.	Jan. 2, 1828	Adverse		Laid on table.		
Martin, Charles, (Pa)	Bounty land for revolutionary services.	14	1	Petition	236	Pens. & Rev. Cl'ms.						Leave to withdraw Feb. 28, 1817.
Martin, Chauncey R.	Bounty land for services in the last war with Great Britain.	31	1	Petition	681	Public Lands.						
Martin, Edward, (R. I.)	Release from imprisonment upon judgment of the United States.	13	3	Senate bill	746	Whole House	Mar. 2, 1815	With't amend.	84	Passed	Passed	App'd March 3, 1815
Martin, Edward, administrator of.	Release from payment of bond due the United States.	19	2	Petition	240	Claims.						
Martin, Edward, administrator of.	Release from payment of bond due the United States.	21	1	Petition	260	Ways and Means.				Discharged; laid on table.		
Martin, Edward, administrator of.	Release from payment of bond due the United States.	23	2	Petition	247	Judiciary	421	Adverse		Referred to Committee Whole House.		

List of private claims presented to the House of Representatives of the United States from the 1st to the 31st Congress, inclusive—Continued.

Names of claimants.	Nature or object of the claim.	Congress.	Session.	How brought before the House of Reps.	Page of journal.	To what committee of the House referred.	No. or date of the report.	Nature of the report.	No. of the bill.	How disposed of by the House of Reps.	How disposed of by the Senate.	Date of the act of Congress, and remarks.
Martin, Edward, administrator of.	Release from payment of bond due the United States.	24	1	Petition	476	Judiciary	455	Adverse		Laid on table.		
Martin, Edward B	(See Edward Martin, administrator of.)	19	2		240							
Martin, Elizabeth	(See George Martin, widow of)	29	1		86							
Martin, Francis	Permission to make final payment for land, and a grant for the same.	24	2	Petition	107	Public Lands.						
Martin, Francis	Permission to make final payment for land, and a grant for the same	25	1	Petition	365	Priv. Land Claims.	96	Favorable; bill	92	Passed	Passed	App'd July 20, 1840
Martin, Lieut. Francis	Compensation for services in the navy.	29	1	Petition	70	Naval Affairs	146	Favorable; bill	150	Referred to Committee Whole House.		
Martin, George, (Va.)	Revolutionary pension	23	1	Petition	308	Rev. Pensions.						
Martin, George, widow of.	Revolutionary pension	29	1	Petition	86	Rev. Pensions	783	Adverse		Laid on table.		
Martin, George, widow of.	Revolutionary pension	30	1	Petition	156	Rev. Pensions	302	Adverse		Laid on table.		
Martin, George, (Tenn.)	Revolutionary pension	24	2	Resolution	97	Rev. Pensions				Discharged; laid on table.		
Martin, Hannah	(See Jeret Martin, widow of, &c.)	29	1		465							
Martin, Henry L	For maps and documents furnished United States commissioners.	30	1	Petition	738	Claims.						
Martin, Henry, (N. C.)	Pension	14	1	Petition	309	Pens. & Rev. Cl'ms.	Mar. 3, 1816	Adverse		Rejected.		
Martin, Henry	Compensation for services on Cumberland road.	23	1	Res. and papers.	589	Claims	456	Rep. and res. to refer to Sec. of War.		Adopted		See report No. 449.
Martin, Hudson, executors of.	Commutation of half-pay for revolutionary services.	25	3	Petition	283	Rev. Claims.						
Martin, Hudson, executors of.	Commutation of half pay for revolutionany services.	26	1	Petition	166, 361	Rev. Claims.						
Martin, Hudson, executors of.	Commutation of half-pay for revolutionary services.	27	2	Petition	61	Rev. Claims	391	Adverse		Laid on table.		
Martin, Jacob	Revolutionary pension	22	1	Petition	36	Rev. Pensions				Discharged; laid on table.		
Martin, Jacob L	Compensation for services as acting chargé de affaires.	30	1	Memorial	306	Foreign Affairs	516	Favorable; bill	444	Referred to Committee Whole House.		See act Aug. 12, 1848
Martin, Jacob L	Compensation for services as acting chargé de affaires.	30	2	Bill of last sess.	318	Whole House	Jan. 26, 1849	Adverse	444	Laid on table.		
Martin, James	Compensation for work done on Cumberland road.	23	1	Res. and papers.	589	Claims	456	Rep. and res. to refer to Sec. of War.		Adopted.		
Martin, James, widow of.	Revolutionary pension	30	2	Petition	274	Rev. Pensions	Feb. 13, 1849			Discharged; laid on table.		
Martin, James, widow of.	Revolutionary pension	31	1	Petition	1043	Rev. Pensions.						
Martin, James C	Pension	24	2	Resolution	384	Invalid Pensions.						
Martin, Jeret, heirs of the widow of.	For five years' pension due deceased.	29	1	Petition	465	Rev. Pensions.						
Martin, Jeret, heirs of the widow of.	For five years' pension due deceased.	29	2	Petition	150	Rev. Pensions	5	Adverse		Laid on table.		
Martin, Joel	Payment for property lost while in public service.	25	3	Petition	120	Claims	46	Adverse		Laid on table.		
Martin, John, (Va.)	Invalid pension	11	2	House bill	283	Whole House	Mar. 24, 1810	With amends.	107	Passed	Passed	App'd April 27, 1810
Martin, John, (Va.)	Invalid pension	12	1	Petition	122	Claims	June 12, 1812	Adverse		Laid on table.		
Martin, John	Invalid pension	12	1	House bill	361	Whole House	June 15, 1812	With amends.	138	Passed	Passed	App'd July 5, 1812
Martin, John W	(See Samuel Allen and J. H. Leonard, by attorney.)	17	1		388							

List of private claims presented to the House of Representatives of the United States from the 1st to the 31st Congress, inclusive—Continued.

Names of claimants.	Nature or object of the claim.	Congress.	Session.	How brought before the House of Reps.	Page of journal.	To what committee of the House referred.	No. or date of the report.	Nature of the report.	No. of the bill.	How disposed of by the House of Reps.	How disposed of by the Senate.	Date of the act of Congress, and remarks.
Martin, John, (Pa.)	Indemnity for property destroyed, war of 1812.	15	2	Petition	117	Claims				Discharged; laid on table.		
Martin, John, (Pa.)	Indemnity for property destroyed war of 1812.	16	1	Petition	136	Claims	Jan. 14, 1820	Adverse		Laid on table.		
Martin, John, (Pa.)	Indemnity for property destroyed, war of 1812.	16	2	Rep. of last sess.	119	Claims				Discharged; laid on table.		
Martin, John, (Pa.)	Indemnity for property destroyed, war of 1812.	17	1	Petition	201	Claims	April 5, 1822	Favorable; bill	154	Passed	Postponed.	
Martin, John, (Pa.)	Indemnity for property destroyed, war of 1812.	17	2	Senate bill	179	Claims	Jan. 31, 1823	With't amend.	S. 27	Passed		App'd March 3, 1823
Martin, Capt. John, (Mich.)	Payment for horses and wagon lost in the war of 1812.	28	2	Petition	167	Claims	159	Adverse		Laid on table.		
Martin, Capt. John, (Mich.)	Payment for horses and wagon lost in the war of 1812.	29	1	Petition	192	Claims	413	Adverse		Laid on table.		
Martin, Capt. John, (Mich.)	Payment for horses and wagon lost in the war of 1812.	30	1	Petition	77	Claims	203	Adverse		Laid on table		
Martin, John, (Tenn.)	Pension	21	1	Resolution	254	Military Pensions				Discharged; laid on table.		
Martin, John, (Tenn.)	Pension	21	2	Petition	110	Military Pensions.						
Martin, John	Arrears of pension	28	1	Petition	289	Invalid Pensions	304	Adverse		Laid on table.		
Martin, John	Arrears of pension	28	2	Petition	83, 187	Invalid Pensions	82	Adverse		Laid on table.		
Martin, John	Arrears of pension	29	1	Petition	70	Invalid Pensions	69	Adverse		Laid on table.		
Martin, John L.	Confirmation of title to land in Louisiana.	22	1	Petition	170	Priv. Land Claims.	166	Favorable; bill	243	Referred to Committee Whole House.		
Martin, John L.	Confirmation of title to land in Louisiana.	22	2	House bill of last session.	92	Whole House	Dec. 26, 1832	Favorable; bill	243	Passed	Passed	App'd Jan. 28, 1833
Martin, Joseph S., & others	Indemnity for losses by the seizure of vessel Sally, by the United States.	6	2	Petition	842					Laid on table.		
Martin, Joseph S., & others	Indemnity for losses by the seizure of vessel Sally, by the United States.	7	1	Petition	105	Com. and Manuf.	March 8, 1802	Adverse		Leave to withdraw.		
Martin, Joseph J.	Invalid pension	27	2	Petition	68	Invalid Pensions	144	Favorable; bill	191	Passed	Passed	App'd July 27, 1842
Martin, Joseph	(See representatives of John Donaldson.)	15	1		184							
Martin, Knott, 3d, and Arnold Martin.	Fishing bounty on schooner Only Son.	26	1	Petition	290	Commerce.						
Martin, Knott, 3d, and Arnold Martin.	Fishing bounty on schooner Only Son.	26	2	Petition	37	Commerce.						
Martin, Knott, 3d, and Arnold Martin.	Fishing bounty on schooner Only Son.	27	2	Petition	95	Commerce	1021	Favorable; bill	594	Referred to Committee Whole House.		
Martin, Knott, 3d, and Arnold Martin.	Fishing bounty on schooner Only Son.	27	3	Bill of last sess.	91	Whole House	Dec. 23, 1842	With't amend.	594	Passed	Passed	App'd March 3, 1843
Martin, Lemuel	(See Thomas West, heirs of)	23	1		376							
Martin, Lucy	(See William Martin, widow of)	18	1		250							
Martin, Martha	(See James Martin, widow of)	30	2		274							
Martin, Mary	(See Robert Lindsay, widow of.)	25	2		407							
Martin, Mary	(See Salathiel, Martin, widow of.)	30	1		558							
Martin, Michael S.	Compensation as collector of militia fines in Dutchess county New York in 1812.	23	1	Petition	355	Claims.						

List of private claims presented to the House of Representatives of the United States from the 1st to the 31st Congress, inclusive—Continued.

Names of claimants.	Nature or object of the claim.	Congress.	Session.	How brought before the House of Reps.	Page of journal.	To what committee of the House referred.	No. or date of the report.	Nature of th report.	No. of the bill.	How disposed of by the House of Reps.	How disposed of by the Senate.	Date of the act of Congress, and remarks.
Martin, Michael S	Compensation as collector of militia fines in Dutchess county New York in 1812.	23	2	Petition	83	Claims	Dec. 22, 1834	Adverse	......	Laid on table.		
Martin, Michael S	Compensation for services as deputy United States marshal.	25	2	Petition	121	Claims.						
Martin, Michael S	Compensation for services as deputy United States marshal.	26	1	Petition	169	Claims.						
Martin, Nancy	(See Jeret Martin, heirs of the widow of.)	29	1	....	465							
Martin, Nathaniel	Invalid pension	7	1	Petition	164	Claims	Mar. 31, 1802	Adverse	......	Leave to withdraw.		
Martin, Nathaniel	Pension	19	2	Petition	31	Military Pensions.						
Martin, Nathaniel, representatives of.	Compensation for revolutionary services	21	1	Petition	298	Rev. Claims	....	....	......	Discharged; laid on table.		
Martin, Nathaniel, representatives of.	Pension	22	1	Resolution	138	Rev. Claims	July 3, 1832	Adverse	......	Laid on table.		
Martin, Nicholas L	(See Hudson Martin's executors.)	25	3	....	283							
Martin & Norris	(See Norris & Martin.)	13	3	....	606							
Martin, Peter	Confirmation of title to land in Missouri.	22	1	Petition	263	Priv. Land Claims.	Feb. 17, 1832	Favorable; bill	380	Referred to Committee Whole House.		
Martin, Richard, and others	Compensation for services against the Indians in 1778.	3	1	Petition	58	Select.						
Martin, Richard, and others	Compensation fer services against the Indians in 1778.	4	1	Petition	424	Claims	May 7, 1796	Adverse	......	Leave to withdraw.		
Martin, Richard, (Pa.)	(See Hugh White and R. Martin.)	6	1	....	673							
Martin, Richard	Revolutionary pension	25	2	Petition	402	Invalid Pensions	....	....	......	Discharged; laid on table.		
Martin, Richard	Revolutionary pension	24	1	Petition	57	Rev. Pensions	207	Favorable; bill	211	Passed	Passed	App'd June 28, 1836
Martin, Robert	Revolutionary pension	23	2	Resolution	204	Rev. Pensions.						
Martin, Robert, (Mo.)	Compensation for wagon and mules lost in United States services.	26	1	Petition	623	Claims.						
Martin, Salathiel, widow of.	Revolutionary pension	30	1	Petition	558	Rev. Pensions	Jan. 20, 1848	....	......	Discharged; laid on table.		
Martin, Salathiel, widow of.	Revolutionary pension	30	2	Petition	96	Rev. Pensions.						
Martin, Salathiel, widow of.	Revolutionary pension	31	1	Petition	815	Rev. Pensions	357	Favorable; bill	321	Referred to Committee Whole House.		
Martin, Samuel, (R. I.)	(See Charles De Wolf and others.)	8	1	....	428							
Martin, Samuel	(See Nathaniel Martin, heirs of.)	22	1	....	138							
Martin, Susan W	(See Thomas Martin, widow of.)	16	1	....	59							
Martin Thomas	(See Richard Martin and others.)	3	1	....	58							
Martin, Thomas, (Va.)	For difference of pay between captain and lieutenant for services revolutionary war.	7	2	Petition	279	Claims	Feb. 23, 1803	Adverse	......	Referred to Committee Whole House.		
Martin, Thomas	Compensation for services on Cumberland road.	23	1	Res. and papers.	589	Claims	456	Rep. and res. to refer to Sec. War.	......	Report adopted.		
Martin, Thomas, (Ohio.)	Additional compensation for services, revolutionary war.	15	1	Petition	72	....	....	....	......	Referred to Secretary War.		
Martin, Thomas, (Ohio.)	Additional compensation for services, revolutionary war.	23	1	Res. and papers.	589	Claims	456	Rep. and res. to refer to Sec. War.	......	Report adopted	....	See Report No. 449
Martin, Thomas, widow of.	Compensation for revolutionary services.	16	1	Petition	59	Pens. & Rev. Cl'ms.	Feb. 25, 1820	Adverse	......	Rejected.		

List of private claims presented to the House of Representatives of the United States from the 1st to the 31st Congress, inclusive—Continued.

Names of claimants.	Nature or object of the claim.	Congress.	Session.	How brought before the House of Reps.	Page of journal.	To what committee of the House referred.	No. or date of the report.	Nature of the report.	No. of the bill.	How disposed of by the House of Reps.	How disposed of by the Senate.	Date of the act of Congress, and remarks.
Martin, Thomas, widow of.	Compensation for revolutionary services.	20	1	Petition	367	Rev. Claims......	....	....	......	Discharged; laid on table.		
Martin, Thomas, widow of.	Compensation for revolutionary services.	22	1	Petition	568	Rev. Claims.						
Martin, Thomas, heirs of..	Commutation and bounty land for revolutionary services.	28	1	Petition	738	Rev. Pensions.						
Martin, William	Invalid pension...............	3	1	Rep. of Secretary War.	131	Select	May 26, 1794	Favorable; bill	62	Passed	Passed	App'd June 7, 1794
Martin, William, (Mass.)	Relief for the seizure of the schooner Fox for breach of revenue laws.	3	2	Petition	295	Claims	Mar. 22, 1795	Adverse	......	Laid on table.		
Martin, William, (Mass.)	Relief for the seizure of the schooner Fox for breach of revenue laws.	4	1	Petition	598	Claims	May 31, 1796	Adverse	......	Laid on table.		
Martin, William, (Vt.)...	Invalid pension...............	3	2	Rep. of Secretary War.	337	Claims	Feb. 28, 1795	Favorable; bill	130	Passed	Postponed.	
Martin, William, (Vt.)...	Invalid pension...............	4	1	Rep. of Secretary War.	447	Claims	Feb. 18, 1796	Favorable; bill	156	Passed	Passed	App'd April 20, 1796
Martin, William	Bounty land for revolutionary services.	17	1	Petition	200	Priv. Land Claims.						
Martin, William, widow of.	Continuation of pension	18	1	Petition	250	Pens. & Rev. Cl'ms.	Mar. 3, 1824	Adverse	......	Laid on table.		
Martin, William F.......	Indemnity for seizure of vessel by United States.	30	1	Petition	980	Commerce.						
Martin, Zadock	Privilege to buy land in Missouri at minimum prices.	22	2	Petition	246	Public Lands.						
Martin, Zadock	Pre-emption right to land on which he resides.	24	2	Petition	312	Public Lands.						
Martin, Zadock	Pre-emption right to land on which he resides.	25	3	Petition	134	Priv. Land Claims.						
Martin, Zadock	Pre emption right to land on which he resides.	26	1	Senate bill	813	Public Lands	June 17, 1840	Adverse	S. 203	Referred to Committee Whole House.		
Martinique, Favel de la Gourand.	Remission of duties on goods taken from wrecked vessels.	25	2	Memorial	923	Commerce.						
Martinique, Favel de la Gourand.	Remission of duties on goods taken from wrecked vessels.	25	3	Memorial	118	Ways and Means..	217	Adverse	......	Laid on table.		
Martinure, Julius........	Confirmation of French land grant.	24	2	Petition	107	Public Lands.						
Martlings, Barnet........	Compensation for revolutionary services.	1	2	Rep. of Secretary War.	163	....	....	....	......	Laid on table.		
Marvin, Benjamin	Invalid pension...............	3	2	Rep. of Secretary War.	337	Claims...........	Feb. 28, 1795	Favorable; bill	130	Passed	Postponed.	
Marvin, Benjamin.......	Invalid pension...............	4	1	Petition	445	Claims.						
Marvin, Benjamin.......	Invalid pension...............	4	2	Petition	614	Claims.						
Marvin, Benjamin.......	Land and compensation for revolutionary services.	15	2	Petition	121	Pens. & Rev. Cl'ms.	Dec. 30, 1818	Adverse	......	Rejected.		
Marvin, Clarissa	(See John C. Marvin, widow of.)	31	1	....	1454							
Marvin, John C., widow of.	Pension on account of services as seaman in revolution.	31	1	Petition	1454	Rev. Pensions.						
Marvin, John C., widow of.	Pension on account of services as seaman in revolution.	31	2	Petition	431	Rev. Pensions.....	48	Adverse	......	Laid on table.		
Marvin, William	Confirmation of title to land	24	1	Petition	672	Priv. Land Claims.						
Marvin, William	Confirmation of title to land	25	3	Petition	133	Priv. Land Claims.						
Marvin, William	Confirmation of title to land	26	1	Petition	179	Priv. Land Claims.						
Marvin, William	Confirmation of title to land.....	29	2	Senate bill	380	Priv. Land Claims.	....	....	S. 111			
Marvin, William	Confirmation of title to land	30	1	Senate bill	389	Priv. Land Claims.	....	....	S. 67			
Marx, Elizabeth	(See George Marx, widow of.)...	2	1	....	474							

List of private claims presented to the House of Representatives of the United States from the 1st to the 31st Congress, inclusive—Continued.

Names of claimants.	Nature or object of the claim.	Congress.	Session.	How brought before the House of Reps.	Page of journal.	To what committee of the House referred.	No. or date of the report.	Nature of the report.	No. of the bill.	How disposed of by the House of Reps.	How disposed of by the Senate.	Date of the act of Congress, and remarks.
Marx, George, widow of..	Renewal of lost loan office certificates.	2	1	Petition and rep Sec. Treasury.	474	Select.						
Marx, George, widow of..	Renewal of lost loan office certificates.	4	1	Petition	511	Claims.						
Marx, George, widow of..	Renewal of lost loan office certificates.	4	2	Petition	614	Claims.						
Mary, owners of the ship..	Indemnity for capture of their vessel by Holland, in 1800.	25	2	Res. and President's message.	979, 1015	Foreign Affairs....	1041	Adverse	......	Laid on table.		
Mary, schooner	(See Benjamin B. Swasey)......	27	3	....	59							
Mary, Theresa, barque...	(See N. Rogers & Co.).........	30	1	....	1000							
Marye, R. A. and C. E. Greneaux.	Compensation for taking testimony under resolution of the House of Representatives of the U. S.	27	2	Petition	131	Accounts.						
Maryland, inspectors of customs at Baltimore.	Increase of compensation........	1	3	Petition	363	....	....	....	......	Referred to Secretary Treasury.		
Maryland, inspectors of customs at Baltimore.	Increase of compensation........	2	2	Rep. of Secretary Treasury.	626	....	....	....	......	Laid on table.		
Maryland, inspectors of customs at Baltimore.	Increase of compensation........	3	2	Petition	299	Select.						
Maryland, inspectors of customs at Baltimore.	Increase of compensation........	9	1	Petition and rep't Sec. War.	209, 235	Ways and Means.						
Maryland, inspectors of customs at Baltimore.	Increase of compensation........	9	2	Petition	600	Ways and Means.						
Maryland, inspectors of customs at Baltimore.	Increase of compensation........	10	1	Petition	14	Ways and Means.						
Maryland, inspectors of customs at Baltimore.	Increase of compensation........	10	2	Petition	374	Com. and Manuf.						
Maryland, inspectors of customs at Baltimore.	Increase of compensation........	11	3	Petition	489	Com. and Manuf.						
Maryland line, revolutionary war, officers of.	Indemnity for depreciation of their certificates of pay.	2	2	Memorial	651	....	....	....	......	Laid on table.		
Maryland line, revolutionary war, officers of.	Indemnity for depreciation of their certificates of pay.	10	2	Memorial	375, 467	Select.						
Maryland line, revolutionary war, officers of.	Indemnity for depreciation of their certificates of pay.	11	2	Memorial	195	Select.						
Maryland line, revolutionary war, officers of.	Indemnity for depreciation of their certificates of pay.	11	3	Memorial	460	Select.						
Maryland, sugar refiners of Baltimore.	Remission of duties on sugar.....	7	2	Memorial	323	Ways and Means.						
Maryland, manufacturers of copper in Baltimore.	Remission of duties on copper....	9	1	Petition	315	Com. and Manuf.						
Maryland, merch'ts of Baltimore.	Indemnity for French spoliations prior to 1800.	7	1	Memorial	84	Select	April 22, 1802	Adverse	......	Laid on table.		
Maryland, merch'ts of Baltimore.	Indemnity for French spoliations prior to 1800.	15	1	Petition	121	Select	....	....	......	Discharged; laid on table.		
Maryland, merch'ts of Baltimore.	Indemnity for French spoliations prior to 1800.	16	1	Petition	303	....	....	....	......	Laid on table.		
Maryland, merch'ts of Baltimore.	Indemnity for French spoliations prior to 1800.	18	1	Petition	98	....	....	....	......	Laid on table.		
Maryland, merch'ts of Baltimore.	Indemnity for French spoliations prior to 1800.	26	1	Memorial	182	Foreign Affairs....	343	Favorable	319	Referred to Committee Whole House.		
Maryland, citizens of Baltimore.	Indemnity for French spoliations prior to 1800.	27	3	Documents.....	53	Foreign Affairs.						

List of private claims presented to the House of Representatives of the United States from the 1st to the 31st Congress, inclusive—Continued.

Names of claimants.	Nature or object of the claim.	Congress.	Session.	How brought before the House of Reps.	Page of journal.	To what committee of the House referred.	No. or date of the report.	Nature of the report.	No. of the bill.	How disposed of by the House of Reps.	How disposed of by the Senate.	Date of the act of Congress, and remarks.
Maryland, merch'ts of Baltimore.	Indemnity for their vessels sunk in defence of Baltimore in the war of 1812.	14	1	Petition	284	Claims	....	....	......	Discharged; laid on table.		
Maryland, merch'ts of Baltimore.	Indemnity for their vessels sunk in defence of Baltimore in the war of 1812.	14	2	Petition	147	Claims	....	....	......	Discharged; laid on table.		
Maryland, merch'ts of Baltimore.	Indemnity for their vessels sunk in defence of Baltimore in the war of 1812.	15	1	Petition	155	Naval Affairs	....	....	......	Discharged; laid on table.		
Maryland, merch'ts of Baltimore.	Indemnity for their vessels sunk in defence of Baltimore in the war of 1812.	16	1	Resolution	154	Claims	Jan. 27, 1820	Adverse	......	Recommitted.		
Maryland, merch'ts of Baltimore.	Indemnity for their vessels sunk in defence of Baltimore in the war of 1812.	16	2	Petition and docs.	64	Claims	11	Favorable; bill	166	Referred to Committee Whole House.		
Maryland, merch'ts of Baltimore.	Indemnity for their vessels sunk in defence of Baltimore in the war of 1812.	17	1	Petition	39	Claims	1	Favorable; bill	5	Passed	Passed	App'd April 26, 1822
Maryland, merch'ts of Baltimore.	Explanatory of act of April 26, 1822.	17	1	House bill.....	561	Whole House.....	....	....	187	Passed	Passed	App'd May 7, 1822
Maryland, merch'ts of Baltimore.	For additional pay for their vessels sunk in defence of Baltimore.	17	2	Petition	69	Claims	Jan. 13, 1823	Adverse	......	Referred to Secretary of the Navy.		
Maryland, merch'ts of Baltimore.	For additional pay for their vessels sunk in defence of Baltimore.	18	1	Rep. of Secretary Treasury.	506	....	....	....	......	Laid on table.		
Maryland, merch'ts of Baltimore.	For additional pay for their vessels sunk in defence of Baltimore.	18	2	Rep. of Secretary Navy.	45	Claims	6	Adverse	......	Laid on table.		
Maryland, merch'ts of Baltimore.	For additional pay for their vessels sunk in defence of Baltimore.	19	1	Senate bill	209	Claims	April 17, 1826	Adverse	S. 28	Referred to Committee Whole House.		
Maryland, merch'ts of Baltimore.	For additional pay for their vessels sunk in defence of Baltimore.	20	1	Senate bill	40	Claims	221	Rep. and resl'n to postpone indef.	S. 71	Referred to Committee Whole House.		
Maryland, merch'ts of Baltimore.	For additional pay for their vessels sunk in defence of Baltimore.	20	2	Memorial	55	Commerce	70	Favorable; bill	412	Referred to Committee Whole House.		
Maryland, merch'ts of Baltimore.	For additional pay for their vessels sunk in defence of Baltimore.	21	1	Memorial	82	Commerce	144	Favorable; bill	191	Passed	Passed	App'd May 29, 1830
Maryland, merch'ts of Baltimore.	For additional pay for their vessels sunk in defence of Baltimore.	22	2	Res. and docs...	42, 71	Claims	128	Favo'ble; joint resolution.	19	Passed	Passed	App'd March 2, 1833
Maryland hospital, Baltimore.	Indemnity for damages to property by United States troops in war of 1812.	14	1	Petition	421	Claims.						
Maryland, city of Baltimore	For expenses incurred in putting said city in a state of defence in war of 1812.	14	2	Petition	377	Claims	....	....	......	Discharged; laid on table.		
Maryland, city of Baltimore	For expenses incurred in putting said city in a state of defence in war of 1812.	19	1	Senate bill	515	Claims	May 9, 1826	With't amend.	S. 134	Passed	....	App'd May 20, 1826
Maryland, city of Baltimore	For interest on amount allowed by act of May 20, 1826.	19	2	Memorial	321	....	....	....	......	Referred to Secretary Treasury.		
Maryland, city of Baltimore	For interest on amount allowed by act of May 20, 1826.	20	1	Rep. of Secretary Treasury.	109	Claims	Mar. 31, 1828	Favorable; bill	249	Referred to Committee Whole House.		
Maryland, city of Baltimore	For interest on amount allowed by acs of May 20, 1826.	20	2	Bill of last sess..	284	Whole House.....	Feb. 13, 1829	With't amend.	249	Passed.		

List of private claims presented to the House of Representatives of the United States form the 1st to the 31st Congress, inclusive—Continued.

Names of claimants.	Nature or object of the claim.	Congress.	Session.	How brought before the House of Reps.	Page of journal.	To what committee of the House referred.	No. or date of the report.	Nature of the report.	No. of the bill.	How disposed of by the House of Reps.	How disposed of by the Senate.	Date of the act of Congress, and remarks.
Maryland, city of Baltimore	For interest on amount allowed by act of May 20, 1826.	21	1	Senate bill	139	Claims	Jan. 11, 1830	With't amend.	S. 7	Passed	....	App'd April 2, 1830
Maryland, levy court of Calvert county.	Payment for court-house destroyed by the British in 1814.	15	1	Report of Com. of Claims.	37	Claims	Dec. 18, 1817	Adverse	......	Referred to Committee Whole House.		
Maryland, levy court of Calvert county.	Payment for court-house destroyed by the British in 1814.	16	1	Petition	49	Claims	Jan. 10, 1820	Adverse	......	Referred to Committee Whole House.		
Maryland, levy court of Calvert county.	Payment for court-house destroyed by the British in 1814.	16	2	Rep't of last sess.	37	....	....	....	......	Rejected.		
Maryland, levy court of Calvert county.	Payment for court-house destroyed by the British in 1814.	17	1	Petition	68	Claims	36	Adverse	......	Referred to Committee Whole House.		
Maryland, levy court of Calvert county.	Payment for court-house destroyed by the British in 1814.	18	1	Petition	37	Claims	7	Adverse	......	Leave to withdraw.		
Maryland, levy court of Calvert county.	Payment for court-house destroyed by the British in 1814.	19	1	Petition	110	Claims	Jan. 16, 1826	Adverse	......	Laid on table.		
Maryland, levy court of Calvert county.	Payment for court house destroyed by the British in 1814.	20	1	Petition	127	Claims	Jan. 30, 1828	Adverse	......	Referred to Committee Whole House.		
Maryland, levy court of Calvert county.	Payment for court-house destroyed by the British in 1814.	21	1	Petition	35	Claims	177	Adverse	......	Referred to Committee Whole House.		
Maryland, levy court of Calvert county.	Payment for court-house destroyed by the British in 1814.	24	2	Petition	81	Claims	313	Favorable; bill	969	Referred to Committee Whole House.		
Maryland, levy court of Calvert county.	Payment for court-house destroyed by the British in 1814.	25	2	Petition	36	Claims	70	Favorable; bill	82	Passed	Passed	App'd April 20, 1838
Maryland, levy court of Charles county.	Payment for warehouses destroyed in war of 1812.	25	2	Memorial	574	Claims.						
Maryland, Union Artillery company of Baltimore.	Compensation for guns, &c., destroyed by British in 1814.	16	1	Resolution	322	Military Affairs	Mar. 31, 1820	Adverse	......	Laid on table.		
Maryland, State of	Payment of interest on money borrowed and expended in war of 1812.	19	1	Res. and President's message.	297, 321	Claims	116	Favorable; bill	152	Referred to Committee Whole House.		
Maryland, State of	Payment of interest on money borrowed and expended in war of 1812.	19	1	Senate bill	474	Whole House	May 10, 1826	With't amend.	S. 88	Passed	....	App'd May 13, 1826
Maryland, State of, by agent	For further allowance of interest	19	2	Memorial	240	Claims	....	....	......	Discharged; laid on table.		
Maryland, State of, by agent	For further allowance of interest	20	1	Resolution	185	Claims	189	Adverse	......	Laid on table.		
Maryland, State of, by agent	For further allowance of interest	20	1	Senate bill	487	Claims	May 5, 1828	Resol'n to postpone indef.	S. 101	Referred to Committee Whole House.		
Maryland, State of, by agent	For further allowance of interest	22	1	Resolution	178	Select.						
Maryland, Insurance companies of.	Payment of deficiency in settling their claims under the Florida treaty.	19	1	Petition	313	Foreign Affairs	201	Adverse	......	Laid on table.		
Maryland, Insurance companies of.	Indemnity for French spoliations prior to 1800.	26	1	Memorial	182	Foreign Affairs	343	Favorable; bill	319	Referred to Committee Whole House.		
Maryland, citizens of Baltimore.	To have the value of Danish brig Henrick added to the amount to be distributed to them under the convention with Denmark.	21	2	Memorial	207	Foreign Affairs	100	Adverse	......	Laid on table.		
Maryland, Board of trade of Baltimore.	Indemnity for French spoliations prior to 1800.	25	2	Memorial	580	....	....	....	......	Referred to Committee Whole House on bill No. 449.		
Maryland, Baltimore and Susquehannah railroad company.	For drawback of duty on dog tooth clamps.	24	2	Memorial	213	Ways and Means	224	Favorable; bill	925	Referred to Committee Whole House.		

List of private claims presented to the House of Representatives of the United States from the 1st to the 31st Congress, inclusive—Continued.

Names of claimants.	Nature or object of the claim.	Congress.	Session.	How brought before the House of Reps.	Page of journal.	To what committee of the House referred.	No. or date of the report.	Nature of the report.	No. of the bill.	How disposed of by the House of Reps.	How disposed of by the Senate.	Date of the act of Congress, and remarks.
Maryland, Baltimore and Susquehannah railroad company.	For drawback of duty on dog tooth clamps.	25	2	Memorial	42	Ways and Means	2	Favorable; bill	14	Referred to Committee Whole House.		
Maryland, Baltimore and Susquehannah railroad company.	For drawback of duty on dog tooth clamps.	25	2	Senate bill	1012	Ways and Means	June 30, 1838	With't amend.	237	Passed	Passed	App'd July 7, 1838
Maryland, Baltimore and Susquehannah railroad company.	For exemption from operation of act of July, 1836, of certain railroad fixtures ordered prior to the passage of said act.	24	2	Memorial	396	Ways and Means.						
Masi, Joseph, heirs of	Indemnity for French spoliations prior to 1800.	27	2	Petition	369					Referred to Committee Whole House.		
Mason, Aaron	Invalid pension	3	1	Rep. of Secretary War.	131	Select.	May 26, 1794	Favorable	J.R. 12	Referred to Secretary War.		
Mason, Aaron	Invalid pension	4	1	Rep. of Secretary War.	445	Claims	Feb. 18, 1796	Favorable	J.R. 16	Referred to Secretary War.		
Mason, Alexander, widow of.	Pension: husband killed in war of 1812.	15	1	Petition	226	Pens. & Rev. Cl'ms.	Mar. 27, 1818	Favorable; bill	165	Passed	Passed	App'd April 20, 1818
Mason, Alexander, widow of.	Renewal of pension	29	2	Petition	100	Invalid Pensions.						
Mason, Alexander, widow of.	Renewal of pension	31	2	Petition	216	Invalid Pensions.						
Mason, A. H.	(See heirs of George Brent)	30	1		79							
Mason, Amasa	(See Nicholas Brown, and others)	23	1		273							
Mason, Amasa	Indemnity for French spoliations prior to 1800.	26	1	Memorial	182	Foreign Affairs	343	Favorable; bill	319	Referred to Committee Whole House.		
Mason, Ashbel	Bounty land for revolutionary services.	25	2	Resolution	161	Priv. Land Claims.	409	Favorable; bill	420	Referred to Committee Whole House.		
Mason, Ashbel	Bounty land for revolutionary services.	25	3	Bill of last sess.	378	Whole House	Jan. 25, 1839	With't amend.	420	Passed	Passed	App'd March 3, 1839
Mason, Ashbel	Bounty land for revolutionary services.	26	1	Petition	282	Rev. Claims.						
Mason, Caleb	Revolutionary pension	20	2	Petition	74	Military Pensions				Discharged; laid on table.		
Mason, Caleb	Revolutionary pension	22	1	Petition	412	Rev. Pensions				Discharged; laid on table.		
Mason, Cornelia	(See Alexander Mason, widow of)	15	1		226							
Mason, David, heirs of	Commutation pay for revolutionary services.	23	1	Petition	121	Rev. Claims.						
Mason, David, heirs of	Commutation pay for revolutionary services.	23	2	Petition	398	Rev. Claims	Feb. 16, 1835	Adverse		Laid on table.		
Mason, David, heirs of	Commutation pay for revolutionary services.	24	1	Petition	103	Rev. Claims	816	Adverse		Laid on table.		
Mason, David, (Tenn.)	Revolutionary pension	25	2	Petition	405	Rev. Pensions				Discharged; laid on table.		
Mason, David, (Tenn.)	Revolutionary pension	26	1	Petition	174	Rev. Pensions				Discharged; laid on table.		
Mason, Deborah	Restoration of pension	27	2	Petition	320	Rev. Pensions.						
Mason, Elizabeth, assignee of.	Correction of error in relinquishing certain lands.	22	1	Petition	227	Public Lands	Feb. 7, 1832	Favorable; bill	354	Passed	Passed	App'd May 25, 1832
Mason, George, (S. C.)	Renewal of pension	7	1	Petition	76	Claims	April 3, 1802	Resolution to postpone.		Resolution adopted.		

List of private claims presented to the House of Representatives of the United States from the 1st to the 31st Congress, inclusive—Continued.

Names of claimants.	Nature or object of the claim.	Congress.	Session.	How brought before the House of Reps.	Page of journal.	To what committee of the House referred.	No. or date of the report.	Nature of the report.	No. of the bill.	How disposed of by the House of Reps.	How disposed of by the Senate.	Date of the act of Congress, and remarks.
Mason, George, (S. C.)	Renewal of pension	7	2	Petition	277	Claims	Jan. 28, 1803	Favorable	......	Referred to Committee Whole House.		
Mason, George, (S. C.)	Renewal of pension	8	1	Petition	536	Claims	Jan. 25, 1804	Favorable; bill	177	Passed	Passed	App'd March 3, 1804
Mason, George	Compensation and bounty land for revolutionary services.	19	1	Resolution	267	Rev. Claims	April 5, 1826	Adverse	......	Laid on table.		
Mason, George	Compensation and bounty land for revolutionary services.	19	2	Resolution	69	Rev. Claims	Jan. 9, 1827	Adverse	......	Laid on table.		
Mason, George, (Ala.)	Patent for land for which he has made full payment.	21	2	Petition	325	Public Lands.						
Mason, George M	Compensation for a horse killed in the Creek war.	24	2	Petition and docs.	38	Claims	Mar. 3, 1837	Adverse	......	Laid on table.		
Mason, George M	Compensation for a horse killed in the Creek war.	25	2	Petition	88	Claims.						
Mason, George M	Compensation for a horse killed in the Creek war.	26	1	Petition	339	Claims.						
Mason, James, heirs of	(See James Mayson, heirs of)	27	2	....	142							
Mason, James M., widow and administratrix of.	Confirmation of title to land	27	2	Petition	622	Priv. Land Claims.						
Mason, James M., widow and administratrix of.	Confirmation of title to land	27	3	Petition	45	Priv. Land Claims.						
Mason, John	(See John D. Schweighauser, representatives of, by attorney.)	9	2	....	607							
Mason, John	(See Francis Louis Taney, trustees of.)	10	1	....	216							
Mason, John, (S. C.)	Pension	20	2	Resolution	93	Military Pensions	Jan. 5, 1829	Adverse	......	Laid on table.		
Mason, John, (Va.)	Payment for cannon manufactured for the naval service of the United States.	29	1	Memorial	381	Claims	628	Adverse	......	Laid on table.		
Mason, John, (Va.)	Payment for cannon manufactured for the naval service of the United States.	30	1	Petition	102	Claims.						
Mason, John, (Va.)	Payment for cannon manufactured for the naval service of the United States.	30	2	Petition	175	Claims.						
Mason, Joseph	(See Michael Bowne)	16	1	....	177							
Mason, Joseph	Compensation for horse lost in United States service in 1832.	24	1	Petition	430	Claims	April 5, 1836	Adverse	......	Laid on table.		
Mason, Josiah	(See George Johnson and others).	17	1	....	386							
Mason, Lucretia	(See Noah Mason, widow of)	27	2	....	246							
Mason, Malinda	(See James M. Mason, widow and administratrix of.)	27	2	....	622							
Mason, Noah	Refunding expenses in improving public grounds on Long Island.	26	2	Petition	124	Claims.						
Mason, Noah	Refunding expenses in improving public grounds on Long Island.	27	2	Petition	246	Claims	165	Adverse	......	Laid on table.		
Mason, Noah, widow of	Permission to remove carriage-house from public grounds.	27	2	Memorial	948	Claims.						
Mason, Peter	Confirmation of title to land in Alabama.	19	2	Petition	37	Public Lands	....	....	......	Discharged; laid on table.		
Mason, Richworth	(See Nathaniel Seavy and others.)	14	2	....	278							
Mason, William	Compensation for revolutionary services.	1	2	Petition	163	....	....	....	......	Referred to Secretary of War.		

List of private claims presented to the House of Representatives of the United States from the 1st to the 31st Congress, inclusive—Continued.

2—50

Names of claimants.	Nature or object of the claim.	Congress.	Session.	How brought before the House of Reps.	Page of journal.	To what committee of the House referred.	No. or date of the report.	Nature of the report.	No. of the bill.	How disposed of by the House of Reps.	How disposed of by the Senate.	Date of the act of Congress, and remarks.
Massachusetts line, revolutionary war, officers, &c., of.	Further compensation for revolutionary services.	1	2	Petition	287					Laid on table.		
Massachusetts line, revolutionary war, officers of.	Relief from losses by depreciation of their pay.	2	1	Petition	547					Laid on table.		
Massachusetts line, revolutionary war, officers of.	Relief from losses by depreciation of their pay.	2	2	Petition	657					Laid on table.		
Massachusetts line, revolutionary war, officers of.	Relief from losses by depreciation of their pay.	10	2	Petition	375					Laid on table.		
Massachusetts, soldiers of 3d regiment.	Balance of pay due for revolutionary services.	2	2	Memorial	653	Select				Discharged; laid on table.		
Massachusetts, sundry soldiers of revolutionary war	Pension	19	1	Petition	35	Rev. Pensions	164	Adverse		Laid on table.		Names of petitioners not given in Journal or Report.
Massachusetts, sundry soldiers of revolutionary war	Pension	21	2	Petition	188	Rev. Pensions.						
Massachusetts, sundry citizens of Charlestown.	Indemnity for property destroyed in revolutionary war.	23	1	Petition	220	Rev. Claims.						
Massachusetts, sundry citizens of Charlestown.	Indemnity for property destroyed in revolutionary war.	24	1	Petition	404	Rev. Claims.						
Massachusetts, State of	Payment of expenses of her militia in war of 1812.	14	2	Res. and report of Sec. War.	400, 429					Laid on table.		
Massachusetts, State of	Payment of expenses of her militia in war of 1812.	15	1	Resolution	186	Select	147	Favorable; bill	132	Referred to Committee Whole House.		
Massachusetts, State of	Payment of expenses of her militia in war of 1812.	15	2	Bill of last sess.	115	Whole House			132			
Massachusetts, State of	Payment of expenses of her militia in war of 1812.	18	1	Pres. message	262	Military Affairs	121	Favorable; bill	217	Referred to Committee Whole House.		
Massachusetts, State of	Payment of expenses of her militia in war of 1812.	18	2	Pres. Message	258	Military Affairs.						
Massachusetts, State of	Payment of expenses of her militia in war of 1812.	19	1	Prss. message	81	Military Affairs	18	Favorable; bill	30	Laid on table.		
Massachusetts, State of	Payment of expenses of her militia in war of 1812.	19	2	Resolution	55					Referred to Secretary of War.		
Massachusetts, State of	Payment of expenses of her militia in war of 1812.	20	1	Rep. of Secretary War.	722					Laid on table.		
Massachusetts, State of	Payment of expenses of her militia in war of 1812.	20	2	Rep. of Secretary War.	87	Military Affairs	Jan. 2, 1829	Favorable; bill	354	Referred to Committee Whole House.		
Massachusetts, State of	Payment of expenses of her militia in war of 1812.	21	1	Resolution	322					Laid on table.		
Massachusetts, State of	Payment of expenses of her militia in war of 1812.	21	1	Senate bill	557	Military Affairs	April 24, 1830	With amend.	S. 31	Passed	Passed	App'd May 31, 1830
Massachusetts, State of	Re-examination of accounts, and for balance due.	22	1	Resolution	283					Referred to Secretary War.		
Massachusetts, State of	Re examination of accounts, and for balance due.	24	1	Jt. res., Senate	354	Military Affairs	May 6, 1836	With amends.	J.R. 11	Passed	Passed	App'd May 14, 1836
Massachusetts, State of	Re-examination of accounts, and for balance due.	25	2	Rep. of Secretary of War.	149	Military Affairs.						
Massachusetts, State of	Re examination of accounts, and for balance due.	25	3	Res. and docs	157	Military Affairs.						
Massachusetts, State of	Re-examination of accounts, and for balance due.	26	1	Res. and docs	785	Military Affairs.						

List of private claims presented to the House of Representatives of the United States from the 1st *to the* 31st *Congress, inclusive*—Continued.

Names of claimants.	Nature or object of the claim.	Congress.	Session.	How brought before the House of Reps.	Page of journal.	To what committee of the House referred.	No. or date of the report.	Nature of the report.	No. of the bill.	How disposed of by the House of Reps.	How disposed of by the Senate.	Date of the act of Congress, and remarks.
Massachusetts, State of...	Re-examination of accounts, and for balance due.	27	2	Senate bill	1047	Military Affairs	Jan. 27, 1842	With amend.	S. 112	Referred to Committee Whole House.		
Massachusetts, State of...	Re-examination of accounts, and for balance due.	27	3	Resolution	203	Ways and Means.	Feb. 3, 1843	By bill	757	Referred to Committee Whole House.		
Massachusetts, State of...	Re-examination of accounts, and for balance due.	27	3	Senate bill	516				S. 7			
Massachusetts, citizens of Falmouth and Portland.	Indemnity for spoliations on their commerce by the British and Spaniards.	4	1	Memorial	371					Referred to Committee Whole House.		
Massachusetts, merchants and citizens of.	Indemnity for French spoliations prior to 1800.	7	1	Memorial	153, 171, 173	Select	April 22, 1802	Adverse		Laid on table.		
Massachusetts, merchants and citizens of.	Indemnity for French spoliations prior to 1800.	14	2	Memorial	127	Foreign Affairs				Leave to withdraw.		
Massachusetts, merchants and citizens of.	Indemnity for French spoliations prior to 1800.	15	1	Memorial	121, 222	Select				Discharged; laid on table.		
Massachusetts, merchants and citizens of.	Indemnity for French spoliations prior to 1800.	18	1	Memorial	93	Foreign Affairs	94	Adverse		Laid on table.		
Massachusetts, merchants and citizens of.	Indemnity for French spoliations prior to 1800.	19	1	Memorial	153	Foreign Affairs	202	Adverse		Laid on table.		
Massachusetts, merchants and citizens of.	Indemnity for French spoliations prior to 1800.	22	1	Resolution	95	Foreign Affairs.						
Massachusetts, merchants and citizens of.	Indemnity for French spoliations prior to 1800.	22	2	Memorial & docs.	25, 211, 264	Foreign Affairs.						
Massachusetts, merchants and citizens of.	Indemnity for French spoliations prior to 1800.	23	1	Memorial	186	Foreign Affairs.						
Massachusetts, merchants and citizens of.	Indemnity for French spoliations prior to 1800.	23	2	Senate bill	318	Foreign Affairs	121	Adverse	S. 5	Laid on table.		
Massachusetts, merchants and citizens of.	Indemnity for French spoliations prior to 1800.	24	1	Memorial	127, 142	Foroign Affairs.						
Massachusetts, merchants and citizens of.	Indemnity for French spoliations prior to 1800.	24	2	Memorial	87	Foreign Affairs.						
Massachusetts, merchants and citizens of.	Indemnity for French spoliations prior to 1800.	25	2	Memorial	304	Foreign Affairs	445	Favorable; bill	449	Referred to Committee Whole House.		
Massachusetts, merchants and citizens of.	Indemnity for French spoliations prior to 1800.	26	1	Memorial	182	Foreign Affairs	343	Favorable; bill	319	Referred to Committee Whole House.		
Massachusetts, merchants and citizens of.	Indemnity for French spoliations prior to 1800.	26	2	Bill of last sess.	118	Whole House			319			
Massachusetts, sundry citizens and merchants of.	Indemnity for French spoliations prior to 1800.	27	2	Petition and docs.	104	Foreign Affairs	Dec. 29, 1841	Favorable	57	Referred to Committee Whole House.		
Massachusetts, sundry citizens and merchants of.	Indemnity for French spoliations prior to 1800.	27	3	Bill of last sess.	291	Whole House			57			
Massachusetts, sundry citizens and merchants of.	Indemnity for French spoliations prior to 1800.	28	1	Memorial	439, 450	Foreign Affairs.						
Massachusetts, sundry citizens and merchants of.	Indemnity for French spoliations prior to 1800.	29	1	Memorial	834	Foreign Affairs.						
Massachusetts, sundry citizens and merchants of.	Indemnity for French spoliations prior to 1800.	29	1	Senate bill	924	Foreign Affairs	July 13, 1846	With't amend.	S. 68	Passed	Passed	Vetoed by the President.
Massachusetts, sundry citizens and merchants of.	Indemnity for French spoliations prior to 1800.	30	1	Resolution	121	Foreign Affairs	Jan. 4, 1848	By bill	21	Referred to Committee Whole House.		
Massachusetts, sundry citizens and merchants of.	Indemnity for French spoliations prior to 1800.	31	1	Memorial	216	Foreign Affairs	355	Favorable; bill	318	Referred to Committee Whole House.		

List of private claims presented to the House of Representatives of the United States from the 1st to the 31st Congress, inclusive—Continued.

Names of claimants.	Nature or object of the claim.	Congress.	Session.	How brought before the House of Reps.	Page of journal.	To what committee of the House referred.	No. or date of the report.	Nature of the report.	No. of the bill.	How disposed of by the House of Reps.	How disposed of by the Senate.	Date of the act of Congress, and remarks.
Massachusetts, inhabitants of Newburyport.	Indemnity for spoliations on their commerce by Holland, Naples, and Denmark.	19	1	Memorial	153	Foreign Affairs	202	Adverse		Laid on table.		
Massachusetts, inhabitants of Salem.	Indemnity for spoliations on their commerce by Holland, Naples, and Denmark.	19	2	Memorial	63	Foreign Affairs				Discharged; laid on table.		
Massachusetts, merchants of Salem and Beverly.	Payment of certain certificates of drawback of duties.	14	2	Petition	127	Com. and Manuf.				Discharged; laid on table.		
Massachusetts, citizens of Salem and Boston.	To have value of brig Henrick added to the amount to be distributed to them under convention with Denmark.	21	2	Memorial	231	Foreign Affairs	100	Adverse		Laid on table.		
Massachusetts, citizens of Salem and Boston.	To have value of brig Henrick added to the amount to be distributed to them under convention with Denmark.	22	1	Memorial	132	Foreign Affairs.						
Massachusetts, inhabitants of Brewster.	Reimbursement of amount paid to the British commander for guaranteeing safety of their property.	13	3	Petition	720	Claims				Discharged; laid on table.		
Massachusetts, merchants of.	Relief for unavoidable violation of revenue laws.	14	1	Petition	360	Ways and Means	April 1, 1816	Favorable; bill		Passed	Passed	App'd April 27, 1816
Massachusetts, Phillips Academy, at Andover.	Remission of duty on certain books.	14	1	Petition	681	Ways and Means.						
Massachusetts, Harvard College.	Remission of duty on certain books.	14	1	Petition	235	Ways and Means	Mar. 6, 1816	Favorable; bill		Passed	Passed	App'd April 9, 1817
Massachusetts, Harvard College.	Remission of duty on certain books.	30	1	Petition	170	Ways and Means.						
Massachusetts, Mercantile Insurance Company of Salem.	Remission of duties on rigging brought from the wreck of brig Lydia.	21	1	Senate bill	180	Ways and Means	Jan. 28, 1830	With't amend.	S. 47	Passed		App'd April 15, 1830
Massachusetts, merchants of Newburyport.	Refunding money expended in erecting piers in the Merrimac river.	9	1	Petition	228	Com. and Manuf.	Mar. 4, 1806	Adverse		Referred to Committee Whole House.		
Massachusetts, merchants of Newburyport.	Refunding money expended in erecting piers in the Merrimac river.	9	2	Petition	509	Com. and Manuf.	Jan. 21, 1807	Adverse		Referred to Committee Whole House.		
Massachusetts, sundry citizens of, by agent.	For settlement of their claim to lands ceded by Georgia to the United States.	8	2	Memorial	27	Claims	Jan. 18, 1805	Favorable; bill	49	Referred to Committee Whole House.		
Massachusetts, sundry citizens of, by agent.	For settlement of their claim to lands ceded by Georgia to the United States.	10	1	Memorial	107	Whole House.						
Massachusetts, inspectors of customs at Beverly and Salem.	Increase of compensation	9	1	Petition	281	Ways and Means.						
Massachusetts, inspectors of customs at Beverly and Salem.	Increase of compensation	9	2	Petition	482	Ways and Means.						
Massachusetts, surveyor of the port of Beverly.	Increase of compensation	28	2	Petition	235	Commerce.						
Massachusetts, inspectors of customs at Boston and Charlestown.	Increase of compensation	9	1	Petition	243	Ways and Means.						

List of private claims presented to the House of Representatives of the United States from the 1st to the 31st Congress, inclusive—**Continued.**

Names of claimants.	Nature or object of the claim.	Congress.	Session.	How brought before the House of Reps.	Page of journal.	To what committee of the House referred.	No. or date of the report.	Nature of the report.	No. of the bill.	How disposed of by the House of Reps.	How disposed of by the Senate.	Date of the act of Congress, and remarks.
Massachusetts, inspectors of customs at Boston and Charlestown.	Increase of compensation	9	2	Petition	482	Ways and Means.						
Massachusetts, distillers of Taunton.	Remission of duties on stills	14	2	Petition	353	Ways and Means.				Discharged; laid on table.		
Massachusetts, postmaster at Taunton.	Increase of compensation	17	2	Resolution	58	P. Of. & P. Roads.				Discharged; leave to withdraw.		
Massachusetts, postmaster at Nantucket.	Increase of compensation	15	2	Resolution	174	P. Of. & P. Roads.						
Massachusetts, postmaster at Springfield.	Increase of compensation	19	1	Resolution	449	P. Of. & P. Roads.						
Massachusetts, State of	Refunding duties paid on certain philosophical apparatus.	22	1	Resolution	77	Ways and Means.						
Massachusetts, Springfield Manufacturing Company.	For balance due for arms, with interest.	23	1	Petition	191	Claims				Discharged; referred to Secretary of War.		
Massachusetts, Springfield Manufacturing Company.	For balance due for arms, with interest.	23	2	Petition	37	Claims	Jan. 2, 1835	Favorable; bil	602	Referred to Committee Whole House.		
Massachusetts, Springfield Manufacturing Company.	For balance due for arms, with interest.	25	2	Petition	37	Claims	372	Favorable: bill	395	Ordered to 3d reading.		
Massachusetts, Springfield Manufacturing Company.	For balance due for arms, with interest.	25	3	Bill of last sess.	378				395	Passed [Senate amendment agreed to, and laid on table.]	Passed, with amendment.	
Massachusetts, Springfield Manufacturing Company.	For balance due for arms, with interest.	27	2	Petition	56	Claims	6	Favorable; bill	45	Passed	Passed	App'd Aug. 24, 1842
Massachusetts, armorers at Springfield.	Increase of compensation	23	1	Petition	307	Military Affairs.						
Massachusetts, merchants of Boston.	Refunding excess of duties paid under tariff law of 1833.	23	1	Petition	569	Ways and Means.						
Massachusetts, citizens of Worcester.	Satisfaction of certain bounty land warrant.	26	1	Petition	280	Public Lands.						
Massachusetts, citizens and merchants of Boston.	Indemnity for property seized by the government of Hayti.	26	1	Memorial	280	Foreign Affairs.						
Massachusetts, citizens and merchants of Boston.	Indemnity for property seized by the government of Hayti.	27	2	Memorial	99	Foreign Affairs.						
Massachusetts, clerks in custom-house, Boston.	Arrears of pay and increase of salaries.	26	2	Resolution	162	Commerce						Provided for in civil and diplomatic appropriation bill, Mar. 3, 1841.
Massachusetts, clerks in Boston post office.	Increased compensation	31	2	Petition	210	P. Of. & P. Roads.						
Massachusetts, citizens of Boston.	Drawback on spirits distilled from foreign molasses.	28	1	Memorial	263	Commerce.						
Massachusetts, citizens of	Remission of duties on railroad iron.	28	1	Petition	335	Commerce				Discharged; laid on table.		
Massachusetts, citizens of Charlestown.	Remission of duties on railroad iron.	28	1	Petition	415	Commerce				Discharged; laid on table.		
Massachusetts, Fitchburg Railroad Company.	Remission of duties on railroad iron.	28	1	Memorial	358	Commerce	113	To discharge & refer to Ways and Means.		Resolution adopted.		
Massachusetts, citizens of Rockport.	Compensation for materials furnished Sandy Bay breakwater.	28	1	Petition	362	Claims.						
Massachusetts and Vermont Railroad Company.	(See Vermont and Massachusetts Railroad Company.)	28	1		901							

List of private claims presented to the House of Representatives of the United States from the 1st to the 31st Congress, inclusive—Continued.

Names of claimants.	Nature or object of the claim.	Congress.	Session.	How brought before the House of Reps.	Page of journal.	To what committee of the House referred.	No. or date of the report.	Nature of the report.	No. of the bill.	How disposed of by the House of Reps.	How disposed of by the Senate.	Date of the act of Congress, and remarks.
Massachusetts, State of, by agent.	Reimbursement of expenses in carrying into effect the treaty of Washington.	29	1	Memorial	752	Ways and Means.						
Massachusetts, Church of the Advent, Boston.	Remission of duties on church plate.	31	1	Petition	660	Commerce	....	....	......	Discharged; laid on table.		
Massey, Alston S	Pension	21	2	Petition	366	Military Pensions.						
Massey, Charles, jr......	Indemnity for French spoliations prior to 1800.	26	1	Memorial	182	Foreign Affairs....	343	Favorable; bill	319	Referred to Committee Whole House.		
Massey, Charles, jr., (Philadelphia.)	Refunding excess of duties paid in consequence of error of collector.	31	1	Petition	235	Commerce	....	....	......	Discharged; laid on table.		
Massey, Charles, jr., (Philadelphia.)	Refunding excess of duties paid in consequence of error of collector.	31	2	Petition	69	Commerce.						
Massey & Eyre.........	(See Eyre & Massey)	26	1	... .	605							
Massey, George R., widow of.	Indemnity for French spoliations prior to 1800.	29	2	Memorial	83	Foreign Affairs.						
Masey, John, (N. C.) ...	Pension	22	1	Petition	287	Rev. Pensions.						
Massey, John H	Commutation pay for revolutionary services.	24	1	Petition	672	Rev. Claims......	June 23, 1836	Adverse	......	Laid on table.		
Massey, Joseph, heirs of ..	Indemnity for French spoliations prior to 1800.	29	2	Memorial	83	Foreign Affairs.						
Massey, Samuel.........	Pre-emption right to land in Missouri.	19	2	Memorial	243	Public Lands.						
Massey, or Mussey, Samuel and Thomas James.	Permission to enter certain lands at minimum price.	25	2	Petition	417	Public Lands.....	890	Favorable; bill	789	Referred to Committee Whole House.		
Massey, or Mussey, Samuel and Thomas James.	Permission to enter certain lands at minimmum price.	25	3	Bill of last sess.	431	Whole House.....	Feb. 1, 1839	With't amend.	789	Passed	Passed	App'd March 3, 1839
Massey, Sarah	(See George R. Massey, widow of.)	29	2	....	83							
Massias, Abraham A.	Indemntiy for expenses in military sercice.	22	1	Petition	144	Military Affairs....	176	Favorable; bill	252	Referred to Committee Whole House.		
Massias, Abraham A.	Indemnity for expenses in military services.	22	2	Ho. bill last sess.	92	Whole House.....	Dec. 26, 1832	With't amend.	252	Passed	Passed	App'd March 2, 1833
Massie, Thomas, (Va.) ..	Commutation pay for revolutionary services.	23	1	Petition	71	Rev. Claims.						
Massie, Thomas, (Va.) ..	Commutation pay for revolutionary services.	23	2	Petition	147	Rev. Claims.						
Massie, Thomas, representatives of.	Commutation pay for revolutionary services.	24	1	Petition	63	Rev. Claims......	636	Adverse	......	Laid on table.		
Massie, Thomas, representatives of.	Commutation pay for revolutionary services.	25	3	Petition	125	Rev. Claims.						
Massie, Thomas, representatives of.	Commutation pay for revolutionary services.	26	1	Petition	360	Rev. Claims.						
Massingill, Thomas and James.	Confirmation of title to land in Arkansas.	22	2	Petition	34	Public Lands.....	Feb. 4, 1832	Favorable; bill	347	Passed	Passed	App'd May 31, 1832
Massoletti, Vincent......	Additional compensation for services as clerk to quartermaster of marines.	24	2	Petition	46	Naval Affairs.....	Feb. 22, 1837	By bill	953	Referred to Committee Whole House.		
Massoletti, Vincent......	Additional compensation for services as clerk to quartermaster of marines.	25	2	Petition	113	Naval Affairs.....	Jan. 18, 1838	By bill	421	Referred to Committee Whole House.		
Massoletti, Vincent......	Additional compensation for services as clerk to quartermaster of marines.	25	3	Bill of last sess.	378	Whole House	Jan. 25, 1839	With't amend.	421	Passed	Rept'd without amendment.	

List of private claims presented to the House of Representatives of the United States from the 1st to the 31st Congress, inclusive—Continued.

Names of claimants.	Nature or object of the claim.	Congress.	Session.	How brought before the House of Reps.	Page of journal.	To what committee of the House referred.	No. or date of the report.	Nature of the report.	No. of the bill.	How disposed of by the House of Reps.	How disposed of by the Senate.	Date of the act of Congress, and remarks.
Massoletti, Vincent	Additional compensation for services as clerk to quartermaster of marines.	26	1	Petition	182	Naval Affairs.						
Massoletti, Vincent	Additional compensation for services as clerk to quartermaster of marines.	27	2	Petition	99	Claims	176	Adverse		Laid on table.		
Massy, Andrew, (N. Y.)	Compensation as clerk to commissary's department, revolutionary war.	3	2	Petition	301	Claims.						
Massy, Andrew, (N. Y.)	Compensation as clerk to commissary's department, revolutionary war.	4	1	Petition	373	Claims	Dec. 23, 1795	Adverse		Leave to withdraw.		
Massy, Hart	To be paid his share of proceeds of sale of cattle as collector of New York.	17	1	Resolution	262	Judiciary				Discharged; leave to withdraw.		
Massy, Hart	To be paid his share of proceeds of sale of cattle as collector of New York.	17	2	Docs. of last sess.	60	Judiciary				Discharged; leave to withdraw.		
Masters, Henry, heirs of	Confirmation of title to land in Missouri.	23	1	Senate bill	844	Priv. Land Claims	Jan. 27, 1834	With't amend.	86	Passed	Passed	App'd June 30, 1834
Masters, James	(See James Marsters.)	24	1		1184				746			
Masters, John	Payment for horses purchased by United States in Florida.	25	2	Petition	397	Claims	835	Adverse		Laid on table.		
Masters, Moses	Pension	20	2	Petition	39	Military Pensions				Discharged.		
Masters, Nathaniel	Invalid pension	25	3	Petition	103	Invalid Pensions.						
Masters, Nathaniel	Invalid pension	26	1	Petition	198	Invalid Pensions	553	Adverse		Laid on table.		
Masters, Stephen	(See Stephen Marsters.)	25	2		43							
Masterson, Alexander, and Robert Smith.	Relief for losses on contract to furnish marble for Post Office Department.	26	1	Memorial	612	Public Buildings	April 25, 1840	Favorable; by joint resol'n.	10	Passed	Passed	App'd May 16, 1840
Masterson, Patrick	Revolutionary pension	27	3	Petition	207	Rev. Pensions	134	Favorable; bill	756	Passed.		
Masterson, Patrick	Revolutionary pension	28	1	Petition	278	Rev. Pensions	361	Favorable; bill	274	Passed.		
Masterson, Patrick	Revolutionary pension	28	2	Petition	58	Rev. Pensions	136	Favorable; bill	619	Ref'd to Com. W. H.		
Masterson, Patrick	Revolutionary pension	29	1	Petition	93	Rev. Pensions	457	Favorable; bill	334	Passed	Passed	App'd Aug. 8, 1846
Masterson, Peter	(See Marcellus Eells and others.)	30	2		77							
Masterson & Roberts	(See Roberts & Masterson.)	23	1		589							
Mastic, Benjamin	Increase of pension	11	3	House bill	604	Whole House	Mar. 2, 1811	With amends.	218	Passed	Passed	App'd March 3, 1811
Mastin, Charles H	(See Jeremiah Mastin, heirs of)	29	2		147							
Mastin, Jeremiah, heirs of.	Indemnity for French spoliations prior to 1800.	29	2	Memorial	147	Foreign Affairs.						
Mastin, Jeremiah, heirs of.	Indemnity for French spoliations prior to 1800.	31	1	Petition	196	Foreign Affairs	355	Favorable; bill	318	Referred to Committee Whole House.		
Mastin, Mary B	(See Jeremiah Mastin, heirs of.)	29	2		147							
Matchin, Thomas	Correction of pension	15	1	Resolution	329	Pens. & Rev. Cl'ms.				Discharged; laid on table.		
Matheny, John D., and others.	Payment for horses lost in the service of the United States in 1817.	18	2	Petition	60	Claims.						
Matheny, John D., and others.	Payment for horses lost in the service of the United States in 1817.	22	1	Petition	633	Claims	April 23, 1832	Adverse		Laid on table.		
Matheny, William, (Va.)	Pension	21	1	Petition	260	Military Pensions	April 23, 1830	By bill	439	Referred to Committee Whole House.		
Matheny, William, (Va.)	Pension	22	1	Petition	45	Rev. Pensions	Dec. 21, 1831	By bill	68	Passed	Postponed.	

List of private claims presented to the House of Representatives of the United States from the 1st to the 31st Congress, inclusive—Continued.

Names of claimants.	Nature or object of the claim.	Congress.	Session.	How brought before the House of Reps.	Page of journal.	To what committee of the House referred.	No. or date of the report.	Nature of the report.	No. of the bill.	How disposed of by the House of Reps.	How disposed of by the Senate.	Date of the act of Congress, and remarks.
Matheay, William	Increase of pension	24	1	Resolution	482	Rev. Pensions				Discharged; laid on table.		
Mather, Elias	(See Elbert Anderson, administrator of.)	21	2		45							
Mather, Elihu	Compensation for services in war of 1812.	14	1	Petition	93	Claims				Leave to withdraw.		
Mather, Elisha	(See William H. Bedford, agent).	28	1		262							
Mather, John, widow of	Half-pay, &c., for revolutionary services.	2	1	Petition	521					Laid on table.		
Mather, Stephen, surety of.	Release from liability	21	1	Petition	173	Judiciary.						
Mather, Thomas	(See B. H. Reeves, and others.)	21	1		689							
Mathers, James	Compensation for services in recess of Congress.	1	2	Appropriat'n bill.	169	Whole House	Mar. 15, 1790	With amend.	47	Passed	Passed	App'd Mar. 26, 1790
Mathers, James, & Thomas Claxton.	Increase of compensation as doorkeepers to the House of Representatives.	5	2	Memorial	219	Ways and Means	May 19, 1798	Adverse.				
Mathers, James, and others	Compensation for extra services as doorkeeper.	5	2	Senate bill	122	Whole House	Jan. 15, 1798	Favorable	S. 10	Passed	Passed	App'd Jan. 20, 1798
Mathers, James, and others	Compensation for extra services as doorkeeper.	5	2	Resolution	391	Select	July 14, 1798	Favorable; bill	133	Passed	Passed	App'd July 16, 1798
Mathers, James	Refunding expenses incurred as sergent-at-arms, United States Senate.	5	3	Senate bill	481	Whole House	Feb. 22, 1799	Favorable	S. 44	Passed	Passed	App'd Feb. 25, 1799
Mathers, Thomas	(See Joseph Paxton and Thomas Mathers.)	19	2		243							
Mathiot, George, widow of	Revolutionary pension	27	2	Petition	524	Rev. Pensions	567	Favorable; bill	363	Ordered to 3d reading.		
Mathiot, George, widow of	Revolutionary pension	27	2	Bill of last sess.	87				363	Passed	Passed	App'd March 3, 1843
Mathiot, Ruth	(See George Mathiot widow of)	27	2		524							
Mathis, Marshal A., or Mathias.	Remuneration for a vessel lost in service United States.	29	1	Petition	151	Claims	636	Adverse		Laid on table.		
Mathis, William	Seven years' services as blacksmith for United States.	29	1	Documents	256	Indian Affairs	286	Adverse		Laid on table.		
Matson, Enoch	Permission to change location of land warrant.	25	2	Resolution	85	Public Lands	635	Favorable; bill	609	Referred to Committee Whole House.		
Matson, Enoch	Permission to change location of land warrant.	25	3	Bill of last sess.	380	Whole House	Jan. 26, 1839	With't amend.	609	Passed	Passed	App'd March 3, 1839
Matson, Richard	Refunding money paid on land	17	1	Senate bill	199	Priv. Land Claims.	Feb. 1, 1822	With't amend.	S. 4	Passed	Passed	App'd May 7, 1822
Matson, Richard or Robert	To change a land location	19	1	Senate bill	118	Public Lands	Jan. 13, 1826	Adverse	11	Passed	Passed	App'd Mar. 31, 1836
Matterson, Philip	Pension	19	2	Petition and docs.	72	Military Pensions.						
Matteson, Joel O., and H. Bigelow.	For damages in consequence of seizure of railroad iron by United States.	28	1	Petition	430	Roads and Canals.						
Matteson, John	Release from imprisonment as surety of P. S. Smith.	17	1	Senate bill	164	P. Of. & P. Roads.	Mar. 1, 1822	With't amend.	S. 4	Passed	Passed	App'd May 7, 1822
Matthews, Beckford C.	Renewal of lost bounty land war warrant.	27	2	Senate bill	1064	Public Lands	July 23, 1842	With't amend.	S. 198	Passed	Passed	App'd Aug. 11, 1842
Matthews, Charles, heirs of	For release from judgment in favor of United States.	30	1	Petition	679	P. Of. & P. Roads.	327	Adverse		Laid on table		Leave to withd'w, Feb 28, 1849.
Matthews, Charles L.	Confirmation of title to land in Florida.	17	1	Petition	70	Public Lands.						
Matthews, Charles L.	Confirmation of title to land in Florida.	17	2	Petition	100	Public Lands				Discharged; laid on table.		
Matthews, Charles	Revolutionary pension	24	1	Resolution	666	Rev. Pensions				Disch'd; laid on table.		

List of private claims presented to the House of Representatives of the United States from the 1st *to the* 31st *Congress, inclusive*—Continued

Names of claimants.	Nature or object of the claim.	Congress.	Session.	How brought before the House of Reps.	Page of journal.	To what committee of the House referred.	No. or date of the report.	Nature of the report.	No. of the bill.	How disposed of by the House of Reps.	How disposed of by the Senate.	Date of the act of Congress, and remarks.
Matthews, Charles S.	(See Matthews & Wood, & James Hall.)	24	2	....	119							
Matthews, Elrey, & others	Compensation for horse and other property lost in services of United States in 1832.	24	1	Petition	430	Claims.						
Matthews, Gregory	Compensation for extra services in carrying mail.	25	3	Petition	416	Claims.						
Matthews, Gregory	Compensation for extra services in carrying mail.	26	2	Petition	214	Claims.						
Matthews, Hugh	Revolutionary pension and pay for express riding.	28	2	Petition	374	Rev. Pensions.						
Matthews, James, (Ohio).	To be discharged from prison	14	2	Petition	176	Ways and Means..	....	....	.....	Discharged; laid on table.		
Matthews, James........	Land for losses by Choctaw treaty	24	1	Petition	57	Public Lands.....	208	Favorable; bill	208	Referred to Committee Whole House.		
Matthews, John, and Elijah Bodwell.	Compensation for building blockhouse at Galliopolis and for powder and lead furnished United States.	3	1	Rep. of Secretary War.	41	Select.						
Matthews, John.........	For a new location of land	19	1	Senate bill	466	Public Lands.....	May 4, 1826	With amend..	74	Passed	Passed	App'd May 20, 1826
Matthews, John.........	(See Leighton Wood, and others)	3	1	....	209							
Matthews, John.......	Invalid pension................	4	1	Petition	387	Claims..........	Jan. 26, 1796	Adverse	.....	Leave to withdraw.		
Matthews, John D., and others.	(See John D. Matheny, and others)	18	2	....	60							
Matthews, Littlebury.....	Bounty land for revolutionary services.	15	2	Petition	70	Pens. & Rev. Cl'ms.	Dec. 18, 1818	Adverse	.....	Rejected.		
Matthews, Littlebury.....	Bounty land for revolutionary service.	16	2	Petition	178	Pensions	....	....	.....	Rreferred to Secretary of War.		
Matthews, Littlebury.....	Revolutionary pension..........	21	1	Resolution	394	Military Pensions..	....	....	.....	Discharged; laid on table.		
Matthews, Mary S., and others.	Confirmation of title to certain lands	30	2	Petition	240	Public Lands.						
Matthews, Moses, heirs of	Pay for property destroyed during revolutionary war.	30	1	Memorial	603	Rev. Claims......	679	Adverse	.....	Laid on table.		
Matthews, Moses, heirs of	Pay for property destroyed during revolutionary war.	30	2	Petition	127	Rev. Claims.						
Matthews, Moses, heirs of	Pay for property destroyed during revolutionary war.	31	1	Petition	257	Rev. Claims......	58	Adverse	.....	Laid on table.		
Matthews, Samuel.......	(See executors of Thos. Matthews)	23	2	....	197							
Matthews & Stewart.....	(See Stewart & Matthews)......	20	2	....	60							
Matthews, Thomas	Compensation for loss of schooner and cargo impressed into the U. States service and destroyed by the enemy.	2	2	Petition	701	....	....	....	.....	Referred to Secretary of Treasury.		
Matthews, Thomas	Compensation for loss of schooner and cargo impressed into the U. States service and destroyed by the enemy.	3	2	Rep. of Secretary Treasury.	284	Claims.						
Matthews, Thomas	Compensation for loss of schooner and cargo impressed into the U. States service and destroyed by the enemy.	4	1	Petition	411	Claims.						

List of private claims presented to the House of Representatives of the United States from the 1st to the 31st Congress, inclusive—Continued.

Names of claimants.	Nature or object of the claim.	Congress.	Session.	How brought before the House of Reps.	Page of journal.	To what committee of the House referred.	No. or date of the report.	Nature of the report.	No. of the bill.	How disposed of by the House of Reps.	How disposed of by the Senate.	Date of the act of Congress, and remarks.
Matthews, Thomas	Compensation for loss of schooner and cargo impressed into the U. States service and destroyed by the enemy.	4	2	Petition	614	Claims.						
Matthews, Thomas	Compensation for loss of schooner and cargo impressed into the U. States service and destroyed by the enemy.	5	2	Petition	265	Claims	April 18, 1798	Adverse	......	Rejected.		
Matthews, Thomas	(See Joseph Paxton and Thomas Matthews.)	19	2	....	243							
Matthews, Thomas, executors of.	Commutation of half-pay for revolutionary services.	23	2	Petition	197	Rev. Claims.						
Matthews, Thomas, executors of.	Commutation of half-pay for revolutionary services.	24	1	Petition	431	Rev. Claims	....	....	......	Discharged; laid on table.		
Matthews, William, (Ga.)	Compensation as clerk to commissioners of purchases in Georgia.	2	2	Petition	683	....	....	....	......	Referred to Secretary of War.		
Matthews, William, (Ga.)	Compensation as clerk to commissioners of purchases in Georgia.	3	1	Rep. of Secretary War.	93	Select.						
Matthews, William, (Ga.)	Compensation as clerk to commissioners of purchases in Georgia.	4	2	Petition	647	Claims	Jan. 27, 1797	Adverse	......	Laid on table.		
Matthews, William	Pension	28	2	Petition	64	Invalid Pensions.						
Matthews, William B.	(See L. Muse, trustee of the sureties of.)	21	2	....	214							
Matthews & Wood, and James Hall.	Indemnity for loss on contract with government.	24	2	Memorial	119	Claims	117	Adverse	......	Laid on table.		
Matthews & Wood, and James Hall.	Indemnity for loss on contract with government.	25	2	Memorial	234	Claims.						
Matthews & Wood, and James Hall.	Indemnity for loss on contract with government.	25	3	Memorial	206	Claims.						
Matthews & Wood, and James Hall.	Indemnity for loss on contract with government.	26	1	Memorial	168	Claims	494	Res. to refer to Solicitor of Treasury.	......	Resolution adopted.		
Matthews & Wood, and James Hall.	Indemnity for loss on contract with government.	26	2	Rep. of Solicitor Treasury.	30	Claims.						
Matthews & Wood, and James Hall.	Indemnity for loss on contract with government.	27	1	Petition	107	Claims.						
Matthews & Wood, and James Hall.	Indemnity for loss on contract with government.	27	2	Petition	56	Claims	348	Adverse	......	Laid on table.		
Matthews & Wood, and James Hall.	Indemnity for loss on contract with government.	28	1	Petition	261	Claims	414	Adverse	......	Laid on table.		
Matthews & Wood, and James Hall.	Indemnity for loss on contract with government.	29	1	Petition	273	....	....	....	......	Referred to Solicitor of Treasury.		
Matthews & Wood, and James Hall.	Indemnity for loss on contract with government.	30	1	Rep. of Solicitor Treasury.	158	Claims	231	Favorable; bill	235			
Matthews & Wood, and James Hall.	Indemnity for loss on contract with government.	30	2	Bill of last sess.	368	Whole House	Feb. 3, 1849	Favorable	235	Passed	Ref. to Com'r of Claims.	
Matthews & Wood, and James Hall.	Indemnity for loss on contract with government.	31	1	Petition	255	Claims	240	Favorable; bill	236	Referred to Committee Whole House.		
Matthews & Wood, and James Hall.	Indemnity for loss on contract with government.	31	2	Bill of last sess.	182	Whole House	Jan. 24, 1851	With't amend.	236	Passed.		
Matthewson, Elisha, widow of.	Revolutionary pension	25	2	Petition	231	Rev. Pensions	....	....	......	Discharged; laid on table.		

List of private claims presented to the House of Representatives of the United States from the 1st to the 31st Congress, inclusive—Continued.

Names of claimants.	Nature or object of the claim.	Congress.	Session.	How brought before the House of Reps.	Page of journal.	To what committee of the House referred.	No. or date of the report.	Nature of the report.	No. of the bill.	How disposed of by the House of Reps.	How disposed of by the Senate.	Date of the act of Congress, and remarks.
Matthewson, Elizabeth	(See Elisha Matthewson, widow of.)	25	2		231							
Matthewson, Jeffrey	Payment for wagon and team sold United States in revolutionary.	22	2	Petition	264	Rev. Claims.						
Matthewson, William	Pre-emption right to land in Alabama.	19	1	Petition	155	Public Lands				Discharged; laid on table.		
Matthewson, William	Pre-emption right to land in Alabama.	21	2	Petition	137	Public Lands				Discharged; laid on table.		
Matthias, George	(See William Miller, and others, by agent of.)	14	2		148							
Mattic, Lawrence	Revolutionary pension	29	1	Petition	610	Rev. Pensions	826	Adverse		Laid on table.		
Mattis, Christian	Revolutionary pension	24	2	Petition	45	Rev. Pensions				Discharged; laid on table.		
Mattison, Benjamin, widow of.	Revolutionary pension	29	1	Petition	104	Rev. Pensions	299	Favorable; bill	244	Passed	Passed	App'd Aug. 8, 1846
Mattison, Henry	Revolutionary pension	27	2	Petition	614	Rev. Pensions				Discharged; laid on table.		
Mattison, Lois	(See Benjamin Mattison, widow of.)	29	1		104							
Mattocks, Robert	Compensation for conveying prisoners of war to New York.	19	2	Resolution	176	Claims	Jan. 31, 1827	Adverse		Laid on table.		
Mattocks, Robert	Compensation for conveying prisoners of war to New York.	22	2	Petition	177	Claims.						
Mattocks, William, (Vt.)	Refunding money paid as tax collector for advertising.	8	1	Petition	421	Claims	Nov. 1, 1803	Adverse		Rejected.		
Mattocks, William, (Vt.)	Refunding money paid as tax collector for advertising.	9	1	Petition	188	Claims	Dec. 10, 1805	Adverse		Rejected.		
Mattoon, Abel	Land for services in revolutionary war.	24	1	Petition	672	Rev. Claims.						
Matzanbaugh, Daniel	Invalid pension	31	1	Petition	270	Invalid Pensions	474	Adverse		Laid on table.		
Mauck, Robert	Release from payment of duty bonds on a distillery.	14	2	Petition	69	Ways and Means	Jan. 28, 1817	Adverse		Rejected.		
Maughny, Daniel, widow of.	Increase of pension	30	2	Petition	102	Invalid Pensions.						
Maughny, Elizabeth	(See Daniel Maughny, widow of.)	30	2		102							
Maule, Rachael	(See heirs of Eli Shoemaker)	31	1		1044							
Maund, Thomas, representatives of.	(See George Repold, representatives of.)	26	1		182							
Maunger, Thomas	Compensation for losses on contract with Secretary of War for furnishing rations.	8	1	Memorial	564	Claims	Feb. 28, 1804	Adverse		Postponed.		
Maupin, William and J. F. C. Potts.	Extra compensation as clerks in naval store at Portsmouth, Virginia.	31	1	Petition	416	Ways and Means.						
Maurice, Ann A.	(See John Jennings, heirs of.)	24	1		138							
Maurice, Theadore W.	For an equitable settlement of his accounts.	24	1	Senate bill	602	Claims	532	With't amend	S. 97	Passed	Passed	App'd July 2, 1836
Maury, Eliza	(See John M. Maury, widow of.)	28	1		332							
Maury, Fontaine, (N. Y.)	Drawback of duty on coffee	11	3	Petition	446	Com. and Manuf.						
Maury, Fontaine, (N. Y.)	Drawback of duty on coffee	12	1	Petition	25	Com. and Manuf.	Feb. 24, 1812	Adverse		Leave to withdraw.		
Maury, James	Reimbursement of money expended for relief of American seamen while consul at Liverpool.	4	2	Petition	496	Claims.						

List of private claims presented to the House of Representatives of the United States from the 1st to the 31st Congress, inclusive—Continued.

Names of claimants.	Nature or object of the claim.	Congress.	Session.	How brought before the House of Reps.	Page of journal.	To what committee of the House referred.	No. or date of the report.	Nature of the report.	No. of the bill.	How disposed of by the House of Reps.	How disposed of by the Senate.	Date of the act of Congress, and remarks.
Maury, James	Reimbursement of money expended for relief of American seamen while consul at Liverpool.	5	2	Petition	126	Select.						
Maury, John M., widow of.	Pension, husband died in naval services.	28	1	Petition	332	Naval Affairs.						
Maury, M. F	Extra compensation for various and important services under direction of Navy Department.	26	1	Petition	960	Claims	....	....	.....	....	....	Leave to withdraw, Sept. 6, 1841.
Maury, M. F	Adjustment of accounts and for expenses in services of Navy Department.	27	2	Petition	227	Claims	496	Adverse	.....	Laid on table.		
Maury, Wm. L	(See Exploring Expedition)	27	3	....	149							
Mauzey, Fayette	(See Robert G. Wood and others.)	29	1	....	320							
Maver, William N	Further compensation for work done under contract with government at Bedlow's island.	27	3	Petition	155	Public Buildings.						
Maver, William N	Further compensation for work done under contract with government at Bedlow's island.	28	1	Petition	204	Claims	256	Adverse	.....	Laid on table.		
Maxson, Jonathan, heirs of.	Arrears of pension	30	1	Memorial	459	Rev. Claims.						
Maxson, John, (or Maxon)	Pension	14	1	Resolution	158	Pens. & Rev. Cl'ms.	....	....	.....	Discharged; laid on table.		
Maxson, John, (or Maxon)	Pension	16	1	Petition	284	Pens. & Rev. Cl'ms.						
Maxson, John, (or Maxon)	Pension	18	2	Petition	160	Pens. & Rev. Cl'ms.						
Maxson, John, (or Maxon)	Pension	19	1	Petition	73	Military Pensions.	Feb. 23, 1826	By bill	118	Passed.		
Maxson, John, (or Maxon)	Pension	19	2	House bill	85	Whole House	....	....	314	Passed	....	Became a law omitting petitioner's name.
Maxson, M. M	Additional pay as surgeon during Florida war.	30	1	Petition	589	Claims.						
Maxwell, Charles	(See Guy Maxwell, heirs of)	18	1	....	131							
Maxwell, Cornelius	Additional compensation for services as assistant doorkeeper to Congress last session.	5	2	Senate bill	122	Whole House	Jan. 15, 1798	Favorable	10	Passed	Passed	App'd Jan. 20, 1798
Maxwell, Cornelius	Compensation for services, present session.	5	2	Resolution	391	Select	July 14, 1798	Favorable; bill	133	Passed	Passed	App'd July 20, 1798
Maxwell, David H	Compensation for medical services rendered United States soldiers in 1813 and 1814.	24	1	Petition	97	Claims	759	Favorable; bill	693	Referred to Committee Whole House.		
Maxwell, David H	Compensation for medical services rendered United States soldiers in 1813 and 1814.	25	2	Petition	37	Claims	55	Favorable; bill	67	Passed	Passed	App'd April 6, 1838
Maxwell, Guy, heirs of	Confirmation of title to land in New York.	18	1	Petition	131	Judiciary	....	....	.....	Discharged; leave to withdraw.		
Maxwell, Guy, heirs of	Confirmation of title to land in New York.	21	2	Petition	42	Judiciary	....	....	.....	Discharged; laid on table.		
Maxwell, Hector	(See Guy Maxwell, heirs of)	18	1	....	131							
Maxwell, Hugh	Invalid pension	3	2	Rep. of Secretary War.	337	Claims	Feb. 28, 1795	Favorable; bill	130	Passed	Postponed.	
Maxwell, Hugh	Invalid pension	4	1	Rep. of Secretary War.	447	Claims	Feb. 18, 1796	Favorable; bill	156	Passed	Passed	App'd April 20, 1796
Maxwell, Hugh, heirs of	Compensation for revolutionary services.	25	3	Petition	220	Rev. Claims.						

List of private claims presented to the House of Representatives of the United States from the 1st to the 31st Congress, inclusive—**Continued.**

Names of claimants.	Nature or object of the claim.	Congress.	Session.	How brought before the House of Reps.	Page of journal.	To what committee of the House referred.	No. or date of the report.	Nature of the report.	No. of the bill.	How disposed of by the House of Reps.	How disposed of by the Senate.	Date of the act of Congress, and remarks.
Maxwell, Hugh, heirs of	Compensation for revolutionary services.	30	1	Petition	485	Rev. Pensions	373	Adverse		Laid on table.		
Maxwell, James, heirs of	Permission to inherit lands of deceased; they being aliens.	14	1	Petition	439	Judiciary	Mar. 22, 1816	By bill		Passed	Passed	App'd April 27, 1816
Maxwell, James, (Pa.)	Bounty land for revolutionary services.	23	2	Petition	48	Priv. Land Claims.	109	Adverse		Laid on table.		
Maxwell, James, (Pa.,) legal representatives of.	Bounty land for revolutionary services.	25	2	Petition	868	Priv. Land Claims.	857	Favorable; bill	775	Referred to Committee Whole House.		
Maxwell, James, (Pa.,) legal representatives of.	Bounty land for revolutionary services.	25	3	Bill of last sess.	431	Whole House	Feb. 1, 1839	With amend.	775	Passed	Passed	App'd March 3, 1839
Maxwell, James	Commutation and bounty land for revolutionary services.	19	1	Resolution	317	Rev. Pensions.						
Maxwell, James, (Ind.)	Payment for property destroyed in revolutionary war.	25	2	Petition	915	Rev. Claims				Discharged; laid on table.		
Maxwell, John	Balance of pay as musician in marine corps.	14	2	Petition and rep't Sec. of Navy.	177, 287	Naval Affairs				Referred to Secretary Navy.		
Maxwell, John P. & Hugh H.	(See James Maxwell, heirs of)	14	1		439							
Maxwell, Priscilla	(See Hugh Maxwell, heirs of.)	30	1		485							
Maxwell, Samuel H. and Susan A.	(See Guy Maxwell, heirs of)	18	1		131							
Maxwell, Thomas	Revolutionary pension	24	1	Petition	260	Rev. Pensions				Discharged; laid on table.		
Maxwell, Thomas	Revolutionary pension	25	2	Petition	546	Rev. Pensions	747	Favorable; bill	709	Passed	Passed, third session.	Bill was not sent to Presid't for approval.
Maxwell, Thomas	Revolutionary pension	26	1	Petition	172	Rev. Pensions.						
Maxwell, Thomas	(See Guy Maxwell, heirs of)	18	1		131							
Maxwell, Thompson	Compensation for services and losses under General Hull.	13	1	Petition	19	Claims				Discharged; laid on table.		
Maxwell, Thompson	Compensation for services and losses under General Hull.	13	2	Petition	181	Claims	March 7, 1814	Res. for leave to withdraw.		Resolution adopted.		
Maxwell, Thompson	Compensation for services and losses under General Hull.	13	3	Petition	493	Claims				Discharged; laid on table.		
Maxwell, Thompson	Compensation for services and losses under General Hull.	14	1	Petition	90	Claims				Discharged; laid on table.		
Maxwell, William	For a grant of land as Canadian refugees.	6	2	Resolution	733	Select	Jan. 19, 1801	Favorable; bill	280	Passed	Passed	App'd Feb. 18, 1801
Maxwell, William	(See Isaac Lawrence, and others)	14	1		386							
Maxwell, William, (Ohio)	Pension	14	2	Resolution	77	Pens. & Rev. Cl'ms.	Jan. 9, 1817	Favorable; bill	91	Passed	Passed	App'd March 3, 1817
Maxwell, William	Release from judgment in favor of United States.	31	1	Petition	881	Judiciary	413	Favorable; bill	355	Passed	Passed	App'd Aug. 10, 1850
May, Jacob	Pre-empt on right to certain lands.	25	2	Petition	119	Public Lands.						
May, James, (Mich.)	Compensation for property destroyed, war of 1812.	15	2	Petition	327					Discharged; laid on table.		
May, James, (Mich.)	Compensation for property destroyed, war of 1812.	16	1	Petition	64	Claims				Discharged; laid on table.		
May, James, (Mich.)	Compensation for property destroyed, war of 1812.	16	2	Report of Commissioners.	165	Claims	44	Favorable; bill	218	Referred to Committee Whole House.		
May, James, (Mich.)	Compensation for property destroyed, war of 1812.	17	1	Petition	47, 61	Claims	7	Favorable; bill	16	Passed	Passed	App'd May 1, 1822
May, James	(See John R. Williams and James May.)	20	1		28							

List of private claims presented to the House of Representatives of the United States from the 1st to the 31st Congress, inclusive—Continued.

Names of claimants.	Nature or object of the claim.	Congress.	Session.	How brought before the House of Reps.	Page of journal.	To what committee of the House referred.	No. or date of the report.	Nature of the report.	No. of the bill.	How disposed of by the House of Reps.	How disposed of by the Senate.	Date of the act of Congress, and remarks.
May, James, heirs or assignees of.	Confirmation of title to land in Michigan.	20	1	Report of commissioners.	28, 29	Public Lands	42	Favorable; bill	34	Passed	Passed	App'd April 22, 1828
May, James, heirs of	Other lands in lieu of those heretofore granted to him.	21	1	Petition	202	Priv. Land Claims.	Mar. 5, 1830	Adverse	......	Laid on table.		
May, James, heirs of	Other lands in lieu of those heretofore granted to him.	27	2	Petition	368	Public Lands	481	Favorable; bill	333	Passed	Passed	App'd Aug. 31, 1842
May, James	Compensation as marshal of Michigan, 1805–'06.	18	2	Petition	102	Claims	Feb. 14, 1825	Adverse	......	Laid on table.		
May, James	Compensation as marshal of Michigan, 1805–'06.	19	1	Petition	293	Territories	177	Favorable; bill	231	Passed.		
May, James	Compensation as Marshal of Michigan, 1805–'06.	19	2	Petition	27	Territories	Dec. 14, 1826	Favorable; bill	291	Passed	Passed	App'd March 2, 1827
May, James L	(See James May, heirs of.)	21	1	....	202							
May, James S	(See David Shaver, sen., & others.)	21	2	....	75							
May, James S	(See Samuel May, sen., heirs of.)	28	1	....	987							
May, John, widow of	Revolutionary pension	30	1	Petition	271	Rev. Pensions	226	Adverse	......	Laid on table.		
May, Joseph, (Mass)	Indemnity for French spoliations prior to 1800.	26	1	Memorial	182	Foreign Affairs	343	Favorable; bill	319	Referred to Committee Whole House.		
May, Magaret	(See James May, heirs of.)	21	1	....	202							
May, Oliver	Revolutionary pension	21	2	Resolution	165	Military Pensions.						
May, Oliver	Revolutionary pension	22	1	Resolution	87	Rev. Pensions	120	Favorable; bill	194	Referred to Committee Whole House.		
May, Oliver	Revolutionary pension	22	2	Bill of last sess.	66	Whole House	....	....	194	Laid on table.		
May, Pleasant, jr., and others.	For leave to enter certain lands	25	2	Petition	86	Public Lands.						
May, Pleasant, jr., and others.	For leave to enter certain lands	26	1	Petition	180	Roads and Canals.						
May, Pleasant, jr., and others.	For leave to enter certain lands	26	2	Petition	37	Roads and Canals.						
May, Renolds	Release from payment of judgment in fovor of United States.	30	1	Senate bill	684	Judiciary	May 17, 1848	With't amend.	111	Passed	Passed	App'd May 31, 1848
May, Samuel	(See Nathaniel Goddard & others.)	15	1	....	143							
May, Samuel	Indemnity for property destroyed, war of 1812.	22	1	Senate bill	795	Claims	501	With't amend.	100	Passed	Passed	App'd July 14, 1832
May, Samuel	Indemnity for property destroyed, war of 1812.	23	1	Petition	273	Claims	389	Adverse	......	Laid on table.		
May, Samuel, sen., heirs of.	Refunding money paid on land	28	1	Petition	987	Priv. Land Claims.						
May, Samuel, sen., heirs of.	Refunding money paid on land	29	1	Petition	92	Priv. Land Claims.						
May, Samuel, sen., heirs of.	Refunding money paid on land	30	1	Petition	240	Priv. Land Claims.						
May, Sarah, (of Martin.)	Pension	22	1	Petition	288	Invalid Pensions	Feb. 15, 1832	Adverse	......	Laid on table.		
May, Sarah	(See John May, widow of.)	30	1	....	271							
May, William	(See Exploring Expedition)	27	3	....	149							
Mayberry, Richard, heirs of.	Five years' full pay for revolutionary services.	28	1	Petition	712	Rev. Claims.						
Mayer, Charles	(See William Cole, executors of.)	26	1	....	182							
Mayer, Christian	(See Valck & Co., trustees and agents of.)	26	1	....	182							
Mayer, Frederick	Compensation for revolutionary services.	12	1	Petition	214	Claims.						

List of private claims presented to the House of Representatives of the United States from the 1st to the 31st Congress, inclusive—Continued.

Names of claimants.	Nature or object of the claim.	Congress.	Session.	How brought before the House of Reps.	Page of journal.	To what committee of the House referred.	No. or date of the report.	Nature of the report.	No. of the bill.	How disposed of by the House of Reps.	How disposed of by the Senate.	Date of the act of Congress, and remarks.
Mayer, Handhendrick	Invalid pension	3	2	Rep. of Secretary War.	278	Claims.						
Mayer, Handhendrick	Invalid pension	4	1	Rep. of Secretary War.	445	Claims	Feb. 8, 1796	Rep't and res.	16	Referred to Secretary of War.		
Mayer, John Andrew	Compensation for services and for supplies furnished in revolutionary war.	4	1	Petition	370	Claims	Jan. 20, 1796	Adverse		Leave to withdraw.		
Mayfield, Charles	Confirmation of claim to land	26	1	Petition & docs.	505	Public Lands.						
Mayfield, George	Confirmation of title to land	14	2	Petition	128	Priv. Land Claims.				Discharged; laid on table.		
Mayfield, George	Allowance of six hundred and forty acres of land as Indian interpreter.	20	1	Resolution	476	Priv. Land Claims.						
Mayfield, George	Allowance of six hundred and forty acres of land as Indian interpreter.	21	2	Resolution	60	Priv. Land Claims.	18	Adverse		Laid on table.		
Mayfield, George	That a patent may issue for six hundred and forty acres of land.	22	1	Resolution	126	Public Lands.	182	Favorable; bill	258	Referred to Committee Whole House.		
Mayfield, George	That a patent may issue for six hundred and forty acres of land.	22	2	House bill	92	Whole House	Dec. 28, 1832	With't amend.	258	Passed	Passed	App'd Jan. 30, 1833
Mayfield, George, (Tenn.)	Confirmation of title to land	26	1	Petition	333	Priv. Land Claims.	597	Favorable; bill	455	Referred to Committee Whole House.		
Mayfield, George, (Tenn.)	Confirmation of title to land	27	2	Petition	99	Priv. Land Claims.	Feb. 9, 1842	By bill	125	Passed	Passed	App'd July 27, 1842
Mayfield, George, (Tenn.)	Confirmation of title to land	27	3	Bill on leave	348				783	Passed	Passed	App'd Feb. 24, 1843
Mayfield, George	Invalid pension	26	1	Petition	326	Invalid Pensions	360	Favorable; bill	339	Referred to Committee Whole House.		
Mayfield, George	Invalid pension	27	2	Petition	95	Invalid Pensions	147	Favorable; bill	194	Passed	Passed	App'd July 27, 1842
Mayfield, George	Act amendatory for his relief	29	1	Bill on leave	133	Priv. Land Claims.	Jan. 30, 1846	With't amend.	3	Passed	Passed	App'd May 22, 1846
Mayfield, Micajah	Pension	20	1	Petition	192	Military Pensions	April 29, 1828	Favorable; bill	283	Passed.		
Mayfield, Micajah	Pension	20	2	House bill	55	Whole House	Jan. 15, 1829	With amends.	311	Passed	Laid on table.	
Mayfield, Micajah	Pension	21	1	Petition	48	Military Pensions	Jan. 5, 1830	By bill	72	Passed	Passed	App'd May 20, 1830
Mayfield, Sutherland	Invalid pension	23	2	Petition	87	Invalid Pensions.						
Mayfield, Sutherland	Invalid pension	24	2	Resolution	311	Invalid Pensions.				Discharged; laid on table.		
Mayfield, Sutherland	Invalid pension	26	1	Petition	326	Invalid Pensions	409	Adverse		Laid on table.		
Mayfield, Sutherland	Invalid pension	27	3	Petition	69	Invalid Pensions	71	Adverse		Laid on table.		
Mayfield, Sutherland	Invalid pension	28	2	Petition	187	Invalid Pensions.						
Mayfield, Sutherland	Arrears of pension	29	1	Petition	265	Invalid Pensions.						
Mayfield, Sutherland	Arrears of pension	29	2	Memorial	92	Invalid Pensions.						
Mayfield, Sutherland	Arrears of pension	30	2	Petition	314	Invalid Pensions	75	Favorable; bill	769	Referred to Committee Whole House.		
Mayhen, Peter	Bounty land for revolutionary services.	22	1	Resolution	484	Public Lands.						
Mayhew, Thadeus	Compensation for property destroyed in war of 1812.	15	1	Letter of Com. on Claims.	34	Claims	154	Favorable; bill	137	Referred to Committee Whole House.		
Mayhew, Thadeus	Compensation for property destroyed in war of 1812.	16	1	Documents	102	Claims	54	Adverse		Referred to Committee Whole House.		
Mayhew, Thadeus	Compensation for property destroyed in war of 1812.	17	1	Petition	39	Claims	Jan. 4, 1822	Favorable; bill	23	Referred to Committee Whole House.		
Mayhew, Thadeus	Compensation for property destroyed in war of 1812.	17	2	House bill	37	Whole House			23	Passed.		

List of private claims presented to the House of Representatives of the United States from the 1st to the 31st Congress, inclusive—Continued.

Names of claimants.	Nature or object of the claim.	Congress.	Session.	How brought before the House of Reps.	Page of journal.	To what committee of the House referred.	No. or date of the report.	Nature of the report.	No. of the bill.	How disposed of by the House of Reps.	How disposed of by the Senate.	Date of the act of Congress, and remarks.
Mayhew, Thadeus	Compensation for property destroyed in war of 1812.	18	1	Senate bill	422	Claims	April 21, 1824	With amend.	71	Passed	Passed	App'd May 5, 1824
Maynard John, (Mass.)	Invalid pension	3	2	Rep. of Secretary War.	278	Claims	Feb. 28, 1795	Favorable; bill	130	Passed.	Postponed.	
Maynard, John, (Mass.)	Invalid pension	4	1	Petition	447	Claims	Feb. 8, 1796	Favorable; bill	156	Passed	Passed	App'd April 20, 1796
Maynard, John, (Mass.)	Increase of pension	9	1	Petition	245	Claims	Mar. 28, 1806	Res. to postpone & leave to withdraw.	......	Adopted.		
Maynard, John, (Mass.)	Increase of pension	9	2	House bill	608	Whole House	Mar. 2, 1807	With amends.	216	Passed	Passed	App'd March 3, 1807
Maynard, Needham	Additional compensation for revolutionary services.	21	1	Petition	235	Military Pensions	May 4, 1830	Adverse	......	Laid on table.		
Maynard, Windsor and Alonzo B.	Release from judgment for duties on stills.	18	1	Petition	74	Ways and Means	Jan. 3, 1825	Adverse	......	Rejected.		
Mayhew, Nathan W.	Confirmation of title to land in Arkansas.	22	1	Documents	672	Public Lands.						
Mayo, Daniel	(See Elisha Winters & Sons)	19	2	....	159							
Mayo, Isaac, and others	Remuneration for capture of a piratical vessel in 1830.	23	1	Memorial	838	Naval Affairs.						
Mayo, P.	Compensation for services rendered State Department.	29	1	Petition	890	Judiciary.						
Mayotte, Jacques	Confirmation of title to land in Illinois.	18	1	Documents	331	Whole House.						
Mayrant, Charles, and wife.	(See Francis Kinlock, heirs of.)	19	2	....	189							
Mayrant, Capt. John, heirs of.	Revolutionary pension	29	1	Petition	266	Rev. Pensions.						
Mayrant, John	Prize money as midshipman under Commodore John Paul Jones.	22	1	Petition	415	Naval Affairs.						
Mays, Elizabeth	(See Wilson Mays, mother of.)	20	1	....	309							
Mays, Joseph	Pension	25	2	Petition	404	Invalid Pensions	Mar. 20, 1838	Adverse	......	Laid on table.		
Mays, Mathew	Revolutionary pension	24	2	Petition	93	Rev. Pensions	....	....	......	Discharged; laid on table.		
Mays, Wilson, mother of.	Pension	20	1	Petition	309	Naval Affairs	108	Favorable; bill	209	Passed.		
Mays, Wilson, mother of.	Pension	20	2	House bill	36	Naval Affairs	Feb. 11, 1828	Favorable	310	Referred to Committee Whole House.		
Mays, Wilson, mother of.	Pension	21	1	Petition	50	Naval Affairs	9	Favorable; bill	14	Passed	Passed	App'd Mar. 25, 1830
Mays, Wilson, mother of.	Continuation of pension	23	2	Petition	38	Naval Affairs	Dec. 11, 1834	Favorable; bill	557	Passed.		
Mays, Wilson, mother of.	Continuation of pension	24	1	Petition	100	Naval Affairs	Jan. 12, 1836	By bill	111	Passed	Passed	App'd May 14, 1836
Mays, Wilson, mother of.	Arrears of pension	25	2	Petition	201	Naval Affairs	431	Adverse	......	Laid on table.		
Mays, Wilson, mother of.	Arrears of pension	26	1	Petition	303	Naval Affairs.						
Mays, Wilson, mother of.	Arrears of pension	26	2	Petition	79	Naval Affairs.						
Mays, Wilson, mother of.	Arrears of pension	27	2	Petition	63	Naval Affairs	597	Adverse	......	Laid on table.		
Mays, Wilson, mother of.	Arrears of pension	30	1	Petition	104	Naval Affairs	57	Favorable; bill	60	Passed.		
Mays, Wilson, mother of.	Arrears of pension	30	2	House bill from Senate.	279	....	....	....	60	....	Passed	App'd Jan. 29, 1849
Mayse, Joseph	Invalid pension	26	1	Resolution	552	Invalid Pensions	....	....	......	Discharged; laid on table.		
Mayson, James, heirs of.	Compensation for revolutionary services.	27	2	Petition	142	Rev. Claims	975	Adverse	......	Laid on table.		
Mayson, James, heirs of.	Compensation for revolutionary services.	27	3	Petition	73	Rev. Claims.						
Mayson, James, heirs of.	Compensation for revolutionary services.	31	2	Petition	143	Rev. Claims.						

List of private claims presented to the House of Representatives of the United States from the 1st to the 31st Congress, inclusive—Continued.

Names of claimants.	Nature or object or the claim.	Congress.	Session.	How brought before the House of Reps.	Page of journal.	To what committee of the House referred.	No. or date of the report.	Nature of the report.	No. of the bill.	How disposed of by the House of Reps.	How disposed of by the Senate.	Date of the act of Congress, and remarks.
McAdam, John, (Va.)	Commutation pay due his father for revolutionary services.	22	2	Petition	46	Rev. Claims				Discharged; laid on table.		
McAdams, John, heirs of	Commutation pay for revolutionary services.	31	1	Petition	496	Rev. Claims	421	Adverse		Laid on table.		
McAdams, John, heirs of	Commutation pay for revolutionary services.	31	2	Petition and docs.	394	Rev. Claims.						
McAdams, Joseph	Remuneration for services in Indian wars.	27	1	Petition	116	Rev. Pensions.						
McAdams, Joseph	Revolutionary pension	27	2	Petition	59	Rev. Pensions	784	Adverse		Laid on table.		
McAdoo, William G	Compensation for property lost in service of United States in war with Mexico.	31	1	Petition	1215	Claims.						
McAfee, Joseph, heirs of	Reimbursement of money paid for certain lands which were again sold by United States.	30	2	Senate bill	518	Priv. Land Claims.			333			
McAfee, Robert B., and others.	For a grant of land in Indiana	13	2	Petition	185	Public Lands	Mar. 31, 1814	Adverse		Rejected.		
McAlear, Francis	Remission of fine for violation of the license laws.	15	1	Petition	199	Ways and Means				Discharged; laid on table.		
McAlear, Francis	Remission of fine for violation of the license laws.	17	1	Petition	294	Ways and Means				Discharged; laid on table.		
McAlear, Francis	Remission of fine for violation of the license law.	18	2	Resolution	167					Leave to withdraw.		
McAllen, Captain John	Payment for services of his company of volunteers.	25	2	Documents	274	Claims.						
McAlhany, Allan B	Reissue of a land warrant	20	1	Resolution	432	Priv. Land Claims.	222	Favorable	253	Passed	Passed	App'd May 24, 1828
McAlister, Archibald	Compensation for revolutionary services.	1	1	Petition	97	Select				Discharged; referred to Secretary War.		
McAlister, Archibald	Compensation for revolutionary services.	1	2	Rep. of Secretary War.	141					Leave to withdraw.		
McAlister, A	Renewal of patent	30	1	Petition	593, 752	Patents.						
McAlister, Charles, (Pa.)	Indemnity for French spoliations prior to 1800.	26	1	Memorial	182	Foreign Affairs	343	Favorable; bill	319	Referred to Committee Whole House.		
McAlister, Charles, President of Pennsylvania Insurance Company.	Indemnity for French spoliations prior to 1800.	26	1	Memorial	182	Foreign Affairs	343	Favorable; bill	319	Referred to Committee Whole House.		
McAlister, Hamit	(See heirs of Samuel Hoyt)	28	1		944							
McAllister, John	Bounty for military services	29	1	Documents	311	Judiciary	439	Favorable	312	Passed	Passed	App'd Aug. 8, 1846
McAlister, John	Compensation for carrying the mail	30	1	Petition	461	P. Of. & P. Roads.						
McAllister & Comyn	Compensation for work, &c., done on Cumberland road.	23	1	Res. and Docs	589	Claims	456	Favorable		Referred to Secretary War.		See report No. 449.
McAllister, John, and Foster Cook.	Permission to remain on school lands settled upon by mistake.	14	2	Petition	143	Public Lands	Jan. 8, 1817	Adverse		Rejected.		
McAllister, John	(See John Forbes, representatives of.)	18	1		339							
McAllister, Randal	Invalid pension	10	1	Petition	232	Claims	Mar. 17, 1808	Favorable	78	Passed	Passed with amendment.	App'd April 25, 1808
McAlpine, William J	Increase of compensation as assistant engineer of dry-dock at Brooklyn.	31	1	Petition	741	Naval Affairs.						
McAnally, Jesse	Pension	14	2	Resolution	157	Pens. & Rev. Cl'ms.	Jan. 29, 1817	Favorable	91	Passed	Passed, with amendment.	App'd March 3, 1817

List of private claims presented to the House of Representatives of the United States from the 1st to the 31st Congress, inclusive—Continued.

2—52

Names of claimants.	Nature or object of the claim.	Congress.	Session.	How brought before the House of Reps.	Page of journal.	To what committee of the House referred.	No. or date of the report.	Nature of the report.	No. of the bill.	How disposed of by the House of Reps.	How disposed of by the Senate.	Date of the act of Congress, and remarks.
McAndrew, John	Pension	21	2	Petition	123	Military Pensions				Discharged; laid on table.		
McAndrew, John	Pension	22	1	Petition	193	Rev. Pensions				Discharged.		
McAnulty, Giles, widow of	Permission to sell lands granted by treaty.	20	1	Petition	319	Public Lands.						
McAnulty, Giles, widow of	Permission to sell lands granted by treaty.	21	1	Petition	60	Public Lands	69	Favorable	97	Recommitted.		
						Public Lands	April 28, 1830	With amend	97	Passed	Passed	App'd May 29, 1830
McArthur, Charles	Patent for land located under a Spanish grant.	27	3	Memorial	255	Priv. Land Claims.						
McArthur, Duncan, and others, (Ohio.)	For a compromise of certain claims to land on the Miamie.	15	2	Petition	172	Public Lands.						
McArthur, Duncan, and others, (Ohio.)	For a compromise of certain claims to land on the Miamie.	19	2	Petition	78	Whole House			295	Passed.		
McArthur, Duncan	Compensation for services and losses in late war.	27	2	Petition	618	Claims	690	Adverse		Laid on table.		
McArthur, Duncan, heirs of.	Grant of land for services in last war.	31	1	Petition	588	Public Lands.						
McAtee & Eastman	Compensation for extra mail service	31	2	Petition	74	P. Of. & P. Roads.						
McAuley, Donald, of Great Britain.	Value of loan office certificate to be converted into United States stock.	8	1	Petition	547	Claims				Referred to Committee Whole House.		
McAuley, William, moderator of German church.	Remission of duties on books for seminary in New York.	7	2	Memorial	361	Com. and Munuf.	March 3, 1803	Rep. & res. to postpone.		Adopted.		
McAuley, William, moderator of German church.	Remission of duties on books for seminary in New York.	8	1	Memorial	440	Com. and Manuf	Nov. 14, 1803	Adverse		Leave to withdraw.		
McAvoy, James	Compensation for work done on National road.	28	1	Petition	510	Claims.						
McAvoy, James	Compensation for work done on National road.	28	2	Petition and docs.	45	Claims	129	Favorable	614	Referred to Committee Whole House.		
McAvoy, James	Compensation for work done on National road.	29	1	Petition and docs.	89	Claims.						
McAvoy, James	Compensation for work done on National road.	30	1	Petition and docs.	102	Claims	64	Favorable	46	Passed.		
McBarney, Thomas	Invalid pension	15	2	House bill	41	Whole House	Nov. 26, 1818	Favorable	203	Passed	Passed	App'd March 3, 1819
McBeath, Alexander	(See Captain Robert Kirkwood, administrator of.)	2	2		634							
McBee, Israel	Revolutionary pension	29	1	Bill (on leave)	443	Rev. Pensions			258			
McBeth, George	Pension	15	1	Petition	195	Pens. & Rev. Cl'ms.				Discharged; laid no table.		
McBlair, F. B	For certain credits in settlement of his accounts, which have been rejected by the Fourth Auditor.	30	2	Memorial	127	Naval Affairs.						
McBoy, Diego	(See Diego McVoy)	15	1		243							
McBrager, Hugh	Revolutionary pension	24	1	Resolution	269	Rev. Pensions.						
McBride, Abraham	(See Mathews & Wood, and Jas. Hall.)	24	2		119							
McBride, Hugh	(See Joseph Brown)	24	2		78							
McBride, Hugh	(See William H. Bedford, agent)	28	1		262							
McBride, James	(See Jos. Hough and J. McBride)	13	2		304							
McBride, Joseph	Pension	24	1	Petition	408	Invalid Pensions	June 22, 1836	Adverse, (verbal.)		Laid on table.		
McBride, Robert	(See administ'r of Andrew Mitchell)	19	1		151							
McBride, Robert	Invalid pension	24	1	Petition	533	Invalid Pensions	749	Favorable	690	Passed	Indef. postp'd.	

List of private claims presented to the House of Representatives of the United States from the 1st to the 31st Congress, inclusive—Continued.

Names of claimants.	Nature or object of the claim.	Congress.	Session.	How brought before the House of Reps.	Page of journal.	To what committee of the House referred.	No. or date of the report.	Nature of the report.	No. of the bill.	How disposed of by the House of Reps.	How disposed of by the Senate.	Date of the act of Congress, and remarks.
McBride, Robert	Invalid pension	25	2	Petition	39	Invalid Pensions	219	Favorable	257	Passed	Adverse.	
McBride, Robert	Invalid pension	26	1	Petition	161	Invalid Pensions	March 5, 1840	Adverse		Laid on table.		
McBride, William	Release from United States judgment.	15	1	Petition	225	Ways and Means				Discharged; laid on table.		
McBride, William	Release from United States judgment.	15	2	Petition	54	Ways and Means				Discharged; laid on table.		
McBride, William	Release from United States judgment.	21	2	Petition	270	P. Of. & P. Roads.						
McBride, William	Release from United States judgment.	22	1	Petition	115	P. Of. & P. Roads.	Jan. 24, 1832	Adverse		Laid on table.		
McBride, William, (Ky.)	Reimbursement of money illegally paid twice.	22	1	Petition	49	Claims	Jan. 16, 1842	Adverse		Laid on table.		
McBride, William, (Ky.)	Reimbursement of money illegally paid twice.	24	1	Petition	429	Claims	470	Adverse		Laid on table.		
McBride, Major William	Arrears of pension	29	1	Memorial	440	Invalid Pensions.						
McBrier, Elizabeth	(See heirs of Colonel Archibald Loughrey.)	29	2		67							
McBryde, Samuel	(See William Williams, & others)	21	1		132							
McCabe, William	(See William Flippo, assignee of)	27	3		305							
McCaffery, John, widow of	For share of prize money, &c	28	1	Petition	695	Rev. Claims.						
McCaffery, John, widow of	For share of prize money, &c	28	2	Petition	147	Rev. Claims				Discharged; laid on table.		
McCaffery, John, widow of	For share of prize money, &c	30	1	Petition	624	Rev. Claims.						
McCafferty John, by James Gay, executor of.	Compensation for property destroyed during the revolutionary war.	3	1	Petition	48	Select	Feb. 5, 1794	Reported		Laid on table.		
McCain, Charlotte	(See widow of William McCain).	28	1		61							
McCain, William, widow of	Revolutionary pension	28	1	Petition	61	Rev. Pensions.						
McCain, William, widow of	Revolutionary pension	30	1	Petition	148	Rev. Pensions	206	Adverse		Laid on table.		
McCaleb, David, (Mo.)	Pre-emption right to land	11	2	Petition	271	Public Lands	Mar. 16, 1810	Adverse		Rejected.		
McCaleb, David	Confirmation of Indian title to land in Mississippi.	24	2	Memorial	391	Priv. Land Claims.						
McCaleb, David	Permission to locate certain confirmed claims.	24	2	Petition	210, 391	Priv. Land Claims				Discharged; laid on table.		
McCaleb, David, jr	Confirmation of title to land in Mississippi.	25	3	Memorial	268	Public Lands.						
McCaleb, David	(See assignee of Alexander McCollough.)	11	2		227							
McCall, Archibl'd, administrator of.	Indemnity for French spoliations prior to 1800.	26	1	Memorial	182	Foreign Affairs	343	Favorable; bill	319	Referred to Committee Whole House.		
McCall, Archibl'd, & others	Extension of time for payment of duties on tea.	2	1	Petition	520	Select.						
McCall, Archibl'd, & others	Extension of time for payment of duties on tea, and remission of forfeitures.	10	1	Memorial	28	Com. and Manuf.						
McCall, Archibl'd, & others	Extension of time for payment of duties on tea, and remission of forfeitures.	10	1	Senate bill	277	Whole House			S. 20	Indefinitely postponed.		
McCall, Archibl'd, & others	Extension of time for payment of duties on tea, and remission of forfeitures.	10	2	Memorial	356	Com. and Manuf.						
McCall, Archibl'd, & others	Extension of time for payment of duties on tea, and remission of forfeitures.	11	1	Memorial	34	Com. and Manuf.						

List of private claims presented to the House of Representatives of the United States from the 1st to the 31st Congress, inclusive—Continued.

Names of claimants.	Nature or object of the claim.	Congress.	Session.	How brought before the House of Reps.	Page of journal.	To what committee of the House referred.	No. or date of the report.	Nature of the report.	No. of the bill.	How disposed of by the House of Reps.	How disposed of by the Senate.	Date of the act of Congress, and remarks.
McCall, Archibl'd, & others	Extension of time for payment of duties on tea, and remission of forfeitures.	11	2	Memorial	139	Whole House.						
McCall, Archibl'd, & others	Extension of time for payment of duties on tea, and remission of forfeitures.	11	3	Memorial	444	Com. and Manuf.	Dec. 14, 1810	Favorable; bill	146	Passed	Postponed.	
McCall, Archibl'd, & others	Extension of time for payment of duties on tea, and remission of forfeitures.	12	1	Memorial	25	Com. and Manuf.	Dec. 2, 1811	Favorable; bill	14	Referred to Committee Whole House.		
McCall, Archibl'd, & others	Drawback of duty on tea	13	2	Memorial	233	Com. and Manuf.	Mar. 29, 1814	Favorable; bill	175	Passed	Passed	App'd April 18, 1814
McCall, John	(See Smith, Thurger & Co.	29	1		151							
McCall, Peter, administrator of.	Indemnity for French spoliations prior to 1800.	26	1	Memorial	182	Foreign Affairs	343	Favorable; bill	319	Referred to Committee Whole House.		
McCalla, Andrew	(See sureties of Joseph Crocket)	18	2		268				357			
McCalla, John M.	(See R. G. Edwards, and others)	15	2		209							
McCalla, John M.	For certain fees as United States marshal, disallowed by the Comptroller of the Treasury.	26	1	Petition	957	Judiciary.						
McCalla, John M.	Further compensation for taking the census in Kentucky.	27	2	Petition	77	Judiciary.						
McCalla, Robert, late maj. U. S. army.	Equitable settlement of his accounts, vouchers having been lost.	15	2	Petition	117	Military Affairs	Jan. 25, 1819	Favorable	291	Passed	Passed	App'd March 3, 1819
McCallister, James, (Ohio)	Revolutionary pension	23	1	Petition	333	Rev. Pensions.						
McCallum, Archibald	Compensation for a house destroyed whilst occupied by United States troops.	26	1	Petition	294	Claims	52	Adverse		Laid on table.		
McCallum, Archibald	Compensation for a house destroyed whilst occupied by United States troops.	27	2	Petition	55	Claims	Feb. 9, 1842	By bill	93	Passed	Passed	App'd July 27, 1842
McCally, James, (Va.)	Release from judgment	23	1	Petition	111	Judiciary	82	Adverse		Recommitted.		
McCally, James, (Va.)	Release from judgment	23	2	Petition	388	Judiciary				Discharged; laid on table.		
McCally, James, (Va.)	Release from judgment	24	1	Petition	425	Judiciary	Mar. 21, 1836	Adverse		Laid on table.		
McCally, James, (Va.)	Release from judgment	24	2	Petition	214	Judiciary.						
McCally, James, (Va.)	Release from judgment	25	2	Petition	112	Judiciary	335	Adverse		Laid on table.		
McCalmont, James	Compensation as surgeon in revolutionary war.	3	2	Petition	273	Claims	Feb. 27, 1795	Adverse		Laid on table.		
McCalmont, James	Compensation as surgeon in revolutionary war.	4	2	Petition	629	Claims	Dec. 27, 1796	Adverse		Leave to withdraw.		
McCamont, Samuel, and wife.	(See Thomas Tyler, heirs of)	19	1		134							
McCamont, Isaac	Invalid pension	22	1	Petition	329	Rev. Pensions				Discharged; laid on table.		
McCamont, or McCammont, Isaac.	Pay for services as a private soldier in revolutionary war.	23	2	Petition	345	Rev. Claims.						
McCamont, or McCammont, Isaac.	Pay for services as a private soldier in revolutionary war.	25	2	Petition	269	Rev. Claims				Discharged; laid on table.		
McCanlass, David	Compensation for gun lost in the service of the United States.	24	1	Petition	92	Claims.						
McCandlass, Robert, heirs of.	Indemnity for French spoliations prior to 1800.	26	1	Memorial	182	Foreign Affairs	343	Favorable; bill	318	Referred to Committee Whole House.		
McCandlass, Robert and George, trustees of.	Indemnity for French spoliations prior to 1800.	31	1	Petition	471	Foreign Affairs	355	Favorable; bill	319	Referred to Committee Whole House.		

List of private claims presented to the House of Representatives of the United States form the 1st to the 31st Congress, inclusive—**Continued.**

Names of claimants.	Nature or object of the claim.	Congress.	Session.	How brought before the House of Reps.	Page of journal.	To what committee of the House referred.	No. or date of the report.	Nature of the report.	No. of the bill.	How disposed of by the House of Reps.	How disposed of by the Senate.	Date of the act of Congress, and remarks.
McCanlass, Thomas F....	Payment for a horse lost in service of United States.	24	1	Petition	92, 429	Claims	427	Favorable; bill	430	Referred to Committee Whole House.		
McCanlass, Thomas F....	Payment for a horse lost in service of United States.	25	2	Petition	37	Claims	18	Favorable; bill	30	Passed.		
McCann, Rebecca, widow of Arthur.	Compensation for a horse lost in war of 1812.	23	1	Petition	136	Claims.						
McCann, Rebecca, widow of Arthur.	Compensation for a horse lost in war of 1812.	25	2	Petition	921	Claims	May 25, 1838	Adverse	......	Laid on table.		
McCann, Rebecca, widow of Arthur.	Compensation for a horse lost in war of 1812.	26	1	Petition	340	Claims	....	....	......	....	....	Leave to withdraw.
McCann, Rebecca, widow of Arthur.	Compensation for a horse lost in war of 1812.	27	2	Petition	908	Claims.						
McCann, Rebecca, widow of Arthur.	Compensation for a horse lost in war of 1812.	27	3	Petition	43	Claims	54	Adverse	......	Laid on table.		
McCanna, John.........	Pension	28	1	Petition	1041	Invalid Pensions.						
McCannon, Christopher..	Pension	3	1	Rep. of Secretary War.	131	Select	May 26, 1794	Report by res.	12	Referred to Secretary of War.		
McCarroll, jr., John	For an issue of scrip in lieu of a land warrant.	23	1	Petition	113	Priv. Land Claims.	April 4, 1834	Favorable	406	Referred to Committee Whole House.		
McCarroll, jr., John	For an issue of scrip in lieu of a land warrant.	24	1	Petition	156	Priv. Land Claims.	137	Favorable	146	Passed.		
McCarroll, jr., John	For an issue of scrip in lieu of a land warrant.	25	2	Petition	42	Public Lands	293	Favorable	333	Referred to Committee Whole House.		
McCarroll, jr., John	For an issue of scrip in lieu of a land warrant.	25	3	House bill	377	Whole House	Jan. 5, 1839	With't amend.	333	Passed	Passed	App'd March 3, 1839
McCarslin, Alfred	Redress for having been deprived of pre-emption right to land.	23	2	Petition	278	Public Lands.....	79	Favorable	696	Referred to Committee Whole House.		
McCartney, John, (Ala.).	Payment for cattle taken for use of United States troops in 1817.	16	2	Petition	22	Claims	14	Adverse	......	Referred to Committee Whole House.		
McCartney, John, (Ala.)..	Payment for cattle taken for use of United States troops in 1817.	19	1	Petition	206	Indian Affairs.....	74	Favorable	103	Passed.		
McCartney, John, (Ala.)..	Payment for cattle taken for use of United States troops in 1817.	19	2	Petition	28	Indian Affairs.....	Dec. 12, 1836	Favorable	284	Passed	Rejected.	
McCartney, John, (Ala.)..	Payment for cattle taken for use of United States troops in 1817.	21	1	Petition	360	Indian Affairs.						
McCartney, John, (Ala.)..	Payment for cattle taken for use of United States troops in 1817.	22	1	Petition	47	Indian Affairs.						
McCartney, John, (Ala.)..	Payment for cattle taken for use of United States troops in 1817.	22	2	Petition	33	Indian Affairs.....	....	....	......	Discharged; laid on table.		
McCartney, John, (Ala.)..	Payment for cattle taken for use of United States troops in 1817.	23	1	Petition	145	Indian Affairs.						
McCartney, John, (Ala.)..	Payment for cattle taken for use of United States troops in 1817.	23	1	Senate bill	550	Claims	433	Adverse	S. 15	Laid on table.		
McCartney, John, (Ala.)..	Payment for cattle taken for use of United States troops in 1817.	24	1	Senate bill	559	Claims..........	530	Adverse	9	Referred to Committee Whole House.		
McCartney, John, (Ala.)..	Payment for cattle taken for use of United States troops in 1817.	24	2	Senate bill	549	Claims	Mar. 2, 1837	Adverse	9	Referred to Committee Whole House.		
McCartney, John, (Ala.)..	Payment for cattle taken for use of United States troops in 1817.	25	2	Senate bill	301	Claims..........	976	Adverse	60	Referred to Committee Whole House.		
McCartney, John, (Ala.)..	Payment for cattle taken for use of United States troops in 1817.	26	1	Senate bill	216	Claims..........	....	....	30			
McCartney, John, (Pa.)..	Relief for balance of payment on a quarter section of land in Ohio.	18	2	Resolution	198	Public Lands.						

List of private claims presented to the House of Representatives of the United States from the 1st to the 31st Congress, inclusive—Continued.

Names of claimants.	Nature or object of the claim.	Congress.	Session.	How brought before the House of Reps.	Page of journal.	To what committee of the House referred.	No. or date of the report.	Nature of the report.	No. of the bill.	How disposed of by the House of Reps.	How disposed of by the Senate.	Date of the act of Congress, and remarks.
McCartney, John, (Pa.)	Relief for balance of payment on a quarter section of land in Ohio.	19	2	Resolution	143	Public Lands	....	....	....	Discharged.		
McCartney, John, (Ohio.)	Compensation for work done and materials furnished as contractor on Cumberland road.	23	1	Res. and papers.	589	Claims	455	Adverse	....	....	....	See report No. 449.
McCartney, John, (Ohio.)	Compensation for work done and materials furnished as contractor on Cumberland road.	24	1	Resolution	952	Claims.						
McCartney, John, (Ohio.)	Compensation for work done and materials furnished as contractor on Cumberland road.	25	2	Petition	274	Claims	....	....	....	Discharged; laid on table.		
McCartney, John, (Ohio.)	Compensation for work done and materials furnished as contractor on Cumberland road.	26	1	Petition	169	Claims.						
McCartney, John, (Ohio.)	Compensation for work done and materials furnished as contractor on Cumberland road.	26	2	Petition	135	Claims.						
McCarty, Daniel	Invalid pension	12	1	House bill	361	Whole House	June 15, 1812	Favorable	138	Passed	Passed, with amendment.	App'd July 5, 1812
McCarty, Daniel	Increase of pension	26	1	Petition	705	Rev. Pensions.						
McCarty, Daniel	Increase of pension	26	2	Petition	134	Rev. Pensions	204	Adverse	....	Laid on table.		
McCarty, Edward, heirs of.	Indemnity for losses in the war of 1812.	15	2	Senate bill	270	Claims	Feb. 17, 1819	With't amend.	40	Referred to Committee Whole House.		
McCarty, Edward, heirs of.	Indemnity for losses in the war of 1812.	16	1	Senate bill	429	Claims	....	....	79			
McCarty, Edward, by executors of.	Indemnity for losses in the war of 1812.	16	2	Petition	115	Claims	Jan. 31, 1821	Favorable; bill.	237	Referred to Committee Whole House.		
McCarty, Edwards, by executors and heirs of.	Indemnity for losses in the war of 1812.	17	1	Petition	47	Claims	Jan. 11, 1822	Favorable; bill	33	Passed	Passed	App'd May 7, 1822
McCarty, James	Compensation for horse wounded in battle with Indians in the late war.	23	1	Resolution	99	Claims	168	Adverse	....	Laid on table.		
McCarty, James, (Ky.)	Payment for lime taken for public buildings at Baton Rouge.	19	2	Petition	64	Claims	Jan. 19, 1827	Adverse	....	Laid on table.		
McCarty, James, (Ky.)	Payment for lime taken for public buildings at Baton Rouge.	20	1	Petition	164	Claims	Jan. 21, 1828	Adverse	....	Referred to Committee Whole House.		
McCarty, James, (Ky.)	Payment for lime taken for public buildings at Baton Rouge.	20	2	Petition	30	Claims	....	....	....	Discharged; laid on table.		
McCarty, James, (Ky.)	Payment for lime taken for public buildings at Baton Rouge.	21	1	Petition	35	Claims	215	Favorable	267	Referred to Committee Whole House.		
McCarty, James, (Ky.)	Payment for lime taken for public buildings at Baton Rouge.	21	2	House bill	339	Whole House	Feb. 21, 1831	With't amend	267	Passed.		
McCarty, James, (Ky.)	Payment for lime taken for public buildings at Baton Rouge.	22	1	Petition	31	Claims	Dec. 19, 1831	Favorable	6	Passed	Passed, with amendment.	App'd May 13, 1832
McCarty, John B., by heirs of.	Confirmation of title to land in Louisiana.	18	2	Petition	161	Priv. Land Claims.						
McCarty, John B., by heirs of.	Confirmation of title to land in Louisiana.	20	1	Petition	344	Priv. Land Claims	....	....	....	Discharged; laid on table.		
McCarty, John, (Va.)	Compensation for house dessroyed in war of 1812.	19	2	Petition	159	Claims	....	....	....	Discharged.		
McCarty, John, (Va.)	Compensation for house destroyed in war of 1812.	20	1	Petition	196	Claims	....	....	....	Discharged; laid on table.		

List of private claims presented to the House of Representatives of the United States from the 1st to the 31st Congress, inclusive—Continued.

Names of claimants.	Nature or object of the claim.	Congress.	Session.	How brought before the House of Reps.	Page of journal.	To what committee of the House referred.	No. or date of the report.	Nature of the report.	No. of the bill.	How disposed of by the House of Reps.	How disposed of by the Senate.	Date of the act of Congress, and remarks.
McCarty, John, (Va.)	Compensation for house destroyed in war of 1812.	20	2	Petition	28	Claims	Dec. 16, 1828	Adverse		Laid on table.		
McCarty, John, (Va.)	Compensation for house destroyed in war of 1812.	24	1	Petition	207	Claims	368	Favorable; bill	371	Referred to Committee Whole House.		
McCarty, John, (Va.)	Compensation for house destroyed in war of 1812.	25	2	Petition	37	Claims	10	Favorable; bill	22	Passed	Passed	App'd Feb. 22, 1838
McCarty, John, (Pa.)	Pension	24	1	Petition	407	Invalid Pensions	April 20, 1836	Adverse		Laid on table.		
McCarty, John, (Pa.)	Pension	25	2	Petition	587	Invalid Pensions.						
McCarty, John, (Pa.)	Pension	25	3	Petition	89	Invalid Pensions.						
McCarty, Capt. John	For a grant of land for services in war of 1812.	21	1	Petition	71	Military Affairs				Discharged; laid on table.		
McCarty, John L., (Tenn.)	(See Charles Lewis, assignees of.)	25	2		921							
McCarty, Nathan, (Mo.)	Confirmation of title to land in Missouri.	15	2	Petition	193	Priv. Land Claims				Discharged; laid on table.		
McCarty, Nathan, (Mo.)	Confirmation of title to land in Missouri.	17	1	Petition	54	Public Lands				Discharged; laid on table.		
McCarty, Nathan, (Mo.)	Confirmation of title to land in Missouri.	18	1	Petition	54	Public Lands	Jan. 16, 1824	Favorable	65	Passed	Passed	App'd May 26, 1824
McCarty, Richard, heirs of, by attorney.	Compensation for losses in revolutionary war and confirmation of land title.	11	1	Petition	33	Public Lands.						
McCarty, Richard, heirs of, by attorney.	Compensation for losses in revolutionary war and confirmation of land title.	11	2	Petition	114	Public Lands.						
McCarty, Richard, heirs of, by attorney.	Compensation for losses in revolutionary war and confirmation of land title.	11	3	Petition	438, 515	Public Lands.						
McCarty, Richard, heirs of, by attorney of.	Compensation for losses in revolutionary war and confirmation of land title.	12	1	Petition	139	Public Lands.						
McCarty, Richard, heirs of, by attorney.	Compensation or losses in revolutionary war and confirmation of land title.	13	2	Petition	210	Public Lands.						
McCarty, William, (N. Y.)	Settlement of account for moneys advanced to army of the United States and for donation of land as Canadian refugee.	9	2	Petition	478	Claims	Dec. 31, 1806	Adverse		Rejected.		
McCarty, William, (N. Y.)	Settlement of account for moneys advanced to army of the United States and for donation of land as Canadian refugee.	10	1	Petition	60	Revisal & Unfinished Business.						
McCarty, William, (N. Y.)	Settlement of account for moneys advanced to army of the United States and for donation of land as Canadian refugee.	11	3	Petition	447					Referred to Secretary War.		
McCashen, James, *et al.*	For further time to pay money as pre-emptioners to certain lands.	7	1	Petition	7	Select	Dec. 14, 1801	Favorable		Referred to Committee Whole House.		
McCashen, James, *et al.*	For further time to pay money as pre-emptioners to certain lands.	7	1	Senate bill	225	Whole House	April 30, 1802	With't amend.	10	Passed		App'd April 30, 1802
McCaslin, John	(See William H. Bedford, agent.)	28	1		262							
McCaughan, John J.	Compensation for taking the census in Hancock county, Mississippi.	27	2	Petition	807	Claims.						

List of private claims presented to the House of Representatives of the United States from the 1st *to the* 31st *Congress, inclusive*—Continued.

Names of claimants.	Nature or object of the claim.	Congress.	Session.	How brought before the House of Reps.	Page of journal.	To what committee of the House referred.	No. or date of the report.	Nature of the report.	No. of the bill.	How disposed of by the House of Reps.	How disposed of by the Senate.	Date of the act of Congress, and remarks.
McCauley, Arthur	Confirmation of title to land in Illinois.	15	2	Petition	149	Public Lands				Discharged; laid on table.		
McCauley, Daniel	(See Daniel Macauley)	12	2		706							
McCauley, James, (Tenn.)	Compensation for services in Creek war.	18	1	Petition	454	Pens. & Rev. Cl'ms.				Discharged; laid on table.		
McCauley, James, (Tenn.)	Pension	18	2	Documents	118	Pens. & Rev. Cl'ms.				Discharged; laid on table.		
McCauley, John, (Ill.)	Confirmation of title to land in Illinois.	15	2	Petition	149	Public Lands				Discharged; laid on table.		
McCauley, Matthew	Payment of a certificate for revolutionary services.	15	1	Petition	52	Pens. & Rev. Cl'ms.				Discharged; laid on table.		
McCauley, Matthew	Payment of a certificate for revolutionary services.	15	2	Petition	78	Pens. & Rev. Cl'ms.	Dec. 28, 1818	Adverse		Laid on table.		
McCauley, William	Invalid pension	28	1	Documents	189	Invalid Pensions	450	Favorable	348	Passed.		
McCauley, William	Invalid pension	28	2	Bill on leave	134	Whole House			467			
McCauley, William	Invalid pension	29	1	Petition	81	Invalid Pensions	52	Favorable	41	Passed	Passed	App'd July 15, 1846
McCauley, Francis P.	Payment for his services as purser in the navy.	27	2	Petition	76	Claims	2	Favorable	41	Passed	Passed	App'd June 22, 1833
McCauley, John	Compensation for the capture of the brig Syren during the war with Tripoli.	14	1	Petition and rep't Sec. of Navy.	117, 560	Naval Affairs	April 17, 1816	Adverse		Leave to withdraw.		
McCauley, John	Compensation for the capture of the brig Syren during the war with Tripoli.	15	1	Petition	31	Naval Affairs	Jan. 5, 1818	Adverse		Recommitted.		
							Mar. 2, 1818	Favorable	112	Referred to Committee Whole House.		
McCausland, James, widow of.	Continuation of pension	21	2	Petition	42	Military Pensions.						
McCausland, John	Release from a military fine	15	1	Petition	98	Claims				Discharged; laid on table.		
McCausland, John	Release from a military fine	15	2	Petition	226	Claims	Feb. 2, 1819	Favorable; bill	301	Passed	Passed	App'd March 3, 1819
McCausland, Marcus, administrator of.	Indemnity for French Spoliations prior to 1800.	26	1	Memorial	182	Foreign Affairs	343	Favorable; bill	319	Referred to Committee Whole House.		
McCausland, Marcus	Indemnity for French spoliations prior to 1800.	26	1	Memorial	182	Foreign Affairs	343	Favorable; bill	319	Referred to Committee Whole House.		
McCausland, Marcus, administrator of.	Indemnity for French Spoliations prior to 1800.	31	1	Resolution	476	Foreign Affairs	355	Favorable; bill	318	Referred to Committee Whole House.		
McCausland, Mark	Payment for his land sold by government.	27	2	Documents	328	Priv. Land Claims.						
McCausland, Mary	(See widow of James McCausland.)	21	2		42							
McCausland, Robert	Invalid pension	22	1	Petition	329	Invalid Pensions	345	Favorable	444	Passed.		
McCausland, Robert	Invalid pension	22	2	Petition	27	Invalid Pensions	Dec. 19, 1832	Favorable	626	Passed	Passed as am'd.	App'd March 2, 1833
McCausland, Robert	Payment for his land sold by government.	26	1	Petition	365	Priv. Land Claims.						
McCausland, Robert	Payment for his land sold by government.	26	2	Petition	134	Priv. Land Claims.						
McCausland, Robert	Payment for his land sold by government.	27	2	Petition	331	Priv. Land Claims.						
McCaw, Margaret	(See widow of Michael Downes)	25	2		921							
McCay, Daniel	Invalid pension	14	1	House bill	122	Whole House	April 23, 1816	With amend.	171			Bill became a law, omitting name of applicant.
McCay, Neal, widow of.	(See McCoy)											

List of private claims presented to the House of Representatives of the United States from the 1st *to the* 31st *Congress, inclusive*—Continued.

Names of claimants.	Nature or object of the claim.	Congress.	Session.	How brought before the House of Reps.	Page of journal.	To what committee of the House referred.	No. or date of the report.	Nature of the report.	No. of the bill.	How disposed of by the House of Reps.	How disposed of by the Senate.	Date of the act of Congress, and remarks.
McCay, William	(See William McCoy.)	2	1		475							
McCerren, George W	Compensation for goods destroyed by United States officers in Mexican war.	31	2	Petition	919	Military Affairs.						
McChesney, John, *et al.*	For pay due for revolutionary services by resolution of Congress.	3	1	Petition	38	Select.						
McChesney, John	Invalid pension	3	1	Rep. of Secretary of War.	131	Select	May 26, 1794	Report by res.	12	Referred to Secretary War.		
McChesney, John	Invalid pension	11	2	Petition	283	Claims	Mar. 15, 1810	Favorable	107	Passed	Passed	App'd April 27, 1810
McChesney, John	That his pension may be allowed from date of application.	12	1	Petition	293	Claims.						
McClain, Abijah, (Pa.)	Pension	15	1	Petition	71	Pens. & Rev. Cl'ms.	Feb. 9, 1818	Adverse		Leave to withdraw.		
McClain, Abijah, (Pa.)	Pension	22	1	Resolution	228	Rev. Pensions				Discharged.		
McClain, Charles	Confirmation of title to land	29	1	Petition	680	Priv. Land Claims.						
McClain, Charles	Confirmation of title to land	30	1	Petition	849	Priv. Land Claims.						
McClain, Charles	Confirmation of title to land	30	2	Petition	392	Priv. Land Claims.	Feb. [illegible]8, 1849	Favorable; bill	759	Passed	Passed	App'd March 3, 1849
McClain, Charles, (Ohio)	Pension	20	2	Petition	39	Military Pensions.				Disch'd; laid on table.		
McClain, Charles, (Ohio)	Pension	21	1	Petition	377	Military Pensions.	April 2, 1830	Adverse		Laid on table.		
McClain, Elizabeth	(See widow of Joshua McClain)	29	1		260							
McClain, John	Arrears of pension	25	2	Petition	775	Rev. Pensions				Discharged; laid on table.		
McClain, John	Arrears of pension	25	3	Petition	348	Rev. Pensions				Discharged; laid on table.		
McClain, John	Arrears of pension	27	2	Petition	703	Rev. Pensions	784	Adverse		Laid on table.		
McClain, John	Increase of pension, or compensation for a connon recovered by him in 1781.	23	2	Petition	120	Rev. Pensions.						
McClain, John, (Md.)	Pension	19	2	Petition	98	Military Pensions.				Discharged.		
McClain, John, (Md.)	Pension	20	1	Petition	126	Military Pensions.	April 29, 1828	By bill	283	Passed.		
McClain, John, (Md.)	Pension	20	2	House bill	55	Whole House	Jan. 15, 1829	With amend.	311	Passed	Laid on table.	
McClain, John, (Md.)	Pension	21	1	Petition	37	Military Pensions.	Jan. 5, 1830	By bill	72	Passed	Passed	App'd May 20, 1830
McClain, Joshua, widow of	Revolutionary pension	29	1	Petition	260	Rev. Pensions	528	Adverse		Laid on table.		
McClain, Josiah	(See William H. Bedford, agent.)	28	1		262							
McClane, Charles	Invalid pension	1	3	Petition	382					Referred to Secretary War.		
McClane, Charles	Invalid pension	3	1	Rep. of Secretary War.	131	Select	May 26, 1794	Resolution	12	Passed	Passed	App'd June 9, 1794
McClane, James	Permission to enter certain lands	24	1	Petition	224	Public Lands				Discharged; laid on table.		
McClellan, Arthur	Indemnity for French spoliations prior to 1800.	26	1	Memorial	182	Foreign Affairs	343	Favorable; bill	319	Referred to Committee Whole House.		
McClanahan, John	Indemnity for loss of crop and improvements on land sold by the United States.	18	1	Petition	215	Indian Affairs.						
McClanahan, John	Indemnity for loss of crop and improvements on land sold by the United States.	18	2	Petition	232	Indian Affairs				Discharged; leave to withdraw.		
McClanahan, John	Indemnity for loss of crop and improvements on land sold by the United States.	19	1	Petition	206	Indian Affairs				Discharged; laid on table.		
McClanahan, John	Indemnity for loss of crop and improvements on land sold by the United States.	21	2	Petition	302	Indian Affairs.						

List of private claims presented to the House of Representatives of the United States from the 1st to the 31st Congress, inclusive—Continued

Names of claimants.	Nature or object of the claim.	Congress.	Session.	How brought before the House of Reps.	Page of journal.	To what committee of the House referred.	No. or date of the report.	Nature of the report.	No. of the bill.	How disposed of by the House of Reps.	How disposed of by the Senate.	Date of the act of Congress, and remarks.
McClanahan, John	Indemnity for loss of crop and improvements on land sold by the United States.	22	1	Petition	75	Indian Affairs.						
McClanahan, John	Indemnity for loss of crop and improvements on land sold by the United States.	22	2	Petition	33	Indian Affairs....	31	Favorable; bill	677	Referred to Committee Whole House.		
McClanahan, John	Indemnity for loss of crop and improvements on land sold by the United States.	23	1	Petition	50	Indian Affairs	78	Favorable; bill	85	Passed	Laid on table.	
McClanahan, John	Indemnity for loss of crop and improvements on land sold by the United States.	23	2	Petition	309	Indian Affairs.....	Feb. 25, 1835	Adverse	......	Laid on table.		
McClanahan, John	Indemnity for loss of crop and improvements on land sold by the United States.	24	1	Petition	96	Indian Affairs.....	Jan. 14, 1836	Adverse.	......	Laid on table.		
McClanahan, John	Indemnity for loss of crop and improvements on land sold by the United States.	25	3	Petition	207	Indian Affairs.....	222	Adverse	......	Laid on table.		
McClanahan, John	Pension	26	1	Senate bill	1277	....	....	....	S. 381			
McClanahan, John	Pension	26	2	Senate bill	329	....	....	....	S. 199			
McClanahan, Thomas....	Compensation for revolutionary services.	19	2	Petition	78	Rev. Claims......	25	Adverse	......	Laid on table.		
McClanahan, William ...	(See William Thompson).......	19	1	....	312							
McClanahan, William ...	Invalid pension..............	10	2	Rep. of Secretary War.	480	Claims	Jan. 30, 1809	Favorable; bil	158	Passed	Passed	App'd March 3, 1809
McClannon, Hugh, heirs of.	Restoration of farm at West Point.	30	1	Petition	67	Judiciary	172	Adverse	......	Laid on table.		
McClannon, Hugh, heirs of.	Restoration of farm at West Point.	31	1	Petition	448	Claims.						
McClannon, Hugh, heirs of.	Restoration of farm at West Point.	31	2	Petition	390	Claims	39	Adverse	.....	Laid on table.		
McClary, Mary.........	(See Nathan Speak, heirs of)....	24	1	....	204							
McClary, Andrew, widow of.	Half-pay due for revolutionary services.	2	1	Petition	440	....	....	....	......	Referred to Secretary War.		
McClary, Andrew, widow of	Half pay due for revolutionary services.	2	2	Rep. of Secretary War.	711	....	....	....	......	Laid on table.		
McClary, Michael	Relief for wounds received in revolution.	2	1	Petition	486	....	....	....	......	Referred to Secretary War.		
McClary, Michael	Relief for wounds received in revolution.	2	2	Rep. of Secretary War.	696	....	....	....	......	Laid on table.		
McClaskey, William, widow of.	(See William McCoskry, widow of.)	29	1	....	357							
McClay, Daniel.........	Pension	14	1	Petition	318	Pens. & Rev. Cl'ms.						
McClean, Alexander.....	Pension	30	1	Resolution	181	Invalid Pensions..	579	Adverse	......	Laid on table.		
McClean, John	(See Moses McClean, heirs of)..	29	1	....	571							
McClean, Moses, heirs of .	One years' pay with interest for revolutionary services.	29	1	Memorial	571	Rev. Claims.						
McClean, Moses, heirs of.	One years' pay with interest for revolutionary services.	29	2	Memorial	92	Rev. Claims.						
McClean, Moses, heirs of .	One years' pay with interest for revolutionary services.	30	1	Memorial	575	Rev. Claims.						
McClean, Washington ...	Compensation for losses in Black Hawk war.	23	2	Petition	436	Claims.						

List of private claims presented to the House of Representatives of the United States from the 1st to the 31st Congress, inclusive—Continued.

Names of claimants.	Nature or object of the claim.	Congress.	Session.	How brought before the House of Reps.	Page of journal.	To what committee of the House referred.	No. or date of the report.	Nature of the report.	No. of the bill.	How disposed of by the House of Reps.	How disposed of by the Senate.	Date of the act of Congress, and remarks.
McCleanning, Mary	Extension of her pension during life.	28	1	Petition	72	Rev. Pensions.						
McCleester, Henry & John, and others.	(See Tavlor & McNeal, and others)	14	1	....	284							
McClellan, Charles M.	Confirmation of title to land	28	1	Petition	527	Priv. Land Claims.						
McClelland, Daniel	Compensation for revolutionary services.	21	1	Petition	49	Military Pensions	....	....	....	Laid on table.		
McClelland, Daniel	Revolutionary pension	21	2	Resolution	125	Military Pensions	....	....	....	Laid on table.		
McClel and, Daniel	Revolutionary pension	22	2	Petition	193	Rev. Pensions.						
McClellan, David, (Ark.)	Pemission to locate certain lands	21	2	Petition	302	Public Lands.						
McClellan, Captain George E., officers and men.	Payment for services, subsistence, and forage in Florida, in 1840	31	1	Senate bill	870	Military Affairs	....	....	S. 139			
McClellan, George E.	Confirmation of Spanish land title	29	2	Memorial	169	Public Lands.						
McClellan, George E.	Confirmation of Spanish land title.	30	1	Memorial	138	Public Lands	652	Favorable; bill	519	Referred to Committee Whole House.		
McClelland, J. H., & Co.	(See J. H. McLellan & Co.)	27	2	....	1112							
McClelland, James A.	Reimbursement of expenses and losses as captain during war of 1812.	18	2	Resolution	153	Claims.						
McClelland, James A.	Reimbursement of expenses and losses as captain during war of 1812.	19	1	Resolution	72, 263	Claims.						
McClelland, John	Payment for horses and equipage lost in the Seminole war in 1818.	23	1	Documents	154	Claims.						
McClelland, John, (Me.)	Revolutionary pension	24	2	Petition	44	Rev. Pensions	144	Favorable; bill	874	Referred to Committee Whole House.		
McClelland, John, (Me.)	Revolutionary pension	25	2	Petition	38	Rev. Pensions	172	Favorable; bill	197	Passed	Passed	App'd July 7, 1838
McClelland, John, heirs of.	Seven years' half pay, having died in service.	25	2	Petition	269	Rev. Claims	733	Favorable; bill	700	Passed	Passed	App'd July 7, 1838
McClelland, John, sureties of.	Refunding of certain moneys paid by them to United States.	25	2	Petition	169	P. Of. and P. Roads.	1058	Adverse	....	Laid on table.		
McClelland, Robert, (Md.)	Pension	22	1	Petition	120	Rev. Pensions.						
McClelland, Thomas, (Pa.)	Payment for equipments taken by the British in revolutionary war.	21	2	Resolution	199	Rev. Claims.						
McClelland, Thomas, (Pa.,) and James Smith.	Release as surety of Samuel Smith.	23	1	Petition	119	Judiciary	430	Favorable; bill	456	Referred to Committee Whole House.		
McClelland, Thomas, (Pa.,) and James Smith.	Release as surety of Samuel Smith.	24	1	Petition	53	Judiciary	91	Favorable; bill	90	Passed.		
McClelland, Thomas, (Pa.,) and James Smith.	Release as surety of Samuel Smith.	24	2	Petition	48	Judiciary	Feb. 28, 1837	Favorable; bill	961	Referred to Committee Whole House.		
McClelland, Thomas, (Pa.,) and James Smith.	Release as surety of Samuel Smith.	25	2	Petition	41	Judiciary	357	Favorable; bill	386	Referred to Committee Whole House.		
McClelland, Thomas, (Pa.,) and James Smith.	Release as surety of Samuel Smith	25	3	House bill	378	Whole House	Jan. 25, 1839	With't amend.	386	Passed	Passed	App'd March 2, 1839
McClellan, Wm., (Pa.)	Compensation for services against the Indians in 1764.	8	2	Petition	58	Claims	Dec. 28, 1804	Adverse	....	Rejected.		
McClellan, Wm., (Pa.)	Compensation for services against the Indians in 1764.	21	1	Petition	191	Claims	Jan. 25, 1831	Adverse	....	Laid on table.		
McClendon, Simon	(See William H. Bedford, agent.)	28	1	....	262							
McClenachan, Blair	(See Thomas Stone, assignee of.)	4	1	....	448							
McClenahan, John	(See McClanahan.)											
McClenahan, John	Arrears of pension	27	2	Petition	458	Invalid Pensions	984	Adverse	....	Laid on table.		
McClenan, John, (Va.)	Increase of pension	7	2	Petition	302	Whole House.						

List of private claims presented to the House of Representatives of the United States from the 1st to the 31st Congress, inclusive—Continued.

Names of claimants.	Nature or object of the claim.	Congress.	Session.	How brought before the House of Reps.	Page of journal.	To what committee of the House referred.	No. or date of the report.	Nature of the report.	No. of the bill.	How disposed of by the House of Reps.	How disposed of by the Senate.	Date of the act of Congress, and remarks.
McClenan, John, (Va.)	Increase of pension	8	2	Petition	6	Claims				Discharged; referred to Com. Whole House.		
McClenan, John, (Va.)	Increase of pension	13	3	Petition	740	Claims	Feb. 20, 1815	Favorable; bill	303	Passed	Passed, with amendment.	App'd March 3, 1815
McClenden, James	(See Joshua W. Prout, administrator of.)	17	1		380							
McClenden, Stanly, representatives of.	(See Thomas Owens and others)	12	1		66							
McClintic, Moses	Allowance of pay while sick on furlough as lieutenant of militia.	14	2	Petition	156	Military Affairs				Discharged; laid on table.		
McClintic, William, heirs of.	For the benefit of the act of March 2, 1821, in relation to public lands.	17	1	Petition	48	Public Lands				Discharged; leave to withdraw.		
McClintock, H. J., and others.	Compensation for services rendered at sub-agency for Sacs and Fox Indians.	31	1	Senate bill	970	Indian Affairs			S. 171			
McClintock, H. J., and others.	Compensation for services rendered at sub-agency for Sacs and Fox Indians.	31	2	Senate bill of last session.	207	Indian Affairs	Jan. 29, 1851	With't amend	171	Passed		App'd March 3, 1851
McClintock, John, executor of	Indemnity for French spoliations prior to 1800.	31	1	Petition	348	Foreign Affairs	355	Favorable; bill	318	Referred to Committee Whole House.		
McClintock, John, (Maine.)	Indemnity for French spoliations prior to 1800.	26	1	Memorial	182	Foreign Affairs	343	Favorable; bill	319	Referred to Committee Whole House.		
McCloskey, James, and others.	Pre-emption right to land in Michigan.	14	2	Petition	86	Public Lands	Dec. 23, 1816	Adverse		Rejected.		
McCloskey, William	Invalid pension	25	2	Petition	267	Invalid Pensions	Feb. 20, 1838	Adverse		Laid on table.		
McCloud, James G	Pre-emption right to land	28	2	Petition	183	Public Lands	Feb. 7, 1845	By bill	600	Referred to Committee Whole House.		
McCloud, James G	Pre-emption right to land	29	1	Petition	117	Public Lands	164	Favorable; bill	172	Passed	Passed	App'd Aug. 8, 1846
McCloud, John	Increase of pension	24	1	Senate bill	811	Invalid Pensions	June 9, 1836	With't amend.	201	Referred to Committee Whole House.		
McCloud, John	Increase of pension	24	2	Senate bill	251	Invalid Pensions			96			
McCloud, John	Increase of pension	25	2	Senate bill	1012	Invalid Pensions	July 2, 1838	With't amend.	242	Referred to Committee Whole House.		
McCloud, John	Increase of pension	25	3	Senate bill	499	Invalid Pensions	Feb. 16, 1839	With't amend.	11	Referred to Committee Whole House.		
McCloud, John	Increase of pension	26	1	Senate bill	803	Invalid Pensions	662	Adverse	96	Referred to Committee Whole House.		
McCloud, John	Increase of pension	26	2	Senate bill	506				103			
McClune, Joseph	Settlement of account, vouchers being burnt.	17	2	Petition	186	Claims				Discharged; leave to withdraw.		
McClung, Hugh	Remuneration for lands of his granted to Indians in Tennessee.	19	1	Senate bill	488	Priv. Land Claims	Mar. 6, 1826	With't amend	101	Passed		App'd May 20, 1826
McClung, James, deceased, representatives of.	Payment of a certificate issued for a horse impressed into the United States service.	17	2	Senate bill	174	Pens. & Rev. Cl'ms.	Jan. 21, 1823	With't amend.	29	Passed		App'd March 3, 1823
McClung, Samuel	Revolutionary pension	24	1	Petition	406	Rev. Pensions				Discharged; laid on table.		
McClung, Samuel	Revolutionary pension	27	2	Petition	971	Rev. Pensions				Discharged; laid on table.		
McClure, Abdiel	Compensation for revolutionary services.	15	1	Petition	191	Pens. & Rev. Cl'ms.				Discharged; laid on table.		

List of private claims presented to the House of Representatives of the United States from the 1st *to the* 31*st Congress, inclusive*—Continued.

Names of claimants.	Nature or object of the claim.	Congress.	Session.	How brought before the House of Reps.	Page of journal.	To what committee of the House referred.	No. or date of the report.	Nature of the report.	No. of the bill.	How disposed of by the House of Reps.	How disposed of by the Senate.	Date of the act of Congress, and remarks.
McClure, Abdiel	Compensation for revolutionary services.	23	1	Petition	158	Pens. & Rev. Cl'ms.						
McClure, Abdiel	Compensation for revolutionary services	24	1	Petition	138	Pens. & Rev. Cl'ms.				Discharged; laid on table.		
McClure, James H., & Co.	(See Samuel Perry, and others)	25	3		272							
McClure, James	Compensation for revolutionary services.	2	2	Petition and rep't of Sec. War.	682					Laid on table.		
McClure, James	Invalid pension	6	1	Petition	564	Claims	Jan. 28, 1800	Adverse		Rejected.		
McClure, James, administrator of William.	(See John Thompson, assignee of)	2[illegible]	1		262							
McClure, Janet	(See widow of Thomas McClure)	26	1		386							
McClure, John	Pension	14	2	Resolution	209	Pens & Rev. Clm's.	Jan. 29, 1817	Favorable	91	Passed	Passed, with amendment.	App'd March 3, 1817
McClure, John, (Ala.)	Revolutionary pension	21	2	Petition	118	Military Pensions.						
McClure, John, (Ind.)	Compensation as commissioner under Louisiana convention of 1803.	19	2	Petition	53	Ways and Means				Discharged.		
McClure, John	Balance due as superintendent of Cumberland road.	19	2	Military approp'n bill.	149	Whole House	Feb. 17, 1827	With amend.	372	Passed	Passed	App'd March 2, 1827
McClure, Rachel, of Wm	Bounty land and balance of pay for services in United States army.	18	2	Petition	134	Claims	Jan. 31, 1825	Favorable; bill	308	Passed	Passed	App'd March 3, 1825
McClure, Rebecca	Compensation for services and expenses in aid of United States soldiers in war of 1812.	21	2	Petition	154	Claims.						
McClure, Richard	Equitable settlement of his accounts as Postmaster.	31	2	Petition	87	P. Of. & P. Roads.						
McClure, Samuel, of Va.	Reimbursement of expenses incurred in war of 1812.	15	1	Petition	268	Claims	Feb. 24, 1818	Adverse		Rejected.		
McClure, Samuel, of Va.	Reimbursement of expenses incurred in war of 1812.	15	2	Petition	74	Claims	Jan. 15, 1819	Adverse		Referred to Committee Whole House.		
McClure, Thomas	Indemnity for French spoliations prior to 1800.	26	1	Memorial	182	Foreign Affairs	343	Favorable; bill	319	Referred to Committee Whole House.		
McClure, Thos., widow of	Revolutionary pension	26	1	Resolution	386	Rev. Pensions	664	Adverse		Laid on table		Leave to withdraw; Jan. 22, 1849.
McClure, William	(See Maclure)	20	1		44							
McCobb, Enos	Pension	22	1	Petition	80	Rev. Pensions	Dec. 21, 1831	Adverse		Laid on table.		
McCobb, Parker	For register for bark Liberator	19	2	Petition	49	Commerce	Jan. 9, 1827	Favorable	358	Referred to Committee Whole House.		
McCobb, Parker	For register for bark Liberator	20	1	Petition	29	Commerce	Dec. 17, 1827	Favorable	8	Passed	Passed	App'd Mar. 10, 1828
McCobb, Parker	Remission of duties on brig Liberator.	20	2	Petition	203	Ways and Means				Discharged; laid on table.		
McCobb, Parker	Remission of duties on brig Liberator.	21	1	Petition	412	Ways and Means	395	Favorable	461	Referred to Committee Whole House.		
McCobb, Parker	Remission of duties on brig Liberator.	22	1	Petition	41	Ways and Means	Dec. 23, 1831	Favorable	113	Passed	Passed	App'd July 14, 1832
McCobb, Parker	Remission of duties on brig Liberator.	22	2	Petition	215	Ways and Means.						
McCobb, Parker	Remission of duties on brig Liberator.	23	1	Petition	79	Ways and Means	103	Favorable	197	Passed	Passed	App'd June 30, 1834
McCobb, Thomas	(See Mark Langdon Hill, & Thos. McCobb.)	13	2		195							
McColgan, John	Reimbursement of amount expended in the support of American seamen.	23	1	Petition	334	Foreign Affairs	478	Adverse		Laid on table.		

List of private claims presented to the House of Representatives of the United States from the 1st to the 31st Congress, inclusive—Continued.

Names of claimants.	Nature or object of the claim.	Congress.	Session.	How brought before the House of Reps.	Page of journal.	To what committee of the House referred.	No. or date of the report.	Nature of the report.	No. of the bill.	How disposed of by the House of Reps.	How disposed of by the Senate.	Date of the act of Congress, and remarks.
McColgan, John	Reimbursement of amount expended in the support of American seamen.	24	1	Memorial	662	Foreign Affairs.						
McColgan, John	Reimbursement of amount expended in the support of American seamen.	25	2	Petition.	91	Commerce	153	Favorable; bill	1020	Referred to Committee Whole House.		
McColgan, John	Reimbursement of amount expended in the support of American seamen.	25	3	Petition	112	Commerce.						
McColgan, John	Reimbursement of amount expended in the support of American seamen.	26	1	Petition	176, 292	Commerce	312	Favorable; bill	275	Referredto Committee Whole House.		
McColgan, John	Reimbursement of amount expended in the support of American seamen.	27	2	Petition	96	Commerce	456	Favorable; bill	305	Referredto Committee Whole House.		
McColgan, John	Reimbursement of amount expended in the support of American seamen	27	3	House bill	90	Whole House.	Dec. 23, 1843	With't amend	305	Passed.		
McCollock, Elliott	(See McCulloch)	31	1		436							
McCollom, Andrew	Payment for property lost in the war of 1812.	23	1	Petition	120	Claims	161	Adverse		Laid on table.		
McCollom, Andrew	Payment for property lost in the war of 1812.	24	1	Petition	474	Claims	623	Adverse		Laid on table.		
McCollum, John, heirs of.	Commutation of half pay for revolutionary services.	25	2	Petition	658	Rev. Claims.				Discharged; laid on table.		
McCollum, John, heirs of.	Commutation of half-pay for revolutionary services.	25	3	Petition	348	Rev. Claims.						
McCollum, John, heirs of.	Commutation of half pay for revolutionary services.	26	1	Petition	166	Rev. Claims.	607	Adverse		Laid on table.		
McComas, Aaron	Revolutionary pension	25	2	Petition	664	Rev. Pensions				Laid on table.		
McComas, James S.	Compensation for extra work on Piny Point light-house.	28	2	Petition	176	Claims.						
McComas, Josiah H., and wife.	(See Henry Willis, representatives of.)	13	3		497							
McComb, James	Patent right for a water-mill	1	2	Petition	161					Laid on table.		
McComb, James	Invalid pension	4	2	Petition	614	Claims.						
McComb, John	Invalid pension	3	2	Rep. of Secretary War.	262	Claims.						
McComb, John	Invalid pension	4	1	Res. and docs.	445	Claims	Feb. 18, 1796	Rep. and res.	16	Referred to Secretary of War.		
McComb, John L	Confirmation of title to land in Alabama.	14	2	Petition	72	Public Lands.						
McComb, Samuel	Compensation for superintending the erection of the branch mint in North Carolina.	25	1	Petition	102					Laid on table.		
McComb, Samuel	Compensation for superintending the erection of the branch mint in North Carolina.	25	2	Petition	154	Ways and Means.	464	Favorable; bill	468	Referred to Committee Whole House.		
McComb, Samuel	Compensation for superintending the erection of the branch mint in North Carolina.	25	3	House bill	378	Whole House	Jan. 25, 1839	With't amend.	468	Passed	Passed	App'd March 3, 1839
McComsey, Alexander	Compensation for team and wagon surrendered with Detroit.	14	1	Petition	33	Claims.				Discharged; leave to withdraw.		

List of private claims presented to the House of Representatives of the United States from the 1st to the 31st Congress, inclusive—Continued.

Names of claimants.	Nature or object of the claim.	Congress.	Session.	How brought before the House of Reps.	Page of journal.	To what committee of the House referred.	No. or date of the report.	Nature of the report.	No. of the bill.	How disposed of by the House of Reps.	How disposed of by the Senate.	Date of the act of Congress, and remarks.
McConkle, John, (Ohio)	(See John F. Barr and others)	19	1		68							
McConnell, Hugh	Revolutionary pension	21	1	Petition and docs.	753	Rev. Pensions				Discharged; laid on table.		
McConnell, James	Permission to relinquish lands and enter others in lieu thereof.	24	1	Petition	674	Public Lands.						
McConnell, John	Remission of duties on stills	14	2	Petition	496					Laid on table.		
McConnell, John	Remission of duties on stills	15	1	Petition	30	Ways and Means	Dec. 15, 1817	Adverse		Rejected.		
McConnell, John, widow of	Continuation of pension	27	2	Petition	69	Rev. Pensions	784	Adverse		Laid on table.		
McConnell, Nancy	(See widow of John McConnell)	27	2		69							
McConnell, Samuel, (Vt.)	Invalid pension	12	1	Petition	270	Claims	June 12, 1812	Adverse		Laid on table.		
McConnell, Samuel, (Vt.)	Invalid pension	18	1	Petition	285	Rev. Claims	Mar. 15, 1824	Adverse		Laid on table.		
McConnell, William	Invalid pension	13	3	Petition	693	Pens. & Rev. Cl'ms.						
McConn, Rosanna	(See widow of William McConn)	26	1		961							
McConn, William, widow of.	For five years half pay and commutation of bounty land for services of husband in war of 1812.	26	1	Petition	961	Claims.						
McConn, William, widow of.	For five years half pay and commutation of bounty land for services of husband in war of 1812.	26	2	Petition	79	Military Affairs	195	Adverse		Laid on table.		
McConn, William, widow of.	Pension	27	2	Petition	228	Military Affairs				Discharged; laid on table.		
McCooley, Randolph	(See H. W. Barnes, *et al.*)	30	2		216							
McCord, David	To be allowed a credit for money lost, in settlement of accounts.	23	2	Senate bill	318	Claims	Feb. 6, 1835	With't amend.	S. 69	Referred to Committee Whole House.		
McCord, David	To be allowed a credit for money lost, in settlement of accounts.	24	1	Senate bill	816	Claims	686	Favorable	S. 84	Passed		App'd July 2, 1836
McCord, John	Payment for supplies furnished in Canada in 1778.	1	2	Petition	150	Select	June 2, 1790	By bill	70	Passed	Passed	App'd July 1, 1790
McCoskry, Felicia	(See William McCoskry, widow of.)	29	1		359							
McCoskry, William, widow of.	Warrant for bounty land in lieu of cost.	29	1	Petition	359	Public Lands.						
McCoskry, William, widow of.	Warrant for bounty land in lieu of cost.	29	2	Petition	215	Public Lands.						
McCoskry, William, widow of.	Warrant for bounty land in lieu of cost.	30	1	Petition	110	Public Lands.	263	Favorable; bill	258	Referred to Committee Whole House.		
McCowley, James	Invalid pension	31	1	Petition	23[illegible]	Invalid Pensions	485	Adverse		Laid on table.		
McCorkle, Alexander, and others.	Pre-emption right to land on which they have made improvements.	24	2	Petition	312	Public Lands.						
McCorkle, C. P.	Difference of pay between captain's clerk and purser in navy during the time he acted as such.	30	2	Petition	123	Naval Affairs.						
McCorkle, C. P.	Difference of pay between captain's clerk and pursur in navy during the time he acted as such.	31	1	Petition	983	Naval Affairs.						
McCorkle, Joseph P.	Payment of balance due for services as clerk to navy commissioners.	25	3	Petition	131	Naval Affairs.						
McCorkle, Robert, (Ohio.)	Release of last payment due for land and patent issue.	16	1	Petition	293	Public Lands	Mar. 23, 1820	Adverse		Rejected.		
McCormick, Alex., (D. C.)	Compensation for property destroyed by the British in 1814.	14	2	Petition	75	Claims	Jan. 18, 1817	Adverse		Leave to withdraw.		

List of private claims presented to the House of Representatives of the United States from the 1st to the 31st Congress, inclusive—Continued.

Names of claimants.	Nature or object of the claim.	Congress.	Session.	How brought before the House of Reps.	Page of journal.	To what committee of the House referred.	No. or date of the report.	Nature of the report.	No. of the bill.	How disposed of by the House of Reps.	How disposed of by the Senate.	Date of the act of Congress, and remarks.
McCormick, Alex., (D. C.)	Compensation for property destroyed by the British in 1814.	16	2	Petition	37	Claims	Dec. 19, 1820	Adverse	......	Rejected.		
McCormick, Charles	Compensation for extra services as quarter master in Mexico.	31	2	Petition	247	Military Affairs.						
McCormick, Charles	Compensation for revolutionary services.	2	1	Petition	448	....	....	....	......	Referred to Secretary War.		
McCormick, Charles	Invalid pension	3	1	Rep. of Secretary War.	131	Select	May 26, 1794	Report by res.	12	Passed	Passed	App'd June 9, 1794
McCormick, Charles	Invalid pension	4	1	Petition	445	Claims	Feb. 18, 1896	Report and bill.	156	Passed	Passed	App'd April 20, 1796
McCormick, Cyrus H	Renewal of patent	30	1	Memorial	277	Patents	Mar. 9, 1848	By bill	320	Referred to Committee Whole House.		
McCormick, Cyrus H	Renewal of patent	31	1	Petition	899	Patents.						
McCormick, George, heirs of.	Commutation of half pay and bounty land for revolutionary services	23	2	Petition	66	Rev. Claims.						
McCormick, George, heirs of.	Commutation of half-pay and bounty land for revolutionary services.	24	1	Petition	205	Rev. Claims.						
McCormick, George, heirs of.	Commutation of half-pay and bounty land for revolutionary services	24	2	Petition	215	Rev. Claims.						
McCormick, George, heirs of.	Commutation of half-pay and bounty land for revolutionary services.	25	2	Petition	82	Rev. Claims	740	Adverse	......	Laid on table.		
McCormick, John, (Va).	Confirmation of title to land	20	1	Petition	224	Priv. Land Claims.						
McCormick, John, (Penn.)	Revolutionary pension	24	1	Petition	604	Rev. Pensions.						
McCormick, John, (Penn.)	Revolutionary pension	24	2	Petition	45	Rev. Pensions	127	Favorable	......	Referred to Committee Whole House.		
McCormick, John, (Penn.)	Revolutionary pension	25	2	Petition	182	Rev. Pensions	270	Favorable; bill	313	Passed	Adverse report.	
McCormick, John, (Penn.)	Revolutionary pension	26	1	Petition	172	Rev. Pensions.						
McCormick, John, (Penn.)	Revolutionary pension	29	1	Petition	192	Rev. Pensions.						
McCormick, John heirs of.	Confirmation of title to land in Missouri.	24	1	Petition and docs.	155	Priv. Land Claims.	....	....	......	Discharged; laid on table.		
McCormick, Paul	Permission to enter section of land.	19	2	Petition	189	Public Lands	....	....	......	Discharged.		
McCormick, Paul	Compensation for losses by contract for public surveys.	24	2	Petition	98	Claims	Jan. 13, 1837	Adverse	......	Laid on table.		
McCormick, Peter P	Confirmation of title to land in Missouri.	20	2	Petition	28	Priv. Land Claims.	13	Report and bill.	328	Referred to Committee Whole House.		
McCormick, Peter P	Confirmation of title to land in Missouri.	21	1	Petition	51	Priv. Land Claims.	....	....	......	Discharged; laid on table.		
McCormick, Peter P	Confirmation of title to land in Missouri.	22	1	Petition	177	Priv. Land Claims.	175	Favorable	250	Referred to Committee Whole House.		
McCormick, Peter P	Confirmation of title to land in Missouri.	22	2	House bill of last session.	92	Whole House	Dec. 22, 1832	With amend.	250	Passed	Passed	App'd Jan. 28, 1833
McCormick, Stephen	Renewal of patent	28	1	Petition	247	Patents	431	Adverse	......	Laid on table.		
McCormick, Thomas	Renewal of lost loan office certificate.	20	1	Petition	40	Public Lands	....	....	......	Discharged; laid on table.		
McCormick, William	Correction of error in land entry	22	1	Resolution	450	Public Lands	Mar. 21, 1832	By bill	499	Passed	Passed	App'd July 3, 1832
MCoull, Neil	Payment of a loan office certificate.	15	1	Petition	63	Pens. & Rev. Cl'ms.	....	....	......	Discharged; leave to withdraw.		
McCoy, Archibald	(See William Baker, New York).	22	1	....	288	....	480					
McCoy, A., (Indiana)	(See John Ross, and others)	19	1	....	155							
McCoy, Barnabas, former widow of.	Revolutionary pension	26	1	Petition	282	Rev. Pensions.						
McCoy, Ephriam	Invalid pension	1	2	Petition and rep't Sec. of War.	179	Select	July 16, 1790	Favorable; bill	88	Passed	Passed	App'd Aug. 11, 1790

List of private claims presented to the House of Representatives of the United States from the 1st to the 31st Congress, inclusive—Continued.

Names of claimants.	Nature or object of the claim.	Congress.	Session.	How brought before the House of Reps.	Page of journal.	To what committee of the House referred.	No. or date of the report.	Nature of the report.	No. of the bill.	How disposed of by the House of Reps.	How disposed of by the Senate.	Date of the act of Congress, and remarks.
McCoy, George	For work done and materials furnished as contractor on Cumberland road.	23	1	Res. and papers.	589	Claims	455	Adverse	......	......	......	See report No. 449.
McCoy, Isaac	Compensation for surveying Indian lands.	23	1	House bill	178	Whole House	May 14, 1834	With amend.	182	Passed	Passed	App'd June 26, 1834
McCoy, James	Indemnity for property captured by the French under the Berlin and Milan decrees.	25	2	Petition	407	Foreign Affairs	978	Adverse	......	Laid on table.		
McCoy, James, representatives of.	Confirmation of title to land	27	2	Petition	459, 614	Priv. Land Claims.						
McCoy, James, representatives of.	Confirmation of title to land	27	3	Petition	45	Priv. Land Claims.						
McCoy, John	Increase of pension	10	1	Petition	232	Claims	Mar. 17, 1808	Favorable	78	Passed	Passed, with amendment.	App'd April 25, 1808
McCoy, John, (Pa.)	Compensation for hire of wagon horses to continental army.	10	2	Petition	391	Select						
McCoy, John, (Pa.)	Compensation for hire of wagon horses to continental army.	11	2	Petition	116	Claims	Jan. 24, 1810	Adverse	......	Rejected.		
McCoy, John	(See representatives of Jas. McCoy)	27	2	......	459, 614							
McCoy, John L., and others, Cherokee Indians, old settlers.	Relief in regard to construction of treaty of New Echota.	30	1	Petition	589, 1238	Indian Affairs.						
McCoy, Matthew	Refunding of duties on stills	15	1	Petition	261	Ways and Means	......	......	......	Disch'd; laid on table.		
McCoy, Neal	Compensation for revolutionary services.	15	1	Petition	271	Pens. & Rev. Cl'ms	Mar. 27, 1818	Adverse	......	Rejected.		
McCoy, (or McCay,) Neal, widow of.	Revolutionary pension	25	2	Resolution	975	Rev. Pensions.						
McCoy, (or McCay,) Neal widow of.	Revolutionary pension	26	1	Petition	174	Rev. Pensions.						
McCoy, Rebecca	(See widow of Neal McCoy)	25	2	......	975							
McCoy, Robert, (Md.)	Pension	21	1	Petition	149	Military Pensions	April 2, 1830	Adverse	......	Laid on table.		
McCoy, Samuel	Remuneration for losses by contract.	29	2	Petition	316	Claims.						
McCoy, Walter, and John Vinyard.	Pension for services in Indian wars of 1790, 1792.	27	2	Petition	375	......	......	......	......	Referred to Committee Whole House.		
McCoy, William	Compensation for revolutionary services.	2	1	Petition	475	......	......	......	......	Referred to Secretary War.		
McCoy, William	Compensation for revolutionary services.	4	2	Petition	635	Claims	Jan. 20, 1797	......	......	Laid on table.		
McCracken, David, jr.	Pension	14	1	Petition	450	Pens. & Rev. Cl'ms.	April 11, 1816	Favorable; bill	171	Passed	Passed	App'd April 30, 1816
McCracken, James	Revolutionary pension	11	2	Petition	140	Claims	Jan. 11, 1810	Adverse	......	Rejected.		
McCracken, James	Revolutionary pension	19	1	Resolution	75	Military Pensions	......	......	......	Discharged; laid on table.		
McCracken, Joseph	Compensation for revolutionary services and for money advanced.	3	2	Petition	237	Claims	Feb. 25, 1795	Adverse	......	Referred to Committee Whole House.		
McCracken, Joseph	Compensation for revolutionary services and for money advanced.	4	2	Petition and docs.	628	Claims	Dec. 26, 1796	Adverse	......	Leave to withdraw.		
McCracken, Joseph	Compensation for revolutionary services and for money advanced.	9	2	Petition	473	Claims	Dec. 11, 1806	Adverse	......	Rejected.		
McCraw, Francis, widow of.	Continuation of pension	27	2	Petition	219	Rev. Pensions	306	Favorable; bill	275	Passed	Indef. postp'd.	
McCraw, Francis, widow of.	Continuation of pension	27	3	Petition	139	Rev. Pensions	......	......	......	Discharged; laid on table.		

List of private claims presented to the House of Representatives of the United States from the 1st to the 31st Congress, inclusive—Continued.

Names of claimants.	Nature or object of the claim.	Congress.	Session.	How brought before the House of Reps.	Page of journal.	To what committee of the House referred.	No. or date of the report.	Nature of the report.	No. of the bill.	How disposed of by the House of Reps.	How disposed of by the Senate.	Date of the act of Congress, and remarks.
McCraw, Francis, widow of.	Continuation of pension	28	1	Petition	210	Rev. Pensions	227	Favorable; bill	185	Passed	Indef. postp'd.	
McCraw, Sally	(See widow of Francis McCraw).	27	2		219							
McCray, Ezekiel	(See executor of Kinchen Carr)	28	2		239							
McCray, Henry	Pension	20	2	Petition	204	Military Pensions				Discharged; laid on table.		
McCray, Michael	Invalid pension	25	2	Petition	116	Invalid Pensions	422	Favorable; bill	429	Ref'd to Com. W. H.		
McCray, Michael	Invalid pension	25	2	House bill	378	Whole House	Jan. 25, 1839	With't amend.	429	Passed	Passed	App'd March 3, 1839
McCrea, John, of N. York, a revenue officer.	Compensation for sufferings and losses while in Indian captivity, war of 1812.	14	1	Petition	404	Claims.						
McCrea, John, of N. York, a revenue officer.	Compensation for sufferings and losses while in Indian captivity, war of 1812.	14	2	Petition	38	Claims	Dec. 20, 1816	Adverse		Rejected.		
McCrea, John, of N. York, a revenue officer.	Compensation for sufferings and losses while in Indian captivity, war of 1812.	15	1	Petition	55	Claims	Feb. 24, 1818	Adverse		Laid on table.		
McCrea, John, of N. York, a revenue officer.	Compensation for sufferings and losses while in Indian captivity, war of 1812.	15	2	Petition	167	Claims				Discharged; laid on table.		
McCrea, John, of N. York, a revenue officer.	Compensation for sufferings and losses while in Indian captivity, war of 1812.	16	1	Petition	28	Claims	Dec. 22, 1819	Adverse		Rejected.		
McCrea, John, of N. York, a revenue officer.	Compensation for sufferings and losses while in Indian captivity, war of 1812.	17	1	Petition	331	Claims	Mar. 18, 1822	Adverse		Leave to withdraw.		
McCrea, John, of N. York, a revenue officer.	Compensation for sufferings and losses while in Indian captivity, war of 1812.	24	2	Petition	215	Military Affairs.						
McCrea, John, of N. York, a revenue officer.	Compensation for sufferings and losses while in Indian captivity, war of 1812.	25	2	Petition	52	Claims	368	Adverse		Recommitted.		
McCrea, John, of N. York, a revenue officer.	Compensation for sufferings and losses while in Indian captivity, war of 1812.	25	3	Petition	348	Claims	Feb. 16, 1839	Adverse		Laid on table.		
McCrea, John, of N. York, a revenue officer.	Compensation for sufferings and losses while in Indian captivity, war of 1812.	26	1	Petition	294	Claims.						
McCrea, John, of N. York, a revenue officer.	Compensation for sufferings and losses while in Indian captivity, war of 1812.	26	2	Petition	36	Military Affairs.						
McCrea, John, of N. York, a revenue officer.	Compensation for sufferings and losses while in Indian captivity, war of 1812.	28	1	Petition	145	Claims.						
McCrea, John, of N. York, a revenue officer.	Compensation for sufferings and losses while in Indian captivity, war of 1812.	30	1	Petition	603	Claims.						
McCready, Jeremiah, and Jonathan Brooks.	Allowance of interest on money advanced to pay United States troops in 1815.	14	1	Petition	722					Laid on table.		
McCready, Jeremiah, and Jonathan Brooks.	Allowance of interest on money advanced to pay United States troops in 1815.	14	2	Petition	116	Claims				Discharged; laid on table.		

List of private claims presented to the House of Representatives of the United States from the 1st to the 31st Congress, inclusive—**Continued.**

Names of claimants.	Nature or object of the claim	Congress.	Session.	How brought before the House of Reps.	Page of journal.	To what committee of the House referred.	No. or date of the report.	Nature of the report.	No. of the bill.	How disposed of by the House of Reps.	How disposed of by the Senate.	Date of the act of Congress, and remarks.
McCready, Mary, (or McCurdy.)	(See widow of Jered Mudd)	25	3	....	126							
McCready, Robert	Increase of pension	25	2	Petition	54	Rev. Claims	682	Adverse	......	Laid on table.		
McCreary, James K	Compensation for a slave lost in Mexico.	30	2	Petition	297	Claims.						
McCreary, James K	Compensation for a slave lost in Mexico.	31	1	Petition	383	Claims.						
McCreary, John	Pension	21	1	Senate bill	352	Military Pensions	Mar. 11, 1830	With't amend.	76	Passed	....	App'd May 29, 1830
McCreary, John, (Va.)	Relief for loss of land in Arkansas by non payment of taxes, and error of United States officer.	23	1	Petition	49	Priv. Land Claims.	841	Adverse	......	Laid on table.		
McCreedy, Jeremiah	Refunding of money advanced United States troops in 1815.	26	1	Petition	933	Claims.						
McCreedy, Jeremiah	Refunding of money advanced United States troops in 1815.	26	2	Petition	80	Claims.						
McCreery, or McCrery, John S.	Indemnity for losses in Mexican war.	31	1	Petition	731	Military Affairs.						
McCreery, Joseph, (Pa.)	Pension	21	1	Petition	46	Military Pensions	....	....	......	Discharged; laid on table.		
McCreery, Letitia	(See administratrix of William McCreery.)	26	1	....	142							
McCreery, William, administratrix of.	Indemnity for French spoliations prior to 1800.	29	2	Memorial	142	Foreign Affairs.						
McCreery, William, administratrix of.	Indemnity for French spoliations prior to 1800.	29	2	Memorial	182	Foreign Affairs	343	Favorable; bill	319	Referred to Committee Whole House.		
McCrimmin, Daniel	Pension	14	1	Petition	134	Pens. & Rev. Cl'ms.	April 22, 1816	Adverse	......	Leave to withdraw.		
McCristal, Patrick	Compensation for work done and materials furnished on Cumberland road	23	1	Res. and papers.	624	Claims	455	Adverse	......	....	....	See Report No. 449
McCrory, James	Commutation pay for services as an ensign in revolutionary war	24	1	Petition	727	Rev. Claims.						
McCrory, James	Commutation pay for services as an ensign in revolutionary war.	24	2	Senate bill	250	Rev. Claims	Feb. 8, 1837	With't amend.	S. 52	Referred to Committee Whole House.		
McCrory, James	Commutation pay for services as an ensign in revolutionary war.	25	2	Senate bill	159	Rev. Claims	Jan. 20, 1838	With't amend.	S. 45	Referred to Committee Whole House.		
McCrosson, Patrick	(See John McElroy and others)	3	2	....	267							
McCubbin, Nicholas	Pension	21	1	Petition	231	Military Pensions	April 13, 1830	Adverse	......	Laid on table.		
McCubbin, Nicholas	Pension	21	2	Petition	209	Rev. Claims.						
McCue, Harriett, widow of James.	Arrears of pension	20	1	Petition	417	Military Pensions	April 5, 1828	Adverse	......	Laid on table.		
McCue, Owen	Payment of prize in lottery authorized by Congress.	25	3	Petition	449	Dist. of Columbia.	293	Adverse	......	Laid on table.		
McCullen, Mary, widow of James.	For settlement of claim against the United States.	1	2	Petition	244	....	....	....	......	Referred to Secretary Treasury.		
McCullen, Mary, widow of James.	For settlement of claim against the United States	2	1	Rep. of Secretary Treasury.	580	....	....	....	......	Laid on table.		
McCullen, Mary, widow of James.	For settlement of claim against the United States.	19	1	Petition	61	Rev. Claims	Jan. 5, 1826	Adverse	......	Laid on table.		
McCullers, William	Indemnity for Indian depredations.	23	1	Petition	196	Indian Affairs	....	....	......	Discharged; laid on table.		
McCulloch, Adam	Payment for ground on which the light house at Goat Island is erected.	26	1	Petition	720	Commerce.						

List of private claims presented to the House of Representatives of the United States from the 1st to the 31st Congress, inclusive—Continued.

Names of claimants.	Nature or object of the claim.	Congress.	Session.	How brought before the House of Reps.	Page of journal.	To what committee of the House referred.	No. or date of the report.	Nature of the report.	No. of the bill.	How disposed of by the House of Reps.	How disposed of by the Senate.	Date of the act of Congress, and remarks.
McCulloch, Adam.......	Payment for ground on which the light house at Goat Island is erected.	26	2	Petition	37	Commerce.						
McCulloch, Adam.......	Payment for ground on which the light house at Goat Island is erected.	27	2	Petition	55	Claims.						
McCulloch, Adam.......	Payment for ground on which the light house at Goat Island is erected.	27	3	Petition	43	Commerce	145	Adverse	......	Laid on table.		
McCulloch, Adam.......	Payment for ground on which the light-house at Goat Island is erected.	28	2	Petition	104	Claims	196	Favorable; bill	648	Referred to Committee Whole House.		
McCulloch, Adam.......	Payment for ground on which the light house at Goat Island is erected.	29	1	Petition	124	Claims	129	Favorable; bill	131	Passed	Passed	App'd July 15, 1846
McCullough, Alexander, by assignee of.	Confirmation of title to land in Mississippi.	11	2	Petition	227	Public Lands.						
McCullough, Alexander, by assignee of.	Confirmation of title to land in Mississippi.	17	2	Petition	27	Priv. Land Claims.	71	Adverse	......	Laid on table.		
McCullough, Alexander, by assignee of	Confirmation of title to land in Mississippi.	18	1	Petition	388	Priv. Land Claims.	....	....	......	Discharged; laid on table.		
McCullough, Alexander, by assignee of.	Confirmation of title to land in Mississippi.	21	2	Petition	129	Public Lands.						
McCullough, Alexander, by assignee of.	Confirmation of title to land in Mississippi.	22	2	Petition	178	Public Lands.....	....	....	......	Discharged; laid on table.		
McCulloch, Benjamin....	Invalid pension................	24	1	Petition & docs.	473	Invalid Pensions.						
McCulloch, Benjamin....	Invalid pension................	24	2	Petition	86	Invalid Pensions ..	72	Favorable; bill	818	Referred to Committee Whole House.		
McCulloch, Benjamin....	Invalid pension............ ...	25	2	Petition	119	Invalid Pensions ..	540	Favorable; bill	533	Passed	Adverse.	
McCulloch, Benjamin....	Invalid pension................	26	1	Petition	161	Invalid Pensions ..	217	Favorable; bill	229	Passed	Indef. postp'd.	
McCulloch, Catharine, widow of George.	Pension	15	1	Petition	198	Claims.						
McCulloch, Elliott	Permission to relinquish certain lands and enter others.	31	1	Petition	436	Priv. Land Claims.						
McCulloch, Captain H. E..	(See Capt. B. F. Hill, and others)	31	1	....	1012							
McCullough, Hugh, (N.C.)	Refunding money paid on land...	16	1	Petition	64	Ways and Means..	11	Adverse	......	Referred to Committee Whole House.	....	Leave to withdraw, 2d session, 16th Cong.
McCullough, Hugh, (N.C.)	Refunding money paid on land...	18	1	Petition	155	Ways and Means..	Feb. 18, 1824	Favorable	127	Passed	Passed	App'd May 19, 1824
McCulloch, James H., and others.	Additional compensation as officers of customs for the port of Baltimore.	11	3	Petition	497	Com. and Manuf.						
McCulloch, James H., and others.	Additional compensation as officers of customs for the port of Baltimore.	12	1	Petition	20	Ways and Means..	Dec. 30, 1811	Report and bill.	34	Recommitted.		
							Jan. 6, 1812	Adverse	......	Rejected.		
McCulloch, James H., and others.	Additional compensation as officers of customs for the port of Baltimore.	15	1	Petition	22	Ways and Means..	....	....	......	Discharged; laid on table.		
McCulloch, John, executor	Indemnity for French spoliations prior to 1800.	24	1	Memorial	537	Foreign Affairs.						
McCulloch, John........	Confirmation of title to land in Missouri.	15	1	Petition	50	Priv. Land Claims.						

List of private claims presented to the House of Representatives of the United States from the 1st to the 31st Congress, inclusive—**Continued.**

Names of claimants.	Nature or object of the claim.	Congress.	Session.	How brought before the House of Reps.	Page of journal.	To what committee of the House referred.	No. or date of the report.	Nature of the report.	No. of the bill.	How disposed of by the House of Reps.	How disposed of by the Senate.	Date of the act of Congress, and remarks.
McCulloch, Robert	Pension and arrears of pay for revolutionary services.	2	1	Petition	475					Referred to Secretary of War.		
McCulloch, Robert	Pension and arrears of pay for revolutionary services.	3	1	Rep. of Secretary War.	131	Select	May 26, 1794	Rep. and resl'n	12	Passed	Passed	App'd June 9, 1794
McCulloch, Robert	Invalid pension	13	2	Petition	343	Pens. & Rev. Cl'ms.	Mar. 31, 1814	Favorable	166	Passed	Passed	App'd April 18, 1814
McCulloch, Samuel	(See executor of John McCulloch)	24	1		537							
McCulloch, Samuel and Elliott.	Change of location of land	27	3	Petition	259	Public Lands	160	Favorable; bill	776	Referred to Committee Whole House.		
McCulloh, John W., executor of.	Indemnity for French spoliations prior to 1800.	26	1	Memorial	182	Foreign Affairs	343	Favorable: bill	319	Referred to Committee Whole House.		
McCulloh, Samuel	(See John W. McCulloh, executor of.)	26	1		182							
McCullough, William H., and John S. Harrison.	Additional compensation for mail service.	31	1	Petition	916	P. Of. & P. Roads.						
McCune, Christiana	(See widow of Peter McCune)	27	2	Petition	524							
McCune, Peter, widow of.	Revolutionary pension	27	2	Petition	524	Rev. Pensions.						
McCutcheon, James and James B.	Payment for provisions furnished Kentucky militia in the war of 1812, and for property destroyed.	23	1	Petition	384	Claims	May 16, 1834	Adverse		Laid on table.		
McCutcheon, James and James B.	Payment for provisions furnished Kentucky militia in the war of 1812, and for property destroyed.	25	2	Petition	121	Claims.						
McCutcheon, James and James B.	Payment for provisions furnished Kentucky militia in the war of 1812, and for property destroyed.	26	1	Petition	168	Claims	67	Adverse		Recommitted.		
McCutcheon, James and James B.	Payment for provisions furnished Kentucky militia in the war of 1812, and for property destroyed.	26	2	Petition	52, 131	Claims.						
McCutcheon, James and James B.	Payment for provisions furnished Kentucky militia in the war of 1812, and for property destroyed.	29	1	Petition	275	Claims	355, 749	Adverse		Laid on table.		
McCutchen, William	Confirmation of title to land in Missouri.	16	1	Petition	77	Priv. Land Claims.				Discharged; laid on table.		
McCurdy, Archibald, Lieutenant.	Commutation of half-pay during life for revolutionary services.	24	1	Petition	432	Rev. Claims	748	Adverse		Laid on table.		
McCurdy, Archibald, Lieutenant.	Commutation of half-pay during life for revolutionary services.	25	2	Petition	194	Rev. Claims				Discharged; laid on table.		
McCurdy, Mary	(See widow of Jeremiah Mudd)	35	3		126							
McCurdy, Moses, representatives of.	Extension of time to obtain military land warrant.	8	1	Petition	486	Select.						
McCurtin, Cornelius	Confirmation of title to land in Alabama.	18	1	Petition	116	Public Lands				Discharged, referred to Com. Whole House on bill No. 93.		Leave to withdraw.
McCurtin, Cornelius	Confirmation of title to land in Alabama.	18	2	Petition	43	Public Lands.						
McCurtin, Cornelius, heirs of.	Confirmation of title to land in Alabama.	19	1	Petition	45	Public Lands				Discharged; laid on table.		
McCurtin, Cornelius, heirs of.	Confirmation of title to land in Alabama.	19	2	Petition	157	Public Lands				Discharged.		
McCurtin, Cornelius, assignee.	Confirmation of title to land	26	2	Senate bill	282				S. 82			
McDade, William	Invalid pension	1	3	Rep. of Secretary War.	393					Laid on table.		

List of private claims presented to the House of Representatives of the United States from the 1st to the 31st Congress, inclusive—Continued.

Names of claimants.	Nature or object of the claim.	Congress.	Session.	How brought before the House of Reps.	Page of journal.	To what committee of the House referred.	No. or date of the report.	Nature of the report.	No. of the bill.	How disposed of by the House of Reps.	How disposed of by the Senate.	Date of the act of Congress, and remarks.
McDaniel, Alexander, and others.	Grant of public land	23	2	Petition	348	Public Lands.						
McDaniel, Alfred W., sureties of.	Refunding of interest on debt paid government.	26	1	Petition	605	Ways and Means	710	Adverse		Laid on table		
McDaniel, Alfred W., sureties of.	Refunding of interest on debt paid government.	26	2	Petition	76	Select	50	Favorable; bill	579	Referred to Committee Whole House.		
McDaniel, Alfred W., sureties of.	Refunding of interest on debt paid government.	27	2	Petition	131	Select	585	Favorable; bill	381	Ordered to 3d reading.		
McDaniel, Alfred W., sureties of.	Refunding of interest on debt paid government.	27	3	Bill of last sess.	88				381	Passed	Indef. postp'd.	
McDaniel, Bersheba	Continuance of pension during life	30	1	Petition	198	Rev. Pensions	220	Adverse		Laid on table.		
McDaniel, Clement, Col	Compensation for revolutionary services.	24	1	Resolution	485	Rev. Claims.						
McDaniel, Enoch	Invalid pension	28	1	Petition	128	Invalid Pensions	54	Favorable	77	Passed	Indef. postp'd.	
McDaniel, Enoch	Invalid pension	31	1	Petition	307	Invalid Pensions.						
McDaniel, James K	Compensation for horses, &c., lost in war.	23	1	Documents	154	Claims.						
McDaniel, James K	(See William H. Bedford, agent.)	28	1		262							
McDaniel, James	(See James Mackay)	15	1		288							
McDaniel, John	Confirmation of Spanish land title.	25	3	Petition	462	Priv. Land Claims.						
McDermott, James	Compensation for work on Cumberland road.	22	1	Petition	223	Claims	April 13, 1832	Adverse		Laid on table.		
McDermott, James	Compensation for work on Cumberland road.	23	1	Petition	384, 589	Claims	455	Adverse		Laid on table		See report No. 449.
McDermott, Michael	Pension	14	1	Petition	32	Pens. & Rev. Cl'ms.	April 11, 1816	Favorable; bill	171	Passed	Passed, with amendment.	App'd April 30, 1816
McDole, Mathews	Confirmation of title to land	27	2	Petition	518	Public Lands				Discharged; laid on table.		
McDonald, Alexander, (Ill.)	Pension	29	1	Petition	714	Invalid Pensions.						
McDonald, Alexander, (Ill.)	Pension	29	2	Petition	314	Invalid Pensions.						
McDonald, Alexander, (Ill.)	Pension	30	1	Petition	171	Invalid Pensions	305	Adverse		Recommitted.		
McDonald, Alexander, (Ill.)	Pension	30	2	Petition	322	Invalid Pensions				Discharged; laid on table.		
McDonald, Alexander, (N. C.)	Invalid pension	22	1	Petition	415	Naval Affairs	April 28, 1832	Adverse		Leave to withdraw.		
McDonald, Alex'r, (Ala.)	Invalid pension	25	2	Petition	923	Naval Affairs				Discharged; laid on table.		
McDonald, Alexander	Invalid pension	26	1	Petition	327	Invalid Pensions	557	Adverse		Laid on table.		
McDonald, Alexander, by his brother Francis.	Relief for loss of a depreciation certificate.	4	2	Petition	654	Claims	Feb. 8, 1797	Adverse		Laid on table.		
McDonald, Alex. (D. C.)	Increase of compensation as clerk in Treasury Department.	9	2	Petition	600	Ways and Means.						
McDonald, Alex. (D. C.)	Increase of compensation as clerk in Treasury Department.	10	1	Petition	24	Whole House.						
McDonald, Alex. (D. C.)	Increase of compensation as clerk in Treasury Department.	11	2	Petition	149	Ways and Means.						
McDonald, Alex. (D. C.)	Increase of compensation as clerk in Treasury Department.	22	1	Petition	471	Ways and Means.						
McDonald, Andrew, heirs of.	Payment of a claim for forage furnished in revolutionary war.	23	2	Petition	132	Rev. Claims.						
McDonald, Andrew, heirs of.	Payment of a claim for forage furnished in revolutionary war.	24	1	Petition	205	Rev. Claims.						

List of private claims presented to the House of Representatives of the United States from the 1st to the 31st Congress, inclusive—Continued.

Names of claimants.	Nature or object of the claim.	Congress.	Session.	How brought before the House of Reps.	Page of journal.	To what committee of the House referred.	No. or date of the report.	Nature of the report.	No. of the bill.	How disposed of by the House of Reps.	How disposed of by the Senate.	Date of the act of Congress, and remarks.
McDonald, Andrew, heirs of.	Payment of a claim for forage furnished in revolutionary war.	25	2	Petition	393	Rev. Claims	614	Adverse	......	Laid on table.		
McDonald, Archibald	Compensation as ensign in Capt Boon's Rangers.	14	2	Petition	276	Military Affairs	Feb. 21, 1817	Adverse	......	Laid on table.		
McDonald, Archibald	Compensation as ensign in Capt. Boon's Rangers.	15	1	Petition	115	Military Affairs	....	....	......	Discharged; laid on table.		
McDonald, Augus	Payment for a mare lost in Florida war.	26	1	Petition	338	Claims.						
McDonald, Daniel	Invalid pension	3	1	Rep. of Secretary of War.	186	Claims	May 26, 1794	Report by bill.	62	Passed	Passed	App'd June 7, 1794
McDonald, Dennis	Confirmation of title to land	30	2	Petition	241	Public Lands.						
McDonald, Donald, (N. Y.)	Revolutionary pension	5	3	Petition	424	Claims	Jan. 21, 1799	Adverse	......	Leave to withdraw.		
McDonald, Donald, (N. Y.)	Revolutionary pension	11	2	Petition	283	Claims	Mar. 15, 1810	Favorable	107	Passed	Passed, with amendment.	App'd April 27, 1810
McDonald, Donald, (Del.)	Compensation for revolutionary services.	1	3	Petition and rep't Sec. of War.	350	....	....	....	......	Laid on table.		
McDonald, Donald, (Del.)	Invalid pension	3	1	Rep. of Secretary War.	131	Select	May 26, 1794	Report by res.	12	Passed	Passed	App'd June 9, 1794
McDonald, Donald, (Del.)	Invalid pension	4	1	Rep. of Secretary War.	447	Claims	Feb. 18, 1796	Favorable; bill	156	Passed	Passed	App'd April 20, 1796
McDonald, Donald, (S. C.)	Pension	18	1	Petition	173	Pens. & Rev. Cl'ms.	May 18, 1824	Adverse	......	Laid on table.		
McDonald, E os	(See Enoch McDaniel.)	28	1	....	128							
McDonald, Flora, widow of John.	Compensation for property taken for use of revolutionary army.	23	1	Petition	245	Claims.						
McDonal , Francis, and others.	Increase of compensation as messengers in the department.	5	2	Petition	147	Ways and Means	Feb. 6, 1798	Favorable	......	Referred to Committee Whole House.		
McDonald, Henry B	(See William H. Bedford, agent).	28	1	....	262							
McDonald, Hugh	Payment for horse lost in war of 1812.	21	2	Petition	191	Claims	Jan. 31, 1831	Adverse	......	Laid on table.		
McDonald, Hugh	Payment for horse lost in war of 1812.	22	2	Resolution	273	Claims.						
McDonald, Hugh	Payment for horse lost in war of 1812.	23	2	Resolution	309	Claims.						
McDonald, Hugh	Payment for horse lost in war of 1812.	24	1	Petition	405	Claims.						
McDonald, Hugh	Payment for horse lost in war of 1812.	24	2	Petition	38	Claims	318	Favorable	972	Referred to Committee Whole House.		
McDonald, Hugh	Payment for horse lost in war of 1812.	25	2	Resolution	37	Claims	71	Favorable	83	Passed	Passed	App'd April 20, 1838
McDonald, Hugh	Arrears of pension	24	2	Petition	398	Invalid Pensions	....	....	......	Discharged; laid on table.		
McDonald, Hugh	Arrears of pension	25	2	Petition	920	Invalid Pensions	....	....	......	Discharged; laid on table.		
McDonald, Hugh	Arrears of pension	25	3	Petition	90	Invalid Pensions	....	....	......	Discharged; laid on table.		
McDonald, Jacob	Invalid pension	26	1	Petition	707	Invalid Pensions.						
McDonald, Jacob	Invalid pension	27	2	Petition	749	Invalid Pensions	....	....	......	Discharged; laid on table.		
McDonald, James, administrator of.	For certain credits in settlement of his accounts.	15	1	Petition	411	Claims.						
McDonald, James, administrator of.	For certain credits in settlement of his accounts.	15	2	Petition	24	Claims	96	Favorable; bill	282	Referred to Committee Whole House.		

List of private claims presented to the House of Representatives of the United States from the 1st to the 31st Congress, inclusive—Continued.

Names of claimants.	Nature or object of the claim.	Congress.	Session.	How brought before the House of Reps.	Page of journal.	To what committee of the House referred.	No. or date of the report.	Nature of the report.	No. of the bill.	How disposed of by the House of Reps.	How disposed of by the Senate.	Date of the act of Congress, and remarks.
McDonald, James, administrator of.	For certain credits in settlement of his accounts.	16	1	Petition	24	Claims	4	Favorable; bill	7	Passed	Passed	App'd Feb. 28, 1820
McDonald, James A	Invalid pension	23	2	Petition	47	Invalid Pensions				Discharged; laid on table.		
McDonald, James A	Invalid pension	24	1	Petition	634	Invalid Pensions				Discharged; laid on table.		
McDonald, James, (N. Y.)	(See Anthony Dey and James McDonald.)	17	1		294							
McDonald, James	Bounty land for military services in war of 1812.	29	1	Petition	502	Invalid Pensions.						
McDonald, James, widow of.	Prize-money due deceased	30	2	House bill	157	Whole House	Jan. 23, 1849	With amend.	692	Passed	Passed	App'd March 3, 1849
McDonald, John, (Va.)	Bounty land for services in war of 1812.	16	1	Petition	122	Military Affairs	Jan. 18, 1820	Adverse		Laid on table.		
McDonald, John, heirs of, (Ohio.)	Compensation for revolutionary services.	23	1	Documents	839	Rev. Claims.						
McDonald, John, (Va.)	(See Andrew McDonald, heirs of.)	23	2		132							
McDonald, Malcom	Pension	20	1	Petition	50	Military Pensions				Discharged; laid on table.		
McDonold, Malcom	Pension	22	1	Petition	329	Invalid Pensions				Discharged; laid on table.		
McDonald, Michael, daughter of.	Arrears of pay due	27	2	Petition	202	Rev. Claims	1079	Adverse		Laid on table.		
McDonald, Michael, daughter of.	Arrears of pay due	31	1	Petition	542	Rev. Claims	416	Adverse		Laid on table.		
McDonald, Patrick, widow of.	Pension	25	2	Petition	942	Naval Affairs				Discharged: laid on table.		
McDonald, Rebecca	(See Patrick McDonald, widow of.)	25	2		942							
McDonald, Rebecca	(See Capt. James Wilson, heirs of)	29	1		218							
McDonald, Thomas	Pension for services under General Wayne, 1794.	31	1	Petition	197	Military Affairs	211	Adverse		Laid on table.		
McDonald, William	(See James McDonald, administrator of.)	15	1		411							
McDonald, William	Compensation for forage furnished United States, in war of 1812.	14	1	Petition	77	Claims				Discharged; laid on table.		
McDonnell, Ferdinand D.	Confirmation of title to land	23	2	Petition	250	Priv. Land Claims.	110	Adverse		Laid on table.		
McDonnell, Ferdinand D.	Interest on claim against government.	29	1	Petition	807	Claims.						
McDonnell, John, (Mich.)	Compensation for losses in late war, and expenses in redeeming American prisoners.	15	1	Petition	36	Claims				Discharged; laid on table.		
McDonnell, John, (Mich.)	Compensation for losses in late war, and expenses in redeeming American prisoners.	17	1	Petition	31	Claims	Jan. 14, 1822	Adverse		Laid on table.		
McDonnell, John, (Mich.)	Compensation for losses in late war, and expenses in redeeming American prisoners.	18	2	Petition	187	Ways and Means.						
McDonnell, John, (Mich.)	Compensation for losses in late war, and expenses in redeeming American prisoners.	19	1	Petition	291	Ways and Means				Discharged; laid on table.		
McDonnell, John, (Mich.)	Compensation for losses in late war, and expenses in redeeming American prisoners.	20	1	Petition	105	Ways and Means	69	Adverse		Leave to withdraw.		

List of private claims presented to the House of Representatives of the United States from the 1st *to the* 31*st Congress, inclusive*—Continued.

Names of claimants.	Nature or object of the claim.	Congress.	Session.	How brought before the House of Reps.	Page of journal.	To what committee of the House referred.	No. or date of the report.	Nature of the report.	No. of the bill.	How disposed of by the House of Reps.	How disposed of by the Senate.	Date of the act of Congress, and remarks.
McDonnell, John, (Mich.)	Compensation for losses in late war, and expenses in redeeming American prisoners.	22	1	Petition	125	Public Lands				Discharged; laid on table.		
McDonnell, John, (Mich.)	Compensation for losses in late war, and expenses in redeeming American prisoners.	23	2	Petition	60	Claims.						
McDonnell, John, (Mich.)	Drawback of duty paid on merchandise.	11	3	Petition	565	Com. and Manuf.						
McDonnell, John, (Mich.)	Drawback of duty paid on merchandise.	12	1	Petition	97	Com. and Manuf.						
McDonnell, John	(See sureties of John S. Langham)	22	1		473							
McDonnell, John	(See Pierre Le Blanc, assignee of)	23	1		111							
McDonnell, John	Indemnity for property destroyed during late war.	24	1	Petition	140	Claims	Feb. 4, 1836	Adverse		Laid on table.		
McDonough, John	Confirmation of title to land in Louisiana.	21	1	Petition	51	Priv. Land Claims.	67	General bill authorizing the receiver at St. Helena to receive evidence.	95	Passed	Passed	App'd May 28, 1830
McDonough, John	Confirmation of title to land in Louisiana.	21	2	Report of Com'r Land Office.	341	Public Lands	Feb. 22, 1831	Favorable	643	Passed.		
McDonough, John	Confirmation of title to land in Louisiana.	22	1	Resolution	38	Priv. Land Claims.	13	Favorable	62	Passed	Passed	App'd Mar. 22, 1832
McDonnough, Stace J.	Pension	23	2	Petition	238	Invalid Pensions.						
McDonough, Thomas, Capt.	Remission of duties on sword	17	1	Memorial	50	Ways and Means.	Jan. 22, 1822	By bill	53	Passed	Passed	App'd April 17, 1822
McDonough, Thomas	(See widow of Stephen Decatur and others.)	20	1		295		201		S. 50			
McDonough, Thomas	(See Edward Preble, heirs, widow, and others.)	22	1		164							
McDougall, Elizabeth	(See heirs of Samuel Casten)	31	1		234							
McDougal, George	Confirmation of title to land in Michigan.	16	2	Petition	41	Priv. Land Claims.				Discharged; laid on table.		
McDougal, George	Confirmation of title to land in Michigan.	17	1	Petition	44	Priv. Land Claims.	Jan. 25, 1822	Adverse		Referred to Committee Whole House.		
McDougal, George	Confirmation of title to land in Michigan.	17	2	Petition	57	Priv. Land Claims.				Discharged; leave to withdraw.		
McDougal, George	Confirmation of title to land in Michigan.	18	2	Petition	137	Priv. Land Claims.						
McDougal, George	Confirmation of title to land in Michigan.	19	1	Petition	313	Priv. Land Claims.				Discharged; laid on table.		
McDougal, George	Confirmation of title to land in Michigan.	20	1	Petition	111	Priv. Land Claims.				Discharged; laid on table.		
McDougal, George	Confirmation of title to land in Michigan.	20	2	Petition	83	Priv. Land Claims.				Discharged; laid on table.		
McDougal, George	Confirmation of title to land in Michigan.	21	1	Petition	93	Priv. Land Claims.				Discharged; laid on table.		
McDougal, George	Confirmation of title to land in Michigan.	21	2	Petition	76	Priv. Land Claims.	Feb. 26, 1831	Adverse		Laid on table.		
McDougal, George	Confirmation of title to land in Michigan.	22	1	Petition	125, 294	Priv. Land Claims.	Feb. 7, 1832	Adverse		Laid on table.		

List of private claims presented to the House of Representatives of the United States from the 1st to the 31st Congress, inclusive—Continued.

Names of claimants.	Nature or object of the claim.	Congress.	Session.	How brought before the House of Reps.	Page of journal.	To what committee of the House referred.	No. or date of the report.	Nature of the report.	No. of the bill.	How disposed of by the House of Reps.	How disposed of by the Senate.	Date of the act of Congress, and remarks.
McDougal, George	Indemnity for property destroyed, war of 1812.	15	1	Report of Com'r Claims.	195	Claims.				Discharged; laid on table.		
McDougal, George	Indemnity for property destroyed, war of 1812.	16	1	Petition	106	Claims.				Discharged; laid on table.		
McDougal, George	Indemnity for property destroyed, war of 1812.	16	2	Petition	120	Claims	Jan. 10, 1821	Adverse		Leave to withdraw.		
McDougal, George	Indemnity for property destroyed, war of 1812.	17	1	Petition	47	Claims				Discharged; laid on table.		
MDougal, Hugh	(See heirs of Israel Pearce)	23	1		242							
McDowell, Andrew, Cap	Indemnity for losses in war of 1812	19	1	Petition	150	Claims	Jan. 20, 1826	Adverse		Leave to withdraw.		
McDowell, Andrew, Cap	Indemnity for losses in war of 1812	21	1	Petition	235	Claims	Feb. 5, 1830	Adverse		Laid on table.		
McDowell, Andrew	Invalid pension	28	1	Petition	880	Invalid Pensions.						
McDowell, Andrew	Invalid pension	28	2	Petition	46	Invalid Pensions				Discharged; laid on table.		
McDowell, Hayne, & Co	Remission of duties on certain goods.	27	2	Petition	89	Ways and Means	264	Adverse		Laid on table.		
McDowell, James	To refund excess of duties on goods	21	2	Petition	191	Commerce	Feb. 16, 1831	General bill	634	Passed	Passed	App'd March 2, 1831
McDowell, John, (Ky.)	Commutation pay for revolutionary services.	22	1	Petition	265	Rev. Claims	287	Favorable	371	Referred to Committee Whole House.		
McDowell, John, (Ky.)	Commutation pay for revolutionary services.	23	1	Res. and docs	198	Rev. Claims.						
McDowell, John, (Ky.)	Commutation pay for revolutionary services.	24	1	Petition	152	Rev. Claims	188	Favorable	195	Referred to Committee Whole House.		
McDowell, John, (Ky.)	Commutation pay for revolutionary services.	24	2	Bill of last sess.	62	Whole House			195			
McDowell, John, (Ky.)	Commutation pay for revolutionary services.	25	2	Petition	40	Rev. Claims	197	Favorable	223	Passed.		
McDowell, John, (Ky.)	Commutation pay for revolutionary services.	25	3	Petition	85	Rev. Claims	110	Favorable	985	Referred to Committee Whole House.		
McDowell, John, (Ky.)	Commutation pay for revolutionary services.	26	1	Petition	165	Rev. Claims.						
McDowell, John, (Ky.)	Commutation pay for revolutionary services.	27	2	Petition	581	Rev. Claims	538	Adverse		Laid on table.		
McDowell, John	Commutation pay for revolutionary services.	28	1	Petition	510	Rev. Claims.						
McDowell, John	Commutation pay for revolutionary services.	28	2	Petition	205	Rev. Claims.						
McDowell, John G	Compensation for services, and for horse lost in war of 1790.	31	2	Petition	142	Military Pensions.						
McDowell, Joseph, (N. Y.)	Settlement of account for services, and compensation for property destroyed during revolution.	3	1	Petition	216					Referred to Secretary War.		
McDowell, Joseph, (N. Y.)	Invalid pension	3	2	Rep. of Secretary War.	278					Laid on table.		
McDowell, Mathew	Discount for prompt payment for lands.	18	2	Petition	38	Public Lands				Discharged; leave to withdraw.		
McDowell, Samuel	(See William H. Bedford, agent.)	28	1		262							
McDuff, Daniel	Compensation for revolutionary services.	12	1	Petition	22	Claims	Feb. 21, 1812	Res. for leave to withdraw.		Resolution adopted.		
McDuff, Daniel	Revolutionary pension	16	1	Petition	102	Pens. & Rev. Cl'ms.	Mar. 10, 1820	Adverse		Referred to Committee Whole House.		
McDuff, Daniel	Revolutionary pension	16	2	Petition and docs.	33	Select	9	Favorable; bill	158	Passed.		
McDuff, Daniel	Revolutionary pension	17	2	Petition	31	Pens. & Rev. Cl'ms.	Dec. 16, 1822	By bill	195	Passed	Indef. postp'd.	

2—55

List of private claims presented to the House of Representatives of the United States from the 1st to the 31st Congress, inclusive—Continued.

Names of claimants.	Nature or object of the claim.	Congress.	Session.	How brought before the House of Reps.	Page of journal.	To what committee of the House referred.	No. or date of the report.	Nature of the report.	No. of the bill.	How disposed of by the House of Reps.	How disposed of by the Senate.	Date of the act of Congress, and remarks.
McDuff, Daniel	Revolutionary pension	19	2	Petition	50	Rev. Claims	22	Adverse		Laid on table.		
McDuff, Daniel	Revolutionary pension	20	1	Petition	32	Military Pensions				Discharged; laid on table.		
McDuff, Daniel	Pension and bounty land for revolutionary services.	21	1	Petition	75	Select	58	Favorable; bill	81	Passed	Passed	App'd April 2, 1830
McDuff, Daniel	Permission to locate his land warrant so as include his improvements.	21	1	Senate bill	529	Public Lands	April 16, 1830	With't amend.	176	Passed	Passed	App'd April 24, 1830
McDuffie, Daniel	For the premium offered by engineers department for the best machine for removing snags from rivers.	18	2	Petition	249	Roads and Canals.						
McDuffie, Daniel	For the premium offered by engineers department for the best machine for removing snags from rivers.	19	1	Petition	177	Roads and Canals	Mar. 17, 1826	Adverse		Laid on table.		
McEldrerry, Thomas	(See Thomas, Horatio, and Judson Clagett.)	2	1		511							
McEldrerry, Thomas	(See Thomas, Horatio, and Judson Clagett.)	3	1		78							
McElduff, Daniel	Invalid pension	11	3	Petition	604	Claims	March 1, 1811	Favorable	218	Passed	Passed, with amendment.	App'd March 3, 1811
McElfresh, Philemon, and others.	Bounty land for services in late war.	25	2	Petition	259	Military Affairs	396	Adverse		Laid on table.		
McElhany, R. J., and others	(See sureties of Samuel H. Bunch.)	30	1		738							
McElhatton, William	Relief for wounds received in revolutionary war.	2	1	Petition	474					Referred to Secretary of War.		
McElhose, Samuel	Revolutionary pension	27	2	Petition	219	Invalid Pensions	784	Adverse		Laid on table.		
McElrath, J. P.	Compensation for a horse lost in Seminole war.	30	1	Petition	423	Claims	474	Adverse		Laid on table.		
McElroy, Archibald	For expenses attending to prize-vessel.	19	1	Resolution	462	Naval Affairs	April 27, 1826	Adverse		Laid on table.		
McElroy, Hiram	(See executor of Ed. Willett)	24	2		395							
McElroy, John, and others.	Confirmation of title to land	3	2	Petition	267	Select	Jan. 6, 1795	Favorable		Referred to Committee Whole House.		
McElroy, John, and others.	Confirmation of title to land	4	1	Petition	381	Select.						
McElroy, John, widow of.	Revolutionary pension	27	2	Petition	783	Rev. Pensions	784	Adverse		Laid on table.		
McElroy, Margaret	(See widow of John McElroy)	27	2		783							
McElroy, Sansom	Pre-emption right to land	23	1	Petition	332	Public Lands.						
McElvain, Purdy	Payment for services as register of land office.	29	1	Memorial	798	Public Lands	822	Favorable	547	Referred to Committee Whole House.		
McEney, Henry O., and others.	Compensation for locating military land warrants.	31	2	Petition	177	Ways and Means.						
McEvers, Charles, president of New York Insurance Company.	Indemnity for French spoliations prior to 1800.	26	1	Memorial	182	Foreign Affairs	343	Favorable; bill	319	Referred to Committee Whole House.		
McEvers, Charles	Indemnity for French spoliations prior to 1800.	26	1	Memorial	182	Foreign Affairs	343	Favorable; bill	319	Referred to Committee Whole House.		
McEvers & Bache	Indemnity for French spoliations prior to 1800.	26	1	Memorial	182	Foreign Affairs	343	Favorable; bill	319	Referred to Committee Whole House.		
McEvoy, Michael	Bounty land for services in war of 1812.	15	2	Petition	215	Priv. Land Claims				Discharged; leave to withdraw.		
McEwen, Alexander	Invalid pension	29	2	Petition	54	Invalid Pensions.						

List of private claims presented to the House of Representatives of the United States from the 1st to the 31st Congress, inclusive—Continued.

Names of claimants.	Nature or object of the claim.	Congress.	Session.	How brought before the House of Reps.	Page of journal.	To what committee of the House referred.	No. or date of the report.	Nature of the report.	No. of the bill.	How disposed of by the House of Reps.	How disposed of by the Senate.	Date of the act of Congress, and remarks.
McEwen, Alexander	Invalid pension	30	1	Petition	114	Invalid Pensions	306, 800	Adverse; Favorable; bill	621	Recommitted. Referred to Committee Whole House.		
McEwen, Alexander	Invalid pension	30	3	House bill	363	Whole House	Feb. 2, 1849	With't amend.	621	Passed	Passed	App'd March 3, 1849
McEwen, Duncan, widow of.	Revolutionary pension	25	2	Petition	403					Referred to Committee Whole House on bill No. 456.		
McEwen, Patrick	Arrears of pension	22	2	Petition	74	Rev. Pensions				Discharged; laid on table.		
McEwen, Patrick	Arrears of pension	24	1	Petition	273	Rev. Pensions	391	Favorable; bill	398	Passed	Passed	App'd June 28, 1836
McEwen, Thomas	Liquidation of a certificate of debt.	4	1	Rep. of Secretary Treasury.	388	Claims	May 31, 1796	Adverse.		Laid on table.		
McEwen, Timothy, by attorney of.	Compensation for property destroyed in war of 1812.	16	1	Petition	28	Claims	Jan. 5, 1820	Adverse		Laid on table.		
McEwen, Timothy, by attorney of.	Compensation for property destroyed in war of 1812.	18	1	Petition	158	Claims	Feb. 27, 1824	Adverse		Laid on table.		
McEwen, Timothy, by attorney of.	Compensation for property destroyed in war of 1812.	21	1	Petition	376	Claims	Mar. 15, 1830	Adverse		Laid on table.		
McEwen, Timothy, by attorney of.	Compensation for property destroyed in war of 1812.	22	1	Petition	257	Claims	Feb. 6, 1832	Adverse		Laid on table.		
McEwing, Nancy	(See Nancy Dolan)	20	1		93							
McFaddin, Alexander	Payment of amount of pension stolen from the mail.	25	2	Petition	405	Rev. Pensions				Discharged; laid on table.		
McFadden, George	Arrears of pension	23	1	Petition	308	Rev. Pensions	June 28, 1834	Favorable	555	Referred to Committee Whole House.		
McFadden, George	Arrears of pension	23	2	House bill	336	Whole House	Feb. 6, 1835	With't amend.	555	Passed	Adverse report.	
McFadden, George	Arrears of pension	24	1	Petition	426	Invalid Pensions	722	Favorable; bill	670	Passed	Indef. postp'd.	
McFadden, George	Arrears of pension	25	2	Petition	39	Invalid Pensions	224	Favorable; bill	262	Passed	Adverse report.	
McFadden, George	Arrears of pension	26	1	Petition	161	Invalid Pensions	290	Adverse		Laid on table.		
McFadon, John	Relief for property destroyed by the government of Hayti.	16	1	Petition	85					Referred to Secretary State.		
McFaden, John	(See John A. Jolly, sureties of)	8	2		132							
McFaden, John, and Frances Johonnot.	(See Richard Caton, sureties of)	8	2		132							
McFadon, John, and Richard Caton.	Release from certain bonds	11	2	Petition	228	Com. and Manuf.				Discharged; leave to withdraw.		
McFadon, John, and Richard Caton.	Release from certain bonds	11	3	Petition	476	Com. and Manuf.						
McFadon, John, & Co.	Indemnity for French spoliations prior to 1800.	26	1	Memorial	182	Foreign Affairs	343	Favorable; bill	319	Referred to Committee Whole House.		
McFadon, John	(See Joseph Calman, trustee of.)	26	1		182							
McFadon, William & Co.	Indemnity for French spoliations prior to 1800.	26	1	Memorial	182	Foreign Affairs	343	Favorable; bill	319	Referred to Committee Whole House.		
McFadon, Joseph R., and W. P. Wallace.	Refunding of duties paid on goods furnished United States in Mexican war.	31	1	Petition	425	Military Affairs	121	Favorable; bill	135	Referred to Committee Whole House.		
McFall, George	Pension	19	1	Petition	34	Pens. & Rev. Cl'ms.	164	Adverse		Laid on table.		
McFall, George	Pension	19	2	Resolution	543	Military Pensions	May 11, 1826	Adverse		Rejected.		
McFall, Thomas	Invalid pension	1	2	Petition and rep't Sec. of War.	207					Laid on table.		
McFall, Thomas	Invalid pension	3	1	Petition and rep't Sec. of War.	131	Select	May 26, 1794	Report by res.	12	Passed	Passed	App'd June 9, 1794

List of private claims presented to the House of Representatives of the United States form the 1st to the 31st Congress, inclusive—Continued.

Names of claimants.	Nature or object of the claim.	Congress.	Session.	How brought before the House of Reps.	Page of journal.	To what committee of the House referred.	No. or date of the report.	Nature of the report.	No. of the bill.	How disposed of by the House of Reps.	How disposed of by the Senate.	Date of the act of Congress, and remarks.
McFarland, Andrew	Drawback of duty on rum	4	2	Petition	644	Com. and Manuf.	Jan. 18, 1797	Adverse		Rejected.		
McFarland, Elizabeth	(See widow of Wm. McFarland.)	18	1		250							
McFarland, Jas., and others.	Relief in relation to land	15	2	Petition	200	Public Lands				Discharged; laid on table.		
McFarland, Jas., and others.	Relief in relation to land	16	1	Petition	351					Ref'd to Com. W. H. on bill No. 46.		See act May 11, 1820
McFarland, Jas., and others.	Remission of balance due on lands	16	2	Petition	79	Public Lands	24	Favorable	191	Ref'd to Com. W. H.		
McFarland, Jas., and others.	Remission of balance due on lands	17	1	Petition	40	Public Lands	9	Favorable	20	Passed	Passed with amendment.	App'd April 26, 1822
McFarland, James, (Mass.)	Invalid pension	19	2	Resolution	89	Military Pensions	Feb. 14, 1827	By bill	436	Referred to Committee Whole House.		
McFarland, James, (Mass.)	Invalid pension	20	1	Resolution	43	Military Pensions	April 29, 1828	By bill	283	Passed.		
McFarland, James, (Mass.)	Invalid pension	20	2	House bill	55	Whole House	Jan. 15, 1829	With amends.	311	Passed	Laid on table.	
McFarland, James, (Mass.)	Invalid pension	21	1	Resolution	63	Military Pensions	Jan. 5, 1830	By bill	72	Passed	Passed	App'd May 20, 1830
McFarland, James, (Mass.)	Arrears of pension	23	2	Petition	131	Invalid Pensions	Jan. 23, 1835	Adverse		Laid on table.		
McFarland, James, (Mass.)	Arrears of pension	24	1	Petition	99	Invalid Pensions	477	Favorable; bill	479	Passed	Indef. postp'd.	
McFarland, James, (Mass.)	Arrears of pension	25	2	Petition	39	Invalid Pensions	276	Favorable; bill	319	Passed	Passed	App'd June 28, 1838
McFarland, John	Compensation for horses lost in service, 1779.	20	1	Resolution	73	Rev. Claims	Jan. 7, 1828	Adverse		Laid on table.		
McFarland, John	Compensation for horses lost in service, 1779.	21	1	Petition	92	Rev. Claims				Discharged; laid on table.		
McFarland, John and Jas.	Compensation for Indian depredations.	31	1	Resolution	679	Indian Affairs	279	Favorable	S. 14	Referred to Committee Whole House.		
McFarland, John, (Va.)	Revolutionary pension	23	1	Petition	97	Rev. Pensions				Discharged; laid on table.		
McFarland, John, (Va.)	Revolutionary pension	23	2	Petition	77	Rev. Pensions				Discharged; laid on table.		
McFarland, John	Remuneration for depredations by Winnebago Indians.	26	1	Resolution	1161	Indian Affairs.						
McFarland, John	Remuneration for depredations by Winnebago Indians.	27	2	Documents	333	Indian Affairs.						
McFarland, Moses	Invalid pension	4	1	Petition	447	Claims	Feb. 18, 1796	Favorable	156	Passed	Passed	App'd April 20, 1796
McFarland, Rob't, sen., executors of.	Arrears of pension	25	2	Petition	547	Rev. Pensions	Mar. 30, 1838	By bill	710	Passed.		
McFarland, Rob't, sen., executors of.	Arrears of pension	25	3	Petition	226	Rev. Pensions	Jan. 23, 1839	By bill	1069	Passed	Adverse.	
McFarland, Rob't, sen., executors of.	Arrears of pension	26	1	Petition	339	Claims.						
McFarland, Rob't, sen., executors of.	Arrears of pension	26	2	Petition	135	Rev. Pensions.						
McFarland, Robert	(See Wm. J. Price, assignees of.)	21	2		100							
McFarland, Robert & John	(See executors of Robert McFarland.)	25	2		547							
McFarland, Walter	Compensation for revolutionary services and pension.	16	1	Petition	48	Rev. Pensions	April 22, 1820	Adverse		Laid on table.		
McFarland, Wm., (N. Y.)	Increase of pension	15	1	Petition	132	Pens. & Rev. Cl'ms.				Discharged; referred to Secretary of War.		
McFarland, Wm., (N. Y.)	Increase of pension	16	1	Petition	225	Pens. & Rev. Cl'ms.				Discharged; laid on table.		
McFarland, Wm., (N. Y.)	Increase of pension	17	2	Petition	31	Pens. & Rev. Cl'ms.	Dec. 16, 1822	By bill	195	Passed	Indef. postp'd.	
McFarland, Wm., widow of.	Invalid pension	18	1	Petition	250	Pens. & Rev. Cl'ms.	March 3, 1824	Adverse		Laid on table.		
McFarland, Wm., (Pa.)	Pension	21	2	Petition	270	Military Pensions.						

List of private claims presented to the House of Representatives of the United States from the 1st to the 31st Congress, inclusive—Continued.

Names of claimants.	Nature or object of the claim.	Congress.	Session.	How brought before the House of Reps.	Page of journal.	To what committee of the House referred.	No. or date of the report.	Nature of the report.	No. of the bill.	How disposed of by the House of Reps.	How disposed of by the Senate.	Date of the act of Congress, and remarks.
McFarland, Wm., heirs of	Confirmation of title to land	27	3	Petition	52	Priv. Land Claims.						
McFarland, Wm., heirs of	Confirmation of title to land	29	1	Petition	498	Priv. Land Claims.						
McFarland, Wm., heirs of	Confirmation of title to land	30	1	Petition	258	Priv. Land Claims.	March 9, 1848	By bill	312	Referred to Committee Whole House.		
McFarland, Wm., heirs of	Confirmation of title to land	30	2	House bill	142	Whole House	Dec. 22, 1848	With't amend.	312	Passed.		
McFarlane, Andrew, (N.Y.)	Compensation for timber, &c., destroyed by U. S. army in 1794.	19	2	Petition	287	Claims				Discharged.		
McFarlane, Andrew, (N.Y.)	Compensation for timber, &c., destroyed by U. S. army in 1774.	20	1	Resolution	90	Claims				Discharged; laid on table.		
McFarlane, Andrew, heirs of.	Commutation pay for revolutionary services.	24	1	Petition	404	Rev. Claims.						
McFarlane, Henley	Invalid pension	11	2	Petition and rep't Sec. War.	196, 202					Laid on table.		
McFarlane, Henry	Invalid pension	8	2	Petition	26	Claims.						
McFarlane, Henry	Invalid pension	12	1	Petition	361	Claims	Jan. 8, 1812	Favorable	138	Passed	Passed, with amendment.	App'd July 5, 1812
McFarlane, James, (Mich.)	Confirmation of title to land in Michigan.	17	1	Petition	184	Public Lands				Discharged; laid on table.		
McFarlane, James	Settlement of accounts as hospital surgeon.	28	2	Senate bill	131	Claims	Feb. 7, 1845	With't amend.	42	Passed		App'd Feb. 13, 1845
McFarlane & Player, by their assignees.	Remission of duties on sugars destroyed by fire.	7	2	Petition	258	Com. and Manuf.	Jan. 5, 1803	Adverse		Leave to withdraw.		
McFarlin, Josiah	Pension	22	2	Petition	246	Invalid Pensions				Discharged; laid on table.		
McFarlin, Josiah	Pension	23	1	Petition	44	Invalid Pensions				Laid on table.		
McFee, Gilbert, widow of	Pension	27	2	Papers	218	Invalid Pensions	410	Adverse		Laid on table.		
McFee, Mary	(See widow of Gilbert McFee)	27	2		218							
McGahan, George	Reimbursement for property in Canada confiscated by British government in war of 1812.	29	1	Petition	532	Claims	748	Adverse		Laid on table.		
McGahee, Andrew, late widow of.	Pension and grant of land for revolutionary services.	20	2	Petition	142	Rev. Claims	Jan. 27, 1829	Adverse		Laid on table.		
McGarr, Catharine	(See John McGarr, widow of.)	30	1		967							
McGarr, John Widow of	Arrears of pension	30	1	Joint resolution from Senate.	967				R. 31	Passed		App'd July 5, 1848
McGarrah, John	Compensation for services in revolutionary war.	1	1	Petition	58					Referred to Secretary War.		
McGarrah, John	Compensation for services in revolutionary war.	1	2	Rep. of Secretary War.	141					Laid on table.		
McGary, Eugene	Permission to complete payment on forfeited lands.	19	1	Petition	32	Public Lands				Discharged; leave to withdraw.		
MaGary, John	Compensation for work done on Cumberland road.	23	1	Res. and docs	589	Claims	455	Adverse		Laid on table.		See report No. 449.
McGaughhey, Samuel	Exemption from duties on distilled spirits.	5	3	Petition	487	Com. and Manuf.	Mar. 2, 1799	Res. to postpone to next session.		Resolution adopted.		
McGaw, John A	Demurrage on a vessel employed by government in the Mexican war.	31	2	Senate bill	40	Commerce.			S. 96			
McGee, Daniel, by attorney	Indemnity for Indian depredations in Missouri.	19	2	Petition	134	Indian Affairs	51	Favorable		Referred to Committee Whole House on bill No. 368.		

List of private claims presented to the House of Representatives of the United States from the 1st to the 31st Congress, inclusive—Continued.

Names of claimants.	Nature or object of the claim.	Congress.	Session.	How brought before the House of Reps.	Page of journal.	To what committee of the House referred.	No. or date of the report.	Nature of the report.	No. of the bill.	How disposed of by the House of Reps.	How disposed of by the Senate.	Date of the act of Congress, and remarks.
McGee, David or Davis, (Alabam.)	Pre-emption right to land	23	1	Petition	159	Public Lands				Discharged; laid on table.		
McGee, Henry	Compensation for a horse lost in war of 1812.	15	2	Petition	33	Claims	Dec. 1, 1818	Adverse		Rejected.		
McGee, Henry	Compensation for a horse lost in war of 1812.	18	1	Petition	253	Claims	Mar. 24, 1824	Adverse		Laid on table.		
McGee, Leonard	Confirmation of title to land	15	1	Petition	56	Priv. Land Claims.						
McGee, Mary, and Susan Pierce.	(See George Nelson, heirs of.)	27	2		228							
McGee, Robert	Invalid pension	3	1	Rep. of Secretary War.	131	Select	May 26, 1794	J't. res. to refer to Sec. War.	R. 12	Passed	Passed	App'd June 9, 1794
McGee, Surmie	Confirmation of title to land	15	1	Petition	56	Priv. Land Claims.						
McGee, Thomas	Arrears of Pension	18	1	Petition	43	Rev. Pensions	Jan. 9, 1824	Adverse		Rejected.		
McGehee, Abraham	Correction of error in sale of lands by government purchased by him.	19	2	Petition	243	Public Lands.						
McGehee, John	Compensation for property taken by Indians in war of 1812.	15	1	Petition	222	Claims	Feb. 16, 1818	Adverse; leave to withdraw.		Resolution adopted.		
McGehee, John	Compensation for property takan by Indians in war of 1812.	15	2	Petition	199	Claims.						
McGenley, John, heirs of	Revolutionary pension	25	2	Petition	404	Rev. Claims				Disch'd; laid on table.		
McGenley, Samuel & William.	(See John McGenley's heirs.)											
McGhee, Lynn, (Indian)	(See Samuel Smith, *et al.*)	22	2		228							
McGhee, William, heirs of	Bounty land for revolutionary services.	30	1	Memorial	398	Priv. Land Claims.	543	Adverse		Laid on table.		
McGibbons, Joseph	Payment of claim against government.	1	2	Petition and rep't of Sec. War.	193	Select	July 16, 1790	Favorable; bill	88	Passed	Passed	App'd Aug. 11, 1790
McGibbony, Patrick, representatives of.	Commutation pay for revolutionary services.	24	2	Resolution	270	Rev. Claims.						
McGibbony, Patrick, representatives of.	Commutation pay for revolutionary services.	25	2	Petition	81	Rev. Claims.						
McGibbony, Patrick, representatives of.	Commutation pay for revolutionary services.	25	2	Senate bill	763	Rev. Claims	May 29, 1838	With't amend.	S. 169	Passed		App'd June 13, 1838
McGilbry, Gordon	(See John McGilbry, *et al.*)	22	1		264							
McGilbry, John, *et al*	For other lands in lieu of those to which they are entitled under treaty of Dancing Rabit creek.	22	1	Petition	264	Indian Affairs.						
McGilbry, Turner	(See John McGilbry, *et al.*)	22	1		264							
McGill, James	Confirmation of title to land in Michigan.	12	1	Petition	110	Public Lands.						
McGill, James, assignee of the heirs of.	Confirmation of title to land in Michigan.	27	3	Petition	77	Public Lands	6	Favorable; bill	625	Passed	Passed	App'd March 3, 1843
McGill, John	Compensation for a horse lost in Seminole war, 1818.	23	1	Petition	154	Claims.						
McGill, John	(See William H. Bedford, agent.)	28	1		262							
McGill, Robert	(See William H. Bedford, agent.)	28	1		262							
McGill, T. L., *et al*	(See representatives of Albert Tison.)	27	2		383							
McGill, William	(See James Lloyd and T. Tuttle.)	15	1		320							
McGillis, Randolph	(See John F. Randolph, *et al.*)	7	2		354							
McGilton, William	Compensation for services as assistant commissary, revolutionary war.	2	1	Petition	505					Referred to Secretary Treasury.		

List of private claims presented to the House of Representatives of the United States from the 1st to the 31st Congress, inclusive—Continued.

Names of claimants.	Nature or object of the claim.	Congress.	Session.	How brought before the House of Reps.	Page of journal.	To what committee of the House referred.	No. or date of the report.	Nature of the report.	No. of the bill.	How disposed of by the House of Reps.	How disposed of by the Senate.	Date of the act of Congress, and remarks.
McGilton, William	Compensation for services as assistant commissary, revolutionary war.	2	2	Rep. of Secretary Treasury.	626					Laid on table		Leave to withdraw, 1st sess., 3d Cong.
McGilvray, Alexander	Additional compensation for mail service.	28	1	Petition	431	P. Of. & P. Roads.	Feb. 28, 1844	Adverse		Laid on table.		
McGin, Charles	Pay and bounty land for services in revolutionary war.	19	1	Resolution	267	Rev. Claims	April 5, 1826	Adverse		Laid on table.		
McGinnis, Hugh, representatives.	Compensation for work done on the Cumberland road.	23	1	Senate bill	170	Claims	354	With't amend.	S. 20	Passed		App'd June 30, 1834
McGinnis, Jacob	Revolutionary pension	25	2	Petition	586	Rev. Pensions				Disch'd; laid on table.		
McGinnis, James S	Payment for subsistence furnished Ohio volunteers.	30	1	Petition	522	Military Affairs.						
McGinnis, John	Bounty land for services in last war.	27	3	Resolution	149	Priv. Land Claims.	121	Favorable; bill	739	Passed	Passed	App'd March 3, 1843
McGinnis, Neill	(See Thomas Lancaster, surety of)	12	1		214							
McGinnis, William	Pension	25	2	Resolution	524	Naval Affairs.						
McGinnis, William	Arrears of pension	29	2	Petition	428	Invalid Pensions.						
McGirk, Andrew S	Pension	15	1	Petition	38, 95					Referred to Secretary of War.		
McGirt, Zachariah	Confirmation of title to land	14	2	Petition	72	Public Lands.						
McGirt, Zachariah	Indemnity for losses in war with Creek Indians.	14	2	Petition	71	Ways and Means.						
McGirt, Zachariah	Indemnity for losses in war with Creek Indians.	15	1	Petition	44	Claims	Jan. 28, 1818, Feb. 9, 1818	Adverse Adverse		Recommitted. Laid on table.		
McGirt, Zachariah	Indemnity for losses in war with Creek Indians.	20	1	Petition	57	Claims	Jan. 4, 1828	Adverse		Laid on table.		
McGirt, Zachariah	Permission to sell lands granted him by treaty with indians in 1814.	23	1	Petition	309	Priv. Land Claims.	540	Favorable; bill	547	Referred to Committee Whole House.		
McGirth's, Captain, company of Moun'ed Rangers.	Compensation for services in Seminole war, 1815.	18	2	Senate bill	259	Claims	Feb. 28, 1825	With't amend.	S. 26	Passed		App'd March 3, 1825
McGlaughlin, John, *et al.*	(See heirs of John Higgins)	15	2		28							
McGowan, Jane	Compensation for supplies furnished in revolutionary war.	3	1	Petition	185					Laid on table.		
McGowan, John	Reimbursement of certain expenditures in public service.	2	1	Petition	458					Referred to Secretary Treasury.		
McGowan, John	Reimbursement of certain expenditures in public service.	3	2	Rep. of Secretary Treasury.	284					Laid on table.		
McGowen, John	(See Canadian refugees)	6	2		748							
McGown, James	Pension	28	1	Petition	976	Invalid Pensions.						
McGraw, Thomas	Invalid pension	17	1	Rep. of Secretary War.	200, 278					Leave to withdraw.		
McGready, William	Pension	16	1	Petition	237	Rev. Pensions	April 6, 1820	Adverse		Laid on table.		
McGregor, Alexander	(See Thomas Tupper, assignees of.)											
McGregor, Alexander	(See Isaac Lawrence, and others.)	14	2		101							
McGregor, John, (Va.)	Grant of land for services in revolutionary war.	11	3	Petition	469	Claims.						
McGregor, William	Arrears of pay for revolutionary services.	12	1	Petition	21	Claims				Discharged; leave to withdraw.		
McGregor, William, heirs of.	Arrears of pay for revolutionary services.	24	2	Petition	94	Rev. Claims	Mar. 2, 1837	Adverse		Laid on table.		
McGreenwood, William	(See John B. Smith, alias)	22	1		170							
McGrew, John F	Confirmation of title to land in Mississippi Territory.	13	2	Petition	168, 272	Public Lands.						

List of private claims presented to the House of Representatives of the United States from the 1st to the 31st Congress, inclusive—Continued.

Names of claimants.	Nature or object of the claim.	Congress.	Session.	How brought before the House of Reps.	Page of journal.	To what committee of the House referred.	No. or date of the report.	Nature of the report.	No. of the bill.	How disposed of by the House of Reps.	How disposed of by the Senate.	Date of the act of Congress, and remarks.
McGrew, John F.	Confirmation of title to land in Mississippi Territory.	13	3	Petition	657	Public Lands.						
McGrew, John F.	Confirmation of title to land in Mississippi Territory.	14	1	Petition	66	Public Lands.						
McGrew, John F.	Confirmation of title to land in Mississippi Territory.	14	2	Petition	200, 372	Priv. Land Claims.	Feb. 11, 1817	By bill	123	Referred to Committee Whole House.		
McGrew, John F.	Confirmation of title to land in Mississippi Territory.	15	1	Petition	39	Priv. Land Claims.						
McGrew, John, jr.	Pre-emption right to land in Mississippi.	14	1	Petition	157	Public Lands.						
McGrew, John, jr.	Pre-emption right to land in Mississippi.	14	2	Petition	49	Priv. Land Claims.						
McGrew, John, heirs of.	Confirmation of title to land	15	1	Petition	387	Priv. Land Claims.	Mar. 26, 1818	By bill	160	Ref'd to Com. W. H.		
McGrew, John, *et al.*	Confirmation of Spanish land title.	16	1	Petition	204	Priv. Land Claims.	Feb. 8, 1820	Favorable; bill	69	Passed	Passed	App'd May 8, 1820
McGruder, George, executors of.	(See John Kurtz, *et al.*)	26	1		168		573					
McGuire, Andrew, (Va.)	Invalid pension	7	1	Petition	17	Claims	Dec. 21, 1801	Adverse		Rejected.		
McGuire, Andrew	Increase of pension	10	2	Rep. of Secretary War.	480	Claims	Jan. 30, 1809	By bill	158	Passed	Passed	App'd March 3, 1809
McGuire, Barnabas	Increase of pension	14	2	Resolution	157	Pens. & Rev. Cl'ms						
McGuire, Bartholomew	Pension	19	1	Petition	310	Military Pensions.	164	Adverse		Laid on table.		
McGuire, Edmund, and Daniel Dorney.	Compensation for damages to their house in Norfolk in the war of 1812.	15	2	Petition	62	Claims	Jan. 8, 1819	Adverse.		Laid on table.		
McGuire, George	Compensation for services as acting superintendent of Indian affairs.	30	1	Petition	260	Indian Affairs	544	Adverse		Laid on table.		
McGuire James	Pension	17	2	Petition	142	Pens. & Rev. Cl'ms.	Jan. 24, 1823	Adverse		Rejected.		
MGuire, James	Pension	18	1	Petition	156	Pens. & Rev. Cl'ms	Feb. 9, 1824	Adverse		Laid on table.		
McGuire, Jane	(See Thomas McGuire, widow of.)	27	2		1298							
McGuire, Philip	Release from last payment on land and patent for the same.	16	1	Petition	289	Public Lands.	Mar. 23, 1820	Adverse		Rejected.		
McGuire, Robert	Compensation for sufferings in war of 1812.	26	1	Petition	335	Claims	712	Adverse.		Laid on table.		Leave to withdraw. Dec. 23, 1840.
McGuire, Thomas	Pension	20	2	Petition	39	Military Pensions.	Dec. 23, 1828	Adverse		Laid on table.		
McGuire, Thomas, widow of.	Revolutionary pension	27	2	Petition	1298	Rev. Pensions.						
McGuire, Thomas, widow of.	Revolutionary pension	27	3	Petition	73	Rev. Pensions	83	Favorable; bill	711	Passed	Indef. postp'd.	
McGuire, Thomas, widow of.	Revolutionary pension	28	1	Petition	99	Rev. Pensions.	10	Favorable; bill	37	Passed	Adverse report.	
McGuire, William	Compensation for a horse lost in Seminole war.	23	1	Documents	154	Claims.						
McGuyer, William	(See William H. Bedford, agent.)	28	1		262							
McHam, Thomas and Esther.	(See Philip Treglohan's representatives.)	2	1		501							
McHardy, Robert, heirs of.	Settlement of claim and judgment against United States.	28	1	Petition	1001	Judiciary.						
McHatton & Hernden	Compensation for losses by mail contract.	28	2	Petition	135	P. Of. and P. Roads.						
McHatton & Hernden	Compensation for losses by mail contract.	29	1	Petition	337	P. Of. and P. Roads.	374	Adverse		Laid on table.		
McHatton, James A.	(See McHatton & Hernden.)	28	2		135							

List of private claims presented to the House of Representatives of the United States from the 1st to the 31st Congress, inclusive—Continued

Names of claimants.	Nature or object of the claim.	Congress.	Session.	How brought before the House of Reps.	Page of journal.	To what committee of the House referred.	No. or date of the report.	Nature of the report.	No. of the bill.	How disposed of by the House of Reps.	How disposed of by the Senate.	Date of the act of Congress, and remarks.
McHatton, John	For five years' full pay and bounty land for revolutionary services.	16	2	Petition	105	Pens. & Rev. Cl'ms.	Jan. 17, 1821	Adverse		Laid on table.		
McHatton, John	For five years' full pay and bounty land for revolutionary services.	17	1	Petition	46	Pens. & Rev. Cl'ms.	Jan. 11, 1822	Adverse		Laid on table.		
McHatton, John, administrator of.	Commutation pay and bounty land for revolutionary services.	25	2	Petition	392	Rev. Claims	826	Adverse		Laid on table.		
McHatton, William	For exchange of half-pay for pension.	3	1	Petition and rep't Sec. of War.	50	Select.						
McHatton, William	For exchange of half-pay for pension.	3	2	Petition	278	Claims	Feb. 28, 1795	Favorable; bill	130	Passed.	Postponed.	
McHatton, William	For exchange of half-pay for pension.	4	1	Rep. of Secretary War.	447	Claims.	Feb. 18, 1796	Favorable; bill	156	Passed	Passed	App'd April 20, 1796
McHeath, Josiah	(See sureties of George Brown)	21	1		132							
McHenry, Isaac	Revolutionary pension	25	2	Petition	914	Rev. Pensions.						
McHenry, Isaac	Revolutionary pension	26	1	Petition	171	Rev. Pensions	483	Adverse		Laid on table.		
McHenry, Isaac	Remuneration for services as Indian spy, revolutionary war.	27	2	Petition	699	Rev. Pensions	784	Adverse		Laid on table.		
McHenry, James	(See Andrew Low & Co.)	16	1		194							
McHugh, John, widow of.	Grant of land in consideration of death of her husband in public service, war of 1812.	20	1	Petition	93	Priv. Land Claims.	Mar. 1, 1828	Adverse		Laid on table.		
McHugh, John, widow of.	Grant of land in consideration of death of her husband in public service, war of 1812.	20	2	Petition	50	Priv. Land Claims.	35	Adverse		Laid on table.		
McHugh, John, representatives of.	Confirmation of title to land in Louisiana.	21	1	Petition	51	Priv. Land Claims.	197	Favorable; bill	251	Referred to Committee Whole House.		
McHugh, John, representatives of.	Confirmation of title to land in Louisiana.	21	2	Bill of last sess.	265	Whole House	Dec. 4, 1831	With't amend	251	Passed.		
McHugh, John, representatives of.	Confirmation of title to land in Louisiana.	22	1	Petition	32	Priv. Land Claims.	59	Favorable; bill	119	Passed	Passed	App'd June 15, 1832
McHugh, Susannah	(See John McHugh's representatives.)	21	1		51							
McIlhenny, James	Release from judgment for violation of the slave importation act.	12	1	Petition	242	Com. and Manuf.				Discharged; laid on table.		
McIlvaine, Archibald	Compensation for a horse lost in the public service.	14	1	Petition	223	Claims	Feb. 7, 1817	Adverse		Rejected.		
McIlvaine, Bloomfield, administrator of.	Compensation for services as attorney for United States in certain suits.	19	1	Petition	125	Ways and Means.	Jan. 5, 1827	By bill	344	Referred to Committee Whole House.		
McIlvaine, Ebenezer	Invalid pension	4	1	Rep. of Secretary War.	447	Claims	Feb. 18, 1796	Favorable; bill	156	Passed	Passed	App'd April 20, 1796
McIlvaine, Ebenezer	Increase of pension	12	1	House bill	361	Whole House	June 15, 1812	With amends	138	Passed	Passed	App'd July 5, 1812
McIlvaine, Ebenezer	Further increase of pension	21	1	Petition	19[illegible]	Military Pensions.	April 2, 1830	Adverse		Laid on table.		
McIlvaine, Purdy	Adjustment of accounts as register of land office in Ohio.	28	1	Petition	999	Claims.						
McIlvaine, Purdy	Adjustment of accounts as register of land office in Ohio.	30	1	Petition	78	Public Lands.						
McIntire, John, *et al.*	(See John McIntyre)	16	1		186							
McIntire, Margaret	(See Margaret McIntyre)	26	1		649							
McIntire, M.	(See M. McIntyre)	30	2		126							
McIntosh, Betsey	Payment of award under Cherokee treaty of 1835–'6.	30	1	Senate joint resolution.	389	Indina Affairs	Feb. 29, 1848	With't amend.	S. R. 9	Passed		App'd Mar. 14, 1848

2—56

List of private claims presented to the House of Representatives of the United States from the 1st to the 31st Congress, inclusive—**Continued.**

Names of claimants.	Nature or object of the claim.	Congress.	Session.	How brought before the House of Reps.	Page of journal.	To what committee of the House referred.	No. or date of the report.	Nature of the report.	No. of the bill.	How disposed of by the House of Reps.	How disposed of by the Senate.	Date of the act of Congress, and remarks.
McIntosh, George	(See surety of Wm. Newsom)	16	2	Petition	41					Discharged; leave to withdraw.		
McIntosh, James	Allowance for certain services as commander in the navy.	26	1	Petition	1007	Naval Affairs.						
McIntosh, James	Allowance for certain services as commander in the navy.	27	2	Petition	64	Naval Affairs.						
McIntosh, James	Allowance for certain services as commander in the navy.	28	1	Petition	110	Naval Affairs.						
McIntosh, James	Allowance for certain services as commander in the navy.	28	1	Senate bill	697	Naval Affairs	May 2, 1844	Adverse	S. 64	Laid on table.		
McIntosh, James	Allowance for certain services as commander in the navy.	29	1	Petition	152	Naval Affairs	703	Favorable; bill	478	Referred to Committee Whole House.		
McIntosh, James	Allowance for certain services as commander in the navy.	29	2	Senate bill	375	Naval Affairs	Feb. 24, 1847	With't amend.	S. 102	Referred to Committee Whole House.		
McIntosh, John, (Ky.)	Invalid pension	29	2	Petition	53	Invalid Pensions.						
McIntosh, John, (Ky.)	Invalid pension	30	1	Petition	657	Invalid Pensions.						
McIntosh, John, (Ky.)	Invalid pension	30	2	Petition	76	Invalid Pensions	1	Favorable; bill	679	Passed.		
McIntosh, John, (Ky.)	Invalid pension	31	2	Petition	270	Invalid Pensions.						
McIntosh, John H.	Permission to exchange lands heretofore confirmed for other lands.	24	1	Senate bill	735	Priv. Land Claims.	Jan. 9, 1836	With't amend.	S. 11	Passed		App'd July 2, 1836
McIntosh, John H.	Compensation for property occupied by United States in Florida and destroyed by the enemy.	24	2	Senate bill	579				S. 199			
McIntosh, John H.	Compensation for property occupied by United States in Florida and destroyed by the enemy.	27	2	Documents	382	Claims	470	Favorable; bill	320	Ordered to 3d reading.		
McIntosh, John H.	Compensation for property occupied by United States in Florida and destroyed by the enemy.	27	3	Bill of last sess.	87	Select			320 320	Passed; reconsidered; recommitted.		
McIntosh, John H.	Compensation for property occupied by United States in Florida and destroyed by the enemy.	28	2	Petition	88	Military Affairs	37	Favorable; bill	511	Passed	Passed	App'd March 3, 1845
McIntosh, John M.	(See assignee of John Clute and Jacob Hart.)	27	3		101							
McIntosh, Lachlan	(See executors of John Lawson)	4	1		526							
McIntosh, Lachlan	(See heirs of John Habersham)	8	1		538							
McIntosh, Lachlan, jr., *et al*	Compensation for services as commissioners for surveying lands on the Tennessee river.	15	2	Petit'n of Georgia legislature.	59	Select	31	Favorable; bill	225	Referred to Committee Whole House.		
McIntosh, Lachlan, jr., *et al*	Compensation for services as commissioners for surveying lands on the Tennessee river.	16	1	Petit'n of Georgia legislature.	30	Select	2	Favorable; bill	5	Commit'd to Com. on Priv. Land Claims.		
						Priv. Land Claims.	62	Adverse	5	Referred to Committee Whole House.		
McIntosh, Maria H.	(See heirs of Christopher Hillary)	23	1		335							
McIntosh, Peter	Revolutionary pension	24	1	Petition	662	Rev. Pensions				Discharged; laid on table.		
McIntosh, Peter	Revolutionary pension	27	2	Petition	437	Rev. Pensions				Discharged; laid on table.		
McIntosh, Robert	Invalid pension	28	1	Petition	646	Invalid Pensions				Discharged; laid on table.		
McIntosh, Thomas	Pension	23	2	Petition	164	Rev. Pensions				Discharged; laid on table.		

List of private claims presented to the House of Representatives of the United States from the 1st to the 31st Congress, inclusive—Continued.

Names of claimants.	Nature or object of the claim.	Congress.	Session.	How brought before the House of Reps.	Page of journal.	To what committee of the House referred.	No. or date of the report.	Nature of the report.	No. of the bill.	How disposed of by the House of Reps.	How disposed of by the Senate.	Date of the act of Congress, and remarks.
McIntosh, William	Invalid pension	3	1	Rep. of Secretary War.	131	Select	May 26, 1794	Jt. res. to refer to Sec. War.	Res. 12	Passed	....	App'd June 9, 1794
McIntosh, William, (Ky.)	Permission to change location of a mill seat.	15	1	Petition	56	Public Lands	Dec. 23, 1817	Adverse; leave to withdraw.	......	Report adopted.		
McIntosh, William, (Ky.)	Permission to change location of a mill seat.	16	1	Petition	59	Public Lands	31	Favorable; bill	33	Rejected.		
McIntosh, William, (Ky.)	Permission to change location of a mill seat.	16	2	Petition	20	Public Lands	1	Favorable; bill	150	Passed	Laid on table.	
McIntyre, Alpheus	Increase of pension	23	1	Petition	121	Invalid Pensions	Feb. 21, 1834	Adverse	......	Laid on table.		
McIntyre, Alpheus	Increase of pension	28	1	Petition	218	Invalid Pensions.						
McIntyre, Andrew, widow of.	Settlement of accounts as tax collector in North Carolina.	16	1	Resolution	273	Select	Mar. 6, 1820	By bill	100	Indefinitely postponed		
McIntyre, Ann	(See widow of Andrew McIntyre).	16	1	....	273							
McIntyre, Daniel, heirs of.	Arrears of pension	21	2	Senate bill	217	Military Pensions	Jan. 31, 1831	With't amend	S. 84	Passed	....	App'd March 2, 1831
McIntyre, James	Refunding a fine for breach of revenue laws.	25	1	Petition	122	Commerce	444	Adverse	......	Laid on table.		
McIntyre, John	Relief from error in location of land.	7	1	Petition	29	Claims	April 15, 1802	Res. to post'p'n	......	Resolution adopted.		
McIntyre, John	Relief from error in location of land.	7	2	Petition	271	Claims	Feb. 9, 1803	Adverse	......	Laid on table.		
McIntyre, John	Relief from error in location of land.	8	1	Petition	505	Claims	Jan. 23, 1804	Adverse	......	Rejected	....	Leave to withdraw.
McIntyre, John	Relief from error in location of land.	8	2	Memorial	79	Claims.						
McIntyre, John	Relief from error in location of land.	9	1	Memorial	198	Public Lands	Dec. 30, 1805	Adverse	......	Leave to withdraw.		
McIntyre, John	Confirmation of title to land	10	2	Memorial	424	Public Lands.						
McIntyre, John	Confirmation of title to land	11	2	Memorial	114	Public Lands	May 1, 1810	Adverse	......	Laid on table.		
McIntyre, John	Confirmation of title to land	11	3	Memorial	438	Public Lands	Dec 12, 1810	Adverse	......	Laid on table	....	Leave to withdraw.
McIntyre, John, et al	Indemnity for losses under contract with government.	16	1	Petition	186	Claims	Feb. 9, 1820	Adverse	......	Laid on table.		
McIntyre, John, et al.	Indemnity for losses under contract with government.	18	1	Petition	315	Claims.						
McIntyre, John, et al.	Indemnity for losses under contract with government.	23	2	Petition	94	Claims	Mar. 2, 1835	Adverse	......	Laid on table.		
McIntyre, John, et al.	Indemnity for losses under contract with government.	25	3	Petition	121	Claims.						
McIntyre, John, et al.	Indemnity for losses under contract with government.	26	1	Petition	167	Claims	59	Adverse	......	Laid on table.		
McIntyre, John, et al.	Indemnity for losses under contract with government.	26	1	Petition (2)	702	Claims.						
McIntyre, John, et al.	Indemnity for losses under contract with government.	26	2	Petition	80	Claims.						
McIntyre, Magaret	Revolutionary pension	26	1	Resolution	649	Rev. Pensions.						
McIntyre, M.	For same commissions on land warrants as are allowed on money entries.	30	2	Petition	126	Public Lands.						
McIntyre, Niel	Draw of duty on fish and salt	4	1	Petition	570	....	....	....	......	Laid on table.		
McIntyre, Thomas	Commutation pay for revolutionary services.	1	3	Petition and rep't Sec. of War.	336	....	....	....	......	Laid on table.		
McIntyre, Thomas	Commutation pay for revolutionary services.	2	1	House bill	463	Whole House	Nov. 9, 1791	With amend.	152	Passed	Passed	App'd Mar. 27, 1792

List of private claims presented to the House of Representatives of the United States from the 1st to the 31st Congress, inclusive—Continued.

Names of claimants.	Nature or object of the claim.	Congress.	Session.	How brought before the House of Reps.	Page of journal.	To what committee of the House referred.	No. or date of the report.	Nature of the report.	No. of the bill.	How disposed of by the House of Reps.	How disposed of by the Senate.	Date of the act of Congress, and remarks.
McIver, John, (Fla)	To be allowed to locate land in Florida.	19	2	Petition	217	Public Lands.						
McIver, John, (Tenn.)...	Payment for his land granted to an Indian chief by Cherokee treaty.	20	2	Petition	229	Priv. Land Claims.						
McIver, John, (Tenn.)...	Payment for his land granted to an Indian chief by Cherokee treaty.	21	1	Petition	40	Claims	3	Adverse	......	Recommitted.		
McJimsey, Robert, surviving partner of Jackson & McJimsey.	Drawback of duty on sugar......	22	1	Petition	124	Commerce.						
McJimsey, Robert, surviving partner of Jackson & McJimsey.	Drawback of duty on sugar......	23	1	Petition	386	Ways and Means..	331	Favorable; bill	359	Referred to Committee Whole House.		
McJimsey, Robert, surviving partner of Jackson & McJimsey.	Drawback of duty on sugar......	24	1	Petition	54	Ways and Means..	Jan. 12, 1836	By bill	107	Passed	Passed	App'd June 28, 1836
McJimsey, Robert.......	Revolutionary pension..........	25	2	Petition	730	Rev. Pensions	....	....	......	Discharged; laid on table.		
McJunkin, Joseph.......	Invalid pension................	10	2	Rep. of Secretary War.	480	Claims	Jan. 30, 1809	By bill	158	Passed	Passed	App'd March 3, 1809
McKavett, Captain Henry, and company.	Remuneration for losses in Florida	27	2	Petition	622	Claims.						
McKavett, Captain Henry, and company.	Remuneration for losses in Florida	28	1	Petition	451	Claims	338	Adverse	......	Laid on table.		
McKay, George.........	Payment of amount due from Ottoway Indians.	29	1	Memorial	160	Indian Affairs.....	278	Adverse	......	Laid on table.		
McKay, Middleton	For other lands in lieu of those granted by treaty of Dancing Rabbit Creek.	22	1	Senate bill	502	Public Lands	Jan. 8, 1832	With amends.	S. 55	Passed............	Passed	App'd July 14, 1832
McKay, Neal...........	Revolutionary pension..........	22	1	Petition	265	Rev. Pensions.						
McKay, Sarah D........	(See S. D. Macay)	31	2	....	146							
McKay, Thomas	Compensation for a horse lost in service of United States.	27	2	Petition	935	Claims.						
McKay, Thomas	Compensation for a horse lost in service of United States.	27	3	Petition	73	Claims	209	Adverse	......	Laid on table.		
McKean, William K.....	Additional compensation for services in Mexican war.	31	1	Petition	862	Public Lands.						
McKean, Robert, agent of.	Indemnity for French spoliations prior to 1800.	26	1	Memorial	182	Foreign Affairs....	343	Favorable; bill	319	Referred to Committee Whole House.		
McKee, Andrew, son of ..	Compensation for corn taken by revolutionary army.	3	1	Petition	51	....	....	....	......	Laid on table.		
McKee, Andrew, son of ..	Compensation for corn taken by revolutionary army.	3	2	Petition	306	Claims.						
McKee, Andrew, son of ..	Compensation for corn taken by revolutionary army.	4	1	Petition	389	Claims	Dec. 28, 1795	Adverse	......	Leave to withdraw.		
McKee, Barnabas	Pension	19	1	Petition	310	Military Pensions..	164	Adverse	......	Laid on table.		
McKee, Henry..........	Pension for services in war of 1812.	21	1	Resolution	405	Military Pensions.						
McKee, Henry..........	Pension for services in war of 1812.	21	2	Petition	336	Military Pensions.						
McKee, Henry..........	Pension for services in war of 1812.	22	1	Petition	143	Invalid Pensions ..	Feb. 15, 1832	Adverse.	......	Laid on table.		
McKee, J. H...........	(See widow of W. R. McKee)...	30	1	....	485	Invalid Pensions.						
McKee, John, and H. Leef	Indemnity for losses by the seizure of the barque Maria Theresa.	30	1	Memorial	1025	Commerce.						

List of private claims presented to the House of Representatives of the United States from the 1st to the 31st Congress, inclusive—Continued.

Names of claimants.	Nature or object of the claim.	Congress.	Session.	How brought before the House of Reps.	Page of journal.	To what committee of the House referred.	No. or date of the report.	Nature of the report.	No. of the bill.	How disposed of by the House of Reps.	How disposed of by the Senate.	Date of the act of Congress, and remarks.
McKee, John, and H. Lee	Indemnity for losses by the seizure of the barque Maria Theresa.	30	2	Petition	91	Commerce	47	Favorable; bill	740	Referred to Committee Whole House.		
McKee, John, and H. Leef	Indemnity for losses by the seizure of the barque Maria Theresa.	31	1	Petition	392	Commerce	104	Favorable; bill	121	Referred to Committee Whole House.		
McKee, John, heirs of	Compensation for revolutionary services.	31	2	Petition	157	Rev. Claims.						
McKee, Martha	(See widow of Samuel McKee)	23	1		383							
McKee, Samuel, widow of	Payment for bounty land belonging to deceased, sold by government.	23	1	Petition	383	Claims.						
McKee, Samuel, widow of	Payment for bounty land belonging to deceased, sold by government.	23	2	Petition	109	Claims.						
McKee, Samuel, widow of	Payment for bounty land belonging to deceased, sold by government.	24	1	Petition	93	Claims.						
McKee, Samuel, widow of	Payment for bounty land belonging to deceased, sold by government.	24	2	Petition	145	Claims	320	Adverse		Laid on table.		
McKee, William	(See Andrew McKee, son of.)	3	1		51							
McKee, William, & James Gilmore, by attorney.	Further time to locate Virginia military land warrant.	9	2	Petition	560					Referred to Committee Whole House on bill No. 190.		
McKee, Colonel W. R., widow of.	Compensation for a horse lost in battle of Buena Vista.	30	1	Petition	485	Claims	412	Favorable; bill	362	Referred to Committee Whole House.		
McKee, Colonel W. R., widow of.	Compensation for a horse lost in battle of Buena Vista.	31	1	Petition	595	Claims.						
McKeen, John, and H. C. We'd.	(See heirs of Richard Toppan and William Stanwood.)	28	1		514							
McKeever, Lieut. Isaac, U. States army.	For expenses as witness in certain suits.	18	2	Petition	229	Ways and Means.						
McKeever, Lieut. Isaac, U. States army.	For expenses as witness in certain suits.	19	1	Petition	225	Naval Affairs	150	Favorable; bill	199	Passed.		
McKeever, Lieut. Isaac, U. States army.	For expenses as witness in certain suits.	19	2	Senate bill	97	Naval Affairs	Jan. 2, 1827	With't amend.	24	Passed	Passed	App'd Feb. 8, 1827
McKellar, John	For certain credits in payments for land.	18	1	Petition	39	Public Lands				Discharged; laid on table.		
McKellar, John	For certain credits in payments for land.	20	2	Petition	206	Public Lands.						
McKelvy, William	(See William H. Bedford, agent).	28	1		262							
McKenna, John	Invalid pension	25	2	Petition	920	Invalid Pensions.						
McKenna, John	Invalid pension	26	1	Petition	163	Invalid Pensions	289	Adverse		Laid on table.		
McKenney, E. D	(See sureties of Samuel H. Bunch)	30	1		738							
McKenney, John, (Ky.)	Invalid pension	14	2	Resolution	54	Pens. & Rev. Cl'ms.	Jan. 10, 1817	Adverse		Rejected.		
McKennie, John H.	Redress for having been deprived of pre-emption right in purchase of land.	23	2	Petition	278	Public Lands	79	Favorable; bill	696	Referred to Committee Whole House.		
McKennon, William	Invalid pension	1	2	Petition and rep't Sec. of War.	172					Laid on table.		
McKenzie, Charles	For change of land entry	26	1	Senate bill	837	Priv. Land Claims.	May 25, 1840	With't amend.	S. 305	Referred to Committee Whole House.		
McKenzie, Charles M.	Refunding money paid on land erroneously described.	28	1	Petition	610	Public Lands.						
McKenzie, Charles M.	Refunding money paid on land erroneously described.	28	2	Petition and docs.	345	Public Lands.						
McKenzie, Charles M.	Refunding money paid on land erroneously described.	29	1	Petition	141	Public Lands	199	Favorable; bill	190	Passed	Passed	App'd July 18, 1846

List of private claims presented to the House of Representatives of the United States from the 1st to the 31st Congress, inclusive—Continued.

Names of claimants.	Nature or object of the claim.	Congress.	Session.	How brought before the House of Reps.	Page of journal.	To what committee of the House referred.	No. or date of the report.	Nature of the report.	No. of the bill.	How disposed of by the House of Reps.	How disposed of by the Senate.	Date of the act of Congress, and remarks.
McKenzie, Collin, and Jas Smyth.	(See Maryland Hospital, of Baltimore.)	14	1	....	421							
McKenzie, Donald, agent of.	Indemnity for French spoliations prior to 1800.	26	1	Memorial	182	Foreign Affairs ...	343	Favorable; bill	319	Referred to Committee Whole House.		
McKenzie, James	Compensation for the capture of Major Andre.	6	2	House bill......	752	Whole House	Feb. 18, 1801	With amend..	277	Passed	Passed	App'd March 3, 1801
McKenzie, Jane.........	Remission of duties on astronomical apparatus.	21	1	Petition	199	Ways and Means.						
McKenzie, John	Invalid pension...............	1	2	Petition and rep't Sec. of War.	174	....	....	....	......	Laid on table.		
McKenzie, John, (Tenn.).	Pension	22	1	Petition	287	Rev. Pensions.						
McKenzie, Lewis........	Compensation and expenses for transporting volunteers.	30	1	Petition	207	Claims	....	....	......	Discharged; leave to withdraw.		
McKenzie, Robert	Compensation for services in war of 1812.	29	1	Petition	921	Claims.						
McKenzie, William, executors of.	For amount due as seaman in United States navy.	30	1	Petition	145	Judiciary	174	Favorable; bill	183	Passed	Passed	App'd Aug. 5, 1848
McKeon, James..........	Compensation for extra services in defending Fort Niagara.	14	1	Petition	548	Military Affairs ...	....	....	......	Discharged; leave to withdraw.		
McKeon, James..........	Compensation for extra services in defending Fort Niagara.	17	1	Petition	314	Military Affairs....	April 9, 1822	Adverse	......	Leave to withdraw.		
McKeon, James, widow of.	Pension for services in war of 1812.	18	1	Petition	65	Pens. & Rev. Cl'ms.	Jan. 6, 1824	Adverse	.....	Leave to withdraw.		
McKerney, James, William, and John.	Remission of duty on stills.......	13	3	Petition	635	Ways and Means..	Jan. 7, 1815	Adverse	......	Rejected.		
McKerney, James, William, and John.	Remission of duty on stills	14	1	Petition	432	Ways and Means.						
McKessock, Isaac........	Pension	21	1	Petition	46	Military Pensions.						
McKewan, Michael	Compensation for loss of a negro man in service of United States, and for horses and wagons furnished revolutionary war.	12	2	Petition	604	Claims.						
McKewan, Michael	Compensation for loss of a negro man in service of United States, and for horses and wagons furnished revolutionary war.	13	2	Petition	309	Pens. & Rev. Cl'ms.	92	Adverse	......	Referred to Committee Whole House.		
McKewan, Michael	Compensation for loss of a negro man in service of United States, and for horses and wagons furnished revolutionary war.	17	1	Petition	125	Pens. & Rev. Cl'ms.	Feb. 22, 1822	Adverse	......	Rejected.		
McKewan, Michael	Compensation for loss of a negro man in service of United States, and for horses and wagons furnished revolutionary war.	18	1	Petition	215	Pens. & Rev. Cl'ms.						
McKewan, Michael	Compensation for loss of a negro man in service of United States, and for horses and wagons furnished revolutionary war.	18	2	Petition	81	Select	Feb. 26, 1825	Favorable; bill	368	Passed	Passed	App'd March 3, 1825
McKibben, Chambers, and Tobias Myers.	Release from a contract with the Navy Department.	31	2	Petition	36	Naval Affairs.						
McKibbon, Thomas, and John H. Murphy.	Compensation for losses by change of contract by Post Office Department.	26	1	Petition	347	P. Of. & P. Roads.						

List of private claims presented to the House of Representatives of the United States from the 1*st to the* 31*st Congress, inclusive*—Continued.

Names of claimants.	Nature or object of the claim.	Congress.	Session.	How brought before the House of Reps.	Page of journal.	To what committee of the House referred.	No. or date of the report.	Nature of the report.	No. of the bill.	How disposed of by the House of Reps.	How disposed of by the Senate.	Date of the act of Congress, and remarks.
McKibbon, Thomas, and John H. Murphy.	Compensation for losses by change of contract by Post Office Department.	26	2	Petition	56	P. Of. & P. Roads.						
McKibbon, Thomas, and John H. Murphy.	Compensation for losses by change of contract by Post Office Department.	27	2	Petition	331	P. Of. & P. Roads.	874	Adverse	......	Laid on table.		
McKim, Alexander, (Md.)	Indemnity for French spoliations prior to 1800.	26	1	Memorial	182	Foreign Affairs....	343	Favorable; bill	319	Referred to Committee Whole House.		
McKim, Andrew	Pension for services in the Indian wars in 1791.	30	1	Petition	849	Rev. Pensions	781	Adverse	......	Laid on table.		
McKim, Hannah	Confirmation of title to land in Louisiana.	21	1	Petition	237	Priv. Land Claims.	March 5, 1830	Adverse	......	Laid on table.		
McKim, Hannah	Confirmation of title to land in Louisiana.	21	2	Petition	55	Priv. Land Claims.	March 3, 1831	By bill......	658	Laid on table.		
McKim, Hannah	Confirmation of title to land in Louisiana.	22	1	Petition	109	Priv. Land Claims.	69	Favorable; bill	137	Passed	Passed	App'd June 25, 1832
McKim, John, & Son....	Indemnity for French spoliations prior to 1800.	26	1	Memorial	182	Foreign Affairs....	343	Favorable; bill	319	Referred to Committee Whole House.		
McKim, John	Compensation for services as acting quartermaster of marines.	2[illegible]	2	Petition	95	Naval Affairs.....	105	Adverse	......	Laid on table.		
McKim, John...........	Compensation for services as acting quartermaster of marines.	22	1	Petition	29	Naval Affairs.						
McKim, John...........	Compensation for services as acting quartermaster of marines.	22	2	Petition	28	Naval Affairs	126	Adverse......	......	Laid on table.		
McKim, John...........	Compensation for services as acting quartermaster of marines.	23	1	Petition	36	Naval Affairs.						
McKim, Robert, executor of.	Indemnity for French spoliations prior to 1800.	26	1	Memorial	182	Foreign Affairs....	343	Favorable; bill	319	Referred to Committee Whole House.		
McKinley, Archibald.....	Arrears of pay and grant of land for revolutionary services.	11	1	Petition	28	Claims	June 9, 1809	Adverse.	......	Laid on table.		
McKinley, Duncan......	Invalid pension...............	3	1	Petition	100	....	....	....	......			
McKinley, Duncan......	Invalid pension...............	3	2	Petition	274	Claims	Mar. 2, 1795	Adverse......	......	Laid on table.		
McKinley, Duncan......	Invalid pension...............	4	1	Petition	598	Claims	May 31, 1796	Adverse	......	Laid on table.		
McKinley, John, heir of..	Grant of land for revolutionary services.	14	1	Petition	347	Pens. & Rev. Cl'ms.	April 11, 1816	Adverse	......	Laid on table.		
McKinley, John, heir of..	Commutation of half pay for revolutionary services.	23	1	Petition	144	Rev. Claims.						
McKinley, John	(See heirs of Thomas McKinley).	27	2	....	376							
McKinley, Thomas, (Va.)	(See heir of John McKinley)	14	1	....	347							
McKinley, Thomas, (Va.)	(See heir of John McKinley)	23	1	....	144							
McKinley, Thomas, heirs of.	Commutation and bounty land for revolutionary services.	27	2	Petition	376	Rev. Claims......	1064	Adverse	......	Laid on table.		
McKinley, William......	Relief for losses on a contract with the government.	4	2	Petition	704	Claims.						
McKinley, William......	Relief for losses on a contract with government.	5	2	Petition	135	Claims	Jan. 16, 1798	Adverse	......	Rejected.		
McKinley, William, (collector of revenue.)	For his portion of fines imposed upon persons convicted of violating revenue laws.	19	1	Petition	204	Ways and Means..	May 5, 1826	Adverse	......	Laid on table.		
McKinley, William, (collector of revenue.)	For his portion of fines imposed upon persons convicted of violating revenue laws.	22	2	Senate bill	325	Ways and Means..	....	....	S. 70			
McKinley, William......	(See heirs of Thomas McKinley).	27	2	....	376							

List of private claims presented to the House of Representatives of the United States from the 1st to the 31st Congress, inclusive—Continued.

Names of claimants.	Nature or object of the claim.	Congress.	Session.	How brought before the House of Reps.	Page of journal.	To what committee of the House referred.	No. or date of the report.	Nature of the report.	No. of the bill.	How disposed of by the House of Reps.	How disposed of by the Senate.	Date of the act of Congress, and remarks.
McKinne, Colonel John	Compensation for services and expenses in service of Treasury Department.	24	1	Resolution	1084	Claims.						
McKinne, John	Compensation for securing payment of certain custom-house bonds.	24	2	Petition	80	Claims.						
McKinne, John	Compensation for securing payment of certain custom-house bonds.	25	2	Petition	200	Claims.						
McKinne, John	Compensation for securing payment of certain custom-house bonds.	25	3	Petition	86	Claims	129	Adverse	......	Laid on table.		
McKinne, John	Compensation for securing payment of certain custom house bonds.	26	1	Petition	339	Claims.						
McKinney, Augustus, and Laysel Bancroft.	Refunding fines, &c., for importing nitre.	12	2	Petition	598	Ways and Means	Mar. 1, 1813	Adverse	......	Rejected.		
McKinney, Augustus, and Laysel Bancroft.	Refunding fines, &c., for import ing nitre.	13	1	Petition	12	Ways and Means.						
McKinney, Augustus, and Laysel Bancroft.	Refunding fines, &c., for importing nitre.	13	2	Petition	173	Ways and Means	Mar. 11, 1814	By bill	162	Passed	Passed, with amendment.	App'd April 18, 1814
McKinney, Daniel	Revolutionary pension	24	1	Resolution	666	Rev. Pensions	782	Favorable; bill	704	Ref'd to Com. W. H.		
McKinney, Daniel	Revolutionary pension	25	2	Petition	38	Rev. Pensions	325	Favorable; bill	367	Passed.		
McKinney, Daniel	Revolutionary pension	26	1	Petition	172	Rev. Pensions.						
McKinney, Daniel	Revolutionary pension	29	2	Petition & docs.	184	Rev. Pensions.						
McKinney, George, and Warner Lewis.	Compensation for locating bounty land warrants.	31	2	Petition	37	Public Lands.						
McKinney, John	Increase of compensation as surveyor of customs for the port of Alexandria.	10	1	Petition	36	Ways and Means.						
McKinney, John	For certain credits in settlement of his accounts as commissary.	18	2	Resolution	125	Claims	Jan. 3, 1825	Adverse	......	Laid on table.		
McKinney, John, sister & heirs of.	Bounty land for services in war of 1812.	29	1	Petition	592	Rev. Claims.						
McKinney, John, sister & heirs of.	Bounty land for services in war of 1812.	30	2	Petition	204	Rev. Claims.						
McKinney, John, sister & heirs of.	Bounty land for services in wer of 1812.	31	1	Petition	362	Rev. Claims.						
McKinney, William	Compensation for work on Cumberland road.	23	1	Resolution	589	Claims	455	Adverse	......	Laid on table	....	See report No. 449.
McKinsey, John	Compensation for services as seaman in 1814.	16	2	Petition	37	Naval Affairs	....	....	......	Discharged; laid on table.		
McKinstry, Bernice	(See widow of Elijah Eggleston)	28	2	....	146							
McKinstrey, John	Increase of pension	10	1	House bill	232	Whole House	April 19, 1808	With amends.	78	Passed	Passed	App'd April 25, 1808
McKinstrey, John	Increase of pension	10	2	Rep. of Secretary War.	480	Claims	Jan. 30, 1809	By bill	158	Passed	Passed	App'd March 3, 1809
McKinstry, Thomas	Compensation for revolutionary services.	1	2	Petition and rep't of Sec. War.	213	....	....	....	......	Laid on table.		
McKinstry, William	Compensation for a vessel taken by British in late war, recaptured and sold by United States.	18	2	Petition	40	Naval Affairs.						
McKinstry, William	Compensation for a vessel taken by British in late war, recaptured and sold by United States.	19	1	Resolution	227	Ways and Means.						
McKinstry, William	Compensation for a vessel taken by British in late war, recaptured and sold by United States.	20	1	Petition	99	Ways and Means.						

List of private claims presented to the House of Representatives of the United States from the 1st to the 31st Congress, inclusive—Continued.

2—57

Names of claimants.	Nature or object of the claim.	Congress.	Session.	How brought before the House of Reps.	Page of journal.	To what committee of the House referred.	No. or date of the report	Nature of the report.	No. of the bill.	How disposed of by the House of Reps.	How disposed of by the Senate.	Date of the act of Congress, and remarks.
McKinty, John	Compensation for services as seaman and for prize money.	2	1	Petition	492	....	....	....	......	Referred to Secretary Treasury.		
McKissack, or McKissick, Daniel.	Invalid pension	4	1	Rep. of Secretary War.	445	Claims	Feb. 15, 1796	Res. to refer to Sec. War.	R. 16	Passed	Passed	App'd April 18, 1796
McKissack, or McKissick, Daniel.	Invalid pension	4	2	Rep. of Secretary War.	651	Claims	Feb. 6, 1797	Favorable; bill	224	Passed	Postponed.	
McKissack, or McKissick, Daniel.	Invalid pension	5	2	Rep. of Secretary War.	126	Claims	Jan. 9, 1798	Favorable; bill	38	Passed	Passed	App'd Feb. 2, 1798
McKissack, William	Restoration of pension	17	1	Petition	96	Rev. Pensions	....	....	......	Disch'd; laid on table.		
McKissack. William, son of.	Commutation pay for revolutionary services.	22	1	Petition	386	Rev. Claims	Mar. 15, 1832	Adverse	......	Laid on table.		
McKissack, William D.	(See son of William McKissack)	22	1	....	386							
McKissick, Wilson H.	(See William H. Bedford, agent.)	28	1	....	262							
McKnight, Alexander, heirs of.	Payment for slaves captured by Indians in 1794.	22	1	Petition	401	Indian Affairs	525	Favorable; bill	504	Passed as amendment to bill No. 597.	Passed	App'd July 14, 1832
McKnight, Alexander, heirs of.	Payment for slaves captured by Indians in 1794.	22	2	Petition	75	Indian Affairs.	Dec. 21, 1832	Favorable; bill	636	Passed.		
McKnight, Andrew	Correction of error in land entry	20	2	Petition	177	Public Lands.						
MaKnight, Anna	(See Humphrey, Fullerton, late widow of.)	9	1	....	321							
McKnight, Brent, & Wood	Compensation for flour destroyed by United States States troops in conquest of New Mexico.	30	1	Petition	236	Claims	243	Adverse	......	Laid on table.		
McKnight, Charles, administrator of.	Compensation for services as physician, revolutionary war.	23	1	Petition	584	Rev. Claims.						
McKnight, Charles, administrator of.	Compensation for services as physician, revolutionary war.	23	2	Petition	132	Rev. Pensions	119	Adverse	......	Laid on table.		
McKnight, Charles, administrator of.	Compensation for services as physician, revolutionary war.	24	1	Petition	281	Rev. Claims	Feb. 12, 1836	Adverse	......	Laid on table.		
McKnight, John M. S.	(See Charles McKnight, administraton of.)	23	1	....	584							
McKnight, Robert	Revolutionary pension	8	1	Petition	576	Claims	Mar. 13 1804	Res. to postpone	......	Resolution adopted.		
McKnight, Robert	(See widow of Step'n Decater, *et al.*)											
McKnight, Robert, and James Baird.	(See Chonteau, Demun, & Co.)	15	1	....	319							
McKnight, T., and M Mobley.	Compensation for locating bounty land warrants.	31	2	Petition	37	Public Lands.						
McKoin, James, representatives of.	Payment for a piece of artillery furnished revolutionary war.	23	1	Resolution	516	Rev. Claims.						
McKnown, John	Fishing bounty on schooner Enterprise.	15	1	Petition	150	Ways and Means.						
McKnown, John, *et al.*	Redress for seizure of their vessel by British in 1817.	22	2	Memorial	397	Commerce.						
McKnown, Patrick	(See Stephen Smith, *et al.*)	23	1	....	239	....	....	....	261			
McKnown, William	Arrears of pension	24	1	Petition	201	Invalid Pensions	Mar. 24, 1836	Adverse	......	Laid on table.		
McKoy, Ephraim	Compensation for revolutionary services.	1	2	Petition and rep't Sec. of War.	179	....	....	....	......	Laid on table.		
McKoy, John	Pension	10	1	House bill	232	Whole House	April 9, 1808	With amend.	78	Passed	Passed	App'd April 25, 1808
McKoy, Neal	Compensation for revolutionary services—said compensation having been paid to Capt. Knowles without his consent.	5	2	Petition	128	Whole House	Jan. 10, 1798	Adverse	......	Laid on table.		

List of private claims presented to the House of Representatives of the United States from the 1st to the 31st Congress, inclusive—Continued.

Names of claimants.	Nature or object of the claim.	Congress.	Session.	How brought before the House of Reps.	Page of journal.	To what committee of the House referred.	No. or date of the report.	Nature of the report.	No. of the bill.	How disposed of by the House of Reps.	How disposed of by the Senate.	Date of the act of Congress, and remarks.
McLachlin, Colin	For the bounty of $80 under resotion of May 15, 1778.	21	1	Petition	57	Rev. Claims	194	Favorable	249	Referred to Committee Whole House.		
McLachlin, Colin	For the bounty of $80 under resotion of May 15, 1778.	21	2	House bill	265	Whole House			249	Passed.		
McLain, John	(See John McClain)	23	2		120							
McLain, John, (Md.)	Arrears of pension	25	2	Petition	775	Rev. Pensions				Discharged; laid on table.		
McLain, John, (Md.)	Arrears of pension	25	3	Petition	348	Rev. Pensions				Discharged; laid on table.		
McLain, John, (Md.)	Arrears of pension	27	2	Petition	703	Rev. Pensions	784	Adverse		Laid on table.		
McLain, Washington	(See Washington McClean)	23	2		436							
McLain, William, *et al.*, by agent of.	Fishing bounty on schooner Milo	23	1	Petition	184	Commerce	187	Favorable	206	Referred to Committee Whole House.		
McLain, William, *et al.*, by agent of.	Fishing bounty on schooner Milo	23	2	House bill	82	Whole House	Dec. 12, 1834	With't amend.	206	Passed	Indef. postp'd.	
McLaland, William	Invalid pension	10	2	Petition and rep't Sec. War.	480, 500	Claims	Jan. 30, 1809	Favorable	158	Passed	Passed, with amendment.	App'd March 3, 1809
McLanahan, William	Pension	10	2	House bill	499	Whole House	Feb. 20, 1809	With amend.	158	Passed	Passed	App'd March 3, 1809
McLane, Allen	Half pay for revolutionary services	14	1	Petition	112	Pens. & Rev. Cl'ms.	Jan. 11, 1816	Adverse		Leave to withdraw.		
McLane, Allen	Half-pay for revolutionary services	14	2	Petition	198	Pens. & Rev. Cl'ms.	Feb. 7, 1817	Adverse		Rejected, and leave to withdraw.		
McLane, Allen	Half-pay for revolutionary services	15	1	Petition	49, 63	Pens. & Rev. Cl'ms.	Feb. 3, 1818	Adverse		Laid on table.		
McLane, Charles	(See Charles McClain.)											
McLane, Joseph	For a grant of land	24	1	Petition	113	Public Lands.						
McLane, William	(See Wm. McLean)	27	2		611							
McLaughlin, Andrew	Revolutionary pension	28	2	Petition	70	Rev. Pensions.						
McLaughlin, B., and E. P. Guion.	Balance due for mail service	30	2	Petition	262	P. Of. & P. Roads.	49	Adverse		Laid on table.		
McLaughlin, James, (Ga.)	Pension	21	2	Resolution	102	Military Pensions				Discharged; laid on table.		
McLaughlin, James	Increase of pension	25	3	Petition	129	Invalid Pensions				Discharged; laid on table.		
McLaughlin, Jas., assignee of.	Payment of balance due for provisions furnished United States army in 1813.	18	2	Resolution	62	Claims	42	Report and bill	297	Passed	Indef. postp'd.	
McLaughlin, Jas., assignee of.	Payment of balance due for provisions furnished United States army in 1813.	19	1	Resolution	40	Claims	32	Report and bill	50	Passed	Passed	App'd May 18, 1826
McLaughlin, Jesse	(See William H. Bedford, agent.)	28	1		262							
McLaughlin, John	Extra compensation as clerk in General Land Office.	19	2	Petition	72	Public Lands				Discharged.		
McLaughlin, John, (La.)	Confirmation of title to land	23	2	Petition	77	Priv. Land Claims.						
McLaughlin, John	For benefit of acts granting lands to Canadian refugees.	26	1	Petition	701	Priv. Land Claims.	550	Adverse		Laid on table.		
McLaughlin, John	For benefit of acts granting lands to Canadian refugees.	26	2	Petition	36	Priv. Land Claims.						
McLaughlin, John	For benefit of acts granting lands to Canadian refugees.	28	1	Petition	70	Priv. Land Claims.	7	Favorable	33	Passed.		
McLaughlin, John	For benefit of acts granting lands to Canadian refugees.	29	1	Petition	120	Priv. Land Claims.	233	Adverse		Laid on table.		
McLaughlin, John	For benefit of acts granting lands to Canadian refugees.	30	1	Petition	344	Priv. Land Claims.						

List of private claims presented to the House of Representatives of the United States from the 1st to the 31st Congress, inclusive—Continued.

Names of claimants.	Nature or object of the claim.	Congress.	Session.	How brought before the House of Reps.	Page of journal.	To what committee of the House referred.	No. or date of the report.	Nature of the report.	No. of the bill.	How disposed of by the House of Reps.	How disposed of by the Senate.	Date of the act of Congress, and remarks.
McLaughlin & Knox	Compensation for work done on the Ohio river.	29	2	Petition	303	Claims.						
McLaughlin, Owen	Relief for being robbed of his certificate of public debt.	5	3	Petition	444	...	...	...	...	Rejected.		
McLaughlin, Patrick	Compensation for revolutionary services.	1	3	Petition and rep't Sec. of War.	352	...	...	...	...	Laid on table.		
McLaurin, D. B.	Compensation for supplies furnished troops in Florida war.	24	2	Petition	308	Military Affairs.						
McLawchlin, C. A.	Confirmation of title to land	27	2	Petition	622	Priv. Land Claims.						
McLawchlin, C. A.	Confirmation of title to land	27	3	Petition	45	Priv. Land Claims.						
McLean, Alexander	Invalid pension	29	2	Petition	331	Invalid Pensions.						
McLean, Angus	Compensation for revolutionary services.	3	2	Senate bill	334	Select	Feb. 23, 1795	With amend.	26	Passed	Concurred in.	App'd Feb. 27, 1795
McLean, Anna	(See widow of Charles McLean).	29	1	...	613							
McLean, Lieut. Charles, widow of.	Relief, husband died in services of United States.	29	1	Petition	613	Invalid Pensions.						
McLean, Elizabeth	Pension	30	2	Petition	94	...	...	...	...	Leave to withdraw.	...	Referred to Pension Office.
McLean & Evans	(See Taylor & McNeal)	14	1	...	284							
McLean, James, *et al.*	Compensation for revolutionary services.	2	1	Petition	573	Select.						
McLean, John, (Pa.)	Payment of expenses incurred in equipping his company in war of 1812.	18	1	Petition	89	Claims	Dec. 29, 1823	Adverse	...	Rejected.		
McLean, John, (Pa.)	Payment of expenses incurred in equipping his company in war of 1812.	19	1	Resolution	56	Claims	Feb. 24, 1826	Adverse	...	Laid on table.		
McLean, John	Permission to correct an error in entry of land.	24	1	Documents	1021	Priv. Land Claims.						
McLean, John, (S. C.)	Additional compensation as postmaster, Marion court-house.	15	1	Petition	191	P. Of. & P. Roads.	...	...	...	Discharged; laid on table.		
McLean, John, (N. Y.)	Compensation for property destroyed during revolutionary war.	3	1	Petition and rep't Sec. Treasury.	21	...	...	...	...	Laid on table.		
McLean, John, (N. N.)	Compensation for property destroyed during revolutionary war.	3	2	Resolution	359	...	...	...	...	Leave to withdraw.		
McLean, John	Revolutionary pension	16	2	Petition	159	Rev. Pensions	Feb. 15, 1821	Adverse	...	Rejected.		
McLean, Moses, heir of	(See McLean)	29	1	...	571							
McLean, Roger	Compensation for services and expenses in removing artillery of United States.	2	1	Petition and rep't Sec. Treasury.	503	...	...	...	...	Laid on table.		
McLean, William	Increase of pension	27	2	Petition	611	Invalid Pensions	933	Adverse	...	Laid on table.		
McLellan, C. J	Remuneration for expenses incurred by death of honorable F. G. McConnell, at his house.	30	1	Petition	68	Accounts.						
McLellan, John	(See John McClelland)	24	2	...	44							
McLellan, Joseph, *et al*	Reimbursement of tonnage duties on ship Eliza.	7	2	Petition	246	Com. and Manuf.	Jan. 27, 1803	Favorable	...	Referred to Committee Whole House.	...	Leave to withdraw.
McLellan, J. H. and Co.	Refunding duties on molasses destroyed by fire.	27	2	Petition	1112	Commerce.						
McLellan, J. H. and Co.	Refunding duties on molasses destroyed by fire.	27	3	Petition	139	Commerce.						
McLellan, J. H. and Co.	Refunding duties on molasses destroyed by fire.	28	1	Petition	532	Commerce	347	Adverse	...	Laid on table.		
McLellan, Samuel	Refunding duties paid on goods	27	2	Petition	45	Commerce.						

List of private claims presented to the House of Representatives of the United States from the 1st to the 31st Congress, inclusive—Continued.

Names of claimants.	Nature or object of the claim.	Congress.	Session.	How brought before the House of Reps.	Page of journal.	To what committee of the House referred.	No. or date of the report.	Nature of the report.	No. of the bill.	How disposed of by the House of Reps.	How disposed of by the Senate.	Date of the act of Congress, and remarks.
McLellan, Samuel	Refunding duties paid on goods	27	2	Petition	239	Commerce.						
McLellan, Samuel	Refunding duties paid on goods	28	1	Petition	532	Commerce.						
McLemore, John, widow of	Pension for long service in United States army.	25	1	Petition	102					Laid on table.		
McLemore, John, widow of	Pension for long service in United States army	25	2	Petition	91	Invalid Pensions	502	Adverse		Laid on table.		
McLemore, Martha E	(See John McLemore, widow of)	25	1		102							
McLeod, Thomas S	Compensation as clerk in General Post Office.	18	1	Petition	454	Ways and Means.						
McLeod, Thomas S	Compensation as clerk in General Post Office.	18	2	Petition	136	Ways and Means				Discharged; laid on table.		
McLeod, William, senior and junior.	(See Robert Gillispie, *et al*)	18	1		285							
McLeran, John	For expenses in defending suits against him by United States.	25	2	Petition	395	Judiciary				Discharged; laid on table		
McLeran, John	For expenses in defending suits against him by United States.	25	3	Petition	122	Judiciary				Discharged; laid on table.		
McLure, Abdiel, heirs of	Compensation for revolutionary services.	19	1	Petition	153	Rev. Claims	Feb. 26, 1826	Adverse		Leave to withdraw.		
McLure, Abdiel, heirs of	Compensation for revolutionary services.	19	2	Petition	158	Rev. Claims	Jan. 30, 1827	Adverse		Laid on table.		
McLure, James	Invalid pension	9	1	Petition	189	Claims	Mar. 28, 1806	Rep. and res. to postpone.		Leave to withdraw.		
McLure, John, (Va.)	Compensation for labor, &c., on Cumberland road.	18	2	Senate bill	143	Claims	Feb. 25, 1825	With't amend.	27	Passed	Passed	App'd March 3, 1825
McMackin, Thomas C	Redress for having been deprived of pre-emption right	23	2	Resolution	243	Public Lands	79	Favorable	696	Referred to Committee Whole House.		
McMahan, Geo., D., heirs of.	Commutation and pay for revolutionary services.	24	1	Resolution	707	Rev. Claims.						
McMahan, Geo., D., heirs of.	Commutation and pay for revolutionary services	24	2	Petition and docs.	119	Rev. Claims.						
McMahan, George D	Payment for revolutionary services.	25	3	Petition	85	Rev. Claims.						
McMahan, George D	Payment for revolutionary services.	26	1	Petition	166	Rev. Claims.						
McMahan, George D	Payment for revolutionary services.	26	2	Petition	35	Rev. Claims	Jan. 15, 1841	Adverse		Laid on table.		
McMahan, George D	Payment for revolutionary services.	27	2	Petition	1006	Rev. Claims	972	Adverse		Laid on table.		
McMahon, Anna, of William.	Compensation for services against the Indians.	3	2	Petition	317	Claims.						
McMahon, Anna, of William.	Compensation for services against the Indians.	4	1	Petition	373	Claims				Discharged.		
McMahon, Hugh, by heirs of.	Refunding money overpaid for land.	21	1	Petition	264	Public Lands				Discharged; laid on table.		
McMahon, James, (Mo.)	Compensation for Indian depredations.	19	2	Petition	134	Indian Affairs	51	Favorable	368	Referred to Committee Whole House.		
McMahon, James, (N. Y.)	Refunding amount expended in service of Post Office Department.	19	2	Petition	241	P. O. & P. Roads				Discharged.		
McMahon, James, (N. Y.)	Refunding amount expended in service of Post Office Department.	21	1	Petition	206	P. Of. and P. Roads				Discharged; laid on table.		

List of private claims presented to the House of Representatives of the United States from the 1st to the 31st Congress, inclusive—Continued.

Names of claimants.	Nature or object of the claim.	Congress.	Session.	How brought before the House of Reps.	Page of journal.	To what committee of the House referred.	No. or date of the report.	Nature of the report.	No. of the bill.	How disposed of by the House of Reps.	How disposed of by the Senate.	Date of the act of Congress, and remarks.
McMahon, James, (N. Y.)	Refunding amount expended in service of Post Office Department.	22	1	Petition	162	P. Of. and P. Roads.				Discharged; laid on table.		
McMahon, James, (N. Y.)	Refunding amount expended in service of Post Office Department.	24	1	Petition	283	Claims	548	Favorable	539	Referred to Committee Whole House.		
McMahon, James, (N. Y.)	Refunding amount expended in service of Post Office Department.	25	2	Petition	37	Claims	28	Favorable	40	Passed	Passed	App'd April 20, 1838
McMahon, James	For interest on amount expended in service of Post Office Department.	24	1	Petition and docs.	125	Claims	65	Adverse		Laid on table.		
McMahon, John	Invalid pension	17	2	Petition	189	Pens. & Rev. Cl'ms.				Discharged; referred to Com. Whole House, on bill No. 195.		
McMahon, John	Invalid pension	18	1	Resolution	305					Leave to withdraw.		
McMahon, Patrick, (Pa.)	Pension	22	1	Petition	287	Rev. Pensions				Discharged; laid on table.		
McMahon, Thomas, sen.	Compensation for Indian depredations.	19	2	Petition	134	Indian Affairs	51	Favorable	368	Referred to Committee Whole House.		
McMahon, Thomas, jr.	Compensation for Indian depredations.	19	2	Petition	134	Indian Affairs	51	Favorable	368	Referred to Committee Whole House.		
McMahon, William, (Mo.)	Indemnity for Indian depredations.	19	2	Petition	134	Indian Affairs	51	Favorable	368	Referred to Committee Whole House.		
McMaken, Joseph H., and John P. Hodges.	Compensation for mail service	27	3	Petition	103	P. Of. & P. Roads.						
McManomy, Thomas	Invalid pension	24	2	Petition	97	Invalid Pensions.				Discharged; laid on table.		
McManus, John	Permission to enter certain lands.	27	2	Petition	614	Public Lands				Discharged; laid on table.		
McMasters, Hugh, widow of.	Arrears of pension	26	1	Petition	285	Rev. Pensions.						
McMasters, Isaac	Revolutionary pension	26	1	Petition	284	Rev. Pensions.						
McMasters, John	Relief from imprisonment on judgment of the United States.	12	1	Petition	32	Com. and Manuf.						
McMasters, John	Relief from imprisonment on judgment of the United States.	12	2	Petition	686	Select	Feb. 19, 1813	Favorable	265	Postponed.		
McMasters, John	Relief from imprisonment on judgment of the United States.	13	1	Petition	91					Laid on table.		
McMasters, John	Relief from imprisonment on judgment of the United States.	13	3	Petition	712	Select	Feb. 10, 1815	Favorable	292	Referred to Committee Whole House.		
McMasters, Martha	(See Hugh McMasters, widow of)	26	1		285							
McMasters, Michael	Arrears of pension	20	2	Petition	262	Military Pensions.				Disch'd; laid on table.		
McMasters, Thomas, jr.	Relief in relation to his contract.	26	1	Resolution	560	P. Of. & P. Roads.	April 4, 1840	Adverse		Laid on table.		
McMeehan	(See Valentine & McMeehan)	23	1		589							
McMeekin, Martha	(See Robert McMeekin's widow)	25	2		267							
McMeekin, Robert, widow of	Pension	25	2	Petition	267	Rev. Pensions.						
McMichan, John, surety of	Release from liability	17	1	Petition	166	Ways and Means.	Jan. 28, 1822	Adverse		Rejected.		
McMickin, Martha	(See widow of Robert McMickin)	26	1		950							
McMickin, Robert, widow of	Revolutionary pension	26	1	Resolution	950	Rev. Pensions.						
McMickins, Elisha	(See William H. Bedford, agent)	28	1		262							
McMillan, Arthur	Compensation for property destroyed in war of 1812.	22	2	Petition	119	Claims	72	Adverse.		Laid on table.		

List of private claims presented to the House of Representatives of the United States from the 1st to the 31st Congress, inclusive—Continued.

Names of claimants.	Nature or object of the claim.	Congress.	Session.	How brought before the House of Reps.	Page of journal.	To what committee of the House referred.	No. or date of the report.	Nature of the report.	No. of the bill.	How disposed of by the House of Reps.	How disposed of by the Senate.	Date of the act of Congress, and remarks.
McMillan, Benjamin	Payment for horses furnished United States in Florida war.	25	2	Petition	397	Claims.						
McMillan, Daniel	Revolutionary pension	17	1	Resolution	324	Rev. Pensions	....	....	.....	Discharged; leave to withdraw.		
McMillan, John	Pension	14	1	Petition	622	Pens. & Rev. Cl'ms.	April 11, 1816	Favorable	171	Passed	Passed with amendment.	App'd June 30, 1816
McMillan, William	Increase of pension	21	2	Petition	120	Military Pensions.						
McMillan, William	Increase of pension	22	1	Petition	67	Rev. Pensions	147	Favorable	226	Referred to Committee Whole House.		
McMillan, William, heirs of.	Commutation of half-pay for revolutionary services.	25	2	Petition	899	Rev. Claims.						
McMillan, William, heirs of.	Commutation of half-pay for revolutionary services.	25	3	Petition	124	Rev. Claims	441	Adverse	.....	Laid on table.		
McMillan, William, heirs of.	Commutation of half-pay for revolutionary services.	26	1	Petition	166	Rev. Claims	Mar. 13, 1812	Res. for leave to withdraw.	.....	Resolution adopted.		
McMillen, A. B.	Confirmation of title to land	28	2	Petition	300	Priv. Land Claims.	134	Favorable	617	Referred to Committee Whole House.		
McMillen, James, widow of	Remuneration for services in the late war.	27	2	Petition	668	Invalid Pensions	....	....	.....	Discharged; laid on table.		
McMillen, Jane	(See widow of James McMillen)	27	2	....	668							
McMillen, Joseph	Revolutionary pension	26	1	Petition	552	Rev. Pensions	....	....	.....	Discharged; laid on table.		
McMillen, Joseph	Revolutionary pension	26	2	Petition	78	Rev. Pensions	....	....	.....	Discharged; laid on table.		
McMillen, Robert	Pension	19	2	Petition	186	Military Pensions	....	....	.....	Discharged.		
McMoran, Samuel	Relief for land erroneously sold by agent of the United States.	19	1	Petition	37	Public Lands	Dec. 29, 1825	Adverse	.....	Laid on table.		
McMullen, Daniel	Pension	26	1	Petition	797	Invalid Pensions.						
McMullen, David	Revolutionary pension	26	2	Petition	82	Invalid Pensions.						
McMullen, John	Compensation for damages to property rented to United States.	31	1	Petition	1271	Military Affairs.						
McMullen, John, *et al*	Bounty land for revolutionary services.	8	1	Petition	493	Select.						
McMullen, Richard R., mother of (Mary.)	Pension	23	1	Petition	188	Naval Affairs.						
McMullen, Richard R., mother of, (Mary.)	Pension	23	2	Petition	182	Naval Affairs.						
McMurdy, John	Invalid pension	12	1	Petition	28	Claims	Mar. 13, 1812	Res. for leave to withdraw.	.....	Adopted		
McMurphy, Rachael	(See late widow of Benj. Cole)	31	2	....	155							
McMurphy, Sarah	Continuation of pension	28	1	Petition	850	Rev. Pensions.						
McMurry, William	Payment for property destroyed by Creek Indian.	25	2	Memorial	1079	Claims.						
McMurtrie, William B.	For expenses incurred in connexion with the Exploring Expedition in 1837 and 1838.	26	1	Petition	938	Naval Affairs.						
McMurtrie, William B.	For expenses incurred in connexion with the Exploring Expedition in 1837 and 1838.	26	1	Senate bill	1121	Claims	....	....	240			
McMurtrie, William B.	For expenses incurred in connexion with the Exploring Expedition in 1837 and 1838.	28	1	Petition	429	Claims.						

List of private claims presented to the House of Representatives of the United States from the 1st to the 31st Congress, inclusive—Continued.

Names of claimants.	Nature or object of the claim.	Congress.	Session.	How brought before the House of Reps.	Page of journal.	To what committee of the House referred.	No. or date of the report.	Nature of the report.	No. of the bill.	How disposed of by the House of Reps.	How disposed of by the Senate.	Date of the act of Congress, and remarks.
McMurtrie, William B.	For expenses incurred in connexion with the Exploring Expedition in 1837 and 1838.	30	1	Petition	644	Naval Affairs.						
McMurtry, John	Pension	20	2	Petition	55	Military Pensions	Feb. 13, 1829	By bill	440	Passed.		
McMurtry, John	Pension	21	1	Petition	47	Military Pensions	Jan. 5, 1830	By bill	72	Passed	Passed	App'd May 20, 1830
McMurtry, John, widow of	Continuation of pension	27	2	Petition	329	Rev. Pensions	294	Favorable	262	Passed	Indef. postp'd.	
McMurtry, John, widow of.	Continuation of pension	27	3	Petition	74	Rev. Pensions.						
McMurtry, Margaret	(See widow of John McMurtry)	27	2		329							
McMyers, John, widow of.	(See John Myers)	29	1		175							
McNabb, Charles	Bounty land for revolutionary services.	14	1	Petition	66	Pens. & Rev. Cl'ms.	Feb. 13, 1816	Adverse		Rejected.		
McNabb, Charles	Bounty land for revolutionary services.	14	2	Petition	177	Pens. & Rev. Cl'ms.				Discharged; laid on table.		
NcNair, Alexander	Compensation for house destroyed while occupied by United States troops, and increase of pay as paymaster.	18	1	Senate bill	512	Claims	May 19, 1824	Adverse as to increase of compens'n.	96	Passed with amend't.	Passed, with amendment.	App'd May 25, 1824
McNair, David	Pension under Cherokee treaty	24	2	Resolution	384	Indian Affairs.						
McNair, David	Pension under Cherokee treaty	25	3	Resolution	89	Invalid Pensions.						
McNair, David	Compensation for a horse lost in public service.	26	1	Senate bill	1105	Claims			S. 148			
McNair, David, (Ky.)	Pension for services in the war of 1812.	30	1	Petition	740	Rev. Pensions.						
McNair, Dunning R.	Extra compensation for mail service.	27	2	Petition	71	P. Of. & P. Roads.						
McNair, Dunning R.	Extra compensation for mail service.	27	3	Petition	155	P. Of. & P. Roads.				Discharged; laid on table.		
McNair, Dunning R.	Extra compensation for mail service.	28	1	Petition	345	P. Of. & P. Roads.	472	Favorable; bill	362	Referred to Committee Whole House.		
McNair, Dunning R.	Extra compensation for mail service	28	2	House bill	343	Whole House	Feb. 7, 1845	With't amend.	362	Passed	Passed	App'd March 3, 1845
McNair, Dunning R.	Release from fines imposed by Postmaster General.	29	1	Petition	436	P. Of. & P. Roads.	626	Adverse		Laid on table.		
McNair, Dunning R.	Release from fines imposed by Postmaster General.	31	1	Petition	200	P. Of. & P. Roads.	250	Favorable; bill	247	Referred to Committee Whole House.		
McNair, Dunning R.	Release from fines imposad by Postmaster General.	31	2	House bill	181	Whole House	Jan. 24, 1851	With't amend.	247	Passed	Passed	App'd Feb. 27, 1851
McNair, John	Invalid pension	27	2	Petition	720	Invalid Pensions				Discharged; laid on table.		
McNair, John	Invalid pension	28	1	Petition	189	Invalid Pensions				Discharged; laid on table.		
McNair, Margaret	Compensation for Indian depredations.	23	2	Petition	40	Indian Affairs				Discharged; laid on table.		
McNair, Mathew	Payment for vessel impressed into United States service.	15	1	Petition	433	Claims				Discharged; laid on table.		
McNair, Mathew	Payment for vessel impressed into United States service.	16	1	Senate bill	444	Claims			S. 91			
McNair, Mathew	Payment for vessel impressed into United States service.	17	1	Senate bill	374	Claims	Mar. 25, 1822	With't amend.	S. 47	Passed	Passed	App'd May 7, 1822
McNally, Henry	Compensation for revolutionary services.	2	1	Petition	474					Referred to Secretary of War.		
McNamara, Darby	Invalid pension	4	1	Petition	439	Claims	May 7, 1796	Adverse		Leave to withdraw.		
McNamara, Darby	Invalid pension	6	2	Petition	733	Claims	Dec. 4, 1800	Adverse		Rejected.		

List of private claims presented to the House of Representatives of the United States from the 1st to the 31st Congress, inclusive—Continued.

Names of claimants.	Nature or object of the claim.	Congress.	Session.	How brought before the House of Reps.	Page of journal.	To what committee of the House referred.	No. or date of the report.	Nature of the report.	No. of the bill.	How disposed of by the House of Reps.	How disposed of by the Senate.	Date of the act of Congress, and remarks.
McNamer, O'Bryant	Land for disabilities received in the service of the United States.	28	1	Petit'n of Indiana legislature.	288	Public Lands	251	Adverse	......	Laid on table.		
McNatt, Jonathan	Invalid pension	5	3	Memorial	478	Claims	Mar. 2, 1799	Adverse	......	Laid on table.		
McNary, John	To be allowed to dispose of lands granted under Cherekee treaty.	17	1	Petition	234	Public Lands	....	....	......	Discharged; laid on table.		
McNary, John	To be allowed to dispose of lands gran ed under Cherokee treaty.	17	2	Petition	121	Public Lands	....	....	......	Discharged; leave to withdraw.		
McNaught, William	Payment for corn furnished troops in 1838.	26	1	Petition	338	Claims	688	Adverse	......	Laid on table.		
McNaught, William	Payment for corn furnished troops in 1838.	26	2	Petition	125	Claims.						
McNaught, William	Payment for corn furnished troops in 1838.	27	2	Petition	94	Claims.						
McNeal & Evans	(See Evans & McNeal)	14	1	....	284							
McNeal, Gabriel, and Peter Null.	For a change of land entry	15	1	Petition	179	Public Lands	Feb. 3, 1818	Adverse	......	Rejected.		
McNeal, Hugh	(See Lewis, Clark, and companions)	9	2	....	284							
McNeal, James	Invalid pension	13	3	Petition	740	Claims	Feb. 20, 1815	Favorable	303	Passed	Passed, with amendment.	App'd March 3, 1815
McNeal & Taylor	(See Taylor & McNeil.)	14	1	....	284							
McNeil, Daniel, by heirs of.	Commutation pay for revolutionary services.	22	1	Petition	288	Rev. Claims	309	Favorable	389	Referred to Committee Whole House.		
McNeil, Daniel, by heirs of.	Commutation pay for revolutionary services.	23	2	Petition	76	Rev. Claims	....	....	......	Discharged; leave to withdraw.		
McNeil, Daniel, by heirs of.	Commutation pay for revolutionary services.	24	1	Petition	102	Rev. Claims.						
McNeil, Daniel, by heirs of.	Commutation pay for revolutionary services.	25	2	Petition	48	Rev. Claims.						
McNeil, Daniel, by heirs of.	Commutation pay for revolutionary services.	26	1	Petition	166	Rev. Claims	240	Adverse	......	Laid on table.		
McNeil, John	Revolutionary pension	26	2	Senate bill	230	Invalid Pensions	Feb. 12, 1841	With't amend.	S 217	Referred to Committee Whole House.		
McNeil, Gen. John	Arrears of pension	28	1	Petition	333	Invalid Pensions.						
McNeil, Gen. John	Arrears of pension	28	2	Petition	337	Invalid Pensions.						
McNeil, Joseph	Compensation for property used by United States troops at New Orleans, war of 1812.	14	2	Petition	279	Claims	....	....	......	Discharged; leave to withdraw.		
McNeil, Joseph	Compensation for property used by United States troops at New Orleans, war of 1812.	15	1	Petition	72	Claims.						
McNeil, Joseph	Compensation for property used by United States troops at New Orleans, war of 1812.	15	2	Senate bill	316	Claims	....	....	S. 60			
McNeil, Joseph	Compensation for property used by United States troops at New Orleans, war of 1812.	16	1	Senate bill	269	Claims	Mar. 24, 1820	Adverse	47	Laid on table.		
McNeil, Joseph	Compensation for property used by Unit d States troops at New Orleans war of 1812.	16	2	Petition	19	Claims	Dec. 19, 1820	Report and bill.	174	Passed	Passed, with amendment.	App'd March 2, 182
McNeil, Neil	Revolutionary pension	24	1	Resolution	811	Rev. Pensions.						
McNeil, Neil	Revolutionary pension	24	2	Resolution	53	Rev. Pensions	133	Favorable; bill	863	Referred to Committee Whole House.		

List of private claims presented to the House of Representatives of the United States from the 1st to the 31st Congress, inclusive—Continued.

2—58

Names of claimants.	Nature or object of the claim.	Congress.	Session.	How brought before the House of Reps.	Page of journal.	To what committee of the House referred.	No. or date of the report.	Nature of the report.	No. of the bill.	How disposed of by the House of Reps.	How disposed of by the Senate.	Date of the act of Congress, and remarks.
McNeil, Neil	Revolutionary pension	25	2	Resolution	38	Rev. Pensions	154	Favorable; bill	179	Passed	Passed	App'd June 28, 1838
McNeil, Neil	Compensation for a horse taken from his father in the revolutionary war.	23	1	Petition	334	Rev. Claims.						
McNeil, Samuel	(See William Boyd, administrator and attorney of.)	26	1		182							
McNeil, Robert, heirs of.	Pension for revolutionary services.	30	1	Petition	723	Rev. Pensions	700	Adverse		Laid on table.		
McNeil, William, (N. Y.)	Compensation for flour taken for United States army.	3	1	Petition & report Sec. Treasury.	20, 78					Laid on table.		
McNeil, William and Archibald.	Remission of duties on hemp, &c.	3	2	Petition	275	Select	Feb. 9, 1795	Adverse		Laid on table.		
McNeil, William and Archibald.	Remission of duties on hemp, &c.	4	1	Petition	408	Com. and Manuf	Jan. 11, 1796	Adverse		Referred to Committee Whole House.		
McNeil, William Gibbs	Refunding amount paid for certain surveys.	26	1	House bill	230	Whole House	May 2, 1840	With amend.	8	Passed	Passed	App'd May 8, 1840
McNiff, Catharine	Indemnity for damages to property at Detroit during war of 1812.	15	2	Petition	33	Claims	Dec. 4, 1818	Adverse		Rejected.		
McNish, Alexander	Bounty land for revolutionary services.	15	1	Petition	217	Public Lands	Mar. 4, 1818	Adverse		Rejected.		
McNish, Alexander	Increase of pension	7	2	Petition	254	Claims	Jan. 11, 1803	Adverse		Rejected.		
McNish, Alexander	Increase of pension	17	2	Petition	87	Pens. & Rev. Cl'ms.	Jan. 31, 1823	Adverse		Laid on table.		
McNish, Alexander	Increase of pension	18	1	Petition	31	Pens. & Rev. Cl'ms.	Dec. 16, 1823	Adverse		Laid on table.		
McNish, Alexander	Increase of pension	18	2	Petition	86	Pens. & Rev. Cl'ms.	Jan. 18, 1825	By bill	279	Passed.		
McNish, Alexander	Increase of pension	19	1	Petition	57	Military Pensions	164	Adverse		Laid on table.		
McNitt, Alexander	Compensation for revolutionary services.	15	1	Petition	265	Pens. & Rev. Cl'ms.				Discharged; laid on table.		
McNulty, John	Invalid pension	13	3	Petition	468	Pens. & Rev. Cl'ms.	Jan. 27, 1815	Res. for leave to withdraw.		Resolution adopted.		
McNulty, John	Invalid pension	14	1	Petition	622	Pens. & Rev. Cl'ms.	April 11, 1816	Favorable	171	Passed	Passed, with amendment.	App'd April 30, 1816
McNutt, Alexander	Pension	19	2	House bill	85	Whole House	Feb. 3, 1827	With amend.	314	Passed	Passed	App'd March 3, 1827
McNutt, George	Compensation for revolutionary services.	16	1	Petition	42	Pens. & Rev. Cl'ms.				Discharged; laid on table.		
McNutt, Henry	(See William H. Bedford, agent.)	28	1		262							
McNutt, James	Arrears of pay for services in war of 1812.	31	1	Petition	629	Military Affairs				Discharged; laid on table.		
McPherran, James	Revolutionary pension	22	1	Petition	45	Rev. Claims				Disch'd; laid on table.		
McPherrin, Clark	Invalid pension	19	1	Senate bill	520	Military Pensions	May 9, 1826	With amend.	S. 1	Passed		App'd May 13, 1826
McPherson, Alex'r, widow of.	Revolutionary pension	26	1	Resolution	950	Rev. Pensions.						
McPherson, Alex'r, widow of.	Revolutionary pension	26	2	Petition and docs.	272	Rev. Pensions.						
McPherson, Ann	(See Daniel McPherson, estate of.)	26	1		182							
McPherson, Daniel, estate of.	Indemnity for French spoliations prior to 1800.	26	1	Memorial	182	Foreign Affairs	343	Favorable; bill	319	Referred to Committee Whole House.		
McPherson, Elias	(See Wm. McPherson and others.)	24	2		269							
McPherson, James	Confirmation of title to land	8	2	Petition	29	Claims	Dec. 12, 1804	Adverse		Rejected.		
McPherson, James, (Ohio.)	Compensation for expenses in supporting Indians while sub-agent, &c.	23	1	Petition	309	Indian Affairs				Discharged; laid on table.		
McPherson, James, (Ohio.)	Compensation for expenses in supporting Indians while sub agent, &c.	23	2	Petition	238	Claims.						

List of private claims presented to the House of Representatives of the United States form the 1st to the 31st Congress, inclusive—Continued.

Names of claimants.	Nature or object of the claim.	Congress.	Session.	How brought before the House of Reps.	Page of journal.	To what committee of the House referred.	No. or date of the report.	Nature of the report.	No. of the bill.	How disposed of by the House of Reps.	How disposed of by the Senate.	Date of the act of Congress, and remarks.
McPherson, James, (Ohio.)	Compensation for expenses in supporting Indians while sub-agent, &c.	24	1	....	93	Claims	194	Adverse	......	Laid on table.		
McPherson, James, (Ohio.)	Compensation for property destroyed in war of 1812.	14	2	Petition	448	....	....	....	......	Laid on table.		
McPherson, James, (Ohio.)	Compensation for property destroyed in war in 1812.	17	1	Petition	141	Claims	....	....	......	Discharged; laid on table.		
McPherson, James, (Ohio.)	Compensation for property destroyed in war of 1812.	17	2	Petition	40	Claims	....	....	......	Discharged; leave to withdraw.		
McPherson, James, (Ohio.)	Compensati n for property destroyed in war of 1812.	24	2	Documents	394	Claims	267	Adverse	......	Laid on table.		
McPherson, John........	Patent for lightning rods, &c.....	1	1	Petition	75	....	....	....	......	Laid on table.		
McPherson, Joseph S....	Equitable settlement of accounts, vouchers having been stolen.	18	1	Petition	43	Claims	Dec. 29, 1823	Adverse	......	Rejected.		
McPherson, Mark........	Revolutionary pension	19	1	Resolution	342	Military Pensions..	164	Adverse	......	Leave to withdraw.		
McPherson, Mark........	Revolutionary pension	19	2	Resolution	29	Military Pensions..	....	....	......	Discharged.		
McPherson, Mark, (Ky.).	Pension	19	2	Petition	36	Military Pensions..	....	....	......	Discharged.		
McPherson, Mary E.....	Arrears of pension............	23	2	Petition	102	Naval Affairs.....	129	Adverse	......	Laid on table.		
McPherson, Nancy......	(See Andrew Clark, deceased widow of.)	22	1	....	266							
McPherson, Rebecca.....	(See widow of Alexander McPherson.)	26	1	....	950							
McPherson, Stephen.....	(See Wm. McPherson and others.)	24	2	....	269							
McPherson, Wm., heirs of.	Depreciation pay for revolutionary services.	23	1	Petition	306	Rev. Claims......	Mar. 4, 1834	Adverse	......	Laid on table.		
McPherson, William, and others.	Pre-emption right to land on which they reside.	24	2	Petition	269	Public Lands.						
McPherson, William, and others.	Pre-emption right to land on which they reside.	25	2	Petition	95	Public Lands.						
McPherson, William, and others.	Pre-emption right to land on which they reside.	25	3	Petition	92	Public Lands	93	Adverse	......	Laid on table.		
McPherson, William.....	Invalid pension	27	3	Senate bill	413	Invalid Pensions...	Feb. 23, 1843	With't amend.	S. 135	Referred to Committee Whole House.		
McPherson, William.....	Invalid pension..............	28	1	Senate bill	697	Naval Affairs.....	April 20, 1844	With't amend.	S. 104	Passed..........	....	App'd June 17, 1844
McPike, John..........	Increase of pension	25	2	Resolution	78	Rev. Pensions....	....	....	......	Discharged; laid on table.		
McQueen, Robert	Reimbursement of costs, &c., on suit as postmaster Cheraw, S. Carolina.	21	1	Petition	52	P. Of. & P. Roads.	....	....	......	Discharged; laid on table.		
McQueen, William, surety of.	Release from judgment	31	1	Petition	502	Judiciary.						
McQueen, William, surety of.	Release from judgment	31	2	Petition	447	Judiciary	68	Adverse	......	Laid on table.		
McQuesten, Mathew P...	Compensation for services in war of 1812.	16	1	Resolution	351	Claims	April 7, 1820	Adverse	......	Laid on table.		
McQuie, Alexander......	(See John Glass)..............	21	1	....	70							
McQuie, William L	Refunding of over payment for land in Missouri.	22	1	Petition	134	Public Lands.....	....	....	......	Discharged; laid on table.		
McQuillan, Alexander....	Revolutionary pension..........	19	1	Resolution	445	Military Pensions..	May 5, 1826	Favorable; bill	119	Passed.		
McQuillan, Alexander....	Revolutionary pension..........	19	2	Petition	67	Military Pensions..	Dec. 22, 1826	By bill	315	Passed	Laid on table.	
McQuillan, Hugh	Indemnity for French spoliations prior to 1800.	26	1	Memorial	182	Foreign Affairs....	343	Favorable; bill	319	Referred to Committee Whole House.		
McQuilty, David	(See administrator of Wm. Head.	24	1	....	265							

List of private claims presented to the House of Representatives of the United States from the 1st to the 31st Congress, inclusive—Continued.

Names of claimants.	Nature or object of the claim.	Congress.	Session.	How brought before the House of Reps.	Page of journal.	To what committee of the House referred.	No. or date of the report.	Nature of the report.	No. of the bill.	How disposed of by the House of Reps.	How disposed of by the Senate.	Date of the act of Congress, and remarks.
McRea, Duncan	Increase of salary as postmaster Fayetteville, North Carolina.	14	2	Petition	184	P. Of. & P. Roads.				Discharged; laid on table.		
McRea, John	Compensation for arresting mail robber, and expenses in sending express to Charleston by order of the President.	30	1	Petition	524	P. Of. & P. Roads.	375	Adverse		Laid on table.		
McRea, Mary	(See widow of Colonel William McRea.)	23	2		276							
McRea, Col. William, widow of.	Compensation for services in revolutionary war.	23	2	Petition	276	Military Affairs.						
McRea, Col. William, widow of.	Compensation for services in revolutionary war.	29	1	Senate bill	1243	Military Affairs	Aug. 10, 1846	With't amend	S. 23	Referred to Committee Whole House.		
McRea, Col. William, widow of.	Compensation for services in revolutionary war.	29	2	Senate bill	430	Whole House			S. 13			
McRea, Col. William, widow of.	Compensation for services in revolutionary war.	30	1	Senate bill	433	Rev. Pensions	Mar. 30, 1848	Adverse	S. 22	Referred to Committee Whole House.		
McRea, Col. William, widow of.	Compensation for services in revolutionary war.	30	2	Senate bill	625	Whole House	Mar. 3, 1849	With't amend.	S. 22	Passed		App'd March 3, 1849
McRea, William, widow of	Renewal or extension of pension	31	1	Senate bill	774	Rev. Pensions	Aug. 1, 1850	With't amend.	S. 186	Referred to Committee Whole House.		
McReynolds, Joseph	Pension	21	1	Petition	294	Military Pensions				Disch'd, laid on table.		
McReynolds, Joseph	Pension	24	1	Petition	853	Invalid Pensions				Discharged; laid on table.		
McRoberts, James	Relative to a claim for an additional quantity of land.	24	1	Documents	257	Public Lands.						
McRoberts, James	Confirmation of title to land in Illinois.	16	2	Petition	20	Public Lands.						
McShane, Robert	Revolutionary pension	24	1	Res and docs	487	Rev. Pensions				Discharged; laid on table.		
McSherry, Richard	Compensation for extra services in Mexican war.	30	2	Petition	270	Naval Affairs.						
McSherry, Richard	Compensation for extra services in Mexican war.	31	1	Petition	236	Naval Affairs.						
McSigley, John	(See William Baker, N. Y.)	22	1		288		480					
McToksin, Jehoiakim	Compensation for services as interpreter.	1	2	Petition	160	Select	Mar. 3, 1790	Favorable		Referred to Committee Whole House.		See appropriation act, March 26, 1790.
McVey, Allen	For other lands in lieu of those heretofore granted.	23	2	Petition	167	Public Lands.						
McVickar, Archibald, executor of.	Compensation for gin and spirits furnished to the army of the revolution.	5	3	Petition	501					Laid on table.		
McVickar, Archibald, executor of.	Compensation for gin and spirit furnished to the army of the revolution.	6	1	Petition	542	Claims	April 1, 1800	Adverse		Rejected.		
McVickar, Archibald, executor of.	(See Isaac Lawrence, and others).	14	2						36			
McVicar, Duncan	Compensation for revolutionary services.	10	1	Petition	52	Claims				Discharged; referred to Com. Whole House.		
McVicar, John	Liquidation of a certificate of revolutionary debt.	4	1	Rep. of Secretary Treasury.	388	Claims	May 31, 1796	Adverse		Laid on table.		
McVicar, Nathan	(See Isaac Lawrence, and others).	14	2						36			
McVoy, Diego	For further time to establish claim to land in Mobile.	13	3	Petition	561	Public Lands				Discharged.		

List of private claims presented to the House of Representatives of the United States from the 1*st to the* 31*st Congress, inclusive*—Continued.

Names of claimants.	Nature or object of the claim.	Congress.	Session.	How brought before the House of Reps.	Page of journal.	To what committee of the House referred.	No. or date of the report.	Nature of the report.	No. of the bill.	How disposed of by the House of Reps.	How disposed of by the Senate.	Date of the act of Congress, and remarks.
McVoy, Diego	Confirmation of title to land in Mobile.	14	2	Petition	112	Public Lands	Jan. 18, 1817	Res. for leave to withdraw.		Resolution adopted.		
McVoy, Diego	Confirmation of title to land in Mobile.	15	1	Petition	115	Public Lands				Discharged; laid on table.		
McVoy, Diego	Confirmation of title to land in Mobile.	18	2	Petition	43	Public Lands.						
McVoy, Diego	Payment for cattle, &c., taken for use of United States.	15	1	Petition	243	Claims	Feb. 25, 1818	Adverse		Rejected.		
McWain, Josiah	Compensation for wood furnished United States troops at Sackett's harbor in 1816.	18	2	Petition	36	Claims	Dec. 27, 1824	Adverse		Laid on table.		
McWhorter, Aaron	Pension	20	1	Petition	440	Military Pensions				Discharged; laid on table.		
McWhorter, Aaron	Pension	20	2	Petition	74	Military Pensions				Discharged; laid on table.		
McWilliams, Alexander	Compensation for revolutionary services.	2	1	Petition	477					Referred to Secretary War.		
McWilliams, Clara	(See heirs of Joshua McWilliams)	29	2		75							
McWilliams, Clara	(See heirs of Joshua McWilliams)	31	2		36							
McWilliams, Clara	Indemnity for French spoliations prior to 1800.	31	2	Petition	37	Foreign Affairs.						
McWilliams, John, (N. H.)	Pension	26	1	Petition	198	Invalid Pensions	288	Adverse		Laid on table.		
McWilliams, John, (Va.)	Increase of pension	27	3	Petition	58	Rev. Pensions.						
McWilliams, Joshua, heirs of.	Satisfaction of military land warrant.	29	2	Petition	75	Public Lands.						
McWilliams, Joshua, heirs of.	Satisfaction of military land warrant.	30	1	Petition	117	Rev. Claims.						
McWilliams, Joshua, heirs of.	Compensation for revolutionary services	32	2	Petition	36	Rev. Claims.						
McWilliams, Peter	Pension for services in late war	27	3	Petition	251	Invalid Pensions	226	Adverse		Laid on table.		
McWilliams, William A.	(See William H. Hines, sureties of)	29	1		460							
McWilliams, William, widow of.	Arrears of pension	25	2	Petition	70	Rev. Pensions.						
McWilliams, William, widow of.	Arrears of pension	25	3	Petition	130	Rev. Pensions.						
McWilliams, William, administrator of widow of.	Arrears of pension	27	2	Petition	374	Rev. Pensions	784	Adverse		Laid on table.		
Meacham, James	Compensation for horse lost in the service of United States.	24	2	Resolution	98					Referred to 3d Auditor.		
Meacham, Simeon	Arrears of pension	23	1	Petition	54	Rev. Pensions	393	Favorable: bill	411	Referred to Committee Whole House.		
Meacham, Simeon	Arrears of pension	23	2	House bill	336	Whole House			411	Passed	Passed	App'd March 3, 1835
Meacham, Simeon	Arrears of pension	24	1	Petition	56	Invalid Pensions				Discharged; laid on table.		
Meacham, Simeon, widow of	Pension for services of her husband.	30	2	Petition	337	Rev. Pensions.						
Mead, Aaron B., & others.	Payment of claim against Ottowa Indians.	29	1	Petition	160	Indian Affairs	287	Adverse		Laid on table.		
Mead, Dorothy	(See Stephen Mead, widow of)	30	1	Petition	786	Rev. Pensions.						
Mead, Elizabeth	(See John Mead, widow of)	28	1		946							
Mead, Everard, heirs of	Commutation pay for revolutionary services.	22	1	Petition	51	Rev. Claims	504	Favorable; bil	610	Referred to Committee Whole House.		
Mead, Everard, heirs of	Commutation pay for revolutionary services.	23	1	Petition	43	Rev. Claims	54	Favorable; bill	62	Passed	Passed	App'd June 30, 1834

List of private claims presented to the House of Representatives of the United States from the 1st to the 31st Congress, inclusive—Continued.

Names of claimants.	Nature or object of the claim.	Congress.	Session.	How brought before the House of Reps.	Page of journal.	To what committee of the House referred.	No. or date of the report.	Nature of the report.	No. of the bill.	How disposed of by the House of Reps.	How disposed of by the Senate.	Date of the act of Congress, and remarks.
Mead, Everard, heirs of	Further compensation for revolutionary services.	25	1	Memorial	131					Laid on table.		
Mead, Everard, heirs of	Further compensation for revolutionary services.	25	2	Petition	72	Rev. Claims	406	Favorable; bill	417	Referred to Committee Whole House.		
Mead, Everard, heirs of	Further compensation for revolutionary services	25	2	Senate bill	700	Rev. Claims	950	Adverse	164	Laid on table.		
Mead, Everard, heirs of	Further compensation for revolutionary services.	25	3	House bill	378	Whole House			417			
Mead, Everard, heirs of	Further compensation for revolutionary services.	26	1	Petition	165	Rev. Claims	436	Adverse		Laid on table.		
Mead, Everard, heirs of	Further compensation for revolutionary services.	27	2	Petition	61	Rev. Claims	392	Adverse		Laid on table.		
Mead, Everard, heirs of	Further compensation for revolutionary services.	31	1	Petition	715	Rev. Claims.						
Mead, Hewett	(See William Baker, New York)	22	1		288		480					
Mead, Hodijah	(See Peyton Randolph, administrator of)	26	1		175							
Mead, Hugh K	Share of proceeds of sale of vessel for breach of the slave trade law	19	1	Petition	225	Naval Affairs.						
Mead, Hugh K	Share of proceeds of sale of vessel for breach of the slave trade law.	29	1	Memorial	625	Claims	730	Adverse		Laid on table.		
Mead, Israel	Further compensation for revolutionary services.	20	1	Petition	43	Rev. Claims				Discharged; laid on table.		
Mead, Israel	Further compensation for revolutionary services.	21	2	Petition	159	Military Pensions.						
Mead, Jacob, (N. Y.)	Invalid pension	6	1	Petition	557	Claims	Feb. 3, 1800	Adverse		Rejected.		
Mead, James, 2d	Refunding amount paid for medical service while in public service.	11	1	Petition	38	Claims.						
Mead, James, (D. C.)	Compensation for property destroyed by the enemy in war of 1812.	29	1	Memorial	275	Claims	401	Adverse		Laid on table.		
Mead, Jesse	Revolutionary pension	16	2	Petition	65	Rev. Pensions	Dec. 15, 1821	Adverse		Rejected.		
Mead, Jesse, daughter of	Revolutionary pension for services of her father.	28	1	Petition	946	Rev. Pensions.						
Mead, John, widow of	Compensat'n for losses and services in revolutionary war.	28	1	Petition	946	Rev. Claims.						
Mead, Joseph	Pension	23	1	Petition	141	Invalid Pensions	404	Favorable; bill	422	Referred to Committee Whole House.		
Mead, Joseph	Pension	23	2	House bill	336	Whole House			422	Passed	Passed	App'd March 3, 1835
Meads, Joseph	(See John Ross, administrator of)	26	1		182							
Mead, Marston	Compensat'n for property destroyed in 1817, by order of Gen. Andrew Jackson.	22	1	Petition	264	Indian Affairs.						
Mead, Marston	Compensat'n for property destroyed in 1817, by order of Gen. Andrew Jackson.	23	1	Petition	50	Indian Affairs	144	Adverse		Laid on table.		
Mead, Rebecca	(See Jesse Mead, daughter of)	28	1	Petition	946							
Mead, Richard W.	Payment of claim against the Spanish government.	16	2	Memorial	267	Foreign Affairs.						
Mead, Richard W.	Payment of claim against the Spanish government.	18	2	Memorial	123	Not referred.						
Mead, Richard W.	Payment of claim against the Spanish government.	19	1	Memorial	293	Foreign Affairs	174	Favorable; bill	223	Referred to Committee Whole House.		

List of private claims presented to the House of Representatives of the United States from the 1st to the 31st Congress, inclusive—Continued.

Names of claimants.	Nature or object of the claim.	Congress.	Session.	How brought before the House of Reps.	Page of journal.	To what committee of the House referred.	No. or date of the report.	Nature of the report.	No. of the bill.	How disposed of by the House of Reps.	How disposed of by the Senate.	Date of the act of Congress, and remarks.
Mead, Richard W.	Payment of claim against the Spanish government.	20	1	Memorial	46	Foreign Affairs	58	Favorable; bill	51	Rejected.		
Mead, Richard W., heirs of	Payment of claim against the Spanish government.	20	2	Memorial	44	Foreign Affairs	.....	.....	.....	Discharged; laid on table.		
Mead, Richard W., heirs of	Payment of claim against the Spanish government.	21	1	Memorial	75	Foreign Affairs	Feb. 19, 1830	Favorable; bill	263	Referred to Committee Whole House.		
Mead, Richard W., heirs of	Payment of claim against the Spanish government.	22	1	Memorial	144	Foreign Affairs	316	Favorable; bill	366	Referred to Committee Whole House.		
Mead, Richard W., heirs of	Payment of claim against the Spanish government.	23	1	Memorial	37	Foreign Affairs	167	Favorable; bill	183	Referred to Committee Whole House.		
Mead, Richard W., heirs of	Payment of claim against the Spanish government.	23	2	House bill	82	Whole House	.....	.....	183			
Mead, Richard W., heirs of	Payment of claim against the Spanish government.	24	1	Senate bill	1107	.....	.....	.....	165			
Mead, Richard W., heirs of	Payment of claim against the Spanish government.	24	2	Senate bill	438	.....	.....	.....	19	Laid on table.		
Mead, Richard W., heirs of	Payment of claim against the Spanish government.	25	2	Senate bill	303	Foreign Affairs	June 27, 1838	With't amend.	31	Referred to Committee Whole House.		
Mead, Richard W., heirs of	Payment of claim against the Spanish government.	25	3	Memorial	456	Foreign Affairs	.....	.....	.....	Discharged; laid on table.		
Mead, Richard W., heirs of	Payment of claim against the Spanish government.	26	1	Petition	182	Military Affairs.						
Mead, Richard W., heirs of	Payment of claim against the Spanish government.	26	2	Petition	135, 86	Foreign Affairs.						
Mead, Richard W., heirs of	Payment of claim against the Spanish government.	27	2	Petition	63	Foreign Affairs	457	Favorable; bill	306	Referred to Committee Whole House.		
Mead, Richard W., heirs of	Payment of claim against the Spanish government.	28	1	Petition	353	Foreign Affairs	April 17, 1844	By bill	340	Referred to Committee Whole House.		
Mead, Richard W., heirs of	Payment of claim against the Spanish government.	29	1	Memorial	115	Foreign Affairs	April 6, 1846	Favorable; bill	381	Referred to Committee Whole House.		
Mead, Richard W., heirs of	Payment of claim against the Spanish government.	30	1	Petition	208	Foreign Affairs	94	Favorable; bill	67	Laid on table.		
Mead, Richard W., heirs of	Payment of claim against the Spanish government.	31	1	Petition	323	Foreign Affairs.						
Mead, Richard W., representatives of.	(See Andrew Leitch, heirs of)	26	1	.....	946							
Mead, Samuel	Revolutionary pension	23	2	Documents	347	Rev. Pensions	.....	.....	.....	Discharged; laid on table.		
Mead, Stephen, widow of.	Pension	30	1	Petition	786	Rev. Pensions.						
Mead, Tilley	Invalid pension	3	2	Petition and rep't Sec. of War.	337	Claims	Feb. 28, 1795	Favorable; bill	130	Passed	Postponed.	
Mead, Tilley	Invalid pension	4	1	Petition and rep't Sec. of War.	447	Claims	Feb. 18, 1796	Favorable; bill	156	Passed	Passed	App'd April 20, 1796
Mead, Walter, and others.	(See Thompson Price)	26	1	.....	704							
Mead, William	Revolutionary pension	25	3	Resolution	166	Rev. Pensions	.....	.....	.....	Discharged; laid on table.		
Mead, William	Revolutionary pension	26	1	Petition	174	Rev. Pensions	.....	.....	.....	Discharged; laid on table.		
Mead, William	Revolutionary pension	26	2	Petition	78	Rev. Pensions.						
Mead, Hugh	Invalid pension	5	2	Petition	203	Claims	April 17, 1798	Adverse	.....	Referred to Committee Whole House.		
Means, Hugh	Invalid pension	5	3	Petition	432	Whole House.						
Means, Hugh	Invalid pension	10	1	Petition	120	Whole House.						

List of private claims presented to the House of Representatives of the United States from the 1st to the 31st Congress, inclusive—Continued.

Names of claimants.	Nature or object of the claim.	Congress.	Session.	How brought before the House of Reps.	Page of journal.	To what committee of the House referred.	No. or date of the report.	Nature of the report.	No. of the bill.	How disposed of by the House of Reps.	How disposed of by the Senate.	Date of the act of Congress, and remarks.
Means, Hugh, heirs of	Commutation pay for revolutionary services.	24	2	Resolution	77	Rev. Claims.						
Means, Hugh, heirs of	Commutation pay for revolutionary services.	25	2	Petition	658	Rev. Claims.						
Means, Hugh, heirs of	Commutation pay for revolutionary services.	25	3	Petition	189	Rev. Claims.						
Means, Hugh, heirs of	Commutation pay for revolutionary services.	26	1	Petition	166	Rev. Claims.						
Means, Isaac, and other	Refunding proceeds of the sale of schooner Elizabeth wrongfully condemned and sold.	24	1	Senate bill	990	Commerce	June 30, 1836	With't amend.	184	Passed	Passed	App'd July 2, 1836
Means, John, (Ky.)	Revolutionary pension	24	2	Petition	49	Rev. Pensions				Discharged; laid on table.		
Mean, J. O	(See James Tilton and others)	30	1		328				S. 118			
Means, Robert	Pension	20	1	Petition	143	Military Pensions.						
Means, Robert	Pension	21	1	Petition	67	Military Pensions.						
Meany, John, assignee of	Indemnity for French spoliations prior to 1800.	26	1	Memorial	182	Foreign Affairs	343	Favorable; bill	319	Referred to Committee Whole House.		
Mears, Bartholomew	Bounty land as seaman in revolutionary war.	11	2	Petition	179	Public Lands	Jan. 26, 1810	Adverse		Rejected.		
Mears, Samuel, jr	Invalid pension	11	3	Petition	604	Claims	Mar. 1, 1811	Favorable; bill	218	Passed	Passed, with amendment.	App'd March 3, 1811
Mebane, John B	Authority to collect arrears of direct tax in North Carolina.	16	2	Resolution	186	Judiciary	Feb. 3, 1820	Favorable; bill	246	Referred to Committee Whole House.		
Mebane, John B., executor of.	Authority to collect arrears of direct tax in North Carolina.	18	1	Petition	61	Ways and Means	Jan. 9, 1824	Favorable; bill	49	Passed	Passed	App'd April 22, 1824
Mebane, John B., executor of.	(An amendatory act)	18	1	Resolution	439	Ways and Means	April 30, 1824	Favorable; bill	214	Passed	Passed	App'd May 19, 1824
Mechan & Ballentine	(See Ballentine & Mechan)	23	1		589							
Mechlin, Alexander H	Compensation for extra services	30	1	Petition	457	Claims	592	Adverse		Laid on table.		
Mechling, Hyram	Invalid pension	28	2	Petition	435	Invalid Pensions.						
Medearis, John	Liquidation of claims for services as quartermaster in revolutionary war.	5	2	Petition	145	Claims	Jan. 12, 1798	Adverse		Rejected.		
Medearis, John	Liquidation of claims for services as quartermaster in revolutionary war.	9	1	Petition	192					Referred to Committee Whole House on bill No. 108.		
Medearis, John	Liquidation of claims for services as quartermaster in revolutionary war.	9	2	Petition	503	Select.						
Medina, Juan	Confirmation of Spanish land claim	22	1	Petition	64	Priv. Land Claims.	Dec. 27, 1831	Favorable; bill	125	Passed	Passed	App'd June 25, 1832
Medina, Lorenzo	Confirmation of Spanish land claim.	22	1	Petition	64	Priv. Land Claims.	Dec. 27, 1831	Favorable; bill	125	Passed	Passed	App'd June 25, 1832
Medlock, Nathaniel	Increase of pension	24	2	Petition	218	Rev. Pensions				Discharged; laid on table.		
Meeder, Edward S	Arrears of pension	20	2	Petition	229	Military Pensions.				Discharged; laid on table.		
Meeder, Edward S	Arrears of pension	21	1	Petition	260	Invalid Pensions	April 24, 1830	Adverse		Laid on table.		
Meeder, Edward S	Arrears of pension	22	1	Senate bill	119	Invalid Pensions	Jan. 10, 1832	With't amend.	15	Passed	Passed	App'd July 9, 1832
Meek, Abner	Pension	18	2	Petition	159	Pens. & Rev. Cl'ms.				Discharged; leave to withdraw.		

List of private claims presented to the House of Representatives of the United States from the 1st to the 31st Congress, inclusive—Continued.

Names of claimants.	Nature or object of the claim.	Congress.	Session.	How brought before the House of Reps.	Page of journal.	To what committee of the House referred.	No. or date of the report.	Nature of the report.	No. of the bill.	How disposed of by the House of Reps.	How disposed of by the Senate.	Date of the act of Congress, and remarks.
Meek, Elijah	Invalid pension	13	2	Petition	354	Pens. & Rev. Cl'ms.	Mar. 28, 1814	Rep. not found	......	Referred to Committee Whole House.		
Meek John	(See William H. Bedford, agent)	28	1	....	262							
Meek, Robert, mother of	Relief for her son, killed in Black Hawk war.	29	1	Petition	648	Invalid Pensions	831	Adverse	......	Laid on table.		
Meek, William E	(See Zebulon M. Pike and companions.)	10	1	....	189							
Meek, William E	To be allowed his pay and rations while he was a prisoner.	17	1	Petition	52	Military Affairs	Jan. 14, 1822	Favorable; bill	36	Passed	Passed	App'd April 26, 1822
Meeker, Catharine	(See Robert Meeker, widow of.)	27	3	....	102							
Meeker, Hyram L	Compensation for saving wrecked goods, and for patent for raising stranded vessels.	25	2	Petition	656	Commerce	....	....	......	Discharged; laid on table.		
Meeker, Hyram L	Compensation for saving wrecked goods, and for patent for raising stranded vessels.	25	3	Petition	226	Commerce	....	....	......	Discharged; laid on table.		
Meeker, Hyram L	Compensation for saving wrecked goods, and for patent for raising stranded vessels.	26	1	Petition	176, 327	Commerce.						
Meeker, Hyram L	Compensation for saving wrecked goods, and for patent for raising stranded vessels.	27	1	Petition	56	Commerce.						
Meeker, Jonathan, administrator of.	Arrears of pension	29	1	Petition	648	Rev. Pensions.						
Meeker, Moses, and others.	(See David G. Bates)	30	2	....	124							
Meeker, Robert, widow of.	Revolutionary pension	27	3	Petition	102	Rev. Pensions.						
Meeker, Samuel	Payment for supplies furnished United States army.	21	1	Petition	99	Claims	244	Adverse	......	Laid on table.		
Meeker, Samuel	Payment for supplies furnished United States army.	22	1	Petition	414	Claims	Mar. 12, 1832	Adverse	.....	Laid on table.		
Meetkerke, William	Release from payment of money due from him as collector of the internal revenue.	7	1	Petition	86	Claims	April 3, 1802	Rep. and res. to postpone.	......	Resolution adopted.		
Meetkerke, William	Release from payment of money due from him as collector of the internal revenue.	7	2	Petition	297	Claims	Feb. 26, 1803	Rep. and res. to postpone.	......	Resolution adopted.		
Meetkerke, William	Release from payment of money due from him as collector of the internal revenue.	8	1	Petition	485	Claims	Feb. 10, 1804	Adverse	......	Discharged; leave to withdraw.		
Megee, William F	Remission of duties on tea destroyed by fire.	6	2	House bill	825	Whole House	Feb. 28, 1801	With't amend.	320	Passed	Passed	App'd March 3, 1801
Megowan, James T	Payment for horse lost in Mexican war.	30	1	Petition	146	Claims	237	Adverse	......	Laid on table.		
Megowan, S. W	Invalid pension	31	1	Petition	1073	Invalid Pensions.						
Megowan, Thomas B	Compensation for keeping a United States prisoner.	24	1	Petition	157	Judiciary.						
Meiere, Adolphus, & Co.	Refunding duties on goods destroyed by fire.	31	1	Petition	433	Commerce	159	Favorable; bill	177	Referred to Committee Whole House.		
Meiere, Adolphus & Co.	Refunding duties on goods destroyed by fire.	31	2	Bill of last sess.	103	Whole House	Jan. 3, 1851	With't amend.	177	Passed.		
Meigs, John	Restoration of pension	17	2	Petition	91	....	....	....	......	Referred to Committee Whole House on bill No. 195.		

List of private claims presented to the House of Representatives of the United States from the 1st to the 31st Congress, inclusive—Continued.

Names of claimants.	Nature or object of the claim.	Congress.	Session.	How brought before the House of Reps.	Page of journal.	To what committee of the House referred.	No. or date of the report.	Nature of the report.	No. of the bill.	How disposed of by the House of Reps.	How disposed of by the Senate.	Date of the act of Congress, and remarks.
Meigs & Reed	Payment of soldiers certificates	15	2	Petition	144	Military Affairs	Feb. 9, 1819	Favorable; bill	315	Passed	Passed	App'd March 3, 1819
Meigs, Return J. jr	For balance of salary due as judge.	8	1	Memorial	677					Laid on table.		
Miegs, Return, J. jr	For balance of salary due as judge.	8	2	Petition	29	Claims	Feb. 18, 1805	Favorable		Referred to Committee Whole House.		
Meigs, Return, J. jr	For balance of salary due as judge.	9	1	Memorial	198	Claims	Dec. 20, 1805	Favorable	83	Passed	Passed	App'd Feb. 21, 1806
Meigs, Return, J. jr	For additional allowance as a witness.	10	1	Petition	23	Claims.						
Meigs, Return, J. jr	For additional allowance as a witness.	10	2	Petition	363	Select	Dec. 27, 1808	Favorable; bill	128	Referred to Committee Whole House.		
Meigs, Return, J. jr	For additional allowance as a witness.	11	2	Petition	197	Select	Mar. 14, 1810	Favorable; bill	101	Referred to Committee Whole House.		
Meigs, Return, J. jr	For additional allowance as a witness.	11	3	Petition	454	Select	Dec. 24, 1810	Favorable; bill	157	Postponed.		
Meigs, Return, J. jr	For additional allowance as a witness.	12	1	Petition	67	Select.						
Melcher, William, heirs of.	Indemnity for French Spoliations prior to 1800.	31	1	Petition	197	Foreign Affairs	355	Favorable; bill	318	Referred to Committee Whole House.		
Melchior, Isaac, heirs of	Release from indemnity bond	16	1	Petition	39, 160	Ways and Means	Jan. 20, 1822	Favorable; bill	57	Passed	Passed	App'd May 4, 1820
Melchor, William, administrator of.	Indemnity for French Spoliations prior to 1800.	26	1	Memorial	182	Foreign Affairs	343	Favorable; bill	319	Referred to Committee Whole House.		
Meldrum, George, administrator of.	Indemnity for property destroyed in war of 1812.	16	1	Petition	365	Claims				Discharged; laid on table.		
Meldrum, George, administrator of.	Indemnity for property destroyed in war of 1812.	16	2	Petition	142	Claims	35	Adverse		Leave to withdraw.		
Meldrum, George, administrator of.	Indemnity for property destroyed in war of 1812.	18	1	Petition	237	Claims	Feb. 25, 1824	Adverse		Laid on table.		
Meldrum, John	(See George Meldrum, administrator of.)	16	1		365							
Melick and Burgess, and others.	Release from certain forfeitures	12	2	Petition	660	Whole House		General bill	239	Rejected.		
Melick and Burgess, and others.	Release from certain forfeitures	12	2	Senate bill	705	Ways and Means	Feb. 25, 1813	With't amend.	61	Passed	Passed	App'd Feb. 27, 1813
Mellen, Aaron	Invalid pension	26	1	Resolution	1012	Invalid Pensions				Discharged; leave to withdraw.		
Mellen, David, (N. Y.)	Compensation for revolutionary services	24	2	Petition	307	Rev. Claims.						
Mellen, David, (N. Y.)	Pension	25	2	Petition	117	Rev. Claims	570	Favorable; bill	560	Passed	Adverse.	
Mellen, David, (N. Y.)	Revolutionary pension	25	3	Petition	88	Rev. Pensions	146	Favorable; bill	1015	Passed	Adverse.	
Mellen, David, (N. Y.)	Revolutionary pension	26	1	Petition	171	Rev. Pensions	152	Favorable; bill	162	Passed	Indef. postp'd.	
Mellen, David, (N. Y.)	Revolutionary pension	27	2	Petition	268	Rev. Pensions	784	Adverse		Laid on table.		
Mellen, David, (N. Y.)	Revolutionary pension	28	1	Petition	60	Rev. Pensions				Discharged; laid on table.		
Mellen, Gilbert	Revolutionary pension	23	2	Petition	389	Rev. Pensions.						
Mellen, Peggy	(See Alford Stebbins, mother of)	16	2		88							
Mellen, Richard	Invalid pension	10	2	Rep. of Secretary War.	480	Claims	Jan. 30, 1809	Favorable; bill	158	Passed	Passed, with amendment.	App'd March 3, 1809
Mellon, Charles, widow of.	Payment due as captain in Seminole war, Florida.	25	2	Petition	327	Military Affairs	Feb. 17, 1838	Adverse		Laid on table.		
Mellon, Charles, widow of.	Continuation of pension	30	1	Petition	280	Invalid Pensions	447	Favorable; bill	378	Passed.		
Mellon, Charles, widow of	Continuation of pension	30	2	House bill	143	Whole House	Dec. 22, 1848	With't amend.	378	Passed	Passed	App'd Jan. 8, 1849
Mellon, Elizabeth	(See Charles Mellon, widow of).	25	2		327							
Mellon, John	(See Casper B. Cooke and others.	30	1	Petition	272							

2—59

List of private claims presented to the House of Representatives of the United States from the 1st to the 31st Congress, inclusive—Continued.

Names of claimants.	Nature or object of the claim.	Congress.	Session.	How brought before the House of Reps.	Page of journal.	To what committee of the House referred.	No. or date of the report.	Nature of the report.	No. of the bill.	How disposed of by the House of Reps.	How disposed of by the Senate.	Date of the act of Congress, and remarks.
Mellon, Sasanna	Continuation of pension	26	2	Petition	122	Rev. Pensions.						
Mellers, Henry	Pension	20	1	Petition	56	Military Affairs				Discharged; laid on table.		
Mellus, William	Compensation for invention to prevent decay of ships.	18	2	Petition	80	Naval Affairs				Discharged; leave to withdraw.		
Mellus, William	Compensation for invention to prevent decay of ships.	19	1	Petition	176	Naval Affairs	Feb. 7, 1826	Adverse		Leave to withdraw.		
Mellus, William	Compensation for invention to prevent decay of ships.	25	3	Petition	209	Patents				Discharged; laid on table.		
Melone, John, (Tenn.)	Allowance for undrawn rations and clothing while a soldier in United States army.	20	1	Petition	360	Claims	May 5, 1828	Adverse		Laid on table.		
Melone, William	(See Joshua W. Prout, administrator of.)	18	2		284				S. 41			
Melton, Jacob, widow of	Continuation of pension	15	2	Petition	178	Military Affairs.						
Melton, Mildred	(See Jacob Melton, widow of)	15	2		178							
Melton, Colonel William	Compensation for services	21	1	Petition	60	Military Affairs				Discharged; leave to withdraw.		
Melville, David	Refunding expenses incurred a weigher and gauger at Newport, Rhode Island.	24	2	Petition	346	Claims	248	Rep. and res. to refer to Sec. of Treasury.		Report adopted.		
Melville, David	Refunding expenses incurred as weigher and gauger at Newport, Rhode Island.	31	1	Petition	306	Claims				Discharged; laid on table.		
Melville, David	(See Benjamin Fry, administrator of.)	26	2		85							
Melvin, Jonah	(See David Rogers, heirs of.)	26	1		918							
Melvin, Josiah	(See David Rogers, heirs of)	25	3		283							
Menan, Patrick	Bounty land	30	1	Petition	146	Claims	237	Adverse		Laid on table.		
Menan, Patrick	Bounty land	30	2	Petition	181					Leave to withdraw.		
Menard, Joseph	Grant of land for revolutionary services of his father.	25	2	Petition	48	Rev. Claims				Discharged; laid on table.		
Menard, Joseph	Grant of land for revolutionary services of his father.	26	1	Petition	166	Rev. Claims.						
Menard, Joseph	Grant of land for revolutionary services of his father.	26	2	Petition	77	Rev. Claims.						
Menard, Medard, and Nathan Smith.	Additional compensation as inspector of customs at Galveston.	31	1	Petition	425	Claims.						
Menard, Pierre	Reimbursement of money, with interest, advanced in revolutionary war.	23	1	Senate bill	846	Rev. Claims			S. 138			
Menard, Pierre	Reimbursement of money, with interest, advanced in revolutionary war.	25	2	Senate bill	1169	Rev. Claims			S. 128			
Menard, Pierre	Reimbursement of money, with interest, advanced in revolutionary war.	25	3	Senate bill	338	Rev. Claims	Feb. 16, 1839	Adverse	S. 4	Referred to Committee Whole House.		
Menard, Pierre	Reimbursement of money, with interest, advanced in revolutionary war.	26	1	Senate bill	811	Rev. Claims	519	Adverse	S. 39	Referred to Committee Whole House.		
Menard, Pierre	Reimbursement of money, with interest, advanced in revolutionary war.	28	1	Bill on leave	268	Rev. Claims			83			

List of private claims presented to the House of Representatives of the United States from the 1st to the 31st Congress, inclusive—Continued.

Names of claimants.	Nature or object of the claim.	Congress.	Session.	How brought before the House of Reps.	Page of journal.	To what committee of the House referred.	No. or date of the report.	Nature of the report.	No. of the bill.	How disposed of by the House of Reps.	How disposed of by the Senate.	Date of the act of Congress, and remarks.
Menard, Pierre	Reimbursement of money, with interest, advanced in revolutionary war.	30	1	Petition	69	Claims	343	Favorable; bill	324	Referred to Committee Whole House.		
Menard, Pierre	Reimbursement of money, with interest, advanced in revolutionary war.	31	1	Bill on leave	474	Rev. Claims	179	With't amend	45	Referred to Committee Whole House.		
Menard, Pierre	(See surety of Felix St. Vrain)	25	2		426							
Menary, John	Payment for horse impressed into United States service.	21	2	Resolution	156	Claims	38	Favorable; bill	557	Referred to Committee Whole House.		
Menary, John	Payment for horse impressed into United States service.	22	1	Resolution	26	Claims	Dec. 19, 1831	Favorable; bill	34	Passed	Passed	App'd Mar. 31, 1832
Menaugh, Hugh	(See Zebulon M. Pike and companions.)	10	1		189							
Mendenhall, William	Payment for two horses lost in United States service.	18	2	Resolution	93	Claims				Discharged; leave to withdraw.		
Mendenhall, William	Payment for two horses lost in United States service.	19	1	Resolution	205	Claims	99	Favorable; bill	134	Passed.		
Mendenhall, William	Payment for two horses lost in United States service.	19	2	Resolution	31	Claims	Dec. 12, 1826	Favorable; bill	283	Passed	Passed	App'd March 2, 1827
Meneghetty, Anthony C.	Register for sloop Sarah	25	3	Petition	212	Commerce	Jan. 12, 1839	By bill	1030	Passed	Passed	App'd March 2, 1839
Meneles, Anthony	Payment for clothing and other property lost by the capture of the frigate Philadelphia.	24	1	Petition	273	Naval Affairs.						
Meneles, Anthony	Payment for clothing and other property lost by the capture of the frigate Philadelphia.	24	2	Petition	85	Naval Affairs	27	Adverse		Laid on table.		
Meneles, Anthony	Payment for clothing and other property lost by the capture of the frigate Philadelphia.	25	2	Petition	723	Naval Affairs				Discharged; laid on table.		
Meneses, Antonio, successor of.	Confirmation of title to land	22	1	Petition	64	Priv. Land Claims.	Dec. 27, 1831	Favorable; bill	125	Passed	Passed	App'd June 25, 1832
Mennessier, Francis	Extension of time for payment for certain lands.	9	1	Petition	206	Public Lands	Feb. 3, 1806	Adverse		Rejected.		
Mennick, Joseph B.	(See assignees of William and Anthony Buckley.)	12	1		174							
Mennie, James or Joseph	Payment for improvements of public lands taken for public use.	22	2	Petition	138	Claims	39	Adverse		Laid on table.		
Mennie, or Minnie, James, assignee of.	Pre emption right to land	24	1	Petition	751	Priv. Land Claims.						
Mennie, or Minnie, James, assignee of.	Pre-eptimon right to land	24	2	Petition	49	Priv. Land Claims.	95	Favorable; bill	841	Referred to Committee Whole House.		
Mennie, or Minnie, James, assignee of.	Pre-emption right to land	25	2	Petition	43	Priv. Land Claims.	Jan. 10, 1838	Favorable; bill	377	Recommitted.		
Mennie, or Minnie, James, assignee of.	Pre-emption right to land	25	3	Petition	92	Priv. Land Claims.	283	Adverse		Laid on table.		
Mennie, or Minnie, James, assignee of.	Pre-emption right to land	26	1	Petition	827	Priv. Land Claims.						
Menter, Anthony M	(See Anthony M. Minter)	21	1		172							
Mentges, Francis	Extra compensation for military services.	1	2	Petition	210	Select	July 14, 1790	Favorable; jt. resolution.		Passed	Rejected.	
Mentges, Francis	Extra compensation for military services.	3	2	Petition	311	Claims.						

List of private claims presented to the House of Representatives of the United States from the 1st to the 31st Congress, inclusive—Continued.

Names of claimants.	Nature or object of the claim.	Congress.	Session.	How brought before the House of Reps.	Page of journal.	To what committee of the House referred.	No. or date of the report.	Nature of the report.	No. of the bill.	How disposed of by the House of Reps.	How disposed of by the Senate.	Date of the act of Congress, and remarks.
Mentges, Francis	Extra compensation for military services.	4	1	Petition	373	Claims	Jan. 6, 1796	Adverse	......	Recommitted.		
Mentges, Francis	Extra compensation for military services.	4	2	Petition	634	Claims	Jan. 2, 1797	Adverse.				
Mentges, Francis	For balance due as agent for erecting fortification.	7	2	Petition	271	Claims	Jan. 19, 1803	Adverse	......	Rejected.		
Mentges, Francis	For balance due as agent for erecting fortification.	8	1	Petition	482	Claims	Dec. 19, 1803	Adverse	......	Rejected.		
Mentges, Francis	For balance due as agent for erecting fortification.	8	2	Petition	96	Claims	Feb. 16, 1805	Adverse; leave to withdraw.	......	Referred to Committee Whole House.		
Mercer, Hugh	Annuity for services of his father.	2	2	Senate bill	720	Whole House	Feb. 28, 1793	With't amend.	45	Passed	Passed	App'd March 2, 1793
Mercer, Joshua	Pension	14	1	Petition	391	Pens. & Rev. Cl'ms.	April 11, 1816	Favorable; bill	171	Passed	Passed, with amendment.	App'd April 30, 1816
Mercer, Wilson, (Miss.)	Confirmation of title to land in Michigan.	10	2	Petition	347	Public Lands.						
Mercereau, John, sen	Pension	16	1	Petition	32	Pens. & Rev. Cl'ms.	Jan. 15, 1820	Adverse	......	Rejected.		
Merchand, Louis	(See Frederick De Laport, administrator of.)	23	1	....	637							
Merchant, George	Allowance of certain credits in the settlement of his accounts.	16	2	Petition	270	....	....	....	......	Referred to Secretary of War.		
Merchant, George	Allowance of certain credits in the settlement of his accounts.	17	2	Rep. of Secretary War.	191	Claims	....	....	......	Discharged; leave to withdraw.		
Merchant, George	Allowance of certain credits in the settlement of his accounts.	19	1	Petition	131	Claims	146	Favorable; bill	186	Passed.		
Merchant, Gurdon, widow of.	Continuation of pension	27	2	Petition	614	Rev. Pensions	784	Adverse	......	Laid on table.		
Merchant, Hannah	(See Gurden Merchant, widow of.)	27	2	....	614							
Merchant, Joseph	Revolutionary pension	31	1	Petition	383	Rev. Pensions	262	Adverse.	......	Laid on table.		
Mercier, John D.	(See Canadian refugees.)	4	2	....	614							
Mercier, Peter, (Penn.)	Settlement of acceptances under contract with the government.	7	1	Petition	76	Claims	Mar. 18, 1802	Adverse	......	Rejected.		
Meredith, David	(See George & J. Gilbert, sureties of.)	7	1	....	29							
Meredith, John	(See Nicholas Currill, heirs of.)	23	1	....	121							
Meredith, Jonathan	(See George & J. Gilbert, sureties of.)	7	1	....	29							
Meredith, Jonathan	(See William Taylor, trustees of.)	26	1	....	182							
Meredith, Sarah	(See Ezekiel Griffin, late widow of.)	11	2	....	197							
Meredith, Thomas H. executors of.	Benefit of acts in relation to public lands.	19	1	Petition	226	Public Lands.	....	....	......	Referred to Committee Whole House on bill No. 32.	....	See act May 4, 1826
Meredith, William, (Ky.)	Compensation for revolutionary services	21	1	Petition	105	Rev. Claims	Feb. 19, 1828	Adverse	......	Laid on table.		
Meredith, William, heirs of.	Compensation for revolutionary services.	27	3	Petition	109	Rev. Claims	245	Adverse	......	Laid on table.		
Meric, George	Relief for illegal seizure and sale of vessel and cargo by the authorities of St. Domingo.	18	1	Memorial	254	Foroign Affairs.	Mar. 5, 1824	Adverse	......	Leave to withdraw.		
Meriwether, James	Commutation pay for revolutionary services.	1	2	Petition and rep't Sec. of War.	168	....	....	....	......	Laid on table.		

List of private claims presented to the House of Representatives of the United States from the 1st to the 31st Congress, inclusive—Continued.

Names of claimants.	Nature or object of the claim.	Congress.	Session.	How brought before the House of Reps.	Page of journal.	To what committee of the House referred.	No. or date of the report.	Nature of the report.	No. of the bill.	How disposed of by the House of Reps.	How disposed of by the Senate.	Date of the act of Congress, and remarks.
Meriwether, Nicholas	Compensation for revolutionary services.	18	2	Petition	59	Rev. Pensions	Jan. 18, 1825	Adverse		Laid on table.		
Meriwether, Nicholas	Compensation for revolutionary services.	20	2	Petition	33					Ref'd to Com. W. H. on bill No. 317.		
Meriwether, Rogers	Grant of land in lieu of bounty land sold for taxes.	25	2	Petition	327	Priv. Land Claims.	Jan. 31, 1838	Adverse		Laid on table.		
Meriwether, Thomas D.	(See Abel Rawle, and others)	19	2		27							
Meriwether, Thos., heirs of	Five years' full pay	25	2	Petition	393	Rev. Claims				Discharged; laid on table.		
Meriwether, Valentine	Revolutionary pension	22	1	Resolution	535	Rev. Pensions				Discharged; laid on table.		
Meriwether, William	Arrears of pension	26	1	Resolution	547	Rev. Pensions.						
Merkell, Gideon	(See John Stoner)	2	1		500							
Meroney & Milligan	(See Milligan & Meroney)	26	1		331							
Meroney, Philip D.	Compensation for damages to property by U. S. troops in 1832.	24	2	Memorial	110	Claims.						
Meroney, Philip D.	Compensation for damages to property by U. S. troops in 1832.	25	2	Memorial	275	Claims	547	Adverse		Laid on table.		
Merriam, Dersire	(See Ichabod Merriam, widow of.)	26	1		626							
Merriam, Ichabod, widow of.	Continuation of pension	26	1	Petition	626	Rev. Pensions	641	Favorable; bill	474	Referred to Committee Whole House.		
Merriam, William	(See Nathaniel Mitchell)	26	1		201							
Merrick, George	Compensation for services in revolutionary war.	15	2	Petition	31	Pens. & Rev. Cl'ms.	Dec. 7, 1818	Adverse		Rejected.		
Merrick, George	Compensation for services in revolutionary war.	16	1	Petition	213	Pens. & Rev. Cl'ms	Feb. 14, 1820	Adverse		Leave to withdraw.		
Merrick, Joseph P.	(See Joseph P. Mennick)	12	1		174							
Merrifield, Abraham	Invalid pension	3	1	Petition and rep't Sec. of War.	131	Select	Mar. 26, 1794	Rep. and resolution.	12	Passed	Passed	App'd June 9, 1794
Merrifield, Abraham	Invalid pension	4	1	Petition and rep't Sec. of War.	445	Claims	Feb. 18, 1796	Rep. and resolution.	16	Passed	Passed	App'd April 17, 1796
Merrifield, Abraham	Invalid pension	13	1	Petition	56	Claims	Jan. 29, 1813	Favorable; bill	31	Passed	Passed, with amendment.	App'd Aug. 2, 1813
Merrifield, John A., representatives of.	Bounty land for services in the Mexican war.	31	1	Petition	370	Public Lands.						
Merrifield, Samuel	Pension	31	1	Petition	424	Rev. Pensions.	365	Adverse		Laid on table.		
Merrill, Abner	Pension	22	1	Petition	671	Invalid Pensions				Discharged; laid on table.		
Merrill, Abner	Pension	22	2	Petition	27	Invalid Pensions	Feb. 15, 1833	Favorable; bill	738	Referred to Committee Whole House.		
Merrill, Abner	Pension	23	1	Petition	44	Invalid Pensions	1	Favorable; bill	1	Passed	Passed, with amendment.	App'd June 25, 1834
Merrill, Asa	Restoration of pension	17	1	Petition	511					Laid on table.		
Merrill, Asa	Restoration of pension	17	2	Petition	81	Rev. Pensions				Discharged; leave to withdraw.		
Merrill, Asa	Arrears of pension	24	2	Petition	45	Rev. Pensions	152	Adverse		Laid on table.		
Merrill, Asa	Arrears of pension	25	2	Petition	55	Rev. Pensions				Discharged; laid on table.		
Merrill, Benjamin	Increase of pension	10	2	Rep. of Secretary War.	480	Claims	Jan. 30, 1809	Favorable; bill	158	Passed	Passed, with amendment.	App'd March 3, 1809
Merrill, Benjamin, 2d	Invalid pension	15	1	House bill	405	Whole House	April 16, 1818	With amend's.	172	Passed	Postponed.	
Merrill, Benjamin, 2d	Invalid pension	15	2	House bill	41	Whole House	Nov. 26, 1818	With amend's.	203	Passed	Passed	App'd March 3, 1819

List of private claims presented to the House of Representatives of the United States from the 1st to the 31st Congress, inclusive—Continued.

Names of claimants.	Nature or object of the claim.	Congress.	Session.	How brought before the House of Reps.	Page of journal.	To what committee of the House referred.	No. or date of the report.	Nature of the report.	No. of the bill.	How disposed of by the House of Reps.	How disposed of by the Senate.	Date of the act of Congress, and remarks.
Merrill, Benjamin	(See John Derby, executors of)	23	1		186							
Merrill, Benjamin & Alexander, Richards.	Relief for sale of their vessel the Alexandria.	12	1	Memorial	11	Com. and Manuf.						
Merrill, Benjamin, & wife, Cherokee Indians.	For authority to sell their reservation of land.	24	1	Petition	65	Indian Affairs	Dec. 29, 1835	Favorable; bill	64	Passed	Passed	App'd June 23, 1836
Merrill, Daniel, (Mass.)	Renewal of certificates of public debt.	5	3	Petition	495					Laid on table.		
Merrill, Daniel, (Mass.)	Additional compensation for revolutionary services.	22	1	Petition	330	Rev. Claims	Mar. 23, 1822	Adverse		Laid on table.		
Merrill, Daniel, and others	Settlement and payment of accounts against the United States.	1	3	Petition and rep't Sec. of War.	342					Laid on table.		
Merrill, Daniel, and others	Compensation for revolutionary services.	16	1	Petition	135	Pens. & Rev. Cl'ms.	Feb. 4, 1810	Adverse		Laid on table.		
Merrill, Daniel, and others	Compensation for revolutionary services.	16	2	Petition	63	Pens. & Rev. Cl'ms.				Discharged; laid on table.		
Merrill, Daniel, (Me.)	Compensation for revolutionary services.	18	1	Petition	250	Pens. & Rev. Cl'ms.	Mar. 11, 1824	Adverse		Laid on table.		
Merrill, Daniel, (Me.)	Compensation for revolutionary services.	18	2	Petition	183	Pens. & Rev. Cl'ms.	Feb. 23, 1825	Adverse.				
Merrill, Daniel, (Me.)	Compensation for revolutionary services.	19	1	Petition	51	Pens. & Rev. Clm's.						
Merrill, Daniel, (N. C.)	Pension	20	1	Petition	163	Military Pensions	April 14, 1828	Adverse		Laid on table.		
Merrill, Edward	(See Charles W. Morgan, and others.)	31	1		1227							
Merrill, Eli	Permission to locate a quarter section of land.	28	2	Petition	171	Priv. Land Claims.	71	Adverse		Laid on table.		
Merrill, Eli	Bounty land	29	1	Petition	170	Priv. Land Claims.	270	Favorable; bill	236	Passed	Passed	App'd Aug. 8, 1846
Merrill, Elizabeth	Pension	28	2	Resolution	132	Rev. Claims.						
Merrill, Frederick	Payment of claims as officer in the war of 1812.	21	1	Petition	144	Military Affairs				Discharged; laid on table.		
Merrill, James	Naval pension	16	1	Petition	27	Naval Affairs	Jan. 20, 1820	Favorable; bill	53	Passed	Passed	App'd May 4, 1820
Merrill, James	Increase of pension	25	2	Petition	594	Naval Affairs.						
Merrill, John, widow of	Compensation for revolutionary services.	15	2	Petition	199	Pens. & Rev. Cl'ms.				Discharged; laid on table.		
Merrill, John, heirs of	For property used by government in the revolutionary war.	29	1	Petition	280	Rev. Claims.						
Merrill, Joseph	(See John Carman, assignee of)	15	2		167							
Merrill, Joshua	Invalid pension	13	1	Petition	15	Claims				Discharged; laid on table.		
Merrill, Joshua	Invalid pension	13	3	Petition	514	Pens. & Rev. Cl'ms.	Dec. 9, 1814	Favorable; bill	303	Passed	Passed, with amendment.	App'd March 3, 1815
Merrill, Josiah	Pension	21	1	Petition	120	Military Pensions				Discharged; laid on table.		
Merrill, Mehitable	(See John Merrill, widow of)	15	2		199							
Merrill, Moses	For fishing bounty on schooner Fortune.	24	1	Petition	533	Commerce	704	Favorable; bill	657	Referred to Committee Whole House.		
Merrill, Moses	For fishing bounty on schooner Fortune.	25	2	Petition	40	Commerce	85	Favorable; bill	101	Passed	Passed, with amendment.	App'd June 7, 1838
Merrill, Nathaniel	Revolutionary pension	23	1	Petition	190	Rev. Pensions.						
Merrill, Roger	Arrears of pension	18	1	Petition	47	Rev. Pensions	Jan. 12, 1824	Adverse		Laid on table.		
Merrill, Roger	Arrears of pension	20	2	Petition	82	Military Pensions	Feb. 13, 1829	By bill	440	Passed.		
Merrill, Roger	Arrears of pension	21	1	Petition	49	Military Pensions	Jan. 5, 1830	By bill	72	Passed	Passed	App'd May 20, 1830

List of private claims presented to the House of Representatives of the United States from the 1st to the 31st Congress, inclusive—Continued.

Names of claimants.	Nature or object of the claim.	Congress.	Session.	How brought before the House of Reps.	Page of journal.	To what committee of the House referred.	No. or date of the report.	Nature of the report.	No. of the bill.	How disposed of by the House of Reps.	How disposed of by the Senate.	Date of the act of Congress, and remarks.
Merrill, Samuel	Increase of pension	13	1	Petition	56	Claims	Jan. 29, 1813	Favorable; bill	31	Passed	Passed, with amendment.	App'd Aug. 2, 1813
Merrill, Susan	(See William Merrill, widow of)	25	2		920							
Merrill, William	Pension and bounty land	20	2	Memorial	312	Military Pensions.						
Merrill, William, (Ky.)	Invalid pension	25	2	Petition	267	Invalid Pensions				Discharged; laid on table.		
Merrill, William, widow of	Pension	25	2	Memorial	920	Invalid Pensions				Discharged; laid on table.		
Merrill, William S.	Invalid pension	26	1	Petition	163	Invalid Pensions	357	Favorable; bill	336	Referred to Committee Whole House.		
Merritt, Asa	Invalid pension	3	1	Rep. of Secretary War.	131	Select	May 26, 1794	Rep. and res. to refer to Sec. of War.	12	Passed	Passed	App'd June 9, 1794
Merritt, Ebenezer	Pension	19	1	Petition	92	Military Pensions	164	Adverse		Laid on table.		
Merritt, John	Revolutionary pension	21	2	Petition	43	Military Pensions.						
Merritt, John	Revolutionary pension	22	1	Petition	35	Rev. Pensions				Discharged; laid on table.		
Merritt, John S	Compensation for horse lost in services of government.	13	3	Petition	521	Claims				Discharged; laid on table.		
Merritt, Oliver	Renewal of pension	21	2	Petition	136	Judiciary				Discharged; laid on table.		
Merritt, Reuben	Revolutionary pension	20	2	Resolution	46	Military Pensions				Referred to Committee Whole House on bill No. 317.		
Merritt, Stephen, heirs of	Commutation pay for revolutionary services.	25	3	Resolution	271	Rev. Claims	445	Adverse		Laid on table.		
Merritt, Stephen, and Giles Raines.	Commutation pay for revolutionary services.	26	1	Petition	166	Rev. Claims	445	Adverse		Laid on table.		
Merry, Jonathan	Indemnity for French spoliations prior to 1800.	14	1	Petition	170	Claims				Discharged; laid on table.		
Merry, Jonathan, administrator of.	Indemnity for French spoliations prior to 1800.	26	1	Memorial	182	Foreign Affairs	343	Favorable; bill	319	Referred to Committee Whole House.		
Merryman, Josiah	Invalid pension	2	1	Rep. of Secretary War.	131	Select	May 26, 1794	J't. res. to refer to Sec. War.	12	Passed	Passed	App'd June 9, 1794
Merryman, Josiah	Invalid pension	2	2	Rep. of Secretary War.	262	Select	Feb. 28, 1795	Favorable; bill	130	Passed	Postponed.	
Merryman, Josiah	Invalid pension	4	1	Petition	447	Select	Feb. 18, 1796	Favorable; bill	156	Passed	Passed	App'd April 20, 1796
Merryman, Josiah	Increase of pension	10	2	Rep. of Secretary War.	480	Select	Jan. 30, 1709	Favorable; bil	158	Passed	Passed	App'd March 3, 1809
Message. Marie	Confirmation of title to land	22	1	House bill	421				425	Passed	Passed	App'd June 25, 1832
Messenger, B. F.	In relation to survey of public lands	23	2	Documents	103	Public Lands	56	Adverse		Discharged; laid on table.		
Messengers of the department.	Increase of salary	6	2	Petition	745	Select.						
Messengers of the department.	Increase of salary	10	1	Petition	24	Ways and Means.						
Messengers of the department.	Increase of salary	11	2	Petition	173	Ways and Means.						
Messengers of the department.	Increase of salary	14	1	Petition	675					Laid on table.		
Messengers of the department.	Increase of salary	14	2	Petition	197	Ways and Means	Feb. 10, 1817	Favorable; bill	119	Laid on table.		

List of private claims presented to the House of Representatives of the United States from the 1st to the 31st Congress, inclusive—Continued

Names of claimants.	Nature or object of the claim.	Congress.	Session.	How brought before the House of Reps.	Page of journal.	To what committee of the House referred.	No. or date of the report.	Nature of the report.	No. of the bill.	How disposed of by the House of Reps.	How disposed of by the Senate.	Date of the act of Congress, and remarks.
Messengers in the Post Office Department.	Increase of compensation	31	2	Petition	241	P. Of. and P. Roads.						
Messer, Jeremiah	Pension	21	1	Resolution	255	Military Pensions	Mar. 30, 1830	Favorable; bill	248	Passed	Postponed.	
Messer, Timothy	Revolutionary pension	29	1	Petition	1001	Rev. Pensions.						
Messonier, Henry, (Md.)	Refunding of excess of duty on coffee.	4	1	Petition	432	Com. and Manuf.	Mar. 4, 1796	Favorable; bill	157	Passed	Rejected.	
Messonier, Henry, (Md.)	Refunding of excess of duty on coffee.	7	1	Memorial	81	Com. and Manuf	Mar. 8, 1802	Favorable; bill	68	Postponed.		
Messonier, Henry, (Md.)	Refunding of excess of duty on coffee.	7	2	Memorial	247	Com. and Manuf.	Jan. 5, 1803	Favorable; bill	74	Passed	Passed	App'd Feb. 10, 1803
Messonier, Henry	Confirmation of title to land in Louisiana.	15	2	Petition	44	Priv. Land Claims				Discharged; laid on table.		
Metals, Abraham	Compensation for services in late war.	27	2	Petition	383	Claims	721	Adverse		Laid on table.		
Metals, Abraham	Compensation for services in late war.	28	2	Petition	185	Claims.						
Metcalfe, Catharine	(See Simeon Metcalf, widow of.)	4	2		648							
Metcalfe, James	(See Stephen Decatur, widow of, and others.)	18	2		55							
Metcalf, John	Payment for goods on board of schooner Tempest impressed in United States service, 1814.	25	3	Petition	121	Claims	51	Adverse		Laid on table.		
Metcalf, John	Payment for goods on board of schooner Tempest impressed in United States service, 1814.	27	2	Petition	94	Claims	166	Adverse		Laid on table.		
Metcalf, John	Payment for goods on board of schooner Tempest impressed in United States service, 1814.	27	3	Petition	73	Claims	109	Adverse		Laid on table.		
Metcalf, John	Payment for goods on board of schooner Tempest impressed in United States service, 1814.	28	1	Petition	263	Claims.						
Metcalf, John	Payment for goods on board of schooner Tempest impressed in United States service, 1814.	30	2	Petition	385	Claims.						
Metcalf, John	Payment for goods on board of schooner Tempest impressed in United States service, 1814.	31	1	Petition	815	Claims.						
Metcalf, John, (Ohio.)	Additional compensation for carrying United States mail.	19	1	Petition	149	P. Of. and P. Roads.	June 30, 1826	Adverse		Laid on table.		
Metcalf, John E., & others	Permission to locate pre-emption claims in Indiana.	25	2	Senate bill	1052	Public Lands	June 12, 1838	With't amend.	213	Rejected.		
Metcalf, John E., & others	Permission to locate pre-emption claims in Indiana.	25	3	Senate bill	477	Public Lands.	Feb. 25, 1839	With amend.	22	Referred to Committee Whole House.		
Metcalf, John, E., & others	Permission to locate pre-emption claims in Indiana.	26	1	Petition	339	Claims.						
Metcalf, John E., & others	Permission to locate pre-emption claims in Indiana.	26	1	Senate bill	391	Priv. Land Claims.	April 4, 1840	With't amend.	50	Referred to Committee Whole House.		
Metcalf, Ruth	Continuation of pension	28	1	Petition	850	Rev. Pensions.						
Metcalf, Simeon, widow of.	Compensation for revolutionary services.	4	2	Memorial	648	Claims	Jan. 27, 1797	Adverse.		Laid on table.		
Metcalf, Vachel	Pension	25	2	Petition	55	Rev. Pensions				Discharged; laid on table.		

List of private claims presented to the House of Representatives of the United States from the 1st to the 31st Congress, inclusive—Continued.

Names of claimants.	Nature or object of the claim.	Congress.	Session.	How brought before the House of Reps.	Page of journal.	To what committee of the House referred.	No. or date of the report.	Nature of the report.	No. of the bill.	How disposed of by the House of Reps.	How disposed of by the Senate.	Date of the act of Congress, and remarks.
Methany, William	Revolutionary pension	23	1	Petition	493	Rev. Pensions				Discharged; laid on table.		
Metoyer, Benj., and others	(See Benoit Laurent, sureties of.)	29	1		1069							
Metoyer, Francis	Confirmation of title to land in Louisiana.	22	2	Petition	42	Priv. Land Claims.						
Metoyer, Jean Bapt. Louis	Confirmation of title to land in Louisiana.	22	2	Petition	41	Priv. Land Claims.	53	Favorable; bill	696	Referred to Committee Whole House.		
Metoyer, Jean Bapt. Louis	Confirmation of title to land in Louisiana.	23	1	Petition	93	Priv. Land Claims.	Jan. 8, 1834	Adverse		Laid on table.		
Metoyer, Pierre, heirs of	Confirmation of title to land	26	1	Petition	179	Priv. Land Claims.						
Metoyer, Victorin	Confirmation of title to land in Louisiana.	22	1	Petition	133	Priv. Land Claims.						
Metoyer, Victorin	Confirmation of title to land in Louisiana.	23	1	Petition	638	Priv. Land Claims.						
Metoyer, Victorin	Confirmation of title to land in Louisiana.	25	2	Petition	374	Priv. Land Claims.						
Metoyer, Victorin	Confirmation of title to land in Louisiana.	25	3	Petition	134	Priv. Land Claims.						
Mexican claimants	Payment of arrears under convention of 1839.	27	1	Memorial	350							See act Sept. 1, 1841
Meyer, Conrad	Compensation for revolutionary services.	2	1	Petition	474					Referred to Secretary War.		
Meyer, Henry	(See Joackin J. Brandt, administrator of.)	3	2		264							
Meyer, John	Liquidation of certain bills of credit	4	1	Rep. of Secretary Treasury.	388	Claims	May 31, 1796	Favorable		Laid on table.		
Meyer, Peter, widow of	Revolutionary pension	28	1	Petition	69	Rev. Pensions.						
Meyer, Salome	(See Peter Meyer, widow of)	28	1		79							
Meyers, Edward	Revolutionary pension	30	1	Petition	99	Naval Affairs	511	Favorable; bill	438	Referred to Committee Whole House.		
Meyers, John	(See John Myers)	23	1		92							
Miami Indians	(See Indians.)											
Michael, Andrew	Revolutionary pension	22	1	Resolution	84	Rev. Pensions	372	Favorable; bill	468	Passed	Postponed.	
Michael, Andrew	Revolutionary pension	22	2	Resolution	57	Rev. Pensions	Jan. 7, 1833	Favorable; bill	664	Referred to Committee Whole House.		
Michael, Andrew	Revolutionary pension	23	1	Resolution	81	Rev. Pensions.						
Michael, Andrew, widow of	Revolutionary pension	29	1	Petition	192	Rev. Pensions.						
Michael, Ann	(See Andrew Michael, widow of)	29	1		192							
Micheal, Carl	Payment for services and medicines in Mexico war.	31	1	Petition	632	Military Affairs.						
Michael, Catharine	(See Jacob Michael, widow of)	31	1		284							
Michael, Jacob, widow of	Revolutionary pension	31	1	Petition	284	Rev. Pensions	131	Adverse		Laid on table.		
Michael, John, (Pa.)	Arrears of revolutionary pay	4	1	Petition	493	Claims	May 31, 1796	Adverse.				
Michael, John, (Pa.)	Arrears of revolutionary pay	4	2	Petition	614	Claims.						
Micheal, John, of Georgia, representatives and administrator of.	For delivery of land certificate for 20,000 acres issued to Robert Williams, jr.	18	1	Resolution	111	Judiciary	Jan. 20, 1824	Favorable	71	Passed	Passed	App'd Feb. 20, 1824
Michael, Philip	Relinquishment of title by United States, and confirmation of his title to land in Alexandria, D. C.	13	2	Petition	206	Public Lands				Discharged; laid on table.		
Micheaux, Joseph, heirs of	Commutation pay for revolutionary services.	26	1	Petition	361	Rev. Claims.						

List of private claims presented to the House of Representatives of the United States from the 1*st to the* 31*st Congress, inclusive*—Continued.

Names of claimants.	Nature or object of the claim.	Congress.	Session.	How brought before the House of Reps.	Page of journal.	To what committee of the House referred.	No. or date of the report.	Nature of the report.	No. of the bill.	How disposed of by the House of Reps.	How disposed of by the Senate.	Date of the act of Congress, and remarks.
Micheaux, Joseph, heirs of.	Commutation pay for revolutionary services.	26	2	Petition	106, 268	Rev. Claims.....	176	Adverse	.....	Laid on table.		
Micheaux, Joseph, heirs of.	Commutation pay for revolutionary services.	27	2	Pet tion	96, 503	Rev. Claims.....	393	Adverse	.....	Laid on table.		
Micheaux, Joseph, heirs of.	Commutation pay for revolutionary services.	27	3	Petition	44	Rev. Claims.....	244	Adverse	.....	Laid on table.		
Michigan Territory, secretary of.	For additional compensation	10	1	Resolution	23	Select	Nov. 17, 1807	Favorable; bill	4	Passed	Passed	App'd Dec. 5, 1807
Michigan Territory, sundry inhabitants of.	Confirmation of French and British grants to lands, and for pre-emption right.	10	1	Petition	133	Public Lands	Mar. 17, 1308	Favorable; bill	70	Passed	Passed	App'd April 25, 1808
Michigan, citizens of the district of Detroit.	Patents for confirmed grants of land and for a donation of other lands.	12	1	Bill on leave ...	255	Whole House.....	Mar. 31, 1812	With amends.	89	Passed	Passed	App'd April 23, 1812
Michigan, citizens of the district of Detroit.	For further time to file their claims to land under act of April 23, 1812.	14	2	Petition	124	Public Lands.....	Jan. 21, 1817	Favorable; bill	66	Passed	Passed	App'd March 3, 1817
Michigan, inhabitants of the river Raisin.	Indemnity for property destroyed by the enemy in war of 1812.	14	2	Petition	348	Claims	....	....	.....	Discharged; laid on table.		
Michigan, inhabitants of the river Raisin.	Indemnity for property destroyed by the enemy in war of 1812.	15	1	Petition	37	Select	....	....	.....	Discharged; laid on table.		
Michigan, citizens of Detroit	Indemnity for property destroyed, after capitulation, by the enemy, war of 1812.	14	2	Petition	348	....	....	....	.....	Referred to Secretary State.		
Michigan, citizens of Detroit	Indemnity for property destroyed, after capitulation, by the enemy, war of 1812.	15	1	Rep. of Secretary State.	57	Select	....	....	.....	Discharged; laid on table.		
Michigan, citizens of Detroit	Indemnity for property destroyed, after capitulation, by the enemy, war of 1812.	16	1	Petition	144	Claims	....	....	.....	Discharged; laid on table.		
Michigan, sundry inhabitants of.	Permission to exchange their bounty land warrants for land in Illinois, for land in Michigan.	15	2	Petition	247	....	....	....	.....	Laid on table.		
Michigan, sundry inhabitants of.	Permission to exchange their bounty land warrants for land in Illinois, for land in Michigan.	16	1	Petition	123	Public Lands	Jan. 13, 1820	Adverse	.....	Recommitted.		
Michigan, inhabitants of the Bay Settlement.	For a grant of land on which they reside.	16	1	Petition	92	Priv. Land Claims.	....	....	.....	Discharged; laid on table.		
Michigan, sundry inhabitants of.	Confirmation of their titles to land.	17	1	Petition	48	Public Lands.....	....	....	.....	Discharged; laid on table.		
Michigan, sundry inhabitants of.	Confirmation of their titles to land.	17	2	Petition	53	Public Lands.....	....	....	.....	Discharged; leave to withdraw.		
Michigan, sundry inhabitants of.	Confirmation of their titles to land.	20	1	Petition	245	Priv. Land Claims.	....	....	.....	Discharged; laid on table.		
Michigan, citizens of Burlington.	Confirmation of their titles to land.	24	1	Petition	215	Public Lands.						
Michigan, citizens of Dubuque.	Confirmation of their titles to certain lands.	24	1	Petition	435	Public Lands.						
Michigan, church of St. Ann's, at Detroit.	Relief against action of the War Department in relation to a certain lot of ground.	17	2	Petition	44	Military Affairs ...	Feb. 7, 1823	Favorable; bill	281	Referred to Committee Whole House.		
Michigan, church of St. Ann's, at Detroit.	Relief against action of the War Department in relation to a certain lot of ground.	18	1	Petition	106	Military Affairs ...	30	Favorable; bill	63	Passed	Passed	App'd May 26, 1824

List of private claims presented to the House of Representatives of the United States from the 1st to the 31st Congress, inclusive—Continued.

Names of claimants.	Nature or object of the claim.	Congress.	Session.	How brought before the House of Reps.	Page of journal.	To what committee of the House referred.	No. or date of the report.	Nature of the report.	No. of the bill.	How disposed of by the House of Reps.	How disposed of by the Senate.	Date of the act of Congress, and remarks.
Michigan, militia of......	Compensation for services against the Indians in 1832.	22	2	Petition	313	Claims.						
Michigan, militia of......	Compensation for services against the Indians in 1832.	23	1	Resolution	294	Ways and Means.						
Michigan, militia of......	Compensation for horses lost in public service in 1832.	22	2	Senate bill	262	Claims	Feb. 6, 1833	With amends.	S. 20	Passed	Passed	App'd Feb. 19, 1833
Michigan, governor and judges of.	Compensation for adjusting land titles.	23	1	Senate bill	845	Judiciary.........	June 28, 1834	Adverse	S. 124	Referred to Committee Whole House.		
Michigan, sundry citizens of	Indemnity for property destroyed by the enemy, war of 1812.	19	2	Memorial	190	Claims	....	....	......	Discharged; laid on table.		
Michigan, sundry citizens of	Indemnity for property destroyed by the enemy, war of 1812.	20	1	Memorial	77	Claims	268	Adverse	......	Laid on table.		
Michigan, sundry citizens of	Indemnity for property destroyed by the enemy, war of 1812.	23	1	Memorial	438	Claims.						
Michigan, sundry citizens of	Indemnity for property destroyed by the enemy, war of 1812.	24	1	Memorial	153	Claims	....	....	......	Discharged; laid on table.		
Michigan, sundry inhabitants of.	Pre-emption right to certain lands.	20	1	Petition	246	Public Lands.....	167	Favorable; bill	196	Referred to Committee Whole House.		
Michigan, sundry inhabitants of.	Pre-emption right to certain lands.	21	1	Petition	174	Public Lands.						
Michigan, sundry inhabitants of.	Pre-emption right to certain lands.	21	2	Petition	111	Public Lands.....	....	....	......	Discharged; laid on table.		
Michigan, sundry inhabitants of.	Pre-emption right to certain lands.	22	1	Petition	227	....	....	....	......	Referred to Committee Whole House on bill No. 148.		
Michigan, sundry inhabitants of.	For an extension of time for paying for lands in Nottawa reservation.	27	2	Petition	454	Public Lands.						
Michigan, Kalamazoo county.	Pre emption right to certain lands.	26	1	Senate bill	782	Public Lands.....	....	....	S. 102			
Michigan militia, certain companies of.	Compensation for services in maintaining neutrality during the Canadian rebellion.	26	1	Senate bill	886	Militia...........	July 26, 1840	With't amend.	S. 27	Referred to Committee Whole House.		
Michigan militia, certain companies of.	Compensation for services in maintaining neutrality during the Canadian rebellion.	27	2	Resolution	458	Military Affairs.						
Michigan militia, certain companies of.	Compensation for services in maintaining neutrality during the Canadian rebellion.	27	2	Senate bill	1042	Military Affairs...	Aug. 20, 1842	With't amend	S. 33	Referred to Committee Whole House.		
Michigan militia, certain companies of.	Compensation for services in maintaining neutrality during the Canadian rebellion.	27	3	Resolution	71	Military Affairs....	125	Favorable; bill	743	Passed	Passed	App'd Feb. 24, 1843
Michigan, Brady Guards..	(See Michigan militia, certain companies of.)	27	3	....	71							
Michigan board of internal improvements.	Remission of duty on railroad iron.	27	2	Memorial	1050	Commerce.						
Michigan board of internal improvements.	Remission of duty on railroad iron	27	3	Petition	71	Ways and Means.						
Michigan board of internal improvements.	Remission of duty on railroad iron.	28	1	Petition	769	Commerce	90	Favorable; bill	105	Referred to Committee Whole House.		
Michigan	For an extension of time for paying duties on railroad iron.	27	2	Senate bill	1263	Ways and Means..	Aug. 16, 1842	Adverse	S. 311	Laid on table.		
Michigan, State of.......	Reimbursement of expenses in fitting out volunteers.	30	1	Resolution	756	Military Affairs ...	....	....	......	Discharged; laid on table.		

List of private claims presented to the House of Representatives of the United States from the 1st to the 31st Congress, inclusive—Continued.

Names of claimants.	Nature or object of the claim.	Congress.	Session.	How brought before the House of Reps.	Page of journal.	To what committee of the House referred.	No. or date of the report.	Nature of the report.	No. of the bill.	How disposed of by the House of Reps.	How disposed of by the Senate.	Date of the act of Congress, and remarks.
Michigan, State of	Reimbursement of expenses in fitting out volunteers.	31	2	Bill on leave	108	Military Affairs			428			
Michigan, land officers at Sault Ste. Marie.	Compensation for locating bounty land warrants.	31	1	Petition	520	Judiciary						See Senate bill No. 62.
Michigan, land officers at Ionia.	Compensation for locating bounty land warrants.	31	2	Petition	50	Public Lands.						
Mickle, Charles, widow of.	Revolutionary pension	29	2	Petition	54	Rev. Pensions	Jan. 20, 1847			Discharged; laid on table.		
Mickle, Collin	(See David Nagle, executor of)	24	1		115							
Mickle, Etting, and William Tillinghast.	To refund a certain amount of duties illegally collected by United States government.	31	2	Petition	270	Ways and Means.						
Mickle, Reuben	Arrears of pension	20	2	Petition	106	Military Affairs.						
Mickle, Reuben	Arrears of pension	21	1	Petition	83	Military Affairs	April 6, 1830	Adverse		Laid on table.		
Mickle, Reuben	Arrears of pension	22	1	Resolution	141	Rev. Pensions.						
Mickle, Reuben	Arrears of pension	23	1	Resolution	228	Rev. Pensions				Discharged; laid on table.		
Mickle, Reuben	Arrears of pension	24	1	Resolution	137	Rev. Pensions	Jan. 27, 1836			Discharged; laid on table.		
Mickels, Lovel G.	Praying an appropriation to purchase his patent for removing snags in Mississippi.	28	1	Petition	321	Commerce.	281	Adverse		Laid on table.		
Micklin, D. E. W., and others.	(See D. E. W. Nicklin)	29	2		326							
Middleton, Ann	(See Wm. Kinnard, heirs of)	16	2		216							
Middleton, Arthur	Additional compensation for services in a diplomatic capacity.	27	2	Memorial	215	Foreign Affairs	993	To refer to President.		Adopted.		
Middleton, Arthur	Additional compensation for services in a diplomatic capacity.	28	2	Civil & dip. appropriat'n bill.	177				498	Passed	Passed	App'd March 3, 1845
Middleton, Basil	Payment of a claim against the United States.	1	2	Petition and rep't Sec. of War.	191	Select.						
Middleton, Basil	Payment of a claim against the United States.	4	1	Petition	428	Claims	May 7, 1796	Adverse		Leave to withdraw.		
Middleton, Charles & Theodore.	(See Theodore Middleton, heirs of)	28	2		172							
Middleton, Isaac S.	Services as superintendent at Pensacola navy yard.	23	2	Petition	102	Naval Affairs				Discharged; referred to Com. of Claims.		
Middleton, Isaac S.	Services as superintendent at Pensacola navy yard.	24	1	Petition	139	Claims	164	Rep't unfavorable.		Laid on table.		
Middleton, Isaac S.	Services as superintendent at Pensacola navy yard.	26	1	Petition	621	Claims	689	Adverse		Laid on table.		
Middleton, Isaac S.	Services as superintendent at Pensacola navy yard.	26	2	Petition	125	Claims.						
Middleton, Isaac S.	Services as superintendent at Pensacola navy yard.	27	2	Petition	94	Claims	179	Adverse		Laid on table.		
Middleton, John, (Fla.)	Payment for provisions furnished as sutler.	19	2	Petition	134	Claims.						
Middleton, Theodore	Commutation pay for revolutionary services.	23	1	Petition	655	Rev. Claims.						
Middleton, Theodore	Commutation pay for revolutionary services.	23	2	Petition	109	Rev. Claims.						
Middleton, Theodore	Commutation pay for revolutionary services.	24	1	Petition	205	Rev. Claims.						
Middleton, Theodore	Commutation pay for revolutionary services.	24	2	Petition	94	Rev. Claims.						

List of private claims presented to the House of Representatives of the United States from the 1st to the 31st Congress, inclusive—Continued.

Names of claimants.	Nature or object of the claim.	Congress.	Session.	How brought before the House of Reps.	Page of journal.	To what committee of the House referred.	No. or date of the report.	Nature of the report.	No. of the bill.	How disposed of by the House of Reps.	How disposed of by the Senate.	Date of the act of Congress, and remarks.
Middleton, Theodore	Commutation pay for revolutionary services.	25	2	Petition	111	Rev. Claims	509	Report and bill.	507	Recommitted.		
Middleton, Theodore	Commutation pay for revolutionary services.	26	1	Petition	360	Rev. Claims	613	Adverse		Laid on table.		
Middleton, Theodore	Commutation pay for revolutionary services.	26	2	Petition	77	Rev. Claims.						
Middleton, Theodore, heirs of.	Commutation pay for revolutionary services.	28	2	Petition	172	Rev. Claims.						
Middleton, Theodore, heirs of.	Commutation pay for revolutionary services.	29	1	Petition	68	Rev. Claims.						
Middleton, Theodore, heirs of.	Commutation pay for revolutionary services.	30	1	Petition	69	Rev. Claims.						
Middleton, Theodore, heirs of.	Commutation pay for revolutionary services.	31	1	Petition	534	Rev. Claims.						
Middleton, William	Compensation for revolutionary services.	1	3	Petition	388					Referred to Secretary War.		
Midwinter, John	Pension	23	1	Petition	45	Invalid Pensions	Dec. 16, 1833	Adverse		Laid on table.		
Midwinter, John R.	Invalid pension	24	1	Petition	214	Naval Affairs				Discharged; laid on table.		
Midwinter, John R.	Invalid pension	24	2	Petition	86	Invalid Pensions	39	Favorable; bill	786	Referred to Committee Whole House.		
Midwinter, John R.	Invalid pension	25	2	Petition	39	Invalid Pensions	280	Favorable; bill	323	Passed	Postponed.	
Mier, Adolphus, & Co.	Refunding duties on goods burned on steamer Marshall Ney.	31	1	Petition	433	Commerce	159	Favorable; bill	177	Referred to Committee Whole House.		
Mier, Adolphus, & Co.	Refunding duties on goods burned on steamer Marshall Ney.	31	2	Bill of last sess.	103	Whole House	Jan. 3, 1851	With't amend.	177	Passed.		
Miercken, Peter, & Co.	Drawback of duty on exported sugars.	8	2	Memorial	92	Com. and Manuf.						
Miesegaes, Otto H.	(See Henry Delius, *et al.*)	22	2		315							
Mifflin, Benjamin and Andrew.	Extra compensation as clerks in the surveyor's office, Philadelphia.	7	2	Petition	320	Claims	Feb. 18, 1803	Favorable	112	Passed	Passed	App'd March 2, 1803
Mifflin, Benjamin and Andrew.	Reimbursement of expenses incurred in removing books, &c., of the office of the public supplies from Philadelphia to Germantown.	10	1	Petition	248	Claims.						
Mifflin, Charles	(See John R. and Charles Mifflin)	17	1		389							
Mifflin, John H., & others	Compensation for services as United States ranger.	13	3	Petition	681	Claims				Discharged.		
Mifflin, John R., & Charles	Pre emption right to land in Alabama.	17	1	Petition	389	Public Lands				Discharged.		
Mifflin, Samuel, legal representatives of.	Payment of $3,200 with interest loaned to government June 6, 1776.	29	1	Petition	120	Claims.						
Milam, Elijah	Compensation for a horse lost in service of United States.	24	1	Resolution	542	Claims.						
Milam, Elijah	Compensation for a horse lost in service of United States.	24	2	Resolution	79	Claims	Mar. 3, 1837			Referred to 3d Auditor.		
Milam, Elijah	Compensation for a horse lost in service of United States.	30	1	Petition	170	Claims	342	Favorable; bill	322	Referred to Committee Whole House.		
Milam, Elijah	Compensation for a horse lost in service of United States.	31	2	Petition	205	Claims.						
Milam, George W., heirs of.	Compensation for a horse lost in service of United States.	24	1	Resolution	542	Claims.						

of private claims presented to the House of Representatives of the United States from the 1st to the 31st Congress, inclusive—Continued.

Names of claimants.	Nature or object of the claim.	Congress.	Session.	How brought before the House of Reps.	Page of journal.	To what committee of the House referred.	No. or date of the report.	Nature of the report.	No. of the bill.	How disposed of by the House of Reps.	How disposed of by the Senate.	Date of the act of Congress, and remarks.
Milam, George W., heirs of.	Compensation for a horse lost in service of United States.	30	1	Petition	170	Claims	395	Favorable; bill	347	Referred to Committee Whole House.		
Milam, George W., heirs of.	Compensation for a horse lost in service of United States.	30	2	House bill	617				347	Passed	Passed	Bill was sent to the President by whom it does not appear to have been returned.
Milam, Jordon	Increase of pension	31	1	Petition	696	Rev. Pensions	257	Adverse		Laid on table.		
Milbank, Mary	Pension	30	2	Petition	289		Jan. 22, 1849			Leave to withdraw.		
Milbury, Sophia	(See William Milbury, heirs of).	26	1		714							
Milbury, William, heirs of	Indemnity for French spoliations prior to 1800.	26	1	Petition	714	Foreign Affairs	343	Favorable; bill	319	Referred to Committee Whole House.		
Miles, Charles	Bounty land for revolutionary services.	16	1	Petition	88	Pens. & Rev. Cl'ms.	Jan. 19, 1820	Adverse		Rejected.		
Miles, Charles	Bounty land for revolutionary services.	18	1	Petition	48	Pens. & Rev. Cl'ms.	Dec. 23, 1823	Adverse		Laid on table.		
Miles, Charles, (Tenn.)	Pension	19	2	Petition	84	Military Pensions.						
Miles, Charles, (Tenn.)	Pension	20	1	Petition	167	Military Pensions.						
Miles, Clough R	Increase of compensation as postmaster in Massachusetts.	20	2	Petition	266	P. Of. & P. Roads.						
Miles, Elizabeth	(See Frederick Bowman, late widow of.)	4	1		486							
Miles, Hartwell	Pension	23	1	Resolution	250	Invalid Pensions				Discharged; laid on table.		
Miles, Hartwell	Pension	23	2	Petition	110	Invalid Pensions	Jan. 20, 1835	Adverse		Laid on table.		
Miles, John, (N. Y.)	Payment of balance due on contract for furnishing arms to United States.	19	2	Petition	190	Claims.						
Miles, John, (N. Y.)	Payment of balance due on contract for furnishing arms to United States.	20	1	Petition	244	Claims	169	Favorable	198	Passed	Passed	App'd May 24, 1848
Miles, John, (Vt.)	Pension	23	2	Petition	289	Invalid Pensions.						
Miles, John, (Vt.)	Pension	24	1	Petition	52	Invalid Pensions	575	Favorable; bill	559	Passed	Passed	App'd June 28, 1836
Miles, John E	(See guardian of the heirs of Hannah Hale and Polly Jones.)	15	1									
Miles, John, widow of	Pension	25	1	Petition	78					Laid on table.		
Miles, Mary	(See John Miles, widow of)	25	1		78							
Miles, Moses, (Miss.)	Confirmation of title to land in Mississippi.	10	2	Petition	347	Public Lands.						
Miles, Samuel, and others, (Pa.)	Confirmation of grant of land for revolutionary services.	4	2	Memorial	677	Claims.						
Miles, Samuel, and others, (Pa.)	Confirmation of grant of land for revolutionary services.	5	2	Memorial	145	Claims	Jan. 22, 1798	Adverse		Laid on table.		
Miles, Sarah	(See William Miles, widow of)	29	1		104							
Miles, Smith M	Payment for medical services rendered negroes imprisoned by order of the United States.	24	1	Res. and docs	635	Claims	574	Favorable; bill	558	Referred to Committee Whole House.		
Miles, Smith M	Payment for medical services rendered negroes imprisoned by order of the United States.	25	2	Petition	36	Claims	31	Favorable; bill	43	Passed	Passed	App'd March 7, 1838
Miles, Walter	Compensation for revolutionary services.	1	2	Petition and rep't of Sec. War.	222					Laid on table.		
Miles, William, widow of.	Revolutionary pension	29	1	Petition	104	Rev. Pensions.						
Miles, William, widow of.	Revolutionary pension	29	2	Petition	133	Rev. Pensions.						

List of private claims presented to the House of Representatives of the United States from the 1st to the 31st Congress, inclusive—Continued.

Names of claimants.	Nature or object of the claim.	Congress.	Session.	How brought before the House of Reps.	Page of journal.	To what committee of the House referred.	No. or date of the report.	Nature of the report.	No. of the bill.	How disposed of by the House of Reps.	How disposed of by the Senate.	Date of the act of Congress, and remarks.
Miles, William, widow of.	Revolutionary services	30	1	Petition	280	Rev. Pensions	387	Adverse		Laid on table.		
Milford, William	For damages sustained through neglect of a United States officer.	30	1	Petition	470	Commerce	730	Favorable; bill	571	Referred to Committee Whole House.		
Milford, William	For damages sustained through neglect of a United States officer.	30	2	House bill	319	Whole House	Jan. 26, 1849	With't amend.	571	Passed.		
Milhado & Ferguson	(See Ferguson & Milhado)	30	2		254							
Milholland, John	Compensation for a horse lost in war of 1812.	18	1	Resolution	220	Claims	May 3, 1824	Adverse		Laid on table.		
Milhomme, Louis, & others	Confirmation of Spanish land claim.	22	1	Petition	263	Priv. Land Claims.	Feb. 17, 1832	By bill	380	Referred to Committee Whole House.		
Millandon, Laurent	Confirmation of title to land	22	1	Petition	64	Priv. Land Claims.	Dec. 27, 1831	Favorable; bill	125	Passed	Passed	App'd June 25, 1831
Millandon, Laurent	Confirmation of title to land	25	2	Senate bill	1155	Priv. Land Claims.			S. 274			
Millandon, Laurent	Permission to import iron for steamboat.	25	2	Amend't to Sen. bill.	1276	Whole House			147	Passed.	Passed	App'd July 7, 1838
Millandon, Laurent, and others.	Confirmation of certain entries of land.	28	1	Petition	76	Priv. Land Claims.	81	Favorable; bill	98	Referred to Committee Whole House.		
Millandon, Laurent, and others.	Confirmation of certain entries of land.	29	1	Petition	824	Priv. Land Claims.						
Millan, George, (Ind.)	Pension	20	1	Petition	124	Military Pensions.	Feb. 29, 1828	Adverse		Laid on table.		
Millbank, Mary widow of John.	Revolutionary pension	26	1	Resolution	385	Rev. Pensions	644	Adverse		Laid on table.		
Mille, Thomas, heirs of	Indemnity for French spoliations prior to 1800.	31	1	Petition	298	Foreign Affairs	355	Favorable; bill	318	Referred to Committee Whole House.		
Millen, Abraham	(See William Millen, administrator of.)	5	2		164							
Millen, Richard	Invalid pension	3	1	Rep. of Secretary War.	131	Select.	May 26, 1794	Report & res.	12	Passed	Passed	App'd June 9, 1794
Millen, Richard	Invalid pension	9	2	Petition	519	Claims	Feb. 9, 1870	Adverse		Leave to withdraw.		
Millen, Richard	Invalid pension	10	2	Rep. of Secretary War.	480	Claims	Jan. 30, 1809	Favorable	158	Passed	Passed with amendment.	App'd March 3, 1809
Millen, William, administrator of.	Compensation for supplies for revolutionary army.	5	2	Petition	164	Claims				Discharged; postponed		
Millen, William, administrator of.	Compensation for supplies for revolutionary army.	7	2	Petition	246	Claims	Dec. 24, 1802	Adverse		Leave to withdraw.		
Millen, William, administrator of.	Compensation for supplies for revolutionary army.	8	1	Petition	413	Claims	Feb. 27, 1804	Adverse		Referred to Committee Whole House.		
Miller, Aaron	Pension	16	1	Petition	186	Rev. Pensions	April 6, 1820	Adverse		Leave to withdraw.		
Miller, Aaron	Pension	17	1	Petition	109	Rev. Pensions				Discharged; laid on table.		
Miller, Alexander	(See Rufus Spaulding, and others.)	15	2		148							
Miller, Amos, widow of	Compensation for a boat impressed into the service, 1812.	18	2	Petition	46	Claims	5	Favorable	244	Passed	Passed	App'd March 3, 1825
Miller, Benjamin, (Ind.)	Pre-emption right to lands in Indiana.	24	2	Petition	391	Priv. Land Claims.						
Miller, Bryce Wilson	For a grant of land	26	1	Petition	363	Public Lands.						
Miller, Bryce Wilson	For a grant of land	26	2	Petition	106	Public Lands.						
Miller, Bryce Wilson	For a grant of land	28	1	Petition	289	Public Lands.						
Miller, Chad. (or Chadwell.)	Pay and bounty land for services in war of 1812.	19	2	Petition	95	Priv. Land Claims.	52	Favorable	391	Referred to Committee Whole House.		
Miller, Chad. (or Chadwell.)	Pay and bounty land for services in war of 1812.	20	1	Petition	68	Priv. Land Claims.	Mar. 14, 1838	Adverse		Laid on table.		
Miller, Chad. (or Chadwell.)	Pay and bounty land for services in war of 1812.	21	1	Petition	376	Priv. Land Claims.	Mar. 26, 1830	Adverse		Laid on table.		

List of private claims presented to the House of Representatives of the United States from the 1st to the 31st Congress, inclusive—Continued.

Names of claimants.	Nature or object of the claim.	Congress.	Session.	How brought before the House of Reps.	Page of journal.	To what committee of the House referred.	No. or date of the report.	Nature of the report.	No. of the bill.	How disposed of by the House of Reps.	How disposed of by the Senate.	Date of the act of Congress, and remarks.
Miller, Chad. (or Chadwell.)	Pay and bounty land for services in war of 1812.	23	2	Petition	239	Priv. Land Claims.				Discharged; laid on table.		
Miller, Christopher	Compensation for services in 1794.	12	1	Petition	125	Select	Feb. 3, 1812	Favorable	60	Passed	Rejected.	
Miller, Christopher	Compensation for services in 1794.	13	3	Petition	455	Claims				Discharged.		
Miller, Christopher	Compensation for services in 1794.	16	1	Petition	85	Select	37	Favorable	39	Passed	Passed, with amendment.	App'd May 2, 1820
Miller, Chistopher, heirs of.	Compensation for revolutionary services.	28	1	Resolution	113	Rev. Claims.						
Miller, Christopher, heirs of.	Compensation for revolutionary services.	28	1	Senate bill	733	Claims	April 9, 1844	With't amend.	S. 83	Passed	Passed	App'd June 17, 1844
Miller, Christopher, heirs of.	Compensation for revolutionary services.	29	1	Memorial	201	Rev. Claims	412	Adverse		Laid on table.		
Miller, Christopher, heirs of.	Compensation for revolutionary services.	29	2	Memorial	87	Rev. Claims.						
Miller, Conrad, widow of.	Revolutionary pension	27	3	Documents	145	Rev. Pensions.						
Miller, Daniel, representatives of.	Revolutionary pension	2	1	Petition	500					Referred to Secretary of War.		
Miller, Daniel, representatives of.	Revolutionary pension	2	2	Rep. of Secretary War.	696					Laid on table.		
Miller, Daniel, (Ky.)	Compensation for damages to property by United States troops.	9	2	Petition	555	Claims				Discharged; laid on table.		
Miller, Daniel, (Ky.)	Compensation for damages to property by United States troops.	10	1	Petition	177	Claims	Feb. 25, 1808	Favorable		Referredto Committee Whole House.		
Miller, Daniel, (Ky.)	Compensation for damages to property by United States troops.	10	2	Petition	350	Claims	Nov. 18, 1808	Favorable; bill	106	Passed.		
Miller, Daniel, (Ky.)	Compensation for damages to property by United States troops.	11	2	Petition	127	Claims	Dec. 26, 1809	Favorable; bill	51	Referred to Committee Whole House.		
Miller, Daniel, (Ky.)	Compensation for damages to property by United States troops.	13	3	Petition	455	Claims	15	Favorable; bill	242	Passed	Passed	App'd Jan. 28, 1815—Petitioner's name omitted.
Miller, Daniel, (Pa.)	Revolutionary pension	20	2	Petition	109	Military Pensions.		General bill.	317	Passed.		
Miller, Daniel, (Pa.)	Revolutionary pension	21	1	Resolution	280	Military Pensions.				Discharged; laid on table.		
Miller, Daniel, (Pa.)	Revolutionary pension	21	2	Resolution	49	Military Pensions.						
Miller, Daniel, (Pa.)	Revolutionary pension	22	1	Resolution	164	Rev. Pensions.						
Miller, D. H	(See Alexander Wilson, executors of.)	18	2		118							
Miller, Edward	Invalid pension	11	3	House bill	604	Whole House	Mar. 2, 1811	With amends.	218	Passed	Passed, with amendment.	App'd Mar. 3, 1811
Miller, Edward	Increase of pension	16	1	Petition	187	Pens. & Rev. Cl'ms.				Discharged; laid on table.		
Miller, Eleazer	Compensation for use of building by United States troops in war of 1812.	17	1	Petition	259	Claims				Discharged; laid on table.		
Miller, Elisha	(See John Miller, son of)	21	1		412							
Miller, Ephraim	Release from payment of $2,461 68, as collector of taxes.	19	1	Petition	36	Ways and Means.	Dec. 21, 1825	Adverse		Laid on table.		
Miller, Capt. E. P	Further pay for services against the Cherokees.	25	3	Petition	205	Claims.						
Miller, Capt. E. P	Further pay for services against the Cherokees.	26	1	Petition	169	Claims	374	Adverse		Laid on table.		

List of private claims presented to the House of Representatives of the United States from the 1st to the 31st Congress, inclusive—Continued.

2—61

Names of claimants.	Nature or object of the claim.	Congress.	Session.	How brought before the House of Reps.	Page of journal.	To what committee of the House referred.	No. or date of the report.	Nature of the report.	No. of the bill.	How disposed of by the House of Reps.	How disposed of by the Senate.	Date of the act of Congress, and remarks.
Miller, Capt. Elisha, administrator of.	Commutation pay for revolutionary services.	31	2	Petition	393	....	....	....	.....	Laid on table.		
Miller, Frederick	Confirmation of title to land in Missouri.	15	1	Petition	312	Priv. Land Claims.						
Miller, Frederick	Confirmation of title to land in Missouri.	16	1	Petition	71	Priv. Land Claims.						
Miller, Frederick	Confirmation of title to land in Missouri.	17	1	Petition	55	Public Lands.						
Miller, Frederick	Confirmation of title to land in Missouri.	18	1	Petition	55	Public Lands.	Jan. 16, 1824	Favorable; bill	65	Passed	Passed	App'd May 26, 1824
Miller, F. O.	Compensation as assistant surgeon in war with Mexico.	31	1	Petition	809	Claims.						
Miller, George	Pension for services in late war	27	2	Petition	377	Invalid Pensions	633	Adverse	.....	Laid on table.		
Miller, George	Pension for services in late war	29	1	Petition	175	Invalid Pensions	832	Adverse	.....	Laid on table.		
Miller, George, (Pa.)	Remission of duty on stills	8	1	Petition	412	Com. and Manuf.	Jan. 20, 1804	Adverse	.....	Rejected.		
Miller, George and Ferdinand.	Pre-emption right to certain lands.	25	3	Petition	211	Public Lands.						
Miller, George, (Ohio)	Compensation for horses impressed in the service, 1812.	15	2	Petition	62	Claims	....	....	.....	Discharged; laid on table.		
Miller, George, (Ohio)	Compensation for horses impressed in the service, 1812.	16	1	Petition	326	Claims	Mar. 22, 1820	Favorable; bill	112	Passed	Passed	App'd May 8, 1820
Miller, George	Pension	22	1	Resolution	400	Rev. Pensions	....	....	.....	Discharged; laid on table.		
Miller, George, (Ky.)	Payment of his pension for 1837.	25	2	Petition	629	Rev. Pensions	....	....	.....	Discharged; laid on table.		
Miller, George, (Ky.)	Invalid pension	25	3	Resolution	172	Invalid Pensions.						
Miller, George	Invalid pension	26	1	Petition	162	Invalid Pensions.						
Miller, George	Invalid pension	26	2	Petition	134	Invalid Pensions	237	Adverse	.....	Laid on table.		
Miller, Heath, Jones and others.	(See Nathaniel Denby, sureties of)	30	2	....	350							
Miller, Helen	(See Philip P. Clum, widow of)	25	2	....	531							
Miller, Henry	Additional compensation for services in late war.	21	1	Petition	294	Claims	April 20, 1830	Adverse	.....	Laid on table.		
Miller, Henry	Invalid pension	30	1	Petition	575	Invalid Pensions	626	Favorable; bill	501	Referred to Committee Whole House.		
Miller, Henry	Invalid pension	30	2	Bill of last sess.	318	Whole House	Jan. 26, 1849	With't amend.	501	Passed.		
Miller, Henry	Invalid pension	31	1	Petition	486	Invalid Pensions.						
Miller, Henry, assignee of	Patent for land	27	2	Petition	66	Public Lands.						
Miller, Gen'l Henry, heirs of.	Pension for revolutionary services.	24	1	Petition	506	Rev. Pensions	....	....	.....	Discharged; laid on table.		
Miller, Gen'l Henry, heirs of.	Pension for revolutionary services.	25	2	Petition	111	Rev. Pensions	Dec. 28, 1837	Adverse	.....	Discharged; laid on table.		
Miller, Gen'l Henry, heirs of.	Compensation for revolutionary services.	31	1	Petition	449	Rev. Pensions	134	Favorable; bill	15[illegible]	Referred to Committee Whole House.		
Miller, Isaac	Pension	15	1	Petition	277	Pens. & Rev. Cl'ms.	....	....	.....	Discharged; laid on table.		
Miller, Isaac, (Ill.)	For leave to relocate lands entered by mistake.	25	2	Petition	661	Public Lands	....	....	.....	Discharged.		
Miller, Isaac, (Ill.)	For leave to relocate lands	25	3	Documents	93	Public Lands	156	Report and bill	1023	Passed	Passed, with amendment.	App'd March 3, 1839
Miller, Isaac F.	Increase of pension	31	2	Petition	110	Invalid Pensions.						

List of private claims presented to the House of Representatives of the United States form the 1st to the 31st Congress, inclusive—Continued.

Names of claimants.	Nature or object of the claim.	Congress.	Session.	How brought before the House of Reps.	Page of journal.	To what committee of the House referred.	No. or date of the report.	Nature of the report.	No. of the bill.	How disposed of by the House of Reps.	How disposed of by the Senate.	Date of the act of Congress, and remarks.
Miller, Jacob, and others..	(See sureties of Nicholas Shrader)	22	1	....	442							
Miller, Jacob, (Mo.).....	Confirmation of title to land in Missouri.	15	2	Petition	220	Priv. Land Claims.	....	....	.....	Discharged; laid on table.		
Miller, Jacob, (Mo.).....	Confirmation of title to land in Missouri.	17	1	Petition	54	Public Lands.						
Miller, Jacob, (Mo.).....	Confirmation of title to land in Missouri.	18	1	Petition	54	Public Lands.....	Jan. 16, 1824	Favorable; bill	65	Passed	Passed	App'd May 26, 1824
Miller, Jacob, (Tenn.) ...	Revolutionary pension	24	2	Petition	417	Rev. Pensions.						
Miller, Jacob, (N. C.) ...	Revolutionary pension	25	2	Resolution	213	Rev. Pensions	721	Report and bill	691	Passed.		
Miller, Jacob, (N. C.) ...	Revolutionary pension	25	3	Resolution	88	Rev. Pensions	....	....	.....	Discharged.		
Miller, Jacob, (N. C.) ...	Revolutionary pension	26	1	Petition	174	Rev. Pensions	....	....	.....	Discharged; laid on table.		
Miller, Jacob, (N. C.) ...	Revolutionary pension	27	3	Petition	131	Rev. Pensions	63	Report and bill	700	Passed	Indef. postp'd.	
Miller, Jacob	Invalid pension..........	25	2	Petition	84	Invalid Pensions ..	Feb. 6, 1838 April 8, 1838	Adverse ..... Adverse.	.....	Laid on table.		
Miller, Jacob	Invalid pension................	26	1	Petition	602	Invalid Pensions.						
Miller, Jacob	Invalid pension................	26	2	Petition	107	Invalid Pensions ..	220	Adverse	.....	Laid on table.		
Miller, James, and James Love, heirs of.	That the estates of deceased may be released as sureties of Lewis Hunter.	10	2	Petition and rep't Sec. Treasury.	431, 454	Ways and Means.						
Miller, James, and James Love, heirs of.	That the estates of deceased may be released as sureties of Lewis Hunter.	11	2	Petition	195	Ways and Means.						
Miller, James, (Mass.)....	Increase of compensation as collector of customs.	19	1	Petition	203	Commerce.	....	....	.....	Discharged; laid on table.		
Miller, James, (Mass.)....	Increase of compensation as collector of customs.	19	2	Petition	49	Commerce	....	....	.....	Discharged.		
Miller, James, (Mass.)....	Increase of compensation as collector of customs.	20	1	Petition	46	Commerce	35	Adverse	.....	Referred to Secretary of Treasury.		
Miller, James, (Mass.)....	Increase of compensation as collector of customs.	26	1	Petition	290	Commerce.						
Miller, James, (Maine.) ..	Indemnity for French spoliations prior to 1800.	26	1	Memorial	182	Foreign Affairs....	343	Favorable; bill	319	Referred to Committee Whole House.		
Miller, James, and others..	(See John H. Alley, sureties of.) .	17	1	....	128							
Miller, James...........	(See William Dunlap, & Co.)...	26	1	....	182							
Miller, James, late widow of.	Pension for revolutionary services.	25	3	Petition	562	Rev. Pensions.....	....	....	.....	Discharged.		
Miller, James, late widow of.	Pension for revolutionary services.	26	1	Petition	173	Rev. Pensions.....	168	Favorable; bill	179	Passed	Indef. postp'd.	
Miller, James F.........	Relief from the operation of 4th section of act 3d March, 1845.	29	1	Petition	169	Naval Affairs.....	148	Favorable; bill	152	Referred to Committee Whole House.		
Miller, James, (R. I.)	Pension	21	2	Petition	159	Military Pensions						
Miller, James, (R. I.)....	Pension	22	1	Petition	80	Rev. Pensions.....	411	Favorable....	511	Ref'd to Com W. H.		
Miller, James, (R. I.)....	Allowance for depreciation of pay for revolutionary services.	24	1	Petition & docs.	136	Select	337	Favorable; bill	352	Referred to Committee Whole House.		
Miller, James, and wife ..	Release from liability on bond of S. Findley.	20	1	Petition	225	Judiciary	Feb. 11, 1828	Adverse	.....	Laid on table.		
Miller, James, J. heirs of.	Indemnity for French spoliations prior to 1800.	29	2	Memorial	128	Foreign Affairs.						
Miller, James, heirs of....	Indemnity for French spoliations prior to 1800.	31	1	Petition	215	Foreign Affairs ...	335	Favorable; bill	318	Referred to Committee Whole House.		
Miller, James R., and others	Indemnity for French spoliations prior to 1800.	31	1	Petition	661	Foreign Affairs....	355	Favorable; bill	318	Referred to Committee Whole House.		

List of private claims presented to the House of Representatives of the United States from the 1st to the 31st Congress, inclusive—Continued.

Names of claimants.	Nature or object of the claim.	Congress.	Session.	How brought before the House of Reps.	Page of journal.	To what committee of the House referred.	No. or date of the report.	Nature of the report.	No. of the bill.	How disposed of by the House of Reps.	How disposed of by the Senate.	Date of the act of Congress, and remarks.
Miller, Jeremiah, representatives of.	Commutation of half-pay for revolutionary services.	13	1	Petition	19	Claims				Discharged.		
Miller, John	Compensation for revolutionary services.	2	2	Petition	674					Referred to Secretary Treasury.		
Miller, John	Compensation for revolutionary services.	3	2	Rep. of Secretary Treasury.	284	Claims.						
Miller, John, (N. Y.) representatives of.	Compensation for revolutionary services.	3	1	Petition and rep't Sec. of War.	59	Select.						
Miller, John, (N. Y.)	Invalid pension	3	1	Rep. of Secretary War.	131	Select	May 26, 1794	Rep. and res.	12	Passed	Passed	App'd June 9, 1794
Miller, John, (N. Y.)	Invalid pension	14	2	Resolution	237	Pens. & Rev. Cl'ms.	Jan. 29, 1817	Favorable	91	Passed	Passed	App'd March 3, 1817
Miller, John, (N. Y.)	Arrears and increase of pension	15	1	Res. and docs	250, 309	Pens. & Rev. Cl'ms.				Discharged; laid on table.		
Miller, John, (N. Y.)	Arrears and increase of pension	15	2	Petition	177	Pens. & Rev. Cl'ms.				Discharged; laid on table.		
Miller, John, (N. Y.)	Arrears and increase of pension	18	1	Petition	134	Pens. & Rev. Cl'ms.	Jan. 24, 1823	Adverse		Laid on table.		
Miller, John, (N. Y.)	Arrears and increase of pension	19	1	Petition	82	Military Pensions	164	Adverse		Leave to withdraw.		
Miller, John, (N. Y.)	Arrears and increase of pension	22	1	Petition	133	Invalid Pensions	203	Favorable	288	Passed	Passed, with amendment.	App'd July 14, 1832
Miller, John, (Ky.)	Pension	21	1	Petition	197	Military Pensions	April 2, 1830	Adverse		Laid on table.		
Miller, John, (Pa.)	Drawback of duty on merchandise.	5	3	Petition	457	Com. and Manuf.				Discharged; leave to withdraw.		
Miller, John, (Pa.)	Invalid pension	24	2	Petition	48	Invalid Pensions				Discharged; laid on table.		
Miller, John, (Md.)	Remission of duty on stills	13	3	Petition	598	Ways and Means	Jan. 14, 1815	Favorable	262	Passed	Passed	App'd Feb. 4, 1815
Miller, John, captain United States army.	Relief; was robbed of money while acting as paymaster.	13	2	Petition	177	Claims	Feb. 7, 1814	Res. for leave to withdraw.		Adopted.		
Miller, John, captain United States army.	Relief; was robbed of money while acting as paymaster.	17	2	Petition	57	Military Affairs	Jan. 10, 1823	Adverse		Laid on table.		
Miller, John, captain United States army.	Relief; was robbed of money while acting as paymaster.	18	1	Petition	295	Claims	Mar. 17, 1824	Adverse		Laid on table.		
Miller, John, (Fla.)	Compensation for services for examining claims under the 9th article of the treaty with Spain.	18	2	Resolution	56	Ways and Means	Feb. 25, 1825	Favorable	358	Passed	Laid on table.	
Miller, John, (Fla.,) administrator of.	Indemnity for expenditures and per diem as clerk of United States district court of Florida.	20	2	Petition	322	Territories.						
Miller, John, (Fla.,) administrator of.	Indemnity for expenditures and per diem as clerk of United States district court of Florida.	21	1	Petition	236	Territories	April 9, 1830	By bill	416	Referred to Committee Whole House.		
Miller, John, (Fla.,) administrator of.	Indemnity for expenditures and per diem as clerk of United States district court of Florida.	22	1	Petition	66	Territories	Jan. 13, 1832	Favorable	257	Referred to Commitee Whole House.		
Miller, John, (Fla.,) administrator of.	Indemnity for expenditures and per diem as clerk of United States district court of Florida.	22	2	Bill of last sess.	92				257	Passed	Passed	App'd March 2, 1833
Miller, John, son of	Bounty land for services in revolutionary war.	21	1	Petition	412	Rev. Claims				Discharged; laid on table.		
Miller, John, jr., (Pa.)	Indemnity for French spoliations prior to 1800.	26	1	Memorial	182	Foreign Affairs	343	Favorable; bill	319	Referred to Committee Whole House.		
Miller, John	Confirmation of title to land	28	1	Petition	274	Priv. Land Claims.	209	Favorable; bill	164	Passed	Passed	App'd May 23, 1844

List of private claims presented to the House of Representatives of the United States from the 1st to the 31st Congress, inclusive—Continued.

Names of claimants.	Nature or object of the claim.	Congress.	Session.	How brought before the House of Reps.	Page of journal.	To what committee of the House referred.	No. or date of the report.	Nature of the report.	No. of the bill.	How disposed of by the House of Reps.	How disposed of by the Senate.	Date of the act of Congress, and remarks.
Miller, John	Right of pre emption as New Orleans branch pilot.	28	1	Petition	77	Priv. Land Claims.	9	Favorable; bill	35	Passed	Passed	App'd June 17, 1844
Miller, John C., (N. Y.)	Pension	21	2	Petition	43	Military Pensions.						
Miller, John and Daniel	(See Joseph Perry, assignees of)	29	1		1017							
Miller, Joseph, and others	(See Justus Miller, heirs of)	19	1		271							
Miller, Joseph, heirs of	Commutation pay for revolutionary services.	31	1	Petition	500	Rev. Claims.						
Miller, Justus, heirs of	Lands in lieu of those sold by decision of United States court.	19	1	Petition	271	Priv. Land Claims.	Mar. 14, 1826	Adverse		Laid on table.		
Miller, Lemuel	Commutation of half pay for revolutionary services.	1	2	Petition	143					Laid on table.		
Miller, Lewis, (Va.)	Arrears of pension	20	2	Petition	64	Military Pensions	Jan. 28, 1829	Adverse		Laid on table.		
Miller, Mark	Invalid pension	14	2	House bill	307	Whole House	Feb. 21, 1817	With amends.	91	Passed	Passed	App'd March 3, 1817
Miller, Margaret, & others.	Pension, bounty, &c	26	1	Petition	727	Rev. Pensions.						
Miller, Margaret	(See Conrad Miller, widow of)	27	3		145							
Miller, Martin	Pension	21	1	Resolution	244	Military Pensions.						
Miller, Martin	Pension	21	2	Senate bill	185	Military Pensions	Jan. 18, 1831	Adverse	S. 67	Passed		App'd March 3, 1831
Miller, Martin	Pension	22	1	Resolution	251	Rev. Pensions.						
Miller, Mary	(See Amos Miller, widow of)	18	2		46							
Miller, Mary, and others	(See Ludwig Kuhn, heirs of)	19	2		63							
Miller, Meredith R	Compensation for guarding J. L. Meck from Oregon to United States.	31	1	Petition	595	Claims.						
Miller, Michael, (Pa)	Remission of duty on stills	8	1	Petition	411	Com. and Manuf.	Dec. 9, 1803	Adverse		Leave to withdraw.		
Miller, Michael	Pension	21	2	Petition	68	Military Pensions.						
Miller, Moses	Pension	14	2	Resolution	238	Pens. & Rev. Cl'ms.	Jan. 29, 1817	Favorable	91	Passed	Passed, with amendment.	App'd March 3, 1817
Miller, Nancy, widow of David.	Revolutionary pension	27	2	Petition	782	Rev. Pensions				Discharged; laid on table.		
Miller, Nelson	Pension	21	1	Petition	353	Military Pensions	May 29, 1830	By bill	499	Referred to Committee Whole House.		
Miller, Nelson	Pension	21	2	Petition	159	Military Pensions.						
Miller, Nelson	Pension	22	1	Petition	80	Rev. Pensions	123	Favorable	194	Referred to Committee Whole House.		
Miller, Nelson	Pension	22	2	Bill of last sess.	66				194	Laid on table.		
Miller, Nicholas, representatives of.	Compensation for revolutionary services.	3	1	Petition and rep't Sec. of War.	59	Select.						
Miller, Nicholas	(See John Flowars, and others.)	22	1		596							
Miller, Noah, and others	Compensation as Nova Scotia refugees.	4	1	Petition	448					Ref'd to Com. W. H. on bill No. 209.		
Miller, Noah, and others	Compensation as Nova Scotia refugees.	6	2	Resolution	733	Select	Jan. 19, 1801	Favorable	280	Passed	Passed	App'd Feb. 18, 1801
Miller, Noah	Pension	14	1	Petition	558	Pens. & Rev. Cl'ms.						
Miller, Noah	Pension	14	2	Petition	48	Select	Feb. 8, 1817	Favorable	144	Referred to Committee Whole House.		
Miller, Noah	Pension	15	1	Petition	21	Select	Dec. 12, 1817	Favorable	7	Passed	Postponed.	
Miller, Noah	Pension	20	2	Petition	112	Military Pensions				Discharged; laid on table.		
Miller, Noah	Pension	21	1	Petition	143	Military Pensions	May 29, 1830	By bill	499	Referred to Committee Whole House.		
Miller, Noah	Pension	22	1	Petition	36	Invalid Pensions	155	Favorable	234	Passed.		
Miller, Noah	Pension	23	2	Petition	76	Invalid Pensions	43	Favorable; bill	629	Passed	Passed	App'd March 3, 1835
Miller, Noah	Arrears of pension	24	1	Petition	51	Invalid Pensions	354	Favorable; bill	360	Passed	Indef. postp'd.	

List of private claims presented to the House of Representatives of the United States from the 1st to the 31st Congress, inclusive—Continued.

Names of claimants.	Nature or object of the claim.	Congress.	Session.	How brought before the House of Reps.	Page of journal.	To what committee of the House referred.	No. or date of the report.	Nature of the report.	No. of the bill.	How disposed of by the House of Reps.	How disposed of by the Senate.	Date of the act of Congress, and remarks.
Miller, Noah	Arrears of pension	24	2	Petition	72	Invalid Pensions	Jan. 19, 1837	Adverse		Laid on table.		
Miller, Noah, (Me.)	Compensation for capturing British ship and cargo.	16	1	Petition	118	Commerce				Discharged; laid on table.		
Miller, Noah, and others	Compensation for capturing British ship and cargo.	25	2	Senate bill	1011	Commerce	977	With amend.	236	Referred to Committee Whole House.		
Miller, Noah, and others	Compensation for capturing British ship and cargo.	26	1	Senate bill	811	Commerce	June 2, 1840	With amend.	161	Referred to Committee Whole House.		
Miller, Noah, and others	Compensation for capturing British ship and cargo.	28	2	Senate bill	448	Commerce	Mar. 3, 1845	With amend.	89	Referred to Committee Whole House.		
Miller, Peter	Indemnity for damages to property during revolutionary war.	1	3	Petition	376					Referred to Secretary of Treasury.		
Miller, Peter	Indemnity for damages to property during revolutionary war.	2	1	Rep. of Secretary Treasury.	580					Laid on table.		
Miller, Peter, and others	Compensation for losses sustained by them in consequence of moving from their settlement on public lands by order of the War Department.	26	2	Petition	131	Public Lands.						
Miller, Peter W.	(See Archibald Beard, and others)	28	1						478			
Miller, Philip	Revolutionary pension	22	1	Petition	124	Invalid Pensions	Jan. 25, 1832	Adverse		Laid on table.		
Miller, Philip	Revolutionary pension	28	2	Petition	184	Invalid Pensions.						
Miller, Philip	Revolutionary pension	30	1	Petition	606	Invalid Pensions	557	Favorable; bill	457	Referred to Committee Whole House.		
Miller, Philip	Revolutionary pension	30	2	House bill	318	Whole House	Jan. 26, 1849	With't amend.	457	Passed.		
Miller, Philip	Revolutionary pension	31	1	Petition	671	Invalid Pensions.						
Miller, Phineas, heirs of, by attorney.	Settlement of accounts for furnishing live oak for Navy Department.	9	1	Petition	239	Claims	Mar. 18, 1806	Adverse		Leave to withdraw.		
Miller, Phineas, heirs of, by attorney.	Settlement of accounts for furnishing live oak for Navy Department.	9	2	Petition	478	Claims	Feb. 16, 1807	Adverse		Leave to withdraw.		
Miller, R. C.	(See Archibald Beard, and others)	28	1						478			
Miller, Richard	Invalid pension	10	2	House bill	499	Whole House	Feb. 20, 1809	With amends.	158	Passed	Passed	App'd March 3, 1809
Miller, Richard, (Pa.)	Revolutionary pension	20	1	Resolution	465	Military Pensions				Discharged; laid on table.		
Miller, Richard, (Pa.)	Revolutionary pension	21	1	Petition	384	Military Pensions				Discharged; laid on table.		
Miller, Robert, (S. C.)	Refunding of amount of certain duty bonds erroneously exacted from him.	27	2	Petition	611	Judiciary.						
Miller, Robert, (S. C.)	Refunding of amount of certain duty bonds erroneously exacted from him.	27	2	Senate bill	1126	Ways and Means	July 27, 1842	With amends.	S. 253	Passed with amendm't.	Passed	App'd Aug. 11, 1842
Miller, Robert, (Me.)	Indemnity for French spoliations prior to 1800.	26	1	Memorial	182	Foreign Affairs	343	Favorable; bill	319	Referred to Committee Whole House.		
Miller & Robertson	(See John Robertson, executor of)	29	2		184							
Miller, Samuel, (N. Y.)	Invalid pension	3	1	Rep. of Secretary War.	175					Laid on table.		
Miller, Samuel, (N. Y.)	Invalid pension	3	2		240					Referred to Secretary War.		
Miller, Samuel, (N. Y.)	Invalid pension	3	2	Rep. of Secretary War.	262	Claims	Feb. 28, 1795	Favorable; bill	130	Passed	Postponed.	

List of private claims presented to the House of Representatives of the United States from the 1st to the 31st Congress, inclusive—**Continued.**

Names of claimants.	Nature or object of the claim.	Congress.	Session.	How brought before the House of Reps.	Page of journal.	To what committee of the House referred.	No. or date of the report.	Nature of the report.	No. of the bill.	How disposed of by the House of Reps.	How disposed of by the Senate.	Date of the act of Congress, and remarks.
Miller, Samuel, (N. Y.)	Invalid pension	4	1	Rep. of Secretary War.	447	Claims	Feb. 18, 1796	Favorable; bill	156	Passed	Passed	App'd April 20, 1796
Miller, Samuel, (Me.)	Indemnity for French spoliations prior to 1800.	26	1	Memorial	182	Foreign Affairs	343	Favorable; bill	319	Referred to Committee Whole House.		
Miller, Samuel, (N. Y.)	Pension	21	2	Petition	357	Military Pensions.						
Miller, Samuel, (Maine)	Reduction of duty paid on a cargo of salt.	10	1	Petition	158	Com. and Manuf.	Mar. 9, 1808	Adverse	......	Leave to withdraw.		
Miller, Lieut. Col. Samuel.	(See R. D. Wainwright and others)	22	1	....	443							
Miller, Samuel	Compensation for arresting two fugitive Indians.	24	2	Senate bill	205	Claims	155	With't amend.	S. 11	Referred to Committee Whole House.		
Miller, Samuel	Compensation for arresting two fugitive Indians.	25	2	Senate bill	197	Claims	Jan. 5, 1838	With't amend.	51	Referred to Committee Whole House.		
Miller, Simon	Pre-emption right to land in Arkansas.	17	1	Petition	40	Priv. Land Claims.	Jan. 22, 1822	Adverse.	......	Rejected.		
Miller, Simon F.	Indemnity for French spoliations prior to 1800.	26	1	Memorial	182	Foreign Affairs	343	Favorable; bill	319	Referred to Committee Whole House.		
Miller, Theodore	(See Zebulon M. Pike and companions.)	10	1	....	189							
Miller, Thomas, (Va.)	Compensation for use of wagon and team in revolutionary war.	3	1	Petition	106	Select	April 4, 1794	Adverse	......	Laid on table.		
Miller, Thomas, (Va.)	Compensation for use of wagon and team in revolutionary war.	3	2	Rep't of last sess.	261	Claims	Feb. 27, 1795	Adverse	......	Laid on table.		
Miller, Thomas, (Va.)	Compensation for use of wagon and team in revolutionary war.	4	2	Rep't of last sess.	629	Claims	Dec. 27, 1796	Adverse	......	Leave to withdraw.		
Miller, Thomas, and Stephen Baker.	Compensation for house destroyed while occupied by United States troops.	14	1	Petition	491	Claims.	April 15, 1816	Favorable	......	Rejected.		
Miller, Thomas, and Stephen Baker.	Compensation for house destroyed while occupied by United States troops.	14	2	Petition	90	Claims	....	....	......	Discharged; laid on table.		
Miller, Thomas, and Stephen Baker.	Compensation for house destroyed while occupied by United States troops.	15	1	Petition	36	Claims	69	Favorable	64	Passed	Passed, with amendment.	App'd April 18, 1818
Miller, Gen. Thomas C.	Indemnity for violation of contract by the United States, relative to the French'ore bank.	27	2	Petition	75	Claims	1046	Adverse	......	Laid on table.		
Miller, Gen. Thomas C.	Indemnity for violation of contract by the United States, relative to the French'ore bank.	27	3	Additional papers	102	Claims.						
Miller, Gen. Thomas C.	Indemnity for violation of contract by the United States, relative to the French'ore bank.	28	1	Petition	194	Claims.						
Miller, Gen. Thomas C.	Indemnity for violation of contract by the United States, relative to the French'ore bank.	29	1	Petition	320	Claims	629	Adverse	......	Laid on table	....	Leave to withd'w, 31st Cong., 1st session.
Miller, Thomas C., and others.	Compensation for services for trying delinquent militia men in 1815.	17	1	Petition	195	Ways and Means	....	....	......	Discharged; laid on table.		
Miller, T. C. H., and other officers of a company of Tennessee militia.	Compensation for services while in the United States service, in Creek war.	24	2	Memorial	80	Claims	....	....	......	....	....	See Senate bill 171.
Miller, Valentine	Revolutionary pension	25	3	Petition	126	Rev. Pensions	....	....	......	Discharged.		
Miller, Valentine	Revolutionary pension	26	1	Petition	174	Rev. Pensions	....	....	......	Discharged; laid on table.		

List of private claims presented to the House of Representatives of the United States from the 1st to the 31st Congress, inclusive—Continued.

Names of claimants.	Nature or object of the claim.	Congress.	Session.	How brought before the House of Reps.	Page of journal.	To what committee of the House referred.	No. or date of the report.	Nature of the report.	No. of the bill.	How disposed of by the House of Reps.	How disposed of by the Senate.	Date of the act of Congress, and remarks.
Miller, Valentine	Revolutionary pension	28	1	Petition	210	Rev. Pensions.						
Miller, Valentine	Pension and bounty land for revolutionary services.	30	1	Petition	590	Invalid Pensions	626	Favorable	501	Referred to Committee Whole House.		
Miller, Valentine	Pension and bounty land for revolutionary services.	30	2	Petition	192	Rev. Pensions	71	Adverse	......	Laid on table.		
Miller, William	Compensation for revolutionary services.	2	1	Petition	....	......	......	......	......	Referred to Secretary War.		
Miller, William C.	Payment for cotton and lumber taken for public purposes in Florida.	25	3	Petition	205	Claims	204	Adverse	......	Laid on table.		
Miller, W. J., attorney of.	Indemnity for French spoliations prior to 1800.	26	1	Memorial	182	Foreign Affairs	343	Favorable; bill	319	Referred to Committee Whole House.		
Miller, William, and others, agent of.	Confirmation of title to land in Louisiana.	14	2	Petition	148	Public Lands	60	Favorable	90	Rejected.		
Miller, William, and others, agent of.	Confirmation of title to land in Louisiana.	15	1	Petition	76	Priv. Land Claims.	......	......	......	Discharged; laid on table.		
Miller, William	(See John Craig, executor of)	26	1	......	182							
Miller, William, (N. Y.).	Indemnity for damage to proprerty in war of 1812.	22	1	Petition	133	Claims	Jan. 30, 1832	Adverse	......	Laid on table.		
Miller, William, assignee of.	Arrears of pension	19	1	Petition	101	Rev. Claims	Jan. 9, 1826	Adverse	......	Laid on table.		
Miller, William and Philip, assignee of.	Arrears of pension	20	1	Resolution	67	Rev. Claims	Jan. 29, 1828	Adverse	......	Leave to withdraw.		
Miller, William, and others, assignees of.	Arrears of pension	21	1	Resolution	218	Rev. Claims.						
Miller, William	(See Archibald Beard and others)	28	1	......	....	......	......	......	478			
Miller, William S.	Compensation for a horse lost in Seminole war.	23	1	Documents	154	Claims.						
Miller & Wells	Indemnity for French spoliations prior to 1800.	31	1	Petition	840	Foreign Affairs	355	Favorable; bill	318	Referred to Committee Whole House.		
Millet, John	Revolutionary pension	29	2	Petition	100	Rev. Pensions	81	Adverse	......	Laid on table.		
Milligan, Dickson	Donation of certain lands	28	1	Petition	74	Priv. Land Claims.						
Milligan, Jacob, (S. C.).	Compensation for revolutionary services and losses.	3	1	Petition	40	......	......	......	......	Referred to Secretary Treasury.		
Milligan, Jacob, (S. C.).	Compensation for revolutionary services and losses.	3	2	Rep. of Secretary Treasury.	234	Claims.						
Milligan, Jacob, (S. C.).	Compensation for revolutionary services and losses.	4	1	Petition	403	Claims	Jan. 6, 1796	Adverse	......	Leave to withdraw.		
Milligan, Joseph S.	Compensation for property taken for public use in 1832.	24	2	Memorial	110	Claims.						
Milligan, Joseph S.	Compensation for property taken for public use in 1832.	25	2	Memorial	275	Claims	547	Adverse	......	Laid on table.		
Milligan, Joseph S.	Compensation for property taken for public use in 1832.	25	3	Memorial	121	Claims	51	Adverse	......	Laid on table.		
Milligan, Joseph S.	Compensation for property taken for public use in 1832.	26	1	Memorial	331	Military Affairs	......	......	......	Discharged; laid on table.		
Milligan, Joseph S.	Compensation for property taken for public use in 1832.	27	2	Petition	1238	Military Affairs.						
Milligan, Joseph S.	Compensation for property taken for public use in 1832.	28	2	Petition	433	Claims.						
Milligan, Lawrence, representatives of.	Confirmation of title to land in Louisiana.	23	1	Senate bill	390	Public Lands	Mar. 18, 1834	With't amend.	S. 50	Passed	Passed	App'd June 30, 1834

List of private claims presented to the House of Representatives of the United States from the 1st to the 31st Congress, inclusive—Continued.

Names of claimants.	Nature or object of the claim.	Congress.	Session.	How brought before the House of Reps.	Page of journal.	To what committee of the House referred.	No. or date of the report.	Nature of the report.	No. of the bill.	How disposed of by the House of Reps.	How disposed of by the Senate.	Date of the act of Congress, and remarks.
Milligan & Meroney	Compensatiom for property destroyed by United States toops in the Cherokee nation.	26	1	Petition	331	Military Affairs				Discharged; laid on table.		
Milligan, Robert	Pension	21	2	Petition	43	Military Pensions.						
Milligan, Robert	Pension	22	1	Petition	36	Invalid Pensions.						
Milligan, Robert	Pension	22	2	Petition	82	Invalid Pensions	Feb. 15, 1833	Favorable	738	Referred to Committee Whole House.		
Milligan, Robert	Pension	23	1	Petition	44	Invalid Pensions	1	Favorable	1	Passed	Passed, with amendment.	App'd June 25, 1834
Milligan, Robert	Increase of pension	27	2	Petition	218	Invalid Pensions	426, 813	Adverse		Laid on table.		
Milligan, Robert	Increase of pension	30	1	Petition	738	Invalid Pensions	640	Adverse		Laid on table.		
Milligan, Robert	Increase of pension	31	1	Petition	755	Invalid Pensions.						
Milligan, Samuel	Drawback of certain duties	25	2	Petition	583	Ways and Means	Mar. 26, 1838	Report by bill.	693	Passed	Passed	App'd April 6, 1838
Milliken, Abner, widow of.	Pension	25	2	Petition	180					Referred to Committee Whole House on bill No. 436.		
Millikin, Alexander	Increase of compensation as keeper of light-house.	20	2	Petition	116	Commerce				Discharged; laid on table.		
Millikin, Ann	(See Abner Millikin, widow of.)	25	2		180							
Millikin, Daniel	Granting him the right to the old bed of the Great Miami river.	30	2	Petition	192	Public Lands	127	Adverse		Laid on table.		
Millikin, Daniel	Praying that the title to certain land may be vested in him.	26	2	Petition	161	Public Lands.						
Millikin, Daniel	Praying that the title to certain land may be vested in him.	27	2	Petition	98	Public Lands	195	Adverse		Laid on table.		
Millikin, Daniel	Praying that the title to certain land may be vested in him.	28	1	Petition	203	Public Lands.						
Milliken, James	(See administrator of Joshua W. Prout.)	17	1		380							
Millikin, John, (Maine)	Indemnity for French spoliations prior to 1800.	26	1	Memorial	182	Foreign Affairs	343	Favorable	319	Referred to Committee Whole House.		
Millikin, John, (Maine)	Indemnity for French spoliations prior to 1800.	29	2	Memorial	70	Foreign Affairs.						
Millikin, John	(See Elisha Gardner, and others.)	5	2		157							
Millikin, John	Payment as bearer of despatches in the case of Aaron Burr.	25	2	Memorial	1086	Claims	1037	Adverse		Laid on table.		
Millikin, Thomas	(See James Roddy, executor of).	18	1		287							
Millikin, Seth, executor of John Millikin.	Indemnity for French spoliations prior to 1800.	31	1	Petition	256	Foreign Affairs	355	Favorable; bill	318	Referred to Committee Whole House.		
Milling, Hugh	For change of location of his bounty land.	15	2	Petition	163	Public Lands	Jan. 15, 1819	Adverse		Rejected.		
Milling, Hugh, (S. C.)	Commutation of half-pay	23	2	Petition	240	Rev. Claims.						
Milling, Capt. Hugh, heirs of.	Commutation of half-pay	25	2	Petition	683	Rev. Claims	735	Adverse		Laid on table.		
Milling, Capt. Hugh, heirs of.	Commutation of half-pay	26	1	Petition	166	Rev. Claims.						
Millows, Mary	(See Viner Leaycraft, executors of)	5	2		159							
Mills, Adam L	Additional compensation for carrying United States mail.	21	2	Petition	68	P. Of. & P. Roads.				Discharged; referred to Postmaster General.		
Mills, Adam L.	Additional compensation for carrying United States mail.	28	1	Petition	188	P. Of. & P. Roads.	146	Report and bill	134	Passed	Passed	App'd May 31, 1844
Mills, Alexander	Pension	14	2	Petition	406	Pens. & Rev. Cl'ms.				Discharged; laid on table.		

List of private claims presented to the House of Representatives of the United States from the 1st to the 31st Congress, inclusive—Continued.

Names of claimants.	Nature or object of the claim.	Congress.	Session.	How brought before the House of Reps.	Page of journal.	To what committee of the House referred.	No. or date of the report.	Nature of the report.	No. of the bill.	How disposed of by the House of Reps.	How disposed of by the Senate.	Date of the act of Congress, and remarks.
Mills, A. L., and William Y. Wetzell.	Extra compensation for carrying mail between Vincennes and St. Louis.	22	1	Petition	390	P. Of. & P. Roads.						
Mills, A. L., and William Y. Wetzell.	Extra compensation for carrying mail between Vincennes and St. Louis.	28	1	Petition	570	P. Of. & P. Roads.						
Mills, Cornelius	Pension	18	2	Petition	186					Referred to Secretary War.		
Mills, Captain Daniel, heirs of.	Praying for seven years' pay and bounty land for services in revolutionary war.	26	2	Petition	146	Rev. Claims.						
Mills, Captain Daniel, heirs of.	Praying for seven years' pay and bounty land for services in revolutionary war.	27	2	Petition	62	Rev. Claims	274	Report and bill	240	Referred to Committee Whole House.		See Report No. 777.
Mills, Captain Daniel, heirs of.	Praying for seven years' pay and bounty land for services in revo lutionary war.	28	1	Petition	204	Rev. Claims.						
Mills, Captain Daniel, heirs of.	Praying for seven years' pay and bounty land for services in revolutionary war.	29	1	Petition	102	Rev. Claims.						
Mills, David, (La.)	Pension	21	1	Petition	91	Military Pensions	April 7, 1830	Adverse		Laid on table.		
Mills, Elisha	(Journal does not give nature of claim.)	27	3	Documents	474					Laid on table.		
Mills, Elizabeth	(See Col. John Mills, widow of).	22	1		224							
Mills, Major Frederick D., administrator of.	Horse and other property lost in the war with Mexico.	31	1	Senate bill	1430	Claims			312			
Mills, Major Frederick D., administrator of.	Horse and other property lost in the war with Mexico.	31	2	Senate bill	420	Claims	March 3, 1851	With't amend.	S. 312	Passed	Passed	App'd March 3, 1851
Mills, Gideon, widow of	Pension for revolutionary services of her husband.	25	2	Petition	271	Rev. Pensions				Discharged; laid on table.		
Mills, James, Constant P., and Alfred.	Pre-emption right to other quarter-section of land in lieu of other heretofore granted.	24	1	Petition	113	Public Lands.						
Mills, James, heirs of	Indemnity for French spoliations prior to 1800.	31	1	Petition	1008	Foreign Affairs	355	Favorable: bill	318	Referred to Committee Whole House.		
Mills, John	Reimbursement of money advanced United States as recruiting officer.	1	2	Petition and rep't Sec. War.	171					Laid on table.		
Mills, Colonel John, widow of.	Renewal of pension	22	1	Petition	224	Claims	Feb. 16, 1832	Res. to refer to 3d Auditor.		Resolution adopted.		
Mills, John, heirs of	Commutation pay for revolutionary services.	23	2	Petition	84	Rev. Claims	Dec. 29, 1834	Adverse		Laid on table.		
Mills, John, heirs of	Bounty land for services in war of 1812.	31	1	Petition	143	Military Pensions	April 7, 1830	Adverse		Laid on table.		
Mills, John H	Confirmation of title to land in Louisiana.	19	1	Petition	68	Priv. Land Claims.	38	Favorable; bill	56	Passed	Passed	App'd May 20, 1826
Mills, Margaret	An allowance of two years' pension from 4th March, 1841, for revolutionary services of her husband.	28	1	Petition	950	Whole House.						
Mills, Martin	Revolutionary pension	31	1	Petition	412	Rev. Pensions.						
Mills, Nathaniel	(See Capt. Daniel Mills, heirs of)	27	2		62		274		240			
Mills, Nathaniel	Revolutionary pension	28	2	Petition	83	Rev. Pensions.						

List of private claims presented to the House of Representatives of the United States from the 1st to the 31st Congress, inclusive—**Continued.**

Names of claimants.	Nature or object of the claim.	Congress.	Session.	How brought before the House of Reps.	Page of journal.	To what committee of the House referred.	No. or date of the report.	Nature of the report.	No. of the bill.	How disposed of by the House of Reps.	How disposed of by the Senate.	Date of the act of Congress, and remarks.
Mills, Peter, (Ohio)	Reimbursement for losses on contract with Navy Department for building gun-boats.	11	2	Petition	215					Referred to Secretary of Navy.		
Mills, Peter, (Ohio)	Reimbursement for losses on contract with Navy Department for building gun-boats.	11	3	Rep. of Secretary Navy.	495	Claims.						
Mills, Peter, (Ohio)	Reimbursement for losses on contract with Navy Department for building gun-boats.	12	1	Rep. of Secretary Navy.	138					Discharged		Leave to withdraw.
Mills, Peter, (N. Y.)	For half-pay and grant of land as captain in revolutionary war.	11	3	Petition	488	Claims	Jan. 24, 1811	Adverse		Referred to Committee Whole House.		
Mills, Peter, (N. Y.)	For half pay and grant of land as captain in revolutionary war.	12	1	Petition	44, 337	Claims	Jan. 14, 1812	Adverse		Rejected.		
Mills, Peter, (N. Y.)	For half-pay and grant of land as captain in revolutionary war.	12	2	Resolution	607	Claims				Leave to withdraw.		
Mills, Peter, (N. Y.)	For half-pay and grant of land as captain in revolutionary war.	13	1	Petition	37	Claims.				Discharged.		
Mills, Peter, (N. Y.)	For half-pay and grant of land as captain in revolutionary war.	[illegible]	2	Petition	214	Pens. & Rev. Cl'ms.	Feb. 10, 1814	Adverse		Leave to withdraw.		
Mills, Peter, (N. Y.)	For half-pay and grant of land as captain in revolutionary war.	13	3	Petition	484, 530	Pens. & Rev. Cl'ms.						
Mills, Peter, (N. Y.)	Revolutionary pension	14	1	Petition	59	Pens. & Rev. Cl'ms.	April 11, 1816	Favorable; bill	171	Passed	Passed, with amendment.	App'd April 30, 1816
Mills, Peter	(See Jeremiah Daggan, attorney of)	11	2		202							
Mills, Peter	(See Stephen Wockley, attorney of)	5	2		302							
Mills, Peter	(See James Bell, of Canada)	7	1		95							
Mills, Peter	Pay for baggage taken by enemy in war of 1812.	15	1	Petition	394	Claims				Discharged; laid on table.		
Mills, Peter	Pay for baggage taken by enemy in war of 1812.	17	1	Petition	220	Military Affairs	Feb. 14, 1822	Adverse		Referred to Committee Whole House.		
Mills, Peter	For land in lieu of that of which he has been deprived.	23	1	Senate bill	395	Public Lands	Mar. 25, 1834	With't amend.	S. 51	Passed		App'd June 30, 1834
Mills, Peter	Bounty land and arrears of pay for revolutionary services.	17	2	Petition	186	Pens. & Rev. Cl'ms.				Discharged; laid on table.		
Mills, Peter	Bounty land and arrears of pay for revolutionary services.	18	1	Petition	156	Priv. Land Claims.						
Mills, Peter	Compensation for a horse lost in United States service.	26	1	Petition	169	Claims	42	Adverse		Laid on table.		
Mills, Rachael	(See Zachariah Mills, widow of)	18	1		358							
Mills, Rebecca	(See Gideon Mills, widow of)	25	2		271							
Mills, Robert, (D. C.)	Compensation for alterations in House of Representatives.	23	1	Resolution	313	Public Buildings	275	Favorable				Paid out of contingent fund of the House of Representatives.
Mills, Samuel, and others	Settlement of claim for revolutionary services.	4	1	Petition	470	Claims	May 31, 1796	Adverse		Laid on table.		
Mills, Simeon	For payment of account for printing for legislature.	29	2	Petition	245	Ways and Means.						
Mills, Solomon	Restoration of pension	22	1	Petition	187	Rev. Pensions	314	Favorable	397	Passed	Postponed.	
Mills, Thomas	Pension	15	1	Petition	71	Pens. & Rev. Cl'ms.	Feb. 9, 1818	Adverse		Laid on table.		
Mills, William, (Conn.)	Release from imprisonment on judgment of United States.	11	3	Senate bill	499	Select	Feb. 5, 1811	With't amend.	S. 54	Passed		App'd Feb. 7, 1811
Mills, Zachariah, widow of	Continuation of pension	18	1	Petition	358	Pens. & Rev. Cl'ms.						
Millspaugh, Cornelius	(See William Hoag, and others)	27	3		153							

List of private claims presented to the House of Representatives of the United States from the 1st to the 31st Congress, inclusive—Continued

Names of claimants.	Nature or object of the claim.	Congress.	Session.	How brought before the House of Reps.	Page of journal.	To what committee of the House referred.	No. or date of the report.	Nature of the report.	No. of the bill.	How disposed of by the House of Reps.	How disposed of by the Senate.	Date of the act of Congress, and remarks.
Milly, an Indian woman..	Pension..........................	27	3	Petition	482	Indian Affairs....	274	Favorable; bill	826	Referred to Committee Whole House.		
Milly, an Indian woman..	Pension	28	1	Petition	289	Indian Affairs	149	Report and bill	137	Passed	Passed	App'd June 17, 1844
Milsted, John...........	Correction of error in land entry..	28	1	Petition	318	Public Lands.....	400	Report and bill	310	Passed.		
Milsted, John...........	Correction of error in land entry..	18	2	Petition	70	Public Lands.						
Milsted, John...........	Correction of error in land entry..	29	1	Petition	573	Public Lands.....	549	Report and bill	371	Passed	Passed	App'd Aug. 8, 1846
Milstead, Lindsey	Bounty land for services in late war	28	2	Petition	65	Public Lands.						
Milstead, William.......	(See Luis F. Beeler, and others)	30	1	....	115							
Milne, Alexander	Indemnity for property destroyed in war of 1812.	15	1	Petition	179	Claims	....	....	......	Discharged; laid on table.		
Milne, Alexander	Indemnity for property destroyed in war of 1812.	15	2	Senate bill	325	Claims	....	....	S. 73			
Milne, Alexander	Indemnity for property destroyed in war of 1812.	16	1	Senate bill	407	Claims	....	....	S. 72			
Milne, Alexander	Indemnity for property destroyed in war of 1812.	16	2	Petition	20	Claims	Dec. 20, 1820	Favorable; bill	175	Passed	Passed	App'd March 2, 1821
Milne, Joseph	Indemnity for French spoliations prior to 1800.	26	1	Memorial	182	Foreign Affairs....	343	Favorable; bill	319	Referred to Committee Whole House.		
Milner, Amos	Revolutionary pension..........	29	1	Petition	396	Rev. Pensions.						
Milnor, Robert, and John Thomson.	Payment for extra services as gaugers at Philadelphia.	25	2	Petition	409	Commerce	....	....	......	Discharged.		
Milnor, Robert, and John Thomson.	Payment for extra services as gaugers at Philadelphia.	25	3	Petition	92	Commerce	211	Favorable; bill	1066	Passed............	Adverse report.	
Milnor, Robert, and John Thomson.	Payment for extra services as gaugers at Philadelphia.	26	1	Petition	176	Commerce.	70	Favorable; bill	57	Passed	Passed	App'd May 2, 1840
Milnor, Robert..........	Payment for gauging instruments .	25	2	Petition	409	Commerce.	751	Favorable; bill	711	Referred to Committee Whole House.		
Milnor, Robert..........	Payment for gauging instruments.	25	3	House bill	380	Whole House	Jan. 25, 1839	With't amend.	711	Passed.		
Milnor, Robert..........	Payment for gauging instruments.	26	1	Petition	176	Commerce.	71	Favorable; bill	58	Passed	Indef. postp'd.	
Milroy, John...........	(See Rasselas Whitcomb, and others.)	25	2	....	1047							
Milton, Elijah	Increase of pension	23	1	Petition	128	Rev. Pensions.						
Milton, Elijah	Increase of pension	23	2	Petition	114	Rev. Pensions	....	....	......	Disch'd; laid on table.		
Milton, Hannah, widow of Col. John.	Compensation for revolutionary services.	22	1	Petition	333	Rev. Claims.						
Milton, Richard.........	Invalid pension................	9	2	Petition	519	Claims	Feb. 9, 1807	Adverse	......	Leave to withdraw.		
Milton, Robert..........	Pension	19	2	Petition	95	Military Affairs. .	....	....	......	Discharged; leave to withdraw.		
Milton, Robert..........	Pension	20	2	Petition	626	Military Pensions..	....	....	......	Discharged; laid on table.		
Milton, Robert..........	Pension	21	1	House bill	130	Whole House.....	Feb. 12, 1830	With amends.	72	Passed	Passed	App'd May 20, 1830
Milton, Wm., and others.	Compensation for military services in Georgia in 1793-'94.	5	2	Petition	94	....	....	....	......	Referred to Secretary of War.		
Milton, Wm., and others.	Compensation for military services in Georgia in 1793-'94.	6	1	Rep. of Secretary War.	626	Claims	....	....	......	Discharged and postponed.		
Milton, Wm., and others.	Compensation for military services in Georgia in 1793-'94.	6	2	Petition	735	Claims.						
Milton, Wm., and others.	Compensation for military services in Georgia in 1793-'94.	6	2	Memorial	747	Claims..........	Mar. 2, 1801	Res. to postpone.	......	Resolution adopted.		
Milton, Wm., and others.	Compensation for military services in Georgia in 1793-'94.	7	1	Petition	19	Claims..........	April 3, 1802	Res. to postpone.				
Milton, William	Pension	16	1	Petition	33	Pens. & Rev. Cl'ms.	....	....	......	Discharged; referred to Secretary of War.		

List of private claims presented to the House of Representatives of the United States from the 1st to the 31st Congress, inclusive—Continued.

Names of claimants.	Nature or object of the claim.	Congress.	Session.	How brought before the House of Reps.	Page of journal.	To what committee of the House referred.	No. or date of the report.	Nature of the report.	No. of the bill.	How disposed of by the House of Reps.	How disposed of by the Senate.	Date of the act of Congress, and remarks.
Mims, Joseph and Hannah.	(See Samuel Mims, administrator of.)	14	2	....	338							
Mims, Samuel	Confirmation of title to land in Mississippi.	9	2	Petition	499	Public Lands.						
Mims, Samuel	Confirmation of title to land in Mississippi.	10	1	Petition	18	Public Lands.						
Mims, Samuel	Confirmation of title to land in Mississippi.	10	2	Petition	511	Public Lands.						
Mims, Samuel	Confirmation of title to land in Mississippi.	11	2	Petition	117, 173	Public Lands	Mar. 27, 1810	Favorable; bill	137	Laid on table.		
Mims, Samuel	Confirmation of title to land in Mississippi.	11	3	Petition	457	Public Lands	Jan. 7, 1811	Favorable; bill	170	Passed	Passed	Vetoed by the President.
Mims, Samuel	Confirmation of title to land in Mississippi.	11	3	Senate bill	612	....	....	....	S. 68	Passed	Passed	App'd March 3, 1811
Mims, Samuel	Confirmation of title to land in Mississippi.	15	1	Petition	226	Priv. Land Claims.						
Mims, Samuel, administrator of.	Indemnity for property destroyed in war of 1812 by Indians.	14	2	Petition	338	Claims.						
Mims, Samuel, administrator of.	Indemnity for property destroyed in war of 1812 by Indians.	18	1	Petition	32	Claims	Jan. 9, 1824	Favorable; bill	46	Passed	Passed	App'd May 17, 1824
Min, John	Revolutionary pension	18	2	Petition	86	Rev. Pensions	Jan. 26, 1825	Adverse	......	Laid on table.		
Minard, Antoine, heirs of.	Grant of land to Canadian refugees in the revolutionary war.	24	1	Petition	508	Rev. Claims.						
Minard, Pierre	Refunding amount advanced Indian commissioners.	23	1	House bill	796	Whole House	June 26, 1834	With amends.	541	Passed	Passed	App'd June 28, 1834
Mines, Peter	Revolutionary pension	11	2	Petition	316	Claims	....	....	......	Laid on table.		
Mingus, Heironimus	Arrears of pension	18	1	Petition	344	Pens. & Rev. Cl'ms.	....	....	......	Discharged; laid on table.		
Minifee, Charles	For damages on cargo of masts for use of the navy.	8	1	Memorial	556	Claims	Mar. 13, 1804	Res. to post'p'n	......	Adopted.		
Minifee, Charles	For damages on cargo of masts for use of the navy.	8	2	Memorial	12	Claims.						
Minifee, Charles	Compensation for timber delivered at navy-yard, Washington, in 1803.	9	2	Memorial	492	Claims	Feb. 3, 1807	Adverse	......	Leave to withdraw.		
Minifee, Charles	Compensation for timber delivered at navy-yard, Washington, in 1803.	10	1	Memorial	58	Claims	Jan. 30, 1808	Adverse	......	Leave to withdraw.		
Minifee, Charles	Compensation for timber delivered at navy-yard, Washington, in 1803.	10	2	Memorial	368	Claims	Jan. 24, 1809	Adverse	......	Leave to withdraw.		
Minifee, Charles	Compensation for timber delivered at navy-yard, Washington, in 1803.	11	2	Senate bill	267	Claims	Mar. 8, 1810	With't amend.	S. 19	Referred to Committee Whole House.		
Minifee, Charles	Compensation for timber delivered at navy-yard, Washington, in 1803.	11	3	Memorial	462	Claims	Jan. 26, 1811	Favorable; bill	187	Passed	Postponed.	
Minifee, Charles	Compensation for timber delivered at navy-yard, Washington, in 1803.	12	1	Senate bill	272	Claims	April 3, 1812	With't amend.	S. 18	Passed	Passed	App'd May 1, 1812
Minifee, Charles	Interest on balance due for timber.	17	2	Petition	44	Claims	Dec. 20, 1822	Adverse	......	Laid on table.		
Minifee, Charles	Interest on balance due for timber.	18	1	Petition	52	Claims	14	Adverse	......	Rejected.		

List of *private claims presented to the House of Representatives of the United States from the* 1st *to the* 31st *Congress, inclusive*—Continued.

Names of claimants.	Nature or object of the claim.	Congress.	Session.	How brought before the House of Reps.	Page of journal.	To what committee of the House referred.	No. or date of the report.	Nature of the report.	No. of the bill.	How disposed of by the House of Reps.	How disposed of by the Senate.	Date of the act of Congress, and remarks.
Mines & Henry and others.	Refunding money advanced United States troops in war of 1812.	15	2	Petition	144	Military Affairs	Feb. 9, 1819	By bill	315	Passed	Passed	App'd March 3, 1819
Mines, Isaac, and others	(See Mines & Henry and others.)	15	2		144							
Minnesota, Territory of	Grant of land for a university	31	2	Petition	111	Territories.						
Minnie, James, assignees of.	Pre-emption right to land	24	1	Petition	751	Priv. Land Claims.						
Minnie, James, assignees of.	Pre-emption right to land	24	2	Petition	49	Priv. Land Claims.	95	Favorable; bill	841	Referred to Committee Whole House.		
Minnie, James, assignees of.	Pre-emption right to land	25	2	Petition	43	Priv. Land Claims.	346	Favorable; bill	377	Referred to Committee Whole House.		
Minnie, James, assignees of.	Pre emption right to land	25	3	Petition	92	Priv. Land Claims.	283	Adverse		Laid on table.		
Minnie, James, assignees of.	Pre-emption right to land	26	1	Petition	827	Priv. Land Claims.	478	Adverse		Laid on table.		
Minns, William	Compensation for property destroyed during revolution.	3	1	Petition	53					Referred to Secretary of Treasury.		
Minns, William	Compensation for property destroyed during revolution.	3	2	Rep. of Secretary Treasury.	284	Claims	Mar. 9, 1795	Adverse		Laid on table.		
Minns, William	Compensation for property destroyed during revolution.	4	1	Petition	598	Claims	May 31, 1796	Adverse		Laid on table.		
Minor, Amos	Relief for wounds received in the revolutionary war.	2	1	Petition	474					Referred to Secretary War.		
Minor, Amos	Relief for wounds received in the revolutionary war.	2	2	Petition	635	Select.						
Minor, Amos	Invalid pension	3	1	Rep. of Secretary War.	131	Select	May 26, 1794	Report and bill	62	Passed	Passed	App'd June 7, 1794
Minor, Amos	Arrears of pension	3	2	Petition	323	Claims.						
Minor, Amos	Arrears of pension	4	1	Petition	373	Claims	Jan. 6, 1796	Adverse		Leave to withdraw.		
Minor, Andrew	Pension	20	2	Petition	26	Military Pensions	Dec. 29, 1828	Adverse		Laid on table.		
Minor, Clarissa	(See James Rumsey, devisee of)	27	2		80							
Minor, James, (N. Y.)	Settlement of claims for revolutionary services.	3	1	Petition	95					Laid on table.		
Minor, John	(See Reuben Minor, administrator of.)	3	2		244							
Minor, John, sen.	Pension	13	2	Petition	331	Pens. & Rev. Cl'ms.	Mar. 8, 1814	Adverse		Laid on table		Leave to withdraw.
Minor, John, (Mich.)	Confirmation of title to land in Michigan.	16	2	Petition	48	Priv. Land Claims.				Discharged; laid on table.		
Minor, Menassah	Reimbursement of expenses in providing for his son John, wounded in the war of 1812.	14	1	Petition	40	Claims	Jan. 29, 1816	Favorable; bill		Passed	Passed	App'd April 29, 1816
Minor, Peter	(See Ottawa Indians)	24	2		312							
Minor, Rachael	Arrears of pension	28	1	Petition	839					Referred to Committee Whole House.		
Minor, Reuben, administrator of.	Compensation as surgeon in the revolutionary war.	3	2	Petition	244	Claims	Feb. 25, 1795	Adverse		Referred to Committee Whole House.		
Minor, Reuben, administrator of.	Compensation as surgeon in the revolutionary war.	4	2	Petition	628	Claims	Dec. 26, 1796	Adverse		Leave to withdraw.		
Minor, Reuben, administrator of.	Compensation as surgeon in the revolutionary war.	7	1	Petition	224					Laid on table.		
Minor, Reuben, administrator of.	Compensation as surgeon in the revolutionary war.	7	2	Petition	287	Claims	Feb. 23, 1803	Adverse		Referred to Committee Whole House.		
Minor, Reuben, administrator of.	Compensation as surgeon in the revolutionary war.	11	2	Petition	276	Claims	Mar. 24, 1810	Favorable; bill	117	Passed	Postponed.	
Minor, Reuben, administrator of.	Compensation as surgeon in the revolutionary war.	13	2	Petition	195	Pens. & Rev. Cl'ms.	Mar. 8, 1814	Resolution		Leave to withdraw.		

List of private claims presented to the House of Representatives of the United States from the 1st to the 31st Congress. inclusive—Continued.

Names of claimants.	Nature or object of the claim.	Congress.	Session.	How brought before the House of Reps.	Page of journal.	To what committee of the House referred.	No. or date of the report.	Nature of the report.	No. of the bill.	How disposed of by the House of Reps.	How disposed of by the Senate.	Date of the act of Congress, and remarks.
Minor, Reuben, administrator of.	Compensation as surgeon in the revolutionary war.	14	1	Petition	675	Pens. & Rev. Cl'ms.				Discharged; laid on table.		
Minor, Reuben, administrator of.	Compensation as surgeon in the revolutionary war.	14	2	Petition	13	Pens. & Rev. Cl'ms.	Feb. 7, 1817	Adverse		Laid on table.		
Minor, Stephen, (Conn.).	Invalid pension	3	1	Report Secretary of War.	131	Select	May 26, 1794	J't. res. to refer to Sec. War.	12	Passed	Passed	App'd June 9, 1794
Minor, Stephen, (Conn.).	Invalid pension	4	1	Resolution	445	Claims	Feb. 18, 1796	Favorable; bill	156	Passed	Passed	App'd April 20, 1796
Minor, Thomas, (Va.)	Commutation pay for revolutionary services.	21	2	Petition	82	Rev. Claims.						
Minor, Thomas, (Va.)	Commutation pay for revolutionary services.	22	1	Petition	44	Rev. Claims	503	Favorable; bill	608	Referred to Committee Whole House.		
Minor, Thomas, (Va.)	Commutation pay for revolutionary services.	23	1	Petition	43	Rev. Claims	33	Favorable; bill	39	Passed	With amend.	App'd June 30, 1834
Minor, Wilshire	Compensation for horse lost in the war with Mexico.	30	1	Petition	189	Claims	471	Adverse		Laid on table		Leave to withdraw, 1st sess. 31st Congress.
Minor, William, (Conn.).	Pension	21	2	Petition	61	Military Pensions.						
Minor, William, (Conn.).	Pension	22	1	Petition	97	Rev. Pensions				Discharged; laid on table.		
Minor, William B.	Confirmation of title to island in Mississippi river.	24	1	Petition	258	Public Lands.						
Minot, James	(See Joshua Green, and others)	4	1		385							
Minot, John	Remission of duties on goods imported into Castine, Maine.	16	1	Senate bill	108	Ways and Means	Jan. 14, 1820	With mend'ts.	S. 13	Passed	Passed	App'd April 11, 1820
Minot, Jonas C.	(See Canadian refugees.)	6	2		748							
Mintor, Anthony M., and J. Brently.	Relief for error in relinqisuhing certain lands.	21	1	Petition	172	Public Lands				Discharged; laid on table.		
Mintor, Anthony M., and J. Brently.	Relief for error in relinquishing certain lands.	21	1	Senate bill	615	Priv. Land Claims.	May 11, 1830	With amend.	127	Referred to Committee Whole House.		
Mintor, Anthony M., and J. Brently.	Relief for error in relinquishing certain lands.	22	1	Petition	388	Public Lands	Mar. 6, 1832	Adverse		Laid on table.		
Mintor, Anthony M., and J. Brently.	Relief for error in relinquishing certain lands.	22	1	Senate bill	819	Public Lands	June 12, 1832	Adverse	S. 124	Rejected.		
Mintor, Anthony M., and J. Brently.	Relief for error in relinquishing certain lands.	22	2	Senate bill	325	Priv. Land Claims.			S. 11			
Mentor, William	(See John Stephenson, representatives of.)	23	2		47							
Minturn, Benjamin G.	(Minturn & Champlin)	26	1		182							
Minturn & Champlin	Indemnity for French spoliations prior to 1800.	26	1	Memorial	182	Foreign Affairs	343	Favorable; bill	319	Referred to Committee Whole House.		
Minturn & Champlin, sureties of.	For a compromise settlement of the claims of United States against them.	23	1	Senate bill	175	Ways and Means	Jan. 14, 1834	With amend.	37	Passed		App'd Mar. 24, 1834
Minturn, William, executor of.	Indemnity for French spoliations prior to 1800.	26	1	Memorial	182	Foreign Affairs	343	Favorable; bill	319	Referred to Committee Whole House.		
Minturn, William	Indemnity for French spoliations prior to 1800.	26	1	Memorial	182	Foreign Affairs	343	Favorable; bill	319	Referred to Committee Whole House.		
Mirando, Pedro	Reimbursement of duties on sugar.	19	1	Petition	407	Ways and Means	198	Favorable; bill	258	Passed.		
Mirando, Pedro	Reimbursement of duties on sugar.	19	2	Petition	31	Ways and Means	Jan. 3, 1827	Favorable; bill	337	Passed	Passed	App'd March 3, 1827
Mirer	(See Andrew Miser)	21	1		98							
Miser, Andrew	Compensation for revolutionary services.	21	1	Petition	98	Military Pensions				Discharged; laid on table.		
Missionnier, Henry, executor of.	Indemnity for French spoliations prior to 1800.	26	1	Memorial	182	Foreign Affairs	343	Favorable; bill	319	Referred to Committee Whole House.		

List of private claims presented to the House of Representatives of the United States from the 1st to the 31st Congress, inclusive—Continued.

Names of claimants.	Nature or object of the claim.	Congress.	Session.	How brought before the House of Reps.	Page of journal.	To what committee of the House referred.	No. or date of the report.	Nature of the report.	No. of the bill.	How disposed of by the House of Reps.	How disposed of by the Senate.	Date of the act of Congress, and remarks.*
Missions, American Board of Foreign.	Indemnity for loss of property by removal of Choctaw Indians.	22	2	Petition	42	Military Affairs.						
Mississippi, Territory, city of Natchez.	Confirmation of title to certain lots in said city.	8	1	Petition	440	Select.						
Mississippi, legislature of	Grant of land for a hospital at Natchez.	9	2	Memorial	479	Select	Jan. 12, 1807	Favorable; bill	173			Bill became a law, omitting grant to Natchez.
Mississippi, United States judges in.	For increase of salary	9	2	Memorial	479	Select	Jan. 12, 1807	Favorable; bill	173	Passed	Passed	App'd March 3, 1807
Mississippi Land Company, by agent.	For compromise of their claim to to certain lands ceded by Georgia to the United States.	8	2	Memorial	48	Claims	Jan. 18, 1805	Favorable; bill ordered.	49	Referred to Committee Whole House.		
Mississippi, Jefferson college, trustees of.	Confirmation of title to certain lands.	8	2	Petition	7	Select	Feb. 7, 1805	Adverse		Referred to Committee Whole House.		
Mississippi, Jefferson college, trustees of.	Confirmation of title to certain lands.	9	1	Memorial	251	Public Lands	Mar. 4, 1806	Adverse		Referred to Committee Whole House.		
Mississippi, legislature of	For further time for pre-emption claimants to make payment for lands.	9	1	Memorial	188	Select	Mar. 26, 1806	Favorable	135	Passed	Passed	App'd April 21, 1806
Mississippi, legislature of	For revision of land laws and for extension of time for making payment for lands.	9	2	Memorial	555	Public Lands.						
Mississippi, sundry claimants to land.	Extension of time for making payments.	12	1	House bill	43	Whole House	Dec. 2, 1811	With't amend.	13	Passed	Passed	App'd Dec. 12, 1811
Mississippi, sundry claimants to land.	Extension of time for making payments.	14	1	Memorial	35	Public Lands.	16	Favorable; bill		Passed	Passed	App'd April 24, 1816
Mississippi, secretary of	Additional compensation	10	1	Resolution	23	Select	Nov. 17, 1807	Favorable; bill	4	Passed	Passed	App'd Dec. 5, 1807
Mississippi, inhabitants of.	Confirmation of their titles to land.	10	1	Petition	112	Public Lands.						
Mississippi, inhabitants of.	Confirmation of their titles to land.	10	2	Petition	350	Public Lands.						
Mississippi, inhabitants of.	Confirmation of their titles to land.	13	3	Petition	509	Public Lands	37	Favorable; bill	244	Rejected.		
Mississippi, inhabitants of.	Confirmation of their titles to land.	14	1	Petition	60	Public Lands	47	Favorable; bill	76	Rejected.		
Mississippi, inhabitants of.	Confirmation of their titles to land.	14	2	Petition	33	Public Lands				Discharged; laid on table.		
Mississippi, land commissioners in.	Increase of compensation	10	1	Resolution	28	Public Lands.	Jan. 11, 1808	Adverse		Laid on table.		
Mississippi, land commissioners in.	Increase of compensation	11	3	Resolution	460					Referred to Secretary Treasury.		
Mississippi, Baptist church at Salem.	Pre-emption right to the land on which the church stands.	11	2	Petition	119	Public Lands	Mar. 16, 1810	Favorable; bill	137	Laid on table.		
Mississippi, Baptist church at Salem.	Pre-emption right to the land on which the church stands.	11	3	Petition	458	Public Lands	Jan. 7, 1811	Favorable; bill	170	Passed	Passed	Vetoed by the President.
Mississippi, inhabitants of.	Pre-emption right to lands	14	1	Petition	153	Public Lands				Discharged; laid on table.		
Mississippi, inhabitants of.	Pre-emption right to lands	14	2	Petition	60	Public Lands	Dec. 31, 1816	Adverse		Rejected.		
Mississippi, inhabitants of.	Pre-emption right to lands	16	2	Petition	203	Public Lands				Discharged; laid on table.		
Mississippi, sundry citizens of.	Indemnity in land for losses in Creek war.	13	3	Petition	681	Select.						

List of private claims presented to the House of Representatives of the United States from the 1st to the 31st Congress, inclusive—Continued.

Names of claimants.	Nature or object of the claim.	Congress.	Session.	How brought before the House of Reps.	Page of journal.	To what committee of the House referred.	No. or date of the report.	Nature of the report.	No. of the bill.	How disposed of by the House of Reps.	How disposed of by the Senate.	Date of the act of Congress, and remarks.
Mississippi, sundry citizens of.	Indemnity in land for lossos in Creek war.	14	1	Petition	56, 114	Select	38	Adverse.	......	Laid on table.		
Mississippi, sundry citizens of.	Indemnity in land for losses in Creek war.	14	2	Petition	216	Ways and Means	......	......	......	Discharged; laid on table.		
Mississippi, sundry citizens of.	Confirmation of Spanish grants to land.	14	1	Petition	60	Public Lands	47	Favorable; bill	76	Rejected.		
Mississippi, legislature of.	Payment for services of the men who served under Col. Nixon and Major Hinds.	14	1	Petition	106	......	......	......	......	Referred to Secretary of War.		
Mississippi, inhabitants of the counties of Baldwin and Mobile.	Compensation for cattle destroyed by soldiers and militia in the service of the U. S. war of 1812.	14	2	Petition	212	Claims.						
Mississippi cavalry	Compensation for services in war of 1812.	15	1	Petition	287	Military Affairs.	Mar. 10, 1818	Favorable; bill	126	Passed	Passed	App'd April 20, 1818
Mississippi, legislature of.	Pre-emption right to settlers on public lands.	20	1	Resolution	115	Public Lands	Jan. 28, 1828	Favorable; bill	115	Referred to Committee Whole House.		
Mississippi, legislature of.	Pre-emption right to settlers on public lands.	20	2	Petition	322	......	......	......	......	Referred to Committee Whole House.		
Mississippi, legislature of.	Pre-emption right to settlers on public lands.	25	3	Memorial	134	Public Lands	173	Favorable; bill	1036	Referred to Committee Whole House.		
Mississippi, legislature of.	Pre-emption right to settlers on public lands.	26	1	Resolution	608	Public Lands.						
Mississippi, registers and receivers of land offices in.	Extra compensation for acting as commissioners of private land claims.	18	1	Resolution	145	Public Lands.						
Mississippi, registers and receivers of land offices in.	Extra compensation for acting as commissioners of private land claims.	20	1	Resolution	202	Public Lands	Mar. 31, 1828	Favorable; bill	246	Referred to Committee Whole House.		
Mississippi, registers and receivers of land offices in.	Extra compensation for acting as commissioners of private land claims.	20	2	Bill of last sess.	284	Whole House	Feb. 13, 1829	With't amend.	246	Passed.		
Mississippi, registers and receivers of land offices in.	Extra compensation for acting as commissioners of private land claims.	21	2	Res. and docs.	115	Public Lands	Dec. 30, 1830	Favorable; bill	525	Referred to Committee Whole House.		
Mississippi, registers and receivers of land offices in.	Extra compensation for locating bounty land warrants.	30	2	Petition	78	Public Lands.						
Mississippi, registers and receivers of land offices in.	Extra compensation for locating bounty land warrants.	31	1	Petition	337	Public Lands.						
Mississippi, registers and receivers of land offices in.	Extra compensation for locating bounty land warrants.	31	1	Senate bill	970	Public Lands	......	......	S. 62			
Mississippi, registers and receivers of land offices in.	Extra compensation for locating bounty land warrants.	31	2	Petition	179	Public Lands.						
Mississippi, postmaster at Jackson.	Increase of compensation	22	1	Resolution	259	P. Of. & P. Roads.						
Mississippi, postmaster at Jackson.	Increase of compensation	22	2	Resolution	60	P. Of. & P. Roads.	Dec. 20, 1832	Adverse	......	Laid on table.		
Mississippi, postmaster at Doakes.	Increase of compensation	22	1	Resolution	475	P. Of. & P. Roads.						
Mississippi, collector of port Pearlington.	Increase of compensation	23	1	Resolution	252	Commerce.						
Mississippi, State of	Relinquishing to said State the two per cent. fund arising from sales of land in said State.	26	1	Senate bill	185	Public Lands	April 24, 1840	With amends.	S. 4	Referred to Committee Whole House.		

List of private claims presented to the House of Representatives of the United States from the 1st to the 31st Congress, inclusive—Continued.

Names of claimants.	Nature or object of the claim.	Congress.	Session.	How brought before the House of Reps.	Page of journal.	To what committee of the House referred.	No. or date of the report.	Nature of the report.	No. of the bill.	How disposed of by the House of Reps.	How disposed of by the Senate.	Date of the act of Congress, and remarks.
Mississippi, State of	Relinquishing to said State the two per cent. fund arising from sales of land in said State.	26	2	Senate bill	203	Public Lands	Feb. 12, 1841	With't amend.	S. 163	Referred to Committee Whole House.		
Mississippi, State of	Authority to apply two per cent. fund to construction of railroads.	30	1	Resolution	596	Public Lands	May 16, 1848	By bill	490	Passed	Passed	App'd June 16, 1848
Mississippi, State of	Compensation for loss of sixteen sections in Choctaw and Chickasaw cessions of land in said State.	26	1	Resolution	765	Public Lands.						
Mississippi, State of	Compensation for loss of sixteen sections in Choctaw and Chickasaw cessions of land in said State.	27	2	Memorial	792	Public Lands	May 25, 1842	Favorable; bill	434	Passed	Passed	App'd June 13, 1842
Mississippi, State of	Permission to relinquish certain sixteenth sections and enter others.	30	1	Resolution	603	Public Lands.						
Mississippi, Agricultural Bank of.	Remission of interest on debt due United States.	27	2	Petition	130	Select	553	Favorable; bill	345	Passed	Passed	App'd Aug. 16, 1842
Mississippi, Agricultural & Planters' Banks of.	For an extension of time to pay judgment against them.	27	2	Senate bill	1126	Ways and Means	....	....	S. 252			
Mississippi, Agricultural & Planters' Banks of.	For an extension of time to pay judgment against them.	27	3	Senate bill	250	Ways and Means	Feb. 23, 1843	Adverse	S. 59	Rejected.		
Mississippi, citizens of Fulton.	Confirmation of certain pre-emption claims.	27	2	Petition	455	Public Lands.						
Mississippi, State of	Legalizing certain land sales	28	1	Resolution	165	Public Lands	447	Favorable; bill	344	Ref'd to Com. W. H.		
Mississippi, State of	Reimbursement of amount expended on account of the troops called into service of United States in 1836.	30	1	Resolution	312	Claims.						
Mississippi, land claimants east of Pearl river.	Confirmation of certain surveys and locations of land.	30	1	House bill	584	Priv. Land Claims.	522	With't amend.	350	Passed	Passed	App'd Aug. 7, 1848
Mississippi, citizens of Lowndes county.	Relief in relation to a section of school land.	30	1	Petition	678	Public Lands	June 23, 1848	Favorable; bill	574	Referred to Committee Whole House.		
Mississippi, Grand Gulf Railroad and Banking Company.	Reimbursement of duties paid on railroad iron.	27	1	Memorial	97	Ways and Means	....	....	......	Discharged; laid on table.		
Mississippi, Grand Gulf Railroad and Banking Company.	To have bonds given for duties on railroad iron cancelled.	27	1	Memorial	108	Ways and Means.						
Mississippi, Grand Sulphur Railroad Company.	Reimbursement of duties on railroad iron, and for cancellation of bonds for duties	27	2	Memorial	129	Ways and Means	1013	Favorable; bill	586	Referred to Committee Whole House.		
Missouri, inhabitants of Boon's Lick.	Compensation in land for services against hostile Indians.	14	1	Petition	36	Public Lands	38	Adverse	......	Rejected.		
Missouri, inhabitants of Boon's Lick.	Compensation in land for services against hostile Indians.	15	1	Petition	278	Public Lands	....	....	......	Discharged; laid on table.		
Missouri frontier settlers	Compensation in land for erecting and arming forts.	14	1	Resolution	361	Select	April 3, 1816	By bill	164	Indefinitely postponed.		
Missouri rangers	Compensation for military services	14	2	Memorial	453	....	....	....	......	Laid on table.		
Missouri militia	Compensation for services against hostile Indians.	21	1	Res. and docs.	556	Military Affairs	May 10, 1830	Favorable; bill	462	Referred to Committee Whole House.		
Missouri militia	Compensation for services against hostile Indians.	22	2	Res. and docs.	96, 127	Ways and Means.						
Missouri militia	Compensation for services against hostile Indians.	23	1	Res. and docs.	95	Ways and Means.						

List of private claims presented to the House of Representatives of the United States from the 1st to the 31st Congress, inclusive—Continued.

Names of claimants.	Nature or object of the claim.	Congress.	Session.	How brought before the House of Reps.	Page of journal.	To what committee of the House referred.	No. or date of the report.	Nature of the report.	No. of the bill.	How disposed of by the House of Reps.	How disposed of by the Senate.	Date of the act of Congress, and remarks.
Missouri militia	Compensation for services against the Indians in 1832.	24	1	Senate bill	810	Claims	May 17, 1836	With't amend.	S. 131	Passed	....	App'd July 2, 1836
Missouri, sundry citizens of	Confirmation of land titles.......	14	1	Memorial	340	Public Lands.						
Missouri, sundry citizens of	Confirmation of land titles.......	14	2	Memorial	96	Public Lands.						
Missouri, sundry citizens of	Permission to apply payments on lands to such portion as they will cover, and to relinquish the residue.	16	2	Memorial	91	Public Lands.....	Dec. 28, 1820	General bill ..	181	Referred to Committee Whole House.		
Missouri, sundry citizens of	Permission to apply payments on lands to such portion as they will cover, and to relinquish the residue.	16	2	Senate bill	218	Public Lands.....	Feb. 15, 1821	With't amend.	S. 16	Passed	....	App'd March 2, 1821
Missouri, sundry citizens of	Pre emption to lands in consideration of having lost their property by removing from the frontier by order of Gov. Howard.	14	2	Memorial	453	....	....	....	.....	Laid on table.		
Missouri, legislature of ...	Grant of land for public buildings in Lawrence county.	14	1	Petition	180	Public Lands.						
Missouri, New Madrid sufferers.	Grant of land for sufferings and losses by earthquakes.	13	2	Resolution	297	Public Lands.....	Feb. 25, 1814	By bill	138	Referred to Committee Whole House.		
Missouri, New Madrid sufferers.	Grant of land for sufferings and losses by earthquakes.	13	3	House bill	636	Whole House.....	Jan. 14, 1829	With amend'ts	249	Passed	Passed	App'd Feb. 17, 1815
Missouri, New Madrid sufferers.	Permission to exchange lands to which they are entitled under act of February 17, 1815, for other lands.	21	2	Senate bill	185	Public Lands.....	March 2, 1831	With amend'ts	S. 70	Passed	Passed	App'd March 2, 1831
Missouri, New Madrid sufferers.	Confirmaion of title to lands entered under acts of February 17, 1815, and March 2, 1831.	26	1	Senate bill	1132	Public Lands.....	....	....	S. 205			
Missouri, New Madrid sufferers.	Confirmation of title to lands entered under acts of February 17, 1815, and March 2, 1831.	27	2	Senate bill	411	Public Lands.....	March 8, 1842	With't amend.	S. 74	Referred to Committee Whole House.		
Missouri, New Madrid sufferers.	Confirmation of title to lands entered under acts of February 17, 1815, and March 2, 1831.	27	3	Senate bill	334	Public Lands.....	Feb. 14, 1843	With amend'ts	S. 19	Passed	Passed	App'd March 1, 1843
Missouri, citizens of......	Pre-emption right to lands.......	15	2	Petition	220	Public Lands.						
Missouri, citizens of......	Pre emption right to lands.......	16	2	Memorial	123	Public Lands.....	Jan. 25, 1821	Adverse	......	Rejected.		
Missouri, citizens of......	Pre emption right to lands.......	17	1	Memorial	291	Priv. Land Claims.	....	....	......	Discharged; laid on table.		
Missouri, citizens of......	Pre emption right to lands.......	21	1	Petition	200	Public Lands.....	....	....	......	Discharged; laid on table.		
Missouri, citizens of......	Pre emption right to lands.......	23	1	Petition	139	Public Lands.						
Missouri, sundry inhabitants of.	Confirmation of land titles.......	15	1	Petition	353	....	....	....	......	Referred to Secretary Treasury.		
Missouri, sundry inhabitants of.	Confirmation of land titles.......	15	2	Petition	89, 144	....	....	....	......	Referred to Committee Whole House on bill No. 81.		
Missouri, sundry inhabitants of.	Confirmation of land titles.......	16	1	Petition	72	Priv. Land Claims.	....	....	......	Discharged; laid on table.		
Missouri, sundry inhabitants of.	Confirmation of land titles.......	16	2	Petition	95	Priv. Land Claims.	....	....	......	Discharged; laid on table.		
Missouri, sundry inhabitants of St. Geneve.	Confirmation of land titles.......	17	1	Petition	54	Public Lands.						

List of private claims presented to the House of Representatives of the United States from the 1st to the 31st Congress, inclusive—Continued.

Names of claimants.	Nature or object of the claim.	Congress.	Session.	How brought before the House of Reps.	Page of journal.	To what committee of the House referred.	No. or date of the report.	Nature of the report.	No. of the bill.	How disposed of by the House of Reps.	How disposed of by the Senate.	Date of the act of Congress, and remarks.
Missouri, sundry inhabitants of.	Confirmation of land titles.......	18	1	Petition	54	Public Lands.....	Jan. 16, 1824	Favorable; bill	65	Passed	Passed	App'd May 26, 1824
Missouri, sundry inhabitants of.	Confirmation of land titles.......	21	1	Petition	151	....	....	....	......	Referred to Committee Whole House on Senate bill No. 4.		
Missouri, sundry inhabitants of.	Confirmation of land titles.......	22	1	Petition	263	Priv. Land Claims.	303	Favorable; bill	380	Referred to Committee Whole House.		
Missouri, Bank of, by agent	For an equitable settlement of its accounts.	18	1	Memorial	469	Ways and Means.						
Missouri, inhabitants of...	Indemnity for Indian depredations.	19	2	Memorial	243	Indian Affairs.....	....	....	......	Disch'd; laid on table.		
Missouri, inhabitants of Wayne county.	Indemnity for Indian depredations.	21	2	Petition	338	Pubilc Lands.						
Missouri, sundry inhabitants of.	Indemnity for Indian depredations.	22	1	Petition and rep't 3d Auditor.	417	Indian Affairs.						
Missouri, inhabit's of Cote Sans Dessein.	Indemnity for Indian depredations.	23	1	Petition	138	Indian Affairs.....	....	....	......	Discharged; laid on table.		
Missouri, inhabitants of...	Indemnity for Indian depredations.	24	1	Petition	96, 212	Indian Affairs.						
Missouri, trustees of the town of Louisiana.	Confirmation of title to land	23	1	Petition and docs.	568	Public Lands.....	May 13, 1834	By bill	473	Referred to Committee Whole House.		
Missouri, inhabitants of Osage valley.	Right of pre-emption to land on which they reside.	23	1	Petition	568	Public Lands.						
Missouri, sundry inhabitants of.	Right of pre-emption to actual settlers.	24	1	Petition	215	Public Lands.....	Feb. 5, 1836	Favorable; bill	294	Referred to Committee Whole House.		
Missouri, citizens of Pike county.	Right of pre-emption to land on which they reside.	25	2	Petition	179	Public Lands.						
Missouri, inhabitants of...	Indemnity for land purchased of United States, and of which they have been deprived by a decision of the Supreme court.	24	1	Petition	478	Public Lands.						
Missouri, sundry citizens of	Confirmation of title to land cal'ed Dubuque mines in Wisconsin.	24	2	Petition	314	Priv. Land Claims.						
Missouri, citizens of......	Drawback on goods exported to New Mexico.	24	1	Memorial	54	Commerce	Dec. 21, 1835	By bill	48	Referred to Committee Whole House.		
Missouri, citizens of......	Drawback on goods exported to New Mexico.	25	2	Memorial	411	Commerce	....	....	......	Discharged; laid on table.		
Missouri, citizens of......	Drawback on goods exported to New Mexico.	27	2	Petition	372	Commerce.						
Missouri, citizens of......	Drawback on goods exported to New Mexico.	28	1	Petition	240	Commerce	399	Favorable; bill	308	Referred to Committee Whole House.		
Missouri, legislature of....	Payment for services of mounted volunteers called out to protect the frontier.	25	2	Memorial	416	Claims	....	....	......	Discharged; laid on table.		
Missouri, legislature of....	Payment for services of mounted volunteers called out to protect the frontier.	26	1	Senate bill	1147	Claims	....	....	S. 183			
Missouri, legislature of....	Payment for services of mounted volunteers called out to protect the frontier.	27	2	Senate bill	155	Military Affairs....	April 12, 1842	With amends.	S. 67	Passed	Passed	App'd Aug. 31, 1842
Missouri volunteers	Payment for horses lost at Tampa bay.	25	2	Senate bill	785	Claims	968	With't amend.	209	Referred to Committee Whole House.		
Missouri volunteers	Payment for horses lost at Tampa bay.	28	1	Bill on leave....	168	Military Affairs ...	167	With amends.	19	Passed	Passed	App'd June 15, 1844

List of private claims presented to the House of Representatives of the United States from the 1st to the 31st Congress, inclusive—Continued.

Names of claimants.	Nature or object of the claim.	Congress.	Session.	How brought before the House of Reps.	Page of journal.	To what committee of the House referred.	No. or date of the report.	Nature of the report.	No. of the bill.	How disposed of by the House of Reps.	How disposed of by the Senate.	Date of the act of Congress, and remarks.
Missouri, legislature of....	To be reimbursed amount expended in expelling Osage Indians.	26	2	Memorial	74	Military Affairs.						
Missouri, citizens of Jefferson county.	Pre-emption right to certain lands.	26	2	Petition	131	Public Lands.						
Missouri, sundry citizens of	Indemnity for Indian depredations.	28	1	Petition	273	Indian Affairs.						
Missouri, citizens of......	Donation of land or pre-emption right to land for five years, in consideration of having deposited money with the receiver of the land office at Palmyra, which has been misapplied.	28	1	Petition	787	Public Lands.						
Missouri, citizens of Hickory county.	For an exchange of school lands for other lands.	30	1	Petition	676	Public Lands.....	794	Adverse	......	Laid on table.		
Missouri, citizens of Ralls county.	For an exchange of school lands for other lands.	30	1	Petition	723	Public Lands.....	794	Adverse.	......	Laid on table.		
Missouri, citizens of Barry county.	For an exchange of school lands for other lands.	30	1	Petition	594	Public Lands.....	794	Adverse	......	Laid on table.		
Missouri, citizens of Shelby county.	For an exchange of school lands for other lands.	30	1	Petition	111	....	....	....	.....	....	....	Not referred.
Missouri, corporate authorities of Carondelet.	Confirmation of title to the commons of said village according to official survey.	30	1	Petition	580	Priv. Land Claims.	Aug. 8, 1848	Favorable; bill	642	Referred to Committee Whole House.		
Missouri, registers and receivers of land office at Fayette.	Increase of compensation for locating military land warrants.	31	1	Petition	520	Public Lands.						
Missouri, registers and receivers of land office at Fayette.	Increase of compensation for locating military land warrants.	31	2	Petition	53	Public Lands.						
Missouri, registers and receivers of land office at Palmyra.	Increase of compensation for locating military land warrants.	31	1	Petition	392	Public Lands.						
Missouri, registers and receivers of land office at Palmyra.	Increase of compensation for locating military land warrants.	31	2	Petition	110	Public Lands.						
Missouri, registers and receivers of land office at St. Louis.	Increase of compensation for locating military land warrants.	31	2	Petition	110	Public Lands.						
Missouri, registers and receivers of land office at Springfield.	Increase of compensation for locating military land warrants.	31	2	Petition	53	Public Lands.						
Missouri, U. States frigate, officers and crew of.	Indemnity for losses occasioned by the destruction of said vessel.	29	1	Memorial	747	Naval Affairs.....	597	Favorable; bill	420	Referred to Committee Whole House.		
Missouri, U. States frigate, officers and crew of.	Indemnity for losses occasioned by the destruction of said vessel.	30	1	Bill on leave....	1074	Whole House	....	....	608			
Mitchell, Aaron, (Mass.)..	Indemnity for French spoliations prior to 1800.	26	1	Memorial	182	Foreign Affairs....	343	Favorable; bill	319	Referred to Committee Whole House.		
Mitchell, A. W., and others.	Permission to enter other lands in lieu of present location.	19	1	Petition	53	Public Lands.....	Dec. 23, 1825	Adverse	......	Laid on table.		
Mitchell, Adam	Payment of Continental money held by him.	27	2	Petition	77	Judiciary	....	....	......	Discharged; laid on table.		
Mitchell, Adam	Payment of Continental money held by him.	28	1	Petition	109	Judiciary.						

List of private claims presented to the House of Representatives of the United States from the 1st to the 31st Congress, inclusive—Continued.

Names of claimants.	Nature or object of the claim.	Congress.	Session.	How brought before the House of Reps.	Page of journal.	To what committee of the House referred.	No. or date of the report.	Nature of the report.	No. of the bill.	How disposed of by the House of Reps.	How disposed of by the Senate.	Date of the act of Congress, and remarks.
Mitchell, Adam	Payment of Continental money held by him.	29	1	Petition	465	Rev. Claims.						
Mitchell, Albin, and others.	Confirmation of title to land	24	1	Petition and docs.	478	Priv. Land Claims.						
Mitchell, Alexander, heirs of.	Release from certain judgment in favor of United States.	27	2	House bill	208	Whole House	Jan. 28, 1843	With't amend.	682	Laid on table.		
Mitchell, Alexander, heirs of.	Release from certain judgment in favor of United States.	28	1	Petition	610	Claims	566	Favorable; bill	419	Referred to Committee Whole House.		
Mitchell, Alexander, heirs of.	Release from certain judgment in favor of United States.	28	2	Bill of last sess.	344	Whole House	Feb. 7, 1845	With't amend.	419	Passed	Passed	App'd March 3, 1845
Mitchell, Ammi	Arrears of pension	24	1	Petition	187	Invalid Pensions.						
Mitchell, Andrew, (Pa.)	Refunding amount paid for licenses on distillery.	17	1	Senate bill	380	Ways and Means.	April 3, 1822	With't amend.	S. 59	Laid on table.		
Mitchell, Andrew, (Pa.)	Refunding amount paid for licenses on distillery.	17	2	Petition	64	Claims	Jan. 22, 1823	Adverse	......	Laid on table.		
Mitchell, Andrew, representatives of.	Refunding amount paid for licenses on distillery.	18	1	Senate bill	301	Ways and Means.	Mar. 12, 1824	With't amend.	S. 43	Laid on table.		
Mitchell, Andrew, administrator of.	Refunding amount paid for licenses on distillery.	19	1	Petition	151	Claims	97	Adverse	......	Laid on table.		
Mitchell, Anna	(See Reuben Mitchell, widow of.)	26	2	....	52							
Mitchell, Benjamin	Revolutionary pension	25	2	Petition	52	Rev. Pensions.	450	Favorable; bill	453	Passed	Adverse report.	
Mitchell, Benjamin	Revolutionary pension	26	1	Petition	172	Rev. Pensions.	130	Favorable; bill	140	Passed.	Indef. postp'd.	
Mitchell & Clayton	(See Clayton & Mitchell)	26	1	....	323							
Mitchell, David R.	Pre-empt on right to land	23	1	Petition	637	Public Lands.						
Mitchell, David R.	Pre-emption right to land	24	1	Petition	433	Public Lands.						
Mitchell, David R.	Pre-emption right to land	26	1	Peti ion	962	Public Lands.	593	Adverse	......	Laid on table.		
Mitchell, Edward, (Miss.,) wife of	Compensation for learning Choctaw Indians to spin and weave.	23	2	Petition	241	Public Lands.	Feb. 23, 1835	As amendment to bill.	664	Passed.	Passed	App'd March 3, 1835
Mitchell, Eli	Pension	23	1	Senate amendm't to House bill.	878	Whole House	June 28, 1834	Res. to concur.	42	Passed	....	App'd June 30, 1834
Mitchell, Ensign	Revolutionary pension	25	3	Petition	130	Rev. Pensions.	....	....	......	Discharged.		
Mitchell, Ensign	Revolutionary pension	26	1	Petition	174	Rev. Pensions.	....	....	......	Discharged; laid on table.		
Mitchell, George	(See Leighton Wood and others.)	3	1	....	209							
Mitchell, George	Compensation for a horse lost in service of United States.	26	1	Petition	336	Claims.						
Mitchell, George V.	To be released from judgment obtained against him.	29	1	Petition	169	P. Of. & P. Roads.	Mar. 27, 1846	....	......	Discharged; laid on table.		
Mitchell, George V.	To be released from judgment obtained against him.	30	1	Senate bill	957	P. Of. & P. Roads.	....	With't amend.	S. 162	Passed	Passed	App'd Aug. 14, 1848
Mitchell, Ignatius	(See William Thompson)	19	1	....	312							
Mitchell, James	Compensation for property of his father, Adam Mitchell, destroyed in the revolution.	28	1	Petition	533	Rev. Claims.						
Mitchell, James	Compensation for property of his father, Adam Mitchell, destroyed in the revolution.	29	1	Petition	179	Rev. Claims.	399	Adverse	......	Laid on table.		
Mitchell, James	Compensation for property of his father, Adam Mitchell, destroyed in the revolution.	31	1	Petition	1140	Claims.						
Mitchell, James, (Penn.)	Pension	21	1	Petition	231	Military Pensions.						
Mitchell, James, (Penn.)	Pension	21	2	Petition	64	Military Pensions.	....	....	......	Discharged; laid on table.		

List of private claims presented to the House of Representatives of the United States from the 1st to the 31st Congress, inclusive—Continued.

Names of claimants.	Nature or object of the claim.	Congress.	Session.	How brought before the House of Reps.	Page of journal.	To what committee of the House referred.	No. or date of the report.	Nature of the report.	No. of the bill.	How disposed of by the House of Reps.	How disposed of by the Senate.	Date of the act of Congress, and remarks.
Mitchell, James, (Penn.)	Pension	22	1	Resolution	95	Rev. Pensions	121	Favorable; bill	194	Referred to Committee Whole House.		
Mitchell, James	Invalid pension	6	1	Petition	640	Claims	April 24, 1800	Adverse		Leave to withdraw.		
Mitchell, James, (Ill.)	Correction of land entry	18	1	Petition	39	Public Lands	Dec. 15, 1823	Favorable; bill	7	Passed	Passed, with amendment.	App'd May 26, 1824
Mitchell, James, English ship.	(See James Hervey, attorney, &c.)	23	1		189							
Mitchell, James, (N. Y.)	Reimbursement of expenses and costs upon sundry suits as inspector.	13	1	Petition	12	Com. and Manuf.				Leave to withdraw.		
Mitchell, James, (Ga.)	Compensation for services, for horse lost, &c., in Florida expedition.	19	1	Resolution	55	Claims	31	Adverse		Laid on table.		
Mitchell, James, (Ga,)	Compensation for services, for horse lost, &c., in Florida expedition.	20	1	Petition	101	Claims	Feb. 4, 1828	Adverse		Laid on table.		
Mitchell, James, (Ga.)	Compensation for services, for horse lost, &c., in Florida expedition.	20	2	Petition	50	Claims	10	Adverse		Referred to Committee Whole House.		
Mitchell, John, (Maine)	Revolutionary pension	28	1	Petition	195	Rev. Pensions				Discharged; laid on table.		
Mitchell, jr., John	Arrears of interest due on claim	2	2	Petition	636					Laid on table.		
Mitchell, John, (Mass.)	Compensation for removing obstruction in the principal channel of Boston harbor.	28	1	Petition	975	Commerce.						
Mitchell, John, and others	Additional compensation as tobacco inspectors at Georgetown.	7	1	Petition	176	Select.						
Mitchell, John, (Maine)	Pension on account of wounds received while engaged in celebrating Scott and Taylor victory.	30	1	Petition	113, 117	Invalid Pensions	83	Favorable; bill	70	Passed	Passed	App'd May 29, 1848
Mitchell, John	Settlement of accounts and extra compensation for services as agent for prisoners of war at Halifax.	17	1	Petition	511	Judiciary	May 3, 1822	Favorable	186	Laid on table.		
Mitchell, John	Settlement of accounts and extra compensation for services as agent for prisoners of war at Halifax.	18	1	Petition	159	Claims	112	Favorable	194	Passed	Passed	App'd May 26, 1824
Mitchell, John, (Pa.)	Invalid pension, war of 1812	29	1	Petition	82	Invalid Pensions	Mar. 27, 1846	Adverse		Laid on table		Leave to withdraw, Dec. 26, 1849.
Mitchell, John, and B. F. Fox.	Balance due on contract for building mint at New Orleans.	26	1	Senate bill	1226	Claims	July 10, 1840	With amend.	S. 379	Referred to Committee Whole House.		Provided for by act of July 21, 1840. See Statutes at Large, page 814.
Mitchell, John	Increase of naval pension	31	1	Senate bill	1219	Whole House		With amend.	92	Passed	Passed	App'd Aug. 17, 1850
Mitchell, John	Pension	19	2	Petition	59	Military Pensions				Discharged.		
Mitchell, John	Pension	20	1	Petition	84	Military Pensions	Jan. 25, 1828	Adverse		Laid on table.		
Mitchell, John, and others	Compensation for violating contract in building custom-house at New Orleans.	31	2	Petition	74	Claims.						
Mitchell, Mary, widow of James.	Pension	20	1	Petition	310	Military Pensions	May 13, 1828	Adverse		Laid on table.		
Mitchell, Mary	(See Stephen Johnson, late widow of.)	17	2		208							
Mitchell, Morland, *alias* Micholl.	For return of duties paid on silk goods.	26	1	Petition	291	Commerce.						
Mitchell, Nathaniel	Payment for damages in arresting mail robber.	25	2	Memorial	234	Claims	780	Report and bill.	732	Referred to Committee Whole House.		

List of private claims presented to the House of Representatives of the United States from the 1st to the 31st Congress, inclusive—Continued.

Names of claimants.	Nature or object of the claim.	Congress.	Session.	How brought before the House of Reps.	Page of journal.	To what committee of the House referred.	No. or date of the report.	Nature of the report.	No. of the bill.	How disposed of by the House of Reps.	How disposed of by the Senate.	Date of the act of Congress, and remarks.
Mitchell, Nathaniel	Payment for damages in arresting mail robber.	25	3	House bill......	380	Whole House.....	Jan. 25, 1839	With't amend	732	Passed	Passed	App'd March 2, 1839
Mitchell, Nathaniel	Relief from judgment at suit of Wm. Merriam.	26	1	Petition	201	Claims.						
Mitchell, Nathaniel	Relief from judgment at suit of Wm. Merriam.	27	1	Petition	101	Claims.						
Mitchell, Nathaniel	Relief from judgment at suit of Wm. Merriam.	27	2	Petition	55	Claims	156	Report and bill.	95 B.	Passed.............	Passed, with amendment.	App'd July 27, 1842
Mitchell, Nathaniel	Additional allowance in correction of error.	27	2	Senate bill	1277	Whole House.....	....	....	314	Passed	Passed.......	App'd Aug. 23, 1842
Mitchell, Nathaniel, (Ohio.)	Bounty land for revolutionary services.	17	2	Petition	167	Priv. Land Claims.	....	....	.....	Discharged; leave to withdraw.		
Mitchell, Obed, & Sons ..	Refunding of duties paid on oil...	12	1	Petition	136	Com. and Manuf.						
Mitchell, Obed, & Sons ..	Refunding of duties paid on oil...	12	2	Petition	564	Com. and Manuf.						
Mitchell, Peter..........	(See John Carnochan and Peter Mitchell.)	14	1	....	558							
Mitchell, Peter..........	(See Anthony L. Molyneux, by attorney of.)	22	2	....	178							
Mitchell, Rector.........	Pension for death of son employed on Patent Office.	26	1	Petition	350	Public Buildings ..	....	....	.....	Discharged; laid on table.		
Mitchell, Rector.........	Pension for death of son employed on Patent Office.	26	2	Petition	79	Public Buildings.						
Mitchell, Reuben, widow of	Revolutionary pension	25	2	Petition	52	Rev. Pensions	Jan. 25, 1838	By bill	456	Referred to Committee Whole House.		
Mitchell, Reuben, widow of	Revolutionary pension	25	3	Petition	87	Rev. Pensions	....	....	.....	Discharged.		
Mitchell, Reuben, widow of	Revolutionary pension..........	26	1	Petition	174	Rev. Pensions.						
Mitchell, Richard, (Tenn.)	Release from judgment as surety of Ruben Saunders.	12	2	Petition	551	Ways and Means.						
Mitchell, Richard, (Tenn.)	Release from judgment as surety of Ruben Saunders.	13	1	Petition	28	Ways and Means.						
Mitchell, Richard, (Tenn.)	Release from judgment as surety of Ruben Saunders.	13	2	Petition	176	Ways and Means..	29	Favorable.. .	80	Rejected	....	Referred to Comptroller of Treasury.
Mitchell, Richard, (Tenn.)	Release from judgment as surety of Ruben Saunders.	13	3	Petition and rep't Comptroller of Treasury.	707	Ways and Means..	....	....	.....	Discharged.		
Mitchell, Richard, (Tenn.)	Release from judgment as surety of Ruben Saunders.	14	1	Senate bill	427	Ways and Means..	Mar. 30, 1826	With't amend.	24	Passed	....	App'd April 20, 1816
Mitchell, Robert.........	Pension	14	2	Petition	155	Pens. & Rev. Cl'ms.	Jan. 29, 1817	Adverse	.....	Rejected.		
Mitchell, Robert.........	(See Archibald Beard, and others)	28	1	....	....	....	....	....	478			
Mitchell, Robert B.......	Reimbursement of money erroneously paid as sub Indian agent.	30	1	Petition	522	Indian Affairs	737	Favorable; bill	541	Referred to Committee Whole House.		
Mitchell, Robert B.......	Indemnity for property destroyed by Indians.	30	2	Petition	241	Indian Affairs	125	Adverse	.....	Laid on table.		
Mitchell, Robert B.......	Indemnity for property destroyed by Indians.	30	2	Bill...........	319	Whole House	Jan. 26, 1849	With't amend.	541	Passed.		
Mitchell, Robert, & others.	Confirmation of title to land in Florida.	19	1	Petition	74	Select	....	....	.....	Leave to withdraw.		
Mitchell, Robert, & others.	Confirmation of title to land in Florida.	20	1	Petition	100	Priv. Land Claims.	....	....	.....	Discharged; laid on table.		
Mitchell, Robert P	Confirmation of title to land	24	1	Petition	852	Public Lands.						
Mitchell, Robert P	Confirmation of title to land	24	2	Petition	92	Indian Affairs.						
Mitchell, Samuel, daughters of.	Confirmation of title to land to under Choctaw treaty, 1805.	17	1	Resolution	354	Public Lands.....	April 5, 1822	By bill	157	Passed	Passed	App'd March 6, 1822

List of private claims presented to the House of Representatives of the United States from the 1st to the 31st Congress, inclusive—Continued.

Names of claimants.	Nature or object of the claim.	Congress.	Session.	How brought before the House of Reps.	Page of journal.	To what committee of the House referred.	No. or date of the report.	Nature of the report.	No. of the bill.	How disposed of by the House of Reps.	How disposed of by the Senate.	Date of the act of Congress, and remarks.
Mitchell, Samuel, daughters of.	Grant of reservation of land	22	1	Senate bill	806	Priv. Land Claims.	Jan. 6, 1832	Adverse	S. 102	Laid on table.		
Mitchell, Samuel	(See Peter Yarnell, and others)	21	1		262							
Mitchell, Samuel, (Mass.)	Indemnity for French spoliations prior to 1800.	26	1	Memorial	182	Foreign Affairs	343	Favorable; bill	319	Referred to Committee Whole House.		
Mitchell, Thomas, (Va.)	Pension	21	1	Petition	498	Military Pensions	May 4, 1830	Adverse		Laid on table.		
Mitchell, Thomas, (Vt.)	Arrears of pension	22	2	Petition	137	Invalid Pensions	Feb. 15, 1833	Favorable	738	Referred to Committee Whole House.		
Mitchell, Thomas, (Vt.)	Arrears of pension	23	1	Petition	44	Invalid Pensions	69	Favorable	79	Passed	Passed	App'd June 30, 1834
Mitchell, William	(See Wm. Woodward, and others)	24	1		92							
Mitchell, William, (Mich.)	(See Edward Biddle and William Mitchell.)	21	1		146							
Mitchelor, Jacob	Payment for money stolen in revolution.	25	2	Petition	392	Rev. Claims				Discharged; laid on table.		
Mitchum, James	Pension	16	1	Petition and rep't Sec. of War.	272, 350					Laid on table.		
Mitman, Charles	Pension	20	2	Petition	143	Military Pensions				Referred to Committee Whole House on bill No. 317.		
Mitts, Peter, (Ind.)	Payment for a horse lost in the public service.	25	2	Documents	176	Claims				Discharged.		
Mix, Amos, widow of	Pension	28	2	Petition	308	Rev. Claims.						
Mix, Amos, widow of	Pension	29	1	Petition	88	Rev. Pensions.						
Mix, Amos, widow of	Pension	29	2	Petition	69	Rev. Pensions.						
Mix, Amos, widow of	Pension	30	1	Petition	100	Rev. Pensions	308	Adverse		Laid on table.		
Mix, Ann	(See Mervin P. Mix, widow of)	26	1		304							
Mix, Clarinda	(See Amos Mix, widow of)	28	2		308							
Mix, Elihu L.	Register for the brig Neuva Granada.	27	2	Petition	1239	Commerce	1055	Report and bill.	603	Referred to Committee Whole House.		
Mix, Elihu L.	Register for the brig Neuva Granada.	27	3	House bill	90	Whole House			603	Passed	Passed	App'd Feb. 18, 1843
Mix, Esther	Compensation for revolutionary services.	1	3	Petition	378					Referred to Secretary of War.		
Mix, Mervine P., Lieutenant.	Credit of $651 79 in settlement of account for discount on treasury notes.	23	1	Petition	188	Naval Affairs	205	Favorable; bill	218	Referred to Committee Whole House.		
Mix, Mervine P., Lieutenant.	Credit of $651 79 in settlement of account for discount on treasury notes.	23	2	Bill of last sess.	82	Whole House	Jan. 31, 1835	With amends.	218	Passed	Passed	App'd March 3, 1835
Mix, Mervine P., Lieutenant.	Further relief for losses on treasury notes.	24	1	Depositions	405	Claims	May 28, 1836	Res. to refer to Sec. Navy.		Resolution adopted.		
Mix, Mervine P., Lieutenant, widow of.	Compensation for use by government of invention of chain cable.	26	1	Petition	304	Naval Affairs	476	Report and bill.	390	Referred to Committee Whole House.		
Mix, Mervine P., Lieutenant, widow of.	Compensation for use by government of invention of chain cable.	28	2	Petition	213	Naval Affairs.						
Mix, Mervine P., Lieutenant, widow of.	Compensation for use by government of invention of chain cable.	29	1	Petition	209	Naval Affairs	74	Report and bill.	93	Passed	Passed	App'd Aug. 8, 1846
Mix, Mervine P., widow of	Pension	28	2	Petition	229	Naval Affairs				Discharged; laid on table.		
Mix, Ransom	Increase of pension	21	1	Senate bill	646	Military Pensions	May 22, 1830	With amend.	S. 137	Referred to Committee Whole House.		
Mix, Ransom	Increase of pension	21	2	Senate bill	79	Military Pensions			S. 1			
Mix, Ransom	Increase of pension	22	1	Senate bill	715	Invalid Pensions	May 23, 1832	Adverse	80	Laid on table.		

List of private claims presented to the House of Representatives of the United States from the 1st to the 31st Congress, inclusive—Continued.

Names of claimants.	Nature or object of the claim.	Congress.	Session.	How brought before the House of Reps.	Page of journal.	To what committee of the House referred.	No. or date of the report.	Nature of the report.	No. of the bill.	How disposed of by the House of Reps.	How disposed of by the Senate.	Date of the act of Congress, and remarks.
Mix, Ransom	Increase of pension	22	2	Petition	176	Invalid Pensions.						
Mix, Ransom	Increase of pension	23	1	Petition	155	Invalid Pensions	March 4, 1834	Adverse		Laid on table.		
Mix, Ransom	Increase of pension	24	1	Senate bill	811	Invalid Pensions	Jan. 9, 1836	With amend.	S. 201	Referred to Committee Whole House.		
Mix, Ransom	Increase of pension	24	2	Senate bill	251	Invalid Pensions	186	With't amend	77	Referred to Committee Whole House.		
Mix, Ransom	Invalid pension	29	1	Petition	82	Invalid Pensions.						
Mix, Timothy	Pension	1	3	Petition and rep't Sec. of War.	337	Select.	Feb. 26, 1791	Favorable; bill ordered.	139	Passed	Postponed.	
Mix, Timothy	Pension	2	1	House bill	463	Whole House	Nov. 29, 1791	With amends.	152	Passed	Passed	App'd Mar. 27, 1792
Mix, Timothy	Invalid pension	15	1	House bill	405	Whole House	April 16, 1818	With amends.	172	Passed	Postponed.	
Mix, Tim thy	Invalid pension	15	2	House bill	231	Whole House.	March 3, 1819	With amends.	308	Passed	Passed	App'd March 3, 1819
Mobbs, Samuel, heirs of	Permission to locate certain bounty land warrants.	26	1	Petition	954	Public Lands.						
Mobbs, William	(See Samuel Mobbs, heirs of)	26	1		954							
Moddrell, Andrew	Pension	29	1	Petition	107	Invalid Pensions	73	Adverse		Laid on table.		
Moddrell, John	Pension	29	1	Petition	107	Invalid Pensions	73	Adverse		Laid on table.		
Moderwell, Adam	Release from certain judgment	27	2	Petition	77	Judiciary				Discharged; laid on table.		
Modglin, Mary Ann	(See Truman Modglin, widow of)	28	1		632							
Modglin, Truman, widow of.	Pension	28	1	Petition	632	Rev. Pensions.						
Moffit, Daniel	Pension	14	1	Petition	301	Pens. & Rev. Cl'ms.	April 11, 1816	Favorable; bill	171	Passed.		
Moffit, Daniel	Pension	14	2	Petition	284	Pens. & Rev. Cl'ms.	Jan. 29, 1817	Favorable; bill	91	Passed	Passed	App'd March 3, 1817
Moffet, George	Invalid pension	19	1	Petition	34	Pens. & Rev. Cl'ms.	164	Adverse		Laid on table.		
Moffet, George	Invalid pension	20	1	Petition	38	Military Pensions	Feb. 20, 1828	Adverse		Laid on table.		
Moffitt, George, heirs of, (Ohio.)	Confirmation of title to land in Ohio.	22	2	Petition	41	Priv. Land Claims.						
Moffitt, George, heirs of, (Ohio.)	Confirmation of title to land in Ohio.	23	1	Petition	144	Priv. Land Claims.						
Moffitt, George, heirs of, (Ohio.)	Confirmation of title to land in Ohio.	23	2	Petition	57	Priv. Land Claims.						
Moffitt, George, heirs of, (Ohio.)	Confirmation of title to land in Ohio.	25	2	Petition	180, 420	Priv. Land Claims.	493	Adverse		Laid on table.		
Moffitt, George, heirs of, (Ohio.)	Confirmation of title to land in Ohio.	29	1	Petition	276	Priv. Land Claims.	560	Adverse		Laid on table.		
Moffitt, George, heirs of, (Ohio.)	Confirmation of title to land in Ohio.	29	1	House bill	1299	Whole House			555			
Moffitt, John S., (Md.)	Reimbursement of expenses incurred in collecting direct tax.	17	2	Petition	225	Claims.						
Moffitt, John S., (Md.)	Settlement of accounts as collector of taxes.	18	1	Petition	130	Ways and Means.	Feb. 19, 1824	Favorable; bill	130	Passed	Passed, with amendment.	App'd May 21, 1824
Moffitt, John S., (Md.)	Extra compensation for collecting taxes.	18	2	Petition	134	Ways and Means.						
Moffitt, John S., (Md.)	Extra compensation for collecting taxes.	19	1	Petition	313	Ways and Means.				Discharged; laid on table.		
Moffitt, John S., (Md.)	Extra compensation for collecting taxes.	19	2	Petition	134	Ways and Means.				Discharged; laid on table.		
Moffitt, John S., (Md.)	Extra compensation for collecting taxes.	20	1	Petition	245	Ways and Means.	March 3, 1828			Discharged; laid on table.		
Moffitt, John S., (Md.)	Extra compensation for collecting taxes.	21	1	Petition	412	Ways and Means.				Discharged; laid on table.		

List of private claims presented to the House of Representatives of the United States from the 1st to the 31st Congress, inclusive—Continued.

Names of claimants.	Nature or object of the claim.	Congress.	Session.	How brought before the House of Reps.	Page of journal.	To what committee of the House referred.	No. or date of the report.	Nature of the report.	No. of the bill.	How disposed of by the House of Reps.	How disposed of by the Senate.	Date of the act of Congress, and remarks.
Moffitt, John, (S. C.)	Payment of loan office certificates	19	2	Resolution	88	Rev. Claims	65	Favorable; bill	417	Referred to Committee Whole House.		
Moffitt, John, (S. C.)	Payment of loan office certificates	20	1	Petition	90	Rev. Claims	121	Favorable; bill	137	Passed.		
Moffitt, John, (S. C.)	Payment of loan office certificates	21	1	Petition	38	Rev. Claims	91	Favorable; bill	125	Passed	Passed	App'd May 28, 1830
Moffitt, Margaret	(See George Moffitt, heirs of.)	22	2		41							
Moffet, Margaret, & others	Confirmation of title to land in Ohio.	27	2	Petition	378	Priv. Land Claims.						
Maffitt, Matthew	Bounty of $80 for reveolutionary services.	21	1	Petition	74	Rev. Claims.						
Moffat, Nathaniel	Pension	18	1	Resolution	142	Pens. & Rev. Cl'ms.	Jan. 27, 1824	Adverse		Laid on table.		
Moffitt, Solomon, heirs of.	Land for losses by Choctaw treaty.	24	1	Petition	57	Public Lands	208	Favorable; bill	208	Referred to Committee Whole House.		
Moger, Jos., former widow of.	Revolutionary pension	25	3	Petition	127	Rev. Pensions	248	Favorable; bill	1119	Referred to Committee Whole House.		
Moger, Jos., former widow of.	Revolutionary pension	26	1	Petition	171	Rev. Pensions.						
Moger, Jos., former widow of.	Revolutionary pension	26	2	Petition	72	Rev. Pensions	42	Favorable; bill	571	Referred to Committee Whole House.		
Moger, Jos., former widow of.	Revolutionary pension	27	2	Petition	59	Rev. Pensions	95	Favorable; bill	141	Passed	Passed	App'd July 9, 1842
Mohun, Philip	Additional compensation for paving Pennsylvania avenue.	23	1	Petition	637	Dist. of Columbia.						
Moins, James	(See James Mains.)	26	2		55							
Moker, Conrad	Pension	12	2	Petition	553	Claims	Dec. 8, 1812	Adverse		Leave to withdraw.		
Molaison, Piere, and others	Confirmation of title to land	26	1	Petition	501	Priv. Land Claims.	96	Favorable; bill	92	Passed	Passed	App'd July 20, 1840
Molero, Antony, Bartole, and Christoval.	Confirmation of title to land	22	1	Petition	64	Priv. Land Claims.	Dec. 27, 1831	Favorable; bill	125	Passed	Passed	App'd June 25, 1832
Molero, Marquerite	(See Nunez, widow of.)	22	1		107							
Moltier, Chilo	Grant of land for making a certain road.	24	1	Petition	671	Public Lands.						
Molly, Jemima	Repayment of money paid for a patent.	27	3	Petition	137	Patents.						
Molyneaux, Anthony L., attorney, of.	Indemnity for Indian depredations.	22	2	Petition	178	Indian Affairs.						
Molyneaux, Anthony L., attorney of.	Indemnity for Indian depredations.	23	1	Memorial	629	Indian Affairs.						
Molyneaux, William	(See Rufus Spauding and others.)	15	2		148							
Molyneaux, William	Indemnity for property destroyed in war of 1812.	17	1	Petition	164	Claims				Discharged; laid on table.		
Monaghan, James	Invalid pension	29	1	Memorial	193	Invalid Pensions	774	Adverse		Laid on table.		
Monaghan, William	Compensation for work on Cumberland road.	23	1	Res. and papers.	589	Claims	455, 499	Adverse		Laid on table		See report No. 449.
Monaugh, Alexander	(See Zebulon M. Pike and companions.)	10	1		189							
Moncrief, Robert	Invalid pension	26	1	Petition	325	Invalid Pensions	July 21, 1840	Adverse		Laid on table.		
Mona, Brian	Invalid pension	3	1	Petition	103					Referred to Secretary War.		
Mona, Bryian	Liquidation of claim for revolutionary services.	3	1	Petition	115	Select.						
Monday, Thomas	Increase of pension	13	2	Petition	344	Claims	Mar. 15, 1814	Favorable; bill	166	Passed	Passed	App'd April 18, 1814
Monelimar, Catharine	(See Joseph Badon, heirs of.)	20	1		168							
Monell, Robert	Refunding money paid as surety of Charles Josslyn.	21	1	Resolution	133	P. Of. & P. Roads.	167	Favorable; bill	213	Passed.		

List of private claims presented to the House of Representatives of the United States from the 1st to the 31st Congress, inclusive—Continued.

Names of claimants.	Nature or object of the claim.	Congress.	Session.	How brought before the House of Reps.	Page of journal.	To what committee of the House referred.	No. or date of the report.	Nature of the report.	No. of the bill.	How disposed of by the House of Reps.	How disposed of by the Senate.	Date of the act of Congress, and remarks.
Monell, Samuell	Indemnity for loss on contract with quartermasters department.	16	2	Petition	97	Claims				Discharged; laid on table.		
Monette, John W	Confirmation of title to land	26	1	Senate bill	813	Public Lands	June 17, 1840	With amends.	228	Passed	Passed	App'd July 9, 1840
Mongrain, Noel	Confirmation of title to land in Missouri.	15	1	Petition	312	Priv. Land Claims.				Leave to withdraw.		
Mongrain, Noel, heirs of	Confirmation of title to land in Missouri.	24	1	Petition	274	Priv. Land Claims.				Discharged; laid on table.		
Monoghan, John	(See John Stoops, administrator of.)	23	1		493							
Monot, Stephen and others	For a grant of land in Gallipolis, Ohio.	5	2	Senate bill	225	Select	June 13, 1798	Favorable	S. 13	Passed		App'd June 25, 1798
Monroe, A. G	Compensation for a horse lost in service of United States, 1823.	27	2	Memorial	1023	Claims.						
Monroe, A. G	Compensation for a horse lost in service of United States, 1823.	27	3	Petition	73	Claims	106	Adverse		Laid on table.		
Monroe, Barney, heirs of	Bounty land for revolutionary services.	19	1	Resolution	305	Rev. Claims				Laid on table.		
Monroe, Barney, heirs of	Bounty land for revolutionary services.	24	1	Res. and docs	341	Rev. Claims	May 21, 1836	Adverse		Laid on table.		
Monroe, Elizabeth	(See Thos. C. J. Monroe, widow of.)	26	1		632							
Monroe, Elizabeth	Revolutionary pension	27	2	Petition	398	Military Affairs	353	Adverse		Laid on table.		
Monroe, Henry	(See Nathaniel Gladding, & others)	23	1		37							
Monroe, James, schooner	(See Nathan Smith, and others)	27	2		57							
Monroe, James	Compensation for horses lost in war of 1812.	29	1	Petition	713	Claims.						
Monroe, James	Compensation for horses lost in war of 1812.	30	1	Memorial	288	Claims	202	Adverse		Laid on table.		
Monroe, James	Equitable settlement of his accounts	18	2	Memorial	110	Select	79	Stating acc'ts.		Laid on table.		
Monroe, James	Equitable settlement of his accounts	19	1	Resolution	72	Select	136	Favorable; bill	177	Passed	Passed, with amendment.	App'd May 22, 1826
Monroe, James	Further remuneration, &c.	20	2	Petition	216	Select	76 & 96	Favorable; bill	436	Referred to Committee Whole House.		
Monroe, James	Further remuneration, &c.	21	1	Petition	297	Select	276	Favorable; bill	330	Referred to Committee Whole House.		
Monroe, James	Further remuneration, &c.	21	2	House bill	61, 75	Whole House	Dec. 15, 1830	Favorable; bill	330	Passed	Passed	App'd March 2, 1831
Monroe, James, (Ind.)	Compensation for three horses lost in service of United States.	29	1	Petition	713	Claims.						
Monroe, James, (Ind.)	Compensation for three horses lost in service of United States.	30	1	Petition	288	Claims	202	Adverse		Laid on table.		
Monroe, Jemima	(See John Haslett, heirs of)	24	1		811							
Monroe, John, (Va.)	Compensation for wagon and team destroyed by Indians in Florida.	27	2	Petition	226	Claims	173	Adverse		Laid on table.		
Monroe, John, (Va.)	Compensation for wagon and team destroyed by Indians in Florida.	27	3	Petition	43	Claims	88	Adverse		Laid on table.		
Monroe, John, (Va.)	Compensation for wagon and team destroyed by Indians in Florida.	28	1	Letters & petition	75	Claims	413	Adverse		Laid on table.		
Monroe, John, (Va.)	Compensation for wagon and team destroyed by Indians in Florida.	28	2	Petition	89	Claims.						
Monroe, John H.	Invalid pension	29	1	Petition	756	Invalid Pensions	817	Favorable; bill	542	Referred to Committee Whole House.		
Monroe, Robert	Invalid pension	27	2	Petition	218	Invalid Pensions	Feb. 9, 1842	Adverse, verbal		Laid on table.		

List of private claims presented to the House of Representatives of the United States from the 1st to the 31st Congress, inclusive—Continued.

Names of claimants.	Nature or object of the claim.	Congress.	Session.	How brought before the House of Reps.	Page of journal.	To what committee of the House referred.	No. or date of the report.	Nature of the report.	No. of the bill.	How disposed of by the House of Reps.	How disposed of by the Senate.	Date of the act of Congress, and remarks.
Monroe, Robert	Invalid pension	28	1	Petition	428	Invalid Pensions	430	Favorable; bill	331	Passed	Passed	App'd June 17, 1844
Monroe, Thomas C. J.	Pension	26	1	Petition	632	Military Affairs.						
Monroe, William	(See Reuben E. Gentry, & others)	23	1		138							
Monsanto, J. & B., heirs of.	Confirmation of Spanish land claim	18	1	Petition	177	Priv. Land Claims.						
Monsanto, Manuel & Isaac, representatives of.	Confirmation of title to land in Michigan.	17	1	Senate bill	115	Priv. Land Claims.	Feb. 28, 1822	Adverse	S. 7	Laid on table.		
Montague, Abraham	(See Richard Montague, father of)	15	1		45							
Montague, Benj., heirs of.	Compensation for revolutionary services	29	1	Memorial	578	Rev. Claims.						
Montague, Nathaniel	Revolutionary pension	22	1	Petition	441	Rev. Pensions	381	Favorable; bill	472	Passed	Postponed.	
Montague, Richard, father of.	Confirmation of title to land in Kentucky.	15	1	Petition	45	Priv. Land Claims.				Discharged; leave to withdraw.		
Montague, Richard, father of.	Confirmation of title to land in Kentucky.	15	2	Petition	110	Priv. Land Claims.	Jan. 8, 1819	Adverse		Laid on table.		
Montague, Richard, father of.	Confirmation of title to land in Kentucky.	16	1	Petition	286	Priv. Land Claims.	Mar. 6, 1820	Adverse		Leave to withdraw.		
Monteath, Caroline	(See Walter N. Monteath, widow of.)	16	1		172							
Monteath, Walter N., widow of.	Naval pension	16	1	Petition	172	Naval Affairs	Feb. 17, 1820	Adverse		Laid on table.		
Montford, John C.	Reimbursement of money erroneously paid for land in Florida.	20	2	Petition	28	Public Lands				Discharged; laid on table.		
Montgomery, Alex., heirs of.	Confirmation of title to land in Mississippi.	14	1	Petition	454	Public Lands.						
Montgomery, Alex., heirs of.	Confirmation of title to land in Mississippi.	14	2	Petition	50	Priv. Land Claims.	Jan. 17, 1817	Adverse		Rejected.		
Montgomery, Alex., heirs of.	Confirmation of title to land in Mississippi.	15	2	Petition	25	Priv. Land Claims.	32	Favorable; bill	226	Passed	Passed	App'd Jan. 8, 1819
Montgomery, Alex., heirs of.	Land in lieu of that sold by the United States.	17	1	Senate bill	375	Priv. Land Claims.	84	With amend.	21	Referred to Committee Whole House.		
Montgomery, Alex., heirs of.	Land in lieu of that sold by the United States.	17	2	Senate bill	78	Priv. Land Claims.	Dec. 3, 1823	With amend.	12	Passed	Passed	App'd March 1, 1823
Montgomery, Alexander	Remisson of balance due on land.	19	1	Petition	366	Public Lands				Disch'd; laid on table.		
Montgomery, Alexander	Permission to complete payment on forfeited lands.	21	1	Resolution	60, 61	Public Lands	11	Favorable; bill	18	Passed	Passed	App'd May 28, 1830
Montgomery, Capt. A.	Commission for disbursing money in Mexican war.	30	2	Petition	389	Military Affairs				Discharged; laid on table.		
Montgomery, Capt. A.	Commission for disbursing money in Mexican war.	30	2	Senate bill	649	Whole House	Mar. 3, 1849	With't amend.	S. 476	Passed	Passed	App'd March 3, 1849
Montgomery, Andrew	Compensation for a negro and other property lost in United States service.	13	3	Petition	761					Laid on table.		
Montgomery, Andrew	Compensation for a negro and other property lost in United States service.	14	1	Petition	65	Claims	Dec. 29, 1815	Adverse		Rejected.		
Montgomery, Andrew	Compensation for a negro and other property lost in United States service.	15	2	Petition	288	Claims				Discharged; laid on table.		
Montgomery, Charles P.	Refunding duty paid on bell for church.	31	2	Civil & dip. appropriat'n bill.	248	Whole House	Feb. 25, 1851	With amend.	461	Passed	Passed	App'd March 3, 1851
Montgomery, Daniel	Increase of pension	30	2	Petition	465	Invalid Pensions				Discharged; laid on table.		

List of private claims presented to the House of Representatives of the United States form the 1st to the 31st Congress, inclusive—Continued.

Names of claimants.	Nature or object of the claim.	Congress.	Session.	How brought before the House of Reps.	Page of journal.	To what committee of the House referred.	No. or date of the report.	Nature of the report.	No. of the bill.	How disposed of by the House of Reps.	How disposed of by the Senate.	Date of the act of Congress, and remarks.
Montgomery, Daniel	Increase of pension	31	1	Memorial	311	Invalid Pensions.						
Montgomery, Elizabeth	(See Hugh Montgomery, heirs of.)	23	1		55							
Montgomery, Elizabeth, of Delaware.	Liquidation of claim for supplies furnished revolutionary army.	5	3	Petition	501					Laid on table.		
Montgomery, Hugh, heirs of.	Compensation for services and expenses in revolutionary war.	23	1	Petition	55	Rev. Claims.						
Montgomery, Jacob P., and others.	Compensation as surgeons in the Mexican war.	30	2	Petition	584	Military Affairs				Discharged; laid on table.		
Montgomery, Jacob P., and others.	Compensation as surgeons in the Mexican war.	31	1	Petition	450	Military Affairs	Aug. 1, 1850	Favorable; bill	365	Passed.		
Montgomery, James, and others.	Increase of compensation as officers of revenue cutters.	2	2	Petition	688					Referred to Secretary Treasury.		
Montgomery, James, and others.	Increase of compensation as officers of revenue cutters.	3	2	Rep. of Secretary Treasury.	284					Laid on table.		
Montgomery, James, and others.	Increase of compensation as officers of revenue cutters.	3	2	Memorial	333					Laid on table.		
Montgomery, Joanna	(See Nathaniel L. Montgomery, widow of.)	18	2		117							
Montgomery, John	(See Richard Butler, executors of.)	2	1		537							
Montgomery, John	Pension	27	2	Petition	220	Naval Affairs	597	Adverse		Laid on table.		
Montgomery, John, and others.	For expenses as witnesses in the trial of Judge Chase.	9	1	Petition	256	Claims.						
Montgomery, John	Compensation for revolutionary services.	14	1	Petition	525	Pens. & Rev. Cl'ms.				Discharged; laid on table.		
Montgomery, John, (Ohio)	Compensation for a boat impressed into service in war of 1812.	15	2	Petition	217	Claims				Discharged; laid on table.		
Montgomery, John, (Ohio)	Compensation for a boat impressed into service in war of 1812.	20	2	Petition	143	Claims	Jan. 28, 1829	Adverse		Laid on table.		
Montgomery, John, (Ohio)	Compensation for a boat impressed into service in war of 1812.	23	1	Petition	336	Claims	Mar. 19, 1834	Adverse		Laid on table.		
Montgomery, John, widow of.	Renewal of pension	17	2	Petition	186, 208	Pens. & Rev. Cl'ms.	Feb. 22, 1823	Adverse		Laid on table.		
Montgomery, John, widow of.	Renewal of pension	22	2	Petition	266	Naval Affairs.						
Montgomery, John	Confirmation of title to land	19	1	Report of register and receiver of land office.	64	Public Lands	33 May 5, 1826	Adverse By bill	 254	Recommitted. Referredto Committee Whole House.		
Montgomery, John P., and others.	Compensation for services in Mexican war.	30	2	Bill on leave	218	Military Affairs			715			
Montgomery, J. M. C.	Allowance for moneys paid by order of superior officers, and for travelling expenses.	17	1	Petition	156	Claims				Discharged; leave to withdraw.		
Montgomery, J. M. C.	Allowance for moneys paid by order of superior officers, and for travelling expenses.	17	2	Petition	44	Claims	Feb. 19, 1823	Favorable; bill	304	Referred to Committee Whole House.		
Montgomery, J. M. C.	Allowance for moneys paid by order of superior officers, and for travelling expenses.	18	1	Petition	32	Claims	Mar. 18, 1824	Favorable; bill	168	Passed	Passed	App'd May 19, 1824
Montgomery, Lawrence, former widow of.	Pension due him	30	1	Petition	513	Naval Affairs.						
Montgomery, Lemuel P., heirs of.	Pension and bounty land	29	2	Petition	110	Invalid Pensions.						

List of private claims presented to the House of Representatives of the United States from the 1*st to the* 31*st Congress, inclusive*—Continued.

Names of claimants.	Nature or object of the claim.	Congress.	Session.	How brought before the House of Reps.	Page of journal.	To what committee of the House referred.	No. or date of the report.	Nature of the report.	No. of the bill.	How disposed of by the House of Reps.	How disposed of by the Senate.	Date of the act of Congress, and remarks.
Montgomery, Lemuel P., heirs of.	Pension and bounty land	30	1	Petition	835	Rev. Pensions				Discharged; laid on table.		
Montgomery, Lemuel P., heirs of.	Compensation for services in war of 1812.	30	1	Memorial	1008	Invalid Pensions				Discharged; laid on table.		
Montgomery, Mary	(See John Montgomery, widow of)	17	2		186, 208							
Montgomery, L. Nathaniel, widow of.	Naval pension	18	2	Petition	117	Naval Affairs	46	Adverse		Referred to Committee Whole House.		
Montgomery & Newbold	Drawback of duty on certain East India merchandise.	7	1	Petition	12	Com. and Munuf.						
Montgomery, Robert, (Pa.)	Compensation for a horse lost in United States service.	16	1	Petition	407	Claims				Discharged; laid on table.		
Montgomery, Robert and John, assignee of.	Indemnity for French spoliations prior to 1800.	26	1	Memorial	182	Foreign Affairs	343	Favorable; bill	319	Referred to Committee Whole House.		
Montgomery, W. and J	Drawback of duty on coffee	19	1	Senate bill	510	Ways and Means	May 5, 1826	With't amend.	129	Passed		App'd May 20, 1826
Montgomery, William W.	Indemnity for losses as surety of Michael Reynolds.	20	1	Senate bill	772	Judiciary			144			
Montleman, Catharine	(See Joseph Badon, heirs of)	20	1		168							
Montleman, Cattelina	(See Cattelina Badon, heirs of)	31	2		123							
Montour, Montgomery	(See Indians, Delaware, tribe of)	9	2		499							
Montreuil, Madame	Indemnity for property destroyed in war of 1812.	14	2	Petition	142	Claims	Feb. 3, 1817	Favorable; bill	97	Passed	Passed	App'd March 3, 1817
Mantross, Reuben	Bounty land for revolutionary services.	24	2	Petition	397	Rev. Claims.						
Monty, Amable	Compensation for supplies furnished in revolutionary war.	22	2	Petition	67	Rev. Claims.						
Monty, Amable	Compensation for supplies furnished in revolutionary war.	23	1	Petition	43	Rev. Claims.						
Monty, Amable	Compensation for supplies furnished in revolutionary war.	24	1	Petition	205	Rev. Claims.						
Monty, Amable	Compensation for supplies furnished in revolutionary war.	25	2	Petition	48	Rev. Claims	504	Adverse		Laid on table.		
Monty, Amable	Compensation for supplies furnished in revolutionary war.	26	2	Petition	77	Rev. Claims.						
Monty, Francis, & son	Compensation for revolutionary services.	3	1	Petition	132	Select.						
Monty, Francis	Invalid pension	3	1	Rep. of Secretary War.	131	Select	May 26, 1794	Favorable; bill	62	Passed	Passed	App'd June 7, 1794
Monty, Francis	Compensation as a spy in revolutionary war, 1775.	4	1	Petition	384	Claims	Jan. 20, 1796	Adverse		Leave to withdraw.		
Moody & Anderson	(See Anderson & Moody, representatives of.)	24	2		273							
Moody, Edward, (N. C.)	Pension	17	1	Resol'n and rep't Sec. of War.	130, 548					Laid on table.		
Moody, Edward, (N. C.)	Pension	22	1	Resolution	389	Rev. Pensions				Discharged; laid on table.		
Moody, Edward, (N. C.,) widow of.	Arrears of pension	31	1	Petition	439	Rev. Pensions	136	Adverse		Laid on table.		
Moody, George, and others.	Fishing bounty on Mary and Sally	23	1	Petition	212	Commerce.	211	Favorable; bill	231	Referred to Committee Whole House.		
Moody, George, and others.	Fishing bounty on Mary and Sally	23	2	Bill of last sess.	82	Whole House	Dec. 12, 1834	With't amend.	231	Passed	Passed	App'd Jan. 27, 1835
Moody, George B., and others.	Indemnity for French spoliations prior to 1800.	31	1	Petition	406	Commerce	355	Favorable; bill	318	Referred to Committee Whole House.		

List of private claims presented to the House of Representatives of the United States from the 1st to the 31st Congress, inclusive—Continued.

Names of claimants.	Nature or object of the claim.	Congress.	Session.	How brought before the House of Reps.	Page of journal.	To what committee of the House referred.	No. or date of the report.	Nature of the report.	No. of the bill.	How disposed of by the House of Reps.	How disposed of by the Senate.	Date of the act of Congress, and remarks.
Moody, John M., & others, (Mass.)	For fishing bounty on schooner Welcome Return.	10	1	Petition	212	Com. and Manuf.						
Moody, John M., & others, (Mass.)	For fishing bounty on schooner Welcome Return.	17	1	Petition	256	Commerce	April 2, 1822	Favorable; bill	148	Passed	Postponed.	
Moody, John M., & others, (Mass.)	For fishing bounty on schooner Welcome Return.	17	2	Petition	59	Commerce				Discharged; leave to withdraw.		
Moody, John M., & others, (Mass.)	For fishing bounty on schooner Welcome Return.	18	1	Petition	154	Commerce.						
Moody, John M., & others, (Mass.)	For fishing bounty on schooner Welcome Return.	18	2	Petition	91	Commerce	Feb. 5, 1825	Favorable; bill	319	Passed	Passed	App'd March 3, 1825
Moody John	Indemnity for French spoliations prior to 1800.	26	1	Memorial	182	Foreign Affairs	343	Favorable; bill	329	Referred to Committee Whole House.		
Moody, John, (Maine)	Pension	22	1	Petition	631	Invalid Pensions.						
Moody, John, (Maine)	Pension	22	2	Petition	27	Invalid Pensions	Feb. 15, 1833	Favorable; bill	738	Referred to Committee Whole House.		
Moody, John, (Maine)	Pension	23	1	Petition	44	Invalid Pensions	1	Favorable; bill	1	Passed	Passed	App'd June 25, 1834
Moody, John	(See Solomon Hewton, administrators of.)	26	1		182							
Moody, Joseph	Indemnity for French spoliations prior to 1800.	26	1	Memorial	182	Foreign Affairs	343	Favorable; bill	319	Referred to Committee Whole House.		
Moody, Lemuel	Pension	28	2	Petition	71	Rev. Pensions	137	Favorable; bill	620	Referred to Committee Whole House.		
Moody, Lemuel	Pension	29	1	Petition	399	Rev. Pensions.						
Moody, Lydia	(See William Story, widow of.)	25	2		347							
Moody, Martin	Invalid pension	28	1	Petition	602	Invalid Pensions.						
Moody, William	Increase of pension	28	2	Petition	192	Invalid Pensions.						
Mooers, Benjamin H	Refunding money expended as a recruiting officer.	20	1	Petition	397	Claims	April 16, 1828	Adverse		Laid on table.		
Mooers, Benjamin	Indemnity for property destroyed in war of 1812.	22	1	Petition	346	Claims.						
Mooers, Benjamin	Indemnity for property destroyed in war of 1812.	23	1	Petition	55	Claims	Dec. 16, 1833	Adverse		Recommitted.		
Mooers, Benjamin	Indemnity for property destroyed in war of 1812.	24	1	Petition	207	Claims	612	Favorable; bill	601	Referred to Committee Whole House.		
Mooers, Benjamin	Indemnity for property destroyed in war of 1812.	25	2	Petition	37	Claims	36	Report and bill	48	Passed	Passed	App'd March 7, 1838
Mooers, Hazen	(See Martin S. Aiken and others.)	17	1		359							
Mooklar, William T	Invalid pension	22	1	Resolution	263	Invalid Pensions	Feb. 15, 1832	Adverse		Laid on table.		
Moon, Jacob, heirs of	Commutation pay for revolutionary services.	24	1	Petition	204	Rev. Claims.						
Moon, Jacob, heirs of	Pension for revolutionary services.	29	1	Memorial	178	Rev. Pensions	Mar. 5, 1846	Adverse		Laid on table.		
Moon, Jacob, heirs of	Pension for revolutionary services.	30	1	Memorial	744	Rev. Pensions	547	Adverse		Laid on table.		
Mooney, Charles E	Compensation for a horse lost in Mexican war.	30	1	Petition	147	Claims	409	Favorable; bill	359	Passed.		
Mooney, Charles E	Compensation for a horse lost in Mexican war.	30	2	House bill from Senate.	524				359		Passed	App'd March 2, 1849
Moore, Samuel	Restoration of pension	17	1	Petition	51	Rev. Pensions				Discharged; laid on table.		
Moore & Co	(See Peters, Moore, & Co.)	24	2	Senate bill	579				200			
Moore, Abner R., representatives of.	Compensation for wagon and team taken for use of United States army.	15	2	Petition	168	Claims	Dec. 31, 1819	Adverse		Laid on table.		

List of private claims presented to the House of Representatives of the United States from the 1st to the 31st Congress, inclusive—Continued.

Names of claimants.	Nature or object of the claim.	Congress.	Session.	How brought before the House of Reps.	Page of journal.	To what committee of the House referred.	No. or date of the report.	Nature of the report.	No. of the bill.	How disposed of by the House of Reps.	How disposed of by the Senate.	Date of the act of Congress, and remarks.
Moore, Abner R., representatives of.	Compensation for wagon and team taken for use of United States army.	16	1	Petition	92	Claims	Dec. 31, 1819	Adverse		Laid on table.		
Moore, Abner R., representatives of.	Compensation for wagon and team taken for use of United States army.	18	1	Petition	214	Claims	Mar. 5, 1824	Adverse		Referred to Committee Whole House.		
Moore, Abner R., representatives of.	Compensation for wagon and team taken for use of United States army.	19	1	Petition	131	Claims	Jan. 27, 1826	Adverse		Laid on table.		
Moore, Abner R., representatives of.	Compensation for wagon and team taken for use of United States army.	20	2	Petition	230	Claims				Discharged; laid on table.		
Moore, Agustus	Compensation for property lost in Mexico.	30	2	Petition	117	Military Affairs	63	Adverse		Laid on table.		
Moore, Alexander	Increase of compensation as register of wills in Alexandria, D. C.	15	2	Petition	247	Dist. of Columbia				Discharged; laid on table.		
Moore, Alexander, heirs of.	Confirmation of title to land in Mississippi.	19	2	Senate bill	351	Public Lands	Mar. 2, 1825	With't amend.	99	Laid on table.		
Moore, Alexander, heirs of.	Confirmation of title to land in Mississippi.	20	1	Senate bill	249	Priv. Land Claims.	Mar. 1, 1828	With't amend.	23	Referred to Committee Whole House.		
Moore, Alfred	(See Morris Lindsey, assignees of.)	18	1		307							
Moore, Alfred L.	(See L. M. Torrant, surety of)	24	1		206							
Moore, Alpheus, and others.	(See Willard Moore, heirs of)	2	1		458							
Moore, Allen R.	Indemnity for property destroyed in war of 1812.	15	1	Petition	114	Claims				Discharged; laid on table.		
Moore, Allen R.	Indemnity for property destroyed in war of 1812.	17	1	Petition	23	Claims	Jan. 11, 1822	Adverse		Referred to Committee Whole House.		
Moore, Allen R.	Indemnity for property destroyed in war of 1812.	23	2	Petition	308	Select.						
Moore, Allen R.	Indemnity for property destroyed in war of 1812.	24	1	Petition	207	Claims	534	Favorable; bill	528	Referred to Committee Whole House.		
Moore, Allen R.	Indemnity for property destroyed in war of 1812.	25	2	Petition	37	Claims	26	Favorable; bill	38	Passed	Passed	App'd March 7, 1838
Moore, Andrew, (Ky.)	Compensation for horse lost in war of 1812.	17	1	Petition	180	Claims.						
Moore, Andrew, (Ky.)	Compensation for horse lost in war of 1812.	22	1	Petition	114	Claims	189	Favorable; bill	270	Referred to Committee Whole House.		
Moore, Andrew, (Ky.)	Compensation for horse lost in war of 1812.	22	2	House bill	93	Whole House	Dec. 28, 1832	With't amend.	270	Passed	Passed	App'd Feb. 5, 1833
Moore, Andrew, (Ky.)	Pension	24	1	Petition	157	Rev. Pensions	Feb. 4, 1836	Adverse		Laid on table.		
Moore, Andrew, (Ky.)	Pension	29	2	Senate bill	380	Invalid Pensions	Feb. 24, 1847	Favorable; bill	123	Passed		App'd Feb. 25, 1847
Moore, Ann	(See William Moore, widow of.)	31	1		232							
Moore, Anne L.	(See Robert Moore, widow of.)	13	3		683							
Moore, Asa, (N. Y.)	Revolutionary pension	22	1	Petition	574	Rev. Pensions.						
Moore, Ashbel	Revolutionary pension	29	1	Petition	494	Rev. Pensions	609	Adverse		Laid on table.		
Moore, Bede	Confirmation of title to land in Missouri.	15	2	Petition	89	Priv. Land Claims.						
Moore, Bede	Confirmation of title to land in Missouri.	17	1	Petition	54	Public Lands.						
Moore, Bede	Confirmation of title to land in Missouri.	18	1	Petition	54	Public Lands	Jan. 16, 1824	Favorable; bill	65	Passed	Passed	App'd May 26, 1824

List of private claims presented to the House of Representatives of the United States from the 1st to the 31st Congress, inclusive—Continued.

Names of claimants.	Nature or object of the claim.	Congress.	Session.	How brought before the House of Reps.	Page of journal.	To what committee of the House referred.	No. or date of the report.	Nature of the report.	No. of the bill.	How disposed of by the House of Reps.	How disposed of by the Senate.	Date of the act of Congress, and remarks.
Moore, Benjamin, widow of.	Pension for revolutionary services.	29	1	Petition	175	Rev. Pensions.						
Moore, Benjamin, widow of.	Pension for revolutionary services.	29	2	Petition	150	Rev. Pensions	9	Adverse	......	Laid on table.		
Moore, Benjamin, and G. Rust.	Increase of pay of officers at the Harper's Ferry armory.	24	1	Petition	200	Military Affairs.						
Moore, Benjamin	Compensation for improvement in fire-arms.	32	1	Petition	681	Military Affairs	....	....	......	Discharged; laid on table.		
Moore, Christopher, (R. I.)	Invalid pension	3	1	Rep. of Secretary War.	131	Select	May 26, 1794	Favorable; res.	12	Passed	Passed	App'd June 9, 1794
Moore, Christopher	(See Jacob Moore, heirs of)	29	1	....	424							
Moore, Cleon, widow of	Continuation of pension	15	1	Petition	330	Pens. & Rev. Cl'ms.	....	....	......	Discharged; laid on table.		
Moore, Daniel, (N. H.)	Invalid pension	3	2	Rep. of Secretary War.	278	Claims.						
Moore, Daniel, (N. H.)	Invalid pension	4	1	Res. and docs.	373	Claims.						
Moore, Daniel	(See Stockton & Stokes)	24	1	....	32							
Moore, Daniel, (Ohio)	Pension	19	1	Petition	384	Military Pensions	193	Favorable; bill	119	Passed.		
Moore, Daniel, (Ohio)	Pension	19	2	Petition	67	Military Pensions	Dec. 22, 1826	By bill	315	Passed.		
Moore, David A	(See William H. Bedford, agent.)	28	1	....	262							
Moore, David, administrator of.	Compensation for revolutionary services.	8	1	Memorial	523	Claims	....	....	......	Referred to Committee Whole House.		
Moore, David, administrator of.	Compensation for revolutionary services.	8	2	Memorial	78	Whole House.						
Moore, David, administrator of.	Compensation for revolutionary services.	9	1	Memorial	212	Select.						
Moore, David, sureties of.	Release from judgment	21	1	Petition	173	Judiciary	....	....	......	Discharged; laid on table.		
Moore, Diana	(See William Moore, widow of)	26	1	....	546, 857							
Moore, Ebenezer, heirs of.	Bounty land as a Canadian volunteer.	26	1	Petition	701	Priv. Land Claims.	514	Favorable; bill	415	Referred to Committee Whole House.		
Moore, Ebenezer, heirs of.	Bounty land as a Canadian volunteer.	26	2	Petition	49	Public Lands.						
Moore, Ebenezer, heirs of.	Bounty land as a Canadian volunteer.	28	1	Petition	117	Priv. Land Claims.	358	Favorable; bill	271	Passed	Passed	App'd June 17, 1844
Moore, Edward, administrator of.	Payment of prize money due	21	1	Petition	175	Naval Affairs	159	Favorable; bill	203	Passed	Passed, with amendment.	
Moore, Edward, administrator of.	Payment of prize-money due	21	2	Petition	88	Naval Affairs	Dec. 24, 1830	Favorable; bill	512	Passed	Passed	App'd Jan. 27, 1831
Moore, Eleanor S	(See William M. A. Moore, widow of.)	24	1	....	946							
Moore, Elizabeth	(See Major John Moore, widow of.)	27	2	....	219							
Moore, Francis	(See John Moore, executor of)	21	2	....	38							
Moore, Harvey	Pension	14	2	Petition	377	Pens. & Rev. Cl'ms.						
Moore, Henrietta, & others	Continuation of pensions during their natural lives.	30	1	Petition	166	Rev. Pensions	699	Adverse	......	Laid on table.		
Moore, Henry, and others.	(See Freeborn Sisson, and others)	14	1	....	449							
Moore, Hugh, administrator of.	Commutation of five years' full pay.	24	1	Petition	851	Claims.						
Moore, Hiram, and J. Hascall.	Extension of patent for their reaping machine.	31	1	Petition	212	Patents	9	Favorable; bill	11	Passed.		
Moore, Ira	Land for military services	24	2	Petition	47	Rev. Pensions	....	....	......	Discharged; laid on table.		

List of private claims presented to the House of Representatives of the United States from the 1st to the 31st Congress, inclusive—Continued.

Names of claimants.	Nature or object of the claim.	Congress.	Session.	How brought before the House of Reps.	Page of journal.	To what committee of the House referred.	No. or date of the report.	Nature of the report.	No. of the bill.	How disposed of by the House of Reps.	How disposed of by the Senate.	Date of the act of Congress, and remarks.
Moore, Isaac, (Maine)	Restoration of pension	22	1	Petition	509	Rev. Pensions	476	Favorable; bill	578	Referred to Committee Whole House.		
Moore, Isaac K	(See William H. Bedford, agent.)	28	1		262							
Moore, Isidore	(See Thomas Fenwick, assignee of)	15	1		45							
Moore, Isidore	(See J. B. Chartier, assignee of).	19	1		134							
Moore, Isidore	Exchange of land	22	2	Petition	64	Priv. Land Claims.	76	Favorable; bill	719	Referred to Committee Whole House.		
Moore, Isidore	Exchange of land	23	1	Petition	48	Priv. Land Claims.	58	Favorable; bill	68	Referred to Committee Whole House.		
Moore, Jacob, (Tenn.)	Indemnity for loss on improvements on lands.	23	1	Petition	50	Indian Affairs.						
Moore, Jacob, (Tenn.)	Indemnity for loss on improvements on lands.	25	2	Petition	279	Indian Affairs	Mar. 13, 1838	Adverse		Laid on table.		
Moore, Jacob, (Tenn.)	Indemnity for loss on improvements on lands.	28	2	Petition	170	Claims.						
Moore, Jacob, (Tenn.)	Indemnity for loss on improvements on lands.	30	2	Petition	253	Claims	109	Adverse		Laid on table.		
Moore, Jacob, (Tenn.)	Indemnity for loss on improvements on lands.	31	2	Petition	225	Claims.						
Moore, Jacob, heir of	Seven years' half-pay for revolutionary services.	29	1	Petition	424	Rev. Claims.						
Moore, Jacob, heir of	Seven years' half-pay for revolutionary services.	30	1	Petition	316, 358	Rev. Pensions	547	Adverse		Laid on table.		
Moore, James, (Ala.)	Correct error in entry of land	23	2	Petition	85	Priv. Land Claims.	Jan. 6, 1835	Favorable; bill	613	Referred to Committee Whole House.		
Moore, James, (Ala.)	Correct error in entry of land	24	1	Petition	113	Priv. Land Claims.	Jan. 12, 1836	Favorable; bill	136	Passed	Rejected.	
Moore, James, (Ala.)	Correct error in entry of land	24	2	Petition	89	Priv. Land Claims.	Dec. 27, 1836	By bill	778	Referred to Committee Whole House.		
Moore, James, (Ala.)	Correct error in entry of land	25	2	Petition	43	Priv. Land Claims.	136	Favorable; bill	156	Referred to Committee Whole House.		
Moore, James, (Ala.)	Correct error in entry of land	25	3	House bill	375	Whole House			156	Passed	Passed	App'd March 3, 1839
Moore, James, (N. H.)	Invalid pension	3	2	Rep. of Secretary War.	278	Claims	Feb. 28, 1795	Favorable; bill	130	Passed	Postponed.	
Morre, James, (N. H.)	Invalid pension	4	1	Petition	447	Claims	Feb. 18, 1796	Favorable; bill	156	Passed	Passed	App'd April 20, 1796
Moore, James, (Penn.)	Compensation for services and losses in revolutionary war.	15	2	Petition	262	Pens. & Rev. Cl'ms.				Discharged; laid on table.		
Moore, James, (Penn.)	Compensation for services and losses in revolutionary war.	16	1	Petition	96	Pens. & Rev. Cl'ms.	Jan. 3, 1820	Adverse		Laid on table.		
Moore, James, (Penn.)	Revolutionary pension	18	1	Petition	285	Pens. & Rev. Cl'ms.	Mar. 22, 1824	Adverse		Laid on table.		
Moore, James, (Penn.)	Revolutionary pension	21	1	Petition	53	Military Pensions.						
Moore, James, (Penn.)	Revolutionary pension	22	1	Petition	46	Military Pensions.						
Moore, James, (N. Y.)	Restoration of pension	17	1	Petition	30	Rev. Pensions.						
Moore, James, (N. Y.)	Restoration of pension	21	2	Petition	159	Military Pensions.						
Moore, James	Payment of $62 50 due from Post Office Department.	17	2	Petition	224	P. Of. & P. Roads.				Leave to withdraw.		
Moore, James, (N. J.)	Pension	20	2	Petition	175	Military Pensions.				Referred to Committee Whole House on bill No. 317.		
Moore, James, (N. J.)	Pension	21	1	Petition	67	Military Pensions.						
Moore, James, heirs of	Commutation of half-pay for revolutionary services.	24	1	Senate bill	1078	Rev. Claims	June 28, 1836	With't amend	S. 219	Passed		App'd July 2, 1836
Moore, James, heirs of	Compensation for revolutionary services.	25	2	Petition	658	Rev. Claims	911	Adverse		Laid on table.		

List of private claims presented to the House of Representatives of the United States from the 1st to the 31st Congress, inclusive—Continued.

Names of claimants.	Nature or object of the claim.	Congress.	Session.	How brought before the House of Reps.	Page of journal.	To what committee of the House referred.	No. or date of the report.	Nature of the report.	No. of the bill.	How disposed of by the House of Reps.	How disposed of by the Senate.	Date of the act of Congress, and remarks.
Moore, Captain James, (N. Y.)	Compensation for property destroyed in revolutionary war and for services rendered.	22	1	Resolution	250	Rev. Claims......	July 3, 1832	Adverse	......	Laid on table.		
Moore, James, widow of..	Pension	28	1	Petition	944	Rev. Pensions.						
Moore, James, heirs of...	Relief in relation to a lost land warrant.	31	1	Memorial	414	Priv. Land Claims.	346	Adverse	......	Laid on table.		
Moore, Jane............	(See Thomas Moore, mother of.).	18	1	....	212							
Moore, Jane............	(See Capt. Stephen Moore, widow of.)	27	2	....	681							
Moor, John Elias	Renewal of a lost loan office certificate.	2	1	Petition and rep't Sec. Treasury.	458	Select.						
Moore, John............	(See John Okley, executors of.)..	3	2	....	291							
Moore, John, (Mo.)......	Compensation as commissary, Missouri militia.	24	2	Petition	80	Claims.						
Moore, John, (Mo.)......	Compensation as commissary, Missouri militia.	25	3	Petition	206	Claims.						
Moore, John, (Mo.)......	Compensation as commissary, Missouri militia.	26	1	Petition	169	Claims.						
Moore, John, (Mo.)......	Compensation as commissary, Missouri militia.	27	2	Senate bill	1126	Claims	1012	With't amend.	238	Referred to Committee Whole House.		
Moore, John, (N. Y.)....	Pension	22	1	Petition	593	Invalid Pensions.						
Moore, John, (N. Y.)....	Pension	22	2	Petition	26	Invalid Pensions ..	Feb. 15, 1833	Favorable; bill	738	Referred to Committee Whole House.		
Moore, John, (N. Y.)....	Pension	23	2	Petition	68	Invalid Pensions ..	65	Favorable; bill	588	Passed	Passed	App'd March 3, 1835
Moore, John M.........	Compensation for extra services as chief clerk in the General Land Office.	29	2	Senate bill	350	Public Lands.....	Feb. 20, 1847	With't amend.	S. 134	Referred to Committee Whole House.		
Moore, John M.........	Compensation for extra services as chief clerk in the Genaral Land Office.	30	1	Senate bill	389	Public Lands......	493	With't amend.	S. 11	Referred to Committee Whole House.		
Moore, John M.........	Compensation for extra services as chief clerk in the General Land Office.	30	2	Senate bill	319	Whole House	Jan. 26, 1849	With't amend.	S. 11	Passed	Passed	App'd Feb. 1, 1849
Moore, John and Mary ...	(See John Cole, administrators of.)	2	2	....	668							
Moore, John, (N. Y.)....	Arrears of pension............	25	2	Petition	663	Invalid Pensions ..	April 18, 1838	Adverse	......	Laid on table.		
Moore, John R..........	(See John Hamil and Abner A. Moore, representatives of.)	15	2	....	168							
Moore, John	(See administrator of L. Bazadone)	24	1	....	942							
Moore, John, executors of.	Payment of certificates of public debt.	21	2	Petition	38	Rev. Claims......	15	Adverse	......	Laid on table.		
Moore, John, executors of.	Payment of certificates of public debt.	22	1	Petition	121	Rev. Claims......	Jan. 13, 1832	Adverse	......	Laid on table.		
Moore, John, executors of.	Payment of certificates of public debt.	22	2	Petition	110	Rev. Claims.						
Moore, John, executors of.	Payment of certificates of public debt.	23	1	Petition	92	Rev. Claims.						
Moore, John, executors of.	Commutation pay..............	24	1	Petition	431	Rev. Claims......	583	Adverse	......	Laid on table.		
Moore, John, executors of.	Commutation pay..............	25	2	Petition	72	Rev. Claims.						
Moore, John, executors of.	Commutation pay..............	26	1	Petition	164	Rev. Claims.						
Moore, John, executors of.	Commutation pay..............	29	1	Memorial	493	Rev. Claims......	746	Adverse	......	Laid on table.		
Moore, Major John, widow of.	Renewal of pension	27	2	Petition	319	Invalid Pensions ..	784	Adverse	......	Laid on table.		

List of *private claims presented to the House of Representatives of the United States from the 1st to the 31st Congress, inclusive*—**Continued.**

Names of claimants.	Nature or object of the claim.	Congress.	Session.	How brought before the House of Reps.	Page of journal.	To what committee of the House referred.	No. or date of the report.	Nature of the report.	No. of the bill.	How disposed of by the House of Reps.	How disposed of by the Senate.	Date of the act of Congress, and remarks.
Moore, Major John, widow of.	Renewal of pension	28	1	Petition	950	Whole House.						
Moore, John E	(See John Moore, executors of)	21	2		38							
Moore, John F., sureties of	Release from judgment	27	3	Resolution	94	P. Of. & P. Roads.	101	Favorable; bill	728	Passed	Passed	App'd March 3, 1843
Moore, John T	(See William H. Bedford, agent)	28	1		262							
Moore, Jonathan	(See David Moore, administrator of.)	8	1		523							
Moore, Jonathan	Pension for revolutionary services	30	1	Petition	78	Rev. Pensions	133	Favorable; bill	122	Passed	Passed	App'd Aug. 5, 1848
Moore, Joseph	(See John Owens, heirs of)	23	1		47							
Moore, Joseph	(See Hugh Moore, administrator of.)	24	1		851							
Moore, Joseph	Increase of pension	29	2	Memorial	223	Rev. Pensions.						
Moore, Joseph, and others	Payment for horses lost in Mexican war.	30	2	Petition	461	Claims.						
Moore, Lewis, (N. J.)	Drawback of duty on merchandise	18	2	Petition	101	Ways and Means				Referred to Secretary of Treasury.		
Moore, Lewis, *et al*	Compensation for guns lost in war of 1812.	19	2	Documents	105	Claims	Jan. 24, 1827	Adverse		Laid on table.		
Moore, Lucy	(See James Moore, widow of)	28	1		944							
Moore, Magdaline	(See Benj. Moore, widow of)	29	1		175							
Moore, Margaret	(See Cleon Moore, widow of)	15	1		330							
Moore, Mary P.	Pension for services of her husband, father, father in-law, and uncle.	25	2	Petition	664	Rev. Pensions				Discharged; laid on table.		
Moore, Mary, administrator of.	Indemnity for French spoliations prior to 1800.	26	1	Memorial	182	Foreign Affairs	343	Favorable; bill	319	Referred to Committee Whole House.		
Moore, Moses	Compensation for horse lost in war of 1812.	19	1	Resolution	239	Claims				Discharged; laid on table.		
Moore, Moses	(See William Baker, (N. Y.)	22	1		288							
Moore, Nancy	For an exchange of land	21	1	Senate bill	159	Claims	480 Feb. 9, 1830	With't amend.	38	Passed		App'd May 26, 1830
Moore, Nathaniel	(See W. R. Freeman, administrator of.)	27	2		750							
Moore, Newall	Release as surety of Amasa Manley	17	1	Petition	176	P. O. & P. Roads.	Mar. 15, 1822	Adverse		Leave to withdraw.		
Moore, Nicholas R.	Settlement of accounts as agent for the government for purchasing horses.	2	1	Resolution	555	Select	April 4, 1792	Favorable; bill	180	Referred to Committee Whole House.		
Moore, Nicholas R.	Revolutionary pension	23	1	Petition	436	Rev. Pensions				Discharged; laid on table.		
Moore, Nicholas R.	Revolutionary pension	26	1	Petition	322	Rev. Pensions	346	Favorable; bill	325	Referred to Committee Whole House.		
Moore, Nicholas R.	Revolutionary pension	27	2	Petition	59	Rev. Pensions	112	Favorable; bill	158	Passed	Passed	App'd July 27, 1842
Moore, Nicholas	Confirmation of title to land in Missouri.	15	2	Petition	89	Priv. Land Claims				Discharged; laid on table.		
Moore, Nicholas	Confirmation of title to land in Missouri.	17	1	Petition	54	Public Lands				Discharged; laid on table.		
Moore, Nicholas	Confirmation of title to land in Missouri.	18	1	Petition	54	Public Lands	Jan. 16, 1824	Favorable; bill	65	Passed	Passed	App'd May 26, 1824
Moore, Nicholas	Confirmation of title to land	23	1	Petition	49	Priv. Land Claims.						
Moore, Peggy	Grant of land; husband and son killed in late war.	15	1	Petition	344	Public Lands				Discharged; laid on table.		
Moore, Peter, heirs of	Revolutionary pension	26	1	Resolution	770	Rev. Claims.						
Moore, Peter, heirs of	Revolutionary pension	27	2	Petition	58	Rev. Pensions	539	Adverse		Laid on table.		
Moore, Peters, & Co.	(See Peters, Moore & Co.)	24	2		579							

List of private claims presented to the House of Representatives of the United States from the 1st to the 31st Congress, inclusive—Continued

Names of claimants.	Nature or object of the claim.	Congress.	Session.	How brought before the House of Reps.	Page of journal.	To what committee of the House referred.	No. or date of the report.	Nature of the report.	No. of the bill.	How disposed of by the House of Reps.	How disposed of by the Senate.	Date of the act of Congress, and remarks.
Moore, Phebe	(See Stephen Moore, administratrix of.)	15	1	....	218							
Moore, Philip, representatives of.	Reimbursement of money erroneously paid as surety of S. H. Moore.	23	1	Senate bill	811	Judiciary	June 24, 1834	With't amend.	184	Passed	....	App'd June 30, 1834
Moore, Pliny, & Levi Platt	Compensation for damages to property by the United States army at Plattsburg.	13	3	Petition and rep't of Sec. War.	662, 681	Military Affairs.						
Moore, Quintin	Invalid pension	11	2	Petition	283	Claims	Mar. 15, 1810	Favorable; bill	107	Passed	Passed, with amendment.	App'd April 27, 1810
Moore, Ransom	Indemnity for Indian depredations.	21	2	Documents	89	Military Affairs	....	....	......	Discharged; laid on table.		
Moore, Reuben, (Va.)	(See surety of Cyrus W. Murry)	17	1	....	176							
Moore, Reuben, heir of	Continuation of pension	24	1	Petition	506	Rev. Pensions	....	....	......	Discharged; laid on table.		
Moore, Reuben, (N. Y.)	Compensation as surveyor of customs at Hudson, New York.	19	1	Petition	132	Commerce	....	....	......	Discharged; laid on table.		
Moore, Rial C.	(See Reuben Moore, heirs of)	24	1	....	506							
Moore, Richard, (Mass.)	Compensation for revolutionary services.	2	1	Petition	440	....	....	....	......	Referred to Secretary War.		
Moore, Richard, (Mass.)	Compensation for revolutionary services.	3	2	Petition	319	Claims.						
Moore, Richard, (Mass.)	Compensation for revolutionary services.	4	1	Petition	373	Claims	May 31, 1796	Adverse	......	Laid on table.		
Moore, Risdon	(See Wm. W. Foulks, attorney of)	17	1	....	221							
Moore, Robert, (N. Y.)	Invalid pension	25	2	Petition	167	Invalid Pensions	Jan. 9, 1838	Adverse	......	Laid on table.		
Moore, Robert, widow of	Revolutionary pension	13	3	Petition	683	Pens. & Rev. Cl'ms.						
Moore, Robert S., representatives of.	For certain credits in settlement of his accounts as purser.	31	1	Memorial	695	Naval Affairs	287	With't amend.	260	Referred to Commitee Whole House.		
Moore, Robert S., representatives of.	For certain credits in settlement of his accounts as purser.	31	2	House bill	181	Whole House	Jan. 24, 1851	Favorable; bill	260	Passed.		
Moore, Robinson R.	Release from liability as quartermaster for goods stolen by soldiers.	14	1	Petition	220	Claims	....	....	......	Discharged; laid on table.		
Moore, Roxana	(See Simon Moore, widow of)	28	2	....	140							
Moore, Ruth	Pension from March 4, 1841, to March 4, 1843.	28	1	Petition	839	Rev. Pensions.						
Moore, Salmon	Pension and bounty land	31	1	Petition	411	Public Lands.						
Moore, Samuel, collector of revenue at Boston.	Relief from the payment of public money stolen from him.	5	1	Petition	49	....	....	....	......	Referred to Secretary Treasury.		
Moore, Samuel, collector of revenue at Boston.	Relief from the payment of public money stolen from him.	5	2	Rep. of Secretary Treasury.	96	....	....	....	......	Laid on table.		
Moore, Samuel, (N. Y.)	(See Ebenezer Moore, heirs of)	26	1	....	701							
Moore, Sarah	(See Nicholas R. Moore, heirs of)	23	1	....	436							
Moore, Sarah	(See James Moore, heirs of)	31	1	....	414							
Moore, Simon, widow of	Revolutionary pension	28	2	Petition	140	Rev. Pensions.						
Moore, Simon, widow of	Revolutionary pension	29	2	Petition	162	Rev. Pensions	528	Adverse	......	Laid on table.		
Moore, Squire	(See Tibbetts Rathburn, heir of)	27	2	....	238							
Moore, Stephen	Compensation for land at West Point.	1	2	Petition and rep't Sec. Treasury.	208	Select	June 15, 1790	Favorable; bill	76	Passed	Passed	App'd July 5, 1790
Moore, Stephen, Captain, widow of.	Invalid pension	27	2	Petition	681	Invalid Pensions	....	....	......	Discharged; laid on table.		

List of private claims presented to the House of Representatives of the United States from the 1st to the 31st Congress, inclusive—Continued.

Names of claimants.	Nature or object of the claim.	Congress.	Session.	How brought before the House of Reps.	Page of journal.	To what committee of the House referred.	No. or date of the report.	Nature of the report.	No. of the bill.	How disposed of by the House of Reps.	How disposed of by the Senate.	Date of the act of Congress, and remarks.
Moore, Stephen, administrator of.	Compensation for vessel captured by the enemy in 1812.	15	1	Petition	218	Claims	March 6, 1818	Adverse	.....	Referred to Committee Whole House.		
Moore, Stephen, administrator of.	Compensation for vessel captured by the enemy in 1812.	17	2	Resolution	48	....	....	....	.....	Leave to withdraw.		
Moore, Stephen, administrator of.	Compensation for vessel captured by the enemy in 1812.	20	2	Petition	32	Claims	....	....	.....	Laid on table.		
Moore, Stephen, administrator of.	Compensation for vessel captured by the enemy in 1812.	21	1	Petition	369	Claims	Dec. 26, 1830	Adverse	.....	Laid on table.		
Moore, Stephen, administrator of.	Compensation for vessel captured by the enemy in 1812.	21	2	Petition	99	Claims.						
Moore, Thomas Lloyd, attorney of.	Indemnity for French spoliations prior to 1800.	26	1	Memorial	182	Foreign Affairs	343	Favorable; bill	319	Referred to Committee Whole House.		
Moore, Thomas, mother of	Bounty land as a soldier in United States army.	18	1	Petition	212	Priv. Land Claims.						
Moore, Thomas	Compensation for work done on Cumberland road.	23	1	Res. and papers.	589	Claims	455	Adverse	.....	Laid on table	....	See report No. 449.
Moore, Willard, heirs of.	Commutation of half-pay	2	1	Petition	458	....	....	....	.....	Referred to Secretary of War.		
Moore, Willard, heirs of.	Commutation of half-pay	2	2	Rep. of Secretary War.	711	....	....	....	.....	Laid on table.		
Moore, William, (Md.)	Payment of balance due as surgeon's mate.	3	1	Petition	93	Select	April 4, 1794	Adverse	.....	Laid on table.		
Moore, William, (Md.)	Payment of balance due as surgeon's mate.	4	1	Petition & docs.	388	Claims	May 31, 1796	Adverse	.....	Laid on table.		
Moore, William, (Md.)	Payment of balance due as surgeon's mate.	4	2	Petition	676	Claims	Feb. 10, 1797	Adverse	.....	Rejected.		
Moore, William H	(See William and George Gould, sureties of.)	29	1	....	411							
Moore, William H. & Mary	(See John Moore, executor of)	21	2	....	38							
Moore, William, (N. C.)	Invalid pension	3	1	Rep. of Secretary War.	131	Select	May 26, 1794	Favorable; bill	62	Passed	Passed	App'd June 7, 1794
Moore, William, (Ill.)	Bounty land for a long military service.	29	1	Petition	148	Priv. Land Claims.	....	....	.....	Discharged; laid on table.		
Moore, William, & others.	Relief as sureties of William Carothers.	7	2	Petition	293	Claims	Feb. 26, 1803	Res. to postpone.	.....	Adopted.		
Moore, William, & others.	Relief as sureties of William Carothers.	8	1	Petition	549	Claims	....	....	.....	Leave to withdraw.		
Moore, William B	(See James Jackson and W. B Moore.)	27	2	....	792							
Moore, William M. A., widow of.	Relief; husband died in service of United States.	24	1	Petition	946	Commerce.						
Moore, William, (Tenn.)	Pension	15	1	Petition	168	Pens. & Rev. Cl'ms.	....	....	.....	Discharged; laid on table.		
Moore, William, (Mass.)	Increase of pension	26	2	Petition	200	Rev. Pensions	....	....	.....	Discharged; laid on table.		
Moore, William, widow of, (Ind.)	Revolutionary pension	31	1	Petition	232	Rev. Pensions.						
Moore, William	Compensation for revolutionary services and two horses.	15	1	Petition	437	Pens. & Rev. Cl'ms.	....	....	.....	Discharged; laid on table.		
Moore, William	Compensation for revolutionary services and two horses.	16	1	Petition	27	Pens. & Rev. Clm's.	....	....	.....	Discharged; laid on table.		
Moore, William	Correction of error in land entry	23	2	Petition	85	Priv. Land Claims.	Jan. 6, 1835	Favorable; bill	613	Referred to Committee Whole House.		

List of private claims presented to the House of Representatives of the United States from the 1st to the 31st Congress, inclusive—Continued.

Names of claimants.	Nature or object of the claim.	Congress.	Session.	How brought before the House of Reps.	Page of journal.	To what committee of the House referred.	No. or date of the report.	Nature of the report.	No. of the bill.	How disposed of by the House of Reps.	How disposed of by the Senate.	Date of the act of Congress, and remarks.
Moore, William	Correction of error in land entry	24	1	Petition	112	Priv. Land Claims.	Jan. 12, 1836	Favorable; bill	136	Passed	Rejected.	
Moore, William	Correction of error in land entry	24	2	Petition	89	Priv. Land Claims.	Dec. 27, 1836	By bill	778	Referred to Committee Whole House.		
Moore, William	Correction of error in land entry	25	2	Petition	43	Priv. Land Claims.	140	Favorable; bill	158	Referred to Committee Whole House.		
Moore, William	Correction of error in land entry	25	3	House bill	375	Whole House	....	....	158	Passed	Passed, with amendment.	App'd March 3, 1839
Moore, William, widow of	Revolutionary pension	26	1	Resolution	546 857	Rev. Pensions.						
Moorfield, Nancy	(See Benjamin Eaton, heirs of)	26	1	....	706							
Moorhead, Forgus, heirs of	For permission to institute seit for land in Iowa.	24	2	Petition	391	Priv. Land Claims.						
Moorhead, James	Compensation for work done on dam in Ohio river under contract for United States.	30	1	Petition	457	Claims	670	Favorable; bill	531	Referred to Committee Whole House.		
Moorhead, James	Compensation for work done on dam in Ohio river under contract for United States.	30	2	House bill	318	Whole House	Jan. 26, 1849	Favorable; bill	531	Passed	Passed	App'd March 3, 1849
Moorhead, David	Invalid pension	3	1	Rep. of Secretary War.	131	Select	May 26, 1794	Favorable; bill	62	Passed	Passed	App'd June 7, 1794
Moors, Jeremiah	Indemnity for loss on contract with government.	22	1	Petition	471	Commerce.						
Moors, Jeremiah	Indemnity for loss on contract with government.	23	1	Petition	240	Claims	281	Adverse	......	Laid on table.		
Moors, Jeremiah	Indemnity for loss on contract with government.	27	2	Petition	613	Claims	722	Adverse	......	Laid on table.		
Moors, Jeremiah	Indemnity for loss on contract with government.	28	1	Petition	89	Claims.						
Moors, Jeremiah	Indemnity for loss on contract with government.	28	2	House bill	295	Claims	157	Adverse	573	Laid on table.		
Moors, Jeremiah	Indemnity for loss on contract with government.	29	1	House bill	141	Claims	126	Adverse	82	Laid on table.		
Moors, Jeremiah	Indemnity for loss on contract with government.	29	1	Petition	219	Claims.						
Moors, Jeremiah	Indemnity for loss on contract with government.	30	1	Petition	153	Claims	165	Favorable	165	Referred to Committee Whole House.		
Moors, Jeremiah	Indemnity for loss on contract with government.	30	2	House bill	102	Whole House	Dec. 15, 1848	Favorable; bill	165	Passed.		
Moors, Jeremiah	Indemnity for loss on contract with government.	31	1	Petition	192	Claims.						
Moose, Moosekenaugh, H., heirs of.	Pension due deceased	24	2	Resolution	222	Rev. Pensions.						
Moose, Moosekenaugh, H., heirs of.	Pension due deceased	25	2	Petition	198	Rev. Pensions	....	....	......	Discharged; laid on table.		
Mophet, Robert	Back pay as a soldier in war of 1812.	20	1	Resolution	77	Claims	Feb. 13, 1828	Adverse	......	Laid on table.		
Mophet, Robert	Invalid pension	20	1	House bill	645	Whole House	May 16, 1828	With amends.	283	Passed.		
Mophet, Robert	Invalid pension	20	2	House bill	55	Whole House	Jan. 15, 1829	With amends.	311	Passed	Laid on table.	
Mophet, Robert	Invalid pension	21	1	Petition	48	Military Pensions.	Jan. 5, 1830	By bill	72	Passed	Passed	App'd May 20, 1830
Mora, Antonia, representatives of.	Confirmation of title to land in Louisiana.	27	2	Documents	58	Priv. Land Claims.	Feb. 9, 1842	Favorable; bill	124	Referred to Committee Whole House.		
Mora, Antonia, representatives of.	Confirmation of title to land in Louisiana.	27	2	Senate bill	359	Priv. Land Claims.	Feb. 26, 1842	With amends.	76	Passed	Passed	App'd July 6, 1842

List of private claims presented to the House of Representativesthe of United States from the 1st to the 31st Congress, inclusive—Continued.

Names of claimants.	Nature or object of the claim.	Congress.	Session.	How brought before the House of Reps.	Page of journal.	To what committee of the House referred.	No. or date of the report.	Nature of the report.	No. of the bill.	How disposed of by the House of Reps.	How disposed of by the Senate.	Date of the act of Congress, and remarks.
Morain, William	Pension	25	3	Petition	218	Invalid Pensions.						
Morain, William	Pension	26	1	Petition	163	Invalid Pensions	271	Adverse		Laid on table.		
Moran, Blair	(See Edmund Moran, heirs of)	23	1		639							
Moran, Charles, (Mich.)	Indemnity for property destroyed in war of 1812.	17	1	Petition	278	Claims				Discharged; laid on table.		
Moran, Charles, (Mich.)	Indemnity for property destroyed in war of 1812.	17	2	Petition	91	Claims	Jan. 20, 1823	Adverse		Laid on table.		
Moran, Charles, (Mich.)	Indemnity for property destroyed in war of 1812.	21	1	Petition	201	Claims	Mar. 2, 1830	Adverse		Laid on table.		
Moran, Charles, (Mich.)	Indemnity for property destroyed in war of 1812.	22	1	Petition	266	Claims	415	Adverse		Referred to Committee Whole House.		
Moran, Edmund, heirs of.	Commutation of half-pay	23	1	Petition	639	Rev. Claims.						
Moran, Edmund, heirs of.	Commutation of half-pay	23	2	Petition	77	Rev. Claims.						
Moran, Edmund, heirs of.	Commutation of half-pay	24	1	Petition	205	Rev. Claims	Jan. 4, 1836	Adverse		Laid on table.		
Moran, Edmund, heirs of.	Commutation of half-pay	26	1	Petition	360	Rev. Claims.						
Moran, Edmund, heirs of.	Commutation of half-pay	26	2	Petition	212	Rev. Claims.						
Moran, Edmund, heirs of.	Commutation of half-pay	27	2	Petition	62	Rev. Claims	394	Adverse		Laid on table.		
Moran, Maurice	Indemnity for property destroyed in war of 1812.	20	1	Petition	311	Claims	Feb. 25, 1828	Adverse		Laid on table.		
Moran, Thomas	Pension	25	3	Petition	218	Invalid Pensions.						
Moran, Thomas	Pension	26	1	Petition	306	Invalid Pensions	501	Adverse		Laid on table.		
Morass, Victor	Permission to locate land	31	1	Petition	904	Priv. Land Claims.						
Moravian missionaries	For expenses in the Cherokee nation.	23	1	Resolution	326	Indian Affairs.						
Moravian missionaries	For expenses in the Cherokee nation.	24	1	Petition	66	Indian Affairs.						
Morcell, John, daughter of	Compensation for losses in revolutionary war.	27	2	Petition	375	Rev. Claims	April 12, 1842	Adverse		Laid on table.		
Morch, John	(See John March)	23	2		113							
Mordecai, Abraham M.	Grant of land under treaty with Creek Indians.	18	1	Petition	388	Public Lands.						
Mordecai, M. C., & others	Remission of duties on fruit, &c.	27	2	Petition	224	Commerce	892	Adverse		Laid on table.		
Moreau, Celestin	Confirmation of titles to land in Louisiana.	18	1	Senate bill	179	Priv. Land Claims.	Feb. 10, 1824	With't amend.	17	Passed.		
Morehead, Charles S.	(See Fidelia C. Sharp, & others).	19	2		113							
Morehead, T. G.	Indemnity for baggage lost in service in the Mexican war.	30	2	Petition	236	Military Affairs.						
Morland, Catharine	Indemnity for property lost in war with Creek Indians.	29	1	Petition	578	Claims	750	Adverse		Laid on table.		
Moreland, Elisha, & others	Pre-emption right to certain lands in Alabama.	24	2	Petition	88	Public Lands	137	Favorable; bill	866	Referred to Committee Whole House.		
Moreland, Elisha, & others	Pre-emption right to certain lands in Alabama.	25	2	Petition	87	Public Lands	92	Favorable; bill	109	Recommitted.		
Moreland, Elisha, & others	Pre-emption right to certain lands in Alabama.	25	3	Petition	135	Public Lands.	175	Adverse		Laid on table.		
Moreland, Elisha, & others	Pre emption right to certain lands in Alabama.	26	1	Petition	178	Public Lands	591	Favorable; bill	450	Referred to Committee Whole House.		
Moreland, Elisha, & others	Pre-emption right to certain lands in Alabama.	26	1	Petition	604, 784	Public Lands	379	Adverse		Laid on table.		
Moreland, Elisha, & others	Pre-emption right to certain lands in Alabama.	26	2	Petition	37	Public Lands.						
Moreland, Elisha, & others	Pre-emption right to certain lands in Alabama.	27	2	Petition	823	Public Lands	844	Favorable; bill	487	Referred to Committee Whole House.		

List of private claims presented to the House of Representatives of the United States from the 1st to the 31st Congress, inclusive—Continued.

Names of claimants.	Nature or object of the claim.	Congress.	Session.	How brought before the House of Reps.	Page of journal.	To what committee of the House referred.	No. or date of the report.	Nature of the report.	No. of the bill.	How disposed of by the House of Reps.	How disposed of by the Senate.	Date of the act of Congress, and remarks.
Moreland, Elisha, & others	Pre-emption right to certain lands in Alabama.	27	3	House bill	89	Whole House			487	Passed	Passed	App'd Jan. 20, 1843
Moreland, Nicholas	Invalid pension	27	2	Petition	68	Invalid Pensions	144	Favorable; bill	191	Passed	Passed	App'd July 27, 1842
Moreno, Francis, (Fla.)	Payment for use of house rented by United States.	30	2	Petition	196	Judiciary	51	Favorable; bill	749	Referred to Committee Whole House.		
Mores, Savil	Increase of pension	29	1	Petition	284	Invalid Pensions	343	Adverse		Laid on table.		
Morey, Elizabeth	(See Louis Morey, widow of.)	25	2		272							
Morey, Louis, widow of	Revolutionary pension	25	2	Petition	272	Rev. Pensions				Discharged; laid on table.		
Morey, Samuel	Extension of patent	10	2	Petition	371	Select	Feb. 8, 1809	Adverse		Leave to withdraw.		
Morfit, Henry, representatives of.	Revolutionary pension	24	2	Memorial	84	Rev. Pensions	76	Adverse		Laid on table.		
Morfit, Henry, representatives of.	Revolutionary pension	24	2	Senate bill	579				S. 160			
Morfit, Henry, representatives of.	Revolutionary pension	25	2	Senate bill	159	Rev. Claims	521	Favorable	S. 46	Passed		App'd June 12, 1838
Morgan, Abel, executors of.	Arrears of pay for revolutionary services.	19	1	Petition	68	Rev. Pensions	160	Adverse		Referred to Committee Whole House.		
Morgan, Abigail	(See Fbenezer Morgan, widow of.)	24	2		41							
Morgan, Major Abner	Pension	22	1	Petition	130	Rev. Pensions	395	Favorable; bill	495	Referred to Committee Whole House.		
Morgan, Maj. Abner, widow of.	Restoration of pension	26	1	Petition	706	Rev. Pensions.						
Morgan, Maj. Abner, widow of.	Restoration of pension	27	2	Petition	374	Rev. Pensions	784	Adverse		Laid on table.		
Morgan Alexander, (S. C.)	For refunding duties on goods	20	1	Memorial	111	Ways and Means				Referred to Committee Whole House on S. bill No. 52.		App'd May 23, 1828
Morgan, Alexander, heirs of.	Pension	25	2	Petition	1175	Rev. Claims	June 27, 1828	Adverse		Laid on table.		
Morgan, Alexander, heirs of.	Pension	26	1	Petition	163	Rev. Claims.						
Morgan, Alexander G.	Compensation for property destroyed by Sac Indians.	24	1	Petition	534	Claims	701	Favorable; bill	653	Referred to Committee Whole House.		
Morgan, Alexander G.	Compensation for property destroyed by Sac Indians.	25	2	Petition	37	Claims	50	Favorable; bill	62	Passed	Passed	App'd April 20, 1838
Morgan, Ann	(See James Morgan, jr., widow of.)	28	1		983							
Morgan, Asher	Confirmation of title to land in Louisiana.	22	2	Petition	41	Priv. Land Claims.	75	Favorable; bill	718	Referred to Committee Whole House.		
Morgan, Asher	Confirmation of title to land in Louisiana.	23	1	Petition	93	Priv. Land Claims.	77	Favorable; bill	84	Passed	Passed	App'd June 6, 1834
Morgan, Austin, and Gideon Fitz.	Extra compensation for locating bounty land warrants.	31	1	Petition	225	Public Lands.						
Morgan, Benjamin, (N. Y.)	Compensation for supplies furnished in revolutionary war.	3	1	Petition	70	Select	Mar. 11, 1794	Adverse		Laid on table.		
Morgan, Charles	Pension and bounty land	15	1	Petition	198	Military Affairs				Discharged; laid on table.		
Morgan, Charles	Pension and bounty land	17	2	Petition	313					Laid on table.		
Morgan, Charles	(See Joseph Emmet, representatives of.)	25	2		905							
Morgan, Charles	(See Simon Porche, representatives of.)	25	2		548							

List of private claims presented to the House of Representatives of the United States from the 1st to the 31st Congress, inclusive—**Continued.**

Names of claimants.	Nature or object of the claim.	Congress.	Session.	How brought before the House of Reps.	Page of journal.	To what committee of the House referred.	No. or date of the report.	Nature of the report.	No. of the bill.	How disposed of by the House of Reps.	How disposed of by the Senate.	Date of the act of Congress, and remarks.
Morgan, Charles, (La.)	Confirmation of title to land in Louisiana.	25	2	Senate bill	994	Priv. Land Claims.	....	....	S. 220			
Morgan, Charles, (La.)	Confirmation of title to land in Louisiana.	25	3	Senate bill	477	Priv. Land Claims.	....	....	S. 111			
Morgan, Charles, (La.)	Confirmation of title to land in Louisiana.	26	1	Senate bill	419	Priv. Land Claims.	July 21, 1840	With amends.	S. 53	Referred to Committee Whole House.		
Morgan, Charles, (La.)	Confirmation of title to land in Louisiana.	26	2	Senate bill	210	Priv. Land Claims.	....	....	S. 113			
Morgan, Colonel Charles, (La.)	Confirmation of title to land in Louisiana.	25	2	Senate bill	994	Priv. Land Claims.	1031	Adverse	S. 221	Laid on table.		
Morgan, Colonel Charles, (La.)	Confirmation of title to land in Louisiana.	25	3	Senate bill	477	Priv. Land Claims.	Feb. 16, 1839	With't amend.	S. 112	Referred to Committee Whole House.		
Morgan, Colonel Charles, (La.)	Confirmation of title to land in Louisiana.	26	1	Petition	365	Priv. Land Claims.	479	Adverse	......	Laid on table.		
Morgan, Colonel Charles, (La.)	Confirmation of title to land in Louisiana.	26	1	Senate bill	391	Priv. Land Claims.	365	Adverse	S. 52	Referred to Committee Whole House.		
Morgan, Colonel, Charles, (La.)	Confirmation of title to land in Louisiana.	26	2	Senate bill	210	Priv. Land Claims.	Feb. 12, 1841	With't amend.	S. 112	Referred to Committee Whole House.		
Morgan, Charles	(See Perruquier, assignee of.)	26	1	Petition	827							
Morgan, Charles W.	Reimbursement of extra expenses on official duty.	28	1	Senate bill	893	Naval Affairs	May 24, 1844	With't amend.	S. 134	Passed	....	App'd June 17, 1844
Morgan, Charles W., and others.	Relief for violation of government contract.	31	1	Petition	1227	Commerce	495	Favorable	J.R. 25	Referred to Committee Whole House.		
Morgan, Cyrus	Pre-emption right to land as branch pilot.	28	1	Petition	77	Priv. Land Claims.	9	Favorable; bill	35	Passed	Passed	App'd June 17, 1844
Morgan, Ebenezer, widow of.	Pension	24	2	Memorial	41	Naval Affairs	25	Adverse	......	Leave to withdraw.		
Morgan, Elizabeth	(See Abel Morgan, executor of)	19	1	....	68							
Morgan, Elizabeth	(See Zackquelle Morgan, widow of)	14	1	....	112							
Morgan, Evan, (Va.)	Pension	20	2	Petition	112	Military Pensions	....	....	......	Discharged; laid on table.		
Morgan, Evan, (Va.)	Pension	21	1	Petition	471	Military Pensions	....	....	......	Discharged; laid on table.		
Morgan, George, heirs of	For five year full pay in lieu of half pay for life.	23	2	Resolution	204	Rev. Claims.						
Morgan, George, heirs of	For five years full pay in lieu of half pay for life.	24	1	Resolution	105	Rev. Claims.						
Morgan, Colonel Gideon	Invalid pension	23	1	Petition	493	Invalid Pensions	409	Favorable; bill	425	Referred to Committee Whole House.		
Morgan, Colonel Gideon	Invalid pension	23	2	Bill of last sess.	336	Whole House	....	....	425	Passed	Passed, with amendment.	
Morgan, Colonel Gideon	Invalid pension	24	1	Petition	176	Invalid Pensions	130	Favorable; bill	140	Passed	Passed	App'd May 14, 1836
Morgan, Humphrey	Revolutionary pension	27	2	Petition	765	Rev. Pensions	July 21, 1842	Adverse	......	Laid on table.		
Morgan, James, (La.)	Extension of time to locate tract of land.	29	1	Memorial	532	Priv. Land Claims.						
Morgan, James, (La.)	Extension of time to locate tract of land.	29	2	Petition	83	Priv. Land Claims.						
Morgan, James, (La.)	Extension of time to locate tract of land.	30	1	Petition	109	Priv. Land Claims.	Feb. 8, 1848	By bill	196	Passed.		
Morgan, James	Increase of pension	10	2	Rep. of Secretary War.	480	Claims	Jan. 30, 1809	Favorable; bill	158	Passed	Passed, with amendment.	App'd March 3, 1809
Morgan, James, (Ind.)	Deduction in price of tract of land covered by water.	29	1	Petition	568	Public Lands	....	....	......	Discharged; laid on table.		

List of private claims presented to the House of Representatives of the United States from the 1st to the 31st Congress, inclusive—Continued.

Names of claimants.	Nature or object of the claim.	Congress.	Session.	How brought before the House of Reps.	Page of journal.	To what committee of the House referred.	No. or date of the report.	Nature of the report.	No. of the bill.	How disposed of by the House of Reps.	How disposed of by the Senate.	Date of the act of Congress, and remarks.
Morgan, James, (N. Y.)	Revolutionary pension	28	1	Petition	252	Rev. Pensions				Discharged; laid on table.		
Morgan, James, (N. Y.)	Revolutionary pension	28	2	Petition	183	Rev. Pensions.						
Morgan, James, jr., widow of.	Pension for revolutionary services.	28	1	Petition	983	Rev. Claims.						
Morgan, James M	For services as bearer of despatches from the governor of Iowa.	26	1	Senate bill	420	Military Affairs	May 25, 1840	Favorable	S. 227	Referred to Committee Whole House.		
Morgan, James M	For services as bearer of despatches from the governor of Iowa.	27	2	Memorial	686	Claims	841	Favorable; bill	484	Referred to Committee Whole House.		
Morgan, James M	For services as bearer of despatches from the governor of Iowa.	27	3	House bill	89	Whole House			484	Passed	Passed	App'd Jan. 20, 1843
Morgan, James W	Pre-emption right to land as New Orleans branch pilot.	28	1	Petition	77	Priv. Land Claims.	9	Favorable; bill	35	Passed	Passed	App'd June 17, 1844
Morgan, Jane	(See Peter Woolsey, or Oosely, representatives of.)	18	1		307							
Morgan, John, (Iowa)	Invalid pension	26	1	Petition	327	Invalid Pensions				Discharged; laid on table.		
Morgan, John, (Iowa)	Invalid pension	27	2	Petition	63	Invalid Pensions	211	Adverse		Laid on table.		
Morgan, John, (Iowa)	Invalid pension	28	1	Petition	73	Invalid Pensions.						
Morgan, John, (Conn.)	Indemnity for French spoliations prior to 1800.	26	1	Memorial	182	Foreign Affairs	343	Favorable; bill	319	Referred to Committee Whole House.		
Morgan, John, (Conn.)	Compensation for losses by the French in 1800.	26	2	Petition	55	Foreign Affairs	53	Favorable; bill	319	Referred to Committee Whole House.		
Morgan, John, (Conn.)	Compensation for losses by the French in 1800.	28	1	Petition	76	Foreign Affairs.						
Morgan, John, attorney of	(See Francis Buckley, and others)	26	1		182							
Morgan, John, (Va.)	Increase of pension	10	1	Petition	87	Claims	Jan. 22, 1808	Adverse		Leave to withdraw.		
Morgan, John, (Va.)	Increase of pension	10	2	Rep. of Secretary of War.	480	Claims	Jan. 30, 1809	Favorable; bill	158	Passed	Passed, with amendment.	App'd Mar. 3, 1809
Morgan, John	Payment for horse lost in Mexico.	30	1	Petition	146	Claims	233	Favorable; bill	237	Passed.		
Morgan, John, (N. Y.)	Indemnity for French spoliations prior to 1800.	26	1	Memorial	182	Foreign Affairs	343	Favorable; bill	319	Referred to Committee Whole House.		
Morgan, Jonathan, (N. Y.)	Pension	23	2	Petition	164	Rev. Pensions.						
Morgan, Jonathan, (N. Y.)	Pension	24	1	Petition	107	Rev. Pensions				Discharged; laid on table.		
Morgan, Pope, and others.	(See Pope, Morgan, and others)	30	1		838							
Morgan, Peter H	(See J. Arnold, administrator of)	30	2		317							
Morgan & Price	Indemnity for French spoliations prior to 1800.	26	1	Memorial	182	Foreign Affairs	343	Favorable; bill	319	Referred to Committee Whole House.		
Morgan, Reese, widow of.	Revolutionary pension	26	1	Resolution	1011	Rev. Pensions.						
Morgan, Samuel, (Mass.)	Pension	23	1	Petition	190	Rev. Pensions.						
Morgan, Simon	Invalid pension	10	1	House bill	232	Whole House	April 19, 1808	With amends.	78	Passed	Passed, with amendment.	App'd April 25, 1808
Morgan, T. A	(See Chandler Price and others, administrator of.)	26	1		182							
Morgan, T. A	(See Morgan & Price)	26	1		182							
Morgan, Thomas, (Ill.)	Pension	25	2	Petition	85	Invalid Pensions				Discharged; laid on table.		
Morgan, Thomas, (Ill.)	Pension	26	1	Petition	327	Invalid Pensions	416	Adverse		Laid on table.		
Morgan, Thomas, (Ill.)	Pension	29	1	Memorial	418	Invalid Pensions	812	Favorable; bill	527	Referred to Committee Whole House.		
Morgan, Thomas Gibbs, sureties of.	Release from judgment	30	1	Petition	685	Judiciary.						

List of private claims presented to the House of Representatives of the United States from the 1st to the 31st Congress, inclusive—Continued.

Names of claimants.	Nature or object of the claim.	Congress.	Session.	How brought before the House of Reps.	Page of journal.	To what committee of the House referred.	No. or date of the report.	Nature of the report.	No. of the bill	How disposed of by the House of Reps.	How disposed of by the Senate.	Date of the act of Congress, and remarks.
Morgan, Thomas Gibbs, sureties of.	Release from judgment	30	2	Senate bill	162	Claims	Mar. 3, 1849	With amends.	S. 301	Passed with amendm't.	Passed	App'd March 3, 1849
Morgan, William, administrator of.	Payment of certain bills drawn by Gen. Armstrong.	15	1	Petition	135	Ways and Means	Mar. 10, 1818	Favorable; bill	124	Referred to Committee Whole House.		
Morgan, William, administrator of.	Payment of certain bills drawn by Gen. Armstrong.	15	2	House bill	108	Whole House	Dec. 16, 1818	With't amend.	124	Passed	Passed	App'd Feb. 20, 1819
Morgan, Col. William C.	Payment for horse killed in Creek war in 1836.	25	2	Petition	575	Claims.						
Morgan, Col. William C.	Payment for horse killed in Creek war in 1836.	26	1	Petition	339	Claims.						
Morgan, William, (Ky.)	Bounty land for revolutionary services.	17	1	Petition	256	Military Affairs	....	....	......	Discharged; laid on table.		
Morgan, William, (Ky.)	Bounty land for revolutionary services.	23	1	Petition	128	Rev. Claims.						
Morgan, William, (Ky.)	Bounty land for revolutionary services.	24	1	Petition	205	Rev. Claims.						
Morgan, Zackquelle, widow of.	Pension	14	1	Petition	112	Pens. & Rev. Cl'ms.	Jan. 26, 1816	Favorable; bill	......	Passed	Postponed.	
Morgan, Zackquelle, heirs of.	Bounty land and pay for revolutionary services.	24	1	Petition	633	Rev. Claims.						
Morgan, Zedekiah	Settlement of accounts as quartermaster in United States army.	2	2	Petition	494	....	....	....	......	Referred to Secretary of Treasury.		
Morgan, Zedekiah	Settlement of accounts as quartermaster in United States army.	3	2	Rep. of Secretary Treasury.	284	....	....	....	......	Laid on table.		
Morgan, Zedekiah	Settlement of accounts and refunding money recovered from him for acts done in his official capacity.	15	2	Petition	65	Pens. & Rev. Cl'ms.	Dec. 11, 1818	Adverse	......	Rejected.		
Morgan, Zedekiah	Settlement of accounts and refunding money recovered from him for acts done in his official capacity.	17	1	Petition	99	Pens. & Rev. Cl'ms.	Jan. 8, 1822	Adverse	......	Rejected.		
Morley, Daniel, heirs of	Bounty land for revolutionary services.	25	3	Petition	455	Priv. Land Claims.						
Morley, Nancy	(See Jacob Hood)	26	2	....	122							
Morley, Roderick	Pension	27	2	Petition	321	Naval Affairs.						
Morman, James, (Ohio)	Correction of land entry	23	2	Documents	39, 423	Public Lands.						
Mormanry, Emmet G. C.	(See Louis F. Beeler, and others)	30	1	....	115							
Mormon battalion	Travelling expenses—Mexican war.	31	1	Petition	938	Military Affairs.						
Mormon delegates	Compensation for property plundered from them.	27	2	Petition	385	Judiciary.						
Morrell, Abraham	Allowance for losses on contract for soldiers' clothing.	14	1	Petition	300	Claims	....	....	......	Discharged; laid on table.		
Morrell, Abraham	Allowance for losses on contract for soldiers' clothing.	18	1	Petition	237	Military Affairs.						
Morrell, Abraham	Allowance for losses on contract for soldiers' clothing.	22	1	Petition	435	Claims	Jan. 18, 1832	Adverse	......	Laid on table.		
Morrell, Abraham	Allowance for losses on contract for soldiers' clothing.	26	1	Petition	702	Claims.						
Morrell, Abraham	Allowance for losses on contract for soldiers' clothing.	27	2	Petition	49	Claims	170	Adverse	......	Laid on table.		
Morrell, Benning	(See Daniel Huntress, executor of)	26	1	....	182							

List of private claims presented to the House of Representatives of the United States from the 1st to the 31st Congress, inclusive—Continued.

Names of claimants.	Nature or object of the claim.	Congress.	Session.	How brought before the House of Reps.	Page of journal.	To what committee of the House referred.	No. or date of the report.	Nature of the report.	No. of the bill.	How disposed of by the House of Reps.	How disposed of by the Senate.	Date of the act of Congress, and remarks.
Morrell, Benjamin, captain of schooner Antonio.	Reimbursem't of expenses in bringing two natives from the Pacific.	22	1	Petition	105	Commerce.						
Morrell, Benjamin, captain of schooner Antonio.	Reimbursem't of expenses in bringing two natives from the Pacific.	22	2	Memorial	30	Naval Affairs.						
Morrell, Elisha	(See Joseph Icard, administrator of.)	28	1		853							
Morrell, George	(See Solomon Sibley, and others).	22	2		314							
Morrell, John, and others, (Pa.)	Compensation for services as jurors in United States court.	9	2	Petition	524	Select	Feb. 18, 1807	Adverse		Leave to withdraw.		
Morrell, John	Invalid pension	24	1	Petition	924	Invalid Pensions.						
Morrell, Joseph	Payment of a loan office certificate.	14	2	Resolution	455	Pens. & Rev. Cl'ms.				Discharged; laid on table.		
Morrell, Joseph	Payment of a loan office certificate.	22	2	Resolution	185	Rev. Claims.						
Morrell, Joseph	Payment of a loan office certificate.	23	1	Petition	188	Rev. Claims.						
Morrell, Joseph	(See John Carman, assignee of)	23	2		134							
Morrell, Joseph, (N. Y.)	Increase of pension	22	1	Petition	219	Rev. Pensions.						
Morrell, Joseph, (N. Y.)	Increase of pension	22	2	Petition	109	Rev. Pensions				Discharged; laid on table.		
Morrell, Joseph, (N. Y.)	Increase of pension	23	1	Petition	135	Rev. Pensions				Discharged; laid on table.		
Morrell, Samuel, (N. H.)	Invalid pension	3	2	Rep. of Secretary War.	278	Claims	Feb. 28, 1795	Favorable; bill	130	Passed	Postponed.	
Morrell, Samuel, (N. H.)	Invalid pension	4	1	Petition	447	Claims	Feb. 18, 1796	Favorable; bill	156	Passed	Passed	App'd April 20, 1796
Morrell, Samuel, (N. H.)	Arrears of pension	4	2	Memorial	654	Claims	Jan. 26, 1797	Adverse.		Laid on table.		
Morrell, Samuel, (N. H.)	Increase of pension	13	1	House bill	56	Whole House	July 20, 1813	With't amend.	31	Passed	Passed	App'd Aug. 2, 1813
Morrell, Stephen	Invalid pension	24	1	Petition	51	Invalid Pensions				Discharged; laid on table.		
Morrell, Stephen	Invalid pension	25	2	Petition	118	Invalid Pensions.						
Morrell, Stephen	Invalid pension	25	3	Petition	89	Invalid Pensions	Jan. 9, 1838	Adverse		Laid on table.		
Morrey, or Murrey, Anthony	Pension	22	1	Petition	564	Invalid Pensions	April 3, 1832	Favorable; bill	528	Passed	Passed	App'd July 14, 1832
Morrill, Daniel	Compensation for services and clothing in revolutionary war.	15	1	Petition	131	Pens. & Rev. Cl'ms.				Discharged; laid on table.		
Morrill, David	Restoration of pension	17	1	Petition	109	Rev. Pensions				Discharged; laid on table.		
Morrill, Eunice	Revolutionary pension	28	1	Petition	950	Whole House.						
Morrill, John, surety of	Release from judgment	18	1	Petition	131	Judiciary				Discharged; laid on table.		
Morrill, Joseph	Pension	9	2	House bill	608	Whole House	Feb. 28, 1807	With amends.	216	Passed	Passed	App'd March 3, 1807
Morrill, Joseph, (Maine)	Naval pension	26	1	Petition	303	Naval Affairs.						
Morrill, Joseph, (Maine)	Naval pension	26	2	Petition	79	Naval Affairs	127	Favorable; bill	634	Referred to Committee Whole House.		
Morrill, Nahum	Indemnity for French spoliations prior to 1800.	26	1	Memorial	182	Foreign Affairs	343	Favorable; bill	319	Referred to Committee Whole House.		
Morrill, Samuel	Increase of pension	16	1	Petition	240	Pens. & Rev. Cl'ms.				Discharged; laid on table.		
Morrill, Samuel	Restoration of pension	17	1	Petition	60	Rev. Pensions				Discharged; laid on table.		
Morrill, Simon S.	Invalid pension	23	2	Petition	40	Invalid Pensions	18	Favorable; bill	591	Passed.		
Morrill, Simon S.	Invalid pension	24	1	Petition	233	Invalid Pensions	June 28, 1836	Adverse		Laid on table.		
Morrill, Simon S.	Invalid pension	25	2	Petition	57	Invalid Pensions	June 18, 1838	Adverse		Laid on table.		
Morrill, Simon S.	Invalid pension	26	1	Petition	707	Invalid Pensions				Laid on table.		
Morrill, Simon S.	Invalid pension	26	2	Petition	107	Invalid Pensions.						
Morrill, Simon S.	Invalid pension	27	2	Petition	59	Rev. Pensions	232	Adverse		Laid on table.		

List of private claims presented to the House of Representatives of the United States from the 1st to the 31st Congress, inclusive—Continued.

Names of claimants.	Nature or object of the claim.	Congress.	Session.	How brought before the House of Reps.	Page of journal.	To what committee of the House referred.	No. or date of the report.	Nature of the report.	No. of the bill.	How disposed of by the House of Reps.	How disposed of by the Senate.	Date of the act of Congress, and remarks.
Morrill, Simon S.	Invalid pension	27	3	Petition	343					Leave to withdraw.		
Morris, Charles	(See Stephen Decatur, representatives and others.)	20	1		295							
Morris, David	Compensation for revolutionary services.	2	1	Petition	458					Referred to Secretary War.		
Morris, Delila	(See Halloway Morris, widow of.)	26	1		382							
Morris, Edward	Payment for services as a mounted ranger.	29	1	Petition	613	Claims	635	Adverse		Laid on table.		
Morris, Elizabeth P.	(See John Maxwell, daughter of.)	27	2		375							
Morris, Eunis H.	(See William H. Bedford, agent.)	28	1		262							
Morris, George, (Va.)	Revolutionary pension	25	2	Resolution	527	Rev. Pensions				Laid on table.		
Morris, George, (Va.)	Revolutionary pension	26	1	Petition	174	Rev. Pensions	128	Favorable; bil	138	Passed	Postponed.	
Morris, George, (Va.)	Revolutionary pension	26	2	Petition	34	Rev. Pensions.						
Morris, George, (Va.)	Revolutionary pension	27	2	Petition	153	Rev. Pensions.	287	Favorable; bill	255	Passed	Postponed.	
Morris, Henry, heirs of	Payment of two loan office certificates.	14	1	Petition	77, 352	Pens. & Rev. Cl'ms.	Mar. 16, 1814	Adverse		Laid on table.		
Morris, Henry, heirs of	Payment of two loan office certificates.	14	2	Petition	777	Pens. & Rev. Cl'ms.				Discharged; laid on table.		
Morris, Henry, heirs of	Payment of two loan office certificates.	15	1	Petition	21	Pens. & Rev. Cl'ms.	Dec. 15, 1817	Adverse		Laid on table.		
Morris, Henry, heirs of	Payment of two loan office certificates.	16	1	Petition	232	Pens. & Rev. Cl'ms.	Feb. 25, 1820	Adverse		Rejected.		
Morris, Henry, heirs of	Payment of two loan office certificates.	17	1	Petition	24	Pens. & Rev. Cl'ms.	27	Adverse		Referred to Committee Whole House.		
Morris, Henry, heirs of	Payment of two loan office certificates.	18	1	Petition	31	Pens. & Rev. Cl'ms.	16	Adverse		Leave to withdraw.		
Morris, Henry, heirs of	Payment of two loan office certificates.	19	1	Petition	78	Rev. Claims				Discharged; laid on table.		
Morris, Henry, heirs of	Payment of two loan office certificates.	20	1	Petition	105	Rev. Claims	126	Adverse		Laid on table.		
Morris, Henry, heirs of	Payment of two loan office certificates.	20	2	Petition	43	Rev. Claims				Discharged; laid on table.		
Morris, Henry, heirs of	Payment of two loan office certificates.	21	1	Petition	171	Rev. Claims	274	Favorable; bill	328	Referred to Committee Whole House.		
Morris, Henry, heirs of	Payment of two loan office certificates.	21	2	Bill of last sess.	333	Whole House	Feb. 22, 1831	With't amend.	328	Passed.		
Morris, Henry, heirs of	Payment of two loan office certificates.	22	1	Senate bill	521	Rev. Claims	Mar. 30, 1832	With't amend.	70	Passed		App'd May 19, 1832
Morris, Halloway, widow of.	Revolutionary pension	26	1	Resolution	382	Rev. Pensions	424	Adverse		Laid on table.		
Morris, James, representatives of.	Compensation for wood taken by United States troops.	23	1	Resolution	116	Claims.						
Morris, James	Invalid pension	28	2	Petition	176	Invalid Pensions.						
Morris, John, (Miss.)	Confirmation of title to land in Mississippi.	12	1	Petition	13	Public Lands.						
Morris, John, (Ohio)	Grant of land for hardships as a western pioneer.	31	2	Petition	205	Priv. Land Claims.						
Morris, John, (Pa.)	Compensation for revolutionary services.	12	1	Petition	158	Claims.						
Morris, Jonathan, (Pa.)	Invalid pension	13	1	Petition	46	Claims	June 29, 1815	Favorable; bill	31	Passed	Passed	App'd Aug. 2, 1815
Morris, Jonathan, (Pa.)	Increase of pension	14	1	Petition	193	Pens. & Rev. Cl'ms.	Mar. 14, 1816	Adverse		Rejected.		
Morris, Jonathan, (Pa.)	Increase of pension	15	1	Petition	261	Pens. & Rev. Cl'ms.				Discharged; laid on table.		

List of private claims presented to the House of Representatives of the United States from the 1st to the 31st Congress, inclusive—Continued.

Names of claimants.	Nature or object of the claim.	Congress.	Session.	How brought before the House of Reps.	Page of journal.	To what committee of the House referred.	No. or date of the report.	Nature of the report.	No. of the bill.	How disposed of by the House of Reps.	How disposed of by the Senate.	Date of the act of Congress, and remarks.
Morris, Jonathan, (Pa.)	Increase of pension	19	1	Petition	128	Military Pensions	164	Adverse	......	Discharged; laid on table.		
Morris, J., administrator of.	Indemnity for French spoliations prior to 1800.	31	1	Petition	216	Foreign Affairs.	355	Favorable; bill	318	Referred to Committee Whole House.		
Morris, Lester	Restoration of pension	20	1	Petition	39	Rev. Claims	Jan. 7, 1828	Adverse	......	Recommitted.		
							Mar. 28, 1828	Adverse	......	Laid on table.		
Morris, Lester	Restoration of pension	21	1	Petition	144	Military Pensions	May 21, 1830	Favorable; bill	478	Referred to Committee Whole House.		
Morris, Lester	Restoration of pension	21	2	Bill of last sess.	318	Whole House	Feb. 16, 1831	With't amend.	478	Passed.		
Morris, Lester	Restoration of pension	22	1	Petition	51	Rev. Pensions	23	Favorable; bill	70	Passed	Postponed.	
Morris, Nathaniel G	Pension	15	1	Petition	251	Pens. & Rev. Cl'ms.	....	....	......	Discharged; laid on table.		
Morris, Richard G	(See Henry Morris, heirs of)	14	1	....	77, 352							
Morris, R. L., and others	(See A. S. Holleman, sureties of)	27	2									
Morris, Robert	(See Ebenezer Stavens, and others)	15	1	....	143							
Morris, Thomas, (Ky.)	Bounty land for services in revolutionary war.	16	2	Petition	153	Pens. & Rev. Cl'ms.	Jan. 19, 1821	Adverse	......	Rejected.		
Morris, Thomas, heirs of.	Commutation pay for revolutionary services.	24	1	Petition	274	Rev. Claims.						
Morris, Thomas, heirs of.	Commutation pay for revolutionary services.	25	3	Petition	84	Rev. Claims.						
Morris, Thomas, heirs of.	Commutation pay for revolutionary services.	26	1	Petition	166	Rev. Claims.						
Morris, Thomas, heirs of.	Commutation pay for revolutionary services.	26	2	Petition	36	Rev. Claims.						
Morris, Thomas, heirs of.	Commutation pay for revolutionary services.	29	1	Petition	1103	Rev. Claims.						
Morris, Thomas, heirs of.	Commutation pay for revolutionary services.	30	1	Petition	69	Rev. Claims.						
Morris, Thomas, heirs of.	Commutation pay for revolutionary services.	30	2	Petition	466	Rev. Claims.						
Morris, Thomas, heirs of.	Commutation pay for revolutionary services.	31	1	Petition	396	Rev. Claims.						
Morris, Thomas, (Mo.)	Pension	31	2	Petition	334	Rev. Claims.						
Morris, Thomas, (S. C.)	Indemnity for French spoliations prior to 1800.	26	1	Memorial	182	Foreign Affairs	343	Favorable; bill	319	Referred to Committee Whole House.		
Morris, William, & others, representatives of Thos., of Georgia.	Compensation for supplies furnished and for services in revolutionary war.	3	2	Petition	299	Claims.						
Morris, William, & others, representatives of Thos., of Georgia.	Compensation for supplies furnished and for services in revolutionary war.	4	1	Petition	373	Claims	Dec. 28, 1795	Adverse	......	Leave to withdraw.		
Morris, Wm. H., (Tenn.)	Compensation for horse lost in the war with Creek Indians.	23	1	Petition	498	Claims	420	Adverse	......	Laid on table.		
Morris, Wm. H., (Tenn.)	Compensation for horse lost in the war with Creek Indians.	24	1	Petition	508	Claims	June 15, 1836	Adverse	......	Laid on table.		
Morris, William V	For his portion of prize money awarded by Congress.	31	2	Petition	33	Naval Affairs.						
Morris, Zadock	Restoration of pension	17	1	Petition	387	Rev. Pensions	....	....	......	Discharged; laid on table.		
Morris, Zadock	Restoration of pension	20	1	Petition	223	Military Pensions	April 29, 1828	By bill	283	Passed.		
Morris, Zadock	Restoration of pension	20	2	Petition	55	Military Pensions	Dec. 12, 1828	By bill	311	Passed	Laid on table.	

List of private claims presented to the House of Representatives of the United States from the 1st to the 31st Congress, inclusive—Continued.

Names of claimants.	Nature or object of the claim.	Congress.	Session.	How brought before the House of Reps.	Page of journal.	To what committee of the House referred.	No. or date of the report.	Nature of the report.	No. of the bill.	How disposed of by the House of Reps.	How disposed of by the Senate.	Date of the act of Congress, and remarks.
Morris, Zadock	Restoration of pension	21	1	Petition	48	Military Pensions	Jan. 5, 1830	By bill	72	Passed	Passed	App'd May 20, 1830
Morrisett, Cason	Compensation for a horse impressed into United States service in revolutionary war.	18	2	Petition	36	Pens. & Rev. Cl'ms.	Dec. 17, 1824	Adverse		Laid on table.		
Morrisett, Joseph	Bounty land for services in war of 1812.	16	1	Petition	158	Military Affairs	Jan. 24, 1820	Adverse		Rejected.		
Morrisett, William	To refund amount of forfeiture for violation of revenue laws.	14	1	Petition	48	Claims	Dec. 29, 1815	Favorable; bill		Passed	Passed, with amendment.	App'd Feb. 15, 1816
Morrison, Abraham	(See John Webster, surety of)	25	2		279							
Morrison, Alexander, (Pa.)	Compensation for a horse lost in revolutionary war.	10	1	Petition	92	Select.						
Morrison, Alexander, (Pa.)	Compensation for a horse lost in revolutionary war.	11	3	Petition	442	Claims	Jan. 2, 1811	Adverse		Leave to withdraw.		
Morrison, Alexander, (Pa.)	Compensation for a horse lost in revolutionary war.	17	1	Petition	186	Rev. Claims	Mar. 22, 1822	Adverse		Rejected.		
Morrison, Arthur, (Ohio)	Confirmation of title to land in Ohio.	7	1	Petition and rep't Sec. Treasury.	120, 180	Whole House.						
Morrison, Caleb	(See George Ficklin and Daniel Ward.)	22	1		132							
Morrison, David	Restoration of pension	20	2	Petition	59	Military Pensions	Jan. 13, 1829	Adverse.		Laid on table.		
Morrison, D. S	(See Isaac Morrison, executor of)	23	2		38							
Morrison, Edward, senior, (Pa.)	Pension	19	2	Petition	59	Military Pensions.						
Morrison, Edward, senior, (Pa.)	Pension	21	2	Resolution	124	Military Pensions.						
Morrison, Edward, senior, (Pa.)	Pension	22	1	Resolution	70	Military Pensions				Discharged; laid on table.		
Morrison, Evan	Drawback of duty on merchandise.	16	1	Petition	180	Commerce				Discharged; laid on table.		
Morrison, George B	Arrears of pay in war of 1812	19	1	Resolution	425	Claims				Discharged; laid on table.		
Morrison, George B	Arrears of pay in war of 1812	19	2	Petition	31	Claims	Dec. 22, 1826	Adverse		Recommitted.		
Morrison, George W	Invalid pension	20	1	Petition	396	Military Pensions	April 29, 1828	Favorable; bill	283	Passed.		
Morrison, George W	Invalid pension	20	2	Petition	55	Military Pensions	Dec. 12, 1828	Favorable; bill	311	Passed	Laid on table.	
Morrison, George W	Invalid pension	21	1	Petition	37	Military Pensions	Jan. 5, 1830	Favorable; bill	72	Passed	Passed	App'd May 29, 1830
Morrison, George M	Confirmation of title to land in Missouri.	21	1	Petition	524	Public Lands				Discharged; laid on table.		
Morrison, Hans, executors of.	Renewal of lost loan office certificate.	2	2	Petition	653					Laid on table.		
Morrison, Hugh and James	(See Hans Morrison, executors of)	2	2		653							
Morrison, Isaac, executors of.	One year's pay for revolutionary services.	23	2	Petition	38	Rev. Claims.						
Morrison, James	(See sureties of Joseph Crockett)	18	2		223							
Morrison, James	Confirmation of title to land in Missouri.	15	1	Petition	238	Priv. Land Claims				Discharged; laid on table.		
Morrison, James	Confirmation of title to land in Missouri.	16	1	Petition	71	Priv. Land Claims				Discharged; laid on table.		
Morrison, James	Confirmation of title to land in Missouri.	17	1	Petition	54	Priv. Land Claims				Discharged; laid on table.		
Morrison, James	Confirmation of title to land in Missouri.	18	1	Petition	54	Priv. Land Claims	Jan. 16, 1824	Favorable; bill	65	Passed	Passed	App'd May 20, 1824
Morrison, James	Confirmation of title to land in Missouri.	25	2	Documents	179	Priv. Land Claims	395	Adverse		Laid on table.		

List of private claims presented to the House of Representatives of the United States from the 1st to the 31st Congress, inclusive—Continued.

Names of claimants.	Nature or object of the claim.	Congress.	Session.	How brought before the House of Reps.	Page of journal.	To what committee of the House referred.	No. or date of the report.	Nature of the report.	No. of the bill.	How disposed of by the House of Reps.	How disposed of by the Senate.	Date of the act of Congress, and remarks.
Morrison, James	Confirmation of title to 640 acres of land.	24	2	Petition	49	Priv. Land Claims.	Dec. 23, 1836	Adverse		Laid on table.		
Morrison, James	For certain credits in settlement of accounts.	16	2	Petition and rep't Sec. of War.	181, 205	Claims.						
Morrison, James	For certain credits in settlement of accounts.	17	1	Rep. of Secretary Treasury.	202	Claims.						
Morrison, James	For certain credits in settlement of accounts.	17	2	Senate bill	261	Military Affairs	Feb. 22, 1823	With't amend.	62	Passed		App'd March 3, 1823
Morrison, James, representatives of.	(See Taylor, Morrison & Wilkins)	16	1		325							
Morrison, James, executors of.	Equitable settlement of his accounts.	21	1	Petition	122	Claims	133	Favorable; bill	177	Passed	Passed	App'd May 20, 1830
Morrison, James, executors of.	(See Ashton Garrett, sureties of).	22	1		104							
Morrison, James	Relief in settlement of accounts as contractor, vouchers lost.	16	2	Petition	181					Referred to Secretary of War.		
Morrison, James	Relief in settlement of accounts as contractor, vouchers lost.	17	2	Petition	95	Claims	99	Favorable; bill	235	Passed	Passed	App'd March 1, 1823
Morison, James and Jesse.	Indemnity for depredations by Sac and Fox Indians in 1813-'14.	21	1	Petition	196	Claims				Discharged; laid on table.		
Morison, James and Jesse.	Indemnity for depreciations by Sac and Fox Indians in 1813-'14.	21	1	Senate bill	158	Claims	Feb. 24, 1830	With amend's.	S. 18	Passed with amend't.	Passed	App'd May 31, 1830
Morrison, James	Pension	21	2	Petition	103	Military Pensions.						
Morrison, James	Pension	22	1	Petition	68	Rev. Pensions	Dec. 29, 1831	Adverse		Laid on table.		
Morrison, Jesse	Payment for horse lost in service of United States, 1832.	24	1	Petition	430	Claims	787	Adverse		Laid on table.		
Morrison, John	For land as Canadian refugee	12	1	Petition	242	Public Lands.	Mar. 11, 1812	Favorable; bill	85	Passed	Passed	App'd April 23, 1812
Morrison, Lieut. John	Relief for services in battle on Lake Champlain.	25	3	Petition	293	Naval Affairs			J. R. 37			
Morrison, John	(See John Roberts, assignee of.)	26	1		352							
Morrison, John, (N. H.)	Pension for revolutionary services.	30	1	Petition	342	Rev. Pensions	281	Favorable; bill	277	Passed.		
Morrison, John, (N. H.)	Pension for revolutionary services.	30	2	House bill	279					Passed	Passed	App'd Jan. 26, 1849
Morrison, John, (Ohio.)	Revolutionary pension	31	1	Petition	193	Invalid Pensions	224	Favorable; bill	219	Referred to Committee Whole House.		
Morrison, John, (Ohio.)	Revolutionary pension	31	2	House bill	181	Whole House	Jan. 25, 1851	Favorable; bill	219	Passed.		
Morrison, John, (N. Y.)	Arrears of pension	29	1	Petition	515	Invalid Pensions	July 25, 1846	Adverse		Laid on table.		
Morrison, John, (N. Y.)	Arrears of pension	29	2	Petition	68	Rev. Pensions.						
Morrison, John, (N. Y.)	Arrears of pension	30	1	Petition	215	Invalid Pensions	223	Adverse		Laid on table.		
Morrison, John, (N. Y.)	Arrears of pension	30	2	Petition	77	Invalid Pensions				Discharged; laid on table.		
Morrison, John, (N. Y.)	Arrears of pension	31	1	Petition	337	Invalid Pensions.						
Morrison, John, (Penn.)	Pension for services under Gen. A. Wayne.	30	1	Petition	279	Invalid Pensions	311	Adverse		Laid on table.		
Morrison, Joseph, (Maine.)	Release from imprisonment on judgment of United States and balance due on settlement of account.	18	1	Petition	499	Military Affairs				Discharged; laid on table.		
Morrison, Joseph, (Maine.)	Release from imprisonment on judgment of United States and balance due on settlement of account.	22	1	Petition	556	Claims	April 16, 1832	Adverse		Laid on table.		
Morrison, Joseph, (Mo.)	Pension	29	1	Senate bill	1041	Invalid Pensions	Aug. 8, 1846	Favorable	S. 17	Referred to Committee Whole House.		

List of private claims presented to the House of Representatives of the United States from the 1st to the 31st Congress, inclusive—Continued.

Names of claimants.	Nature or object of the claim.	Congress.	Session.	How brought before the House of Reps.	Page of journal.	To what committee of the House referred.	No. or date of the report.	Nature of the report.	No. of the bill.	How disposed of by the House of Reps.	How disposed of by the Senate.	Date of the act of Congress, and remarks.
Morrison, Joseph, (Mo.)	Pension	29	2	Senate bill	306	Invalid Pensions	Feb. 24, 1847	Favorable	S. 12	Passed	Passed	App'd Feb. 25, 1847
Morrison, Joseph, (Mo.)	Arrears of pension	31	1	Petition	257	Invalid Pensions	392	Adverse		Laid on table.		
Morrison, Kaine, heirs of.	Compensation for supplies furnished revolutionary war.	23	1	Petition	334	Rev. Claims.						
Morrison, Margaret	(See Benjamin Marshall, daughter of.)	25	2		231							
Morrison, Robert J.	Correction of entry of land	23	2	Petition	199	Priv. Land Claims.	Jan. 19, 1835	Favorable; bill	652	Passed	Passed	App'd March 3, 1835
Morrison, Robert, & others	Confirmation of title to land	30	1	Senate bill	913	Priv. Land Claims.			S. 147			
Morrison, Robert, & others	Confirmation of title to land	30	2	Senate bill	119	Priv. Land Claims.	Dec. 19, 1848	Favorable	S. 147	Passed	Passed	App'd Dec. 22, 1848
Morrison, Robert, & others	Confirmation of title to land	31	1	Petition	596	Public Lands.						
Morrison, Samuel, (N. Y.)	Revolutionary pension	22	1	Petition	292	Rev. Pensions.						
Morrison, Thomas D.	Payment of money found on British officer killed by him in war of the revolution.	25	2	Petition	724	Claims	1049	Adverse		Laid on table.		
Morrison, Thomas D.	Payment of money found on British officer killed by him in war of the revolution.	27	3	Petition	136	Claims.						
Morrison, Thomas D.	Payment of money found on British officer killed by him in war of the revolution.	28	1	Petition	414	Invalid Pensions.						
Morrison, Thomas D.	Payment of money found on British officer killed by him in war of the revolution.	31	1	Petition	971	Claims.						
Morrison, William, (Ark.)	Confirmation of title to land	19	2	Petition	38	Public Lands				Discharged; laid on table.		
Morrison, Wm., and others	Renewal of pension	28	1	Petition	904	Patents	505	Adverse		Laid on table		
Morrison, William	Compensation for Indian depredations.	19	1	Resolution	308	Indian Affairs	130	Favorable; bill	168	Passed.		
Morrison, William	Compensation for Indian depredations.	19	2	Petition	54	Indian Affairs	Dec. 20, 1826	Favorable; bill	310	Passed	Passed	App'd March 2, 1827
Morrison, William, (Ill.)	Compensation for supplies furnished in late war.	19	2	Documents	105	Claims	64	Favorable; bill	414	Referred to Committee Whole House.		
Morrison, William, (Ill.)	Compensation for supplies furnished in late war.	20	1	Petition	311	Claims	163	Favorable; bill	188	Referred to Committee Whole House.		
Morrison, William, (Ill.)	Compensation for supplies furnished in late war.	20	2	House bill	174	Whole House	Jan. 17, 1829	With't amend.	188	Passed.		
Morrison, William, (Ill.)	Compensation for supplies furnished in late war.	21	1	Petition	76	Claims	63	Favorable; bill	87	Passed	Passed	App'd May 29, 1830
Morrison, William, (Ill.)	Additional compensation for supplies furnished in late war.	23	1	Petition	384	Claims	548	Adverse		Laid on table.		
Morrison, William, (Ill.)	Additional compensation for supplies furnished in late war.	24	1	Petition	474	Claims	June 18, 1836	Adverse		Laid on table.		
Morrison, Wm. W., and others.	(See George M. Morrison, heirs of)	21	1		524							
Morrison & Wheeler	(See John Roberts)	26	1		352							
Morrow, David	Revolutionary pension	25	3	Petition	460	Rev. Pensions.						
Morrow, Isaac, (Ala.)	Permission to enter land in lieu of lot occupied by him.	25	2	Petition	119	Public Lands				Discharged; laid on table.		
Morrow, Isaac, (Ala.)	Permission to enter land in lieu of lot occupied by him.	25	3	Petition	134, 135	Public Lands	227	Adverse		Laid on table.		
Morrow, Isaac, (Ala.)	Permission to enter land in lieu of lot occupied by him.	26	1	Petition	751	Public Lands	323	Favorable; bill	288	Referred to Committee Whole House.		

List of private claims presented to the House of Representatives of the United States from the 1st to the 31st Congress, inclusive—Continued.

Names of claimants.	Nature or object of the claim.	Congress.	Session.	How brought before the House of Reps.	Page of journal.	To what committee of the House referred.	No. or date of the report.	Nature of the report.	No. of the bill.	How disposed of by the House of Reps.	How disposed of by the Senate.	Date of the act of Congress, and remarks.
Morrow, James, and Jonathan Tipton.	Indemnity for losses as agents in Cherokee nation.	26	1	Petition	352	Judiciary	April 4, 1840	Favorable; bill	291	Referred to Committee Whole House.		
Morrow, James, and Jonathan Tipton.	Indemnity for losses as agents in Cherokee nation.	27	2	Petition	268	Judiciary	272	Favorable; bill	238	Passed	Passed	App'd July 27, 1842
Morrow, James	Pension	15	1	Petition	349	Pens. & Rev. Cl'ms.				Referred to Secretary of War.		
Morrow, James	Payment of Continental money	30	1	Petition	77	Claims	14	Adverse		Laid on table.		
Morrow, Richard	(See Jacob Miller, and others)	22	1		442							
Morrow, Thomas, assignee of.	Confirmation of title to land	22	1	Petition	34	Public Lands	Feb. 4, 1832	Favorable; bill	347	Passed	Passed	App'd May 31, 1832
Morrow, William	Back pay as captain in U. States army.	16	1	Petition	284	Military Affairs	Feb. 28, 1820	Adverse		Laid on table.		
Morrow, William, (Pa.)	Pension	21	1	Petition	471	Military Pensions	April 3, 1830	Adverse		Rejected.		
Morrow, Dr. William J. J.	Compensation as surgeon in Cherokee nation in 1836.	25	2	Petition	918	Military Affairs	1024	Adverse		Laid on table.		
Morrow, Dr. William J. J.	Compensation as surgeon in Cherokee nation in 1836.	26	1	Petition	331	Military Affairs				Discharged; laid on table.		
Morrow, Dr. William J. J.	Compensation as surgeon in Cherokee nation in 1836.	27	3	Petition	175	Claims.						
Morse, Andrew, jr.	Extension of patent	31	1	Petition	763	Patents	380	Favorable; bill	328	Referred to Committee Whole House.		
Morse, Asa H	Arrears of pension	25	2	Petition	268	Invalid Pensions				Discharged; laid on table.		
Morse, Asa H	Arrears of pension	26	1	Resolution	1011	Invalid Pensions.						
Morse, B. F., and Samuel Colt.	Remission of duties on certain presents.	31	1	Senate res.	998				S. 19	Referred to Committee Whole House.		
Morse, Daniel, (Vt.)	Invalid pension	25	2	Petition	58	Invalid Pensions				Discharged; laid on table.		
Morse, Daniel, (Vt.)	Invalid pension	25	3	Resolution	161	Rev. Pensions				Discharged; laid on table.		
Morse, Daniel, (Vt.)	Invalid pension	26	1	Petition	163	Invalid Pensions	260	Adverse		Laid on table.		
Morse, Daniel, (Vt.)	Invalid pension	28	2	Petition	236	Invalid Pensions.						
Morse, Daniel, (Vt.)	Invalid pension	29	1	Petition	70	Invalid Pensions	496	Adverse		Laid on table.		
Morse, Eliakim	Indemnity for French spoliations prior to 1800.	26	1	Memorial	182	Foreign Affairs	343	Favorable; bill	319	Referred to Committee Whole House.		
Morse, Eliakin, and others	Indemnity for French spoliations prior to 1800.	31	1	Petition	672	Foreign Affairs	355	Favorable; bill		Adopted.		
Morse, Eliakim	Compensation for four cabouses imported by order of navy agent at Boston.	8	1	Memorial	547	Claims	Mar. 13, 1804	Resolution to postpone.	318	Referred to Committee Whole House.		
Morse, Eliakim	Compensation for four cabouses imported by order of navy agent at Boston.	8	2	Memorial	74	Claims.						
Morse, Elihu	Pension	21	2	Petition	299	Military Pensions.						
Morse, Elihu	Pension	22	1	Petition	56	Rev. Pensions	Mar. 13, 1832	Favorab'e; bill	467	Passed	Postponed.	
Morse, Elihu	Arrears of pension	24	2	Petition	216	Rev. Pensions				Discharged; laid on table.		
Morse, Elijah, (N. H.)	Invalid pension	3	2	Rep. of Secretary War.	278	Claims.						
Morse, Elijah, (N. H.)	Invalid pension	4	1	Petition	445	Claims	Feb. 18, 1796	Favorable	J. R. 16	Passed	Passed	App'd April 17, 1796
Morse, Elijah, (N. H.)	Invalid pension	10	1	House bill	232	Whole House	April 19, 1808	With mend'ts.	78	Passed	Passed, with amendment.	App'd April 25, 1808
Morse, Hannah	Continuation of pension	28	1	Petition	850	Rev. Pensions.						

List of private claims presented to the House of Representatives of the United States form the 1st to the 31st Congress, inclusive—Continued.

Names of claimants.	Nature or object of the claim.	Congress.	Session.	How brought before the House of Reps.	Page of journal.	To what committee of the House referred.	No. or date of the report.	Nature of the report.	No. of the bill.	How disposed of by the House of Reps.	How disposed of by the Senate.	Date of the act of Congress, and remarks.
Morse, Hiram	Indemnity for property destroyed in war of 1812.	14	1	Petition	697	Claims.						
Morse, Isaac, (N. Y.)	Pension	21	2	Petition	299	Military Pensions.						
Morse, Isaac, (N. Y.)	Pension	22	1	Petition	56	Rev. Pensions	Mar. 13, 1832	Favorable; bill	467	Passed	Postponed.	
Morse, Jedediah	Pension for revolutionary services.	29	1	Petition	303	Rev. Pensions				Discharged; laid on table.		
Morse, Jedediah	Pension for revolutionary services.	30	1	Petition	65	Rev. Pensions	140	Adverse		Discharged; laid on table.		
Morse, Jonah	Fishing bounty	25	3	Petition	674					Laid on table.		
Morse, Jonah	Fishing bounty	26	1	Petition	711	Commerce.						
Morse, Jonah	Fishing bounty	27	3	Petition	274	Commerce	275	Favorable; bill	821	Referred to Committee Whole House.		
Morse, Joseph, (N. H.)	Invalid pension	3	2	Rep. of Secretary War.	337	Claims	Feb. 28, 1795	Favorable; bill	130	Passed	Postponed.	
Morse, Joseph, (N. H.)	Invalid pension	4	1	Petition	445	Claims	Feb. 18, 1796	Favorable; bill	156	Passed	Passed	App'd April 20, 1796
Morse, Joseph	Relief for land sold for taxes	15	1	Petition	132	Ways and Means				Discharged; laid on table.		
Morse, Josiah	Revolutionary pension	20	1	Res. and petition	159, 163	Military Pensions	April 29, 1828	Favorable; bill	283	Passed.		
Morse, Josiah	Revolutionary pension	20	2	Petition	55	Military Pensions	Dec. 12, 1828	Favorable; bill	311	Passed	Laid on table.	
Morse, Josiah	Revolutionary pension	21	1	Petition	47	Military Pensions	Jan. 5, 1830	Favorable; bill	72	Passed	Passed	App'd May 20, 1830
Morse, Matthew	Confirmation of title to land in Missouri.	15	2	Petition	89	Priv. Land Claims.						
Morse, Micah	Indemnity for losses and compensation for services in revolutionary war.	19	1	Resolution	229	Claims.				Discharged; laid on table.		
Morse, Moses	Compensation for property lost at the surrender of Detroit.	13	2	Petition	319	Claims				Discharged; leave to withdraw.		
Morse, Nathan	Compensation for a horse lost in United States service.	12	1	Petition	51	Claims	April 22, 1812	Adverse		Laid on table.		
Morse, Noble	Pension	14	1	Petition	32	Pens. & Rev. Cl'ms.	April 11, 1816	Favorable; bill	171	Passed	Passed	App'd April 30, 1816
Morse, Peabody A., and Charles E. Greneaux.	Pre-emption right to land	23	2	Petition	138	Priv. Land Claims.				Discharged; laid on table.		
Morse, Richard, daughter of	Arrears of pension	25	3	Petition	334	Naval Affairs.						
Morse, Richard, daughter of	Arrears of pension	26	1	Petition	180	Naval Affairs.						
Morse, Samuel A.	To refund money paid to John A Balkan as deputy collector.	28	2	Petition	71	Claims	97	Adverse		Laid on table.		
Morse, Sarah B.	(See Richard Morse, daughter of)	25	3		334							
Morse, Thomas, and William Stanwood, jr.	Fishing bounty on schooner Atlas and Betsey.	4	2	Petition	744					Laid on table.		
Morsell, James, heir of	Indemnity for damage to property by United States troops in war of 1812.	31	1	Petition	510	Claims.						
Morsell, James S.	(See James Morsell, heir of)	31	1		510							
Morshon, John, heirs of	Payment for property destroyed by the British during the revolution.	31	1	Petition	1135	Rev. Claims.						
Morsman, Timothy, heirs of.	Compensation for services in revolutionary war.	27	2	Petition	69	Rev. Pensions	784	Adverse		Laid on table.		
Morss, David	Restoration of pension	17	1	Petition	176					Referred to Committee Whole House on bill No. 37.		
Morss, David	Restoration of pension	17	2	Petition	56	Rev. Pensions				Leave to withdraw.		
Mort, Benjamin	Pension	20	2	House bill	55	Whole House	Jan. 15, 1829	With amends.	311	Passed	Laid on table.	

List of private claims presented to the House of Representatives of the United States from the 1st to the 31st Congress, inclusive—Continued.

Names of claimants.	Nature or object of the claim.	Congress.	Session.	How brought before the House of Reps.	Page of journal.	To what committee of the House referred.	No. or date of the report.	Nature of the report.	No. of the bill.	How disposed of by the House of Reps.	How disposed of by the Senate.	Date of the act of Congress, and remarks.
Mortee, Thomas J	For deficiency in land purchase	23	2	Senate bill	244	Priv. Land Claims.	Jan. 26, 1835	Favorable	S. 70	Referred to Committee Whole House.		
Morte, Peter	(See Bennett & Mott.)	21	1		552							
Mortimer, Edwin	For a grant of a quarter section of land in lieu of one lost.	29	2	Petition	352	Public Lands.						
Morton, Aaron	Compensation for property destroyed, revolutionary war.	20	2	Resolution	250	Rev. Claims				Discharged; laid on table.		
Morton, Aaron	Compensation for property destroyed, revolutionary. war	23	1	Petition	438	Rev. Claims.						
Morton, A. H	Compensation for a house used by United States troops at Fort Jessup.	22	2	Petition	244	Military Affairs	101	Adverse		Laid on table.		
Morton, Jackson	(See Jasper Strong, *et al.*)	25	2		1209							
Morton, John	Compensation for property destroyed, war of 1812.	15	2	Petition	24	Claims	Nov. 23, 1818	dverse		Laid on table.		
Morton, John	Compensation for property destroyed, war of 1812.	16	1	Petition	142	Claims	Jan. 17, 1820	Adverse		Laid on table.		
Morton, John H., surety of.	Release of balance due as collector of direct taxes, Kentucky.	23	1	Senate bill	506	Judiciary	April 24, 1834	With't amend.	23	Passed		App'd June 30, 1834
Morton, Joseph, (Mass.)	To fund loan office certificates as administrator.	10	1	Petition	87	Claims.						
Morton, Joseph, (Mass.)	To fund loan office certificates as administrator.	12	1	Petition	137	Claims.						
Morton, Martin T	Increase of compensation as collector of customs in Massachusetts.	17	2	Petition	73	Commerce				Discharged; leave to withdraw.		
Morton, Martin T	Increase of compensation as collector of customs in Massachusetts.	18	1	Petition	81	Commerce.						
Morton, Perez	(See Gideon Granger and others.)	8	2		28							
Morton, Perez, and others.	Indemnity for French spoliations prior to 1800.	24	2	Memorial	117	Foreign Affairs.						
Morton, Quinn	Compensation as an assessor of the third district, Tennessee.	15	1	Petition	195	Ways and Means				Discharged; laid on table.		
Morton, Seth, (N. Y.)	Invalid pension	25	2	Petition	268	Invalid Pensions				Discharged; laid on table.		
Morton, Seth, (N. Y.)	Invalid pension	26	1	Petition	938	Invalid Pensions				Discharged; laid on table.		
Morton, Seth, (N. Y.)	Invalid pension	28	1	Petition	346	Invalid Pensions.						
Morton, Seth, (N. Y.)	Invalid pension	28	2	Petition	145	Invalid Pensions.						
Morton, Seth, (N. Y.)	Invalid pension	29	1	Petition	1000	Invalid Pensions				Discharged; laid on table.		
Morton, Seth, (N. Y.)	Invalid pension	29	2	Petition	54	Invalid Pensions				Discharged; laid on table.		
Morton, Seth, (N. Y.)	Invalid pension	30	1	Petition	356	Invalid Pensions	339	Favorable; bill	317	Passed.		
Morton, Dr. Thomas M	Full pay as surgeon of Col. Doniphan's regiment.	31	1	Petition	1111	Military Affairs.						
Morton, Thomas, (Tenn.)	Pension	23	1	Petition	45, 216	Invalid Pensions	499	Favorable; bill	503	Referred to Committee Whole House.		
Morton, Thomas, (Tenn.)	Pension	23	2	House bill	336	Whole House			503	Passed	Passed	App'd March 3, 1835
Morton, William, and John S. Snead.	Payment of Treasury notes lost in the mail.	14	2	Petition	364	Ways and Means.						
Morton, William, and John S. Snead.	Payment of Treasury notes lost in the mail.	15	1	Petition	84	Ways and Means	Feb. 3, 1818	Favorable; bill	66	Passed.		

List of private claims presented to the House of Representatives of the United States from the 1st to the 31st Congress, inclusive—Continued.

Names of claimants.	Nature or object of the claim.	Congress.	Session.	How brought before the House of Reps.	Page of journal.	To what committee of the House referred.	No. or date of the report.	Nature of the report.	No. of the bill.	How disposed of by the House of Reps.	How disposed of by the Senate.	Date of the act of Congress, and remarks.
Morton, William, (D. C.)	Additional compensation as inspector of customs in Georgetown.	25	2	Petition	395	Claims.						
Morton, William, (D. C.)	Additional compensation as inspector of customs in Georgetown.	26	1	Petition	169	Claims.						
Morton, Dr. W. T. G.	Compensation, for use by government, of his invention to prevent pain in surgical operations.	29	2	Memorial	97	Select	Feb. 23, 1849	Majority report		Ordered to be printed.		
Morton, Dr. W. T. G.	Compensation, for use by government, of his invention to prevent pain in surgical operations.	30	2	Petition	282	Select	114	Minority report		Ordered to be printed; laid on table.		
Moscat, Robert	Invalid pension	3	1	Rep. of Secretary of War.	131	Select	May 26, 1794	Rep't and res.	12	Passed	Passed	App'd June 9, 1794
Moseby, jr., Littlebury	Compensation for money advanced in revolution.	10	1	Petition	209	Whole House.						
Moseby, jr., Littlebury	Compensation for money advanced in revolution.	11	2	Petition	308	Claims.						
Moseby, jr., Littlebury	Compensation for money advanced in revolution.	12	1	Petition	22	Claims.						
Moseby, jr., Littlebury	Compensation for money advanced in revolution.	12	2	Petition	559	Claims	Feb. 12, 1813	Adverse		Rejected.		
Mosely, Robert, (Va.)	Further time to locate land warrant.	17	2	Petition	91					Referred to Committee Whole House on bill No. 196.		
Moseby, William, heirs of	Compensation for revolutionary services.	22	2	Petition	137	Rev. Claims.						
Moseley, Catharine	(See Aaron Rollins, widow of)	24	2		216							
Moseley, Leonard, (Va.)	Invalid pension	4	1	Petition	457	Claims	May 31, 1796	Adverse.		Laid on table.		
Moseley, Samuel	Compensation for damages to property by United States troops.	9	2	Petition	555	Claims				Discharged; laid on table.		
Moseley, Samuel	Compensation for damages to property by United States troops.	10	1	Petition	177	Claims	Feb. 25, 1808	Favorable		Referred to Committee Whole House.		
Moseley, Samuel	Compensation for damages to property by United States troops.	10	2	Petition	350	Claims	Nov. 18, 1808	Favorable; bill	106	Passed.		
Moseley, Samuel	Compensation for damages to property by United States troops.	11	2	Petition	127	Claims	Dec. 26, 1809	Favorable; bill	51	Referred to Committee Whole House.		
Moseley, Samuel	Compensation for damages to property by United States troops.	13	3	Petition	455	Claims	15	Favorable; bill	242	Passed	Passed	App'd Jan. 28, 1815
Moseley, jr., Thomas, and others.	(See Abner S. Holleman, sureties of.)	27	2		783							
Moseley, William, (S. C.)	Additional compensation as deputy marshal for taking the Third Census.	13	3	Petition and rep't of Sec. Treas'y	509, 529	Claims.						
Moseley, William, (S. C.)	Additional compensation as deputy marshal for taking the Third Census.	14	1	Petition	275	Claims	Mar. 1, 1816	Favorable; bill		Passed	Passed	App'd April 27, 1816
Moses, Isaac, (N. Y.)	Payment of a loan office certificate.	18	2	Petition	36	Select	Jan. 27, 1825	Adverse		Laid on table		Referred to Secretary Treasury.
Moses, James	Increase of pension	21	1	Petition	259	Military Pensions				Discharged; laid on table.		
Moses, James	Increase of pension	21	2	Petition	75	Naval Affairs.						
Mosher, Charles, and others	(See John Mosher, heirs of)	20	1		167							
Mosher, John, heirs of	Compensation for revolutionary services.	20	1	Petition	167	Rev. Claims	Feb. 19, 1828	Adverse		Laid on table.		

List of private claims presented to the House of Representatives of the United States from the 1st to the 31st Congress, inclusive—Continued.

Names of claimants.	Nature or object of the claim.	Congress.	Session.	How brought before the House of Reps.	Page of journal.	To what committee of the House referred.	No. or date of the report.	Nature of the report.	No. of the bill.	How disposed of by the House of Reps.	How disposed of by the Senate.	Date of the act of Congress, and remarks.
Mosher, William	Revolutionary pension	20	2	Resolution	46	Military Pensions	Jan. 27, 1829	Favorable	......	Referred to Committee Whole House.		
Mosier, Ebenezer	(See Thomas Howard, representatives of.)	14	2	....	268							
Moss, Daniel	Renewal of land warrant	15	1	Petition	83	Priv. Land Claims	....	....	......	Discharged; laid on table.		
Moss, Daniel	Renewal of land warrant	15	2	Petition	51	Priv. Land Claims	Jan. 8, 1819	Favorable; bill	267	Passed	Passed	App'd March 3, 1819
Moss, Francis, heirs of	Issue of certificates for Virginia military land warrants.	25	2	Petition	178	Priv. Land Claims.						
Moss, Henry J. T.	Correction of error in entries of land.	26	2	Petition	122	Public Lands.						
Moss, Henry J. T.	Correction of error in entries of land.	27	2	Petition	1207	Priv. Land Claims.						
Moss, Henry J. T.	Correction of error in entries of land.	27	3	Petition	175	Priv. Land Claims.	112	Adverse	......	Laid on table.		
Moss, Isaac, (Ohio)	Increase of pension	25	3	Petition	130	Rev. Pensions	....	....	......	Discharged; laid on table.		
Moss, Isaiah	Land in lieu of losses by Choctaw treaty.	24	1	Petition	57	Public Lands	208	Favorable; bill	208	Referred to Committee Whole House.		
Moss, Joseph, (S. C.)	Revolutionary pension	21	1	Resolution	218	Military Pensions	April 26, 1830	Favorable; bill	445	Referred to Committee Whole House.		
Moss, Joseph	Invalid pension	4	1	Petition	447	Claims	Feb. 18, 1796	Favorable; bill	156	Passed	Passed	App'd April 20, 1796
Moss, Judith	(See James Thomas, and others)	27	3	....	240							
Moss, Simeon	Invalid pension	21	2	Petition	67	Military Pensions.						
Moss, Simeon	Invalid pension	24	1	Resolution	923	Rev. Pensions	806	Favorable; bill	722	Referred to Committee Whole House.		
Moss, Simeon	Invalid pension	25	2	Petition	38	Rev. Pensions	178	Favorable; bill	203	Passed.		
Moss, William	Permission to float his land claims	29	1	Petition	88	Public Lands	366	Favorable; bill	278	Passed	Passed	App'd Aug. 8, 1846
Moss, William & Matthew	Extra compensation for carrying the mail.	31	1	Petition	1284	P. Of. & P. Roads.						
Mosser, Abraham & others	Compensation for revolutionary services.	3	2	Petition	330	Claims.						
Mosser, Abraham & others	Compensation for revolutionary services.	4	1	Petition	373	Claims	Jan. 6, 1796	Adverse	......	Leave to withdraw.		
Mothershead, Nathaniel	Revolutionary pension	20	2	Senate bill	192	Military Pensions	Jan. 23, 1829	With't amend.	58	Referred to Committee Whole House.		
Mothershead, Nathaniel	Revolutionary pension	21	1	Petition	59	Military Pensions	....	....	......	Discharged; laid on table.		
Motley, John, heirs and representatives of.	Permission to make the last payment on forfeited land.	21	1	Petition	52	Public Lands	....	....	......	Discharged; laid on table.		
Motlon, Malachiah, heirs of	(See Motlow)	14	1	....	231							
Motlow, John, (S. C.)	Compensation for losses in revolutionary war.	9	2	Petition	593	Claims.						
Motlow, John, (S. C.)	Compensation for losses in revolutionary war.	11	2	Petition	206	Select	....	....	......	Referred to Committee Whole House.		
Motlow, John, (S. C.)	Compensation for losses in revolutionary war.	12	1	Petition	133	Select.						
Motlow, John, (S. C.)	Compensation for losses in revolutionary war.	12	2	Petition	652	Select.						
Motlow, John, (S. C.)	Compensation for losses in revolutionary war.	13	1	Petition	78	Claims.						
Motlow, John, (S. C.)	Compensation for losses in revolutionary war.	13	2	Petition	232	Pens. & Rev. Cl'ms.						

List of private claims presented to the House of Representatives of the United States from the 1st to the 31st Congress, inclusive—Continued.

Names of claimants.	Nature or object of the claim.	Congress.	Session.	How brought before the House of Reps.	Page of journal.	To what committee of the House referred.	No. or date of the report.	Nature of the report.	No. of the bill.	How disposed of by the House of Reps.	How disposed of by the Senate.	Date of the act of Congress, and remarks.
Motlow, John, (S. C.)	Compensation for losses in revolutionary war.	13	3	Petition	543	Select	Dec. 14, 1814	Favorable		Referred to Committee Whole House.		
Motlow, John, (S. C.,) heirs of.	Compensation for negroes, &c., taken by Cherokees in 1792.	14	1	Petition	537	Pens. & Rev. Cl'ms.						
Motlow, John, (S. C.,) heirs of.	Compensation for negroes, &c., taken by Cherokees in 1792.	21	1	Petition	203, 483	Indian Affairs				Discharged; laid on table.		
Motlow, John, (S. C.,) heirs of.	Compensation for negroes, &c., taken by Cherokees in 1792.	22	1	Petition	538	Indian Affairs				Discharged; laid on table.		
Motlow, John, (S. C.,) heirs of.	Compensation for negroes, &c., taken by Cherokees in 1792.	25	2	Petition	630	Claims	845	Adverse		Laid on table.		
Motlow, John, (S. C.,) heirs of.	Compensation for negroes, &c., taken by Cherokees in 1792.	29	1	Petition	279	Indian Affairs	547	Adverse		Laid on table.		
Motlow, Malachiah, heirs of.	Indemnity for depredations by Indians in 1782.	14	1	Petition	231	Pens. & Rev. Cl'ms.				Discharged; laid on table.		
Motlow, Malachiah, heirs of.	Indemnity for depredations by Indians in 1782.	14	2	Petition	80	Pens. & Rev. Cl'ms.						
Motlow, Malachiah, heirs of.	Indemnity for depredations by Indians in 1782.	15	1	Petition	206	Pens. & Rev. Cl'ms.	May 14, 1818	Adverse		Leave to withdraw.		
Motlow, Malachiah, heirs of.	Indemnity for depredations by Indians in 1782.	16	1	Petition	53	Pens. & Rev. Cl'ms.				Discharged; leave to withdraw.		
Motlow, Malachiah, heirs of.	Indemnity for depredations by Indians in 1782.	21	2	Petition	55	Rev. Claims				Discharged; laid on table.		
Motlow, Malachiah, heirs of.	Indemnity for depredations by Indians in 1782.	25	2	Petition	776	Indian Affairs	1067	Adverse		Laid on table.		
Motlow, Malachiab, heirs of.	Indemnity for depredations by Indians in 1782.	29	1	Petition	161	Indian Affairs	803	Adverse		Laid on table.		
Motte, Abraham, (S. C.)	Balance due as collector of taxes	11	1	Petition	15	Claims	June 9, 1809	Adverse		Laid on table.		
Mott, Benjamin	Pension	20	1	Petition	223	Military Pensions	April 29, 1828	Favorable; bill	283	Passed.		
Mott, Bonjamin	Pension	20	2	Petition	55	Military Pensions	Dec. 12, 1828	Favorable; bill	311	Passed	Laid on table.	
Mott, Benjamin	Pension	21	1	Petition	48	Military Pensions	Jan. 5, 1830	Favorable; bill	72	Passed	Passed	App'd May 20, 1830
Motte, Charles, heirs of	For half-pay for revolutionary services.	2	1	Petition and rep't of Sec. War.	440	Select	Nov. 25, 1791	By bill	152	Passed	Passed	App'd Mar. 27, 1792
Mott, G. L	Compensation for property destroyed by Indians.	26	2	Petition	124	Claims.						
Mott, Josiah, (Ohio)	Pension	17	2	Petition	223	Pens. & Rev. Cl'ms.				Referred to Committee Whole House on bill No. 152.		
Mott, Josiah, (Ohio)	Pension	19	1	Petition	203	Military Pensions	Feb. 23, 1826	By bill	118	Passed.		
Mott, Josiah, (Ohio)	Pension	19	2	Petition	44	Military Pensions	Dec. 22, 1826	By bill	314			Bill became a law omitting petitioners name.
Mott, Josiah, (Ohio)	Pension	20	2	Petition	39	Military Pensions				Discharged; laid on table.		
Mott, Josiah, (Ohio)	Pension	21	1	Petition	49	Military Pensions	Jan. 5, 1830	By bill	72	Passed	Passed	App'd May 20, 1830
Mott, Jordon L	Extension of patent	30	1	Petition	948	Patents.						
Mott, Thomas, heirs of	Bounty land for revolutionary services.	27	3	Petition	52	Rev. Claims	246	Adverse		Laid on table.		
Mott, William B	Payment for taking census	29	1	Petition	208	Claims	414	Adverse.		Laid on table.		
Mottas, Sylvester	Pre-emption right to land in Mississippi.	14	1	Petition	498	Public Lands	Mar. 19, 1816	Adverse		Rejected.		
Mottas, Sylvester	Confirmation of title to land in Mississippi.	14	2	Petition	216	Public Lands				Discharged; laid on table.		
Mottas, Sylvester	Confirmation of title to land in Alabama.	15	1	Petition	212	Priv. Land Claims				Leave to withdraw.		

List of private claims presented to the House of Representatives of the United States from the 1st to the 31st Congress, inclusive—Continued.

Names of claimants.	Nature or object of the claim.	Congress.	Session.	How brought before the House of Reps.	Page of journal.	To what committee of the House referred.	No. or date of the report.	Nature of the report.	No. of the bill.	How disposed of by the House of Reps.	How disposed of by the Senate.	Date of the act of Congress, and remarks.
Motter, Andrew	Payment for property lost in war with Sioux and Fox Indians.	29	1	Petition	450	Military Affairs.						
Mougban, Matthias	Compensation for a slave carried off by the British.	20	1	Petition	195	Judiciary				Discharged; laid on table.		
Moulon, Jacques, heirs of.	Confirmation of title to land in Louisiana.	29	2	Senate bill	307	Priv. Land Claims.			S. 53			
Moulon, Jacques, heirs of.	Confirmation of title to land in Louisiana.	30	1	Senate bill	455	Priv. Land Claims.			S. 74			
Moulton, Ferdinand	Pre-emption right to land	26	1	Petition	934	Public Lands.						
Moulton, Ferdinand	Pre-emption right to land	26	2	Petition	37, 50, 131	Public Lands.						
Moulton, Ferdinand	Pre-emption right to land	27	2	Petition	66	Public Lands	502	Adverse		Laid on table.		
Moulton, Joseph	Compensation as corporal in United States marine service.	25	2	Petition	594	Naval Affairs				Discharged; laid on table.		
Moulton, Joshua, widow of	Revolutionary pension	25	2	Petition	729	Rev. Pensions				Discharged; laid on table.		
Moulton, Mary	(See Joshua Moulton, widow of).	25	2		729							
Moulton, Samuel	Compensation for revolutionary services.	20	1	Resolution	374	Rev. Claims				Discharged; laid on table.		
Moulton, Simeon	Restoration of pension	21	1	Resolution	248	Military Pensions				Discharged; laid on table.		
Moulton, Simeon	Restoration of pension	21	2	Petition	113	Military Pensions.						
Moulton, Simeon	Restoration of pension	22	1	Petition	68	Rev. Pensions	365	Favorable; bill	460	Passed	Postponed.	
Moulton, William	Release from certain bonds for goods destroyed by fire.	2	2	Petition	699					Referred to Secretary Treasury.		
Moultrie, Alexander	Confirmation of title to land in Mississippi.	7	2	Petition	352	Select.						
Moultrie, Alexander	Confirmation of title to land in Mississippi.	8	1	Petition	504	Select	Jan. 7, 1804	Adverse		Recommitted.		
Mounsey, Thomas	Remission of duties on merchandise.	14	2	Petition	353	Ways and Means				Discharged; laid on table.		
Mount, Adam D	Compensation for services rendered and provision furnished Continental army.	26	1	Petition	701	Rev. Claims.						
Mount, Adam D., heirs of.	Compensation for services rendered and provision furnished Continental army.	27	2	Petition	236	Rev. Claims.						
Mount, Adam D., heirs of.	Compensation for services rendered and provision furnished Continental army.	28	1	Petition	99	Rev. Claims	685	Adverse		Laid on table.		
Mount, James	Increase and arrears of pension	26	1	Petition	330	Naval Affairs.						
Mount, James	Increase and arrears of pension	26	2	Petition	79	Naval Affairs.						
Mount, James	Increase and arrears of pension	27	2	Petition	860	Naval Affairs	758	Favorable; bill	442	Referred to Committee Whole House.		
Mount, James	Increase and arrears of pension	27	3	House bill	88	Whole House			442	Passed	Indef. postp'd.	
Mount, John F	Indemnity for French spoliations prior to 1800.	26	1	Memorial	182	Foreign Affairs	343	Favorable; bill	319	Referred to Committee Whole House.		
Mount, John W	(See Louis F. Beeler, and others)	30	1		115							
Mountcastle, George E	(See George B. Russell, & others)	29	2		210							

List of private claims presented to the House of Representativesthe of United States from the 1st to the 31st Congress, inclusive—Continued.

Names of claimants.	Nature or object of the claim.	Congress.	Session.	How brought before the House of Reps.	Page of journal.	To what committee of the House referred	No. or date of the report.	Nature of the report.	No. of the bill.	How disposed of by the House of Reps.	How disposed of by the Senate.	Date of the act of Congress, and remarks.
Mountford, Matthew W	Release from judgment of United States.	21	2	Petition	337	P. Of. & P. Roads.						
Mountford, Matthew W	Release from judgment of United States.	23	1	Petition	153	P. Of. & P. Roads.				Discharged; laid on table.		
Mountford, Timothy	Compensation for revolutionary services.	2	1	Petition and rep't Sec. War.	448					Laid on table.		
Mountjoy, John, Captain, heirs of.	Commutation pay for revolutionary services.	28	1	Petition	944	Rev. Claims.						
Mountjoy, John, Captain, heirs of.	Commutation pay for revolutionary services.	28	2	Petition	150	Rev. Claims.						
Mountjoy, John, Captain, heirs of.	Commutation pay for revolutionary services.	29	1	Petition	310	Rev. Claims.						
Mountjoy, John, Captain, heirs of.	Commutation pay for revolutionary services.	30	1	Petition	405	Rev. Claims	770	Favorable; bill	604	Referred to Committee Whole House.		
Mountjoy, John, Captain, heirs of.	Commutation pay for revolutionary services.	31	1	Petition	472	Rev. Claims.						
Mountjoy, John	Renewal of lost land warrant	6	1	Petition	593	Select	Feb. 21, 1800	Favorable		Recommitted.		
Mountjoy, John	(See Zebulon M. Pike, and companions.)	10	1		189							
Mountjoy, William, heirs of.	Commutation pay for revolutionary services.	24	1	Petition	664	Rev. Claims	646	Adverse		Laid on table.		
Mountjoy, William, heirs of.	Commutation pay for revolutionary services.	25	2	Petition	178	Rev. Claims	May 18, 1838	Adverse		Laid on table.		
Mour, George, (N. Y.)	Invalid pension	3	1	Rep. of Secretary War.	131	Select	May 26, 1794	Favorable; bill	62	Passed	Passed	App'd June 7, 1794
Mourer, Mathias, by attorney.	Compensation for revolutionary services.	3	1	Petition	132	Select.						
Mourns, Thomas	Invalid pension	18	1	Petition	250	Pens. & Rev. Cl'ms.	Feb. 25, 1284	Adverse		Laid on table.		
Mouton, Jean	Confirmation of title to land in Louiaiana.	27	2	Documents	58	Priv. Land Claims.	Feb. 9, 1842	Favorable; bill	124	Referred to Committee Whole House.		
Mouton, Jean	Confirmation of title to land in Louisiana	27	2	Senate bill	359	Priv. Land Claims.	Feb. 26, 1842	With amends.	S. 76	Passed	Passed	App'd July 6, 1842
Mowatt, John, jr	Payment of certain bills of credit	4	1	Report of Secretary Treasury	388	Claims	May 31, 1796	Adverse		Laid on table.		
Mowatt, John	(See Edenezer Stevens and others.)	15	1		143							
Mower, Peter	Pension	21	2	Petition	80	Military Pensions.						
Mowry Conrad	For relief	31	2	Notice of bill	124							Bill was not introd'd.
Mowry, George	Relief as deputy marshal of west district of Pennsylvania.	30	1	Petition	114	Claims.						
Mowry, George	Relief as deputy marshal of west district of Pennsylvania.	30	2	Petition	362	Claims	105	Favorable; bill	787	Referred to Committee Whole House.		
Mowry, George	Relief as deputy marshal of west district of Pennsylvania.	31	1	Petition	643	Claims.						
Mowry, Jabez and, others.	Indemnity against certain bonds captured by the enemy in late war.	14	1	Petition	242	Select	Feb. 22, 1816	Favorable; bill		Passed	Passed, with amendment.	App'd April 29, 1816
Mowry, Jabez, and others.	Refund sales of sugar, forfeited	19	1	Petition	175	Ways and Means	May 8, 1826	Adverse		Laid on table.		
Mowry, John, heirs of	Bounty land for services in war of 1812.	29	1	Petition	591	Priv. Land Claims.						
Mowry, John, heirs of	Bounty land for services in war of 1812.	30	1	Petition	204	Priv. Land Claims.						
Mowry, Fillinghast	(See John Mowry, heirs of)	29	1		591							
Moxa, Sefexino	Confirmation of title to land	28	1	Petition	108	Priv. Land Claims.				Disch'd: laid on table.		

List of private claims presented to the House of Representatives of the United States from the 1st to the 31st Congress, inclusive—Continued

Names of claimants.	Nature or object of the claim.	Congress.	Session.	How brought before the House of Reps.	Page of journal.	To what committee of the House referred.	No. or date of the report.	Nature of the report.	No. of the bill.	How disposed of by the House of Reps.	How disposed of by the Senate.	Date of the act of Congress, and remarks.
Moxley, John, widow of.	Pension for revolutionary services.	29	1	Petition	913	Invalid Pensions.						
Moxley, John, widow of.	Pension for revolutionary services.	29	2	Petition	87	Invalid Pensions.						
Moxley, Joseph	Increase of pension	10	2	Rep. of Secretary War.	480	Claims	Jan. 30, 1809	Favorable; bill	158	Passed	Passed, with amendment.	App'd March 3, 1809
Moyer, Elizabeth	(See Joseph Wilcox, mother and guardian of.)	15	1		85							
Moyer, John	Compensation for revolutionary services.	2	1	Petition	474					Referred to Secretary War.		
Moyer, John, widow of	Revolutionary pension	26	1	Petition	937	Rev. Pensions.						
Moyer, John, and others	Indemnity for lands bought of the United States, the titles of which are invalid.	31	1	Petition	656	Public Lands				Leave to withdraw, Jan. 21, 1851.		
Moyer, Samuel M	Compensation for loss on Continental money in revolutionary war.	26	1	Petition	358	Ways and Means.						
Moyers, George	Revolutionary pension	18	1	Petition	250	Rev. Pensions	Mar. 01, 1824	Adverse		Laid on table.		
Moylan, Stephen, (Pa.)	Increase of compensation as commissioner of loans.	4	2	Petition	624	Select.						
Moylan, Stephen, heirs of.	Commutation of half-pay	23	2	Petition	47	Rev. Claims.						
Moylan, Stephen, heirs of.	Commutation of half-pay	24	1	Petition	62	Rev. Claims	487	Adverse		Laid on table.[1]		
Moylan, Stephen, heirs of.	Commutation of half-pay	25	2	Petition	201	Rev. Claims				Discharged; laid on table.		
Moylan, Stephen, heirs of.	Commutation of half-pay	26	1	Petition	77	Rev. Claims.						
Moynihan, James	(See Morgan Connor, heirs of)	11	2		176							
Mozart, John G	Payment for extra services as captain's clerk in United States naval service.	25	2	Petition	657	Naval Affairs	998	Favorable; bill	860	Referred to Committee Whole House.		
Mozart, John G	Payment for extra services as captain's clerk in United States naval service.	25	3	House bill	432	Whole House			860	Passed.		
Mozart, John G	Payment for extra services as captain's clerk in United States naval service.	26	1	Petition	180	Naval Affairs.						
Muckelroy, James	Arrears of pay for revolutionary services.	2	1	Petition	450					Laid on table.		
Mudd, Barbara	(See Jeremiah Mudd, representatives of.)	23	1		494							
Mudd, Bennett	Pension	15	1	Petition	23	Pens. & Rev. Cl'ms.						
Mudd, Henry, heirs of	Bounty land and bounty in money for revolutionary services.	23	1	Petition	494	Rev. Claims.						
Mudd, Henry, heirs of	Bounty land and bounty in money for revolutionary services.	23	2	Petition	239	Rev. Claims.						
Mudd, Hezekiah, heirs of	Bounty land and bounty in money for revolutionary services.	23	1	Petition	494	Rev. Claims.						
Mudd, Hezekiah, heirs of.	Bounty land and bounty in money for revolutionary services.	23	2	Petition	239	Rev. Claims.						
Mudd, Jeremiah, heirs of	Bounty land and bounty in money for revolutionary services.	23	1	Petition	494	Rev. Claims.						
Mudd, Jeremiah, heirs of	Bounty land and bounty in money for revolutionary services.	23	2	Petition	239	Rev. Claims.						
Mudd, Jeremiah, widow of.	Arrears of pension	25	3	Petition	126	Rev. Claims.						
Mudd, Jeremiah, widow of.	Arrears of pension	26	1	Petition	174	Rev. Claims	457	Favorable; bill	828	Referred to Committee Whole House.		

List of private claims presented to the House of Representatives of the United States from the 1st to the 31st Congress, inclusive—Continued.

Names of claimants.	Nature or object of the claim.	Congress.	Session.	How brought before the House of Reps.	Page of journal.	To what committee of the House referred.	No. or date of the report.	Nature of the report.	No. of the bill.	How disposed of by the House of Reps.	How disposed of by the Senate.	Date of the act of Congress, and remarks.
Mudd, Jeremiah, widow of.	Arrears of pension	27	2	Petition	58	Rev. Pensions	784	Adverse	......	Laid on table.		
Mudd, Jeremiah, widow of	Arrears of pension	28	2	Petition	70	Rev. Pensions.						
Mudd, Martin, heirs of	Bounty land and bounty in money for revolutionary services.	23	1	Petition	494	Rev. Claims.						
Mudd, Martin, heirs of	Bounty land and bounty in money for revolutionary services.	23	2	Petition	239	Rev. Claims.						
Mugford, James, former widow of	Compensation for revolutionary services.	4	2	Memorial	645	Claims	Jan. 25, 1797	Adverse	......	Rejected.		
Mugford, James, former widow of.	Compensation for revolutionary services.	9	2	Memorial	471	Select.						
Mugford, James, former widow of.	Compensation for revolutionary services.	12	1	Memorial	358	Claims.						
Mugford, James, former widow of.	Compensation for revolutionary services	12	2	Memorial	575	Claims.						
Mugford, James, former widow of.	Compensation for revolutionary services.	13	1	Memorial	11	Claims.						
Mugford, James, former widow of.	Compensation for revolutionary services.	13	2	Memorial	234	Pens. & Rev. Cl'ms.	March 3, 1814	....	......	Leave to withdraw.		
Mugford, James, sister and heir of.	Allowance of prize money as commander of schooner Franklin.	28	1	Petition	516	Rev. Claims.						
Mugford, James, sister and heir of.	Allowance of prize money as commander of schooner Franklin.	29	1	Petition	126	Rev. Claims.						
Muhlenberg, Frederick Augustus, representatives of.	Release as sureties of George and Jacob Gilbert.	7	1	Petition	26	Claims	Dec. 31, 1801	Adverse	......	Rejected.		
Muhlenberger, Michael	Compensation for property taken by revolutionary army.	6	2	Petition	733	Claims	Dec. 4, 1800	Adverse	......	Rejected.		
Muir, Jane	(See William Muir, widow of)	21	1	....	35							
Muir, Jane	(See William Muir, administrator of.)	26	1	....	182							
Muir, Thomas	Revolutionary pension	22	1	Petition	533	Rev. Pensions	....	....	......	Discharged; laid on table.		
Muir, William, widow of.	Indemnity for property destroyed during war of 1812.	21	1	Petition	35	Claims	303	Favorable	358	Referred to Committee Whole House.		
Muir, William, widow of.	Indemnity for property destroyed during war of 1812.	22	1	Petition	47	Claims	Dec. 19, 1831	Favorable	14	Passed	Passed	App'd March 7, 1832
Muir, William, administratrix of.	Indemnity for French spoliations prior to 1800.	26	1	Memorial	182	Foreign Affairs	343	Favorable; bill	319	Referred to Committee Whole House.		
Muirhead, George	Compensation for revolutionary services.	21	1	Documents	203	Military Pensions	....	....	......	Discharged; laid on table.		
Muirhead, John	Pension	21	1	Petition	36	Military Pensions	April 6, 1830	Adverse	......	Laid on table.		
Mulady, Robert, (Ga.)	Revolutionary pension	8	1	Petition	582	Claims	....	....	......	Ref'd to Com. W. H on bill No. 184.		
Mulford, Charles	Credit of $810 in settlement of account as agent.	17	1	Petition	276	Military Affairs	....	....	......	Discharged; laid on table.		
Mulford, Clarence	Credit of $800 in settlement of account as military agent.	17	1	Senate bill	483	Military Affairs	May 7, 1822	With't amend.	82	Laid on table.		
Mulhollan, Hugh	Confirmation of title to land in Louisiana.	14	2	Petition	96	Priv. Land Claims.						
Mulhollan, Hugh	Confirmation of title to land in Louisiana.	15	1	Petition	173	Priv. Land Claims.						
Mulhollan, Hugh	Confirmation of title to land in Louisiana.	27	2	Petition and docs.	140	Priv. Land Claims	Feb. 9, 1842	Favorable; bill	124	Referred to Committee Whole House.		

List of private claims presented to the House of Representatives of the United States from the 1st to the 31st Congress, inclusive—Continued.

Names of claimants.	Nature or object of the claim.	Congress.	Session.	How brought before the House of Reps.	Page of journal.	To what committee of the House referred.	No. or date of the report.	Nature of the report.	No. of the bill.	How disposed of by the House of Reps.	How disposed of by the Senate.	Date of the act of Congress, and remarks.
Mulhollan, Hugh	Confirmation of title to land in Louisiana.	27	2	Senate bill	359	Priv. Land Claims.	Feb. 26, 1842	With amends.	S. 76	Passed	Passed	App'd July 6, 1842
Mulke, Moses	Invalid pension	27	2	Petition	218	Invalid Pensions				Discharged; laid on table.		
Mullanphy, John, heirs of.	Confirmation of land titles	24	1	Petition	64	Priv. Land Claims.						
Mullany, James R.	Additional compensation as quartermaster general in 1812.	17	1	Petition	432	Claims				Discharged; laid on table.		
Mullany, James R.	Additional compensation as quartermaster general in 1812.	17	2	Petition	40	Claims				Discharged; laid on table.		
Mullany, James R.	Additional compensation as quartermaster general in 1812.	18	1	Petition	197	Claims				Discharged; laid on table.		
Mullany, James R.	Additional compensation as quartermaster general in 1812.	18	2	Petition	253	Military Affairs				Discharged; laid on table.		
Mullany, James R.	Additional compensation as quartermaster general in 1812.	19	1	Petition	82	Military Affairs	15	Favorable	31	Passed	Passed	App'd May 18, 1826
Mullenheim, Ferdinand	Indemnity for a libelled vessel	6	2	Petition	730	Com. and Manuf.	Dec. 8, 1800	Adverse		Leave to withdraw.		
Mullenheim, Ferdinand	Indemnity for a libelled vessel	7	1	Petition and rep't Sec. Treasury.	136, 225					Laid on table.		
Mullenheim, Ferdinand	Indemnity for a libelled vessel	9	1	Petition	338	Claims	April 11, 1806	Resolution to postpone.		Resolution adopted.		
Mullenheim, Ferdinand	Indemnity for a libelled vessel	9	2	Petition	560	Claims.						
Mullenheim, Ferdinand	Indemnity for a libelled vessel	10	1	Petition	32	Claims	Jan. 30, 1808	Adverse		Rejected.		
Muller, A. A., heirs of	Commutation pay for revolutionary services.	25	2	Resolution	523	Rev. Claims.						
Muller, A. A., heirs of	Commutation pay for revolutionary services.	26	1	Petition	349	Select.						
Muller, A. A., heirs of	Commutation pay for revolutionary services.	29	1	Petition	220	Rev. Claims.						
Muller, A. A., heirs of	Commutation pay for revolutionary services.	30	1	Petition	162	Rev. Claims.						
Mullican, J. N., administrator of.	Compensation for work done on Cumberland road.	29	1	Petition	125	Claims	282	Adverse		Laid on table.		
Mullican, J. N., administrator of.	Compensation for work done on Cumberland road.	29	2	Petition	59	Claims.						
Mullican, J. N., administrator of.	Compensation for work done on Cumberland road.	30	1	Petition	305	Claims.						
Mulligan, Bernard	(See Elias De Butts and others)	9	2		606							
Mulligan, John E	Pension	28	1	Petition	449	Rev. Pensions				Discharged; laid on table.		
Mulligan, John M	(See Hector Craig, and others)	22	1		447							
Mulligan, Patrick	Pension	19	1	Petition	381	Military Pensions	164	Adverse		Laid on table.		
Mulligan, Patrick	Pension	19	2	Petition	36	Military Pensions	Dec. 22, 1826	By bill	314	Passed	Passed	App'd March 3, 1827
Mullin, Daniel, assignee of	Confirmation of title to land in Missouri.	15	1	Petition	50	Rev. Claims.						
Mullin, Daniel, assignee of	Confirmation of title to land in Missouri.	16	1	Petition	71	Rev. Claims.						
Mullin, Daniel, assignee of	Confirmation of title to land in Missouri.	17	1	Petition	55	Public Lands.						
Mullin, Daniel, assignee of	Confirmation of title to land in Missouri.	18	1	Petition	55	Public Lands.						
Mullings, James	Revolutionary pension	23	2	Petition	58	Rev. Pensions.						
Mullings, James	Revolutionary pension	24	1	Petition	57	Rev. Pensions	274	Favorable; bill	281	Passed	Passed	App'd Jan. 28, 1836

List of private claims presented to the House of Representatives of the United States from the 1st to the 31st Congress, inclusive—Continued.

Names of claimants.	Nature or object of the claim.	Congress.	Session.	How brought before the House of Reps.	Page of journal.	To what committee of the House referred.	No. or date of the report.	Nature of the report.	No. of the bill.	How disposed of by the House of Reps.	How disposed of by the Senate.	Date of the act of Congress, and remarks.
Mullings, John	Confirmation of title to land in Mississippi.	28	1	Petition	75	Indian Affairs	36	Favorable; bill	66	Passed	Passed	App'd Mar. 26, 1844
Mullins, Susan	Indemnity for Indian depredations.	24	1	Petition	477	Indian Affairs.						
Mullowney, John	Redress for capture of his brig by the French.	9	2	Petition	592	Claims.						
Mullowney, John	Redress for capture of his brig by the French.	10	1	Petition	248	Claims.						
Mullowney, John	Redress for capture of his brig by the French.	10	2	Petition	410	Claims.						
Mullowney, John	Redress for capture of his brig by the French.	11	2	Petition	116	Claims	Mar. 2, 1810	Adverse		Leave to withdraw.		
Mullony, John, administrator of.	Settlement of his accounts as consul at Tangiers.	23	1	Petition	568	Foreign Affairs.	460	Favorable; bill	474	Referred to Committee Whole House.		
		23	2	Bill of last sess.	93				474	Passed	Passed	App'd Jan. 13, 1834
Mulloy, Hugh	Invalid pension	13	1	Petition	12	Claims				Disch'd; laid on table.		
Mulloy, Hugh	Invalid pension	13	2	Petition	196	Pens. & Rev. Cl'ms.				Leave to withdraw.		
Mulloy, Hugh	Invalid pension	15	1	Petition	71	Pens. & Rev. Cl'ms.	Feb. 11, 1818	Adverse		Laid on table.		
Mulloy, Hugh	Invalid pension	20	2	Petition	70	Military Pensions	Jan. 13, 1829	Adverse		Laid on table.		
Mulloy, Hugh	Arrears of pension	24	2	Petition	398	Rev. Pensions.						
Mulloy, Hugh	Arrears of pension	26	1	Petition	626	Invalid Pensions.						
Mulloy, Hugh	Arrears of pension	26	2	Petition	82	Invalid Pensions	214	Adverse		Laid on table.		
Mumbower, Henry, and others.	Refunding of certain fines	7	1	Petition	12	Select	April 12, 1802	Adverse		Rejected.		
Mumford, Benjamin	Compensation for services as a post-rider in 1775–'76.	3	1	Petition	113	Select				Referred to Postmaster General.		
Mumford, Benjamin	Compensation for services as a post-rider in 1775–'76.	3	2	Petition	314	Claims.						
Mumford, Benjamin	Compensation for services as a post-rider in 1775–'76.	4	1	Docs. and report.	403	Claims	Jan. 6, 1796	Adverse		Leave to withdraw.		
Mumford, Benjamin, executors of.	For pro rata of award in the case of the ship Mary Ann.	25	2	Petition	542	Claims	830	Adverse		Laid on table.		
Mumford, C. F	Payment for attendance as witness in case of contested election.	30	2	Petition	77	Accounts.						
Mumford, Hannah R.	(See Benjamin Mumford, executors of.)	25	2		542							
Mumford, Mehitable	(See Charles Handy, daughter of.)	25	3		126							
Mumford & Murray	(See Murray & Mumford.)	5	2		319							
Mumford, Robert.	(See William G. Mumford, heirs of.)	4	2		666							
Mumford, Robert, assignee of.	For lands in lieu of others granted by government.	9	1	Petition	346	Public Lands	April 9, 1806	Res. to postpone indef.		Resolution adopted.		
Mumford, Robert, assignee of.	For lands in lieu of others granted by government.	9	2	Petition	564	Whole House.						
Mumford, Robert, assignee of.	For lands in lieu of others granted by government.	11	2	Petition	257	Public Lands	Mar. 15, 1810	Adverse		Rejected.		
Mumford, Sylvester, and Wm. H. Tison.	Land in lieu of that purchased from government, covered by private grant.	30	1	Petition	918	Public Lands.						
Mumford, Thomas	Compensation for vessel wrecked with government stores.	22	1	Petition	98	Claims	Dec. 28, 1831	Adverse		Laid on table.		
Mumford, Wm. G., heirs of.	Compensation for services as deputy commissary general, revolutionary war.	4	2	Petition	666	Claims	Feb. 8, 1797	Adverse.		Rejected.		

List of private claims presented to the House of Representatives of the United States from the 1st to the 31st Congress, inclusive—Continued.

Names of claimants.	Nature or object of the claim.	Congress.	Session.	How brought before the House of Reps.	Page of journal.	To what committee of the House referred.	No. or date of the report.	Nature of the report.	No. of the bill.	How disposed of by the House of Reps.	How disposed of by the Senate.	Date of the act of Congress, and remarks.
Mumford, Wm. G., heirs of.	Compensation for services as deputy commissary general, revolutionary war.	5	2	Petition	264	Claims	May 14, 1798	Adverse.	......	Laid on table.		
Mumford, Wm. G., heirs of.	Compensation for services as deputy commissary general, revolutionary war.	5	3	Petition	443	Claims	Feb. 13, 1799	Adverse	......	Referred to Committee Whole House.		
Mumford, William, and others.	Confirmation of title to land.....	19	2	Petition	286	Public Lands.....	....	....	......	Discharged.		
Mumford, William, and others.	Confirmation of title to land.....	20	1	Petition	51	Public Lands	....	....	......	Laid on table.		
Mumford, William, and others.	Confirmation of title to land.....	20	2	Petition	263	Public Lands.....	....	....	......	Laid on table.		
Mumford, William, and others.	Confirmation of title to land	22	1	Petition	115	Public Lands	May 1, 1822	Adverse	......	Laid on table.		
Mumford, William......	Compensation for services as clerk to the commissioners for settling account between United States and Pennsylvania.	1	2	Petition and rep't Sec. Treasury.	169	....	....	....	......	Laid on table.		
Munday, Leap..........	(See William Munday, widow of.)	26	1	....	714							
Munday, William, (Md.).	Revolutionary pension..........	9	2	Petition	473	Claims	Dec. 16, 1806	Adverse	......	Leave to withdraw.		
Munday, William	Increase of pension	14	1	Senate bill	441	Whole House.....	April 12, 1816	Favorable....	44	Passed	Passed	App'd April 16, 1816
Munday, William, widow of.	Revolutionary pension..........	26	1	Petition	714	Rev. Pensions	638	Favorable; bill	471	Referred to Committee Whole House.		
Munday, William, widow of.	Revolutionary pension..........	30	2	Petition	125	Rev. Pensions.						
Mundell, Henry & James,	(See Robert Ferguson, executors and attorneys of.)	26	1	....	182							
Munger, Asa	(See John Mahon & Asa Munger.)	24	1	....	173							
Munger, Charles	Invalid pension...............	24	1	Resolution	951	Invalid Pensions.						
Munger, Lorane	Pension	28	1	Petition	839	Whole House.						
Munger, Philip	Invalid pension	19	1	Petition	310	Military Pensions..	164	Adverse	......	Laid on table.		
Munger, Sally..........	(See Noah Wiseman, heirs and widow of.)	26	1	....	296							
Munn, David..........	Revolutionary pension..........	27	3	Petition	112	Rev. Pensions....	64	Favorable; bill	701	Passed	Indef. postp'd.	
Munn, James	Invalid pension...............	11	1	House bill	283	Whole House.....	Mar. 24, 1810	With amend's.	107	Passed	Passed, with amendment.	App'd April 27, 1810
Munn, John G.........	Increase of compensation as keeper of light-house at New London.	25	2	Petition	46	Commerce.						
Munn, John G.........	Increase of compensation as keeper of light-house at New London.	26	1	Petition	177	Commerce.	388	Adverse	......	Laid on table.		
Munn, Justus	Invalid pension...............	4	1	Rep. of Secretary War.	447	Claims	Feb. 18, 1796	Favorable; bill	156	Passed	Passed	App'd April 20, 1796
Munn, Neal............	For certain credits in payment for land.	18	1	Petition	39	Public Lands	....	....	......	Discharged; laid on table.		
Munn, Neal............	For certain credits in payment for land.	20	2	Petition	206	Public Lands.						
Munnel, Peter..........	(See Stephen Decatur, widow of.)	23	1	....	36	....	45	....	50			
Munnikhuysen, John, heris of.	Indemnity for French spoliations prior to 1800.	31	1	Petition	233	Foreign Affairs ...	355	Favorable; bill	318	Referred to Committee Whole House.		
Munoz, Alonzo B.......	Indemnity for vessel and cargo during war of 1812.	17	1	Petition	432	Judiciary.........	May 4, 1822	Adverse	......	Laid on table.		

List of private claims presented to the House of Representatives of the United States from the 1st to the 31st Congress, inclusive—Continued.

Names of claimants.	Nature or object of the claim.	Congress.	Session.	How brought before the House of Reps.	Page of journal.	To what committee of the House referred.	No. or date of the report.	Nature of the report.	No. of the bill.	How disposed of by the House of Reps.	How disposed of by the Senate.	Date of the act of Congress, and remarks.
Munroe, Andrew	Pension	23	1	Petition	190	Rev. Pensions				Discharged; laid on table.		
Munroe, Barney, heirs of.	Bounty land for revolutionary services.	19	2	Petition	133	Rev. Claims				Discharged; laid on table.		
Munroe, Barney, heirs of.	Bounty land for revolutionary services.	20	1	Petition	58	Rev. Claims				Discharged; laid on table.		
Munroe, Elizabeth	Permission to exchange lands erroneously entered.	27	3	Senate bill	171	Public Lands	Jan. 14, 1843	With't amend.	S. 41	Passed		App'd Jan. 28, 1843
Mnnroe, Henry	(See Nathaniel Gladding & others)	23	1		37							
Munroe, Robert	Invalid pension	27	2	Petition	218	Invalid Pensions	Feb. 9, 1842	Adverse, verbal		Laid on table.		
Munroe, Robert	Invalid pension	28	1	Petition	428	Invalid Pensions	430	Favorable; bill	331	Passed	Passed	App'd June 17, 1844
Munroe, Walter, (colored)	Revolutionary pension	28	1	Petition	550	Rev. Pensions				Discharged; laid on table.		
Munroe, William	(See Reuben E. Gentry, *et al*)	24	1		96							
Munsee, John	Pension	23	1	Petition	332	Invalid Pensions	June 28, 1834	Adverse		Laid on table.		
Munsee, John	Pension	23	2	Petition	101	Invalid Pensions	Jan. 20, 1835	Adverse		Laid on table.		
Munsee, John	Pension	24	1	Petition	53	Invalid Pensions				Discharged; laid on table.		
Munsell, Elisha	Invalid pension	3	2	Report of Secretary of War.	337	Claims	Feb. 28, 1795	Favorable; bill	130	Passed	Postponed.	
Munsell, Elisha	Invalid pension	4	1	Report and docs.	447	Claims	Feb. 18, 1796	Favorable; bill	156	Passed	Passed	App'd April 20, 1796
Munson, Æneas	Commutation pay for revolutionary services.	24	2	Senate bill	260	Rev. Claims	259	Adverse	S. 110	Referred to Committee Whole House.		
Munson, Moses	Revolutionary pension	17	1	Petition	389					Referred to Committee Whole House on bill No. 37.		
Munson, Nehemiah	Pension	21	1	Resolution	572	Military Pensions.						
Munson, Samuel	Pension	22	1	Resolution	497	Rev. Pensions				Discharged; laid on table.		
Munson, Samuel	Pension	23	1	Petition	491	Rev. Pensions				Discharged; laid on table.	Passed	Leave to withdraw.
Murain, Josiah	(See Thos. Tupper, assignees of)	22	2		142							
Murch, Hiram	Refunding of a certain fine	27	2	Petition	756	Commerce.						
Murch, Hiram	Refunding of a certain fine	27	3	Petition	45	Commerce.						
Murch, Hiram	Refunding of a certain fine	28	1	Senate bill	868	Commerce	May 15, 1844	With't amend.	S. 74	Passed		App'd June 17, 1844
Murcheson, John	Compensation for revolutionary services.	25	2	Petition	392	Rev. Claims.						
Murcheson, John	Compensation for revolutionary services.	26	1	Petition	360	Rev. Claims.						
Murcheson, John	Compensation for revolutionary services.	26	2	Petition	131	Rev. Claims.						
Murcheson, John	Compensation for revolutionary services.	30	1	Petition	383	Rev. Pensions	208	Adverse.		Laid on table.		
Murcia, or Mercia, Julian.	Confirmation of title to land	16	2	Petition	24	Priv. Land Claims.	Dec. 20, 1819	Adverse		Rejected.		
Murdock, Elisha	Pension	21	1	Petition	143	Military Pensions.	April 2, 1830	Adverse		Laid on table.		
Murdock, Ellis	(See Thos. Tupper, assignees of)	22	2		142							
Murdock, Fry & Co.	(See Thos. Tupper, assignees of)	22	2		142							
Murdock, George L.	Compensation for services in war of 1812.	18	2	Petition	161	Priv. Land Claims.						
Murdock, George L.	Compensation for services in war of 1812.	19	1	Petition	67	Priv. Land Claims.	Jan. 16, 1826	Adverse		Laid on table.		
Murdock, George L.	Compensation for services in war of 1812.	19	2	Petition	105	Military Affairs				Discharged; laid on table.		

List of private claims presented to the House of Representatives of the United States from the 1st to the 31st Congress, inclusive—Continued.

Names of claimants.	Nature or object of the claim.	Congress.	Session.	How brought before the House of Reps.	Page of journal.	To what committee of the House referred.	No. or date of the report.	Nature of the report.	No. of the bill.	How disposed of by the House of Reps.	How disposed of by the Senate.	Date of the act of Congress, and remarks.
Murdock, George L.	Compensation for services in war of 1812.	21	1	Petition	175	Military Affairs				Discharged; laid on table.		
Murdock, J. G.	(See William H. Bedford, agent.)	28	1		262							
Muren, Francis W. C.	(See F. B. Gamble, widow of)	23	2		96							
Murian, Joseph	(See Thomas Tupper, assignees of.)	22	2		142							
Murphy, Barnabas	Compensation for revolutionary services.	2	1	Petition	475					Referred to Secretary War.		
Murphy, Barnabas	Compensation for revolutionary services.	3	1	Rep. of Secretary War.	131	Select	May 26, 1794	Res. to refer to Sec. War.		Resolution adopted.		
Murphy, Benjamin	Payment for corn, cattle, &c., taken by Cherokee Indians.	24	1	Senate bill	146	Indian Affairs	162	Adverse	S. 36	Referred to Committee Whole House.		
Murphy, Benjamin	Payment for corn, cattle, &c., taken by Cherokee Indians.	24	2	Senate bill	250	Whole House			S. 43			
Murphy, Benjamin	Payment for corn, cattle, &c., taken by Cherokee Indians.	25	2	Senate bill	301	Indian Affairs	549	With't amend.	S. 85	Referred to Committee Whole House.		
Murphy, Benjamin	Payment for corn, cattle, &c., taken by Cherokee Indians.	25	3	Senate bill	636				S. 204			
Murphy, Benjamin	Payment for corn, cattle, &c., taken by Cherokee Indians.	26	1	Senate bill	189	Claims	364	Adverse	S. 23	Referred to Committee Whole House.		
Murphy, Benjamin	Payment for corn, cattle, &c., taken by Cherokee Indians.	26	2	Senate bill	113	Claims	186	Adverse	S. 55	Referred to Committee Whole House.		
Murphy, Benjamin	Payment for corn, cattle, &c., taken by Cherokee Indians.	27	2	Petition	130	Indian Affairs.						
Murphy, Benjamin	Payment for corn, cattle, &c., taken by Cherokee Indians.	27	2	Senate bill	938	Indian Affairs	June 22, 1842	With't amend.	S. 183	Referred to Committee Whole House.		
Murphy, Benjamin	Payment for corn, cattle, &c., taken by Cherokee Indians.	27	3	Senate bill	147	Indian Affairs	Feb. 16, 1843	With't amend.	S. 45	Referred to Committee Whole House.		
Murphy, Benjamin	Payment for corn, cattle, &c., taken by Cherokee Indians.	28	1	Senate bill	448	Indian Affairs	307	Favorable, with amendments.	S. 47	Passed	Passed	App'd June 17, 1844
Murphy, David	Invalid pension	29	1	Memorial	466	Invalid Pensions	810	Favorable; bill	535	Referred to Committee Whole House.		
Murphy, David	Invalid pension	30	1	Petition	666	Invalid Pensions	716	Favorable; bill	561	Referred to Committee Whole House.		
Murphy, David	Invalid pension	30	2	Bill of last sess.	319	Whole House	Jan. 26, 1849	With't amend.	561	Passed.		
Murphy, David	Invalid pension	31	1	Petition	32	Invalid Pensions.						
Murphy, Edward, heirs of.	Confirmation of title to land	21	1	Petition	297	Priv. Land Claims.						
Murphy, Edward, heirs of.	Confirmation of title to land	22	1	Petition	65	Priv. Land Claims.	Jan. 25, 1832	By bill	311	Referred to Committee Whole House.		
Murphy, Edward, heirs of.	Confirmation of title to land	23	1	Petition	714	Public Lands.						
Murphy, Edward, heirs of.	Confirmation of title to land	23	2	Senate bill	159	Priv. Land Claims.	Jan. 15, 1835	With amends.	S. 42	Referred to Committee Whole House.		
Murphy, Elizabeth	Permission to redeem land sold for taxes.	17	1	Petition	22	Public Lands				Discharged; laid on table.		
Murphy, Francis D.	Compensation for discoveries in the art of surveying.	29	1	Memorial	226	Public Lands				Discharged; laid on table.		
Murphy, Greenbury H., heirs of.	Reimbursement of expenses in collecting militia fines.	17	1	Senate bill	465	Ways and Means	April 19, 1822	With't amend.	S. 81	Passed	Passed	App'd May 7, 1822
Murphy, Isaac	Pre-emption right to land	15	2	Petition	34	Priv. Land Claims.						
Murphy, James, heirs of.	Compensation for revolutionary services.	23	1	Petition	439	Rev. Claims.						
Murphy, James, heirs of.	Compensation for revolutionary services.	23	2	Petition	37	Rev. Claims.						

List of private claims presented to the House of Representatives of the United States from the 1st to the 31st Congress, inclusive—Continued.

Names of claimants.	Nature or object of the claim.	Congress.	Session.	How brought before the House of Reps.	Page of journal.	To what committee of the House referred.	No. or date of the report.	Nature of the report.	No. of the bill.	How disposed of by the House of Reps.	How disposed of by the Senate.	Date of the act of Congress, and remarks.
Murphy, James, heirs of	Compensation for revolutionary services.	24	1	Petition	205	Rev. Claims				Discharged; laid on table.		
Murphy, Jeremiah	Invalid pension	29	1	Petition	189	Invalid Pensions						Leave to withdraw, 2d session.
Murphy, Jesse	Revolutionary pension	18	1	Resolution	122	Rev. Pensions	Jan. 14, 1824	Adverse		Laid on table.		
Murphy, John	(See James Murphy, heir of)	23	1		439							
Murphy, John	Restoration to pension roll	29	1	Petition	298	Rev. Pensions	429	Adverse		Laid on table.		
Murphy, John H	(See Thomas McKibbon and John H. Murphy.)	26	1		347							
Murphy, John	(See William H. Bedford, agent)	28	1		262							
Murphy, Martin	Pension	21	2	Petition	80	Military Pensions.						
Murphy, Nicholas	Invalid pension	2	1	Petition	527					Rreferred to Secretary of War.		
Murphy, Sarah	Compensation for services in Arch street prison, Philadelphia, by order of quartermaster general.	24	1	Petition	430	Claims	572	Favorable; bill	556	Referred to Committee Whole House.		
Murphy, Sarah	Compensation for services in Arch street prison, Philadelphia, by order of quartermaster general.	25	2	Petition	37	Claims	29	Favorable; bill	41	Passed	Passed	App'd March 7, 1838
Murphy, William	Invalid pension	29	2	Petition	74	Invalid Pensions.						
Murray, Alexander	Refunding amount of judgment, &c., against him in case of the schooner Betsey.	8	2	Memorial	22	Claims	Jan. 8, 1805	Favorable; bill	38	Passed	Passed	App'd Jan. 31, 1805
Murray, Alexander	Payment of loan office certificate	15	1	Petition	156	Pens. & Rev. Cl'ms.				Discharged		Leave to withdraw.
Murray, Anthony	Invalid pension	22	1	Resolution	328	Invalid Pensions	426	Favorable; bill	528	Passed	Passed	App'd July 16, 1832
Murray, Anthony	Compensation for services on board frigate Philadelphia at Tripoli.	27	2	Petition	534	Claims	646	Adverse		Laid on table.		
Murray, Charles	Pre-emption right to land	14	1	Petition	113	Public Lands.						
Murray, Cyrus W., surety of.	Release from liability	17	1	Petition	176	Ways and Means	Jan. 28, 1822	Adverse		Rejected.		
Murray, Cyrus W., surety of.	Release from liability	17	2	Petition	231	P. Of. & P. Roads				Discharged; leave to withdraw.		
Murray, Cyrus W., surety of.	Release from liability	18	1	Petition	42	P. Of. & P. Roads	Jan. 20, 1824	Adverse		Laid on table.		
Murray, Daniel	Compensation for revolutionary services.	3	1	Petition	103					Referred to Secretary War.		
Murray, Daniel	Compensation for revolutionary services.	3	2	Rep. of Secretary War.	278					Laid on table.		
Murray, Elizabeth	(See Matthew Murray, widow of)	21	1		231							
Murray, Fountaine	Drawback on coffee	8	2	Petition and rep't Sec. of War.	86, 90	Claims.						
Murray, George	(See Stephen Decatur's widow and others.)	23	1						50			
Murray, Hamilton, administrator of.	Indemnity for French spoliations prior to 1800.	26	1	Memorial	182	Foreign Affairs	343	Favorable; bill	319	Referred to Committee Whole House.		
Murray, Henry, representatives of.	Payment of loan office certificates	10	1	Petition	159					Referred to Committee Whole House on bill No. 20.		
Murray, Henry, representatives of.	Payment of loan office certificates.	10	2	Petition	463					Referred to Committee Whole House on bill No. 129.		
Murray, Henry, representatives of.	Payment of loan office certificates.	11	1	Petition	31	Claims	June 17, 1809	Adverse		Laid on table.		

List of private claims presented to the House of Representatives of the United States from the 1*st to the* 31*st Congress, inclusive*—Continued.

Names of claimants.	Nature or object of the claim.	Congress.	Session.	How brought before the House of Reps.	Page of journal.	To what committee of the House referred.	No. or date of the report.	Nature of the report.	No. of the bill.	How disposed of by the House of Reps.	How disposed of by the Senate.	Date of the act of Congress, and remarks.
Murray, Henry, representatives of.	Payment of loan office certificates.	11	2	Petition	122	Claims	Dec. 15, 1809	Adverse; bill ordered.	108	Passed	Rejected.	
Murray, Henry, representatives of.	Payment of loan office certificates.	11	3	Petition	438	Claims.						
Murray, Henry, representatives of.	Payment of loan office certificates.	12	1	Petition	49	Claims	Dec. 17, 1811	Favorable; bill	141	Referred to Committee Whole House.		
Murray, Henry, representatives of.	Payment of loan office certificates.	12	2	Petition	571	Claims	Dec. 15, 1812	Favorable; bill	207	Passed	Passed	App'd Feb. 25, 1813
Murray, James	(See Abraham Mosser, and others)	3	2		330							
Murray, James	(See James Murray, heirs of)	22	2		57							
Murray, James, heirs of	Pay and bounty land for revolutionary services.	22	2	Resolution	57	Rev. Claims.						
Murray, James, heirs of	Pay and bounty land for revolutionary services.	23	1	Resolution	54	Rev. Claims.						
Murray, James, heirs of	Pay and bounty land for revolutionary services.	24	1	Resolution	247	Rev. Claims	Feb. 5, 1836	Adverse		Laid on table.		
Murray, James, heirs of	Pay and bounty land for revolutionary services.	26	1	Petition	166	Rev. Claims.						
Murray, James, heirs of	Pay and bounty land for revolutionary services.	26	2	Petition	77	Rev. Claims	170	Adverse		Laid on table.		
Murray, James, heirs of	Pay and bounty land for revolutionary services.	27	2	Petition	110	Rev. Claims	520	Adverse		Laid on table.		
Murray, James, heirs of	Pay and bounty land for revolutionary services.	28	1	Petition	361	Rev. Claims.						
Murray, James, heirs of	Pay and bounty land for revolutionary services.	28	2	Petition	104	Rev. Claims.						
Murray, James, heirs of	Pay and bounty land for revolutionary services.	29	1	Petition	435	Rev. Claims.						
Murray, James B.	(See New York city, claimants of)	26	1		182							
Murray, John	(See James Swan, agent of)	8	1		540							
Murray, John B., and son.	Drawback on certain goods	18	2	Petition	101					Referred to Secretary Treasury.		
Murray, John	Compensation for extra work on Cumberland road.	23	1	Res. and docs.	589	Claims	455	Adverse		Laid on table		See report No. 449.
Murray, John	Compensation for extra work on Cumberland road.	24	1	Resolution	891	Claims	757	Adverse		Laid on table.		
Murray, John	Grant of land in lieu of losses by Choctaw treaty.	24	1	Petition	57	Public Lands	208	Favorable; bill	208	Referred to Committee Whole House.		
Murray, John	(See Henry Murray, representatives of.)	10	1		159							
Murray, John R., and William Ogden.	Drawback of duties on sugars	11	1	Petition	83	Com. and Manuf.						
Murray, John R., and William Ogden.	Drawback of duties on sugars	11	2	Petition	209	Com. and Manuf.						
Murray, John R., and William Ogden.	Drawback of duties on sugars	14	2	Petition	101	Com. and Manuf.	Dec. 31, 1816	Favorable; bill	36	Passed	Passed	App'd March 3, 1817
Murray, John R	(See Joseph Lindley, executor of)	26	1		182							
Murray, Lackey, heirs of	Compensation for services and for property destroyed in revolutionary war.	16	1	Petition	76	Pens. & Rev. Cl'ms.	Jan. 3, 1830	Adverse		Laid on table.		
Murray, Lackey, heirs of	Compensation for services and for property destroyed in revolutionary war.	26	1	Petition	630	Rev. Claims.						

List of private claims presented to the House of Representatives of the United States from the 1st *to the* 31st *Congress, inclusive*—Continued.

Names of claimants.	Nature or object of the claim.	Congress.	Session.	How brought before the House of Reps.	Page of journal.	To what committee of the House referred.	No. or date of the report.	Nature of the report.	No. of the bill.	How disposed of by the House of Reps.	How disposed of by the Senate.	Date of the act of Congress, and remarks.
Murray, Lackey, heirs of..	Compensation for services and for property destroyed in revolutionary war.	31	1	Petition	628	Rev. Claims.....	343	Adverse	......	Laid on table.		
Murray, Margaret C	(See Thomas Murray, widow of).	24	2	....	391							
Murray, Matthew, widow of.	Revolutionary pension..........	21	1	Petition	231	Military Pensions..	April 2, 1830	Adverse	......	Laid on table.		
Murray & Mumford......	Remission of duties on iron cannon.	5	2	Petition	319	Com. and Manuf.						
Murray, Nicholas, *et al* .	(See James Murray, heirs of)....	22	2	....	57							
Murray, Reuben	Refunding expenses incurred in public service.	2	1	Petition	458	....	....	....	.....	Referred to Secretary Treasury.		
Murray, Reuben	Refunding expenses incurred in public service.	2	2	Rep. of Secretary Treasury.	626	....	....	....	.....	Laid on table.		
Murray, Reuben	Revolutionary pension..........	25	2	Petition	585	Rev. Pensions	919	Favorable; bill	805	Passed	Adverse.	
Murray, Reuben	Revolutionary pension..........	25	3	Petition	87	Rev. Pensions	212	Favorable; bill	1070	Passed.		
Murray, Reuben	Revolutionary pension..........	26	1	Petition	172	Rev. Pensions	131	Favorable; bill	141	Passed	Indef. postp'd.	
Murray, Reuben	Revolutionary pension..........	27	2	Petition	153	Rev. Pensions	784	Adverse	......	Laid on table.		
Murray, Robert	Permission to relinquish certain lands and enter others.	24	1	Petition	114	Public Lands	April 22, 1836	Favorable; bill	585	Passed.		
Murray, Robert	Permission to relinquish certain lands and enter others.	24	2	Petition	107	Public Lands.....	Jan. 3, 1837	By bill......	805	Referred to Committee Whole House.		
Murray, Robert	Permission to relinquish certain lands and enter others.	25	2	Petition	42	Public Lands.....	204	Favorable; bill	239	Referred to Committee Whole House.		
Murray, Robert	Permission to relinquish certain lands and enter others.	25	3	Bill of last sess.	376	Whole House.....	Jan. 23, 1839	With't amend.	239	Passed	Passed	App'd March 2, 1839
Murray, Thomas	Compensation for revolutionary services.	2	1	Petition	517	....	....	....	.....	Referred to Secretary War.		
Murray, Thomas	Payment of balance due as master cooper at navy yard, Brooklyn.	14	2	Petition	65	....	....	....	.....	Referred to Secretary War.		
Murray, Thomas	Payment of balance due as master cooper at navy yard, Brooklyn.	15	1	Petition	101	Claims.						
Murray, Thomas	Payment of balance due as master cooper at navy yard, Brooklyn.	24	1	Petition	94	Claims	371	Adverse	......	Laid on table.		
Murray, Thomas, jr......	Compensation for services as secretary to Cherokee delegation in 1828.	22	2	Resolution	182	Indian Affairs.....	Feb. 15, 1833	Adverse	......	Laid on table.		
Murray, Thomas, jr......	Compensation for services as secretary to Cherokee delegation in 1828.	23	1	Res. and docs...	163	Indian Affairs.....	....	....	.....	Discharged; laid on table.		
Murray, Thomas, jr., widow of.	Compensation for services as secretary to Cherokee delegation in 1828.	24	2	Petition	391	Indian Affairs.						
Murray, Thomas, jr., widow of.	Compensation for services as secretary to Cherokee delegation in 1828.	25	2	Petition	278	Indian Affairs.....	696	Favorable; bill	668	Referred to Committee Whole House.		
Murray, Thomas, jr., widow of.	Compensation for services as secretary to Cherokee delegation in 1828.	25	3	Bill of last sess..	380	Whole House.....	Jan. 25, 1839	With't amend.	668	Passed	Adverse.	
Murray, Thomas, jr., widow of.	Compensation for services as secretary to Cherokee delegation in 1828.	26	1	Petition	180	Claims.						
Murray, Thomas, jr., widow of.	Compensation for services as secretary to Cherokee delegation in 1828.	27	3	Petition	71	Indian Affairs.....	137	Adverse	......	Laid on table.		

List of private claims presented to the House of Representatives of the United States from the 1*st to the* 31*st Congress, inclusive*—Continued.

Names of claimants.	Nature or object of the claim.	Congress.	Session.	How brought before the House of Reps.	Page of journal.	To what committee of the House referred.	No. or date of the report.	Nature of the report.	No. of the bill.	How disposed of by the House of Reps.	How disposed of by the Senate.	Date of the act of Congress, and remarks.
Murray, Thomas, jr., widow of.	Compensation for services as secretary to Cherokee delegation in 1828.	29	1	Memorial	175	Indian Affairs	446	Favorable; bill	320	Passed.		
Murray, William	Pension	22	1	Petition	122	Rev. Pensions	Dec. 29, 1831	Adverse		Laid on table.		
Murray, William	Pension	30	1	Petition	1198	Invalid Pensions				Discharged; laid on table.		
Musehett, James, heir of.	Indemnity for French spoliations prior to 1800.	26	1	Memorial	182	Foreign Affairs	343	Favorable; bill	319	Referred to Committee Whole House.		
Muse, James W.	Compensation for services as captain's clerk in United States navy.	22	1	Petition	144	Naval Affairs.						
Muse, James W.	Compensation for services as captain's clerk in United States navy.	22	2	Petition	31	Naval Affairs.						
Muse, James W.	Compensation for services as captain's clerk in United States navy.	23	1	Petition	213	Naval Affairs	Feb. 25, 1834	Adverse		Laid on table.		
Muse, J. Fort, and wife	Confirmation of title to land	26	1	Petition	611	Priv. Land Claims.						
Muse, J. Fort, and wife	Confirmation of title to land	26	2	Petition	134	Priv. Land Claims.	121	Favorable; bill	626	Referred to Committee Whole House.		
Muse, J. Fort, and wife	Confirmation of title to land	27	2	Petition	155	Priv. Land Claims.	281	Favorable; bill	247	Passed.		
Muse, Lawrence, trustee of the sureties of.	Refunding money erroneously paid into the Treasury.	21	2	Senate bill	214	Claims	69	With't amend.	S. 82	Passed		App'd March 3, 1831
Muse, Lawrence	Indemnity for a house and tobacco destroyed by the enemy in war of 1812.	15	1	Report of Commissioners.	37	Claims	116	Adverse		Referred to Committee Whole House.		
Muse, Lawrence	Indemnity for a house and tobacco destroyed by the enemy in war of 1812.	16	1	Report of Commissioners.	46	Claims	Jan. 7, 1820	Adverse		Laid on table.		
Muse, Lawrence	Indemnity for a house and tobacco destroyed by the enemy in war of 1812.	16	2	Rep't of last sess.	36	Whole House.						
Muse, Lawrence	Indemnity for a house and tobacco destroyed by the enemy in war of 1812.	17	1	Resolution	237	Claims				Leave to withdraw.		
Muse, Lawrence	Indemnity for a house and tobacco destroyed by the enemy in war of 1812.	17	2	Petition	60	Claims	Dec. 31, 1822	Adverse		Laid on table.		
Muse, Lawrence	Indemnity for a house and tobacco destroyed by the enemy in war of 1812.	18	1	Petition	52	Claims	Dec. 19, 1823	Adverse		Referred to Committee Whole House.		
Muse, Lawrence, (Va.)	Increase of compensation as collector at Tappahannock, Va.	4	1	Petition	454	Com. and Manuf.						
Muse, Lawrence, (Va.)	Increase of compensation as collector at Tappahannock, Va.	4	2	Petition	627	Select.						
Muse, Lawrence, (Va.)	Increase of compensation as collector at Tappahannock, Va.	5	2	Petition	331	Com. and Manuf.						
Muse, Lawrence, (Va.)	Further time to pay balance due government.	14	2	Petition	337	Ways and Means				Discharged; laid on table.		
Muse, Lawrence, (Va.)	Further time to pay balance due government.	15	1	Petition	44	Ways and Means	Mar. 23, 1818	Adverse		Laid on table.		
Muse, Lawrence, (Va.)	Further time to pay balance due government.	15	2	Rep't of last sess.	234	Ways and Means				Discharged; laid on table.		

List of private claims presented to the House of Representatives of the United States from the 1st to the 31st Congress, inclusive—Continued.

Names of claimants.	Nature or object of the claim.	Congress.	Session.	How brought before the House of Reps.	Page of journal.	To what committee of the House referred.	No. or date of the report.	Nature of the report.	No. of the bill.	How disposed of by the House of Reps.	How disposed of by the Senate.	Date of the act of Congress, and remarks.
Muse, Marguerite Adelaide	(See J. Fort Muse and wife)	26	2	....	134							
Muse, Wm., passed midshipman.	Compensation for services as lieutenant during the time he acted as such.	31	1	Petition	338	Naval Affairs.						
Musgenug, Anthony	(See Nicholas Haugendobler)	1	3	....	351							
Musgrove, Samuel.......	To apply money paid for certain lands to other lands.	16	1	Petition	434	Public Lands.....	May 3, 1820	Adverse	......	Rejected.		
Musick, Lewis..........	Compensation for property destroyed by Sioux Indians.	22	2	Petition	347	Indian Affairs.						
Musser, George, & others.	(See Jeremiah Buckley, heirs of).	19	1	....	61							
Musser, George, & others.	(See Jeremiah Buckley, heirs of).	19	2	....	65							
Mussey, Samuel.........	(See Samuel Massey and Thomas James.)	25	2	....	417							
Mussi, Joseph, heirs of...	Indemnity for French spoliations prior to 1800.	25	1	Petition	80	....	....	....	......	Laid on table.		
Mussi, Joseph, heirs of...	Indemnity for French spoliations prior to 1800.	26	1	Memorial	182	Foreign Affairs....	343	Favorable; bill	319	Referred to Committee Whole House.		
Mussi, Joseph, heirs of, by attorney.	Indemnity for French spoliations prior to 1800.	31	1	Petition	233	Foreign Affairs....	355	Favorable; bill	318	Referred to Committee Whole House.		
Mu-ta-ma-go-qua........	(See Angelica Cutaw)..........	20	1	....	197							
Mutterspack, John.......	Relief for wounds received in revolutionary war.	2	1	Petition	474	....	....	....	......	Referred to Secretary War.		
Muzzy, Amos...........	Release upon suit of the United States.	17	1	Petition	177	P. Of. & P. Roads.	Feb. 11, 1822	Favorable....	83	Passed.		
Muzzy, Amos...........	Release upon suit of the United States.	17	2	Petition	26	P. Of. & P. Roads.						
Muzzy, Robert..........	Invalid pension................	12	2	Petition	615	Claims	Feb. 26, 1813	Adverse	......	Laid on table.		
Myerle, David	Compensation for losses on contract for hemp for navy.	28	1	Petition	631	Naval Affairs	....	....	......	Discharged; laid on table.		
Myerle, David	Compensation for losses on contract for hemp for navy.	28	2	Petition	45	Naval Affairs.						
Myerle, David	Compensation for losses on contract for hemp for navy.	29	1	Petition	74	Naval Affairs	702	Favorable; bill	477	Referred to Committee Whole House.		
Myerle, David	Compensation for losses on contract for hemp for navy.	29	2	House bill	382	Whole House	Feb. 19, 1847	Favorable....	477	Passed.		
Myerle, David	Compensation for losses on contract for hemp for navy.	30	1	Petition	97	Naval Affairs.....	169	Favorable; bill	32	Passed.		
Myerle, David	Compensation for losses on contract for hemp for navy.	30	2	House bill from Senate.	410	....	....	....	......	....	Passed, with amendment.	Laid on table.
Myerle, David	Compensation for losses on contract for hemp for navy.	31	1	Petition	216	Naval Affairs.....	204	Favorable; bill	212	Referred to Committee Whole House.		
Myers, Abraham	(See Samuel Delp, heirs and attorney of.)	17	1	....	86							
Myers, Edward	Pension	28	1	Petition	274	Invalid Pensions ..	188	Adverse	......	Laid on table.		
Myers, Edward	Pension	30	1	Petition	99	Naval Affairs.....	511	Favorable; bill	438	Referred to Committee Whole House.		
Myers, Edward	Pension	30	2	House bill	318	Whole House.....	Jan. 26, 1849	With't amend.	438	Passed.		
Myers, Elizabeth	(See John, Myers, widow of.) ...	29	1	....	175							
Myers, George, (Mo.)....	Confirmation of title to land.....	15	1	Petition	312	Priv. Land Claims.	....	....	......	Discharged; laid on table.		
Myers, George, (Mo.)....	Confirmation of title to land.....	16	1	Petition	71	Priv. Land Claims.	....	....	......	Discharged; laid on table.		

List of private claims presented to the House of Representatives of the United States from the 1st to the 31st Congress, inclusive—Continued.

Names of claimants.	Nature or object of the claim.	Congress.	Session.	How brought before the House of Reps.	Page of journal.	To what committee of the House referred.	No. or date of the report.	Nature of the report.	No. of the bill.	How disposed of by the House of Reps.	How disposed of by the Senate.	Date of the act of Congress, and remarks.
Myers, George, (Mo.)	Confirmation of title to land	17	1	Petition	54	Priv. Land Claims.						
Myers, George, (Mo.)	Confirmation of title to land	18	1	Petition	54	Priv. Land Claims.	Jan. 16, 1824	Favorable; bill	65	Passed	Passed	App'd May 26, 1824
Myers, George, and others.	(See William R. Campbell.)	30	2		358							
Myers, Hans	Pre-emption right, New Orleans branch pilot.	28	1	Petition	77	Priv. Land Claims.	9	Favorable; bill	35	Passed	Passed	App'd June 17, 1844
Myers, Henry	Arrears of pension	23	1	Petition	309	Invalid Pensions	Feb. 21, 1834	Adverse		Laid on table.		
Myers, Isaac	Grant of land for losses by Choctaw treaty.	24	1	Petition	57	Public Lands	208	Favorable; bill	208	Referred to Committee Whole House.		
Myers, Jacob, (N. J.)	Compensation for revolutionary services.	11	2	Petition	215	Claims.						
Myers, Jacob, (N. J.)	Compensation for revolutionary services.	11	3	Petition	443	Claims.						
Myers, Jacob, (Ark.)	Pre-emption right to land	19	2	Petition	113	Public Lands				Discharged; leave to withdraw.		
Myers, Jacob, (Baltimore).	Indemnity for French spoliations prior to 1800.	26	1	Memorial	182	Foreign Affairs	343	Favorable; bill	319	Referred to Committee Whole House.		
Myers, John, (Pa.)	Revolutionary pension	21	2	Resolution	125	Military Pensions.						
Myers, John, (Pa.)	Revolutionary pension	22	1	Resolution	45	Rev. Pensions.						
Myers, John, (Pa.)	Revolutionary pension	23	1	Resolution	202	Rev. Pensions				Discharged; laid on table.		
Myers, John, widow of	Revolutionary pension	25	2	Petition	231	Rev. Pensions	Feb. 17, 1838	Adverse		Laid on table.		
Myers, or McMyers, John, widow of, (Md.)	Revolutionary pension	29	1	Petition	175	Rev. Pensions	617	Adverse		Laid on table.		
Myers, John, (Ill.)	Pension	14	2	Resolution	103	Pens. & Rev. Cl'ms.	Jan. 29, 1817	Favorable; bill	91	Passed	Passed, with amendment.	App'd March 3, 1817
Myers, John, (Mo.)	Confirmation of title to land	15	1	Petition	312	Priv. Land Claims.				Discharged; laid on table.		
Myers, John, (Mo.)	Confirmation of title to land	16	1	Petition	71	Priv. Land Claims.				Discharged; laid on table.		
Myers, John, (Mo.)	Confirmation of title to land	17	1	Petition	54	Priv. Land Claims.				Discharged; laid on table.		
Myers, John, (Mo.)	Confirmation of title to land	18	1	Petition	54	Priv. Land Claims.	Jan. 16, 1824	Favorable; bill	65	Passed	Passed	App'd May 26, 1824
Myers, John	Compensation for horse lost in military services United States.	20	1	Resolution	54	Claims	Feb. 13, 1828	Adverse		Laid on table.		
Myers, John	Compensation for horse lost in military services United States.	23	1	Resolution	92	Claims	Jan. 26, 1834	Adverse		Laid on table.		
Myers, John	Compensation for horse lost in military services United States.	23	2	Resolution	106	Claims.						
Myers, John, (Md.)	Release from suit of the United States.	16	2	Petition	88	Judiciary.						
Myers, Lawrence, widow of.	(See Nathaniel Hunt, and others.)	19	2		242							
Myers, Mary	(See John Myers, widow of)	25	2		231							
Myers, Moses, (Va.)	Increase of compensation as collector of customs.	20	1	Petition	192	Commerce.						
Myers, Moses, (Va.)	Allowance of commissions on certain bonds.	21	2	Petition	211	Ways and Means.						
Myers, Moses, (Va.)	Allowance of commissions on certain bonds.	22	1	Petition	41	Ways and Means.						
Myers, Moses, (Va.)	Exoneration from payment of duties on goods sunk at Norfolk, Va.	3	2	Petition	225	Select	Nov. 21, 1794	Report not extant.		Laid on table.		
Myers, Moses, (Va.)	Exoneration from payment of duties on goods sunk at Norfolk, Va.	4	1	Petition	384	Com. and Manuf.	Jan. 11, 1796	Adverse		Leave to withdraw.		

List of private claims presented to the House of Representatives of the United States from the 1st to the 31st Congress, inclusive—Continued.

Names of claimants.	Nature or object of the claim.	Congress.	Session.	How brought before the House of Reps.	Page of journal.	To what committee of the House referred.	No. or date of the report.	Nature of the report.	No. of the bill.	How disposed of by the House of Reps.	How disposed of by the Senate.	Date of the act of Congress, and remarks.
Myers, Moses, (Va.).....	Exoneration from payment of duties on goods sunk at Norfolk, Va.	4	1	Rep. of last sess.	386	Com. and Munuf..	May 4, 1796	Favorable; bill	180	Passed	Rejected.	
Myers, Moses, (Va.,) heirs of.	Indemnity for French spoliations prior to 1800.	26	1	Memorial	182	Foreign Affairs....	343	Favorable; bill	319	Referred to Committee Whole House.		
Myers, Peter A	Pension	25	3	Resolution	161	Invalid Pensions.						
Myers, Peter H., or A....	Invalid pension................	26	1	Petition	163	Invalid Pensions ..	169	Favorable; bill	180	Passed	Passed	App'd July 20, 1840
Myers, Peter, (Pa.)......	Invalid pension................	29	1	Petition and docs.	499	Invalid Pensions.						
Myers, Peter, (Pa)......	Invalid pension................	29	2	Petition	89	Invalid Pensions.						
Myers, Peter, (Pa.)......	Invalid pension................	30	1	Resolution	182	Invalid Pensions ..	799	Favorable; bill	620	Referred to Committee Whole House.		
Myers, Peter, (Pa.)......	Invalid pension................	30	2	House bill	362	Whole House	Feb. 2, 1849	With't amend.	620	Passed.		
Myers, Peter, (Pa.)......	Invalid pension................	31	1	Petition	643	Invalid Pensions.						
Myers, Samuel..........	For authority to purchase land which he improved.	25	3	Petition	495	Public Lands.						
Myers, Samuel..........	Pre emption right to certain lands in Ohio.	26	1	Petition	504	Priv. Land Claims.	....	....	......	Discharged; laid on table.		
Myers, T. Bailey	Compensation as special commissioner in taking testimony.	30	1	Petition	422	Accounts.........	Mar. 13, 1848	Res. to pay out of contingent fund.	......	Resolution adopted.		
Myers, Tobias, and Chambers McKibbin.	(See Chambers McKibbin, and Tobias Myers.)	31	2	....	36							
Myler, Catherine, widow of Robert.	Compensation for revolutionary services.	3	1	Petition and rep't Sec. of War.	32, 93	Select.						
Myles, John E., guardian of.	(See Hannah Hall, heirs of).....	14	2	....	71							
Myles, John E., guardian of.	(See Hannah Hall, heirs of).....	15	1	....	44							
Myles, John E., and others	Confirmation of title to land in Alabama.	14	2	Petition	72	Public Lands.....	....	....	......	Discharged; laid on table.		
Mylne, William C.......	(See H. and R. Use, assignee of).	26	1	....	362							
Mynard, John Henry	Compensation for property taken for use of revolutionary army.	3	1	Petition	48	....	....	....	......	Laid on table.		
Myotte, Jacques, & others.	Confirmation of titles to land in Illinois.	18	1	Petition	177	Public Lands.....	Mar. 12, 1824	Favorable	155	Postponed.		
Myotte, Jacques, & others.	Confirmation of titles to land in Illinois.	19	1	Resolution	331	Public Lands.....	April 28, 1826	Favorable	241	Passed.		
Myotte, Jacques, & others.	Confirmation of titles to land in Illinois.	19	2	Resolution	136	Public Lands.						
Myotte, Jacques, & others.	Confirmation of titles to land in Illinois.	20	1	Resolution	154	Public Lands.....	....	....	......	Discharged; laid on table.		
Myrick, Samuel.........	Pension	19	2	Resolution	103	Military Pensions.						

List of private claims presented to the House of Representatives of the United States form the 1st to the 31st Congress, inclusive—Continued.

Names of claimants.	Nature or object of the claim.	Congress.	Session.	How brought before the House of Reps.	Page of journal.	To what committee of the House referred.	No. or date of the report.	Nature of the report.	No. of the bill.	How disposed of by the House of Reps.	How disposed of by the Senate.	Date of the act of Congress, and remarks.
Nadaun, or Nadaux, Martin.	Indemnity for land sold by United States.	21	1	Petition	151	Public Lands.						
Nadaun, or Nadaux, Martin.	Indemnity for land sold by United States.	22	2	Petition	219	Public Lands.						
Nadaun, or Nadaux, Martin.	Indemnity for land sold by United States.	23	2	Petition	276	Priv. Land Claims.						
Nadean, James, heirs of	Confirmation of titles to land in Alabama.	26	1	Petition	962	Priv. Land Claims.						
Naff, John H., and W. W. Rockhold.	Compensation for clothing furnished Tennessee volunteers.	31	2	Petition	58	Military Affairs	82	Favorable; bill	486	Referred to Commitee Whole House.		
Nagle, David, executor of.	Indemnity for the seizure of slave ship.	24	1	Petition	115	Foreign Affairs	209	Adverse		Laid on table.		
Nagle, Peter	Pension for revolutionary services.	3	1	Petition	103					Referred to Secretary War.		
Nagle, Peter	Pension for revolutionary services.	3	2	Rep. of Secretary War.	278					Laid on table.		
Nagle, Philip	Pension for revolutionary services.	20	1	Petition	365	Military Pensions	April 29, 1828	By bill	283	Passed.		
Nagle, Philip	Pension for revolutionary services.	20	2	Pension bill	55	Whole House	Jan. 15, 1829	With amend.	311	Passed	Laid on table.	
Nagle, Philip	Pension for revolutionary services.	21	1	Petition	48	Military Pensions	Jan. 5, 1830	By bill	72	Passed	Passed	App'd May 20, 1830
Nagle, Richard	Pension	20	1	Resolution	465	Military Pensions	April 29, 1828	By bill	283	Passed.		
Nagle, Richard	Pension	20	2	Pension bill	55	Whole House	Jan. 15, 1829	With amend.	311	Passed	Laid on table.	
Nagle, Richard	Pension	21	1	Petition	48	Military Pensions	Jan. 5, 1830	By bill	72	Passed	Passed	App'd May 20, 1830
Naif, Jonathan	Pension	30	1	Petition	440	Invalid Pensions.						
Naif, Jonathan	Pension	30	2	Petition	174	Invalid Pensions	76	Favorable	770	Referred to Committee Whole House.		
Naif, Jonathan	Pension	31	1	Petition	276	Invalid Pensions.						
Nail, Henry, representatives of.	Confirmation of title to land	8	2	Petition	106	Select.						
Nail, Henry, representatives of.	Confirmation of title to land	9	1	Petition	188	Public Lands	Mar. 11, 1806	Report not of record.		Referred to Committee Whole House.		
Nail, Henry, representatives of.	Confirmation of title to land	9	2	Petition	479	Public Lands.						
Nail, Henry, representatives of.	Confirmation of title to land	10	1	Petition	18	Public Lands.						
Nail, Henry, and others	Right of pre emption	15	1	House bill	218	Whole House	Feb. 6, 1818	With't amend.	70	Referred to Committee Whole House.		
Nail, Mary, late Mary Wilson.	Five years' half-pay and land, for services of husband in revolutionary war.	23	1	Petition	45	Invalid Pensions	Jan. 21, 1834	Adverse		Laid on table.		
Nail, Mathew	(See Mathew Neale)	21	1		74							
Nailor, Dixon	(See assignee of administrator of John Nailor.)	2	1		475							
Nailor, John, assignee of administrator.	Pension for revolutionary services.	2	1	Petition	475					Referred to Secretary of War.		
Naismith, Alexander	Invalid pension	13	3	Pension bill	740	Whole House	Mar. 1, 1815	With amend.	303	Passed	Passed	App'd March 3, 1815
Naismith, Alexander	Arrears of pension	22	1	Petition	415	Invalid Pensions.						
Naismith, Alexander	Arrears of pension	22	1	Senate bill	779	Invalid Pensions	June 1, 1832	With't amend.	S. 153	Referred to Committee Whole House.		
Nance, Eaton	Confirmation of title to land	28	1	House bill	268	Public Lands	Feb. 28, 1844	With't amend.	82	Passed	Passed	App'd June 15, 1844
Nance, Richard	For correction of name in land patent.	23	1	Petition	67	Priv. Land Claims.	79	Favorable; bill	86	Passed	Passed	App'd June 26, 1834

2—70

List of private claims presented to the House of Representatives of the United States from the 1st to the 31st Congress, inclusive—**Continued.**

Names of claimants.	Nature or object of the claim.	Congress.	Session.	How brought before the House of Reps.	Page of journal.	To what committee of the House referred.	No. or date of the report.	Nature of the report.	No. of the bill.	How disposed of by the House of Reps.	How disposed of by the Senate.	Date of the act of Congress, and remarks.
Nancy, (ship,) owners of	Indemnity for vessel sunk in defence of Baltimore.	21	1	Memorial	82	Commerce	Feb. 2, 1830	Favorable; bill	191	Passed	Passed	App'd May 29, 1830
Nanna, Abraham	Indemnity for damages to his farm by American troops.	4	1	Rep. of Secretary Treasury.	388	Claims	May 31, 1796	Adverse	......	Laid on table.		
Nanna, Abraham, heirs of.	Payment for supplies furnished U. States army.	12	1	Petition	11	Claims	Nov. 27, 1811	Favorable	......	Recommitted.		
Nanna, Abraham, heirs of.	Payment for supplies furnished U. States army.	14	1	Petition	339	Pens. & Rev. Cl'ms.						
Nanna, Abraham, heirs of.	Payment for supplies furnished U. States army.	15	2	Petition	65	Pens. & Rev. Cl'ms.						
Nanna, Abraham, heirs of.	Payment for supplies furnished U. States army.	18	1	Petition	297	Pens. & Rev. Clm's.	Mar. 22, 1824	Adverse	......	Laid on table.		
Nanna, Abraham, heirs of.	Payment for supplies furnished U. States army.	24	1	Petition	205	Claims.						
Nanna, Reese	(See Abraham Nanna, heirs of)	12	1	....	11							
Nantucket Steamboat Company.	Compensation for carrying the mail.	25	2	Senate bill	301	P. Of. & P. Roads.	641	Adverse	S. 71	Referred to Committee Whole House.		
Nantucket Steamboat Company.	Compensation for carrying the mail.	25	3	Senate bill	546	P. Of. & P. Roads.	Mar. 2, 1839	With't amend.	S. 129	Referred to Committee Whole House.		
Nantucket Steamboat Company.	Compensation for carrying the mail.	26	1	Senate bill	811	Commerce	May 16, 1840	With't amend.	S. 130	Referred to Committee Whole House.		
Nantucket Steamboat Company.	Compensation for carrying the mail.	26	2	Senate bill	256	....	....	....	S. 167			
Nantucket Steamboat Company.	Compensation for carrying the mail.	27	2	Senate bill	1194	P. Of. & P. Roads.	....	....	S. 69			
Nantucket Steamboat Company.	Compensation for carrying the mail.	27	3	Senate bill	118	P. Of. & P. Roads.	Jan. 19, 1843	With't amend.	S. 18	Passed	Passed	App'd Feb. 6, 1843
Nantz, John	Arrears of pension	26	1	Petition	330	Naval Affairs.						
Nantz, John	Arrears of pension	26	2	Petition	79	Naval Affairs.						
Napier, Benjamin A., *et al.*	Remuneration for schooner Tempest impressed into U. S. service.	25	3	Petition	121	Claims.						
Napier, Benjamin A., *et al.*	Remuneration for schooner Tempest impressed into U. S. service.	30	1	Petition	270	Claims.						
Napier, Benjamin A., *et al.*	Remuneration for schooner Tempest impressed into U. S. service.	30	2	Petition	322	Claims	136	Adverse	......	Laid on table.		
Napier, James R.	(See William H. Bedford, agent)	28	1	....	262							
Napier, John S., surety of.	Release from bond to Post Office Department.	29	1	Resolution	492	P. Of. and P. Roads.						
Napier, John S., surety of.	Release from bond to Post Office Department.	29	2	Petition	55	P. Of. and P. Roads.	....	....	......	....	....	Leave to withdraw, 2d sess., 30th Cong.
Napier, Rapellye & Bennett, *et al.*	Remission of duties on muskets and pistols.	18	1	Senate bill	328	Whole House	April 30, 1824	With't amend.	S. 58	Passed	....	App'd May 5, 1824
Napier, Thomas	Compensation for revolutionary services.	2	1	Petition	452	....	....	....	......	Referred to Secretary of War.		
Napier, Thomas	Compensation for revolutionary services.	2	2	Rep. of Secretary War.	735	....	....	....	......	Laid on table.		
Napier, Thomas, *et al.*	To have certain duties refunded	17	2	Petition	142	Ways and Means.						
Napier, Thomas, *et al.*	To have certain duties refunded	18	1	Petition	109	Ways and Means.						
Napier, Thomas, *et al.*	To have certain duties refunded	18	1	Senate bill	328	Whole House	April 30, 1824	With't amend.	S. 58	Passed	Passed	App'd April 29, 1824
Napier, Thomas J.	Payment for horses lost in Mexican war.	30	2	Memorial	461	Claims.						
Napp, Joshua	Pension for revolutionary services.	21	2	Resolution	203	Military Pensions.						

List of private claims presented to the House of Representatives of the United States from the 1st to the 31st Congress, inclusive—Continued.

Names of claimants.	Nature or object of the claim.	Congress.	Session.	How brought before the House of Reps.	Page of journal.	To what committee of the House referred.	No. or date of the report.	Nature of the report.	No. of the bill.	How disposed of by the House of Reps.	How disposed of by the Senate.	Date of the act of Congress, and remarks.
Napertandy, John	Pension for services in war of 1812.	28	2	Petition	64	Invalid Pensions				Discharged; laid on table.		
Napertandy, John	Pension for services in war of 1812.	29	1	Petition	118	Invalid Pensions	Dec. 31, 1845	Adverse		Laid on table.		
Napton, William, *et al*	Compensation for supplies furnished New Jersey volunteers.	30	1	Resolution	627					Laid on table.		
Narney, Andrew	Liquidation of certificates of public debt.	4	1	Rep. of Secretary Treasury.	388	Claims	May 31, 1796	Adverse		Laid on table.		
Narrows, James	Pension	27	3	Petition	471	Invalid Pensions.						
Nash, Dempsey	(See Thomas Bressie, heirs of)	30	1		879							
Nash, Ebenezer	Invalid pension	1	3	Petition and rep't of Sec. War.	355, 393					Laid on table.		
Nash, Francis	Renewal of loan of office certificates.	3	2	Petition	290	Select	Feb. 23, 1795	By bill	122	Referred to Committee Whole House.		
Nash, Francis, representatives of.	Seven years' half pay for revolutionary service.	23	1	Senate bill	846	Rev. Claims	June 28, 1834	With't amend.	S. 179	Passed		App'd June 30, 1834
Nash, Ira	Remuneration for Indian depredations.	24	1	Petition	65	Indian Affairs	131	Favorable; bill	141	Passed	Passed	App'd July 1, 1836
Nash, James	Remuneration for Indian depredations.	24	1	Petition	65	Indian Affairs.						
Nash, Joana	(See William Nash, widow of)	13	2		241							
Nash, John	Pension	21	2	Petition	222	Military Pensions.						
Nash, John, jr	Pension	21	2	Petition	372	Military Pensions.						
Nash, Joseph	Pension for revolutionary services.	2	1	Petition	451					Referred to Secretary of War.		
Nash, Michael	Balance due him for revolutionary services.	18	2	Petition	136	Pens. & Rev. Cl'ms.	Jan. 26, 1825	Adverse		Laid on table.		
Nash, Michael, widow of.	Pension	28	1	Petition	362	Rev. Pensions.						
Nash, Nancy	(See Michael Nash, widow of.)											
Nash, Phineas	Permission to enter land at minimum price.	24	1	Petition	435	Public Lands.						
Nash, Sylvester	Invalid pension	23	1	Petition	80	Invalid Pensions				Discharged; laid on table.		
Nash, Sylvester	Invalid pension	24	1	Petition	98	Invalid Pensions				Discharged; laid on table.		
Nash, Sylvester	Invalid pension	24	2	Petition	311	Invalid Pensions				Discharged; laid on table.		
Nash, Sylvester	Invalid pension	25	2	Petition	560	Invalid Pensions	644	Favorable; bill	620	Passed	Adverse report.	
Nash, Sylvester	Invalid pension	25	3	Petition	90	Invalid Pensions	131	Favorable; bill	998	Passed	Adverse report.	
Nash, Sylvester	Invalid pension	26	1	Petition	161	Invalid Pensions.	676	Adverse		Laid on table.		
Nash, Sylvester	Invalid pension	26	1	Petition	1001	Invalid Pensions	676	Adverse		Laid on table.		
Nash, Sylvester	Invalid pension	27	2	Petition	268	Invalid Pensions	433	Adverse.		Laid on table.		
Nash, Sylvester	Invalid pension	31	1	Petition	307	Invalid Pensions.						
Nash, Thomas, heirs of	Indemnity for French spoliations prior to 1800.	26	1	Memorial	182	Foreign Affairs	343	Favorable	319	Referred to Committee Whole House.		
Nash, Thornton and John.	(See Winder Nash, heirs of.)	23	1		639							
Nash, William, widow of.	Pension	13	2	Petition	241	Pens. & Rev. Cl'ms.				Discharged; referred to Secretary War.		
Nash, Winder, heirs of	Compensation for revolutionary services.	23	1	Petition	639	Rev. Claims.						
Nason, Richard	(See Hugh Milling, heirs of.)	25	2		683							
Natchez, city of	Confirmation of title to land	8	1	Petition	440	Select	Dec. 15, 1803	Favorable		Recommitted.		
							Mar. 10, 1804	Favorable; bill ordered.	212	Referred to Committee Whole House.		

List of private claims presented to the House of Representatives of the United States from the 1st to the 31st Congress, inclusive—Continued.

Names of claimants.	Nature or object of the claim.	Congress.	Session.	How brought before the House of Reps.	Page of journal.	To what committee of the House referred.	No. or date of the report.	Nature of the report.	No. of the bill.	How disposed of by the House of Reps.	How disposed of by the Senate.	Date of the act of Congress, and remarks.
Natchez, city of	Confirmation of title to vacant land within said city.	8	2	Memorial and petition.	7	Select.						
Natchez, city of	Confirmation of title to vacant land within said city.	12	1	Petition	115	Public Lands.						
Nathan, Simon	Liquidation of his claim against the United States.	1	2	Petition	285					Referred to Secretary Treasury.		
Nathan, Simon	Liquidation of his claim against the United States.	2	1	Rep. of Secretary Treasury.	580					Laid on table.		
Nations, Baylis	Pre-emption right to certain land	23	2	Petition	278							Not referred.
Nations, Christopher	Pre-emption right to certain land	28	1	Petition	433	Public Lands.						
Nations, Christopher, widow of.	Confirmation of title to certain land	29	1	Petition	220	Priv. Land Claims.	493	Adverse		Laid on table.		
Nations, Mary	(See Christopher Nations, widow of.)	29	1		220							
Naudi, Xaverio	Settlement of accounts as chargé de affairs at Tripoli.	14	1	Senate bill	252	Com. and Manuf.	April 11, 1816	With't amend.		Passed		App'd April 20, 1816
Naught, George	Pre emption right to certain land	23	1	Petition	447					Referred to Committee Whole House on bill No. 104.		
Navarre, Francis, *et al.*	Compensation for property destroyed in war of 1812.	16	1	Report of Com'r Claims.	85	Claims.						
Navarre, Francis, *et al.*	Compensation for property destroyed in war of 1812.	17	1	Petition	78	Claims	Jan. 17, 1822	Adverse		Referred to Committee Whole House.		
Navarre, Francis, *et al.*	Compensation for property destroyed in war of 1812.	17	2	Petition and docs.	83	Whole House.						
Navarre, Isadore	Pay for batteau taken for the use of the United States army in 1813.	22	1	Petition	266	Claims	418	Adverse		Referred to Committee Whole House.		
Navarre, Touissant	Grant of certain lands	22	1	Petition	294	Public Lands.						
Navy, officers of, in revolutionary war.	For the same compensation allowed to officers of the army.	1	2	Petition	182	Select	May 13, 1790	Adverse		Rejected.		
Navy, boatswains, gunners, carpenters, and sailmakers, of.	For an increase of pay	24	1	Petition	61	Naval Affairs	511	Favorable	508	Referred to Committee Whole House.		
Navy, junior surgeons of the.	Increase of compensation	26	1	Petition	627	Naval Affairs	July 2, 1840			Laid on table.		
Navy, marine guard of Exploring Expedition.	Extra compensation for services beyond enlistment.	27	3	Petition	150	Naval Affairs				Discharged; laid on table.		
Navy, Moses	(See Joseph Stewart, *et al*)	13	3		751							
Navy officers of schooner Shark.	Indemnity for losses by shipwreck.	30	1	Petition & memorial.	334	Naval Affairs.						
Navy, petty officers and seamen of the Cyane.	Increase of pay	26	1	Petition & memorial.	938	Naval Affairs.						
Navy, professors of mathematics.	Increase of pay	30	1	Petition	380	Naval Affairs.						
Navy, sailing-masters	Increase of pay	24	1	Petition	99	Naval Affairs	511	Favorable	508	Referred to Committee Whole House.		
Navy, sailing-masters	Increase of pay	25	2	Petition	593	Naval Affairs.						
Navy, seamen of	Arrearages of revolutionary pay	2	1	Petition	466					Referred to Secretary War.		
Navy, surgeons of	Increase of compensation	10	1	Memorial and petition.	219	Select	April 21, 1808	Favorable	98	Laid on table.		

List of private claims presented to the House of Representatives of the United States from the 1st to the 31st Congress, inclusive—Continued.

Names of claimants.	Nature or object of the claim.	Congress.	Session.	How brought before the House of Reps.	Page of journal.	To what committee of the House referred.	No. or date of the report.	Nature of the report.	No. of the bill.	How disposed of by the House of Reps.	How disposed of by the Senate.	Date of the act of Congress, and remarks.
Navy, warrant officers of..	Increase of compensation........	24	1	Memorial	61	Naval Affairs.....	511	Favorable....	508	Referred to Committee Whole House.		
Navy, warrant officers of..	Increase of compensation........	26	1	Petition	304	Naval Affairs.						
Navy, warrant officers of..	Increase of compensation........	27	2	Petition	63	Naval Affairs.						
Navy yards, clerks in	Increase of compensation........	24	1	Petition	214	Naval Affairs.						
Navy yard, N. York, boatswain, gunner, carpenter, and sailmaker of.	Increase of compensation........	24	1	Petition	188	Naval Affairs.....	511	Favorable....	508	Referred to Committee Whole House.		
Navy yard, Washington city, mechanics in.	Pay for lost time by suspension of of work during the year 1843.	28	2	Petition	391	Naval Affairs.....	Feb. 7, 1845	Adverse	......	Recommitted.		
Naylor, John C.........	Compensation for services in surveyor's office, Mississippi.	22	1	Petition	172	Claims.						
Naylor, John C.........	Compensation for services in surveyor's office, Mississippi.	22	2	Resolution	58	Public Lands.....	Jan. 11, 1833	Favorable....	682	Recommitted to Ways and Means.		
Naylor, John C.........	Compensation for services in surveyor's office, Mississippi.	23	1	Petition	139	Public Lands.....	Jan. 9, 1834	Favorable....	166	Passed	Passed	App'd June 30, 1834
Naylor, W. H..........	Pay for labor on Cumberland road.	30	1	Petition	657	Claims.						
Nayson, Nathaniel, widow of.	For duplicate land warrant, the original being lost.	29	1	Senate bill	865	Public Lands.....	June 17, 1846	With't amend.	S. 166	Passed	Passed	App'd June 19, 1846
Neaff, John	(See Conrad Houseman, *et al.*)											
Neagle, Philip	(See Philip Nagle)	20	2	....	365							
Neagle, Richard.........	Pension for revolutionary services.	20	1	Resolution	465	Military Pensions..	April 29, 1828	Favorable....	283	Passed.		
Neagle, Richard.........	Pension for revolutionary services.	20	2	Pension bill	55	Whole House.....	Jan. 15, 1829	With amend..	311	Passed	Laid on table.	
Neagle, Richard.........	Pension for revolutionary services.	21	1	Petition	48	Military Pensions.						
Neal, Benjamin.........	Remission of duty accruing on stills	7	1	Petition	63	Claims	Jan. 29, 1802	Adverse	......	Rejected.		
Neal, Benjamin, widow of	Pension	27	3	Petition	222	Naval Affairs......	68	Favorable....	737	Passed	Adverse report.	See joint res., No. 32.
Neal, Hosea, heirs of	Land for services in war of 1812.	23	2	Resolution	276	Military Affairs.						
Neal, Hosea, widow of...	Compensation for services	25	2	Documents.....	171	Military Affairs....	391	Adverse	......	Laid on table.		
Neal, Hosea, widow of...	Compensation for services	25	2	Documents.....	1028	Claims.						
Neal, James, (Maine.)....	Indemnity for French spoliations prior to 1800.	26	1	Memorial	182	Foreign Affairs....	343	Favorable....	319	Referred to Committee Whole House.		
Neal, James, administrator of.	Indemnity for French spoliations prior to 1800.	29	2	Memorial	53	Foreign Affairs.						
Neal, John, *et al.*.......	Indemnity for French spoliations prior to 1800.	31	1	Petition	337	Foreign Affairs....	355	Favorable....	318	Referred to Committee Whole House.		
Neal, Jonathan, *et al*, owners of brig Osprey.	Indemnity for Brazilian spoliations	20	1	Memorial	222	Foreign Affairs....	....	....	......	Leave to withdraw.		
Neal, Jonathan, *et al*, owners of brig Osprey.	Indemnity for Brazilian spoliations	20	2	Petition	49	Foreign Affairs....	Dec. 30, 1828	Adverse	......	Laid on table.		
Neal, Mary	(See Benjamin Neal, widow of).	27	3	....	222							
Neal, Samuel, widow of ..	Pension	26	1	Senate bill	836	Rev. Pensions	May 25, 1840	Favorable....	S. 257	Referred to Committee Whole House.		
Neal, Samuel, widow of ..	Pension	26	2	Senate bill	334	Rev. Pensions	....	....	S. 201			
Neal, Susan, *et al.*......	Continuation of pension	22	2	Petition	40	Naval Affairs.						
Neal, William A........	Pension	22	2	Petition	176	Invalid Pensions ..	....	....	......	Discharged; laid on table.		
Neal, William, *et al.*....	Compensation for services in war of 1812.	31	1	Petition	730	Rev. Pensions	216	Adverse	......	Laid on table.		
Neale, Armistead	Increase of compensation as postmaster.	31	1	Petition	691	P. Of. & P. Roads.	....	....	......	Discharged; laid on table.		
Neale, Augustus and Austin.	(See Ghent, claimants under treaty of.)	30	1	....	398							

List of private claims presented to the House of Representatives of the United States from the 1st to the 31st Congress, inclusive—Continued.

Names of claimants.	Nature or object of the claim.	Congress.	Session.	How brought before the House of Reps.	Page of journal.	To what committee of the House referred.	No. or date of the report.	Nature of the report.	No. of the bill.	How disposed of by the House of Reps.	How disposed of by the Senate.	Date of the act of Congress, and remarks.
Neale, Christopher	Increase of fees as coroner of Alexandria county, D. C.	17	1	Petition	332	Dist. of Columbia.						
Neale, Christopher	Increase of salary as judge of orphan's court, Alexandria county, D. C.	24	1	Petition	197	Dist. of Columbia.	Jan. 30, 1836	Favorable; bill	268	Referred to Committee Whole House.		
Neale, Christopher	Increase of salary as judge of orphan's court, Alexandria county, D. C.	25	2	Petition	113	Dist. of Columbia.	Jan. 4, 1838	Favorable; bill	282	Passed	Passed	App'd June 28, 1838
Neale, Christopher	Indemnity for property destroyed in war of 1812.	31	1	Petition	809	Claims.						
Neale, Mathew, *alias* Mathew Nail.	Pension	21	1	Petition	74	Military Pensions.						
Neale, Seeley, *et al.*	Compensation in land for laying out St. Joseph's road, in Michigan.	22	1	Petition	264	Public Lands	Feb. 24, 1832	Adverse	......	Referred to Committee Whole House.		
Neale, Thomas, surety of.	Release from liability	18	2	Petition	159	P. Of. & P. Roads.	Feb. 21, 1825	Adverse	......	Laid on table.		
Nealy, Henry	Pension for services in war of 1812	28	2	Petition	207	Invalid Pensions.						
Neamathla, a Seminole Indian.	Fee simple of a treaty grant of land.	18	2	Petition	231	Public Lands.						
Neapolitan Indemnity Stock Proprietors.	For purchase of said stock by the United States.	25	2	Memorial	303	Ways and Means.	441	Adverse	......	Laid on table.		
Nebinger, George, heirs of.	Payment of certain final-settlement certificates.	12	1	Petition	288	Whole House.						
Nebinger, George, heirs of.	Payment of certain final settlement certificates.	12	2	Petition	579	Claims	Feb. 9, 1813	Favorable	252	Referred to Committee Whole House.		
Nebinger, George, heirs of.	Payment of certain final-settlement certificates.	13	1	Petition	36	Claims.						
Nebinger, George, heirs of.	Payment of certain final-settlement certificates.	14	1	Petition	126	Pens. & Rev. Cl'ms.	Jan. 11, 1816	Favorable; bill	......	Passed.		
Nebinger, George, heirs of.	Payment of certain final-settlement certificates.	14	2	Petition	123	Pens. & Rev. Cl'ms.	Feb. 3, 1816	Favorable	96	Referred to Committee Whole House.		
Nebinger, George, heirs of.	Payment of certain final-settlement certificates.	15	1	Petition	171	Pens. & Rev. Cl'ms.	....	....	......	Discharged; leave to withdraw.		
Nedean, Martin, *alias* Martin Nideon.	Confirmation of title to land	23	2	Petition	78	Priv. Land Claims.	Jan. 15, 1835	Adverse	......	Laid on table.		
Needham, Jeremiah	Pension for revolutionary services.	26	1	Petition and docs.	936	Rev. Pensions	714	Adverse	......	Laid on table.		
Needham, John D., *et al.*	Relief for imprisonment by United States.	15	1	Petition	136	Select.						
Needs, James	Pension for revolutionary services.	20	2	Resolution	224	Military Pensions.	Feb. 15, 1829	Pension bill.	440	Passed.		
Needs, James	Pension for revolutionary services.	21	1	Petition	49	Military Pensions.	Jan. 5, 1830	Pension bill.	72	Passed	Passed, with amendment.	App'd May 20, 1830
Neel, John M	Pension	23	1	Petition	333	Invalid Pensions	....	....	......	Discharged; laid on table.		
Neel, William	Pension for revolutionary services.	26	1	Petition	173	Rev. Pensions	Mar. 5, 1840	Favorable	178	Passed	Indef. postp'd.	
Neel, William, heirs of	Pension for revolutionary services.	26	2	Petition	78	Rev. Pensions.						
Neeley, James C	Payment for a horse lost in Mexican war.	30	1	Petition	305	Claims	Feb. 29, 1848	Favorable	238	Referred to Committee Whole House.		
Neely, Abraham	Invalid pension	6	1	Petition	583	Claims	Feb. 18, 1800	Adverse	......	Leave to withdraw.		
Neely, Caleb	Payment for a horse lost in Mexican war.	30	1	Petition	305	Claims	Feb. 29, 1848	Favorable	238	Referred to Committee Whole House.		
Neely, Henry	Invalid pension	30	1	Petition	522	Invalid Pensions	April 28, 1848	....	......	Discharged; laid on table.		
Neely, Capt. R. P	Extra pay for services of his company in Cherokee nation.	25	3	Resolution	171	Claims.						

List of private claims presented to the House of Representatives of the United States from the 1st to the 31st Congress, inclusive—Continued.

Names of claimants.	Nature or object of the claim.	Congress.	Session.	How brought before the House of Reps.	Page of journal	To what committee of the House referred.	No. or date of the report.	Nature of the report.	No. of the bill.	How disposed of by the House of Reps.	How disposed of by the Senate.	Date of the act of Congress, and remarks.
Neely, Capt. R. P.	Extra pay for services of his company in Cherokee nation.	26	1	Petition	170	Claims.						
Neely, Capt. R. P.	Extra pay for services of his company in Cherokee nation.	26	2	Petition	38	Claims.						
Neely, Samuel	Invalid pension	18	2	Petition	127	Pens. & Rev. Cl'ms.				Rejected, and leave to withdraw.		
Neely, Samuel	Invalid pension	23	1	Petition	141	Invalid Pensions	Feb. 14, 1834	Adverse		Laid on table.		
Neely, Samuel	Invalid pension	26	2	Resolution	63	Invalid Pensions	63	Adverse.		Laid on table.		
Neely, Samuel	Invalid pension	27	2	Petition	60	Invalid Pensions	802	Favorable	456	Ref'd to Com. W. H.		
Neely, Samuel	Invalid pension	27	3	House bill	89				456	Passed	Indef. postp'd.	
Neely, Samuel	Invalid pension	28	1	Petition	646	Invalid Pensions	517	Favorable	392	Referred to Committee Whole House.		
Neely, Samuel	Invalid pension	28	2	House bill	344	Whole House			392	Passed	Passed, with amendment.	App'd March 1, 1845
Neely, William	Pension for revolutionary services.	22	1	Petition	558	Rev. Pensions.						
Neely, or Neley, William.	Pension for revolutionary services.	9	2	Pension bill	608	Whole House	Feb. 28, 1807	With amend.	216	Passed	Passed, with amendment.	App'd March 3, 1807
Neereamer, Jonathan	Pension for services in 1812	29	1	Petition	169	Invalid Pensions.						
Neese, Peter	Pension	22	1	Petition	330	Rev. Pensions.						
Neevis, Daniel, widow of.	Pension for revolutionary services.	26	1	Petition	950	Rev. Pensions.						
Neevis, Mary	(See Daniel Neevis, widow of)	26	1		950							
Negus, Samuel	Compensation for revolutionary services.	2	1	Petition	464					Referred to Secretary War.		
Neibert, Joseph, assignee of.	Confirmation of title to land	23	2	Petition	438	Priv. Land Claims.						
Neibert, Joseph, assignee of	Confirmation of title to land	24	1	Petition	121, 266	Priv. Land Claims.	142	Favorable	149	Passed	Rejected.	
Neibert, Joseph, assignee of.	Confirmation of title to land	25	2	Petition	374	Priv. Land Claims.	665	Favorable	639	Recommitted.		
							Mar. 21, 1838	With't amend.	639	Passed	Passed	App'd Mar. 28, 1838
Neigaman, John	Pre-emption right to land	18	1	House bill	151	Whole House	May 13, 1824	With amend.	65	Passed	Passed	App'd May 26, 1824
Neil, Daniel, heirs of.	Seven years' half-pay	22	1	Petition	288	Rev. Claims	309	Favorable	389	Referred to Committee Whole House.		
Neil, Daniel, heirs of.	Seven years' half-pay	23	1	Petition	39	Rev. Claims	64	Favorable	74	Passed	Laid on table.	
Neil, Daniel, heirs of.	Seven years' half-pay	23	2	Petition	76	Rev. Claims.						
Neil, Daniel, heirs of.	Seven years' half pay	24	1	Petition	102	Rev. Claims.						
Neil, Daniel, heirs of.	Seven years' half-pay	25	2	Petition	48	Rev. Claims.						
Neil, Daniel, heirs of.	Seven years' half-pay	26	1	Petition	166	Rev. Claims	240	Adverse		Laid on table		Leave to withdraw, 2d session.
Neil, Robert	Pension	13	2	Petition	175	Claims	Mar. 29, 1814	As an amend't to H. bill.	166	Passed	Passed	App'd April 18, 1814
Neil, William	Pension for revolutionary services.	25	2	Resolution	527	Rev. Pensions				Laid on table.		
Neil, William	Pension for revolutionary services.	25	2	Petition	547	Rev. Pensions				Laid on table.		
Neil, William	Pension for revolutionary services.	25	3	Petition	88	Rev. Pensions.						
Neill, Alexander	(See Luke Tiernan, executor of)	29	2		489							
Neill, Bernard O.	(See Bernard O'Neill)	29	1		618							
Neill, John, *alais* John Neile	Pension for revolutionary services.	18	2	Petition	183	Pens. & Rev. Cl'ms.				Discharged; laid on table.		Leave to withdraw.
Neill, or Neil, Robert	Relief against the decesion of the Auditor and Comptroller of the Treasury on his claim.	1	3	Petition	358					Referred to Secretary Treasury.		
Neill, or Neil, Robert	Relief against the decision of the Auditor and Comptroller of the Treasury on his claim.	2	1	Rep. of Secretary Treasury.	585	Whole House	April 24, 1792	Adverse		Rejected.		

List of private claims presented to the House of Representatives of the United States from the 1st to the 31st Congress, inclusive—Continued.

Names of claimants.	Nature or object of the claim.	Congress.	Session.	How brought before the House of Reps.	Page of journal.	To what committee of the House referred.	No. or date of the report.	Nature of the report.	No. of the bill.	How disposed of by the House of Reps.	How disposed of by the Senate.	Date of the act of Congress, and remarks.
Neiler, John, heirs of	Release from liability on certain bond.	19	2	Petition	134	Ways and Means.						
Neilly, Charles	Pension	15	1	Petition	199	Pens. & Rev. Cl'ms.				Discharged; referred to Secretary of War.		
Neilson, George, heirs of	Renewal of bounty land warrant	27	2	Petition	228	Priv. Land Claims.	849	Favorable	492	Ordered to 3d reading.		
Neilson, George, heirs of	Renewal of bounty land warrant	27	3	House bill	89				492	Passed	Passed	App'd March 3, 1843
Neilson, Joseph	Pension	19	2	Petition	111	Military Pensions.						
Neilson, Joseph	Pension	20	2	Pension bill	55	Whole House	Jan. 15, 1829	With amend.	311	Passed	Laid on table.	
Neilson, Joseph	Pension	21	1	Petition	47	Military Pensions	April 5, 1830	By bill	72	Passed	Passed	App'd May 20, 1830
Neilson, William	Reimbursement of medical expenses while in United States service.	28	1	Petition	62	Claims	6	Adverse		Laid on table.		
Neilson, William	Reimbursement of medical expenses while in United States service.	29	1	Petition	465	Claims.						
Neilson, William	Indemnity for French spoliations prior to 1800.	26	1	Memorial	182	Foreign Affairs	343	Favorable	319	Referred to Committee Whole House.		
Neiswanger, Jacob	That patents may issue for certain lands.	28	1	Petition	107	Public Lands				Discharged; laid on table.		
Nell, Elizabeth	(See Jacob Nell, widow of.)	20	1		417							
Nell, Jacob, widow of	Pension	20	1	Petition	417	Military Pensions	April 1, 1828	Adverse		Laid on table.		
Nellis, Henry W	Invalid pension	3	1	Rep. of Secretary War.	131	Select	May 26, 1794	Jt. res. to refer to Sec. War.	J. R. 12	Passed	Passed	App'd June 9, 1794
Nelmes, Jeremiah, widow of.	Renewal of lost certificate	2	2	Petition	626	Whole House						See act of April 21, 1794.
Nelmes, Thomas, administrator of.	Payment of claim	2	1	Petition	539					Referred to Secretary of Treasury.		
Nelson, Alexander, attorney in fact for others.	Compensation for revolutionary services.	1	3	Petition and rep't Sec. of War.	342, 385					Laid on table.		
Nelson, Andrew, heirs of	Payment of certain prize-money	21	1	Petition	606	Naval Affairs	May 25, 1830	Favorable	488	Referred to Committee Whole House.		
Nelson, Andrew, administrator of.	Payment of certain prize-money	22	1	Petition	42	Claims	330	Favorable	414	Referred to Committee Whole House.		
Nelson, Andrew, administrator of.	Payment of certain prize-money	22	1	Senate bill	745	Naval Affairs	June 2, 1832	Favorable	S. 85	Passed with amend't.	Passed	App'd July 14, 1832
Nelson, Ann	Pension for revolutionary services.	27	2	Resolution	399	Rev. Pensions.						
Nelson, Hans	Compensation for services on frigate President.	29	1	Memorial	847	Naval Affairs.						
Nelson, Heman	Release from certain judgment	18	2	Petition	210	Judiciary.						
Melson, Hugh	Pension for revolutionary services.	19	1	Resolution	70	Military Pensions	164	Adverse		Laid on table.		
Nelson, Hugh	Pension for revolutionary services.	19	2	Petition	67	Military Pensions.						
Nelson, Hugh, wife, *et al.*	(See Francis Kinlock, heirs of.)	19	2		189							
Nelson, Jeremiah	Indemnity for French spoliations prior to 1800.	26	1	Memorial	182	Foreign Affairs	343	Favorable	319	Referred to Committee Whole House.		
Nelson, Major John	For land in lieu of land ceded to Chicasaw Indians.	4	2	Petition	656	Claims.						
Nelson, Major John	For land in lieu of land ceded to Chicasaw Indians.	5	2	Petition	146	Claims	Jan. 23, 1798	Favorable		Rejected.		
Nelson, Captain John	Commutation of half-pay	22	1	Petition	333	Rev. Claims	Feb. 24, 1832	Adverse		Laid on table.		
Nelson, Captain John, *et al.*	Additional compensation while prisoner of war, 1812.	26	1	Resolution	392	Claims.						

List of private claims presented to the House of Representatives of the United States from the 1st to the 31st Congress, inclusive—Continued.

Names of claimants.	Nature or object of the claim.	Congress.	Session.	How brought before the House of Reps.	Page of journal.	To what committee of the House referred.	No. or date of the report.	Nature of the report.	No. of the bill.	How disposed of by the House of Reps.	How disposed of by the Senate.	Date of the act of Congress, and remarks.
Nelson, John, (Ky.)	Compensation for revolutionary services.	19	2	Petition	199	Rev. Claims.						
Nelson, John, (Va.)	Compensation for revolutionary services.	10	2	Petition	463	Claims.						
Nelson, John, (Va.)	Compensation for revolutionary services.	11	1	Petition	28	Claims.						
Nelson, John, (Va.)	Compensation for revolutionary services.	11	2	Petition	120	Claims	April 12, 1810	Adverse		Referred to Committee Whole House.		
Nelson, John, (Va.)	Compensation for revolutionary services.	11	3	Petition	442	Claims	Feb. 1, 1811	Adverse		Referred to Committee Whole House.		
Nelson, John, (Va.)	Compensation for revolutionary services.	12	1	Petition	40	Claims.						
Nelson, John, (Va.)	Compensation for revolutionary services.	12	2	Petition	676	Claims.						
Nelson, John, (Va.)	Arrears of pay	11	2	Petition	220	Claims.						
Nelson, John, (Va.)	Arrears of pay	14	2	Petition	80	Pens. & Rev. Cl'ms.	Jan. 10, 1817	Adverse		Laid on table.		
Nelson, John, heirs of	Compensation as surgeon in revolutionary war.	31	1	Petition	595	Rev. Claims.						
Nelson, John, heirs of	Commutation pay for revolutionary services.	31	2	Petition	122	Rev. Pensions.						
Nelson, Joseph	Pension for revolutionary services.	20	1	Resolution	90	Military Pensions.						
Nelson, Joseph	Arrears of revolutionary pay	22	1	Resolution	228	Rev. Claims.						
Nelson, Magnus	Release from imprisonment	14	2	Petition	136	Ways and Means.						
Nelson, Mary, (Ill.)	(See Col. William Nelson, widow of.)	27	2		375							
Nelson, Oliver	(See Exploring Expedition)	27	3		149							
Nelson, Robert	Pension for revolutionary services.	15	2	Petition	215	Rev. Pensions	Feb. 11, 1819	Adverse		Laid on table.		
Nelson, Seth	(See Samuel Brown, attorney of)	6	1		530							
Nelson, General Thomas, heirs of.	Remuneration for money advanced and losses sustained during revolutionary war.	23	1	Memorial and petition.	41	Select.						
Nelson, General Thomas, heirs of.	Remuneration for money advanced and losses sustained during revolutionary war.	24	1	Petition	665	Select	847	Favorable	749	Referred to Committee Whole House.		
Nelson, General Thomas, heirs of.	Remuneration for money advanced and losses sustained during revolutionary war.	25	2	Petition	40	Rev. Claims				Discharged; leave to withdraw.		
Nelson, Tyrey	Pension for services in war of 1812.	29	1	Petition	353	Invalid Pensions.						
Nelson, William	(See Andrew Nelson, widow of).	21	1		606							
Nelson, William	Invalid pension	10	1	House bill	232	Whole House	April 19, 1808	With amends.	78	Passed	Passed	App'd April 25, 1808
Nelson, Colonel William, heirs of.	Commutation of half-pay for revolutionary services.	23	1	Memorial	524	Rev. Claims.						
Nelson, Colonel William, heirs of.	Commutation of half-pay for revolutionary services.	24	1	Memorial	697	Rev. Claims.						
Nelson, Colonel William, heirs of.	Commutation of half-pay for revolutionary services.	24	2	Memorial	216	Rev. Claims.						
Nelson, Colonel William, heirs of.	Commutation of half-pay for revolutionary services.	25	2	Memorial	111	Rev. Claims	603	Adverse		Laid on table.		
Nelson, Colonel William, heirs of.	Commutation of half-pay for revolutionary services.	26	1	Petition	164	Rev. Claims	442	Adverse		Laid on table.		
Nelson, Colonel William, heirs of.	Commutation of half-pay for revolutionary services.	26	2	Petition	134	Rev. Claims.						

List of private claims presented to the House of Representatives of the United States from the 1st to the 31st Congress, inclusive—Continued.

Names of claimants.	Nature or object of the claim.	Congress.	Session.	How brought before the House of Reps.	Page of journal.	To what committee of the House referred.	No. or date of the report.	Nature of the report.	No. of the bill.	How disposed of by the House of Reps.	How disposed of by the Senate.	Date of the act of Congress, and remarks.
Nelson, Colonel William, heirs of.	Commutation of half-pay for revolutionary services.	27	2	Petition	61	Rev. Claims	395	Adverse		Laid on table.		
Nelson, Colonel William, heirs of.	Commutation of half-pay for revolutionary services.	31	1	Petition	588	Rev. Claims	423	Adverse		Laid on table.		
Nelson, William, heirs of.	Half-pay for revolutionary services.	24	2	Petition	269	Rev. Claims.						
Nelson, William, widow of	Pension for revolutionary services.	27	2	Petition	375	Rev. Pensions	784	Adverse		Laid on table.		
Nelson, Colonel William, widow of.	Pension for revolutionary services.	27	2	Petition	1356	Rev. Pensions	1002	Favorable	581	Referred to Committee Whole House.		
Neppes, Abraham, heirs of	Further remuneration for arms furnished under contract.	16	1	Senate bill	274	Claims	Mar. 17, 1820	Adverse	S. 47	Referred to Committee Whole House.		
Neptune and Fox, (privateer,) owners of.	Bounty on prisoners captured by them.	24	1	Senate bill	810	Claims	May 18, 1836	Favorable	S. 148	Passed	Passed	App'd July 2, 1836
Nes, Hon. Henry, heirs of.	Per diem to end of session be paid Charles Nes, in trust for children.	31	1	Resolution	1545							Paid out of contingent fund.
Nesbit, Samuel	Invalid pension	10	1	House bill	232	Whole House	April 19, 1808	With amends.	78	Passed	Passed	App'd April 25, 1808
Nesbit, William	Compensation for work at La Plaisance bay.	28	1	Petition	239	Claims	131	Favorable	121	Passed	Passed	App'd June 15, 1844
Nesbit, William, *et al.*	Right to purchase certain lands	4	1	Petition	443					Referred to Committee Whole House on bill No. 134.		
Nesbit & Co	Indemnity for French spoliations prior to 1800.	26	1	Memorial	182	Foreign Affairs	343	Favorable	319	Referred to Committee Whole House.		
Nestler, Cutlip	Invalid pension	4	2	Petition	615	Claims	Jan. 19, 1797	Adverse		Laid on table.		
Nestle, Gotleib	Invalid pension	3	1	Rep. of Secretary War.	131	Select	July 26, 1794	J't. res. to refer to Sec. War.	J.R. 12	Passed	Passed	App'd June 9, 1794
Nestle, Gotleib	Invalid pension	5	2	Petition	220	Claims	April 17, 1798	Adverse		Laid on table.		
Nestle, Gotleib	Invalid pension	5	3	Petition and rep't Sec. of War.	434	Whole House.						
Neth, Lewis, jr	(See James Williams, executors of)	19	1		492							
Neth, Lewis, trustee of	Indemnity for French spoliations prior to 1800.	31	1	Petition	629	Foreign Affairs	355	By bill	318	Referred to Committee Whole House.		
Nettles, Captain William	Pension	20	2	Resolution	259	Military Pensions.						
Nettles, Captain William	Pension	21	1	Resolution	78	Military Pensions	April 2, 1830	Adverse		Laid on table.		
Nettleton, Roger, *et al*	Compensation for services in war of 1812.	25	3	Petition	121	Claims.						
Neufville, John de	Reimbursement of advances in support of American cause, and in negotiating treaty with Holland.	2	1	Memorial	573					Referred to Secretary State.		
Neufville, John de	Reimbursement of advances in support of American cause, and in negotiating treaty with Holland.	2	2	Rep. of Secretary State.	627					Laid on table.		
Neufville, John De, and son.	(See John DeNeufvilles, heir of).	31	1		1035							
Nevelling, John	Compensation for services rendered	4	1	Petition	384	Claims	Jan. 19, 1796	Adverse		Leave to withdraw.		
Neves, Jonathan	(See Canadian refugees)	4	2		614							
Neves, Phineas	(See Canadian refugees)	4	2		614							
Neves, William	Pension for revolutionary services.	25	2	Resolution	525	Rev. Pensions				Discharged; laid on table.		
Nevett, John B	Confirmation of title to land	30	2	Petition	78	Priv. Land Claims	Feb. 8, 1849	Joint resolut'n.	50	Passed	Passed	App'd Feb. 22, 1849
Neville, Joseph	Payment of loan office certificate	13	3	Petition	506	Pens. & Rev. Cl'ms.	Jan. 21, 1815	Adverse		Laid on table.		
Nevils, James	Patent for certain lands	25	2	Resolution	1176	Priv. Land Claims.						
Nevins, John	Pension for revolutionary services.	24	1	Petition	274	Rev. Pensions	Feb. 19, 1836	Adverse		Laid on table.		
Nevins, Peter	Invalid pension	10	1	House bill	232	Whole House	April 19, 1808	With amends.	78	Passed	Passed	App'd April 25, 1808

List of private claims presented to the House of Representatives of the United States from the 1st to the 31st Congress, inclusive—Continued.

Names of claimants.	Nature or object of the claim.	Congress.	Session.	How brought before the House of Reps.	Page of journal.	To what committee of the House referred.	No. or date of the report.	Nature of the report.	No. of the bill.	How disposed of by the House of Reps.	How disposed of by the Senate.	Date of the act of Congress, and remarks.
New, John	Pension for revolutionary services	27	2	Petition	105	Rev. Pensions	784	Adverse		Laid on table.		
Newberry, James	Pension	14	2	House bill	307	Whole House	Feb. 21, 1817	With amends.	91	Passed	Passed, with amendment.	App'd March 3, 1817
Newberry, O. and W., *et al.*	Reimbursement of advances made to Indians.	21	1	Petition	151	Indian Affairs.						
Newbit, Christopher, widow of.	Continuation of pension	26	1	Petition	198	Invalid Pensions	413	Adverse.		Laid on table.		
Newbold, Caleb, executors of.	Compensation for supplies furnished revolutionary army.	2	2	Petition	706					Referred to Secretary of Treasury.		
Newbold, Caleb, executors of.	Compensation for supplies furnished revolutionary army.	3	2	Petition and rep't Sec. Treasury.	284	Claims	Mar. 2, 1795	Favorable		Laid on table.		
Newbold, Caleb, executors of.	Compensation for supplies furnished revolutionary army.	4	1	Petition and docs.	409	Claims.						
Newbold, Caleb, executors of.	Compensation for supplies furnished revolutionary army.	4	2	Petition and docs.	614	Claims.						
Newbold, Caleb, executors of.	Compensation for supplies furnished revolutionary war.	5	2	Petition & docs.	265	Claims	April 18, 1798	Adverse		Laid on table.		
Newbold, Samuel, *et al.*	Salvage on amount of duties paid on articles saved from wreck of barque Ann.	24	1	Petition	506	Commerce.						
Newby, Pichard	Remission of duties on stills and distilled spirits.	13	3	Petition	668	Ways and Means	Jan. 23, 1815	Adverse		Rejected.		
New Castle & Frenchtown Railroad Company.	Drawback of duties on railroad iron	25	2	Senate bill	1012	Whole House	June 30, 1838	Favorable	S. 238	Passed	Passed	App'd July 7, 1838
Newcomb Bethsheba, *et al.*	(See Isaac Peirson, heirs of.)	8	2		71							
Newcomb, Charlotte S. or J.	(See Thomas Lincoln, heir of the widow of.)	30	1		713							
Newcomb, Francis D., sureties of.	Authority to the Secretary of the Treasury to compromise and settle his accounts as surveyor general of Louisiana.	30	1	Senate bill	1046	Whole House	July 22, 1848	With't amend.	S. 231	Passed		App'd July 25, 1848
Newcomb, Henry S., *et al*	Confirmation of title to land in Florida.	15	1	Petition	157	Priv. Land Claims				Leave to withdraw.		
Newcomb, Lieut. Henry, widow of.	Arrears of pension	23	2	Resolution	204	Naval Affairs.						
Newcomb, Jonathan, *et al.*	Payment for stone for dry-dock at Gosport, Virginia.	22	1	Petition	257	Claims	Feb. 6, 1832	Res. to refer to Sec. of Navy for settlem't.		Adopted.		
Newcomb, Joseph Warren.	(See Major Gen. Joseph Warren, heirs of.)	26	1		280							
Newcomb, Kinner	Bounty land for revolutionary services.	16	1	Petition	197, 214	Priv. Land Claims.						
Newcomb, Kinner	Payment for provender furnished United States troops in 1813.	22	1	Petition	26	Claims	Feb. 27, 1832	Adverse		Laid on table.		
Newcomb, Obediah	Pension for revolutionary services.	28	1	Petition	76, 259	Rev. Pensions				Discharged; laid on table.		
Newcomb, Rhoda	(See Lieutenant Henry Newcomb, widow of.)	23	2		204							
Newel, Andrew, *et al.*	Settlement of accounts as assistant commissaries of issues.	1	1	Petition	26					Laid on table.		
Newell, Daniel	Invalid pension	26	1	Memorial	728	Invalid Pensions.						
Newell, Daniel	Invalid pension	27	2	Petition	97	Invalid Pensions	429	Adverse		Laid on table.		
Newell, Daniel	Invalid pension	27	3	Petition	72	Invalid Pensions	27	Adverse		Laid on table.		

List of private claims presented to the House of Representativesthe of United States from the 1st to the 31st Congress, inclusive—Continued.

Names of claimants.	Nature or object of the claim.	Congress.	Session.	How brought before the House of Reps.	Page of journal.	To what committee of the House referred.	No. or date of the report.	Nature of the report.	No. of the bill.	How disposed of by the House of Reps.	How disposed of by the Senate.	Date of the act of Congress, and remarks.
Newell, Daniel	Invalid pension	28	1	Petition	509	Invalid Pensions.						
Newell, James	Pension	21	1	Petition	149	Military Pensions	April 7, 1830	Adverse	......	Laid on table.		
Newell, James	Pension	24	1	Petition	942	Rev. Claims.						
Newell, Col. John, heirs of.	Commutation pay for revolutionary services.	31	1	Petition	661	Rev. Claims.						
Newell, John	Indemnity for French spoliations prior to 1800.	26	1	Memorial	182	Foreign Affairs	343	Favorable	319	Referred to Committee Whole House.		
Newell, Joseph	(See Wyandot Indians.)	27	3	....	259	....	160	....	771			
Newell, Joseph	Permission to relinquish land granted by an Indian treaty and to enter other lands.	31	1	Petition	436	Priv. Land Claims.						
Newell, Joseph S.	Correction of an error of survey in locating land.	14	1	Petition	492	Public Lands	April 6, 1816	Favorable; bill	......	Passed	Passed	App'd April 27, 1816
Newell, Samuel	Invalid pension	12	1	House bill	361	Whole House	June 15, 1812	With amends.	138	Passed	Passed	App'd July 5, 1812
Newell, Stewart	Compensation for transcribing and indexing records at Galveston, Texas.	30	2	Petition	93	Claims.						
Newell, Thomas	Pension	14	2	Petition	70	Pens. & Rev. Cl'ms.						
Newell, Thomas M.	Reimbursement of money paid on custom-house bonds.	29	1	Memorial	238	Claims.						
Newell, Thomas M.	Reimbursement of money paid on custom-house bonds.	29	2	Memorial	74	Claims.						
Newell, Thomas M.	Reimbursement of money paid on custom-house bonds.	30	1	Memorial	214	Claims.						
Newell, Thomas M.	Reimbursement of money paid on custom-house bonds.	31	1	Memorial	624	Commerce	....	....	......	Discharged; laid on table.		
Newell, Thomas M.	Reimbursement of expenses incurred whilst disabled on board U. S. frigate Java.	29	1	Memorial	400	Naval Affairs	706	Favorable; bil	481	Referred to Committee Whole House.		
Newell, Thomas M.	Reimbursement of expenses incurred whilst disabled on board U. S. frigate Java.	29	2	House bill	212	....	....	....	481	Passed	Passed	App'd March 3, 1847
Newell, Thomas M.	Reimbursement of expenses incurred whilst disabled on board U. S. frigate Java.	30	1	Petition	115	Claims.						
Newell, Thomas M.	Full leave pay during period of suspension from command.	31	1	Petition	654	Naval Affairs.						
New England Mississippi Land Company.	Final adjustment of claim to land in Mississippi Territory.	10	1	Petition	107, 175	Whole House.						
New England Mississippi Land Company.	Final adjustment of claim to land in Mississippi Territory.	11	2	Memorial	133	Claims	....	....	......	Discharged; laid on table.		
New Enlgand Mississippi Land Company.	Indemnity for lands ceded by Georgia to the United States.	25	2	Senate bill	785	Judiciary	956	With't amend.	S. 208	Referred to Committee Whole House.		
New England Mississippi Land Company, directors of.	Indemnity for land ceded by Georgia to the United States.	28	1	Senate bill	941	Judiciary	June 6, 1844	With't amend.	S. 66	Referred to Committee Whole House.		
New England Mississippi Land Company, directors of.	Indemnity for land ceded by Georgia to the United States.	28	1	Petition	1087	Judiciary.						
New England Mississippi Land Company, directors of.	Indemnity for land ceded by Georgia to the United States.	30	1	Petition	110	Judiciary	765	Favorable; bill	601	Referred to Committee Whole House.		

List of private claims presented to the House of Representatives of the United States from the 1st to the 31st Congress, inclusive—Continued.

Names of claimants.	Nature or object of the claim.	Congress.	Session.	How brought before the House of Reps.	Page of journal.	To what committee of the House referred.	No. or date of the report.	Nature of the report.	No. of the bill.	How disposed of by the House of Reps.	How disposed of by the Senate.	Date of the act of Congress, and remarks.
New England Mississippi Land Company, directors of.	Indemnity for land ceded by Georgia to the United States.	31	1	Memorial	584	Judiciary.						
Neugent, or Nugent, Jacob.	Revolutionary pension	26	1	Petition	625	Rev. Pensions	490	Adverse	......	Laid on table.		
New Hampshire, legislature of.	Payment of claims of her invalid soldiers, barred by Statute of Limitations.	2	1	Memorial	466	Select.						
New Hampshire, officers and soldiers of.	Compensation for losses by depreciation of certificate of public debt.	2	2	Memorial	656	Whole House.....	Jan. 16, 1793	Adverse	......	Rejected.		
New Hampshire, merchants of Portsmouth.	Indemnity for French spoliations prior to 1800.	7	1	Memorial	162	Select.						
New Hampshire, merchants of Portsmouth.	Remission of duties on goods destroyed by fire.	9	2	Petition	542	Com. and Manuf.						
New Hampshire, merchant of Portsmouth.	Indemnity for French spoliations prior to 1800.	14	2	Petition	405	....	....	....	......	Laid on table.		
New Hampshire, merchants of Portsmouth.	Indemnity for French spoliations prior to 1800.	15	1	Petition	121, 222	Select.						
New Hampshire, merchants of Portsmouth.	Indemnity for French spoliations prior to 1800.	27	3	Petition	184	....	....	....	......	Referred to Committee Whole House on bill No. 57.		
New Hampshire, State of..	Final settlement of the claim of her militia for services, war of 1812.	18	1	Resolution	67	Military Affairs.						
New Hampshire, State of..	Payment for services of her militia, and for disbursements for military purposes in war of 1812.	31	2	Bill on leave....	95	Military Affairs ...	....	....	425	Discharged; laid on table.		
New Hampshire, State of..	Payment for military expenses incurred in repelling invasion and suppressing insurrection at Indian stream.	25	3	Documents.....	91	Foreign Affairs....	176	Favorable; bill	1038	Referred to Committee Whole House.		
New Hampshire, State of..	Payment for military expenses incurred in repelling invasion and suppressing insurrection at Indian stream.	26	1	Senate bill	853	Military Affairs ...	July 2, 1840	With't amend	S. 210	Referred to Committee Whole House.		
New Hampshire, State of..	Payment for military expenses incurred in repelling invasion and suppressing insurrection at Indian stream.	29	2	Bill on leave....	104	Military Affairs ...	Jan. 20, 1847	With't amend.	582	Referred to Committee Whole House.		
New Hampshire, State of..	Payment for military expenses incurred in repelling invasion and suppressing insurrection at Indian stream.	30	1	Bill on leave ...	175	Military Affairs ...	149	With't amend.	15	Referred to Committee Whole House.		
New Hampshire, State of..	Payment for military expenses incurred in repelling invasion and suppressing insurrection at Indian stream.	30	2	Bill of last sess..	396	Whole House.....	Feb. 8, 1849	With't amend.	15	Passed	Passed	App'd March 2, 1849
New Hampshire, State of..	Payment of interest on amount allowed by act of March 2, 1849.	31	1	Bill on leave....	981	Ways and Means..	....	....	309			
New Hampshire, State of..	Payment of interest on amount allowed by act of March 2, 1849.	31	2	Bill on leave....	206	Judiciary	63	With't amend.	449	Referred to Committee Whole House.		
New Hampshire, citizens of.	Remission of duty on iron for Fitchburgh railroad.	28	1	Petition	371, 376	Ways and Means..	....	....	......	Discharged; laid on table.		
New Hampshire, Dartmouth College.	Remission of duties on astronomical and mathematical instruments.	30	1	Memorial	393	Ways and Means.						

List of private claims presented to the House of Representatives of the United States from the 1st to the 31st Congress, inclusive—**Continued.**

Names of claimants.	Nature or object of the claim.	Congress.	Session.	How brought before the House of Reps.	Page of journal.	To what committee of the House referred.	No. or date of the report.	Nature of the report.	No. of the bill.	How disposed of by the House of Reps.	How disposed of by the Senate.	Date of the act of Congress, and remarks.
New Hampshire, citizens of Hillsborough.	Pension for revolutionary services.	19	1	Petition	98	Military Pensions	164	Adverse	......	Laid on table	....	Names of claimants not given in the Journal or Report.
New Haven Insurance Co.	Indemnity for French spoliations prior to 1800.	26	1	Memorial	182	Foreign Affairs	343	Favorable; bill	319	Referred to Committee Whole House.		
New Haven and Hartford Railroad Company.	Remission of du y on railroad iron.	28	1	Petition	252	Ways and Means.						
New Haven and Hartford Railroad Company.	Remission of duty on railroad iron.	28	2	Petition	187	Commerce.						
Newhouse, Philip	Compensation for revolutionary services.	2	1	Petition	474	....	....	....	......	Referred to Secretary of War.		
Newhouse, Philip	Compensation for revolutionary services.	3	1	Petition	49	....	....	....	......	Referred to Secretary of Treasury.		
Newhouse, Philip	Compensation for revolutionary services.	3	2	Petition and rep't Sec. Treasury.	284	....	....	....	......	Laid on table.		
Newingham, Daniel, heirs of.	Bounty land f r revolutionary services.	18	1	Petition	157	Priv. Land Claims.	Feb. 18, 1824	Adverse	......	Laid on table.		
Newingham, Daniel, heirs of.	Bounty land for revolutionary services.	19	1	Petition	225	Priv. Land Claims.	Feb. 14, 1826	Adverse	......	Laid on table.		
Newingham, Henry	(See Daniel Newingham, heirs of.)											
Newingham, Henry	(See William Marshal, heirs of)	22	1	....	165							
New Jersey, sundry citizens of.	Compensation for depreciation of their revolutionary pay.	1	2	Petition	153	....	....	....	......	Laid on table.		
New Jersey, Presbyterian church of Elizabethtown.	Indemnity for an academy burnt by the enemy in consequence of its being occupied by U. States as an arsenal.	2	1	Memorial	578	....	....	....	......	Laid on table.		
New Jersey, Presbyterian church of Elizabethtown.	Compensation for property destroyed by the enemy, revolutionary war.	27	3	Memorial	271	Rev. Claims	259	Adverse	......	Laid on table.		
New Jersey, citizens of Newark.	Indemnity for an academy burnt by the enemy in consequence of its occupation as a barracks by United States troops.	2	1	Petition	573	Select.						
New Jersey, owners of the ship.	Indemnity for their vessel and cargo captured by the French.	9	1	Memorial	312	Claims.						
New Jersey college, trustees of.	Remission of duties on books imported for the use of the college.	8	2	Memorial	19	Com. and Manuf.	Dec. 4, 1804	Adverse	......	Leave to withdraw.		
New Jersey, citizens of	To be relieved from half pilotage.	27	2	Petition	57	Commerce.						
New Jersey Steam Navigation company.	Compensation for supporting a light-boat on Eel Grass shoals in Fisher Island sound.	30	1	Petition	355	Commerce.						
Newkirk, Chs., *alias* Chs. Nukirk.	Payment for baggage and money lost at the battle of Oswego.	26	1	Petition	296	Military Affairs	420	Adverse	......	Laid on table.		
Newkirk, Jacob	Pension	1	2	House bill	271	Whole House	July 16, 1790	With't amend.	88	Passed	Passed	App'd Aug. 11, 1790
Newkirk, William	Pension for revolutionary services.	25	2	Petition	404, 775	Rev. Pensions	....	....	......	Discharged; laid on table.		
Newland, John	Pension for services, war of 1812.	27	2	Petition	714	Invalid Pensions	820	Adverse	......	Laid on table.		
Newland, John H.	Invalid pension	24	1	Petition	52	Invalid Pensions	Jan. 15, 1836	Adverse	......	Laid on table.		
Newland, John H.	Invalid pension	25	2	Petition	401	Invalid Pensions.						
Newland, John H.	Invalid pension	26	1	Petition	163	Invalid Pensions	269	Adverse	......	Laid on table.		
Newland, William, and D. M. Rice.	Compensation for supplies and for services rendered to sick soldiers.	23	2	Resolution	234	Claims.						

List of private claims presented to the House of Representatives of the United States from the 1st to the 31st Congress, inclusive—Continued.

Names of claimants.	Nature or object of the claim.	Congress.	Session.	How brought before the House of Reps.	Page of journal.	To what committee of the House referred.	No. or date of the report.	Nature of the report.	No. of the bill.	How disposed of by the House of Reps.	How disposed of by the Senate.	Date of the act of Congress, and remarks.
Newlin, James, heirs of...	Commutation of half pay for revolutionary services.	29	1	Memorial	283	Rev. Claims.						
New London Insurance Co.	Indemnity for French spoliations prior to 1800.	26	1	Memorial	182	Foreign Affairs....	343	Favorable....	319	Referred to Committee Whole House.		
New Madrid...........	(See Missouri—New Madrid sufferers.)	13	2	....	297							
Newman, Daniel	Compensation for servant killed in expedition against Seminole Indians.	13	1	Petition	15	Claims.						
Newman, Daniel	Compensation for servant killed in expedition against Seminole Indians.	13	2	Petition	203	Claims	Jan. 19, 1814	Adverse	......	Laid on table.		
Newman, Daniel	Arrears of pension	25	2	Petition	406	Military Affairs....	674	Adverse	......	Laid on table.		
Newman, Capt. Daniel, of Tennessee.	Pension for services in war of 1812	28	2	Petition	332	Invalid Pensions.						
Newman, Col. Daniel, of Georgia.	Invalid pension................	23	2	Memorial	219	Military Affairs....	50	Favorable; bill	641	Passed	Passed, with amendment.	Amendment not acted on.
Newman, Erasmus	Right of pre-emption as New Orleans branch pilot.	28	1	Petition	77	Priv. Land Claims.	9	Favorable....	35	Passed	Passed	App'd June 17, 1844
Newman, Francis, executor of.	Release of interest on debt due U. States.	24	1	Petition	753	Judiciary.						
Newman, Francis, executor of.	Release of interest on debt due U. States.	24	2	Petition	89	Judiciary	....	....	......	Discharged; leave to withdraw.		
Newman, Francis, heirs of	Release from interest on debt due United States.	25	2	Senate bill	332	Ways and Means..	July 4, 1832	Adverse	S. 95	Laid on table.		
Newman, Francis, heirs of	Release from interest on debt due United States.	25	3	Senate bill	657	Ways and Means..	....	....	S. 147			
Newman, Francis, heirs of	Release from interest on debt due United States.	26	1	Senate bill	803	Judiciary	....	....	S. 128			
Newman, Francis, heirs of	Release from interest on debt due United States.	26	2	Senate bill	203	Judiciary	....	....	S. 59			
Newman, Francis, heirs of	Release from interest on debt due United States.	27	2	Senate bill	1116	Judiciary	July 29, 1842	With't amend.	S. 114	Passed	....	App'd Aug. 11, 1842
Newman, Gustavus......	(See Exploring Expedition)	27	3	....	149							
Newman, Henry........	Payment of certain bills of credit.	4	1	Rep. of Secretary Treasury.	388	Claims	May 31, 1796	Adverse	......	Laid on table.		
Newman, Henry	Confirmation of title to land	27	2	Senate bill	1126	Public Lands.....	Aug. 20, 1842	With amend..	S. 263	Laid on table.		
Newman, Henry	Confirmation of title to land	28	1	Senate bill	868	Public Lands.....	June 7, 1844	With't amend.	S. 3	Referred to Committee Whole House.		
Newman, Henry	Confirmation of title to land	29	1	Senate bill	1075	Public Lands.....	....	....	S. 92			
Newman, Henry, *et al* ...	Correction of errors in surveys of land.	24	1	Senate bill	1078	Public Lands.....	July 1, 1836	With't amend	S. 227	Passed	....	App'd July 2, 1836
Newman, John	(See Stephen Decatur, widow of, *et al.*)	20	1	....	295							
Newman, John	Compensation as companion of Lewis & Clark in exploration of western waters.	9	2	Resolution	507	Select...........	Jan. 23, 1807	By bill	183	Passed	Passed	App'd March 3, 1807
Newman, John	Invalid pension................	11	2	House bill......	283	Whole House	Mar. 24, 1810	With amend'ts	107	Passed	Passed	App'd April 27, 1810
Newman, Joseph, widow of.	Pension	20	1	Petition	84	Military Pensions..	....	....	......	Discharged; laid on table.		
Newman, Owen	Compensation as commissory of issues, revolutionary war.	10	1	Petition	112	....	....	....	......	Referred to Committee Whole House on bill No. 20.		

List of private claims presented to the House of Representatives of the United States from the 1st to the 31st Congress, inclusive—Continued

Names of claimants.	Nature or object of the claim.	Congress.	Session.	How brought before the House of Reps.	Page of journal.	To what committee of the House referred.	No. or date of the report.	Nature of the report.	No. of the bill.	How disposed of by the House of Reps.	How disposed of by the Senate.	Date of the act of Congress, and remarks.
Newman, Samuel	Indemnity for French spoliations prior to 1800.	26	1	Memorial	182	Foreign Affairs	343	Favorable; bill	319	Referred to Committee Whole House.		
Newman, Samuel	(See Samuel Brown, jr., administrator of.)	26	1		182		343		319			
Newman, S. C.	(See George B. Russell, *et al.*)	28	2		136							
Newman, Samuel	(See Samuel Bayley, executors of)	26	1		182		343		319			
Newman, Samuel	(See John Davenport, admisistrator of.)	26	•1		182		343		319			
Newman, Samuel	(See William Boardman, administrator of.)	26	1		182		343		319			
Newman, Samuel	(See Samuel Chase, administrator of.)	26	1		182		343		319			
Newman, Timothy, widow of.	Pension for naval services	24	2	Petition	45	Naval Affairs	Dec. 27, 1836	Adverse		Laid on table.		
Newman, W. D.	(See Exploring Expedition)	27	3		149							
New Orleans, surviving defenders of in 1814, '15.	For one section of public land	31	1	Petition	1009	Rev. Pensions	369	Adverse		Laid on table.		
Newsom, Joshua	Payment for two horses impressed and lost in United States service.	16	1	Petition	186	Claims	April 26, 1820	Favorable; bill	141	Passed	Passed	App'd May 15, 1820
Newsom, Lorenzo D.	Payment for a horse lost in United States service.	20	1	Petition	226	Claims	Feb. 4, 1828	Adverse		Laid on table.		
Newsom, Lorenzo D.	Payment for a horse lost in United States service.	20	2	Petition	118	Claims	Jan. 14, 1829	Adverse		Laid on table.		
Newsom, Lorenzo D.	Payment for a horse lost in United States service.	21	1	Petition	117	Claims	Feb. 22, 1830	Adverse		Laid on table.		
Newsom, Lorenzo D.	Payment for a horse lost in United States service.	21	1	Petition	294	Claims	Feb. 22, 1832	Adverse		Laid on table.		
Newsom, Randolph	Pension for revolutionary services.	22	1	Resolution	228	Rev. Pensions	395	Favorable	494	Referred to Committee Whole House.		
Newsom, Richard W	Confirmation of title to land	28	2	Petition	303	Public Lands.						
Newsom, William, surety of.	Release from liability and for moiety of fine as informer.	16	2	Petition	41	P. Of. & P. Roads.				Discharged		Leave to withdraw.
Newsom, William, sen.	Compensation for clerks' hire, fuel, lights, &c., as postmaster at Norfolk.	20	1	Petition	166	P. Of. & P. Roads.	Feb. 20, 1828	Adverse		Laid on table.		
Newsom, William, sen.	Compensation for clerks' hire, fuel, lights, &c., as postmaster at Norfolk.	20	2	Petition	83	P. Of. & P. Roads.	Jan. 14, 1829	Adverse		Laid on table.		
Newsom, William, sen.	Compensation for clerks' hire, fuel, lights, &c., as postmaster at Norfolk.	21	2	Petition	82	P. Of. & P. Roads.	Dec. 29, 1830	Adverse		Laid on table.		
Newsom, William, sen.	Compensation for clerks' hire, fuel, lights, &c., as postmaster at Norfold.	22	1	Petition	412	P. Of. & P. Roads.	April 11, 1832	Adverse		Laid on table.		
Newton, Betsey	(See Daniel Newton, widow of.)											
Newson	(See Newsom.)											
Newton, David	Invalid pension	3	2	Rep. of Secretary War.	278	Claims				Laid on table.		
Newton, Daniel, widow of	Pension	25	2	Petition	54	Rev. Pensions	Feb. 6, 1838	Adverse		Laid on table.		
Newton, Francis	Renewal of pension	17	1	Petition	132	Rev. Pensions.						
Newton, Francis	Invalid pension	19	2	Petition	215	Military Pensions.	Feb. 14, 1827	By bill	436	Referred to Committee Whole House.		
Newton, Francis	Invalid pension	20	1	Petition	193	Military Pensions.						

List of private claims presented to the House of Representatives of the United States from the 1st to the 31st Congress, inclusive—Continued.

Names of claimants.	Nature or object of the claim.	Congress.	Session.	How brought before the House of Reps.	Page of journal.	To what committee of the House referred.	No. or date of the report.	Nature of the report.	No. of the bill.	How disposed of by the House of Reps.	How disposed of by the Senate.	Date of the act of Congress, and remarks.
Newton, Francis	Invalid pension	20	2	House bill	55	Whole House	Jan. 15, 1829	Favorable	311	Passed	Laid on table.	
Newton, Francis	Invalid pension	21	1	Petition and docs.	47	Military Pensions	Jan. 5, 1830	Report and bill.	72	Passed	Passed, with amendment.	App'd May 20, 1830
Newton, George	Restoration of pension	26	1	Petition	287	Invalid Pensions	Mar. 5, 1840	Adverse		Laid on table.		
Newton, George	Restoration of pension	28	1	Petition	109	Invalid Pensions.						
Newton, George	Restoration of pension	29	1	Petition	203	Invalid Pensions	497	Adverse		Laid on table.		
Newton, George	Restoration of pension	29	2	Petition	69	Invalid Pensions.						
Newton, George	Arrears of pension	27	2	Petition	68	Invalid Pensions	135	Favorable	181	Passed	Indef. postp'd.	
Newton, George	Arrears of pension	28	1	Petition	102	Invalid Pensions				Discharged; laid on table.		
Newton, George	Arrears of pension	30	1	Petition	65	Invalid Pensions	20	Favorable; bill	24	Passed	Passed, second session.	App'd Feb. 22, 1849
Newton, George	(See William Pennock, administrator of.)	26	1		182		343		319			
Newton, George, widow of	Payment for flour furnished United States army.	14	2	Petition	45	Pens. & Rev. Cl'ms.						
Newton, George, widow of	Payment for flour furnished United States army.	15	2	Petition	46	Pens. & Rev. Cl'ms.	Dec. 9, 1818	Adverse		Leave to withdraw.		
Newton, George, (Va.)	Indemnity for French spoliations prior to 1800.	26	1	Memorial	182	Foreign Affairs	343	Favorable	319	Referred to Committee Whole House.		
Newton, John	Compensation for a horse lost in United States service.	24	1	Documents	806	Claims.						
Newton, John	Land in lieu of other land heretofore granted, but which is unfit for cultivation.	25	3	Senate bill	107	Public Lands	Jan. 15, 1839	Favorable	S. 42	Passed	Passed	App'd Feb. 6, 1839
Newton, John	Permission to exchange bounty land for other lands.	29	1	Documents	276	Public Lands				Discharged; laid on table.		
Newton, John	Permission to exchange bounty land for other lands.	30	1	Petition	154	Public Lands	812	Adverse		Laid on table.		
Newton, John	Permission to exchange bounty land for other lands.	30	2	Petition & papers	252					Leave to withdraw.		
Newton, John	Permission to exchange bounty land for other lands.	30	2	Memorial	296	Public Lands.						
Newton, Mary	(See George Newton, widow of)	14	2		45							
Newton, Obediah, widow of	For relief for revolutionary services of late husband.	4	2	Petition	645	Claims	Jan. 27, 1797	Adverse		Laid on table.		
Newton, Stephen, widow of	Pension for revolutionary services.	25	2	Petition	53	Rev. Pensions	Feb. 6, 1838	Adverse		Laid on table.		
Newton, Susannah	(See Stephen Newton, widow of.)											
Newton, Thomas W.	(See Robert Crittendon, assignee of.)	21	1		464							
Newton, William	Increase of pension	25	3	Petition	294	Invalid Pensions.						
Newton, William	Increase of pension	26	1	Petition	163	Invalid Pensions.						
Newton, William	Increase of pension	26	2	Petition	135	Military Pensions	234	Adverse		Laid on table.		
Newton, William	Increase of pension	27	2	Petition	60	Military Pensions	220	Adverse		Laid on table.		
Newton, William	Increase of pension	27	3	Petition	193	Invalid Pensions.						
Newton, William	Increase of pension	28	1	Resolution	310	Invalid Pensions	273	Adverse		Laid on table.		
New York, Agriculture, Board of.	To refund duties paid on books and seeds.	16	2	Petition	170	Ways and Means.						
New York, Albany, merchants of.	Relief from certain penalty	12	2	Petition	170	Ways and Means.						
New York, Alleghany co., assistant marshals and citizens of.	Additional compensation for taking seventh census.	31	2	Petition	335, 343, 365	Judiciary				Discharged.		

List of private claims presented to the House of Representatives of the United States from the 1st to the 31st Congress, inclusive—Continued.

Names of claimants.	Nature or object of the claim.	Congress.	Session.	How brought before the House of Reps.	Page of journal.	To what committee of the House referred.	No. or date of the report.	Nature of the report.	No. of the bill.	How disposed of by the House of Reps.	How disposed of by the Senate.	Date of the act of Congress, and remarks.
New York American	(See Theodore Dwight, *et al.*)	19	1	....	221							
New York American insurance Company.	Indemnity for illegal seizure of goods by marshal of Pennsylvania.	22	1	Memorial	473	Ways and Means	May 29, 1832	Favorable	590	Passed	Passed	App'd July 14, 1832
New York Atlantic Insurance Company.	Indemnity for illegal saizure of goods by marshal of Pennsylvania.	22	1	Memorial	473	Ways and Means	May 29, 1832	Favorable	590	Passed	Passed	App'd July 14, 1832
New York, Brown's county, marshal of.	Additional compensation for taking seventh census.	31	2	Petition	314	Judiciary	....	....	......	Discharged.		
New York Daily Advertiser	(See Theodore Dwight, *et al.*)	19	1	....	221	....	....	....	264			
New York, citizens of Buffalo.	Payment for property destroyed in war of 1812.	14	2	Petition	89	Select	July 23, 1817	Favorable	70	Laid on table.		
New York, citizens of Buffalo.	Payment for property destroyed in war of 1812.	15	1	Report of Com'r Claims.	389	Claims	177	Favorable	162	Rejected.		
New York, citizens of Buffalo.	Payment for property destroyed in war of 1812.	17	2	Petition	163	Claims.						
New York, Cataraugus co., marshal of.	Additional compensation for taking seventh census.	31	2	Petition	326, 365, 387	Judiciary	....	....	......	Discharged.		
New York, Cayuga county, marshals of.	Additional compensation for taking seventh census.	31	2	Petition	314	Judiciary	....	....	......	Discharged.		
New York, Chautauque co., marshals of.	Additional compensation for taking seventh census.	31	2	Petition	326, 352	Judiciary	....	....	......	Discharged.		
New York, Chemung county, marshals of.	Additional compensation for taking seventh census.	31	2	Petition	280, 282	Judiciary	....	....	......	Discharged.		
New York, Chenango co., marshals of.	Additional compensation for taking seventh census.	31	2	Petition	282	Judiciary	....	....	......	Discharged.		
New York, citizens of	Confirmation of title to land	20	1	Petition	33	Public Lands.						
New York, citizens of	Confirmation of title to land	20	1	Petition	419	Public Lands.						
New York, city of	Payment of expense incurred in defence of said city in late war.	15	1	Petition	140	Claims.						
New York, city of	That certain lands be reconveyed to said city.	16	2	Senate bill	300	Whole House	....	....	S. 48	Indefinitely postponed.		
New York, city of	That certain lands be reconveyed to said city.	17	1	Memorial	33	Military Affairs	Dec. 27, 1821	Favorable	11	Passed	Passed	App'd Mar. 30, 1822
New York, city of	Compensation for property taken and used by revolutionary army.	1	2	Petition	143	....	....	....	.....	Laid on table.		
New York, city of	Reconveyance of Castle Clinton and lands.	18	1	Memorial	65	Military Affairs	Jan. 9, 1824	Adverse	......	Laid on table.		
New York, city of	That site of North Battery be retroceded to said city.	21	1	Petition	144	Military Affairs	Jan. 20, 1830	Favorable	137	Passed	Passed	App'd May 10, 1830
New York, city of	That title of United States to Fort Gansevoort be released to said city.	22	1	Senate bill	844	Military Affairs	June 7, 1832	Favorable	S. 109	Laid on table.		
New York city, citizens of	Confirmation of title to land	20	1	Petition	33, 419	Public Lands.						
New York city, assistant marshals of.	Additional compensation for taking seventh census.	31	2	Petition	247	Ways and Means.						
New York city, mechanics and laborers of.	Compensation for work done on custom-house.	27	2	Petition	836	Select.						
New York city and State.	Indemnity for French spoliations prior to 1800.	7	1	Memorial	106	Select.						
New York city, merchants of.	Extension of time for payment of bonds and benefit of drawback.	10	1	Memorial	144	Com. and Manuf.						

List of private claims presented to the House of Representatives of the United States from the 1st to the 31st Congress, inclusive—Continued.

Names of claimants.	Nature or object of the claim.	Congress.	Session.	How brought before the House of Reps.	Page of journal.	To what committee of the House referred.	No. or date of the report.	Nature of the report.	No. of the bill.	How disposed of by the House of Reps.	How disposed of by the Senate.	Date of the act of Congress, and remarks.
New York city, merchants of.	Permission to export flax seed . . .	10	1	Memorial	221	Whole House.						
New York city, merchants of.	Release from penalties incurred by importing British goods.	12	2	Petition	549	Ways and Means. .	. . . .	. . . .	. . . . .	. . . .	. . . .	See act Jan. 2, 1813
New York city, merchants of.	That copper bars and copper bottoms be exempt from duties, also for drawback on copper.	9	1	Petition	297	Com. and Manuf.						
New York city, merchants of.	That copper bars and copper bottoms be exempt from duties, also for drawback on copper.	10	1	Memorial	34	Com. and Manuf.						
New York city, merchants of.	That copper bars and copper bottoms be exempt from duties, also for drawback on copper.	10	1	Memorial	86	Com. and Manuf. .	Jan. 21, 1808	Favorable	. . . . . .	Referred to Committee Whole House.		
New York city, sundry claimants of.	Indemnity for French spoliations prior to 1800.	26	1	Memorial	182	Foreign Affairs. . . .	343	Favorable	319	Referred to Committee Whole House.		
New York city, sundry merchants of.	Payment of debenture of drawback for goods exported to New Orleans.	14	1	Petition	386	Com. and Manuf. .	April 12, 1816	Favorable	. . . . . .	Indefinitely postponed.		
New York city, sundry merchants of.	Payment of debenture of drawback for goods exported to New Orleans.	14	2	Petition	127	Com. and Manuf.						
New York city, merchants of.	Drawback of duties on certain goods.	23	1	Petition	584	Ways and Means.						
New York city, merchants of.	Drawback of duties levied under the act of 1828.	23	1	Memorial	47	Ways and Means. .	Jan. 3, 1834	Favorable. . . .	129	Referred to Committee Whole House.		
New York city, merchants of.	Remission of excess of duties imposed under act of 1828.	24	1	Petition	53	Ways and Means.						
New York city, merchants of.	Remission of excess of duties imposed under act of 1828.	25	2	Memorial	579	Commerce.						
New York city, merchants of.	Drawback of duties on coal	25	3	Memorial	213	Whole House.						
New York city, merchants of.	(See Goodhue & Co., *et al.*)	26	1	. . . .	291							
New York city, merchants of.	Drawback on goods exported to Canada.	27	2	Memorial	438	Commerce.						
New York, United Insurance Company of.	Indemnity for French spoliations prior to 1800.	26	1	Memorial	182	Foreign Affairs. . . .	343	Favorable	319	Referred to Committee Whole House.		
New York city, merchants of, *et al.*	Payment of certain certificates of drawback.	14	2	Petition	127	Com. and Manuf.						
New York city, Merchant's Exchange Company.	Permission to import statue of Gen. Hamilton, duty free.	19	1	Petition	73	Ways and Means. .	Dec. 23, 1825	Favorable	18	Passed	Passed, with amendment.	App'd May 20, 1826
New York city, society for reforming of juvenile delinquents.	Relief from payment of debt to United States.	21	1	Memorial	596	Ways and Means.						
New York city, society for reforming of juvenile delinquents.	Relief from payment of debt to United States.	30	1	Senate bill	936	Judiciary	July 19, 1848	Favorable. . . .	S. 209	Passed	Passed	App'd July 25, 1848
New York city, citizens of.	Relief of sufferers by fire in said city.	24	1	Senate bill	182	Whole House	Feb. 18, 1836	Favorable. . . .	S. 65	Passed	Passed	App'd Mar. 19, 1836
New York city, citizens of.	Remission of duties on goods destroyed by fire.	24	1	Petition	77	Ways and Means.	41	Favorable	41	Referred to Committee Whole House.		
New York city, citizens of.	Remission of duties on goods destroyed by fire.	25	2	Senate bill	125	Ways and Means. .	Dec. 22, 1837	Favorable	S. 18	Passed with amend't.	Passed	App'd July 7, 1838

List of private claims presented to the House of Representatives of the United States from the 1st to the 31st Congress, inclusive—Continued.

Names of claimants.	Nature or object of the claim.	Congress.	Session.	How brought before the House of Reps.	Page of journal.	To what committee of the House referred.	No. or date of the report.	Nature of the report.	No. of the bill.	How disposed of by the House of Reps.	How disposed of by the Senate.	Date of the act of Congress, and remarks.
New Yow city, citizens of.	Remission of duties on goods destroyed by fire.	25	2	Petition	42	Ways and Means..	June 27, 1838	Adverse	......	Laid on table.		
New York Clinton Company, citizens of.	Payment of due bills for materials furnished trroops during the late war.	24	1	Memorial	91	Claims.						
New York, Clinton county, supervisors of.	Indemnity for destruction of court-house, &c., by Gen. Macomb, in 1814.	14	1	Petition	65	Claims	April 1, 1816	Favorable.....	......	Passed	Passed, with amendment.	App'd April 26, 1816
New York, Columbia county, assistant marshals of.	Additional compensation for taking Seventh Census.	31	2	Petition	236	Judiciary	....	....	......	Discharged.		
New York, Courtland county, marshals of.	Additional compensation for taking Seventh Census.	31	2	Petition	308, 326	Judiciary.........	....	....	......	Discharged.		
New York, custom-house clerks.	Compensation for extra services in 1841.	29	1	Memorial	517	Claims	722	Adverse	......	Laid on table.		
New York custom-house, clerks.	Compensation for extra services in 1814.	30	1	Petition	481	Commerce	501	Favorable	416	Referred to Committee Whole House.		
New York custom-house, gaugers of.	Compensation for services in said custom-house in collection of duties.	26	1	Petition	292	Commerce.						
New York custom-house, inspectors in.	Relief by reason of personal danger, and expense incurred during the epidemic.	8	1	Petition	523	Claims.						
New York custom-house, inspectors in.	Increase of compensation........	9	1	Petition	190	Ways and Means.						
New York custom-house, inspectors in.	Increase of compensation........	9	2	Resolution	482	Ways and Means.						
New York custom-house, inspectors in.	Increase of compensation........	10	1	Petition and rep't Sec. Treasury.	30	Ways and Means..	Nov. 23, 1807	Report not of record.	......	Referred to Committee Whole House.		
New York custom-house, inspectors in.	Increase of compensation........	11	2	Petition	490	Com. and Manuf.						
New York custom-house, inspectors in.	Increase of compensation........	24	1	Petition	272	Commerce.						
New York custom-house measurers of coal and salt.	Increase of compensation........	9	1	Memorial	199	Ways and Means.						
New York custom-house measurers of coal and salt.	Increase of compensation........	9	2	Resolution	482	Ways and Means.						
New York custom-house measurers of coal and salt.	Increase of compensation........	10	1	Petition and rep't of Sec. Treas'y	30	Ways and Means..	Nov. 23, 1807	Report not of record.	......	Referred to Committee Whole House.		
New York custom-house weighers.	Increase of compensation........	7	1	Petition	100	Com. and Manuf.						
New York custom-house weighers.	Increase of compensation........	11	3	Petition	559	Com. and Manuf.						
New York, Delaware county, marshals of.	Additional compensation for taking Seventh Census.	31	2	Petition	360	Judiciary.........	....	....	......	Discharged.		
New York, revolutionary soldiers living in Durham.	That depreciated revolutionary pay be made good to them.	21	1	Petition	57	Claims.						
New York, Erie county, marshals of.	Additional compensation for taking Seventh Census.	31	2	Petition	314	Judiciary	....	....	......	Discharged.		

List of private claims presented to the House of Representatives of the United States from the 1st to the 31st Congress, inclusive—Continued.

Names of claimants.	Nature or object of the claim.	Congress.	Session.	How brought before the House of Reps.	Page of journal.	To what committee of the House referred.	No. or date of the report.	Nature of the report.	No. of the bill.	How disposed of by the House of Reps.	How disposed of by the Senate.	Date of the act of Congress, and remarks.
New York, Essex county, marshals of.	Additional compensation for taking Seventh Census.	31	2	Petition	393	Judiciary				Discharged.		
New York, Foreign Missionary Society of.	For a grant of land on which they have erected a mission house, on Lake Superior.	19	1	Petition	270	Indian Affairs	Mar. 6, 1826	Favorable	137	Passed.		
New York, (French's Mills,) inhabitants of.	Remuneration for damages to property by United States army.	13	3	Petition	640	Claims.						
New York, Fulton county, marshals of.	Additional compensation for taking Seventh Census.	31	2	Petition	321	Judiciary				Discharged.		
New York, General Assembly of.	Provision for sufferers at Niagara frontier during late war.	18	1	Resolution	298					Laid on table.		
New York, Genesee county, marshals of.	Additional compensation for taking Seventh Census.	31	2	Petition	334	Judiciary				Discharged.		
New York, Green county, marshals of.	Additional compensation for taking Seventh Census.	31	2	Petition	253	Judiciary				Discharged.		
New York, Green county, revolutionary soldiers of.	That depreciated revolutionary pay be made good to them.	21	1	Petition	117	Military Pensions	April 2, 1830	Adverse		Laid on table.		
New York and Harlem railroad company.	Refunding certain duties on railroad iron.	25	2	Senate bill	763	Com. and Manuf.	May 10, 1838	Favorable	S. 176	Passed	Passed	App'd July 7, 1838
New York, Herkemer county, marshals of.	Additional compensation for taking Seventh Census.	31	2	Petition	321	Judiciary				Discharged.		
New York, Hopkinton co., marshals of.	Additional compensation for taking Seventh Census.	31	2	Petition	365	Judiciary				Discharged.		
New York, hospital, governors of.	For payment for support of seamen	13	2	Petition	185	Claims Com. and Manuf.	44 Mar. 29, 1814	Adverse Favorable		Com. to Com. & Man. Ref'd to Com. W. H.		
New York, hospital, governors of.	For payment for support of seamen	17	1	Petition	85	Commerce.						
New York, hospital, governors of.	For payment for support of seamen	18	1	Memorial	172	Commerce.						
New York, hospital, governors of.	For payment for support of seamen	19	1	Memorial	150	Commerce.						
New York, hospital, governors of.	For payment for support of seamen	19	2							Leave to withdraw.		
New York, surveyor of Port of Hudson.	Adequate compensation	19	2	Resolution	40	Commerce.						
New York, inspectors of customs for the State of.	Increase of compensation	1	3	Petition	366					Laid on table.		
New York, inspectors of customs for the State of.	Increase of compensation	2	2	Rep. of Secretary Treasury.	626					Laid on table.		
New York, Insurance Company.	For distribution of proceeds of Danish brig Henrick.	21	2	Memorial	190	Foreign Affairs	Feb. 23, 1831	Adverse	523	Passed	Passed	App'd Feb. 19, 1831
New York Insurance Company.	Indemnity for French spoliations prior to 1800.	26	1	Memorial	182	Foreign Affairs	343	Favorable; bill	319	Referred to Committee Whole House.		
New York Insurance Company.	Indemnity for illegal seizure of the ships Superior, Addison, and Woodross, &c.	22	2	Memorial	215	Ways and Means	103	Favorable	744	Referred to Committee Whole House.		
New York Insurance Companies.	Indemnity for certain expenses in prosecuting suits for damages for illegal seizures.	23	1	Memorial	47	Ways and Means				Discharged; laid on table.		
New York, Jefferson county, marshals of.	Additional compensation for taking Seventh Census.	31	2	Petition	287	Judiciary				Discharged.		
New York, Kings county, marshals of.	Additional compensation for taking Seventh Census.	31	2	Petition	193	Judiciary				Discharged.		

List of private claims presented to the House of Representatives of the United States from the 1st to the 31st Congress, inclusive—Continued.

Names of claimants.	Nature or object of the claim.	Congress.	Session.	How brought before the House of Reps.	Page of journal.	To what committee of the House referred.	No. or date of the report.	Nature of the report.	No. of the bill.	How disposed of by the House of Reps.	How disposed of by the Senate.	Date of the act of Congress, and remarks.
New York, Kingston, citizens of.	Indemnity for damage done property during the revolutionary war.	3	1	Petition	216					Referred to Secretary War.		
New York, Lewis county, marshals of.	Additional compensation for taking Seventh Census.	31	2	Petition	326, 365	Judiciary				Discharged.		
New York, line of revolution.	For the difference of interest on their funded certificates and commutation certificates, (deferred stock.)	10	2	Memorial	381					Laid on table.		
New York, Livingston co., marshals of.	Additional compensation for taking Seventh Census.	31	2	Memorial	321	Judiciary				Discharged.		
New York, mayor, &c., of city of.	Compensation for arms, &c., taken for use of revolutionary army.	3	1	Petition	95	Select.						
New York, Madison county, marshals of.	Additional compensation for taking the Seventh Census.	31	2	Petition	314, 343	Judiciary				Discharged.		
New York, sundry insurance companies of.	Indemnity for illegal seizure of goods by marshal of Penn.	22	1	Memorial	473	Ways and Means	May 29, 1832	Favorable	590	Passed	Passed	App'd July 14, 1832
New York, Monroe county, marshals of.	Additional compensation for taking the Seventh Census.	31	2	Memorial	287, 387	Ways and Means				Discharged.		
New York, Montgomery county, marshals of.	Additional compensation for taking the Seventh Census.	31	2	Memorial	321, 334	Ways and Means				Discharged.		
New York, Niagara county, citizens of.	Indemnity for property destroyed in war of 1812.	14	1	Petition	156	Select.						
New York, Niagara county, citizens of.	Indemnity for property destroyed in war of 1812.	14	1	Petition	459	Claims.						
New York, Niagara county, citizens of.	Indemnity for property destroyed in war of 1812.	14	2	Petition	85	Select	48	Favorable	70	Laid on table.		
New York, Niagara county, citizens of.	Indemnity for property destroyed in war of 1812.	15	1	Rep't of Comm'r of Claims.	288	Claims	Mar. 27, 1818	Favorable	162	Rejected.		
New York, Niagara county, citizens of.	Indemnity for property destroyed in war of 1812.	15	1	Petition	349	Claims.						
New York, Niagara county, citizens of.	Indemnity for property destroyed in war of 1812.	16	2	Petition	57	Claims	31	Adverse		Referred to Committee Whole House.		
New York, Niagara county, citizens of.	Indemnity for property destroyed in war of 1812.	17	1	Petition	39	Claims	Dec. 26, 1821	Adverse		Rejected.		
New York, Niagara county, citizens of.	Indemnity for property destroyed in war of 1812.	18	1	Petition	316	Select.						
New York, officers and soldiers of the army.	That depreciation certificates may be made good to them.	2	2	Memorial	650					Laid on table.		
New York, officers of the army and navy in revolutionary war.	Interest on certificates for revolutionary services.	10	2	Memorial	381, 467	Select.						
New York, Oneida county, marshals of.	Additional compensation for taking the Seventh Census.	31	2	Petition	283	Judiciary				Discharged.		
New York, Onondaga county, marshals of.	Additional compensation for taking the Seventh Census.	31	2	Petition	334	Judiciary				Discharged.		
New York, Orange county, marshals of.	Additional compensation for taking the Seventh Census.	31	2	Petition	287	Judiciary				Discharged.		
New York, Ontario county, marshals of.	Additional compensation for taking the Seventh Census.	31	2	Petition	314	Judiciary				Discharged.		
New York, Orleans county, marshals of.	Additional compensation for taking the Seventh Census.	31	2	Petition	365	Judiciary				Discharged.		
New York, Oswego county, marshals of.	Additional compensation for taking the Seventh Census.	31	2	Petition	352	Judiciary				Discharged.		

List of private claims presented to the House of Representatives of the United States from the 1*st to the* 31*st Congress, inclusive*—Continued.

Names of claimants.	Nature or object of the claim.	Congress.	Session.	How brought before the House of Reps.	Page of journal.	To what committee of the House referred.	No. or date of the report.	Nature of the report.	No. of the bill.	How disposed of by the House of Reps.	How disposed of by the Senate.	Date of the act of Congress, and remarks.
New York, Oswego, merchants and ship owners of.	Drawback of duties on goods exported to Canada.	27	3	Petition	85	Commerce.						
New York, Otsego county, marshals of.	Additional compensation for taking the Seventh Census.	31	2	Petition	282	Judiciary	....	....	......	Discharged.		
New York, Pacific Insurance Company.	Indemnity for illegal seizure of goods by marshal of Penn.	22	1	Memorial	473	Ways and Means	May 29, 1832	Favorable	590	Passed	Passed	App'd July 14, 1832
New York, Pacific Insurance Company.	Indemnity for damages sustained by them in suits against James Connard.	30	1	Memorial	457	Claims	757	Adverse	......	Laid on table.		
New York, pensioners of	Increase of pension	25	2	Memorial	54	Rev. Pensions.						
New York, pilots of the port of.	Refunding certain fees paid into the public treasury.	22	1	Memorial	220	Commerce.						
New York, Plattsburg, inhabitants of.	Payment for houses and other property at Plattsburg destroyed by order of General Macomb, late war.	13	3	Petition	723	Claims	Feb. 15, 1815	Favorable	297	Passed	Passed	App'd March 3, 1815
New York, Long Island, Railroad Company.	Remission of duty on railroad iron	28	1	Petition	277	Commerce.						
New York, Providence and Boston Railroad Company.	Compensation for supporting a light on Eel Grap shoal.	29	1	Petition	269	Commerce.						
New York, Providence and Boston Railroad Company.	Compensation for supporting a light on Eel Grap shoal.	30	1	Petition	355	Commerce.						
New York, Queens county, marhals of.	Additional compensation for taking Seventh Census.	31	2	Petition	247	Judiciary	....	....	......	Discharged.		
New York, Richmond co., marshals of.	Additional compensation for taking Seventh Census.	31	2	Petition	221	Judiciary	....	....	......	Discharged.		
New York, Sacketts Harbor, city of.	Indemnity for losses sustained in late war.	14	2	Petition	198	Claims.						
New York, Saratoga county, marshals of.	Additional compensation for taking Seventh Census.	31	2	Petition	321	Judiciary	....	....	......	Discharged.		
New York, Senaca county, marshals of.	Additional compensation for taking Seventh Census.	31	2	Petition	287	Judiciary	....	....	......	Discharged.		
New York, Schenectady county, marshals of.	Additional compensation for taking Seventh Census.	31	2	Petition	283	Judiciary	....	....	......	Discharged.		
New York, Schoharie co., marshals of.	Additional compensation for taking Seventh Census.	31	2	Petition	343	Judiciary	....	....	......	Discharged.		
New York, State of	Payment of interest on money advanced, late war.	19	1	Senate bill	541	Claims	May 15, 1826	Favorable	S. 140	Passed	Passed	App'd May 22, 1826
New York, State of	Payment in full of expenditures, late war.	22	1	Resolution	228	Military Affairs.						
New York, State of	Payment for services of militia	25	2	House bill	1205	Military Affairs	July 2, 1838	Favorable	869	Passed	Passed	App'd July 9, 1838
New York, State of	Interest on balance due on advances in late war.	20	1	Senate bill	486	Claims	326	Adverse	S. 101	Indefinitely postponed.		
New York, State Bank	Payment of interest on money loaned United States during late war.	19	2	Petition	59	Claims.						
New York State, citizens of.	Redemption of certain bills of credit.	2	1	Petition	453	....	....	....	......	Laid on table.		
New York State, citizens of.	Indemnity for British spoliations	4	1	Memorial	386	Whole House.						

List of private claims presented to the House of Representatives of the United States from the 1st to the 31st Congress, inclusive—Continued.

Names of claimants.	Nature or object of the claim.	Congress.	Session.	How brought before the House of Reps.	Page of journal.	To what committee of the House referred.	No. or date of the report.	Nature of the report.	No. of the bill.	How disposed of by the House of Reps.	How disposed of by the Senate.	Date of the act of Congress, and remarks.
New York State, citizens of.	Compensation for lands ceded to United States by Georgia.	10	1	Memorial	168	Whole House.						
New York State, citizens of.	Relief from effects of the embargo act.	12	1	Petition	299					Postponed.		
New York State, citizens of.	Indemnity for arms and equipments lost in service.	18	1	Petition	195	Claims.						
New York State, citizens of.	Drawback of duties on goods exported in original packages.	28	1	Petition	294	Commerce.						
New York State, citizens of.	Indemnity for French spoliations prior to 1800.	27	3	Memorial	100	Whole House.						
New York State, citizens of.	Indemnity for French spoliations prior to 1800.	28	1	Memorial	124	Foreign Affairs.						
New York State, citizens of.	Indemnity for French spoliations prior to 1800.	31	2	Petition	37	Foreign Affairs.						
New York State, 103 claimants of.	Indemnity for property destroyed by the enemy, late war.	15	1	Rep't of commissioner claims.	288	Claims	Mar. 27, 1818	Favorable	162	Rejected.		
New York State, 56 claimants of.	Indemnity for property destroyed by the enemy, late war.	15	1	Rep't of commissioner claims.	380	Claims	Mar. 27, 1818	Favorable	162	Rejected.		
New York State, marshals of.	Additional compensation for taking Fifth Census.	21	2	Petition	232					Laid on table.		
New York State, marshals of northern district.	Increase of compensation	15	1	Resolution	74	Judiciary	Jan. 2, 1818	Adverse		Rejected.		
New York State, (Morrisville,) revolutionary soldiers of.	Pension	22	1	Petition	66	Rev. Pensions.						
New York State, sugar refiners of.	Relief from act to repeal the internal taxes.	8	1	Petition	498	Whole House.						
New York, Steuben county, marshals of.	Additional compensation for taking Seventh Census.	31	2	Petition	314, 283	Judiciary				Discharged.		
New York, St. Lawrence county, marshals of.	Additional compensation for taking Seventh Census.	31	2	Petition	352	Judiciary				Discharged.		
New York, Suffolk county, marshals of.	Additional compensation for taking Seventh Census.	31	2	Petition	225	Judiciary				Discharged.		
New York, Sullivan county, marshals of.	Additional compensation for taking Seventh Census.	31	2	Petition	287	Judiciary				Discharged.		
New York, Tioga county, marshals of.	Additional compensation for taking Seventh Census.	31	2	Petition	326	Judiciary				Discharged.		
New York, Tompkins county, marshals of.	Additional compensation for taking Seventh Census.	31	2	Petition	326	Judiciary				Discharged.		
New York, Troy, citizens of.	Remission of duties on certain railroad iron.	28	1	Petition	527	Ways and Means.						
New York, Ulster county, inhabitants of.	Indemnity for damage done property during the revolutionary war.	3	1	Petition	215	Secretary War, with instructions.						
New York, Ulster county, marshals of.	Additional compensation for taking Seventh Census.	31	2	Petition	236	Judiciary				Discharged.		
New York, Washington county, marshals of.	Additional compensation for taking Seventh Census.	31	3	Petition	360	Judiciary				Discharged.		
New York, Wayne county, marshals of.	Additional compensation for taking Seventh Census.	31	2	Petition	283, 315	Judiciary				Discharged.		
New York, Yorktown Presbyterian church.	Indemnity for destruction of buildings by the British in revolutionary war.	23	1	Petition	354	Rev. Claims.						

List of private claims presented to the House of Representatives of the United States from the 1st to the 31st Congress, inclusive—Continued.

Names of claimants.	Nature or object of the claim.	Congress.	Session.	How brought before the House of Reps.	Page of journal.	To what committee of the House referred	No. or date of the report.	Nature of the report.	No. of the bill.	How disposed of by the House of Reps.	How disposed of by the Senate.	Date of the act of Congress, and remarks.
New York, Yorktown Presbyterian church.	Indemnity for destruction of buildings by the British in revolutionary war.	24	1	Petition	281	Rev. Claims	807	Favorable	723	Referred to Committee Whole House.		
New York, Yorktown Presbyterian church.	Indemnity for destruction of buildings by the British in revolutionary war.	25	2	Petition	39	Rev. Claims	433	Favorable	441	Referred to Committee Whole House.		
New York, Yorktown Presbyterian church.	Indemnity for destruction of buildings by the British in revolutionary war.	25	3	House bill	378	Whole House	....	....	441			
New York, Yorktown Presbyterian church.	Indemnity for destruction of buildings by the British in revolutionary war.	26	1	Petition	165	Rev. Claims.						
New York, Yorktown Presbyterian church.	Indemnity for destruction of buildings by the British in revolutionary war.	27	2	Petition	105	Rev. Claims	1081	Adverse	......	Laid on table.		
New York, Yorktown Presbyterian church.	Indemnity for destruction of buildings by the British in revolutionary war.	27	3	Petition	44	Rev. Claims	262	Adverse	......	Laid on table.		
New York, Yorktown Presbyterian church.	Indemnity for destruction of buildings by the British in revolutionary war.	30	1	Petition	506	Claims.						
New York, Yorktown Presbyterian church.	Indemnity for destruction of buildings by the British in revolutionary war.	31	1	Petition	232	Claims	492	Favorable	393	Referred to Committee Whole House.		
New York, White Plains, Presbyterian church of.	Indemnity for property destroyed in revolutionary war.	24	2	Petition	307	Rev. Claims.						
New York, White Plains, Presbyterian church of.	Indemnity for property destroyed in revolutionary war.	25	2	Petition	333	Rev. Claims	514	Adverse	......	Laid on table.		
New York, White Plains, Presbyterian church of.	Indemnity for property destroyed in revolutionary war.	26	1	Petition	282	Rev. Claims.						
New York, Wyoming county, marshals of.	Additional compensation for taking Seventh Census.	31	2	Petition	360	Judiciary	....	....	......	Discharged.		
Nexen, jr., William	Release from imprisonment, judgment, and cost.	12	2	Senate bill	711	Ways and Means	Mar. 3, 1833	With amend's.	S. 65	Passed with amendm't.	Passed	App'd March 3, 1813
Nexen, jr., William	Released from costs, &c	13	1	Petition	11	Ways and Means.						
Nexen, jr., William	Released from costs, &c	13	1	Senate bill	21	Ways and Means	June 15, 1813	With amends.	S. 1	Passed with amendm't.	Passed	App'd June 19, 1813
Nexren, Elias, *et al*	Compensation for services as gaugers at New York.	27	2	Petition	633	Commerce.						
Ney, Michael	Pension	17	1	Resolution	268	Pens. & Rev. Cl'ms.						
Ney, Thomas	Change of location of bounty-land warrant.	26	1	Petition	608	Public Lands.						
Niblah, Johns	Pension	3	1	Rep. of Secretary War.	131	Select	May 26, 1794	Favorable	62	Passed	Passed	App'd June 7, 1794
Nicholas, Amos	Compensation for services as clerk in Navy Department.	17	1	Petition	184	Ways and Means.						
Nicholas, Amos	Compensation for services as clerk in Navy Department.	17	2	Senate bill	106	Naval Affairs	Jan. 17, 1823	With amends.	S. 19	Passed	Passed	App'd March 1, 1823
Nicholas, Cary, sureties of	Release from liability	30	2	Petition	204	Judiciary	27	Favorable	718	Referred to Committee Whole House.		
Nicholas, Cary, sureties of	Release from liability	31	1	Petition	236	Judiciary.						
Nicholas, Edmund	Pension	22	1	Petition	443	Invalid Pensions.						
Nicholas, Edward	Arrears of pension	23	1	Petition	45	Invalid Pensions	Jan. 27, 1834	Adverse	......	Laid on table.		
				Recommitted	821	Invalid Pensions	June 24, 1834	Favorable	545	Ref'd to Com. W. H.		

List of private claims presented to the House of Representatives of the United States from the 1st *to the* 31*st Congress, inclusive*—**Continued.**

Names of claimants.	Nature or object of the claim.	Congress.	Session.	How brought before the House of Reps.	Page of journal.	To what committee of the House referred.	No. or date of the report.	Nature of the report.	No. of the bill.	How disposed of by the House of Reps.	How disposed of by the Senate.	Date of the act of Congress, and remarks.
Nicholas, Edward	Arrears of pension	23	2	House bill	336	Whole House	....	....	545	Passed	Adverse report.	
Nicholas, Edward	Pension	24	1	Petition	52	Invalid Pensions	46	Favorable	58	Passed	Passed	App'd May 14, 1836
Nicholas, Francis, *et al.*	Redress from merchandise seized by the French government in 1809.	18	1	Petition	330	Foreign Affairs.						
Nicholas, John, *alias* Canous.	Pension for revolutionary services.	19	2	Petition	43	Military Pensions.						
Nicholas, John	Pension for revolutionary services.	24	2	Petition	90	Rev. Pensions	Feb. 14, 1837	Adverse	......	Laid on table.		
Nicholas, John	Indemnity for sufferings while in captivity with Indians.	28	1	Petition	74, 204	Rev. Claims.						
Nicholas, William	Payment for two horses taken by the Indians in 1814.	25	2	Petition	397	Claims.						
Nicholas, William	Payment for two horses taken by the Indians in 1814.	26	1	Petition	170, 621	Claims	36	Adverse	......	Laid on table.		
Nicholl, William	Warrant to locate bounty land	29	1	Petition	995	Priv. Land Claims.						
Nichols, Benjamin	Pension for revolutionary services.	19	2	Petition	91	Military Pensions.						
Nichols, or Nicholls, Caleb	Indemnity for damages done property at Plattsburg in 1814.	14	1	Petition	220	Claims.						
Nichols, or Nicholls, Caleb, and others.	Indemnity for damages done property at Plattsburg in 1814.	14	2	Petition	123	Claims	61	Favorable	81	Passed	Passed	App'd March 3, 1817
Nichols, Elizabeth	(See Isaac Nichols, widow of)	25	2	....	272							
Nichols, Ezekiel, *et al.*	Renewal of patent	14	2	Petition	76	Select.						
Nichols, Ezekiel, *et al.*	Renewal of paten	15	1	Petition	211	Select	Feb. 25, 1818	Adverse.	......	Laid on table.		
Nichols, Ichabod	Indemnity for French spoliations prior to 1800.	26	1	Memorial	182	Foreign Affairs	343	Favorable; bill	319	Referred to Committee Whole House.		
Nichols, Isaac, widow of	Continuation of pension	25	2	Petition	272	Rev. Pensions	Mar. 7, 1838	Adverse	......	Laid on table.		
Nichols, James, sureties of	Release from liability	15	1	Petition	394	Ways and Means.						
Nichols, John	Indemnity for boats detained in 1815 by order of Gen. Thomas.	16	1	Senate bill	300	Claims	Mar. 24, 1820	Favorable	S. 32	Passed	Passed	App'd April 5, 1820
Nichols, John	Payment for supplies furnished 36th regiment, New York militia, in 1838.	26	1	Petition	621	Claims.						
Nichols, John	Payment for supplies furnished 36th regiment, New York militia, in 1838.	27	2	Petition	618	Claims.						
Nichols, Jonah, *et al*	Renewal of patent	14	2	Petition	76	Select.						
Nichols, Jonah, or Josiah, *et al.*	Renewal of patent	15	1	Petition	211	Select	Feb. 25, 1818	Adverse.	......	Laid on table.		
Nichols, Levi, (Ohio)	Pension for revolutionary services.	28	2	Petition	332	Rev. Pensions.						
Nichols, Levi, (Ohio)	Pension for revolutionary services.	29	1	Petition	87	Rev. Pensions	529	Adverse	......	Laid on table.		
Nichols, Levi, (Ohio)	Pension for revolutionary services.	30	1	Petition	277	Rev. Pensions	June 20, 1848	....	......	Discharged; laid on table.		
Nichols, Levi, (Ohio)	Pension for revolutionary services.	31	1	Petition	582	Rev. Pensions	458	Adverse	......	Laid on table.		
Nichols, Moses, *et al.*	For extension to them of act of Congress for relief of purchasers of public lands.	18	2	Petition	161	Priv. Land Claims.						
Nichols, Sturges	Reimbursement of the amount of a certain fine.	20	2	Petition	203	Commerce.						
Nichols, Sturges	Reimbursement of the amount of a certain fine.	21	1	Petition	294	Commerce	....	....	......	Discharged; laid on table.		
Nichols, Thomas	Compensation for a horse and other property lost in United States service in 1832.	24	1	Petition	430	Claims.						

List of private claims presented to the House of Representatives of the United States from the 1st to the 31st Congress, inclusive—Continued.

Names of claimants.	Nature or object of the claim.	Congress.	Session.	How brought before the House of Reps.	Page of journal.	To what committee of the House referred.	No. or date of the report.	Nature of the report.	No. of the bill.	How disposed of by the House of Reps.	How disposed of by the Senate.	Date of the act of Congress, and remarks.
Nichols, Thompson, (Ky.)	Indemnity for damage to property by United States troops.	9	2	Petition	555	Claims	....	....	......	Discharged; laid on table.		
Nichols, Thompson, (Ky.)	Indemnity for damage to property by United States troops.	10	1	Petition	177	Claims	Feb. 25, 1808	Favorable	......	Referred to Committee Whole House.		
Nichols, Thompson, (Ky.)	Indemnity for damage to property by United States troops.	10	2	Petition	350	Claims	Nov. 18, 1808	Favorable	106	Passed.		
Nichols, Thompson, (Ky.)	Indemnity for damage to property by United States troops.	11	2	Memorial	127	Claims	Dec. 26, 1809	Favorable	51	Referred to Committee Whole House.		
Nichols, Thompson, (Ky.)	Indemnity for damage to property by United States troops.	13	3	Petition	455	Claims	15	Favorable; bill	242	Passed	Passed	App'd Jan. 28, 1815
Nichols, William, (Mass.)	Indemnity for French spoliations prior to 1800.	26	1	Memorial	182	Foreign Affairs	343	Favorable; bill	319	Referred to Committee Whole House.		
Nichols, William	Reimbursement of money paid by him as marshal of Pennsylvania.	6	1	Petition	555	Claims	April 9, 1800	Favorable	273	Referred to Committee Whole House.		
Nichols, William	Reimbursement of money paid by him as marshal of Pennsylvania.	6	2	Petition & report of Committee.	730	Claims	Dec. 17, 1800	Favorable	273	Postponed to next session.		
Nichols, Woodbury S., heirs of.	Indemnity for French spoliations prior to 1800.	31	1	Petition	323	Foreign Affairs	355	Favorable	318	Referred to Committee Whole House.		
Nicholls, James	(See William Miller, assignee of).	19	1	....	101							
Nicholls, William	Pension	28	1	Petition	277	Invalid Pensions.						
Nicholson, Lieut. A. A.	For the same compensation allowed assistant quartermasters of the army while acting as such of marines.	23	1	Petition	568	Naval Affairs.						
Nicholson, Lieut. A. A.	For the same compensation allowed assistant quartermasters of the army while acting as such of marines.	23	2	Petition	199	Naval Affairs.						
Nicholson, Lieut. A. A.	For the same compensation allowed assistant quartermasters of the army while acting as such of marines.	24	1	Senate bill	320	Naval Affairs	Mar. 3, 1836	Adverse	S. 55	Referred to Committee Whole House.		
Nicholson, Elizabeth R.	(See Samuel Nicholson, heirs of)	24	2	....	45							
Nicholson, Francis	Pension	3	1	Rep. of Secretary War.	131	Select	May 26, 1794	Ref'd back to Sec. War.	R. 12	Passed	Passed	App'd June 9, 1794
Nicholson, Francis	Pension	4	1	Res. and docs.	445	Claims.						
Nicholson, Henry, *et al*	Permission for their ship to proceed on her voyage.	12	1	Petition	331	Whole House	....	....	......	Postponed to the 4th of July next.		
Nicholson, James	Patent for gas apparatus	24	1	Petition	427	Select.						
Nicholson, John	Compensation for services as Indian interpreter, &c.	1	3	Petition	381	....	....	....	......	Referred to Secretary Treasury.		
Nicholson, John	Compensation for services as Indian interpreter, &c.	2	2	Rep. of Secretary Treasury.	626	....	....	....	......	Laid on table.		
Nicholson, John	Redemption of Continental bills	4	1	Rep. of Secretary War.	388	Claims	74	Adverse.	......	Laid on table.		
Nicholson, John	Reimbursement of expenses for supporting captured Africans.	21	2	Senate bill	384	Claims	Mar. 2, 1831	Favorable	S. 168	Passed	Passed	App'd March 3, 1831
Nicholson, John	Extra compensation for taking the Fifth Census.	22	1	Petition	266	Judiciary.						
Nicholson, John, *et al.*	Payment for arrears of interest, and annual interest on certain claims.	2	2	Memorial	636	....	....	....	......	Laid on table.		
Nicholson, John, *et al.*	(See Abner L. Duncan, executors of.)	23	1	....	338							

List of private claims presented to the House of Representatives of the United States from the 1st to the 31st Congress, inclusive—Continued.

Names of claimants.	Nature or object of the claim.	Congress.	Session.	How brought before the House of Reps.	Page of journal.	To what committee of the House referred.	No. or date of the report.	Nature of the report.	No. of the bill.	How disposed of by the House of Reps.	How disposed of by the Senate.	Date of the act of Congress, and remarks.
Nicholson, John, jr., *et al.*	Compensation for revolutionary services.	3	1	Petition	132	Select.						
Nicholson, John, and wife.	(See Walker Baylor, assignee of.)	12	1		139							
Nicholson, John B	(See Lewis Warrington, & others)	28	1		285							
Nicholson, Maria	(See Samuel Nicholson, heirs of.)	24	2		45							
Nicholson, Com. Samuel, heirs of.	Compensation for revolutionary services.	24	2	Petition	45	Rev. Claims.						
Nicholson, Com. Samuel, heirs of.	Arrears of pay for revolutionary services.	24	2	Petition	214	Naval Affairs.						
Nicholson, Com. Samuel, heirs of.	Compensation for revolutionary services.	25	2	Petition	48	Rev. Claims				Discharged; laid on table.		
Nicholson, Com. Samuel, heirs of.	Additional compensation for revolutionary services.	26	1	Petition	632	Rev. Claims.						
Nicholson, Com. Samuel, heirs of.	Compensation for revolutionary services.	28	2	Petition	117, 687	Rev. Claims				Discharged; laid on table.		
Nicholson, Com. Samuel, heirs of.	Compensation for revolutionary services.	28	2	Petition	66	Rev. Claims.						
Nicholson, Com. Samuel, heirs of.	Compensation for revolutionary services	29	1	Petition	115	Rev. Claims.						
Nicholson, Com. Samuel, heirs of.	Compensation for revolutionary services.	31	1	Petition	1043	Rev. Pensions	460	Adverse		Laid on table.		
Nicholson, Richard	Pension for services in 1791	17	2	Petition	209	Pens. & Rev. Cl'ms.						
Nick, John	Pension for revolutionary services.	3	1	Petition	103					Referred to Secretary War.		
Nick, John	Reimbursement of money advanced to United States.	21	1	Senate bill	387	Claims	Mar. 2, 1831	With amend'ts	S. 135	Passed	Passed	App'd March 3, 1831
Nickels, William, executor of.	Indemnity for French spoliations prior to 1800.	26	1	Memorial	182	Foreign Affairs.	343	Favorable; bill	319	Referred to Committee Whole House.		
Nickerson, Ebenezer, *et al.*	Indemnity for a vessel captured by the French.	12	1	Petition	315					Referred to Secretary of State.		
Nickerson, Eleazer	Bounty on fishing vessel	14	1	Petition	531	Com. and Manuf.						
Nickerson, Eleazer	Bounty on fishing vessel	14	2	Petition	278	Com. and Manuf.						
Nickerson, Eleazer	Bounty on fishing vessel	15	1	Petition	293	Com. and Manuf.	Mar. 17, 1818	Adverse		Rejected.		
Nickerson, Eleazer	Bounty on fishing vessel	17	1	Petition	280	Commerce.						
Nickerson, Jonathan, *et al.*	Bounty on vessels engaged in cod fishing.	14	1	Petition	558	Com. and Manul.						
Nickerson, Jonathan, *et al.*	Bounty on vessels engaged in cod fishing.	14	2	Petition	155	Com. and Manuf.						
Nickerson, Salathiel	Bounty on fishing schooner Nine Sisters.	15	1	Petition	157	Com. and Manuf.						
Nickerson, Salathiel	Bounty on fishing schooner Nine Sisters.	17	1	Petition	199	Commerce.						
Nickerson, Salathiel C., administrator of.	Bounty on fishing schooner Martha	25	3	Petition	214	Commerce.						
Nickerson, Salathiel C., administrator of.	Bounty on fishing schooner Martha	26	1	Petition	177	Commerce	311	Favorable	274	Referred to Committee Whole House.		
Nickerson, Salathiel C., administrator of.	Bounty on fishing schooner Martha	27	2	Petition	470	Commerce	April 12, 1842	Favorable	390	Referred to Committee Whole House.		
Nickerson, Salathiel C., administrator of.	Bounty on fishing schooner Martha	27	3	House bill	88	Whole House			390	Passed	Indef. postp'd.	
Nickerson, Salathiel C., administrator of.	Bounty on fishing schooner Martha	29	1	Memorial	336	Commerce.						

List of private claims presented to the House of Representatives of the United States form the 1st to the 31st Congress, inclusive—Continued.

Names of claimants.	Nature or object of the claim.	Congress.	Session.	How brought before the House of Reps.	Page of journal.	To what committee of the House referred.	No. or date of the report.	Nature of the report.	No. of the bill.	How disposed of by the House of Reps.	How disposed of by the Senate.	Date of the act of Congress, and remarks.
Nickerson, Seth, *et al.*	Bounty on vessels engaged in cod fishing.	14	1	Petition	558	Com. and Manuf.						
Nickerson, Seth, *et al.*	Bounty on vessels engaged in cod fishing.	14	2	Petition	155	Com. and Manuf.	....	....	......	Discharged; laid on table.		
Nickless, John	Increase of pension	4	2	Petition	651	Claims	Jan. 27, 1797	Adverse	......	Rejected.		
Nicklin, D. E. W., *et al.*	Indemnity for loss by destruction of steam frigate Missouri.	29	2	Memorial	326	Naval Affairs.						
Nicklin, Joseph M	Reimbursement of mon y due Post Office Department at time his store was destroyed by fire, which has been paid over by him.	29	2	Petition	232	P. Of. & P. Roads.						
Nicklin & Griffith	Register for ship America	8	2	Memorial	122	Com. and Manuf.	Feb. 12, 1805	Favorable; bill	58	Ref'd to Com. W. H.		
Nicklin & Griffith	Register for ship America	9	1	Memorial	281	Com. and Manuf.	Feb. 18, 1806	By bill	106	Passed	Rejected.	
Nicklin & Griffith	Register for ship America	9	1	Petition	379	Claims	April 11, 1806	Adverse	......	Indef. postponed.		
Nicklin & Griffith	Indemnity for French spoliations prior to 1800.	19	1	Memorial	312	Foreign Affairs.						
Nicoll, Agnes C	Indemnity for Indian depredations.	25	2	Petition	541	Claims.						
Nicoll, Francis H	(See John Conard)	21	1	....	394							
Nicoll, James	(See William Miller, assignee of.)	19	1	....	101							
Nicoll, S. T., & Co	Compensation for tea furnished the navy.	30	2	Petition	76	Claims	38	Favorable	728	Referred to Committee Whole House.		
Nicoll, S. T., & Co	Compensation for tea furnished the navy.	31	1	Petition	213	Claims	31	Favorable	59	Passed.		
Nicolls, Simon	Pension	3	1	Rep. of Secretary War.	131	Select	May 26, 1794	Referred to Sec. War.	R. 12	Passed	Passed	App'd June 9, 1794
Nicolls, Simon	Pension	5	2	Petition	224	Claims	....	....	......	Laid on table.		
Nicolls, Simon	Pension	5	3	Petition & docs	432	....	....	....	......	Ref'd to Com W. H		
Nicols, Jeremiah	Increase of salary as collector of customs.	3	1	Petition	27	....	....	....	......	Referred to Secretary Treasury.		
Nicols, Jeremiah	Increase of salary as collector of customs.	3	2	Petition and rep't Sec. Treasury.	284	....	....	....	......	Laid on table.		
Nicols, Jeremiah	Increase of salary as collector of customs.	4	2	Petition	649	Com. and Manuf.						
Nieves, Antonio	Confirmation of title to land	22	1	House bill	107	Whole House	Mar. 23, 1832	With't amend.	125	Passed	Passed	App'd June 25, 1832
Nieves, Joseph	Confirmation of title to land	22	1	House bill	107	Whole House	Mar. 23, 1832	With't amend.	125	Passed	Passed	App'd June 25, 1832
Nightingale & Clark	(See Nathaniel West and others.)	4	1	....	383							
Niles, Elisha	Pension	21	2	Petition	61	Military Pensions.						
Niles, Lucy	Continuation of pension	28	1	Petition	72	Rev. Pensions.						
Niles, Nathaniel	Compensation as chargé to France	23	1	Memorial	418	Foreign Affairs	April 3, 1834	Favorable	404	Passed	Passed	App'd June 30, 1834
Niles, Nathaniel	For outfit as chargé and for expenses incurred in that capacity.	23	2	Memorial	83	Foreign Affairs	Jan. 13, 1835	Favorable	634	Referred to Committee Whole House.		
Niles, Nathaniel	For outfit as chargé and for expenses incurred in that capacity.	26	1	Senate bill	1156	Foreign Affairs	....	....	S. 366			
Niles, Nathaniel	For outfit as chargé and for expenses incurred in that capacity.	26	1	House bill	471	Whole House	Mar. 20, 1840	With't amend.	27	Passed	Passed	App'd July 21, 1840
Niles, Nathaniel, (R. I.)	Restoration and continuation of pension.	27	2	Petition	818	Naval Affairs.						
Niles, Robert	Indemnity for losses by depreciation of paper money in revolutionary war, and by the non-fulment of engagements by public agents.	15	1	Petition	83	Pens. & Rev. Cl'ms.	....	....	......	Leave to withdraw.		

List of private claims presented to the House of Representatives of the United States from the 1st to the 31st Congress, inclusive—Continued.

Names of claimants.	Nature or object of the claim.	Congress.	Session.	How brought before the House of Reps.	Page of journal.	To what committee of the House referred.	No. or date of the report.	Nature of the report.	No. of the bill.	How disposed of by the House of Reps.	How disposed of by the Senate.	Date of the act of Congress, and remarks.
Nimblet, Joseph	Pension	26	1	Petition	287	Invalid Pensions	523	Favorable	420	Referred to Committee Whole House.		
Nimblet, Joseph	Pension	27	2	Petition	60	Invalid Pensions	149	Favorable	196	Rejected.		Reconsideration pending.
Nimblet, Joseph	Pension	27	3	House bill	126	Whole House	Dec. 31, 1842	With't amend.	196	Passed	Passed	App'd March 3, 1843
Nimmo, Henry	Remission of duties on cotton	13	3	Senate bill	686	Ways and Means	Feb. 4, 1814	Favorable	S. 75	Passed	Passed	App'd Feb. 23, 1815
Nimmo, Henry	Indemnity for ship Rebecca captured by Spanish government.	19	1	Petition	77					Laid on table.		
Nimmo, William T., *et al.*	Indemnity for house destroyed by the British.	15	1	Rep't of commissioner claims.	37	Claims.						
Nimmo, William T., *et al.*	Indemnity for house destroyed by the British.	15	2	Rep't of commissioner claims.	24	Claims	Nov. 25, 1818	Favorable	202	Referred to Committee Whole House.		
Nimmo, William T., *et al.*	Indemnity for house destroyed by the British.	16	2	Rep't of commissioner claims.	66	Claims	Dec. 12, 1820	Favorable	169	Rejected.		
Nimmo, William T., *et al.*	Indemnity for house destroyed by the British.	17	1	Rep't of commissioner claims.	195	Claims.						
Nimmo, William T., *et al.*	Indemnity for house destroyed by the British.	17	2	Petition	31	Claims	40	Favorable	200	Laid on table.		
Nimmo, William T., *et al.*	Indemnity for house destroyed by the British.	18	1	Petition	70	Claims	Dec. 29, 1823	Favorable	33	Passed	Passed	App'd May 17, 1824
Nine Sisters, schooner	(See Seth Sprague)	15	1		26							
Nippes, Abraham, executor of.	(See Winner, Nippes & Stemman)	19	1		78							
Nisewanger, Christopher, and Wm. S. Sullivant.	Indemnity for supplies lost on passage to Fort Towson.	26	1	Memorial	940	Claims.						
Nisewanger, Christopher, and Wm. S. Sullivant.	Indemnity for supplies lost on passage to Fort Towson.	26	2	Petition	167	Claims.						
Nisewanger, Christopher, and Wm. S. Sullivant.	Indemnity for supplies lost on passage to Fort Towson.	28	2	Petition	141	Claims.						
Nisewanger, David, *et al.*	To be released from judgment recovered against them as sureties for David Moore.	21	1	Petition	173	Judiciary.						
Nisewanger, Joseph, sen., and Joseph, jr., *et al.*	Confirmation of title to land	15	1	Petition	267	Priv. Land Claims.						
Nisewanger, Joseph, sen., and Joseph, jr., *et al.*	Confirmation of title to land	15	2	Petition	207	Priv. Land Claims.						
Nisewanger, Joseph, sen.	Confirmation of title to land	16	1	Petition	71	Priv. Land Claims.						
Nisewanger, Joseph, sen.	Confirmation of title to land	17	1	Petition	54	Public Lands						
Nisewanger, Joseph, sen.	Confirmation of title to land	18	1	Petition	54	Public Lands						
Nisewanger, Joseph, jr.	Confirmation of title to land	16	1	Petition	71	Priv. Land Claims.						
Nithercut, William, widow of.	Pension	19	2	Senate amendm't to House bill.	376	Whole House	March 2, 1827		314	Passed		App'd March 3, 1827
Nix, George	Pre-emption right to certain lands.	27	2	Senate bill	673	Public Lands	June 10, 1842	With't amend.	S. 134	Passed	Passed	App'd June 22, 1842
Nix, George	Relief for error of entry of land	31	1	Petition	1074	Public Lands.						
Nix, George	Relief for error of entry of land	31	2	Petition	445	Public Lands	102	Adverse		Laid on table.		
Nixon, George, *et al.*	Extra pay as clerks in Treasury Department.	3	1	Petition	88	Select	47	Favorable	69	Passed	Rejected.	
Nixon, Colonel, and Major Hinds.	Compensation for the services of the men who served under them.	14	1	Petition	106					Referred to Secretary War.		
Nixon, John	Pension	3	1	Rep. of Secretary War.	131	Select	May 26, 1794	Res. to refer to Sec'y War.	R. 12	Passed	Passed	App'd June 9, 1794
Nixon, John	Pension	3	2	Rep. of Secretary War.	278	Claims	Feb. 27, 1795	Adverse		Laid on table.		

List of private claims presented to the House of Representatives of the United States from the 1st to the 31st Congress, inclusive—Continued.

Names of claimants.	Nature or object of the claim.	Congress.	Session.	How brought before the House of Reps.	Page of journal.	To what committee of the House referred.	No. or date of the report.	Nature of the report.	No. of the bill.	How disposed of by the House of Reps.	How disposed of by the Senate.	Date of the act of Congress, and remarks.
Nixon, John	Pension	4	1	Res. and docs.	445	Claims	Feb. 18, 1796	Favorable	156	Passed	Passed	App'd April 20, 1796
Nixon, Captain Thomas, widow of.	Pension for revolutionary services.	30	1	Petition	116	Rev. Pensions	26	Adverse	......	Laid on table.		
Nixon, William	(See Caleb Thornley, sen., and others.)	4	1	....	388							
Nixon, Robert	Pension	4	1	Petition	438	Claims	May 7, 1796	Adverse	......	Leave to withdraw.		
Noah, Mordecai M., *et al.*	Portion of proceeds of goods sold for violation of revenue laws.	24	1	Memorial	945	Ways and Means.						
Noakes, Ephraim	Pension for revolutionary services.	20	2	Resolution	68	Military Pensions.						
Noble, Alanson	Pension	28	1	Petition	518	Invalid Pensions.						
Noble, David, heirs of	Compensation for revolutionary services.	24	2	Documents	119	Rev. Claims.						
Noble, David, heirs of	Compensation for revolutionary services.	26	1	Petition	167	Rev. Claims.						
Noble, David, heirs of	Compensation for revolutionary services.	26	1	Add'l evidence	701	Rev. Claims.						
Noble, David, heirs of	Compensation for revolutionary services.	26	2	Petition	36	Rev. Claims	49	Favorable	578	Referred to Committee Whole House.		
Noble, David, heirs of	Compensation for revolutionary services.	27	2	Petition	96	Rev. Claims.						
Noble, David, heirs of	Compensation for revolutionary services.	27	2	Petition	237	Rev. Claims	287	Favorable	244	Referred to Committee Whole House.		
Noble, David, heirs of	Compensation for revolutionary services.	28	1	Petition	300	Rev. Claims.						
Noble, Elijah	Continuation of pension	17	2	Petition	78	....	....	....	......	Laid on table.		
Noble, Elizabeth	(See William Noble, widow of.)	8	1	....	482							
Noble, Gideon	Pension	3	1	Report of Secretary of War.	131	Select	May 26, 1794	Favorable	J.R. 12	Passed	Passed	App'd June 9, 1794
Noble, Gideon	Pension	4	1	Res. and docs.	445	Claims.						
Noble, Goodman or Godman.	Continuation of pension	22	1	Petition	287	Rev. Pensions	379	Favorable	473	Passed	Indef. postp'd.	
Noble, James	Compensation for services as acting lieutenant on the Dolphin.	23	1	Senate bill	845	Naval Affairs	June 27, 1834	Favorable	S. 133	Passed	Passed	App'd June 30, 1834
Noble, Jeremiah and Moses	Fishing bounty on schooner Privado.	26	1	Petition	710	Commerce.						
Noble, Jeremiah and Moses	Fishing bounty on schooner Privado.	26	2	Petition	181	Commerce.						
Noble, Jeremiah and Moses	Fishing bounty on schooner Privado.	27	3	Petition	108	Commerce	129	Favorable	751	Referred to Committee Whole House.		
Noble, Jeremiah and Moses	Fishing bounty on schooner Privado.	28	1	Petition	414	Commerce	383	Favorable	281	Passed	Passed	App'd June 17, 1844
Noble, Jeremiah and Moses, and others.	Fishing bounty on schooner Privado.	30	1	Petition	317	Commerce	259	Favorable	252	Referred to Committee Whole House.		
Noble, John	(See Jeremiah and Moses Noble.)	30	1	....	317	....	259	....	252			
Noble, Joseph, heirs of	Permission to enter certain lands.	21	2	Senate bill	387	Public Lands	March 2, 1831	Adverse	S. 124	Laid on table.		
Noble, Mary and Philemon	(See Philemon Noble, heirs of.)	27	2	....	48							
Noble, Moses	Fishing bounty on schooner Ruth	29	1	Petition	632	Commerce	540	Favorable	362	Referred to Committee Whole House.		
Noble, Moses	Fishing bounty on schooner Ruth.	30	1	Petition	289	Commerce.						
Noble, Noah	Reimbursement of money paid J. F. Polk for services in the land office in Indiana.	19	1	Senate bill	520	Public Lands.	May 9, 1826	With amend.	S. 141	Passed	Amend't disagreed to.	

List of private claims presented to the House of Representatives of the United States from the 1st to the 31st Congress, inclusive—Continued.

Names of claimants.	Nature or object of the claim.	Congress.	Session.	How brought before the House of Reps.	Page of journal.	To what committee of the House referred.	No. or date of the report.	Nature of the report.	No. of the bill.	How disposed of by the House of Reps.	How disposed of by the Senate.	Date of the act of Congress, and remarks.
Noble, Noah	Reimbursement of money paid J. F. Polk for services in the land office in Indiana.	19	2	Senate bill	266	Public Lands	Feb. 14, 1827	Favorable	S. 62	Passed	Passed	App'd Feb. 22, 1827
Noble, Philemon, heirs of.	Arrears of pay for services on board frigate Congress in 1800.	27	2	Petition	48, 255	Naval Affairs	597	Adverse		Laid on table.		
Noble, Seth	Land in satisfaction of claim for revolutionary services.	6	2	Report of Commissioners.	748	Select	Jan. 19, 1801	By bill	280	Passed	Passed	App'd Feb. 18, 1801
Noble, Seth	(See Canadian refugees.)											
Noble, Thomas H.	Payment for charcoal furnished the United States at Fort Leavenworth.	26	1	Petition	623	Claims.						
Noble, Thomas H.	Payment for charcoal furnished the United States at Fort Leavenworth.	29	2	Senate bill	375	Claims	Mar. 1, 1847	With't amend.	S. 98	Referred to Secretary Treasury.		
Noble, Thomas H.	Payment for charcoal furnished the United States at Fort Leavenworth.	30	1	Report of Third Auditor.	76	Claims	742	Favorable; bill	583	Referred to Committee Whole House.		
Noble, Thomas H.	Payment for charcoal furnished the United States at Fort Leavenworth.	30	2	House bill	319	Whole House	Jan. 26, 1849	With't amend.	583	Passed	Passed	App'd March 3, 1849
Noble, William, widow of	Compensation for revolutionary services.	8	1	Petition	482	Claims				Discharged; leave to withdraw.		
Nock, Joseph	Remuneration for damages by violation of contracts by the Postmaster General.	27	2	Petition	110	Claims.						
Nock, Joseph	Remuneration for damages by violation of contracts by the Postmaster General.	27	3	Petition	49	Claims	290	Resolution		Referred to Solicitor of Treasury.		
Nock, Joseph	Remuneration for damages by violation of contracts by the Postmaster General.	28	1	Petition	964	Claims	493	Favorable	376	Referred to Committee Whole House.		
Nock, Joseph	Remuneration for damages by violation of contracts by the Post master General.	29	1	Memorial	58	Claims	377	Adverse		Leave to withdraw.		
Nock, Joseph	Remuneration for damages by violation of contracts by the Post master General.	30	2	Petition	227	P. Of. & P. Roads.						
Nock, Joseph	Remuneration for damages by violation of contracts by the Postmaster General.	31	1	Petition	1446	P. Of. & P. Roads.						
Nock, Joseph	Renewal of patent	30	1	Petition	228	Patents	114	Adverse		Laid on table.		
Noe, Marsh	Pension for revolutionary services.	22	1	Petition	109	Rev. Pensions				Discharged; laid on table.		
Noeks, Jonathan	Continuation of pension	21	2	Petition	158	Military Pensions.						
Noeks, Jonathan	Continuation of pension	22	1	Petition	68	Rev. Pensions	365	Favorable	460	Passed	Indef. postp'd.	
Noel, Alexander	Pension for revolutionary services.	23	2	Petition	303	Rev. Pensions.						
Noel, Alexander	Pension for revolutionary services.	24	1	Petition	108	Rev. Pensions	Jan. 13, 1836	Adverse. Res. of minority, favorable.		Referred to Committee Whole House.		
Noel, Alexander	Pension for revolutionary services.	27	2	Petition	375	Rev. Pensions	784	Adverse		Laid on table.		
Noel, Alexander	Pension for revolutionary services.	28	1	Petition	324	Rev. Pensions.						
Noel, James, C., *et al*	Patent for land located and paid for in Missouri.	28	2	Resolution	133	Public Lands.						

List of private claims presented to the House of Representatives of the United States from the 1st to the 31st Congress, inclusive—Continued.

Names of claimants.	Nature or object of the claim.	Congress.	Session.	How brought before the House of Reps.	Page of journal.	To what committee of the House referred.	No. or date of the report.	Nature of the report.	No. of the bill.	How disposed of by the House of Reps.	How disposed of by the Senate.	Date of the act of Congress, and remarks.
Noel, Richard, heirs of	Compensation for revolutionary services.	25	3	Petition	221	Rev. Claims.						
Noel, Richard, heirs of	Compensation for revolutionary services.	26	1	Petition	167	Rev. Claims.						
Noel, Richard, heirs of	Compensation for revolutionary services.	27	2	Petition	62	Rev. Claims	1027	Adverse		Leave to withdraw.		
Noel, Richard, heirs of	Compensation for revolutionary services.	28	1	Petition	276	Rev. Claims.						
Noel, Richard, heirs of	Compensation for revolutionary services.	29	1	Memorial	160	Rev. Claims.						
Noeles, Jonathan	(See Jonathan Noeks)	22	1		68		365		460			
Noland, James	Pension	19	2	Resolution	101	Military Pensions	Feb. 14, 1827	Favorable	436	Referred to Committee Whole House.		
Noland, William, *et al.*	Increase of compensation as registers and receivers of the land office.	18	2	Petition	55	Public Lands.						
Noland, William, *et al.*	Increase of compensation as registers and receivers of the land office.	19	2	Petition	137	Public Lands.						
Nollert, Philip	(See Philip Nullert)	13	3		593							
Nolton, Charles	(See Canadian refugees)	4	2		614							
Nones, A. B.	(See Benjamin Nones, heirs of)	26	1		182		343		319			
Nones, Benjamin, heirs of	Indemnity for French spoliations prior to 1800.	26	1	Memorial	182	Foreign Affairs	343	Favorable	319	Referred to Committee Whole House.		
Nones, Benjamin, heirs of	Indemnity for French spoliations prior to 1800.	31	1	Memorial	414	Foreign Affairs	355	Favorable	318	Referred to Committee Whole House.		
Nones, David B.	Indemnity for French spoliations prior to 1800.	26	1	Memorial	182	Foreign Affairs	343	Favorable	319	Referred to Committee Whole House.		
Noon, John	Pension	14	1	Petition	535	Naval Affairs.						
Nooner, John	Indemnity in land for losses by Choctaw treaty.	24	1	Petition	57	Public Lands	208	Favorable	208	Referred to Committee Whole House.		
Noot, William, (Minn.)	That improvements on certain lands may be secured to him.	31	2	Petition	184	Territories.						
Norcoos, Samuel, widow of.	Five years' half pay for services of deceased, who was killed in war of 1812.	22	1	Petition	441	Invalid Pensions.						
Norcoos, Samuel, widow of.	Five years' half-pay for services of deceased, who was killed in war of 1812.	22	2	Petition	142	Invalid Pensions.						
Norcoos, Samuel, widow of	Five years' half-pay for services of deceased, who was killed in war of 1812.	23	1	Petition	45	Invalid Pensions.						
Norcoos, Samuel, widow of.	Five years' half-pay for services of deceased, who was killed in war of 1812.	24	1	Petition	201	Invalid Pensions	Feb. 16, 1836	Favorable	343	Passed	Indef. postp'd.	
Norcoos, Samuel, widow of.	Five years' half-pay for services of deceased, who was killed in war of 1812.	27	2	Petition	97	Invalid Pensions	May 26, 1842	Adverse		Laid on table.		
Norcoss, Samuel, widow of.	Five years' half-pay for services of deceased, who was killed in war of 1812.	31	1	Petition	333	Invalid Pensions.						
Noreigo, Joseph	Indemnity for vessel condemned and sold by the United States.	17	2	Petition	167	Judiciary	Feb. 15, 1823	Favorable	297	Passed	Passed, with amendment.	App'd March 1, 1823

2—74

List of private claims presented to the House of Representatives of the United States from the 1st to the 31st Congress, inclusive—Continued.

Names of claimants.	Nature or object of the claim.	Congress.	Session.	How brought before the House of Reps.	Page of journal.	To what committee of the House referred.	No. or date of the report.	Nature of the report.	No. of the bill.	How disposed of by the House of Reps.	How disposed of by the Senate.	Date of the act of Congress, and remarks.
Norman, Aaron	(See William H. Bedford, agent.)	28	1	....	262							
Norman, Berryman	Pay for horses lost in Seminole war, 1818.	23	1	Documents	154	Claims.						
Norman, Berryman	Pay for horses lost in Seminole war, 1818.	28	1	Petition	262	Claims.						
Norman, George	Compensation for work on Cumberland road.	23	1	Resolution	589	Claims	455	Adverse	......	Laid on table		
Norman, Joseph	Pension for revolutionary services.	25	2	Petition	707	Rev. Pensions	....	....	......	Discharged; laid on table.		
Norman, Joseph	Pension for revolutionary services.	26	1	Petition	174	Rev. Pensions.						
Norman, Obediah, *et al.*	Pension for revolutionary services.	17	2	Petition	47	Pens. & Rev. Cl'ms.	Dec. 20, 1822	Adverse	......	Rejected.		
Norman, Patrick	Pension and bounty land for services and injuries in late war.	17	1	Petition	195	Military Affairs	Feb. 5, 1822	Adverse	......	Laid on table.		
Norman, Patrick	Pension and bounty land for services and injuries in late war.	18	1	Petition	135	Military Affairs	....	....	......	Discharged; leave to withdraw.		
Norman, Reuben	Confirmation of title to land in Missouri.	15	1	Petition	73	Priv. Land Claims.						
Norman, Reuben	Confirmation of title to land in Missouri.	16	1	Petition	71	Priv. Land Claims.						
Norman, Thomas W	Pension for revolutionary services.	24	2	Petition	90	Rev. Pensions.						
Norman, Thomas W	Pension for revolutionary services.	25	2	Petition	38	....	....	....	......	Referred to Committee Whole House on bill No. 176.		
Norman, Thomas W	Pension for revolutionary services.	25	3	Petition	349	Rev. Pensions.						
Norman, Thomas W	Pension for revolutionary services.	26	1	Petition	174	Rev. Pensions.						
Norman, Thomas W., heirs of.	Indemnity for French spoliations prior to 1800.	31	1	Petition	271	Foreign Affairs	355	Favorable	318	Referred to Committee Whole House.		
Norman, William	Invalid pension	28	1	Petition	429	Invalid Pensions.						
Norman, William	Invalid pension	28	1	Petition	56	Invalid Pensions	23	Adverse	......	Laid on table.		
Norrill, Joseph, *et al.*	Payment of witnesses fees in the case of the contested seat of D. S. Jackson.	30	2	Petition	77	Accounts.						
Norris, Benjamin	(See John W. Russell, administrator of)	31	1	....	197							
Norris, Eliphalet, widow of	Pension for revolutionary services.	28	1	Petition	289	Rev. Pensions.						
Norris, Eliphalet, widow of	Pension for revolutionary services.	29	1	Petition	255	Rev. Pensions	525	Adverse	......	Laid on table.		
Norris G. F., *et al.*, Cherokees.	Enforcement of treaty stipulations.	27	3	Memorial	257	Indian Affairs.						
Norris, Isaac W	(See Joseph Summerl, administrator of,)	15	2	....	182							
Norris, James	Compensation for revolutionary services.	1	3	Petition and rep't Sec. War.	370	....	....	....	......	Laid on table.		
Norris, James	Compensation for revolutionary services.	12	1	Petition	188	Claims	....	....	......	....	....	Leave to withdraw, 2d session.
Norris, James	Pension	30	1	Petition	975	Invalid Pensions.						
Norris, James	Pension	30	2	Petition	239	Invalid Pensions	83	Favorable	779	Passed	Passed, with amendment.	App'd March 3, 1849
Norris, Lieut. James, widow of.	For arrearages of pay	18	1	Resolution	369	Pens. & Rev. Cl'ms.	May 4, 1824	Adverse	......	Rejected.		
Norris, Cap. James F	Compensation for military services.	17	2	Resolution	213	Military Affairs	May 4, 1824	Adverse	......	Rejected.		
Norris, John	Release from liability to United States.	25	2	Memorial	1118	Judiciary.						

List of private claims presented to the House of Representatives of the United States from the 1st to the 31st Congress, inclusive—Continued.

Names of claimants.	Nature or object of the claim.	Congress.	Session.	How brought before the House of Reps.	Page of journal.	To what committee of the House referred.	No. or date of the report.	Nature of the report.	No. of the bill.	How disposed of by the House of Reps.	How disposed of by the Senate.	Date of the act of Congress, and remarks.
orris, John	Release from liability to United States.	25	2	Report of the Solicitor of the Treasury.	46	Judiciary				Discharged; laid on table		
Norris, John, executors of.	Release from judgment	28	2	Petition	333	Claims.						
Norris, John, executors of.	Release from judgment	29	1	Petition	373	Claims	195	Favorable; bill	186	Referred to Committee Whole House.		
Norris, John, executors of.	Release from judgment	29	2	House bill	337	Claims			186			
Norris, John, executors of.	Release from judgment	30	1	Petition	153	Claims	101	Adverse		Laid on table.		
Norris, John, administrator of.	Indemnity for French spoliations prior to 1800.	26	1	Memorial	182	Foreign Affairs	343	Favorable; bill	319	Referred to Committee Whole House.		
Norris, Robert T.	Indemnity for injuries received while pilot to New Yory.	26	1	Petition	708	Commerce.						
Norris, Robert T.	Indemnity for injuries received while pilot at New York.	26	2	Petition	53	Commerce.						
Norris, Robert T.	Indemnity for injuries received while pilot at New York.	27	2	Petition	57	Commerce	672	Favorable	404	Ordered to 3d reading.		
Norris, Robert T.	Indemnity for injuries reveived while pilot at New York.	27	3	House bill	88				404	Passed	Indef. postp'd.	
Norris, Robert T.	Indemnity for injuries reveived while pilot at New York.	28	2	Petition	134	Commerce.						
Norris, Robert T.	Indemnity for injuries received while pilot at New York.	29	1	Petition	314	Commerce	197	Favorable	188	Referred to Commitee Whole House.		
Norris, Robert T.	Indemnity for injuries received while pilot at New York.	29	2	House bill	381	Whole House	Feb. 19, 1847	Adverse	188	Rejected		
Norris, Robert T.	Indemnity for injuries received while pilot at New York.	30	1	Petition	111	Invalid Pensions				Discharged; laid on table.		
Norris, Samuel	Confirmation of title to land in Louisiana.	18	2	Report of land officers.	182	Public Lands				Discharged; referred to Sec'ry Treasury.		
Norris, Samuel	Confirmation of title to land in Louisiana.	19	1	Resolution	64	Public Lands.						
Norris, Samuel	Confirmation of title to land in Louisiana.	24	2	House bill	149	Whole House			797			
Norris, Samuel	Confirmation of title to land in Louisiana.	25	3	Petition	451	Public Lands				Discharged; laid on table.		
Norris, Samuel	Confirmation of title to land in Louisiana.	26	1	Petition	366	Priv. Land Claims.	338	Favorable	310	Referred to Committee Whole House.		
Norris, Samuel	Confirmation of title to land in Louisiana.	26	2	Petition	89	Priv. Land Claims.				Discharged; laid on table.		
Norris, Samuel	Confirmation of title to land in Louisiana.	26	2	Senate bill	334				S. 161			
Norris, Samuel	Confirmation of title to land in Louisiana.	27	2	Add'al evidence.	80	Indian Affairs	Aug. 20, 1842	Favorable	18	Passed	Passed	App'd Aug. 30, 1842
Norris, Theophilus	Pension for revolutionary services.	22	1	Petition	89	Rev. Pensions	Mar. 26, 1832	Favorable	512	Referred to Committee Whole House.		
Norris, William B.	(See John Norris, executor of.)	28	2		333							
Norris, William & Co.	Refunding of duties paid on iron.	28	2	Memorial	113	Ways and Means				Discharged; laid on table.		
Norris, William & Co.	Debenture on iron exported	29	2	Memorial	58	Commerce.						
Norris, William & Co.	Debenture on iron exported	30	1	Memorial	215	Ways and Means.						
Norris & Martin	Renewal of two certificates of United States stock lost.	13	3	Petition	606	Ways and Means				Discharged.		
North America Insurance Company.	Indemnity for French spoliations prior to 1800.	26	1	Memorial	182	Foreign Affairs	343	Favorable; bill	319	Referred to Committee Whole House.		

List of private claims presented to the House of Representativesthe of United States from the 1st to the 31st Congress, inclusive—Continued.

Names of claimants.	Nature or object of the claim.	Congress.	Session.	How brought before the House of Reps.	Page of journal.	To what committee of the House referred.	No. or date of the report.	Nature of the report.	No. of the bill.	How disposed of by the House of Reps.	How disposed of by the Senate.	Date of the act of Congress, and remarks.
North, Daniel	Pension for revolutionary services.	12	1	Petition	201	Claims	Mar. 19, 1812	Adverse		Laid on table.		
North, Hicks	Compensation for capture of vessel in war of 1812.	14	2	House bill	236	Whole House	Jan. 21, 1817	With't amend.	65	Passed	Passed	App'd Feb. 8, 1817
North, James H.	(See Exploring Expedition)	27	3		149		270		818			
North, Joseph, administratrix of.	Payment of award in the case of the schooner Postboy.	25	2	Petition	574	Claims.						
North, Joseph, administratrix of.	Payment of award in the case of the schooner Postboy.	26	1	Petition	170	Claims.						
North, Joseph E.	Invalid pension	29	1	Petition	233	Invalid Pensions.						
North, Sarah	(See Joseph North, administratrix of.)	25	2		574							
North, Thomas	Compensation for use of and restoration of property at West Point.	4	1	Petition	385					Referred to Secretary of War.		
North, Treviah	(See Septa Filmore, heirs of.)	22	2		151							
North & Vesey	Remission of duties on goods destroyed by fire.	4	2	Memorial	668	Com. and Manuf.	Feb. 23, 1797	Favorable		Referred to Committee Whole House.		
North & Vesey	Remission of duties on goods destroyed by fire.	5	2	Petition	83	Com. and Manuf.	Dec. 18, 1797	Favorable	24	Passed	Passed, with amendment.	App'd Jan. 15, 1798
Northam, Stephen T.	(See Samuel and John G Whitehorn, *et al.*)	14	1		449							
Northam, Timothy	Invalid pension	4	1	Rep. of Secretary War.	445	Claims	Feb. 18, 1796	Favorable	156	Passed	Passed	App'd April 20, 1796
Northam, Timothy	Increase of pension	15	1	Petition	265	Pens. & Rev. Cl'ms.						
North Carolina, citizens of Beaufort.	Salvage on cargo of the Spanish schooner Lucy.	16	1	Petition	428	Ways and Means.						
North Carolina, citizens of Cherokee county.	Remuneration for property destroyed by United States troops while removing Cherokee Indians.	26	1	Petition	340	Claims.						
North Carolina, merchants of Wilmington.	Release from the payment of certain duties.	1	2	Petition	222					Referred to Secretary Treasury.		
North Carolina, merchants of Wilmington.	Release from the payment of certain duties.	2	2	Rep. of Secretary War.	626					Laid on table.		
North Carolina line, revolutionary war, officers & soliers of.	Payment of arrearages due them in 1782–'83.	1	2	Resolution	210	Select	May 14, 1790	Favorable	Jt. R.	Passed	Passed	App'd June 7, 1790
North Carolina line, revolutionary war, officers of.	Indemnity for loss on their certificates of pay for services.	10	2	Petition	375					Laid on table.		
North Carolina line, revolutionary war, officers of.	Indemnity for loss on their certificates of pay for services.	11	2	Petition	195	Select.						
North Carolina line, revolutionary war, officers of.	Indemnity for loss on their certificates of pay for services.	11	3	Petition	460	Select.						
North Carolina, Quakers of.	Relief from laws of the State depriving them of right of preemption.	1	2	Petition	215	Select.						
North Carolina, State of	Payment of claims against the U. States settled by said State.	3	1	Resolution	102	Select	April 30, 1794	Favorable		Referred to Committee Whole House.		
North Carolina, State of	Remission of duties on statue of Washington.	16	1	Senate bill	201	Ways and Means.	Feb. 10, 1820	With't amend.	S. 28	Passed	Passed	App'd Feb. 24, 1820
North, Carolina, State of	That all valid claims for lands against said State be satisfied out of lands ceded to the United States in 1798.	18	1	Petition	287	Select.						

List of private claims presented to the House of Representatives of the United States from the 1st to the 31st Congress, inclusive—Continued.

Names of claimants.	Nature or object of the claim.	Congress.	Session.	How brought before the House of Reps.	Page of journal.	To what committee of the House referred.	No. or date of the report.	Nature of the report.	No. of the bill.	How disposed of by the House of Reps.	How disposed of by the Senate.	Date of the act of Congress, and remarks.
North Carolina, State of..	Reimbursement of money paid Cherokee Indians.	19	1	Resolution	235	Indian Affairs.						
North Carolina, State of..	Reimbursement of money paid Cherokee Indians.	19	2	Resolution	101	Indian Affairs.						
North Carolina, State of..	Reimbursement of money paid Cherokee Indians.	20	1	Resolution	35	Indian Affairs.	92	Favorable; bill	102	Referred to Committee Whole House.		
							April 23, 1828	As an amend' to bill.	120	Passed	Passed	App'd May 9, 1828
North Carolina, State of.,	Payment of money advanced during the late war.	24	1	Resolution.....	734	Claims.						
North Carolina, State of..	Payment of money advanced during the war with Mexico.	31	1	Senate bill	475	Military Affairs ...	Feb. 13, 1850	Adverse	S. 25	Referred to Committee Whole House.		
North Carolina, trustees of University of.	Reimbursemen for land ceded by United States to the Indians.	2	1	Memorial	528	....	....	....	......	Laid on table.		
Northen, Robert	Pre-emption right to lands in Indiana.	25	3	Petition	451	Public Lands.						
Northrop, Andrew, widow of.	Increase of pension	27	3	Petition	59	Rev. Pensions.						
Northrop, Andrew, widow of.	Increase of pension	28	1	Petition	99	Rev. Pensions.						
Northrop, Andrew, widow of.	Increase of pension	28	2	Add'l evidence..	172	Rev. Pensions.						
Northup, Henry	For relief as assignee of Nancy White.	17	2	Petition	78	Claims	....	....	......	Leave to withdraw.		
Northup, Henry	Payment for a horse lost in war of 1812.	23	1	Petition	80	Claims	95	Adverse	......	Laid on table.		
Northup, Henry	Indemnity for land scrip sold by Treasury Department.	23	1	Petition	220	Rev. Claims......	Mar. 13, 1834	Adverse	......	Laid on table.		
Northup, Henry	Indemnity for land scrip sold by Treasury Department.	24	1	Petition	431	Rev. Claims.						
Northup, Henry	Indemnity for land scrip sold by Treasury Department.	24	2	Petition	91	Rev. Claims.						
Northup, Henry	Indemnity for land scrip sold by Treasury Department.	25	2	Petition	49	Rev. Claims......	412	Adverse	......	Laid on table.		
Northup, Henry	(See Barnet Eichelberger, executors of.)	29	2	....	86							
Northup, Henry	(See James Armstrong Wilson, widow of.)	29	2	....	162							
Northrop, Joel	(See Henry S. Whiting, executors of.)	18	2	....	158							
Northrop, Stephen, heirs of	Arrears of revolutionary pension ..	29	1	Petition	618	Rev. Pensions.						
Northrop, Stephen, heirs of.	Arrears of revolutionary ension...	30	1	Petition	886	Rev. Pensions.						
Northway, Zenas	Pension	21	2	Petition	43	Military Pensions.						
Northwestern Territory, inhabitants of.	Confirmation of their titles to land.	2	1	Petition	574	Select.						
Northwestern Territory, inhabitants of.	Confirmation of their titles to land.	2	2	Resolution	628	Whole House.....	Dec. 31, 1792	Favorable; bill ordered.				
Northwestern Territory, inhabitants of.	Confirmation of their titles to land.	6	1	Petition	591	Select...........	April 16, 1800	Favorable....	249	Passed	Postponed.	
Northwestern Territory, inhabitants of.	Confirmation of their titles to land.	6	2	Memorial	745	Select.						

List of private claims presented to the House of Representatives of the United States from the 1st to the 31st Congress, inclusive—Continued

Names of claimants.	Nature or object of the claim.	Congress.	Session.	How brought before the House of Reps.	Page of journal.	To what committee of the House referred.	No. or date of the report.	Nature of the report.	No. of the bill.	How disposed of by the House of Reps.	How disposed of by the Senate.	Date of the act of Congress, and remarks.
Northwest'n Territory, sundry inhabitants of.	Indemnity for land ceded to Indians.	3	1	Petition	57	Select.						
Norton, Comfort	(See Timothy T. Norton, widow of.)	24	1		409							
Norton, Daniel D	Pay and boun y land for revolutionary services in war of 1812.	16	1	Petition and rep't Sec. of War.	188, 224					Laid on table.		
Nortcn, Daniel D	Paym nt for two horses taken by British in war of 1812.	18	2	Petition	55	Claims.						
Norton, Elnathan	Invalid pension	3	1	Rep. of Secretary War.	131	Select	Mar. 26, 1794	Res. to refer to Sec. War.	R. 12	Passed	Passed	App'd June 9, 1794
Norton, Elnathan	Invalid pension	3	2	Rep. of Secretary War.	337	Claims	Feb. 28, 1795	Favorable	130	Passed	Postponed.	
Nort n, Eln than	Inva id pension	4	1	Reps. of Secretary War.	445	Claims	Feb. 18, 1796	Favorable	156	Passed	Passed	App'd April 20, 1796
Norton, Garr t	Reimburs ment of illegal payment for public land.	28	1	Petition	75	Public Lands	144	Favorable	132	Passed	Passed, with amendment.	Amendmnent not concurred in by House.
Norton, G. W. and P. E.	Payment of Texas bonds and treasury n tes.	30	2	Petition	338	Claims.						
Norton, Hannah	(See Nathaniel Norton, widow of)	29	1		856							
Norton, Hunn B., *et al*	(See Oliver Norton, heirs of)	29	2		54							
Norton, John	Pension for injuries received in the army.	13	3	Petition	484	Pens. & Rev. Cl'ms.	Feb. 20, 1815	Favorable	303	Passed	Pas ed, with amendment.	App'd March 3, 1815
Norton, John	Renewal of pension	17	1	Petition	45	Rev Pensions.						
Norton, John	Arrearages of pension	22	1	Petition	381	Rev. Pensions				Discharged; laid on table.		
Norton, John P	Compensation for collecting certain duties.	26	2	Petition	121	Commerce.						
Norton, John P	Compensation for collecting certain duties.	27	2	Petition	56	Commerce				Discharged; laid on table.		
Norton, John P	Compensation for collecting certain du ies.	28	2	Petition	381	Commerce.						
Norton, John P	Compensation for collecting certain duties.	31	1	Petition	518	Commerce.						
Norton, Martha	(See heirs of Oliver Norton)	29	2		54							
Nort n, Nathaniel	Pension for revolutionary services.	22	1	Petition	556	Rev. Pensions.						
Norton, Nathaniel, widow of.	Pension	29	1	Petition	856	Rev. Pensions	786	Adverse		Laid on table.		
Norton, Nathaniel, widow of.	Extension of pension	30	1	Petition	637	Rev. Pensions	526	Adverse		Laid on table.		
Norton, Oliver, heirs of	Pension for revolutionary services.	29	2	Petition	54	Rev. Pensions	83	Adverse		Laid on table.		
Norton, Stephen, *et al*	(See Peter Bargy, jr., *et al*)	21	1		201							
Norton, Lieut. Thos., heirs of.	Arrearages of pay and expenditures while in public service.	19	1	Resolution	297	Rev. Claims	April 12, 1826	Adverse		Laid on table.		
Norton, Timothy T., widow of.	Bounty land for services in war of 1812.	24	1	Petition	409	Public Lands				Discharged; laid on table.		
Norton, Timothy T., widow of.	Bounty land for services in war of 1812.	24	2	Add'l evidence	390	Public Lands.						
Norvell, Benjamin	Payment for a horse lost in the late war.	15	2	Petition	74	Claims.						
Norvell, Edward B	(See Thomas Norvell, executor of.)	19	1		366							
Norvell, James	Pension	14	1	Petition	416	Pens. & Rev. Clm's.						
Norvell, Thomas, executors of.	Aid in locating land warrants	19	1	Petition	366	Public Lands.						

List of private claims presented to the House of Representatives of the United States from the 1st to the 31st Congress, inclusive—Continued.

Names of claimants.	Nature or object of the claim.	Congress.	Session.	How brought before the House of Reps.	Page of journal.	To what committee of the House referred.	No. or date of the report.	Nature of the report.	No. of the bill.	How disposed of by the House of Reps.	How disposed of by the Senate.	Date of the act of Congress, and remarks.
Norwood, Samuel	(See Jas. Daily, guardian of children of.)	15	2		78							
Notler, Benjamin	Pension	20	1	Petition	163	Military Affairs				Discharged; laid on table.		
Nott, William, *et al.*	That certain bonds may be cancelled.	17	1	Senate bill	374	Commerce	April 5, 1822	With amend.	S. 40	Referred to Committee Whole House.		
Nott, William, *et al.*	That certain bonds may be cancelled.	17	2	Petition	60	Commerce				Referred to 1st Comptrolles of Treasury.		
Nourse, Benjamin F., widow of.	Five years' half pay, in consideration of death of husband in Seminole war.	25	2	Petition	114	Military Affairs	510	Favorable	509	Rejected.		
Nourse, Benjamin F., widow of.	Pension	25	3	Senate bill	657				S. 180			
Nourse, Benjamin F., widow of.	Pension	27	2	Petition	63	Military Affairs	353	Adverse		Laid on table.		
Nourse, Benjamin F., widow of.	Pension	27	3	Petition	134	Military Affairs.						
Nourse, Benjamin F., widow of.	Pension	28	1	Petition	80	Military Affairs	425	Favorable	327	Referred to Committee Whole House.		
Nourse, Benjamin F., widow of.	Pension	29	1	Memorial	87	Naval Affairs				Discharged; laid on table.		Leave to withdraw.
Nourse, Elizabeth	(See James Nourse, widow of)	37	2		255							
Nourse, James	Pension	14	1	House bill	622	Whole House	April 11, 1816	Favorable	171	Passed	Passed, with amendment.	App'd April 30, 1816
Nourse, James	Increase of pension	15	1	Pension bill	405	Whole House	April 16, 1818	With amend.	172	Passed	Postponed.	
Nourse, James	Arrearages of pension	16	1	Petition	76	Pens. & Rev. Cl'ms.	Dec. 31, 1819	Adverse		Rejected.		
Nourse, James	Increase of pension	19	1	Petition	203	Military Pensions	164	Adverse		Laid on table.		
Nourse, James, widow of	Continuation of pension	27	2	Petition	255	Rev. Pensions.						
Nourse, James, widow of	Continuation of pension	28	1	Petition	541	Rev. Pensions.						
Nourse, Joseph	Increase of compensation as Register of Treasury.	4	2	Memorial	627	Select.						
Nourse, Joseph	Increase of compensation as Register of Treasury.	5	2	Senate bill	258	Whole House	May 18, 1798	Favorable	S. 17	Passed with amendm'.	Passed	App'd May 22, 1798
Nourse, Joseph	Payment of amount found due him by United States court.	21	2	Memorial	160	Claims.						
Nourse, Joseph	Payment of amount found due him by United States court.	22	1	Memorial	384	Claims.						
Nourse, Joseph	Payment of amount found due him by United States court.	23	1	Petition	34	Claims	372	Favorable	396	Referred to Committee Whole House.		
Nourse, Joseph	Payment of amount found due him by United States court.	24	1	Petition	50	Claims	844	Favorable	745	Referred to Committee Whole House.		
Nourse, Joseph	Payment of amount found due him by United States court.	25	2	Petition	37	Claims	58	Favorable	70	Referred to Committee Whole House.		
Nourse, Joseph	Payment of amount found due him by United States court.	25	3	House bill	375	Whole House			70			
Nourse, Joseph	Payment of amount found due him by United States court.	25	3	Add'l evidence	455	Whole House			70			
Nourse, Joseph	Payment of amount found due him by United States court.	26	1	Memorial	168, 340	Claims.						
Nourse, Joseph, widow of.	Settlement of the accounts of her late husband.	27	2	Petition	75	Claims.						
Nourse, Joseph, widow of.	Settlement of the accounts of her late husband.	27	2	Senate bill	1063	Judiciary	July 13, 1842	Favorable	S. 184	Referred to Committee Whole House.		

List of private claims presented to the House of Representatives of the United States from the 1st to the 31st Congress, inclusive—Continued.

Names of claimants.	Nature or object of the claim.	Congress.	Session.	How brought before the House of Reps.	Page of journal.	To what committee of the House referred.	No. or date of the report.	Nature of the report.	No. of the bill.	How disposed of by the House of Reps.	How disposed of by the Senate.	Date of the act of Congress, and remarks.
Nourse, Joseph, widow of.	Settlement of the accounts of her late husband.	27	3	Memorial	59	Judiciary.						
Nourse, Joseph, widow of.	Settlement of the accounts of her late husband.	27	3	Senate bill	209	Judiciary	July 31, 1843	Adverse	S. 25	Referred to Committee Whole House.		
Nourse, Joseph, widow of.	Settlement of the accounts of her late husband.	28	1	Petition	274	Judiciary	548	Adverse	......	Laid on table.		
Nourse, Joseph, widow of.	Settlement of the accounts of her late husband.	28	2	Petition	171	Claims.						
Nourse, Joseph, widow of.	Settlement of the accounts of her late husband.	29	1	Petition	120	Judiciary	375	Adverse	......	Laid on table.		
Nourse, Joseph, widow of.	Settlement of the accounts of her late husband.	29	2	Senate bill	375	Claims	Feb. 26, 1847	Favorable	S. 106	Referred to Committee Whole House.		
Nourse, Joseph, widow of.	Settlement of the accounts of her late husband.	30	1	Senate bill	308	Claims	Feb. 9, 1848	Favorable	S. 64	Passed with amend't.	Passed	App'd June 28, 1848
Nourse, Joseph P.	Fishing bounty on schooner Girls.	29	1	Petition	385	Commerce	542	Favorable	364	Ref'd to Com. W. H		
Nourse, Joseph P.	Fishing bounty on schooner Girls.	30	1	Petition	289	Commerce.						
Nourse, Joseph P.	Fishing bounty on schooner Girls.	30	2	Petition	203	Commerce.						
Nourse, Joseph P.	Fishing bounty on schooner Girls.	31	1	Petition	731	Commerce.						
Nourse, Josephine.	(See Benjamin Nourse, widow of.)	25	2	....	114							
Nourse, Maria L.	(See Joseph Nourse, widow of.)	27	2	....	75							
Nourse, Michael	Compensation for services in Treasury Department.	29	1	Memorial	498	Claims	579	Favorable	397	Referred to Committee Whole House.		
Nourse, Michael	Compensation for services in Treasury Department.	30	1	Petition	154	Claims.						
Nourse, William	Bounty land for naval service in revolutionary war.	11	2	Petition	243	Public Lands.						
Nourse, William	Compensation for naual service in revolutionary war.	19	2	Petition	333	Rev. Claims.						
Nourse, William	Pension	21	2	Petition	110	Military Pensions.						
Nourse, William	Pension	22	1	Petition	120	Rev. Pensions.						
Nourse, William	Pension	24	1	Petition	213	Invalid Pensions	254 June 28, 1836	Adverse Adverse.	....	Recommitted. Laid on table.		
Nowe, Lewis	To be restored to pension roll	17	2	Petition	36	Rev. Pensions.						
Nowell, Henry H.	Pension	19	1	Petition	66	Military Pensions.	164	Adverse	......	Laid on table.		
Nowell, Henry H.	Pension	19	2	Petition	84	Military Pensions.						
Nowell, James.	Invalid pension	14	1	House bill	622	Whole House.	April 23, 1816	With amend.	......	Passed	Passed	App'd April 30, 1816
Nowell, Samuel.	Pension	21	1	Senate bill	686	Military Pensions.	May 25, 1830	Favorable	S. 160	Referred to Committee Whole House.		
Nowell, Samuel.	Pension	21	2	Senate bill	106	Military Pensions.	Jan. 3, 1831	Adverse	S. 30	Passed	Passed	App'd March 2, 1831
Nowland, Mary M.	Release from a suit of the United States court.	30	1	Petition	114, 120	P. Of. & P. Roads.	327	Adverse	......	Laid on table.		
Nowland, Mary M.	Release from a suit of the United States court.	31	2	Petition	353	Judiciary.						
Noyes, Elihu	Pension for wounds in revolutionary war.	24	2	Petition	41	Naval Affairs	22	Adverse	......	Leave to withdraw.		
Noyes, Elihu	Pension for wounds in revolutionary war.	27	2	Petition	238	Invalid Pensions.						
Noyes, Enoch J.	(See John L. Bowman, *et al*)	26	1	....	199							
Noyes, John M.	(See John Chickring and John M. Noyes.)	16	1	....	160							
Noyes, Joseph	Invalid pension	11	2	House bill	283	Whole House	Mar. 24, 1810	With amends.	107	Passed	Passed	App'd April 27, 1810
Noyes, St. Joseph	Pension for revolutionary services.	10	2	Petition and rep't Sec. of War.	521	....	....	....	......	Laid on table.		

List of private claims presented to the House of Representatives of the United States from the 1st to the 31st Congress, inclusive—Continued.

Names of claimants.	Nature or object of the claim.	Congress.	Session.	How brought before the House of Reps.	Page of journal.	To what committee of the House referred.	No. or date of the report.	Nature of the report.	No. of the bill.	How disposed of by the House of Reps.	How disposed of by the Senate.	Date of the act of Congress, and remarks.
Noyes, Lieut. Joseph	Increase of pension	15	1	Petition	132							
Noyes, Joseph C.	Payment of three Treasury notes destroyed by fire which he had received as compensation for services as a member of Congress.	25	2	Resolution	152	Accounts	291	Favorable		Adopted		Paid out of contingent fund of House.
Noyes, Moses	(See Wadleigh Noyes, representatives of.)	2	1		448							
Noyes, Paul	Payment for equipments furnished army.	8	2	Memorial	13	Claims.						
Noyes, Paul, heirs of	Compensation for revolutionary services.	24	1	Petition	136	Rev. Pensions	May 10, 1836	Adverse		Laid on table.		
Noyes, Paul, heirs of	Compensation for revolutionary services.	25	2	Petition	200	Claims.						
Noyes, Paul, heirs of	Compensation for revolutionary services.	26	1	Petition	167	Rev. Claims.						
Noyes, Peter	Pension for services in war of 1812.	30	1	Resolution	182	Invalid Pensions	April 28, 1848	Adverse		Laid on table.		
Noyes, Rebecca	(See Paul Noyes, heirs of)	24	1		136							
Noyes, Samuel	Remission of duties on goods imported into Castine at the time it was in possession of the British.	16	1	Senate bill	108	Ways and Means	Jan. 14, 1820	With amend.	S. 13	Passed with amendm't.	Passed as am'd.	App'd April 11, 1820
Noyes, or Noes, Simeon	Invalid pension	1	3	Petition and rep't of Sec. War.	350, 393					Laid on table.		
Noyes, or Noes, Simeon	Invalid pension	3	1	Rep. of Secretary War.	131	Select	May 26, 1794	J't. res. to refer to Sec. War.	J. R. 12	Passed	Passed	App'd June 9, 1794
Noyes, or Noes, Simeon	Invalid pension	8	2	Memorial	13	Claims				Discharged; referred to Com. Whole House.		
Noyes, or Noes, Simeon	Invalid pension	9	1	Memorial	191	Claims				Leave to withdraw.		
Noyes, or Noes, Simeon	Invalid pension	15	1	House bill	405	Whole House	April 16, 1818	With amends.	172	Passed	Postponed.	
Noyes, Wadleigh, representatives.	For the benefit of the act for the relief of widows and heirs of those who died in the service.	2	1	Petition and rep't Sec. of War.	448	Select.						
Noyes, Wadleigh, representatives of.	For the benefit of the act for the relief of widows and heirs of those who died in the service.	16	2	Petition	145	Pens. & Rev. Cl'ms.	Jan. 31, 1821	Adverse		Laid on table.		
Noyes, Wadleigh, widow of	Continuation of pension	23	1	Memorial	73	Naval Affairs.						
Noyes, Wadleigh, representatives of.	Seven years' half pay for revolutionary services.	23	1	Memorial	354	Rev. Claims.						
Noyes, Wadleigh, representatives of.	Seven years' half-pay for revolutionary services.	23	2	Memorial	196	Rev. Claims.						
Noyes, Wadleigh, representatives of.	Seven years' half pay for revolutionary services.	24	1	Memorial	383	Rev. Claims	634	Favorable	614	Referred to Committee Whole House.		
Noyes, Wadleigh, representatives of.	Seven years' half-pay for revolutionary services.	25	2	Memorial	40	Rev. Claims	192	Favorable	218	Passed		
Noyes, Wadleigh, representatives of.	Seven years' half-pay for revolutionary services.	26	1	Memorial	165	Rev. Claims.						
Noyes, Wadleigh, representatives of.	Seven years' half-pay for revolutionary services.	30	1	Memorial	559	Rev. Claims.						
Noyes, Wadleigh, representatives of.	Compensation for revolutionary services.	28	1	Memorial	115	Rev. Claims.						
Noyes, Wadleigh, representatives of.	Compensation for revolutionary services.	28	2	Memorial	84	Rev. Pensions.						
Noyes, Wadleigh, representatives of.	Compensation for revolutionary services.	29	1	Memorial	227	Rev. Claims.						

List of private claims presented to the House of Representatives of the United States from the 1st to the 31st Congress, inclusive—Continued.

Names of claimants.	Nature or object of the claim.	Congress.	Session.	How brought before the House of Reps.	Page of journal.	To what committee of the House referred.	No. or date of the report.	Nature of the report.	No. of the bill.	How disposed of by the House of Reps.	How disposed of by the Senate.	Date of the act of Congress, and remarks.
Noyes, Wadleigh, representatives of.	Compensation for revolutionary services.	29	1	Memorial	984	Rev. Claims.						
Noyes, Wadleigh, representatives of.	Compensation for revolutionary services.	30	1	Memorial	111	Rev. Claims.						
Noyes, Wadleigh, representatives of.	Compensation for revolutionary services.	30	2	Memorial	86	Rev. Claims	22	Favorable	708	Referred to Committee Whole House.		
Noyes, Wadleigh, representatives of.	Compensation for revolutionary services.	31	1	Memorial	234	Rev. Claims.						
Noyrit, or Noyvit, Charles Francois.	For a grant of a section of land	26	1	Memorial	798	Priv. Land Claims.	July 21, 1840	Adverse	......	Laid on table.		
Noyrit, or Noyvit, Charles Francois	For a grant of a section of land	27	2	Petition	58	Priv. Land Claims.						
Noyrit, or Noyvit, Charles Francois.	Permission to exchange a tract of land	27	3	Petition	136	Priv. Land Claims.						
Nugent, or Newgent, Jacob	Revolutionary pension	26	1	Petition	625	Rev. Pensions	490	Adverse	......	Laid on table.		
Nukerck, Charles	Payment for baggage and money lost at battle of Oswego.	26	1	Petition	296	Military Affairs	420	Adverse	......	Laid on table.		
Null, Henry	Indemnity for losses sustained by contract on Cumberland road.	23	1	Petition	336	Roads and Canals.						
Null, Henry	Indemnity for losses sustained by contract on Cumberland road	23	2	Petition	248	Claims.						
Null, Henry	Indemnity for losses sustained by contract on Cumberland road.	24	1	Petition	207	Claims	283	Adverse	......	Laid on table.		
Null, Peter	Permission to correct an error in entries of land.	15	1	Petition	179	Public Lands	Feb. 3, 1818	Adverse	......	Rejected.		
Null, Peter	Permission to correct an error in entries of land.	15	2	Petition	122	Public Lands	....	....	......	Leave to withdraw.		
Nullert, Philip	Compensation for revolutionary services.	13	3	Petition	593	Public Lands.						
Nullert, Philip	Compensation for revolutionary services.	15	1	Petition	265	....	....	....	......	Laid on table.		
Nullert, Philip	Land for services in French war, 1755.	15	1	Petition	265	Pens. & Rev. Cl'ms.						
Numond, Joseph	(See Stephen Decatur, widow of, and others.)	20	1	....	295	....	201	....	S. 50			
Nunes, Henry A.	Reimbursement of money expended for repairing roads in Florida.	23	1	Petition	446	P. Of. & P. Roads.	....	....	......	Discharged; laid on table.		
Nunez, Widow	Confirmation of title to land in Louisiana.	22	1	House bill	107	Whole House	62	With't amend.	125	Passed	Passed	App'd June 25, 1832
Nunnally, Moses	Pension	23	1	Petition	113	Rev. Pensions	Feb. 10, 1834	Adverse	......	Laid on table.		
Nute, Jotham	Invalid pension	3	2	Rep. of Secretary War.	278	Claims	Feb. 28, 1795	Favorable; bill	130	Passed	Postponed.	
Nute, Jotham	Invalid pension	4	1	Rep. of Secretary War.	445	Claims	Feb. 18, 1796	Favorable; bill	156	Passed	Passed, with amendment.	App'd April 20, 1796
Nute, Jotham	Increase of pension	12	1	Petition	136	Claims	June 12, 1812	Adverse	......	Laid on table.		
Nute, Jotham	Increase of pension	12	1	House bill	361	Whole House	June 15, 1812	With amend.	138	Passed	Passed	App'd July 5, 1812
Nute, Jotham	Further increase of pension	19	2	Petition	49	Military Pensions.						
Nute, Jotham	Further increase of pension	21	1	Petition	83	Military Pensions.						
Nute, William	Pension for revolutionary services.	25	2	Resolution	767	Rev. Pensions	....	....	......	Laid on table.		
Nutt, William D.	Compensation for services in office of Treasurer of United States.	30	1	Petition	624	Claims	658	Adverse	......	Laid on table.		
Nutt, William D.	Compensation for services in office of Treasurer of United States.	30	2	Petition	313	Claims.						

List of private claims presented to the House of Representatives of the United States from the 1st to the 31st Congress, inclusive—Continued.

Names of claimants.	Nature or object of the claim.	Congress.	Session.	How brought before the House of Reps.	Page of journal.	To what committee of the House referred.	No. or date of the report.	Nature of the report.	No. of the bill.	How disposed of by the House of Reps.	How disposed of by the Senate.	Date of the act of Congress, and remarks.
Nutter, David, widow of	Pension for revolutionary services	24	2	Petition	84	Rev. Pensions				Discharged; laid on table.		
Nutter, David, widow of	Pension for revolutionary services	26	1	Resolution	385	Rev. Pensions	664	Adverse		Laid on table.		
Nutter, David, widow of	Pension for revolutionary services	30	2	Resolution	289					Leave to withdraw.		
Nutter, Elizabeth	(See David Nutter, widow of)	24	2		84							
Nutter, Jacob, heirs of	For prize money as seaman on board the Alliance.	30	1	Petition	635	Rev. Claims	April 26, 1848			Discharged; laid on table.		
Nutter, James P., *et al.*	(See Jacob Nutter, heirs of)	30	1		635							
Nutter, John	Invalid pension	12	1	Petition	193	Claims	June 12, 1812	Adverse		Laid on table.		
Nutter, John	Invalid pension	15	1	Petition	23	Pens. & Rev. Cl'ms.				Leave to withdraw.		
Nye, Ichabob	Pension for revolutionary services	21	2	Petition	209	Rev. Claims.						
Nye, John	Increase of pension	31	2	Petition	225	Invalid Pensions.						
Nye, John W	Compensation for horses and carryalls for use of House of Representatives, United States.	28	2	Memorial	275	Accounts	March 3, 1845	Adverse		Laid on table.		
Nye, John W	Compensation for horses and carryalls for use of House of Representatives, United States.	30	1	Petition	1047	Judiciary.						
Nye, John W	Indemnity for non-fulfilment of contract by House of Representatives, United States.	29	2	Petition	135	Claims.						
Nye, John W	Indemnity for non-fulfilment of contract by House of Representatives, United States.	29	2	Petition	227	Claims	March 1, 1847			Discharged; laid on table.		
Nye, John W	Payment of his accounts against House of Representatives, United States.	30	1	Petition	108	Accounts.						
Nye, John W	Payment of his accounts against House of Representatives, United States.	30	2	Petition	77	Judiciary	Feb. 8, 1849	Favorable		Laid on table.		
Nye, John W	Payment of his accounts against House of Representatives, United States.	31	1	Petition	324	Claims	167	Favorable		Referred to Committee Whole House.		
Nye, John W	Payment of his accounts against House of Representatives, United States.	31	2	Resolution	420	Whole House.						
Nye, John W	(See assignee of Peter Bargy, jr.)	26	1		294							
Nye, Samuel	Pension for revolutionary services	23	1	Petition	454	Rev. Pensions				Discharged; laid on table.		
Nyman, Henry	(See Ezra Slifer, administrator of)	26	1		278							

List of private claims presented to the House of Representatives of the United States from the 1st to the 31st Congress, inclusive—**Continued.**

Names of claimants.	Nature or object of the claim.	Congress.	Session.	How brought before the House of Reps.	Page of journal.	To what committee of the House referred.	No. or date of the report.	Nature of the report.	No. of the bill.	How disposed of by the House of Reps.	How disposed of by the Senate.	Date of the act of Congress, and remarks.
Oakes, Ephraim	Pension	21	1	Petition	49	Military Pensions	Jan. 3, 1830	Favorable	72	Passed	Passed	App'd May 14, 1830, name of petitioner omitted in act.
Oakes, Henry	(See Aaron M. Ogden, surety of.)	23	1	.....	37							
Oakey, Daniel	(See Richard & Charles A. Pullan.)	14	2	.....	136							
Oakley, Aulay	(See James Oakley, widow of.)	25	2	.....	914							
Oakley, Cornelius, widow of.	Pension for revolutionary services.	25	3	Petition	127	Rev. Pensions	.....	.....	.....	Discharged; laid on table.		
Oakley, Cornelius, widow of.	Pension for revolutionary services.	26	1	Petition	171	Rev. Pensions	137	Favorable	147	Passed	Indef. postp'd.	
Oakley, Cornelius, executors of.	Pension for revolutionary services.	29	2	Petition	141	Rev. Pensions.						
Oakley, James, widow of.	Pension for revolutionary services.	25	2	Petition	914	Rev. Pensions	.....	.....	.....	Discharged; laid on table.		
Oakley, Sarah	(See Cornelius Oakley, widow of.)	25	3	.....	127							
Oakman, Constance B.	Pension	22	1	Petition	55	Rev. Pensions	.....	.....	.....	Discharged; laid on table.		
O'Bannon, Andrew, widow of.	Compensation for property lost and for revolutionary services.	24	2	Petition	91	Rev. Claims	173	Adverse	.....	Laid on table.		
O'Bannon, Andrew, widow of.	Compensation for property lost and for revolutionary services.	25	2	Petition	546	Rev. Claims	973	Adverse	.....	Laid on table.		
O'Bannon, Andrew, widow of.	Compensation for property lost and for revolutionary services.	25	3	Petition	117	Rev. Claims	.....	.....	.....	Leave to withdraw.		
O'Bannon, Andrew, widow of.	Compensation for property lost and for revolutionary services.	26	1	Petition	362	Rev. Claims	.....	.....	.....	Discharged; laid on table.		
O'Bannon, Andrew, heirs of.	Compensation for revolutionary services.	31	1	Petition	714	Rev. Claims.						
O'Bannon, Jennings	Indemnity for expenses of a certain suit.	16	1	Petition	35	Claims	28	Adverse	.....	Laid on table.		
O'Bannon, Jennings	Indemnity for expenses of a certain suit.	16	1	Senate bill	201	Whole House	Mar. 30, 1820	With't amend.	S. 27	Passed	.....	App'd April 5, 1820
O'Bannon, John	(See Reuben E. Gentry, *et al.*)	24	1	.....	65							
O'Bannon, Mary	(See Andrew O'Bannon, widow of)	24	2	.....	91							
O'Bannon, Presley N.	Compensation for horse lost in the public service.	19	1	Petition	99	Claims	Jan. 6, 1826	Adverse	.....	Laid on table.		
O'Bannon, Presley N.	Compensation for horse lost in the public service.	21	1	Petition	135	Claims	Jan. 11, 1830	Adverse	.....	Laid on table.		
O'Bannon, Presley N.	Compensation for horse lost in the public service.	22	2	Petition	89	Claims	Jan. 28, 1832	Adverse	.....	Laid on table.		
O'Bannon, Presley N.	Compensation for horse lost in the public service.	24	1	Petition	49	Claims	586	Favorable	567	Referred to Committee Whole House.		
O'Bannon, Presley N.	Compensation for horse lost in the public service.	25	2	Petition	37	Claims	34	Favorable	46	Passed	Passed	App'd March 7, 1838
Obannon, Thomas	Correction of error in entry of land	11	3	Petition	457	Public Lands.						
Obannon, Thomas	Correction of error in entry of land	12	1	Senate bill	52	Public Lands	Feb. 21, 1812	With't amend.	S. 3	Passed	Passed	App'd Feb. 24, 1812
Obert, John	Invalid pension	3	1	Rep. of Secretary War.	131	Select	May 26, 1794	Res. to refer to Sec. of War.	J.R. 12	Passed	Passed	App'd June 9, 1794
Obert, John	Invalid pension	3	2	Rep. of Secretary War.	262	Claims.						
Obert, John	Invalid pension	4	1	Resolution	445	Claims.						
Obert, John	Invalid pension	4	2	Resolution	614	Claims.						

List of private claims presented to the House of Representatives of the United States from the 1st to the 31st Congress, inclusive—Continued.

Names of claimants.	Nature or object of the claim.	Congress.	Session.	How brought before the House of Reps.	Page of journal.	To what committee of the House referred.	No. or date of the report.	Nature of the report.	No. of the bill.	How disposed of by the House of Reps.	How disposed of by the Senate.	Date of the act of Congress, and remarks.
Oblenis, Garret	Invalid pension	3	1	Rep. of Secretary War.	175	....	....	....	......	Laid on table.		
Oblenis, Garret	Invalid pension	3	2	Rep. of Secretary War.	262	Claims.						
Oblenis, Garret	Invalid pension	4	1	Resolution	545	Claims.						
Oblenis, Garret	Invalid pension	4	2	Resolution	614	Claims	Feb. 6, 1797	Pension bill	224	Passed	Postponed.	
Oblenis, Garret	Invalid pension	5	2	Pension bill	127	Whole House	Jan. 9, 1798	With amends.	38	Passed	Passed	App'd Feb. 2, 1798
Oblenis, Garret	(See Hendrick Oblenis, executor of)	14	2	....	90							
Oblenis, Hendrick, executor of.	Payment of revolutionary certificate.	14	2	Petition	90	Pens. & Rev. Cl'ms.	....	....	......	Discharged; laid on table.		
O'Brien, Christopher, heirs of.	Land in lieu of a Spanish grant	25	2	Petition	373	Priv. Land Claims.	....	....	......	Discharged; laid on table.		
O'Brien, Christopher, heirs of.	Land in lieu of a Spanish grant	25	3	Petition	134	Priv. Land Claims.						
O'Brien, Christopher, heirs of.	Land in lieu of a Spanish grant	26	1	Petition	179	Priv. Land Claims.						
O'Brien, Daniel	Invalid pension	23	2	Petition	150	Invalid Pensions.						
O'Brien, Dennis	(See Stephen Decatur, widow of, *et al.*)	20	1	....	295	....	201	....	S. 50			
O'Brien, James, and James Aylyard.	Remission of tonnage duties on two vessels.	4	2	Petition	716	Com. and Manuf.	115	Favorable	244	Passed	Passed	App'd March 3, 1797
O'Brien, Jeremiah	Compensation for supplies on public account.	13	1	Petition and rep't of Sec. War.	32, 138	Military Affairs.						
O'Brien, Jeremiah	Compensation for supplies on public account.	13	2	Petition	201	Military Affairs	....	....	......	Discharged; laid on table.		
O'Brien, Jeremiah	Compensation for supplies on public account.	14	1	Petition	238	Military Affairs.						
O'Brien, Lucius, widow of.	Pension for military services	27	2	Petition	228	Military Affairs	July 8, 1842	Adverse	......	Laid on table.		
O'Brien, Lucius, widow of.	Pension for military services	29	2	Petition	112	Invalid Pensions.						
O'Brien, Reuben	(See Stephen Decatur, widow of, *et al.*)	20	1	....	295	....	201	....	S. 50			
O'Brien, Richard	Settlement of account as United States consul at Algiers.	16	1	Senate bill	429	Foreign Affairs	May 9, 1820	With amend.	S. 90	Passed with amendm't.	Concurred in.	App'd May 15, 1820
O'Brien, Richard	Additional compensation	16	2	Petition	78	Claims	Jan. 31, 1821	Favorable	239	Referred to Committee Whole House.		
O'Brien, Richard	Additional compensation	17	1	Petition	68	Claims	Jan. 21, 1822	Favorable	49	Passed	Passed	App'd May 6, 1822
O'Brien, Richard, heirs of.	Compensation for losses sustained in public service.	27	3	Petition	151	Claims.						
O'Brien, Richard, heirs of.	Indemnity for French spoliations prior to 1800.	29	2	Petition	136	Foreign Affairs.						
O'Brien, Richard, heirs of.	Indemnity for French spoliations prior to 1800.	30	1	Petition	117	Foreign Affairs	....	General bill	21	Referred to Committee Whole House.		
O'Brien, Richard, heirs of.	Indemnity for French spoliations prior to 1800.	31	1	Petition	299	Foreign Affairs	355	Favorable	318	Referred to Committee Whole House.		
O'Brien, Shadrach	Arrears of pension	25	2	Petition	181	Invalid Pensions	....	....	......	Discharged; laid on table.		
O'Brien, Shadrach	Arrears of pension	29	1	Petition	1103	Invalid Pensions.						
O'Brien, Thomas M	Compensation for loss of time as a stonecutter.	31	1	Petition	742	Claims	....	....	......	Discharged; laid on table.		
O'Brien, William	Compensation for naval service	28	2	Petition	405	Naval Affairs.						
O'Bryan, John	Release from judgment for violating revenue laws.	11	3	Petition	527	Com. and Manuf.	....	....	......	....	....	See act June 2, 1813

List of private claims presented to the House of Representatives of the United States from the 1st to the 31st Congress, inclusive—Continued.

Names of claimants.	Nature or object of the claim.	Congress.	Session.	How brought before the House of Reps.	Page of journal.	To what committee of the House referred.	No. or date of the report.	Nature of the report.	No. of the bill.	How disposed of by the House of Reps.	How disposed of by the Senate.	Date of the act of Congress, and remarks.
O'Bryan, William, heirs of.	Pension for disabilities in Florida war.	29	1	Petition	82	Invalid Pensions...	50	Adverse	......	Laid on table.		
O'Bryan, William, heirs of.	Pension for disabilities in Florida war.	29	2	Petition	86	Invalid Pensions.						
Obuchon, Francis M.....	Permission to locate land........	25	2	Petition	418	Priv. Land Claims.	....	....	......	Discharged; laid on table.		
O'Cairn, Jeremiah.......	Indemnity for vessel lost in public service.	1	2	Petition	173	....	....	....	......	Referred to Secretary of War.		
Ochiltree, David, heirs of.	Compensation for property taken for public use.	23	1	Petition	41	Rev. Claims......	Dec. 17, 1833	Adverse	......	Laid on table.		
Ochiltree, James	Pre-emption right to land in Illinois.	24	2	Petition	268	Public Lands.						
O'Conner, John, heirs of..	Confirmation of title to land	12	2	Petition	611	Public Lands.....	....	....	......	Discharged; laid on table.		
O'Conner, John, heirs of..	Confirmation of title to land	13	2	Petition	251	Public Lands.....	....	....	......	Discharged; laid on table.		
O'Conner, John, heirs of..	Confirmation of title to land	13	3	Petition	681	Public Lands.....	....	....	......	Discharged; laid on table.		
O'Conner, John, heirs of..	Confirmation of title to land	14	1	Petition	60	Public Lands.....	....	....	......	Discharged; laid on table.		
O'Conner, John, heirs of..	Confirmation of title to land	14	2	Petition	41	Priv. Land Claims.	....	....	......	Discharged; laid on table.		
O'Conner, John, heirs of..	Confirmation of title to land	15	1	Petition	173	Priv. Land Claims.	....	....	......	Discharged; laid on table.		
O'Conner, John, heirs of..	Confirmation of title to land	16	1	Senate bill	237	Priv. Land Claims.	Feb. 25, 1820	With't amend.	S. 33	Passed	....	App'd April 5, 1820
O'Conner, Nicholas, widow of.	Continuation of pension	17	2	Petition	208	Military Affairs....	....	....	......	Discharged; laid on table.		
O'Conner, Nicholas, widow of.	Continuation of pension	18	1	Petition	97	Military Affairs....	Mar. 29, 1824	Adverse	......	Laid on table.		
O'Conner, Sarah	(See Nicholas O'Conner, widow of.)	17	2	....	208							
O'Conner, Thomas	Invalid pension................	22	1	Petition	383	Invalid Pensions...	....	....	......	Discharged; laid on table.		
Odam, Seybert...........	Increase of pension	11	3	Pension bill	604	Whole House	Mar. 2, 1811	With amend..	218	Passed	Passed	App'd March 3, 1811
Odell, Azariah W., heirs of.	Compensation for services in war of 1812.	26	1	Petition	294	Invalid Pensions.						
Odell, Azariah W., heirs of.	Compensation for services in war of 1812.	26	2	Petition	77	Invalid Pensions ..	Jan. 8, 1841	Adverse	......	Laid on table.		
Odell, Catharine	(See Jonathan Odell, widow of)..	27	2	....	1239							
Odell, Elizabeth.........	Payment of money under treaty of 1837.	31	1	Petition	312	Indian Affairs.						
Odell, Elizabeth.........	Payment of money under treaty of 1837.	31	2	Petition	207	Indian Affairs.....	19	Favorable....	451	Referred to Committee Whole House.		
Odell, James M.........	(See Marcellus Eells)..........	30	2	....	77							
Odell, Jeremiah	Pension for revolutionary services.	25	2	Petition	914	Rev. Pensions.....	....	....	......	Discharged; laid on table.		
Odell, Jeremiah	Pension for revolutionary services.	26	1	Petition	173	Rev. Pensions	....	....	......	Discharged; laid on table.		
Odell, Jeremiah	Pension for revolutionary services.	26	2	Petition	78	Rev. Pensions.						
Odell, Jeremiah	Pension for revolutionary services.	27	2	Petition	153	Rev. Pensions	784	Adverse	......	Laid on table.		
Odell, Jonathan, widow of.	Continuation of pension	27	2	Petition	1239	Rev. Pensions	....	....	......	Discharged; laid on table.		
Odell, Joseph G.........	Arrears of pension	23	1	Petition	309	Invalid Pensions...	Mar. 20, 1834	Adverse	......	Laid on table.		
Odell, Joseph G.........	Arrears of pension	28	1	Petition	366	Claims.						

List of private claims presented to the House of Representatives of the United States from the 1st to the 31st Congress, inclusive—Continued.

Names of claimants.	Nature or object of the claim.	Congress.	Session.	How brought before the House of Reps.	Page of journal.	To what committee of the House referred.	No. or date of the report.	Nature of the report.	No. of the bill.	How disposed of by the House of Reps.	How disposed of by the Senate.	Date of the act of Congress, and remarks.
Odell, Nathan	Compensation for supplies furnished United States army.	4	1	Rep. of Secretary Treasury.	388	Claims	74	Adverse	......	Laid on table.		
Oden, Benjamin	Bounty land for military services of slave.	22	1	Petition	582	Claims.						
Oden, Benjamin	Bounty land for military services of slave.	22	2	Petition	186	Claims	Mar. 2, 1833	Favorable	762	Referred to Committee Whole House.		
Oden, Benjamin	Bounty land for military services of slave.	23	1	Resolution	96	Priv. Land Claims.	392	Favorable	408	Referred to Committee Whole House.		
Oden, Benjamin	Bounty land for military services of slave.	24	1	Resolution	459	Priv. Land Claims.	425	Adverse	......	Laid on table.		
Odle, Perry	(See William H. Bedford, agent.)	28	1	....	262							
Odler, or Outler, Francis	Pension for military services	21	2	Petition	209	Military Pensions.						
Odem, Jacob, representatives of.	Confirmation of title to land in Missouri.	15	1	Petition	312	Priv. Land Claims.						
Odom, Sion	Compensation for revolutionary services.	21	1	Petition	74	Military Pensions.						
Odom, Sion	Compensation for revolutionary services.	22	1	Petition	454	Rev. Pensions.						
O'Donnell, Bernard, widow of.	Pension for services of husband as naval hospital steward.	26	1	Petition	627	Naval Affairs.						
O'Donnell, Bernard, widow of.	Pension for services of husband as naval hospital steward.	26	2	Petition	181	Naval Affairs.						
O'Donnell, Bernard, widow of.	Pension for services of husband as naval hospital steward.	27	2	Petition	308	Naval Affairs	597	Adverse	......	Laid on table.		
O'Donnell, Eleanor	(See Bernard O'Donnell, widow of.)											
O'Donnell, or O'Donald, John.	Invalid pension	31	1	Petition	988	Invalid Pensions.						
O'Fallon, John	(See Elias T. Laugham, sureties of.)	25	3	....	176							
Offerrals, or Ferralls, Denis	Increase of pension	15	1	Petition	49	Pens. & Rev. Cl'ms.	....	....	......	Discharged; leave to withdraw.		
Offert, Theodore	Compensation for a mare taken for public use.	31	1	Senate bill	1161	Claims	419	With't amend	S. 6	Referred to Committee Whole House.		
Officers of the war of 1756.	Confirmation of title to land granted by the King of Great Britain.	9	1	Petition	357	Public Lands	April 9, 1806	Res. to postpone indef.	......	Resolution adopted.		
Officers of the war of 1756.	Confirmation of title to land granted by the King of Great Britain.	9	2	Petition	485	Public Lands	Feb. 3, 1807	Report not of record.	......	Referred to Committee Whole House.		
Officers of the war of 1756.	Confirmation of titles to land granted by the King of Great Britain.	10	1	Petition	185	Public Lands.						
Officers of the war of 1756, heirs of.	Bounty land	12	1	Petition	32	Claims.						
Officers of the revolutionary war.	Confirmation of their locations of bounty land warrants.	3	2	Petition	291	Select.						
Officers of the revolutionary war.	Permission to include their improvements in locating their bounty land warrants.	4	1	Petition	503	....	....	....	......	Referred to Committee Whole House on bill No. 147.	....	See act June 1, 1796
Officers and soldiers, war of 1812.	Bounty land for services on the Wabash.	12	1	President's mess.	8	Select	Feb. 10, 1812	Favorable; bill	76	Passed	Passed	App'd April 10, 1812
Officers at Fort Bowyer	(See Wm. Lawrence and others.)	14	1	....	375							
Officers, &c., Barney's flotilla.	Indemnity for property destroyed by the blowing up of said flotilla.	14	1	Petition	146	Naval Affairs	Mar. 18, 1816	Adverse	......	Laid on table.		

List of private claims presented to the House of Representatives of the United States from the 1st to the 31st Congress, inclusive—Continued.

Names of claimants.	Nature or object of the claim.	Congress.	Session.	How brought before the House of Reps.	Page of journal.	To what committee of the House referred.	No. or date of the report	Nature of the report.	No. of the bill.	How disposed of by the House of Reps.	How disposed of by the Senate.	Date of the act of Congress, and remarks.
Officers of Governor Edward's staff.	(See Illinois, staff of the governor.)	14	2	....	340							
Officers and soldiers of the Seminole war.	Payment for horses and other property lost in said war.	16	1	Resolution	25	Select	Dec. 15, 1819	By bill	8	Rejected.		
Officers and soldiers of the Seminole war.	Payment for horses and other property lost in said war.	16	1	Senate bill	326	Claims	Mar. 27, 1820	Adverse	S. 29	Laid on table.		
Officers and soldiers of the Seminole war.	Payment for horses and other property lost in said war.	17	1	Documents.....	47	Select	April 3, 1822	By bill	152	Passed............	Passed	App'd May 4, 1822
Officers and soldiers of the Seminole war.	Explanatory act	18	1	Senate bill	164	Military Affairs ...	Jan. 21, 1824	With amend'ts	S. 11	Passed	Passed	App'd May 26, 1824
Officers and soldiers of Fort Delaware.	Indemnity for destruction of their property by the burning of said fort.	21	2	Senate bill	381	Military Affairs ...	Feb. 28, 1831	Adverse	S. 163	Referred to Committee Whole House.		
Officers and soldiers of Fort Delaware.	Indemnity for destruction of their property by the burning of said fort.	22	1	Senate bill	521	Military Affairs ...	Mar. 27, 1832	With't amend.	S. 73	Passed	....	App'd July 14, 1832
Officers and soldiers of Hancock barracks.	Indemnity for destruction of their property by the accidental burning of said barracks.	22	2	Petition	397	Claims.						
Officers and soldiers of Hancock barracks.	Indemnity for destruction of their property by the accidental burning of said barracks.	23	1	Petition	35	Military Affairs ...	Dec. 31, 1833	Adverse	......	Laid on table.		
Offield, Lewis D	Reimbursement of expenses in preparing two sons to enter United States service.	30	1	Petition	480	Claims	419	Adverse	......	Laid on table.		
O'Flyng, Abigail........	Bounty land for military services of husband and three sons.	14	1	Petition	257	Claims	Feb. 26, 1816	Favorable; bill	......	Passed	Passed	App'd April 24, 1816
O'Flyng, Edmund and Patrick.	Bounty land for military services .	14	1	House bill......	401	Whole House.....	April 9, 1816	With amend's.	......	Passed	Passed	App'd April 24, 1816
O'Flyng, Patrick, (2d)...	(See Abigail O'Flyng.)											
O'Flyng, Temple E......	(See Abigail O'Flyng.)											
Ogden, Aaron, and others.	For settlement of their claim against government for services in revolutionary war.	19	1	Petition	31	Select	....	....	......	Discharged; laid on table.		
Ogden, Aaron, and others.	For settlement of their claim against government for services in revolutionary war.	20	1	Petition	10	Select	136	Favorable; bill	160	Referred to Committee Whole House.		
Ogden, Aaron, and others.	For settlement of their claim against government for services in revolutionary war.	20	1	Senate bill	646	Whole House.....	May 1, 1828	With amend'ts	S. 44	Passed with amendm't.	Passed	App'd May 15, 1828
Ogden, Aaron M., surety of.	Release from judgment on custom-house bond.	23	1	Petition	37	Judiciary.........	142	Favorable; bill	155	Passed	Passed	App'd May 10, 1834
Ogden, Aaron N........	(See Samuel Langdon, and others)	12	1	....	138							
Ogden, Abraham........	(See Isaac Lawrence, and others).	14	1	....	386							
Ogden, Abraham, & others	Remuneration for losses by detention by Spanish government of their schooner Mary, chartered by United States.	19	1	Petition	248	Commerce.......	....	....	......	Discharged; laid on table.		
Ogden, Abraham, & others	Remuneration for losses by detention by Spanish government of their schooner Mary, chartered by United States.	20	1	Petition	51	Commerce	....	....	......	Discharged; laid on table.		
Ogdee, Albert, & Co	For drawback on goods exported..	14	1	Petition	366	Com. and Manuf..	....	....	......	Disch'd; laid on table.		

List of private claims presented to the House of Representatives of the United States from the 1st to the 31st Congress, inclusive—Continued.

Names of claimants.	Nature or object of the claim.	Congress.	Session.	How brought before the House of Reps.	Page of journal.	To what committee of the House referred.	No. or date of the report.	Nature of the report.	No. of the bill.	How disposed of by the House of Reps.	How disposed of by the Senate.	Date of the act of Congress, and remarks.
Ogden, Albert, & Co	For drawback on goods exported	14	2	Petition	185	Com. and Manuf.	....	....	......	Discharged; laid on table.		
Ogden, Andrew, and Thos. C. Butler.	Remission of forfeiture of ship Koran libelled for smuggling.	15	1	Petition	90	Ways and Means	....	....	......	Discharged; laid on table.		
Ogden & Curtis	(Sea Michael Gratz, heir of)	23	1	....	42	....	71	....	81			
Ogden, David B	(See John Shaw, executor of)	29	1	....	124	....	170					
Ogden, Edward, and E. York, representatives of.	Refunding money paid for land	27	2	Memorial	829	Priv. Land Claims.						
Ogden, Edmund	(See Joseph Hover)	27	3	....	484							
Ogden & Harrison	Permission to import brass wire and machinery.	12	1	Petition	63	Com. and Manuf.						
Ogden, Samuel G	For new register for American built ship Indostan.	8	2	Petition	22	Com. and Manuf.	Nov. 29, 1804	Report not on record.	......	Leave to withdraw.		
Ogden, Stephen	Pension	9	2	House bill	608	Whole House	Feb. 28, 1807	With amends.	216	Passed	Passed	App'd March 3, 1807
Ogden, Thomas	Compensation for use and damage to property, at Sacketts' Harbor, by United States during war of 1812.	16	1	Senate bill	444	Claims	....	....	S. 58			
Ogden, Thomas	Compensation for use and damage to property, at Sacketts' Harbor, by United States during war of 1812.	16	2	Senate bill	102	Claims	Feb. 12, 1821	With amends.	S. 12	Referred to Committee Whole House.		
Ogden, Thomas	Compensation for use and damage to property, at Sacketts' Harbor, by United States during war of 1812.	17	1	Petition	38	Claims	....	....	......	Discharged; laid on table.		
Ogden, Thomas	Compensation for use and damage to property, at Sacketts' Harbor, by United States during war of 1812.	17	2	Petition	30	Claims	Jan. 22, 1823	Favorable; bill	245	Referred to Committee Whole House.		
Ogden, Thomas	Compensation for use and damage to property, at Sacketts' Harbor, by United States during war of 1812.	18	1	Petition	37	Claims	86	Favorable; bill	160	Passed	Rejected.	
Ogden, Thomas	Compensation for use and damage to property, at Sacketts' Harbor, by United States during war of 1812.	18	2	Senate bill	109	Claims	Jan. 12, 1825	With't amend.	S. 12	Passed	Passed	App'd March 3, 1825
Ogden, William	(See John R. Murray.)	11	1	....	83							
Ogden, William, (N. Y.)	Indemnity for French spoliations prior to 1800.	26	1	Memorial	182	Foreign Affairs	343	Favorable; bill	319	Referred to Committee Whole House.		
Ogh, George	Invalid pension	4	1	Petition	425	Claims	May 7, 1692	Adverse	......	Leave to withdraw.		
Oglesby, Elijah	Indemnity for Indian depredations.	28	2	Petition	84	Claims.						
Oglesby, Richard, widow of.	Revolutionary pension	27	2	Resolution	791	Rev. Pensions	....	....	......	Discharged; laid on table.		
Oglesby, Richard, widow of.	Revolutionary pension	27	3	Documents	190	Rev. Pensions	....	....	......	Discharged; laid on table.	....	Leave to withdraw, 1st session, 28th Cong.
Oglesby, Richard, widow of.	Revolutionary pension	28	2	Petition	135	Rev. Pensions.						
Oglesby, Richard, widow of.	Revolutionary pension	30	1	Petition	358	Rev. Pensions	....	....	......	Discharged; laid on table.		
Oglesby, Susan	(See Richard Oglesby, widow of.)											

2—76

List of private claims presented to the House of Representatives of the United States from the 1st to the 31st Congress, inclusive—Continued.

Names of claimants.	Nature or object of the claim.	Congress.	Session.	How brought before the House of Reps.	Page of journal.	To what committee of the House referred.	No. or date of the report.	Nature of the report.	No. of the bill.	How disposed of by the House of Reps.	How disposed of by the Senate.	Date of the act of Congress, and remarks.
Ogg, Isaac	Invalid pension; wounded in Indian war, 1790.	27	3	Petition	166	Rev. Pensions.						
O'Hara, Daniel, & Son	Indemnity for French spoliations prior to 1800.	26	1	Memorial	182	Foreign Affairs	343	Favorable; bill	319	Referred to Committee Whole House.		
O'Harra, James	Compensation for services in revolutionary war.	3	1	Petition	132	Select.						
O'Harra, James	Authority to locate certain confirmed land claims.	24	1	Senate bill	492	Public Lands	Mar. 24, 1836	With't amend.	163	Passed	Passed	App'd July 2, 1836
O'Harra, John	Arrears of pension.	10	2	Petition	395	Claims.						
O'Harra, John	Arrears of pension	11	2	Petition	282	Claims	Mar. 21, 1810	Adverse	......	Laid on table.		
O'Harra, John	Arrears of pension	12	1	Petition	64	Select.						
O'Harra, Patrick	Invalid pension	26	1	Petition	938	Invalid Pensions.						
O'Harra, Patrick	Invalid pension	26	2	Petition	36	Invalid Pensions	62	Adverse	......	Laid on table.		
O'Harra, Thomas	Extra compensation for services as clerk during the prevalence of the yellow fever, 1793.	3	1	Resolution	209	Select	47	Favorable	69	Passed	Rejected.	
Ohe, Andrew	Settlement of claim against United States.	1	3	Petition	370	....	....	....	......	Referred to Solicitor of Treasury.		
Ohe, Andrew	Settlement of claim against United States.	4	1	Petition	451	Claims	May 7, 1796	Adverse	......	Laid on table.		
Ohe, Andrew	Settlement of claim against United States.	4	2	Petition	614	Claims.						
Ohio, Company of Associates.	Confirmation of title to land	2	1	Memorial	525	Select	Mar. 8, 1792	Favorable; bill ordered.	174	Passed	Passed	App'd April 21, 1792
Ohio, citizens of Galiopolis.	Confirmation of title to land	2	2	Petition	697	Select	Feb. 14, 1793	Favorable; bill	238	Passed	Rejected.	
Ohio, inhabitants of Fairfield.	Indemnity for deficiency in land purchased of United States.	8	1	Petition	456	Claims.						
Ohio, settlers between the Miamies.	Remission of interest and extension of time for payments of land.	9	2	Petition	206	Public Lands	April 16, 1806	Favorable; bill	137	Passed	Passed	App'd April 21, 1806
Ohio, sundry inhabitants of.	Extension of time for making payments for land.	8	2	Petition	106	Select.						
Ohio, sundry inhabitants of.	Extension of time for making payments for land.	10	1	Petition	262	Public Lands.						
Ohio, sundry inhabitants of.	Extension of time for making payments for land.	10	2	Petition	357	Public Lands	Jan. 19, 1809	Favorable; bill	150	Referred to Committee Whole House.		
Ohio, sundry inhabitants of.	Extension of time for making payments for land.	14	1	Petition	253	Public Lands.						
Ohio, sundry inhabitants of.	Extension of time for making payment for land.	15	1	Petition	350	Public Lands.						
Ohio, sundry inhabitants of.	Extension of time for making payments for land.	15	2	Petition	178	Public Lands.						
Ohio, sundry inhabitants of.	Extension of time for making payments for land.	16	1	Petition	77	Public Lands.						
Ohio, sundry inhabitants of.	Extension of time for making payments for land.	16	2	Petition	159	....	....	....	......	Referred to Committee Whole House on bill No. 181.		
Ohio, sundry inhabitants of.	Extension of time for making payments for land.	19	1	Petition	197	....	....	....	......	Referred to Committee Whole House on bill No. 32.	....	See act May 4, 1826
Ohio, sundry inhabitants of.	For further indulgence in making payments for land.	20	1	Petition	75	Public Lands.						
Ohio, sundry inhabitants of.	Correction of error in surveys of land.	9	2	Petition	582	Public Lands.						

List of private claims presented to the House of Representatives of the United States from the 1st to the 31st Congress, inclusive—Continued.

Names of claimants.	Nature or object of the claim.	Congress.	Session.	How brought before the House of Reps.	Page of journal.	To what committee of the House referred.	No. or date of the report.	Nature of the report.	No. of the bill.	How disposed of by the House of Reps.	How disposed of by the Senate.	Date of the act of Congress, and remarks.
Ohio, State of	Pre-emption to certain quarter-sections of land.	16	1	Senate bill	435	Public Lands	May 11, 1820	With't amend.	81	Passed		App'd May 15, 1820
Ohio, sundry citizens of	Indemnity for deficiency in land purchase.	17	1	Petition	134	Public Lands	43	Adverse		Laid on table.		
Ohio, sundry citizens of	Permission to relinquish certain lands and enter others.	17	1	Petition	221					Referred to Committee Whole House on bill No. 7.		
Ohio, sundry citizens of	Permission to relinquish certain lands and enter others.	20	2	Petition	177	Public Lands.						
Ohio, sundry citizens of Champaign county.	Pre emption to certain lands	9	2	Petition	493	Public Lands				Discharged; laid on table.		
Ohio, sundry citizens of Champaign county, *et al.*	Indemnity for land of which they have been deprived by decision of the Supreme Court of United States.	21	1	Petition	297					Referred to Committee Whole House on bill No. 141.		See act May 26, 1830
Ohio, sundry citizens of Clark county.	(See Ohio, sundry citizens of Champaign county, *et al.*)	21	1		297							
Ohio, sundry citizens of Logan county.	(See Ohio, sundry citizens of Champaign county, *et al.*)	21	1		297							
Ohio, sundry citizens of	Pre-emption right to certain lands on which they reside.	14	1	Petition	250	Public Lands.						
Ohio, sundry citizens of	Pre-emption right to certain lands on which they reside.	21	2	Petition	111, 375	Public Lands.						
Ohio, sundry citizens of Maumee county.	Pre emption right to certain lands on which they reside.	27	2	Petition	75	Public Lands	April 1, 1842	Adverse		Laid on table.		
Ohio, inhabitants of Perrysburgh.	Pre-emption right to certain lots	23	1	Petition	381	Public Lands.						
Ohio, inhabitants of Perrysburgh.	Pre-emption right to certain lots	24	1	Petition	59	Public Lands.						
Ohio, inhabitants of Perrysburgh.	Pre-emption right to certain lots	25	1	Petition	78					Laid on table.		
Ohio, inhabitants of Perrysburgh.	Pre-emption right to certain lots	25	2	Petition	173	Public Lands	895	Favorable; bill	795	Referred to Committee Whole House.		
Ohio, inhabitants of Perrysburgh.	Pre emption right to certain lots	26	1	Petition	177	Public Lands	78	Favorable; bill	66	Passed.		
Ohio, inhabitants of Perrysdurgh.	Pre-emption right to certain lots	26	2	Petition	37	Public Lands.						
Ohio, inhabitants of Perrysburgh.	Pre-emption right to certain lots	27	2	Petition	63	Public Lands	70	Favorable	106	Passed	Passed	App'd July 27, 1842
Ohio, inhabitants of Dublin.	Indemnity for loss of school lands.	25	3	Documents	352	Public Lands	241	Favorable; bill	1104	Referred to Committee Whole House.		
Ohio, inhabitants of Dublin.	Indemnity for loss of school lands.	26	1	Petition	178	Public Lands	320	Favorable; bill	285	Referred to Committee Whole House.		
Ohio, inhabitants of Dublin.	Indemnity for loss of school lands.	27	2	Petition	62	Public Lands	483	Favorable; bill	335	Referred to Committee Whole House.	Passed	App'd Aug. 16, 1842
Ohio, citizens of Oxford	For other lands in lieu of those set apart for schools.	25	2	Petition	661	Public Lands	938	Favorable; bill	819	Referred to Committee Whole House.		
Ohio, citizens of Oxford	For other lands in lieu of those set apart for schools.	25	3	Bill of last sess.	433	Whole House	Feb. 1, 1839	With't amend.	819	Passed	Passed	App'd March 3, 1839
Ohio, trustees of Mercer county.	Indemnity for school lands sold by government.	28	1	Petition	516	Public Lands.						
Ohio, trustees of Seneca county.	Indemnity for school lands sold by government.	28	1	Petition	526	Public Lands.						

List of private claims presented to the House of Representatives of the United States from the 1st to the 31st Congress, inclusive—Continued.

Names of claimants.	Nature or object of the claim.	Congress.	Session.	How brought before the House of Reps.	Page of journal.	To what committee of the House referred.	No. or date of the report.	Nature of the report.	No. of the bill.	How disposed of by the House of Reps.	How disposed of by the Senate.	Date of the act of Congress, and remarks.
Ohio, land officers at Marietta.	Increase of compensation	15	1	Resolution	169	Public Lands.						
Ohio, land officer at Defiance.	Extra compensation for locating military bounty land warrants.	31	2	Petition	77	Public Lands.						
Ohio, land officers at Chillicothe.	Extra compensation for locating military bounty land warrants.	31	2	Petition	32	Public Lands.						
Ohio, inhabitants of Allen county.	Refunding money overpaid for land	25	1	Petition	54	....	....	....	.....	Laid on table.		
Ohio, inhabitants of Allen county.	Refunding money overpaid for land	25	2	Petition	88	Public Lands	....	....	.....	Discharged; laid on table.		
Ohio, Hamilton county	Indemnity for destruction of court-house while occupied by United States troops.	14	1	Resolution	234	Claims	Mar. 11, 1816	Favorable; bill	.....	Passed	Passed	App'd April 26, 1816
Ohio, sundry officers of the revolutionary war residing in.	Indemnity for depreciation of their certificates of pay.	10	2	Memorial	369	Select.						
Ohio, sundry officers of the revolutionary war residing in.	Indemnity for depreciation of their certificates of pay.	11	2	Memorial	195	Select.						
Ohio, sundry officers of the revolutionary war residing in.	Indemnity for depreciation of their certificates of pay.	11	3	Memorial	460	Select.						
Ohio, citizens on Lake Erie	Compensation for supplies furnished United States troops.	13	2	Petition	294	Claims	Mar. 25, 1814	Adverse	.....	Leave to withdraw.		
Ohio, inhabitants of Sandusky.	Indemnity in land for privations in war of 1812.	13	2	Petition	176	Public Lands	Jan. 13, 1814	Adverse	.....	Laid on table.		
Ohio volunteers, (Cincinnati.)	Compensation for horses lost at Detroit.	13	2	Petition	241	....	....	....	.....	Referred to Committee Whole House on bill No. 62.		
Ohio volunteers, (Cincinnati.)	Compensation for horses lost at Detroit.	13	3	Petition	472	Claims	Nov. 14, 1814	Favorable; bill	228	Passed	Indef. postp'd.	
Ohio volunteers, (Cincinnati.)	Compensation for horses lost at Detroit.	14	1	Petition	41	Claims	....	....	.....	Discharged; laid on table.		
Ohio volunteers, survivors of.	Land for military services, war of 1812.	24	1	Petition	257	Public Lands.						
Ohio, Bank of Chillicothe.	Interest on loan to government and for an equitable adjustment of their accounts.	18	2	Petition	96	Claims	....	....	.....	Discharged.	....	Leave to withdraw.
Ohio, Bank of Chillicothe.	Interest on loan to government and for an equitable adjustment of their accounts.	19	1	Petition	177	Claims.						
Ohio, Bank of Chillicothe.	Interest on loan to government and for an equitable adjustment of their accounts.	19	2	Petition	50	Claims	48	Favorable; bill	386	Referred to Committee Whole House.		
Ohio, Bank of Chillicothe.	Interest on loan to government and for an equitable adjustment of their accounts.	20	1	Petition	31	Claims.						
Ohio, Bank of Chillicothe.	Interest on loan to government and for an equitable adjustment of their accounts.	21	1	Petition	69	Claims	45	Favorable; bill	69	Passed	Passed	App'd April 24, 1830
Ohio, Miami Exporting Co.	Indemnity for loss on advances to United States officers.	19	1	Petition	249	Claims.						

List of private claims presented to the House of Representatives of the United States form the 1st to the 31st Congress, inclusive—Continued.

Names of claimants.	Nature or object of the claim.	Congress.	Session.	How brought before the House of Reps.	Page of journal.	To what committee of the House referred.	No. or date of the report.	Nature of the report.	No. of the bill.	How disposed of by the House of Reps.	How disposed of by the Senate.	Date of the act of Congress, and remarks.
Ohio, Miami Exporting Co.	Indemnity for loss on advances to United States officers.	19	2	Petition	44	Claims.						
Ohio, Miami Exporting Co.	Indemnity for loss on advances to United States officers.	20	1	Petition	164	Claims.						
Ohio, Miami Exporting Co.	Indemnity for loss on advances to United States officers.	20	2	Petition	143	Claims.						
Ohio, Miami Exporting Co.	Indemnity for loss an advances to United States officers.	21	1	Petition	70	Claims..........	373	Favorable; bill	434	Referred to Committee Whole House.		
Ohio, Miami Exporting Co.	Indemnity for loss on advances to United States officers.	22	1	Petition	43	Claims	Dec. 19, 1831	Favorable; bill	23	Passed	Passed	App'd May 19, 1832
Ohio, Miami Exporting Co.	For further relief	24	2	Petition and docs.	395	Claims	310	Adverse	......	Laid on table.		
Ohio, Theological Seminary, Keyon College.	Remission of duties on donations from England.	19	2	Resolution	126	Ways and Means.						
Ohio, Theological Seminary, Keyon College.	Remission of duties on donations from England.	20	1	Resolution	87	Ways and Means..	Feb. 28, 1828	Favorable; bill	191	Referred to Committee Whole House.		
Ohio, Theological Seminary, Keyon College.	Remission of duties on donations from England.	20	2	Bill of last sess..	198	Whole House	Jan. 23, 1829	With amend..	191	Passed.		
Ohio, Theological Seminary, Keyon College.	Remission of duties on donations from England.	21	1	Resolution	95	Ways and Means..	Feb. 26, 1830	Favorable; bill	300	Referred to Committee Whole House.		
Ohio, Theological Seminary, Keyon College.	Remission of duties on donations from England.	21	2	Bill of last sess..	132	Whole House.....	Feb. 19, 1831	With't amend.	300	Passed.		
Ohio, Church of St. James, Piqua county.	Remission of duty on church bell.	21	1	Resolution	384	Ways and Means..	....	....	......	Discharged; laid on table.		
Ohio, inhabitants of Lucas and Wood counties.	Payment of claim against Ottowa Indians.	25	3	Petition	207	Indian Affairs.....	Mar. 2, 1839	Adverse	......	Laid on table.		
Ohio, inhabitants of Lucas and Wood counties.	Payment of claim against Ottowa Indians.	26	1	Petition	180	Claims.						
Ohio, inhabitants of Lucas and Wood counties.	Payment of claim against Ottowa Indians.	26	2	Petition	248	Claims.						
Ohio, inhabitants of Lucas and Wood counties.	Payment of claim against Ottowa Indians.	27	2	Petition	56	....	....	....	......	....	....	See bill No. 86.
Ohio, inhabitants of Maumee Valley.	Payment of claim against Ottowa Indians.	30	1	Petition	173	Indian Affairs.....	442	Favorable; bill	374	Referred to Committee Whole House.		
Ohio and Mississippi Mail Line Company.	(See John D. Colmesnil & Co.)..	31	1	....	298							
Ohio and Lexington Railroad Company.	Reimbursement of duties on railroad iron.	21	1	Petition	95	Ways and Means..	152	Favorable; bill	160	Passed	Passed	App'd July 2, 1836
Ohl, John F	Remission of duties on goods destroyed by fire.	19	2	Petition	322	Ways and Means..	....	....	......	Discharged; laid on table.		
Ohl, John F	Remission of duties on goods destroyed by fire.	20	1	Resolution	205	Ways and Means..	170	Favorable; bill	195	Referred to Committee Whole House.		
Ohl, John F	Remission of duties on goods destroyed by fire.	20	2	House bill	198	Whole House	Jan. 23, 1829	With't amend.	195	Passed.		
Ohl, John F	Remission of duties on goods destroyed by fire.	21	1	Petition	145	Ways and Means..	406	Favorable; bill	469	Referred to Committee Whole House.		
Ohl, John F	Remission of duties on goods destroyed by fire.	22	1	Petition	50	Ways and Means.						
Ohl, John F	Remission of duties on goods destroyed by fire.	23	1	Petition	300	Ways and Means..	344	Favorable; bill	371	Referred to Committee Whole House.		
Ohl, John F	Remission of duties on goods destroyed by fire.	24	1	Petition	277	Ways and Means.						
Ohl, John F	Remission of duties on goods destroyed by fire.	25	3	Petition	118	Ways and Means.						

List of private claims presented to the House of Representatives of the United States from the 1st to the 31st Congress, inclusive—Continued.

Names of claimants.	Nature or object of the claim.	Congress.	Session.	How brought before the House of Reps.	Page of journal.	To what committee of the House referred.	No. or date of the report.	Nature of the report.	No. of the bill.	How disposed of by the House of Reps.	How disposed of by the Senate.	Date of the act of Congress, and remarks.
Ohl, John F	Remission of duties on goods destroyed by fire.	26	1	Petition	179	Ways and Means.						
Ohl, John F	Remission of duties on goods destroyed by fire.	30	1	Petition	100	Ways and Means	725	Favorable; bill	566	Referred to Committee Whole House.		
Ohl, John F	Remission of duties on goods destroyed by fire.	30	2	House bill	319	Whole House	Jan. 26, 1849	With't amend.	556	Passed	Passed	App'd March 3, 1849
Oings, Acy	Compensation for revolutionary services.	4	1	Petition	425	Claims	May 7, 1796	Adverse		Leave to withdraw.		
Ojeda, Marie	Confirmation of title to land in Louisiana.	22	1	House bill	107	Whole House	Mar. 23, 1832	With't amend.	125	Passed	Passed	App'd June 25, 1832
Okely, John, executors of.	Adjustment of accounts as deputy quartermaster general.	3	2	Petition	291	Claims	March 2, 1795	Adverse		Laid on table.		
Okely, John, executors of.	Adjustment of accounts as deputy quartermaster general.	4	1	Petition	598	Claims	May 31, 1796	Adverse		Laid on table.		
Okely, John, executors of.	Adjustment of accounts as deputy quartermaster general.	4	2	Resolution	635					Leave to withdraw.		
O'Kelly, Ebenezer, or widow of.	Bounty land as Canadian volunteer, war of 1812.	22	1	Petition	224	Priv. Land Claims.	Mar. 6, 1832	Adverse		Laid on table.		
O'Kelly, *alias* Kelly, Henry, assignee of.	Arrears of pay for service in revolutionary war.	2	2	Petition	697					Laid on table.		
O'Koy, (Chickasaw Indian)	For amount due him under treaty stipulations.	9	1	House bill	380	Whole House	April 12, 1806	With amends.	139	Passed	Passed, with amendment.	Amendment disagreed to by House.
O'Koy, (Chickasaw Indian)	For amount due him under treaty stipulations.	9	2	Resolution	517	Ways and Means	Jan. 22, 1807	Favorable; bill ordered.	187	Passed	Passed	App'd March 3, 1807
Olcott, Isaac	Revolutionary pension	22	1	Resolution	137	Rev. Pensions	410	Favorable; bill	510	Referred to Committee Whole House.		
Olcott, Samuel	Indemnity for French spoliations prior to 1800.	26	1	Memorial	182	Foreign Affairs	343	Favorable; bill	319	Referred to Committee Whole House.		
Old Fourth Regiment	(See army, fourth regiment)	25	2		461							
Olden, James, assignee of.	Indemnity for French spoliations prior to 1800.	26	1	Memorial	182	Foreign Affairs	343	Favorable; bill	319	Referred to Committee Whole House.		
Oldham, Conwary, heirs of	Commutation pay for revolutionary services.	23	1	Petition	110	Rev. Claims.						
Oldham, Conway	Transfer of pre-emption right to land.	23	2	Resolution	243	Public Lands.	79	Favorable; bill	696	Passed.		
Oldham, Goodman, sureties of.	Release from liability	20	1	Petition	365	P. Of. & P. Roads.						
Oldham, James	Revolutionary pension	29	2	Petition	162	Rev. Pensions.						
Oldham, James	Revolutionary pension	30	1	Petition	414	Rev. Pensions				Discharged; laid on table.		
Oldham, Jesse D	Increase of pension	26	1	Petition	960	Rev. Pensions	671	Adverse		Laid on table.		
Oldham, Jesse D	Increase of pension	28	1	Petition	435	Invalid Pensions.						
Oldham, John	Restoration of pension	17	1	Petition	67	Rev. Pensions				Discharged; laid on table.		
Oldham, John, heirs of	Commutation pay for revolutionary services.	28	1	Petition	828	Rev. Claims.						
Oldham, John, heirs of	Commutation pay for revolutionary services.	29	1	Petition	256	Rev. Claims.						
Oldham, John, heirs of	Commutation pay for revolutionary services.	30	1	Petition	698	Rev. Pensions	687	Adverse		Laid on table		Leave to withdraw, 2d session.
Oldham, Moses, heirs of	Compensation for wagon and team taken for public use, revolutionary war.	20	1	Resolution	113	Rev. Claims	Jan. 3, 1828	Adverse		Laid on table.		

List of private claims presented to the House of Representatives of the United States from the 1st to the 31st Congress, inclusive—Continued.

Names of claimants.	Nature or object of the claim.	Congress.	Session.	How brought before the House of Reps.	Page of journal.	To what committee of the House referred.	No. or date of the report.	Nature of the report.	No. of the bill.	How disposed of by the House of Reps.	How disposed of by the Senate.	Date of the act of Congress, and remarks.
Oldham, Moses, heirs of	Compensation for wagon and team taken for public use, revolutionary war.	20	2	Resolution	104	Rev. Claims	Jan. 29, 1828	Adverse	......	Laid on table.		
Oldham, Moses, heirs of	Compensation for wagon and team taken for public use, revolutionary war.	22	1	Petition	333	Rev. Claims.						
Oldham, Moses, heirs of	Compensation for wagon and team taken for public use, revolutionary war.	25	2	Petition	270	Rev. Claims.						
Oldham, Moses, heirs of	Compensation for wagon and team taken for public use, revolutionary war.	26	1	Petition	166	Rev. Claims.						
Oldham, Moses, heirs of	Compensation for wagon and team taken for public use, revolutionary war.	26	2	Petition	248	Rev. Claims.						
Oldham, Moses, heirs of	Compensation for wagon and team taken for public use, revolutionary war.	27	1	Petition	106	Rev. Claims.						
Oldham, Moses, heirs of	Compensation for wagon and team taken for public use, revolutionary war.	27	2	Petition	96	Rev. Claims	203	Adverse	......	Laid on table.		
Oldham, Richard	Compensation for revolutionary services.	9	2	Petition	498	Claims.						
Olds, Hannah	(See Thomas Stevenson, widow of.)	25	3	....	124							
Olds, Marcay	(See John Stewart, former widow of.)	26	2	....	82							
Oldwine, Charles	To be restored to pension roll	17	1	Petition	51	Rev. Pensions.						
Oldwine, Charles	To be restored to pension roll	17	2	Petition	69	Rev. Pensions	....	....	......	Discharged; leave to withdraw.		
Olinger, Jacob	Revolutionary pension	26	1	Petition	392	Rev. Pensions	424	Adverse	......	Laid on table.		
Olinger, Jacob	Revolutionary pension	29	1	Petition	254	Rev. Pensions	785	Adverse	......	Laid on table.		
Olinger, Jacob	Revolutionary pension	30	1	Petition	78	Rev. Pensions	221	Adverse	......	Laid on table.		
Oliphant, David	Additional compensation for services as director of hospitals.	1	2	Petition and rep't Sec. of War.	170, 181	....	....	....	......	Laid on table.		
Olivella, Cayetano, representatives of.	Confirmation of title to land in Louisiana.	22	1	Petition	388	Priv. Land Claims	....	....	......	Discharged; laid on table.		
Oliver, Edward D.	Invalid pension	26	1	Petition	326	Invalid Pensions	419	Adverse	......	Laid on table.		
Oliver, Edward D.	Invalid pension	27	2	Petition	869	Invalid Pensions	938	Adverse	......	Laid on table.		
Oliver, Edward D.	Invalid pension	28	1	Petition	117	Invalid Pensions.						
Oliver, Isabella	(See John Oliver, widow of.)											
Oliver, John, widow of	Arrears of pay for naval services, and for a pension.	18	2	Petition	80	Naval Affairs	Jan. 19, 1825	Adverse	......	Laid on table.		
Oliver, John	Redemption of Continental money held by him.	31	2	Petition	50	Claims.						
Oliver, John and Robert	Indemnity for damages to their property by order of United States officers, at Baltimore, war of 1812.	13	3	Petition	756	Claims	....	....	......	Discharged; laid on table.		
Oliver, John and Robert	Indemnity for French spoliations prior to 1800.	26	1	Memorial	182	Foreign Affairs	343	Favorable; bill	319	Referred to Committee Whole House.		
Oliver, John M.	Compensation for work on Cumberland road.	24	1	Petition	405	Claims	620	Favorable; bill	607	Referred to Committee Whole House.		
Oliver, John M.	Compensation for work on Cumberland road.	25	2	Petition	37	Claims	Dec. 14, 1837	Favorable; bill	51	Passed	Passed	App'd May 7, 1838

List of private claims presented to the House of Representatives of the United States from the 1*st to the* 31*st Congress, inclusive*—Continued.

Names of claimants.	Nature or object of the claim.	Congress.	Session.	How brought before the House of Reps.	Page of journal.	To what committee of the House referred.	No. or date of the report.	Nature of the report.	No. of the bill.	How disposed of by the House of Reps.	How disposed of by the Senate.	Date of the act of Congress, and remarks.
Oliver, Madame	Confirmation of titles to land in Louisiana.	22	1	House bill	107	Whole House	Mar. 23, 1832	With't amend.	125	Passed	Passed	App'd June 25, 1832
Oliver, Phineas R.	(See Robert G. Ford, assignee of)	27	2	....	515							
Oliver, Richard	Invalid pension	23	2	Petition	58	Invalid Pensions	Jan. 31, 1835	Adverse	......	Laid on table.		
Oliver, Richard	Invalid pension	24	1	Petition	52	Invalid Pensions	June 2, 1836	Adverse	......	Laid on table.		
Oliver, Richard	Invalid pension	24	2	Petition	48	Invalid Pensions	....	....	......	Discharged; laid on table.		
Oliver, Richard	Invalid pension	25	3	Petition	218	Invalid Pensions.						
Oliver, Richard	Invalid pension	26	1	Petition	163	Invalid Pensions.						
Oliver, Richard	Invalid pension	27	2	Petition	377	Invalid Pensions	614	Adverse	......	Laid on table.		
Oliver, Robert	(See Ohio Company of associates)	2	1	....	525							
Oliver, Robert	(See Abraham M. Scott, & others)	13	3	....	533							
Oliver, Robert	(See John and Robert Oliver)	13	3	....	756							
Oliver, Robert	(See John and Robert Oliver)	26	1	....	182							
Oliver, Robert & Brothers.	Indemnity for French spoliations prior to 1800.	26	1	Memorial	182	Foreign Affairs	343	Favorable; bill	319	Referred to Committee Whole House.		
Oliver & Thompson	For correction of error in payment of certain duties.	3	1	Petition	115	Select.						
Oliver & Thompson	For correction of error in payment of certain duties.	3	2	Petition	315	Select.						
Oliver, West, & Co	(See Cooke, Anthony, Mahon, and others.)	30	1	....	826	....	....	....	S. 113			
Oliver, William	Pension	1	2	Petition and rep't Sec. of War.	171, 199	....	....	....	......	Rejected.		
Oliver, William	Pension	3	2	Resolution	352	Claims	Feb. 28, 1795	Favorable; bill	130	Passed	Postponed.	
Oliver, William	Pension	4	1	Resolution	447	Claims	Feb. 18, 1796	Favorable; bill	156	Passed	Passed	App'd April 20, 1796
Oliver, William	For drawback of certain duties	7	1	Petition	13	Com. and Manuf.	Dec. 10, 1801	Adverse	......	Leave to withdraw.		
Oliver, William	Indemnity for property destroyed by order of United States officers, war of 1812.	14	2	Petition	191	Claims	Feb. 12, 1817	Favorable; bill	131	Passed	Passed	App'd March 3, 1817
Oliver, William, (Maine).	Revolutionary pension	21	2	Petition	9	Pensions Military.						
Oliver, William, (Maine).	Revolutionary pension	25	2	Petition	180	Rev. Pensions	....	....	......	Discharged; laid on table.		
Oliver, William, (Maine).	Revolutionary pension	26	1	Petition	174	Rev. Pensions	551	Adverse	......	Laid on table.		
Oliver, William, (Maine).	Revolutionary pension	27	2	Petition	320	Rev. Pensions	784	Adverse	......	Laid on table.		
Oliver, William, heirs of.	Commutation pay for revolutionary services.	23	1	Petition	81	Rev. Claims.						
Oliver, William, heirs of.	Commutation pay for revolutionary services.	23	2	Petition	84	Rev. Claims.						
Oliver, William, heirs of.	Commutation pay for revolutionary services.	24	1	Petition	103	Rev. Claims	818	Adverse	......	Laid on table.		
Oliver, William, heirs of.	Commutation pay for revolutionary services.	25	2	Petition	94	Rev. Claims	277	Adverse	......	Laid on table.		
Oliver, Wilson	Compensation for services in war of 1812.	31	1	Petition	582	Claims.						
Olmstead, Ebenezer, widow of.	Continuation of pension	27	2	Petition	375	Rev. Pensions	784	Adverse	......	Laid on table.		
Olmstead, Edward, widow of.	Revolutionary pension	13	2	Petition	329	Pens. & Rev. Cl'ms.						
Olmstead, Esther	(See Ebenezer Olmsted, widow of)	27	2	....	375							

List of private claims presented to the House of Representativesthe of United States from the 1st to the 31st Congress, inclusive—Continued.

Names of claimants.	Nature or object of the claim.	Congress.	Session.	How brought before the House of Reps.	Page of journal.	To what committee of the House referred.	No. or date of the report.	Nature of the report.	No. of the bill.	How disposed of by the House of Reps.	How disposed of by the Senate.	Date of the act of Congress, and remarks.
Olmstead, James	(See Thomas Tupper, assignees of)	22	2		142							
Olmstead, John	(See Thomas Tupper, assignees of)	22	2		142							
Olmstead, Jonathan	Indemnity for property destroyed by the British, war of 1812.	15	2	Petition	148	Claims				Discharged; laid on table.		
Olmstead, Lewis	Release from imprisonment	14	2	Senate bill	351	Whole House	Feb. 6, 1817	With't amend.		Passed	Passed	App'd Feb. 22, 1817
Olmstead, Sarah	(See Edward Olmstead, widow of)	13	2		329							
Olmstead, S. B	Payment for a horse lost in United States service.	30	1	Petition	594	Claims	754	Adverse		Laid on table.		
Olney, Amasa	Arrears of pension	27	2	Petition	381	Claims	500	Adverse		Laid on table.		
Olney, Joseph, heir of	Compensation for revolutionary services.	24	2	Petition	271	Rev. Pensions				Discharged; laid on table.		
Olney, Joseph, heir of	Compensation for revolutionary services.	25	2	Petition	270	Rev. Claims	784	Adverse		Laid on table.		
Olney, Joseph, heir of	Compensation for revolutionary services	25	3	Petition	561	Rev Claims.						
Olney, Joseph, heir of	Compensation for revolutionary services.	26	1	Petition	167	Rev. Claims.						
Olney, Martha	(See Stephen Olney, widow of)	27	2		524							
Olney, Stephen, (R. I.)	Bounty land and commutation pay for revolutionary services.	15	1	Petition	242	Pens. & Rev. Cl'ms.				Discharged; leave to withdraw.		
Olney, Stephen, (R. I.)	Additional compensation for revolutionary services.	20	2	Petition	95	Military Pensions.	Mar. 2, 1829	Favorable; bill	462	Laid on table.		
Olney, Stephen, (R. I.)	Additional compensation for revolutionary services.	21	1	Petition	75	Rev. Claims	53	Favorable; bill	74	Passed	Passed	App'd May 28, 1830
Olney, Stephen, (Pa.)	Revolutionary pension	24	2	Petition	154	Rev. Pensions				Discharged; laid on table.		
Olney, Stephen, (Pa.)	Revolutionary pension	25	2	Petition	405	Rev. Pensions	705	Favorable; bill	679	Passed	Adverse.	
Olney, Stephen, (Pa.)	Revolutionary pension	25	3	Petition	88	Rev. Pensions	Jan. 9, 1839	Favorable; bill	996	Passed	Adverse.	
Olney, Stephen, (Pa.)	Revolutionary pension	26	1	Petition	171	Rev. Pensions	162	Favorable; bill	172	Passed	Indef. postp'd.	
Olney, Stephen, widow of.	Revolutionary pension	27	2	Petition	524	Rev. Pensions	784	Adverse		Laid on table.		
O'Neal, Barnett, heirs of	Reimbursement of advances on public account.	21	1	Resolution	432	Rev. Claims				Discharged; laid on table.		
O'Neal, Barnett, heirs of	Reimbursement of advances on public account.	28	2	Documents	250	Rev. Claims.						
O'Neal, Benjamin, administratrix of.	Indemnity for Indian depredations.	19	2	Petition	37	Claims	Jan. 24, 1827	Adverse		Laid on table.		
O'Neal, Benjamin, administratrix of.	Indemnity for Indian depredations.	20	1	Petition	342	Claims	Mar. 18, 1828	Adverse		Laid on table.		
O'Neal, or O'Neil, Bernard.	Compensation for use of land by government, and for wood and sand.	29	1	Petition	618	Claims	688	Favorable; bill	460	Referred to Committee Whole House.		
O'Neal, or O'Neil, Bernard.	Compensation for use of land by government, and for wood and sand.	29	2	Bill of last sess.	211				460	Passed	Passed	App'd March 3, 1847
O'Neal, Catharine	(See Constantine O'Neal, widow of.)	29	2		54							
O'Neal, Constantine, widow of.	Revolutionary pension	29	2	Petition	54	Rev. Claims.						
O'Neal, Constantine, widow of.	Revolutionary pension	30	1	Petition	422	Rev. Pensions	701	Adverse		Laid on table.		
O'Neal, Constantine, widow of.	Revolutionary pension	30	2	Petition	117	Rev. Pensions	73	Adverse		Laid on table.		

List of private claims presented to the House of Representatives of the United States from the 1st to the 31st Congress, inclusive—Continued.

Names of claimants.	Nature or object of the claim.	Congress.	Session.	How brought before the House of Reps.	Page of journal.	To what committee of the House referred.	No. or date of the report.	Nature of the report.	No. of the bill.	How disposed of by the House of Reps.	How disposed of by the Senate.	Date of the act of Congress, and remarks.
O'Neal, Elizabeth	Indemnity for losses in war of 1812	23	2	Petition	147	Indian Affairs				Discharged; laid on table.		
O'Neal, Elizabeth	(See George O'Neal, widow of.)	28	1		707							
O'Neal, George, widow of.	Revolutionary pension	28	1	Petition	707	Rev. Pensions.						
O'Neal, John, (Md.)	Pension	18	1	Petition	250	Pens. & Rev. Cl'ms.				Discharged; laid on table.		
O'Neal, John, (Md.)	Pension	21	1	Petition	231	Military Pensions.						
O'Neal, John, (Md.)	Pension	23	1	Petition	72	Invalid Pensions	Jan. 8, 1834	Adverse		Laid on table.		
O'Neal, John, (Penn.)	Invalid pension	22	1	Petition	383	Invalid Pensions	477	Favorable; bill	576	Passed.		
O'Neal, John, (Penn.)	Invalid pension	23	1	Petition	54	Invalid Pensions	37	Favorable; bill	42	Passed	Passed	App'd June 30, 1834
O'Neal, Wm., and Robert Taylor.	Compensation for a vessel lost in public service, 1814.	14	1	Petition	33	Claims	Jan. 5, 1816	Adverse		Rejected.		
O'Neal, William	Invalid pension	14	1	Petition	367	Pens. & Rev. Cl'ms.	April 11, 1816	Favorable; bill		Passed	Passed	App'd April 30, 1816
O'Neal, William, (Ind.)	For correction of error in land entry.	23	1	Resolution	390	Priv. Land Claims.	Mar. 11, 1834	Favorable; bill	358	Passed.		
O'Neal, William, (Ind.)	For correction of error in land entry.	23	2	Resolution	199	Priv. Land Claims.	Jan. 19, 1835	Favorable; bil	652	Passed	Passed	App'd March 3, 1835
O'Neal, William	(See Henry Ashton and others.)	23	1		337							
Ongin, Elizabeth	(See Isaac Ongin, widow of.)											
Ongin, Isaac, widow of	Continuation of pension	28	1	Petition	541	Rev. Pensions.						
Onion, Caroline	Continuation of pension	27	2	Petition	256	Rev. Pensions.						
Onion, Juliet	(See William Pendergrast widow of.)	26	1		322							
Only Son, schooner	(See Knott & Arnold Martin)	27	2		95							
Onstine, Frederick	Indemnity for confiscation of his property by the British.	15	2	Petition	182	Military Affairs.						
Onstine, Frederick	Indemnity for confiscation of his property by the British.	19	2	Petition	50	Priv. Land Claims.	33	Favorable; bil	347	Referred to Committee Whole House.		
Onstine, Frederick	Indemnity for confiscation of his property by the British.	20	1	Petition	64	Priv. Land Claims.	108	Favorable; bill	124	Passed	Passed	App'd May 24, 1828
Onwarenccake, R.	(See Archibald Beard and others.)	18	2		252							
Osely, Peter, heirs of	(See Peter Woosely, heirs of.)	18	1		307							
Oothoudt, Richard	Arrears of pension	27	2	Petition	1158	Invalid Pensions.						
Oothoudt, Richard	Arrears of pension	28	1	Petition	333	Invalid Pensions	Mar. 7, 1844	Adverse		Laid on table.		
Oothoudt, Richard	Arrears of pension	31	1	Petition	537	Invalid Pensions	467	Adverse		Laid on table.		
Opie, Elizabeth S.	(See Le Roy Opie, widow of)	18	2		117							
Opie, Le Roy, sureties of	For extension of time for settlement of his accounts as paymaster.	16	2	Petition	137	Claims	Jan. 19, 1821	Favorable; bill	212	Passed	Passed	App'd March 3, 1821
Opie, Le Roy, sureties of	Reimbursement of money paid as surety.	27	2	Petition	747	Claims	703	Adverse		Laid on table.		
Opie, Le Roy, widow of	Pension	18	2	Petition	117	Pens. & Rev. Cl'ms.				Discharged; leave to withdraw.		
Opp, Conrad	(See John Kaul and Conrad Opp.)	20	1		398							
Oram, Abigail or Rebecca	(See Cooper Oram, widow of.)											
Oram, Cooper, widow of	Revolutionary pension	23	2	Petition	389	Rev. Claims.						
Oram, Darby	Compensation for revolutionary services.	1	2	Petition	195					Laid on table.		
Oram, Darby	Compensation for revolutionary services.	2	1	Petition	517					Laid on table.		
Oran, Darby, (N. J.)	Revolutionary pension	21	2	Resolution	258	Military Pensions.						
Oran, Darby, (N. J.)	Revolutionary pension	22	1	Resolution	140	Rev. Pensions.						

List of private claims presented to the House of Representatives of the United States from the 1st to the 31st Congress, inclusive—Continued.

Names of claimants.	Nature or object of the claim.	Congress.	Session.	How brought before the House of Reps.	Page of journal.	To what committee of the House referred.	No. or date of the report.	Nature of the report.	No. of the bill.	How disposed of by the House of Reps.	How disposed of by the Senate.	Date of the act of Congress, and remarks.
Oramos, Joseph	Confirmation of title to land in Louisiana.	22	1	House bill	107	Whole House	Mar. 23, 1832	With't amend.	125	Passed	Passed	App'd June 25, 1832
Oramos, Geronimo	Confirmation of title to land in Louisiana.	22	1	House bill	107	Whole House	Mar. 23, 1832	With't amend.	125	Passed	Passed	App'd June 25, 1832
Orcutt, David	Increase of pension	11	2	House bill	283	Whole House	Mar. 24, 1810	With amends.	107	Passed	Passed	App'd April 27, 1810
Orcutt, Ephraim	To be restored to pension roll	17	2	Petition	24	Rev. Pensions.						
Orcutt, Micah, (*alias* Druett.)	Pension	21	2	Petition	42	Military Pensions				Discharged; laid on table.		
Orcutt, Micah, (*alias* Druett.)	Pension	22	1	Petition	66, 93	Rev. Pensions.						
Orchard, J. & S. M.	Release from mail contract	31	2	Petition	220	P. Of. & P. Roads.						
Ord, James, (D. C.)	Compensation for extra services as clerk in Solicitors office.	22	1	Petition	836	Claims.						
Ord, James, (D. C.)	Compensation for extra services as clerk in Solicitors office.	23	1	Senate bill	873	Claims	June 28, 1834	With't amend.	141	Passed	Passed	App'd June 30, 1834
Ord, Pacificus, D. C.)	Compensation for services as clerk in the Solicitors office.	26	2	Petition	124	Claims.						
Ord, Pacificus, (D. C.)	Compensation for services as clerk in the Solicitors office.	27	2	Petition	56	Claims	10	Favorable; bill	49	Laid on table.		
Ord, Pacificus, (D. C.)	Compensation for services as clerk in the Solicitors office.	28	1	Petition	368	Claims	289	Favorable; bill	201	Referred to Committee Whole House.		
Ord, Pacificus, D. C.)	Compensation for services as clerk in the Solicitors office.	29	1	Petition	75	Claims	274	Adverse		Laid on table.		
Ordway, Enoch	Compensation for revolutionary services.	27	2	Petition	423	Rev. Pensions.						
Ordway, John	(See Lewis Clark & companions.)	9	2		284							
Ore, Major James	Payment for horses stolen by Indians.	4	2	Petition	624	Claims	Jan. 12, 1797	Adverse		Laid on table.		
Ore, Major James	Payment for horses stolen by Indians.	5	2	Resolution	270	Select	April 24, 1798	Favorable; bill	85	Passed	Passed	App'd May 8, 1798
Ore, James, (Indian)	Permission to lease land ceded him by treaty.	18	1	Petition	82	Public Lands.						
Ore, James, (Indian)	For relinquishment by United States of reversionary interest in certain lands.	21	1	Petition	85	Public Lands	69	Favorable; bill	97	Passed	Passed	App'd May 29, 1830
Orear, Daniel	Pension	20	2	Petition	229	Military Pensions.						
Orear, Daniel	Pension	21	1	Petition	47	Military Pensions	May 4, 1830	Adverse		Laid on table.		
Orear, N. C	Compension for corn furnished volunteers at Santa Fe, Mexican war.	30	1	House bill	238	Claims			78			
O'Reily, Elizabeth	(See Clement Sewell, daughter of)	24	1		404, 405							
O'Reily, Henry	For right of way for telegraph company.	31	1	Petition	973	P. Of. & P. Roads.						
Orendorff, Christian	Commutation pay for revolutionary services.	12	1	Petition	43	Select				Leave to withdraw.		
Orendorff, Christian, heirs of.	Payment of final settlement certificate.	27	2	Petition	908	Rev. Claims	866	Adverse		Laid on table.		
Orendorff, Christian, heirs of.	Payment of final settlement certificate.	27	3	Petition	350	Rev. Claims	252	Adverse		Laid on table.		
Orendorff, Christian, heirs of.	Payment of final settlement certificate.	28	1	Petition	975	Rev. Claims.						

List of private claims presented to the House of Representatives of the United States from the 1st to the 31st Congress, inclusive—Continued.

Names of claimants.	Nature or object of the claim.	Congress.	Session.	How brought before the House of Reps.	Page of journal.	To what committee of the House referred.	No. or date of the report.	Nature of the report.	No. of the bill.	How disposed of by the House of Reps.	How disposed of by the Senate.	Date of the act of Congress, and remarks.
Orendorff, Christian, heirs of.	Payment of final settlement certificate.	28	2	Petition	150	Rev. Claims	133	Favorable; bill	616	Referred to Committee Whole House.		
Orendorff, Christian, heirs of.	Payment of final settlement certificate.	29	1	Petition	302	Rev. Claims.						
Orendorff, Christian, heirs of.	Payment of final settlement certificate.	30	1	Petition	405	Rev. Claims.						
Orendorff, Christian, heirs of.	Payment of final settlement certificate.	31	1	Petition	472	Rev. Claims	422	Adverse	......	Laid on table.		
Organ, David	Compensation for medicines furnished Virginia troops, revolutionary war.	3	2	Petition	320	Claims.						
Organ, David	Compensation for medicines furnished Virginia troops, revolutionary war.	4	1	Petition	403	Claims	Jan. 6, 1796	Adverse	......	Laid on table	....	Leave to withdraw, 2d session.
Organ, Elizabeth	Continuation of pension	27	2	Petition	255	Rev. Pensions.						
Orgain, Sterling	(See Morris Lindsey, assignee of)	18	1	....	307							
Orillon, Don Louis Rosamond.	Patent for certain lots of land in Louisiana.	24	1	Petition	65	Priv. Land Claims.	79	Favorable; bill	95	Postponed.		
Orillon, Don Louis Rosamond.	Patent for certain lots of land in Louisiana.	24	2	Bill of last sess.	157	Whole House	....	....	95			
Orillon, Don Louis Rosamond.	Patent for certain lots of land in Louisiana.	25	2	Petition	43	Priv. Land Claims.	554	Favorable; bill	543	Referred to Committee Whole House.		
Orillon, Don Louis Rosamond.	Patent for certain lots of land in Louisiana.	25	3	Bill of last sess.	380	Whole House	Jan. 25, 1839	With't amend.	543			
Orillon, Don Louis Rosamond.	Patent for certain lots of land in Louisiana.	26	1	Petition	179	Priv. Land Claims.						
Oriskany Manufacturing Company.	For permission to import card wire	12	1	Petition	164	....	....	....	......	Referred to Committee Whole House on bill No. 46.		
Orleans Territory	(See Louisiana, inhabitants of Point Coupee.)	11	2	....	142							
Ormond, James	Compensation for negroes taken by Indians, in Florida, prior to 1819.	26	1	Petition	397	Claims.						
Ormond, James	Compensation for negroes taken by Indians, in Florida, prior to 1819.	26	2	Petition	135	Claims.						
Ormond, James, heirs of.	Compensation for negroes taken by Indians, in Florida, prior to 1819.	27	2	Petition	94	Claims	723	Adverse	......	Laid on table.		
Ormond, Richard	(See Stephen Decatur, widow of, and others.)	20	1	....	295	....	201	....	S. 50			
Ormond, William	Pension	3	1	Rep. of Secretary War.	175	....	....	....	......	Laid on table.		
Ormond, William	Pension	3	2	Rep. of Secretary War.	262	Claims.						
Ormond, William	Pension	4	1	Petition & docs.	445	Claims	Feb. 15, 1796	Favorable; bill	156	Passed	Passed	App'd April 20, 1796
Ormond, William	Relief for having been deprived of pre-emption right by decision of land officers.	23	2	Petition	278	....	....	....	......	....	....	Not referred.
Orms, Jonathan	Pension	22	1	Resolution	160	Rev. Pensions	....	....	......	Discharged; laid on table.		
Ormsby, Oliver	For certain credits in settlement of his accounts as army contractor.	13	2	Petition	182	Claims	Mar. 7, 1814	Adverse	......	Laid on table.		
Ormsby, Oliver	For certain credits in settlement of his accounts as army contractor.	14	1	Petition	139	Select.						

List of private claims presented to the House of Representatives of the United States from the 1st to the 31st Congress, inclusive—Continued.

Names of claimants.	Nature or object of the claim.	Congress.	Session.	How brought before the House of Reps.	Page of journal.	To what committee of the House referred.	No. or date of the report.	Nature of the report.	No. of the bill.	How disposed of by the House of Reps.	How disposed of by the Senate.	Date of the act of Congress, and remarks.
Ormsby, Stephen	Indemnity for damages to his wagon and team while in public service, war of 1812.	15	2	Petition	227	Claims.						
Ormsby, Stephen	Indemnity for damages to his wagon and team while in public service, war of 1812.	16	1	Petition	401	Claims	April 12, 1820	Adverse	......	Laid on table.		
Ormsby, Stephen	Indemnity for damages to his wagon and team while in public service, war of 1812.	17	1	Petition	145	Claims.						
Ormsby, Stephen	Indemnity for damages to his wagon and team while in public service, war of 1812.	18	1	Petition	214	Military Affairs.						
Orne, Joshua, and others	For settlement of claim against United States.	1	3	Petition and rep't Sec. of War.	342, 380	......	......	......	......	Laid on table.		
Orner, Michael	Pension	3	1	Rep. of Secretary War.	131	Select	May 26, 1794	Jt. res. to refer to Sec. War.	J. R. 12	Passed	Passed	App'd June 9, 1794
Orner, Michael	Pension	4	1	Rep. of Secretary War.	373	Claims	Feb. 18, 1796	Favorable; bill	156	Passed	Passed	App'd April 20, 1796
Orr, B. G.	(See William Boone, et al)	19	2	......	91							
Orr, James	Payment for vessel sunk for defence of Baltimore, war of 1812.	14	2	Petition	155	Claims	Feb. 12, 1817	Favorable; bill	132	Passed	Rejected.	
Orr, James	Payment for vessel sunk for defence of Baltimore, war of 1812.	15	1	Petition	297	Claims	April 1, 1818	Favorable; bill	169	Referred to Committee Whole House.		
Orr, James	Payment for vessel sunk for defence of Baltimore, war of 1812.	15	2	Bill of last sess.	326	Whole House	Feb. 27, 1819	With't amend	169	Passed	Passed	App'd March 3, 1819
Orr, James	Increase of pension	31	1	Petition	437	Invalid Pensions	......	......	......	Leave to withdraw.		
Orr, John, and J. Pierce.	Remission of certain fines and costs.	26	2	Petition	54	Judiciary.						
Orr, Robert	Increase of compensat on as master armorer at Springfield, Mass.	5	2	Petition	82	......	......	......	......	Referred to Secretary War.		
Orr, Thomas	Pre-emption right to land on which he has erected a mill.	8	2	Petition	106	Select.						
Orr, Thomas	Pre-emption right to land on which he has erected a mill.	9	1	Petition	224	Public Lands.						
Orr, Thomas	Pre-emption right to land on which he has erected a mill.	12	1	Petition	165	Public Lands	Feb. 14, 1812	Favorable; bill	72	Passed	Passed	App'd April 8, 1812
Orr, William	Compensation for work on Cumberland road.	24	2	Petition	208	Claims	Feb. 14, 1837	Adverse	......	Laid on table.		
Orso, Zenon, et al	Remission of certain duties	12	1	Petition	176	Com. and Manuf.						
Orso, Zenon, et al	Remission of certain duties	13	2	Petition	210	Com. and Manuf.	91	Adverse	......	Laid on table.		
Orso, Zenon, et al	Remission of certain duties	13	3	Petition	684	Com. and Manuf.						
Orso, Zenon, et al	Remission of certain duties	14	1	Petition	220	Com. and Manuf.	Feb. 2, 1816	Adverse	......	Laid on table.		
Orsen, Matthew	Compensation for services and for supplies furnished in revolutionary war.	3	2	Petition	323	Claims.						
Orsen, Matthew	Compensation for services and for supplies furnished in revolutionary war.	4	1	Resolution	373	Claims	Jan. 6, 1796	Adverse	......	Laid on table.		
Ortman, John	Pension	21	1	Petition	59	Military Pensions.						
Ortman, John	Pension	21	2	Petition	159	Military Pensions.						
Orvis, Asenath	(See Gershom Orvis, widow of)	28	1	......	436							
Orvis, Gershom, widow of.	Revolutionary pension	28	1	Petition	436	Rev. Pensions	429	Favorable; bil	330	Passed.		
Orvis, Gershom, widow of.	Revolutionary pension	28	2	Petition	57	Rev. Pensions	19	Favorable; bill	487	Passed.		
Osborne, Charles F	(See Nathaniel Deuby, sureties of)	30	2	......	350							

List of private claims presented to the House of Representatives of the United States from the 1st to the 31st Congress, inclusive—Continued.

Names of claimants.	Nature or object of the claim.	Congress.	Session.	How brought before the House of Reps.	Page of journal.	To what committee of the House referred	No. or date of the report.	Nature of the report.	No. of the bill.	How disposed of by the House of Reps.	How disposed of by the Senate.	Date of the act of Congress, and remarks.
Osborn, or Osburn, James	Compensation for revolutionary services.	2	1	Petition	493					Referred to Secretary War.		
Osborne, James, (Maine)	Increase of pension	22	1	Petition	254	Rev. Pensions	Mar. 26, 1832	Favorable; bill	512	Referred to Committee Whole House.		
Osborne, James, (Maine)	Increase of pension	24	1	Petition	475	Rev. Pensions				Discharged; laid on table.		
Osborne, James, (N. Y.)	Additional compensation for revolutionary services.	22	2	Petition	46	Rev. Claims.						
Osborne, James W	Refunding duties paid on Spanish tobacco.	23	2	Petition	102	Ways and Means.						
Osborne, James W	Refunding duties paid on Spanish tobacco.	24	1	Petition	95	Ways and Means	537	Favorable; bill	532	Referred to Committee Whole House.		
Osborne, James W	Refunding duties paid on Spanish tobacco.	25	2	Petition	42	Ways and Means	Dec. 28, 1837	Favorable; bill	229	Referred to Committee Whole House.		
Osborne, James W	Refunding duties paid on Spanish tobacco.	25	3	Bill of last sess.	375	Whole House	Jan. 25, 1839	With't amend.	229	Passed.		
Osborne, James W	Refunding duties paid on Spanish tobacco.	26	1	Petition	172	Ways and Means	Feb. 29, 1840	Favorable; bill	21	Passed	Indef. postp'd.	
Osborne, James W	Refunding duties paid on Spanish tobacco.	27	2	Petition	55	Ways and Means.						
Osborne, James W	Refunding duties paid on Spanish tobacco.	29	2	Petition	55	Ways and Means.						
Osborne, James W	Revolutionary pension	26	1	Petition	172	Rev. Pensions.						
Osborne, Jeremiah	Pension	3	1	Rep. of Secretary War.	131	Select	May 26, 1794	Adverse		Referred to Committee Whole House.		
Osborne, Jeremiah	Pension	3	2	Petition and rep't Sec. of War.	262	Claims.						
Osborn, or Osburn, John, (Pa.)	Compensation for services as wagoner, revolutionary war.	21	1	Petition	523	Rev. Claims.						
Osborne, John	Pension for disabilities incurred in Mexican war.	30	1	Petition	136	Invalid Pensions.						
Osborne, Maria F., (Ga.)	Confirmation of title to land in Florida.	21	1	Petition	547	Priv. Land Claims.						
Osborne, Noble, and William Doake.	Pre-emption right to land on which they reside.	17	1	Senate bill	283	Priv. Land Claims.	Feb. 28, 1822	With't amend.	S. 29	Passed		App'd May 7, 1822
Osborne, Richard	Revolutionary pension	13	3	Petition	643	Pens. & Rev. Cl'ms.	Feb. 20, 1815	Favorable; bill	303	Passed	Passed	App'd March 3, 1815
Osborn, or Osburn, Sherwood.	(See Lieutenant John L. Cline)	26	1		623							
Osborne, Stephen	Revolutionary pension	22	1	Resolution	338	Rev. Claims.						
Osborn, or Osburn, William (R. I.)	Indemnity for injuries received whilst employed as boatman by the collector.	8	2	Petition	54	Claims				Leave to withdraw.		
Osborne, W., and others	Pre-emption right to certain lots in Albany, Illinois.	25	2	Petition	85	Public Lands				Discharged; laid on table.		
Osborne, William, (N. Y.)	For debenture on claret wine exported.	13	1	Petition	12	Com. and Manuf.						
Osborne, William, (N. Y.)	For debenture on claret wine exported.	13	2	Petition	232	Com. and Munuf.	Mar. 25, 1814	Adverse		Laid on table.		
Osborne, William, (N. Y.)	For debenture on claret wine exported.	14	2	Petition	116	Com. and Manuf.				Discharged; laid on table.		
Osborne, William, (N. Y.)	For debenture on claret wine exported.	15	1	Petition	165	Com. and Manuf.	Mar. 30, 1818	Adverse		Laid on table.		

List of private claims presented to the House of Representatives of the United States from the 1st to the 31st Congress, inclusive—Continued.

Names of claimants.	Nature or object of the claim.	Congress.	Session.	How brought before the House of Reps.	Page of journal.	To what committee of the House referred.	No. or date of the report.	Nature of the report.	No. of the bill.	How disposed of by the House of Reps.	How disposed of by the Senate.	Date of the act of Congress, and remarks.
Osborne, William, (N. Y.)	For depenture on claret wine exported.	21	1	Petition	412	Ways and Means	....	....	......	Discharged; laid on table.		
Osborne, William, (N. Y.)	For debenture on claret wine exported.	21	2	Petition	67	Ways and Means.						
Osborne, William, (N. Y.)	For debenture on claret wine exported.	22	1	Petition	186	Ways and Means	Jan. 21, 1832	Favorable; bill	301	Referred to Committee Whole House.		
Osborne, William, (N. Y.)	For debenture on claret wine exported.	22	2	Bill of last sess.	171	Whole House	Feb. 15, 1833	With't amend.	301	Passed	Passed	App'd March 2, 1833
Osborne, William, (Ill.)	Revolutionary pension	22	1	Resolution	97	Rev. Pensions	....	....	......	Discharged; laid on table.		
Osborne, William S	Compensation for services and losses in Indian wars.	31	1	Petition	231	Claims	24	Adverse	......	Laid on table.		
Osgood, John	(See Wadleigh Noyes, representatives of.)	2	1	....	448							
Osgood, Joseph H	Pension	22	2	Petition	81	Invalid Pensions.						
Osgood, Joseph H	Pension	23	1	Petition	44	Invalid Pensions	Jan. 7, 1834	Favorable; bill	154	Passed.		
Osgood, Lemuel H	Equitable settlement of his accounts as lieutenant in the army.	15	1	Petition	30	Claims	Mar. 19, 1818	Adverse	......	Rejected.		
Osgood, Lemuel H	Equitable settlement of his accounts as lieutenant in the army.	15	1	Senate bill	414	Claims	April 6, 1818	With't amend.	S. 60	Passed	Passed	App'd April 11, 1818
O'Sheals, Jethro	Revolutionary pension	25	2	Petition	406	Rev. Pensions	....	....	......	Discharged; laid on table.		
O'Sheals, Jethro	Revolutionary pension	26	1	Petition	174	Rev. Pensions.						
Oslum, Samuel	Confirmation of title to land in Ohio.	23	1	Petition	114	Priv. Land Claims.						
Osteen, William	Correction of error in land entry	26	1	Senate bill	811	Priv. Land Claims.	May 25, 1840	With't amend.	S. 193	Referred to Committee Whole House.		
Osteen, William	Correction of error in land entry	27	2	Senate bill	1126	Public Lands	July 29, 1842	With't amend.	S. 246	Passed	....	App'd Aug. 11, 1842
Osterman, Christian	Pension	19	2	Petition	91	Military Pensions	....	....	......	Disch'd; laid on table.		
Ostertrout, Isaac, widow of	Revolutionary pension	31	1	Petition	519	Rev. Claims.						
Ostertrout, Isaac, widow of	Revolutionary pension	31	2	Petition	175	Rev. Claims	50	Adverse	......	Laid on table.		
Ostrander, A. D	For balance due him as clerk in the pursers office, New York.	22	2	Petition	28	Claims.						
Ostrander, A. D	For balance due him as clerk in the pursers office, New York.	23	1	Petition	36	Naval Affairs.						
Ostrander, A. D	For balance due him as clerk in the pursers office, New York.	24	1	Senate bill	390	Naval Affairs	458	Adverse	S. 74	Referred to Committee Whole House.		
Ostrander, A. D	For balance due him as clerk in the pursers office, New York.	24	1	Petition	945	Naval Affairs	....	....	......	Discharged; laid on table.		
Ostrander, John	For the depreciation of pay and other emoluments for revolutionary services.	3	1	Petition	88	Select	Mar. 31, 1794	Adverse	......	Laid on table.		
Ostrander, John	For the depreciation of pay and other emoluments for revolutionary services.	3	2	Petition	313	Claims.						
Ostrander, John	For the depreciation of pay and other emoluments for revolutionary services.	4	1	Petition	403	Claims	Jan. 6, 1796	Adverse	......	Leave to withdraw.		
Ostrander, Maria	(See William Ostrander, widow of.)	27	2	....	1041							
Ostrander. William	Arrears of pension	24	1	Petition	406	Rev. Pensions	....	....	......	Discharged; laid on table.		
Ostrander, William, widow of.	Arrears of pension	27	2	Petition	1041	Rev. Pensions.						

List of private claims presented to the House of Representatives of the United States from the 1st to the 31st Congress, inclusive—Continued

Names of claimants.	Nature or object of the claim.	Congress.	Session.	How brought before the House of Reps.	Page of journal.	To what committee of the House referred.	No. or date of the report.	Nature of the report.	No. of the bill.	How disposed of by the House of Reps.	How disposed of by the Senate.	Date of the act of Congress, and remarks.
Ostrander, William, widow of.	Arrears of pension	28	1	Petition	313	Rev. Pensions	330	Favorable; bill	238	Passed	Adverse report.	
Ostrander, William, widow of.	Arrears of pension	28	2	Petition	134	Rev. Pensions.						
O'Sullivan, John, widow of.	Indemnity for arrest and detention of vessel by United States agent at Buenos Ayres.	20	1	Petition	365	Claims	....	....	......	Discharged; laid on table.		
O'Sullivan, John, widow of.	Indemnity for arrest and detention of vessel by United States agent at Buenos Ayres.	21	1	Petition	321	Foreign Affairs	....	....	......	Discharged; laid on table.		
O'Sullivan, John, widow of.	Indemnity for arrest and detention of vessel by United States agent at Buenos Ayres.	22	2	Petition	54	Foreign Affairs	Feb. 6, 1833	Favorable; bill	726	Referred to Committee Whole House.		
O'Sullivan, John, widow of.	Indemnity for arrest and detention of vessel by United States agent Buenos Ayres.	23	1	Petition	37	Foreign Affairs	Jan. 14, 1834	Favorable; bill	184	Passed.		
O'Sullivan, John, widow of.	Indemnity for arrest and detention of vessel by United States agent at Buenos Ayres.	23	2	Memorial	56	Foreign Affairs	Dec. 16, 1835	Favorable; bill	512	Referred to Committee Whole House.		
O'Sullivan, John, widow of.	Indemnity for arrest and detention of vessel by United States agent at Buenos Ayres.	23	2	Senate bill	476	Whole House	....	....	S. 116			
O'Sullivan, John, widow of.	Indemnity for arrest and detention of vessel by United States agent at Buenos Ayres.	24	1	Senate bill	320	Foreign Affairs	Feb. 16, 1836	With't amend.	S. 53	Passed	....	App'd July 2, 1836
O'Sullivan, Mary	(See John O'Sullivan, widow of.)											
Otis, James	Pension	21	2	Petition	299	Military Pensions.						
Otis, John, (Mass.)	Restoration of United States stock taken from him at suit of United States as surety of W. Otis late collector of customs.	19	1	Petition	204	Ways and Means	May 4, 1826	Adverse.	......	Laid on table.		
Otis, John, (Mass.)	Compensation for improvements in loading and firing gunpowder.	27	2	Petition	629	Military Affairs.						
Otis, John, (Mass.)	Compensation for improvements in loading and firing gunpowder.	28	1	Petition	623	Military Affairs	April 3, 1844	Adverse	......	Laid on table.		
Otis, John, (Mass.)	Compensation for improvements in loading and firing gunpowder.	29	1	Petition	487	Patents.						
Otis, John, (N. Y.)	Compensation for services and expenses incurred in the war of 1812.	27	2	Petition	535	Claims	724	Adverse	......	Laid on table.		
Otis, John, (N. Y.)	Compensation for services and expenses incurred in the war of 1812.	27	3	Petition	142	Claims.						
Otis, John, (N. Y.)	Compensation for services and expenses incurred in the war of 1812.	28	1	Petition	552	Claims.						
Otis, John, (N. Y.)	Compensation for services and expenses incurred in the war of 1812.	28	2	Petition	46	Claims.						
Otis, John, (N. Y.)	Compensation for services and expenses incurred in the war of 1812.	29	1	Petition	116	Claims	149	Adverse	......	Laid on table.		

List of private claims presented to the House of Representatives of the United States from the 1st to the 31st Congress, inclusive—Continued.

Names of claimants.	Nature or object of the claim.	Congress.	Session.	How brought before the House of Reps.	Page of journal.	To what committee of the House referred.	No. or date of the report.	Nature of the report.	No. of the bill.	How disposed of by the House of Reps.	How disposed of by the Senate.	Date of the act of Congress, and remarks.
Otis, Joseph	Pension	3	2	Report of Secretary of War.	337	Claims.						
Otis, Joseph	Pension	4	1	Resolution	373	Claims	Feb. 18, 1796	Favorable; bill	156	Passed	Passed	App'd April 20, 1796
Otis, William, (Mass.) late collector of customs.	Indemnity for losses arising from his efforts to execute embargo laws.	18	2	Petition	118	Claims	....	....	......	Discharged; leave to withdraw.		
Otis, William, (Mass.) late collector of customs.	Indemnity for losses arising from his efforts to execute embargo laws.	19	2	Petition	157	Ways and Means	Jan. 27, 1827	Favorable; bill	400	Referred to Committee Whole House.		
Otis, William, (Mass.) late collector of customs.	Equitable settlement of his accounts	20	1	Senate bill	471	Claims	244	With't amend.	S. 107	Referred to Committee Whole House.		
Otis, William, (Mass.) late collector of customs.	Equitable settlement of his accounts	20	2	Petition	28	Claims	Dec. 10, 1810	Favorable; bill	309	Referred to Committee Whole House.		
Otis, William, (Mass.) late collector of customs	Equitable settlement of his accounts	20	2	Senate bill	354	Whole House	Mar. 2, 1829	With't amend.	S. 93	Passed	....	App'd March 2, 1829
Otis, William, (Mass.) late collector of customs.	Additional allowance for losses in executing embargo laws.	24	1	Petition	1054	Claims.						
Otman, Nicholas, (N. Y.)	Revolutionary pension	23	1	Petition	80	Rev. Pensions.						
Otman, Nicholas, (N. Y.)	Revolutionary pension	23	2	Petition	101	Rev. Pensions.						
Otman, Nicholas, (N. Y.)	Revolutionary pension	29	1	Petition	275	Rev. Pensions	488	Adverse	......	Laid on table.		
Otman, Peter	Revolutionary pension	29	1	Petition	275	Rev. Pensions	488	Adverse	......	Laid on table.		
Otman, William	Revolutionary pension	29	1	Petition	275	Rev. Pensions	488	Adverse	......	Laid on table.		
Otway & Fletcher	(See Fletcher & Otway)	26	1	....	182	....	343	....	319			
Ott, Adam, (Md.)	To be restored to pension roll	17	1	Petition	45	Rev. Pensions.						
Ott, Adam, (Md.)	To be restored to pension roll	17	2	Petition	65	Rev. Pensions.						
Ott, Adam, (Md.)	To be restored to pension roll	19	2	Petition	186	Military Pensions.						
Ottawa Indians	(See Indians.)											
Otter, Thomas	Compensation for services rendered in taking fort at Baton Rouge.	25	1	Petition	180	....	....	....	......	Laid on table.		
Otter, Thomas	Compensation for services rendered in taking fort at Baton Rouge.	25	2	Petition	282	Priv. Land Claims	....	....	......	Discharged; laid on table.		
Otterson, Samuel	Pension	10	2	Rep. of Secretary War.	480	Claims	Jan. 30, 1809	By bill	158	Passed	Passed	App'd March 3, 1809
Ottramare, I., of France	Remission of forfeiture of jewelry condemned at New Orleans.	16	1	Petition	519	....	....	....	......	Laid on table.		
Ottramare, I., of France	Remission of forfeiture of jewelry condemned at New Orleans.	16	2	Petition	75	Ways and Means	Jan. 5, 1821	Favorable; bill	186	Referred to Committee Whole House.		
Ottramare, I., of France	Remission of forfeiture of jewelry condemned at New Orleans.	18	1	Petition	213	Ways and Means	Feb. 17, 1824	Favorable; bill	121	Passed	Passed	App'd May 24, 1824
Oury, Augustus, (Va.)	Additional compensation as postmaster.	21	2	Petition	301	P. Of. & P. Roads.						
Oury, Augustus, (Va.)	Additional compensation as postmaster.	22	1	Petition	41	P. Of. & P. Roads.						
Oury, Augustus, (Va.)	Additional compensation as postmaster.	23	1	Petition	57	P. Of. & P. Roads.						
Oury, Eve	(See Francis Oury, heirs of.)											
Oury, Francis, heirs of	Compensation for property destroyed in revolutionary war, and for a pension.	29	2	Petition	172	Rev. Pensions.						
Oury, George	Increase of compensation as mail carrier.	16	1	Resolution	62	P. Of. & P. Roads	....	....	......	Discharged; laid on table.		
Oury, George, sureties of	Indemnity for carrying the mail for nine months.	17	1	Resolution	223	P. Of. & P. Roads	....	....	......	Discharged; leave to withdraw.		

2—77

List of private claims presented to the House of Representatives of the United States from the 1st to the 31st Congress, inclusive—Continued.

Names of claimants.	Nature or object of the claim.	Congress.	Session.	How brought before the House of Reps.	Page of journal.	To what committee of the House referred.	No. or date of the report.	Nature of the report.	No. of the bill.	How disposed of by the House of Reps.	How disposed of by the Senate.	Date of the act of Congress, and remarks.
Ousley, John	Additional compensation as gardener to President's grounds.	31	2	Petition	185	Public Buildings & Grounds.						
Overall, John	(See Nathaniel Overall, representatives of.)	13	3		510							
Overall, John	Permission to locate certain land warrants.	19	1	Petition	225	Priv. Land Claims.						
Overall, John	Permission to locate certain land warrants.	19	2	Petition	45	Priv. Land Claims.	42	Adverse		Referred to Committee Whole House.		
Overall, John	Permission to locate certain land warrants.	20	1	Petition	64	Priv. Land Claims.	Jan. 11, 1828	Adverse		Laid on table.		
Overall, John	Permission to locate certain land warrants.	21	2	Petition	162	Priv. Land Claims.	Feb. 11, 1831	Adverse		Laid on table.		
Overall, John	Permission to locate certain land warrants.	22	1	Petition	78	Priv. Land Claims.	Jan. 4, 1832	Adverse		Laid on table.		
Overall, Nathaniel, representatives of.	Compensation for revolutionary services.	13	3	Petition	510	Pens. & Rev. Cl'ms.	Nov. 4, 1814	Adverse		Leave to withdraw.		
Overbaugh, Jeremiah, widow of.	Revolutionary pension	28	1	Petition	441	Rev. Pensions.						
Overbaugh, Sarah	(See Jeremiah Overbaugh, widow of.)											
Overly, Henry	Pension	10	2	House bill	499	Whole House	Feb. 28, 1809	With't amend.	158	Passed	Passed	App'd March 3, 1809
Overly, Henry	Arrears of pension	25	2	Petition	588	Invalid Pensions.						
Overly, Henry	Arrears of pension	26	1	Resolution	768	Invalid Pensions	665	Adverse		Laid on table.		
Overshire, John	Pension	19	2	Petition	156	Military Pensions.						
Overstreet, John H., heirs of.	Compensation for revolutionary services.	24	2	Petition	397	Rev. Claims.						
Overstreet, John H., heirs of.	Compensation for revolutionary services.	25	2	Petition	178	Rev. Claims	520	Adverse		Laid on table.		
Overstreet, John H., heirs of.	Compensation for revolutionary services.	27	2	Petition	226	Rev. Claims	396	Adverse		Laid on table.		
Overstreet, John H	(See Benjamin J. Harrison, sureties of.)	27	2		77							
Overton, Cornelius	Correction of error in land entry	22	1	Petition	47	Public Lands	Dec. 28, 1831	Favorable; bill	150	Passed	Passed	App'd Feb. 24, 1832
Overton, John H	(See Wm. H. Bedford, agent, &c.)	28	1		262							
Overton, Samuel	Compensation for a horse lost in public service.	22	2	Resolution	25	Claims.						
Overton, Samuel	Compensation for a horse lost in public service.	23	1	Resolution	386	Claims	477	Adverse		Laid on table.		
Overton, Samuel	Compensation for a horse lost in public service.	23	2	Resolution	299	Claims	131	Adverse		Laid on table.		
Overton, Samuel	Compensation for a horse lost in public service.	24	1	Resolution	512	Claims	June 21, 1836	Adverse		Laid on table.		
Overton, Seth	Compensation for revolutionary service	27	2	Petition	47	Rev. Pensions	784	Adverse		Laid on table.		
Overton, Seth	Compensation for revolutionary services.	28	1	Petition	370	Rev. Pensions.						
Overton, Seth	Compensation for revolutionary services.	29	1	Petition	189	Rev. Pensions.	239	Adverse		Laid on table.		
Overton, William	(See Saltmarsh & Overton)	27	2		757							
Ovington, William	(See James Alexander, heirs of)	21	1		202							
Owen, Abel	Indemnity for property taken by United States troops, war of 1812.	29	1	Petition	673	Claims.						

List of private claims presented to the House of Representatives of the United States from the 1st to the 31st Congress, inclusive—Continued.

Names of claimants.	Nature or object of the claim.	Congress.	Session.	How brought before the House of Reps.	Page of journal.	To what committee of the House referred.	No. or date of the report.	Nature of the report.	No. of the bill.	How disposed of by the House of Reps.	How disposed of by the Senate.	Date of the act of Congress, and remarks.
Owen, Abel	Indemnity for property taken by United States troops, war of 1812.	29	2	Petition	164	Claims.						
Owen, Abraham, widow of	Pension	14	2	Petition	45	Pens. & Rev. Cl'ms.	Jan. 10, 1817	Favorable; bill	44	Passed	Passed	App'd March 3, 1817
Owens, Arthur R	Compensation for a horse lost in removing Creek Indians.	25	2	Petition	724	Claims				Discharged; laid on table.		
Owens, Arthur R	Compensation for a horse lost in removing Creek Indians.	26	1	Petition	170	Claims	703	Adverse		Laid on table.		
Owens, Bailey, widow of	Revolutionary pension	29	1	Petition	292	Rev. Pensions	527	Adverse		Laid on table.		
Owens, Benjamin, assignees of.	Relinquishment of United States title or lien to a certain lot of ground.	19	1	Resolution	429	Judiciary				Discharged; laid on table.		
Owens, Benjamin, assignees of.	Relinquishment of United States title or lien to a certain lot of ground.	20	2	Petition	84	Judiciary	Dec. 22, 1828	Favorable; bill	323	Passed	Passed	App'd Feb. 5, 1829
Owens, Eleazer, (Mass.)	Pension	21	2	Petition	372	Military Pensions.						
Owens, Eleazer, (Mass.)	Pension	22	1	Petition	329	Rev. Pensions	439	Favorable; bill	543	Referred to Committee Whole House.		
Owens, Elizabeth	(See James Shirley, heirs of)	21	2		62							
Owens, Elizabeth	(See H. Yeager, daughter of)	26	1		937							
Owen, Ephraim	Revolutionary pension	26	1	Petition	706	Rev. Pensions.						
Owen, James	(See Col. James Porterfield, heirs of.)	29	2		352							
Owen, Jeannet	(See John Owens, heirs of)	23	1		47							
Owen, John	Invalid pension	24	2	Petition	124	Invalid Pensions	Jan. 19, 1837	Adverse		Laid on table.		
Owen, John	Invalid pension	27	3	Petition and docs.	69, 72	Invalid Pensions	191	Adverse		Laid on table.		
Owen, John	Invalid pension	28	1	Petition	143	Invalid Pensions	107	Adverse		Laid on table.		
Owen, John	Invalid pension	29	1	Petition	194	Invalid Pensions	177	Adverse		Laid on table.		
Owens, John	Compensation for a horse lost in public service, war of 1812.	28	1	Petition	609	Claims.						
Owens, John, heirs of	Compensation for two slaves killed on public works, Norfolk, Va.	23	1	Petition	47	Claims.						
Owen, Martha	(See Abraham Owen, widow of)	14	2		45							
Owens, Mary	(See John Owens, heirs of)	23	1		47							
Owens, Polly	(See Bailey Owens, widow of)	29	1		292							
Owens, Robert	For difference of pay between chief boatswain's mate and boatswain.	31	1	Petition	313	Naval Affairs.						
Owens, Theodore	Additional compensation for taking the Fifth Census, Florida.	21	2	Petition	342	Ways and Means.						
Owens, Theodore	Additional compensation for taking the Fifth Census, Florida.	22	1	Petition	224	Judiciary	245	Favorable; bill	333	Referred to Committee Whole House.		
Owens, Theodore	Additional compensation for taking the Fifth Census, Florida.	23	1	Petition	163	Judiciary	Feb. 4, 1834	Favorable; bill	271	Referred to Committee Whole House.		
Owens, Theodore	Additional compensation for taking the Fifth Census, Florida.	23	2	Bill of last sess.	300	Whole House	Jan. 31, 1835	With't amend	271	Passed	Passed	App'd March 3, 1835
Owens, Thomas, and others	Indemnity for Indian depredations.	12	1	Petition	66	Claims.						
Owen, Thomas, (an alien)	Patent for a new and useful discovery.	13	2	Petition	181	Select	Mar. 29, 1814			Leave to withdraw.		
Owen, Thomas, and John W. Skidmore.	Compensation for mail service	25	2	Senate bill	994	P. Of. & P. Roads.	June 27, 1838	Adverse	S. 171	Laid on table.		
Owen, Thomas J. V	Compensation for use and occupation of property by United States troops in 1832.	30	1	Senate bill	1143	Military Affairs	Aug. 8, 1848	With't amend.	S. 256	Passed		App'd Aug. 14, 1848

List of private claims presented to the House of Representatives of the United States form the 1st to the 31st Congress, inclusive—Continued.

Names of claimants.	Nature or object of the claim.	Congress.	Session.	How brought before the House of Reps.	Page of journal.	To what committee of the House referred.	No. or date of the report.	Nature of the report.	No. of the bill.	How disposed of by the House of Reps.	How disposed of by the Senate.	Date of the act of Congress, and remarks.
Owen, William, (N. Y.)	Arrears of pension	19	1	Petition	82	Military Pensions				Discharged; laid on table.		
Owen, William, (Ind.)	Pension	21	1	Petition	66	Military Pensions.						
Owen, William, (Ind.)	Pension	21	2	Documents	209	Military Pensions.						
Owen, William	Invalid pension	26	1	Petition	288	Invalid Pensions	Mar. 5, 1840	Adverse		Laid on table.		
Owen, William H.	Compensation for services as express rider.	31	1	Petition	864	Military Affairs	435	Favorable; bill	366	Referred to Committee Whole House.		
Owens, William	Pension	21	2	Resolution	209	Military Pensions.						
Owens, William	(See heir of James Shirley)	21	2		62		42		572			
Owens, William J.	Compensation for horse lost in public service.	25	2	Documents	396	Claims.						
Owens, William J.	Compensation for horse lost in public service.	25	3	Documents	207	Claims	215	Adverse		Laid on table.		
Owings, Bale, representative of.	Indemnity for French spoliations prior to 1800.	29	2	Petition	224	Foreign Affairs.						
Owings, Caleb D., *et al*	(See Nicholas Owings, representatives of.)											
Owings, Caleb D.	Indemnity for French spoliations prior to 1800.	31	1	Petition	647	Foreign Affairs	355	General bill	318	Referred to Committee Whole House.		
Owings, C. D.	Indemnity for loss of slaves	31	1	Petition	313	Judiciary.						
Owings, Cornelius H.	Indemnity for French spoliations prior to 1800.	31	1	Petition	647	Foreign Affairs	355	General bill	318	Referred to Committee Whole House.		
Owings, David	(See Z. M. Pike and his companions)	10	1		189							
Owings, David	Confirmation of title to land	24	1	Petition		Priv. Land Claims.	March 3, 1836	Adverse		Laid on table		Name does not appear on the Journal.
Owings, George W., heirs of.	Pension for revolutionary services.	28	1	Petition	432	Rev. Pensions.						
Owings, Nicholas, heirs of.	Indemnity for French spoliations prior to 1800.	29	2	Petition	224	Foreign Affairs.						
Owings, Sarah R.	Indemnity for French spoliations prior to 1800.	31	1	Petition	647	Foreign Affairs	355	General bill	318	Referred to Committee Whole House.		
Owings, Thomas	Indemnity for Indian depredations.	14	1	Petition	406	Claims.						
Owings, Thomas	Indemnity for Indian depredations.	14	2	Petition	137	Priv. Land Claims.						
Owings, Thomas	Indemnity for Indian depredations.	15	1	Petition	173	Select	Feb. 2, 1818	Adverse		Leave to withdraw.		
Owings & Rogers	(See Rogers & Owings)	26	1		182		343		319			
Ownbey, James, and others.	Payment of pension stolen from mail.	25	2	Petition	405	Rev. Pensions				Discharged; laid on table.		
Owsly, Jona. D., heirs of.	Confirmation of title to land in Missouri.	15	1	Petition	232	Priv. Land Claims.						See John Calleway.
Owsly, Jona. D., heirs of.	Confirmation of title to land in Missouri.	16	1	Petition	72	Priv. Land Claims.						
Owsly, Jona. D., heirs of.	Confirmation of title to land in Missouri.	17	1	Petition	53	Public Lands.						
Owsly, Jona. D., heirs of.	Confirmation of title to land in Missouri.	18	1	Petition	53	Public Lands	Jan. 16, 1824	Favorable	65	Passed	Passed	App'd May 26, 1824
Ozias, John	Reimbursement of a land payment.	28	1	Petition	547	Claims.						
Ozias, John	Reimbursement of a land payment	28	2	Petition	124	Public Lands.						
Ozias, John	Reimbursement of a land payment.	30	1	Petition	299	Public Lands	264	Favorable	259	Passed.		
Ozias, John	Reimbursement of a land payment.	31	1	Petition	234	Public Lands	247	Favorable	2	Referred to Committee Whole House.		

DIGESTED SUMMARY

AND

ALPHABETICAL LIST OF PRIVATE CLAIMS

WHICH HAVE BEEN

PRESENTED TO THE HOUSE OF REPRESENTATIVES

FROM THE FIRST TO THE THIRTY-FIRST CONGRESS,

EXHIBITING

THE ACTION OF CONGRESS ON EACH CLAIM,

WITH

REFERENCES TO THE JOURNALS, REPORTS, BILLS, &c.,

ELUCIDATING ITS PROGRESS.

COMPILED BY ORDER OF THE HOUSE OF REPRESENTATIVES.

VOL. III.

From P to Z inclusive.

GENEALOGICAL PUBLISHING CO., INC.
Baltimore 1970

Originally Printed for the
House of Representatives of the United States
32d Congress, 1st Session
as House Miscellaneous Documents, unnumbered, Series 653-655
Washington, D. C., 1853

Reprinted with added Publisher's Preface
Genealogical Publishing Company
Baltimore, 1970

Library of Congress Catalog Card Number 79-135476
International Standard Book Number 0-8063-0447-2

The publisher gratefully acknowledges
the loan of the original of this book
by the
George Peabody Branch
Enoch Pratt Free Library
Baltimore, Maryland

NOTICE

This work was reproduced by the photo-offset process from the original edition. A characteristic of this copy, from which the offset printer worked, was that the image was uneven. Every effort has been made by our photo-offset printer to produce as fine a reprint of the original edition as possible.

Genealogical Publishing Company

Made in the United States of America

In the House of Representatives U. S.,
January 27, 1848.

Resolved, That the Clerk of the House be directed to cause to be prepared an Alphabetical List of Private Claims which have been before the House of Representatives from the commencement of the First Congress to the close of the Twenty-ninth Congress, with the proceedings of the House of Representatives and Senate thereon: showing the names of the claimants; the nature or object of each claim; at what session, and in what manner, it was brought before the House; to what committee it was referred; the nature of the report, and the number of the report if printed, and, if not, the date of the report; the number of the bills, distinguishing between the Senate and House bills; the manner in which the claim was disposed of in the House, and, in cases where it passed both Houses, the date of the act of Congress:—the whole to be compiled from the Journals of the House of Representatives, and by reference, when necessary, to the Journals of the Senate, the reports of committees, the bills of the two Houses, and the laws of the United States. And that the Clerk be authorized to employ James Young, of the city of Washington, with a compensation not exceeding the sum now paid the engrossing clerks of this House, to be paid out of the contingent fund of the House; and that the Clerk of the House furnish such aid, by the clerks of his office, as may not be inconsistent with the discharge of their ordinary duties.

In the House of Representatives U. S.,
September 2, 1850.

Resolved, That the more effectually to carry out the intention of the House, as expressed in a resolution passed on the 27th day of January, 1848, the Clerk of this House be, and he is hereby, directed to employ such number of experienced clerks (in addition to his own clerks, whose duty it shall be to assist thereat, without additional compensation when not otherwise officially employed) as will insure the completion, within twelve months, of an alphabetical list of all claims submitted to this House from the day of its organization to the end of the present Congress, according to the plan indicated in the above resolution. Their compensation shall be the same as that allowed the engrossing clerks of the House. The clerk shall cause the work to be printed as a public document, and, to insure *accuracy,* shall take care, to have the clerks carefully compare the proofsheets with their manuscript copy.

In the House of Representatives U. S.,
December 22, 1851.

Resolved, That the Clerk of this House be, and he is hereby, directed to have completed, in the shortest possible time consistent with accuracy, the digest of claims authorized by the resolutions of the House of the 27th of January, 1848, and the 2d of September, 1850, in the manner and at the rate of compensation therein authorized to the extra clerks employed upon the same; and that he pay the compensation due for services already performed on the work, which has been withheld in consequence of the restriction as to time in the resolution of 1850.

Resolved, further, That the Clerk be, and he is hereby, required to withhold the work from the press until the whole of it shall have been completed and subjected to a re-examination with the journals, reports, laws, &c.; and to have reprinted so much of that now printed as shall, by the discovery of errors in it, connected with that now incomplete or otherwise, be deemed necessary; and that the work, when ready for the press, be printed by the printer now engaged upon it.

An Alphabetical list of Private Claims presented to the House of Representatives of the United States from the commencement of the 1st to the close of the 31st Congress.

Names of claimants.	Nature or object of the claim.	Congress.	Session.	How brought before the House of Reps.	Page of journal.	To what committee of the House referred.	No. or date of the report.	Nature of the report.	No. of the bill.	How disposed of by the House of Reps.	How disposed of by the Senate.	Date of the act of Congress, and remarks.
Pace, Thomas, *et al.*	Compensation for horses lost in public service.	13	3	Petition	460	Claims	Nov. 14, 1814	By bill	228	Passed	Indef. postp'd.	
Pachard, Jonah B.	Pension	14	1	House bill	622	Whole House	April 23, 1816	With amend.	171	Passed	Passed	App'd April 30, 1816
Pacheco, Antonio, administrator of.	Compensation for a negro slave lost in service of United States.	26	1	Petition	337	Claims.						
Pacheco, Antonio, administrator of.	Compensation for a negro slave lost in service of United States.	26	2	Petition	135	Claims.						
Pacheco, Antonio, administrator of.	Compensation for a negro slave lost in service of United States.	27	2	Petition	94	Claims	472	Favorable; bill	322	Referred to Committee Whole House.		
Pacheco, Antonio, administrator of.	Compensation for a negro slave lost in service of United States.	28	1	Petition	132	Claims	523	Favorable; bill	398	Referred to Committee Whole House.		
Pacheco, Antonio, administrator of.	Compensation for a negro slave lost in service of United States.	29	1	Petition	474	Military Affairs.						
Pacheco, Antonio, administrator of.	Compensation for a negro slave lost in service of United States.	30	1	Petition	162	Military Affairs	187	Favorable; bill, also minority report.	197	Referred to Committee Whole House.		
Pacheco, Antonio, administrator of.	Compensation for a negro slave lost in service of United States.	30	2	Bill of last sess.	149	Whole House	Dec. 23, 1848	Favorable	197	Passed	Reported without amend't.	
Pacheco, Antonio, administrator of.	Compensation for a negro slave lost in service of United States.	31	1	Petition	396	Military Affairs.						
Pacheco, Antonio, administrator of.	Compensation for a negro slave lost in service of United States.	31	2	Petition	241	Military Affairs.	Feb. 7, 1851	Favorable; bill	458	Referred to Committee Whole House.		
Pack, Phoebe	(See William Pack, widow of.)	28	2		193							
Pack, Ruth	Relief: husband killed by Indians in revolutionary war.	3	1	Petition	82					Laid on table.		
Pack, William, widow of.	Revolutionary pension	28	2	Petition	193	Rev. Pensions				Discharged; laid on table.		
Packard, Absalom, and others.	Relief from penalties for trespassing on public lands.	22	1	Petition	514	Public Lands.				Discharged; laid on table.		
Packard, John	Revolutionary pension	24	1	Petition	56	Rev. Pensions				Discharged; laid on table.		
Packard, Jonah B.	Arrears of pension	20	2	Petition	143	Military Pensions.	Jan. 23, 1829	Adverse		Laid on table.		
Packard, Mark	Pension	19	2	Petition	242	Military Pensions.				Discharged; laid on table.		
Packard, Mark	Pension	20	1	Petition	124	Military Pensions.				Discharged; laid on table.		
Packard, Shepherd	Pension	10	1	House bill	232	Whole House	April 19, 1808	With amends.	78	Passed	Passed	App'd April 23, 1808
Packard, Shepherd	Increase of pension	16	1	Resolution	268	Pens. & Rev. Cl'ms.						
Packer, James	Compensation for risk and hardships in purchasing hides for the American army in revolutionary war.	2	2	Petition	697					Laid on table.		

List of private claims presented to the House of Representatives of the United States from the 1st to the 31st [illegible] *inclusive*—Continued.

Names of claimants.	Nature or object of the claim.	Congress.	Session.	How brought before the House of Reps.	Page of journal.	To what committee of the House referred.	No. or date of the report.	Nature of the report.	No. of the bill.	How disposed of by the House of Reps.	How disposed of by the Senate.	Date of the act of Congress, and remarks.
Packer, Job	Payment for hides furnished revolutionary army.	23	1	Petition	368	Rev. Claims.						
Packer, Job	Payment for hides furnished revolutionary army.	23	2	Petition	147	Rev. Claims.						
Packwood, Joseph	Liquidation of claim against the United States.	1	2	Petition	245					Referred to Secretary Treasury.		
Packwood, Joseph	Liquidation of claim against the United States.	3	1	Rep. of Secretary Treasury.	78					Laid on table.		
Paddock, Cains, widow of	Revolutionary pension	25	3	Petition	562	Rev. Pensions.						
Paddock, Cains, widow of	Revolutionary pension	26	1	Petition	174	Rev. Pensions.						
Paddock, James	To be allowed the amount paid for advertising as collector of the direct tax in Vermont.	8	1	Petition	421	Claims	Nov. 1, 1803	Res.; adverse.		Resolution adopted.		
Paddock, James	To be allowed the amount paid for advertising as collector of the direct tax in Vermont.	8	2	Petition	163					Laid on table.		
Paddock, Loveland	(See assignees of Thomas Tupper)	22	2		142							
Paddock, Peter	Revolutionary pension	23	1	Petition	273	Rev. Pensions.						
Paddock, Polly	(See Cains Paddock, widow of)	25	3		562							
Paddy, William	Pension for long services in United States army.	30	1	Petition	137	Invalid Pensions	457	Favorable; bill	387	Passed	Rept'd without amendment.	
Paddy, William	Pension for long services in United States army.	31	1	Petition	193	Invalid Pensions	8	Favorable; bill	10	Passed	Passed	App'd Sept. 28, 1850
Padget, John	Payment of the amount of his pension which was stolen from the mail.	25	2	Petition	405	Rev. Pensions				Discharged; laid on table.		
Page, Carter	Relief from an error in locating a land warrant granted by the State of Virginia.	6	1	Petition	665					Referred to Committee Whole House.		
Page, Carter, executor of	Commutation pay for revolutionary services.	31	1	Petition	449	Rev. Pensions				Discharged; laid on table.		
Page, Daniel	Arrears of pension	23	1	Petition	46	Rev. Pensions	66	Favorable; bill	76	Passed	Rejected.	
Page, Daniel	Arrears of pension	23	2	Petition	41	Rev. Pensions	Dec. 11, 1834	Favorable; bill	559	Passed	Passed	App'd March 3, 1835
Page, Enoch	Pension	22	1	Petition	631	Rev. Pensions.						
Page, Ephraim	Pension	24	1	Senate bill	1107	Invalid Pensions	July 1, 1836	With't amend.	293	Passed	Passed	App'd July 2, 1836
Page, Eunice	(See Stephen Page, widow of)											
Page, Gad	Revolutionary pension	20	2	Resolution	72	Military Pensions				Discharged; laid on table.		
Page, George	Payment for a machine for cutting paper envelopes, ordered by the House of Representatives.	28	1	Petition	483	Accounts	268	Favorable; and res. directing clerk to pay.		Referred to Committee Whole House.		
Page, James, widow of	Increase of pension	30	1	Petition	440	Naval Affairs.						
Page, Jerry L	(See Samuel Upton and Jerry L. Page.)	12	1		94							
Page, John	Pension for wounds received in the naval service, revolutionary war.	11	3	Petition	464					Referred to Secretary War.		
Page, John, and Joseph Ray.	Reduction of duties on a quantity of goat skins, they having been invoiced too high.	14	1	Petition	63	Com. and Manuf.				Discharged; laid on table.		
Page, John, heir of	Payment for boarding United States soldiers in 1813.	27	2	Petition	1111	Claims.						
Page, J. W	(See Timothy Page, only son of)	25	2		404							

List of private claims presented to the House of Representatives of the United States from the 1st to the 31st Congress, inclusive—Continued.

Names of claimants.	Nature or object of the claim.	Congress.	Session.	How brought before the House of Reps.	Page of journal.	To what committee of the House referred.	No. or date of the report.	Nature of the report.	No. of the bill.	How disposed of by the House of Reps.	How disposed of by the Senate.	Date of the act of Congress, and remarks.
Page, Joseph Wellington	To be exonerated from paying a certain bond to the United States.	12	1	Petition	276	Com. and Manuf.						
Page, Joseph Wellington	To be exonerated from paying a certain bond to the United States.	13	2	Petition	226	Ways and Means	48	Favorable; bill	92	Passed	Passed	App'd Mar. 31, 1814
Page, Joseph Wellington	Compensation for procuring testimony in the case of the United States *vs.* B. Lafon.	15	1	Petition and rep't Sec. of War.	127	Claims	Feb. 20, 1818	Res. adverse		Resolution adopted		Leave to withdraw, February 25, 1818.
Page, Joseph Wellington	Compensation for procuring testimony in the case of the United States *vs.* B. Lafon.	25	2	Petition	554	Ways and Means				Discharged; laid on table.		
Page, Joseph W	For his share of the forfeiture in the case of the brig Belona.	24	1	Petition	943	Claims.						
Page, Lewis B	Equitable settlement of his accounts as sailing-master in the navy.	18	2	Petition	136	Naval Affairs				Discharged		Leave to withdraw.
Page, Maria	(See James Page, widow of)	30	1		440							
Page, Mary	(See William Hall, widow of.)											
Page, Robert	(See John Page, heir of)	27	2		1111							
Page, Samuel	Invalid pension	27	2	Petition	836	Invalid Pensions.						
Page, Samuel	Invalid pension	28	1	Petition	428	Invalid Pensions.						
Page, Samuel	Invalid pension	29	1	Petition	462	Invalid Pensions				Disch'd; laid on table.		
Page, Samuel	Invalid pension	30	1	Petition	154	Invalid Pensions				Discharged; laid on table.		
Page, Samuel	Invalid pension	30	2	Petition	174	Invalid Pensions	99	Adverse		Laid on table.		
Page, Samuel	Invalid pension	31	2	Petition	164	Invalid Pensions.						
Page, Samuel, heirs of	Indemnity for French spoliations prior to 1800.	26	1	Memorial	182	Foreign Affairs	343	Favorable; bill	319	Referred to Committee Whole House.		
Page, Samuel, (Mass.,) administrator of.	Indemnity for French spoliations prior to 1800.	26	1	Memorial	182	Foreign Affairs	343	Favorable; bill	319	Referred to Committee Whole House.		
Page, Samuel, administrator of.	Indemnity for French spoliations prior to 1800.	31	1	Petition	681	Foreign Affairs	355	Favorable; bill	318	Referred to Committee Whole House.		
Page, Stephen, widow of	Pension to which he was entitled	31	1	Petition	904	Rev. Pensions	359	Adverse		Laid on table.		
Page, Thomas	(See Seth Webber and Thomas Page.)	15	2		186							
Page, Thomas	(See Robert Kid, and others)	15	2		168							
Page, Timothy, only daughter of.	Gratuity from government for the loss of her father in the service of his country.	25	2	Petition	347	Rev. Claims	972	Adverse		Laid on table.		
Page, Timothy, only son of.	Pension for services in revolutionary war.	25	2	Petition	404	Rev. Claims	April 10, 1838	Adverse		Laid on table.		
Page, William	(See J. Ramsay, administrator of)	31	1		256							
Page, William Byrd	Arrears of pay due for services as clerk in the treasurer's office.	30	2	Petition	361	Claims.						
Page, William P	Indemnity for French spoliations prior to 1800.	26	1	Memorial	182	Foreign Affairs	343	Favorable; bill	319	Referred to Committee Whole House.		
Paimbouef, Lewis	Further compensation for services as lieutenant colonel in the service of the United States.	20	1	Petition	168	Military Affairs				Discharged; laid on table.		Leave to withdraw, Feb. 29, 1828.
Pain, Abigail	Continuation of pension	27	2	Petition	93	Rev. Pensions	784	Adverse		Laid on table.		
Pain, Christian	(See Canadian refugees)	4	2		614							
Pain, Elizabeth	(See Thomas Paine, widow of)	28	1		901							
Pain, Captain Joel's company of volunteers, survivors of.	Relief for services under General Perkins in Ohio.)	31	2	Petition	283	Military Affairs.						

List of private claims presented to the House of Representatives of the United States from the 1st to the 31st Congress, inclusive—Continued.

Names of claimants.	Nature or object of the claim.	Congress.	Session.	How brought before the House of Reps.	Page of journal.	To what committee of the House referred.	No. or date of the report.	Nature of the report.	No. of the bill.	How disposed of by the House of Reps.	How disposed of by the Senate.	Date of the act of Congress, and remarks.
Paine, Jonathan	(See John Alden and Jonathan Paine.)	17	1		32							
Paine, Joseph	Restoration to pension roll	17	1	Petition	67	Pens. & Rev. Cl'ms.						
Paine, Raphael, and Elias Arnold.	Exchange of land scrip	22	2	Senate bill	441	Public Lands	Mar. 2, 1833	With't amend.	393	Passed		App'd March 2, 1833
Paine, Raphael, and Elias Arnold.	To amend act of March 2, 1833, for their relief.	25	2	House bill	484	Priv. Land Claims.	Feb. 20, 1838	With't amend.	570	Passed	Passed	App'd June 28, 1838
Paine, Thomas	Compensation for various services in the revolutionary war.	10	1	Petition	160	Claims.						
Paine, Thomas	Compensation for various services in the revolutionary war.	10	2	Petition	391	Claims	Feb. 1, 1809	Rep. and resl'n for leave to withdraw.		Laid on table.		
Paine, Thomas	Compensation for various services in the revolutionary war.	11	1	Petition	29	Claims.						
Paine, Thomas, widow of.	Revolutionary pension	28	1	Petition	901	Rev. Pensions.						
Paine, Thomas, widow of.	Revolutionary pension	29	1	Petition	1203	Rev. Pensions.						
Paine, Thomas, widow of	Revolutionary pension	29	2	Petition	86	Rev. Pensions				Discharged; laid on table.		
Paine, Thomas	Indemnity for losses sustained by the wreck of the revenue cutter Crawford, under his command.	21	1	Petition	145	Ways and Means.	224	Favorable bill	283	Referred to Committee Whole House.		
Paine, Thomas	Indemnity for losses sustained by the wreck of the revenue cutter Crawford, under his command.	21	2	Bill of last sess.	332	Whole House	Feb. 10, 1831	With't amend.	283	Passed.		
Paine, Thomas	Indemnity for losses sustained by the wreck of the revenue cutter Crawford, under his command.	22	1	Petition	53	Ways and Means.	14	Favorable; bill	64	Passed	Passed	App'd Mar. 22, 1832
Paine, Thomas	Arrears of pension	23	1	Petition	638	Naval Affairs.						
Paine, Thomas	Arrears of pension	24	1	Petition	52	Invalid Pensions				Discharged; laid on table.		
Paine, Thomas	Arrears of pension	25	2	Petition	52	Rev. Pensions.						
Paine, William	Compensation for services and losses in revolutionary war.	1	3	Petition and rep't Sec. of War.	346					Laid on table.		
Paine, William	Renewal of a certerficate of indebtedness which had been defaced and destroyed.	1	3	Petition	346					Referred to Secretary Treasury.		
Paine, William	Compensation for services as assistant commissary general of issues to the army, and for saddlery furnished, rev. war.	13	3	Petition	512	Pens. & Rev. Cl'ms.						
Painter, John	Compensation for services in revolutionary war.	25	2	Petition	85	Public Lands				Discharged; laid on table.		
Pairo, B.	Confirmation of title to land	19	1	Report of register and receiver of land office.	64	Public Lands	33	Favorable; bill	254	Referred to Committee Whole House.		
Paira, Henry T	(See John Laub, administrator of)	31	1		390							
Palacios, Captain J. J. Dos.	Relief on account of servives as captain of Native Spy company in Mexican war.	31	1	Petition	406	Military Affairs.						
Palao, Don Pedro, heirs of.	Confirmation of Spanish land title.	24	1	Petition	672	Priv. Land Claims.	727	Adverse		Laid on table.		
Palao, Don Pedro, heirs of.	Confirmation of Spanish land title.	24	2	Petition	122	Priv. Land Claims.				Discharged; laid on table.		
Palmer, Archibald, *et al.*	Permission to enter certain lands.	28	1	Petition	683	Priv. Land Claims.	461	Adverse		Laid on table.		

List of private claims presented to the House of Representatives of the United States from the 1st to the 31st Congress, inclusive—Continued.

Names of claimants.	Nature or object of the claim.	Congress.	Session.	How brought before the House of Reps.	Page of journal.	To what committee of the House referred.	No. or date of the report.	Nature of the report.	No. of the bill.	How disposed of by the House of Reps.	How disposed of by the Senate.	Date of the act of Congress, and remarks.
Palmer, Asher	Indemnity for loss of schooner in attempting to retake British prisoners in late war.	14	1	Petition	317	Claims	April 1, 1816	Favorable; bill		Passed	Passed	App'd April 27, 1816
Palmer, Barnabas	To have $150, overpaid by him as collector of customs, refunded with interest.	27	1	Petition	99	Claims.						
Palmer, Barnabas	To have $150, overpaid by him as collector of customs, refunded with interest.	27	2	Petition	55	Claims	57	Favorable; bill	92	Passed	Indef. postp'd.	
Palmer, Caleb	Indemnity for a house destroyed by the army in late war in consequence of its occupation by United States troops.	16	1	Petition	232	Claims	April 5, 1820	Adverse		Laid on table.		
Palmer, Daniel	Increase of pension	16	1	Petition	350	Pens. & Rev. Cl'ms.						
Palmer, Daniel	Increase of pension	17	1	Petition	45	Pens. & Rev. Cl'ms.	Feb. 15, 1822	Adverse		Rejected.		
Palmer, Daniel	Increase of pension	17	2	Petition	104	Pens. & Rev. Cl'ms.	Jan. 13, 1823	Rep. and res. for leave to withdraw.		Resolution adopted.		
Palmer, Daniel	Increase of pension	18	1	Petition	312					Referred to Committee Whole House.		
Palmer, Daniel	Increase of pension	20	2	Petition	39	Military Pensions				Discharged; laid on table.		
Palmer, Daniel	Increase of pension	21	2	Petition	270	Military Pensions.						
Palmer, Daniel	Increase of pension	22	2	Petition	30	Invalid Pensions.						
Palmer, Daniel	Increase of pension	23	2	Petition	68	Invalid Pensions	Dec. 23, 1834	Adverse		Laid on table.		
Palmer, Daniel	Increase of pension	24	1	Petition	140	Invalid Pensions	Jan. 14, 1836	Adverse		Laid on table.		
Palmer, Daniel	Increase of pension	25	2	Petition	269	Invalid Pensions				Discharged; laid on table.		
Palmer, Daniel	Increase of pension	30	2	Petition	224	Invalid Pensions				Discharged; laid on table.		
Palmer, Daniel	Increase of pension	31	1	Petition	324	Invalid Pensions	468	Adverse		Laid on table.		
Palmer, Daniel	(See Thomas Cox and Daniel Palmer.)	18	1		105							
Palmer, Daniel	Arrears of pension	16	2	Petition	65	Pens. & Rev. Cl'ms.				Discharged; laid on table.		
Palmer, Daniel	Arrears of pension	17	2	Petition	22	Pens. & Rev. Cl'ms.	Dec. 16, 1822	Adverse		Laid on table.		
Palmer, Daniel	Arrears of pension	21	1	Petition	67	Military Pensions	April 24, 1830	Adverse		Laid on table.		
Palmer, Daniel	Arrears of pension	22	1	Petition	165	Invalid Pensions	235	Favorable; bill	344	Passed.		
Palmer, Daniel	Arrears of pension	23	1	Petition	155	Invalid Pensions	160	Favorable; bill	175	Passed	Passed	App'd June 30, 1834
Palmer, Daniel	Remuneration for services rendered and misfortunes sustained in war of 1812.	24	1	Petition	62	Invalid Pensions				Discharged; laid on table.		
Palmer, Daniel	Remuneration for services rendered and misfortunes sustained in war of 1812.	24	2	Petition	87	Invalid Pensions.						
Palmer, Daniel	Remuneration for services rendered and misfortunes sustained in war of 1812.	27	2	Petition	1070	Invalid Pensions	967	Adverse		Laid on table.		
Palmer, Daniel, (Penn.)	Revolutionary pension	26	1	Petition	625	Rev. Pensions.						
Palmer, Daniel	Renewal of pension and bounty land for services in the Mexican war.	30	1	Petition	300	Invalid Pensions						Leave to withdraw.

List of private claims presented to the House of Representatives of the United States from the 1st to the 31st Congress, inclusive—Continued.

Names of claimants.	Nature or object of the claim.	Congress.	Session.	How brought before the House of Reps.	Page of journal.	To what committee of the House referred.	No. or date of the report.	Nature of the report.	No. of the bill.	How disposed of by the House of Reps.	How disposed of by the Senate.	Date of the act of Congress, and remarks.
Palmer, Daniel	Compensation for services and commutation of rations while acting as recruiting officer during the Mexican war.	30	2	Petition	255	Military Affairs.						
Palmer, Daniel	Invalid pension	31	2	Petition	58	Invalid Pensions.						
Palmer, Elijah, and Solomon Porter.	Increase of compensation as surveyors of customs.	14	2	Petition	346	Ways and Means.						
Palmer, Elizabeth & Mary Whitemore.	(See Jonathan Whitemore, sisters of.)	23	2		197							
Palmer, George, executors of.	Compensation for revolutionary services.	22	1	Petition	442	Rev. Claims	April 9, 1832	Adverse		Laid on table.		
Palmer, George M	Extension of time to take out a patent for his spark arrester.	27	3	Petition	206	Patents.						
Palmer, Gilbert	(See Samuel Gibbs, heirs of)	22	2		91							
Palmer, Innis B	Payment of claim against United States for $1,117 40.	18	2	Petition	160	Claims.						
Palmer, Innis B	Payment of claim against United States for $1,117 40.	20	2	Petition	118	Claims.						
Palmer, Isaac	Invalid pension	3	1	Rep. of Secretary War.	131	Select	May 26, 1794	Jt. res. to refer to Sec. War.	R. 12	Passed	Passed	App'd June 9, 1794
Palmer, Isaac	Invalid pension	4	1	Rep. of Secretary War.	445	Claims	Mar. 4, 1796	Jt. res. to refer to Sec. War.	R. 16	Passed	Passed	App'd April 18, 1796
Palmer, Jacob	(See George Palmer, executors of.)	22	1		442							
Palmer, James C	(See Exploring Expedition)	27	3		149							
Palmer, Jared	Invalid pension	3	2	Rep. of Secretary War.	278	Claims	Mar. 2, 1795	Rep. and res. to refer to Sec. of War.		Resolution adopted.		
Palmer, Jared	Invalid pension	4	1	Rep. of Secretary War.	445	Claims	Feb. 18, 1796	Favorable; bill	156	Passed	Passed	App'd April 20, 1796
Palmer, Jonathan W., heirs of.	Bounty land for revolutionary services.	21	1	Petition	260	Rev. Claims.						
Palmer, Mary	Relief, husband drowned while attending to his duties as inspector of customs.	12	1	Petition	204	Select	April 7, 1812	Res. adverse		Rejected.		
Palmer, Mary, (Ohio)	Pension for services of husband in revolutionary war.	27	3	Petition	78	Rev. Pensions				Discharged; laid on table.		
Palmer, Orion S	(See Robert Swan and O. S. Palmer.)	29	2		227							
Palmer, Philo B	(See sureties of Chas. Josslyn)	21	1		133							
Palmer, Richard	Back pay, or arrears of pension	29	1	Petition	517	Invalid Pensions				Discharged; laid on table.		
Palmer, Stephen	Revolutionary pension	21	1	Petition	59	Military Pensions	May 4, 1830	Adverse		Laid on table.		
Palmer, Stephen	Revolutionary pension	26	1	Petition	759	Rev. Pensions	424	Adverse		Laid on table.		
Palmer, Sybil	Continuation of pension	28	1	Petition	850	Rev. Pensions.						
Palmer, Thomas, guardian, &c.	(See Mary M. Van Drieson)	27	2		526							
Palmer, Thomas	Pension	22	1	Petition	105	Rev. Pensions				Discharged; laid on table.		
Palmer, Thomas H	Indemnity for property lost in the Florida war, and for bounty land.	31	1	Petition	810	Military Affairs.						
Palmer, William	(See Daniel Haselton.)	22	1		378							
Palmer, William	Naval pension	23	2	Petition	199	Naval Affairs	Feb. 10, 1835	Adverse		Laid on table.		

List of private claims presented to the House of Representatives of the United States from the 1st to the 31st Congress, inclusive—Continued.

Names of claimants.	Nature or object of the claim.	Congress.	Session.	How brought before the House of Reps.	Page of journal.	To what committee of the House referred.	No. or date of the report.	Nature of the report.	No. of the bill.	How disposed of by the House of Reps.	How disposed of by the Senate.	Date of the act of Congress, and remarks.
Palmer, William, widow of.	Revolutionary pension	27	3	Petition	190	Rev. Pensions	295	Adverse	......	Laid on table.		
Palmer, Wyatt, sen	(See Jonathan W. Palmer, heirs of.)	21	1	....	260							
Palmetto, (brig) owners of.	Register for brig	30	1	Senate bill	664	Commerce	April 18, 1848	With't amend.	204	Passed	....	App'd April 19, 1848
Palmitter, Phineas	Pension	20	1	Petition	338	Military Pensions	Mar. 18, 1828	Adverse	......	Laid on table.		
Palmitter, Phineas	Pension	21	1	Petition	198	Military Pensions	....	....	......	Discharged; laid on table.		
Palmitter, Phineas	Pension	21	2	Petition	208	Military Pensions.						
Palms, William	Pay as a revenue officer during the time he was a prisoner.	26	1	Petition	335	Claims.						
Palms, William	Pay as a revenue officer during the time he was a prisoner.	26	2	Petition	79	Claims	247	Adverse	......	Laid on table.		
Pancake, Joseph	Confirmation of title to land in district of Vincennes.	12	2	House bill	609	Whole House	Jan. 18, 1813	With't amend.	222	Passed	Passed	App'd Feb. 13, 1813
Pancoast, William	Confirmation of title to a tract of land in the District of Columbia, derived from the State of Maryland prior to its cession to the United States.	8	1	Petition	422	Select	....	....	......	Discharged; laid on table.		
Pancoast, William	Confirmation of title to a tract of land in the District of Columbia, derived from the State of Maryland prior to its cession to the United States.	16	1	Petition	177	Dist. of Columbia	April 1, 1820	By bill	123	Passed	Indef. postp'd.	
Panfield, Hiram	Indemnity for French spoliations prior to 1800.	26	1	Memorial	182	Foreign Affairs	343	Favorable; bill	319	Referred to Committee Whole House.		
Pangburn, William	(Nature of claim not stated.)	27	2	Petition	55	Claims.						
Pankey, Hampton	(See James McFarland and others.)	15	2	....	200							
Pannell, Edward, heirs of.	Amount due on a certificate signed by Lord Berkley, assistant deputy quartermaster general in revolutionary army.	24	1	Resolution	541	Rev. Claims	....	....	......	Discharged; laid on table.		
Pannell, Edward, heirs of.	Amount due on a certificate signed by Lord Berkley, assistant deputy quartermaster general in revolutionary army.	24	2	Resolution	77	Rev. Claims.						
Pannell, Edward, heirs of.	Amount due on a certificate signed by Lord Berkley, assistant deputy quartermaster general in revolutionary army.	25	2	Resolution	108	Rev. Claims	....	....	......	Discharged; laid on table.		
Pannell, Edward, heirs of.	Amount due on a certificate signed by Lord Berkley, assistant deputy quartermaster general in revolutionary army.	25	3	Resolution	166	Rev. Claims	....	....	......	Discharged; laid on table.		
Pannell, Edward, heirs of.	Amount due on a certificate signed by Lord Berkley, assistant deputy quartermaster general in revolutionary army.	26	1	Petition	167	Rev. Claims.						
Pannell, Edward, heirs of.	Amount due on a certificate signed by Lord Berkley, assistant deputy quartermaster general in revolutionary army.	26	2	Petition	182	Rev. Claims	....	....	......	Discharged; laid on table.		

List of private claims presented to the House of Representatives of the United States from the 1st to the 31st Congress, inclusive—Continued.

Names of claimants.	Nature or object of the claim.	Congress.	Session.	How brought before the House of Reps.	Page of journal.	To what committee of the House referred.	No. or date of the report.	Nature of the report.	No. of the bill.	How disposed of by the House of Reps.	How disposed of by the Senate.	Date of the act of Congress, and remarks.
Pannell, Joseph	Compensation for services in revolutionary war.	1	2	Petition	269					Referred to Secretary of War.		
Pannell, Joseph	Settlement of his accounts as a deranged officer.	2	1	House bill	463	Whole House	Nov. 29, 1791	With amend.	152	Passed	Passed	App'd Mar. 27, 1792
Pannell, Joseph, *et al.*	Confirmation of title to land in the Territory of Mississippi.	7	2	Petition	283	Select	Feb. 19, 1803	By bill	120	Passed.		
Pantry, John	Compensation for supplies furnished a detachment of United States troops in 1799.	8	2	Petition	26	Claims	Dec. 13, 1804	Report and res. for leave to withdraw.		Resolution adopted.		
Paoly, Paolo, (a Dane,) by attorney.	Reimbursed the amount of expenses incurred in recovering his vessel, captured by the United States schooner, in 1800.	7	1	Petition	153	Select	May 26, 1802	Favorable; bill	47	Passed	Passed	App'd April 14, 1802
Papin, Joseph, *et al.*	Confirmation of title to land in Missouri.	15	1	Petition	280	Priv. Land Claims.						
Papy, Don Michael	(See Don Mates Solano and others.)	28	2		84							
Paranque, Step'n, of France.	Permission to land goods on condition of his giving bond, without security.	3	1	Petition	83	Select	Mar. 6, 1794	Favorable; bill	21	Passed	Passed	App'd April 2, 1794
Parcell, Jacob and Paul	(See William Parcell, heirs of)	19	1		336							
Parcell, William, heirs of.	Balance of pay for revolutionary services.	19	1	Petition	336	Rev. Claims.						
Pardee, Chandler	Invalid pension	3	1	Rep. of Secretary War.	131	Select	May 26, 1794	Jt. res. to refer to Sec. War.	R. 12	Passed	Passed	App'd June 9, 1794
Pardee, Chandler	Invalid pension	3	2	Rep. of Secretary War.	350	Claims	Feb. 28, 1795	Favorable; bill	130	Passed	Postp'd to next session.	
Pardee, Chandler	Invalid pension	4	1	Rep. of Secretary War.	445	Claims	Feb. 18, 1796	Favorable; bill	156	Passed	Passed	App'd April 20, 1796
Pardee, Lemuel	Pension	19	1	Resolution	144	Military Pensions	Feb. 23, 1826	By bill	119	Passed.		
Pardee, Lemuel	Pension	19	2	Resolution	66	Military Pensions	Dec. 22, 1826	By bill	315	Passed	Laid on table.	
Pardee, Lemuel	Pension	20	1	Petition	243	Military Pensions	April 29, 1828	By bill	283	Passed.		
Pardee, Lemuel	Pension	20	2	Petition	229	Military Pensions	Dec. 12, 1828	By bill	311	Passed	Laid on table.	
Pardee, Lemuel	Pension	21	1	Petition	48	Military Pensions	Jan. 5, 1830	By bill	72	Passed	Passed	App'd May 20, 1830
Pardue, William	Pension	22	1	Petition	171	Rev. Pensions	367	Favorable; bill	462	Passed	Indef. postp'd.	
Pardy, Samuel	Pension	22	1	Petition	219	Rev. Pensions.						
Parent, Charles, heirs of	Confirmation of title to two tracts of land.	18	2	Senate bill	92	Priv. Land Claims.	Mar. 1, 1825	With't amend.	S. 8	Laid on table.		
Parent, Charles, heirs of	Permission to locate lands in lieu of lands which belonged to them, and were sold by the U. States.	31	1	Petition	496	Priv. Land Claims.						
Parent, David	Pension	20	2	Petition	49	Military Pensions	Jan. 15, 1829	Adverse		Laid on table.		
Parent, Etienne, heirs of	Confirmation of title to land in Missouri.	15	2	Petition	28	Priv. Land Claims.						
Parent, Etienne, heirs of	Confirmation of title to land in Missouri.	17	1	Petition	54	Public Lands.						
Parent, Etienne, hiers of	Confirmation of title to land in Missouri.	18	1	Petition	55	Public Lands	Jan. 16, 1824	By bill, giving the courts jurisdiction of such cases.	65	Passed	Passed	App'd May 26, 1824
Parham, John	(See William Avery, administrator of.)	23	2		177							
Parke, Erastus	(See Rufus Spalding and others)	15	2		148							

List of private claims presented to the House of Representatives of the United States from the 1*st to the* 31*st Congress, inclusive*—Continued.

Names of claimants.	Nature or object of the claim	Congress.	Session.	How brought before the House of Reps.	Page of journal.	To what committee of the House referred.	No. or date of the report	Nature of the report.	No. of the bill.	How disposed of by the House of Reps.	How disposed of by the Senate.	Date of the act of Congress, and remarks.
Parke, Capt. E. E.	Payment for services of his company of mounted volunteers against the Indians in 1837.	26	1	Petition	340	Claims.						
Park, George	Renewal of patent	31	1	Petition	955	Patents.						
Park, Henry	Revolutionary pension	23	1	Petition	333	Rev. Pensions.						
Parke, Hervey, or Harvey.	Balance due for services as deputy surveyor in Michigan.	27	2	Documents	382	Claims	1049	Adverse	......	Laid on table.		
Parke, Hervey, or Harvey.	Balance due for services as deputy surveyor in Michigan.	27	3	Petition	73	Claims.						
Parke, Hervey, or Harvey.	Balance due for services as deputy surveyor in Michigan.	28	1	Petition	526	Claims	312	Favorable; bill	220	Passed	Adverse report.	
Parke, Hervey, or Harvey.	Balance due for services as deputy surveyor in Michigan.	28	2	Petition	104	Claims	156	Favorable; bill	628	Referred to Committee Whole House.		
Parke, Hervey, or Harvey.	Balance due for services as deputy surveyor in Michigan.	29	1	Petition	207	Claims	801	Adverse	......	Laid on table.		
Parke, Jane	(See Mathew Parke, widow and heirs of, and William Earle.)	15	1	....	286							
Park, Jonathan, widow of.	Revolutionary pension	26	1	Petition	706	Rev. Pensions.						
Park, Jonathan, widow of.	Revolutionary pension	28	1	Petition	861	Rev. Pensions.						
Park, Jonathan, widow of.	Revolutionary pension	29	1	Petition	623	Rev. Pensions	784	Adverse	......	Laid on table.		
Park, Jonathan, widow of.	Revolutionary pension	30	1	Petition	156	Rev. Pensions	137	Favorable; bill	126	Passed	Reported with't amendment.	
Parke, Mathew, widow and heirs of, and Wm. Earle.	For their portion of the prize money out of vessels captured by the frigate Alliance, in revolutionary war.	15	1	Petition	286	Naval Affairs	....	....	......	Discharged; laid on table.		
Parke, Mathew, widow and heirs of.	For prize money	19	2	Petition	83	Naval Affairs	....	....	......	Discharged; laid on table.		
Parke, Mathew, widow and heirs of.	For prize money	23	1	Petition	109	Foreign Affairs	....	....	......	Discharged; laid on table.		
Parke, Mathew, widow and heirs of.	For prize money	24	1	Petition	661	Foreign Affairs.						
Pa ke, Mathew, widow and heirs of.	For prize money	25	2	Petition	50	Foreign Affairs	389	Report and res. to refer to the President.	......	Resolution adopted.		
Park, Thomas	(See Philadelphia Library Company.)	8	2	....	18							
Park, Thomas	Invalid pension	3	1	Rep. of Secretary War.	131	Select	May 26, 1794	J't. res. to refer to Sec. War.	R. 12	Passed	Passed	App'd June 9, 1794
Park, Thomas	Invalid pension	4	1	Rep. of Secretary War.	445	Claims	Mar. 4, 1796	Jt. res. to refer to Sec. War.	R. 16	Passed	Passed	App'd April 18, 1796
Park, Thomas	Compensation for sails and rigging of a vessel sold to an agent of the government during the revolutionary war.	19	2	Petition	133	Rev. Claims	Feb. 9, 1827	Adverse	......	Laid on table.		
Park, Thomas	Compensation for sails and rigging of a vessel sold to an agent of the government during the revolutionary war.	20	1	Petition	126	Rev. Claims	Jan. 23, 1828	Adverse	......	Laid on table.		
Park, Thomas	Compensation for sails and rigging of a vessel sold to an agent of the government during the revolutionary war.	20	2	Petition	40	Rev. Claims	Jan. 5, 1829	Adverse	......	Laid on table.		

List of private claims presented to the House of Representatives of the United States from the 1st to the 31st Congress, inclusive—Continued.

Names of claimants.	Nature or object of the claim.	Congress.	Session.	How brought before the House of Reps.	Page of journal.	To what committee of the House referred.	No. or date of the report.	Nature of the report.	No. of the bill.	How disposed of by the House of Reps.	How disposed of by the Senate.	Date of the act of Congress, and remarks.
Park, Thomas	Compensation for sails and rigging of a vessel sold to an agent of the government during the revolutionary war.	21	1	Petition	70	Rev. Claims	72	Favorable; bill	103	Passed	Indef. postp'd.	
Park, Thomas	Compensation for sails and rigging of a vessel sold to an agent of the government during the revolutionary war.	21	2	Petition	82	Rev. Claims	33	Favorable; bill	551	Referred to Committee Whole House.		
Park, Thomas	Compensation for sails and rigging of a vessel sold to an agent of the government during the revolutionary war.	22	1	Petition	73	Rev. Claims	....	....	......	Discharged; laid on table.		
Park, Thomas	Compensation for sails and rigging of a vessel sold to an agent of the government during the revolutionary war.	23	1	Petition	377	Rev. Claims.						
Park, Thomas	Compensation for sails and rigging of a vessel sold to an agent of the government during the revolutionary war.	25	2	Petition	112	Rev. Claims	....	....	......	Discharged; laid on table.		
Park, Thomas	Compensation for sails and rigging of a vessel sold to an agent of the government during the revolutionary war.	26	1	Petition	281	Rev. Claims	512	Favorable; bill	413	Referred to Committee Whole House.		
Park, Thomas	Compensation for sails and rigging of a vessel sold to an agent of the government during the revolutionary war.	27	2	Petition	96	Rev. Claims	651	Adverse	......	Laid on table.		
Park, Thomas	Compensation for sails and rigging of a vessel sold to an agent of the government during the revolutionary war.	28	1	Petition	246	Rev. Claims.						
Park, Thomas	Compensation for sails and rigging of a vessel sold to an agent of the government during the revolutionary war.	31	2	Petition	71	Rev. Claims.						
Park, Thomas, (Ind.)	Compensation for private property taken for the use of government in revolutionary war.	24	1	Petition	62	Rev. Claims.						
Park, Thomas, (Ind.)	Compensation for private property taken for the use of government in revolutionary war.	24	2	Petition	119	Rev. Claims.						
Park, William	Pension	21	1	Petition	143	Military Pensions.						
Park, William C	(See M. Parke, widow and heirs of)	19	2	....	83							
Parke, Zebulon	Balance due for services as sergeant in revolutionary war.	21	1	Petition	57	Claims.						
Parker, Abraham	Pension	21	1	Petition	407	Military Pensions	April 23, 1830	By bill	439	Referred to Committee Whole House.		
Parker, Abraham	Pension	21	2	House bill	278	Whole House	Feb. 16, 1831	With amends.	439	Passed.		
Parker, Abraham	Pension	22	1	Petition	51	Rev. Pensions	Dec. 21, 1831	By bill	68	Passed	Indef. postp'd.	
Parker, Alexander	Restoration to pension roll	21	2	Resolution	49	Military Pensions.						
Parker, Amasa, widow of	Pension for services in war of 1812	31	1	Petition	512	Invalid Pensions.						
Parker, Archibald, heirs of	Bounty land for services in late war.	27	2	Senate bill	841	Public Lands	Aug. 20, 1842	With't amend.	S. 149	Laid on table.		

List of private claims presented to the House of Representatives of the United States from the 1st to the 31st Congress, inclusive—Continued.

Names of claimants.	Nature or object of the claim.	Congress.	Session.	How brought before the House of Reps.	Page of journal.	To what committee of the House referred.	No. or date of the report.	Nature of the report.	No. of the bill.	How disposed of by the House of Reps.	How disposed of by the Senate.	Date of the act of Congress, and remarks.
Parker, Austin	(See Zebulon and Austin Parker.)	30	2		91							
Parker, Benjamin, & John Cundiff.	To be placed on same footing with regular troops, they having served in the militia in revolutionary war.	16	2	Petition	136	Pens. & Rev. Cl'ms.	Feb. 15, 1821	Adverse		Rejected.		
Parker, Dr. Benjamin	Remuneration for professional services rendered to a corps of recruits in 1813.	24	2	Petition	260	Claims.						
Parker, Dr. Benjamin	Remuneration for professianal services rendered to a corps of recruits in 1813.	25	2	Petition	51	Claims	492	Adverse		Laid on table.		
Parker, Copeland	Increase of compensation as surveyor of customs and inspector of the revenue.	14	2	Petition	206	Com. and Manuf.						
Parker, Copeland	Increase of compensation as surveyor of customs and inspector of the revenue.	17	2	Petition	142	Ways and Means.						
Parker, Copeland	Increase of compensation as surveyor of customs and inspector of the revenue.	18	1	Petition	177	Commerce.						
Parker, Daniel	Relief for losses sustained under contract to supply the American army with provisions in 1783.	3	1	Petition and rep't Sec. Treasury.	25	Select.						
Parker, Daniel P., *et al*	Relief from penalties and forfeitures incurred on importations from Great Britain.	13	1	Petition	91					Laid on table.		
Parker, Daniel P., *et al*	Relief from penalties and forfeitures incurred on importations from Great Britain.	13	2	Petition	214	Com. and Manuf.	Feb. 1, 1814	(Not found)		Laid on table.		
Parker, Daniel	Settlement of his accounts as inspector and paymaster general in the army on principles of equity.	23	2	Petition	49	Claims	77	Adverse		Laid on table.		
Parker, Daniel	Settlement of his accounts as inspector and paymaster general in the army on principles of equity.	24	1	Petition	93	Military Affairs	731	Favorable; bill	676	Referred to Committee Whole House.		
Parker, Daniel	Settlement of his accounts as inspector and paymaster general in the army on principles of equity.	25	2	Petition	41	Military Affairs	296	Favorable; bill	336	Referred to Committee Whole House.		
Parker, Daniel	Settlement of his accounts as inspector and paymaster general in the army on principles of equity.	25	3	Bill of last sess.	377	Whole House	Jan. 25, 1829	With't amend.	336			
Parker, Daniel	Settlement of his accounts as inspector and paymaster general in the army on principles of equity.	26	1	Petition	182	Military Affairs	104	Favorable; bill	107	Laid on table.		
Parker, Daniel	Settlement of his accounts as inspector and paymaster general in the army on principles of equity.	26	2	Petition	79	Military Affairs	124	Favorable; bill	629	Referred to Committee Whole House.		
Parker, Daniel	Additional compensation as pay master general from January 1 to May 9, 1822.	30	1	Letter of Secretary of War.	760	Claims.						
Parker, Daniel	Additional compensation as pay master general from January 1 to May 9, 1822.	30	2	Petition	93	Military Affairs.						

List of private claims presented to the House of Representatives of the United States from the 1st to the 31st Congress, inclusive—Continued.

Names of claimants.	Nature or object of the claim.	Congress.	Session.	How brought before the House of Reps.	Page of journal.	To what committee of the House referred.	No. or date of the report.	Nature of the report.	No. of the bill.	How disposed of by the House of Reps.	How disposed of by the Senate.	Date of the act of Congress, and remarks.
Parker, Daniel, executors of	Balance due for services as paymaster general.	31	1	Civil and dip. appropriation bill.	1034	Whole House	Aug. 26, 1850	With amend's.	334	Passed	Passed	App'd Sept. 30, 1850
Parker, Edmund	Revolutionary pension	18	1	Petition	73	Pens. & Rev. Cl'ms.				Discharged; laid on table.		
Parker, Edmund	Revolutionary pension	19	1	Petition	334	Military Pensions	164	Adverse		Laid on table.		
Parker, Edmund	Revolutionary pension	19	2	Petition	245	Military Pensions						Leave to withdraw.
Parker, Elias, heirs of	Bounty land for military services	24	2	Petition	390	Public Lands.						
Parker, Eliphalet	Reimbursement of duties paid on importations into Castine, Maine.	16	1	Senate bill	108	Ways and Means	Jan. 14, 1820	With't amend.	S. 13	Passed	Passed	App'd April 11, 1820
Parker, Elizabeth	Compensation for supplies furnished and for losses in revolutionary war.	1	3	Petition	378					Referred to Secretary Treasury.		
Parker, Elizabeth	Compensation for supplies furnished and for losses in revolutionary war.	2	2	Rep. of Secretary Treasury.	735					Laid on table.		
Parker, Elizabeth, (Va.)	Compensation for use and occupation of her land by United States, near Portsmouth, Virginia.	31	2	Petition	108	Naval Affairs.						
Parker, Foxhall A., (U. S. navy.)	Indemnity for expenses incurred in conveying a bearer of despatches to the Mediteranean.	23	1	Petition	303	Naval Affairs				Discharged; laid on table.		
Parker, Foxhall A., (U. S. navy.)	Indemnity for expenses incurred in conveying a bearer of despatches to the Mediteranean.	23	2	Petition	110	Naval Affairs.						
Parker, Foxhall A., (U. S. navy.)	Indemnity for expenses incurred in conveying a bearer of despatches to the Mediteranean.	24	1	Petition	99	Naval Affairs	279	Favorable; bill	286	Referred to Committee Whole House.		
Parker, Foxhall A., (U. S. navy.)	Indemnity for expenses incurred in conveying a bearer of despatches to the Mediteranean.	24	2	Bill of last sess.	200	Whole House	Jan. 13, 1837	With't amend.	286	Passed	Passed	App'd March 3, 1837
Parker, Foxhall A., (U. S. navy.)	Indemnity for expenses incurred in conveying United States commissioner to China, to his destination, in United States ship Brandywine.	30	1	Senate bill	678	Naval Affairs			S. 30			
Parker, Isaiah	Restoration of pension, and for arrears of pension.	24	2	Petition	48	Invalid Pensions	264	Favorable; bill	961	Referred to Committee Whole House.		
Parker, Isaiah	Restoration of pension, and for arrears of pension.	25	2	Petition	39	Invalid Pensions	187	Favorable; bill	213	Passed	Adverse report.	
Parker, Isaiah	Restoration of pension, and for arrears of pension.	25	3	Petition	89	Invalid Pensions	83	Favorable; bill	962	Passed	Adverse report.	
Parker, Isaiah	Restoration of pension, and for arrears of pension.	26	1	Petition	162	Invalid Pensions.						
Parker, Isaiah	Restoration of pension, and for arrears of pension.	27	2	Petition	680	Invalid Pensions.						
Parker, Isaiah	Restoration of pension, and for arrears of pension.	29	1	Petition	118	Invalid Pensions	159	Favorable; bill	162	Passed	Passed	App'd Aug. 8, 1846
Parker, James	Payment for services in investigating accounts of collector at Amboy.	21	2	Appropriat'n bill.	528	Whole House	Jan. 11, 1831	With amends.	528	Passed	Passed	App'd March 2, 1831
Parker, James, (Lawrence county, Ky.)	Invalid pension	29	1	Petition	326	Invalid Pensions	351	Adverse		Laid on table.		

List of private claims presented to the House of Representatives of the United States from the 1*st to the* 31*st Congress, inclusive*—Continued.

Names of claimants.	Nature or object of the claim.	Congress.	Session.	How brought before the House of Reps.	Page of journal.	To what committee of the House referred.	No. or date of the report.	Nature of the report.	No. of the bill.	How disposed of by the House of Reps.	How disposed of by the Senate.	Date of the act of Congress, and remarks.
Parker, James, (Floyd co., Ky.)	Increase of pension	29	1	Petition	589	Invalid Pensions.						
Parker, Lieut. James, and others.	Indemnity for losses by the upsetting of the United States brig Somers while blockading Vera Cruz.	30	1	Petition	116	Naval Affairs.						
Parker, Jane	(See Southey Parker, widow of.)	27	2		155							
Parker, John, (New Orleans pilot.)	Pre-emption to certain lands at the mouth of the Mississippi river.	28	1	Petition	77	Priv. Land Claims.	9	Favorable; bill	35	Passed	Passed	App'd June 17, 1844
Parker, John, sureties of.	Release from judgment	22	1	Petition	558	Judiciary				Discharged; laid on table.		
Parker, John, (Ind.)	Increase of pension	23	2	Petition	58	Invalid Pensions	Jan. 14, 1835	Adverse		Laid on table.		
Parker, John, (Iowa.)	Remuneration for expenses incurred in equipping a company of volunteers raised under a requisition of Gov. Clark in 1846.	29	2	Memorial	198	Military Affairs.						
Parker, John A., *et al.*	(See W. Forbes, heirs of.)	15	1		316							
Parker, Jonathan, widow of.	Revolutionary pension	27	2	Petition	238	Rev. Pensions	898	Favorable; bill	520	Referred to Committee Whole House.		
Parker, Jonathan, widow of.	Revolutionary pension	27	3	Bill of last sess.	89				520	Passed.		
Parker, Jonathan, widow of.	Revolutionary pension	28	1	Petition	114	Rev. Pensions	152	Favorable; bill	140	Passed.		
Parker, Joseph	Extra compensation for services as clerk in the War Department during the prevalence of the yellow fever in Philadelphia in 1793.	3	1	Petition	93	Select	May 16, 1794	Favorable; bill	69	Passed.	Rejected.	
Parker, Joseph	(See Stephen Decatur, widow of, *et al.*)	20	1		295							
Parker, Joseph	Revolutionary pension	23	1	Resolution	237	Rev. Pensions.						
Parker, Joseph	Revolutionary pension	23	2	Resolution	150	Rev. Pensions.						
Parker, Joseph	Revolutionary pension	24	1	Resolution	107	Rev. Pensions.						
Parker, Joseph	Revolutionary pension	25	2	Resolution	55	Rev. Pensions	April 13, 1838	Adverse		Laid on table.		
Parker, Joseph	Revolutionary pension	25	3	Resolution	216	Rev. Pensions				Discharged; laid on table.		
Parker, Joseph	Revolutionary pension	26	1	Resolution	174	Rev. Pensions	636	Favorable; bill	470	Referred to Committee Whole House.		
Parker, Joseph	Revolutionary pension	27	2	Petition	581	Rev. Pensions	568	Favorable; bill	364	Passed	Passed	App'd Aug. 27, 1842
Parker, Joseph, widow of.	Revolutionary pension	22	1	Petition	265	Rev. Pensions				Discharged; laid on table.		
Parker, Joshua	Revolutionary pension	19	1	Resolution	239	Military Pensions	164	Adverse		Laid on table.		
Parker, Joshua	Pension for injuries received on board frigate Constitution.	29	1	Petition	201	Naval Affairs	741	Adverse		Laid on table.		
Parker, Lemuel, heirs of the late widow of.	Back pension to which the late widow was entitled.	29	1	Petition	268	Rev. Claims				Discharged; laid on table.		
Parker, Lemuel, heirs of the late widow of.	Back pension to which the late widow was entitled.	30	1	Petition	66	Rev. Pensions.						
Parker, Lemuel	Arrears of pension	30	1	Petition	513	Invalid Pensions	584	Adverse		Laid on table.		
Parker, Martin	Pension	21	1	Petition	46	Military Pensions	May 3, 1830	By bill	454	Referred to Committee Whole House.		
Parker, Martin	Pension	21	2	Bill of last sess.	318	Whole House	Feb. 16, 1831	With amend.	454	Passed.		
Parker, Martin	Pension	22	1	Petition	537	Invalid Pensions	424	Favorable; bill	524	Passed	Laid on table.	

List of private claims presented to the House of Representativesthe of United States from the 1st to the 31st Congress, inclusive—Continued.

Names of claimants.	Nature or object of the claim.	Congress.	Session.	How brought before the House of Reps.	Page of journal.	To what committee of the House referred.	No. or date of the report.	Nature of the report.	No. of the bill.	How disposed of by the House of Reps.	How disposed of by the Senate.	Date of the act of Congress, and remarks.
Parker, Martin	Pension	22	2	Petition	83	Invalid Pensions	Feb. 15, 1833	Favorable; bill	738	Referred to Committee Whole House.		
Parker, Martin	Pension	23	1	Petition	60	Invalid Pensions	69	Favorable; bill	128	Passed	Passed	App'd June 30, 1834
Parker, Mary	(See Joseph Parker, widow of)	22	1		265							
Parker, Mary	(See Robert Parker, widow of)	23	1		494							
Parker, Mary	(See Amasa Parker, widow of.)											
Parker, Mary S	(See Joshua O. Alley, heirs of)	26	1		199							
Parker, M., *et al*	Bounty land for services in the war of 1812.	31	1	Petition	511	Public Lands.						
Parker, Col. Moses, widow of.	Pension	1	1	Petition	26					Laid on table.		
Parker, Col. Moses, widow of.	Pension	2	1	Petition	467					Referred to Secretary War.		
Parker, Col. Moses, widow of.	Pension	2	2	Rep. of Secretary War.	711					Laid on table.		
Parker, Col. Moses, widow of.	Pension	3	1	Petition	32					Referred to Secretary Treasury.		
Parker, Col. Moses, widow of.	Pension	3	2	Petition and rep' Sec. Treasury.	284	Claims.						
Parker, Col. Moses, widow of.	Pension	4	1	Petition	598					Laid on table.		
Parker, Paul	Relief, (is illiterate and did not know of the direct tax until his land was sold.)	15	1	Petition	132	Ways and Means				Discharged; laid on table.		
Parker, Peter	Compensation for acting as chargé de affairs to China.	30	1	Petition	306	Foreign Affairs	516	Favorable; bill	444	Referred to Committee Whole House.		Provided for in civil and diplomatic appropriation bill, Aug. 14, 1848.
Parker, Peter	Compensation for acting as chargé de affairs to China.	30	2	Bill of last sess.	318				444	Laid on table.		
Parker, Richard	(See Philip Lefavour, *et al.*)	16	1		271							
Parker, Robert	Pension	20	2	Petition	204	Military Pensions.						
Parker, Robert, widow of.	Half pay for life after deducting five years' full pay due deceased for revolutionary services.	23	1	Petition	494	Rev. Claims.						
Parker, Robert, widow of.	Half pay for life after deducting five years' full pay due deceased for revolutionary services.	25	2	Petition	629					Referred to Committee Whole House on bill No. 456.		
Parker, Rufus	Arrears of pension	22	2	Petition	53	Invalid Pensions				Discharged; laid on table.		
Parker, Rufus	Arrears of pension	23	1	Petition	44	Invalid Pensions				Discharged; laid on table.		
Parker, Rufus	Arrears of pension.	23	2	Petition	86	Invalid Pensions	Dec. 29, 1835	Adverse		Laid on table.		
Parker, Rufus	Arrears of pension	25	2	Petition	773	Invalid Pensions				Discharged; laid on table.		
Parker, Rufus	Arrears of pension	25	3	Petition	89	Invalid Pensions	Jan. 9, 1839	Adverse		Laid on table.		
Parker, Samuel	Renewal of a patent for currying leather.	16	2	Senate bill	299	Judiciary	Mar. 2, 1821	With't amend.	S. 55	Passed		App'd March 2, 1821
Parker, Sarah	(See Moses Parker, widow of.)	1	1		26							
Parker, Sarah	(See widow of Jonathan Parker)	27	2		238							
Parker, Sharod H.	Permission to correct an error in the entry of lands.	19	1	Petition	313	Public Lands				Discharged; laid on table.		Leave to withdraw.

List of private claims presented to the House of Representatives of the United States from the 1st to the 31st Congress, inclusive—Continued.

Names of claimants.	Nature or object of the claim.	Congress.	Session.	How brought before the House of Reps.	Page of journal.	To what committee of the House referred.	No. or date of the report.	Nature of the report.	No. of the bill.	How disposed of by the House of Reps.	How disposed of by the Senate.	Date of the act of Congress, and remarks.
Parker, Southey	Increase of compensation as superintendent of the Navy Department.	23	1	Petition	303	Claims				Discharged; laid on table.		
Parker, Southey	Increase of compensation as superintendent of the Navy Department.	25	2	Petition	544	Public Buildings				Discharged; laid on table.		
Parker, Southey, widow of.	Increase of compensation as superintendent of the Navy Department.	27	2	Petition	155	Claims	33	Adverse		Laid on table.		
Parker, Southey, widow of.	Increase of compensation as superintendent of the Navy Department.	28	1	Petition	570	Claims.						
Parker, Southey, widow of.	Increase of compensation as superintendent of the Navy Department.	28	2	Petition	169	Claims	31	Adverse		Laid on table.		
Parker, Southey, widow of.	Increase of compensation as superintendent of the Navy Department.	30	1	Petition	414	Claims				Discharged; laid on table.		
Parker, Lieut. Col. Thomas	Extra expenses incurred in the service of the United States.	6	2	Petition	824	Claims	Mar. 2, 1801	Res. to postpone to next session.		Adopted.		
Parker, Lieut. Col. Thomas	Extra expenses incurred in the service of the United States.	7	1	Petition	19	Claims						Leave to withdraw. April 30, 1802.
Parker, William	Revolutionary pension	16	1	Petition	32	Pens. & Rev. Cl'ms.				Discharged; laid on table.		
Parker, Wm., *et al.*, (Seneca Indians.)	Invalid pension	17	2	Petition	187	Military Affairs	Feb. 24, 1823	Favorable		Referred to Committee Whole House on bill No. 195.		
Parker, Wm., *et al.*, (Seneca Indians.)	Invalid pension	18	1	Petition	135					Referred to Committee Whole House on bill No. 35.		See act May 19, 1824
Parker, Wm., *et al.*, (Seneca Indians.)	Increase of pension	26	1	Petition	288	Invalid Pensions	Mar. 5, 1840	Adverse		Laid on table.		
Parker, Wm., *et al.*, (Seneca Indians.)	Increase of pension	26	2	Petition	36	Invalid Pensions	239	Adverse		Laid on table.		
Parker, Wm., *et al.*, (Seneca Indians.)	Increase of pension	27	2	Petition	268	Invalid Pensions	445	Adverse		Laid on table.		
Parker, William, (Mass.).	Revolutionary pension	30	1	Petition	264	Rev. Pensions	445	Favorable; bill	376	Passed	Reported with't amendment.	
Parker, William B	(See Samuel Patch, attorney of).	26	2		51							
Parker, William B., and D. Devereneny.	(See Pickering Dodge, executors of.)	29	2		135							
Parker, William B	For difference of pay and rations between first lieutenant and captain for thirteen and half months.	25	2	Petition	114	Military Affairs	Jan. 18, 1838	Adverse		Laid on table.		
Parker, Zebulon and Austin	Renewal and extension of certain patents.	30	2	Petition	91	Patents.						
Parker, Zebulon and Austin	Renewal and extension of certain patents.	31	1	Petition	276	Patents	308	Favorable; bill	278	Referred to Committee Whole House.		
Parkerson, Lieut. James, heirs of.	Seven years' half-pay for services.	24	1	Senate bill	907	Rev. Claims	Jan. 7, 1836	With't amend	S. 128	Passed	Passed	App'd July 2, 1836
Parkerson, John S	Additional compensation for work done on the Cumberland road.	23	1	Resolution	589	Claims	456	Rep. and res. to refer to Sec. of War.		Resolution adopted.		

List of private claims presented to the House of Representatives of the United States from the 1st to the 31st Congress, inclusive—Continued.

Names of claimants.	Nature or object of the claim.	Congress.	Session.	How brought before the House of Reps.	Page of journal.	To what committee of the House referred.	No. or date of the report.	Nature of the report.	No. of the bill.	How disposed of by the House of Reps.	How disposed of by the Senate.	Date of the act of Congress, and remarks.
Parkerson, John S	Additional compensation for work on the Cumberland road.	25	2	Memorial	397	Claims				Discharged; laid on table.		
Parkerson, John S	Additional compensation for work on the Cumberland road.	25	3	Petition	457	Claims.						
Parkerson, John S.	Additional compensation for work on the Cumberland road.	26	1	Petition	170	Claims.						
Parkerson, John S	Additional compensation for work on the Cumberland road.	26	2	Petition	167	Claims.						
Parkerson, John S	Additional compensation for work on the Cumberland road.	27	2	Petition	517	Claims.						
Parkerson, John S	Additional compensation for work on the Cumberland road.	27	3	Petition	43	Claims	9	Adverse			Laid on table.	
Parkerson, William	Revolutionary pension	31	1	Petition	891	Rev. Pensions.						
Parkhurst, Aaron and Sally	Confirmation of title to land	31	1	Petition	471	Priv. Land Claims.						
Parkhurst, Benjamin	Revolutionary pension	24	1	Resolution	285	Rev. Pensions	498	Favorable; bill	498	Passed	Passed	App'd June 28, 1836
Parkhurst, Lydia	(See Phineas Parkhurst, widow of)	16	1		252							
Parkhurst, Phineas	Invalid pension	3	2	Rep. of Secretary War.	350	Claims	March 2, 1795	Res. to refer to Sec. War.		Resolution adopted.		
Parkhurst, Phineas	Invalid pension	4	1	Rep. of Secretary War.	447	Claims	Feb. 18, 1796	Favorable; bill	156	Passed	Passed	App'd April 20, 1796
Parkhurst, Phineas, widow of.	Payment for services as surgeon in the navy in revolutionary war, and for his share of three prizes consigned to the United States agent at Martinico.	16	1	Petition	252	Pens. & Rev. Cl'ms.				Discharged; laid on table.		
Parkhurst, Phineas, widow of.	Payment for services as surgeon in the navy in revolutionary war, and for his share of three prizes consigned to the United States agent at Martinico.	23	1	Petition	36	Rev. Claims.						
Parkhurst, Phineas, widow of.	Payment for services as surgeon in the navy in revolutionary war, and for his share of three prizes consigned to the United States agent at Martinico.	23	2	Petition	193	Rev. Claims.						
Parkhurst, Phineas, widow of.	Payment for services as surgeon in the navy in revolutionary war, and for his share of three prizes consigned to the United States agent at Martinico.	24	1	Petition	63, 102	Rev. Claims.						
Parkhurst, Phineas, widow of.	Payment for services as surgeon in the navy in revolutionary war, and for his share of three prizes consigned to the United States agent at Martinico.	24	2	Petition	73	Rev. Claims.						
Parkhurst, Phineas, widow of.	Payment for services as surgeon in the navy in revolutionary war, and for his share of three prizes consigned to the United States agent at Martinico.	25	2	Petition	48	Rev. Claims				Discharged; laid on table.		

List of private claims presented to the House of Representatives of the United States from the 1st to the 31st Congress, inclusive—Continued.

Names of claimants.	Nature or object of the claim.	Congress.	Session.	How brought before the House of Reps.	Page of journal.	To what committee of the House referred.	No. or date of the report.	Nature of the report.	No. of the bill.	How disposed of by the House of Reps.	How disposed of by the Senate.	Date of the act of Congress, and remarks.
Parkhurst, Phineas, widow of.	Payment for services as surgeon in the navy in revolutionary war, and for his share of three prizes consigned to the United States agent at Martinico.	25	3	Petition	85	Rev. Claims	....	....	......	Discharged; laid on table.		
Parkhurst, Phineas, widow of.	Payment for services as surgeon in the navy in revolutionary war, and for his share of three prizes consigned to the United States agent at Martinico.	26	1	Petition	167	Rev. Claims.						
Parkinson, Daniel	Pre-emption to land on which he has erected mills and other valuable improvements.	17	1	Petition	22	Public Lands	Dec. 20, 1821	Adverse	......	Rejected.		
Parkinson, H.	Permission to change entry of land	27	2	Petition	383	Priv. Land Claims.						
Parkinson, William	Compensation for the use of his machine for rifling gun barrels, and for other purposes.	27	3	Petition	100	Claims.						
Parkman, John	(See Sturges & Parkman)	10	2	....	414							
Parkman, William E., *et al.*	Arrears of pension for 1841–'2	31	1	Petition	733	Rev. Pensions	459	Adverse	......	Laid on table.		
Parks, Aaron	Revolutionary pension	22	1	Resolution	261	Rev. Pensions	365	Favorable; bill	460	Passed	Indef. postp'd.	
Parks, Benjamin	(See John D. Needham, & others)	15	1	....	136							
Parks, Elias	Compensat'n for merchandise which fell into the hands of the British at Oswego, his means of transportation having been impressed by United States officers.	14	1	Petition	323	Claims	Mar. 15, 1816	Adverse	......	Laid on table.		
Parks, Elias	Compensat'n for merchandise which fell into the hands of the British at Oswego, his means of transportation having been impressed by United States officers.	14	2	Petition	24	Claims	Dec. 20, 1816	Rep. not found	......	Laid on table.		
Parks, Elias	Compensat'n for merchandise which fell into the hands of the British at Oswego, his means of transportation having been impressed by United States officers.	15	1	Petition	48	Claims	....	....	......	Discharged; laid on table.		
Parks, Elias	Compensat'n for merchandize which fell into the hands of the British at Oswego, his means of transportation having been impressed by United States officers.	15	2	Petition	44	Claims	43	Adverse	......	Laid on table.		
Parks, Elias	Compensat'n for merchandize which fell into the hands of the British at Oswego, his means of transportation having been impressed by United States officers.	16	1	Petition	28	Claims	Dec. 29, 1819	Adverse	......	Referred to Committee Whole House.		
Parks, Elias	Compensat'n for merchandise which fell into the hands of the British at Oswego, his means of transportation having been impressed by United States officers.	16	2	Rep't of last sess.	31	Whole House	Mar. 23, 1820	Bill ordered	155	Passed	Passed	App'd Dec. 29, 1820
Parks, Henry	Invalid pension	14	1	Resolution	212	Pens. & Rev. Cl'ms.	April 11, 1816	By bill	171	Passed	Passed	App'd April 30, 1816

List of private claims presented to the House of Representatives of the United States from the 1st to the 31st Congress, inclusive—Continued.

Names of claimants.	Nature or object of the claim.	Congress.	Session.	How brought before the House of Reps.	Page of journal.	To what committee of the House referred.	No. or date of the report.	Nature of the report.	No. of the bill.	How disposed of by the House of Reps.	How disposed of by the Senate.	Date of the act of Congress, and remarks.
Parks, Jacob	Confirmation of title to land in Missouri.	15	1	Petition	267	Priv. Land Claims.				Discharged; laid on table.		
Parks, Jacob	Confirmation of title to land in Missouri.	16	1	Petition	71	Priv. Land Claims.				Discharged; laid on table.		
Parks, Jacob	Confirmation of title to land in Missouri.	17	1	Petition	55	Public Lands				Discharged; laid on table.		
Parks, Jacob	Confirmation of title to land in Missouri.	18	1	Petition	55	Public Lands.						
Parks, James, and Robert Lucas.	Remission of duties on two stills destroyed by fire.	8	1	Petition	488	Claims	Dec. 21, 1803	Adverse		Rejected.		
Parks, Jonas	Invalid pension	3	2	Rep. of Secretary War.	350	Claims	Mar. 2, 1795	Res. to refer to Sec. War.		Resolution adopted.		
Parks, Jonas	Invalid pension	4	1	Rep. of Secretary War.	445	Claims	Mar. 4, 1796	J't. res. to refer to Sec. War.	R. 16	Passed	Passed	App'd April 18, 1795
Parks, Joseph	Increase of pension	28	1	Petition	879	Invalid Pensions.						
Parks, Leonard	Pension	21	1	Petition	31	Military Pensions.				Discharged; laid on table.		
Parks, Levi	Invalid pension	24	1	Petition	507	Invalid Pensions.	April 12, 1836	Adverse		Laid on table.		
Parks, Michael	Restoration to pension roll	17	1	Petition	291					Referred to Committee Whole House on bill No. 37.		
Parlent, William	Revolutionary pension	7	2	Petition	321	Claims				Discharged; laid on table.		
Parlin, Josiah	Payment of the amount found due him by a jury in a suit by the United States.	18	1	Petition	129	Claims	May 7, 1824	Adverse		Laid on table.		
Parlin, Josiah	Payment of the amount found due him by a jury in a suit by the United States.	18	2	Petition	117	Claims.						
Parlin, Josiah	Payment of the amount found due him by a jury in a suit by the United states.	19	1	Petition	57	Claims	April 26, 1826	Adverse		Laid on table.		
Parmlee, Thomas	Invalid pension	3	2	Rep. of Secretary War.	278	Claims	Feb. 28, 1795	Favorable; bill	130	Passed	Postp'd to next session.	
Parmlee, Thomas	Invalid pension	4	1	Rep. of Secretary War.	445	Claims	Feb. 18, 1796	Favorable; bil	156	Passed	Passed	App'd April 20, 1796
Parmeter, Welcome	Revolutionary pension	30	1	Senate bill	826	Rev. Pensions	July 19, 1848	With't amend.	S. 133	Passed		App'd Aug. 14, 1848
Parnel, John	Pension	26	1	Petition	326	Invalid Pensions	414	Adverse		Laid on table.		
Parnell, Wiley B	Permission to correct error in entry of land.	29	1	Petition	88	Public Lands	136	Favorable; bill	142	Passed	Passed	App'd Aug. 8, 1846
Parr, Henry	Pre-emption to land on which he resides.	11	3	Petition	495	Public Lands.						
Parr, Henry	Pre-emption to land on which he resides.	13	2	Petition	172	Public Lands.						
Parr, James S	Confirmation of title to land in Arkansas.	22	2	Petition and docs.	284	Public Lands.						
Parris, Richard S	Remuneration for depredations by Miami Indians.	28	1	Petition	351	Indian Affairs.						
Parrish, Aaron, administrator of.	Arrears of pension	30	1	Petition	625	Rev. Pensions				Discharged; laid on table.		
Parnish, Betsy	(See Oliver Parrish's heirs)	24	1		406							
Parrish, Chester	Arrears of pension	28	2	Petition	72	Invalid Pensions				Discharged; laid on table.		

List of private claims presented to the House of Representatives of the United States from the 1st to the 31st Congress, inclusive—Continued

Names of claimants.	Nature or object of the claim.	Congress.	Session.	How brought before the House of Reps.	Page of journal.	To what committee of the House referred.	No. or date of the report.	Nature of the report.	No. of the bill.	How disposed of by the House of Reps.	How disposed of by the Senate.	Date of the act of Congress, and remarks.
Parrish, Chester	Arrears of pension	29	2	Petition	86	Invalid Pensions.						
Parrish, Chester	Arrears of pension	30	1	Petition	136	Invalid Pensions				Discharged; laid on table.		
Parrish, Chester	Arrears of pension	31	1	Petition	1272	Invalid Pensions				Discharged; laid on table.		
Parrish, Clinton	(See heirs of Oliver Parrish)	24	1		406							
Parrish, Ebenezer	Half-pay as a sergeant for wounds received in revolutionary war.	23	1	Petition	215	Invalid Pensions				Discharged; laid on table.		
Parrish, Eliza	(See heirs of Oliver Parrish)	24	1		406							
Parrish, Humphrey	Payment of the amount of his pension, which was stolen from the mail.	25	2	Petition	405	Rev. Pensions				Discharged; laid on table.		
Parrish, Jasper	Grant of land for services as Indian interpreter.	15	1	Petition	184	Public Lands				Discharged; laid on table.		
Parrish, Jasper	Indemnity for property taken, used, and destroyed by United States troops in late war.	15	1	Petition	386	Claims				Discharged; laid on table.		
Parrish, Jasper	Indemnity for property taken, used, and destroyed by United States troops in late war.	18	1	Petition	158	Claims	Feb. 11, 1824	Adverse		Referred to Committee Whole House.		
Parrish, Jasper	Indemnity for property taken, used, and destroyed by United States troops in late war.	18	2	Petition and rep't of last session.	50	Claims						Leave to withdraw.
Parrish, Jasper	Indemnity for property taken, used, and destroyed by United States troops in late war.	19	1	Petition	442	Claims						Leave to withdraw.
Parrish, Jasper	Indemnity for property taken, used, and destroyed by United States troops in late war.	21	1	Petition	83	Claims	163	Favorable; bill	197	Passed	Passed	App'd May 29, 1830
Parrish, Jasper	Indemnity for house destroyed by the British, on the Niagara frontier, in late war.	15	2	Petition	32	Claims	Dec. 2, 1818	Adverse		Laid on table.		
Parrish, John T.	(See administrator of Aaron Parrish.)	30	1		625							
Parrish, Joseph, widow and children of.	For the same relief they would have been entitled if deceased had died in service, he having died of disease contracted in service.	14	2	Resolution	83	Pens. & Rev. Clm's.				Discharged; laid on table.		
Parrish, Levi H.	Increase of pension	22	1	Res. and docs.	389	Invalid Pensions				Discharged; laid on table.		
Parrish, Levi H.	Increase of pension	23	1	Petition	44	Invalid Pensions	Dec. 20, 1833	Adverse		Laid on table.		
Parrish, Levi H.	Increase of pension	23	2	Resolution	149	Invalid Pensions	Jan. 12, 1835	Adverse		Laid on table.		
Parrish, Levi H.	Increase of pension	28	1	Petition	338	Invalid Pensions	392	Adverse		Laid on table.		
Parrish, Levi H.	Increase of pension	29	1	Petition	192	Invalid Pensions				Discharged; laid on table.		
Parrish, Oliver	Pension	22	1	Petition	51	Rev. Pensions	395	Favorable	494	Referred to Committee Whole House.		
Parrish, Oliver, heirs of	Arrears of pension due at the time of his death.	24	1	Petition	406	Rev. Pensions.						
Parrish, Oliver, heirs of	Arrears of pension due at the time of his death.	24	2	Petition	161	Rev. Pensions	55	Favorable; bill	804	Referred to Committee Whole House.		
Parrish, Oliver, heirs of	Arrears of pension due at the time of his death.	25	2	Petition	38	Rev. Pensions				Discharged; laid on table.		

List of private claims presented to the House of Representatives of the United States from the 1st to the 31st Congress, inclusive—Continued.

Names of claimants.	Nature or object of the claim.	Congress.	Session.	How brought before the House of Reps.	Page of journal.	To what committee of the House referred.	No. or date of the report.	Nature of the report.	No. of the bill.	How disposed of by the House of Reps.	How disposed of by the Senate.	Date of the act of Congress, and remarks.
Parrish, Oliver, heirs of	Arrears of pension at the time of his death.	27	2	Petition	415	Rev. Pensions	301	Favorable; bill	270	Passed	Indef. postp'd.	
Parrish, Oliver, jr	(See heirs of Oliver Parrish)	24	1		406							
Parrish, Samuel B	Permission to enter land in lieu of that to which he was entitled, under act of March 2, 1833.	23	2	Petition	243	Public Lands	79	Favorable; bill	696	Postponed.		
Parrish, William, (Ohio)	Permission to purchase the land on which he resides.	30	2	Petition	87	Public Lands.						
Parrish, Zenas	(See heirs of Oliver Parrish)	24	1		406							
Parrott, Esther	(See widow of Jonathan Wakelee)	25	3		126							
Parrott, John	Pension	27	2	Resolution	398	Invalid Pensions	631	Adverse		Laid on table.		
Parrott, John, heirs of	Pension for revolutionary services.	28	1	Resolution	406	Rev. Pensions.						
Parrott, John	Compensation for tobacco, mules and horses, seized by the Mexican authorities.	31	2	Petition	343	Foreign Affairs.						
Parrott, Joseph	Reissue of bounty land scrip for revolutionary services.	29	2	Petition	89	Rev. Claims.						
Parrott, Joseph	Reissue of bounty land scrip for revolutionary services.	30	1	Petition	360	Rev. Claims.						
Parrott, Marstin	Pension	21	2	Petition	43	Military Pensions.						
Parrott, Marstin	Pension	22	1	Petition	164	Rev. Pensions				Disch'd; laid on table.		
Parrott, Silas	Pension	10	1	House bill	232	Whole House	April 19, 1808	With amends.	78	Passed	Passed	App'd April 25, 1808
Parrott, William S.	Payment of claim against Mexico.	27	2	Memorial	215	Foreign Affairs.						
Parry, Bridget	Compensation for services as hospital nurse; also for services of her husband in revolutionary war.	2	2	Petition	665					Laid on table.		
Parry, Bridget	Compensation for services as hospital nurse; also for services of her husband in revolutionary war.	3	1	Petition	132	Select.						
Parry, Martain, administrator of.	Indemnity for French spoliations prior to 1800.	26	1	Memorial	182	Foreign Affairs	343	Favorable; bill	319	Referred to Committee Whole House.		
Parshall, David	Pension	22	1	Petition	533	Rev. Pensions	479	Favorable; bill	580	Referred to Committee Whole House.		
Parshall, Rachael	(See Samuel Parshall, widow of)	27	3		259							
Parshall, Samuel, widow of	Revolutionary pension	27	3	Petition	259	Rev. Pensions				Discharged		Leave to withdraw.
Parsons, Benjamin	Bounty land for services in war of 1812.	26	1	Senate bill	811	Public Lands			S. 156			
Parsons, Eli	Allowance for depreciation of pay as commissary of issues in revolutionary war.	4	1	Petition	451	Claims	May 7, 1796	Adverse		Rejected		Leave to withdraw.
Parsons, Eli	Compensation for services as officer in revolutionary war.	15	1	Petition	160	Pens. & Rev. Cl'ms.	Feb. 19, 1818	Adverse		Laid on table.		
Parsons, Eli, heirs of	For the amount due as commissary general in revolutionary war.	25	3	Petition	124	Rev. Claims				Discharged; laid on table.		
Parsons, Eli, heirs of	For the amount due as commissary general in revolutionary war.	26	1	Petition	166	Rev. Claims.						
Parsons, Eli, heirs of	For the amount due as commissary general in revolutionary war, and for interest on a certificate for $1,800.	27	2	Petition	174	Rev. Claims	1062	Adverse		Laid on table.		
Parsons, George	Payment for timber furnished for the breakwater at Plattsburg, N. York.	28	1	Petition	999	Claims.						

List of private claims presented to the House of Representatives of the United States form the 1st to the 31st Congress, inclusive—Continued.

Names of claimants.	Nature or object of the claim.	Congress.	Session.	How brought before the House of Reps.	Page of journal.	To what committee of the House referred.	No. or date of the report.	Nature of the report.	No. of the bill.	How disposed of by the House of Reps.	How disposed of by the Senate.	Date of the act of Congress, and remarks.
Parsons, George	Payment for timber furnished for the breakwater at Plattsburg, N. York.	29	1	Petition	175, 984	Claims	337	Adverse		Laid on table.		
Parsons, George	Payment for timber furnished for the breakwater at Plattsburg, N. York.	29	2	Petition	56	Claims	2	Favorable; bill	580	Referred to Committee Whole House.		
Parsons, George	Payment for timber furnished for the breakwater at Plattsburg, N. York.	30	1	Petition	68	Claims.						
Parsons, George	Payment for timber furnished for the breakwater at Plattsburg, N. York.	30	2	Petition	223	Claims.						
Parsons, Gustavus A.	Compensation for raising and organizing volunteers for Mexican war.	31	1	Petition	357	Military Affairs.						
Parsons, Isaac, by guardian	Permission to fund certain loan office certificates.	5	2	Petition	99					Referred to Committee Whole House.		
Parsons, Israel	Restoration to pension roll	25	2	Petition	273	Rev. Pensions	738	Favorable; bill	704	Passed	Adverse report.	
Parsons, Israel	Restoration to pension roll	26	1	Petition	172	Rev. Pensions	155	Favorable; bill	165	Passed	Passed	App'd July 20, 1840
Parsons, Jabez	Commutation of half-pay for services in revolutionary war.	15	1	Petition	283	Claims	May 11, 1818	Adverse		Rejected.		
Parsons, Jabez	Compensation for services in revolutionary war.	24	1	Petition	105	Rev. Claims	Feb. 5, 1836	Adverse		Laid on table.		
Parsons, John, widow of	Continuation of pension	25	2	Petition	405	Rev. Pensions				Disch'd; laid on table.		
Parsons, John, widow of	Continuation of pension	26	1	Petition	174	Rev. Pensions				Disch'd; laid on table		
Parsons, John	Compensation for extra services in the land office in Florida.	28	1	Petition	840	Pubilc Lands.						
Parsons, John, *et al*	Compensation for extra services in the land office in Florida.	29	1	Petition	573	Public Lands.						
Parsons, John G.	Permission to correct error in the entry of land.	25	2	Petition	1030	Public Lands				Discharged; laid on table.		
Parsons, John G.	Permission to correct error in the entry of land.	25	3	Petition	98	Public Lands				Discharged; laid on table.		
Parson, Nehemiah, & Israel Thordike.	Renewal of registry of their ship Isis, forfeited in late war, and that extra duties paid on said vessel be refunded.	19	2	Petition	155	Commerce				Discharged; laid on table.		
Parsons, Nehemiah, & Israel Thordike.	Renewal of registry of their ship Isis, forfeited in late war, and that extra duties paid on said vessel be refunded.	20	1	Petition	270	Commerce	132	Favorable; bill	151	Referred to Committee Whole House.		
Parsons, Nehemiah, & Israel Thordike.	Renewal of registry of their ship Isis, forfeited in late war, and that extra duties paid on said vessel be refunded.	21	1	Petition	67	Commerce				Discharged; laid on table.		
Parsons, Nehemiah, & Israel Thordike.	Renewal of registry of their ship Isis, forfeited in late war, and that extra duties paid on said vessel be refunded.	21	2	Petition	66	Commerce.						
Parsons, Nehemiah, & Israel Thordike.	Renewal of registry of their ship Isis, forfeited in late war, and that extra duties paid on said vessel be refunded.	22	1	Petition	105	Commerce.	300	Adverse		Laid on table.		

List of private claims presented to the House of Representatives of the United States from the 1st to the 31st Congress, inclusive—Continued.

Names of claimants.	Nature or object of the claim.	Congress.	Session.	How brought before the House of Reps.	Page of journal.	To what committee of the House referred.	No. or date of the report.	Nature of the report.	No. of the bill.	How disposed of by the House of Reps.	How disposed of by the Senate.	Date of the act of Congress, and remarks.
Parsons, Osborne	Renewal of a bounty land warrant lost or mislaid.	18	1	Petition	38	Priv. Land Claims.						
Parsons, Portius F.	(See Eli Parsons, heirs of.)	25	3		124							
Parsons, Sally	(See Theodosius Parsons, widow of.)	31	1		348							
Parsons, Sarah	(See John Parsons, widow of.)	25	2		40							
Parsons, Theodosius	Increase of compensation as postmaster at Holme's Hole.	19	1	Petition	220	P. Of. & P. Roads				Discharged; laid on table.		
Parsons, Theodosius	Increase of compensation as postmaster at Holme's Hole.	19	2	Petition	64	P. Of. & P. Roads				Discharged; laid on table.		
Parsons, Theodosius, widow of.	Revolutionary pension	31	1	Petition	348	Rev. Pensions.						
Parsons, Thomas	(See Nathaniel Goddard, *et al.*)	15	1		143							
Parsons, Thomas, (Mass.)	Indemnity for French spoliations prior to 1800.	26	1	Memorial	182	Foreign Affairs	343	Favorable; bill	319	Referred to Committee Whole House.		
Parsons, Thomas A.	Compensation for services as surgeon in the navy.	25	2	Petition	544	Naval Affairs				Discharged; laid on table.		
Parsons, Thomas B.	Pension for disabilities incurred in the naval service.	24	1	Petition	127	Naval Affairs	609	Favorable; bill	598	Passed	Laid on table.	
Parsons, Thomas B.	Pension for disabilities incurred in the naval service.	24	2	Petition	75	Naval Affairs.						
Parsons, Thomas B.	Pension for disabilities incurred in the naval service.	24	2	Senate bill	578				S. 155			
Parsons, Thomas B.	Pension for disabilities incurred in the naval service.	25	2	Petition	41	Naval Affairs	148	Favorable; bill	170	Passed	Reported with't amendment.	
Parsons, Thomas B.	Pension for disabilities incurred in the naval service.	27	1	Petition	106	Invalid Pensions.						
Parsons, Thomas B.	Pension for disabilities incurred in the naval service.	27	2	Petition	60	Invalid Pensions.						
Parsons, Thomas B.	Pension for disabilities incurred in the naval service.	27	2	Senate bill	1364	Naval Affairs	Aug. 20, 1842	With't amend.	S. 307	Passed		App'd Aug. 30, 1842
Parsons, Usher	Increase of pension	24	1	Petition	140	Naval Affairs.						
Parsons, Warren	Land for services in the war of 1812.	26	2	Petition	52	Public Lands.						
Parsons, William, by attorney.	Compensation for services as a seaman in revolutionary war.	3	1	Petition	122	Select.						
Parsons, William, by attorney.	Compensation for services as a seaman in revolutionary war.	3	2	Petition	286	Claims.						
Parsons, William, by attorney.	Compensation for services as a seaman in revolutionary war.	4	1	Resolution	373	Claims.						
Parsons, William, by attorney.	Compensation for services as a seaman in revolutionary war.	4	2	Resolution	614	Claims	Dec. 26, 1796	Favorable		Referred to Committee Whole House.		
Parsons, William, by attorney.	Compensation for services as a seaman in revolutionary war.	5	2	Petition and rep't	273	Whole House				Rejected.		
Parsons, William	(See William Flannagan and Wm. Parsons.)	14	2		176							
Parson, William, (Boston)	(See Nathaniel Goddard, *et al.*)	15	1		143				76			
Parten, John	Land for services in late war	22	1	Petition	227	Invalid Pensions.						
Partenay, Amable	Confirmation of title to land in Missouri.	15	1	Petition	353	Priv. Land Claims.						
Partenay, Amable	Confirmation of title to land in Missouri.	16	1	Petition	72	Priv. Land Claims.	Jan. 19, 1820	By bill	49	Postponed to next session.		

List of private claims presented to the House of Representatives of the United States from the 1st to the 31st Congress, inclusive—Continued.

Names of claimants.	Nature or object of the claim.	Congress.	Session.	How brought before the House of Reps.	Page of journal.	To what committee of the House referred.	No. or date of the report.	Nature of the report.	No. of the bill.	How disposed of by the House of Reps.	How disposed of by the Senate.	Date of the act of Congress, and remarks.
Partenay, Amable	Confirmation of title to land in Missouri.	16	2	Bill of last sess..	28	Priv. Land Claims.	....	....	49			
Partenay, Amable	Confirmation of title to land in Missouri.	22	1	Petition	263	Priv. Land Claims.	Feb. 17, 1832	By bill	380	Referred to Committee Whole House.		
Partington, Richard, administrator of.	Balance due from Post Office Department.	29	1	Petition	340	Claims.						
Partridge, Abel	Continuation of pension granted by act of March 18, 1818.	16	2	Petition	96	Pens. & Rev. Cl'ms	Feb. 15, 1821	Res. for leave to withdraw.	......	Adopted.		
Partridge, James	Confirmation of title to land	22	1	Petition	134	Public Lands.....	94	Favorable; bill	184	Passed	Passed	App'd July 14, 1832
Paschal, George W......	Expenses incurred in defending suit against him, for acts done in his official capacity.	26	1	Senate bill	794	Claims	488	With amends.	S. 192	Referred to Committee Whole House.		
Paschal, George W......	Expenses incurred in defending suit against him, for acts done in his official capacity.	26	2	Senate bill	99	Claims	....	....	S. 27			
Paschal, George W......	Expenses incurred in defending suit against him, for acts done in his official capacity.	27	2	Senate bill	232	Claims	April 12, 1842	With amends.	S. 15	Passed	Passed	App'd Aug. 12, 1842
Pascauet, Lewis.........	Indemnity for French spoliations prior to 1800.	26	1	Memorial	182	Foreign Affairs....	343	Favorable....	319	Referred to Committee Whole House.		
Pasco, Jonathan.........	Revolutionary pension..........	21	2	Resolution	48	Military Pensions.						
Pasgrove, James	(See Stephen Decatur, widow of, *et al.*)	20	1	....	295							
Paskell, John...........	(See Canadian refugees)........	6	2	....	748							
Pasko, Abel A., and others	Release from judgment as surety of Orson Crane.	25	2	Petition	51	Claims	544	Favorable; bil	535	Referred to Committee Whole House.		
Pasko, Abel A., and others	Release from judgment as surety of Orson Crane.	25	3	Bill of last sess..	379	Whole House	Jan. 25, 1839	With't amend.	535	Passed	Passed	App'd March 3, 1839
Paslay, Thomas.........	Compensation for services and for clothing furnished in revolutionary war.	16	2	Petition	72	Pens. & Rev. Cl'ms.	....	....	......	Discharged; laid on table.		
Pasquet, W...........	Permission to import goods from Martinique.	12	1	Petition	211	....	....	....	......	Ref'd to Com. W. H. on bill No. 46.		
Pass, Francis, administrator of.	Indemnity for property destroyed by United States troops in Florida in 1812-'13.	30	1	Petition	1008	Judiciary	766	As an amend't to S. bill.	S. 48	Passed	Passed	App'd March 3, 1849
Patch, Hannah	Continuation of pension	22	2	Petition	40	Naval Affairs.						
Patch, Hannah	Continuation of pension	23	1	Memorial	73	Naval Affairs.....	Dec. 19, 1833	Favorable....	49	Passed	Passed	App'd June 18, 1834
Patch, James...........	Pension	21	2	Petition	299	Military Pensions.						
Patch, Jonathan	Pension	10	1	House bill......	232	Whole House	April 19, 1808	With amend..	78	Passed	Passed	App'd April 25, 1808
Patch, Jonathan	Arrearages of pension	18	2	Petition	35	Pens. & Rev. Cl'ms.	Dec. 23, 1824	Adverse	......	Laid on table.		
Patch, Samuel, by attorney	Revolutionary pension	26	2	Petition	51	Rev. Pensions	136	Favorable; bill	644	Referred to Committee Whole House.		
Patch, Samuel, by attorney	Revolutionary pension	27	2	Petition	97	Rev. Pensions	117	Favorable; bil	163	Passed	Indef. postp'd.	
Patcham, Ralph.........	Indemnity for damage done to property by United States troops in late war.	15	1	Petition	247	Claims	....	....	......	Discharged; laid on table.		
Patcham, Ralph.........	Indemnity for damage done to property by United States troops in late war.	15	2	Petition	40	Claims	Jan. 5, 1819	Adverse......	......	Laid on table.		
Patcham, Ralph.........	Indemnity for damage done to property by United States troops in late war.	18	2	Petition	160	Claims.						

List of private claims presented to the House of Representatives of the United States from the 1st to the 31st Congress, inclusive—Continued.

Names of claimants.	Nature or object of the claim.	Congress.	Session.	How brought before the House of Reps.	Page of journal.	To what committee of the House referred.	No. or date of the report.	Nature of the report.	No. of the bill.	How disposed of by the House of Reps.	How disposed of by the Senate.	Date of the act of Congress, and remarks.
Patcham, Ralph	Indemnity for damage done to property by United States troops in late war.	22	1	Petition	511	Claims	Jan. 28, 1832	Adverse	......	Laid on table.		
Patchin, Ebenezer	Invalid pension	3	1	Rep. of Secretary War.	131	Select	May 26, 1794	Jt. res. to refer to Sec. War.	R. 12	Passed	Passed	App'd June 9, 1794
Patchin, Ebenezer	Invalid pension	3	2	Rep. of Secretary War.	337	Claims	March 2, 1795	Res. to refer to Sec. War.	......	Adopted.		
Patchin, Ebenezer	Invalid pension	4	1	Rep. of Secretary War.	445	Claims	March 4, 1796	Jt. res. to refer to Sec. War.	R. 16	Passed	Passed	App'd April 18, 1796
Patchin, Freegift	Compensation for services in the New York militia, revolutionary war.	11	2	Petition	280	Claims.						
Patchin, Freegift	Compensation for services in the New York militia, revolutionary war.	11	3	Petition	444	Claims	Dec. 29, 1810	Adverse	......	Rejected.	....	Dec. 10, 1811, leave to withdraw.
Patchin, Isaac	Compensation for services in revolutionary army.	15	1	Petition	184	Select	....	....	......	Discharged; laid on table.		
Patchin, Samuel	Increase of pension	27	2	Petition	238	Rev. Pensions	784	Adverse	......	Laid on table.		
Patchin, Samuel	Increase of pension	28	1	Petition	526	Rev. Pensions.						
Pate, John, David, & William.	Relief on account of back rations due them.	31	2	Petition	51	Military Affairs	Feb. 18, 1851	Adverse	......	Laid on table.		
Patentees, sundry	Renewal of patents for a second term.	9	2	Petition	481	Select	Jan. 2, 1807	By bill	188	Referred to Committee Whole House.		
Patentees, sundry, of Philadelphia.	Renewal and extension of their patents.	10	1	Petition	207	....	....	....	......	Referred to Committee Whole House on bill No. 72.		
Patfield, Joshua, former widow of.	Pension	28	2	Petition	212	Naval Affairs.						
Patfield, Joshua, former widow of.	Pension	30	1	Petition	116	Naval Affairs.						
Patin, Antoine, assignee of.	Confirmation of title to land	19	1	Petition	444	Priv. Land Claims.						
Patin, Antoine, assignee of.	Confirmation of title to land	22	1	Petition	32	Priv. Land Claims.	37	Favorable; bill	82	Passed	Passed	App'd May 19, 1832
Patinotte, Amable	Patent for land held under Spanish grant.	22	1	Petition	263	Priv. Land Claims.	Feb. 17, 1832	By bill	380	Referred to Committee Whole House.		
Patrick, Alexander, widow of.	Settlement of his accounts	24	1	Petition	64	Military Affairs	....	....	......	Discharged; laid on table.		
Patrick, Alexander H.	Payment for a horse and equipage turned over to the government in Florida war.	26	1	Petition	1023	Military Affairs.						
Patrick, Alexander H.	Payment for a horse and equipage turned over to the government in Florida war.	26	2	Petition	79	Military Affairs	93	Favorable; bill	599	Referred to Committee Whole House.		
Patrick, Jacob	Pension	21	1	Petition	377	Military Pensions	....	....	......	Disch'd; laid on table.		
Patrick, Jacob	Pension	21	2	Resolution	41	Military Pensions.						
Patrick, Jacob	Increase of pension	29	1	Petition	254	Rev. Pensions	491	Adverse	......	Laid on table.		
Patrick, John	To be exempt from the payment of foreign duties on his ship Eugenia.	7	2	Memorial	287	Com. and Manuf.	Feb. 21, 1803	Res. to postpone to next session.	......	Adopted.		
Patrick, John	Release from foreign duties on wines brought in a British vessel from the wreck of his ship at Nassau.	15	1	Petition	283	Com. and Munuf.	....	....	......	Discharged; laid on table.		

List of private claims presented to the House of Representatives of the United States from the 1st to the 31st Congress, inclusive—Continued.

Names of claimants.	Nature or object of the claim.	Congress.	Session.	How brought before the House of Reps.	Page of journal.	To what committee of the House referred.	No. or date of the report.	Nature of the report.	No. of the bill.	How disposed of by the House of Reps.	How disposed of by the Senate.	Date of the act of Congress, and remarks.
Patrick, John	Payment of claim against Ottawa Indians.	29	1	Memorial	160	Indian Affairs.	287	Adverse		Laid on table.		
Patrick, Johnson	Compensation for boarding certain Pottawatomie chiefs and their families.	27	2	Petition & docs.	382	Claims	106	Favorable; bill	589	Referred to Committee Whole House.		
Patrick, Johnson	Compensation for boarding certain Pottawatomie chiefs and their families.	27	3	Bill of last sess.	91	Whole House	Dec. 23, 1842	With't amend	589	Passed	Passed	App'd March 3, 1843
Ratrick, Joshua	Pension for losses while a volunteer under General Hull.	13	1	Petition	28	Claims	June 29, 1813	By bill	31	Passed	Passed	App'd Aug. 2, 1813
Patrick, Joshua	Increase of pension	14	2	Rep. of Secretary War.	218	Pens. & Rev. Cl'ms.	Jan. 17, 1817	Res. for leave to withdraw.		Adopted.		
Patrick, Joshua	Increase of pension	17	2	Petition	119	Pens. & Rev. Cl'ms.				Discharged; laid on table.		
Patrick, Joshua	Payment for a horse lost in United States service late war.	16	1	Petition	125	Claims	Jan. 17, 1820	Adverse		Laid on table.		
Patrick, Mary A.	(See Matew A. Patrick, widow of.)	25	2		58							
Patrick, Matthew A., widow of.	Arrears of pay for services in the United States army.	25	2	Petition	58	Military Affairs	512	Favorable; bill	510	Referred to Committee Whole House.		
Patrick, Matthew A., widow of.	Arrears of pay for services in the United States army.	25	2	Senate bill	523	Military Affairs	April 13, 1838	With't amend.	S. 127	Passed		App'd July 7, 1838
Patrick, William, widow of.	Compensation for services rendered and injuries received in revolutionary war.	2	1	Petition	447					Referred to Secretary War.		
Patrick, William	Payment for a horse lost in the public service.	25	2	Petition and docs.	396	Claims.				Discharged; laid on table.		
Patrick, William	Payment for a horse lost in the public service.	25	3	Petition	207	Claims	224	Adverse		Laid on table.		
Patterson, Alexander	Pension	14	1	Petition	632	Pens. & Rev. Cl'ms.				Discharged; laid on table.		
Patterson, A. H.	(See Gid. Peters & Co.)	28	1		218							
Patterson, Andrew H.	Compensation for mail bags destroyed by fire before delivery to Post Office Department.	29	1	Petition	451	Claims	720	Adverse		Laid on table.		
Patterson, Andrew H.	Compensation for mail bags destroyed by fire before delivery to Post Office Department.	29	2	Petition	74	Claims.						
Patterson, Andrew H.	For damages sustained by sudden termination of contract with Post Office Department for the manufacture of mail bags.	30	1	Petition	724	Claims	749	Favorable; bill	588	Referred to Committee Whole House.		
Patterson, Andrew H.	For damages sustained by sudden termination of contract with Post Office Department for the manufacture of mail bags.	31	1	Petition	486	Claims	500	Adverse		Laid on table.		
Pattison, A. N.	Pre-emption right to land	26	1	Petition	600	Public Lands.						
Patterson, Barnard M.	Repayment of money recovered from him by United States by suit, he having previously paid over the amount to an officer of the government.	21	1	Petition	116	Claims	April 26, 1836	Adverse		Laid on table.		

List of private claims presented to the House of Representatives of the United States from the 1st to the 31st Congress, inclusive—Continued.

Names of claimants.	Nature or object of the claim.	Congress.	Session.	How brought before the House of Reps.	Page of journal.	To what committee of the House referred.	No. or date of the report.	Nature of the report.	No. of the bill.	How disposed of by the House of Reps.	How disposed of by the Senate.	Date of the act of Congress, and remarks.
Patterson, Barnard M.	Repayment of money recovered from him by United States by suit, he having previously paid over the amount to an officer of the government.	22	1	Petition	49	Claims	248	Adverse		Laid on table.		
Patterson, Barnard M.	Repayment of money recovered from him by United States by suit, he having previously paid over the amount to an officer of the government.	23	1	Petition	155	Claims	Jan. 29, 1834	Adverse		Laid on table.		
Patterson, Daniel T., and George T. Ross, *et al.*	Prize-money arising from the expedition against the pirates at Barataria.	14	1	Petition	42	Ways and Means	April 18, 1816	By bill	191	Passed	Passed	App'd April 27, 1816
Patterson, Daniel T., and George T. Ross, *et al.*	Act amendatory for their relief	14	1	Senate bill	345	Naval Affairs	Feb. 13, 1817	With't amend.		Passed		App'd Feb. 22, 1817
Patterson, Daniel T.	For certain credits in the settlement of his accounts.	18	2	Memorial	52	Claims	Jan. 19, 1825	Favorable; bill	282	Passed	Passed	App'd March 3, 1825
Patterson, Daniel T.	For the difference of pay between a captain in command of a squadron and a captain on other duty, from October 25, 1835, to March 9, 1836.	24	1	Petition	840	Claims.						
Patterson, Daniel T.	Allowance of certain commissions.	24	2	Petition	37	Claims	37	Favorable; bill	785	Referred to Committee Whole House.		
Patterson, Daniel T.	For necessary expenses while commanding United States naval forces in the Mediterranean.	25	2	Petition	37	Claims	7	Favorable; bill	20	Passed	Passed	App'd July 9, 1838
Patterson, Daniel T.	For necessary expenses while commanding United States naval forces in the Mediterranean.	25	3	Petition	130	Naval Affairs.						
Patterson, David	To be reimbursed money advanced on public account, and for pay and bounty land for his services from 1790 to 1794.	15	2	Petition	202	Claims				Discharged; laid on table.		
Patterson, David	To be reimbursed money advanced on public account, and for pay and bounty land for his services from 1790 to 1794.	16	1	Petition	199	Claims	Feb. 7, 1820	Adverse		Laid on table.		
Patterson, Elizabeth	(See James Patterson, widow of).	30	2		322							
Patterson, Elizabeth, heirs of.	Arrears of pension	30	1	Petition	794	Rev. Pensions.						
Patterson, Elizabeth, heirs of.	Arrears of pension	30	2	Petition	239							
Patterson, or Pattison, Granville S.	Remission of duties on his anatomical museum.	16	1	Petition	148	Ways and Means				Discharged; laid on table.		
Patterson, Hannah	(See Samuel and Hannah Peterson)	15	2		117							
Patterson, Isaac	(See Joseph Brown)	24	2		78							
Patterson, James, widow of	Revolutionary pension	30	2	Petition	322	Rev. Pensions.						
Patterson, James, widow of	Revolutionary pension	31	1	Petition	323	Rev. Pensions	67	Adverse		Laid on table.		
Patterson, James	(See William H. Bedford, agent.)	28	1		262							
Patterson, or Pattison, Jas. J.	Indemnity for a house destroyed by the British in the war of 1812.	21	1	Petition	50	Claims				Discharged; laid on table.		

List of private claims presented to the House of Representatives of the United States from the 1st to the 31st Congress, inclusive—Continued.

Names of claimants.	Nature or object of the claim.	Congress.	Session.	How brought before the House of Reps.	Page of journal.	To what committee of the House referred.	No. or date of the report.	Nature of the report.	No. of the bill.	How disposed of by the House of Reps.	How disposed of by the Senate.	Date of the act of Congress, and remarks.
Patterson, or Pattison, Jas. J.	Indemnity for a house destroyed by the British in the war of 1812.	22	1	Petition	288	Claims	Feb. 24, 1832	Adverse	......	Laid on table.		
Patterson, or Pattison, Jas. J.	Indemnity for a house destroyed by the British in the war of 1812.	22	2	Petition	265	Claims.						
Patterson, or Pattison, Jas. J.	Indemnity for a house destroyed by the British in the war of 1812.	23	1	Petition	111	Claims.						
Patterson, or Pattison, Jas. J.	Indemnity for a house destroyed by the British in the war of 1812.	23	2	Petition	59	Claims.						
Patterson, or Pattison, Jas. J.	Indemnity for a house destroyed by the British in the war of 1812.	24	1	Petition	92	Claims	406	Favorable; bill	444	Referred to Committee Whole House.		
Patterson, or Pattison, Jas. J.	Indemnity for a house destroyed by the British in the war of 1812.	25	2	Petition	37	Claims	14	Favorable; bill	26	Passed	Passed	App'd Mar. 28, 1838
Patterson, or Pattison, Jas. J.	Additional compensation for his house destroyed by the British in the war of 1812.	27	3	Petition	140	Claims	199	Adverse	......	Laid on table.		
Patterson, or Pattison, Jas. J.	Additional compensation for his house destroyed by the British in the war of 1812.	28	1	Petition	926	Claims.						
Patterson, John.........	Further time to complete payment for land.	12	2	Petition	597	Public Lands.						
Patterson, John.........	Further time to complete payment for land.	13	2	Petition	197	Public Lands.....	....	....	......	Discharged; laid on table.		
Patterson, John, 1st......	Invalid pension............ ...	14	1	House bill......	622	Whole House	April 23, 1816	With amends.	171	Passed	Passed	App'd April 30, 1816
Patterson, John, 2d......	Invalid pension...............	14	1	Petition	401	Pens. & Rev. Cl'ms.	April 11, 1816	By bill	171	Passed	Passed	App'd April 30, 1816
Patterson, John, 2d......	Increase of pension	15	2	Petition	153	Pens. & Rev. Cl'ms.	Feb. 5, 1819	By bill	308	Passed	Postponed.	
Patterson, John, 2d......	Increase of pension	16	1	Petition	148	Pens. & Rev. Cl'ms.						
Patterson, John, (Maine).	Fishing bounty on schooner Alexander.	25	2	Memorial	579	Commerce	....	....	......	Discharged; laid on table.		
Patterson, John, (Maine).	Fishing bounty on schooner Alexander.	25	3	Memorial	457	Commerce	....	....	......	Discharged; laid on table.		
Patterson, John, (Maine).	Fishing bounty on schooner Alexander.	26	1	Memorial	177	Commerce	386	Adverse	......	Laid on table.		
Patterson, John, (Ohio) ..	Indemnity against a judgment rendered against him.	28	1	Petition	428	Judiciary	....	....	......	Discharged; laid on table.		
Pattison, John J	Indemnity for a building destroyed by the British in 1814.	15	1	Rep't of Comm'r of Claims.	37	Claims	14	Adverse	......	Rejected.		
Patterson, Joseph	Invalid pension...............	3	2	Rep. of Secretary War.	278	Claims	Mar. 2, 1795	Res. to refer to Sec. War.	......	Res. adopted.		
Patterson, Joseph........	Invalid pension...............	4	1	Rep. of Secretary War.	445	Claims	Mar. 4, 1796	J't. res. to refer to Sec. War.	R. 16	Passed	Passed	App'd April 18, 1796
Patterson, Joseph	Invalid pension	4	2	Rep. of Secretary War.	651	Claims	Feb. 6, 1797	Favorable; bill	224	Passed	Postp'd to next session.	
Patterson, Joseph........	Invalid pension...............	5	2	House bill	127	Whole House.....	Jan. 11, 1798	With amends.	38	Passed	Passed	App'd Feb. 2, 1798
Patterson, Margaret, by attorney.	(See William McMillan, heirs of.)	25	2	....	899							
Patterson, Martin L......	Compensation for services as clerk in the office of the Solicitor of the Treasury.	27	2	Petition	382	Claims..........	1047	Adverse	......	Laid on table.		
Patterson, Martin L......	Compensation for services as clerk in the office of the Solicitor of the Treasury.	27	3	Petition	73	Claims.						

List of private claims presented to the House of Representatives of the United States from the 1st to the 31st Congress, inclusive—Continued.

Names of claimants.	Nature or object of the claim.	Congress.	Session.	How brought before the House of Reps.	Page of journal.	To what committee of the House referred.	No. or date of the report.	Nature of the report.	No. of the bill.	How disposed of by the House of Reps.	How disposed of by the Senate.	Date of the act of Congress, and remarks.
Patterson, Martin L.	Compensation for services as clerk in the office of the Solicitor of the Treasury.	28	1	Petition	429	Claims.						
Patterson, Martin L.	Compensation for services as clerk in the office of the Solicitor of the Treasury.	28	2	Petition	53	Claims.						
Patterson, Martin L.	Compensation for services as clerk in the office of the Solicitor of the Treasury.	29	1	Petition	148	Claims.						
Patterson, Martin L., heirs of.	Compensation for services as clerk in the office of the Solicitor of the Treasury.	30	1	Petition	77	Claims	50	Adverse		Laid on table.		
Patterson, Martin L., heirs of.	Compensation for services as clerk in the office of the Solicitor of the Treasury.	31	1	Petition	361	Claims.						
Patterson, Peter	Pension	21	2	Petition	270	Military Pensions.						
Patterson, Richard	Reissue of land warrant, the original being lost.	30	1	Petition and docs.	598	Rev. Claims.						
Patterson, Richard	Reissue of land warrant, the original being lost.	30	2	Petition and docs.	433	Rev. Claims				Discharged; laid on table.		
Patterson, Robert	Invalid pension	12	1	Petition	29	Claims	July 12, 1812	Adverse		Laid on table		Leave to withdraw.
Patterson, Robert, (2d)	Invalid pension	12	1	House bill	361	Whole House	June 15, 1812	Favorable	138	Passed	Passed	App'd July 5, 1812
Patterson, Robert, (2d)	Arrears of pension	16	1	Petition	53	Pens. & Rev. Cl'ms.	Dec. 27, 1819	Adverse		Laid on table.		
Patterson, Robert, (Ohio)	Pension to take effect from the time he was wounded.	19	1	Resolution	72	Military Pensions	164	Adverse		Laid on table.		
Patterson, Robert, (Ky.)	Pension	20	2	Petition	49	Military Pensions	Jan. 20, 1829	Adverse		Laid on table.		
Patterson, Robert, (Ky.)	Pension	22	1	Petition	89	Invalid Pensions	Feb. 9, 1832	Adverse		Laid on table.		
Patterson, Robert, (Ky.)	Pension	22	2	Petition	509	Invalid Pensions.						
Patterson, Robert, (Tenn.)	Increase of pension	28	1	Petition	318	Rev. Pensions.						
Patterson, Rowena	(See heirs of Martin L. Patterson.)	30	1		77							
Patterson, Samuel, representatives of.	Compensation for services of deceased as loan office commissioner, revolutionary war.	4	2	Rep. Com. Ways and Means.	675	Whole House	Jan. 31, 1797	Favorable; bill corded.	223	Passed	Passed	App'd March 3, 1797
Patterson, Samuel	Payment for work and material on Cumberland road.	23	1	Resolution	589	Claims	455	Adverse		Laid on table.		
Patterson, Sherman	Restoration of pension	25	2	Petition	272	Rev. Pensions				Discharged; laid on table.		
Patterson, Captain Thomas, heirs of.	Seven years' half-pay; died in service.	23	1	Petition	71	Rev. Claims.						
Patterson, Captain Thomas, heirs of.	Donation of lands under the act of 1828.	24	1	Petition and docs.	58	Public Lands.						
Patterson, Thos. L., surety of.	Release from liability	19	1	Petition	68	Judiciary	30	Favorable	44	Passed	Passed	App'd May 13, 1826
Patterson, Thomas & William, representatives of.	Commutation pay for revolutionary services.	24	1	Petition	259	Rev. Claims	Jan. 28, 1836	Adverse		Laid on table.		
Patterson, William, *et al.*	Further relief for the French emigrants from St. Domingo.	3	1	Memorial	25	Select	Jan. 10, 1794	Favorable		Referred to Committee Whole House.		
Patterson, William	Arrears of pension	13	2	Petition	317	Pens. & Rev. Cl'ms.	92	Adverse; leave to withdraw.		Referred to Committee Whole House.		
Patterson, William	Grant of land on Perdido river for opening a road.	17	1	Petition	267	Public Lands				Discharged; laid on table.		
Patterson, William	Confirmation of title to land in Arkansas.	22	1	House bill	421	Whole House	Feb. 29, 1832	Favorable	425	Passed	Passed	App'd June 25, 1832

List of private claims presented to the House of Representatives of the United States from the 1st to the 31st Congress, inclusive—Continued.

Names of claimants.	Nature or object of the claim.	Congress.	Session.	How brought before the House of Reps.	Page of journal.	To what committee of the House referred.	No. or date of the report.	Nature of the report.	No. of the bill.	How disposed of by the House of Reps.	How disposed of by the Senate.	Date of the act of Congress, and remarks.
Patterson, Wm., (Ireland)	Patent for improvement in tanning hides.	24	1	Petition	625	Patent Laws.						
Patterson, William	Invalid pension	27	2	Petition	421	Invalid Pensions.						
Patterson, Wm., & Sons, *et al.*	Relief from illegal seizure of their property by the ruler of St. Domingo.	16	1	Petition	85	Foreign Affairs				Discharged; referred to Secretary of State.		
Patterson, William	For a sum of money in lieu of his bounty land.	27	2	Petition	421	Public Lands.						
Patterson, William	For a sum of money in lieu of his bounty land.	27	3	Petition	193	Public Lands	85	Favorable; bill	713	Passed	Indef. postp'd.	
Patterson, William D.	Compensation for services as captain's clerk in U. States navy.	25	3	Petition	224	Naval Affairs.						
Patterson, William J., *et al.*	(See heirs of Elizabeth Patterson).	30	1		794							
Patterson, (Md.)	Indemnity for French spoliations prior to 1800.	26	1	Memorial	182	Foreign Affairs	343	Favorable	319	Referred to Committee Whole House.		
Pattie, William, (Va.)	Revolutionary pension	23	1	Petition	493	Rev. Pensions				Discharged; laid on table.		
Pattie, William, (Va.)	Revolutionary pension	24	1	Petition	137	Rev. Pensions	591	Favorable; bill	575	Passed	Passed	App'd June 28, 1836
Pattie, William	Revolutionary pension	25	2	Petition	70	Rev. Pensions				Discharged; laid on table.		
Pattie, William	Revolutionary pension	25	3	Petition	87	Rev. Pensions				Discharged; laid on table.		
Pattie, William	Revolutionary pension	26	1	Petition	171	Rev. Pensions				Discharged; laid on table.		
Pattie, William	Revolutionary pension	27	2	Petition	58	Rev. Pensions	784	Adverse		Laid on table.		
Patton, David	Restoration of pension	17	1	Petition	67	Pens. & Rev. Cl'ms.				Discharged; laid on table.		
Patton, David, representatives of.	Revolutionary pension	29	1	Petition	498	Rev. Pensions.						
Patton, Edward	Additional compensation as butcher in revolutionary army.	10	2	Petition	509					Referred to Committee Whole House on bill No. 129.		
Patton, Eliza A.	(See widow of Nathaniel Patton).	25	2		425							
Patton, James	Increase of pension	11	3	House bill	604	Whole House	Mar. 2, 1811	With amend.	218	Passed	Passed	App'd March 3, 1811
Patton, James	Release from judgment as surety on a revenue bond.	13	2	Petition	201	Ways and Means	67	Favorable; bill	128	Referred to Committee Whole House.		
Patton, or Patten, James	(See Captain Martin J. Aiken)	17	1		359							
Patton, James, sen	Increase of pension	28	1	Petition	729	Rev. Pensions				Discharged; laid on table.		
Patton, James, (Ky.)	Release from payment of a balance held against him by the Post Office Department.	27	2	Petition	747	P. Of. & P. Roads.				Discharged; laid on table.		
Patton, James, (Va.)	Indemnity for French spoliations prior to 1800.	26	1	Memorial	182	Foreign Affairs	343	Favorable		Referred to Committee Whole House.		
Patton, John	Invalid pension	22	2	Petition	26	Invalid Pensions				Discharged; laid on table.		
Patton, John	Invalid pension	25	2	Petition	167	Invalid Pensions				Discharged; laid on table.		
Patton, John	Invalid pension	25	3	Petition	89	Invalid Pensions.						
Patton, John	Invalid pension	26	1	Petition	161	Invalid Pensions	258	Adverse		Laid on table.		
Patton, John	Invalid pension	29	1	Petition	86	Invalid Pensions	300	Favorable; bill	245	Passed	Passed	App'd Aug. 8, 1846
Patton, John, widow of	Continuation of her husband's pension.	30	1	Petition	78	Rev. Pensions	24	Adverse		Laid on table.		

List of private claims presented to the House of Representatives of the United States from the 1st to the 31st Congress, inclusive—Continued.

Names of claimants.	Nature or object of the claim.	Congress.	Session.	How brought before the House of Reps.	Page of journal.	To what committee of the House referred.	No. or date of the report.	Nature of the report.	No. of the bill.	How disposed of by the House of Reps.	How disposed of by the Senate.	Date of the act of Congress, and remarks.
Patton, John, jr.	Fishing bounty for schooner Credit	27	2	Petition	319	Commerce	1000	Favorable; bill	579	Referred to Committee Whole House.		
Patton, John, jr.	Fishing bounty for schooner Credit	27	3	Bill of last sess.	91	Whole House	Dec. 23, 1842	With't amend.	579	Passed	Indef. postp'd.	
Patton, John, and James Dykes.	Indemnity for French spoliations prior to 1800.	26	1	Memorial	182	Foreign Affairs	343	Favorable; bill	319	Referred to Committee Whole House.		
Patton, Joseph	Revolutionary pension	18	2	Petition	41	Rev. Pensions	Jan. 12, 1825	Adverse	......	Laid on table.		
Patton, Mary	(See David Patton, representatives of.)	29	1	....	498							
Patton, Mary	(See John Patton, widow of)	30	1	....	78							
Patton, Nathaniel, postmaster in Missouri.	To be exempted from repaying $800; public money of which he was robbed.	16	1	Petition	260	Claims	....	....	......	Discharged; laid on table.		
Patton, Nathaniel, postmaster in Missouri.	To be exempted from repaying $800; public money of which he was robbed.	17	1	Petition	129	Claims	Mar. 18, 1822	Adverse	......	Laid on table	....	Leave to withdraw.
Patton, Nathaniel, postmaster in Missouri.	To be exempted from repaying $800; public money of which he was robbed.	20	1	Senate bill	96	P. Of. & P. Roads.	Jan. 7, 1828	With't amend.	S. 25	Laid on table.		
Patton, Nathaniel, postmaster in Missouri.	To be exempted from repaying $800; public money of which he was robbed.	20	2	Senate bill	94	Claims	Mar. 2, 1829	With't amend.	S. 9	Laid on table.		
Patton, Nathaniel, postmaster in Missouri.	To be exempted from repaying $800; public money of which he was robbed.	21	1	Petition	132	P. Of. & P. Roads.	59	Favorable; bill	80	Referred to Committee Whole House.		
Patton, Nathaniel, postmaster in Missouri.	To be exempted from repaying $800; public money of which he was robbed.	21	2	Bill of last sess.	150	Whole House	Jan. 6, 1831	With't amend.	80	Postponed.		
Patton, Nathaniel, postmaster in Missouri.	Release from judgment for money stolen from him.	22	1	Petition	292	Judiciary	335	Favorable; bill	426	Referred to Committee Whole House.		
Patton, Nathaniel, postmaster in Missouri.	Release from judgment for money stolen from him.	23	1	Petition	73	Judiciary	52	Favorable; bill	60	Rejected.		
Patton, Nathaniel, postmaster in Missouri.	Release from judgment for money stolen from him.	24	2	Petition	85	P. Of. & P. Roads.	271	Adverse	......	Laid on table.		
Patton, Nathaniel, widow of.	For the allowance of the amount stolen from him in the settlement of his accounts.	25	2	Petition	425	P. Of. & P. Roads.						
Patton, Nathaniel, widow of.	For the allowance of the amount stolen from him in the settlement of his accounts.	26	1	Petition	183	P. Of. & P. Roads.						
Patton, Nathaniel, widow of.	For the allowance of the amount stolen from him in the settlement of his accounts.	29	1	Petition	317	P. Of. & P. Roads.	376	Adverse	......	Laid on table.		
Patton, Pilcher, & Co.	Settlement of their accounts for transporting the United States mails.	27	2	Joint resolution from Senate.	1231	P. Of. & P. Roads.	Aug. 30, 1842	With't amend.	R. 16	Passed	Passed	App'd Aug. 31, 1842
Patton, Rachael	(See William Patton, heirs of)	29	1	....	446							
Patton, Richard	Debentures on a number of straw-hats exported to South America.	18	2	Petition	148	Ways and Means.						
Patton, Richard	Payment for instruments, charts, &c., furnished United States.	27	2	Senate bill	680	Claims	May 25, 1842	With't amend.	S. 136	Laid on table.		
Patton, Richard	Payment for instruments, charts, &c., furnished United states.	27	3	Senate bill	477	Claims	Mar. 2, 1843	With't amend.	S. 79	Passed	....	App'd March 3, 1843
Patton, Richard T.	(See William H. Bedford, agent)	28	1	....	262							

List of private claims presented to the House of Representatives of the United States from the 1st to the 31st Congress, inclusive—Continued.

Names of claimants.	Nature or object of the claim.	Congress.	Session.	How brought before the House of Reps.	Page of journal.	To what committee of the House referred.	No. or date of the report.	Nature of the report.	No. of the bill.	How disposed of by the House of Reps.	How disposed of by the Senate.	Date of the act of Congress, and remarks.
Patton, Robert, & Co., *et al.*	Reimbursement of foreign duties in the case of the schooner Iris and her cargo.	8	2	Petition	127	Com. and Manuf.	Feb. 15, 1805	By bill	62	Passed	Passed	App'd March 3, 1805
Patton, Robert, (Va.)	Indemnity for French spoliations prior to 1800.	26	1	Memorial	182	Foreign Affairs	344	Favorable; bill	319	Referred to Committee Whole House.		
Patton, Samuel	Pension	21	1	Petition	411	Military Pensions	April 7 1830	Adverse	......	Laid on table.		
Patton, Samuel	Pension	21	2	Petition	230	Military Pensions	Feb. 8, 1831	Favorable; bill	607	Passed	Reported with't amendment.	
Patton, Samuel	Pension	22	1	Petition	45	Rev. Pensions	127	Favorable; bill	72	Passed	Indef. postp'd.	
Patton, Susan	Pension and bounty land; husband killed in battle in 1814.	25	3	Petition	129	Rev. Pensions	......	......	......	Discharged; laid on table.		
Patton, Susan	Pension and bounty land; husband killed in battle in 1814.	26	1	Petition	163	Invalid Pensions	......	......	......	Discharged; laid on table.		
Patton, Thomas	Pension	20	1	Petition	64	Military Pensions.						
Patton, William	Relief from prosecution for selling spirituous liquors without license.	4	2	Petition	637	......	......	......	......	Rejected.		
Patton, William, heirs of.	Pension for services in revolutionary war.	29	1	Petition	446	Rev. Claims.						
Patton, William H	Payment for a horse and equipage lost in the Seminole campaign in 1818.	23	1	Petition & docs.	154	Claims.						
Patton, Williamson and Meeker.	(See Samuel Meeker)	21	1	......	99							
Paul & Livezey	(See Thomas Livezey)	4	2	......	627							
Paul, Hugh	(See John Peck)	22	1	......	394							
Paul, James	Restoration of pension	17	1	Petition	163	......	......	......	......	Referred to Committee Whole House on bill No. 37.		
Paul, James	(See Paul & Watson)	26	1	......	182							
Paul & Watson	Indemnity for French spoliations prior to 1800.	26	1	Memorial	182	Foroign Affairs.	343	Favorable	319	Referred to Committee Whole House.		
Paulding, John	Satisfaction of grant and annnity.	6	2	House bill	752	Whole House	Jan. 5, 1801	Favorable	277	Passed	Passed	App'd March 3, 1801
Paulding, John, and James Minor.	Compensation for collecting provisions and impressing teams for the use of the revolutionary army.	3		Petition	95	......	......	......	......	Laid on table.		
Paulding, John	Increase of pension for arresting Major Andre.	14	2	Petition	70	Pens. & Rev. Cl'ms.	Jan. 13, 1817	Adverse	......	Rejected.		
Paulding, John	Increase of pension for arresting Major Andre.	15	1	Petition	265	Pens. & Rev. Cl'ms.	......	......	......	Discharged; laid on table.		
Paulding, John, widow and children.	Extension to them for five years the pension of deceased for capturing Major Andre.	15	1	Resolution	310	Pens. & Rev. Cl'ms.						
Paulding, John, heirs of.	Pension in consideration of eminent services of deceased.	19	2	Petition	242	Military Pensions.						
Paulding, John, heirs of.	Pension in consideration of eminent services of deceased.	20	1	Petition	45	Military Pensions.	......	......	......	Discharged; laid on table.		
Paulding, John, heirs of.	Pension in consideration of eminent services of deceased.	20	2	Petition	211	Military Pensions.						
Paulding, John, daughter of.	Donation for services of deceased in arresting Major Andre.	28	1	Petition	272	Rev. Claims.						
Paulding, Marcus	Invalid pension	27	2	Petition	125	Invalid Pensions.						
Paulett, Richard	Commutation of half-pay as lieutenant in revolutionary war.	22	2	Petition	180	Rev. Claims.						

List of private claims presented to the House of Representatives of the United States from the 1st to the 31st Congress, inclusive—Continued.

Names of claimants.	Nature or object of the claim.	Congress.	Session.	How brought before the House of Reps.	Page of journal.	To what committee of the House referred.	No. or date of the report.	Nature of the report.	No. of the bill.	How disposed of by the House of Reps.	How disposed of by the Senate.	Date of the act of Congress, and remarks.
Paulett, Richard	Commutation of half-pay as lieutenant in revolutionary war.	23	1	Petition	158	Rev. Claims.						
Paulett, Richard	Commutation of half pay as lieutenant in revolutionary war.	23	2	Petition	48	Rev. Claims.						
Paulett, Richard	Commutation of half pay as lieutenant in revolutionary war.	24	1	Petition	259	Rev. Claims.						
Paulett, Richard	Commutation of half pay as lieutenant in revolutionary war.	24	2	Petition	39	Rev. Claims.						
Paulett, Richard	Commutation of half pay as lieutenant in revolutionary war.	25	2	Petition	70	Rev. Claims				Discharged; laid on table.		
Paulett, Richard	Commutation of half-pay as lieutenant in revolutionary war.	25	3	Petition	84	Rev. Claims				Discharged; laid on table.		
Paulett, Richard	Commutation of half-pay as lieutenant in revolutionary war.	26	1	Petition	164	Rev. Claims	608	Adverse		Laid on table.		
Paulett, Richard, heirs of	Commutation of half-pay as lieutenant in revolutionary war.	27	2	Petition	61	Rev. Claims	397	Adverse		Laid on table.		
Paulett, William W.	Remuneration for depredations by Creek Indians.	25	2	Petition and docs.	770	Claims	841	Adverse		Laid on table.		
Paulett, William W.	Remuneration for depredations by Creek Indians.	26	1	Petition and docs.	340	Claims.						
Paulling, William K.	Pre-emption right to land in Alabama.	23	1	Petition	139	Public Lands	163	Favorable; bil	178	Passed	Passed	App'd June 30, 1834
Paulas, Barbara	(See John Zeabold, mother of)	18	1		175							
Paulus, Jacob.	Revolutionary pension	2	1	Petition	465					Referred to Secretary War.		
Pavenstedt, E., and F. A. Shumacker, *et al.*	Release of themselves and sureties, and cancellation of custom house bonds.	31	1	Petition	202	Commerce	35	Favorable; bill	63	Passed	Reported with't amendment.	
Pavenstedt, E , and F. A. Shumacker, *et al.*	Release of themselves and sureties, and cancellation of custom house bonds.	31	2	Senate bill	40	Commerce			S. 72			
Pawling, Albert	Relief in consideration of services as an officer of the revolutionary army.	19	1	Petition	43	Select				Discharged; laid on table.		
Pawling, Albert	Relief in consideration of services as an officer of the revolutionary army.	20	1	Petition	223	Rev. Claims				Discharged; laid on table.		Leave to withdraw.
Pawling, Albert	Additional compensation for services in revolutionary war.	21	1	Petition	57	Military Pensions	April 2, 1830	Adverse		Laid on table.		
Pawling, Albert	Additional compensation for services in revolutionary war.	21	2	Petition	54	Select.						
Pawling, Albert, and others	For the benefits of the several acts for the relief of those who served in the revolutionary war.	22	1	Petition	72	Rev. Pensions.						
Pawling, Albert	Land for revolutionary services	24	1	Petition	62	Rev. Claims				Disch'd; laid on table.		
Pawling, Col. Albert	Payment for revolutionary services, in obedience to act of May 15, 1828.	24	1	Senate bill	811	Rev. Pensions	May 17, 1836	With't amend.	S. 193	Passed		App'd June 15, 1836
Pawling, Albert and Sila	(See executors of Henry Rawling.)	29	2		161							
Pawling, Henry, executors of.	Five years' full pay in lieu of commutation, with interest.	29	2	Petition	161	Rev. Claims.						
Pawling, Henry, executors of.	Five years' full pay in lieu of commutation, with interest.	30	1	Petition	117	Rev. Claims	830	Adverse		Laid on table		March 3, 1849, leave to withdraw.

List of private claims presented to the House of Representatives of the United States from the 1st to the 31st Congress, inclusive—Continued.

Names of claimants.	Nature or object of the claim.	Congress.	Session.	How brought before the House of Reps.	Page of journal.	To what committee of the House referred.	No. or date of the report.	Nature of the report.	No. of the bill.	How disposed of by the House of Reps.	How disposed of by the Senate.	Date of the act of Congress, and remarks.
Pawlings, Susan, and Janet Wilson, heirs of.	Permission to locate land warrant bequeathed to them on any vacant land of the United States.	24	1	Petition	152	Rev. Claims.						
Pawlings & Wilson......	(See heirs of Susan Pawlings and Janet Wilson.)	24	1	....	152							
Pawling, William	(See heirs of Adam Wallace)....	23	1	....	243							
Paxton, James..........	(See executors of John Jordon) ..	24	1	....	138							
Paxton, Joseph, and Thomas Matthews.	Compensation for services as commissioners under act of January, 1824, for surveying a road from Memphis to Little Rock.	19	2	Petition	243	Public Lands.....	....	....	......	Discharged; laid on table.		
Paxton, Joseph, and Thomas Matthews.	Compensation for services as commissioners under act of January, 1824, for surveying a road from Memphis to Little Rock.	24	1	Petition and docs.	206	Claims	Jan. 27, 1836	Adverse......	......	Laid on table.		
Paxton, Joseph	Payment for arms and clothing lost while in the service of the United States.	26	1	Senate bill	803	Claims	516	Adverse	S. 134	Referred to Committee Whole House.		
Paxton, Joseph	Payment for arms and clothing lost while in the service of the United States.	26	2	Senate bill	231	Claims..........	....	....	S. 159			
Paxton, Joseph	Payment for arms and clothing lost while in the service of the United States.	28	1	Petition	707	Claims.						
Paxton, Joseph	Payment for arms and clothing lost while in the service of the United States.	28	2	Petition	104	Claims.						
Payett, John, legal representatives of.	Confirmation of title to land	39	1	Petition	236	Priv. Land Claims.						
Payne, Adams	Increase of pension	27	2	Petition	443	Invalid Pensions ..	....	....	......	Disch'd; laid on table.		
Payne, Adams	Increase of pension	28	1	Petition	193	Invalid Pensions.						
Payne, Adams	Increase of pension	28	2	Petition	214	Invalid Pensions.						
Payne, Adams, widow of.	Revolutionary pension...........	31	1	Petition	449	Invalid Pensions.						
Payne, B. O...........	Pension for wounds received while acting ordnance officer in the army.	30	2	Petition	192	Invalid Pensions ..	31	Favorable; bill	725	Passed	Passed	App'd March 3, 1849
Payne, Dorothea	(See Adam Payne, widow of.)...	31	1	....	449							
Payne, Edward.........	Payment of claim arising under treaty of Ghent.	20	2	Petition	23, 231	Foreign Affairs....	79	Adverse	......	Laid on table.		
Payne, John	(See administrator of Jacob Rasor.)	18	1	....	330							
Payne, John, jr.........	Pension for loss of an arm by an explosion of cannon while a cadet at West Point.	16	1	Petition	53	Pens. & Rev. Cl'ms.	Jan. 7, 1820	Adverse	......	Laid on table.......	....	Leave to withdraw.
Payne, John	Pension	31	1	Petition	730	Rev. Pensions	216	Adverse	......	Laid on table.		
Payne, John C..........	Invalid pension................	29	1	Memorial	1102	Invalid Pensions.						
Payne, John H., *et al*...	Compensation for services as fireman on United States ship Alleghany.	31	1	Petition	255	Claims	410	Adverse	......	Laid on table.		
Payne, Joseph	Confirmation of title to land in Missouri.	15	1	Petition	102	Priv. Land Claims.	....	....	......	Discharged; laid on table.		
Payne, Matthew	Permission to locate lands granted by the State of Georgia, or that scrip may issue for the same.	27	2	Petition	66	Priv. Land Claims.						

List of private claims presented to the House of Representatives of the United States from the 1st to the 31st Congress, inclusive—Continued.

Names of claimants.	Nature or object of the claim.	Congress.	Session.	How brought before the House of Reps.	Page of journal.	To what committee of the House referred.	No. or date of the report.	Nature of the report.	No. of the bill.	How disposed of by the House of Reps.	How disposed of by the Senate.	Date of the act of Congress, and remarks.
Payne, Maj. M. M.	Indemnity for expenses incurred in defending a suit brought against him for acts done in his official cspacity.	21	1	Petition	238	Military Affairs	Feb. 8, 1830	Favorable; bill	212	Passed	Passed	App'd May 29, 1830
Payne, N., and B. H.	Pre-emption right to land	27	2	Petition	129	Public Lands.						
Payne, Roswell	Invalid pension	27	3	Petition	156	Invalid Pensions.						
Payne, Silas	Revolutionary pension	15	1	Petition	184	Select				Discharged; laid on table.		
Payne, Solomon	Land for revolutionary services	29	1	Petition	939	Claims.						
Payne, Solomon	Land for revolutionary services	29	2	Petition	87	Claims.						
Payne, Thomas J.	(See Alfred Tracy, and others)	23	2		201							
Payne, Wm., and others	Confirmation of title to land in Mississippi Territory.	7	2	Documents	361					Referred to Committee Whole House on bill No. 120.		
Payne, Wm, and others	Confirmation of title to certain lot in Milwaukie.	26	1	Petition	709	Commerce.						
Payne, William H.	(See Isaac Bush and others.)	30	1		740							
Payne, William S.	Refunding of a fine for an alleged violation of the coasting laws.	31	1	Petition	349	Commerce				Discharged; laid on table.		
Payson, Asa	Pre-emption to land as a New Orleans branch pilot.	28	1	Petition	77	Priv. Land Claims.	9	Favorable; bill	35	Passed	Passed	App'd June 17, 1844
Payson, Henry	(See William Patterson and sons, and others.)	16	1		85							
Payson, Henry	Indemnity for French spoliations prior to 1800.	26	1	Memorial	182	Foreign Affairs	343	Favorable	319	Referred to Committee Whole House.		
Payson, Henry	(See George Sears, executors of.)	26	1		182							
Payson, Samuel	Pension	20	1	Petition	163	Military Pensions				Discharged; laid on table.		
Payson, Samuel	Pension	20	2	Petition	26	Military Pensions				Discharged; laid on table.		
Payson, Samuel	Pension	21	1	Petition	36	Military Pensions	Jan. 5, 1830	By bill	72	Passed	Passed	App'd May 20, 1830
Pazos, Vincent, agent for Venezuela, New Grenada, and Mexico.	Indemnity for losses and injuries sustained by the United States taking possession of Amelia Island.	15	1	Memorial	320					Not received by the House.		
Pazos, Vincent, *et al.*	Indemnity for private property taken by the United States troops with possession of Amelia Island.	15	1	Memorial	411	Claims				Discharged; laid on table.		
Peabody, Andrew	Pension	20	1	Petition	223	Military Pensions				Discharged; laid on table.		
Peabody, Andrew	Pension	20	2	Petition	82					Referred to Committee Whole House on bill No. 137.		
Peabody, Andrew	Pension	21	1	Petition	128	Military Pensions	May 4, 1830	Adverse		Laid on table.		
Peabody & Huntingdon	Indemnity for French spoliations prior to 1800.	26	1	Memorial	182	Foreign Affairs	343	Favorable; bill	319	Referred to Committee Whole House.		
Peabody, John, assignee of.	Indemnity for French spoliations prior to 1800.	26	1	Memorial	182	Foreign Affairs	343	Favorable; bill	319	Referred to Committee Whole House.		
Peabody, Jonathan	Pension	22	1	Resolution	136	Military Pensions.						
Peabody, Joseph	Invalid pension	3	1	Rep. of Secretary War.	131	Select	May 26, 1794	Jt. res. to refer to Sec. War.	R. 12	Passed	Passed	App'd June 9, 1794
Peabody, Joseph	Invalid pension	3	2	Rep. of Secretary War.	262	Claims	Mar. 2, 1795	Res. to refer to Sec. War.		Resolution adopted.		

List of private claims presented to the House of Representatives of the United States from the 1st to the 31st Congress, inclusive—Continued.

Names of claimants.	Nature or object of the claim.	Congress.	Session.	How brought before the House of Reps.	Page of journal.	To what committee of the House referred.	No. or date of the report.	Nature of the report.	No. of the bill.	How disposed of by the House of Reps.	How disposed of by the Senate.	Date of the act of Congress, and remarks.
Peabody, Joseph	Invalid pension	4	1	Rep. of Secretary War.	445	Claims	Feb. 18, 1796	Favorable; bill	156	Passed	Passed	App'd April 20, 1796
Peabody, Joseph, *et al.*	Assumption by Congress of Neapolitan indemnity stock.	25	2	Memorial	172	Ways and Means	Jan. 20, 1838	Adverse	......	Laid on table.		
Peabody, Joseph, *et al.*	Assumption by Congress of Neapolitan indemnity stock.	25	2	Petition & report Ways & Means.	341	Foreign Affairs						
Peabody, Joseph	Indemnity for French spoliations prior to 1800.	26	1	Memorial	182	Foreign Affairs	343	Favorable; bill	319	Referred to Committee Whole House.		
Peabody, N. P., heirs of	Indemnity for French spoliations prior to 1800.	26	1	Memorial	182	Foreign Affairs	343	Favorable; bill	319	Referred to Committee Whole House.		
Peabody, Samuel, Jeremiah and John, by attorney.	Half of the proceeds of the sale of a quantity of cotton found by them upon the high seas.	12	1	Petition	262	Com. and Manuf.						
Peabody, Samuel, Jeremiah and John, by attorney.	Half of the proceeds of the sale of a quantity of cotton found by them upon the high seas.	15	2	Petition	32	Claims	Dec. 9, 1818	Adverse	......	Rejected.		
Peachy, Thomas G., representatives of.	Compensation for property destroyed in revolutionary war.	25	2	Petition	391	Rev. Claims	....	....	......	Discharged; laid on table.		
Peachy, Thomas G., representatives of.	Compensation for property destroyed in revolutionary war.	26	1	Petition	630	Rev. Claims.						
Peachy, Thomas G., representatives of.	Compensation for property destroyed in revolutionary war.	26	2	Petition	212	Rev. Claims.						
Peachy, Thomas G., representatives of.	Compensation for property destroyed in revolutionary war.	28	1	Petition	332	Rev. Claims.						
Peacock, Richard	Compensation for services in revolutionary war.	20	1	Petition	243	Rev. Claims	193	Adverse	......	Laid on table	....	Leave to withdraw.
Peacock, Richard	Pension	22	1	Petition	66	Rev. Pensions	Dec. 28, 1831	Adverse	......	Laid on table.		
Peacock, Sarah	Compensation for a saw mill burnt by Indians in Florida.	26	1	Petition	170	Claims.						
Peacock, U. S. ship, officers and crew of.	(See Charles Wilkes, and others)	28	1	....	515							
Peacock, William A.	(Claim not stated)	20	1	Documents	244	Claims.						
Peacock, Wyandott Indian	Permission to change location of lands.	27	3	Petition	259	Public Lands	160	Favorable; bill	776	Referred to Committee Whole House.		
Peairs, John	Compensation for supplies furnished United States troops in revolutionary war.	23	1	Petition	157	Rev. Claims	Jan. 23, 1834	Adverse	......	Laid on table.		
Peak, John	Invalid pension	24	2	Documents	267	Invalid Pensions	....	....	......	Disch'd; laid on table		
Peak, John	Invalid pension	26	1	Petition	938	Invalid Pensions.						
Peak, John	Invalid pension	27	2	Petition	342	Invalid Pensions	922	Favorable; bill	534	Ordered to 3d reading.		
Peak, John	Invalid pension	27	3	Bill of last sess.	89	....	....	....	534	Passed	Indef. postp'd.	
Peak, John, agent of A. B. West.	(See Major Chs. West, widow of)	8	2	....	87							
Peake, Thomas	(See heirs of John K. Latimer)	24	2	....	308							
Peak, William	Settlement of his accounts as quartermaster in revolutionary army, and for increase of pension.	2	1	Petition	573	....	....	....	......	Referred to Secretary War.		
Peak, William	Settlement of his accounts as quartermaster in revolutionary army, and for increase of pension.	2	2	Report of Secretary of War.	696	....	....	....	......	Laid on table.		
Peake, William H	Reimbursement of money advanced United States, and for invalid pension.	11	3	Petition	489	Claims.						

List of private claims presented to the House of Representatives of the United States from the 1st to the 31st Congress, inclusive—Continued.

Names of claimants.	Nature or object of the claim.	Congress.	Session.	How brought before the House of Reps.	Page of journal.	To what committee of the House referred.	No. or date of the report	Nature of the report.	No. of the bill.	How disposed of by the House of Reps.	How disposed of by the Senate.	Date of the act of Congress, and remarks.
Peake, William H	Reimbursement of money advanced United States, and for invalid pension.	13	2	Petition	181	Pensions				Discharged; leave to withdraw.		
Peale, Titian R	Indemnity for losses sustained by the wreck of the United States ship Peacock, and for arrears of salary.	29	2	Memorial	57	Naval Affairs.	59	Favorable; bill	663	Referred to Committee Whole House.		
Peale, Titian R	Indemnity for losses sustained by the wreck of the United States ship Peacock, and for arrears of salary.	30	1	Petition	79	Naval Affairs	July 19, 1848	By bill	608	Referred to Committee Whole House.		
Peale, Titian R	Indemnity for losses sustained by the wreck of the United States ship Peacock, and for arrears of salary.	31	1	Petition	192	Naval Affairs.						
Pearce, Abigail	(See widow of Shubal Pearce.)	24	2		313							
Pearce, Cromwell	Compensation for services against Indians in 1763.	8	2	Petition	80	Claims	Jan. 24, 1805	Adverse		Rejected.		
Pearce, C. R. and David, jr.	(See David Pearce, heirs of.)	26	1		182							
Pearce, David, *et al*	Drawback on salt used in curing fish.	4	1	Memorial	441	Com. and Manuf.	April 5, 1796	Adverse		Laid on table.		Leave to withdraw.
Pearce, David	Compensation for clothing furnished troops, revolutionary war.	11	1	Petition	71	Claims.						
Pearce, David	Compensation for property destroyed in public service.	13	2	Petition	239	Pens. & Rev. Cl'ms.	92	Adverse, leave to withdraw.		Referred to Committee Whole House.		
Pearce, David, heirs of	Indemnity for French spoliations prior to 1800.	26	1	Memorial	182	Foreign Affairs	343	Favorable; bill	319	Referred to Committee Whole House.		
Pearce, Dutee J., widow of.	To set off certain items against claim of government, and deceased's estate discharged from balance.	31	1	Petition	502	Judiciary	161	Favorable; bill	181	Referred to Committee Whole House.		
Pearce, Elizabeth	(See heirs of Israel Pearce)	23	1		242							
earce, Elizabeth	(See widow of Squire Ambler)	28	1		99							
Pearce, George, widow and children of.	Naval pension	17	2	Resolution	49					Referred to Commissioners of Naval Pension Fund.		
Pearce, George, widow and children of.	Naval pension	21	1	Petition	175	Naval Affairs				Discharged; laid on table.		
Pearce, George, widow and children of.	Naval pension	21	2	Petition	62	Naval Affairs.						
Pearce, George, widow and children of.	Naval pension	22	1	Petition	187	Naval Affairs.						
Pearce, Israel, heirs of	Payment of final settlement certificates and bounty land warrants due deceased as assignee of ten revolutionary soldiers.	23	1	Petition	242	Rev. Claims.						
Pearce, Israel, heirs of	Payment of final settlement certificates and bounty land warrants due deceased as assignee of ten revolutionary soldiers.	25	3	Petition	124	Rev. Claims				Discharged; laid on table.		
Pearce, Israel, heirs of	Payment of final settlement certificates and bounty land warrants due deceased as assignee of ten revolutionary soldiers.	26	1	Petition	167	Rev. Claims	439	Adverse as to certif's; bill for land warrants.	358	Referred to Committee Whole House.		

List of private claims presented to the House of Representatives of the United States from the 1st to the 31st Congress, inclusive—Continued.

Names of claimants.	Nature or object of the claim.	Congress.	Session.	How brought before the House of Reps.	Page of journal.	To what committee of the House referred.	No. or date of the report.	Nature of the report.	No. of the bill.	How disposed of by the House of Reps.	How disposed of by the Senate.	Date of the act of Congress, and remarks.
Pearce, Israel, heirs of....	Payment of final settlement certificates and bounty land warrants due deceased as assignee of ten revolutionary soldiers.	27	1	Petition	106	Rev. Claims.						
Pearce, Israel, heirs of....	Payment of final settlement certificates and bounty land warrant due deceased as assignee of ten revolutionary soldiers.	27	2	Petition	96	Rev. Claims......	79	Former report adopted; bill	119	Passed	Passed	App'd June 4, 1842
Pearce, Israel, heirs of....	Payment of ten final settlement certificates and two bounty land warrants due deceased as assignee of revolutionary soldiers.	28	1	Petition	240	Rev. Claims......	459	Report and bill for two warrants and one certificate.	355	Passed	Passed	App'd June 17, 1844
Pearce, Israel, heirs of....	Payment of ten final settlement certificates and two bounty land warrants due deceased as assignee of revolutionary soldiers.	30	1	Petition	422	Rev. Claims......	768	Favorable; bill	602	Referred to Committee Whole House.	....	This bill reprovides for those embraced in the previous acts among others.
Pearce, Israel, heirs of....	Payment of ten final settlement certificates and two bounty land warrants due deceased as assignee of revolutionary soldiers.	31	1	Petition	496	Rev. Claims......	427	Adverse	......	Laid on table.		
Pearce, Jonathan	Pension	21	2	Petition	159	Military Pensions.						
Pearce, Jonathan	Pension	22	1	Petition	80	Rev. Claims......	122	Favorable; bill	194	Referred to Committee Whole House.		
Pearce, Jonathan	Pension	22	2	Bill of last sess..	66	....	....	....	194	Laid on table.		
Pearce, Jonathan, administra'rix of.	Arrears of pension	24	1	Petition	136	Rev. Pensions	Jan. 29, 1836	Adverse	......	Referred to Committee Whole House.		
Pearce, Mathew.........	Indemnity for French spoliations prior to 1800.	26	1	Memorial	182	Foreign Affairs....	343	Favorable....	319	Referred to Committee Whole House.		
Pearce, Nathaniel........	To refund amount of insurance of vessel.	18	1	Petition	109	Ways and Means..	Jan. 4, 1824	Adverse	......	Laid on table.		
Pearce, Philip	Pre-emption right to land........	27	2	Petition	66	Public Lands.						
Pearce, Pliny...........	Increase of pension	29	1	Petition	175	Invalid Pensions.						
Pearce, Richard	Compensation for naval services in revolutionary war.	2	1	Petition	492	....	....	....	......	Referred to Secretary of War.		
Pearce, Robert...........	Pension	19	2	Petition	215	Military Pensions..	....	....	......	Discharged; laid on table.		
Pearce, Robert S........	(See John H. Robinson, *et al*) ..	26	1	....	363	....	378					
Pearce, Silas	Pension	23	1	Petition	493	Rev. Pensions	....	....	......	Discharged; laid on table.		
Pearce, Silas	Pension	23	2	Petition	147	Rev. Pensions.....	....	....	......	Discharged; laid on table.		
Pearce, Shubal, widow of.	Pension for services of husband...	24	2	Petition	313	Rev. Pensions.						
Pearce, William, 2d.....	(See Richard Smith and others)..	21	1	....	376							
Pearce, William, (Mass.).	Indemnity for French spoliations prior to 1800.	26	1	Memorial	182	Foreign Affairs....	343	Favorable; bil	319	Referred to Committee Whole House.		
Pearcey, Ann...........	(See Jonathan Pearcey, widow of)	28	1	....	901							
Pearcey, Jonathan, widow of.	Revolutionary pension	28	1	Petition	901	Rev. Pensions.						
Pearcey, Jonathan, widow of.	Revolutionary pension..........	29	1	Memorial	386, 889	Rev. Pensions	525 and 786	Adverse	......	Laid on table.		
Pearcey, Jonathan, widow of.	Revolutionary pension..........	30	1	Petition	169	Rev. Pensions	148	Adverse	......	Laid on table.		
Pearis, Jeremiah.........	Pension	25	2	Resolution	756	Rev. Pensions	....	....	......	Disch'd; laid on table.		

List of private claims presented to the House of Representatives of the United States from the 1st to the 31st Congress, inclusive—Continued.

Names of claimants.	Nature or object of the claim.	Congress.	Session.	How brought before the House of Reps.	Page of journal.	To what committee of the House referred.	No. or date of the report.	Nature of the report.	No. of the bill.	How disposed of by the House of Reps.	How disposed of by the Senate.	Date of the act of Congress, and remarks.
Pearl, Abegail	(See Stephen Pearl, widow of)	17	1		323							
Pearl, Frederick	Arrears of pension	25	2	Petition	54	Rev. Pensions				Discharged; laid on table.		
Pearl, Frederick	Arrears of pension	25	3	Petition	674					Laid on table.		
Pearl, Frederick	Arrears of pension	28	2	Petition	57	Rev. Pensions				Discharged; laid on table.		
Pearl, John	Pension	21	1	Petition	36	Military Pensions	Jan. 5, 1830	By bill	72	Passed	Passed	App'd May 20, 1830
Pearl, John	Pension	31	1	Petition	623	Invalid Pensions	486	Adverse		Laid on table.		
Pearl, Stephen, widow of.	Estate to be released from liability as surety.	17	1	Petition	323	Ways and Means	Mar. 18, 1822	Adverse		Laid on table.		
Pearson, Abel	To change location of land	25	2	Resolution	188	Public Lands.						
Pearson, Ann	(See Benjamin Pearson, widow of)	21	1		234							
Pearson, Amos	Invalid pension	3	1	Rep. of Secretary War.	131	Select.						
Pearson, Amos	Invalid pension	3	2	Rep. of Secretary War.	262	Claims.						
Pearson, Amos	Invalid pension	4	1	Rep. of Secretary War.	445	Claims	Feb. 18, 1796	Favorable; bill	156	Passed	Passed	App'd April 20, 1796
Pearson, Amos	Indemnity for French spoliations prior to 1800.	26	1	Memorial	182	Foreign Affairs	343	Favorable; bill	319	Referred to Committee Whole House.		
Pearson, Benjamin, widow of.	Indemnity for losses caused by seizure of schooner Dolphin by U. States officers.	21	1	Petition	234	Commerce	Feb. 9, 1830	Adverse		Laid on table.		
Pearson, David	Pension	22	1	Petition	89, 509	Invalid Pensions	474	Favorable; bill	576	Passed	Laid on table.	
Pearson, David	Pension	22	2	House bill	334	Whole House			738			
Pearson, David	Pension	23	1	Resolution	587	Invalid Pensions	545	Favorable; bill	550	Referred to Committee Whole House.		
Pearson, David	Pension	23	2	Bill of last sess.	336	Whole House	Feb. 6, 1835	With't amend.	550	Passed	Passed	App'd March 3, 1835
Pearson, George	Benefit of act of 31st March, 1814, in relation to claimants to land in Mississippi Territory.	15	1	Petition	22	Public Lands	52	Favorable; bill	42	Passed	Passed	App'd April 16, 1818
Pearson, James, executors of.	Compensation for services in revolutionary war.	13	2	Petition	246	Pens. & Rev. Cl'ms.				Discharged; leave to withdraw.		
Pearson, John	Correction of error in date of loan certificate.	3	1	Petition	77					Referred to Secretary Treasury.		
Pearson, John	Correction of error in date of loan certificate.	3	2	Rep. of Secretary Treasury.	284					Laid on table.		
Pearson, John	Indemnity for French spoliations prior to 1800.	26	1	Memorial	182	Foreign Affairs	343	Favorable; bill	319	Referred to Committee Whole House.		
Pearson, John, *et al.*	Indemnity for French spoliations prior to 1800.	23	1	Petition	310	Foreign Affairs.						
Pearson, John, executors of	Indemnity for French spoliations prior to 1800.	28	1	Petition	245	Foreign Affairs.						
Pearson, Capt. John, representatives of.	Remuneration for revolutionary services and losses.	26	1	Petition	360	Claims.						
Pearson, Joshua	Revolutionary pension	31	2	Petition	447	Rev. Pensions	Mar. 3, 1851	Adverse		Laid on table.		
Pearson, Meshac	Arrears of pension	22	1	Petition	509	Rev. Pensions.						
Pearson, Meshac	Arrears of pension	23	1	Petition	216	Rev. Pensions	Feb. 18, 1834	Adverse		Laid on table.		
Pearson, Moses	Compensation for a horse lost in public service.	24	2	Petition	208	Claims				Discharged; laid on table.		
Pearson, Paul, *et al*	To refund duties paid on Holland gin.	23	1	Petition	328	Ways and Means	Mar. 7, 1834	Adverse		Laid on table.		

List of private claims presented to the House of Representatives of the United States from the 1st to the 31st Congress, inclusive—Continued.

Names of claimants.	Nature or object of the claim.	Congress.	Session.	How brought before the House of Reps.	Page of journal.	To what committee of the House referred.	No. or date of the report.	Nature of the report.	No. of the bill.	How disposed of by the House of Reps.	How disposed of by the Senate.	Date of the act of Congress, and remarks.
Pearson, Samuel	(See Robert Patton & Co., and others.)	8	2	....	127							
Pearson, Simon T.	(See John Pearson, executors of.)	28	1	....	245							
Pearson, Thomas	Increase of pension	9	2	House bill	608	Whole House	Feb. 28, 1807	With amend.	216	Passed	Passed	App'd March 3, 1807
Pearson, Thomas, (Ky.)	Invalid pension, wounded in revolu ionary war.	12	1	Petition	172	Claims	June 12, 1812	Adverse	......	Laid on table.		
Pearson, Thomas, (Ky.)	Invalid pension	16	1	Petition	26	Pens. & Rev. Cl'ms.	....	....	......	Discharged; laid on table.		
Pearson, Thomas, (Ky.)	Invalid pension	19	1	Petition	364	Military Pensions	164	Adverse	......	Laid on table.		
Pearson, Thomas, widow of.	Pension	19	2	Petition	285	Military Pensions	....	....	......	Discharged; laid on table.		
Pearson, Thomas, widow of.	Pension	20	1	Petition	243	Military Pensions	May 13, 1828	Adverse	......	Laid on table.		
Pearson, Thomas, widow of.	Commutation of half-pay	21	2	Petition	191	Rev. Claims	....	....	......	Discharged; laid on table.		
Pearson, Thomas, widow of.	Commutation of half-pay	22	1	Petition	210	Rev. Claims.						
Pearson, Thomas, heirs of.	Commutation of half pay	23	1	Petition	158	Rev. Claims.						
Pearson, Thomas, heirs of.	Pension for services of deceased	28	1	Petition	687	Rev. Pensions.						
Pearson, William	Indemnity for French spoliations prior to 1800.	26	1	Memorial	182	Foreign Affairs	343	Favorable; bill	319	Referred to Committee Whole House.		
Pease, Bartlett	Invalid pension	30	1	Petition	166	Invalid Pensions	359	Adverse	......	Discharged.		
Pease, Daniel, jr.	Renewal of patent for smut machine	23	1	Petition	656	Patents.						
Pease, Daniel, jr.	Renewal of patent for smut machine	23	2	Petition	102	Judiciary.						
Pease, Daniel, jr.	Renewal of patent for smut machine	24	1	Petition	106	Patents	May 11, 1836	Adverse	......	Laid on table.		
Pease, Daniel, jr.	Renewal of patent for smut machine	24	2	Petition	155	Patents	Jan. 5, 1837	Adverse	......	Laid on table.		
Pease, David	Pension	21	2	Petition	208	Military Affairs.						
Pease, John H.	Remission of fine incurred under coasting act of 1795.	25	2	Petition	113	Commerce	233	Favorable; bill	273	Referred to Committee Whole House.		
Pease, John H.	Remission of fine incurred under coasting act of 1795.	25	3	Bill of last sess.	376	Whole House	Jan. 25, 1839	With't amend.	273	Passed	Passed	App'd March 2, 1839
Pease, John H.	(See Pope, Morgan, and others)	30	1	....	838							
Pease, L. T., and J. M. Smith.	For travelling expenses as commissioner to Creek and Seminole Indians	28	2	Petition	135	Indian Affairs	March 1, 1845	By bill	92	Referred to Committee Whole House.		
Pease, L. T., and J. M. Smith.	For travelling expenses as commissioner to Creek and Seminole Indians.	29	1	Petition	93	Indian Affairs	88	Adverse	......	Laid on table.		
Pease, Silas	Pension	21	1	Petition	49	Military Pensions	Jan. 5, 1830	By bill	72	Passed	Passed	App'd May 20, 1830
Pease, William	Invalid pension	25	2	Petition	57	Invalid Pensions	Dec. 22, 1837	Adverse	......	Laid on table.		
Peaslee, John H., *et al.*	Release from imprisonment on judgments at suit of United States.	13	3	Petition	484	Ways and Means	Oct. 31, 1814	Adverse	......	Recommitted.		
Peaslee, John H., *et al.*	Release from imprisonment on judgments at suit of United States.	14	1	Petition	93	Select	Mar. 28, 1816	By bill	......	Indefinitely postponed.		
Peasner, William	(See Louis F. Beeler, and others)	30	1	....	115	....	482					
Peck, Aaron	Invalid pension	12	1	House bill	361	Whole House	June 15, 1812	With amend.	138	Passed	Passed	App'd July 5, 1812
Peck, Adam	For an equitable settlement of his accounts.	19	1	Petition	223	Claims	....	....	......	Discharged; laid on table.		
Peck, Adam	For an equitable settlement of his accounts.	19	2	Petition	26	Claims	....	....	.....	Discharged; laid on table.		
Peck, Adam	For an equitable settlement of his accounts.	20	1	Petition	226	Claims.						

List of private claims presented to the House of Representatives of the United States from the 1st to the 31st Congress, inclusive—Continued.

Names of claimants.	Nature or object of the claim.	Congress.	Session.	How brought before the House of Reps.	Page of journal.	To what committee of the House referred.	No. or date of the report.	Nature of the report.	No. of the bill.	How disposed of by the House of Reps.	How disposed of by the Senate.	Date of the act of Congress, and remarks.
Peck, Adam	For an equitable settlement of his accounts.	21	2	Petition	88	Claims	32	Favorable; bill	549	Referred to Committee Whole House.		
Peck, Adam	For an equitable settlement of his accounts.	22	1	Petition	26	Claims	Dec. 19, 1831	Favorable; bill	33	Passed	Passed	App'd Feb. 18, 1832
Peck, Alexander D. wife of.	Confirmation of title to land	29	1	Petition	502	Priv. Land Claims.						
Peck, Alexander D. wife of.	Confirmation of title to land	29	2	Petition	83	Priv. Land Claims.						
Peck, Alexander D. wife of.	Confirmation of title to land	30	1	Petition	240	Priv. Land Claims.	334	Favorable; bill	311	Passed	Passed	App'd June 28, 1848
Peck, Charles	Payment for articles furnished soldiers as sutler to 12th regiment of United States infantry in 1814.	20	1	Petition	57	Claims	Jan. 4, 1828	Adverse	......	Laid on table.		
Peck, Christopher	Revolutionary pension	19	2	Petition	91	Military Pensions.						
Peck, Elizabeth	Continuation of pension	28	1	Petition	72	Rev. Pensions.						
Peck, George, widow of	Revolutionary pension	25	2	Petition	198	Rev. Pensions.						
Peck, George, widow of	Revolutionary pension	25	3	Petition	126	Rev. Pensions	....	....	......	Discharged; laid on table.		
Peck, George, widow of	Revolutionary pension	26	1	Petition	174	Rev. Pensions	....	....	......	Discharged; laid on table.		
Peck, Capt. G. W.	Pension for services in Mexican war.	31	1	Petition	672	Invalid Pensions.						
Peck, Ichabod, widow of	Payment for property destroyed by United States troops.	25	3	Petition	206	Claims	282	Adverse	......	Laid on table.		
Peck, Ichabod, widow of	Compensation for revolutionary services.	29	1	Petition	102	Rev. Claims	120	Adverse	......	Laid on table.		
Peck, Jacob, heirs of	Compensation for wagons and teams impressed into United States service in revolutionary war.	23	2	Petition	84	Claims.						
Peck, Jacob, heirs of	Compensation for wagons and teams impressed into United States service in revolutionary war.	24	1	Petition	138	Rev. Claims	Feb. 16, 1836	Adverse	......	Laid on table.		
Peck, John	Payment of three final settlement certificates.	22	1	Resolution	394	Rev. Claims	March 9, 1832	Favorable; bill	455	Passed	Passed	App'd July 14, 1832
Peck, John	Interest on amount allowed on above certificates.	22	2	Resolution	61	Claims	38	Favorable; bill	681	Referred to Committee Whole House.		
Peck, John	Interest on amount allowed on above certificates.	23	1	Petition	396	Claims.						
Peck, John	Interest on amount allowed on above certificates.	23	1	Senate bill	845	Rev. Claims	Jan. 28, 1834	With't amend.	S. 126	Passed	Passed	App'd June 30, 1834
Peck, Jonathan	Pension	20	2	Petition	262	Military Pensions	....	....	......	Discharged; laid on table.		
Peck, Jonathan	Pension	21	1	Petition	144	Military Pensions	....	....	......	Discharged; laid on table.		
Peck, Joseph	Increase of pension	28	1	Petition	434	Naval Affairs.						
Peck, Mary	(See Ichabod Peck, widow of)	25	3	....	206							
Peck, Oliver	Revolutionary pension	24	2	Petition	271	Rev. Pensions	221	Favorable; bill	928	Referred to Committee Whole House.		
Peck, Oliver	Revolutionary pension	25	2	Petition	38	Rev. Pensions	158	Favorable; bill	183	Passed	Adverse report.	
Peck, Oliver	Revolutionary pension	25	3	Petition	88	Rev. Pensions	29	Favorable; bill	929	Passed	Adverse report	
Peck, Oliver	Revolutionary pension	26	1	Petition	172	Rev. Pensions	....	....	......	Discharged; laid on table.		
Peck, Peter	Payment for a horse lost in United States service.	21	1	Petition	262	Claims	408	Favorable; bill	475	Referred to Committee Whole House.		
Peck, Peter	Payment for a horse lost in United States service.	21	2	Bill of last sess.	265	Whole House	Feb. 4, 1831	Favorable	475	Passed	Report'd with't amendment.	

List of private claims presented to the House of Representatives of the United States from the 1st to the 31st Congress, inclusive—Continued.

Names of claimants.	Nature or object of the claim.	Congress.	Session.	How brought before the House of Reps.	Page of journal.	To what committee of the House referred.	No. or date of the report.	Nature of the report.	No. of the bill.	How disposed of by the House of Reps.	How disposed of by the Senate.	Date of the act of Congress, and remarks.
Peck, Peter	Payment for a horse lost in United States service.	22	1	Petition	43	Claims	Dec. 19, 1831	Favorable; bill	29	Passed	Passed	App'd Feb. 24, 1832
Peck, Phœbe	(See George Peck, widow of)	25	2		198							
Peck, Thomas M., assignee of.	Arrears of pay and travelling expenses.	19	1	Petition	407	Claims	165	Favorable; bill	217	Passed.		
Peck, Thomas M., assignee of.	Arrears of pay and travelling expenses.	19	2	Petition	82	Claims	Dec. 22, 1826	By bill	313	Passed	Passed	App'd Feb. 22, 1827
Peck, Ward	Increase of pension	25	2	Petition	53	Rev. Pensions				Discharged; laid on table.		
Peck, Ward	Increase of pension	26	1	Petition	174	Rev. Pensions				Discharged; laid on table.		
Peck, William	Release from prison where he is confined at suit of United States, being insolvent.	12	1	Petition	351	Select.	June 1, 1812	By bill	136	Passed	Passed	App'd June 26, 1812
Peckett, William R.	Confirmation of Spanish land title.	22	1	Petition	263	Priv. Land Claims.	Feb. 17, 1823	By bill	380	Referred to Committee Whole House.		
Peckham, Benedict, widow of.	Release of deceased's estate from judgment for duties on rum.	8	2	Petition	133	Com. and Manuf.						
Peckham, Benedict, widow of.	Release of deceased's estate from judgment for duties on rum.	9	1	Petition	195	Com. and Manuf.	Jan. 20, 1806	Res. for leave to withdraw.		Resolution adopted.		
Peckham, Elizabeth	(See Benedict Peckham, widow of)	8	2		133							
Peckham, Philip	Compensation for building and repairing boats for the American army.	3	1	Petition and rep't Sec. of War.	50	Select.						
Peckham, Samuel, jr., inspector of customs.	Fees on seles of seized goods	15	2	Petition	262	Ways and Means.						
Peckham, Samuel, jr.	Fees on sales of seized goods	16	1	Petition	141	Ways and Means.						
Peckham, Samuel, jr.	Fees on sales of seized goods	16	2	Petition	32	Ways and Means.	Nov. 24, 1820	Adverse		Laid on table.		
Peckham, William	Revolutionary pension	24	1	Petition	662	Rev. Pensions				Discharged; laid on table.		
Peckham, William	Revolutionary pension	24	2	Petition	70	Rev. Pensions.						
Peckham, William	Revolutionary pension	25	2	Petition	117	Rev. Pensions	581	Adverse		Laid on table.		
Peden, or Pedru, William W., *et al.*	Compensation for services as volunteers in Cherokee country in 1838, and for wagon and team.	26	1	Petition	340	Claims				Discharged; leave to withdraw.		
Peden, or Pedru, William W., *et al.*	Compensation for services as volunteers in Cherokee country in 1838, and for wagon and team.	26	2	Petition	205	Claims.						
Peden, or Pedru, William W., *et al.*	Compensation for services as volunteers in Cherokee country in 1838, and for wagon and team.	27	2	Petition	94	Claims	1017	Adverse as to Peden.				
Pedesclaux, Peter	Compensation for losses by being deprived of certain rights by the cession of Louisiana to the United States.	8	2	Petition	77	Claims	Jan. 24, 1805	Adverse; leave to withdraw.		Report adopted.		
Pedesclaux, Peter	Compensation for losses by being deprived of certain rights by the cession of Louisiana to the United States.	11	2	Petition	193	Select	April 10, 1810	Res. for leave to withdraw.		Resolution adopted.		
Pedrick, Samuel	(See Barney Tisdale, and others)	22	1		868							
Pedrick, William	(See Philip B. Holmes, *et al.*)	28	1		517							
Peebles, Abner	Revolutionary pension	22	1	Petition	44	Rev. Claims	102	Favorable; bill	190	Referred to Committee Whole House.		

List of private claims presented to the House of Representatives of the United States from the 1st to the 31st Congress, inclusive—Continued.

Names of claimants.	Nature or object of the claim.	Congress.	Session.	How brought before the House of Reps.	Page of journal.	To what committee of the House referred.	No. or date of the report.	Nature of the report.	No. of the bill.	How disposed of by the House of Reps.	How disposed of by the Senate.	Date of the act of Congress, and remarks.
Peebles, Abner	Revolutionary pension	22	2	House bill	66				190	Laid on table		
Peebles, John	(See William Peebles, heir of)	23	2		38							
Peebles, John	Payment for services as collector of the revenue.	25	2	Petition	416	Claims.						
Peebles, John	Payment for services as collector of the revenue.	25	3	Petition	107	Claims	64	Adverse		Laid on table.		
Peebles, John	Payment for services as collector of the revenue.	26	1	Petition	337	Claims.						
Peebles, John	Payment for services as collector of the revenue.	27	2	Petition	56	Claims	183	Adverse		Laid on table.		
Peebles, Robert H.	Permission to correct error in entry of land.	22	2	Petition	110	Public Lands	Jan. 4, 1833	Favorable; bill	659	Passed.		
Peebles, Robert, and James Graham.	Settlement of accounts arising from non fulfillment of contract with War Department.	24	1	Petition	662	Claims	680	Favorable; bill	640	Referred to Committee Whole House.		
Peebles, Robert, and James Graham.	Settlement of accounts arising from non-fulfillment of contract with War Department.	25	2	Petition	37	Claims	46	Favorable; bill	58	Passed	Passed	App'd Mar. 19, 1838
Peebles, William, heir of.	Bounty land for revolutionary services.	23	2	Petition	38	Rev. Claims	Dec. 15, 1834	Adverse		Laid on table.		
Peebles, William, heir of.	Bounty land for revolutionary services.	24	1	Petition	104	Rev. Claims.						
Peebles, William, heir of.	Bounty land for revolutionary services.	25	2	Petition	49	Rev. Claims				Discharged; laid on table.		
Peebles, William, heir of.	Bounty land for revolutionary services.	25	3	Petition	84	Rev. Claims.						
Peebles, William, heir of.	Bounty land for revolutionary services.	26	1	Petition	165	Rev. Claims.						
Peed, Nathaniel, and John Brooks.	Reimbursement of cost of suit against them by United States.	8	1	Petition	565	Claims	Mar. 7, 1804	Adverse		Leave to withdraw.		
Peery, William	Liquidation of claims against United States.	1	2	Petition	244					Referred to Secretary of Treasury.		
Peery, William	Land for services under General Clarke, revolutionary war.	20	2	Petition	119	Priv. Land Claims.				Discharged; laid on table.		
Peery, William	Land for services under General Clark, revolutionary war.	21	1	Petition	91	Rev. Claims				Discharged; laid on table.		
Pegg, Benjamin	Land for revolutionary services	26	1	Petition	333	Public Lands				Disch'd; laid on table.		
Pegg, Benjamin	Land for revolutionary services	27	2	Petition	98	Public Lands.						
Pegg, Benjamin	Land for revolutionary services	27	3	Petition	71	Public Lands	98	Adverse		Laid on table.		
Pegg, Elias	Arrears of pension	24	1	Resolution	513	Rev. Pensions				Discharged; laid on table.		
Pegion, John	Pension	19	2	Petition	85	Military Pensions.				Discharged; laid on table.		
Pegman, John G.	Compensation for losses sustained in the late war.	27	2	Petition	613	Claims	Mar. 20, 1842	Adverse		Laid on table.		
Peirratt, Valentine	Revolutionary pension	24	1	Resolution	216	Rev. Pensions	Mar. 3, 1836	Adverse		Laid on table.		
Peixotto, Raphael	Drawback on goods lost at sea	22	1	Petition	1063	Ways and Means.						
Pelaskie, Charles G.	Payment of certain bills of credi issued by the State of Virginia in revolutionary war.	4	1	Rep. of Secretary Treasury.	388	Claims	May 31, 1796	Adverse		Laid on table.		
Pelfrey, William	Revolutionary pension	30	1	Petition	597	Rev. Pensions	533	Adverse		Laid on table.		
Pelham, Maj. Charles, widow of.	Commutation of half-pay for life.	23	2	Petition	240	Rev. Claims.						

List of private claims presented to the House of Representativesthe of United States from the 1st to the 31st Congress, inclusive—Continued.

Names of claimants.	Nature or object of the claim.	Congress.	Session.	How brought before the House of Reps.	Page of journal.	To what committee of the House referred.	No. or date of the report.	Nature of the report.	No. of the bill.	How disposed of by the House of Reps.	How disposed of by the Senate.	Date of the act of Congress, and remarks.
Pelham, Isabella	(See Charles Pelham, widow of).	23	2	....	240							
Peling, Robert	Compensation for services and injuries in revolutionary war.	3	2	Petition	239	Claims	Jan. 6, 1795	Adverse	......	Referred to Committee Whole House.		
Peling, Robert	Compensation for services and injuries in revolutionary war.	4	2	Petition	700	Claims	Feb. 15, 1797	Adverse	......	Rejected.		
Peling, Robert	Compensation for services and injuries in revolutionary war.	24	1	Petition	137	Claims	Mar. 25, 1836	Adverse	......	Laid on table.		
Pell, Joseph Simon, heirs of.	Further compensation as surgeon in State navy of Virginia in revolutionary war.	25	2	Petition	269	Rev. Claims	962	Adverse	......	Laid on table.		
Pell, Joseph Simon, heirs of.	Further compensation as surgeon in State navy of Virginia in revolutionary war.	26	1	Petition	167	Rev. Claims.						
Pell, Joseph Simon, heirs of.	Further compensation as surgeon in State navy of Virginia in revolutionary war.	26	2	Petition	212	Rev. Claims.						
Pell, Joseph Simon, heirs of.	Further compensation as surgeon in State navy of Virginia in revolutionary war.	27	2	Petition	309	Rev. Claims	540	Adverse	......	Laid on table.		
Pellardie, Pierre, & C. Lamarch.	Indemnity for Indian depredations.	24	2	Petition	49	Priv. Land Claims.						
Pellardie, Pierre, & C. Lamarch.	Indemnity for Indian depredations.	25	2	Petition	398	Claims.						
Pellerin, Barthelemy	Compensation for a quantity of timber and wood furnished United States troops in 1812.	20	1	Petition	38	Claims.						
Pellerin, Barthelemy	Compensation for a quantity of timber and wood furnished United States troops in 1812.	21	1	Petition	170	Claims	Feb. 1, 1830	Adverse	......	Laid on table.		
Pelleron, Barthlomew, heirs of.	Confirmation of land title and the issuance of patent.	27	2	Petition	106, 1457	Priv. Land Claims.	282	Favorable; bill	248	Passed	Passed	App'd Aug. 1, 1842
Pelleron, Lewis, heirs of.	Confirmation of title to land	20	1	Petition	33	Priv. Land Claims.	....	....	......	Discharged; laid on table.		
Pelleron, Lewis, heirs of.	Confirmation of title to land	20	2	Petition	34	Priv. Land Claims.	....	....	......	Discharged; laid on table.		
Pelleron, Lewis, heirs of.	Confirmation of title to land	21	1	Petition	40	Priv. Land Claims.	Jan. 18, 1830	Adverse	......	Laid on table.		
Pelleron, Lewis, heirs of.	Confirmation of title to land	21	2	Petition	55	Priv. Land Claims.	....	....	......	Discharged; laid on table.		
Pelleron, Lewis, heirs of.	Confirmation of title to land	22	1	Petition	66	Priv. Land Claims.	284	Favorable; bill	369	Referred to Committee Whole House.		
Pelleron, Lewis, heirs of.	Confirmation of title to land	23	1	Petition	76	Priv. Land Claims.						
Pelleron, Lewis, heirs of.	Confirmation of title to land	23	2	Petition	166	Priv. Land Claims.	40	Favorable; bill	624	Referred to Committee Whole House.		
Pellett, John	Indemnity for damage to his land by British and American armies, near New Orleans.	15	1	Petition	72	Claims	....	....	......	Discharged; laid on table.		
Pellett, John	Indemnity for damage to his land by British and American armies, near New Orleans.	15	2	Senate bill	325	Claims	....	....	S. 71			
Pellett, John	Indemnity for damage to his land by British and American armies, near New Orleans.	16	1	Senate bill	290	Claims	Mar. 24, 1820	Adverse	S. 50	Laid on table.		

List of private claims presented to the House of Representatives of the United States from the 1st to the 31st Congress, inclusive—Continued.

Names of claimants	Nature or object of the claim.	Congress.	Session.	How brought before the House of Reps.	Page of journal.	To what committee of the House referred.	No. or date of the report.	Nature of the report.	No. of the bill.	How disposed of by the House of Reps.	How disposed of by the Senate.	Date of the act of Congress, and remarks.
Pellett, John	Indemnity for damage to his land by British and American armies, near New Orleans.	17	1	Petition	47	Claims	Jan. 30, 1822	Favorable; bill	65	Passed	Passed	App'd May 7, 1822
Pellicer, Francis, representatives of.	Revisal of decision of the Secretary of Treasury on certain claims.	26	1	Petition	339	Claims	57	Adverse	......	Laid on table.		
Pellicer, Francis, representatives of.	Revisal of decision of the Secretary of Treasury on certain claims.	27	2	Petition	390	Claims	908	Favorable; bill	525	Referred to Committee Whole House.		
Pellicer, Francis, representatives of.	Revisal of decision of the Secretary of Treasury on certain claims.	27	3	Bill of last sess.	91	Whole House	Dec. 23, 1842	Favorable	525	Passed	Indef. postp'd.	
Pellieu, Antonio, Frances, and James.	Indemnity for Indian depredations in East Florida.	25	3	Petition	121	Claims	162	Adverse	......	Laid on table.		
Pelot, James	Compensation for services as assessor, and for a negro taken by the British.	15	1	Petition	272	Ways and Means.						
Pelot, Joseph S.	Increase of compensation as naval officer at Savannah.	21	1	Memorial	58	Commerce.						
Pelot, Joseph S.	Increase of compensation as naval officer at Savannah.	22	1	Memorial	74	Commerce.						
Peltier, Antoine, heirs of.	Indemnity for advances to the regiment of General Clarke.	23	1	Senate bill	846	Rev. Claims	....	....	S. 139			
Peltier, Antoine, heirs of.	Indemnity for advances to the regiment of General Clarke.	24	2	Senate bill	250	Rev. Claims	....	....	S. 18			
Peltier, Antoine, heirs of.	Indemnity for advances to the regiment of General Clarke.	26	1	Senate bill	811	Rev. Claims	519	Adverse	S. 39	Referred to Committee Whole House.		
Peltier, Antoine, heirs of.	Indemnity for advances to the regiment of General Clarke.	28	1	House bill	268	Rev. Claims	....	....	83			
Peltier, Antoine, heirs of.	Indemnity for advances to the regiment of General Clarke.	30	1	Petition	69	Claims	343	Favorable; bill	323	Referred to Committee Whole House.		
Peltier, Antoine, heirs of.	Indemnity for advances to the regiment of General Clarke.	31	1	Petition	472	Claims	179	Favorable; bill	46	Referred to Committee Whole House.		
Peltier, Louis	Confirmation of title to land in Missouri.	15	1	Petition	102	Priv. Land Claims.	....	....	......	Discharged; laid on table.		
Peltier, Francis, heirs of.	Confirmation of title to land in the district of Vincennes.	12	2	House bill	609	Whole House	Jan. 18, 1813	With't amend.	222	Passed	Passed	App'd Feb. 13, 1813
Pelton, Samuel	Pension	21	1	Petition	260	Military Pensions.	....	....	......	Discharged; laid on table.		
Pelton, Samuel	Pension	21	2	Petition	127	Military Pensions.						
Pember, Eli	Compensation for services in the last war.	29	1	Petition	315	Priv. Land Claims.						
Pemberton, John, widow of.	Revolutionary pension	24	2	Resolution	222	Rev. Pensions	139	Favorable; bill	868	Referred to Committee Whole House.		
Pemberton, John, widow of.	Revolutionary pension	25	2	Petition	58	Rev. Pensions	456	Favorable; bill	459	Passed	Passed	App'd July 7, 1838
Pemberton, Sarah	(See John Pemberton, widow of).	24	2	....	222							
Pemberton, William	Compensation for a horse lost in United States service in 1813.	16	1	Resolution	314	Claims.						
Pemberton, William	Compensation for a horse lost in United States service in 1813.	18	2	Resolution	85	Claims	16	Favorable; bill	257	Passed	Passed	App'd March 3, 1835
Pembleton, Jabez	Increase of pension	9	2	House bill	608	Whole House	Feb. 28, 1807	With amend.	216	Passed	Passed	App'd March 2, 1807
Pendergast, William, widow of.	Revolutionary pension	26	1	Petition	322	Rev. Pensions.						
Pendergast, William, widow of.	Revolutionary pension	26	2	Petition	78	Rev. Pensions	....	....	......	Discharged; laid on table.		

List of private claims presented to the House of Representatives of the United States from the 1st to the 31st Congress, inclusive—Continued.

Names of claimants.	Nature or object of the claim.	Congress.	Session.	How brought before the House of Reps.	Page of journal.	To what committee of the House referred.	No. or date of the report.	Nature of the report.	No. of the bill.	How disposed of by the House of Reps.	How disposed of by the Senate.	Date of the act of Congress, and remarks.
Pendergrass, Ellen	(See Michael Pendergrass, widow of.)	27	3		206							
Pendergrass, G. J	Allowance for medical expenses incurred as commandant of navy-yard, Memphis.	31	1	Petition	827	Naval Affairs.						
Pendergrass, Michael	Pension	14	2	Rep. of Secretary War.	131	Pens. & Rev. Cl'ms.	Jan. 17, 1817	Report and res. for leave to withdraw.		Resolution adopted.		
Pendergrass, Michael, widow of.	Pension	27	3	Petition	206	Invalid Pensions.						
Pendergrass, Robert	Pension	31	1	Petition	944	Invalid Pensions.						
Pendergrass, Thomas	Bounty land for revolutionary services.	17	1	Senate bill	482	Public Lands			S. 83			
Pendergrass, Thomas	(See represent's of James Albert)	18	1		76							
Pendexter, Thomas	Pension	19	2	House bill	85	Whole House	Feb. 2, 1827	With amend.	314	Passed	Passed	App'd March 3, 1837
Pendleton, Benjamin	Refunding money paid for cancelling charter party and outfit and demurrage of brig Seraph.	21	2	House bill	129	Whole House	Feb. 17, 1831	With amend.	531	Passed	Passed	App'd March 2, 1831
Pendleton, Benjamin	Compensation for services and damages as pilot.	21	2	Petition	84	Naval Affairs	418	Favorable; bill	498	Referred to Committee Whole House.		
Pendleton, Benjamin	Compensation for services and damages as pilot.	22	1	Petition	106	Naval Affairs.						
Pendleton, Benjamin, *et al.*	Compensation for certain benefits to the trade of the United States, and for an outfit for expedition to the South sea	22	1	Petition	78	Naval Affairs.						
Pendleton, Benjamin, *et al.*	Compensation for certain benefits to the trade of the United States.	22	2	Memorial	30	Commerce.						
Pendleton, Benjamin, *et al.*	Compensation for certain benefits to the trade of the United States.	23	1	Memorial	37	Naval Affairs				Discharged; laid on table.		
Pendleton, David	Invalid pension	3	1	Rep. of Secretary War.	131	Select	May 26, 1794	Jt. res. to refer to Sec. War.	R. 12	Passed	Passed	App'd June 9, 1794
Pendleton, David	Invalid pension	4	1	Rep. of Secretary War.	445	Claims	Mar. 4, 1796	Jt. res. to refer to Sec. War.	R. 16	Passed	Passed	App'd April 18, 1796
Pendleton, David	Invalid pension	10	2	House bill	499	Whole House	Feb. 20, 1809	With amend.	158	Passed	Passed	App'd March 3, 1809
Pendleton, James	Pre-emption right to land in Alabama.	18	2	Petition	211	Public Lands.						
Pendleton, Libeus, *et al.*	Fishing bounty on schooner Mary Elizabeth.	10	1	Petition	238	Com. and Manuf.						
Pendleton, Otis and Harris, *et al.*	Fishing bounty on a vessel lost at sea.	18	1	Petition	153	Commerce.						
Pendleton, Otis and Harris, *et al.*	Fishing bounty on a vessel lost at sea.	18	2	House bill	243	Whole House	Feb. 17, 1825	Favorable	340	Passed	Passed	App'd March 3, 1825
Pendleton, Zebulon E	Pre-emption right to land	28	1	Petition	333	Public Lands.						
Penhallow, Daniel	Pension	21	2	Petition	127	Military Pensions.						
Penhallow, Daniel	Pension	22	1	Petition	114	Invalid Pensions	Jan. 11, 1832	Adverse		Laid on table.		
Penhallow, Daniel	Pension	26	2	Petition	84	Invalid Pensions.						
Penhallow, Daniel	Pension	27	2	Petition	60	Invalid Pensions	982	Favorable; bill	563	Referred to Committee Whole House.		
Penhallow, Daniel	Pension	27	3	Bill of last sess.	91	Whole House	Dec. 23, 1842	Favorable	563	Passed	Passed	App'd March 3, 1843
Penland, Noble A	Back pension	28	2	Petition	141	Invalid Pensions	83	Adverse		Laid on table.		
Penland, Noble A	Back pension	29	1	Petition	189	Invalid Pensions	294	Adverse		Laid on table.		
Penley, Joseph	Invalid pension	24	1	Petition	73	Invalid Pensions	May 17, 1836	Adverse		Laid on table.		

3—7

List of private claims presented to the House of Representatives of the United States from the 1st to the 31st Congress, inclusive—Continued.

Names of claimants.	Nature or object of the claim.	Congress.	Session.	How brought before the House of Reps.	Page of journal.	To what committee of the House referred.	No. or date of the report.	Nature of the report.	No. of the bill.	How disposed of by the House of Reps.	How disposed of by the Senate.	Date of the act of Congress, and remarks.
Penley, Joseph	Invalid pension	25	2	Petition	722	Invalid Pensions	May 25, 1838	Adverse	......	Laid on table.		
Penley, Thankful	Benefit of act of July 7, 1838	30	1	Petition	406	Rev. Pensions	385	Adverse	......	Laid on table.		
Penn, Alexander G	Increase of salary as receiver of public money.	21	2	Petition	232	Public Lands.						
Penn, Alexander G	Increase of salary as receiver of public money.	22	1	Petition	75	Public Lands.						
Penn, Alexander G	Extra expenses incurred as postmaster at New Orleans.	31	1	Petition	742	P. Of. and P. Roads.						
Penn, Joshua H	(See Benjamin Ray.)	24	1	....	477							
Penn, Margaret	(See Shadrack Penn, widow of.)	26	1	....	385							
Penn, Shadrac, widow of	Revolutionary pension	26	1	Resolution	385	Rev. Pensions	664	Adverse	......	Laid on table	....	Jan. 22, 1849, leave to withdraw.
Pennell, Jacob, *et al.*	Refunding fine imposed for violating revenue laws.	26	1	Senate bill	836	Commerce.	June 2, 1840	With't amend.	S. 258	Referred to Committee Whole House.		
Pennell, Jocob, *et al.*	Refunding fine imposed for violating revenue laws.	26	2	Senate bill	256	....	....	....	S. 165			
Pennell, Jacob, *et al.*	Refunding fine imposed for violating revenue laws.	27	2	Senate bill	232	Commerce.	Jan. 18, 1842	With't amend.	S. 92	Passed	....	App'd June 27, 1842
Pennell, Thomas	Compensation for occupancy of houses and lots by United States troops, from February, 1813, to February, 1815.	20	1	Resolution	387	Claims	Mar. 25, 1828	Adverse	......	Laid on table.		
Penny, Joshua	Compensation for imprisonment and bad treatment by the British.	13	3	Petition	656	Claims	Jan. 18, 1815	Res.; adverse.	......	Resolution adopted.		
Penny, Joshua	Compensation for imprisonment and bad treatment by the British.	14	2	Petition	354	Pens. & Rev. Cl'ms.	Jan. 29, 1817	Favorable; bill	91	Passed	Passed	App'd March 3, 1817
Penney, J. P. and E. B., (Mexico.)	Refunding duties on jalap	21	2	Petition	44	Ways and Means.	88	Favorable; bill	636	Referred to Committee Whole House.		
Penney, J. P. and E. B., (Mexico.)	Refunding duties on jalap	22	1	Petition	41	Ways and Means.	4	Favorable; bill	49	Passed	Passed	App'd Mar. 15, 1832
Pennington, J	(See James Clark, administrator of.)	29	2	....	129							
Pennington, William, assignee of.	Permission to correct error in land patent.	23	2	Petition	91	Public Lands.	Jan. 12, 1835	Favorable; bill	626	Passed	Passed.	App'd March 3, 1835
Pennock, Abraham S. and George.	(See James Sellers, *et al.*)	28	1	....	707							
Pennock, Moses	Renewal of patent	24	1	Petition	211	Patents	....	....	......	Discharged; laid on table.		
Pennock, William, administrator of.	Indemnity for French spoliations prior to 1800.	26	1	Memorial	182	Foreign Affairs.	343	Favorable; bill	319	Referred to Committee Whole House.		
Pennoyer, James	Payment for services and loss of steamboat Dolphin.	25	3	Petition	205	Claims.						
Pennoyer, James	Payment for services and loss of steamboat Dolphin.	26	1	Petition	170	Claims.						
Pennoyer, James	Compensation for assistance to United States brig Porpoise in 1836.	26	2	Petition	135	Claims	104	Adverse	......	Laid on table.		
Pennoyer, James	Compensation for assistance to United States brig Porpoise in 1836.	29	1	Memorial	890	Naval Affairs.	704	Favorable; bill	479	Referred to Committee Whole House.		
Pennoyer, James	Compensation for assistance to United States brig Porpoise in 1836.	29	2	Bill of last sess.	382	Whole House	Feb. 19, 1847	With't amend.	479	Passed	Passed	App'd March 3, 1847
Pennquite, John	(See William Thompson)	19	1	....	312							
Pennsylvania, merchants of Philadelphia.	Further time for the payment of duties on merchandise.	2	1	Memorial	547, 560	....	....	....	......	Referred to Committee Whole House.		

List of private claims presented to the House of Representatives of the United States from the 1st to the 31st Congress, inclusive—Continued.

Names of claimants.	Nature or object of the claim.	Congress.	Session.	How brought before the House of Reps.	Page of journal.	To what committee of the House referred.	No. or date of the report.	Nature of the report.	No. of the bill.	How disposed of by the House of Reps.	How disposed of by the Senate.	Date of the act of Congress, and remarks.
Pennsylvania, merchants of Philadelphia.	(See William Davy and others)...	10	1	....	48							
Pennsylvania, commissioners of city and county of Philadelphia.	Compensation for use of jail for prisoners in revolutionary war.	2	1	Petition	573	....	....	....	.....	Referred to Secretary Treasury.		
Pennsylvania, wardens of churches in Chester co.	Compensation for damages to churches by revolutionary army.	2	1	Rep. of Secretary Treasury.	538	....	....	....	.....	Laid on table.		
Pennsylvania flying camp, Watt's regiment.	For pay while prisoners of war...	2	1	Petition	507	....	....	....	.....	Referred to Secretary War.		
Pennsylvania line, revolutionary army.	(See Philip Clamberg and others.)											
Pennsylvania navy, revolutionary war, officers of.	Compensation for services	1	3	Memorial	353	Select	Jan. 14, 1791	Adverse	.....	Rejected.	....	Leave to withdraw.
Pennsylvania line, revolutionary army, officers of.	Allowance for depreciation on certificate of debt.	2	2	Memorial	650	....	....	....	.....	Laid on table.		
Pennsylvania line, revolutionary army, officers of.	Allowance for depreciation of pay.	3	1	Petition and rep't Sec. of War.	60	Select.						
Pennsylvania line, revolutionary army, officers of.	Allowance for depreciation of pay.	10	2	Petition	375	Select.						
Pennsylvania line, revolutionary army, officers of.	Further compensation	12	1	Petition	149	Select.						
Pennsylvania line, revolutionary army, officers of.	Further compensation	14	1	Petition	416	Pens. & Rev. Cl'ms.						
Pennsylvania line, revolutionary army, officers of.	For whole amount of half-pay, deducting five years' full pay.	15	1	Petition	71	Select.						
Pennsylvania line, revolutionary army, officers of.	For some relief from government..	19	2	Petition	43	Military Pensions..	....	....	.....	Discharged; laid on table.		
Pennsylvania, citizens of western counties.	Indemnity for damages to property during the insurrection of 1792.	3	2	Presid'ts message.	233	Select	Dec. 11, 1794	Favorable; bill	90	Passed	Passed	App'd Feb. 27, 1795
Pennsylvania, citizens of western counties.	Compensation for property destroyed in 1792.	4	1	Petition	477	Claims.						
Pennsylvania, citizens of western counties.	Compensation for property destroyed in 1792.	4	2	Petition	614	Claims.						
Pennsylvania, citizens of western counties.	Compensation for property destroyed in 1792.	5	2	Petition	153	Claims	May 11, 1798	Adverse	.....	Leave to withdraw.		
Pennsylvania, citizens of western counties.	Compensation for property destroyed in 1792.	11	2	Petition	192	....	....	....	.....	Referred to Secretary War.		
Pennsylvania, citizens of Philadelphia.	Indemnity for French spoliations in 1793, 1794, and 1795.	4	1	Memorial......	524	Select.						
Pennsylvania, inspector of customs for the district of.	Increase of compensation	2	2	Rep of Secretary Treasury.	626	....	....	....	.....	Laid on table.		
Pennsylvania, inspector of customs for the district of.	Extra compensation for services during the prevalence of the yellow fever in 1793.	4	1	Memorial......	476	Claims	May 17, 1796	Favorable; bill	38	Referred to Committee Whole House.		
Pennsylvania, inspector of customs for the district of.	Increase of compensation	4	2	Memorial	636	Com. and Manuf..	Jan. 23, 1797	By bill	210	Referred to Committee Whole House.		
							Feb. 6, 1797	Amendat'y bill.	211	....	Passed	App'd March 3, 1797
Pennsylvania, inspector of customs for the district of.	Further increase of compensation.	9	1	Petition and rep't Sec. Treasury.	231	Ways and Means.						
Pennsylvania, inspector of customs for the district of.	Further increase of compensation.	9	2	Petition and rep't Sec. Treasury.	482	Ways and Means.						

List of private claims presented to the House of Representatives of the United States from the 1st to the 31st Congress, inclusive—Continued.

Names of claimants.	Nature or object of the claim	Congress.	Session.	How brought before the House of Reps.	Page of journal.	To what committee of the House referred.	No. or date of the report.	Nature of the report.	No. of the bill.	How disposed of by the House of Reps.	How disposed of by the Senate.	Date of the act of Congress, and remarks.
Pennsylvania, inspector of customs for the district of.	Further increase of compensation.	10	1	Petition	51	....	....	....	......	Referred to Committee Whole House.		
Pennsylvania, inspector of customs for the district of.	Further increase of compensation.	11	3	Petition and rep't Sec. Treasury.	535	....	....	....	......	Laid on table.		
Pennsylvania, inspector of customs for the district of.	Further increase of compensation.	14	1	Petition and rep't Sec. Treasury.	54	Ways and Means..	April 6, 1816	Favorable; bill	......	Passed	Passed	App'd April 27, 1816
Pennsylvania, measurers of salt and coal for the district of Philadelphia.	Increase of compensation........	9	1	Petition	256	Ways and Means.						
Pennsylvania, measurers of salt and coal for the district of Philadelphia.	Increase of compensation........	10	1	Petition	43	....	....	....	......	Referred to Committee Whole House.		
Pennsylvania, manufacturers and importers of copper, Philadelphia.	Remission of duties on copper and for refunding of duties paid.	9	1	Petition	315	Com. and Manuf.						
Pennsylvania, merchants of Philadelphia.	Extension of time for taking oath and giving bond in case of goods exported for drawback.	9	1	Petition	215	....	....	....	......	Referred to Committee Whole House on bill No. 80.		
Pennsylvania, merchants of Philadelphia.	Extension of time for taking oath and giving bond in case of goods exported for drawback.	9	2	Petition	555	....	....	....	......	Referred to Committee Whole House on bill No. 171.		
Pennsylvania, merchants of Philadelphia.	Release from operation of embargo act.	10	1	Memorial	106	Com. and Manuf..	Jan. 11, 1808	Rep. not found	......	Referred to Committee Whole House.		
Pennsylvania, merchants of Philadelphia.	Permission to import goods ordered prior to the President's proclamation in 1810.	12	1	Petition	261, 269, 295	....	....	....	......	Referred to Committee Whole House on bill No. 46.		
Pennsylvania, merchants of Philadelphia.	Release from penalties incurred by importing goods from Great Britain.	12	2	Petition	551, 556	Ways and Means..	Jan. 29, 1813	By bill......	239	Referred to Committee Whole House.	....	See act Feb. 27, 1813
Pennsylvania, merchants & underwriters of Philadelphia.	Indemnity for French spoliations prior to 1800.	15	1	Petition	115	Select	....	....	.....	Discharged; laid on table.		
Pennsylvania, merchants & insurance companies of Philadelphia.	Indemnity for French spoliatinos prior to 1800.	18	1	Memorial	33, 81	....	....	....	......	Laid on table.		
Pennsylvania, merchants of Philadelphia.	Indemnity for spoliations on their commerce by foreign nations.	19	2	Memorial	133	Foreign Affairs ...	....	....	......	Discharged; laid on table.		
Pennsalvania, merchants of Philadelphia.	Remission of additional duties imposed by new tariff.	20	2	Memorial	177	Whole House.....	....	....	......	Laid on table.		
Pennsylvania, merchants of Philadelphia.	Refunding duties paid on goods ..	23	1	Petition	48	Ways and Means.						
Pennsylvania, inhabitants of Marcus Hook.	Compensation for ground on which the public piers are erected.	11	1	Petition	16	Com. and Manuf.						
Pennsylvania, inhabitants of Marcus Hook.	Compensation for ground on which the public piers are erected.	11	2	Petition	119	Com. and Manuf.						
Pennsylvania, Bible Society of Philadelphia.	Remission of duties on a set of stereotype plates.	12	2	Petition	619	Ways and Means..	Jan. 18, 1813	By bill	232	Referred to Committee Whole House.		
Pennsylvania, Bible Society of Philadelphia.	Remission of duties on a set of stereotype plates.	12	2	Senate bill	623	Whole House.....	Jan. 29, 1813	With't amend.	S. 51	Passed	....	App'd Feb. 2, 1813

List of private claims presented to the House of Representatives of the United States from the 1st to the 31st Congress, inclusive—Continued.

Names of claimants.	Nature or object of the claim.	Congress.	Session.	How brought before the House of Reps.	Page of journal.	To what committee of the House referred.	No. or date of the report.	Nature of the report.	No. of the bill.	How disposed of by the House of Reps.	How disposed of by the Senate.	Date of the act of Congress, and remarks.
Pennsylvania, Bible Society of Philadelphia.	Remission of duties on a set of stereotype plates.	17	1	Petition	142	Ways and Means				Discharged; laid on table.		
Pennsylvania, Academy of Fine Arts.	Remission of duties on box of paintings and engravings.	13	1	Senate bill	107	Whole House	July 20, 1813	With't amend.	S. 23	Passed		App'd July 22, 1813
Pennsylvania, Susquehanna Bridge Company.	Exemption from law taxing bank notes.	13	2	Petition	190	Ways and Means	Jan. 10, 1814	Adverse		Rejected.		
Pennsylvania, Council of the City of Philadelphia.	For the admission of iron conduits free of duty.	15	2	Petition	267	Com. and Manuf.				Discharged; laid on table.		
Pennsylvania, citizens of Westmoreland.	(See Robert Campbell)											
Pennsylvania Hospital, managers of.	Exemption from property tax	14	1	Petition	543	Ways and Means				Discharged; laid on table.		
Pennsylvania Hospital, managers of.	Remission of duty on painting, by West.	15	1	Petition	22	Com. and Manuf.	Dec. 16, 1817	By bill	5	Passed	Passed	App'd Jan. 14, 1818
Pennsylvania, inhabitants of Lebanon county.	Release from fines for non-performance of military duty.	15	1	Petition	226					Referred to Secretary of War.		
Pennsylvania, General Assembly of.	Transfer of military fines, with power to collect.	17	1	Resolution	476	Select				Discharged; laid on table.		
Pennsylvania, distillers of Lancaster.	Refunding of duties on distilleries.	15	1	Petition	284	Ways and Means				Discharged; laid on table.		
Pennsylvania, distillers of Lancaster.	Refunding of duties on distilleries.	17	1	Petition	32	Ways and Means	Jan. 23, 1822	Favorable; bill	57	Passed	Passed	App'd April 26, 1822
Pennsylvania, distillers of Berks county.	Remission of duties on globes of stills.	17	2	Petition	165	Ways and Means				Discharged; laid on table.		
Pennsylvania, distillers of Berks county.	Remission of duties on globes of stills.	18	1	Petition	74	Ways and Means	13	Favorable; bill	26	Passed	Passed	App'd Jan. 19, 1824
Pennsylvania, Insurance companies of Philadelphia.	Relief from seizure of vessels and cargoes by France, under Berlin decree.	18	1	Memorial	33					Laid on table.		
Pennsylvania, Insurance companies of Philadelphia.	Relief from seizure of vessels and cargoes by France, under Berlin decree.	19	1	Memorial	109	Foreign Affairs				Discharged; laid on table.		
Pennsylvania, Insurance companies of Philadelphia.	Distribution of amount due on account of the Danish brigantine Herrick.	21	2	Memorial	190	Foreign Affairs	Feb. 23, 1831	Adverse		Laid on table.		
Pennsylvania, Insurance companies of Philadelphia.	Distribution of amount due on account of the Danish brigantine Herrick.	22	1	Memorial	260	Foreign Affairs.						
Pennsylvania, Insurance companies of Philadelphia.	Relative to the insurance of the brig Josephine	24	1	Petition	59	Foreign Affairs.						
Pennsylvania, Insurance companies of Philade'i'a.	Indemnity for spoliations by the Hatien government in 1811.	26	1	Memorial	599	Foreign Affairs.						
Pennsylvania, State of	Payment of interest on money advanced to United States.	19	2	Senate bill	312	Claims	Feb. 22, 1827	Favorable	S. 36	Passed		App'd March 3, 1827
Pennsylvania, State of	Payment of interest on money advanced to United States.	20	1	Senate bill	486	Claims	May 5, 1828	Adverse	S. 101	Indef. postponed.		
Pennsylvania, State of	Payment of money due, as appears by the books of the Treasury Department.	20	1	Resolution	175	Claims	April 4, 1828	Favorable; bil	254	Referred to Committee Whole House.		
Pennsylvania, State of	Payment of money due, as appears by the books of the Treasury Department.	20	2	Bill of last sess.	284	Whole House	Feb. 13, 1829	Favorable	254	Passed	Reported without amend't.	

List of private claims presented to the House of Representatives of the United States form the 1st to the 31st Congress, inclusive—Continued.

Names of claimants.	Nature or object of the claim.	Congress.	Session.	How brought before the House of Reps.	Page of journal.	To what committee of the House referred.	No. or date of the report.	Nature of the report.	No. of the bill.	How disposed of by the House of Reps.	How disposed of by the Senate.	Date of the act of Congress, and remarks.
Pennsylvania, State of....	Payment of money due, as appears by the books of the Treasury Department.	21	1	Petition	35	Claims..........	Dec. 21, 1829	Favorable; bill	8	Passed	Passed	App'd Feb. 11, 1830
Pennsylvania, marshal of eastern district.	(See New York Insurance Companies.)	22	1	....	473							
Pennsylvania, Little Schuylkill Railroad Company.	Remission of duties on two engines.	22	2	Petition	268	Ways and Means.						
Pennsylvania, Commercial Exchange Company, Philadelphia.	Remission of duties on sculptured marble.	20	1	Memorial	48	Ways and Means..	Dec. 3, 1833	Favorable; bill	111	Rejected.		
Pennsylvania, vestry of Christ church.	Remission of duty on bells......	24	1	Memorial	277	Ways and Means..	Feb. 5, 1836	By bill	299	Referred to Committee Whole House.		
Pennsylvania, vestry of Christ church.	Remission of duty on bells......	24	1	Senate bill	899	Ways and Means..	June 7, 1836	With't amend	S. 124	Passed	....	App'd July 2, 1886
Pennsylvania, custom-house officers of Philadelphia.	Increase of compensation........	24	1	Memorial	663	Commerce.						
Pennsylvania, custom-house officers of Philadelphia.	Increase of compensation........	26	1	Petition	712	Ways and Means.						
Pennsylvania, vestry of St Peter's church, Philadelphia.	Permission to import bells free of duty.	27	2	Petition	1239	Ways and Means.						
Pennsylvania, vestry of St. Peter's church, Philadelphia.	Permission to import bells free of duty.	27	3	Petition	120	Ways and Means..	19	Favorable; bill	643	Referred to Committee Whole House.		
Pennsylvania, insurance companies of Philadelphia.	Indemnity for French spoliations prior to 1800.	26	1	Memorial	182	Foreign Affairs....	343	Favorable; bill	319	Referred to Committee Whole House.		
Pennsylvania, citizens of..	Indemnity for French spoliations prior to 1800.	26	1	Petition	1219	Foreign Affairs....	343	Favorable; bill	319	Referred to Committee Whole House.		
Pennsylvania, citizens of..	Indemnity for French spoliations prior to 1800.	27	3	Memorial	69	....	....	....	......	Referred to Committee Whole House.		
Pennsylvania, citizens of..	Indemnity for French spoliations prior to 1800.	28	1	Petition	141	Foreign Affairs.						
Pennsylvania, members of the bar, Western court.	Increase of compensation of judge of Western district.	26	1	Memorial	629	Judiciary.						
Pennsylvania, members of the bar, Western court.	Increase of compensation of judge of Western district.	27	2	Memorial	581	Judiciary.						
Pennsylvania, citizens of..	Compensation to judge of eastern district for extra duties.	29	1	Memorial	1001	Judiciary.						
Pennsylvania, Summit Coal and Railroad Company.	Remission of duty on railroad iron	27	2	Petition	67	Ways and Means..	514	Adverse	......	Recommitted.		
Pennsylvania, Summit Coal and Railroad Company.	Remission of duty on railroad iron.	27	3	Petition	125	Ways and Means.						
Pennsylvania, citizens of Philadelphia.	Repeal of duty on railroad iron...	28	1	Memorial	483	Ways and Means.						
Pennsylvania, citizens of Philadelphia.	Drawback on spirits distilled from molasses.	28	1	Petition	144	Commerce.						
Pennsylvania, Saving Fund Society of Philadelphia.	Payment of certain treasury notes.	28	1	Memorial	317	Ways and Means.						
Pennsylvania, Delaware Insurance Company, Philadelphia.	Payment of certain treasury notes.	28	1	Petition	335	Ways and Means.						

List of private claims presented to the House of Representatives of the United States from the 1st to the 31st Congress, inclusive—Continued.

Names of claimants.	Nature or object of the claim.	Congress.	Session.	How brought before the House of Reps.	Page of journal.	To what committee of the House referred.	No. or date of the report.	Nature of the report.	No. of the bill.	How disposed of by the House of Reps.	How disposed of by the Senate.	Date of the act of Congress, and remarks.
Pennsylvania, Norristown and Valley Railroad Company.	Permission to remove iron from custom-house on giving bonds for duties.	26	2	Petition	120	Ways and Means.						
Pennsylvania, Norristown and Valley Railroad Company.	Permission to remove iron from custom-house on giving bonds for duties.	27	2	Petition	55	Ways and Means..	463	Favorable; bill	314	Ordered to 3d reading.		
Pennsylvania, Norristown and Valley Railroad Company.	Permission to remove iron from custom-house on giving bonds for duties.	27	3	Bill of last sess..	87	....	....	....	314	Laid on table.		
Pennsylvania, Norristown and Valley Railroad Company, assignee of.	Remission of duty on railroad iron.	28	1	Memorial	357	Ways and Means.						
Pennsylvania, Norristown and Valley Railroad Company, sureties of.	(See Thomas Weaver, and others)	27	3	....	254	....	....	....	725			
Pennsylvania, Philadelphia, Wilmington, and Baltimore Railroad Company.	Remission of duty on railroad iron.	28	1	Petition	317	Ways and Means.						
Pennsylvania, Philadelphia and Reading Railroad Company.	Remission of duty on railroad iron.	28	2	Petition	112	Ways and Means.						
Pennyman, Huldah......	(See Barnabas Hollis, widow of).	24	2	....	346							
Penrose, Clement B	Further compensation for services as a land commissioner.	12	1	Petition and rep't Sec. Treasury.	253	Claims..........	April 28, 1817	Favorable; bill	116	Passed	Passed	App'd June 20, 1812
Penrose, Clement B	Further compensation for services as a land commissioner.	14	1	Petition	258	Public Lands.						
Penrose, Clement B	Further compensation for services as a land commissioner.	15	2	Petition	52	Select	Dec. 15, 1818	Favorable; bill	228	Indefinitely postponed.		
Penrose, Clement B	Further compensation for services as a land commissioner.	16	1	Petition	40, 49	Public Lands.....	Dec. 27, 1819	Favorable; bill	24	Rejected.		
Penrose, Clement B	Further compensation for services as a land commissioner.	16	2	Petition	32	Public Lands.....	Jan. 2, 1821	Favorable; bill	182	Referred to Committee Whole House.		
Penrose, Clement B	Further compensation for services of dec'd, as a land commissioner.	18	1	Petition	116	Public Lands.....	April 13, 1824	....	......	Discharged	....	Leave to withdraw.
Penrose, Clement B., widow of.	Further compensation for services of dec'd, as a land commissioner.	21	1	Petition	60	Public Lands.....	....	....	......	Discharged; laid on table.		
Penrose, Clement B., widow of.	Further compensation for services of dec'd, as a land commissioner.	21	2	Petition	121	Public Lands.....	23	Adverse	......	Laid on table.		
Penrose, Clement B., widow of.	Further compensation for services of dec'd, as a land commissioner.	23	1	Senate bill	395	Claims	355	With amend..	S. 56	Passed	Passed	App'd June 30, 1834
Penrose, Clement B	Confirmation of title to land in Missouri.	15	2	Petition	89	Priv. Land Claims.	....	....	......	Discharged; laid on table.		
Penrose, Clement B	Confirmation of title to land in Missouri.	17	1	Petition	55	Public Lands.....	46	Favorable; bill	93	Laid on table.		
Penrose, Clement B	Confirmation of title to land in Missouri.	18	1	Petition	55	Public Lands.....	....	....	......	Discharged	....	Leave to withdraw.
Penrose, Mary	Ransom of her husband from Algerine slavery.	3	1	Memorial	82	....	....	....	......	Laid on table.		
Pensacola Academy, Florida, trustees of.	Grant of public lands in the city of Pensacola for use of.	23	1	Memorial	382	Public Lands.						
Pensacola Academy, Florida, trustees of.	Grant of public lands in the city of Pensacola for use of.	23	2	Memorial	85	Public Lands.....	Jan. 20, 1835	....	......	Discharged; laid on table.		

List of private claims presented to the House of Representatives of the United States from the 1st to the 31st Congress, inclusive—Continued.

Names of claimants.	Nature or object of the claim.	Congress.	Session.	How brought before the House of Reps.	Page of journal.	To what committee of the House referred.	No. or date of the report.	Nature of the report.	No. of the bill.	How disposed of by the House of Reps.	How disposed of by the Senate.	Date of the act of Congress, and remarks.
Pensinger, Henry	Pension for wounds received in revolutionary war.	6	2	Petition	770	Claims	Jan. 26, 1801	Adverse		Rejected.		
Penticost, Dorsey	Pre-emption to land in the western territory.	1	3	Petition	391					Referred to Secretary Treasury.		
Penticost, Dorsey	Pre-emption to land in the western territory.	3	2	Rep. of Secretary Treasury.	284					Laid on table.		
Penticost, Dorsey, heirs of	Grant of other public lands in lieu of those taken by United States.	15	1	Petition	192	Priv. Land Claims.				Discharged; laid on table.		
Penticost, Dorsey, heirs of	Grant of other public lands in lieu of those taken by United States.	16	1	Petition	145	Priv. Land Claims.				Discharged		Leave to withdraw.
Penticost, Dorsey, heirs of	Grant of other public lands in lieu of those taken by United States	19	1	Resolution	232	Public Lands				Discharged; laid on table.		
Pentland, Hegins & Steele, army contractors.	Relief from import duties on flour imported from Canada for United States troops.	14	2	Petition and rep't Sec. Treasury.	32, 67	Claims.						
Pentland, Hegins & Steele, army contractors.	Relief from import duties on flour imported from Canada for United States troops	15	1	Petition	90	Ways and Means.	Jan. 23, 1818	Adverse		Laid on table.		
Pentland, Noble A.	(See Noble A. Penland.)											
Pepin, Andrew	Relief for wounds and injuries received in revolutionary war.	2	2	Petition and rep't Sec. War.	621, 735					Laid on table		March 3, 1795, leave to withdraw.
Pepin, Andrew	Relief for wounds and injuries received in revolutionary war.	5	2	Petition and rep't Sec. War.	90	Claims	Dec. 7, 1797	Adverse				Leave to withdraw.
Pepin, Francis	Compensation for services in revolutionary war.	11	2	Petition	325	Claims.						
Pepper, James, *et al*, (La.)	Confirmation of title to land	27	3	Petition	136	Priv. Land Claims.	161	Favorable; bill	777	Laid on table.		
Pepper, James, and others.	Confirmation of title to land	28	1	Petition	351	Priv. Land Claims.	208	Favorable; bill	163	Passed	Passed	App'd June 17, 1844
Pepper, William	(See widow of Stephen Decatur, and others.)	20	1		295							
Pepper, William, (Va.)	Restoration of pension	26	1	Resolution	774	Rev. Pensions.						
Peppin, Joseph	(See Mississippi Land Company.)	8	2		48							
Percival, Henry	(See S. Morris Waln & Co.)	23	1		214							
Percival, John	Revolutionary pension	18	2	Petition	210	Pens. & Rev. Cl'ms.				Discharged; laid on table.		
Percival, John	Revolutionary pension	21	2	Petition	336	Military Pensions.						
Percival, John	Revolutionary pension	22	1	Petition	124	Rev. Pensions	395	Favorable; bill	494	Referred to Committee Whole House.		
Percival, John, commandant U. S. navy.	Remuneration for extraordinary expenses in voyage to Mulgrave and Sandwich Islands.	22	2	Memorial	179	Naval Affairs	86	Favorable; bill	731	Referred to Committee Whole House.		
Percival, John, commandant U. S. navy.	Remuneration for extraordinary expenses in voyage to Mulgrave and Sandwich Islands.	23	1	Petition	74	Claims	30	Favorable; bill	35	Passed		App'd June 19, 1834
Percival, John	(See Lewis Warrington, & others)	28	1		285							
Percival, John, (U. States navy.)	Allowance of money paid to naturalist.	30	1	Memorial	473	Naval Affairs	275	Favorable; bill	270	Referred to Committee Whole House.		
Percival, John, (U. States navy.)	Allowance of money paid to naturalist.	30	2	House bill	342	Whole House	Jan. 30, 1849	Favorable	270	Passed	Passed	App'd Feb. 1, 1849
Percy, Robert, widow of.	Confirmation of title to land in Louisiana.	18	1	Petition	287	Public Lands.						
Percy, Robert, widow of.	Confirmation of title to land in Louisiana.	18	2	Petition	42	Priv. Land Claims.						
Percy, Robert, widow of.	Confirmation of title to land in Louisiana.	20	1	Petition	344	Priv. Land Claims.				Discharged; laid on table.		

List of private claims presented to the House of Representatives of the United States from the 1st to the 31st Congress, inclusive—Continued.

Names of claimants.	Nature or object of the claim.	Congress.	Session.	How brought before the House of Reps.	Page of journal.	To what committee of the House referred.	No. or date of the report.	Nature of the report.	No. of the bill.	How disposed of by the House of Reps.	How disposed of by the Senate.	Date of the act of Congress, and remarks.
Percy, Robert, widow of	Confirmation of title to land in Louisiana.	21	2	Petition	83	Priv. Land Claims				Discharged; laid on table.		
Percy, Robert, widow of	Confirmation of title to land in Louisiana.	22	1	Petition	32	Priv. Land Claims	Jan. 13, 1832	Adverse		Laid on table.		
Perez, Juan	Confirmation of title to land	22	1	House bill	107	Whole House	Mar. 23, 1832	With't amend.	125	Passed	Passed	App'd June 25, 1832
Perham, Benjamin	Compensation for services in late war.	28	1	Petition	927	Claims.						
Perham, Benjamin	Compensation for services in late war.	29	1	Petition	592	Priv. Land Claims.						
Perham, Benjamin	Compensation for services in late war.	29	2	Petition	87	Priv. Land Claims.						
Perham, Benjamin	Compensation for services in late war.	30	1	Petition	399	Claims	Mar. 15, 1848	Adverse		Laid on table.		
Perham, Benjamin	Compensation for services in late war.	30	2	Petition	204	Priv. Land Claims.						
Perham, Benjamin	Compensation for services in late war.	31	1	Petition	361	Priv. Land Claims.						
Perham, Ezekiel, widow of	Pension for revolutionary services.	29	1	Petition	1000	Rev. Pensions.						
Perham, John	Invalid pension	23	1	Petition	436	Invalid Pensions	April 11, 1834	Adverse		Laid on table.		
Perham, John	Invalid pension	23	2	Petition	236	Invalid Pensions.						
Perham, John	Invalid pension	24	1	Petition	285	Invalid Pensions.						
Perham, John	Invalid pension	24	2	Petition	72	Invalid Pensions	Dec. 30, 1836	Favorable; bill	793	Ref'd to Com. W. H.		
Perham, John	Invalid pension	25	2	Petition	39	Invalid Pensions	474	Adverse		Discharged; laid on table.		
Perham, John	Invalid pension	25	3	Petition	219	Invalid Pensions				Discharged; laid on table.		
Perham, John	Invalid pension	26	1	Petition	198	Invalid Pensions	282	Adverse		Laid on table.		
Perham, John	Invalid pension	27	2	Petition	320	Invalid Pensions	955	Adverse		Laid on table.		
Perham, John	Invalid pension	28	1	Petition	236	Invalid Pensions	405	Favorable; bill	313	Passed	Passed	App'd June 17, 1844
Periam, Mary Eliza	Payment for property used by government.	28	1	Petition	60	Claims	45	Adverse		Laid on table.		
Perien, Francois	Adjustment of land claim	26	1	Memorial	610	Priv. Land Claims	July 21, 1840	Adverse		Laid on table.		
Perit, John W., attorney, &c.	(See D. Wheeler & S. Cock)	15	1		261							
Perker, Samuel	Pension for services in revolutionary war.	3	1	Rep. of Secretary War.	131	Select	May 26, 1794	Joint resolut'n.	12	Passed	Passed	App'd June 9, 1794
Perker, Samuel	Pension for services in revolutionary war	4	1	Resolution	445	Claims	Mar. 4, 1796	Joint resolut'n.	16	Passed	Passed	App'd April 18, 1796
Perkins, Abraham	Revolutionary pension	23	1	Petition	242	Rev. Pensions				Discharged; laid on table.		
Perkins, Andrew and Joseph	Indemnity for French spoliations prior to 1800.	26	1	Memorial	182	Foreign Affairs	343	Favorable; bill	319	Referred to Committee Whole House.		
Perkins, Angier March	Patent for warming buildings	25	2	Senate bill	785	Patents	May 11, 1838	With't amend	S. 210	Passed		App'd May 31, 1838
Perkins, Augustus	Relief from payment of duties on distillery.	14	2	Petition	190	Ways and Means				Discharged; laid on table.		
Perkins, Augustus	Relief from payment of duties on distillery.	15	1	Petition	202	Ways and Means				Discharged; laid on table.		
Perkins, Benjamin, and Frances M., his wife.	Confirmation of title to land	19	2	Petition	27	Public Lands				Discharged; laid on table.		
Perkins, Benjamin G	Invalid pension	28	1	Petition	783	Invalid Pensions.						
Perkins, Benjamin G	Invalid pension	28	2	Petition	207	Invalid Pensions.						
Perkins, Benjamin G	Invalid pension	29	1	Petition	192	Invalid Pensions	Mar. 27, 1846			Discharged; laid on table.		

List of private claims presented to the House of Representatives of the United States from the 1st to the 31st Congress, inclusive—**Continued.**

Names of claimants.	Nature or object of the claim.	Congress.	Session.	How brought before the House of Reps.	Page of journal.	To what committee of the House referred.	No. or date of the report.	Nature of the report.	No. of the bill.	How disposed of by the House of Reps.	How disposed of by the Senate.	Date of the act of Congress, and remarks.
Perkins, Benjamin G	Invalid pension	29	2	Add'l evidence	133	Invalid Pensions.						
Perkins, Benjamin G	Invalid pension	30	1	Petition	339	Invalid Pensions	453	Favorable; bill	383	Passed.		
Perkins, Daniel	Arrears of pay due for revolutionary services.	3	2	Petition	289	Claims	Mar. 2, 1795	Adverse	......	Laid on table.		
Perkins, Daniel	Arrears of pay due for services, revolutionary war.	4	1	Petition	598	Claims	May 31, 1796	Adverse	......	Laid on table.		
Perkins, Daniel B	Compensation for services in extinguishing a fire at Springfield, Massacusetts, in 1819.	24	2	Petition	36	Invalid Pensions	89	Favorable; bill	832	Referred to Committee Whole House.		
Perkins, Daniel B	Invalid pension	25	2	Petition	39	Invalid Pensions	354	Favorable; bill	383	Passed	Rejected.	
Perkins, Daniel B	Invalid pension	26	1	Petition	162, 287	Invalid Pensions	248	Adverse	......	Laid on table.		
Perkins, Daniel B	Invalid pension	28	2	Petition	57	Invalid Pensions.						
Perkins, Daniel B	Invalid pension	29	1	Petition	265	Invalid Pensions	Mar. 27, 1846	....	......	Discharged; laid on table.		
Perkins, Ebenezer	Increase of compensation as mate on revenue cutter Argus.	4	1	Petition and rep't Sec. Treasury.	472	Select	April 12, 1796	By bill	167	Passed	Passed	App'd May 6, 1796
Perkins, Ebenezer	Increase of pension	10	1	House bill	232	Whole House	April 19, 1808	With amends.	78	Passed	Passed	App'd April 25, 1808
Perkins, Enoch	Revolutionary pension	28	1	Petition	85	Rev. Pensions.						
Perkins, Enoch	Revolutionary pension	29	1	Petition	59	Rev. Pensions	727	Adverse	......	Laid on table.		
Perkins, Enoch	Revolutionary pension	29	2	Petition	82	Rev. Pensions.						
Perkins, Hector	Pension	19	1	Petition	66	Military Pensions	164	Adverse	......	Laid on table.		
Perkins, Hector	Pension	29	1	Memorial	233	Invalid Pensions.						
Perkins, Hector	Increase of pension	30	1	Petition	752	Invalid Pensions	797	Favorable; bill	619	Ref'd to Com. W. H		
Perkins, Hector	Increase of pension	30	2	House bill	362	Whole House	Feb. 2, 1849	With't amend.	619	Passed.		
Perkins, Hector	Increase of pension	31	1	Petition	973	Invalid Pensions.						
Perkins, Jacob, assignees of	Renewal of patent right for cutting nails.	9	1	Petition	232	Com. and Manuf.	Mar. 17, 1806	Adverse	......	Leave to withdraw.		
Perkins, Jacob	Renewal of patent right for cutting nails.	13	1	Petition	32	Select.						
Perkins, Jacob	Renewal of patent right for cutting nails.	13	3	Petition	686	Select.						
Perkins, James and Thomas	(See Nathaniel Goddard)	16	1	....	27							
Perkins, James, & Son	Indemnity for French spoliations prior to 1800.	26	1	Memorial	182	Foreign Affairs	343	Favorable; bill	319	Referred to Committee Whole House.		
Perkins, Jonathan	Pension	11	2	House bill	283	Whole House	Mar. 24, 1810	With amend.	107	Passed	Passed	App'd April 27, 1810
Perkins, John, and others	Relief from imprisonment by the United States.	15	1	Petition	136	Select.						
Perkins, John	(See assignee of Thomas Tupper)	22	2	....	142							
Perkins, John	To be exonerated from bonds as surety for S. F. Donaldson, pay master of United States army.	17	1	Petition	172	Military Affairs	....	....	......	Discharged; laid on table.		
Perkins, John B	Payment for services and horse lost in Seminole war.	17	1	By letter	267	Whole House.						
Perkins, John B	Payment for services and horse lost in Seminole war.	23	1	Documents	154	Claims.						
Perkins, John B	Payment for services and horse lost in Seminole war.	24	1	Resolution	542	Claims	668	Favorable; bill	627	Referred to Committee Whole House.		
Perkins, John B	Payment for services and horse lost in Seminole war.	25	2	Petition	37	Claims	43	Favorable; bill	55	Passed	Passed	App'd Feb. 22, 1838
Perkins, Joseph and Ebenezer.	Remission of penalties incurred by illegal importation of goods from British West Indies.	12	2	Petition	713	Ways and Means	....	....	......	Discharged; laid on table.		

List of private claims presented to the House of Representatives of the United States from the 1st to the 31st Congress, inclusive—Continued.

Names of claimants.	Nature or object of the claim.	Congress.	Session.	How brought before the House of Reps.	Page of journal.	To what committee of the House referred.	No. or date of the report.	Nature of the report.	No. of the bill.	How disposed of by the House of Reps.	How disposed of by the Senate.	Date of the act of Congress, and remarks.
Perkins, Joseph and Ebenezer.	Remission of penalties incurred by illegal importation of goods from British West Indies.	13	2	Petition	266	Ways and Means				Discharged; laid on table.		
Perkins, Joseph	Compensation for destruction of ship Liverpool Trader.	13	3	Petition	559	Claims	Jan. 9, 1815	Favorable; bill	253	Passed	Passed	App'd Feb. 16, 1815
Perkins, Joseph	Pension	19	2	Petition	26	Military Pensions				Discharged; laid on table.		
Perkins, Joseph	Pension	20	2	Resolution	185	Military Pensions				Discharged; laid on table.		
Perkins, Joseph, James, and John G.	Damages to vessel ($163 10) in Florida reef.	24	1	Petition	48	Claims	Dec. 21, 1835	Adverse		Laid on table.		
Perkins, Joseph, James, and John G.	Damages to vessel ($163 10) in Florida reef.	25	2	Petition	398	Claims				Discharged; laid on table.		
Perkins, Joseph, James, and John G.	Damages to vessel ($163 10) in Florida reef.	26	1	Petition	169	Claims.						
Perkins, Joseph, James, and John G.	Damages to vessel ($163 10) in Florida reef.	26	2	Petition	37	Claims	25	Adverse		Laid on table.		
Perkins, Joseph, James, and John G.	Damages to vessel ($163 10) in Florida reef.	27	2	Petition	55	Commerce	11	Favorable; bill	50	Passed	Indef. postp'd.	
Perkins, Luke, widow of	Revolutionary pension	25	2	Petition	405	Rev. Pensions				Discharged; laid on table.		
Perkins, Mary, widow of Sebastian Sroufe.	Pre-emption right to land in Ohio.	26	1	Petition	179	Priv. Land Claims.	102	Favorable; bill	98	Passed.	Passed	App'd July 20, 1840
Perkins, Moses	Compensation for damages to his property by United States troops.	26	1	Petition	335	Claims.						
Perkins, Nicholas	Confirmation of title to land in Alabama.	16	2	Senate bill	174	Priv. Land Claims.						
Perkins, Nicholas, Lieut.	Compensation for revolutionary services.	31	2	Petition	365	Priv. Land Claims.						
Perkins, Obadiah	Pension for services in revolutionary war.	3	2	Rep. of Secretary War.	278	Claims	Mar. 2, 1795	Res. to refer to Sec. War.		Resolution adopted.		
Perkins, Obadiah	Pension for services in revolutionary war.	4	1	Resolution	415	Claims	Mar. 4, 1796	Joint resolut'n.	16	Passed	Passed	App'd April 18, 1796
Perkins, Obadiah	Pension	5	2	House bill	127	Whole House	Jan. 11, 1798	With't amend.	38	Passed	Passed	App'd Feb. 2, 1798
Perkins, Obadiah	Increase of pension	10	2	House bill	499	Whole House	Feb. 20, 1809	With amends.	158	Passed	Passed	App'd March 3, 1809
Perkins, Samuel G., & Co.	(See Nathaniel Goddard, & others)	16	1		27							
Perkins, Simon	Increase of pension	10	2	House bill	499	Whole House	Feb. 20, 1809	With amends.	158	Passed	Passed	App'd March 3, 1809
Perkins, Stover	Remission of penalties incurred by importation of goods from British West Indies.	12	2	Petition	713	Ways and Means				Discharged; laid on table.		
Perkins, Stover	Remission of penalties incurred by importation of goods from British West Indies.	13	2	Petition	266	Ways and Means				Discharged; laid on table.		
Perkins, Thomas	Liquidation of certain bills of credit	4	1	Rep. of Secretary Treasury.	388	Claims	May 31, 1796	Adverse		Laid on table.		
Perkins, Thomas H	(See Nathaniel Goddard, *et al.*)	16	1		27							
Perkins, Thomas H., surviving partner of J. and T. H. Perkins.	Release from payment of bond for excessive duties, 1818.	21	2	Memorial	40	Ways and Means	43	Favorable; bill	790	Referred to Committee Whole House.		
Perkins, Thomas H., surviving partner of J. and T. H. Perkins.	Release from payment of bond for excessive duties, 1818.	24	2	Senate bill	251	Ways and Means	Jan. 24, 1837	With amend.	101	Referred to Committee Whole House.		

List of private claims presented to the House of Representatives of the United States from the 1st to the 31st Congress, inclusive—Continued.

Names of claimants.	Nature or object of the claim.	Congress.	Session.	How brought before the House of Reps.	Page of journal.	To what committee of the House referred.	No. or date of the report.	Nature of the report.	No. of the bill.	How disposed of by the House of Reps.	How disposed of by the Senate.	Date of the act of Congress, and remarks.
Perkins, Thomas H., surviving partner of J. and T. H. Perkins.	Release from payment of bond for excessive duties, 1818.	25	2	Petition	42	Ways and Means..	Jan. 5, 1838	Favorable; bill	331	Referred to Committee Whole House.		
Perkins, Thomas H., surviving partner of J. and T. H. Perkins.	Release from payment of bond for excessive duties, 1818.	25	3	House bill......	377	Whole House.....	Jan. 25, 1839	With't amend.	331	Passed.		
Perkins, Thomas, executors of.	Indemnity for French spoliations prior to 1800.	26	1	Memorial	182	Foreign Affairs....	343	Favorable; bill	319	Referred to Committee Whole House.		
Perkins, William........	Pension	21	2	Petition	159	Military Pensions..	....	....	......	Discharged.		
Perkins, Zophar, heirs of .	Revolutionary pension..........	28	2	Petition	420	Rev. Pensions.						
Perkins Zophar, heirs of..	Revolutionary pension..........	31	2	Petition	177	Rev. Pensions.						
Perkinson, William......	Issue of patent for grooving rifle barrels.	23	1	Petition	590	Patents..........	June 17, 1834	Favorable; bill	530	Referred to Committee Whole House.		
Perkinson, William......	Issue of patent for grooving rifle barrels.	24	1	Petition	271	Judiciary	July 1, 1836	Favorable; bill	739	Referred to Committee Whole House.		
Perkinson, William......	Issue of patent for grooving rifle barrels.	25	2	Petition	41	Patents..........	667	Favorable; bill	643	Referred to Committee Whole House.		
Perkinson, William......	Issue of patent for grooving rifle barrels.	25	3	House bill	380	Whole House.....	Jan. 26, 1839	With't amend.	643	Passed.		
Perkinson, William......	Issue of patent for grooving rifle barrels.	26	1	Petition	181	Dist. of Columbia						
Perley, Frederick........	Indemnity for loss by breach of contract with United States.	17	1	Petition	474	Claims	....	....	......	Discharged; laid on table.		
Perley, Frederick........	Indemnity for loss by breach of contract with United States.	18	1	Petition	77	Claims	40	Adverse	......	Recom'itted to Claims.		
							Feb. 19, 1824	Favorable; bill	171	Passed	Passed	App'd May 18, 1824
Perleins, John P.........	(See William H. Bedford, agent.)	28	1	....	262							
Perot, Elliston and John..	(See Jared Shattuck, attorney of.)	9	1	....	349							
Perpall, Gabriel W......	To be allowed part of claim under ninth article of treaty with Spain, rejected by commissioners.	19	1	Petition	313	Indian Affairs.....	210	Adverse	......	Referred to Secretary War.		
Perpall, Gabriel W., for self, and as attorney for M. Sans Berta.	Compensation for losses sustained by United States army in Florida, in 1818.	21	1	Petition	150	Foreign Affairs ...	Mar. 5, 1830	Adverse	......	Laid on table.		
Perpall, Gabriel W., for self, and as attorney for M. Sans Berta.	Compensation for losses sustained by United States army in Florida, in 1818.	22	1	Petition	192	Claims...........	May 7, 1832	Adverse	......	Laid on table.		
Perrault, P. H..........	Balance due for surveying the harbor of St. Augustine, Florida.	23	1	House bill	283	Whole House.....	April 8, 1834	With amends.	283	Passed	Passed	App'd June 27, 1834
Perrera, Gabriel.........	Confirmation of title to land	22	1	Petition	107	Priv. Land Claims.	Dec. 27, 1831	Favorable; bill	125	Passed	Passed	App'd June 25, 1832
Perrigo, Frederick	Pension	21	2	Petition	143	Military Pensions.						
Perrigo, Frederick	Pension	25	2	Petition	633	Invalid Pensions ..	....	....	......	Discharged; laid on table.		
Perrigo, Frederick	Invalid pension...............	27	2	Petition	93	Invalid Pensions ..	133	Favorable; bill	179	Passed	Passed	App'd Aug. 27, 1842
Perrigo, Frederick	Invalid pension...............	30	1	Petition	619	Invalid Pensions..	570	Adverse	......	Laid on table.		
Perrine, Ann F.........	(See Dr. Henry Perrine, widow and heirs of.)	26	2	....	51							
Perrine, Daniel	Pre-emption right to land on which he has made improvements.	12	1	Petition	22	Public Lands.						
Perrine, Daniel	Pre-emption right to land on which he has made improvements.	12	2	Petition	549	Public Lands.						
Perrine, Daniel	Pre-emption right to land on which he has made improvements.	13	2	Petition	194	Public Lands.....	....	....	......	Discharged; laid on table.		

List of private claims presented to the House of Representatives of the United States from the 1st to the 31st Congress, inclusive—Continued.

Names of claimants.	Nature or object of the claim.	Congress.	Session.	How brought before the House of Reps.	Page of journal.	To what committee of the House referred.	No. or date of the report.	Nature of the report.	No. of the bill.	How disposed of by the House of Reps.	How disposed of by the Senate.	Date of the act of Congress, and remarks.
Perrine, Daniel	Pre-emption right to land on which he has made improvements.	13	3	Petition	469	Public Lands	Nov. 12, 1814	By bill	227	Passed	Passed	App'd Feb. 24, 1815
Perrine, Dr. Henry	Compensation for services and expenses as American consul at Campeachy, &c.	22	1	Memorial & letter Sec. Treasury.	295, 572	Agriculture	April 24, 1832	Favorable; bill	555	Referred to Committee Whole House.		
Perrine, Dr. Henry	Compensation for services aud expenses as American consul at Campeachy, &c.	23	1	Petition	162	Agriculture	....	....	......	Discharged; laid on table.		
Perrine, Dr. Henry	Grant of land to cultivate tropical plants.	23	2	Memorial	393	Agriculture.						
Perrine, Dr. Henry	Grant of land to cultivate tropical plants.	25	2	Senate bill	1085	Agriculture	June 28, 1838	With't amend.	S. 241	Passed	....	App'd July 7, 1838
Perrine, Dr. Henry, widow and heirs of.	Confirmation of title to land in Florida.	26	2	Petition	51	Agriculture	73	Favorable; bill	587	Referred to Committee Whole House.		
Perrine, Dr. Henry, widow and heirs of.	Confirmation of title to land in Florida.	26	2	Senate bill	195	Public Lands	Feb. 12, 1841	With't amend.	S. 175	Passed	....	App'd Feb. 18, 1841
Perrine, Dr. Henry, widow and heirs of.	Extension of time to locate land	30	1	Petition	724	Public Lands.						
Perrine, Dr. Henry, widow and heirs of.	Extension of time to locate land	30	2	Petition	285	Public Lands.						
Perrine, Dr. Henry, widow and heirs of.	Extension of time to locate land	31	1	Petition	308	Priv. Land Claims.						
Perrine, John	(See John Hamilton, executors of.)	14	1	....	300							
Perrin, John	Pre-emption right to land as branch pilot, New Orleans.	28	1	Petition	77	Priv. Land Claims.	9	Favorable; bill	35	Passed	Passed	App'd June 17, 1844
Perrin, Nathan	Increase of pension	27	2	Petition	614	Rev. Pensions	....	....	......	Disch'd; laid on table		
Perrin, Oliver, and others.	Authorize issue of patent	25	3	Resolution	116	Patents	Feb. 16, 1839	Favorable; bill	1159	Referred to Committee Whole House.		
Perrin, Oliver, and others.	Authorize issue of patent	26	1	Petition	18[illegible]	Patents	May 25, 1840	By bill	428	Passed	Passed	App'd July 20, 1840
Perrin, Payton	Drawback on cotton exported	20	1	Senate bill	453	Ways and Means	....	....	S. 99			
Perrin, Payton	Drawback on cotton exported	20	2	Senate bill	312	Ways and Means	Feb. 23, 1829	With amends.	S. 56	Ref'd to Com. W. H.		
Perrin, Payton	Drawback on cotton exported	21	1	Senate bill	258	Ways and Means	Feb. 22, 1830	With't amend.	S. 41	Passed	....	App'd May 26, 1830
Perrit, Peter	Payment as captain in Connecticut line.	2	2	Petition and rep't Sec. of War.	668	....	....	....	......	Laid on table.		
Perrit, Peter	Payment as captain in Connecticut line.	3	1	Petition and rep't Sec. of War.	53	Select	April 22, 1794	Adverse	......	Referred to Secretary War.		
Perrit, Peter	Payment as captain in Connecticut line.	3	2	Petition and rep't of Sec. War.	239	Claims	Jan. 6, 1795	Adverse	......	Referred to Committee Whole House.		
Perrit, Peter	Payment as captain in Connecticut line.	4	1	Memorial & rep't of Att'y Gen.	37	....	....	....	......	Rejected.		
Perruquier, assignee of	Confirmation of title to land	26	1	Petition	827	Priv. Land Claims.	April 25, 1840	Adverse	......	Laid on table.		
Perryman, Anthony M., postmas'r at Holmesville, Mississippi.	Additional compen ation as postmaster, to enable him to employ a clerk.	23	1	Petition	379	P. Of. & P. Roads.	....	....	......	Discharged; laid on table.		
Perry, Andrew T.	To be credited amount of uncurrent money received by him for public lands.	22	1	Petition	266	Judiciary	Mar. 20, 1832	Adverse	......	Laid on table.		
Perry, Asaph	Compensation for services in late war.	28	1	Petition	1021	Military Affairs.						
Perry, Benjamin	Compensation as clerk to board of assessors for State of Pennsylvania, under act of January 9, 1815.	15	1	Petition	30	Ways and Means	Jan. 2, 1818	Adverse	......	Leave to withdraw.		

List of private claims presented to the House of Representatives of the United States from the 1st to the 31st Congress, inclusive—Continued.

Names of claimants.	Nature or object of the claim.	Congress.	Session.	How brought before the House of Reps.	Page of journal.	To what committee of the House referred.	No. or date of the report.	Nature of the report.	No. of the bill.	How disposed of by the House of Reps.	How disposed of by the Senate.	Date of the act of Congress, and remarks.
Perry, Christop'r Raymond	(See O. H. Perry, family of)	16	1		236							
Perry, David	Pension	15	2	Petition	39	Pens. & Rev. Cl'ms.	Jan. 15, 1819	Adverse		Laid on table.		
Perry, David	Revolutionary pension	24	1	Petition	801	Rev. Pensions	May 10, 1836			Discharged; laid on table.		
Perry, Elizabeth C.	(See O. H. Perry, family of)	16	1		236							
Perry, Elizabeth M.	(See O. H. Perry, family of)	16	1		236							
Perry, Gideon A.	Invalid pension	26	1	Petition	938	Invalid Pensions.						
Perry, Gideon A.	Invalid pension	26	2	Petition	148	Invalid Pensions	217	Adverse		Laid on table.		
Perry, Gideon A.	Invalid pension	27	2	Resolution	421	Invalid Pensions	806	Favorable; bill	460	R'f'd to Com. W. H.		
Perry, Gideon A.	Invalid pension	27	3	House bill	89	Whole House			460	Passed	Indef. postp'd.	
Perry, Gideon A.	Invalid pension	28	1	Petition	60	Invalid Pensions.						
Perry, Gideon A.	Invalid pension	28	2	Petition	145	Invalid Pensions	Jan. 28, 1845			Discharged; laid on table.		
Perry, Gideon A.	Invalid pension	29	1	Petition	298	Invalid Pensions	334	Favorable; bill	269	Laid on table.		
Perry, Gideon A.	Invalid pension	30	1	Petition	575	Invalid Pensions	627	Favorable; bill	502	Passed.		
Perry, Grant Mason	(See O. H. Perry, family of)	16	1		236							
Perry, Hardy	Confirmation of title to land in Mississippi.	15	1	House bill	387	Priv. Land Claims.	Mar. 26, 1818	With't amend.	160	Referred to Committee Whole House.		
Perry, Hardy	Confirmation of title to land in Mississippi.	15	2	Documents	84	Whole House.						
Perry, Hardy	Confirmation of title to land in Mississippi.	16	1	Petition	204	Priv. Land Claims.	64	By bill	69	Passed	Passed	App'd May 8, 1820
Perry, Hardy, and others	Grant of land under the treaty of Dancing Rabbit Creek.	23	1	Petition	523	Indian Affairs.						
Perry, Hardy, and others	(See Richard Cravat, and others)	25	2		100							
Perry, Hannah	(See Ezekiel Harlin, widow of)	23	1		79							
Perry, Israel	Revolutionary pension	28	1	Petition	484	Rev. Pensions.						
Perry, James, and Thomas Hays, (England.)	Payment for property taken from them for the use of United States army in New Jersey.	1	2	Petition	160					Referred to Secretary Treasury.		
Perry, James, and Thomas Hays, (England.)	Payment for property taken from them for the use of United States army in New Jersey.	3	2	Rep. of Secretary Treasury.	284					Laid on table.		
Perry, James, and Thomas Hays, (England.)	Payment for property taken from them for the use of United States army in New Jersey.	5	2	Memorial	227	Claims	Mar. 22, 1798	Adverse		Rejected.		
Perry, James	Grant of land for services in late war.	22	2	Petition	30	Public Lands.						
Perry, James, and others	Remuneration for services in defending the frontiers in January, 1838.	26	1	Petition	294	Claims.						
Perry, Jean F., heirs of, & others.	Confirmation of title to land	30	1	Senate bill	913	Priv. Land Claims.			S. 147			
Perry, Jean F., heirs of, & others.	Confirmation of title to land	30	2	Senate bill	119	Priv. Land Claims.	Dec. 19, 1848	With't amend.	S. 147	Passed		App'd Dec. 22, 1848
Perry, Jesse	Pension	21	2	Petition	104	Military Pensions.						
Perry, Joseph, assignees of	Authority to locate land	29	1	Petition	1017	Indian Affairs.						
Perry, Joseph, assignees of	Authority to locate land	30	1	Petition	155	Indian Affairs	129	Favorable; bill	120	Passed	Passed	App'd Aug. 11, 1848
Perry, John	Compensation for provisions furnished United States troops.	14	1	Petition	473	Claims.						
Perry, John	Indemnity for property destroyed by a mob of United States soldiers.	15	2	Petition	225	Claims				Discharged; laid on table.		

List of private claims presented to the House of Representatives of the United States from the 1st to the 31st Congress, inclusive—Continued.

Names of claimants.	Nature or object of the claim.	Congress.	Session.	How brought before the House of Reps.	Page of journal.	To what committee of the House referred.	No. or date of the report.	Nature of the report.	No. of the bill.	How disposed of by the House of Reps.	How disposed of by the Senate.	Date of the act of Congress, and remarks.
Perry, John	Indemnity for property destroyed by a mob of United States soldiers.	16	1	Petition	136	Claims	Jan. 14, 1820	Adverse	.....	Referred to Committee Whole House.		
Perry, John	Indemnity for property destroyed by a mob of United States soldiers.	16	2	Petition	216	Claims	.....	.....	.....	Discharged; laid on table.		
Perry, John	Indemnity for property destroyed by a mob of United States soldiers.	17	1	Petition	38	Claims	Dec. 21, 1821	Adverse	.....	Rejected.		
Perry, John	Indemnity for property destroyed by a mob of United States soldiers.	18	1	Petition	214	Claims	April 5, 1824	Adverse	.....	Leave to withdraw.		
Perry, John	Invalid pension	19	1	House bill	282	Whole House	May 9, 1826	With amends.	119	Passed.		
Perry, John	Invalid pension	19	2	House bill	85	Whole House	Feb. 2, 1827	With amends.	315	Passed.		
Perry, John, (2d)	Pension as a revolutionary soldier.	18	1	Resolution	276	Rev. Pensions.						
Perry, John, (2d)	Pension as a revolutionary soldier.	19	1	Resolution	144	Military Pensions	.....	.....	.....	Discharged; laid on table.		
Perry, John, (2d)	Pension as a revolutionary soldier.	19	2	Petition	64	Military Pensions	.....	.....	.....	Discharged; laid on table.		
Perry, John, (2d)	Pension as a revolutionary soldier.	20	1	Resolution	95	Military Pensions	.....	.....	.....	Discharged; laid on table.		
Perry, John, (2d)	Pension as a revolutionary soldier.	21	1	Petition	48	Military Pensions	Jan. 5, 1830	Favorable; bill	72	Passed	Passed	App'd May 20, 1830
Perry, John W	Grant of public land in consideration of his wife producing three sons at a birth.	21	2	Petition	338	Public Lands.						
Perry, Luke	Return of money paid into land office.	30	1	Petition	439	Public Lands	.....	.....	.....	Discharged; laid on table.		
Perry, Luke	Return of money paid into land office.	31	1	Petition	198	Public Lands.						
Perry, Martha, widow	Pension	15	1	Petition	106	Pens. & Rev. Cl'ms.	Feb. 24, 1818	Adverse	.....	Rejected.		
Perry, Mary B., and others	(See John Donnell, heirs of.)	28	1	.....	263							
Perry, Mary	Revolutionary pension	28	2	Petition	83	Rev. Pensions.						
Perry, Margaret	(See O. H. Perry, family of.)	16	1	.....	236							
Perry, Margaret	(See William Valiant, mother of.)	16	1	.....	334							
Perry, Mathew C., master commandant U. States navy.	Indemnity for extra expenses incurred in taking out J. Randolph, minister to Russia.	23	1	Petition	89	Naval Affairs.	Jan. 31, 1834	Favorable; bill	263	Referred to Committee Whole House.		
Perry, Matthew C., master commandant U. States navy.	Indemnity for extra expenses incurred in taking out J. Randolph, minister to Russia.	23	2	House bill	300	Whole House	Jan. 31, 1835	With't amend.	263	Passed	Passed	App'd March 3, 1835
Perry, Moses, (Choctaw Indian.)	Confirmation of title to reservation of land under treaty of Dancing Rabbit Creek.	23	2	Petition	68	Priv. Land Claims.						
Perry, Nathaniel	Restoration of pension	17	1	Petition	118	Rev. Pensions	.....	.....	.....	Discharged.	.....	Leave to withdraw.
Perry, Nathaniel	Restoration of pension	17	2	Petition	43	Rev. Pensions	.....	.....	.....	Discharged.	.....	Leave to withdraw.
Perry, Oliver H., family of.	That provision be made for support and education of children.	16	1	Resolution	236	Select	Feb. 28, 1820	Favorable; bill	93	Referred to Committee Whole House.		
Perry, Oliver H., family of.	That provision be made for support and education of children.	16	2	Bill of last sess.	73	Whole House	Jan. 23, 1821	With amends.	93	Passed	Passed	App'd March 2, 1821
Perry, O. H. and James Alexander, mother of.	Pension	17	2	Petition	122	Naval Affairs	65	Favorable; bill	243	Referred to Committee Whole House.		
Perry, O. H. and James Alexander, mother of.	Pension during natural life	18	1	Resolution	30	Naval Affairs	Dec. 16, 1823 68	By bill Adverse	8 8	Recommitted. Laid on table.		
Perry, O. H	(See Exploring Expedition)	27	3	.....	149							
Perry, Paul	Additional allowance as assistant marshal.	22	1	Resolution	499	Claims.						

List of private claims presented to the House of Representatives of the United States from the 1st to the 31st Congress, inclusive—Continued.

Names of claimants.	Nature or object of the claim.	Congress.	Session.	How brought before the House of Reps.	Page of journal.	To what committee of the House referred.	No. or date of the report	Nature of the report.	No. of the bill.	How disposed of by the House of Reps.	How disposed of by the Senate.	Date of the act of Congress, and remarks.
Perry, Paul	Additional allowance as assistant marshal.	22	2	Resolution	91	Claims	35	Adverse		Laid on table.		
Perry, Richard	Arrears of pension	26	2	Petition	55	Invalid Pensions	55	Adverse		Laid on table.		
Perry, Robert	Pension for wounds received in 1794.	30	1	Petition	713	Rev. Pensions	785	Adverse		Laid on table.		
Perry, Robert	Payment for provisions furnished United States troops in 1818 and 1819.	22	1	Petition	193	Claims	Feb. 6, 1832	Adverse		Laid on table.		
Perry, Reuben, and others	Extra work on United States mint at Charlotte, N. C.	25	2	Petition	724	Claims	1000	Adverse		Laid on table.		
Perry, Reuben, and others	Extra work on United States mint at Charlotte, N. C.	29	2	Memorial	82	Claims.						
Perry, Reuben, and others	Extra work on United States mint at Charlotte, N. C.	30	1	Petition	169	Claims	119	Favorable; bill	110	Passed.		
Perry, Reuben, and others	Extra work on United States mint at Charlotte, N. C.	30	2	House bill from Senate.	143				110		Passed	App'd Jan. 8, 1849
Perry, Samuel, *et al.*	Compensation for boat lost in United States service.	14	1	Petition	433	Claims.				Discharged; laid on table.		
Perry, Samuel, *et al.*	Compensation for boat lost in United States service.	15	1	Petition	90	Claims				Discharged; laid on table.		
Perry, Samuel, heirs of	Compensation for losses and services in war of 1812.	24	2	Petition	209	Claims	212	Adverse		Laid on table.		
Perry, Samuel, *et al.*	Compensation for transportation of Indian stores and for losses.	25	3	Resolution	272	Claims.						
Perry, Samuel, *et al.*	Payment for transportation of Indian stores and for losses.	28	2	Resolution	89	Claims	173	Favorable; bill	643	Referred to Committee Whole House.		
Perry, Samuel, *et al.*	Payment for transportation of Indian stores and for losses.	29	1	Resolution	411	Claims	691	Favorable; bill	463	Referred to Committee Whole House.		
Perry, Samuel, *et al.*	Payment for transportation of Indian stores and for losses.	30	1	Petition	154	Claims.						
Perry, Samuel, *et al.*	Payment for transportation of Indian stores and for losses.	30	2	Petition	86	Claims	11	Favorable; bill	704	Passed.		
Perry, Samuel, *et al.*	Payment for transportation of Indian stores and for losses.	31	1	Petition	213	Claims.						
Perry, Sarah	(See O. H. and James Alexander Perry, mother of.)	17	2		122							
Perry, William	Revolutionary pension	26	1	Petition	1001	Rev. Pensions	673	Adverse		Laid on table.		
Perron, Charles	(See William Teas, administrator of.)	22	2		88							
Persico, Luigi	Compensation for two statues for the Capitol.	24	2	Senate bill	399	Public Buildings			S. 243			Provided for in civil and diplomatic appropriation bill, Mar. 3, 1839.
Pescud, Edward	Salary as surveyor for port of Petersburg, Virginia, from 1831 to 1840.	26	2	Petition	53	Commerce	Feb. 6, 1841			Discharged; laid on table.		
Pescud, Edward	Salary as surveyor for port of Petersburg, Virginia, from 1831 to 1840.	27	2	Petition	76	Claims	352	Adverse		Laid on table.		
Peteille, Louis	Compensation for houses, &c., destroyed by United States troops.	15	2	Petition	300					Laid on table.		
Peterkin, Thomas	Confirmation of title to land in Arkansas.	17	1	Petition	299	Public Lands				Discharged; laid on table.		

List of private claims presented to the House of Representatives of the United States from the 1st to the 31st Congress, inclusive—Continued.

Names of claimants.	Nature or object of the claim.	Congress.	Session.	How brought before the House of Reps.	Page of journal.	To what committee of the House referred.	No. or date of the report.	Nature of the report.	No. of the bill.	How disposed of by the House of Reps.	How disposed of by the Senate.	Date of the act of Congress, and remarks.
Peters, Adrain	Pension	20	1	Petition	124	Military Pensions	May 19, 1828	Favorable; bill	283	Passed.		
Peters, Adrain	Pension	21	1	Petition	48	Military Pensions	Jan. 5, 1830	Favorable; bill	72	Passed	Passed	App'd May 20, 1830
Peters, Alexander A., widow of.	Pension for services of husband	7	2	Petition	260	Claims	Jan. 5, 1803	Adverse		Leave to withdraw.		
Peter, David, executors of.	(See W. Bowie, Kurtz, and others)	19	1		150							
Peters, Lieut. Gabriel	Commutation pay for revolutionary services.	31	1	Petition	310	Rev. Claims.						
Peters, George	(See W. Bowie, Kurtz, and others)	19	1		150							
Peters, George P., (late captain.)	To be exonerated from deficiency in settlement of accounts.	15	2	Petition	296	Claims				Discharged; laid on table.		
Peters, Gideon & Co	Payment for mail bags destroyed by fire.	28	1	Petition	218	P. Of. & P. Roads.	Feb. 15, 1844			Discharged; laid on table.		
Peters, John, and Sabin Pond.	To refund proceeds of sale of brig Anna and cargo.	19	1	Petition	174	Commerce	179	Favorable; bill	233	Rejected.		
Peters, John, and Sabin Pond.	To refund proceeds of sale of brig Anna and cargo.	20	1	Petition	191	Commerce.	110	Favorable; bill	122	Passed.		
Peters, John, and Sabin Pond.	To refund proceeds of sale of brig Anna and cargo.	20	2	Petition	25	Commerce				Discharged; laid on table.		
Peters, John, and E. Q Sheaffe.	Remission of duties on imported rum.	21	1	Petition	619	Ways and Means.				Discharged; laid on table.		
Peters, John	Increase of compensation as clerk United States court.	25	2	Petition	75	Judiciary	356	Favorable; bill	385	Referred to Committee Whole House.		
Peters, John, widow of	Pension	26	1	Resolution	950	Rev. Pensions.						
Peters, John	(See Henry Gibson and John Peters.)	26	1		175							
Peters, John, heirs of	Renewal of land warrant	27	3	Petition	168	Priv. Land Claims.	123	Favorable; bill	742	Passed	Passed	App'd March 3, 1843
Peters, Joseph	Revolutionary pension	23	1	Petition	53	Rev. Pensions.						
Peters, Joseph	Revolutionary pension	24	1	Petition	213	Rev. Pensions.						
Peters, Joseph	Revolutionary pension	25	2	Petition	180	Rev. Pensions				Referred to Committee Whole House.		
Peters, Joseph P.	Increase of pension	27	3	Petition	345	Rev. Pensions.						
Peters, Joseph P.	Increase of pension	28	1	Petition	70	Rev. Pensions.						
Peters, Landon C.	Damages to his property by volunteers under Brig. Gen. Wool.	26	1	Petition	940	Claims.						
Peters, Landon C.	Damages to his property by volunteers under Brig. Gen. Wool.	26	2	Petition	38	Claims	34	Adverse		Laid on table.		
Peters, Moore & Co.	Compensation for extra mail service.	24	2	Senate bill	579				S. 200			
Peters, Moore & Co.	Compensation for extra mail service	24	2	Petition	214	P. Of. & P. Roads.						
Peters, Moore & Co.	Compensation for extra mail service.	25	2	Memorial	169	P. Of. & P. Roads.				Discharged; laid on table.		
Peters, Moore & Co.	Compensation for extra mail service.	25	2	Senate bill	301	P. Of. and P. Roads.	745	With amends.	S. 20	Ref'd to Com. W. H.		
Peters, Moore & Co.	Compensation for extra mail service.	25	3	Petition	132	P. Of. & P. Roads	144	Favorable; bill	1012	Recommitted.		
Peters, Moore & Co.	Compensation for extra mail service.	26	1	Petition and Senate bill.	183, 227	P. Of. & P. Roads.	324	Favorable	S. 289	Referred to Committee Whole House.		
Peters, Moore & Co.	Compensation for extra mail service,	27	2	Petition	98	P. Of. & P. Roads.	927	Favorable; bill	545	Referred to Committee Whole House.		
Peters, Moore & Co.	Additional compensation for carrying mail.	27	3	House bill	89	Whole House.			545	Passed	Passed	App'd March 3, 1843
Peters, Moore & Co.	Compensation for extra mail service.	28	1	Petition	345	P. Of. & P. Roads.	May 10, 1844	Favorable; bill	361	Referred to Committee Whole House.		
Peters, Moore & Co.	Additional compensation for extra mail service.	29	1	Petition	115, 471	P. Of. & P. Roads.	Feb. 28, 1846	Favorable; bill	283	Referred to Commitee Whole House.		

List of private claims presented to the House of Representatives of the United States from the 1st to the 31st Congress, inclusive—Continued.

Names of claimants.	Nature or object of the claim.	Congress.	Session.	How brought before the House of Reps.	Page of journal.	To what committee of the House referred.	No. or date of the report.	Nature of the report.	No. of the bill.	How disposed of by the House of Reps.	How disposed of by the Senate.	Date of the act of Congress, and remarks.
Peters, Moore & Co.	Additional compensation for extra mail service.	30	1	Petition	229	P. Of. and P. Roads	494	Adverse	......	Laid on table.		
Peters, Moore & Co.	Additional compensation for extra mail service.	31	1	Petition	389	P. Of. & P. Roads.						
Peters, Osmond	Pay as lieutenant in the navy while acting as such.	26	1	Petition	330	Military Affairs	July 2, 1840	Favorable; bill	462	Referred to Committee Whole House.		
Peters, Osmond	Payment for time while improperly dismissed from revenue service.	31	1	Petition	201	Commerce	May 16, 1850	....	......	Discharged; laid on table.		
Peters & Pond	Indemnity for French spoliations prior to 1800.	26	1	Memorial	182	Foreign Affairs	343	Favorable; bill	319	Referred to Committee Whole House.		
Peters, Dr. Samuel	(See Jonathan Carver, assignee of.)	18	2	....	74							
Peters, Sarah	(See Alexander A. Peters, widow of.)	7	2	....	260							
Peters, Susannah	Continuance of pension	28	1	Petition	850	Rev. Pensions.						
Peter, Thomas	(See W. Bowie, Kurtz, and others)	19	1	....	150							
Peterson, A. A.	(See Exploring Expedition.)	27	2	....	149							
Peterson, Andrew, heir of.	Bounty land for his services	28	2	Petition	206	Rev. Claims.						
Peterson, Andrew, heir of.	Bounty land for his services	30	1	Petition	627	Public Lands.						
Peterson, Ezekiel, heirs and representatives of.	Compensation for revolutionary services.	19	1	Petition	57	Priv. Land Claims.	Feb. 15, 1826	Adverse	......	Laid on table.		
Peterson, Falck J.	Drawback on willow hats	20	1	Petition	276	Commerce	....	....	.....	Discharged; laid on table.		
Peterson, Gabriel.	Pension for wounds received in revolutionary war.	11	2	Petition and rep't Sec. of War.	236	....	....	....	......	Laid on table.		
Peterson, John	Compensation for revolutionary services.	25	2	Petition	390	Rev. Claims	684	Adverse	......	Laid on table.		
Peterson, John H., surveyor and inspector of customs, (Va.)	Increase of compensation	20	1	Petition	276	Commerce	....	....	......	Discharged; laid on table.		
Peterson, John H., executor of.	Salary due deceased as surveyor and inspector of customs, Va.	24	1	Petition	212	Commerce	805	Favorable; bill	721	Referred to Committee Whole House.		
Peterson, John H., executor of.	Salary due deceased as surveyor and inspector of customs, Va.	25	2	Petition	40	Commerce	90	Favorable; bill	106	Passed	Passed	App'd July 7, 1838
Peterson, M. C., and P. W. Law.	Benefit of law for armed occupation of Florida.	30	1	Petition	678	Public Lands.						
Peterson, Nicholas	Confirmation of land title erroneously patented.	26	1	Petition	365	Claims.						
Peterson, Samuel and Hannah.	Indemnity for damages to property by United States troops in late war.	15	2	Petition	117	Claims	....	....	......	Discharged; laid on table.		
Peterson, Samuel and Hannah.	Indemnity for damages to property by United States troops in late war.	16	1	Petition	136	Claims	Jan. 14, 1820	Adverse	......	Laid on table.		
Peterson, Samuel and Hannah.	Indemnity for damages to property by United States troops in late war.	16	2	Petition and rep't of last session.	119	Claims	....	....	......	Discharged; laid on table.		
Peterson, Samuel and Hannah.	Indemnity for damages to property by United States troops in late war.	17	1	Petition	201	Claims	April 5, 1822	Favorable; bill	154	Passed	Indef. postp'd.	
Peterson, Samuel and Hannah.	Indemnity for damages to property by United States troops in late war.	17	2	Senate bill	179	Claims	Jan. 31, 1823	With't amend.	S. 27	Passed	....	App'd March 3, 1823

List of private claims presented to the House of Representatives of the United States from the 1st to the 31st Congress, inclusive—Continued.

Names of claimants.	Nature or object of the claim.	Congress.	Session.	How brought before the House of Reps.	Page of journal.	To what committee of the House referred.	No. or date of the report.	Nature of the report.	No. of the bill.	How disposed of by the House of Reps.	How disposed of by the Senate.	Date of the act of Congress, and remarks.
Peterson, Teye T.	Right to enter land at minimum price.	25	2	Petition	372	Priv. Land Claims.	727	Adverse	......	Laid on table.		
Peterson, Teye T.	Right to enter land at minimum price.	25	3	Petition	133	Priv. Land Claims.	143	Adverse	......	Laid on table.		
Peterson, Teye T.	Right to purchase land not yet surveyed.	27	1	Petition	99	Priv. Land Claims.						
Pe igru, ——	(See Pettigrew.)											
Petray, Louis A., and Just Viel.	To refund duties paid on sugar	18	1	Petition	30	Ways and Means.						
Petray & Viel	To refund duties paid on sugar	18	1	Senate bill	328	Whole House	April 30, 1824	With't amend.	S. 58	Passed	....	App'd May 5, 1824
Pettibone, Daniel	Compensation for use, by United States, of machine for boring gun barrels.	14	1	Petition	153	Claims	....	....	......	Discharged; laid on table.		
Pettibone, Daniel	Compensa ion for use, by United States, of machine for boring gun barrels.	14	2	Petition	58	Claims	Jan. 27, 1817	Adverse	......	Leave to withdraw.		
Pettibone, Daniel, for self and E. and J. Nichols.	Renewal of patent for welding and working cast steel.	14	2	Petition	76	Select.						
Pettibone, Daniel, for self and E. and J. Nichols.	Renewal of patent for welding and working cast steel.	15	1	Petition	211	Select	Feb. 25, 1818	Adverse	......	Rejected.		
Pettibone, Daniel, for self and E. and J. Nichols.	Renewal of patent for welding and working cast steel.	16	1	Petition	66	Judiciary.						
Pettibone, Daniel	Renewal of patent for forming edged tools.	15	2	Senate bill	259	Select	March 2, 1819	Adverse	S. 33	Laid on table.		
Pettibone, Daniel, heirs of.	Compensa ion for use of machine for making iron balls.	26	2	Senate bill	248	Whole House	....	....	S. 202			
Pettibone, Daniel, heirs of.	Renewal of patent right	26	2	Petition	132	Patents	160	Favorable; bill	672	Referred to Committee Whole House.		
Pettibone, Daniel, heirs of.	Compensation for use by United States of circular bullet moulds.	27	2	Senate bill	155	Military Affairs	Mar. 8, 1842	Favorable; bill	S. 10	Passed	Passed	App'd July 6, 1842
Pettibone, Daniel, heirs of.	(See John Pettibone and others)	30	1	....	109	....	806	....	627			
Pettibone, John	Extension of patent	29	1	Petition	68	Patents.						
Pettibone, John, for self and heirs of Daniel.	Compensation for use of patent for rarefying air stove.	29	1	Memorial	315	Patents.						
Pettibone, John, for self and heirs of Daniel.	Compensation for use of patent for rarefying air stove.	30	1	Petition	109	Patents	806	Favorable; bill	627	Referred to Committee Whole House.		
Pettibone, John, for self and heirs of Daniel.	Compensation for use of patent for rarefying air stove.	31	1	Petition	212	Claims.						
Pettibone, Sylvester	Relief as surety of Wm. Pettibone.	31	1	Petition	938	Judiciary	412	Favorable; bill	354	Ref'd to Com. W. H.		
Pettigrew, James	Renewal of certain Continental certificates which had been lost or destroyed.	2	1	Petition	459	....	....	....	......	Referred to Secretary Treasury.		
Pettigrew, James and Alexander, heirs and representatives of.	Compensation for property taken by Cherokee Indians.	18	2	Petition	46	Claims	Jan. 5, 1825	Adverse	......	Laid on table.		
Pettigrew, James and Alexander, heirs and representatives of.	Compensation for property taken by Cherokee Indians.	19	2	Petition	156	Indian Affairs.						
Pettigrew, James and Alexander, heirs and representatives of.	Compensation for property taken by Cherokee Indians.	21	1	Petition	116	Indian Affairs	April 16, 1830	Adverse	......	Referred to Committee Whole House.		
Pettigrew, James and John.	(See Alexander Scott and others.)	8	2	....	74							

List of private claims presented to the House of Representatives of the United States from the 1st to the 31st Congress, inclusive—Continued.

Names of claimants.	Nature or object of the claim.	Congress.	Session.	How brought before the House of Reps.	Page of journal.	To what committee of the House referred.	No. or date of the report.	Nature of the report.	No. of the bill.	How disposed of by the House of Reps.	How disposed of by the Senate.	Date of the act of Congress, and remarks.
Pettigrew, James and John, attorney for heirs of.	Compensation for certain slaves captured by Cherokee Indians.	22	1	Petition	401	Indian Affairs	406	Favorable; bill	504	Passed	Passed	App'd July 14, 1832
Pettigrew, James and John, agent for heirs of.	Additional compensation for certain slaves taken by Cherokee Indians.	22	2	Petition	75	Indian Affairs.						
Pettigrew, Timothy and Robert.	(See James and Alexander Pettigrew.)	18	2	....	46							
Pettingel, John	Indemnity for French spoliations prior to 1800.	26	1	Memorial	182	Foreign Affairs	343	Favorable; bill	319	Referred to Committee Whole House.		
Pettingel, J., executor of.	Indemnity for French spoliations prior to 1800.	26	1	Memorial	182	Foreign Affairs	343	Adverse	319	Referred to Committee Whole House.		
Pettingill, Abraham	Pension for services in the late war.	24	1	Petition	98	Invalid Pensions	Feb. 4, 1836	Adverse	......	Laid on table.		
Pettingill, A. M.	One months' extra pay for transporting mail.	28	2	Petition	332	P. Of. & P. Roads.						
Pettingill, Samuel	Revolutionary pension	24	1	Resolution	923	Rev. Pensions.						
Pettingill, Samuel	Revolutionary pension	25	2	Petition	177	Rev. Pensions	....	....	......	Discharged; laid on table.		
Pettingill, Samuel	Revolutionary pension	26	1	Petition	172	Rev. Pensions.						
Pettingill, Sarah	(See Joshua O. Alley, heirs of.)	26	1	....	199							
Pettit & Bayard, assignee of.	Indemnity for French spoliations prior to 1800.	26	1	Memorial	182	Foreign Affairs	343	Favorable	319	Referred to Committee Whole House.		
Pettit, Charles, surviving partner of Major General Green and John Cox.	Allowance of further credits in the settlement of the accounts of Gen. Green, and that the balance found to be due be paid to him.	4	1	Memorial	395	....	....	....	......	Referred to Secretary of Treasury.		
Pettit, Charles, surviving partner of Major General Green and John Cox.	Allowance of further credits in the settlement of the accounts of Gen. Green, and that the balance found to be due be paid to him.	6	1	Petition and rep't Sec. Treasury.	547	Claims	April 29, 1800	Adverse	......	Referred to Committee Whole House.		
Pettit, Charles, surviving partner of Major General Green and John Cox.	Allowance of further credits in the settlement of the accounts of Gen. Green, and that the balance found to be due be paid to him.	7	1	Petition and docs.	95	....	....	....	......	Referred to Secretary Treasury.		
Pettit, Charles, surviving partner of Major General Green and John Cox.	Allowance of further credits in the settlement of the accounts of Gen. Green, and that the balance found to be due be paid to him	7	2	Petition, docs., & reports.	306	....	....	....	......	Referred to Secretary Treasury.		
Pettit, Charles, administrator of.	Indemnity for French spoliations prior to 1800.	26	1	Memorial	182	Foreign Affairs	343	Favorable	319	Referred to Committee Whole House.		
Pettit, Enos	Pension	11	2	House bill	283	Whole House	Mar. 24, 1810	With amends.	107	Passed	Passed	App'd April 27, 1810
Pettit, John	Pension	15	2	Resolution	136	Rev. Claims	Jan. 5, 1819	Adverse	......	Laid on table.		
Pettit, John	Pension	16	1	Petition	23	Rev. Pensions	April 22, 1820	Adverse	......	Leave to withdraw.		
Petit, Peter, and A. Cavalier.	Confirmation of title to tract of land.	15	1	Senate bill	440	Priv. Land Claims.	....	....	S. 71	Laid on table.		
Petit, Peter, and A. Cavalier.	Confirmation of title to tract of land.	15	2	Senate bill	252	....	....	....	S. 32			
Petit, Peter, and A. Cavalier.	Confirmation of title to tract of land.	16	1	Senate bill	207	Priv. Land Claims.	Feb. 18, 1820	Favorable	S. 21	Passed	Passed	App'd Feb. 28, 1820
Pettit, William McD.	Permission to enter land at minimum price, and return donation claims.	25	2	Petition	38	Priv. Land Claims.						
Petrie, Daniel	(See Nehemiah Huntington, postmaster.)	17	1	....	150							
Petrie, George	Restoration of pension	17	1	Petition	45	Rev. Pensions	....	....	......	Discharged; laid on table.		
Petre, John Baptiste, attorney of.	Compensation for provisions taken by United States troops in 1813.	16	1	Petition	49	Claims	....	....	......	Discharged; laid on table.		

List of private claims presented to the House of Representatives of the United States from the 1st to the 31st Congress, inclusive—Continued.

Names of claimants.	Nature or object of the claim.	Congress.	Session.	How brought before the House of Reps.	Page of journal.	To what committee of the House referred.	No. or date of the report.	Nature of the report.	No. of the bill.	How disposed of by the House of Reps.	How disposed of by the Senate.	Date of the act of Congress, and remarks.
Petrie, Joseph Pierre	That grants of land be made to officers of United States army who served in late war.	23	1	Petition	298	Public Lands.						
Petre, Joseph Pierre	Refunding money paid on land	22	2	House bill	223	Whole House			701			
Petre, Joseph Pierre	Refund ng money paid on land	23	1	Petition	93	Priv. Land Claims.	Dec. 24, 1833	Favorable; bill	89	Passed	Passed	App'd June 28, 1834
Petroline, P., attorney of	Indemnity for French spoliations prior to 1800.	26	1	Memorial	182	Foreign Affairs	343	Favorable; bill	319	Referred to Committee Whole House.		
Petry, William	Relief for wound received in revolutionary war.	9	1	Petition	191	Claims	Mar. 28, 1806	Report		Indefinitely postponed.		Leave to withdraw.
Pettrick, Ferdinand	Paym nt for models of statuary	25	2	Petition	173	Public Buildings				Discharged.		
Pettrick, Ferdinand	Payment for finishing sta ue of Washington.	27	2	Senate joint resolution.	1014	Library	July 27, 1842	With't amend.	S. 15	Passed	Passed	App'd Aug. 29, 1842
Pettrick, Ferdinand	Remuneration for repairing illustrations on pedestal of sta'ue of Washington.	30	1	Petition	136	Public Buildings.						
Pettus, Samuel O., heir of.	Commutation of half-pay due as an officer in the revolutionary war.	23	1	Petition	121	Rev. Claims.						
Pettus, Samuel O., heir of.	Commutation of half-pay due as an officer in the revolutionary war.	23	2	Petition	48	Rev. Claims.						
Pettus, Samuel O., heir of.	Commutation of half-pay due as an officer in the revolutionary war.	24	2	Petition	119	Rev. Claims.						
Pettus, Samuel O., heir of.	Commutation of half-pay due as an officer in the revolutionary war.	25	2	Petition	82	Rev. Claims.	208	Favorable; bill	243	Passed.		
Pettus, Samuel O., heir of.	Commutation of half-pay due as an officer in the revolutionary war.	25	3	Petition	84	Rev. Claims	20	Favorable; bill	918	Referred to Committee Whole House.		
Pettus, Samuel O., heir of.	Commutation of half-pay due as an officer in the revolutionary war.	26	1	Petition	165	Rev. Claims	436	Adverse		Laid on table.		
Pettus, William G	(See George Collier and William G. Pettus.)	26	1		623							
Petty, Alexander	(See William H. Bedford, agent.)	28	1		262							
Petty, Elijah, and wife	(See John Beardon, heirs of)	30	1		361							
Pettypool, Joseph, late paymaster U. S. army.	Relief from judgment obtained against him by United States for $70,000.	17	1	Petition	288	Judiciary				Discharged; laid on table.		
Pettypool, Joseph, sureties of.	Relief in settlement of accounts	17	1	Senate bill	430	Judiciary	April 9, 1822	Favorable	63	Passed	Passed	App'd May 7, 1822
Peurifoy, Telman D	Compensation for slaves murdered by Indians.	25	3	Petition	205	Claims	203	Adverse		Laid on table.		
Pevey, Lucy	Continuance of pension	28	1	Petition	850	Rev. Pensions.						
Pew, William	Revolutionary pension	18	1	Petition	30	Pens. & Rev. Cl'ms.	Dec. 16, 1823	Adverse		Laid on table.		
Pew, William	Revolutionary pension	20	2	Resolution	268	Military Pensions				Discharged; laid on table.		
Pew, William	Revolutionary pension	21	1	Petition	49	Military Pensions	Jan. 5, 1830	Favorable; bill	72	Passed	Passed	App'd May 20, 1830
Peyster, ——	(See De Peyster)	26	1		182							
Peyton, Craven T	For an American registry for his vessel.	14	1	Petition	587	Com. and Manuf.				Discharged; laid on table.		
Peyton, Lieut. Dade, heirs and representatives of.	Commutation of half-pay for life for services as an officer in revolutionary war.	23	1	Petition	188	Rev. Claims.						
Peyton, Lieut. Dade, heirs and representatives of.	Commutation of half-pay for life for services as an officer in revolutionary war.	23	2	Petition	147	Rev. Claims.						

List of private claims presented to the House of Representatives of the United States from the 1st to the 31st Congress, inclusive—Continued.

Names of claimants.	Nature or object of the claim.	Congress.	Session.	How brought before the House of Reps.	Page of journal.	To what committee of the House referred.	No. or date of the report.	Nature of the report.	No. of the bill.	How disposed of by the House of Reps.	How disposed of by the Senate.	Date of the act of Congress, and remarks.
Peyton, Lieut. Dade, heirs and representatives of.	Commutation of half-pay for life for services as an officer in revolutionary war.	24	1	Petition	138	Rev. Claims.						
Peyton, Lieut. Dade, heirs and representatives of.	Commutation of half-pay for life for services as an officer in revolutionary war.	25	2	Petition	76	Rev. Claims	....	....	......	Discharged; laid on table.		
Peyton & Hargrove, (captains of Indiana Rangers.)	Compensation for military services.	13	2	Petition	251	Military Affairs.						
Peyton, Henry, heirs and representatives of.	Commutation of half-pay for life as major in Continental line, revolutionary war.	23	1	Petition	188	Rev. Claims.						
Peyton, Henry, heirs and representatives of.	Commutation of half-pay for life as major in Continental line, revolutionary war.	23	2	Petition	147	Rev. Claims.						
Peyton, Henry, heirs and representatives of.	Commutation of half pay for life as major in Continental line, revolutionary war.	24	1	Petition	138	Rev. Claims.						
Peyton, Henry, heirs and representatives of.	Commutation of half-pay for life as major in Continental line, revolutionary war.	25	2	Petition	76	Rev. Claims	....	....	......	Discharged; laid on table.		
Peyton, Henry, (of Cabell county, Va.)	Arrears of pension	25	2	Petition	664	Rev. Pensions.						
Peyton, Henry, (of Cabell county, Va.)	Arrears of pension	25	3	Petition	225	Rev. Pensions	Feb. 16, 1839	Favorable; bill	1150	Referred to Committee Whole House.		
Peyton, Henry, (of Cabell county, Va.)	Arrears of pension	26	1	Petition	172	Rev. Pensions	....	....	......	Discharged; laid on table.		
Peyton, Valentine R., administrator of.	Commutation pay	24	1	Petition	152	Rev. Claims.						
Pezant, John L., & Co., representatives of.	Remission of duties on fruit	27	2	Petition	224	Commerce	892	Adverse	......	Laid on table.		
Pfrimmer, John George	Release from judgment as surety of William Branham.	16	2	Petition	189	P. Of. & P. Roads.						
Phagan, John	Compensation for services as Indian agent in Florida.	24	2	Petition	210	Indian Affairs	....	....	......	Discharged; laid on table.		
Phagan, John	Compensation for services as Indian agent in Florida.	27	3	Resolution	296	Claims.						
Phagan, John	Compensation for services in removing Indians from Florida.	28	1	Petition	131	Claims.						
Phagan, John	Compensation for services in removing Indians from Florida.	30	1	Petition	819	Indian Affairs	....	....	......	Discharged; laid on table.		
Pharoah, Joshua	Increase of pension	25	1	Petition	80	....	....	....	......	Laid on table.		
Pharoah, Joshua	Increase of pension	25	2	Petition	273	Rev. Pensions	....	....	......	Disch'd; laid on table.		
Pharr, Ephraim, attorney, &c.	(See Daniel Davis, administrator of.)											
Phelan, John, widow of	Assistance from government on account of services in revolutionary war.	18	2	Petition	230	Pens. & Rev. Cl'ms.	....	....	......	Discharged; laid on table.		
Phelan, John, widow of	Assistance from government on account of services in revolutionary war.	19	1	Petition	224	....	....	....	......	Referred to Secretary War.		
Phelan, John, widow of	Assistance from government on account of services in revolutionary war.	19	2	Petition	188	Rev. Claims	....	....	......	Discharged; laid on table.		

List of private claims presented to the House of Representatives of the United States from the 1st to the 31st Congress, inclusive—Continued.

Names of claimants.	Nature or object of the claim.	Congress.	Session.	How brought before the House of Reps.	Page of journal.	To what committee of the House referred.	No. or date of the report.	Nature of the report.	No. of the bill.	How disposed of by the House of Reps.	How disposed of by the Senate.	Date of the act of Congress, and remarks.
Phelan, John, heir of	Script or bounty land for services in revolutionary war.	25	3	Petition	133	Pens. & Rev. Cl'ms.	142	Favorable; bill	1011	Passed	Passed	App'd March 3, 1839
Phelan, Nicholas	(See John Phelan, heir of)	25	3		133							
Phelps, Alexander	Increase of pension	11	1	Petition	60	Claims				Discharged; laid on table.		
Phelps, Alexander	Increase of pension	24	1	Petition	137	Invalid Pensions				Discharged; laid on table.		
Phelps, Alexander	Increase of pension	24	2	Petition	72	Invalid Pensions				Discharged; laid on table.		
Phelps, Arminda	(See Obadiah Phelps, widow of)	26	2		146							
Phelps, Bissell	Compensation for services as wagon master in revolutionary war.	15	2	Petition	121	Pens. & Rev. Cl'ms.	Jan. 4, 1819	Adverse		Rejected		Leave to withdraw.
Phelps, Bissell	Compensation for services as wagon master in revolutionary war.	18	2	Petition	69	Pens. & Rev. Cl'ms.	Jan. 26, 1825	Adverse		Laid on table.		
Phelps, Bissell, (Vt.)	Restoration of pension	27	3	Petition	69	Rev. Pensions	295	Adverse		Laid on table.		
Phelps, Cornelius	Arrears of pension	25	3	Petition	127	Rev. Pensions	Jan. 16, 1839	Adverse		Laid on table.		
Phelps, Cornelius, widow of.	Extension of provisions of acts granting pensions to widows.	30	1	Petition	264	Rev. Pensions	385	Adverse		Laid on table.		
Phelps, Cornelius, widow of.	Extension of provisions of acts granting pensions to widows.	31	2	Petition	50	Rev. Pensions	Mar. 3, 1851	Adverse		Laid on table.		
Phelps, Eleazer W., widow of.	Compensation for boarding sundry cadets at West Point who were unable to pay.	15	2	Petition	209	Claims.						
Phelps, Eleazer W., widow of.	Compensation for boarding sundry cadets at West Point who were unable to pay.	17	1	Petition	133	Claims	Feb. 20, 1822	Adverse		Laid on table.		
Phelps, Elnathan	Bounty land for services in war of 1812.	31	1	Petition	661	Invalid Pensions				Discharged; laid on table.		
Phelps, Epaphras L.	Indemnity for property destroyed in Upper Canada while occupied by United States troops.	14	2	Petition	372	Claims				Discharged		Leave to withdraw.
Phelps, Epaphras L., administrators of.	Indemnity for property destroyed in Upper Canada while occupied by United States troops.	19	1	Petition	252	Claims	May 15, 1826	Adverse		Laid on table.		
Phelps, Hannah	(See Samuel Phelps, widow of)	31	1		865							
Phelps, James, (N.Y.)	Revolutionary pension	26	1	Petition	286	Rev. Pensions	113	Favorable; bill	124	Passed	Indef. postp'd.	
Phelps, James	Pension for services as guard of public stores in revolutionary war.	27	2	Petition	73	Rev. Pensions	108	Favorable; bill	154	Passed	Indef. postp'd.	
Phelps, James, heirs of	Pension for services in revolutionary war.	30	1	Petition	339	Rev. Pensions				Discharged; laid on table.		
Phelps, James, heirs of	Pension for services in revolutionary war.	30	2	Petition	164	Rev. Pensions				Leave to withdraw.		
Phelps, Joel	Invalid pension	1	3	Petition & report Sec. of War.	364					Laid on table.		
Phelps, Joel	Invalid pension	2	1	Petition & report Sec. of War.	464					Referred to Committee Whole House.		
Phelps, Joel	Invalid pension	3	1	Rep. of Secretary War.	131	Select	May 26, 1794	Joint resolut'n.	12	Passed	Passed	App'd June 9, 1794
Phelps, Joel	Invalid pension	3	2	Rep. of Secretary War.	262	Claims	Feb. 28, 1795	Favorable; bill	130	Passed	Postponed.	
Phelps, Joel	Invalid pension	4	1	Rep. of Secretary War.	445	Claims	Feb. 18, 1796	Favorable; bill	156	Passed	Passed	App'd April 20, 1796

List of private claims presented to the House of Representatives of the United States from the 1st to the 31st Congress, inclusive—Continued.

Names of claimants.	Nature or object of the claim.	Congress.	Session.	How brought before the House of Reps.	Page of journal.	To what committee of the House referred.	No. or date of the report.	Nature of the report.	No. of the bill.	How disposed of by the House of Reps.	How disposed of by the Senate.	Date of the act of Congress, and remarks.
Phelps, John, in behalf of minor son.	Extra pay and bounty land for services of James Malary in Mexican war.	31	2	Petition	78	Military Affairs	....	....	......	Discharged; laid on table.		
Phelps, John D	(See Fidelius C. Sharp and others)	19	2	....	113							
Phelps, Lyman and James.	(See James Phelps, heirs of)	30	1	....	339							
Phelps, Mary	(See Reuben Phelps, widow of)	25	2	....	52							
Phelps, Mary	(See Richard Austin, widow of)	29	1	....	266							
Phelps, Major Matthew, widow of.	Revolutionary pension	14	1	Petition	47	Pens. & Rev. Cl'ms.	....	....	......	Discharged; laid on table.		
Phelps, Noah	Compensation for services in revolutionary war.	2	2	Petition	634	....	....	....	......	Rejected.		
Phelps, Noah A	Payment of amount awarded by United States district court of Connecticut.	29	2	Petition	99	Claims	67	Favorable; bill	673	Referred to Committee Whole House.		
Phelps, Noah A	Payment of amount awarded by United States district court of Connecticut.	30	1	Petition	154	Claims	214	Favorable; bill	214	Referred to Committee Whole House.		
Phelps, Noah A	Payment of amount awarded by United States district court of Connecticut.	30	2	Bill of last sess.	368	Whole House	Feb. 3, 1849	With't amend.	214	Passed	Passed	App'd March 3, 1849
Phelps, Obadiah, widow of.	Pension	26	2	Petition	146	Invalid Pensions.						
Phelps, Oliver	(See Nathaniel Gordon and others.)	1	1	....	66							
Phelps, Oliver	(See Comfort Sands, *et al.*)	1	3	....	358							
Phelps, Oliver	To be placed on the pension roll	21	2	Resolution	65	Military Pensions.						
Phelps, Oliver	To be placed on the pension roll	22	1	Resolution	141	Rev. Pensions	....	....	......	Disch'd; laid on table.		
Phelps, Peleg B	Increase of compensation as surveyor and inspector of the revenue.	30	1	Petition	414	Claims	....	....	......	Discharged; laid on table.		
Phelps, Philemon	(See Cornelius Phelps, widow of)	30	1	....	264							
Phelps, Phoebe	Compensation for boarding cadets at West Point.	17	1	Petition	133	Claims	Jan. 24, 1822	Adverse	......	Laid on table.		
Phelps, Reuben, widow of.	Benefit of the act of July 4, 1836.	25	2	Petition	52	Rev. Pensions	609	Favorable; bill	589	Passed.		
Phelps, Samuel, widow of.	Revolutionary pension	31	1	Petition	865	Rev. Pensions	360	Adverse	......	Laid on table.		
Phelps, Seth	Pension, or other relief	18	2	Petition	36	Pens. & Rev. Cl'ms.						
Phelps, Susannah	(See Epaphras L. Phelps, administrators of.)	19	1	....	252							
Phelps, Sylvester, and Chas. Landon.	Indemnity for property destroyed by the enemy while in possession of United States troops.	14	1	Petition	76	Claims	Jan. 15, 1816	Adverse	......	Laid on table.	....	Leave to withdraw.
Phelps, Sylvester, and Chas. Landon.	Indemnity for property destroyed by the enemy while in possession of United States troops.	15	1	Petition	222	Claims	Feb. 24, 1818	Adverse	......	Rejected.		
Phelps, Sylvester, and Chas. Landon.	Indemnity for property destroyed by the enemy while in possession of United States troops.	23	1	Petition	35	Claims	....	....	......	Discharged; laid on table.		
Phelps, Sylvester, surviving partner of Phelps & Landon.	Indemnity for property destroyed by the enemy while in possession of United States troops.	24	1	Petition	93	Claims.						
Phelps, Sylvester, surviving partner of Phelps & Landon.	Indemnity for property destroyed by the enemy while in possession of United States troops.	24	2	Petition	110	Claims.						
Phelps, Sylvester, surviving partner of Phelps & Landon.	Indemnity for property destroyed by the enemy while in possession of United States troops.	25	2	Petition	51	Claims	442	Favorable; bill	446	Referred to Committee Whole House.		

List of private claims presented to the House of Representatives of the United States from the 1st to the 31st Congress, inclusive—Continued.

Names of claimants.	Nature or object of the claim.	Congress.	Session.	How brought before the House of Reps.	Page of journal.	To what committee of the House referred.	No. or date of the report.	Nature of the report.	No. of the bill.	How disposed of by the House of Reps.	How disposed of by the Senate.	Date of the act of Congress, and remarks.
Phelps, Sylvester, surviving partner of Phelps & Landon.	Indemnity for property destroyed by the enemy while in possession of United States troops.	25	3	Bill of last sess.	378	Whole House	Jan. 25, 1839	With't amend.	446	Passed.		
Phelps, Sylvester, surviving partner of Phelps & Landon.	Indemnity for property destroyed by the enemy while in possession of United States troops.	26	1	Petition	168	Claims	26	Favorable; bill	45	Passed	Indef. postp'd.	
Phelps, Sylvester, surviving partner of Phelps & Landon.	Indemnity for property destroyed by the enemy while in possession of United States troops.	26	2	House bill	101	Whole House			55			
Phelps, Sylvester, surviving partner of Phelps & Landon.	Indemnity for property destroyed by the enemy while in possession of United States troops.	27	2	Petition	55	Claims	13	Favorable; bill	52	Passed	Passed	App'd Aug. 1, 1842
Phelps, Sylvester	Indemnity for property impressed into United States service and destroyed.	22	1	Petition	165	Claims.						
Phelps, Sylvester	Indemnity for property impressed into United States service and destroyed.	22	2	Petition	151	Claims.						
Phelps, Thaddeus, & others.	(See Bogart & Kneeland, & others)	29	2		142							
Phelps, Thaddeus, & Co.	Benefit of drawback on one hundred and eighty bales of Cuba cotton shipped to Liverpool.	19	1	Petition	334	Ways and Means	May 3, 1826	Adverse		Laid on table.		
Phelps, Thaddeus, & Co.	Benefit of drawback on one hundred and eighty bales of Cuba cotton shipped to Liverpool.	22	1	Petition	186	Ways and Means	Jan. 25, 1832	Favorable; bill	316	Referred to Committee Whole House.		
Phelps, Thaddeus, & Co.	Benefit of drawback on one hundred and eighty bales of Cuba cotton shipped to Liverpool.	22	2	Bill of last sess.	171	Whole House	Feb. 15, 1833	With amend.	316	Passed	Passed	App'd March 2, 1833
Phelps, Thaddeus, & others.	Assumption by United States of Neapolitan indemnity stock.	25	2	Petition	192	Claims	597	Adverse		Laid on table.		
Phelps, Thaddeus, & others.	Assumption by United States of Neapolitan indemnity stock.	25	2	Petition and rep't No. 597.	341	Foreign Affairs.						
Phelps, Thomas W., and W. Cotton.	Release from liability as sureties for Enoch M. Granger in a bond to secure duties on a distillery.	14	2	Petition	342	Ways and Means				Discharged; laid on table.		
Phelps, Thomas W., W. Cotton, and E. M. Granger.	(See S. Blakeslee, sureties of)	15	1		211							
Phelps, Timothy	Indemnity for injuries sustained by the action of the authorities of Vermont during the territorial controversy with New York.	8	2	Petition	23	Claims	Dec. 13, 1814	Adverse		Rejected.		
Phelps, William	Revolutionary pension	24	2	Petition	271	Rev. Pensions				Discharged; laid on table.		
Philadelphia Library Company, by Thomas Parke, and others.	Remission of duties on books and prints imported for use of said company.	8	2	Petition	18	Com. and Manuf.	Dec. 4, 1804	Adverse		Leave to withdraw.		
Philadelphia frigate, officers and crew.	Prize money for capturing ship Mirboha returned to Emperor of Morocco.	8	1	House bill	525	Whole House	Jan. 11, 1804	With amend'ts	160	Passed	Passed	App'd Mar. 19, 1804
Philadelphia frigate, crew of.	Compensation for allowance withheld, also for stoppages from their pay.	9	1	Petition	192	Claims	Dec. 17, 1805	Adverse		Leave to withdraw.		

List of private claims presented to the House of Representatives of the United States from the 1st to the 31st Congress, inclusive—Continued.

Names of claimants.	Nature or object of the claim.	Congress.	Session.	How brought before the House of Reps.	Page of journal.	To what committee of the House referred.	No. or date of the report.	Nature of the report.	No. of the bill.	How disposed of by the House of Reps.	How disposed of by the Senate.	Date of the act of Congress, and remarks.
Philadelphia frigate, crew of.	(See Christopher Simmons, and others.)	9	1	....	257							
Philadelphia frigate, captors of.	Pensions to survivors...........	30	1	Resolution	326	Rev. Pensions.....	520	Favorable; bill	448	Referred to Committee Whole House.		
Philadelphia frigate, captors of.	Prize money for her destruction ..	30	1	Resolution	326	Claims	....	....	......	Discharged; laid on table.		
Philadelphia, frigate, captors of.	Reward for recapturing the same..	31	1	Petition	192	Naval Affairs.....	14	Favorable; bill	17	Referred to Committee Whole House.		
Philadelphia, citizens of...	Indemnity for French spoliations prior to 1800.	26	1	Memorial	182	Foreign Affairs....	343	Favorable; bill	319	Referred to Committee Whole House.		
Philadelphia Gas Company, trustees of.	Refunding duties on telescope gas-holder.	31	1	Memorial	1253	Ways and Means.						
Philadelphia, Wilmington, and Baltimore Railroad Company.	Remission of duties on railroad iron	25	3	Senate bill	149	Manufactures	Jan. 3, 1839	With amend'ts	77	Passed	Passed	App'd Feb. 6, 1839
Philbrook, Joseph	Revolutionary pension	23	1	Petition	69	Rev. Pensions	Dec. 24, 1833	Adverse	......	Laid on table.		
Phillips, Benjamin.......	For value of five slaves captured by the British.	19	2	By message from President.	171	Foreign Affairs....	Jan. 26, 1827	By bill	395	Referred to Committee Whole House.		
Phillips, Bradford	Pension for services in the navy in the late war.	25	3	Petition	130	Naval Affairs.						
Phillips, Charles	Restoration to pension roll.......	20	2	Petition	55	Military Pensions..	....	....	......	Discharged; laid on table.		
Phillips, Charles	Restoration to pension roll.......	21	1	Petition	99	Military Pensions..	April 6, 1830	Adverse	......	Laid on table.		
Phillips, Charles	Increase of pension	22	2	Petition	310	Rev. Pensions.						
Phillips, Cramond & Co., attorney of.	Indemnity for French spoliations prior to 1800.	26	1	Memorial	182	Foreign Affairs....	343	Favorable	319	Referred to Committee Whole House.		
Phillips, Ebenezer	Restoration of pension..........	17	2	Petition	99	....	....	....	......	Referred to Committee Whole House.		
Phillips, Ebenezer, & others	Bounty on a fishing vessel fitted out and lost at sea.	24	1	Petition	54	Commerce	49	Favorable; bill	61	Passed	Passed	App'd June 23, 1836
Phillips, Lieutenant E....	Pay for extra services rendered out of the line of his duty.	23	1	Petition	222	Military Affairs....	Feb. 7, 1834	Adverse	......	Laid on table.		
Phillips, George T., syndics of the creditors of.	Cancellation of bonds given for the safe landing of merchandise in foreign ports.	17	2	Petition	60	....	....	....	......	Ref'd to First Comptroller of Treasury.		
Phillips, George L.	Compensation for services in Florida war.	24	2	Documents.....	308	Claims	220	Adverse	......	Laid on table.		
Phillips, George.........	Pension	19	1	Resolution	55	Military Pensions..	164	Adverse	......	Laid on table.		
Phillips, Henry, sureties of	Release from judgment..........	17	1	Petition	221	Judiciary	Feb. 12, 1822	Favorable; bill	84	Passed	Rejected.	
Phillips, H. G...........	(See James Steel, and others)....	17	2	....	232							
Phillips, Horatio G.......	(See Joseph Pierce, heirs of)....	17	2	....	232							
Phillips, Israel	Pension	21	2	Petition	255	Military Pensions.						
Phillips, Jacob..........	Reimbursement of money advanced United States in revolutionary war.	3	2	Rep. of Secretary Treasury.	284	....	....	....	......	Laid on table.		
Phillips, Jacob..........	Reimbursement of money advanced United States in revolutionary war.	4	1	Rep. of Secretary Treasury.	510	Claims	May 31, 1796	Adverse	......	Laid on table.		
Phillips, Jacob..........	Revolutionary pension	25	3	Petition	216	Rev. Pensions	....	....	......	Discharged; laid on table.		
Phillips, Jacob..........	Revolutionary pension..........	26	1	Petition	174	Rev. Pensions.						
Phillips, Jacob..........	Revolutionary pension..........	26	2	Petition	78	Rev. Pensions.						
Phillips, Jacob, executors of	Reissue of land warrant.........	30	2	Petition	224	Public Lands.....	Feb. 28, 1849	Favorable; bill	799	Passed	Passed	App'd March 3, 1849

List of private claims presented to the House of Representatives of the United States from the 1st to the 31st Congress, inclusive—Continued.

Names of claimants.	Nature or object of the claim.	Congress.	Session.	How brought before the House of Reps.	Page of journal.	To what committee of the House referred.	No. or date of the report.	Nature of the report.	No. of the bill.	How disposed of by the House of Reps.	How disposed of by the Senate.	Date of the act of Congress, and remarks.
Phillips, James	Invalid pension	3	1	Rep. of Secretary War.	131	Select	May 26, 1794	J't. res. to refer to Sec. War.	R. 12	Passed	Passed	App'd June 9, 1794
Phillips, James	Invalid pension	3	2	Rep. of Secretary War.	262	Claims.						
Phillips, James	Invalid pension	4	1	Rep. of Secretary War.	445	Claims	Mar. 4, 1796	J't. res. to refer to Sec. War.	R. 16	Passed	Passed	App'd April 18, 1796
Phillips, James	Invalid pension	10	2	House bill	499	Whole House	Feb. 20, 1809	With amendt's	158	Passed	Passed	App'd March 3, 1809
Phillips, James	Compensation for wounds received on western frontier in 1777.	10	1	Petition	155	Select.						
Phillips, James, (N. Y.)	Revolutionary pension	26	2	Petition	133	Rev. Pensions.						
Phillips, Jeremiah	(See Wiseman Walker, & J. Phillips, administrator of.)	24	2		160							
Phillips, Job	Pension	22	1	Resolution	498	Rev. Pensions	438	Favorable; bill	542	Referred to Committee Whole House.		
Phillips, John	Payment of certain bills of credit issued by Massachusetts during revolutionary war.	4	1	Rep. of Secretary Treasury.	388	Claims	May 31, 1796	Adverse		Laid on table.		
Phillips, John	(See Wiseman Walker, administrator of.)	20	2		103							
Phillips, John, administrator of John.	Remuneration for property destroyed by Creek Indians in the late war.	20	2	Resolution	103	Ways and Means				Discharged; laid on table.		
Phillips, John, administrator of John.	Remuneration for property destroyed by Creek Indians in the late war.	21	2	Resolution	112	Claims	Dec. 29, 1830	Adverse		Laid on table.		
Phillips, John, administrator of John.	Remuneration for property destroyed by Creek Indians in the late war.	22	1	Petition	25	Claims	Dec. 28, 1831	Adverse		Laid on table.		
Phillips, John, administrator of.	Remuneration for property destroyed by Creek Indians in the late war.	24	1	Petition and docs.	96	Indian Affairs.						
Phillips, John, administrator of.	Remuneration for property destroyed by Creek Indians in the late war.	24	2	Petition	160	Indian Affairs.						
Phillips, John	To relinquish his present pension for benefit of the act of May 15, 1828.	25	3	Petition	571	Rev. Pensions				Discharged; laid on table.		
Phillips, John, (Va.)	Revolutionary pension	26	1	Petition	323	Rev. Pensions	414	Adverse		Laid on table.		
Phillips, John L.	(See Isaac Bush and others.)	30	1		740							
Phillips, John L., & company.	Compensation for services in Florida war prior to being mustered into service.	30	1	Petition	859	Military Affairs.						
Phillips, Capt. John L., & company.	Compensation for services in Florida war.	31	1	Petition	257	Military Affairs.						
Phillips, Lewis	Confirmation of title to land	5	2	Senate bill	225	Select	Jan. 22, 1798	With't amend.	S. 13	Passed		App'd June 25, 1798
Phillips, Nathaniel	Pension and compensation for lost property.	29	1	Senate bill	968	Naval Affairs	July 13, 1846	With't amend.	S. 54	Passed		App'd July 29, 1846
Phillips, Nehemiah	Arrears of pension	25	3	Petition	127	Rev. Pensions				Discharged; laid on table.		
Phillips, Olive A.	Extension of provisions of pension acts for relief of widows.	28	1	Petition	850	Rev. Pensions.						
Phillips, Richard	Pension	1	1	Petition	64					Laid on table.		

List of private claims presented to the House of Representatives of the United States from the 1st to the 31st Congress, inclusive—Continued.

Names of claimants.	Nature or object of the claim.	Congress.	Session.	How brought before the House of Reps.	Page of journal.	To what committee of the House referred.	No. or date of the report.	Nature of the report.	No. of the bill.	How disposed of by the House of Reps.	How disposed of by the Senate.	Date of the act of Congress, and remarks.
Phillips, Richard	Payment of claim against United States.	1	2	Petition	218					Referred to Secretary Treasury.		Provided for in civil and diplomatic bill, app'd Aug. 12, 1790
Phillips, Richard	Payment of claim against United States.	3	2	Rep. of Secretary Treasury.	284					Laid on table.		
Phillips, Robert	Extra pay for services in State Department.	3	1	Petition	93	Select	54	Favorable; bill	69	Passed	Rejected.	
Phillips, Samuel	Liquidation of a certificate of revolutionary debt.	4	1	Rep. of Secretary Treasury.	388	Claims	May 31, 1796	Adverse		Laid on table.		
Phillips, Samuel, (Va.)	Payment for a vessel captured by the British in war of 1812.	20	9	Petition	27	Claims	Dec. 15, 1828	Adverse		Laid on table.		
Phillips, Samuel	Revolutionary pension	25	2	Resolution	765	Rev. Pensions				Discharged; laid on table.		
Phillips, Samuel	Revolutionary pension	26	1	Petition	174	Rev. Pensions	714			Laid on table.		
Phillips, Samuel, collector of Newburyport, Mass.	Payment for service as superintendent of light-houses.	26	1	Resolution	372	Commerce.						
Phillips, Samuel, collector of Newburyport, Mass.	Payment for service as superintendent of light-houses.	26	2	Resolution	134	Commerce.						
Phillips, Samuel, collector of Newburyport, Mass.	Payment for service as superintendent of light-houses.	27	2	Petition	57	Commerce	64	Favorable; bill	99	Passed	Passed	App'd July 27, 1842
Phillips, Samuel, collector of Newburyport, Mass.	For interest on amount allowed by act of July 27, 1842.	28	1	Resolution	146	Commerce				Discharged; laid on table.		
Phillips, Samuel C.	(See Jonathan P. Felt, administrator of.)	26	2		86							
Phillips, Samuel H.	Pension	16	1	Petition	42	Pens. & Rev. Cl'ms.	Jan. 4, 1820	Adverse		Laid on table.		
Phillips, Samuel H.	Pension	21	1	Senate bill	352	Military Pensions	Mar. 11, 1830	With't amend.	S. 76	Passed		App'd May 29, 1830
Phillips, Samuel S.	Remuneration for Indian depredations.	25	2	Petition	192	Claims	597	Adverse		Laid on table.		
Phillips, Solomon C.	Confirmation of title to land in Mississippi.	16	2	Petition	171	Priv. Land Claims				Discharged; laid on table.		
Phillips, Solomon C.	Confirmation of title to land in Mississippi.	17	[illegible]	Petition	146	Priv. Land Claims				Discharged; laid on table.		
Phillips, Solomon C.	Confirmation of title to land in Mississippi.	17	2	Petition	27	Priv. Land Claims				Discharged; leave to withdraw.		
Phillips, Stephen, late widow of.	Revolutionary pension	27	2	Petition	239	Rev. Pensions	573	Favorable; bill	369	Referred to Committee Whole House.		
Phillips, Stephen	(See Wm. Robinson and others)	9	2		555							
Phillips, Stephen C.	Remuneration for expenses incurred in support and transportation of wrecked American seamen.	23	1	Senate bill	754	Commerce	Jan. 28, 1834	With't amend.	S. 103	Passed		App'd June 30, 1834
Phillips, Sylvanus	Confirmation of title to land in Arkansas.	22	1	House bill	421	Whole House	Feb. 28, 1832	Favorable	425		Passed	App'd June 25, 1832
Phillips, Sylvanus	(See Henry Curter, assignee of.)											
Phillips, Sylvanus	(See Peter Edwards, assignee of.)											
Phillips, Sylvanus	(See Baptiste Socia, assignee of.)											
Phillips, Thomas, (Ind.)	Pension	22	1	Petition	556	Invalid Pensions	Jan. 1, 1832	Favorable; bill	593	Passed.		
Phillips, Thomas, (Ind.)	Pension	22	2	Petition	40	Invalid Pensions	Dec. 19, 1832	Favorable; bill	626	Passed	Passed	App'd March 2, 1833
Phillips, Thomas, administrator of.	Indemnity for French spoliations prior to 1800.	26	1	Memorial	182	Foreign Affairs	343	Favorable; bill	319	Referred to Committee Whole House.		
Phillips, Walter	Revolutionary pension	23	2	Petition	114	Rev. Pensions	51	Favorable; bill	643	Passed.		

List of private claims presented to the House of Representativesthe of United States from the 1st to the 31st Congress, inclusive—Continued.

Names of claimants.	Nature or object of the claim.	Congress.	Session.	How brought before the House of Reps.	Page of journal.	To what committee of the House referred.	No. or date of the report.	Nature of the report.	No. of the bill.	How disposed of by the House of Reps.	How disposed of by the Senate.	Date of the act of Congress, and remarks.
Phillips, William, (Conn.)	Revolutionary pension	17	1	Petition	199	Rev. Pensions				Disch'd; laid on table		
Phillips, William, (Va.)	Pension	17	2	Petition	165	Pens. & Rev. Cl'ms.				Discharged; laid on table.		
Phillips, William, (Va.)	Pension	18	1	Petition	61	Pens. & Rev. Cl'ms.	Mar. 24, 1824	Adverse		Laid on table.		
Phillips, William	(See William Baker, N. Y.)	22	1		288		480					
Phillips, Zachariah	Payment of property destroyed by Creek Indians.	25	2	Resolution	195	Claims	1027	Adverse		Laid on table.		
Phillipson, Joseph	Permission to surrender certain lands and enter others at the minimum price, or to receive the value of the same in money.	24	1	Petition	435	Public Lands.						
Phillipson, Simon	Drawback on a cargo shipped at St. Iago de Cuba.	8	1	Petition	571	Com. and Manuf.	Mar. 1, 1804	Res. to postp'ne to Dec. next.		Adopted.		
Phillipson, Simon	Drawback on a cargo shipped at St. Iago de Cuba.	8	2	Petition	58	Com. and Manuf.	Feb. 20, 1805	Favorable		Referred to Committee Whole House.		
Phillipson, Simon	Drawback on a cargo shipped at St. Iago de Cuba.	9	1	Petition	193	Com. and Manuf.	Dec. 24, 1805	Favorable		Referred to Committee Whole House.		
Phillipson, Simon	Drawback on a cargo shipped at St. Iago de Cuba.	10	1	Senate bill	277	Whole House			S. 20	Indefinitely postponed.		
Phinizy, Ferdinand	Payment of balance due as contractor for supplying troops in Georgia.	10	2	Army & navy appropriation bill.	525	Whole House	Feb. 25, 1809	With amends.	164	Passed	Passed	App'd March 3, 1809
Phinney, Alanson	Confirmation of title to land	28	2	Petition	88	Public Lands.						
Phinney, Ebenezer	Pension for services in revolutionary war.	3	2	Rep. of Secretary War.	278	Claims	Mar. 2, 1795	Res. to refer to Sec. War.		Adopted.		
Phinney, Ebenezer	Pension for services in revolution ary war.	4	1	Rep. of Secretary War.	445	Claims	Feb. 18, 1796	Favorable; bill	156	Passed	Passed	App'd April 20, 1796
Phinney, Elisha, executors of.	Payment of a certificate of revolutionary debt.	22	1	Petition	559	Rev. Claims.						
Phiole, Gaspard, heirs of the widow of.	Permission to enter land in lieu of claim recommended for confirmation.	26	2	Senate bill	225	Priv. Land Claims.			S. 123			
Phiole, Gaspard, heirs of the widow of.	Permission to locate land in lieu of their claim recommended for confirmation.	27	2	Senate bill	1125	Priv. Land Claims.	Aug. 6, 1842	With't amend.	S. 78	Passed		App'd Aug. 29, 1842
Phiole, Gaspard, heirs of the widow of.	Amendatory of the act of August 29, 1842.	29	1	Petition	266	Priv. Land Claims.	555	Favorable; bill	378	Referred to Committee Whole House.		
Phoenix, Alexander	Release from prison, where he is confined at suit of United States	12	2	Senate bill	711	Ways and Means.	Mar. 3, 1813	With't amend.	S. 65	Passed		App'd March 3, 1813
Phoenix, Alexander	Amendatory of act of March 3, 1813	13	1	Senate bill	21	Ways and Means.	June 15, 1813	With't amend.	S. 1	Passed		App'd June 19, 1813
Phoenix, Dawson	For expenses incurred as passed midshipman.	31	1	Petition	629	Naval Affairs.						
Phoenix Insurance Company, Philadelphia.	Payment of certain treasury notes.	28	1	Petition	335	Ways and Means.						
Phouto, John, and others,	Grant of land in consideration of their blindness and extreme poverty.	11	2	Petition	249	Public Lands.						
Piatt, Frances L	(See William Piatt, daughter of).	26	1		547							
Piatt, Jacob, late Captain United States army.	Revolutionary pension	21	1	Resolution	464	Military Pensions.				Discharged; laid on table.		
Piatt, John H.	Relief as contractor to supply provisions to the Northwest army in war of 1812.	15	1	Petition	280	Military Affairs.				Discharged; laid on table.		

List of private claims presented to the House of Representatives of the United States from the 1st to the 31st Congress, inclusive—Continued.

Names of claimants.	Nature or object of the claim.	Congress.	Session.	How brought before the House of Reps.	Page of journal.	To what committee of the House referred.	No. or date of the report.	Nature of the report.	No. of the bill.	How disposed of by the House of Reps.	How disposed of by the Senate.	Date of the act of Congress, and remarks.
Piatt, John H.	Relief as contractor to supply provisions to the Northwest army in war of 1812.	15	2	Resolution	84	Military Affairs				Discharged; laid on table.		
Piatt, John H.	Relief as contractor to supply provisions to the Northwest army in war of 1812.	16	1	Senate bill	401	Claims	April 26, 1820	With't amend.	S. 51	Passed		App'd May 8, 1820
Piatt, John H., assignee of	Payment of claim growing out of act for his relief.	17	1	Petition	387	Ways and Means				Discharged; laid on table.		
Piatt, John H., administrator of.	Payment of claim growing out of act for his relief.	17	2	Petition	87	Select	Mar. 3, 1823	Favorable		Laid on table.		
Piatt, John H., administrator of.	Payment of claim growing out of act for his relief.	18	1	Petition and rep't of last session.	44	Select	21	Favorable; bill	48	Passed	Passed	App'd May 24, 1824
Piatt, John H., heirs of	Compensation for provisions furnished United States army in 1814 and 1815.	27	2	Petition	110	Claims.						
Piatt, John H., heirs of	Compensation for provisions furnished U. S. army in 1814 & 1815	30	1	Petition	912	Claims	747	Favorable; bill	586	Referred to Committee Whole House.		
Piatt, John H., heirs of	Compensation for provisions furnished United States army in 1814 and 1815.	31	1	Petition	923	Claims	325	Favorable; bill	282	Referred to Committee Whole House.		
Piatt, Martha	(See Joshua Huddy, heir of.)											
Piatt & Riddle	Extension of time for paying certain bonds.	14	2	Petition	69	Ways and Means.						
Piatt, Sarah	(See William Piatt, widow of.)	3	1		70							
Piatt, William, widow of	Relief; husband killed by the Indians in 1794 in an expedition under General St. Clair.	3	1	Petition	70	Select.						
Piatt, William, (Ky.)	Compensation for services as quartermaster general in the army under General Harrison.	13	1	Petition and rep't Sec. of War.	46	Claims				Discharged; laid on table.		
Piatt, William, (Ky.)	Compensation for services as quartermaster general in the army under General Harrison.	13	2	Petition	194	Claims	Jan. 19, 1814	Favorable; bill	86	Passed	Passed	App'd Feb. 19, 1814
Piatt, William, (Ky.)	For difference of pay between a major of the line and quartermaster general, and compensation for clerk hire.	23	1	Documents	310	Military Affairs	292	Favorable; bill	328	Referred to Committee Whole House.		
Piatt, William, (Ky.)	For difference of pay between a major of the line and quartermaster general, and compensation for clerk hire.	24	1	Petition	425	Military Affairs	528	Favorable; bill	521	Referred to Committee Whole House.		
Piatt, William, (Ky.)	For difference of pay between a major of the line and quartermaster general, and compensation for clerk hire.	25	2	Petition	41	Military Affairs.						
Piatt, William, (Ky.)	For difference of pay between a major of the line and quartermaster general, and compensation for clerk hire.	26	1	Petition	306	Military Affairs	331	Favorable; bill	430	Referred to Committee Whole House.		
Piatt, William, (Ky.)	For difference of pay between a major of the line and quartermaster general, and compensation for clerk hire.	27	2	Petition	99	Military Affairs	85 B.	Favorable; bill	127	Passed	Passed	App'd July 9, 1842

List of private claims presented to the House of Representatives of the United States from the 1st to the 31st Congress, inclusive—Continued.

Names of claimants.	Nature or object of the claim.	Congress.	Session.	How brought before the House of Reps.	Page of journal.	To what committee of the House referred.	No. or date of the report.	Nature of the report.	No. of the bill.	How disposed of by the House of Reps.	How disposed of by the Senate.	Date of the act of Congress, and remarks.
Piatt, William, heirs of, (N. Y.)	Seven years' half-pay for services in revolutionary war.	25	2	Petition	231	Rev. Claims	695	Adverse		Laid on table.		
Piatt, William, heirs of, (N. Y.)	Seven years' half-pay for services in revolutionary war.	29	1	Memorial	88	Rev. Claims				Discharged; laid on table.		
Piatt, William F.	(See heirs of William Piatt)	25	2		231							
Piatt, Col. William, daughter of.	Pension for services in revolutionary war.	26	1	Resolution	547	Invalid Pensions	486	Adverse		Laid on table.		
Piatt, Col. William, daughter of.	Pension for services in revolutionary war.	27	2	Petition	256	Rev. Pensions	April 1, 1842	Adverse		Laid on table.		
Pick, Hannah	Restoration of pension	27	2	Petition	614	Rev. Pensions	May 24, 1842	Adverse		Laid on table.		
Pickard, Adolphus	Revolutionary pension	20	2	Petition	142					Referred to Committee Whole House on bill No. 311.		
Pickard, Alexander	Pension	21	2	Petition	95	Military Pensions.						
Pickard, Alexander	Pension	22	2	Petition	68	Rev. Pensions	Jan. 11, 1832	Adverse		Laid on table.		
Pickard, Alexander	Grant of land for benefit of his mills.	28	1	Petition	683	Public Lands.						
Pickard, Henry H.	Payment for boats impressed in U. States service in war of 1812.	22	1	Resolution	97	Claims	Jan. 10, 1832	Adverse		Laid on table.		
Pickard, Henry H.	Payment for boats impressed in U. States service in war of 1812.	23	2	Petition	109	Claims.						
Pickard, John	Revolutionary pension	23	2	Petition	271	Rev. Pensions.						
Pickard, John	Revolutionary pension	24	1	Petition	184	Rev. Pensions	206	Favorable; bill	210	Passed	Passed	App'd June 28, 1836
Pickell, John, of U. States army.	To be allowed certain expenditures in the settlement of his accounts.	22	2	Petition	96	Military Affairs.						
Pickell, John, of U. States army.	To be allowed certain expenditures in the settlement of his accounts.	23	1	Petition	35	Military Affairs	Feb. 10, 1834	Adverse		Laid on table.		
Pickell, Joseph, assignee of	Arrears of pay and travelling expenses as soldier in war of 1812.	19	1	Petition	407	Claims	165	Favorable; bill	217	Passed.		
Pickell, Joseph, assignee of	Arrears of pay and travelling expenses as soldier in war of 1812.	19	2	Petition	82	Claims	Dec. 22, 1826	By bill	313	Passed	Passed	App'd Feb. 22, 1827
Pickens, Israel, and W. Crawford.	Compensation for certain surveys made by them as land officers at St. Stephen's.	19	1	Petition	206	Public Lands.						
Pickens, John	Revolutionary pension	22	1	Petition	710	Rev. Pensions				Discharged; laid on table.		
Pickering, Charles W.	Extra pay for doing duty as lieutenant on United States ship Falmouth on Pacific station.	24	1	Petition	188	Naval Affairs	293	Favorable; bill	301	Referred to Committee Whole House.		
Pickering, Charles W.	Extra pay for doing duty as lieutenant on United States ship Falmouth on Pacific station.	24	2	House bill	200				301	Passed	Passed	App'd March 2, 1837
Pickering, Henry J.	Remission of duty on machine for making paper.	24	2	Petition	98	Ways and Means.						
Pickering, Henry J.	Refunding of duties paid on machine for making paper, with interest.	25	2	Memorial	60	Ways and Means.						
Pickering, Henry J.	Refunding of duties paid on machine for making paper, with interest.	25	2	Senate bill	130	Ways and Means	Jan. 4, 1838	With amend.	41	Referred to Committee Whole House.		
Pickering, Henry J.	Refunding of duties paid on machine for making paper, with interest.	25	3	Memorial	465	Ways and Means.						

List of private claims presented to the House of Representatives of the United States from the 1st to the 31st Congress, inclusive—Continued.

Names of claimants.	Nature or object of the claim.	Congress.	Session.	How brought before the House of Reps.	Page of journal.	To what committee of the House referred.	No. or date of the report.	Nature of the report.	No. of the bill.	How disposed of by the House of Reps.	How disposed of by the Senate.	Date of the act of Congress, and remarks.
Pickering, Henry J.	Refunding of duties paid on machine for making paper, with interest.	26	1	Memorial	179	Ways and Means				Discharged; laid on table.		
Pickering, Jacob	(See James Sheaf, executor of)	26	1		182		343		319			
Pickering, James	Pension for revolutionary services.	3	1	Rep. of Secretary War.	131	Select	May 26, 1796	Favorable; bill	62	Passed	Passed	App'd June 7, 1794
Pickering, John	Permission to register certificate for a pre emption right to land.	9	2	Petition	549	Public Lands.						
Pickering, John	Permission to register certificate for a pre-emption right to land.	10	1	Petition	18	Public Lands.						
Pickering, Joseph	Grant of land for services of his father in revolutionary war.	17	2	Petition	21	Rev. Pensions				Discharged; laid on table.		
Pickering, Timothy, by Peter Auspach, attorney.	Liquidation and settlement of claim against United States.	1	2	Petition	254					Referred to Secretary of Treasury.		
Pickering, Timothy, by Peter Auspach, attorney.	Liquidation and settlement of claim against United States.	3	1	Rep. of Secretary Treasury.	78					Laid on table.		
Pickering, Timothy	Balance due for services as commissioner to negotiate treaties with the Indians.	4	2	Appropriat'n bill.	675	Whole House	Jan. 31, 1797	With amend'ts	223	Passed	Passed	App'd March 3, 1797
Pickering, Timothy, Bev. Randolph, and Benjamin Lincoln.	Balance due for making treaties with the northwestern Indians.	4	2	Resolution	675	Ways and Means	Jan. 31, 1797	Favorable; bill	223	Passed	Passed	App'd March 3, 1794
Pickett, A. J., and G. W. Gayle.	Compensation for services as aid de-camp to the governor of Alabama, in organizing volunteers in 1836.	25	2	Resolution	647	Claims	894	Favorable; bill	793	Referred to Committee Whole House.		
Pickett, A. J., and G. W. Gayle.	Compensation for services as aid-de-camp to the govenor of Alabama, in organizing volunteers in 1836.	25	3	Bill of last sess.	431	Whole House	Feb. 1, 1839	With't amend.	793	Passed	Passed	App'd March 3, 1839
Pickett, James C.	Compensation as acting chargé to Bogota.	23	1	House bill	474	Whole House	June 27, 1834	With't amend.	404	Passed	Passed	App'd June 30, 1834
Pickett, John, and others.	Indemnity for illegal seizure and detention of brig Albert by the United States consul at Bahai, Brazil.	29	1	Petition	331	Claims	690	Favorable; bill	462	Referred to Committee Whole House.		
Pickett, John, and others.	Indemnity for illegal seizure and detention of brig Albert by the United States consul at Bahai, Brazil.	29	2	Bill of last sess.	211	Whole House	Jan. 22, 1847	Favorable	462	Passed	Passed	App'd Mar 3, 1847; act directs Solicitor of Treasury to examine case and report to House.
Pickett, John, and others.	Indemnity for illegal seizure and detention of brig Albert by the United States consul at Bahai, Brazil.	30	1	Report of the Solicitor of the Treasury.	159	Claims.						
Picket, T., widow of	Pension for services in revolutionary war.	23	2	Petition	128	Rev. Pensions				Discharged; laid on table.		
Pickett, William R.	Renewal of certificate of forfeited land stock, lost.	22	1	Petition	173	Public Lands.	Feb. 17, 1832	Favorable; bill	385	Passed	Passed	App'd Mar. 31, 1832
Pickman, B., and others.	Permission to land bandannah handkerchiefs upon their giving bond to reship them without the United States.	10	1	Petition	29					Referred to Committee Whole House on bill No. 16.		See act Feb. 27, 1808

List of private claims presented to the House of Representatives of the United States from the 1st to the 31st Congress, inclusive—Continued.

Names of claimants.	Nature or object of the claim.	Congress.	Session.	How brought before the House of Reps.	Page of journal.	To what committee of the House referred.	No. or date of the report.	Nature of the report.	No. of the bill.	How disposed of by the House of Reps.	How disposed of by the Senate.	Date of the act of Congress, and remarks.
Pickman, Benjamin	(See Elias H. Derby, executors of.)	26	1	....	182							
Pickman, Benjamin	(See John Derby, executor of.)	23	1	....	186							
Pickman, Dudley L.	(See P. Dodge, executor of.)	26	1	....	182							
Pickman, D. L.	Indemnity for French spoliations prior to 1800.	26	1	Memorial	182	Foreign Affairs	343	Favorable; bill	319	Referred to Committee Whole House.		
Pickman, W. D., executors of.	Indemnity for French spoliations prior to 1800.	31	1	Petition	216	Foreign Affairs	355	Favorable; bill	318	Referred to Committee Whole House.		
Pickrell, Eliza	(See John Pickrell, widow of.)											
Pickrell, John, widow of	Payment of claims against United States bought by her late husband of the Shawnee Indians.	28	1	Petition	211	Indian Affairs	369	Adverse	......	Laid on table.		
Picotte, Joseph	Compensation for a horse lost in service of United States.	15	2	Petition	33	Claims	Dec. 1, 1818	Adverse	......	Laid on table.		
Picton, Thomas	Pay for services as chaplain and professor of Ethics in West Point academy.	20	2	Petition	118	Claims	....	....	......	Discharged; laid on table.		
Picton, Thomas	Pay for services as chaplain and professor of Ethics in West Point academy.	21	1	Petition	358	Claims	Mar. 10, 1830	Adverse	......	Laid on table.		
Pidgeon, John	Pension	14	1	Petition	84	Pens. & Rev. Cl'ms.	April 11, 1816	Favorable; bill	......	Passed	Passed	App'd April 30, 1816
Pier, Abner	Compensation for supplies furnished, and for services and losses, in revolutionary war.	1	3	Petition and rep't Sec. of War.	352	....	....	....	......	Laid on table.		
Pier, Abner	Pension for revolutionary services.	3	1	Rep. of Secretary War.	131	Select	May 26, 1794	Joint resolut'n.	12	Passed	Passed	App'd June 9, 1794
Pier, Abner	Pension for revolutionary services.	4	1	Rep. of Secretary War.	445	Claims	Feb. 18, 1796	Favorable; bill	156	Passed	Passed	App'd April 20, 1796
Pierce, Aaron	Compensation for two horses killed by a party of hostile Indians in 1832.	24	1	Resolution	679	Claims	756	Adverse	......	Laid on table.		
Pierce, Amos	Pension for services in revolutionary war.	3	2	Rep. of Secretary War.	278	Claims	Feb. 28, 1795	Favorable; bill	130	Passed.	Postponed.	
Pierce, Amos	Pension for services in revolutionary war.	4	1	Rep. of Secretary War.	445	Claims	Feb. 18, 1796	Favorable; bill	156	Passed	Passed	App'd April 20, 1796
Pierce, Anna	Pension for services of her husband during revolutionary war.	24	2	Petition	153	Rev. Pensions	....	....	......	Discharged; laid on table.		
Pierce, Benjamin	Revolutionary pension	25	2	Petition	729	Rev. Pensions	....	....	......	Discharged; laid on table.		
Pierce, Benjamin	Revolutionary pension	26	1	Petition	174	Rev. Pensions	....	....	......	Discharged; laid on table.		
Pierce, Charles S.	(See James Deerick and Charles S. Pierce.)	22	2	....	312							
Pierce, David Z.	(See heirs of Joseph Pierce)	17	2	....	232							
Pierce, Ebenezer	Commutation pay and other aid in consideration of revolutionary services.	24	2	Petition	311	Invalid Pensions	....	....	......	Discharged; laid on table.		
Pierce, Ebenezer	Invalid pension	26	2	Petition	55	Invalid Pensions	61	Adverse	......	Laid on table.		
Pierce, Erasmus	Permission to secure certain property to the United States in payment of excise duties.	3	1	Petition	29	....	....	....	......	Referred to Secretary Treasury.		
Pierce, Erasmus	Relief in case of certain bond given for excise duties.	4	1	Petition	455	....	....	....	......	Referred to Secretary Treasury.		
Pierce, Erasmus J.	Refunding duties on umbrellas	25	2	House bill	637	Whole House	....	....	669			

List of private claims presented to the House of Representatives of the United States from the 1st to the 31st Congress, inclusive—Continued.

Names of claimants.	Nature or object of the claim.	Congress.	Session.	How brought before the House of Reps.	Page of journal.	To what committee of the House referred.	No. or date of the report.	Nature of the report.	No. of the bill.	How disposed of by the House of Reps.	How disposed of by the Senate.	Date of the act of Congress, and remarks.
Pierce, Gad	Indemnity for property destroyed at Niagara by the British in war of 1812.	15	2	Petition	148	Claims	Jan. 16, 1819	Adverse		Laid on table.		
Pierce, Gad	Indemnity for property destroyed at Niagara by the British in war of 1812.	17	1	Petition	46	Claims	Jan. '21, 1822	Adverse		Referred to Committee Whole House.		
Pierce, Gad	Indemnity for property destroyed at Niagara by the British in war of 1812.	22	1	Petition	54	Claims	Mar. 14, 1832	Adverse		Laid on table.		
Pierce, Ignatius	Fishing bounty on schooner Fortune.	29	1	Petition	198	Commerce	546	Favorable; bill	368	Referred to Committee Whole House.		
Pierce, Ignatius	Fishing bounty on schooner Fortune.	30	1	Petition	288	Commerce.						
Pierce, James	Payment for a wagon and team lost at the surrender of Detroit.	15	2	Petition	281	Claims				Discharged; laid on table.		
Pierce, James	Payment for a wagon and team lost at the surrender of Detroit.	17	1	Petition	73	Claims	Feb. 25, 1822	Favorable; bill	97	Passed	Passed	App'd May 7, 1822
Pierce, James	(See William H. Bedford, agent).	28	1		262							
Pierce, James, administrator of.	Indemnity for French spoliations prior to 1800.	26	1	Memorial	182	Foreign Affairs	343	Favorable; bill	319	Referred to Committee Whole House.		
Pierce, James, executors of.	Indemnity for French spoliations prior to 1800.	31	1	Petition	337	Foreign Affairs	318	Favorable; bill	318	Referred to Committee Whole House.		
Pierce, Jerathamael	Drawback on goods exported to New Orleans.	6	2	Memorial	788	Com. and Manuf.	Feb. 23, 1801	Adverse		Rejected.		
Pierce, Jeremiah	(See Joseph Pierce, heirs of.)	17	2		232							
Pierce, Job	Revolutionary pension	22	1	Resolution	436	Rev. Pensions.						
Pierce, John	(See John Orr and John Pierce.)	26	2		54							
Pierce, John	Pension	16	1	Petition	27	Pens. & Rev. Cl'ms.	Dec. 14, 1819	Adverse		Rejected.		
Pierce, John	(See State of Georgia, by agent.)	23	2		308							
Pierce, John, jr., Professor of Mathematics, United States navy.	Pay for time and expenses while waiting order of the Secretary of Navy.	30	2	Petition	285	Naval Affairs.						
Pierce, John, jr., Professor of Mathematics, United States navy.	Pay for time and expenses while waiting order of the Secretary of Navy.	31	1	Petition	277	Naval Affairs	437	Adverse		Laid on table.		
Pierce, John B., and others	Salvage money on brig Rob Roy and cargo.	27	2	Petition	45	Commerce	466	Favorable; bill	316	Passed	Passed	App'd Aug. 11, 1842
Pierce, John, and Daniel Van Voorheis.	Indemnity for losses sustained under contract to furnish glass and lime to the navy-yard at New York.	23	1	Petition	188	Claims	277	Favorable; bill	315	Referred to Committee Whole House.		
Pierce, John, and Daniel Van Voorheis.	Indemnity for losses sustained under contract to furnish glass and lime to the navy-yard at N. York.	24	1	Petition	50	Claims	Dec. 21, 1835	Adverse		Laid on table.		
Pierce, John, and Daniel Van Voorheis.	Indemnity for losses under contract to furnish iron mongery to navy-yard at New York.	23	1	Petition	188	Claims	277	Favorable; bill	315	Referred to Committee Whole House.		
Pierce, John, and Daniel Van Voorheis.	Indemnity for losses under contract to furnish iron mongery to navy-yard at New York.	24	1	Petition	50	Claims	2	Favorable; bill	2	Passed	Passed	App'd June 14, 1836
Pierce, John and William.	Indemnity for destruction of property by Cherokee Indians in war of 1812.	18	1	Petition	75	Claims	Dec. 22, 1823	Adverse		Laid on table.		

List of private claims presented to the House of Representatives of the United States from the 1st to the 31st Congress, inclusive—Continued.

Names of claimants.	Nature or object of the claim.	Congress.	Session.	How brought before the House of Reps.	Page of journal.	To what committee of the House referred.	No. or date of the report.	Nature of the report.	No. of the bill.	How disposed of by the House of Reps.	How disposed of by the Senate.	Date of the act of Congress, and remarks.
Pierce, John and William.	Indemnity for destruction of property by Cherokee Indians in war of 1812.	19	2	Petition	82	Claims	Jan. 24, 1827	Adverse	......	Laid on table.		
Pierce, John and William.	Indemnity for destruction of property by Cherokee Indians in war of 1812.	20	1	Petition	38	Claims	25	Adverse	.....	Laid on table.	....	Leave to withdraw.
Pierce, Jonathan	(See John McKown and others)..	22	2	....	397							
Pierce, Jonathan	Fishing bounty on his vessel the Ramble.	15	1	Petition	150	....	....	....	......	Discharged; laid on table.		
Pierce, Jonathan, widow of	Arrears of pension due at the time of his death.	22	2	Petition	29	Rev. Pensions	....	....	......	Discharged; laid on table.		
Pierce, Joseph	Commutation of half-pay and bounty land for revolutionary services.	15	1	Petition	165	Pens. & Rev. Cl'ms.	....	....	......	Discharged; laid on table.		
Pierce, Joseph	Pension	19	1	Petition	98	Military Pensions.	164	Adverse	......	Laid on table.		
Pierce, Joseph, heirs of, and D. Hubbard.	Compensation for land for which they have made payment, but which was again sold.	17	2	Petition	232	Priv. Land Claims.						
Pierce, Joseph, heirs of, and D. Hubbard.	Compensation for land for which they have made payment, but which was again sold.	18	1	Petition	137	Priv. Land Claims.						
Pierce, Joseph, heirs of, and D. Hubbard.	Compensation for land for which they have made payment, but which was again sold.	19	1	Petition	316	Priv. Land Claims.	May 17, 1826	Favorable; bill	274	Referred to Committee Whole House.		
Pierce, Joseph, heirs of, and D. Hubbard.	Compensation for land for which they have made payment, but which was again sold.	20	1	Resolution	153	Priv. Land Claims.	Feb. 5, 1828	Favorable; bill	147	Passed	Reported, with amendm'nts.	
Pierce, Joseph, heirs of, and D. Hubbard.	Compensation for land for which they have made payment, but which was again sold.	20	2	Petition	50	Priv. Land Claims.	Dec. 29, 1828	Favorable; bill	337	Referred to Committee Whole House.		
Pierce, Joseph, heirs of, and D. Hubbard.	Compensation for land for which they have made payment, but which was again sold.	22	2	Petition	46	Priv. Land Claims.						
Pierce, Joseph, heirs of, and D. Hubbard.	Compensation for land for which they have made payment, but which was again sold.	25	2	Petition	282	Priv. Land Claims.	Mar. 9, 1838	Favorable; bill	640	Referred to Committee Whole House.		
Pierce, Joseph, heirs of, and D. Hubbard.	Compensation for land for which they have made payment, but which was again sold.	25	3	Bill of last sess.	380	Whole House	Jan. 25, 1839	With't amend.	640	Passed	Passed	App'd March 3, 1839
Pierce, Joseph, heirs of, (Ohio.)	Permission to complete payment for land purchased in 1814, and that patents issue.	24	1	Petition	671	Public Lands.						
Pierce, Joseph, heirs of, (Ohio.)	Permission to complete payment for land purchased in 1814, and that patents issue.	25	2	Petition	282	Priv. Land Claims.	....	....	......	Discharged; laid on table.		
Pierce, Josiah	Pension	21	1	Petition	546	Military Pensions.	....	....	......	Discharged; laid on table.		
Pierce, Levi	Pension for services in revolutionary war.	3	1	Rep. of Secretary War.	131	Select	May 26, 1794	By bill	62	Passed	Passed	App'd June 7, 1794
Pierce, Leonard	(See Elias Bates, and others)	15	2	....	109							
Pierce, Mary	(See heirs of Joseph Pierce)	17	2	....	232							
Pierce, Moses	Invalid pension	24	1	Petition	74	Invalid Pensions	....	....	......	Discharged; laid on table.		
Pierce, Moses	Invalid pension	24	2	Petition	303	Public Lands	....	....	......	Disch'd; laid on table.		

List of private claims presented to the House of Representatives of the United States from the 1*st to the* 31*st Congress, inclusive*—Continued.

Names of claimants.	Nature or object of the claim.	Congress.	Session.	How brought before the House of Reps.	Page of journal.	To what committee of the House referred.	No. or date of the report.	Nature of the report.	No. of the bill.	How disposed of by the House of Reps.	How disposed of by the Senate.	Date of the act of Congress, and remarks.
Pierce, Moses	Bounty land for twelve years' military services.	25	2	Resolution	108	Military Affairs	Jan. 18, 1838	Adverse		Laid on table.		
Pierce, M. W.	Indemnity for French spoliations prior to 1800.	26	1	Memorial	182	Foreign Affairs	343	Favorable; bill	319	Referred to Committee Whole House.		
Pierce, Nehemiah	Increase of pension	12	1	House bill	361	Whole House	June 15, 1812	With amends.	138	Passed	Passed	App'd July 5, 1812
Pierce, Nicholas, heir of	Indemnity for French spoliations prior to 1800.	26	1	Memorial	182	Foreign Affairs	343	Favorable; bill	319	Referred to Committee Whole House.		
Pierce, Otis	Invalid pension	24	2	Resolution	387	Invalid Pensions	Feb. 22, 1837	Adverse		Laid on table.		
Pierce, Pliny	Increase of pension	29	1	Petition	322	Invalid Pensions	186	Adverse		Laid on table.		
Pierce, Richard and Elizabeth.	(See Isaac Howard, representatives of.)	26	1		166							
Pierce, Robert	Invalid pension	19	2	Petition	298	Military Pensions	Feb. 14, 1827	By bill	436	Referred to Committee Whole House.		
Pierce, Sherman	Invalid pension	28	1	Petition	368	Invalid Pensions	372	Favorable; bill	276	Passed.		
Pierce, Sherman	Invalid pension	28	2	Petition	229	Invalid Pensions.						
Pierce, Sherman	Invalid pension	29	1	Petition	389	Invalid Pensions	May 4, 1846			Discharged; laid on table.		
Pierce, Sherman	Invalid pension	31	1	Petition	578	Invalid Pensions.						
Pierce, Silas, (N. H.)	Pension	2	1	Petition	486					Referred to Secretary of War.		
Pierce, Silas, (N. H.)	Pension	4	1	Rep. of Secretary War.	445	Claims	Feb. 18, 1796	Favorable; bill	156	Passed	Passed	App'd April 20, 1796
Pierce, Silas	Invalid pension	10	1	House bill	232	Whole House	April 9, 1808	With amend.	78	Passed	Passed	App'd April 25, 1808
Pierce, Silas, (Ohio)	Revolutionary pension	23	1	Petition	440	Rev. Pensions.						
Pierce, Solomon	Pension	15	2	Petition	87	Pens. & Rev. Cl'ms.	Jan. 5, 1819	Adverse		Laid on table.		
Pierce, Stephen, widow of.	Revolutionary pension	25	2	Petition	1209	Rev. Pensions				Discharged; laid on table.		
Pierce, Stephen, widow of.	Revolutionary pension	25	3	Petition	86	Rev. Claims				Discharged; laid on table.		
Pierce, Stephen, widow of.	Revolutionary pension	26	1	Petition	167	Rev. Pensions	714	Adverse		Laid on table.		
Pierce, Stephen, widow of.	Revolutionary pension	26	2	Petition	212	Rev. Claims.						
Pierce, Stephen, widow of.	Revolutionary pension	27	2	Petition	308	Rev. Claims	653	Adverse		Laid on table.		
Pierce, Susan	(See George Neilson, heirs of)	27	2		228							
Pierce, Thomas	Renewal of patent	30	2	Petition	264	Patents	91	Adverse		Laid on table.		
Pierce, Lieut. Timothy, administrator of.	Settlement of accounts for services in revolutionary war, and for five years' half-pay, he having been killed in battle.	2	1	Petition	471					Referred to Secretary of War.		
Pierce, William and John, and Thomas J. Strong.	Relief for unlawful seizure and sale of their vessel and cargo by the Spanish authorities on the river Mobile.	9	1	Petition	260					Referred to Secretary of State.		
Pierce, William and John.	Relief for unlawful seizure and sale of their vessel and cargo by the Spanish authorities at Mobile.	12	1	Petition	14					Referred to Secretary of State.		
Pierce, William, (Penn.).	Revolutionary pension	31	1	Petition	628	Rev. Pensions	318	Adverse		Laid on table.		
Piercy, Henry, widow of.	Grant of land for services in revolutionary war.	11	2	Petition and rep't of Sec. War.	163	Public Lands	Mar. 13, 1810	Adverse		Leave to withdraw.		
Piercy, Henry, widow of.	Grant of land for services in revolutionary war.	11	3	Petition	471	Public Lands.						
Piercy, Marinus W.	Invalid pension	31	1	Petition	385	Public Lands.						
Piercy, Mary	(See Henry Piercy, widow of)	11	2		163							

List of private claims presented to the House of Representatives of the United States from the 1st to the 31st Congress, inclusive—Continued.

Names of claimants.	Nature or object of the claim.	Congress.	Session.	How brought before the House of Reps.	Page of journal.	To what committee of the House referred.	No. or date of the report.	Nature of the report.	No. of the bill.	How disposed of by the House of Reps.	How disposed of by the Senate.	Date of the act of Congress, and remarks.
Piercy, Lieut. William P.	Compensation for extra services rendered by order of his superior officer.	23	1	Petition	302	Naval Affairs.						
Piercy, Lieut. William P.	Compensation for extra services rendered by order of his superior officer.	23	2	Petition	56	Naval Affairs.						
Piercy, Lieut. William P.	Compensation for extra services rendered by order of his superior officer.	24	1	Petition	214	Naval Affairs	310	Adverse		Laid on table.		
Pierie, John G.	Refunding of foreign tonnage duties paid under protest at New York.	29	1	Memorial	124	Claims	59	Favorable; bill	56	Passed	Passed	App'd July 15, 1846
Piernas, Madame Lecompte	Indemnity for property destroyed and articles furnished United States army at New Orleans in late war with Great Britain.	18	2	Resolution	103	Claims.						
Piernas, Madame Lecompte	Indemnity for property destroyed and articles furnished United States army at New Orleans in late war with Great Britain.	19	1	Resolution	39	Claims	Dec. 16, 1825	Adverse		Referred to Committee Whole House.		
Piernas, Madame Lecompte	Indemnity for property destroyed and articles furnished United States army at New Orleans in late war with Great Britain.	19	2	Petition	160	Claims	Jan. 15, 1827	Adverse		Laid on table.		
Piernas, Madame Lecompte	Indemnity for property destroyed and articles furnished United States army at New Orleans in late war with Great Britain.	20	1	Petition	31	Claims	8	Adverse		Laid on table.		
Piernas, Madame Lecompte	Indemnity for property destroyed and articles furnished United States army at New Orleans in late war with Great Britain.	21	2	Petition	143	Claims	Jan. 12, 1831	Adverse		Laid on table.		
Pierpont, Hezekiah, and others.	Refunding of duties paid on the heads of their stills.	18	1	Petition	213	Ways and Means	Feb. 18, 1824	By bill	126	Passed	Passed	App'd May 26, 1824
Pierpoint, Hezekiah B	Indemnity for French spoliations prior to 1800.	26	1	Memorial	182	Foreign Affairs	343	Favorable; bill	319	Referred to Committee Whole House.		
Pierpoint, Hezekiah	(See Seffingwell & Pierpoint)	26	1		182							
Pierpont, ——	(See William and James Constable, executors of.)	26	1		182							
Pierpont, John	Revolutionary pension	18	1	Resolution	323	Rev. Pensions	Mar. 24, 1824	Adverse		Laid on table.		
Pierpont, Thomas	Revolutionary pension	16	1	Petition	51	Rev. Pensions	Jan. 14, 1820	Adverse		Laid on table.		
Pierro, ——	Indemnity for damages sustained by reservation of land by government.	30	2	Petition	313	Claims.						
Pierson, Amos	Pension for services in revolutionary war.	3	1	Rep. of Secretary War.	131	Select	May 17, 1794	Joint resolut'n.	12	Passed.	Passed	App'd June 9, 1794
Pierson, Amos	Pension for services in revolutionary war.	3	2	Rep. of Secretary War.	262	Claims	Feb. 28, 1795	Favorable; bill	130	Passed	Postponed.	
Pierson, Amos	Pension for services in revolutionary war.	4	1	Rep. of Secretary War.	447	Claims	Feb. 18, 1796	Favorable; bill	156	Passed	Passed	App'd April 20, 1796
Pierson, Amos	Increase of pension	15	1	House bill	405	Whole House	April 16, 1818	With't amend.	172	Passed	Postponed.	
Pierson, Amos, (Ohio)	Revolutionary pension	22	1	Petition	187	Rev. Pensions				Discharged; laid on table.		
Pierson, Erastus, heirs of	Pension for revolutionary services	24	2	Petition	90	Rev. Pensions	41	Favorable; bill	788	Referred to Committee Whole House.		

List of private claims presented to the House of Representatives of the United States from the 1st to the 31st Congress, inclusive—Continued.

Names of claimants.	Nature or object of the claim.	Congress.	Session.	How brought before the House of Reps.	Page of journal.	To what committee of the House referred.	No. or date of the report.	Nature of the report.	No. of the bill.	How disposed of by the House of Reps.	How disposed of by the Senate.	Date of the act of Congress, and remarks.
Pierson, Erastus, heirs of..	Pension for revolutionary services.	25	2	Petition	117	Rev. Pensions....	538	Favorable; bill	531	Passed.		
Pierson, Erastus, heirs of..	Pension for revolutionary services.	26	1	Petition	172	Rev. Pensions ...	166	Favorable; bill	176	Passed	Passed	App'd July 20, 1840
Pierson, Eunice........	(See Moses Pierson, widow of.)..	25	2	....	546							
Pierson, George........	Invalid pension............ ...	12	1	House bill	361	Whole House....	June 15, 1812	With amends.	138	Passed	Passed	App'd July 5, 1812
Pierson, George........	Increase of pension	15	2	House bill.....	41	Whole House....	Nov. 26, 1818	With amends.	203	Passed	Passed	App'd March 3, 1819
Pierson, Harry..........	(See Thomas Tynes, and others).	24	1	....	497							
Pierson, Harry..........	Payment for extra work on the Cumberland road in Indiana.	24	1	Petition	497	Claims	Mar. 25, 1836	Adverse	......	Laid on table.		
Pierson, Harry..........	Payment for extra work on the Cumberland road in Indiana.	24	2	Petition	267	Claims	Feb. 2, 1837	Adverse	......	Laid on table.		
Pierson, Harry..........	Payment for extra work on the Cumberland road in Indiana.	25	3	Petition	188	Claims	201	Adverse	......	Laid on table.		
Pierson, Harry..........	Payment for extra work on the Cumberland road in Indiana.	27	2	Petition	428	Claims	1050	Adverse	......	Laid on table.		
Pierson, Harry..........	Payment for extra work on the Cumberland road in Indiana.	27	3	Petition	274	Claims.						
Pierson, Harry..........	Payment for extra work on the Cumberland road in Indiana.	28	1	Petition	117	Claims	560	Adverse	......	Laid on table.		
Pierson, Morris	(See Thomas Tyner, and others).	24	1	....	497							
Pierson, Moses, widow of.	Revolutionary pension	25	2	Petition	546	Rev. Pensions ...	816	Favorable; bill	757	Passed	Adverse report.	
Pierson, Moses, widow of.	Revolutionary pension..........	26	1	Petition	172	Rev. Pensions.						
Piesch, Abraham........	Drawback on claret, which he is prevented from reshipping by the embargo act.	10	2	Petition	487	Com. and Manuf..	Feb. 18, 1809	....	......	Laid on table.		
Piesch, Abraham, assignees of.	Remission of bonds for security of duties on goods captured by the enemy in war of 1812.	13	3	Petition	693	Ways and Means..	....	....	......	Discharged.		
Piesch, Abraham, assignees of.	Remission of bonds for security of duties on goods captured by the enemy in war of 1812.	14	1	Petition	43	Ways and Means..	Feb. 14, 1816	Adverse......	......	Laid on table.		
Piesch, Abraham, assignees of.	Remission of bonds for security of duties on goods captured by the enemy in war of 1812.	14	2	Petition	48	Ways and Means.						
Piety, Robert D.........	Pre-emption right in the purchase of section No. 16, and that other lands be assigned for the use of schools.	24	1	Petition	913	Public Lands.						
Piety, Thomas	Increase of pension	23	2	Petition	58	Invalid Pensions...	Jan. 14, 1835	Adverse	......	Laid on table.		
Pigeon-in the-Water, (Indian.)	Pension for services in war of 1812, pursuant to treaty stipulations.	24	2	Resolution	384	Invalid Pensions.						
Pigeon-in-the-Water, (Indian.)	Pension for services in war of 1812, pursuant to treaty stipulations.	25	3	Resolution	89	Invalid Pensions ..	....	....	......	Discharged; laid on table.		
Pigg, Samuel...........	Payment for a horse lost in Mexican war.	30	1	Petition	147	Claims	238	Favorable; bill	238	Referred to Committee Whole House.		
Piggott, Isaac N.........	Compensation for services of his father in revolutionary war.	24	1	Petition	62	Rev. Claims.						
Piggott, Isaac N	Compensation for services of his father in revolutionary war.	25	2	Petition	771	Rev. Claims......	970	Adverse	......	Laid on table.		
Pigot, Jochonias, and Benjamin Lecraft.	Release from liability as sureties of James Manney, collector at Beaufort, S. C.	25	2	Senate bill	612	Commerce	Mar. 20, 1838	With't amend.	S. 148	Referred to Committee Whole House.		

List of private claims presented to the House of Representatives of the United States from the 1st to the 31st Congress, inclusive—Continued.

Names of claimants.	Nature or object of the claim.	Congress.	Session.	How brought before the House of Reps.	Page of journal.	To what committee of the House referred.	No. or date of the report.	Nature of the report.	No. of the bill.	How disposed of by the House of Reps.	How disposed of by the Senate.	Date of the act of Congress, and remarks.
Pigot, Jochonias, and Benjamin Lecraft.	Release from liability as sureties of James Manney, collector at Beaufort, S. C.	25	3	Senate bill	149	Claims	Jan. 14, 1839	With't amend.	S. 76	Passed	Passed	App'd Feb. 6, 1839
Piggott, Mason	(See Lewis Ratcliff and others)	26	1	....	606							
Pike, Daniel, (Mass.)	Indemnity for French spoliations prior to 1800.	26	1	Memorial	182	Foreign Affairs	343	Favorable; bill	319	Referred to Committee Whole House.		
Pike, Elijah	Invalid pension	12	1	Petition	204	Claims	Feb. 28, 1812	Adverse	......	Laid on table.		
Pike, Ezra, widow of	Revolutionary pension	29	1	Petition	397	Rev. Pensions.						
Pike, Ezra, widow of	Revolutionary pension	30	1	Petition	460	Rev. Pensions	624	Favorable; bill	499	Passed.		
Pike, Ezra, widow of	Revolutionary pension	31	1	Petition	383	Rev. Pensions	139	Favorable; bill	153	Referred to Committee Whole House.		
Pike, Ezra, widow of	Revolutionary pension	31	2	Bill of last sess.	103	Whole House	Jan. 3, 1851	With't amend.	153	Passed.		
Pike, Joseph S	Indemnity for French spoliations prior to 1800.	26	1	Memorial	182	Foreign Affairs	343	Favorable; bill	319	Referred to Committee Whole House.		
Pike, Mary	(See Ezra Pike, widow of)	29	1	Petition	397							
Pike, Nicholas	Copyright	1	1	....	46	Select.						
Pike, Phebe	Continuance of pension	28	1	Petition	849	Rev. Pensions.						
Pike, Richard	Indemnity for French spoliations prior to 1800.	26	1	Memorial	182	Foreign Affairs	343	Favorable; bill	319	Referred to Committee Whole House.		
Pike, Simeon, by Mary, widow of.	Pension, husband killed at battle of Bunker Hill.	25	2	Petition	349	....	....	....	......	Referred to Committee Whole House on bill No. 456.		
Pike, Simeon, by Mary, widow of.	Pension, husband killed at battle of Bunker Hill.	26	1	Petition	172	Rev. Pensions	....	....	......	Discharged; laid on table.		
Pike, Simeon, by Mary, widow of.	Pension, husband killed at battle of Bunker Hill.	26	2	Petition	51	Rev. Pensions	Feb. 2, 1841	Adverse	......	Laid on table.		
Pike, Simeon, by Mary, widow of.	Pension, husband killed at battle of Bunker Hill.	27	2	Petition	97	Rev. Pensions	307	Favorable; bill	276	Passed	Indef. postp'd.	
Pike, Simeon, by Mary, widow of.	Pension, husband killed at battle of Bunker Hill.	27	3	Petition	74	Rev. Pensions	45	Favorable; bill	673	Passed	Ref'd to Pensions.	
Pike, Simeon, by Mary, widow of.	Pension, husband killed at battle of Bunker Hill.	28	1	Petition	414	Rev. Pensions.						
Pike, Simeon, daughter of.	Pension	30	2	Petition	101	Rev. Pensions.						
Pike, Captain Zebulon M., and companions.	Compensation for explorations beyond the western frontier.	10	1	Resolution	189	Select	Mar. 10, 1808	By bill	74	Referred to Committee Whole House.		
Pike, Captain Zebulon M., and companions.	Compensation for explorations beyond the western frontier.	10	2	Resolution	352	Select	Dec. 16, 1808	Favorable; bill	114	Referred to Committee Whole House.		
Pike, Captain Zebulon M., and companions.	Compensation for explorations beyond the western frontier.	11	1	Resolution	35	Select	June 12, 1809	Favorable; bill	17	Laid on table.		
Pike, Captain Zebulon M., and companions.	Compensation for explorations beyond the western frontier.	12	1	Petition	415	....	....	....	......	Laid on table.		
Pike, Lieut. Col. Zebulon M., and others.	Compensation for explorations beyond the western frontier.	12	2	Petition	669	Claims.						
Pike, Zebulon, widow of	Compensation for explorations beyond the western frontier.	29	1	Senate bill	831	Military Affairs	Jan. 17, 1846	With amend.	50	Passed	Passed	App'd Aug. 1, 1846
Pike, Zebulon	Pension	18	2	House bill	315	Rev. Pensions	Mar. 3, 1825	Favorable; bill	307	Passed	Passed	App'd March 3, 1825
Pike, Zebulon, widow of	Pension	28	2	Petition	170	Invalid Pensions.						
Pilcher & Co	(See Patton, Pilcher, & Co.)	27	2	....	1231							
Pilcher, Josiah P	Compensation for services as a volunteer in Mexican war.	30	1	Petition	146	Military Affairs	676	Favorable; bill	542	Referred to Committee Whole House.		

List of private claims presented to the House of Representatives of the United States form the 1st to the 31st Congress, inclusive—Continued.

Names of claimants.	Nature or object of the claim.	Congress.	Session.	How brought before the House of Reps.	Page of journal.	To what committee of the House referred.	No. or date of the report.	Nature of the report.	No. of the bill.	How disposed of by the House of Reps.	How disposed of by the Senate.	Date of the act of Congress, and remarks.
Pilcher, Josiah P.	Compensation for services as a volunteer in Mexican war.	30	2	Bill of last sess.	319	Whole House	Jan. 26, 1849	With't amend.	542	Passed.		
Pilcher, Josiah P.	Compensation for services as a volunteer in Mexican war.	31	1	Petition	595	Military Affairs	251	Favorable; bill	248	Referred to Committee Whole House.		
Pilcher, Josiah P.	Compensation for services as a volunteer in Mexican war.	31	2	Bill of last sess.	181	Whole House	Jan. 24, 1851	With't amend.	248	Passed.		
Piles, Zachariah, surety of	Release from certain bond	29	1	Petition	284	Judiciary						Leave to withdraw, 2d session.
Pilgrim, owners of schooner	To be paid fishing bounty	19	1	Resolution	230	Commerce				Discharged; laid on table.		
Pilmore, Catharine	(See P. Surgett, and others, representatives of.)	22	1		205							
Pillsbury, Merrill	Invalid pension	25	2	Petition	984	Invalid Pensions.						
Pillsbury, Merrill	Arrears of pension	25	3	Petition	128	Invalid Pensions.						
Pillsbury, Merrill	Invalid pension	26	1	Petition	708	Invalid Pensions.						
Pillsbury, T. and William Billings.	Bounty on fishing vessel	18	2	Petition	157	Commerce.						
Pillsbury, T. and William Billings.	Bounty on fishing vessel	19	1	Petition	92	Commerce.						
Pilsipher, Oliver	Revolutionary pension	15	1	Resolution	275	Rev. Pensions.						Leave to withdraw.
Pimion, Benjamin	Invalid pension	15	1	House bill	405	Whole House	April 16, 1818	With amends.	172	Passed	Postponed.	
Pinchin, William	Balance due for services as a measurer at the port of Philadelphia.	4	2	Petition	634	Com. and Manuf.	Jan. 18, 1797	Adverse		Rejected.		Leave to withdraw.
Pincin, Benjamin	Invalid pension	15	1	Petition	131	Pens. & Rev. Cl'ms.				Discharged; laid on table.		
Pincin, Benjamin	Invalid pension	15	2	House bill	41	Whole House	Nov. 26, 1818	With amend's.	203	Passed	Passed	App'd March 3, 1819
Pincin, William	Restoration of pension	17	2	Petition	99	Whole House				Discharged; laid on table.		
Pinckney, Ninian	To be relieved from refunding money received for services as brigade inspector.	12	1	Petition	110	Select	Jan. 18, 1812	By bill	52	Rejected.		
Pinckney, Ninian	To be relieved from refunding money received for services as brigade inspector.	12	1	Senate bill	334	Claims	May 15, 1812	With't amend	S. 35	Passed		App'd May 28, 1812
Pinckney, Richard F.	(See Exploring Expedition)	27	3		149							
Pinckney, Somerville	(See James Williams, administrator of.)	23	1		213							
Pinckney, Susannah H. and Roger.	(See Capt. Richard Shubrick, heirs of.)	23	1		639							
Pinckney, Thomas	Payment for supplies furnished revolutionary army.	3	1	Petition	75					Laid on table.		
Pinckney, Thomas	Payment for supplies furnished revolutionary army.	4	1	Petition	422	Claims	May 7, 1796	Adverse				Leave to withdraw.
Pinckney, William, widow of.	Balance due deceased as minister plenipotentiary to England.	22	1	Memorial	472	Foreign Affairs.						
Pinckney, Wm., daughter of.	Revolutionary pension	28	1	Petition	946	Rev. Pensions.						
Pindle, Thomas	Pension	14	1	Petition	450	Pens. & Rev. Cl'ms.				Discharged; laid on table.		
Pindle, Thomas	Permission to complete payment on forfeited land.	19	1	Petition	133	Whole House				Discharged; laid on table.		
Pingree, David, executor of.	Indemnity for French spoliations prior to 1800.	26	1	Memorial	182	Foreign Affairs.	343	Favorable; bill	319	Referred to Committee Whole House.		

List of private claims presented to the House of Representatives of the United States from the 1st to the 31st Congress, inclusive—Continued.

Names of claimants.	Nature or object of the claim.	Congress.	Session.	How brought before the House of Reps.	Page of journal.	To what committee of the House referred.	No. or date of the report.	Nature of the report.	No. of the bill.	How disposed of by the House of Reps.	How disposed of by the Senate.	Date of the act of Congress, and remarks.
Pinkerton, Andrew	Pension for wounds received in revolutionary war.	11	2	Petition	239	Claims	Mar. 15, 1810	By bill	107	Passed	Passed	App'd April 27, 1810
Pinkham, Calvin, (Mo.)	Restoration of pension	22	1	Petition	509	Rev. Pensions	472	Favorable; bill	574	Referred to Committee Whole House.		
Pinkham, Emily	(See Daniel Grant, and others)	28	1		130							
Pinkham, Paul	Increase of compensation as light-house keeper.	4	1	Petition	402	Referred to Secretary of Treasury.	Mar. 25, 1796	Report		Laid on table.		
Pinkham, Silas, heirs of	(See Daniel Grant, and others)	28	1		130							
Pinny, Isaac	Restoration of pension	17	1	Petition	72	Rev. Pensions				Discharged; laid on table.		
Pinny, Isaac	Restoration of pension	17	2	Petition	119	Whole House				Discharged; laid on table.		Leave to withdraw.
Pinny, Isaac	Restoration of pension	21	1	Senate bill	732	Military Pensions	Mar. 29, 1830	With't amend.	S. 174	Passed	Passed	App'd May 31, 1830
Pinney, Levi	Indemnity for property destroyed in late war.	23	1	Petition	348	Claims	440	Adverse		Laid on table.		
Pinney, Levi	Indemnity for property destroyed in the war of 1812.	31	1	Petition	192	Claims.						
Pino, Mary, and Philip Réviere, heirs of.	Confirmation of title to land	24	1	Petition	799	Priv. Land Claims.						
Pinson, George	Increase of pension	15	1	House bill	405	Whole House	April 16, 1818	With't amends	172	Passed	Postponed.	
Pintard, Lewis	Drawback on wines exported to the East Indies.	2	2	Petition	700	Select	Feb. 26, 1793	Favorable		Referred to Committee Ways and Means.		
Pintard, Lewis	Balance due as agent for American prisoners during the revolutionary war.	4	1	Resolution	421	Ways and Means	Jan. 18, 1796	By bill	142	Passed	Passed	App'd Feb. 5, 1796
Pion, Jean Baptiste	Pay for a horse lost in United States service.	22	2	Petition	397	Claims.						
Piper, Daniel	Pension	16	2	Petition	68	Rev. Pensions	Feb. 15, 1821	Adverse				Leave to withdraw.
Piper, David, (N. H.)	Restoration of pension	17	1	Petition	106	Rev. Pensions				Discharged; laid on table.		
Piper, James, heirs of	Amount due for revolutionary services of deceased, and for the bounty land to which he was entitled.	25	2	Petition	575	Rev. Claims				Discharged; laid on table.		
Piper, James, heirs of	Amount due for revolutionary services of deceased, and for the bounty land to which he was entitled.	26	1	Petition	360	Rev. Claims.						
Piper, John	Arrears of pay and emoluments as a soldier of the revolutionary war.	4	1	Petition	487	Claims	May 31, 1796	Adverse		Laid on table.		
Piper, John, heirs of	Commutation pay for revolutionary services.	24	2	Petition	39	Rev. Claims.						
Piper, John, heirs of	Commutation pay for revolutionary services.	25	3	Petition and docs.	85	Rev. Claims				Discharged.		
Piper, John, (N. Y.)	Invalid pension	26	1	Petition	166	Rev. Claims	170	Favorable; bill	181	Passed	Indef. postp'd.	
Piper, John, (N. Y.)	Invalid pension	26	2	Petition	134	Invalid Pensions	153	Favorable; bill	664	Referred to Committee Whole House.		
Piper, John, (N. Y.)	Commutation of half-pay	27	2	Petition	61	Invalid Pensions	27	Adverse		Laid on table.		
Piper, John, (N. Y.)	Pension	28	2	Petition	57	Invalid Pensions.						
Pipes, Abner, and Delilah.	(See Gustavus Campbell, heirs of.)	13	2		387							
Pipes, Abner	Confirmation of title to land in Mississippi.	18	1	Petition	136	Priv. Land Claims.	Feb. 13, 1824	Adverse		Laid on table.		

3—12

List of private claims presented to the House of Representatives of the United States from the 1st to the 31st Congress, inclusive—Continued.

Names of claimants.	Nature or object of the claim.	Congress.	Session.	How brought before the House of Reps.	Page of journal.	To what committee of the House referred.	No. or date of the report.	Nature of the report.	No. of the bill.	How disposed of by the House of Reps.	How disposed of by the Senate.	Date of the act of Congress, and remarks.
Pishen, Isaac, widow of	Five years' half-pay, he having died in service of the United States in late war.	32	2	Resolution	143	Invalid Pensions	89	Favorable; bill	712	Passed.		
Pishen, Isaac, widow of	Five years' half-pay, he having died in service of the United States in late war.	24	1	Resolution	99	Invalid Pensions	97	Favorable; bill	110	Passed	Indef. postp'd.	
Pishen, Isaac, widow of	Five years' half-pay, he having died in service of the United States in late war.	27	2	Resolution	47	Invalid Pensions	Feb. 9, 1842	Adverse	......	Laid on table.		
Pistole, Charles, widow of.	Revolutionary pension	29	2	Senate bill	375	Rev. Pensions	Feb. 24, 1847	With't amend.	S. 96	Referred to Committee Whole House.		
Pistole, Char'es, widow of.	Revolutionary pension	30	1	Senate bill	683	Rev. Pensions	....	....	S. 78	Passed	....	App'd Aug. 14, 1848
Pistole, Elizabeth	(See Charles Pistole, widow of.)	29	2	....	375							
Pitcher, Joshua	To be reimbursed amount paid an interpreter while acting as sub-agent for Sioux Indians.	24	1	Petition	244	Indian Affairs	230	Favorable; bill	242	Passed	Passed	App'd July 1, 1836
Pitchlyn, John, by A. Foster, attorney.	Compensation for services as interpreter to the Choctaw Indians from 1786 to July, 1792.	5	3	Petition	433	Claims	....	....	......	Postp'd to next sess.		
Pitchlyn, John, by A. Foster, attorney.	Compensation for services as interpreter to the Choctaw Indians from 1786 to July, 1792.	6	1	Petition	535	Claims	Jan. 24, 1800	Adverse	......	Laid on table	....	Mar. 24, 1804, leave to withdraw.
Pitchlyn, John, by Silas Dismore, attorney.	Compensation for services as interpreter to the Choctaw Indians from February, 1786, to March 3, 1789.	10	1	Petition	40	Claims.						
Pitchlyn, John	Compensation for services as interpreter to Choctaw Indians.	13	1	Petition	37	Claims	....	....	......	Discharged.		
Pitchlyn, John	Compensation for services as interpreter to Choctaw Indians.	13	2	Petition	196	Claims	32	Adverse; bill ordered.	196	Passed	Passed	App'd April 18, 1814
Pittman, Col. Dempsey, & staff.	Payment for services rendered by order of an officer of the regular army.	26	1	Resolution	963	Military Affairs.						
Pittman, George	To be allowed a deficiency in the pension heretofore granted him.	12	2	Petition	591	Claims	Feb. 26, 1836	Adverse	......	Laid on table.		
Pitman, James	Increase of pension	31	1	Petition	898	Rev. Pensions	370	Adverse	......	Laid on table.		
Pitman, John	Renewal of patent for the manufacture of cordage.	11	1	Petition	30	Select.						
Pitman, John	Renewal of patent for the manufacture of cordage.	11	2	Petition	165	Select.						
Pittman, John	Invalid pension	24	1	Petition	157	Invalid Pensions	Jan. 26, 1836	Adverse	......	Laid on table.		
Pitman, Joshua	Invalid pension	28	2	Petition	435	Invalid Pensions.						
Pitman, Joshua	Invalid pension	29	1	Petition	257	Invalid Pensions	289	Adverse	......	Laid on table.		
Pitman, Joshua	Invalid pension	31	1	Petition	827	Invalid Pensions.						
Pitman, William	Invalid pension	27	2	Petition	218, 1157	Invalid Pensions	....	....	......	Discharged; laid on table.		
Pitman, William	Invalid pension	28	1	Petition	875	Invalid Pensions.						
Pitman, William	Invalid pension	28	2	Petition	207	Invalid Pensions	....	....	......	Discharged; laid on table.		
Pitman, William	Invalid pension	29	1	Petition	397	Invalid Pensions.						
Pitman, William	Invalid pension	30	1	Petition	740	Invalid Pensions	711	Favorable; bill	556	Passed	Passed	App'd Aug. 14, 1848
Pitner, Adam, sen.	Pay for a horse lost in the war of 1812.	16	2	Petition	173	Claims	Feb. 2, 1821	Adverse	......	Laid on table.		

List of private claims presented to the House of Representatives of the United States from the 1st to the 31st Congress, inclusive—Continued.

Names of claimants.	Nature or object of the claim.	Congress.	Session.	How brought before the House of Reps.	Page of journal.	To what committee of the House referred.	No. or date of the report.	Nature of the report.	No. of the bill.	How disposed of by the House of Reps.	How disposed of by the Senate.	Date of the act of Congress, and remarks.
Pitray, Lewis, and Just Veil.	Remission of duties on goods brought to the United State from St. Augustine, Florida, after the treaty of peace.	17	2	Memorial	136	Ways and Means				Discharged		Leave to withdraw.
Pix, Christopher H	Rent of house in Galveston, used by United States.	30	1	Petition	270	Claims	344	Favorable; bill	325	Passed.		
Pix, Christopher H	Rent of house in Galveston, used by United States.	31	1	Petition	308	Judiciary	Feb. 13, 1850	Favorable; bill	101	Referred to Committee Whole House.		
Pix, Christopher H	Rent of house in Galveston, used by United States.	31	2	Bill of last sess.	183				101	Passed.		
Pix, Peter	Increase of pension	31	1	Petition	501	Invalid Pensions.						
Place, John, mother of	Pension, son killed in naval engagement in late war.	21	2	Petition	137	Naval Affairs.						
Place, John, mother of	Pension, son killed in naval engagement in late war.	22	1	Petition	49	Naval Affairs.						
Place, John, mother of	Pension, son killed in naval engagement in late war.	23	1	Petition	273	Naval Affairs.						
Place, John, mother of	Pension, son killed in naval engagement in late war.	25	2	Petition	56	Naval Affairs				Discharged; laid on table.		
Place, John, mother of	Pension, son killed in naval engagement in late war.	25	3	Petition	131	Naval Affairs.						
Place, John, mother of	Pension, son killed in naval engagement in late war.	26	1	Petition	180	Naval Affairs.	July 21, 1840	By bill	522	Referred to Committee Whole House.		
Place, John, mother of	Pension, son killed in naval engagement in late war.	27	2	Petition	63	Naval Affairs	April 12, 1842	By bill	357	Referred to Committee Whole House.		
Place, John, mother of	Pension, son killed in naval engagement in late war.	27	3	Bill of last sess.	87				357	Passed	Indef. postp'd.	
Place, John, mother of	Pension, son killed in naval engagement in late war.	30	1	Petition	103	Naval Affairs	76	Favorable; bill	61	Passed.		
Place, John, mother of	Pension, son killed in naval engagement in late war.	30	2	Bill of last sess.	466				61		Passed	App'd Feb. 22, 1849
Placet, John B	Confirmation of title to land in Missouri.	15	2	Petition	28	Priv. Land Claims.				Discharged; laid on table.		
Placet, John B	Confirmation of title to land in Missouri.	17	1	Petition	54	Public Lands				Discharged; laid on table.		
Placet, John B	Confirmation of title to land in Missouri.	18	1	Petition	55	Public Lands	Jan. 16, 1824	By bill	65	Passed	Passed	App'd May 26, 1824. The act gives the courts jurisdiction.
Placet, John B	Confirmation of Spanish land title.	22	1	Petition	263	Priv. Land Claims.	Feb. 17, 1832	By bill	380	Referred to Committee Whole House.		
Placey, Joseph, assignee of.	Payment, with interest, for supplies furnished, regiment of General Clarke.	23	1	Senate bill	846	Rev. Claims			S. 139			
Placey, Joseph, assignee of.	Payment, with interest, for supplies furnished, regiment of General Clarke.	24	2	Senate bill	250	Rev. Claims			S. 22			
Placey, Joseph, assignee of.	Payment, with interest, for supplies furnished, regiment of General Clarke.	25	2	Senate bill	1169	Rev. Claims			S. 128			
Placey, Joseph, assignee of.	Payment, with interest, for supplies furnished, regiment of General Clarke.	25	3	Senate bill	338	Rev. Claims	Feb. 16, 1839	Adverse	S. 4	Referred to Committee Whole House.		

List of private claims presented to the House of Representatives of the United States from the 1st to the 31st Congress, inclusive—Continued.

Names of claimants.	Nature or object of the claim.	Congress.	Session.	How brought before the House of Reps.	Page of journal.	To what committee of the House referred.	No. or date of the report.	Nature of the report.	No. of the bill.	How disposed of by the House of Reps.	How disposed of by the Senate.	Date of the act of Congress, and remarks.
Placey, Joseph, assignee of.	Payment, with interest, for supplies furnished, regiment of General Clarke.	26	2	Senate bill	811	Rev. Claims	519	Adverse	S. 39	Referred to Committee Whole House.		
Placey, Joseph, assignee of.	Payment, with interest, for supplies furnished, regiment of General Clarke.	28	1	Bill on leave	268	Rev. Claims	....	....	83			
Placey, Joseph, assignee of.	Payment, with interest, for supplies furnished, regiment of General Clarke.	30	1	Petition	69	Claims	343	Favorable; bill	324	Referred to Committee Whole House.		
Placey, Joseph, assignee of.	Payment, with interest, for supplies furnished, regiment of General Clarke.	31	1	Bill on leave	474	Rev. Claims	179	With't amend	45	Referred to Committee Whole House.		
Placide, Louis	Confirmation of title to land	22	1	House bill	421	Whole House	Feb. 28, 1832	Favorable	425	Passed	Passed	App'd June 25, 1832
Plane, Catharine	(See David Plane, widow of)	21	1	....	377							
Plane, David, widow of	Revolutionary pension	21	1	Petition	377	Military Pensions.						
Plant, Ebenezer	Arrears of pension	31	1	Petition	994	Invalid Pensions.						
Plant, Eli	Revolutionary pension	25	2	Resolution	466	Rev. Pensions	....	....	......	Discharged; laid on table.		
Plant, John, widow of	Compensation for his services in revolutionary war.	23	2	Petition	390	Rev. Claims.						
Plant, John, widow of	Compensation for services in revolutionary war.	24	1	Petition	753	Rev. Claims.						
Plant, Mary A	(See John Plant, widow of)	24	1	....	753							
Plants, William	Land for revolutionary services	16	1	Petition	88	Pens. & Rev. Cl'ms.	Jan. 5, 1820	Adverse	......	Laid on table.		
Plantau, A	Renewal of patent for producing steam.	20	2	Petition	33	Judiciary	Dec. 16, 1825	Adverse	......	Laid on table.		
Planters' Bank, New Orleans.	Reimbursement of advances to United States officers.	17	1	Senate bill	316	Ways and Means	Mar. 6, 1822	With't amend.	S. 30	Passed	....	App'd May 7, 1822
Plater, John R	To be exonerated from tax on slaves which had been stolen by the British.	13	3	Petition	519	Ways and Means	....	....	......	Discharged; laid on table.		
Platner, Henry	(See Killian Van Rensellaer and others.)	3	1	....	21							
Plato, brig	(See George Lee)	29	1	....	198							
Plato, Charles and Huldah.	(See Sawney York, representatives of.)	24	2	....	73							
Platt, Charles, and others.	Indemnity for damages to their property by United States troops, in Plattsburg, in late war.	15	1	Petition	207	Claims.						
Platt, Charles, and others.	Indemnity for damages to their property by United States troops, in Plattsburg, in late war.	17	1	Petition	92	Claims	....	....	......	Discharged; laid on table.		
Platt, Charles, and others.	Indemnity for damages to their property by United States troops, in Plattsburgh, in late war.	17	2	Petition	26	Claims	....	....	......	Discharged; laid on table.	....	Leave to withdraw.
Platt, David	Revolutionary pension	22	1	Resolution	634	Rev. Pensions.						
Platt, Ebenezer S	Relief in consideration of sufferings and hardships while a prisoner in revolutionary war.	9	2	Petition	581	Claims.						
Platt, Frederick	Pension for services in revolutionary war.	4	1	Rep. of Secretary of War.	445	Claims	Feb. 18, 1796	Favorable; bill	156	Passed	Passed	App'd April 20, 1796
Platt, Henry	Compensation for property destroyed by order of General Macomb.	13	3	Petition	751	Claims	Feb. 15, 1815	By bill	297	Passed	Passed	App'd March 3, 1815

List of private claims presented to the House of Representatives of the United States from the 1st to the 31st Congress, inclusive—Continued.

Names of claimants.	Nature or object of the claim.	Congress.	Session.	How brought before the House of Reps.	Page of journal.	To what committee of the House referred.	No. or date of the report.	Nature of the report.	No. of the bill.	How disposed of by the House of Reps.	How disposed of by the Senate.	Date of the act of Congress, and remarks.
Platt, Jonas D.	Invalid pension	28	1	Petition	83	Invalid Pensions				Discharged; laid on table.		
Platt, Jonas D.	Invalid pension	28	2	Petition	54	Invalid Pensions				Discharged; laid on table.		
Platt, Jonas D.	Invalid pension	29	1	Petition	233	Invalid Pensions	498	Adverse		Laid on table.		
Platt, Jonas D.	Invalid pension	31	1	Petition	311	Invalid Pensions	228	Favorable; bill	223	Referred to Committee Whole House.		
Platt, Jonas D.	Invalid pension	31	2	Bill of last sess.	182	Whole House	Jan. 24, 1851	With't amend.	223	Passed.		
Platt, Levi, (N. Y.)	Compensation for property destroyed by order of Gen. Macomb.	13	3	Petition	751	Claims	Feb. 15, 1815	By bill	297	Passed	Passed	App'd March 3, 1815
Platt, Levi, (N. Y.)	Increase of compensation as postmaster at Plattsburg.	30	1	Petition	558	P. Of. & P. Roads.						
Platt, Nathaniel	Compensation for supplies furnished and for use of buildings by United States troops at Plattsburg, in late war.	23	1	Petition	217	Claims	514	Adverse		Recommit'd to Claims.		
Platt, Nathaniel	Compensation for supplies furnished and for use of buildings by United States troops at Plattsburg, in late war.	24	1	Petition	93	Claims	185	Favorable; bill	190	Passed	Passed	App'd July 2, 1836
Platt, N. Z.	Payment for wharf and store-house destroyed by the British at Plattsburg in late war.	13	3	Petition	528					Referred to Committee Whole House on bill No. 228.		Leave to withdraw; Feb. 23, 1815.
Platt, N. Z.	Payment for wharf and store-house destroyed by the British at Plattsburg in late war.	14	1	Petition	459					Laid on table.		
Please, George	Revolutionary pension	17	1	Petition	30	Pens. & Rev. Cl'ms.	Dec. 21, 1821	Adverse		Laid on table.		
Please, George	Revolutionary pension	17	2	Petition	47	Pens. & Rev. Cl'ms.	Dec. 20, 1822	Adverse		Rejected.		
Pleasonton, Stephen, Third Auditor.	Compensation for extra services as agent of United States Treasury.	21	1	Petition	55	Claims.						
Pleasonton, Stephen, Third Auditor.	Compensation for extra services as agent of United States Treasury.	22	1	Petition	49	Claims.						
Pleasonton, Stephen, Third Auditor.	Compensation for extra services as agent of United States Treasury.	22	1	Senate bill	715	Claims	511	Adverse	S. 75	Laid on table.		
Pleasonton, Stephen, Third Auditor.	Compensation for extra services as agent of United States Treasury.	22	2	Petition	110	Claims	79	Adverse		Laid on table.		
Pleasonton, Stephen, Third Auditor.	Compensation for extra services as agent of United States Treasury.	23	1	Petition	38	Judiciary.						
Pleasonton, Stephen, Third Auditor.	Compensation for extra services as agent of United States Treasury.	23	1	Senate bill	844	Judiciary	June 27, 1834	Adverse	S. 115	Rejected.		
Pleasants, Thomas S. and Joseph J.	Compensation for loss of certain lands.	26	1	Petition	954	Public Lands.						
Pleasants, Thomas S. and Joseph J.	Compensation for loss of certain lands.	26	2	Petition	79	Public Lands.						
Please, George	Pension	17	1	Petition	30	Pens. & Rev. Cl'ms.	Dec. 21, 1821	Adverse		Laid on table.		
Please, George	Pension	17	2	Petition	47	Pens. & Rev. Cl'ms.	Dec. 20, 1822	Adverse		Laid on table.		
Plumb, Elisha	Increase of pension	26	2	Petition	77	Rev. Pensions	138	Favorable; bill	645	Referred to Committee Whole House.		
Pumb Island Bridge and Turnpike Company.	Indemnity for destruction of bridge	26	1	Senate bill	882	Roads and Canals.	July 21, 1840	With't amend.	S. 173	Referred to Committee Whole House.		
Plumb Island Bridge and Turnpike Company.	Indemnity for destruction of bridge	26	2	Senate bill	151	Claims			S. 84			

List of private claims presented to the House of Representatives of the United States from the 1st to the 31st Congress, inclusive—Continued.

Names of claimants.	Nature or object of the claim.	Congress.	Session.	How brought before the House of Reps.	Page of journal.	To what committee of the House referred.	No. or date of the report.	Nature of the report.	No. of the bill.	How disposed of by the House of Reps.	How disposed of by the Senate.	Date of the act of Congress, and remarks.
Plumb Island Bridge and Turnpike Company.	Indemnity for destruction of bridge	27	2	Senate bill	232	Commerce		With't amend.	S. 94	Passed		App'd June 4, 1842
Plumb, James	(See assignees of Thomas Tupper)	22	2		142							
Plumb, Joseph	Revolutionary pension	23	1	Petition	197	Rev. Pensions.						
Plumb, Joseph, heirs of	Pension due him at the time of his death.	26	1	Petition	936	Rev. Pensions	714	Adverse		Laid on table.		
Plumb, Joseph, heirs of	Pension due him at the time of his death.	26	2	Petition	77	Rev. Pensions	138	Favorable; bill	645	Referred to Committee Whole House.		
Plumb, Joseph, heirs of	Pension due him at the time of his death.	27	2	Petition	153	Rev. Pensions	100	Favorable; bill	146	Passed	Indef. postp'd.	
Plumb, Joseph, heirs of	Pension due him at the time of his death.	30	1	Petition	619	Rev. Pensions	786	Adverse		Laid on table.		
Plumb, Joseph, heirs of	Pension due him at the time of his death.	31	1	Petition	536	Rev. Pensions	450	Adverse		Laid on table.		
Plumb, Nathaniel	Bounty land for revolutionary services.	25	2	Petition	59	Priv. Land Claims.	408	Favorable; bill	419	Referred to Committee Whole House.		
Plumb, Nathaniel	Bounty land for revolutionary services.	25	3	House bill	378	Whole House	Jan. 25, 1839	With't amend.	419	Passed	Passed	App'd March 3, 1839
Plumb, Samuel	Indemnity for property destroyed by United States troops in late war.	15	1	Petition	247	Claims.						
Plumb, Samuel	Indemnity for property destroyed by United States troops in late war.	15	2	Petition	40	Claims	Jan. 5, 1819	Adverse		Laid on table.		
Plumb, Samuel	Indemnity for property destroyed by United States troops in late war.	18	2	Petition	160	Claims.						
Plumb, Samuel A	(See heirs of James and John Pettigrew.)	22	1		401							
Plumer, Addison	(See David Plumer, estate of)	26	1		182							
Plumer, David, estate of	Indemnity for French spoliations prior to 1800.	26	1	Memorial	182	Foreign Affairs	343	Favorable	319	Referred to Committee Whole House.		
Plummer, Alpheus	For losses by depreciation of Continental money.	28	1	Petition	106	Claims.						
Plummer, Elizabeth	Compensation for boarding and clothing United States sailors.	18	1	Petition	214	Claims.						
Plummer, Elizabeth	Compensation for boarding and clothing United States sailors.	19	1	Petition	57	Claims.						
Plummer, Elizabeth	Compensation for boarding and clothing United States sailors.	20	1	Petition	311	Claims	Feb. 25, 1828	Adverse		Laid on table.		Leave to withdraw.
Plummer, Isaac	Pension	19	1	Resolution	172	Military Pensions	May 5, 1826	Favorable		Referred to Committee Whole House on bill No. 118.		
Plummer, Isaac	Pension	20	1	Petition	125	Military Pensions	April 29, 1828	By bill	283	Passed.		
Plummer, Isaac	Pension	20	2	House bill	55	Whole House	Jan. 15, 1829	With amends.	311	Passed	Laid on table.	
Plummer, Isaac	Pension	21	1	Petition	36	Military Pensions	Jan. 5, 1830	By bill	72	Passed	Passed	App'd May 20, 1830
Plummer, Isaac	Increase of pension	26	1	Petition	198	Invalid Pensions	351	Favorable; bill	330	Referred to Committee Whole House.		
Plummer, Isaac	Increase of pension	27	2	Petition	154	Invalid Pensions	317	Favorable; bill	286	Ordered to 3d reading;		
Plummer, Isaac	Increase of pension	27	3	House bill	87				286	Passed	Indef. postp'd.	
Plummer, Isaac	Increase of pension	28	1	Petition	116	Invalid Pensions	12	Favorable; bill	39	Passed	Indef. postp'd.	
Plummer, Isaac	Increase of pension	29	1	Petition	261	Invalid Pensions	506	Adverse		Laid on table.		
Plummer, Isaac	Increase of pension	31	1	Petition	472	Invalid Pensions	469	Adverse		Laid on table.		

List of private claims presented to the House of Representatives of the United States from the 1st to the 31st Congress, inclusive—Continued.

Names of claimants.	Nature or object of the claim.	Congress.	Session.	How brought before the House of Reps.	Page of journal.	To what committee of the House referred.	No. or date of the report.	Nature of the report.	No. of the bill.	How disposed of by the House of Reps.	How disposed of by the Senate.	Date of the act of Congress, and remarks.
Plummer, Jeremiah	(See executors of Jonathan Libbey)	17	1	....	83							
Plummer, Jerome and Girard, assignees of.	Indemnity for property destroyed in late war.	31	1	Petition	809	Claims.						
Plummer, Jones W.	Compensation for services as surgeon on U. States ship Ontario.	26	1	Petition	627	Naval Affairs.						
Plumer, Joshus, Portland, Maine.	Indemnity for French spoliations prior to 1800.	26	1	Memorial	182	Foreign Affairs	343	Favorable; bill	319	Referred to Committee Whole House.		
Plumer, Joshua, Scarboro', Maine.	Indemnity for French spoliations prior to 1800.	26	1	Memorial	182	Foreign Affairs	343	Favorable; bill	319	Referred to Committee Whole House.		
Plummer, Moses	Permission to change entry of land.	18	2	Petition	81	Public Lands	Feb. 7, 1825	Favorable; bill	321	Passed	Passed	App'd March 3, 1825
Plummer, Prudence	Compensation for property destroyed by United States troops in 1812.	19	1	Memorial	252	Foreign Relations	112	Adverse	......	Laid on table.		
Plummer, Prudence	Compensation for property destroyed by United States troops in 1812.	20	2	Memorial	339	Foreign Affairs	99	Favorable; bill	385	Referred to Committee Whole House.		
Plummer, Prudence	Compensation for property destroyed by United States troops in 1812.	23	1	Memorial	67	Foreign Affairs	368	Favorable; bill	395	Passed	Passed	App'd June 26, 1834
Plummer, William	(See executors of Starkey Armistead)	30	2	....	167							
Plumstead, George, administrator of.	Indemnity for French spoliations prior to 1800.	26	1	Memorial	182	Foreign Affairs	343	Favorable; bill	319	Referred to Committee Whole House.		
Plunkett, James, heirs of.	Payment for a horse and accoutrements lost in war of 1812.	23	1	Petition	567	Claims.						
Plunkett, James, heirs of.	Payment for a horse and accoutrements lost in war of 1812.	24	1	Petition	51	Claims	Dec. 21, 1835	Favorable; bill	26	Passed	Passed	App'd Feb. 9, 1836
Plunket, John	Compensation for injuries received in United States arsenal in North Carolina.	30	1	Petition	685	Claims.						
Plunket, John	Compensation for injuries received in United States arsenal in North Carolina.	31	1	Petition	347	Claims	75	Favorable; bill	90	Passed.		
Plunket, Penelope	(See Joseph Davis, widow of)	26	1	....	556							
Plunket, Reuben	Invalid pension	12	1	House bill	361	Whole House	June 15, 1812	With amends.	138	Passed	Passed	App'd July 5, 1812
Plympton, Ebenezer	Pension	21	1	Petition	99	Military Pensions	April 7, 1830	Adverse	......	Laid on table.		
Plympton, Ebenezer	Pension	22	1	Petition	31	Rev. Pensions	160	Favorable; bill	237	Referred to Committee Whole House.		
Plympton, Ebenezer	Pension	22	2	House bill	123	....	....	....	237	Laid on table.		
Plympton, William	Payment for Holland gin seized illegaly and sold for benefit of United States.	21	2	Petition	336	Commerce.						
Plympton, William	Payment for Holland gin seized illegaly and sold for benefit of United States.	22	1	Petition	132	Commerce	April 13, 1832	Adverse	......	Laid on table.		
Poe, David, widow of.	Payment for forage supplied American army by deceased, as quartermaster gen. in revolutionary war	16	1	Petition	135	Pens. & Rev. Cl'ms.	Jan. 24, 1820	Adverse	......	Rejected.		
Poe, Elizabeth	(See David Poe, widow of.)	16	1	....	135							
Poe, John, (Ohio)	Compensation for services in revolutionary war.	22	2	Petition	64	Rev. Claims.						
Poe, John, (Ohio)	Compensation for services in revolutionary war.	23	1	Petition	377	Rev. Claims.						

List of private claims presented to the House of Representatives of the United States from the 1st to the 31st Congress, inclusive—Continued.

Names of claimants.	Nature or object of the claim.	Congress.	Session.	How brought before the House of Reps.	Page of journal.	To what committee of the House referred.	No. or date of the report.	Nature of the report.	No. of the bill.	How disposed of by the House of Reps.	How disposed of by the Senate.	Date of the act of Congress, and remarks.
Poe, John, (Ky)	Compensation for services in purchasing horses and mules for United States army.	30	1	Petition	773	Claims.						
Poe, John, (Ky)	Compensation for services in purchasing horses and mules for United States army.	30	2	Petition	77	Claims	5	Favorable; bill	681	Referred to Committee Whole House.		
Poe, John, (Ky)	Compensation for services in purchasing horses and mules for United States army.	31	1	Petition	624	Claims	154	Favorable; bill	172	Referred to Committee Whole House.		
Poe, John, (Ky)	Compensation for services in purchasing horses and mules for United States army.	31	2	Bill of last sess.	103	Whole House	Jan. 3, 1851	With't amend.	172	Passed	Reported without amend't.	
Poe, Virgil	Invalid pension	12	1	House bill	361	Whole House	June 15, 1812	With amend.	138	Passed	Passed	App'd July 5, 1812
Poelzel, Lorenzo	Pension for wounds in Mexican war.	30	2	Petition	123	Invalid Pensions	....	....	......	Discharged; laid on table.		
Pogue, Robert	(See administrator of Daniel Clark)											
Pohon, William	Revolutionary pension	26	1	Petition	1001	Rev. Pensions.						
Poidevin, Madame	Refunding amount advanced A. Vail, United States consul at L'Orient, for relief of shipwrecked American seamen.	15	1	Petition and rep't Sec. Treasury.	161	Claims	99	Favorable; bill	88	Passed	Passed	App'd April 20, 1818
Poindexter, Chapman	Revolutionary pension	22	1	Resolution	581	Rev. Pensions.						
Poindexter, George	Compensation for damages to property by Kentucky volunteers.	31	1	Senate bill	1029	Military Affairs	....	....	S. 221			
Poindexter, Robert	Invalid pension	27	2	Petition	182	Invalid Pensions	947	Favorable; bill	551	Ordered to 3d reading.		
Poindexter, Robert	Invalid pension	27	3	House bill	89	....	....	....	551	Passed	Indef. postp'd.	
Poindexter, Robert	Invalid pension	28	1	Petition	122	Invalid Pensions	47	Adverse	......	Laid on table.		
Poindexter, Robert, (Ky)	Revolutionary pension	28	1	Petition	76	Rev. Pensions.						
Poineer, W. H.	(See Lewis F. Beeler, *et al.*)	30	1	....	112	....	482					
Poissot, Paul	Confirmation of title to land in Louisiana.	23	1	Petition	76	Priv. Land Claims.	109	Favorable; bill	119	Passed.		
Poissot, Paul	Confirmation of title to land in Louisiana.	24	1	Petition	208	Priv. Land Claims.	241	Favorable; bill	247	Referred to Committee Whole House.		
Poissot, Paul	Confirmation of title to land in Louisiana.	24	2	Bill of last sess.	63	Whole House	....	....	247			
Poissot, Paul	Confirmation of title to land in Louisiana.	25	2	Petition	43	Priv. Land Claims.	654	Favorable; bill	631	Referred to Committee Whole House.		
Poissot, Paul	Confirmation of title to land in Louisiana.	25	3	Bill of last sess.	380	Whole House	Jan. 25, 1839	With amend.	631	Passed	Passed	App'd March 3, 1819
Poissot, Remy	Pre-emption right to certain lands, and that others be set apart for schools.	23	1	Petition	587	Public Lands.						
Poissot, Remy	Pre-emption right to certain lands, and that others be set apart for schools.	23	2	Petition	49	Public Lands.						
Poissot, Remy	Pre-emption right to certain lands, and that others be set apart for schools.	24	1	Petition	121	Public Lands.						
Poissot, Remy	Pre-emption right to certain lands, and that others be set apart for schools.	25	2	Petition	374	Priv. Land Claims.						
Poirey, Monsieur, aid to General Lafayette.	Settlement of accounts for revolutionary services.	4	1	Petition and rep't Sec. of War.	436	....	....	....	......	Laid on table.		

List of private claims presented to the House of Representatives of the United States from the 1st to the 31st Congress, inclusive—Continued.

Names of claimants.	Nature or object of the claim.	Congress.	Session.	How brought before the House of Reps.	Page of journal.	To what committee of the House referred.	No. or date of the report.	Nature of the report.	No. of the bill.	How disposed of by the House of Reps.	How disposed of by the Senate.	Date of the act of Congress, and remarks.
Poirey, Monsieur, aid to General Lafayette.	Settlement of accounts for revolutionary services.	4	2	Petition	640	Whole House	Jan. 9, 1797	Bill ordered	213	Passed	Rejected.	
Poirey, Monsieur, aid to General Lafayette.	Settlement of accounts for revolutionary services.	15	1	Petition	140	Pens. & Rev. Cl'ms.	Mar. 28, 1818	By bill	166	Referred to Committee Whole House.		
Poirey, Monsieur, aid to General Lafayette.	Settlement of accounts for revolutionary services.	15	2	House bill	185	Whole House	Jan. 25, 1819	With't amend.	166	Passed	Passed	App'd Feb. 24, 1819
Pol, Joseph, heirs of	Confirmation of Spanish land title.	19	1	Petition	381	Public Lands	April 14, 1826	By bill	214	Passed.		
Poland, exiles from	Grant of land for their relief	23	1	Senate bill	617	Public Lands	June 5, 1836	With't amend.	S. 158	Passed	....	App'd June 30, 1834
Poland, exiles from	Further relief from government	23	2	Memorial	307	Public Lands.						
Poland, exiles from	For a modification of the act of June 30, 1834.	24	1	Memorial	478	Public Lands	Mar. 25, 1836	By bill	488	Referred to Committee Whole House.		
Poland, exiles from	For enforcement of act of June 30, 1834.	24	2	Memorial	107	Public Lands.						
Poland, exiles from	An act extending and enforcing act of June 30, 1834.	27	2	Senate bill	550	Public Lands	April 1, 1842	With't amend	S. 120	Passed	....	App'd April 14, 1842
Polander, Adam	Invalid pension	3	1	Petition	26	....	....	....	......	Referred to Secretary War.		
Polander, Adam	Invalid pension	3	2	Rep. of Secretary War.	278	....	....	....	......	Laid on table.		
Polereczky, J. L., a French officer in the service of the United States, revolutionary war.	For the benefit of the acts for the relief of those who served in the land and naval forces in revolutionary war.	15	2	Petition	46	Pens. & Rev. Cl'ms.	Jan. 14, 1819	Adverse	......	Leave to withdraw.		
Polereczky, J L., a French officer in the service of the United States, revolutionary war.	For the benefit of the acts for the relief of those who served in the land and naval forces in revolutionary war.	16	1	Petition	176	Pens. & Rev. Cl'ms.	59	Adverse	......	Laid on table.		
Polereczky, J. L., a French officer in the service of the United States, revolutionary war.	For the benefit of the acts for the relief of those who served in the land and naval forces in revolutionary war.	16	2	Petition	88	Rev. Claims	Feb. 15, 1821	Adverse	......	Rejected.	....	Leave to wi hdraw
Polereczky, J. L., a French officer in the service of the United States, revolutionary war.	For the benefit of the acts for the relief of those who served in the land and naval forces in revolutionary war.	17	1	Petition	234	Pens. & Rev. Cl'ms.	Feb. 12, 1822	Adverse	......	Laid on table.		
Polereczky, J. L., a French officer in the service of the United States, revolutionary war.	For the benefit of the acts for the relief of those who served in the land and naval forces in revolutionary war.	17	2	Resolution	197	Rev. Claims	Feb. 5, 1823	By bill	274	Laid on table.		
Polereczky, J. L., a French officer in the service of the United States, revolutionary war.	For the benefit of the acts for the relief of those who served in the land and naval forces in revolutionary war.	18	1	Resolution	35	Rev. Pensions	Feb. 3, 1824	Adverse	......	Laid on table.		
Polereczky, J. L., a French officer in the service of the United States, revolutionary war.	For the benefit of the acts for the relief of those who served in the land and naval forces in revolutionary war.	19	1	Petition	52, 399	Military Pensions	May 5, 1826	Favorable	......	Referred to Committee Whole House on bill No. 119.		
Polereczky, J. L., a French officer in the service of the United States, revolutionary war.	For the benefit of the acts for the relief of those who served in the land and naval forces in revolutionary war.	19	2	Resolution	66	Military Pensions	....	....	......	Discharged; laid on table.		

List of private claims presented to the House of Representativesthe of United States from the 1st to the 31st Congress, inclusive—Continued.

Names of claimants.	Nature or object of the claim.	Congress.	Session.	How brought before the House of Reps.	Page of journal.	To what committee of the House referred.	No. or date of the report.	Nature of the report.	No. of the bill.	How disposed of by the House of Reps.	How disposed of by the Senate.	Date of the act of Congress, and remarks.
Polereczky, J. L., a French officer in the service of the United States, revolutionary war.	For the benefit of the acts for the relief of those who served in the land and naval forces in revolutionary war.	20	1	Petition	124	Military Pensions..	April 29, 1828	By bill	283	Passed.		
Polereczky J. L., a French officer in the service of the United States, revolutionary war.	For the benefit of the acts for the relief of those who served in the land and naval forces in revolutionary war.	21	1	Petition	36	Military Pensions..	Mar. 2, 1830	By bill	311	Passed	Indef. postp'd.	Provided for in act of May 20, 1830.
Polereczky, Nancy	Revolutionary pension..........	27	3	Senate bill	495	Rev. Pensions	Mar. 3, 1843	With't amend.	S. 96	Passed	....	App'd March 3, 1843
Polhemus, Jacob	Payment for wood and timber furnished American army in revolutionary war.	4	1	Rep. of Secretary War.	388	Claims	May 31, 1796	Adverse	......	Laid on table.		
Polhemus, John.........	Renewal of lost loan office certificate.	2	1	Petition and rep'. Sec. Treasury.	500	Select.						
Polhemus, Capt. John....	Reimbursement of money advanced to arm and equip a company under his command in revolutionary war.	14	1	Petition	47	Pens. & Rev. Cl'ms.						
Polhemus, Capt. John....	Reimbursement of money advanced to arm and equip a company under his command in revolutionary war.	14	2	Petition	199	Pens. & Rev. Cl'ms.						
Polhemus, Capt. John....	Reimbursement of money advanced to arm and equip a company under his command in revolutionary war.	15	2	Petition	31	Pens. & Rev. Cl'ms.	Dec. 30, 1818	Adverse	......	Laid on table.		
Polhemus, Capt. John....	Reimbursement of money advanced to arm and equip a company under his command in revolutionary war.	18	2	Petition	148	Pens. & Rev. Cl'ms.	....	....	......	Discharged; laid on table.	....	Leave to withdraw.
Polhemus, Capt. John....	Reimbursement of money advanced to arm and equip a company under his command in revolutionary war.	21	1	Petition	356	Rev. Claims.						
Polhemus, Capt. John....	Reimbursement of money advanced to arm and equip a company under his command in revolutionary war.	22	1	Petition	90	Rev. Claims......	275	Favorable; bill	353	Referred to Committee Whole House.		
Polhemus, Capt. John....	Reimbursement of money advanced to arm and equip a company under his command in revolutionary war.	23	1	Petition	111	Rev. Claims......	80	Favorable; bill	87	Passed.		
Polhemus, Rachael	(See John Van Orden.).........	26	1	....	286							
Polk, Ephraim, widow of.	Pension for services in revolutionary war.	26	1	Petition	386	Pens. & Rev. Cl'ms.	664	Adverse	......	Laid on table	....	Leave to withdraw, January 22, 1849, 2d sess., 30th Cong
Polk, Rhody	(See Ephraim Polk, widow of) ..	26	1	....	386							
Polk, William, and others.	Confirmation of title to land in Tennessee, granted by North Carolina, or compensation for the same.	7	1	Petition and docs.	55	Select	May 24, 1802	Favorable....	......	Referred to Committee Whole House.		

List of private claims presented to the House of Representatives of the United States from the 1st to the 31st Congress, inclusive—Continued.

Names of claimants.	Nature or object of the claim.	Congress.	Session.	How brought before the House of Reps.	Page of journal.	To what committee of the House referred.	No. or date of the report.	Nature of the report.	No. of the bill.	How disposed of by the House of Reps.	How disposed of by the Senate.	Date of the act of Congress, and remarks.
Polk, William, and others.	Confirmation of title to land in Tennessee, granted by North Carolina, or compensation for the same.	8	1	Petition and docs.	459	Select.	Jan. 9, 1804	Favorable....	......	Petition rejected.		
Polk, William..........	Compensation for forage and provisions furnished militia in 1836.	27	2	Senate bill	1063	Claims..........	1011	Adverse	S. 192	Passed.............	....	App'd Aug. 30, 1842
Pollan, (*alias* Paulding,) William, heirs of.	Compension for services in revolutionary war.	29	1	Petition	510	Rev. Claims.						
Pollard, Absalom, widow of	Revolutionary pension..........	28	1	Petition	744	Rev. Pensions.						
Pollard, Braxton	Pension	21	1	Petition	75	Military Pensions..	Mar. 30, 1830	Favorable; bill	248	Passed	Indef. postp'd.	
Pollard, Calvin, and others.	Payment for their plans and estimates for a custom-house at New York, burnt with the Treasury building.	23	1	Petition	523	Commerce	....	....	......	Discharged; laid on table.		
Pollard, Calvin, and others.	Payment for their plans and estimates for a custom house at New York, burnt with the Treasury building.	24	1	Petition	283	Commerce	384	Adverse	......	Laid on table.		
Pollard, Calvin, and others.	Payment for their plans and estimates for a custom-house at New York, burnt with the Treasury building.	25	2	Petition	408, 412	Commerce........	March 6, 1838	Adverse	......	Laid on table.		
Pollard, George, administrators of.	Indemnity for French spoliations prior to 1800.	31	1	Petition	413	Foreign Affairs ...	355	Favorable; bill	318	Referred to Committee Whole House.		
Pollard, James..........	Compensation for services in revolutionary war.	20	1	Petition	39	Rev. Claims......	Dec. 24, 1827	Adverse	......	Laid on table.		
Pollard, James..........	Compensation for services in revolutionary war.	21	1	Resolution	434	Military Pensions..	....	....	......	Discharged; laid on table.		
Pollard, John, widow of ..	Pension; her husband having died from wounds received in the war of 1812.	30	1	Petition	954	Invalid Pensions ..	802	Favorable; bill	623	Referred to Committee Whole House.		
Pollard, John, widow of ..	Pension; her husband having died from wounds received in the war of 1812.	30	2	Bill of last sess..	363	Whole House	Feb 2, 1849	With't amend.	623	Passed.		
Pollard, Joseph, (Ky.) ...	Pension	22	1	Petition	387	Rev. Pensions.						
Pollard, Leaner	(See Absalom Pollard, widow of).	28	1	....	744							
Pollard, Mary Ann	(See John Pollard, widow of)....	30	1	....	954							
Pollard, Philip..........	For benefit of the act of February 6, 1839, confirming the sale of certain reservations of land.	29	1	Petition	261	Indian Affairs.						
Pollard, Richard, late chargé d'affairs to Chili.	Indemnity for certain losses sustained.	28	1	Petition	83	Foreign Affairs.						
Pollard, Robert	(See Wharton Quarles, administrator of.)	24	1	....	105							
Pollard, Robert, and others.	(See Byrd Chamberlayn, representatives of.)	27	2	....	545							
Pollard, Thomas	Additional compensation for taking the Second Census in Virginia	7	1	Petition	164	Claims..........	Mar. 30, 1802	Adverse	......	Rejected.		
Pollard, William, heirs of.	Confirmation of Spanish land title.	22	1	Petition	193	Priv. Land Claims.	299	Favorable; bill	378	Referred to Committee Whole House.		
Pollard, William, heirs of.	Confirmation of Spanish land title.	23	1	Petition	220	Priv. Land Claims.	226	Favorable; bill	247	Referred to Committee Whole House.		
Pollard, William, heirs of.	Confirmation of Spanish land title.	23	2	House bill......	299	Whole House.....	Jan. 31, 1835	With't amend.	247	Passed.		

List of private claims presented to the House of Representatives of the United States from the 1st to the 31st Congress, inclusive—Continued.

Names of claimants.	Nature or object of the claim.	Congress.	Session.	How brought before the House of Reps.	Page of journal.	To what committee of the House referred.	No. or date of the report.	Nature of the report.	No. of the bill.	How disposed of by the House of Reps.	How disposed of by the Senate.	Date of the act of Congress, and remarks.
Pollard, William, heirs of.	Confirmation of Spanish land title.	24	1	Petition	425	Priv. Land Claims.	496	Favorable; bill	496	Passed	Passed	App'd July 2, 1836
Pollen, George P., and R. Colgate.	Return of duties paid on goods destroyed by fire, and release from payment of duties due.	26	1	Petition	291	Commerce.						
Pollen, George P., and R. Colgate.	Return of duties paid on goods destroyed by fire, and release from payments of duties due.	27	2	Petition	96	Commerce	900	Favorable; bill	521	Engrossed.		
Pollen, George P., and R Colgate.	Return of duties paid on goods destroyed by fire, and release from payment of duties due.	27	3	Ho. bill last sess	89	....	....	....	521	Passed	Indef. postp'd.	
Pollen, George P., and R. Colgate.	Return of duties paid on goods destroyed by fire, and release from payment of duties due.	30	1	Petition	388	Commerce.						
Polley, Samuel	Revolutionary pension	22	1	Petition	556							
Pollock, Carlisle	Additional compensation as surveyor of the revenue.	7	2	Memorial	245	Claims	Dec. 15, 1802	Adverse	.....	Rejected.		
Pollock, Carlisle, assignee of.	Indemnity for French spoliations prior to 1800.	26	1	Memorial	182	Foreign Affairs	343	Favorable; bill	319	Referred to Committee Whole House.		
Pollock, George, executor of.	Indemnity for French spoliations prior to 1800.	27	3	Petition	425	....	....	....	.....	Referred to Committee Whole House.		
Pollock, Hugh, assignee of.	Indemnity for French spoliations prior to 1800.	26	1	Memorial	182	Foreign Affairs	343	Favorable; bill	319	Referred to Committee Whole House.		
Pollock, John, (Ohio)	Permission to change location of land warrant.	13	3	Petition	756	Public Lands.						
Pollock, John, (Ohio)	Permission to change location of land warrant.	14	1	Petition	66	Public Lands	Jan. 4, 1816	By bill	.....	Passed	Passed	App'd Feb. 6, 1816
Pollock, John, (N. Y.)	Revolutionary pension	17	1	Petition	165	Rev. Pensions	....	....	.....	Disch'd; laid on table.		
Pollock, John, (Pa.)	Payment for a boat and cargo taken for the use of the Kentucky troops in 1814.	23	1	Petition	192	Claims	505	Favorable; bill	510	Referred to Committee Whole House.		
Pollock, John, (Pa.)	Payment for a boat and cargo taken for the use of the Kentucky troops in 1814.	24	1	Petition	51	Claims	21	Favorable; bill	21	Passed	Passed	App'd Feb. 17, 1836
Pollock, Oliver	Compensation for expenses and advances made as United States commercial agent at Havana, from 1783 to 1788.	3	1	Petition	113	....	....	....	.....	Referred to Secretary of Treasury.		
Pollock, Oliver	Compensation for expenses and advances made as United States commercial agent at Havana, from 1783 to 1788.	3	2	Rep. of Secretary Treasury.	284	Claims.						
Pollock, Oliver	Compensation for expenses and advances made as United States commercial agent at Havana, from 1783 to 1788.	4	1	Resolution	373	Claims	May 26, 1796	Report not of record.	.....	Referred to Committee Whole House.		
Pollock, Oliver	Compensation for expenses and advances made as United States commercial agent at Havana, from 1783 to 1788.	4	2	Memorial	656	....	....	....	.....	Referred to Committee Whole House.		
Pollock, Oliver	Compensation for expenses and advances made as United States commercial agent at Havana, from 1783 to 1788.	5	2	Petition and rep't, former.	106	Whole House	Feb. 1, 1798	Favorable; bill ordered.	47	Rejected.		

List of private claims presented to the House of Representatives of the United States from the 1st to the 31st Congress, inclusive—Continued.

Names of claimants.	Nature or object of the claim.	Congress.	Session.	How brought before the House of Reps.	Page of journal.	To what committee of the House referred.	No. or date of the report.	Nature of the report.	No. of the bill.	How disposed of by the House of Reps.	How disposed of by the Senate.	Date of the act of Congress, and remarks.
Pollock, Oliver	Compensation for expenses and advances made as United States commercial agent at Havana, from 1783 to 1788.	6	1	Petition	634	Claims	April 18, 1800	Adverse; leave to withdraw.	......	Referred to Committee Whole House.		
Pollock, Oliver	Compensation for expenses and advances made as United States commercial agent at Havana, from 1783 to 1788.	6	2	Petition	732	......	......	......	......	Laid on table.		
Pollock, Oliver	Liquidation and settlement of claim for services and expenses as public agent at New Orleans during revolutionary war.	7	1	Petition	90	Claims	April 3, 1802	Adverse, leave to withdraw.	......	Postponed to November 4, next.		
Pollock, Oliver	Liquidation and settlement of claim for services and expenses as public agent at New Orleans during revolutionary war.	7	2	Petition and docs.	336	Claims	Feb. 26, 1803	Adverse	......	Referred to Committee Whole House.		
Pollock, Oliver	Liquidation and settlement of claim for services and expenses as public agent at New Orleans during revolutionary war.	8	1	Petition, docs., & report, former.	533	......	......	......	......	Referred to Committee Whole House on bill No. 184.		
Pollock, Oliver	Liquidation and settlement of claim for services and expenses as public agent at New Orleans during revolutionary war.	8	2	Petition and docs.	77	Claims	Feb. 20, 1805	Favorable	......	Referred to Committee Whole House.		
Pollock, Oliver	Liquidation and settlement of claim for services and expenses as public agent at New Orleans during revolutionary war.	9	1	Petition	250	Claims	Feb. 17, 1806	Rep. and resl'n for leave to withdraw.	......	Resolution adopted.		
Pollock, Oliver	Authority for Treasury Department to settle his accounts for services rendered and supplies furnished in revolutionary war.	9	1	Petition	312	Claims	April 11, 1806	Res. to postpone indef.	......	Resolution adopted.		
Pollock, Oliver	Authority for Treasury Department to settle his accounts for services rendered and supplies furnished in revolutionary war.	9	2	Petition	493	Claims	Jan. 23, 1807	Favorable; bill	213	Passed	Passed	App'd March 3, 1807
Pollock, Oliver	For moneys expended by him as public agent in revolutionary war.	13	1	Petition	20	Claims	June 16, 1813	Adverse	......	Referred to Committee Whole House.		
Pollock, Oliver	For moneys expended by him as public agent in revolutionary war.	13	2	Petition	234	Pens. & Rev. Cl'ms.	60	Report and res. adverse.	......	Referred to Committee Whole House.		
Pollock, Oliver	For moneys expended by him as public agent in revolutionary war.	14	2	Petition	397	Pens. & Rev. Cl'ms.	......	......	......	Discharged; laid on table.		
Pollock, Oliver	For moneys expended by him as public agent in revolutionary war.	15	2	Petition	23	Pens. & Rev. Cl'ms.	50	Adverse	......	Laid on table.		
Pollock, Oliver	For an appointment in New Orleans custom-house in consideration of services and expenses in revolutionary war.	17	1	Petition	320	......	......	......	......	Laid on table.		
Polly, Joseph, widow of	Revolutionary pension	31	2	Petition	50	Rev. Pensions.						
Polly, Rebecca	(See Jos. Polly, widow of)	31	2	......	50							
Pomar, E., and Jose Pons.	(See D. R. Denham and others)	25	3	......	121							
Pomar, Joseph E.	Payment for cattle taken by the Indians during the Florida war.	25	2	Memorial	630	Claims	842	Adverse	......	Laid on table.		

List of private claims presented to the House of Representatives of the United States from the 1st to the 31st Congress, inclusive—Continued.

Names of claimants.	Nature or object of the claim.	Congress.	Session.	How brought before the House of Reps.	Page of journal.	To what committee of the House referred.	No. or date of the report.	Nature of the report.	No. of the bill.	How disposed of by the House of Reps.	How disposed of by the Senate.	Date of the act of Congress, and remarks.
Pomeroy, Eleazer	(See Joel W. White and E. Pomeroy.)	33	1	....	379							
Pomeroy, Grove	Renewal of final settlement certificate destroyed by fire.	5	2	Petition	107	Claims	Mar. 9, 1798	Adverse	......	Referred to Committee Whole House.		
Pomeroy, Grove	Renewal of final settlement certificate destroyed by fire.	10	1	Petition	116	....	....	....	......	Referred to Committee Whole House on bill No. 20.		
Pomeroy, Grove	Renewal of final settlement certificate destroyed by fire.	11	2	Petition	289	Claims	Mar. 31, 1810	By bill	121	Referred to Committee Whole House.		
Pomeroy, Grove	Renewal of final settlement certificate destroyed by fire.	11	2	Amend'nt to Ho. bill.	350	Whole House	April 6, 1810	Favorable	108	Passed	Rejected.	
Pomeroy, Grove	Renewal of final settlement certificate destroyed by fire.	11	3	Petition	454	Claims.						
Pomeroy, Grove	Renewal of final settlement certificate destroyed by fire.	12	2	Petition	582	Claims.						
Pomeroy, Grove, heirs of	Renewal of final settlement certificate destroyed by fire.	23	1	Petition	42	Rev. Claims	126	Favorable; bill	135	Passed	Passed	App'd June 28, 1834
Pomroy, John	Release from a judgment as bail of Fowler Crane.	29	1	Petition	291	P. Of. and P. Roads						
Pomeroy, Phoebus	Pension	22	1	Petition	329	Rev. Pensions	....	....	......	Discharged; laid on table.		
Pomeroy, Pliny	Pension	3	2	Rep. of Secretary War.	337	Claims.						
Pomeroy, Pliny	Pension	4	1	Rep. of Secretary War.	447	Claims	Feb. 18, 1796	Favorable; bill	156	Passed	Passed	App'd April 20, 1796
Pomeroy, Ralph M.	Compensation for property destroyed by United States troops.	13	1	Petition	36	Claims	....	....	......	Discharged; laid on table.		
Pomeroy, Ralph M.	Compensation for property destroyed by United States troops.	13	2	Petition	275	Claims	Feb. 12, 1814	Rep. not found	......	Laid on table.		
Pomeroy, Ralph M.	Compensation for property destroyed by United States troops.	14	1	Petition	156	Claims	Feb. 4, 1815	Adverse	......	Rejected.		
Pomeroy, Ralph M.	Compensation for property destroyed by United States troops.	15	1	Petition	168	Claims	Jan. 26, 1818	Adverse	......	Laid on table.		
Pomeroy, Ralph M.	Compensation for property destroyed by United States troops.	15	2	Petition	36	Claims	Dec. 11, 1818	Adverse	......	Laid on table.		
Pomeroy, Ralph M.	Compensation for property destroyed by United States troops.	16	1	Petition	35	Claims	Jan. 31, 1820	Adverse	......	Laid on table.		
Pomeroy, Samuel W., and others.	Indemnity for French spoliations prior to 1800.	24	2	Petition	87	Foreign Affairs.						
Pomeroy, Samuel W.	Indemnity for French spoliations prior to 1800.	26	1	Memorial	182	Foreign Affairs	343	Favorable; bill	319	Referred to Committee Whole House.		
Pomeroy & White	(See Joel W. White and E. Pomeroy.)	23	1	....	379							
Pompilly, Barnard	Invalid pension	24	1	Petition	51	Invalid Pensions	149	Favorable; bill	157	Passed	Passed	App'd June 28, 1836
Pon John W.	Payment for merchandise sold to Creek Indians out of their annuity.	29	2	Petition	59	Indian Affairs.						
Ponce, John	Payment for a horse furnished for United States service in Florida war.	25	2	Petition	397	Claims	828	Adverse	......	Laid on table.		
Pond, Adam	Revolutionary pension	27	3	Petition	68, 78	Rev. Pensions.						
Pond, Beriah, widow of	Revolutionary pension	26	1	Petition	706	Rev. Pensions.						

List of private claims presented to the House of Representatives of the United States from the 1st to the 31st Congress, inclusive—Continued.

Names of claimants.	Nature or object of the claim.	Congress.	Session.	How brought before the House of Reps.	Page of journal.	To what committee of the House referred.	No. or date of the report.	Nature of the report.	No. of the bill.	How disposed of by the House of Reps.	How disposed of by the Senate.	Date of the act of Congress, and remarks.
Pond, Beriah, widow of	Continuation of pension	30	1	Petition	69	Rev. Pensions	....	....	......	Discharged; laid on table.		
Pond, Elihu	Revolutionary pension	16	2	Petition	32	Pens. & Rev. Cl'ms.	Dec. 17, 1819	Adverse	......	Rejected.		
Pond, Elihu	Revolutionary pension	20	2	Petition	95	Military Pensions	Jan. 13, 1825	Adverse	......	Laid on table.		
Pond, Elihu	Revolutionary pension	21	1	Petition	63	Military Pensions	....	....	......	Discharged; laid on table.		
Pond, Elihu	Revolutionary pension	21	2	Petition	120	Military Pensions.						
Pond, Elihu	Revolutionary pension	22	1	Resolution	93	Rev. Pensions	371	Favorable; bill	466	Passed	Indef. postp'd.	
Pond, Elihu	Revolutionary pension	23	2	Petition	38	Rev. Claims	Feb. 2, 1835	Adverse	......	Laid on table.		
Pond, Ira, widow of	Revolutionary pension	25	3	Petition	216	Rev. Pensions	....	....	......	Discharged; laid on table.		
Pond, Ira, widow of	Revolutionary pension	26	1	Petition	174	Rev. Pensions	714	Adverse	......	Laid on table.		
Pond, Ira, widow of	Revolutionary pension	28	1	Petition	60, 429	Rev. Pensions.						
Pond, Ira, widow of	Revolutionary pension	29	1	Petition	298	Rev. Pensions.						
Pond, Ira, widow of	Revolutionary pension	30	1	Petition	576	Rev. Pensions	....	....	......	Disch'd; laid on table.		
Pond, Lettis	(See Ira Pond, widow of)	25	3	....	216							
Pond, Sabin	(See John Peters and Sabin Pond)	19	1	....	174							
Pond, Sylvia	(See Beriah Pond, widow of)	26	1	....	706							
Ponderman, Sabina	Restoration of pension	27	2	Petition	614	Rev. Pensions	May 24, 1842	....	......	Laid on table.		
Pons, Jose	(See David R. Denham, *et al.*)	25	3	....	121	....	162					
Pontius, Frederick	Permission to change location of land.	11	2	Petition	145	Public Lands	Jan. 3, 1810	Adverse	......	Rejected.		
Ponvert, Eli	(See Julian Chastelain and E. Ponvert.)	22	1	....	90							
Pool, Alanson	Invalid pension	30	2	Petition	116	Invalid Pensions	....	....	......	Discharged; laid on table.		
Pool, Alanson	Invalid pension	31	1	Petition	270	Invalid Pensions	236	Favorable; bill	231	Referred to Committee Whole House.		
Pool, Alanson	Invalid pension	31	2	Bill of last sess.	182	Whole House	Jan. 24, 1851	With amend.	231	Passed.		
Poole, Benjamin	Indemnity against damages on account of suits brought against him for acts done in his official capacity.	14	2	Petition	495	....	....	....	......	Laid on table.		
Poole, Benjamin	Indemnity against damages on account of suits brought against him for acts done in his official capacity.	15	1	Petition	167	Ways and Means	117	Favorable; bill	110	Referred to Committee Whole House.		
Poole, Benjamin	Indemnity against damages on account of suits brought against him for acts done in his official capacity.	15	2	Bill of last sess.	180	Whole House	Jan. 13, 1819	With't amend.	110	Passed	Passed	App'd Feb. 20, 1819
Poole, David	Invalid pension	1	2	Petition & report Sec. of War.	164	Select	July 16, 1790	By bill	88	Passed	Passed	App'd Aug. 11, 1790
Pool, Elizabeth	(See John Pool, widow of)	30	1	....	264							
Pool, George	Invalid pension	25	2	Petition	154	Invalid Pensions	Jan. 18, 1838	Adverse	......	Laid on table.		
Pool, George	Invalid pension	27	3	Petition	268	Invalid Pensions	116	Adverse	......	Laid on table.		
Pool, Isaac, commander of schooner Evergreen.	Indemnity for being captured by a piratical vessel in revolutionary war, and recapturing the same.	18	1	Petition	113	Claims	Jan. 28, 1838	Adverse	......	Laid on table.		
Pool, Isaac, commander of schooner Evergreen.	Indemnity for being captured by a piratical vessel in revolutionary war, and recapturing the same.	18	2	Resolution	93	Commerce.						

List of private claims presented to the House of Representatives of the United States from the 1st to the 31st Congress, inclusive—Continued.

Names of claimants.	Nature or object of the claim.	Congress.	Session.	How brought before the House of Reps.	Page of journal.	To what committee of the House referred.	No. or date of the report.	Nature of the report.	No. of the bill.	How disposed of by the House of Reps.	How disposed of by the Senate.	Date of the act of Congress, and remarks.
Pool, Isaac, commander of schooner Evergreen.	Indemnity for being captured by a piratical vessel in revolutionary war, and recapturing the same.	19	1	Resolution	86	Select	Jan. 16, 1826	Favorable; bill	53	Referred to Committee Whole House.		
Pool, Isaac, commander of schooner Evergreen.	Indemnity for being captured by a piratical vessel in revolutionary war, and recapturing the same.	19	2	Resolution	184	Ways and Means				Discharged; laid on table.		
Pool, Isaac, commander of schooner Evergreen.	Indemnity for being captured by a piratical vessel in revolutionary war, and recapturing the same.	20	1	Petition	125	Claims	Mar. 14, 1828	Adverse		Laid on table.		
Pool, Isaac, commander of schooner Evergreen.	Indemnity for being captured by a piratical vessel in revolutionary war, and recapturing the same.	21	1	Petition	39	Ways and Means	Jan. 28, 1830	Adverse		Laid on table.		
Pool, Isaac, commander of schooner Evergreen.	Indemnity for being captured by a piratical vessel in revolutionary war, and recapturing the same.	22	1	Petition	553	Commerce				Discharged; laid on table.		
Poole, Isaac	Invalid pension	27	3	Petition	170	Invalid Pensions.						
Poole, Jacob	Invalid pension	1	2	Petition & report Sec. of War.	164	Select.						
Pool, John, widow of	Revolutionary pension	30	1	Petition	264	Rev. Pensions	312	Adverse		Laid on table.		
Pool, Rebecca	(See Thomas Pool, heirs of the widow of.)	29	1		476							
Poole, Richard	Balance due for services as captain in United States army, and pension for disabilities received in late war.	21	2	Petition	233	Claims	Feb. 18, 1831	Adverse		Laid on table.		
Poole, Richard	Balance due for services as captain in United States army, and pension for disabilities received in late war.	22	1	Petition	73	Claims	Dec. 30, 1831	Adverse		Laid on table.		
Poole, Richard	Balance due for services as captain in United States army, and pension for disabilities received in late war.	22	2	Petition	245	Claims.						
Poole, Richard	Balance due for services as captain in United States army, and pension for disabilities received in late war.	23	1	Petition	556	Claims	517	Adverse		Laid on table.		
Pool, Richard	Relief on account of wounds received in the war with Mexico.	31	1	Petition	501	Military Affairs				Discharged; laid on table.		
Pool, Samuel	Pension for services in the army on the frontier for three years from 1791.	30	1	Petition	137	Rev. Pensions	210	Adverse		Laid on table.		
Pool, Thomas, heirs of the widow of.	Pension for the revolutionary services of said Thomas.	29	1	Petition	476	Rev. Pensions.						
Poole, William	Invalid pension	24	1	Petition	98	Invalid Pensions.						
Poole, William	Invalid pension	24	2	Petition	219	Invalid Pensions	Feb. 2, 1837	Adverse		Laid on table.		
Poole, William	Invalid pension	25	2	Petition	118	Invalid Pensions	589	Favorable; bill	576	Passed	Adverse report.	
Poole, William	Invalid pension	25	3	Petition	88	Invalid Pensions	261	Favorable; bill	1132	Referred to Committee Whole House.		
Poole, William	Invalid pension	26	1	Petition	162	Invalid Pensions	221	Favorable; bill	233	Passed	Indef. postp'd.	
Poole, William	Invalid pension	27	2	Petition	97	Invalid Pensions	Feb. 9, 1842	Adverse		Laid on table.		
Poole, William	Invalid pension	27	3	Petition	72	Invalid Pensions	26	Adverse		Laid on table.		

List of private claims presented to the House of Representatives of the United States from the 1st to the 31st Congress, inclusive—Continued.

Names of claimants.	Nature or object of the claim.	Congress.	Session.	How brought before the House of Reps.	Page of journal.	To what committee of the House referred.	No. or date of the report.	Nature of the report.	No. of the bill.	How disposed of by the House of Reps.	How disposed of by the Senate.	Date of the act of Congress, and remarks.
Poole, William	Invalid pension	28	1	Petition	117	Invalid Pensions				Discharged; laid on table.		
Poole, William	Invalid pension	29	1	Petition	175	Invalid Pensions	333	Favorable; bill	268	Passed	Passed	App'd Aug. 8, 1846
Poole, William	Arrears of pension	30	1	Petition	112	Invalid Pensions	195	Favorable; bill	205	Passed.		
Pool, William W	(See Thomas Pool, heirs of the widow of.	29	1		476							
Poor, A., and other widows of officers of revolutionary war.	For extension to them of the act of May 24, 1827.	20	2	Memorial	289					Referred to Committee Whole House.		
Poor, A., and other widows of officers of revolutionary war.	For extension to them of the act of May 24, 1827.	21	1	Memorial	36	Military Pensions	May 4, 1830	Adverse		Laid on table.		
Poor, Edward L	Compensation for services as inspector of customs at Portland and Falmouth, Maine.	28	2	Petition	382	Claims.						
Poor, Edward L	Compensation for services as inspector of customs at Portland and Falmouth, Maine.	30	2	Petition	193	Claims				Discharged; laid on table.		
Poor, John H	Settlement of his accounts as purser in the navy.	30	1	Senate bill	328	Naval Affairs	Feb. 29, 1848	With't amend.	S. 118	Referred to Committee Whole House.		
Poor, Paul	Revolutionary pension	24	1	Petition	213	Rev. Pensions	April 12, 1836	Adverse		Laid on table.		
Poore, Robert	Compensation for a horse lost in service of United States in 1807.	10	1	Petition	216	Claims.						
Poore, Robert	Compensation for a horse lost in service of United States in 1807.	10	2	Petition	417	Claims.						
Poore, Robert	Compensation for a horse lost in service of United States in 1807.	11	2	Petition	268	Claims	Mar. 24, 1810	Adverse		Laid on table.		
Poore, Robert	Compensation for a horse lost in service of United States in 1807.	24	1	Petition	429	Claims.						
Poor, William A	For his pay as purser in the navy during his journey home from the Pacific by land, he having been ordered home by his commander.	24	1	Petition	214	Naval Affairs.						
Poor, William A	For his pay as purser in the navy during his journey home from the Pacific by land, he having been ordered home by his commander.	24	2	Petition	155	Naval Affairs	171	Adverse.		Laid on table		July 17, 1848, leave to withdraw.
Poorman, Christian	Pension for services in the war of 1812.	28	1	Petition	217	Invalid Pensions.				Discharged; laid on table.		
Pope, Benjamin S	(See Andrew Knox, & B. S. Pope)	12	1		137							
Pope, Benjamin S., and O. Jones.	Compensation fore xtra services as lando fficers at Huntville, Ala.	19	1	Petition	179	Public Lands				Discharged; laid on table.		
Pope, Benjamin S., and Samuel Cruse.	Allowance for office rent as register and receiver of land office at Huntsville, Alabama.	19	2	Petition	287	Public Lands				Discharged; laid on table.		
Pope, James	Donation of land for losses by Choctaw treaty.	24	1	Petition	57	Public Lands	208	Favorable; bill	208	Referred to Committee Whole House.		
Pope, Lemuel, jr	(See William Gray, and others)	14	2		310							
Pope, LeRoy	Remission of interest on second instalment on land and extension of time for payment.	12	1	Petition and rep't Sec. Treasury.	20					Laid on table.		

List of private claims presented to the House of Representatives of the United States from the 1st to the 31st Congress, inclusive—Continued.

Names of claimants.	Nature or object of the claim.	Congress.	Session.	How brought before the House of Reps.	Page of journal.	To what committee of the House referred.	No. or date of the report.	Nature of the report.	No. of the bill.	How disposed of by the House of Reps.	How disposed of by the Senate.	Date of the act of Congress, and remarks.
Pope, Morgan, and others, owners of the ship Chandler Price.	Compensation for ransoming the crew of the whale ship Columbia.	30	1	Petition	838	Commerce	751	Favorable; bill	590	Referred to Committee Whole House.		
Pope, Morgan, and others, owners of the ship Chandler Price.	Compensation for ransoming the crew of the whale ship Columbia.	31	1	Petition	596	Commerce	177	Favorable; bill	190	Referred to Committee Whole House.		
Pope, Morgan, and others, owners of the ship Chandler Price.	Compensation for ransoming the crew of the whale ship Columbia.	31	2	Bill of last sess.	103	Whole House	Jan. 3, 1851	With't amend.	190	Passed.		
Pope, Nathaniel	(See Thomas H. Pope, heirs of).	23	1		439							
Pope, Ruth	(See Samuel Pope, widow of)	29	1		704							
Pope, Samuel, widow of	Pension for services in the wars of the revolution and of 1812.	29	1	Petition	704	Rev. Pensions	606	Adverse		Laid on table.		
Pope, Thomas	Compensation for services in revolutionary war.	2	1	Petition	455					Rreferred to Secretary of War.		
Pope, Thomas H., heirs of.	Compensation for services in revolutionary war.	23	1	Petition	439	Rev. Claims.						
Pope, Thomas H., heirs of.	Compensation for services in revolutionary war.	23	2	Petition	147	Rev. Claims	Feb. 11, 1835	Adverse		Laid on table.		
Pope, William, jr	For patents on land warrants issued to sundry Canadian volunteers, purchased by him.	16	2	Petition	75	Public Lands	27	Favorable; bill	194	Passed	Passed	App'd March 3, 1821
Pope, Worden, and others.	Release from liability as sureties of Charles M. Taylor, receiver of public money in Indiana.	20	1	Petition	168	Judiciary				Discharged; laid on table.		May 26, 1828, leave to withdraw.
Pope, Worden, and others.	Release from liability as sureties of Charles M. Taylor, receiver of public money in Indiana.	23	1	Petition	219	Judiciary.						
Popham, Francis, heir of	Bounty land for services in revolutionary war.	29	2	Petition	85, 161	Rev. Claims.						
Popkin, John, widow of	Pension for services in revolutionary war.	25	3	Petition	367	Rev. Pensions				Discharged; laid on table.		
Popkin, John, widow of	Pension for services in revolutionary war.	28	2	Petition	49	Rev. Pensions.						
Popkin, Sarah	(See John Popkin, widow of)	25	3		367							
Popple, George	Pension for services in revolutionary war.	3	1	Rep. of Secretary War.	131	Select	May 26, 1794	J't. res. to refer to Sec. War, with instructions.	R. 12	Passed	Passed	App'd June 9, 1794
Popple, George	Pension for services in revolutionary war.	3	2	Rep. of Secretary War.	352	Claims	Feb. 28, 1795	Favorable; bill	130	Passed	Postponed.	
Popple, George	Pension for services in revolutionary war.	4	1	Resolution	445	Claims	Feb. 18, 1796	Favorable; bill	156	Passed	Passed	App'd April 20, 1796
Porche, Marcha	(See Michael Booth, daughter of.)	28	2		234							
Porche, Simon, representatives of.	Confirmation of title to land	25	2	Petition	548	Public Lands	731	Favorable; bill	698	Referred to Commitee Whole House.		
Porche, Simon, representatives of.	Confirmation of title to land	25	3	Bill of last sess.	380	Whole House	Jan. 25, 1839	With't amend.	698	Passed.	Passed	App'd March 3 1839
Porcher, Peter	Payment for a negro slave lost in the service of the United States.	23	1	Petition	498	Claims.						
Porcher, Peter, or Poucher	Compensation for medical services rendered Capt. Smuch, United States army in Florida, 1834.	24	1	Petition	430	Claims	772	Adverse		Laid on table.		

List of private claims presented to the House of Representatives of the United States from the 1st to the 31st Congress, inclusive—Continued.

Names of claimants.	Nature or object of the claim.	Congress.	Session.	How brought before the House of Reps.	Page of journal.	To what committee of the House referred.	No. or date of the report.	Nature of the report.	No. of the bill.	How disposed of by the House of Reps.	How disposed of by the Senate.	Date of the act of Congress, and remarks.
Poret, John	Compensation for property destroyed by the United States troops in 1811.	22	2	Petition	32	Claims.						
Poret, John	Compensation for property destroyed by the United States troops in 1811.	23	1	Petition	23	Claims	85	Favorable; bill	91	Recom'itted to Claims.		
Poret, John	Compensation for property destroyed by the United States troops in 1811.	23	2	Petition	68	Claims.						
Porham, John	For certificates for his pay and other emoluments for services in revolutionary war; for which service one John Bregor has fraudulently obtained certificates.	4	1	Petition	371	Claims	Jan. 29, 1796	Adverse & res. for leave to withdraw.	......	Resolution adopted.		
Porie, Francis, & Stephen Carpenter.	Drawback on wines exported to St. Croix.	3	1	Petition	194	....	....	....	......	Referred to Secretary Treasury.		
Porie, Francis, & Stephen Carpenter.	Drawback on wines exported to St Croix.	3	2	Rep. of Secretary Treasury.	284	Claims	Mar. 2, 1795	Adverse	......	Laid on table.		
Porie, Francis, & Stephen Carpenter.	Drawback on wines exported to St. Croix.	4	1	Report of Com'r of claims.	598	....	....	....	......	Laid on table.		
Porlier, Jacques, and others	Confirmation of title to land in Wisconsin.	20	2	Petition	64	Public Lands	40	Favorable; bill	357	Referred to Committee Whole House.		
Porlier, Jacques, and others	Confirmation of title to land in Wisconsin.	21	1	Petition	93	Public Lands	81	Favorable; bill	114	Rejected.		
Porlier, Jacques, and others	Confirmation of title to land in Wisconsin.	22	1	Petition	125	Public Lands	Mar. 12, 1832	Adverse	......	Laid on table.		
Porlier, Jacques, and others	Confirmation of title to land in Wisconsin.	23	1	Petition	450	Priv. Land Claims.	396	Favorable; bill	415	Referred to Committee Whole House.		
Porlier, Jacques, and others	Confirmation of title to land in Wisconsin.	24	1	House bill	219	Whole House	....	....	172			
Porlier, Jacques, and others	Confirmation of title to land in Wisconsin.	25	2	Senate bill	508	Priv. Land Claims.	782	Adverse	S. 17	Referred to Committee Whole House.		
Porte, John A., (Mexico,)	Indemnity for seizure of his property during Mexican war.	31	1	Petition	826	Foreign Affairs.						
Porte, John A., (Mexico.)	Indemnity for seizure of his property during Mexican war.	31	2	Petition	445	Foreign Affairs	104	Adverse	......	Laid on table.		
Portel, John	Patent for land held under Spanish grant.	22	1	Petition	263	Priv. Land Claims.	Feb. 17, 1832	By bill	380	Referred to Committee Whole House.		
Porter, Aaron	Compensation for professional services to a wounded seaman in a private armed vessel in the late war.	15	2	Petition	36	Claims	Dec. 8, 1818	Adverse	......	Rejected.		
Porter, Aaron	Compensation for professional services to a wounded seaman in a private armed vessel in the late war.	16	1	Petition & docs.	194	Claims	Feb. 9, 1820	Adverse	......	Laid on table.		
Porter, Abner, heirs of	Payment for corn furnished revolutionary army.	18	1	Resolution	122	Pens. & Rev. Cl'ms.	Jan. 20, 1824	Adverse	......	Laid on table.		
Porter, Abner, heirs of	Payment for corn furnished revolutionary army.	18	2	Rep't of Comm'r of Claims.	200	....	....	....	......	Referred to Committee Whole House.		
Porter, Abner, heirs of	Payment for corn furnished revolutionary army.	19	1	Petition	41	Rev. Claims.						

List of private claims presented to the House of Representatives of the United States from the 1st to the 31st Congress, inclusive—Continued.

Names of claimants.	Nature or object of the claim.	Congress.	Session.	How brought before the House of Reps.	Page of journal.	To what committee of the House referred.	No. or date of the report.	Nature of the report.	No. of the bill.	How disposed of by the House of Reps.	How disposed of by the Senate.	Date of the act of Congress, and remarks.
Porter, Abner, heirs of...	Payment for corn furnished revolutionary army.	24	1	Petition	205	Rev. Claims......	June 21, 1836	Adverse	......	Laid on table.		
Porter, Amos, widow of ..	Pension and arrears of pension...	29	1	Petition	74, 670	Rev. Pensions	826	Adverse	......	Laid on table.		
Porter, Andrew.........	Additional compensation for services as deputy surveyor general.	25	2	Petition	541	Claims..........	869 960	Adverse. Supplementary report.	......	Referred to Secretary Treasury.		
Porter, Asbell	Invalid pension................	24	1	Petition and docs.	708	Invalid Pensions...	....	....	......	Discharged; laid on table.		
Porter, Augustus........	Compensation for property destroyed on the Niagara frontier in 1813 by the British.	15	2	Petition	66, 148	Claims	Jan. 6, 1819	Adverse	......	Laid on table.		
Porter, Bazlee	Invalid pension...............	22	2	Petition	27	Invalid Pensions...	Feb. 5, 1833	Favorable; bill	738	Ref'd to Com. W. H.		
Porter, Bazlee	Invalid pension...............	23	1	Petition	141	Invalid Pensions...	122	Favorable; bill	128	Passed	Passed	App'd June 30, 1834
Porter, Benjamin........	(See assignee of Thomas Tupper)	22	2	....	142							
Porter, Benjamin, (N. Y.)	Revolutionary pension..........	19	1	Petition	149	Military Pensions..	164	Adverse	......	Laid on table.		
Porter, Benjamin, (N. Y.)	Revolutionary pension..........	19	2	Petition	132	Rev. Pensions.						
Porter, Benjamin........	Compensation for property lost during the late war.	24	1	Petition and docs.	708	Claims.						
Porter, Benjamin Jones...	Commutation pay for services as surgeon in revolutionary army.	24	1	Resolution	339	Rev. Claims.						
Porter, Benjamin Jones...	Commutation pay for services as surgeon in revolutionary army.	24	2	Senate bill	260	Rev. Claims......	259	Adverse......	S. 106	Referred to Committee Whole House.		
Porter, Benjamin Jones...	Commutation pay for services as surgeon in revolutionary army.	28	2	Petition	250	Rev. Claims......	165	Favorable; bill	632	Referred to Committee Whole House.		
Porter, Benjamin Jones...	Commutation pay for services as surgeon in revolutionary army.	29	1	Petition	175	Rev. Pensions	....	....	......	Discharged; laid on table.		
Porter, Candace.........	(See Amos Porter, widow of)....	29	1	....	74, 670							
Porter, David...........	Reimbursement of money advanced to seamen in the revenue service in 1792 and 1793.	3	1	Memorial......	109	Select...........	April 8, 1794	Adverse; leave to withdraw.	......	Laid on table.		
Porter, David, (commodore)	Remission of duty on monument to the officers of the navy killed in the attack upon Tripoli.	10	1	Petition	46	Ways and Means..	Dec. 3, 1807	By bill	11	Passed	Passed	App'd Mar. 13, 1808
Porter, David...........	Pension......................	21	2	Petition	43	Military Pensions.						
Porter, David, and others.	Relinquishment by United States of nett proceeds of sales of certain vessels captured by them.	13	2	Senate bill	366	Whole House.....	April 12, 1814	With't amend.	S. 40	Passed	Passed	App'd April 13, 1814
Porter, David, widow of..	Pension for services in United States navy.	28	1	Petition	374, 718	Naval Affairs.						
Porter, David, widow of..	Payment of outfit as resident minister to Sublime Porte.	28	1	Petition	567	Foreign Affairs....	....	....	......	....	....	See civil and diplomatic appropriation act, June 17, 1844.
Porter, David, widow of..	Payment of outfit as resident minister to Sublime Porte.	28	2	Petition	272	Foreign Affairs.						
Porter, David, heirs of....	Relief against claim of accounting officers of the treasury against estate of deceased.	30	2	Petition	75	Naval Affairs.						
Porter, David, heirs of....	Relief against claim of accounting officers of the treasury against estate of deceased.	31	1	Petition	271	Naval Affairs.						
Porter, David B.........	Compensation for services as diplomatic agent of the United States.	31	1	Petition	215	Foreign Affairs.						

List of private claims presented to the House of Representatives of the United States form the 1st to the 31st Congress, inclusive—Continued.

Names of claimants.	Nature or object of the claim.	Congress.	Session.	How brought before the House of Reps.	Page of journal.	To what committee of the House referred.	No. or date of the report.	Nature of the report.	No. of the bill.	How disposed of by the House of Reps.	How disposed of by the Senate.	Date of the act of Congress, and remarks.
Porter, Edwin & Co.	Payment of certain moneys withheld by the Post Office Department.	28	1	Petition	76	P. Of. & P. Roads.	237	Adverse	......	Laid on table.		
Porter, Edwin & Co.	Payment of certain moneys withheld by the Post Office Department.	30	1	Petition	299	P. Of. & P. Roads.	267	Adverse	......	Laid on table.		
Porter, Eleazer	Revolutionary pension	15	2	Petition	26	Pens. & Rev. Cl'ms.	Dec. 24, 1818	Res. adverse; leave to withdraw.	......	Adopted.		
Porter, Eleazer	Arrears of pension	22	1	Petition	35	Rev. Pensions	Dec. 28, 1831	Adverse	......	Laid on table.		
Porter, Elias	Revolutionary pension	20	1	Petition	310	Military Pensions.						
Porter, Elias	Revolutionary pension	20	2	House bill	55	Whole House	Dec. 23, 1828	Favorable	311	Passed	Laid on table.	
Porter, Elias	Revolutionary pension	21	1	Petition	48	Military Pensions	Jan. 5, 1830	By bill	72	Passed	Passed	App'd May 20, 1830
Porter, Elizabeth C.	Arrears of pension	23	2	Petition	102	Naval Affairs	Feb. 25, 1835	Adverse	......	Laid on table.		
Porter, Evelina	(See David Porter, widow of.)	28	1	....	567							
Porter, Isaac	Redemption of continental money.	27	2	Petition	684	Rev. Claims	942	Adverse	......	Laid on table.		
Porter, Isaac	Redemption of continental money.	30	1	Petition	188	Rev. Claims	186	Adverse	......	Laid on table.		
Porter, Jacob	Revolutionary pension	15	2	Petition	62	Rev. Pensions	Aug. 1, 1818	Adverse	......	Rejected.		
Porter, Jacob	Remuneration for losses sustained and services rendered in revolutionary war.	24	1	Petition	942	Rev. Claims.						
Porter, James	Increase of pension	14	1	House bill	622	Whole House	April 11, 1816	Favorable	171	Passed	Passed	App'd April 30, 1816
Porter, James, and Tunstall Quarles.	Release from liability as sureties of W. J. Sallee, late Postmaster at Somerset, Kentucky.	18	2	Petition	209	P. Of. and P. Roads.	Feb. 24, 1825	Favorable; bill	356	Passed	Passed	App'd March 3, 1825
Porter, James, (Tenn.)	Revolutionary pension	20	1	Resolution	267	Military Pensions	April 29, 1828	By bill	283	Passed.		
Porter, James, (Tenn.)	Revolutionary pension	20	2	House bill	55	Whole House	Dec. 23, 1828	Favorable	311	Passed	Laid on table	
Porter, James, (Tenn.)	Revolutionary pension	21	1	Petition	48	Military Pensions	Jan. 5, 1830	By bill	72	Passed	Passed	App'd May 20, 1830
Porter, James	(See William H. Bedford, agent.)	28	1	....	262							
Porter, James, (Ala.)	Arrears of pension	21	2	Petition	68	Military Pensions.						
Porter, Major James P. H.	Pension for disabilities and sufferings incurred in war of 1812.	29	1	Petition	279	Invalid Pensions	329	Favorable; bill	264	Laid on table.		
Porter, Joel	Invalid pension	3	2	Rep. of Secretary War.	350	Claims	Mar. 2, 1795	Rep. and res. to refer to Sec. of War, with instructions.	......	Resolution adopted.		
Porter, Joel	Invalid pension	4	1	Resolution	445	Claims	Feb. 18, 1796	Favorable; bill	156	Passed	Passed	App'd April 20, 1796
Porter, John	Compensation for work on Cumberland road.	23	1	Resolution	589	Claims	456	Statem't of facts	......	Referred to Secretary War.	....	See report No. 449.
Porter, jr., John	Compensation for services as wagon conductor in revolutionary war.	4	1	Rep. of Secretary Treasury.	388	Claims	May 31, 1796	Adverse	......	Laid on table.		
Porter, jr., John	Compensation for services as wagon conductor in revolutionary war.	4	2	Petition	629	Claims	Jan. 6, 1797	Adverse	......	Rejected.		
Porter, jr., John	Compensation for services as wagon conductor in revolutionary war.	6	1	Petition	551	Claims	Jan. 16, 1800	Adverse	......	Rejected.		
Porter, jr., John	Compensation for services as wagon conductor in revolutionary war.	7	1	Petition	164	Claims	....	....	......	Discharged; laid on table.	....	Leave to withdraw, Jan. 4, 1803.
Porter, John, (Va.)	Compensation for services rendered and injuries received as wagon conductor, and as sergeant of infantry in revolutionary war.	10	1	Petition	175	....	....	....	......	Referred to Committee Whole House on bill No. 20.		

List of private claims presented to the House of Representatives of the United States from the 1st to the 31st Congress, inclusive—Continued.

Names of claimants.	Nature or object of the claim.	Congress.	Session.	How brought before the House of Reps.	Page of journal.	To what committee of the House referred.	No. or date of the report.	Nature of the report.	No. of the bill.	How disposed of by the House of Reps.	How disposed of by the Senate.	Date of the act of Congress, and remarks.
Porter, John, (Va.)......	Compensation for services rendered and injuries received as wagon conductor, and as sergeant of infantry in revolutionary war.	12	1	Petition	60	Claims.						
Porter, John, (Va.)......	Compensation for services rendered and injuries received as wagon conductor, and as sergeant of infantry in revolutionary war.	12	2	Petition	560	Claims.						
Porter, John, (Va.)......	Compensation for services rendered and injuries received as wagon conductor, and as sergeant of infantry in revolutionary war.	13	3	Petition	573	Pens. & Rev. Cl'ms.	Jan. 24, 1815	Adverse	......	Rejected.		
Porter, John, (Va.)......	Compensation for services rendered and injuries received as wagon conductor, and as sergeant of infantry in revolutionary war.	14	1	Petition	32	Pens. & Rev. Cl'ms.						
Porter, John, (Va.)......	Compensation for services rendered and injuries received as wagon conductor, and as sergeant of infantry in revolutionary war.	15	1	Petition	172	Pens. & Rev. Cl'ms.	March 2, 1818	Adverse	......	Referred to Committee Whole House.		
Porter, John, (Va.)......	Compensation for services rendered and injuries received as wagon conductor, and as sergeant of infantry in revolutionary war.	15	2	Petition	87	Whole House	Dec. 11, 1818	Adverse	......	Rejected.		
Porter, John, (Va.)......	Compensation for services rendered and injuries received as wagon conductor, and as sergeant of infantry in revolutionary war.	16	1	Petition	186	Rev. Pensions	April 22, 1820	Adverse	......	Laid on table	....	Leave to withdraw.
Porter, John............	(See Henry Develin and others)..	23	1	....	589							
Porter, John, of Tolland county, Conn.	Pension for services in 1780	25	3	Petition	217, 291	Invalid Pensions.						
Porter, John, of Tolland county, Conn.	Pension for services in 1780	26	1	Petition	284	Invalid Pensions.						
Porter, John, of Tolland county, Conn.	Pension for services in 1780	26	2	Petition	35	Invalid Pensions ..	20	Favorable; bill	561	Referred to Committee Whole House.		
Porter, John, of Tolland county, Conn.	Pension for services in 1780	27	2	Petition	59	Invalid Pensions ..	784	Adverse	......	Laid on table.		
Porter, John............	Pension for injuries received while on board revenue cutter Van Buren 1840.	29	1	Petition	151	Invalid Pensions...	157	Favorable; bill	160	Rejected.		
Porter, John, *et al.*......	Indemnity for French spoliations prior to 1800.	31	1	Petition	370	Foreign Affairs....	355	Favorable; bill	318	Referred to Committee Whole House.		
Porter, J. N., executors of.	For lands in lieu of those granted him by North Carolina in Tennessee.	20	1	Petition	457	....	....	....	......	Referred to Committee Whole House on bill No. 27.		
Porter, Joseph B........	For land in lieu of those granted by North Carolina in Tennessee.	20	1	Petition	457	....	....	....	......	Referred to Committee Whole House on bill No. 27.		
Porter, Moses...........	Renewal of land warrant granted..	15	1	Petition and rep't Sec. of War.	25	Priv. Land Claims.	Mar. 17, 1818	By bill	148	Passed	Passed	App'd April 14, 1818
Porter, Nathaniel........	Compensation for supplies and services in revolutionary war.	1	3	Petition and rep't Sec. of War.	346	....	....	....	......	Laid on table.		

List of private claims presented to the House of Representatives of the United States from the 1st *to the* 31st *Congress, inclusive*—Continued.

Names of claimants.	Nature or object of the claim.	Congress.	Session.	How brought before the House of Reps.	Page of journal.	To what committee of the House referred.	No. or date of the report.	Nature of the report.	No. of the bill.	How disposed of by the House of Reps.	How disposed of by the Senate.	Date of the act of Congress, and remarks.
Porter, Nathaniel P.	Commissions on imports, &c., as inspector of the port at Louisville.	31	1	Petition	1003	Claims.						
Porter, Robert L	Indemnity for losses sustained by destruction of Chesapeake flotilla by order of Commodore Barney in 1814.	28	2	Petition	316	Naval Affairs.						
Porter, Robert L	Indemnity for losses sustained by destruction of Chesapeake flotilla by order of Commodore Barney in 1814.	29	1	Petition	398	Naval Affairs.						
Porter, Roseman	(See John Brady, widow of.)	31	1		415							
Porter, Samuel	Revolutionary pension	26	1	Petition	106	Rev. Pensions.						
Porter, Solomon	Increase of compensation as surveyor of customs.	14	2	Petition	346	Ways and Means.						
Porter, Solomon, jr	Refunding of duties paid on low wines.	16	2	Petition	205	Ways and Means.						
Porter, Solomon, jr	Refunding of duties paid on low wines.	17	1	Petition	173	Ways and Means.	Jan. 22, 1822	By bill	52	Passed	Passed	App'd April 17, 1822
Porter, Solomon, widow of	Revolutionary pension	25	3	Petition	563	Rev. Pensions.						
Porter, Stephen	Compensation for supplies furnished, and for property impressed into the service of United States, revolutionary war.	2	1	Petition	521	....	....	....	......	Referred to Secretary Treasury.		
Porter, Stephen	Compensation for supplies furnished, and for property impressed into the service of United States, revolutionary war.	3	1	Rep. of Secretary Treasury.	64	Select	Feb. 25, 1794	Favorable	......	Referred to Committee Whole House.		
Porter, Stephen	Compensation for supplies furnished, and for property impressed into the service of United States, revolutionary war.	9	1	Petition	309	Claims	Mar. 8, 1806	Rep. and res. for leave to withdraw.	......	Resolution adopted.		
Porter, Stephen	Compensation for supplies furnished, and for property impressed into the service of United States, revolutionary war.	13	2	Petition	305	Pens. & Rev. Cl'ms.	92	Avderse; leave to withdraw.	......	Referred to Committee Whole House.		
Porter, Stephen, heirs of	Compensation for supplies furnished, and for property impressed into the service of United States, revolutionary war.	22	2	Resolution	34	Rev. Claims.						
Porter, Stephen, heirs of	Compensation for supplies furnished, and for property impressed into the service of United States, revolutionary war.	23	1	Petition	272	Rev. Claims.						
Porter, Stephen, heirs of	Compensation for supplies furnished, and for property impressed into the service of United States, revolutionary war.	24	1	Petition	205	Rev. Claims.						
Porter, Stephen, heirs of	Compensation for supplies furnished, and for property impressed into the service of United States, revolutionary war.	24	2	Petition	91	Rev. Claims.						

List of private claims presented to the House of Representatives of the United States from the 1st to the 31st Congress, inclusive—Continued.

Names of claimants.	Nature or object of the claim.	Congress.	Session.	How brought before the House of Reps.	Page of journal.	To what committee of the House referred.	No. or date of the report.	Nature of the report.	No. of the bill.	How disposed of by the House of Reps.	How disposed of by the Senate.	Date of the act of Congress, and remarks.
Porter, Stephen, heirs of..	Compensation for supplies furnished, and for property impressed into the service of United States, revolutionary war.	25	2	Petition	49	Rev. Claims......	....	....	.....	Discharged; laid on table.		
Porter, Stephen, heirs of..	Compensation for supplies furnished, and for property impressed into the service of United States, revolutionary war.	25	3	Petition	84	Rev. Claims......	....	....	.....	Discharged; laid on table.		
Porter, Stephen, heirs of..	Compensation for supplies furnished, and for property impressed into the service of United States, revolutionary war.	26	1	Petition	164	Rev. Claims.						
Porter, Stephen, heirs of..	Compensation for supplies furnished, and for property impressed into the service of United States, revolutionary war.	26	2	Petition	36	Rev. Claims.						
Porter, Stephen, heirs of..	Compensation for supplies furnished, and for property impressed into the service of United States, revolutionary war.	29	1	Petition	623	Rev. Claims.						
Porter, Thomas, (S. C.)..	Bounty land and bounty money for services in war of 1812.	16	2	Petition	159	....	....	....	.....	Referred to Secretary of War.		
Porter, Thomas, (S. C.)..	Bounty land and bounty money for services in war of 1812.	17	1	Petition	119	Military Affairs....	Jan. 28, 1822	Adverse	.....	Laid on table	....	Leave to withdraw.
Porter, Thomas, (S. C.)..	Bounty land and bounty money for services in war of 1812.	18	1	Petition	105, 250	Pens. & Rev. Cl'ms.						
Porter, Thomas, (Ind.)...	Invalid pension................	21	2	Resolution	118	Military Pensions..	....	....	.....	Discharged; laid on table.		
Porter, Thomas, (Ind.)...	Invalid pension................	21	2	Senate bill	305	Military Pensions..	Feb. 22, 1831	Adverse	S. 107	Passed	Passed	App'd March 2, 1831
Porter, William.........	(See assignees of Thomas Tupper)	22	2	....	142							
Porter, William, (N. Y.).	For register for his vessel William of New York, built out of the wreck of a foreign vessel.	18	1	Petition	154	Commerce.	51	Favorable; bill	98	Passed	Passed	App'd May 21, 1824
Porter, William, heirs of..	(See John McClelland, sureties of)	25	2	....	169							
Porter, William R.......	(See William Estis, sureties of)..	21	1	....	70							
Porter, Winey..........	(See Solomon Porter, widow of).	25	3	....	563							
Porterfield, Colonel James, heirs of.	For amount due him for services in revolutionary war.	29	2	Memorial	352	Rev. Claims.						
Porterfield, Colonel James, heirs of.	For amount due him for services in revolutionary war.	30	1	Petition	369	Claims	239	Favorable; bill	239	Passed	Adverse report.	
Porterfield, James, *et al* ..	(See James Young, heirs of)	31	1	....	743	....	....	....	315			
Portius, Alexander	Land in lieu of a tract which belonged to him, and has been assigned to the Cherokee Indians by the United States.	17	1	Petition	196	Priv. Land Claims.	....	....	.....	Discharged; laid on table.		
Posey, Jubilee	Refunding of money overpaid on land.	25	2	Petition and docs.	547	Public Lands.						
Posey, Jubilee	Refunding of money overpaid on land.	25	3	Petition	93	Public Lands.						
Posey, Jubilee	Refunding of money overpaid on land.	26	1	Petition	803	Public Lands.....	....	....	.....	Discharged; laid on table.		
Posey, Jubilee	Refunding of money overpaid on land.	28	1	Petition	850	Public Lands.						

List of private claims presented to the House of Representatives of the United States from the 1st to the 31st Congress, inclusive—Continued.

Names of claimants.	Nature or object of the claim.	Congress.	Session.	How brought before the House of Reps.	Page of journal.	To what committee of the House referred.	No. or date of the report.	Nature of the report.	No. of the bill.	How disposed of by the House of Reps.	How disposed of by the Senate.	Date of the act of Congress, and remarks.
Posey, Jubilee	Refunding of money overpaid on land.	28	2	Petition	70	Public Lands.						
Posey, Micajah	Increase of pension	19	2	Petition	156	Military Pensions.						
Posey, Pharos T.	(See Wm. Atwood, administrator of.)	26	1		1162							
Posey, William J.	Compensation for a horse lost in service of United States.	23	2	Petition	200	Claims	Feb. 10, 1835	Adverse		Laid on table.		
Posey, William J.	Compensation for a horse lost in service of United States.	24	1	Petition	49	Claims	Dec. 21, 1835	Adverse		Laid on table.		
Posner, Joseph G., executors of.	Compensation for houses destroyed by fire while in possession of United States troops.	19	2	Petition	82	Claims	37	Adverse		Referred to Committee Whole House.		
Posner, Joseph G., executors of.	Compensation for houses destroyed by fire while in psssession of United States troops.	21	1	Petition	35	Claims	Dec. 21, 1829	Adverse		Laid on table.		
Posner, Joseph G., heirs of	Compensation for houses destroyed by fire while in possession of United States troops.	22	1	Senate bill	521	Claims	489	With amend.	S. 72	Passed	Passed	App'd July 14, 1832
Posner, Silvia	(See Joseph G. Posner, heirs of).	22	1		521							
Post, Joel	Grant of land in late Winnebago reservation.	30	1	Petition	989	Priv. Land Claims.						
Post, John	Compensat'n for supplies furnished, or for services and losses in revolutionary war.	1	3	Petition and rep't Sec. War.	350					Laid on table.		
Post, John	Revolutionary pension	16	2	Petition	78	Pens. & Rev. Cl'ms.	Feb. 15, 1821	Adverse		Laid on table.		
Post, John	Revolutionary pension	19	1	Petition	224	Rev. Pensions	April 7, 1826	Adverse		Laid on table.		
Post, John, and F. Fuller.	Release from liability as sureties of Robert Dickson, postmaster at Ripiey, New York.	17	1	Petition	160	P. Of. & P. Roads.	March 8, 1822	Favorable; bill	111	Passed	Passed	App'd May 7, 1822
Post, Stephen	Compensation for loss of property in the British dominions, withheld from him in consequence of his attachment to his country.	13	2	Petition	196	Pens. & Rev. Cl'ms.				Discharged; laid on table.		
Post, Stephen	Compensation for loss of property in the British dominions, withheld from him in consequence of his attachment to his country.	14	1	Petition	64	Select	March 2, 1816	Adverse		Rejected.		
Post, Stephen	Compensation for loss of property in the British dominions, with held from him in consequence of his attachment to his country.	14	2	Petition	45	Pens. & Rev. Cl'ms.				Discharged; laid on table.		
Postell, William	(See Exploring Expedition.)	27	3		149							
Postmaster General	Increase of compensation	15	1	House bill	345				141	Referred to Committee Whole House.		
Postmaster General	Increase of compensation	19	2	Senate bill	162	Ways and Means.	Jan. 19, 1827	With't amend.	53 *a*.	Passed		App'd March 2, 1827
Postmaster General, assistants of.	Increase of compensation	15	2	Resolution	22	P. Of. & P. Roads.	Jan. 6, 1819	Favorable; bill	266	Referred to Committee Whole House.		Provided for by act of February 20, 1819.
Post Office Department, messengers of.	Increase of compensation	31	2	Petition	241	P. Of. & P. Roads.						
Potash & Cairn	(See New York, sundry inhab'tants of Ptattsburgh.)	13	3		723							
Pote, Greenleaf, administrator of.	Indemnity for French spoliations prior to 1800.	26	1	Memorial	182	Foreign Affairs	343	Favorable; bill	319	Referred to Committee Whole House.		

List of private claims presented to the House of Representatives of the United States from the 1st to the 31st Congress, inclusive—**Continued.**

Names of claimants.	Nature or object of the claim.	Congress.	Session.	How brought before the House of Reps.	Page of journal.	To what committee of the House referred.	No. or date of the report.	Nature of the report.	No. of the bill.	How disposed of by the House of Reps.	How disposed of by the Senate.	Date of the act of Congress, and remarks.
Potens, Mary	(See Matthew Potens, widow of)	3	2		276							
Potens, Matthew, widow of	For one years' pay due as a deranged officer.	3	2	Petition	276	Claims	Mar. 2, 1795	Adverse		Laid on table.		
Potens, Matthew, widow of	For one years' pay due as a deranged officer.	4	1	Rep. of Secretary Treasury.	388	Claims	May 31, 1796	Adverse		Laid on table.		
Potter, Abel	Revolutionary pension	23	1	Resolution	90, 190	Rev. Pensions.						
Potter, Barret, agent of	Indemnity for French spoliations prior to 1800.	26	1	Memorial	182	Foreign Affairs	343	Favorable; bill	319	Referred to Committee Whole House.		
Potter, Charles	Refunding of duties which he was compelled to pay in consequence of a want of timely notice of the passage of the act of May 19, 1828.	27	2	Petition	1003	Commerce.						
Potter, Charles	Refunding of duties which he was compelled to pay in consequence of a want of timely notice of the passage of the act of May 19, 1828.	27	3	Petition	108	Commerce.	196	Adverse		Laid on table.		
Potter, Charles	Refunding of duties which he was compelled to pay in consequence of a want of timely notice of the passage of the act of May 19, 1828.	28	1	Petition	159	Commerce.						
Potter, Daniel	Settlement of his accounts for military service in 1794.	9	1	Petition	224	Claims	Jan. 17, 1790	Report and res. for leave to withdraw.		Resolution adopted.		
Potter, David	Invalid pension	29	1	Petition	617	Invalid Pensions.						
Potter, Earl	Compensation for revolutionary service.	23	1	Petition	215	Rev. Pensions				Discharged; laid on table.		
Potter, Ebenezer	Pension	19	1	Petition	175	Military Pensions	164	Adverse		Laid on table.		
Potter, Elisha R.	Payment as a member of Congress while contesting a seat in the United States Senate.	23	1	Civil and diplomatic appropriation bill.	283	Whole House	April 8, 1834	With amend.	283	Passed	Passed	App'd June 27, 1834
Potter, Herman B.	Indemnity for property destroyed by the British, war of 1812.	15	2	Petition	32	Claims	Dec. 16, 1818	Adverse		Laid on table.		
Potter, Herman B.	Indemnity for property destroyed by the British, war of 1812.	17	1	Petition	178	Claims	Jan. 23, 1822	Adverse		Laid on table.		
Potter, Herman B.	Indemnity for property destroyed by the British, war of 1812.	19	1	Petition	46	Claims	23	Adverse		Referred to Committee Whole House.		
Potter, Joel	(See William H. Bedford, agent.)	28	1		262							
Potter, John	(See Robert Munford, assignee of.)	9	1		346							
Potter, John, (Va.)	Compensation for services and injuries in revolutionary war as wagon conductor.	10	1	Petition	175					Referred to Committee Whole House on bill No. 20.		
Potter, John, widow of	Pension: husband died of disease contracted in service of United States.	15	1	Petition	38	Military Affairs				Discharged; laid on table.		
Potter, John, widow of	Pension: husband died of disease contracted in service of United States.	16	1	Petition and rep't Sec. of War.	60, 159	Pens. & Rev. Cl'ms.	Feb. 25, 1820	Adverse		Rejected.		
Potter, John, (S. C.)	Indemnity for French spoliations prior to 1800.	26	1	Memorial	182	Foreign Affairs	343	Favorable; bill	319	Referred to Committee Whole House.		

List of private claims presented to the House of Representatives of the United States from the 1*st to the* 31*st Congress, inclusive*—Continued.

Names of claimants.	Nature or object of the claim.	Congress.	Session.	How brought before the House of Reps.	Page of journal.	To what committee of the House referred.	No. or date of the report	Nature of the report.	No. of the bill.	How disposed of by the House of Reps.	How disposed of by the Senate.	Date of the act of Congress, and remarks.
Potter, John	Correction of error in entry of lands	30	1	Petition	300	Public Lands	262	Favorable; bill	257	Passed	Passed	App'd July 17, 1848
Potter, John	(See William H. Bedford, agent.)	28	1		262							
Potter, John	Release from penalties incurred by importing British manufactures.	12	2	Petition	567					Referred to Committee Whole House on bill No. 239.		See act Feb. 27, 1813
Potter, John, (Conn.)	Payment for supplies furnished army in revolutionary war.	22	1	Petition	333	Rev. Claims				Discharged; laid on table.		
Potter, John, (Penn.)	Payment for provisions furnished revolutionary army.	17	1	Petition	119	Claims				Discharged; laid on table.		
Potter, John, (Penn.)	Payment for provisions furnished revolutionary army.	18	1	Petition	332	Claims.						
Potter, John, (Penn)	Payment for provisions furnished revolutionary war.	19	1	Petition	67	Claims.						
Potter, John, *et al.*	Correction of errors in entry of lands.	30	1	House bill	466	Whole House	July 6, 1848	Favorable	257	Passed	Passed	App'd July 17, 1848
Potter, Joseph	Compensation for stores lost as sutler, and for use of his house in Vermont for a hospital.	16	2	Petition	54	Claims	Dec. 14, 1820	Adverse		Laid on table.		
Potter, Joseph	Compensation for stores lost as sutler, and for use of his house in Vermont for a hospital.	28	1	Petition	334	Claims.						
Potter, Joseph, widow of.	Pension	19	1	Petition	365	Naval Affairs	Mar. 29, 1826	Adverse		Laid on table.		
Potter, John	Indemnity for French spoliations prior to 1800.	26	1	Memorial	182	Foreign Affairs	343	Favorable; bill	319	Referred to Committee Whole House.		
Potter, Milton	Revolutionary pension	25	2	Petition	913	Rev. Pensions				Discharged; laid on table.		
Potter, Milton	Revolutionary pension	25	3	Petition	87	Rev. Pensions				Discharged; laid on table.		
Potter, Milton	Revolutionary pension	26	1	Petition	284	Rev. Pensions	714	Adverse		Laid on table.		
Potter, Nathan, *et al.*	Fishing bounty for schooner Lucy.	10	1	Petition	238	Com. and Manuf.						
Potter, Robinson, (R. I.)	Remission of duty on iron imported into Newport.	21	1	Petition	412	Ways and Means				Discharged; laid on table.		
Potter, Robinson, (R. I.)	Remission of duty on iron imported into Newport.	21	2	Petition	63	Ways and Means.						
Potter, Rowena	(See Peter Cabet, widow of.)	21	1		144							
Potter, Samuel, & J. Cassidy.	Register for their barque Calypso	25	2	Petition	410	Commerce	Mar. 2, 1838	By bill	600	Passed	Passed	App'd July 7, 1838
Potter, Samuel	Invalid pension	3	2	Rep. of Secretary War.	278	Claims	Mar. 2, 1795	Res. to refer to Sec. War.		Resolution adopted.		
Potter, Samuel	Invalid pension	4	1	Rep. of Secretary War.	445	Claims	Feb. 18, 1796	Favorable; bill	156	Passed	Passed	App'd April 20, 1796
Potter, Samuel	Renewal of pension	26	1	Petition	797	Rev. Pensions.						
Potter, Thaddeus	Revolutionary pension	24	1	Petition	282	Rev. Pensions	323	Favorable; bill	337	Passed	Passed	App'd June 28, 1836
Potter, Thomas	Confirmation of title to land	29	1	Memorial	592	Public Lands.						
Potter, Woodburn	Compensation for service as clerk to General Gaines.	25	2	Memorial	397	Claims	1044	Favorable; bill	878	Referred to Committee Whole House.		
Potter, Woodburn	Compensation for service as clerk to General Gaines.	25	3	Bill of last sess.	432	Whole House	Feb. 1, 1839	With't amend.	878	Passed.	Passed	App'd March 3, 1839
Potterfield, Joseph	Confirmation of title to land	30	1	Petition	236	Public Lands	328	Adverse		Laid on table.		
Pottinger, Frances	Continuation of pension	28	2	Petition	172	Naval Affairs				Discharged; laid on table.		
Pottinger, Thomas B	(See administ'r of Jonathan Hudson.)	26	1		182							

List of private claims presented to the House of Representatives of the United States from the 1st to the 31st Congress, inclusive—**Continued.**

Names of claimants.	Nature or object of the claim.	Congress.	Session.	How brought before the House of Reps.	Page of journal.	To what committee of the House referred.	No. or date of the report.	Nature of the report.	No. of the bill.	How disposed of by the House of Reps.	How disposed of by the Senate.	Date of the act of Congress, and remarks.
Pottle, Bemsley, administrator of.	Renewal of lost final settlement certificate.	2	2	Petition	652					Laid on table.		
Pottle, Elizabeth	(See heir of Abner Dow)	29	1		1204							
Pottle, Priscilla	(See administ'r of Bemsley Pott'e)	2	2		652							
Potts, A. K	Compensation as assistant commissary of subsistance.	31	1	Petition	1286	Military Affairs.						
Potts, Isaac	Compensation for damages to house and mills by revolutionary army.	2	2	Petition	636					Laid on table.		
Potts, Jesse	Commutation pay under resolution of 1783.	23	2	Resolution	178	Rev. Claims.						
Potts, Jesse	Commutation pay under resolution of 1783.	24	1	Petition	63	Rev. Claims	173	Adverse		Laid on table.		
Potts, Jesse	Commutation pay under resolution of 1783.	24	2	Petition	92	Rev. Claims	275	Adverse		Laid on table		
Potts, Jesse	Commutation pay under resolution of 1783.	25	2	Petition	49	Rev. Claims				Discharged; laid on table.		
Potts, Jesse	Commutation pay under resolution of 1783.	25	3	Petition	84	Rev. Claims				Discharged; laid on table.		
Potts, John	(See William Wilson, *et al.*)	7	2		291							
Potts, John	(See Lewis, Clark and companions)											
Potts, John	Land for revolutionary services	17	1	Petition	256	Public Lands				Discharged; laid on table.		
Potts, John F. C	Increase of compensation as clerk in naval store, Portsmouth, Va.	31	1	Petition	416	Ways and Means.						
Potts, Nathaniel, *et al.*	(See Jacob Clements, assignee of)	19	1		312							
Potts, Samuel J	Compensation for services in the bounty land bureau.	24	2	Civil and diplomatic bill.	137	Whole House	Feb. 3, 1837	With amend.	776	Passed	Passed	App'd March 3, 1837
Potts, Sarah B., and others	(See Capt. William Rogers, representatives of.)	29	1		199							
Potts, Thomas	Revolutionary pension	22	1	Petition	470	Rev. Pensions				Discharged; laid on table.		
Potts, Thomas	Revolutionary pension	23	1	Petition	333	Rev. Pensions.						
Poucher, Jacob	Amount due for clothing as a volunteer in 1812.	23	1	Petition	491	Claims				Discharged; laid on table.		
Pound, John M	Compensation for a horse lost in United States service.	25	2	Documents	396	Claims				Discharged; laid on table.		
Pound, John M	Compensation for a horse lost in United States service.	25	3	Documents	207	Claims	316	Adverse		Laid on table.		
Povet, Francis	Confirmation of title to land	23	2	Petition	49	Priv. Land Claims.						
Power, Abner	Indemnity for damages sustained by him in consequence of government having included in a military reserve land on which he had made improvements.	30	2	Petition	313	Claims.						
Powell, Allen H., representatives of.	Compensation for a horse and equipage lost in the service of United States.	25	2	Resolution	758	Claims				Discharged; laid on table.		
Powell, Dempsey	Payment for two guns impressed into service of United States in late war.	18	1	Resolution	240	Claims.						
Powell, Elisha, (N. Y.)	Revolutionary pension	22	1	Petition	441	Rev. Pensions.						
Powell, Henry	Invalid pension	30	1	Petition	1037	Invalid Pensions				Discharged; laid on table.		

List of private claims presented to the House of Representatives of the United States from the 1st to the 31st Congress, inclusive—Continued.

Names of claimants.	Nature or object of the claim.	Congress.	Session.	How brought before the House of Reps.	Page of journal.	To what committee of the House referred.	No. or date of the report.	Nature of the report.	No. of the bill.	How disposed of by the House of Reps.	How disposed of by the Senate.	Date of the act of Congress, and remarks.
Powell, James	Renewal of certain loan office certificates captured by the enemy in revolutionary war.	4	1	Petition	428	Claims.						
Powell, James	Renewal of certain loan office certificates captured by the enemy in revolutionary war.	4	2	Petition	614	Claims	Feb. 1, 1797	Adverse	......	Rejected.		
Powell, James, collector at Savannah.	Reimburse money advanced for commissions.	10	2	Army & navy appropriation bill.	525	Whole House	Feb. 25, 1809	With amends.	164	Passed	Passed	App'd March 3, 1809
Powell, James	Compensation for military services in 1794.	21	1	Petition	363	Military Affairs	......	......	......	Discharged; laid on table.		
Powell, James	Payment for property lost in last war.	25	2	Petition	299	Military Affairs	Feb. 7, 1838	Adverse	......	Laid on table.		
Powell, Jesse	Bounty land for services in war of 1812.	16	2	Petition	51	Priv. Land Claims.	51	Favorable; bill	238	Referred to Committee Whole House.		
Powell, Jesse	Proportion of the indemnity paid by the Brazilian government for capture of brig Sarah George.	23	1	Resolution	84	Ways and Means	149	Favorable; bill	158	Passed	Passed	App'd June 30, 1834
Powell, John, (an alien)	Patent for machine for separating gold from other matter.	21	2	Petition	46	Judiciary	Dec. 27, 1830	Favorable; bill	515	Passed	Passed	App'd Feb. 3, 1831
Powell, John	Revolutionary pension	15	2	Petition	217	Rev. Pensions	Feb. 11, 1819	Adverse	......	Laid on table.		
Powell, John	Revolutionary pension	17	1	Petition	128	Rev. Pensions.						
Powell, John	Revolutionary pension	17	2	Petition	119	......	......	......	......	Ref'd to Com. W. H	......	Leave to withdraw.
Powell, John	Revolutionary pension	18	1	Petition	193	Rev. Pensions.						
Powell, John	Revolutionary pension	20	1	Petition	338	Military Pensions.	April 29, 1828	By bill	283	Passed	Laid on table.	
Powell, John	Revolutionary pension	21	1	Petition	48	Military Pensions.	Jan. 5, 1830	By bill	72	Passed	Passed	App'd May 20, 1830
Powell, John	Revolutionary pension	24	1	Senate bill	811	Rev. Pensions	June 3, 1836	Adverse	S. 195	Rejected.		
Powell, Joseph	Revolutionary pension	24	1	Petition	107	Rev. Pensions	Jan. 13, 1836	Adverse	......	Laid on table.		
Powell, J. R.	Compensation for extra service rendered Post Office Department.	31	1	Petition	944	P. Of. & P. Roads.						
Powell, Levin, executors of.	Indemnity for French spoliations prior to 1800.	23	1	Petition	162	Foreign Affairs.						
Powell, Margaret	Confirmation of title to land	14	1	Petition	114	Public Lands.						
Powell, Margaret	Confirmation of title to land	14	2	Petition	81	Public Lands	......	......	......	Discharged; laid on table.		
Powell, Margaret	Confirmation of title to land	15	1	Petition	56	Public Lands	......	......	......	Discharged; laid on table.		
Powell, Robert, heirs of	Commutation of half pay for revolutionary services.	23	1	Petition	42, 81	Rev. Claims.						
Powell, Robert, heirs of	Commutation of half-pay for revolutionary services.	24	1	Resolution	485	Rev. Claims	760	Adverse	......	Laid on table.		
Powell, Robert, heirs of	Commutation of half-pay for revolutionary services.	24	2	Resolution	42	Rev. Claims	Jan. 19, 1837	Adverse	......	Laid on table.		
Powell, William	Patent for certain lands	25	2	Resolution	1176	Priv. Land Claims.	......	......	......	Discharged; laid on table.		
Powell, William A.	Pre-emption right to enter lands	26	1	Petition	603	Public Lands.						
Power, Alexander, attorney, &c.	Compensation to the officers of Col. Ben. Flowers' regiment, revolutionary war.	1	1	Petition	110	......	......	......	......	Referred to Secretary of War.		
Power, Alexander, attorney, &c.	Compensation to the officers of Col. Ben. Flowers' regiment, revolutionary war.	1	2	Rep. of Secretary War.	178	......	......	......	......	Laid on table.		
Power, Alexander, attorney, &c.	Compensation to the officers of Col. Ben. Flowers' regiment, revolutionary war.	5	3	Rep. of Secretary War.	464	Claims	......	......	......	Discharged; laid on table.	......	Leave to withdraw.

List of private claims presented to the House of Representatives of the United States from the 1st to the 31st Congress, inclusive—Continued.

Names of claimants.	Nature or object of the claim.	Congress.	Session.	How brought before the House of Reps.	Page of journal.	To what committee of the House referred.	No. or date of the report.	Nature of the report.	No. of the bill.	How disposed of by the House of Reps.	How disposed of by the Senate.	Date of the act of Congress, and remarks.
Power, Alexander	(See Edward Bryan, *et al.*)	5	2		207							
Powers, Charles	Pension	15	2	Petition	148	Rev. Pensions	Jan. 5, 1819	Adverse		Laid on table.		
Powers, David	Payment for a horse lost in the Black Hawk war.	25	2	Petition	397	Claims				Discharged; laid on table.		
Powers, David	Payment for a horse lost in the Black Hawk war.	25	3	Petition & docs	87	Claims	107	Adverse		Laid on table.		
Powers, Eslee, (Penn.)	Compensation for four horses stolen by Indians in 1792.	22	2	Petition	313	Claims.						
Powers, Henry	Compensation for property destroyed by order of Gen. Macomb.	13	3	Report of Com'r Claims.	751	Claims	Feb. 15, 1815	By bill	297	Passed	Passed	App'd March 3, 1815
Powers, Hiram	Protection in his copy-right of busts, &c.	24	1	Petition	537	Judiciary.						
Powers, James	Compensation for revolutionary services.	20	1	Petition	58	Rev. Claims	Jan. 7, 1828	Adverse		Laid on table.		
Powers, Joshua	Arrears of pay and grant of land for revolutionary services.	11	1	Petition	51	Claims.						
Powers, Joshua P.	Indemnity for capture of vessel by a Texan cruiser.	30	2	Petition	78	Claims.						
Powers, Joshua P.	Indemnity for capture of vessel by a Texan cruiser.	31	1	Petition	324	Claims.						
Powers, Joseph	Revolutionary pension	22	1	Petition	35	Rev. Pensions	Dec. 28, 1831	Adverse		Laid on table.		
Powers, Justus, or Justin.	Arrears of pension	31	1	Petition	977	Claims.						
Power, Robert	Pension for disabilities incurred in revolutionary war.	7	1	Petition	120	Cliams	Mar. 8, 1802	Adverse		Laid on table.		
Power, Robert, heirs of	Compensation for services in revolutionary war.	23	2	Petition	38	Rev. Claims.						
Powers, Stephen	Balance of pay for revolutionary services withheld by paymaster of Massachusetts line.	5	3	Petition	501					Laid on table.		
Powers, Timothy	Revolutionary pension	26	1	Petition	286	Rev. Pensions.						
Powers, Timothy, widow of.	Revolutionary pension	27	2	Petition	684	Rev. Pensions	784	Adverse		Laid on table.		
Powers, Timothy, widow of.	Revolutionary pension	27	3	Petition	73	Rev. Pensions	37	Favorable; bill	666	Passed	Passed	App'd March 3, 1842
Powers, William	Invalid pension	12	1	House bill	361	Whole House	June 15, 1812	With amends.	138	Passed	Passed	App'd July 5, 1812
Powers, William	Increase of pension	14	2	House bill	307	Whole House	Feb. 29, 1817	With amends.	91	Passed	Passed	App'd March 3, 1817
Powers, William	(See Joseph Stewart, *et al*)	14	2		56							
Poythriss, William, heirs of	Commutation pay for revolutionary services.	23	1	Petition	127	Rev. Claims.						
Poythriss, William, heirs of.	Commutation pay for revolutionary services.	23	2	Petition	48	Rev. Claims.						
Poythriss, William, heirs of.	Commutation pay for revolutionary services.	24	1	Petition	942	Rev. Claims.						
Pragers, Mark, & Co., assignee of.	Indemnity for French spoliations prior to 1800.	26	1	Memorial	182	Foreign Affairs	343	Favorable	319	Referred to Committee Whole House.		
Prahl, Lewis	Compensation for services and supplies furnished in revolutionary war.	1	3	Petition and rep't Sec. War.	346					Laid on table.		
Prahl, Lewis	Compensation for a quantity of muskets made for American army, captured by the enemy.	8	1	Petition	408	Claims	Nov. 2, 1803	Adverse		Referred to Committee Whole House.		
Pratt, Asa	Pension	20	1	Resolution	720	Military Pensions				Discharged; laid on table.		
Pratt, Asa	Pension	21	1	Resolution	48	Military Pensions				Discharged; laid on table.		

List of private claims presented to the House of Representatives of the United States from the 1st to the 31st Congress, inclusive—Continued.

Names of claimants.	Nature or object of the claim.	Congress.	Session.	How brought before the House of Reps.	Page of journal.	To what committee of the House referred.	No. or date of the report.	Nature of the report.	No. of the bill.	How disposed of by the House of Reps.	How disposed of by the Senate.	Date of the act of Congress, and remarks.
Pratt, Benjamin	Restoration to pension roll	17	1	Petition	67	Rev. Pensions	....	....	.....	Discharged; laid on table.		
Pratt, Bernard	(See Sylvester Labadié's heirs)	15	2	....	118							
Pratt, Bernard	Confirmation of title to land in Missouri.	15	2	Petition	47	Priv. Land Claims.	....	....	.....	Discharged; laid on table.		
Pratt, Bernard	Confirmation of title to land in Missouri.	17	1	Petition	55	Priv. Land Claims.						
Pratt, Bernard	Confirmation of title to land in Missouri.	18	1	Petition	55	Priv. Land Claims.						
Pratt, brig, owners of	Indemnity for French spoliations prior to 1800.	26	1	Memorial	182	Foreign Affairs	343	Favorable; bill	319	Referred to Committee Whole House.		
Pratt, Carey	Pension	19	1	Petition	88	Military Pensions	164	Adverse	.....	Laid on table.		
Pratt, Carey	Pension	20	1	Petition	126	Rev. Claims	....	....	.....	Discharged; laid on table.	....	March 26, 1828, leave to withdraw.
Pratt, Carey	Increase of pension	25	3	Petition	215	Rev. Pensions	....	....	.....	Discharged; laid on table.		
Pratt, Carey	Increase of pension	26	1	Petition	174	Rev. Pensions.						
Pratt, Carey, (Dist. Col.)	Compensation for services as naval officer in revolutionary war.	23	1	Petition	242	Rev. Claims.						
Pratt, Charles	Invalid pension	14	1	Petition	391	Pens. & Rev. Cl'ms.	April 11, 1816	By bill	171	....	....	Bill became a law omitting petitioner's name.
Pratt, Charles	Invalid pension	29	1	Petition and docs.	806	Invalid Pensions.						
Pratt, Daniel	Invalid pension	26	1	Petition	602	Invalid Pensions	May 25, 1840	By bill	422	Referred to Committee Whole House.		
Pratt, Daniel	Invalid pension	28	1	Petition	84	Invalid Pensions	109	Adverse	.....	Laid on table.		
Pratt, Daniel	Invalid pension	28	2	Petition	532	Invalid Pensions.						
Pratt, Daniel	Invalid pension	29	1	Petition	74	Invalid Pensions	468	Favorable; bill	346	Passed	Passed	App'd Aug. 8, 1846
Pratt, David	Pension for services in revolutionary war.	3	1	Rep. of Secretary War.	131	Select	May 26, 1794	Jt. res. to refer to Sec. War.	R. 12	Passed	Passed	App'd June 9, 1794
Pratt, David	Pension for services in revolutionary war.	4	1	Rep. of Secretary War.	445	Claims	Mar. 4, 1796	Jt. res. to refer to Sec. War.	R. 16	Passed	Passed	App'd April 18, 1796
Pratt, David, (N. Y.)	Invalid pension	25	2	Petition	401	Invalid Pensions.						
Pratt, David, (N. Y.)	Invalid pension	25	3	Petition	90	Invalid Pensions.						
Pratt, Elijah	Indemnity for encroachments by government on his patent.	30	1	Petition	785	Patents.						
Pratt, Elizabeth	(See John Pratt, widow of)	25	3	....	217							
Pratt, Esther	(See Samuel Pratt, widow of)	15	2	....	66							
Pratt, Fielding	Invalid pension	24	2	Petition	103	Invalid Pensions	68	Favorable; bill	814	Referred to Committee Whole House.		
Pratt, Fielding	Invalid pension	25	2	Petition	39	Invalid Pensions	182	Favorable; bill	208	Passed	Adverse report.	
Pratt, Fielding	Invalid pension	25	3	Petition	89	Invalid Pensions	34	Favorable; bill	934	Passed	Adverse report.	
Pratt, Fielding	Invalid pension	26	1	Petition	160	Invalid Pensions	174	Favorable; bill	185	Passed	Indef. postp'd.	
Pratt, Fielding	Invalid pension	26	2	Petition	168	Invalid Pensions	149	Favorable; bill	660	Referred to Committee Whole House.		
Pratt, Fielding	Invalid pension	27	2	Petition	60	Invalid Pensions	218	Adverse	.....	Laid on table.		
Pratt, Fielding	Invalid pension	27	3	House bill	96	Invalid Pensions	....	....	618			
Pratt, Fielding	Invalid pension	27	3	Petition	429	Invalid Pensions	265	Adverse	.....	Laid on table.		
Pratt, Fielding	Invalid pension	28	1	Petition	324	Invalid Pensions.						
Pratt, Fielding	Invalid pension	28	2	Petition	209	Invalid Pensions.						
Pratt, Fielding	Invalid pension	29	2	Petition	84	Invalid Pensions.						
Pratt, Henry, (Pa.)	Indemnity for French spoliations prior to 1800.	26	1	Memorial	182	Foreign Affairs	343	Favorable; bill	319	Referred to Committee Whole House.		
Pratt, Hiram, and G. Burt	(See guardian of Augustus C. Fox)	22	1	....	224							

List of private claims presented to the House of Representatives of the United States from the 1st to the 31st Congress, inclusive—Continued.

Names of claimants.	Nature or object of the claim.	Congress.	Session.	How brought before the House of Reps.	Page of journal.	To what committee of the House referred.	No. or date of the report.	Nature of the report.	No. of the bill.	How disposed of by the House of Reps.	How disposed of by the Senate.	Date of the act of Congress, and remarks.
Pratt, James, widow of	Pension for services in the war of 1812.	26	2	Petition	55	Invalid Pensions.						
Pratt, James, widow of	Pension for services in the war of 1812.	27	3	Petition	106	Invalid Pensions	188	Adverse		Laid on table.		
Pratt, James, widow of	Pension for services in the war of 1812.	28	1	Petition	986	Invalid Pensions.						
Pratte, Jean Baptiste	(See heirs of Francis Vallé)	19	1		133							
Pratt, Joel	Continuation of pension	16	2	Petition	95	Rev. Pensions	Feb. 15, 1821	Adverse		Laid on table		Leave to withdraw.
Pratt, John, widow of	Revolutionary pension	25	3	Petition	217	Rev. Pensions				Disch'd; laid on table.		
Pratt, John, widow of	Revolutionary pension	26	1	Petition	174	Rev. Pensions	714	Adverse		Laid on table.		
Pratt, John, representatives of.	Confirmation of title to land	26	1	Petition	365	Priv. Land Claims.	452	Favorable; bill	364	Referred to Committee Whole House.		
Pratt, John, representatives of.	Confirmation of title to land	27	2	Petition	99	Priv. Land Claims.	85 *a*	Favorable; bill	126	Passed	Passed	App'd Aug. 27, 1842
Pratt, John H., representatives of.	(Journal nor files show nature of claim.)	31	1	Petition	192	Claims.						
Pratt, Joseph, Mary, Joan, and Jean Baptiste.	(See heirs of Francis Vallé)	19	1		133							
Pratt, John	Patent for certain lands held under Spanish grant.	22	1	Petition	263	Priv. Land Claims.	Feb. 17, 1832	By bill	380	Referred to Committee Whole House.		
Pratt, Joseph	Confirmation of title to land in Missouri.	15	2	Petition	67	Priv. Land Claims.				Discharged; laid on table.		
Pratt, Joseph	Confirmation of title to land in Missouri.	17	1	Petition	55	Public Lands.				Discharged; laid on table.		
Pratt, Joseph	Confirmation of title to land in Missouri.	18	1	Petition	55	Public Lands.						
Pratt, Joseph	Confirmation of land claim	22	1	Petition	263	Priv. Land Claims.	Feb. 17, 1832	Favorable; bill	380	Referred to Committee Whole House.		
Pratt & Kintzing	Debenture for drawback on imported merchandise.	5	3	Petition	431	Com. and Manuf.				Discharged; laid on table.		Leave to withdraw.
Pratt, Martha	(See daughter of Johnathan Huddy)	26	1		165							
Pratt, Martha	(See Moses Pratt, widow of)	28	2		240							
Pratt, Moses, widow of	Revolutionary pension	28	2	Petition	240	Rev. Pensions.						
Pratt, Moses, widow of	Revolutionary pension	29	1	Petition	75	Rev. Pensions.						
Pratt, Moses, widow of	Revolutionary pension	29	2	Petition	164	Rev. Pensions.						
Pratt, Nathan	Refunding duties paid on wool, purchased prior to passage of tariff act of 1828.	24	1	Memorial	94	Ways and Means	Jan. 27, 1836	By bill	233	Referred to Committee Whole House.		
Pratt & Putnam	(See Putnam & Pratt)	22	1		383							
Pratt, Sally	(See Thomas Pratt, widow of)	21	1		323							
Pratt, Sarah	(See James Pratt, widow of)	26	2		55							
Pratt, Samuel, (Vt.)	Compensation for property destroyed by the British on the Niagara frontier, late war.	15	2	Petition	36	Claims	Dec. 16, 1818	Adverse		Laid on table.		
Pratt, Samuel, assignee of.	Compensation for property destroyed by the British on the Niagara frontier, late war.	22	1	Senate bill	795	Claims	501	Fav'ble.; without amend.	S. 100	Passed		App'd July 14, 1832
Pratt, Samuel, assignee of.	Compensation for property destroyed by the British on the Niagara frontier, late war.	23	1	Petition	273	Claims	389	Adverse		Laid on table.		
Pratt, Samuel, widow of, (N. Y.)	Compensation for property destroyed by the British on the Niagara frontier.	15	2	Petition	66	Claims	Jan. 6, 1819	Adverse		Laid on table.		

List of private claims presented to the House of Representatives of the United States from the 1st to the 31st Congress, inclusive—Continued.

Names of claimants.	Nature or object of the claim.	Congress.	Session.	How brought before the House of Reps.	Page of journal.	To what committee of the House referred.	No. or date of the report.	Nature of the report.	No. of the bill.	How disposed of by the House of Reps.	How disposed of by the Senate.	Date of the act of Congress, and remarks.
Pratt, Thomas	Pension for services in revolutionary war.	3	2	Rep. of Secretary War.	278	Claims	Feb. 28, 1795	Favorable; bill	130	Passed	Postponed.	
Pratt, Thomas	Pension for services in revolutionary war.	4	1	Rep. of Secretary War.	445	Claims	Feb. 18, 1796	Favorable; bill	156	Passed	Passed	App'd April 20, 1796
Pratt, Thomas, widow of.	Revolutionary pension	21	1	Petition	323	Rev. Pensions.						
Pratt, Thomas, widow of.	Revolutionary pension	27	2	Petition	356	Rev. Pensions	310	Favorable; bill	279	Passed	Indef. postp'd.	
Pratt, Thomas, widow of.	Revolutionary pension	27	3	Petition	154	Rev. Pensions	295	Adverse		Laid on table.		
Pratt, William	Restoration of pension and for arrears of pension.	29	1	Petition	162	Rev. Pensions	618	Adverse		Laid on table.		
Pratt, William, Col., daughter of.	(See Col. William Piatt, daughter of.)	26	1		547							
Pray, Abraham	Arrears of pension	22	1	Petition	287	Rev. Pensions				Discharged; laid on table.		
Pray, Abraham	Arrears of pension	22	2	Petition	81	Rev. Pensions				Disch'd; laid on table.		
Pray, Abraham	Arrears of pension	23	2	Resolution	155	Rev. Pensions	Feb. 2, 1835	Adverse		Laid on table.		
Pray, Abraham	Arrears of pension	26	1	Petition	198	Invalid Pensions	568	Adverse		Laid on table.		
Pray, John	Increase of compensation as collector of the revenue, New York.	2	2	Memorial	628					Referred to Secretary Treasury.		
Pray, John	Increase of compensation as collector of the revenue, New York.	3	2	Rep. of Secretary Treasury.	284	Select	Jan. 26, 1795	By bill	75	Passed	Passed	App'd Feb. 14, 1795
Pray, John, (Ohio)	Pre-emption right in purchasing land.	18	2	Petition	231	Public Lands.						
Pray, John, (Ohio)	Pre-emption right in purchasing land.	19	1	Petition	178	Public Lands.						
Pray, John G	Compensation for services in transporting cannon to the lakes in late war.	23	1	Petition	102	Claims	508	Adverse		Laid on table.		
Pray, John G	Compensation for services rendered in connection with Navy Department in 1814 and 1815.	24	1	Petition	534	Claims	584	Adverse		Laid on table.		
Pray, Richard, & Co.	Permission to purchase land on an extended credit.	15	1	Petition	353	Public Lands	Mar. 21, 1818	Adverse		Rejected.		
Pray, Samuel	Pension	22	1	Petition	122	Rev. Pensions	Dec. 29, 1831	Adverse		Laid on table.		
Pray, Welcome	Payment of claim against Maumee Indians.	29	1	Memorial	160	Indian Affairs	287	Adverse		Laid on table.		
Pray, William, *et al.*, Maumee city, (Ohio.)	Payment of claim against Ottawa Indians.	29	1	Memorial	160	Indian Affairs.						
Preble, Edward, heirs of, *et al.*	Distribution of prize money for capture of brig Transfer.	15	1	House bill	289				112	Referred to Committee Whole House.		
Preble, Edward, heirs of, *et al.*	Distribution of prize money for capture of brig Transfer.	15	2	Bill of last sess.	87	Whole House	Dec. 11, 1818	With't amend.	112	Passed	Passed	App'd Feb. 11, 1819
Preble, Edward, heirs and widow of, *et al.*	Portion of prize money due for destruction of the frigate Philadelphia.	19	2	Petition	154	Naval Affairs.						
Preble, Edward, heirs and widow of, *et al.*	Portion of prize money due for destruction of the frigate Philadelphia.	20	1	Petition	45	Naval Affairs				Discharged; laid on table.		
Preble, Edward, heirs and widow of, *et al.*	Portion of prize money due for destruction of the frigate Philadelphia.	22	1	Petition	161					Referred to Committee Whole House on bill No 98.		
Preble, Edward, heirs and widow of, *et al.*	Portion of prize money due for destruction of the frigate Philadelphia.	23	1	Petition	36	Naval Affairs	Dec. 19, 1833	Favorable; bill	50	Referred to Committee Whole House.		

List of private claims presented to the House of Representativesthe of United States from the 1st to the 31st Congress, inclusive—Continued.

Names of claimants.	Nature or object of the claim.	Congress.	Session.	How brought before the House of Reps.	Page of journal.	To what committee of the House referred.	No. or date of the report.	Nature of the report.	No. of the bill.	How disposed of by the House of Reps.	How disposed of by the Senate.	Date of the act of Congress, and remarks.
Preble, Edward, heirs and widow of, *et al.*	Portion of prize money due for destruction of the frigate Philadelphia.	24	1	Petition	100	Naval Affairs.....	Jan. 11, 1836	By bill	225	Referred to Committee Whole House.		
Preble, Edward, heirs and widow of, *et al.*	Portion of prize money due for destruction of the frigate Philadelphia	24	1	Senate bill	928	Naval Affairs.....	June 4, 1836	With't amend.	S. 138	Referred to Committee Whole House.		
Preble, Henry	(See William Fullerton, *et al.*) ..	26	1	....	710							
Preble, Mary	(See heirs, &c., of Edward Preble)	15	1	....	289							
Prentice, David, heirs of..	Compensation for use by government of his plan for removing snags from Mississippi river.	30	2	Petition	102	Claims.						
Prentiss, Edgecomb......	Land for services of his father in revolutionary war.	23	1	Petition	491	Public Lands.						
Prentiss, Hannah........	Continuat'n of pension from March, 1841, to March, 1843.	28	1	Petition	850	Rev. Pensions.						
Prentiss, Joshua	Increase of compensation as collector of customs.	20	1	Petition	37	....	....	....	.....	Referred to Secretary of Treasury.		
Prentiss, Manaseph, widow of.	Pension; husband died in service of United States.	29	2	Petition	53	Invalid Pensions ..	....	....	.....	Discharged; laid on table.		
Prentiss, Manaseph, widow of.	Pension; husband died in service of United States.	30	1	Petition	886	Invalid Pensions ..	777	Favorable; bill	614	Referred to Committee Whole House.		
Prentiss, Manaseph, widow of.	Pension; husband died in service of United States.	30	2	House bill	362	Whole House.....	Feb. 2, 1849	With't amend.	614	Passed.		
Prentiss, Orin, *et al*......	Fishing bounty on schooner Lilly.	27	2	Petition	318	Commerce	737	Favorable; bill	414	Referred to Committee Whole House.		
Prentiss, Orin, *et al*......	Fishing bounty on schooner Lilly.	27	3	Bill of last sess.	88	....	....	....	414	Passed	Indef. postp'd.	
Prentiss, Susannah	(See widow of Manaseph Prentiss)	29	2	....	53							
Prentiss, William H.....	Compensation for extra service in Department of State.	30	1	Senate bill	826	Rev. Claims......	....	....	S. 117			
Prentiss, William H.....	Compensation for extra service in Department of State.	30	2	Senate bill	82	Claims..........	Dec. 12, 1848	With't amend.	S. 117	Referred to Committee Whole House.		
Prentiss, William H.....	Compensation for extra service in Department of State.	31	1	Petition	193	Claims..........	4	Adverse	.....	Laid on table	....	Leave to withdraw, Dec. 10, 1850.
Prescott, Benjamin, widow of.	Indemnity for French spoliations prior to 1800.	31	1	Petition	196	Foreign Affairs....	355	Favorable; bill	318	Referred to Committee Whole House.		
Prescott, D. W	Remission of duties on goods destroyed by fire.	27	2	Petition	72	Commerce.						
Prescott, Hannah........	(See Benjamin Prescott's widow).	31	1	....	196							
Prescott, Henry N. and William.	Drawback on cotton and cocoa exported to Batavia.	7	2	Petition	372	Com. and Manuf..	Mar. 3, 1803	Res. to postpone to Nov. next.	.....	Resolution adopted.		
Prescott, Henry N. and William.	Drawback on cotton and cocoa exported to Batavia.	8	1	Petition	436	Com. and Manuf..	Nov. 15, 1803	Res. for leave to withdraw.	.....	Resolution adopted.		
Prescott, Jeremiah, and Thomas Canny, heirs of.	Bounty land for services in late war.	31	1	Petition	611	Public Lands.						
Prescott, Joseph, (Maine).	Pension	22	2	Petition	63	Invalid Pensions ..	112	Favorable; bill	748	Referred to Committee Whole House.		
Prescott, Joseph, (Maine).	Pension	23	1	Petition	44	Invalid Pensions ..	1	Favorable; bill	1	Passed	Passed	App'd June 25, 1834
Prescott, Dr. Joseph	Commutation, with interest, as surgeon in revolutionary war.	24	1	Memorial	62	Rev. Claims.......	251	Favorable; bill	261	Referred to Committee Whole House.		
Prescott, Dr. Joseph	Commutation, with interest, as surgeon in revolutionary war.	24	2	Bill of last sess..	200	Whole House.....	....	....	261			

List of private claims presented to the House of Representatives of the United States from the 1st to the 31st Congress, inclusive—Continued.

Names of claimants.	Nature or object of the claim.	Congress.	Session.	How brought before the House of Reps.	Page of journal.	To what committee of the House referred.	No. or date of the report.	Nature of the report.	No. of the bill.	How disposed of by the House of Reps.	How disposed of by the Senate.	Date of the act of Congress, and remarks.
Prescott, Dr. Joseph	Commutation, with interest, as surgeon in revolutionary war.	25	2	Memorial	48	Rev. Claims	314	Favorable; bill	355	Passed	Passed	App'd July 7, 1838
Prescott, Moses	Pre emption to land on which he resides.	18	2	Petition	137	Public Lands.						
Prescott, P.	Increase of compensation as Indian interpreter.	29	1	Petition	274	Indian Affairs	229	Adverse	......	Laid on table.		
Pressy, Benjamin	Revolutionary pension	3	1	Rep. of Secretary War.	131	Select	May 26, 1794	Jt. res. to refer to Sec. War.	R. 12	Passed	Passed	App'd June 9, 1794
Pressy, Benjamin	Revolutionary pension	4	1	Rep. of Secretary War.	445	Claims	March 4, 1796	Jt. res. to refer to Sec. War.	R. 16	Passed	Passed	App'd April 18, 1796
Prestler, Peter	(See John Conner, heirs of)	15	2	....	234							
Preston, Amariah	Balance due for revolutionary services and for arrears of pension.	25	2	Petition	394	....	....	....	......	Laid on table.		
Preston, Benjamin	Pension	25	2	Petition	197	Invalid Pensions.						
Preston, Bonker, *et al.*	(See John Hook's heirs.)											
Preston, Daniel	Revolutionary pension	3	2	Rep. of Secretary War.	278	Claims	Feb. 28, 1795	Favorable; bill	130	Passed	Postponed.	
Preston, Daniel	Revolutionary pension	4	1	Rep. of Secretary War.	445	Claims	Feb. 18, 1796	Favorable; bill	156	Passed	Passed	App'd April 20, 1796
Preston, Frances and Hannah.	(See William Campbell, heirs of)	10	2	....	381							
Preston, Isaac, heirs of	Commutation pay due for revolutionary services.	8	2	Memorial	71	Claims	Jan. 4, 1815	Report and res. for leave to withdraw.	......	Resolution adopted.		
Preston, Joel, widow of	Revolutionary pension	28	1	Petition	683	Rev. Claims	....	....	......	Discharged; laid on table.		
Preston, John	(See Louis F. Beeler, *et al.*)	30	1	....	115							
Preston, John	Increase of pension	25	2	Petition	913	Rev. Pensions	....	....	......	Discharged; laid on table.		
Preston, John	Increase of pension	26	2	Petition	49	Rev. Pensions.						
Preston, Jonas, *et al*	Bounty on account of confinement in British prisons in war of 1812.	28	1	Petition	101	Claims.						
Preston, Lucy	(See widow of Joel Preston.)	28	1	....	683							
Prettyman, Mary	(See Thomas G. Prettyman, widow of.)	26	1	....	1277							
Prettyman, Thomas G.	Pension for injuries received while a prisoner of war.	24	2	Petition	398	Invalid Pensions	Feb. 22, 1837	Adverse	......	Laid on table.		
Prettyman, Thomas G.	Pension for injuries received while a prisoner of war.	25	2	Memorial	71	Invalid Pensions	Mar. 7, 1838	Adverse	......	Laid on table.		
Prettyman, Thos. G., widow of.	Pension	26	1	Senate bill	1277	....	....	....	S. 360			
Prettyman, Thos. G., widow of.	Pension	26	2	Senate bill	165	Rev. Pensions	Feb. 12, 1841	With't amend.	S. 85	Referred to Committee Whole House.		
Prettyman, Thos. G., widow of.	Pension	27	2	Senate bill	1194	Whole House	Aug. 5, 1842	With't amend.	S. 19	Passed	....	App'd Aug. 11, 1842
Prevost, Stanhope	Compensation for services as acting chargé at Lima.	30	1	Civil and Diplomatic Appropriation bill.	523	Whole House	July 18, 1848	With't amend.	298	Passed	Passed	App'd Aug. 2, 1848
Prewitt, R. C.	Additional compensation for mail service.	30	1	Petition	757	Claims	756	Adverse	......	Laid on table.		
Prewitt, Solomon, (Ky.)	Restoration of pension	23	1	Petition	379	Rev. Pensions.						
Prewitt, Solomon, (Ky.)	Restoration of pension	24	1	Resolution	992	Rev. Pensions.						
Prewitt, Solomon, (Ky.)	Restoration of pension	24	2	Resolution	78	Rev. Pensions.						
Prewitt, Solomon, (Ky.)	Restoration of pension	25	2	Resolution	93	Rev. Pensions	451	Favorable; bill	451	Passed	Reported with't amendment.	

List of private claims presented to the House of Representatives of the United States from the 1*st to the* 31*st Congress, inclusive*—Continued.

Names of claimants.	Nature or object of the claim.	Congress.	Session.	How brought before the House of Reps.	Page of journal.	To what committee of the House referred.	No. or date of the report.	Nature of the report.	No. of the bill.	How disposed of by the House of Reps.	How disposed of by the Senate.	Date of the act of Congress, and remarks.
Prewitt, Solomon, (Ky.)	Restoration of pension	25	3	Resolution	87	Rev. Pensions	26	Favorable; bill	925	Passed	Passed	App'd March 3, 1839
Price, Alexander H	(See assignee of Wm. J. Price.)	21	2		100							
Price, Anna	Further compensation for a horse impressed into the service of the United States in revolutionary war.	15	2	Petition	268	Pens. & Rev. Cl'ms.				Discharged; laid on table.		
Price, Anna	Further compensation for a horse impressed into the service of the United States in revolutionary war.	24	1	Petition	103	Rev. Claims.						
Price, Anna	Further compensation for a horse impressed into the service of the United States in revolutionary war.	24	2	Petition	94	Rev. Claims				Discharged; leave to withdraw.		
Price, Benjamin, daughter of.	Pension for services in revolutionary war.	19	1	Petition	407	Military Pensions	April 26, 1826	Rep. and Res. adverse.		Res. adopted.		
Price, Captain Benjamin, heirs of.	Five years' half pay—killed in battle, 1791.	23	1	Petition	80	Claims.						
Price, Benjamin	Five years' half-pay—killed in battle, 1791.	23	2	Petition	56	Rev. Claims.						
Price, Benjamin, (N. J.)	Revolutionary pension	21	2	Petition	230	Military Pensions.						
Price, Benjamin, (N. J.)	Revolutionary pension	24	1	Petition	213	Rev. Pensions	305	Favorable; bill	319	Passed	Indef. postp'd.	
Price, Benjamin, (N. J.)	Revolutionary pension	25	2	Petition	38	Rev. Pensions	267	Favorable; bill	310	Passed	Adverse report.	
Price, Benjamin, (N. J.)	Revolutionary pension	25	3	Petition	216	Rev. Pensions	179	Favorable; bill	1042	Passed.		
Price, Benjamin, (N. J.)	Revolutionary pension	26	1	Petition	172	Rev. Pensions	144	Favorable; bill	154	Passed.		
Price, Benjamin, (N. J.)	Revolutionary pension	27	2	Petition	268	Rev. Pensions	784	Adverse		Laid on table.		
Price, Chandler, administrator of.	Indemnity for French spoliations prior to 1800.	26	1	Memorial	182	Foreign Affairs	343	Favorable; bill	319	Referred to Committee Whole House.		
Price, Daniel B	(See Joseph Crockett, heirs of.)	26	1		332							
Price, Francis	Pension	18	1	Petition	89	Pens. & Rev. Clm's.				Discharged; laid on table.		
Price, George	Pension	19	1	Petition	442	Military Pensions	May 9, 1826	Adverse		Rejected.		
Price, Howell	(See Henry Davis, assignee of)											
Price, Isaac, widow of	Revolutionary pension	26	1	Resolution	950	Rev. Pensions.						
Ptice, James	Payment for supplies furnished the American army in Canada.	1	2	Petition	145	Select	May 7, 1790	Rep. not of record.		Laid on table.		
Price, James	Payment of loan office certificate, also compensation for services as assistant commissary and forage master revolutionary war.	4	1	Rep. of Secretary Treasury.	388	Claims	May 31, 1796	Adverse		Laid on table.		
Price, James	Compensation for services as keeper of public stores in revolutionary war.	5	2	Petition	220	Claims	May 4, 1798	Adverse; leave to withdraw.		Referred to Committee Whole House.		
Price, James	(See Canadian refugees.)	6	2		748							
Price, James, heirs of, by James, jr.	Compensation for services, injuries, and loss of property by deceased in revolutionary war.	7	2	Petition	328	Claims	Feb. 26, 1803	Res. to postpone to November next.		Adopted.		
Price, James, heirs of, by James, jr.	Compensation for services, injuries, and loss of property by deceased in revolutionary war.	9	1	Petition	223	Select.						
Price, James, heirs of, by James, jr.	Compensation for services, injuries, and loss of property by deceased in revolutionary war.	24	1	Petition	851	Rev. Claims.						

List of private claims presented to the House of Representatives of the United States from the 1st to the 31st Congress, inclusive—Continued.

Names of claimants.	Nature or object of the claim.	Congress.	Session.	How brought before the House of Reps.	Page of journal.	To what committee of the House referred.	No. or date of the report.	Nature of the report.	No. of the bill.	How disposed of by the House of Reps.	How disposed of by the Senate.	Date of the act of Congress, and remarks.
Price, James, heirs of, by James, jr.	Compensation for services, injuries, and loss of property by deceased in revolutionary war.	25	2	Petition	270	Rev. Claims......	....	....	......	Discharged; laid on table.		
Price, James, heirs of....	To be reimbursed the amount advanced General Gates in revolutionary war on public account.	12	2	Petition	553	Claims.						
Price, James, heirs of....	To be reimbursed the amount advanced General Gates in revolutionary war.	15	1	Petition	43	Pens. & Rev. Cl'ms.	....	....	......	Discharged; leave to withdraw.	....	Claim adjusted by the Treas'y Department.
Price, James, heirs of....	For interest on amount advanced General Gates.	15	2	Petition	23	Pens. & Rev. Cl'ms.	Feb. 5, 1819	By bill	309	Referred to Committee Whole House.		
Price, James, heirs of....	For interest on amount advanced General Gates.	16	1	Petition	142	Pens. & Rev. Cl'ms.	Jan. 17, 1820	Adverse	......	Rejected.		
Price, James, executors of.	Indemnity for French spoliations prior to 1800.	26	1	Memorial	182	Foreign Affairs....	343	Favorable; bill	319	Referred to Committee Whole House.		
Price, James, widow of...	Compensation for advances and for losses by being compelled to abandon property in Canada.	27	2	Petition	154	Rev. Claims......	867	Adverse	......	Laid on table.		
Price, James, (Md.).....	Indemnity for French spoliations prior to 1800.	26	1	Memorial	182	Foreign Affairs....	343	Favorable....	319	Referred to Committee Whole House.		
Price, John	(See William Somersall & Son, and J. Price.)	4	1	....	591							
Price, John, (S. C.).....	(See Tunno & Cox, and others.).	7	1	....	82							
Price, John, heirs of.....	Bounty land for services in revolutionary war.	26	1	Petition	361	Rev. Claims.						
Price, John, heirs of.....	Bounty land for services in revolutionary war.	26	2	Petition	212	Rev. Claims.						
Price, John, heirs of.....	Bounty land for services in revolutionary war.	27	2	Petition	62	Rev. Claims......	1080	Adverse	......	Laid on table.		
Price, John, heirs of.....	Pension: deceased lost his life in the naval service.	27	3	Petition	132	Invalid Pensions.						
Price, John, heirs of.....	Pension: deceased lost his life in the naval service.	28	1	Petition	284	Naval Affairs.						
Price, Capt. John, *et al.*.	Compensation for services of themselves and companions in Florida war.	30	1	Memorial	838	Military Affairs ...	740	Favorable; bill	582	Referred to Committee Whole House.		
Price, Capt. John, *et al.*.	Compensation for services of themselves and companions in Florida war	31	1	Petition	338	Military Affairs.						
Price, Capt. John, *et al.*.	Compensation for services of themselves and companions in Florida war.	31	2	Petition	241	Military Affairs ...	Feb. 7, 1851	Favorable; bill	456	Referred to Committee Whole House.		
Price, Joseph F., *et al.*...	(See heirs of J. Winston).......	22	1	....	470							
Price, Looney	Confirmation of title to land	22	1	House bill......	421	Whole House	Feb. 29, 1832	With't amend.	425	Passed	Passed	App'd June 25, 1832
Price, M. A., and E. A. White.	Compensation for carrying the mail under contract with the Post Office Department.	27	2	Petition	383	Claims.						
Price, M. A., and E. A. White.	Compensation for carrying the mail under contract with the Post Office Department.	29	1	Petition	701	P. Of. & P. Roads.	July 6, 1846	By joint res...	R. 43	Referred to Committee Whole House.		
Price, M. A., and E. A. White.	Compensation for carrying the mail under contract with the Post Office Department.	29	2	Jt. resolution of last session.	305	Whole House.....	Feb. 5, 1847	With't amend.	R. 43	Passed	Passed	App'd March 3, 1847

List of private claims presented to the House of Representatives of the United States from the 1st to the 31st Congress, inclusive—Continued.

Names of claimants.	Nature or object of the claim.	Congress.	Session.	How brought before the House of Reps.	Page of journal.	To what committee of the House referred.	No. or date of the report.	Nature of the report.	No. of the bill.	How disposed of by the House of Reps.	How disposed of by the Senate.	Date of the act of Congress, and remarks.
Price, Mary	(See James Price, widow of)	27	2	....	154							
Price, Nathan, sureties of.	Release from a bond to the United States.	26	1	Petition	348	Judiciary.						
Price, Olivia	(See widow of Isaac Price)	26	1	....	950							
Price, P. B	(See administrator of George Mansell.)	19	2	....	100							
Price, Risdon H	(See Don Jacques Clamorgan)	15	1	....	144							
Price, Risdon H	Indemnity for French spoliations prior to 1800.	26	1	Memorial	182	Foreign Affairs	343	Favorable; bill	319	Referred to Committee Whole House.		
Price, Rodman M	For certain credits in settlement of his accounts.	28	2	Petition	405	Naval Affairs	Feb. 52, 1845	Favorable; jt. resolution.	R. 76	Referred to Committee Whole House.		
Price, Samuel	Pension	20	1	Petition	310	Military Pensions.						
Price, Sarah	(See William Price's widow)	22	2	....	94							
Price, Siter, & Co	Refunding duties paid on goods	24	1	Memorial	143	Ways and Means.						
Price, Solomon	(See administrator of Richard Partington.)	29	1	....	340							
Price, Spencer	Compensation for a slave lost in service of United States.	27	2	Petition	382	Claims	1048	Adverse	......	Laid on table.		
Price, Spencer	Compensation for a slave lost in service of United States.	28	1	Petition	157	Claims	246	Adverse	......	Laid on table.		
Price, Spencer	Compensation for a slave lost in service of United States.	28	2	Petition	71	Claims.						
Price, Thomas, by attorney.	Compensation for services rendered or injuries sustained in revolutionary war.	3	1	Petition	132	Select.						
Price, Thompson, *et al.*	Remission of taxes which have accrued on the Arredondo grant.	26	1	Petition	704	Judiciary.						
Price, William J., assignees of.	Pre-emption right to land	21	2	Petition	100	Public Lands	....	....	......	Discharged; laid on table.		
Price, William	To be released from imprisonment without the payment of costs.	18	1	Petition	213	Judiciary.						
Price, William, (Va.)	Release from a judgment in favor of United States.	19	1	Petition	407	P. Of. & P. Roads.	April 27, 1826	Adverse	......	Laid on table.		
Price, William, (Va.)	Release from a judgment in favor of United United.	19	2	Petition	105	P. Of. & P. Roads.	Jan. 9, 1827	Adverse	......	Laid on table.		
Price, jr., William, (S. C.)	(See Jos. L. Weyman, surety of.)	20	1	....	39							
Price, jr., William, administrator of.	Remission of interest due United States on certain custom house bonds.	22	1	Petition	484	Ways and Means.						
Price, William	Five years' full pay in lieu of half pay for life for revolutionary services.	21	1	Petition	36	Military Pensions	352	Favorable; bill	414	Passed	Passed	App'd May 29, 1830
Price, William, widow of.	Interest on commutation pay granted deceased.	22	2	Petition	94	Rev. Claims	Jan. 3, 1833	Favorable; bill	655	Referred to Committee Whole House.		
Price, William, widow of.	Interest on commutation pay granted deceased.	22	2	Senate bill	466	Rev. Claims	Mar. 2, 1833	With't amend.	105	Passed	....	App'd March 2, 1833
Price, jr., William	Relinquishment by United States of reversionary interest in a section of land in Alabama.	28	2	Petition	144	Indian Affairs.						
Price, jr., William	Relinquishment by United States of reversionary interest in a section of land in Alabama.	29	1	Memorial	87	Indian Affairs	Feb. 21, 1846	By bill	255	Referred to Committee Whole House.		

List of private claims presented to the House of Representatives of the United States from the 1st to the 31st Congress, inclusive—Continued.

Names of claimants.	Nature or object of the claim.	Congress.	Session.	How brought before the House of Reps.	Page of journal.	To what committee of the House referred.	No. or date of the report.	Nature of the report.	No. of the bill.	How disposed of by the House of Reps.	How disposed of by the Senate.	Date of the act of Congress, and remarks.
Price, jr., William	Relinquishment by United States of reversionary interest in a section of land in Alabama.	29	2	House bill	71	Whole House	Dec. 18, 1846	With't amend.	255	Passed.		
Price, jr., William	Relinquishment by United States of reversionary interest in a section of land in Alabama.	30	1	Petition	664	Public Lands	814	Favorable; bill	633	Referred to Committee Whole House.		
Price, jr., William	Relinquishment by United States of reversionary interest in a section of land in Alabama.	31	1	Petition	325	Public Lands	81	Favorable; bill	98	Referred to Committee Whole House.		
Price, jr., William	Relinquishment by United States of reversionary interest in a section of land in Alabama.	31	2	House bill	154	Whole House	Jan. 18, 1851	With't amend.	98	Passed.		
Price, William	Compensation for services as captain in Florida war.	30	1	Petition	740	Claims.						
Price, William, and Joseph Wilson.	Release from prison, (insolvents)	16	2	Petition	131	Judiciary	....	....	......	Discharged; laid on table.		
Prichard, John R.	Increase of pension for loss of sight, &c.	31	2	Petition	220	Invalid Pensions.						
Priddy, Mathew	Pre-emption right in the purchase of land on which he has made improvements.	26	1	Petition	934	Public Lands.						
Priddy, Thomas	Invalid pension	29	2	Petition	100	Invalid Pensions.						
Pridmore, John	Payment of Continental bills received for services and supplies furnished revolutionary army.	13	2	Petition	173	Pens. & Rev. Cl'ms.	92	Adverse; res. for leave to withdraw.	......	Referred to Committee Whole House.		
Priest, Captain Gabriel	Compensation for property destroyed by the Indians in Florida, in 1835.	24	1	Petition	475	Claims	669	Adverse	......	Laid on table.		
Priest, Job	Compensation for supplies furnished, or for services and losses in revolutionary war.	1	3	Petition and rep't Sec. of War.	352	....	....	....	......	Laid on table.		
Priest, Job	Pension for services in revolutionary war.	3	1	Rep. of Secretary War.	131	Select	May 26, 1794	Jt. res. to refer to Sec. War.	R. 12	Passed	Passed	App'd June 9, 1794
Priest, Job	Pension for services in revolutionary war.	4	1	Rep. of Secretary War.	445	Claims	Feb. 18, 1796	Favorable; bill	156	Passed	Passed	App'd April 20, 1796
Priest, Mary	Continuation of her pension from March, 1841, to March, 1843.	28	1	Petition	850	Rev. Pensions.						
Priestly, Mary Ann Elizabeth.	Compensat'n for nursing and boarding sick soldiers in revolutionary war.	19	1	Petition	153	Rev. Claims	....	....	......	Discharged; laid on table.		
Priestly, Mary Ann Elizabeth.	Compensat'n for nursing and boarding sick soldiers in revolutionary war.	19	2	Petition	64	Rev. Claims	Jan. 4, 1827	Adverse	......	Laid on table.		
Priestly, Mary Ann Elizabeth.	Compensat'n for nursing and boarding sick soldiers in revolutionary war.	22	1	Petition	91	Rev. Claims	Jan. 31, 1832	Adverse	......	Laid on table.		
Priestman, Thomas	(See William Priestman, administrator of.)	26	1	....	182							
Priestman, William, administrator of.	Indemnity for French spoliations prior to 1800.	26	1	Memorial	182	Foreign Affairs	343	Favorable	319	Referred to Committee Whole House.		
Prim, Abraham, & others.	Remuneration for Indian depredations in 1836.	29	2	Petition	87	Indian Affairs.						

List of private claims presented to the House of Representatives of the United States from the 1st to the 31st Congress, inclusive—Continued.

Names of claimants.	Nature or object of the claim.	Congress.	Session.	How brought before the House of Reps.	Page of journal.	To what committee of the House referred.	No. or date of the report.	Nature of the report.	No. of the bill.	How disposed of by the House of Reps.	How disposed of by the Senate.	Date of the act of Congress, and remarks.
Prim, Abraham, & others.	Remuneration for Indian depredations in 1836.	30	1	Petition	485	Claims.						
Prime, Mark	Revolutionary pension	21	2	Resolution	124	Military Pensions	....	....	......	Discharged; laid on table.		
Prime, Mark	Revolutionary pension	22	1	Resolution	70	Rev. Pensions	Dec. 29, 1831	Adverse	......	Laid on table.		
Prime, Nathaniel	Payment of bills of credit issued by the State of New Hampshire during revolutionary war.	4	1	Rep. of Secretary Treasury.	388	Claims	May 31, 1796	Adverse	......	Laid on table	....	Leave to withdraw, 2d session, 5th Cong.
Primeau & Chapman, surviving partner of.	Compensation for Indian depredations.	29	1	Petition	302	Indian Affairs.	596	Favorable; bill	417	Referred to Committee Whole House.		
Primeau & Chapman, surviving partner of.	Compensation for Indian depredations.	29	2	House bill	382	Whole House	Feb. 19, 1847	With't amend.	417	Passed	Passed	App'd March 3, 1847
Primm, Wilson	(See Alfred Tracy, and others)	23	2	....	201							
Prince, Cynthia Holland	Permission to purchase land at minimum price.	24	1	Petition	258	Public Lands.						
Prince, Cynthia Holland	Permission to purchase land at minimum price.	25	2	Petition	418	Priv. Land Claims	....	....	......	Discharged; laid on table.		
Prince, Hezekiah	Compensation for services rendered in the quartermaster's department, United States army.	14	1	Petition	33	Claims	....	....	......	Discharged; laid on table.		
Prince, James	Grant of land as a refugee from Canada.	6	2	House bill	766	Whole House	Jan. 26, 1801	Favorable	280	Passed	Passed	App'd Feb. 18, 1801
Prince, James, executors of, (Mass.)	Indemnity for French spoliations prior to 1800.	26	1	Memorial	182	Foreign Affairs	343	Favorable; bill	319	Referred to Committee Whole House.		
Prince, James	Indemnity for French spoliations prior to 1800.	26	1	Memorial	182	Foreign Affairs	343	Favorable; bill	319	Referred to Committee Whole House.		
Prince, James, (U. States marshal.)	To be allowed amount paid district attorney of Massachusetts, and which has been rejected in settlement of his accounts.	14	2	Petition	38	Claims.						
Prince, James, (U. States marshal.)	To be allowed amount paid district attorney of Massachusetts, and which has been rejected in settlement of his accounts.	15	1	Petition	44	Claims	Dec. 29, 1817	Adverse	......	Rejected.		
Prince, John, jr	(See John and Samuel G. Derby.)											
Prince, John, & John Pickman.	(See John Derby, executors of.)	23	1	....	186							
Prince, Nicholas	Revolutionary pension	22	1	Petition	265	Rev. Pensions.						
Prindall, Mary	(See daughter of John Burnham.)	26	2	....	99							
Prindle, Martin	Compensation for a horse lost in United States service.	24	1	Senate bill	602	Claims	April 5, 1836	With't amend.	96	Passed	....	App'd July 2, 1836
Pringle, Benjamin	Damages done to his farm by American army in 1778.	4	1	Rep. of Secretary Treasury.	388	Claims	May 31, 1796	Adverse	......	Laid on table.		
Pringle, Benj., by William Thorne.	Payment for supplies furnished revolutionary army.	5	2	Petition	218	Claims	Mar. 13, 1798	Adverse	......	Rejected.		
Pringle, Mark, administrator of.	Indemnity for French spoliations prior to 1800.	26	1	Memorial	182	Foreign Affairs	343	Favorable; bill	319	Referred to Committee Whole House.		
Prioleau, Samuel, jr.	Compensation for certain wharves and houses in the city of Charleston, used by the American army at its seige.	1	3	Petition	337	....	....	....	......	Referred to Secretary of Treasury.		

List of private claims presented to the House of Representatives of the United States from the 1st to the 31st Congress, inclusive—Continued.

Names of claimants.	Nature or object of the claim.	Congress.	Session.	How brought before the House of Reps.	Page of journal.	To what committee of the House referred.	No. or date of the report.	Nature of the report.	No. of the bill.	How disposed of by the House of Reps.	How disposed of by the Senate.	Date of the act of Congress, and remarks.
Prioleau, Samuel, jr.	Compensation for certain wharves and houses in the city of Charleston, used by the American army at its seige.	3	1	Rep. of Secretary Treasury.	78	Select	Jan. 6, 1794	By bill	67	Passed	Postp'd to next session.	
Prioleau, Samuel, jr.	Compensation for certain wharves and houses in the city of Charleston, used by the American army at its seige.	3	2	Senate bill	287	Claims	Jan. 20, 1795	With amend.	S. 23	Passed	....	App'd Jan. 28, 1795
Prioleau, Samuel	(See Samuel Legare, and others.)	4	1	....	493							
Prior, Abner	(See John Elliott)	2	1	....	463							
Prior, Abner, heirs of	Commutation pay for services in revolutionary war.	23	1	Petition	189	Rev. Claims.						
Prior, Abner, heirs of	Commutation pay for services in revolutionary war.	24	1	Petition	1108	Rev. Claims	June 27, 1836	Adverse	......	Laid on table.		
Prior, Abner, heirs of	Commutation pay for services in revolutionary war.	25	2	Petition	49	Rev. Claims	856	Report and bill	774	Referred to Committee Whole House.		
Prior, Abner, heirs of	Commutation pay for services in revolutionary war.	25	3	Bill of last sess.	431	Whole House	....	....	774			
Prior, Abner, heirs of	Commutation pay for services in revolutionary war.	26	1	Petition	165	Rev. Claims.						
Prior, Nathaniel	(See Lewis&Clarke,&companions)	9	2	....	....	....	....	....	......	....	....	App'd March 3, 1807
Prior, Simon	Revolutionary pension	22	1	Petition	381	Rev. Pensions	....	....	......	Disch'd; laid on table		
Pritchard, A. P.	(See A. Avery, and others)	25	2	....	478							
Pritchard, Jeremiah	Compensation for services, &c., in revolutionary war.	2	1	Petition	490	....	....	....	......	Referred to Secretary of War.		
Pritchard, Jeremiah	Pension for services in revolutionary war.	3	1	Rep. of Secretary War.	131	Select	May 26, 1794	Jt. res. to refer to Sec. War.	J. R. 12	Passed	Passed	App'd June 9, 1794
Pritchard, Jeremiah	Pension for services in revolutionary war.	3	2	Rep. of Secretary War.	262	Claims	Feb. 28, 1795	Favorable; bill	130	Passed	Postponed.	
Pritchard, Jeremiah	Pension for services in revolutionary war.	4	1	Rep. of Secretary War.	445	Claims	Feb. 18, 1796	Favorable; bill	156	Passed	Passed	App'd April 20, 1796
Pritchard, Jeremiah	Increase of pension	10	1	House bill	232	Whole House	April 19, 1808	With amendt's	78	Passed	....	App'd April 25, 1808
Pritchard, John	Pension	18	1	Petition	81	Pens. & Rev. Cl'ms.	....	....	......	Discharged; laid on table.	....	March 1, 1824, leave to withdraw.
Pritchard, Thomas, (Md.)	Revolutionary pension	15	2	Petition	51	Pens. & Rev. Cl'ms.	Dec. 4, 1818	Res. for leave to withdraw.	......	Adopted.		
Pritchard, Thomas, (Tenn.)	Revolutionary pension	30	1	Petition	439	Rev. Pensions	....	....	......	Discharged; laid on table.		
Pritchett, John	Pension	14	1	Petition	32	Rev. Pensions	....	....	......	Discharged.		
Pritchett, Samuel M.	(See John Harris, and others.)											
Probasco, Henry	(See surety of John C. Jones)	15	2	....	246							
Prock, John	Increase of compensation as mail contractor.	25	3	Petition	569	P. Of. & P. Roads.	....	....	......	Discharged.		
Prock, John	Increase of compensation as mail contractor.	26	1	Petition	1012	P. Of. and P. Roads	549	Adverse	......	Laid on table.		
Prock, John	Increase of compensation as mail contractor.	26	2	Petition	56	P. Of. and P. Roads.	....	....	......	Discharged; laid on table.		
Proctor, Amos	Indemnity against act of Congress and return of certain forfeitures.	26	1	Memorial	289	Commerce.						
Proctor, Amos	Indemnity against act of Congress, and return of certain forfeitures.	27	2	Memorial	95	Commerce.						
Proctor, Amos	Indemnity against act of Congress, and return of certain forfeitures.	28	1	Memorial	117	Commerce	474	Favorable; bill	364	Passed	Passed	App'd June 17, 1844

List of private claims presented to the House of Representatives of the United States from the 1st to the 31st Congress, inclusive—Continued.

Names of claimants.	Nature or object of the claim.	Congress.	Session.	How brought before the House of Reps.	Page of journal.	To what committee of the House referred.	No. or date of the report.	Nature of the report.	No. of the bill.	How disposed of by the House of Reps.	How disposed of by the Senate.	Date of the act of Congress, and remarks.
Proctor, Francis	Compensation for revolutionary services.	1	3	Petition	375					Referred to Secretary War.		
Practor, Francis	Compensation for revolutionary services.	3	2	Rep. of Secretary War.	278					Laid on table.		
Proctor, Francis, Captain	Compensation for services in revolutionary war, and for hardships endured whilst a prisoner.	3	2	Petition	296	Claims.						
Proctor, Francis, Captain	Compensation for services in revolutionary war, and for hardships endured whilst a prisoner.	4	1	Resolution	373	Claims	Dec. 28, 1795	Res. for leave to withdraw.		Resolution adopted.		
Proctor, Isaac	(Nature of claim not stated)	27	3	Petition	107	Commerce.						
Proctor, John	Correction of an error in the entry of land.	22	1	Senate bill	152	Public Lands	Jan. 18, 1832	With't amend.	14	Passed		App'd Feb. 18, 1832
Proctor, Samuel	Compensation for services, &c., in revolutionary war.	2	1	Petition	464					Referred to Secretary War.		
Proctor, William	Pension for services in revolutionary war.	3	2	Rep. of Secretary War.	350	Claims	Mar. 2, 1795	Res. to refer to Sec. War.		Resolution adopted.		
Proctor, William	Pension for services in revolutionary war.	4	2	Rep. of Secretary War.	445	Claims	Mar. 2, 1796	Jt. res. to refer to Sec. War.	16	Passed	Passed	App'd April 18, 1796
Promis, Eulalie and Leopold	(See Guilliaume Promis, heirs of)	24	1		434							
Promis, Guilliaume, heirs of.	Permission to complete payment for a certain tract of land, and that a grant issue to them for the same.	24	1	Petition	434	Public Lands.						
Promis, Guilliaume, heirs of.	Permission to complete payment for a certain tract of land, and that a grant to issue them for the same.	25	2	Petition	87	Public Lands				Discharged; laid on table.		
Protestant University of U. States, trustees of.	Donation of public lands	30	1	Memorial	78	Public Lands	16	Adverse		Laid on table.		
Prout, Ebenezer	For ballance of his accounts as assistant commissory during late war.	2	1	Petition	448					Referred to Secretary Treasury.		
Prout, Ebenezer	For balance of his accounts as assistant commissory during late war.	2	2	Rep. of Secretary Treasury.	626					Laid on table.		
Prout, Holden W	(See Joshua W. Prout, administrator of.)	17	1		380							
Prout, Joshua W., adminitrator of.	Payment to him as assignee, of money due soldiers.	17	1	Senate bill	380	Claims	April 10, 1822	Adverse	S. 54	Laid on table.		
Prout, Joshua W., administrator of.	Payment to him as assignee, of money due soldiers.	17	2	Petition	95	Claims	Feb. 3, 1823	Adverse		Laid on table.		
Prout, Joshua W., administrator of.	Payment to him as assignee, of money due soldiers.	18	1	Petition	66	Military Affairs				Discharged.		Leave to withdraw.
Prout, Joshua W., administrator of.	Payment to him as assignee, of money due soldiers.	18	2	Senate bill	284	Military Affairs	Mar. 1, 1825	With't amend:	S. 41	Passed		App'd March 3, 1825
Prout, William	Authority to institute a bill in equity against Commissioner of Public Buildings in the circuit court, District of Columbia.	15	2	Senate bill	280	Judiciary	Feb. 23, 1819	With't amends	S. 51	Passed		App'd March 2, 1819
Provandie, Louis	Payment of amount of sundry due bills received for services in revolutionary war.	22	2	Petition	346	Rev. Claims.						

List of private claims presented to the House of Representatives of the United States from the 1st to the 31st Congress, inclusive—Continued.

Names of claimants.	Nature or object of the claim.	Congress.	Session.	How brought before the House of Reps.	Page of journal.	To what committee of the House referred.	No. or date of the report.	Nature of the report.	No. of the bill.	How disposed of by the House of Reps.	How disposed of by the Senate.	Date of the act of Congress, and remarks.
Providence Insurance Company.	(See Rhode Island.)	26	1		182							
Proveaux, Adrien	Compensation for services and expenses in revolutionary war.	2	1	Petition	505					Referred to Secretary War.		
Proveaux, Adrien	Compensation for services and expenses in revolutionary war.	2	2	Rep. of Secretary War.	696					Laid on table.		
Province, William, & Co.	Right of pre-emption to land in Indiana.	13	1	Petition	74	Public Lands				Discharged.		
Province, William, & Co.	Right of pre-emption to land in Indiana.	13	2	Petition	175	Public Lands	Jan. 13, 1816	Adverse		Rejected.		
Provost, Nicholas, assignee of.	Confirmation of title to land in Louisiana.	27	2	Senate bill	359	Priv. Land Claims.	Feb. 26, 1842	With't amend.	S. 76	Passed	Passed	App'd July 6, 1842
Provost, Robert	Compensation for military services in revolutionary war.	1	2	Petition	286					Referred to Secretary War.		
Provost, Solomon	Compensation for property taken for United States army in late war.	15	2	Senate bill	325	Claims			S. 69			
Provost, Solomon	Compensation for property taken for United States army in late war.	16	1	Senate bill	407	Claims			S. 70			
Provost, Solomon	Compensation for property taken for United States army in late war.	16	2	Petition	115	Claims	Jan. 31, 1821	By bill	236	Referred to Committee Whole House.		
Provost, Solomon	Compensation for property taken for United States army in late war.	17	1	Petition	47	Claims	Jan. 29, 1822	By bill	62	Passed	Passed	App'd May 7, 1842
Pruden, E.	(See Joel Hill, heirs and representatives of.)											
Prudhomme, Antoine, and others.	Confirmation of title to land in Louisiana.	20	1	Petition	368	Priv. Land Claims.				Discharged; laid on table.		
Prudhomme, Antoine, and others.	Confirmation of title to land in Louisiana.	20	2	Petition	34	Priv. Land Claims.				Discharged; laid on table.		
Prudhomme, Antonie, and others.	Confirmation of title to land in Louisiana.	21	1	Petition	40	Priv. Land Claims.	31	Report and bill	44	Passed	Passed	App'd Mar. 23, 1830
Prudhomme, Emanuel	Confirmation of title to land	26	1	Petition	365	Priv. Land Claims.						
Prudhomme, Jean Baptiste, widow of.	Confirmation of title to land	25	2	Petition	373	Priv. Land Claims.				Discharged; laid on table.		
Prudhomme, Jean Baptiste, widow of.	Confirmation of title to land	25	3	Petition	134	Priv. Land Claims.	145	Report and bill	1013	Passed	Passed	App'd March 3, 1839
Prudhomme, Rosalie	(See Jean Baptiste Prudhomme, widow of.)	25	2		373							
Pruett, William	Pension	14	1	Petition	42	Pens. & Rev. Cl'ms.				Disch'd; laid on table.		
Pruit, Martin	Revolutionary pension	22	1	Petition	36	Rev. Pensions.						
Pruitt, Solomon	Revolutionary pension	23	1	Petition	379	Rev. Pensions.						
Pryor, Green, for self and heirs of Peter Pryor.	Patent for lands sold by United States, and for which they have made payment.	20	1	Petition	367	Priv. Land Claims.				Discharged; laid on table.		
Pryor, Green, for self and heirs of Peter Pryor.	Patent for lands sold by United States, and for which they have made payment.	21	1	Petition	100	Public Lands	May 5, 1830	Adverse		Laid on table.		
Pryor, Green, for self and heirs of Peter Pryor.	Patent for lands sold by United States, and for which they have made payment.	21	2	Petition	56	Public Lands	Dec. 29, 1830	Adverse		Laid on table.		

List of private claims presented to the House of Representatives of the United States from the 1st to the 31st Congress, inclusive—Continued.

Names of claimants.	Nature or object of the claim.	Congress.	Session.	How brought before the House of Reps.	Page of journal.	To what committee of the House referred.	No. or date of the report.	Nature of the report.	No. of the bill.	How disposed of by the House of Reps.	How disposed of by the Senate.	Date of the act of Congress, and remarks.
Pryor, Green, for self and heirs of Peter Pryor.	Patent for lands sold by United States, and for which they have made payment.	23	1	Petition	75	Priv. Land Claims.						
Pryor, Green, for self and heirs of Peter Pryor.	Patent for lands sold by United States, and for which they have made payment.	23	2	Petition	49	Public Lands.						
Pryor, Green, for self and heirs of Peter Pryor.	Patent for lands sold by United States, and for which they have made payment.	24	1	Petition	59	Public Lands.	284	Report and bill	287	Referred to Committee Whole House.		
Pryor, Green, for self and heirs of Peter Pryor.	Patent for lands sold by United States, and for which they have made payment.	24	2	House bill	200	Whole House.....	Jan. 13, 1837	With't amend.	287	Passed	Passed	App'd March 3, 1837
Pryor, Green..........	Confirmation of title to land.....	22	2	Petition	219							
Pryor, Nathaniel, representatives of.	Indian depredations	26	2	Senate bill	229	Claims	....	....	S. 143			
Pryor, Nathaniel, representatives of.	Indian depredations	27	2	Senate bill	782	Indian Affairs.....	June 1, 1842	With't amend.	52	Referred to Committee Whole House.		
Pryor, Norton	For arrears of interest on money loaned United States.	2	2	Petition	636	....	....	....	.....	Laid on table.		
Pryor, Peter, heirs of	(See Green Pryor, for self and heirs of.)	20	1	....	367							
Puckett, Benjamin.......	Compensation for services in revolutionary war.	19	2	Petition	84	Rev. Claims.						
Puckett, Benjamin.......	Compensation for services in revolutionary war.	22	2	Petition	74	Claims	Jan. 4, 1833	Adverse	.....	Laid on table.		
Puckett, Benjamin.......	Revolutionary pension..........	21	2	Resolution	85	Military Pensions.						
Puckett, Benjamin.......	Revolutionary pension..........	24	1	Petition	213	Rev. Pensions.						
Puckett, Charles J.......	Pre-emption right to land	23	2	Petition	241	Public Lands.						
Puckett, William........	Invalid pension................	23	1	Petition	308	Invalid Pensions.						
Pue, Edward	(See Richard Ridgely)..........	13	3	....	679							
Pugh, David	(See Robert Watkins, heirs of the widow of.)	29	1	....	340							
Pugh, Littlejohn	Indemnity for costs of suit about Roanoke light-house.	26	1	Petition	621	Claims.						
Pugh, William, heirs of ..	Compensation for property destroyed by enemy in revolutionary war.	23	1	Petition	494	Rev. Claims.						
Pugh, William, heirs of ..	Compensation for property destroyed by enemy in revolutionary war.	23	2	Petition	77	Rev. Claims.						
Pugh, William, heirs of ..	Compensation for property destroyed by enemy in revolutionary war.	24	2	Memorial	215	Rev. Claims.						
Pugh, William, heirs of ..	Compensation for property destroyed by enemy in revolutionary war.	25	2	Petition	49	Rev. Claims......	621	Adverse	.....	Laid on table.		
Puig, John.............	(See Puscareo & Puig).........	27	3	....	285							
Puitzman, Isaac, sureties of.	Release from bond as postmaster..	31	2	Petition	192	P. Of. & P. Roads.						
Pulah, Francis..........	Payment of claim against Ottowa Indians.	29	1	Petition	160	Indian Affairs.....	287	Adverse	.....	Laid on table.		
Pullan, Rich'd and Charles A.	Remission of forfeiture of goods ..	14	2	Petition	136	....	....	....	.....	Referred to Secretary Treasury.		
Pulliam, Thomas........	Confirmation of title to land	26	1	Petition	365	Priv. Land Claims.						
Pulsifer, David, and others.	Release of cargo of ship Restitution.	12	2	Petition	552	Ways and Means..	....	....	.....	Discharged; laid on table.	....	See act Feb. 27, 1813
Pulsifer, Joseph.	Arrears of pension.............	26	1	Petition	198	Invalid Pensions ..	569	Adverse	.....	Laid on table.		
Pulsifer, Joseph.........	Arrears of pension.............	27	2	Petition	47	Invalid Pensions ..	436	Adverse	.....	Laid on table.		

List of private claims presented to the House of Representatives of the United States form the 1st to the 31st Congress, inclusive—Continued.

Names of claimants.	Nature or object of the claim.	Congress.	Session.	How brought before the House of Reps.	Page of journal.	To what committee of the House referred.	No. or date of the report.	Nature of the report.	No. of the bill.	How disposed of by the House of Reps.	How disposed of by the Senate.	Date of the act of Congress, and remarks.
Pulsifer, Joseph	Arrears of pension	29	1	Petition	107	Invalid Pensions	174	Adverse		Laid on table.		
Pumphrey, William	Confirmation of title to land	28	2	Petition	327	Priv. Land Claims				Discharged; laid on table.		
Punch, John Smith, sureties of.	Exemption from payment of bond to United States.	24	1	Petition	762	Judiciary				Discharged; laid on table.		
Puntenny, Nancy, (Ind.)	Grant of land on which she resides.	19	1	Petition	102	Priv. Land Claims	Jan. 5, 1826	Adverse		Laid on table.		
Purcel, Dennis, (Pursell)	Compensation for a boat taken for use of revolutionary army.	11	2	Petition	145	Claims	Mar. 14, 1810	Adverse		Rejected.		
Purcel, Dennis, (Pursell)	Compensation for a boat taken for use of revolutionary army.	12	1	Petition	110	Claims.						
Purcel, Dennis, (Pursell)	Compensation for a boat taken for use of revolutionary army.	24	1	Petition	924	Claims.						
Purcel, Dennis, (Pursell)	Compensation for a boat taken for use of revolutionary army.	24	2	Petition	91	Rev. Claims.						
Purcel, Dennis, (Pursell)	Compensation for a boat taken for use of revolutionary army.	25	2	Petition	82	Rev. Claims				Discharged; laid on table.		
Purcel, Dennis, (Pursell)	Compensation for a boat taken for use of revolutionary army.	26	1	Petition	166	Rev. Claims	624	Adverse		Laid on table.		
Purcell, Dennis	Compensation for a boat taken for use of revolutionary army.	28	1	Petition	79	Rev. Claims.						
Purcell, Dennis	Compensation for a boat taken for use of revolutionary army.	30	1	Petition	664	Rev. Claims	793	Adverse		Laid on table.		
Purcell, George, heirs of	Allowance of amount due as lieutenant revolutionary army to close of the war.	27	3	Petition	257	Rev. Claims	248	Adverse		Laid on table.		
Purcell, Henry D., heirs of	Commutation of half-pay	25	2	Petition	69	Rev. Claims	867	Adverse		Laid on table.		
Purcell, Pierce	Compensation for a fence taken for use of the army.	13	3	Petition	729	Claims				Discharged; laid on table.		
Purcell, William	Compensation for two horses lost in military service United States.	14	1	Petition	355	Claims				Discharged; laid on table.		
Purcell, William	Compensation for two horses lost in military service United States.	23	1	Senate bill	845	Claims	558	Adverse	S. 128	Rejected.		
Purcell, William	Compensation for two horses lost in military service United States.	24	1	Petition	430	Claims.						
Purcell, William	Compensation for two horses lost in military service United States.	24	2	Petition	368	Claims	268	Adverse		Laid on table.		
Purcell, William	Compensation for two horses lost in military service United States.	25	2	Petition	121	Claims				Discharged; laid on table.		
Purcell, William	Compensation for two horses lost in military service United States.	27	2	Petition	745	Claims.						
Purcell, William F., *et al.*	(See Henry D. Purcell's heirs)	25	2		69							
Purcell, William F	(See Andrew Russell's heirs)	29	1		218							
Purdon, Richard B	(See attorney for the heirs of John Sevier.)	15	1		184							
Purdon & Storkes	(See Stokes & Purdon)	27	2		129							
Purdon, Richard D	For the benefits of the acts in relation to purchasers of public lands.	19	1	Petition	252					Referred to Committee Whole House on bill No. 32.		Leave to withdraw.
Purdon, Richard D	For the benefit of the acts in relation to purchasers of public lands.	19	2	Petition	113	Public Lands.						
Purdy, Daniel	Pension	21	2	Petition	43	Military Pensions.						

List of private claims presented to the House of Representatives of the United States from the 1st to the 31st Congress, inclusive—Continued.

Names of claimants.	Nature or object of the claim.	Congress.	Session.	How brought before the House of Reps.	Page of journal.	To what committee of the House referred.	No. or date of the report.	Nature of the report.	No. of the bill.	How disposed of by the House of Reps.	How disposed of by the Senate.	Date of the act of Congress, and remarks.
Purdy, Daniel	Pension	22	1	Petition	67	Military Pensions	51	Favorable; bill	104	Passed.		
Purdy, Elijah	Bounty land for services in late war.	25	2	Petition	577	Military Affairs				Discharged; laid on table.		
Purdy, Jacob	Relief from loss of continental certificate taken from him by the enemy.	1	2	Petition	186					Referred to Secretary Treasury.		
Purdy, Nathaniel	Bounty land for services in late war.	25	2	Petition	577	Military Affairs				Discharged; laid on table.		
Purdy, Robert	For costs of suit against him for official acts.	15	1	Senate bill	183	Claims	Mar. 4, 1818	Adverse		Rejected.		
Purdy, Robert	For costs of suit against him for official acts.	16	1	Senate bill	269	Claims	Mar. 16, 1826	Adverse	S. 43	Laid on table.		
Purdy, Robert	For costs of suit against him for official acts.	16	2	Petition	115	Military Affairs	Jan. 12, 1821	With amend's.	S. 2	Indef. postponed.		
Purdy, Robert	For costs of suit against him for official acts.	17	1	Petition	129	Military Affairs	Jan. 28, 1822	By bill	60	Laid on table.		
Purdy, Robert	For costs of suit against him for official acts.	17	2	Senate bill	106	Military Affairs	Jan. 15, 1823	With amend's.	S. 17	Passed	Passed	App'd March 3, 1823
Purit, Archibald	Revolutionary pension	29	2	Petition	387	Rev. Pensions.						
Purkill, Jacob	Compensation for a slave impressed into service of United States and lost to owner.	15	2	Senate bill	302	Claims	Feb. 27, 1819	Adverse	S. 41	Referred to Committee Whole House.		
Purkill, Jacob	Compensation for a slave impressed into service of United States and lost to owner.	16	1	Petition	46	Claims	Jan. 6, 1820	Adverse		Rejected.		
Purkill, Jacob	Compensation for a slave impressed into service of United States and lost to owner.	20	1	Petition	51	Claims	Dec. 19, 1827	Adverse		Laid on table.		
Purkill, Jacob	Compensation for a slave impressed into service of United States and lost to owner.	21	1	Petition	128	Claims				Discharged; laid on table.		
Purkis, Robert	Compensation for capturing four prisoners of war.	13	3	Petition	720	Naval Affairs.						
Purkis, Robert	Compensation for capturing four prisoners of war.	28	2	Senate bill	469	Claims			S. 138			
Purkis, Robert	Compensation for recapturing a vessel taken by the enemy.	29	2	Senate bill	375	Claims	Feb. 26, 1847	With't amend.	S. 89	Referred to Committee Whole House.		
Purkis, Robert	Compensation for recapturing a vessel taken by the enemy.	30	1	Senate bill	814	Claims	May 30, 1848	With't amend.	S. 21	Passed		App'd Aug. 14, 1848
Purnell, John	(See Burnell Boyce's heirs)	22	1		42							
Purse, Agnes	(See James Purse's widow.)	25	2		87							
Purse, James, widow of	Relief—husband and son killed in battle at Buffalo.	25	2	Petition	87	Claims				Discharged; laid on table.		
Purse, James, widow of	Relief—husband and son killed in battle at Buffalo.	26	1	Petition	170	Claims.						
Purtle, Jacob	(See Jacob Purkill)	15	2		302							
Purviance, John	Revolutionary pension	22	1	Resolution	535	Rev. Pensions.				Discharged; laid on table.		
Purvis, James, executors of.	Benefit of act of July 5, 1832, for payment of Virginia claims.	22	2	Petition	96	Select.						
Purvis, James, executors of.	Commutation of half-pay for revolutionary services.	23	1	Petition	188	Rev. Claims.						

List of private claims presented to the House of Representatives of the United States from the 1st to the 31st Congress, inclusive—Continued.

Names of claimants.	Nature or object of the claim.	Congress.	Session.	How brought before the House of Reps.	Page of journal.	To what committee of the House referred.	No. or date of the report.	Nature of the report.	No. of the bill.	How disposed of by the House of Reps.	How disposed of by the Senate.	Date of the act of Congress, and remarks.
Purvis, James, executors of.	Commutation of half-pay for revolutionary services.	24	1	Petition	942	Rev. Claims.						
Purvis, James, executors of.	Commutation of half-pay for revolutionary services.	24	2	Petition	92	Rev. Claims	295	Favorable; bill	964	Referred to Committee Whole House.		
Purvis, James, executors of.	Commutation of half-pay for revolutionary services.	25	2	Petition	40	Rev. Claims	135	Favorable; bill	153	Passed	Reported without amend't.	
Purvis, James, executors of.	Commutation of half-pay for revolutionary services.	25	3	Petition	84	Rev. Claims	23	Favorable; bill	921	Referred to Committee Whole House.		
Purvis, James, executors of.	Commutation of half-pay for revolutionary services.	26	1	Petition	165	Rev. Claims.						
Purvis, James, executors of.	Commutation of half-pay for revolutionary services.	26	2	Petition	36	Rev. Claims	80	Adverse		Laid on table.		
Puscareo & Puig	Refunding tonnage duties on Spanish brig Restourador.	27	3	Petition	285	Commerce.						
Puscareo & Puig	Refunding tonnage duties on Spanish brig Restourador.	29	1	Petition	436	Commerce	371	Favorable; bill	389	Referred to Committee Whole House.		
Puscareo & Puig	Refunding tonnage duties on Spanish brig Restourador.	30	1	Petition	235	Commerce	123	Favorable; bill	113	Passed.		
Puscareo & Puig	Refunding tonnage duties on Spanish brig Restourador.	30	2	House bill from Senate.	283						Passed	App'd Feb. 1, 1849
Pushee, David	Revolutionary pension	22	1	Petition	533	Rev. Claims				Disch'd; laid on table		
Putnam, Aaron	Patent for improvement in distilleries.	1	2	Petition	149	Select.						
Putnam, Benjamin	Compensation for services in late war.	21	2	Petition	90	Claims.						
Putnam, Daniel	Pension	20	2	Petition	26	Military Pensions	Jan. 15, 1829	Adverse		Laid on table.		
Putnam, David, widow and heirs of.	Compensation for services in revolutionary war.	11	3	Petition	444	Claims	Dec. 29, 1810	Adverse		Rejected.		
Putnam, Edward	Revolutionary pension	26	1	Petition	706	Rev. Pensions	537	Favorable; bill	436	Referred to Committee Whole House.		
Putnam, Edward	Revolutionary pension	27	2	Petition	390	Rev. Pensions	784	Adverse		Laid on table.		
Putnam, Garret	Compensation for services as guide in revolutionary war.	5	3	Petition	434	Claims	Jan. 23, 1799	Adverse		Rejected.		
Putnam, Garret'	Compensation for services as guide in revolutionary war.	16	2	Petition	212	Pens. & Rev. Cl'ms.	Feb. 16, 1821	Adverse		Laid on table.		
Putnam, Garret	Revolutionary pension	16	1	Resolution	63	Rev. Pensions	Jan. 14, 1820	Adverse		Laid on table.		
Putnam, Garret	(See administrator of Abr. Garrison.)	18	1		315							
Putnam, Henry	Payment for a horse lost in service of United States.	27	2	Petition	883	Claims.						
Putnam, Henry	Payment for a horse lost in service of United States.	27	3	Petition	73	Claims	108	Adverse		Laid on table.		
Putnam, Howard	Pension	21	2	Resolution	209	Military Pensions.						
Putnam, Jesse	Compensation for services in revolutionary war.	23	1	Petition	110	Rev. Pensions	Jan. 23, 1834	Adverse		Laid on table.		
Putnam, Justice	Revolutionary pension	24	1	Petition	296	Rev. Pensions				Discharged; laid on table.		
Putnam, Nathan	Pension	3	1	Rep. of Secretary War.	131	Select	May 26, 1794	Favorable; bill	62	Passed	Passed	App'd June 7, 1794
Putnam, Nathan	Increase of pension	8	2	Petition	138	Claims.						
Putnam, Nathan	Increase of pension	9	1	Petition	191	Claims	Mar. 28, 1806	Res'n to postpone; leave to withdraw.		Resolution adopted.		

List of private claims presented to the House of Representatives of the United States from the 1st to the 31st Congress, inclusive—Continued.

Names of claimants.	Nature or object of the claim.	Congress.	Session.	How brought before the House of Reps.	Page of journal.	To what committee of the House referred.	No. or date of the report.	Nature of the report.	No. of the bill.	How disposed of by the House of Reps.	How disposed of by the Senate.	Date of the act of Congress, and remarks.
Putnam & Pratt	Refunding duties paid on wool	22	1	Petition	383	Ways and Means				Disch'd; laid on table.		
Putnam, Perley	(See John Saunders and Perley Putnam.)	24	1		51							
Putnam, Rebecca	(See David Putnam's widow, and heirs of.)	11	3		444							
Putnam, Rufus	Compensation for clothing, supplies and services in revolutionary war.	10	1	Petition	241					Referred to Committee Whole House on bill No. 20.		
Putnam, Rufus	(See Ohio Company of Associates)											
Putnam, Samuel	For proceeds of sale of cotton found on the high seas.	11	1	Petition	37	Claims.						
Putnam, William	(See heir of William Scott)	26	1		332							
Putney, Asa	Pension	3	2	Rep. of Secretary War.	278	Claims	Feb. 28, 1795	Favorable; bill	130	Passed	Postponed.	
Putney, Asa	Pension	4	1	Rep. of Secretary War.	445	Claims	Feb. 18, 1796	Favorable; bill	156	Passed	Passed	App'd April 20, 1796
Putney, Caleb	Pension	14	1	Petition	99					Referred to Secretary War.		
Putney, John	Pension	20	1	Petition	68	Military Pensions	Feb. 13, 1828	By bill	166	Passed.		
Putney, John	Pension	20	2	House bill	55	Whole House	Jan. 15, 1829	With amend'ts	311	Passed	Laid on table.	
Putney, John	Pension	21	1	Petition	48	Military Pensions	Jan. 5, 1830	By bill	72	Passed	Passed	App'd May 20, 1830
Putney, True, and Hugh Riddle.	Compensation for losses in erecting a public warehouse in Baltimore.	27	3	Petition	153	Claims.						
Putney, True, and Hugh Riddle.	Compensation for losses in erecting a public warehouse in Baltimore.	28	1	Petition	100	Commerce	288	Favorable; bill	200	Passed	Passed	App'd June 17, 1844
Putney, True, and Hugh Riddle.	Re-examination of their accounts	28	2	Senate joint resolution.	515				R. 25	Referred to Committee Whole House.		
Putney, True, and Hugh Riddle.	Re-examination of their accounts	29	1	Senate joint resolution.	859	Claims	692	Favorable	R. 14	Passed	Passed	App'd Aug. 4, 1846
Putney, Thomas	Pension	20	1	Petition	223	Military Pensions	April 29, 1828	By bill	283	Passed.		
Putney, Thomas	Pension	20	2	House bill	55	Whole House	Jan. 15, 1829	Favorable	311	Passed	Laid on table.	
Putney, Thomas	Pension	21	1	Petition	47	Military Pensions	Jan. 5, 1830	Favorable	72	Passed	Passed	App'd May 20, 5830
Pye, Edward	Refunding money paid as surety of Edward Sangster.	21	2	Petition	303	P. Of. & P. Roads.						
Pye, Edward	Refunding money paid as surety of Edward Sangster.	22	1	Petition	582	P. Of. & P. Roads.						
Pyke, Abraham	Invalid pension	2	1	Petition	451					Referred to Secretary War.		
Pyke, Abraham	Invalid pension	3	1	Rep. of Secretary War.	131	Select	May 26, 1794	Jt. res. to refer to Sec. War.	R. 12	Passed	Passed	App'd June 9, 1794
Pyke, Abraham	Invalid pension	4	1	Rep. of Secretary War.	445	Claims	Mar. 4, 1796	J't. res. to refer to Sec. War.	R. 16	Passed	Passed	App'd April 18, 1796
Pyke, William	Renewal of patent for lock	22	1	Petition	632	Patent laws	June 22, 1823	Adverse		Laid on table.		
Pyles, Joseph	Pension	19	1	Petition	57	Rev. Claims	April 28, 1826	Adverse		Laid on table.		
Pyles, Joseph	Pension	20	2	Petition	203	Military Pensions				Discharged; laid on table.		
Pynchen, E. E.	Indemnity for two negroes killed in United States service.	28	1	Petition	610	Claims.						

List of private claims presented to the House of Representatives of the United States from the 1st *to the* 31st *Congress, inclusive*—Continued.

Names of claimants.	Nature or object of the claim.	Congress.	Session.	How brought before the House of Reps.	Page of journal.	To what committee of the House referred.	No. or date of the report.	Nature of the report.	No. of the bill.	How disposed of by the House of Reps.	How disposed of by the Senate.	Date of the act of Congress, and remarks.
Quackenboss, David C.	Revolutionary pension	23	1	Petition	419	Rev. Pensions				Discharged; laid on table.		
Quackenboss, David C.	Revolutionary pension	24	1	Petition	753	Rev. Pensions				Discharged; laid on table.		
Quackenboss, John H.	Revolutionary pension	23	1	Petition	418	Rev. Pensions				Discharged; laid on table.		
Quackenboss, John H.	Revolutionary pension	24	1	Petition	753	Rev. Pensions				Discharged; laid on table.		
Quackenboss, Mangle M., and others.	Release from liability as surety of Samuel Swartwout.	29	1	Senate bill	388	Judiciary	Mar. 14, 1846	With't amend.	S. 10	Recommitted.		
Quackenboss, Mangle M., and others.	Release from liability as surety of Samuel Swartwout.	30	1	Senate bill	683	Judiciary			S. 4			
Quackenboss, Mangle M., and others.	Release from liability as surety of Samuel Swartwout.	30	2	Senate bill	545	Judiciary	Feb 28, 1849	With't amend.	S. 4	Referred to Committee Whole House.		
Quackenboss, Mangle M., and others.	Release from liability as surety of Samuel Swartwout.	31	1	Senate bill	591	Judiciary	May 22, 1850	With't amend.	S. 125	Referred to Committee Whole House.		
Quackenbush, James	Revolutionary pension	25	2	Petition	629	Rev. Pensions.						
Quackenbush, James	Revolutionary pension	26	1	Petition	830	Rev. Pensions				Discharged; laid on table.		
Quackenbush, Rindert	For wood furnished United States army, revolutionary war.	4	1	Rep. of Secretary Treasury.	388	Claims	May 31, 1796	Adverse		Laid on table.		
Quait, William	Pension	31	1	Petition	731	Rev. Pensions	366	Adverse		Laid on table.		
Quait, William	Pension	31	2	Petition	110	Invalid Pensions.						
Quaker, U. States schooner, representatives of officers, &c., of.	Arrears of pay and six months' extra pay.	21	1	Senate bill	685				S. 158	Referred to Committee Whole House.		
Quantrill, Thomas	Pension, war of 1812	26	1	Petition	325	Invalid Pensions.						
Quantrill, Thomas	Pension, war of 1812	28	1	Petition	272	Invalid Pensions	Feb. 1, 1844	Adverse		Laid on table		Leave to withd'w, 31st Cong., 2d session.
Quarles, James	Depreciation of revolutionary pay and for pension.	3	1	Petition	62	Select	Mar. 24, 1794	Fovorable, in part.		Laid on table.		
Quarles, James	Commutation of revolutionary pay and depreciation.	3	1	Petition	100					Laid on table.		
Quarles, James	Revolutionary pension	10	2	Petition	352	Claims				Discharged.		Leave to withdraw.
Quarles, James, heirs and representatives of.	Commutation of half-pay	22	2	Petition	54	Rev. Claims.						
Quarles, James, heirs and representatives of.	Commutation of half pay	23	1	Petition	54	Rev. Claims	75	Adverse		Laid on table.		
Quarles, Martha	(See Robert Quarles, widow of.)	23	1		306							
Quarles, Robert, widow of.	Commutation pay	23	1	Petition	306	Rev. Claims.						
Quarles, Robert, widow of.	Commutation pay	23	2	Petition	55	Rev. Claims.						
Quarles, Robert, widow of.	Commutation pay	24	1	Report of Commissioners.	800	Rev. Claims	639	Adverse		Laid on table.		
Quarles, Robert, widow of.	Commutation pay	25	2	Petition	49	Rev. Claims	Jan. 10, 1838	Adverse		Laid on table.		
Quarles, R. G.	(See Drake & Quarles.)	27	3		141							
Quarles, Roger, and Richard Drummond, *et al.*, owners of the privateer Roger.	Bounty for capture of British prisoners.	14	1	Petition	587	Judiciary	April 6, 1816	Favorable; bill ordered.		Passed.	Passed	App'd April 29, 1816
Quarles, Roger	(See Richard Drummond, *et al.*)	20	1		195							
Quarles, Samuel	Compensation for extra mail service.	26	1	Petition	342	P. Of. & P. Roads.						

3—18

List of private claims presented to the House of Representatives of the United States from the 1st to the 31st Congress, inclusive—Continued.

Names of claimants.	Nature or object of the claim.	Congress.	Session.	How brought before the House of Reps.	Page of journal.	To what committee of the House referred.	No. or date of the report.	Nature of the report.	No. of the bill.	How disposed of by the House of Reps.	How disposed of by the Senate.	Date of the act of Congress, and remarks.
Quarles, Samuel	Compensation for extra mail service.	26	2	Petition	263	P. Of. & P. Roads.	Feb. 12, 1841	Adverse		Laid on table.		
Quarles, Tunstall	(See James Porter and Turnstall Quarle..)	18	2		209							
Quarles, Wharton, administrator of.	Commutation of half-pay	24	1	Petition	105	Rev. Claims	Jan. 19, 1836	Adverse		Recommitted.		
							June 2, 1836	Suplementary report.	674	Referred to Committee Whole House.		
Quarles, Wharton, administrator of.	Commutation of half-pay	25	2	Petition	40	Rev. Claims	106	Report and bill	123	Passed	Passed	App'd July 9, 1838
Quartermasters general's department, clerks of.	For increased compensation	24	1	Documents.	118	Military Affairs.	81	Favorable; bill	97	Referred to Committee Whole House.		
Quenaudon, D. V	For grant of land in Oregon for the purpose of establishing a military colony.	29	2	Memorial	246	Territories.						
Quenaudon, D. V	For grant of land in Oregon for the purpose of establishing a military coloney.	30	2	Petition	146	Military Affairs.						
Queret, Pierre	(See Louis Mallet and others.)	12	2		609							
Querry, William	Revolutionary pension	28	1	Petition	322	Rev. Pensions.						
Quertier, A. and Albert	To re-export cards free of duty	25	2	Memorial	232	Ways and Means	Jan. 20, 1838	Report by bill.	443	Passed	Passed	App'd July 7, 1838
Quick, George	Pension	23	1	Petition	308	Invalid Pensions	June 28, 1834	Adverse		Laid on table.		
Quick, George	Pension	24	2	Petition	398	Invalid Pensions.						
Quick, Jacob, and Jacob Sluyter, assignee of.	Bounty land for services in revolutionary war.	17	2	Petition	91	Rev. Claims.						
Quick, James	Pension	21	2	Petition	120	Military Pensions				Discharged; laid on table.		
Quick, James	Pension	22	1	Petition	90	Rev. Pensions				Discharged; laid on table.		
Quick, Lewis	Revolutionary pension	26	1	Petition	830	Rev. Pensions				Discharged; laid on table.		
Quigley, Barnabas	Pension	16	1	Petition	95	Pens. & Rev. Cl'ms.	Jan. 14, 1820	Adverse		Rejected.		
Quigley, William	Revolutionary pension	11	2	Petition	248	Claims	Mar. 14, 1810	Adverse		Laid on table.		
Quimby, Diadame S. L.	(See James Quimby, widow of)	17	1		188							
Quimby, James, widow of.	Relief; husband died of wounds received in battle.	17	1	Petition	188	Priv. Land Claims.				Discharged; laid on table.		
Quinn, Benjamin, widow of.	Pension	26	1	Petition	386	Rev. Pensions.	664	Adverse		Laid on table.		
Quinn, Edward	Naval pension	29	2	Petition	180	Naval Affairs	61	Favorable; bill	666	Referred to Committee Whole House.		
Quinn, Edward	Naval pension	30	1	Petition	81	Naval Affairs	17	Favorable; bill	20	Passed.		
Quinn, Edward	Naval pension	30	2	House bill from Senate.	279						Passed	App'd Jan. 29, 1849
Quinn, Franky	(See Benjamin Quinn, widow of)	26	1		386							
Quin, John, sailingmaster U. S. navy.	Full pay and rations from date of appointment to date of orders to Pensacola station.	24	1	Petition	1101	Claims.						
Quin, John, sailingmaster U. S. navy.	Full pay and rations from date of appointment to date of orders to Pensacola station.	24	2	Petition	37	Claims	33	Adverse		Laid on table.		
Quin, John	(See Stephen Decatur, widow of)	20	1		295							
Quin, Michael	Relief for injuries received in erection of fortification at Newport.	24	1	Petition	51	Invalid Pensions	Feb. 11, 1836	Adverse		Referred to Committee Whole House.		

List of private claims presented to the House of Representatives of the United States from the 1st to the 31st Congress, inclusive—Continued.

Names of claimants.	Nature or object of the claim.	Congress.	Session.	How brought before the House of Reps.	Page of journal.	To what committee of the House referred.	No. or date of the report.	Nature of the report.	No. of the bill.	How disposed of by the House of Reps.	How disposed of by the Senate.	Date of the act of Congress, and remarks.
Qninn, Thomas F., assignee of soldiers.	Payment for money due soldiers for services in late war.	18	2	Petition	229	Claims.						
Quinby, Elizabeth U.	Payment for lumber furnished United States by her father.	31	1	Petition	1240	Claims.						
Quinby, Samuel	Payment for extra services as receiver of public moneys.	25	2	Petition	919	Public Lands				Discharged.		
Quincy, Academy	(See Florida)	27	3		237							
Quincy, Charles E. and William J.	Payment of a debenture certificate.	20	1	Resolution	202	Ways and Means	161	Report and bill	188	Passed.		
Quincy, Charles E. and William J.	Payment of a debenture certificate.	20	2	Petition	25	Ways and Means	Dec. 10, 1828	Report by bill.	306	Referred to Committee Whole House.		
Quincy, Charles E. and William J.	Payment of a debenture certificate.	21	1	Petition	142	Ways and Means	Feb. 15, 1830	Report by bill.	246	Referred to Committee Whole House.		
Quincy, Charles E. and William J.	Payment of a debenture certificate.	21	2	Report and bill of last session.	265	Whole House	Feb. 4, 1831	With't amend.	246	Passed.		
Quincy, Charles E. and William J.	Payment of a debenture certificate.	22	2	Petition	24	Ways and Means	Dec. 15, 1831	Report and bill.	3	Passed	Passed	App'd Jan. 18, 1832
Quincy, Marcus, and William Gorham.	Reimbursement of foreign duties paid on brig Neptune.	22	2	Petition	73	Commerce	Dec. 26, 1832	Report by bill.	640	Referred to Committee Whole House.		
Quincy, Marcus, and William Gorham.	Reimbursement of foreign duties paid on brig Neptune.	23	1	Petition	58	Commerce	Jan. 24, 1834	Report and bill.	235	Referred to Committee Whole House.		
Quincy, Marcus, and William Gorham.	Reimbursement of foreign duties paid on brig Neptune.	23	2	House bill	82	Whole House	Dec. 15, 1835	With't amend.	235	Passed.		
Quincy, Marcus, and William Gorham.	Refunding forfeiture for violating revenue laws.	25	2	Petition	199	Commerce	305	Report and bill	342	Referred to Committee Whole House.		
Quincy, Marcus, and William Gorham.	Refunding forfeiture for violating revenue laws.	25	3	House bill of last session.	377	Whole House			342	Passed	Adverse report.	
Quincy, Marcus, and William Gorham.	Refunding forfeiture for violating revenue laws.	26	1	Petition	176	Commerce.						
Quinlivan, Dennis	Compensation for horse lost	26	1	Senate bill	1105	Claims			S. 145			
Quinton, John	Revolutionary pension	3	1	Petition	840	Rev. Pensions.						
Quinton, Samuel	Revolutionary pension	31	2	Petition	447	Rev. Pensions	73	Adverse		Laid on table.		
Quirk, Major Thomas, widow of.	Pension	26	1	Petition	808	Rev. Pensions.						
Quirk, Major Thomas, widow of.	Pension	27	2	Petition	153	Rev. Pensions	May 24, 1842	Adverse		Laid on table.		
Quivy, Asa, or Quiry	Pension	20	1	Petition	30	Military Pensions	Feb. 13, 1828	By bill	166	Passed.		
Quivy, Asa, or Quiry	Pension	20	2	House bill	55	Whole House	Dec. 23, 1828	With amends.	311	Passed	Laid on table.	
Quivy, Asa, or Quiry	Pension	21	1	Petition	48	Military Pensions	Jan. 5, 1830	By bill	72	Passed	Passed	App'd May 20, 1830

List of private claims presented to the House of Representatives of the United States from the 1st to the 31st Congress, inclusive—Continued.

Names of claimants.	Nature or object of the claim.	Congress.	Session.	How brought before the House of Reps.	Page of journal.	To what committee of the House referred.	No. or date of the report.	Nature of the report.	No. of the bill.	How disposed of by the House of Reps.	How disposed of by the Senate.	Date of the act of Congress, and remarks.
Raab, Christian	Remedy for purchase of a fraudulent land warrant.	31	2	Petition	107	Priv. Land Claims.						
Rabb, James	Compensation for horses taken for public use.	16	1	Petition	288	Claims	Mar. 31, 1820	Adverse	......	Laid on table.		
Rabb, James	Compensation for horses taken for public use.	16	1	Resolution	443	Claims	April 26, 1820	Favorable	141	Passed	Passed	App'd May 15, 1820
Raberg, Andrew	Arrears of pay and pension for revolutionary services.	2	1	Petition	498	....	....	....	......	Referred to Secretary of War.		
Raborg, Mary	(See Conrad Eiselen, administrator of.)	26	1	....	182	....	343	....	319			
Race, John	Payment of claim against Ottowa Indians.	29	1	Memorial	160	Indian Affairs	287	Adverse	......	Laid on table.		
Rachal, Antoine Barthelemy.	Confirmation of title to land in Louisiana.	22	2	Petition	41	Priv. Land Claims.	53	Favorable	696	Referred to Committee Whole House.		
Rachal, Antoine Barthelemy.	Confirmation of title to land in Louisiana.	23	1	Petition	93	Priv. Land Claims.	Jan. 8, 1834	Adverse	......	Laid on table.		
Rachal, Barthelemy	Confirmation of title to land in Louisiana.	22	2	Petition	42	Priv. Land Claims.	53	Favorable	696	Referred to Committee Whole House.		
Rachal, Barthelemy	Confirmation of title to land in Louisiana.	23	1	Petition	93	Priv. Land Claims.	Jan. 8, 1834	Adverse	......	Laid on table.		
Rachal, Eloi J	Confirmation of title to land in Louisiana.	23	1	Petition	76	Priv. Land Claims.						
Rachal, Eloi J	Confirmation of title to land in Louisiana.	24	1	Petition	208	Priv. Land Claims.	240	Favorable	246	Referred to Committee Whole House.		
Rachal, Eloi J	Confirmation of title to land in Louisiana.	24	2	House bill	63	Whole House	....	....	246			
Rachal, Eloi J	Confirmation of title to land in Louisiana.	25	2	Petition	42	Priv. Land Claims.	653	Favorable	630	Referred to Committee Whole House.		
Rachal, Eloi J	Confirmation of title to land in Louisiana.	25	3	House bill	380	Whole House	Jan. 26, 1839	With amend.	630	Passed	Passed	App'd March 3, 1839
Rachal, Jean Baptiste Julian.	Confirmation of title to land in Louisiana.	22	2	Petition	42	Priv. Land Claims.	53	Favorable	696	Referred to Committee Whole House.		
Rachal, Jean Baptiste Julian.	Confirmation of title to land in Louisiana.	23	1	Petition	93	Priv. Land Claims.	Jan. 8, 1834	Adverse	......	Laid on table.		
Rachal, Julian	Confirmation of title to land in Louisiana.	22	2	Petition	41	Priv. Land Claims.	53	Favorable	696	Referred to Committee Whole House.		
Rachal, Julian	Confirmation of title to land in Louisiana.	23	1	Petition	76	Priv. Land Claims.	Jan. 8, 1834	Adverse	......	Laid on table.		
Racine, Athanasse	Confirmation of title to land in Arkansas.	22	1	House bill	421	Whole House	Feb. 28, 1832	Favorable	425	Passed	Passed	App'd June 25, 1832
Rack, John	(See executors of Wm. Stewart)	21	2	....	120							
Rackliff, James, and others.	Indemnity for loss of schooner Enterprise, condemned for breach of revenue laws.	20	1	Petition	162	Commerce.						
Radcliff, Joseph, (D. C.)	Compensation for timber furnished for United States navy, but which was burnt, before measurement, with the navy-yard, in 1814.	18	1	Petition	130	Claims	Feb. 25, 1824	Adverse	......	Laid on table.		
Radcliff, Joseph, (D. C.)	Compensation for timber furnished for United States navy, but which was burnt, before measurement, with the navy-yard, in 1814.	23	1	Petition	384	Claims	521	Adverse	......	Laid on table.		

List of private claims presented to the House of Representatives of the United States from the 1st to the 31st Congress, inclusive—Continued.

Names of claimants.	Nature or object of the claim.	Congress.	Session.	How brought before the House of Reps.	Page of journal.	To what committee of the House referred.	No. or date of the report.	Nature of the report.	No. of the bill.	How disposed of by the House of Reps.	How disposed of by the Senate.	Date of the act of Congress, and remarks.
Radcliff, Joseph, (D. C.)..	Compensation for timber furnished for United States navy, but which was burnt, before measurement, with the navy-yard, in 1814.	24	1	Petition	405	Claims.						
Radcliff, Joseph, (D. C.)..	Compensation for timber furnished for United States navy, but which was burnt, before measurement, with the navy-yard, in 1814.	24	2	Petition	81	Claims..........	266	Favorable....	954	Referred to Committee Whole House.		
Radcliff, Joseph, (D. C.)..	Compensation for timber furnished for United States navy, but which was burnt (before measurement) with the navy yard in 1814.	25	2	Petition	37	Claims	75	Favorable	87	Passed	Indef. postp'd.	
Radcliff, Joseph, (D. C.)..	Compensation for timber furnished for United States navy, but which was burnt (before measurement) with the navy yard in 1814.	31	1	Petition	467	Naval Affairs.....	540	Favorable....	370	Referred to Committee Whole House.		
Radcliff, William........	(See Isaac Lawrence, and others).	14	2	....	101							
Radcliff, William........	(See attorney of D. S. Kennedy, and others.)	15	2	....	209							
Radcliff, William........	Settlement of accounts for diplomatic services at Lima.	21	1	House bill	326	Foreign Affairs....	Feb. 28, 1830	Favorable....	275	Passed	Passed	App'd May 20, 1820
Radcliffe, William D.....	(See A. C. Bryan, and others)...	30	1	....	621							
Rady, Daniel	Revolutionary pension	12	1	Petition	57	Claims	June 8, 1812	Pension bill ..	138	Passed	Passed	App'd July 5, 1812
Ragan, Elizabeth........	(See Robert Ragan, widow of)...	28	1	....	218	....	101					
Ragan, John A	(See Francois Perien)	26	1	....	610							
Ragan, John A	(See Joseph Lauligne, assignees of)	26	1	....	1346							
Ragan, John A	Compensation as counsel in case of United States *vs.* J. Brooks.	29	1	Petition	101	Claims.						
Ragan, Richard, widow of.	Compensation for revolutionary services.	25	2	Petition	391	Rev. Pensions	819	Favorable....	759	Passed.		
Ragan, Richard, widow of.	Compensation for revolutionary services.	25	3	Petition	446	Rev. Pensions	251	Favorable....	1122	Referred to Committee Whole House.		
Ragan, Richard, widow of.	Compensation for revolutionary services.	26	1	Petition	172	Rev. Pensions.						
Ragan, Richard, widow of.	Compensation for revolutionary services.	28	2	Petition	328	Rev. Pensions.						
Ragan, Robert, widow of..	Compensation for services in war of 1812.	28	1	Petition	218	Invalid Pensions...	101	Adverse	......	Laid on table.		
Ragan, Samuel	Exchange of bounty land unfit for cultivation.	23	2	Petition	426	Priv. Land Claims.						
Ragland, Evan..........	Pension	10	2	House bill	499	Whole House.....	Jan. 30, 1809	Favorable....	158	Passed	Passed	App'd March 3, 1809
Ragsdale, Edward	(See William H. Bedford, agent, &c.)	28	1	....	262							
Ragsdale, Godfrey, widow of.	Continuation of pension for revolutionary services.	28	1	Petition	685	Rev. Pensions.						
Ragsdale, Samuel........	Compensation for corn furnished United States, war of 1812.	20	1	Petition	342	Claims	April 9, 1828	Adverse	......	Laid on table.		
Ragsdale, Samuel........	Compensation for provisions and for services in war of 1812.	27	2	Petition	703	Claims.						
Raguet, Condy, widow of.	Compensation for services while consul at Rio de Janeiro.	28	1	Petition	582	Foreign Affairs....	....	....	......	Discharged; laid on table.		
Raimbaux & Basmarin...	(See Basmarin & Raimbaux)...	21	2	....	245							

List of private claims presented to the House of Representatives of the United States from the 1st to the 31st Congress, inclusive—Continued.

Names of claimants.	Nature or object of the claim.	Congress.	Session.	How brought before the House of Reps.	Page of journal.	To what committee of the House referred.	No. or date of the report.	Nature of the report.	No. of the bill.	How disposed of by the House of Reps.	How disposed of by the Senate.	Date of the act of Congress, and remarks.
Raines, George	Pension for disabilities in war of 1812.	26	2	Petition	133	Invalid Pensions.						
Raines, George	Pension for disabilities in war of 1812.	27	1	Petition	108	Invalid Pensions.						
Raines, George	Pension for disabilities in war of 1812.	27	2	Petition	60	Invalid Pensions	160	Adverse	......	Laid on table.		
Raines, George	Pension for disabilities in war of 1812.	27	3	Petition	44	Invalid Pensions	25	Adverse	......	Laid on table.		
Raines, George	Pension for disabilities in war of 1812.	27	3	Petition, (2)	151	Invalid Pensions.						
Raines, Giles, heirs of	Commutation pay for revolutionary services.	25	3	Resolution	272	Rev. Claims.						
Raines, Giles, heirs of	Commutation pay for revolutionary services.	26	1	Petition	166	Rev. Claims.						
Raines, Giles, heirs of	Commutation pay for revolutionary services.	27	2	Petition	356	Rev. Claims	1086	Adverse	......	Laid on table.		
Raines, Richard	Pension for revolutionary services.	26	1	Petition	323	Rev. Pensions	....	....	......	Discharged; laid on table.		
Rainey, Stephen	Commutation pay for revolutionary services.	25	2	Petition	554	Rev. Claims.						
Rainey, Stephen	Commutation pay for revolutionary services.	26	1	Petition	166	Rev. Claims.						
Rake, Daniel P	(See Joseph F. Rake, heirs of.)	26	1	....	332							
Rake, Joseph F., heirs of	Change location of land warrant	26	1	Petition	332	Public Lands.						
Ralls, Isaac	Compensation for horses lost in public service.	16	2	Petition	181	Claims.						
Ralston, Ashbel & Girard	Remission of duty on railroad iron imported under act of May 28, 1830.	22	1	Petition	258	Ways and Means.						
Ralston, A. and G., & Co.	Refunding duties paid on railroad iron.	25	2	Petition	416	Ways and Means	Mar. 6, 1838	Favorable	606	Referred to Committee Whole House.		
Ralston, A. and G., & Co.	Refunding duties paid on railroad iron.	25	3	Petition	450	Com. and Manuf.						
Ralston, A. and G., & Co.	Remission of duties on railroad iron.	28	1	Petition	193	Ways and Means.						
Ralston, A. and G., & Co.	Remission of duties on railroad iron.	28	2	Petition	144	Ways and Means.						
Ralston, George, widow of	Compensation for services of husband as inspector at Philadelphia.	8	1	Petition	617	Claims	....	....	......	Postponed.		
Ralston, George, widow of	Compensation for services of husband as inspector at Philadelphia.	8	2	Petition	6	Claims	....	....	......	Laid on table	....	Leave to withdraw.
Ralston, Girard	(See A. and G. Ralston)	22	1	....	258							
Ralston, James H	Compensation for horse and gun lost in public services.	25	3	Senate bill	661	....	....	....	S. 127			
Ralston, Lewis	Indemnity for damages under treaty with Cherokees.	29	1	Petition	425	Judiciary.						
Ralston, Robert	(See assignee of Thomas Barclay.)	2	2	....	652							
Ralston, Samuel	Release from penalties for importing British goods.	12	2	Petition	684	Ways and Means	....	....	......	Discharged.		
Ralston, Samuel	Release from penalties for importing British goods.	13	1	Petition	24	Ways and Means.						
Ralston, Samuel	Release from penalties for importing Briting goods.	13	2	Petition	189	Ways and Means	Feb. 1, 1814	Favorable	102	Passed	Passed	App'd April 6, 1814
Ralston, Sarah	Compensation for two slaves drowned in public service.	26	1	Petition	338	Claims.						

List of private claims presented to the House of Representatives of the United States from the 1st to the 31st Congress, inclusive—Continued.

Names of claimants.	Nature or object of the claim.	Congress.	Session.	How brought before the House of Reps.	Page of journal.	To what committee of the House referred.	No. or date of the report.	Nature of the report.	No. of the bill.	How disposed of by the House of Reps.	How disposed of by the Senate.	Date of the act of Congress, and remarks.
Ralston, William	Compensation for services as chaplain in Mexico.	30	1	Petition	137	Claims	72	Favorable	54	Passed	Passed	App'd June 27, 1848
Ramay, J. administrator of.	Indemnity for French spoliations prior to 1800.	31	1	Petition	256	Foreign Affairs	355	Favorable	318	Referred to Committee Whole House.		
Rambo, Peter	Payment of money taken by the British at Fort Niagara.	21	1	Petition	170	Claims	Jan. 25, 1830	Adverse	......	Laid on table.		
Rambo, Peter	Payment of money taken by the British at Fort Niagara.	23	1	Petition	383	Claims	516	Adverse	......	Laid on table.		
Rambo, Peter	Payment of money taken by the British at Fort Niagara.	29	1	Petition	616	Claims	619	Adverse	......	Laid on table.		
Ramay, Catherine	Compensation for loss of a horse by her son killed in Mexico.	30	1	Petition	147	Claims	238	Favorable	238	Passed.		
Ramey, Edith	(See John Ramey, widow of.)	29	1	....	147							
Ramey, George	Confirmation of title to land in Missouri.	15	1	Petition	312	Priv. Land Claims.						
Ramey, George	Confirmation of title to land in Missouri.	16	1	Petition	71	Priv. Land Claims.						
Ramey, George	Confirmation of title to land in Missouri.	17	1	Petition	55	Public Lands.						
Ramey, George	Confirmation of title to land in Missouri.	18	1	Petition	55	Public Lands.						
Ramey, George	Confirmation of title to land in Missouri.	29	1	Petition	588	Public Lands	585	Favorable	403	Referred to Committee Whole House.		
Ramey, George	Confirmation of title to land in Missouri.	29	2	House bill	211	....	....	....	403	Indefinitely postponed.		
Ramey, George	(See William Ramey and others.)	29	1	....	160							
Ramey, John, widow of	Pension for revolutionary services of her husband.	29	1	Petition	147	Rev. Pensions	710	Favorable	485	Referred to Committee Whole House.		
Ramey, John, widow of	Pen ion for revolutionary services of her husband.	29	2	House bill	212	....	....	....	485	Passed	Passed	App'd March 3, 1847
Ramey, Joseph	(See William Ramey and others.)	29	1	....	160							
Ramey, Matthew, assignee of heirs of.	Confirmation of title to land in Missouri.	22	1	Petition	514	Priv. Land Claims.	428	Favorable	529	Referred to Committee Whole House.		
Ramey, Matthew, assignee of heirs of.	Confirmation of title to land in Missouri.	23	1	House bill	321	Priv. Land Claims.	Feb. 14, 1834	Favorable	305	Passed	Passed	App'd June 30, 1834
Ramey, Moses	(See William Ramey and others.)	29	1	....	160							
Ramey, Wm., and others.	Pre-emption right to land in Missouri.	29	1	Petition	160	Public Lands	61	Favorable	58	Referred to Committee Whole House.		
Ramirez, ———, widow of.	Confirmation of title to land in Louis ana.	22	1	Petition	64	Priv. Land Claims.	Dec. 27, 1831	Favorable	125	Passed	Passed	App'd June 25, 1832
Ramsay, Andrew	Compensation for services as express rider in 1782.	3	2	Memorial	244	Claims	Feb. 27, 1795	Adverse	......	Laid on table.		
Ramsay, Andrew	Compensation for services as express rider in 1782.	4	2	Rep. of last Cong.	633	Claims	Dec. 30, 1796	Adverse.				
Ramsay, Andrew, jr	Confirmation of title to land in Missouri.	15	2	Petition	28	Priv. Land Claims.						
Ramsay, Andrew, jr	Confirmation of title to land in Missouri.	17	1	Petition	55	Public Lands.						
Ramsay, Andrew, jr	Confirmation of title to land in Missouri.	18	1	Petition	55	Public Lands.						
Ramsay, Archibald	Pension for revolutionary services.	25	3	Resolution	275	Rev. Pensions.						
Ramsay, George D	Arrears of pay as lieutenant in the United States army.	22	2	Petition	46	Military Affairs	Dec. 29, 1832	Favorable	647	Passed	Passed	App'd March 2, 1833

List of private claims presented to the House of Representatives of the United States from the 1*st to the* 31*st Congress, inclusive*—Continued.

Names of claimants.	Nature or object of the claim.	Congress.	Session.	How brought before the House of Reps.	Page of journal.	To what committee of the House referred.	No. or date of the report.	Nature of the report.	No. of the bill.	How disposed of by the House of Reps.	How disposed of by the Senate.	Date of the act of Congress, and remarks.
Ramsay, H. G.	Compensation for services for quartermasters department in Florida.	26	1	Documents	338	Claims				Discharged; referred to Sec. Treasury.		
Ramsay, John	Pension	5	2	House bill	127	Whole House	Jan. 19, 1798	Favorable	38	Passed	Passed	App'd Feb. 2, 1798
Ramsay, John, heirs of	Commutation pay for revolutionary services.	24	2	Senate bill	260	Rev. Claims	Feb. 8, 1837	With't amend.	S. 109	Referred to Committee Whole House.		
Ramsay, John, heirs of	Commutation pay for revolutionary services.	25	2	Senate bill	197	Rev. Claims	Jan. 22, 1838	With't amend.	S. 48	Referred to Committee Whole House.		
Ramsay, John, executors of.	Indemnity for French spoliations prior to 1800.	26	1	Memorial	182	Foreign Affairs	343	Favorable	319	Referred to Committee Whole House.		
Ramsay, John, administrator of.	Indemnity for French spoliations prior to 1800.	31	1	Memorial	256	Foreign Affairs	355	Favorable	318	Referred to Committee Whole House.		
Ramsay, Joseph, widow of.	Pension for revolutionary services of her husband.	29	2	Petition	352	Rev. Pensions.						
Ramsay, Joseph	Release from judgment of United States against him.	26	1	Petition	352	Judiciary	609	Adverse		Referred to Committee Whole House.		
Ramsay, Joseph	Release from judgment of United States against him.	27	2	Petition	77	Judiciary	857	Adverse		Laid on table.		
Ramsay, Joseph	Release from judgment of United States against him.	28	1	Petition	104	Judiciary	122	Favorable	116	Passed	Indef. postp'd.	
Ramsay, Joseph	Release from judgment of United States against him.	28	2	House bill	93	Judiciary	Jan. 28, 1845	Favorable	441	Passed	Passed	App'd March 1, 1845
Ramsay, Nathaniel	Additional compensation as naval officer at Baltimore.	11	3	Petition	497	Com. and Manuf.						
Ramsay, Robert	Pension for injuries in revolutionary naval service.	15	1	Petition	171					Referred to Secretary of Navy.		
Ramsay, Robert	Pension for injuries in revolutionary naval service.	23	2	Petition	40	Invalid Pensions.						
Ramsay, Robert	Pension for injuries in revolutionary naval service.	25	2	Petition	171	Naval Affairs	486	Favorable	482	Passed.		
Ramsay, Robert	Pension for injuries in revolutionary naval service.	25	3	Petition	91	Naval Affairs.						
Ramsay, Robert	Pension for injuries in revolutionary naval service.	26	1	House bill	560	Naval Affairs	Mar. 9, 1840	Favorable	248	Referred to Committee Whole House.		
Ramsay, Robert	Pension for injuries in revolutionary naval service.	27	2	House bill	418	Naval Affairs	881	Favorable	209	Ord'd to be engrossed.		
Ramsay, Robert	Pension for injuries in revolutionary naval service.	27	3	Bill of last sess.	87				209	Passed	Passed	App'd March 3, 1843
Ramsay, Robert	Increase of pension	30	1	Petition	406	Invalid Pensions	561	Favorable	461	Passed.		
Ramsay, Robert	Increase of pension	30	2	House bill	648				461	Passed	Passed	App'd March 3, 1849
Ramsay, Robert	Increase and arrears of pension	31	1	Petition	623	Invalid Pensions	465	Adverse		Laid on table.		
Ramsey, Thomas	Arrearages of revolutionary pension.	24	2	Petition	126	Rev. Pensions				Disch'd; laid on table.		
Ramsey, Thomas	Arrearages of revolutionary pension.	25	2	Resolution	671	Rev. Pensions.						
Ramsey, Thomas	Arrearages of revolutionary pension.	26	1	Petition	174	Rev. Pensions				Discharged; laid on table.		
Ramsey, Thomas, heirs of.	Arrears of pension	28	2	Petition	206	Rev. Pensions.						
Ramsey, William	Confirmation of title to land in Missouri.	15	1	Petition	367	Priv. Land Claims				Discharged; laid on table.		
Ramsey, William	Confirmation of title to land in Missouri.	16	1	Petition	71	Priv. Land Claims				Discharged; laid on table.		
Ramsey, William	Confirmation of title to land in Missouri.	17	1	Petition	55	Priv. Land Claims.						
Ramsey, William	Confirmation of title to land in Missouri.	18	1	Petition	55	Public Lands.						

List of private claims presented to the House of Representatives of the United States from the 1st to the 31st Congress, inclusive—Continued.

Names of claimants.	Nature or object of the claim.	Congress.	Session.	How brought before the House of Reps.	Page of journal.	To what committee of the House referred.	No. or date of the report.	Nature of the report.	No. of the bill.	How disposed of by the House of Reps.	How disposed of by the Senate.	Date of the act of Congress, and remarks.
Ramsey, William, United States navy.	To be credited with $700 standing charged to him on books of Navy Department.	22	2	Petition	178	Public Lands.						
Ramsey, William, United States navy.	To be credited with $700 standing charged to him on books of Navy Department.	23	1	Petition	303	Naval Affairs.						
Ramsey, William, representatives of.	Commutation pay for revolutionary services.	24	1	Senate bill	928	Rev. Claims	798	Adverse	S. 91	Referred to Committee Whole House.		
Ramsey, Dr. William, heirs of.	Bounty land for medical services during revolutionary war.	25	2	Senate bill	496	Rev. Claims	May 11, 1838	With amend	S. 110	Referred to Committee Whole House.		
Ramsdell, Joseph	Grant of land for services against Indians, war of 1812.	15	1	Petition	184	Public Lands.						
Ramyau, Peter L	(Nature of claim not stated)	26	2	Petition	123	Claims.						
Rand, A., and others	Payment of balance due on bills of credit.	3	1	Memorial	69					Referred to Secretary Treasury.		
Rand, Benjamin H	Remission of duty on plate engraved in London for publishing farewell address of Washington.	16	2	Petition	77	Ways and Means	Jan. 18, 1821	Favorable	209	Referred to Committee Whole House.		
Rand, Benjamin H	Remission of duty on plate engraved in London for publishing farewell address of Washington.	17	1	Petition	31	Ways and Means	Jan. 28, 1822	Favorable	59	Passed	Passed	App'd April 26, 1822
Rand, Edward S	Indemnity for French spoliations prior to 1800.	26	1	Memorial	182	Foreign Affairs	343	Favorable	319	Referred to Committee Whole House.		
Rand, Hannah	Pension for services of her late husband, Thomas Hoyt, who died in the naval service in 1799.	25	2	Petition	846	Naval Affairs				Discharged; laid on table.		
Rand, Walter, widow of.	Half-pay and pension for revolutionary services.	26	1	Resolution	964	Rev. Pensions.						
Rand, Walter, widow of.	Half pay and pension for revolutionary services.	27	2	Petition	345	Rev. Pensions	301	Favorable	269	Passed	Passed	App'd Aug. 27, 1842
Rand, William	Pension for revolutionary services.	26	1	Senate bill	1277				S. 348			
Rand, William	Pension for revolutionary services.	26	2	Senate bill	334				S. 206			
Rand, William	Pension for revolutionary services.	27	2	Senate bill	115	Rev. Pensions	Mar. 5, 1842	With't amend.	S. 18	Passed	Passed	App'd Mar. 19, 1842
Randall, Alexander	Right of pre emption to land in Alabama.	24	2	Documents	275	Whole House.						
Randall, Archibald, widow and executors of.	Payment for services as acting circuit judge during vacancy in judgship.	30	1	Petition	204	Judiciary	269	Favorable	262	Referred to Committee Whole House.		
Randall, Archibald, widow and executors of.	Payment for services as acting circuit judge during vacancy in judgship.	31	1	Petition	325	Judiciary	175	Favorable	186	Referred to Committee Whole House.		
Randall, Benjamin	Pension	12	1	Petition	142	Claims				Leave to withdraw.		
Randall, Benjamin	Pension	12	2	Petition	620	Claims.						
Randall, Benjamin	Pension	13	1	House bill	56	Whole House	July 20, 1813	With amends.	31	Passed	Passed	App'd Aug. 2, 1813
Randall, Benjamin	Increase of pension	14	1	Petition	92	Pens. & Rev. Cl'ms.	Mar. 23, 1816	Adverse		Leave to withdraw.		
Randall, Benjamin	Increase of pension	15	2	Petition	150	Pens. & Rev. Cl'ms.	Feb. 5, 1819	Favorable	308	Passed	Postponed.	
Randall, Benjamin	Increase of pension	16	1	Petition	268	Pens. & Rev. Cl ms.				Discharged; laid on table.		
Randall, Elijah	Confirmation of title to land in Missouri.	15	1	Petition	157	Priv. Land Claims.						
Randall, George, and others.	Compensation as contractors to open channel at Big Sodus Bay.	26	1	Petition	1256	Claims	652	Favorable	488	Referred to Committee Whole House.		

List of private claims presented to the House of Representatives of the United States from the 1st to the 31st Congress, inclusive—Continued.

Names of claimants.	Nature or object of the claim.	Congress.	Session.	How brought before the House of Reps.	Page of journal.	To what committee of the House referred.	No. or date of the report.	Nature of the report.	No. of the bill.	How disposed of by the House of Reps.	How disposed of by the Senate.	Date of the act of Congress, and remarks.
Randall, George, and others	Compensation for excavating channel in the harbor at Saybrook, Connecticut.	27	2	Petition	56	Claims	5	Favorable	44	Passed.		
Randall, George, and others.	Compensation for excavating channel in the harbor at Saybrook, Connecticut.	27	3	Petition	43	Claims	14	Favorable	637	Passed	Passed	App'd March 1, 1843
Randall, James, and wife.	(See representatives of Jos. Jean.)	17	1		100							
Randall, Jediah	(See Silas Bebee and others)	20	2		48							
Randall, Jethro	Pension	15	1	Petition	35	Pens. & Rev. Cl'ms.				Discharged; leave to withdraw.		
Randall, John, late collector, Annapolis, Md.	Release from judgment against him for seizure of vessel libelled and condemned for violation of non intercourse act.	11	1	Petition	59	Com. and Manuf.						
Randall, John, (Ohio)	Pension	20	1	Resolution	421	Military Pensions.						
Randall, John W	Payment of damages for being detached from U. States Exploring Expedition, without cause.	26	1	Petition	330	Naval Affairs.						
Randall, John, and Charles York.	(See Silas Holmes, sureties of)	26	2		249							
Randall, John, and Jacob M. Van Winkle.	Relief on account of goods destroyed by fire in the public store, in the city of New York.	26	2	Petition	196	Commerce.						
Randall, Jonas	Pension	19	1	Petition	175	Military Pensions	164	Adverse		Laid on table.		
Randall, Jonas	Pension	20	1	Petition	223	Military Pensions				Discharged; laid on table.		
Randall, Jonas	Pension	21	2	Petition	80	Military Pensions.						
Randall, Joseph, (Ohio)	Pension	20	2	Petition	39	Military Pensions	Feb. 13, 1829	Pension bill	440	Passed.		
Randall, Joseph, (Ohio)	Pension	21	1	Petition	49	Military Pensions	Jan. 5, 1830	Pension bill	72	Passed	Passed	App'd May 20, 1830
Randall, Nathaniel, widow of.	Pension for revolutionary services.	26	1	Petition	707	Rev. Pensions	423	Adverse		Laid on table.		
Randall, Richard P., heirs of.	Payment of loan office certificates.	31	1	Petition	623	Rev. Claims.						
Randall, Richard P., heirs of.	Payment of loan office certificates.	31	2	Petition	174	Rev. Claims				Discharged; laid on table.		
Randall, Samuel	(See Thomas Tupper, assignees of.)	22	2		142							
Randall, Susan C.	(See Archibald Randall, widow and executors of.)	30	1		204		269		262			
Randall, Thomas	Compensation for vessel impressed into public service.	1	3	Petition	337					Referred to Secretary Treasury.		
Randall, Thomas	Compensation for vessel impressed into public service.	2	2	Rep of Secretary Treasury.	626	Whole House.						
Randall, Thankful	(See Isaac Pishon, widow of)	23	2		143							
Randall, Wheeler	Compensation as surgeon in public service.	26	1	Documents	338	Claims	51	Adverse		Laid on table.		
Randall, William, (Penn.)	Pension	29	1	Petition	85	Rev. Pensions	203	Adverse		Laid on table.		
Randall, William	(See Richard P. Randall, heir of.)	31	1		623							
Randall, & Clayton	(See Margaret Dowell, *et al.*)	14	1		236							
Randall, Gideon	Pension for revolutionary services.	25	2	Petition	273	Rev. Pensions.						
Randolph, Alfred F	Leave to enter certain land	30	1	Petition	625	Public Lands	611	Adverse		Laid on table.		
Randolph, David Meade	(See Richard Randolph, executors of.)	2	1		449							

List of private claims presented to the House of Representativesthe of United States from the 1st to the 31st Congress, inclusive—Continued.

Names of claimants.	Nature or object of the claim.	Congress.	Session.	How brought before the House of Reps.	Page of journal.	To what committee of the House referred.	No. or date of the report.	Nature of the report.	No. of the bill.	How disposed of by the House of Reps.	How disposed of by the Senate.	Date of the act of Congress, and remarks.
Randolph, David Meade	(See Gurdon Backus and others.)	3	1	....	163							
Randolph, David Meade	Compensation as marahal in taking Second Census.	7	1	Petition	48	Claims	Mar. 11, 1802	Favorable	33	Passed	Passed	App'd April 6, 1802
Randolph, David Meade	Compensation for revolutionary services.	19	2	Memorial	26	Military Pensions.						
Randolph, David Meade	Compensation for revolutionary services.	20	1	Petition	30	Military Pensions	Dec. 24, 1827	Adverse	......	Laid on table.		
Randolph, David Meade	Compensation for revolutionary services.	20	2	Petition	33	Rev. Claims	Feb. 24, 1829	Favorable	440	Passed.		
Randolph, David Meade	Compensation for revolutionary services.	21	1	Senate bill	308	Military Pensions	....	....	S. 33	Laid on table.		
Randolph, David Meade	Pension for revolutionary services.	21	1	Pension bill	130	Whole House	Feb. 12, 1830	With amends.	72	Passed	Passed	App'd May 20, 1830
Randolph, Ichabod	Pension for revolutionary services.	24	2	Petition	313	Rev. Pensions	....	....	......	Discharged; laid on table.		
Randolph, John F., and others.	Compensation for services against Indians in 1793.	5	2	Petition	145	....	....	....	......	Referred to Secretary of War.		
Randolph, John F., and others.	Compensation for services against Indians in 1793.	6	1	Rep. of Secretary War.	626	....	....	....	......	Referred to Committee Whole House.		
Randolph, John F., and others.	Compensation for services against Indians in 1793.	7	2	Petition	354	Claims	....	....	......	Postponed.		
Randolph, John F., and others.	Compensation for services against Indians in 1793.	8	1	Petition and rep't Sec. of War.	436	Claims	Dec. 16, 1803	Adverse	......	Referred to Committee Whole House.		
Randolph, John F., and others.	Compensation for services against Indians in 1793.	8	2	Petition and rep't Sec. of War.	89	Claims	Feb. 23, 1805	Adverse	......	Referred to Committee Whole House.		
Randolph, John F., and others.	Compensation for services against Indians in 1793.	9	1	Petition	196	Claims	Dec. 24, 1805	Adverse	......	Referred to Committee Whole House.		
Randolph, John F., and others.	Compensation for services against Indians in 1793	9	2	Petition	486	Claims.						
Randolph, Malachiah, widow of.	Pension for revolutionary services of her husband.	28	1	Petition	436	Rev. Pensions	....	....	......	Discharged; laid on table.		
Randolph, Malachiah, widow of.	Pension for revolutionary services of her husband.	29	1	Petition	358	Rev. Pensions	527	Adverse	......	Laid on table.		
Randolph, Peyton, representatives of.	Renewal of copy-right	25	2	Petition	655	Judiciary	1052	Favorable	884	Referred to Committee Whole House.		
Randolph, Peyton, representatives of.	Renewal of copy-right	25	3	House bill	432	Whole House	Feb. 1, 1839	With't amend.	884	Passed.		
Randolph, Peyton, administrator of.	Renewal of copy-right	26	1	Petition	175	Judiciary	Mar. 5, 1840	Adverse	......	Laid on table.		
Randolph, Richard, executors of.	Compensation for flour furnished revolutionary army.	2	1	Petition	449	....	....	....	......	Referred to Secretary Treasury.		
Randolph, Richard, executors of.	Compensation for flour furnished revolutionary army.	2	2	Rep. of Secretary Treasury.	626	....	....	....	......	Laid on table.		
Randolph, Richard Bland	For wages and prize money as midshipman on the L'Insurgent, an for a pension.	18	1	Petition	432	Naval Affairs	May 17, 1824	Adverse	......	Laid on table.		
Randolph, Richard Bland	For wages and prize money as midshipman on the L'Insurgent, and for a pension.	27	3	Petition	71	Naval Affairs.						
Randolph, Richard Bland	Pension for services in the navy of the United States.	28	1	Petition	883	Naval Affairs.						
Randolph, Richard Bland	Pension for services in the navy of the United States.	28	2	Petition	145	Naval Affairs.						
Randolph, Thomas F	Pension for revolutionary services.	25	2	Petition	54	Rev. Pensions	398	Adverse	......	Laid on table.		

List of private claims presented to the House of Representatives of the United States from the 1st to the 31st Congress, inclusive—Continued.

Names of claimants.	Nature or object of the claim.	Congress.	Session.	How brought before the House of Reps.	Page of journal.	To what committee of the House referred.	No. or date of the report.	Nature of the report.	No. of the bill.	How disposed of by the House of Reps.	How disposed of by the Senate.	Date of the act of Congress, and remarks.
Randon, Daniel, and others, (half breed Creek Indians.)	Confirmation of title to land in Alabama.	15	2	Petition	56	Priv. Land Claims.						
Randon, David	(See Peter and David Randon)	14	2		213							
Randon, John, representatives of.	Indemnity for property destroyed by Indians.	28	2	House bill	326	Claims			581			
Randon, John, representatives of.	Indemnity for property destroyed during Creek Indian war.	30	2	Memorial	362	Indian Affairs.						
Randon, John, representatives of.	Indemnity for property destroyed during Creek Indian war.	31	1	Petition	745	Indian Affairs.						
Randon, John, representatives of.	Indemnity for property destroyed during Creek Indian war.	31	2	Petition	206	Indian Affairs	16	Adverse		Laid on table.		
Randon, Peter	(See John Randon, representatives of.)	28	2		213							
Randon, Peter and David, (half breed Creek Indians.)	Survey and designate lands granted to them by treaty of Fort Jackson.	14	2	Petition	213	Public Lands				Discharged; laid on table.		
Randon, Peter	(Not stated.)	21	1	Petition	111	Indian Affairs.						
Randon, Peter	Confirmation of title to land	26	1	Petition	365	Priv. Land Claims.						
Randon, Peter	Confirmation of title to land	26	2	Petition	80	Priv. Land Claims.				Discharged; laid on table.		
Range, James	Issue of script in lieu of bounty land granted to him as a soldier of Virginia line, revolutionary war.	22	2	Resolution	169	Public Lands	Jan. 11, 1833	Favorable	683	Passed	Passed	App'd March 2, 1833
Rankin, Alexander	(See Smith, Thurgar, & Co.)	29	1		151							
Rankin, Daniel, widow of.	Pension for services of her husband during revolutionary war.	31	1	Petition	542	Rev. Pensions.						
Rankin, James	Compensation as interpreter to Wyandott Indians.	28	1	Petition	533	Indian Affairs.						
Rankin, Margaret	(See heirs of John Whitsett)	29	1		353							
Rankin, Richard, widow of	Pension for services of her husband in revolutionary war.	29	1	Petition	283	Rev. Pensions	826	Adverse		Laid on table.		
Rankin, Robert	Continuation of pension after removal to Mexican province of Texas.	22	1	Petition	381	Rev. Pensions.						
Rankin, Robert, widow of.	Pension for revolutionary services of her husband.	27	3	Petition	170	Rev. Pensions	295	Adverse		Laid on table.		
Ranny, David	Pension for revolutionary services.	3	1	Rep. of Secretary War.	131	Select	May 26, 1794	J't. res. to refer to Sec. War.	J. R. 12	Passed	Passed	App'd June 9, 1794
Ranny, David	Pension for revolutionary services.	3	2	Rep. of Secretary War.	262	Claims.						
Ranny, David	Pension for revolutionary services.	4	1	Rep. of Secretary War.	445	Claims	Feb. 18, 1796	Favorable; bill	156	Passed	Passed	App'd April 20, 1796
Ranney, David	Increase of pension	10	1	Pension bill	252	Whole House	Mar. 17, 1808	Favorable	78	Passed	Passed	App'd April 25, 1808
Ransom, Elias	Indemnity for property destroyed by the British at Buffalo, in 1813.	15	2	Petition	163	Claims				Discharged; laid on table.		
Ransom, Elias	Indemnity for property destroyed by the British at Buffalo, in 1813.	16	1	Petition	245	Claims	April 7, 1820	Adverse		Laid on table.		
Ransom, Elisha	Compensation for use of his house at Chazy, New York, as an arsenal during war of 1812.	21	1	Petition	235	Claims				Discharged; leave to withdraw.		

List of private claims presented to the House of Representatives of the United States from the 1st to the 31st Congress, inclusive—Continued.

Names of claimants.	Nature or object of the claim.	Congress.	Session.	How brought before the House of Reps.	Page of journal.	To what committee of the House referred.	No. or date of the report.	Nature of the report.	No. of the bill.	How disposed of by the House of Reps.	How disposed of by the Senate.	Date of the act of Congress, and remarks.
Ransom, Ely, representatives of.	Payment of final settlement certificate in his favor, dated March 22, 1782.	24	1	Resolution	707	Rev. Claims	822	Adverse		Laid on table.		
Ransom, George P.	Compensation for military services during revolutionary war.	2	1	Petition	575					Referred to Secretary of War.		
Ransom, Joseph	Arrears of pension	1	2	Petition and rep't Sec. War.	207, 249					Laid on table.		
Ransom, Luther	Indemnity for damages to farm during war of 1812.	15	1	Petition	25	Claims				Discharged; laid on table.		
Ransom, Luther	Indemnity for damages to farm during war of 1812.	17	1	Petition	92	Claims.						
Ransom, Luther	Indemnity for damages to farm during war of 1812.	21	1	Petition	147	Claims	Jan. 29, 1830	Adverse		Laid on table.		
Ransom, Richard, widow of.	Pension for revolutionary services of her husband.	26	2	Petition	82	Rev. Pensions	208	Adverse		Laid on table.		
Ransom, Roswell	Indemnity for property destroyed by British at Plattsburg, while absent in military service of United States.	14	1	Petition	309	Claims	March 1, 1816	Adverse.		Laid on table.		
Ransom, Samuel	(See William Baker, &c.)	22	1		288		480					
Ransom, Sam'l, representatives of.	Payment of seven years' half pay for revolutionary services.	29	1	Petition	515	Rev. Claims.						
Ransom, Sam'l, representatives of.	Payment of seven years' half-pay for revolutionary services.	30	1	Petition	258	Rev. Claims	823	Favorable	640	Referred to Committee Whole House.		
Ransom, Sam'l, representatives of.	Payment of seven years' half-pay for revolutionary services.	31	1	Petition	520	Rev. Claims	187	Favorable	194	Referred to Committee Whole House.		
Rape, Nicholas	Settlement of account for vessel chartered to United States for revenue service.	12	1	Petition	252	Claims				Leave to withdraw.		
Rapelye, George B., and others, merchants of New York.	Payment of drawback upon exported merchandise.	12	1	Petition	64	Com. and Manuf.				Leave to withdraw.		
Rapelye, Jacob, and others, merchants of Charleston, South Carolina.	Refund duties paid on merchandise at St. Augustine.	17	2	Petition	142	Ways and Means.						
Rapelye, John R.	(See John R. Rappelye)	13	3		671							
Rapelye, Napier and Bennett.	Refunding certain duties	18	1	Senate bill	329	Whole House	April 30, 1824	With't amend.	S. 58	Passed	Passed	App'd May 5, 1824
Rapelyea, Mary	Renewal of loan office certificate destroyed by fire.	3	2	Petition	332	Select	Feb. 24, 1795	Favorable		Referred to Committee Whole House on bill No. 122.		
Rapelyea, Mary, administrator of.	Renewal of loan office certificate destroyed by fire.	12	1	Petition	98	Claims.						
Rapelyea, Mary, administrator of.	Renewal of loan office certificate destroyed by fire.	12	2	Petition	580	Claims	Feb. 9, 1813	Favorable	252	Referred to Committee Whole House.		
Rapelyea, Mary, administrator of.	Renewal of loan office certificate destroyed by fire.	13	2	Petition	325	Pens. & Rev. Cl'ms.				Discharged.		Leave to withdraw.
Rapelyea, Mary, administrator of.	Renewal of loan office certificate destroyed by fire.	13	3	Petition	557	Pens. & Rev. Cl'ms.	42	Favorable	258	Passed	Passed	App'd Feb. 2, 1815
Raper, Leonard	Confirmation of title to land in Missouri.	15	2	Petition	28	Priv. Land Claims.				Discharged; laid on table.		
Raper, Leonard	Confirmation of title to land in Missouri.	17	1	Petition	55	Public Lands.						

List of private claims presented to the House of Representatives of the United States from the 1st to the 31st Congress, inclusive—Continued.

Names of claimants.	Nature or object of the claim.	Congress.	Session.	How brought before the House of Reps.	Page of journal.	To what committee of the House referred.	No. or date of the report.	Nature of the report.	No. of the bill.	How disposed of by the House of Reps.	How disposed of by the Senate.	Date of the act of Congress, and remarks.
Raper, Leonard	Confirmation of title to land in Missouri.	18	1	Petition	55	Public Lands.						
Rapp, George	To empower him and associates of the Society of Harmony to purchase certain public lands.	9	1	Senate bill	251	Whole House	Feb. 18, 1806	With amend'ts	S. 17	Rejected.		
Rapp, John	Bounty land for military services in war of 1812.	25	2	Petition	577	Military Affairs				Discharged; laid on table.		
Rapp, Michael	Compensation for advances and supplies furnished during revolutionary war.	2	1	Petition	459					Laid on table.		
Rappelye, John R.	Pension for wounds in war of 1812.	13	3	Petition	671	Pens. & Rev. Cl'ms.	Feb. 20, 1815	Favorable	303	Passed	Passed	App'd March 3, 1815
Rappelye, John R.	Arrears of pension	21	1	Petition	411	Military Pensions.						
Rappelye, John R.	Arrears of pension	21	2	Petition	260	Military Pensions	59	Favorable	597	Passed.		
Rappelye, John R.	Arrears of pension	22	1	Resolution	176	Invalid Pensions	211	Favorable	288	Passed	Passed	App'd July 14, 1832
Rardon, Daniel	Increase of pension	24	2	Petition	86	Invalid Pensions	292	Favorable	963	Re 'd to Com. W. H.		
Rardon, Daniel	Increase of pension	25	2	Petition	39	Invalid Pensions	186	Favorable	212	Passed	Passed	App'd June 28, 1848
Rardin, John W.	Pension for military services during war of 1812.	26	1	Petition	326	Invalid Pensions	Mar. 5, 1840	Adverse		Laid on table.		
Rareshide, John, and others	Compensation for services as volunteers in Texas in 1845.	29	1	Memorial	339	Military Affairs						
Raser, Adam Frederick	Compensation for military services during revolutionary war.	4	1	Petition	384	Claims	Jan. 20, 1796	Adverse		Leave to withdraw.		
Rash, Jacob	For duplicates of certificates of public debt, originals destroyed by fire.	1	2	Petition	253					Referred to Secretary Treasury.		
Rasmussen, Andrew, widow of.	Navy pension in consideration of her husband being killed while pilot in naval service of United States.	22	2	Petition	266	Naval Affairs.						
Rasmussen, Andrew, widow of.	Navy pension in consideration of her husband being killed while pilot in naval service of United States.	23	1	Petition	74, 302	Naval Affairs.						
Rasor, Jacob, administrator of.	Arrears of pension	18	1	Memorial	330	Pens. & Rev. Cl'ms.	April 2, 1824	Adverse		Laid on table.		
Ratcliff, John	Increase of compensation as deputy postmaster at Fairfax courthouse, Virginia.	11	3	Petition and rep't P. M. General.	457					Laid on table.		
Ratcliff, John	Pension for revolutionary services.	22	1	Resolution	810	Rev. Pensions				Discharged; laid on table.		
Ratcliff, Lewis, and others.	Increase of compensation as guard to penitentiary of the District of Columbia.	26	1	Petition	606	Dist. of Columbia.						
Ratcliffe, William D.	Payment for horse lost in war with Mexico.	30	1	Petition	146	Claims	409	Favorable	359	Passed.		
Rathbone, John W	Pension for disabilities in the naval service.	20	1	Petition	224	Naval Affairs				Discharged; laid on table.		
Rathbone, John W.	Pension for disabilities in the naval service.	20	2	Petition	71	Naval Affairs				Discharged; laid on table.		
Rathbone, John W.	Increase of pension	22	1	Petition	187	Naval Affairs				Discharged; laid on table.		
Rathbone, Jonathan	Pension	21	2	Petition	143	Military Pensions.						

List of private claims presented to the House of Representatives of the United States from the 1st to the 31st Congress, inclusive—Continued.

Names of claimants.	Nature or object of the claim.	Congress.	Session.	How brought before the House of Reps.	Page of journal.	To what committee of the House referred.	No. or date of the report.	Nature of the report.	No. of the bill.	How disposed of by the House of Reps.	How disposed of by the Senate.	Date of the act of Congress, and remarks.
Rathbone, William P	(See representatives of Caleb Wood)	15	1	....	142							
Rathbone, William P	Payment of judgment against United States, awarded to him by district court United States for the southern district of N. York.	23	2	Petition	114	Claims.						
Rathbone, William P	Payment of judgment against United States, awarded to him by district court United States for the southern district of N. York.	24	1	Senate bill	1078	Claims	813	With't amend.	S. 223	Passed	Passed	App'd July 2, 1836
Rathbone, William P	Payment of balance due as paymaster and contractor to supply rations for United States troops.	25	2	Petition	234	Claims	....	....	......	Discharged; laid on table.		
Rathbone, William P	Payment of balance due as paymaster and contractor to supply rations for United States troops.	25	3	Petition	640	Claims	300	Favorable	1163	Referred to Committee Whole House.		
Rathbone, William P	Payment of balance due as paymaster and contractor to supply rations for United States troops.	26	1	Petition	169	Claims.						
Rathbone, William P	Payment of balance due as contractor to furnish rations under contract with War Department.	26	1	Senate bill	1121	Claims	657	With't amend.	S. 249	Referred to Committee Whole House.		
Rathbone, William P	Payment of balance due as contractor to furnish rations under contract with War Department.	26	2	Petition	80	Claims	Dec. 23, 1840	Favorable	547	Referred to Committee Whole House.		
Rathbone, William P	Payment of balance due as contractor to furnish rations under contract with War Department.	26	2	Senate bill	113	Claims	Jan. 4, 1841	With't amend.	S. 50	Passed	Passed	App'd March 2, 1841
Rathburn, Tibbitts, heir of	Pension for revolutionary services of her husband.	27	2	Petition	238	Rev. Pensions	May 24, 1842	Adverse	......	Laid on table.		
Raugh, Michael	Payment for military services during revolutionary war.	3	1	Petition	81	....	....	....	......	Laid on table.		
Raven, James	Bounty land for military services during revolutionary war.	19	2	Petition	49	Priv. Land Claims.	Dec. 29, 1826	Adverse	......	Laid on table.		
Raven, James	Bounty land for military services during revolutionary war.	21	2	Petition	272	Rev. Claims	....	....	......	Discharged; laid on table.		
Ravenscroft, Thomas, administrator of.	Commutation pay as an officer of Virginia line, revolutionary war.	23	1	Petition	189	Rev. Claims.						
Ravenscroft, Thomas, administrator of.	Commutation pay as an officer of Virginia line, revolutionary war.	23	2	Petition	196	Rev. Claims.						
Ravenscroft, Thomas, administrator of.	Commutation pay as an officer of Virginia line, revolutionary war.	24	1	Petition	152	Rev. Claims	856	Adverse	......	Laid on table.		
Ravette, Catharine	(See heirs and representatives of Francis Gigo.)	31	2	....	365							
Rawle, Abel, and T. D. Merriwether.	Pre-emption right to enter land	19	2	Petition	27	Public Lands	....	....	......	Discharged; laid on table.		
Rawlings, Asahel, representatives of.	Compensation for property stolen or destroyed by Cherokees.	29	1	Petition	274	Indian Affairs	481	Adverse	......	Laid on table.		
Rawlings, Daniel	Payment for supplies furnished United States troops, late Creek Indian war.	17	1	Petition	129	Claims.						
Rawlings, George W	Pension for revolutionary services.	25	2	Petition	914	Rev. Pensions	....	....	......	Discharged; laid on table.		
Rawlings, George W	Pension for revolutionary services.	25	3	Petition	188	Rev. Pensions	....	....	......	Disch'd; laid on table.		

List of private claims presented to the House of Representatives of the United States from the 1st to the 31st Congress, inclusive—Continued.

Names of claimants.	Nature or object of the claim.	Congress.	Session.	How brought before the House of Reps.	Page of journal.	To what committee of the House referred.	No. or date of the report.	Nature of the report.	No. of the bill.	How disposed of by the House of Reps.	How disposed of by the Senate.	Date of the act of Congress, and remarks.
Rawlings, James E.	(See representatives of Asahel Rawlings.)	29	1	....	274							
Rawlings, Michael	(See representatives of Asahel Rawlings.)	29	1	....	274							
Rawlings, Moses	Compensation for military services during revolutionary war.	1	2	Petition	287	....	....	....	.....	Referred to Secretary War.		
Rawlings, Moses	Compensation for military services during revolutionary war.	1	3	Rep. of Secretary War.	379	....	....	....	.....	Laid on table.		
Rawlings, Moses	Difference of pay as lieutenant colonel and colonel in revolution.	8	1	Memorial	445	Claims	Dec. 6, 1803	....	.....	Referred to Committee Whole House.		
Rawlings, Thomas	(See Crutcher & Rawlings.)	15	2	....	24							
Rawlings, Thos., & others	Payment for horses and accoutrements lost in military service of United States in war of 1812.	19	1	Petition	337	Claims	April 10, 1826	Adverse	.....	Laid on table.		
Rawlings, Thos., & others	Payment for horses and accoutrements lost in military service of United States in war of 1812.	20	1	Petition	127	Judiciary.						
Rawls, John H. B.	Payment for property lost in service of the United States in Florida in 1836.	27	3	Documents	423	Claims.						
Rawson, Abel	Confirmation of title to land in Ohio.	30	1	Memorial	807	Public Lands	650	Favorable	517	Referred to Committee Whole House.		
Rawson, Abner	Renewal of pension	17	1	Petition	92	Rev. Pensions.						
Rawson, Edmund	Pension	15	2	Petition	70	Pens. & Rev. Cl'ms.	Dec. 11, 1818	Adverse	.....	Laid on table.		
Rawson, Joseph, widow of	Pension for revolutionary services of her husband.	25	2	Petition	116	Rev. Pensions	Jan. 25, 1837	General bill	456	Referred to Committee Whole House.		
Rawson, Joseph, widow of	Pension for revolutionary services of her husband.	27	3	Petition	137	Rev. Pensions.						
Rawson, Samuel	Pension	20	1	Resolution	283	Military Pensions	....	....	.....	Discharged; laid on table.		
Ray, Alexander	(See guardian of children of T. W. Ross.)	31	1	....	720							
Ray, Benjamin	Arrears of revolutionary pension	24	1	Petition	477	Rev. Pensions	454	Adverse	.....	Laid on table.		
Ray, Beverley	(See Beverley Roy)	21	2	....	110							
Ray, Cornelius	(See Thomas L. Ogden, and others)	18	1	....	37							
Ray, David, and others	Reimburse money loaned to American consul at Cadiz to fit out vessel for conveyance of American seamen to United States.	13	2	Petition	172	Claims.						
Ray, George	Pension	26	1	Petition	602	Invalid Pensions	....	....	.....	Leave to withdraw.		
Ray, James, and others	Redress for capture, detention, and condemnation, in 1823, by Spanish authorities, of their brig James Lawrence.	18	1	Petition	431	Foreign Affairs.						
Ray, James, and others	Redress for capture, detention, and condemnation, in 1823, by Spanish authorities, of their brig James Lawrence.	18	2	Memorial	74	Naval Affairs.						
Ray, James, and others	Redress for capture, detention, and condemnation, in 1823, by Spanish authorities, of their brig James Lawrence.	20	1	Petition	93	Foreign Affairs	....	....	.....	Discharged; laid on table.		

List of private claims presented to the House of Representatives of the United States from the 1st to the 31st Congress, inclusive—Continued.

Names of claimants.	Nature or object of the claim.	Congress.	Session.	How brought before the House of Reps.	Page of journal.	To what committee of the House referred.	No. or date of the report.	Nature of the report.	No. of the bill.	How disposed of by the House of Reps.	How disposed of by the Senate.	Date of the act of Congress, and remarks.
Ray, James, and others...	Redress for capture, detention, and condemnation, in 1823, by Spanish authorities, of their brig James Lawrence.	20	1	Memorial	280	Foreign Affairs....	247	Rep. and resl'n	......	Referred to President United States.		
Ray, James, and others...	Redress for capture, detention, and condemnation, in 1823, by Spanish authorities, of their brig James Lawrence.	20	2	Petition	83	Foreign Affairs....	....	....	......	Discharged; laid on table.		
Ray, James, and others...	Redress for capture, detention, and condemnation, in 1823, by Spanish authorities, of their brig James Lawrence.	21	1	Petition	339	Foreign Affairs....	....	....	......	Discharged; laid on table.		
Ray, John	Grant of public land............	19	1	Petition	68	Priv. Land Claims.	Dec. 23, 1825	Adverse	......	Laid on table.		
Ray, Joseph, & John Page	Reduction of duty on importation of goat skins.	14	1	Petition	63	Com. and Manuf.						
Ray, Joseph...........	Confirmation of title to land	27	2	Documents.....	681	Priv. Land Claims.						
Ray, Silas	Patent for a land warrant issued to him for revolutionary services.	24	2	Petition	83	Priv. Land Claims.	....	....	......	Discharged; laid on table.		
Ray, William, and John Follawell.	Compensation for military services during revolutionary war.	6	2	Petition	768	Claims	....	....	......	Discharged; laid on table.		
Ray, William, and John Follawell.	Compensation for military services during revolutinnary war.	7	1	Petition	19	Claims	April 3, 1802	Favorable....	......	Postponed.		
Ray, William, and John Follawell.	Compensation for military services during revolutionary war.	7	2	Petition	248	Claims	Jan. 20, 1803	Favorable....	86	Passed	Rejected.	
Ray, William	Pension as a sailor on board frigate Philadelphia, captured at Tripoli in 1803.	18	2	Petition	65	Pens. & Rev. Cl'ms.	....	....	......	Discharged; laid on table.		
Ray, William	Pension as a sailor on board frigate Philadelphia, captured at Tripoli in 1803.	19	1	Petition	57	Military Pensions..	164	Adverse	......	Laid on table.		
Ray, William, widow of..	Pension for services of her husband as a sailor on board frigate Philadelphia, captured at Tripoli in 1803.	19	2	Petition	133	Naval Affairs.....	Jan. 19, 1827	Adverse	......	Laid on table.		
Ray, William, widow of..	Pension for services of her husband as a sailor on board frigate Philadelphia, captured at Tripoli in 1803.	20	1	Memorial	100	Naval Affairs.....	Feb. 15, 1828	Adverse	......	Laid on table.		
Ray, William, widow of..	Pension for services of her husband as a sailor on board frigate Philadelphia, captured at Tripoli in 1803.	20	2	Petition	44	Naval Affairs.....	103	Adverse	......	Laid on table.		
Ray, William, widow of..	Pension for services of her husband as a sailor on board frigate Philadelphia, captured at Tripoli in 1803.	21	1	Petition	58	Naval Affairs.....	....	....	......	Discharged; laid on table.		
Ray, William, widow of..	Pension for services of her husband as a sailor on board frigate Philadelphia, captured at Tripoli in 1803.	22	1	Petition	29	Naval Affairs.....	Dec. 27, 1831	Adverse......	......	Laid on table.		
Ray, William, widow of..	Pension for services of her husband as a sailor on board frigate Philadelphia, capt'd at Tripoli in 1803.	23	1	Petition	160	Naval Affairs.	329	Favorable	356	Referred to Committee Whole House.		

Names of claimants.	Nature or object of the claim.	Congress.	Session.	How brought before the House of Reps.	Page of journal.	To what committee of the House referred.	No. or date of the report.	Nature of the report.	No. of the bill.	How disposed of by the House of Reps.	How disposed of by the Senate.	Date of the act of Congress, and remarks.
Ray, William, widow of..	Pension for services of her husband as a sailor on board frigate Philadelphias captured at Tripoli in 1803.	24	1	Memorial	61	Naval Affairs.						
Ray, William, widow of..	Pension for services of her husband as a sailor on board frigate Philadelphia, captured at Tripoli in 1803.	25	2	Petition	276	Naval Affairs	774	Favorable	727	Passed	Passed	App'd July 9, 1838
Ray, William, widow of..	Continuation of pension.........	27	2	Petition	376	Naval Affairs.....	597	Adverse	......	Laid on table.		
Ray, William	Payment of balance due as captains' clerk on board United States ship Essex, in war with Tripoli.	15	2	Petition	116	Claims.						
Ray, William	Payment of balance due as captains' clerk on board United States ship Essex, in war with Tripoli.	16	1	Petition	355	Claims...........	Mar. 31, 1820	Adverse	......	Laid on table.		
Ray, William	Pension	21	2	Resolution	209	Military Pensions.						
Ray, William	Payment for work and materials furnished as contractor on Cumberland road.	23	[illegible]	Res. and papers.	589	Claims..........	455	Adverse	......	....	....	See report No. 449.
Raybold, Jacob, and others	Compensation for military services during revolutionary war.	12	1	Petition	72	Claims.						
Rayburn, Samuel K.....	Payment for horse lost in war with Mexico.	31	2	Petition	107	Military Affairs ...	Jan. 4, 1851	Favorable	431	Referred to Committee Whole House.		
Rayland, Rane C., administrator of.	Payment for provisions furnished United States for militia in service in Georgia in 1837.	27	2	Memorial	1186	Claims.						
Raymer, Frederick	Compensation for revolutionary services and losses.	16	2	Petition	155	Pens. & Rev. Cl'ms.	Feb. 16, 1821	Adverse.....	......	Leave to withdraw.		
Raymer, Frederick	Compensation for revolutionary services and losses.	17	2	Petition	24	Pens. & Rev. Cl'ms.	Dec. 13, 1822	Adverse	......	Laid on table.		
Raymer, Frederick	Compensation for revolutionary service and losses.	19	1	Petition	176	Rev. Claims......	....	....	......	Discharged; laid on table.		
Raymer, Frederick	Compensation for revolutionary services and losses.	20	1	Petition	167	Rev. Claims......	Jan. 29, 1828	Adverse	......	Laid on table.		
Raymer, Frederick	Compensation for revolutionary services and losses.	21	1	Petition	50	Rev. Claims......	46	Favorable....	70	Passed.		
Raymer, Frederick	Compensation for revolutionary services and losses.	21	2	Petition	82	Rev. Claims......	17	Favorable....	532	Referred to Committee Whole House.		
Raymer, Frederick	Compensation for revolutionary services and losses.	22	1	Petition	73	Rev. Claims......	93	Favorable....	183	Referred to Committee Whole House.		
Raymer, Frederick	Compensation for revolutionary services and losses	22	2	House bill......	66	Whole House	Dec. 15, 1832	With amends.	183	Passed.		
Raymer, Frederick	Compensation for revolutionary services and losses.	23	1	Petition	117	Rev. Claims......	104	Favorable....	112	Passed	Passed	App'd June 28, 1834
Raymond, Elizabeth, and others, widows of revolutionary soldier.	Renewal of pension act of July 7, 1838.	27	2	Petition	853	Rev. Pensions	784	Adverse	......	Laid on table.		
Raymond, Elizabeth, and others, widows of revolutionary soldier.	Renewal of pension act of July 7, 1838.	27	3	Petition	284	Rev. Pensions.						
Raymon, George	Grant of public land............	21	1	Petition	173	Priv. Land Claims.	Feb. 18, 1830	Adverse	......	Laid on table.		
Raymond, Jesse.........	Renewal of loan office certificate issued in 1778.	3	1	Petition	27	Whole House.						

List of private claims presented to the House of Representatives of the United States from the 1st to the 31st Congress, inclusive—Continued.

Names of claimants.	Nature or object of the claim.	Congress.	Session.	How brought before the House of Reps.	Page of journal.	To what committee of the House referred.	No. or date of the report.	Nature of the report.	No. of the bill.	How disposed of by the House of Reps.	How disposed of by the Senate.	Date of the act of Congress, and remarks.
Raymond, Jesse, administrator of.	Renewal of loan office certificate issued in 1778.	29	1	Petition	625	Ways and Means.						
Raymond, Jesse, administrator of.	Renewal of loan office certificate issued in 1778.	30	1	Petition	115	Ways and Means.						
Raymond, Jesse, administrator of.	Renewal of loan office certificate issued in 1778.	31	1	Memorial	496	Ways and Means.						
Raymond, Joshua, widow of.	Pension for revolutionary services of her husband.	28	1	Petition	318	Rev. Pensions				Discharged; laid on table.		
Raymond, Joshua, heirs of.	Payment for revolutionary services.	28	1	Petition	713	Rev. Pensions.						
Raymond, Lemuel	Payment for military services during revolutionary war.	4	1	Petition	425	Claims	May 7, 1796	Adverse		Laid on table.		
Raymond, Moses	Increase of pension	12	1	House bill	361	Whole House	June 15, 1812	With amends.	138	Passed	Passed	App'd July 5, 1812
Raymond, Nathaniel L.	Renewal of pension	19	1	Petition	268	Military Pensions	164	Adverse		Laid on table.		
Raymond, Nathaniel L.	Renewal of pension	20	2	Petition	294	Military Pensions				Discharged; laid on table		
Raymond, Nathaniel L.	Renewal of pension	21	1	Petition	83	Military Pensions	April 2, 1830	Adverse		Laid on table.		
Raymond, Nathan	Payment of fees due him as late deputy marshal of the United States for the State of Connecticut.	22	1	Petition	413	Claims.						
Raymond, Phineas	Pension for revolutionary services.	30	1	Petition	104	Rev. Pensions	217	Adverse		Laid on table.		
Raymond, Solomon, representatives of.	Bounty land due for revolutionary services.	17	1	Petition	99	Pens. & Rev. Clm's.	Mar. 5, 1822	Adverse		Rejected.		
Raymond, Stephen	(See Solomon Raymond, representatives of.)	17	1		99							
Raymond, Warren	Pension for disabilities incurred in war of 1812.	29	1	Petition	425	Invalid Pensions.						
Raymond, Warren	Pension for disabilities incurred in war of 1812.	29	2	Petition	245	Invalid Pensions				Discharged; laid on table.		
Raymond, Warren	Pension for disabilities incurred in war of 1812.	30	1	Petition	575	Invalid Pensions	555	Favorable	455	Referred to Committee Whole House.		
Raymond, Warren	Pension for disabilities incurred in war of 1812.	30	2	House bill	318	Whole House	Jan. 26, 1849	With't amend.	455	Passed.		
Raymond, Warren	Pension for disabilities incurred in war of 1812.	31	1	Papers and res.	493	Invalid Pensions	148	Favorable	164	Referred to Committee Whole House.		
Raymore, Edward	Pension for injuries in public services.	29	1	Petition	578	Invalid Pensions	815	Favorable	510	Referred to Committee Whole House.		
Raynsford, Joseph	Pension	20	1	Resolution	120	Military Pensions.						
Raynsford, Joseph	Pension	20	1	Petition	124	Military Pensions	April 29, 1828	Pension bill	283	Passed.		
Raynsford, Joseph	Pension	20	2	Pension bill	55	Whole House	Dec. 12, 1828	Favorable	311	Passed	Laid on table.	
Raynsford, Joseph	Pension	21	1	Petition	48	Military Pensions	Jan. 5, 1830	Pension bill—	72	Passed	Passed	App'd May 20, 1830
Rea, Alexander, widow of.	Extension of time to pay purchase money on pre-emption right.	27	3	Petition	344	Public Lands.						
Rea, Matthew, heirs of.	Pension for revolutionary services.	30	1	House bill	327	Rev. Pensions	Feb. 9, 1848		150	Discharged; laid on table.		
Rea, Wallace, sureties of.	Release of sureties from their liabilities.	23	1	Petition	570	P. Of. & P. Roads.				Discharged; laid on table.		
Reab, George	Increase of pension	24	1	Resolution	541	Rev. Pensions.						
Read, ——	(See Reid or Reed.)											
Read, Daniel	Refunding money paid for rent of wharfs and warehouses.	21	1	Petition	201	Claims	Feb. 1, 1830	Adverse		Laid on table.		
Read, David, widow of.	Pension for revolutionary services of her husband.	28	1	Petition	839	Whole House.						

List of private claims presented to the House of Representatives of the United States from the 1st to the 31st Congress, inclusive—Continued.

Names of claimants.	Nature or object of the claim.	Congress.	Session.	How brought before the House of Reps.	Page of journal.	To what committee of the House referred.	No. or date of the report.	Nature of the report.	No. of the bill.	How disposed of by the House of Reps.	How disposed of by the Senate.	Date of the act of Congress, and remarks.
Read, Edmund, executor of widow of.	Arrears of pension due widow....	29	1	Petition	1103	Rev. Pensions.						
Read, Edmund, executor of widow of.	Arrears of pension due widow....	29	2	Petition	128	Rev. Pensions	66	Adverse	......	Laid on table.		
Read, Edmund, executor of widow of.	Arrears of pension due widow....	30	1	Petition	306	Rev. Pensions	276	Favorable....	272	Passed.		
Read, Edmund, executor of widow of.	Arrears of pension due widow ...	30	2	House bill.....	648	....	....	....	272	....	Passed	App'd March 3, 1849
Read, George..........	For settlement of accounts as United States district attorney.	23	1	Senate bill	844	Judiciary	Jan. 27, 1834	With amend..	S. 114	Passed	Passed	App'd June 30, 1834
Read, George, attorney of..	Payment of loan office certificate lost or destroyed.	5	2	Petition	134	Claims..........	March 9, 1798	Adverse	......	Laid on table.		
Read, jr., George........	Increase of fees as marshal of Delaware.	5	2	Memorial	220	Select.						
Read, George B.........	Arrears of pay as inspector at Richmond, Virginia.	29	1	Petition	234	Claims..........	781	Adverse	......	Laid on table.		
Read. George B., heirs of.	Arrears of pay as inspector at Richmond, Virginia.	30	1	Petition	219	Claims.						
Read, George B., heirs of.	Arrears of pay as inspector at Richmond, Virginia.	31	1	Petition	214	Claims	156	Favorable....	174	Referred to Committee Whole House.		
Read, Henry, assignee of..	Compensation for revolutionary services.	9	1	Petition	192	Claims..........	....	....	......	Discharged; leave to withdraw.		
Read, Henry, assignee of..	Compensation for revolutionary services.	10	2	Petition	459	Claims.						
Read, Henry, assignee of..	Compensation for revolutionary services.	11	2	Petition	127	Claims.						
Read, Henry, assignee of..	Compensation for revolutionary services.	12	1	Petition	39	Claims.						
Read, Henry, assignee of..	Compensation for revolutionary services.	14	1	Petition	146	Pens. & Rev. Cl'ms.						
Read, Henry, assignee of..	Compensation for revolutionary services.	16	1	Petition	139	Pens. & Rev. Cl'ms.	Jan. 21, 1820	Adverse	......	Laid on table		
Read, Henry, assignee of..	Compensation for revolutionary services.	19	2	Petition	158	Rev. Claims......	....	....	......	Discharged.		
Read, Henry, assignee of..	Compensation for revolutionary services.	20	1	Petition	126	Rev. Claims......	Feb. 8, 1828	Adverse	......	Laid on table.		
Read, Henry, assignee of..	Compensation for revolutionary services.	21	2	Petition	74	Rev. Claims.						
Read, Henry, assignee of..	Compensation for revolutionary services.	22	1	Petition	190	Rev. Claims......	Jan. 28, 1832	Adverse	......	Laid on table.		
Read, Henry, assignee of..	Compensation for revolutionary services.	22	2	Petition	137	Rev. Claims......	Jan. 11, 1833	Adverse	......	Laid on table.		
Read, James	Compensation for revolutionary services.	1	1	Petition	90	Select..........	....	....	......	Laid on table.		
Read, James	Compensation for revolutionary services.	1	2	Petition	137	Select..........	....	....	......	Laid on table.		
Read, James	Compensation for revolutionary services.	3	1	Rep. of Secretary Treasury.	78	....	....	....	......	Laid on table.		
Read, James	Pension	1	2	Petition	123	Select..........	Sept. 25, 1789	Favorable....	......	Ref'd to Com. W. H.		
Read, James B.........	Right of pre-emption as New Orleans branch pilot.	28	1	Petition	77	Priv. Land Claims.	9	Favorable....	35	Passed	Passed	App'd June 17, 1844
Read, James W. E......	(See Exploring Expedition)	27	3	....	149							
Read & Johnson	Remission of certain duties	10	2	Memorial	463	Com. and Manuf..	Feb. 18, 1809	Adverse.....	......	Laid on table.		

List of private claims presented to the House of Representatives of the United States form the 1st to the 31st Congress, inclusive—Continued.

Names of claimants.	Nature or object of the claim.	Congress.	Session.	How brought before the House of Reps.	Page of journal.	To what committee of the House referred.	No. or date of the report.	Nature of the report.	No. of the bill.	How disposed of by the House of Reps.	How disposed of by the Senate.	Date of the act of Congress, and remarks.
Read, Joel	Pension for revolutionary services.	22	1	Petition	66	Rev. Pensions.						
Read, John	Increase of compensation as register of land office in Alabama.	15	2	Petition	200	Public Lands.						
Read, John	Reimburse expenses paid for clerk hire.	20	2	Senate bill	349	Public Lands	Feb. 28, 1829	With't amend.	S. 69	Referred to Committee Whole House.		
Read, John	Reimburse expenses paid for clerk hire.	21	1	Senate bill	109	Public Lands			S. 22			
Read, John	Reimburse expenses paid for clerk hire.	21	2	Senate bill	134	Public Lands	Feb. 24, 1831	Adverse	S. 28	Laid on table.		
Read, John	Increase of pension	15	2	Petition	160	Pens. & Rev. Cl'ms.	Feb. 5, 1819	Favorable	308	Passed	Postponed.	
Read, John	Increase of pension	16	1	Petition	174	Pens. & Rev. Cl'ms.				Discharged; laid on table.		
Read, John	Pension for revolutionary services.	26	1	Petition	174	Rev. Pensions.				Discharged; laid on table.		
Read, John jr.	(See attorney of George Read)	5	2		134							
Read, John P.	Pension	22	1	Petition	532	Invalid Pensions.	426	Favorable	528	Passed	Passed	App'd July 16, 1832
Read, John P.	Increase of pension	28	1	Petition	194	Invalid Pensions	170	Adverse		Laid on table.		
Read, John W.	Compensation for services rendered to United States.	26	1	Resolution	436	Claims.						
Read, John, and others	Bounty land for services during the war of 1812.	31	1	Petition	755	Public Lands						See act Sept. 28, 1850
Read, John	(See sureties of Joseph Boyd)	31	1		1095							
Read, Joseph S.	Increase of compensation as postmaster.	15	2	Petition	177	P. Of. & P. Roads.				Discharged; laid on table.		
Read, Joseph E., *et al.*, owners of the schooner Minerva.	Redress for capture of schooner by Venezuelan cruiser, while on a voyge from Cuba to Philadelphia.	16	2	Memorial	248	Foreign Affairs				Discharged; referred to Secretary of State.		
Read, Nathan	Patent	1	2	Petition	154	Select.						
Read, Samuel F	Payment for horse taken for United States service in Florida war in 1836.	29	1	Memorial	903	Claims.						
Read, Samuel F	Payment for horse taken for United States service in Florida war in 1836.	29	2	Memorial	133	Claims.						
Read, Squire, widow of	Payment for timber, &c., belonging to her husband, destroyed by American troops during war of 1812.	18	1	Petition	176	Claims	Feb. 27, 1824	Adverse		Laid on table.		
Read, Squire, widow of	Payment for timber, &c., belonging to her husband, destroyed by American troops during war of 1812.	19	1	Petition	204	Claims	Feb. 17, 1826	Adverse		Laid on table.		
Read, Squire, widow of	Payment for timber, &c., belonging to her husband, destroyed by American troops during war of 1812.	21	1	Petition	170	Claims				Discharged; laid on table.		
Read, William & Co.	Indemnity for French spoliations prior to 1800.	26	1	Memorial	182	Foreign Affairs	343	Favorable	319	Referred to Committee Whole House.		
Read, William	Settlement of accounts *vs.* United States.	2	1	Petition	539					Referred to Secretary Treasury.		
Read, William	Payment for services in revolutionary war.	3	1	Rep. of Secretary Treasury.	78					Laid on table.		

List of private claims presented to the House of Representatives of the United States from the 1st to the 31st Congress, inclusive—Continued.

Names of claimants.	Nature or object of the claim.	Congress.	Session.	How brought before the House of Reps.	Page of journal.	To what committee of the House referred.	No. or date of the report.	Nature of the report.	No. of the bill.	How disposed of by the House of Reps.	How disposed of by the Senate.	Date of the act of Congress, and remarks.
Read, William	(See Archibald McCall, administrator of.)	26	1		182		343		319			
Read, William, widow of.	Pension for revolutionary services.	28	1	Petition	405	Rev. Pensions	463	Favorable	358	Passed.		
Read, William	(See George Plumsted, administrator of.)	26	1		182							
Read, William	Indemnity for French spoliations prior to 1800.	26	1	Memorial	182	Foreign Affairs	343	Favorable	319	Referred to Committee Whole House.		
Readpath, John, heirs of.	Pension for revolutionary services.	3	1	Petition	68	Select	June 3, 1794	Adverse		Leave to withdraw.		
Reagan, Philip	Pension	21	1	Petition	59	Military Pensions	April 24, 1830	Adverse		Laid on table.		
Reagan, Ralph	Confirmation of title to salt spring lands in Louisiana.	17	2	Petition	27	Priv. Land Claims				Discharged; leave to withdraw.		
Reagan, Ralph	Confirmation of title to salt spring lands in Louisiana.	18	1	Petition	28	Priv. Land Claims.						
Ream, George	(See George Rheam)	16	2		59							
Ream, Jacob	Pension for wounds received in war of 1812.	30	2	Petition	296	Invalid Pensions.						
Reandeau, Antoine	Confirmation of title to land in Missouri.	15	1	Petition	102	Priv. Land Claims				Discharged; laid on table.		
Reandeau, Joseph	Confirmation of title to land in Missouri.	15	1	Petition	102	Priv. Land Claims				Discharged; laid on table.		
Reap, Michael	Pension	12	1	Pension bill	361	Whole House	June 15, 1812	With amend'ts	138	Passed	Passed	App'd July 5, 1812
Reardin, Timothy	Pension	11	2	Petition	284	Claims				Discharged; leave to withdraw.		
Reardon, John	Arrears of pension	4	2	Petition	627	Claims	Feb. 25, 1797	Adverse		Laid on table.		
Reasons, William	Pension	14	2	Resolution	104	Pens. & Rev. Cl'ms.				Disch'd; laid on table		
Reass, Michael	Pension for revolutionary services.	12	1	Petition	23	Claims.						
Reassnyder, Benjamin	Pension for services in war of 1812.	24	1	Petition	407	Invalid Pensions	Mar. 24, 1836	Adverse		Laid on table.		
Reaud, P. & Oliver, brothers.	Confirmation of title to land in Louisiana.	22	1	House bill	107	Whole House	Mar. 23, 1832	With't amend.	125	Passed	Passed	App'd June 25, 1832
Reaum, Charles	Indemnity for depredations committed on his property by British and Indians in war of 1812.	15	1	Petition	115	Select				Discharged; laid on table.		
Reaume, Paul, heirs of	For land and money due from Virginia for revolutionary services in Clarks' Illinois regiment.	26	1	Petition	359	Rev. Claims.						
Re Beck, William	Pension	9	2	House bill	608	Whole House	Mar. 2, 1807	With amends.	216	Passed	Passed	App'd March 3, 1807
Rebutaille, Francois, widow of.	Compensation for military services of her husband in the revolutionary war.	2	1	Petition	581					Rreferred to Secretary of War.		
Reckless, Joseph W., attorney of.	To be allowed commissions on duty bonds collected while collector of customs at Perth Amboy.	27	2	Petition	916	Judiciary	1023	Favorable	596	Referred to Committee Whole House.		
Reckless, Joseph W., attorney of.	To be allowed commissions on duty bonds collected while collector of customs at Perth Amboy.	27	3	Bill of last sess.	91	Whole House	Dec. 23, 1842	With't amend.	596	Passed.		
Record, Simeon	Increase of pension	25	2	Petition	327	Rev. Pensions				Discharged; laid on table.		
Rector, Elias and William.	Payment for services as surveyors of public lands under direction of board of land commissioners.	11	2	Petition	123	Claims	Dec. 13, 1809	Favorable	37	Passed	Passed	App'd Jan. 3, 1810
Rector, Elias	Payment for services in selecting lands for seminary of learning in Arkansas.	22	1	Senate bill	502	Public Lands	Mar. 16, 1832	With't amend.	S. 98	Referred to Committee Whole House.		

List of private claims presented to the House of Representatives of the United States from the 1st to the 31st Congress, inclusive—Continued.

Names of claimants.	Nature or object of the claim.	Congress.	Session.	How brought before the House of Reps.	Page of journal.	To what committee of the House referred.	No. or date of the report.	Nature of the report.	No. of the bill.	How disposed of by the House of Reps.	How disposed of by the Senate.	Date of the act of Congress, and remarks.
Rector, Elias	Payment for services in selecting lands for seminary of learning in Arkansas.	22	2	Petition	89	Ways and Means						
Rector, William	Increase of compensation as surveyor general of Illinois and Missouri, and for services rendered as deputy serveyor.	15	1	Petition	254	Ways and Means				Discharged; laid on table.		
Reddick, Thomas F	Compensation for services as clerk to board of land commissioners in Louisiana.	12	1	Petition	242	Claims	April 3, 1812	By bill	98	Passed	Passed	App'd May 14, 1812
Reddick, Thomas F	Confirmation of title to land	20	1	Petition	33	Priv. Land Claims.				Discharged; laid on table.		
Reddick, Thomas F., heirs of.	Confirmation of title to land	23	2	Petition	49	Public Lands	31	Favorable	611	Referred to Committee Whole House.		
Reddick, Thomas F., heirs of.	Confirmation of title to land	24	1	Petition	65	Priv. Land Claims.	117	Favorable	137	Passed	Passed, with amendment.	App'd July 1, 1836
Reddick, Thomas F., heirs of.	For amendment to act for their relief.	24	2	Resolution	79	Priv. Land Claims.	Dec. 30, 1836	Adverse		Laid on table.		
Reddick, Col. Willis, representatives of.	(See Col Willis Riddick.)	30	1		513							
Redding, John	Pension for revolutionary services.	3	2	Rep. of Secretary War.	278	Claims.						
Redding, John	Pension for revolutionary services.	4	1	Rep. of Secretary War.	373	Claims.						
Redding, John	Pension for revolutionary services.	4	2	Rep. of Secretary War.	614	Claims.						
Redding, Joseph	Compensation for naval services in war of 1812.	25	2	Petition	58	Invalid Pensions.						
Redding, Joseph	Compensation for naval services in war of 1812.	28	2	Petition	72	Claims.						
Redenour, Jacob	Pension	10	2	Pension bill	499	Whole House	Jan. 30, 1809	Favorable	158	Passed	Passed	App'd March 3, 1809
Redfield, Daniel	Compensation for a vessel destroyed by the enemy.	25	2	Petition	399	Rev. Claims				Discharged; laid on table.		
Redfield, Daniel	Compensation for a vessel destroyed by the enemy.	26	1	Petition	165	Rev. Claims.						
Redfield, Daniel	Compensation for a vessel destroyed by the enemy.	26	2	Petition	35	Rev. Claims.						
Redfield, John, jr	To be discharged from prison at suit of United States.	12	2	Senate bill	664	Claims	Feb. 18, 1813	With't amend.	S. 57	Passed	Passed	App'd Feb. 24, 1813
Redfield, Levi	Pension	21	2	Petition	43	Military Affairs.						
Redgran, J., and others	Indemnity for French spoliations prior to 1800.	31	1	Petition	416	Foreign Affairs	355	Favorable	318	Referred to Committee Whole House.		
Redington, Daniel	Pension	17	2	Petition	143	Pens. & Rev. Cl'ms.	Jan. 24, 1823	Adverse		Rejected.		
Redington, Daniel	Pension	18	2	Petition	97	Pens. & Rev. Cl'ms.	Jan. 3, 1826	Adverse		Laid on table.		
Redington, Jacob	Restoration of revolutionary pension.	18	2	Petition	186	Rev. Pensions	Feb. 22, 1825	Adverse		Laid on table.		
Redington, Jacob	Restoration of revolutionary pension.	20	1	Petition	50	Military Pensions.	Feb. 13, 1828	By bill	166	Passed.		
Redington, Jacob	Restoration of revolutionary pension.	20	2	Petition	55	Military Pensions.	Dec. 12, 1828	By bill	311	Passed	Laid on table.	
Redington, Jacob	Restoration of revolutionary pension.	21	1	Petition	48	Military Pensions.	Jan. 5, 1830	By bill	72	Passed	Passed	App'd May 20, 1830
Redington, Jacob	Arrears of pension	23	1	Petition	272	Rev. Pensions				Disch'd; laid on table.		

List of private claims presented to the House of Representatives of the United States from the 1st to the 31st Congress, inclusive—Continued.

Names of claimants.	Nature or object of the claim.	Congress.	Session.	How brought before the House of Reps.	Page of journal.	To what committee of the House referred.	No. or date of the report.	Nature of the report.	No. of the bill.	How disposed of by the House of Reps.	How disposed of by the Senate.	Date of the act of Congress, and remarks.
Redington, Jacob	Arrears of pension	24	1	Resolution	285	Rev. Pensions	342	Adverse		Laid on table.		
Redington, Jacob	Arrears of pension	25	2	Petition	273	Rev. Pensions				Discharged; laid on table.		
Redington, Jacob	Arrears of pension	26	1	Petition	285	Rev. Pensions				Discharged; laid on table.		
Redington, Jacob	Arrears of pension	26	2	Petition	34	Rev. Pensions.						
Redington, Jacob	Arrears of pension	27	3	Petition	60	Invalid Pensions.						
Redington, Jocob, widow of.	Arrears of pension	28	2	Petition	187	Rev. Pensions.						
Redington, James	Pension	22	2	Res. and docs.	91	Invalid Pensions	Feb. 7, 1833	Adverse		Laid on table.		
Redington, John, widow of.	Pension due her husband for revolutionary services.	28	1	Petition	223	Rev. Pensions.						
Redington, John, widow of.	Pension due her husband for revolutionary services.	28	2	Petition	111	Rev. Pensions.						
Redington, John, widow of.	Pension due her husband for revolutionary services.	29	1	Petition	162	Rev. Pensions	489	Adverse.		Laid on table.		
Redmond, Catharine, (executors and trustees of.).	Relinquishing the right of the United States to certain lots in Georgetown, D. C., for purposes mentioned.	20	2	Petition	61	Judiciary	Feb. 25, 1829	Favorable	457	Passed.		
Red Pepper, Capt. (Choctaw Indian.)	(See Hishe Homa.)	23	1		501							
Redway, Preserved	Pension for revolutionary services.	21	2	Resolution	108	Military Pensions				Discharged; laid on table.		
Redway, Preserved	Pension for revolutionary services.	22	1	Resolution	82	Rev. Pensions				Discharged; laid on table.		
Reed, ———,	(See Read or Reid.)											
Reed, Andrew	Pension for revolutionary services.	24	1	Resolution	926	Rev. Pensions.						
Reed, Ben. Franklin, widow of.	To be placed on navy pension list.	18	1	Petition	195	Naval Affairs	Feb. 25, 1824	Adverse		Laid on table.		
Reed, Ben. Franklin, widow of.	Relief for services of her husband as commandant in the navy of United States.	24	2	Petition	46	Naval Affairs	24	Adverse		Laid on table.		
Reed, Benjamin	Pension for revolutionary services.	22	1	Resolution	116	Rev. Pensions.						
Reed, B. F.	Refund duties paid on cargo shipped from California.	30	2	Petition	87	Commerce.						
Reed, Charles	Compensation for property lost in public service.	13	3	Petition	607	Claims.						
Reed, Charles	Compensation for property lost in publice service.	14	1	Petition	78	Whole House.						
Reed, Ebenezer	Pension	19	2	Petition	84	Military Pensions				Discharged; laid on table.		
Reed, Ebenezer	Pension	20	1	Petition	243	Military Pensions				Discharged; laid on table.		
Reed, Ebenezer	Pension	21	1	Petition	260	Military Pensions				Discharged; laid on table.		
Reed, Ebenezer	Pension	22	1	Petition	77	Rev. Pensions				Discharged; laid on table.		
Reed, Ebenezer Z.	(See Wyandot Indians.)	27	3		259		160		776			
Reed, Elias	Payment of soldiers certificates for arrears of pay for services in war of 1812 purchased by him.	15	2	Petition	144	Military Affairs.						

List of private claims presented to the House of Representatives of the United States from the 1st to the 31st Congress, inclusive—Continued.

Names of claimants.	Nature or object of the claim.	Congress.	Session.	How brought before the House of Reps.	Page of journal.	To what committee of the House referred.	No. or date of the report.	Nature of the report.	No. of the bill.	How disposed of by the House of Reps.	How disposed of by the Senate.	Date of the act of Congress, and remarks.
Reed, Elias	Payment of soldiers certificates for arrears of pay for services in war of 1812 purchased by him.	16	2	Petition	89	Claims				Discharged; leave to withdraw		
Reed, George, *et al.*	Payment of balance due for work done at Big Sodus bay.	26	1	Petition	702	Claims.						
Reed, George	(See Read.)											
Reed, Giles	Pension for revolutionary services.	18	1	Petition	134	Pens. & Rev. Cl'ms.	Mar. 10, 1824	Adverse		Laid on table.		
Reed, Giles	Pension for revolutionary services.	18	2	Petition	234	Pens. & Rev. Cl'ms.						
Reed, Hardy	Confirmation of title to land in Alabama.	15	1	Petition	56	Priv. Land Claims.				Discharged; laid on table.		
Reed, Isaac G.	(See Charles and George Cramer, and others.)	21	1		375							
Reed, Jacob	Compensation for revolutionary services.	2	1	Petition	578					Referred to Secretary War.		
Reed, James, (Penn.)	Pension for revolutionary services.	22	1	Petition	113	Rev. Pensions				Discharged; laid on table.		
Reed, James, (Penn.)	Pension for revolutionary services.	25	2	Petition	392	Rev. Pensions.						
Reed, James, (Penn.)	Pensien for revolutionary services.	26	1	Petition	174	Rev. Pensions				Discharged; laid on table.		
Reed, James, heirs of	Pension for revolutionary services.	27	3	Petition	260	Rev. Pensions				Discharged; leave to withdraw.		
Reed, James	Compensation for horse lost in public service.	22	1	Resolution	535	Claims	April 13, 1832	Adverse		Laid on table.		
Reed, Jibs, representatives of.	Arrears of pension	20	1	Resolution	715	Military Pensions.				Discharged; laid on table.		
Reed, John	Pension for revolutionary services.	3	1	Rep. of Secretary War.	131	Select	May 26, 1794	Jt. res. to refer to Sec. War.	J.R. 12	Passed	Passed	App'd June 9, 1794
Reed, John	Pension for revolutionary services.	3	2	Rep. of Secretary War.	262	Claims.						
Reed, John	Pension for revolutionary services.	4	1	Rep. of Secretary War.	445	Claims.						
Reed, John	Pension for revolutionary services.	4	2	Rep. of Secretary War.	614	Claims.						
Reed, John	Pension	11	2	Pension bill	283	Whole House	Mar. 24, 1810	With amend.	107	Passed	Passed	App'd April 27, 1810
Reed, John	(See Joseph Boyd, sureties of)	31	1		1095							
Reed, John	Pension	12	1	Petition	165	Claims	June 12, 1812	Adverse		Laid on table.		
Reed, John	(See John Read)	15	2		200							
Reed, John, (Va.)	To be restored to pension roll	24	2	Memorial	84	Rev. Pensions				Laid on table.		
Reed, John, (Va.)	To be restored to pension roll	25	2	Petition	984	Rev. Pensions				Discharged; laid on table.		
Reed, John, (Va.)	To be restored to pension roll	26	1	Petition	175	Rev. Pensions				Discharged; laid on table.		
Reed, John, (Ind.)	Pension for revolutionary services.	29	1	Petition	280	Rev. Pensions	521	Adverse		Laid on table.		
Reed, John M.	Compensation for services in taking testimony.	25	2	Resolution	1065	Claims				Discharged.		
Reed, John M.	Compensation for services in taking testimony.	26	1	Petition	169	Claims.						
Reed, John M.	Compensation for services in taking testimony.	26	2	Letter from Solicitor of Traasury.	114	Claims.						
Reed, J. P.	Compensation for publishing laws of United States.	27	3	Petition	284	Claims.						
Reed John P.	(See John P. Read)	22	1		532							
Reed, Joseph	Pension	11	2	Pension bill	283	Whole House	Mar. 24, 1810	With amend.	107	Passed	Passed	App'd April 27, 1810

List of private claims presented to the House of Representatives of the United States from the 1st to the 31st Congress, inclusive—**Continued.**

Names of claimants.	Nature or object of the claim.	Congress.	Session.	How brought before the House of Reps.	Page of journal.	To what committee of the House referred.	No. or date of the report.	Nature of the report.	No. of the bill.	How disposed of by the House of Reps.	How disposed of by the Senate.	Date of the act of Congress, and remarks.
Reed, Joseph	Arrears of pension	15	1	Petition	182	Pens. & Rev. Cl'ms.				Discharged; laid on table.		
Reed, Joseph, (Pa.)	Pension	19	1	Petition	290	Military Pensions	164	Adverse.				
Reed, Joseph, (Pa.)	Pension	20	2	Resolution	125	Military Pensions				Discharged; laid on table.		
Reed, Josiah	(See surety of Wm. Markham)	26	1		875							
Reed, Mary	(See widow of Francis Ryan)	26	1		282							
Reed, Michael, by his mother, Eleanor Wills.	Relief for loss of her son killed on board the L'Insurgent.	20	1	Petition	46	Naval Affairs	Jan. 25, 1828	Adverse		Laid on table.		
Reed, Michael, by his mother, Eleanor Wills.	Relief for loss of her son killed on board the L'Insurgent.	20	2	Petition	27	Naval Affairs	103	Adverse		Laid on table.		
Reed, Nancy	Pension for revolutionary services.	28	1	Resolution	557	Rev. Pensions.						
Reed, Rufus F., and Daniel Dobbin.	Compensation for vessel taken for public use.	13	1	Petition	18	Claims				Discharged.		
Reed, Rufus F., and Daniel Dobbin.	Compensation for vessel taken for public use.	13	2	Petition	169	Claims				Discharged; leave to withdraw.		
Reed, Rufus F., and Daniel Dobbin.	Compensation for vessel taken for public use.	14	1	Petition	138	Claims	Mar. 15, 1816	Favorable		Passed	Passed	App'd April 27, 1816
Reed, Samuel C	Compensation for beef and pork furnished United States troops.	28	1	Petition	913	Claims.						
Reed, Samuel, (Ohio)	Compensation for land bought of United States, the title to which he has not been able to maintain.	29	1	Memorial	279	Priv. Land Claims.	674	Adverse		Laid on table.		
Reed, Samuel, (Ohio)	Compensation for land bought of United States, the title to which he has not been able to maintain.	29	2	Memorial	67	Priv. Land Claims.						
Reed, Samuel, (Ohio)	Compensation for land bought of United States, the title to which he has not been able to maintain.	30	1	Petition	99	Claims	49	Adverse		Laid on table.		
Reed, Samuel, (Ohio)	Compensation for land bought of United States, the title to which he has not been able to maintain.	30	2	Petition	109	Priv. Land Claims.						
Reed, Samuel, (Ohio)	Compensation for land bought of United States, the title to which he has not been able to maintain.	31	1	Petition	338	Public Lands				Leave to withdraw.		
Reed, Samuel, (Ohio)	Compensation for land bought of United States, the title to which he has not been able to maintain.	31	2	Petition	361	Public Lands				Leave to withdraw.		
Reed, Samuel	Compensation for revolutionary services.	29	1	Petition	446	Rev. Claims.						
Reed, Stephen	To be allowed to pay for land purchased of the United States at 37½ per cent.	17	2	Petition	145	Public Lands	Feb. 5, 1823	Favorable	271	Passed	Passed	App'd March 3, 1823
Reed, Thaddeus	Pension	1	3	Petition	392					Referred to Secretary War.		
Reed, Thaddeus	Pension for revolutionary services.	3	1	Rep. of Secretary War.	131	Select	May 26, 1794	Jt. res. to refer to Sec. War.	J.R.12	Passed	Passed	App'd June 9, 1794
Reed, Thaddeus	Pension for revolutionary services.	3	2	Rep. of Secretary War.	262	Claims.						
Reed, Thaddeus	Pension for revolutionary services.	4	1	Rep. of Secretary War.	445	Claims.						
Reed, Thaddeus	Pension for revolutionary services.	4	2	Rep. of Secretary War.	614	Claims.						

List of private claims presented to the House of Representatives of the United States from the 1st to the 31st Congress, inclusive—Continued.

Names of claimants.	Nature or object of the claim.	Congress.	Session.	How brought before the House of Reps.	Page of journal.	To what committee of the House referred.	No. or date of the report.	Nature of the report.	No. of the bill.	How disposed of by the House of Reps.	How disposed of by the Senate.	Date of the act of Congress, and remarks.
Reed, Thomas, and Wm. Gates.	Payment for horses lost in military service of United States.	13	3	Petition	493	Claims	Nov. 14, 1814	Favorable	228	Passed	Indef. postp'd.	
Reed, Thomas B.	Increase of pension	24	1	Petition	281	Invalid Pensions	648	Adverse		Laid on table.		
Reed, Thomas, heirs of	Pension for revolutionary services.	27	3	Petition	260	Rev. Pensions.						
Reed, Thomas, heirs of	Pension for revolutionary services.	29	1	Petition	1203	Rev. Pensions				Discharged; laid on table.		
Reed, Thomas, heirs of	Pension for revolutionary services.	29	2	Petition	86	Rev. Pensions				Discharged; laid on table.		
Reed, Thomas, (La.)	Pension for wounds received in war of 1812.	29	1	Memorial	381	Invalid Pensions	521	Adverse		Laid on table.		
Reed, Thos. C., and others, soldiers of the war of 1212	To be placed on same footing in regard to pensions, as soldiers of the revolution.	31	1	Petition	369	Invalid Pensions.						
Reed, Upton	Renewal of patent	17	2	Petition	210	Judiciary				Discharged; laid on table.		
Reed, Upton	Renewal of patent	18	1	Petition	132	Judiciary	Jan. 16, 1824	Adverse.				
Reed, William, heirs of	Grant of land to make up deficiency, confirmed to them in Missouri by board of commissioners.	15	1	Petition	39	Priv. Land Claims.				Discharged; laid on table.		
Reed, William, heirs of	Grant of land to make up deficiency, confirmed to them in Missouri by board of commissioners.	16	1	Petition	72	Priv. Land Claims.				Discharged; laid on table.		
Reed, William, heirs of	Grant of land to make up deficiency, confirmed to them in Missouri by board of commissioners.	17	1	Petition	55	Public Lands.						
Reed, William, heirs of	Grant of land to make up deficiency, confirmed to them in Missouri by board of commissioners.	18	1	Petition	55	Public Lands.						
Reed, William, widow of	For bounty land due her husband, who died previous to joining his regiment in war of 1812.	15	2	Petition	109	Military Affairs	Feb. 20, 1819	Favorable	324	Laid on table.		
Reed, William, and others, attorney of.	Remuneration for losses sustained by Indian depredations.	19	2	Petition	134	Indian Affairs.						
Reed, ——	(See Rice, Reed & Co.)	12	1		248							
Reed & Meigs, merchants of Savannah.	Payment of soldiers' certificates, for services in war of 1812, purchased by them.	15	2	Petition	144	Military Affairs.						
Reed & Dunham, merchants of Savannah.	Payment of soldiers' certificates, for services in war of 1812, purchased by them.	15	2	Petition	144	Military Affairs.						
Reed & Dunham, merchants of Savannah.	Payment of soldiers' certificates, for services in war of 1812, purchased by them.	16	2	Petition	89	Claims				Discharged; leave to withdraw.		
Reeder, Benjamin, late marshal western district of Virginia.	To transfer to his successor a treasury warrant against collector of 5th district of Virginia.	23	2	Resolution	90	Judiciary				Discharged; laid on table.		
Reeder, Charles	Payment for services in making experimental trials to prevent explosions of steam boilers.	29	1	Memorial	284	Naval Affairs.						
Reeder, Charles	Payment for services in making experimental trials to prevent explosions of steam boilers.	30	1	Petition	111	Naval Affairs	79	Favorable	65	Passed	Reported with amendment.	

List of private claims presented to the House of Representatives of the United States from the 1st to the 31st Congress, inclusive—Continued.

Names of claimants.	Nature or object of the claim.	Congress.	Session.	How brought before the House of Reps.	Page of journal.	To what committee of the House referred.	No. or date of the report.	Nature of the report.	No. of the bill.	How disposed of by the House of Reps.	How disposed of by the Senate.	Date of the act of Congress, and remarks.
Reeder, Charles	Payment for services in making experimental trials to prevent explosions of steam boilers.	31	1	Senate bill	1438	Claims			S. 7			
Reeder, Charles	Payment for services in making experimental trials to prevent explosions of steam boilers.	31	1	Petition	534	Naval Affairs.						
Reeder, George	Payment for losses sustained and injuries received in the war of 1812.	30	1	Petition	116	Claims	45	Adverse		Laid on table.		
Reeder, Richard Henry	(See William and Richard Henry Reeder.)	26	1		622							
Reeder, Simon	Compensation for use of house as barracks by United States troops.	13	1	Petition	28	Claims				Discharged.		
Reeder, Wm. and Richard Henry.	Compensation for property destroyed by the British during the war of 1812.	26	1	Petition	622	Claims.						
Reeder, Wm. and Richard Henry.	Compensation for property destroyed by the British during the war of 1812.	27	2	Petition	441	Claims	732	Adverse		Laid on table.		
Reeder, Wm. and Richard Henry.	Compensation for property destroyed by the British during the war of 1812.	27	3	Petition	370	Claims.						
Reeder, Wm. and Richard Henry.	Compensation for property destroyed by the British during the war of 1812.	28	1	Petition	110	Claims.						
Reeder, Wm. and Richard Henry.	Compensation for property destroyed by the British during the war of 1812.	29	2	Memorial	135	Claims.						
Reeder, Wm. and Richard Henry.	Compensation for property destroyed by the British during the war of 1812.	30	1	Petition	589	Claims.						
Reeks, Augustus	(See Henry Reeks)	30	1		80							
Reeks, Henry	Grant of land for services of Augustus Reeks, a volunteer of first Ohio regiment.	30	1	Petition	80	Priv. Land Claims.	185	Adverse		Laid on table.		
Reel, Henry	Donation of land in lieu of losses by Choctaw Indians.	24	1	Petition	57	Public Lands	208	Favorable	208	Referred to Committee Whole House.		
Reel, Henry, heirs of	Payment for services of deceased, and grant of land to which he was entitled as a soldier of revolutionary war.	15	1	Petition	257	Pens. & Rev. Cl'ms.				Discharged; referred to Secretary War.		
Reeper, Francisco	Right of pre-emption as New Orleans branch pilot.	28	1	Petition	77	Priv. Land Claims.	9	Favorable	35	Passed	Passed	App'd June 17, 1844
Rees, Griffith	Compensation for military services in revolutionary war.	2	1	Petition	469					Referred to Secretary of War.		
Rees, Griffith	Pension for revolutionary services.	3	1	Rep. of Secretary War.	131	Select	May 26, 1794	J't. res. to refer to Sec. War.	J. R. 12	Passed	Passed	App'd June 9, 1794
Rees, Griffith	Pension for revolutionary services.	3	2	Rep. of Secretary War.	262	Claims	Feb. 28, 1795	Pension bill	130	Passed	Postponed.	
Rees, Griffith	Pension for revolutionary services.	4	1	Rep. of Secretary War.	445	Claims	Feb. 18, 1796	Pension bill	156	Passed	Passed	App'd April 20, 1796
Rees, O. S.	(See David R. Denham, *et al.*)	25	3		121							

List of private claims presented to the House of Representatives of the United States from the 1st to the 31st Congress, inclusive—Continued.

Names of claimants.	Nature or object of the claim.	Congress.	Session.	How brought before the House of Reps.	Page of journal.	To what committee of the House referred.	No. or date of the report.	Nature of the report.	No. of the bill.	How disposed of by the House of Reps.	How disposed of by the Senate.	Date of the act of Congress, and remarks.
Rees, Orlando S	Compensation for losses sustained by Indian war in Florido.	29	1	Petition	315	Claims	633	Adverse	......	Laid on table.		
Rees, Henry J., and John P. Converse.	Payment of interest on protested drafts drawn on Post Office Department, United States.	24	2	Petition	394	Claims	246	Favorable	945	Referred to Committee Whole House.		
Rees, Henry J., and John P. Converse.	Payment of interest on protested drafts drawn on Post Office Department, United States.	25	2	Petition	37	Claims	Dec. 14, 1837	Favorable	79	Passed	Passed.	
Rees, Henry J., and John P. Converse.	Payment of interest on protested drafts drawn on Post Office Department, United States.	26	1	Petition and additional docs.	337	Claims.						
Rees, Henry J., and John P. Converse.	Payment of interest on protested drafts drawn on Post Office Department, United States.	26	2	Senate bill	334	Whole House	....	....	S. 207			
Rees, Henry J., and John P. Converse.	Payment of interest on protested drafts drawn on Post Office Department, United States.	26	2	Petition	....	P. Of. & P. Roads.						
Rees, Henry J., and John P. Converse.	Payment of interest on protested drafts drawn on Post Office Department, United States.	27	2	Petition	334	Claims	Feb. 9, 1842	Favorable	82	Passed	Passed	App'd Aug. 1, 1842
Reese, James	(See Joseph Reese, surety of)	17	2	....	143							
Reese, James	(See surety of Joseph H. Reese)	18	2	....	94							
Reese, John A	(See Louis F. Beeler)	30	1	....	115							
Reese, John M	(See Emanuel Berri)	29	1	....	324							
Reese, Joseph, surety of	For settlement of accounts of said Joseph.	17	2	Petition	143	Claims	Feb. 10, 1823	Favorable	285	Passed	Passed	App'd March 3, 1823
Reese, Joseph H., surety of	Exoneration from liability	18	2	Petition	94	Military Affairs	....	....	......	Discharged; leave to withdraw.		
Reese, Thomas	Payment for slave captured by the British.	2	1	Petition	528	....	....	....	......	Referred to Secretary War.		
Reese, Thomas	Payment for slave captured by the British.	2	2	Rep. of Secretary War.	696	....	....	....	......	Laid on table.		
Reeser, Caspar	Payment of loan office certificates, not founded.	9	2	Petition	473	Claims	....	....	......	Discharged; referred to Com. Whole House.		
Reeser, Urich, executor of.	Payment of loan office certificates, not founded.	10	1	Petition	42	Select.						
Reeser, Urich, executor of.	Payment of loan office certificates, not founded.	12	2	Petition	583	Claims	....	....	......	Referred to Committee Whole House on bill No. 252.		
Reeser, Urich, executor of.	Payment of loan office certificates, not founded.	20	2	Petition	142	Rev. Claims	....	....	......	Discharged; laid on table.		
Reeser, Urich, heirs and executor of.	Payment of loan office certificates, not founded.	21	1	Petition	50	Rev. Claims	104	Favorable	148	Referred to Committee Whole House.		
Reeside, James	Payment of judgment obtained as mail contractor against U. States.	27	2	Memorial	1110	Judiciary.						
Reeside, James, widow and executor of.	Payment of judgment obtained as mail contractor against U. States.	27	3	Petition	85	Judiciary.						
Reeside, James, widow and executor of.	Payment of judgment obtained as mail contractor against U. States.	28	1	Petition	59	Judiciary	163	Indefinite	......	Discharged; referred to Select Committee.		
Reeside, James, widow and executor of.	Payment of judgment obtained as mail contractor against U. States.	28	1	Senate bill	1097	P. Of. & P. Roads.	....	....	S. 99			
Reeside, James, widow and executor of.	Payment of judgment obtained as mail contractor against U. States.	28	2	Memorial	532	Judiciary.						

List of private claims presented to the House of Representatives of the United States from the 1st to the 31st Congress, inclusive—Continued.

Names of claimants.	Nature or object of the claim.	Congress.	Session.	How brought before the House of Reps.	Page of journal.	To what committee of the House referred.	No. or date of the report.	Nature of the report.	No. of the bill.	How disposed of by the House of Reps.	How disposed of by the Senate.	Date of the act of Congress, and remarks.
Reeside, James, widow and executor of.	Payment of judgment obtained as mail contractor against U. States.	28	2	Senate bill	174	P. Of. & P. Roads.			S. 22			
Reeside, James, widow and executor of.	Payment of judgment obtained as mail contractor against U. States.	29	1	Memorial & pet'n	74, 177	P. Of. & P. Roads.						
Reeside, James, widow and executor of.	Payment of judgment obtained as mail contractor against U. States.	31	1	Petition	499	P. Of. & P. Roads.						
Reeside, Mary	(See James Reeside, widow and executrix of.)	27	3		85							
Reeside, Robinson & Co.	Payment for two horses drowned while carrying U. States mail.	20	2	Petition	266	P. Of. & P. Roads.				Discharged; laid on table.		
Reeside, Robinson & Co.	Payment for two horses drowned while carrying U. States mail.	22	2	Petition	89	P. Of. and P. Roads	Feb. 6, 1833	Adverse		Laid on table.		
Reeves, Benjamin H., and others.	Payment of balance due for services rendered as commissioners to locate road from Missouri to New Mexico.	21	1	Letter of Secretary of War.	689	Claims	416	Adverse		Referred to Commitee Whole House.		
Reeves, Benjamin H., and others.	Payment of balance due for services rendered as commissioners to locate road from Missouri to New Mexico.	22	2	Resolution	247	Ways and Means.						
Reeves, Cornelius A.	Pension for services in war of 1812.	28	1	Petition	79	Invalid Pensions	169	Adverse		Laid on table.		
Reeves, Cornelius A.	Pension for services in war of 1812.	29	1	Petition	83	Invalid Pensions.						
Reeves, Henry	Pension for services rendered and wounds received in war of 1812.	18	2	Petition	278					Laid on table.		
Reeves, Isaac S. K., adjutant at West Point.	To be placed on same footing as officers of the same grade in the United States army.	29	2	Petition	141	Military Affairs.						
Reeves, Isaac S. K., adjutant at West Point.	To be placed on same footing as officers of the same grade in the United States army.	30	1	Petition	171	Military Affairs				Discharged; laid on table.		
Reeves, Isaac S. K., adjutant at West Point.	To be placed on same footing as officers of the same grade in the United States army.	30	2	Petitions	91, 121, 225	Military Affairs.						
Reeves, Israel	Increase of pension	21	1	Petition	46	Military Pensions	Mar. 26, 1830	Adverse		Laid on table.		
Reeves, Israel	Increase of pension	23	1	Petition	655	Rev. Pensions				Discharged; laid on table.		
Reeves, Joshua	Pension for revolutionary services.	22	1	Petition	66	Rev. Pensions	Dec. 29, 1831	Favorable	166	Passed	Indef. postp'd.	
Reeves, Minor, administrator of.	Compensation for poperty lost in Seminole campaign.	18	2	Resolution	131	Claims	Jan. 31, 1825	Favorable	306	Passed	Passed	App'd March 3, 1825
Reeves, Samuel	Compensation for services in war of 1812.	14	1	Petition	425	Military Affairs				Discharged; leave to withdraw.		
Reeves, William, widow of	Pension for revolutionary services.	26	1	Petition	625	Rev. Pensions				Discharged; laid on table.		
Reeves, William, widow of	Pension for revolutionary services.	26	2	Petition	77	Rev. Pensions				Discharged; laid on table.		
Reewalk, Barbara	Pension for revolutionary services of her husband.	27	3	Petition	482	Rev. Pensions	295	Adverse		Laid on table.		
Refeld, Charles	Confirmation of title to land in Arkansas.	22	1	House bill	421	Public Lands	Feb. 28, 1832	Favorable	425	Passed	Passed	App'd June 25, 1832
Refeld, Charles, heirs of.	Confirmation of title to land in Arkansas.	22	1	House bill	421	Public Lands	Feb. 28, 1832	Favorable	425	Passed	Passed	App'd June 25, 1832
Refugees	(See Canadian refugees.)											

List of private claims presented to the House of Representatives of the United States from the 1st to the 31st Congress, inclusive—Continued.

Names of claimants.	Nature or object of the claim.	Congress.	Session.	How brought before the House of Reps.	Page of journal.	To what committee of the House referred.	No. or date of the report.	Nature of the report.	No. of the bill.	How disposed of by the House of Reps.	How disposed of by the Senate.	Date of the act of Congress, and remarks.
Reggio, Augustin	Confirmation of title to land in Louisiana.	22	1	House bill	107	Whole House	Mar. 23, 1832	With't amend.	125	Passed	Passed	App'd June 25, 1832
Regnier, John B.	(See John B. Reigner)	15	2		25							
Reib, Nicholas	Compensation for services as an artificer, also for pay due for services of his son Peter.	3	1	Memorial	26	Select	April 25, 1794	By bill	37	Passed	Passed	App'd June 7, 1794
Reid, Alexander	Revolutionary pension	28	1	Documents	75	Invalid Pensions	48	Adverse		Laid on table.		
Reid, Edmond	(See executor of the widow of Edmund Read.)	29	1		1103							
Reid, Jacob	Pension	3	2	Petition & report Sec. of War.	278					Laid on table.		
Reid, James	(See Henry Miller, assignee of)	27	2		66							
Reid, James, (Ill.)	Pension for services in war of 1812	28	1	Petition	76	Invalid Pensions	55	Favorable	78	Passed	Passed	App'd May 23, 1844
Reid, Joseph	(See representatives of Sam'l Farr)	18	1		134							
Reid, Samuel C., & others	Compensation for important services on board privateer General Armstrong.	15	1	Petition	63	Naval Affairs	135	Favorable	115	Referred to Committee Whole House.		
Reid, Samuel C., & others	Compensation for important services on board privateer General Armstrong.	16	1	Petition	393	Naval Affairs	April 10, 1820	Adverse		Laid on table.		
Reid, Samuel C., & others	Compensation for important services on board privateer General Armstrong.	23	1	Senate bill	845	Naval Affairs	June 27, 1834	With amend.	S. 131	Passed	Passed	App'd June 30, 1834
Reid, William, (N. H.)	Indemnity for French spoliations prior to 1800.	26	1	Memorial	182	Foreign Affairs	343	Favorable	319	Referred to Committee Whole House.		
Reid, ——	(See Read, or Reed.)											
Reid, William	(See John Ferguson & Wm. Reid)	27	3		421							
Reider, Adam	Pension for revolutionary services.	4	2	Petition	625	Claims.						
Reider, Adam	Pension	5	2	Petition	264	Claims	April 17, 1798	Adverse		Laid on table.		
Reider, Adam	Pension	5	3	Petition	432	Whole House.						
Reifsynder, Benjamin	Pension for disabilities incurred in war of 1812.	29	1	Petition	797	Invalid Pensions.						
Reifsynder, Benjamin	Pension for disabilities incurred in war of 1812.	29	2	Petition	110	Invalid Pensions.						
Reifsynder, Benjamin	Pension for disabilities incurred in war of 1812.	30	1	Petition	199, 611	Invalid Pensions	449	Favorable	379	Passed.		
Reigner, John B.	Grant of land under act of March 3, 1795.	15	2	Petition	25	Priv. Land Claims.	Dec. 30, 1818	Favorable	257	Referred to Committee Whole House.		
Reigner, John B.	Grant of land under act of March 3, 1795.	16	1	Petition	184	Priv. Land Claims.	55	Favorable	63	Passed	Passed	App'd May 2, 1820
Reiley, George, (Va.)	Pension for revolutionary services.	25	3	Petition	563	Rev. Pensions.						
Reilsy, George, (Va.)	Pension for revolutionary services.	26	2	Petition	133	Invalid Pensions.						
Reiley, George, (Va.)	Pension for revolutionary services.	28	1	Petition	144	Invalid Pensions	176	Adverse		Laid on table.		
Reilly, George, (Va.)	Pension for revolutionary services.	28	2	Petition	87	Invalid Pensions.						
Reilly, Boyd	Compensation for use of his vapor bath by United States.	24	2	Senate bill	549				S. 97	Referred to Committee Whole House.		
Reilly, Boyd	Compensation for use of his vapor bath by United States.	25	2	Petition	187	Select	543	Favorable	534	Referred to Committee Whole House.		
Reilly, Boyd	Compensation for use of his vapor bath by United States.	26	1	Memorial	859	Naval Affairs	497	Favorable	398	Referred to Committee Whole House.		
Reilly, Boyd	Compensation for use of his vapor bath by United States.	27	2	Petition	63	Claims	729	Adverse		Laid on table.		

List of private claims presented to the House of Representatives of the United States from the 1st to the 31st Congress, inclusive—Continued.

Names of claimants.	Nature or object of the claim.	Congress.	Session.	How brought before the House of Reps.	Page of journal.	To what committee of the House referred.	No. or date of the report.	Nature of the report.	No. of the bill.	How disposed of by the House of Reps.	How disposed of by the Senate.	Date of the act of Congress, and remarks.
Reilly, Boyd	Compensation for use of his vapor bath by United States.	27	2	Senate bill	1073	Military Affairs	July 12, 1842	Favorable	S. 179	Referred to Committee Whole House.		
Reilly, Boyd	Compensation for use of his vapor bath by United States.	27	3	Petition	45	Military Affairs	Dec. 29, 1842	Favorable	635	Passed	Passed	App'd March 3, 1843
Reilly, James, and others	Compensation for revolutionary services.	3	1	Petition	132	Select.						
Reilly, John, (Ga.)	Compensation for property lost during Creek war.	24	2	Petition	80	Claims	32	Adverse	......	Laid on table.		
Reily, Jacob	Release from duty on distillery	14	1	Petition	386	Ways and Means.						
Reily, James	(See executor of James Purvis)	22	2	....	96							
Reily, John, (Ohio)	For location of land warrant	21	1	Senate bill	615	Public Lands	May 29, 1830	With't amend.	S. 132	Passed	Passed	App'd May 31, 1830
Reily, John, (Ohio)	To amend act for his relief of May 31, 1830.	24	1	Petition	112	Priv. Land Claims	Jan. 12, 1836	Adverse	......	Laid on table.		
Reily, Wm., widow of	Arrears of pension and bounty land for revolutionary services.	21	2	Petition	189	Military Pensions.						
Reily, Wm., widow of	Arrears of pension and bounty land for revolutionary services.	22	1	Petition	120	Rev. Pensions.						
Reily, Wm., widow of	Arrears of pension and bounty land for revolutionary services.	23	1	Petition	71	Rev. Pensions.						
Reily, Wm., widow of	Arrears of pension and bounty land for revolutionary services.	24	1	Petition	106	Rev. Pensions	....	....	......	Discharged; laid on table.		
Reily, Wm., widow of	Arrears of pension and bounty land for revolutionary services.	24	2	Petition	90	Rev. Pensions	....	....	......	Discharged; laid on table.		
Reily, Wm., widow of	Arrears of pension and bounty land for revolutionary services.	25	2	Petition	312	Rev. Pensions	....	....	......	Discharged; laid on table.		
Reinholt, George	Indemnity for French spoliations prior to 1800.	26	1	Memorial	182	Foreign Affairs	343	Favorable	319	Referred to Committee Whole House.		
Reintzel, George	Increase of pension	21	1	Petition	120	Military Pensions	....	....	......	Discharged; laid on table.		
Reintzel, George	Increase of pension	22	1	Petition	225	Invalid Pensions	....	....	......	Discharged; laid on table.		
Reintzel, George	Increase of pension	25	2	Petition	1209	Invalid Pensions	....	....	......	Discharged; laid on table.		
Reissor, or Reizer, John	Pension	20	1	Petition	45	Military Pensions	April 29, 1828	By bill	283	Passed.		
Reissor, or Reizer, John	Pension	20	2	Petition	55	Military Pensions	Dec. 12, 1828	By bill	311	Passed.		
Reissor, or Reizer, John	Pension	21	1	Pension bill	130	Whole House	Feb. 12, 1830	With amend.	72	Passed	Passed	App'd May 20, 1830
Relf & Chew	(See heirs of Marquis de Maison Rouge.)	14	2	....	73							
Relf, James H.	Compensation for executing order of War Department.	26	1	Senate bill	837	Claims	July 10, 1840	With't amend.	S. 307	Referred to Committee Whole House.		
Relf, James H.	Compensation for executing order of War Department.	26	2	Senate bill	178	Claims	187	With't amends	S. 140	Referred to Committee Whole House.		
Relf, James H.	Compensation for executing order of War Department.	27	2	Senate bill	215	Claims	April 2, 1842	With amend.	S. 50	Passed	....	App'd April 14, 1842
Reliquet, Monsieur, attorney of.	Relief from penalty for shipping wine to Baltimore without a permit.	4	1	Petition	466	Com. and Manuf.						
Reliquet, Monsieur, attorney of.	Relief from penalty for shipping wine to Baltimore without a permit.	4	2	Petition	631	Com. and Manuf.	Dec. 29, 1796	Adverse	......	Leave to withdraw.		
Relyea, John	Pension	20	1	Petition	37	Military Pensions	....	....	......	Discharged; laid on table.		

List of private claims presented to the House of Representatives of the United States from the 1st to the 31st Congress, inclusive—Continued.

Names of claimants.	Nature or object of the claim.	Congress.	Session.	How brought before the House of Reps.	Page of journal.	To what committee of the House referred.	No. or date of the report.	Nature of the report.	No. of the bill.	How disposed of by the House of Reps.	How disposed of by the Senate.	Date of the act of Congress, and remarks.
Rembert, Andrew	Payment for horses lost in Creek war of 1836.	25	2	Memorial	922	Claims	....	....	......	Discharged; laid on table.		
Rembert, Andrew	Payment for services as quartermaster to Alabama volunteers in 1837.	25	2	Memorial	922	Claims	966	Favorable	838	Referred to Committee Whole House.		
Rembert, Andrew	Payment for services as quartermaster to Alabama volunteers in 1837.	25	3	House bill	432	Whole House	Feb. 1, 1839	With't amend.	838	Passed	Passed	App'd March 3, 1839
Remf, or Kemf, Jacob	Change location of entry of land	20	2	Petition	264	Priv. Land Claims.	Feb. 16, 1829	Favorable	443	Passed.		
Remf, or Kemf, Jacob	Change location of entry of land	22	1	Petition	388	Public Lands	Mar. 2, 1832	Favorable	438	Passed	Passed	App'd June 15, 1832
Remick, Samuel	Pension for revolutionary services.	24	1	Petition	613	Invalid Pensions.						
Remick, Samuel	Pension for revolutionary services.	25	2	Petition	39	Invalid Pensions	Dec. 28, 1837	Favorable	253	Postponed.		
Remick, Samuel	Pension for revolutionary services.	25	3	House bill	155	Whole House	Jan. 26, 1839	....	253	The name of Samuel Remick stricken out.		
Remick, Samuel	Pension for revolutionary services.	26	1	Petition	161	Invalid Pensions.						
Remick, Samuel	Pension for revolutionary services.	27	2	Petition	459	Invalid Pensions.						
Remick, Samuel	Pension for revolutionary services.	27	3	Petition	335	Invalid Pensions.						
Remington, Benedict	Pension for revolutionary services.	14	2	Petition	283	Pens. & Rev. Cl'ms.						
Remington, Benedict	Pension for revolutionary services.	23	2	Memorial	67	Select	Feb. 25, 1835	By bill	769	Referred to Committee Whole House.		
Remington, Benedict	Pension for revolutionary services.	24	1	Documents	136	Select	337	Favorable	352	Referred to Committee Whole House.		
Remington, Jabez	(See heirs of Israel Pearce)	27	2	....	96	....	79					
Remington, Stephen	Renewal of lost loan office certificate.	2	1	....	511	....	....	....	......	Referred to Secretary of Treasury.		
				Rep. of Secretary Treasury.	583	Select.						
Remington, Z. W., and John B. McFadden.	Leave to import, free of duty, scientific instruments.	25	2	Petition	629	Com. and Manuf.						
Remmel, Francis	Pension for revolutionary services.	29	1	Petition	151	Rev. Pensions.						
Remsen, Garret, widow of.	Pension for revolutionary services of her husband.	28	1	Petition	753	Rev. Pensions.						
Remsen, Henry, and Evander Childs.	Possession of land purchased of United States or others in lieu thereof.	13	3	Petition	668	Claims.						
Remsen, Henry, and Evander Childs.	Possession of land purchased of United States or others in lieu thereof.	14	1	Petition	231	Claims	Feb. 26, 1816	Adverse	......	Laid on table.		
Remsen, Henry, and Evander Childs.	Possession of land purchased of United States or others in lieu thereof.	14	2	Petition	79	Claims.						
Remson, Henry	(See Isaac Clason, executors of.)	26	1	....	182	....	343	....	319			
Remsin, Johannis, & William Konwenhoven.	Compensation for board, &c., furnished revolutionary officers during captivity on Long Island.	7	1	Memorial	59	Claims	Mar. 8, 1802	Adverse	......	Leave to withdraw.		
Remson, J., and Holmes & Co.	Remission of duties secured to be paid on cargo of goods imported to New Orleans, and burned on passage to Natchez.	14	2	Petition	....	....	....	....	......	Laid on table.		
Remus, William	(See William Thompson.)	19	1	....	312							
Renason, William	Balance of pay due for revolutionary services.	21	2	Petition	96	Rev. Claims	Jan. 7, 1831	Adverse	......	Laid on table.		

3—22

List of private claims presented to the House of Representatives of the United States from the 1st to the 31st Congress, inclusive—Continued.

Names of claimants.	Nature or object of the claim.	Congress.	Session.	How brought before the House of Reps.	Page of journal.	To what committee of the House referred.	No. or date of the report.	Nature of the report.	No. of the bill.	How disposed of by the House of Reps.	How disposed of by the Senate.	Date of the act of Congress, and remarks.
Renaut, Philip, heirs of...	Confirmation of title to land in Illinois under Spanish grant.	14	2	Petition	337	Priv. Land Claims.						
Renaut, Philip, heirs of...	Confirmation of title to land in Illinois under Spanish grant.	19	1	Resolution	228	Priv. Land Claims.	....	....	......	Discharged; leave to withdraw.		
Renaut, Philip, heirs of...	Confirmation of title to land in Illinois under Spanish grant.	19	2	Resolution	173	Priv. Land Claims.	....	....	......	Discharged; laid on table.		
Renaut, Philip, heirs of...	Confirmation of title to land in Illinois under Spanish grant.	20	1	Resolution	50	Priv. Land Claims.	120	Favorable	138	Referred to Committee Whole House.		
Renaut, Philip, heirs of...	Confirmation of title to land in Illinois under Spanish grant.	21	1	Resolution	42	Priv. Land Claims.	....	....	......	Discharged; laid on table.		
Renaut, Philip, heirs of...	Confirmation of title to land in Illinois under Spanish grant.	22	1	Petition	55	Priv. Land Claims.						
Renaut, Philip, heirs of...	Confirmation of title to land in Illinois under Spanish grant.	22	2	Petition	398	Public Lands.						
Renaut, Philip, heirs of...	Confirmation of title to land in Illinois under Spanish grant.	23	1	Petition	385	Priv. Land Claims.	Mar. 28, 1834	Adverse	......	Laid on table.		
Renaut, Philip, heirs of...	Confirmation of title to land in Illinois under Spanish grant.	23	1	Petition	156	Priv. Land Claims.	377	Adverse; bill	399	Referred to Committee Whole House.	....	Directing sale of the lands.
Renaut, Philip, heirs of...	Confirmation of title to land in Illinois under Spanish grant.	27	2	Memorial	182	Priv. Land Claims.	951	Favorable	555	Referred to Committee Whole House.		
Renaut, Philip, heirs of...	Confirmation of title to land in Illinois under Spanish grant.	27	3	House bill......	91	Whole House.....	Dec. 23, 1842	With't amend.	555	Rejected.		
Renaut, Philip..........	(See Philip Renant, heirs of.)....	14	2	....	337							
Rendall, Wm., and others.	Change location of entry of land..	14	1	Petition	257	Public Lands	....	....	......	Discharged; laid on table.		
Reneau, George	Pension	22	2	Petition	39	Invalid Pensions ..	....	....	......	Discharged; laid on table.		
Renquenet, B...........	Remission of duties on importation of goods from Cadiz.	13	1	Petition	35	Ways and Means.						
Renquenet, B...........	Remission of duties on importation of goods from Cadiz.	13	2	Petition	188	Ways and Means..	45	Adverse.	......	Laid on table.		
Renner, Daniel, and Nathaniel H. Heath.	Indemnity for losses by burning of rope-walk by British, in the city of Washington, Aug. 25, 1814.	13	3	Petition	480	Claims	Nov. 19, 1814	Adverse	......	Leave to withdraw.		
Renner, Daniel, and Nathaniel H. Heath.	Indemnity for losses by burning of rope-walk by British, in the city of Washington, Aug. 25, 1814.	14	2	Petition	58	Claims	41	Adverse.	......	Laid on table.		
Renner, Daniel, and Nathaniel H. Heath.	Indemnity for losses by burning of rope-walk by British, in the city of Washington, Aug. 25, 1814.	15	1	Petition	31	Claims	158	Favorable	142	Referred to Committee Whole House.		
Renner, Daniel, and Nathaniel H. Heath.	Indemnity for losses by burning of rope-walk by British, in the city of Washington, Aug. 25, 1814.	15	2	Bill of last sess..	121	Whole House	Dec. 21, 1818	With amend..	142	Passed	Passed, with amendment.	App'd Feb. 15, 1819
Renner, Daniel, surviving partner of Renner & Heath.	Additional compensation for losses by burning rope-walk by British, in August, 1814.	18	1	Petition	345	Claims.						
Renner, Daniel, surviving partner of Renner & Heath.	Additional compensation for losses by burning rope-walk by British, in August, 1814.	19	1	Petition	62	Claims	Feb. 24, 1826	Adverse	......	Laid on table.		
Renner, Daniel, surviving partner of Renner & Heath.	Additional compensation for losses by burning rope-walk by British, in August, 1814.	19	2	Petition	54	Claims	Jan. 5, 1827	Adverse	......	Laid on table; leave to withdraw.		

List of private claims presented to the House of Representatives of the United States from the 1st to the 31st Congress, inclusive—Continued.

Names of claimants.	Nature or object of the claim.	Congress.	Session.	How brought before the House of Reps.	Page of journal.	To what committee of the House referred.	No. or date of the report.	Nature of the report.	No. of the bill.	How disposed of by the House of Reps.	How disposed of by the Senate.	Date of the act of Congress, and remarks.
Renner, Daniel, surviving partner of Renner & Heath.	Additional compensation for losses by burning rope-walk by British, in August, 1814.	20	1	Petition	342	Claims	Mar. 10, 1828	Adverse	......	Laid on table.		
Renner, Daniel, surviving partner of Renner & Heath.	Additional compensation for losses by burning rope-walk by British, in August, 1814.	20	2	Petition	106	Claims	....	....	......	Discharged; laid on table.		
Renner, Daniel, surviving partner of Renner & Heath.	Additional compensation for losses by burning rope-walk by British, in August, 1814.	21	1	Petition	116	Claims	Jan. 7, 1830	Adverse	......	Laid on table.		
Renner, Daniel, widow of.	Indemnity for property of Renner & Heath, destroyed by British in 1814.	29	1	Petition	208	Claims	804	Favorable	525	Referred to Committee Whole House.		
Renner, Daniel, widow of.	Indemnity for property of Renner & Heath, destroyed by British in 1814.	30	1	Petition	109	Claims..........	213	Favorable	213	Passed.		
Renner, Daniel, widow of.	Indemnity for property of Renner & Heath, destroyed by British in 1814.	31	1	Petition	628	Claims..........	....	....	......	Leave to withdraw.		
Renner, Daniel, widow of.	Indemnity for property of Renner & Heath, destroyed by British in 1814.	31	2	Petition	88	Claims.						
Rennehan, Martin	Compensation for services as door-keeper to Executive mansion.	29	1	Petition	440	Dist. of Columbia.						
Renshaw, Elijah	(See William H. Bedford, agent.)	28	1	....	262							
Renshaw, Elisha	Payment for horse and equipage lost in Seminole campaign in 1818.	23	1	Petition	154	Claims.						
Renshaw, Francis	Pre-emption right to purchase land claimed by Isaac Keys under Indian treaty.	21	2	Petition	100	Public Lands.....	....	....	......	Discharged; laid on table.		
Renshaw, Capt. James ...	Indemnity for damages by suits for acts in discharge of official duty.	23	1	Memorial	190	Naval Affairs.....	....	....	......	Discharged; laid on table.		
Renshaw, Josiah	Payment for horse and equipage lost in Seminole campaign in 1818.	23	1	Petition	154	Claims.						
Renshaw, Josiah	(See William H. Bedford, agent.)	28	1	....	262							
Renshaw, Wm., and John Cook.	(See Kennedy, Lampas & Co., assignees of.)	14	2	....	59							
Renter, Elizabeth........	(See W. Seavey, executors of)...	31	1	....	425							
Rentleman, Jacob........	Relinquish land entered by mistake, and select others in lieu thereof.	20	2	Senate bill	209	Public Lands.....	Jan. 26, 1829	With't amend.	S. 61	Passed	Passed	App'd Feb. 24, 1829
Rentleman, John & others.	Compensation for losses in Black Hack war.	23	2	Petition	436	Claims.						
Rentrope, Peter H........	Reimburse money paid for land bought of United States, previously sold.	18	1	Petition	109	Public Lands.....	Feb. 3, 1824	Favorable	99	Referred to Committee Whole House.		
Repentigney, D., heirs of .	(See heirs of Chevalier De Repentigney.)	31	1	....	1044							
Repold, George, representatives of.	Indemnity for French spoliations prior to 1800.	26	1	Memorial	182	Foreign Affairs ...	343	Favorable	319	Referred to Committee Whole House.		
Repshere, Leon'd, late wife of, now Margaret Daniels.	Benefit of certain acts of Congress.	18	1	Petition	130	Rev. Claims.						
Repshere, Leon'd, late wife of, now Margaret Daniels.	Benefit of certain acts of Congress.	19	1	Petition	52	Claims	Feb. 22, 1826	Adverse	......	Committed to Private Land Claims.		

List of private claims presented to the House of Representatives of the United States from the 1st to the 31st Congress, inclusive—Continued.

Names of claimants.	Nature or object of the claim.	Congress.	Session.	How brought before the House of Reps.	Page of journal.	To what committee of the House referred.	No. or date of the report.	Nature of the report.	No. of the bill.	How disposed of by the House of Reps.	How disposed of by the Senate.	Date of the act of Congress, and remarks.
Repshere, Leon'd, late wife of, now Margaret Daniels.	Benefit of certain acts of Congress.	19	2	Petition	53	Priv. Land Claims.	Jan. 2, 1827	Adverse	......	Laid on table.		
Respass, Robert C., surety of.	Release of W. E. Boswell from liability as surety.	18	1	Petition	176	Claims	Feb. 26, 1824	Adverse	......	Referred to Committee Whole House.		
Respass, William, attorney of.	Indemnity for French spoliations prior to 1800.	26	1	Memorial	182	Foreign Affairs	343	Favorable	319	Referred to Committee Whole House.		
Respass, William, heirs of.	Indemnity for French spoliations prior to 1800.	29	2	Petition	100	Foreign Affairs.						
Respass, William, heirs of.	Indemnity for French spoliations prior to 1800.	31	1	Petition	413	Foreign Affairs	355	Favorable	318	Referred to Committee Whole House.		
Restaurador, Spanish brig, owners of.	Refund duties on cargo of flour	29	1	Petition	678	Commerce	571	Favorable	389	Referred to Committee Whole House.		
Restaurador, Spanish brig, owners of.	Refund duties on cargo of flour	30	1	Petition	235	Commerce	123	Favorable	113	Passed	Passed 2d sess.	App'd Feb. 1, 1849
Retman, or Ritman, Francis.	Increase of pension	30	2	Petition	217	Invalid Pensions	....	....	......	Discharged; laid on table.		
Reviere, Francis V	(See attorney of Benj. Desoby.)	17	1	....	387							
Reviere, Henry L	Pre emption right in purchase of land.	24	1	Petition	672	Priv. Land Claims.	June 17, 1836	Favorable	706	Referred to Committee Whole House.		
Reviere, Henry L	Pre-emption right in purchase of land.	25	2	Petition	42	Priv. Land Claims.	Dec. 22, 1837	Favorable	162	Referred to Committee Whole House.		
Reviere, Henry L	Pre emption right in purchase of land.	25	3	Bill of last sess.	375	Whole House	Jan. 25, 1839	With't amend	162	Passed	Passed	App'd March 3, 1839
Reviere, Philip, heirs of	Confirmation of title to land	24	1	Petition	799	Priv. Land Claims.						
Reviere, Philip, heirs of	Confirmation of title to land	25	2	Senate bill	523	Priv. Land Claims.	Mar. 21, 1838	With't amend.	S. 129	Passed	Passed	App'd March 3 1838
Rewalt, John, widow of	Compensation for revolutionary services of her husband.	25	2	Petition	111	Rev. Pensions	567	Favorable	557	Passed.		
Reynault, Philip, heirs of	(See heirs of Philip Renaut)	14	2	....	337							
Reynes, Joseph	Leave to locate land in lieu of that claimed under Spanish title.	30	2	Memorial	91	Priv. Land Claims.	15	Favorable	710	Referred to Committee Whole House.		
Reynes, Joseph	Leave to locate land in lieu of that claimed under Spanish title.	31	1	Memorial	197	Priv. Land Claims.	275	Adverse	......	Laid on table.		
Reynolds, Aaron	Pension	21	1	Petition	36	Military Pensions	153	Favorable	195	Laid on table.		
Reynolds, Allen	(See P. and J. S. Crary, & Co.)	21	1	....	38							
Reynolds, Archibald	(See William Baker, &c.)	22	1	....	288	....	480					
Reynolds, Benedict	Restoration of pension	17	2	Petition	75	Rev. Pensions	....	....	......	Discharged; leave to withdraw.		
Reynolds, Benedict	Restoration of pension	31	1	Petition	533	Claims.						
Reynolds, Benjamin	(See Canadian refugees.)											
Reynolds, Benj., (Tenn.)	Commutation of pension for land and money.	20	2	Senate bill	216	Public Lands	Feb. 4, 1829	With't amend.	S. 62	Laid on table.		
Reynolds, Benj., (N. Y.)	Compensation for timber furnished United States troops in war of 1812.	24	1	Petition	91	Claims.						
Reynolds, Benj., (N. Y.)	Compensation for timber furnished United States troops in war of 1812.	24	2	Documents	72	Claims.						
Reynolds, Benj, (N. Y.)	Compensation for timber furnished United States troops in war of 1812.	25	2	Petition	51	Claims	339	Adverse	......	Laid on table.		
Reynolds, Benj., (N. Y.)	Compensation for timber furnished United States troops in war of 1812.	26	2	Petition	80	Claims	Jan. 4, 1841	Adverse	......	Laid on table.		

List of private claims presented to the House of Representatives of the United States from the 1st to the 31st Congress, inclusive—Continued.

Names of claimants.	Nature or object of the claim.	Congress.	Session.	How brought before the House of Reps.	Page of journal.	To what committee of the House referred.	No. or date of the report.	Nature of the report.	No. of the bill.	How disposed of by the House of Reps.	How disposed of by the Senate.	Date of the act of Congress, and remarks.
Reynolds, Benj., (N. Y.)	Compensation for timber furnished United States troops in war of 1812.	30	1	Petition	480	Claims.						
Reynolds, Charlotte, and others.	(See Samuel Lucas, children of.)	27	2		613							
Reynolds, Clement, and others.	Payment for rifles impressed into and lost in service of the United States.	20	1	Petition	382	Claims	Mar. 22, 1828	Adverse		Laid on table.		
Reynolds, Clement, and others.	Payment for rifles impressed into and lost in service of the United States.	21	1	Petition	201	Claims	Feb. 22' 1830	Adverse		Laid on table.		
Reynolds, Daniel, (Maine) widow of.	Pension for revolutionary services of her husband.	27	2	Senate bill	550	Rev. Pensions	April 12, 1842	With amend's.	S. 26	Passed		App'd Aug. 11, 1842
Reynolds, Daniel, (Maine) widow of.	Continuation of pension	29	1	Petition	766	Rev. Pensions	769	Favorable	508	Referred to Committee Whole House.		
Reynolds, Daniel, (Maine) widow of.	Continuation of pension	29	2	House bill	212				508	Passed	Passed	App'd March 3, 1847
Reynolds, David, representatives of.	Compensation as commissary of purchases and for supplies furnished army of United States in revolutionary war.	27	2	Senate bill	236	Rev. Claims.						
Reynolds, David, representatives of.	Compensation as commissary of purchases and for supplies furnished army of United State in revolutionary war.	28	1	Petition	983	Rev. Claims.						
Reynolds, Elisha	Pension for revolutionary services.	3	1	Rep. of Secretary War.	131	Select	May 26, 1794	Jt. res. to refer to Sec. War.	J. R. 12	Passed	Passed	App'd June 9, 1794
Reynolds, Elisha	Increase of pension	13	3	House bill	344	Whole House	Mar. 31, 1814	Favorable	166	Passed	Passed	App'd April 18, 1814
Reynolds, Elisha, (Vt.)	Increase and arrears of pension	22	2	Petition	264	Invalid Pensions.						
Reynolds, Elizabeth	(See Major W. Bailey, heirs of.)	23	2		165							
Reynolds, Ezra	Pension	16	2	Petition	24		Feb. 15, 1820	Adverse		Leave to withdraw.		
Reynolds, George	Payment for services as an officer in the revolutionary war.	12	1	Petition	196	Claims.						
Reynolds, George	Payment and grant of land for services in revolutionary war.	13	2	Petition	325	Public Lands and Rev. Claims.	Mar. 23, 1814	Adverse; from Pub. Lands.				
Reynolds, George	Payment and grant of land for services in revolutionary war.	13	3	Petition	529	Rev. Claims				Discharged; laid on table.		
Reynolds, George	Payment and grant of land for services in revolutionary war.	14	1	Petition	60	Rev. Claims	Feb. 13, 1816	Adverse		Rejected.		
Reynolds, George	Payment and grant of land for services in revolutionary war.	14	2	Petition	206	Rev. Claims.						
Reynolds, George	Commutation pay, depreciation of pay, and bounty land for revolutionary services.	15	2	Petition	226	Select				Discharged; laid on table.		
Reynolds, George	Commutation pay, depreciation of pay, and bounty land for revolutionary services.	16	1	Petition	177	Rev. Pensions				Discharged; leave to withdraw.		
Reynolds, George	Indemnity for property confiscated in Canada on leaving it for United States during war of 1812.	15	2	Petition	182	Military Affairs				Discharged; laid on table.		
Reynolds, George	Indemnity for property confiscated in Canida on leaving it for United States during war of 1812.	23	1	Petition	154	Claims	Jan. 10, 1834	Adverse		Laid on table.		

List of private claims presented to the House of Representatives of the United States from the 1st to the 31st Congress, inclusive—Continued.

Names of claimants.	Nature or object of the claim.	Congress.	Session.	How brought before the House of Reps.	Page of journal.	To what committee of the House referred.	No. or date of the report.	Nature of the report.	No. of the bill.	How disposed of by the House of Reps.	How disposed of by the Senate.	Date of the act of Congress, and remarks.
Reynolds, George	Indemnity for losses sustained during war of 1812.	31	1	Petition	213	Claims.						
Reynolds, Gideon	Additional compensation as contractor for carrying United States mail.	22	1	Petition	130	P. Of. & P. Roads.	....	....	......	Discharged; laid on table.		
Reynolds, Harvey	Increase of pension	23	1	Resolution	81	Invalid Pensions	283	Favorable	319	Ref'd to Com. W H		
Reynolds, Harvey	Increase of pension	23	2	Bill of last sess.	336	Whole House	Feb. 6, 1835	With amend's.	319	Passed	Passed, with amendment.	Amendment not acted on by the House.
Reynolds, Harvey	Increase of pension	24	1	Petition	201	Invalid Pensions	June 23, 1836	Adverse	......	Laid on table.		
Reynolds, Harvey	Increase of pension	25	2	Petition	714	Invalid Pensions	770	Favorable	724	Passed	Adverse report.	
Reynolds, Harvey	Increase of pension	25	3	Resolution	89	Invalid Pensions	130	Favorable	997	Passed	Passed	App'd March 3, 1839
Reynolds, Harvey	Increase of pension in consequence of increase of disability.	28	1	Petition	857	Invalid Pensions.						
Reynolds, Harvey	Increase of pension in consequence of increase of disability.	28	2	Petition	236	Invalid Pensions.						
Reynolds, Harvey	Increase of pension in consequence of increase of disability.	29	1	Petition	70	Invalid Pensions	708	Favorable	483	Referred to Committee Whole House.		
Reynolds, Harvey	Increase of pension in conseqnence of increase of disability.	29	2	House bill	212	....	....	....	483	Passed	Passed	App'd March 3, 1847
Reynolds, Henry	Payment for flour furnished American army during revolutionary war.	4	1	Rep. of Secretary Treasury.	388	Claims	74	Adverse	......	Laid on table.		
Reynolds, Isaac	Pension for disabilities incurred in war of 1812.	24	2	Petition	41	Invalid Pensions.						
Reynolds, Israel	Revolutionary pension	23	2	Petition	272	Rev. Pensions	Feb. 17, 1835	Adverse	......	Laid on table.		
Reynolds, Dr. James, heirs of.	Payment for a horse taken by the British after deceased was killed in battle at Detroit, during war of 1812.	16	1	Resolution	164	Claims	Jan. 31, 1820	Adverse	......	Laid on table.		
Reynolds, Dr. James, heirs of.	Payment for a horse taken by the British after deceased was killed in battle at Detroit, during war of 1812.	22	1	Resolution	672	Claims.						
Reynolds, Dr. James, heirs of.	Payment for a horse taken by the British after deceased was killed in battle at Detroit, during war of 1812.	22	2	Petition	64	Claims	44	Adverse	......	Laid on table.		
Reynolds, Dr. James, heirs of.	Payment for a horse taken by the British after deceased was killed in battle at Detroit, during war of 1812.	23	1	Petition	97	Claims.						
Reynolds, Dr. James, heirs of.	Payment for a horse taken by the British after deceased was killed in battle at Detroit, during war of 1812.	23	2	Petition	114	Claims.						
Reynolds, Dr. James, heirs of.	Payment for a horse taken by the British after deceased was killed in battle at Detroit, during war of 1812.	25	3	Resolution	411	Claims.						
Reynolds, Dr. James, heirs of.	Payment for a horse taken by the British after deceased was killed in battle at Detroit, during war of 1812.	26	1	Petition	168	Claims	38	Adverse	......	Laid on table.		

List of private claims presented to the House of Representatives of the United States from the 1st to the 31st Congress, inclusive—Continued.

Names of claimants.	Nature or object of the claim.	Congress.	Session.	How brought before the House of Reps.	Page of journal.	To what committee of the House referred.	No. or date of the report.	Nature of the report.	No. of the bill.	How disposed of by the House of Reps.	How disposed of by the Senate.	Date of the act of Congress, and remarks.
Reynolds, James, (R. I.)	Revolutionary pension	22	1	Petition	66	Rev. Pensions	Dec. 29, 1831	Favorable	166	Passed	Indef. postp'd.	
Reynolds, Jane	Payment for property destoyed by Sac and Fox Indians, 1812–'13.	21	2	Petition	107	Claims	Jan. 7, 1831	Adverse	......	Laid on table.		
Reynolds, Jeremiah	Release from penalty for violation of law prohibiting importation of slaves.	11	2	Petition	174	Com. and Manuf.	Jan. 16, 1810	Favorable	50	Passed	Passed	App'd Feb. 6, 1810
Reynolds, Jesse	Compensation for property destroyed by Sac and Fox Indians in 1812–'13.	21	2	Petition	107	Claims	Jan. 7, 1831	Adverse	......	Laid on table.		
Reynolds, John	Pension	12	1	House bill	361	Whole House	June 15, 1812	Favorable	138	Passed	Passed	App'd July 5, 1812
Reynolds, John	Confirmation of title to land in Missouri.	14	2	Petition	200	Priv. Land Claims.						
Reynolds, John and others.	(See Samuel B. Magraw.)	17	1	....	248							
Reynolds, John, widow and executrix of.	Amount due as commissary in revolutionary war.	18	2	Petition	69	Pens. & Rev. Cl'ms.						
Reynolds, John, widow and executrix of.	Amount due as commissary in revolutionary war.	19	1	Petition	67	Rev. Claims	....	....	......	Discharged.		
Reynolds, John, widow and executrix of.	Amount due as commissary in revolutionary war.	19	2	Petition	128	Rev. Claims	....	....	......	Discharged.		
Reynolds, John, widow and executrix of.	Amount due as commissary in revolutionary war.	20	1	Petition	38	Rev. Claims	89	Favorable	97	Passed	Passed	App'd May 24, 1828
Reynolds, John, representatives of.	Amount due as commissary in revolutionary war.	21	1	Petition	37	Rev. Claims	Jan. 29, 1830	Adverse	......	Laid on table.		
Reynolds, John, representatives of.	Amount due as commissary in revolutionary war.	21	1	Petition	497	Rev. Claims.						
Reynolds, John, representatives of.	Payment of money wrongfully paid under act for relief of, passed in 1828.	22	1	Petition	570	Rev. Claims.						
Reynolds, John, representatives of.	Payment of money wrongfully paid under act for relief of, passed in 1828.	22	2	Petition	124	Rev. Claims.						
Reynolds, John, representatives of.	Payment of money wrongfully paid under act for relief of, passed in 1828.	23	1	Petition	39	Rev. Claims.						
Reynolds, John, representatives of.	Payment of money wrongfully paid under act for relief of, passed in 1828.	23	2	Petition	55	Rev. Claims.						
Reynolds, John, representatives of.	Payment of money wrongfully paid under act for relief of, passed in 1828.	24	1	Petition	63	Rev. Claims.						
Reynolds, John, representatives of.	Payment of money wrongfully paid under act for relief of, pessed in 1828.	24	2	Petition	39	Rev. Claims	160	Adverse	......	Laid on table.		
Reynolds, John, representatives of.	Payment of money wrongfully paid under act for relief of, passed in 1828.	26	1	Petition	163	Rev. Claims.						
Reynolds, John, (Ohio)	Pension	21	2	Petition	114	Military Pensions.						
Reynolds, John, (Ohio)	Pension	22	1	Petition	561	Rev. Pensions	....	....	......	Discharged; laid on table.		
Reynolds, John, (Ohio)	Indemnity for costs of suit to recover land purchased of United States by him.	20	2	Memorial	321	....	....	....	......	Referred to Committee Whole House on bill No. 450.		

List of private claims presented to the House of Representativesthe of United States from the 1st to the 31st Congress, inclusive—Continued.

Names of claimants.	Nature or object of the claim.	Congress.	Session.	How brought before the House of Reps.	Page of journal.	To what committee of the House referred.	No. or date of the report.	Nature of the report.	No. of the bill.	How disposed of by the House of Reps.	How disposed of by the Senate.	Date of the act of Congress, and remarks.
Reynolds, John, & H. Van Metre.	Relief in case of land bought of United States, of which they have been dispossessed.	21	1	Petition	236	....	....	....	......	Referred to Committee Whole House on bill No. 141.		
Reynolds, John G.	Compensation for extra services as assist't quartermaster of marines.	22	2	Petition	109	Naval Affairs	47	Favorable	692	Referred to Committee Whole House.		
Reynolds, John G.	Compensation for extra services as assist't quartermaster of marines.	23	1	Petition	36	Naval Affairs	29	Favorable	34	Passed	Passed	App'd June 30, 1834
Reynolds, John G., (Ky.)	Compensation for a horse lost in public service.	23	2	Petition	102	Claims.						
Reynolds, John C.	Credit for money stolen while in discharge of official duty.	26	1	Senate bill	811	Indian Affairs	April 30, 1840	With't amend.	S. 191	Referred to Committee Whole House.		
Reynolds, John C.	Credit for money stolen while in discharge of official duty.	26	2	Senate bill	178	Claims	188	Adverse	S. 145	Laid on table.		
Reynolds, John C.	Credit for money stolen while in discharge of official duty.	27	2	Senate bill	782	Indian Affairs	Aug. 5, 1842	With't amend	S. 145	Passed	Passed	App'd Aug. 11, 1842
Reynolds, Jonathan, widow of.	Pension for revolutionary services of her husband.	25	3	Petition	459	Rev. Pensions	....	....	......	Discharged.		
Reynolds, Jonathan, widow of.	Pension for revolutionary services of her husband.	26	1	Petition	171	Rev. Pensions	....	....	......	Discharged; laid on table.		
Reynolds, Joseph, surety of	Release from liability	17	2	Petition	185	P. Of. and P. Roads.	Feb. 6, 1823	Adverse	......	Laid on table.		
Reynolds, Margaret	(See widow of Samuel Norcross).	22	1	....	441							
Reynolds, Mary	(See widow and executrix of John Reynolds.)	18	2	....	69							
Reynolds, Mary	(See widow of Jonathan Reynolds)	25	3	....	459							
Reynolds, Michael, surety of.	Release from liability	20	1	Senate bill	772	Judiciary	....	....	S. 144			
Reynolds, Nathaniel	Grant of land under act for relief of refugees from Canada and Nova Scotia.	12	1	House bill	242	Whole House	Mar. 22, 1812	With amend'ts	85	Passed	Passed	App'd April 23, 1812
Reynolds, Nathaniel	Pension	20	2	Petition	39	Military Pensions	Jan. 15, 1829	Adverse	......	Laid on table.		
Reynolds, Richard	Pension	23	1	Petition	190	Invalid Pensions	Feb. 21, 1834	Adverse	......	Laid on table.		
Reynolds, Richard	Pension	25	2	Petition	268	Invalid Pensions	....	....	......	Discharged; laid on table.		
Reynolds, Richard	Pension	25	3	Petition	89	Invalid Pensions	Jan. 9, 1839	Adverse	......	Laid on table.		
Reynolds, Richard	Pension	26	1	Petition	602	Invalid Pensions.						
Reynolds, Richard	Pension	28	1	Petition	117	Invalid Pensions	25	Adverse	......	Laid on table.		
Reynolds, Richard	Pension	30	1	Petition	117	Invalid Pensions	280	Favorable	276	Passed	Passed	App'd Aug. 14, 1848
Reynolds, Richard	Arrears of pension	30	2	Petition	322	Invalid Pensions	94	Adverse	......	Laid on table.		
Reynolds, Robert	Confirmation of title to land in Missouri.	15	1	Petition	267	Priv. Land Claims	....	....	......	Discharged; laid on table.		
Reynolds, Robert	Confirmation of title to land in Missouri.	16	1	Petition	72	Priv. Land Claims	....	....	......	Discharged; laid on table.		
Reynolds, Robert	Pension for revolutionary services.	21	1	Resolution	303	Military Pensions.						
Reynolds, Robert	Pension for revolutionary services.	21	2	Petition	88	Military Pensions.						
Reynolds, Robert	Pension for revolutionary services.	22	1	Petition	35	Rev. Pensions	400	Favorable	500	Referred to Committee Whole House.		
Reynolds, Robert	Pension for revolutionary services.	23	1	Resolution	99	Rev. Pensions	99	Favorable	103	Passed	Passed	App'd June 30, 1834
Reynolds, Solomon	Pension for revolutionary services.	3	2	Rep. of Secretary War.	278	Claims	Feb. 25, 1795	Pension bill	130	Passed	Postponed.	
Reynolds, Solomon	Pension for revolutionary services.	4	1	Rep. of Secretary War.	445	Claims	Feb. 18, 1796	Pension bill	156	Passed	Passed	App'd April 20, 1796
Reynolds, Solomon	Increase of pension	11	3	Pension bill	604	Whole House	Mar. 1, 1811	With amend'ts	218	Passed	Passed	App'd March 3, 1811

List of private claims presented to the House of Representatives of the United States from the 1st to the 31st Congress, inclusive—Continued.

Names of claimants.	Nature or object of the claim.	Congress.	Session.	How brought before the House of Reps.	Page of journal.	To what committee of the House referred.	No. or date of the report.	Nature of the report.	No. of the bill.	How disposed of by the House of Reps.	How disposed of by the Senate.	Date of the act of Congress, and remarks.
Reynolds, Sylvanus......	Indemnity for destruction of property in revolution.	3	1	Petition	124	....	....	....	......	Laid on table.		
Reynolds, Thankful	(See Daniel Reynolds, widow of)	29	1	....	766							
Reynolds, Thomas, and others, attorney of.	Indemnity for Indian depredations.	19	2	Petition	134	Indian Affairs.						
Reynolds, Thomas, (Fla.)	Confirmation of title to land in Florida.	22	1	Petition	227	Priv. Land Claims.	Feb. 6, 1832	Favorable....	349	Referred to Committee Whole House.		
Reynolds, Thomas, (Fla.)	Confirmation of title to land in Florida.	23	1	Petition	158	Priv. Land Claims.	Jan. 14, 1834	Favorable....	189	Passed	Passed	App'd June 30, 1834
Reynolds, Thomas, (N.Y.)	Arrears of pension............	22	1	Petition	164	Rev. Pensions.....	....	....	......	Discharged; laid on table.		
Reynolds, Thomas, (N.Y.)	Arrears of pension............	23	1	Petition	353	Invalid Pensions ..	....	....	......	Discharged; laid on table.		
Reynolds, Thomas, (N.Y.)	Arrears of pension....	24	1	Petition	201	Invalid Pensions ..	....	....	......	Laid on table.		
Reynolds, Thomas, (N.Y.)	Arrears of pension............	25	2	Petition	57	Invalid Pensions ..	....	....	......	Discharged; laid on table.		
Reynolds, William	Pension	1	3	Petition and rep't of Sec. War.	347, 393	....	....	....	......	Laid on table.		
Reynolds, William	Pension for revolutionary services.	3	1	Petition and rep't Sec. of War.	131	Select..........	May 26, 1794	Jt. res. to refer to Sec. War.	J. R. 12	Passed	Passed	App'd June 9, 1794
Reynolds, William, widow of.	Pension for death of her husband in naval service.	18	1	Petition	115	Naval Affairs.						
Reynolds, William	Compensation as bearer of report of land commissioners.	18	2	Resolution	245	Public Lands.....	Feb. 28, 1825	Favorable....	313	Passed	Passed	App'd March 3, 1825
Reynolds, William	Bounty land for services in war of 1812.	30	1	Memorial	558	Claims..........	654	Adverse	......	Laid on table.		
Reynolds, William	(See Exploring Expedition)	27	3	....	149							
Rezé, Frederick, (Mich.) .	Remission of duty on importation of books.	24	1	Petition	924	Commerce	735	Favorable....	678	Referred to Committee Whole House.		
Rezé, Frederick, (Mich.) .	Remission of duty on importation of books.	24	2	Petition and docs.	93, 214	Judiciary.						
Rezé, Frederick, (Mich.) .	Remission of duty on importation of books.	25	2	Petition	40	Commerce	79	Favorable....	94	Passed.		
Rezé, Frederick, (Mich.) .	Compensation for expenses in establishing Indian missions in Northwest Territory.	24	1	Petition	943	Judiciary.						
Rezé, Frederick, (Mich.) .	Compensation for expenses in establishing Indian missions in Northwest Territory.	26	1	Petition	957	Commerce.						
Rhea, John	Indemnity for relinquishing title to tract of land to the United States.	22	1	Memorial	192	Judiciary	Feb. 9, 1832	Adverse	......	Laid on table.		
Rhea, Joseph M.........	Pension for disability incurred in war of 1812.	24	2	Memorial	120	Invalid Pensions ..	Jan. 5, 1837	Adverse	......	Laid on table.		
Rhea, Joseph M.........	Pension for disability incurred in war of 1812.	25	2	Petition	920	Invalid Pensions ..	....	....	......	Discharged; laid on table.		
Rhea, Joseph M.........	Pension for disability incurred in war of 1812.	25	3	Petition	89	Invalid Pensions ..	....	....	......	Discharged; laid on table.		
Rhea, Joseph M.........	Pension for disability incurred in war of 1812.	26	1	Petition	162	Invalid Pensions.						
Rhea, Joseph M.........	Pension for disability incurred in war of 1812.	26	2	Petition	36	Invalid Pensions...	47	Favorable....	576	Referred to Committee Whole House.		
Rhea, Joseph M.........	Pension for disability incurred in war of 1812.	27	2	Petition	97	Invalid Pensions ..	634	Adverse	......	Laid on table.		

List of private claims presented to the House of Representatives of the United States from the 1st to the 31st Congress, inclusive—Continued.

Names of claimants.	Nature or object of the claim.	Congress.	Session.	How brought before the House of Reps.	Page of journal.	To what committee of the House referred.	No. or date of the report.	Nature of the report.	No. of the bill.	How disposed of by the House of Reps.	How disposed of by the Senate.	Date of the act of Congress, and remarks.
Rhea, Joseph M.	Pension for disability incurred in war of 1812.	27	3	Petition	107	Invalid Pensions	268	Adverse		Laid on table.		
Rhea, Joseph M.	Pension for disability incurred in war of 1812.	28	1	Petition	622	Invalid Pensions	June 7, 1844	Favorable	414	Referred to Committee Whole House.		
Rhea, Joseph M.	Pension for disability incurred in war of 1812.	28	2	Bill of last sess.	344	Whole House	Feb 8, 1845	With amend.	414	Passed.	Indef. postp'd.	
Rhea, Joseph M.	Pension for disability incurred in war of 1812.	29	2	Petition	93	Invalid Pensions	56	Favorable	45	Passed.	Passed	App'd July 15, 1846
Rhea, Joseph M.	Pension for disability incurred in war of 1812.	30	1	Petition	603	Invalid Pensions				Discharged; laid on table.		
Rhea, Joseph M.	Pension for disability incurred in war of 1812.	31	1	Petition	276	Invalid Pensions.						
Rhea, Lund	Increase of pension	23	2	Petition	198	Invalid Pensions	Feb. 2, 1835	Adverse		Disch'd; laid on table.		
Rhea, Samuel	Pension	23	1	Petition	569	Invalid Pensions				Discharged; laid on table.		
Rhea, Stephen	Pension	20	2	Pension bill	280	Military Pensions	Feb. 13, 1829	Favorable	440	Passed.		
Rheam, George	Compensation for services of his servant as a soldier in revolutionary war.	16	2	Petition	59	Pens. & Rev. Cl'ms.	Jan. 9, 1821	Adverse		Rejected.		
Rheams, Tobias	Confirmation of title to land under Spanish grant.	15	1	House bill	108	Whole House	Mar. 23, 1818	With't amend.	31	Passed	Passed, with amendment.	App'd April 9, 1818
Rhind, Charles	Compensation for negotiating treaty with the Turkish government.	27	2	Petition	237	Foreign Affairs.						
Rhind, Charles	Payment of balance due for bringing Arabian horses to U. States.	27	2	Petition	237	Foreign Affairs.						
Rhind, Charles	Payment of balance due for bringing Arabian horses to U. States.	28	1	Petition	294	Foroign Affairs.						
Rhinelander, William	Indemnity for French spoliations prior to 1800.	26	1	Memorial	182	Foreign Affairs	343	Favorable	319	Referred to Committee Whole House.		
Rhinelanders, Hartshorn, & Co.	Indemnity for French spoliations prior to 1800.	26	1	Memorial	182	Foreign Affairs	343	Favorable	319	Referred to Committee Whole House.		
Rhinevault, Mary, widow of	Pension for revolutionary services.	27	3	Petition	108	Rev. Pensions	96	Favorable	719	Passed.		
Rhodes, Arnold	Patents for lands purchased of Stockbridge Indians.	31	1	Petition	520	Judiciary.						
Rhodes, Catherine	Pension for revolutionary services of her husband.	25	3	Resolution	168	Rev. Pensions	Jan. 16, 1839	Adverse		Laid on table.		
Rhodes, Daniel	Compensation for revolutionary services.	20	2	Petition	119	Rev. Claims	Jan. 29, 1829	Adverse		Laid on table.		
Rhodes, George T.	Compensation for extra service as clerk in the Engineer Department.	24	1	Memorial	1054	Claims.						
Rhodes, George T.	Compensation for extra service as clerk in the Engineer Department.	24	2	Memorial	124	Claims	84	Adverse		Laid on table.		
Rhodes, Mary, and Lucy Forbes.	Pension or other relief as widows of revolutionary soldiers.	22	2	Petition	40	Rev. Claims				Discharged; laid on table.		
Rhodes, Nicholas	Commutation pay for revolutionary services.	9	1	Petition	309	Whole House.						
Rhodes, Nicholas	Commutation pay for revolutionary services.	10	1	Petition	59	Whole House.						
Rhodes, Solomon	Refund purchase money paid United States for lands since forfeited.	20	1	Resolution	425	Public Lands				Discharged; laid on table.		

List of private claims presented to the House of Representatives of the United States from the 1st to the 31st Congress, inclusive—Continued.

Names of claimants.	Nature or object of the claim.	Congress.	Session.	How brought before the House of Reps.	Page of journal.	To what committee of the House referred.	No. or date of the report.	Nature of the report.	No. of the bill.	How disposed of by the House of Reps.	How disposed of by the Senate.	Date of the act of Congress, and remarks.
Rhodes, Thomas, and Jeremiah Austill.	Reimbursement of amount expended in opening and keeping in repair a post road.	23	1	Senate bill	165	P. Of. & P. Roads.	Jan. 16, 1834	With amend..	S. 12	Rejected.		
Rhodes, Thomas, and Jeremiah Austill.	Reimbursement of amount expended in opening and keeping in repair a post road.	23	2	Petition	147	P. Of. & P. Roads.						
Rhodes, Thomas, and Jeremiah Austill.	Reimbursement of amount expended in opening and keeping in repair a post road.	24	2	Senate bill	579	....	....	....	S. 200			
Rhodes, Thomas, and Jeremiah Austill.	Reimbursement of amount expended in opening and keeping in repair a post road.	25	2	Senate bill	301	P. Of. & P. Roads.	745	With amends.	S. 20	Referred to Committee Whole House.		
Rhodes, Thomas, and Jeremiah Austill.	Reimbursement of amount expended in opening and keeping in repair a post road.	26	1	Senate bill......	227	P. Of. & P. Roads.	325	Adverse	29			
Rhodes, Thomas	Reimbursement of amount expended in opening and keeping in repair a post road.	29	1	Senate bill	1075	P. Of. & P. Roads.	Aug. 10, 1846	With't amend.	S. 100	Referred to Committee Whole House.		
Rhodes, Thomas	Reimbursement of amount expended in opening and keeping in repair a post road.	29	2	Senate bill	307	P. Of. & P. Roads.	Feb. 16, 1847	With't amend.	S. 58	Referred to Committee Whole House.		
Rhodes, Thomas	Reimbursement of amount expended in opening and keeping in repair a post road.	30	1	Senate bill	203	P. Of. & P. Roads.	131	Adverse	S. 28	Laid on table.		
Rhodes, Thomas	Reimbursement of amount expended in opening and keeping in repair a post road.	30	2	Senate bill	111	P. Of. & P. Roads.	Jan. 25, 1849	With't amend.	S. 28	Laid on table.		
Rhodes, Thomas	Reimbursement of amount expended in opening and keeping in repair a post road.	31	2	Senate bill	191	Whole House.....	....	....	S. 104			
Rhodes, William........	Pension	14	1	House bill	622	Whole House	April 23, 1816	With amends.	......	Passed	Passed with amendments	App'd April 30, 1816
Rhode Island, citizens of Newshoreham.	Bounty on vessels engaged in cod fisheries.	8	1	Petition	441	Com. and Manuf..	Nov. 25, 1803	Adverse	......	Rejected	....	Leave to withdraw.
Rhode Island, claim'ts under convention with Denmark.	Compensation for capturing brigantine Henrick.	21	2	Memorial	235	Foreign Affairs....	Feb. 23, 1831	Adverse	......	Laid on table.		
Rhode Island College, corporation of.	Indemnity for damages to buildings occupied by American troops, revolutionary war.	2	2	Petition	657	....	....	....	......	Referred to Secretary Treasury.		
Rhode Island College, corporation of.	Indemnity for damages to buildings occupied by American troops, revolutionary war.	3	2	Rep. of Secretary Treasury.	312	Whole House.						
Rhode Island College, corporation of.	Indemnity for damages to buildings occupied by American troops, revolutionary war.	4	1	Rep. of Secretary Treasury.	384	Claims.						
Rhode Island College, corporation of.	Indemnity for damages to buildings occupied by American troops, revolutionary war.	5	2	Rep. of Secretary Treasury.	102	Whole House.						
Rhode Island College, corporation of.	Indemnity for damages to buildings occupied by American troops, revolutionary war.	6	1	Petition	563	Claims	Feb. 17, 1800	Favorable; bill	222	Passed	Passed	App'd April 16, 1800
Rhode Island, manufacturers of Providence.	Drawback of duty on imported hemp.	3	2	Memorial	312	Select	Feb. 9, 1895	Adverse	......	Laid on table.		

List of private claims presented to the House of Representatives of the United States form the 1st to the 31st Congress, inclusive—**Continued.**

Names of claimants.	Nature or object of the claim.	Congress.	Session.	How brought before the House of Reps.	Page of journal.	To what committee of the House referred.	No. or date of the report.	Nature of the report.	No. of the bill.	How disposed of by the House of Reps.	How disposed of by the Senate.	Date of the act of Congress, and remarks.
Rhode Island, citizens of..	Indemnity for French spoliations prior to 1800.	19	2	Petition	241	Foreign Affairs....	....	....	.....	Discharged; laid on table.		
Rhode Island, citizens of..	Indemnity for French spoliations prior to 1800.	28	1	Petition	104	Foreign Affairs.						
Rhode Island, New Haven Insurance Company.	Indemnity for French spoliations prior to 1800.	26	1	Memorial	182	Foreign Affairs....	343	Favorable....	319	Referred to Committee Whole House.		
Rhode Island, New London In-urance Company.	Indemnity for French spoliations prior to 1800.	26	1	Memorial	182	Foreign Affairs....	343	Favorable....	319	Referred to Committee Whole House.		
Rhode Island, citizens of Newport.	Indemnity for French spoliations prior to 1800.	28	1	Petition	343	Foreign Affairs.						
Rhode Island, Providence Insurance Company.	Ind mnity for French spoliations prior to 1800.	26	1	Memorial	182	Foreign Affairs....	343	Favorable....	319	Referred to Committee Whole House.		
Rhode Island, Warren Insurance Company.	Indemnity for French spoliations prior to 1800.	26	1	Memorial	182	Foreign Affairs....	343	Favorable....	319	Referred to Committee Whole House.		
Rhode Island, Warren Insurance Company.	Indemnity for French spoliations prior to 1800.	31	1	Petition	307	Foreign Affairs....	355	Favorable....	318	Referred to Committee Whole House.		
Rhode Island brigade, revolutionary army, officers, &c., of.	Indemnity for depreciation of pay.	2	2	Memorial	692	....	....	....	.....	Laid on table.		
Rhode Island brigade, revolutionary army, officers, &c., of.	Half-pay for life...............	11	3	Petition	494	Select.						
Rhode Island brigade, revolutionary army, officers, &c., of.	Half pay for life...............	14	2	Petition	283	Pens. & Rev. Cl'ms.						
Rhode Island brigade, revolutionary army, officers, &c., of.	Half-pay for life...............	20	1	Petition	124	Military Pensions..	....	....	.....	Discharged; laid on table.		
Rhode Island brigade, revolutionary army, officers, &c., of.	Half-pay for life...............	22	1	Petition	163	Select	....	....	.....	Discharged.		
Rhode Island brigade, revolutionary army, officers, &c., of.	Indemnity for depreciation of pay and for arrears of pay.	24	1	Memorial	136	Select	337	Favorable; bill	352	Referred to Committee Whole House.		
Rhode Island brigade, revolutionary army, officers, &c., of.	Indemnity for depreciation of pay and for arrears of pay.	25	2	Memorial	40	Rev. Claims.						
Rhode Island, United States marshal of.	For a fixed salary in lieu of present compensation.	20	2	Resolution	164	Judiciary	....	....	.....	Discharged; laid on table.		
Rhode Island, United States marshal of.	Increase of compensation..	20	2	Senate bill	249	Judiciary	....	....	S. 70			
Rhode Island, United States marshal of.	Increase of compensation........	21	1	Senate bill	271	Judiciary.........	Feb. 12, 1830	With't amend.	S. 12	Referred to Committee Whole House.		
Rhode Island, United States marshal of.	Increase of compensation........	21	2	Resolution	41	Judiciary.						
Rhode Island, United States marshal of.	Increase of compensation........	21	2	Senate bill	134	Judiciary.........	Jan. 4, 1831	With't amend.	S. 2	Passed	Passed	App'd March 2, 1831
Rhode Island, merchants of Providence.	Refunding of duties wrongfully paid.	4	1	Memorial	444	Com. and Manuf.						
Rhode Island, merchants of Providence.	Remission of duties on tea destroyed by fire.	6	2	Petition	804	Com. and Manuf..	Feb. 23, 1801	Favorable; bill	320	Passed	Passed	App'd March 3, 1801
Rhode Island, merchants of Providence.	Release from penalties incurred by importing British manufactures.	12	2	Petition	575	Whole House.....	....	....	.....	....	....	See act Feb. 27, 1813

List of private claims presented to the House of Representatives of the United States from the 1st to the 31st Congress, inclusive—Continued.

Names of claimants.	Nature or object of the claim.	Congress.	Session.	How brought before the House of Reps.	Page of journal.	To what committee of the House referred.	No. or date of the report.	Nature of the report.	No. of the bill.	How disposed of by the House of Reps.	How disposed of by the Senate.	Date of the act of Congress, and remarks.
Rhode Island, Merchants Bank of Newport.	Repayment of certain stamp duties.	15	1	Senate bill	397	Ways and Means..	April 13, 1818	With't amend.	S. 53	Referred to Committee Whole House.		
Rhode Island, Merchants Bank of Newport.	Repayment of certain stamp duties.	16	1	Senate bill	212	Ways and Means..	Feb. 14, 1820	With't amend.	S. 30	Laid on table.		
Rhode Island, Merchants Bank of Newport.	Repayment of certain stamp duties.	18	1	Senate bill	187	Ways and Means..	Feb. 9, 1824	Adverse	S. 26	Referred to Committee Whole House.		
Rhode Island, postmaster at Newport.	Compensation for mailing and receiving ship letters.	20	1	Resolution	202	P. Of. & P. Roads.	....	....	......	Discharged; laid on table.		
Rhode Island, surveyor of the customs at Patuxent.	Increase of compensation........	15	2	Senate bill	91	Com. and Manuf..	Feb. 24, 1819	With't amend.	S. 10	Laid on table.		
Ricaud, John	To be released from imprisonment at suit of United States.	14	1	Petition	689	Ways and Means..	....	....	......	Discharged; laid on table.		
Ricaud, John...........	To be released from imprisonment at suit of United States.	14	2	Petition	39	Ways and Means..	Dec. 18, 1816	Favorable....	17	Passed	Passed, with amendment.	App'd Jan. 23, 1817
Ricaud, John, surety of ..	Release from liability...........	14	2	Petition	128	Ways and Means.						
Ricaud, John, surety of ..	For resettlement of accounts	17	2	Petition	184	Claims..........	Feb. 24, 1823	Favorable....	293	Passed	Passed	App'd Mar. 23, 1823
Ricaud, John, surety of ..	To be released from payment of balance claimed.	18	1	Petition	176	Claims..........	71	Adverse	......	Referred to Committee Whole House.		
Ricaud, John, surety of ..	To be released from payment of balance claimed.	18	2	Petition	66	Claims	Feb. 25, 1825	Adverse	......	Laid on table.		
Ricaud, John, surety of ..	To be released from payment of balance claimed.	19	1	Petition	57	Claims	123	Adverse	......	Referred to Committee Whole House.		
Ricaud, John, surety of ..	To be released from payment of balance claimed.	20	1	Petition	47	Claims	Dec. 21, 1827	Adverse	......	Laid on table.		
Ricaud, John, surety of ..	To be released from payment of balance claimed.	20	2	Petition and rep't of last session.	50	Whole House.						
Ricand, John, surety of ..	To be released from payment of balance claimed.	21	1	Petition	56	Claims	Mar. 3, 1830	Adverse	......	Referred to Committee Whole House.		
Ricaud, John, surety of ..	To be released from payment of balance claimed.	22	1	Petition	384	Claims.						
Ricaud, John, surety of ..	To be released from payment of balance claimed.	22	2	Petition	74	Military Affairs. ..	....	....	......	Discharged; laid on table.		
Ricaud, John, surety of ..	To be released from payment of balance claimed.	23	1	Petition	162	Claims.						
Ricaud, John, surety of ..	To be released from payment of balance claimed.	23	2	Petition	95	Military Affairs.						
Ricaud, John, surety of ..	To be released from payment of balance claimed.	24	1	Petition	64	Military Affairs....	257	Favorable....	265	Referred to Committee Whole House.		
Rice, Benjamin.........	Restoration of pension discontinued under act of May, 1820.	17	1	Petition	45	Rev. Pensions.						
Rice, Charles	Pension.................... ...	3	2	Rep. of Secretary War.	352	Claims	Feb. 28, 1795	Favorable; bill	130	Passed	Postponed.	
Rice, Charles...........	Pension	4	1	Rep. of Secretary War.	445	Claims	Feb. 18, 1796	Favorable; bill	156	Passed	Passed	App'd April 20, 1796
Rice, Chauncey.........	Revolutionary pension..........	23	1	Petition	617	Rev. Pensions	....	....	......	Discharged; laid on table.		
Rice, Chauncey.........	Revolutionary pension..........	24	1	Declaration.....	506	Rev. Pensions	....	....	......	Discharged; laid on table.		
Rice, Chauncey.........	Revolutionary pension..........	24	2	Petition	90	Rev. Pensions.....	58	Favorable....	808	Referred to Committee Whole House.		
Rice, Chauncey.........	Revolutionary pension..........	25	2	Petition	38	Rev. Pensions.....	180	Favorable....	205	Passed	Adverse.	
Rice, Chauncey.........	Revolutionary pension..........	25	3	House bill	383	Rev. Pensions	231	Favorable....	1082	Passed	Adverse.	
Rice, Chauncey.........	Revolutionary pension..........	26	1	Petition	170	Rev. Pensions	122	Favorable....	132	Passed	Passed	App'd July 20, 1840

List of private claims presented to the House of Representatives of the United States from the 1st to the 31st Congress, inclusive—Continued.

Names of claimants.	Nature or object of the claim.	Congress.	Session.	How brought before the House of Reps.	Page of journal.	To what committee of the House referred.	No. or date of the report.	Nature of the report.	No. of the bill.	How disposed of by the House of Reps.	How disposed of by the Senate.	Date of the act of Congress, and remarks.
Rice, Christian	Pension for revolutionary services	25	2	Petition	984	Rev. Pensions				Discharged; laid on table.		
Rice, D. M	(See Newland & Rice)	23	2		234							
Rice, Edmund	Increase of pension	25	2	Petition	913	Rev. Pensions				Discharged; laid on table.		
Rice, Edmund	Increase of pension	25	3	Petition	189	Rev. Pensions	Jan. 16, 1839	Adverse		Laid on table.		
Rice, Edmund	Increase of pension	26	1	Petition	603	Rev. Pensions.						
Rice, Edmund	Increase of pension	26	2	Petition	222	Rev. Pensions.						
Rice, Elijah	Pension for revolutionary services	3	1	Rep. of Secretary War.	131	Select	May 26, 1794	Jt. res. to refer to Sec. War.	J. R. 12	Passed	Passed	App'd June 9, 1794
Rice, Elijah	Pension for revolutionary services	3	2	Rep. of Secretary War.	262	Claims.						
Rice, Elijah	Pension for revolutionary services	4	1	Rep. of Secretary War.	445	Claims.						
Rice, Elijah	Pension for revolutionary services	4	2	Rep. of Secretary War.	614	Claims.						
Rice, Elisha	Pension	3	1	Petition and rep't Sec. War.	49, 93					Laid on table.		
Rice, Elisha	Increase of pension	11	3	Pension bill	604	Whole House	Mar. 2, 1811	With amends.	218	Passed	Passed	App'd March 3, 1811
Rice, Frederick	Papment for revolutionary services	24	1	Petition	204	Rev. Claims	May 10, 1836	Adverse		Laid on table.		
Rice, George, heirs of	Commutation pay for revolutionary services.	23	2	Petition	239	Rev. Claims.						
Rice, George, heirs of	Commutation pay for revolutionary services.	24	1	Petition	431	Rev. Claims	Mar. 25, 1836	Adverse		Laid on table.		
Rice, George, heirs of	Commutation pay for revolutionary services.	24	2	Petition	94	Rev. Claims.						
Rice, George, heirs of	Commutation pay for revolutionary services.	25	2	Petition	393	Rev. Claims	908	Adverse		Laid on table.		
Rice, George, heirs of	Commutation pay for revolutionary services.	27	2	Petition	62	Rev. Claims	398	Adverse		Laid on table.		
Rice, Henry, and others, merchants of Boston.	To be refunded duties paid on goods, and exonerated from bonds.	14	2	Petition	176	Ways and Means				Discharged; laid on table.		
Rice, Henry, and others	To be refunded duties paid on goods, and exonerated from bonds.	15	1	Petition	165	Ways and Means.						
Rice, Henry, and others	To be refunded duties paid on goods, and exonerated from bonds.	15	2	Petition	61	Ways and Means				Discharged; laid on table.		
Rice, Henry, and others	To be refunded duties paid on goods, and exonerated from bonds.	16	1	Senate bill	108	Ways and Means	Jan. 14, 1820	With't amend.	13	Passed	Passed	App'd April 11, 1820
Rice Henry, attorney for merchants of Boston.	For interposition of government for seizure and confiscation of vessels at St Domingo in 1810.	16	1	Petition	38	Foreign Affairs				Discharged; referred to Secretary State.		
Rice, Henry, merchant of Boston.	For debenture on goods reshipped to Leghorn.	16	2	Petition	140	Commerce.				Discharged; laid on table.		
Rice, Henry G., merchant of Boston.	Reimburse duties paid on East India goods reshipped to Leghorn.	19	2	Petition	26	Ways and Means	32	Favorable	334	Referred to Committee Whole House.		
Rice, Henry G., merchant of Boston.	Reimburse duties paid on East India goods reshipped to Leghorn.	20	1	Petition	31	Ways and Means	7	Favorable	10	Passed	Passed	App'd Mar. 10, 1828
Rice, Holeman	Commutation pay for revolutionary services.	22	2	Petition	94	Rev. Claims.						
Rice, Holeman	Commutation pay for revolutionary services.	23	1	Petition	138	Rev. Claims.						
Rice, Hopkins	To correct an error in the entry of land.	21	2	Petition	75	Priv. Land Claims.	22	Favorable	537	Referred to Committee Whole House.		

List of private claims presented to the House of Representatives of the United States from the 1st to the 31st Congress, inclusive—Continued.

Names of claimants.	Nature or object of the claim.	Congress.	Session.	How brought before the House of Reps.	Page of journal.	To what committee of the House referred.	No. or date of the report.	Nature of the report.	No. of the bill.	How disposed of by the House of Reps.	How disposed of by the Senate.	Date of the act of Congress, and remarks.
Rice, Hopkins	To correct an error in the entry of land.	22	1	Petition	64	Rev. Claims	Dec. 23, 1831	Favorable	115	Passed	Passed	App'd June 15, 1832
Rice, Hopkins, and Benjamin Carpenter.	To correct an error in the entry of land.	22	1	Petition	107	......	......	......	......	Laid on table.		
Rice, Jacob	(See Wm. H. Bedford, agent)	28	1	......	262							
Rice, Jacob	(See Jacob Eyerly, administrator of.)	22	2	......	321							
Rice, James	(See heirs of John Neiler)	19	2	......	134							
Rice, James B.	Pension for revolutionary services.	24	1	Petition	432	Rev. Claims.						
Rice, James B.	Pension for revolutionary services.	24	1	Resolution	912	Rev. Pensions.						
Rice, James B.	Pension for revolutionary services.	24	2	Petition	126	Rev. Pensions	185	Favorable	907	Referred to Committee Whole House.		
Rice, James B.	Pension for revolutionary services.	25	2	Petition	312	Rev. Pensions	454	Favorable	457	Passed.		
Rice, James B.	Pens on for revolutionary services.	25	2	Resolution	74	Rev. Pensions.						
Rice, James B.	Pension for revolutionary services.	25	3	Petition	88	Rev. Pensions	232	Favorable	1013	Passed.		
Rice, James B.	Pension for revolutionary services.	25	3	Resolution	136	Rev. Pensions.						
Rice, James B.	Pension for revolutionary services.	26	1	Petition	172	Rev. Pensions	484	Adverse	......	Laid on table.		
Rice, James B.	Pension for revolutionary services.	27	2	Petition	59	Rev. Pensions	May 20, 1842	Adverse	......	Laid on table.		
Rice, John P.	Arrears of pension	17	1	Petition	256	Pens. & Rev. Cl'ms.	Feb. 15, 1822	Adverse	......	Rejected.		
Rice, John	Compensation for military services in revolutionary war.	24	2	Documents	397	Rev. Claims.						
Rice, Joseph	(See Jacob Eyerly, &c.)	22	2	......	321							
Rice, Joseph H.	Relief on account of military land warrant granted to him by State of North Carolina for services in revolutionary war.	31	1	Petit on	827	Public Lands.						
Rice, Luther	Payment of money in lieu of land.	24	1	Indian appropriation bill.	1012	......	......	......	695	Passed	Passed	App'd July 2, 1836
Rice, Owen	(See Jacob Eyerly, administrator of.)	22	2	Petition	321							
Rice, Philip R.	Payment for vessel pressed into and lost in public service during revolutionary war.	27	2	Petition	328	Rev. Claims	781	Adverse	......	Laid on table.		
Rice, Philip R.	Payment for vessel pressed into and lost in public service during revolutionary war.	28	1	Petition	72	Rev. Claims.						
Rice, Philip R., heirs of	Payment for vessel pressed into and lost in public service during revolutionary war.	28	1	Petition	745	Rev. Claims.						
Rice, Philip R., heirs of	Payment for vessel pressed into and lost in public sesvice during revolutionary war.	28	2	Petition	54	Rev. Claims	107	Favorable	590	Referred to Committee Whole House.		
Rice, Philip R., heirs of	Payment for vessel pressed into and lost in public service during revolutionary war.	29	1	Petition	75	Rev. Claims.						
Rice, Philip R., heirs of	Payment for vessel pressed into and lost in public service during revolutionary war.	29	2	Petition	54	Rev. Claims.						
Rice, Philip R., heirs of	Payment for vessel pressed into and lost in public service during revolutionary war.	31	1	Petition	653	Rev. Claims	429	Favorable	356	Referred to Committee Whole House.		
Rice, Richard	Pension for services in Cherokee war.	31	1	Petition	904	Public Lands.						

List of private claims presented to the House of Representatives of the United States from the 1st to the 31st Congress, inclusive—Continued.

Names of claimants.	Nature or object of the claim.	Congress.	Session.	How brought before the House of Reps.	Page of journal.	To what committee of the House referred.	No. or date of the report.	Nature of the report.	No. of the bill.	How disposed of by the House of Reps.	How disposed of by the Senate.	Date of the act of Congress, and remarks.
Rice, Solomon	(See Elias Bates and others)	15	2		109							
Rice, Thomas, and J. P. Williamson.	(See sureties of Benjamin Wall)	13	2		209							
Rice, Warren	(See Wm. Nickels, executor of)	26	1		182		343		319			
Rice, William	Pension for revolutionary services.	10	1	Petition	99	Select.						
Rice, William	Pension for revolutionary services.	10	2	Petition	476					Referred to Secretary War.		
Rice, William, and others.	Release from penalty incurred by importation of goods from British colonies.	13	1	Petition	18	Com. and Manuf.						
Rice, William	Payment for vessel destroyed by British at Bangor, during war of 1812.	14	2	Petition	154	Claims				Discharged; laid on table.		
Rice, William	Payment for vessel destroyed by British at Bangor, during war of 1812.	15	2	Petition	227	Claims				Discharged; laid on table.		
Rice, William	Payment for vessel destroyed by British at Bangor, during war of 1812.	16	1	Petition	52	Claims	Jan. 5, 1820	Adverse		Laid on table.		
Rice, William, and others.	Restoration of proceeds of sale of cargo from West Indies, seized and sold under non-intercourse act of 1812.	17	1	Petition	114	Ways and Means	Mar. 12, 1822	Adverse		Laid on table.		
Rice, William, and others.	Restoration of proceeds of sale of cargo from West Indies, seized and sold under non-intercourse act of 1812.	18	1	Petition	358	Claims.						
Rice, William, (Mass.)	Payment for losses on contract to build monument on Bourditch's ledge.	26	1	Petition	293	Claims	371	Adverse		Laid on table.		
Rice, William, (Mass.)	Payment for losses on contract to build monument on Bourditch's ledge.	27	2	Petition	94	Claims	765	Adverse		Laid on table.		
Rice, William, (Mass.)	Payment for losses on contract to build monument on Bourditch's ledge.	27	3	Petition	73	Claims	90	Adverse		Laid on table.		
Rice, William, widow of	Pension for his services in war with Mexico.	31	1	Petition	369	Invalid Pensions	391	Adverse		Laid on table.		
Rice, Reed & Co	Permission to import goods ordered from England previous to proclamation of 1810.	12	1	Petition	248					Referred to Committee Whole House on bill No. 46.		
Rich, Mary	Pension	22	1	Petition	124	Rev. Pensions				Discharged; laid on table.		
Rich, Mary	(See heirs of Samuel Jones)	25	2		403							
Rich, S. and M	(See sureties of John F. Moore)	27	3		94							
Rich, William	Payment for services in detecting smugglers.	23	1	Petition	155	Judiciary.						
Rich, William	Payment for services in detecting smugglers.	23	2	Petition	214	Judiciary.						
Rich, William	Payment for services and expenses incurred in seizing goods imported in violation of revenue laws.	28	1	Petition	802	Claims.						

List of private claims presented to the House of Representatives of the United States from the 1st to the 31st Congress, inclusive—Continued.

Names of claimants.	Nature or object of the claim.	Congress.	Session.	How brought before the House of Reps.	Page of journal.	To what committee of the House referred.	No. or date of the report.	Nature of the report.	No. of the bill.	How disposed of by the House of Reps.	How disposed of by the Senate.	Date of the act of Congress, and remarks.
Rich, William	Payment for services and expenses incurred in seizing goods imported in violation of revenue laws.	28	2	Petition	57	Claims	15	Favorable	477	Passed	Passed	App'd March 3, 1845
Rich, William	Compensation for services as clerk in the office of the paymaster general.	28	2	Senate bill	156	Claims	Jan. 11, 1845	Adverse	S. 41	Referred to Committee Whole House.		
Rich, Zacheus	Restoration of pension, discontinued under act May 15, 1820.	17	1	Petition	45	Rev. Pensions.						
Rich, Zacheus	Restoration of pension, discontinued under act May 15, 1820.	19	1	Petition	98	Military Pensions	164	Adverse	......	Laid on table.		
Rich, Zacheus	Restoration of pension, discontinued under act May 15, 1820.	19	1	Resolution	467	Military Pensions	May 5, 1826	Favorable	......	Referred to Committee Whole House.		
Rich, Zacheus	Restoration of pension, discontinued under act May 15, 1820.	19	2	Petition	67	Military Pensions	Dec. 22, 1826	Favorable	315	Passed.		
Rich, Zacheus	Restoration of pension, discontinued under act May 15, 1820.	20	1	Resolution	409	Military Pensions	....	....	......	Discharged; laid on table.		
Rich, Zacheus	Restoration of pension, discontinued under act May 15, 1820.	21	1	Petition	48	Military Pensions	Jan. 5, 1830	Pension bill	72	....	Passed	App'd May 20, 1830
Richard, Dominique	Confirmation of title to land in Louisiana.	21	2	Petition	189	Priv. Land Claims	....	....	......	Discharged; laid on table.		
Richard, Dominique	Confirmation of title to land in Louisiana.	22	1	Petition	65	Priv. Land Claims	Dec. 27, 1831	Adverse	......	Laid on table.		
Richard, Gabriel, & others.	Payment for land granted to, and taken by War Department.	17	2	Petition	44	Military Affairs	Feb. 7, 1823	Favorable	281	Referred to Committee Whole House.		
Richard, Gabriel, & others.	Payment for land granted to, and taken by War Department.	18	1	Petition	106	Claims	30	Favorable	63	Passed	Passed	App'd May 26, 1824
Richard, Jeremiah	Pension for revolutionary services.	3	2	Rep. of Secretary War.	278	Claims.						
Richard, Jeremiah	Pension for revolutionary services.	4	1	Rep. of Secretary War.	373	Claims.						
Richard, Jeremiah	Pension for revolutionary services.	4	2	Rep. of Secretary War.	614	Claims.						
Richard, Lewis and Pierre.	Confirmation of title to land in Louisiana.	14	1	Petition	422	Public Lands.						
Richard, Lewis and Pierre.	Confirmation of title to land in Louisiana.	14	2	Petition	133	Priv. Land Claims.						
Richard, Lewis and Pierre.	Confirmation of title to land in Louisiana.	15	1	Petition	173	Priv. Land Claims.						
Richard, Maria A.	(See Gabriel Giard, heirs of.)	30	1	....	606							
Richard, Pierre, widow of.	Confirmation of title to land in Louisiana.	26	1	Petition	365	Priv. Land Claims.						
Richards, Abraham	Remission of duties on merchandise carried off by the enemy in 1812.	14	2	Petition	377	Ways and Means.						
Richards, Abraham	Remission of duties on merchandise carried off by the enemy in 1812.	15	1	Petition	44	Ways and Means	Jan. 19, 1818	Adverse	......	Laid on table.		
Richards, Alexander	(See Benjamin Merrill and Alexander Richards.)	12	1	....	11							
Richards, Benjamin	Pension	20	1	Petition	598	Military Pensions.						
Richards, Benjamin, representatives of.	Arrears of pension due for naval services.	26	1	Petition	738	Rev. Pensions.						

List of private claims presented to the House of Representatives of the United States from the 1st to the 31st Congress, inclusive—Continued.

Names of claimants.	Nature or object of the claim.	Congress.	Session.	How brought before the House of Reps.	Page of journal.	To what committee of the House referred.	No. or date of the report.	Nature of the report.	No. of the bill.	How disposed of by the House of Reps.	How disposed of by the Senate.	Date of the act of Congress, and remarks.
Richards, Benjamin, representatives of.	Arrears of pension due for naval services.	27	2	Petition	251	Naval Affairs.....	April 12, 1482	Adverse	......	Laid on table.		
Richards, Benjamin, representatives of.	Arrears of pension due for naval services.	28	1	Petition	912	Naval Affairs.						
Richards, Benjamin, representatives of.	Arrears of pension due for naval services.	28	2	Petition	216	Naval Affairs.						
Richards, B. W.........	(See J. and W. Lippencott & Co.)	22	1	....	440							
Richards, Daniel, and Jos. Humphrey.	Indemnity for loss of schooner captured by British while fishing off Nova Scotia.	14	2	Petition	278	Ways and Means..	....	....	......	Discharged; laid on table.		
Richards, Daniel, widow of.	Pension for revolutionary services.	25	2	Petition	230	Rev. Pensions	550	Favorable....	537	Passed.		
Richards, Daniel, widow of.	Pension for revolutionary services.	26	1	Petition	172	Rev. Pensions.....	....	....	......	Discharged; laid on table.		
Richards, Edmund.......	Pension for revolutionary services.	22	1	Petition	56	Rev. Pensions	Dec. 28, 1831 Mar. 13, 1832	Adverse ..... Favorable; bill	 467	Recommitted. Passed	 Indef. postp'd.	
Richards, Elisha F......	Indemnity for property sold by United States for an alleged violation of revenue laws.	28	1	Petition	533	Claims.						
Richards, Elisha F......	Indemnity for property sold by United States for an alleged violation of revenue laws.	28	2	Petition	117	Claims.						
Richards, Elisha F......	Indemnity for property sold by United States for an alleged violation of revenue laws.	29	1	Petition	75	Claims	580	Favorable....	398	Passed.		
Richards, Elisha F......	Indemnity for property sold by United States for an alleged violation of revenue laws.	29	2	Petition	49	Claims	3	Favorable....	581	Referred to Committee Whole House.		
Richards, Elisha F......	Indemnity for property sold by United States for an alleged violation of revenue laws.	30	1	Petition	154	Claims	164	Favorable....	164	Passed.		
Richards, Gabriel........	(See Michigan, rector of St. Ann's church, Detroit.)	17	2	....	44							
Richards, George........	Pension	16	2	Petition	238	Rev. Pensions	Feb. 15, 1821	Adverse	......	Rejected.		
Richards, Isaac..........	Compensation for revolutionary services.	2	1	Petition	444	....	....	....	......	Referred to Secretary of War.		
Richards, Isaac..........	Pension for revolutionary services.	3	1	Rep. of Secretary War.	131	Select	May 26, 1794	Jt. res. to refer to Sec. War.	J. R. 12	Passed	Passed	App'd June 9, 1794
Richards, Isaac..........	Pension for revolutionary services.	3	2	Rep. of Secretary War.	262	Claims	Feb. 28, 1795	Favorable....	130	Passed	Postponed.	
Richards, Isaac..........	Pension for revolutionary services.	4	1	Report Secretary of War.	445	Claims	Feb. 18, 1796	Favorable; bill	156	Passed............	Passed	App'd April 20, 1796
Richards, Isaac..........	Increase of pension	11	3	Pension bill	604	Whole House	Mar. 2, 1811	With amends.	218	Passed	Passed	App'd March 3, 1811
Richards, John, (Ohio)...	Pension	21	1	Resolution	79	Military Pensions..	April 6, 1830	Adverse	......	Laid on table.		
Richards, John, (Ohio)...	Pension	22	1	Petition	104	Rev. Pensions	....	....	......	Discharged; laid on table.		
Richards & Jones........	(See Bordman & Pope and others.)	12	1	....	136							
Richards, Joseph, and others	Payment for stone delivered under contract with government for construction of dry-dock at Gosport, Virginia.	22	1	Petition	257	Claims	....	....	......	Discharged; laid on table.		
Richards, Joseph	(See Henry Hutchinson, representatives of.)	31	1	Petition	277	....	83	....	103			

List of private claims presented to the House of Representatives of the United States from the 1st to the 31st Congress, inclusive—Continued.

Names of claimants.	Nature or object of the claim.	Congress.	Session.	How brought before the House of Reps.	Page of journal.	To what committee of the House referred.	No. or date of the report.	Nature of the report.	No. of the bill.	How disposed of by the House of Reps.	How disposed of by the Senate.	Date of the act of Congress, and remarks.
Richards, Josephus, representatives of.	Payment for horse lost in Florida war.	29	1	Memorial	515	Claims	738	Adverse		Laid on table.		
Richards, Nancy Ermine	(See representatives of Josephus Richards.)	29	1		515							
Richards, Nathaniel	(See Richards, Upson & Co.)	11	2		173							
Richards, Paul	Pension	12	2	Petition	713	Claims.						
Richards, Samuel	(See executor of Wm. T. Smith.)	24	2		95							
Richards, Samuel, executor of.	Commutation pay for revolutionary services.	29	2	Petition	75	Rev. Claims.						
Richards, Samuel, executors of.	Commutation pay for revolutionary services.	30	1	Petition	439	Rev. Claims.						
Richards, Samuel, executors of.	Commutation pay for revolutionary services.	30	2							Leave to withdraw.		
Richards, Thomas C.	Indemnity for property destroyed by Indians in 1817.	22	1	Petition	575	Indian Affairs.						
Richards, Thomas, heirs of	Compensation for revolutionary services.	26	1	Petition	630	Rev. Claims				Discharged; laid on table.		
Richards, Upson & Co.	Release from bond for double duties imposed for violation of non-importation act	11	2	Petition	173	Com. and Manuf.						
Richards, Upson & Co.	To be exonerated from payment of double duties.	11	2	Petition	173	Com. and Manuf.						
Richards, Upson & Co.	To be exonerated from payment of double duties.	12	1	Petition	50	Com. and Manuf.	Dec. 9, 1811	Adverse		Leave to withdraw.		
Richards & Van Wart	Payment for stone delivered for dry-dock at navy-yard, New York.	30	2	Petition	164	Claims				Discharged; laid on table.		
Richards, Wyatt	To change location of bounty land	30	1	Petition	260	Public Lands.	812	Adverse		Laid on table.		
Richardson, A., widow of.	Payment for medical services in revolutionary war.	12	1	Petition	236	Claims.						
Richardson, A., widow of.	Payment for medical services in revolutionary war.	13	2	Petition	270	Claims	Feb. 7, 1814	Adverse		Leave to withdraw.		
Richardson, Abijah	Restoration of pension	17	1	Petiti n	45	Rev. Pensions.						
Richardson, Andrew H.	(See executors of Valentine Richardson.)	21	1		547							
Richardson, Booker	(See Wm. H. Bedford, agent, &c.)	28	1		262							
Richardson, Charles, capt. of brig Leontine.	Compensation for losses arising under alleged misconduct of American consul at Havana.	27	2	Petition	321	Commerce				Discharged; referred to Claims.		
Richardson Elizabeth	Extension of pension	28	1	Petition	850	Rev. Claims.						
Richardson, Ellis, attorney of.	Pay for military services in revolutionary war.	4	1	Petition	394	Claims	Jan. 26, 1796	Adverse		Leave to withdraw.		
Richardson, George, administrator of.	Renewal of final settlement certificate.	2	1	Petition and rep't Sec. Treasury.	490, 583	Select.						
Richardson, George	Invalid pension	3	1	Petition	197					Laid on table.		
Richardson, George	Invalid pension	10	1	House bill	232	Whole House	April 19, 1808	With amend'ts	78	Passed	Passed	App'd April 25, 1808
Richardson, Hannah	(See Wadleigh Noyes)	2	1		448							
Richardson, Hannah	(See Mary Elliott, *et al.*)	23	1		73							
Richardson, Harry	Payment of portion of judgment obtained against John French, detected in smuggling.	26	1	Petition	885	Claims.						
Richardson, Harry	Payment of portion of judgment obtained against John French, detected in smuggling.	26	2	Petition	214	Claims.						

List of private claims presented to the House of Representatives of the United States from the 1st to the 31st Congress, inclusive—Continued.

Names of claimants.	Nature or object of the claim.	Congress.	Session.	How brought before the House of Reps.	Page of journal.	To what committee of the House referred.	No. or date of the report.	Nature of the report.	No. of the bill.	How disposed of by the House of Reps.	How disposed of by the Senate.	Date of the act of Congress, and remarks.
Richardson, Harry.......	Paymant of portion of judgment obtained against John French, detected in smuggling.	27	2	Petition	55	Claims	24	Adverse	......	Laid on table.		
Richardson, Harry.......	Payment of portion of judgment obtained against John French, detected in smuggling.	28	1	Petition	109	Claims	556	Adverse	......	Laid on table.		
Richardson, Harry.......	Payment of portion of judgment obtained against John French, detected in smuggling.	28	2	Petition	57	Judiciary	....	....	......	Discharged; laid on table.		
Richardson, Harry.......	Payment of portion of judgment obtained against John French, detected in smuggling.	29	1	Petition	83	Judiciary	138	Adverse	......	Laid on table.		
Richardson, Harry.......	Payment of portion of judgment obtained against J hn French, detected in smuggling.	30	1	Petition	77	Claims	401	Adverse	......	Laid on table.		
Richardson, Harry......	Payment of portion of judgment obtained against John French, detected in smuggling.	31	1	Petition	191	Claims	....	....	......	Discharged; laid on table.		
Richardson, Henry, widow of.	Payment of wages and prize money as a United States marine in 1812.	24	1	Petition	408	Naval Affairs.....	Mar. 21, 1836	Favorable....	456	Referred to Committee Whole House.		
Richardson, Henry, widow of.	Payment of wages and prize money as a United States marine in 1812.	24	1	Senate bill	811	Naval Affairs.....	May 17, 1836	With amend..	S. 186	Passed	Passed	App'd July 2, 1836
Richardson, Henry, representatives of.	Payment of wages and prize money for naval services.	25	2	Petition	41	Naval Affairs.....	149	Favorable	171	Referred to Committee Whole House.		
Richardson, Henry, representatives of.	Payment of wages and prize money for naval services.	25	3	Bill of last sess..	375	Whole House	Jan. 25, 1839	With't amend.	171	Passed	Passed.......	App'd March 2, 1839
Richardson, Holt, heirs of.	Commutation pay for revolutionary services.	23	2	Petition	109	Rev. Claims......	Jan. 2, 1835	Adverse	......	Laid on table.		
Richardson, Holt, heirs of.	Commutation pay for revolutionary services.	24	1	Petition	536	Rev. Claims......	....	....	......	Discharged; laid on table.		
Richardson, Holt, heirs of.	Commutation pay for revolutionary services.	24	2	Petition	92	Rev. Claims.						
Richardson, Holt, heirs of.	Commutation pay for revolutionary services.	30	2	Petition	175	Rev. Claims.						
Richardson, Holt, heirs of	Commutation pay for revolutionary services.	31	1	Petition .... Documents	225 437	Rev. Claims. Rev. Claims.						
Richardson, Humphrey...	Payment for property lost while a soldier in the revolutionary war.	25	2	Petition	47	Rev. Claims......	438	Adverse	......	Laid on table.		
Richardson, Isaac, and J. Thompson.	For further time to complete payment on land purchased of United States	16	2	Petition	249	Public Lands.						
Richardson, Isaac	Pension for revolutionary services.	22	1	Petition	219	Rev. Pensions....	381	Favorable	472	Passed	Indef. postp'd.	
Richardson, James.......	Reimburse money expended, and compensation for revolutionary services.	3	1	Petition	65	....	....	....	......	Rreferred to Secretary of War.		
Richardson, James.......	Reimburse money expended, and compensation for revolutionary services.	3	2	Rep. of Secretary War.	290	Claims	....	....	......	Laid on table.		
Richardson, James.......	Reimburse money expended, and compensation for revolutionary services.	4	1	Resolution	373	Claims	Dec. 24, 1795	Adverse	......	Leave to withdraw.		

List of private claims presented to the House of Representatives of the United States from the 1st to the 31st Congress, inclusive—Continued.

Names of claimants.	Nature or object of the claim.	Congress.	Session.	How brought before the House of Reps.	Page of journal.	To what committee of the House referred.	No. or date of the report.	Nature of the report.	No. of the bill.	How disposed of by the House of Reps.	How disposed of by the Senate.	Date of the act of Congress, and remarks.
Richardson, James D	Pension	19	2	Resolution	70	Military Pensions	Feb. 14, 1827	Pension bill	436	Referred to Committee Whole House.		
Richardson, James D	Pension	20	1	Petition	38	Military Pensions.						
Richardson, James D	Pension	20	2	Petition	55	Military Pensions	Dec. 12, 1828	Favora le	311	Passed	Laid on table.	
Richardson, James D	Pension	21	1	Petition	48	Military Pensions	Jan. 5, 1830	Pension bill	72	Passed	Passed	App'd May 20, 1830
Richardson, James, widow of.	Pension for revolutionary services of her husband.	28	1	Petition	718	Rev. Pensions				Discharged; laid on table.		
Richardson, Jesse	Confirmation of title to land in Missouri.	15	2	Petition	114	Priv. Land Claims.				Discharged; laid on table.		
Richardson, Jesse	Confirmation of title to land in Missouri.	16	1	Petition	36	Priv. Land Claims.				Discharged; laid on table.		
Richardson, Jesse	Confirmation of title to land in Missouri.	17	1	Petition	55	Public Lands.						
Richardson, Jesse	Confirmation of title to land in Missouri.	18	1	Petition	55	Public Lands.						
Richardson, Jesse, heirs of.	Indemnity for Indian depredations.	24	2	Documents	315	Indian Affairs.						
Richardson, John	Compensation for extra services as captain's clerk on board United States ship Portsmouth.	30	2	Petition	86	Naval Affairs.						
Richardson, John	Compensation for extra services as captain's clerk on board United States ship Portsmouth.	31	1	Petition	944	Naval Affairs.						
Richardson, Joseph	(See Wadleigh Noyes, guardian of children of.)	2	1		448							
Richardson, Joseph	Pension	10	2	Pension bill	449	Whole House	Feb. 20, 1809	With amends.	158	Passed	Passed	App'd March 3, 1809
Richardson, Joseph	Increase of pension	11	1	Petition	84	Claims.						
Richardson, Joseph	Increase of pension	11	2	Petition	190	Claims.						
Richardson, Joseph	Arrears of pension	15	1	Petition	236	Pens. & Rev. Cl'ms.				Discharged; laid on table.		
Richardson, Joseph	Renewal of land warrant lost or mislaid or leave to locate land without warrant.	15	2	Petition	104	Military Affairs				Discharged; laid on table.		
Richardson, Joseph	Renewal of land warrant lost or mislaid or leave to locate land without warrant.	16	1	Petition	66	Priv. Land Claims.				Discharged; laid on table.		
Richardson, Landie	Compensation for a horse lost in public service.	18	1	Petition	214	Claims	March 9, 1824	Favorable	151	Passed	Passed	App'd May 21, 1824
Richardson, Mathew	Confirmation of title to land in Alabama.	18	1	Petition	255	Priv. Land Claims.						
Richardson, Matthew	Confirmation of title to land in Alabama.	20	1	Petition	197	Priv. Land Claims.				Discharged; laid on table.		
Richardson, Nathan	(See Sergeant & Richardson)	3	2		289							
Richardson, Oliver	Pension for revolutionary services.	21	2	Petition	120	Military Pensions.						
Richardson, Oliver	Pension for revolutionary services.	22	1	Resolution	93	Rev. Pensions				Discharged; laid on table.		
Richardson, Richard	Pension for revolutionary services.	3	1	Rep. of Secretary War.	131	Select	May 26, 1796	Jt. res. to refer Sec. War.	J.R. 12	Passed	Passed	App'd June 9, 1794
Richardson, Richard	Pension for revolutionary services.	3	2	Rep. of Secretary War.	262	Claims.						
Richardson, Richard	Pension for revolutionary services.	4	1	Rep. of Secretary War.	445	Claims.						
Richardson, Richard	Pension for revolutionary services.	4	2	Rep. of Secretary War.	614	Claims.						

List of private claims presented to the House of Representatives of the United States from the 1*st to the* 31*st Congress, inclusive*—Continued.

Names of claimants.	Nature or object of the claim.	Congress.	Session.	How brought before the House of Reps.	Page of journal.	To what committee of the House referred.	No. or date of the report.	Nature of the report.	No. of the bill.	How disposed of by the House of Reps.	How disposed of by the Senate.	Date of the act of Congress, and remarks.
Richardson, Robert R....	Additional compensation as assistant marshal in taking census.	7	1	Petition	43	Claims	Jan. 13, 1802	Adverse	......	Laid on table.		
Richardson, Robert D., representatives of.	Payment of money due by verdict against United Stetes.	25	2	Memorial	88	Claims	....	....	......	Discharged.		
Richardson, Robert D., representatives of.	Payment of money due by verdict against United States.	25	3	Petition	87	Claims	164	Adverse	......	Laid on table.		
Richardson, Robert D., representatives of.	Payment of money due by verdict against United States.	26	1	Petition	339	Claims.						
Richardson, Robert D., representatives of.	Payment of money due by verdict against United States.	26	2	Petition	167	Claims.						
Richardson, Robert D., representatives of.	Paynent of money due by verdict against United States.	27	2	Petition	58	Claims	34	Adverse	......	Laid on table.		
Richardson, Samuel Q., & John Haley.	Compensation for property lost in public service.	15	2	Petition	24	Claims	Nov. 24, 1818	Adverse	......	Referred to Committee Whole House.		
Richardson, Samuel Q., & John Haley.	Compensation for property lost in public service.	16	1	Petition	142	Claims	Jan. 17, 1820	Adverse	......	Leave to withdraw.		
Richardson, Samuel Q., & John Haley.	Compensation for property lost in public service.	19	1	Petition	337	Claims	April 10, 1826	Adverse	......	Laid on table.		
Richardson, Samuel Q., & John Haley.	Compensation for property lost in public service.	20	1	Petition	127	Claims	....	....	......	Discharged; laid on table.		
Richardson, Samuel Q., & John Haley.	Compensation for property lost in public service.	20	2	Petition	218	Claims	....	....	......	Discharged; laid on table.		
Richardson, Samuel Q., & John Haley.	Compensation for property lost in public service.	22	1	Petition	288	Claims	Feb. 17, 1832	Adverse	......	Referred to Committee Whole House.		
Richardson, Samuel	(See Wm. H. Bedford, agent, &c.)	28	1	....	262							
Richardson, Stephen	Pension	25	2	Petition	946	Invalid Pensions ..	....	....	......	Referred to Secretary War.		
Richardson, Stephen	Arrears of pension............	26	1	Petition	547	Invalid Pensions ..	571	Adverse	......	Laid on table.		
Richardson, Thomas, and William Staylor.	Permission to enter public land lying within the city of Mobile.	18	1	Petition	178	Public Lands.....	....	....	......	Discharged; laid on table.		
Richardson, Thomas	Payment to him as assignee, amount due certain soldiers of the war of 1812.	22	1	Petition	422	Claims	353	Favorable....	450	Referred to Committee Whole House.		
Richardson, Thomas	Payment to him as assignee, amount due certain soldiers of the war of 1812.	23	1	Petition	34	Claims	6	Favorable....	6	Passed	Passed	App'd April 15, 1834
Richardson, Thomas L...	Pension for wounds received in war of 1812.	30	1	Memorial	867	Invalid Pensions ..	....	....	......	Discharged; laid on table.		
Richardson, Valentine, executor of.	For commissions on money paid to United States, and for relief from costs of suits.	21	1	Petition	547	Claims	349	Favorable....	450	Referred to Committee Whole House.		
Richardson, Valentine, executor of.	For commissions on money paid to United States, and for relief from costs of suits.	22	1	Petition	43	Claims	Dec. 19, 1831	Favorable....	26	Passed	Passed	App'd Feb. 18, 1832
Richardson, William S...	(See William H. Bedford, agent).	28	1	....	262							
Richardson, William.....	Pension	14	1	House bill	622	Whole House	April 23, 1816	With amends.	......	Passed............	Passed	App'd April 30, 1816
Richardson, William.....	Confirmation of title to land in Alabama.	18	1	Petition	255	Priv. Land Claims.						
Richardson, William.....	Pre-emption right to purchase land.	19	2	Petition	287	Public Lands.....	....	....	......	Discharged; laid on table.		
Richardson, William.....	Pre-emption right to purchase land.	20	1	Petition	40	Public Lands.....	....	....	......	Discharged; laid on table.		

List of private claims presented to the House of Representatives of the United States from the 1st to the 31st Congress, inclusive—Continued.

Names of claimants.	Nature or object of the claim.	Congress.	Session.	How brought before the House of Reps.	Page of journal.	To what committee of the House referred.	No. or date of the report.	Nature of the report.	No. of the bill.	How disposed of by the House of Reps.	How disposed of by the Senate.	Date of the act of Congress, and remarks.
Richardson, William, of Maryland, heirs of.	Payment for revolutionary services	25	2	Memorial	391	Rev. Claims	617	Adverse	......	Laid on table.		
Richardson, W. H. and W.	To refund to them excess of duties paid on umbrella stretchers.	25	2	House bill	637	Commerce	697	Favorable	669	Referred to Committee Whole House.		
Richardson, ——	(See Herring & Richardson)	23	1	....	255							
Richart, Henry, and others.	Change location of land entries	14	1	Petition	257	Public Lands	....	....	......	Discharged; leave to withdraw.		
Richart, Henry, and others.	Change location of land entries	14	2	Petition	117	Priv. Land Claims.						
Richart, Henry, and others.	Change location of land entries	15	2	Petition	220	Public Lands	....	....	......	Leave to withdraw.		
Richart, Thomas	Pension for revolutionary services	3	2	Rep. of Secretary of War.	352	Claims	Feb. 28, 1795	Favorable	130	Passed	Postponed.	
Richart, Thomas	Pension for revolutionary services	4	1	Rep. of Secretary of War.	445	Cliams	Feb. 18, 1796	Favorable	156	Passed	Passed	App'd April 20, 1796
Richaud, John	(See Jas. Caze and John Richaud.)	14	1	....	171							
Richcreek, Humphrey, assignee of.	Indemnity for failure of a land entry.	26	1	Petition	954	Public Lands.						
Richcreek, Humphrey, assignee of.	Indemnity for failure of a land entry.	28	1	Petition	122	Priv. Land Claims.	417	Favorable	321	Passed	Passed	App'd June 17, 1844
Richers, Reuben	Pension for revolutionary services.	20	1	Pension bill	300	Whole House	May 16, 1828	With amends.	166	Passed.		
Richeson, Holt	(See Holt Richardson.)											
Richey, David	Increase of pension	10	1	Pension bill	232	Whole House	April 19, 1808	With amends.	78	Passed	Passed	App'd April 25, 1808
Richey, John	Compensation for guns taken for public service.	25	3	Senate bill	656	....	....	....	S. 121			
Richey, John	Compensation for guns taken for public service.	26	1	Senate bill	1105	Claims	July 10, 1840	Adverse	S. 150	Referred to Committee Whole House.		
Richmond, Charles	Compensation for services as assistant marshal during Canadian disturbances, in 1839 and 1840.	30	1	Senate bill	957	Claims	July 12, 1848	With amend.	S. 153	Passed	Passed	App'd Aug. 14, 1848
Richmond, David	Pre-emption right to enter land	23	2	Resolution	243	Public Lands	79	Favorable	696	Referred to Committee Whole House.		
Richmond, Frederick	Payment for services rendered and property lost during war of 1812.	22	2	Petition	397	Claims.						
Richmond, Frederick	Payment for services rendered and property lost during war of 1812.	23	1	Petition	192	Claims.						
Richmond, Frederick	Payment for services rendered and property lost during war of 1812.	23	2	Petition	37	Claims.						
Richmond, Frederick	Payment for services rendered and property lost during war of 1812.	24	1	Petition	93	Claims	543	Adverse	......	Laid on table.		
Richmond, Frederick	Payment for services rendered and property lost during war of 1812.	25	2	Petition	121	Claims	860	Adverse	......	Laid on table.		
Richmond, Frederick	Payment for services rendered and property lost during war of 1812.	25	3	Petition	86	Claims	99	Favorable	973	Passed	Passed	App'd March 3, 1839
Richmond, George	Revolutionary pension	16	2	Petition	27	Rev. Pensions	Feb. 15, 1821	Adverse	......	Laid on table.		
Richmond, Isaac, and others	Pre-emption right to enter lands	23	2	Resolution	243	Public Lands	79	Favorable	696	Referred to Committee Whole House.		
Richmond, James	Pension	21	2	Petition	159	Military Pensions.						
Richmond, James	Pension	22	1	Petition	80	Rev. Pensions	132	Favorable	202	Referred to Committee Whole House.		
Richmond, James	Pension	22	2	House bill	66	....	....	....	202	Laid on table.		
Richmond, John W	(See Aaron Sheffield, attorney of.)	26	1	....	182	....	343	....	319			
Richmond, Lem. C., owner of schooner La Bruce.	Refund foreign tonnage exacted of master of said vessel.	24	2	Petition	389	Commerce.						

List of private claims presented to the House of Representatives of the United States from the 1st to the 31st Congress, inclusive—**Continued.**

Names of claimants.	Nature or object of the claim.	Congress.	Session.	How brought before the House of Reps.	Page of journal.	To what committee of the House referred.	No. or date of the report.	Nature of the report.	No. of the bill.	How disposed of by the House of Reps.	How disposed of by the Senate.	Date of the act of Congress, and remarks.
Richmond, Lem. C., owner of schooner La Bruce.	Refund foreign tonnage exacted of master of said vessel.	25	2	Petition	412	Commerce	....	....	......	Discharged.		
Richmond, Lem. C., owner of schooner La Bruce.	Refund foreign tonnage exacted of master of said vessel.	25	3	Petition	118	Commerce	264	Adverse	......	Laid on table.		
Richoux, Pierre	(See Pierre Molaison, *et al*)	26	1	....	501							
Rickard, Abner	Pension for revolutionary services.	22	1	Resolution	266	Rev. Pensions	381	Favorable	472	Passed	Indef. postp'd.	
Rickard, Elijah	Pension for revolutinnary services.	22	1	Resolution	436	Rev. Pensions	Mar. 17, 1832	Favorable	46	Passed	Indef. postp'd.	
Rickard, William	To be reimbursed expenses incurred during revolutionary war.	6	2	Petition	736	Claims	Jan. 12, 1801	Adverse	......	Laid on table.		
Rickard, William	To be reimbursed expenses incurred during revolutionary war.	8	1	Petition	579	Claims	Feb. 29, 1804	Adverse	......	Laid on table.		
Rickard, William	To be reimbursed expenses incurred during revolutionary war.	9	1	Petition	235	Claims	....	....	......	Discharged.		
Rickard, William	Payment of expenses incurred and services rendered while in command of a detachment of United States troops at Knoxville, Tennessee.	12	1	Petition	98	Claims.						
Ricke, John, heirs of	Redemption of Continental money paid deceased for revolutionary services.	29	1	Petition	1103	Claims.						
Ricker, Abraham, widow of.	(See Abraham Riker, widow of.)	2	1	....	500							
Ricker, Isaac	Payment for horse and equipments surrendered with Detroit in 1812.	16	1	Petition	169	Claims	Feb. 4, 1820	Adverse	......	Laid on table.		
Ricker, Isaac	Payment for horse and equipmen s surrendered with Detroit in 1812.	18	2	Petition	46	Claims	Jan. 3, 1825	Adverse	......	Laid on table.		
Ricker, Isaac	Payment for horse and equipments surrendered with Detroit in 1812.	19	1	Petition	67	Claims	200	Adv.; bill ord'd	261	Passed.		
Ricker, Isaac	Payment for horse and equipments surrendered with Detro t in 1812.	19	2	Petition	59	Claims	Dec. 20, 1826	Favorable	307	Passed	Passed	App'd March 2, 1827
Ricker, Jacob	Pension	19	2	Petition	78	Military Pensions	....	....	......	Discharged.		
Ricker, Reuben	Restoration and arrearages of pension.	19	1	Resolution	331	Military Pensions	May 5, 1826	Favorable	......	Referred to Committee Whole House.		
Ricker, Reuben	Restoration and arrearages of pension.	19	2	Petition	67	Military Pensions	Dec. 22, 1826	Pension bill	315	Passed.		
Ricker, Reuben	Restoration and arrearages of pension.	20	1	Petition	57	Military Pensions	....	....	......	Discharged; laid on table.		
Ricker, Reuben	Restoration and arrearages of pension.	20	2	Petition	55	Military Pensions	Dec. 12, 1828	Favorable	311	Passed	Laid on table	
Ricker, Reuben	Restoration and arrearages of pension.	21	1	Petition	36	Military Pensions	Jan. 5, 1830	Pens'on bill	72	Passed	Passed	App'd May 20, 1830
Ricketson, Barton	Compensation for removal of wreck at Delaware breakwater.	30	1	Petition	524	Commerce.						
Ricketson, Daniel, heirs of.	Indemnity for French spoliations prior to 1800.	26	1	Memorial	182	Foreign Affairs	343	Favorable	319	Referred to Committee Whole House.		
Ricketson, Daniel, heirs of.	Indemnity for French spoliations prior to 1800.	31	1	Petition	196	Foreign Affairs	355	Favorable	318	Referred to Committee Whole House.		
Ricketson, Joseph	Indemnity for French spoliations prior to 1800.	26	1	Memorial	182	Foreign Affairs	343	Favorable	319	Referred to Committee Whole House.		
Ricketts, Benjamin	Payment of prize money due as a marine on board the Bon Homme Richard.	3	1	Petition	95	....	....	....	......	Referred to Secretary of War.		

List of private claims presented to the House of Representatives of the United States from the 1st to the 31st Congress, inclusive—Continued.

Names of claimants.	Nature or object of the claim.	Congress.	Session.	How brought before the House of Reps.	Page of journal.	To what committee of the House referred.	No. or date of the report.	Nature of the report.	No. of the bill.	How disposed of by the House of Reps.	How disposed of by the Senate.	Date of the act of Congress, and remarks.
Ricketts, Benjamin	Payment of prize money due as a marine on board the Bon Homme Richard.	3	2	Report of Secretary of War.	278					Laid on table.		
Ricketts, Benjamin	Payment of prize-money due as a marine on board the Bon Homme Richard.	6	2	Petition	736	Claims	Dec. 12, 1800	Adverse		Laid on table.		
Ricketts, Micajah	Pension	24	1	Resolution	809	Invalid Pensions	692	Favorable	650	Passed	Passed	App'd June 28, 1836
Ricketts, William	Pension	21	1	Resolution	207	Military Pensions				Disch'd; laid on table.		
Ricketts, William	Pension	21	2	Resolution	285	Military Pensions.						
Ricketts, William	Pension	22	1	Resolution	148	Invalid Pensions	Feb. 9, 1832	Adverse		Laid on table.		
Ricketts, William	Pension	22	2	Pension bill	79	Whole House	Dec. 22, 1832	With amends.	626	Passed	Passed	App'd March 2, 1833
Rickman, Dr. Wm., heirs of.	Commutation pay due deceased for services in revolutionary war.	26	1	Petition	706	Rev. Claims	June 23, 1840	Adverse		Laid on table.		
Rickman, Dr. Wm., heirs of.	Commutation pay due deceased for services in revolutionary war.	27	2	Petition	61	Rev. Claims	May 25, 1842	Adverse		Laid on table.		
Ricks, John W	Change location of entry of land.	20	2	Petition	177	Public Lands				Disch'd; laid on table.		
Ricotte, Joseph	Compensation for a horse lost in public service.	15	2	Petition	33	Claims	Dec. 1, 1818	Adverse		Laid on table.		
Riddall, John	Revolutionary pension	18	1	Petition	155	Pens. & Rev. Cl'ms.	Feb. 25, 1824	Adverse		Laid on table.		
Riddick, Mills	(See Richard Taylor, representatives of.)	22	2		127							
Riddick, Thoms F	(See Thomas F. Reddick)	12	1		242							
Riddick, Col. Willis, heirs of.	Payment for loss and destruction of property during revolutionary war.	23	1	Petition	127	Rev. Claims.	412	Favorable	430	Referred to Committee Whole House.		
Riddick, Col. Willis, heirs of.	Payment for loss and destruction of property during revolutionary war.	24	1	Petition	62	Rev. Claims	273	Favorable	280	Referred to Committee Whole House.		
Riddick, Col. Willis, heirs of.	Payment for loss and destruction of property during revolutionary war.	24	2	Bill of last sess.	200	Whole House			280			
Riddick, Col. Willis, heirs of.	Payment for loss and destruction of property during revolutionary war.	25	2	Petition	40	Rev. Claims	119	Favorable	137	Referred to Committee Whole House.		
Riddick, Col. Willis, heirs of.	Payment for loss and destruction of property during revolutionary war.	26	1	Petition	165	Rev. Claims.						
Riddick, Col. Willis, heirs of.	Payment for loss and destruction of property during revolutionary war.	28	1	Petition	288	Rev. Claims.						
Riddick, Col. Willis, heirs of.	Payment for loss and destruction of property during revolutionary war.	28	2	Petition	57	Rev. Claims.						
Riddick, Col. Willis, heirs of.	Payment for loss and destruction of property during revolutionary war.	30	1	Petition	513	Rev. Claims	Aug. 8, 1848	Favorable	638	Referred to Committee Whole House.		
Riddick, Col. Willis, heirs of.	Payment for loss and destruction of property during revolutionary war.	31	1	Petition	194	Rev. Claims	41	Favorable	70	Referred to Committee Whole House.		
Riddick, Col. Willis, heirs of.	Payment for loss and destruction of property during revolutionary war.	31	2	Bill of last sess.	75	Whole House	Dec. 20, 1850	With't amend.	70	Passed.		
Riddle, Hugh	(See True Putney & Hugh Kiddle)	27	3		153							

List of private claims presented to the House of Representatives of the United States from the 1st to the 31st Congress, inclusive—Continued.

Names of claimants.	Nature or object of the claim.	Congress.	Session.	How brought before the House of Reps.	Page of journal.	To what committee of the House referred.	No. or date of the report.	Nature of the report.	No. of the bill.	How disposed of by the House of Reps.	How disposed of by the Senate.	Date of the act of Congress, and remarks.
Riddle, Hugh	Bounty land for services during the war of 1812.	25	2	Resolution	1067	Priv. Land Claims.						
Riddle, Hugh	Bounty land for services during the war of 1812.	25	3	Petition	348	Public Lands.						
Riddle, Hugh	Bounty land for services during the war of 1812.	26	1	Petition	178	Public Lands	June 23, 1840	Favorable	459	Referred to Committee Whole House.		
Riddle, Hugh	Bounty land for services during the war of 1812.	27	2	Petition	390	Priv. Land Claims.	1030	Favorable	599	Referred to Committee Whole House.		
Riddle, Hugh	Bounty land for services during the war of 1812.	27	3	Bill of last sess.	91	Whole House	Dec. 23, 1842	With't amend.	599	Passed	Passed	App'd March 3, 1843
Riddle, Hugh, (N. Y.)	Pension for disabilities incurred in war of 1812.	29	1	Petition	396	Invalid Pensions.						
Riddle, Hugh, (N. Y.)	Pension for disabilities incurred in war of 1812.	29	2	Petition	128	Invalid Pensions.						
Riddle, Hugh, (N. Y.)	Pension for disabilities incurred in war of 1812.	30	1	Petition	65	Invalid Pensions	138	Favorable	127	Passed.		
Riddle, Hugh, (N. Y.)	Pension for disabilities incurred in war of 1812.	30	2	House bill	166	....	....	....	127	....	Passed	App'd Jan. 8, 1849
Riddle & Hunt	(See Hunt, Riddle, & Piatt)	14	2	....	69							
Riddle, James	Indemnity for French spoliations prior to 1800.	26	1	Memorial	182	Foreign Affairs	343	Favorable	319	Referred to Committee Whole House.		
Riddle, James, and Henry Becktel, surviving partners of Riddle, Becktel, and Headington.	Payment for damages by the protest of a bill of exchanges.	19	1	Resolution	86	Claims	....	....	....	Discharged; laid on table.		
Riddle, James, and Henry Becktel, surviving partners of Riddle, Becktel, and Headington.	Payment for damages by the protest of a bill of exchange.	20	1	Petition	226	Claims	173	Favorable	199	Referred to Committee Whole House.		
Riddle, James, and Henry Becktel, surviving partners of Riddle, Becktel, and Headington.	Payment for damages by the protest of a bill of exchange.	20	2	Bill of last sess.	198	Whole House	Jan. 23, 1829	With amend.	199	Passed.		
Riddle, James, and Henry Becktel, surviving partners of Riddle, Becktel, and Headington.	Payment for damages by the protest of a bill of exchange.	21	1	Petition	117	Claims	....	....	....	Discharged; laid on table.		
Riddle, James, and Henry Becktel, surviving partners of Riddle, Becktel, and Headington.	Payment for damages by the protest of a bill of exchange.	22	1	Petition	104	Claims	135	Favorable	204	Referred to Committee Whole House.		
Riddle, James, and Henry Becktel, surviving partners of Riddle, Becktel, and Headington.	Payment for damages by the protest of a bill of exchange.	22	2	Bill of last sess.	66	Whole House	Dec. 15, 1832	With amend.	204	Passed	Passed	App'd Feb. 27, 1833
Riddle, James, and Henry Becktel, surviving partners of Riddle, Becktel, and Headington.	For explanation of and decision upon act passed at last session for their relief.	23	1	Resolution	259	Claims	239	Favorable	266	Referred to Committee Whole House.		
Riddle, James, and Henry Becktel, surviving partners of Riddle, Becktel, and Headington.	For explanation of and decision upon act passed at last session for their relief.	23	2	Bill of last sess.	300	Whole House	Jan. 31, 1835	With't amend.	266	Passed	Passed	App'd March 3, 1835

List of private claims presented to the House of Representatives of the United States from the 1st to the 31st Congress, inclusive—Continued.

Names of claimants.	Nature or object of the claim.	Congress.	Session.	How brought before the House of Reps.	Page of journal.	To what committee of the House referred.	No. or date of the report.	Nature of the report.	No. of the bill.	How disposed of by the House of Reps.	How disposed of by the Senate.	Date of the act of Congress, and remarks.
Riddle, James K., widow of.	Pension for services and death of her husband in war with Mexico.	30	1	Petition	414	Rev. Pensions	536	Adverse	......	Laid on table.		
Riddle, James, administrator of.	Payment of a sum of money allowed deceased by Treasury Department.	27	2	Petition	227	Claims	730	Adverse	......	Laid on table.		
Riddle, John	Pension	21	1	Senate bill	401	Military Pensions..	May 21, 1830	With amend..	S. 65	Referred to Committee Whole House.		
Riddle, John	Pension	21	2	Senate bill	156	Military Pensions..	Jan. 13, 1831	Adverse	S. 46	Laid on table.		
Riddles, Thomas	Increase of pension	13	3	Petition and rep't Sec. Navy.	618, 697	....	....	....	......	Laid on table.		
Rideout, William........	Compensation for services during revolutionary war.	4	1	Petition	384	Claims	Jan. 20, 1796	Adverse	......	Leave to withdraw.		
Rideout, William........	Increase of pension	15	2	Petition	36	Pens. & Rev. Cl'ms.	....	....	......	Discharged; laid on table.		
Rider, Jeremiah	Pension for revolutionary services.	21	2	Resolution	90	Military Pensions.						
Rider, Jeremiah.........	Pension for revolutionary services.	22	1	Resolution	540	Rev. Pensions	....	....	......	Discharged; laid on table.		
Rider, Peter............	Pension for revolutionary services.	3	2	Rep. of Secretary War.	337	Claims.						
Rider, Peter............	Pension for revolutionary services.	4	1	Rep. of Secretary War.	373	Claims.						
Rider, Peter............	Pension for revolutionary services.	4	2	Rep. of Secretary War.	614	Claims.						
Rider, Peter............	Pension for revolutionary services	5	2	House bill......	127	Whole House.....	Jan. 11, 1798	With amend'ts	38	Passed	Passed	App'd Feb. 2, 1798
Rider, Seneca...........	Pension for services in war of 1812.	26	1	Petition	288	Invalid Pensions ..	223	Favorable	235	Passed	Passed	App'd July 20, 1840
Rider, Thomas, (subject of Great Britain.)	Indemnity for arrest and imprisonment by United States military authorities in Mexico.	31	1	House bill......	636	Foreign Affairs ...	Mar. 6, 1850	Favorable	146	Referred to Committee Whole House.		
Rider, Thomas, (subject of Great Britain.)	Indemnity for arrest and imprisonment by United States military authorities in Mexico.	31	2	Bill of last sess..	103	Whole House	Jan. 3, 1851	With't amend	146	Passed.		
Ridge, David	(See Joseph Broun.)...........	24	2	....	78							
Ridge, John, and David Vann.	Compensation as secretaries to the delegation of Creek Indians in 1826.	23	1	Petition	196	Indian Affairs.....	....	....	......	Discharged; laid on table.		
Ridgely, Charles G......	To be allowed expenses and commissions as commander on West India naval station.	22	2	Petition	82	Naval Affairs.						
Ridgely, Charles G......	To be allowed expenses and commissions as commander on West India station.	23	1	Petition	190	Naval Affairs.						
Ridgely, Charles G......	To be allowed expenses and commissions as commander on West India naval station.	24	1	Petition	408	Naval Affairs.						
Ridgely, Charles G......	To be allowed expenses and commissions as commander on West India naval station.	24	2	Petition	87	Foreign Affairs....	113	Favorable	846	Referred to Committee Whole House.		
Ridgely, Charles G......	To be allowed expenses and commissions as commander on West India naval station.	25	2	Petition	39	Foreign Affairs....	489	Favorable	486	Referred to Committee Whole House.		
Ridgely, Charles G......	To be allowed expenses and commissions as commander on West India naval station.	25	3	House bill	379	Whole House.....	....	....	486			

List of private claims presented to the House of Representatives of the United States from the 1st to the 31st Congress, inclusive—Continued.

Names of claimants.	Nature or object of the claim.	Congress.	Session.	How brought before the House of Reps.	Page of journal.	To what committee of the House referred.	No. or date of the report.	Nature of the report.	No. of the bill.	How disposed of by the House of Reps.	How disposed of by the Senate.	Date of the act of Congress, and remarks.
Ridgely, Charles G......	To be allowed expenses and commissions as commander on West India naval station.	26	1	Petition	182	Foreign Affairs....	498	Favorable....	399	Referred to Committee Whole House.		
Ridgely, Charles G......	To be all wed expenses and commissions as commander on West India naval station.	27	2	Petition	63	Foreign Affairs.						
Ridgely, Charles G......	To be allowed expenses and commissions as commander on West India naval station.	27	3	Petition	72	ForeignAffai s.						
Ridgely, Charles G......	To be allowed expenses and commissions as commander on West India naval station.	29	1	Petition	292	Foreign Affairs ...	Feb. 10, 1846	Favorable....	214	Referred to Committee Whole House.		
Ridgely, Charles G......	To be allowed expens s and commissions as commander on West India naval station.	29	2	House bill......	73	Foreign Affairs ...	....	....	214			
Ridgely, Charles G......	To be allowed expenses and commissions as commander on West India naval station.	30	1	Petition	76	Foreign Affairs ...	191	Favorable....	7	Passed.		
Ridgely, Charles G......	To be allowed expenses and commissions as commander on West India naval station.	30	2	House bill......	237	....	....	....	7	....	Rejected.	
Ridgely, Charles G......	To be allowed expenses and commissions as commander on West India naval station	31	1	Petition	500	Naval Affairs.						
Ridgeley, Elizabeth, and Catharine Dorsey.	(See John Dumesti, heirs of.)....	31	1	....	647							
Ridgeley, James L......	(See Edward Moore, administrator of.)	21	1	....	175							
Ridgeley, Richard, & others	Compensation for damages to their farms by United States militia, war of 1812.	13	3	Petition	679	Claims..........	....	....	......	Discharged.		
Ridgeley, Richard, & others	Compensation for damage to their farms by United States militia, war of 1812.	14	1	Petition	179	Claims..........	Mar. 11, 1816	Favorable....	123	Indefinitely postponed.		
Ridgeley, William A.....	(See John Dumesti, heirs of)....	29	2	....	70							
Ridgley, Wm. G., (D. C.)	To cancel bonds given on importation of British goods in 1812.	14	1	Petition	442	Ways and Means..	....	....	......	Discharged; laid on table.		
Ridgeway, Maria, widow of Captain.	Naval pension	27	2	Petition	690	Naval Affairs.....	597	Adverse	......	Laid on table.		
Ridgeway, Matthew, surety of.	Release from liability..........	17	1	Petition	164	P. Of. & P. Roads.						
Ridgeway, Thomas	Continuation of pension, and to be placed on same footing as commissioned officers of the revolutionary army.	24	1	Petition	258	Rev. Claims......	396	Adverse	......	Laid on table.		
Ridler, George..........	Change location of entry of land..	29	1	Memorial	1162	Public Lands.						
Ridley, George..........	(See William H. Bedford, agent.)	28	1	....	262							
Reib, Nicholas..........	Compensation for services during revolutionary war and for pay and emoluments due his son, who was taken prisoner.	2	1	Petition	464	....	....	....	......	Referred to Secretary War.		

List of private claims presented to the House of Representatives of the United States from the 1st to the 31st Congress, inclusive—Continued.

Names of claimants.	Nature or object of the claim.	Congress.	Session.	How brought before the House of Reps.	Page of journal.	To what committee of the House referred.	No. or date of the report.	Nature of the report.	No. of the bill.	How disposed of by the House of Reps.	How disposed of by the Senate.	Date of the act of Congress, and remarks.
Reib, Nicholas	Compensation for services during revolutionary war and for pay and emoluments due his son, who was taken prisoner.	2	2	Memorial	658		Feb. 8, 1793	Rep't Secretary of War.		Laid on table.		
Reib, Nicholas	Compensation for services during revolutionary war and for pay and emoluments due his son, who was taken prisoner.	3	1	Memorial	26	Select	Feb. 19, 1794	Favorable	37	Passed	Passed	App'd June 7, 1794
Reib, Nicholas	Additional compensation for services in revolutionary war.	4	1	Petition	447	Claims	May 11, 1796	Adverse		Laid on table.		
Reib, Nicholas	On behalf of himself and son, and for a resettlement of his accounts for services during revolutionary war.	6	1	Petitions	662, 698					Laid on table.		
Rieb, Peter	(See Nicholas Reib)	2	1		464							
Riensch, Ruchner, & Co., (subjects of Prussia.)	Indemnity for injuries to their commerce during Mexican war.	31	2	Petition	142	Commerce.						
Rife, Peter	Revolutionary pension	29	1	Petition	86	Rev. Pensions	213	Favorable	207	Passed	Passed	App'd Aug. 8, 1846
Rife, Peter	Increase of pension	30	1	Petition	100	Rev. Pensions				Disch'd; laid on table.		
Rife, Peter	Increase of pension	30	2	Petition	103	Rev. Pensions	21	Adverse		Laid on table.		
Riffle, Susannah	To be allowed five years' half-pay due her husband for military services in war of 1812.	23	1	Petition	45	Military Affairs	Jan. 21, 1834	Adverse		Laid on table.		
Rifford, Frederick	Restoration of pension, discontinued under act of May, 1820.	17	1	Petition	92	Rev. Pensions.						
Rigden, James	Compensation for services rendered and losses sustained while in the army of the United States.	24	1	Petition	64	Military Affairs				Discharged; laid on table.		
Rigden, James	Compensation for services rendered and losses sustained while in the army of the United States.	25	2	Petition	83	Military Affairs	232	Adverse		Laid on table.		
Rigg, Hosea	Pension	20	1	Petition	417	Military Pensions	April 18, 1828	Adverse		Laid on table.		
Rigg, Hosea	Pension	21	1	Petition	67	Military Pensions				Discharged; laid on table.		
Riggs, Cyrus, widow of	Pension for death of her husband from disease contracted in public service.	14	2	Petition	243	Pens. & Rev. Clm's.				Discharged; laid on table.		
Riggs, Daniel	Pension	25	1	Petition	205					Laid on table.		
Riggs, Gideon	Pension	19	2	Documents	95	Military Pensions				Disch'd; laid on table.		
Riggs, Stephen, heirs of	Pension for services in Seminole war.	31	1	Petition	653	Rev. Pensions	312	Adverse		Laid on table.		
Riggins, Joel	Pension	20	2	Petition	31	Military Pensions	Feb. 13, 1829	Pension bill	440	Passed.		
Riggins, Joel	Pension	21	1	Pension bill	130	Whole House	Feb. 12, 1830	With amends.	72	Passed	Passed	App'd May 20, 1830
Riker, Abraham, widow of	Half pay for revolutionary services.	2	1	Petition	500					Referred to Secretary War.		
Riker, Abraham, widow of	Half pay for revolutionary services.	2	2	Rep. of Secretary War.	711					Laid on table.		
Riker, Abraham, widow of	Half-pay for revolutionary services.	3	1	Petition and rep't Sec. of War.	73, 93	Select	April 22, 1794	Adverse		Laid on table.		
Riker, Abraham, widow of	Half pay for revolutionary services.	23	1	Resolution	142	Rev. Claims	139	Favorable; bill	150	Passed	Passed	App'd June 30, 1834
Riker, Abraham, and J. Ward, owners of privateer Saratoga.	(See Jasper Ward and others)	14	1		295							

List of private claims presented to the House of Representatives of the United States from the 1st to the 31st Congress, inclusive—Continued.

Names of claimants.	Nature or object of the claim.	Congress.	Session.	How brought before the House of Reps.	Page of journal.	To what committee of the House referred.	No. or date of the report.	Nature of the report.	No. of the bill.	How disposed of by the House of Reps.	How disposed of by the Senate.	Date of the act of Congress, and remarks.
Riker, Gerardus	Pension	22	1	Petition	56	Rev. Pensions	Dec. 28, 1831	Adverse	......	Laid on table.		
Riker, Maturin	Pension for revolutionary services.	22	1	Petition	122	Rev. Pensions	Dec. 29, 1831	Adverse	......	Laid on table.		
Riley, Major Bennett, and others.	Payment for horses stolen by Indians while conducting traders to Santa Fe.	21	2	Petition	192	Claims.						
Riley, Major Bennett, and others.	Payment for horses stolen by Indians while conducting traders to Santa Fe.	21	2	Senate bill	245	Military Affairs	Feb. 8, 1831	With't amend.	S. 102	Passed	Passed	App'd March 3, 1831
Riley, Catharine, & others, (half-breed Indians.)	Permission to sell lands reserve to them under treaty of 1817, between United States and the Cherokees	20	1	Petition	319	Public Lands	......	......	......	Discharged; laid on table.		
Riley, Dayton	For payment of claim against Ottawa Indians.	29	1	Memorial	160	Indian Affairs.	287	Adverse	......	Laid on table.		
Riley, James	(See James Simpson, attorney of.)	16	1	......	157							
Riley, James, (Mass.)	Pension	20	1	Petition	37	Military Pensions.	April 29, 1828	Pension bill	283	Passed.		
Riley, James, (Mass.)	Pension	20	2	Pension bill	55	Whole House	Jan. 15, 1829	With amends.	311	Passed	Laid on table.	
Riley, James, (Mass.)	Pension	21	1	Petition	48	Military Pensions.	Jan. 5, 1830	By bill	72	Passed	Passed	App'd May 20, 1830
Riley, James, and widow of James Watson.	Redress for seizure and condemnation of ship Two Marys under the Milan decree.	20	1	Petition	40	Foreign Affairs	1	Adverse	......	Laid on table.		
Riley, John	Bounty land for revolutionary services.	9	1	Petition	192	Claims	......	......	......	Referred to Committee Whole House.		
Riley, Justus, executors and heirs of.	Indemnity for French spoliations prior to 1800.	26	1	Memorial	182	Foreign Affairs	343	Favorable	319	Referred to Committee Whole House.		
Riley, Justus, executors and heirs of.	Indemnity for French spoliations prior to 1800.	31	1	Petition	537	Foreign Affairs	355	Favorable	318	Referred to Committee Whole House.		
Riley, Justus, (Conn.)	Indemnity for French spoliations prior to 1800.	26	1	Memorial	182	Foreign Affairs	343	Favorable	319	Referred to Committee Whole House.		
Riley, Miles, *et al.*	For balance of pay due for services in western army of Pennsylvania in 1794.	6	2	Petition	814	Claims	March 2, 1801	To disch'ge & postpone.	......	Report adopted.		
Riley, Miles, *et al.*	For balance of pay due for services in western army of Pennsylvania in 1794.	7	1	Petition	19	Claims	April 3, 1802	Rep. and resl'n adverse.	......	Resolution adopted.		
Riley, Philip	Payment for injuries to horse, received while in public service.	30	1	Petition	891	Claims.						
Riley, Philip	Payment for injuries to horse, received while in public service.	30	2	Petition	224	Naval Affairs.						
Rimick, Samuel	(See Josiah Strong.)	24	2	......	198							
Rinaldi, Charles	Compensation for maintenance of sailors during act of Embargo.	11	2	Petition	220	Claims	Feb. 20, 1810	Adverse	......	Laid on table.		
Rinaldi, John	To be exonerated from payment of bond given to collector at Charleston, South Carolina.	11	1	Petition	85	......	......	......	......	Referred to Committee Whole House on S. bill No. 8.	......	See act June 28, 1809
Rind, Edmund	Bounty land for services in Mexican war.	31	1	Petition	611	Priv. Land Claims.						
Rind, Francis	Pension	25	2	Petition	486	Invalid Pensions	Feb. 20, 1838	Adverse	......	Laid on table.		
Rind, Samuel S	Compensation for extra services as clerk in Third Auditors office.	31	1	Petition	324	Claims	27	Adverse	......	Laid on table.		
Rinensio, Isidore	Permission to locate land warrant in Bayou La Fourche, La.	14	1	Petition	210	Military Affairs	Feb. 27, 1816	Adverse	......	Laid on table.		

List of private claims presented to the House of Representatives of the United States from the 1st to the 31st Congress, inclusive—Continued.

Names of claimants.	Nature or object of the claim.	Congress.	Session.	How brought before the House of Reps.	Page of journal.	To what committee of the House referred.	No. or date of the report.	Nature of the report.	No. of the bill.	How disposed of by the House of Reps.	How disposed of by the Senate.	Date of the act of Congress, and remarks.
Rinensio, Isidore	Permission to locate land warrant in Bayou La Fourche, La.	14	2	Petition	133	Military Affairs	Feb. 21, 1817	Adverse		Laid on table.		
Ring, Abijah	Pension	21	1	Petition	66	Military Pensions	Mar. 26, 1830	Favorable	390	Referred to Committee Whole House.		
Ring, Abijah	Pension	21	2	Bill of last sess.	318	Whole House	Feb. 16, 1831	With't amend.	390	Passed.		
Ring, Abijah	Arrears of pension	23	1	Petition	155	Invalid Pensions	252	Favorable	289	Referred to Committee Whole House.		
Ring, Abijah	Arrears of pension	23	2	Bill of last sess.	300	Whole House	Jan. 31, 1835	With't amend.	289	Postponed.		
Ring, Abijah	For scrip in lieu of bounty land warrant for services in the war of 1812.	27	3	Petition	107	Public Lands.						
Ring, Abijah	Pension for wounds received and disabilities incurred in the war of 1812.	30	2	Petition	116	Invalid Pensions				Discharged; laid on table.		
Ring, Jonathan, wife of	Pension for revolutionary services of her husband, (who is bereft of reason.)	15	2	Petition	39	Rev. Pensions	57	Favorable	249	Passed	Passed, with amendment.	App'd March 3, 1819
Ring, Thomas, widow of	Indemnity for French spoliations prior to 1800.	31	1	Petition	232	Foreign Affairs	355	Favorable	318	Referred to Committee Whole House.		
Ringgold, Benjamin	Payment for superintending erection of the custom-house at New York.	25	2	Memorial	656	Commerce	943	Rep. and resolution.		Referred to Secretary Treasury.		
Ringgold, Cadwallader	(See Exploring Epedition.)	27	3		149							
Ringgold, Cadwallader	Compensation for extra duty on United States Exploring expedition.	29	1	Memorial	400	Naval Affairs.						
Ringgold, Samuel G.	(Not stated.)	21	1	Letter from Secretary War.	501	Judiciary				Discharged; laid on table.		
Ringgold, Tench, late marshal of the District of Columbia.	Payment of poundage fees on certain executions levied at instance of United States	23	1	Senate bill	873	Judiciary			S. 145	Discharged; laid on table.		
Ringgold, Tench, late marshal of the District of Columbia.	Payment of claim growing out of proceedings instituted by United States against John Gates an insolvent debtor.	24	1	Memorial	211	Judiciary				Discharged; laid on table.		
Ringgold, Tench, late marshal of the District of Columbia.	To be allowed in settlement of his accounts a sum assigned him by the United States Supreme Court.	24	2	Senate bill	496	Whole House			S. 78			
Ringlang, Thos. & others.	Additional bounty lands for extra services during the war of 1812.	31	2	Petition	155	Public Lands.						
Ringo, Burtgis	Payment for a horse, and for revolutionary services.	19	1	Petition	153	Rev. Claims	Feb. 1, 1826	Adverse		Laid on table.		
Ringo, Burtgis	Pension	21	1	Petition	479	Military Pensions				Discharged; laid on table.		
Ringo, Burtgis	Pension	21	2	Petition	115	Military Pensions.						
Rinker, Jacob, widow of	Pension for revolutionary services.	27	2	Petition	153	Rev. Pensions	784	Adverse		Laid on table.		
Rinker, Jacob, widow of	Pension for revolutionary services.	27	3	Petition	266	Rev. Pensions	295	Adverse		Laid on table.		
Rinker, James, surviving partner of Bailey and Rinker, and administrator of said Bailey.	Indemnity for damages to property near New Orleans by U. States troops during the war of 1812.	16	1	Petition	323	Claims	April 3, 1820	Adverse		Referred to Commitee Whole House.		

List of private claims presented to the House of Representatives of the United States from the 1st to the 31st Congress, inclusive—Continued.

Names of claimants.	Nature or object of the claim.	Congress.	Session.	How brought before the House of Reps.	Page of journal.	To what committee of the House referred.	No. or date of the report.	Nature of the report.	No. of the bill.	How disposed of by the House of Reps.	How disposed of by the Senate.	Date of the act of Congress, and remarks.
Rinker, James, surviving partner of Bailey and Rinker, and administrator of said Bailey.	Indemnity for damages to property near New Orleans by U. States troops during the war of 1812.	17	1	Petition	78	Claims	Jan. 28, 1822	Adverse	......	Laid on table.		
Rinker, James, surviving partner of Bailey and Rinker, and administrator of said Bailey.	Indemnity for damages to property near New Orleans by U. States troops during the war of 1812.	18	1	Petition	360	Claims.						
Rinker, James, surviving partner of Bailey and Rinker, and administrator of said Bailey.	Indemnity for damages to property near New Orleans by U. States troops during the war of 1812.	18	2	Petition	47	Claims.						
Rinker, James, surviving partner of Bailey and Rinker, and administrator of said Bailey.	Indemnity for damages to property near New Orleans by U. States troops during the war of 1812.	19	1	Petition	38	Claims	Mar. 22, 1826	Adverse	......	Referred to Committee Whole House.		
Rinker, James, surviving partner of Bailey and Rinker, and administrator of said Bailey.	Indemnity for damages to property near New Orleans by U. States troops during the war of 1812.	19	2	Petition	44	Claims	Jan. 8, 1827	Adverse	......	Laid on table.		
Rinker, James, surviving partner of Bailey and Rinker, and administrator of said Bailey.	Indemnity for damages to property near New Orleans by U. States troops during the war of 1812.	20	1	Petition	64	Claims	Dec. 27, 1827	Adverse	......	Referred to Committee Whole House.		
Rinker, Samuel, widow of.	Pension for revolutionary services of her husband.	18	2	Petition	251	Pens. & Rev. Cl'ms.	Feb. 22, 1825	Adverse	......	Laid on table.		
Rinker, Samuel, widow of.	Pension for revolutionary services of her husband.	23	2	Petition	40	Naval Affairs	Feb. 17, 1835	Adverse	......	Laid on table.		
Rinker, Samuel, widow of.	Pension for revolutionary services of her husband.	26	1	Petition	322	Rev. Pensions	....	....	......	Discharged; laid on table.		
Rinker, Samuel, widow of.	Pension for revolutionary services of her husband.	28	1	Petition	176	Rev. Pensions.						
Rinker, Samuel, widow of.	For re-enactment of navy pension laws.	28	1	Petition	1042	Naval Affairs.						
Rinker, Samuel, widow of.	For re enactment of navy pension laws.	30	1	Petition	380	Naval Affairs.						
Riopelle, Ambrose, heirs and assignees of.	Patent for a tract of land	31	1	Petition	1001	Judiciary.						
Riopelle, Ambrose, heirs and assignees of.	Patent for a tract of land	31	2	Petition	48	Judiciary	1	Favorable	412	Referred to Committee Whole House.		
Ripley, Eleazer W.	Pension	24	1	Senate bill	1151	Whole House	....	....	S. 284	Passed	....	App'd July 4, 1836
Ripley, Major Eleazer W., widow of.	Payment of amount due deceased by the United States on the verdict of a jury.	29	1	Memorial	812	Claims.						
Ripley, Major Eleazer W., widow of.	Payment of amount due deceased by the United States on the verdict of a jury.	30	1	Petition	108	Claims.						
Ripley, Eliphalet, heirs of.	Arrears of pension	30	1	Petition	217	Invalid Pensions.						
Ripley, Jabez, widow of	Pension for revolutionary services.	26	1	Petition	283	Rev. Pensions.						
Ripley, Jabez, widow of	Pension for revolutionary services.	26	2	Petition	35	Rev. Pensions	129	Favorable	636	Referred to Committee Whole House.		
Ripley, Jabez, widow of	Pension for revolutionary services.	27	2	Petition	59	Rev. Pensions	110	Favorable	156	Passed	Indef. postp'd.	
Ripley, Jabez, widow of	Pension for revolutionary services.	27	3	Petition	43	Rev. Pensions	Jan. 10, 1842	Adverse	......	Laid on table.		

List of private claims presented to the House of Representatives of the United States from the 1st to the 31st Congress, inclusive—Continued.

Names of claimants.	Nature or object of the claim.	Congress.	Session.	How brought before the House of Reps.	Page of journal.	To what committee of the House referred.	No. or date of the report.	Nature of the report.	No. of the bill.	How disposed of by the House of Reps.	How disposed of by the Senate.	Date of the act of Congress, and remarks.
Ripley, Jerusha	(See widow of Samuel Sturtevant.)	24	2		132							
Ripley, John, and others	Extra compensation as clerks in the Treasury Department, at Philadelphia.	3	1	Petition	88	Select	47	Adverse		Laid on table.		
Ripley, John A.	Pension for revolutionary services.	23	1	Petition, (1)	419	Rev. Pensions				Discharged; laid on table.		
Ripley, John A.	Pension for revolutionary services.	23	1	Petition, (2)	419	Rev. Pensions				Discharged; laid on table.		
Ripley, John A.	Pension for revolutionary services.	23	2	Petition	114	Rev. Pensions	Feb. 17, 1835	Adverse		Laid on table.		
Ripley, John A.	Pension for revolutionary services.	24	1	Petition	213	Rev. Pensions.	Feb. 4, 1836	Adverse		Laid on table.		
Ripley, John A.	Pension for revolutionary services.	27	2	Petition	836	Rev. Pensions.				Discharged; laid on table.		
Ripley, Major John, heirs of.	Commutation pay for revolutionary services.	31	2	Petition	36	Rev. Claims.						
Ripley, Mary	Compensation for services rendered and injuries sustained during the revolutionary war.	1	3	Petition	378					Referred to Secretary War.		
Ripley, Perum	Pension	22	1	Petition	131	Rev. Pensions.	395	Favorable	498	Ref'd to Com. W. H		
Ripley, Tilson	(See Dodd & Barnard)	20	1		111							
Ripley, William	Restoration of pension, discontinued under act of May, 1820.	17	1	Petition	132	Rev. Pensions.						
Risdon, Daniel	Arrears and increase of pension	31	1	Petition	653	Rev. Pensions.	368	Adverse		Laid on table.		
Rising, Josiah	Restoration of pension, discontinued by act of May, 1820.	17	1	Petition	51	Rev. Pensions.						
Risley, Charles	Pension	25	2	Petition	268	Invalid Pensions	616	Favorable	594	Passed.		
Risley, Charles	Pension	25	3	Petition	98	Invalid Pensions	182	Favorable	1045	Passed.		
Risley, Charles	Pension	26	1	Petition	162	Invalid Pensions	200	Favorable	212	Passed	Indef. postp'd.	
Risley, Stephen	Restoration of pension, discontinued by act of May, 1820.	17	1	Petition	106	Rev. Pensions.						
Risley, Timothy	Correction of error in location of patent for land.	21	1	Petition	200	Public Lands	238	Favorable	303	Referred to Committee Whole House.		
Risley, Timothy	Correction of error in location of patent for land.	21	2	Bill of last sess.	333	Whole House	Feb. 19, 1831	With amend.	303	Passed.		
Risley, Timothy	Correction of error in location of patent for land.	22	1	Senate bill	816	Public Lands	June 21, 1832	With amend.	S. 123	Passed	Passed	App'd July 9, 1832
Rist, Samuel, guardian of	Pension for revolutionary services of said Rist, who is now insane.	18	1	Petition	31	Rev. Pensions	Feb. 3, 1824	Favorable	100	Passed	Indef. postp'd.	
Ritchey, Esau	Pension for services in war of 1812.	20	1	Resolution	348	Military Pensions	April 29, 1828	Pension bill	283	Passed.		
Ritchey, Esau	Pension for services in war of 1812.	20	2	Pension bill	55	Whole House	Jan. 15, 1829	With amends.	311	Passed	Laid on table.	
Ritchey, Esau	Pension for services in war of 1812.	21	1	Petition	48	Military Pensions	Jan. 5, 1830	Pension bill	72	Passed	Passed	App'd May 20, 1830
Ritchie, James	Compensation for materials furnished and work done on Cumberland road.	23	1	Resolution	623	Claims	455	Adverse		Laid on table		See report No. 449.
Ritchie, James	Payment of balance found due upon settlement of his accounts.	28	1	Senate bill	980	Claims	June 14, 1844	With't amend.	S. 105	Referred to Committee Whole House.		
Ritchie, James	Payment of balance found due upon settlement of his accounts.	28	2	Senate bill	131	Claims	Dec. 31, 1844	With't amend.	S. 19	Passed		App'd Feb. 13, 1845
Ritchie, Thomas, assignee of Wm. M. Belt and John H. Trenholm.	Relief for losses by contract for the congressional printing.	31	1	Amend. of Senate to civil and dip. bill of House.	1509	Ways and Means.				Rejected.		
Ritchie, Thomas, assignee of Wm. M. Belt and John H. Trenholm.	Relief for losses by contract for the congressional printing.	31	2	Petition	125	Printing	Feb. 12, 1851	Favorable	J. R. 36	Passed.		

List of private claims presented to the House of Representatives of the United States from the 1st to the 31st Congress, inclusive—Continued.

Names of claimants.	Nature or object of the claim.	Congress.	Session.	How brought before the House of Reps.	Page of journal.	To what committee of the House referred.	No. or date of the report.	Nature of the report.	No. of the bill.	How disposed of by the House of Reps.	How disposed of by the Senate.	Date of the act of Congress, and remarks.
Ritchey, William	Pension	27	2	Petition	526	Invalid Pensions	611	Adverse		Laid on table.		
Rite, Peggy	Pension for loss of husband in the public service	12	2	Petition	634	Claims	Feb. 26, 1813	Adverse		Laid on table.		
Ritson, Thomas, heirs of	Indemnity for French spoliations prior to 1800.	26	1	Memorial	182	Foreign Affairs	343	Favorable	319	Referred to Committee Whole House.		
Rittenhouse, Joseph	Release from imprisonment	4	2	Petition	613	Select	Mar. 3, 1797	Adverse		Laid on table.		
Rittenhouse, Joseph	Release from imprisonment	5	2	Petition and rep't	159	Whole House.						
Ritter, Jacob, widow of	Compensation for supplies, expenses, and services in the revolution.	9	1	Petition	189	Claims				Discharged; referred to Com. Whole House.		
Ritter, Jacob, widow of	Compensation for supplies, expenses, and services in the revolution.	10	2	Petition	410	Select.						
Ritter, Jacob, widow of	Compensation for supplies, expenses, and services in the revolution.	11	3	Petition	461	Claims.						
Ritter, Jacob, widow of	Compensation for supplies, expenses, and services in the revolution.	12	1	Petition	25	Claims.						
Ritter, Jacob, widow of	Compensation for supplies, expenses, and services in the revolution.	13	2	Petition	201	Pens. & Rev. Cl'ms.	92	Adverse		Referred to Committee Whole House.		
Ritter, Jacob, widow of	Compensation for supplies, expenses, and services in the revolution.	13	3	Petition	614	Pens. & Rev. Cl'ms.	Jan. 27, 1815	Adverse		Laid on table.		
Ritter, Jacob, widow of	Compensation for supplies, expenses, and services in the revolution.	14	1	Petition	221	Pens. & Rev. Cl'ms.	Mar. 19, 1816	Adverse		Laid on table.		
Ritter, Jacob, widow of	Compensation for supplies, expenses, and services in the revolution.	14	2	Petition	305	Pens. & Rev. Cl'ms.				Discharged; laid on table.		
Ritter, Jacob, widow of	Compensation for supplies, expenses, and services in the revolution.	15	1	Petition	101	Pens. & Rev. Cl'ms.	Feb. 18, 1818	Adverse		Leave to withdraw.		
Ritter, Jacob, widow of	Compensation for supplies, expenses, and services in the revolution.	16	1	Petition	232	Pens. & Rev. Cl'ms.	Feb. 28, 1820	Adverse		Rejected.		
Ritter, Jacob, widow of	Compensation for supplies, expenses, and services in the revolution.	16	2	Petition	188	Claims				Discharged; laid on table.		
Ritter, Jacob, widow of	Compensation for supplies, expenses, and services in the revolution.	17	1	Petition	200	Claims.						
Ritter, Jacob, widow of	Compensation for supplies, expenses, and services in the revolution.	17	2	Petition	26	Pens. & Rev. Cl'ms.	Dec. 13, 1822	Adverse		Rejected.		
Ritter, Jacob, widow of	Compensation for supplies, expenses, and services in the revolution.	18	1	Petition	215	Pens. & Rev. Cl'ms.				Discharged; laid on table.		
Ritter, Jacob, widow of	Compensation for supplies, expenses, and services in the revolution.	19	1	Petition	74	Rev. Claims	Jan. 23, 1826	Adverse		Laid on table.		

List of private claims presented to the House of Representatives of the United States from the 1st to the 31st Congress, inclusive—Continued.

Names of claimants.	Nature or object of the claim.	Congress.	Session.	How brought before the House of Reps.	Page of journal.	To what committee of the House referred.	No. or date of the report.	Nature of the report.	No. of the bill.	How disposed of by the House of Reps.	How disposed of by the Senate.	Date of the act of Congress, and remarks.
Ritter, Jacob, widow of	Compensation for supplies, expenses, and services in the revolution.	20	2	Petition	61	Rev. Claims				Discharged; laid on table.		
Ritter, Jacob, widow of	Compensation for supplies, expenses, and services in the revolution.	21	1	Petition	261	Rev. Claims				Discharged; laid on table.		
Ritter, Jacob, jr	Drawback of duties on sugar exported in 1806.	9	2	Petition	471	Com. and Manuf.	Jan. 5, 1807	Adverse		Laid on table.		
Ritter, Jacob, jr	Drawback of duties on sugar exported in 1806.	10	1	Petition	30	Com. and Manuf.						
Ritter, Jacob, jr	Drawback of duties on sugar exported in 1806.	10	2	Petition	356	Com. and Manuf.	Feb. 16, 1809	Adverse		Leave to withdraw.		
Ritter, Jacob, jr	Drawback of duties on sugar exported in 1806	14	1	Petition	89	Com. and Manuf.				Leave to withdraw.		
Ritter, Jacob, jr	Drawback of duties on sugar exported in 1806.	15	1	Petition	135	Com. and Manuf	Mar. 30, 1818	Adverse		Leave to withdraw.		
Ritter, Jacob, jr., & others.	(See Abraham Piesch, assignee of.)	13	3		693							
Ritter, Jacob, jr	Drawback of duty on merchandise.	26	1	Petition	292	Commerce	30	Favorable	49	Passed	Passed	App'd July 20, 1840
Rivard, Francis, heirs and representatives of.	Confirmation of title to land on Mississippi river.	25	2	Senate bill	736	Priv. Land Claims.	April 13, 1838	With amends.	S. 295	Referred to Committee Whole House.		
Rivard, Francis, heirs and representatives of.	Confirmation of title to land on Mississippi river.	25	3	Senate bill	477	Priv. Land Claims.			S. 44			
Rivard, Francis, heirs and representatives of.	Confirmation of title to land on Mississippi river.	26	1	Senate bill	270	Priv. Land Claims.	April 25, 1840	With't amend.	S. 47	Referred to Committee Whole House.		
Rivard, Francis, heirs and representatives of.	Confirmation of title to land on Mississippi river.	26	2	Senate bill	165	Priv. Land Claims.	Feb. 13, 1841	With't amend.	S. 74	Referred to Committee Whole House.		
Rivard, Francis, heirs and representatives of.	Confirmation of title to land on Mississippi river.	27	2	Senate bill	1116	Priv. Land Claims.	Aug. 6, 1842	With't amend.	S. 96	Passed	Passed	App'd Aug. 30, 1842
River, Joseph, administrator of.	Payment for Indian depredation	25	3	Petition	124	Indian Affairs	225	Adverse		Laid on table.		
Rives & Blair	(See Blair & Rives)	27	2		108							
Rives, S. S., widow of	Compensation for extra services of her husband as acting master's mate in the navy of the U. States.	31	2	Petition	123	Naval Affairs.						
Riviere, Philip	(See Philip Reviere, heirs of)	24	1		799							
Rix, James, heirs of	Payment for revolutionary services.	23	1	Petition	306	Rev. Claims.						
Rix, James, heirs of	Payment for revolutionary services.	23	2	Petition	55	Rev. Claims.						
Rix, Nathaniel	Compensation for revolutionary services.	23	1	Petition	306	Rev. Claims.						
Rix, Nathaniel	Compensation for revolutionary services.	23	2	Petition	55	Rev. Claims.						
Roach, Benjamin	Change location of entry of land	23	1	Petition	215	Public Lands				Discharged; laid on table.		
Roach, Benjamin	Change location of entry of land	23	2	Petition	242	Public Lands	Jan. 31, 1835	Adverse		Laid on table.		
Roach, Christian	Pension	21	1	Petition	584	Military Pensions	April 29, 1830	Adverse		Laid on table.		
Roach, Edward	Pension for revolutionary services.	28	1	Petition	901	Military Pensions.						
Roach, Frederick, widow of.	Continuation of pension allowed her husband for revolutionary services.	26	2	Petition	131	Rev. Claims.						
Roach, Frederick, widow of.	Continuation of pension allowed her husband for revolutionary services.	27	2	Petition	105	Rev. Pensions	784	Adverse		Laid on table.		
Roach, James	Pension	20	1	Petition	365	Military Pensions				Disch'd; laid on table		

List of private claims presented to the House of Representatives of the United States from the 1st to the 31st Congress, inclusive—Continued.

Names of claimants.	Nature or object of the claim.	Congress.	Session.	How brought before the House of Reps.	Page of journal.	To what committee of the House referred.	No. or date of the report.	Nature of the report.	No. of the bill.	How disposed of by the House of Reps.	How disposed of by the Senate.	Date of the act of Congress, and remarks.
Roach, Samuel	Pension	21	1	Resolution	254	Military Pensions	....	....	.....	Discharged; laid on table.		
Roach, Sassnct	Pension for revolutionary services	20	2	Resolution	46	Military Pensions	....	....	.....	Discharged; laid on table.		
Roach, Stephen J., and Joseph Russ.	Payment of claim arising under contract to repair mail road in Florida.	23	1	Petition	447	Claims	529	Favorable	531	Referred to Committee Whole House.		
Roach, Stephen J., and Joseph Russ.	Payment of claim arising under contract to repair mail road in Florida.	24	1	Petition	51	Claims	Dec. 21, 1835	Favorable	25	Passed	Passed	App'd Feb. 17, 1836
Roach, Thomas	Pension for wound received in revolutionary war.	13	2	Petition	328	Pens. & Rev. Cl'ms.	....	....	.....	Referred to Committee Whole House on bill No. 166.		
Roach, Thomas	Pension for wound received in revolutionary war.	13	3	Petition	671	Pens. & Rev. Cl'ms.						
Roades, Abiel, and others.	Fishing bounty on schooner Mary.	22	1	Petition	137	Commerce.						
Roades, Abiel, and others.	Fishing bounty on schooner Mary.	23	1	Petition	656	Commerce	495	Favorable	500	Referred to Committee Whole House.		
Roades, Abiel, and others.	Fishing bounty on schooner Mary.	24	1	Petition	54	Commerce	48	Favorable	60	Passed	Passed	App'd May 14, 1836
Roades, John	(See Abiel Roads, and others)	22	1	....	137							
Roades, Mark	For benefits of act for relief of revolutionary officers and soldiers.	20	2	Petition	33	Rev. Claims	....	....	.....	Discharged; laid on table.		
Roan, James	Change location of entry of land	26	1	Petition	610	Priv. Land Claims.						
Roane, De Lafayette, representatives of.	(Not stated)	18	2	Resolution	219	Claims.						
Roane, James P	Confirmation of title to land	28	2	Petition	84	Priv. Land Claims.						
Roane, James P	Confirmation of title to land	30	1	Petition	682	Priv. Land Claims.						
Roane, James P	Confirmation of title to land	31	1	Petition	257	Priv. Land Claims.	345	Favorable	306	Referred to Committee Whole House.		
Roane, Samuel C	Compensation for extra services as United States attorney.	20	2	Petition	33	Judiciary.						
Roan, Woodward	Pre-emption right to enter land	23	2	Petition	278	Not referred.						
Roath, Ebenezer, widow of.	Continuation of pension	25	2	Petition	587	Naval Affairs.	....	....	.....	Discharged; laid on table.		
Robards, Jesse	Increase of pension	27	2	Petition	1031	Rev. Pensions.						
Robards, Jesse	Increase of pension	28	2	Petition	382	Rev. Pensions.						
Robards, Jesse	Increase of pension	29	1	Petition	257	Rev. Pensions.						
Robards, William	(See Pollard Keene, administrator of.)	15	2	....	24, 27							
Robart, Francis	(See John Anderson and others.)	16	1	....	85							
Robb, David	Compensation for services rendered and expenses incurred as Indian agent.	28	1	Senate bill	868	Indian Affairs	533	Adverse	S. 154	Referred to Committee Whole House.		
Robb, David	Compensation for services rendered and expenses incurred as Indian agent.	30	1	Documents	81	Indian Affairs	171	Adverse	.....	Laid on table.		
Robb, John, (Md.)	Indemnity for French spoliations prior to 1800.	26	1	Memorial	182	Foreign Affairs	343	Favorable	319	Referred to Committee Whole House.		
Robb, John	Increase of compensation as superintendent of the United States armory at Springfield, Massachusetts.	24	1	Petition	200	Military Affairs.						

List of private claims presented to the House of Representatives of the United States from the 1st to the 31st Congress, inclusive—Continued.

Names of claimants.	Nature or object of the claim.	Congress.	Session.	How brought before the House of Reps.	Page of journal.	To what committee of the House referred.	No. or date of the report.	Nature of the report.	No. of the bill.	How disposed of by the House of Reps.	How disposed of by the Senate.	Date of the act of Congress, and remarks.
Robb, John, executors of	Indemnity for French spoliations prior to 1800.	26	1	Memorial	182	Foreign Affairs	343	Favorable	319	Referred to Committee Whole House.		
Robbe, John	Pension	3	1	Petition	46	Select	May 30, 1794	Favorable	60	Passed	Passed	App'd June 4, 1794
Robbins, Asher	(See Thomes Tupper, assignees of.)	22	2	....	142							
Robbins, Benjamin	Pension	21	1	Petition	143	Military Pensions	April 2, 1830	Adverse	.....	Laid on table.		
Robbins, Brintnel	Compensation for boats furnished United States on Lake Erie, and for boats lost and condemned during war of 1812.	15	1	Petition	272	Military Affairs	....	....	.....	Discharged; referred to Secretary war, Mar. 14, 1848, reported from Sec. War, laid on the table.		
Robbins, Brintnel	Compensation for boats furnished United States on Lake Erie, and for boats lost and condemned during war of 1812.	17	1	Petition	388	Claims.						
Robbins, Brintnel	Compensation for boats furnished United States on Lake Erie, and for boats lost and condemned during war of 1812.	17	2	Petition	196	Indian Affairs	....	....	.....	Discharged; leave to withdraw.		
Robbins, Brintnel	Compensation for boats furnished United States on Lake Erie, and for boats lost and condemned during war of 1812.	18	1	Petition	60	Claims	9	Favorable	18	Passed	Passed	App'd Jan. 19, 1824
Robbins, Brintnel	Compensation for boats, &c., built for United States for the use of the army, under contract with proper officers.	19	1	Petition	130	Claims	Jan. 30, 1826	Adverse	.....	Laid on table.		
Robbins, Brintnel	Compensation for boats, &c., built for United States for the use of the army, under contract with proper officers.	20	1	Petition	311	Claims	Mar. 12, 1828	Adverse	.....	Laid on table.		
Robbins, Daniel	Renewal of loan office certificate.	2	1	Petition	447							
				Rep. of Secretary Treasury.	583	Select.						
Robbins, David	Pension for revolutionary services.	3	2	Rep. of Secretary War.	350	Claims.						
Robbins, David	Pension for revolutionary services.	4	1	Rep. of Secretary War.	373	Claims.						
Robbins, David	Pension for revolutionary services.	4	2	Rep. of Secretary War.	614	Claims.						
Robbins, Jeremiah	Increase of pension	11	2	House bill	283	Whole House	Mar. 24, 1810	With amends.	107	Passed	Passed	App'd April 27, 1810
Robbins, John, heirs of	Commutation pay due deceased as an officer in the revolutionary army.	23	1	Petition	40	Rev. Claims	Jan. 2, 1834	Favorable	125	Laid on table.		
Robbins, Joseph	Pension for revolutionary services.	24	2	Petition	106	Rev. Pensions	....	....	.....	Discharged; laid on table.		
Robbins, Joseph	Pension for revolutionary services.	25	2	Petition	55	Rev. Pensions	Jan. 12, 1838	Adverse	.....	....	....	Committee report that he is entitled to pension under existing laws.
Robbins, Mercy	Continuation of pension for revolutionary services of her husband.	28	1	Petition	850	Rev. Pensions.						
Robbins, Robert	Arrearages of pension	18	2	Petition	159	Pens. & Rev. Cl'ms.	....	....	.....	Disch'd; laid on table.		

List of private claims presented to the House of Representativesthe of United States from the 1st to the 31st Congress, inclusive—Continued.

Names of claimants.	Nature or object of the claim.	Congress.	Session.	How brought before the House of Reps.	Page of journal.	To what committee of the House referred.	No. or date of the report.	Nature of the report.	No. of the bill.	How disposed of by the House of Reps.	How disposed of by the Senate.	Date of the act of Congress, and remarks.
Robbins, Samuel	Pension	9	1	Petition	52	Military Pensions	164	Adverse		Laid on table.		
Robbins, William H., and James Gillespie.	(See John S. Punch, sureties of.)	24	1		672							
Robeno, Lewis	Payment for a horse lost in public service.	19	1	Petition	83	Claims	Jan. 13, 1826	Adverse		Laid on table.		
Robert, A. D	(See A. Boudouin and A. D. Robert.)	30	1		102							
Robert, Charles	(See Hipolite Robert)	22	1		372							
Robert, Hipolite	Confirmation of title to land in Missouri.	22	1	Petition	263	Priv. Land Claims.	303	Favorable	380	Referred to Committee Whole House.		
Robert, John	(See Hipolite Robert)	22	1		263							
Robert, Louis D	(See heirs of Peter Dominick Robert.)	27	2		75							
Robert, Peter Dominick	Confirmation of title to land in Illinois.	9	1	Petition	236	Public Lands	April 10, 1806	Adverse		Laid on table.		
Robert, Peter Dominick	Confirmation of title to land in Illinois.	14	2	Petition	518					Laid on table.		
Robert, Peter Dominick	Confirmation of title to land in Illinois.	15	1	Petition	39	Priv. Land Claims.				Discharged.		
Robert, Peter Dominick	Confirmation of title to land in Illinois.	16	2	Petition	22	Priv. Land Claims.				Discharged; laid on table.		
Robert, Peter Dominick	Confirmation of title to land in Illinois.	17	1	Petition	41	Priv. Land Claims.						
Robert, Peter Dominick	Confirmation of title to land in Illinois.	19	2	Petition	112	Priv. Land Claims.				Discharged; laid on table.		
Robert, Peter Dominick	Confirmation of title to land in Illinois.	22	1	Petition	190	Priv. Land Claims.	Feb. 6, 1832	Adverse		Laid on table.		
Robert, Peter Dominick	Confirmation of title to land in Illinois.	23	1	Petition	439	Public Lands.						
Robert, Peter Dominick	Confirmation of title to land in Illinois.	23	2	Petition	48	Priv. Land Claims.						
Robert, Peter Dominick	Confirmation of title to land in Illinois.	24	1	Petition	65	Priv. Land Claims.				Discharged; laid on table.		
Robert, Peter Dominick	Confirmation of title to land in Illinois.	27	2	Petition	75	Priv. Land Claims.						
Robert, Peter Dominick	Confirmation of title to land in Illinois.	27	3	Petition	386					Leave to withdraw.		
Robert, Peter Dominick	Confirmation of title to land in Illinois.	29	2	Petition	132	Priv. Land Claims.				Leave to withdraw.		
Robertail, Robert	(See Indians, Wyandott.)											
Roberts, Benjamin	(See William G. Roberts, *et al*)	17	1		238							
Roberts, Benjamin P., heirs of.	Compensation for quarters and fuel furnished British prisoners during war of 1812.	24	2	Petition	209	Claims.						
Roberts, Benjamin P., heirs of.	Compensation for quarters and fuel furnished British prisoners during war of 1812.	26	1	Petition	169	Claims	29	Favorable	48	Passed	Indef. postp'd.	
Roberts, Benjamin P., heirs of.	Compensation for quarters and fuel furnished British prisoners during war of 1812.	26	2	Petition	80	Claims	16, 39	Favorable	554, 567	Referred to Committee Whole House.		
Roberts, Benjamin P., heirs of.	Compensation for quarters and fuel furnished British prisoners during war of 1812.	27	2	Petition	154	Claims	326	Favorable	297	Passed	Passed	App'd Aug. 11, 1842

List of private claims presented to the House of Representatives of the United States from the 1st to the 31st Congress, inclusive—Continued.

Names of claimants.	Nature or object of the claim.	Congress.	Session.	How brought before the House of Reps.	Page of journal.	To what committee of the House referred.	No. or date of the report.	Nature of the report.	No. of the bill.	How disposed of by the House of Reps.	How disposed of by the Senate.	Date of the act of Congress, and remarks.
Roberts, Benjamin S.	Release from judgment obtained against him by United States.	27	2	Petition	247	Judiciary.						
Roberts, Benjamin S.	Release from judgment obtained against him by United States.	27	3	Petition	107	Judiciary.						
Roberts, Benjamin S.	Release from judgment obtained against him by United States.	28	1	Petition	70	Judiciary	572	Favorable	427	Referred to Committee Whole House.		
Roberts, Benjamin S.	Release from judgment obtained against him by United States.	28	2	Bill of last sess.	344	Whole House	Feb. 7, 1845	With amends.	427	Passed	Passed	App'd March 1, 1845
Roberts, Benjamin S.	Release from judgment obtained against him by United States.	29	1	Petition	172	Judiciary	....	....	......	Discharged; laid on table.		
Roberts, Boas	(See sureties of Wm. Whitsett)	17	2	....	228							
Roberts, Charles, & others.	Confirmation of title to land in Louisiana.	16	1	Petition	182	Select.						
Roberts, Charles, & others.	Confirmation of title to land in Louisiana.	17	1	Petition	389	Public Lands.						
Roberts, Charles, & others.	Confirmation of title to land in Louisiana.	18	2	Petition	70	Priv. Land Claims.						
Roberts, Charles W., assignee of.	Payment of one-half of proceeds of sale of the brig Josefa Segunder, condemned and sold for violation of law.	19	2	Petition	216	Judiciary.						
Roberts, Charles W., assignee of.	Payment of one half of proceeds of sale of the brig Josefa Segunper, condemned and sold for violation of law.	20	1	Petition	99	Judiciary	....	....	......	Discharged; laid on table.		
Roberts, Cyrus L., heirs of.	Commutation pay for revolutionary services.	24	1	Petition	281	Rev. Claims	Mar. 26, 1836	Adverse	......	Laid on table.		
Roberts, Edmund	Additional compensation for diplomatic services.	23	2	Petition	36	Foreign Affairs	25	Favorable	589	Referred to Committee Whole House.		
Roberts, Edmond, representatives of.	Additional pay for services as diplomatic agent in Asia.	25	2	Resolution	160	Foreign Affairs	317	Favorable	359	Referred to Committee Whole House.		
Roberts, Edmond, representatives of.	Additional pay for services as diplomatic agent in Asia.	25	2	Bill of last sess.	377	Whole House	Jan. 25, 1839	With't amend.	359	Passed	Passed, with amendment.	App'd March 3, 1839
Roberts, Edmund	(See Felix St. Vrain, sureties of).	25	2	....	426							
Roberts, Edward, widow of	Pension	10	1	Petition	248	Claims.						
Roberts, Eliza S	(See widow of Moses A. Roberts).	30	1	....	111							
Roberts, Elvington	Correction of error in entry of land.	17	2	Petition	207	Priv. Land Claims.	....	....	......	Discharged; leave to withdraw.		
Roberts, Elvington	Correction of error in entry of land.	20	1	Senate bill	97	Public Lands	Jan. 11, 1828	With't amend.	S. 29	Passed	Passed	App'd May 9, 1828
Roberts, Ephriam	Pension	21	1	Petition	377	Military Pensions.	....	....	......	Discharged; laid on table.		
Roberts, Ephriam	Pension	22	1	Petition	287	Rev. Pensions	....	....	......	Discharged; laid on table.		
Roberts, Ezekiel	Compensation for military services during revolutionary war.	4	1	Petition	494	Claims	May 31, 1796	Adverse	......	Laid on table.		
Roberts, George	(See administrator of W. Roberts)	24	1	....	152							
Roberts, Henry	Payment for military services in revolutionary war.	3	2	Petition	247	Claims	Feb. 25, 1795	Adverse	......	Referred to Committee Whole House.		
Roberts, Henry	Payment for military services in revolutionary war.	4	2	Petition	631	Claims	Dec. 29, 1796	Adverse	......	Rejected.		
Roberts, Henry	Payment for services as officer in the revolutionary army.	15	1	Petition	307	Pens. & Rev. Cl'ms.	....	....	......	Discharged; laid on table.		
Roberts, Hopestell	(See widow of Ishmael Handy)	30	1	....	822							

List of private claims presented to the House of Representatives of the United States from the 1st to the 31st Congress, inclusive—Continued.

Names of claimants.	Nature or object of the claim.	Congress.	Session.	How brought before the House of Reps.	Page of journal.	To what committee of the House referred.	No. or date of the report.	Nature of the report.	No. of the bill.	How disposed of by the House of Reps.	How disposed of by the Senate.	Date of the act of Congress, and remarks.
Roberts, Hough	(See Joseph Stewart, and others)	14	2		56							
Roberts, Ishmael, widow of	Payment for revolutionary services of her husband in United States navy.	25	2	Petition	399	Naval Affairs				Discharged; laid on table.		
Roberts, Ishmael, widow of	Payment for revolutionary services of her husband in United States navy.	30	1	Petition	822					Leave to withdraw.		
Roberts, James	Additional compensation for carrying the United States mail in the years 1803 and 1804.	22	1	Petition	473	P. Of. & P. Roads.						
Roberts, James	Increase of pension	26	1	Resolution	551	Invalid Pensions.						
Roberts, Jesse	Pension	21	1	Petition	411	Military Pensions	May 18, 1830	Adverse		Laid on table.		
Roberts, Jesse	Pension	27	3	Petition	384					Leave to withdraw.		
Roberts, Jesse	Increase of pension	29	2	Petition	150	Rev. Pensions	7	Adverse		Laid on table.		
Roberts, John	Pension for revolutionary services	3	1	Rep. of Secretary War.	131	Select.						
Roberts, John	Pension for revolutionary services	3	2	Rep. of Secretary War.	262	Claims	Feb. 28, 1795	Favorable	130	Passed	Postponed.	
Roberts, John	Pension for revolutionary services	4	1	Rep. of Secretary War.	445	Claims.						
Roberts, John	Payment for revolutionary services	4	2	Rep. of Secretary War.	614	Claims.						
Roberts, John	Compensation for services rendered, and property destroyed during war of 1813.	14	1	Petition	667					Laid on table.		
Roberts, John	(See Richard C. Langdon)	23	1		362							
Roberts, John	(See sureties of William Whitsett)	17	2		228							
Roberts, John, (Pa.)	Commutation pay for revolutionary services.	18	1	Petition	284	Pens. & Rev. Cl'ms.						
Roberts, John, (Pa.,) heirs of.	Compensation for revolutionary services.	18	2	Resolution	193	Pens. & Rev. Cl'ms.				Discharged; laid on table.		
Roberts, John, (Pa.,) heirs of.	Compensation for revolutionary services.	19	1	Resolution	80	Claims				Discharged; laid on table.		
Roberts, Dr. John, heirs of.	Commutation pay for revolutionary services.	22	1	Petition	470	Rev. Claims				Discharged; laid on table.		
Roberts, Dr. John, heirs of.	Commutation pay for revolutionary services.	23	2	Petition	165	Rev. Claims.						
Roberts, Dr. John, heirs of.	Commutation pay for revolutionary services.	24	1	Petition	431	Rev. Claims	640	Adverse		Laid on table.		
Roberts, Dr. John, heirs of	Commutation pay for revolutionary services.	25	2	Petition	70	Rev. Claims	Jan. 10, 1838	Adverse		Laid on table.		
Roberts, Dr. John, heirs of.	Commutation pay for revolutionary services.	26	1	Petition	164	Rev. Claims	390	Adverse		Laid on table.		
Roberts, Dr. John, heirs of.	Commutation pay for revolutionary services.	26	1	Petition	1144					Recommitted to Rev. Claims.		
Roberts, Dr. John, heirs of.	Commutation pay for revolutionary services.	27	2	Petition	96	Rev. Claims	871	Adverse		Laid on table.		
Roberts, Dr. John, administrator of.	Commutation pay for revolutionary services.	29	1	Memorial	389	Rev. Claims	Mar. 27, 1846	Res.; adverse		Laid on table.		
Roberts, Dr. John, administrator of.	Commutation pay for revolutionary services.	30	1	Memorial	799	Rev. Claims.						
Roberts, Dr. John, administrator of.	Commutation pay for revolutionary services.	31	1	Petition	648	Rev. Claims.						

List of private claims presented to the House of Representatives of the United States from the 1st to the 31st Congress, inclusive—Continued.

Names of claimants.	Nature or object of the claim.	Congress.	Session.	How brought before the House of Reps.	Page of journal.	To what committee of the House referred.	No. or date of the report.	Nature of the report.	No. of the bill.	How disposed of by the House of Reps.	How disposed of by the Senate.	Date of the act of Congress, and remarks.
Roberts, John, heirs of....	Half-pay and bounty land for revolutionary services in Virginia line.	24	1	Resolution	269	Rev. Claims.						
Roberts, Captain J.......	(See Capt. B. F. Hill and others.)	31	1	....	1012							
Roberts, Major John, (Va.)	Pay and emoluments for services as an officer in the revolutionary war.	21	2	Petition	63	Rev. Claims......	6	Favorable; bill	505	Referred to Committee Whole House.		
Roberts, Major John, (Va.)	Pay and emoluments for services as an officer in the revolutionary war.	22	1	Petition	28	Rev. Claims......	45	Favorable; bill	94	Passed	Passed	App'd May 25, 1832
Roberts, Major John, (Va.)	For interest on amount allowed by act of May 25, 1832.	23	1	Petition	42	Rev. Claims.						
Roberts, Major John, (Va.)	For interest on amount allowed by act of May 25, 1832.	24	1	Petition	942	Rev. Claims.						
Roberts, Major, John, (Va.)	For interest on amount allowed by act of May 25, 1832.	25	3	Petition	221	Rev. Claims.						
Roberts, Major, John, (Va.)	For interest on amount allowed by act of May 25, 1832.	27	2	Petition	390	Rev. Claims......	541	Adverse	......	Laid on table.		
Roberts, Major, John, (Va.)	Pension to his wife in the event of her surviving him.	27	2	Petition	374	Rev. Pensions	784	Adverse	......	Laid on table.		
Roberts, Major, John, (Va.) widow of.	Revolutionary pension	31	1	Petition	647	Rev. Pensions.						
Roberts, John, (Conn.)...	Revolutionary pension..........	21	2	Petition	159	Military Pensions.						
Roberts, John, (Conn.)...	Revolutionary pension..........	22	1	Petition	35	Rev. Pensions.						
Roberts, John, (Ky.)	Payment for a horses lost in war of 1812.	22	1	Petition	288	Claims	Feb. 15, 1832	Adverse	......	Laid on table.		
Roberts, John	Release from liability as surety of Morrison & Wheeler in a contract to supply government with arms.	26	1	Petition	352	Judiciary	329	Favorable; bill	296	Passed	Indef. postp'd.	
Roberts, John	Release from liability as surety of Morrison & Wheeler in a contract to supply government with arms.	26	2	Petition	38	Judiciary.						
Roberts, John, assignee of.	Relinquishment by government of a lien on land.	26	1	Petition	352	Judiciary.						
Roberts, John, assignee of.	Relinquishment by government of a lien on land.	26	2	Petition	38	Judiciary.						
Roberts, John, assignee of.	Relinquishment by government of a lien on land.	27	1	Petition	104	Judiciary.						
Roberts, John, (N. Y.)...	Bounty land for military services..	25	2	Petition	59	Priv. Land Claims.	Dec. 28, 1837	Adverse	......	Referred to Committee Whole House.		
Roberts, Joseph.........	Pension	3	1	Report Secretary of War.	131	Select...........	May 26, 1794	Favorable; bill	62	Passed	Passed	App'd June 7, 1794
Roberts, Joseph G., Surgeon	For his share of prize-money for capture of British fleet on Lake Erie.	13	3	Petition	462	Naval Affairs.....	Jan. 30, 1815	Adverse......	......	Laid on table.		
Roberts, Joseph G., Surgeon	For his share of prize-money for capture of British fleet on Lake Frie.	17	2	Petition	122	Naval Affairs.....	Jan. 29, 1823	Adverse	......	Laid on table.		
Roberts, Joseph G., Surgeon	For certain credits in settlement of his accounts.	23	1	Petition	384	Claims.						

List of private claims presented to the House of Representatives of the United States from the 1st *to the* 31st *Congress, inclusive*—Continued.

Names of claimants.	Nature or object of the claim.	Congress.	Session.	How brought before the House of Reps.	Page of journal.	To what committee of the House referred.	No. or date of the report.	Nature of the report.	No. of the bill.	How disposed of by the House of Reps.	How disposed of by the Senate.	Date of the act of Congress, and remarks.
Roberts, Joseph, (N. H.)	Compensation for services in revolutionary war.	21	1	Petition	49	Rev. Claims				Discharged; laid on table.		
Roberts, Joseph	Arrears of pension	25	3	Petition	217	Rev. Pensions				Discharged; laid on table.		
Roberts, Joseph	Script in lieu of land granted by Kentucky to Wm. Armstead.	31	1	Petition	234	Priv. Land Claims.						
Roberts, Judah	Pension	21	2	Senate bill	79	Military Pensions	Dec. 29, 1830	Adverse	S. 21	Laid on table.		
Roberts, Levi M.	Pension for injuries while express rider in war of 1812.	17	2	Petition	24	Pens. & Rev. Cl'ms.	Dec. 13, 1822	Adverse.		Laid on table.		
Roberts, Levi M.	Pension for loss of a leg in war of 1812.	20	1	Resolution	304	Military Pensions				Discharged; laid on table.		
Roberts, Levi M.	Pension for loss of a leg in war of 1812.	20	2	Resolution	55	Military Pensions	Dec. 12, 1828	By bill	311	Passed	Laid on table.	
Roberts, Levi M.	Pension for loss of a leg in war of 1812.	21	1	Res. and docs	130	Military Pensions	Jan. 5, 1830	By bill	72	Passed	Passed	App'd May 20, 1830
Roberts, Levi M.	Arrearages of pension	23	1	Petition	241	Invalid Pensions	Feb. 18, 1834	Adverse		Laid on table.		
Roberts, Levi M.	Arrearages of pension	24	1	Petition	98	Invalid Pensions	Jan. 28, 1836	Adverse		Laid on table.		
Roberts, Levi M.	Arrearages of pension	25	2	Petition	57	Invalid Pensions	571	Favorable	561	Passed.		
Roberts, Levi M.	Increase and arrearages of pension.	25	3	Petition	89	Invalid Pensions.	84	Favorable	963	Passed.		
Roberts, Levi M.	Increase and arrearages of pension.	25	3	Petition, (2)	90	Invalid Pensions	147	Favorable	1016	Referred to Committee Whole House.		
Roberts, Levi M.	Increase and arrearages of pension.	26	1	Petition	162	Invalid Pensions	207	Favorable	219	Passed	Indef. postp'd.	
Roberts, Levi M.	Increase and arrearages of pension.	26	2	Petition	77	Invalid Pensions	156	Favorable	668	Referred to Committee Whole House.		
Roberts, Levi M.	Increase and arrearages of pension.	27	2	Petition	60	Invalid Pensions	226	Adverse		Laid on table.		
Roberts, Levi M.	Increase and arrearages of pension.	27	3	Petition	106	Invalid Pensions.						
Roberts, Levi M.	Increase and arrearages of pension.	28	1	Petition	123	Invalid Pensions	239	Adverse		Laid on table.		
Roberts, Levi M.	Increase and arrearages of pension.	29	2	Petition	82	Invalid Pensions.				Discharged; laid on table.		
Roberts, Levi M.	Increase and arrearages of pension.	30	1	Petition	82	Invalid Pensions				Discharged; laid on table.		
Roberts, Levi M.	Increase and arrearages of pension.	30	2	Petition	76	Invalid Pensions	2	Favorable	680	Passed.		
Roberts, Levi M.	Increase and arrearages of pension.	31	1	Petition	486	Invalid Pensions.						
Roberts, Lewis	Payment of balance due him as artificer in war of 1812.	30	1	Petition	172	Claims	204	Adverse		Laid on table.		
Roberts, Lewis	Payment of balance due him as artificer in war of 1812.	31	1	Petition	1209	Claims.						
Roberts, Lucy Ann	(See John Roberts, of Virginia, widow of.)	31	1		647							
Roberts, Mark R.	Pension for wounds received in Seminole war.	18	2	Petition	183	Pens. & Rev. Cl'ms.				Discharged; leave to withdraw.		
Roberts, Mark R.	Pension for services during war of 1812.	19	1	Resolution	197	Military Pensions	Feb. 23, 1826	Pension bill	118	Passed.		
Roberts, Mark R.	Pension for services during war of 1812.	19	2	House bill	85	Whole House	Feb. 2, 1827	With amend'ts	314	Passed	Passed	App'd March 3, 1827
Roberts & Masterson	Payment for work and materials done on Cumberland road.	23	1	Res. and papers.	589	Claims	455	Adverse				See report No. 449.
Roberts, Moses A., widow of.	Pension; husband died of disease contracted in public service.	30	1	Petition	111	Invalid Pensions	338	Favorable	316	Passed.		
Roberts, Moses A., widow of.	Pension; husband died of disease contracted in public service.	31	1	Petition	433	Invalid Pensions				Leave to withdraw.		
Roberts, Namon	Pension for services during revolutionary war.	17	1	Petition	39	Pens. & Rev. Cl'ms.	Dec. 21, 1821	Adverse		Laid on table.		

List of private claims presented to the House of Representatives of the United States from the 1*st to the* 31*st Congress, inclusive*—Continued.

Names of claimants.	Nature or object of the claim.	Congress.	Session.	How brought before the House of Reps.	Page of journal.	To what committee of the House referred.	No. or date of the report.	Nature of the report.	No. of the bill.	How disposed of by the House of Reps.	How disposed of by the Senate.	Date of the act of Congress, and remarks.
Roberts, Owen, representatives of.	Seven years' half-pay	2	1	House bill	463	Whole House	Nov. 28, 1791	Favorable	152	Passed	Passed	App'd Mar. 27, 1792
Roberts, Patrick	(See John McElroy, *et al*)	3	2		267							
Roberts, Perley, widow of.	Arrears of pension for revolutionary services of her husband.	27	3	Petition	365	Rev. Pensions.						
Roberts, Perley, widow of.	Arrears of pension for revolutionary services of her husband.	28	1	Petition	839	Whole House.						
Roberts, Perley, widow of.	Extension of pension act of June, 1844.	30	1	Petition	230	Rev. Pensions	Jan. 25, 1848	Adverse		Laid on table		
Roberts, Reuben, (Tenn.).	Grant of land in lieu of that for revolutionary services, of which he has been defrauded.	19	2	Petition	286	Priv. Land Claims.				Discharged; laid on table.		
Roberts, Reuben, (Tenn.).	Grant of land in lieu of that for revolutionary services, of which he has been defrauded.	20	1	Petition	100	Priv. Land Claims.	March 4, 1828	Adverse		Laid on table.		
Roberts, Reuben	Increase of pension	23	2	Petition	198	Invalid Pensions				Discharged; laid on table.		
Roberts, Reuben	Arrears of pension	25	2	Resolution	605	Rev. Pensions				Discharged; laid on table.		
Roberts, Reuben	Arrears of pension	26	1	Petition	759	Rev. Pensions	424	Adverse		Recommitted.		
Roberts, Robert	Debenture on coffee exported to Holland.	16	1	Petition	101	Commerce				Discharged; laid on table.		
Roberts, Robert	Indemnity for the capture of ship Experiment by a French privateer in 1805.	24	1	Petition	508	Foreign Affairs				Discharged; laid on table.		
Roberts, Robert	Indemnity for the capture of ship Experiment by a French privateer in 1805.	25	2	Memorial	584	Foreign Affairs	874	Adverse		Laid on table.		
Roberts, Robert	Indemnity for the capture of ship Experiment by a French privateer in 1805.	26	1	Petition	298	Judiciary.						
Roberts, Robert	Indemnity for the capture of ship Experiment by a French privateer in 1805.	28	1	Memorial	59	Claims.						
Roberts, Robert	Indemnity for the capture of ship Experiment by a French privateer in 1805.	29	1	Memorial	340	Claims	805	Favorable	527	Referred to Committee Whole House.		
Roberts, Robert	Indemnity for the capture of ship Experiment by a French privateer in 1805.	30	1	Petition	66	Claims	2	Favorable	2	Referred to Committee Whole House.		
Roberts, Robert	Indemnity for the capture of ship Experiment by a French privateer in 1805.	30	2	Petition and bill of last session.	87	Claims	Jan. 17, 1849	With amend.	2	Referred to Committee Whole House.		
Roberts, Robert	Indemnity for the capture of ship Experiment by a French privateer in 1805.	31	1	Petition	255	Claims	164	Adverse.		Laid on table.		
Roberts, Robert M.	Permission to enter lands reserved for schools, and appropriation of others in lieu thereof.	24	2	Petition	210	Priv. Land Claims.						
Roberts, Robert M.	Permission to enter lands reserved for schools, and appropriation of others in lieu thereof.	25	2	Petition	374	Priv. Land Claims.	936	Favorable	817	Referred to Committee Whole House.		

List of private claims presented to the House of Representatives of the United States from the 1st to the 31st Congress, inclusive—Continued.

Names of claimants.	Nature or object of the claim.	Congress.	Session.	How brought before the House of Reps.	Page of journal.	To what committee of the House referred.	No. or date of the report.	Nature of the report.	No. of the bill.	How disposed of by the House of Reps.	How disposed of by the Senate.	Date of the act of Congress, and remarks.
Roberts, Robert M.	Permission to enter lands reserved for schools, and appropriation of others in lieu thereof.	25	3	Bill of last sess.	431	Whole House	Feb. 1, 1839	With't amend.	817	Passed	Passed	App'd March 3, 1839
Roberts, Ruth	Compensation for revolutionary losses and injuries sustained by her late husband.	1	2	Petition and rep't Sec. of War.	142, 153	....	....	....	......	Laid on table.		
Roberts, Samuel E.	Bounty land services in Mexican war.	30	1	Petition	147	Military Affairs.						
Roberts, Stephen	Pension	19	1	Petition	175	Military Pensions	164	Adverse	......	Laid on table.		
Roberts, Submit	(See Perley Roberts, widow of.)	27	3	....	365							
Roberts, Thomas, widow of.	Same annuity allowed her husband by Pennsylvania for revolutionary services.	24	1	Petition	137	Rev. Claims.						
Roberts, William	Increase of pension	3	1	Petition	19	....	....	....	......	Referred to Secretary of War.		
Roberts, William, administrator of.	Commutation pay for revolutionary services.	24	1	Petition	152	Rev. Claims	July 2, 1836	Adverse	......	Laid on table.		
Roberts, Wm., jr., (N. J.)	Payment of promissory notes held by him against the United States which he purchased during war of 1812.	25	2	Petition	111	Rev. Claims	936	Adverse	......	Laid on table.		
Roberts, William, (Conn.) widow of.	Pension for revolutionary services of her husband.	25	2	Petition	403	Rev. Pensions	....	....	......	Discharged; referred to Com. Whole House, on bill No. 456.		
Roberts, William G. and Benjamin, (N. Y.)	Indemnity for property destroyed by United States troops during the war of 1812.	17	1	Petition	238	Claims	March 4, 1822	Adverse	......	Laid on table.		
Roberts, William G. and Benjamin, (N. Y.)	Indemnity for property destroyed by United States troops during the war of 1812.	17	2	Petition	89	Claims.						
Roberts, William J	(See John Roberts, assignee of.)	26	1	....	352							
Roberts, William	Pension	29	1	Petition	1150	Invalid Pensions	....	....	......	Discharged; laid on table.		
Roberts, William	Pension	29	2	Petition	89	Invalid Pensions.						
Roberts, William	Pension	30	1	Petition	625	Invalid Pensions	580	Adverse	......	Laid on table.		
Roberts, William	Pension	31	1	Petition	298	Invalid Pensions	....	....	......	Discharged; laid on table.		
Roberts, William	Permission to enter land under act to provide for armed occupation of Florida.	30	1	Petition	740	Public Lands.						
Roberts, Zachariah	Compensation for services as a militia officer.	13	2	Petition	240	Claims	72	Adverse	......	Laid on table.		
Roberts, Zachariah	Pension	16	1	Petition	26	Pens. & Rev. Cl'ms.	Dec. 16, 1819	Adverse	......	Recommitted	....	Leave to withdraw.
Roberston, Archibald	Payment for a horse and equipage lost in Seminole campaign in 1818	23	1	Documents	154	Claims.						
Robertson, Archibald	Payment for a gun lost in public service in 1818.	24	1	Petition	534	Claims.						
Robertson & Barnwell	Remission of duty on playing cards	20	1	Petition	419	Ways and Means	Mar. 24, 1828	Favorable	239	Referred to Committee Whole House.		
Robertson & Barnwell	Remission of duty on playing cards	20	2	Bill of last sess.	269	Whole House	Feb. 9, 1829	With't amends	239	Passed.		
Robertson & Barnwell	Remission of duty on playing cards	21	2	Petition	44	Ways and Means	Dec. 30, 1830	Favorable	527	Referred to Committee Whole House.		

List of private claims presented to the House of Representatives of the United States form the 1st to the 31st Congress, inclusive—Continued.

Names of claimants.	Nature or object of the claim.	Congress.	Session.	How brought before the House of Reps.	Page of journal.	To what committee of the House referred.	No. or date of the report.	Nature of the report.	No. of the bill.	How disposed of by the House of Reps.	How disposed of by the Senate.	Date of the act of Congress, and remarks.
Robertson & Barnwell....	Remission of duty on playing cards	22	1	Petition	24	Ways and Means..	Dec. 15, 1831	Favorable....	2	Passed	Passed	App'd Jan. 18, 1832
Robertson, Catharine.....	(See Catharine Robinson.)	9	1	....	189							
Robertson, David........	(See Wm. H. Bedford, agent, &c.)	28	1	....	262							
Robertson, David & others.	Compensation for services during war of 1812.	23	1	Senate bill	845	Commerce	....	....	S. 119			
Robertson, Elizabeth.....	(See Elizabeth Ribinson)........	24	1	....	602							
Robertson, George.......	Pension	14	1	Petition	497	Pensions.						
Robertson, George.......	Confirmation of title to land in Missouri.	15	1	Petition	312	Priv. Land Claims.	....	....	......	Discharged; laid on table.		
Robertson, George.......	Confirmation of title to land in Missouri.	16	1	Petition	72	Priv. Land Claims.	....	....	......	Discharged; laid on table.		
Robertson, George.......	Confirmation of title to land in Missouri.	17	1	Petition	54	Public Lands.						
Robertson, George.......	Confirmation of title to land in Missouri.	18	1	Petition	55	Public Lands.						
Robertson, George.......	(See John Robertson, executors of)	29	2	....	184							
Robertson, Henry	(See Louis F. Beeler, *et al.*).....	30	1	....	115							
Robertson, Ica	Payment for rifle pressed into service, war of 1812.	18	1	Resolution	276, 367	Claims	Feb. 27, 1824	Adverse	......	Laid on table.		
Robertson, Isaac	Compensation for military services during revolutionary war.	2	1	Petition	452	....	....	....	......	Referred to Secretary of War.		
Robertson, Isaac	Compensation for military services during revolutionary war.	2	2	Rep. of Secretary War.	696	....	....	....	......	Laid on table.		
Robertson, Isaac S.......	Remission of penalty incurred for selling spirituous liquors without license.	14	2	Petition	222	Ways and Means..	....	....	......	Discharged; laid on table.		
Robertson, James........	To be reimbursed advances made to Chickasaw Indians in 1778.	2	1	Petition	554	....	....	....	......	Referred to Secretary of War.		
Robertson, James........	To be reimbursed advances made to Chickasaw Indians in 1778.	2	2	Rep. of Secretary of War.	735	....	....	....	......	Laid on table.		
Robertson, James, collector of customs, Va.	For an alteration of the mode and amount of his compensation.	19	1	Petition	268	Commerce	....	....	......	Discharged; laid on table.		
Robertson, James, collector of customs, Va.	For an alteration of the mode and amount of his compensation.	19	2	Petition	112	Commerce	....	....	......	Discharged; laid on table.		
Robertson, James, collector of customs, Va.	For an alteration of the mode and amount of his compensation.	20	1	Petition	37	Commerce	35	Adverse	......	Referred to Secretary Treasury.		
Robertson, James M., executor of.	Payment for stone furnished by him in 1801 for construction of Fort McHenry.	21	2	Petition	212	Claims	Feb. 8, 1831	Adverse	......	Laid on table.		
Robertson, James, Charleston, S. C.	Refund excess of duties on importation of goods under tariff of 1832.	23	1	Petition	569	Ways and Means.						
Robertson, James, Charleston, S. C.	Refund excess of duties on importation of goods under tariff of 1832.	24	1	Petition	95	Ways and Means..	Jan. 21, 1836	Favorable....	200	Passed	Passed	App'd June 28, 1836
Robertson, James, jr., surety of.	Release from liability...........	21	2	Petition	110	Ways and Means.						
Robertson, John.........	Reimburse amount paid as ransom from slavery among the Algerines.	2	1	Petition	580	Select	....	....	......	Referred to Committee Whole House.		
Robertson, John.........	Reimburse amount paid as ransom from slavery among the Algerines.	4	2	Memorial and report of Secretary of State.	704	Com. and Manuf..	Mar. 1, 1797	Favorable....	242	Passed	Passed	App'd March 3, 1797

List of private claims presented to the House of Representatives of the United States from the 1st to the 31st Congress, inclusive—Continued.

Names of claimants.	Nature or object of the claim.	Congress.	Session.	How brought before the House of Reps.	Page of journal.	To what committee of the House referred.	No. or date of the report.	Nature of the report.	No. of the bill.	How disposed of by the House of Reps.	How disposed of by the Senate.	Date of the act of Congress, and remarks.
Robertson, John A.	Extension of time for payment of bonds given for duties.	8	2	Petition	89	Com. and Manuf.	Jan. 18, 1805	Favorable	35	Laid on table.		
Robertson, John, (Del.)	Arrearages of pay, bounty land, &c., for revolutionary services.	15	1	Petition	76	Claims	Mar. 18, 1818	Adverse		Laid on table.		
Robertson, John	Compensation for services as navy agent at Charleston, South Carolina.	18	2	Petition	229	Claims.						
Robertson, John	Refund certain discounts upon treasury notes disbursed by him.	19	1	Petition	36	Ways and Means				Discharged; laid on table.		
Robertson, John	Refund certain discounts upon treasury notes disbursed by him.	20	1	Petition	30	Claims	Dec. 17, 1827	Adverse		Leave to withdraw.		
Robertson, John T.	(See surety of James Robertson, jr.)	21	2		110							
Robertson, John, (Va.)	Compensation for revolutionary services.	24	2	Petition	39	Rev. Claims.						
Robertson, John, (Va.)	Compensation for revolutionary services.	25	2	Petition	72	Rev. Claims				Discharged; laid on table.		
Robertson, John, (Va.)	Compensation for revolutionary services.	25	3	Petition	85	Rev. Claims.						
Robertson, John, (Va.)	Compensation for revolutionary services.	26	1	Petition	167	Rev. Claims.						
Robertson, John, (Va.)	Compensation for revolutionary services.	27	2	Petition	61	Rev. Claims	663	Adverse		Laid on table.		
Robertson, John, executors of.	Indemnity for French spoliations prior to 1800.	29	2	Memorial	184	Foreign Affairs.						
Robertson, John T.	Pension for wounds received in public service.	31	1	Petition	223	Invalid Pensions.						
Robertson & Miller	(See executors of John Robertson.)	29	2		184							
Robertson, Joseph M.	(See A. Scott Brownlee)	28	1		189							
Robertson, Lambert	Pension for revolutionary services.	14	2	Petition	40	Pens. & Rev. Cl'ms.	Dec. 30, 1816	Adverse		Leave to withdraw.		
Robertson, Mack, C. C.	(See William H. Bedford, agent).	28	1		262							
Robertson, Margaret	(See widow of Wm. Robertson)	22	1		33							
Robertson, Mitchell	Payment of certificate for services in foraging department of the revolutionary army.	22	1	Petition	260	Rev. Claims	499	Favorable	607	Referred to Committee Whole House.		
Robertson, Moses	Confirmation of title to land in Louisiana.	19	1	Report Reg'r and Receiver Land Office.	64	Public Lands	33	Favorable	254	Referred to Committee Whole House.		
Robertson, Peter	Pension for wounds received at Bunker Hill.	8	2	Petition	81	Claims				Discharged.		
Robertson, Peter	Right of pre-emption as New Orleans branch pilot.	28	1	Petition	77	Priv. Land Claims.	9	Favorable	35	Passed	Passed	App'd June 17, 1844
Robertson, Richard	Payment for horse lost in Creek war of 1813 and 1814.	25	3	Senate bill	657				S. 166			
Robertson, Robert	(See Martin Hurley)	9	1		330							
Robertson, Robert O.	(See Hiram L. Meeker)	26	1		327							
Robertson, R. C.	Pre-emption right to enter land	26	1	Petition	608	Public Lands.						
Robertson, Samuel	Payment for property lost in public service.	23	1	Documents	154	Claims.						
Robertson, Samuel	(See William H. Bedford, agent).	28	1		262							
Robertson, Stephen	Grant of land for revolutionary services.	16	2	Petition	153	Pens. & Rev. Cl'ms.	Jan. 29, 1821	Adverse		Laid on table.		

List of private claims presented to the House of Representatives of the United States from the 1st to the 31st Congress, inclusive—Continued.

Names of claimants.	Nature or object of the claim.	Congress.	Session.	How brought before the House of Reps.	Page of journal.	To what committee of the House referred.	No. or date of the report.	Nature of the report.	No. of the bill.	How disposed of by the House of Reps.	How disposed of by the Senate.	Date of the act of Congress, and remarks.
Robertson, Thomas B.	Compensation for bearing report of land commissioners of Louisiana to Washington city.	14	1	Senate amend'mt to House bill.	715	Whole House	April 26, 1816	Concurred in	127	Passed	....	App'd April 29, 1816
Robertson, William H.	(See attorney of Francisco H. De Hevia.)	18	1	....	177							
Robertson, W. W.	(See James M. Robertson.)	21	2	....	212							
Robertson, William	(See William H. Bedford, agent).	28	1	....	262							
Robertson, Wm. H., and others.	Release from judgment obtained against them at suit of United States.	19	1	Petition	36	Ways and Means	....	....	......	Discharged; referred to President U. States.		
Robertson, Wm. H., and others.	Release from judgment obtained against them at suit of United States.	24	1	Senate bill	1157	Claims	July 2, 1836	Adverse	S. 263	Referred to Committee Whole House.		
Robertson, Wm. H., and others.	Release from judgment obtained against them at suit of United States.	24	2	Senate bill	250	Judiciary	Feb. 28, 1837	With amend.	S. 50	Referred to Committee Whole House.		
Robertson, Wm. H., and others.	Release from judgment obtained against them at suit of United States.	25	2	Senate bill	483	Judiciary	Mar. 9, 1838	With't amend.	S. 101	Referred to Committee Whole House.		
Robertson, Wm. H., and others.	Release from judgment obtained against them at suit of United States.	25	3	Senate bill	372	Judiciary	Feb. 6, 1839	With amend.	S. 241	Referred to Committee Whole House.		
Robertson, Wm. H., and others.	Release from judgment obtained against them at suit of United States.	26	1	Senate bill	189	Claims	504	Adverse	S. 1	Referred to Committee Whole House.		
Robertson, Wm. H., and others.	Release from judgment obtained against them at suit of United States.	27	2	Senate bill	1169	Judiciary	Aug. 4, 1842	With amend.	S. 271	Passed	Passed	App'd Aug. 29, 1842
Robertson, William, widow of.	Leave to pay sum due on land forfeited by non-payment.	22	1	Petition	33	Public Lands	Dec. 19, 1831	Favorable	42	Passed	Passed, with amendment.	App'd Feb. 24, 1832
Robertson, William	Compensation for services to commissioners under treaty with Denmark.	24	1	Petition	66	Claims	....	....	......	Discharged; referred to President of U. S.		
Robeson, Joseph	Pension for revolutionary services.	22	1	Resolution	263	Rev. Pensions	....	....	......	Disch'd; laid on table.		
Robieu, Francis	(See Julian Rachal)	22	2	....	41							
Robin, Martin	Confirmation of title to land in Louisiana.	22	1	House bill	107	Whole House	Mar. 23, 1832	With't amend.	125	Passed	Passed	App'd June 25, 1832
Robin, (Indian)	(See Robin Loyd)	26	1	....	324							
Robinet, Elemuel	Increase of pension	28	1	Petition	696	Invalid Pensions.						
Robinet, Elemuel	Increase of pension	28	2	Petition	120	Invalid Pensions	....	....	......	Discharged; laid on table.		
Robinet, Elemuel	Increase of pension	30	1	Petition	200	Invalid Pensions.						
Robinet, Isaac H	Confirmation of title to land	14	2	Petition	60	Priv. Land Claims.						
Robins, Gurdon	Indemnity for vessel destroyed by British in war of 1812.	24	1	Petition	943	Claims	June 21, 1836	Adverse	......	Laid on table.		
Robins, Gurdon	Indemnity for vessel destroyed by British in war of 1812.	24	2	Petition	72	Claims	169	Adverse	......	Laid on table.		
Robins, Michael	Back pay as a pensioner	29	1	Petition	418	Invalid Pensions	295	Adverse	......	Laid on table.		
Robins, Richard	Pension	29	1	Petition	418	Invalid Pensions	Feb. 17, 1846	Adverse	......	Laid on table.		
Robinson, Alexander	(See Henry Rutgers, and others).	6	2	....	783							
Robinson, Dr. Alexander	Compensation for services as physician to emigrating Creek Indians.	22	2	Petition	86	Indian Affairs	30	Favorable	676	Referred to Committee Whole House.		

List of private claims presented to the House of Representatives of the United States from the 1st to the 31st Congress, inclusive—Continued.

Names of claimants.	Nature or object of the claim.	Congress.	Session.	How brought before the House of Reps.	Page of journal.	To what committee of the House referred.	No. or date of the report.	Nature of the report.	No. of the bill.	How disposed of by the House of Reps.	How disposed of by the Senate.	Date of the act of Congress, and remarks.
Robinson, Dr. Alexander	Compensation for services as physician to emigrating Creek Indians.	23	1	Petition	138	Indian Affairs	172	Favorable	188	Passed	Passed	App'd June 30, 1834
Robinson, Amos, (Cherokee Indian.)	(See William Wilson, and other Cherokees.)	17	2		96							
Robinson, Beverly	(See representatives of Wm. Alexander, earl of Sterling.)	22	1		142							
Robinson, Carr, & Co	(See John Jones, and others)	25	2		952							
Robinson, Carr, & Co	Payment for work done on the Pea Patch island.	25	2	Letter of Secretary of War.	518	Claims	922	Favorable	807	Referred to Committee Whole House.		
Robinson, Catherine	(See widow of Jacob Ritter)	9	1		189							
Robinson, Charles, widow of.	Grant of land for revolutionary services.	15	2	Petition	263	Whole House				Discharged; laid on table.		
Robinson, Charles, widow of.	Grant of land for revolutionary services.	16	1	Petition	91	Priv. Land Claims.				Discharged; laid on table.		
Robinson, Charles, widow of.	Grant of land for revolutionary services.	16	2	Petition	178	Priv. Land Claims.	Jan. 24, 1821	Adverse		Laid on table.		
Robinson, Charles P.	(See William H. Bedford, agent, &c.)	28	1		262							
Robinson, Charles	(See widow of Stephen Decatur, *et al.*)	20	1		39		201		S. 50			
Robinson, Charles	Pension for revolutionary services.	23	1	Petition	308	Rev. Pensions				Discharged; laid on table.		
Robinson, Charles	Pension for revolutionary services.	23	2	Petition	77	Rev. Pensions	Feb. 17, 1835	Adverse		Laid on table.		
Robinson, Daniel, (N. Y.)	Increase of pension	21	2	Petition	43	Military Pensions.						
Robinson, Daniel, (N. Y.)	Increase of pension	22	1	Petition	219	Rev. Pensions				Discharged; laid on table.		
Robinson, Daniel, (N. Y.)	Arrearages of pension	23	1	Petition	46	Rev. Pensions				Discharged; laid on table.		
Robinson, Daniel	Compensation for losses by contract for delivery of sand.	28	1	Petition	983	Military Affairs.						
Robinson, Daniel	Compensation for losses by contract for delivery of sand.	28	2	Petition	110	Commerce.						
Robinson, Daniel	Compensation for losses by contract for delivery of sand.	30	1	Petition	108	Claims	11	Favorable	13	Referred to Committee Whole House.		
Robinson, Daniel	Compensation for losses by contract for delivery of sand.	30	2	House bill	647	Whole House	Mar. 3, 1849	With't amend.	13	Passed	Passed	App'd Marc
Robinson, David, & John, heirs of.	Payment for information given by deceased of frauds upon the revenue, in 1812.	21	1	Petition	169	Military Pensions.				Discharged; laid on table.		
Robinson, David, (N. H.)	Pension for revolutionary services.	22	1	Resolution	499	Rev. Pensions				Discharged; laid on table.		
Robinson, David, & others.	Remuneration as captors of privateer Lydia.	24	1	Senate bill	1158	Claims	July 2, 1836	With't amend.	S. 268	Referred to Committee Whole House.		
Robinson, David, & others.	Remuneration as captors of privateer Lydia.	24	2	Senate bill	551	Commerce	Mar. 2, 1837	With't amend.	S. 71	Referred to Committee Whole House.		
Robinson, David, & others.	Remuneration as captors of privateer Lydia.	25	2	Senate bill	700	Naval Affairs	April 17, 1838	With't amend.	S. 123	Referred to Committee Whole House.		
Robinson, David, & others.	Remuneration as captors of privateer Lydia.	25	3	Senate bill	149	Commerce	Jan. 4, 1839	With't amend.	S. 57	Passed		App'd Feb. 6, 1839
Robinson, Ebenezer	(See heirs of David and John Robinson.)	21	1		169							

List of private claims presented to the House of Representatives of the United States from the 1st to the 31st Congress, inclusive—Continued.

Names of claimants.	Nature or object of the claim.	Congress.	Session.	How brought before the House of Reps.	Page of journal.	To what committee of the House referred.	No. or date of the report.	Nature of the report.	No. of the bill.	How disposed of by the House of Reps.	How disposed of by the Senate.	Date of the act of Congress, and remarks.
Robinson, Ebenezer	(See David Robinson and others, privateer Lydia.)	25	3		149							
Robinson, Elizabeth	(See daughter of Lieutenant Richard Wilde.)	24	1		602							
Robinson, Elizabeth and James.	(See represent's of Richard Wilde)	25	3		124							
Robinson, Franklin & Co.	Indemnity for French spoliations prior to 1800.	26	1	Memorial	182	Foreign Affairs	343	Favorable; bill	319	Referred to Committee Whole House.		
Robinson, George H.	(See William Robinson, jr.)	26	1		182		343		319			
Robinson, George	Pension	3	1	Rep. of Secretary War.	131	Select	May 26, 1794	Jt. res. to refer to Sec. War.	J. R. 12	Passed	Passed	App'd Jan. 9, 1794
Robinson, George	Pension for revolutionary services.	12	1	Petition	23	Claims	Feb. 21, 1812	Adverse		Leave to withdraw.		
Robinson & Hartshorne, assignees of.	Permission to import certain goods.	12	1	Petition	295					Referred to Committee Whole House on bill No. 46.		
Robinson, Henry	Bounty land for services during war of 1812.	31	1	Petition	596	Public Lands	246	Favorable	244	Referred to Committee Whole House.		
Robinson, N. N., & others	(See heirs of James Williams)	31	1		271							
Robinson, Isaac and Lewis, administrators of.	Compensation for their services as soldiers of the revolutionary war.	13	2	Petition	307	Pens. & Rev. Cl'ms.	92	Adverse		Leave to withdraw.		
Robinson, Isaac and Lewis, administrators of.	Bounty land due as soldiers of the revolutionary war.	21	1	Petition	171	Rev. Claims	131	Favorable	175	Rejected.		
Robinson, James	Pension for revolutionary services.	4	1	Petition	471	Claims	May 31, 1796	Adverse		Laid on table.		
Robinson, James and Catharine.	(See widow of Jacob Ritter)	9	1		189							
Robinson, James	Pension for revolutionary services.	19	1	Resolution	189	Military Pensions	Feb. 23, 1826	Pension bill	119	Passed.		
Robinson, James	Pension for revolutionary services.	19	2	Petition	66	Military Pensions	Dec. 27, 1826	Pension bill	315	Passed.		
Robinson, James	Pension for revolutionary services.	20	1	Petition	243	Military Pensions	April 29, 1828	Pension bill	283	Passed.		
Robinson, James	Pension for revolutionary services.	20	2	House bill	55	Whole House	Jan. 15, 1829	With amends.	311	Passed	Laid on table.	
Robinson, James	Pension for revolutionary services.	21	1	Petition	47	Military Pensions	Jan. 5, 1830	Pension bill	72	Passed	Passed	App'd May 20, 1830
Robinson, James	(See widow of Stephen Decatur, and others.)	20	1		295		201		S. 50			
Robinson, James	Compensation for a horse lost in public service.	24	1	Resolution	486	Claims.						
Robinson, James	Compensation for a horse lost in public service.	26	1	Petition	169	Claims.						
Robinson, James, (Tenn.).	Pension for disabilities incurred in war of 1812.	25	2	Petition	267	Invalid Pensions	Feb. 23, 1838	Adverse		Laid on table.		
Robinson, Jim	(See William Parker and others, Seneca Indians.)	17	2		187							
Robinson, J. P. and others, (appraisers of Boston.)	Increase of compensation	23	1	Petition	32	Commerce.						
Robinson, John	Compensation for revolutionary services.	3	1	Petition	103					Laid on table.		
Robinson, John, representatives of.	Payment for revolutionary services of deceased.	23	1	Petition	54	Rev. Pensions.						
Robinson, John, widow of.	Pension for revolutionary services of her husband.	26	1	Resolution	950	Rev. Pensions.						
Robinson, John	(See Isaac and Lewis Robinson, administrator of.)	13	2		307							
Robinson, John	(See Lewis and Mark Robinson, representatives of.)	13	2		302							

List of private claims presented to the House of Representatives of the United States from the 1st to the 31st Congress, inclusive—Continued.

Names of claimants.	Nature or object of the claim.	Congress.	Session.	How brought before the House of Reps.	Page of journal.	To what committee of the House referred.	No. or date of the report.	Nature of the report.	No. of the bill.	How disposed of by the House of Reps.	How disposed of by the Senate.	Date of the act of Congress, and remarks.
Robinson, John	(See David and John Robinson, heirs of.)	21	1		169							
Robinson, John	(See George M. Lavender, administrator of.)	28	2		102							
Robinson, John	(See George B. Russell.)	29	1		87							
Robinson, John, and others	Remission of penalty incurred by master of ship William for a breach of the revenue laws.	4	2	Petition	636	Com. and Manuf.	Jan. 30, 1797	Favorable		Referred to Committee Whole House.		
Robinson, John, (Tenn.)	Payment for property taken from his father in 1780, for the use of the United States troops.	22	1	Petition	49	Claims	Jan. 30, 1832	Adverse		Laid on table.		
Robinson, John, (N. Y.)	Payment for property destroyed by the British, December 19, 1813	22	1	Petition	63	Claims	Jan. 11, 1832	Adverse		Laid on table.		
Robinson, John, (N. Y.)	Payment for property destroyed by the British, December 19, 1813.	24	1	Petition	405	Claims	April 6, 1836	Adverse		Laid on table.		
Robinson, John, (N. Y.)	Payment for property destroyed by the British, December 19, 1813.	28	1	Petition	345	Claims	499	Adverse		Laid on table.		
Robinson, John, (N. Y.)	Pension	25	3	Resolution	398	Invalid Pensions				Discharged; laid on table.		
Robinson, John H.	Payment for horses and wagon impressed into and lost in service of the United States in war of 1812.	16	1	Petition	153	Claims	Feb. 11, 1820	Adverse		Laid on table.		
Robinson, John H.	Payment for horses and wagon impressed into and lost in service of the United States in war of 1812.	22	2	Petition	335	Claims.						
Robinson, John H.	Payment for horses and wagon impressed into and lost in service of the United States in war of 1812.	23	1	Petition	142	Claims	146	Adverse		Laid on table.		
Robinson, John H.	Payment for horses and wagon impressed into and lost in service of the United States in war of 1812.	25	3	Petition	122	Claims	61	Adverse		Laid on table.		
Robinson, John H., and others.	Pre-emption right to enter land	26	1	Petition	363	Priv. Land Claims.	378	Adverse		Laid on table.		
Robinson, John W.	Pension for services during war of 1812.	27	2	Petition	360	Invalid Pensions				Discharged; laid on table.		
Robinson, John W.	Pension for services during war of 1812.	31	1	Petition	918	Invalid Pensions	376	Favorable	324	Referred to Committee Whole House.		
Robinson, John, (N. C.)	Payment for extra services in transportation of United States mail.	28	2	Petition	309	P. Of. and P. Roads.	161	Adverse		Laid on table.		
Robinson, Jonathan, jr.	Indemnity for French spoliations prior to 1800.	26	1	Memorial	182	Foreign Affairs	343	Favorable	319	Referred to Committee Whole House.		
Robinson, Jona., jr., heirs of.	Indemnity for French spoliations prior to 1800.	31	1	Petition	232	Foreign Affairs.	355	Favorable	318	Referred to Committee Whole House.		
Robinson, Joseph	Bounty land for services during war of 1812.	29	1	Petition	592	Priv. Land Claims.						
Robinson, Joseph	Bounty land for services during war of 1812.	29	2	Petition	87	Priv. Land Claims.						
Robinson, Joseph	Remission of penalty for violation of laws regulating distilleries.	18	1	Petition	155	Ways and Means.				Discharged; leave to withdraw.		

List of private claims presented to the House of Representatives of the United States from the 1st to the 31st Congress, inclusive—Continued.

Names of claimants.	Nature or object of the claim.	Congress.	Session.	How brought before the House of Reps.	Page of journal.	To what committee of the House referred.	No. or date of the report.	Nature of the report.	No. of the bill.	How disposed of by the House of Reps.	How disposed of by the Senate.	Date of the act of Congress, and remarks.
Robinson, Laban R.	Pension for disabilities incurred in war of 1812.	25	2	Petitions	117, 268	Invalid Pensions				Discharged; laid on table.		
Robinson, Levi	Pension for disabilities incurred in war of 1812.	24	1	Petition	1054	Invalid Pensions.						
Robinson, Lewis and Mark, representatives of.	Compensation for revolutionary services.	13	2	Petition	302	Pens. & Rev. Cl'ms.	92	Adverse		Leave to withdraw.		
Robinson, Lewis	(See administrator of Isaac and Lewis Robinson.)	13	2		307							
Robinson, Manoah D.	Compensation for services rendered and articles furnished U. States commissioners.	31	1	Petition	668	Claims	242	Favorable	239	Referred to Committee Whole House.		
Robinson, Manoah D.	Compensation for services rendered and articles furnished U. States commissioners.	31	2	Bill of last sess.	182	Whole House	Jan. 24, 1851	With amend.	239	Passed.		
Robinson, Mark	(See representatives of Lewis and Mark Robinson.)	13	2		302							
Robinson, Matthew	Pension	23	1	Petition	113	Rev. Pensions				Discharged; laid on table.		
Robinson, Michael	Arrearages of pension	28	2	Petition	141	Military Pensions.						
Robinson, Michael	Arrearages of pension	29	1	Petition	189	Invalid Pensions	295	Adverse		Laid on table.		
Robinson, Moses	Pension for revolutionary services.	22	1	Petition	187	Rev. Pensions				Discharged; laid on table.		
Robinson, Moses	Pension for revolutionary services.	22	2	Petition	119	Rev. Pensions				Discharged; laid on table.		
Robinson, N. P., surety of.	Release from liability	26	1	Petition	619	P. Of. & P. Roads.						
Robinson, Noah	Pension	9	2	House bill	608	Whole House	Feb. 28, 1807	With amend'ts	216	Passed	Passed	App'd March 3, 1807
Robinson, Paul	Compensation for rum left in his charge and used by United States troops.	14	2	Petition	127	Claims	70	Adverse		Laid on table.		
Robinson, Paul	Compensation for rum left in his charge and used by United States troops.	15	1	Petition	31	Claims	Feb. 6, 1818	Adverse		Laid on table.		
Robinson, Peggy		19	1	Petition	295	Public Lands				Discharged; laid on table.		Nature of this case not upon Journal, and no papers found.
Robinson, Peter	Right of pre-emption as New Orleans branch pilot.	28	1	Petition	77	Priv. Land Claims.	9	Favorable	35	Passed	Passed	App'd June 17, 1844
Robinson, Rich'd and Peggy		19	1	Petition		Public Lands				Discharged; laid on table.		Nature of this case not upon Journal, and no papers found.
Robinson, Richard	Pension for naval service	31	1	Petition	534	Invalid Pensions	476	Adverse		Laid on table.		
Robinson, Rix	Payment of money in lieu of land.	24	1	Indian appropriation bill.	1012	Whole House	June 30, 1836	With amends.	695	Passed	Passed	App'd July 2, 1836
Robinson, Robert	Compensation for services as clerk to land commissioners at Kaskaskia.	11	2	Senate bill	402	Whole House	May 1, 1810	With't amend	S. 37	Passed	Passed	App'd May 1, 1810
Robinson, Shubaiel, assignee of.	Grant of bounty land	18	1	Petition	69	Public Lands	Jan. 20, 1824	Adverse		Laid on table.		
Robinson, Susannah	(See widow of Alva West)	25	2		116							
Robinson, Thomas C.	To be placed on navy pension list.	16	1	Petition	334	Indian Affairs	May 8, 1820	With't amend.		Laid on table.		
Robinson, Thomas, representatives of.	(See surety of Sharp Dulany)	17	1		118							

List of private claims presented to the House of Representatives of the United States from the 1st to the 31st Congress, inclusive—Continued.

Names of claimants.	Nature or object of the claim.	Congress.	Session.	How brought before the House of Reps.	Page of journal.	To what committee of the House referred.	No. or date of the report.	Nature of the report.	No. of the bill.	How disposed of by the House of Reps.	How disposed of by the Senate.	Date of the act of Congress, and remarks.
Robinson, Wallace	Correction of error in title to a tract of land purchased of the United States.	20	1	Petition	367	Public Lands	Mar. 28, 1828	Favorable	245	Referred to Committee Whole House.		
Robinson, Wallace	Correction of error in title to a tract of land purchased of the United States.	20	2	Bill of last sess.	283	Whole House	Feb. 13, 1829	With't amend.	245	Passed.		
Robinson, Wallace	Correction of error in title to a tract of land purchased of the United States.	21	1	Petition	129	Public Lands	70	Favorable	98	Passed	Passed	App'd May 28, 1830
Robinson, jr., William	Indemnity for French spoliations prior to 1800.	26	1	Memorial	182	Foreign Affairs	343	Favorable; bill	319	Referred to Committee Whole House.		
Robinson, William	Renewal of final settlement certificate lost in 1783.	1	3	Petition	339	Select	....	....	......	Referred to Secretary Treasury.		
Robinson, William	Renewal of final settlement certificate lost in 1783.	2	1	Petition and rep't Sec. Treasury.	583	Select.						
Robinson, Wm. T., and others.	Release of ship Ontario from operation of embargo act.	3	1	Petition	134	Select.						
Robinson, William, *et al*	Compensation for damages from United States troops.	9	2	Petition	555	Claims	....	....	......	Discharged; laid on table.		
Robinson, William, *et at*	Compensation for damages from United States troops.	10	1	Petition	177	Claims	Feb. 25, 1808	Favorable	......	Referred to Committee Whole House.		
Robinson, William, *et al*	Compensation for damages from United States troops.	10	2	Petition	350	Claims	Nov. 18, 1808	Favorable	106	Passed.		
Robinson, William, *et al*	Compensation for damages from United States troops.	11	2	Petition	127	Claims	Dec. 26, 1809	Favorable	51	Passed.		
Robinson, William, *et al*	Compensation for damages from United States troops.	13	3	Petition	455	Claims	15	Favorable	248	Passed	Passed	App'd Jan. 28, 1815
Robinson, William	Compensation for services during war of 1812.	14	1	Petition	405	Claims	....	....	......	Discharged.		
Robinson, William	Pension for revolutionary services.	24	1	Petition	282	Rev. Pensions	313	Adverse	......	Laid on table.		
Robinson, William	Payment for a horse lost in Black Hawk war.	25	2	Petition	397	Claims	....	....	......	Discharged; laid on table.		
Robinson, William	Payment for a horse lost in Black Hawk war.	26	1	Petition	170	Claims.						
Robinson, William M.	(See Joseph Stewart, *et al*)	14	2	....	236							
Robinson, Winthrop	Pension for revolutionary services.	17	1	Petition	31	Rev. Pensions.						
Robinson, Zadock, widow of.	Bounty land and five years' half-pay due him as an artificer in the army of the United States.	22	2	Petition	347	Military Affairs.						
Robinson, Zadock, widow of.	Bounty land and five years' half-pay due him as an artificer in the army of the United States.	23	1	Petition	144	Priv. Land Claims.	Jan. 9, 1834	Adverse	......	Laid on table.		
Robinson, Zadock, widow of.	Bounty land and five years' half-pay due him as an artificer in the army of the United States.	27	3	Petition	271	Rev. Pensions.						
Robinson, Zophar, representatives of.	Bounty land for revolutionary services.	25	2	Petition	721	Rev. Claims	926	Adverse	......	Laid on table.		
Robinson, ———	(See Reeside, Robinson & Co.)	20	2	....	266							
Robinson, Joseph	Bounty land for services in war of 1812.	29	1	Petition	592	Priv. Land Claims.						
Robinson, Joseph	Bounty land for services in war of 1812.	30	2	Petition	204	Priv. Land Claims.						

List of private claims presented to the House of Representatives of the United States from the 1st to the 31st Congress, inclusive—Continued.

Names of claimants.	Nature or object of the claim.	Congress.	Session.	How brought before the House of Reps.	Page of journal.	To what committee of the House referred.	No. or date of the report.	Nature of the report.	No. of the bill.	How disposed of by the House of Reps.	How disposed of by the Senate.	Date of the act of Congress, and remarks.
Robinson, Joseph	Bounty land for services in war of 1812.	31	1	Petition	362	Priv. Land Claims.						
Roby, Charles G., and others.	Payment of claims against Ottawa Indians.	29	1	Documents	167	Indian Affairs	103	Adverse	......	Laid on table.		
Roby, James	Compensation for horse impressed into public service.	13	3	Petition	513	Claims	Nov. 14, 1814	Favorable	228	Passed	Indef. postp'd.	
Roby, James	Compensation for horse impressed into public service.	14	1	Petition	41	Claims	....	....	......	Discharged; laid on table.		
Roby, Joseph	Pension for revolutionary services.	15	2	Petition	297	Pens. & Rev. Cl'ms.						
Roby, Joseph	Pension for revolutionary services.	16	1	Petition	147	Rev. Pensions	April 6, 1820	Adverse	......	Laid on table.		
Roby, Samuel	Arrears and increase of pension	25	2	Petition	350	Invalid Pensions	....	....	......	Disch'd; laid on table.		
Rochambeau, Count de Marshal.	(See De Rochambeau, heirs of.)	23	2	....	38							
Roche, George F. D. L.	(See George F. De La Roche.)	28	2	....	266							
Roche, Thomas	Arrears of pay for revolutionary services.	3	2	Petition	274	Claims.						
Roche, Thomas	Pension for revolutionary services.	4	1	Rep. of Secretary War.	445	Claims.						
Roche, Thomas	Pension for revolutionary services.	4	2	Rep. of Secretary War.	614	Claims.						
Rochester, Nicholas	Pension for revolutionary services.	17	1	Petition	51	Rev. Pensions.						
Rochester, Nicholas	Pension for revolutionary services.	21	1	Resolution	94	Military Pensions	May 3, 1830	Pension bill	454	Passed.		
Rochon, Augustine	Pre-emption right to enter land	12	1	Petition	20	Public Lands.						
Rochon, Augustine	Pre-emption right to enter land	12	2	Petition	663	Public Lands.						
Rock, (a Seneca Indian.)	Pension	18	1	Pension bill	153	Whole House	Jan. 16, 1824	With amends.	35	Passed	Passed	App'd May 19, 1824
Rock, (a Seneca Indian.)	(See William Parker and others.)	17	2	....	187							
Rock, Joseph, *alias* Jarott, heirs of.	Payment for provisions destroyed by Indians in 1812.	24	1	Petition	95	Indian Affairs	....	....	......	Discharged; laid on table.		
Rock, Joseph, *alias* Jarott, heirs of.	Payment for provisions destroyed by indians in 1812.	24	2	Documents	392	Indian Affairs.						
Rock, Michael	To be restored to pension roll	25	2	Resolution	240	Rev. Pensions	....	....	......	Discharged; laid on table.		
Rockafellow, Peter	Refund expenses for medicine furnished during the revolution.	2	2	Petition	697	....	....	....	......	Referred to Secretary of Treasury.		
Rockafellow, Peter	Refund expenses for medicine furnished during the revolution.	3	1	Rep. of Secretary Treasury.	78	....	....	....	......	Laid on table.		
Rockhill, William	Pension for revolutionary services.	2	2	Petition	628	Select.						
Rockhold, W. W.	(See John H. Naff, and W. W. Rockhold.)	31	2	....	58							
Rockwell, Charles	(See James Dickson, attorney of.)	12	2	....	634							
Rockwell, Charles	Indemnity for French spoliations prior to 1800.	26	1	Memorial	182	Foreign Affairs	343	Favorable	319	Referred to Committee Whole House.		
Rockwell, Charles	Payment for performing duties of chaplain in the United States navy.	25	2	Petition	56	Naval Affairs	996	Favorable	858	Referred to Committee Whole House.		
Rockwell, Charles	Payment for performing duties of chaplain in the United States navy.	25	3	House bill	432	Whole House	Feb. 1, 1839	With't amend.	858	Passed	Passed	App'd March 3, 1839
Rockwell, Jabez	Pension for wounds received in the revolutionary war.	17	1	Petition	128	Pens. & Rev. Cl'ms.	Mar. 1, 1822	Adverse	......	Rejected.		
Rockwell, John A.	Patents for lands purchased of pre-emption claimants, whose claims had been rejected.	27	2	Senate bill	1126	Public Lands	July 29, 1842	With amend.	S. 244	Passed	Passed	App'd Aug. 2, 1842

List of private claims presented to the House of Representatives of the United States from the 1st to the 31st Congress, inclusive—Continued.

Names of claimants.	Nature or object of the claim.	Congress.	Session.	How brought before the House of Reps.	Page of journal.	To what committee of the House referred.	No. or date of the report.	Nature of the report.	No. of the bill.	How disposed of by the House of Reps.	How disposed of by the Senate.	Date of the act of Congress, and remarks.
Rockwell, Merrit, widow of.	Continuation of pension of deceased.	7	1	Petition	79	Claims	Feb. 5, 1802	Adverse	......	Laid on table.		
Rockwell, Samuel, representatives of.	Compensation for professional services rendered the Cherokee Indians.	26	1	Petition	623	Claims.						
Rockwell, Samuel, representatives of.	Compensation for professional services rendered the Cherokee Indians.	26	2	Petition	80	Claims.						
Rockwell, Samuel, representatives of.	Compensation for professional services rendered the Cherokee Indians.	27	2	Petition	225	Claims	733	Adverse	......	Laid on table.		
Rockwell, Samuel, representatives of.	Compensation for professional services rendered the Cherokee Indians.	29	1	Petition	358	Indian Affairs.						
Rockwell, Samuel, representatives of.	Compensation for professional services rendered the Cherokee Indians.	30	1	Petition	962	Claims.						
Rockwell, Samuel, representatives of.	Compensation for professional services rendered the Cherokee Indians.	30	2	Petition	127	Claims.						
Rockwell, Samuel, representatives of.	Compensation for professional services rendered the Cherokee Indians.	31	1	Petition	1047	....	....	....	......	Leave to withdraw.		
Rockwell, William, administratrix of.	Payment for naval services of deceased during the revolutionary war.	1	2	Petition	190	....	....	....	......	Referred to Secretary Treasury.		
Rockwell, William, administratrix of.	Payment for naval services of deceased during the revolutionary war.	2	2	Petition	626	....	....	....	......	Laid on table.		
Rockwell, William	Pension for revolutionary services.	20	2	Resolution	68	Military Pensions..	....	....	......	Discharged; laid on table.		
Rockwell, William	Pension for revolutionary services.	21	1	Petition	49	Military Pensions..	Jan. 5, 1830	Pension bill ..	72	Passed	Passed	App'd May 20, 1830
Rockwell, William, widow of.	Continuation of her husbands pension.	26	1	Petition	705	Rev. Pensions	551	Adverse	......	Laid on table.		
Rockwood, Cephas L.....	Payment of money advanced to recruiting officers in war of 1812.	15	2	Petition	23	Military Affairs ...	....	....	......	Discharged; laid on table.		
Rockwood, Cephas L....	Payment of money advanced to recruiting officers in war of 1812.	20	1	Petition	52	Claims	26	Adverse	......	Laid on table.		
Rockwood, Cephas L.....	Payment of money advanced to recruiting officers in war of 1812.	23	1	Petition	442	Priv. Land Claims.	....	....	......	Discharged; laid on table.		
Rockwood, Cephas L.....	Payment of money advanced to recruiting officers in war of 1812.	23	2	Petition	165	Military Affairs.						
Rockwood, Cephas L.....	Payment of money advanced to recruiting officers in war of 1812.	25	2	Petition	406	Military Affairs....	Mar. 3, 1838	Adverse	......	Laid on table.		
Roddy, Alexander, (S. C.)	Compensation as deputy marshal, Third Census.	15	2	Petition	139	Ways and Means.						
Roddy, Alexander, (S. C.)	Compensation as deputy marshal, Third Census.	16	1	Petition	130	Ways and Means..	66	Adverse	......	Laid on table.		
Roddy, Alexander, (S. C.)	Compensation as deputy marshal, Third Census.	16	2	Petition	178	Claims..........	Feb. 27, 1821	Favorable....	265	Referred to Committee Whole House.		
Roddy, Alexander, (S. C.)	Compensation as deputy marshal, Third Census.	17	1	Petition	26	Claims	Jan. 7, 1822	Favorable....	27	Passed	Passed	App'd May 7, 1822
Roddy, James, executors of.	(See Robert C. Jennings).......	22	1	....	745							

List of private claims presented to the House of Representatives of the United States from the 1st to the 31st Congress, inclusive—Continued.

Names of claimants.	Nature or object of the claim.	Congress.	Session.	How brought before the House of Reps.	Page of journal.	To what committee of the House referred.	No. or date of the report.	Nature of the report.	No. of the bill.	How disposed of by the House of Reps.	How disposed of by the Senate.	Date of the act of Congress, and remarks.
Roddy, James, executors of.	(See Robert P. Carter, administrator of.)	23	2	....	275							
Roddy, James, executors of.	Equitable settlement of account for supplies.	18	1	Petition	287	Claims	113	Adverse	......	Laid on table.		
Roddy, James, executors of.	Balance due as surety for S. Champlin.	22	1	Senate bill	745	Claims..........	487	With amend..	96	Passed with amend't.	Passed as am'd.	App'd July 14, 1832
Roddy, James, executors of.	Extension of the act of July, 1832	22	2	Resolution	70	Claims	10	Favorable	629	Passed	Passed	App'd Feb. 5, 1833
Roddy, James, executors of.	Further extension of act of July, 1832.	23	1	Petition	55	Claims..........	206	Adverse	227	Referred to Committee Whole House.		
Roddy, James, executors of.	Further extension of act of July, 1832.	23	2	House bill......	93	Whole House.....	....	....	227			
Roddy, James, executors of.	Fur her extension of act of July, 1832.	24	1	Petition	507	Claims.						
Roddy, James, executors of.	Further extension of act of July, 1832.	26	1	Petition	175	Judiciary	July 21, 1840	Favorable	519	Referred to Committee Whole House.		
Roddy, James, executors of.	Further extension of act of July, 1832.	27	2	Petition	56	Claims.						
Roddy, James, executors of.	Further extension of act of July, 1832.	27	3	Petition	73	Claims	128	Favorable	750	Referred to Committee Whole House.	....	See Journal, page 476
Roddy, James, executors of.	Further extension of act of July, 1832.	28	1	Rep. of Secretary Treasury.	408	Claims.						
Roddy, James, executors of.	Balance due deceased, erroneously credited to R. C. Jennings.	21	1	Petition	146	Judiciary.						
Roddy, James, executors of.	Balance due deceased, erroneously credited to R. C. Jennings.	22	1	Petition	191	Judiciary.						
Roddy, James, executors of.	Balance due deceased, erroneously credited to R. C. Jennings.	23	1	Petition	311	Claims.						
Roddy, James, executors of.	(See sureties of Sam'l Champlin).	21	1	....	146							
Roderick, Anthony, and others.	Compensation for arresting pirates.	17	1	Petition	77	Claims.						
Roderick, Anthony, and others.	Compensation for arresting pirates.	18	1	Petition	98	Claims	Mar. 22, 1824	Favorable	173	Passed	Passed	App'd May 19, 1824
Rodgers, Alexander A....	Confirmation of title to land erroneously entered in name of his son.	25	2	Petition	696	Priv. Land Claims.	April 12, 1838	Adverse	......	Laid on table.		
Rodgers, Ann	(See Nicholas Cruger, administratrix of)	26	1	....	182	....	343	....	319			
Rodgers, Benjamin W., & Co.	Permission to export merchandise from Great Britain.	12	1	Petition	88	Com. and Manuf.						
Rodgers, Charles	Payment of a revolutionary loan certificate.	4	1	Rep. of Secretary Treasury.	388	Claims	74	Adverse	......	Laid on table.		
Rodgers, David, & Sons..	(See David Rogers & Sons)	21	1	....	142							
Rodgers, Francis	Increase of pension	31	1	Petition	501	Invalid Pensions.						
Rodgers, Francis	Increase of pension	31	2	Petition	155	Invalid Pensions.						
Rodgers, Geo. W., widow of.	Naval pension	22	2	Petition	123	Naval Affairs.....	123	Favorable	751	Referred to Committee Whole House.		
Rodgers, Geo. W., widow of.	Naval pension	23	1	Petition	74	Naval Affairs.						
Rodgers, George.........	(See Canadian refugees.)											
Rodgers, Jas., (Cherokee.)	Compensation for negotiating treaty with Cherokee nation of Indians.	22	1	Petition	596	Indian Affairs.....	464	Favorable	561	Referred to Committee Whole House.		
Rodgers, Jas., (Cherokee.)	Compensation for negotiating treaty with Cherokee nation of Indians.	23	1	Petition	50	Indian Affairs.....	....	....	......	Discharged; laid on table.		

List of private claims presented to the House of Representatives of the United States from the 1st to the 31st Congress, inclusive—Continued.

Names of claimants.	Nature or object of the claim.	Congress.	Session.	How brought before the House of Reps.	Page of journal.	To what committee of the House referred.	No. or date of the report.	Nature of the report.	No. of the bill.	How disposed of by the House of Reps.	How disposed of by the Senate.	Date of the act of Congress, and remarks.
Rodgers, John, and others.	Prize money for capturing the armed ship Meshouda.	8	1	House bill	525	Whole House	Jan. 11, 1804	With't amend.	160	Passed	Passed	App'd Mar. 19, 1804
Rodgers, John, and others.	Compensation for capture of a midshipman and two seamen of British navy during war of 1812.	14	1	Petition	416	Naval Affairs	April 17, 1816	Favorable	185	Passed with amendm't.	Passed	App'd April 27, 1816
Rodgers, Captain John, U. States navy.	Release from judgment obtained against him for detaining at sea schooner Eleanor.	14	1	Letter	267	Select	Feb. 7, 1816	Favorable	J. R. 5	Passed	Passed	App'd Feb. 15, 1816
Rodgers, Captain John, U. States navy.	Indemnity for expenses incurred in defending suit for acts done in discharge of duty.	15	1	Petition	107	Select	Jan. 20, 1818	Favorable	48	Passed	Passed	App'd April 11, 1818
Rodgers, Captain John, U. States navy.	Payment of extra rations allowed to commanding officers United States navy under act of February 25, 1799.	23	1	Memorial	74	Naval Affairs.						
Rodgers, Captain John, U. States navy.	Payment of extra rations allowed to commanding officers United States navy under act of February 25, 1799.	23	2	Petition	95	Naval Affairs.						
Rodgers, Captain John, U. States navy.	Payment of extra rations allowed to commanding officers United States navy under act of February 25, 1799.	24	1	Petition	99	Naval Affairs.						
Rodgers, Captain John, U. States navy, widow and executrix of.	Payment of extra rations allowed to commanding officers United States navy under act of February 25, 1799.	26	1	Petition	713	Naval Affairs.						
Rodgers, John, assignee of.	Grant of bounty land	18	1	Petition	69	Public Lands	Jan. 20, 1824	Adverse	......	Laid on table.		
Rodgers, John, (Cherokee)	Grant of land under treaty of 1818 with Cherokee Indians.	21	2	Petition	46	Indian Affairs	12	Favorable	518	Referred to Committee Whole House.		
Rodgers, John, (Cherokee)	Grant of land under treaty of 1818 with Cherokee Indians.	22	1	Petition	31	Indian Affairs	10	Favorable	59	Passed	Passed	App'd Mar. 31, 1832
Rodgers, John	Pension	21	2	Resolution	209	Military Pensions.						
Rodgers, John, (Conn.)	Pension	25	2	Resolution	466	Rev. Pensions	....	....	......	Discharged; laid on table.		
Rodgers, John A	Pension	24	1	Senate bill	811	Invalid Pensions	June 9, 1836	With't amend.	S. 212	Passed	Passed	App'd June 15, 1836
Rodgers, John A	Arrearages of pension	29	1	Petition	124	Invalid Pensions	....	....	......	Disch'd; laid on table.		
Rodgers, John A	Arrearages of pension	31	1	Petition	1166	Claims	July 23, 1850	Adverse	......	Leave to withdraw.		
Rodgers, John Baker	Refund amount paid for United States stamps issued during the war of 1812.	23	2	Petition	57	Ways and Means.						
Rodgers, John Baker	Refund amount paid for United States stamps issued during the war of 1812.	25	2	Petition	95	Ways and Means	Mar. 6, 1838	Favorable	607	Referred to Committee Whole House.		
Rodgers, John Baker	Refund amount paid for United States stamps issued during the war of 1812.	25	3	House bill	380	Whole House	....	....	607			
Rodgers, John Baker	Refund amount paid for United States stamps issued during the war of 1812.	26	1	Petition	179	Ways and Means	April 30, 1840	Favorable	397	Referred to Committee Whole House.		
Rodgers, John Baker	Refund amount paid for United States stamps issued during the war of 1812.	28	2	Petition	302	Ways and Means.						

List of private claims presented to the House of Representatives of the United States from the 1st to the 31st Congress, inclusive—Continued.

Names of claimants.	Nature or object of the claim.	Congress.	Session.	How brought before the House of Reps.	Page of journal.	To what committee of the House referred.	No. or date of the report.	Nature of the report.	No. of the bill.	How disposed of by the House of Reps.	How disposed of by the Senate.	Date of the act of Congress, and remarks.
Rodgers, John Baker	Refund amount paid for United States stamps issued during the war of 1812.	30	1	Petition	398	Claims	254	Favorable	247	Passed.		
Rodgers, Joseph	(See John W. Flowers, and others, Cherokees.	22	1		596							
Rodgers, Minerva	(See widow and executrix of John Rodgers, captain U. S. navy.)	26	1		713							
Rodgers, Major Robert, representatives of.	Confirmation of title to land	26	2	Petition & papers	196, 213	Priv. Land Claims.						
Rodgers, Samuel	(See Canadian refugees.)											
Rodgers, Stephen	Restoration of pension; discontinued under act of May, 1820.	17	1	Petition	314	Rev. Pensions.						
Rodgers, Stephen	Restoration of pension; discontinued under act of May, 1820.	17	2	Petition	257					Laid on table.		
Rodgers, Thomas, (S. C.)	Pension	20	2	Petition	288	Military Pensions.				Discharged; laid on table.		
Rodgers, Wm., and others.	Compensation for horses killed, and injury to wagons while in public service.	4	1	Petition	384	Claims	May 31, 1796	Adverse		Laid on table.		
Rodgers, William	(See widow of Stephen Decatur, and others.	20	1		295		201		S. 50			
Rodman, Jane, assignee of.	Payment for services of deceased as nurse in military hospital at Philadelphia.	2	1	Petition	477					Referred to Secretary War.		
Rodman, Jane, administratrix of.	Payment for services of deceased as nurse in military hospital a Philadelphia.	2	2	Petition	712					Laid on table.		
Rodman, Michael and Jane, assignee of.	Payment for services in military hospital at Philadelphia.	2	2	Petition	712					Laid on table.		
Rodman, Samuel, jr., and others.	Remission of duties on imported whale oil.	14	1	Petition	82	Com. and Manuf.	Mar. 15, 1816	Favorable; bill		Passed	Passed	App'd April 29, 1816
Rodman, Samuel	Indemnity for French spoliations prior to 1800.	26	1	Memorial	182	Foreign Affairs	343		319	Referred to Committee Whole House.		
Rodman, Wm. and Samuel	(See Samuel Rodman, jr., and others.)	14	1		82							
Rodman, William R	(See Cha's W. Morgan and others)	31	1		1227							
Rodney, John	Confirmation of title to land in Missouri.	15	1	Petition	73	Priv. Land Claims.						
Rodney, John	Confirmation of title to land in Missouri.	16	1	Petition	72	Priv. Land Claims.				Discharged; laid on table.		
Rodney, John	Confirmation of title to land in Missouri.	17	1	Petition	54	Public Lands.						
Rodney, John	Confirmation of title to land in Missouri.	18	1	Petition	55	Public Lands.						
Rodney, Martin	Confirmation of title to land in Missouri.	15	1	Petition	102	Priv. Land Claims.				Discharged; laid on table.		
Rodney, Martin	Confirmation of title to land in Missouri.	16	1	Petition	72	Priv. Land Claims.				Discharged; laid on table.		
Rodney, Martin	Confirmation of title to land in Missouri.	17	1	Petition	54	Public Lands.						
Rodney, Martin	Confirmation of title to land in Missouri.	18	1	Petition	55	Public Lands.						

List of private claims presented to the House of Representatives of the United States from the 1st to the 31st Congress, inclusive—Continued.

Names of claimants.	Nature or object of the claim.	Congress.	Session.	How brought before the House of Reps.	Page of journal.	To what committee of the House referred.	No. or date of the report.	Nature of the report.	No. of the bill.	How disposed of by the House of Reps.	How disposed of by the Senate.	Date of the act of Congress, and remarks.
Rodney, Thomas S	Confirmation of title to land in Missouri.	15	1	Petition	85	Priv. Land Claims.						
Rodney, Thomas S	Confirmation of title to land in Missouri.	16	1	Petition	72	Priv. Land Claims.	....	....	....	Discharged; laid on table.		
Rodney, Thomas S	Confirmation of title to land in Missouri.	17	1	Petition	54	Public Lands.						
Rodney, Thomas S	Confirmation of title to land in Missouri.	18	1	Petition	55	Public Lands.						
Rodney, William, & others	Bounty land for services in General Wayne's army in 1787.	24	2	Petition	47	Rev. Pensions	....	....	....	Discharged; laid on table.		
Rodney, William	Pension	23	2	Resolution	205	Invalid Pensions	Feb. 3, 1835	Adverse	....	Laid on table.		
Rodriguez, Francisca	Confirmation of title to land in Louisiana.	22	1	House bill	107	Whole House	Mar. 23, 1832	With't amend	125	Passed	Passed	App'd June 25, 1832
Rodriguez, John	Indemnity for damages to plantation by U. S. troops, near New Orleans, during the war of 1812.	15	1	Petition	294	Claims	....	....	....	Discharged; laid on table.		
Rodriguez, John	Indemnity for damages to plantation by U. S. troops, near New Orleans, during the war of 1812.	15	2	Senate bill	316	Claims	....	....	S. 64			
Rodriguez, John	Indemnity for damages to plantation by U. S. troops, near New Orleans, during the war of 1812.	16	1	Senate bill	416	Claims	....	....	S. 71			
Rodriguez, John	Indemnity for damages to plantation by U. S. troops, near New Orleans, during the war of 1812.	16	2	Petition	20	Claims	Dec. 20, 1820	Favorable	177	Passed	Passed	App'd March 2, 1821
Rodriguez, John	Indemnity for damages to plantation by U. S. troops, near New Orleans, during the war of 1812.	18	2	Petition	47	Claims	Dec. 20, 1824	Adverse	....	Laid on table.		
Rodriguez, John	Indemnity for damages to plantation by U. S. troops, near New Orleans, during the war of 1812.	19	1	Petition	38	Claims	Feb. 6, 1826	Adverse	....	Laid on table.		
Rodriguez, John	Indemnity for damages to plantation by U. S. troops, near New Orleans, during the war of 1812	19	2	Petition	44	Claims	27	Favorable	329	Referred to Committee Whole House.		
Rodriguez, John	Indemnity for damages to plantation by U. S. troops, near New Orleans, during the war of 1812.	20	1	Petition	31	Claims	19	Favorable	14	Passed	Rejected.	
Rodriguez, John	Indemnity for damages to plantation by U. S. troops, near New Orleans, during the war of 1812.	21	1	Petition	84	Claims	27	Favorable	35	Passed	Passed	App'd April 7, 1830
Rodriguez, John	Payment for property destroyed during military operations near New Orleans, in January, 1815.	23	1	Petition	131	Claims	526	Adverse	....	Laid on table.		
Rodriguez, Peter	Arrearages and increase of pension.	21	1	Petition	168	Military Pensions.	....	....	....	Discharged; laid on table.		
Rodriguez, Peter	Arrearages and increase of pension.	21	2	Petition	62	Military Pensions.						
Rodriguez, Peter	Arrearages and increase of pension.	22	1	Petition	165	Invalid Pensions.	....	....	....	Discharged; laid on table.		
Rodriguez, Santiago	Confirmation of title to land in Louisiana.	22	1	House bill	107	Priv. Land Claims.	Dec. 27, 1831	Favorable	125	Passed.	Passed	App'd June 25, 1834
Rodriguez, Simon	Confirmation of title to land in Louisiana.	21	2	Petition	162	Priv. Land Claims.						

List of private claims presented to the House of Representatives of the United States from the 1st to the 31st Congress, inclusive—Continued.

Names of claimants.	Nature or object of the claim.	Congress.	Session.	How brought before the House of Reps.	Page of journal.	To what committee of the House referred.	No. or date of the report.	Nature of the report.	No. of the bill.	How disposed of by the House of Reps.	How disposed of by the Senate.	Date of the act of Congress, and remarks.
Rodriguez, Simon	Confirmation of title to land in Louisiana.	22	1	Petition	75	Priv. Land Claims.						
Rodriguez, Simon	Confirmation of title to land in Louisiana.	22	2	Petition	54	Priv. Land Claims.						
Rodriguez, Simon	Confirmation of title to land in Louisiana.	23	1	Petition	249	Priv. Land Claims.	....	....	......	Discharged; laid on table.		
Rodriguez, Simon	Confirmation of title to land in Louisiana.	30	1	Petition	198	Priv. Land Claims.	184	Favorable....	194	Passed	Passed, second session.	App'd Jan. 8, 1849
Roe, John, widow of.....	(See widow of John Rowe)	25	2	....	469							
Roe, Joseph, administrator of.	Payment of prize-money due deceased as a boatswain in United States navy during war of 1812.	22	1	Petition	222	Naval Affairs.....	477	Favorable....	579	Referred to Committee Whole House.		
Roe, Joseph, administrator of.	Payment of prize-money due deceased as a boatswain in United States navy during war of 1812.	23	1	Petition	74	Naval Affairs.....	Dec. 17, 1833	Favorable....	32	Passed	Passed	App'd June 18, 1834
Roe, Orpha............	(See representatives of John Durnell.)	27	3	....	260							
Roe, Robert, administrator of.	Authority to sell or transfer land warrants issued to deceased.	31	1	Petition	197	Priv. Land Claims.						
Roe, Robert, administrator of.	Authority to sell or transfer land warrants issued to deceased.	31	2	Petition	177	Priv. Land Claims.						
Roe, Susanna...........	(See widow of John Rowe)......	25	2	....	469							
Roff, Christopher.......	Increase of pension	25	2	Resolution	466	Rev. Pensions	....	....	......	Discharged; laid on table.		
Roff, John	Payment for property destroyed by United States troops during revolutionary war.	2	2	Petition	682	....	....	....	.....	Laid on table.		
Roff, John	Payment for property destroyed by United States troops during revolutionary war.	3	2	Petition	301	Claims.						
Roff, John	Payment for property destroyed by United States troops during revolutionary war.	4	1	Resolution	373	Claims	Dec. 24, 1795	Adverse	......	Laid on table.		
Roff, John	Payment for property destroyed by United States troops during revolutionary war.	4	2	Petition	615	Claims	Jan. 6, 1797	Adverse	......	Leave to withdraw.		
Rogan, Bernard, and others.	Grants of land to make up deficiency to which they are entitled under existing laws.	15	1	Petition	344	Priv. Land Claims.	....	....	......	Discharged; laid on table.		
Rogan, Bernard, and others.	Grants of land to make up deficiency to which they are entitled under existing laws.	16	1	Petition	72	Priv. Land Claims.	....	....	......	Discharged; laid on table.		
Rogan, Bernard, and others.	Grants of land to make up deficiency to which they are entitled under existing laws.	17	1	Petition	55	Public Lands.						
Rogan, Bernard, and others.	Grants of land to make up deficiency to which they are entitled under existing laws.	18	1	Petition	55	Public Lands.....	Jan. 16, 1824	Bill to enable claimants to try validity of claims.	65	Passed	Passed	App'd May 26, 1824
Rogan, Bernard	Relief in consequence of deficiency in land.	24	1	Petition	207	Priv. Land Claims.						
Rogan, Bernard	Relief in consequence of deficiency in land.	24	2	Petition	93	Priv. Land Claims.						

List of private claims presented to the House of Representatives of the United States from the 1*st to the* 31*st Congress, inclusive*—Continued.

Names of claimants.	Nature or object of the claim.	Congress.	Session.	How brought before the House of Reps.	Page of journal.	To what committee of the House referred.	No. or date of the report.	Nature of the report.	No. of the bill.	How disposed of by the House of Reps.	How disposed of by the Senate.	Date of the act of Congress, and remarks.
Rogan, Bernard	Relief in consequence of deficiency in land.	25	2	Petition	97	Priv. Land Claims.						
Roger, privateer schooner, officers and owners of.	(See Richard Drummond and others)	24	1	....	95							
Roger, privateer	(See Roger Quarles and Richard Drummond.	14	1	....	587							
Rogers, Absalom	Restoration of pension	24	1	Resolution	647	Rev. Pensions	....	....	......	Discharged; laid on table.		
Rogers, Allen	Payment of expenses incurred by the detention of his vessel, having on board a part of the United States Exploring Expedition.	26	1	Petition	702	Naval Affairs	534	Favorable	433	Referred to Committee Whole House.		
Rogers, Allen	Payment of expenses incurred by the detention of his vessel, having on board a part of the United States Exploring Expedition.	27	2	Petition	155	Claims	April 12, 1842	Favorable	388	Ordered to 3d reading.		
Rogers, Allen	Payment of expenses incurred by the detention of his vessel, having on board a part of the United States Exploring Expedition.	27	3	Bill of last sess.	88	....	....	....	388	Passed	Passed	App'd March 3, 1843
Rogers, Baptiste, heirs of	Payment of pension to which deceased was entitled under act of April 16, 1816.	25	3	Petition	569	Military Affairs.						
Rogers, Baptiste, heirs of	Payment of pension to which deceased was entitled under act of April 16, 1816.	26	2	Petition	168	Military Affairs	193	Adverse	......	Laid on table.		
Rogers, Benjamin W.	(See Thomas L. Ogdon & others.)	17	1	....	38							
Rogers, Charles, and Thos. Burnham.	Fishing bounty on sloop Cyrus	10	1	Petition and rep't Sec. Treasury.	213, 230	....	....	....	......	Laid on table.		
Rogers, Charles	Payment for distillery destroyed by Indians.	24	2	Indian appropriation bill.	....	Ways and Means	Dec. 21, 1836	Favorable	757	Passed	Passed	App'd March 3, 1837
Rogers, Chester	Pension	19	2	Petition	131	Military Pensions	Feb. 14, 1827	Pension bill	436	Referred to Committee Whole House.		
Rogers, David S., & others	Payment for horses and forage furnished while in service of the United States.	25	2	Petition	84	Military Affairs	....	....	......	Discharged; laid on table.		
Rogers, David S., & others	Payment of depreciation of money paid them for their services in Indian war of 1836'-37.	29	1	Memorial	380	Military Affairs	642	Adverse	......	Laid on table.		
Rogers, David, & Son	Payment of drawback on exportation of teas.	20	2	Petition	40	Ways and Means	36	Favorable	355	Referred to Commitee Whole House.		
Rogers, David, & Son	Payment of drawback on exportation of teas.	21	1	Petition	142	Ways and Means	114	Favorable	154	Passed	Passed	App'd May 29, 1830
Rogers, David, heirs of	Compensation for services rendered by deceased as a colonel in the revolutionary army.	25	3	Documents	283	Rev. Claims.						
Rogers, David, heirs of	Compensation for services rendered by deceased as a colonel in the revolutionary army.	26	1	Petition	918	Rev. Claims.						
Rogers, Ebenezer	Restoration of pension discontinued under act of May, 1820.	17	1	Petition	259	Whole House.						
Rogers, Ebenezer	Restoration of pension discontinued under act of May, 1820.	17	2	Petition	36	Rev. Pensions.						

List of private claims presented to the House of Representatives of the United States from the 1st to the 31st Congress, inclusive—Continued.

Names of claimants.	Nature or object of the claim.	Congress.	Session.	How brought before the House of Reps.	Page of journal.	To what committee of the House referred.	No. or date of the report.	Nature of the report.	No. of the bill.	How disposed of by the House of Reps.	How disposed of by the Senate.	Date of the act of Congress, and remarks.
Rogers, Ebenezer P.	Indemnity for French spoliations prior to 1800.	31	1	Petition	451	Foreign Affairs	355	Favorable	318	Referred to Committee Whole House.		
Rogers, Elizabeth	Indemnity for French spoliations prior to 1800.	31	1	Petition	451	Foreign Affairs	355	Favorable	318	Referred to Committee Whole House.		
Rogers, Elizabeth	(See widow of Robert Rogers)	28	1		329							
Rogers, George, heirs of	For certificates of script on Virginia land warrants belonging to deceased.	23	2	Petition	140	Public Lands.						
Rogers, George, heirs of	For certificates of script on Virginia land warrants belonging to dec'd.	24	1	Petition	114	Public Lands.						
Rogers, H. Gold	Payment of outfit and travelling expenses as late chargé de affairs to Sardinia.	29	1	Petition	68	Foreign Affairs	308	Adverse		Laid on table.		
Rogers, H. Gold	Payment of outfit and travelling expenses as late chargé de affairs to Sardinia.	31	1	Petition	370	Foreign Affairs.						
Rogers, Henry A.	(See heirs of Baptiste Rogers)	25	3		569							
Rogers, Hezekiah, widow of.	Pension for revolutionary services of her husband.	16	2	Petition	50	Pens. & Rev. Cl'ms.	Jan. 22, 1821	Adverse		Laid on table.		
Rogers, Isaac, widow of	Continuation of revolutionary pension.	27	2	Petition	255	Rev. Pensions	784	Adverse		Laid on table.		
Rogers, Isaiah	(See Calvin Pollard, and others).	23	1		523							
Rogers, Isaiah, and Richard Bond.	Payment for drawings and specifications for the custom-house at New York.	25	3	Petition	335	Claims	278	Adverse		Laid on table.		
Rogers, Isaiah, and Richard Bond.	Payment for drawings and specifications for the custom-house at New York.	27	2	Petition	49	Claims	182	Adverse		Laid on table.		
Rogers, Ithamar	Release of his son from military services of the United States.	30	1	Petitions	159, 215	Military Affairs				Discharged; laid on table.		
Rogers, Jabez, jr	Remmission of duties on spirits destroyed by fire.	3	1	Senate bill	98	Whole House	June 5, 1794	With't amend.	S. 6	Passed	Passed	App'd June 7, 1794
Rogers, James	Indemnity for French spoliations prior to 1800.	26	1	Memorial	182	Foreign Affairs	343	Favorable	319	Referred to Committee Whole House.		
Rogers, James, (a Cherokee Indian.)	Compensation as a witness in the trial of James Blount at Philadelphia in 1798.	17	2	Petition	196	Indian Affairs				Discharged; leave to withdraw.		
Rogers, James	Compensation for the attendance of his father as a witness in the trial of Wm. Blout at Philadelphia in 1798.	20	1	Petition	680	Ways and Means				Discharged; laid on table.		
Rogers, James	(See administrator and attorney of Moses Garland.)	19	2		293							
Rogers, James	(See William H. Bedford)	28	1		262							
Rogers, James H	Compensation for services in removing Cherokee Indians.	26	1	Petition	1162	Claims.						
Rogers, James H	Compensation for services in Florida war.	30	2	Petition	327	Military Affairs				Discharged; laid on table.		
Rogers, James H	Compensation for services in Florida war.	31	1	Petition	595	Military Affairs				Discharged; laid on table.		
Rogers, John	Indemnity for lands ceded to Chickasaw Indians.	2	2	Petition Rep. of Secretary State.	692 706					Laid on table.		

List of private claims presented to the House of Representatives of the United States from the 1st to the 31st Congress, inclusive—Continued.

Names of claimants.	Nature or object of the claim.	Congress.	Session.	How brought before the House of Reps.	Page of journal.	To what committee of the House referred.	No. or date of the report.	Nature of the report.	No. of the bill.	How disposed of by the House of Reps.	How disposed of by the Senate.	Date of the act of Congress, and remarks.
Rogers, John	Indemnity for lands ceded to Chickasaw Indians.	5	2	Rep. of Secretary State.	146	Whole House.						
Rogers, John	Indemnity for lands ceded to Chickasaw Indians.	5	3	Petition	406	Claims	Feb. 27, 1799	Adverse	.....	Laid on table.		
Rogers, John	Pension for revolutionary services.	3	1	Rep. of Secretary War.	178	.....	.....	.....	.....	Laid on table.		
Rogers, John	Pension for revolutionary services.	3	2	Rep. of Secretary War.	262	Claims	Feb. 28, 1795	Pension bill	130	Passed	Postponed.	
Rogers, John	Pension for revolutionary services.	4	1	Rep. of Secretary War.	445	Claims	Feb. 18, 1796	Pension bill	156	Passed	Passed	App'd April 20, 1796
Rogers, John	(See William H Bedford.)	28	1	.....	262							
Rogers, John	To be restored to pension roll	17	1	Petition	67	Rev. Pensions.						
Rogers, John, and others	Commutation pay for revolutionary services.	1	2	Petition and rep't Sec. of War.	168, 181, 247	Select	.....	.....	.....	Laid on table.		
Rogers, John, and others	Compensation for capturing a midshipman and two seamen of the British navy.	14	1	Petition	416	Naval Affairs	Mar. 5, 1816	Favorable	185	Passed	Passed	App'd April 27, 1816
Rogers, Capt. John, heirs of.	Half pay under act of July 5, 1832.	30	1	Petition	574	Judiciary.						
Rogers, Capt. John, heirs of.	Compensation for revolutionary services.	30	1	Petition	711	Rev. Claims.						
Rogers, John	Correction of erroneous entry of land.	28	1	Petition	532	Public Lands	Mar. 29, 1844	Favorable	286	Passed.		
Rogers, John	Correction of erroneous entry of land.	29	1	Petition	463	Public Lands.						
Rogers, John	Correction of erroneous entry of land.	31	1	Petition	325	Public Lands.						
Rogers, Jonathan	Pension for revolutionary services.	26	1	Petition	936	Rev. Pensions	714	Adverse	.....	Laid on table.		
Rogers, Jonathan, jr	Release from imprisonment on debt due United States.	14	1	Petition	134	Select	Jan. 13, 1816	Favorable	34	Passed	Passed	App'd Feb. 22, 1816
Rogers, J. K., and others.	For commission to adjust Cherokee claims.	29	1	Memorial	198	Indian Affairs.						
Rogers, Joseph	(See Mathews, Wood, & Hall)	24	2	.....	119							
Rogers, Joseph, heirs of	Indemnity for French spoliations prior to 1800.	26	1	Memorial	182	Foreign Affairs	343	Favorable	319	Referred to Committee Whole House.		
Rogers, Kinsley, widow of.	Pension for revolutionary services.	26	1	Resolution	386	Rev. Pensions	664	Adverse	.....	Laid on table.		
Rogers, Mary G. H	Indemnity for French spoliations prior to 1800.	31	1	Petition	384	Foreign Affairs	355	Favorable	318	Referred to Committee Whole House.		
Rogers, Moses	Relief in consequence of the sale of land for direct tax.	15	1	Petition	132	Ways and Means	.....	.....	.....	Discharged; laid on table.		
Rogers, N., and J. Bell	Indemnity for French spoliations prior to 1800.	26	1	Memorial	182	Foreign Affairs	343	Favorable	319	Referred to Committee Whole House.		
Rogers, Nathan	Payment for horse and equipage lost in Seminole campaign of 1818.	23	1	Petition	154	Claims.						
Rogers, Nathaniel	(See W. H. Bedford, agent, &c.)	28	1	.....	262	Claims.						
Rogers, Nicholas	(See Philip and Nicholas Rogers.)	11	2	.....	169							
Rogers, Notley, and others	(See heirs of William Rogers)	23	1	.....	376							
Rogers, N., & Co	Register for barque Mary Teresa	30	1	Petition	1000	Commerce	Aug. 3, 1848	Favorable	630	Passed	Passed	App'd Aug. 7, 1838
Rogers & Owings	Indemnity for French spoliations prior to 1800.	26	1	Memorial	182	Foreign Affairs	343	Favorable	319	Referred to Committee Whole House.		
Rogers, Peter	Pension	19	2	Petition	59	Military Pensions	.....	.....	.....	Discharged.		
Rogers, Phebe	(See widow of William Rogers)	25	2	.....	58							

List of private claims presented to the House of Representativesthe of United States from the 1*st to the* 31*st Congress, inclusive*—Continued.

Names of claimants.	Nature or object of the claim.	Congress.	Session.	How brought before the House of Reps.	Page of journal.	To what committee of the House referred.	No. or date of the report.	Nature of the report.	No. of the bill.	How disposed of by the House of Reps.	How disposed of by the Senate.	Date of the act of Congress, and remarks.
Rogers, Philip, and Nicholas.	Release from penalty as surety for bonds to prevent violation of embargo act.	11	2	Petition thro' Sec. of Treasury.	169	Com. and Manuf.						
Rogers, Philip, and Nicholas.	Release from penalty as surety for bonds to prevent violation of embargo act.	11	2	Petition	350	Com. and Manuf..	....	....	......	Referred to Committee Whole House.		
Rogers, Philip, heirs of...	Indemnity for French spoliations prior to 1800.	31	1	Petition	384	Foreign Affairs.						
Rogers, Philip	(See Jeremiah Tellott, executors of.)	26	1	....	182	....	343	....	319			
Rogers, Robert, representatives of.	Confirmation of title to Chippewa land.	26	2	Petition and docs.	196, 213	Priv. Land Claims.						
Rogers, Robert, representatives of.	Confirmation of title to Chippewa land.	27	2	Petition	327	Priv. Land Claims.	....	....	......	Discharged; leave to withdraw.		
Rogers, Robert, widow of.	Pension	28	1	Petition	329	Invalid Pensions ..	Jan. 31, 1844	Adverse	......	Laid on table.		
Rogers, Samuel	(See Canadian refugees.)											
Rogers, Samuel	Indemnity for unavailable right of pre-emption.	22	1	Petition	98	Public Lands.						
Rogers, Samuel	Pension for revolutionary services.	27	3	Petition	190	Rev. Pensions	295	Adverse	......	Laid on table.		
Rogers, Sarah	(See widow of Isaac Rogers.)....	27	2	....	255							
Rogers, Susan	(See widow of Dr. Wm. Rogers).	25	2	....	729							
Rogers, S. G	Indemnity for French spoliations prior to 1800.	26	1	Memorial	182	Foreign Affairs....	343	Favorable....	319	Referred to Committee Whole House.		
Rogers, Thomas	Confirmation of title to land	9	2	Petition	536	Public Lands.....	....	....	......	Leave to withdraw.		
Rogers, Thomas	(See Charles Binns, surety of)...	25	2	....	396							
Rogers, Thomas	Pension	12	1	Pension bill	361	Whole House.....	June 15, 1812	Favorable....	138	Passed	Passed	App'd July 5, 1812
Rogers, Thomas	(See heirs of George Rogers)	24	1	....	114							
Rogers, Thomas	(See attorney of Charles Binns)..	25	2	....	396							
Rogers, Thomas, and L. A. Thomas.	Compensation for legal services in defending Sioux Indians charged with murder.	29	1	Memorial	1054	Claims.						
Rogers, Thomas, and L. A. Thomas.	Compensation for legal services in defending Sioux Indians charged with murder.	29	2	Memorial	56	Claims.						
Rogers, Thomas, and L. A. Thomas.	Compensation for legal services in defending Sioux Indians charged with murder	31	1	Senate bill	1219	Indian Affairs.....	....	....	S. 82			
Rogers, Thomas, and L. A. Thomas.	Compensation for legal services in defending Sioux Indians charged with murder.	31	2	Senate bill	207	Indian Affairs.....	Jan. 29, 1851	Adverse	S. 82	Laid on table.		
Rogers, Willard.........	(See heirs of Baptiste Rogers)....	25	3	....	569							
Rogers, William S., purser United States navy.	Release from payment of money of which he was robbed upon the capture of the frigate Adams.	14	1	Petition	76	Claims	Jan. 3, 1816	Adverse.	......	Laid on table.		
Rogers, Captain William, representatives of Sarah B. Potts, Priscilla B. Harman, and others.	Compensation for revolutionary services.	23	1	Petition	40	Rev. Claims	156	Favorable....	171	Passed.		
Rogers, Captain William, representatives of Sarah B. Potts, Priscilla B. Harman, and others.	Compensation for revolutionary services.	29	1	Memorial	199	Rev. Claims.						

List of private claims presented to the House of Representatives of the United States from the 1st to the 31st Congress, inclusive—Continued.

Names of claimants.	Nature or object of the claim.	Congress.	Session.	How brought before the House of Reps.	Page of journal.	To what committee of the House referred.	No. or date of the report.	Nature of the report.	No. of the bill.	How disposed of by the House of Reps.	How disposed of by the Senate.	Date of the act of Congress, and remarks.
Rogers, Captain William, representatives of Sarah B. Potts, Priscilla B. Harman, and others.	Compensation for revolutionary services.	30	1	Petition	575	Rev. Claims.						
Rogers, Captain William, representatives of Sarah B. Potts, Priscilla B. Harman, and others.	Compensation for revolutionary services.	31	1	Petition	472	Rev. Claims.						
Rogers, William, heirs of.	Commutation pay for revolutionary services.	23	1	Petition	376	Rev. Claims.						
Rogers, William, heirs of.	Commutation pay for revolutionary services.	23	2	Petition	....	Rev. Claims......	....	....	......	....	....	Omitted in Journal.
Rogers, William, heirs of.	Commutation pay for revolutionary services.	24	1	Petition	63	Rev. Claims......	Jan. 12, 1836	Adverse	......	Laid on table.		
Rogers, William, heirs of.	Commutation pay for revolutionary services.	24	2	Petition	39	Rev. Claims......	Dec. 30, 1837	Adverse	......	Laid on table.		
Rogers, William, heirs of.	Commutation pay for revolutionary services.	25	2	Petition	72	Rev. Claims......	337	Adverse	......	Laid on table.		
Rogers, William, heirs of.	Commutation pay for revolutionary services.	26	1	Petition	630	Rev. Claims.						
Rogers, William, heirs of.	Commutation pay for revolutionary services.	26	2	Petition	148	Rev. Claims.						
Rogers, William, heirs of.	Commutation pay for revolutionary services.	27	2	Petition	61	Rev. Claims......	542	Adverse	......	Laid on table.		
Rogers, William C	Relief as mail contractor	24	1	Petition	535	P. Of. & P. Roads.						
Rogers, William	Donation of land for services as chaplain in revolutionary army.	6	1	Petition	555	Claims	April 16, 1800	Adverse	......	Laid on table.		
Rogers, Dr. William, widow of.	Pension for services of her husband as a chaplain in revolutionary army.	25	2	Petition	729	Rev. Pensions	....	....	......	Discharged; laid on table.		
Rogers, Dr. William, widow of.	Pension for services of her husband as a chaplain in revolutionary army.	26	1	Petition	283	Rev. Pensions	490	Adverse	......	Laid on table.		
Rogers, Dr. William, widow of.	Pension for services of her husband as a chaplain in revolutionary army.	26	2	Petition	35	Rev. Pensions.						
Rogers, Dr. William, widow of.	Pension for services of her husband as a chaplain in revolutionary army.	27	2	Petition	58	Rev. Pensions	784	Adverse	......	Laid on table.		
Rogers, Dr. William, widow of.	Pension for services of her husband as a chaplain in revolutionary army.	28	1	Petition	144	Rev. Pensions	....	....	......	Discharged; laid on table.		
Rogers, Dr. William, widow of.	Pension for services of her husband as a chaplain in revolutionary army.	28	2	Petition	67	Rev. Pensions	....	....	......	Discharged; laid on table.		
Rogers, William, widow of.	Payment for services of her husband as a rigger at navy-yard, Charleston, Massachusetts.	25	2	Petition	58	Invalid Pensions ..	....	....	......	Discharged; laid on table.		
Rogers, William, widow of.	Payment for services of her husband as a rigger at navy-yard, Charleston, Massachusetts.	26	1	Petition	739	Naval Affairs.						
Rogers, William H......	Pension for injuries received while acting as chaplain in Mexican war.	31	1	Petition	1273	Invalid Pensions.						

List of private claims presented to the House of Representatives of the United States from the 1st to the 31st Congress, inclusive—Continued.

Names of claimants.	Nature or object of the claim.	Congress.	Session.	How brought before the House of Reps.	Page of journal.	To what committee of the House referred.	No. or date of the report.	Nature of the report.	No. of the bill.	How disposed of by the House of Reps.	How disposed of by the Senate.	Date of the act of Congress, and remarks.
Roget, Isaac	(See Isaac Lawrence and others.)	14	2		101							
Rohrer, Marein	Increase of pension	21	1	Petition	411	Military Pensions	April 24, 1830	Adverse		Laid on table.		
Roice, Jeremiah	Indemnity for property lost during the war of 1812.	31	1	Petition	809	Claims.						
Roland, William	(See H. Boswell and others.)	19	1		64							
Rolette, Joseph	Confirmation of title to land in Michigan.	17	1	Petition	184	Public Lands.						
Rolette, Joseph	(See John Camp, assignee of heirs of.)	23	1		249							
Rolette, Joseph	(See John Campbell, heirs of.)	27	2		132							
Roll, Matthias	For duplicate bounty land warrant.	20	1	Petition	100	Priv. Land Claims.	Jan. 17, 1828	Favorable	89	Passed.		
Roll, Matthias	For duplicate bounty land warrant.	20	2	Petition	41	Priv. Land Claims.	Dec. 12, 1828	Favorable	314	Referred to Committee Whole House.		
Roll, Matthias	For duplicate bounty land warrant.	21	2	Petition	112	Priv. Land Claims.	Dec. 30, 1830	Favorable	526	Passed	Passed, with amendment.	App'd Feb. 3, 1831
Rollins, Aaron, widow of	Bounty land due to, and continuation of pension of, deceased for revolutionary services.	24	2	Petition	216	Rev. Pensions	Feb. 23, 1837	Favorable	937	Referred to Committee Whole House.		
Rollins, Aaron, widow of	Bounty land due to, and continuation of pension, of deceased for revolutionary services.	25	2	Petition	38	Rev. Pensions	273	Favorable	316	Passed	Passed	App'd June 28, 1838
Rollins, Aaron, (Maine)	Arrears of pension for services in war of 1812.	28	1	Petition	73	Claims.						
Rollins, Aaron, (Maine)	Arrears of pension for services in war of 1812.	28	2	Petition	46	Invalid Pensions	45	Adverse		Laid on table.		
Rollins, Aaron, (Maine)	Arrears of pension for services in war of 1812.	29	1	Petition	93	Invalid Pensions	43	Adverse		Laid on table.		
Rollins, Catharine, *alias* Catharine Moseley.	(See Aaron Rollins, widow of.)	25	2		38							
Rollins, Daniel G.	(See John Rollins, administrator of)	26	1		182		343		319			
Rollins, David	Pension	25	2	Petition	57	Invalid Pensions.	572	Favorable	562	Passed	Adverse report.	
Rollins, David	Pension	25	3	Petition	89	Invalid Pensions	133	Favorable	1000	Passed	Passed	App'd March 3, 1839
Rollins, Ebenezer	Debenture on cargo of coffee	11	3	Senate bill	487	Whole House.			S. 50			
Rollins, Ebenezer	Debenture on cargo of coffee	12	1	Petition	61	Com. and Manuf.				Leave to withdraw.		
Rollins, Ebenezer	Debenture on cargo of coffee	17	1	Petition	180	Commerce.						
Rollins, Ebenezer	Debenture on cargo of coffee	21	2	Senate bill	134	Commerce	Jan. 4, 1831	With't amend.	S. 20	Passed	Passed	App'd March 2, 183
Rollins, George W.	Remuneration for services rendered United States.	27	2	Petition	369	Claims						
Rollins, James, (Maine)	Indemnity for French spoliations prior to 1800.	26	1	Memorial	182	Foreign Affairs	343	Favorable	319	Referred to Committee Whole House.		
Rollins, James, (N. H.)	Indemnity for French spoliations prior to 1800.	26	1	Memorial	182	Foreign Affairs	343	Favorable	319	Referred to Committee Whole House.		
Rollins, John	Indemnity for French spoliations prior to 1800.	15	1	Petition	297	Claims	Mar. 26, 1818	Adverse		Laid on table.		
Rollins, John, administrator of.	Indemnity for French spoliations prior to 1800.	26	1	Memorial	182	Foreign Affairs	343	Favorable	319	Referred to Committee Whole House.		
Rollins, John, attorney of.	Indemnity for French spoliations prior to 1800.	26	1	Memorial	182	Foreign Affairs	343	Favorable	319	Referred to Committee Whole House.		
Rollins, Moses	Pension	14	1	Petition	90	Pens. & Rev. Cl'ms.				Discharged; laid on table.		
Rolls, John H. B.	Payment for horse and saddle converted to public use, Florida war.	31	1	Petition	224	Military Affairs	353	Favorable	315	Referred to Committee Whole House.		

List of private claims presented to the House of Representatives of the United States form the 1st to the 31st Congress, inclusive—Continued.

Names of claimants.	Nature or object of the claim.	Congress.	Session.	How brought before the House of Reps.	Page of journal.	To what committee of the House referred.	No. or date of the report.	Nature of the report.	No. of the bill.	How disposed of by the House of Reps.	How disposed of by the Senate.	Date of the act of Congress, and remarks.
Rolls, Sally, *et al*	Arrears of pension due to Elijah Green.	24	1	Petition	433	Rev. Pensions	May 17, 1836	Favorable	645	Passed	Passed	App'd June 28, 1836
Romans, Bernard, widow of.	Pension for revolutionary services of her husband.	31	1	Petition	1467	Rev. Pensions.						
Romer, Henry	Pension for military services in the revolutionary war.	20	1	Resolution	303	Military Pensions	April 29, 1828	Pension bill	283	Passed.		
Romer, Henry	Pension for military services in the revolutionary war.	21	1	Petition	48	Military Pensions	Jan. 5, 1830	Pension bill	72	Passed	Passed	App'd May 20, 1830
Romero, Antonio	(See Antonio Segura, *et al.*)	24	1		907							
Romero, Julia	(See Charles Vallean, widow of.)	25	2		373							
Romine, John	Pension	31	1	Petition	233	Invalid Pensions.						
Ronaldson, James	(See Archibald Binney and James Ronaldson.)	6	2		782							
Rooke, Amos	Pension for revolutionary services.	24	1	Petition	944	Rev. Pensions.						
Rooke, Amos	Pension for revolutionary services.	25	3	Petition	126	Rev. Pensions				Discharged; laid on table.		
Rooke, Amos	Pension for revolutionary services.	26	1	Petition	285	Rev. Pensions	424	Adverse		Laid on table.		
Rook, Thomas, and others, wreckers.	Remission of duties on portion of cargo of British ship Britannia, assigned to them as salvage, and to be allowed part of duties on remainder of cargo.	21	1	Petition	558	Commerce.				Discharged; laid on table.		
Roosa, Dr. Cornelius	Pension for revolutionary services.	15	2	Petition	186	Pens. & Rev. Cl'ms.	Jan. 28, 1819	Adverse.		Laid on table.		
Roosa, Dr. Cornelius	Pension for revolutionary services.	16	1	Petition	139	Rev. Pensions	April 22, 1820	Adverse		Laid on table.		
Roosa, Dr. Cornelius	Pension for revolutionary services.	17	1	Petition	141	Pens. & Rev. Cl'ms.				Discharged; referred to Com. Whole House.		
Roosa, Dr. Cornelius	Pension for revolutionary services.	21	1	Petition	128	Military Pensions				Discharged; laid on table.		
Roosa, Dr. Cornelius	Pension for revolutionary services.	21	2	Petition	74	Select.						
Roosa, Dr. Cornelius	Pension for revolutionary services.	23	1	Petition	90	Rev. Pensions.						
Roosevelt, James, *et al.*	Reimburse duties on refined sugars.	7	1	Petition	86	Com. and Manuf.	Mar. 3, 1802	Adverse		Leave to withdraw.		
Roosevelt, James J	(See Jacob Mark & Co.)	26	1		182		343		319			
Root, Azariah	Payment for property destroyed by the United States troops during war of 1812.	13	2	Petition	183	Claims	Jan. 25, 1814	Adverse		Laid on table.		
Root, Phebe	(See widow of Lieut. Colonel Colburn)	15	1		142							
Root, Phebe	Revolutionary pension	22	1	Resolution	137	Rev. Claims.						
Ropes, Benjamin	Indemnity for French spoliations prior to 1800.	28	2	Petition	103	Foreign Affairs.						
Ropemakers, &c., of New York.	For an allowance of drawback on exported American cordage.	23	2	Petition	307	Ways and Means.						
Rosati, Joseph	Confirmation of title to land	26	1	Petition	365	Priv. Land Claims.						
Rose, Abner	Increase of pension	13	2	Pens on bill	344	Whole House	Mar. 31, 1814	With amend's.	166	Passed	Passed	App'd April 18, 1814
Rose, Abraham	Payment for military services in revolutionary war.	25	3	Petition	334	Rev. Claims				Discharged.		
Rose, Abraham, (N. H.)	Increase of revolutionary pension	29	2	Petition	146	Rev. Pensions.						
Rose, Alexander, heirs of	Commutation pay as an officer in revolutionary war.	23	1	Petition	81	Rev. Claims.						
Rose, Alexander, heirs of	Commutation pay as an officer in revolutionary war.	23	2	Petition	84	Rev. Claims.						

List of private claims presented to the House of Representatives of the United States from the 1st to the 31st Congress, inclusive—Continued.

Names of claimants.	Nature or object of the claim.	Congress.	Session.	How brought before the House of Reps.	Page of journal.	To what committee of the House referred.	No. or date of the report.	Nature of the report.	No. of the bill.	How disposed of by the House of Reps.	How disposed of by the Senate.	Date of the act of Congress, and remarks.
Rose, Alexander, heirs of	Commutation pay as an officer in revolutionary war.	24	1	Petition	103	Rev. Claims	817	Adverse		Laid on table.		
Rose, David	(See Jacob Serross, administrator of.)	26	1		182		343		319			
Rose, Elijah	Payment for military services in war of 1812.	29	1	Petition	493	Claims	620	Adverse		Laid on table.		
Rose, Elizabeth	(See representatives of Francis and John Kline.	29	2		169							
Rose, Henry	Pension	22	1	Resolution	97	Rev. Pensions				Discharged; laid on table.		
Rose, Jacob	Pension	19	1	Petition	423	Military Pensions	April 20, 1826	Adverse		Laid on table.		
Rose, Jacob, widow of	Pension for revolutionary services of her husband.	26	1	Petition	324	Rev. Pensions.						
Rose, Jacob, widow of	Continuation of her husband's pension.	27	2	Petition	375	Rev. Pensions	784	Adverse		Laid on table.		
Rose, Jesse	Pension for revolutionary services.	29	1	Petition	939	Invalid Pensions	1150	Adverse		Laid on table.		
Rose, Jesse	Pension for revolutionary services.	29	2	Petition	86	Invalid Pensions	82	Adverse		Laid on table.		
Rose, Jesse	Pension for revolutionary services.	30	1	Petition	625	Invalid Pensions				Discharged; laid on table.		
Rose, John	Payment for drawings, models, &c., destroyed by burning of navy yard.	13	2	Petition	668	Claims.						
Rose, John	Payment for drawings, models, &c., destroyed by burning of navy yard.	14	2	Petition	319	Claims				Discharged; laid on table.		
Rose, John, heirs of	Payment for drawings, models, &c., destroyed by burning of navy yard.	23	1	Senate bill	592	Claims	454	With't amend.	S. 71	Passed	Passed	App'd June 30, 1834
Rose, John, widow of	Continuation of pension	20	2	Resolution	68	Military Pensions	Feb. 16, 1829	Adverse		Laid on table.		
Rose, John, (Ky.)	Pension for revolutionary services.	26	1	Petition	1001	Invalid Pensions.						
Rose, John, (Ky.)	Pension for revolutionary services	27	3	Petition	110	Rev. Pensions	Feb. 16, 1843	Favorable	796	Referred to Committee Whole House.		
Rose, John, (Ky.)	Pension for revolutionary services.	28	1	Petition	118	Rev. Pensions	154	Favorable	142	Passed.		
Rose, John, (Ky.)	Pension for revolutionary services.	28	2	Petition	58	Rev. Pensions.						
Rose, John, (Ky.)	Pension for revolutionary services.	29	1	Petition	292	Rev. Pensions	530	Adverse		Laid on table.		
Rose, John, (Ky.)	Pension for revolutionary services.	30	1	Petition	798	Rev. Pensions				Discharged; laid on table.		
Rose, John, heirs of	Compensation for the use by the United States, of an invention of the deceased.	31	1	Petition	787	Claims.						
Rose, Joseph	Increase of pension	25	2	Resolution	534	Invalid Pensions				Discharged; laid on table.		
Rose, Joseph	Arrears of pension	25	3	Petition	219	Invalid Pensions				Discharged; laid on table.		
Rose, Justus	Pension for revolutionary services.	25	3	Petition	217	Rev. Pensions				Discharged; laid on table.		
Rose, Levi	Pension	21	2	Petition	158	Military Pensions.						
Rose, Levi	Pension	22	1	Petition	123	Rev. Pensions.						
Rose, Lisa	(See widow of Jacob Rose)	27	2		375							
Rose, Marie, *et al.*	To reinstate on docket of Supreme Court of United States, an appeal from superior court of East Florida.	30	1	Senate bill	682	Claims	April 26, 1848 July 12, 1848	With't amend With amends.	S. 215 S. 215	Recommitted. Passed with amendm't	Passed as am'd	App'd July 20, 1848

List of private claims presented to the House of Representatives of the United States from the 1st to the 31st Congress, inclusive—Continued.

Names of claimants.	Nature or object of the claim.	Congress.	Session.	How brought before the House of Reps.	Page of journal.	To what committee of the House referred.	No. or date of the report.	Nature of the report.	No. of the bill.	How disposed of by the House of Reps.	How disposed of by the Senate.	Date of the act of Congress, and remarks.
Rose, Martha	(See widow of John Rose)	20	2		68							
Rose, Mary W	Arrears of pension	23	2	Petition	102	Naval Affairs	Feb. 25, 1835	Adverse		Laid on table.		
Rose, Orpha	Pension	29	1	Petition	1261	Rev. Pensions	826	Adverse		Laid on table.		
Rose, Orpha	Pension	30	1	Petition	406	Rev. Pensions.						
Rose, Robert H	Payment of money expended while sick in United States service in Florida.	25	2	Petition	396	Claims	859	Adverse		Laid on table.		
Rose, Robert	Pension for military services during war of 1812.	29	1	Petition	939	Invalid Pensions	July 25, 1846	Adverse		Laid on table.		
Rose, Robert	Pension for military services during war of 1812.	29	2	Petition	86	Invalid Pensions.						
Rose, Robert	Pension for military services during war of 1812.	30	1	Petition	625	Invalid Pensions				Discharged; laid on table.		
Rose, Robert	Pension for military services during war of 1812.	30	2	Petition	118	Invalid Pensions	101	Adverse		Laid on table.		
Rose, Robert	Pension for military services during war of 1812.	31	1	Petition	298	Invalid Pensions	71	Adverse		Laid on table.		
Rose, Samuel D	Refunding money lost in mail, 1834	26	1	Petition	941	P. Of. & P. Roads.						
Rose, Samuel D	Refunding money lost in mail, 1834	27	2	Petition	308	P. Of. & P. Roads.	846	Favorable	489	Ordered to 3d reading.		
Rose, Samuel D	Refunding money lost in mail, 1834	27	3	House bill	89				489	Passed	Passed	App'd Feb. 24, 1843
Rose, William H	Discharge from enlistment as a soldier in thirty-eighth regiment of infantry of United States.	14	2	Petition	41	Military Affairs	Feb. 21, 1817	Adverse		Laid on table.		
Rose, William H.	Discharge from enlistment as a soldier in thirty-eighth regiment of infantry of United States.	15	1	Petition	102	Military Affairs				Discharged; laid on table.		
Rose, William, (Ohio)	Payment for military services during revolutionary war.	19	2	Petition	158	Rev. Claims				Discharged; laid on table.		
Roseberry, James, widow and administratrix of.	Payment for a horse lost by deceased in public service.	16	1	Petition	188	Claims	Feb. 7, 1820	Adverse		Laid on table.		
Roseberry, John	Pension for revolutionary services.	27	3	Petition	95	Rev. Pensions	295	Adverse		Laid on table.		
Roseberry, John	Pension for revolutionary services.	28	1	Petition	296	Rev. Pensions.						
Roseberry, John	Pension for revolutionary services.	31	1	Petition	193	Invalid Pensions.						
Roseberry, John	Pension for revolutionary services.	31	2	Petition	143					Leave to withdraw.		
Roseberry, John M	Pension for revolutionary services.	28	1	Petition	195	Rev. Pensions				Disch'd; laid on table.		
Roseberry, John M	Pension for revolutionary services.	30	1	Petition	339	Rev. Pensions	789	Adverse		Laid on table.		
Roseberry, John M	Pension for revolutionary services.	31	1	Petition	449	Rev. Pensions.	143	Favorable	159	Referred to Committee Whole House.		
Roseberry, John M	Pension for revolutionary services.	31	2	Bill of last sess.	104	Whole House	Jan. 3, 1851	With amends.	159	Passed.		
Roseboom, John	Pension for revolutionary services.	22	1	Resolution	262	Rev. Pensions				Discharged; laid on table.		
Rosebrough, Samuel	Settlement for certain loan office certificates.	11	1	Petition	55	Claims.						
Roseman, Edward	(See William Baker, &c.)	22	1		288		480					
Rosenberger, Christian	(See executors of John Kerlin)	19	1		131							
Rosvelt, C., and others	Additional compensation for locating military bounty land warrants.	31	2	Petition	107	Public Lands.						
Rosilias, Christian	(See surety of Wm. McQueen)	31	1		502							
Ross, Abner	Renewal of loan office certificate destroyed by fire.	3	1	Petition	11					Laid on table.		
Ross, Andrew, widow of	Pension for death of her husband in public services.	24	2	Petition	314	Naval Affairs.						

List of private claims presented to the House of Representatives of the United States from the 1st to the 31st Congress, inclusive—Continued.

Names of claimants.	Nature or object of the claim.	Congress.	Session.	How brought before the House of Reps.	Page of journal.	To what committee of the House referred.	No. or date of the report.	Nature of the report.	No. of the bill.	How disposed of by the House of Reps.	How disposed of by the Senate.	Date of the act of Congress, and remarks.
Ross, Andrew, widow of..	Pension for death of her husband in public service.	25	2	Petition	75	Invalid Pensions ..	462	Favorable....	465	Passed.		
Ross, Andrew, widow of..	Pension for death of her husband in public service.	25	3	Petition	188	Invalid Pensions ..	139	Favorable....	1006	Passed.		
Ross, Andrew, widow of..	Pension for death of her husband in public service.	26	1	Petition	163	Invalid Pensions ..	Mar. 5, 1840	Adverse	......	Laid on table.		
Rose, Andrew, widow of..	Pension for death of her husband in public serviee.	28	2	Petition	135	Rev. Pensions.						
Ross, Anthony B	Release from prison at suit of United States.	13	3	Petition	725	Select...........	Feb. 15, 1815	Favorable....	298	Passed	Rejected.	
Ross, David, and others...	(See representatives of Geo. Webb)	13	1	....	89							
Ross, Eli R	(See heirs of Robert Knox)......	12	1	....	316							
Ross, Eli K. W.........	Confirmation of title to land in Louisiana	29	2	Petition	232	Priv. Land Claims.						
Ross, George T., Captain United States navy, and D. T. Patterson, Colonel army.	Payment of prize money	14	1	Petition	42	Ways and Means..	April 18, 1816	Favorable ...	190	Passed............	Passed	App'd April 27, 1816
Ross, Hugh	Pension for wound received in the naval service of United States during revolutionary war.	13	2	Petition	174	Pens. & Rev. Clm's.	Jan. 10, 1814	Adverse	......	Laid on table.		
Ross, Hugh	(See surety of Matthew Ridgeway)	17	1	....	164							
Ross, Hugh, (Maine.)....	Pension for disability incurred in the war of 1812.	25	2	Petition	268	Invalid Pensions ..	....	....	......	Discharged; laid on table.		
Ross, Isaac, and D. McCaleb.	Pre-emption rights to enter land..	11	2	Petition	271	Public Lands.....	Mar. 16, 1810	Adverse	......	Laid on table.		
Ross, Jack F	Payment for supplies furnished, and services rendered in war of 1812.	16	1	Petition	153	Claims	Mar. 25, 1820	Adverse	......	Laid on table.		
Ross, Jack F	Payment for supplies furnished, and services rendered in war of 1812.	18	1	Petition	315	Claims.						
Ross, James, and others, commissioners.	Grant of land for site of town, (Pulaski, Tennessee.)	11	3	Petition	444	Public Lands	Jan. 18, 1811	Favorable....	186	Passed	Passed	App'd Feb. 25, 1811
Ross, James............	Refund duties paid on molasses destroyed by fire.	16	2	Petition	48	Ways and Means..	Dec. 8, 1820	Adverse.	......	Laid on table.		
Ross, James............	Refund duties paid on molasses destroyed by fire.	17	1	Petition	32	Ways and Means..	16	Favorable....	45	Referred to Committee Whole House.		
Ross, James............	Refund duties paid on molasses destroyed by fire.	17	2	Bill of last sess..	276	Whole House.....	Feb. 27, 1823	With't amend.	45	Laid on table.		
Ross, James............	Reimburse money paid on judgment in favor of the United States.	19	1	Senate bill	488	Claims	May 3, 1826	With't amend.	S. 122	Referred to Committee Whole House.		
Ross, James, and Stephen Donohoe.	Indemnity for Indian depredations.	20	1	Petition	92	Claims	Jan. 23, 1828	Adverse	......	Laid on table.		
Ross, James, and Stephen Donohoe.	Indemnity for Indian depredations.	23	1	Petition	451	Indian Affairs.....	....	....	......	Discharged; laid on table.		
Ross, John, (Penn.).....	Payment of balance due on merchandize purchased on commission for the Government.	2	2	Petition	712	Select...........	....	....	......	Referred to Secretary of Treasury.		
Ross, John, and others, of Baltimore.	Payment for vessel and cargo captured by French privateer, and condemned by court of admiralty.	11	2	Petition	235	Com. and Manuf.						

List of private claims presented to the House of Representatives of the United States from the 1st to the 31st Congress, inclusive—Continued.

Names of claimants.	Nature or object of the claim.	Congress.	Session.	How brought before the House of Reps.	Page of journal.	To what committee of the House referred.	No. or date of the report.	Nature of the report.	No. of the bill.	How disposed of by the House of Reps.	How disposed of by the Senate.	Date of the act of Congress, and remarks.
Ross, John, executors of	Indemnity for damages to property in Georgia by U. States troops during war of 1812.	14	1	Petition	53	Claims	Jan. 5, 1816	Favorable; bill	......	Passed	Passed	App'd April 27, 1816
Ross, John, and others, (Cherokees.)	Payment of money withheld by the War Department out of annuities due the Cherokee nation of Indians.	19	1	Memorial	155	Indian Affairs.						
Ross, John, and others, (Cherokees.)	Payment of interest on annuities, and license money collected from traders and deducted by Secretary of War.	20	2	Memorial	292	Indian Affairs.						
Ross, John T., (Mass.)	Reimburse drawback on goods exported by him in brig William, in 1822.	20	1	Petition	220	Commerce	Feb. 14, 1828	Favorable	167	Passed	Passed	App'd May 26, 1828
Ross, John, (Pa.)	Pension for revolutionary services.	20	2	Resolution	213	Military Pensions	....	....	......	Discharged; laid on table.		
Ross, John, (Pa.)	Pension for revolutionary services.	21	1	Petition	83	Military Pensions	April 7, 1830	Adverse	......	Laid on table.		
Ross, John, (Pa.)	Pension for revolutionary services.	22	1	Petition	187	Rev. Pensions	....	....	......	Discharged; laid on table.		
Ross, John, (Pa.)	Pension for revolutionary services.	29	1	Petition	133	Rev. Pensions.						
Ross, John G	Payment for property destroyed by United States troops while removing intruders from Cherokee lands.	21	1	Petition	524	Claims	....	....	......	Discharged; laid on table.		
Ross, John G	(See Anthony Foreman and others)	22	1	....	43							
Ross, John, (Ky.,) administrator of.	Indemnity for French spoliations prior to 1800.	26	1	Memorial	182	Foreign Affairs	343	Favorable	319	Referred to Committee Whole House.		
Ross, John	Compensation for military services in 1794 and 1795.	26	1	Petition	963	Military Affairs.						
Ross, John, (Md.)	Indemnity for French spoliations prior to 1800.	26	1	Memorial	182	Foreign Affairs	343	Favorable	319	Referred to Committee Whole House.		
Ross, John, heirs of	Indemnity for French spoliations prior to 1800.	29	2	Memorial	136	Foreign Affairs.						
Ross, John, heirs of	Indemnity for French spoliations prior to 1800.	31	1	Petition	216	Foreign Affairs	355	Favorable	318	Referred to Committee Whole House.		
Ross, Joseph W	Pension for services in war of 1812.	25	2	Documents	991	Invalid Pensions	....	....	......	Discharged; laid on table.		
Ross, Joseph W	Pension for services in war of 1812.	26	1	Petition	163	Invalid Pensions	410	Adverse	......	Laid on table.		
Ross, Joseph W	Pension for services in war of 1812.	28	1	Petition	684	Invalid Pensions.						
Ross, Joseph W	Pension for services in war of 1812.	30	2	Petition	137	....	....	....	......	Referred to Commissioner of Pensions.		
Ross, Joshua, heirs of	Bounty land for revolutionary services.	24	2	Petition	102	Priv. Land Claims	....	....	......	Discharged; laid on table.		
Ross, Joshua, heirs of	Bounty land for revolutionary services.	25	2	Petition	270	Rev. Claims	....	....	......	Discharged; laid on table.		
Ross, Joshua, heirs of	Bounty land for revolutionary services.	25	3	Petition	221	Rev. Claims	....	....	......	Discharged.		
Ross, Matthias J	To purchase on credit public lands in Illinois for salt-works.	22	1	Petition	189	Public Lands	....	....	......	Discharged; laid on table.		
Ross, Robert P	Pension	15	2	Petition	172	Pens. & Rev. Cl'ms	....	....	......	Discharged; referred to Secretary War.		
Ross, Sally	(See widow of William Ross)	26	1	....	950							
Ross, Samuel	Navy pension for services in 1812.	24	2	Petition	97	Naval Affairs.						

List of private claims presented to the House of Representatives of the United States from the 1st to the 31st Congress, inclusive—Continued.

Names of claimants.	Nature or object of the claim.	Congress.	Session.	How brought before the House of Reps.	Page of journal.	To what committee of the House referred.	No. or date of the report.	Nature of the report.	No. of the bill.	How disposed of by the House of Reps.	How disposed of by the Senate.	Date of the act of Congress, and remarks.
Ross, Samuel	Navy pension for disabilities incurred in war of 1812.	24	2	Resolution	166	Naval Affairs.						
Ross & Surisson, assignee of.	Indemnity for French spoliations prior to 1800.	26	1	Memorial	182	Foreign Affairs	343	Favorable	319	Referred to Committee Whole House.		
Ross, Templin W., guardian of the children of.	Reimbursing for Indian reservations.	31	1	Petition	720	Indian Affairs.						
Ross, Templin W., guardian of the children of.	Reimbursing for Indian reservations.	31	2	Petition	207	Indian Affairs	Jan. 29, 1851	Adverse	......	Laid on table.		
Ross, Thomas	(See William Baker, &c.)	22	1	....	288	....	480					
Ross, Thomas	Increase of pension	23	2	Petition	489	Rev. Pensions.						
Ross, Wm., widow of	Pension for revolutionary services.	26	1	Resolution	950	Rev. Claims.						
Ross, Wm., and others	(See Wyoming sufferers, heirs of.)	26	1	....	630							
Ross, William, assignee of.	Indemnity for French spoliations prior to 1800.	26	1	Memorial	182	Foreign Affairs	343	Favorable	319	Referred to Committee Whole House.		
Ross, William, heirs of	Indemnity for French spoliations prior to 1800.	29	2	Memorial	171	Foreign Affairs.						
Ross, William, heirs of	Indemnity for French spoliations prior to 1800.	31	1	Petition	413	Foreign Affairs.						
Ross, Wm. B., and others.	Confirmation of titles to land in Florida.	29	2	Memorial	169	Public Lands.						
Ross, Wm. B., and others.	Confirmation of titles to land in Florida.	30	1	Petition	138	Public Lands	652	Favorable	519	Referred to Committee Whole House.		
Ross, Wm. S	Issue of scrip in his name in lieu of Virginia land warrant given to Capt. Thos. Warman, deceased, for revolutionary services.	30	1	Petition	674	Priv. Land Claims.						
Ross, Wm. S	Issue of scrip in his name in lieu of Virginia land warrant given to Capt. Thos. Warman, deceased, for revolutionary services.	30	2	Petition	210	Public Lands.						
Ross, Wm. S	Issue of scrip in his name in lieu of Virginia land warrant given to Capt. Thos. Warman, deceased, for revolutionary war.	31	1	Petition	216	Public Lands.						
Ross, Zephaniah	Pension for revolutionary services.	19	2	Petition	59	Military Pensions.						
Ross, Zephaniah	Pension for revolutionary services.	20	1	Petition	38	Military Pensions	....	....	......	Discharged; laid on table.		
Ross, Zephaniah	Pension for revolutionary services.	20	2	House bill	55	Whole House	Jan. 15, 1829	With amend'ts	311	Passed	Laid on table.	
Ross, Zephaniah	Pension for revolutionary services.	21	1	Petition	48	Military Pensions	Jan. 5, 1830	Pension bill	72	Passed	Passed	App'd May 20, 1830
Ross, Zephaniah	Arrears of pension	23	2	Petition	87	Rev. Pensions	Dec. 27, 1834	Adverse	......	Laid on table.		
Ross & Shropshire	(See Shropshire & Ross)	23	2	....	52							
Rosseau, James A	(See Rasselas Whitcomb, and others.)	25	2	....	1047							
Rossell, Thomas	Pension	21	2	Petition	43	Military Pensions.						
Rosser, Ephraim	Extension of a patent	31	1	Petition	1345	Patents.						
Rosser, J. Travis	Increase of compensation as collector, Petersburg, Virginia.	29	2	Memorial	322	Commerce.						
Rosser, J. Travis	Increase of compensation as collector, Petersburg, Virginia.	30	1	Petition	260	Commerce.						
Rosset, D. D	Indemnity for French spoliations prior to 1800.	29	2	Memorial	163	Foreign Affairs.						
Rossetter, Abby	(See representatives of Jeremiah Miller.)	13	1	....	19							

List of private claims presented to the House of Representatives of the United States from the 1st to the 31st Congress, inclusive—Continued.

Names of claimants.	Nature or object of the claim.	Congress.	Session.	How brought before the House of Reps.	Page of journal.	To what committee of the House referred.	No. or date of the report.	Nature of the report.	No. of the bill.	How disposed of by the House of Reps.	How disposed of by the Senate.	Date of the act of Congress, and remarks.
Rossetter, Benjamin	(See representatives of Jeremiah Miller.)	13	1	....	19							
Rosetter, Samuel	Pension	3	1	Rep. of Secretary War.	131	Select	May 26, 1796	Jt. res. to refer to Sec. War.	R. 12	Passed	Passed	App'd June 9, 1796
Rosetter, Samuel	Pension	3	2	Rep. of Secretary War.	262	Claims.						
Rosetter, Samuel	Pension	4	1	Rep. of Secretary War.	445	Claims	Feb. 18, 1796	Favorable; bill ordered.	156	Passed	Passed	App'd April 20, 1796
Rosetter, Samuel	Increase of pension	10	1	House bill	234	Whole House	April 19, 1808	With amends.	78	Passed	Passed	App'd April 25, 1808
Rosetter, Samuel	Arrears of pension	11	2	Petition	226	Select	Mar. 27, 1810	Adverse	......	Rejected.		
Rossetter, Timothy	Restoration of pension discontinued under act of May, 1820.	17	1	Petition	45	Rev. Pensions.						
Rossetter, Timothy	Restoration of pension discontinued under act of May, 1820.	17	2	Petition	25	Rev. Pensions.						
Rossier, George and Roseles	Drawback on goods and merchandise exported.	14	1	Petition	386	Com. and Manuf.	April 12, 1816	Favorable	172	Indefinitely postponed.		
Rossier, George and Roseles	Drawback on goods and merchandise exported.	14	2	Petition	101	Com. and Manuf.	Dec. 31, 1816	Favorable	36	Passed	Passed	App'd March 3, 1817
Rossier, George and others.	Renewal of treasury notes lost or miscarried in United States mail.	14	1	Senate bill	484	Whole House	....	....	......	Laid on table.		
Rosson, Joseph	Payment for a rifle impressed into United States service during war of 1812.	18	1	Resolution	176	Claims	Feb. 27, 1824	Adverse	......	Laid on table.		
Rotch, William, & Sons	Release from payment of duties on goods imported in foreign vessels not registered.	3	2	Petition	261	Select.						
Rotch, William, & Sons	Release from payment of duties on goods imported in foreign vessels not registered.	4	1	Petition	388	Com. and Manuf.	April 5, 1796	Adverse	......	Leave to withdraw.		
Rotch, William, jr., & Sons.	Damage and other expenses incurred by detention of vessels employed to bring home prisoners of war from England.	13	2	Petition	299	Claims	Mar. 23, 1814	Adverse	......	Leave to withdraw.		
Rotch, William, and Wm. Handy.	Indemnity for French spoliations prior to 1800.	29	2	Memorial	57	Foreign Affairs.						
Rotch, William, jr., executor of William, deceased.	Indemnity for French spoliations prior to 1800.	26	1	Memorial	182	Foreign Affairs	343	Favorable	319	Referred to Committee Whole House.		
Rotch, William, jr., executor of William, deceased.	Indemnity for French spoliations prior to 1800.	31	1	Petition	197	Foreign Affairs	355	Favorable	318	Referred to Committee Whole House.		
Roubieu, Francois	Confirmation of title to land in Louisiana.	22	2	Petition	41	Priv. Land Claims.	53	Favorable	696	Referred to Committee Whole House.		
Roubieu, Francois	Confirmation of title to land in Louisiana.	23	1	Petition	93	Priv. Land Claims.	Jan. 8, 1834	To be dischar'd	......	Laid on table.		
Rouerie, Marquis	(See Major Gen. Duportail, *et al.*)	27	2	....	62							
Rough, Ludwick, heirs of.	(See Ludwick Rowe, heirs of.)	24	1	....	261							
Roulet, and G. Rozier	(See Isaac Lawrence and others.)	14	2	....	101							
Roulet, John S.	(See Isaac Lawrence and others.)	14	2	....	101							
Roulet, John S., sureties of.	Refunding amount paid on certain bond.	25	2	Memorial	408	Commerce.						
Roulet, John S., sureties of.	Refunding amount paid on certain bond.	26	1	Memorial	176	Commerce.						
Roumfort, A. L., military storekeeper.	Increase of compensation	24	1	Petition	773	Military Affairs.						

List of private claims presented to the House of Representatives of the United States from the 1st to the 31st Congress, inclusive—Continued.

Names of claimants.	Nature or object of the claim.	Congress.	Session.	How brought before the House of Reps.	Page of journal.	To what committee of the House referred.	No. or date of the report.	Nature of the report.	No. of the bill.	How disposed of by the House of Reps.	How disposed of by the Senate.	Date of the act of Congress, and remarks.
Round, Amos	Change location of bounty land	25	2	Petition	421	Public Lands				Discharged; laid on table.		
Rounds, Mary	Pension	26	1	Petition	1252	Rev. Pensions				Discharged; leave to withdraw.		
Rounds, Reuben	Pension	22	1	Resolution	194	Invalid Pensions.						
Rounds, Reuben	Pension	23	2	Resolution	215	Invalid Pensions	Feb. 2, 1835	Adverse		Laid on table.		
Rounds, Sally, and Hannah Wyatt.	(See John Price, heirs of.)	28	1		284							
Roundtree, Gracy	Patent for land purchased of United States and assigned to him.	22	1	Petition	514	Public Lands				Discharged; laid on table.		
Roundtree, Francis	Indemnity for losses in carrying United States mail.	25	2	Petition	514	P. Of. & P. Roads.	627	Adverse		Laid on table.		
Rouse, Anna	(See Jocob Rouse, widow of.)	26	1		950							
Rouse, Casper	Compensation for supplies in money furnished the army during revolutionary war.	11	2	Petition	149	Claims	Jan. 26, 1810	Adverse		Leave to withdraw.		
Rouse, Casper, heirs of	Remuneration for losses sustained by deceased upon continental money.	25	3	Petition	561	Rev. Claims				Discharged.		
Rouse, Casper, heirs of	Remuneration for losses sustained by deceased upon continental money.	26	1	Petition	164	Rev. Claims.						
Rause, Casper, heirs of	Remuneration for losses sustained by deceased upon continental money.	27	2	Petition	509	Rev. Claims	942	Adverse		Laid on table.		
Rouse, Casper, heirs of	Remuneration for losses sustained by deceased upon continental money.	29	2	Petition	172	Rev. Claims.						
Rouse, Casper, heirs of	Remuneration for losses sustained by beceased upon continental money.	31	1	Petition	511	Rev. Claims	426	Adverse		Laid on table.		
Rouse, Jacob, widow of	Pension for revolutionary services.	26	1	Resolution	950	Rev. Pensions.						
Rouse, James Jaques, heirs of.	Payment for services of deceased during the war of 1812.	25	2	Petition	274	Claims	598	Adverse		Laid on table.		
Rouse, Lewis	Payment for whiskey taken for U. States troops.	17	1	Petition	194	Claims.						
Rouse, Lewis	Payment for whiskey taken for U. States troops.	17	2	Petition	119	Claims.						
Rouse, Lewis	Payment for whiskey taken for U. States troops.	18	1	Petition	130	Claims	Mar. 12, 1824	Adverse		Leave to withdraw.		
Rouse, Lewis	Payment for whiskey taken for U. States troops.	19	1	Petition	43	Claims	76	Adverse		Recommitted.		
Rouse, Lewis	Payment for whiskey taken for U. States troops.	19	2	Petition	59	Claims	68	Adverse		Laid on table.		
Rouse, Lewis	Payment for whiskey taken for U. States troops.	20	1	Petition	58	Claims	45	Adverse		Laid on table.		
Rouse, Lewis	Payment for whiskey taken for U. States troops.	20	2	Petition	40	Claims				Discharged; laid on table.		
Rouse, Lewis	Payment for whiskey taken for U. States troops.	21	1	Petition	35	Claims	110	Favorable	151	Passed	Passed	App'd May 30, 1830
Rouse, Lewis	For further compensation for whiskey taken for U. States troops.	22	2	Petition	218	Claims.						
Rouse, Louis	Confirmation of title to land	22	2	Petition	219	Priv. Land Claims.	104	Adverse		Laid on table.		

List of private claims presented to the House of Representatives of the United States from the 1st to the 31st Congress, inclusive—Continued.

Names of claimants.	Nature or object of the claim.	Congress.	Session.	How brought before the House of Reps.	Page of journal.	To what committee of the House referred.	No. or date of the report.	Nature of the report.	No. of the bill.	How disposed of by the House of Reps.	How disposed of by the Senate.	Date of the act of Congress, and remarks.
Rouse, Nicholas	Increase of pension	14	2	Petition	40	Pens. & Rev. Cl'ms.				Discharged, laid on table.		
Rouse, Peter	Pension for revolutionary services.	22	1	Petition	594	Rev. Pensions						
Roush, George	Pension for revolutionary services.	27	2	Petition	935	Rev. Pensions	912	Favorable	528	Ordered to 3d reading.		
Roush, George	Pension for revolutionary services.	27	3	House bill	89				528	Passed	Indef. postp'd.	
Roush, George	Pension for revolutionary services.	28	1	Petition	296	Rev. Pensions.						
Roush, George	Pension for revolutionary services.	28	2	Petition	59	Rev. Pensions	116	Favorable	595	Referred to Committee Whole House.		
Roush, George	Pension for revolutionary services.	29	1	Petition	104	Rev. Pensions	215	Favorable	209	Passed.		
Roush, George	Pension for revolutionary services.	29	2	Senate bill	375	Rev. Pensions	Feb 24, 1847	With't amend.	S. 103	Passed	Passed	App'd Feb. 25, 1847
Rousseau, Eugene, attorneys of.	Refund purchase money for lands entered in St. Helena land district.	27	2	Petition	934	Public Lands.						
Rousseau, Lawrence, U. S. navy.	To be allowed extra compensation while in command of naval station at New Orleans.	21	1	Petition	100	Naval Affairs				Discharged; laid on table.		
Routzoun, Conrad	Reimburse money paid to redeem himself from Indian captivity in the war of 1812.	23	1	Petition	656	Claims				Discharged; referred to Third Auditor of the Treasury.		
Roux, Albert	Pension	1	3	Petition and rep't Sec. of War.	363, 373					Laid on table.		
Row, Zebulon	(See Canadian refugees.)											
Rowand, Thomas	Renewal of patent	23	1	Petition	221	Patents, &c.						
Rowark, William	Compensation and land for services as a soldier during revolutionary war.	19	1	Resolution	266	Rev. Claims	April 5, 1826	Adverse		Laid on table.		
Rowe, Abel, widow of	Pension for revolutionary services.	26	1	Petition	171	Rev. Pensions.						
Rowe, Benjamin	Pension for services in war of 1812.	27	2	Petition	90	Invalid Pensions	227	Adverse		Laid on table.		
Rowe, Benjamin	Pension for services in war of 1812.	29	1	Petition	436	Invalid Pensions	510	Adverse		Laid on table		Leave to withd'w, 31st Cong., 2d session.
Rowe, Ebenezer	Invalid pension	10	1	House bill	234	Whole House	April 9, 1808	With amend'ts	78	Passed	Passed	App'd April 25, 1808
Rowe, Edward	Relief for wounds received by bursting of a blunderbuss on board of vessel in service of United States.	4	2	Petition	701	Claims.						
Rowe, Edward	Relief for wounds received by bursting of a blunderbuss on board of vessel in service of United States.	5	2	Petition	204	Claims	Mar. 3, 1798	Adverse		Laid on table.		
Rowe, Elizabeth	(See widow of Squire Ambler)	25	3		217							
Rowe, Elizabeth	(See widow of Abel Rowe)	26	1		171							
Rowe, George	Change location of land entry	23	2	Petition	40	Priv. Land Claims.	Dec. 19, 1834	Adverse		Recommitted to Priv. Land Claims.		
Rowe, George	Change location of land entry	24	1	Petition	121	Priv. Land Claims.	729	Favorable	675	Referred to Committee Whole House.		
Rowe, George	Change location of land entry	25	2	Petition	42	Priv. Land Claims.	483	Favorable	479	Referred to Committee Whole House.		
Rowe, George	Change location of land entry	25	3	Bill of last sess.	378	Whole House	Jan. 25, 1839	With't amend.	479	Passed	Passed	App'd March 3, 1839
Rowe, John	(See widow of Stephen Decatur and others.)	20	1		295		201		S. 50			
Rowe, John	(See widow of Stephen Decatur and others.)	21	1		137				82			
Rowe, John	Restoration of pension, discontinued under act of May, 1820.	17	1	Petition	37	Rev. Pensions.						
Rowe, John, widow of	Pension	25	2	Resolution	469	Rev. Pensions	Mar. 23, 1838	Favorable	683	Passed.		

List of private claims presented to the House of Representatives of the United States from the 1st to the 31st Congress, inclusive—Continued.

Names of claimants.	Nature or object of the claim.	Congress.	Session.	How brought before the House of Reps.	Page of journal.	To what committee of the House referred.	No. or date of the report.	Nature of the report.	No. of the bill.	How disposed of by the House of Reps.	How disposed of by the Senate.	Date of the act of Congress, and remarks.
Rowe, John, widow of	Pension	25	3	Resolution	88	Rev. Pensions	30	Favorable	930	Passed	Passed	App'd March 3, 1839
Rowe, John	(See heirs of Ludwick Rowe)	24	1		261							
Rowe, Johnson, daughter of	Pension for revolutionary services.	25	2	Petition	271	Rev. Pensions	Feb. 23, 1838	Adverse		Laid on table.		
Rowe, Joseph, widow of	Payment for provender taken for use of United States during war of 1812.	19	2	Petition	300	Claims				Discharged; laid on table.		
Rowe, Joseph, representatives of.	Payment of prize-money as a boatswain in the navy during the war of 1812.	22	1	Petition	222	Naval Affairs	May 17, 1832	Favorable	579	Referred to Committee Whole House.		
Rowe, Joseph, representatives of.	Payment of prize-money as a boatswain in the navy during the war of 1812.	23	1	Petition	74	Naval Affairs	Dec. 17, 1833	Favorable	32	Passed	Passed	App'd June 18, 1834
Rowe, Ludwick, heirs of	Indemnity for lost military bounty-land warrant.	24	1	Petition	261	Priv. Land Claims.	521	Favorable	516	Referred to Committee Whole House.		
Rowe, Ludwick, heirs of	Indemnity for lost military bounty-land warrant.	25	2	Petition	43	Priv. Land Claims.	316	Favorable	357	Referred to Committee Whole House.		
Rowe, Ludwick, heirs of	Indemnity for lost military bounty-land warrant.	25	3	Bill of last sess.	377	Whole House	Jan. 25, 1839	With't amend.	357	Passed	Passed	App'd March 3, 1839
Rowe, Peter	Pension as a marine and for loss of an arm while firing a salute.	18	2	Petition	80	Naval Affairs	Jan. 20, 1825	Adverse		Laid on table.		
Rowe, Samuel, widow of	Continuation of pension	27	2	Petition	1066	Rev. Pensions.						
Rowe, Samuel	(See heirs of Ludwick Rowe)	24	1		261							
Rowe, Submit	(See widow of Samuel Rowe)	27	2		1066							
Rowe, Susannah	(See widow of John Rowe)	25	2		469							
Rowe, Mrs. S.	(See heir of Oliver Bucklin)	26	1		280							
Rowe, Zebulon	Compensation for losses sustained during revolutionary war.	9	1	Petition	236	Select.						
Rowell, Enoch, widow of	Arrears of pension for revolutionary services.	28	1	Petition	839, 950	Rev. Pensions.						
Rowell, Enoch, heirs of	Arrears of pension for revolutionary services.	31	1	Petition	917	Rev. Pensions	371	Adverse		Laid on table.		
Rowell, Hubert, representatives of.	Confirmation of title to land	14	1	Petition	90	Public Lands.						
Rowell, Hubert, representatives of.	Confirmation of title to land	14	2	Petition	49	Priv. Land Claims.						
Rowell, Hubert, representatives of.	Confirmation of title to land	15	1	Petition	192	Priv. Land Claims.	Feb. 18, 1818	Favorable; bill	94	Passed	Passed	App'd April 11, 1818
Rowell & Haskell	Repayment of duties paid on goods imported into Castine.	16	1	Senate bill	108	Ways and Means	Jan. 14, 1830	With't amend.	13	Passed	Passed	App'd April 11, 1820
Rowell, Rachel	(See widow of Enoch Rowell)	28	1		839, 950							
Rowell, Rachel, heirs of	(See heirs of Enoch Rowell)	31	1		917							
Rowell, Samuel	Restoration of pension, discontinued under act of May, 1820.	17	1	Petition	109	Rev. Pensions.						
Rowell, Sarah	(See heirs of Hubert Rowell)	14	1		90							
Rowland, Edward	Payment for a horse lost in military service of the United States in 1814.	15	2	Petition	52	Claims				Discharged; laid on table.		
Rowland, Edward	Payment for a horse lost in military service of the United States in 1814.	16	1	Petition	24	Claims	Dec. 13, 1819	Adverse		Discharged; laid on table.		
Rowland, James	(See executors of William R land)	3	2		247							
Rowland, John	Pension for revolutionary services.	2	2	Petition	660					Laid on table.		

List of private claims presented to the House of Representatives of the United States from the 1st to the 31st Congress, inclusive—**Continued.**

Names of claimants.	Nature or object of the claim.	Congress.	Session.	How brought before the House of Reps.	Page of journal.	To what committee of the House referred.	No. or date of the report.	Nature of the report.	No. of the bill.	How disposed of by the House of Reps.	How disposed of by the Senate.	Date of the act of Congress, and remarks.
Rowland, Thomas	Renewal of patent	23	1	Petition	56	Judiciary	Dec. 23, 1833	Adverse		Laid on table.		
Rowland, Thomas	Additional pay for services as a soldier in the war of 1812.	27	2	Petition	1298	Claims.						
Rowland, Thomas	Additional pay for services as a soldier in the war of 1812.	28	1	Petition	371	Claims.						
Rowland, Thomas	Additional pay for services as a soldier in the war of 1812.	28	2	Petition	84	Claims.						
Rowland, Thomas	Additional pay for services as a soldier in the war of 1812.	29	1	Petition	326	Invalid Pensions				Discharged; laid on table.		
Rowland, William, executors of.	Compensation for use of teams in government service in 1780.	3	2	Petition	247	Claims	Feb. 25, 1795	Adverse		Referred to Committee Whole House.		
Rowland, William, executors of.	Compensation for use of teams in government service in 1780.	4	2	Petition	631	Claims	Dec. 29, 1796	Adverse.		Laid on table.		
Rowland, William, executors of.	Compensation for use of teams in government service in 1780.	5	3	Petition	424	Claims.	Jan. 22, 1799	Adverse.		Laid on table.		
Rowles, George	Pension	14	2	Petition	103	Pens. & Rev. Cl'ms.				Discharged; laid on table.		
Rowles, George	Pension	15	1	Petition	150	Pens. & Rev. Cl'ms.				Discharged; laid on table.		
Rowlett, E. W	Relief relative to lands purchased from the holder of receiver's certificates.	31	1	Petition	629	Public Lands.						
Rowlett, John	Copyright for tables of discount	20	1	Senate bill	781	Judiciary	Mar. 22, 1828	With't amend.	S. 141	Passed	Passed	App'd May 24, 1828
Rowlett, John	For amendment to act of May 24, 1828, in his favor.	20	2	Letter	83	Judiciary.	Jan. 9, 1829	Favorable	359	Passed.		
Rowlett, John	For amendment to act of May 24, 1828, in his favor.	21	1	Petition	39	Judiciary.	Dec. 21, 1829	Favorable	7	Passed.	Passed	App'd Feb. 11, 1830
Rowlett, John	For an extension of copyright	27	2	Memorial	540	Judiciary	652	Adverse		Laid on table.		
Rowlett, John	For an extension of copyright	27	3	Petition	113	Judiciary	Jan. 7, 1843	Favorable	657	Passed	Passed	App'd March 3, 1843
Rowlett, William M.	Payment for a horse lost and other property destroyed by the Seminole Indians in 1840.	26	1	Petition	1009	Claims.						
Rowlett, William M	Payment for a horse lost and other property destroyed by the Seminole Indians in 1840.	26	2	Petition	135	Claims.						
Rowlett, William M	Payment for a horse lost and other property destroyed by the Seminole in 1840.	27	2	Petition	94	Claims	172	Adverse		Laid on table.		
Rowley, Nathan	Pension for military services in war of 1812.	29	1	Petition	1139	Invalid Pensions.						
Rowse, Thomas	Arrearages of pay and rations for services in revolutionary war.	11	2	Petition	200	Claims	Mar. 14, 1810	Adverse.		Laid on table.		
Roxas, J. D.	(See Jose De Roxas)	26	1		947							
Roxburgh, Maj. Alexander.	Renewal of final settlement certificates lost or destroyed.	3	2	Petition	311	Select	Feb. 3, 1795	Favorable; res.		Referred to Committee Whole House.		
Roxburgh, Maj. Alexander.	Renewal of final settlement certificates lost or destroyed.	5	2	Petition	224	Claims	100	Adverse.		Laid on table.		
Roxburgh, Maj. Alexander.	Renewal of final settlement certificates lost or destroyed.	6	1	Petition	610	Claims	Jan. 26, 1801	Adverse.		Laid on table.		
Roxburgh, Maj. Alexander.	Renewal of final settlement certificates lost or destroyed.	7	1	Petition	76	Claims	Mar. 18, 1802	Report not of record.		Referred to Committee Whole House.		
Roxburgh, Maj. Alexander.	Renewal of final settlement certificates lost or destroyed.	9	1	Petition	238	Claims.						

List of private claims presented to the House of Representatives of the United States from the 1st to the 31st Congress, inclusive—Continued.

Names of claimants.	Nature or object of the claim.	Congress.	Session.	How brought before the House of Reps.	Page of journal.	To what committee of the House referred.	No. or date of the report.	Nature of the report.	No. of the bill.	How disposed of by the House of Reps.	How disposed of by the Senate.	Date of the act of Congress, and remarks.
Roxburgh, Maj. Alexander, representatives of.	Renewal of final settlement certificates lost or destroyed.	12	1	Petition	263	Claims.						
Roxburgh, Maj. Alexander, representatives of.	Renewal of final settlement certificates lost or destroyed.	12	2	Petition	570	Claims.						
Roxburgh, Maj. Alexander, representatives of.	Renewal of final settlement certificates lost or destroyed.	13	1	Petition	15	Claims	....	....	......	Discharged.		
Roxburgh, Maj. Alexander, representativos of.	Renewal of final settlement certificates lost or destroyed.	14	1	Petition	55	Pens. & Rev. Cl'ms.	Jan. 23, 1816	Favorable	49	Passed	Passed	App'd April 26, 1816
Roxburgh, Elizabeth.....	(See representatives of Maj. Alexander Roxburgh.)	12	1	....	263							
Roy, Beverley	Pension	21	2	Petition	110	Military Pensions.						
Roy, Beverley	Pension	22	1	Petition	36	Invalid Pensions.						
Roy, Beverley	Pension	22	2	Petition	321	Invalid Pensions.						
Roy, Beverley	Pension	23	1	Petition	112	Invalid Pensions ..	Mar. 15, 1834	Favorable	367	Referred to Committee Whole House.		
Roy, Beverley	Pension	23	2	Bill of last sess.	336	Whole House	Feb. 6, 1835	With't amend.	367	Passed.		
Roy, Beverley	Pension	24	1	Petition	52	Invalid Pensions ..	Dec. 29, 1835	Favorable	58	Passed	Passed	App'd May 14, 1826
Roy, Francis	(See Reuben E. Gentry, and others)	25	2	....	155							
Roy, Jean Baptiste	(See Reuben E. Gentry, and others)	25	2	....	155							
Roy, Joseph............	(See Reuben E. Gentry, and others)	25	2	....	155							
Roy, Lonis	Grant of land for services against Indians.	15	2	Petition	28	Priv. Land Claims.						
Roy, Louis.............	Confirmation of title to land in Missouri.	17	1	Petition	51	Public Lands.						
Roy, Louis.............	Confirmation of title to land in Missouri.	18	1	Petition	55	Public Lands.						
Roy, Louis, administrator of.	Indemnity for Indian depredations.	25	3	Petition	124	Indian Affairs.....	184	Adverse	......	Laid on table.		
Roy, Seymour	(See William Baker, &c.)......	22	1	....	288	....	480					
Roy, ——	(See Searle, Roy & Co)	25	2	....	425							
Royall, Anne...........	(See heirs and widow of William Royall.)	21	1	....	597							
Royal, James...........	Pension for loss of eyes by bursting of a cannon at a public rejoicing.	15	1	Petition	182	Pens. & Rev. Cl'ms.	....	....	......	Discharged; laid on table.		
Royal, James...........	Pension for loss of eyes by bursting of a cannon at a public rejoicing.	16	1	Petition	115	Pens. & Rev. Cl'ms.	Jan. 7, 1820	Adverse.	......	Laid on table.		
Royal, James...........	Pension for loss of eyes by bursting of a cannon at a public rejoicing	17	2	Petition	44	Select	Dec. 23, 1822	Favorable	205	Passed.		
Royal, James...........	Pension for loss of eyes by bursting of a cannon at a public rejoicing	18	1	Petition	31	Pens. & Rev. Cl'ms.	Dec. 31, 1823	Favorable	35	Passed	Pas'd amended	Petitionr's name stricken out.
Royal, James...........	Pension for loss of eyes by bursting of a cannon at a public rejoicing.	20	2	Petition	288	Military Pensions..	89	Favorable	451	Referred to Committee Whole House.		
Royal, James...........	Pension for loss of eyes by bursting of a cannon at a public rejoicing.	21	1	Petition	49	Military Pensions..	Aug. 5, 1830	Pension bill ..	72	Passed	Passed	App'd May 20, 1830
Royall, John	Pension for revolutionary services.	20	2	Resolution	52	Military Pensions..	....	....	......	Disch'd; laid on table		
Royall, Joseph..........	Pre-emption right to enter land...	24	1	Petition	946	Public Lands.						
Royall, Major Wm., widow and heirs of.	Commutation pay for revolutionary services.	21	1	Petition	597	Rev. Claims.						
Royall, Major Wm., widow and heirs of.	Commutation pay for revolutionary services.	22	2	Petition	184	Military Affairs.						
Royall, Major Wm., widow and heirs of.	Commutation pay for revolutionary services.	23	1	Senate bill	846	Rev. Claims......	Jan. 28, 1834	With't amend.	S. 156	Passed	Passed	App'd June 30, 1834

List of private claims presented to the House of Representatives of the United States from the 1st to the 31st Congress, inclusive—Continued.

Names of claimants.	Nature or object of the claim.	Congress.	Session.	How brought before the House of Reps.	Page of journal.	To what committee of the House referred.	No. or date of the report.	Nature of the report.	No. of the bill.	How disposed of by the House of Reps.	How disposed of by the Senate.	Date of the act of Congress, and remarks.
Royall, Major Wm., widow of.	Pension for revolutionary services of her husband.	25	3	Petition	293	Rev. Pensions	267	Adverse	......	Laid on table.		
Royall, Major Wm., widow of.	Pension for revolutionary services of her husband.	26	1	Petition	283	Rev. Pensions	491	Adverse	......	Laid on table.		
Royall, Major Wm., widow of.	Pension for revolutionary services of her husband.	26	2	Petition	212	Rev. Pensions.						
Royall, Major Wm., widow of.	Pension for revolutionary services of her husband.	27	2	Petition	97	Rev. Pensions	796	Favorable	450	Ordered to 3d reading.		
Royall, Major Wm., widow of.	Pension for revolutionary services of her husband.	27	3	Bill of last sess.	88	....	....	....	450	Passed	Rejected.	
Royall, Major Wm., widow of.	Pension for revolutionary services of her husband.	28	1	Petition	102	Rev. Pensions	....	....	......	Discharged; laid on table.		
Royall, Major Wm., widow of.	Pension for revolutionary services of her husband.	28	2	Petitions	68	Rev. Pensions.						
Royall, Major Wm., widow of.	Pension for revolutionary services of her husband.	29	1	Petitions	118, 162, 227	Rev. Pensions	524	Adverse	......	Laid on table.		
Royall, Major Wm., widow of.	Pension for revolutionary services of her husband.	29	2	Petition	68	Rev. Pensions.						
Royall, Major Wm., widow of.	Pension for revolutionary services of her husband.	30	1	Petitions	682	Rev. Pensions	....	....	......	Discharged; laid on table.		
Royce, Elijah	Pension for revolutionary services.	4	1	Rep. of Secretary War.	445	Claims	Feb. 18, 1796	Favorable	156	Passed	Passed	App'd April 20, 1796
Royer, Samuel	Indemnity for losses in purchase of cattle for public use.	3	1	Petition	115	....	....	....	......	Laid on table.		
Royer, Samuel	Payment for supplies purchased for the army during the revolutionary war.	16	1	Petition	288	Select.						
Royer, Samuel, heirs and representatives of.	Payment for provisions purchased by deceased as commissary in the revolution.	27	3	Petition	103	Rev. Claims	249	Adverse	......	Laid on table.		
Royer, Samuel, heirs and representatives of.	Payment for provisions purchased by deceased as commissary in the revolution.	30	1	Petition	959	....	....	....	......	Leave to withdraw.		
Royston, James	Pension	8	2	Petition	108	Claims.						
Royston, Jesse F	Payment for a horse lost in the public service in war of 1812.	19	1	Senate bill	520	Claims	May 9, 1826	With amend.	S. 139	Passed	Passed	App'd May 20, 1826
Rozier, George	(See Isaac Lawrence and others.)	14	2	....	101							
Rubey, James	Grant of land as remuneration for destruction of house by fire.	23	2	Petition	39	Public Lands	....	....	......	Discharged.		
Rubin, Levi	Settlement of claim *vs.* United States.	1	3	Petition	380	....	....	....	......	Referred to Secretary Treasury.		
Ruble, Hannah	Grant of land in lieu of Continental money in her possession.	26	1	Petition	630	Rev. Claims.						
Ruble, Hannah	Grant of land in lieu of Continental money in her possession.	26	2	Petition	48	Rev. Claims	Jan. 4, 1841	Adverse	......	Laid on table.		
Rucker, Agnes	(See Julius Rucker, heirs of)	22	2	....	142							
Rucker, Angus	Payment of interest on commutation pay allowed and paid him by Virginia for services as a captain in revolutionary war.	22	1	Petition	714	Rev. Claims.						
Rucker, Angus, representatives of.	Commutation pay for revolutionary services.	29	1	Petition	389	Rev. Pensions.						

List of private claims presented to the House of Representatives of the United States from the 1st to the 31st Congress, inclusive—Continued.

Names of claimants.	Nature or object of the claim.	Congress.	Session.	How brought before the House of Reps.	Page of journal.	To what committee of the House referred.	No. or date of the report.	Nature of the report.	No. of the bill.	How disposed of by the House of Reps.	How disposed of by the Senate.	Date of the act of Congress, and remarks.
Rucker, Elliott	(See surety of E. F. Vawter)	18	1	....	89							
Rucker, Eizaphen	Pension	27	2	Petition	1129	Invalid Pensions	....	....	......	Discharged; laid on table.		
Rucker, Elzaphen	Pension	28	1	Petition	547	Invalid Pensions.						
Rucker, Elzaphen	Pension	28	2	Petition	199	Invalid Pensions.						
Rucker, Elzaphen	Pension	29	2	Petition	89	Invalid Pensions.						
Rucker, Julius, heirs of	Commutation pay for revolutionary services.	22	2	Petition	142	Rev. Claims.						
Rucker, Riensch & Co	Indemnity for injury to their commerce during the Mexican war.	31	2	Petition	142	Commerce.						
Rudd, John, United States navy.	Payment of prize money for capture of piratical felucca in West Indies.	24	1	Petition	214	Naval Affairs	Feb. 4, 1836	Favorable	276	Referred to Committee Whole House.	....	Provided for in act for relief of the heirs of Mary Richardson—app'd July 2, 1836.
Rudd, Stephen	Compensation for the use of his invention for propelling vessels in the navy of the United States.	17	2	Petition	47	Naval Affairs	Jan. 29, 1823	Adverse	......	Laid on table.		
Rudder, David, attorney of.	Payment for loss of a horse in military services of the U. States in 1817.	18	2	Petition	60	Military Affairs.						
Ruddle, John, representatives of.	Change location of land erroneously entered.	28	2	Petition	213	Priv. Land Claims.	Feb. 25, 1845	Favorable	635	Referred to Committee Whole House.		
Buddle, John, representatives of.	Change location of land erroneously entered.	29	1	Petition	193	Priv. Land Claims.	April 6, 1846	Favorable	377	Passed	Passed	App'd Aug. 8, 1846
Rude, Asa	Pension for revolutionary services.	20	1	Resolution	89	Military Pensions	Jan. 31, 1828	Adverse	......	Laid on table.		
Rudolph, Jacob	Bounty land for services as a soldier in the war of 1812.	20	1	Resolution	160	Priv. Land Claims.	Feb. 15, 1828	Adverse	......	Laid on table.		
Rudolph, Jacob	Arrearages of pension for services in war of 1812.	20	1	Resolution	160	Claims	....	....	......	Discharged.		
Rudolph, Jacob	Arrearages of pension for services in war of 1812.	21	1	Resolution	536	Military Pensions.						
Rudolph, Jacob	Arrearages of pension for services in war of 1812.	21	2	Resolution	48	Military Pensions.						
Rudolph, Jacob	Arrearages of pension for services in war of 1812.	22	1	Petition	45	Military Pensions.						
Rudolph, Jacob	Increase of pension	24	2	Petition	399	Rev. Pensions.						
Rudolph, John, representatives of.	Reimbursement of advances on public account.	3	1	Memorial	124	Select.						
Rudolph, John, representatives of.	Reimbursement of advances on public account.	3	2	Resolution	264	Select	Dec. 15, 1794	Favorable	88	Recom'itted to Claims.		
					348	Claims	Feb. 27, 1795	Adverse	......	Laid on table.		
Rudolph, John, representatives of.	Reimbursement of advances on public account.	6	1	Petition	556	Claims	Mar. 6, 1800	Adverse	......	Laid on table.		
Rudolph, John, representatives of.	Reimbursement of advances on public account.	6	2	Resolution & rep.	770	Whole House	....	....	......	Rejected.		
Rudolph, John	To be allowed extra price for rations furnished United States troops in Delaware during war of 1812.	15	2	Petition	155	Claims	....	....	......	Discharged.		
Rudolph, John	To be allowed extra price for rations furnished United States troops in Delaware during war of 1812.	18	2	Petition	134	Claims.						

List of private claims presented to the House of Representatives of the United States from the 1st to the 31st Congress, inclusive—Continued.

Names of claimants.	Nature or object of the claim.	Congress.	Session.	How brought before the House of Reps.	Page of journal.	To what committee of the House referred.	No. or date of the report.	Nature of the report.	No. of the bill.	How disposed of by the House of Reps.	How disposed of by the Senate.	Date of the act of Congress, and remarks.
Rudolph, John	To be allowed extra price for rations furnished United States troops in Delaware during war of 1812.	20	1	Petition	164	Claims	Feb. 11, 1828	Adverse.	......	Laid on table.		
Rudolph, John	To be allowed extra price for rations furnished United States troops in Delaware during war of 1812.	21	1	Petition	472	Claims.						
Rudolph, John	To be allowed evtra price for rations furnished United States troops in Delaware during war of 1812.	22	1	Petition	188	Claims.						
Rudolph, John	To be allowed extra price for rations furnished United States troops in Delaware during war of 1812.	22	2	Petition	245	Claims.						
Rudolph, John	To be allowed extra price for rations furnished United States troops in Delaware during war of 1812.	29	1	Petition	262	Claims	623	Adverse	......	Laid on table.		
Rudolph, Thomas C., captain in revenue service.	Remuneration for services on the coast of Florida during the Indian difficulties in 1836.	26	1	Petition	330	Naval Affairs.						
Rudolph, Thomas C., captain in revenue service.	Remuneration for services on the coast of Florida during the Indian difficulties in 1836.	26	1	Resolution	773	Claims.						
Rudolph, Thomas C., and others, officers of the revenue service.	To be allowed the same pro-rata compensation as officers of the navy, during their service in the navy in Florida war.	30	2	Petition	86	Naval Affairs.						
Ruff, Samuel W	Additional compensation as a surgeon in the navy of the United States.	23	2	Petition	139	Naval Affairs	78	Favorable	698	Referred to Committee Whole House.		
Ruff, Samuel W	Additional compensation as a surgeon in the navy of the United States.	24	1	Petition	61	Indian Affairs	66	Favorable	81	Passed	Passed	App'd June 14, 1836
Ruffener, Simon	Increase of pension	28	1	Petition	811	Rev. Pensions.						
Ruggles, James	Pension for revolutionary services.	24	1	Petition	433	Rev. Pensions	....	....	......	Discharged; laid on table.		
Ruggles, Lazarus	Pension for revolutionary services.	3	1	Rep. of Secretary War.	131	Select	Mar. 26, 1794	General bill	62	Passed	Passed	App'd June 7, 1794
Ruggles, Mary	(See widow of Timothy Ruggles).	31	1	....	348							
Ruggles, Nathaniel	Relief from apprehended seizure of merchandise on voyage from Calcutta.	12	1	Petition	21	Com. and Manuf.						
Ruggles, Nathaniel	Permission to import merchandise from Great Britain, ordered previous to non-importation act.	12	1	Petition	28	Com. and Manuf.						
Ruggles, Timothy, widow of.	Pension for revolutionary services of her husband.	31	1	Petition	348	Rev. Pensions.						
Ruland, Isaac	Pension for wounds received in the war of 1812.	24	1	Petition	295	Invalid Pensions	503	Favorable	503	Passed	Passed	App'd June 28, 1836

List of private claims presented to the House of Representatives of the United States from the 1st to the 31st Congress, inclusive—Continued.

3—32

Names of claimants.	Nature or object of the claim.	Congress.	Session.	How brought before the House of Reps.	Page of journal.	To what committee of the House referred.	No. or date of the report.	Nature of the report.	No. of the bill.	How disposed of by the House of Reps.	How disposed of by the Senate.	Date of the act of Congress, and remarks.
Ruland, Isaac	Payment for property lost during the war of 1812.	24	1	Petition	64	Claims.						
Ruland, Isaac	Payment for property lost during the war of 1812.	25	2	Petition	275	Claims	556	Adverse		Laid on table.		
Ruland, Isaac	Payment for property lost during the war of 1812.	25	3	Petition	462	Claims.						
Ruland, Isaac	Payment for property lost during the war of 1822.	26	1	Petition	169	Claims	58	Adverse		Laid on table.		
Ruland, Israel	For land under acts for relief of refugees from Canada and Nova Scota.	12	1	House bill	242	Whole House	Mar. 22, 1812	With amends.	85	Passed	Passed	App'd April 23, 1812
Ruland, James	(See Canadian refugees.)											
Rulufson, Herman	Revolutionary pension	25	2	Petition	586	Rev. Pensions				Disch'd; laid on table.		
Ruminer, Daniel	Pension	14	1	Pension bill	622	Whole House	April 11, 1816	Favorable	171	Passed amended.	Passed, with amendment.	App'd April 30, 1816
Rumage, Jones	(See William H. Bedford, agent, &c.)	28	1		262							
Rummel, George	Payment for services as a militia officer in the war of 1812.	15	1	Petition	294	Claims				Discharged.		
Rummel, George	Payment for services as a militia officer in the war of 1812.	15	2	Petition	52	Claims				Discharged.		
Rumney, William, representatives of.	For an appropriation of land scrip for the redemption of a bounty land warrant held by them.	27	3	Petition	140	Rev. Claims	250	Adverse		Laid on table.		
Rumsey, Charles	Pension	13	3	House bill	740	Whole House	Mar. 2, 1815	With amends.	303	Passed	Passed	App'd March 3, 1815
Rumsey, Charles	Donation of land in lieu of pension	28	2	Petition	69	Public Lands.						
Rumsey, David	Interposition of Congress in relation to the impressment of his son by British ship-of-war.	9	1	Letter to Speaker.	227					Referred to Secretary of State.		
Rumsey, James	Remuneration in consideration of his being the original inventor of the art of propelling vessels by steam.	24	1	Memorial	538	Select.						
Rumsey, James	Remuneration in consideration of his being the original inventor of the art of propelling vessels by steam.	25	3	Memorial	119	Select	265	Favorable	J. R. 46	Passed.		
Rumsey, James	Remuneration in consideration of his being the original inventor of the art of propelling vessels by steam.	26	1	Memorial	350	Select	650	Favorable	483	Referred to Committee Whole House.		
Rumsey, James	Remuneration in consideration of his being the original inventor of the art of propelling vessels by steam.	27	2	Memorial	80	Select	324	Favorable	294	Referred to Committee Whole House.		
Rumsey, James D.	(See James Rumsey)	24	1		538							
Rumsey, John	Pension for revolutionary services.	16	2	Petition	21	Rev. Pensions	Feb. 15, 1821	Adverse		Leave to withdraw.		
Rumsey, John	Pension for revolutionary services.	27	2	Petition	80	Select	324	Favorable	294	Referred to Committee Whole House.		
Rumsey, Jonas	Pension for revolutionary services.	16	1	Petition	245	Rev. Pensions	April 6, 1820	Adverse		Laid on table.		
Rumsey, Jonas	Pension for revolutionary services.	18	1	Petition	314	Rev. Pensions	Mar. 24, 1824	Adverse		Laid on table.		
Rumsey, Willis	Pension for revolutionary services.	13	3	Petition	455	Pens. & Rev. Cl'ms.				Discharged; referred to Secretary of War.		

List of private claims presented to the House of Representatives of the United States from the 1st to the 31st Congress, inclusive—Continued.

Names of claimants.	Nature or object of the claim.	Congress.	Session.	How brought before the House of Reps.	Page of journal.	To what committee of the House referred.	No. or date of the report.	Nature of the report.	No. of the bill.	How disposed of by the House of Reps.	How disposed of by the Senate.	Date of the act of Congress, and remarks.
Rundle, George	(See agents of Scholfield & Taylor)	16	1	....	212							
Rundlet, James	Compensation for losses on treasury notes.	24	2	Petition	36	Claims	5	Adverse	......	Laid on table.		
Rundlet, Jonathan	Pension	21	2	Petition	52	Military Pensions.						
Rundlet, Jonathan	Pension	22	1	Petition	51	Military Pensions	Dec. 29, 1831	Favorable	166	Passed	Indef. postp'd.	
Rundlet, Hannah	Continuation of pension	28	1	Petition	849	Rev. Pensions.						
Runk, Samuel	Pension for revolutionary services.	25	1	Petition	94	....	....	....	......	Laid on table.		
Runk, Samuel	Pension for revolutionary services.	25	2	Petition	84	Rev. Pensions	....	....	......	Discharged; laid on table.		
Runnells, Isaac	Pension	24	2	Petition	197	Invalid Pensions	Jan. 13, 1837	Adverse	......	Laid on table.		
Runnells, Isaac	Pension	26	2	Petition	119	Invalid Pensions.						
Runnells, Issac	Pension	27	2	Petition	47	Invalid Pensions	237	Adverse	......	Leave to withdraw.		
Runnells, James	Compensation for services by impressment.	31	2	Petition	216	Claims.						
Runnells, Thomas	Compensation for services by impressment.	31	2	Petition	216	Claims.						
Runness, Nathaniel	(See Canadian refugees.)											
Runyon, George W.	Compensation for a horse lost in public service.	30	1	Petition	147	Claims	236	Adverse	......	Laid on table.		
Rusco, Albert P.	For additional compensation for building a bridge in Florida.	21	2	Petition	88	Claims	Jan. 5, 1831	Adverse	......	Laid on table.		
Rusco, Albert P.	For additional compensation for building a bridge in Florida.	23	1	Petition	273	Claims	519	Adverse	......	Laid on table.		
Rush, Benjamin	Compensation as chargé d' affairs at London.	31	1	Petition	633	Foreign Affairs	291	Adverse	......	Laid on table.		
Rush, Jacob, widow of	Indemnity for depreciation pay, &c., due deceased as a baker in the revolutionary army.	2	1	Petition	486	....	....	....	......	Referred to Secretary of War.		
Rush, Jacob, widow of	Indemnity for depreciation pay, &c., due deceased as a baker in the revolutionary army.	2	2	Rep. of Secretary War.	735	....	....	....	......	Laid on table.		
Rush, John	Remission of balance of payment due on land purchased of United States for revolutionary services	17	2	Petition	144	Priv. Land Claims.	Jan. 29, 1823	Adverse	......	Laid on table.		
Rush, John	Grant of land for revolutionary services.	18	1	Petition	215	Priv. Land Claims.						
Rush, John	Grant of land for revolutionary services.	18	2	Petition	142	Priv. Land Claims.	Jan. 18, 1825	Adverse	......	Laid on table.		
Rush, John	Grant of land for revolutionary services.	19	1	Petition	78	Rev. Claims	Feb. 1, 1826	Adverse	......	Laid on table.		
Rush, John	Grant of land for revolutionary services.	19	2	Petition	91	Rev. Claims	Jan. 16, 1827	Adverse	......	Laid on table.		
Rush, Richard	Compensation for services rendered the United States in recovering the Smithsonian legacy.	27	2	Memorial	611	Claims	Jan. 8, 1842	Favorable	479	Ordered to 3d reading.		
Rush, Richard	Compensation for services rendered the United States in recovering the Smithsonian legacy.	27	3	House bill	89	....	....	....	479	Passed	Passed	App'd March 3, 1843
Rushing, Bryant	Permission to enter public lands	23	1	Petition	637	Public Lands.						
Rushing, Bryant	Permission to enter public lands	23	2	Petition	85	Public Lands.						
Rushton, Jeremiah	To be reimbursed money paid for public lands which had been previously entered.	30	1	Petition	288	Claims	380	Adverse	......	Laid on table.		

List of private claims presented to the House of Representatives of the United States from the 1st to the 31st Congress, inclusive—Continued.

Names of claimants.	Nature or object of the claim.	Congress.	Session.	How brought before the House of Reps.	Page of journal.	To what committee of the House referred.	No. or date of the report.	Nature of the report.	No. of the bill.	How disposed of by the House of Reps.	How disposed of by the Senate.	Date of the act of Congress, and remarks.
Rusk, James	Restoration of pension discontinued under act of May, 1820.	17	1	Petition	30	Rev. Pensions.						
Russ, Joseph, and S. J. Roach.	Payment of claim arising under contract to repair mail road in Florida.	23	1	Petition	447	Claims	529	Favorable	531	Referred to Committee Whole House.		
Russ, Joseph, and S. J. Roach.	Payment of claim arising under contract to repair mail road in Florida.	24	1	Petition	51	Claims	Dec. 21, 1835	Favorable	25	Passed	Passed	App'd Feb. 17, 1836
Russ, Joseph, and S. J. Roach.	Payment of claim arising under contract to repair mail road in Florida	25	1	Documents	205							
Russ, John P.	(See executors of Wiley Jones.)	27	2		617							
Russ, Thomas	Confirmation of title to land in Missouri.	22	1	House bill	372	Priv. Land Claims.	303	Favorable	380	Referred to Committee Whole House.		
Russell, Albert	Pension for revolutionary services.	3	1	Petition and rep't Sec. of War.	17, 93	Select.						
Russell, Albert	Pension for revolutionary services.	4	1	Petition	546	Claims	Feb. 13, 1797	Adverse		Rejected.		
Russell, Albert, and others	Indemnity for loss of Virginia land warrants and surveys of lands granted them for revolutionary services.	7	1	Petition	60	Select.						
Russell, A. W.	Payment for property lost in public service.	24	1	Petition	430	Claims.						
Russell, Captain Andrew, heirs of.	Compensation for revolutionary services.	29	1	Memorial	218	Rev. Claims.						
Russell, Captain Andrew, heirs of.	Compensation for revolutionary services.	29	2	Memorial	164	Rev. Claims.						
Russell, Captain Andrew, heirs of.	Compensation for revolutionary services.	30	1	Petition	575	Rev. Claims.						
Russell, Captain Andrew, heirs of.	Compensation for revolutionary services.	31	1	Petition	472	Rev. Claims.						
Russell, Charles, widow & administratrix of.	Payment for lands granted to deceased for revolutionary services which have been ceded to the Chickasaw Indians.	4	2	Petition	691	Claims.						
Russell, Charles, widow & administratrix of.	Payment for lands granted to deceased for revolutionary services which have been ceded to the Chickasaw Indians.	5	2	Petition	146	Claims	Jan. 23, 1798	Favorable		Referred to Committee Whole House.		
Russell, Charles, heirs of.	For grant of land, pay and emoluments, and commutation of half-pay to which deceased was entitled as a captain in the revolutionary army.	15	1	Petition	223	Pens. & Rev. Cl'ms.	Feb. 13, 1818	Adverse		Laid on table.		
Russell, Charles, heirs of.	Commutation pay due deceased as revolutionary officer.	23	1	Petition	41	Rev. Claims.						
Russell, Charles, heirs of.	Commutation pay due deceased as revolutionary officer.	24	1	Petition	104	Rev. Claims	233	Adverse		Laid on table.		
Russell, Charles H., & Co., importers of New York.	Refund additional duties paid by them for want of timely notice of passage of act of May 19, 1828.	27	2	Memorial	1003	Commerce.						
Russell, Charles H., & Co., importers of New York.	Refund additional duties paid by them for want of timely notice of passage of act of May 19, 1828.	27	3	Petition	108	Commerce	196	Adverse		Laid on table.		

List of private claims presented to the House of Representatives of the United States from the 1st to the 31st Congress, inclusive—Continued.

Names of claimants.	Nature or object of the claim.	Congress.	Session.	How brought before the House of Reps.	Page of journal.	To what committee of the House referred.	No. or date of the report.	Nature of the report.	No. of the bill.	How disposed of by the House of Reps.	How disposed of by the Senate.	Date of the act of Congress, and remarks.
Russell, Charles H., & Co., importers of New York.	Refund additional duties paid by them for want of timely notice of passage of act of May 19, 1828.	28	1	Petition	159	Commerce				Discharged; laid on table.		
Russell, Charles	Pension for services rendered during the war with Mexico.	30	2	Petition	116	Invalid Pensions.						
Russell, Cornelius, heirs of.	Commutation pay and bounty land for revolutionary services.	24	1	Resolution	540	Rev. Claims	522	Adverse		Laid on table.		
Russell, Daniel	Increase of pension	12	1	Pension bill	361	Whole House	June 15, 1812	With amend'ts	138	Passed	Passed	App'd July 5, 1812
Russell, Daniel M	Additional compensation for revolutionary services.	21	1	Petition	497	Rev. Claims				Discharged.		
Russell, David	Arrears of revolutionary pension	24	2	Petition	44	Rev. Pensions				Discharged; laid on table.		
Russell, David B	(See Josiah Blackman)	29	1		624							
Russell, Edmund, daughter of.	Pension for naval services during revolutionary war.	26	1	Petition	713	Naval Affairs.						
Russell, Elizabeth	(See sister and heir of James Mugford.)	28	1		516							
Russell, Elmore	Compensation for revolutionary services.	22	1	Petition	55	Rev. Claims				Discharged.		
Russell, Esther	(See Dr. Philip Russell, widow of.)	29	1		198							
Russell, George B., and others.	Compensation for advances to Cherokee Indians.	28	2	Petition	136	Indian Affairs	70	Favorable	553	Passed.		
Russell, George B., and others.	Compensation for advances to Cherokee Indians.	29	1	Memorial	87	Indian Affairs	589	Favorable	415	Referred to Committee Whole House.		
Russell, George B., and others.	Compensation for advances to Cherokee Indians.	29	2	House bill	210				415	Passed	Passed	App'd March 3, 1847
Russell, Gilbert C	Reimbursement of advances on public account.	9	1	Senate bill	362	Whole House	April 12, 1806	With't amend.	S. 29	Passed	Passed	App'd April 15, 1806
Russell, Gilbert C	Indemnity for property taken for public use.	18	2	Petition	42	Claims	62	Favorable	324	Passed	Passed	App'd March 3, 1825
Russell, Gilbert C	For amendment to act for his relief.	19	1	Petition	294	Claims	149	Favorable	197	Passed	Passed	App'd May 20, 1826
Russell, Gilbert C	Indemnity for breach of contract, and for property seized by the government of United States.	31	1	Petition	255	Claims.						
Russell, Col. Giles, representatives of.	Bounty land for revolutionary services.	22	1	Petition	133	Rev. Claims.						
Russell, Col. Giles, representatives of.	Bounty land for revolutionary services.	22	2	Petition	29	Rev. Claims	Jan. 7, 1833	Adverse		Laid on table.		
Russell, Col. Giles, representatives of.	Bounty land for revolutionary services.	23	1	Petition	54	Rev. Claims.						
Russell, H. W	Indemnity for advances on public account.	24	2	Petition	68	Claims	87	Favorable	830	Referred to Committee Whole House.		
Russell, H. W	Indemnity for advances on public account.	25	2	Resolution	37	Claims	61	Favorable	73	Passed	Passed	App'd April 20, 1838
Russell, James	Pension	13	1	Pension bill	56	Whole House	July 20, 1813	With amends	31	Passed	Passed	App'd Aug. 2, 1813
Russell, James, (Ark.)	Compensation for lands ceded to Cherokee Indians.	20	1	Petition	343	Priv. Land Claims.	206	Favorable	238	Referred to Committee Whole House.		
Russell, James, (Mo.)	Confirmation of title to land	31	1	Petition	235	Priv. Land Claims.						
Russell, Jeremiah	(See Seth Nickerson and others)	14	1		558							
Russell, John	Pension for services as a United States marine.	16	1	Petition	27	Naval Affairs	Jan. 27, 1820	Adverse		Laid on table.		

List of private claims presented to the House of Representatives of the United States from the 1st to the 31st Congress, inclusive—Continued.

Names of claimants.	Nature or object of the claim.	Congress.	Session.	How brought before the House of Reps.	Page of journal.	To what committee of the House referred.	No. or date of the report.	Nature of the report.	No. of the bill.	How disposed of by the House of Reps.	How disposed of by the Senate.	Date of the act of Congress, and remarks.
Russell, John, (Penn.)	Pension	21	1	Petition	120	Military Pensions	Mar. 3, 1830	Adverse		Laid on table.		
Russell, John, (Penn.)	Pension	21	2	Petition	44	Military Pensions.						
Russell, John, (N. Y.)	Arrears of pension	22	1	Petition	287	Rev. Pensions				Discharged.		
Russell, John	Increase of pension	23	1	Petition	216	Invalid Pensions	Jan. 20, 1834	Adverse		Laid on table.		
Russell, John	Pension	31	1	Petition	307	Invalid Pensions.						
Russell, John, (Tenn.)	Pension	23	2	Petition	58	Invalid Pensions	Dec. 22, 1834	Adverse		Laid on table.		
Russell, John, (Tenn.)	Increase of pension	26	1	Petition	326	Invalid Pensions				Discharged; laid on table.		
Russell, John, (N. Y.)	Pension for wounds and disabilities in war of 1812.	29	2	Petition	164	Invalid Pensions.						
Russell, John, (Md.)	Pension for wounds and disabilities in Mexican war.	31	2	Petition	112	Invalid Pensions				Leave to withdraw.		
Russell, John	(See John Barr, guardian of)	26	1		182		343		319			
Russell, John H	Bounty on fishing schooner Lucy Ann.	25	3	Petition	214	Commerce	233	Adverse		Laid on table.		
Russell, John H	Bounty on fishing schooner Lucy Ann.	26	1	Petition	290	Commerce	385	Adverse		Laid on table.		
Russell, John H	Bounty on fishing schooner Lucy Ann.	26	2	Petition	60	Judiciary.						
Russell, John H	Bounty on fishing schooner Lucy Ann.	27	2	Petition	95	Commerce	1019	Favorable	592	Referred to Committee Whole House.		
Russell, John H	Bounty on fishing schooner Lucy Ann.	27	3	Bill of last sess.	91	Whole House	Dec. 23, 1842	With't amend.	592	Passed	Indef. postp'd.	
Russell, John H	Bounty on fishing schooner Lucy Ann.	28	1	Petition	361	Commerce	385	Favorable	283	Passed.		
Russell, John H	Bounty on fishing schooner Lucy Ann.	28	2	Petition	176	Commerce.						
Russell, John H	Bounty on fishing schooner Lucy Ann.	29	1	Petition	177	Commerce	263	Favorable	225	Referred to Committee Whole House.		
Russell, John H	Bounty on fishing schooner Lucy Ann.	30	1	Petition	157	Commerce.						
Russell, John H	Bounty on fishing schooner Lucy Ann.	30	2	Petition	203	Commerce.						
Russell, John H	Bounty on fishing schooner Lucy Ann.	31	1	Petition	451	Commerce.						
Russell, John Miller	Reimbursement of duty paid on hemp.	1	3	Petition	340					Referred to Secretary Treasury.		
Russell, John Miller	Reimbursement of duty paid on hemp.	3	2	Rep. of Secretary Treasury.	284					Laid on table.		
Russell, John W., administrator of.	Indemnity for French spoliations prior to 1800.	31	1	Petition	197	Foreign Affairs	355	Favorable	318	Referred to Committee Whole House.		
Russell, Joseph	(See Thomas Russell, and others.)	3	1		67							
Russell, Joshua	Land patent improperly withheld	16	1	Petition	24	Priv. Land Claims.				Leave to withdraw.		
Russell, Joshua	Patent for land on completing payment.	17	1	Petition	101	Priv. Land Claims.						
Russell, Joshua	Confirmation of title to land in Ohio.	17	2	Senate bill	117	Priv. Land Claims.	Jan. 17, 1823	With t amend.	S. 23	Passed	Passed	App'd March 1, 1823
Russell, Joshua	Pension for services, war of 1812.	30	1	Petition	619	Invalid Pensions				Discharged; laid on table.		
Russell, Mary F	(See Edmund Russell, daughter of.)	26	1		713							
Russell, Nathaniel	(See assignees of Robert Hazelhurst.)	11	3		559							

List of private claims presented to the House of Representatives of the United States from the 1st to the 31st Congress, inclusive—Continued.

Names of claimants.	Nature or object of the claim.	Congress.	Session.	How brought before the House of Reps.	Page of journal.	To what committee of the House referred.	No. or date of the report.	Nature of the report.	No. of the bill.	How disposed of by the House of Reps.	How disposed of by the Senate.	Date of the act of Congress, and remarks.
Russell, Oliver	Invalid pension	12	1	Pension bill	361	Whole House	June 15, 1812	With amend.	138	Passed	Passed	App'd July 5, 1812
Russell, Paul, widow of	Continuation of pension	28	2	Petition	356	Rev. Pensions.						
Russell, Dr. Philip M., widow of.	Increase of pension for revolutionary services.	29	1	Petition	198	Rev. Pensions	826	Adverse	......	Laid on table.		
Russell, Dr. Philip M., widow of.	Increase of pension for revolutionary services.	29	2	Petition	74	Rev. Pensions.						
Russell, Dr. Philip M., widow of.	Increase of pension for revolutionary services.	30	1	Petition	198	Rev. Pensions	112	Favorable	101	Passed	Passed, second session.	App'd Jan. 8, 1849
Russell, Robert	Pension for revolutionary services.	22	1	Petition	287	Rev. Pensions	....	....	......	Discharged.		
Russell, Samuel	Compensation for services as commissary, war of 1812.	15	1	Petition	166	Military Affairs	....	....	......	Discharged; leave to withdraw.		
Russell, Samuel	Compensation for services as commissary, war of 1812.	18	2	Senate bill	181	Claims	Feb. 25, 1825	With amend.	S. 32	Passed	Passed	App'd March 3, 1825
Russell, Samuel, administrator of.	Additional compensation for services as commissary, war of 1812.	25	3	Petition	516	Claims.						
Russell, Samuel, administrator of.	Additional compensation for services as commissary, war of 1812.	26	1	Petition	168	Claims.						
Russell, Samuel, administrator of.	Additional compensation for services as commissary, war of 1812.	26	2	Petition	38	Claims.						
Russell, Samuel, administrator of.	Additional compensation for services as commissary, war of 1812.	27	2	Petition	94	Claims	331	Adverse	......	Laid on table.		
Russell, Samuel, administrator of.	Additional compensation for services as commissary, war of 1812.	27	3	Petition	43	Claims	55	Adverse	......	Laid on table.		
Russell, Samuel, (Va.)	To be restored to pension roll	17	1	Petition	30	Rev. Pensions.						
Russell, Samuel	Confirmation of title to land	27	2	Resolution	400	Indian Affairs.						
Russell, Samuel, and John Parsons.	Additional compensation as land officers.	28	1	Petition	840	Public Lands.						
Russell, Samuel P.	(See representatives of Samuel Davenport.)	21	1	....	297							
Russell, Seth	Indemnity for French spoliations prior to 1800.	26	1	Memorial	182	Foreign Affairs	343	Favorable	319	Referred to Committee Whole House.		
Russell, Seth, & Sons	Remission of duty on fish oil	12	1	Petition	351	Com. and Manuf.						
Russell, Seth, & Sons	Remission of duty on fish oil	12	2	Petition	564	Com. and Manuf.						
Russell, Seth, & Sons	Remission of duty on fish oil	13	2	Petition	296	Com. and Manuf.	Mar. 11, 1814	Favorable	160	Passed	Passed	App'd April 9, 1814
Russell, Seth, & Sons	Indemnity for French spoliations prior to 1800.	26	1	Memorial	182	Foreign Affairs	343	Favorable	319	Referred to Committee Whole House.		
Russell, Solomon	Bounty land for revolutionary services.	27	2	Petition	48	Public Lands	511	Adverse	......	Laid on table.		
Russell, Solomon	Bounty land for revolutionary services.	28	2	Petition	140	Public Lands.						
Russell, Solomon	Bounty land for revolutionary services.	29	1	Petition	193	Priv. Land Claims.	317	Favorable	254	Passed	Passed	App'd Aug. 8, 1846
Russell, Susannah	(See widow and administratrix of Charles Russell.)	4	2	....	691							
Russell, Thomas	Compensation for revolutionary services.	12	2	Petition	623	Claims.						
Russell, Thomas, & others.	For the balance due on sundry bills of credit.	3	1	Memorial	67	....	....	....	......	Referred to Secretary Treasury.		
Russell, Thomas, & others	For the balance due on sundry bills of credit.	3	2	Rep. of Secretary Treasury.	312	....	....	....	......	Laid on table.		
Russell, Thomas, & others.	For the balance due on sundry bills of credit.	4	1	Rep. of Secretary Treasury.	388	Claims	74	Adverse	......	Laid on table.		

List of private claims presented to the House of Representatives of the United States from the 1st to the 31st Congress, inclusive—Continued.

Names of claimants.	Nature or object of the claim.	Congress.	Session.	How brought before the House of Reps.	Page of journal.	To what committee of the House referred.	No. or date of the report.	Nature of the report.	No. of the bill.	How disposed of by the House of Reps.	How disposed of by the Senate.	Date of the act of Congress, and remarks.
Russell, Thomas A	Compensation for property taken for public use.	27	2	Petition	76	Claims	31	Adverse		Laid on table.		
Russell, Thomas A	Compensation for property taken for public use.	27	3	Petition	113	Claims.						
Russell, Thomas A	Compensation for property taken for public use.	28	1	Petition	122	Claims.						
Russell, Thomas T., and W. H. Simmons.	Additional compensation as land officers for locating military land warrants.	31	1	Petition	448	Public Lands.						
Russell, William	(See John Eli Tholozan)	23	1		845							
Russell, William	Increase of pension	23	1	Petition	333	Invalid Pensions.						
Russell, William, (N. Y.)	Compensation for property taken and supplies furnished for public use, war of 1812.	23	1	Petition	437	Claims.						
Russell, William, (N. Y.)	Compensation for property taken and supplies furnished for public use, war of 1812.	23	2	Petition	199	Claims.						
Russell, William, (N. Y.)	Compensation for property taken and supplies furnished for public use, war of 1812.	24	1	Res. and docs	174	Claims	794	Adverse		Laid on table.		
Russell, William	Bounty on fishing schooner Perch.	27	3	Petition	69	Commerce.						
Russell, William, & others.	Bounty on fishing schooner Perch	27	3	Senate bill	276	Commerce	Feb. 14, 1843	With't amend.	S. 74	Ref'd to Com. W. H.		
Russell, William, & others.	Bounty on fishing schooner Perch.	28	2	Senate bill	156	Commerce	Jan. 28, 1845	With't amend.	S. 25	Ref'd to Com. W. H.		
Russell, William H	Reimbursem't of moneys disbursed by him as late marshal of Missouri.	30	1	Petition	589	Claims	678	Adverse		Laid on table.		
Russell, William H	Reimbursem't of moneys disbursed by him as late marshal of Missouri.	30	2	Petition	127	Claims.						
Russell, William O	Compensation for services and reimbursement of expenses incurred in arresting pirates.	28	1	Petition	596	Claims.						
Russell, William W	Drawback on Spanish playing cards.	19	1	Petition	93	Ways and Means	April 12, 1826	Favorable	211	Passed.		
Russell, William W	Drawback on Spanish playing cards.	19	2	Senate bill	81	Ways and Means	Dec. 27, 1826	With't amend.	S. 113	Passed	Passed	App'd March 2, 1827
Russum, Joseph	(See sureties of Algernon S. Stanford)	17	1		334							
Russum, William	(See sureties of Algernon S. Stanford.)	16	1		182							
Russwurm, Lieut. William, heirs of.	Commutation pay for revolutionary services.	25	2	Senate bill	496	Rev. Claims	May 15, 1838	With amends.	S. 116	Passed	Passed	App'd June 12, 1838
Rust, George, and others	Increase of compensation as officers at the armory at Harper's Ferry.	22	2	Petition	138	Military Affairs.						
Rust, George, and others	Increase of compensation as officers at the armory at Harper's Ferry.	24	1	Petition	200	Military Affairs.						
Rust, Sally	(See heirs of James Liblee)	8	2		30							
Rutledge, Edward	(See heirs and widow of Edward Preble and others)	23	1		36							
Rutledge, Joshua	Payment of a lost loan office certificate.	15	2	Petition	253	Pens. & Rev. Cl'ms.				Discharged.		
Rutledge, Joshua	Payment of a lost loan office certificate.	16	1	Petition	102	Pens. & Rev. Cl'ms.	60	Adverse		Laid on table.		
Rutledge, Pleasant	(See Wm. H. Bedford, agent, &c.)	28	1		262							

List of private claims presented to the House of Representativesthe of United States from the 1st to the 31st Congress, inclusive—Continued.

Names of claimants.	Nature or object of the claim.	Congress.	Session.	How brought before the House of Reps.	Page of journal.	To what committee of the House referred.	No. or date of the report.	Nature of the report.	No. of the bill.	How disposed of by the House of Reps.	How disposed of by the Senate.	Date of the act of Congress, and remarks.
Rutledge, Thomas, administrator of.	Compensation for services as commissary in revolutionary war.	3	3	Memorial	332	....	....	....	......	Referred to Secretary Treasury.		
Rutledge, Thomas, administrator of.	Payment of a lost loan office certificate.	25	2	Memorial	699	Rev. Claims	946	Favorable	824	Referred to Committee Whole House.		
Rutledge, Thomas, administrator of.	Payment of a lost loan office certificate.	25	3	House bill	432	Whole House	....	....	824			
Rutledge, Thomas, administrator of.	Payment of a lost loan office certificate.	26	1	Petition	165	Rev. Claims.						
Rutledge, Thomas, administrator of.	Payment of a lost loan office certificate.	26	2	Petition	76	Rev. Claims	177	Adverse	......	Laid on table.		
Rutledge, William, administrator of.	Arrears of revolutionary pay	3	2	Memorial	313	Claims.						
Rutledge, William, administrator of.	Arrears of revolutionary pay	4	1	Resolution	373	Claims	Jan. 26, 1796	Adverse	......	Leave to withdraw.		
Rutten, Edmund	Right of pre-emption to land	24	1	Petition	852	Public Lands.						
Rutter & Etting	Indemnity for French spoliations prior to 1800.	26	1	Memorial	182	Foreign Affairs	343	Favorable; bill	319	Referred to Committee Whole House.		
Rutter & Etting	Indemnity for French spoliations prior to 1800.	30	1	Memorial	79	Foreign Affairs	Jan. 4, 1848	General bill	21	Referred to Committee Whole House.		
Rutter, Thomas	Release from the repayment of money paid a purser in United States navy, having lost his vouchers.	14	1	Petition	98	Claims.						
Rutter, Thomas, heirs of	Indemnity for French spoliations prior to 1800.	29	2	Memorial	58	Foreign Affairs.						
Rutter, Thomas, heirs of	Indemnity for French spoliations prior to 1800.	31	1	Petition	416	Foreign Affairs	355	General bill	318	Referred to Committee Whole House.		
Rutan, Paul	Pension for revolutionary services.	23	1	Resolution	618	Rev. Pensions.						
Rutan, Peter	Arrears and depreciation of revolutionary pay.	3	1	Petition	88	Select	Mar. 31, 1794	Adverse	......	Laid on table.		
Rutan, Peter	Arrears and depreciation of revolutionary pay.	3	2	Petition and rep't	313	Claims.						
Rutan, Peter	Arrears and depreciation of revolutionary pay.	4	1	Resolution	373	Claims	Jan. 6, 1796	Adverse	......	Leave to withdraw.		
Ruter, Alanson	Compensation for services by impressment at New Orleans.	31	2	Petition	216	Claims.						
Ruter, Calvin W	Compensation for services by impressment at New Orleans.	31	2	Petition	216	Claims.						
Rutgers, Arend	(See assignee of William Dunn.)	15	1	....	133							
Rutgers, N. G	Indemnity for French spoliations prior to 1800.	26	1	Memorial	182	Foreign Affairs	343	Favorable; bill	319	Referred to Committee Whole House.		
Rutgers, Henry, and others.	Release as surety of John Lamb.	6	2	Petition	783	Select.						
Rutgers, Henry, and others.	Release as surety of John Lamb.	7	1	Petition	132	Claims.						
Rutherford, Griffith	Compensation for horses and equipments lost in Seminole war.	23	1	Documents	154	Claims.						
Rutherford, Griffith	(See Wm. H. Bedford, agent, &c.)	28	1	....	262							
Rutherford, John, attorney of.	Permission to bring slaves from Bahama to the United States.	12	1	Petition	167	Select	Feb. 17, 1812	Favorable	71	Rejected.		
Rutherford, Larkin, heirs of.	Bounty land and pay for revolutionary services.	26	1	Petition	359	Rev. Claims.						
Rutherford, Robert	Pension	31	1	Petition	424	Invalid Pensions.						
Ryall, David	Reimbursement of money paid for public land.	17	1	Petition	93	Public Lands	....	....	......	Discharged.		

List of private claims presented to the House of Representatives of the United States from the 1st to the 31st Congress, inclusive—Continued.

Names of claimants.	Nature or object of the claim.	Congress.	Session.	How brought before the House of Reps.	Page of journal.	To what committee of the House referred.	No. or date of the report.	Nature of the report.	No. of the bill.	How disposed of by the House of Reps.	How disposed of by the Senate.	Date of the act of Congress, and remarks.
Ryall, David	Reimbursement of money paid for public land.	18	1	Petition	135	Public Lands				Discharged.		
Ryan, Francis, widow of	Pension for revolutionary services.	26	1	Petition	282	Rev. Pensions.						
Ryan, Francis, widow of	Pension for revolutionary services.	26	2	Petition	78	Rev. Pensions	135	Favorable	643	Referred to Committee Whole House.		
Ryan, James J	Reimbursement of expenses incurred in raising and equiping a company of volunteers, war of 1812.	14	2	Petition	279	Military Affairs				Discharged.		
Ryan, Jeremiah	Compensation for revolutionary losses and injuries.	1	2	Petition	142	Select	July 16, 1790	Favorable	18	Passed	Passed	App'd Aug. 11, 1790
Ryan, Jeremiah	Increase of pension	15	1	Petition	199	Pens. & Rev. Cl'ms.				Discharged.		
Ryan, John, assignee of	Compensation for military services.	9	1	Petition	192	Claims.						
Ryan, John, assignee of	Compensation for military services.	10	2	Petition	459	Claims.						
Ryan, John, assignee of	Compensation for military services	11	2	Petition	127	Claims.						
Ryan, John, assignee of	Compensation for military services	12	1	Petition	39	Claims.						
Ryan, John, assignee of	Compensation for military seevice	14	1	Petition	146	Pens. & Rev. Cl'ms.						
Ryan, John, assignee of	Compensation for military services.	16	1	Petition	139	Pens. & Rev. Cl'ms.	Jan. 21, 1820	Adverse		Laid on table.		
Ryan, John, assignee of	Compensation for military services.	9	2	Petition	158	Rev. Claims				Discharged.		
Ryan, John, assignee of	Compensation for military services.	20	1	Petition	126	Rev. Claims	Feb. 8, 1828	Adverse		Laid on table.		
Ryan, John, assignee of	Compensation for military services	21	2	Petition	74	Rev. Claims.						
Ryan, John, assignee of	Compensation for military services.	22	1	Petition	190	Rev. Claims	Jan. 28, 1832	Adverse		Laid on table.		
Ryan, John, assignee of	Compensation for military services.	22	2	Petition	137	Rev. Claims	Jan. 11, 1833	Adverse		Laid on table.		
Ryan, Lawrence	(See Lieut. William Scott, heirs of.)	24	1		106							
Ryan, Samuel	Compensation for services at the Indian agency Green Bay.	26	2	Petition	52	Claims.						
Ryan, William	Additional compensation for services, United States navy.	22	2	Petition	313	Naval Affairs.						
Ryan, William	Additional compensation for services, United States navy.	23	1	Petition	386	Claims	520	Adverse.		Laid on table.		
Ryan, William	Additional compensation for services, United States navy.	24	1	Petition	674	Claims	June 15, 1836	Adverse		Laid on table.		
Ryan, William	Additional comdensation for services, United States navy.	26	2	Petition	162	Naval Affairs.						
Rybecker, John	Increase of pension	10	1	Pension bill	232	Whole House	April 19, 1808	With amends.	78	Passed	Passed	App'd April 25, 1808
Ryburn, James	Pension for revolutionary services.	19	1	Resolution	338	Military Pensions	164	Adverse		Laid on table.		
Ryder, Richard G	Right of pre-emption	18	2	Petition	137	Public Lands.						
Ryder, Richard G	Right of pre-emption	19	1	Petition	45	Priv. Land Claims.	Dec. 20, 1825	Adverse		Laid on table.		
Ryder, Samuel	Bounty on fishing schooner Union	30	1	House bill	465	Commerce	259	Favorable	252	Referred to Committee Whole House.		
Ryder, Stephen	Bounty on fishing schooner Friendship.	10	2	Petition and rep't Sec. Treasury	524, 530					Laid on table.		
Ryder, Stephen	Bounty on fishing schooner Friendship.	11	2	Petition and rep't Sec. Treasury.	198	Com. and Manuf.						
Ryder, Stephen	Bounty on fishing schooner Friendship.	11	3	Petition and rep't Sec. Treasury	459	Com. and Manuf.						
Ryer, John M	Reimbursement of expenses incurred in fitting out private armed vessel in war of 1812.	14	2	Petition	242	Naval Affairs	Feb. 5, 1817	Adverse		Laid on table.		
Ryker, Philip	Indemnity for property destroyed by enemy in war of 1812.	24	2	Petition	208	Claims	March 1, 1837	Adverse		Laid on table.		

3—33

List of private claims presented to the House of Representatives of the United States form the 1st to the 31st Congress, inclusive—Continued.

Names of claimants.	Nature or object of the claim.	Congress.	Session.	How brought before the House of Reps.	Page of journal.	To what committee of the House referred.	No. or date of the report.	Nature of the report.	No. of the bill.	How disposed of by the House of Reps.	How disposed of by the Senate.	Date of the act of Congress, and remarks.
Ryker, Philip	Indemnity for property destroyed by enemy in war of 1812.	26	1	Petition	337	Claims.						
Ryland, Edwin M.	(See Thomas Talbot and others)	20	1		312							
Ryneason, Isaac	Arrears of pension	22	2	Petition	245	Rev. Pensions				Discharged; laid on table.		
Ryneason, Minny	Pension	13	3	Pension bill	740	Whole House	March 1, 1815	With amend'ts	303	Passed	Passed	App'd March 3, 1815
Ryneason, Minny	Continuation of pension	20	1	Petition	310	Military Pensions				Discharged.		
Ryneason, Minny	Continuation of pension	20	2	Petition	55	Military Pensions	Dec. 12, 1828	By bill	311	Passed	Laid on table.	
Ryneason, Minny	Continuation of pension	21	1	Petition	48	Military Pensions	Jan. 5, 1830	By bill	72	Passed	Passed	App'd May 20, 1830
Rynsel, Valentine	Pension for revolutionary services.	21	1	Resolution	536	Military Pensions				Discharged; laid on table.		
Rynsel, Valentine	Pension for revolutionary services.	21	2	Resolution	48	Military Pensions				Discharged; laid on table.		
Rynsel, Valentine	Pension for revolutionary services.	22	1	Petition	45	Rev. Pensions.						
Sabate, Pablo	(See F. M. Arredondo, *et al*)	19	1		252							
Sabin, Elihu	Pension	3	1	Rep. of Secretary War.	131	Select	May 26, 1794	Res. to refer to Sec. of War.	J. R. 12	Passed	Passed	App'd June 9, 1794
Sabin, Elihu	Pension	3	2	Rep. of Secretary War.	262	Claims	Feb. 28, 1795	Favorable	130	Passed	Postponed.	
Sabin, Elihu	Pension	4	1	Rep. of Secretary War.	445	Claims	Feb. 18, 1796	Favorable	156	Passed	Passed	App'd April 20, 1796
Sabin, Elihu	Increase of pension	11	2	Pension bill	283	Whole House	April 9, 1810	With amend.	107	Passed	Passed, with amendment.	App'd April 27, 1810
Sabin, Eliphalet Y.	Remission of duty on damaged iron.	23	1	Petition	380	Ways and Means				Discharged; laid on table.		
Sabin, Flavil	Equitable settlement of his accounts.	14	2	Senate bill	291	Claims	Feb. 3, 1817	With't amend.	S. 17	Passed	Passed	App'd March 3, 1817
Sabin, Lemuel D.	Arrears of pension	30	1	Petition	65	Invalid Pensions.						
Sabin, Timothy	Pension for revolutionary services.	22	1	Petition	412	Rev. Pensions.						
Sabin, Timothy	Pension for revolutionary services.	23	2	Petition	66	Rev. Pensions				Discharged; laid on table.		
Sabina, Spanish ship	Reimbursement of expenses in supporting shipwrecked American seamen.	27	2	President's mess.	734	Foreign Affairs						See Ex. Doc. No. 191
Sackett, Augustus	Indemnity for destruction of property at Buffalo.	17	1	Petition	110	Claims	Mar. 6, 1822	Adverse		Laid on table.		Leave to withdraw.
Sackett, Augustus	Indemnity for destruction of property at Buffalo.	18	1	Petition	158	Claims	Feb. 27, 1824	Adverse		Laid on table.		
Sackett, Augustus	Indemnity for destruction of property at Buffalo.	24	1	Petition	140	Claims	Jan. 19, 1836	Adverse		Laid on table.		
Saddler, Benjamin	Compensation for revolutionary sufferings and disability.	9	2	Petition	473	Claims	Dec. 18, 1806	Adverse		Laid on table.		
Saddler, Benjamin	Pension	10	1	Pension bill	232	Whole House	April 19, 1808	With amend.	78	Passed.	Passed, with amendment.	App'd April 25, 1808

List of private claims presented to the House of Representatives of the United States from the 1st to the 31st Congress, inclusive—Continued.

Names of claimants.	Nature or object of the claim.	Congress.	Session.	How brought before the House of Reps.	Page of journal.	To what committee of the House referred.	No. or date of the report.	Nature of the report.	No. of the bill.	How disposed of by the House of Reps.	How disposed of by the Senate.	Date of the act of Congress, and remarks.
Saddler, Christopher	Remission of the forfeiture of vessel and cargo.	1	2	Petition and rep't Sec. Treasury.	137, 143	Select	Jan. 26, 1790	Favorable; bill ordered.	57	Passed	Passed	App'd May 26, 1790
Saddler, Emory, and wife	(See representatives of William Wright.)	4	1	....	503							
Saddler, Henry, & Co	Indemnity for French spoliations prior to 1800.	26	1	Memorial	182	Foreign Affairs	343	Favorable; bill	319	Referred to Committee Whole House.		
Saddler, John, widow of	Pension for revolutionary services.	27	3	Petition	77	Rev. Pensions	....	....	......	Discharged; leave to withdraw.		
Saddler, Matthias	Compensation for revolutionary services.	2	1	Petition	451	....	....	....	......	Referred to Secretary War.		
Saddler, Matthias	Compensation for revolutionary services.	3	2	Rep. of Secretary War.	278	....	....	....	......	Laid on table.		
Saddler, Thomas S., administrator of.	Renewal of a lost revolutionary certificate.	2	1	Petition	573	....	....	....	......	Referred to Secretary Treasury.		
Saddler, Warren	Indemnity for destruction of property by the enemy.	15	2	Petition	148	Claims	Jan. 16, 1819	Adverse	......	Laid on table.		
Safford, David	Pension for revolutionary services.	24	2	Petition	102	Rev. Pensions	....	....	......	Discharged; laid on table.		
Safford, Edwin, and Archibald Hay.	Release from excise bonds	14	2	Petition	84	Ways and Means	Jan. 25, 1817	General bill	72	Passed	Passed	App'd March 3, 1817
Safford, Gideon	Pension for revolutionary services.	24	2	Documents	102	Rev. Pensions	....	....	......	Discharged; laid on table.		
Safford, John, and others	Bounty on fishing shooner Volney.	31	1	Petition	863	Commerce.						
Safford, Joseph, heirs of	Duplicate land warrant	25	2	House bill	317	Whole House	....	....	478			
Safford, Joseph, heirs of	Duplicate land warrant	25	3	Bill of last sess.	375	Whole House	Jan. 25, 1839	With't amend.	478	Passed	Passed	App'd March 3, 1839
Safford, Samuel, and others.	Settlement of accounts as agent for Warner's regiment.	2	2	Memorial	706	....	....	....	......	Referred to Secretary War.		
Rofford, Samuel, and others.	Settlement of accounts as agent for Warner's regiment.	3	1	Rep. of Secretary War.	93	Select	April 22, 1794	Adverse	......	Laid on table.		
Sagathey, Jacob	Invalid pension	30	2	Petition	239	Invalid Pensions	....	....	......	Discharged; laid on table.		
Sagathey, Jacob	Invalid pension	31	1	Petition	193, 432	Invalid Pensions.						
Sage, David	Pension	29	1	Petition	74	Invalid Pensions	....	....	......	Discharged; laid on table.		
Sage, Nathan, representatives of.	Share of judgment for breach of revenue laws.	25	2	Petition	165	Commerce	374	Favorable	397	Referred to Committee Whole House.		
Sage, Nathan, representatives of.	Share of judgment for breach of revenue laws.	25	3	Bill of last sess.	378	Whole House	Jan. 25, 1839	With't amend.	397	Passed	Passed	App'd March 2, 1839
Sage, Robert	Reimbursement of the value of merchandize improperly seized for breach of revenue laws.	4	2	Petition	668	Com. and Manuf.	Feb. 6, 1797	Adverse	......	Rejected.		
Sailly, Peter	Indemnity for destruction of property at Plattsburgh.	14	1	Petition	64	Claims.						
Sailly, Peter	Indemnity for destruction of property at Plattsburgh.	15	1	Petition	207	Claims.						
Sailly, Peter, and others	Indemnity for destruction of property at Plattsburgh.	17	1	Petition	92	Claims.						
Sailor, Elizabeth	(See Jacob Sailor, widow of.)											
Sailor, Jacob, widow of, (Pa.)	Pension for revolutionary services.	29	1	Petition	310	Rev. Claims	....	....	......	Discharged; laid on table.		

List of private claims presented to the House of Representatives of the United States from the 1st to the 31st Congress, inclusive—Continued.

Names of claimants.	Nature or object of the claim.	Congress.	Session.	How brought before the House of Reps.	Page of journal.	To what committee of the House referred.	No. or date of the report.	Nature of the report.	No. of the bill.	How disposed of by the House of Reps.	How disposed of by the Senate.	Date of the act of Congress, and remarks.
Sailor, Jacob, (Ohio.)….	Pension for services in the war of 1812.	31	2	Petition …….	143	Invalid Pensions.						
Sailor, Thomas, and others.	Compensation for improvement on public lands.	27	2	Petition …….	132	Public Lands…..	513	Adverse …….	……	Laid on table.		
Sains, John …………	Pension ………………..	21	1	Petition …….	36	Military Pensions.						
Salady, John and George .	Compensation for a deficit in land purchased.	17	2	Petition …….	209	Public Lands.						
Salady, John and George .	Compensation for a deficit in land purchased.	18	1	Petition …….	66	Public Lands…..	Jan. 7, 1824	Adverse …….	……	Laid on table.		
Salady, John and George .	Compensation for a deficit in land purchased.	21	1	Petition …….	123	Public Lands…..	Jan. 19, 1830	Adverse …….	……	Laid on table.		
Salady, John and George .	Compensation for a deficit in land purchased.	24	2	Petition …….	146	Public Lands…..	…………	…………	……	Discharged; laid on table.		
Sale, John B……….	(See William Tee, and others)…	22	1	…………..	61							
Salem Marine Insurance Company.	(See merchants and citizens of Massachusetts.)	26	1	…………..	182							
Salger, Jacob ……….	(See J. G. Wacksmith, executor of.)	26	1	…………..	182							
Salisbury, Simon, widow of.	Pension for military services …..	19	2	Petition …….	26	Miiltary Pensions.						
Salisbury, Simon, widow of.	Pension for military services…..	20	1	Petition …….	163	Military Pensions..	Feb. 19, 1828	Adverse …….	……	Laid on table		
Salisbury, Thomas…….	Pension ………………..	19	2	Petition …….	36	Military Pensions.						
Salisbury, Thomas…….	Pension ………………..	20	1	Petition …….	163	Military Pensions.						
Salisbury, Thomas…….	Pension ………………..	20	2	Pension bill ….	55	Whole House ….	Jan. 15, 1829	With't amend.	311	Passed …………	Laid on table.	
Salisbury, Thomas…….	Pension ………………..	21	1	Resolution …..	4	Military Pensions..	Jan. 5, 1830	Pension bill..	72	Passed …………	Passed ……	App'd May 20, 1830
Salisbury, Thomas…….	Increase of pension …………	21	1	Petition …….	68	Military Pensions..	April 6, 1830	Adverse …….	……	Laid on table.		
Sally, brig, owners of….	Compensation for taking her for	21	1	House bill …..	248	Whole House…..	April 30, 1830	With't amend.	191	Passed …………	Passed ……	App'd May 29, 1830
Salmon, George, executor of.	Indemnity for French spoliations prior to 1800.	26	1	Memorial ……	182	Foreign Affairs….	343	Favorable….	319	Referred to Committee Whole House.		
Salmon, Joseph………	Compensation for services in Indian war.	3	1	Petition …….	54	Select ……….	Feb. 19, 1794	Favorable….	……	Laid on table.		
Salmon, William H …..	(See John Thompson and wife) ..	19	1	…………..	206							
Salmon, William H …..	Indemnity for loss of a certain tract of land.	31	1	Petition …….	880	Priv. Land Claims.						
Salmonds, Joseph …….	Pension ………………..	25	2	Petition …….	236	Invalid Pensions ..	460	Favorable….	463	Passed …………	Passed ……	App'd July 7, 1838
Salno, Mateo……….	Indemnity for property destroyed by United States troops.	19	1	Memorial ……	252	Foreign Relations..	112	Adverse …….	……	Laid on table.		
Salno, Mateo……….	Indemnity for property destroyed by United States troops.	20	2	Petition …….	339	Foreign Affairs….	99	Favorabie ….	385	Referred to Committee Whole House.		
Salno, Moteo……….	Indemnity for property destroyed by United States troops.	23	1	Petition …….	67	Foreign Affairs….	368	Favorable ….	395	Passed …………	Psssed ……	App'd June 26, 1834
Salomon, Haym M., heirs of.	Reimbursement of advances on public account.	29	1	Petition …….	171	Rev. Claims……	…………	…………	……	Discharged; laid on table.		
Salomon, Haym M., heirs of.	Reimbursement of advances on public account.	30	1	Petition …….	110	Rev. Claims……	504	Favorable ….	425	Referred to Committee Whole House.		
Salomon, Haym M., heirs of.	Reimbursement of advances on public account.	31	1	Petition …….	500	Rev. Claims……	…………	…………	……	…………	…………	Leave to withdraw 2d session.
Salomon, Lewis……..	(See executors of Peter Benani) . public use.	18	1	…………..	70							
Saltmarsh & Avery …..	(See Avery, Saltmarsh, & Co.)..	24	2	…………..	85							

List of private claims presented to the House of Representatives of the United States from the 1st to the 31st Congress, inclusive—Continued.

Names of claimants.	Nature or object of the claim.	Congress.	Session.	How brought before the House of Reps.	Page of journal.	To what committee of the House referred.	No. or date of the report.	Nature of the report.	No. of the bill.	How disposed of by the House of Reps.	How disposed of by the Senate.	Date of the act of Congress, and remarks.
Saltmarsh, A	Reimbursement of office rent at Cahaba, Alabama, as register of land office.	29	2	Petition	99	Claims.						
Saltmarsh, Orlando, & W. Fuller.	Compensation for mail service under contract with Reesides & Co.	27	2	Petition and res.	757, 801	Claims.						
Saltmarsh, Orlando, & W. Fuller.	Compensation for mail services under contract with Reesides & Co.	27	3	Petition	59	P. Of. & P. Roads.						
Saltmarsh, Orlando, & W. Fuller.	Compensation for mail services under contract with Reesides & Co.	28	1	Petition	183	Claims	201	Favorable	R. 10	Passed	Adverse report.	
Saltmarsh, Orlando, & W. Fuller.	Compensation for mail services under contract with Reesides & Co.	29	1	Senate joint resolution.	972	P. Of. & P. Roads.	July 24, 1846	With't amend.	S. R. 7	Referred to Committee Whole House.		
Saltmarsh, Orlando, & W. Fuller.	Compensation for mail services under contract with Reesides & Co.	29	2	Senate joint resolution.	307	P. Of. & P. Roads.	Feb. 16, 1847	With't amend.	S. R. 6	Referred to Committee Whole House.		
Saltmarsh, Orlando, & W. Fuller.	Compensation for mail services under contract with Reesides & Co.	30	1	Petition	80	P. Of. & P. Roads.	102	Favorable	92	Passed	Passed, second session.	App'd Feb. 12, 1849
Saltmarsh, Orlando, and William Overton.	Compensation for mail service between Milledgeville and Ellerslie, Georgia.	27	2	Petition	757, 801	Claims.						
Saltmarsh, Orlando, and William Overton.	Compensation for mail service between Milledgeville and Ellerslie, Georgia.	27	3	Petition	59	P. Of. & P. Roads.	180	Favorable	791	Referred to Committee Whole House.		
Saltmarsh, Orlando, and William Overton.	Compensation for mail service between Milledgeville and Ellerslie, Georgia.	28	1	Petition	202	P. Of. & P. Roads.	Feb. 28, 1844	Res. to refer to 6th Auditor.	J. R. 12	Passed	Passed	App'd June 17, 1844
Saltmarsh, Orlando, and William Overton.	Compensation for mail service between Milledgeville and Ellerslie, Georgia.	30	1	Petition	80	P. Of. & P. Roads.	102	Report and bill.	92	Passed.		
Saltmarsh, William	Pension for disability in war of 1812.	17	2	Petition	56	Pens. & Rev. Cl'ms.	....	....	......	Discharged; laid on table.		
Saltmarsh, William	Pension for disability in war of 1812.	18	2	Petition and rep't Sec. War.	36, 122	....	....	....	......	Laid on table.		
Saltonstall, G. F	Renewal of patent for improvement in cotton gin.	22	1	Petition	226	Patent laws	May 26, 1832	Adverse	......	Laid on table.		
Saltonstall, Winthrop	Indemnity for destruction of property by fire.	4	2	Petition	649	Claims	Jan. 30, 1797	Adverse	......	Rejected.		
Salts, John, widow of	Pension	30	1	Petition	164	Invalid Pensions	356	Adverse	......	Laid on table.		
Saltsman, Daniel	(See Casper B. Cook and others.)	30	1	....	272							
Saltsman, Frederick	(See Casper B. Cook and others.)	30	1	....	272							
Saltsman, Peter J.	(See Casper B. Cook and others.)	30	1	....	272							
Saltus, Francis	Indemnity for French spoliations prior to 1800.	26	1	Memorial	182	Foreign Affairs	343	Favorable; bill	319	Referred to Committee Whole House.		
Saltus, Solomon	(See Francis Nicholas and others.)	18	1	....	330							
Saltus, Son & Co	Remission of duty on damaged glass.	13	2	Petition	602	Ways and Means	Jan. 23, 1815	Favorable; bill	267	Passed	Passed	App'd Feb. 22, 1815
Saltus, Son & Co	Indemnity for French spoliations prior to 1800.	26	1	Memorial	182	Foreign Affairs	343	Favorable; bill	319	Referred to Committee Whole House.		
Sammons, Allen	(See sureties of Reddick Dishough.)	25	3	....	369							
Sammons, Frederick	Pension and compensation for revolutionary services.	15	1	Petition	287	Pens. & Rev. Cl'ms.						
Sammons, Frederick	Pension and compensation for revolutionary services.	23	1	Petition	352	Invalid Pensions	....	....	......	Discharged; leave to withdraw.		
Sammons, Frederick	Pension and compensation for revolutionary services.	24	2	Petition	311	Invalid Pensions	....	....	......	Discharged; leave to withdraw.		

List of private claims presented to the House of Representatives of the United States from the 1st to the 31st Congress, inclusive—Continued.

Names of claimants.	Nature or object of the claim.	Congress.	Session.	How brought before the House of Reps.	Page of journal.	To what committee of the House referred.	No. or date of the report.	Nature of the report.	No. of the bill.	How disposed of by the House of Reps.	How disposed of by the Senate.	Date of the act of Congress, and remarks.
Sammons, Frederick	Pension and compensation for revolutionary services.	25	2	Petition	198	Invalid Pensions	525	Favorable	515	Passed	Adverse report.	
Sammons, Jacob, heirs of	Reimbursement of advances on public account.	23	1	Petition	439	Rev. Claims.						
Sammons, Jacob, heirs of	Reimbursement of advances on public account.	23	2	Petition	308	Rev. Claims.						
Sammons, Jacob, heirs of	Reimbursement of advances on public account.	24	1	Petition	404	Rev. Claims.						
Sammons, Jacob, heirs of	Reimbursement of advances on public account.	24	2	Petition	73	Rev. Claims	228	Adverse		Laid on table.		
Sampas, Wm. and Kennedy, assignee of.	Reimbursement of overpayment of tax on still.	18	1	Petition	330	Whole House	May 24, 1824	With't amend.	126	Passed	Passed	App'd May 26, 1824
Sample, John	Compensation for services in war of 1812.	29	1	Memorial	354	Claims.						
Sample, John	Compensation for services in war of 1812.	29	2	Memorial	82	Claims.						
Sample, Nathaniel, attorney of.	Pension for revolutionary services.	23	2	Petition	77	Rev. Pensions	Feb. 17, 1835	Adverse		Laid on table.		
Sampley, John, heirs of	Indemnity for property destroyed by the enemy.	31	2	Petition	158	Rev. Claims.						
Sampson, Asa	(See Phineas Sprague and others.)	21	1		232				215			
Sampson, Colson	Pension for revolutionary services.	21	1	Resolution	302	Military Pensions.						
Sampson, Crocker, heirs of.	Renewal of a military land warrant.	23	1	Petition	156	Rev. Claims	179	Favorable	197	Passed	Laid on table.	
Sampson, Crocker, heirs of.	Renewal of a military land warrant.	24	1	Petition	404	Rev. Claims	553	Favorable	544	Referred to Committee Whole House.		
Sampson, Crocker, heirs of.	Renewal of a military land warrant.	25	2	Petition	40	Rev. Claims	134	Favorable	152	Passed.		
Sampson, Crocker, heir of	Reneawal of a military land warrant.	25	3	House bill	436	Whole House	Feb 1, 1839	With't amend.	1093	Passed	Passed	App'd March 3 1839
Sampson, Crocker, heirs of.	Renewal of a military land warrant.	29	1	Senate bill	1108	Rev. Claims			S. 165			
Sampson, Crocker, heirs of.	Renewal of a military land warrant.	29	2	Senate bill	199	Rev. Claims	Feb. 16, 1846	With't amend	S. 46	Referred to Committee Whole House.		
Sampson, Daniel	Indemnity for loss of sight in the public service.	29	1	Petition	70	Naval Affairs				Discharged; laid on table.		
Sampson, Daniel	Indemnity for loss of sight in the public service.	30	2	Petition	75	Naval Affairs	29	Favorable	722	Referred to Committee Whole House.		
Sampson, James	(See William Harris, and others.)	20	1		51							
Samson, James, widow of.	Pension for revolutionary services of her husband.	28	1	Petition	368	Rev. Pensions				Discharged; laid on table.		
Sampson, Mary	(See James Sampson, widow of.)											
Samson, Peleg, widow of.	Pension for revolutionary services of her husband.	30	1	Petition	482	Rev. Pensions				Discharged; laid on table.		
Sampson, Rebecca	(See Crocker Sampson, heirs of).	23	1		156							
Simpson, Sarah	(See Peleg Simpson, widow of.)	30	1		482							
Samsing, J.	Release of a Danish vessel from embargo.	3	1	Petition	131	Select.						
Samuel, William	Pension	15	1	Resolution	40					Referred to Secretary War.		
Sanborn, Benjamin	To be restored to pension roll	17	2	Petition	162	Whole House.						
Sanborn, Coffin	Pension for services in the war of 1812.	25	2	Petition	400	Invalid Pensions	647	Favorable	263	Passed	Passed	App'd July 7, 1838

List of private claims presented to the House of Representatives of the United States from the 1st to the 31st Congress, inclusive—Continued.

Names of claimants.	Nature or object of the claim.	Congress.	Session.	How brought before the House of Reps.	Page of journal.	To what committee of the House referred.	No. or date of the report.	Nature of the report.	No. of the bill.	How disposed of by the House of Reps.	How disposed of by the Senate.	Date of the act of Congress, and remarks.
Sanborn, Coffin	Arrears of pay or pension	26	1	Resolution	289	Rev. Pensions.						
Sanborn, Coffin	Arrears of pension	26	2	Petition	36	Invalid Pensions	Feb. 12, 1841	Adverse		Laid on table.		
Sanborne, Dolly	Pension for revolutionary services of her husband.	28	1	Petition	849	Rev. Pensions.						
Sanborn, Matthew N.	To be restored to pension roll	18	1	Petition	42	Rev. Pensions	Jan. 9, 1824	Adverse		Laid on table.		
Sanborn, Nathan	Increase of pension	6	2	Petition	738	Claims	Dec. 15, 1800	Adverse		Rejected.		
Sanborn, Peter	Pension	22	1	Petition	55	Rev. Pensions	367	Favorable	462	Passed	Indef. postp'd.	
Sanchez, Diego	Confirmation of title to land at Terre aux Bœuf.	22	1	House bill	107	Whole House	Mar. 23, 1832	With't amend.	125	Passed	Passed	App'd June 25, 1832
Sanchez, Francis R.	Compensation for hogs taken for public use.	28	1	Petition	571	Claims.						
Sanchez, Francis Z	Indemnity for Indian depredations in Florida.	25	3	Petition	121	Claims	162	Adverse		Laid on table.		
Sanchez, Francisco	Confirmation of title to land at Terre aux Bœuf.	22	1	House bill	107	Whole House	Mar. 23 1832	With't amend.	125	Passed	Passed	App'd Jan. 25, 1832
Sanchez, John M.	Indemnity for Indian depredations in Florida.	25	3	Petition	121	Claims	162	Adverse		Laid on table.		
Sanchez, Jose E.	Indemnity for Indian depredations in Florida.	25	3	Petition	121	Claims	162	Adverse		Laid on table.		
Sanchez, Joseph	Confirmation of title to land at Terre aux Bœuf.	22	1	House bill	107	Whole House	Mar. 23, 1832	With't amend.	125	Passed	Passed	App'd June 25, 1832
Sanchez, Maurice	Indemnity for Indian depredations in Florida.	25	3	Petition	121	Claims	162	Adverse.		Laid on table.		
Sanchez, Remsen	Indemnity for Indian depredations in Florida.	25	3	Petition	121	Claims	162	Adverse		Laid on table.		
Saunders, Alexander H.	Compensation for military services	13	3	Petition	729	Claims				Discharged.		
Saunders, Alexander H.	Compensation for military services	14	1	Petition	77	Pens. & Rev. Cl'ms.						
Saunders, Alexander H.	Arrears of pay for revolutionary services.	19	2	Petition	189	Military Affairs.						
Saunders, Alexander H.	Arrears of pay for revolutionary services.	26	1	Resolution	549	Claims.						
Saunders, Alexander H.	Arrears of pay for revolutionary services.	27	2	Petition	297	Claims	647	Adverse		Laid on table.		
Sanders, Benjamin	Pension	20	2	Petition	26	Military Pensions				Discharged; laid on table.		
Saunders, Celey, heirs of.	Commutation pay for revolutionary services	23	1	Petition	55	Rev. Claims.						
Saunders, Celey, heirs of.	Commutation pay for revolutionary services.	23	2	Petition	84	Rev. Claims.						
Saunders, Celey, heirs of.	Commutation pay for revolutionary services.	24	1	Petition	104	Rev. Claims	139	Adverse		Laid on table.		
Saunders, Celey, heirs of.	Commutation pay for revolutionary services.	24	2	Petition	94	Rev. Claims.						
Sanders, Chancellor, and Manuel Judah.	Remission of duty on merchandise destroyed by fire.	14	1	Petition	180	Ways and Means	Feb. 24, 1816	Rep. not found		Referred to Committee Whole House.		
Sanders, Chancellor, and Manuel Judah.	Remission of duty on merchandise destroyed by fire.	14	2	Petition	69	Ways and Means	Jan. 21, 1816	Adverse		Rejected.		
Saunders, Charles	(See James Devereux, and others)	20	1		222							
Sanders, Davis, widow of.	Reimbursement of expenses while in command of a public vessel.	31	1	Petition	391	Naval Affairs.						
Saunders, Elizabeth	(See heir of George Guthrie)	23	1		98							
Saunders, Eunice	(See widow of Moses Pierson)	25	2		546							

List of private claims presented to the House of Representatives of the United States from the 1st to the 31st Congress, inclusive—Continued.

Names of claimants.	Nature or object of the claim.	Congress.	Session.	How brought before the House of Reps.	Page of journal.	To what committee of the House referred.	No. or date of the report.	Nature of the report.	No. of the bill.	How disposed of by the House of Reps.	How disposed of by the Senate.	Date of the act of Congress, and remarks.
Saunders, Isaac D	(See assignee of Edward Berins.)	26	1		951							
Saunders, Isaac D	Bounty land for military services.	25	2	Documents	590	Priv. Land Claims.	814	Favorable	756	Referred to Committee Whole House.		
Saunders, Isaac D	Bounty land for military services.	25	3	Bill of last sess.	381	Whole House	Jan. 26, 1839	With't amend.	756	Passed	Passed	App'd March 3, 1839
Saunders, Isaac D	Increase of pension	27	2	Petition	377	Invalid Pensions	621	Adverse		Laid on table.		
Saunders, James, widow of	To be restored to pension roll	27	3	Petition	60	Naval Affairs				Discharged; laid on table.		
Saunders, John	Increase of compensation as revenue officer, Massachusetts.	19	2	Memorial	91	Commerce.						
Sanders, John	Pension	23	1	Petition	381	Invalid Pensions	399	Favorable	418	Referred to Committee Whole House.		
Sanders, John	Pension	23	2	House bill	336	Whole House	Feb. 6, 1835	With't amend.	418	Passed.		
Saunders, John, and P. Putnam.	Compensation for services, superintending building of custom house at Salem, Mass.	23	1	Petition	74	Claims.						
Saunders, John, and P. Putnam.	Compensation for services, superintending building of custom-house at Salem, Mass.	23	2	House bill	169	Claims	29	Favorable	609	Referred to Commitee Whole House.		
Saunders, John, and P. Putnam.	Compensation for services, superintending building of custom house at Salem, Mass.	24	1	Petition	51	Claims	31	Favorable	31	Passed.	Passed	App'd Feb. 17, 1836
Saunders, John H	Compensation for military services.	31	1	Petition	715	Military Affairs.						
Saunders, John L	Reimbursement of expenses in commanding ship St. Mary's.	31	1	Petition	487	Naval Affairs.						
Saunders, John W	(See Samuel Upton and others)	12	1		94							
Saunders, Joseph	A special act of insolvency	7	1	Petition	176	Select.						
Saunders, Joseph	Increase of pension	10	1	Pension bill	234				78	Passed	Passed	App'd April 25, 1808
Saunders, Joseph	(See Joseph Stewart and others)	14	2		56				65			
Saunders, Joseph	Additional compensation as revolutionary seaman.	22	2	Petition	88	Rev. Claims.						
Saunders, Luke	Pension for revolutionary services.	22	1	Petition	46	Rev. Pensions	Dec. 21, 1831	Adverse		Laid on table.		
Saunders, Lydia	Pension for revolutionary services of her husband.	28	1	Petition	839	Whole House.						
Sanders, Mivard	Compensation for a horse lost in public service.	16	1	Resolution	289	Claims.						
Sanders, Nathaniel, widow of.	Pension for revolutionary services.	26	1	Resolution	385	Rev. Pensions	664	Adverse		Laid on table.		
Sanders, Peter	Renewal of revolutionary land warrant.	22	2	Petition	264	Priv. Land Claims.						
Sanders, Peter	Renewal of revolutionary land warrant.	23	1	Petition	48	Priv. Land Claims.						
Saunders, Presly	Credit for money stolen from his post office.	19	2	Resolution	174	Claims	Jan. 29, 1827	Adverse		Laid on table.		
Saunders Reuben, and surety.	Release of a judgment	12	1	Senate bill	302	Claims			S. 26			
Sanders, Robert	Indemnity for destruction of property by a government party.	7	1	Petition	86	Claims	Mar. 24, 1802	Adverse		Rejected.		
Saunders, Robert	(See William Finnie, administrator of.)	30	1		740							
Saunders, Robert Hyde	Compensation for revolutionary services.	19	2	Petition	112	Rev. Claims.						

List of private claims presented to the House of Representatives of the United States from the 1st to the 31st Congress, inclusive—Continued.

Names of claimants.	Nature or object of the claim.	Congress.	Session.	How brought before the House of Reps.	Page of journal.	To what committee of the House referred.	No. or date of the report.	Nature of the report.	No. of the bill.	How disposed of by the House of Reps.	How disposed of by the Senate.	Date of the act of Congress, and remarks.
Saunders, Robert Hyde	Compensation for revolutionary services.	20	1	Petition	193	Rev. Claims	....	....	......	Discharged; laid on table.		
Saunders, Robert Hyde	Pension for revolutionary services.	20	2	Petition	121	Whole House.						
Saunders, Robert Hyde	Commutation pay for revolutionary services.	21	1	Petition	50	Rev. Claims.						
Saunders, Robert Hyde	Commutation pay for revolutionary services.	21	2	Petition	226	Rev. Claims.						
Saunders, Robert Hyde	Commutation pay for revolutionary services.	22	1	Petition	113	Rev. Claims	Mar 6, 1832	Adverse	......	Laid on table.		
Sanders, Sally	(See Nathaniel Sanders, widow of.)	26	1	....	385							
Sanders, Samuel, widow of.	To be restored to pension roll	27	2	Petition	320	Rev. Pensions.						
Sanders, Samuel, widow of.	To be restored to pension roll	27	3	Petition	365	Rev. Pensions.						
Saunders, Thomas	Pension	29	1	Petition	872	Invalid Pensions	....	....	......	Discharged; laid on table.		
Saunders, Thomas R.	Pension	30	1	Petition	912	Invalid Pensions	778	Favorable	615	Referred to Committee Whole House.		
Saunders, Thomas R.	Pension	30	2	Bill of last sess.	362	Whole House	Feb. 2, 1849	With't amend.	615	Passed.		
Saunders, Thomas R.	Pension	31	1	Petition	275	Invalid Pensions	145	Favorable	161	Referred to Committee Whole House.		
Saunders, Thomas R.	Pension	31	2	Bill of last sess.	104	Whole House	Jan. 3, 1851	With't amend.	161	Passed.		
Saunders, William	(See William Estes, sureties of)	21	1	....	70							
Saunders, W.	(See Justice Forbes and others.)	24	1	....	914							
Sanders, William	Right of pre-emption to land in Missouri.	25	3	Petition	211	Public Lands.						
Sanders, William G.	(See Seminole Indians.)	27	2	....	369							
Sanders, William G.	Indemnity for property destroyed by a public officer.	24	2	Memorial	80	Claims	216	Adverse.	......	Laid on table.		
Sanders, William G.	Indemnity for property destroyed by a public officer.	25	3	Memorial	122	Claims	Feb. 16, 1839	Adverse	......	Laid on table.		
Sanders, William G.	Indemnity for property destroyed by a public officer.	26	1	Memorial	339	Claims	677	Adverse	......	Laid on table.		
Sanders, William G.	Indemnity for property destroyed by a public officer.	27	2	Petition	381	Claims	590	Favorable	389	Ordered to 3d reading.		
Sanders, William G.	Indemnity for property destroyed by a public officer.	27	3	House bill	88	....	....	....	389	Passed	Passed	App'd March 1, 1843
Sanders, William G.	Further indemnity for property, &c.	28	2	Petition	171	Claims.						
Sanders, William G.	Further indemnity for property, &c.	29	1	Memorial	151	Claims	840	Adverse	......	Laid on table.		
Sanders, William G.	Further indemnity for property, &c.	30	1	Petition	69	Claims.						
Sanders, Zachariah	Pension	21	2	Petition	230	Military Pensions.						
Sanders, Zachariah	Pension	22	1	Petition	473	Rev. Pensions	381	Favorable	472	Passed	Indef. postp'd.	
Saunderson, David	Bounty land for revolutionary services.	21	1	Petition	353	Rev. Claims.						
Saunderson, David	Bounty land for revolutionary services.	21	2	Petition	67	Rev. Claims	....	....	......	Discharged; laid on table.		
Saunderson, David	Bounty land for revolutionary services.	22	1	Petition	51	Rev. Pensions.						
Saunderson, David	Bounty land for revolutionary services.	22	2	Petition	244	Rev. Claims	....	....	......	Discharged; laid on table.		
Saunderson, David	Bounty land for revolutionary services.	23	1	Petition	242	Rev. Claims	Jan. 3, 1834	Adverse	......	Laid on table.		

List of private claims presented to the House of Representatives of the United States from the 1st to the 31st Congress, inclusive—Continued.

Names of claimants.	Nature or object of the claim.	Congress.	Session.	How brought before the House of Reps.	Page of journal.	To what committee of the House referred.	No. or date of the report.	Nature of the report.	No. of the bill.	How disposed of by the House of Reps.	How disposed of by the Senate.	Date of the act of Congress, and remarks.
Saunderson, David	Bounty land for revolutionary services.	23	2	Petition	196	Rev. Claims.						
Saunderson, David	Bounty land for revolutionary services.	24	1	Petition	102	Rev. Claims	830	Adverse		Laid on table.		
Saunderson, David	Bounty land for revolutionary services.	24	2	Petition	47	Rev. Pensions				Discharged; laid on table.		
Saunderson, James, and others.	Remission of certain foreign tonnage duty.	14	1	Petition	292	Com. and Manuf.						
Saunderson, James, and others.	Remission of certain foreign tonnage duty.	14	2	Petition	41	Com. and Manuf.						
Saunderson, James, and others.	Remission of certain foreign tonnage duty.	17	1	Petition	78	Commerce	Jan. 15, 1822	Favorable	38	Passed	Passed, with amendment	App'd May 1, 1822
Saunderson, Moses, agent of	Compensation for revolutionary services and injuries.	1	3	Petition	378					Referred to Secretary of War.		
Saunderson, Moses, agent of	Compensation for revolutionary services and injuries.	3	2	Rep. of Secretary War.	337	Claims	Feb. 28, 1795	Favorable; bill ordered.	130	Passed	Postponed.	
Saunderson, Moses	Invalid pension	4	1	Rep. of Secretary War.	445	Claims	Feb. 13, 1796	Favorable; bill ordered.	156	Passed	Passed	App'd April 20, 1796
Saunderson, Moses	Increase of pension	15	1	Petition	206	Pens. & Rev. Cl'ms.						
Sanderson, Samuel	Compensation for rescuing African slaves.	23	2	Petition	138	Claims.						
Sanderson, Samuel	Compensation for rescuing African slaves.	24	1	Petition	50	Claims	268	Favorable	274	Referred to Committee Whole House.		
Sanderson, Samuel	Compensation for rescuing African slaves.	24	2	Bill of last sess.	199	Whole House	Jan. 13, 1837	With't amend.	274	Postponed.		
Sanderson, Samuel	Compensation for rescuing African slaves.	25	2	Petition	37	Claims	4	Favorable	16	Passed	Passed	App'd Mar. 28, 1838
Sanderson, Sylvanus	Pension for revolutionary services.	21	2	Resolution	165	Military Pensions.						
Sanderlin, Robert	Compensation for property lost at Honduras.	28	2	Memorial	84	Claims.						
Saundery, Luke	Pension	27	2	Petition	799	Invalid Pensions.						
Sandon, Laban	Pension for revolutionary services.	20	2	House bill	55	Whole House			311	Passed	Laid on table.	
Sandwich Islands, commissioner to.	Allowance of outfit	29	1	Resolution	238	Judiciary	288	Adverse		Laid on table.		
Sands, Austin L	(See heirs of Walter Livingston and others.)	14	2		147							
Sands, Austin L	(See Ebenezer Stevens and others)	15	1		143							
Sands, Comfort, and others.	Confirmation and payment of certain claims.	1	3	Petition	358							
				Rep. of Secretary Treasury.	391	Select				Laid on table.		
Sands, Comfort, and others.	Confirmation and payment of certain claims.	2	1	Resolution	479	Select	Feb. 8, 1792	Favorable; bill ordered.	193	Ordered to 3d reading.		
Sands, Comfort, and others.	Confirmation and payment of certain claims.	3	1	Petition	31	Whole House.						
Sands, Comfort, and others.	Confirmation and payment of certain claims.	4	1	Documents	455	Claims.						
Sands, Comfort, and others.	Confirmation and payment of certain claims.	4	2	Petition	687	Claims	Feb. 9, 1797	To refer to arbitration.		Referred to Committee Whole House.		
Sands, Comfort, and others.	Confirmation and payment of certain claims.	5	2	Petition	112	Claims	Dec. 29, 1797	Favorable; bill ordered.	46	Postponed to next session.		
Sands, Comfort, and others.	Confirmation and payment of certain claims.	5	3	Petition	445	Claims	Feb. 12, 1799	Favorable; bill ordered.	163	Passed	Passed	App'd March 2, 1799

List of private claims presented to the House of Representatives of the United States from the 1st to the 31st Congress, inclusive—Continued.

Names of claimants.	Nature or object of the claim.	Congress.	Session.	How brought before the House of Reps.	Page of journal.	To what committee of the House referred.	No. or date of the report.	Nature of the report.	No. of the bill.	How disposed of by the House of Reps.	How disposed of by the Senate.	Date of the act of Congress, and remarks.
Sands, Comfort, and others.	Damages sustained under a government contract.	7	1	Documents	183	Select	Feb. 14, 1802	Favorable; bill ordered.	62	Postponed.		
Sands, Comfort	(See Ebenezer Stevens and others)	15	1		143							
Sands, Comfort	Indemnity for French spoliations prior to 1800.	26	1	Memorial	182	Foreign Affairs	343	Favorable; bil	319	Referred to Committee Whole House.		
Sand, Hart	Reimbursement of the amount of a certain bond.	17	1	Petition	110	Ways and Means	Feb. 28, 1822	Adverse		Laid on table.		
Sands, John	Remission of a certain fine	27	3	Petition	206	Commerce.	144	Favorable	763	Referred to Committee Whole House.		
Sands, John	Remission of a certain fine	28	1	Petition	159	Commerce	446	Favorable	343	Passed	Passed, with amendment.	App'd June 17, 1844
Sands, Joshua	(See Comfort Sands, and others).	1	3		358							
Sands, Joshua	(See heirs of Walter Livingston, and others.	14	2		147							
Sands, Joshua	(See Ebenezer Stevens, and others.)	15	1		143							
Sands, Joshua	Reimbursement of sundry debentures, &c.	9	2	Petition	574	Com. and Manuf.						
Sands, Joshua	Reimbursement of sundry debentures, &c.	11	2	Petition	284	Com. and Manuf.						
Sands, Joshua	Reimbursement of sundry debentures, &c.	13	2	Petition	231	Com. and Manuf.	53	Favorable	103	Passed	Passed	App'd Mar. 28, 1814
Sands, Joshua	Indemnity for damages on account of certain seizures as a public officer.	13	3	Petition	686	Ways and Means	Feb. 4, 1815	Favorable	284	Passed	Passed	App'd Feb. 27, 1815
Sands, Joshua	Indemnity for French spoliations prior to 1800.	26	1	Memorial	182	Foreign Affairs	343	Favorable; bill	319	Referred to Committee Whole House.		
Sands, Joshua R.	Reimbursement of expenses on public account.	30	1	Memorial	559	Naval Affairs.						
Sands, Joshua R.	Reimbursement of expenses on public account.	30	2	Petition	327	Naval Affairs.						
Sands, Joseph	(See trustees of Francis S. Taney.)	10	1		216							
Sands, Joseph	Indemnity for French spoliations prior to 1800.	26	1	Memorial	182	Foreign Affairs	343	Favorable; bill	319	Referred to Committee Whole House.		
Sands, Lucretia	(See Ebenezer Stevens, and others.)	15	1		143							
Sands, Richardson	(See Comfort Sands, and others).	1	3		358							
Sands, Richardson	(See heirs of Walter Livingston, and others.)	14	2		147							
Sands, Richardson	(See Ebenezer Stevens, and others.)	15	1		143							
Sanerheber, Valentine	Compensation for services in Indian war.	31	1	Petition	768	Invalid Pensions.						
Sanford, Edward	Arrears of pension	23	1	Memorial	137	Rev. Pensions				Discharged; laid on table.		
Sanford, Elihu, and others.	To be placed on the same footing with commissioned officers of the revolutionary war.	19	1	Petition	82	Military Pensions	April 1, 1826	Adverse		Laid on table.		
Sanford, Elihu	Compensation for extra revolutionary services.	21	2	Petition	44	Rev. Claims.						
Sanford, Elihu	Compensation for extra revolutionary services.	22	1	Petition	67	Rev. Pensions.						
Sanford, Elihu	Compensation for extra revolutionary services.	22	2	Petition	94	Rev. Claims.						
Sanford, Elihu	Compensation for extra revolutionary services.	23	1	Petition	220	Rev. Claims.						

List of private claims presented to the House of Representatives of the United States from the 1st to the 31st Congress, inclusive—Continued.

Names of claimants.	Nature or object of the claim.	Congress.	Session.	How brought before the House of Reps.	Page of journal.	To what committee of the House referred.	No. or date of the report.	Nature of the report.	No. of the bill.	How disposed of by the House of Reps.	How disposed of by the Senate.	Date of the act of Congress, and remarks.
Sanford, Elihu	Compensation for extra revolutionary services.	24	2	Petition	73	Rev. Claims.						
Sanford, Elihu	(See Atwater & Daggett, and others)	22	1		30							
Sanford, F. C	Reimbursement of certain tonnage duties.	26	2	Petition	121	Commerce	98	Favorable	604	Referred to Committee Whole House.		
Sanford, F. C	Reimbursement of certain tonnage duties.	27	2	Petition	56	Commerce.	61	Favorable	96	Passed	Indef. postp'd.	
Sanford, James	Compensation for military services.	21	1	Petition	497	Rev. Claims.						
Sanford, Jonathan	Pension for revolutionary services.	21	2	Resolution	65	Military Pensions.						
Sanford, J. P	(See Exploring Expedition)	27	3		149		278		818			
Sanford, Thomas	Indemnity for a vessel illegally condemned.	23	1	Petition	239	Ways and Means	360	Adverse		Laid on table.		
Sanford, Thomas	Indemnity for a vessel illegally condemned.	29	1	Petition	275	Commerce	515	Adverse		Laid on table.		
Sanford, Thomas	Indemnity for a vessel illegally condemned.	31	1	Petition	899	Commerce.						
Sanford, Thomas, (Ga.,) assignee of.	Indemnity for French spoliations prior to 1800.	26	1	Memorial	182	Foreign Affairs	343	Favorable; bill	319	Referred to Committee Whole House.		
Sanford, Thomas, attorney of.	Indemnity for French spoliations prior to 1800	26	1	Memorial	182	Foreign Affairs	343	Favorable; bill	319	Referred to Committee Whole House.		
Sanford, William, heir of.	Commutation pay for revolutionary services.	25	2	Senate bill	994	Rev. Claims	June 7, 1838	Adverse	S. 215	Laid on table.		
Sanford, Zachariah	Pension	3	1	Rep. of Secretary War.	131	Select	May 26, 1794	Res. to refer to Sec. War.	J.R. 12	Passed	Passed	App'd June 9, 1794
Sanger, L. P	Compensation for mail service	30	1	Petition	122	P. Of. & P. Roads.						
Sanger, W. P. S	Credit for disbursements on public account.	29	1	Petition	470	Naval Affairs	367	Favorable	280	Referred to Committee Whole House.		
Sanger, W. P. S	Credit for disbursements on public account.	29	2	Bill of last sess.	71	Whole House	Dec. 18, 1846	With't amend.	280	Passed	Passed	App'd March 3, 1847
Sanger, W. P. S	Credit for disbursements on public account.	30	1	Memorial	161	Naval Affairs	130	Favorable	121	Passed	Passed 2d sess.	App'd Jan. 26, 1849
Sanger, W. P. S	Increase of salary as an engineer	31	1	Petition	1096	Naval Affairs.						
Sanger, W. P. S	Increase of salary as an engineer	31	2	Petition	165	Naval Affairs.						
Sangster, Alexander, surety of.	Reimbursement of moneys paid to government.	21	2	Petition	303	P. Of. & P. Roads.						
Sanguinett, Charles	Permission to record evidence of land title in Louisiana.	11	2	Resolution	175	Public Lands.						
Sanguinett, Charles	Confirmation of title to land in Missouri.	14	2	Petition	428	Priv. Land Claims.						
Sanguinette, Charles	(See Henry Duchuquette, representatives of.)	23	2		353							
Sanmiguel, C	(See H. Fredieu, and others)	30	1		976							
Sans, Berta Marianna	(See Gabriel W. Perpall, & others)	22	1		192							
Santalistra, Matthias	Confirmation of title to land in Mississippi.	11	1	Petition	34	Public Lands.						
Santalistra, Matthias	Confirmation of title to land in Mississippi.	11	2	Resolution	112	Public Lands.						
Santangelo, Orazio de Attelis.	Indemnity for claims against Mexico.	29	2	Memorial	224	Foreign Affairs				Discharged; laid on table.		
Santeer, William	Compensation for a horse lost in public service.	15	1	Petition	81	Claims.						
Sapp, Benjamin	Pension	23	1	Petition	45	Invalid Pensions.						
Sapp, Benjamin	Pension	23	2	Petition	76	Invalid Pensions	Dec. 23, 1824	Adverse		Laid on table.		

List of private claims presented to the House of Representatives of the United States from the 1st to the 31st Congress, inclusive—Continued.

Names of claimants.	Nature or object of the claim.	Congress.	Session.	How brought before the House of Reps.	Page of journal.	To what committee of the House referred.	No. or date of the report.	Nature of the report.	No. of the bill.	How disposed of by the House of Reps.	How disposed of by the Senate.	Date of the act of Congress, and remarks.
Sapp, John	Compensation for a horse lost in public service.	21	1	Petition	262	Claims	192	Favorable	245	Referred to Committee Whole House.		
Sapp, John	Compensation for a horse lost in public service.	21	2	Bill of last sess.	265	Whole House	Feb. 4, 1831	With't amend.	245	Passed.		
Sapp, John	Compensation for a horse lost in public service.	22	1	Petition	43	Claims	Dec. 19, 1831	Favorable	5	Passed	Passed	App'd Feb. 24, 1832
Sapp, Joseph	Bounty land for revolutionary services.	12	2	Petition	671	Public Lands.						
Sapp, Joseph	Bounty land for revolutionary services.	13	1	Petition	28	Public Lands				Discharged.		
Sapp, Joseph	Bounty land for revolutionary services.	13	2	Petition	259	Pens. & Rev. Cl'ms				Discharged.		
Sapp, Joseph	Pension for revolutionary services.	24	2	Petition	212	Invalid Pensions	Feb. 14, 1837	Adverse		Laid on table.		
Sappington, Dr. Richard	Compensation for revolutionary surgeon.	2	1	Petition	604					Referred to Secretary War.		
Sappington, Dr. Richard	Compensation for revolutionary surgeon.	3	2	Rep. of Secretary War.	278					Laid on table.		
Sappington, Thomas	Payment of a lost revolutionary certificate.	16	1	Petition	323	Pens. & Rev. Clm's.	April 3, 1820	Adverse		Laid on table.		
Sappington, Thomas	Pension for revolutionary services.	20	2	Petition	89	Military Pensions.						
Sappington, Thomas	Pension for revolutionary services.	21	1	Petition	294	Military Pensions	April 23, 1830	Favorable	439	Referred to Committee Whole House.		
Sarazin, Bartholomew	Indemnity for sufferings at Cape François.	4	2	Petition	613	Select	Jan. 3, 1797	Adverse		Rejected.		
Sarazin, John B	Relief from decision of Secretary of Treasury.	11	1	Petition	11	Com. and Manuf.						
Sarazin, John B	Relief from decision of Secretary of Treasury.	11	2	Resolution and rep. of Secretary Treasury.	119 413					Laid on table.		
Sarazzin, Jonathan	(See executor of Thomas Washington.)	10	1		166							
Sarchet, John	Discharge as an insolvent debtor to United States.	23	2	Memorial	388	Judiciary				Discharged; laid on table.		
Sarchet, J. F. and E.	Release from judgment on revenue bond.	23	2	Petition	164	Judiciary.						
Sardina, Bisente	Confirmation of title to land in Louisiana.	22	1	House bill	107	Whole House	Mar. 23, 1832	With't amend.	125	Passed.	Passed	App'd June 25, 1832
Sargent, Daniel, administrator of.	Indemnity for French spoliations prior to 1800.	26	1	Memorial	182	Foreign Affairs	343	Favorable; bill	318	Referred to Committee Whole House.		
Sargent, Daniel	(See Marine Insurance Company of Boston.)	26	1		182							
Sargent, Eli	(See Smith & Hersey)	31	1		406							
Sargent, James	Compensation for team lost in public service.	28	1	Petition	429	Claims.						
Sargent, John	Pension	15	2	House bill	41				203	Passed	Passed	App'd March 3, 1819
Sargent, John	Arrears of pension	23	1	Petition	45	Invalid Pensions.						
Sargent, Paul Dudley	To be restored to pension roll	18	1	Petition	314	Rev. Pensions.						
Sargent, S. A. and J. H.	Payment of amount due from Ottowa Indians.	29	1	Memorial	160	Indian Affairs	287	Adverse		Laid on table.		
Sargent, Solomon	Continuation of pension	16	2	Petition	119	Rev. Pensions	Feb. 15, 1821	Adverse		Leave to withdraw.		
Sargent, Winthrop	Increase of compensation as secretary of Western Territory.	1	3	Petition	344					Referred to Secretary of Treasury.		

List of private claims presented to the House of Representatives of the United States from the 1st to the 31st Congress, inclusive—Continued.

Names of claimants.	Nature or object of the claim.	Congress.	Session.	How brought before the House of Reps.	Page of journal.	To what committee of the House referred.	No. or date of the report.	Nature of the report.	No. of the bill.	How disposed of by the House of Reps.	How disposed of by the Senate.	Date of the act of Congress, and remarks.
Sargent, Winthrop	Increase of compensation as secretary of Western Territory.	3	1	Rep. of Secretary Treasury.	53	Select	Feb. 13, 1794	Rep. not found	......	Laid on table.		
Sargent, Winthrop	Increase of compensation as secretary of Western Territory.	4	1	Memorial	423	Claims	April 25, 1796	Favorable	......	Referred to Committee Whole House.		
Sargent, Winthrop	Compensation as adjutant general.	2	2	Appropriat'n bill.	294	Whole House	....	....	100	Passed	Passed	App'd March 2, 1793
Sargent, Winthrop	Renewal of a lost revolutionary certificate.	14	1	Petition	356	Pens. & Rev. Cl'ms						
Sargent, Winthrop	Renewal of a lost revolutionary certificate.	14	2	Petition	133	Pens. & Rev. Cl'ms.	Jan. 31, 1817	Adverse	......	Leave to withdraw.		
Sargent, Winthrop	Renewal of a lost revolutionary certificate.	16	1	Petition	47	Priv. Land Claims.						
Sargent, Winthrop	Indemnity for French spoliations prior to 1800.	26	1	Petition	182	Foreign Affairs	343	Favorable; bill	319	Referred to Committee Whole House.		
Sarpey, Gregoire	Indemnity for the loss of certain privileges as an Indian trader.	13	1	Petition	37	Claims	....	....	......	Discharged.		
Sarpey, Gregoire	Indemnity for the loss of certain privileges as an Indian trader.	13	2	Petition	246	Claims	79	Adverse	......	Leave to withdraw.		
Sarpey, Gregoire	Indemnity for the loss of certain privileges as an Indian trader.	14	1	Petition	417	Claims.						
Sarpey, Gregoire	Indemnity for the loss of certain privileges as an Indian trader.	14	2	Petition	163	Claims.						
Sarpey, Gregoire	Indemnity for the loss of certain privileges as an Indian trader.	15	1	Petition	324	Claims	Mar. 26, 1818	Adverse	......	Leave to withdraw.		
Sarpey, Gregoire	Confirmation of title to land in Missouri.	15	1	Petition	280	Priv. Land Claims.						
Sarpey, Gregoire, representatives of.	Confirmation of title to land in Missouri.	21	1	Senate bill	419	Priv. Land Claims.	Mar. 30, 1830	With't amend.	S. 70	Referred to Committee Whole House.		
Sarpey, Gregoire, heirs of.	Patent from United States for a Spanish grant of land.	24	1	Resolution	514	Public Lands.						
Sarpey, Gregoire, heirs of.	Patent from United States for a Spanish grant of land.	24	2	Petition	93	Public Lands.						
Sarpey, Gregoire, heirs of.	Patent from United States for a Spanish grant of land.	25	2	Resolution	418	Public Lands.						
Sarpey, Gregoire, heirs of.	Patent from United States for a Spanish grant of land.	26	1	Petition	179	Priv. Land Claims.	....	....	......	Discharged; laid on table.		
Sarpey, Gregoire, heirs of.	Patent from United States for a Spanish grant of land.	26	2	Senate bill Senate bill	813 197	Public Lands Priv. Land Claims.	....	....	S. 216 S. 75			
Sarpey, Gregoire, heirs of.	Patent from United States for a Spanish grant of land.	27	2	Senate bill	634	Priv. Land Claims.	July 27, 1842	With't amend.	S. 127	Passed	Passed	App'd Aug. 11, 1842
Sartori, Joel	Compensation for a horse lost in public service.	22	2	Petition	218	Claims.						
Sartori, Joel	Compensation for a horse lost in public service.	23	2	Petition	132	Claims	34	Favorable	615	Referred to Committee Whole House.		
Sartori, Joel	Compensation for a horse lost in public service.	24	1	Petition	51	Claims	36	Favorable	36	Passed	Passed	App'd Feb. 17, 1836
Sartori, Lewis C	Compensation for scientific services, United States navy.	27	3	Petition	78	Naval Affairs	276	Favorable	827	Referred to Committee Ways and Means.		
Sartori, Lewis C	Compensation for scientific services, United States navy.	28	1	Petition	483	Naval Affairs	454	Adverse	......	Laid on table.		
Sartori, Lewis C	Compensation for scientific services, United States navy.	28	2	Petition	176	Naval Affairs.						

List of private claims presented to the House of Representatives of the United States from the 1st to the 31st Congress, inclusive—Continued.

Names of claimants.	Nature or object of the claim.	Congress.	Session.	How brought before the House of Reps.	Page of journal.	To what committee of the House referred.	No. or date of the report.	Nature of the report.	No. of the bill.	How disposed of by the House of Reps.	How disposed of by the Senate.	Date of the act of Congress, and remarks.
Sartori, Lewis C	Compensation for scientific services, United States navy.	29	1	Petition	315	Naval Affairs	763	Favorable	502	Referred to Committee Whole House.		
Sartori, Lewis C	Compensation for scientific services, United States navy.	29	2	House bill	382				502	Passed	Passed	App'd March 3, 1847
Sasportas, Abraham, widow of.	Indemnity for French spoliations prior to 1800.	26	1	Memorial	182	Foreign Affairs	343	Favorable; bill	319	Referred to Committee Whole House.		
Sasportas, Abraham, widow of.	Indemnity for French spoliations prior to 1800.	31	2	Petition	222	Foreign Affairs.						
Sasportas, Charlotte	(See William Sarportas, widow of.)											
Sasser, Isaac	Arrears of pay for military services.	26	1	Petition	622	Claims	578	Adverse		Laid on table.		
Satterlee, Elisha	Pension for revolutionary services.	17	1	Petition	195	Whole House.						
Satterly, Isaac	Compensation for secret services in revolutionary war.	24	2	Petition	145	Rev. Claims	120	Adverse		Laid on table.		
Satterly, Isaac	Compensation for secret services in revolutionary war.	25	2	Petition	112	Rev. Claims	Dec. 18, 1837	Adverse		Laid on table.		
Satterly, Isaac	Compensation for secret services in revolutionary war.	28	1	Petition	365	Rev. Claims.						
Sattley, Archibald	Compensation for horse lost in Indian war.	21	1	Petition	262	Claims	Mar. 10, 1830	Adverse		Laid on table.		
Satterwhite, Edwin T	Equitable settlement of accounts as purser.	13	1	Petition	33	Claims	June 19, 1813	Favorab'e	32	Passed	Passed	App'd July 22, 1813
Satterwhite, Edwin T	Explanatory act	13	2	Petition	259	Claims	Feb. 28, 1814	Favorable	144	Passed	Passed	App'd Mar. 31, 1814
Satterwhite, John	Compensation for revolutionary services.	2	1	Petition	466					Referred to Secretary of War.		
Sancier, Francois	Confirmation of title to land in Missouri.	15	1	Petition	280	Priv. Land Claims.						
Sancier, Francois	Confirmation of title to land in Missouri.	16	1	Petition	36	Priv. Land Claims.						
Sancier, Francois	Confirmation of title to land in Missouri.	17	1	Petition	55	Public Lands.						
Sancier, Francois	Confirmation of title to land in Missouri.	18	1	Petition	55	Public Lands.						
Sancier, Jean Baptiste	Confirmation of title to land in Louisiana.	22	1	Petition	78	Priv. Land Claims.	90	Favorable	175	Referred to Committee Whole House.		
Sancier, Jean Baptiste	Confirmation of title to land in Louisiana.	22	2	Bill of last sess.	66	Whole House	Dec. 13, 1832	With't amend	175	Passed	Passed	App'd Jan. 30, 1833
Sangrain, Antoine F	Confirmation of title to land in Missouri.	15	1	Petition	157	Priv. Land Claims.						
Sangrain, Antoine F	Confirmation of title to land in Missouri.	15	2	Petition	118	Priv. Land Claims.						
Sangrain, Frederick	Confirmation of an entry of land.	25	3	Petition	451	Public Lands.						
Sangrain, Frederick	Confirmation of an entry of land.	26	2	Petition	89	Priv. Land Claims.				Discharged; laid on table.		
				Senate bill	334	Whole House			S. 161	Laid on table.		
Sanguayunk, Cornelius, widow of.	Pension for revolutionary services.	23	1	Petition	333	Rev. Pensions.						
Saul, Hiram	Pension	22	2	Petition	245	Invalid Pensions.						
Saul, Hiram	Pension	23	2	Resolution	207	Invalid Pensions.						
				Documents	237	Invalid Pensions	Feb. 3, 1835	Adverse		Laid on table.		
Saul, Hiram	Pension	24	1	Petition	97	Invalid Pensions	Mar. 24, 1836	Adverse		Laid on table.		
Saul, Hiram	Pension	24	2	Petition	267	Invalid Pensions	205	Favorable	924	Referred to Committee Whole House.		

List of private claims presented to the House of Representatives of the United States from the 1st to the 31st Congress, inclusive—Continued.

Names of claimants.	Nature or object of the claim.	Congress.	Session.	How brought before the House of Reps.	Page of journal.	To what committee of the House referred.	No. or date of the report.	Nature of the report.	No. of the bill.	How disposed of by the House of Reps.	How disposed of by the Senate.	Date of the act of Congress, and remarks.
Saul, Hiram	Pension	25	2	Petition	39	Invalid Pensions	590	Favorable	577	Passed	Adverse report.	
Saul, Hiram	Pension	26	1	Petition	162	Invalid Pensions	183	Favorable	195	Passed	Indef. postp'd.	
Sauligne, Joseph, assignees of.	Confirmation of title to land in Louisiana.	27	2	Petition	58	Priv. Land Claims.						
Savage, Charles	Compensation for diplomatic services.	22	1	House bill	426	Foreign Affairs.						
Savage, Charles	(See William Fuller and Charles Savage.)	30	2		142				261			
Savage & Dugan	Indemnity for French spoliations prior to 1800.	26	1	Memorial	182	Foreign Affairs		Favorable	319	Referred to Committee Whole House.		
Savage, Ebenezer	Pension for revolutionary services.	22	1	Petition	381	Rev. Pensions.						
Savage, Ebenezer	Pension for revolutionary services.	24	1	Res. and docs.	914	Rev. Pensions.						
Savage, Henry R.	(See heirs of Timothy Savage)	31	1		232							
Savage, James	Bounty land for revolutionary services.	11	2	Petition	216	Public Lands.						
Savage, James, *et al*	Indemnity for destruction of property at Plattsburgh.	13	3	Petition	723	Claims	Feb. 15, 1815	Favorable	297	Passed	Passed	App'd March 3, 1815
Savage, John	Pension	26	1	Petition	326	Invalid Pensions	551	Adverse		Laid on table.		
Savage, John	Pension	27	2	Petition	130	Invalid Pensions	229	Adverse		Laid on table.		
Savage, John	Pension	30	1	Petition	339	Invalid Pensions	455	Favorable	385	Passed	Passed, second session.	App'd March 3, 1849
Savage, Joseph	Arrears of pay as sergeant major	4	1	Petition	469	Claims	May 31, 1796	Adverse		Laid on table.		
Savage, Joseph	Additional compensation for transmitting electoral vote of Massachusetts.	11	1	Petition	19	Claims	May 31, 1809	Adverse.		Rejected.		
Savage, Dr. Joseph	Commutation pay for services as surgeon.	24	1	Documents	851	Rev. Claims.						
Savage, Dr. Joseph, heirs of.	Commutation pay for services as surgeon.	25	2	Petition	177	Rev. Claims	855	Favorable	773	Referred to Committee Whole House.		
Savage, Dr. Joseph, heirs of.	Commutation pay for services as surgeon.	25	3	House bill	431	Whole House			773			
Savage, Dr. Joseph, heirs of.	Commutation pay for services as surgeon.	26	1	Petition	166	Rev. Claims.						
Savage, Dr. Joseph, heirs of.	Commutation pay for services as surgeon.	30	1	Petition	198	Rev. Claims	330	Favorable	307	Referred to Committee Whole House.		
Savage, Dr. Joseph, heirs of.	Commutation pay for services as surgeon.	30	2	Bill of last sess.	142	Whole House	Dec. 22, 1849	With't amend.	307	Passed.		
Savage, Dr. Joseph, heirs of.	Commutation pay for services as surgeon.	31	1	Petition	225	Rev. Claims	189	Favorable	195	Referred to Committee Whole House.		
Savage, Josiah, and others	Refunding certain tonnage duties, and to be exonerated from further duties.	18	1	Memorial	27	Ways and Means	Mar. 17, 1824	Adverse		Laid on table.		
Savage, Nathaniel L., executor of.	Indemnity for destruction of property by United States troops.	5	2	Petition	291					Laid on table.		
Savage, Nathaniel L., executor of.	Indemnity for destruction of property by United States troops.	5	3	Petition	478	Claims	Mar. 2, 1799	Adverse		Leave to withdraw.		
Savage, Teackle, *et al*	Compensation for capture of a British vessel.	14	1	Petition	548					Referred to Secretary Navy.		
				Rep. of Secretary Navy.	618					Laid on table.		
Savage, Teackle, *et al*	Compensation for capture of a British vessel.	14	2	Petition	91	Naval Affairs.	Feb. 17, 1817	Favorable	139	Passed	Passed	App'd March 3, 1817
Savage, Teackle, *et al*	(See administrator of Bolitha Laws)	22	2		124							

List of private claims presented to the House of Representatives of the United States from the 1st to the 31st Congress, inclusive—Continued.

3—35

Names of claimants.	Nature or object of the claim.	Congress.	Session.	How brought before the House of Reps.	Page of journal.	To what committee of the House referred.	No. or date of the report.	Nature of the report.	No. of the bill.	How disposed of by the House of Reps.	How disposed of by the Senate.	Date of the act of Congress, and remarks.
Savage, Timothy	Indemnity for French spoliations prior to 1800.	26	1	Memorial	182	Foreign Affairs	343	Favorable; bill	319	Referred to Committee Whole House.		
Savage, Timothy	Indemnity for French spoliations prior to 1800.	29	2	Memorial	199	Foreign Affairs.						
Savage, Timothy, heirs of.	Indemnity for French spoliations prior to 1800.	31	1	Petition	232	Foreign Affairs	355	General bill	318	Referred to Committee Whole House.		
Savage, William, by attorney.	Indemnity for Indian depredations.	19	2	Petition	134	Indian Affairs	51	Favorable	......	Referred to Committee Whole House.		
Savage, William Henry	Reimbursement of office rent and stationery.	12	2	Petition	582	Claims	Feb. 12, 1813	Adverse	......	Laid on table.		
Savage, William Henry	Reimbursement of office rent and stationery.	13	2	Petition	226	Claims	Feb. 24, 1814	Favorable	137	Passed	Passed	App'd April 9, 1814
Saveak, John	Duplicate land warrant	21	1	Resolution	510	Judiciary.						
Savings Institution, Louisville.	Reimbursement of money improperly paid.	25	2	Documents	176	Claims	466	Favorable	470	Referred to Committee Whole House.		
Savourys, Moses, assignee of.	Indemnity for French spoliations prior to 1800.	26	1	Memorial	182	Foreign Affairs	343	Favorable; bill	319	Referred to Committee Whole House.		
Sawers, Michael	Bounty land f r revolutionary services.	12	1	Petition	57	Claims	April 15, 1812	Adverse	......	Referred to Committee Whole House.		
Sawtell, Hezekiah	Pension for revolutionary services.	10	2	Pension bill	499	....	....	....	158	Passed	Passed, with amendment.	App'd March 3, 1809
Sawyer, Abraham	Pension	11	2	Pension bill	283	....	....	....	107	Passed	Passed, with amendment.	App'd April 27, 1810
Sawyer, Ansel	Confirmation of title to land in Alabama.	24	1	Documents	212	Indian Affairs.						
Sawyer, Azariah, widow of	Pension for revolutionary services.	26	1	Petition	283	Rev. Pensions.						
Sawyer, Azariah, widow of	Pension for revolutionary services.	26	2	Petition	35	Rev. Pensions.						
Sawyer, Azariah, widow of	Pension for revolutionary services.	27	2	Petition	59	Rev. Pensions	111	Favorable	157	Passed	Indef. postp'd.	
Sawyer, Azariah, widow of	Pension for revolutionary services.	27	3	Petition	107	Rev. Pensions	163	Favorable	779	Referred to Committee Whole House.		
Sawyer, Enoch	Increase of salary as revenue officer	4	1	Petition	466	Com. and Manuf.						
Sawyer, Esther	(See Azariah Sawyer, widow of.)	26	1	....	283							
Sawyer, Horace B.	Pension	25	2	Petition	113	Naval Affairs	....	....	......	Discharged; laid on table.		
Sawyer, Isaac	Bounty on fishing schooner Betsey.	7	1	Petition and rep't Sec. Treasury.	111	....	....	....	......	Referred to Committee Whole House.		
Sawyer, Isaac, (Maine)	Pension	26	1	Petition	708	Invalid Pensions.						
Sawyer, Isaac, (Maine)	Pension	27	2	Petition	98	Invalid Pensions	635	Adverse	......	Laid on table.		
Sawyer, Jabez	Arrears of pension	21	2	Senate bill	217	Military Pensions	Jan. 28, 1831	Adverse	S. 92	Laid on table.		
Sawyers, James	Compensation for revolutionary services.	11	2	Petition	134	Claims	Feb. 7, 1810	Adverse	......	Referred to Committee Whole House.		
Sawyers, James	Compensation for revolutionary services.	13	2	Petition	206	Pens. & Rev. Cl'ms.	92	Adverse	......	Referred to Committee Whole House.		
Sawyers, James	Compensation for revolutionary services.	15	1	Petition	203	Pens. & Rev. Cl'ms.						
Sawyer, James	Pension for revolutionary services.	16	1	Resolution	200	....	....	....	......	Rreferred to Secretary of War.		
Sawyer, James Lucius	Compensation for services in the war of 1812.	21	2	Resolution	77	Claims	16	Favorable	530	Referred to Committee Whole House.		
Sawyer, James Lucius	Compensation for services in the war of 1812.	22	1	Resolution	26	Claims	Dec. 19, 1831	Favorable	32	Passed	Passed	App'd Feb. 18, 1832
Sawyer, Joseph	Arrears of pay as captain in revenue service.	29	1	Petition	255	Claims	279	Adverse	......	Laid on table.		

List of private claims presented to the House of Representatives of the United States from the 1st to the 31st Congress, inclusive—Continued.

Names of claimants.	Nature or object of the claim.	Congress.	Session.	How brought before the House of Reps.	Page of journal.	To what committee of the House referred.	No. or date of the report.	Nature of the report.	No. of the bill.	How disposed of by the House of Reps.	How disposed of by the Senate.	Date of the act of Congress, and remarks.
Sawyer, Luke	Pay due him for revolutionary service.	24	1	Petition	633	Rev. Claims	824	Adverse		Laid on table.		
Sawyer, Mary	Recovery of land sold for taxes	15	1	Petition	132	Ways and Means.						
Sawyier, Nathan'l & others	Right to purchase certain public lands.	14	1	Petition	153	Public Lands	Jan. 23, 1816	Adverse		Rejected.		
Sawyer, Oramel	Increase of compensation as postmaster.	19	1	Petition	407	P. Of. & P. Roads.						
Sawyer, Robert, representatives of.	Commutation pay for revolutionary services.	22	2	Resolution	121	Rev. Claims				Discharged; laid on table.		
Sawyer, Samuel	Pension for revolutionary services.	3	1	Rep. of Secretary War.	131	Select	May 26, 1794	Res. to refer to Sec'ry War.	J.R. 12	Passed	Passed	App'd June 9, 1794
Sawyer, Samuel	Pension for revolutionary services.	3	2	Rep. of Secretary War.	262	Claims	Feb. 28, 1795	Favorable; bill ordered.	130	Passed	Postponed.	
Sawyer, Samuel	Pension for revolutionary services.	4	1	Rep. of Secretary War.	445	Claims	Feb. 18, 1796	Favorable; bill ordered.	156	Passed	Passed	App'd April 20, 1796
Sawyer, Samuel	Pension for revolutionary services.	13	1	Pension bill	56	Whole House	July 20, 1813	Favorable	31	Passed	Passed	App'd Aug. 2, 1813
Sawyer, William	Pension for revolutionary services	3	1	Rep. of Secretary War.	131	Select	May 26, 1794	Res. to refer to Sec. War.	J. R. 12	Passed	Passed	App'd June 9, 1794
Sawyer, William	Pension for revolutionary services.	4	1	Rep. of Secretary War.	445	Claims	Feb. 18, 1796	Res. to refer to Sec. War.	J. R. 16	Passed	Passed	App'd April 18, 1796
Saxton, Huldah	(See James Saxton, widow of.)	27	2		756							
Saxton, James, widow of	Pension for revolutionary services.	27	2	Petition	756	Rev. Pensions	784	Adverse		Laid on table.		
Saxton, James, widow of	Pension for revolutionary services.	28	1	Petition	116	Rev. Pensions				Discharged; laid on table.		
Saxton, James, widow of	Pension for revolutionary services.	28	2	Petition	68	Rev. Pensions.						
Saxton, James, widow of	Pension for revolutionary services.	29	1	Petition	118	Rev. Pensions	526	Adverse		Laid on table.		
Saxton, John	Pension	20	1	Petition	37	Military Pensions				Discharged; laid on table.		
Saxon, William	Compensation for extra work on Cumberland road.	24	1	Petition	851	Claims.						
Sayers, Benjamin	Pension for naval services	22	1	Petition	37	Naval Affairs.						
Sayers or Sayre, Benjamin	Indemnity for loss on Cumberland road contract.	24	1	Petition	430	Claims.						
Sayers or Sayer, Benjamin	Indemnity for loss on Cumberland road contract.	24	2	Petition	267	Claims.						
Sayers or Sayer, Benjamin	Indemnity for loss on Cumberland road contract.	25	2	Petition	88	Claims.						
Sayers or Sayer, Benjamin	Indemnity for loss on Cumberland road contract.	25	3	Petition	86	Claims	206	Adverse		Referred to Committee Whole House.		
Sayers or Sayer, Benjamin	Indemnity for loss on Cumberland road contract.	26	2	Petition	135	Claims.						
Sayers or Sayer, Benjamin	Indemnity for loss on Cumberland road contract.	28	1	Petition	124	Claims.						
Sayers or Sayer, Benjamin	Indemnity for loss on Cumberland road contract.	29	1	Petition	90	Claims	280	Adverse		Laid on table.		
Sayers or Sayer, Benjamin	Indemnity for loss on Cumberland road contract.	30	1	Petition	172	Claims	361	Adverse		Laid on table.		
Sayers or Sayer, Benjamin	Indemnity for loss on Cumberland road contract.	31	1	Petition	390	Claims.						
Sayers, Robert, representatives of.	Commutation pay for revolutionary services.	25	2	Resolution	528	Rev. Claims				Discharged; laid on table.		
Sayles, Samuel S	Compensation for services as a seaman.	25	2	Petition	395	Claims.						

List of private claims presented to the House of Representatives of the United States from the 1st to the 31st Congress, inclusive—Continued.

Names of claimants.	Nature or object of the claim.	Congress.	Session.	How brought before the House of Reps.	Page of journal.	To what committee of the House referred.	No. or date of the report.	Nature of the report.	No. of the bill.	How disposed of by the House of Reps.	How disposed of by the Senate.	Date of the act of Congress, and remarks.
Sayles, Samuel S.	Compensation for services as a seaman.	26	1	Petition	170	Claims	576	Adverse	......	Laid on table.		
Sayles, William	Release from imprisonment at suit of United States.	17	2	Petition	22	P. Of. & P. Roads.	Dec. 11, 1822	Favorable	188	Passed	Laid on table.	
Sayre, James	Pension for revolutionary services.	25	2	Petition	629	Rev. Pensions	882	Favorable	788	Passed	Passed	App'd July 7, 1838
Sayre, Nathan	Pension for revolutionary services.	20	2	Resolution	67	Whole House.						
Sayre, Stephen	Compensation for services and expenses as diplomatic agent.	3	1	Petition and rep't Sec. of War.	54, 128	Select.						
Sayre, Stephen	Compensation for services and expenses as diplomatic agent.	3	2	Petition	261	Whole House.						
Sayre, Stephen	Compensation for services and expenses as diplomatic agent.	6	1	Petition	554	Claims	April 14, 1800	Adverse	......	Leave to withdraw.		
Sayre, Stephen	Compensation for services and expenses as diplomatic agent.	7	1	Memorial	110	Claims	Mar. 24, 1802	Adverse	......	Leave to withdraw.		
Sayre, Stephen	Compensation for services and expenses as diplomatic agent.	7	2	Memorial	329	Claims	....	....	......	Discharged; leave to withdraw.		
Sayre, Stephen	Compensation for services and expenses as diplomatic agent.	8	1	Memorial	518	Claims	....	....	......	Referred to Committee Whole House.		
Sayre, Stephen	Compensation for services and expenses as diplomatic agent.	8	2	Memorial & docs. and rep. of Secretary of State.	58, 116	....	....	....	......	Referred to Committee Whole House.		
Sayre, Stephen	Compensation for services as secretary, &c.	4	1	Petition	486	Claims.						
Sayre, Stephen	Compensation for services as secretary, &c.	4	2	Resolution	614	Claims.						
Sayre, Stephen	Compensation for services as secretary, &c.	5	2	Petition	133	Claims	Jan. 15, 1798	Adverse	......	Referred to Committee Whole House.		
Sayre, Stephen	Compensation for services as secretary, &c.	5	3	Petition and rep't	445	....	....	....	......	Referred to Committee Whole House.		
Sayre, Stephen	Compensation for services as secretary, &c.	9	1	Memorial	192	....	....	....	......	Referred to Committee Whole House.		
Sayre, Stephen	Compensation for services as secretary, &c.	9	2	Memorial	494	Claims	Feb. 12, 1807	Favorable; bill ordered.	201	Passed	Passed, with amendment.	App'd March 3, 1807
Sayre, Stephen	Additional compensation for services in Europe.	10	2	Memorial	347	....	....	....	......	Rejected.		
Sayward, Joseph	Indemnity for French spoliations prior to 1800.	26	1	Memorial	182	Foreign Affairs	343	Favorable; bill	319	Referred to Committee Whole House.		
Sayward, Henry, surety of.	Release from liability on a certain bond.	11	3	Petition	505	Com. and Manuf.						
Sayward, Joseph	Indemnity for French spoliations prior to 1800.	31	1	Petition	196	Foreign Affairs	355	General bill	318	Referred to Committee Whole House.		
Scales, Nathaniel	Compensation for services of his team and driver, rev. war.	25	2	Petition	269	Rev. Pensions	....	....	......	Discharged; laid on table.		
Scalf, John	Pension for revolutionary services.	26	1	Petition	962	Rev. Pensions.						
Scalf, John	Bounty land for revolutionary services.	29	1	Petition	948	Rev. Claims.						
Scannon, Nicholas, administrator of.	(See Thomas Cutts, jr.)	22	1	....	226	....	310	....	390			
Scantland, James M	Pension for disability, Mexican war.	30	1	Senate bill	1163	....	....	....	S. 337	Passed	Passed	App'd Aug. 7, 1848
Scantland, James M	Pension for disability, Mexican war.	30	2	Senate bill	203	....	....	....	S. 377	Passed	Passed	App'd Jan. 19, 1849
Scantling, Thomas	Compensation for military and naval services.	25	2	Petition	594	Naval Affairs	....	....	......	Discharged; laid on table.		

List of private claims presented to the House of Representatives of the United States from the 1st to the 31st Congress, inclusive—Continued.

Names of claimants.	Nature or object of the claim.	Congress.	Session.	How brought before the House of Reps.	Page of journal.	To what committee of the House referred.	No. or date of the report.	Nature of the report.	No. of the bill.	How disposed of by the House of Reps.	How disposed of by the Senate.	Date of the act of Congress, and remarks.
Scarborough, John, heirs of.	Commutation pay for revolutionary services.	24	1	Petition	432	Rev. Claims.						
Scarborough, John, heirs of.	Commutation pay for revolutionary services.	25	3	Petition	125	Rev. Claims.						
Scarborough, Silas S	(See William H. Bedford, agent).	28	1		262							
Scause, Barbary	Pension for revolutionary services of her husband.	27	2	Petition	1437	Rev. Pensions.						
Schaeffer, Elizabeth	(See William Seavey, executrix of)	26	1		182							
Schaeffer, F	Reimbursem't of medical expenses.	30	1	Petition	1093	Claims.						
Schafer, Henry	Pension for revolutionary wounds and disability.	3	1	Rep. of Secretary War.	131	Select	May 26, 1794	Res. to refer to Sec. War.	J. R. 12	Passed	Passed	App'd June 9, 1794
Schafer, Henry	Pension for revolutionary wounds and disability.	4	1	Rep. of Secretary War.	445	Claims.						
Schafer, Henry	Pension for revolutionary wounds and disability.	4	2	Rep. of Secretary War.	614	Claims.						
Schaeffer, John	Compensation for revolutionary services.	23	1	Petition	368	Rev. Claims.						
Schafer, Peter	Pension for revolutionary disability.	3	1	Rep. of Secretary War.	131	Select	May 26, 1794	Res. to refer to Sec. War.	J. R. 12	Passed	Passed	App'd June 9, 1794
Schammburg, Bartholo'w, administrator of.	Reimbursement of money paid Major Riddle.	30	1	Petition	644	Military Affairs				Discharged; laid on table.		
Schammburg, James W	(See Bartholomew Schammburg, administrator of.)	30	1		644							
Scheib, Catharine	(See Catharine Schieb.)	27	2		614							
Scheifflin, Jacob	Permission to import certain merchandise.	12	1	Petition	63	Com. and Manuf.						
Scheifflin, Jacob and son	Indemnity for confiscation of a cargo of sugar.	14	2	Petition	122					Referred to Secretary of State.		
Scheifflin, Jacob and son	Indemnity for confiscation of a cargo of sugar.	16	1	Petition	65							
				Rep. of Secretary State.	137	Claims	Jan. 19, 1820	Adverse		Laid on table.		
Scheifflin, Jacob and son	Indemnity for confiscation of a cargo of sugar.	16	2	Rep't of last sess.	153	Whole House.						
Scheifflin, Jacob and son	Indemnity for confiscation of a cargo of sugar.	17	1	Petition	77	Foreign Relations	85	Adverse		Referred to Committee Whole House.		
Scheifflin, Jacob and son	Indemnity for confiscation of a cargo of sugar.	17	2	Petition	227					Referred to President of United States.		
Scheifflin, Jacob and son	Indemnity for French spoliations in 1809.	18	1	Petition	344	Foreign Affairs.						
Scheifflin, Jacob, executors of.	Indemnity for British seizure	30	1	Petition	187	Claims	473	Adverse		Laid on table.		
Scheifflin, Jonathan	Compensation for services as agent of Indian affairs.	9	1	Petition	351					Laid on table.		
Scheifflin, Jonathan	Compensation for services as agent of Indian affairs.	9	2	Petition	529	Claims.						
Scheifflin, Richard L	(See Jacob Scheifflin)	30	1		187							
Schell, George	Pension	1	2	House bill	271	Whole House	July 11, 1790	With't amend.	88	Passed	Passed	App'd Aug. 11, 1790
Schell, Johannes	Pension for revolutionary disabilities.	3	1	Rep. of Secretary War.	131	Select.	May 26, 1794	Res. to refer to Sec. War.	J. R. 12	Passed	Passed	App'd June 9, 1794
Schell, Johannes	Pension for revolutionary disabilities.	4	1	Rep. of Secretary War.	445	Claims.						

List of private claims presented to the House of Representatives of the United States from the 1st to the 31st Congress, inclusive—Continued.

Names of claimants.	Nature or object of the claim.	Congress.	Session.	How brought before the House of Reps.	Page of journal.	To what committee of the House referred.	No. or date of the report.	Nature of the report.	No. of the bill.	How disposed of by the House of Reps.	How disposed of by the Senate.	Date of the act of Congress, and remarks.
Schell, Johannes	Pension for revolutionary disabilities.	4	2	Rep. of Secretary War.	614	Claims.						
Schell, John, jr	Increase of compensation as postmaster.	17	2	Petition	82	P. Of. & P. Roads.						
Scheller, Ludwick, widow of.	Pension	20	1	Petition	310	Military Pensions	April 8, 1828	Adverse		Laid on table.		
Scheller, Rosanna	(See Ludwick Scheller, widow of.)											
Schellinger, George	Indemnity for destruction of property by United States troops.	31	1	Petition	762	Claims.						
Scheltz, Christopher	Right of pre-emption as branch pilot New Orleans.	28	1	Petition	77	Priv. Land Claims.	9	Favorable	35	Passed	Passed	App'd June 17, 1844
Schenck, Ann	(See Ralph Schenck, widow of.)	25	2		272							
Schenck, John H	Pension for revolutionary services.	25	2	Petition	231	Rev. Pensions				Discharged; laid on table.		
Schenck, John H	Pension for revolutionary services.	25	3	Petition	367	Rev. Pensions.						
Schenck, John H	Pension for revolutionary services.	26	1	Petition	175	Rev. Pensions				Discharged; laid on table.		
Schenck, John H	Pension for revolutionary services.	26	2	Petition	82	Rev. Pensions.						
Schenck, John H	Pension for revolutionary services.	27	2	Petition	69	Rev. Pensions.						
Schenck, John H	Pension for revolutionary services.	27	2	Memorial	553	Rev. Pensions	784			Laid on table.		
Schenck, Paul	Compensation for revolutionary supplies.	3	1	Petition	185					Laid on table.		
Schenck, Paul	Compensation for revolutionary supplies.	3	2	Petition	250	Claims	Jan. 5, 1795	Adverse		Leave to withdraw.		
Schenck, Peter A	Liquidation of a revolutionary certificate.	4	1	Rep. of Secretary Treasury.	388	Claims	May 31, 1796	Adverse		Laid on table.		
Schenck, Peter A	(See David Gelston and P. A. S.)	14	1		538							
Schenck, Ralph	Compensation for revolutionary services.	19	2	Petition	44	Rev. Claims	Dec. 19, 1826	Adverse.		Laid on table.		
Schenck, Ralph	Compensation for a horse lost in revolutionary war.	23	1	Petition	157	Rev. Claims	Feb. 25, 1834	Adverse		Laid on table.		
Schenck, Ralph	Compensation for revolutionary services and losses.	23	2	Petition	331	Rev. Claims.						
Schenck, Ralph, widow of.	Pension for revolutionary services.	25	2	Petition	272	Rev. Pensions				Referred to Committee Whole House on bill No. 456.		
Schenck, Robert	Remission of certain tonnage duties.	21	1	Petition	171	Ways and Means	Feb. 2, 1830	Adverse		Laid on table.		
Schermerhorn, Daniel	Renewal of a lost certificate	2	1	Petition and rep't Sec. Treasury.	583	Select.						
Schermerhorn, Jane	(See William W. Schermerhorn, widow of.)											
Schermerhorn, Jane, and others.	Lands in consideration of the loss of their husbands in Indian wars.	24	1	Memorial	113	Public Lands	Feb. 10, 1836	Adverse		Laid on table.		
Schermerhorn, Jane, and others.	Lands in consideration of the loss of their husbands in Indian wars.	24	2	Memorial	95	Priv. Land Claims.				Discharged; laid on table.		
Schermerhorn, John F	Reimbursement of expenditure on public account.	30	1	Petition	440	Indian Affairs.						
Schermerhorn, John F	Reimbursement of expenditure on public account.	31	1	Petition	763	Indian Affairs.						
Schermerhorn, John L	Pension for revolutionary services.	23	1	Petition	191	Rev. Pensions.						
Schermerhorn, Wm. W., widow of.	Indemnity for property destroyed by Indians.	24	1	Petition	153	Claims	Jan. 27, 1836	Adverse		Laid on table.		
Schieb, Catharine	To be restored to pension roll	27	2	Petition	614	Rev. Pensions	784	Adverse		Laid on table.		

List of private claims presented to the House of Representatives of the United States from the 1st to the 31st Congress, inclusive—Continued.

Names of claimants.	Nature or object of the claim.	Congress.	Session.	How brought before the House of Reps.	Page of journal.	To what committee of the House referred.	No. or date of the report.	Nature of the report.	No. of the bill.	How disposed of by the House of Reps.	How disposed of by the Senate.	Date of the act of Congress, and remarks.
Schindler, Theresa, and M. A. Fisher.	Exchange of a grant of land at Mackinaw.	20	1	Petition	485	Public Lands.						
Schley, William	(See executor of J. G. Posner)	19	2		82							
Schliecker, P. F	(See administrator of John M. Burt)	31	1		215		355		318			
Schmidt, J. S	(See Louis F. Beeler, and others.)	30	1		115		482					
Schmiemeyer, John F	Confirmation of title to land in Missouri.	30	2	Petition	240	Public Lands.						
Schmuck, Ellen A	(See Jacob Schmuck, widow of.)											
Schmuck, Jacob, widow of	Pension for military services	24	1	Petition	201	Invalid Pensions	335	Favorable	350	Passed	Passed	App'd June 28, 1836
Schmuck, Jacob, widow of	Pension for military services	26	2	Petition	54	Invalid Pensions	230	Adverse		Laid on table.		
Schnabel, George, and A. Green.	Reimbursement of money paid for public lands.	26	1	Petition	332	Public Lands.						
Schnabel, George, and A. Green.	Reimbursement of money paid for public lands.	26	2	Resolution	61	Public Lands.						
Schnabel, George	Reimbursement of money paid for public land.	27	2	Petition	534	Priv. Land Claims.	682	Favorable	J. R. 9	Passed	Passed	App'd July 27, 1842
Schnebly, Henry C	Payment of works made by T. B. Hall.	24	1	Resolution	514	Judiciary.						
Schnebly, Henry C	Payment of works made by T. B. Hall.	24	2	Resolution	48	Judiciary.						
Schnebly, Henry C	Payment of works made by T. B. Hall.	25	2	Documents	233	Judiciary.						
Schneider, Casper	Remission of duty on a still	7	1	Petition	25	Ways and Means.	Dec. 29, 1801	Adverse		Rejected.		
Schnell, Philip	Pension for revolutionary services.	28	1	Petition	289	Rev. Pensions.						
Schoedde, Theodore A	(See Minis & Henry, and others)	15	2		144							
Scholfield, Asahel	Pension for revolutionary services.	22	1	Petition	255	Rev. Pensions.						
Scholfield & Taylor, agent of.	Remission of certain illegal duties.	16	1	Petition	212	Ways and Means.						
Schoner, or Shoner, Henry.	Pension	21	1	Petition	478	Military Pensions.	April 13, 1830	Adverse		Laid on table.		
Schoolcraft, Col. Lawrence.	Compensation in land for revolutionary services and losses.	18	2	Resolution	146	Public Lands.						
Schooler, John, widow of.	Pension for disabilities	28	1	Petition	714	Invalid Pensions				Discharged; laid on table.		
Schoolfield, J. N	(See administrator of Robert Roe)	31	1		197							
Schoonmaker, Frederick, heirs of.	Reimbursement of revolutionary expenditures.	31	1	Petition	1135	Rev. Claims.						
Schoonmaker, Henry	Increase of pension	19	1	Petition	43	Rev. Pensions	164	Adverse		Laid on table.		
Schoonmaker, Johannes	Pension for revolutionary services.	21	2	Resolution	48	Military Pensions.						
Schoonmaker, Thomas F	(See heirs of Frederick Schoonmaker.)	31	1		1135							
Schoonmaker, Zachariah	Indemnity for money lost while paymaster.	13	2	Petition	185	Claims	Mar. 10, 1814	Indefinite		Laid on table.		
Schoonmaker, Zachariah	Indemnity for money lost while paymaster.	14	1	Petition	70	Claims	Jan. 29, 1816	Adverse		Laid on table.		
Schoonmaker, Zachariah, administrator of.	Indemnity for money lost while paymaster.	17	1	Petition	38	Claims	Mar. 29, 1822	Adverse		Referred to Committee Whole House.		
Schoonover, James	Pension	14	1	Resolution	514	Pens. & Rev. Cl'ms.						
Schoonover, James	Pension	25	3	Petition	570	Invalid Pensions.						
Schoonover, James	Pension	26	1	Petition	163	Invalid Pensions.						
Schoonover, James	Pension	31	1	Petition	436	Invalid Pensions.						
Schoonover, Samuel	Pension	14	1	Pension bill	622	Whole House	April 23, 1823	With amend.	171	Passed	Passed	App'd April 30, 1816
Schovil, Asahel	Compensation for horses lost in public service.	13	3	Petition	514	Claims	Nov. 14, 1814	Favorable	228	Indefinitely postponed.		

List of private claims presented to the House of Representatives of the United States from the 1st to the 31st Congress, inclusive—Continued.

Names of claimants.	Nature or object of the claim.	Congress.	Session.	How brought before the House of Reps.	Page of journal.	To what committee of the House referred.	No. or date of the report.	Nature of the report.	No. of the bill.	How disposed of by the House of Reps.	How disposed of by the Senate.	Date of the act of Congress, and remarks.
Schott, James	(See Frederick Dawson, and others)	30	1		617							
Schott, John Paul	Compensation for services as revolutionary officer.	1	3	Petition	396					Referred to Secretary of War.		
Schrack, Lewis	Compensation for gun-stocks made on contract.	18	1	Petition	115	Military Affairs.						
Schrack, Lewis	Compensation for gun-stocks made on contract.	19	1	Petition	249	Claims.						
Schrack, Lewis	Compensation for gun-stocks made on contract.	19	2	Petition	134	Claims	Jan. 12, 1827	Adverse		Laid on table.		
Schrack, Lewis	Compensation for gun-stocks made on contract.	20	1	Petition	99	Claims.	231	Favorable	260	Referred to Committee Whole House.		
Schrack, Lewis	Compensation for gun-stocks made on contract.	20	2	House bill	284	Whole House	Feb. 13, 1829	With amend.	260	Passed.		
Schrack, Lewis	Compensation for gun-stocks made on contract.	21	1	Petition	35	Claims	4	Favorable	4	Passed	Passed	App'd Jan. 30, 1830
Schrader, or Schroder, John	Pension	16	1	Petition	325	Rev. Pensions	April 6, 1820	Adverse		Laid on table.		
Schram, Frederick	Pension for revolutionary services.	22	1	Petition	470	Rev. Pensions.						
Schreffwar, George	Compensation for services as revolutionary surgeon.	3	2	Petition	283	Claims.	Jan. 30, 1795	Adverse		Leave to withdraw.		
				Petition, (2)	353		March 2, 1795	Adverse		Laid on table.		
Schreinmaker, Catharine	(See Francis Schreinmaker)	2	1		461							
Schreinmaker, Francis, widow of.	Depreciation pay due deceased)	2	1	Petition	461					Referred to Secretary War.		
Schroeder, Henry, & others.	Indemnity for damage to Lutheran church in 1814.	14	1	Petition	146	Claims.						
Schroeder, John	(See John Schrader, or Schroder.)	16	1		325							
Schroyer, Christian	Indemnity for six hundred dollars lost in mail.	26	1	Petition	341	P. Of. & P. Roads.						
				Petition, (2)	618	P. Of. & P. Roads.	394	Adverse		Laid on table.		
Schultze, Charles	(See John Bowers, administrator of.)	26	1		182							
Schultz, Jacob	Exchange of an entry of land	16	2	Petition	249	Public Lands				Discharged; laid on table.		
Schultz, Jacob	Exchange of an entry of land	17	1	Petition	101	Public Lands						Leave to withdraw, 2d sess., 18th Cong.
Schultz, John	(See H. Silliman, and others)	12	1		98							
Schultz, John	Pension for revolutionary services.	22	1	Petition	538	Rev. Pensions.						
Schultz, John	Compensation for rifle and equipments.	22	1	Petition	538	Rev. Claims				Discharged; laid on table.		
Schultz, Nicholas	Bounty land for entering public service.	2	1	Petition	464	Select.						
Schultz, Nicholas	Compensation for revolutionary services.	2	2	Petition	474					Referred to Secretary of War.		
Schultz and Vogeler	(See Jacob Shinnick, and others.)	13	3		522							
Schumaker, F. A.	(See E. Pavenstedt, and F. A. S.)	31	1		202		35					
Schumann, Franz	Pension and bounty land for military services.	31	1	Petition	617	Military Affairs				Discharged; laid on table.		
Schureman, Hercules	Pension for revolutionary services.	2	1	Petition	936	Rev. Pensions.						
Schutt, C. C., heir of	Indemnity for French spoliations prior to 1800.	26	1	Memorial	182	Foreign Affairs	343	Favorable; bill	319	Referred to Committee Whole House.		
Schutt, Casper C., son of.	Release of sundry judgments	13	3	Petition	563	Com. and Manuf.						
Schutt, Casper C., son of.	Release of sundry judgments	14	1	Petition	148	Com. and Manuf	Mar. 19, 1816	Favorable		Passed	Passed	App'd April 29, 1816
Schutt, Lewis H. C	(See son of Casper C. Schutt)	13	3		563							
Schuyler, Catharine	(See John S. Schuyler)	24	1		275							
Schuyler, David A.	Pension for revolutionary services and sufferings.	21	1	Resolution	431	Military Pensions	April 27, 1830	Adverse		Laid on table.		

List of private claims presented to the House of Representatives of the United States from the 1st to the 31st Congress, inclusive—Continued.

Names of claimants.	Nature or object of the claim.	Congress.	Session.	How brought before the House of Reps.	Page of journal.	To what committee of the House referred.	No. or date of the report.	Nature of the report.	No. of the bill.	How disposed of by the House of Reps.	How disposed of by the Senate.	Date of the act of Congress, and remarks.
Schuyler, John P	Pension for services in war of 1812.	18	1	Petition	196	Pens. & Rev. Cl'ms.	Feb. 25, 1824	Adverse	......	Leave to withdraw.		
Schuyler, John P	Pension for services in war of 1812.	22	2	Petition	245	Invalid Pensions.						
Schuyler, John P	Pension for services in war of 1812.	23	1	Petition	96	Invalid Pensions ..	Mar. 31, 1834	Adverse......	......	Laid on table.		
Schuyler, John P	Arrears of pension under act of April 24, 1816.	27	3	Petition	150	Invalid Pensions...	183	Favorable	798	Passed	Adverse report.	
Schuyler, John P	Arrears of pension under act of April 24, 1816.	28	1	Petition	73	Invalid Pensions ..	14	Favorable	41	Passed	Indef. postp'd.	
Schuyler, John P	Arrears of pension under act of April 24, 1816.	29	1	Petition	82	Invalid Pensions.						
Schuyler, John S., widow of.	Compensation for revolutionary services.	24	1	Petition	275	Rev. Claims......	....	....	......	Discharged; laid on table.		
Schuyler, Nicholas	Compensation for extra services as revolutionary surgeon.	3	1	Petition	59	....	....	....	......	Referred to Secretary War.		
Schuyler, Nicholas	Compensation for extra services as revolutionary surgeon.	3	2	Rep. of Secretary War.	278	Claims	Mar. 2, 1795	Adverse	......	Laid on table.		
Schuyler, Nicholas	Compensation for ext a services as revolutionary surgeon.	4	1	Rep. of Secretary War.	445	Claims	May 31, 1796	Adverse	......	Laid on table.		
Schuyler, Nicholas	Pension	21	1	Petition	36	Military Pensions..	April 24, 1830	Adverse	......	Laid on table.		
Schuyler, Peter P	Credit for money lost in the mail.	14	1	Petition	156	Claims	Feb. 4, 1814	Adverse	......	Rejected.		
Schwartzaver, Mary Eve..	Indemnity for damage to property in 1814.	19	1	Petition	151	Claims	Feb. 22, 1826	Adverse	......	Laid on table.		
Schwartze, August J.....	Indemnity for French spoliations prior to 1800.	26	1	Memorial	182	Foreign Affairs....	343	Favorable; bill	319	Referred to Committee Whole House.		
Schwartztrauber, Philip...	Compensation for work on Red river improvement.	28	1	Petition	683	Claims	408	Favorable	314	Passed	Adverse report.	
Schwartztrauber, Philip...	Compensation for work on Red river improvement.	28	2	Petition	117	Claims	13	Favorable	475	Passed	Passed	App'd March 3, 1845
Schweighauser, John D., representatives of.	Compensation for revolutionary services and supplies.	9	2	Petition	607	....	....	....	......	Referred to Secretary Treasury.		
Schweighauser, John D., representatives of.	Compensation for revolutionary services and supplies.	10	1	Rep. of Secretary Treasury.	71	Claims.						
Schweighauser, John D., representatives of.	Compensation for revolutionary services and supplies.	10	1	Petition	455	Claims	Feb. 27, 1809	Favorable	171	Referred to Committee Whole House.		
Schwenck, Jacob........	(See executors of John Kerlin)...	19	1	....	131							
Schwenck, Jacob........	Pension for revolutionary services.	24	2	Petition	399	Rev. Pensions.						
Schweyer, Margaret......	(See administrator of Henry Allis.)	2	1	....	461							
Scioto, ship, owners of....	Compensation for use of said ship.	21	1	House bill	248	Whole House.						
Scison, Nicholas	Pension for revolutionary services.	29	1	Petition	385	Rev. Pensions.....	April 30, 1830	With't amend.	191	Passed	Passed	App'd May 29, 1830
Scoby, John..	(See son of Matthew Scoby).....	25	3	....	220							
Scoby, Matthew, son of ..	Compensation for slave and team .	25	3	Petition	220	Rev. Claims.						
Scoby, Matthew, son of ..	Compensation for slave and team .	26	1	Petition	167	Rev. Claims.						
Scoby, Matthew, son of ..	Compensation for slave and team .	26	2	Petition	76	Rev. Claims.						
Scoby, Matthew, son of...	Compensation for slave and team .	28	2	Petition	303	Rev. Claims.						
Scoby, Matthew, son of...	Compensation for slave and team .	29	1	Petition	176	Rev. Claims......	394	Adverse	......	Laid on table.		
Scofield, Josiah W.......	Pension for revolutionary services.	22	1	Petition	381	Rev. Pensions.						
Scoggins, Jonah........	Compensation for revolutionary services.	28	1	Petition	335	Rev. Claims.						
Scolacuttaw, (Indian,) widow of.	Indemnity for losses and injuries by armed men.	4	2	Petition	637	Claims	Jan. 17, 1797	Adverse	......	Referred to Committee Whole House.		
Scollay, Esther	(See John Scollay)	30	1	....	166							
Scollay, John, widow of..	Pension for revolutionary services.	30	1	Petition	166	Rev. Pensions	89	Adverse	......	Laid on table.		
Scollay, John, widow of ..	Pension for revolutionary services.	30	2	Petition	322	Rev. Pensions.						
Scoone, George	Pension for revolutionary services.	8	2	Senate bill	165	Whole House.....	Mar. 2, 1805	With't amend.	S. 14	Passed	Passed	App'd March 3, 1805

List of private claims presented to the House of Representatives of the United States from the 1st to the 31st Congress, inclusive—Continued.

Names of claimants.	Nature or object of the claim.	Congress.	Session.	How brought before the House of Reps.	Page of journal.	To what committee of the House referred.	No. or date of the report.	Nature of the report.	No. of the bill.	How disposed of by the House of Reps.	How disposed of by the Senate.	Date of the act of Congress, and remarks.
Scotland, Thomas	Indemnity for revolutionary sufferings and services.	9	1	Petition	309	Claims	Mar. 28, 1806	Adverse		Indef. postponed.		
Scotland, Thomas	Indemnity for revolutionary sufferings and services.	11	3	Petition	438	Claims.						
Scotland, Thomas	Indemnity for revolutionary sufferings and services.	12	1	Petition	349	Claims	June 8, 1812	General bill	138	Passed	Passed, with amendment.	App'd July 5, 1812
Scott, Abraham M., and others.	Right of pre-emption	13	3	Petition	533	Public Lands.						
Scott, Abraham M., and others.	Right of pre-emption	14	1	Petition	61, 113	Public Lands.						
Scott, Abraham M., and others.	Right of pre-emption	14	2	Petition	50	Priv. Land Claims.						
Scott, Abraham M., and others.	Right of pre-emption	15	2	Petition	192	Priv. Land Claims.						
Scott, Alexander, and others	Indemnity for slaves captured by Indians.	8	2	Petition	74	Claims	Jan. 22, 1805	Adverse		Leave to withdraw.		
Scott, Alexander, and others	Indemnity for slaves captured by Indians.	11	2	Petition	196	Select	Mar. 14, 1810	Favorable		Referred to Committee Whole House.		
Scott, Alexander, and others	Indemnity for slaves captured by Indians.	11	3	Petition	445	Select	Dec. 20, 1810	Favorable		Referred to Committee Whole House.		
Scott, Alexander, and others	Indemnity for slaves captured by Indians.	12	1	Petition	44	Select.						
Scott, Alexander, and others	Indemnity for slaves captured by Indians.	13	2	Petition	307	Claims.						
Scott, Alexander, and others	Indemnity for slaves captured by Indians.	20	1	Petition	164	Claims.						
Scott, Alexander, and others	Indemnity for slaves captured by Indians.	21	1	Petition	116	Indian Affairs.						
Scott, Alex'r, assignee of.	Pay and bounty land	9	1	Petition	192	Claims				Discharged; leave to withdraw.		
Scott, Alex'r, assignee of.	Pay and bounty land	10	2	Petition	459	Claims.						
Scott, Alex'r, assignee of.	Pay and bounty land	11	2	Petition	127	Claims.						
Scott, Alex'r, assignee of.	Pay and bounty land	12	1	Petition	39	Claims.						
Scott, Alex'r, assignee of.	Pay and bounty land	14	1	Petition	146	Pens. & Rev. Cl'ms.						
Scott, Alex'r, assignee of.	Pay and bounty land	16	1	Petition	139	Pens. & Rev. Cl'ms.	Jan. 21, 1820	Adverse		Laid on table.		
Scott, Alex'r, assignee of.	Pay and bounty land	19	2	Petition	158	Rev. Claims				Discharged.		
Scott, Alex'r, assignee of.	Pay and bounty land	20	1	Petition	126	Rev. Claims	Feb. 28, 1828	Adverse		Laid on table.		
Scott, Alex'r, assignee of.	Pay and bounty land	21	2	Petition	74	Rev. Claims.						
Scott, Alex'r, assignee of.	Pay and bounty land	22	1	Petition	190	Rev. Claims	Jan. 25, 1832	Adverse		Laid on table.		
Scott, Alex'r, assignee of.	Pay and bounty land	22	2	Petition	137	Rev. Claims	Jan. 11, 1833	Adverse		Laid on table.		
Scott, Alexander	Compensation for release and transportation of seamen.	13	1	Senate bill	55	Claims	June 29, 1813	With't amend.	12	Passed with amendm't	Passed as am'd	App'd July 22, 1813
Scott, Alexander	(See Abr'm M. Scott and others).	13	3		533							
Scott, Alexander	Increase of salary as a revenue officer.	18	1	Petition	172	Commerce				Discharged; leave to withdraw.		
				Senate bill	531	Commerce	May 21, 1824	With't amend	S. 105	Passed	Passed	App'd May 26, 1824
Scott, Alexander, and others	Indemnity for non fulfilment of a government contract.	19	1	Petition and docs.	254	P. Of. & P. Roads.						
Scott, Alexander, (D. C.).	Compensation for services as government agent.	19	1	Petition	337	Foreign Affairs	Mar. 23, 1826	Adverse		Leave to withdraw.		
Scott, Alexander, (D. C.).	Compensation for services as government agent.	20	1	Petition	245	Foreign Affairs	182	Adverse		Laid on table.		

List of private claims presented to the House of Representatives of the United States from the 1st to the 31st Congress, inclusive—**Continued.**

Names of claimants.	Nature or object of the claim.	Congress.	Session.	How brought before the House of Reps.	Page of journal.	To what committee of the House referred.	No. or date of the report.	Nature of the report.	No. of the bill.	How disposed of by the House of Reps.	How disposed of by the Senate.	Date of the act of Congress, and remarks.
Scott, Alexander, (D. C.)	Compensation for services as government agent.	20	2	Petition	79	Foreign Affairs	72	Favorable	428	Referred to Committee Whole House.		
Scott, Alexander, (D. C.)	Compensation for services as government agent.	21	1	Petition	40	Foreign Affairs	20	Favorable	27	Passed	Passed	App'd May 29, 1830
Scott, Alexander, (D. C.)	Reimbursement of advances and expenses.	22	2	Petition	82	Foreign Affairs.						
Scott, Alexander, (D. C.)	Interest on advances	23	1	Petition	37	Foreign Affairs	427	Favorable	453	Referred to Committee Whole House.		
Scott, Alexander, (D. C.)	Interest on advances	24	1	Petition	59	Foreign Affairs	550	Favorable	541	Referred to Committee Whole House.		
Scott, Alexander, (D. C.)	Interest on advances	25	2	Petition	267	Foreign Affairs	518	Favorable	512	Ref'd to Com. W. H.		
Scott, Alexander, (D. C.)	Interest on advances	25	3	House bill	379	Whole House			512			
Scott, Alexander, (D. C.)	Interest on advances	26	1	Petition	182	Foreign Affairs.						
Scott, Alexander, (D. C.)	Interest on advances	26	2	Petition	148	Foreign Affairs	201	Adverse		Laid on table.		
Scott, Alexander, widow of.	Equitable settlement of the accounts of deceased.	29	1	Memorial	701	Foreign Affairs.						
Scott, Alexander, jr	Unpaid salary as inspector of customs.	20	1	Petition	30	Claims	Feb. 11, 1828	Adverse		Rejected.		
Scott, Alexander, jr., assignee of.	Unpaid salary as inspector of customs.	20	2	Petition	100	Ways and Means				Discharged; laid on table.		
Scott, Alexander, jr., assignee of.	Unpaid salary as inspector of customs.	21	1	Senate bill	686	Ways and Means			S. 182			
Scott, Alexander, jr., assignee of.	Unpaid salary as inspector of customs.	22	1	Senate bill	816	Commerce	July 7, 1832	Adverse	S. 121	Laid on table.		
Scott, Alexander, jr., assignee of.	Unpaid salary as inspector of customs.	22	2	Senate bill	441	Claims	Mar. 1, 1833	With't amend.	S. 96	Passed	Passed	App'd March 3, 1833
Scott, Alexander, jr., assignee of.	Interest on appropriation	23	2	Petition	164	Judiciary.						
Scott, Alexander, jr., mother of.	Interest on appropriation	24	2	Petition	80	Claims				Leave to withdraw.		
Scott, Alexander, jr., mother of.	Interest on appropriation	25	2	Petition	71	Judiciary				Discharged; laid on table.		
Scott, Alexander	(See William Knox and others.)	23	2		275							
Scott, Alexander	Pension	27	2	Resolution	216	Invalid Pensions.						
Scott, Almedeus	Re-issue of land patent	30	1	Petition	276	Claims	411	Favorable	361	Passed.		
Scott, Amasa	Invalid pension	3	2	Rep. of Secretary War.	337	Claims	Feb. 28, 1795	Favorable	130	Passed	Postponed.	
Scott Amasa	Invalid pension	4	1	Rep. of Secretary War.	445	Claims	Feb. 18, 1796	Favorable	156	Passed	Passed	App'd April 20, 1796
Scott, Anna	(See Major Samuel Scott, widow of)	28	1		74							
Scott, Anna L	(See James Scott, widow of)	31	1		712							
Scott, Axum	Pension	6	1	Petition	59	Rev. Pensions	April 6, 1820	Adverse		Laid on table.		
Scott, Charles	Increase of pension	9	2	Pension bill	608				216	Passed	Passed	App'd March 3, 1807
Scott, Charles	Increase of pension	25	2	Petition	399	Invalid Pensions				Discharged; laid on table.		
Scott, Charles	Increase of pension	25	3	Petition	128	Invalid Pensions.						
Scott, Charles J., executor of.	Indemnity for French spoliations prior to 1800.	26	1	Memorial	182	Foreign Affairs	343	Favorable; bill	319	Referred to Committee Whole House.		
Scott, Christopher	Pension for services in revolutionary navy.	20	1	Petition	56	Military Affairs				Discharged; laid on table.		
Scott, Clarissa	(See J. & B. Monsarto, heir of.)	18	1		177							
Scott, Cyrus C	Compensation for transportation of the mail.	24	2	Petition	395	Claims.						

List of private claims presented to the House of Representatives of the United States from the 1st to the 31st Congress, inclusive—Continued.

Names of claimants.	Nature or object of the claim.	Congress.	Session.	How brought before the House of Reps.	Page of journal.	To what committee of the House referred.	No. or date of the report.	Nature of the report.	No. of the bill.	How disposed of by the House of Reps.	How disposed of by the Senate.	Date of the act of Congress, and remarks.
Scott, Cyrus C	Compensation for transportation of the mail.	25	2	Memorial	88	Claims	439	Fovorable, in part.	......	Discharged; referred to P. O. Department.		
Scott, Cyrus C	Compensation for transportation of the mail.	26	1	Petition	339	Claims	372	Adverse	......	Recommitted.		
Scott, Cyrus C	Compensation for transportation of the mail.	26	2	Petition	81	Claims.						
Scott, Cyrus C	Compensation for transportation of the mail.	27	2	Petition	94	Claims.						
Scott, Cyrus C	Compensation for transportation of the mail.	28	1	Petition	371	Claims	241	Adverse	......	Laid on table.		
Scott, David	Renewal of a loan office certificate.	3	2	Petition	273	Claims	Feb. 25, 1795	Adverse	......	Referred to Committee Whole House.		
Scott, David	Renewal of a loan office certificate.	4	2	Petition	667	Claims	Jan. 30, 1797	Adverse	......	Rejected.		
Scott, David	Pension	13	2	Petition	199	Pens. & Rev. Cl'ms.						
Scott, David	Pension	14	1	Pension bill	622	Whole House.	April 23, 1816	With amend.	171	Passed	Passed	App'd April 29, 1816
Scott, David, heirs of	Commutat on pay for revolutionary services.	29	1	Petition	1256	Rev. Claims.						
Scott, Dennis	Pension for revolutionary services.	18	1	Petition	52	Pens. & Rev. Cl'ms.	Dec. 16, 1823	Adverse	......	Laid on table.		
Scott, Drucilla	(See Joseph Scott, widow of)	29	2	....	223							
Scott, Edward	Pension	1	2	House bill	271	Whole House	July 19, 1790	With amend.	88	Passed	Passed	App'd Aug. 11, 1790
Scott, Eleazer	Pension	17	2	Petition	117	Whole House.						
Scott, Eleazer	Pension	18	1	Petition	74	Pens. & Rev. Cl'ms.	Dec. 31, 1823	G neral pension bill.	35	Name stricken out	....	Leave to withdraw.
Scott, Eleazer	Pension	18	2	Petition	36	Pens. & Rev. Cl'ms.						
Scott, Eleazer	Pension	19	1	Petition	129	Military Pensions	May 5, 1826	Favorable	118	Passed.		
Scott, Eleazer	Pension	19	2	Pension bill	85	Whole House.	Feb. 3, 1827	With amend.	314	Passed	Passed, with amendment.	App'd March 3, 1827
Scott, Elizabeth	(See heirs of Joseph Scott)	11	2	....	127							
Scott, Elizabeth	(See assignee of Alex'r Scott, jr.)	20	2	....	100							
Scott, Elizabeth	(See mother of Alex'r Scott, jr.)	24	2	....	80							
Scott, Elizabeth	(See heirs of William Blackwell)	22	1	....	263							
Scott, Elizabeth B	(See Alexander Scott, deceased)	29	1	....	701							
Scott, Ezekiel	Pay and emolument as a revolutionary officer.	2	2	Petition	631	Select	Jan. 18, 1793	Not found	......	Referred to Committee Whole House.		
Scott, Ezekiel	Pay and emolument as a revolutionary officer.	4	1	Petition	427	Claims	May 7, 1796	Adverse.	......	Rejected.		
Scott, Ezekiel	Pay and emolument as a revolutionary officer.	8	1	Petition	452	Claims	....	....	......	Referred to Committee Whole House.		
Scott, Ezekiel	Pension	21	1	Petition	260	Military Pensions	April 2, 1830	Adverse	......	Laid on table.		
Scott, Gabriel	(See heirs of William Scott)	15	2	....	25							
Scott, George	(See William Thompson, Va.)	20	1	....	38	....	....	....	......	....	....	See act for relief of W. Thompson.
Scott, George	Compensation for services as an Indian spy.	29	1	Petition	85	Rev. Pensions.						
Scott, George	(See B. Marshall and others)	30	1	....	809							
Scott, George, sureties of.	Remission of forfeiture for violation of non-intercourse act.	15	1	Petition	30	Ways and Means	Feb. 3, 1818	By bill	67	Passed	Passed	App'd April 18, 1818
Scott, Gustavus	(See William Patterson & others)	3	1	....	25							
Scott, Hector	Payment of a certificate of debenture.	15	1	Petition	76	Com. and Manuf.	Mar. 30, 1818	Adverse	......	Leave to withdraw.		
Scott, Hector	(See D. S. Kennedy and others)	15	2	....	209							
Scott, Hector	(See James Lenox and others)	17	1	....	32							

List of private claims presented to the House of Representatives of the United States from the 1st to the 31st Congress, inclusive—Continued.

Names of claimants.	Nature or object of the claim.	Congress.	Session.	How brought before the House of Reps.	Page of journal.	To what committee of the House referred.	No. or date of the report.	Nature of the report.	No. of the bill.	How disposed of by the House of Reps.	How disposed of by the Senate.	Date of the act of Congress, and remarks.
Scott, James	Compensation for revolutionary services and losses.	3	1	Petition	132	Select.						
Scott, James	Compensation for revolutionary services and losses.	9	1	Petition	351					Laid on table.		
Scott, James	Compensation for revolutionary services and losses.	24	1	Petition	405	Rev. Pensions	437	Favorable	452	Passed	Passed	App'd June 28, 1836
Scott, James	Remission of duty on still and liquors.	6	2	Petition	775					Referred to Secretary of Treasury.		
				Rep. of Secretary Treasury.	835					Laid on table.		
Scott, James	Remission of duty on still and liquors.	7	1	Petition & docs.	76	Claims	Feb. 5, 1802	Adverse		Rejected.		
Scott, James	Reimbursement of duty paid on stills.	7	2	Petition	304	Ways and Means	Jan. 27, 1803	Adverse		Rejected.		
Scott, James, (Pa.)	Compensation for services and disabilities.	24	2	Petition	85	Invalid Pensions	Dec. 30, 1837	Adverse		Laid on table.		
Scott, James, (Pa.)	Compensation for services and disabilities.	25	2	Petition	56	Invalid Pensions				Discharged.		
Scott, James, (Pa.)	Compensation for services and disabilities.	26	1	Petition	327	Invalid Pensions	418	Adverse		Laid on table.		
Scott, James	Right of pre-emption as New Orleans branch pilot.	28	1	Petition	77	Priv. Land Claims.	9	Favorable	35	Passed	Passed	App'd June 17, 1844
Scott, James A.	Invalid pension	23	2	Petition	131	Invalid Pensions	Jan. 12, 1835	Adverse		Laid on table.		
Scott, James A.	Invalid pension	24	2	Petition	159	Invalid Pensions.						
Scott, James, and others	Compensation for locating land warrants.	31	1	Petition	198	Public Lands.						
Scott, James, widow of	Pension for revolutionary services.	31	1	Petition	712	Rev. Pensions	258	Adverse		Laid on table.		
Scott, John	(See executor of Charles Yates)	20	1		846							
Scott, John	Pension	21	1	Resolution	255	Military Pensions.						
Scott, John	Pension	21	2	Petition	61	Military Pensions.						
Scott, John, (Pa.)	Pension	22	1	Petition	260	Invalid Pensions	297	Favorable	377	Passed.		
Scott, John, (Pa.)	Pension	22	2	Petition	93	Invalid Pensions	Feb. 13, 1833	Favorable	738	Referred to Committee Whole House.		
Scott, John, (Pa.)	Pension	24	1	Petition	407	Invalid Pensions	602	Favorable	583	Passed	Passed	App'd June 28, 1836
Scott, John	Pension for revolutionary services.	22	1	Resolution	338	Rev. Pensions				Discharged; laid on table.		
Scott, John	Compensation for horse lost in public service.	23	2	Petition	132	Rev. Claims.						
Scott, John	Compensation for horse lost in public service.	24	1	Petition	104	Rev. Claims	Jan. 12, 1836	Adverse		Laid on table.		
Scott, John	Compensation for horse lost in public service.	28	1	Petition	516	Rev. Claims.						
Scott, John	Compensation for horse lost in public service.	28	2	Petition	169	Rev. Claims.						
Scott, John	Indemnity for destruction of property by Indians.	25	2	Petition	255	Indian Affairs.						
Scott, John, repsesentatives of.	Indemnity for destruction of property by Indians.	26	1	Senate bill	837	Claims			S. 270			
Scott, John, representatives of.	Indemnity for destruction of property by Indians.	26	2	Senate bill	327	Whole House			S. 171			
Scott, John, representatives of.	Indemnity for destruction of property by Indians.	27	2	Senate bill	1042	Indian Affairs	July 21, 1842	With't amend.	S. 55	Passed	Passed	App'd Aug. 11, 1842

List of private claims presented to the House of Representatives of the United States from the 1st to the 31st Congress, inclusive—Continued.

Names of claimants.	Nature or object of the claim.	Congress.	Session.	How brought before the House of Reps.	Page of journal.	To what committee of the House referred.	No. or date of the report.	Nature of the report.	No. of the bill.	How disposed of by the House of Reps.	How disposed of by the Senate.	Date of the act of Congress, and remarks.
Scott, John	(See representatives of Nimrod Farrow and Richard Harris.)	29	1		75							
Scott, John	Indemnity for injuries sustained in Creek war.	31	1	Memorial	653	Military Affairs.						
Scott, John B.	Liquidation of revolutionary certificate.	4	1	Rep. of Secretary Treasury.	388	Claims						
Scott, John E., administratrix of.	Commutation pay for revolutionary services.	30	1	Petition	625	Rev. Claims				Discharged; laid on table.		
Scott, John H.	Compensation for work and materials on Cumberland road.	23	1	Res. and docs.	589	Claims	455	Adverse		Laid on table		See report No. 449.
Scott, John L.	Compensation for arms furnished mounted volunteers.	25	3	Senate bill	657				S. 122			
Scott, John L.	Compensation for arms furnished mounted volunteers.	26	1	Senate bill	813	Claims	658	Adverse	S. 143	Referred to Committee Whole House.		
Scott, Jonathan	Compensation for a horse lost in public service.	26	1	Memorial	939	Claims.						
Scott, Jonathan	Compensation for a horse lost in public service.	28	1	Petition	241	Claims.						
Scott, Jonathan	Compensation for a horse lost in public service.	28	2	Petition	46	Claims.						
Scott, Jonathan	Compensation for a horse lost in public service.	29	1	Petition	116	Claims	340	Adverse		Laid on table.		
Scott, Joseph, heirs of	Compensation for ferriage of American troops.	11	2	Petition	127	Claims.						
Scott, Joseph, (Va.)	Pay and subsistence as a revolutionary captain.	12	1	Petition	28	Claims	Mar. 13, 1812	Adverse		Leave to withdraw.		
Scott, Joseph, (Va.)	Pension for revolutionary services.	14	2	Petition	65	Pens. & Rev. Cl'ms.				Discharged; laid on table.		
Scott, Joseph, widow of	Pension for revolutionary services.	29	2	Petition	223	Rev. Pensions.						
Scott, Joseph, heirs of	Commutation pay for revolutionary services.	24	1	Petition	105	Rev. Claims	506	Adverse		Laid on table.		
Scott, Joseph	(See heirs of William Scott)	26	1		332							
Scott, Joseph O.	Release from payment of public money destroyed by fire.	31	2	Petition	179	P. Of. & P. Roads.						
Scott, Josiah	Correction of error in land entry.	28	2	Petition	65	Public Lands.	121	Favorable	604	Referred to Committee Whole House.		
Scott, Mary Ann	Payment of a revolutionary certificate.	14	2	Petition	438	Pens. & Rev. Cl'ms.				Leave to withdraw.		
Scott, Mary, administratrix.	(See John E. Scott)	30	1		625							
Scott, Obidiah	Remission of payment on a distillery license.	6	1	Petition and rep't Sec. Treasury.	624					Laid on table.		
Scott, Obidiah	Confirmation of title to land in Missouri.	13	1	Petition	28	Public Lands				Discharged.		
Scott, Obidiah	Confirmation of title to land in Missouri.	13	2	Petition	168	Public Lands	April 9, 1814	Adverse		Leave to withdraw.		
Scott, Presley	Balance due for piles at St. Louis.	26	1	Petition	338	Cliams	653	Favorable	489	Referred to Committee Whole House.		
Scott, Richard	Pension for revolutionary services.	10	1	Pension bill	232	Whole House			78	Passed	Passed, with amendment.	App'd April 25, 1808
Scott, Robert	Increase of salary as engraver for United States mint.	4	2	Petition	644	Select.						
Scott, Robert	Compensation for military services	18	1		330	Military Affairs				Discharged; laid on table.		
Scott, Robert	Compensation for military services.	19	1	Petition	53	Priv. Land Claims.	Jan. 31, 1826	Adverse		Laid on table.		

List of private claims presented to the House of Representatives of the United States from the 1st to the 31st Congress, inclusive—Continued.

Names of claimants.	Nature or object of the claim.	Congress.	Session.	How brought before the House of Reps.	Page of journal.	To what committee of the House referred.	No. or date of the report.	Nature of the report.	No. of the bill.	How disposed of by the House of Reps.	How disposed of by the Senate.	Date of the act of Congress, and remarks.
Scott, Robert	Payment of reserved military bounty	19	1	Resolution	265	Claims				Discharged; laid on table.		
Scott, Robert, (Ky.)	Compensation for rifle lost in Indian wars.	22	2	Petition	313	Claims.						
Scott, Robert	Compensation for a horse lost in Seminole war.	23	1	Documents	154	Claims.						
Scott, Robert	(See Wm. H. Bedford, agent)	28	1		262							
Scott, Robert G.	(See sureties of Nathaniel Denby)	30	2		350							
Scott, R. C., and E. K. Wilson.	Confirmation of title to land in Louisiana.	23	1	Petition	93	Priv. Land Claims.						
Scott, R. C., and E. K. Wilson.	Confirmation of title to land in Louisiana.	23	2	Petition	49	Priv. Land Claims.	Dec. 24, 1834	Adverse		Laid on table.		
Scott, R. T.	(See agent of the State of Alabama)	31	1		909							
Scott, Samuel	Pension	14	1	Pension bill	622	Whole House	April 23, 1816	With amend.	171	Passed	Passed	App'd April 30, 1816
Scott, Samuel, widow of.	Bounty land and commutation pay for revolutionary services.	28	1	Memorial	74	Rev. Claims.						
Scott, Samuel, widow of.	Bounty land and commutation pay for revolutionary services.	28	2	Memorial	135	Rev. Claims.						
Scott, Samuel, widow of.	Bounty land and commutation pay for revolutionary services.	29	1	Petition	126	Rev. Claims	121	Adverse		Laid on table.		
Scott, Samuel P.	Indemnity for damages in a suit for assault.	24	1	Petition	127	Claims	128	Adverse		Laid on table.		
Scott, Seybert, and others.	Indemnity for Indian depredations.	19	2	Petition	134	Indian Affairs	51	Favorable		Referred to Committee Whole House.		
Scott, Susanna	(See William Scott, Connecticut)	28	1		61							
Scott, Thomas	(See heirs of William Scott)	15	2		25							
Scott, Thos., *als.* T. Knox	Pension	20	1	House bill	645	Military Pensions	April 29, 1828	Favorable	283	Passed.		
Scott, Thos., *als.* T. Knox	Pension	20	2	Pension bill	55	Whole House	Jan. 15, 1829	With amend.	311	Passed	Laid on table.	
Scott, Thos., *als.* T. Knox	Pension	21	1	Pension bill	130	Whole House	Feb. 13, 1830	With amend.	72	Passed	Passed, with amendment.	App'd May 20, 1830
Scott, Thomas	Extra compensation as a land officer	28	1	Petition	713	Public Lands.						
Scott, Thomas	Extra compensation as a land officer	29	1	Petition	297	Public Lands	588	Favorable	406	Referred to Committee Whole House.		
Scott, Thomas	Extra compensation as a land officer	29	2	Documents	98	Whole House.						
				Documents	236	Whole House.						
Scott, Thomas	Extra compensation as a land officer	30	1	Petition	99	Claims	59	Favorable	44	Passed	Passed	App'd June 28, 1848
Scott, Thomas, B., *et al.*	Confirmation of title to land in Louisiana.	29	1	Petition	440	Priv. Land Claims.	697	Favorable	471	Referred to Committee Whole House.		
Scott, William	Pension for revolutionary disabilities	1	2	Petition	153					Referred to Secretary War.		
Scott, William	Pension for revolutionary disabilities	3	2	Rep. of Secretary War.	278	Claims.						
Scott, William	Pension for revolutionary disabilities	4	1	Rep. of Secretary War.	445	Claims	Feb. 18, 1796	Res. to refer to Sec. War.	J. R. 16	Passed	Passed	App'd April 18, 1796
Scott, William	Pension for revolutionary disabilities	4	2	Rep. of Secretary War.	614	Claims	Feb. 6, 1797	Favorable; bill ordered.	224	Passed	Postponed.	
Scott, William	Pension for revolutionary disabilities	5	2	Pension bill	127	Whole House	Jan. 11, 1798	With amend.	38	Passed	Passed	App'd Feb. 2, 1798
Scott, William	Indemnity for losses as a revolutionary officer.	2	1	Petition	554					Referred to Secretary War.		
Scott, William	Indemnity for losses as a revolutionary officer.	2	2	Rep. of Secretary War.	735					Laid on table.		
Scott, William, administrator of.	Indemnity for losses as a revolutionary officer.	3	1	Rep. of Secretary War.	131	Select.						

List of private claims presented to the House of Representatives of the United States from the 1st to the 31st Congress, inclusive—Continued.

Names of claimants.	Nature or object of the claim.	Congress.	Session.	How brought before the House of Reps.	Page of journal.	To what committee of the House referred.	No. or date of the report.	Nature of the report.	No. of the bill.	How disposed of by the House of Reps.	How disposed of by the Senate.	Date of the act of Congress, and remarks.
Scott, William	Pension for revolutionary services.	10	1	Pension bill	232	Whole House	....	....	78	Passed	Passed, with amendment.	App'd April 25, 1808
Scott, William	(See heirs of Joseph Scott)	11	2	....	127							
Scott, William	Increase of pension	14	2	Petition	377	Pens. & Rev. Cl'ms.						
Scott, William	Equ table settlement of his accounts.	17	1	Petition	47	Claims.						
Scott, William	Bounty land due his father	18	1	Petition	283	Pens. & Rev. Cl'ms.						
Scott, William, (Penn.)	Pension for revolutionary services.	19	2	Resolution	116	Military Pensions.						
				Petition	131	Military Pensions.						
Scott, William, (Penn.)	Pension for revolutionary services.	20	1	Resolution	160	Military Pensions.	April 29, 1828	Favorable	283	Passed.		
Scott, William, (Penn.)	Pension for revolutionary services.	20	2	Pension bill	55	Whole House	Jan. 15, 1829	With amend.	311	Passed	Laid on table.	
Scott, William, (Penn.)	Pension for revolutionary services.	21	1	Pension bill	130	Whole House	Feb. 13, 1830	With amend.	72	Passed.	Passed, with amendment.	App'd May 20, 1830
Scott, William, (Conn.)	Pension for revolutionary services.	20	1	Resolution	314	Military Pensions.	April 29, 1828	Favorable	283	Passed.		
Scott, William, (Conn.)	Pension for revolutionary services.	21	1	Petition	49	Military Pensions.	Jan. 5, 1830	Pension bill	72	Passed	Passed, with amendment.	App'd May 20, 1830
Scott, William, (Conn.,) widow of.	Pension for revolutionary services.	28	1	Petition	61	Rev. Pensions	223	Favorable	177	Passed	Indef. postp'd.	
Scott, William, (Conn.,) widow of.	Pension for revolutionary services.	28	2	Petition	82	Rev. Claims	7	Favorable	457	Passed	Indef. postp'd.	
Scott, William, (Tenn.)	Pension for disabilities	21	2	Senate bill	225	Military Pensions.	Feb. 2, 1831	Adverse	S. 97	Laid on table.		
Scott, William, (Tenn.)	Pension for disabilities	22	1	Senate bill	521	Invalid Pensions	Mar. 31, 1832	With't amend.	S. 71	Passed	Passed	App'd July , 1832
Scott, William, administrator of.	Indemnity for Indian depredations.	21	2	Resolution	157	Indian Affairs.						
Scott, William, (Penn.)	Pension for disabilities, in the war of 1812.	25	3	Petition	128	Invalid Pensions	....	....	......	Discharged; laid on table.		
Scott, William, (Penn.)	Pension for disabilities, in the war of 1812.	26	1	Petition	327	Invalid Pensions	359	Favorable	338	Referred to Committee Whole House.		
Scott, William, (Penn.)	Pension for disabilities, in the war of 1812.	27	2	Petition	63	Invalid Pensions	142	Favorable	189	Laid on table.		
Scott, William, (Penn.)	Pension for disabilities, in the war of 1812.	27	3	Petition	44	Invalid Pensions	73	Adverse	......	Laid on table.		
Scott, William, (Penn.)	Pension for disabilities, in the war of 1812.	28	1	Petition	79	Invalid Pensions	303	Adverse	......	Laid on table.		
Scott, William, (Penn.)	Pension for disabilities, in the war of 1812.	28	2	Petition	141	Invalid Pensions.						
Scott, William, (Penn.)	Pension for disabilities, in the war of 1812.	31	1	Petition	1072	Invalid Pensions.						
Scott, William, heirs of, (Va.)	Bounty land for revolutionary services.	26	1	Petition	332	Public Lands.						
Scott, William, heirs of, (Va.)	Bounty land for revolutionary services.	27	2	Petition	297	Public Lands	510	Adverse	......	Laid on table.		
Scott, William B	Increase of compensation as a revenue officer.	23	1	Petition	369	Commerce	April 1, 1834	Favorable	401	Referred to Committee Whole House.		
Scott, William H	Indemnity for loss of a contract with Postmaster General.	30	1	Petition	438	P. Of. & P. Roads.						
Scott, William H	Indemnity for loss of a contract with Postmaster General.	31	1	Petition	808	P. Of. & P. Roads.						
Scott, William H	Indemnity for loss of a contract with Postmaster General.	31	2	Petition	444	P. Of. & P. Roads.	94	Favorable	491	Referred to Committee Whole House.		
Scott, William M	Indemnity for destruction of property at Detroit.	13	2	Petition	329	Claims	....	....	......	Discharged.		
Scott, William M	Indemnity for destruction of property at Detroit.	13	3	Petition	570	Claims	....	....	......	Discharged.		

List of private claims presented to the House of Representatives of the United States from the 1st to the 31st Congress, inclusive—Continued.

Names of claimants.	Nature or object of the claim.	Congress.	Session.	How brought before the House of Reps.	Page of journal.	To what committee of the House referred.	No. or date of the report.	Nature of the report.	No. of the bill.	How disposed of by the House of Reps.	How disposed of by the Senate.	Date of the act of Congress, and remarks.
Scott, William M	Indemnity for destruction of property at Detroit.	14	1	Petition	485	Claims.						
Scott, William W	Compensation for a horse lost in public service.	25	2	Petition	396	Claims.						
Scott, William W	Compensation for a horse lost in public service.	25	3	Petition	86	Claims	126	Adverse		Laid on table.		
Scott, William, heirs of	Confirmation of title to land in Mississippi Territory.	14	2	Petition	285	Priv. Land Claims.						
Scott, William, heirs of	Confirmation of title to land in Mississippi Territory.	15	1	Petition	25	Priv. Land Claims.	Jan. 29, 1819	Favorable	298	Referred to Committee Whole House.		
Scott, William, representatives of.	Exchange of an entry of public land.	19	2	Senate bill	351	Priv. Land Claims.			S. 104			
Scott, William, representatives of.	Exchange of an entry of public land.	20	1	Senate bill	332	Priv. Land Claims.	Feb. 26, 1828	With't amend.	S. 59	Referred to Committee Whole House.		
Scott, William, representatives of.	Exchange of an entry of public land.	20	2	Senate bill	349	Public Lands	Feb. 28, 1829	With't amend.	S. 74	Referred to Committee Whole House.		
Scott, William, heirs of	Commutation pay for revolutionary services.	24	1	Petition	106	Rev. Claims	282	Adverse		Laid on table.		
Scott, Winfield	Increased rate of pension	24	1	Resolution	343	Invalid Pensions	Jan. 9, 1836	Adverse		Laid on table.		
Scovel, Jonah	Pension for revolutionary services.	3	1	Rep. of Secretary War.	131	Select	May 26, 1794	Res. to refer to Sec. of War.	J. R. 12	Passed	Passed	App'd June 9, 1794
Scovel, Jonah, widow of	Pension for revolutionary services.	27	3	Petition	252	Rev. Pensions	295	Adverse		Laid on table.		
Scovel, Jonah, widow of	Pension for revolutionary services.	28	1	Petition	776	Rev. Pensions				Discharged; laid on table.		
Scovel Jonah, widow of	Pension for revolutionary services.	28	2	Petition	118	Rev. Pensions.						
Scovel, Jonah, widow of	Pension for revolutionary services.	29	1	Petition	104	Rev. Pensions	526	Adverse		Laid on table.		
Scovel, Sarah	(See Jonah Scovel)	27	3		252							
Scovil, James M. L	(See surety of William K. Lamson.)	21	1		234							
Scraggs, E. D. H	Exchange of an entry of land	24	1	Petition	671	Public Lands.						
Scranton, Abraham	Indemnity for loss on Continental money.	18	1	Petition	155	Pens. & Rev. Cl'ms.				Leave to withdraw.		
Scranton, Abraham	Indemnity for loss on Continental money.	19	2	Petition	158	Rev. Claims	Feb. 28, 1827	Adverse		Laid on table.		
Scranton, John	(See Martin Blatchley and J. S	22	1		671							
Scranton, John	Indemnity for loss of vessel captured by the French in 1779.	25	2	Petition	50	Foreign Affairs				Discharged; laid on table.		
Scranton, John	Indemnity for French spoliations prior to 1800.	26	1	Memorial	182	Foreign Affairs	343	Favorable; bill	319	Referred to Committee Whole House.		
Screven, Gen. James, executrix of.	Renewal of revolutionary certificates.	2	2	Petition	621	Whole House.						
Screven, R. B	Indemnity for property lost in Mexican war.	31	1	Petition	1003	Claims.						
Screven, Thomas	(See General James Sereven)	2	2		621							
Scriba, George	Permission to purchase a tract of public land.	1	2	Petition	166					Referred to Secretary Treasury.		
Scriba, George	Permission to purchase a tract of public land.	1	2	Memorial	173					Referred to Secretary Treasury.		
Scribel, To tengen	(See Marshall Sled, and others)	30	1		236							
Scribner, Abraham and Thomas Cabel.	Indemnity for a vessel taken for public use.	1	2	Petition	214					Referred to Secretary Treasury.		
Scribner, Abraham and Thomas Cabel.	Indemnity for a vessel taken for public use.	2	2	Rep. of Secretary Treasury.	636					Laid on table.		

List of private claims presented to the House of Representatives of the United States from the 1st to the 31st Congress, inclusive—Continued.

3—37

Names of claimants.	Nature or object of the claim.	Congress.	Session.	How brought before the House of Reps.	Page of journal.	To what committee of the House referred.	No. or date of the report.	Nature of the report.	No. of the bill.	How disposed of by the House of Reps.	How disposed of by the Senate.	Date of the act of Congress, and remarks.
Scribner, Nathaniel	Pension	3	1	Rep. of Secretary War.	135	Select	May 26, 1794	Res. to refer to Sec. War.	J. R. 12	Passed	Passed	App'd June 9, 1794
Scribner, Nathaniel	Pension	4	1	Rep. of Secretary War.	445	Claims	Feb. 18, 1796	Favorable; bill ordered.	156	Passed	Passed	App'd April 20, 1796
Scribner, Thaddeus	Pension	21	1	Petition	168	Military Pensions.						
Scribner, Thaddeus	Pension	21	2	Petition	53	Military Pensions.						
Scribner, Thaddeus	Pension	22	1	Petition	56	Rev. Pensions	Dec. 28, 1831	Adverse	......	Laid on table.		
Scrivener, James	Reimbursement of certain traveling expenses.	22	1	Petition	187	Naval Affairs	290	Favorable	375			
				Senate bill	745	Naval Affairs	June 2, 1831	With't amend.	S. 85	Passed with amendm't.	Passed as am'd.	App'd July 14, 1833
Scrivener, John	Indemnity for property destroyed by the enemy.	24	1	Petition	751	Claims	795	Adverse	......	Laid on table.		
Scrivener, John	Indemnity for property destroyed by the enemy.	25	2	Petition	1085	Claims	1046	Favorable	880	Referred to Committee Whole House.		
Scrivener, John	Indemnity for property destroyed by the enemy.	25	3	House bill	432	Whole House	Feb. 1, 1839	With't amend.	880	Passed	Adverse report.	
Scrivener, John	Indemnity for property destroyed by the enemy.	27	2	Petition	106	Claims	55	Favorable	90	Passed	Passed	App'd Aug. 27, 1842
Scrivener, John	Compensation for extra services in General Land Office.	29	1	Memorial	588	Claims	631	Adverse	......	Laid on table.		
Scrouf, Mary	Right of pre-emption to land in Ohio.	24	1	Petition	156	Priv. Land Claims	....	....	......	Discharged; laid on table.		
Scruder, Elizabeth	Continuation of pension	28	1	Petition	144	Rev. Pensions.						
Scudder, David & Eleazer.	Bounty on fishing schooners Polly and Dolphin.	4	1	Petition	516	Com. and Manuf.						
Scudder, David & Eleazer.	Bounty on fishing schooners Polly and Dolphin.	4	2	Petition	614	Com. and Manuf.	Dec. 25, 1797	Adverse	......	Rejected.		
Scudder, Mazor	Compensation for revolutionary services.	2	1	Petition	494	....	....	....	......	Referred to Secretary War.		
Scudder, schooner, owners of.	Indemnity for vessel destroyed at Baltimore.	21	1	House bill	248	Whole House	April 30, 1830	With't amend.	191	Passed	Passed	App'd May 29, 1830
Scudder, Wm. Smith	Pension for revolutionary services.	3	1	Rep. of Secretary of War.	175	....	....	....	......	Laid on table.		
Scudder, Wm. Smith	Pension for revolutionary services.	3	2	Rep. of Secretary of War.	262	Claims	Feb. 28, 1795	Favorable; bill	130	Passed	Postponed.	
Scudder, Wm. Smith	Pension for revolutionary services.	4	1	Report Secretary of War.	445	Claims	Feb. 18, 1796	Favorable; bill	156	Passed	Passed	App'd April 20, 1796
Scuggs, Israel B.	Compensation for a horse lost in the war 1812.	18	1	Petition	130	Claims.						
Scull, James, and others	Confirmation of claim to land under Quapaw treaty.	19	2	Petition	137	Public Lands	60	Favorable	401	Laid on table.		
Scull, James	Money in lieu of land allotted by treaty.	20	2	Resolution	49	Ways and Means	5	Adverse	......	Laid on table.		
Scull, James	Confirmation of claim to land in Arkansas.	22	1	House bill	421	Whole House	Feb. 28, 1832	With't amend.	425	Passed	Passed	App'd June 25, 1832
Scull, James	(See John B. Dachasein, assignee of.)	22	1	....	421							
Scull, James	(See LaCource, assignee of.)	22	1	....	421							
Scull, James	(See Michael Gimblet, assignee of.)	22	1	....	421							
Scull, Manette	(See Joseph Vallieries DeHauterive.)	31	2	....	270							

List of private claims presented to the House of Representatives of the United States from the 1st to the 31st Congress, inclusive—Continued.

Names of claimants.	Nature or object of the claim.	Congress.	Session.	How brought before the House of Reps.	Page of journal.	To what committee of the House referred.	No. or date of the report.	Nature of the report.	No. of the bill.	How disposed of by the House of Reps.	How disposed of by the Senate.	Date of the act of Congress, and remarks.
Scull, William	(See Thomas Dure, administrator of.)	18	1		130							
Scurloc, James, widow of.	Commutation pay for revolutionary services.	23	1	Petition	306	Rev. Claims.						
Scurloc, Lucy	(See James Scurloc, widow of.)											
Scurlock, Terry	Indemnity for loss on bank notes.	27	2	Petition	1006	Claims.						
Scurlock, Terry	Indemnity for loss on bank notes.	31	2	Petition	211	Claims.						
Scutt, William, widow of.	Pension for revolutionary services of her husband.	30	1	Resolution	122	Rev. Pensions	282	Favorable	278	Passed.		
Seabody, Jonathan	Pension	22	1	House bill	478	Rev. Pensions	367	Favorable	462	Passed	Indef. postp'd.	
Seaburn, James	Reimbursement of duty on a cargo of salt.	26	1	Petition	358	Ways and Means.						
Seaburn, James	Reimbursement of duty on a cargo of salt.	26	2	Petition	148	Ways and Means.						
Seaburn, James	Reimbursement of duty on a cargo of salt	27	2	Petition	55	Ways and Means	465	Favorable	315	Passed	Passed	App'd Aug. 11, 1842
Scager, Nathaniel	Release from imprisonment	7	2	Petition	245	Select	Dec. 20, 1802	General bill	69	Referred to Committee Whole House.		See bill No. 75.
Seagle, Frederick, representatives of.	Compensation for revolutionary services.	4	1	Petition	524	Claims	Jan. 4, 1794	Adverse		Rejected.		See Federick Seigle.
Seagrove, Robert, administrator of.	Indemnity for Indian depredations.	22	1	Memorial	416, 473	Public Lands.						
Seagrove, Robert, administrator of.	Indemnity for Indian depredations.	23	1	Memorial	132	Indian Affairs.						
Seal, Joseph	Pension for revolutionary services.	23	1	Resolution	251	Rev. Pensions				Discharged; laid on table.		
Seaman, Benjamin, & Co	Indemnity for French spoliations prior to 1800.	26	1	Memorial	182	Foreign Affairs	343	Favorable; bill	319	Referred to Committee Whole House.		
Seamans, Gilbert, heirs of.	Indemnity for losses as a Nova Scotia refugee.	12	1	Petition	214	Public Lands	Mar. 11, 1812	Favorable	85	Passed	Passed	App'd April 23, 1812
Seman, James, widow of.	Pension for revolutionary services.	27	2	Petition	443	Rev. Pensions.						
Seman, James, widow of.	Pension for revolutionary services.	27	3	Petition	139	Rev. Pensions.						
Seaman, John E., representatives of.	Indemnity for French spoliations prior to 1800.	29	1	Memorial	984	Foreign Affairs.						
Seaman & Rhind	(See John E. Seaman, representatives of.)	29	1		984							
Seaman, Robert	(See John E. Seaman, representatives of.)	29	1		984							
Seaman, William C.	Indemnity for a vessel erroneously conditioned.	28	1	Petition	774	Judiciary.						
Seamen of frigate Philadelphia.	Indemnity for losses, &c., while captives at Tripoli.	18	2	Memorial	116	Naval Affairs	Feb 1, 1825	Adverse		Laid on table		
Searcy & Allen, (captains)	(See Missouri militia)	22	2		96							
Searcy, Jeremiah	Pension for revolutionary services.	13	3	Petition	459	Pens. & Rev. Cl'ms.	Feb. 20, 1815	Favorable	303	Passed	Passed	App'd March 3, 1815
Searcy, Jeremiah	Bounty land for revolutionary services.	13	3	Petition and rep't Sec. of War.	459, 478					Laid on table.		
Searcy, John	Payment for pension stolen from mail.	25	2	Petition	405	Rev. Pensions.						
Searcy, William, administrator of.	Indemnity for French spoliations prior to 1800.	31	1	Petition	425	Foreign Affairs	355	General bill	318	Referred to Committee Whole House.		
Seargeant, John, or James.	Pension	23	1	Petition	234	Invalid Pensions	Jan. 24, 1834	Adverse		Laid on table.		
Searle, Daniel	Compensation for extra mail service.	27	2	Resolution	1037	P. Of. & P. Roads.						

List of private claims presented to the House of Representatives of the United States from the 1st to the 31st Congress, inclusive—Continued.

Names of claimants.	Nature or object of the claim.	Congress.	Session.	How brought before the House of Reps.	Page of journal.	To what committee of the House referred.	No. or date of the report.	Nature of the report.	No. of the bill.	How disposed of by the House of Reps.	How disposed of by the Senate.	Date of the act of Congress, and remarks.
Searle, Daniel	Compensation for extra mail service.	27	3	Resolution	44	P. Of. & P. Roads.						
Searle, David	(See assignee of Jona. Wheelock.)	25	3		162							
Searle, George	(See Lewis Tappan and George Searle.)	12	2		612							
Searle, Roy, & Co.	Increase of pay for mail transportation.	25	2	Petition	425	P. Of. & P. Roads.	March 1, 1838	Adverse		Laid on table.		
Sears, Artridge	(See heirs of William Sears)	14	1		485							
Sears, David	Pension for revolutionary services.	22	1	Petition	164	Rev. Pensions.						
Sears, Elnathan	Increase of pension	25	2	Petition	197	Rev. Pensions.						
Sears, Elnathan	Increase of pension	25	3	Rep. and res.	87, 161	Rev. Pensions	303	Favorable	1172	Referred to Committee Whole House.		
Sears, Elnathan	Increase of pension	26	1	Petition	171	Rev. Pensions	348	Favorable	327	Ref'd to Com. W. H		
Sears, Elnathan	Increase of pension	27	2	Petition	153	Rev. Pensions	784	Adverse		Laid on table.		
Sears, George, administrator of.	Indemnity for French spoliations prior to 1800.	26	1	Memorial	182	Foreign Affairs	343	Favorable; bill	319	Referred to Commitee Whole House.		
Sears, Grace	(See Iseac Sears, widow of.)	26	2		49							
Sears, Isaac	(See E. Brewer, deceased, surety of.)	8	2		145							
Sears, Isaac, widow of	Continuation of pension	26	2	Petition	49	Rev. Pensions.						
Sears, Isaac, widow of	Continuation of pension	27	2	Petition	97	Rev. Pensions	114	Favorable	160	Passed	Indef. postp'd.	
Sears, John	Compensation for revolutionary services.	3	2	Memorial	309	Claims.						
Sears, John	Compensation for revolutionary services.	4	1	Rep't and res.	373	Claims	Jan. 8, 1796	Favorable; bill ordered.	143	Passed	Rejected.	
Sears, John	Compensation for revolutionary services.	4	2	Memorial	625	Claims	Dec. 26, 1796	Favorable; bill ordered.	208	Passed	Rejected.	
Sears, John	(See heirs of William Sears)	14	1		485							
Sears, Mary	Indemnity for property destroyed by the enemy.	13	1	Petition	45	Claims.						
Sears, Mary	Indemnity for property destroyed by the enemy.	14	1	Petition	392	Claims				Discharged.		
Sears, Mary	Indemnity for property destroyed by the enemy.	14	2	Petition	207	Claims				Leave to withdraw.		
Sears, Mary	Indemnity for property destroyed by the enemy.	15	1	Rep't of Comm'r of Claims.	87	Claims	Feb. 10, 1818	Adverse		Referred to Committee Whole House.		
Sears, Mary	Indemnity for property destroyed by the enemy.	16	1	Res. and docs.	91, 102	Claims	Jan. 10, 1820	Adverse		Laid on table.		
Sears, Mary	Indemnity for property destroyed by the enemy.	16	2	Petition and rep't	85	Whole House.						
Sears, Mary	Indemnity for property destroyed by the enemy.	17	2	Petition	164	Claims	Feb. 21, 1822	Adverse		Laid on table.		
Sears, Mary	Indemnity for property destroyed by the enemy.	18	1	Resolution Documents	345 432	Claims. Claims.						
Sears, Mary	Indemnity for property destroyed by the enemy.	18	2	Petition	89	Claims.						
Sears, Mary	Indemnity for property destroyed by the enemy.	19	1	Petition Documents	131 189	Claims. Claims	May 15, 1826	Adverse		Laid on table.		
Sears, Mary	Indemnity for property destroyed by the enemy.	20	1	Petition	51	Claims	Dec. 19, 1827	Adverse.		Laid on table.		
Sears, Mary	Indemnity for property destroyed by the enemy.	21	1	Petition	75	Claims	Dec. 28, 1829	Adverse.		Laid on table.		
Sears, Mary, executors of.	Indemnity for property destroyed by the enemy.	23	2	Petition	199	Claims.						

List of private claims presented to the House of Representatives of the United States from the 1st to the 31st Congress, inclusive—Continued.

Names of claimants.	Nature or object of the claim.	Congress.	Session.	How brought before the House of Reps.	Page of journal.	To what committee of the House referred.	No. or date of the report.	Nature of the report.	No. of the bill.	How disposed of by the House of Reps.	How disposed of by the Senate.	Date of the act of Congress, and remarks.
Sears, Mary, executors of	Indemnity for property destroyed by the enemy.	24	1	Petition	141	Claims	176	Adverse	......	Laid on table.		
Sears, Mary	Interest on amount paid her husband.	13	3	Petition	652	Pens. & Rev. Cl'ms.						
Sears, Mary	Interest on amount paid her husband.	14	1	Petition	89	Pens. & Rev. Cl'ms.	April 22, 1816	Adverse	......	Rejected.		
Sears, Nathan	To be restored to pension roll	17	1	Petition	67	Rev. Pensions.						
Sears, Peter	Bounty on fishing schooner Reliance.	4	2	Petition	615	....	....	....	......	Referred to Secretary of Treasury.		
Sears, Snow Y	Reimbursement of a fine	27	2	Petition	633	Commerce	986	Favorable	567	Ordered to 3d reading		
Sears, Snow Y	Reimbursement of a fine	27	3	House bill	89	....	....	....	567	Passed	Passed	App'd Jan. 20, 1843
Sears, Stephen	Liquidation of a revolutionary certificate.	4	1	Report of Secretary Treasury	388	Claims	May 31, 1796	Adverse.	......	Laid on table.		
Sears, William, heirs of	Indemnity for losses, war of 1812.	14	1	Petition	485	Select.						
Sears, Winthrop, and others	Bounty on fishing schooner Laban.	24	1	Petition	283	Commerce	501	Favorable	501	Referred to Committee Whole House.		
Sears, Winthrop, and others	Bounty on fishing schooner Laban.	25	2	Petition	41	Commerce	77	Favorable	92	Passed	Passed with amendments	App'd April 20, 1838
Seas, Michael	Pension for revolutionary services.	26	2	Petition	82	Rev. Pensions	Jan. 7, 1841	Favorable	589	Referred to Committee Whole House.		
Seaton, Augustine	Reimbursement of advances on public account, and indemnity for property destroyed.	3	1	Petition	111	....	....	....	......	Laid on table.		
Seaton, George C	Increase of pension	23	1	Petition	73	Invalid Pensions	Dec. 24, 1833	Adverse.	......	Laid on table.		
Seaton, George C	Increase of pension	23	2	Petition	68, 86	Invalid Pensions	26	Favorable	606	Passed	Passed	App'd March 3, 1835
Seaton, Richard	Reimbursement of outlay on piers in Delaware river over contract.	9	1	Petition	234	Claims	Feb. 19, 1806	Adverse	......	Rejected.		
Seaver, Benjamin F	Reimbursement of money paid for ransom.	10	2	Memorial	414	Select.						
Seaver, Benjamin F	Reimbursement of money paid for ransom.	11	1	Petition	20	Select.						
Seaver, Mary	Continuation of pension	28	1	Petition	827	Whole House.						
Seavey, Dorcas	(See Ebenezer Seavey, widow of.)											
Seavey, Ebenezer, widow of	Pension	29	2	Petition	198	Invalid Pensions.						
Seavey, Nath'l, and others	Compensation for recapture of schooner Pink.	14	2	Petition	278	Naval Affairs	Feb. 11, 1817	Favorable	125	Passed	Passed	App'd March 3, 1817
Seavey, William, executrix of.	Indemnity for French spoliations prior to 1800.	26	1	Memorial	182	Foreign Affairs	243	Favorable; bill	319	Referred to Committee Whole House.		
Seavey, William, executrix of.	Indemnity for French spoliations prior to 1800.	31	1	Petition	425	Foreign Affairs	355	Favorable; bill	318	Referred to Committee Whole House.		
Seaward, John H	Indemnity for French spoliations prior to 1800.	26	1	Memorial	182	Foreign Affairs	343	Favorable; bill	319	Referred to Committee Whole House.		
Seaward, Swain	Arrears of pension	23	1	Petition	235	Invalid Pensions	....	....	......	Discharged; laid on table.		
Seawell, Washington	Credit for public money lost	23	1	Petition	587	Claims	525	Favorable	525	Referred to Committee Whole House.		
Seawell, Washington	Credit for public money lost	24	1	Petition and docs.	51	Claims	24	Favorable	24	Passed	Passed	App'd Feb. 17, 1836
Seawell, Washington	Compensation for services as secretary to Indian commissioners.	25	2	Documents	1041	Indian Affairs.						
Seawright, Lt. J. D	(See Bennett Riley and others)	21	2	....	245							
Seay, Jacob	Invalid pension	12	1	House bill	361	Whole House	June 15, 1812	With amend.	138	Passed	Passed	App'd July 5, 1812

List of private claims presented to the House of Representatives of the United States from the 1st to the 31st Congress, inclusive—Continued.

Names of claimants.	Nature or object of the claim.	Congress.	Session.	How brought before the House of Reps.	Page of journal.	To what committee of the House referred.	No. or date of the report.	Nature of the report.	No. of the bill.	How disposed of by the House of Reps.	How disposed of by the Senate.	Date of the act of Congress, and remarks.
Seay, John	Compensation for a negro slave murdered by United States soldiers.	18	2	Petition	38	Claims.						
Sebon, Jacob	Indemnity for French spoliations prior to 1800.	29	2	Memorial	83	Foreign Affairs.						
Sebree, Uriel	Correction of erroneous charge at Treasury Department.	26	1	Petition	620	Claims				Discharged; laid on table.		
Sechler, or Sichler, Michael.	Compensation for services as revolutionary artificer.	18	1	Petition	214	Pens. & Rev. Cl'ms.	Feb. 25, 1824	Adverse		Laid on table.		
Sechler, or Sichler, Michael.	Compensation for services as revolutionary artificer.	25	2	Petition	178	Rev. Claims	Jan. 27, 1836	Adverse		Laid on table.		
Secor, Halstead	Pension	19	2	Petition	156	Military Pensions.						
Secor, Jacob	Pension	15	2	Petition	322					Laid on table.		
Secrett, John H.	Pension for revolutionary services.	22	1	Petition	509	Rev. Pensions				Disch'd; laid on table		
Seddon, Thos., and others.	Payment of claim, 1st article, treaty of Ghent.	20	2	Petition	231	Foreign Affairs	79	Adverse		Laid on table.		
Sedgley, Daniel	Pension	15	1	Petition	21	Pens. & Rev. Cl'ms.	Dec. 18, 1817	Adverse		Recommitted.		
Sedgwick, Asher	Pension	20	2	Petition	31	Military Pensions.						
Sedgwick, Asher	Pension	21	1	Petition	197	Military Pensions						
Sedgwick, Asher	Pension	21	2	Petition	127	Military Pensions.						
Sedgwick, John	Commutation pay for revolutionary services.	15	2	Petition	132	Pens. & Rev. Cl'ms.	Dec. 30, 1818	Adverse				Withdrawn, 1st sess., 16th Congress.
Sedgwick, R	(See New York Insurance Company.)	26	1		182							
See, James	Pension for revolutionary services.	3	1	Rep. of Secretary War.	175					Laid on table.		
See, James	Pension for revolutionary services.	3	2	Rep. of Secretary War.	265	Claims.						
See, James	Pension for revolutionary services.	4	1	Rep. of Secretary War.	445	Claims.						
See, James	Pension for revolutionary services.	4	2	Rep. of Secretary War.	614	Claims.						
Seecamp, Albert, administrator of.	Indemnity for French spoliations prior to 1800.	26	1	Memorial	182	Foreign Affairs	343	Favorable	319	Referred to Committee Whole House.		
Seeds, Edward	Compensation for revolutionary services.	16	1	Petition	38	Pens. & Rev. Cl'ms.	Dec. 22, 1819	Adverse		Rejected.		
Seeds, William, attorney of	Pay and emolument for revolutionary services.	14	1	Documents	521	Pens. & Rev. Cl'ms.						
Seeley, Benjamin	Pension for revolutionary services.	3	1	Rep. of Secretary War.	131	Claims	May 26, 1794	Favorable; bill ordered.	62	Passed	Passed	App'd June 7, 1794
Seelye, Ebenezer	Pension for revolutionary services.	21	1	Resolution	208	Military Pensions.						
Seelye, Ebenezer	Pension for revolutionary services.	22	1	Resolution	178	Rev. Pensions	365	Favorable	460	Passed	Indef. postp'd.	
Seely, Isaac, widow of	Bounty land and compensation for revolutionary services.	9	1	Petition	246	Select.						
Seely, Isaac, heir of	Compensation for revolutionary services.	31	1	Petition	1095	Rev. Pensions	457	Adverse		Laid on table.		
Seely, Joab	Reimbursement of an overpayment.	26	2	Senate bill	113	Claims	Jan. 4, 1841	With't amend.	S. 30	Passed	Passed	App'd March 2, 1841
Seely, Samuel	Compensation for revolutionary services.	2	1	Petition	448					Referred to Secretary of War.		
Seely, Thaddeus	Pension for revolutionary services.	10	1	Pension bill	232	Whole House			78	Passed	Passed, with amendment.	App'd April 25, 1808
Sees, John	Compensation for transporting prisoners.	13	2	Petition	174	Pens. & Rev. Cl'ms.	Jan. 10, 1814	Adverse		Rejected.		

List of private claims presented to the House of Representatives of the United States from the 1st to the 31st Congress, inclusive—Continued.

Names of claimants.	Nature or object of the claim.	Congress.	Session.	How brought before the House of Reps.	Page of journal.	To what committee of the House referred.	No. or date of the report.	Nature of the report.	No. of the bill.	How disposed of by the House of Reps.	How disposed of by the Senate.	Date of the act of Congress, and remarks.
Segeran, Frederick	Pension for revolutionary services	8	2	Petition	149					Laid on table.		
Segeran, Frederick	Pension for revolutionary services.	9	1	Petition	193	Claims	Mar. 28, 1806	Adverse		Indefinitely postponed.		Leave to withdraw.
Seger, Ebenezer, widow of.	Pension	15	1	Petition	156	Pens. & Rev. Cl'ms.	Feb. 20, 1818	Adverse		Rejected.		
Seger, Ebenezer, widow of.	Pension	20	1	Petition	417	Rev. Claims				Discharged; laid on table.		
Seger, Mary	(See Peter Seger, widow of.)	30	1		962							
Seger, Mehetable	(See Ebenezer Seger, widow of.)	15	1		156							
Seger, Moses	(See heir of Peter Seger)	30	1		394							
Seger, Nathaniel	Pension	17	2	Petition	187	Claims.						
Seger, Peter, heir of	Additional compensation for revolutionary services.	30	1	Petition	394	Rev. Pensions.						
Seger, Peter, heir of	Additional compensation for revolutionary services.	30	2	Petition	296	Rev. Pensions.						
Seger, Peter, widow of	Pension for revolutionary services.	30	1	Petition	962	Rev. Pensions				Discharged; laid on table.		
Segur, Peter, widow of	Pension for revolutionary services.	26	1	Petition	705	Rev. Pensions.						
Segur, Peter, widow of	Pension for revolutionary services.	28	1	Petition	346	Rev. Pensions.						
				Petition (2)	706	Rev. Pensions.						
Segur, Peter, widow of	Pension for revolutionary services.	29	1	Petition	149	Rev. Pensions	460	Favorable	337	Passed	Passed	App'd Aug. 8, 1846
Segur, Peter, widow of	Correction of the act of August 8, 1846.	29	2	House bill	438				692	Passed	Passed	App'd March 3, 1847
Segura, Antonio, and others	Permission to locate a quarter section of land.	24	1	Senate bill	907	Priv. Land Claims.	June 9, 1836	With't amend.	S. 133	Passed	Passed	App'd July 2, 1836
Segura, Eloy	(See representatives of Francis Segura.)	22	1		417				475			
Segura, Francis, representatives of.	Indemnity in land for certain losses.	22	1	Petition	417	Priv. Land Claims.	383	Favorable	475	Referred to Committee Whole House.		
Segura, Francis, representatives of.	Indemnity in land for certain losses.	23	1	Petition	144	Priv. Land Claims.	Jan. 21, 1834	Adverse		Laid on table.		
Segura, Francis, representatives of.	Indemnity in land for certain losses.	23	2	Petition	48	Priv. Land Claims.				Discharged; laid on table.		
Segura, Louis	(See representatives of Francis Segura.)	22	1		417				475			
Segura, Matildo	(See representatives of Francis Segura.)	22	1		417				475			
Segura, Rafael	(See representatives of Francis Segura.)	22	1		417				475			
Segura, St. Jago	(See representatives of Francis Segura.)	22	1		417				475			
Seigle, Frederick, heirs of.	Commutation pay for revolutionary services.	24	2	Senate bill	373	Rev. Claims			S. 54			
Seigle, Frederick, heirs of.	Commutation pay for revolutionary services.	25	2	Senate bill	197	Rev. Claims	Jan. 22, 1838	With't amend.	S. 49	Referred to Committee Whole House.		
Seigle, Frederick, heirs of.	Commutation pay for revolutionary services.	29	1	Petition	654	Rev. Claims.						
Seigle, Frederick, heirs of.	Commutation pay for revolutionary services.	29	2	Petition	244	Rev. Claims.						
Seigle, Frederick, heirs of.	Commutation pay for revolutionary services.	31	1	Petition	324	Rev. Claims.						
Seitsenger, Michael	Pension for revolutionary services.	25	2	Petition	984	Rev. Pensions.						
Seitsenger, Michael	Pension for revolutionary services.	26	1	Petition	175	Rev. Pensions	167	Favorable	177	Passed	Indef. postp'd.	
Seixas, Solomon	Pension	15	1	Petition	371	Pens. & Rev. Cl'ms.				Discharged; referred to Secretary War.		

List of private claims presented to the House of Representatives of the United States from the 1st to the 31st Congress, inclusive—Continued.

Names of claimants.	Nature or object of the claim.	Congress.	Session.	How brought before the House of Reps.	Page of journal.	To what committee of the House referred.	No. or date of the report.	Nature of the report.	No. of the bill.	How disposed of by the House of Reps.	How disposed of by the Senate.	Date of the act of Congress, and remarks.
Seixas, Solomon	Pension	16	1	Petition	28	Pens. & Rev. Cl'ms.	Feb. 3, 1820	Adverse	.....	Rejected.		
elby, James	Remission of duty on the Sea Flower.	10	1	Memorial	58	Com. and Manuf.						
Selby, James	Remission of duty on the Sea Flower.	10	2	Memorial	519	Com. and Manuf.						
Selby, James	Remission of duty on the Sea Flower.	22	1	Petition	162	Commerce	April 3, 1832	Favorable	527	Referred to Committee Whole House.		
Selby, James	Remission of duty on the Sea Flower.	23	1	Petition	92	Commerce.						
Selby, James	Remission of duty on the Sea Flower.	24	1	Petition	403	Commerce.						
Selby, James	Remission of duty on the Sea Flower.	25	2	Petition	230	Commerce	602	Favorable	583	Referred to Committee Whole House.		
Selby, James	Remission of duty on the Sea Flower.	25	3	Bill of last sess.	380	Whole House	Jan. 26, 1839	With't amend.	583	Passed	Passed	App'd March 3, 1839
Selby, Samuel, 3d	Relief from imprisonment at suit of the United States.	6	1	Petition	544	Select	April 28, 1800	Favorable; bill ordered.	261	....	....	See act Jan. 6, 1800
Selden, Carey	(See administrator of Charles C. B. Thompson.)	23	1	....	129							
Selden, Joseph D	Compensation for erecting a light-house.	23	1	Appropriation bill	283	....	....	....	283	....	....	App'd June 27, 1834
Selfridge, Thomas O	Increase of pay as an officer in United States navy.	26	1	Memorial	303	Naval Affairs	631	Adverse	.....	Laid on table.		
Selfridge, Thomas O	Increase of pay as an officer in United States navy.	27	2	Memorial	254	Naval Affairs	....	....	.....	Discharged; laid on table.		
Selfridge, Thomas O	Increase of pay as an officer in United States navy.	30	1	Petition	607	Naval Affairs.						
Selfridge, Thomas O	Increase of pay as an officer in United States navy.	31	1	Petition	191	Naval Affairs	87	Favorable	108	Referred to Committee Whole House.		
Selin, Anthony, orphan children of.	Renewal of a land warrant	6	1	Petition	636	Select.						
Sellers, Daniel	Pension for revolutionary services.	24	2	Petition	271	Rev. Pensions	167	Adverse	.....	Laid on table.		
Sellers, Hamilton, (mother of.)	Continuation of pension	21	1	Petition	58	Naval Affairs	Dec. 21, 1821	Adverse	.....	Laid on table.		
Sellers, James, and others.	Indemnity for non-fulfillment of a contract by government.	28	1	Petition	707	P. Of. and P. Roads.	491	Favorable	J.R.30	Passed	Adverse report.	
Sellers, James, and others.	Indemnity for non-fulfillment of a contract by government.	28	2	Petition	278	P. Of. & P. Roads.	67	Favorable	J. R. 67	Passed	Indef. postp'd.	
Sellers, James, and others.	Indemnity for non-fulfillment of a contract by government.	29	1	Memorial	208	P. Of. & P. Roads.	220	Favorable	J. R. 15	Laid on table.		
Sellers, James, and others.	Indemnity for non-fulfillment of a contract by government.	30	1	Memorial	239	P. Of. & P. Roads.						
Sellers, Juliet E., guardian of.	Indemnity for property destroyed by the enemy.	15	1	Documents.	256	Claims.						
Sellers, Robert B	(See Hall and Sellers)	10	2	....	495							
Sellers, William	(See Hall and Sellers)	10	2	....	495							
Selma and Tennessee Railroad Company.	(See Tennessee.)											
Seminole war, officers of.	(See officers, &c.)	16	1	....	25							
Semmes, Virginia	(See guardian of the heirs of Francis Iardella.)	22	1	....	98							
Semoice, (Creek Indian).	Reservation of land under treaty.	22	2	Senate bill	228	Public Lands	....	....	S. 32			

List of private claims presented to the House of Representatives of the United States from the 1st to the 31st Congress, inclusive—Continued.

Names of claimants.	Nature or object of the claim.	Congress.	Session.	How brought before the House of Reps.	Page of journal.	To what committee of the House referred.	No. or date of the report.	Nature of the report.	No. of the bill.	How disposed of by the House of Reps.	How disposed of by the Senate.	Date of the act of Congress, and remarks.
Semoice, (Creek Indian)	Reservation of land under treaty	23	2	Senate bill	126	Public Lands	June 2, 1835	Favorable	S. 2	Referred to Committee Whole House.		
Semoice, (Creek Indian,) heirs of.	Bounty land for valuable public services.	29	2	Memorial	172	Priv. Land Claims.						
Semoice, (Creek Indian,) heirs of.	Bounty land for valuable public services.	30	1	Petition	156	Priv. Land Claims.						
Semoice, (Creek Indian,) heirs of.	Bounty land for valuable public services.	30	2	Petition	257	Priv. Land Claims.	28	Favorable	719			
Semoice, (Creek Indian,) heirs of.	Bounty land for valuable public services.	31	1	Petition	451	Priv. Land Claims.	Mar. 28, 1850	Favorable	200	Referred to Committee Whole House.		
Semoice, (Creek Indian,) heirs of.	Bounty land for valuable public services.	31	2	Bill of last sess.	181	Whole House	Jan. 24, 1851	With't amend.	200	Passed.		
Semple, John	(See executors of Hans Morrison.)	2	2		653							
Semple, Nathaniel	Invalid pension	8	1	Petition	586					Laid on table.		
Senet, Eugene, heirs of	Confirmation of title to land in Alabama.	23	1	Petition	220	Priv. Land Claims.	271	Favorable	309	Referred to Committee Whole House.		
Sengstack, Charles P	Reimbursement of money paid for surplus glass for Post Office buillding.	28	1	Petition	188	Claims	315	Favorable	222	Passed	Passed	App'd June 17, 1844
Senter, George W	Indemnity for non-fulfilment of government contract.	27	2	Petition	548	Claims	726	Adverse		Laid on table.		
Seon, Thomas	(See administrator of Thomas S. Saddler.)	2	1		573							
Sergeant, James	Pension	22	1	Petition	219	Rev. Pensions.						
Sergeant, James, widow of.	Pension	28	1	Petition	550	Rev. Pensions.						
Sergeant, John	Pensions	3	1	Rep. of Secretary War.	131	Select	May 26, 1794	Res. to refer to Sec. War.	J. R. 12	Passed	Passed	App'd June 9, 1794
Sergeant, John	Pensions	4	1	Rep. of Secretary War.	445	Claims.						
Sergeant, John	Pensions	4	2	Rep. of Secretary War.	614	Claims.						
Sergeant, Lemuel	Pension for revolutionary services.	15	2	Petition	182	Rev. Pensions	Feb. 11, 1819	Adverse.		Laid on table.		
Sergeant, William H., and N. Richardson.	Drawback on wine	3	2	Petition	289	Select	Jan. 22, 1795	Adverse.		Laid on table.		
Sergeant, Sarah	(See James Sergeant, widow of)	28	1		550							
Serpas, Antonio	Confirmation of title to land in Louisiana.	22	1	Petition	64	Priv. Land Claims.	62	Favorable	125	Passed	Passed	App'd June 25, 1832
Serpas, Joseph	Confirmation of title to land in Louisiana.	22	1	Petition	64	Priv. Land Claims.	62	Favorable	125	Passed	Passed	App'd June 25, 1832
Serpas, Succession of	Confirmation of title to land in Louisiana.	22	1	Petition	64	Priv. Land Claims.	62	Favorable	125	Passed	Passed	App'd June 25, 1832
Serrill, George	(See executor of James Pearson)	13	2		246							
Serro, Augustus	Pension	25	2	Petition	74	Naval Affairs.						
Serross, Jacob, administrator of.	Indemnity for French spoliations prior to 1800.	26	1	Memorial	182	Foreign Affairs	343	Favorable; bill	319	Referred to Committee Whole House.		
Serry, Augustine	Balance due for services as boatswain.	10	1	Petition	264	Claims.						
Serry, Augustine	Balance due for services as boatswain.	10	2	Petition	350	Claims	Dec. 19, 1808	Favorable	117	Passed.	Passed	App'd Jan. 12, 1809
Servoss, Christopher, son of.	Restoration of the confiscated estate of deceased.	21	1	Petition	199	Rev. Claims	Feb. 12, 1830	Adverse		Laid on table.		
Servoss, John	(See Chistopher Servoss, son of.)	21	1		199							
Seton,	(See Hoffinan & Seton)	26	1		182							

List of private claims presented to the House of Representatives of the United States from the 1st to the 31st Congress, inclusive—Continued.

3—38

Names of claimants.	Nature or object of the claim.	Congress.	Session.	How brought before the House of Reps.	Page of journal.	To what committee of the House referred.	No. or date of the report.	Nature of the report.	No. of the bill.	How disposed of by the House of Reps.	How disposed of by the Senate.	Date of the act of Congress, and remarks.
Sevar, Isaac	Pension	30	1	Resolution	245					Leave to withdraw		
Seveaney, Benj. W., representatives of.	(See Alexander Sweeney, heirs of.)	25	3		451							See p. 178, 1st sess. 26th Cong.
Severance, Benjamin	Pension	21	2	Resolution	123	Military Pensions.						
Severance, Benjamin	Pension	22	1	Petition	142	Invalid Pensions.						
Severson, Derick or Richard	Pension for revolutionary services.	24	1	Petition	406	Rev. Pensions	438	Favorable	452	Passed	Passed	App'd June 28, 1836
Sevier, Alexander	Indemnity for property lost in public service.	13	2	Petition	242	Claims				Discharged.		
Sevier, Alexander	Indemnity for property lost in public service.	13	3	Petition	466	Claims	Oct. 17, 1814	Adverse		Rejected.		
Sevier, Alexander	Indemnity for property lost in public service.	17	2	Petition	187	Claims.						
Sevier, Alexander, widow of.	Half-pay for naval service	22	2	Petition	143	Invalid Pensions.						
Sevier, Alexander, widow of.	Half-pay for naval service	23	1	Petition	247	Naval Affairs.						
Sevier, Alexander, widow of.	Half pay for naval service	26	1	Petition	331	Naval Affairs.						
Sevier, A. H	Confirmation of title to land in Arkansas.	22	1	Petition	64	Priv. Land Claims.	62	Favorable	425	Passed	Passed	App'd June 25, 1832
Sevier, A. H	(See Solomon Bodwell, assignee of)	22	1		64		62		425			
Sevier, A. H	(See Sylvanus Phillips, assignee of)	22	1		421		62		425			
Sevier, Charles	(See Robert Sevier, heirs of.)	31	1		857							
Sevier, Elizabeth	(See widow of Alexander Sevier.)	22	2		143							
Sevier, Lieut. Frederick S.	Indemnity for property lost on the Ondiacker.	31	1	Petition	857	Claims.						
Sevier, George W	(See John Sevier, heirs of.)	15	1		184							
Sevier, James	(See John Sevier, heirs of.)	18	2		96							
Sevier, John, heirs of	Compensation in land for services in laying out a new county in Tennessee.	15	1	Petition	184	Select	86	Favorable	74	Laid on table.		
Sevier, John, heirs of	Compensation in land for services in laying out a new county in Tennessee.	15	2	Documents	59	Select	31	Favorable	225	Referred to Committee Whole House.		
Sevier, John, heirs of	Compensation in land for services in laying out a new county in Tennessee.	18	1	House bill	162	Whole House	April 24, 1824	With't amend.	73	Rejected.		
Sevier, John, heirs of	Permission to locate land under act of last session on certain forfeited lands.	18	2	Senate bill Petition	518 96	Public Lands Public Lands.	May 20, 1824	With't amend.	S. 106	Passed with amendm't.	Passed as am'd.	App'd May 24, 1824
Sevier, John, attorney for heirs of.	Extension of time for locating land	22	1	Petition	173	Public Lands	Jan. 20, 1832	Favorable	299	Passed	Passed	App'd May 19, 1832
Sevier, John, attorney for heirs of.	Continuing in force, act of May 24, 1824.	24	1	Senate bill	320	Public Lands	Feb. 19, 1836	With't amend.	S. 20	Passed	Passed	App'd June 23, 1836
Sevier, Robert, heirs of	Compensation for revolutionary services.	31	1	Petition	857	Rev. Pensions	396	Adverse		Laid on table.		
Sevier, Valentine	(See Robert Sevier, heirs of.)	31	1		857							
Sewall, Clement	Commutation pay for revolutionary services.	12	2	Petition	633	Claims						Leave to withdraw, Mar. 13, 1813.
Sewall, Clement	Commutation pay for revolutionary services.	13	2	Petitions	270	Pens. & Rev. Cl'ms.	Feb. 23, 1814	Adverse		Leave to withdraw, p. 309.		

List of private claims presented to the House of Representatives of the United States from the 1st to the 31st Congress, inclusive—Continued.

Names of claimants.	Nature or object of the claim.	Congress.	Session.	How brought before the House of Reps.	Page of journal.	To what committee of the House referred.	No. or date of the report.	Nature of the report.	No. of the bill.	How disposed of by the House of Reps.	How disposed of by the Senate.	Date of the act of Congress, and remarks.
Sewall, Clement, daughter of.	Commutation pay for revolutionary services.	24	1	Petitions	404	Rev. Claims.						
Sewall, Clement, daughter of.	Commutation pay for revolutionary services.	29	1	Petition	102	Military Affairs.						
Sewall, Clement, daughter of.	Commutation pay for revolutionary services.	30	1	Petitions	110	Rev. Claims.						
Sewall, Clement, daughter of.	Compensation for ferriage of American troops.	24	1	Petition	405	Claims	697	Adverse	......	Laid on table.		
Sewall, Daniel	(See guardian of Isaac Parsons)	5	2	....	99							
Sewall, David	Increase of compensation as judge in Mississippi.	13	1	Petition	31	Ways and Means.						
Sewall, David	Increase of compensation as judge in Mississippi.	13	2	Petition	190	Judiciary.						
Sewall, Henry	(See heirs of Nicholas Sewall.)	22	2	....	42							
Sewall, Lewis, and Sam'l Smith.	Compensation for removing books from land office at St. Stephens	13	2	Petition	414	....	....	....	......	Referred to Committee of the Land Office.		
Sewall, Lewis	Compensation for extra services as land officer.	14	1	Petition	722	....	....	....	......	Laid on table.		
Sewall, Lewis	Compensation for extra services as land officer.	14	2	Petition	133	Public Lands.						
Sewell, James	Pension	3	2	Rep. of Secretary War.	350	Claims.						
Sewell, James	Pension	4	1	Rep. of Secretary War.	445	Claims	Feb. 15, 1796	Res. to refer to Sec. War.	J. R. 16	Passed	Passed	App'd April 18, 1796
Sewell, James	Pension	4	2	Rep. of Secretary War.	614	Claims.						
Sewall, Joseph, and others.	Reimbursement of duty on goods destroyed by fire.	19	1	Petition	291	Ways and Means.	166	Favorable	215	Postponed.		
Sewall, Joseph, and others.	Reimbursement of duty on goods destroyed by fire.	20	1	Petition	38	Ways and Means.	Dec. 24, 1827	Favorable	22	Referred to Committee Whole House.		
Sewall, Joseph, and others.	Reimbursement of duty on goods destroyed by fire.	28	2	Petition	69	Ways and Means.	....	....	......	Discharged; laid on table.		
Sewall, Mary	(See Nicholas Sewall, widow of.)	16	2	....	181							
Sewall, Moses	(See administrator of D. Doane.)	20	1	....	339							
Sewall, Nicholas, widow of.	Indemnity for destruction of property by the enemy.	16	2	Petition	181	Claims	Feb. 9, 1821	Adverse	......	Laid on table.		
Sewall, Nicholas, heirs of.	Indemnity for destruction of property by the enemy.	22	2	Petition	42	Claims.						
Sewall, Nicholas, heirs of.	Indemnity for destruction of property by the enemy.	23	1	Petition	35	Claims	148	Favorable	157	Passed	Passed	App'd June 30, 1834
Sewall, Robert	(See heirs of Nicholas Sewall)	22	2	....	42							
Sewall, Robert	Indemnity for destruction of property by the enemy.	14	2	Petition	59							
				Rep. of Secretary War.	86	Select	....	....	......	Discharged; leave to withdraw.		
Sewall, Robert	Indemnity for destruction of property by the enemy.	15	1	Petition	81	....	....	....	......	Referred to Commissioner of Claims.	....	See report 177 and bill No. 162.
Sewall, Robert	Indemnity for destruction of property by the enemy.	16	1	Petition	181	Claims	April 7, 1820	Adverse	......	Laid on table.		
Sewall, Robert, representatives of.	Indemnity for destruction of property by the enemy.	21	1	Petition	358	Claims	Mar. 19, 1830	Adverse	......	Laid on table.		
Sewall, Robert, representatives of.	Indemnity for destruction of property by the enemy.	25	2	Petition	176	Claims.						

List of private claims presented to the House of Representatives of the United States from the 1st to the 31st Congress, inclusive—Continued.

Names of claimants.	Nature or object of the claim.	Congress.	Session.	How brought before the House of Reps.	Page of journal.	To what committee of the House referred.	No. or date of the report.	Nature of the report.	No. of the bill.	How disposed of by the House of Reps.	How disposed of by the Senate.	Date of the act of Congress, and remarks.
Sewall, Robert, representatives of.	Indemnity for destruction of property by the enemy.	25	3	Petition	87	Claims.						
Sewall, Robert, representatives of.	Indemnity for destruction of property by the enemy.	26	1	Petition	170	Claims.						
Sewall, Robert, representatives of.	Indemnity for destruction of property by the enemy.	26	2	Petition	167	Claims.						
Sewall, Robert, representatives of.	Indemnity for destruction of property by the enemy.	27	2	Petition	764	Claims.						
Sewall, Robert, representatives of.	Indemnity for destruction of property by the enemy.	28	1	Petition	76	Claims	254	Adverse	......	Laid on table.		
Sewall, Robert, representatives of.	Indemnity for destruction of property by the enemy.	28	2	Petition	250	Claims.						
Sewall, Robert, representatives of.	Indemnity for destruction of property by the enemy.	29	1	Petition	75	Claims.						
				Petitions.......	90	Claims	98	Adverse......	......	Laid on table.		
Sewall, Thomas R.......	(See Joseph Sewall and others)...	19	1	....	291							
Seybold, John	Transfer of a land entry.........	15	1	Resolution	333	Public Lands.....	April 10, 1818	Favorable....	187	Passed	Passed, with amendment.	App'd April 20, 1818
Seymour, ——	(See Abraham Prim and others)..	30	1	....	485							
Seymour, Daniel M......	(See Thomas S. Seymour)	30	2	....	78							
Seymour, Henry R......	(See sureties of Pierre A. Barker.)	27	2	....	972							
Seymour, Isaac..........	Pension	31	1	Petition	994	Invalid Pensions ..	483	Favorable....	380	Passed	Passed	App'd Aug. 10, 1850
Seymour, Jesse, representatives of.	Further time to present claim for prize money.	25	2	Petition	594	Naval Affairs.....	995	Favorable....	857	Referred to Committee Whole House.		
Seymour, Jesse, representatives of.	Further time to present claim for prize money.	25	3	Bill of last sess.	434	Whole House	Feb. 1, 1835	With't amend.	857	Passed	Passed	App'd March 3, 1839
Seymour, Mabel.........	(See Moses Seymour, jr., widow of)	21	2	....	106							
Seymour, jr., Moses......	Indemnity for damages in defending a certain suit.	19	1	Petition	224	Judiciary	Mar. 4, 1826	Adverse	......	Leave to withdraw.		
Seymour, jr., Moses, widow of.	Indemnity for damages in defending a certain suit.	21	2	Memorial	106	Judiciary.						
Seymour, jr., Moses, widow of.	Indemnity for damages in defending a certain suit.	23	1	Memorial	418	Judiciary	....	....	......	Discharged; laid on table.		
Seymour, Nathan	Pension for revolutionary services.	20	1	Resolution	200	Military Pensions.						
Seymour, Thomas S., heirs of.	Bounty land for military services..	30	2	Petition	78	Priv. Land Claims.						
Seymour, William.......	Relief, in consideration of revolutionary disabilities.	2	2	Petition	662	Select	June 15, 1793	Favorable	......	Laid on table.		
Seymour, William.......	Relief, in consideration of revolutionary disabilities.	3	1	Petition	91	Select	Mar. 12, 1794	Favorable; bill ordered.				
Seymour, William.......	Relief, in consideration of revolutionary disabilities.	3	2	Petition	297	Claims	Feb. 14, 1795	Favorable; bill ordered.	115	Passed	Passed	App'd March 2, 1795
Sexton, Aaron, widow of..	Pension for revolutionary services.	30	2	Petition	477	Rev. Pensions.						
Sexton, Aaron, widow of..	Pension for revolutionary services.	31	1	Petition	935	Rev. Pensions	372	Adverse	......	Laid on table.		
Sexton, Charles	Confirmation of title to land in Missouri.	15	1	Petition	102	Priv. Land Claims.						
				Petition, (2)....	367	Priv. Land Claims.						
Sexton, Charles	Confirmation of title to land in Missouri.	16	1	Petition	71	Priv. Land Claims.						
Sexton, Charles	Confirmation of title to land in Missouri.	17	1	Petition	55	Public Lands.						
Sexton, Charles	Confirmation of title to land in Missouri.	18	1	Petition	55	Public Lands.						

List of private claims presented to the House of Representatives of the United States from the 1st to the 31st Congress, inclusive—Continued.

Names of claimants.	Nature or object of the claim.	Congress.	Session.	How brought before the House of Reps.	Page of journal.	To what committee of the House referred.	No. or date of the report.	Nature of the report.	No. of the bill.	How disposed of by the House of Reps.	How disposed of by the Senate.	Date of the act of Congress, and remarks.
Sexton, George	Increase of compensation for mail service.	29	1	Memorial	731	P. Of. & P. Roads.						
Sexton, George	Increase of compensation for mail service.	30	1	Petition	679	P. Of. & P. Roads.						
Sexton, James P., and J. Holden.	Permission to purchase a sixteenth section of land.	30	1	Petition	137	Priv. Land Claims.	180	Favorable	190	Passed	Passed, with amendment, 2d session.	App'd Feb. 19, 1849
Sexton, Jane	(See Aaron Sexton, widow of)	30	2		477							
Sexton, Richard	Reimbursement of money expended on government contract.	9	1	Petition	234	Claims	Feb 19, 1806	Adverse		Rejected.		
Shackerly, Peter, heirs of	Compensation for services in U. States navy.	25	2	Resolution	981					Referred to President of United States.		
Shackerly, Peter, heirs of	Compensation for services in U. States navy.	25	3	Memorial	461	Claims.						
Shackerly, Peter, heirs of	Compensation for services in U. States navy.	26	1	Petition	168	Claims.						
Shackford, John	Compensation for a horse taken for public use.	23	1	Senate bill	592	Claims	June 30, 1834	With't amend.	S. 72	Passed	Passed	App'd June 30, 1834
Shackleford, B	Right of pre emption	19	2	Petition	113	Public Lands				Discharged.		
Shackleford, James T	Confirmation of title to land in Alabama.	31	1	House bill	465	Priv. Land Claims.	May 22, 1850	Favorable	303	Passed	Passed	App'd June 17, 1850
Shackleford, John	Compensation for prosecuting certain offenders.	21	1	Petition	411	P. Of. & P. Roads.				Discharged; referred to Postmaster General.		
Shackleford, Robert	(See William Thompson)	19	1		312							
Shade, Henry	Pension for revolutionary services.	3	2	Memorial	306	Claims				Referred to Secretary War.		
Shade, Henry	Pension for revolutionary services.	4	1	Rep. of Secretary War.	445	Claims	Dec. 28, 1795	Adverse		Leave to withdraw.		
Shade, Jacob	Pension for disability in the war of 1812.	24	1	Petition	140	Invalid Pensions				Discharged; laid on table.		
Shade, Jacob	Pension for disability in the war of 1812.	24	2	Petition	213	Invalid Pensions	316	Favorable	971	Referred to Committee Whole House.		
Shade, Jacob	Pension for disability in the war of 1812.	25	2	Petition	39	Invalid Pensions	222	Favorable	260	Passed	Adverse.	
Shade, Jacob	Pension for disability in the war of 1812.	26	1	Petition	162	Invalid Pensions	525	Favorable	421	Referred to Committee Whole House.		
Shade, Jacob	Pension for disability in the war of 1812.	27	2	Documents	68	Invalid Pensions.						
				Petition	154	Invalid Pensions	444	Adverse		Laid on table.		
Shade, Jacob	Pension for disability in the war of 1812.	29	1	Petition	358	Invalid Pensions	665	Adverse		Laid on table.		
Shade, Jacob	Pension for disability in the war of 1812.	31	1	Petition	337	Invalid Pensions.						
Shaeffer, Christain	Compensation for provisions on public account.	19	1	Petition	130	Claims	April 1, 1826	Adverse		Laid on table.		
Shafer, Dewald, widow of	Pension for revolutionary services.	29	1	Petition	1163	Rev. Pensions.						
Shafer, Elizabeth	(See Dewald Shafer, widow of.)											
Shaeffer, Frederick	Reimbursement of expenditure for medical aid.	30	2	Petition	253	Claims.						
Shaeffer, Frederick	Reimbursement of expenditure for medical aid.	31	1	Petition	672	Claims.						
Shaffer, Henry	Pension for revolutionary services.	29	2	Petition	315	Rev. Pensions.						
Shaffer, Henry	Pension for revolutionary services.	30	1	Petition	204	Rev. Pensions	440	Adverse		Laid on table.		

List of private claims presented to the House of Representatives of the United States from the 1st to the 31st Congress, inclusive—Continued.

Names of claimants.	Nature or object of the claim.	Congress.	Session.	How brought before the House of Reps.	Page of journal.	To what committee of the House referred.	No. or date of the report.	Nature of the report.	No. of the bill.	How disposed of by the House of Reps.	How disposed of by the Senate.	Date of the act of Congress, and remarks.
Shafer, Jacob	Bounty land for military services	16	1	Petition	34	Priv. Land Claims	46	Adverse	......	Referred to Committee Whole House.		
Shafer, Jacob	Bounty land for military services	16	2	Petition	40	Priv. Land Claims	Nov. 28, 1820	With't amend.	......	Leave to withdraw.		
Shafer, Jacob	Bounty land for military services	17	1	Petition	331	Priv. Land Claims.						
Shafer, Jocob	Bounty land for military services	17	2	Petition	82	Claims	Jan. 10, 1833	Favorable	223	Referred to Committee Whole House.		
Shafer, Jacob	Bounty land for military services	18	1	Petition	38	Priv. Land Claims	2	Favorable	10	Rejected.		
Shafer, Jacob	Bounty land for military services	19	1	Petition	251	Priv. Land Claims	April 26, 1826	Favorable	230	Passed.		
Shafer, Jacob	Bounty land for military services	19	2	Petition	37	Priv. Land Claims	Dec. 19, 1826	Favorable	302	Passed	Passed with amendment.	App'd March 2, 1827
Shafer, John	Arrears of pay and bounty land	31	1	Petition	583	Military Affairs	269	Adverse	......	Laid on table.		
Shafer, Jonathan	(See Christain Orendorff.)	27	2	....	908	....	866					
Shaffer, Michael	Pension for revolutionary services	17	2	Petition	86	Whole House.						
Shaffer, Peter	Allowance of forfeited land payment on account of new location.	22	1	Petition	106	Public Lands.						
Shaffer, Peter	Balance due for work on Cumberland road.	28	1	Petition	910	Claims.						
Shaffer, Peter	Balance due for work on Cumberland road.	28	2	Petition	89	Claims	128	Favorable	613	Referred to Committee Whole House.		
Shaffer, Peter	Balance due for work on Cumberland road.	29	1	Petition	90	Claims	97	Adverse	......	Referred to Committee Whole House.		
				Documents	519	Claims.						
Shaffer, Peter	Balance due for work on Cumberland road.	30	1	Petition	108	Claims	215	Favorable	215	Passed	Passed, second session.	App'd March 3, 1849
Shafer, Philip	Pension for revolutionary services	19	2	Resolution	203	Military Pensions.						
Shafer, Philip	Pension for revolutionary services	20	1	Petition	192	Military Pensions.						
Shaff, William	Pension	20	2	Petition	78	Military Pensions	....	....	......	Disch'd; laid on table.		
Shaffner, Francis	Compensation for revolutionary services.	1	3	Petition	368	....	....	....	......	Referred to Secretary War.		
Shaffner, Francis	Compensation for revolutionary services.	2	2	Rep. of Secretary of War.	735	....	....	....	......	Laid on table.		
Shaffner, Peter	Pension for revolutionary disabilities.	1	3	Petition	371	....	....	....	......	Leave to withdraw.		
Shafly, Adam, heirs of	Compensation for revolutionary services.	26	1	Petition	167	Rev. Claims.						
Shakers Society, trustees of	Indemnity for damage to property by United States troops.	14	1	Petition	433	Public Lands.						
Shakers Society, trustees of	Indemnity for damage to property by United States troops.	16	1	Petition	33	Claims	Jan. 17, 1820	Adverse	......	Laid on table.		
Shakers Society, trustees of	Indemnity for damage to property by United States troops.	17	1	Petition	47	Claims	Jan. 3, 1822	Adverse	......	Laid on table.		
Shakers Society, trustees of	Indemnity for damage by United States troops.	17	2	Memorial	22	Claims.						
Shakers Society, trustees of	Indemnity for damage by United States troops.	18	1	Petition	214	Claims	Feb. 19, 1824	Adverse	......	Laid on table.		
Shaler, Ephraim	Arrears of pension	20	2	Petition	39	Military Pensions.						
Shaler, Ephraim	Arrears of pension	21	1	Petition	47	Military Pensions	Dec. 24, 1829	Adverse	......	Laid on table.		
Shaler, Ephraim	Arrears of pension	22	1	Petition	56	Rev. Pensions.						
Shaler, Ephraim	Arrears of pension	22	2	Petition	27	Invalid Pensions	Feb. 25, 1833	Favorable	748	Referred to Committee Whole House.		
Shaler, Ephraim	Arrears of pension	23	1	Petition	46	Invalid Pensions	1	Favorable	1	Passed	Passed, with amendment.	App'd June 25, 1834

List of private claims presented to the House of Representatives of the United States from the 1st to the 31st Congress, inclusive—Continued.

Names of claimants.	Nature or object of the claim.	Congress.	Session.	How brought before the House of Reps.	Page of journal.	To what committee of the House referred.	No. or date of the report.	Nature of the report.	No. of the bill.	How disposed of by the House of Reps.	How disposed of by the Senate.	Date of the act of Congress, and remarks.
Shaler, Ephraim	Arrears of pension.............	23	2	Petition	147	Invalid Pensions ..	Jan. 16, 1835	Adverse	......	Laid on table.		
Shaler, Ephraim	Arrears of pension.............	24	1	Petition	98	Invalid Pensions...	832	Favorable....	735	Referred to Committee Whole House.		
Shaler, Ephraim	Increase of pension	24	2	Petition	120	Invalid Pensions...	....	....	......	Discharged; laid on table.		
Shaler, Ephraim	Increase of pension	25	2	Petition .... Documents	39 722	Invalid Pensions. Invalid Pensions.						
Shaler, Ephraim	Increase of pension.............	25	3	Petition	89	Invalid Pensions ..	....	....	......	Discharged; laid on table.		
Shaler, Ephraim	Arrears of pension.............	29	1	Petition	381	Invalid Pensions ..	Jan. 25, 1846	Adverse	......	Laid on table.		
Shaler, Ephraim, and others	Bounty land for military services..	25	2	Petition	420	Public Lands.						
Shaler, Ephraim	Right of pre-emption to land in Wisconsin.	31	1	Petition	1179	Public Lands.						
Shaler, Joseph	Pension for revolutionary services.	11	2	Pension bill	283	Whole House.....	Mar. 24, 1810	With amend..	107	Passed	Passed	App'd April 27, 1810
Shallus, Elizabeth	(See heirs of Baron de Ulrick) ...	16	1	....	39							
Shamburger, John	Allowance of a forfeited land payment.	17	2	Petition	122	Public Lands.						
Shamburger, John	Allowance of a forfeited land payment.	19	1	Petition	155	Public Lands.						
Shamburger, John	Allowance of a forfeited land payment.	22	1	Petition	294	Public Lands.....	Mar. 6, 1832	Adverse	......	Laid on table.		
Shane, Anthony.........	Compensation in land for public services.	13	3	Resolution	510	Public Lands	Jan. 23, 1815	Favorable	269	Passed.............	Passed	App'd Feb. 24, 1815
Shane, Anthony.........	Pension for military services	18	1	Petition	285	Pens. & Rev. Cl'ms.	Mar. 24, 1824	Adverse	......	Laid on table.		
Shane, Daniel, widow of..	Pension for services, war of 1812.	26	1	Petition	602	Invalid Pensions.						
Shane, Daniel, widow of..	Pension for services, war of 1812	26	2	Petition	77	Invalid Pensions ..	213	Adverse	......	Laid on table.		
Shane, Elizabeth	(See Daniel Shane, widow of)...	26	1	....	602							
Shankland, Joseph.......	(See John King and Joseph Shankland.)	15	1	....	130							
Shanks, John...........	Increase of pension	12	1	Petition	248	Claims	June 12, 1812	Adverse	......	Laid on table.		
Shanley, Patrick	Pension for revolutionary services.	3	1	Rep't of Secretary War.	131	Select	May 26, 1794	Res. to refer to Sec. War.	J. R. 12	Passed	Passed	App'd June 9, 1794
Shanley, Patrick	Pension for revolutionary services.	4	1	Rep't of Secretary War.	445	Claims.						
Shanley, Patrick	Pension for revolutionary services	4	2	Rep't of Secretary War.	614	Claims.						
Shannon, Catharine......	(See Robert Shannon, widow of).	26	1	....	546							
Shannon, Chloe.........	(See Canadian refugees)........	12	1	....	242	....	....	....	85			
Shannon, George........	(See Lewis and Clark and companions.)	9	2	....	470, 507	....	....	....	183	....	....	App'd March 3, 1807
Shannon, George........	Renewal of a land warrant	13	2	Petition	199	Public Lands.....	Jan. 31, 1814	Favorable....	95	Passed............	Passed, with amendment.	App'd April 16, 1814
Shannon, George........	(See George Nebinger, heirs of)..	12	2	....	579							
Shannon, George........	Pension for revolutionary services.	12	2	Petition	567	Claims.						
Shannon, George........	Pension for revolutionary services.	13	1	Pension bill....	56	Whole House	July 20, 1813	Favorable....	31	Passed	Passed	App'd Aug. 2, 1813
Shannon, George........	Increase of pension.............	14	1	Resolution	575	Pens. & Rev. Cl'ms.						
Shannon, George........	Increase of pension.............	14	2	Petition	32	Pens. & Rev. Cl'ms.	Jan. 29, 1817	Favorable....	91	Passed	Passed, with amendment.	App'd March 3, 1817
Shannon, George W.....	(See Michael L. Sullivant)......	27	2	....	66	....	74					
Shannon, Isaac..........	Compensation for a horse carried off by Indians.	22	1	Documents.....	514	Indian Affairs....	April 28, 1832	Adverse	......	Laid on table.		
Shannon, James Noble...	(See relict of Obediah Ayer).....	12	1	....	242							

List of private claims presented to the House of Representatives of the United States from the 1*st to the* 31*st Congress, inclusive*—Continued.

Names of claimants.	Nature or object of the claim.	Congress.	Session.	How brought before the House of Reps.	Page of journal.	To what committee of the House referred.	No. or date of the report.	Nature of the report.	No. of the bill.	How disposed of by the House of Reps.	How disposed of by the Senate.	Date of the act of Congress, and remarks.
Shannon, James	Equitable settlement of his accounts.	18	2	Resolution	107	Claims.						
Shannon, John	(See Exploring Expedition)	27	3		149		270		818			
Shannon, Neil	Pension	20	1	Petition	396	Military Pensions				Discharged; laid on table.		
Shannon, Neil	Pension	24	2	Petition	86	Invalid Pensions				Discharged; laid on table.		
Shannon, Neil	Pension	25	2	Petition	401	Invalid Pensions	739	Favorable	705	Passed	Adverse report.	
Shannon, Neil	Pension	25	3	Petition	89	Invalid Pensions	260	Favorable	1131	Referred to Committee Whole House.		
Shannon, Neil	Pension	26	1	Petition	161	Invalid Pensions	177	Favorable	188	Passed	Indef. postp'd.	
Shannon, Neil	Pension	26	2	Petition	77	Invalid Pensions	155	Favorable	667	Referred to Committee Whole House.		
Shannon, Neil	Pension	27	2	Petition	297	Invalid Pensions	415	Adverse		Laid on table.		
Shannon, Neil	Pension	29	1	Petition	269	Invalid Pensions	816	Favorable	514	Referred to Committee Whole House.		
Shannon, Robert	Pension for revolutionary services.	22	1	Resolution	301	Rev. Pensions.						
Shannon, Robert	Pension for revolutionary services.	25	3	Petition	220	Rev. Claims.						
Shannon, Robert	Pension for revolutionary services.	26	1	Petition	170	Rev. Claims.						
Shannon, Robert	Pension for revolutionary services.	26	2	Petition	38	Claims.						
Shannon, Robert, widow of.	Pension for revolutionary services.	26	1	Resolution	546	Rev. Pensions				Discharged; laid on table.		
Shannon, Samuel, executor of.	Equitable settlement of his accounts.	27	2	Petition	382	Claims	1102	Favorable	612	Referred to Committee Whole House.		
Shannon, Samuel, executor of.	Equitable settlement of his accounts.	27	3	House bill	91	Whole House	Dec. 23, 1842	With't amend.	612	Passed	Passed	App'd Jan. 20, 1843
Shannon, Samuel, executor of.	Equitable settlement of his accounts.	28	1	House bill	502	Whole House	Mar. 22, 1844	With't amend.	156	Passed	Passed	App'd May 23, 1844
Shannon, Wm. and Hugh, administrator of.	Further compensation for fire-arms.	19	1	Petition	269	Claims.						
Shannon, Wm. and Hugh, administrator of.	Further compensation for fire-arms.	20	1	Petition	68	Claims	Jan. 9, 1828	Favorable; bill	61	Passed	Passed	App'd May 24, 1828
Shannon, Wilson, assignee of.	Patents for certain lands	28	1	Petition	300	Public Lands	187	Favorable		Laid on table.		
Shapendoshia and other Indians.	Permission to purchase public lands.	29	1	Petition	309	Indian Affairs	Mar. 27, 1846	Adverse		Laid on table.		
Shapley, Adam, representatives of.	Bounty land and commutation pay for revolutionary services.	25	3	Petition	220	Rev. Claims.						
Shapley, Ann, executrix of, by assignees of.	Indemnity for French spoliations prior to 1800.	26	1	Memorial	182	Foreign Affairs	343	Favorable; bill	319	Referred to Committee Whole House.		
Shapley, Ann	(See Peter Clark, administratrix of.)	30	1		118							
Shapley, James,	(See Edward Cutts, administrator of.)	26	1		182							
Shapley, James,	(See Thomas Manning, administrator of.)	26	1		182							
Shapley, Reuben	Indemnity for French spoliations prior to 1800.	26	1	Memorial	182	Foreign Affairs	319	Favorable; bill	319	Referred to Committee Whole House.		
Shapley, William	Redemption of Continental money	29	1	Memorial	340	Claims	670	Adverse		Laid on table.		
Sharadon, James, widow of	Pension for revolutionary services.	25	2	Petition	1210	Rev. Pensions.						
Sharadon, Mary	(See James Sharadon, widow of.)											
Sharer, Peter	Arrears of pay, &c., due claimant's son.	14	1	Petition	70	Claims				Discharged; laid on table.		

List of private claims presented to the House of Representatives of the United States from the 1st to the 31st Congress, inclusive—Continued.

Names of claimants.	Nature or object of the claim.	Congress.	Session.	How brought before the House of Reps.	Page of journal.	To what committee of the House referred.	No. or date of the report.	Nature of the report.	No. of the bill.	How disposed of by the House of Reps.	How disposed of by the Senate.	Date of the act of Congress, and remarks.
Shark, U. States schooner, officers, &c., of.	Indemnity for loss by shipwreck	30	1	Petition	334	Naval Affairs.						
Sharon, Samuel	Pension	13	3	Pension bill	740	Whole House	Mar. 3, 1815	With't amend	303	Passed	Passed	App'd March 3, 1815
Sharpe, Edmund	(See heirs of Linchfield Sharpe	24	1	.....	274							
Sharp, Fidelis C., & others	Right of pre-emption	19	2	Petition	113	Public Lands	...	...	...	Discharged.		
Sharp, Fidelis C., & others	Right of pre-emption	20	1	Petition	310	Public Lands.						
Sharp, George	Compensation for revolutionary services and supplies.	3	2	Petition	317	Claims.						
Sharp, George	Compensation for revolutionary services and supplies.	4	1	Rep. of Secretary War.	273	Claims	Jan. 6, 1796	Adverse	...	Leave to withdraw.		
Sharp, James, by attor'y	Compensation for horses lost in revolutionary war.	4	1	Rep. of Secretary Treasury.	388	Claims	May 31, 1796	Adverse	...	Laid on table.		
Sharp, James, heirs of	Compensation for horses lost in revolutionary war.	17	2	Petition	26	Pens. & Rev. Cl'ms.	Dec. 13, 1822	Adverse	...	Rejected.		
Sharp, James	Additional compensation for work on Cumberland road.	21	1	Petition	174	Internal Improv'nt.						
Sharp, James	Additional compensation for work on Cumberland road.	21	2	Petition	138	Internal Improv'nt.						
Sharp, James	Additional compensation for work on Cumberland road.	23	1	Petition	218	Claims	247	Adverse	...	Laid on table.		
Sharp, Jesse	Pension for revolutionary services.	19	1	Petition	525	Military Pensions.						
Sharpe, John, heirs of	Commutation pay for revolutionary services.	28	1	Memorial	927	Rev. Pensions.						
Sharp, Joseph	(See Canadian refugees)	4	2	.....	614							
Sharp, Joseph	Compensation for work on Cumberland road.	23	1	Res. and docs.	589	Claims	455	Adverse	...	Laid on table	...	See report No. 449.
Sharpe, Lincefield, heirs of	Commutation pay for revolutionary services.	24	1	Petition	274	Rev. Claims	561	Adverse	...	Laid on table.		
Sharpe, Lincefield, heirs of	Commutation pay for revolutionary services.	25	2	Petition	76	Rev. Claims.						
Sharp, Linchfield	Pension for services in Indian wars	29	1	Petition	399	Rev. Pensions.						
Sharp, Linchfield	Pension for services in Indian wars	30	1	Petition	485	Invalid Pensions	568	Adverse	...	Laid on table.		
Sharp, Matthew	(See Canadian refugees)	4	2	.....	614							
Sharpe, Reuben	Pension	21	1	Petition	471	Military Pensions	May 4, 1830	Adverse	...	Laid on table.		
Sharp, Robert	(See Canadian refugees)	11	2	.....	115							
Sharp, Robert	Benefit of the act of February 24, 1810.	12	1	House bill	242	Whole House	Mar. 22, 1812	With't amend.	85	Passed	Passed, with amendment.	App'd April 23, 1812
Sharp, Robert	Pension	28	2	Documents	304	Rev. Pensions.						
Sharp, Salmon	Bounty land for military services.	22	2	Petition	31	Military Affairs.						
Sharp, Salmon	Bounty land for military services.	23	1	Petition	298	Public Lands	...	...	...	Disch'd; laid on table.		
Shartell, Jacob	Pension for revolutionary services.	3	1	Rep. of Secretary War.	131	Select	May 26, 1794	Res. to refer to Sec. War.	J. R. 12	Passed	Passed	Appd June 9, 1794
Shartell, Jacob	Pension for revolutionary services.	4	1	Rep. of Secretary War.	445	Claims.						
Shartell, Jacob	Pension for revolutionary services.	4	2	Rep. of Secretary War.	614	Claims.						
Shatto, Sarah	(See John Walker, heir of.)	29	1	.....	592							
Shattuck, Jared	Indemnity for illegal capture and condemnation of his vessel.	9	1	Petition	349							
				Rep. of Secretary War.	384	...	...	...	...	Laid on table.		
Shattuck, Jared	Indemnity for illegal capture and condemnation of his vessel.	9	2	Petition	486	Claims.						

List of private claims presented to the House of Representatives of the United States from the 1st to the 31st Congress, inclusive—Continued.

Names of claimants.	Nature or object of the claim.	Congress.	Session.	How brought before the House of Reps.	Page of journal.	To what committee of the House referred.	No. or date of the report.	Nature of the report.	No. of the bill.	How disposed of by the House of Reps.	How disposed of by the Senate.	Date of the act of Congress, and remarks.
Shattuck, Jared	Indemnity for illegal capture and condemnation of his vessel.	10	1	Petition	28	Claims	Feb. 17, 1808	Favorable	......	Referred to Committee Whole House.		
Shattuck, Jared	Indemnity for illegal capture and condemnation of his vessel.	10	2	Petition	367	Claims.						
Shattuck, Jared	Indemnity for illegal capture and condemnation of his vessel.	11	1	Petition	20	Claims.						
Shattuck, Jared	Indemnity for illegal capture and condemnation of his vessel.	11	2	Petition	111	Claims	Dec. 28, 1809	Favorable	55	Passed	Postponed.	
Shattuck, Jared	Indemnity for illegal capture and condemnation of his vessel.	11	3	Petition	446	Claims	Jan. 31, 1811	Favorable	194	Referred to Committee Whole House.		
Shattuck, Jared	Indemnity for illegal capture and condemnation of his vessel.	12	1	Petition	41	Claims	234	Favorable	140	Referred to Committee Whole House.		
Shattuck, Jared	Indemnity for illegal capture and condemnation of his vessel.	12	2	Petition	552	Claims	Nov. 25, 1812	Favorable	198	Passed	Passed	App'd Feb. 2, 1813
Shattuck, Jared	Payment of an award of Supreme Court.	18	1	Petition	42	Claims	Jan. 2, 1824	Adverse	......	Laid on table.		
Shattuck, Williams	Compensation for revolutionary services and reimbursement of expenses.	3	1	Petition	75	....	....	....	......	Referred to Secretary War.		
Shattuck, Williams	Compensation for revolutionary services and reimbursement of expenses.	3	2	Rep. of Secretary War.	....	....	....	....	......	Laid on table.		
Shattuck, William	(See Timothy Stewart, surety of.)	17	2	....	120							
Shaumburgh, Bartholomew	Reimbursement of advances on public account.	13	2	Petition	295	Claims	Feb. 28, 1814	Adverse	......	Laid on table.		
Shaumburgh, Bartholomew	Reimbursement of advances on public account.	22	1	Senate bill	540	Claims	April 6, 1832	With't amend.	S. 77	Passed	Passed	App'd July 14, 1832
Shaumburgh, Bartholomew	Credit for money lost in transmission.	17	1	Petition	172	Claims.						
Shaumburgh, Bartholomew	Credit for money lost in transmission.	17	2	Petition	122	Military Affairs	Jan. 17, 1823	Adverse	......	Referred to Committee Whole House.		
Shauntee, Henry	Pension for revolutionary services.	23	1	Res. and docs.	512	Rev. Pensions.						
Shaver, David, sen., and others.	Commutation of their land claims.	21	2	Memorial	75	Priv. Land Claims.	....	....	......	Discharged; laid on table.		
Shaver, David, sen., and others.	Commutation of their land claims.	22	1	Petition	50	Judiciary	236	Adverse	......	Referred to Committee Whole House.		
Shaver, George	Bounty pay, &c., for military services.	15	1	Petition	161	Military Affairs	Mar. 31, 1818	General bill	168	Laid on table.		
Shaver, John, executor of widow of.	Payment of pension due deceased.	26	2	Petition	49	Rev. Pensions.						
Shaver, Nathaniel, representatives of.	Authority to locate a tract of land.	24	1	Senate bill	1055	Priv. Land Claims.	Ju'y 1, 1836	With't amend.	S. 121	Passed	Passed	App'd July 2, 1836
Shaw, Archibald	Pension	21	1	Petition	231	Military Pensions.						
Shaw, Archibald	Pension	21	2	Resolution	49	Military Pensions.						
Shaw, Archibald	Pension	22	1	Petition	164	Rev. Pensions	372	Favorable	467	Passed	Indef. postp'd.	
Shaw, Basil	Compensation for a slave killed in battle.	15	1	Petition	168	Claims	Feb. 3, 1818	Adverse	......	Laid on table.		
Shaw, Basil	Compensation for a slave killed in battle.	16	1	Petition	35	Claims	Dec. 31, 1819	Adverse	......	Rejected.		
Shaw, Charles, and Joseph Sumner.	Bounty on fishing schooner Fox.	19	1	Petition	108	Commerce.						
Shaw, David, and Solomon T. Corser.	Extra compensation for mail service.	28	2	Senate resolution.	162	P. Of. & P. Roads.	Feb. 7, 1845	With't amend.	S. R. 1	Referred to Committee Whole House.		

List of private claims presented to the House of Representatives of the United States from the 1st to the 31st Congress, inclusive—Continued.

Names of claimants.	Nature or object of the claim.	Congress.	Session.	How brought before the House of Reps.	Page of journal.	To what committee of the House referred.	No. or date of the report.	Nature of the report.	No. of the bill.	How disposed of by the House of Reps.	How disposed of by the Senate.	Date of the act of Congress, and remarks.
Shaw, David, and Solomon T. Corser.	Extra compensation for mail service.	29	1	Senate resolution.	808	P. Of. & P. Roads.	July 24, 1846	With't amend.	S. R. 2	Referred to Committee Whole House.		
Shaw, David, and Solomon T. Corser.	Extra compensation for mail service.	29	2	Senate resolution.	307	P. Of. & P. Roads.	Feb. 24, 1847	With't amend.	S. R. 1	Referred to Committee Whole House.		
Shaw, David, and Solomon T. Corser.	Extra compensation for mail service.	30	1	Senate resolution.	203	P. Of. and P. Roads.	Feb. 29, 1848	With't amend.	S. R. 1	Passed wi h amendm't.	Passed as am'd	App'd June 26, 1848
Shaw, David, and Solomon T. Corser.	Extra compensation for mail service.	30	2	Rep't of Postmaster General.	544	P. Of. and P. Roads	121	Adverse	......	Laid on table.		
Shaw, Elijah, daughter of.	Pension for revolutionary services.	28	1	Petition	946	Rev. Pensions.						
Shaw, Gilman B........	Arrears of pension............	22	2	Petition	246	Invalid Pensions ..	Feb. 15, 1833	Favorable....	738	Referred to Committee Whole House.		
Shaw, Gilman B........	Arrears of pension............	23	1	Petition	46	Rev. Pensions	1	Favorable....	1	Passed	Passed, with amendment.	App'd June 25, 1834
Shaw, Gilman B........	Pension for services in the war of 1812.	24	1	Petition	98	Invalid Pensions.						
Shaw, Gilman B........	Pension for services in the war of 1812.	24	2	Petition	504	Invalid Pensions...	Feb. 22, 1837	Adverse	......	Laid on table.		
Shaw, Giiman B........	Pension for services in the war of 1812.	29	1	Petition	541	Invalid Pensions ..	....	....	......	Discharged; laid on table.		
Shaw, Henry...........	Pension	11	2	Pension bill	283	....	....	....	107	Passed	Passed, with amendment.	App'd April 27, 1810
Shaw, Henry...........	(See David Jewett)	19	1	....	127							
Shaw, Hillyard	Pension	27	2	Petition	320	Invalid Pensions ..	934	Adverse	......	Laid on table.		
Shaw, Hillyard	Pension	27	3	Petition	76	Invalid Pensions ..	....	....	......	Leave to withdraw.		
Shaw, James	Compensation for revolutionary services and supplies.	4	1	Petition	472	Claims	....	....	......	Laid on table.		
Shaw, James	Pension	14	1	Pension bill....	622	Whole House.....	April 23, 1816	With't amend.	171	Passed	Passed, with amendment.	App'd April 30, 1816
Shaw, John	(See Isaac Lawrence and others)..	14	2	....	101							
Shaw, John, (Elizabeth,) widow of.	Balance of pension............	19	1	Resolution	115	Military Pensions..	164	Adverse	......	Laid on table.		
Shaw, John, (Elizabeth,) widow of.	Balance of pension............	19	2	Resolution	57	Military Pensions..	34	Favorable....	349	Referred to Committee Whole House.		
Shaw, John, (Elizabeth,) widow of.	Balance of pension............	20	2	Petition	32	Military Pensions..	81	Favorable....	83	Passed	Passed	App'd May 24, 1828
Shaw, John, executor of..	Balance due on the books of the Treasury.	29	1	Petition	124	Claims	170	Adverse.	......	Laid on table.		
Shaw, John C..........	Liquidation of a revolutionary certificate.	4	1	Rep. of Secretary Treasury.	388	Claims	May 31, 1796	Adverse	......	Laid on table.		
Shaw, John Robert......	Compensation for military services and suffering.	10	1	Petition	142	Select.						
Shaw, John Robert......	Pension for revolutionary services.	10	2	Pension bill	499	Whole House.....	....	....	158	Passed	Passed, with amendment.	App'd March 3, 1809
Shaw, John R., widow of.	Pension for naval services.......	24	1	Petition	432	Naval Affairs.						
Shaw, John R., widow of.	Indemnity for property taken by the enemy.	25	3	Memorial	486	Naval Affairs.						
Shaw, John R., widow of.	Indemnity for property taken by the enemy.	26	1	Petition	180	Naval Affairs.						
Shaw, Joseph..........	Pension	12	1	Pension bill	361	Whole House.....	June 15, 1812	With amend..	138	Passed	Passed, with amendment.	App'd July 5, 1812
Shaw, Joseph..........	Arrears of pension	21	1	Petition	260	Military Pensions..	Feb. 19, 1830	Adverse	......	Laid on table.		
				Senate bill	646	Military Pensions..	May 21, 1830	With't amend.	S. 138	Passed	Passed......	App'd May 28, 1830

List of private claims presented to the House of Representatives of the United States from the 1st to the 31st Congress, inclusive—Continued.

Names of claimants.	Nature or object of the claim.	Congress.	Session.	How brought before the House of Reps.	Page of journal.	To what committee of the House referred.	No. or date of the report.	Nature of the report.	No. of the bill.	How disposed of by the House of Reps.	How disposed of by the Senate.	Date of the act of Congress, and remarks.
Shaw, Joseph	Indemnity for property destroyed in the public service.	23	1	Petition	191	Claims	June 18, 1834	Adverse	—	Laid on table.		
Shaw, Joshua	Compensation for sundry experiments in fire-arms.	28	1	Memorial	868	Military Affairs.						
Shaw, Joshua	Compensation for use of improvement in fire-arms.	28	2	Petition	56	Claims	53	Favorable	533	Referred to Committee Whole House.		
				Senate bill	249	Military Affairs	Feb. 15, 1845	With amend.	S. 52	Referred to Committee Whole House.		
Shaw, Joshua	Compensation for use of improvement in fire-arms.	29	1	Petition	266	Patents	212	Favorable	206	Referred to Committee Whole House.		
Shaw, Joshua	Compensation for use of improvement in fire-arms.	29	2	House bill	71				206	Passed	Passed	App'd Feb. 20, 1847
Shaw, Joshua, widow of	Compensation for right of dower	13	2	Petition	190	Claims				Discharged; leave to withdraw.		
Shaw, Juliana	(See Nathan Shaw, widow of)	28	1		351							
Shaw, Margaret E	(See John R. Shaw, widow of)	24	1		432							
Shaw, Nathan, widow of	Pension for revolutionary services.	28	1	Petition	351	Rev. Pensions				Discharged; laid on table.		
Shaw, Neill, widow of	Compensation for property taken for public use.	23	1	Petition	334	Rev. Claims.						
Shaw, Noah	Remission of penalty under non-importation act.	13	3	Petition	471	Ways and Means	27	Adverse		Laid on table.		
Shaw, Noah	Remission of penalty under non-importation act.	14	1	Petition	432	Ways and Means.						
Shaw, Robert, jr	Equitable settlement of his accounts.	19	1	Petition	177	Claims				Discharged; leave to withdraw.		
Shaw, Samuel	Exemption from duty on teas, &c.	2	2	Petition	628	Select	Dec. 12, 1792	Adverse		Laid on table.		
Shaw, Samuel	Pension	3	2	Rep. of Secretary War.	278	Claims.						
Shaw, Samuel	Pension	4	1	Rep. of Secretary War.	445	Claims	Feb. 18, 1796	Res. to refer to Sec. War.	R. 16	Passed	Passed	App'd April 18, 1796
Shaw, Samuel	Pension	4	2	Rep. of Secretary War.	614	Claims.						
Shaw, Samuel	Pension	10	1	Pension bill	232	Whole House			78	Passed	Passed	App'd April 25, 1808
Shaw, Samuel	Increase of pension	18	1	Petition	81	Pens. & Rev. Clm's.				Discharged; laid on table.		Leave to withdraw.
Shaw, Samuel	Increase of pension	20	1	Pension	192	Military Pensions	May 13, 1828	Adverse		Leave to withdraw.		
Shaw, Thomas M	Indemnity for French spoliations prior to 1800.	21	1	Petition	116	Claims.						
Shaw, Thomas M	Indemnity for French spoliations prior to 1800.	26	1	Memorial	182	Foreign Affairs	343	Favorable; bill	319	Referred to Committee Whole House.		
Shaw, Thomas M	Indemnity for French spoliations prior to 1800.	31	1	Petition	197	Foreign Affairs	355	General bill	318	Referred to Committee Whole House.		
Shaw, William	Indemnity for French spoliations prior to 1800.	26	1	Memorial	182	Foreign Affairs	343	Favorable; bill	319	Referred to Committee Whole House.		
Shaw, William	Indemnity for destruction of property at Baltimore.	24	2	Petition	209	Claims	282	Adverse		Laid on table.		
Shaw, William	Indemnity for destruction of property at Baltimore.	25	2	Petition	73	Claims	Feb. 31, 1838	Adverse		Laid on table.		
Shaw, William D	Compensation for supplies on public account.	31	1	Petition	231	Claims	30	Adverse		Laid on table.		
Shawnee Indians	(See Indians)	31	1		544							

List of private claims presented to the House of Representatives of the United States from the 1st to the 31st Congress, inclusive—**Continued.**

Names of claimants.	Nature or object of the claim.	Congress.	Session.	How brought before the House of Reps.	Page of journal.	To what committee of the House referred.	No. or date of the report.	Nature of the report.	No. of the bill.	How disposed of by the House of Reps.	How disposed of by the Senate.	Date of the act of Congress, and remarks.
Shay, Timothy	(See Timothy Shey or Shay)	24	1		107							
Shayler, Ephraim	Equitable settlement of accounts	14	1	Petition	231	Claims	Feb. 24, 1816	Favorable; bill		Passed	Passed	App'd April 27, 1816
				Petition, (2)	296	Military Affairs.						
Shaylor, Joseph	Pension for disabilities incurred in revolutionary war.	6	2	Petition	830	Claims				Discharged; laid on table.		
Shaylor, Joseph	Pension for disabilities incurred in revolutionary war.	7	1	Petition	135					Laid on table.		
Shea, Stephen	Pension	20	2	Petition	143	Military Pensions.						
Shea, Stephen	Pension	21	1	Petition	49	Military Pensions	Jan. 5, 1830	By bill	72	Passed	Passed	App'd May 20, 1830
Shead, Oliver, surety of	Release from liability	14	1	Petition	722	Judiciary.						
Shead, Oliver, surety of	Release from liability	16	1	Petition	77	Judiciary	Jan. 6, 1820	Adverse		Laid on table.		
Shead, Oliver, surety of	Release from liability	17	1	Petition	68	P. Of. & P. Roads.	Jan. 29, 1823	Favorable; bill	261	Passed	Passed	App'd Mar. 23, 1823
Sheafe, Edmund Q	(See John Peters, and E. Q. S.)	21	1		619							
Sheafe, Edmund Q	(See Joseph and Jacob Sheafe, & Co.)	26	1		182							
Sheafe, George, widow of.	Arrears of revolutionary pension	26	1	Petition	937	Rev. Pensions	714	Adverse		Laid on table.		
Sheafe, Henry, heirs of	Compensation for revolutionary services.	7	1	Petition	110	Claims	Mar. 2, 1802	Adverse		Rejected.		
Sheafe, Henry	(See Conrad Wile, and others)	16	1		39							
Sheafe, Jacob, executor of.	Indemnity for French spoliations prior to 1800.	26	1	Memorial	182	Foreign Affairs	343	Favorable; bill	319	Referred to Committee Whole House.		
Sheafe, James	Indemnity for French spoliations prior to 1800.	26	1	Memorial	182	Foreign Affairs	343	Favorable; bill	319	Referred to Committee Whole House.		
Sheafe, James, executor and attorney of.	Indemnity for French spoliations prior to 1800	26	1	Memorial	182	Foreign Affairs	343	Favorable; bill	319	Referred to Committee Whole House.		
Sheafe, John H	Indemnity for French spoliations prior to 1800.	26	1	Memorial	182	Foreign Affairs	343	Favorable; bill	319	Referred to Committee Whole House.		
Sheafe, John H	(See Thomas Sheafe, executor of)	26	1		182							
Sheafe, John H	(See James Sheafe, &c.)	26	1		182							
Sheafe, Joseph, executor of	Indemnity for French spoliations prior to 1800.	26	1	Memorial	182	Foreign Affairs	343	Favorable; bill	319	Referred to Committee Whole House.		
Sheafe, Samuel	Indemnity for French spoliations prior to 1800.	26	1	Memorial	182	Foreign Affairs	343	Favorable; bill	319	Referred to Committee Whole House.		
Sheafe, Thomas	Indemnity for French spoliations prior to 1800.	19	2	Petition	157	Foreign Affairs.						
Sheafe, Thomas, executor of.	Indemnity for French spoliations prior to 1800.	26	1	Memorial	182	Foreign Affairs	343	Favorable; bill	319	Referred to Committee Whole House.		
Sheafe, Thomas	Indemnity for French spoliations prior to 1800.	31	1	Petition	348	Foreign Affairs	355	General bill	318	Referred to Committee Whole House.		
Sheafe, Thomas and Wm.	Indemnity for French spoliations prior to 1800.	26	1	Memorial	182	Foreign Affairs	343	Favorable; bill	319	Referred to Committee Whole House.		
Sheafe, W. M	Indemnity for French spoliations prior to 1800.	26	1	Memorial	182	Foreign Affairs	343	Favorable; bill	319	Referred to Committee Whole House.		
Sheafe, William	Indemnity for French spoliations prior to 1800.	26	1	Memorial	102	Foreign Affairs	343	Favorable; bill	319	Referred to Committee Whole House.		
Shearer, Joseph	Reimbursement of expenditures on public account.	24	1	Petition	48	Claims	264	Adverse		Laid on table.		
Shearer, Joseph	Reimbursement of expenditures on public account.	24	2	Petition	260	Claims.						

List of private claims presented to the House of Representatives of the United States from the 1st to the 31st Congress, inclusive—Continued.

Names of claimants.	Nature or object of the claim.	Congress.	Session.	How brought before the House of Reps.	Page of journal.	To what committee of the House referred.	No. or date of the report.	Nature of the report.	No. of the bill.	How disposed of by the House of Reps.	How disposed of by the Senate.	Date of the act of Congress, and remarks.
Shearer, Sextus	Compensation for goods furnished Indians.	28	1	Appropriat'n bill.	196				32	Passed	Passed	App'd June 17, 1844
Shearman, F. W	Compensation for services in Indian department.	26	1	Petition	1147	Indian Affairs				Discharged; laid on table.		
Shearman, Job	Pension	21	1	Petition	377	Military Pensions	May 18, 1830	Adverse		Laid on table.		
Shears, William, assignee of.	Arrears of pay for military services.	19	1	Petition	407	Claims	165	Favorable	217	Passed.		
Shears, William, assignee of.	Arrears of pay for military services.	19	2	Petition	82	Claims	Dec. 22, 1826	Favorable	313	Passed	Passed	App'd Feb. 22, 1827
Sheather, John	Increase of pension	22	1	Petition	287	Rev. Pensions.						
Sheckler, Frederick	Pension for revolutionary services.	20	1	Resolution	704	Military Pensions	Feb. 13, 1828	By bill	166	Passed.		
Sheckler, Frederick	Pension for revolutionary services.	20	2	Pension bill	55	Whole House	Jan. 15, 1829	With amend.	311	Passed	Laid on table.	
Sheckler, Frederick	Pension for revolutionary services.	21	1	Petition	49	Military Pensions	Jan. 5, 1830	By bill	72	Passed	Passed	App'd May 20, 1830
Sheckler, Frederick	Pension for revolutionary services.	21	2	Resolution	85	Military Pensions.						
Sheckler, Frederick	Pension for revolutionary services.	22	1	Resolution	251	Rev Pensions.						
Shedlate, O., surety of	Release from liability on a bond	15	2	Petition	103	Judiciary	Dec. 29, 1818	Adverse		Rejected.		
Shee, Elizabeth	(See administratrix of Geo. Gooding.)	18	1		176							
Sheehey, Edward	Indemnity for loss on a government contract.	23	2	Petition	309	Claims.						
Sheets, Matthias	(See Matthias Shirts)	21	1		95							
Sheets, Zebulon	Correction of a land entry	24	1	Petition	261	Priv. Land Claims.	309	Favorable	324	Referred to Committee Whole House.		
Sheets, Zebulon	Correction of a land entry	25	2	Petition	42	Priv. Land Claims.	348	Favorable	379	Referred to Committee Whole House.		
Sheets, Zebulon	Correction of a land entry	25	3	Bill of last sess.	378	Whole House	Jan. 25, 1839	With't amend.	379	Passed	Passed	App'd March 3, 1839
Sheffield, Aaron	Remission of penalty on a certain bond.	4	1	Petition	541	Com. and Manuf.	Dec. 27, 1796	Adverse		Recommitted.		
Sheffield, Aaron	Remission of penalty on a certain bond.	4	2	Petition	720	Com. and Munuf.	Feb. 24, 1797	Adverse		Laid on table.		
Sheffield, Aaron, widow of	Reimbursement of a moiety of the proceeds of the sale of sloop Speedwell and cargo.	8	2	Petition	149	Com. and Manuf.						
Sheffield, Aaron, widow of	Reimbursement of a moiety of the proceeds of the sale of sloop Speedwell and cargo.	9	2	Petition	493	Com. and Manuf.	Jan. 9, 1807	Adverse		Leave to withdraw.		
Sheffield, Aaron, att'ney of	Indemnity for French spoliations prior to 1800.	26	1	Memorial	182	Foreign Affairs	343	Favorable; bill	319	Referred to Committee Whole House.		
Sheffield, Amos, & others.	Bounty on fishing schooner Three Sisters.	22	1	Petition	471	Commerce	433	Favorable	532	Referred to Committee Whole House.		
Sheffield, Amos, & others.	Bounty on fishing schooner Three Sisters.	23	1	Petition	32	Commerce	Dec. 16, 1833	Favorable	30	Passed	Passed	App'd June 27, 1834
Sheffield, Geo., widow of.	Pension for revolutionary services.	28	2	Petition	53	Rev. Pensions.						
Sheffield, Geo., widow of.	Pension for revolutionary services.	30	1	Petition	115	Rev. Pensions	346	Adverse		Laid on table.		
Sheffield, Ichabod	(See Otis Harris, Pendleton & others.)	18	1		153							
Sheffield, Mary	(See Aaron Sheffield, widow of)	8	2		149							
Sheffield, Mary	(See George Sheffield, widow of)	28	2		53							
Sheffler, George	Compensation for military services	27	2	Petition	68	Invalid Pensions	128	Favorable	174	Passed	Passed	App'd Aug. 16, 1842
Sheftall, Frances	(See Mordecai Sheftall, widow of)	7	1		136							

List of private claims presented to the House of Representatives of the United States from the 1st to the 31st Congress, inclusive—Continued.

Names of claimants.	Nature or object of the claim.	Congress.	Session.	How brought before the House of Reps.	Page of journal.	To what committee of the House referred.	No. or date of the report.	Nature of the report.	No. of the bill.	How disposed of by the House of Reps.	How disposed of by the Senate.	Date of the act of Congress, and remarks.
Sheftall, Mordecai	Settlement of accounts as revolutionary commissary.	2	1	Petition	554					Referred to Secretary Treasury.		
Sheftall, Mordecai	Settlement of accounts as revolutionary commissary.	3	1	Rep. of Secretary Treasury.	78					Laid on table.		
Sheftall, Mordecai	Settlement of accounts as revolutionary commissary.	4	1	Rep. of Secretary Treasury.	451	Claims.						
Sheftall, Mordecai	Settlement of accounts as revolutionary commissary.	4	2	Petition	691	Claims	Feb. 11, 1797	Adverse		Referred to Committee Whole House.		
Sheftall, Mordecai, widow of.	Settlement of accounts as revolutionary commissary.	7	1	Petition	136	Claims	April 3, 1802	Recommend to postpone.		Postponed.		
Shelby, Abraham, assignee of.	Bounty land for revolutionary services.	6	1	Senate bill	649	Select	May 7, 1800	With't amend.	59	Passed	Passed	App'd May 10, 1800
Shelby, C. W.	Confirmation of title to land in De Bastrop grant.	30	1	Petition	119	Priv. Land Claims.						
Shelby, William	(See Bryant R. Young, & others)	23	1		449							
Sheldon, Elijah	Pension for revolutionary services.	10	2	Pension bill	499	Whole House			158	Passed	Passed	App'd March 3, 1809
Sheldon, Gideon	Pension for disabilities in the war of 1812.	24	2	Petition	311	Invalid Pensions	207	Adverse		Laid on table.		
Sheldon, Gideon	Pension for disabilities in the war of 1812.	25	2	Petition	118	Invalid Pensions	499	Favorable	502	Passed.		
Sheldon, Gideon	Pension for disabilities in the war of 1812.	25	3	Petition	89	Invalid Pensions	86	Favorable	965	Passed.		
Sheldon, Gideon	Pension for disabilities in the war of 1812.	26	1	Petition	162	Invalid Pensions	195	Favorable	207	Passed	Passed	App'd July 20, 1840
Sheldon, Ichabod	Pension for disability, war of 1812.	24	2	Petition	41	Invalid Pensions.				Discharged; laid on table.		
Sheldon, James	Balance due on a loan office certificate.	20	1	Resolution	313	Rev. Claims				Discharged; laid on table.		
Sheldon, Job	Bounty land for revolutionary services.	10	2	Petition	380	Public Lands.	Feb. 27, 1809	Adverse		Leave to withdraw.		
Sheldon, John	Increase of pension	12	2	Petition	678	Claims	Feb. 26, 1813	Adverse		Laid on table.		
Sheldon, Joseph	Invalid pension	3	1	Rep. of Secretary War.	131	Select	May 26, 1794	Res. to refer to Sec. War.	J. R. 12	Passed	Passed	App'd June 9, 1794
Sheldon, Joseph	Invalid pension	4	1	Rep. of Secretary War.	445	Claims.						
Sheldon, Joseph	Invalid pension	4	2	Rep. of Secretary War.	614	Claims.						
Sheldon, Ptolemy	Pension	14	1	Resolution	158	Pens. & Rev. Cl'ms.	April 23, 1816	Favorable	171	Passed	Passed, with amendment.	App'd April 30, 1816
Sheldon, Thomas C.	Reimbursement of amount paid for clerk hire.	29	2	Senate bill	380	Public Lands	Feb. 24, 1847	With't amend.	S. 119	Referred to Committee Whole House.		
Sheldon, Thomas C.	Reimbursement of amount paid for clerk hire.	30	2	Senate bill	518	Whole House	Feb. 28, 1849	With't amend.	S. 225	Passed	Passed	App'd March 2, 1849
Sheldon, Walter, sureties of.	Discharge from liability to the United States.	18	1	Resolution	204	Cliams				Discharged; laid on table.		
Sheldon, Whiting	Pension for revolutionary services.	24	1	Petition	663	Rev. Pensions				Discharged; laid on table.		
Shelton, Clough, heirs of.	Commutation pay for revolutionary services.	25	3	Petition	125	Rev. Claims.						
Shelton, Clough, heirs of.	Commutation pay for revolutionary services.	26	1	Petition	164	Rev. Claims	237	Adverse		Laid on table.		
Shelton, Edward P.	Military bounty land	31	1	Petition	215	Military Affairs.						

List of private claims presented to the House of Representatives of the United States from the 1st to the 31st Congress, inclusive—Continued.

Names of claimants.	Nature or object of the claim.	Congress.	Session.	How brought before the House of Reps.	Page of journal.	To what committee of the House referred.	No. or date of the report.	Nature of the report.	No. of the bill.	How disposed of by the House of Reps.	How disposed of by the Senate.	Date of the act of Congress, and remarks.
Shelton, Medley	To be restored to pension roll	18	1	Petition	81	Rev. Pensions	....	....	......	Discharged; laid on table.		
Shell, Benjamin and Casper.	Confirmation of title to land in Missouri.	15	1	Petition	180	Priv. Land Claims.						
Shell, Benjamin and Casper.	Confirmation of title to land in Missouri.	16	1	Petition	71	Priv. Land Claims.						
Shell, Benjamin and Casper.	Confirmation of title to land in Missouri.	17	1	Petition	55	Public Lands.						
Shell, Benjamin and Casper.	Confirmation of title to land in Missouri.	18	1	Petition	55	Public Lands.						
Shell, Christian	Indemnity for hogs destroyed by Indians.	24	1	Petition	95	Indian Affairs	....	....	......	Discharged; laid on table.		
Shell, George	Pension for revolutionary services.	11	3	Rep. of Secretary War.	604	Whole House	Mar. 2, 1811	With amend.	218	Passed	Passed, with amendment.	App'd March 3, 1811
Shell, John, heirs of	Compensation for military services, &c.	22	1	Documents	575	Rev. Claims.						
Shell, John, heirs of	Compensation for military services, &c.	23	2	Petition	120	Rev. Claims.						
Shell, John, heirs of	Compensation for military services, &c.	24	1	Petition	138	Rev. Claims.						
Shell, John, heirs of	Compensation for military services, &c.	24	2	Petition	119	Claims.						
Shell, John, heirs of	Compensation for military services, &c.	25	2	Documents	111	Rev. Claims	411	Adverse	......	Laid on table.		
Shell, John, heirs of	Reimbursement of expenses incurred in public service.	23	1	Petition	156	Rev. Claims.						
Shelley, Medad	Pension for revolutionary services.	29	1	Petition	162	Rev. Pensions	562	Adverse	......	Laid on table.		
Shellhorn, Baltzer H.	Arrears of pension	25	3	Petition	129	Invalid Pensions.						
Shellhorn, Baltzer H.	Arrears of pension	27	2	Petition	130	Invalid Pensions	233	Adverse	......	Laid on table.		
Shellman, John	Cancellation of a revenue bond	16	1	Petition	238	Ways and Means.						
Shellman, John	(See John Stevens and others)	21	1	....	58							
Shelmerdine, Samuel	Pension	23	1	Petition	388	Invalid Pensions	450	Favorable	467	Referred to Committee Whole House.		
Shelmerdine, Samuel	Pension	23	2	Bill of last sess.	336	Whole House	Feb. 6, 1835	With't amend.	467	Passed	Passed	App'd March 3, 1835
Shenfessell, Andrew	(See William Zoll and others)	15	2	....	190							
Shenkele, Jacob	Compensation for military services, war of 1812.	24	1	Petition	64	Military Affairs	....	....	......	Discharged; laid on table.		
Shepard, Aaron	Increase of compensation as collector of direct tax.	8	2	Petition	133	Claims.						
Shepard, Andrew	Renewal of a certificate of public debt.	6	2	Petition	738	Claims	Dec. 15, 1800	Adverse	......	Rejected.		
Shepard, Michi	(See Thomas Perkins, executors of)	26	1	....	182							
Shepherd, David	Compensation for work on Cumberland road.	17	1	Documents	422	Roads and Canals	....	....	......	Discharged.		
Shepherd, David	Bounty land for military services.	17	1	Resolution	237	Military Affairs	Feb. 14, 1822	Adverse	......	Rejected.		
Shepherd, David	Right of pre-emption as New Orleans branch pilot.	28	1	Petition	77	Priv. Land Claims.	9	Favorable	35	Passed	Passed	App'd June 17, 1844
Shepherd, David	Compensation for a horse lost in Mexican war.	30	1	Petition	146	Claims	408	Favorable	358	Passed.		
Shepherd, Edward S.	(See Amos Jones and others)	24	1	....	411							
Shephard, Edward	Pension for revolutionary services.	30	1	Petition	798	Rev. Pensions	790	Adverse	......	Laid on table.		
Shephard, George	Pay and bounty land for revolutionary services.	16	1	Petition	237	Pens. & Rev. Cl'ms.	April 17, 1820	Adverse	......	Rejected.		

List of private claims presented to the House of Representatives of the United States from the 1st to the 31st Congress, inclusive—Continued.

Names of claimants.	Nature or object of the claim.	Congress.	Session.	How brought before the House of Reps.	Page of journal.	To what committee of the House referred.	No. or date of the report.	Nature of the report.	No. of the bill.	How disposed of by the House of Reps.	How disposed of by the Senate.	Date of the act of Congress, and remarks.
Shepherd, Isaac	Compensation for a horse lost in Mexican war.	30	1	Petition	147	Claims	407	Favorable	357	Passed.		
Shepherd, Israel	Pension for revolutionary services.	22	1	Petition	219	Rev. Pensions.						
Shepherd, James	Pension	3	1	Rep. of Secretary War.	131	Select	May 26, 1795	Favorable; bill ordered.	62	Passed	Passed	App'd June 7, 1795
Shepherd, John	Confirmation of title to land in Missouri.	15	1	Petition	50	Priv. Land Claims.						
Shepherd, John	Confirmation of title to land in Missouri.	16	1	Petition	71	Priv. Land Claims.						
Shepherd, John	Confirmation of title to land in Missouri.	17	1	Petition	55	Priv. Land Claims.						
Shepherd, John	Confirmation of title to land in Missouri.	18	1	Petition	55	Public Lands.						
Shepherd, John	Pension for revolutionary services.	22	1	Petition	441	Rev. Pensions	....	....	....	Discharged; laid on table.		
Shepherd, John, heirs of	Commutation pay for revolutionary services.	23	1	Petition	305	Rev. Claims.						
Shepherd, John H	Credit for moneys of which he was robbed.	21	1	Petition	205	P. Of. & P. Roads.						
Shepherd, John H	(See Abiel Wood, administrator of.)	24	1	....	53							
Shepherd, Joseph	Pre-emption right as New Orleans branch pilot.	28	1	Petition	77	Priv. Land Claims.	9	Favorable	35	Passed	Passed	App'd June 17, 1844
Shepherd, Joseph M	Compensation for a horse lost in public service.	25	3	Documents	121	Claims.						
Shepherd, Joseph M	Compensation for a horse lost in public service.	26	1	Petition	1257	Claims	701	Adverse	....	Laid on table.		
Shepherp, Joseph M	(Farrow & Harris, representa's of)	29	1	....	75							
Shepherd, John and others.	Compensation for transportation of the mail.	25	2	Petition	591	P. Of. & P. Roads.						
Shepherd, Mary	(See Frederick M. Bell, heirs of.)	25	2	....	160							
Shepherd, Moses	Compensation for extra work on Cumberland road.	18	1	Petition	316	Select	May 10, 1824	Adverse	....	Referred to Secretary of War.		
Shepherd, Moses	Compensation for extra work on Cumberland road.	18	2	Rep. of Secretary War.	175	Claims	63	Favorable	325	Passed	Passed	App'd March 3, 1825
Shepherd, Moses	Equitable settlement of accounts as contractor.	19	1	Petition	249	Claims	133	Favorable	175	Referred to Secretary Treasury.		
Shepherd, Moses	Equitable settlement of accounts as contractor.	20	1	Memorial	91	Claims	....	....	....	Discharged; leave to withdraw.		
				Senate bill	473	Claims	253	Adverse	S. 112	Laid on table.		
Shepherd, Moses, representatives of.	Additional pay for work on Cumberland road.	25	2	Petition	542	Claims.						
Shepherd, Moses, representatives of.	Additional pay for work on Cumberland road.	27	3	Petition	43	Claims.						
Shepherd, Moses, representatives of.	Additional pay for work on Cumberland road.	28	1	Petition	337	Claims.						
Shepherd, Noadiah	Confirmation of title to land	24	1	Petition	1165	Priv. Land Claims.	....	....	....	Discharged; laid on table.		
Shepherd, Noadiah	Confirmation of title to land	24	2	Petition	587	Priv. Land Claims.	....	....	....	Discharged; laid on table.		
Shephard, Phinehas	Pension	22	1	Petition	330	Rev. Pensions.						
Shepherd, Peletiah	(See Isaac Cook and others.)	25	3	....	121							

List of private claims presented to the House of Representatives of the United States from the 1st to the 31st Congress, inclusive—Continued.

Names of claimants.	Nature or object of the claim.	Congress.	Session.	How brought before the House of Reps.	Page of journal.	To what committee of the House referred.	No. or date of the report.	Nature of the report.	No. of the bill.	How disposed of by the House of Reps.	How disposed of by the Senate.	Date of the act of Congress, and remarks.
Shepherd, Peletiah	Compensation for a vessel taken for public use.	25	3	Petition	121	Claims.						
Shepherd, Peletiah	Compensation for a vessel taken for public use.	26	1	Petition	336	Claims.						
Shepherd, Peletiah	Compensation for a vessel taken for public use.	26	2	Petition	38	Claims.						
Shepherd, Peletiah	Compensation for a vessel taken for public use.	27	2	Petition	56	Claims.						
Shepherd, Peletiah	Compensation for a vessel taken for public use.	27	3	Petition	73	Claims	107	Adverse	......	Laid on table.		
Shepherd, Peletiah	Compensation for a vessel taken for public use.	30	1	Petition	270	Claims.						
Shepherd, Peletiah	Compensation for a vessel taken for public use.	30	2	Petition	322	Claims	136	Adverse	......	Laid on table.		
Shepherd, Peletiah	Compensation for a vessel taken for public use.	31	1	Petition	756	Claims.						
Shepherd, Peter, heirs of..	Payment of a Virginia military warrant.	29	1	Petition	626	Public Lands.						
Sheppard, Samuel	Pension for revolutionary disabilities	1	3	Petition and rep't Sec. of War.	368, 378	....	....	....	......	Laid on table.		
Shepard, Sarah	(See William Shepard, widow of.)	15	2	....	153							
Shepherd, Silas	(See heirs of John Shepherd)....	23	1	....	305							
Sheppard, Thomas.......	Pension for revolutionary services.	3	1	Rep. of Secretary War.	131	Select	May 26, 1794	res. to refer to Sec. of War.	J.R. 12	Passed	Passed	App'd June 9, 1794
Sheppard, Thomas.......	Pension for revolutionary services.	3	2	Rep. of Secretary War.	262	Claims...........	Feb. 28, 1795	Favorable; bill ordered.	130	Passed	Postponed.	
Shepherd, Thomas	Pension for revolutionary services.	4	1	Rep of Secretary War.	445	Claims...........	Feb. 18, 1796	Favorable; bill ordered.	156	Passed	Passed	App'd April 20, 1796
Shepherd, William	Pension for revolutionary services.	3	1	Petition and rep't Sec. of War.	39, 93	Select.						
Sheppard, William	(See Leighton Wood and others).	3	1	....	88							
Shepard, William, widow of.	Pension for revoluntioary services.	15	2	Petition	153	Pens. & Rev. Cl'ms.	Feb. 6, 1819	Adverse	......	Rejected.		
Shepard, William A	(See Foster Henshaw)	28	1	....	375							
Shepley, Ether..........	(See administ'r of Thomas Buckminster.)	16	1	....	28	....	15	....	25			
Sheppey, Daniel	Arrears of pension..............	25	3	Petition	219	Invalid Pensions ..	....	....	......	Discharged; laid on table.		
Sheppie, William	Pay and bounty land for military services.	24	2	Petition	390	Public Lands.						
Sherbrooke, Miles	(See attorney of James Perry and Thomas Hayes.)	5	2	....	227							
Sherburne, Andrew......	Bounty land for revolutionary services.	17	2	Petition	209	Public Lands.						
Sherburne, Andrew......	Pension for revolutionary services.	29	1	Petition	1000	Rev. Pensions.						
Sherburn, Henry........	Relief in consideration of revolutionary disabilities.	2	1	Petition	490	....	....	....	......	Laid on table.		
Sherburn, Job, (See Job Shurboon.)	Arrears of pension	22	1	Resolution	89	Rev. Pensions.						
Sherburne, John H	(See Robert Blunt, heirs and attorney of.)	26	1	....	182							

List of private claims presented to the House of Representatives of the United States from the 1st to the 31st Congress, inclusive—**Continued.**

Names of claimants.	Nature or object of the claim.	Congress.	Session.	How brought before the House of Reps.	Page of journal.	To what committee of the House referred.	No. or date of the report.	Nature of the report.	No. of the bill.	How disposed of by the House of Reps.	How disposed of by the Senate.	Date of the act of Congress, and remarks.
Sherburne, Jonathan W., widow of.	Naval pension	22	1	Petition	387	Naval Affairs.						
Sherburne, Jonathan W., widow of.	Naval pension	23	1	Petition	74	Naval Affairs.						
Sherburne, Jonathan W., widow of.	Naval pension	23	2	Petition	389	Rev. Pensions.						
Sherburne, Jonathan W., widow of.	Naval pension	24	1	Petition	99	Naval Affairs.						
Sherburne, Jonathan W., administrator of.	Compensation for constructing a buoy.	24	1	Petition	750	Claims	623	Adverse		Laid on table.		
Sherburne, Jonathan W., administrator of.	Compensation for constructing a buoy.	29	1	Memorial	283	Claims	638	Adverse		Laid on table.		
Sherburne, Louisa	(See Jonathan W. Sherburne, widow of.)	22	1		387							
Sherburne, Samuel, daughter of.	Pension for revolutionary services.	25	2	Petition	273	Rev. Pensions	Feb. 2, 1838	Adverse		Laid on table.		
Sherer, David	Arrears of pension	26	1	Petition	728	Rev. Pensions	642	Favorable	475	Referred to Committee Whole House.		
Sherer, David	Arrears of pension	27	2	Petition	97	Rev. Pensions	784	Adverse		Laid on table.		
Sherer, David	Arrears of pension	27	3	Petition	73	Rev. Pensions.						
Sherfey, Benjamin	Reimbursement of a military fine	14	2	Petition	353	Ways and Means.						
Sherfey, Benjamin	Reimbursement of a military fine	21	2	Petition	74	Claims.						
Sherfey, Benjamin	Reimbursement of a military fine	22	1	Petition	50	Claims	333	Favorable	420	Referred to Committee Whole House.		
Sherfey, Benjamin	Reimbursement of a military fine	23	1	Petition	34	Claims	4	Favorable	4	Passed	Passed	App'd Feb. 26, 1834
Sherley, Abiathar	(See Benijah Wolcott and others.)	15	1		184							
Sherlock, Patrick	Compensation for work, &c., on Cumberland road.	23	1	Res. and docs	589	Claims	455	Adverse		Laid on table		See report No. 449.
Sherman, Abiel	Increase of pension	23	1	Petition	190	Invalid Pensions.						
Sherman, Abner	Compensation for services, &c., war of 1812.	24	1	Petition	205	Claims	Jan. 27, 1836	Adverse		Laid on table.		
Sherman, Abner	Compensation for services, &c., war of 1812.	25	2	Petition	398	Claims	899	Adverse		Laid on table.		
Sherman, Abner	Compensation for services, &c., war of 1812.	26	1	Petition	624	Claims.						
Sherman, Benjamin	Pension	21	2	Petition	158	Military Pensions.						
Sherman, Benjamin	Pension	22	1	Petition	123	Rev. Pensions	367	Favorable	462	Passed	Indef. postp'd.	
Sherman, Charles E	Compensation for detention as a witness.	31	1	Petition	1251	Judiciary.						
Sherman, Curtis	(See Absalom Packard and others)	22	1		514							
Sherman, Isaac	Additional compensation as assistant surveyor, &c.	1	2	Petition	153					Referred to Secretary of Treasury.		
Sherman, Isaac	Additional compensation as assistant surveyor, &c.	3	2	Rep. of Secretary Treasury.	284					Laid on table.		
Sherman, Isaac	Additional compensation as assistant surveyor, &c.	4	1	Petition	389	Claims	Dec. 28, 1795	Adverse		Leave to withdraw.		
Sherman, Ivory, heirs of	Commutation pay in lieu of bounty land.	16	1	Petition	217	Military Affairs	Mar. 20, 1820	Adverse		Rejected.		
Sherman, Lemuel	Compensation for revolutionary services.	1	2	Petition	269							
				Rep. of Secretary War.	385	Select	Feb. 28, 1791	Favorable; bill ordered.	139	Passed	Postponed.	
Sherman, Lemuel	Compensation for revolutionary services.	2	1	House bill	463	Whole House			152	Passed	Passed	App'd Mar. 27, 1792

List of private claims presented to the House of Representatives of the United States from the 1st to the 31st Congress, inclusive—Continued.

Names of claimants.	Nature or object of the claim.	Congress.	Session.	How brought before the House of Reps.	Page of journal.	To what committee of the House referred.	No. or date of the report.	Nature of the report.	No. of the bill.	How disposed of by the House of Reps.	How disposed of by the Senate.	Date of the act of Congress, and remarks.
Sherman, Richard	Increase of pension	10	1	Pension bill	232	Whole House			78	Passed	Passed, with amendment.	App'd April 25, 1808
Sherman, William T.	Increase of pay as a military officer	31	1	Petition	880	Military Affairs.						
Sherman, William T.	Increase of pay as a military officer	31	2	Petition	291	Military Affairs	27	Adverse		Laid on table.		
Sherod, Samuel	Right of pre-emption	23	2	Petition	437	Public Lands.						
Sherrod, William	Pension	29	1	Petition	675	Invalid Pensions.						
Sherwin, Daniel, widow of	Pension for revolutionary services	27	2	Petition	524	Rev. Pensions	784	Adverse		Laid on table.		
Sherwood, Asa	Compensation for supplies furnished, war of 1812.	22	1	Petition	54	Claims	June 18, 1832	Adverse		Laid on table.		
Sherwood, Daniel	Compensation for a horse lost in public service.	24	1	Petition	368	Claims	469	Adverse		Laid on table.		
Sherwood, Eliphalet	Pension for revolutionary services	10	2	Pension bill	499	Whole House			158	Passed	Passed, with amendment.	App'd March 3, 1809
Sherwood, Moses	To be restored to pension roll	22	1	Petition	130	Rev. Pensions	314	Favorable	397	Passed.		
Sherwood, Salmon	Pension for services in Indian war	24	1	Petition	265					Laid on table.		
Sherwood, Samuel	Increase of pay as messenger	27	3	Petition	285	P. Of. & P. Roads.						
Sherwood, Samuel	Compensation for extra services	29	1	Memorial	149	P. Of. & P. Roads.						
Sherwood, Samuel	Compensation for extra services	29	2	Memorial	76	P. Of. & P. Roads.						
Sherwood, Sarah	Relief—wounded in escaping from a party of British in 1776.	8	1	Petition	605					Laid on table.		
Sherwood, Zachariah	Pension	13	1	Pension bill	56	Whole House	July 20, 1813	Favorable	31	Passed	Passed	App'd Aug. 2, 1813
Sherwood, Zachariah	Arrears of pension	21	1	Petition	377	Military Pensions	April 13, 1830	Adverse		Laid on table.		
Shetler, Henry	(See Moses McCurdy, representatives of.)	8	1		486							
Shey or Shay, Timothy	Pension for revolutionary services	24	1	Petition	107	Rev. Pensions	Jan. 13, 1836	Adverse		Laid on table.		
Shey or Shay, Timothy	Pension for revolutionary services	24	2	Petition	271	Rev. Pensions				Discharged; laid on table.		
Shey or Shay, Timothy	Increase of pension	25	2	Petition	177	Rev. Pensions.						
Shey or Shay, Timothy	Increase of pension	26	1	Petition	171	Rev. Pensions	Mar. 5, 1840	Adverse		Laid on table.		
Sheyer, Conrad	Compensation for revolutionary services.	2	1	Petition	474					Referred to Secretary of War.		
Shibles, James	Pension for services, war of 1812	26	1	Petition	708	Invalid Pensions.						
Shields, David L.	Pension for revolutionary services	16	2	Petition	279	Pens. & Rev. Cl'ms.						
Shields, James	Compensation for revolutionary services.	2	1	Petition and rep't Secretary War	490, 500					Laid on table.		
Sheilds, James	Right of pre-emption to land in Indiana.	16	1	Petition	221	Public Lands	73	Favorable	96	Passed	Passed	App'd May 12, 1820
Shields, James	Permission to enter a certain section of land.	26	1	Petition	827	Priv. Land Claims.	451	Favorable	363	Referred to Committee Whole House.		
Shields, John	(See Lewis & Clarke, and companions.)	9	2		470, 507							
Shields, John	Pension, &c., for revolutionary services.	15	2	Petition	138	Pens. & Rev. Cl'ms.	Jan. 4, 1819	Adverse		Rejected.		
Shields, Joseph B.	Remission of fine imposed by revenue officer.	24	1	Petition	1057	Commerce.						
Shields, Meedy W.	Compensation for a horse lost in public service.	25	2	Documents	396	Claims.						
Shields, Meedy W.	Compensation for a horse lost in public service.	25	3	Documents	207	Claims.						
Shields, Thomas	Credit for disbursement on public account.	14	1	Petition	485	Claims.						
Shields, Thomas	Credit for disbursement on public account.	14	2	Petition	112	Naval Affairs.						

List of private claims presented to the House of Representatives of the United States from the 1st to the 31st Congress, inclusive—Continued.

Names of claimants.	Nature or object of the claim.	Congress.	Session.	How brought before the House of Reps.	Page of journal.	To what committee of the House referred.	No. or date of the report.	Nature of the report.	No. of the bill.	How disposed of by the House of Reps.	How disposed of by the Senate.	Date of the act of Congress, and remarks.
Shields, Thomas	Credit for disbursement on public account.	15	1	Petition	187	Ways and Means				Discharged; leave to withdraw.		
Shields, Thomas	Credit for disbursement on public account.	15	2	Petition	89	Naval Affairs	66	Favorable	258	Referred to Committee Whole House.		
Shields, Thomas	Compensation for capture of prisoner of war.	15	2	Petition	104	Naval Affairs	Dec. 29, 1818	Favorable	255	Referred to Committee Whole House.		
Shields, Thomas	Compensation for capture of prisoner of war.	16	2	Senate bill	190	Naval Affairs	Feb. 28, 1821	With't amend.	S. 38	Passed	Passed	App'd March 3, 1821
Shields, Thomas	Indemnity for naval stores destroyed by Captain Jones.	16	1	Petition	494	Naval Affairs	May 8, 1820	Adverse		Laid on table.		
Shields, Thomas	Indemnity for naval stores destroyed by Captain Jones.	17	1	Senate bill	123	Claims	Jan. 23, 1823	With amend.	S. 10	Passed with amendm't	Pas'd amended	App'd May 7, 1822
Shields, Thomas	Prize money due self and associates	15	1	Petition	188	Naval Affairs.						
Shields, Thomas	Prize money due self and associates	15	2	Petition	168	Naval Affairs.						
Shields, Thomas	Prize money due self and associates	16	1	Petition	99	Judiciary.						
Shields, Thomas	Prize money due self and associates	18	2	Senate bill	430	Naval Affairs	May 4, 1822	With't amend.	S. 90	Laid on table.		
Shields, Thomas, heirs of.	Pension under act of March 3, 1837	29	1	Memorial	70	Naval Affairs	454	Favorable	331	Referred to Committee Whole House.		
Shields, Thomas, heirs of.	Pension under act of March 3, 1837	29	2	Bill of last sess.	71				331	Passed	Passed	App'd March 3, 1847
Shields, Wilmer	(See heirs of Thomas Shields)	29	1		70							
Shields, William L.	Compensation for services as assistant surgeon.	30	1	Petition	276	Claims.						
Shiflett, Nathaniel	Pension	28	1	Petition	128	Invalid Pensions				Discharged; laid on table.		
Shiflett, Nathaniel	Pension	28	2	Petition	64	Invalid Pensions.						
Shiflett, Nathaniel	Pension	29	1	Petition	118	Invalid Pensions	187	Adverse		Laid on table.		
Shiflett, Nathaniel	Pension	30	1	Petition	111	Invalid Pensions	290	Favorable	286	Passed.		
Shiflett, Nathaniel	Pension	31	1	Petition	696	Invalid Pensions.						
Shilleto, Sarah	Indemnity for destruction of a house while in public use.	13	2	Petition	226	Claims	Jan. 28, 1814	Adverse		Rejected.		
Shilleto, Sarah	Indemnity for destruction of a house while in public use.	18	1	Petition	98	Claims	Jan. 9, 1824	Adverse		Laid on table.		
Shilleto, Sarah	Indemnity for destruction of a house while in public use.	18	2	Documents, &c.	101	Claims	26	Favorable	275	Passed	Passed	App'd March 3, 1825
Shillito, George	(See heirs of James Sharp)	17	2		26							
Shilling, Polsor, executors of.	Confirmation of title to land in Mississippi Territory.	11	2	Petition	116	Public Lands.						
Shinalt, James	Right of pre-emption to land in Arkansas.	26	1	Petition	366	Priv. Land Claims.	332	Favorable	304	Referred to Committee Whole House.		
Shindle, John C	Compensation for extra naval services.	14	2	Petition	106	Naval Affairs				Discharged; laid on table.		
Shinks, John and Joseph	Permission to redeem land sold for taxes.	19	1	Petition	68	Whole House.						
Shinn, Isaac, or Isaac S	Pension	24	2	Petition	84	Rev. Pensions				Discharged; laid on table.		
Shinn, Isaac, or Isaac S	Pension	25	2	Petition	974	Rev. Pensions.						
Shinn, Isaac, or Isaac S	Pension	26	1	Petition	175	Rev. Pensions	March 5, 1840	Adverse		Laid on table.		
Shinnick, Jacob, & others.	Indemnity for destruction of a rope-walk.	13	3	Petition	522	Claims	Dec. 4, 1814	Favorable	235	Passed	Passed	App'd Feb. 27, 1815
Shinnick, Jacob	Arrears of pension	23	1	Petition	640	Invalid Pensions				Discharged; laid on table.		
Shinnick, Jacob	Arrears of pension	23	2	Petition	198	Invalid Pensions				Discharged; laid on table.		

List of private claims presented to the House of Representatives of the United States from the 1st to the 31st Congress, inclusive—Continued.

Names of claimants.	Nature or object of the claim.	Congress.	Session.	How brought before the House of Reps.	Page of journal.	To what committee of the House referred.	No. or date of the report.	Nature of the report.	No. of the bill.	How disposed of by the House of Reps.	How disposed of by the Senate.	Date of the act of Congress, and remarks.
Shipe, Elizabeth	Compensation for services as baker in revolutionary war.	3	1	Petition	75					Laid on table.		
Shipley, Shelby T.	Compensation for services as a Tennessee volunteer.	25	2	Documents	274	Claims.						
Shipley, Thomas	(See assignees of W. and A. M. Buckley.)	12	1		174							
Shipman, Benoni	Compensation for revolutionary supplies.	1	3	Petition	371							
				Rep. of Secretary War.	385					Laid on table.		
Shipman, Charles	Indemnity for Indian depredations.	26	1	Petition	351	Claims.						
Shipman, Charles	Indemnity for Indian depredations.	27	2	Petition	92	Priv. Land Claims.	282	Favorable	282	Passed	Passed	App'd Aug. 4, 1842
Shipman, David	Pension for revolutionary services.	24	2	Petition	313	Rev. Pensions.						
Shipman, Dennison & Co.	Permission to import certain merchandise.	12	1	Petition	39	Com. and Manuf.						
Shipman, Stephen	Arrears of pension	27	2	Resolution	70	Claims	727	Adverse	727	Laid on table.		
Shipp, William	Permission to locate a certain claim.	24	1	Resolution	47	Priv. Land Claims.						
Shippen, William, representatives of.	Payment of a revolutionary certificate.	29	1	Memorial	369	Ways and Means.						
Shippen, William, representatives of.	Payment of a revolutionary certificate.	30	1	Petition	235	Rev. Claims	546	Adverse		Laid on table.		
Shippey, Daniel	Arrears of pension	20	1	Petition	599	Military Pensions.						
Shippey, Daniel	Arrears of pension	21	2	Petition	342	Invalid Pensions.						
Shircliff, John	Pension	29	1	Petition	903	Invalid Pensions.						
Shirkey, John	Pension for disability in public service.	19	2	Resolution	310	Military Pensions.						
Shirkey, John	Pension for disability in public service.	20	1	Petition	45	Military Pensions.	40	Favorable	33	Passed	Passed	App'd April 17, 1828
Shirley, James, heir of	Pay and emolument due for military service.	21	2	Petition	62	Claims	42	Favorable	572	Referred to Committee Whole House.		
Shirley, James, heir of	Pay and emolument due for military service.	22	1	Petition	26	Claims	Dec. 19, 1831	Favorable	36	Passed	Passed	App'd Mar. 15, 1832
Shirlock, William, heirs of.	Bounty land for revolutionary services.	31	1	Petition	500	Rev. Claims.						
Shirtliff, William	(See H. Silliman and others)	12	1		98							
Shirts, Matthias	Pension for revolutionary services.	17	1	Petition	31	Rev. Pensions.						
Shirts, Matthias	Pension for revolutionary services.	21	1	Resolution	95	Military Pensions.	May 25, 1830	Favorable	490	Referred to Committee Whole House.		
Shirts, Matthias	Arrears of pension	21	2	Petition	43	Military Pensions				Discharged; laid on table.		
Shirts, Matthias	Increase of pension	22	1	Petition	45	Rev. Pensions				Discharged; laid on table.		
Shite, Peter	Pension	20	2	Petition	203	Military Pensions.						
Shite, Peter	Pension	21	1	Petition	49	Military Pensions.	Jan. 5, 1830	General bill	72	Passed	Passed	App'd May 20, 1830
Shiverick, Thomas	Reimbursement of a coasting license penalty.	20	2	Petition	175	Commerce	53	Favorable	387	Referred to Committee Whole House.		
Shiverick, Thomas	Reimbursement of a coasting license penalty.	21	1	Petition	68	Commerce	Dec. 29, 1829	Favorable	39	Passed	Passed	App'd April 7, 1830
Shober, John	Confirmation of title to lots in Washington city.	13	3	Petition	659	Public Lands				Discharged.		
Shockley, Davis	Pension for revolutionary services.	24	2	Petition	93	Rev. Pensions				Discharged; laid on table.		
Shockley, Davis	Pension for revolutionary services.	25	2	Petition	82	Rev. Pensions				Disch'd; laid on table.		

List of private claims presented to the House of Representatives of the United States from the 1st to the 31st Congress, inclusive—Continued.

Names of claimants.	Nature or object of the claim.	Congress.	Session.	How brought before the House of Reps.	Page of journal.	To what committee of the House referred.	No. or date of the report.	Nature of the report.	No. of the bill.	How disposed of by the House of Reps.	How disposed of by the Senate.	Date of the act of Congress, and remarks.
Shockley, Davis	Pension for revolutionary services	26	1	Petition	325	Rev. Pensions	424	Adverse	......	Laid on table.		
Shockley, Nehemiah, widow of.	Arrears of pension	31	2	Petition	74	Invalid Pensions.						
Shockley, Phebe Ann	(See Nehem'h Shockley, widow of)	31	2	....	74							
Shody, Thomas	Indemnity for imprisonment	29	1	Resolution	404	Judiciary.						
Shoemaker, Daniel	Pension	24	2	Petition	398	Invalid Pensions	....	....	......	Discharged; laid on table.		
Shoemaker, Daniel	Pension	25	2	Petition	168	Invalid Pensions.						
Shoemaker, Eli, heir of	Indemnity for French spoliations prior to 1800.	31	1	Petition	1044	Foreign Affairs	355	General bill	318	Referred to Committee Whole House.		
Shoemaker, George R., widow of.	Pay due deceased for services in United States navy.	30	1	Petition	260	Claims	157	Favorable	161	Passed	Passed, second session.	App'd March 3, 1849
Shoemaker, George R., representatives of.	Pay due deceased for services in United States navy.	31	1	Petition	470	Claims	106	Favorable	123	Passed.		
Shoemaker, Indiana	(See widow of Geo. R. Shoemaker.)	30	1	....	260							
Shoemaker, Jacob	(See attorney of John Eberly)	3	2	....	305							
Shoemaker, Jacob	Drawback on merchandise exported in 1815.	14	1	Petition Documents	42 275	Com. and Manuf. Com. and Manuf.						
Shoemaker, Jacob, widow of.	Drawback on merchandise exported in 1815.	24	1	Petition	141	Commerce	219	Favorable	228	Passed	Passed	App'd July 2, 1836
Shoemaker, Mercy	(See Jacob Shoemaker, widow of)	24	1	....	141							
Shoemaker, Peter	Pension	15	1	Petition	182	Pens. & Rev. Cl'ms.						
Shoemaker, W. R	Increase of pay and compensation for extra services.	31	2	Petition	144	Military Affairs.						
Shoemate, Spencer	Pension	14	2	Resolution	209	Pens. & Rev. Cl'ms.	Jan. 29, 1817	General bill	91	Name stricken out.		
Sholes, Abel	Increase of pension	15	2	Petition	36	Pens. & Rev. Cl'ms.						
Sholes, Abel	Pension for disabilities in the war of 1812.	24	2	Petition	41	Invalid Pensions.						
Sholes, Abel	Pension for disabilities in the war of 1812.	25	2	Petition	57	Invalid Pensions	Jan. 25, 1838	Adverse	......	Laid on table.		
Sholes, Stanton	Indemnity for bagage lost in public service.	15	1	Petition	258	Military Affairs	Mar. 16, 1818	Adverse	......	Laid on table.		
Sholes, Stanton	Indemnity for bagage lost in public service.	15	2	Petition	61	Military Affairs	39	Favorable	232	Referred to Committee Whole House.		
Sholes, Stanton	Indemnity ror bagage lost in public service.	16	1	Petition	99	Military Affairs	Jan. 3, 1820	Favorable	32	Passed	Passed	App'd May 2, 1820
Sho-mac-hah, (Indian.)	(See Elbert W. Stephenson, and others.)	22	1	....	529							
Shomo, Joseph	Reimbursement of advances to recruits.	18	2	Petition	95	Claims.						
Shomo, Joseph	Reimbursement of advances to recruits.	19	1	Petition	44	Claims	5	Favorable	12	Passed	Passed	App'd May 16, 1826
Shoner, John	Pension for revolutionary services	22	1	Petition	219	Rev. Pensions.						
Shook, John	Pension	19	2	Petition	131	Military Pensions.						
Shook, John	Pension	20	2	Petition	26	Military Pensions	Dec. 24, 1828	Adverse	......	Laid on table.		
Shorb, Andreas, administrator of.	Compensation for revolutionary services.	3	2	Petition	269	Claims	Feb. 27, 1795	Adverse	......	Laid on table.		
Shorb, Andreas, administrator of.	Compensation for revolutionary services.	4	2	Petition	629	Claims	Dec. 27, 1796	Adverse	......	Leave to withdraw.		
Shorb, Joseph	(See Andreas Shorb, administrator of.)	3	2	....	269							
Shore, Thomas	Increase of salary as postmaster	14	2	Petition	184	P. Of. & P. Roads.						
Shorey, Samuel	Arrears of pension	22	2	Petition	246	Invalid Pensions	....	....	......	Disch'd; laid on table.		

List of private claims presented to the House of Representatives of the United States from the 1st to the 31st Congress, inclusive—Continued.

Names of claimants.	Nature or object of the claim.	Congress.	Session.	How brought before the House of Reps.	Page of journal.	To what committee of the House referred.	No. or date of the report.	Nature of the report.	No. of the bill.	How disposed of by the House of Reps.	How disposed of by the Senate.	Date of the act of Congress, and remarks.
Shorey, Samuel	Arrears of pension	23	1	Petition	44	Invalid Pensions	Jan. 24, 1834	Adverse	......	Laid on table.		
Shorey, Samuel	Arrears of pension	24	1	Petition	128	Invalid Pensions	June 28, 1836	Adverse	......	Laid on table.		
Shorey, Samuel	Arrears of pension	24	1	Petition	128	Invalid Pensions	June 28, 1836	Adverse	......	Laid on table.		
Short, Eli	Pension	13	3	Pens on bill	740	Whole House	Mar. 1, 1815	With't amend	303	Passed	Passed	App'd March 3, 1815
Short, Jacob	Reimbursement of expenditure on public account.	18	1	Petition	320	Claims.						
Short, Martin	Pension for revolutionary services.	22	2	Petition	66	Rev. Pensions.						
Short, Peter W	Arrears of pension	25	3	Petition and docs.	219	Invalid Pensions	257	Favorable	1128	Referred to Committee Whole House.		
Short, Peter W	Arrears of pension	26	1	Petition	161	Invalid Pensions	224	Favorable	236	Passed	Passed	App'd July 20, 1840
Short, Peter W	Increase of pension	27	3	Petition	95	Invalid Pensions	70	Adverse.				
Short, Peter W	Increase of pension	28	1	Documents	313	Invalid Pensions.						
				Petition	317	Invalid Pensions.						
Short, Peyton, & J. Smith.	(See Northwestern Territory, inhabitants of.)	6	2	....	745							
Short, Peyton	Release of a judgment at suit of the United States.	14	1	Petition	428	Claims.						
Short, Peyton	Release of a judgment at suit of the United States.	14	2	Petition & docs	198	Claims	Feb. 13, 1817	Favorable	137	Passed	Passed	App'd March 3, 1817
Short, Robert	Pension	16	1	Petition	49	Pens. & Rev. Cl'ms.	Dec. 17, 1819	Adverse	......	Rejected.		
Short, Samuel	Pension	21	2	Petition	159	Military Pensions.						
Short, Samuel	Pension	22	1	Petition	80	Rev. Pensions	....	....	......	Discharged; laid on table.		
Short, Siloam	Pension for revolutionary services.	22	1	Petition	254	Rev. Pensions	411	Favorable	511	Referred to Committee Whole House.		
Short, Zachariah	Pension for revolutionary services.	21	1	Resolution	431	Military Pensions	May 3, 1830	Adverse	......	Laid on table.		
Shorthouse, Thomas	(See H. Silliman, and others.)	12	1	....	98							
Shott, Mary	(See Richard Shott, widow of.)	16	1	....	153							
Shott, Richard	Pension for revolutionary services.	5	1	Petition	100	Claims	Dec. 15, 1797	Adverse	......	Rejected.		
Shott, Richard	Pension for revolutionary services.	15	1	Petition	203	Pens. & Rev. Cl'ms.						
Shott, Richard, widow of.	Pension for revolutionary services.	16	1	Petition	153	Rev. Pensions	April 22, 1820	Adverse	......	Laid on table.		
Shover, John	Pension for revolutionary services.	22	1	Resolution	300	Rev. Pensions	410	Favorable	510	Referred to Committee Whole House.		
Shrader, Nicholas, sureties of.	Release of a judgment at suit of United States.	22	1	Petition	442	Claims	401	Adverse	......	Laid on table.		
Shrantz, John	(See assignees of Michael Pear)	17	2	....	100							
Shreiner, Christopher	Compensation for revolutionary services.	2	1	Petition	466	....	....	....	......	Referred to Secretary War.		
Shreve, Henry M.	Compensation in land for inventing snag boat.	23	1	Documents	137	Roads and Canals.						
				Petition	600	Public Lands	509	Favorable	513	Referred to Committee Whole House.		
Shreve, Henry M	Compensation in land for inventing snag boat.	24	1	Petition	54	Public Lands.						
				Petition 2	57	Public Lands	383	Favorable	388	Referred to Committee Whole House.		
Shreve, Henry M	Compensation in land for inventing snag boat.	25	2	Petition	42	Public Lands.						
Shreve, Henry M	Compensation in land for inventing snag boat.	25	3	Memorial	131	Patents.						
Shreve, Henry M	Compensation in land for inventing snag boat.	26	1	Petition	181	Patents.						
Shreve, Henry M	Compensation in land for inventing snag boat.	27	2	Memorial	93	Select	556	Favorable	348	Referred to Committee Whole House.		
				Resolution	393	....	....	....	......	Laid on table.		

List of private claims presented to the House of Representatives of the United States from the 1st to the 31st Congress, inclusive—Continued.

Names of claimants.	Nature or object of the claim.	Congress.	Session.	How brought before the House of Reps.	Page of journal.	To what committee of the House referred.	No. or date of the report.	Nature of the report.	No. of the bill.	How disposed of by the House of Reps.	How disposed of by the Senate.	Date of the act of Congress, and remarks.
Shreve, Henry M	For an appropriation to purchanse snag boat.	28	1	Memorial	256	Select	538	Favorable	416	Referred to Committee Whole House.		
Shreve, Henry M	Compensation for use of his invention.	29	1	Petition	68	Patents	369	Favorable	282	Referred to Committee Whole House.		
Shreve, Henry M	Compensation for use of his invention.	30	1	Petition	109	Patents	30	Favorable	29	Laid on table.		
Shreve, Henry M	Compensation for use of his invention.	31	1	Petition	537	Claims.						
Shreve, Israel, heirs of	Commutation pay for revolutionary services.	29	2	Petition	489	Rev. Claims.						
Shreve, Israel, heirs of	Commutation pay for revolutionary services.	30	1	Petition	413	Rev. Claims.						
Shreve, Israel, heirs of	Commutation pay for revolutionary services.	30	2	Petition	117	Rev. Claims.						
Shreve, Israel, heirs of	Commutation pay for revolutionary services.	31	1	Petition	348	Rev. Claims.						
Shreve, John	Commutation pay for revolutionary services.	21	2	Resolution	60	Rev. Claims.						
Shreve, John	Commutation pay for revolutionary services.	29	2	Petition	489	Rev. Pensions.						
Shrieve, George	Increase of pension	15	1	Petition	23	Pens. & Rev. Cl'ms.						
Shriver, David, jr.	(See sureties of Joseph Crockett.)	18	2		223							
Shriver, David, jr.	Balance due him at Treasury Department.	19	1	Resolution	56	Ways and Means						Appropriation bill, No. 42.
Shrofe, Emanuel	(See Emanuel Shroufe.)	24	2		384							
Shropshire & Ross	Compensation for supplies furnished on public account.	23	2	Resolution	52	Claims.						
Shropshire & Ross	Compensation for supplies furnished on public account.	24	1	Petition	429	Claims.						
Shropshire & Ross	Compensation for supplies furnished on public account.	26	1	Petition	339	Claims	711	Adverse		Laid on table.		
Shroufe, Emanuel	Pension	24	2	Petition	384	Invalid Pensions				Discharged; laid on table.		
Shroufe, Emanuel	Pension	25	2	House bill	156	Whole House	May 26, 1838	With't amend.	258	Passed	Adverse report.	
Shroufe, Emanuel	Pension	25	3	Resolution	349	Invalid Pensions	254	Favorable	1125	Referred to Committee Whole House.		
Shroufe, Emanuel	Pension	26	1	Petition	162	Invalid Pensions	214	Favorable	226	Passed.		
Shroufe, Emanuel	Pension	26	2	Petition	107	Invalid Pensions	46	Favorable	575	Referred to Committee Whole House.		
Shroufe, Emanuel	Pension	27	2	Petition	97	Invalid Pensions.						
Shroufe, Emanuel	Pension	28	1	Petition	344	Invalid Pensions	220	Favorable	174	Passed	Passed	App'd June 17, 1844
Shroufe, Sebastian, widow of.	Right of pre-emption to land in Ohio.	24	2	Petition	122	Priv. Land Claims.	147	Favorable	877	Referred to Committee Whole House.		
Shroufe, Sebastian, widow of.	Right of pre-emption to land in Ohio.	25	2	Petition	43	Priv. Land Claims.	285	Favorable	328	Referred to Committee Whole House.		
Shroufe, Sebastian, widow of.	Right of pre-emption to land in Ohio.	25	3	Bill of last sess.	377	Whole House	June 25, 1839	With amend.	328	Passed	Passed	App'd Mar. 3, 1839
Shroufe, Sebastian, widow of.	Right of pre-emption to land in Ohio.	26	1	Petition	179	Priv. Land Claims.	102	Favorable	98	Passed	Passed	App'd July 20, 1840. Title amended to read Mary Perkins.
Shroyer, Mary	(See Matthias Shroyer, widow of.)	25	2		984							
Shroyer, Matthias, widow of.	Revolutionary pension	25	2	Memorial	984	Rev. Pensions.						

List of private claims presented to the House of Representatives of the United States from the 1st to the 31st Congress, inclusive—Continued.

Names of claimants.	Nature or object of the claim.	Congress.	Session.	How brought before the House of Reps.	Page of journal.	To what committee of the House referred.	No. or date of the report.	Nature of the report.	No. of the bill.	How disposed of by the House of Reps.	How disposed of by the Senate.	Date of the act of Congress, and remarks.
Shrum, Johnson, *et al.*	Pension	31	1	Petition	730	Rev. Pensions	216	Adverse	......	Laid on table.		
Shuaton, Elizabeth	(See O. B. A. Deman, administratrix of.)	26	1	....	182							
Shubrick, Edward R.	Reimbursement of certain expenses.	22	2	Petition	335	Naval Affairs	124	Favorable	759	Referred to Committee Whole House.		
Shubrick, Edward R.	Reimbursement of certain expenses.	23	1	Resolution	115	Naval Affairs	237	Favorable	264	Referred to Committee Whole House.		
Shubrick, Edward R.	Reimbursement of certain expenses.	23	2	House bill	300	Whole House	Jan. 31, 1835	With't amend.	264	Passed	Passed	App'd March 3, 1835
Shubrick, Elizabeth Matilda	(See Captain John T. Shubrick, widow of.)	14	2	....	106							
Shubrick, E. T.	(See Exploring Expedition)	27	3	....	149	....	270	....	818			
Shubrick, Irvine	For the pay of a lieutenant in United States navy.	24	1	Senate bill	146	Naval Affairs	Feb. 5, 1836	With't amend.	S. 34	Passed; reconsidered.		
Shubrick, Irvine	For the pay of a lieutenant in United States navy.	24	2	Senate bill	251	Naval Affairs	Jan. 24, 1837	With't amend.	S. 92	Referred to Committee Whole House.		
Shubrick, Irvine	For the pay of a lieutenant in United States navy.	25	2	Senate bill	605	Naval Affairs	Mar. 29, 1838	With't amend.	S. 139	Referred to Committee Whole House.		
Shubrick, John T., widow of.	Provision for relief, &c	14	2	Petition	106	Naval Affairs	Jan. 22, 1817	General bill	68	Passed	Passed	App'd March 3, 1817
Shubrick, Richard, heirs of.	Half-pay due deceased for revolutionary services.	2	1	Petition	440							
				Rep. of Secretary War.	459	Select	Nov. 25, 1791	General bill	152	Passed	Passed	App'd Mar. 23, 1792
Shubrick, Richard, heirs of.	Half-pay due deceased for revolutionary services.	23	1	Petition	639	Rev. Claims.						
Shubrick, Richard, heirs of.	Half-pay due deceased for revolutionary services.	23	2	Petition	120	Rev. Claims.						
Shubrick, Richard, heirs of.	Half-pay due deceased for revolutionary services.	24	2	Petition	270	Rev. Claims.						
Shubrick, Richard, heirs of.	Half-pay due deceased for revolutionary services.	25	2	Petition	315	Rev. Claims	468	Favorable	475	Passed.		
Shubrick, Richard, heirs of.	Half-pay due deceased for revolutionary services.	25	3	Petition	226	Rev. Claims	160	Favorable	1025	Referred to Committee Whole House.		
Shubrick, Richard, heirs of.	Half-pay due deceased for revolutionary services.	26	1	Petition	165	Rev. Claims.						
Shubrick, Richard, heirs of.	Half-pay due deceased for revolutionary services.	26	2	Petition	182	Rev. Claims	119	Favorable	624	Referred to Committee Whole House.		
Shubrick, Richard, heirs of.	Half-pay due deceased for revolutionary services.	27	2	Petition	154	Rev. Claims	Feb. 9, 1842	Favorable	118	Rejected; reconsidered.		
				House bill	744	Judiciary	777	Adverse	118	Laid on table.		
Shubrick, Thomas	Indemnity for loss on naval contract.	7	2	Petition	259							
				Rep. of Secretary Navy.	313	....	....	....	......	Referred back to Secretary of Navy.		
Shubrick, Thomas	Indemnity for loss on naval contract.	9	1	Petition	313							
				Rep. of Secretary Navy.	361	Claims	April 8, 1806	Adverse	......	Leave to withdraw.		
Shufelt, John	(See William Baker, N. Y.)	22	1	....	288	....	480					
Shull, Jesse W	Compensation in land for public services.	24	1	Petition	775	Public Lands.						
Shull, John	Pension for revolutionary services.	24	2	Petition	272	Rev. Pensions	....	....	......	Discharged; laid on table.		
Shulz, George, executors of.	Compensation for use of tenement by medical department.	2	1	Petition	459	....	....	....	......	Laid on table.		

List of private claims presented to the House of Representatives of the United States from the 1st to the 31st Congress, inclusive—**Continued.**

Names of claimants.	Nature or object of the claim.	Congress.	Session.	How brought before the House of Reps.	Page of journal.	To what committee of the House referred.	No. or date of the report.	Nature of the report.	No. of the bill.	How disposed of by the House of Reps.	How disposed of by the Senate.	Date of the act of Congress, and remarks.
Shulz, George, executors of	Compensation for use of tenement by medical department.	3	1	Petition	92	Select.						
Shumate, Spencer	Pension	14	2	House bill	307				91			Omitted in the act.
Shumate, William J	Pension	14	1	House bill	622	Whole House	April 23, 1816	With amend.	171	Passed	Passed, with amendment.	App'd April 30, 1816
Shumate, William J	Pension	19	1	Petition	175	Military Pensions	164	Adverse		Laid on table.		
Shurborn, Job	Reimbursement of expenditure on public account.	21	1	Petition	56	Claims	Feb. 17, 1830	Adverse		Laid on table.		
Shurley, Bennett, widow of	Pension for revolutionary services.	24	2	Petition	39	Rev. Claims.						
Shurley, Bennett, widow of.	Renewal of bounty land certificate.	25	2	Petition	72	Rev. Claims	511	Favorable	508	Referred to Committee Whole House.		
Shurley, Bennett, heirs of.	Renewal of bounty land certificate.	25	3	Bill of last sess.	379	Whole House	Jan. 25, 1839	With't amend.	508	Passed	Passed	App'd March 2, 1839
Shurley, Susannah	(See Bennett Shurley, widow of.)	24	2		39							
Shurtleff, Gideon	Pension	16	1	Petition	33	Rev. Pensions	April 22, 1820	Adverse		Rejected.		
Shurtleff, Lydia	Benefit of the act of July 7, 1838.	30	1	Petition	406	Rev. Pensions	537	Adverse		Laid on table.		
Shurtleff, Robert	(See Deborah Gannett)	5	2		90							
Shurts, Mathias	(See Mathias Shirts)	17	1		31							
Shurtz, Gerhart, and others	Authority to select certain school lands.	29	1	Petition	181	Public Lands	10	Favorable	22	Passed	Passed	App'd Aug. 8, 1846
Shuster, Andrew	Pension for revolutionary services.	22	1	Petition	808	Rev. Pensions.						
Shute, John	(See John Harding and others)	16	1		300							
Shute, William	(See Aaron Smith and W. S., representatives of.)	21	2		91							
Shute, William	Arrears of pension	21	2	Petition	222	Military Pensions.						
Shute, William	Arrears of pension	22	1	Petition	72	Rev. Pensions.						
Shute, William	Arrears of pension	22	2	Petition	176	Rev. Pensions				Discharged; laid on table.		
Shutler, Lewis	Reimbursement of excessive duty on scissors.	27	3	Petition	206	Ways and Means.						
Shuttlief, Joseph	Pension	1	2	House bill	271	Whole House	July 19, 1790	With amend.	88	Passed	Passed, with amendment.	App'd Aug. 11, 1790
Shutts, Hannah	(See heirs of John Shutts)	30	2		284							
Shutts, Henry G	Pension	28	2	Petition	209	Invalid Pensions.						
Shutts, John, heirs of	Pension for revolutionary services.	30	2	Petition	284	Rev. Pensions.						
Shutts, Peter	(See John Shutts, heirs of.)	30	2		284							
Shy, Jacob	Compensation in land for military services.	31	1	Petition	234	Public Lands.						
Shy, Jacob	Compensation in land for military services	31	2	Petition	445	Public Lands	100	Adverse		Laid on table.		
Sibbald, Charles F	Confirmation of title to land in Florida.	20	1	Petition	225	Public Lands.						
Sibbald, Charles F	Indemnity for depredations of United States troops.	22	2	Petition	143	Claims.						
Sibbald, Charles F	Indemnity for depredations of United States troops.	24	1	Memorial	603	Judiciary.						
Sibbald, Charles F	Indemnity for depredations of United States troops.	24	2	Petition	38	Claims	323	Indefinite		Referred to Secretary Treasury.		
Sibbald, Charles F	Indemnity for depredations of United States troops.	25	2	Documents	378	Claims	July 2, 1838	Indefinite		Referred to Treasury officers.		
Sibbald, Charles F	Indemnity for depredations of United States troops.	25	3	Rep. of Treasury officers.	703					Laid on table.		
Sibbald, Charles F	Indemnity for depredations of United States troops.	26	1	Petition	169	Claims.						

List of private claims presented to the House of Representatives of the United States from the 1st to the 31st Congress, inclusive—Continued.

Names of claimants.	Nature or object of the claim.	Congress.	Session.	How brought before the House of Reps.	Page of journal.	To what committee of the House referred.	No. or date of the report.	Nature of the report.	No. of the bill.	How disposed of by the House of Reps.	How disposed of by the Senate.	Date of the act of Congress, and remarks.
Sibbald, Charles F.	Indemnity for depredations of United States troops.	26	2	Petition	38	Claims.						
				Senate bill	334	Whole House			S. 265			
Sibbald, Charles F.	Indemnity for depredations of United States troops.	27	2	Petition	55	Claims	473	Favorable	323	Passed	Passed with amendment.	App'd Aug. 23, 1842
Sibbald, Charles F.	Explanatory act	29	1	Petition	713	Judiciary.						
Sibbald, Charles F.	Indemnity for acts of public agents	31	1	Senate res.	1013	Judiciary	July 24, 1846	With't amend.	R. 19	Passed	Passed	App'd Aug. 10, 1846
				Senate res.	1413	Claims			R. 15	Referred to Secretary Treasury.		
Sibbald, Charles F.	Indemnity for acts of public agents	31	2	Senate res.	390	Claims	31	Adverse	R. 15	Laid on table.		
Sibbald, Charles F.	(See John Birely, assignee of.)	31	2		123							
Sibery, William	Pension	21	1	Petition	74	Military Pensions.						
Sibley, Cyrus	(See George M. Brooke, agent of.)	20	1		604							
Sibley, Cyrus	Payment of Mexican indemnity	29	1	Memorial	525	Foreign Affairs.						
Sibley, George C.	Authority to pay a government debt in land.	23	1	Petition	48	Ways and Means.						
Sibley, George C.	(See B. H. Reeves, and others.)	21	1		689							
Sibley, John	(See Canadian Refugees.)	4	2		614							
Sibley, John	(See Louis Tregarie., assignee of.)	24	1		362							
Sibley, John	Confirmation of title to land in Louisiana.	24	2	Letter of Secre'y Treasury.	88	Priv. Land Claims.						
Sibley, John	Confirmation of title to land in Louisiana.	25	2	Letter of Secre'y Treasury.	374	Priv. Land Claims.						
Sibley, Solomon	(See widow of Joseph Harrison)	12	1		22							
Sibley, Solomon	Indemnity for the depredation of United States troops.	17	2	Petition	30	Claims.						
Sibley, Solomon	Indemnity for the depredation of United States troops.	18	1	Petition	214	Pens. & Rev. Cl'ms.	18	Favorable	163	Passed	Passed	App'd May 17, 1824
Sibley, Solomon, and others	Additional compensation as judges in Michigan.	22	2	Petition	314	Territories.						
Sibley, Solomon, and others	Additional compensation as judges in Michigan.	23	1	Petition	93	Territories.						
Sickles & Cook	To purchase patent known as "Sickle's cut off."	29	1	Petition	577	Naval Affairs	834	Favorable	551	Referred to Committee Whole House.		
Sickles, *alias* Ackerly, Dan'l	Pension for revolutionary services.	27	2	Petition	426	Rev. Pensions.						
				Documents	525	Rev. Pensions.	784	Adverse		Laid on table.		
Sickles, J. F.	(See Exploring Expedition)	27	3		149		270		818			
Siddall, Joseph	(See Issachar Thorpe and others.)	14	2		191							
Siddle, George	Pension for revolutionary services.	19	1	Petition	387	Military Pensions.	May 5, 1826	Favorable		Referred to Committee Whole House.		
Siddle, George	Pension for revolutionary services.	19	2	Petition	66	Military Pensions.	Dec. 22, 1826	General pension bill.	314	Passed	Passed, with amendment.	App'd March 3, 1827
Sidebottom, Agnes	(See Joseph Sidebottom, widow of.)	28	1		794							
Sidebottom, Joseph, widow of.	Continuation of revolutionary pension.	28	1	Petition	794	Rev. Pensions.						
Sidman, John	Pension for revolutionary services.	26	1	Petition	286	Rev. Pensions	July 21, 1840	Favorable	502	Referred to Committee Whole House.		
Sierra, Eugenio	Indemnity for a slave killed in public service.	19	2	Petition	105	Claims.						
Sierra, Joseph	Rent of United States court-room in Florida.	30	1	Petition	679	Claims.						
Sight, David	(See executors of John Doyle)	22	1		512							

List of private claims presented to the House of Representatives of the United States from the 1st to the 31st Congress, inclusive—Continued.

Names of claimants.	Nature or object of the claim.	Congress.	Session.	How brought before the House of Reps.	Page of journal.	To what committee of the House referred.	No. or date of the report.	Nature of the report.	No. of the bill.	How disposed of by the House of Reps.	How disposed of by the Senate.	Date of the act of Congress, and remarks.
Sights, Jacob	Compensation for services in revolutionary war.	19	2	Petition	73	Rev. Claims	Jan. 2, 1827	Adverse		Laid on table.		
Sigourney, Charles, and J. H. Wells.	Remission of penalty for breach of non importation act.	12	2	Petition	564	Ways and Means				Referred to Committee Whole House.		
Sikes, Henry	Arrears of pension	22	2	Resolution	172	Invalid Pensions.						
Sikes, Henry	Arrears of pension	23	1	Petition	44	Invalid Pensions	217	Adverse		Laid on table.		
Silby, James	(See James Selby)	23	1		92							
Silence, Joseph	Pension	14	1	Petition	126	Pens. & Rev. Cl'ms.						
Silence, William	Pension	15	1	Petition	166					Referred to Secretary War.		
Sill, Jabez	Pension for revolutionary services.	24	2	Petition	158	Rev. Pensions				Discharged; laid on table.		
Sill, Joseph	Indemnity for destruction of property by the enemy.	17	1	Petition	46	Claims	Jan. 13, 1822	Adverse		Referred to Committee Whole House.		
Sill, Joseph	(See Lucius Storrs and others)	22	1		220							
Sillaway, Reuben	Pension	9	1	Petition	249	Claims	Mar. 28, 1806	Adverse		Indefinitely postponed.		Leave to withdraw.
Sillcock, Joseph	(See guardian of the children of Caleb Crews.)	20	2		54							
Sillcock, Joseph, widow of.	Pension for revolutionary services.	28	1	Petition	947	Rev. Pensions.						
Sillcock, Mary	(See Joseph Sillcock, widow of.)	28	1		947							
Silliman, H., and others.	Indemnity for the illegal seizure of the ship Golden Fleece by British government.	12	1	Documents	98					Referred to Secretary State.		
Silliman, John	Military bounty land	31	1	Petition	276	Public Lands.						
Sillivent, William	(See William W. Byers & others)	23	2		278							
Silsbee, John	Increase of pension	15	2	Petition	234	Pens. & Rev. Cl'ms.						
Silsbee, John	Increase of pension	19	1	Petition	102	Military Pensions.						
Silsbee, John	Commutation of pension for land	21	1	Petition	51	Public Lands	Jan. 13, 1830	Adverse		Laid on table.		
Silsbee, Z. F	Indemnity for French spoliations prior to 1800.	26	1	Memorial	182	Foreign Affairs	343	Favorable; bill	319	Referred to Committee Whole House.		
Silva, Joze Roiz	Exemption of ship King David from the operation of embargo.	3	1	Petition	115					Laid on table.		
Silva, Joze Roiz	Reimbursement of duty on wine	3	2	Memorial	233	Select	90	Favorable; bill ordered.	105	Passed	Rejected.	
Silva, Joze Roiz	Reimbursement of duty on wine	4	1	Memorial	424	Com. and Manuf.	Feb. 12, 1796	Favorable; bill ordered.	150	Passed	Passed	App'd Mar. 23, 1796
Silva, Joao José da	(See Jose Joaquim Da Costa)	5	2		215							
Silvey, Isaac	(See William Thompson, Va.)	19	1		312							
Simes, Mark	(See Martin Parry, administrator of.)	26	1		182							
Simes, Mark	Indemnity for French spoliations prior to 1800.	26	1	Memorial	182	Foreign Affairs	343	Favorable; bill	319	Referred to Committee Whole House.		
Simeson, John	Pension for revolutionary services.	16	1	Petition	365	Rev. Pensions	April 20, 1820	Adverse		Rejected.		
Simison, Robert	Reimbursement of money paid for public land.	7	1	Petition	95	Claims	March 8, 1802	Adverse		Laid on table.		
Simkins, Carrington, administrator of.	Indemnity for French spoliations prior to 1800.	26	1	Memorial	182	Foreign Affairs	343	Favorable; bill	319	Referred to Committee Whole House.		
Simmons, ———	(See Swain, Abel & Simmons)	28	1		317							
Simmons, B. Louisa	(See William Broadfoot, heirs of)	29	2		87							
Simmons, Benjamin	Payment of two revolutionary certificates.	15	1	Petition	265	Pens. & Rev. Cl'ms.				Discharged; leave to withdraw.		
Simmons, Benjamin	Payment of two revolutionary certificates.	16	1	Petition	130	Pens. & Rev. Cl'ms.	April 3, 1820	Adverse		Laid on table.		

List of private claims presented to the House of Representatives of the United States from the 1st to the 31st Congress, inclusive—Continued.

Names of claimants.	Nature or object of the claim.	Congress.	Session.	How brought before the House of Reps.	Page of journal.	To what committee of the House referred.	No. or date of the report.	Nature of the report.	No. of the bill.	How disposed of by the House of Reps.	How disposed of by the Senate.	Date of the act of Congress, and remarks.
Simmons, Benjamin	Payment of two revolutionary certificates.	17	1	Petition	26	Pens. & Rev. Cl'ms	April 19, 1822	Adverse	......	Laid on table.		
Simmons, Benjamin	Payment of two revolutionary certificates.	19	1	Petition	176	Rev. Claims.						
Simmons, Benjamin	Payment of two revolutionary certificates.	19	2	Petition	133	Rev. Claims	Feb. 6, 1827	Adverse	......	Laid on table.		
Simmons, Benjamin	Payment of two revolutionary certificates.	20	1	Petition	69	Rev. Claims	103	Favorable	......	Rejected.		
Simmons, Benjamin	Compensation for revolutionary services.	15	2	Petition	46	Pens. & Rev. Cl'ms.	Dec. 4, 1818	Adverse.				
				Recommitted	184	Pens. & Rev. Cl'ms.	Feb. 1, 1819	Bill ordered	300	Referred to Committee Whole House.		
Simmons, Benjamin	Compensation for revolutionary services.	26	1	Resolution	374	Rev. Pensions.						
Simmons, Benoni	Correction of error relating to pension.	9	2	Petition	496	Claims	Feb. 16, 1807	Adverse	......	Leave to withdraw.		
Simmons, Benoni	Arrears of pension	21	1	Petition	121	Military Pensions	April 7, 1830	Adverse	......	Laid on table.		
Simmons, Berer, or Bezer.	Compensation for mail services	30	2	Petition	308	P. Of. & P. Roads.	....	....	......	Discharged; laid on table.		
Simmons, Christopher, and crew of brig Philadelphia.	Indemnity for sufferings while captive in Tripoli.	9	1	Petition	257	Select.						
Simmons, Edward	(See Joseph Stewart, and others.)	14	2	....	56	....	....	....	65			
Simmons, Elijah	Confirmation of title to land	23	2	Senate bill	126	Public Lands	Jan. 2, 1835	With amend.	S. 9	Referred to Committee Whole House.		
Simmons, Elijah	Confirmation of title to land	24	1	Senate bill	602	Public Lands	May 6, 1836	With't amend.	S. 16	Passed	Passed	App'd July 2, 1836
Simmons, George	Right of pre-emption to land in Alabama.	20	1	Resolution	386	Public Lands.						
Simmons, George	Right of pre-emption to land in Alabama.	20	2	Petition	106	Public Lands.						
Simmons, George	Right of pre-emption to land in Alabama.	23	2	Resolution	243	Public Lands	79	Favorable	696	Postponed.		
Simmons, Hannah	(See Joshua Simmons, widow of)	27	2	....	525							
Simmons, James	Balance due on the books of the government.	11	3	Appropriation bill	....	....	....	....	177	....	....	App'd Feb. 20, 1811
Simmons, James, (Tenn.)	Pension	24	2	Resolution	384	Invalid Pensions	....	....	......	Discharged; laid on table.		
Simmons, James, (Tenn.)	Pension	25	2	Resolution	773	Invalid Pensions.						
Simmons, James, (Tenn.)	Pension	25	3	Resolution	89	Invalid Pensions	....	....	......	Discharged; laid on table.		
Simmons, James, (Tenn.)	Back pension	31	1	Petition	955	Invalid Pensions.						
Simmons, James W	(See William Broadfoot, heirs of)	29	2	....	87							
Simmond, John	Indemnity for wounds and disabilities.	9	2	Petition	607	....	....	....	......	Laid on table.		
Simmons, John	(See Joseph Stewart, and others).	14	2	....	56	....	....	....	65			
Simmons, Joseph	Payment of drawback withheld	12	1	Petition	20	Com. and Manuf.						
Simmons, Joseph	Payment of drawback withheld	26	1	Petition	292	Commerce	30	Favorable	49	Passed	Passed	App'd July 20, 1840
Simmons, Joseph	Pension	28	2	Senate bill	275	Invalid Pensions	Mar. 3, 1845	With't amend.	S. 69	Passed	Passed	App'd March 3, 1845
Simmons, Joshua, widow of.	Pension for revolutionary services.	27	2	Petition	525	Rev. Pensions	784	Adverse	......	Laid on table.		
Simmons, Moses	(See Joseph Stewart, and others).	14	2	....	56	....	....	....	65			
Simmons, Stephen G.	Compensation for horse lost in public service.	6	1	Petition	640	Claims	May 2, 1800	Adverse.	......	Rejected.		

List of private claims presented to the House of Representatives of the United States from the 1st to the 31st Congress, inclusive—Continued.

Names of claimants.	Nature or object of the claim.	Congress.	Session.	How brought before the House of Reps.	Page of journal.	To what committee of the House referred.	No. or date of the report.	Nature of the report.	No. of the bill.	How disposed of by the House of Reps.	How disposed of by the Senate.	Date of the act of Congress, and remarks.
Simmons, Lieutenant S. G.	Compensation for service as secretary to Indian commissioners.	26	1	Petition	557	Claims.						
Simmons, Lieutenant S. G.	Compensation for service as secretary to Indian commissioners.	26	2	Petition	182	Claims.						
Simmons, Sylvanus	Pension for revolutionary services.	22	1	Petition	381	Rev. Pensions	410	Favorable	510	Referred to Committee Whole House.		
Simmons, William	Increase of salary as treasury clerk.	1	3	Petition	350							
				Report of Secretary Treasury.	388	Select.						
Simmons, William	Increase of salary as treasury clerk.	3	1	Petition	91	Select	April 3, 1794	Favorable; bill ordered.		Laid on table.		
Simmons, William	Increase of salary as treasury clerk.	5	2	Memorial	235	Revisal and Unfinished Business.	May 7, 1798	Favorable; bill ordered.	95	Passed	Postponed.	
Simmons, William	Increase of salary as treasury clerk.	13	2	Petition	343	Ways and Means	April 7, 1814	Favorable	186	Referred to Committee Whole House.		See Senate bill 50.
Simmons, William	Pension for revolutionary services.	15	2	Petition	628	Pens. & Rev. Cl'ms.						
Simmons, William H	(See Edward R. Gibson, and W. H. S.)	19	1		170							
Simmons, William, sureties of.	Release from judgment	20	1	Petition	448	Ways and Means.						
Simmons, William	(See Jacob Thompson)	23	1		523							
Simmons, William	Pension for services in U. States navy.	23	2	Petition	436	Invalid Pensions.						
Simmons, William W	Indemnity for Indian depredations.	25	3	Petition	121	Claims	162	Adverse		Laid on table.		
Simmons, William H.	Compensation for locating land warrants.	31	1	Petition	448	Public Lands.						
Simmons, William	Pension for disabilities, in Creek war.	31	1	Petition	653	Invalid Pensions.						
Simmons, Zachariah	Pension	28	2	House bill	173	Invalid Pensions			495			
Simmons, Zachariah	Pension	29	1	Petition	118	Invalid Pensions	330	Favorable	265	Referred to Committee Whole House.		
Simmons, Zachariah	Pension	29	2	House bill	71				265	Passed	Passed	App'd March 3, 1847
Simons, Ann C	(See Francis Kinlock, heirs of)	19	2		189							
Simonds, Daniel	Pension for revolutionary services.	3	2	Rep. of Secretary War.	337	Claims	Mar. 3, 1795	To postpone		Laid on table.		
Simonds, Daniel	Pension for revolutionary services.	4	1	Rep. of Secretary War.	445	Claims.						
Simonds, Daniel	Pension for revolutionary services.	4	2	Rep. of Secretary War.	614	Claims.						
Simonds, Daniel	Pension for revolutionary services.	14	2	Petition	267	Pens. & Rev. Cl'ms.						
Simonds, Daniel	Pension for revolutionary services.	15	1	Petition	23	Pens. & Rev. Cl'ms.						
Simons, Faulkner	Pension	15	2	Documents	84	Pens. & Rev. Cl'ms.						
Simons, James	Compensation for revolutionary services.	2	1	Petition	527					Referred to Secretary War.		
Simons, James	Compensation for revolutionary services.	2	2	Rep. of Secretary War.	697					Laid on table.		
Simonds, Jeduthun	Pension for revolutionary services.	23	1	Petition	490	Rev. Pensions.						
Simonds, Jeduthun	Pension for revolutionary services.	24	1	Petition	213	Rev. Pensions				Discharged; laid on table.		
Simonds, John	Increase of compensation as marshal of Missouri.	20	2	Resolution	93	Judiciary				Discharged; laid on table.		
Simonds, Lewis, & Co.	Permission to import Jamaica rum.	12	1	Petition	75	Com. and Manuf.						

List of private claims presented to the House of Representatives of the United States from the 1st to the 31st Congress, inclusive—Continued.

Names of claimants.	Nature or object of the claim.	Congress.	Session.	How brought before the House of Reps.	Page of journal.	To what committee of the House referred.	No. or date of the report.	Nature of the report.	No. of the bill.	How disposed of by the House of Reps.	How disposed of by the Senate.	Date of the act of Congress, and remarks.
Simons, Matthew, assignee of.	Compensation for military services.	24	1	Petition	1077	Claims.						
Simons, Maurice R.	Pension for disability, in Mexican war.	30	1	Petition	590	Invalid Pensions	558	Favorable	458	Passed	Passed, second session.	App'd March 3, 1849
Simons, Maurice R.	Increase of pension	31	1	Petition	233	Invalid Pensions	307	Favorable	277	Referred to Commitee Whole House.		
Simons, Nathan	Pension for revolutionary services.	20	2	Resolution	107	Military Pensions.	Jan. 20, 1820	Adverse	......	Laid on table		
Simons, Nathan	Pension for revolutionary services.	21	1	Res. and docs.	134	Military Pensions.	April 2, 1830	Adverse	......	Laid on table.		
Simons, Richard	(See Richard Simms, or Simons).	26	2	....	182							
Simons, Lieut. Robert	Compensation for revolutionary services.	5	2	Petition	98	Claims	Jan. 4, 1798	Adverse	......	Rejected.		
Simonton, Alexander	Pension	8	2	Memorial	98	Claims.						
Simonton, Isaac B., heirs of	Moneys due under Chippawa treaty.	29	2	Petition	128	Indian Affairs.						
Simonton, John W.	(See William H. Robertson and others.)	24	2	....	250							
Simonton, John W., and others.	Indemnity for property taken for naval purposes.	26	1	Memorial	304	Naval Affairs.						
Simonton, John W., and others.	Indemnity for property taken for naval purposes.	27	3	Petition	109	Naval Affairs	....	....	......	Discharged; laid on table.		
Simonton, John W., and others.	Indemnity for property taken for naval purposes.	28	1	Memorial	105	Naval Affairs.						
Simonton, John W., and others.	Indemnity for property taken for naval purposes.	30	1	Petition	115	Naval Affairs	189	Favorable	199	Referred to Committee Whole House.		
Simonton, Samuel	(See heirs of Isaac P. Simonton).	29	2	....	128							
Simonton, Lieut. S. P.	Moneys due him by treaty stipulations.	31	2	Petition	193	Claims	83	Favorable	......	Laid on table.		
Simonton, William	Indemnity for injury to property, revolutionary war.	3	1	Memorial	86	Select	Mar. 31, 1794	Adverse	......	Leave to withdraw.		
Simms, Arthur L.	Confirmation of a Spanish grant of land.	24	1	Petition	946	Priv. Land Claims	....	....	......	Discharged; laid on table.		
Sims, Cuthbert	Compensation for revolutionary disabilities.	8	2	Petition	105	Whole House.						
Sims, Cuthbert	Compensation for revolutionary disabilities.	9	1	Petition	275	Claims	....	....	......	Discharged; referred to Com. Whole House.		
Sims, Cuthbert	To be restored to pension roll	18	1	Petition	525	Rev. Pensions	....	....	......	Discharged; leave to withdraw.		
Sims, Cuthbert	To be restored to pension roll	21	1	Petition	168	Military Pensions.	April 27, 1830	General bill	248	Passed	Indef. postp'd.	
Sims, Cuthbert	To be restored to pension roll	21	2	Petition	189	Military Pensions.						
Sims, Edward	(See George Park)	31	1	....	955							
Sims, James	(See sureties of David Moore)	21	1	....	173							
Sims, Jeremiah	Pension for revolutionary services.	24	1	Petition	213	Rev. Pensions	Feb. 4, 1836	Adverse	......	Laid on table.		
Sims, Jeremiah	Increase of pension	28	2	Petition	208	Rev. Pensions.						
Sims, Jeremiah	Increase of pension	29	1	Resolution	413	Rev. Pensions.						
Sims, John	Release from liabilities on revenue bond.	13	2	Petition	250	Ways and Means	Jan. 28, 1814	Adverse	......	Leave to withdraw.		
Sims, Joseph	(See Francis Coppinger, assignee of.)	26	1	....	182							
Sims, Joseph	Reimbursement of expenses transporting American prisoners.	14	1	Petition	48	Claims	Feb. 24, 1816	Adverse	......	Leave to withdraw.		
Sims, Joseph	Indemnity for French spoliations prior to 1800.	26	1	Memorial	182	Foreign Affairs	343	Favorable; bill	319	Referred to Committee Whole House.		
Sims, Lewis, and wife	(See heirs of Jacob Doggitt.)	15	2	....	28							
Sims,	(See Woodrup & Sims.)	26	1	....	182							

List of private claims presented to the House of Representatives of the United States from the 1st to the 31st Congress, inclusive—Continued.

Names of claimants.	Nature or object of the claim.	Congress.	Session.	How brought before the House of Reps.	Page of journal.	To what committee of the House referred.	No. or date of the report.	Nature of the report.	No. of the bill.	How disposed of by the House of Reps.	How disposed of by the Senate.	Date of the act of Congress, and remarks.
Simms, Richard	Bounty land for revolutionary services.	25	2	Petition	719	Public Lands.						
Simms, Richard	Bounty land for revolutionary services.	25	3	Petition	98	Public Lands.						
Simms or Simons, Richard	Bounty land for revolutionary services.	26	2	Petition	182	Public Lands.						
Sims, William O	Pension for services in the war of 1812.	26	2	Petition	118	Invalid Pensions	219	Adverse	......	Laid on table.		
Sims, William	Pension	27	2	Petition	308	Invalid Pensions	423	Adverse	......	Laid on table.		
Sims, William	Pension	28	1	Petition	417	Invalid Pensions.						
Simms, Woodrop, & Jos.,	Remission of duties on salt and wine	2	1	Petition	579	Select	April 24, 1792	Favorable; bill ordered.	189	Passed	Rejected.	
Simms, Woodrop & Jos.,	Remission of duties on salt and wine.	2	2	Petition	615	Select	Dec. 6, 1792	Favorable; bill ordered.	228			
Simpkins, Covington, administrator of.	Indemnity for French spoliations prior to 1800.	29	2	Petition	100	Foreign Affairs.						
Simpkins, Covington, administrator of.	Indemnity for French spoliations prior to 1800.	31	1	Petition	196	Foreign Affairs	355	General bill	318	Referred to Committee Whole House.		
Simpkins, Gilbert	(See William Baker, N. Y.)	22	1	....	288	....	840					
Simkins, John	(See Covington Simpkins.)	29	2	....	100							
Simpsion, Charles	(See Charles Sumption.)	26	2	....	135							
Simpson, Edward, & others	Remissionn of duty on salt destroyed in a gale.	4	1	Petition	428	Com. and Manuf.	Mar. 7, 1796	Adverse	......	Laid on table.		
Simpson, Elizabeth	(See John Simpson, widow of.)	30	1	....	358							
Simpson, George	Compensation for services in negotiating a loan.	14	1	Petition	71	Ways and Means.						
Simpson, George	Compensation for services in negotiating a loan.	14	2	Petition	101	Ways and Means	Feb. 13, 1817	Adverse	......	Rejected.		
Simpson, George	Compensation for services in negotiating a loan.	15	1	Petition	59	Ways and Means	Feb. 3, 1818	Adverse	......	Rejected.		
Simpson, George	Compensation for services in negotiating a loan.	16	1	Petition	95	Ways and Means.						
Simpson, George	Compensation for services in negotiating a loan.	17	1	Petition Rep. of Secretary Treasury.	234 380	....	....	....	......	Laid on table.		
Simpson, George	Compensation for services in negotiating a loan.	17	2	Petition and rep't Sec. Treasury.	187	Claims.						
Simpson, George, widow of.	Commission on a loan obtained by deceased.	17	2	Memorial	119	Claims	Feb. 10, 1823	Adverse	......	Laid on table.		
Simpson, George, widow of.	Compensation for services in effecting a loan.	19	1	Petition	151	Claims	Mar. 13, 1826	Adverse	......	Laid on table.		
Simpson, George, widow of.	Compensation for services in effecting a loan.	19	2	Petition	159	Claims	Jan. 24, 1827	Adverse	......	Laid on table.		
Simpson, George, widow of.	Compensation for services in effecting a loan.	20	1	Petition	68	Ways and Means	Feb. 25, 1828	Adverse	......	Leave to withdraw.		
Simpson, George, widow of.	Compensation for services in effecting a loan.	20	2	Petition	57	Claims	Jan. 28, 1829	Adverse	......	Laid on table.		
Simpson, George, widow of.	Compensation for services in effecting a loan.	24	1	Memorial	206	Claims	746	Adverse	......	Laid on table.		
Simpson, George, administrator of.	Compensation for services in effecting a loan.	28	2	Petition	46	Ways and Means.						
Simpson, George, administrator of.	Compensation for services in effecting a loan.	30	1	Memorial	68	Ways and Means	662	Adverse	......	Laid on table.		

List of private claims presented to the House of Representatives of the United States from the 1st to the 31st Congress, inclusive—Continued.

Names of claimants.	Nature or object of the claim.	Congress.	Session.	How brought before the House of Reps.	Page of journal.	To what committee of the House referred.	No. or date of the report.	Nature of the report.	No. of the bill.	How disposed of by the House of Reps.	How disposed of by the Senate.	Date of the act of Congress, and remarks.
Simpson, George, heir of	Compensation for services in effecting a loan.	31	1	Petition	955	Claims.						
Simpson, Henry	Compensation for writing two months for government.	29	1	Memorial	823	Ways and Means.						
Simpson, Henry	Balance of salary as appraiser at Philadelphia.	31	1	Petition	425	Claims.						
Simpson, Henry	(See administrator of George Simpson.)	28	2		46							
Simpson, James	Reimbursement of expenses in the public service.	2	1	Petition	464					Referred to Secretary of Treasury.		
Simpson, James	Reimbursement of expenses in the public service.	3	2	Rep. of Secretary Treasury.	284					Laid on table.		
Simpson, James	Additional compensation as consul at Tangiers.	15	1	Petition	203	Foreign Affairs.						
Simpson, James, attorney of.	Additional compensation as consul at Tangiers.	16	1	Petition	157	Claims	April 7, 1820	Adverse		Laid on table.		
Simpson, John W	Right of pre-emption to Creek lands.	14	2	Petition	91	Public Lands	Dec. 31, 1816	Adverse		Rejected.		
Simpson, John	Pension	15	1	Petition	74	Pens. & Rev. Cl'ms.	Feb. 9, 1818	Adverse		Leave to withdraw.		
Simpson, John	Pension	19	1	Petition	175	Military Pensions.	164	Adverse		Laid on table.		
Simpson, John	Confirmation of title to land in Wisconsin.	27	2	Petition	1204	Public Lands.						
Simpson, John, widow of.	Pension under the act of July 4, 1836.	30	1	Petition	358	Rev. Pensions				Discharged; laid on table.		
Simpson, John, & William Ross.	Indemnity for French spoliations prior to 1800.	31	1	Petition	413	Foreign Affairs	355	General bill	318	Referred to Committee Whole House.		
Simpson, Joseph	Pension for revolutionary services.	23	1	Petition	379	Rev. Pensions				Discharged; laid on table.		
Simpson, Joseph	(See John Simpson)	27	2		1204							
Simpson, Josiah	(See attorney of Dorcas Frost)	1	3		337							
Simpson, Josiah	Arrears of pension	23	2	Petition	391	Invalid Pensions.						
Simpson, Lawrence	Compensation for revolutionary services.	24	2	Petition	39	Rev. Claims				Discharged; laid on table.		
Simpson, Mark	Compensation for military services.	28	1	Senate bill	1025	Invalid Pensions			S. 50			
Simpson, Mark	Pension	28	2	Senate bill	177	Invalid Pensions	Jan. 28, 1845	With't amend.	S. 7	Passed	Passed	App'd Feb. 13, 1845
Simpson, Mark	Increase of pension	29	1	Petition	86	Rev. Pensions	July 25, 1846	Adverse		Laid on table.		
Simpson, Mary	(See Rezin Simpson, widow of)	20	2		229							
Simpson, Morgan	Indemnity for loss on contract for transportation	25	2	Petition	273	Claims	657	Adverse		Laid on table.		
Simpson, Morgan	Indemnity for loss on contract for transportation.	27	2	Petition	94	Claims	769	Adverse		Laid on table.		
Simpson, Moses W	(See James H. Grant, and others.)	25	2		279							
Simpson, M. H	Extension of a certain patent	31	2	Petition	254	Patents.						
Simpson, Rezin, widow of.	Pension for revolutionary services.	20	2	Petition	229	Military Pensions.				Discharged; laid on table.		
Simpson, Rezin, widow of.	Pension for revolutionary services.	21	1	Petition	260	Military Pensions.	April 24, 1830	Adverse		Laid on table.		
Simpson, Samuel	Indemnity for French spoliations prior to 1800.	22	2	Petition	31	Foreign Affairs.						
Simpson, Samuel	Indemnity for French spoliations prior to 1800.	26	1	Memorial	182	Foreign Affairs	343	Favorable; bill	319	Referred to Committee Whole House.		
Simpson, Sarah	Continuation of pension	28	1	Petition	827	Whole House.						
Simpson, Stephen	(See heirs of George Simpson)	24	1		206							
Simpson, Stephen	(See heir of George Simpson)	31	1		955							

List of private claims presented to the House of Representatives of the United States from the 1st to the 31st Congress, inclusive—Continued.

Names of claimants.	Nature or object of the claim.	Congress.	Session.	How brought before the House of Reps.	Page of journal.	To what committee of the House referred.	No. or date of the report.	Nature of the report.	No. of the bill.	How disposed of by the House of Reps.	How disposed of by the Senate.	Date of the act of Congress, and remarks.
Simpson, Thomas	Compensation or relief in consideration of revolutionary services.	1	2	Petition Rep. of Secretary War.	188 198					Laid on table.		
Simpson, Thomas	Compensation or relief in consideration of revolutionary services.	3	1	Petition	98	Select	April 2, 1794	Favorable		Laid on table.		
Simpson, Thomas	Compensation or relief in consideration of revolutionary services.	10	2	Petition Rep. of Secretary War.	512 525					Laid on table.		
Simpson, Thomas	Indemnity for risk in depositing public money.	25	3	Resolution Documents.	457 462	Claims. Claims.						
Simpson, Thomas	Indemnity for risk in depositing public money.	26	1	Petition	170	Claims	49	Adverse		Laid on table.		
Simpson, Thomas	Increase of pension	10	1	Pension bill	232	Whole House			78	Passed	Passed with amendment.	App'd April 25, 1808
Simpson, Thomas	Arrears of pension	11	3	Petition Rep. of Secretary War.	536 607	Claims.						
Simpson, Thomas	Arrears of pension and bounty land.	12	2	Petition	626	Priv. Land Claims.	Feb. 26, 1813	Adverse		Laid on table.		
Simpson, Thomas	To be restored to pension roll	23	2	Petition	327	Invalid Pensions	Feb 5, 1835	Favorable	711	Passed.		
Simpson, Thomas	Correction of an entry of land	23	1	Documents	215	Public Lands.						
Simpson, William	Pension for revolutionary disabilities.	3	1	Rep. of Secretary War.	175					Laid on table.		
Simpson, William	Pension for revolutionary disabilities.	3	2	Rep. of Secretary War.	262	Claims.						
Simpson, William	Pension for revolutionary disabilities.	4	1	Rep. of Secretary War.	445	Claims.						
Simpson, William	Pension for revolutionary disabilities.	4	2	Rep. of Secretary War.	614	Claims	Feb. 6, 1797	Favorable; bill ordered.	224	Passed	Postponed.	
Simpson, William	Pension for revolutionary disabilities.	5	2	General bill	127				38	Passed	Passed	App'd Feb. 2, 1798
Simpson, William	Pension for revolutionary disabilities.	15	2	Pension bill	61				203	Passed	Passed, with amendment.	App'd March 3, 1819
Simpson, William	Indemnity for losses, war of 1812.	28	1	Petition	483	Claims.						
Simpson, William	Indemnity for losses, war of 1812.	28	2	Petition	53	Claims.						
Simpson, ——	(See Sympson.)											
Simpton, Capt. George	Compensation for loss of schooner Alert.	31	1	Petition	192	Claims	402	Favorable	339	Referred to Committee Whole House.		
Simrall, Colonel, (Ky.)	Compensation for horses lost by his regiment, war of 1812.	12	2	Petition	691	Claims.						
Sinclair, Arthur	Prize-money for destruction of a store-ship.	14	2	Petition	192	Naval Affairs	Feb. 5, 1817	Adverse		Laid on table.		
Sinclair, Arthur	Compensation for naval services	25	2	Petition	58	Claims	599	Adverse		Laid on table.		
Sinclair, Arthur	Compensation for naval services	28	2	Petition	72	Claims.						
Sinclair, George T.	Extra compensation as a naval officer.	30	1	Petition	236	Naval Affairs.						
Sinclair, George T.	(See Exploring Expedition)	27	3		149		270		818			
Sinclair, Jacob, widow of	Pension for revolutionary services.	25	2	Petition	846	Rev. Pensions.						
Sinclair, John	Compensation for revolutionary services.	2	1	Petition	502					Referred to Secretary War.		
Sinclair, John	Compensation for revolutionary services.	2	2	Petition	623					Laid on table.		
Sinclair, Mary	Continuation of pension	22	2	Petition	266	Naval Affairs.						

List of private claims presented to the House of Representatives of the United States from the 1st to the 31st Congress, inclusive—Continued.

Names of claimants.	Nature or object of the claim.	Congress.	Session.	How brought before the House of Reps.	Page of journal.	To what committee of the House referred.	No. or date of the report.	Nature of the report.	No. of the bill.	How disposed of by the House of Reps.	How disposed of by the Senate.	Date of the act of Congress, and remarks.
Sinclair, Noah	Increase of pension	10	1	Pension bill	232	Whole House			78	Passed	Passed, with amendment.	App'd April 25, 1808
Sinclair, Rachel	(See Jacob Sinclair, widow of)	25	2		846							
Sinclair, Thomas	Pension	29	1	Petition	623	Invalid Pensions				Discharged; laid on table.		
Singley, George	Pension for revolutionary services	28	1	Resolution	534	Rev. Pensions	322	Favorable	230	Passed.		
Singley, George	Pension for revolutionary services	28	2	Resolution	57	Rev. Pensions				Discharged; laid on table.		
Singletary, Ithamar	Pension for revolutionary services	4	1	Rep. of Secretary War.	445	Claims	Feb. 18, 1796	Res. to refer to Sec. War.	J.R. 16	Passed	Passed	App'd April 18, 1796
Singletary, Ithamar	Pension for revolutionary services	4	2	Rep. of Secretary War.	651	Claims	Feb. 6, 1797	Favorable; bill ordered.	224	Passed	Postponed.	
Singletary, Ithamar	Pension for revolutionary services	5	2	Pension bill	127				38	Passed	Passed	App'd Feb. 2, 1898
Singletary, Joseph, jr	Invalid pension	3	1	Rep. of Secretary War.	13	Select	May 26, 1794	Favorable; bill ordered.	62	Passed	Passed	App'd June 7, 1794
Singletary, Joseph, jr	Invalid pension	4	1	Rep. of Secretary War.	445	Claims	Feb. 18, 1796	Res. to refer to Sec. War.	J. R. 16	Passed	Passed	App'd April 18, 1796
Singletary, Joseph, jr	Invalid pension	4	2	Rep. of Secretary War.	651	Claims	Feb. 6, 1797	Favorable; bill ordered.	224	Passed	Postponed.	
Singleton, Elizabeth	(See heirs of Flanders Thompson)	31	1		1003							
Singleton, James	Pension	25	2	Petition	401	Invalid Pensions.						
Singleton, James	Pension	25	3	Resolution	89	Invalid Pensions	Jan. 9, 1839	Adverse		Laid on table.		
Singleton, Joshua	Commutation pay for naval services.	22	2	Petition	114	Rev. Claims.						
Singleton, Joshua	Land for Virginia scrip, 3,834 acres.	22	1	Petition	107	Public Lands.						
Singleton, Joshua	Land for Virginia scrip, 3,834 acres.	23	1	Petition	70	Rev. Claims.						
Singleton, Mary Ann	(See heirs of Flanders Thompson)	31	1		1003							
Singleton, Robert	Bounty land for services in Indian war.	8	2	Petition	131	Claims.						
Singleton, Robert	Bounty land for services in Indian war.	9	1	Petition	310	Public Lands	April 9, 1806	Adverse		Indefinitely postponed.		
Singleton, Robert	Bounty land for services in Indian war.	9	2	Petition	472	Public Lands.						
Singleton, Stephen	Remission of duty on damaged merchandise.	13	2	Petition	188	Ways and Means	Mar 11, 1814	Adverse		Rejected.		
Singleton, Stephen	Reimbursement of duty on damaged merchandise.	15	1	Petition	261	Ways and Means.						
Singleton, William, (Pa.)	Pension for revolutionary services.	26	1	Petition	322	Rev. Pensions.						
Singleton, Wyatt, *et al.*	Confirmation of title to land in Louisiana.	22	1	Petition	133	Priv. Land Claims.	221	Favorable	293	Referred to Committee Whole House.		
Singleton, Wyatt, *et al.*	Confirmation of title to land in Louisiana.	22	2	House bill	171	Whole House	Jan. 11, 1833	With amend.	293	Passed	Ref. to Com. on Priv. Land Claims.	
Singleton, Wyatt, *et al.*	Conrfimation of title to land in Louisiana.	23	1	Petition	93	Priv. Land Claims.	76	With amend.	83	Passed.		
Sinnard, Thomas	Compensation for work on Cumberland road.	23	2	Petition	163	Claims						See Journal, Linnard.
Sinnard, Thomas	Compensation for work on Cumberland road.	24	1	Petition	94	Claims.						
Sinnard, Thomas	Compensation for work on Cumberland road.	24	2	Petition	120	Claims.						
Sinnard, Thomas	Compensation for work on Cumberland road.	25	2	Petition	89	Claims	340	Favorable	370	Referred to Committee Whole House.		

List of private claims presented to the House of Representatives of the United States from the 1st to the 31st Congress, inclusive—Continued.

Names of claimants.	Nature or object of the claim.	Congress.	Session.	How brought before the House of Reps.	Page of journal.	To what committee of the House referred.	No. or date of the report.	Nature of the report.	No. of the bill.	How disposed of by the House of Reps.	How disposed of by the Senate.	Date of the act of Congress, and remarks.
Sinnard, Thomas	Compensation for work on Cumberland road.	25	3	House bill	377	Whole House	Jan. 25, 1839	With't amend.	370	Passed	Passed	App'd March 3, 1839
Sinnell, Israel T	Naval pension	25	2	Petition	399	Naval Affairs.						
Sinkler, James	Permission to fund certificates	2	1	Petition	450	....	....	....	....	Laid on table.		
Sinks, Charles	Right of pre-emption to land in Indiana.	15	1	Petition	195	Public Lands	Feb. 16, 1818	Adverse	....	Rejected	....	Leave to withdraw.
Sintz, Nicholas	(See Conrad Houseman.)											
Siscoe, Nicholas	Pension for revolutionary services.	29	2	Petition	150	Rev. Pensions	20	Adverse	....	Laid on table.		
Sisson, Freeborn, & others.	Remission of duty on molasses	14	1	Petition	449	Ways and Means.						
Sitcher, Andrew	Pay and emolument as commissary of a regiment.	13	2	Petition	246	Select	Feb. 17, 1814	Favorable	103	Passed	Passed	App'd Mar. 28, 1814
Sites, Christopher	Pension	13	3	Pension bill	740	Whole House	Mar. 1, 1815	With't amend.	303	Passed	Passed	App'd March 3, 1815
Sitgreaves, Samuel, executors of.	Settlement of his accounts as government agent.	20	2	Resolution	124	Foreign Affairs	54	Favorable	391	Referred to Committee Whole House.		
Sitgreaves, Samuel, executors of.	Settlement of his accounts as government agent.	21	1	Resolution	90	Foreign Affairs	105	Favorable	92	Passed	Passed, with amendment.	App'd May 29, 1830
Sithens, Jesse	Compensation for extra work on Cumberland road.	24	1	Petition	851	Claims.						
Sithin, John	Pension	19	2	Petition	36	Military Pensions.						
Sits, Henry	Arrears of pension	28	1	Petition	853	Rev. Pensions.						
Sizemoor, Absalom	Confirmation of title to land in Alabama.	15	1	Petition	56	Priv. Land Claims.						
Sizemoor, Arthur	Confirmation of title to land in Mississippi Territory.	14	1	Petition	114	Public Lands.						
Sizemoor, Arthur	Indemnity for losses during Creek war.	14	2	Petition	71	Ways and Means	Jan. 29, 1817	Favorable	93	Passed	Passed	App'd March 3, 1817
Sizemoor, Arthur	Confirmation of title to land in Alabama.	15	1	Petition	56	Priv. Land Claims.						
Sizemoor, Arthur	Confirmation of title to land in Mississippi.	15	1	Petition	56	Priv. Land Claims.	Jan. 20, 1818	Favorable	49	Passed	Passed	App'd April 20, 1818
Sizemore, Arthur	Release of government title to Indian reservation.	21	1	Petition	378	Public Lands	Jan. 11, 1830	General bill	97	Passed	Passed	App'd May 29, 1830
Sizemoor, Mary	Confirmation of title to land in Mississippi.	14	1	Petition	113	Public Lands.						
Sizemoor, Mary	Confirmation of title to land in Mississippi.	15	1	Petition	59	Priv. Land Claims.	Jan. 20, 1818	Favorable	49	Passed	Passed	App'd April 20, 1818
Sizemore, William	Confirmation of title to land in Alabama.	15	1	Petition	56	Priv. Land Claims.						
Sizer, Jonathan	Pension for revolutionary services.	22	1	Resolution	59	Rev. Pensions	26	Favorable	71	Passed.	Indef. postp'd.	
Skeel, Amos	Pension for revolutionary services.	4	1	Rep. of Secretary War.	445	Claims	Feb. 18, 1796	Favorable; bill ordered.	156	Passed	Passed	App'd April 20, 1796
Skeel, Amos	Increase of pension	12	1	Pension bill	361	Whole House	June 15, 1812	With't amend.	138	Passed	Passed, with amendment.	App'd July 5, 1812
Skeel, Amos	Pension for revolutionary services.	10	2	Pension bill	499	Whole House	....	....	158	Passed	Passed	App'd March 3, 1809
Skelton, Medley	Pension for revolutionary services.	17	2	Petition	36	Rev. Pensions.						
Skelton, Robert	Exchange of military bounty land.	24	1	Petition	207	Priv. Land Claims.	....	....	....	Discharged; laid on table.		
Skidmore, John W.	(See Thomas H. Owen and others)	25	2	....	994	....	....	....	S. 171			
Skidmore, John W.	Compensation for transportation of the mail.	27	2	Senate bill	1291	P. Of. & P. Roads.	Aug. 30, 1842	With't amend.	S. 287	Referred to Committee Whole House.		
Skimmer, Rich'd, and others	Increase of compensation as custom-house boatmen.	19	1	Petition	222	Commerce.						

List of private claims presented to the House of Representatives of the United States from the 1st to the 31st Congress, inclusive—Continued.

Names of claimants.	Nature or object of the claim.	Congress.	Session.	How brought before the House of Reps.	Page of journal.	To what committee of the House referred.	No. or date of the report.	Nature of the report.	No. of the bill.	How disposed of by the House of Reps.	How disposed of by the Senate.	Date of the act of Congress, and remarks.
Skinker, Samuel W	(See administrator of Dr. John Julian.)	31	2		36							
Skiles, Elizabeth	Compensation for horse killed in Indian war.	22	1	Petition	557	Claims	April 23, 1832	Adverse		Laid on table.		
Skillman, John, or Samuel	Renewal of a lost certificate	2	1	Petition and rep't Sec. of War.	517, 583	Select.						
Skinner, Abraham	Reimbursement of advances on public account.	1	2	Petition	166	Select				Referred to Secretary Treasury.		See appropriation bill, Aug. 11, 1790.
Skinner, Abraham	Reimbursement of advances on public account.	1	3	Petition	370					Referred to Secretary Treasury.		
Skinner, Abraham	Reimbursement of advances on public account.	3	2	Rep. of Secretary Treasury.	284					Laid on table.		
Skinner, Albert	Back pension for services in Indian war.	27	2	Petition	757	Invalid Pensions.						
Skinner, Alfred	(See representatives of James Mackay.)	24	1		671							
Skinner, Charles	(See assignees of Thomas Tupper)	22	2		142							
Skinner, Daniel G	Compensation for stores taken for public use.	26	2	Senate bill	210	Claims	Feb. 12, 1841	With't amend.	S. 208	Referred to Committee Whole House.		
Skinner, Daniel G	Compensation for stores taken for public use.	27	2	Senate bill	1064	Claims			S. 212			
Skinner, Daniel G	Compensation for stores taken for public use.	27	3	Senate bill	496	Claims			S. 99	Discharged.		
Skinner, Daniel G	Compensation for stores taken for public use.	28	1	Senate bill	539	Claims	May 25, 1844	With't amend.	S. 60	Passed	Passed	App'd June 10, 1844
Skinner, Eli	Renewal of a loan office certificate.	3	1	Petition	111					Laid on table.		
Skinner, Elisha	To be restored to pension roll	17	1	Petition	92	Rev. Pensions.						
Skinner, George, administrator of.	Compensation for a wagon taken for public use.	16	1	Petition	135	Claims	Jan. 28, 1820	Favorable	61	Passed	Passed	App'd May 4, 1820
Skinner, George D	Bounty lands for military services.	24	1	Petition	409	Public Lands				Discharged; laid on table.		
Skinner, George D	Bounty lands for military services.	24	2	Documents	390	Public Lands.						
Skinner, Henry	Compensation for revolutionary services.	2	1	Petition and rep't Sec. of War.	490, 500					Laid on table.		
Skinner, Ichabod Lord	Indemnity for loss by change of a contract on the Cumberland road.	18	1	Senate bill	422	Roads and Canals.	April 24, 1824	Favorable	75	Passed	Passed	App'd May 5, 1824
Skinner, Jedediah	Pension	24	2	Petition	132	Invalid Pensions				Discharged; laid on table.		
Skinner, Jedediah	Pension	25	2	Petition	920	Invalid Pensions.						
Skinner, Jedediah	Pension	26	1	Petition	163	Invalid Pensions	407	Adverse		Laid on table.		
Skinner, John, administrator of.	Indemnity for French spoliations prior to 1800.	26	1	Memorial	182	Foreign Affairs	343	Favorable; bill	319	Referred to Committee Whole House.		
Skinner, John	Compensation for services as U. States commissioner, &c.	7	1	Petition	63	Claims	March 8, 1802	Adverse		Laid on table.		
Skinner, John	Compensation for services as U. States commissioner, &c.	7	2	Petition and docs.	292	Claims				Discharged; leave to withdraw.		
Skinner, John, (Va.)	To be restored to pension roll	17	1	Petition	249	Whole House.						
Skinner, John, & Son, surviving partner of.	Indemnity for French spoliations prior to 1800.	26	1	Petition	714	Foreign Affairs	343	Favorable; bill	319	Referred to Committee Whole House.		
Skinner, John	(See John Skinner & Son)	26	1		182							
Skinner, John L. B	(See Martin S. Atkin)	17	1		359							
Skinner, John P	(See sureties of Thomas Emerson)	27	2		100		992		575			

List of private claims presented to the House of Representatives of the United States from the 1st to the 31st Congress, inclusive—Continued.

Names of claimants.	Nature or object of the claim.	Congress.	Session.	How brought before the House of Reps.	Page of journal.	To what committee of the House referred.	No. or date of the report.	Nature of the report.	No. of the bill.	How disposed of by the House of Reps.	How disposed of by the Senate.	Date of the act of Congress, and remarks.
Skinner, Jonathan, heirs of.	Compensation for property destroyed by the enemy.	29	2	Petition	172	Rev. Claims.						
Skinner, Joseph M	(See administrator of George Skinner.)	16	1		135							
Skinner, Josiah	Pension for revolutionary services.	22	1	Petition	412	Rev. Pensions.						
Skinner, J. S	(See assignee of John Mullings)	28	1		75							
Skinner, Micah	Pension for revolutionary services.	22	1	Petition	265	Rev. Pensions	381	Favorable	472	Passed	Indef. postp'd.	
Skinner, Richard	Indemnity for French spoliations prior to 1800.	26	1	Memorial	182	Foreign Affairs	343	Favorable; bill	319	Referred to Committee Whole House.		
Skinner, Samuel W	(See representatives of Dr. John Julian.)	23	1		494							
Skinner, Solomon	Reimbursement of duty on merchandise imported to Castine.	16	1	Senate bill	108	Ways and Means	Jan. 14, 1820	With't amend.	S. 13	Passed with amendm't	Passed as am'd.	App'd April 11, 1820
Skinner, Thomas	Pension	27	2	Declaration	458	Rev. Pensions	784	Adverse		Laid on table.		
Skinner, William	Increase of salary as commissioner of loans.	4	1	Memorial	467	Select.						
Skipwith, Fulwar	Reimbursement of advances to American prisioners.	3	1	President's mess.	102	Select	May 10, 1794	Favorable; bill ordered.	44	Passed	Passed, with amendment.	App'd May 19, 1794
Skipwith, Fulwar	Reimbursement of advances as consul general at Paris.	7	1	Memorial & rep't Sec. of State.	54, 184	Whole House	April 12, 1802	Favorable; bill ordered.	59	Passed	Passed	App'd May 3, 1802
Skipwith, Fulwar, administrator of.	Indemnity for seizures by British government.	31	1	Petition	742	Claims.						
Skipwith, Fulwar	Indemnity for French spoliations prior to 1800.	26	1	Memorial	182	Foreign Affairs	343	Favorable; bill	319	Referred to Committee Whole House.		
Skipwith, G. G., and others.	Indemnity for French spoliations prior to 1800.	31	1	Petition	692	Foreign Affairs	355	General bill	318	Referred to Committee Whole House.		
Skirving, John	Compensation for services in examining public buildings.	27	2	Petition	618	Public Buildings	Aug. 20, 1842	Favorable	600	Referred to Committee Whole House.		
Skirving, John	Compensation for services in examining public buildings.	27	3	House bill	91	Whole House	Dec. 23, 1842	With't amend.	600	Passed	Passed, with amendment.	App'd March 3, 1842
Skirving, John	Compensation for work on furnaces in the Treasury.	27	3	Petition	102	Public Buildings	Jan. 28, 1843	Favorable	733	Passed	Passed	App'd March 3, 1843
Skirving, John	Compensation for plan of a public building.	28	1	Petition	369	Public Buildings.						
Skirving, John	Compensation for sundry services.	29	1	Petition	172	Public Buildings.						
Skirving, John	Compensation for sundry services.	30	1	Petition	80	Public Buildings.						
Skirvin, Joel	Pension	21	1	Petition	377	Military Pensions	April 2, 1830	Adverse		Laid on table.		
Sky, Peter	Pension for military services during the war of 1812.	26	2	Petition	55	Invalid Pensions	86	Adverse		Laid on table.		
Sky, Peter	Pension for military services during the war of 1812.	27	2	Petition	46	Invalid Pensions	18	Favorable	59	Passed	Passed	App'd July 9, 1842
Skyrin, John, heirs of	Indemnity for French spoliations prior to 1800.	31	1	Petition	312	Foreign Affairs	355	General bill	318	Referred to Committee Whole House.		
Slacke, Agnes	(See John Slacke, widow of)	19	2		59							
Slack, John	Bounty land for revolutionary services.	9	1	Petition	280					Referred to Secretary of War.		
Slacke, John, widow of	Confirmation of title to land in Michigan.	19	2	Memorial	59	Priv. Land Claims.	Jan. 2, 1827	Adverse		Laid on table.		
Slacke, John, widow of	Confirmation of title to land in Michigan.	23	1	Petition	103	Priv. Land Claims.						
Slacke, John, widow of	Confirmation of title to land in Michigan.	23	2	Memorial	110	Priv. Land Claims.						

List of private claims presented to the House of Representatives of the United States from the 1st to the 31st Congress, inclusive—Continued.

Names of claimants.	Nature or object of the claim.	Congress.	Session.	How brought before the House of Reps.	Page of journal.	To what committee of the House referred.	No. or date of the report.	Nature of the report.	No. of the bill.	How disposed of by the House of Reps.	How disposed of by the Senate.	Date of the act of Congress, and remarks.
Slacke, John, widow of	Confirmation of titles to land in Michigan.	24	1	Petition	143	Priv. Land Claims				Discharged; laid on table.		
Slacke, John, widow of	Confirmation of title to land in Michigan.	31	1	Petition	1044	Priv. Land Claims.						
Slack, Joseph	Pension	11	2	Pension bill	283	Whole House	Mar. 24, 1810	With't amend.	107	Passed	Passed, with amendment.	App'd April 27, 1810
Slack, Joseph	Arrears of pension	11	3	Petition	510	Claims.						
Slacum, George W	Diplomatic services at Buenos Ayres.	22	2	Appropriat'n bill.	145				669			App'd March 2, 1833
Slacum, William A	Reimbursement of certain expenses, &c.	29	1	Senate bill	1075	Foreign Affairs	July 24, 1846	With't amend.	S. 104	Referred to Committee Whole House.		
Slacum, William A	Reimbursement of certain expenses, &c.	29	2	Senate bill	307	Foreign Affairs	Feb. 24, 1847	With't amend.	S. 61	Referred to Committee Whole House.		
Slacum, William A	Reimbursement of certain expenses, &c.	30	1	Senate bill	936	Foreign Affairs	Aug. 8, 1848	With amend.	S. 251	Referred to Committee Whole House.		
Slacum, William A	Reimbursement of certain expenses, &c.	30	2	Senate bill of last session.	363	Whole House	Feb. 2, 1849	With amend.	S. 251	Passed with amendm't.	Amendm't disagreed to.	House insists.
Slade, Abner	To be restored to pension roll	21	2	Senate bill	305	Military Pensions	Feb. 17, 1821	Adverse	S. 114	Laid on table.		
Slade, Alfred M., widow of.	Compensation for services as acting consul.	27	2	Memorial	617	Foreign Affairs	958	Adverse		Laid on table.		
Slade, Eliza A	(See Alfred M. Slade, widow of.)	27	2		617							
Slade, William, heirs of	(Claim not stated)	23	2	Documents	85	Rev. Claims.						
Slagg, ——	(See Harvey & Slagg)	26	1		708							
Slater, George	(See Charles Cramer, and others.)	21	1		375							
Slater, James	Pension for revolutionary services.	3	1	Rep. of Secretary War.	131	Select	May 26, 1794	Res. to refer to Sec. War.	J. R. 12	Passed	Passed	App'd June 9, 1794
Slater, James	Pension for revolutionary services.	4	1	Rep. of Secretary War.	445	Claims	Feb 18, 1796	Favorable; bill ordered.	156	Passed	Passed	App'd April 20, 1796
Slater, Lemuel	Compensation for services in obtaining statistics.	23	2		176				616			App'd Mar. 3, 1835
Slater, Persis	(See widow of Samuel Graves)	24	2		397							
Slatton, Joseph, representative of.	Compensation for services in the war of 1812.	24	1	Petition	776	Military Affairs				Discharged; laid on table.		
Slatton, Joseph, administrator of.	Reimbursement of money paid as surety.	24	2	Petition	89	Military Affairs				Discharged; laid on table.		
Slaughter, Arthur	(See heirs of James Slaughter)	24	1		152							
Slaughter, Augustine, administrator of.	Commutation pay for revolutionary services.	23	2	Petition	94	Rev. Claims.						
Slaughter, Augustine, administrator of.	Commutation pay for revolutionary services.	24	1	Petition	104	Rev. Claims.						
Slaughter, Augustine, administrator of.	Commutation pay for revolutionary services.	24	2	Petition	39	Rev. Claims.						
Slaughter, Francis L	Pension for revolutionary wounds and disabilities.	7	2	Petition	283	Claims				Discharged; leave to withdraw.		
Slaughter, Francis L	Pension for revolutionary wounds and disabilities.	9	2	Pension bill	608				216	Passed	Passed	App'd March 3, 1807
Slaughter, George H	Exchange of an entry of land in Wisconsin.	26	2	House bill	156	Whole House			585			
Slaughter, James, heir of	Compensation for revolutionary services.	24	1	Petition	152	Rev. Claims	856	Adverse		Laid on table.		
Slaughter, John S., heirs of.	Compensation for revolutionary services.	22	1	Petition	289	Rev. Claims.						

List of private claims presented to the House of Representatives of the United States from the 1st to the 31st Congress, inclusive—Continued.

Names of claimants.	Nature or object of the claim.	Congress.	Session.	How brought before the House of Reps.	Page of journal.	To what committee of the House referred.	No. or date of the report.	Nature of the report.	No. of the bill.	How disposed of by the House of Reps.	How disposed of by the Senate.	Date of the act of Congress, and remarks.
Slaughter, John, heirs of	Commutation pay for revolutionary services.	29	1	Petition	523	Rev. Claims.						
Slaughter, John, heirs of	Commutation pay for revolutionary services.	29	2	Memorial	335	Rev. Claims.						
Slaughter, John, heirs of	Commutation pay for revolutionary services.	30	1	Petition	379	Rev. Claims.						
Slaughter, John, heirs of	Commutation pay for revolutionary services.	30	2	Petition and docs.	137	Rev. Claims.						
Slaughter, Philip	Compensation for rev. services	20	1	Resolution	60	Rev. Claims	Feb. 15, 1828	Favorable	168	Referred to Committee Whole House.		
Slaughter, Philip	Relief from proviso of act May 26, 1828.	20	2	Petition	27	Rev. Claims.						
Slaughter, Philip	Relief from proviso of act May 26, 1828.	21	1	Petition.	171	Rev. Claims	Feb. 26, 1830	Favorable	301	Passed	Passed	App'd May 29, 1830
Slaughter, Philip	Interest on commutation pay	21	2	Petition.	190	Rev. Claims	...	...	...	Disch'd; laid on table.		
Slaughter, Philip	Interest on commutation pay	22	1	Petition.	28	Rev. Claims	Feb. 21, 1832	Favorable	403	Ref'd to Com. W. H.		
Slaughter, Philip	Interest on commutation pay	22	2	House bill	126	Whole House	...	...	403			
				Senate bill	466	Rev. Claims	Mar. 2, 1833	With amend.	S. 105	Passed wtth amendm't.	Passed as am'd.	App'd March 2, 1833
Slaughter, Philip	Arrears of commutation pay	30	1	Petition	656	Rev. Claims.						
Slaughter, Philip I	Compensation for military services in Mexico.	30	1	Petition	109	Priv. Land Claims.						
Slaughter, Reuben	(See William H. Bedford, agent.)	28	1	...	262							
Slaughter, Robert	Half or commutation pay for revolutionary services.	18	2	Resolution	125	Pens. & Rev. Cl'ms.						
Slaughter, Thomas S	(See sureties of Wm. H. Whitsitt.)	17	2	...	228							
Slaughter, William, executor of.	Commutation pay for revolutionary services.	22	1	Petition	538	Rev. Claims.						
Slaughter, William, executor of.	Commutation pay for revolutionary services.	22	2	Petition	29	Rev. Claims.						
Slaughter, William, executor of.	Commutation pay for revolutionary services.	22	2	Petition	216	Select.						
Slaughter, William, executor of.	Commutation pay for revolutionary services.	23	1	Petition & docs.	242	Rev. Claims.						
Slaughter, William, executor of.	Commutation pay for revolutionary services.	24	1	Petition	152	Rev. Claims	358	Adverse	...	Laid on table.		
Slaughter, William, executor of.	Commutation pay for revolutionary services.	25	2	Petition	1080	Rev. Claims	...	...	...	Discharged; laid on table.		
Slaughter, William, executor of.	Commutation pay for revolutionary services.	25	3	Petition	125	Rev. Claims.						
Slaughter, William, executor of.	Commutation pay for revolutionary services.	26	1	Petition	163	Rev. Claims	623	Adverse	...	Laid on table.		
Slaughter, William, executor of.	Commutation pay for revolutionary services.	27	2	Petition	308	Rev. Claims	863	Adverse	...	Laid on table.		
Slaughter, William B	Correction of an entry of land	26	1	Petition	1004	Public Lands.						
Slaughter, William B	Equitable settlement of his accounts.	30	1	Senate bill	232	Territories	132	With amend.	S. 49	Passed with amend't.	Passed as am'd.	App'd June 26, 1836
Slaughter, William B	Explanatory legislation	30	1	Senate resolution.	961	...	...	...	S. 30	Passed	Passed	App'd June 26, 1848
Slaven, John	Compensation for revolutionary services.	19	2	Petition	26	Rev. Claims	15	Adverse	...	Laid on table.		
Slaven, John	Compensation for revolutionary services.	20	1	Petition	32	Rev. Claims	38	Adverse	...	Rejected.		
Slaven, John	Compensation for revolutionary services.	21	1	Petition	199	Military Pensions	April 23, 1830	Favorable	439	Referred to Committee Whole House.		
Slaven, John	Pension for revolutionary services.	22	1	Petition	45	Rev. Pensions	Dec. 21, 1831	Favorable	68	Passed	Postponed.	

List of private claims presented to the House of Representatives of the United States from the 1st to the 31st Congress, inclusive—Continued.

3—43

Names of claimants.	Nature or object of the claim.	Congress.	Session.	How brought before the House of Reps.	Page of journal.	To what committee of the House referred.	No. or date of the report.	Nature of the report.	No. of the bill.	How disposed of by the House of Reps.	How disposed of by the Senate.	Date of the act of Congress, and remarks.
Slaves captured by the enemy, owners of.	Indemnity for slave captured by British.	27	2	House bill	939	Whole House			483			
Slaves captured by the enemy, owners of.	Indemnity for slaves captured by British.	27	3	Senate bill	167	Whole House			S. 11			
				House bill	312	Whole House	Feb. 3, 1843 269	With amend.	483	Passed	Passed	App'd Feb. 18, 1843
Slavin, Parmela	(See late widow of John Blue)	28	1		217							
Slawson, Ebenezer	Indemnity for destruction of property, and compensation for revolutionary services.	3	1	Memorial	124					Laid on table		Leave to withdraw, 4th Cong., 1st session.
Slaymaker, Samuel R.	Compensation for transportation of the mail.	26	1	Senate bill	240	P. Of. & P. Roads.	May 25, 1840	With't amend.	S. 98	Referred to Committee Whole House.		
Slaymaker, Samuel R.	Compensation for transportation of the mail.	26	2	Senate bill	301	Whole House			S. 256			
Slaymaker, Samuel R.	Compensation for transportation of the mail.	27	2	Petition	153	P. Of. & P. Roads.	845	Favorable	488	Passed	Passed	App'd Aug. 27, 1842
Slaymaker, John	Pension for revolutionary services.	21	1	Resolution	432	Military Pensions.						
Slaymaker, John	Pension for revolutionary services.	21	2	Resolution	77	Military Pensions.						
Slaymaker, John	Pension for revolutionary services.	22	1	Petition	46	Rev. Pensions.						
Slayton, Thomas	Indemnity for destruction of property at Niagara.	19	2	Petition	159	Claims	Jan. 22, 1827	Adverse		Laid on table.		
Sled, Marshall, and others.	Right of pre-emption to land in Missouri.	30	1	Petition	236	Public Lands	328	Adverse		Laid on table.		
Sleeker, George	Pension	14	1	House bill	622	Whole House	April 11, 1816	With amend.	171	Passed	Passed, with amendment.	App'd April 30, 1816
Sleeth, David W.	Pension	25	2	Resolution	526	Rev. Pensions	762	Favorable	721	Passed	Adverse report.	
Sleeth, David W.	Pension	26	1	Petition	172	Rev. Pensions	145	Favorable	155	Referred to Committee Whole House.		
Slessman, John	(See Godfrey Haga and others)	7	1		12							
Slick, William	Pension	26	1	Petition	936	Rev. Pensions	714	Adverse		Laid on table.		
Slifer, Dr. Ezra, administrator of.	Extension of a patent	26	1	Memorial	278	Patents				Discharged; aid on table.		
Slingerland, Jacob	Increase of pension	31	1	Petition	719	Rev. Pensions	315	Adverse		Laid on table.		
Sliver, Henry	Naval pension	25	2	Petition	234	Naval Affairs	399	Adverse		Laid on table.		
Sliver, Henry	Naval pension	28	2	Petition	302	Invalid Pensions.						
Sliver, Henry	Pension for disability incurred in public service.	27	2	Petition	218	Invalid Pensions.						
Sliver, Henry	Pension for disability incurred in public service.	27	3	Petition	154	Invalid Pensions.						
Sliver, Henry	Pension for disability incurred in public service.	29	1	Petition	199	Invalid Pensions	345	Adverse		Laid on table.		
Sliver, Henry	Pension for disability incurred in public service.	30	2	Petition	328	Invalid Pensions	95	Adverse		Laid on table.		
Sloan, Bryant	Pension for revolutionary services.	3	1	Rep. of Secretary War.	131	Select	May 26, 1794	Res. to refer to Sec. of War.	J. R. 12	Passed	Passed	App'd June 9, 1794
Sloan, Bryant	Pension for revolutionary services.	4	1	Rep. of Secretary War.	445	Claims.						
Sloan, Bryant	Pension for revolutionary services.	4	2	Rep. of Secretary War.	614	Claims.						
Sloan, Bryant	Increase of pension	27	2	Resolution	566	Invalid Pensions				Discharged; laid on table.		
Sloan, Bryant	Increase of pension	28	1	Petition	317	Invalid Pensions.						
Sloane, Elizabeth	Compensation for revolutionary services.	23	1	Petition	73	Rev. Pensions.						
Sloane, George	Pension for revolutionary services.	16	1	Petition	212	Rev. Pensions	April 6, 1820	Adverse				Leave to withdraw.

List of private claims presented to the House of Representatives of the United States from the 1st to the 31st Congress, inclusive—Continued.

Names of claimants.	Nature or object of the claim.	Congress.	Session.	How brought before the House of Reps.	Page of journal.	To what committee of the House referred.	No. or date of the report.	Nature of the report.	No. of the bill.	How disposed of by the House of Reps.	How disposed of by the Senate.	Date of the act of Congress, and remarks.
Sloan, James	Prize-money for capture of Caledonia.	29	1	Petition	567	Claims	732	Adverse	......	Laid on table.		
Sloan, James	Prize-money for capture of Caledonia.	30	1	Petition	387	Claims.						
				Documents	589	Claims	659	Adverse	......	Laid on table.		
Sloan, John	Pension	21	1	Resolution	254	Military Pensions.						
Sloan, John	Pension	21	2	Petition	110	Military Pensions.						
Sloan, Joseph	Pension for services in Indian wars.	30	1	Petition	891	Rev. Pensions	....	....	......	Discharged; laid on table.		
Sloan, Philip	Reimbursement of money paid for his ransom.	6	2	Memorial	824	Claims	....	....	......	Postponed.		
Sloan, Philip	Reimbursement of money paid for his ransom.	7	1	Memor'l and rep't of Sec. State.	16, 26	Whole House	Jan. 14, 1802	Favorable; bill ordered.	19	Passed	Postponed.	
Sloan, Philip	Reimbursement of money paid for his ransom.	8	1	Memorial	605	Claims	May 13, 1804	To postpone	......	Postponed.		
				Senate bill	682	Whole House						
Sloan, Temperance	To be restored to pension roll	27	2	Petition	320	Rev. Pensions.	....	....	S. 33	Passed	Passed	App'd Mar. 26, 1804
Sloan, William	Pension for revolutionary services.	3	1	Rep. of Secretary War.	131	Select	May 26, 1794	Res. to refer to Sec. War.	J. R. 12	Passed	Passed	App'd June 9, 1794
Sloan, William	Pension for revolutionary services.	4	1	Rep. of Secretary of War.	445	Claims.						
Sloan, William	Pension for revolutionary services.	4	2	Rep. of Secretary of War.	614	Claims.						
Sloan, William	Pension	18	1	Petition	243	Pens. & Rev. Cl'ms.	April 12, 1824	Adverse	......	Laid on table.		
Sloan, William	Pension	24	2	Petition	159	Invalid Pensions	Jan. 13, 1837	Adverse	......	Laid on table.		
Sloan, William	Increase of pension	25	2	Petition	400	Invalid Pensions	648	Favorable	624	Passed.		
Sloan, William	Increase of pension	25	3	Petition	187	Invalid Pensions	134	Favorable	1001	Passed.	Adverse report	
Sloan, William	Increase of pension	26	1	Petition	162	Invalid Pensions	204	Favorable	216	Passed	Indef. postp'd.	
Sloat, John D.	Reimbursement of certain expenses as naval captain.	22	1	President's Message	567	Foreign Affairs	471	Favorable	572	Referred to Committee Whole House.		
Sloat, John D.	Indemnity for depreciation of Treasury notes.	22	2	Senate bill	277	Claims	Feb. 11, 1833	With amend.	S. 61	Passed with amendm't.	Passed as am'd.	App'd Feb. 19, 1833
Slocomb, Cora Ann	(See Samuel B. Slocomb, widow of)	29	1	....	353							
Slocomb, Samuel B., widow of.	Adjustment of claim under convention with Mexico.	29	1	Memorial	353	Foreign Affairs.						
Slocum, Frances	Payment of her annuity at Fort Wayne	28	2	Petition	273	Indian Affairs	Jan. 28, 1845	Favorable	J. R. 63	Passed	Passed	App'd March 3, 1845
Slocum, Frances	Extension of the provision of act of March 3, 1845	31	1	Senate resolution	613	Indian Affairs	281	With't amend.	S. 11	Passed	Passed	App'd Feb. 12, 1850
Slocum, Giles, sureties of.	Release from liability to government	15	2	Petition	215	Ways and Means.						
Slocum, Giles, sureties of.	Release from liability to government	16	2	Petition	43	Ways and Means.	Nov. 30, 1820	Adverse.	......	Rejected.		
Slocum, G. W.	Compensation for diplomatic services	22	1	House bill	426	Foreign Affairs	....	....	437			
Slocum, Holder	(See surety of Giles Slocum)	15	2	....	215							
Slocum, Isaac	(See John Church and others)	25	2	....	391							
Slocum, John	Pension	19	1	Petition	52	Military Pensions.	164	Adverse.	......	Laid on table.		
Slocum, Smith P.,	Pension	16	1	Petition	76	Pens. & Rev. Cl'ms.	Jan. 7, 1820	Adverse	......	Rejected.		
Slocum William	Pension	22	1	Petition	260	Invalid Pensions	April 3, 1832	Favorable	528	Passed	Passed, with amendment.	
Slocum, William	Pension	22	2	Petition	40	Invalid Pensions	Dec. 19, 1832	Favorable	626	Passed	Passed, with amendment.	
Slocum, William	Pension	23	1	Petition	60	Invalid Pensions	380	Favorable	400	Referred to Committee Whole House.		

List of private claims presented to the House of Representatives of the United States from the 1st to the 31st Congress, inclusive—Continued.

Names of claimants.	Nature or object of the claim.	Congress.	Session.	How brought before the House of Reps.	Page of journal.	To what committee of the House referred.	No. or date of the report.	Nature of the report.	No. of the bill.	How disposed of by the House of Reps.	How disposed of by the Senate.	Date of the act of Congress, and remarks.
Slocum, William	Pension	23	2	House bill	336	Whole House	Feb. 6, 1835	With't amend	400	Passed	Indef. postp'd.	
Slocum, William	Pension	24	1	Resolution	52	Invalid Pensions	Mar. 25, 1836	Adverse		Laid on table.		
Slocum, William	Pension	24	2	Petition	42	Invalid Pensions	Jan. 3, 1837	Adverse		Laid on table.		
Slocum, William	Pension	26	1	Petition	163	Invalid Pensions	July 21, 1840	Adverse		Laid on table.		
Slocum, William	Pension	27	2	Petition	268	Invalid Pensions	311	Favorable	280	Passed	Indef. postp'd.	
Slocum, William	Pension	28	1	Petition	115	Invalid Pensions	24	Adverse.		Laid on table.		
Slocum, William	Pension	29	1	Petition	82	Invalid Pensions				Discharged; laid on table.		
Slocum, William	Pension	30	1	Petition	104	Invalid Pensions						
Slocum, William	Pension	30	2	Petition	76	Invalid Pensions	3	Adverse		Laid on table.		
Slocum, William	Pension	31	1	Petition	193	Invalid Pensions	53	Favorable	83	Referred to Committee Whole House.		
Slocum, William	Pension	31	2	House bill	75	Whole House	Dec. 20, 1850	With amend.	83	Passed.		
Sloo, A. G.	(See S. W. Fullerton, and others.)	27	2		686							
Sloo, Thomas	Additional compensation as land commissioner, Kaskaskia.	13	1	Senate bill	25	Claims	June 14, 1813	With't amend.	S. 4	Passed	Passed	App'd July 5, 1813
Sloo, Thomas, and J. Caldwell.	Compensation for extra services as register and receiver.	16	2	Petition	200	Public Lands				Discharged; laid on table.		
Sloo, William, executor of.	Payment of revolutionary certificates.	15	2	Petition	154	Pens. & Rev. Cl'ms.						
Sloo, William, executor of.	Payment of revolutionary certificates.	16	1	Petition	92	Pens. & Rev. Cl'ms.	Dec. 31, 1819	Adverse		Rejected		Leave to withdraw, p. 539.
Sloop, Michael	Pension	22	1	Petition	329	Rev. Claims.						
Sloop, Michael	Pension	22	2	Petition	152	Invalid Pensions				Discharged; laid on table.		
Sloop, Michael	Pension	24	1	Petition	507	Invalid Pensions.						
Sloop Peacock	(See Lewis Warrington, and others)	28	1		285							
Slough, Jacob	Equitable settlement of his accounts.	18	1	Petition	158	Military Affairs	97	Favorable	182	Passed	Passed	App'd May 19, 1824
Slough, Jabob	Arrears of pension	23	2	Petition	128	Invalid Pensions	Jan. 5, 1835	Adverse.		Laid on table.		
Slough, Jacob	Increase of pension	24	1	Senate bill	811	Invalid Pensions	June 1, 1836	With't amend.	S. 241	Passed	Passed	App'd June 15, 1836
Sloughborough, John	Correction of a land entry	22	1	Petition	336	Priv. Land Claims.	322	Favorable	404	Referred to Committee Whole House.		
Sluthour, Anthony	Pension	20	2	Petition	143	Military Pensions	Feb. 13, 1829	Favorable	440	Passed.		
Sluthour, Anthony	Pension	21	1	Petition	49	Military Pensions	Jan. 5, 1830	Favorable	72	Passed	Passed, with amendment.	App'd May 20, 1830
Sluyter, Jacob, assignee of.	Bounty land for revolutionary services.	17	2	Petition	91	Priv. Land Claims.						
Slyter, Jonathan	Pension	29	1	Documents	284	Invalid Pensions	Aug. 8, 1846	Adverse		Laid on table.		
Slyter, Jonathan	Pension	30	1	Petition	457	Invalid Pensions	394	Favorable	346	Passed.		
Slye, William	Pension for revolutionary wounds and disability.	7	1	Petition	189					Laid on table.		
Small, Andrew, and others.	Confirmation of claim to land in Northwest Territory.	6	1	Petition	544	Select.						
Small, Andrew	Pension for revolutionary services.	15	2	Petition	74	Rev. Pensions	Jan. 21, 1819	Adverse				Leave to withdraw.
Small, Andrew	Pension for revolutionary services.	19	2	Petition	242	Military Pensions.						
Small, Andrew	Pension for revolutionary services.	20	1	Petition	38	Military Pensions	Feb. 15, 1828	Favorable	166	Passed.		
Small, Andrew	Pension for revolutionary services.	20	2	Pension bill	55	Whole House	Jan. 15, 1829	Favorable	311	Passed	Laid on table.	
Small, Andrew	Pension for revolutionary services.	21	1	Petition	49	Military Pensions	Jan. 5, 1830	Favorable	72	Name stricken out		App'd May 20, 1830
Small, Andrew	Pension for revolutionary services.	22	1	Petition	143	Rev. Pensions.						
Small, Archibald	Correction of an entry of land	23	1	Petition	49	Priv. Land Claims.	50	Favorable	58	Passed	Laid on table.	
Small, Archibald	Correction of an entry of land	24	1	Petition	65	Priv. Land Claims.	Dec. 21, 1835	Favorable	43	Passed	Passed	App'd June 23, 1836
Small, Daniel	To be restored to pension roll	17	2	Petition	25	Rev. Pensions.						

List of private claims presented to the House of Representatives of the United States from the 1st to the 31st Congress, inclusive—Continued.

Names of claimants.	Nature or object of the claim.	Congress.	Session.	How brought before the House of Reps.	Page of journal.	To what committee of the House referred.	No. or date of the report.	Nature of the report.	No. of the bill.	How disposed of by the House of Reps.	How disposed of by the Senate.	Date of the act of Congress, and remarks.
Small, Daniel	To be restored to pension roll	18	2	Petition	54	Rev. Pensions	54	Adverse		Laid on table.		
Small, Denne	Bounty on fishing schooner Lydia	24	1	Petition	715	Commerce				Dischraged; laid on table.		
Small, Henry	To be restored to pension roll	17	2	Petition	25	Rev. Pensions.						
Small, James	(See Louis F. Beeler and others)	30	1		115							
Small, John	Indemnity for expenses, &c., incurred on public account.	6	1	Petition	612	Select.						
Small, John	Confirmation of title to land in Indiana.	14	1	Petition	433	Public Lands.						
Small, John	Confirmation of title to land in Indiana.	15	1	Senate bill	358	Priv. Land Claims.	Mar. 26, 1818	With't amend.	S. 36	Passed	Passed	App'd April 3, 1818
Small, John	Indemnity for loss by an inundation.	25	2	Petition	731	P. Of. & P. Roads.	813	Adverse		Laid on table.		
Small, Matthew	Pension	31	2	Petition	50	Invalid Pensions.						
Small, Nehemiah	Bounty on fishing schooner Argus.	28	2	Petition	428	Commerce.						
Small, Nehemiah	Bounty on fishing schooner Argus.	29	1	Petition	235	Commerce.						
Small, Zebina H., & others.	Bounty on fishing schooner Medium.	30	2	Petition	285	Commerce.						
Smalley, Isaac, (N. J.)	Pension	19	2	Petition	285	Military Pensions.						
Smalley, Isaac, (N. J.)	Pension	20	1	Petition	124	Military Pensions.						
				Petition	278	Military Pensions	April 29, 1828	General pension bill.	283	Passed.		
Smalley, Isaac, (N. J)	Pension	20	2	Pension bill	55	Whole House	Jan. 15, 1829	With amend.	311	Passed	Laid on table.	
Smalley, Isaac, (N. J.)	Pension	21	1	Petition	47	Military Pensions	Jan. 5, 1830	General pension bill.	72	Passed	Passed	App'd May 20, 1830
Smalley, Joseph	Permission to enter a Spanish land claim in Arkansas.	28	1	Petition	274	Public Lands.						
Smallwood, James	Pension for services in Black Hawk war.	25	3	Petition	218	Invalid Pensions				Discharged; laid on table.		
Smallwood, James	Pension for services in Black Hawk war.	26	1	Petition	327	Invalid Pensions	415	Adverse		Laid on table.		
Smallwood, Leonard	Pension	23	2	Petition	40	Invalid Pensions.						
Smallwood, Samuel	Compensation for sand taken for public use.	24	2	Petition	266	Claims	Feb. 22, 1837	Adverse		Laid on table.		
Smart, Elijah	Pension for revolutionary services.	3	2	Rep. of Secretary War.	278	Claims.						
Smart, Elijah	Pension for revolutionary services.	4	1	Rep. of Secretary War.	445	Claims	Feb. 18, 1796	Res. to refer to Sec. War.	J. R. 16	Passed	Passed	App'd April 18, 1796
Smart, Ephraim K	(See Watson Hopkins)	27	2		319							
Smart, Robert	Indemnity for property taken for public use.	16	1	Resolution	351	Claims	April 5, 1820	Adverse		Laid on table.		
Smart, Robert	Indemnity for property taken for public use.	18	1	Petition	432	Claims.						
Smart, Robert	Indemnity for property taken for public use.	21	1	Petition	69	Claims	366	Favorable	424	Referred to Committee Whole House.		
Smart, Robert	Indemnity for property taken for public use.	22	1	Petition	43	Claims	Dec. 19, 1831	Favorable	47	Passed	Passed	App'd Mar. 31, 1832
Smart, Sarah	(See widow of Benajah Carpenter.)	3	1		68							
Smart, William	Pension for revolutionary services.	4	1	Rep't of Secretary War.	445	Claims.						
Smart, William	Pension for revolutionary services.	11	2	Pension bill	283				107	Passed	Passed, with amendment.	App'd April 27, 1810

List of private claims presented to the House of Representatives of the United States from the 1st to the 31st Congress, inclusive—Continued.

Names of claimants.	Nature or object of the claim.	Congress.	Session.	How brought before the House of Reps.	Page of journal.	To what committee of the House referred.	No. or date of the report.	Nature of the report.	No. of the bill.	How disposed of by the House of Reps.	How disposed of by the Senate.	Date of the act of Congress, and remarks.
Smelley, John R.	Permission to locate a land warrant.	23	2	Petition	242	Military Affairs				Discharged; laid on table.		
Smiley, Hugh B.	(See William H. Bedford, agent.)	28	1		262							
Smiley, William	(See surety of Henry Phillips)	17	1		221							
Smith, Aaron	Pension for revolutionary services.	4	1	Rep't of Secretary War.	445	Claims	Feb. 18, 1790	General pension bill.	156	Passed	Passed	App'd April 20, 1796
Smith, Aaron	Indemnity for loss on Continental money.	20	2	Petition	27	Rev. Claims	Jan. 5, 1829	Adverse		Laid on table.		
Smith, Aaron	Pension	21	2	Petition	159	Military Pensions.						
Smith, Aaron	Pension	22	1	Petition	104	Rev. Pensions.						
Smith, Aaron, and William Shute, representatives of.	Compensation for use and destruction of property.	21	2	Resolution	91	Claims	Dec. 29, 1830	Adverse		Laid on table.		
Smith, Aaron, and William Shute, representatives of.	Compensation for use and destruction of property.	22	2	Petition	151	Claims.						
Smith, Aaron, and William Shute, representatives of.	Compensation for use and destruction of property.	23	1	Petition	141	Claims	248	Favorable as to Smith. Adverse as to Shute.	284	Referred to Committee Whole House. Laid on table.		
Smith, Aaron, representatives of.	Compensation for use and destruction of property.	23	2	House bill	300	Whole House	Jan. 31, 1835	With't amend.	284	Passed	Passed	App'd March 3, 1835
Smith, Aaron, widow of.	To be restored to pension roll	27	2	Petition	320	Rev. Pensions.						
Smith, Abiel	Indemnity for revolutionary losses.	1	3	Petition	362					Referred to Secretary Treasury.		
Smith, Abiel	Indemnity for revolutionary losses.	2	1	Rep. of Secretary Treasury.	580					Laid on table.		
Smith, Abigail P.	Indemnity for French spoliations prior to 1800.	26	1	Memorial	182	Foreign Affairs	343	Favorable; bill	319	Referred to Committee Whole House.		
Smith, Abner	Pension for revolutionary services.	22	1	Petition	44	Rev. Pensions	133	Favorable	202	Referred to Committee Whole House.		
Smith, Abner	Pension for revolutionary services.	22	2	Bill of last sess.	66	Whole House			202	Laid on table.		
Smith, Abraham	Remission of tax on a distillery	15	1	Petition	90	Ways and Means	Feb. 18, 1818	Adverse		Rejected.		
Smith, Abraham	(See Bird & Abraham Smith)	19	1		293							
Smith, Abram, widow of.	Pension for revolutionary services.	26	2	Petition	82	Rev. Pensions				Discharged; laid on table.		See 26th Congress, 1st session, p. 1012.
Smith, Abram, widow of.	Pension for revolutionary services.	27	2	Petition	239	Rev. Pensions	299	Favorable	267	Passed	Passed	App'd Aug. 24, 1842
Smith, Adah	(See James Smith, widow of)	28	1		901							
Smith, Adam	Compensation for work, &c., on Cumberland road.	23	1	Res. and docs.	589	Claims	455	Adverse				See report No. 449.
Smith, Adam	Compensation for work, &c., on Cumberland road.	23	2	Documents	410					Referred to Secretary of War.		
Smith, Adam	Compensation for work, &c., on Cumberland road.	25	2	Resolution	78	Claims	467	Favorable	471	Referred to Committee Whole House.		
Smith, Adam, representatives of.	Compensation for work, &c., on Cumberland road.	25	3	Bill of last sess.	378	Whole House	Jan. 25, 1839	With't amend.	471	Passed	Passed	App'd March 3, 1839
Smith, Adam	Compensation for revolutionary services.	23	1	Petition	353	Rev. Pensions.						
Smith, Adam	Pension for wounds in the naval service.	28	1	Petition	903	Invalid Pensions.						
Smith, Adam	Pension for wounds in the naval service.	29	1	Petition	834	Invalid Pensions.						
Smith, Alba C., widow of.	Pension for services in Mexican war.	31	1	Petition	996	Invalid Pensions.						
Smith, Albert J.	(See heirs of Jacob Smith)	23	2		392							

List of private claims presented to the House of Representatives of the United States from the 1st to the 31st Congress, inclusive—Continued.

Names of claimants.	Nature or object of the claim.	Congress.	Session.	How brought before the House of Reps.	Page of journal.	To what committee of the House referred.	No. or date of the report.	Nature of the report.	No. of the bill.	How disposed of by the House of Reps.	How disposed of by the Senate.	Date of the act of Congress, and remarks.
Smith, Allen	Compensation for military supplies.	24	1	Petition	91	Claims.						
Smith, Allen	Compensation for military supplies.	26	1	Petition	623	Claims.						
Smith, Allen	Compensation for military supplies.	26	2	Petition	80	Claims.						
Smith, Allen	Compensation for military supplies.	31	1	Petition	633	Claims.						
Smith, Alexander	(See Louis F. Beeler, and others.)	30	1		115		485					
Smith, Alexander L., heirs of.	Commutation pay for revolutionary services.	25	1	Petition	771	Rev. Claims.						
Smith, Alexander L., heirs of.	Commutation pay for revolutionary services.	25	2	Petition	85	Rev. Claims.						
Smith, Alexander L., heirs of.	Commutation pay for revolutionary services.	26	3	Petition	16	Rev. Claims.						
Smith, Alexander L., heirs of.	Commutation pay for revolutionary services.	27	1	Petition	268	Rev. Claims	664	Adverse		Laid on table.		
Smith, Alexander L., heirs of.	Commutation pay for revolutionary services.	28	2	Petition	228	Rev. Claims.						
Smith, Alexander L., heirs of.	Commutation pay for revolutionary services.	31	2	Petition	588	Rev. Claims.						
Smyth, Alexander	(See Henry Devlin, and others.)	23	1		589		456					
Smith, Ambrose	Pension for revolutionary services.	3	1	Rep. of Secretary War.	131	Select	May 26, 1794	Res. to refer to Sec. War.	J.R. 12	Passed	Passed	App'd June 9, 1794
Smith, Ambrose	Pension for revolutionary services.	4	1	Rep. of Secretary War.	445	Claims.						
Smith, Ambrose	Pension for revolutionary services.	4	2	Rep of Secretary War.	614	Claims.						
Smith, Ambrose D., representatives of.	Equitable settlement of account for for supplies.	15	2	Resolution	63	Military Affairs.						
Smith, Ambrose D., representatives of.	Equitable settlement of account for for supplies.	16	2	Petition	43	Claims	Dec. 7, 1820	Adverse		Laid on table.		
Smith, Ambrose D., representatives of.	Equitable settlement of account for for supplies.	17	1	Petition	165	Claims	Mar. 4, 1822	Adverse		Laid on table		Leave to withdraw.
Smith, Amos, heirs of	Arrears of pension	27	2	Petition	320	Rev. Pensions.						
Smith, Amy	(See Job T. Smith, widow of)	24	2		217							
Smith, Andrew, (Ga.)	Payment of treasury notes stolen from mail.	31	1	Petition	502	Judiciary	173	Favorable	182	Referred to Committee Whole House.		
Smith, Andrew, (Ga.)	Payment of treasury notes stolen from mail.	31	2	Bill of last sess.	103	Whole House	Jan. 3, 1851	With't amend.	182	Passed.		
Smith, Andrew	(See William H. Bedford, agent.)	28	1		262							
Smith, Ann	Pension	16	1	Petition	117	Rev. Pensions	April 22, 1820	Adverse		Laid on table.		
Smith, Anna	Renewal of pension act	30	1	Petition	117	Rev. Pensions	91	Adverse		Laid on table.		
Smyth, Anna M	(See widow of Maj. Thos. Smyth.)	20	2		82							
Smith, Arnold	(See Remington Arnold, jr.)	22	1		441							
Smith, Asa, and others	Bounty on fishing vessels	10	2	Petition	519	Whole House.						
Smith, Asa	Pension	21	2	Petition	158	Military Pensions.						
Smith, Asa	Pension	22	1	Petition	123	Rev. Pensions	367	Favorable	462	Passed	Indef. postp'd.	
Smith, Asahael	(See assignees of Thomas Tupper.)	22	2		142							
Smith, Atarah	(See Anna Guild, and others)	27	2		256							
Smith, Ballard, representatives of.	Commutation pay for revolutionary services.	23	1	Petition	306	Rev. Claims.						
Smith, Ballard, representatives of.	Commutation pay for revolutionary services.	24	1	Petition	431	Rev. Claims.						
Smith, Ballard, representatives of.	Commutation pay for revolutionary services.	24	2	Petition	94	Rev. Claims.						

List of private claims presented to the House of Representatives of the United States from the 1st to the 31st Congress, inclusive—Continued.

Names of claimants.	Nature or object of the claim.	Congress.	Session.	How brought before the House of Reps.	Page of journal.	To what committee of the House referred.	No. or date of the report.	Nature of the report.	No. of the bill.	How disposed of by the House of Reps.	How disposed of by the Senate.	Date of the act of Congress, and remarks.
Smith, Ballard, representatives of.	Commutation pay for revolutionary services.	25	2	Petition	49	Rev. Claims	715	Adverse	......	Laid on table.		
Smith, Benjamin, (N. J.)	Indemnity for property destroyed during revolution.	3	1	Petition	91	....	....	....	......	Laid on table.		
Smith, Benjamin, (N. J.)	Indemnity for property destroyed during revolution.	8	2	Petition	133	Claims.						
Smith, Benjamin, (N. J.)	Indemnity for property destroyed during revolution.	9	2	Petition	507	Claims.						
Smith, Benjamin, (N. J.)	Indemnity for property destroyed during revolution.	10	1	Petition	59	Select.						
Smith, Benjamin, (N. J.)	Indemnity for property destroyed during revolution.	11	2	Petition	132	Claims	....	....	......	Discharged.		
Smith, Benjamin, (N. J.)	Indemnity for property destroyed during revolution.	13	3	Petition	696	Pens. & Rev. Cl'ms.						
Smith, Benjamin, (N. J.)	Indemnity for property destroyed during revolution.	15	1	Petition	63	Pens. & Rev. Cl'ms.	Jan. 19, 1818	Adverse	......	Rejected.		
Smith, Benjamin	Pension for revolutionary services.	9	2	Pension bill	608	Whole House	....	....	216	Passed	Passed	App'd March 3, 1807
Smith, Benjamin, (Ohio).	Compensation for property taken for public use.	13	2	Petition	303	Claims	March 7, 1814	Adverse	......	....	....	Leave to withdraw.
Smith, Benjamin, (Ohio).	Compensation for property taken for public use.	13	3	Petition	471	Claims	Nov. 14, 1814	Favorable	228	Passed	Indef. postp'd.	
Smith, Benjamin, (Ohio).	Compensation for property taken for public use.	14	1	Petition	355	Pens. & Rev. Cl'ms.	Mar. 13, 1816	Adverse.	......	Laid on table.		
Smith, Benjamin, (Ohio).	Compensation for property taken for public use.	18	1	Petition	98	Claims	Jan. 16, 1824	Adverse	......	Laid on table.		
Smith, Benjamin	Pension for revolutionary services.	21	1	Resolution	510	Military Pensions.						
Smith, Benjamin	Pension for revolutionary services.	22	1	Resolution	146	Rev. Pensions.						
Smith, Benjamin	Pension for revolutionary services.	23	1	Petition	491	Rev. Pensions	....	....	......	Discharged; laid on table.		
Smith, Benjamin	Pension for revolutionary services.	23	2	Petition	237	Rev. Pensions.						
Smith, Benjamin	Pension for revolutionary services.	24	1	Petition	213	Rev. Pensions	April 12, 1836	Adverse	......	Laid on table.		
Smi h, Benj., and others.	Indemnity for French spoliations prior to 1800.	26	1	Memorial	182	Foreign Affairs	343	Favorable; bill	319	Referred to Committee Whole House.		
Smith, Benjamin A.	Confirmation of title to land in Louisiana.	14	1	Petition	422	Public Lands.						
Smith, Benjamin A.	Confirmation of title to land in Louisiana.	14	2	Petition	60	Priv. Land Claims.						
Smith, Benjamin A	Confirmation of title to land in Louisiana.	15	1	Petition	173	Priv. Land Claims.						
Smith, Benjamin P.	Pension	30	1	Petition	261	Invalid Pensions	....	....	......	Discharged; laid on table.		
Smith, Benjamin P.	Pension	30	2	Petition	263	Invalid Pensions	81	Favorable	777	Referred to Committee Whole House.		
Smith, Benjamin P.	Pension	31	1	Petition	223	Invalid Pensions	48	Favorable	78	Passed	Passed	App'd Aug. 10, 1850
Smith, Bernard	(See H. Boswell, and others.)	18	2	....	55							
Smith, Bernard, and B Desha.	Credit for office rent and fuel	21	1	Petition	378	Public Lands	Mar. 22, 1830	Adverse	......	Laid on table.		
Smith, Beverly	(See heirs of William Smith)	17	2	....	25							
Smith, Bird and Ab'm	Indemnity for Indian depredations.	19	1	Petition	293	Indian Affairs	208	Adverse	......	Laid on table	....	Leave to withdraw, 2d session.
Smith, Bird and Ab'm	Indemnity for Indian depredations.	20	1	Petition	64	Indian Affairs	Jan. 3, 1828	Adverse	......	Laid on table.		
				Petition	419	Claims.						

List of private claims presented to the House of Representatives of the United States from the 1st to the 31st Congress, inclusive—Continued.

Names of claimants.	Nature or object of the claim.	Congress.	Session.	How brought before the House of Reps.	Page of journal.	To what committee of the House referred.	No. or date of the report.	Nature of the report.	No. of the bill.	How disposed of by the House of Reps.	How disposed of by the Senate.	Date of the act of Congress, and remarks.
Smith, Bird and Ab'm	Indemnity for Indian depredations	21	1	Petition	170	Claims.						
				Senate bill	158	Claims	Feb. 24, 1830	With amend.	S. 18	Passed with amendm't.	Passed as am'd	App'd May 31, 1830
Smith, Bird and Ab'm	Indemnity for Indian depredations	22	2	Petition	313	Indian Affairs.						
Smith, Byrd	(See Eppler Smith, and others)	19	2		132							
Smith, Bryant	Pension	28	2	Resolution	132	Rev. Pensions.						
Smith, Caleb	Reimbursement of certain payments	31	1	Petition	1189	Claims.						
Smith, Caleb	Reimbursement of certain payments	31	2	Petition	69	Claims.						
Smith, Calvin	Confirmation of title to land in Mississippi.	19	1	Senate bill	474	Priv. Land Claims.	May 17, 1826	With't amend.	S. 79	Laid on table.		
Smith, Calvin	Confirmation of title to land in Mississippi.	19	2	Senate bill	77	Priv. Land Claims.			S. 12			
Smith, Calvin	Confirmation of title to land in Mississippi.	22	2	Senate bill	228	Claims			S. 52			
Smith, Calvin	Confirmation of title to land in Mississippi.	23	1	Senate bill	390	Priv. Land Claims.	Jan. 27, 1834	With't amend.	S. 35	Rejected.		
Smith, Campbell	Compensation for judicial services.	5	2	Memorial	478	Claims	March 2, 1799	Adverse				Leave to withdraw.
Smith, Campbell	Compensation for judicial services.	6	1	Petition	535	Claims	Feb. 21, 1800	Favorable; bill ordered.	209	Passed	Passed	App'd Mar. 29, 1800
Smith, Catharine	(See Ebenezer Smith, widow of.)	25	2		1209							
Smith, Catharine M.	(See Thomas D. Smith, widow of)	24	1		507							
Smith, Charles	Compensation for revolutionary services.	15	1	Petition	26	Pens. & Rev. Cl'ms.	Dec. 23, 1817	Adverse		Rejected.		
Smith, Charles	(See executors of Larkin Smith).	23	1		40							
Smith, Charles	Indemnity for sufferings in Turkey	29	1	Memorial	682	Naval Affairs	740	Adverse		Laid on table.		
Smith, Charles	Indemnity for sufferings in Turkey	30	1	Petition	206	Naval Affairs.						
Smith, Charles, widow of.	Pension	28	2	Resolution	292	Invalid Pensions						Leave to withdraw, 30th Con., 1st sess., page 671.
Smith, Charles, representatives of.	Commutation pay for revolutionary services.	30	1	Petition	263	Rev. Claims	769	Favorable	603	Referred to Committee Whole House.		
Smith, Charles, & others.	Compensation for horses taken for public use.	25	2	Petition	397	Claims	838	Adverse		Laid on table.		
Smith, Charles, (Mass.)	Indemnity for French spoliations prior to 1800.	26	1	Memorial	182	Foreign Affairs	343	Favorable; bill	319	Referred to Committee Whole House.		
Smith, Charles H.	Compensation for his land sold by government.	26	1	Petition	333	Public Lands				Discharged; laid on table.		
Smith, Charles K.	(See Nathan and C. K. Smith)	29	1		89							
Smith, Charles P., & others	Bounty land for services in Florida war.	31	1	Petition	996	Public Lands	246	Favorable	244	Referred to Committee Whole House.		
Smith, Christian	Pension for revolutionary services.	10	2	Pension bill	499	Whole House			158	Passed	Passed, with amendment.	App'd March 3, 1809
Smith, Daniel	(See Abijah Barnum and others).	8	1		446							
Smith, Daniel	Pension	20	2	Petition	26	Military Pensions				Discharged; laid on table.		
Smith, Daniel	Pension	21	1	Petition	36	Military Pensions				Discharged; laid on table.		
Smith, Daniel	Patent for land he has paid for	23	1	Petition	499	Priv. Land Claims.	543	Favorable	546	Ref'd to Com. W. H.		
Smith, Daniel	Patent for land he has paid for	24	1	Petition	65	Priv. Land Claims.	69	Favorable	84	Passed	Passed	App'd June 23, 1836
Smith, Daniel, (Pa.)	(See Pennsylvania Insurance Company.)	26	1		182							
Smith, Daniel	(See heirs of Amos Smith)	27	2		320							
Smith, Daniel	Indemnity for French spoliations prior to 1800.	26	1	Memorial	182	Foreign Affairs	343	Favorable; bill	319	Referred to Committee Whole House.		

List of private claims presented to the House of Representatives of the United States from the 1st to the 31st Congress, inclusive—Continued.

Names of claimants.	Nature or object of the claim.	Congress.	Session.	How brought before the House of Reps.	Page of journal.	To what committee of the House referred.	No. or date of the report.	Nature of the report.	No. of the bill.	How disposed of by the House of Reps.	How disposed of by the Senate.	Date of the act of Congress, and remarks.
Smith, David, jr	Permission to import merchandise ordered prior to president's proclamation.	12	1	Petition	97	Com. and Manuf.						
Smith, David	Confirmation of title to land in Missouri.	15	1	Petition	157	Priv. Land Claims.						
Smith, David, (N. H.)	Pension	20	1	Petition	92	Military Pensions.				Discharged; laid on table.		
Smith, David, (Ohio)	Pension	21	1	Petition	294	Military Pensions.						
Smith, David, (Ohio)	Pension	21	2	Petition	95	Military Pensions.	48	Favorable	582	Passed.		
Smith, David, (Ohio)	Pension	22	1	Petition	45	Rev. Pensions	Dec. 21, 1831	Favorable	66	Passed	Indef. postp'd.	
Smith, David, (N. Y.)	Bounty land for revolutionary services.	21	1	Petition	84	Rev. Claims	Feb. 15, 1830	Adverse		Laid on table.		
Smith, David	(See represent's of Robert Smith)	23	1		128							
Smith, David	Arrears of pension	24	1	Petition	127	Invalid Pensions	June 23, 1836	Adverse		Laid on table.		
Smith, David N	Pension	30	1	Senate bill	913	Invalid Pensions	July 19, 1848	With't amend	S. 135	Passed	Passed	App'd Aug. 11, 1848
Smith, David N	Arrears of pension	31	1	Senate bill	1206	Rev. Pensions			S. 236	Referred to Committee Whole House.		
Smith, Desassure & Darrell	Indemnity for French spoliations prior to 1800.	26	1	Memorial	182	Foreign Affairs	343	Favorable; bill	319	Referred to Committee Whole House.		
Smith, Ebenezer A	Compensation for revolutionary services and supplies.	1	3	Petition and rep't Sec. of War.	349, 385					Laid on table.		
Smith, Ebenezer	Pension	15	1	Petition	230	Pens. & Rev. Cl'ms.				Discharged; referred to Secretary War.		
Smith, Ebenezer	Pension	23	1	Petition	436	Invalid Pensions				Discharged; laid on table.		
Smith, Ebenezer	Pension	23	2	Petition	147	Invalid Pensions				Discharged; laid on table.		
Smith, Ebenezer	Pension	24	1	Petition	98	Invalid Pensions				Discharged; laid on table.		
Smith, Ebenezer, (Catharine,) widow of.	Pension for revolutionary services.	25	2	Petition	1209	Rev. Pensions.						
Smith, Ebenezer, (Catharine,) widow of.	Pension for revolutionary services.	26	1	Petition	175	Rev. Pensions				Discharged; laid on table.		
Smith, Ebenezer, (Jenny,) widow of.	Pension for revolutionary services.	26	1	Petition	198	Rev. Pensions				Discharged; laid on table.		
Smith, Edmond	Increase of pension	21	1	Senate bill	646	Military Pensions	May 22, 1830	With amend	S. 137	Referred to Committee Whole House.		
Smith, Edmond	Increase of pension	21	2	Senate bill	79	Military Pensions			S. 1			
Smith, Edmund	Pension for revolutionary disabilities.	3	1	Rep. of Secretary War.	131	Select	May 26, 1794	Res. to refer to Sec'ry War.	J. R. 12	Passed	Passed	App'd June 9, 1794
Smith, Edmund	Pension for revolutionary disabilities.	3	2	Report Secretary of War.	262	Claims	Feb. 28, 1795	Pension bill	130	Passed	Postponed.	
Smith, Edmund	Pension for revolutionary disabilities.	4	1	Rep. of Secretary of War.	445	Claims	Feb. 18, 1796	Pension bill	156	Passed	Passed	App'd April 20, 1796
Smith, Edner, or Edna	(See Richard Smith, widow of)	27	2		320							
Smith, Edward	(See Conrad Houseman.)											
Smith, Edward	(See executors of Philip Bush)	15	2		138							
Smith, Edward	Compensation for work, &c., on Cumberland road.	23	1	Res. and docs	589	Claims	455	Adverse				See report No. 449.
Smith, Edward	(See Smith & Wood)	26	1		182							
Smith, Edward	Pension for services in Indian wars.	29	1	Petition	226	Rev. Pensions	431	Adverse		Laid on table.		
Smith, Eli	Pension for revolutionary services.	20	2	Petition	64	Military Pensions	Feb. 13, 1839	Favorable	440	Passed	Reported with amendment.	

List of private claims presented to the House of Representatives of the United States from the 1st to the 31st Congress, inclusive—Continued.

Names of claimants.	Nature or object of the claim.	Congress.	Session.	How brought before the House of Reps.	Page of journal.	To what committee of the House referred.	No. or date of the report.	Nature of the report.	No. of the bill.	How disposed of by the House of Reps.	How disposed of by the Senate.	Date of the act of Congress, and remarks.
Smith, Eli	Pension for revolutionary services.	21	2	Resolution	42	Military Pensions.	58	Favorable	596	Passed.		
Smith, Eli	Pension for revolutionary services.	22	1	Resolution	93	Rev. Pensions	365	Favorable	460	Passed	Indef. postp'd.	
Smith, Elijah	Confirmation of title to land in Missouri.	15	1	Petition	280	Priv. Land Claims.						
Smith, Elijah	(See heirs of John Ellis)	19	1		134							
Smith, Elijah	Pension for revolutionary services.	28	1	Petition	435	Rev. Pensions.						
Smith, Elijah, heirs of	Compensation for revolutionary services and losses.	30	1	Petition	264	Rev. Pensions.						
Smith, Elisha	Indemnity for loss in transportation of the mail.	23	1	Petition	217	P. Of. & P. Roads.	Feb. 14, 1834	Adverse		Laid on table.		
Smith, Elisha	Indemnity for loss in transportation of the mail.	24	1	Petition	210	P. Of. & P. Roads.						
Smith, Elisha	Extra compensation for mail service.	24	2	Petition	42	P. Of. & P. Roads.	231	Adverse		Laid on table.		
Smith, Elisha	Extra compensation for mail service.	25	2	Petition	93	P. Of. & P. Roads.				Discharged; laid on table.		
Smith, Elliott	Compensation for saving the lives of United States troops.	25	2	Petition	408	Commerce.						
Smith, Elliott	Compensation for saving the lives of United States troops.	25	3	Petition	118	Commerce.	239	Favorable	1101	Referred to Committee Whole House.		
Smith, Elliott	Compensation for saving the lives of United States troops.	26	1	Petition	176	Commerce	35	Favorable	55	Passed	Indef. postp'd.	
Smith, Elliott	Compensation for saving the lives of United States troops.	26	2	Petition	38	Claims.						
Smith, Elliott	Compensation for saving the lives of United States troops.	27	2	Petition	57	Commerce	474	Favorable	324	Passed.		
Smith, Elliott	Compensation for saving the lives of United States troops.	27	3	Petition	45	Commerce.						
Smith, Elliott	Compensation for saving the lives of United States troops.	28	1	Petition	117	Commerce	195	Favorable	152	Referred to Committee Whole House.		
Smith, Elliott	Compensation for saving the lives of United States troops.	28	2	Bill of last sess.	343	Whole House	Feb. 7, 1845	With't amend.	152	Passed	Indef. postp'd.	
Smith, Elliott	Compensation for saving the lives of United States troops.	30	1	Petition	1025	Commerce	811	Favorable	632	Referred to Committee Whole House.		
Smith, Elliott	Compensation for saving the lives of United States troops.	31	1	Petition	500	Commerce	268	Adverse		Laid on table.		
Smith, Elevily	Pension for revolutionary services.	22	2	Resolution	186	Rev. Pensions				Discharged; laid on table.		
Smith, E. Goodrich	Compensation for extra services as clerk in patent office.	29	2	Petition	49	Patents	74	Favorable	686	Referred to Committee Whole House.		
Smith, E. Goodrich	Compensation for extra services as clerk in patent office.	30	1	Petition	66	Patents	31	Favorable	31	Passed	Passed	App'd Aug. 5, 1848
Smith, E. Kirby, widow of.	Increase of pension	31	1	Petition	595	Rev. Pensions	206	Favorable	215	Referred to Committee Whole House.		
Smith, E. Kirby, widow of.	Increase of pension	31	2	Bill of last sess.	181	Whole House	Jan. 24, 1851	With't amend.	215	Passed.		
Smith, E. W. & H	Compensation for erecting a custom-house.	25	2	Senate bill	785	Claims	April 20, 1838	With't amend.	S. 193	Referred to Committee Whole House.		
Smith, E. W. & H	Compensation for erecting a custom-house.	26	1	Senate bill	811	Claims	April 24, 1840	With't amend.	S. 104	Referred to Committee Whole House.		
Smith, Elvira T	(See Maj. Henry Smith, widow of)	30	1		111							
Smith, Eppler, and others.	(Nature of claim not stated)	19	2	Petition	132	Claims.						
Smith, Erastus	Indemnity for French spoliations prior to 1800.	26	1	Memorial	182	Foreign Affairs	343	Favorable; bill	319	Referred to Committee Whole House.		

List of private claims presented to the House of Representatives of the United States from the 1st to the 31st Congress, inclusive—Continued.

Names of claimants.	Nature or object of the claim.	Congress.	Session.	How brought before the House of Reps.	Page of journal.	To what committee of the House referred.	No. or date of the report.	Nature of the report.	No. of the bill.	How disposed of by the House of Reps.	How disposed of by the Senate.	Date of the act of Congress, and remarks.
Smith, Eunice	(See Preserved Smith, widow of)	27	2		612							
Smith, Ezra	Indemnity for losses during revolutionary war.	1	2	Petition & report Sec. of War.	142, 153	Select	April 5, 1790	General bill	53	Passed.		
Smith, Francis N., widow of.	Compensation due to widows of soldiers dying in the public service.	15	1	Petition	237	Military Affairs	Mar. 13, 1818	Legislation unnecessary.		Report adopted.		
Smith, Francis, (Va.)	Indemnity for French spoliations prior to 1800.	26	1	Memorial	182	Foreign Affairs	343	Favorable; bill	319	Referred to Committee Whole House.		
Smith, Frederick W	Pay and emolument for services, United States navy.	19	2	Petition	154	Naval Affairs.						
				Petition	216	Naval Affairs	Feb. 5, 1827	Adverse		Laid on table.		
Smith, Frederick W	Indemnity for loss on treasury notes.	26	1	Petition	1007	Naval Affairs.						
Smith, Frederick W	Indemnity for loss on treasury notes.	26	2	Petition	79	Claims.						
Smith, Frederick W., heirs of.	Indemnity for loss on treasury notes.	27	2	Petition	669	Claims	1014	Favorable	587	Referred to Committee Whole House.		
Smith, Frederick W., heirs of.	Indemnity for loss on treasury notes.	27	3	Bill of last sess.	91	Whole House	Dec. 23, 1842	With't amend.	587	Passed	Indef. postp'd.	
Smith, Frederick W., heirs of.	Indemnity for loss on treasury notes.	28	1	Petition	1024	Claims	562	Adverse		Laid on table.		
Smith, Frederick	(See heirs of Jeremiah Goodall)	25	2		178							
Smith, Frederick	Exchange of a bounty land location.	26	1	Petition	797	Public Lands.						
Smith, Frederick	Exchange of a bounty land location.	27	3	Petition	351	Priv. Land Claims.						
Smith, Gamaliel E	Additional compensation for building light-house.	23	3	Petition	163	Claims.						
Smith, Gamaliel E	Additional compensation for building light-house.	24	1	Petition	474	Claims	567	Adverse; recommitted.		Discharged; laid on table.		
Smith, Gamaliel E	Additional compensation for building light-house.	24	2	Petition	72	Claims.						
Smith, Gamaliel E	Additional compensation for building light-house.	25	2	Petition	121	Claims	1065	Favorable		Referred to Secretary Treasury.		
Smith, Gamaliel E	Additional compensation for building light-house.	25	3	Rep. of Secretary Treasury.	249	Claims.						
Smith, Gamaliel E	Additional compensation for building light-house.	26	1	Petition	168	Claims	18	Favorable	37	Passed	Passed	App'd May 2, 1840
Smith, Gamaliel E	Additional compensation for building light-house.	27	1	Petition	95	Commerce.						
Smith, Gamaliel E	Additional compensation for building light-house.	27	2	Petition	313	Commerce.						
Smith, Gamaliel E	Additional compensation for building light-house.	27	3	Petition	43	Claims	78	Favorable	706	Passed	Passed	App'd March 3, 1843
Smith, George	Indemnity for revolutionary losses.	1	2	Petition	173					Laid on table.		
Smith, George	Reimbursement of money paid for ransom.	4	2	Memorial & rep't Sec. of State.	704, 725	Select	Feb. 28, 1797	Favorable; bill ordered.	242	Passed	Passed	App'd March 3, 1797
Smith, George	Arrears of pay due for revolutionary services.	15	1	Petition	89	Pens. & Rev. Cl'ms.	Feb. 18, 1818	Adverse		Rejected.		
Smith, George	(See executors of William Findley)	17	1		388							
Smith, George	Pension for revolutionary services.	23	2	Petition	272	Rev. Pensions				Discharged; laid on table.		
Smith, George, administrator of.	Correction of an error in award under Florida treaty.	24	2	Memorial	399	Foreign Affairs.						
Smith, George B	(See Lewis Ratcliffe, and others.)	26	1		606							

List of private claims presented to the House of Representatives of the United States from the 1st to the 31st Congress, inclusive—**Continued.**

Names of claimants.	Nature or object of the claim.	Congress.	Session.	How brought before the House of Reps.	Page of journal.	To what committee of the House referred.	No. or date of the report.	Nature of the report.	No. of the bill.	How disposed of by the House of Reps.	How disposed of by the Senate.	Date of the act of Congress, and remarks.
Smith, George R	Additional compensation for mail service.	29	1	Memorial	752	P. Of. & P. Roads.	717	Favorable	R. 39	Referred to Committee Whole House.		
Smith, George R	Additional compensation for mail service.	30	1	Petition	110	P. Of. & P. Roads.	103	Favorable	R. 7	Passed	Passed, second session.	App'd March 3, 1849
Smith, George R	Additional compensation for mail service.	31	1	Petition	858	P. Of. & P. Roads.						
Smith, George P	Credit for vouchers lost in Mexico.	30	1	Petition	676	Military Affairs.						
Smith, George P	Credit for vouchers lost in Mexico.	31	1	Petition	971	Military Affairs.						
Smith, George P	Credit for vouchers lost in Mexico.	31	2	Petition	145	Military Affairs	25	Favorable	469	Referred to Committee Whole House.		
Smith, George W	Compensation for extra services at the navy-yard, Memphis.	31	1	Petition	836	Naval Affairs.						
Smith, Gerard D	Arrears of pension	18	1	Petition	134	Pens. & Rev. Cl'ms	Jan. 27, 1824	Adverse	......	Laid on table.		
Smith, Gerard D	Arrears of pension	18	2	Petition	36	Pens. & Rev. Cl'ms.	Dec. 20, 1814	Adverse	......	Laid on table.		
Smith, Gerard D	Arrears of pension	21	1	Petition	67	Military Pensions.						
Smith, Gideon, widow of	Pension for revolutionary services.	25	3	Petition	127	Rev. Pensions	Jan. 16, 1839	Adverse	......	Laid on table.		
Smith, Gilbert A., & others.	Bounty on fishing schooner Lilly.	23	2	Petition	272	Commerce	87	Favorable	709	Referred to Committee Whole House.		
Smith, Gilbert A., & others.	Bounty on fishing schooner Lilly.	24	1	House bill	130	Whole House	Feb. 27, 1836	With't amend.	77	Passed	Indef. postp'd.	
Smith, Gilbert A., & others.	Bounty on fishing schooner Lilly.	25	2	Petition	41	Commerce.						
				Petition	165	Commerce	234	Favorable	274	Referred to Committee Whole House.		
Smith, Gilbert A., & others.	Bounty on fishing schooner Lilly.	25	3	Bill of last sess.	376	Whole House	Jan. 25, 1839	With't amend.	274	Passed	Adverse report.	
Smith, Gilbert A., & others.	Bounty on fishing schooner Lilly.	26	1	Petition	176	Commerce	75	Favorable	62	Passed	Passed, with amendment.	App'd July 20, 1840
Smith, Green, & Co	Payment of claims against Ottawa Indians.	29	1	Memorial	160	Indian Affairs.	287	Adverse	......	Laid on table.		
Smith, Guy	(See Eppler Smith, and others.)	19	2	....	132							
Smith, Guy W	Indemnity for losses while land officer.	22	1	Senate bill	745	Claims	May 28, 1832	With amend.	S. 92	Passed with amendm't	Passed as am'd	App'd July 14, 1832
Smith, Hannah	(See heir of John Wain)	27	3	....	259							
Smyth, Harold	Equitable settlement of accounts as quartermaster.	15	1	Resolution	308	Military Affairs	Mar. 16, 1818	Favorable	144	Referred to Committee Whole House.		
Smyth, Harold	Equitable settlement of accounts as quartermaster.	15	2	Bill of last sess.	142	Whole House	Dec. 29, 1818	With't amend.	144	Passed	Passed	App'd March 3, 1819
Smith, Harriet M	(See heirs of Jacob Smith)	23	2	....	392							
Smith, Harry	Compensation for revolutionary services.	22	2	Petition	219	Rev. Claims.						
Smith, Heber	Pension	3	1	Rep. of Secretary War.	131	Select	May 26, 1794	res. to refer to Sec. of War.	R. 12	Passed	Passed	App'd June 9, 1794
Smith, Heber	Pension	4	1	Rep. of Secretary War.	445	Claims	Feb. 18, 1796	Favorable	156	Passed	Passed	App'd April 20, 1796
Smith, Heber	Pension	12	1	House bill	361	Whole House	June 15, 1812	With amend.	138	Passed	Passed, with amendment.	App'd July 5, 1812
Smith, Henry, and others.	Remission of duty on tea destroyed by fire.	6	2	House bill	825	Whole House	....	....	320	Passed	Passed	App'd March 3, 1801
Smith, Henry, (Md.)	Pension	23	1	Petition	128	Invalid Pensions	Feb. 21, 1834	Adverse	......	Laid on table.		
Smith, Captain Henry	Compensation for disbursing public money.	24	1	Petition	354	Military Pensions.						
Smith, Henry, widow of	Pension for services of deceased in Mexico.	30	1	Petition	111	Invalid Pensions.						
Smith, Henry, heir of	Compensation for revolutionary services.	30	1	Petition	397	Rev. Claims	739	Favorable	540	Referred to Committee Whole House.		

List of private claims presented to the House of Representatives of the United States from the 1st to the 31st Congress, inclusive—Continued.

Names of claimants.	Nature or object of the claim.	Congress.	Session.	How brought before the House of Reps.	Page of journal.	To what committee of the House referred.	No. or date of the report.	Nature of the report.	No. of the bill.	How disposed of by the House of Reps.	How disposed of by the Senate.	Date of the act of Congress, and remarks.
Smith, Henry, heir of....	Compensation for revolutionary services.	30	2	Bill of last sess..	319	Whole House	Jan. 26, 1849	With't amend.	540	Passed.		
Smith, Henry, heir of....	Compensation for revolutionary services.	31	1	Petition	680	Rev. Claims......	431	Favorable....	359	Referred to Committee Whole House.		
Smith & Henry.........	Remission of duty on molasses...	30	2	Petition	530	Commerce.						
Smith & Henry.........	Remission of duty on molasses...	31	1	Petition	406	Commerce	80	Favorable....	96	Passed	Passed	App'd May 24, 1850
Smith, Hopkin..........	Indemnity for property destroyed, revolutionary war.	3	1	Memorial	124	....	....	....	......	Laid on table.		
Smith, Hopkin..........	Indemnity for property destroyed, revolutionary war.	6	1	Petition	578	Claims	Feb. 14, 1800	Adverse.	......	Leave to withdraw.		
Smith, Horace..........	Indemnity for enlisment of his minor son.	31	1	Petition	1081	Judiciary.						
Smith, Hugh...........	Release from liability as surety ...	11	2	Petition	169	Com. and Manuf..	April 7, 1810	Favorable.				
Smith, Hugh...........	Release from liability as surety ...	12	1	Petition	39	Com. and Manuf.						
Smith, Hugh, heirs of....	Bounty land for revolutionary services.	18	1	Petition	82	Public Lands.						
Smith, Hugh, heirs of....	Bounty land for revolutionary services.	19	2	....	78	Priv. Land Claims.	Dec. 26, 1826	Adverse	......	Laid on table.		
Smith, Hugh, heirs of....	Bounty land for revolutionary services.	20	1	Petition	40	Priv. Land Claims.	54	Favorable....	50	Passed	Passed	App'd April 17, 1828
Smith, Hugh G.........	Pension	30	1	Petition	148	Invalid Pensions ..	....	....	......	Discharged; laid on table.		
Smith, Hugh...........	(See Joseph Dean, executor and attorney of.)	26	1	....	182							
Smith, Huldah..........	(See Aaron Smith, widow of.)...	27	2	....	320							
Smith, Ichabod	Pension for revolutionary services.	21	2	Resolution	124	Military Pensions.						
Smith, Ichabod	Pension for revolutionary services.	22	1	Resolution	70	Rev. Pensions.						
Smith, Isaac...........	Indemnity for French spoliations prior to 1800.	26	1	Memorial	182	Foreign Affairs....	343	Favorable; bill	319	Referred to Committee Whole House.		
Smith, Isaac............	Release from a judgment as surety.	13	2	Petition	336	Ways and Means.						
Smith, Isaac............	Release from a judgment as surety.	13	3	Petition	509	Ways and Means..	43	Favorable....	261	Passed	Passed	App'd Feb. 22, 1815
Smith, Isaac, surety of ...	Release from judgment on a duty bond.	25	3	Petition	265	Ways and Means.						
Smith, Isaac, surety of ...	Release from judgment on a duty bond.	26	1	Petition	178	Ways and Means..	579	Adverse	......	Laid on table.		
Smith, Israel	Credit for erroneous charge of four hundred dollars.	15	1	Petition	84	Claims	Jan. 28, 1818	Favorable....	60	Passed	Passed	App'd Mar. 18, 1818
Smith, Jabez	Indemnity for destruction of property on frontier.	15	2	Petition	58	Pens. & Rev. Cl'ms.	....	....	......	Discharged; referred to Secretary of War.		
Smith, Jabez, (Conn)....	Pension	19	1	Petition	105	Military Pensions..	164	Adverse	......	Laid on table.		
Smith, Jabez	Pension	29	1	Documents.....	68	Claims	395	Adverse......	......	Laid on table.		
Smith, Jacob	Relief in consideration of revolutionary disability.	1	2	Petition and rep't of Sec. War.	234, 247	....	....	....	......	Laid on table.		
Smith, Jacob	(See heirs of Maj. Charles Motte.)	2	1	....	440							
Smith, Jacob, (Ohio)....	(See Lewis Moore, and others)...	19	2	Documents.....	105	Claims	Jan. 24, 1827	Adverse	......	Laid on table.		
Smith, Jacob, (La.)......	Equitable adjustment of a claim..	23	1	Petition	438	Claims..........	557	Adverse	......	Laid on table.		
Smith, Jacob, heirs of....	Confirmation of title to land in Michigan.	23	2	Petition	392	Priv. Land Claims.	Feb. 24, 1835	Favorable....	762	Passed	Reported with amendment.	
Smith, Jacob, heirs of....	Confirmation of title to land in Michigan.	24	1	Petition	168	Priv. Land Claims.	101	Favorable....	116	Passed	Passed	App'd June 23, 1836
Smith, Jacob, son of.....	Compensation for goods furnished Chippewa Indians.	28	1	Petition	482	Indian Affairs.						

List of private claims presented to the House of Representatives of the United States from the 1st to the 31st Congress, inclusive—Continued.

Names of claimants.	Nature or object of the claim.	Congress.	Session.	How brought before the House of Reps.	Page of journal.	To what committee of the House referred.	No. or date of the report.	Nature of the report.	No. of the bill.	How disposed of by the House of Reps.	How disposed of by the Senate.	Date of the act of Congress, and remarks.
Smith, James, heirs of....	Indemnity for slaves stolen by Indians.	3	1	Petition	32	Select..........	Jan. 20, 1794	Adverse	......	Laid on table.		
Smith, James..........	Pension for revolutionary services.	3	2	Rep. of Secretary War.	337	Claims	Feb. 28, 1795	Favorable; bill ordered.	130	Passed	Postponed.	
Smith, James..........	Pension for revolutionary services.	4	1	Rep't of Secretary War.	445	Claims	Feb. 18, 1796	Favorable; bill ordered.	156	Passed	Passed	App'd April 20, 1796
Smith, James..........	(See assignee of William Ballard.)	7	1	....	109							
Smyth, James	(See Maryland hospital at Baltimore.)	14	1	....	421							
Smith, James..........	Compensation for horse taken for public use.	14	1	Petition	83	Claims.						
Smith, James..........	Compensation for horse taken for public use.	20	2	Petition	230	Claims.						
Smith, James..........	Compensation for horse taken for public use.	21	1	Petition	99	Claims	64	Favorable	88	Passed	Passed	App'd May 28, 1830
Smith, James.........	Pension for revolutionary services.	15	2	Petition	168	Rev. Pensions.						
Smith, James P.........	(See representatives of Ambrose D. Smith.)	15	2	....	63							
Smith, James..........	Equitable settlement of accounts as paymaster.	17	1	Petition	114	Claims.						
Smith, James..........	Equitable settlement of accounts as paymaster.	17	2	Petition	26	Claims	Dec. 20, 1822	Favorable	203	Passed in Committee Whole House.		
Smith, James..........	Equitable settlement of accounts as paymaster.	18	1	Petition	145	Claims..........	....	....	......	Discharged; leave to withdraw.	....	See MS. report, vol. 5, p. 374.
Smith, James..........	Indemnity for losses while government vaccine agent.	19	1	Documents.....	90	Select	Mar. 9, 1826	Bill to encourage vaccination.	145	Referred to Committee Whole House.		
Smith, James..........	(See sureties of Samuel Smith) ..	24	1	....	53							
Smith, James F.........	Indemnity for destruction of property in Black Hawk war.	24	1	Documents.....	206	Claims.						
Smith, James F.........	Indemnity for destruction of property in Black Hawk war.	24	2	Petition and docs.	48	Judiciary.........	Feb. 28, 1837	Favorable	961	Referred to Committee Whole House.		
Smith, James F.........	(See Thomas McClelland and J. Smith.)	25	2	....	41							
Smith, James Y.........	Compensation for steamboat service.	26	1	Petition	337	Claims.						
Smith, James Y.........	Compensation for steamboat service.	30	1	Petition	711	Claims..........	666	Favorable	530	Referred to Committee Whole House.		
Smith, James Y.........	Compensation for steamboat service.	30	2	Bill of last sess..	318	Whole House.....	Jan. 26, 1849	With't amend.	530	Passed	Passed	App'd Feb. 26, 1849
Smith, James..........	Pension	25	2	Res. and docs...	188	Invalid Pensions ..	424	Favorable....	431	Passed	Adverse report.	
Smith, James..........	Pension	26	1	Petition	162	Invalid Pensions ..	203	Favorable	215	Passed	Indef. postp'd.	
Smith, James, widow of ..	Pension for revolutionary services.	28	1	Petition	901	Rev. Pensions.						
Smith, James, widow of ..	Pension for revolutionary services.	29	1	Petition	1139	Rev. Pensions.						
Smith, James, widow of ..	Pension for revolutionary services.	29	2	Petition	86	Rev. Pensions.....	44	Adverse	......	Laid on table.		
Smith, James, widow of ..	Pension for revolutionary services	30	1	Petition	628	Rev. Pensions	697	Adverse	......	Laid on table.		
Smith, James, widow of ..	Pension for revolutionary services.	31	1	Petition	361	Rev. Pensions.						
Smith, James..........	(See Thomas McClelland and J. J. Smith.)	25	2	....	41	....	....	....	......	....	....	See James F. Smith.
Smith, James, (Ark.)	Right of pre-emption to land in Arkansas.	26	1	Senate bill	813	Priv. Land Claims.	June 23, 1840	With't amend.	S. 197			

List of private claims presented to the House of Representatives of the United States from the 1st to the 31st Congress, inclusive—Continued.

Names of claimants.	Nature or object of the claim.	Congress.	Session.	How brought before the House of Reps.	Page of journal.	To what committee of the House referred.	No. or date of the report.	Nature of the report.	No. of the bill.	How disposed of by the House of Reps.	How disposed of by the Senate.	Date of the act of Congress, and remarks.
Smith, James, (Ark.)	Right of pre-emption to land in Arkansas.	26	2	Senate bill	99	Priv. Land Claims.	....	....	S. 20			
Smith, James, (Ark.)	Right of pre-emption to land in Arkansas.	27	2	Senate bill	87	Public Lands	Feb. 9, 1842	With amend.	S. 16	Passed with amendm't.	Passed as am'd.	App'd April 14, 1842
Smith, James	Further compensation for services as a spy.	27	2	Petition	376	Military Affairs.						
Smith, James	Further compensation for services as a spy.	28	1	Petition	136	Rev. Pensions.						
Smith, James	(See Benjamin Kerlin)	28	2	....	420							
Smith, James	(See Samuel and James Smith)	31	1	....	644							
Smith, James, and others	Additional compensation for naval services.	28	2	Petition	60	Naval Affairs.						
Smith, Jared, widow of	Pension for revolutionary services.	26	1	Resolution	386	Rev. Pensions.						
				Documents	624	Rev. Pensions	664	Adverse	....	Laid on table.		
Smith, J. M	(See L. T. Pease and J. M. Smith.)	28	2	....	135	....	191					
Smith, Capt. J. M	(See Capt. B. F. Hill, *et al*)	31	1	....	1012							
Smith, Jedediah	Pension for revoluntioary services.	3	1	Rep. of Secretary War.	131	Select	May 26, 1794	Res. to refer to Sec. War.	J. R. 12	Passed	Passed	App'd June 9, 1794
Smith, Jedediah	Pension for revolutionary services.	4	1	Rep. of Secretary War.	156	Claims	Feb. 18, 1796	General pension bill.	156	Passed	Passed	App'd April 20, 1796
Smith, Jennett	(See Capt. Eben'r Smith, widow of)	26	1	....	198							
Smith, Jeremiah	(See attorney of David Grant)	4	1	....	383							
Smith, Jeremiah	(See attorney of William Laken)	4	1	....	383							
Smith, Jeremiah	(See Wm. Tilghman and others.)	7	2	....	307							
Smith, Jeremiah	Restoration to pension roll	17	1	Petition	30	Rev. Pensions.						
Smith, Jeremiah, jr	Compensation for a house destroyed while in public use.	25	2	Memorial	402	Territories.						
Smith, Jeremiah, jr	Compensation for a house destroyed while in public use.	26	1	Memorial	352	Territories	Mar. 5, 1840	Favorable	117	Referred to Committee Whole House.		
Smith, Jeremiah, jr	Compensation for a house destroyed while in public use.	26	2	Documents	124	Claims.						
				Bill of last sess.	194	Whole House	Jan. 16, 1841	Adverse	117	Rejected.		
Smith, Jeremiah, jr	Compensation for a house destroyed while in public use.	27	2	Memorial	713	Claims.						
Smith, Jeremiah, jr	Compensation for a house destroyed while in public use.	27	3	Memorial	73	Territories.						
Smith, Jeremiah, jr	Compensation for a house destroyed while in public use.	28	1	Memorial	449	Territories.						
Smith, Jeremiah, jr	Payment of $4,000 by terms of Indian treaty.	28	2	Petition	144	Claims	148	Adverse	....	Laid on table	....	See schedule to Sac & Fox treaty, June 17, 1844.
Smith, Jeremiah	Pension for revolutionary services.	31	2	Petition	53	Rev. Pensions	54	Adverse	....	Laid on table.		
Smith, Jerusha	(See children of the widow of Samuel Lucas.)	27	2	....	613							
Smith, Lt. Jesse, widow of	Relief in consideration of the services of deceased.	22	1	Petition	114	Naval Affairs.						
Smith, Lt. Jesse, widow of	Pension	23	1	Memorial	73	Naval Affairs.						
Smith, Jesse	(See assignees of Thomas Tupper)	22	2	....	142							
Smith, Joanna	(See Shadrach Smith, widow of)	25	3	....	216							
Smith, Job T	Arrears of pension	22	2	Petition	310	Rev. Pensions	....	....	....	Discharged; laid on table.		
Smith, Job T., widow of	Arrears of pension	24	2	Petition	217	Rev. Pensions	....	....	....	Discharged; laid on table.		

List of private claims presented to the House of Representatives of the United States from the 1st to the 31st Congress, inclusive—Continued.

Names of claimants.	Nature or object of the claim.	Congress.	Session.	How brought before the House of Reps.	Page of journal.	To what committee of the House referred.	No. or date of the report.	Nature of the report.	No. of the bill.	How disposed of by the House of Reps.	How disposed of by the Senate.	Date of the act of Congress, and remarks.
Smith, Job T., attorney of	Indemnity for French spoliations prior to 1800.	26	1	Memorial	182	Foreign Affairs	343	Favorable; bill	319	Referred to Committee Whole House.		
Smith, Joel M.	Compensation for services as pension agent.	27	2	Petition	524	Rev. Pensions.						
Smith, John, executor of, (Philadelphia.)	Indemnity for French spoliations prior to 1800.	26	1	Memorial	182	Foreign Affairs	343	Favorable; bill	319	Referred to Committee Whole House.		
Smith, John	Extension of the period of payment.	1	2	Petition	173	Select.						
Smith, John	Pension for revolutionary services.	4	1	Rep. of Secretary War.	445	Claims	Feb. 18, 1796	Res. to refer to Sec. War.	R. 16	Passed	Passed	App'd April 18, 1796
Smith, John, (Pa.)	Compensation for team captured by the enemy.	2	1	Petition	518							
				Rep. of Secretary Treasury.	518	....	....	....	......	Laid on table.		
Smith, John	Pension for revolutionary services.	4	1	Rep of Secretary War.	445	Claims.						
Smith, John	Pension for revolutionary services.	4	2	Rep. of Secretary War.	614	Claims.						
Smith, John	Pension for revolutionary services.	11	2	Pension bill	283	....	....	....	107	Passed	Passed, with amendment.	App'd April 27, 1810
Smith, John	(See heirs of Francis Koontz)	5	2	....	210							
Smith, John, agent of, (Ga.)	Indemnity for French spoliations prior to 1800.	26	1	Memorial	182	Foreign Affairs	343	Favorable; bill	319	Referred to Committee Whole House.		
Smith, John, administrator of, (Ala.)	Indemnity for French spoliations prior to 1800.	26	1	Memorial	182	Foreign Affairs	343	Favorable; bill	319	Referred to Committee Whole House.		
Smith, John C.	(See Robert Waln, assignee of)	26	1	....	182							
Smith, John, President of.	(See North American Insurance Company.)	26	1	....	182							
Smith, John	Pension for revolutionary services.	2	2	Petition	623	Select.						
Smith, John	Pension for revolutionary services.	3	1	Rep. of Secretary War.	131	Select	May 26, 1794	Res. to refer to Sec. War.	R. 12	Passed	Passed	App'd June 9, 1794
Smith, John	Pension for revolutionary services.	4	1	Rep. of Secretary War.	445	Claims	Feb. 18, 1796	General pension bill.	156	Passed	Passed	App'd April 20, 1796
Smith, John	(See Northwestern Territory, inhabitants of.)											
Smith, John	Right of pre-emption	7	1	Memorial	164	Select.						
Smith, John	Pension for revolutionary services.	10	2	Pension bill	499	Whole House	....	....	158	Passed	Passed with amendment.	App'd March 3, 1809
Smith, John, (Ky)	Pension for disability in Indian wars.	10	1	Petition	209	Select.						
Smith, John, (Ky)	Pension for disability in Indian wars.	10	2	Petition	376	Claims	....	....	......	Discharged; laid on table.		
Smith, John, (Ky)	Bounty land for services in Indian wars.	23	1	Petition	73	Military Affairs	Jan. 21, 1834	Adverse	......	Laid on table.		
Smith, John, (Ky)	Bounty land for services in Indian wars.	23	2	Petition	164	Rev. Claims.						
Smith, John	Confirmation of title to land in Mississippi Territory.	13	3	Petition	720	Public Lands	....	....	......	Discharged.		
Smith, John	Confirmation of title to land in Mississippi Territory.	14	1	Petition	75	Public Lands.						
Smith, John	Confirmation of title to land in Mississippi Territory.	14	2	Petition	51	Priv. Land Claims.	Jan. 17, 1817	....	......	Discharged; leave to withdraw.		
Smith, John	Remission of an excise penalty	14	1	Petition	71	Ways and Means	....	....	......	Discharged; referred to Secretary Treasury.		

List of private claims presented to the House of Representatives of the United States from the 1st to the 31st Congress, inclusive—Continued.

Names of claimants.	Nature or object of the claim.	Congress.	Session.	How brought before the House of Reps.	Page of journal.	To what committee of the House referred.	No. or date of the report.	Nature of the report.	No. of the bill.	How disposed of by the House of Reps.	How disposed of by the Senate.	Date of the act of Congress, and remarks.
Smith, John	Pay and bounty land, war of 1812.	14	2	Petition	315	Military Affairs				Discharged; referred to Secretary of War.		
Smith, John	Equitab'e settlement of account for supplies.	15	2	Petition	63	Military Affairs.						
Smith, John, (Ohio)	Credit for a forfeited land payment.	19	1	Petition	78	Public Lands				Discharged; leave to withdraw.		
Smith, John, (Ala)	Pension	19	1	Petition	250	Military Pensions	164	Adverse		Laid on table.		
Smith, John, (Ohio)	Pension	19	1	Petition	464	Military Pensions	May 3, 1826	Adverse		Rejected.		
Smith, John, (Ohio)	Pension	19	2	Petition	44	Military Pensions.						
Smith, John, (Ohio)	Pension	20	2	Petition	39	Military Pensions	Dec. 23, 1828	Adverse		Laid on table.		
Smith, John, (S. C.)	Pension	20	1	Petition	56	Military Pensions	Feb. 19, 1828	Adverse		Laid on table		
Smith, John, (S. C.)	Arrears of pension	21	2	Petition	120	Military Pensions.						
Smith, John, (S. C.)	Arrears of pension	22	1	Petition	35	Rev. Pensions				Discharged; laid on table.		
Smith, John, (S. C.)	Arrears of pension	22	2	Petition	74	Rev. Pensions				Discharged; laid on table.		
Smith, John, (S. C.)	Arrears of pension	23	1	Petition	53	Rev. Pensions				Discharged; laid on table.		
Smith, John, (S. C.)	Arrears of pension	23	2	Petition	110	Rev. Pensions				Discharged; laid on table.		
Smith, John, (Maine)	Compensation for revolutionary services.	20	1	Petition	110	Rev. Claims	Jan. 18, 1828	Adverse		Laid on table.		
Smith, John, (Miss.)	Compensation for horse lost in public service.	21	2	Petition	301	Claims.						
Smith, John, administrator of.	Indemnity for French spoliations prior to 1800.	26	1	Memorial	182	Foreign Affairs	343	Favorable; bill	319	Referred to Committee Whole House.		
Smith, John	Compensation for work on Cumberland road.	23	1	Resolution	589	Claims	455	Adverse		Laid on table		See report No. 449.
Smith, John	Compensation for work on Cumberland road.	23	2	Resolution	320					Referred to Secretary War.		
Smith, John	(See representative of Ballard Smith.)	23	1		306							
Smith, John, (N. C.)	Compensation for cattle furnished by his father.	23	1	Petition	334	Rev. Claims.						
Smith, John, (Pa.)	Commutation pay for revolutionary services.	24	1	Resolution	144	Rev. Claims.						
Smith, John, (Pa.)	Commutation pay for revolutionary services.	25	3	Resolution	285	Invalid Pensions.						
Smith, John, (Pa.)	Commutation pay for revolutionary services.	26	1	Petition	359	Rev. Claims.						
Smith, John, (Pa.)	Commutation pay for revolutionary services.	26	2	Petition	77	Rev. Claims.						
Smith, John, (Pa.,) administrator of.	Commutation pay for revolutionary services.	29	1	Petition	68	Rev. Pensions	40	Adverse		Laid on table.		
Smith, John, (Va.)	Compensation for services, war of 1812.	24	1	Petition	97	Invalid Pensions	218	Favorable	227	Passed	Passed	Appd June 28, 1836
Smith, John	Permission to purchase land in North Carolina.	25	2	Petition	914	Indian Affairs				Laid on table.		
Smith, John, (N. Y.)	Pension	25	3	Documents	219	Invalid Pensions.						
Smith, John, (N. Y.)	Pension	26	1	Petition	172	Rev Pensions.						
Smith, John, (Va.)	Pension for revolutionary services.	25	2	Petition	405	Rev. Pensions.						
Smith, John, (Va.)	Pension for revolutionary services.	25	3	Petition	88	Rev. Pensions	Jan. 2, 1839	Favorable	944	Passed	Adverse.	
Smith, John, (Va.)	Pension for revolutionary services.	26	2	Petition	78	Rev. Pensions.						

List of private claims presented to the House of Representatives of the United States from the 1st to the 31st Congress, inclusive—Continued.

Names of claimants.	Nature or object of the claim.	Congress.	Session.	How brought before the House of Reps.	Page of journal.	To what committee of the House referred.	No. or date of the report.	Nature of the report.	No. of the bill.	How disposed of by the House of Reps.	How disposed of by the Senate.	Date of the act of Congress, and remarks.
Smith, John, (Pa.)......	Pension for revolutionary services.	23	2	Petition	58	Rev. Pensions.						
Smith, John, (Pa.)......	Pension for revolutionary services.	24	2	Petition	97	Rev. Claims.						
Smith, John, (Pa.)......	Pension for revolutionary services.	25	2	Petition	111	Rev. Claims.						
Smith, John, (Pa.)......	Compensation for revolutionary services.	25	3	Petition	561	Rev. Claims.						
Smith, John, (Pa.)......	Compensation for revolutionary services.	26	1	Petition	167	Rev. Claims.						
Smith, John, (Pa.,) heirs of.	Compensation for revolutionary services.	26	2	Resolution	97	Rev. Claims.						
Smith, John............	(See heirs of Amos Smith)......	27	2	....	320							
Smith, John, (Ky.)......	Pension for revolutionary services.	29	2	Petition	195	Rev. Pensions	42	Adverse	......	Laid on table.		
Smith, Rev. John, widow of.	Renewal and extension of copy right.	14	1	Petition	46	Select.						
Smith, Rev. John, widow of.	Extension of a copy-right.......	15	2	Petition	132	Select.						
Smith, John, (Agnes,) widow of.	Pension for revolutionary services.	26	1	Petition	625	Rev. Pensions	511	Adverse	......	Laid on table	....	Leave to withdraw, 2d sess. 27th Congress, p. 89.
Smith, John, (Ann,) widow of.	Pension for revolutionary services.	29	1	Petition	625	Rev. Pensions	786	Adverse	......	Laid on table.		
Smith, John, daughter of .	Pension for revolutionary services.	25	2	Petition	585	Rev. Pensions	....	Adverse	......	Laid on table		
Smith, John, daughter of .	Pension for revolutionary services.	25	3	Petition	215	Rev. Pensions.....	....	....	......	Laid on table.		
Smith, John, daughter of .	Pension for revolutionary services.	26	1	Petition	324	Rev. Pensions.						
Smith, John, surety of ...	Revision of accounts as army contractor.	17	2	Senate bill	174	Cliams	Feb. 5, 1823	With amend..	S. 31	Passed with amend'mt	Passed as am'd	App'd March 3, 1823
Smith, John, heir of	Pension and bounty land for revolutionary services.	29	1	Petition	1189	Rev. Pensions.						
Smith, John, heir of	Pension and bounty land for revolutionary services.	29	2	Petition	151	Priv. Land Claims.						
Smith, John, heir of	Pension and bounty land for revolutionary services.	30	1	Petition	407	Priv. Land Claims.						
Smith, John, heir of	Pension and bounty land for revolutionary services.	30	2	Petition	204	Priv. Land Claims.						
Smith, John, heir of	Pension and bounty land for revo lutionary services.	31	1	Petition	362	Rev. Claims.						
Smith, John............	(See heir of Parke Smith.)	29	2	....	49							
Smith, John............	Pension	31	2	Petition	36	Invalid Pensions.						
Smith, John, (Ind.)......	Compensation for services by impressment at New Orleans.	31	2	Petition	216	Claims.						
Smith, John Adams......	(See Nathaniel Niles.)..........	23	1	....	418	....	....	....	404			
Smith, John Adams......	Outfit as chargé to London, &c ..	23	2	Petition	199	Foreign Affairs.						
Smith, John Adams......	Outfit as chargé to London, &c ..	24	1	Petition	115	Foreign Affairs ...	841	Favorable	743	Referred to Committee Whole House.		
Smith, John Adams......	Compensation for diplomatic services.	25	2	Petition	39							
				Petition	50	Foreign Affairs....	638	Favorable	615	Referred to Committee Whole House.		
Smith, John Adams......	Compensation for diplomatic services.	25	3	Bill of last sess..	380	Whole House.....	Jan. 25, 1839	With't amend.	615	Passed	Adverse report.	
Smith, John Adams......	Compensation for diplomatic services.	26	1	Petition	182	Foreign Affairs.						
Smith, John Adams......	Compensation for diplomatic services.	27	2	Petition	390	Foreign Affairs....	743	Favorable	421	Ordered to 3d reading.		

List of private claims presented to the House of Representatives of the United States from the 1st to the 31st Congress, inclusive—Continued.

Names of claimants.	Nature or object of the claim.	Congress.	Session.	How brought before the House of Reps.	Page of journal.	To what committee of the House referred.	No. or date of the report.	Nature of the report.	No. of the bill.	How disposed of by the House of Reps.	How disposed of by the Senate.	Date of the act of Congress, and remarks.
Smith, John Adams	Compensation for diplomatic services.	27	3	House bill	88				421	Passed	Laid on table.	
Smith, John B	Indemnity for loss on a government contract.	19	1	Petition	223	Claims.						
Smith, John B	Indemnity for loss on a government contract.	20	1	Petition	164	Claims	Jan. 21, 1828	Adverse		Laid on table.		
Smith, John B., *alias* Wm. McGreenwood.	Compensation for a horse lost in the war of 1812.	22	1	Report of Com'r Claims.	170		Jan. 10, 1832	Adverse		Laid on table.		
Smith, John B	Indemnity for hides destroyed at Niagara.	15	1	Petition	247	Claims.						
Smith, John B	Indemnity for hides destroyed at Niagara.	16	1	Petition	106	Claims	Jan. 14, 1820	Adverse		Laid on table.		
Smith, John B	Indemnity for hides destroyed at Niagara.	17	2	Petition	74	Claims	Jan. 22, 1823	Adverse		Laid on table.		
Smith, John B	Indemnity for hides destroyed at Niagara.	18	1	Petition	101	Claims	38	Adverse		Referred to Committee Whole House.		
Smith, John B., and S. Darden.	Compensation for arresting mail robber.	30	1	Bill on leave	556	Claims	508	Favorable	328	Passed	Passed, second session.	App'd Jan. 10, 1849
Smith, John C., and W. H., surety of.	Release for liability on custom-house bond.	20	2	Petition	89	Ways and Means.						
Smith, John E., (Md.)	Indemnity for an illegal capture of vessel by British.	22	2	Memorial	119	Foreign Affairs				Discharged; referred to Secretary of State.		
Smith, John E., (Md.)	Indemnity for an illegal capture of vessel by British.	23	2	Petition	106	Foreign Affairs				Discharged; referred to Secretary of State.		
Smith, John E., (Md.)	Indemnity for an illegal capture of vessel by British.	25	2	Petition	172	Foreign Affairs				Discharged; leave to withdraw.		
Smith, John G	Right of pre-emption to land in Florida.	22	1	Petition	134	Public Lands	94	Favorable; bill	184	Passed	Passed	App'd July 14, 1832
Smith, John G	Payment of a certificate of Colonel Harney.	30	1	Petition	877	Claims.						
Smith, John G	Payment of a certificate of Colonel Harney.	31	1	Petition	432	Commerce.						
Smith, John H	(See heirs of Larkin Smith)	24	1		105							
Smith, John J	Right of pre-emption	23	2	Petition	320					Laid on table.		
Smith, John J	Increase and arrears of pension	26	1	Petition	325	Invalid Pensions	417	Adverse		Laid on table.		
Smith, John J	Increase and arrears of pension	29	1	Petition	337	Invalid Pensions				Discharged; laid on table.		
Smith, John K	(See widow of Wm. Hawkins)	18	1		253							
Smith, John P	(See heir of John Smith)	29	1		1189							
Smith, John P., (Pa.)	Compensation for disability in Mexican war.	31	1	Petition	396	Invalid Pensions.						
Smith, John R	(See Philip Sloane)	8	1		605							
Smith, John R	(See Rufus Spalding and others)	15	2		148							
Smith, John R., and others.	Bounty land as Canadian volunteers.	16	1	Petition	197	Military Affairs	Feb. 21, 1820	Adverse		Rejected.		
Smith, John Spear	(See representatives of Sam. Smith)	29	2		75							
Smith, John T	(See sureties of Alpha Kingsley)	19	1		488							
Smith, John T	Permission to enter certain lands	29	1	Petition	311	Public Lands	Feb. 10, 1846	Favorable	189	Referred to Committee Whole House.		
Smith, John T., representatives of.	Right of pre-emption	25	2	Senate bill	1155	Public Lands	July 6, 1838	With't amend.	S. 271	Referred to Committee Whole House.		
Smith, John T., representatives of.	Right of pre-emption	29	1	House bill	374	Public Lands	198	Favorable	189	Referred to Committee Whole House.		

List of private claims presented to the House of Representatives of the United States from the 1st to the 31st Congress, inclusive—Continued.

Names of claimants.	Nature or object of the claim.	Congress.	Session.	How brought before the House of Reps.	Page of journal.	To what committee of the House referred.	No. or date of the report.	Nature of the report.	No. of the bill.	How disposed of by the House of Reps.	How disposed of by the Senate.	Date of the act of Congress, and remarks.
Smith, John T., representatives of.	Right of pre emption	29	2	Bill of last sess.	305	Whole House	Feb. 5, 1847	With amend.		Passed	Passed	App'd March 3, 1847
Smith, John U.	(See Caleb Stanley and John W. Smith.)	14	1		70							
Smith, John W	Balance due him on settlement at Treasury.	23	1	Appropriat'n bill.								Stat. at Large, vol. 4, p. 697.
Smith, John Y	Compensation for services as librarian, Territory of Wisconsin.	28	1	Petition	927	Claims.						
Smith, John H. D. W., attorney for executrix of.	Settlement of a claim in favor of deceased.	1	3	Petition	346					Referred to Secretary Treasury.		
Smith, John H. D. W., attorney for executrix of.	Settlement of a claim in favor of deceased.	3	2	Rep. of Secretary Treasury.	284	Claims				Laid on table.		
Smith, John H. D. W., attorney for executrix of.	Settlement of a claim in favor of deceased.	4	1	Rep. of Secretary Treasury.	436	Claims	May 7, 1796	Adverse		Leave to withdraw.		
Smith, John, and others	Right of pre emption	3	1	Petition	53					Laid on table.		
Smith, John, and others	Right of pre emption	6	1	Petition	544	Select.						
Smith, Jonathan, (N. J.)	Further compensation for revolutionary services.	12	1	Petition	12	Select	Feb. 18, 1812	Adverse		Rejected.		
Smith, Jonathan S.	Indemnity for coffee abandoned at Algiers.	13	2	Petition	307	Ways and Means.	Mar. 29, 1814			Laid on table.		
Smith, Jonathan S.	Indemnity for coffee abandoned at Algiers.	14	2	Petition	191	Com. and Manuf.	Jan. 27, 1817	Adverse		Laid on table.		
Smith, Jonathan S.	Indemnity for coffee abandoned at Algiers.	15	2	Petition	95	Ways and Means.						
Smith, Jonathan S.	Indemnity for coffee abandoned at Algiers.	17	1	Petition	99	Ways and Means.	78	Adverse		Referred to Committee Whole House.		
Smith, Jonathan S.	Indemnity for coffee abandoned at Algiers.	18	1	Petition	27	Foreign Affairs	95	Adverse		Laid on table.		
Smith, Jonathan S.	Indemnity for coffee abandoned at Algiers.	18	2	Petition and docs.	45	Claims.						
Smith, Jonathan S.	Indemnity for coffee abandoned at Algiers.	19	2	Petition	189	Foreign Affairs.						
Smith, Jonathan S.	Indemnity for coffee abandoned at Algiers.	20	1	Petition	196	Foreign Affairs	239	Adverse		Laid on table.		
Smith, Johnathan, (Mass.)	Pension for revolutionary services.	22	1	Petition	44	Rev. Pensions.						
Smith, Jonathan	Commutation pay for revolutionary services.	30	1	Petition	565	Rev. Claims				Discharged; laid on table.		
Smith, Joseph	Compensation for revolutionary services.	2	2	Petition and rep't Sec. of War.	678, 735					Laid on table.		
Smith, Joseph	Indemnity for French exactions on cargo of tobacco.	12	1	Petition	339					Referred to Secretary of State.		
Smith, Joseph, and others.	Confirmation of title to land in Missouri.	15	1	Petition	50	Priv. Land Claims.						
Smith, Joseph, and others.	Confirmation of title to land in Missouri.	17	1	Petition	55	Public Lands.						
Smith, Joseph, and others.	Confirmation of title to land in Missouri.	18	1	Petition	55	Public Lands.						
Smith, Joseph	Confirmation of title to land in Missouri.	15	1	Petition	312	Priv. Land Claims.						
Smith, Joseph	Confirmation of title to land in Missouri.	16	1	Petition	71	Priv. Land Claims.						
Smith, Joseph	Confirmation of title to land in Missouri.	17	1	Petition	55	Public Lands.						

List of private claims presented to the House of Representatives of the United States from the 1st to the 31st Congress, inclusive—Continued.

Names of claimants.	Nature or object of the claim.	Congress.	Session.	How brought before the House of Reps.	Page of journal.	To what committee of the House referred.	No. or date of the report.	Nature of the report.	No. of the bill.	How disposed of by the House of Reps.	How disposed of by the Senate.	Date of the act of Congress, and remarks.
Smith, Joseph	Confirmation of title to land in Missouri.	18	1	Petition	55	Public Lands.						
Smith, Joseph, (Alex.)	Pay and prize money due slave	17	2	Petition	91	Claims	Jan. 24, 1823	Favorable	249	Referred to Committee Whole House.		
Smith, Joseph, (Alex.)	Pay and prize money due slave	18	1	Petition	134	Claims	Jan. 30, 1834	Favorable	89	Passed	Passed	App'd May 19, 1824
Smith, Joseph, (Alex.)	Appropriation pursuant to act of last session.	18	2	Resolution	99	Claims	12	Favorable	255	Passed	Passed	App'd March 3, 1825
Smith, Joseph, (Alex.)	Compensation for slave lost in public service.	19	1	Petition	102	Claims	Jan. 4, 1826	Adverse	......	Laid on table	....	Leave to withdraw.
Smith, Joseph, (Alex.)	For the benefit of a certain act	17	2	Petition	96	Public Lands	Feb. 5, 1823	General bill	271	Passed	Passed	App'd March 3, 1823
Smith, Joseph, (Alex.)	For the benefit of a certain act	18	1	Petition	136	Public Lands	....	....	......	Discharged; laid on table.		
Smith, Joseph	(See assignee of John B. Dupuis)	19	2	....	49							
Smith, Joseph, jr.	Indemnity for French spoliations prior to 1800.	26	1	Memorial	182	Foreign Affairs	343	Favorab'e; bill	319	Referred to Committee Whole House.		
Smith, Joseph P.	Reimbursement of expenditures on public account.	29	2	Memorial	181	Military Affairs	....	....	......	Discharged; laid on table.		
Smith, Josiah	Compensation for revolutionary services.	4	1	Petition	425	Claims	May 7, 1796	Adverse	......	Leave to withdraw.		
Smith, Josiah, executors of	Indemnity for French spoliations prior to 1800.	26	1	Memorial	182	Foreign Affairs	343	Favorable; bill	319	Referred to Committee Whole House.		
Smith, Josiah	Increase of pension	10	1	Pension bill	232	Whole House	....	....	78	Passed	Passed, with amendment.	App'd April 25, 1808
Smith, Josiah	(See Smith, Dessasure & Darrell)	26	1	....	182							
Smith, Josiah	Compensation for a horse lost in public service.	23	1	Documents	115	Claims	Jan. 3, 1834	Adverse	......	Laid on table.		
Smith, Josiah, (Mass.)	Indemnity for French spoliations prior to 1800.	26	1	Memorial	182	Foreign Affairs	343	Favorable; bill	319	Referred to Committee Whole House.		
Smith, Josias	Pension	11	2	Pension bill	283	....	....	....	107	Passed	Passed, with amendment.	App'd April 27, 1810
Smith, Kenderton, agent of	(See John Smith, &c.)	26	1	....	182							
Smith, Laban	Arrears of pension	22	1	Petition	130	Rev. Pensions	365	Favorable	460	Passed	Indef. postp'd.	
Smith, Larkin	Increase of compensation as collector, Norfolk, Va.	12	1	Petition	23	Ways and Means	Dec. 30, 1811	General bill	34	Referred to Committee Whole House.		
Smith, Larkin, executors of.	Commutation pay for revolutionary services.	23	1	Petition	40	Rev. Claims.						
Smith, Larkin, executors of.	Commutation pay for revolutionary services.	23	2	Petition	56	Rev. Claims.						
Smith, Larkin, executors of.	Commutation pay for revolutionary services.	24	1	Petition	103	Rev. Claims.						
Smith, Larkin, heirs of	Commutation pay for revolutionary services.	24	1	Petition	105	Rev. Claims.						
Smith, Larkin, heirs of	Commutation pay for revolutionary services.	24	2	Petition	39	Rev. Claims	285	Adverse	......	Laid on table.		
Smith, Larkin, executors of.	Commutation pay for revolutionary services.	25	2	Petition	74	Rev. Claims	672	Favorable	650	Postponed.		
Smith, Larkin, executors of.	Commutation pay for revolutionary services.	25	3	Bill of last sess.	265	Whole House	Jan. 12, 1839	With amend.	650	Rejected.		
Smith, Larkin, executors of.	Commutation pay for revolutionary services.	26	1	Petition	164	Rev. Claims.						
Smith, Larkin, executors of.	Commutation pay for revolutionary services.	26	2	Petition	35	Rev. Claims.						

List of private claims presented to the House of Representatives of the United States from the 1st to the 31st Congress, inclusive—Continued.

Names of claimants.	Nature or object of the claim.	Congress.	Session.	How brought before the House of Reps.	Page of journal.	To what committee of the House referred.	No. or date of the report.	Nature of the report.	No. of the bill.	How disposed of by the House of Reps.	How disposed of by the Senate.	Date of the act of Congress, and remarks.
Smith, Larkin, executors of.	Commutation pay for revolutionary services.	27	2	Petition	61	Rev. Claims	976	Adverse		Laid on table.		
Smith, Larkin, executors of.	Commutation pay for revolutionary services	28	1	Petition	117	Rev. Claims.						
Smith, Larkin, executors of.	Commutation pay for revolutionary services.	29	1	Petition	115	Rev. Claims	67	Favorable	62	Rejected.		
Smith, Larkin, executors of.	Commutation pay for revolutionary services.	30	1	Petition	79	Rev. Claims	673	Favorable	537	Referred to Committee Whole House.		
Smith, Larkin, executors of.	Commutation pay for revolutionary services.	31	1	Petition	270	Rev. Claims	113	Favorable	126	Referred to Committee Whole House.		
Smith, Lawrence, (Ga.)	Pension for revolutionary services.	28	1	Petition	99	Rev. Pensions				Discharged; laid on table.		
Smith, Levi, & Co	Remission of duty on distillery	14	2	Petition	390	Ways and Means.						
Smith, Leonard	Pension for revolutionary services.	24	1	Petition	56	Rev. Pensions				Discharged; laid on table.		
Smith, Leonard	Pension for revolutionary services.	25	2	Petition	198	Rev. Pensions	698	Favorable	672	Passed.		
Smith, Leonard	Pension for revolutionary services.	25	3	Petition	88	Rev. Pensions	102	Favorable	977	Passed	Adverse.	
Smith, Leonard	Pension for revolutionary services.	26	1	Petition	170	Rev. Pensions	135	Favorable	145	Passed	Passed, with amendment.	App'd July 20, 1840
Smith, Lewis M	Increase of compensation as postmaster.	17	1	Petition	326	P. Of. & P. Roads.	Mar. 15, 1822	Adverse		Rejected.		
Smith, Lois	Pension as widow of a revolutionary officer.	26	1	Resolution	556	Rev. Pensions	April 4, 1840	Adverse		Laid on table.		
Smith, Louis	Pension for revolutionary services.	26	1	Petition	867	Rev. Pensions	714	Adverse		Laid on table.		
Smith, Louisa L	(See heirs of Jacob Smith)	23	2		392							
Smith, Luther L	Confirmation of title to land in Louisiana.	20	1	Petition	312	Priv. Land Claims.						
Smith, Luther L	Confirmation of title to land in Louisiana.	21	2	Petition	55	Priv. Land Claims.	Dec. 24, 1830	Adverse		Laid on table.		
Smith, Luther L	Confirmation of title to land in Louisiana.	22	1	Petition	32	Priv. Land Claims.	228	Favorable	342	Referred to Committee Whole House.		
Smith, Luther L	Confirmation of title to land in Louisiana	23	1	Petition	48	Priv. Land Claims.	39	Favorable	45	Passed	Passed	App'd May 14, 1834
Smith, Luther, representatives of.	Confirmation of title to land in Louisiana.	21	1	Petition	297	Priv. Land Claims.						
Smith, Margaret	(See Jared Smith, widow of)	26	1		386							
Smith, Maria G.	(See heirs of Jacob Smith)	23	2		392							
Smith, Marshall	Compensation for property lost while in public use.	18	2	Petition	210	Claims						
Smith, Marshall	Compensation for property lost while in public use.	21	1	Petition	262	Claims	Mar. 10, 1830	Adverse		Laid on table.		
Smith, Mary	(See Claudius Besse, heirs of)	29	2		163							
Smith, Mary	(See heirs of James P. Wallace)	24	1		425							
Smith, Mary K.	(See E. Kerby Smith, widow of)	31	1		595							
Smith, Mary	(See widow of Zachariah Hall)	25	3		217							
Smith, Mary	(See William Smith, widow of)	27	2		375							
Smith, Martin	Arrears of pension	22	1	Petition	67	Rev. Pensions	234	Favorable	344	Passed.		
Smith, Martin	Arrears of pension	22	2	Petition	53	Rev. Claims	7	Favorable	626	Passed	Passed, with amendment.	App'd Mar. 2, 1833
Smith, Matthew, and others.	Reimbursement of money paid for lands.	10	1	Petition	145	Claims	Feb. 5, 1808	Favorable	53	Passed	Passed	App'd April 21, 1808
Smith, Mehitabel	(See widow of Lieut. Jesse Smith)	22	1		114							
Smith Melancton	(See Henry Rutgers and others)	7	1		132							

List of private claims presented to the House of Representatives of the United States from the 1st to the 31st Congress, inclusive—Continued.

Names of claimants.	Nature or object of the claim.	Congress.	Session.	How brought before the House of Reps.	Page of journal.	To what committee of the House referred.	No. or date of the report.	Nature of the report.	No. of the bill.	How disposed of by the House of Reps.	How disposed of by the Senate.	Date of the act of Congress, and remarks.
Smith, Melancton	Indemnity for damage to property at Plattsburg.	15	1	Petition	207	Claims.						
Smith, Melancton	Indemnity for damage to property at Plattsburg.	17	1	Petition	92	Claims.						
Smith, Melancton	Indemnity for damage to property at Plattsburg.	17	2	Petition	26	Claims.						
Smith, Moses	Pension for revolutionary services.	3	1	Rep. of Secretary War.	131	Select	May 26, 1794	Res. to refer to Sec. War	R. 12	Passed	Passed	App'd June 9, 1694
Smith, Moses	Pension for revolutionary services.	4	1	Rep. of Secretary War.	445	Claims.						
Smith, Moses	Pension for revolutionary services.	4	2	Rep. of Secretary War.	614	Claims.						
Smith, Moses	Pension for revolutionary services.	11	2	Pension bill	283	...	...	...	107	Passed	Passed, with amendment.	App'd April 27, 1810
Smith, Moses	Increase of pension	15	2	Petition	192	Pens. & Rev. Cl'ms.	Feb. 5, 1819	General bill	308	Passed	Postponed.	
Smith, Moses	Increase of pension	16	1	Petition	268	Pens. & Rev. Cl'ms.	...	...	...	Discharged; laid on table.		
Smith, Moses	Increase of pension	18	1	Petition	234	Pens. & Rev. Cl'ms.						
Smith, Moses	Increase of pension	18	2	Petition	53	Pens. & Rev. Cl'ms.						
Smith, Moses	Increase of pension	19	1	Petition	43	Rev. Pensions	164	Adverse	...	Laid on table.		
Smith, Moses, (D. C.)	Pension	22	1	Petition	509	Rev. Pensions.						
Smith, Moses, (D. C.)	Arrears of pension	22	2	Petition	206	Rev. Pensions.						
Smith, Moses	Compensation for improvement in mariners' compass.	22	1	Memorial	145	Commerce	Feb. 20, 1832	Favorable				
Smith, Moses	Compensation for improvement in mariners' compass.	22	2	Memorial	30	Naval Affairs	84	Indefinite	...	Laid on table.		
Smith, Moses, (R. I.)	Arrears of pension	23	1	Petition	47	Rev. Pensions	...	...	...	Disch'd; laid on table		
Smith, Moses, (R. I.)	Arrears of pension	24	2	Resolution	129	Invalid Pensions	...	...	...	Discharged; laid on table.		
Smith, Moses, (R. I.)	Arrears of pension	26	1	Petition	163	Invalid Pensions	266	Adverse	...	Laid on table.		
Smith, Moses, (Maine)	Pension	25	2	Petition	165	Invalid Pensions.						
Smith, Moses, (Maine)	Pension	25	3	Petition	89	Invalid Pensions.						
Smith, Munday	Pension for services under Comodore Barney.	14	1	Petition	59	Naval Affairs.						
Smith, Rev. M.	Indemnity for losses as a Canadian refugee.	14	2	Petition	207	Claims.						
Smith, Mursden	Indemnity for French spoliations prior to 1800.	26	1	Memorial	182	Foreign Affairs	313	Favorable; bill	319	Referred to Committee Whole House.		
Smith, Nancy	(See Charles Smith, widow of)	28	2	...	292							
Smith, Nathan	Commutation pay for revolutionary services.	3	1	Memorial	18	Select.						
Smith, Nathan	Commutation pay for revolutionary services.	3	2	Memorial	247	Claims	Feb. 25, 1795	Adverse	...	Referred to Committee Whole House.		
Smith, Nathan	Commutation pay for revolutionary services.	4	2	Petition	247	Claims	Dec. 30, 1796	Adverse	...	Rejected.		
Smith, Nathan, administrator of.	Commutation pay and bounty land, revolutionary.	17	2	Petition	215	Pens. & Rev. Cl'ms.	...	...	...	Discharged.		
Smith, Nathan, heirs of	Commutation pay and bounty land, revolutionary.	21	2	Petition	112	Rev. Claims.						
Smith, Nathan, heirs of	Commutation pay and bounty land, revolutionary.	22	1	Petition	809	...	...	...	...	Laid on table.		

List of private claims presented to the House of Representatives of the United States from the 1st to the 31st Congress, inclusive—Continued.

Names of claimants.	Nature or object of the claim.	Congress.	Session.	How brought before the House of Reps.	Page of journal.	To what committee of the House referred.	No. or date of the report.	Nature of the report.	No. of the bill.	How disposed of by the House of Reps.	How disposed of by the Senate.	Date of the act of Congress, and remarks.
Smith, Nathan, executrix of.	Commutation pay and bounty land, revolutionary.	23	1	Petition	144	Rev. Claims.						
Smith, Nathan, executrix of.	Commutation pay and bounty land, revolutionary.	23	2	Petition	55	Rev. Claims.						
Smith, Nathan, executrix of.	Commutation pay and bounty land, revolutionary.	24	2	Petition	94	Rev. Claims.						
Smith, Nathan, executrix of.	Commutation pay and bounty land, revolutionary.	25	2	Petition	49	Rev. Claims......	968	Favorable	840	Referred to Committee Whole House.		
Smith, Nathan, executrix of.	Commutation pay and bounty land, revolutionary.	25	3	Bill of last sess..	432	Whole House.....	....	....	840			
Smith, Nathan, executrix of.	Commutation pay and bounty land, revolutionary.	26	1	Petition	164	Rev. Claims.						
Smith, Nathan, executrix of.	Commutation pay and bounty land, revolutionary.	26	2	Petition	36	Rev. Claims.						
Smith, Nathan..........	Right of pre-emption to land in Mississippi.	25	3	Petition	368	Priv. Land Claims.						
Smith, Nathan..........	Bounty on fishing schooner James Monroe.	24	1	Petition	198	Commerce	502	Favorable	502	Referred to Committee Whole House.		
Smith, Nathan..........	Bounty on fishing schooner James Monroe.	25	2	Petition	41	Commerce	83	Favorable	99	Passed	Indef. postp'd.	
Smith, Nathan.	Bounty on fishing schooner James Monroe.	25	3	Petition	213	Commerce	234	Adverse	......	Laid on table.		
Smith, Nathan..........	Bounty on fishing schooner James Monroe.	26	1	Petition	291	Commerce	314	Favorable	277	Referred to Committee Whole House.		
Smith, Nathan..........	Bounty on fishing schooner James Monroe.	27	2	Petition	57	Commerce	66	Favorable	101	Passed	Passed	App'd Aug. 27, 1842
Smith, Nathan, and C. K.	Bounty on fishing schooner Washington.	29	1	Petition	89	Claims	128	Favorable	130	Passed	Passed.......	App'd Aug. 8, 1846
Smith, Nathan..........	Additional compensation as revenue officer, Texas.	31	1	Petition	425	Claims.						
Smith, Nathaniel, and Wm.	Drawback on sugars...........	8	1	Petition	484	Com. and Munuf..	Dec. 15, 1803	Adverse	......	Rejected.		
Smith, Nathaniel, (Mass.).	Indemnity for French spoliations prior to 1800.	26	1	Memorial	182	Foreign Affairs....	343	Favorable; bill	319	Referred to Committee Whole House.		
Smith, Nathaniel P......	(See Ephraim W. Burr, and others.)	26	2	....	99							
Smith, Neal............	(See administrator of Theo. Bright well.	19	2	....	57							
Smith, Noah	Pension for revolutionary services.	18	1	Senate bill	328	Rev. Pensions	Mar. 24, 1824	With amend..	S. 73	Passed wtth amendm't.	Passed as am'd	App'd May 5, 1844
Smith, Noah	Pension for revolutionary services.	25	2	Petition	546	Rev. Pensions	....	....	......	Discharged; laid on table.		
Smith, Noah	Pension for revolutionary services.	26	1	Petition	175	Rev. Pensions	....	....	......	Discharged; laid on table.		
Smith, Noah	Pension for revolutionary services.	27	3	Petition	260	Rev. Pensions	....	....	......	Discharged; leave to withdraw.		
Smith, Noah	Pension for revolutionary services.	29	2	Petition	85	Rev. Claims.						
Smith, Noah	Pension for revolutionary services.	30	1	Petition	405	Rev. Claims......	680	Adverse	......	Laid on table.		
Smith, Noah	Pension for revolutionary services.	30	2	Petition	117	Rev. Claims.						
Smith, Noah	Pension for revolutionary services.	31	1	Petition	348	Rev. Claims.						
Smith, N. R............	(See sureties of Samuel H. Bunch.)	30	1	....	738							
Smith, Oziel...........	Compensation for use of buildings.	19	2	Petition	132	Claims	Jan. 30, 1827	Adverse	......	Laid on table.		
Smith, Paca...........	(See Mark Pringle, administrator of.	26	1	....	182							

List of private claims presented to the House of Representatives of the United States from the 1st to the 31st Congress, inclusive—Continued.

Names of claimants.	Nature or object of the claim.	Congress.	Session.	How brought before the House of Reps.	Page of journal.	To what committee of the House referred.	No. or date of the report.	Nature of the report.	No. of the bill.	How disposed of by the House of Reps.	How disposed of by the Senate.	Date of the act of Congress, and remarks.
Smith, Parsons	Pension	23	1	Petition	141	Invalid Pensions	Mar. 15, 1834	Favorable	367	Referred to Committee Whole House.		
Smith, Parsons	Pension	23	2	Bill of last sess.	336	Whole House	Feb. 6, 1835	With't amend.	367	Passed.		
Smith, Parsons	Pension	24	1	Petition	74	Invalid Pensions	46	Favorable	58	Passed	Passed	App'd May 14, 1836
Smith, Paschal N., executor of.	Indemnity for French spoliations prior to 1800.	26	1	Memorial	182	Foreign Affairs	343	Favorable	319	Referred to Committee Whole House.		
Smith, Parke, heir of	Pension for revolutionary services.	29	2	Petition	49	Rev. Pensions	42	Adverse	......	Laid on table.		
Smith, Patience	(See Gideon Smith, widow of)	25	3	....	127							
Smith, Patrick	(See Z. M. Pike and others)	10	1	....	189							
Smith, Patrick	Compensation for repairing guns at Buffalo.	27	2	Petition	535	Claims	643	Adverse	......	Laid on table.		
Smith, Patrick	Compensation for repairing guns at Buffalo.	27	3	Petition	72	Claims.						
Smith, Patrick	Compensation for repairing guns at Buffalo.	28	2	Petition	82	Claims.						
Smith, Patrick	Compensation for repairing guns at Buffalo.	29	1	Pension	58	Claims	72	Adverse	......	Laid on table.		
Smith, Patrick	Compensation for repairing guns at Buffalo.	29	2	Documents	49	Claims.						
Smith, Phebe	(See widow of Ebenezer Eaton)	25	3	....	217							
Smith, Philander, heirs of.	Confirmation of title to land in Mississippi.	27	3	Petition	52	Priv. Land Claims.	58	Favorable	691	Passed	Passed	App'd March 3, 1843
Smith, Preserved, widow of.	Continuation of pension	27	2	Petition	612	Rev. Pensions	784	Adverse	......	Laid on table.		
Smith, Peleg	Pension	11	2	Pension bill	283	....	....	....	107	Passed	Passed, with amendment.	App'd April 27, 1810
Smith, Peter	To be placed on revolutionary pension roll.	1	2	Petition and rep't Secretary War.	196, 199	....	....	....	......	Laid on table.		
Smith, Peter	To be placed on revolutionary pension roll.	10	2	Pension bill	232	Whole House	....	....	78	Passed.	Passed, with amendment.	App'd April 25, 1808
Smith, Peter	Reimbursement of medical expenses, revolutionary war.	12	1	Petition	193	Claims.						
Smith, Peter	(See William Jessup and others)	20	1	....	191							
Smith, Peter, (N. Y.)	Pension	22	1	Petition	120	Rev. Pensions.						
Smith, Peter, (Tenn.)	Balance due for use of team, &c.	25	2	Petition	541	Claims	1005	Indefinite	......	Referred to Secretary of War.		
Smith, Peter S., sureties of.	Exemption from imprisonment on a judgment.	17	1	Petition	164	P. Of. & P. Roads.	Mar. 8, 1822	Favorable	114	Passed	Laid on table.	
Smith, Peter, widow of	Pension for revolutionary services.	24	1	Senate bill	1107	Rev. Pensions	July 1, 1836	With't amend.	S. 291	Passed	Passed	App'd July 2, 1836
Smith, Randall	Pension for revolutionary services.	28	1	Petition	481	Rev. Pensions	....	....	......	Discharged; laid on table.		
Smith, Raphael	Confirmation of title to land in Louisiana.	14	1	Petition	422	Public Lands.						
Smith, Raphael	Confirmation of title to land in Louisiana.	14	2	Petition	60	Priv. Land Claims.						
Smith, Raphael	Confirmation of title to land in Louisiana.	15	1	Petition	173	Priv. Land Claims.						
Smith, Reuben, and N. Strong.	Remission of foreign tonnage duty.	3	1	Petition	149	Select	May 11, 1794	Favorable; bill ordered.	45	Passed	Passed	App'd May 19, 1794
Smith, Reuben, and N. Strong.	Bounty on beef exported to France.	4	2	Petition	715	Com. and Manuf.						

3—46

List of private claims presented to the House of Representatives of the United States from the 1st to the 31st Congress, inclusive—Continued.

Names of claimants.	Nature or object of the claim.	Congress.	Session.	How brought before the House of Reps.	Page of journal.	To what committee of the House referred.	No. or date of the report.	Nature of the report.	No. of the bill.	How disposed of by the House of Reps.	How disposed of by the Senate.	Date of the act of Congress, and remarks.
Smith, Reuben, and N. Strong, *et al.*	Bounty on beef exported to France.	5	2	Petition	184	Com. and Manuf.	April 9, 1798	Favorable; bill ordered.	82	Passed	Postponed.	
Smith, Richard, *et al.*	Compensation for horses lost at Detroit.	15	2	Petition	33	Claims	Dec. 1, 1818	Adverse		Rejected.		
Smith, Richard, *et al.*	Compensation for horses lost at Detroit.	21	1	Petition	376	Claims	Mar. 15, 1830	Adverse		Laid on table.		
Smyth, Richard	Release from liability for money of which he was robbed.	15	2	Petition	330	Ways and Means						
Smyth, Richard	Release from liability for money of which he was robbed.	16	1	Senate bill	449	Ways and Means	April 26, 1820	With't amend.	S. 96	Passed	Passed	App'd May 15, 1820
Smyth, Richard	(See Antoine Dequindre and R. Smith.)	21	1		318							
Smyth, Richard	(See sureties of John S. Langham)	22	1		473							
Smith, Richard	Increase of pension	26	1	Petition	602	Invalid Pensions.						
Smith, Richard, executor of	Payment of claims as officer of marines.	23	2	Senate bill	194	Claims	60	With't amend.	S. 25	Referred to Committee Whole House.		
Smith, Richard, executor of	Balaance due deceased under act July 14, 1832.	24	1	Senate bill	128	Claims	Jan. 6, 1836	With't amend.	S. 30	Passed	Passed	App'd April 9, 1836
Smith, Richard, widow of.	To be restored to pension roll	27	2	Petition	320	Rev. Pensions.						
Smith, Robert, (Phila.)	Indemnity for French spoliations prior to 1800.	26	1	Memorial	182	Foreign Affairs	343	Favorable; bill	319	Referred to Committee Whole House.		
Smith, Robert	(See James Yard, assignee of)	26	1		182							
Smith, Robert, (Pittsburg)	Annuity in consideration of military services.	19	1	Petition	84	Claims.						
Smith, Robert	Pension for revolutionary services.	3	2	Rep. of Secretary War.	337	Claims	Feb. 28, 1795	General pension bill.	130	Passed	Postponed.	
Smith, Robert	Pension for revolutionary services.	4	1	Rep. of Secretary War.	445	Claims	Feb. 18, 1796	General pension bill.	156	Passed	Passed	App'd April 20, 1796
Smith, Robert, (Tenn.)	For the return of title deeds	21	2	Petition	68	Judiciary	Feb. 1, 1831	Adverse		Laid on table.		
Smith, Robert, (Ala.)	Compensation for horses lost in public service.	21	2	Petition	112	Rev. Claims	Jan. 13, 1831	Adverse		Laid on table.		
Smith, Robert	Reimbursement of $250 paid Cahaba land office.	23	2	Petition	140	Public Lands				Discharged; laid on table.		
Smith, Robert	Reimbursement of $250 paid Cahaba land office.	24	2	Petition	83	Priv. Land Claims.				Discharged; laid on table.		
Smith, Robert, (Conn.)	Pension for revolutionary services.	24	1	Petition	282	Rev. Pensions	547	Favorable	537	Passed	Passed	App'd June 28, 1836
Smith, Robert	(See Philadelphia, citizens of)	26	1		182							
Smith, Robert	(See Alex. Masterson and Robert Smith.)	26	1		612							
Smith, Robert, & Co.	Indemnity for French spoliations prior to 1800.	26	1	Memorial	182	Foreign Affairs	343	Favorable; bill	319	Referred to Committee Whole House.		
Smith, Robert, (Va.)	Pension for revolutionary services.	31	2	Petition	155	Rev. Pensions.						
Smith, Robert H.	(See executor of Robert Smith)	29	2		50							
Smith, Robert M.	Grant of land for military services.	22	1	Petition	65	Public Lands.						
Smith, Robert S.	Extra compensation as collector, New Bedford.	26	1	Petition	709	Commerce.						
Smith, Robert S.	Extra compensation as collector, New Bedford.	26	2	Petition	200	Commerce.						
Smith, Robert S.	Extra compensation as collector, New Bedford.	27	2	Petition	56	Commerce				Discharged; laid on table.		
Smith, Robert, heirs of	Compensation for revolutionary services.	15	1	Petition	26	Pens. & Rev. Cl'ms.	Dec. 23, 1817	Adverse		Rejected.		

List of private claims presented to the House of Representatives of the United States from the 1st to the 31st Congress, inclusive—Continued.

Names of claimants.	Nature or object of the claim.	Congress.	Session.	How brought before the House of Reps.	Page of journal.	To what committee of the House referred.	No. or date of the report.	Nature of the report.	No. of the bill.	How disposed of by the House of Reps.	How disposed of by the Senate.	Date of the act of Congress, and remarks.
Smith, Robert, representative of.	Compensation for horse taken for public use.	23	1	Petition	128	Rev. Claims.						
Smith, Robert, heir of	Arrears of pay for revolutionary services.	28	1	Petition	987	Rev. Claims.						
Smith, Robert, heir of	Arrears of pay for revolutionary services.	29	1	Petition	172	Rev. Claims	Feb. 19, 1846	Adverse		Laid on table.		
Smith, Robert, executor of.	Indemnity for French spoliations prior to 1800.	29	2	Memorial	50	Foreign Affairs.						
Smith, Robert, assignee of.	Indemnity for French spoliations prior to 1800.	30	1	Petition	262	Foreign Affairs	Jan. 4, 1848	General bill	21	Referred to Committee Whole House.		
Smith, Robert, executors of	Indemnity for French spoliations prior to 1800.	31	1	Petition	270	Foreign Affairs	355	General bill	318	Referred to Committee Whole House.		
Smith, Russell L.	Indemnity for destruction of property at Buffalo.	21	1	Petition	235	Claims	Mar. 10, 1830	Adverse		Laid on table.		
Smith, Samuel	(See Lewis Sewall and S. Smith).	13	2		414							
Smith, Samuel	Confirmation of title to land in Alabama.	15	1	Petition	56	Priv. Land Claims.						
Smith, Samuel, (Ky.)	Compensation for a horse lost, war of 1812.	18	1	Petition	109	Claims	Jan. 15, 1824	Adverse		Laid on table.		
Smith, Samuel, (Ky.)	Compensation for a horse lost, war of 1812.	19	2	Resolution	51	Claims	Dec. 15, 1826	Adverse		Laid on table.		
Smith, Samuel, (Ky.)	Compensation for a horse lost, war of 1812.	20	2	Resolution	225	Claims	Feb. 9, 1829	Adverse		Laid on table.		
Smith, Samuel	(See administrator of John Young)	18	2		229							
Smith, Samuel, N. Y.	Pension	20	2	Petition	228	Military Pensions				Discharged; referred to Com. Whole House.		
Smith, Samuel	(See representat's of Luther Smith)	21	1		297							
Smith, Samuel	Compensation for work, &c., on Cumberland road.	23	1	Res. and docs.	589	Claims	455	Adverse				See report No. 449.
Smith, Samuel	(See administrator of John Fleming.)	26	1		621							
Smith, Samuel, (Maine)	Arrears of pension	31	1	Petition	623	Invalid Pensions	473	Adverse		Laid on table.		
Smith, Samuel, representatives of.	Reimbursement of advances on public account.	12	1	Petition	95	Claims.						
Smith, Samuel, representatives of.	Reimbursement of advances on public account.	13	2	Petition	196	Pens. & Rev. Cl'ms.	Jan. 25, 1814	Adverse		Rejected.		
Smith, Samuel, representative of.	Indemnity for French spoliations prior to 1800.	29	2	Memorial	75	Foreign Affairs.						
Smith, Samuel, heirs of	Commutation pay for revolutionary services.	23	2	Petition	47	Rev. Claims	Dec. 22, 1834	Adverse		Laid on table.		
Smith, Samuel, heirs of	Commutation pay for revolutionary services.	24	1	Petition	213	Rev. Claims.						
Smith, Samuel, and others.	Permission to return with vessel and cargo to Beverly, Mass.	13	2	Petition	266	Foreign Relations.						
Smith, Samuel, administratrix of.	Credit for money lost in mail	19	1	Petition	251	Ways and Means.						
Smith, Samuel, administratrix of.	Credit for money lost in mail	20	1	Petition	51	Ways and Means				Discharged.		
				Rep. of Postmaster General.	109					Laid on table.		
Smith, Samuel, and others.	Confirmation of title to certain lands.	22	2	Senate bill	228	Public Lands			S. 32			

List of private claims presented to the House of Representatives of the United States from the 1st to the 31st Congress, inclusive—Continued.

Names of claimants.	Nature or object of the claim.	Congress.	Session.	How brought before the House of Reps.	Page of journal.	To what committee of the House referred.	No. or date of the report.	Nature of the report.	No. of the bill.	How disposed of by the House of Reps.	How disposed of by the Senate.	Date of the act of Congress, and remarks.
Smith, Samuel, and others.	Confirmation of title to certain lands.	23	2	Senate bill	126	Public Lands	Jan. 20, 1835	With't amend.	S. 2	Referred to Committee Whole House.		
Smith, Samuel, and others.	Confirmation of title to certain lands.	24	1	Senate bill	552	Public Lands	May 6, 1836	With't amend.	S. 17	Passed	Passed	App'd July 2, 1836
Smith, Samuel, and others.	To amend act of July 2, 1836	24	2	Senate bill	551				S. 118	Passed	Passed	App'd March 3, 1837
Smith, Samuel, and others.	Exchange of certain lands	31	1	Petition	390	Priv. Land Claims.	195	Favorable	201	Referred to Committee Whole House.		
Smith, Samuel, and others.	Exchange of certain lands	31	2	Bill of last sess.	181	Whole House	Jan. 24, 1851	With't amend.	201	Passed.		
Smith, Samuel, sureties of.	To be exonerated from liability	24	1	Petition	53	Judiciary	91	Favorable	90	Passed.		
Smith, Samuel, sureties of.	To be exonerated from liability	24	2	Petition	48	Judiciary	Feb. 28, 1837	Favorable	961	Referred to Committee Whole House.		
Smith, Samuel, sureties of.	To be exonerated from liability	25	2	House bill	254	Whole House			386			
Smith, Samuel, sureties of.	To be exonerated from liability	25	3	Bill of last sess.	378	Whole House	Jan. 25, 1839	With't amend.	386	Passed	Passed	App'd March 2, 1839
Smith, Samuel J	Pension	24	1	Petition	473	Invalid Pensions.						
Smith, Samuel J	Pension	24	2	Petition	72	Invalid Pensions	51	Favorable	800	Referred to Committee Whole House.		
Smith, Samuel J	Pension	25	2	Petition	39	Invalid Pensions	218	Favorable	256	Passed	Adverse report.	
Smith, Samuel J	Pension	30	1	Petition	624	Invalid Pensions				Discharged; laid on table.		
Smith, Samuel J	Pension	31	1	Petition	1221	Invalid Pensions.						
Smith, Samuel S	(See administrator of John Smith, Penn.)	29	1		68							
Smith, Sam'l, or Sam'l C.	Pension	23	1	Petition	72	Invalid Pensions	Jan. 7, 1834	Adverse		Laid on table.		
Smith, Samuel, and James.	(Not stated.)	31	1	Documents	644	Claims.						
Smith, Sarah	(See heirs of Elisha Alford)	27	3		260							
Smith, Sarah	(See Alba C. Smith, widow of)	31	1		996							
Smith, Sarah H	(See Francis N. Smith, widow of)	15	1		237							
Smith, Shadrach, widow of.	Pension for revolutionary services.	25	3	Petition	216	Rev. Pensions.						
Smith, Simeon	Confirmation of title to land in Missouri.	15	1	Petition	312	Priv. Land Claims.						
Smith, Simeon	Confirmation of title to land in Missouri.	16	1	Petition	71	Priv. Land Claims.						
Smith, Simeon	Confirmation of title to land in Missouri.	17	1	Petition	55	Public Lands.						
Smith, Simeon	Confirmation of title to land in Missouri.	18	1	Petition	55	Public Lands	Jan. 16, 1824	Favorable	65	Passed	Passed	App'd May 26, 1824
Smith, Simeon	Pension	24	2	Petition	74	Rev. Pensions	154	Favorable	882	Ref'd to Com. W. H.		
Smith, Simeon	Pension	25	2	Petition	38	Rev. Pensions	167	Favorable	192	Passed	Passed	App'd June 28, 1838
Smith, Simon, (N. H.)	Pension for disabilities, war of 1812.	26	2	Petition	100	Invalid Pensions	81	Adverse		Laid on table.		
Smith, Stephen	Increase of compensation as collector of customs.	6	1	Memorial	586	Com. and Manuf.				Postponed.		
Smith, Stephen	(See Wm. W. Byers, and others.)	23	2		278							
Smith, Stephen	(See William H. Bedford)	28	1		262							
Smith, Stevens, and others.	Bounty on fishing schooner Rising States.	23	1	Petition	239	Commerce	235	Favorable	261	Referred to Committee Whole House.		
Smith, Stevens, and others.	Bounty on fishing schooner Rising States.	23	2	Bill of last sess.	299	Whole House	Jan. 31, 1835	With't amend.	261	Passed	Passed	App'd March 3, 1835
Smith	(See Gurney & Smith)	26	1		182							
Smith, Stevenson, agent of	(See Conrad Eiselen, administrator of.)	26	1		182							
Smith, Susan, or Susannah.	(See widow of Rev. John Smith.)	14	1		46							
Smith, Sylvanus	(See executors of Judah Alden)	29	2		131							

List of private claims presented to the House of Representatives of the United States from the 1st to the 31st Congress, inclusive—Continued.

Names of claimants.	Nature or object of the claim.	Congress.	Session.	How brought before the House of Reps.	Page of journal.	To what committee of the House referred.	No. or date of the report.	Nature of the report.	No. of the bill.	How disposed of by the House of Reps.	How disposed of by the Senate.	Date of the act of Congress, and remarks.
Smith, Thomas	Settlement of account as commissary.	2	1	Petition	471	....	....	....	......	Referred to Secretary War.		
Smith, Thomas	(See execu'ors of General Richard Butler.)	2	1	....	537							
Smith, Thomas	Liquidation of twenty-seven tax notes.	4	1	Rep. of Secretary Treasury.	388	Claims	May 31, 1796	Adverse	......	Laid on table.		
Smith, Thomas	Pension for wounds received at Dartmoor.	14	1	Petition	125	Naval Affairs.						
Smith, Thomas	Payment of pension stolen from mail.	25	2	Petition	405	Rev. Pensions.						
Smith, Thomas	Remission of fine for violation of revenue laws.	28	2	Senate bill	243	Commerce.	Feb. 25, 1845	With't amend.	S. 58	Referred to Committee Whole House.		
Smith, Thomas, representatives of.	Interest on claim as commissioner of loans.	4	1	Petition	457	Claims	....	....	......	....	....	See appropriation bill, No. 142.
Smith, Thomas, representatives of.	Interest on claim as commissioner of loans.	5	2	Petition	318	Claims	May 29, 1798	Legislation inexpedient.	......	Report concurred in.		
Smith, Thomas, representatives of.	Indemnity for French spoliations prior to 1800.	29	2	Memorial	136	Foreign Affairs.						
Smyth, Thomas, widow of.	Pension for revolutionary services.	20	2	Petition	82	Military Pensions.						
Smyth, Thomas, widow of.	Arrears of pay and pension for revolutionary services.	24	2	Petition	119	Rev. Claims......	Jan. 19, 1837	Adverse	......	Laid on table.		
Smith, Thomas D., widow of.	Compensation for horse lost in public service	24	1	Memorial	507	Claims	775	Adverse	......	Laid on table.		
Smith, Thomas D., widow of.	Compensation for horse lost in public service.	24	2	Memorial	266	Claims	Jan. 28, 1837	Adverse	......	Laid on table.		
Smith, Thomas D., widow of.	Compensation for horse lost in public service.	25	2	Petition	51	Claims	Feb. 21, 1838	Adverse	......	Laid on table.		
Smith, Thomas, executrix of.	Pay for naval services...........	21	2	Petition	106	Naval Affairs.						
Smith, Thomas, heir of...	Bounty land for military services..	28	1	Petition	195	Priv. Land Claims.						
Smith, Thomas A.......	Indemnity for loss of public moneys.	21	2	Senate bill	301	Claims...........	471	Adverse	S. 76			
Smith, Thomas G	Pension	22	1	Petition	287	Rev. Pensions.						
Smith, Thomas Gregory..	Land warrant.................	26	1	Petition	364	Priv. Land Claims.	625	Adverse	......	Leave to withdraw.		
Smith, Thomas George...	Indemnity for his land sold by government.	31	1	Petition	400	Rev. Claims.						
Smith, Thomas H., & Son.	(See George B. Rapelye and others)	12	1	....	64							
Smith, Thos. H., & Son, surety of.	Release from custom-house bonds.	20	2	Petition	142	Ways and Means.						
Smith, Thos. H., & Son, surety of.	Compromise of liability.........	22	1	Senate bill	701	Judiciary	482	With't amend.	S. 183	Passed	Passed	App'd June 15, 1832
Smith, Thorowgood, trustee of.	Indemnity for French spoliations prior to 1800.	26	1	Memorial	182	Foreign Affairs....	343	Favorable; bill	319	Referred to Committee Whole House.		
Smith, Thurgar, & Co...	Reimbursement of duties paid on carpeting.	29	1	Memorial	151	Claims	57	Favorable	54	Passed	Passed, with amendment.	App'd Aug. 8, 1846
Smith, Thurgar, & Co...	Reimbursement of duties paid on wool.	29	1	Petition	358	Commerce........	407	Adverse	......	Laid on table.		
Smith, Thurgar, & Co...	Reimbursement of duties paid on wool.	29	2	Petition	357	Claims	54	Favorable	656	Referred to Committee Whole House.		
Smith, Thurgar, & Co...	Reimbursement of duties paid on wool.	30	1	Petition	97	Commerce	65	Favorable....	47	Passed	Passed	App'd June 28, 1848
Smith, Timothy S.......	Indemnity for destruction of property at Niagara.	20	2	Petition	71	Claims	Dec. 24, 1828	Adverse......	......	Laid on table.		

List of private claims presented to the House of Representatives of the United States from the 1st to the 31st Congress, inclusive—Continued.

Names of claimants.	Nature or object of the claim.	Congress.	Session.	How brought before the House of Reps.	Page of journal.	To what committee of the House referred.	No. or date of the report.	Nature of the report.	No. of the bill.	How disposed of by the House of Reps.	How disposed of by the Senate.	Date of the act of Congress, and remarks.
Smith, Timothy S.	Indemnity for destruction of property at Niagara.	21	1	Petition	318	Claims	Mar. 15, 1830	Adverse.		Laid on table.		
Smith & Town	Drawback on merchandise	25	2	Documents	113	Commerce	July 6, 1838	Favorable	883	Ordered to 3d reading.		
Smith & Town	Drawback on merchandise	25	3	Bill of last sess.	264				883	Passed	Passed	App'd Mar. 2, 1839
Smith, Valentine	Pension	21	2	Petition	230	Military Pensions.						
Smith, Valentine	Pension	22	1	Petition	187	Rev. Pensions.						
Smith, Walter	Compensation for medical supplies, revolutionary war.	2	2	Petition	634					Motion to refer, rejected.		
Smith, Walter	Balance due on books of Fourth Auditor.	22	1	Appropriation bill	101				116			App'd May 5, 1832
Smith, Waters, assignee of.	Payment of balance due him from government.	22	1	Petition	258	Ways and Means.						
Smith, Willard	(See Rufus Spalding, and others.)	15	2		148							
Smith, William, (Balt.)	Permission to fund revolutionary certificate.	1	3	Memorial & rep't Sec. of War.	376, 380					Laid on table.		
Smith, William, (Balt.)	Permission to fund revolutionary certificate.	2	1	Petition and rep't Sec. Treasury.	481, 554					Laid on table.		
Smith, William, (Balt.)	Permission to fund revolutionary certificate.	3	1	Petition	27	Select	Feb. 10, 1794	Adverse		Laid on table.		
Smith, William, (Balt.)	Permission to fund revolutionary certificate.	4	1	Rep. of Secretary Treasury.	388	Claims.						
				Petition	427	Claims	May 31, 1796	Adverse		Laid on table.		
Smith, William, (Balt.)	Permission to fund revolutionary certificate.	4	2	Petition	656	Claims	Jan. 24, 1797	Adverse		Rejected.		
Smith, William, (Balt.)	Permission to fund revolutionary certificate.	5	2	Petition	221	Claims	Mar. 12, 1798	Adverse		Laid on table		Leave to withdraw, p. 261.
Smith, William, (Balt.)	Permission to fund revolutionary certificate.	8	2	Petition	89	Claims.						
Smith, William, (Balt.)	Permission to fund revolutionary certificate.	9	1	Petition	187	Claims				Discharged; referred to Com. Whole House.		
Smith, William, (Balt.)	Permission to fund revolutionary certificate.	9	2	Petition	474	Claims				Discharged; referred to Com. Whole House.		
Smith, William, (Balt.)	Permission to fund revolutionary certificate.	10	1	Petition	38	Select.						
Smith, William, (Balt.)	Permission to fund revolutionary certificate.	13	2	Petition	201	Pens. & Rev. Clm's.				Discharged.		
Smith, William	(See heirs of James Smith)	3	1		32							
Smith, William, (Phila)	Pension for revolutionary services.	4	1	Petition	451	Claims	May 7, 1796	Adverse		Leave to withdraw.		
Smith, William, (Pa.)	Pension	4	1	Petition	543	Claims	May 31, 1796	Adverse		Leave to withdraw.		
Smith, William	Reimbursement of money paid for public land.	7	1	Petition	95	Claims	Mar. 8, 1802	Adverse		Laid on table.		
Smith, William, (S. C.)	Release from imprisonment at suit of United States.	14	2	Petition	279	Select	Feb. 1, 1817	Favorable	94	Laid on table.		
				Senate bill	329	Whole House	Feb. 27, 1817	With't amend.	S. 18	Passed	Passed	App'd March 3, 1817
Smith, William	Bounty land for revolutionary services.	14	2	Petition	422	Claims.						
Smith, William, (heirs of)	Bounty land for revolutionary services.	17	2	Petition	25	Public Lands	Dec. 17, 1822	General bill	196	Laid on table.		
Smith, William, (Va.)	Exchange of location of Virginia military lands.	15	1	Petition	279	Select				Discharged; leave to withdraw.		
Smith, William, (Va.)	Exchange of location of Virginia military lands.	16	1	Petition	92	Priv. Land Claims.	Mar. 6, 1820	Adverse		Rejected.		

List of private claims presented to the House of Representatives of the United States from the 1st to the 31st Congress, inclusive—Continued.

Names of claimants.	Nature or object of the claim.	Congress.	Session.	How brought before the House of Reps.	Page of journal.	To what committee of the House referred.	No. or date of the report.	Nature of the report.	No. of the bill.	How disposed of by the House of Reps.	How disposed of by the Senate.	Date of the act of Congress, and remarks.
Smith, William, (Ohio)	Pension for services in the war of 1812.	18	2	Petition	86	Pens. & Rev. Cl'ms.						
Smith, William	(See administrator of John Taylor)	21	2		178							
Smith, William, (Va.)	Compensation for a horse lost in public service.	22	1	Petition	63	Claims	456	Favorable	557	Referred to Committee Whole House.		
Smith, William	(See assignees Thomas Tupper)	22	2		142							
Smith, William	Pension for revolutionary services.	24	1	Petition	107	Invalid Pensions	Feb. 16, 1836	Adverse		Laid on table.		
Smith, William, (S. C.)	Indemnity for Indian depredations in 1793.	25	2	Petition	632	Indian Affairs.						
Smith, William, (S. C.)	Indemniay for Indian depredations in 1793.	25	3	Petition	130	Indian Affairs.						
Smith, William	Indemnity for French spoliations prior to 1800.	27	3	Petition	191	Commerce.						
Smith, William	(See Exploring Expedition)	27	3		149		270		818			
Smith, Major William	Increase of pension	24	1	Res. and docs.	267	Rev. Pensions				Discharged; laid on table.		
Smith, Major William	Increase of pension	24	2	Res. and docs.	90	Rev. Pensions	42	Favorable	789	Referred to Committee Whole House.		
Smith, Major William	Increase of pension	25	2	Petition	38	Rev. Pensions	274	Favorable	317	Passed	Adverse report.	
Smith, Major William	Increase of pension	25	3	Petition	88	Rev. Pensions	87	Favorable	966	Passed	Adverse report.	
Smith, Major William	Increase of pension	26	1	Petition	172	Rev. Pensions.						
Smith, Major William	Increase of pension	26	2	Petition	248	Rev. Pensions.						
Smith, Major William	Increase of pension	27	2	Petition	97	Rev. Pensions	784	Adverse		Laid on table.		
Smith, William	(See heir of Thomas Smith)	28	1		195							
Smith, William	Pension for disabilities in Indian wars.	28	1	Petition	912	Invalid Pensions.						
Smith, William, jr.	(See Henry Ingraham, and others)	16	1		35							
Smith, William, jr.	Remission of the interest on a judgment.	16	2	Petition	63	Ways and Means	Jan. 9, 1821	Favorable	188	Referred to Committee Whole House.		
Smith, William, jr.	Remission of the interest on a judgment.	17	1	Petition	125	Ways and Means.						
Smith, William, widow of	Pension for revolutionary services.	27	2	Petition	375	Rev. Pensions				Laid on table.		
Smith, Wm. W., & others	Compensation for services as revolutionary surgeons.	2	1	Petition	458					Referred to Secretary of Treasury.		
Smith, Wm. W., & others	Compensation for services as revolutionary surgeons.	2	2	Rep. of Secretary Treasury.	78					Laid on table.		
Smith, William W.	(See administrator of Gilbert Tennent.)	2	1		458							
Smith, William, and others.	Compensation for extra services on exploring expedition.	28	2	Petition	70	Naval Affairs.						
Smith, William, and others.	Indemnity for loss of ship Friendship.	4	1	Petition	371	Com. and Manuf.	Jan. 11, 1796	Adverse		Leave to withdraw.		
Smith, William A.	Pension	30	1	Petition	406	Invalid Pensions	Mar. 30, 1848	Adverse		Laid on table.		
Smith, William H., heirs of.	Commutation pay for revolutionary services as surgeon.	23	2	Petition	38	Rev. Claims.						
Smith, William H., heirs of.	Commutation pay for revolutionary services as surgeon.	24	1	Petition	102	Rev. Claims	495	Favorable	495	Referred to Committee Whole House.		
Smith, William H., representatives of.	Commutation pay for revolutionary services.	25	2	Petition	48	Rev. Claims	112	Favorable	130	Passed	Passed	App'd July 7, 1838
Smith, William M., daughter of.	Commutation pay for revolutionary services.	28	1	Resolution	305	Rev. Claims.						
Smith, William S., heirs of.	Commutation pay for revolutionary services.	22	2	Petition	89	Rev. Claims.						

List of private claims presented to the House of Representatives of the United States from the 1st to the 31st Congress, inclusive—Continued.

Names of claimants.	Nature or object of the claim.	Congress.	Session.	How brought before the House of Reps.	Page of journal.	To what committee of the House referred.	No. or date of the report.	Nature of the report.	No. of the bill.	How disposed of by the House of Reps.	How disposed of by the Senate.	Date of the act of Congress, and remarks.
Smith, William T., (Philadelphia.)	Permission to fund loan office certificates.	8	1	Memorial	569	Select.						
Smith, William T., (Philadelphia.)	Permission to fund loan office certificates.	8	2	Memorial	60	Select.						
Smith, William T., executor of.	Permission to fund loan office certificates.	24	2	Petition	95	Rev. Claims	315	Favorable	970	Referred to Committee Whole House.		
Smith, William T., executor of.	Permission to fund loan office certificates.	25	2	Petition	40	Rev. Claims	103	Favorable	124	Postponed.		
Smith, William T., executor of.	Permission to fund loan office certificates.	26	1	Petition	164	Rev. Claims	330	Favorable	302	Referred to Committee Whole House.		
Smith, William T., executor of.	Permission to fund loan office certificates.	27	2	Petition	61	Rev. Claims	80	Favorable	120	Passed.		
Smith, William T., executor of.	Permission to fund loan office certificates.	27	3	Petition	70	Rev. Claims	16	Favorable	639	Passed.		
Smith, William T., executor of.	Permission to fund loan office certificates.	28	1	Petition	79	Rev. Claims	318	Favorable	226	Referred to Committee Whole House.		
Smith, William T., executor of.	Permission to fund loan office certificates.	29	1	Memorial	115	Rev. Claims.						
Smith, William T., executor of.	Permission to fund loan office certificates.	31	1	Petition	348	Rev. Claims	190	Favorable	196	Referred to Committee Whole House.		
Smith, William T	Right of pre-emption as New Orleans branch pilot.	28	1	Petition	77	Priv. Land Claims.	9	Favorable; bill	35	Passed	Passed	App'd June 17, 1844
Smith, William W., (Ala.)	Compensation for military stores for public use.	18	1	Petition	358	Claims	May 5, 1824	Adverse		Laid on table.		
Smith, William, (Boston).	Indemnity for French spoliations prior to 1800.	26	1	Memorial	182	Foreign Affairs	343	Favorable; bill	319	Referred to Committee Whole House.		
Smith, Wm. W., mother of.	Pension for loss of her son in battle.	21	2	Petition	43	Military Pensions.						
Smith, William, executor of.	Indemnity for French spoliations prior to 1800.	26	1	Memorial	182	Foreign Affairs	343	Favorable; bill	319	Referred to Commitee Whole House.		
Smith, Williamson	Indemnity for non-fulfilment of a government contract.	26	1	Petition	808	Judiciary	588	Indefinite		Discharged; referred to Secretary of War.		
Smith, Williamson	Indemnity for non-fulfilment of a government contract.	26	2	Petition	166	Ways and Means.						
Smith, Williamson, assignees of.	Indemnity for non-fulfilment of a government contract.	28	1	Petition	515	Judiciary.						
Smith, Williamson, assignees of.	Indemnity for non-fulfilment of a government contract.	29	1	Petition	310	Claims.						
Smith, Williamson, assignee of.	Payment of ascertained balance due him.	27	2	Petition	514	Judiciary				Discharged; leave to withdraw.		
Smith, Williamson, assignee of.	Payment of ascertained balance due him.	27	3	Petition	44	Judiciary	177	Adverse		Laid on table		Minority report favorable.
Smith, Wilson	Indemnity for destruction of property, Niagara.	22	1	Resolution	178	Claims	Mar. 14, 1832	Adverse		Laid on table.		
Smith & Wood	Indemnity for French spoliations prior to 1800.	26	1	Memorial	182	Foreign Affairs	343	Favorable; bill	319	Referred to Committee Whole House.		
Smith, Zebedee	Increase of pension	24	1	Resolution	750	Invalid Pensions	June 28, 1836	Adverse		Laid on table.		
Smith, Zebedee	Increase of pension	25	2	Petition	93	Invalid Pensions.						
Smock, John Q	Compensation for a horse lost in Indian wars.	24	1	Petition	430	Claims.						
Smoot, S. Alexander, and William Thornton.	Indemnity for a vessel sunk for defence of Baltimore.	13	3	Petition	561							
				Rep. of Secretary of War.	713	Claims	Feb. 27, 1815	Adverse		Rejected.		

List of private claims presented to the House of Representatives of the United States from the 1st to the 31st Congress, inclusive—Continued.

Names of claimants.	Nature or object of the claim.	Congress.	Session.	How brought before the House of Reps.	Page of journal.	To what committee of the House referred.	No. or date of the report.	Nature of the report.	No. of the bill.	How disposed of by the House of Reps.	How disposed of by the Senate.	Date of the act of Congress, and remarks.
Smoot, Benjamin S......	Compensation for services as United States marshal.	12	2	Petition	648	Claims.						
Smoot, Benjamin S......	(See Denni-on Darling and others)	15	2	....	139							
Smoot, Benjamin S., (Ala.)	Indemnity for injuries to property in public service.	18	2	Petition	229	Claims.						
Smoot, Benjamin S., (Ala.)	Indemnity for injuries to property in public service.	19	1	Petition	44	Claims	Jan. 30, 1826	Adverse......	......	Laid on table.		
Smoot, Benjamin S......	Indemnity for destruction of property at Fort Bowyer.	21	2	Senate bill	217	Claims	61	Adverse	S. 91	Passed	Passed	App'd March 3, 1831
Smoot, Benjamin S......	Further indemnity, &c.........	22	1	Senate bill	1076	Claims	July 5, 1832	With't amend	S. 58	Ref'd to Com. W. H.		
Smoot, Benjamin S......	Compensation for services as marshal, Alabama.	21	2	Petition	178	Judiciary	....	....	......	Discharged; laid on table.		
Smoot, Benjamin S......	Adjustment of his accounts as sutler.	21	2	Petition	235	Claims.						
Smoot, Benjamin S......	Adjustment of his accounts as sutler.	22	2	Senate bill	211	Claims	89	Adverse.	S. 33			
Smothers, Joseph........	Increase of revolutionary pension.	25	3	Resolution	275	Rev. Pensions.						
Smuck, John...........	(See Conrad Houseman & others.)											
Smuck, John...........	(See Francis Loonzs.)	5	2	....	210							
Smylie & Patterson......	(See H. Silliman and others.)....	12	1	....	98							
Snagg, Henry	Pension for revolutionary services.	3	1	Rep. of Secretary War.	131	Select	May 26, 1794	Res. to refer to Sec. War.	R. 12	Passed	Passed	App'd June 9, 1794
Snagg, Henry	Pension for revolutionary services.	3	2	Rep. of Secretary of War.	262	Claims.						
Snagg, Henry	Pension for revolutionary services.	4	1	Rep. of Secretary War.	445	Claims.						
Snagg, Henry	Pension for revolutionary services.	4	2	Rep. of Secretary War.	614	Claims.						
Snapp, Lewis, and others.	Reimbursement of fine imposed by Postmaster General.	29	1	Petition	873	P. Of. & P. Roads.						
Snapp, Lewis, and others.	Reimbursement of fine imposed by Postmaster General.	31	1	Petition	390	P. Of. & P. Roads.	110	Adverse	......	Laid on table.		
Snavely, William	Reimbursement of money paid for public land.	26	1	Petition	504	Claims.						
Snavely, William	Reimbursement of money paid for public land.	27	2	Petition	379	Priv. Land Claims.						
Snavely, William	Reimbursement of money paid for public land.	27	3	Petition	228	Priv. Land Claims.						
Snavely, William	Reimbursement of money paid for publie land.	29	1	Memorial	648	Priv. Land Claims.						
Snavely, William	Reimbursement of money paid for public land.	30	1	Petition	524	Claims	647	Favorable....	514	Referred to Committee Whole House.		
Snavely, William	Reimbursement of money paid for public land.	30	2	Bill of last sess..	318	Whole House	Jan. 26, 1849	With't amend.	514	Passed.		
Snavely, William	Reimbursement of money paid for public land.	31	1	Petition	486	Claims.						
Sneed, Archibald H., surety of.	Release from a judgment at suit of United States.	24	1	Petition	537	Judiciary.........	....	....	......	Discharged; laid on table.		
Sneed, Archibald H., surety of.	Release from a judgment at suit of United States.	25	2	Senate bill	605	Judiciary.........	Mar. 28, 1838	With't amend.	S. 142	Referred to Committee Whole House.		
Sneed, Archibald H., surety of.	Release from a judgment at suit of United States.	26	1	Senate bill	1152	Judiciary.........	....	....	S. 252			

3—47

List of private claims presented to the House of Representatives of the United States from the 1st to the 31st Congress, inclusive—Continued.

Names of claimants.	Nature or object of the claim.	Congress.	Session.	How brought before the House of Reps.	Page of journal.	To what committee of the House referred.	No. or date of the report.	Nature of the report.	No. of the bill.	How disposed of by the House of Reps.	How disposed of by the Senate.	Date of the act of Congress, and remarks.
Sneed, Archibald H., surety of	Release from a judgment at suit of United States.	27	3	Petition	176	Judiciary	99	Favorable	723	Passed	Passed	App'd March 3, 1843
Sneed, Archibald H., surety of.	Release from a judgment at suit of United States.	28	1	Petition and docs.	228	Judiciary	354	Favorable	267	Passed	Passed	App'd June 17, 1844
Snead, Charles, heirs of	Commutation pay for revolutionary services.	23	1	Petition	40	Rev. Claims.						
Snead, Charles, heirs of	Commutation pay for revolutionary services.	23	2	Petition	113	Rev. Claims.						
Snead, Charles, heirs of	Commutation pay for revolutionary services.	24	1	Petition	103	Rev. Claims	708	Favorable	661	Referred to Committee Whole House.		
Snead, Charles, heirs of	Commutation pay for revolutionary services.	25	2	Petition	40	Rev. Claims	111	Favorable	129	Passed	Passed	App'd July 7, 1838
Snead, Harrison	Exchange of bounty land	25	2	Petition	417	Public Lands.						
Snead, Harrison	Exchange of bounty land	25	3	Petition	92	Public Lands.						
Snead, John S.	(See William Morton and J. S. Snead.)	14	2		364							
Sneed, Richard	(See sureties of A. H. Sneed)	24	1		537							
Sneed, Stephen, executors of.	(See sureties of A. H Sneed)	24	1		537							
Sneed, Stephen K.	(See sureties of A. H. Sneed)	24	1		37							
Sneed, William M.	(See sureties of A. H. Sneed)	24	1		537							
Sneathen, John	(See Jacob Groom and others)	25	3		124							
Snell, George, (Pa.)	Compensation for military supplies.	18	1	Petition	286	Military Affairs				Discharged; laid on table.		Leave to withdraw 2d session.
Snell, Jacob	Pension	12	1	Petition	183	Claims	June 12, 1812	Adverse		Laid on table.		
Snell, Jacob	Pension	16	1	Petition	117	Pens. & Rev. Cl'ms.						
Snell, Jacob	Arrears of pension	22	2	Petition	318	Invalid Pensions.						
Snell, Jacob	Arrears of pension	23	1	Petition	60	Invalid Pensions				Discharged; leave to withdraw.		
Snell, Job	Pension for revolutionary services.	3	1	Rep. of Secretary War.	131	Select	May 26, 1794	Res. to refer to Sec. War.	J. R. 12	Passed	Passed	App'd June 9, 1794
Snell, Job	Pension for revolutionary services.	3	2	Rep. of Secretary War.	262	Claims	Feb. 28, 1795	Favorable; bill ordered.	130	Passed	Postponed.	
Snell, Job	Pension for revolutionary services.	4	1	Rep. of Secretary War.	445	Claims	Feb. 18, 1796	Favorable; bill ordered.	156	Passed	Passed	App'd April 20, 1796
Snell, John	Indemnity in land for loss by Choctaw treaty.	24	1	Petition	57	Public Lands	208	Favorable	208	Referred to Committee Whole House.		
Snell, Joseph	To be restored to pension roll	17	1	Petition	60	Rev. Pensions.						
Snells, Samuel, and others.	Fee simple title to lands in Alabama.	14	2	Petition	72	Public Lands.						
Snell, Thomas	(See Thomas Stagg, jr., and Thos. Snell.)	7	1		27							
Snelling, Joseph	Additional compensation for services in commissary department.	12	1	Petition	190	Claims	Mar. 2, 1812	Adverse		Laid on table.		
Snelling, Joseph, & others	Depreciation pay for revolutionary services.	5	3	Memorial	452							Not referred.
Snelling, N. G.	(See Massachusetts, merchants and citizens of.)	26	1		182							
Snelson, Robert L., father of.	Prize money due deceased	16	1	Petition	81	Naval Affairs	Feb. 10, 1820	Adverse		Laid on table.		
Snethen, W. G.	(See Thomas Copeland)	29	2		89							
Sniffen, Thomas	Pension for revolutionary services.	24	2	Petition	74	Rev. Pensions.						
Snipes, William Clay	(See representatives of John Wood)	5	3		429							

List of private claims presented to the House of Representatives of the United States from the 1st to the 31st Congress, inclusive—Continued.

Names of claimants.	Nature or object of the claim.	Congress.	Session.	How brought before the House of Reps.	Page of journal.	To what committee of the House referred.	No. or date of the report.	Nature of the report.	No. of the bill.	How disposed of by the House of Reps.	How disposed of by the Senate.	Date of the act of Congress, and remarks.
Snively, Henry	Indemnity for an erroneous entry of land.	31	1	Petition	198	Public Lands.						
Snodgrass, company S. C. volunteers.	Compensation as guards to emigrating Indians.	26	1		332	Military Affairs	April 4, 1840	Favorable	314	Referred to Committee Whole House.		
Snodgrass, company S. C. volunteers.	Reimbursement of expenses	26	1	Senate bill	640	Claims			S. 32			
Snodgrass, John	(See heirs of Alex. Montgomery)	14	1		454							
Snodgrass, Thomas	Compensation for escorting emigrating Indians.	31	1	Senate bill	1105	Indian Affairs			S. 227			
Snodgrass, William	Payment of a quartermaster's draft	14	1	Petition	40	Claims.						
Snow, Aaron	Compensation for revolutionary services.	21	1	Petition	199	Rev. Claims	171	Favorable	216	Referred to Committee Whole House.		
Snow, Aaron	Compensation for revolutionary services.	21	2	Bill of last sess.	264	Whole House	Feb. 4, 1831	With't amend.	216	Passed.		
Snow, Aaron	Compensation for revolutionary services.	22	1	Petition	62	Rev. Claims	187	Favorable	170	Passed	Passed	App'd July 4, 1832
Snow, Abner	Compensation for revolutionary services and injuries.	8	1	Petition	502	Claims				Disch'd; postponed.		
Snow, Abner	Compensation for revolutionary services and injuries.	8	2	Petition	69	Claims				Discharged; referred to Com. Whole House.		
Snow, Abner	Pension for revolutionary services, &c.	10	1	Pension bill	232	Whole House			78	Passed	Passed, with amendment.	App'd April 25, 1808
Snow, Amos	Pension for revolutionary services.	3	2	Rep. of Secretary War.	337	Claims				Discharged; laid on table.		
Snow, Amos	Pension for revolutionary services.	4	1	Rep. of Secretary War.	445	Claims	Feb. 15, 1796	Res. to refer to Sec. War.	R. 16	Passed	Passed	App'd April 16, 1796
Snow, Amos	Pension for revolutionary services.	4	2	Rep. of Secretary War.	614	Claims.						
Snow, Benjamin	(See Woodbridge & Snow)	26	1		182							
Snow, Benjamin, widow of	Indemnity for French spoliations prior to 1800.	31	1	Petition	285	Foreign Affairs	355	General bill	318	Referred to Committee Whole House.		
Snow, Ebenezer	To be restored to pension roll	17	1	Petition	67	Rev. Pensions.						
Snow, Elisha, jr	Reimbursement of forfeiture paid to United States.	18	1	Petition	297	Judiciary	May 1, 1824	Favorable	216	Referred to Committee Whole House.		
Snow, Elisha, jr	Reimbursement of forfeiture paid to United States.	18	2	Bill of last sess.	250	Whole House	Feb. 19, 1825	With't amend.	216	Passed	Passed	App'd March 3, 1825
Snow, Freelove	(See James Vanuxem.)	3	1		185							
Snow, Isaac, heirs of	Indemnity for vessel destroyed by the enemy.	28	1	Petition	745	Claims	565	Adverse		Laid on table.		
Snow, James, (Mass)	Pension for revolutionary services.	22	1	Petition	105	Rev. Pensions.						
Snow, John	Redemption of a Continental note.	25	2	Petition	270	Rev. Claims				Discharged; laid on table.		
Snow, John	Pension for revolutionary services.	25	2	Petition	403	Rev. Pensions				Discharged; referred to Com. Whole House.		
Snow, John	Pension for revolutionary services.	26	1	Petition	174	Rev. Pensions				Discharged; laid on table.		
Snow, Jonas, widow of	Pension for revolutionary services.	25	2	Petition	116	Rev. Pensions	763	Favorable	722	Ref'd to Com. W. H.		
Snow, Jonas, widow of	Pension for revolutionary services.	26	1	Senate bill	1277				S. 359			
Snow, Jonas, widow of	Pension for revolutionary services.	26	2	Senate bill	327	Whole House			S. 186			
Snow, Jonas, widow of	Pension for revolutionary services.	27	2	Senate bill	550	Rev. Pensions	April 12, 1842	With't amend.	S. 41	Passed	Passed	App'd Aug. 11, 1842
Snow, Lemuel	Arrears of pay for revolutionary services.	4	1	Petition	445	Claims.						

List of private claims presented to the House of Representatives of the United States from the 1st to the 31st Congress, inclusive—**Continued.**

Names of claimants.	Nature or object of the claim.	Congress.	Session.	How brought before the House of Reps.	Page of journal.	To what committee of the House referred.	No. or date of the report.	Nature of the report.	No. of the bill.	How disposed of by the House of Reps.	How disposed of by the Senate.	Date of the act of Congress, and remarks.
Snow, Lemuel	Arrears of pay for revolutionary services.	4	2	Documents	709	Claims	Feb. 21, 1797	Favorable		Referred to Committee Whole House.		
Snow, Lemuel	Arrears of pay for revolutionary services.	5	2	Petition	89	Whole House	Mar. 19, 1798	Favorable		Rejected.		
Snow, Loring	Confirmation of title to land in Illinois.	28	1	Petition	945	Public Lands.						
Snow, Loring	Right of pre-emption	30	1	Petition	103	Priv. Land Claims.	Feb. 8, 1848	Adverse		Laid on table.		
Snow, Mary	(See Jonas Snow, widow of.)	25	2		116							
Snow, Samuel	Pension for revolutionary services.	20	1	Resolution	265	Military Pensions.	April 29, 1828	Favorable	283	Passed.		
Snow, Samuel	Pension for revolutionary services.	20	2	Pension bill	55	Whole House	Jan. 15, 1840	With amend.	311	Passed	Laid on table.	
Snow, Samuel	Pension for revolutionary services.	21	1	Petition	49	Military Pensions.	Jan. 5, 1830	Favorable	72	Passed	Passed	App'd May 20, 1830
Snow, Sarah	(See Benjamin Snow, widow of.)	31	1		285							
Snow, Solomon	Pension	21	2	Petition	158	Military Pensions.						
Snow, Solomon	Pension	22	1	Petition	123	Rev. Pensions.						
Snow, Sylvanus	Pension for revolutionary services.	4	1	Rep. of Secretary War.	445	Claims	Feb. 18, 1796	Favorable; bill ordered.	156	Passed	Passed	App'd April 20, 1796
Snow, William, heirs of.	Pension	25	2	Petition	406	Invalid Pensions.						
Snow, William, heirs of.	Pension	26	1	Petition	163	Invalid Pensions	April 4, 1840	Favorable	331	Referred to Committee Whole House.		
Snow, Zephaniah D	(See heirs of William Snow.)	25	2		406							
Snowbush, Joseph	Confirmation of title to land in Missouri.	15	2	Petition	88	Priv. Land Claims.						
Snowbush, Joseph	Confirmation of title to land in Missouri.	17	1	Petition	55	Public Lands.						
Snowbush, Joseph	Confirmation of title to land in Missouri.	18	1	Petition	55	Public Lands.						
Snowden, Jonathan	Pension for revolutionary disabilities.	7	1	Petition	89	Claims	March 5, 1802	Adverse.		Laid on table.		
Snowden, Jonathan	Pension for revolutionary disabilities.	7	2	Petition and rep.	285	Claims				Discharged; leave to withdraw.		
Snowden, Jonathan	Pension for revolutionary disabilities.	8	1	Petition	542	Claims	Jan. 25, 1804	Adverse		Referred to Committee Whole House.		
Snowden, Jonathan	Pension for revolutionary disabilities.	9	1	Petition and rep.	252	Claims	Feb. 26, 1806	Adverse		Referred to Committee Whole House.		
Snowden, Jonathan	Pension for revolutionary disabilities.	9	2	Petition	489	Claims	Jan. 19, 1807	Adverse		Referred to Committee Whole House.		
Snowden, Jonathan	Pension for revolutionary disabilities.	10	1	Petition	17	Claims.						
Snowden, Jonathan B., heir of.	Commutation pay for revolutionary services.	24	1	Petition	274	Claims.						
Snowden, Jonathan B., heir of.	Commutation pay for revolutionary services.	24	2	Petition	40	Rev. Claims.						
Snowden, Jonathan B., heir of.	Commutation pay for revolutionary services.	25	2	Petition	70	Rev. Claims.						
Snowden, Jonathan B., heir of.	Commutation pay for revolutionary services.	25	3	Petition	85	Rev. Claims.						
Snowden, Jonathan B., heir of.	Commutation pay for revolutionary services.	26	1	Petition	164	Rev. Claims	391	Adverse		Laid on table.		
Snowden, Jonathan B., heir of.	Commutation pay for revolutionary services.	2[illegible]	2	Petition	134	Claims	Feb. 12, 1841	Adverse		Laid on table.		
Snowden, Jonathan B., heir of.	Commutation pay for revolutionary services.	27	2	Petition	96	Rev. Claims	399	Adverse		Laid on table.		

List of private claims presented to the House of Representatives of the United States from the 1st to the 31st Congress, inclusive—Continued.

Names of claimants.	Nature or object of the claim.	Congress.	Session.	How brought before the House of Reps.	Page of journal.	To what committee of the House referred.	No. or date of the report.	Nature of the report.	No. of the bill.	How disposed of by the House of Reps.	How disposed of by the Senate.	Date of the act of Congress, and remarks.
Snowden, Thomas	Relief in consideration of revolutionary disabilities.	9	1	Petition	210	Claims	Mar. 28, 1806	Adverse		Indefinitely postponed.		Leave to withdraw.
Snowden, Thomas J	Compensation for services, &c., campaign of 1818.	22	1	Resolution	390	Claims.						
Snyder, Abraham	Release from imprisonment at suit of United States.	17	2	Petition and rep't Sec. of War.	60, 135	Judiciary	Feb. 3, 1823	Favorable	264	Passed	Passed	App'd March 3, 1823
Snyder, Andrew, heirs of	Pension for revolutionary services.	29	1	Petition	731	Rev. Pensions.						
Snyder, Andrew, heirs of	Pension for revolutionary services.	29	2	Petition	128	Rev. Claims.						
Snyder, Andrew, heirs of	Pension for revolutionary services.	30	1	Petition	698	Rev. Pensions	784	Adverse		Laid on table.		
Snyder, Conrad	Release from liability to account for certain moneys.	17	2	Petition	144	Judiciary				Leave to withdraw.		
Snyder, David, or Daniel	Compensation for property lost in public service.	25	2	Petition	192	Claims	788	Favorable	738	Referred to Committee Whole House.		
Snyder, David, or Daniel	Compensation for property lost in public service.	25	3	Bill of last sess.	381	Whole House	Jan. 25, 1839	With't amend.	738	Passed	Adverse report.	
Snyder, David, or Daniel	Compensation for property lost in public service.	26	1	Petition	168	Claims.						
Snyder, Daniel	Exchange of a certain location	31	1	Petition	1492	Public Lands.						
Snyder, Elias	Increase of pension	23	1	Petition	128	Rev. Pensions.						
Snyder, Elias	Increase of pension	24	1	Petition	56	Rev. Pensions				Discharged; laid on table.		
Snyder, Elias	Increase of pension	24	2	Petition	44	Rev. Pensions				Discharged; laid on table.		
Snyder, Elias	Further compensation for revolutionary services.	25	2	Petition	111	Rev. Pensions				Discharged; laid on table.		
Snider, George, or Christopher, widow of.	Pension for revolutionary services.	26	1	Petition	322	Rev. Pensions	714	Adverse		Laid on table.		
Snyder, Jacob	Compensation for horse lost in public service.	17	2	Petition	164	Claims.						
Snyder, Jacob	Compensation for horse lost in public service.	18	1	Petition	60	Claims	100	Adverse		Referred to Committee Whole House.		
Snyder, Jacob	Compensation for horse lost in public service.	19	1	Petition	57	Claims	Dec. 22, 1825	Adverse		Laid on table.		
Snyder, Jacob	Compensation for horse lost in public service.	20	1	Petition	31	Claims.						
Snyder, Jacob	Indemnity for French spoliations prior to 1800.	28	1	Petition	78	Foreign Affairs.						
Snyder, John, attorney of.	Relief in consideration of revolutionary services.	2	1	Petition Rep. of Sec. War	477, 696					Laid on table.		
Snyder, John	(See heirs of Andrew Snyder.)	29	1		731							
Snyder, John, and others	Indemnity for illegal capture of schooner Henry.	12	1	Petition	335					Referred to Secretary State.		
Snyder, John, (Ill.)	Pension	21	2	Petition	270	Military Pensions.						
Snyder, John, (Ohio.)	Pension for revolutionary services.	23	1	Petition	436	Rev. Pensions.						
Snyder, John, heirs of	Pension	29	1	Petition	1261	Rev. Pensions	826	Adverse		Laid on table.		
Snyder, John	Pension for disabilities in the war of 1812.	24	1	Petition	281	Invalid Pensions	June 28, 1836	Adverse		Laid on table.		
Snyder, John, heirs of	Extension of time to locate land warrant.	30	1	Petition	162	Claims	58	Favorable	43	Passed	Passed	App'd June 26, 1848
Snyder, Peter	Land for services as Indian interpreter.	14	2	Petition	49	Priv. Land Claims.	Jan. 8, 1817	Adverse		Rejected.		

List of private claims presented to the House of Representatives of the United States from the 1st to the 31st Congress, inclusive—Continued.

Names of claimants.	Nature or object of the claim.	Congress.	Session.	How brought before the House of Reps.	Page of journal.	To what committee of the House referred.	No. or date of the report.	Nature of the report.	No. of the bill.	How disposed of by the House of Reps.	How disposed of by the Senate.	Date of the act of Congress, and remarks.
Snyder, Peter	Land for services as Indian interpreter.	15	1	Petition	130	Public Lands	Jan. 23, 1818	Adverse		Rejected.		
Snyder, Peter	Compensation for services as cooper in revolutionary war.	15	2	Petition	297	Pens. & Rev. Cl'ms.						
Snyder, William	Increase of pension	29	1	Petition	199	Invalid Pensions				Discharged; laid on table.		
Socie, Battiste, assignee of.	Confirmation of title to land in Arkansas.	22	1	House bill	421				425	Passed	Passed	App'd June 25, 1832
Soder, John	Pension for revolutionary services.	23	1	Petition	379	Rev. Pensions.						
Soderstrom, Richard	(See attorney of Paolo Paoly.)	7	1		153							
Soher, Solomon	Reimbursement of drawback on goods wrecked.	22	1	Petition	1062	Ways and Means.						
Soileau, Noel, heirs of	Confirmation of title to land in Louisiana.	18	2	Petition	92	Priv. Land Claims.	32	Favorable	286	Passed	Passed	App'd March 3, 1825
Sojourner, Gabriel	Confirmation of title to land in Mississippi Territory.	12	1	Petition	26	Public Lands.						
Sojourner, Gabriel	Confirmation of title to land in Mississippi Territory.	12	2	Petition	663	Public Lands.						
Sojourner, Gabriel	Confirmation of title to land in Mississippi Territory.	14	2	Petition	285	Priv. Land Claims.						
Solis, Juan	Confirmation of title to land in Louisiana.	22	1	House bill	107	Whole House	Mar. 23, 1832	With't amend.	125	Passed	Passed	App'd June 25, 1832
Solis, Manuel	Confirmation of title to land in Louisiana.	22	1	House bill	107	Whole House	Mar. 23, 1832	With't amend.	125	Passed	Passed	App'd June 25, 1832
Solomo, Jonathan	Indemnity for Indian depredations in Florida.	25	3	Petition	121	Claims	162	Adverse		Laid on table.		
Solana, Mateo	(See F. M. Arredondo, *et al*)	19	1		252							
Solana, Don Mates, and others.	Confirmation of claim for loss of a negress.	28	2	Memorial	84	Claims.						
Sole-Emarthla, (Seminole Indian.)	Indemnity for property stolen by United States soldiers.	31	1	Appropriat'n bill.	1034				324			App'd Sept. 30, 1850
Solomon, John	Release of merchandise seized by revenue officers.	3	1	Memorial	59					Laid on table.		
Soltan, Alexander	Reimbursement of duties illegally collected.	29	1	Appropriat'n bill.	206				50			App'd Aug. 10, 1846
Somers, brig, officers, &c., of.	Increase of pay	30	1	Senate bill	826	Naval Affairs	June 14, 1848	With't amend.	S. 110	Passed with amendm't	Passed as am'd.	App'd Aug. 14, 1848
Sommers, Hugh, (Vt.)	(Not stated)	19	2	Petition	37	Ways and Means	Dec. 29, 1846	Adverse		Laid on table.		
Somers, James	Pension	29	1	Petition	947	Invalid Pensions.						
Somers, James	Pension	29	2	Petition	469	Invalid Pensions.						
Somers, James	Pension	30	1	Petition	406	Invalid Pensions				Discharged; aid on table.		
Somers, James	Arrears of pension	31	1	Petition	224	Invalid Pensions.						
Somers, Mary	Pension	26	2	Petition	182	Rev. Pensions.						
Sommers, Simon	Confirmation of title to military lands.	6	1	Petition	564	Claims	Feb. 25, 1800	Adverse		Report disagreed to		Select committee, page 668.
Sommers, Simon, heirs of.	Commutation pay for revolutionary services.	27	2	Petition	96	Rev. Claims	1083	Adverse		Laid on table.		
Somerby, Theophilus	Pension	25	3	Petition	334	Invalid Pensions.						
Somerby, Theophilus	Pension	26	1	Petition	161	Invalid Pensions	665	Adverse		Laid on table.		
Somerby, Theophilus	Pension	28	1	Petition	88	Invalid Pensions	119	Adverse		Laid on table.		
Somerby, Theophilus	Pension	28	2	Petition	66	Invalid Pensions.						
Somerby, Theophilus	Pension	29	1	Petition	119	Invalid Pensions	48	Adverse		Laid on table.		

List of private claims presented to the House of Representatives of the United States from the 1st to the 31st Congress, inclusive—Continued.

Names of claimants.	Nature or object of the claim.	Congress.	Session.	How brought before the House of Reps.	Page of journal.	To what committee of the House referred.	No. or date of the report.	Nature of the report.	No. of the bill.	How disposed of by the House of Reps.	How disposed of by the Senate.	Date of the act of Congress, and remarks.
Sommeraner, Francis	Pension	27	2	Petition	377	Invalid Pensions.						
				Documents	611	Invalid Pensions.						
Sommeraner, Francis	Pension	28	1	Petition	211	Invalid Pensions	298	Favorable	208	Passed.		
Sommeraner, Francis	Pension	28	2	Petition	177	Invalid Pensions	81	Favorable	562	Passed.		
Sommeraner, Francis	Pension	29	1	Senate bill	1075	Invalid Pensions	Aug. 8, 1846	With amend't.	S. 95	Referred to Committee Whole House.		
Sommeraner, Francis	Pension	29	2	Senate bill	307	Invalid Pensions	Feb. 24, 1847	With amend.	S. 67	Passed	Passed	App'd March 3, 1847
Somersal, Wm., and Son, and John Price.	Indemnity for capture, &c., of sloop Electa.	4	1	Memorial & rep' Sec. Treasury.	591, 596	......	......	......	......	Laid on table.		
Sommersett, Levi	Pension	25	2	Petition	577	Naval Affairs.						
Sommersett, Levi	Pension	26	1	Petition	180	Naval Affairs.						
Somervell, James	(See guardian of heirs of A. Trueman.)	5	3	......	431							
Somerville, Alex., (Md.)	Compensation for property destroyed by the enemy.	23	2	Petition	163	Claims.						
Somerville, Alex., (Md.)	Compensation for property destroyed by the enemy.	24	1	Petition	474	Claims.						
Somerville, Alex., (Md.)	Compensation for property destroyed by the enemy.	24	2	Petition	81	Claims.						
Somerville, Alex., (Md.)	Compensation for property destroyed by the enemy.	25	2	Petition	121	Claims.						
Somerville, Alex., (Md.)	Compensation for property destroyed by the enemy.	25	3	Petition	121	Claims.						
Somerville, Alex., (Md.)	Compensation for property destroyed by the enemy.	26	1	Petition	170	Claims.						
Sommerville, John	Balance due on supplies furnished on public account.	25	2	Petition	542	Claims	May 11, 1838	Indefinite	......	Discharged; referred to Third Auditor.		
Sommerville, Wm., surety of.	Release from liability	19	1	Petition	129	P. Of. and P. Roads.	May 16, 1826	Adverse	......	Laid on table.		
Somes, Nehemiah	Remission of duties on salt	3	2	Petition	276	Select	74	Adverse	......	Laid on table.		
Somes, Nehemiah	Remission of duties on salt	4	1	Petition	430	Com. and Manuf.	Feb. 8, 1796	Adverse	......	Laid on table.		
Somes, Nehemiah	Remission of duties on salt	5	2	Petition	179	Com. and Manuf.	Feb 26, 1798	Adverse	......	Rejected.		
Sontag, Wm. L. & Co.	Indemnity for French spoliations prior to 1800.	26	1	Memorial	182	Foreign Affairs	343	Favorable; bill	319	Referred to Committee Whole House.		
Soper, Amasa	Commutation pay for revolutionary services.	11	2	Petition	289	Claims	May 21, 1810	Adverse	......	Recommitted.		
Soper, Amasa	Commutation pay for revolutionary services.	23	1	Petition	39	Rev. Claims	127	Favorable	136	Passed	Laid on table.	
Soper, Amasa	Commutation pay for revolutionary services.	23	2	Petition	94	Rev. Claims.						
Soper, Amasa	Commutation pay for revolutionary services.	24	1	Petition	63	Rev. Claims	......	......	......	Laid on table.		
Soper, Amasa	Commutation pay for revolutionary services.	25	2	Petition	48	Rev. Claims	1009	Adverse	......	Laid on table.		
Soper, Amos	(See Martin S. Aikin *et al*.)	7	1	......	359							
Soper, Enos	Compensation for services as a military volunteer.	25	2	Petition	657	Military Affairs	801	Adverse	......	Rejected.		
Soper, Enos	Compensation for services as a military volunteer.	26	1	Petition	338	Claims	574	Adverse	......	Laid on table.		
Soper, Enos, heirs of	Bounty land and reimbursement of expenditure.	30	1	Petition	607	Public Lands	612	Adverse	......	Laid on table.		
Soper, Evander M.	(See Enos Soper, heirs of.)	30	1	......	607	......	612					

List of private claims presented to the House of Representatives of the United States from the 1st to the 31st Congress, inclusive—Continued.

Names of claimants.	Nature or object of the claim.	Congress.	Session.	How brought before the House of Reps.	Page of journal.	To what committee of the House referred.	No. or date of the report.	Nature of the report.	No. of the bill.	How disposed of by the House of Reps.	How disposed of by the Senate.	Date of the act of Congress, and remarks.
Sorin, Jos. als. Larochelle	Confirmation of title to land in Missouri.	24	1	Senate bill	928	Priv. Land Claims	June 21, 1836	With't amend.	S. 47	Passed	Passed	App'd July 2, 1836
Sorrell, Francis	Cancellation of bond for the slave vessel Antelope.	20	1	House bill	76	Whole House			17			
				Senate bill	123	Judiciary	Jan. 14, 1828	With't amend.	S. 35	Pass'd with amendm't.	Passed as am'd.	App'd May 2, 1828
Sorrell, John	Pension for revolutionary services.	21	1	Documents	128	Military Pensions	April 2, 1830	Adverse		Laid on table.		
Sorrell, John	Pension for revolutionary services.	21	2	Resolution	86	Military Pensions.						
Sorton, Peter	Pension for revolutionary services.	22	1	Petition	470	Rev. Pensions				Discharged; laid on table.		
Sothoron, James F	Indemnity for destruction of property by the enemy.	24	1	Senate bill	899	Claims	June 2, 1836	With't amend.	S. 118	Passed.	Passed	App'd July 2, 1836
Sothoron, James F	Indemnity for destruction of property by the enemy.	29	2	Senate bill	381	Claims	May 1, 1847	With't amend.	S. 150	Referred to Committee Whole House.		
Sothoron, James F	Indemnity for destruction of property by the enemy.	30	1	Senate bill	913	Claims	July 12, 1848	With amend.	S. 129	Referred to Committee Whole House.		
Sothoron, James F	Indemnity for destruction of property by the enemy.	30	2	Bill of last sess.	626	Whole House	Mar. 3, 1849	With amend.	S. 129	Passed with amendm't.	Passed as am'd	App'd March 3, 1849
Soudard, Charles	(See John Jones and others.)	24	1		1185							
Soulard, Antoine	(See John Watkins, heirs of.)	15	1		85							
Soulard, Antoine	Confirmation of title to land	15	1	Petition	280	Priv. Land Claims.						
Soulard, Antoine, widow of.	Reimbursement of costs in land suits.	25	2	Petition	416	Judiciary				Discharged; laid on table.		
Soule, Jahiel	Pension	24	1	Petition	187	Invalid Pensions	751	Favorable	691	Passed.		
Soulard, Julia	(See Antoine Soulard, widow of.)	25	2		416							
Sountaz, Wm. L., & Co., representatives of.	Indemnity for French spoliations prior to 1800.	31	1	Petition	416	Foreign Affairs	355	General bill	318	Referred to Committee Whole House.		
Southall, George W	(See Peyton A. Southall, sureties of.)	27	2		807							
Southall, Peyton A., surety of.	Release from liability to the United States.	27	2	Petition	807	Judiciary	928	Favorable	546	Ordered to 3d reading.		
Southall, Peyton A., surety of.	Release from liability to the United States.	27	3	House bill	89				546	Passed	Passed	App'd March 3, 1843
Southard, Benjamin	Pension	24	2	Petition	398	Invalid Pensions				Discharged; laid on table.		
Southard, Benjamin	Pension	25	2	Petition	168	Invalid Pensions	Feb. 6, 1838	Adverse		Laid on table.		
Southard, Eli	Compensation for services by impression at New Orleans.	31	2	Petition	216	Claims.						
South Carolina line, revolutionary army, officers of.	For the six months pay granted by certain resolutions of late Congress.	1	2	Memorial	168					Laid on table.		
South Carolina line, revolutionary army, officers and soldiers of.	Relief for depreciation of their certificates of pay.	2	2	Petition	695					Laid on table.		
South Carolina, merchants of Charleston.	Indemnity for French spoliations prior to 1800.	7	1	Memorial	127	Select.						
South Carolina, merchants of Charleston.	Indemnity for French spoliations prior to 1800.	9	2	Petition	499	Select	Feb. 18, 1807	Favorable		Referred to Committee Whole House.		
South Carolina, merch'ts & underwriters of Charleston.	Indemnity for French spoliations prior to 1800.	15	1	Petition	115	Select.						
South Carolina, merch'ts & underwriters of Charleston.	Indemnity for French spoliations prior to 1800.	16	1	Petition	401					Laid on table.		

List of private claims presented to the House of Representatives of the United States from the 1*st to the* 31*st Congress, inclusive*—Continued.

Names of claimants.	Nature or object of the claim.	Congress.	Session.	How brought before the House of Reps.	Page of journal.	To what committee of the House referred.	No. or date of the report.	Nature of the report.	No. of the bill.	How disposed of by the House of Reps.	How disposed of by the Senate.	Date of the act of Congress, and remarks.
South Carolina, merchants of Charleston.	Remission of penalty for violation of non-importation act.	12	2	Petition	567	Ways and Means	Nov. 25, 1812	Favorable; bill ordered.	239	Rejected	....	See acts Jan. 2, and Feb. 27, 1813.
South Carolina, inspector of customs at Charleston.	Increase of compensation	11	1	Petition	37	Com. and Manuf.						
South Carolina, inspector of customs at Charleston.	Increase of compensation	11	2	Petition	127	Com. and Manuf.						
South Carolina, city council of Charleston.	Refunding amount expended in support of sick seamen in marine hospital.	14	2	Petition	179	Com. and Manuf.						
South Carolina, city council of Charleston.	Refunding amount expended in support of sick seamen at marine hospital.	21	1	Petition	38	Commerce	Feb. 4, 1830	By bill	194	Referred to Committee Whole House.	....	See Senate bill 71.
South Carolina, city council of Charleston.	Refunding amount expended in support of sick seamen at marine hospital.	21	1	Senate bill	401	Commerce	Mar. 19, 1830	With amend's.	S. 71	Passed	Passed	App'd May 14, 1830
South Carolina, St. Andrew's Society of Charleston.	Remission of duties on chandeliers.	15	2	Petition	125	Com. and Manuf.						
South Carolina, light-house keeper at Charleston.	Increase of compensation	18	2	Resolution	234	Commerce.						
South Carolina, comptroller general of.	Refunding amount expended in arming and equiping her militia in war of 1812.	19	2	Memorial	134	Claims.						
South Carolina, comptroller general of.	Balance due for military works and arms purchased in war of 1812	20	1	Memorial	111	Military Affairs.						
South Carolina, comptroller general of.	Balance due for military works and arms purchased in war of 1812.	20	1	Senate bill	405	Claims	246	Adverse	S. 65	Referred to Committee Whole House.		
South Carolina, comptroller general of.	Balance due for military works and arms purchased in war of 1812.	21	1	Memorial	122	Military Affairs	66	Favorable; bill	91	Referred to Committee Whole House.		
South Carolina, comptroller general of.	Balance due for military works and arms purchased in war of 1812.	21	2	Bill of last sess.	261	Whole House	....	....	91			
South Carolina, comptroller general of.	Balance due for military works and arms purchased in war of 1812.	22	1	Memorial	34	Military Affairs	141	Favorable; bill	4	Passed	Passed	App'd March 5, 1832
South Carolina, State of	For a retrocession of the land occupied by the late arsenal at Mt. Dearborn.	19	1	Resolution	255	Military Affairs	128	Favorable; bill	169	Referred to Committee Whole House.		
South Carolina, State of	For a retrocession of the land occupied by the late arsenal at Mt. Dearborn.	20	1	Resolution	91	Military Affairs	Jan. 30, 1828	Favorable; bill	127	Referred to Committee Whole House.		
South Carolina, State of	For a retrocession of the land occupied by the late arsenal at Mt. Dearborn.	20	2	Bill of last sess.	185	Whole House	Jan. 20, 1829	With amends.	127	Passed	Passed	App'd March 3, 1829
South Carolina, postmaster at Edgefield.	Increase of compensation	15	2	Petition	84	P. Of. & P. Roads.						
South Carolina, postmaster at Georgetown.	Increase of compensation	15	2	Resolution	174	P. Of. & P. Roads.						
South Carolina, postmaster at Georgetown.	Increase of compensation	16	1	Resolution	318	P. Of. & P. Roads.						
South Carolina, postmaster at Georgetown.	Increase of compensation	17	1	Resolution	341	P. Of. & P. Roads.	Mar. 25, 1822	Adverse	......	Laid on table.		
South Carolina, postmaster at Georgetown.	Increase of compensation	17	2	Resolution	108	P. Of. and P. Roads.	....	....	......	Discharged; leave to withdraw.		

List of private claims presented to the House of Representatives of the United States from the 1st to the 31st Congress, inclusive—**Continued.**

Names of claimants.	Nature or object of the claim.	Congress.	Session.	How brought before the House of Reps.	Page of journal.	To what committee of the House referred.	No. or date of the report.	Nature of the report.	No. of the bill.	How disposed of by the House of Reps.	How disposed of by the Senate.	Date of the act of Congress, and remarks.
South Carolina, Postmaster at Marion C. H.	Increase of compensation	15	2	Resolution	80	P. Of. & P. Roads.						
South Carolina, Postmaster at Marion C. H.	Increase of compensation	17	2	Resolution	71	P. Of. & P. Roads.	....	....	......	Discharged; leave to withdraw.		
South Carolina, State of.	Refunding expenses incurred in fitting out a battalion of militia for Seminole war, 1837.	25	2	Resolution	981	Military Affairs.						
South Carolina, State of.	Refunding expenses incurred in fitting out a battalion of militia for Seminole war, 1837.	31	1	Resolution	620	Military Affairs	201	Favorable; bill	208	Referred to Committee Whole House.		
South Carolina, Episcopal church of Charleston.	Remission of duty on an organ	26	1	Petition	328	Commerce	307	Favorable; bill	269	Referred to Committee Whole House.		
South Carolina, Episcopal church of Charleston.	Remission of duty on an organ	26	1	Senate bill	811	Ways and Means.	....	....	S. 188			
South Carolina, Episcopal church of Charleston.	Remission of duty on an organ	27	2	Petition	268	Commerce	April 1, 1842	By bill	325	Ordered to 3d reading.		
South Carolina, Episcopal church of Charleston.	Remission of duty on an organ	27	3	Bill of last sess.	87	....	....	....	325	Passed	Indef. postp'd.	
South Carolina, Episcopal church of Charleston.	Remission of duty on an organ	28	1	Petition	74	Commerce.						
South Carolina, Southern Steam Packet Company of Charleston.	Compensation for mail transportation.	26	1	Memorial	942	P. Of. & P. Roads.						
South Carolina, Railroad Company.	Remission of duty on railroad iron	28	1	Memorial	142	Ways and Means.						
South Carolina, Railroad Company.	Permission to import machinery for railroad free of duty.	28	2	Memorial	111	Ways and Means.						
South Carolina, Railroad Company.	Permission to import machinery for railroad free of duty.	28	2	Senate bill	408	Commerce	Feb. 25, 1845	With't amend.	127	Passed	....	App'd March 1, 1845
South Carolina, clerks in the post office at Charleston.	Increase of compensation	31	2	Petition	199	P. Of. & P. Roads.						
Southerland, Samuel, heirs of.	Pension under act of 1828	23	1	Resolution	333	Rev. Pensions	465	Favorable	479	Referred to Committee Whole House.		
Southerland, Sam'l, heirs of.	Pension under act of 1828	23	2	Bill of last sess.	337	Whole House	Feb. 6, 1835	With t amend.	479	Passed	Adverse report.	
Southgate, John	(See Marcus McCausland, administrator of.)	26	1	....	182							
Southgate, Wright	Indemnity for French spoliations prior to 1800.	26	1	Memorial	182	Foreign Affairs	343	Favorable; bill	319	Referred to Committee Whole House.		
Southmayd, John B., sureties of.	Release from liability	24	1	Petition	476	Judiciary.						
Southwestern steamboat	(See steamboats Compte and S. W.	27	2	....	327							
Southwick, Sol'n, surety of	Release from liability	21	1	Petition Petition, (2)	66 104	P. Of. & P. Roads. P. Of. & P. Roads.	388	Adverse	......	Referred to Committee Whole House.		
Southwick, Sol'n, surety of	Reimbursement of certain moneys	23	1	Petition	192, 217	Claims	....	....	......	Discharged; laid on table.		
Southworth, Samuel W.	(See James W. Law, and others).	15	1	....	366							
Soward, Wm., (Mo.)	Compensation for revolutionary services.	26	1	Petition	946	Rev. Claims.						
Soward, Wm., (Mo.)	Compensation for revolutionary services.	26	2	Petition	305	Rev. Claims.						
Soyars, James	Depreciation pay, &c., for revolutionary services.	5	2	Petition	150	Claims	Feb. 7, 1798	Adverse	......	Rejected.		

List of private claims presented to the House of Representatives of the United States from the 1st to the 31st Congress, inclusive—Continued.

Names of claimants.	Nature or object of the claim.	Congress.	Session.	How brought before the House of Reps.	Page of journal.	To what committee of the House referred.	No. or date of the report.	Nature of the report.	No. of the bill.	How disposed of by the House of Reps.	How disposed of by the Senate.	Date of the act of Congress, and remarks.
Soyars, James	Depreciation pay, &c., for revolutionary services.	20	2	Petition	177	Military Pensions	91	Favorable	452	Passed.		
Soyars, James	Depreciation pay, &c., for revolutionary services.	21	1	Petition	261	Rev. Claims	275	Favorable	327	Referred to Committee Whole House.		
Soyars, James	Depreciation pay, &c., for revolutionary services.	21	2	House bill	318	Whole House			327	Passed.		
Soyars, James	Depreciation pay, &c., for revolutionary services.	22	1	Petition	29	Rev. Claims	66	Favorable	129	Passed	Indef. postp'd.	
Spafford, Amos	Pension for revolutionary services	10	2	Pension bill	499	Whole House			158	Passed	Passed, with amendment.	App'd March 3, 1809
Spafford, Amos	Right of pre-emption to land in Ohio.	14	1	Petition	250	Public Lands	Feb. 22, 1816	Favorable	91	Passed	Passed	App'd April 27, 1816
Spafford, Bernard	Exchange of a location of land	19	1	Petition	58	Public Lands	54	Favorable	77	Passed	Passed	App'd May 22, 1826
Spafford, Eliphalet	Pension	24	2	Petition	398	Invalid Pensions				Discharged; laid on table.		
Spafford, Eliphalet	Pension	25	2	Petition	58	Invalid Pensions	384	Favorable	407	Passed.		
Spafford, Eliphalet	Pension	25	3	Petition	89	Invalid Pensions	138	Favorable	1005	Passed	Passed	App'd March 3, 1839
Spafford, Eliphalet, daughter of.	Bounty land due deceased for revolutionary services.	25	3	Petition	124	Rev. Claims.						
Spafford, Horatio Gates	A special copy-right for Gazetteer.	18	2	Memorial	101	Judiciary				Discharged; laid on table.		
Spafford, Horatio Gates	A special act to authorize a patent.	22	1	Petition	260	Patent Laws	351	Favorable	449	Passed	Passed with amendment.	App'd July 2, 1832
Spalding, Basil	Indemnity for property destroyed by the enemy.	22	2	Petition	379	Claims	109	Adverse		Laid on table.		
Spalding, Basil	Indemnity for property destroyed by the enemy.	23	1	Petition	55	Claims.						
Spalding, Basil, administrator of.	Indemnity for property destroyed by the enemy.	24	1	Documents	753	Foreign Affairs.						
Spalding, Basil, administrator of.	Indemnity for property destroyed by the enemy.	24	2	Petition	81	Claims.						
Spalding, Basil, administrator of.	Indemnity for property destroyed by the enemy.	25	3	Petition	111	Foreign Affairs.						
Spalding, Basil, administrator of.	Indemnity for property destroyed by the enemy.	26	2	Petition	80	Foreign Affairs	69	Adverse		Laid on table		Leave to withdraw.
Spaulding, Ebenezer	Reimbursement of patent fees	24	1	Senate bill	956	Claims	June 7, 1836	With't amend.	S. 162	Passed	Passed	App'd April 2, 1836
Spaulding, Ebenezer, heirs of.	Compensation for revolutionary services.	29	1	Petition	184	Rev. Pensions	24	Adverse		Laid on table.		
Spalding, Elextius	Reimbursement of expenses incurred as a witness.	9	2	Petition	485	Select	Feb. 4, 1807	Favorable	193	Referred to Committee Whole House.		
Spalding, Erastus	Indemnity for damage to property in public use.	13	3	Petition	618	Claims				Discharged.		
Spalding, Erastus	Indemnity for damage to property in public use.	15	1	Petition	355	Claims.						
Spaulding, Ezekiel	Invalid pension	3	1	Rep. of Secretary War.	131	Select	May 26, 1794	Res. to refer to Sec. War.	R. 12	Passed	Passed	App'd June 9, 1794
Spaulding, Ezekiel	Invalid pension	4	1	Rep. of Secretary War.	445	Claims.						
Spaulding, Ezekiel	Invalid pension	4	2	Rep. of Secretary War.	614	Claims.						
Spaulding, Ezra	Pension	25	2	Resolution	466	Rev. Pensions				Discharged; laid on table.		
Spalding, George, widow of.	Pension for revolutionary services.	31	1	Petition	647	Rev. Pensions.						

List of private claims presented to the House of Representatives of the United States from the 1st to the 31st Congress, inclusive—Continued.

Names of claimants.	Nature or object of the claim.	Congress.	Session.	How brought before the House of Reps.	Page of journal.	To what committee of the House referred.	No. or date of the report.	Nature of the report.	No. of the bill.	How disposed of by the House of Reps.	How disposed of by the Senate.	Date of the act of Congress, and remarks.
Spalding, George, & others.	Reimbursement of duties on silk thread.	23	1	Petition	47	Ways and Means	137	Adverse		Laid on table.		
Spaulding & Irwin	Compensation for extra work on Potomac bridge.	24	1	Petition	534	Claims				Referred to Secretary Treasury.		
Spaulding, James	Indemnity for disability incurred in public service.	14	2	Petition	183	Pens. & Rev. Cl'ms.	Jan. 29, 1817	Favorable	91	Omitted in the act.		
Spaulding, James	Pension	15	1	Petition	23					Referred to Secretary War.		
Spalding, John	Settlement of a claim against United States.	2	1	Petition	540					Referred to Secretary Treasury.		
Spalding, John	Settlement of a claim against United States.	2	2	Rep. of Secretary Treasury.	626					Laid on table.		
Spalding, John	(See administrator of Basil Spalding.)	24	1		753							
Spalding, Josiah	Pension for revolutionary services.	3	2	Rep. of Secretary War.	337	Claims	Feb. 28, 1795	Favorable; bill ordered.	130	Passed	Postponed.	
Spalding, Josiah	Pension for revolutionary services.	4	1	Rep. of Secretary War.	445	Claims	Feb. 18, 1796	Favorable; bill ordered.	156	Passed	Passed	App'd April 30, 1796
Spalding, Josiah	Compensation for work on Cumberland road.	23	1	Res. and docs.	589	Claims	455	Adverse				See report No. 449.
Spalding, Lyman	Compensation for medical attendance on United States prisoners.	10	2	Petition	484	Claims.						
Spalding, Lyman	Compensation for medical attendance on United States prisoners.	11	2	Petition	120	Claims.						
Spalding, Marcus	Compensation for services, war of 1812.	25	2	Petition	574	Claims	June 7, 1838	Adverse		Laid on table.		
Spalding, Marcus	Compensation for services, war of 1812.	25	3	Petition	132	Priv. Land Claims.	200	Adverse		Laid on table.		
Spalding, Marcus	Benefit of Canadian volunteer act.	27	2	Petition	68	Invalid Pensions.						
Spalding, Marcus	Pension for services, war of 1812.	29	1	Petition	82	Invalid Pensions.						
Spalding, Marcus	Pension for services, war of 1812.	31	1	Petition	307	Invalid Pensions.						
				Documents	821	Invalid Pensions				Discharged; laid on table.		
Spalding, Marcus	Bounty land for military services.	29	1	Petition	103	Priv. Land Claims.	Feb. 10, 1846	Adverse		Laid on table.		
Spalding, Marcus	Bounty land for military services.	31	1	Petition	308	Priv. Land Claims.	115	Adverse		Laid on table.		
Spalding, Marcus	Pension	25	2	Petition	406	Military Affairs	Mar. 20, 1838	Adverse		Laid on table.		
Spalding, Micah, (Ohio.)	Pension	27	2	Memorial	869	Invalid Pensions.						
				Documents	939	Invalid Pensions.						
Spalding, Nehemiah	Pension	21	1	Petition	411	Military Pensions.						
Spalding, Noah	Indemnity for property destroyed by militia.	13	2	Petition	183	Claims	Jan. 25, 1814			Laid on table.		
Spalding, Richard	Increase of compensation as bailiff, superior court.	14	2	Petition	378	Judiciary	Feb. 18, 1817	Adverse		Rejected.		
Spalding, Rufus, and others.	Indemnity for property destroyed by the enemy.	15	2	Petition	148	Claims	Jan. 16, 1819	Adverse		Laid on table.		
Spalding, Rufus, and others.	Indemnity for property destroyed by the enemy.	17	2	Petition	74	Claims.						
Spalding, Rufus, and others.	Indemnity for property destroyed by the enemy.	19	2	Petition	240	Claims.						
Spalding, Rufus	(See sureties of Jonas Harrison)	16	2		170							
Spalding, Samuel	Pension for services, &c., war of 1812.	24	1	Petition	945	Invalid Pensions	July 1, 1836	Adverse		Laid on table.		

List of private claims presented to the House of Representatives of the United States from the 1st to the 31st Congress, inclusive—Continued.

Names of claimants.	Nature or object of the claim.	Congress.	Session.	How brought before the House of Reps.	Page of journal.	To what committee of the House referred.	No. or date of the report.	Nature of the report.	No. of the bill.	How disposed of by the House of Reps.	How disposed of by the Senate.	Date of the act of Congress, and remarks.
Spalding, Samuel	Pension for services, &c., war of 1812.	25	3	Petition	218	Invalid Pensions.						
Spalding, Samuel	Arrears of pension	30	2	Petition	385	Invalid Pensions	Feb. 13, 1849	Adverse		Laid on table.		
Spalding, Samuel	Pension	31	1	Petition	696	Invalid Pensions	386	Adverse		Laid on table.		
Spalding, Samuel, (Vt.)	Pension	21	2	Petition	270	Military Pensions.						
Spalding, Simon	Payment of a lost commutation certificate.	11	3	Petition	490	Claims.						
Spalding, Simon, administrator of.	Compensation for revolutionary services.	28	2	Petition Documents	227 235	Rev. Claims. Rev. Claims.						
Spalding, Simon, administrator of.	Compensation for revolutionary services.	29	1	Petition	202	Rev. Claims	168	Favorable	177	Referred to Committee Whole House.		
Spalding, Simon, representatives of.	Payment of a lost certificate	29	2	House bill					177	Passed	Passed	App'd March 3, 1847
Spaulding, Stephen	Reimbursement of advances on public account.	31	1	Petition	1003	Rev. Claims.						
Spaulding, Stephen	Reimbursement of advances on public account.	31	2	Petition	175	Claims.						
Spalding, Susan	(See George Spalding, widow of.)	31	1		647							
Spaulding, Thaddeus	(See executor of John Hart)	28	1		516							
Spalding, ——	(See Fry & Spalding)	17	1		124							
Spaugenberg, Conrad	Compensation for revolutionary services.	2	1	Petition	474					Referred to Secretary of War.		
Spangler, Daniel	(See heirs of George Nebinger)	12	1	Petition	288	Whole House		General bill	104	Referred to Committee Whole House.		
Spanish brig Lion	(See Leon, Spanish brig.)	22	1		53							
Spanish brig Restaurada	(See William Howill & Son)	27	3		285							
Spann, James, sen	Pension	21	1	Petition	36	Military Pensions	March 6, 1830	Favorable	390	Referred to Committee Whole House.		
Spann, James, sen	Pension	21	2	Bill of last sess.	318	Whole House	Feb. 16, 1831	With't amend.	390	Passed.		
Sparding, John, attorney of.	Compensation for transporting United States troops.	13	1	Petition	12	Claims.						
Sparhawk, Timothy	Pension	15	2	Petition	46	Rev. Claims	Dec. 24, 1818	Adverse		Leave to withdraw.		
Sparks, Jesse	(See administrator of Matthew Sparks.)	22	1		293							
Sparks, John	(See Z. M. Pike, and companions.)	10	1		189							
Sparks, Leah	Continuation of pension	28	1	Petition	72	Rev. Pensions.						
Sparks, Matthew, administrator of.	Indemnity for Indian depredations.	22	1	Petition	293	Indian Affairs.						
Sparks, Matthew, administrator of.	Indemnity for Indian depredations.	23	1	Petition	121	Indian Affairs				Discharged; laid on table.		
Sparks, Michael	(See Michael Spatz)	15	2		190							
Sparks, Nimrod	Pension for services in Indian war.	25	2	Petition	401	Invalid Pensions.						
Sparks, Nimrod	Pension for services in Indian war.	25	3	Petition	89	Invalid Pensions	Jan. 22, 1839			Laid on table.		
Sparks, Orson	Compensation for horses lost in public service.	20	1	Resolution	43	Claims	33	Adverse		Referred to Committee Whole House.		
Sparks, Orson	Compensation for horses lost in public service.	20	2	Rep't of last sess.	81	Claims	27	Favorable	343	Referred to Committee Whole House.		
Sparks, Orson	Compensation for horses lost in public service.	21	1	Resolution	44	Claims	3	Favorable	3	Passed	Passed	App'd Feb. 11, 1830
Sparks, Richard	Confirmation of title to land	9	1	Petition	296	Public Lands	Mar. 18, 1806	Favorable	135	Passed	Passed	App'd April 21, 1806
Sparks, Richard	Indemnity for property lost in the public service.	10	1	Senate bill	300				S. 27	Indefinitely postponed.		
Sparks, Stephen	Indemnity for Indian depredations.	25	2	Petition	396	Claims.						

List of private claims presented to the House of Representatives of the United States from the 1st to the 31st Congress, inclusive—Continued.

Names of claimants.	Nature or object of the claim.	Congress.	Session.	How brought before the House of Reps.	Page of journal.	To what committee of the House referred.	No. or date of the report.	Nature of the report.	No. of the bill.	How disposed of by the House of Reps.	How disposed of by the Senate.	Date of the act of Congress, and remarks.
Spark, U. S. brig	(See Jesse Wilkinson, commissioner, &c.	20	1		168							
Sparks, William	Pension	21	2	Petiti n	61	Military Pensions.						
Sparks, William	Pension	29	1	Petition	947	Invalid Pensions.						
Sparks, William	Pension	30	1	Petition	82	Invalid Pensions.						
				Documents	162	Invalid Pensions	147	Adverse		Laid on table.		
Sparks, William	Pension	31	1	Petition	194	Invalid Pensions	294	Favorable	167	Referred to Committee Whole House.		
Sparks, William	Pension	31	2	Bill of last sess.	104	Whole House	Jan. 3, 1851	With amend.	167	Passed.		
Sparnell, William	Premium for plan and estimate of New York custom-house.	23	1	Petition	522	Claims.						
Sparr, Enoch	Payment of arrears due for revolutionary services.	19	1	Petition	34	Pens. & Rev. Cl'ms.	Jan. 9, 1826	Adverse		Laid on table.		
Sparrow, Thos., & others.	Increase of compensation for repairs to light-boat.	21	1	Petition	169	Commerce	Feb. 9, 1830	Adverse		Laid on table.		
Spartz or Spatz, Mich'l.	To be restored to pension roll	22	1	Resolution	561	Rev. Pensions	472	Adverse	574	Referred to Committee Whole House.		
Spatz, Michael	Pension for services as revolutionary marine.	15	2	Petition	190	Pens. & Rev. Cl'ms.						
Spatz, Michael	To be restored to pension roll	28	2	Petition	59	Rev. Pensions				Discharged; laid on table.		
Spatz, Michael	Increase of pension	29	1	Petition	435	Rev. Pensions	826	Adverse		Laid on table.		
Spatz, Michael	Pension for revolutionary services.	30	1	Petition	415	Rev. Pensions				Discharged; laid on table.		
Spaulding, ——	(See Spalding.)											
Spaur, Valentine	Pension for disabilities in Indian wars.	29	1	Petition	648	Invalid Pensions.						
Spaur, Valentine	Pension for disabilities in Indian wars	29	2	Petition	86	Invalid Pensions.						
Spaur, Valentine	Pension for disabilities in Indian wars.	30	1	Petition	397	Invalid Pensions	466	Adverse		Laid on table.		
Speak, Nathan, heirs of	Bounty land and commutation pay	24	1	Petition	204	Rev. Claims.						
Speakman, John	Indemnity for suspension of a government contract.	29	1	Memorial	362	Claims	537	Favorable	359	Passed in Committee Whole House.		
Speakman, John	Indemnity for suspension of a government contract.	29	2	Bill of last sess.	73	Whole House	Dec. 18, 1846	With't amend.	359	Passed	Passed	App'd March 3, 1847
Speer, or Spear, Alexander	(See S uth Carolina)	19	2		134							
Spear, Adre	(See John Spear, widow of)	27	2		47							
Spear, David	(See Thomas Russell, and others).	3	1		67							
Spears, Dixon	Correction of a land entry	22	1	Senate bill	119	Public Lands	Dec. 30, 1831	With't amend.	S. 13	Passed	Passed	App'd Jan. 18, 1832
Spear, Lieutenant Edward, former widow of.	Support of children of	14	2	Petition	46	Pens. & Rev. Cl'ms.						
Spear, Lieutenant Edward, former widow of.	Support of children of	15	1	Petition	115	Pens. & Rev. Cl'ms.				Discharged; referred to Secretary of War.		
Spear, Edward N., heirs of	Compensation for horses lost, war of 1812.	29	1	Petition	756	Claims.						
Spear, Harmanus	Pension for revolutionary services.	23	1	Petition	617	Rev. Pensions.						
Spear, Henry D.	(See heirs of Edward N. Spear.)	29	1		756							
Spears and Hutchinson	Payment of amount due from Ottawa Indians.	29	1	Memorial	160	Indian Affairs	287	Adverse		Laid on table.		
Spears, John	Pension for services in Indian wars.	26	1	Petition	322	Invalid Pensions.						
Spears, John	Pension for services in Indian wars.	26	2	Petition	55	Invalid Pensions	228	Adverse		Laid on table.		
Spears, John	Pension for services in Indian wars.	27	2	Petition	68	Invalid Pensions	437	Adverse		Laid on table.		

List of private claims presented to the House of Representatives of the United States from the 1st to the 31st Congress, inclusive—Continued.

Names of claimants.	Nature or object of the claim.	Congress.	Session.	How brought before the House of Reps.	Page of journal.	To what committee of the House referred.	No. or date of the report.	Nature of the report.	No. of the bill.	How disposed of by the House of Reps.	How disposed of by the Senate.	Date of the act of Congress, and remarks.
Spears, John	Pension for services in Indian wars.	28	1	Petition	353	Rev. Pensions.						
Spear, John, widow of	Arrears of pension	27	2	Petition	47	Invalid Pensions.						
Spear, Joshua	Bounty land and pension for revolutionary services.	16	2	Petition	50	Rev. Pensions	Feb. 15, 1821	Adverse	......	Leave to withdraw.		
Spears, Joshua	To be restored to pension roll	18	1	Resolution	141	Rev. Pensions	....	....	......	Discharged; leave to withdraw.		
Spears, Joshua	To be restored to pension roll	20	1	Resolution	715	Military Pensions.						
Spears, Joshua	To be restored to pension roll	20	2	Pension bill	55	Whole House	Jan. 15, 1829	With't amend.	311	Passed	Laid on table.	
Spears, Joshua	To be restored to pension roll	21	1	Petition	49	Military Pensions	Jan. 6, 1830	Pension bill	72	Passed	Passed	App'd May 20, 1830
Spear, Joshua	Pension for revolutionary services.	23	1	Petition	308	Rev. Pensions	Feb. 24, 1834	Adverse	......	Laid on table.		
Spear, Samuel	Invalid pension	3	2	Rep. of Secretary War.	337	Claims	....	....	......	Laid on table.		
Spear, Samuel	Invalid pension	4	1	Rep. of Secretary War.	445	Claims	Feb. 15, 1796	Res. to refer to Sec. War	J. R. 16	Passed	Passed	App'd April 18, 1796
Spear, Samuel	Invalid pension	4	2	Rep. of Secretary War.	614	Claims.						
Spear, William	Pension for revolutionary services.	21	1	Resolution	249	Military Pensions	April 6, 1830	Adverse	......	Laid on table.		
Spear, William	Pension for revolutionary services.	21	2	Resolution	77	Military Pensions.						
Spear, William	Pension for revolutionary services.	22	1	Petition	46	Rev. Pensions	395	Favorable	494	Referred to Committee Whole House.		
Spearing, James	Naval pension	17	1	Petition	33	Naval Affairs	Dec. 20, 1821	Adverse	......	Rejected.		
Spedden, Robert	Pension	23	2	Petition	41	Naval Affairs.						
Spedden, Robert	Pension	24	1	Petition	43	Invalid Pensions.						
Spedden, Robert	Pension	24	2	Petition	85	Rev. Pensions.						
Speed, Diana	(See Henry Speed, widow & heirs of.)											
Speed, Elizabeth	(See Henry Speed, widow & heirs of.)	19	1	....	68							
Speed, Henry, widow and heirs of	Remission of forfeiture of public land.	19	1	Petition	68	Priv. Land Claims	....	....	......	Leave to withdraw.		
Speed, Henry	(See Henry Speed, widow & heirs of.)											
Speed, James	Pension for revolutionary services.	4	1	Rep. of Secretary War.	445	Claims	Feb 18, 1796	Pension bill	156	Passed	Passed	App'd April 20, 1796
Speed, Maria and Nancy	(See Henry Speed, widow & heirs of.)	19	1	....	68							
Speed, Thomas	(See Henry Speed, widow & heirs of.)	19	1	....	68							
Speedwell, Sloop	(See Aaron Sheffield, widow of.)	8	2	....	149							
Speiden, William	Indemnity for stores lost on ship Peacock.	27	3	Memorial	78	Naval Affairs	....	....	......	Discharged; laid on table.		
Speiden, William	Indemnity for stores lost on ship Peacock.	28	1	Petition	415	Naval Affairs.						
Speiden, William	Indemnity for stores lost on ship Peacock.	30	1	House resolution.	382	Whole House	Mar. 24, 1848	With't amend.	R. 14	Passed	Passed, second session.	App'd Feb. 22, 1849
Speiden, William	Compensation for extra services as purser.	31	1	Petition	258	Naval Affairs	284	Favorable	259	Referred to Committee Whole House.		
Speiden, William	(See Exploring Expedition)	27	3	....	149	....	270	....	818			
Spellman & Fraser	(See Cook, Anthony, Mahon, and others.)	30	1	....	826							
Spellman, Oliver, (R. I).	Release from imprisonment at suit of United States.	14	2	Petition	64	Ways and Means	Jan. 4, 1817	Favorable	39	Passed	Passed	A

List of private claims presented to the House of Representatives of the United States from the 1st to the 31st Congress, inclusive—Continued.

Names of claimants.	Nature or object of the claim.	Congress.	Session.	How brought before the House of Reps.	Page of journal.	To what committee of the House referred.	No. or date of the report.	Nature of the report.	No. of the bill.	How disposed of by the House of Reps.	How disposed of by the Senate.	Date of the act of Congress, and remarks.
Spence, Groeme Keith ...	Reimbursement of discount paid on treasury notes.	16	1	Petition	445	Ways and Means..	April 27, 1820	Favorable....	142	Passed	Indef. postp'd.	
Spence, Groeme Keith ...	Reimbursement of discount paid on treasury notes.	18	1	Petition	526	Naval Affairs.						
Spence, Groeme Keith ...	Reimbursement of discount paid on treasury notes.	22	2	Petition	312	Naval Affairs.						
Spence, Mary F	(See heirs-at-law of John Tebbs).	22	2	....	88							
Spence, Mary Clare Carroll.	(See Robert T. Spence, widow of.)											
Spence, Robert T., widow of.	Release from a judgment against him.	26	2	Petition	79	Naval Affairs.						
Spence, Robert T., widow of.	Release from a judgment against him.	27	2	Petition	382	Claims	750	Favorable....	428	Ordered to 3d reading.		
Spence, Robert T., widow of.	Release from a judgment against him.	27	3	House bill......	....	....	....	....	428	Passed	Passed	App'd March 3, 1843
Spence, Abner..........	(See Eleazer Spencer)	10	2	....	510							
Spence, Ann	(See widow of Hosea Hamilton)..	30	1	....	886							
Spencer, Charles	(See executors of William Carter).	8	1	....	489							
Spencer, Christopher.....	(See son of John Spencer)	27	1	....	107							
Spencer, Daniel.........	Pension for revolutionary services.	23	1	Petition	655	Rev. Pensions....	....	....	......	Discharged; laid on table.		
Spencer, Daniel.........	Pension for revolutionary services.	24	1	Petition	127	Rev. Pensions	....	....	......	Discharged; laid on table.		
Spencer, Daniel.........	Compensation for military services, &c.	27	1	Petition	622	Claims	763	Adverse	......	Discharged; laid on table.		
Spencer, Daniel.........	Compensation for military services, &c.	27	3	Petition	155	Rev. Pensions	295	Adverse	......	Discharged; laid on table.		
Spencer, Daniel.........	Compensation for military services, &c.	28	2	Petition	141	Claims.						
Spencer, Daniel.........	Compensation for military services, &c.	29	1	Petition	255	Claims..........	362	Adverse	......	Laid on table.		
Spencer, Dennis, widow of.	Compensation for revolutionary services.	21	2	Petition	63	Rev. Claims......	....	....	......	Discharged; laid on table.		
Spencer, Dennis, widow of.	Pension for revolutionary services.	22	2	Petition	119	Rev. Pensions.						
Spencer, Eleazer	Reimbursement of money paid as security for a minor soldier of the revolutionary army.	10	2	Petition	510	Whole House.....	....	....	......	....	....	Leave to withdraw, 1st session, 12th Cong.
Spencer, George D......	Reimbursement of expenditure in a certain suit.	27	2	Petition	669	Cliams	728	Adverse	......	Laid on table.		
Spencer, George D......	Reimbursement of expenditure in a certain suit.	28	2	Petition	71	Claims	127	Favorable....	612	Referred to Committee Whole House.		
Spencer, George D......	Reimbursement of expenditure in a certain suit.	29	1	Petition	90	Claims..........	18	Favorable....	32	Passed	Passed	App'd July 15, 1846
Spencer, Ichabod, & others	Relief in consideration of revolutionary losses.	1	2	Petition	186							
				Rep. of Secretary War.	251	....	....	....	......	Laid on table.		
Spencer, Jabes..........	Pension for revolutionary services.	20	1	Resolution	272	Military Pensions.						
Spencer, Jared, widow of .	Pension for revolutionary services.	25	2	Petition	403	Rev. Pensions	....	....	......	Discharged; referred to Com. Whole House.		
Spencer, Capt. John.....	Compensation for horse lost in the public service.	23	1	Resolution	155	Claims	183	Adverse	......	Laid on table.		
Spencer, John, son of....	Compensation for revolutionary arms.	27	1	Petition	170	Rev. Claims.						

List of private claims presented to the House of Representatives of the United States from the 1st to the 31st Congress, inclusive—Continued.

Names of claimants.	Nature or object of the claim.	Congress.	Session.	How brought before the House of Reps.	Page of journal.	To what committee of the House referred.	No. or date of the report.	Nature of the report.	No. of the bill.	How disposed of by the House of Reps.	How disposed of by the Senate.	Date of the act of Congress, and remarks.
Spencer, John, son of	Compensation for revolutionary arms.	27	3	Petition	193	Rev. Claims	251	Adverse	......	Laid on table		
Spencer, John	Further compensation as receiver at Fort Wayne.	28	1	Memorial & docs.	787	Public Lands.						
Spencer, John	Further compensation as receiver at Fort Wayne.	29	1	Petition	772	Public Lands	758	Favorable	496	Referred to Committee Whole House.		
Spencer, John	Further compensation as receiver at Fort Wayne.	29	2	Bill of last sess.	212	Whole House	Jan. 22, 1847	With't amend.	496	Passed	Passed	App'd March 3, 1847
Spencer, Joseph, executors of.	Adjustment and payment of claim due deceased.	1	2	Petition	199	....	....	....	......	Referred to Secretary Treasury.		
Spencer, Joseph, executors of.	Adjustment and payment of claim due deceased.	3	2	Rep. of Secretary Treasury.	284	....	....	....	......	Laid on table.		
Spencer, Joseph, heirs of	Commutation pay due deceased	23	1	Petition	42	Rev. Claims.						
Spencer, Joseph, heirs of	Commutation pay due deceased	24	1	Petition	152	Rev. Claims.						
Spencer, Joseph, heirs of	Commutation pay and bounty land	30	1	Petition	909	Rev. Pensions	....	....		....	....	Leave to withdraw, 2d session.
Spencer, Margaret	(See Jared Spencer, widow of.)	25	2	....	403							
Spencer, O	(See E. Winter & Sons, representatives of.)	19	2	....	159							
Spencer, Oliver	Pension	24	1	Petition	406	Invalid Pensions	June 28, 1836	Adverse	......	Laid on table.		
Spencer, Oliver	Pension	25	2	Petition	268	Invalid Pensions	....	....	......	Discharged; laid on table.		
Spencer, Oliver M	Indemnity for deficiency in public land.	25	2	Petition	282	Public Lands	....	....	......	Discharged; referred to Com. Whole House		
Spencer, Peleg	Compensation for team lost in Indian war.	23	1	Senate bill	175	Claims	Jan. 14, 1834	With't amend.	S. 42	Passed with amend'mt	Passed as am'd	App'd April 15, 1834
Spencer, Polly	(See Micha Whitmarsh, widow of.)	27	3	....	58							
Spencer, Rebecca	(See Dennis Spencer, widow of.)	21	2	....	63							
Spencer, Reuben	Increase of pension	1	3	Petition	380	....	....	....	......	Referred to Secretary War.		
Spencer, Reuben	Increase of pension	2	2	Rep. of Secretary War.	696	....	....	....	......	Laid on table.		
Spencer, Samuel B	Compensation for a horse lost in Mexican war.	30	2	Petition	102	Claims	133	Adverse	......	Laid on table.		
Spencer, Thomas, (Ill)	Pension for services in Indian wars.	31	1	Petition	232	Rev. Pensions.						
Spencer, Truman	Bounty land for revolutionary services.	23	1	Petition	354	Rev. Claims.						
Spencer, William A	Credit for discount on treasury notes.	23	1	Petition	274	Naval Affairs.						
Spencer, William A	Credit for discount on treasury notes.	23	2	Petition	199	Claims.						
Sperry, Sally	(See Truman Sperry, widow of.)											
Sperry, Truman, widow of	Pay and bounty land due deceased	22	2	Petition	69	Priv. Land Claims	Jan. 7, 1833	Adverse	......	Laid on table.		
Speyer, John	Liquidation of a revolutionary certificate.	4	1	Rep. of Secretary Treasury.	388	Claims	May 31, 1796	Adverse	......	Laid on table.		
Spicer, Elizabeth	(See heirs of Joseph Donaldson)	12	1	....	112							
Spicer, Jeremiah	(See Joseph Stewart, and others)	13	3	....	751							
Spicer, Thomas	Compensation for services as clerk, district court Maryland.	23	2	Memorial	37	Claims	Jan. 22, 1835	Adverse	......	Laid on table.		
Spicer, Thomas	Compensation for services as clerk, district court Maryland.	24	1	Memorial	106	Judiciary.						
Spicer, Thomas	Compensation for services as clerk, district court Maryland.	25	2	Memorial	71	Claims	829	Adverse	......	Laid on table.		
Spicer, Travers	(See Joseph Stewart, and others)	13	3	....	751							

List of private claims presented to the House of Representatives of the United States from the 1st to the 31st Congress, inclusive—Continued.

Names of claimants.	Nature or object of the claim.	Congress.	Session.	How brought before the House of Reps.	Page of journal.	To what committee of the House referred.	No. or date of the report	Nature of the report.	No. of the bill.	How disposed of by the House of Reps.	How disposed of by the Senate.	Date of the act of Congress, and remarks.
Spikes, Jonas	(See John D. Matheny, and others.)	18	2		60							
Spiller, Collin	Compensation for a horse lost in public service.	19	2	Resolution	88	Claims.						
Spiller, William	Bounty land for services in Indian war.	30	2	Petition	295	Public Lands.						
Spiller, William H	Compensation for a horse lost in public service.	24	1	Resolution	368	Claims	544	Adverse		Laid on table.		
Spiller, William H	Compensation for a horse lost in public service.	25	3	Documents	205	Claims	317	Adverse		Laid on table.		
Spillman, James	Indemnity for property taken by the enemy.	14	1	Petition	89	Claims.						
Spindler, Sebastian	Relief in consideration of revolutionary disability.	8	1	Memorial	458	Claims.						
Spitfathom, John	Arrears of pension	25	2	Resolution	240	Rev. Pensions.	660	Adverse.		Laid on table.		
Spitfathom, John	Commutation pay for revolutionary services.	25	2	Senate bill	496	Rev. Claims	Mar. 9, 1838	With amend.	S. 111	Passed	Passed	App'd June 12, 1838
Spitfire, slaver	(See Henry Bruce)	29	1		591							
Spivey, Joseph W	(See heirs of Alexander Sweeny).	25	3		451							
Sponcelar, Frederick	Balance of pay due for revolutionary services.	11	1	Petition	52	Claims.						
Sponcelar, Frederick	Balance of pay due for revolutionary services.	11	2	Resolution	181	Claims	Mar. 5, 1810	Adverse		Rejected.		
Spooner, Eliakim & Alfred.	Remission of distillery duties	14	1	Petition	275	Ways and Means.	Feb. 24, 1846	Adverse		Rejected.		
Spooner, Eliakim & Alfred.	Remission of distillery duties	15	1	Petition	237	Ways and Means.						
Spooner, Eliakim & Alfred.	Remission of distillery duties	15	2	Petition	90	Ways and Means.	Dec. 14, 1818	Adverse		Rejected		Leave to withdraw.
Spooner, Ephraim	(See Sylvanus Bartlett)	5	2		145							
Spoor, Ephraim	Pension and bounty land, military service.	30	1	Petition	723	Invalid Pensions	639	Adverse		Laid on table.		
Spoor, John	Compensation for revolutionary services.	3	1	Petition and rep't Sec. War.	57, 93	Select.						
Sport, Eli	Pension	14	1	Resolution	417	Pens. & Rev. Cl'ms.						
Spotts, Samuel	Benefit of an act for the relief of purchasers of public lands.	18	1	Petition	198	Priv. Land Claims.				Discharged; laid on table.		
Spottswood, Alexander	Grant of land for revolutionary services.	5	3	Petition	501					Discharged; laid on table.		
Spottswood, Alexander	Grant of land for revolutionary services.	6	1	Petition	545	Claims				Referred to Committee Whole House.		
Spotswood, George W.	(See heirs of John Spotswood)	25	2		915							
Spotswood, John, heirs of.	Commutation pay for revolutionary services.	25	2	Petition	915	Rev. Claims	934	Favorable	814	Postponed.		
Spotswood, John, heirs of.	Commutation pay for revolutionary services.	27	2	Petition	61	Rev. Claims	977	Adverse		Laid on table.		
Spotswood, John, heirs of.	Commutation pay for revolutionary services.	28	1	Petition	99	Rev. Claims.						
Spottswood, John, heirs of.	Half-pay for revolutionary services.	24	2	Resolution	78	Rev. Claims	Dec. 28, 1836	Adverse		Laid on table.		
Spotswood, Norborn B.	Compensation for services as hospital surgeon.	19	2	Petition	218	Military Affairs.						
Spotswood, Norborn B.	Compensation for services as hospital surgeon.	20	1	Petition	168	Military Affairs.						
Spotswood, Norborn B.	Compensation for services as hospital surgeon.	21	1	Petition	501	Military Affairs.						
Spotswood, Norborn B.	Compensation for services as hospital surgeon.	23	2	Petition	49	Claims	Dec. 19, 1834	Adverse		Laid on table.		

List of private claims presented to the House of Representatives of the United States from the 1st to the 31st Congress, inclusive—Continued.

Names of claimants.	Nature or object of the claim.	Congress.	Session.	How brought before the House of Reps.	Page of journal.	To what committee of the House referred.	No. or date of the report.	Nature of the report.	No. of the bill.	How disposed of by the House of Reps.	How disposed of by the Senate.	Date of the act of Congress, and remarks.
Spotswood, Norborn B.	Compensation for services as hospital surgeon.	24	1	Petition	93	Claims	159	Adverse	......	Laid on table.		
Spraggins, Samuel	(See John Thompson and others).	19	1	....	413							
Sprague, Andrew	Pension for revolutionary services.	22	1	Petition	381	Rev. Pensions	....	....	......	Discharged; laid on table.		
Sprague, Asa	Compensation for military services.	29	1	Petition	90	Invalid Pensions	....	....	......	Discharged; laid on table.		
Sprague, Bela	Pension	25	2	Petition	268	Invalid Pensions	....	....	......	Discharged; laid on table.		
Sprague, Bela	Pension	31	1	Petition	1219	Invalid Pensions	466	Adverse	......	Laid on table.		
Sprague, Ceasar	Pension for revolutionary services.	3	1	Rep. of Secretary War.	131	Select	May 26, 1794	Res. to refer to Sec. of War.	J. R. 12	Passed	Passed	App'd June 9, 1794
Sprague Ceasar	Pension for revolutionary services.	4	1	Rep. of Secretary War.	445	Claims	Feb. 18, 1796	Pension bill	156	Passed	Passed	App'd April 20, 1796
Sprague, Daniel	Pension	28	1	Petition	484	Invalid Pensions.	374	Adverse	......	Laid on table.		
Sprague, Ephraim	Compensation for horse, &c., lost in public service.	24	1	Resolution	368	Claims.						
Sprague, Ephraim	Compensation for horse, &c., lost in public service.	25	3	Senate bill	499	Claims	....	....	S. 74			
Sprague, Ephraim	Compensation for horse, &c., lost in public service.	27	2	Senate bill	411	Claims	642	Adverse	S. 61	Rejected.		
Sprague, Ezra, or Lazaras.	Pension for disabilities, in public service.	24	1	Petition	407	Invalid Pensions.						
Sprague, Ezra, or Lazaras.	Pension for disabilities, in public service.	24	2	Petition	219	Invalid Pensions	Feb. 2, 1837	Adverse	......	Laid on table.		
Sprague, Horatio	Reimbursement of advances to consul at Tangiers.	27	3	Petition	84	Foreign Affairs.						
Sprague, Horatio	Reimbursement of advances to consul at Tangiers.	28	1	Petition	435	Foreign Affairs	....	....	......	Discharged; laid on table.		
Sprague, Horatio	Reimbursement of advances to consul at Tangiers.	30	1	Petition	161	Foreign Affairs	205	Adverse.	......	Laid on table.		
Sprague, James	Benefit of acts for relief of Canadian refugees.	12	1	House bill	242	Whole House	Mar. 22, 1812	With't amend.	85	Passed	Passed	App'd April 23, 1812
Sprague, James	Location of a certain land claim	21	2	Senate bill	225	Priv. Land Claims.	Feb. 9, 1831	Adverse	S. 80	Passed	Passed	App'd March 2, 1831
Sprague, James, heirs of.	Half-pay for revolutionary services.	24	2	Petition	92	Rev. Claims.						
Sprague, Joseph E	Increase of compensation as post master.	15	2	Petition	331	P. Of. & P. Roads.						
Sprague, Joseph E	Increase of compensation as postmaster.	16	1	Petition	280	P. Of. & P. Roads.	Mar. 3, 1820	Adverse	......	Laid on table.		
Sprague, Joseph E	Compensation for certain legal services.	16	1	Petition	279	Claims.						
Sprague, Joseph E	Compensation for certain legal services.	21	1	Senate bill	401	Judiciary	April 12, 1830	With't amend	S. 67	Referred to Committee Whole House.		
Sprague, Joseph E	Compensation for certain legal services.	21	2	Senate bill	164	Judiciary	Jan. 11, 1831	With't amend.	S. 19	Passed	Passed	App'd March 2, 1831
Sprague, Joseph E	(See Sarah W. Steavens, executor and attorney of.)	26	1	....	182							
Sprague, Joshua, heirs of.	Benefit of act of February 24, 1810.	12	1	N. S. refugee bill.	242	Whole House	Mar. 22, 1812	With amend.	85	Passed	Passed	App'd April 23, 1812
Sprague, Joshua	(See Peter Mills.)	23	1	....	395							
Sprague, Margaret, executrix of.	Indemnity for French spoliations prior to 1800.	26	1	Memorial	182	Foreign Affairs	343	Favorable; bill	319	Referred to Committee Whole House.		
Sprague, Phineas, & others.	Bounty on fishing schooner Two Brothers.	21	1	Petition	232	Commerce	Feb. 9, 1830	Favorable	215	Referred to Committee Whole House.		

List of private claims presented to the House of Representatives of the United States from the 1st to the 31st Congress, inclusive—**Continued.**

Names of claimants.	Nature or object of the claim.	Congress.	Session.	How brought before the House of Reps.	Page of journal.	To what committee of the House referred.	No. or date of the report.	Nature of the report.	No. of the bill.	How disposed of by the House of Reps.	How disposed of by the Senate.	Date of the act of Congress, and remarks.
Sprague, Phineas, & others.	Bounty on fishing schooner Two Brothers.	21	2	House bill	264	Whole House	Feb. 4, 1831	With't amend.	215	Passed.		
Sprague, Phineas, & others.	Bounty on fishing schooner Two Brothers.	22	1	Petition	253	Commerce	268	Favorable	346	Referred to Committee Whole House.		
Sprague, Phineas, & others.	Bounty on fishing schooner Two Brothers.	23	1	Senate bill	175	Commerce	Mar. 26, 1834	With amend.	S. 24	Passed	Passed	App'd June 30, 1834
Sprague, Seth	Fishing bounty	14	2	Petition	415					Laid on table.		
Sprague, Seth	Fishing bounty	15	1	Petition	26	Com. and Manuf.	April 6, 1818	General bill	181	Passed	Passed	App'd April 18, 1818
Sprague, Seth, jr	(See Phineas Sprague, and others)	21	1		232				215			
Sprague, William	(See Phineas Sprague, and others)	21	1		232				215			
Sprague, Lieutenant	Journal does not state nature of claim.	25	2	Documents	947	Indian Affairs.						
Sprigg, Ann, representatives of.	Compensation for team lost, war of 1812.	16	1	Documents	218	Claims.						
Sprigg, Jenifer T	Compensation for extra services as deputy surveyor.	15	2	Petition	193	Public Lands.						
Sprigg, Jenifer T	Compensation for extra services as deputy surveyor.	16	1	Petition	333	Public Lands	Mar. 19, 1820	General bill	121	Rejected.		
Sprigg, Jenifer T	Compensation for extra services as deputy surveyor.	17	1	Petition	90	Public Lands.						
Sprigg, Jenifer T	Compensation for extra services as deputy surveyor.	17	2	Petition	36	Public Lands.						
Sprigg, Jenifer T	Compensation for extra services as deputy surveyor.	20	2	Petition	178	Public Lands.						
Sprigg, Samuel, (Ohio)	Reimbursement of payment for public land in Ohio.	15	1	Petition	135	Public Lands	Feb. 18, 1818	Adverse		Laid on table.		
Sprigg, Samuel, (Ohio)	Reimbursement of payment for public land in Ohio.	19	2	Petition	112	Priv. Land Claims.	59	Favorable	402	Referred to Committee Whole House.		
Sprigg, Samuel, (Ohio)	Reimbursement of payment for public land in Ohio.	20	1	Petition	79	Priv. Land Claims.	84	Favorable	88	Passed	Indef. postp'd.	
Sprigg, Samuel, (Ohio)	Reimbursement of payment for public land in Ohio.	21	1	Petition	161	Priv. Land Claims.	124	Favorable	163	Passed	Passed	App'd May 29, 1830
Sprigg, Samuel, (Md.)	Pension for revolutionary services.	17	1	Petition	45	Rev. Pensions.						
Sprigg, Thomas	Indemnity for destruction of property by public officer.	13	3	Petition	644	Claims	Feb. 15, 1815	Favorable	296	Passed	Passed	App'd March 3, 1815
Sprigg, William B	(See Louis F. Beeler and others).	30	1		115		482					
Spring, Daniel, administrator of.	Indemnity for a Danish capture	23	1	Petition	186	Foreign Affairs				Discharged; laid on table.		
Spring, Seth	Arrears of pension	25	2	Petition	52	Rev. Pensions.						
Spring, Setto	Indemnity for French spoliations prior to 1800.	26	1	Memorial	182	Foreign Affairs	343	Favorable; bill	319	Referred to Committee Whole House.		
Spring, ———	(See Wells & Spring)	31	1		434							
Springer, Abraham	Compensation for revolutionary services.	2	1	Petition and rep't Sec. of War.	442, 500					Laid on table.		
Springer, Charles, widow of.	Pension for military services	18	1	Petition	69	Naval Affairs	April 22, 1824	Adverse		Leave to withdraw.		
Springer, Edward, (N. Y.)	Arrears of pension	22	1	Petition	164	Invalid Pensions.						
Springer, Edward, (N. Y.)	Arrears of pension	31	1	Petition	193	Invalid Pensions.						
Springer, Mary Ann	(See Charles Springer, widow of.)	18	1		69							
Springer, Moses	(See executors of Wm. Springer.)	19	2		189							
Springer, Sylvester	Compensation for services as revolutionary surgeon's mate.	1	3	Petition	371					Referred to Secretary War.		

List of private claims presented to the House of Representatives of the United States from the 1st to the 31st Congress, inclusive—Continued.

Names of claimants.	Nature or object of the claim.	Congress.	Session.	How brought before the House of Reps.	Page of journal.	To what committee of the House referred.	No. or date of the report.	Nature of the report.	No. of the bill.	How disposed of by the House of Reps.	How disposed of by the Senate.	Date of the act of Congress, and remarks.
Springer, Sylvester	Compensation for services as revolutionary surgeon's mate.	2	2	Rep. of Secretary War.	696	....	....	....	......	Laid on table.		
Springer, Uriah, widow of.	Continuation of pension	19	2	Petition	156	Military Pensions.						
Springer, Uriah, widow of.	Continuation of pension	20	2	Petition	319	Military Pensions.						
Springer, Uriah, widow of.	Continuation of pension	21	1	Petition	83	Military Pensions.	April 27, 1830	Adverse	......	Laid on table.		
Springer, Uriah, widow of.	Continuation of pension	22	1	Petition	513	Rev. Pensions	Mar. 31, 1832	Adverse	......	Laid on table.		
Springer, William, executors of.	Indemnity for French capture in 1799.	19	2	Petition	189	Foreign Affairs	....	....	......	Discharged; laid on table.		
Springfield Manufacturing Company.	Indemnity for loss on a government contract.	23	1	Petition	191	Claims.						
Springfield Manufacturing Company.	Indemnity for loss on a government contract.	24	1	Petition	48	Claims	40	Favorable	40	Passed		
Springfield Manufacturing Company.	Indemnity for loss on a government contract.	25	2	Petition	37	Claims	372	Favorable; bill	395	Ordered to 3d reading.		
Springfield Manufacturing Company.	Indemnity for loss on a government contract.	25	3	Bill of last sess.	378	....	....	....	395	Passed	Passed, with amendment.	Laid on table H. R.
Springfield Manufacturing Company.	Indemnity for loss on a government contract.	26	1	Petition	168	Claims	305	Favorable	267	Referred to Committee Whole House.		
Springfield Manufacturing Company.	Indemnity for loss on a government contract.	27	2	Petition	56	Ways and Means	6	Favorable	45	Passed	Passed	App'd Aug. 24, 1842
Springfield Manufacturing Company.	Balance due on manufacture of muskets.	30	1	Petition	165	Claims.						
Sprinkle, Henry	Benefit of an act relative to public lands.	18	1	Petition	43	Public Lands.						
Sprinkle, Henry	Benefit of an act relative to public lands.	19	1	Petition	272	Public Lands	....	....	......	Discharged; referred to Com. W. House.		
Sproston, Dr. G. S. widow of	Continuation of navy pension	29	2	Memorial	302	Naval Affairs.						
Sprott, Thomas	Pension for revolutionary services.	24	1	Petition	107	Rev. Pensions	....	....	......	Discharged; laid on table.		
Sproul, William	Indemnity for French spoliations prior to 1800.	26	1	Memorial	182	Foreign Affairs	343	Favorable; bill	319	Referred to Committee Whole House.		
Sproull, James	Credit for lost vouchers	16	1	Petition	158	Claims	Feb. 9, 1820	Adverse	......	Laid on table.		
Sprout, Ebenezer, heirs of	Compensation for revolutionary services.	27	2	Petition	684	Rev. Pensions	784	Adverse	......	Laid on table.		
Sprout, Nathaniel	(See heirs of Ebenezer Sprout)	27	2	....	684							
Sprout, Samuel	(See heirs of Ebenezer Sprout)	27	2	....	684							
Squeendeptee	(See Indians, Wyandot)	27	3	....	339	....	160	....	776			
Squin, Suly	Pension for revolutionary services.	21	2	Resolution	65	Military Pensions.						
Squire, Abiathar	Pension for revolutionary services.	27	2	Resolution	64	Rev. Pensions	784	Adverse	......	Laid on table.		
Squires, Elizabeth	(See executrix of Thomas Smith).	21	2	....	106							
Squier, John	Compensation for revolutionary services.	20	1	Petition	484	Military Pensions.						
Squier, Nathaniel	Pension for services in Indian wars	28	1	Petition	868	Rev. Pensions.						
Squires, Samuel, widow of	Pension for revolutionary services.	25	3	Petition	127	Rev. Pensions	Feb. 6, 1839	Favorable	1116	Referred to Committee Whole House.		
Squires, Samuel, widow of	Pension for revolutionary services.	26	1	Petition	171	Rev. Pensions.						
Squires, Samuel, widow of	Pension for revolutionary services.	26	2	House bill	139	Whole House	....	....	572			
Squires, Samuel, widow of	Pension for revolutionary services.	27	2	Petition	59	Rev. Pensions	88	Favorable	134	Passed	Passed	App'd July 9, 1842
Squirrell, Amariah	(See administrator of Jacob Squirrell.)	21	2	....	88							
Squirrell, Jacob, administrator of.	Pay and emolument due deceased.	21	2	Petition	88	Claims	39	Favorable	558	Referred to Committee Whole House.		

List of private claims presented to the House of Representatives of the United States from the 1st to the 31st Congress, inclusive—Continued.

Names of claimants.	Nature or object of the claim.	Congress.	Session.	How brought before the House of Reps.	Page of journal.	To what committee of the House referred.	No. or date of the report.	Nature of the report.	No. of the bill.	How disposed of by the House of Reps.	How disposed of by the Senate.	Date of the act of Congress, and remarks.
Squirrell, Jacob, administrator of.	Pay and emolument due deceased.	22	1	Petition	26	Claims	Dec. 19, 1831	Favorable	35	Passed	Passed	App'd Mar. 15, 1832
Srofe, Adam	Pension	25	2	Resolution	78	Invalid Pensions						
Sruofe, Emanuel	(See Emanuel Shroufe)	24	2		384							
Sruofe, Sebastian	(See widow of Sebastian Shroufe)	24	2		122							
St. Ann's Church, Detroit.	Indemnity for a lot taken by government.	17	2	Petition	44	Military Affairs.						
St. Clair, Arthur	For certain credits in the settlements in his accounts.	2	2	Memorial	712	Select	Mar. 1, 1793	Favorable		Laid on table.		
St. Clair, Arthur	For certain credits in the settlements in his accounts.	3	1	Rep. of last Congress.	64	Select	April 22, 1794	Favorable; bill ordered.	47	Passed	Passed	App'd May 31, 1794
St. Clair, Arthur	For certain credits in the settlements in his accounts.	3	2	General appropriation bill.	261				81 B.	Passed	Passed	App'd Jan. 2, 1795
St. Clair, Arthur	Compensation for horses killed by Indians.	3	1	Letter of claimant	178					Laid on table.		
St. Clair, Arthur	Compensation for horses killed by Indians.	4	1	Documents	438	Claims	April 6, 1796	Favorable; bill ordered.	173	Passed	Passed	App'd May 12, 1796
St. Clair, Arthur	Reimbursement of advances on public account.	8	2	Petition	66	Claims.						
St. Clair, Arthur	Reimbursemen of advances on public account.	9	1	Petition	236	Select				Indef. postponed.		
St. Clair, Arthur	Reimbursement of advances on public account.	10	1	Petition	50	Select.						
St. Clair, Arthur	Reimbursement of advances on public account.	11	1	Memorial	16	Claims	June 20, 1809	Adverse		Laid on table.		
St. Clair, Arthur	Reimbursement of advances on public account.	11	2	Petition	154	Claims	Feb. 23, 1810	Adverse		Referred to Committee Whole House.		
St. Clair, Arthur	For the full amount of advances	11	3	Resolution	350	Whole House	April 6, 1810	Favorable; bill	108	Passed	Passed	App'd May 1, 1810
				Petition	488	Select	Jan. 24, 1811	Favorable	204	Referred to Committee Whole House.		
St. Clair, Arthur	For the full amount of advances	12	1	Petition	159	Select	Feb. 11, 1812	Favorable	65	Passed	Rejected.	
St. Clair, Arthur	Annuity for revolutionary services.	12	1	Senate bill	326	Whole House	May 12, 1812	With't amend.	S. 33	Rejected.		
St. Clair, Arthur	Compensation for services in Indian expedition.	12	1	Resolution	339	Select	May 12, 1812	Favorable	127	Rejected.		
St. Clair, Arthur	Reimbursement of advances on public account.	15	1	Petition	187	Select	Jan. 30, 1818	Favorable	63	Passed	Passed	App'd Mar. 9, 1818
St. Clair, Arthur, daughter of.	Balance due deceased for revolutionary services.	18	1	Petition	37	Rev. Claims	Dec. 31, 1823	Adverse		Laid on table.		
St. Clair, Arthur, executor of.	(See Elisha Winter & Sons, representatives of.)	19	2		159							
St. Clair, Arthur & Daniel	Confirmation of title to land south of the Ohio river.	3	2	Memorial	291	Select.						
St. Clair, Arthur & Daniel	Confirmation of title to land south of the Ohio river.	4	1	Memorial	381	Select.						
St. Clair, Daniel	Credit for public money lost in transmission.	7	2	Petition	356	Claims	Feb. 26, 1803	Adverse		Postponed.		
St. Clair, Daniel	Credit for public money lost in transmission.	8	1	Petition	484	Claims	Dec. 23, 1803	Adverse		Rejected.		
St. Clare, George	Compensation for fuel furnished House of Representatives.	13	2	Petition	209	Select	Jan. 28, 1814	Favorable		Referred to Committee Whole House.		
St. Cyr, Francis F	Pension	23	1	Petition	309	Invalid Pensions	April 8, 1834	Favorable	413	Referred to Committee Whole House.		
St. Cyr, Francis F	Pension	23	2	Bill of last sess.	336	Whole House	Feb. 6, 1835	With't amend.	413	Passed	Indef. postp'd.	

List of private claims presented to the House of Representatives of the United States from the 1st to the 31st Congress, inclusive—Continued.

Names of claimants.	Nature or object of the claim.	Congress.	Session.	How brought before the House of Reps.	Page of journal.	To what committee of the House referred.	No. or date of the report.	Nature of the report.	No. of the bill.	How disposed of by the House of Reps.	How disposed of by the Senate.	Date of the act of Congress, and remarks.
St. Cyr, Francis F.	Pension	24	1	Petition	202	Invalid Pensions	277	Favorable	284	Passed	Passed	App'd June 28, 1836
St. Cyr, Hyacinthe	Confirmation of title to land in Missouri.	18	1	Petition	212	Priv. Land Claims.						
St. George, George	To be restored to pension roll	17	1	Petition	388	Whole House				Leave to withdraw.		
St. Germain, Francis	Confirmation of title to land in Louisiana.	23	1	Petition	76	Priv. Land Claims.	Jan. 2, 1834	Adverse		Laid on table.		
St. Germain, Martial	Confirmation of title to land in Louisiana.	22	1	General bill	107	Whole House	Mar. 23, 1832	With't amend.	125	Passed	Passed, with amendment.	App'd June 25, 1832
St. Peter's church, Philadelphia.	Remission of duty on church bells.	27	3	Memorial	120	Ways and Means	19	Favorable	643	Referred to Committee Whole House.		
St. Romain, Zenon, wife of.	Pre-emption right	30	2	Petition	78	Priv. Land Claims.	24	Favorable	678	Passed	Passed	App'd March 3, 1849
St. German, Leon L., assignee of.	Confirmation of title to land in Michigan.	20	1	Resolution	28	Public Lands.	42	Favorable	34	Passed	Passed	App'd April 22, 1828
St. John, Adonijah	Pension	21	2	Petition	80	Military Pensions.						
St. John, Ezra	Indemnity for property destroyed by the enemy.	15	2	Petition	105	Claims	Dec. 16, 1818	Adverse		Laid on table.		
St. John, Ezra	Indemnity for property destroyed by the enemy.	16	2	Petition	93	Claims.						
St. John, Ezra	Indemnity for property destroyed by the enemy.	22	2	Petition	177	Priv. Land Claims.						
St. John, Ezra	Indemnity for property destroyed by the enemy.	23	1	Petition	567	Claims	June 20, 1834	Adverse		Laid on table.		
St. John, Hannah	(See John St. John, widow of.)	20	2		144							
St. John, Henry	Compensation for a horse lost in public service.	23	2	Petition	344	Claims.						
St. John, Henry	Compensation for a horse lost in public service.	24	1	Petition	93	Claims	615	Adverse		Laid on table.		
St. John, John	Pension for revolutionary services.	10	1	Pension bill	232	Whole House			78	Passed	Passed, with amendment.	App'd April 25, 1808
St. John, John	Increase of pension	15	1	Petition	21	Pens. & Rev. Cl'ms						
St. John, John, widow of.	Continuation of pension	16	2	Petition	177	Pens. & Rev. Cl'ms.						
St. John, John, widow of.	Continuation of pension	17	1	Petition	52	Military Affairs				Discharged; laid on table.		
St. John, John	To be restored to pension roll	17	1	Petition	432	Rev. Pensions.						
St. John, John, widow of.	Continuation of pension	20	2	Petition	144	Military Pensions				Discharged; laid on table.		
St. John, Lois	(See John St. John, widow of.)	16	2		177							
St. John, Margaret	Indemnity for damage to property, war of 1812.	17	1	Petition	186	Claims.						
St. John, Samuel	Pension for revolutionary services.	28	2	Petition	53	Rev. Pensions				Discharged; laid on table.		
St. Vrain, Bent & Co.	(See Bent, St. Vrain & Co.)	28	2		180							
St. Vrain, Felix, sureties of.	Release from certain bond	25	2	Petition	426	Indian Affairs.						
St. Vrain, Felix, sureties of.	Release from certain bond.	28	1	Senate bill	948	Whole House			S. 155			
St. Vrain, Felix, sureties of.	Release from certain bond	28	2	Senate bill	131	Judiciary	Jan. 31, 1845	With't amend.	S. 13	Referred to Committee Whole House.		
St. Vrain, Felix, sureties of.	Release from certain bond	29	1	Senate bill	372	Claims	298	With amend.	S. 7	Passed with amendm't.	Passed	App'd Aug. 3, 1846
Staats, Anne	(See executors of Barent J. Staats)	4	2		613							
Staats, Barent J.	Payment of the note of a revolutionary commissary.	4	1	Rep. of Secretary Treasury.	388	Claims	May 31, 1796	Adverse		Laid on table.		
Staats, Barent J., executors of.	Payment of the note of a revolutionary commissary.	4	2	Petition	631	Claims.						

List of private claims presented to the House of Representatives of the United States from the 1st to the 31st Congress, inclusive—Continued.

Names of claimants.	Nature or object of the claim.	Congress.	Session.	How brought before the House of Reps.	Page of journal.	To what committee of the House referred.	No. or date of the report.	Nature of the report.	No. of the bill.	How disposed of by the House of Reps.	How disposed of by the Senate.	Date of the act of Congress, and remarks.
Staats, Barent J., executors of.	Payment of the note of a revolutionary commissary.	5	2	Petition	282	Claims	May 20, 1798	Adverse	......	Referred to Committee Whole House.		
Staats, Barent J., representatives of.	Reimbursement of advances on public account.	19	1	Petition	407	Rev. Claims.						
Staats, Barent J., heirs of.	Reimbursement of advances on public account.	19	2	Petition	112	Rev. Claims	Jan. 23, 1827	Adverse	......	Laid on table	....	Leave to withdraw.
Staats, Nicholas	(See executors of Barent J. Staats.)	4	2	....	613							
Staats, Philip	(See executors of Barent J. Staats.)	4	2	....	613							
Stacy, James	(See John D. Needham, and others.)	15	1	....	136							
Stacy, Mary	Pension for revolutionary services.	28	1	Petition	975	Rev. Pensions.						
Stacy, Nathan, and others.	Compensation for revolutionary services.	1	3	Petition	378							
Stacy, Rebecca	Continuation of pension	28	1	Petition	850	Rev. Pensions.						
Stacy, Richard	(See John D. Needham, and others.)	15	1	....	136							
Stacy, Samuel	Prize-money as sailingmaster under Paul Jones.	30	1	Petition	344	Rev. Claims	....	....	......	Discharged; laid on table.		
Stack, Richard	Relief in consideration of revolutionary disability.	2	1	Petition	474	....	....	....	......	Referred to Secretary of War.		
Stack, Richard	Pension for revolutionary disability.	3	1	Rep. of Secretary War.	186	Whole House.						
Stack, Richard	Pension for revolutionary disability.	3	2	Rep. of Secretary War.	262	Claims.						
Stack, Richard	Pension for revolutionary disability.	4	1	Rep. of Secretary War.	445	Claims.						
Stack, Richard	Pension for revolutionary disability.	4	2	Rep. of Secretary War.	614	Claims.						
Stadden, Richard	Extra compensation for services in Mexico.	30	2	Petition	459	Military Affairs.						
Stadtler, John	Confirmation of title to an anterior revolutionary grant.	4	2	Petition	634							
Stadtler. John	Confirmation of title to an ante-revolutionary grant.	5	2	Petition	145	Claims	Jan. 22, 1798	Adverse	......	Referred to Committee Whole House.		
Stafford, Aaron	Pension	14	2	Resolution	237	Pens. & Rev. Cl'ms.	Jan. 29, 1817	Favorable	91	Passed	Passed, with amendment.	App'd March 3, 1817
Stafford, Aaron	Increase of pension	15	1	Resolution Documents	257 261	 Pens. & Rev. Cl'ms.						
Stafford, Aaron	Increase of pension	15	2	Pension bill	41	....	....	....	203	Passed	Passed, with amendment.	App'd March 3, 1819
Stafford, Aaron	Pension for services, war of 1812.	30	1	Petition Documents	100 271	Invalid Pensions. Invalid Pensions	 780	 Favorable	 617	 Referred to Committee Whole House.		
Stafford, Aaron	Pension for services, war of 1812.	30	2	Bill of last sess.	362	Whole House	Feb. 2, 1849	With't amend.	617	Passed.		
Stafford, Aaron	Pension for services, war of 1812.	31	1	Res'n and docs.	493	Invalid Pensions.						
Stafford, Aaron	Pension for services, war of 1812.	31	2	Petition	412	Invalid Pensions	41	Favorable	477	Referred to Committee Whole House.		
Stafford, Abigail	(See heirs of Henry Smith)	30	1	....	397							
Stafford, Abraham	Pension	22	1	Petition	171	Invalid Pensions.						
Stafford, Abraham	Pension	24	1	Petition	71	Invalid Pensions	....	....	......	Disch'd; laid on table.		
Stafford, Benjamin	Pension	21	2	Petition	193	Military Pensions.						
Stafford, Benoni	Exchange of bounty land	19	1	Petition	58	Public Lands	54	Favorable	77	Passed	Passed	App'd May 22, 1826
Stafford, Gideon	Pension for revolutionary services.	24	1	Resolution	667	Rev. Pensions.						
Stafford, James B., widow of.	Pension for revolutionary services.	27	1	Petition	107	Rev. Pensions.						

List of private claims presented to the House of Representatives of the United States from the 1st to the 31st Congress, inclusive—Continued.

Names of claimants.	Nature or object of the claim.	Congress.	Session.	How brought before the House of Reps.	Page of journal.	To what committee of the House referred.	No. or date of the report.	Nature of the report.	No. of the bill.	How disposed of by the House of Reps.	How disposed of by the Senate.	Date of the act of Congress, and remarks.
Stafford, James B., widow of.	Pension for revolutionary services	27	2	Petition	153	Rev. Pensions				Discharged; laid on table.		
Stafford, Joab	Pension for revolutionary services	3	1	Rep. of Secretary War.	131	Select	May 26, 1794	Res. to refer to Sec. War.	J.R. 12	Passed	Passed	App'd June 9, 1794
Stafford, Joab	Arrears of pension	3	2	Petition	231	Claims	Jan. 2, 1795	Adverse		Laid on table.		
Stafford, Joab	Pension for revolutionary services	4	1	Rep. of Secretary War.	445	Claims.						
Stafford, Joab	Pension for revolutionary services	4	2	Rep't of Secretary War.	614	Claims.						
Stafford, Joab	Reconsideration of former petition	5	2	Petition	159	Claims	April 17, 1798	Adverse		Laid on table.		
Stafford, Joab	Reconsideration of former petition	5	3	Petition	432	Whole House.						
Stafford, John	Confirmation of title to land in Mississippi.	13	2	Petition	312	Public Lands	April 5, 1814	Adverse		Rejected.		
Stafford, John, executors of.	(See sureties of Solo. Southwick.)	21	1		104							
Stafford, Nathaniel	Pension	29	1	Senate bill	1016	Rev. Pensions	July 13, 1846	With't amend.	S. 188	Passed	Passed	App'd July 18, 1846
Stafford, Spencer	(See sureties of Solo. Southwick.)	21	1		66							
Stafford, Spencer	(See sureties of Samuel Edmonds.)	24	2		400							
Stafford, ——	(See Abraham Prim and others)	30	1		485							
Stager, Peter	Pension for revolutionary services	29	2	Petition	292	Rev. Pensions.						
Stagg, Daniel	Pension	14	1	Petition	450	Pens. & Rev. Cl'ms.	April 11, 1816	Pension bill	171	Passed	Passed, with amendment.	App'd April 30, 1816
Stagg, John, jr.	Increase of salary as chief clerk in War Department.	2	1	Petition	480	Select				Laid on table.		
Stagg, Thomas, jr., and others.	Remission of forfeiture on schooner Virago.	7	1	Petition	27	Com. and Manuf				Disch'd; postponed.		
Stagg, ——	(See Harvey & Stagg)	27	3		108							
Staley, George	Exchange of location of land	23	1	Senate bill	170	Priv. Land Claims.	Jan. 14, 1834	With't amend.	S. 32	Passed	Passed	App'd Mar. 24, 1834
Staley, Noah	Exchange of location of land	23	1	Senate bill	170	Priv. Land Claims.	Jan. 14, 1834	With't amend.	S. 31	Passed.	Passed	App'd Mar. 24, 1834
Stalker, Gilbert, & Hill	Compensation for steamboat lost in public service.	27	2	Senate bill	1126	Claims			S. 248			
Stalker, Gilbert, & Hill	Compensation for steamboat lost in public service.	27	3	Senate bill Petition	115 228	Claims Claims.	119	Adverse	S. 4	Referred to Committee Whole House.		
Stalker, Gilbert, & Hill	Compensation for steamboat lost in public service.	28	1	Petition	80	Claims	1	Adverse		Laid on table.		
Stalker, Gilbert, & Hill	Compensation for steamboat lost in public service.	29	1	Petition	591	Claims	755	Favorable	493	Referred to Committee Whole House.		
Stalker, Gilbert, & Hill	Compensation for steamboat lost in public service.	30	1	Petition Senate bill	99 956	Claims Claims	118	Favorable	109 S. 161	Passed	Passed	App'd July 5, 1848 Returned to Senate.
Stalker, Gilbert, administrator of.	Remuneration for steamboat service.	30	2	Petition	127	Claims.						
Stalker, Gilbert, administrator of.	Remuneration for steamboat service.	31	1	Petition	719	Claims	498	Adverse		Laid on table.		
Stall, George W., widow of.	Pension for military services	28	1	Petition	975	Claims.						
Stall, George W., widow of.	Pension for military services	29	1	Petition	395	Claims	564	Adverse		Laid on table.		
Stall, Maria B	(See George W. Stall, widow of.)	28	1		975							
Stallings, Thomas	Remission of duty on still destroyed by fire.	7	1	Petition	27	Ways and Means	Dec. 30, 1801	Adverse		Rejected.		
Stam, George	Compensation for services as drummer, Maryland line.	2	1	Petition	498					Referred to Secretary of War.		
Stamford, Hannah	(See heirs of Wm. Kinnard)	16	2		216							
Stamford, William	(See heirs of Wm. Kinnard)	16	2		216							
Stamps, Nathan D.	Compensation for a horse lost in Florida.	26	2	Petition	130	Claims.						

List of private claims presented to the House of Representatives of the United States from the 1st to the 31st Congress, inclusive—Continued.

Names of claimants.	Nature or object of the claim.	Congress.	Session.	How brought before the House of Reps.	Page of journal.	To what committee of the House referred.	No. or date of the report.	Nature of the report.	No. of the bill.	How disposed of by the House of Reps.	How disposed of by the Senate.	Date of the act of Congress, and remarks.
Stanberry, Job	Indemnity for property destroyed in public service.	13	2	Petition	299	Claims	Mar. 1, 1814	Adverse	......	Leave to withdraw.		
Stanberry, Job	Duplicate for land warrant lost in mail.	16	1	Petition	314	Public Lands.						
Standifer, Abraham	Indemnity for an illegal seizure of property.	23	1	Petition	248	Indian Affairs	....	....	......	Discharged; laid on table.		
Standefer, Wm. H.	Compensation for team lost in public service.	26	2	Documents	960	Claims.						
Standefer, Wm. H.	Compensation for team lost in public service.	27	2	Documents	823	Claims.						
Standiford, Vincent	Additional compensation for work on Cumberland road.	23	1	Petition	335	Claims	455	Adverse	......	....	....	See report No. 449.
Standiford, Vincent	Additional compensation for work on Cumberland road.	23	2	Petition Res. and docs.	276 589	Claims. Claims	 455	 Adverse		 Laid on table.		
Standish, Amos, widow of.	Continuation of deceased's pension.	28	1	Petition	360	Rev. Pensions.						
Standish, Amos, widow of.	Continuation of deceased's pension.	28	2	Petition	56	Rev. Pensions.						
Standish, Esther	(See Amos Standish, widow of.)	28	1	....	360							
Standish, George A	(See heirs of Prudent La Jeanesse)	29	2	....	92							
Standish, Nathaniel	To be restored to pension roll	17	1	Petition	227	Rev. Pensions.						
Standish, Nathaniel	Pension for revolutionary services.	20	1	Res and docs.	415	Military Pensions.						
Standish, Nathaniel	Pension for revolutionary services.	20	2	Resolution	57	Military Pensions.	Feb. 13, 1829	Favorable	440	Passed.		
Standish, Nathaniel	Pension for revolutionary services	21	1	Resolution Pension bill	63 130	Military Pensions. Whole House	414 Feb. 12, 1830	Favorable With amend.	489 72	Referred to Committee Whole House. Name omitted in act.		
Standish, Nathaniel	Pension for revolutionary services.	21	2	House bill	318	Whole House	Feb. 16, 1831	With't amend.	489	Passed.		
Standish, Nathaniel	Pension for revolutionary services.	22	1	Petition Resolution	45 422	Rev. Pensions. Rev. Pensions	 Dec. 20, 1831	 Favorable	 52	 Passed	 Indef. postp'd.	
Standley, Andrew	(See John Pickett and others)	29	1	....	331	....	690	....	462			
Standley, Hannah	(See Robert Standley, widow of.)	25	2	....	351							
Standley, Robert, widow of.	Pension for naval services of son	25	2	Petition	351	Naval Affairs.						
Stanert, John	Increase of revolutionary pension	29	1	Petition	315	Invalid Pensions	....	....	......	Discharged; laid on table.		
Stanert, John	Increase of revolutionary pension	30	1	Petition	207	Invalid Pensions	465	Adverse	......	Laid on table.		
Stanford, Alg. S., surety of.	Release from liability	16	1	Petition	182	Ways and Means.						
Stanford, Alg. S., surety of.	Release from liability	16	2	Petition	35	Ways and Means.	Nov. 27, 1820	Adverse	......	Rejected.		
Stanford, Alg. S., surety of.	Release from liability	17	1	Petition	334	Ways and Means.						
Stanford, Alg. S., surety of.	Release from liability	17	2	Petition	60	Ways and Means.	Dec. 30, 1822	Adverse	......	Rejected.		
Stanford, Alg. S., surety of.	Release from liability	18	1	Petition	198	Ways and Means.	May 17, 1824	Adverse	......	Rejected.		
Stanford, Clement	(See sureties of Alg S. Stanford)	16	1	....	182							
Stanford, Elizabeth	(See widow of John McCaffery)	28	1	....	695							
Staniford, Daniel	Compensation for property damaged by United States troops.	22	1	Petition	777	Claims.						
Staniford, Daniel	Compensation for property damaged by United States troops.	23	1	Petition	33	Claims	523	Adverse	......	Laid on table.		
Staniford, Thomas	Equitable settlement of his accounts.	16	1	Petition	203	Claims	Feb. 28, 1820	Adverse	......	Laid on table.		
Staniford, Thomas	Equitable settlement of his accounts.	16	2	Rep. of last sess.	121	Whole House	....	....	......	Discharged.		
Staniford, Thomas	Equitable settlement of his accounts.	18	1	Senate bill	339	Claims	April 21, 1824	With amend.	S. 60	Passed with amend't.	Passed	App'd May 5, 1824
Stanley, Adin	Pension for revolutionary disabilities.	24	1	Documents	661	Invalid Pensions	....	....	......	Discharged; laid on table.		
Stanley, Adin	Pension for revolutionary disabilities.	24	2	Petition	72	Invalid Pensions	Dec. 30, 1836	Adverse	......	Laid on table.		

List of private claims presented to the House of Representatives of the United States from the 1st to the 31st Congress, inclusive—Continued.

Names of claimants.	Nature or object of the claim.	Congress.	Session.	How brought before the House of Reps.	Page of journal.	To what committee of the House referred.	No. or date of the report.	Nature of the report.	No. of the bill.	How disposed of by the House of Reps.	How disposed of by the Senate.	Date of the act of Congress, and remarks.
Stanley, Caleb, & Smith..	Reimbursement of duty on distillery.	14	1	Petition	70	Ways and Means..	....	....	......	Discharged; referred to Com. Whole House.		
Stanley, Elisha	Pension for revolutionary services.	19	1	Petition	423	Military Pensions..	....	....	......	Discharged; leave to withdraw.		
Stanley, Elisha	Pension for revolutionary services.	19	2	Petition	132	Military Pensions.						
Stanley, Elisha	Pension for revolutionary services.	20	2	Resolution	212	Military Pensions..	....	....	......	Discharged; laid on table.		
Stanley, Elisha	(See Thomas Talbot and others)..	20	1	....	312							
Stannard, Benjamin	(See Wm. Stannard. and others).	23	2	....	320							
Stannard, Job	(See Wm. Stannard, and others).	23	2	....	320							
Stannard, Wm., and others	Bounty on a fishing voyage......	23	2	Memorial	320	Commerce	115	Favorable	744	Referred to Committee Whole House.		
Stannard, Wm., and others	Bounty on a fishing voyage......	24	1	Petition	55	Commerce	80	Favorable	96	Passed.		
Stansbury, Dixon	Compensation for baggage lost in public service.	22	1	Petition	387	Military Affairs ...	May 8, 1832	Adverse	......	Laid on table.		
Stansbury, Dixon	Compensation for baggage lost in public service	23	2	Petition	106	Claims	Jan. 2, 1835	Adverse	......	Laid on table.		
Stansbury, Dixon	Compensation for baggage lost in public service.	25	2	Petition	114	Military Affairs....	Mar. 30, 1838	Adverse	......	Laid on table.		
Stansbury, Dixon	Compensation for baggage lost in public service.	26	2	Petition	130	Claims.						
Stansbury, Job	(See Job Stanberry)	13	2	....	299							
Stansbury, Jonas........	Liquidation of a revolutionary certificate.	4	1	Rep. of Secretary Treasury.	388	Claims	May 31, 1796	Adverse	......	Laid on table.		
Stansbury, Luke	Increase of pension............	29	1	Petition	280	Rev. Pensions	357	Adverse......	......	Laid on table.		
Stansberry, Recompense ..	Pension	21	2	Petition	270	Military Pensions.						
Stansbury, Tobias, E. & W.	Indemnity for property destroyed by the enemy.	14	2	Petition	410	Claims.						
Stansbury, Tobias, E. & W.	Indemnity for property destroyed by the enemy.	15	1	Report of Com'r Claims.	256	Claims	March 2, 1818	Adverse......	......	Referred to Committee Whole House.		
Stansbury, Tobias, E. & W.	Indemnity for property destroyed by the enemy.	19	2	Petition	132	....	....	....	......	Laid on table.		
				Rep. of Secretary Navy.	197	Claims	45	Adverse	......	Referred to Secretary of the Navy.		
Stansbury, Tobias, E. & W.	Indemnity for property destroyed by the enemy.	22	2	Petition	32	Claims	9	Adverse	......	Laid on table.		
Stansbury, Tobias, E. & W.	Indemnity for property destroyed by the enemy.	23	1	Petition	154	Claims.						
Stansbury, Tobias, E. & W.	Indemnity for property destroyed by the enemy.	23	2	Petition	114	Claims	Jan. 7, 1835	Adverse	......	Laid on table.		
Stansbury, Tobias E.....	Pension for revolutionary services.	29	1	Memorial	573	Rev. Pensions.						
Stanton, Aaron	(See Thomas Brown, and A. S.).	20	1	....	186							
Stanton, Adam & John ..	Bounty on fishing schooner Viper.	10	1	Petition	205	Com. and Manuf.						
Stanton, Amos, daughter of	Pension for revolutionary services.	25	2	Petition	586	Rev. Claims......	....	....	......	Discharged; laid on table.		
Staunton, Charles	Additional pay as boatswain's mate	24	1	Petition	405	Claims.						
Staunton, Daniel........	Increase of pension	12	1	Pension bill	361	Whole House.....	June 15, 1812	With amend..	138	Passed	Passed, with amendment.	App'd July 6, 1812
Stanton, Edward........	Increase of pension	10	2	Pension bill	499	Whole House	....	....	158	Passed	Passed, with amendment.	App'd March 3, 1809
Stanton, Edward, widow of	Continuation of pension	24	2	Petition	41	Invalid Pensions.						

List of private claims presented to the House of Representatives of the United States from the 1st to the 31st Congress, inclusive—Continued.

Names of claimants.	Nature or object of the claim.	Congress.	Session.	How brought before the House of Reps.	Page of journal.	To what committee of the House referred.	No. or date of the report.	Nature of the report.	No. of the bill.	How disposed of by the House of Reps.	How disposed of by the Senate.	Date of the act of Congress, and remarks.
Stanton, Eldridge, widow of.	Pension for military services	29	1	Petition	298	Invalid Pensions.						
Stanton, Eldridge, widow of.	Pension for military services	30	1	Petition	274	Invalid Pensions	702	Adverse		Laid on table.		
Stanton, Enoch, heirs of.	Back pay, &c., for revolutionary services.	30	1	Petition	277	Rev. Claims.						
Stanton, Enoch, heirs of.	Back pay, &c., for revolutionary services.	30	2	Petition	121	Rev. Claims.						
Stanton, John	(See Adam and John Stanton)	10	1		205							
Stanton, John	(See heirs of Enoch Stanton)	30	1		277							
Stanton, Martha	(See Edward Stanton, widow of.)	24	2		41							
Stanton, Mary	(See Eldridge Stanton, widow of.)	29	1		298							
Stanwood, Abel, attorney of.	Indemnity for French spoliations prior to 1800.	26	1	Memorial	182	Foreign Affairs	343	Favorable; bill	319	Referred to Committee Whole House.		
Stanwood, Eben	Indemnity for French spoliations prior to 1800.	26	1	Memorial	182	Foreign Affairs	343	Favorable; bill	319	Referred to Committee Whole House.		
Stanwood, Theodore, and others.	Bounty on two fishing vessels	21	2	Petition	54	Commerce				Discharged; laid on table.		
Stanwood, Theodore, and others.	Bounty on two fishing vessels	22	1	Petition	114	Commerce.						
Stanwood, Theodore, and others.	Bounty on two fishing vessels	24	1	Petition	200	Commerce	198	Favorable	202	Passed.		
Stanwood, William, jr	(See Thomas Morse, *et al.*)	4	2		744							
Stanwood, William, and others.	Restitution of land sold for tax	15	1	Petition	132	Ways and Means.						
Stanwood, William, heirs of.	Compensation for naval services	25	3	Petition	563	Naval Affairs.						
Stanwood, William, heirs of.	Pension for revolutionary services.	28	2	Petition	71	Rev. Pensions				Dischraged; laid on table.		
Stanwood, William, heirs of.	Pension for revolutionary services.	29	1	Petition	1001	Rev. Pensions.						
Stanwood, William, heirs of.	Indemnity for French spoliations prior to 1800.	28	1	Petition	514	Foreign Affairs.						
Staples, Charles	Bounty on a fishing vessel	16	1	Petition	180	Commerce.						
Staples, Charles	Pension	25	2	Petition	56	Invalid Pensions.						
Staples, David	Pension	16	1	Petition	147	Pens. & Rev. Cl'ms.				Referred to Secretary War.		
Staples, James	Pension	22	2	Petition	26	Invalid Pensions.	Jan. 15, 1833	Adverse		Laid on table.		
Staples, Joanna	Revolutionary pension	30	1	Petition	460	Rev. Pensions.	372	Adverse		Laid on table.		
Staples, John	Arrears of pay due for revolutionary services.	3	1	Petition and rep't Sec. of War.	48, 93	Select.						
Staples, John	Compensation for revolutionary services.	15	1	Petition	191	Pens. & Rev. Cl'ms.						
Staples, John	Compensation for revolutionary services.	15	2	Petition	32	Pens. & Rev. Cl'ms.	Nov. 30, 1818	Adverse		Leave to withdraw.		
Staples, Mark, widow of.	Continuance of his pension	21	2	Petition	54	Military Pensions				Discharged; laid on table.		
Staples, Sally	(See Mark Staples, widow of.)	21	2		54							
Staples, Samuel	Bounty on fishing schooner Harp.	31	2	Petition	101	Commerce.						
Staples & Williams	(See Williams, Staples & Williams.)	30	2		241							
Stapp, J. T. B., and others.	Bounty land for services, Mexican war.	31	1	Petition	544	Public Lands.						

List of private claims presented to the House of Representatives of the United States from the 1st to the 31st Congress, inclusive—Continued.

Names of claimants.	Nature or object of the claim.	Congress.	Session.	How brought before the House of Reps.	Page of journal.	To what committee of the House referred.	No. or date of the report.	Nature of the report.	No. of the bill.	How disposed of by the House of Reps.	How disposed of by the Senate.	Date of the act of Congress, and remarks.
Starboard, Anthony......	Pension for revolutionary services.	3	1	Rep. of Secretary War.	131	Select..........	May 26, 1794	Res. to refer to Sec. War..	R. 12	Passed...........	Passed......	App'd June 9, 1794
Starboard, Anthony......	Pension for revolutionary services.	4	1	Rep. of Secretary War.	445	Claims.						
Starboard, Anthony......	Pension for revolutionary services.	4	2	Rep. of Secretary War.	614	Claims.						
Stark, Caleb............	Compensation for revolutionary services.	19	1	Senate bill.....	478	Rev. Claims.....	May 4, 1826	Adverse.....	S. 103	Laid on table.		
Stark, Caleb............	Half-pay and bounty land.......	20	1	Senate bill.....	410	Rev. Claims......	Mar. 18, 1828	With amend..	S. 73	Passed with amendm't.	Passed as am'd	App'd May 24, 1828
Starks, David, widow of..	Pension for military services.....	24	2	Petition.......	72	Invalid Pensions..	Dec. 30, 1836	Adverse.....	......	Laid on table.		
Starks, David, widow of..	Pension for military services.....	27	2	Petition.......	415	Invalid Pensions..	821	Adverse.....	......	Laid on table.		
Stark, Major General John.	Government bounty for revolutionary services.	15	1	Petition.......	306	Select.....	Mar. 18, 1818	With't amend.	123	Passed.		
Stark, Major General John.	Pension for revolutionary services.	15	2	Resolution.....	42	Select..........	Nov. 30, 1818	Favorable....	208	Passed...........	Passed, with amendment.	App'd Dec. 28, 1818
Stark, John...........	Pension for revolutionary services.	3	2	Rep. of Secretary War.	350	Claims.........	Mar. 2, 1795	Pension bill..	130	Passed...........	Postponed.	
Stark, John...........	Pension for revolutionary services.	4	1	Rep. of Secretary War.	445	Claims.........	Feb. 18, 1796	Pension bill..	156	Passed...........	Passed......	App'd April 20, 1796
Stark, Jonathan, administrator of.	Pension....................	29	2	Petition......	162	Invalid Pensions.						
Stark, Jonathan, heir of..	Pension....................	30	1	Petition.......	636	Invalid Pensions..	....	....	......	Discharged; laid on table.		
Stark, Joseph, widow of..	Pension for revolutionary services.	28	1	Petition.......	344	Rev. Claims.						
Stark, Nathan..........	(See Gilbert A. Smith, and others)	24	1	....	130							
Stark, Phœbe...........	(See Joseph Stark, widow of.)...	28	1	....	344							
Stark, Soloman.........	Invalid pension..............	11	2	Pension bill....	283	....	....	....	107	Passed...........	Passed, with amendment.	App'd May 24, 1828
Stark, William E.......	Additional compensation as assistant quartermaster.	29	2	Petition.......	56	Naval Affairs.						
Starkefelt, William.....	(Not stated)................	28	2	Petition.......	82	Rev. Claims.						
Starkey, John..........	Pension....................	15	1	Petition.......	59	Pens. & Rev. Cl'ms.						
Starkes, Josiah.........	(See Stothard and Starkey)......	13	1	....	78							
Starman, Frederick, and others.	Exchange and renewal of public certificate.	1	3	Petition.......	383	....	....	....	......	Referred to Secretary Treasury.		
Starman, Frederick, and others.	Exchange and renewal of public certificate.	3	1	Rep. of Secretary Treasury.	78	....	....	....	......	Laid on table.		
Starr, J. B............	Compensation for supplies furnished Tennessee volunteers.	27	3	Memorial......	395	Claims.						
Starr, Daniel, heirs of....	Pension for revolutionary services.	25	3	Petition.......	217	Rev. Pensions....	Jan. 16, 1839	Adverse.....	......	Laid on table.		
Starr, Daniel, heirs of....	Pension for revolutionary services.	26	2	Petition.......	134	Rev. Claims.						
Starr, Daniel, heirs of....	Pension for revolutionary services.	27	2	Petition.......	62	Rev. Claims......	785	Adverse.....	......	Referred to Committee Whole House.		
Starr, Daniel, heirs of....	Pension or half-pay for revolutionary services.	28	1	Petition.......	99	Rev. Claims.						
Starr, Daniel, heirs of....	Pension or half-pay for revolutionary services.	29	1	Petition.......	89	Rev. Claims.						
Starr, Daniel, heirs of....	Pension or half-pay for revolutionary services.	30	2	Petition.......	87	Rev. Claims.						
Starr, Daniel, heirs of....	Pension or half-pay for revolutionary services.	31	1	Petition.......	526	Rev. Pensions.						
Starr, Eunice, widow of William.	Pension....................	29	1	Petition.......	175	Rev Pensions.....	617	Adverse.....	......	Laid on table.		
Starr, John............	Bounty land as a Canadian refugee.	6	2	House bill.....	766	Whole House....	Jan. 26, 1801	With't amend	280	Passed...........	Passed......	App'd Feb. 18, 1801
Starr, Robert..........	Release from imprisonment at New York.	14	2	Petition.......	162	Ways and Means						

List of private claims presented to the House of Representatives of the United States from the 1st to the 31st Congress, inclusive—Continued.

Names of claimants.	Nature or object of the claim.	Congress.	Session.	How brought before the House of Reps.	Page of journal.	To what committee of the House referred.	No. or date of the report.	Nature of the report.	No. of the bill.	How disposed of by the House of Reps.	How disposed of by the Senate.	Date of the act of Congress, and remarks.
Starr, Thaddeus	Pension	21	2	Petition	43	Military Pensions.						
Starr, Thomas	Pension for revolutionary services.	3	1	Rep. of Secretary War.	131	Select	May 26, 1794	Pension bill	62	Passed	Passed	App'd June 7, 1794
Starr, William	Increase of pension	10	2	Pension bill	499	Whole House			158	Passed	Passed, with amendment.	App'd March 3, 1809
Starr, William, widow of	Continuation of deceased's pension.	29	1	Petition	175	Rev. Pensions	617	Adverse		Laid on table.		
Starring, jr., Henry	Pension	19	2	Petition	82	Military Pensions.						
Starring, jr., Henry	Pension	20	1	Petition	99	Military Pensions.	April 29, 1828	Pension bill	283	Passed.		
Starring, jr., Henry	Pension	20	2	House bill	55	Whole House	Jan. 15, 1829	With amends.	311	Passed	Laid on table.	
Starring, jr., Henry	Pension	21	1	Petition	36	Military Pensions.	Jan. 5, 1830	Pension bill	72	Passed	Passed	App'd May 20, 1830
Starritt, or Stanitt, B.	Increase of revolutionary pension.	27	2	Petition	268	Rev. Pensions	784	Adverse		Laid on table.		
Staser, John F.	Bounty land for services in Mexican war.	30	1	Petition	436	Military Affairs	622	Adverse		Laid on table.		
Statesman, Peter	Compensation for services by impressment at New Orleans.	31	2	Petition	216	Claims.						
Statesman, Samuel	Compensation for services by impressment at New Orleans.	31	2	Petition	216	Claims.						
Statler, John	Compensation for revolutionary supplies.	13	2	Petition	210	Pens. & Rev. Cl'ms.	Mar. 3, 1814	Adverse		Leave to withdraw.		
Staylor, William	(See Thomas Richardson and William Staylor.)	18	1		178							
Stayner, Roger	Commutation pay for revolutionary services.	24	2	Petition	215	Rev. Claims.						
Stayner, Roger	Commutation pay for revolutionary services.	25	2	Petition	49	Rev. Claims	593	Favorable	580	Passed	Adverse report.	
Stayner, Roger	Commutation pay for revolutionary services.	25	3	Petition	84	Rev. Claims	12	Favorable	909	Referred to Committee Whole House.		
Steads, Richard	Pension for revolutionary services.	10	1	Pension bill	232	Whole House			78	Passed	Passed, with amendment.	App'd April 25, 1808
Stead, William, heirs of	(Not stated)	23	2	Documents	85	Rev. Claims.						
Steadley, John	(See Charles Cramer and others)	21	1		375							
Steadman, Aaron	Extension of patent	31	2	Petition	185	Patents.						
Steadman, Emanuel	Compensation for revolutionary services.	31	2	Petition	343	Claims.						
Steadman, William, (Ala.)	Indemnity for losses in war of 1812.	17	2	Petition	64	Claims.						
Steadman, William, (Ala.)	Indemnity for losses in war of 1812.	19	2	Petition	240	Claims.						
Steadman, William, (Ala.)	Indemnity for losses in war of 1812.	20	1	Petition	638	Claims	May 7, 1828	Adverse		Laid on table.		
Stealey, John, (Indiana)	Indemnity for deficiency in public land.	17	2	Petition	122	Priv. Land Claims.	Jan. 17, 1823	Adverse		Laid on table.		
Stealey, John, (Indiana)	Indemnity for deficiency in public land.	18	1	Petition	28	Public Lands.						
Steamboats Compte and S. Western.	Compensation for services and expenses.	26	2	Petition	81	Claims.						
Steamboats Compte and S. Western.	Compensation for services and expenses.	27	2	Petition	327	Claims.						
Steamboat Gen. Brady	Payment due from Ottowa Indians.	29	1	Memorial	160	Indian Affairs	287	Adverse		Laid on table.		
Steamboat Jas. Boatwright.	(See Stalker, Gilbert, & Hill)	27	2		1126							
Steamboat Company, Nantucket.	Compensation for transportation of the mail.	26	2	Senate bill	256	Whole House			S. 167			
Steamboat Company, Nantucket.	Compensation for transportation of the mail.	27	3	Senate bill	118	P. Of. and P. Roads.	Jan. 19, 1843	With't amend.	S. 18	Passed	Passed	App'd Feb. 4, 1843
Steamboat Company, New Haven.	Remission of certain fines	27	2	Petition	532	Select.						

List of private claims presented to the House of Representatives of the United States from the 1st to the 31st Congress, inclusive—Continued.

Names of claimants.	Nature or object of the claim.	Congress.	Session.	How brought before the House of Reps.	Page of journal.	To what committee of the House referred.	No. or date of the report.	Nature of the report.	No. of the bill.	How disposed of by the House of Reps.	How disposed of by the Senate.	Date of the act of Congress, and remarks.
Steamboat Phenix	(See William W. Street)	27	2	....	227							
Stearns, Catharine	(See David Stearns, widow of)	19	2	....	156							
Stearns, Charles	Indemnity for an illegal prosecution.	30	1	Petition	444	Judiciary.						
Stearns Charles	Reimbursement of expenses of government prosecution.	31	2	Petition	164	Judiciary.						
Stearns, Charles	Pension	20	1	Petition	98	Military Pensions	Feb. 13, 1828	Pension bill	[illegible]6	Passed.		
Stearns, Charles	Pension	20	2	Pension bill	55	Whole House	Jan. 15, 1829	With't amend.	311	Passed	Laid on table.	
Stearns, Charles	To be restored to pension roll	21	1	Petition	49	Military Pensions	Jan. 5, 1830	Pension bill	72	Passed	Passed	App'd May 20, 1830
Stearns, David, widow of	Compensation for dower in Charlestown navy-yard.	19	2	Petition	156	Judiciary.						
Stearns, David, widow of	Compensation for dower in Charlestown navy-yard.	20	1	Rep. of Secretary Navy.	27	Claims	2	Favorable	3	Passed	Passed, with amendment.	App'd April 3, 1828
Stearns, John	(See William Bartlett and others.)	16	2	....	149							
Stearns, Peleg, administrator of.	Indemnity for property destroyed by the enemy.	2	2	Petition	668	....	....	....	......	Referred to Secretary Treasury.		
Stearns, Peleg, administrator of.	Indemnity for property destroyed by the enemy.	3	1	Rep. of Secretary Treasury.	78	....	....	....	......	Laid on table.		
Stearns, Squier	Indemnity for certain forfeitures	23	1	Petition	386	Ways and Means.						
Stearns, Squier	Indemnity for certain forfeitures	24	1	Petition	200	Commerce	644	Favorable	619	Referred to Committee Whole House.		
Stearns, Squier	Indemnity for certain forfeitures	25	2	Petition	41	Commerce	80	Favorable	95	Passed	Indef. postp'd.	
Steavens, Sarah W., executrix and attorney of.	Indemnity for French spoliations prior to 1800.	26	1	Memorial	182	Foreign Affairs	343	Favorable; bill	319	Referred to Committee Whole House.		
Stebbins, Alfred, mother of	Pay and bounty land due deceased.	16	2	Petition	88	Priv. Land Claims.	23	Favorable	189	Referred to Committee Whole House.		
Stebbins, Alfred, mother of	Bounty land warrant	17	1	Petition	44	Priv. Land Claims.	2	Favorable	10	Passed	Passed	App'd Feb. 4, 1822
Stebbins, Chester	Revival of a certain act	30	1	Petition	148	Public Lands	....	....	......	Discharged; laid on table.	....	Leave to withdraw, 2d session.
Stebbins, Isaac	Pension	15	2	Resolution	251	Pens. & Rev. Cl'ms.						
Steed, Henry	Compensation for subsisting United States troops.	14	2	Petition	156	....	....	....	......	Rreferred to Secretary of War.		
Steele, Ashbel	Pension	22	1	Resolution	140	Rev. Pensions.						
Steele, Augustus, (Fla.)	Moneys due him as inspector of customs.	26	2	Memorial	124	Claims.						
Steele, Augustus, (Fla.)	Moneys due him as inspector of customs.	27	2	Memorial	94	Claims.						
				Documents	1023	Claims	761	Adverse	......	Laid on table.		
Steele, Augustus, (Fla.)	Moneys due him as inspector of customs.	28	1	Petition	526	Claims.						
Steele, Augustus, (Fla.)	Moneys due him as inspector of customs.	30	1	Petition	647	Claims	....	....	......	Discharged; laid on table.		
Steele, Augustus, (Fla.)	Moneys due him as inspector of customs.	31	1	Petition	612	Claims.						
Steele, Augustus, (Fla.)	Moneys due him as inspector of customs.	31	2	Petition	443	Claims	80	....	484	Referred to Committee Whole House.		
Steele, Betsy Brooke	(See Robert Beale, representative of.)	10	2	....	367							
Steele, Bradford	Pension for revolutionary services.	22	1	Senate bill	830	Rev. Pensions	June 20, 1832	With't amend.	S. 126	Referred to Committee Whole House.		
Steele, Daniel S., widow of.	Pension	25	3	Petition	216	Rev. Pensions	....	....	......	Discharged; laid on table.		

List of private claims presented to the House of Representatives of the United States from the 1st to the 31st Congress, inclusive—Continued.

Names of claimants.	Nature or object of the claim.	Congress.	Session.	How brought before the House of Reps.	Page of journal.	To what committee of the House referred.	No. or date of the report.	Nature of the report.	No. of the bill.	How disposed of by the House of Reps.	How disposed of by the Senate.	Date of the act of Congress, and remarks.
Steele, David	Relief in consideration of revolutionary disability.	1	2	Petition	189							
				Rep. of Secretary War.	198	Select	July 16, 1790	By bill	88	Passed	Passed	App'd Aug. 11, 1790
Steele, Eliphalet	Release from imprisonment at suit of United States.	14	2	Petition	448	Ways and Means.						
Steele, Elizabeth	Pension	24	1		107							
Steele, El zur	(See James Steele, widow of.)	15	1	Petition	246					Referred to Secretary War.		
Steele, Francis, widow of.	Pension for revolutionary services.	27	2	Documents	614	Rev. Pensions				Discharged; laid on table.		
Steele, Frederick	Credit of public money stolen	31	1	Petition	763	Military Affairs.						
Steele, Frederick	Credit of public money stolen	31	2	Petition	239	Military Affairs				Discharged; laid on table.		
Steele, George	Compensation for a horse lost in Indian wars.	28	1	Petition	714	Claims	497	Adverse		Laid on table.		
Steele, George Boone	Confirmation of title to land in Kentucky.	26	1	Resolution	547	Priv. Land Claims.	334	Favorable	306	Referred to Committee Whole House.		
Steele, Hiram	Additional compensation for services at Sackett's Harbor.	22	2	Petition	94	Claims	57	Adverse		Laid on table.		
Steele, James, and others	Revocation of a grant of land to S. Ewing.	17	2	Petition	232	Priv. Land Claims.						
Steele, James, and others	Revocation of a grant of land to S. Ewing.	20	1	Resolution	153	Priv. Land Claims.	Feb. 28, 1828	Favorable	147	Passed.		
Steele, Margaret	(See Daniel S. Steele, widow of.)	25	3		216							
Steele, Margaret	(See Francis Steele, widow of.)	27	2		614							
Steel, James	Pension for revolutionary services.	3	1	Rep. of Secretary War.	131	Select	May 36, 1794	Res to refer to Sec. War.	R. 12	Passed	Passed	App'd June 9, 1794
Steel, James	Pension for revolutionary services.	4	1	Rep't of Secretary War.	445	Claims.						
Steel, James	Pension for revolutionary services.	4	2	Rep. of Secretary War.	614	Claims.						
Steel, James	Pension for revolutionary services.	6	1	Petition	548	Claims	Jan. 28, 1800	Adverse		Rejected.		
Steel, James, wife of	Pension for revolutionary services of said James.	24	1	Petition	107	Rev. Pensions	158	Favorable	168	Passed	Passed	App'd June 28, 1836
Steele, James, daughter of.	Authority to receive pension of deceased.	25	2	Petition	71	Rev. Pensions	Jan. 13, 1838	Favorable	410	Passed	Passed	App'd Feb. 15, 1838
Steele, James	Pension for revolutionary services.	25	2	Petition	1029	Rev. Pensions.						
Steele, Jason	(See Chester Baxter and others)	27	3		68							
Steele, John	Compensation for services as governor of Mississippi Territory.	8	1	Petition	496	Claims	Jan. 4, 1804	Favorable		Referred to Committee Whole House.		
Steele, John	Compensation for services as governor of Mississippi Territory.	8	2	Petition	10	Claims	Dec. 13, 1804	Favorable; bill ordered.	25	Passed	Passed	App'd Jan. 31, 1805
Steele, John	(See executors of Polser Shilling).	11	2		116							
Steele, John	Additional compensation as a revenue officer, Philadelphia.	11	3	Petition	474					Laid on table.		
Steele, John	Additional compensation as a revenue officer, Philadelphia.	12	1	Petition	25	Ways and Means.	Dec. 30, 1811	Favorable	34	Referred to Committee Whole House.		
Steele, John	Release from a certain judgment.	16	1	House bill	381	Whole House	April 6, 1820	With't amend.	127	Passed	Passed, with amendment.	App'd May 1, 1820
Steele, John, representative of.	Redemption of $50; Continental note.	24	2	Petition	397	Rev. Claims.						

List of private claims presented to the House of Representatives of the United States from the 1st to the 31st Congress, inclusive—Continued.

Names of claimants.	Nature or object of the claim.	Congress.	Session.	How brought before the House of Reps.	Page of journal.	To what committee of the House referred.	No. or date of the report.	Nature of the report.	No. of the bill.	How disposed of by the House of Reps.	How disposed of by the Senate.	Date of the act of Congress, and remarks.
Steele, John, representative of.	Redemption of $50; Continental note.	25	2	Petition	178	Rev. Claims	480	Adverse		Laid on table.		
Steele, John, executor of	Reimbursement of expenditure on public account.	21	2	Petition	191	Claims	Feb. 25, 1831	Adverse		Laid on table.		
Steele, John, executor of	Additional compensation to be credited on account.	22	1	Memorial	90	Commerce	441	Adverse		Laid on table.		
Steele, Lydia	(See daughter of John Sullivan)	25	3		334							
Steele, Richard W	Settlement of claim for military services.	19	1	Petition	66	Claims	142	Adverse		Recommitted.		
Steele, Richard W	Settlement of claim for military services.	19	2	Petition	159	Claims	67	Favorable	419	Passed	Passed, with amendment.	App'd March 2, 1827
Steele, Richard W	Settlement of claim for military services.	20	1	Petition	46	Priv. Land Claims	229	Favorable	258	Referred to Committee Whole House.		
Steele, Richard W	Settlement of claim for military services.	20	2	Bill of last sess.	284	Whole House	Feb. 13, 1829	With't amend.	258	Passed.		
Steele, Richard W	Settlement of claim for military services.	21	1	Petition	146	Priv. Land Claims	326	Favorable	381	Referred to Committee Whole House.		
Steele, Richard W	Bounty land for military services.	22	1	Petition	64	Priv. Land Claims	68	Favorable	136	Passed	Passed	App'd June 25, 1832
Steele, Stephen	Liquidation and settlement of a claim.	1	2	Petition	236					Referred to Secretary of Treasury.		
Steele, Stephen	Liquidation and settlement of a claim.	2	2	Rep. of Secretary Treasury.	626					Laid on table.		
Steele, William	Pension for revolutionary services	25	2	Petition	54	Rev. Pensions	421	Favorable	428	Passed	Adverse report.	
Steele, William	Pension for revolutionary services.	25	3	Petition	163	Invalid Pensions				Discharged; laid on table.		
Steele, William	Pension for revolutionary services.	27	2	Petition	525	Rev. Pensions	784	Adverse		Laid on table.		
Steele, William	Pension for revolutionary services.	27	3	Petition	43	Rev. Pensions	295	Adverse		Laid on table		Leave to withd'w, 30th Con. 1st ses., p. 1044.
Steele, ———	(See Pentland, Hegins & Steele).	14	2		32							
Steele, William	Payment of claim as deputy collector, Florida.	25	2	Documents	543	Priv. Land Claims.						
Steele, Zadock	To be restored to pension roll	17	1	Petition	72	Rev. Pensions.						
Steele, Zadock	To be restored to pension roll	17	2	Petition	119	Whole House.						
Steen, James	Relief in consideration of disability	23	1	Petition	525	Naval Affairs				Discharged; laid on table.		
Steen, James	Relief in consideration of disability.	24	1	Petition	945	Naval Affairs				Discharged; laid on table.		
Steen, James	Relief in consideration of disability	25	2	Petition	113	Naval Affairs				Discharged; laid on table.		
Steen, John, and Thomas Thompson.	Arrears of pay for military services.	28	2	Petition	307	Claims	99	Adverse		Laid on table.		
Steen, Robert	Pension	22	2	Petition	369	Invalid Pensions.						
Steeniker, Hieronymus	(See James W. Low, and others.)	15	1		366							
Steenrod, Daniel	Compensation for repairing bridge on Cumberland road.	19	1	Petition	177	Roads and Canals.	56	Favorable	78	Referred to Committee Whole House.		
Steenrod, Daniel	Compensation for repairing bridge on Cumberland road.	19	2	Bill of last sess.	107	Roads and Canals	Jan. 21, 1827	With't amend.	78	Leave to withdraw.		
Steenrod, Daniel	Compensation for repairing bridge on Cumberland road.	24	1	Senate bill	990	Claims	835	Adverse	S. 107	Referred to Committee Whole House.		
Steenrod, Daniel	Compensation for repairing bridge on Cumberland road.	24	2	Senate bill	280	Claims			S. 93			
Steenrod, Daniel	Compensation for repairing bridge on Cumberland road.	25	2	Petition	71	Claims				Discharged.		
				Senate bill	455	Claims	583	With amend.	S. 99	Ref'd to Com. W. H.		

List of private claims presented to the House of Representatives of the United States from the 1st to the 31st Congress, inclusive—Continued.

Names of claimants.	Nature or object of the claim.	Congress.	Session.	How brought before the House of Reps.	Page of journal.	To what committee of the House referred.	No. or date of the report.	Nature of the report.	No. of the bill.	How disposed of by the House of Reps.	How disposed of by the Senate.	Date of the act of Congress, and remarks.
Steenrod, Daniel	Compensation for repairing bridge on Cumberland road.	25	3	Petition	640	Claims	298	Favorable	1162	Referred to Committee Whole House.		
Steenrod, Daniel	Compensation for repairing bridge on Cumberland road.	26	2	Senate bill	178	Claims			S. 137			
Steenrod, Daniel	Compensation for repairing bridge on Cumberland road.	27	2	Petition	90	Claims.						
Steenrod, Daniel	Compensation for repairing bridge on Cumberland road.	27	3	Petition	43	Claims.						
Steenrod, Daniel	Compensation for repairing bridge on Cumberland road.	28	1	Petition	70	Claims	87	Favorable	102	Referred to Committee Whole House.		
Steenrod, Daniel	Compensation for repairing bridge on Cumberland road.	29	1	Petition	67	Claims	255	Favorable	219	Referred to Commitee Whole House.		
Steenrod, Daniel	Compensation for repairing bridge on Cumberland road.	30	1	Petition	77	Claims	251	Favorable	244	Referred to Committee Whole House.		
Steenrod, Daniel	Compensation for repairing bridge on Cumberland road.	31	1	Petition	192	Claims	78	Favorable	94	Referred to Committee Whole House.		
Steenrod, Daniel	Compensation for repairing bridge on Cumberland road.	31	2	Bill of last sess.	154	Whole House	Jan. 18, 1851	Adverse	94	Laid on table.		
Steenrod, Stephen	Pension	31	1	Petition	1269	Invalid Pensions.						
Steers, Hugh	Pension	20	2	Resolution	57	Military Pensions.						
Steers, John	Pension	24	2	Petition	120	Invalid Pensions				Discharged; laid on table.		
Steers, John	Pension	25	2	Memorial	85	Invalid Pensions	Jan. 29, 1828	Adverse		Laid on table.		
Steers, John	Pension	25	3	Resolution	57	Military Pensions.						
Steers, John	Pension	26	1	Petition	162	Invalid Pensions.						
Steers, John	Pension	26	2	Petition	134	Invalid Pensions	235	Adverse		Laid on table.		
Steers, John	Pension	28	2	Petition	170	Invalid Pensions.						
Steeves, Jeremiah	Compensation for a vessel taken for public use.	3	1	Petition	98					Laid on table.		
Steeves, Jeremiah, representatives of.	Compensation for property taken for public use.	22	2	Petition	109	Rev. Claims.						
Steeves, Jeremiah, representatives of.	Compensation for property taken for public use.	23	1	Pension	440	Rev. Claims.						
Steeves, Jeremiah, representatives of.	Compensation for property taken for public use.	23	2	Petition	196	Rev. Claims.						
Steeves, Jeremiah, representatives of.	Compensation for property taken for public use.	24	2	Petition	216	Rev. Claims.						
Steeves, Jeremiah, representatives of.	Compensation for property taken for public use.	25	2	Petition	112	Rev. Claims				Discharged; laid on table.		
Steeves, Reuben	(See representatives of Jeremiah Steeves.)	22	2		109							
Steffey, H., and A. Hewitt, assignee of.	Bounty land warrants	30	2	Petition	361	Priv. Land Claims.						
Stegagnini, L.	Compensation for the use of drawings.	28	2	Petition	141	Public Buildings.						
Steger, William, executor of.	Payment of moneys due from Government.	2	2	Petition	622	Select	Feb. 18, 1793	Adverse		Leave to withdraw.		
Steger, William, executor of.	Payment of moneys due from Government.	4	1	Report of Secretary Treasury.	388	Claims	May 31, 1796	Adverse		Laid on table.		
Steigleman, John	Pension	25	3	Petition	285	Invalid Pensions.						
Stein, Henry	(See representatives of Joseph Fenwick.)	15	1		45							

List of private claims presented to the House of Representatives of the United States from the 1st to the 31st Congress, inclusive—Continued.

Names of claimants.	Nature or object of the claim.	Congress.	Session.	How brought before the House of Reps.	Page of journal.	To what committee of the House referred.	No. or date of the report.	Nature of the report.	No. of the bill.	How disposed of by the House of Reps.	How disposed of by the Senate.	Date of the act of Congress, and remarks.
Steinback, John	Indemnity for damage to property, war of 1812.	20	1	Petition	195	Claims	Feb. 13, 1828	Adverse	......	Laid on table.		
Steinback, J. L.	(See Isaac Lawrence, and others)	14	2	....	101							
Steinfelt, John	Permission to import property from Jamaica.	12	1	Petition	175	Com. and Manuf.						
Steinman, John	(See James Winner, and others)	19	1	....	36							
Steinmetz, Daniel, heir of.	Indemnity for French spoliations prior to 1800.	26	1	Memorial	182	Foreign Affairs	343	Favorable; bill	319	Referred to Committee Whole House.		
Stell, George W	Bounty land for disability in public service.	20	2	Petition	230	Public Lands	....	....	......	Discharged; laid on table.		
Stell, George W	Bounty land for disability in public service.	21	1	Petition	238	Public Lands.						
Stell, George W	Pension for military services	21	1	Resolution	246	Military Pensions	April 27, 1830	Adverse	......	Laid on table.		
Stellwagen, Daniel, widow of.	Re-enactment of navy pension act.	27	3	Petition	309	Naval Affairs	....	....	......	Discharged.		
Stellwagen, Daniel, widow of.	Re-enactment of navy pension act.	28	1	Petition	1020	Naval Affairs.						
Stellwagen, Mary	(See Daniel Stellwagon, widow of)	27	3	....	309							
Stellwyer, Daniel, widow of.	Arrears of pension	24	2	Petition	314	Naval Affairs.						
Stellwyer, Mary	(See Daniel Stellwyer, widow of.)	24	2	....	314							
Stembel, Henry	(See surety of Leonard Littlejohn.)	18	2	....	41							
Stene, Enoch E	(See William McPherson, *et al.*)	24	2	....	269							
Stengel, Catharine	(See Conrad Stengel, widow of.)	20	1	....	310							
Stengel, Conrad, widow of.	Pension	20	1	Petition	310	Military Pensions	....	....	......	Discharged; laid on table.		
Stephens, Ebenezer	Indemnity for unlawful seizure of a ship.	7	1	Petition	52	Com. and Manuf.	Feb. 12, 1802	Adverse	......	Leave to withdraw.		
Stephens, George	(See executor of James Busten)	23	1	....	99							
Stephens, Hanson	Pension for revolutionary services	30	1	Petition	78	Rev. Pensions.						
Stephens, Isaac	Indemnity for losses and suffering in Algiers.	5	2	Petition	97	Com. and Manuf.	Jan. 2, 1798	Adverse	......	Rejected.		
Stephens, James	Compensation for horse lost in public service.	16	1	Petition	369	Claims	April 7, 1820	Adverse	......	Laid on table.		
Stephens, James	Pension for revolutionary services.	21	2	Resolution	65	Military Pensions.						
Stephens, John	Half-pay as a revolutionary officer.	1	2	Petition and rep't Sec. of War.	150, 199	Select	July 16, 1790	Pension bill	88	Passed	Passed, with amendment.	App'd Aug. 11, 1790
Stephens, John, and others.	Increase of compensation as revenue officer, New York.	4	2	Petition	687	....	....	General bill	211	Passed	Passed	App'd March 3, 1797
Stephen, John	Reimbursement of expenses as a witness.	9	1	Petition	256	Claims.						
Stephens, John	(See Joseph Brown.)	24	2	....	78							
Stephens, Jonathan L.	Reimbursement of duties paid at Castine.	15	1	Petition	93	Ways and Means.						
Stephens, Jonathan L.	Reimbursement of duties paid at Castine.	16	1	Senate bill	108	Ways and Means	Jan. 14, 1820	With't amend.	S. 13	Passed with amendm't.	Pass'd as am'd.	App'd April 11, 1820
Stephens, Moses K	Indemnity for property destroyed at Buffalo.	23	1	Petition	131	Claims.						
Stephens, Sutton	Authority to convey an Indian reservation.	23	1	Petition	215	Public Lands	Jan. 28, 1834	Favorable	248	Referred to Committee Whole House.		
Stephens, Sutton	Authority to convey an Indian reservation.	23	2	Bill of last sess.	299	Whole House	Jan. 31, 1835	With't amend.	248	Passed	Passed, with amendment.	

List of private claims presented to the House of Representatives of the United States from the 1st to the 31st Congress, inclusive—Continued.

Names of claimants.	Nature or object of the claim.	Congress.	Session.	How brought before the House of Reps.	Page of journal.	To what committee of the House referred.	No. or date of the report.	Nature of the report.	No. of the bill.	How disposed of by the House of Reps.	How disposed of by the Senate.	Date of the act of Congress, and remarks.
Stephens, Sutton	Authority to convey an Indian reservation.	25	2	Petition	282	Public Lands	Feb. 9, 1838	Favorable	542	Referred to Committee Whole House.		
Stephens, Sutton	Authority to convey an Indian reservation.	25	3	Bill of last sess.	379	Whole House			542			
Stephens, Sutton	Authority to convey an Indian reservation.	26	1	Petition	177	Public Lands	Mar. 4, 1840	Favorable	69	Passed	Passed	App'd April 10, 1840
Stephens, Truman	Indemnity for provisions captured by the enemy.	22	1	Petition	188	Claims	Feb. 6, 1832	Adverse		Laid on table.		
Stephens, Wheelright	Indemnity for French spoliations prior to 1800.	26	1	Memorial	182	Foreign Affairs	343	Favorable; bill	319	Referred to Committee Whole House.		
Stephens, Willis	Right of pre-emption to land in Alabama.	24	1	Petition	840	Indian Affairs.						
Stephens, Willis	Right of pre-emption to land in Alabama.	24	2	Petition	47	Indian Affairs.						
Stephens, Willis	Right of pre-emption to land in Alabama.	25	2	Petition	95	Indian Affairs	210	Favorable	246	Referred to Committee Whole House.		
Stephens, Willis	Right of pre-emption to land in Alabama.	25	3	Bill of last sess.	376	Whole House	Jan. 26, 1839	With't amend.	246	Passed	Adverse report.	
Stephens, Willis	Right of pre-emption to land in Alabama.	28	1	Petition	433	Public Lands.						
Stephens, Willis	Right of pre-emption to land in Alabama.	28	2	Petition	303	Public Lands.						
Stephens, Willis	Right of pre-emption to land in Alabama.	29	1	Petition	100	Indian Affairs	102	Adverse		Laid on table.		
Stephenson, Alex'r, heirs of.	Compensation for revolutionary services.	25	2	Petition	180	Rev. Claims				Discharged; laid on table.		
Stephenson, Alex'r, heirs of.	Compensation for revolutionary services.	28	2	Petition	120	Rev. Claims.						
Stephenson, Alex'r, heirs of.	Compensation for revolutionary services.	29	1	Petition	89	Rev. Claims.						
Stephenson, Alex'r, heirs of.	Compensation for revolutionary services.	31	1	Petition	1251	Rev. Claims.						
Stephenson, Alexander	Confirmation of title to land in Indiana.	28	2	Petition	406	Public Lands.						
Stephenson, Ann C.	Compensation for repairs to a tenement in public use.	24	2	Petition	395	Claims.						
Stephenson, Ann C.	Compensation for repairs to a tenement in public use.	25	2	Petition, (2) Petition	395 73	Military Affairs. Military Affairs	712	Adverse		Rejected.		
Stephenson, Ann C.	Compensation for repairs to a tenement in public use.	25	3	Petition, (2) Petition	76 212	Claims Military Affairs	Mar. 21, 1838 266	Adverse Adverse		Laid on table. Laid on table.		
Stephenson, Benjamin	(See legal representatives of George Hite.)	16	2		61							
Stephenson, Elbert W., and others.	Reimbursement of costs in a certain suit.	22	1	Resolution	529	Indian Affairs.						
Stephenson, James	(See heirs of Alexander Stephenson.)	25	2		180							
Stephenson, John	Pension for revolutionary services.	4	2	Petition	645	Claims	Jan. 19, 1797	Adverse		Rejected.		
Stephenson, John	(See surety of Thomas Neale)	18	2		159							
Stephenson, John	Pension	20	2	Resolution	213	Military Pensions				Discharged; laid on table.		

List of private claims presented to the House of Representatives of the United States from the 1st to the 31st Congress, inclusive—Continued.

Names of claimants.	Nature or object of the claim.	Congress.	Session.	How brought before the House of Reps.	Page of journal.	To what committee of the House referred.	No. or date of the report.	Nature of the report.	No. of the bill.	How disposed of by the House of Reps.	How disposed of by the Senate.	Date of the act of Congress, and remarks.
Stephenson, John, representative of.	Commutation pay for revolutionary services.	23	2	Petition	47	Rev. Claims.						
Stephenson, John, representative of.	Commutation pay for revolutionary services.	24	1	Petition	103	Rev. Claims.						
Stephenson, John, representative of.	Commutation pay for revolutionary services.	25	2	Petition	82	Rev. Claims.						
Stephenson, John, representative of.	Commutation pay for revolutionary services.	25	3	Petition	86	Rev. Claims.						
Stephenson, John, representative of.	Commutation pay for revolutionary services.	28	2	Petition	199	Rev. Claims.						
Stephenson, Moses, widow of.	Pension for revolutionary services.	28	1	Petition	632	Rev. Pensions.						
Stephenson, William	Balance due as contractor on Cumberland road.	19	1	Appropriation bill	142				42			App'd Mar. 14, 1826
Stephenson, William, heirs of.	Compensation for revolutionary services.	23	1	Resolution	70	Rev. Claims.						
Stephenson, William, heirs of.	Compensation for revolutionary services.	23	2	Resolution	66	Rev. Claims.						
Stephenson, William, heirs of.	Compensation for revolutionary services.	24	1	Petition	205	Rev. Claims.						
Steptoe, James, sen., and others.	Permission to file claims to Yazoo lands.	17	2	Memorial	74	Public Lands.						
Sterling, Comfort	(See heirs of Seth Sterling)	30	1		807							
Sterling, Isaac	(See heirs of Seth Sterling)	30	1		807							
Sterling, John T	Confirmation of title to land in Louisiana.	27	2	Petition	622	Priv. Land Claims.						
Sterling, John T	Confirmation of title to land in Louisiana.	27	3	Petition	45	Priv. Land Claims.						
Sterling, Josiah	Permission to redeem land sold for tax.	16	1	Petition	237	Whole House.						
Sterling, Seth, heirs of	Arrears of pension	30	1	Petition	807	Rev. Pensions.						
Sterling, Silas	Pension	28	2	Resolution	132	Rev. Pensions.						
Stern, Richard	(See Benjamin Farrar and others.)	11	1		41							
Sterne, Samuel	Pension for revolutionary services.	11	2	Pension bill	283				107	Passed	Passed, with amendment.	App'd April 27, 1816
Sterrett, Adam	Indemnity for loss of bounty land.	27	2	Petition	223	Priv. Land Claims.	1094	Adverse		Laid on table.		
Sterrett, Adam	Indemnity for loss of bounty land.	27	3	Petition	346	Priv. Land Claims.						
Sterrett, Adam	Indemnity for loss of bounty land.	28	1	Petition	131	Priv. Land Claims.	33	Adverse		Laid on table.		
Sterrett, James, and others.	Permission to locate on certain lands.	4	1	Petition	446	Select.						
Sterrett, Lieut. John	Compensation for horse lost in public service.	19	2	Resolution	40	Claims	Dec. 27, 1826	Adverse		Leave to withdraw.		
Sterrett, Samuel	(See Wm. Patterson and others)	3	1		25							
Sterrett, Samuel	(See Maryland, citizens of Baltimore.)	26	1		182							
Sterrett, William, heirs of.	Adjustment of claim under 9th article, Spanish treaty.	31	1	Petition	259	Judiciary	96	Adverse		Laid on table.		
Stetson, Abner	Compensation for services in Indian wars.	23	2	Petition	331	Claims	120	Favorable	757	Referred to Committee Whole House.		
Stetson, Abner	Compensation for services in Indian wars.	24	1	Petition	51	Claims	39	Favorable	39	Passed	Passed	App'd Feb. 17, 1836
Stetson, Amasa	Interest on money borrowed on public account.	17	1	Petition	186	Claims	Mar. 2, 1822	Adverse		Laid on table.		

List of private claims presented to the House of Representatives of the United States from the 1st to the 31st Congress, inclusive—Continued.

Names of claimants.	Nature or object of the claim.	Congress.	Session.	How brought before the House of Reps.	Page of journal.	To what committee of the House referred.	No. or date of the report.	Nature of the report.	No. of the bill.	How disposed of by the House of Reps.	How disposed of by the Senate.	Date of the act of Congress, and remarks.
Stetson, Amasa	Interest on money borrowed on public account.	17	2	Rep't of last sess.	132	Claims	Feb. 21, 1823	Adverse		Leave to withdraw.		
Stetson, Amasa	Interest on money borrowed on public account.	18	1	Senate bill	309	Claims	April 1, 1824	With't amend.	S. 24	Passed wtth amendm't.	Passed as am'd.	App'd May 4, 1824
Stetson, Amasa	Interest on money borrowed on public account.	19	1	Senate bill	474	Claims			S. 75	Discharged; laid on table.		
Stetson, Ebenezer	Naval pension	4	1	Petition	381	Claims	Jan. 20, 1796	Adverse		Leave to withdraw.		
Stetson, Ebenezer	Pension	15	1	Petition	35	Pens. & Rev. Cl'ms				Discharged; leave to withdraw.		
Stetson, Ebenezer	Increase of pension	20	2	Petition	26	Military Pensions	Jan. 16, 1829	Adverse		Laid on table.		
Stetson, Ebenezer	Increase of pension	22	1	Petition	67	Invalid Pensions	Jan. 13, 1832	Adverse		Laid on table.		
Stetson, Ebenezer	Increase of pension	22	2	Petition	176	Invalid Pensions.						
Stetson, Ebenezer	Increase of pension	23	1	Petition	54	Invalid Pensions	Dec. 24, 1833	Adverse		Laid on table.		
Stetson, Ebenezer	Increase of pension	23	2	Petition	119	Invalid Pensions				Discharged; laid on table.		
Stetson, Ebenezer	Increase of pension	24	1	Petition	282	Invalid Pensions	Mar. 3, 1836	Adverse		Laid on table.		
Stettinius, John W	(See Louis F. Beeler, and others.)	30	1		115		482					
Steuben, Baron	(See Baron De Steuben)	1	1		110							
Stevelie, Frederick, assignee	Compensation for services of certain militia.	14	2	Petition	38	Select				Leave to withdraw.		
Stevelie, Frederick, assignee	Compensation for services of certain militia.	15	1	Petition	31	Claims.						
Stevens, Aaron	Pension for revolutionary services.	10	1	Pension bill	232	Whole House			78	Passed	Passed, with amendment.	App'd April 25, 1808
Stevens, Albert, heir of	Pension for revolutionary services.	24	2	Petition	119	Rev. Claims	66	Adverse		Laid on table.		
Stevens, Amos	Compensation as a revolutionary teamster.	24	2	Petition	397	Rev. Claims.						
Stevens, Benjamin	To be restored to pension roll	17	1	Petition	77	Rev. Pensions.						
Stevens, Benjamin	Pension	23	1	Petition	309	Invalid Pensions				Discharged; laid on table.		
Stevens, Benjamin	Pension	24	1	Petition	188	Invalid Pensions	Feb. 5, 1836	Adverse		Laid on table.		
Stevens, Caleb	Pension	24	1	Petition	98	Invalid Pensions				Discharged; laid on table.		
Stevens, Caleb	Pension	29	1	Petition	569	Invalid Pensions.						
Stevens, Cyprian	Pension	21	2	Petition	372	Military Pensions.						
Stevens, Daniel	Increase of compensation as a revenue officer, South Carolina.	5	3	Memorial	458	Ways and Means	Feb. 7, 1799	Adverse		Laid on table.		
Stevens, Daniel	Pension	27	3	Petition	240	Invalid Pensions	154	Adverse		Laid on table.		
Stevens, Ebenezer, & others	Compensation for revolutionary supplies.	15	1	Petition	143	Pens. & Rev. Cl'ms.	159	Favorable	143	Referred to Committee Whole House.		
Stevens, Ebenezer, & others	Compensation for revolutionary supplies.	15	2	Bill of last sess.	127	Whole House	Dec. 28, 1818	With amend.	143	Laid on table.		
Stevens, Ebenezer, & others	Payment of an award for revolutionary supplies.	16	1	Senate bill	429	Pens. & Rev. Cl'ms.	Mar. 1, 1820	With't amend.	S. 87	Laid on table.		
Stevens, Ebenezer, & others	Payment of an award for revolutionary supplies.	16	2	Senate bill	52	Pens. & Rev. Cl'ms.	Jan. 17, 1821	With't amend.	S. 4	Referred to Committee Whole House.		
Stevens, Ebenezer, & others	Payment of an award for revolutionary supplies.	17	2	Senate bill	174	Pens. & Rev. Cl'ms.	Feb. 7, 1823	With't amend.	S. 15	Passed with amendm't.	Passed as am'd	App'd March 3, 1823
Stevens, Lieutenant Colonel Ebenezer.	Benefit of the act of February 28, 1779.	1	3	Petition	376					Referred to Secretary War.		
Stevens, Ebenezer, & others	Remission of certain tonnage duties.	16	2	Petition	30	Commerce	Dec. 6, 1820	General bill	162	Passed	Passed, with amendment.	App'd March 3, 1821
Stevens, Elijah, heir of	Bounty land for military services.	27	2	Senate bill	1063	Public Lands			S. 188			

List of private claims presented to the House of Representatives of the United States from the 1st to the 31st Congress inclusive—Continued.

Names of claimants.	Nature or object of the claim.	Congress.	Session.	How brought before the House of Reps.	Page of journal.	To what committee of the House referred.	No. or date of the report.	Nature of the report.	No. of the bill.	How disposed of by the House of Reps.	How disposed of by the Senate.	Date of the act of Congress, and remarks.
Stevens, Eliza	(See Thomas Holdup Stevens, widow of.)	27	3		184							
Stevens, Elkanah, daughter of.	Compensation for revolutionary services.	30	1	Petition	780	Rev. Pensions.						
Stevens, Holdup	(See Thomas Holdup Stevens)	29	2		70							
Stevens, James	Pension	24	1	Petition	98	Invalid Pensions	262	Favorable	271	Passed	Passed	App'd Jan. 28, 1836
Stevens, James	Pension	27	3	Petition	76	Invalid Pensions	Jan. 19, 1843	Adverse		Laid on table.		
Stevens, Jeduthun	Pension for revolutionary services.	20	2	Petition	120	Whole House.						
Stevens, Jeduthun	Pension for revolutionary services.	21	2	Petition	126	Military Pensions.						
Stevens, Jeduthun	Pension for revolutionary services.	25	2	Petition	53	Rev. Pensions.						
Stevens, John	Pension for revolutionary services.	3	1	Rep. of Secretary War.	131	Select	May 26, 1794	Res. to refer to Sec. War.	R. 12	Passed	Passed	App'd June 9, 1794
Stevens, John	Pension for revolutionary services.	4	1	Rep. of Secretary War.	445	Claims	Feb. 15, 1796	Res. to refer to Sec. War.	R. 16	Passed	Passed	App'd April 18, 1796
Stevens, John	Pension for revolutionary services.	4	2	Rep. of Secretary War.	614	Claims.						
Stevens, John, (Hoboken.)	Extension of patent for improvement in application of steam.	14	1	Petition	405	Select.						
Stevens, John, and others.	Increase of compensation as revenue officers, Georgia.	21	1	Memorial	58	Commerce.						
Stevens, John, and others.	Increase of compensation as revenue officers, Georgia.	22	1	Memorial	74	Commerce.						
Stevens, John, (Maine)	Pension for revolutionary services.	29	1	Petition	823	Rev. Pensions	785	Adverse		Laid on table.		
Stevens, Jonas	Compensation for revolutionary services.	2	2	Petition	662					Referred to Secretary War.		
Stevens, Jonas	Compensation for revolutionary services.	3	1	Rep. of Secretary War.	93	Select.						
Stevens, Jonathan	Increase of pension	12	1	Pension bill	361	Whole House	June 15, 1812	With amend.	138	Passed	Passed, with amendment.	App'd July 5, 1812
Stevens, Jonathan	Pension	18	2	Petition	207	Rev. Pensions	Feb. 5, 1825	Adverse		Laid on table.		
Stevens, Jonathan L.	Remission of duty on imports to Castine.	16	1	Senate bill	108	Ways and Means.	Jan. 14, 1820	With amend.	S. 13	Passed with amendm't	Passed as am'd.	App'd April 11, 1820
Stevens, Jonathan L.	Indemnity for property plundered by the enemy.	20	1	Petition	456	Ways and Means.						
Stevens, Lucretia	(See Ebenezer Stevens and others.)	15	1		143							
Stevens, Moses K.	Indemnity for property destroyed at Niagara.	24	1	Memorial	430	Claims.						
Stevens, Nathaniel	Liquidation of a revolutionary certificate.	4	1	Rep. of Secretary Treasury.	388	Claims	May 31, 1796	Adverse		Laid on table.		
Stevens, Paul, (Ohio)	Pension	20	1	Petition	163	Military Pensions.	Mar. 6, 1828	Adverse		Laid on table.		
Stevens, Paul, (Ohio)	Pension	21	1	Petition	67	Military Pensions.	May 18, 1830	Adverse		Laid on table.		
Stevens, Phydelia	(See heirs of Elijah Stevens)	27	2		1063							
Stevens, Roger	Pension	3	2	Rep. of Secretary War.	337	Claims	Mar. 3, 1795	To postpone.		Laid on table.		
Stevens, Roger	Pension	4	1	Rep. of Secretary War	445	Claims.						
Stevens, Samuel	Indemnity for French spoliations prior to 1800.	2	1	Memorial	182	Foreign Affairs	343	Favorable; bill	319	Referred to Committee Whole House.		
Stevens, Stephen	Pension	21	1	Petition	35	Military Pensions.	April 7, 1830	Adverse		Laid on table.		
Stevens, Stephen	Pension	21	2	Petition	127	Military Pensions.						
Stevens, Sutton, (Ind.)	(See Joseph Elliott, and others)	20	2		64							
Stevens, Thomas H., and others.	Compensation for capture of a privateer vessel.	22	1	Senate bill	779	Naval Affairs	June 5, 1832	With't amend	S. 152	Passed	Passed	App'd July 14, 1832

List of private claims presented to the House of Representatives of the United States from the 1st to the 31st Congress, inclusive—Continued.

Names of claimants.	Nature or object of the claim.	Congress.	Session.	How brought before the House of Reps.	Page of journal.	To what committee of the House referred.	No. or date of the report.	Nature of the report.	No. of the bill.	How disposed of by the House of Reps.	How disposed of by the Senate.	Date of the act of Congress, and remarks.
Stevens, Thomas H., widow of.	Continuation of pension	27	3	Resolution	184	Naval Affairs.						
Stevens, Thomas H., widow of.	Extension of pension for five years	29	1	Memorial	398	Naval Affairs				Discharged; laid on table.		
Stevens, Thomas H., widow of.	Extension of pension for five years	29	2	Petition	70	Naval Affairs.						
Stevens, William	Right of pre-emption as New Orleans branch pilot.	28	1	Petition	77	Priv. Land Claims.	9	Favorable	35	Passed	Passed	App'd June 17, 1844
Stevens, William, *et al.*	Pension	31	1	Petition	730	Rev. Pensions	216	Adverse		Laid on table.		
Stevens, Zachariah	Indemnity for French spoliations prior to 1800.	26	1	Memorial	182	Foreign Affairs	343	Favorable; bill	319	Referred to Committee Whole House.		
Stevenson, Ann	(See Wm. Stevenson, widow of.)	28	1		1042							
Stevenson, Atchison, Capt., *et als.*	(See Missouri, legislature of)	25	2		416							
Stevenson, Catharine	(See George Stevenson, widow of)	28	2		272							
Stevenson, Charles	Arrears of pay for revolutionary services.	21	2	Resolution	56	Military Pensions.						
Stevenson, Edmond	Increase of pension	14	1	House bill	622	Pens. & Rev. Cl'ms.	April 11, 1818	Favorable	171	Passed	Passed, with amendment.	App'd April 30, 1816
Stevenson, Elizabeth	(See Peter Stevenson, widow of)	30	1		240							
Stevenson, Frederick P.	Pension	14	2	Documents	314	Pens. & Rev. Cl'ms.	Jan. 29, 1817	Favorable	91	Passed	Passed, with amendment.	App'd March 3, 1817
Stevenson, Fred'k, P. widow of.	Pension	29	1	Petition	151	Rev. Pensions	525	Adverse		Laid on table.		
Stevenson, Fred'k P. widow of.	Pension	29	2	Petition	93	Rev. Pensions	45	Adverse		Laid on table.		
Stevenson, George, widow of.	Pension for revolutionary services	28	2	Petition	272	Rev. Pensions.						
Stevenson, George, widow of.	Pension for revolutionary services	29	1	Petition	87	Rev. Pensions	709	Favorable	484	Referred to Committee Whole House.		
Stevenson, George, widow of.	Pension for revolutionary services	29	2	Bill of last sess.	212	Whole House	Jan. 22, 1847	With't amend.	484	Passed	Passed	App'd March 3, 1847
Stevenson, George Pitt	Compensation for services as judge advocate.	30	1	Petition	717	Naval Affairs.						
Stevenson, George Pitt	Compensation for services as judge advocate.	30	2	Petition	313	Naval Affairs.						
Stevenson, Hannah	(See Frederick P. Stevenson, widow of.)	29	1		151							
Stevenson, Hugh	Pension for military services	18	1	Petition	65	Pens. & Rev. Cl'ms.						
Stevenson, Hugh	Pension for military services	19	1	Petition	52	Military Pensions	164	Adverse		Laid on table.		
Stevenson, James, (Ind.)	Pension	22	1	Petition	36	Rev. Pensions	528	General bill	528	Omitted in the act.		
Stevenson, John	(See sureties of Joseph Kinkaid)	19	1		181							
Stevenson, Peter, widow of	Arrears of pension	30	1	Petition	240	Rev. Pensions.						
Stevenson, Samuel	(See John Carr, and others)	27	3		423							
Stevenson, Thomas	(See sureties of Jos. Kinkaid)	19	1		181							
Stevenson, Thomas, widow of.	Half pay due deceased	25	3	Petition	124	Rev. Claims.						
Stevenson, William	Pension	31	2	Petition	192	Invalid Pensions.						
Stevenson, William, widow of.	Compensation for revolutionary services.	4	1	Petition	409	Claims	Feb. 18, 1796	Adverse		Leave to withdraw.		
Stevenson, William, heirs of.	Commutation pay for revolutionary services.	25	2	Petition	392	Rev. Claims	May 18, 1838	Adverse		Laid on table.		

List of private claims presented to the House of Representatives of the United States from the 1st to the 31st Congress, inclusive—Continued.

Names of claimants.	Nature or object of the claim.	Congress.	Session.	How brought before the House of Reps.	Page of journal.	To what committee of the House referred.	No. or date of the report.	Nature of the report.	No. of the bill.	How disposed of by the House of Reps.	How disposed of by the Senate.	Date of the act of Congress, and remarks.
Stevenson, William, widow of.	Re-enactment of navy pension act.	28	1	Petition	1042	Naval Affairs.						
Stevenson, William W.	Indemnity for loss of a pre-emption right.	23	1	Petition	382	Public Lands	528	Favorable	528	Referred to Committee Whole House.		
Stevenson, William W.	Indemnity for loss of a pre-emption right.	24	1	Petition	58	Public Lands	201	Favorable	205	Referred to Committee Whole House.		
Stevenson, William W.	Indemnity for loss of a pre-emption right.	24	2	Bill of last sess.	62	Whole House			205			
Stevenson, William W.	Indemnity for loss of a pre-emption right.	25	2	Petition	42	Public Lands	Dec. 28, 1837	Favorable	237	Referred to Committee Whole House.		
Stevenson, William W.	Indemnity for loss of a pre-emption right.	25	3	Bill of last sess.	376	Whole House	Jan. 25, 1839	With't amend.	237	Passed	Passed	App'd May 30, 1816
Steves, Jeremiah, representatives of.	(See representatives of Jeremiah Steeves.)	22	2		109							
Stewart, Ann, (N. York,) heir of.	Indemnity for French spoliations prior to 1800.	26	1	Memorial	182	Foreign Affairs	343	Favorable; bill	319	Referred to Committee Whole House.		
Stewart, Ann, administratrix of.	Indemnity for French spoliations prior to 1800.	26	1	Memorial	182	Foreign Affairs	343	Favorable; bill	319	Referred to Committee Whole House.		
Steuart, A. L.	(See Isaac Lawrence and others)	14	2		101							
Steuart, Robert	(See Isaac Lawrence and others)	14	2		101							
Stewart Aaron	Pension	14	1	Petition	257	Pens. & Rev. Clm's.	April 11, 1816	Pension bill	171	Passed	Passed, with amendment.	App'd April 30, 1816
Stewart, Adam D	Reimbursement of money expended in suit.	26	2	Senate bill	282	Whole House			S. 174			
Stewart, Alexander	Compensation for revolutionary services.	2	1	Petition	500					Referred to Secretary War.		
Stewart, Alexander	Compensation for revolutionary services.	24	1	Petition	433	Rev. Pensions	457	Adverse		Referred to Committee Whole House.		
Stewart, Alexander	Compensation for horses lost, war of 1812.	16	1	Petition	209	Claims.						
Stewart, Alfred	Indemnity for slaves stolen by Indians.	23	1	Petition	67	Indian Affairs	369	Adverse		Laid on table.		
Stewart, Allen, and others.	Reimbursement of expenditure in placing buoy.	24	1	Petition	641	Commerce.						
Stewart, Andrew, widow of.	Half-pay pension for five years	22	1	Resolution	112	Invalid Pensions				Discharged; laid on table.		
Stewart, Andrew, widow of.	Half-pay pension for five years	24	1	Resolution	267	Claims.						
Stewart, Archibald	Indemnity for French spoliations prior to 1800.	17	1	Petition	40	Foreign Affairs	32	Adverse		Referred to Committee Whole House.		
Stewart, Archibald	Indemnity for French spoliations prior to 1800.	29	2	Memorial	142	Foreign Affairs.						
Stewart, Archibald	Pension for revolutionary services.	20	2	Resolution	250	Military Pensions				Discharged; laid on table.		
Stewart, Archibald, attorney of.	Indemnity for French spoliations prior to 1800.	26	1	Memorial	182	Foreign Affairs	343	Favorable; bill	319	Referred to Committee Whole House.		
Stewart & Barr, executors of.	Indemnity for French spoliations prior to 1800.	31	1	Petition	298	Foreign Affairs	355	General bill	318	Referred to Committee Whole House.		
Stewart, Charles, *et al.*	Prize money for the capture of the Levant by the frigate Constitution.	14	1	Petition	116	Naval Affairs	Feb. 4, 1816	Favorable; bill		Passed	Passed	App'd April 27, 1816
Stewart, Charles, U. S. N.	Prize money due officers and crew of Constitution.	14	1	Senate bill	562	Naval Affairs	April 15, 1816	Adverse		Laid on table.		

List of private claims presented to the House of Representatives of the United States from the 1st to the 31st Congress, inclusive—Continued.

Names of claimants.	Nature or object of the claim.	Congress.	Session.	How brought before the House of Reps.	Page of journal.	To what committee of the House referred.	No. or date of the report.	Nature of the report.	No. of the bill.	How disposed of by the House of Reps.	How disposed of by the Senate.	Date of the act of Congress, and remarks.
Stewart, Charles, U. S. N	(See Edward Preble, representatives of.)	15	1	....	289	....	....	....	112			
Stewart, Charles, U. S. N.	(See Syren, officers and crew of.)	20	1	....	309							
Stewart, Charles	(See surety of Samuel Lewis.)	17	1	....	281							
Stewart, Charles, heirs of.	Confirmation of title to land in Florida.	24	1	Petition	155	Priv. Land Claims.	Jan. 19, 1836	Adverse	......	Laid on table.		
Stewart, Charles, heirs of.	Confirmation of title to land in Florida.	24	2	Petition	107	Priv. Land Claims.	....	....	......	Discharged; laid on table.		
Stewart, Charles	(See Charles Stuart)	31	1	....	269	....	103					
Stewart, Charles B	(See Louis F. Beeler, and others.)	30	1	....	115	....	482					
Stewart, Christopher, widow of.	Compensation for revolutionary services.	23	1	Petition	215	Rev. Pensions	....	....	......	Discharged; laid on table.		
Stewart, Daniel	Reimbursement of expenditures on public account.	13	2	Petition	176	Claims	Mar. 7, 1814	Adverse	......	Leave to withdraw.		
Stewart, David	Pension	31	1	Petition	898	Invalid Pensions.						
Stewart, David, & Son, trustees of.	Indemnity for French spoliations prior to 1800.	26	1	Memorial	182	Foreign Affairs	343	Favorable; bill	319	Referred to Committee Whole House.		
Stewart, Dorcas	(See Lemuel H. Stewart, widow of)	27	2	....	611							
Stewart, Duncan, daughter of.	Compensation for military services.	19	1	Petition	364	Military Pensions.	April 1, 1826	Adverse	......	Laid on table.		
Stewart, Eliphalet	Pension for revolutionary services.	18	2	Petition	81	Rev. Pensions	Jan. 24, 1825	Adverse	......	Laid on table.		
Stewart, Eliphalet	Pension for revolutionary services.	20	1	Petition	338	Military Pensions.	Mar. 18, 1828	Adverse	......	Laid on table.		
Stewart, Eliphalet	Pension for revolutionary services.	20	2	Petition	99	Whole House.						
Stewart, Eliphalet	Pension for revolutionary services.	21	2	Petition	208	Military Pensions.						
Stewart, Eliphalet	Pension for revolutionary services.	22	1	Petition	255	Rev. Pensions.						
Stewart, Elizabeth	(See James Stewart, widow of.)	4	2	....	676							
Stewart, Elizabeth	(See Christopher Stewart, widow of.)	23	1	....	215							
Stewart, Findley	Pension for revolutionary services.	3	1	Rep. of Secretary War.	131	Select	May 26, 1794	Res. to refer to Sec. War.	R. 12	Passed	Passed	App'd June 9, 1848
Stewart, Findley	Pension for revolutionary services.	4	1	Rep. of Secretary War.	445	Claims	Feb. 18, 1796	Res. to refer to Sec. War.	R. 16	Passed	Passed	App'd April 18, 1796
Stewart, Findley	Pension for revolutionary services.	4	2	Rep. of Secretary War.	614	Claims	Feb. 6, 1797	Favorable; bill ordered.	224	Passed	Postponed.	
Stewart, Findley	Pension for revolutionary services.	5	2	Pension bill	127	....	....	....	38	Passed	Passed	App'd Feb. 2, 1798
Stewart, Frederick A	Relief as a purchaser of public land.	17	1	Petition	134	Public Lands.	....	....	......	Discharged; laid on table.		
Stewart, George	(See Conrad Houseman, and others)											
Stewart, George, heirs of.	Pension for revolutionary services.	30	1	Petition	263	Rev. Claims	Feb. 29, 1848	Adverse	......	Laid on table.		
Stewart, George H	(See administrator of Hugh Thompson.)	29	2	....	171							
Stewart, Henrietta M	(See heirs of Aquilla Stinchecomb)	31	1	....	1141	....	444					
Stewart, Henry	Reimbursement of expenses on public account.	20	2	Petition	116	Military Affairs.	....	....	......	Discharged; laid on table.		
Stewart, Henry	Reimbursement of expenses on public account.	21	1	Petition	85	Military Affairs.						
Stewart, Hugh	Indemnity for loss on a contract.	26	2	Petition	133	Public Buildings	161	Favorable	673	Referred to Committee Whole House.		
Stewart, Hugh	Indemnity for loss on a contract.	27	2	Petition	56	Public Buildings	253	Favorable	219	Passed	Passed	App'd Aug. 31, 1842
Stewart, Hugh	Indemnity for loss on a contract.	28	1	Petition	941	Select	525	Favorable	400	Referred to Committee Whole House.		
Stewart, Hugh	Indemnity for loss on a contract.	29	1	Petition	105	Dist. of Columbia.	106	Favorable	118	Rejected.		
Stewart, Hugh	Indemnity for loss on a contract.	30	2	Petition	118	Dist. of Columbia.						

List of private claims presented to the House of Representatives of the United States from the 1st to the 31st Congress, inclusive—Continued.

Names of claimants.	Nature or object of the claim.	Congress.	Session.	How brought before the House of Reps.	Page of journal.	To what committee of the House referred.	No. or date of the report.	Nature of the report.	No. of the bill.	How disposed of by the House of Reps.	How disposed of by the Senate.	Date of the act of Congress, and remarks.
Stewart, Jacob, (Ky.)	Pension	23	1	Petition	72	Invalid Pensions	Dec. 24, 1833	Adverse	......	Laid on table.		
Stewart, Jacob, (Ky.)	Pension	23	2	Petition	68	Invalid Pensions	83	Favorable	702	Passed	Adverse report.	
Stewart, Jacob, (Ky.)	Pension	24	1	Petition	98	Invalid Pensions	Jan. 15, 1836	Favorable	161	Passed	Passed	App'd June 28, 1836
Stewart, James	Permission to import merchandise from Great Britain.	12	1	Petition	292	....	....	....	......	Referred to Committee Whole House.		
Stewart, James	(See John McIntyre, and others)	16	1	....	186							
Stewart, James	Bounty land for services, Mexican war.	31	1	Petition	344	Public Lands.						
Stewart, James, widow of.	Payment of a lost revolutionary certificate.	4	2	Petition	676	Claims	Feb. 1, 1797	Adverse	......	Rejected.		
Stewart, James, representatives of.	Indemnity for French spoliations prior to 1800.	23	2	Petition	354	Foreign Affairs.						
Stewart, James, executors of.	Indemnity for French spoliations prior to 1800.	26	1	Memorial	182	Foreign Affairs	343	Favorable	319	Referred to Committee Whole House.		
Stewart, James, or James A., sureties of.	Release from liability	11	2	Petition	115	Com. and Manuf.	Mar. 23, 1810	Favorable; bill	124	Referred to Committee Whole House.	....	See act Mar. 3, 1817
Stewart, James E	Extra pay while serving as colonel.	30	1	Petition	115	Military Affairs.						
Stewart, James E	Extra pay while serving as colonel.	31	2	Petition	177	Military Affairs.						
Stewart, James W., and others.	Special pre-emption to their improved lands.	24	1	Petition	741	Public Lands.						
Stewart, James W., and others.	Special pre-emption to their improved lands.	24	2	Petition	211	Priv. Land Claims.						
Stewart, John	(See Matthew Crozier, and others.)	10	2	....	363							
Stewart, John	Pension for revolutionary services.	23	1	Petition	494	Rev. Pensions	....	....	......	Discharged; laid on table.		
Stewart, John	Pension	30	2	Petition	127	Invalid Pensions	78	Favorable	774	Referred to Committee Whole House.		
Stewart, John, heirs of	Commutation pay for revolutionary services.	23	2	Petition	157	Rev. Claims.						
Stewart, John, heirs of	Commutation pay for revolutionary services.	24	1	Petition	664	Rev. Claims	687	Adverse	......	Laid on table.		
Stewart, John, heirs of	Commutation pay for revolutionary services.	31	1	Petition	748	Rev. Claims.						
Stewart, John	(See Canadian refugees)	4	2	....	614							
Stewart, John, administrator of.	Settlement of unliquidated accounts.	1	2	Petition	185	Select.						
				Rep. of Secretary War.	255	Select	....	....	......	Discharged; referred to Secretary of War.		
Stewart, John, widow of.	Pension for revolutionary services.	21	1	Petition	82	Military Pensions.	May 7, 1830	Adverse	......	Laid on table.		
Stewart, John, widow of.	Pension for revolutionary services.	21	2	Petition	73	Military Pensions.						
Stewart, John, former widow of.	Pension for revolutionary services.	26	2	Petition	82	Rev. Pensions.						
Stewart, John, former widow of.	Pension for revolutionary services.	27	2	Petition	59	Rev. Pensions	784	Adverse.	......	Leave to withdraw.		
Stewart, John, former widow of.	Pension for revolutionary services.	28	1	Petition	696	Rev. Pensions	464	Favorable	359	Passed	Passed	App'd June 17, 1844
Stewart, John C., and others	Compensation for services as Treasury watchmen.	29	1	Memorial	208	Claims	756	Favorable	494	Referred to Committee Whole House.		
Stewart, John C., and others	Compensation for services as Treasury watchmen.	29	2	House bill	212	....	....	....	494	Passed	Passed	App'd March 3, 1847
Stewart, John, and J. Davidson.	Remission of duty on a cargo of salt.	1	2	Petition	256	Select	July 24, 1790	Favorable; bill ordered.	90	Passed	Passed	App'd Aug. 4, 1790
Stewart, Joseph, and others.	Proceeds of the capture of a British vessel.	13	3	Petition	751	Ways and Means	....	....	......	Discharged.		

List of private claims presented to the House of Representatives of the United States from the 1st to the 31st Congress, inclusive—Continued.

Names of claimants.	Nature or object of the claim.	Congress.	Session.	How brought before the House of Reps.	Page of journal.	To what committee of the House referred.	No. or date of the report.	Nature of the report.	No. of the bill.	How disposed of by the House of Reps.	How disposed of by the Senate.	Date of the act of Congress, and remarks.
Stewart, Joseph, and others.	Proceeds of the capture of a British vessel.	14	1	Petition	249	Naval Affairs	April 17, 1816	Favorable		Passed	Passed	App'd April 29, 1816
Stewart, Joseph, and others.	Amendment to act of last session.	14	2	Resolution	56	Naval Affairs	Jan. 20, 1817	Favorable	65	Passed	Passed	App'd Feb. 8, 1817
Stewart, Lemuel H., widow of.	Compensation for military services.	27	2	Petition	611	Invalid Pensions.						
Stewart, Levi B	Pension	15	2	Petition	46	Pens. & Rev. Cl'ms.				Discharged; referred to Secretary of War.		
Stewart, Margaret	(See late wife of Leonard Repsher)	18	1		130							
Stewart & Matthews	Reimbursement of forfeiture of whiskey.	20	2	Petition	60	Ways and Means.						
Stewart & Matthews	Reimbursement of forfeiture of whiskey.	21	1	Petition	58	Ways and Means				Discharged; laid on table.		
Stewart & Matthews	Reimbursement of forfeiture of whiskey.	22	1	Petition	62	Ways and Means.						
Stewart & Matthews	Reimbursement of forfeiture of whiskey.	22	2	Petition	45	Ways and Means.						
Stewart & Matthews	Reimbursement of forfeiture of whiskey.	23	1	Petition	48	Ways and Means				Discharged; laid on table.		
Stewart & Matthews	Reimbursement of forfeiture of whiskey.	23	2	Petition	84	Ways and Means.						
Stewart & Matthews	Reimbursement of forfeiture of whiskey.	24	1	Petition	215	Ways and Means				Discharged; laid on table.		
Stewart, Matthew	Compensation for extra work on Cumberland road.	24	2	Petition	208	Claims	Feb. 2, 1837	Indefinite		Referred to Secretary War.		
Stewart, Matthew	Compensation for extra work on Cumberland road.	25	2	Documents	820	Claims.						
Stewart, Matthew	Compensation for extra work on Cumberland road.	27	2	Petition	1204	Claims.						
Stewart, Matthew	Compensation for extra work on Cumberland road.	29	1	Documents	282	Claims	94	Favorable	523	Referred to Committee Whole House.		
Stewart, Matthew, heirs of.	Compensation for extra work on Cumberland road.	30	1	Petition	154	Claims	69	Favorable	51	Passed	Passed	App'd Aug. 5, 1848
Stewart, Nancy	(See Blue Jacket, daughter of)	23	1		249							
Stewart, Nancy Anne	(See James W. Stewart and others)	24	1		741							
Stewart, Nathaniel	Pension	16	1	Petition	174	Rev. Pensions	April 6, 1820	Adverse		Laid on table.		
Stewart, Nathaniel	Pension	22	1	Petition	120	Rev. Pensions	369	Pension bill	464	Referred to Committee Whole House.		
Stewart & Plunkett	Remission of duty on coffee destroyed by fire.	3	1	Senate bill	137				S. 9	Passed	Passed	App'd May 9, 1794
Stewart, Ralph	Pension	28	2	Petition	184	Rev. Pensions.						
Stewart, Robert, (Va.)	Pension	22	2	Petition	26	Invalid Pensions				Discharged; laid on table.		
Stewart, Robert, (Ind.)	Bounty land and pay for services in Mexico.	31	1	Petition	495	Claims.						
Stewart, Samuel	(See William H. Bedford, agent).	28	1		262							
Stewart, Susannah	Return of land certificate from State Department.	16	1	Petition	373	Judiciary	April 8, 1820	Favorable	131	Passed	Passed	App'd May 12, 1820
Stewart, Thomas	Grant of land	23	1	Petition	523	Indian Affairs.						
Stewart, Timothy, surety of.	Release from judgment at suit of United States.	17	2	Petition	120	Military Affairs				Discharged; leave to withdraw.		
Stewart, Timothy, surety of.	Release from judgment at suit of United States.	18	1	Petition	214	Claims	Mar. 4, 1824	Adverse		Laid on table.		
Stewart, William	(See William H. Bedford, agent).	28	1		262							

List of private claims presented to the House of Representatives of the United States from the 1st *to the* 31*st Congress, inclusive*—Continued.

Names of claimants.	Nature or object of the claim.	Congress.	Session.	How brought before the House of Reps.	Page of journal.	To what committee of the House referred.	No. or date of the report.	Nature of the report.	No. of the bill.	How disposed of by the House of Reps.	How disposed of by the Senate.	Date of the act of Congress, and remarks.
Stewart, William, (Ohio).	Indemnity for deficit in public land	20	1	Resolution	356	Public Lands.....	Mar. 22, 1828	Favorable	237	Referred to Committee Whole House.		
Stewart, William, (Ohio).	Indemnity for deficit in public land	20	2	Bill of last sess..	261	Whole House.....	Feb. 9, 1829	With amend..	237	Passed.		
Stewart, William, (Ohio).	Indemnity for deficit in public land	21	1	Petition	473	Public Lands.....	398	Favorable	465	Ref'd to Com. W. H.		
Stewart, William, executors of.	Indemnity for deficit in public land	21	2	Petition	120	Public Lands.....	....	....	......	Discharged; laid on table.		
Stewart, William, executors of.	Indemnity for deficit in public land	22	1	Petition	173	Public Lands.....	Jan. 4, 1832	Favorable	303	Referred to Committee Whole House.		
Stewart, William, executors of.	Indemnity for deficit in public land	22	2	Bill of last sess..	171	Whole House.....	Jan. 12, 1833	With't amend.	303	Passed	Passed	App'd March 2, 1833
Stewart, William F......	Indemnity for imprisonm't in Dartmoor.	28	1	Petition	310	Claims.						
Stewart, William T......	Compensation for services as messenger, House Representatives.	30	1	Resolution	552	....	....	....	......	Laid on table.		
Stibbins, Samuel	To be restored to pension roll....	17	2	Petition	142	Whole House.						
Stickell, Valentine.......	Pension for revolutionary services.	20	2	Petition	109	Military Pensions..	Feb. 13, 1829	Favorable	440	Passed.		
Stickell, Valentine	Pension for revolutionary services.	21	1	Pension bill	130	Whole House	Feb. 12, 1830	With amend..	72	Passed	Passed, with amendment.	App'd May 20, 1830
Stickney, Benjamin F....	Compensation for services in Indian department.	23	1	Petition	246	Claims	487	Favorable	496	Referred to Committee Whole House.		
Stickney, Benjamin F....	Compensation for services in Indian department.	24	1	Petition	50	Claims	18	Favorable	18	Passed	Passed	App'd Feb. 17, 1836
Stickney, Elizabeth......	Pension for revolutionary services of deceased husband.	28	1	Petition	950	Whole House.						
Stickney, Henry R.	Reimbursement of duties on shipwrecked goods.	25	2	Petition	327	Ways and Means..	1029	Adverse	......	Laid on table.		
Stickney, Henry R.	Reimbursement of duties on shipwrecked goods.	27	1	Petition	95	Commerce.						
Stickney, Henry R.	Reimbursement of duties on shipwrecked goods.	27	2	Petition	56	Commerce	1052	Adverse	......	Laid on table.		
Stickney, John	Additional compensation as Postmaster.	28	1	Petition	622	P. Of. & P. Roads.						
Stickney, Robert C.......	Compensation for mail service....	26	1	Petition	200	P. Of. & P. Roads.	397	Adverse	......	Laid on table.		
Stickney, Sarah.........	Extension of pension act........	30	1	Petition	230	Rev. Pensions.....	Jan. 25, 1848	Adverse	......	Laid on table.		
Stidger, George	Resurvey of public land, and credit for deficiency, &c.	13	3	Petition	702	Public Lands.						
Stidger, George	Resruvey of public land, and credit for deficiency, &c.	14	1	Petition	210	Public Lands.....	Mar. 12, 1816	Adverse	......	Rejected.		
Stidham, G. W.........	(See B. Marshall and others)....	30	1	....	809							
Stiff, William F	(See Louis F. Beeler and others).	30	1	....	115	....	482					
Stigermire, Hiner........	Correction of an entry of land....	24	2	Petition	47	Public Lands.....	57	Favorable	807	Referred to Committee Whole House.		
Stigermire, Hiner........	Correction of an entry of land....	25	2	Petition	42	Public Lands.....	311	Favorable	348	Ref'd to Com. W. H.		
Stigermire, Hiner........	Correction of an entry of land....	25	3	Bill of last sess..	377	Whole House.....	Jan. 25, 1839	With t amend.	348	Passed	Passed	App'd March 2, 1839
Stiggins, George	Confirmation of title to land in Alabama.	15	1	Petition	56	Priv. Land Claims.						
Stiggins, George	Confirmation of title to land in Alabama.	20	1	Petition	40	Public Lands.....	May 13, 1828	Favorable	299	Referred to Committee Whole House.		
Stiggins, George	Authority to sell certain land in fee.	21	1	Petition	53	Public Lands	69	Favorable	97	Passed	Passed	App'd May 29, 1830
Stiggins, George	Authority to sell certaln land in fee.	23	1	Petition	386	Priv. Land Claims.						
Stiles, Aaron	Increase of pension............	12	1	Pension bill....	361	Whole House.....	June 12, 1812	With amend..	138	Passed	Passed	App'd July 5, 1812
Stiles, Benjamin, & others.	Confirmation of title to certain lands.	2	1	Petition	543							

List of private claims presented to the House of Representatives of the United States from the 1*st to the* 31*st Congress, inclusive*—Continued.

Names of claimants.	Nature or object of the claim.	Congress.	Session.	How brought before the House of Reps.	Page of journal.	To what committee of the House referred.	No. or date of the report.	Nature of the report.	No. of the bill.	How disposed of by the House of Reps.	How disposed of by the Senate.	Date of the act of Congress, and remarks.
Stiles, Benjamin	Conpensation for supplies furnished on public account.	6	1	Petition	614	Claims	April 3, 1800	Adverse		Rejected.		
Stiles, Beriah	Pension	21	2	Petition	188	Military Pensions.						
Stiles, Beriah	Pension	22	1	Petition	188	Rev. Pensions	365	Favorable	460	Passed	Indef. postp'd.	
Stiles, David	(See Wm. H. Hoag [Hoey] and others.)	27	3		153							
Stiles, Ezra	(See Yale College, President of).	1	2		148							
Stiles, George, executor of.	Indemnity for vessels sunk in defence of Baltimore.	17	2	Petition	210	Claims				Discharged; leave to withdraw.		
Stiles, George, executor of.	Indemnity for vessels sunk in defence of Baltimore.	18	2	Senate bill	278	Judiciary	March 1, 1825	With't amend.	S. 36	Passed	Passed	App'd March 3, 1825
Stiles, George, executor of.	Indemnity for vessels sunk in defence of Baltimore.	20	1	Memorial	167	Ways and Means.	Feb. 29, 1828	Adverse		Laid on table.		
Stiles, George, executor of.	Additional indemnity for vessels sunk, &c.	22	2	Petition	42	Claims	128	Favorable	R. 19	Passed	Passed	App'd March 2, 1833
Stiles, George, executor of.	Additional indemnity for vessels sunk, &c.	23	1	Petition	335	Claims	532	General bill	532	Passed	Passed	App'd June 27, 1834
Stiles, John	To locate land warrant on the Great Miami.	4	1	Petition	386	Select.						
Stiles, John S	(See executor of George Stiles)	17	2		210							
Stiles, John S	Indemnity for loss on naval contract.	24	1	Senate resolution.	497	Claims	625	Changed to bill	S. 313	Passed with amendm't.	Passed as am'd.	App'd July 2, 1836
Stiles, Joseph	(See administrators of Joseph Clay)	15	1		165							
Stiles, Samuel	Renewal of a revolutionary certificate.	4	1	Petition	524					Referred to Secretary Treasury.		
Still, Bartlett	Remission of a certain penalty	15	2	Petition	190	Ways and Means.	Feb. 9, 1819	Favorable	313	Referred to Committee Whole House.		
Still, Samuel H	Pension	31	1	Petition	519	Invalid Pensions.						
Stille, James	Indemnity for costs, &c., in a trespass suit.	7	2	Petition	246	Claims				Discharged; leave to withdraw.		
Stille, James	Indemnity for costs, &c., in a trespass suit.	8	1	Petition	468	Claims	Dec. 28, 1803	Adverse		Leave to withdraw.		
Stiller, John	Pension for revolutionary disabilities.	1	2	Petition and rep't Secretary War.	214, 221					Laid on table.		
Stiller, John	Compensation for revolutionary services.	2	1	Petition	539					Referred to Secretary of War.		
Stiller, John	Pension for disability incurred	3	1	Rep. of Secretary War.	131	Select	May 26, 1794	Favorable; bill ordered.	62	Passed	Passed	App'd June 7, 1794
Stillman, Charles, & Bro.	Indemnity for detention of property in Texas.	31	1	Petition	835	Commerce.						
Sillman, Ethan	Extra price for manufactured arms.	14	2	Petition						Referred to Secretary of War.		
Stillman, Samuel	Pension for revolutionary services.	4	1	Rep. of Secretary of War.	445	Claims	Feb. 18, 1796	Pension bill	156	Passed	Passed	App'd April 20, 1796
Stillman, Samuel	Pension for revolutionary services.	13	1	Pension bill	56	Whole House	July 20, 1813	With amend.	31	Passed	Passed, with amendment.	App'd Aug. 2, 1813
Stillwell, Harold	Confirmation of title to land in Arkansas Territory.	16	1	Petition	291	Priv. Land Claims.						
Stillwell, Harold	Confirmation of title to land in Arkansas Territory.	22	1	House bill	421				425	Passed	Passed, with amendment.	App'd June 25, 1832
Stillwell, Jarrett	Pension	21	2	Petition	299	Military Pensions.						
Stillwell, Jeremiah	Pension for services in Indian wars.	31	1	Petition	269	Rev. Pensions	263	Adverse		Laid on table.		

List of private claims presented to the House of Representatives of the United States from the 1st to the 31st Congress, inclusive—Continued.

ames of claimants.	Nature or object of the claim.	Congress.	Session.	How brought before the House of Reps.	Page of journal.	To what committee of the House referred.	No. or date of the report.	Nature of the report.	No. of the bill.	How disposed of by the House of Reps.	How disposed of by the Senate.	Date of the act of Congress, and remarks.
Stillwell, John	Confirmation of title to land in Arkansas Territory.	16	1	Petition	291	Priv. Land Claims.						
Stillwell, John	Confirmation of title to land in Arkansas Territory.	22	1	House bill	421				425	Passed	Passed, with amendment.	App'd June 25, 1832
Stillwell, Joseph	Confirmation of title to land in Arkansas Territory.	16	1	Petition	291	Priv. Land Claims.						
Stillwell, Joseph	Confirmation of title to land in Arkansas Territory.	22	1	House bill	421				425	Passed	Passed, with amendment.	App'd June 25, 1832
Stillwell, Samuel	(See George B. Rapelye, & others.)	12	1		64							
Stillwell, Savage	(See attorney for John Addison)	6	1		676							
Stilt, Elizabeth	(See heirs of Thomas Mott)	27	3		52							
Stilt, John M.	(See heirs of Thomas Mott)	27	3		52							
Stimmell, Philip	Remission of duty on snuff	4	1	Petition	390	Com. and Manuf.						
Stimmell, Philip	Remission of duty on snuff	4	2	Petition	633	Com. and Manuf.						
Stinchecomb, Aquilla, heirs of.	Compensation for services as revolutionary officer.	31	1	Petition	1141	Rev. Pensions	444	Adverse		Laid on table.		
Stiner, Thomas	Payment of a loan office certificate.	15	2	Petition	150	Pens. & Rev. Cl'ms.						
Stipp, Abraham	Scrip in lieu of land warrant	25	2	Petition	417	Public Lands	757	Favorable	716	Referred to Committee Whole House.		
Stipp, Abraham	Scrip in lieu of land warrant	25	3	Bill of last sess.	380	Whole House	Jan. 25, 1839	With't amend.	716	Passed	Passed	App'd March 3, 1839
Stipp, jr., John	Remission of duty on distillery	16	1	Petition	250	Ways and Means.						
Stipp, jr., John	Remission of duty on distillery	16	2	Petition	32	Ways and Means.	Nov. 24, 1820	Adverse		Rejected.		
Stipp, jr., John	Release from judgment at suit of United States.	16	2	Petition	78	Select.						
Stirling, Earl of	(See William Alexander)	5	2		81							
Stirman, William, assignee of.	Payment of draft for services as Choctaw teacher.	24	1	Resolution	347	Claims	Feb. 19, 1836	Adverse		Laid on table.		
Stirman, William	Salary as Choctaw teacher	24	1	Petition	672	Indian Affairs				Discharged; laid on table.		
Stites, John, and others	To change location of military warrants.	4	1	Petition	387	Select.						
Stith, Ann	(See Richard Stith, widow of)	19	1		93							
Stith, Catharine	(See Townsend Stith, widow of)	19	1		128							
Stith, John, widow of	Remission of balance due for public land.	22	1	Petition	537	Judiciary				Discharged; laid on table.		
Stith, John, widow of	Remission of balance due for public land.	22	2	Petition	45	Judiciary.						
Stith, John, widow of	Remission of balance due for public land.	23	1	Petition	121	Judiciary.						
Stith, John, widow of	Remission of balance due for public land.	23	2	Petition	164							
				Memorial	211	Judiciary	Feb. 21, 1835	Favorable	760	Passed.		
Stith, John, widow of	Remission of balance due for public land.	24	1	Memorial	106	Judiciary	June 28, 1836	Favorable	731	Referred to Committee Whole House.		
Stith, John, widow of	Remission of balance due for public land.	25	2	Petition	74	Judiciary	732	Favorable	699	Referred to Committee Whole House.		
Stith, John, widow of	Remission of balance due for public land.	25	3	Bill of last sess.	380	Whole House	June 25, 1839	With't amend.	699	Passed	Adverse report.	
Stith, John, widow of	Remission of balance due for public land.	26	1	House bill	499	Whole House			83			
Stith, John, widow of	Remission of balance due for public land.	26	2	Bill of last sess.	194	Whole House	Jan. 16, 1841	With't amend.	83			
Stith, John, widow of	Remission of balance due for public land.	27	2	Petition	63	Judiciary				Discharged; laid on table.		

List of private claims presented to the House of Representatives of the United States from the 1st to the 31st Congress, inclusive—Continued.

Names of claimants.	Nature or object of the claim.	Congress.	Session.	How brought before the House of Reps.	Page of journal.	To what committee of the House referred.	No. or date of the report.	Nature of the report.	No. of the bill.	How disposed of by the House of Reps.	How disposed of by the Senate.	Date of the act of Congress, and remarks.
Stith, John, widow of	Remission of balance due for public land.	28	1	Petition	145	Judiciary				Discharged; laid on table.		
Stith, John, widow of	Remission of balance due for public land.	28	2	Petition	141	Judiciary	190	Favorable	647	Referred to Committee Whole House.		
Stith, John, widow of	Remission of balance due for public land.	29	1	Petition	147	Judiciary	304	Adverse		Laid on table.		
Stith, Richard, widow of	Confirmation of title to land in Arkansas.	19	1	Petition	93	Public Lands	Jan. 18, 1826	Adverse		Laid on table.		
Stith, Sarah B	(See John Stith, widow of)	22	1		537							
Stith, Townsend, widow of.	Arrears of pension	19	1	Petition	128	Military Pensions	164	Adverse		Laid on table.		
Stivers, Ann Maria	(See Stephen D. Stives, widow of)	28	1		1042							
Stiver, Edward	Pension	14	2	Petition	116	Pens. & Rev. Cl'ms.						
Stivers, Stephen D., widow of.	Re-enactment of naval pension act.	28	1	Petition	1042	Naval Affairs.						
Stoaks, Christopher	Balance due for revolutionary services.	8	1	Petition	421	Claims	Nov. 20, 1803	Adverse		Leave to withdraw.		
Stobo, Jane, heirs of	Compensation for supplies furnished in revolutionary war.	4	1	Petition	518	Claims	May 31, 1796	Adverse		Laid on table.		
Stockbridge Indians	(See Indians.)											
Stockbridge, John, (Mary,) widow of.	Pension for revolutionary services.	25	2	Petition	230	Rev. Pensions				Discharged; laid on table.		
Stocker, Ebenezer, administrator of.	Indemnity for French spoliations prior to 1800.	26	1	Memorial	182	Foreign Affairs	343	Favorable; bill	319	Referred to Committee Whole House.		
Stocker, jr., John Clements.	Remission of duties on wine	12	2	Petition	689	Com. and Manuf.						
Stocker, Samuel	Pension for revolutionary services.	3	2	Rep. of Secretary War.	278	Claims	Feb. 28, 1795	Pension bill	130	Passed	Postponed.	
Stocker, Samuel	Pension for revolutionary services.	4	1	Rep. of Secretary War.	445	Claims	Feb. 18, 1796	Pension bill	156	Passed	Passed	App'd April 20, 1796
Stocker, Susannah	(See Peter Surget and others)	22	1		205							
Stocking, Horace	(See Josiah Savage and others)	18	1		27							
Stocking & Bull	Indemnity for destruction of property by the enemy.	15	2	Petition	148	Claims.						
Stockley, John	Compensation for revolutionary services.	12	2	Petition	579	Claims	Feb. 26, 1813	Adverse		Laid on table.		
Stockman, Christopher	To be restored to pension roll	24	2	Petition	158	Rev. Pensions				Discharged; laid on table.		
Stockman, Henry	Confirmation of title to land on Rio Hondo and Sabine.	19	1	House bill	516	Whole House			254			
Stockman, Peter	Confirmation of title to land on Rio Hondo and Sabine.	19	1	House bill	516	Whole House			254			
Stocks, William	Compensation for team taken for public use.	29	1	Petition	161	Claims.						
Stocks, William	Compensation for team taken for public use.	29	2	Petition	56	Claims.						
Stocks, William	Compensation for team taken for public use.	30	1	Petition	169	Claims	201	Adverse		Laid on table.		
Stockton, Charles	Pension	15	1	Petition	156					Referred to Secretary War.		
Stockton, Francis B	Reimbursement of expenditure on public account.	31	1	Senate bill	1075	Naval Affairs	Aug. 1, 1850	With't amend.	S. 188	Referred to Committee Whole House.		
Stockton, Falls & Co	Reimbursement of expenses in extra mail service.	27	2	Resolution	870	P. Of. & P. Roads.						

List of private claims presented to the House of Representatives of the United States from the 1st to the 31st Congress, inclusive—Continued.

3—53

Names of claimants.	Nature or object of the claim.	Congress.	Session.	How brought before the House of Reps.	Page of journal.	To what committee of the House referred.	No. or date of the report.	Nature of the report.	No. of the bill.	How disposed of by the House of Reps.	How disposed of by the Senate.	Date of the act of Congress, and remarks.
Stockton, George	Indemnity for property lost in public service.	20	2	Resolution	238	Claims.						
Stockton, George	Indemnity for property lost in public service.	21	2	Petition	38	Claims	19	Adverse	......	Referred to Committee Whole House.		
Stockton, George	Indemnity for property lost in public service.	22	1	Petition	190	Claims	Jan. 23, 1832	Adverse	......	Laid on table.		
Stockton, George	Indemnity for property lost in public service.	22	2	Petition	152	Claims.						
Stockton, George	Indemnity for property lost in public service.	23	1	Petition	33	Claims	April 9, 1834	Adverse	......	Laid on table.		
Stockton, George	Reimbursement of interest on a judgment.	23	1	Petition	305	Claims	401	Adverse	......	Laid on table.		
Stockton, Henry	Confirmation of title to land	19	1	Rep. of land officers.	64	Public Lands	33	Favorable	254	Referred to Committee Whole House.		
Stockton, John	Indemnity for loss by invasion of Upper Canada.	28	2	Petition	206	Military Affairs	Jan. 24, 1845	Favorable	R. 66	Referred to Committee Whole House.		
Stockton, John	Indemnity for loss by invasion of Upper Canada.	29	1	Petition	74	Military Affairs	553	Favorable	146	Referred to Committee Whole House.		
Stockton, John	Indemnity for loss by invasion of Upper Canada.	29	2	Senate bill	381	Military Affairs	Feb. 24, 1847	With't amend.	S. 36	Passed	Passed	App'd March 3, 1847
Stockton, J. N. C.	Balance due for transportation of the mail.	25	2	Memorial	576	Judiciary	....	....	......	Leave to withdraw.		
Stockton, J. N. C., & Co.	Compensation for mail service	28	2	Petition	46	P. Of. & P. Roads.	145	Favorable	R. 73	Referred to Committee Whole House.		
Stockton, J. N. C., & Co.	Compensation for mail service	29	1	Petition	68	P. Of. & P. Roads.	315	Favorable	R. 21	Referred to Committee Whole House.		
Stockton, J. N. C., & Co.	Compensation for mail service	29	2	House resolution.	71	....	....	....	R. 21	Passed	Passed	App'd March 3, 1847
Stockton, J. N. C., & Co.	Compensation for mail service	30	1	Senate bill	957	P. Of. & P. Roads.	764	With't amend.	S. 154	Passed with amendm't.	Passed as am'd	App'd Aug. 14, 1848
Stockton, J. N. C., & Co.	Same allowance as for prior service.	30	2	Petition	126	P. Of. & P. Roads.	Jan. 3, 1849	Adverse	......	Laid on table.		
Stockton, Lewis	(See Louis F. Beeler and others).	30	1	....	115	....	482					
Stockton, Lucius W.	Reimbursement of expenditure on Cumberland road.	22	1	Appropriat'n bill.	195	....	....	....	267	....	....	App'd July 2, 1832
Stockton, Lucius W.	(See Wm. B. Stokes, and others.)	24	1	....	832							
Stockton, Peter	Confirmation of title to land	19	1	Report of land officer.	64	Public Lands	33	Favorable	254	Referred to Committee Whole House.		
Stockton, Richard C.	(See Wm. B. Stokes, and others.)	24	1	....	832							
Stockton, Richard C.	(See Octavo De La Houpoje)	30	1	....	387							
Stockton, Robert F.	Reimbursement of expenses in defending certain suits.	17	2	Senate bill	378	Whole House	Mar. 1, 1823	With't amend.	S. 6[illegible]	Passed	Passed	App'd March 3, 1823
Stockton, W. T.	Indemnity for annulment of mail contract.	28	1	Petition Documents	288 332	 P. Of. & P. Roads.						
Stockton, W. T.	Indemnity for annulment of mail contract.	29	1	Petition	122	P. Of. & P. Roads.						
Stoddard, Amos, and others.	Increase of pay for military services.	10	1	Petition	69	Whole House						
Stoddert, Benjamin	(See trustees of Francis L. Taney)	10	1	....	216							
Stoddert, Benjamin	(See Robert G. Harper, & others)	11	3	....	458							
Stoddert, Benjamin, heirs of.	Balance of pay due for revolutionary services.	23	2	Petition	197	Rev. Claims.						
Stoddert, Benjamin, heirs of.	Balance of pay due for revolutionary services.	24	1	Petition	205	Rev. Claims.						
Stoddert, Benjamin, heirs of.	Balance of pay due for revolutionary services.	25	2	Petition	111	Rev. Claims	1010	Adverse	......	Laid on table.		

List of private claims presented to the House of Representatives of the United States from the 1st to the 31st Congress, inclusive—Continued.

Names of claimants.	Nature or object of the claim.	Congress.	Session.	How brought before the House of Reps.	Page of journal.	To what committee of the House referred.	No. or date of the report.	Nature of the report.	No. of the bill.	How disposed of by the House of Reps.	How disposed of by the Senate.	Date of the act of Congress, and remarks.
Stoddert, Benjamin, heir of.	Balance of pay due for revolutionary services.	27	3	Petition	155	Rev. Claims	....	....	......	Discharged; leave to withdraw.		
Stoddard, Charles	Reimbursement of duties on chain cables.	26	2	Petition	181	Commerce.						
Stoddard, Charles	Reimbursement of duties on chain cables.	27	3	Petition	193	Commerce.						
Stoddard, Charles	Reimbursement of duties on chain cables.	28	1	Petition	631	Commerce	....	....	......	Discharged; laid on table.		
Stoddard, Daniel	Pension	15	1	Petition	113	Pens. & Rev. Cl'ms.						
Stoddard, Daniel	Pension	21	2	Petition	188	Military Pensions.						
Stoddard, Daniel	Pension	22	1	Petition	51	Invalid Pensions	209	Pension bill	288	Passed	Passed, with amendment.	App'd July 14, 1832
Stoddard, Daniel	Increase of pension	23	2	Petition	447	Invalid Pensions	126	Favorable	767	Referred to Committee Whole House.		
Stoddard, Daniel	Increase of pension	24	1	Senate bill	810	Invalid Pensions	July 1, 1836	With't amend.	S. 149	Passed	Passed	App'd June 15, 1836
Stoddard, Francis	Compensation for services as clerk in custom house, Massachusetts.	28	1	Petition	204	Ways and Means.						
Stoddard, Henry	Patent for an Indian grant of land.	23	1	Petition	138	Priv. Land Claims.	330	Favorable	357	Referred to Committee Whole House.		
Stoddard, Henry	Patent for an Indian grant of land.	24	1	Petition	112	Priv. Land Claims.	114	Favorable	131	Passed	Passed	App'd June 23, 1836
Stoddard, Henry, & Co	Compensation for supplies, Mexican war.	31	1	Petition	857	Claims.						
Stoddard, Nathan A	Land due his father killed in revolutionary war.	6	1	Petition	684	....	....	....	......	Laid on table.		
Stoddart, Philo	Increase of pension	12	1	Pension bill	361	Whole House	June 15, 1812	With't amend.	138	Passed	Passed, with amendment.	App'd July 5, 1812
Stoddart, Philo	Bounty land for revolutionary services.	14	2	Petition	64	Pens. & Rev. Cl'ms.	....	....	......	Leave to withdraw.		
Stoddart, Philo	Increase of pension	22	2	Petition	74	Rev. Pensions	....	....	......	Disch'd; laid on table.		
Stoddart, Philo	Increase of pension	23	1	Petition	44	Invalid Pensions	June 28, 1834	Adverse	......	Laid on table.		
Stoddart, Philo	Increase of pension	23	2	Petition	86	Invalid Pensions	Dec. 30, 1834	Adverse	......	Laid on table.		
Stoddart, Philo	Increase of pension	24	1	Petition	201	Invalid Pensions	July 1, 1836	Adverse	......	Laid on table.		
Stoddart, Philo	Increase of pension	25	2	Petition	57	Invalid Pensions.						
Stoddart, Philo	Increase of pension	28	1	Petition	481	Invalid Pensions.						
Stoddard, Robert W	Compensation for digest of evidence in certain cases.	15	2	Documents	140	Claims.						
Stoddard, Robert W	Compensation for digest of evidence in certain cases.	18	1	Petition	213	Ways and Means	Feb. 23, 1824	Adverse	......	Laid on table.		
Stoddard, Robert W	Compensation for digest of evidence in certain cases.	20	1	Petition	163	Claims	Feb. 5, 1828	Adverse	......	Laid on table.		
Stoddard, Robert W	Compensation for digest of evidence in certain cases.	22	1	Petition	288	Claims	Feb 29, 1832	Adverse	......	Laid on table.		
Stodder, Eber	Pension for revolutionary services.	21	1	Resolution	63	Military Pensions.						
Stogdill, Robert	Compensation for revolutionary services.	4	1	Petition	425	Claims	May 7, 1796	Adverse	......	Leave to withdraw.		
Stokeley, Joseph	(See Nehemiah Stokely, heirs of.)	29	1	....	352							
Stokeley, Nehemiah, widow of.	Commutation pay for revolutionary services.	19	2	Petition	308	Rev. Claims.						
Stokeley, Nehemiah, widow of.	Commutation pay for revolutionary services.	20	1	Petition	105	Rev. Claims.						
				Petition, (2)	311	Rev. Claims	Mar. 26, 1828	Adverse	......	Laid on table.		
Stokeley, Nehemiah, widow of.	Commutation pay for revolutionary services.	21	1	Petition	147	Rev. Claims	Mar. 5, 1830	Adverse	......	Laid on table.		

List of private claims presented to the House of Representatives of the United States from the 1st to the 31st Congress, inclusive—Continued.

Names of claimants.	Nature or object of the claim.	Congress.	Session.	How brought before the House of Reps.	Page of journal.	To what committee of the House referred.	No. or date of the report.	Nature of the report.	No. of the bill.	How disposed of by the House of Reps.	How disposed of by the Senate.	Date of the act of Congress, and remarks.
Stokeley, Nehemiah, heirs of.	Commutation pay for revolutionary services.	29	1	Petition	352	Rev. Claims.						
Stokeley, Nehemiah, heirs of.	Commutation pay for revolutionary services.	29	2	Petition	75	Rev. Claims.						
Stokeley, Nehemiah, heirs of.	Commutation pay for revolutionary services.	30	1	Petition	270	Rev. Claims	617	Favorable	496	Referred to Committee Whole House.		
Stokeley, Nehemiah, heirs of.	Commutation pay for revolutionary services.	30	2	Bill of last sess.	318	Whole House	Jan. 26, 1849	With't amend.	496	Passed.		
Stokeley, Nehemiah, heirs of.	Commutation pay for revolutionary services.	31	1	Petition	610	Rev. Claims	339	Adverse	......	Laid on table.		
Stokeley, Susannah	(See Nehemiah Stokely, widow of.)	19	2	....	308							
Stoker, Henry	Confirmation of title to land in Louisiana.	20	2	Petition	34	Priv. Land Claims.	597	Favorable	579	Referred to Committee Whole House.		
Stoker, Henry	Confirmation of title to land in Louisiana.	21	1	Petition	40	Priv. Land Claims.						
Stoker, Henry	Confirmation of title to land in Louisiana.	21	2	Petition	55	Priv. Land Claims.	Jan. 31, 1831	Adverse	......	Laid on table.		
Stoker, Henry	Confirmation of title to land in Louisiana.	22	1	Petition	65	Priv. Land Claims.	Dec. 27, 1831	Adverse	......	Laid on table.		
Stoker, Henry	Confirmation of title to land in Louisiana.	23	1	Petition	381	Public Lands	420	Favorable	442	Referred to Committee Whole House.		
Stoker, Henry	Confirmation of title to land in Louisiana.	24	1	Petition	121	Public Lands.						
Stoker, Henry	Confirmation of title to land in Louisiana.	25	2	Petition	42, 373	Priv. Land Claims.	Mar. 7, 1838	Favorable	632	Referred to Committee Whole House.		
Stoker, Henry	Confirmation of title to land in Louisiana.	25	3	Petition	134	Priv. Land Claims.						
Stoker, Henry	Confirmation of title to land in Louisiana.	25	3	Bill of last sess.	376	Whole House	Jan. 25, 1839	With't amend.	632	Passed	Passed	App'd Mar. 3, 1839
Stoker, Henry	Compensation for slave killed by United States soldiers.	23	1	Petition	305	Claims	537	Adverse	......	Laid on table.		
Stoker, Henry	Compensation for slave killed by United States soldiers.	23	2	Petition	49	Claims.						
Stoker, Henry	Compensation for slave killed by United States soldiers.	24	1	Petition	121	Claims.						
Stoker, Henry	Compensation for slave killed by United States soldiers.	25	2	Petition	372	Claims	1003	Adverse	......	Laid on table.		
Stoker, Henry	Compensation for slave killed by United States soldiers.	28	1	Petition	602	Claims	336	Adverse	......	Laid on table.		
Stoker, Mary	(See late widow of Apollos Cooper	15	2	....	220							
Stoker, William	Compensation for revolutionary wounds and disabilities.	9	1	Petition	224	Claims	Mar. 28, 1796	Adverse	......	Indefinitely postponed.		
Stokes, David, heirs of	Payment of loan office certificate.	23	1	Petition	569	Rev. Claims.						
Stokes, Hampton	Pension for revolutionary services.	25	3	Petition	673	....	....	....	......	Laid on table.		
Stokes, James L.	Permission to purchase school section.	22	1	Petition	189	Priv. Land Claims.	225	Favorable	300	Referred to Committee Whole House.		
Stokes, James L.	Permission to purchase school section.	22	2	Bill of last sess.	171	Whole House	Jan. 12, 1833	With't amend.	300	Passed.		
Stokes, James L.	Permission to purchase school section.	23	1	Petition	93	Priv. Land Claims.	89	Favorable	97	Passed.		
Stokes, James L.	Permission to purchase school section.	24	1	Petition	208	Priv. Land Claims.	214	Favorable	220	Passed.		

List of private claims presented to the House of Representatives of the United States from the 1st to the 31st Congress, inclusive—Continued.

Names of claimants.	Nature or object of the claim.	Congress.	Session.	How brought before the House of Reps.	Page of journal.	To what committee of the House referred.	No. or date of the report.	Nature of the report.	No. of the bill.	How disposed of by the House of Reps.	How disposed of by the Senate.	Date of the act of Congress, and remarks.
Stokes, James L.	Permission to purchese school section.	25	2	Petition	42	Priv. Land Claims.	1026	Favorable	853	Referred to Committee Whole House.		
Stokes, James L.	Permission to purchase school section.	25	3	Bill of last sess.	432	Whole House	Feb. 1, 1839	With't amend.	853	Passed	Passed	App'd March 3, 1839
Stokes, John, heirs of	Commutation pay for revolutionary services.	24	1	Petition	474	Rev. Claims.						
Stokes, John, heirs of	Commutation pay for revolutionary services.	24	2	Petition	73	Rev. Claims	165	Adverse	......	Laid on table.		
Stokes, John, heirs of	Commutation pay for revolutionary services.	25	2	Petition	48	Rev. Claims.						
Stokes, John, widow of	Benefit of certain pension acts	30	1	Petition	164	Rev. Pensions	111	Favorable	100	Passed	Passed	App'd Aug. 5, 1848
Stokes, John, widow of	Benefit of certain pension acts	31	1	Petition	632	Rev. Pensions	222	Favorable	R. 11	Passed	Passed	App'd Sept. 28, 1850
Stokes, John, widow of	Benefit of certain pension acts	31	2	Petition	95	....	....	....	......	Leave to withdraw.		
Stokes & Purdom	Indemnity for loss on mail contract	27	2	Petition	129	P. Of. & P. Roads.	858	Adverse	......	Laid on table.		
Stokes, Richard	Bounty land for military services	28	1	Resolution	422	Priv. Land Claims.						
Stokes, William B.	Indemnity for property destroyed by the enemy.	15	1	Petition	87	Claims	Feb. 10, 1818	Adverse	......	Referred to Committee Whole House.		
Stokes, William B.	Indemnity for property destroyed by the enemy.	17	2	Petition	164	Claims	Feb. 21, 1823	Adverse	......	Laid on table.		
Stokes, Wm. B., & others	Compensation for extra mail service	24	1	Senate bill	832	Judiciary	June 17, 1836	With't amend.	S. 258	Passed	Passed	App'd July 2, 1836
Stokes, Wm. B., & others	Settlement of claims under mail contract.	24	2	Rep. of Solicitor Treasury.	124	Judiciary.						
Stokes, Wm. B., & others	Interest on their claims	25	2	Petition	1029	P. Of. & P. Roads.						
Stokes, Wm. B., & others	Payment of judgment against Postmaster General.	27	2	Memorial	765	Judiciary	June 21, 1842	Adverse	......	Leave to withdraw.		
Stokes, William B.	(See J. N. C. Stockton & Co.)	28	2	....	46							
Stokes, William M.	(See heirs of John Stokes)	24	1	....	474							
Stokes, William, administrator of.	Indemnity for French spoliations prior to 1800.	26	1	Memorial	182	Foreign Affairs	343	Favorable; bill	319	Referred to Committee Whole House.		
Stone, Asahel	(See surety of Asa Lord)	20	1	....	39							
Stone, A.	Indemnity for property destroyed at Plattsburgh.	13	3	Petition	723	Claims	Feb. 15, 1815	Favorable	297	Passed	Passed	App'd March 3, 1815
Stone, Bannister	(See sureties of Adam Carruth)	17	2	....	225							
Stone, Benjamin	Commutation pay for revolutionary services.	12	1	Petition	326	Claims	....	....	......	Leave to withdraw.		
Stone, Benjamin, widow of.	Pension for services of deceased; died in Mexico.	31	1	Petition	383	Invalid Pensions	304	Favorable	274	Referred to Committee Whole House.		
Stone, Benjamin F.	Remission of fine for breach of revenue laws.	20	1	Petition	101	Commerce	105	Favorable	120	Passed	Passed	App'd June 23, 1836
Stone, Charles S., & others.	Bounty on fishing schooner Defiance.	29	1	Petition	390	Commerce.						
Stone, Charles S., & others.	Bounty on fishing schooner Defiance.	30	1	Petition	157	Commerce.						
Stone, Charles S., & others.	Bounty on fishing schooner Defiance.	30	2	Petition	209	Commerce.						
Stone, Daniel	(See executors of Anthony Wright)	17	1	....	195							
Stone, David, (Mass.)	Pension for disability, war of 1812.	17	1	Petition	474	Pens. & Rev. Cl'ms.						
Stone, David, (Mass)	Pension for military service in United States army.	18	1	Petition	113	Pens. & Rev. Cl'ms.	....	....	......	Discharged; laid on table.		
Stone, David, (Mass.)	Pension for military service in United States army.	18	2	Petition	51	Military Affairs.						
Stone, David, (Mass.)	Pension for military service in United States army.	19	1	Petition	175	Military Pensions	164	Adverse	......	Leave to withdraw.		

List of private claims presented to the House of Representatives of the United States from the 1st to the 31st Congress, inclusive—Continued.

Names of claimants.	Nature or object of the claim.	Congress.	Session.	How brought before the House of Reps.	Page of journal.	To what committee of the House referred.	No. or date of the report.	Nature of the report.	No. of the bill.	How disposed of by the House of Reps.	How disposed of by the Senate.	Date of the act of Congress, and remarks.
Stone, David, (N. H)	Payment of the claims of sundry assignees.	20	1	Petition	164	Claims.						
Stone, David, (N. H)	Payment of the claims of sundry assignees.	24	2	Senate bill	552	Claims	Mar. 2, 1837	With't amend	S. 135	Referred to Committee Whole House.		
Stone, David, (N. H)	Payment of the claims of sundry assignees.	25	2	Senate bill	197	Claims	541	With amend.	S. 52	Referred to Committee Whole House.		
Stone, David	(See F. and W. Brewster)	21	1		151							
Stone, David, (Ohio)	Compensation for goods delivered Indians on public account.	22	1	Petition	414	Claims	April 12, 1832	Adverse		Laid on table.		
Stone, David, and J. Bellows.	Remission of penalty for violation of non-importation act.	13	2	Petition	386	Ways and Means	April 9, 1814	Adverse		Leave to withdraw.		
Stone, Ebenezer	(See Jonathan Coolidge, heirs of, by attorney.)	26	1		182							
Stone, Ebenezer	(See Moses Brown, executor of.)	26	1		182							
Stone, Ellis, (Indiana.)	Confirmation of title to land	20	1	Petition	310	Public Lands.						
Stone, Emily	(See Benjamin Stone, widow of)	31	1		383							
Stone, Fauntley R.	(See William Thompson)	19	1		312							
Stone, Hannah	(See widow of John Stone)	23	1		714							
Stone, Henry	(See Charles M. Kellar and H. S.)	25	2		763							
Stone, Isaac	Indemnity for French spoliations prior to 1800.	26	1	Memorial	182	Foreign Affairs	343	Favorable; bill	319	Referred to Committee Whole House.		
Stone, Israel P.	(See Daniel Grant, and others)	28	1		130							
Stone, James E.	(See administrator of John Lindsay.)	26	1		323							
Stone, John, widow of	Pension for naval services	23	1	Senate bill	714	Naval Affairs	June 28, 1834	With't amend.	S. 94	Passed	Passed	Appd June 30, 1834
Stone, John	Pension	28	1	Petition	571	Invalid Pensions.						
Stone, John	Pension	28	2	Petition	60	Invalid Pensions	21	Adverse		Laid on table.		
Stone, John	Pension	29	1	Petition	83	Invalid Pensions	42	Adverse		Laid on table.		
Stone, John H., heirs of	Bounty land for revolutionary services and sufferings.	9	1	Petition	249	Public Lands	Feb. 24, 1806	Adverse		Leave to withdraw.		
Stone, John H., heirs of	Bounty land for revolutionary services and sufferings.	9	2	Petition	524	Whole House,						
Stone, John H., heirs of	Commutation pay	15	2	Petition	73	Pens. & Rev. Cl'ms.	Dec. 28, 1818	Adverse		Rejected.		
Stone, John H., heirs of	Commutation pay	17	2	Petition	100	Pens. & Rev. Cl'ms.	Jan. 24, 1823	Adverse		Laid on table.		
Stone, John H., heirs of	Commutation pay	22	2	Petition	29	Claims				Discharged; laid on table.		
Stone, John H., heirs of	Balance of pension	24	1	Petition Petition	52 56	Invalid Pensions Rev. Pensions.	801	Favorable	717	Referred to Committee Whole House.		
Stone, John H., heirs of	Commutation pay and bounty land	24	1	Petition	62	Rev. Pensions	138	Adverse		Laid on table.		
Stone, John H., heirs of	Balance of pension	25	2	Petition	57	Invalid Pensions	458	Favorable	461	Passed.		
Stone, John H., heirs of	Balance of pension	26	1	Resolution	775	Rev. Pensions	520	Favorable	417	Referred to Committee Whole House.		
Stone, John H., heirs of	Balance of pension	27	2	Petition	59	Rev. Pensions	308	Favorable	277	Passed	Indef. postp'd.	
Stone, John H., heirs of	Balance of pension	30	1	Petition	198	Rev. Claims	821	Favorable	638	Referred to Committee Whole House.		
Stone, John H., heirs of	Balance of pension	31	1	Petition	270	Rev. Claims	40	Favorable	69	Referred to Committee Whole House.		
Stone, John H., heirs of	Balance of pension	31	2	Bill of last sess.	75	Whole House	Dec. 20, 1850	With't amend.	69	Postponed.		
Stone, John, (Baltimore)	Payment of money lost in transmission.	18	1	Petition & report Sec. of War.	237, 259	Ways and Means.						
Stone, John, (Baltimore)	Payment of money lost in transmission.	18	2	Petition	41	Ways and Means.						

List of private claims presented to the House of Representatives of the United States from the 1st to the 31st Congress, inclusive—Continued.

Names of claimants.	Nature or object of the claim.	Congress.	Session.	How brought before the House of Reps.	Page of journal.	To what committee of the House referred.	No. or date of the report.	Nature of the report.	No. of the bill.	How disposed of by the House of Reps.	How disposed of by the Senate.	Date of the act of Congress, and remarks.
Stone, John, (Baltimore)..	Payment of money lost in transmission.	19	1	Petition	58	Claims	Feb. 10, 1826	Adverse	......	Laid on table.		
Stone, John, (Baltimore)..	Payment of money lost in transmission.	19	2	Petition	131	Military Pensions.						
Stone, John, (Baltimore)..	Payment of money lost in transmission.	20	1	Petition	58	Ways and Means..	29	Adverse	......	Laid on table.		
Stone, Jonas A..........	Increase of pension	23	2	Petition	304	Invalid Pensions ..	....	....	......	Discharged; laid on table.		
Stone, Jonas A..........	Increase of pension	28	2	Petition	172	Invalid Pensions.						
Stone, Jonathan.........	Indemnity for French spoliations prior to 1800.	26	1	Memorial	182	Foreign Affairs....	343	Favorable; bill	319	Referred to Committee Whole House.		
Stone, Josiah, widow of ..	Benefit of a certain pension act...	30	1	Petition	387	Rev. Pensions.						
Stone, Leman, and others, owners of sloop Polly.	Indemnity for French spoliations prior to 1800.	26	1	Memorial	182	Foreign Affairs....	343	Favorable; bill	319	Referred to Committee Whole House.		
Stone, Leman	Indemnity for French spoliations prior to 1800.	29	2	Memorial ...... Memorial ...... Memorial	198 215 317	Foreign Affairs. Foreign Affairs. Foreign Affairs.						
Stone, Leman, heirs of ...	Indemnity for French spoliations prior to 1800.	31	1	Petition	425	Foreign Affairs....	355	General bill...	318	Referred to Committee Whole House.		
Stone, Lydia	Continuation of a pension.......	28	1	Petition	850	Rev. Pensions.						
Stone, Noyce, (Ohio)	Pension	22	1	Petition	532	Invalid Pensions ..	April 11, 1832	Adverse	......	Laid on table.		
Stone, Robert...........	(See executor of Pickering Dodge.)	31	1	....	215							
Stones, Samuel..........	(See attorney for Benjamin Gott & Son)	16	1	....	284							
Stone, Samuel B.........	Indemnity for French spoliations prior to 1800.	26	1	Memorial	182	Foreign Affairs....	343	Favorable; bill	319	Referred to Committee Whole House.		
Stone, Samuel	Pension for revolutionary services.	27	2	Petition	525	Rev. Pensions	784	Adverse	......	Laid on table.		
Stone, Sardins, widow of .	Pension for revolutionary services.	25	3	Petition	564	Rev. Pensions.						
Stone, Silas	Renewal of pension............	12	1	Petition	42	Select...........	....	....	......	Discharged.		
Stone, Thomas J........	Compensation for a horse lost in public service.	22	1	Petition	384	Claims	Feb. 29, 1832	Adverse	......	Laid on table.		
Stone, Thomas J........	Compensation for a horse lost in public service.	27	2	Petition	56	Claims	342	Adverse	......	Laid on table	....	Leave to withdraw.
Stone, Thomas, assignee of.	Permission to fund loan office certificates.	4	1	Petition	448	Claims.						
Stone, Thomas, assignee of.	Permission to fund loan office certificates.	5	2	Petition	248	Claims	March 3, 1798	Adverse	......	Laid on table.		
Stone & Todd	Remission of certain extra duties..	16	1	Petition	212	Ways and Means.						
Stone, William D.......	To locate 1,000 acres in lieu of a British grant.	18	2	Petition	60	Priv. Land Claims.						
Stone, ———	(See W. and S. Lawrence and others.)	22	1	....	333							
Stoner, Abraham........	Pension for revolutionary services.	25	2	Resolution	976	Rev. Pensions.						
Stoner, John	Compensation for revolutionary services.	2	1	Petition	500	....	....	....	......	Referred to Secretary of War.		
Stoner, John	Compensation for revolutionary services.	3	1	Petition	132	Select.						
Stoney, John...........	(See H. Silliman and others)	12	1	....	98							
Stonisfert, Jacob, (Pa.)...	Compensation for a horse lost in public service.	17	2	Petition	119	Claims	Feb. 26, 1823	Adverse	......	Laid on table.		
Stonisfert, Jacob, (Pa.)...	Compensation for a horse lost in public service.	29	1	Petition	198	Claims	634	Adverse	......	Laid on table.		

List of private claims presented to the House of Representatives of the United States from the 1st to the 31st Congress, inclusive—Continued.

Names of claimants.	Nature or object of the claim.	Congress.	Session.	How brought before the House of Reps.	Page of journal.	To what committee of the House referred.	No. or date of the report.	Nature of the report.	No. of the bill.	How disposed of by the House of Reps.	How disposed of by the Senate.	Date of the act of Congress, and remarks.
Stonisfert, Jacob, (Pa.)	Compensation for a horse lost in public service.	29	2	Petition	56	Claims.						
Stoop, James	Compensation for a horse lost in Seminole war.	23	1	Documents	154	Claims.						
Stoop, James	(See William H. Bedford, agent.)	28	1	....	262							
Stoop, John	Compensation for revolutionary services.	23	1	Petition	493	Rev. Pensions	....	....	......	Discharged; laid on table.		
Stoop, John, administrator of.	Compensation for revolutionary services.	24	1	Petition	613	Rev. Pensions	....	....	......	Discharged; laid on table.		
Stopinal, Widow	Confirmation of title to land in Louisiana.	22	1	General bill	107	Whole House	Mar. 23, 1832	With't amend.	125	Passed	Passed	App'd June 25, 1832
Storer, Dorothy	(See representatives of Robert Hanson Harrison.)	13	3	....	560							
Storer, Ebenezer	Compensation for revolutionary services.	2	2	Senate bill	726	Whole House	....	....	S. 46	Postponed.		
Storer, Ebenezer	Arrears of pension	25	3	Petition	460	Rev. Pensions.						
Storer, Ebenezer	Arrears of pension	26	1	Petition	707	Rev. Pensions	490	Adverse	......	Laid on table.		
Storer, Ebenezer	Arrears of pension	27	2	Petition	47	Rev. Pensions	784	Adverse	......	Laid on table.		
Storer, Ebenezer, widow of.	Pension for revolutionary services.	29	1	Memorial	399	Rev. Pensions	....	....	......	Discharged; laid on table.		
Storer, Eliphalet G	(See William Storer and others)	16	2	....	112							
Storer, George W	Reimbursement of expenses for accompanying Commodore Porter.	22	2	Appropriat'n bill.	69	....	....	....	621	....	....	App'd March 2, 1833
Storer, John, heirs of	Indemnity for French spoliations prior to 1800.	31	1	Petition	285	Foreign Affairs	355	General bill	318	Referred to Committee Whole House.		
Storer, Joseph	Increase of compensation as collector of customs.	14	1	Petition	466	Ways and Means.						
Storer, Joseph	Increase of compensation as collector of customs.	14	2	Petition	39	Ways and Means	Feb. 17, 1817	General bill	112	Passed	Passed	App'd March 3, 1817
Storer, William, and others	Release from a judgment at suit of United States.	16	2	Petition	112	Ways and Means	Jan. 19, 1821	Adverse	......	Laid on table.		
Storer, W., attorney of	(See Lemuel Denniti)	26	1	....	182							
Storer, Woodbury	Indemnity for French spoliations prior to 1800.	26	1	Memorial	182	Foreign Affairs	343	Favorable; bill	319	Referred to Committee Whole House.		
Storrer, John	Indemnity for French spoliations prior to 1800.	26	1	Memorial	182	Foreign Affairs	343	Favorable; bill	319	Referred to Committee Whole House.		
Storke, Thomas	Payment of sundry Virginia bills of credit.	16	1	Petition	42	Pens. & Rev. Cl'ms.	Feb. 7, 1820	Adverse	......	Rejected.		
Storms, Abraham	Compensation for wood supplied during revolutionary war.	4	1	Rep. of Secretary Treasury.	388	Claims	May 31, 1796	Adverse	......	Laid on table.		
Storm, Chauncey, G.	Pension	27	2	Petition	518	Invalid Pensions	623	Adverse	......	Laid on table.		
Storm, Chauncey, G.	Pension	27	3	Petition	137	Invalid Pensions	269	Adverse	......	Laid on table.		
Storm, Chauncey, G.	Pension	28	1	Petition	101	Invalid Pensions.						
				Documents	115	Invalid Pensions	Jan. 31, 1844	Adverse	......	Laid on table.		
Storm, Jacob	Pension for revolutionary services.	28	1	Petition	250	Rev. Pensions	....	....	......	Discharged; laid on table.		
Storm, Thomas H., representatives of.	Balance due him as agent of prisoners.	29	1	Appropriat'n bill.	206	....	....	....	50	....	....	App'd Aug. 10, 1846
Storrs, Lucius, and others.	Compensation for services as revenue officers.	22	1	Petition	220	Commerce.						
Storrs, Lucius, and others.	Compensation for services as revenue officers.	23	1	Petition	156	Ways and Means	....	....	......	Discharged; laid on table.		
Story, Abraham	Pension	24	2	Petition	311	Invalid Pensions	Feb. 14, 1837	Adverse	......	Laid on table.		
Story, Abraham	Pension	25	2	Petition	167	Invalid Pensions	Feb. 17, 1838	Adverse	......	Laid on table.		

List of private claims presented to the House of Representatives of the United States from the 1st to the 31st Congress, inclusive—Continued.

Names of claimants.	Nature or object of the claim.	Congress.	Session.	How brought before the House of Reps.	Page of journal.	To what committee of the House referred.	No. or date of the report.	Nature of the report.	No. of the bill.	How disposed of by the House of Reps.	How disposed of by the Senate.	Date of the act of Congress, and remarks.
Story, Benijah	Compensation for revolutionary services.	27	2	Petition	73	Rev. Claims	1054	Adverse		Laid on table.		
Story, Daniel	Pension for revolutionary services.	26	2	Petition	34	Rev. Pensions	5	Favorable	542	Referred to Committee Whole House.		
Story, Daniel	Pension for revolutionary services.	27	2	Petition	70	Rev. Pensions	105	Favorable	151	Passed	Indef. postp'd.	
Story, Daniel	Pension for revolutionary services.	31	1	Petition	396	Rev. Pensions	62	Adverse		Laid on table.		
Storey, John	(See Charles Fitzimmons & others, attorney of.)	26	1		182							
Storey, John	Compensation for revolutionary services and injuries.	4	1	Petition	406	Claims	Jan. 26, 1796	Adverse		Leave to withdraw.		
Storey, John	Pension	23	1	Petition	129	Invalid Pensions				Discharged; laid on table.		
Storey, Joseph	(See New England Mississippi Land Company.)	10	1		175							
Story, Samuel	Confirmation of title to land in Missouri.	15	1	Petition	262	Priv. Land Claims.						
Story, Samuel	Confirmation of title to land in Missouri.	16	1	Petition	72	Priv. Land Claims.						
Story, Samuel	Confirmation of title to land in Missouri.	17	1	Petition	55	Public Lands.						
Story, William	Settlement of accounts as paymaster, &c.	2	2	Petition	627					Referred to Secretary Treasury.		
Storey, William, widow of	Pension	25	2	Memorial	347	Rev. Pensions				Discharged; referred to Com. Whole House on bill No. 456.		
Story, William	Compensation for services as clerk, revolutionary war.	2	1	Petition	626					Referred to Secretary Treasury.		
Story, William	Compensation for services as clerk, revolutionary war.	3	2	Petition	264	Claims	Feb. 27, 1795	Adverse		Laid on table.		
Story, William	Compensation for services as clerk, revolutionary war.	4	1	Rep. of Secretary War.	445	Claims.						
Story, William	Compensation for services as clerk, revolutionary war.	4	2	Rep. of Secretary War.	614	Claims	Jan. 2, 1797	Adverse		Rejected.		
Stotesbury, John	Indemnity for revolutionary disabilities.	5	2	Petition	246	Claims	April 17, 1798	Adverse		Laid on table.		
Stotesbury, John	Indemnity for revolutionary disabilities.	5	3	Petition	432					Referred to Committee Whole House.		
Stotesbury, John	Indemnity for revolutionary disabilities.	6	1	Petition	551	Claims	Feb. 11, 1800	Adverse		Rejected.		
Stotesbury, Sarah	(See children of Hugh Hughes)	15	1		293							
Stothart and Starkey	Remission of penalty under non-importation act.	13	1	Petition	78	Ways and Means.						
Stothart and Starkey	Remission of penalty under non-importation act.	13	2	Senate bill	276	Ways and Means.	Feb. 10, 1814	With't amend.	S. 33	Passed	Passed	App'd Feb. 12, 1814
Stothart, William	Reimbursement of duty on defective merchandise.	15	2	Petition	70	Ways and Means.	Dec. 16, 1818	Adverse		Rejected.		
Stott, Ebenezer, & Co., attorney of.	Indemnity for French spoliations prior to 1800.	26	1	Memorial	182	Foreign Affairs	343	Favorable; bill	319	Referred to Committee Whole House.		
Stott, Robert	(See Robert Scott.)	18	1		330							
Stouf, Isidore	Reimbursement of expenses as temporary engineer.	7	1	Petition	136	Claims				Discharged; and postponed.		
Stouf, Isidore	Reimbursement of expenses as temporary engineer.	7	2	Petition	297	Claims	Feb. 19, 1803	Adverse		Leave to withdraw.		

List of private claims presented to the House of Representatives of the United States from the 1st to the 31st Congress, inclusive—Continued.

Names of claimants.	Nature or object of the claim.	Congress.	Session.	How brought before the House of Reps.	Page of journal.	To what committee of the House referred.	No. or date of the report.	Nature of the report.	No. of the bill.	How disposed of by the House of Reps.	How disposed of by the Senate.	Date of the act of Congress, and remarks.
3—54 Stouffer & Cross	Indemnity for French spoliations prior to 1800.	26	1	Memorial	182	Foreign Affairs	343	Favorable; bill	319	Referred to Committee Whole House.		
Stouffer, Henry	(See heirs of John Stouffer.)	29	2		70							
Stouffer, Henry	(See Stouffer & Cross)	26	1		182							
Stouffer, John, heirs of	Indemnity for French spoliations prior to 1800.	29	2	Petition	70	Foreign Affairs.						
Stoughton, Gustavus	Pension	21	2	Petition	270	Military Pensions.						
Stoule, Freegift	(See Z. M. Pike, and companions)	10	1		189							
Stout, Aaron	Bounty land for military services.	24	1	Petition	261	Priv. Land Claims.	595	Favorable	578	Referred to Committee Whole House.		
Stout, Aaron	Bounty land for military services.	25	2	Petition	42	Priv. Land Claims.	Jan. 4, 1838	Favorable	296	Referred to Committee Whole House.		
Stout, Aaron	Bounty land for military services.	25	3	Bill of last sess.	376	Whole House	Jan. 25, 1839	With't amend.	296	Passed	Passed	App'd March 3, 1839
Stout, Abraham	Pension for revolutionary services.	5	3	Petition	472	Claims	Mar. 2, 1799	Indefinite.				
Stout, Abraham	Pension for revolutionary services.	7	2	Petition	283	Claims				Discharged; leave to withdraw.		
Stout, Caleb	Pension for revolutionary services.	22	1	Resolution	178	Rev. Pensions	367	Pension bill	462	Passed	Indef. postp'd.	
Stout, David R	(See assignee of Matthew Simons)	24	1		1077							
Stout, John N	Compensation for support of a prisoner, (Barnaby.)	10	1	Petition	119	Claims.						
Stout, John N	Compensation for support of a prisoner, (Barnaby.)	10	2	Petition	354	Claims	Feb. 4, 1809	Favorable	160	Referred to Committee Whole House.		
Stout, John N	Compensation for support of a prisoner, (Barnaby.)	11	2	Petition	114	Claims	Dec. 21, 1809	Favorable	47	Passed	Passed	App'd Feb. 14, 1810
Stout, John N	Compensation for support of a prisoner, (Hamilton.)	12	1	Petition	183	Claims	Mar. 6, 1812	Favorable	82	Passed	Passed	App'd May 20, 1812
Stout, John	Pension for revolutionary services.	20	1	Resolution	200	Military Pensions.						
				Resolution	303	Military Pensions.	April 29, 1828	Pension bill	283	Passed.		
Stout, John	Pension for revolutionary services.	20	2	Pension bill	55	Whole House	Jan. 15, 1829	With amend.	311	Passed	Laid on table.	
Stout, John	Pension for revolutionary services.	21	1	Petition	48	Military Pensions.	Jan. 5, 1830	Pension bill	72	Passed	Passed	App'd May 20, 1833
Stout, John	Pension for revolutionary services.	29	1	Petition	625	Rev. Pensions.						
Stout, John	Pension for revolutionary services.	29	2	Petition	150	Rev. Pensions	12	Adverse		Laid on table.		
Stout, Joseph	Compensation for revolutionary services.	2	1	Petition	451					Referred to Secretary of War.		
Stout, Joseph	Compensation for revolutionary services.	3	2	Rep. of Secretary War.	278					Laid on table.		
Stout, Samuel, representatives of.	Prize-money for an Algerine capture.	24	1	Petition	214	Naval Affairs	Feb. 4, 1836	Favorable	276	Referred to Committee Whole House.		
				Senate bill	811	Naval Affairs	May 17, 1836	With amend.	S. 186	Passed with amendm't.	Passed as am'd	App'd July 2, 1836
Stout, William	Compensation for a horse captured by Indians.	25	3	Petition	12	Claims	128	Adverse		Laid on table.		
Stoval, Archelaus H.	Compensation for mail service	31	1	Petition	623	P. Of. & P. Roads						
Stoval, Archelaus H.	Compensation for mail service	31	2	Petition	445	P. Of. & P. Roads.				Discharged; laid on table.		
Stow, Amos	Pension	21	1	Resolution	207	Military Pensions.						
Stow, Clark	Pension for revolutionary services.	25	2	Petition	54	Rev. Pensions	Feb. 2, 1838	Adverse		Laid on table.		
Stow, George	Indemnity for property destroyed by the enemy.	15	2	Petition	148	Claims	Jan. 16, 1819	Adverse		Laid on table.		
Stow, Samuel	Compensation for revolutionary services and supplies.	4	1	Petition	566	Claims.						
Stow, Samuel	Compensation for revolutionary services and supplies.	4	2	Petition	614	Claims	Jan. 5, 1797	Adverse		Rejected.		
Stowell, Nathaniel	Pension	15	1	Petition	23	Pens. & Rev. Cl'ms.						

List of private claims presented to the House of Representatives of the United States from the 1st to the 31st Congress, inclusive—**Continued.**

Names of claimants.	Nature or object of the claim.	Congress.	Session.	How brought before the House of Reps.	Page of journal.	To what committee of the House referred.	No. or date of the report.	Nature of the report.	No. of the bill.	How disposed of by the House of Reps.	How disposed of by the Senate.	Date of the act of Congress, and remarks.
Stoy Peter	Pension for revolutionary disabilities	1	3	Petition	388					Referred to Secretary War.		
Stoy, Samuel	Confirmation of title to land in Missouri.	18	1	Petition	55	Public Lands.						
Straber, Peter, heirs of	Compensation for revolutionary services	31	2	Petition	36	Rev. Claims	6	Adverse		Laid on table.		
Strachan, Wm., and others	Increase of compensation as inspector of customs.	3	2	Petition	274	Select	Jan. 26, 1795	Favorable	75	Passed	Passed, with amendments.	App'd Feb. 14, 1795
Strader, George	Pension	23	2	Petition	140	Rev. Pensions				Discharged; laid on table.		
Strader, John M	Compensation for mail service	26	2	Senate bill	229	P. Of. & P. Roads			S. 149			
Strahan, Charles	(See Gregory Strahan, heirs of.)	13	1		18							
Strahan, Gregory, heir of	Indemnity for losses as Canadian refugee.	13	1	Petition	18	Claims.						
Strahan, Gregory, heir of	Indemnity for losses as Canadian refugee.	19	1	Petition	44	Pens. & Rev. Cl'ms.	17	Adverse		Recommitted		
				Petition	278	Rev. Claims	Feb. 22, 1846	Bill as per instruction.	114	Passed.		
Strahan, Gregory, heir of	Indemnity for losses as Canadian refugee.	19	2	Petition	32	Rev. Claims	9	Favorable	298	Passed	Passed	App'd March 2, 1827
Strahan, Gregory, heir of	Indemnity for losses as Canadian refugee.	22	2	Petition	172	Rev. Claims.						
Strahan, Gregory, heir of	Indemnity for losses as Canadian refugee.	23	1	Petition	70	Rev. Claims.						
Strahan, Gregory, heir of	Indemnity for losses as Canadian refugee.	23	2	Petition	55	Rev. Claims.						
Strahan, Joseph	(See heirs of Gregory Strahan)	13	1		18							
Strains, Robert, (Tenn)	Compensation for two rifles taken for public use.	18	1	Petition	114	Claims	Feb. 18, 1824	Favorable	129	Passed	Passed	App'd May 20, 1824
Stranaghan, James	(See administrator of William and Hugh Shannon.)	19	1		269							
Stranahan, William	Exchange of an entry of land	15	1	Petition	360	Public Lands.						
Stranahan, William	Exchange of an entry of land	15	2	Petition	89	Public Lands	Dec. 17, 1818	Adverse		Laid on table.		
Strange, James	Remission of duty on shipwrecked salt.	3	2	Petition	332	Select	Feb. 21, 1795	Not found		Referred to Committee Whole House.		
Strange, James	Remission of duty on shipwrecked salt.	4	1	Petition	422	Com. and Manuf.	Feb. 8, 1796	Not found		Laid on table.		
Strange, James	(See heir of John Strange)	21	1		497							
Strange, James	Compensation for forage on public account.	30	1	Petition	435	Claims.						
Strange, John, heir of	Bounty land	21	1	Petition	497	Rev. Claims.						
Strange, Lucy	(See daughter of Eliphalet Spafford)	25	3	Petition	124	Rev. Claims.						
Strange, Washington	Grant of land for military services.	28	1	Petition	357	Public Lands	255	Adverse		Laid on table.		
Stratton, Aaron	Compensation for revolutionary services.	2	1	Petition	483					Referred to Secretary of War.		
				Petition	490					Referred to Secretary of War.		
Stratton, Aaron	Compensation for revolutionary services.	2	2	Rep. of Secretary War.	711					Laid on table.		
Stratton, Aaron	Compensation for revolutionary services	3	2	Rep. of Secretary War.	278					Laid on table.		
Stratton, Aaron	(See administrator of Samuel Gilbert.)	4	1		45							

List of private claims presented to the House of Representatives of the United States from the 1st to the 31st Congress, inclusive—Continued.

Names of claimants.	Nature or object of the claim.	Congress.	Session.	How brought before the House of Reps.	Page of journal.	To what committee of the House referred.	No. or date of the report.	Nature of the report.	No. of the bill.	How disposed of by the House of Reps.	How disposed of by the Senate.	Date of the act of Congress, and remarks.
Stratton, Franklin	Confirmation of title to land in Illinois.	28	1	Petition	787	Priv. Land Claims.						
Stratton, Jonathan	To be restored to pension roll	17	1	Petition	26	Rev. Pensions.						
Stratton, Jonathan F., and others.	Compensation for laying out a road.	22	1	Petition	264	Public Lands	Feb. 24, 1832	Adverse		Referred to Committee Whole House.		
Stratton, Polly	Continuation of pension	28	1	Petition	850	Rev. Pensions.						
Stratton, Thomas	Compensation for revolutionary services.	26	1	Petition	359	Rev. Claims	447	Adverse		Laid on table.		
Stratton, Thomas	Compensation for revolutionary services.	27	2	Petition	73	Rev. Claims	358	Adverse		Laid on table.		
Stratton, Thomas	Compensation for revolutionary services.	28	1	Petition	251	Rev. Claims.						
Stratton, Thomas	Compensation for revolutionary services.	28	2	Petition	57	Rev. Pensions.						
Straughan, John	Pay and rations as quartermaster.	26	2	Petition	78	Naval Affairs.						
Straw, Jacob	(See heirs of Wm. Marshall)	30	1		287							
Straw, Heziah	(See heirs of Wm Marshall)	30	1		287							
Straw, Nicholas	Pension for revolutionary services.	20	2	Resolution	124	Military Pensions.						
Straw, Nicholas	Pension for revolutionary services	22	1	Petition	412	Rev. Pensions.						
Strawn, Joel	Indemnity for property destroyed to public use.	13	2	Petition	298	Claims				Discharged; referred to Com. W. House.		
Strawn, Joel	Indemnity for property destroyed in public use.	13	3	Petition	509	Claims	Nov. 14, 1814	Favorable	228	Passed	Indef. postp'd.	Leave to withdraw, March 2, 1815.
Strawn, Joel	Indemnity for property destroyed in public use.	17	1	Petition	206	Claims	Feb. 22, 1822	Adverse		Laid on table.		
Strayer, Jacob, (Va.)	Pension for revolutionary services.	23	1	Petition	242	Rev. Pensions				Discharged; laid on table.		
Streegle, Nicholas, (Ga.)	Pension	21	2	Petition	270	Military Pensions.						
Street, Joseph M	(See Jonathan Taylor and J. M. Street)	16	1		102							
Street, Joseph M	(See David E. Twiggs and others)	22	1		540							
Street, Joseph M	Reimbursement of attorney's fees in a certain suit.	23	1	Appropriat'n bill.	253	Whole House	June 26, 1834	With amends.	238	Passed	Passed	App'd June 28, 1834
Street, Solomon	Pension	30	1	Petition	738	Invalid Pensions	720	Adverse		Laid on table.		
Street, William W	Compensation for steamboat service.	27	2	Petition	227	Claims.						
Street, William W	Compensation for steamboat service.	27	3	Petition	176	Claims	77	Favorable	707	Passed	Passed	App'd Feb. 4, 1843
Streper, William	Pension for revolutionary services.	20	1	Resolution	272	Military Pensions.						
				Petition	278	Military Pensions				Discharged; laid on table.		
Streshley, Thomas	Release from a judgment at suit of United States.	9	1	Petition	250	Claims	Feb. 28, 1806	Adverse		Leave to withdraw.		
Streshley, Thos. and Wm.	Equitable settlement of their account.	12	1	Senate bill	294	Claims	May 15, 1812	With amend.	S. 24	Passed with amend't.	Passed as am'd	App'd May 22, 1812
Stretch, Joseph	(See Leighton Wood and others).	3	1		88							
Stretch, Joseph	(See administrator of Jos. Wright)	3	2		261							
Strickland, Lot	Pension	25	2	Petition	83	Rev. Pensions.						
Strickland, Samuel	Pension for revolutionary services.	28	1	Petition	632	Rev. Pensions.						
Strickland, Titus	(See guardian of heirs of N. Holcum.)	15	1		65							
Strickland, Vincent J	Compensation for cattle taken by soldiers.	26	2	Petition	135	Claims.						

List of private claims presented to the House of Representatives of the United States from the 1st to the 31st Congress, inclusive—Continued.

Names of claimants.	Nature or object of the claim.	Congress.	Session.	How brought before the House of Reps.	Page of journal.	To what committee of the House referred.	No. or date of the report.	Nature of the report.	No. of the bill.	How disposed of by the House of Reps.	How disposed of by the Senate.	Date of the act of Congress, and remarks.
Strickland, Vincent J	Compensation for cattle taken by soldiers.	27	2	Petition	94	Claims	641	Adverse	......	Laid on table.		
Strickler, John, and others.	Further compensation for services, war of 1812.	31	1	Petition	638	Rev. Pensions	138	General bill	152	Referred to Committee Whole House.		
Strider, William	Indemnity for non-fulfilment of a government contract.	25	2	Petition	575	Claims	810	Adverse	......	Laid on table.		
Strider, William	Indemnity for non-fulfilment of a government contract.	25	3	Petition	212	Military Affairs.						
Strider, William	Indemnity for non-fulfilment of a government contract.	27	2	Petition	764	Claims.						
Striker, John	(See George Sears, administrator of.)	26	1	Petition	18							
Stringer, Francis, & others	Confirmation of a Spanish grant of land.	12	1	Petition	13	Public Lands.						
Stringer, Francis, & others	Confirmation of a Spanish grant of land	12	2	Petition	663	Public Lands.						
Stringer, Francis, & others	Confirmation of a Spanish grant of land.	13	3	Petition	762	......	......	......	......	Laid on table.		
Stringer, Francis, & others	Confirmation of a Spanish grant of land.	14	1	Petition	66	Public Lands.						
Stringer, Francis, & others	Location of confirmed title on unlocated land.	14	1	Petition	147	Public Lands.						
Stringer, Francis, & others	Location of confirmed title on unlocated land.	14	2	Petition	50	Priv. Land Claims.	Jan. 17, 1817	Adverse	......	Rejected.		
Stringer, Francis, representatives of.	Right of pre-emption to land in Alabama.	16	1	Petition	170	Priv. Land Claims.						
Stringer, Francis, administrator of.	Right of pre-emption to land in Alabama.	16	1	Petition	105	Public Lands.						
Stringer, Francis, administrator of	Indemnity for land of deceased sold by government.	24	2	Petition	391	Priv. Land Claims.						
Stringer, Francis, administrator of.	Indemnity for land of deceased sold by government.	25	2	Petition	179	Priv. Land Claims.						
Stringer, Francis, administrator of.	Indemnity for land of deceased sold by government.	25	3	Petition	133	Priv. Land Claims.						
Stringer, William	(See Francis Stringer, representatives of.)	16	1	......	170							
Stringham, S. H	Money in lieu of quarters navy-yard, New York.	25	2	Documents	398	Naval Affairs.						
Strohecker, John, & others	Reimbursement of money paid by insurance company.	28	2	Petition	145	Foreign Affairs.						
Strohecker, John, & others	Reimbursement of money paid by insurance company.	29	1	Petition	220	Foreign Affairs.						
Strohecker, John, & others	Reimbursement of money paid by insurance company.	30	1	Petition	290	Foreign Affairs.						
Strohm, Hon. John	(See Richard E. Cockran, heirs of.)	29	2	......	181							
Stroman, John	Additional compensation for revolutionary services.	23	1	Petition	305	Rev. Pensions.	......	......	......	Discharged; laid on table.		
Strong, Adonijah	Compensation for services as a revolutionary officer.	10	1	Petition	23	Select.						
Strong, Chloe	(See David Strong, widow of.)											
Strong, David, widow of	Compensation for revolutionary services and losses.	9	1	Petition	248	Claims	Jan. 31, 1806	Adverse	......	Leave to withdraw.		

List of private claims presented to the House of Representatives of the United States from the 1st to the 31st Congress, inclusive—Continued.

Names of claimants.	Nature or object of the claim.	Congress.	Session.	How brought before the House of Reps.	Page of journal.	To what committee of the House referred.	No. or date of the report.	Nature of the report.	No. of the bill.	How disposed of by the House of Reps.	How disposed of by the Senate.	Date of the act of Congress, and remarks.
Strong, David, widow of	Compensation for revolutionary services and losses.	10	1	Petition	213	Claims.						
Strong, David, widow of	Compensation for revolutionary services and losses.	11	2	Petition	123	Claims	Dec. 28, 1809	Adverse	......	Rejected.		
Strong, David, widow of	Compensation for revolutionary services and losses.	13	1	Petition	18	Claims	....	....	......	Discharged.		
Strong, David, widow of	Compensation for revolutionary services and losses.	13	2	Petition	202	Pens. & Rev. Cl'ms.	Jan. 25, 1814	Adverse	......	Laid on table.		
Strong, Eben	To be placed on the pension roll	27	2	Resolution	64	Rev. Pensions.						
Strong, Eleazer	Pension	21	2	Petition	158	Military Pensions.						
Strong, Elijah, widow of	Half pay due widow of deceased officers.	12	1	Petition	85	Select.						
Strong, Harriet	(See Benjamin W. Hopkins, heirs of.)	21	1	Senate bill	118	Claims	....	....	S. 14			
Strong, Jasper, and others	Compensation for slaves lost in public service	25	2	Petition	1209	Naval Affairs.						
Strong, John	(See representatives of Charles & James Knowles.)	18	1	....	113							
Strong, John	Remission of fine as a mail contractor.	23	1	Petition	353	P. Of. & P. Roads.	Mar. 4, 1834	Adverse	......	Laid on table.		
Strong, John, representative of.	Pension for revolutionary services.	28	1	Petition	944	Rev. Pensions.						
Strong, John, wife of	(See heir of Charles Knowles)	9	2	....	471							
Strong, John, widow of	Pension for revolutionary services.	25	2	Petition	54	Rev. Pensions	542	Favorable	536	Passed	Adverse report.	
Strong, John, widow of	Pension for revolutionary services.	25	3	Petition	88	Rev. Pensions	Jan. 2, 1839	Favorable	970	Passed	Adverse report	
Strong, John, widow of	Pension for revolutionary services.	26	1	Petition	172	Rev. Pensions	143	Favorable	153	Passed	Indef. postp'd.	
Strong, John B., attorney for heirs of.	Confirmation of title to land in Florida.	22	2	Petition	185	Priv. Land Claims.						
Strong, Joseph	(See representative of John Strong)	28	1	....	944							
Strong, Josiah	Pension for revolutionary services.	24	1	Petition	56	Invalid Pensions	478	Favorable	480	Referred to Committee Whole House.		
Strong, Josiah	Pension for revolutionary services.	24	2	Bill of last sess	198	Whole House	Jan. 13, 1837	With't amend.	480	Passed	Indef. postp'd.	
Strong, Josiah	Pension for revolutionary services.	25	2	Petition	39	Invalid Pensions	302	Favorable	253	Postponed.		
Strong, Josiah	Pension for revolutionary services.	25	3	House bill	155	....	....	....	253	Laid on table.		
Strong, Josiah	Pension for revolutionary services.	26	1	Petition	161	Invalid Pensions	222	Favorable	234	Passed	Indef. postp'd.	
Strong, Levi	Pension	22	1	Petition	329	Rev. Pensions	348	Pension bill	444	Passed	Passed, with amendment	
Strong, Levi	Pension	22	2	Petition	89	Invalid Pensions	Feb. 13, 1833	Pension bill	738	Referred to Committee Whole House.		
Strong, Levi	Pension	23	1	Petition	51	Invalid Pensions	37	Pension bill	42	Passed	Passed, with amendment.	App'd June 30, 1834
Strong, Martha	(See John Strong, widow of)	25	2	....	54							
Strong, Martha	(See representatives of Charles & James Knowles.	18	1	....	113							
Strong, Moses M.	Compensation for public services.	27	2	Petition	385	Claims	748	Favorable	426	Rejected.		
Strong, Nathan	(See Reuben Smith & N. S.)	3	1	....	149							
Strong, Rev. Nathan	Liquidation of three revolutionary certificates.	4	1	Rep. of Secretary Treasury.	388	Claims	May 31, 1796	Adverse	......	Laid on table.		
Strong, Nathan & Sibel	(See widow of Thomas Barnes)	25	3	....	87							
Strong, Robert, (Mass.)	Indemnity for French spoliations prior to 1800.	26	1	Memorial	182	Foreign Affairs	343	Favorable; bill	319	Referred to Committee Whole House.		
Strong, Roger	Pension for revolutionary services.	22	1	Petition	44	Rev. Pensions	53	Favorable	104	Passed.		
Strong, Roger	Pension for revolutionary services.	22	2	Petition	142	Invalid Pensions	Feb. 7, 1833	Adverse	......	Laid on table.		

List of private claims presented to the House of Representatives of the United States from the 1st to the 31st Congress, inclusive—Continued.

Names of claimants.	Nature or object of the claim.	Congress.	Session.	How brought before the House of Reps.	Page of journal.	To what committee of the House referred.	No. or date of the report.	Nature of the report.	No. of the bill.	How disposed of by the House of Reps.	How disposed of by the Senate.	Date of the act of Congress, and remarks.
Strong, Roger	Pension for revolutionary services.	24	1	Petition	107	Invalid Pensions				Discharged; laid on table.		
Strong, Submit R.	(See Elijah Strong, widow of)	12	1		85							
Strong, Wolcott A.	(See Pierre S. Durbanne)	28	1		107		148		136			
Strother, Benjamin	Reimbursement of expenditure on recruiting service.	4	1	Petition	384	Claims	Feb. 5, 1796	Favorable; bill ordered.	146	Passed	Passed	App'd Feb. 26, 1796
Strother, Benjamin	Pension for revolutionary services.	11	2	Pension bill	283				107	Passed	Passed, with amendment.	App'd April 17, 1810
Strother, Daniel, (Ind.)	Pension	23	1	Resolution	501	Rev. Pensions				Discharged; laid on table.		
Strother, Daniel, (Ind.)	Pension	25	3	Resolution	128	Rev. Pensions.						
Strother, Francis	Redemption of Continental money.	29	1	Petition	96	Rev. Claims.				Discharged; laid on table.		
Strother, George F	Equitable settlement of accounts as receiver.	24	1	Senate bill	1128	Claims	836	Adverse	S. 240	Referred to Committee Whole House.		
Strother, George F	Equitable settlement of accounts as receiver.	24	2	Senate bill	260	Judiciary	Feb. 14, 1837	With't amend.	S. 24	Passed	Passed	App'd March 3, 1837
Strother, Jane	To be placed on pension roll	27	2	Resolution	81	Rev. Pensions				Discharged; laid on table.		
Stroud, Hampton	Pension	20	1	Petition	417	Military Pensions	May 13, 1828	Adverse		Laid on table.		
Stroud, Joseph	Indemnity for revolutionary sufferings.	9	1	Petition	268	Claims				Discharged; referred to Com. Whole House.		
Stroud, Joseph	Pension for sundry revolutionary services.	10	2	Petition	367	Claims.						
Stroud, Joseph	Pension for sundry revolutionary services.	12	1	Petition	172	Claims.						
Stroud, Joseph	(See daughter of Jonathan Carver)	18	1		252							
Stroud, Martha	(See daughter of Jonathan Carver)	18	1		252							
Strowman, Henry	(See heirs and executor of Ulrick Reeser.)	21	1		50				142			
Stroyer, Matthias	Relief in consideration of destruction of armory.	6	1	Petition	809	Claims				Postponed.		
Stroyer, Matthias	Relief in consideration of destruction of armory.	7	1	Petition	19	Claims				Postponed.		
Stroyer, Matthias, widow of.	Pension for revolutionary services.	25	2	Petition	984	Rev. Pensions.						
Strullen, Louis	Reimbursement of duties illegally exacted.	28	1	Petition	188	Commerce.						
Struthers, John	Pension for revolutionary services.	27	2	Petition	790	Rev. Pensions				Discharged; laid on table		
Stryker, Barent	Extra compensation for mail service.	27	2	Resolution	856	P. Of. and P. Roads	847	Favorable	490	Referred to Committee Whole House.		
Stryker, Barent	Extra compensation for mail service.	27	3	Bill of last sess.	89	Whole House	Dec. 23, 1842	With't amend.	490	Passed	Passed	App'd Feb. 4, 1843
Stryker, Dennis, widow of.	Pension for revolutionary services.	28	1	Petition	256	Rev. Pensions				Discharged; laid on table.		
Stryker, John	(See Johannes E. Lott and others).	5	2		144							
Stryker, Mary	(See Dennis Stryker, widow of)	28	1		256							
Stryker, Michael	(See Johannes E. Lott and others).	5	2		144							
Stuart, Alexander	(See surety of John Ricaud)	14	2		128							
Stuart, Catharine	(See William Stuart, widow of)	25	2		1119							
Stuart, Charles	Indemnity for disability incurred in public service.	30	1	Petition	899	Claims.						

List of private claims presented to the House of Representatives of the United States from the 1st to the 31st Congress, inclusive—**Continued.**

Names of claimants.	Nature or object of the claim.	Congress.	Session.	How brought before the House of Reps.	Page of journal.	To what committee of the House referred.	No. or date of the report.	Nature of the report.	No. of the bill.	How disposed of by the House of Reps.	How disposed of by the Senate.	Date of the act of Congress, and remarks.
Stuart, Charles	Indemnity for disability incurred in public service.	30	2	Petition	116	Claims	106	Favorable	788	Referred to Committee Whole House.		
Stuart, Charles	Indemnity for disability incurred in public service.	31	1	Petition	269	Claims	103	Favorable	120	Passed	Passed	**App'd Sept. 28, 1850**
Stuart, Elizabeth	Pension	27	3	Documents	421	Rev. Pensions.						
Stuart, James, & J. Barr	Remission of duties on salt destroyed.	4	1	Petition	556	Com. and Manuf.						
Stuart, James, & J. Barr	Remission of duties on salt destroyed.	4	2	Memorial	629	Com. and Manuf.	Dec. 27, 1796	Adverse	......	Rejected.		
Stuart, James, widow of	Pension for military services	15	2	Petition	163	Select	Jan. 25, 1819	Favorable	290	Passed	Passed	**App'd March 3, 1819**
Stuart, Phœbe	(See James Stuart, widow of.)											
Stuart, Silas	Pension	25	2	Petition	400	Invalid Pensions	......	......	......	Discharged; laid on table.		
Stuart, William, widow of.	Pension for revolutionary services.	25	2	Petition	1119	Rev. Claims	......	......	......	Discharged; laid on table.		
Stubblefield, Seth	Pension for revolutionary services.	17	1	Petition	50	Pens. & Rev. Cl'ms.	Dec. 21, 1821	Adverse	......	Laid on table.		
Stubblefield, William	(See Benjamin Farrar, and others)	11	1	......	41							
Stubblefield, William	Pension for services in Indian wars.	28	1	Petition	443	Rev. Pensions	......	......	......	Discharged; laid on table.		
Stubblefield, William	Pension for services in Indian wars	28	2	Petition	72	Rev. Pensions.						
Stubblefield, William	Pension for services in Indian wars.	29	1	Petition	399	Rev. Pensions	608	Adverse	......	Laid on table.		
Stubbs, Benjamin, heirs of.	Pension for revolutionary services.	29	1	Memorial	821	Rev. Pensions	826	Adverse	......	Laid on table.		
Stubbs, Joel H.	(See heir of Benjamin Stubbs)	29	1	......	82							
Stubbs, John G	Compensation for services as surveyor.	15	1	Senate bill	104	Whole House	Mar. 21, 1818	With't amend.	S. 5	Passed	Passed	**App'd April 3, 1818**
Stubbs, Joseph	Pension	22	1	Petition	103	Invalid Pensions.						
Studley, John	(See Charles Cramer, and others.)	21	1	......	375							
Studley, William	(See Wm. L. Hupper, and others.)	14	2	......	39							
Stull, Frederick	Pension for revolutionary services.	20	1	Resolution	382	Military Pensions.	April 29, 1828	Favorable	283	Passed.		
Stull, Frederick	Pension for revolutionary services.	20	2	Pension bill	55	Whole House	Jan. 15, 1829	With amend.	311	Passed	Laid on table.	
Stull, Frederick	Pension for revolutionary services	21	1	Petition	49	Military Pensions.	Jan. 5, 1830	Pension bill.	72	Passed	Passed	**App'd May 20, 1830**
Stump, Christopher, widow of.	Compensation for revolutionary services.	27	1	Petition	107	Rev. Claims.						
Stump, Elizabeth	(See Christopher Stump, widow of.)											
Stump, John	Correction of a public survey	15	2	Petition	250	Public Lands.						
Stump, John	Correction of a public survey	16	1	Petition	59	Public Lands.						
Sturdevant, James	Pension for revolutionary services.	22	1	Petition	46	Rev. Claims	Dec. 28, 1831	Adverse	......	Laid on table.		
Sturdevant, John	Compensation for horses captured by Indians.	16	1	Petition	8	Claims	Jan. 17, 1820	Adverse	......	Laid on table.		
Sturdevant, Jonathan	Pension for revolutionary services.	22	1	Petition	124	Rev. Pensions	Mar. 13, 1832	Favorable	467	Passed	Indef. postp'd.	
Sturgeon, Hance	Compensation for horse, &c., lost in Indian wars.	24	1	Petition	430	Claims.						
Sturgeon, Robert	Release from imprisonment	5	2	Petition	414	Select	Feb. 13, 1799	Favorable; bill ordered.	165	Passed	Rejected.	
Sturgeon, Robert	Release from imprisonment	6	1	Petition	53	Select	Jan. 17, 1800	Favorable; bill ordered.	189	Passed	Passed, with amendment.	App'd April 5, 1800
Sturgeon, William, (Va.)	Retained bounty, &c., for military services.	21	2	Petition	55	Priv. Land Claims	......	......	......	Referred to Secretary War.		
Sturges, Benjamin	Pension for revolutionary services.	3	2	Rep. of Secretary War.	337	Claims	Feb. 28, 1795	Favorable; bill ordered.	130	Passed	Postponed.	
Sturges, Benjamin	Pension for revolutionary services.	4	1	Rep. of Secretary War.	445	Claims	Feb. 18, 1796	Favorable; bill ordered.	156	Passed	Passed	App'd April 20, 1796
Sturges, Benjamin	Increase of pension	10	2	Pension bill	499	Whole House	......	......	158	Passed	Passed	**App'd March 3, 1809**

List of private claims presented to the House of Representatives of the United States from the 1st to the 31st Congress, inclusive—Continued.

Names of claimants.	Nature or object of the claim.	Congress.	Session.	How brought before the House of Reps.	Page of journal.	To what committee of the House referred.	No. or date of the report.	Nature of the report.	No. of the bill.	How disposed of by the House of Reps.	How disposed of by the Senate.	Date of the act of Congress, and remarks.
Sturges, David	Indemnity for revolutionary wounds and disability.	1	1	Petition	60					Laid on table.		
Sturges, David	Indemnity for revolutionary wounds and disability.	1	2	Resol'n and rep't Sec. of War.	143, 176					Laid on table.		
Sturges, Doane, & Co.	(See George Brown, and others)	22	1		253							
Sturges, Hill	Pension for revolutionary services.	11	1	Petition	30	Claims.						
Sturges, J. S.	(See Wm. H Hoag, and others)	27	3		153							
Sturges, Jonathan, children of.	Compensation for revolutionary supplies.	2	1	Petition	503					Referred to Secretary Treasury.		
Sturgis, Jonathan, children of.	Compensation for revolutionary supplies.	3	2	Rep. of Secretary Treasury.	284					Laid on table.		
Sturges, Josiah	Indemnity for property sunk in revenue cutter.	25	2	Petition	165	Commerce.						
Sturges, Josiah	Indemnity for property sunk in revenue cutter.	26	1	Petition	177	Commerce	383	Adverse		Laid on table.		
Sturges, Josiah	Indemnity for property sunk in revenue cutter.	29	1	Petition	450	Commerce	404	Adverse		Laid on table		Leave to withdraw.
Sturges & Parkman	Permission to import Irish linen	10	2	Petition	414	Com. and Manuf.						
Sturges, Solomon	(See assignee of Rezin Frazier)	24	1		215							
Sturges, Solomon	(See assignee of Humphrey Rich creek.)	26	1		954							
Sturges, William, (Md)	Indemnity for destruction of property on the Patuxent.	14	1	Petition	467	Naval Affairs	Mar. 28, 1816	Does not appear.				
Sturgett, Francis	(See James C. Wilkins, and others)	21	2		47							
Sturtevant, Ephraim	(See Silas Sturtevant, heirs of.)	16	2		246							
Sturtevant, Hannah	(See Isaac Sturtevant, widow of.)	26	1		324							
Sturtevant, Isaac, widow of.	Continuation of pension	26	1	Petition	324	Rev. Pensions	424	Adverse		Laid on table.		
Sturtevant, Isaac, widow of.	Continuation of pension	26	2	Petition	55	Invalid Pensions.						
Sturtevant, Jonathan	Pension	21	1	Petition	143	Military Pensions	May 3, 1830	Favorable	454	Referred to Committee Whole House.		
Sturtevant, Samuel, widow of.	Revolutionary pension	24	2	Petition	132	Rev. Pensions	Jan. 7, 1837	Favorable	822	Referred to Committee Whole House.		
Sturtevant, Silas, heir of.	Balance of pay for revolutionary services.	16	2	Petition	244	Pens. & Rev. Cl'ms.	Feb. 26, 1821	Adverse		Rejected.		
Stutes, Peter, heirs of.	Confirmation of title to land in Louisiana.	14	2	Petition	32	Priv. Land Claims.						
Suarez, Thomas	Compensation for services in Florida war.	30	1	Petition	838	Military Affairs	740	Favorable	582	Referred to Committee Whole House.		
Suarez, Thomas	Compensation for services in Florida war.	31	1	Petition	338	Military Affairs.						
Suarez, Thomas	Compensation for services in Florida war.	31	2	Petition	241	Military Affairs	Feb. 6, 1851	Favorable	456	Referred to Committee Whole House.		
Sudler, Emory	(See Emory Sudler and wife)	4	1		503							
Suffolk, ship	(See Augustus V. Van Horn and others.)	18	1		387							
Sugart, Eli	Pension for revolutionary services.	19	1	Resolution	77	Military Pensions	Feb. 14, 1827	Pension bill	436	Referred to Committee Whole House.		
Sugart, Eli	Pension for revolutionary services.	20	2	Pension bill	55	Whole House	Jan. 15, 1829	With amend.	311	Passed	Laid on table.	
Sugart, Eli	Pension for revolutionary services.	21	1	Petition	47	Military Pensions	Jan. 5, 1830	Pension bill	72	Passed	Passed, with amendment.	App'd May 20, 1830
Sulcer, Jane	(See William Sulcer, widow of.)											
Sulcer, William, widow of.	Pension for revolutionary services.	30	1	Petition	171	Rev. Pensions				Discharged; laid on table.		

List of private claims presented to the House of Representatives of the United States from the 1st to the 31st Congress, inclusive—Continued.

3—55

Names of claimants.	Nature or object of the claim.	Congress.	Session.	How brought before the House of Reps.	Page of journal.	To what committee of the House referred.	No. or date of the report.	Nature of the report.	No. of the bill.	How disposed of by the House of Reps.	How disposed of by the Senate.	Date of the act of Congress, and remarks.
Sullivan, Daniel	Confirmation of title to land in Vincennes district.	12	2	House bill	609	Whole House	Jan. 18, 1813	With't amend.	222	Passed	Passed	App'd Feb. 13, 1813
Sullivan, George	(See Wm. H. Bedford, agent)	28	1		262							
Sullivan, James B	Confirmation of pre-emption to a sixteenth section.	27	2	Memorial	328	Public Lands	950	Favorable	554	Ordered to 3d reading.		
Sullivan, James B	Confirmation of pre-emption to a sixteenth section.	27	3	House bill	89				554	Passed	Passed	App'd March 3, 1843
Sullivan, John	Compensation for horse sold public officer.	25	2	Petition	1118	Claims.						
Sullivan, John, daughter of.	Compensation for revolutionary services.	25	3	Petition	334	Rev. Pensions.						
Sullivan, John H	Right of pre emption to land in Wisconsin.	25	2	Petition	422	Public Lands.						
Sullivan, John T	Balance due for stationery	30	1	Resolution	1106							Paid out of contingent fund.
Sullivan, Mary	Indemnity for property taken for public use.	12	2	Petition	591	Claims.						
Sullivan, Mary	Indemnity for property taken for public use.	15	1	Petition	49	Pens. & Rev. Cl'ms.	Feb. 9, 1818	Adverse; re-commit'd & bill ordered.	185	Passed	Passed	App'd April 18, 1818
Sullivan, Mary	Interest on claim allowed	16	2	Petition	172	Pens. & Rev. Cl'ms.						
Sullivan, Patrick	Compensation for services as assistant commissary.	1	3	Petition	396					Referred to Secretary of War.		
Sullivan, Patrick	Compensation for services as assistant commissary.	2	2	Petition	656					Laid on table.		
Sullivan, William S	(See Christopher Niswanger and W. S. Sullivan.)	26	1		940							
Sullivan, Wilson	Pension	28	1	Petition	723	Invalid Pensions.						
Sullivan, Wilson	Pension	28	2	Petition	145	Invalid Pensions.						
Sullivant, Michael L	Patents for three sections of land in Ohio.	27	2	Petition	66	Public Lands	74	Favorable	110	Referred to Committee Whole House.		
Sullivant, Michael L	Patents for three sections of land in Ohio.	27	3	Bill of last sess.	91	Whole House			110	Left on Speaker's table.		
Sullivant, Michael L	Patents for three sections of land in Ohio.	28	1	Petition	364	Public Lands	238	Adverse		Laid on table.		
Summerl, Joseph	Drawback of duty on merchandise	10	1	Senate bill	277	Whole House			S. 20	Indef. postponed.		
Summerl, Joseph, administrator of.	Drawback of duty on merchandise.	15	2	Petition	182	Com. and Manuf.						
Summerl, Joseph, administrator of.	Drawback of duty on merchandise.	16	1	Petition	186	Commerce				Discharged; laid on table.		
Summerl, Joseph, administrator of.	Drawback of duty on merchandise.	20	1	Petition	163	Commerce	101	Favorable	112	Passed	Passed	App'd May 24, 1828
Summerl, Joseph, administrator of.	Indemnity for French spoliations prior to 1800.	26	1	Memorial	182	Foreign Affairs	343	Favorable; bill	319	Referred to Committee Whole House.		
Summerl & Brown	(See administrator of Joseph Summerl.)	15	2		182							
Summers, Andrew, assignee of.	Indemnity for French spoliations prior to 1800.	26	1	Memorial	182	Foreign Affairs	343	Favorable; bill	319	Referred to Committee Whole House.		
Summers, Andrew, jr.	Liquidation of a revolutionary certificate.	4	1	Rep. of Secretary Treasury.	388	Claims	May 31, 1796	Adverse		Laid on table.		
Summers, Andrew, assignee of.	Indemnity for French spoliations prior to 1800.	26	1	Memorial	182	Foreign Affairs	343	Favorable; bill	319	Referred to Committee Whole House.		
Summers, George	Pension for revolutionary services.	25	3	Petition	218	Rev. Pensions.						

List of private claims presented to the House of Representatives of the United States from the 1st to the 31st Congress, inclusive—Continued.

Names of claimants.	Nature or object of the claim.	Congress.	Session.	How brought before the House of Reps.	Page of journal.	To what committee of the House referred.	No. or date of the report.	Nature of the report.	No. of the bill.	How disposed of by the House of Reps.	How disposed of by the Senate.	Date of the act of Congress, and remarks.
Summers, George, widow of.	Pension for revolutionary services.	27	2	Petition	58	Rev. Pensions	113	Favorable	159	Passed	Indef. postp'd.	
Summers, James	Pension for revolutionary services.	22	1	Petition	115	Military Pensions.						
Summers, Joseph........	Correction of an erroneous entry of land.	14	2	Petition	107	Public Lands	Jan. 16, 1817	Favorable	59	Passed	Indef. postp'd.	
Summers, Mary.........	(See George Summers, widow of)	27	2	....	58							
Summers, Simon........	Compensation for revolutionary services.	1	3	Petition	341							
				Rep't of Secretary War.	385	....	....	....	......	Laid on table.		
Summers, Simon........	Commutation pay for revolutionary services.	22	2	Petition	54	Rev. Claims.						
Summers, Simon........	Commutation pay for revolutionary services.	23	1	Petition	65	Rev. Claims.						
Summers, Simon........	Commutation pay for revolutionary services.	23	2	Petition	84	Rev. Claims.						
Summers, Simon........	Commutation pay for revolutionary services.	24	1	Petition	103	Rev. Claims......	205	Favorable	209	Referred to Committee Whole House.		
Summers, Simon........	Commutation pay for revolutionary services.	24	2	Bill of last sess..	62	Whole House.....	Dec. 19, 1836	With't amend.	209			
Summers, Simon........	Commutation pay for revolutionary services.	25	2	Petition	70	Rev. Claims......	358	Favorable	387	Passed.		
Summers, Simon........	Commutation pay for revolutionary services.	28	2	Petition	83	Rev. Pensions.						
Summers, Thomas	Compensation for a horse lost in public service.	21	1	Petition	83	Claims	Dec. 30, 1829	Adverse	......	Laid on table.		
Summers, Zebadee	(See William H. Bedford, agent).	28	1	....	262							
Summerville, Alexander ..	Balance of pay as revolutionary lieutenant.	8	1	Petition	445	Claims	....	....	......	Discharged.		
Summit Coal and Railroad Company.	Extension of time—duty on iron..	27	2	Petition	649	Ways and Means..	514	Adverse	......	Laid on table.		
Summit Coal and Railroad Company.	Remission of duty on railroad iron	27	3	Petition	125	Ways and Means.						
Summer, Ebenezer	Indemnity for French spoliations prior to 1800.	26	1	Memorial	182	Foreign Affairs....	343	Favorable; bill	319	Referred to Committee Whole House.		
Summer, John, heirs of...	Payment of two revolutionary certificates.	30	1	Petition	759	Rev. Claims.						
Summer, Joseph	(See Charles Shaw & J. S.)	19	1	....	108							
Sumpsion, Charles	Indemnity for destruction of property by Indians.	25	3	Resolution	173	Claims	281	Adverse	......	Laid on table.		
Sumpsion, Charles	Indemnity for destruction of property by Indians.	26	1	Petition	339	Claims	373	Adverse	......	Laid on table.		
Sumpsion, Charles	Indemnity for destruction of property by Indians.	26	2	Petition	135	Claims.						
Sumpsion, Charles	Indemnity for destruction of property by Indians.	28	1	Resolution	429	Claims.						
Sumpsion, Charles	Indemnity for destruction of property by Indians.	28	2	Resolution	134	Claims.						
Sumpsion, Charles	Indemnity for destruction of property by Indians.	29	1	Petition	148	Claims	346	Adverse	......	Laid on table.		
Sumpsion, Charles	Indemnity for destruction of property by Indians.	31	1	Petition	390	Claims.						
Sumpter, Henry, heirs of.	Exchange of an entry of land....	24	1	House bill......	641	....	....	....	540	Passed	Passed	App'd May 14, 1836

List of private claims presented to the House of Representatives of the United States from the 1st to the 31st Congress, inclusive—Continued.

Names of claimants.	Nature or object of the claim.	Congress.	Session.	How brought before the House of Reps.	Page of journal.	To what committee of the House referred.	No. or date of the report.	Nature of the report.	No. of the bill.	How disposed of by the House of Reps.	How disposed of by the Senate.	Date of the act of Congress, and remarks.
Sumpter, John	Compensation for making clothing, revolutionary army.	3	2	Petition	315	Claims.						
Sumpter, John	Compensation for making clothing, revolutionary army.	4	1	Rep. of Secretary War.	445	Claims	Jan. 6, 1795	Adverse		Leave to withdraw.		
Sumpter, Thomas	Compensation for diplomatic services.	25	2	Senate bill	763	Foreign Affairs	May 11, 1838	With't amend	S. 168	Referred to Committee Whole House.		
Sumpter, Thomas	Compensation for diplomatic services.	25	3	Senate bill	49	Foreign Affairs	Jan. 4, 1839	With't amend.	S. 15	Passed	Passed	App'd Feb. 6, 1839
Sumter, Francis	(See Thomas Sumpter, administrator of.)	28	1		352							
Sumter, Thomas, representatives of.	Reimbursement of advances on public accounts.	25	2	Petition	177	Rev. Claims	359	Favorable	388	Postponed.		
Sumter, Thomas, administrator of.	Reimbursement of advances on public accounts.	28	1	Petition	352	Rev. Claims.						
Sumter, Thomas, administrator of.	Reimbursement of advances on public accounts.	28	2	Pension	172	Claims	166	Favorable	634	Referred to Committee Whole House.		
Sumter, Thomas, administrator of.	Reimbursement of advances on public accounts.	29	1	Petition	88	Rev. Claims	440	Favorable	313	Referred to Committee Whole House.		
Sumter, Thomas, administrator of.	Reimbursement of advances on public accounts.	29	2	Bill of last sess.	71	Whole House	Dec. 18, 1846	With't amend.	313	Passed.		
Sumter, Thomas, administrator of.	Reimbursement of advances on public accounts.	30	1	Petition	99	Rev. Claims.						
Sumter, Thomas, heirs of.	Payment of lost loan office certificate.	26	1	Petition	165	Rev. Claims	331	Favorable	303	Referred to Committee Whole House.		
Sumter, Thomas, heirs of.	Payment of lost loan office certificate.	27	2	Petition	61	Rev. Claims	1082	Adverse		Laid on table.		
Sumter, Thomas, heirs of.	Payment of lost loan office certificate.	31	1	Petition	234	Rev. Claims	39	Favorable	68	Referred to Committee Whole House.		
Sumter, Thomas, heirs of.	Payment of lost loan office certificate.	31	2	Bill of last sess.	54	Whole House	Dec. 13, 1850	With amend.	68	Laid on table.		
Supplee, Abraham and Petu	Compensat'n for revolutionary supplies	2	1	Petition	494					Referred to Secretary of Treasury.		
Supplee, Abraham and Petu	Compensat'n for revolutionary supplies.	3	2	Report of Secretary Treasury	284					Laid on table.		
Surgeons, (naval)	(See Edward Cutbush.)	14	2		163							
Surget, Cath. and Charles	(See Peter Surget and others, representatives of.)	22	1		205							
Surgett, Francis	Permission to locate land for rejected claim.	21	2	Petition	47	Priv. Land Claims.						
Surget, Peter, and others, representatives of.	Exchange of lands	22	1	Petition	205	Priv. Land Claims.	Jan. 25, 1832	With't amend.	S. 45	Passed	Passed	App'd July 16, 1832
Surison,	(See Ross & Surison.)	26	1		182							
Susee, Francis	Bounty land for services as Canadian refugee.	12	1	Petition	40					Referred to Secretary War.		
Susee, Francis	(See Canadian Refugees)	4	2		614							
Suthards, William	Pension	21	1	Resolution	383	Military Pensions.						
Sutherland, George	Pension	27	2	Petition	219	Invalid Pensions	288	Favorable	256	Passed	Indef. postp'd.	
Sutherland, Isaac	(See Richard C. Langdon.)	23	1		362							
Sutherland, James & wife.	(See James Parkerson, heir of.)	24	1		907							
Sutherland, John	Pension for services in Indian war.	29	1	Petition	673	Rev. Pensions	826	Adverse		Laid on table.		
Sutherland, John	Pension for services in Indian war.	29	2	Petition	86	Rev. Pensions.						
Sutherland, John	Pension for services in Indian war.	30	1	Petition	460	Rev. Pensions	386	Adverse		Laid on table.		
Sutherland, Rebecca	(See James Sutherland and wife.)	24	1		907							

List of private claims presented to the House of Representatives of the United States from the 1st to the 31st Congress, inclusive—Continued.

Names of claimants.	Nature or object of the claim.	Congress.	Session.	How brought before the House of Reps.	Page of journal.	To what committee of the House referred.	No. or date of the report.	Nature of the report.	No. of the bill.	How disposed of by the House of Reps.	How disposed of by the Senate.	Date of the act of Congress, and remarks.
Sutherland, Samuel, heirs of.	Arrears of pension	23	1	Resolution	333	Rev. Pensions	465	Favorable	479	Referred to Commitee Whole House.		
Surrage, Isaac	Pension for revolutionary disabilities.	3	1	Petition	64							
				Rep. of Secretary War.	93	Select.						
Surveyors General, United States.	To equalize compensation	29	1	Petition	633		567	Favorable	373	Passed	Passed	App d Aug. 8, 1846
Sutliff, Deborah	Indemn ty for loss by mistake of land officer.	20	2	Petition	60	Public Lands	Jan. 7, 1829	Adverse		Laid on table.		
Sutliff or Sutlief, John	Compensation for revolutionary services.	2	2	Petition	650					Referred to Secretary Treasury.		
Sutliff or Sutlief, John	Compensation for revolutionary services.	3	1	Rep. of Secretary Treasury.	78					Laid on table.		
Sutphen, Gilbert	(See William Baker, N. York.)	22	1		288		480					
Suts, Peter P.	(See Casper B. Cook, and others)	30	1		272							
Sutton, Abraham	Reimbursement of advances for certificates not received.	2	1	Petition	539					Laid on table.		
Sutton, Abraham	Reimbursement of advances for certificates not received.	3	1	Rep. of Secretary War.	93	Select.						
Sutton, Abraham	Reimbursement of advances for certificates not received.	3	2	Rep. of Secretary War.	250	Claims	Feb. 25, 1795	Adverse.		Laid on table.		
Sutton, Abraham	Reimbursement of advances for certificates not received.	4	2	Petition	703	Claims	Feb. 21, 1797	Adverse		Referred to Committee Whole House.		
Sutton, Abraham	Reimbursement of advances for certificates not received.	5	2	Report of Com'r Claims.	89	Whole House	Mar. 19, 1798	Res.; favorable		Rejected.		
Sutton, Abraham	(See John Bennett)	3	1		93							
Sutton, Ephraim	Pay and bounty land for revolutionary services.	18	1	Petition	130	Military Affairs	Feb. 4, 1824	Adverse		Leave to withdraw.		
Sutton, Ephraim	Pay and bounty land for revolutionary services.	19	1	Petition	223	Claims	April 18, 1826	Adverse		Laid on table.		
Sutton, George	Pension for revolutionary services.	18	1	Petition	74	Whole House.						
Sutton, James	Right of pre-emption to certain lands.	8	1	Memorial	460	Select				Discharged; leave to withdraw.		
Sutton, Jesse	Compensation for services as blacksmith to Indians.	30	1	Petition	647	Indian Affairs	619	Favorable	498	Referred to Committee Whole House.		
Sutton, Jesse	Compensation for services as blacksmith to Indians.	30	2	Bill of last sess.	318	Whole House	Jan. 26, 1849	With't amend.	498	Passed.		
Sutton, Jesse	Compensation for services as blacksmith to Indians.	31	1	Petition	216	Indian Affairs	15	Favorable	19	Passed	Passed	App'd June 5, 1850
Sutton, John	Commutation pay for revolutionary services.	23	1	Petition	71	Rev. Claims.						
Sutton, John	Commutation pay for revolutionary services.	23	2	Petition	77	Rev. Claims.						
Sutton, John	Commutation pay for revolutionary services.	24	1	Petition	103	Rev. Claims	655	Adverse		Laid on table.		
Sutton, John	Commutation pay for revolutionary services.	24	2	Petition	95	Rev. Claims	99	Adverse		Laid on table.		
Sutton, J. S.	(See Captain B. F. Hill)	31	1		1012							
Sutton, Mary	(See William Sutton, widow of)	28	1		947							
Sutton, Moses	Compensation for horse lost in public service.	24	1	Documents	152	Claims	256	Adverse		Laid on table.		
Sutton, Philip	Pension for revolutionary services.	26	2	Petition	248	Rev. Pensions.						

List of private claims presented to the House of Representatives of the United States from the 1st to the 31st Congress, inclusive—Continued.

Names of claimants.	Nature or object of the claim.	Congress.	Session.	How brought before the House of Reps.	Page of journal.	To what committee of the House referred.	No. or date of the report.	Nature of the report.	No. of the bill.	How disposed of by the House of Reps.	How disposed of by the Senate.	Date of the act of Congress, and remarks.
Sutton, Philip	Pension for revolutionary services.	27	2	Petition	97	Rev. Pensions	784	Adverse	......	Laid on table.		
Sutton, Philip	Pension for revolutionary services.	27	3	Petition	73	Rev. Pensions.						
Sutton, Thomas	Compensation for extinguishing fire on board Raritan.	30	1	Petition	738	Naval Affairs.						
Sutton, Thomas	Compensation for extinguishing fire on board Raritan.	31	1	Petition	416	Naval Affairs.						
Sutton, William, widow of.	Pension for revolutionary services.	28	1	Petition	947	Rev. Pensions.						
Suydam, Hendrick	(See Johannes E. Lott and others)	5	2	....	144							
Suzor, Françáise	(See Louis Suzor, widow of.)											
Suzor, Louis, widow of	Compensation for property taken for public use.	23	1	Petition	131	Claims	145	Favorable	156	Passed	Passed	App'd June 30, 1834
Swaggart, John, & others.	Indemnity for their lands sold by government.	18	1	Petition	101	Public Lands.						
Swails, Robert	Compensation for military services in 1791.	8	1	Petition	555	Claims	Feb. 15, 1804	Adverse	......	Rejected.		
Swaim, Meriam	Continuation of pension	28	1	Petition	849	Rev. Pensions.						
Swaim, Abell, and Simmons	Payment of certain treasury notes.	28	1	Petition	317	Ways and Means.						
Swain, Charles, wife of	Pension for revolutionary services of insane husband.	22	2	Petition	53	Claims	....	....	......	Discharged; laid on table.		
Swain, Charles, wife of	Pension for revolutionary services of insane husband.	23	1	Petition	162	Rev. Claims	221	Favorable	242	Referred to Committee Whole House.		
wain, Charles, wife of	Pension for revolutionary services of insane husband.	23	2	Bill of last sess.	299	Whole House	Jan. 31, 1835	With't amend.	242	Passed	Adverse report.	
Swain, Charles, wife of	Pension for revolutionary services of insane husband.	24	1	Petition	670	Rev. Pensions	681	Favorable	642	Passed	Passed	App'd June 28, 1836
Swain, Elizabeth	(See Charles Swain, wife of.)	22	2	....	53							
Swain, Elizabeth, attorney of.	Indemnity for French spoliations prior to 1800.	26	1	Memorial	182	Foreign Affairs	343	Favorable; bill	319	Referred to Committee Whole House.		
Swain, Isaac	Indemnity for property destroyed by the enemy.	19	2	Petition	240	Claims.						
Swain, Isaac	Indemnity for property destroyed by the enemy.	20	1	Petition	727	Claims.						
Swain, Isaac	Indemnity for property destroyed by the enemy.	22	1	Petition	120	Claims	Mar. 16, 1832	Adverse	......	Laid on table.		
Swain, Isaac	Indemnity for property destroyed by the enemy.	23	2	Petition	489	Claims.						
Swain, Isaac	Indemnity for property destroyed by the enemy.	24	1	Petition	284	Claims.						
Swain, James	Compensation for revolutionary services.	1	3	Petition	368	....	....	....	......	Referred to Secretary War.		
Smain, James	Compensation for revolutionary services.	2	1	Rep. of Secretary War.	500	....	....	....	......	Laid on table.		
Swain, Shubael	Remission of a penalty	1	3	Petition	344	Select	Jan. 3, 1791	Favorable; bill ordered.	111	Passed	Rejected.	
Swain, Thomas G	Release from liability for official acts.	25	3	Petition	461	Claims.						
Swallow, brig, owners of	Indemnity for vessel sunk in defence of Baltimore.	21	1	General bill	248	Whole House	April 30, 1830	With't amend.	191	Passed	Passed	App'd May 29, 1830
Swallow, Larnard	Pension	23	2	Petition	131	Invalid Pensions	28	Favorable	608	Passed	Passed	App'd March 3, 1835
Swallow, Larnard	Pension	24	1	Petition	127	Invalid Pensions	Jan. 28, 1836	Adverse	......	Recommitted.		
				Senate bill	1084	Invalid Pensions	July 1, 1836	With't amend.	S. 292	Passed	Passed	App'd July 2, 1836
Swallow, Larnard	Increase of pension	27	2	Petition	91	Invalid Pensions	412	Adverse	......	Laid on table.		
Swallow, Larnard	Pension	28	1	Petition	428	Invalid Pensions	453	Adverse	......	Laid on table.		

List of private claims presented to the House of Representatives of the United States from the 1st to the 31st Congress, inclusive—Continued.

ames of claimants.	Nature or object of the claim.	Congress.	Session.	How brought before the House of Reps.	Page of journal.	To what committee of the House referred.	No. or date of the report.	Nature of the report.	No. of the bill.	How disposed of by the House of Reps.	How disposed of by the Senate.	Date of the act of Congress, and remarks.
Swan, Benjamin L	Release from penalty under non-importation act.	12	2	Petition	566	Ways and Means.						
Swan, Benjamin L	Release from penalty under non-importation act.	14	2	Petition	410	Ways and Means	Feb. 28, 1817	Adverse	......	Rejected.		
Swan, Catharine	(See Charles Swan, widow of.)											
Swan, Charles, widow of	Pension for revolutionary services.	27	2	Petition	1067	Rev. Pensions	....	....	......	Discharged; laid on table.		
Swan, Charles, widow of	Pension for revolutionary services.	27	3	Petition	257	Rev. Pensions	....	....	......	Discharged; referred to Com'r of Pensions.		
Swann, Elijah	Pension	14	1	Petition	28	Pens. & Rev. Cl'ms.						
Swann, Francis	(See widow of Wm. T. Swann)	28	1	....	993							
Swan, James	Payment of a certain bill of exchange.	5	2	Memorial	113	Claims	May 28, 1798	Adverse	......	Rejected.		
Swan, James, agent of	Reimbursement of duty on arms for public use.	8	1	Petition	540	Claims	Feb. 9, 1804	Adverse	......	Rejected.		
Swan, James	(See trustees of Francis L. Taney)	10	1	....	216							
Swan, James	Redemption of continental money.	23	1	Petition	221	Rev. Claims.						
Swann, John	Compensation for services, war of 1812.	27	2	Petition	68	Invalid Pensions	240	Adverse	......	Laid on table.		
Swan, Nathan	Pension for revolutionary services.	22	1	Petition	533	Rev. Pensions.						
Swan, Peter	Indemnity for forfeiture of a British pension.	2	1	Petition	478	....	....	....	......	Referred to Secretary War.		
Swan, Robert, and O. S. Palmer.	Compensation for work at Twin Islands.	29	2	Memorial	227	Ways and Means.						
Swann, William T., widow of.	Compensation for tobacco destroyed by the enemy.	28	1	Petition	993	Claims.						
Swann, William T., widow of.	Compensation for tobacco destroyed by the enemy.	28	2	Petition	118	Claims	158	Adverse	......	Laid on table.		
Swann, William T., widow of.	Compensation for tobacco destroyed by the enemy.	29	1	Petition	103	Claims.						
Swann, William T., widow of.	Compensation for tobacco destroyed by the enemy.	30	1	Petition	77	Claims.						
Swann, William T., widow of.	Compensation for tobacco destroyed by the enemy.	30	2	Memorial	235	Commerce.						
Swann, William T., widow of.	Compensation for tobacco destroyed by the enemy.	31	1	Memorial	661	Claims.						
Swart, Adam	Compensation for revolutionary services.	29	1	Petition	327	Claims.						
Swart, Adam	Pension for revolutionary services.	29	1	Memorial	525	Rev. Claims.						
Swart, Adam	Pension for revolutionary services.	31	1	Petition	672	Rev. Claims.						
Swart, Dirck	Compensation for property destroyed by public officer.	3	2	Petition	286	Claims	Mar. 2, 1795	Adverse	......	Laid on table.		
Swart, Dirck	Compensation for property destroyed by public officer.	4	1	Report of Com'r Claims.	598	....	....	Adverse	......	Laid on table.		
Swart, Tunis	Pension	20	2	Petition	262	Military Pensions.						
Swart, Tunis	Pension	22	1	Resolution	337	Rev. Pensions.						
Swart, Tunis	Pension	25	2	Resolution	618	Rev. Pensions.						
Swartz, John	(See John Crane.)	15	1	....	132							
Swartwood, Daniel	Pension	21	2	Petition	43	Miltary Pensions.						
Swartwood, James	Pension	21	2	Petition	43	Military Pensions.						
Swartwood, John	Pension	21	2	Petition	43	Military Pensions.						
Swartwood, J[illegible]	Arrears of pension	23	1	Petition	640	Invalid Pensions	542	Favorable	544	Referred to Committee Whole House.		

List of private claims presented to the House of Representatives of the United States from the 1st to the 31st Congress, inclusive—Continued.

Names of claimants.	Nature or object of the claim.	Congress.	Session.	How brought before the House of Reps.	Page of journal.	To what committee of the House referred.	No. or date of the report.	Nature of the report.	No. of the bill.	How disposed of by the House of Reps.	How disposed of by the Senate.	Date of the act of Congress, and remarks.
Swartwood, Joseph	Arrears of pension............	23	2	Bill of last sess..	336	Whole House.....	Feb. 6, 1835	With't amend.	544	Passed......... ...	Passed	App'd March 3, 1835
Swartwout, Jacobus......	Pension for revolutionary services.	25	2	Resolution	162	Rev. Pensions.						
Swartwout, Melanc. S....	Increase of compensation as custom house officer.	21	2	Petition	230	....	....	....	......	Referred to Secretary of Treasury.		
Swartwout, Robert.......	Indemnity from effect of a certain judgment.	15	2	Petition	117	Military Affairs...	58	Favorable....	252			
Swartwout, Robert.......	Indemnity from effect of a certain judgment.	16	1	Petition	30	Claims.						
				Petition	38	Claims.						
				Documents.....	325	Claims	Mar. 22, 1820	Adverse	......	Referred to Committee Whole House.	....	Leave to withdraw, 2d session.
Swartwout, Robert.......	Indemnity from effect of a certain judgment.	16	2	Senate bill	287	Claims	Mar. 3, 1821	With't amend.	32	Passed	Passed	App'd March 3, 1821
Swartwout, Robert.......	Equitable settlement of accounts and indemnity, &c.	16	1	Senate bill	309	Ways and Means..	May 17, 1820	With't amend.	63	Passed	Passed	App'd April 5, 1820
Swartwout, Samuel, and others.	Share of the proceeds of a custom-house seizure.	24	1	Memorial	945	Ways and Means.						
Swartwout, Samuel, sureties of.	Compromise of their liability.....	26	2	Senate bill	203	Judiciary	Feb. 12, 1841	With't amend.	S. 211	Laid on table.		
Swartwout, Samuel, sureties of.	Compromise of their liability.....	27	2	Senate bill	1116	Judiciary	July 29, 1842	With't amend.	S. 218	Laid on table.		
Swartwout, Samuel, sureties of.	Compromise of their liability.....	27	3	Senate bill	115	Judiciary	Jan. 10, 1843	With't amend.	S. 24	Laid on table.		
Swartwout, Samuel, sureties of.	Compromise of their liability.....	28	2	Senate bill	140	Whole House.....	....	....	S. 35	Laid on table.		
Swartwout, Samuel, sureties of.	Compromise of their liability.....	30	1	Senate bill	683	Judiciary.........	....	....	S. 4			
Swartwout, Samuel, sureties of.	Compromise of their liability.....	30	2	Senate bill	545	Judiciary	Feb. 28, 1849	With't amend.	S. 4	Referred to Committee Whole House.		
Swartwout, Samuel, sureties of.	Compromise of their liability.....	31	1	Senate bill	591	Judiciary	May 22, 1850	With't amend.	S. 125	Referred to Committee Whole House.		
Swasey, Benjamin B.....	Bounty on fishing schooner Mary.	27	3	Petition	59	Commerce.						
Swasey, Benjamin B.....	Bounty on fishing schooner Mary.	28	1	Petition	183	Commerce.						
Swasey, Benjamin B.....	Bounty on fishing schooner Mary.	28	2	Petition	88	Commerce	....	....	......	Discharged; leave to withdraw.		
Swazey & Folsom.......	Reimbursement of duties paid at Castine.	16	1	Senate bill	108	Ways and Means..	Jan. 14, 1820	With't amend.	S. 13	Passed with amendm't.	Passed as am'd.	App'd April 11, 1820
Swazey, John N.........	Reimbursement of duties paid at Castine.	16	1	Senate bill	108	Ways and Means..	Jan. 14, 1820	With't amend.	S. 13	Passed with amendm't	Passed as am'd.	App'd April 11, 1820
Swayze, C. L...........	Confirmation of title to land in Louisiana.	28	1	Petition	449	Public Lands.						
Swearingen, Benoni	Compensation for horse taken for public use.	19	1	Resolution	186	Claims	Feb. 24, 1826	Adverse	......	Laid on table.		
Swearingen, Charles A...	Compensation for horse taken for public use.	17	1	Petition	180	Judiciary	Jan. 28, 1822	Favorable....	61	Passed.............	Indef. postp'd.	
Sweatt, Elizabeth........	(See representatives of Benjamin Richards.)	27	2	....	254	....	597					
Sweazey, Hiram, attorney, &c.	Confirmation of a Spanish land title.	12	1	Petition	13	Public Lands.						
Sweazey, Hiram, attorney, &c.	Confirmation of a Spanish land title.	14	2	Petition	338	Priv. Land Claims.						
Swedish subjects	Indemnity for acts of United States ship Erie.	22	2	President's mess.	129	Foreign Affairs.						

List of private claims presented to the House of Representatives of the United States from the 1st to the 31st Congress, inclusive—Continued.

Names of claimants.	Nature or object of the claim.	Congress.	Session.	How brought before the House of Reps.	Page of journal.	To what committee of the House referred.	No. or date of the report	Nature of the report.	No. of the bill.	How disposed of by the House of Reps.	How disposed of by the Senate.	Date of the act of Congress, and remarks.
Sweeney, Alexander, heirs of.	Right of pre-emption to a tract of land.	25	3	Petition	451	Public Lands	....	....	......	Discharged; laid on table.		
Sweeney, Doyle, and others	Extra compensation as government clerks.	4	1	Petition	477	Claims.						
Sweeney, Doyle, and others	Extra compensation as government clerks.	4	2	Resolution	614	Claims.						
Sweeney, Doyle	Compensation for services as clerk.	12	2	Petition	623	Ways and Means.						
Sweeney, James	Increase of compensation as postmaster.	16	1	Petition	623	Ways and Means.						
Sweeney, John	Pension for disabilities in the war of 1812.	13	1	Petition	15	Claims	....	....	......	Discharged.		
Sweeney, John	Pension for disabilities in the war of 1812.	13	3	Petition	464	Pens. & Rev. Cl'ms.	Feb. 20, 1815	Favorable	303	Passed	Passed	App'd March 3, 1815
Sweeney, John	Remission of duty on a pipe of gin.	28	1	Petition	73	Ways and Means	439	Adverse	......	Laid on table.		
Sweeney, John M	Patent for land in Illinois	31	1	House bill	462	Public Lands	....	....	......	Discharged; laid on table.		
Sweet, Amos, and others	Additional compensation for muskets.	19	1	Petition	442	Claims.						
Sweet, Amos, and others	Additional compensation for muskets.	20	1	Petition	78	Claims	Feb. 29, 1828	Favorable	197	Passed	Passed	App'd May 24, 1828
Sweet, Benajah	Pension	21	2	Resolution	165	Military Pensions.						
Sweet, Godfrey	Pension for revolutionary services.	5	2	Petition	87	Claims	Jan. 9, 1798	Pension bill	38	Passed	Passed	App'd Feb. 2, 1798
Sweet, Thomas R	Pension	22	1	Petition	287	Military Pensions	....	....	......	Discharged; laid on table.		
Sweetland, Elizabeth	(See Bailey & De Lord	23	2	....	83							
Sweetland, William	Pension	22	1	Petition	66	Rev. Pensions.						
Sweetman, James	Pension	27	2	Petition	239	Invalid Pensions	803	Favorable	457	Ordered to 3d reading.		
Sweetman, James	Pension	27	3	House bill	89	....	....	....	457	Passed	Passed	App'd March 3, 1843
Sweetser, Seth	Compensation for diplomatic services in Ecuador.	27	3	Petition	77	Foreign Affairs	131	Favorable	753	Passed	Indef. postp'd.	
Sweetser, Seth	Compensation for diplomatic services in Ecuador.	28	1	Petition	83	Foreign Affairs	37	Favorable	68	Laid on table.		
Sweetser, Seth	Compensation for diplomatic services in Ecuador.	28	2	Petition	170	Foreign Affairs.						
Sweetser, Seth	Compensation for diplomatic services in Ecuador.	29	1	Petition	102	Foreign Affairs	36	Adverse	......	Laid on table		
Sweetzer, S	Indemnity for French spoliations prior to 1800.	26	1	Memorial	182	Foreign Affairs	343	Favorable; bill	319	Referred to Committee Whole House.		
Swem, Jesse	Pension for revolutionary services.	21	1	Resolution	213	Military Pensions	....	....	......	Discharged; laid on table.		
Swem, Jesse	Pension for revolutionary services.	22	1	Petition	104	Rev. Pensions	....	....	......	Discharged; laid on table.		
Swift, Alex., J., administrator of.	Compensation for horses lost in public service.	30	1	Petition	644	Claims.						
Swift, Ann P	Indemnity for French spoliations prior to 1800.	31	1	Petition	311	Foreign Affairs	355	General bill	318	Referred to Committee Whole House.		
Swift, Charles	Bounty land for military services.	17	1	Resolution	215	Military Affairs	Feb. 12, 1822	Adverse	......	Rejected.		
Swift, Foster	Release from a balance due to United States.	9	1	Petition	327	Claims	April 1, 1806	Adverse	......	Leave to withdraw.		
Swift, Jonathan W	Pension	31	1	Petition	337	Invalid Pensions.						
Swift, Joseph G	Exchange of public securities	22	1	Memorial	732	Public Lands.						

List of private claims presented to the House of Representatives of the United States from the 1st to the 31st Congress, inclusive—Continued.

Names of claimants.	Nature or object of the claim.	Congress.	Session.	How brought before the House of Reps.	Page of journal.	To what committee of the House referred.	No. or date of the report.	Nature of the report.	No. of the bill.	How disposed of by the House of Reps.	How disposed of by the Senate.	Date of the act of Congress, and remarks.
Swift, Joseph G.	(See administrator of Alexander J. Swift.)	30	1	....	644							
Swift, Socrates	Pension	14	1	House bill	622	Whole House	April 23, 1816	With amend.	171	Passed	Passed, with amendment.	App'd April 30, 1816
Swigert, George	Compensation for horses lost in public services.	28	1	Petition	687	Claims.						
Swiler, John	Right of pre emption as New Orleans branch pilot.	28	1	Petition	77	Priv. Land Claims.	9	Favorable	35	Passed	Passed	App'd June 17, 1844
Swinerton, Anna	(See Benjamin Swinerton, widow of.)											
Swinerton, Benjamin, widow of.	Pension for military services	25	2	Petition	1028	Invalid Pensions.						
Swinerton, Benjamin, widow of.	Pension for military services	26	1	Petition	163	Invalid Pensions	280	Adverse	......	Laid on table.		
Swinerton, Benjamin, widow of.	Pension for military services	26	2	Petition	59	Invalid Pensions	59	Adverse	......	Laid on table.		
Swink, Edwin	Right of pre-emption to an Indian reservation.	21	2	Petition	100	Public Lands.						
Swope, Dr. John, sister of.	Authority to locate land warrants of deceased.	20	2	Petition	230	Public Lands.						
Swope, Dr. John, sister of.	Authority to locate land warrants of deceased.	21	1	Petition	53	Public Lands.						
Syfat, or Sybert, Adam	Indemnity for revolutionary disabilities.	2	1	Petition	524	....	....	....	......	Referred to Secretary War.		
Syfat, or Sybert, Adam	Indemnity for revolutionary disabilities.	3	1	Rep. of Secretary War.	131	Select	May 26, 1794	Favorable; bill ordered.	62	Passed	Passed	App'd June 7, 1794
Sykes, George	Reimbursement of public money of which he was robbed.	30	2	Petition	263	Military Affairs.						
Sykes, James	Pension for revolutionary services.	19	2	Resolution	52	Military Pensions.						
Sykes, James	Pension for revolutionary services.	20	1	Resolution	356	Military Pensions	....	....	......	Discharged; laid on table.		
Sykes, James	Pension for revolutionary services.	20	2	Petition	31	Military Pensions.						
				Petition, (2)	144	Military Pensions	....	....	......	Discharged; laid on table.		
Sykes, James	Pension for revolutionary services.	21	2	Petition	255	Military Pensions	....	....	......	Discharged; laid on table.		
Sykes, Jesse	Pension	23	2	Petition	200	Rev. Pensions	114	Favorable	743	Referred to Committee Whole House.		
Sykes, Jesse	Pension	24	1	Petition	108	Rev. Pensions	143	Favorable	150	Passed	Passed	App'd May 14, 1836
Sykes, Samuel	Pension for revolutionary services.	19	2	Resolution	70	Military Pensions	Feb. 14, 1827	Pension bill	436	Referred to Committee Whole House.		
Sykes, Samuel	Pension for revolutionary services.	20	1	Res'n and docs.	201	Military Pensions	April 29, 1828	Pension bill	283	Passed.		
Sykes, Samuel	Pension for revolutionary services.	20	2	Pension bill	55	Whole House	Jan. 15, 1829	With amend.	311	Passed	Laid on table.	
Sykes, Samuel	Pension for revolutionary services.	21	1	Petition	49	Military Pensions	Jan. 5, 1830	Pension bill	72	Passed	Passed, with amendment.	App'd May 20, 1830
Sylph, U. S. schooner, representatives of officers, &c., of.	Six months extra pay and arrears of pay.	22	2	Senate bill	85	Naval Affairs	Jan. 4, 1833	With't amend.	S. 18	Passed	Passed	App'd March 2, 1833
Sylvester, Joel	To be restored to pension roll	17	1	Petition	67	Rev. Pensions.						
Sylvester, Joseph	Arrears of pension	29	1	Petition	199	Invalid Pensions	....	....	......	Discharged; laid on table.		
Syne, John	Compensation for revolutionary supplies, (flour.)	7	1	Petition	122	Claims	....	....	......	Discharged; postponed		

3—56

List of private claims presented to the House of Representatives of the United States from the 1st to the 31st Congress, inclusive—Continued.

Names of claimants.	Nature or object of the claim.	Congress.	Session.	How brought before the House of Reps.	Page of journal.	To what committee of the House referred.	No. or date of the report.	Nature of the report.	No. of the bill.	How disposed of by the House of Reps.	How disposed of by the Senate.	Date of the act of Congress, and remarks.
Syne, John, administrator of.	Compensation for revolutionary supplies, (flour.)	22	1	Petition	143	Rev. Claims	190	Favorable	272	Referred to Committee Whole House.		
Syne, John, administrator of.	Compensation for revolutionary supplies, (flour.)	22	2	Bill of last sess.	93	Whole House	Dec. 26, 1832	With't amend.	272	Rejected.		
Syne, John, administrator of.	Compensation for revolutionary supplies, (flour.)	23	1	Petition	43	Rev. Claims	97	Favorable	101	Passed	Passed	App'd May 23, 1834
Symington, James F	(See assignees of Waters Smith)	22	1		258							
Symington, John	Indemnity for damages, &c., recovered against him.	24	1	Petition	94	Claims.						
Symington, Theophilus, heirs of.	Compensation for revolutionary services.	17	1	Petition	460	Pens. & Rev. Cl'ms.						
Symmes, John Cleves	Purchase of lands on Miami river.	2	1	President's Message	453	Select	Mar. 22, 1794	Favorable; bill	172	Passed	Passed, with amendment.	App'd April 12, 1792
Symmes, John Cleves	Grant and conveying of certain lands.	2	1	House bill	586				186	Passed	Passed, with amendment.	App'd May 5, 1792
Symmes, John Cleves	(See Northwestern Territory, inhabitants of.)	6	1		591							
Symmes, John Cleves	Authority to relinquish certain lands.	7	1	Petition Memorial	52 224	Select				Discharged.		
Symmes, John Cleves	Compensation for military services.	20	2	Petition	320	Claims.						
Symmes, John C., widow of.	Settlement of accounts	28	1	Petition	84	Claims.						
Symmes, Mary Ann	(See John Cleves Symmes, widow of.)	28	1		84							
Symms, William	Pension for revolutionary services.	3	1	Rep. of Secretary War.	131	Select	May 26, 1794	Favorable; bill ordered.	62	Passed	Passed	App'd June 7, 1794
Symmes, W	(See attorney of Henry Green)	4	1		451							
Sympson, James, heirs of.	Confirmation of title to land in Louisiana.	26	1	Petition	200	Priv. Land Claims.	98	Favorable; bill	94	Passed	Postponed.	
Sympson, James, heirs of.	Confirmation of title to land in Louisiana.	27	2	Senate bill	1126	Priv. Land Claims.	April 12, 1842	With't amend.	237	Passed	Passed	App'd Aug. 29, 1842
Sype, Christopher	Pension	20	2	Petition	99	Military Pensions.	Feb. 13, 1829	Favorable	440	Passed.		
Sype, Christopher	Pension	21	1	Petition	49	Military Pensions.	Jan. 5, 1830	Pension bill	72	Passed.	Passed, with amendment.	App'd May 20, 1830
Sypert, William L.	Pension	14	1	Pension bill	622	Whole House	April 23, 1816	With't amend.	171	Passed	Passed, with amendment.	App'd April 30, 1816
Syren, brig, officers, &c., of.	(See heirs of Edward Preble, and others.)	15	1		289							
Syren, brig, officers, &c., of, by agent.	Portion of the prize-money for the destruction of the frigate Philadelphia.	20	1	Memorial	309	Naval Affairs	Mar. 18, 1828	Adverse		Referred to Committee Whole House.		

List of private claims presented to the House of Representatives of the United States from the 1st to the 31st Congress, inclusive—Continued.

Names of claimants.	Nature or object of the claim.	Congress.	Session.	How brought before the House of Reps.	Page of journal.	To what committee of the House referred.	No. or date of the report.	Nature of the report.	No. of the bill.	How disposed of by the House of Reps.	How disposed of by the Senate.	Date of the act of Congress, and remarks.
Tabb, William, (Va.)	(See Henry Cheeseman, heir of)	27	3		77							
Taber, Constant	(See Daniel Marcy, surety of)	8	1		428							
Taber, Constant	(See Caleb Gardner, executors of)	9	2		554							
Taber, Constant, *et al.*	Indemnity for French spoliations prior to 1800.	10	1	Petition	28	Com. and Manuf.						
Taber, John	(See John Bagley, *et al.*	5	2		113							
Taber, Philip	Arrears of pension	4	2	Petition	627	Claims	Feb. 25, 1797	Favorable, (in part.)		Referred to Committee Whole House.		
Taber, Philip	Arrears of pension	5	1	Resolution	13					Leave to withdraw.		
Taber, Philip	Arrears of pension	21	2	Petition	159	Military Pensions.						
Taber, Philip	Arrears of pension	23	1	Petition	273	Invalid Pensions	Mar. 16, 1824	Adverse		Laid on table.		
Taber, Philip	Arrears of pension	28	1	Petition	950	Rev. Pensions.						
Taber, Philip	Arrears of pension	30	1	Petition	780	Rev. Pensions.						
Taber, Philip	Arrears of pension	31	1	Petition	719	Rev. Pensions	358	Adverse		Laid on table.		
Taber, James A.	(See Miguel Eslava, heirs of)	24	1		436							
Taber, Daniel	(See Joseph McLellan, *et al.*)	7	2		246							
Taber, John	(See Joseph McLellan, *et al.*)	7	2		246							
Taber, Thomas	Revolutionary pension	22	1	Report	516					Discharged; laid on table.		
Tadlock, Andrew	Compensation for services rendered and indemnity for clothing lost during war of 1812.	25	2	Petition	542	Claims	April 21, 1838	Adverse		Laid on table.		
Taft, Daniel, *et al.*	Payment for extra work on Cumberland road.	33	1	Res. and papers.	589	Claims	455	Adverse		Laid on table		See report No. 449.
Taft, Nathaniel	Release from imprisonment at suit of United States.	14	2	Petition	69	Ways and Means.	Dec. 20, 1816	Favorable; bill	19	Passed	Passed	App'd Jan. 14, 1817
Taft, William S.	Indemnity for French spoliations prior to 1800.	31	1	Petition	1035	Foreign Affairs	355	Favorable; bill	318	Referred to Committee Whole House.		
Tager, Jacob	Invalid pension	6	1	Petition	626	Claims	April 4, 1800	Adverse		Rejected.		
Tagert, Joseph, *et al.*	(See Edward Simpson, *et al.*)	4	1		428							
Tagert, Joseph	(See Gray & Taylor, *et al.*)	26	1		327							
Taggart, Arthur	(See Peter Cornyn & A. Taggart)	24	1		349							
Taggert, Arthur, *et al.*	Payment for extra work on Cumberland road.	23	1	Res. and papers.	589	Claims	455	Adverse		Laid on table		See report No. 449.
Taggart, Arthur	Payment for extra work on Cumberland road.	25	2	Res. and papers.	88	Claims.						
Taggart, Arthur	Payment for extra work on Cumberland road.	25	3	Res. and papers.	457	Claims.						
Taggart, Arthur	Payment for extra work on Cumberland road.	26	1	Res. and papers.	170	Claims.						
Taggart, Arthur	Payment for extra work on Cumberland road.	26	2	Res. and papers.	167	Claims.						
Taggart, Arthur	Payment for extra work on Cumberland road.	27	2	Res. and papers.	517	Claims.						
Taggart, Arthur	Payment for extra work on Cumland road.	30	1	Petition	513	Claims.						
Taggart, James	Revolutionary pension	16	1	Petition	117	Rev. Pensions				Discharged; laid on table.		
Taggart, John	Indemnity for French spoliations prior to 1800.	26	1	Memorial	182	Foreign Affairs	343	Favorable; bill	319	Referred to Committee Whole House.		
Taggart, John, (Pa.)	To refund duties paid on merchandise destroyed by fire.	8	1	Petition	429	Com. and Manuf.	Nov. 7, 1803	Adverse		Leave to withdraw.		

List of private claims presented to the House of Representatives of the United States from the 1st to the 31st Congress, inclusive—Continued.

Names of claimants.	Nature or object of the claim.	Congress.	Session.	How brought before the House of Reps.	Page of journal.	To what committee of the House referred.	No. or date of the report.	Nature of the report.	No. of the bill.	How disposed of by the House of Reps.	How disposed of by the Senate.	Date of the act of Congress, and remarks.
Taggart, John	(See John Wilmot, *et al.*)	11	2	....	350							
Taggart, William	Revolutionary pension	2	2	Rep. of Secretary War.	649	Whole House.						
Taggart, William	Revolutionary pension	3	1	Rep of Secretary War.	131	Select.						
Taggart, William	Revolutionary pension	3	2	Rep. of Secretary War.	262	Claims.						
Taggart, William	Revolutionary pension	4	1	Res. and docs.	373	Claims	Feb. 18, 1796	General bill	156	Passed	Passed	App'd April 20, 1796
Tailer, Edward N.	(See John P. Austin and E. N. Tailer.)	23	2	....	304							
Teitte, Jean B	Invalid pension	25	2	Petition	401	Invalid Pensions.						
Tait, Adam	(See Adam Tate)	15	2	....	196							
Tait, Alexander	Compensation for time lost whilst employed on the Patent Office in 1840.	28	1	Petition	685	Claims.						
Tait, Robert L	Revolutionary pension	21	1	Resolution	275	Military Pensions	May 3, 1830	Favorable; bill	454	Referred to Committee Whole House on bill No. 362.		
Tait, Robert L	Revolutionary pension	21	2	Resolution	310	Military Pensions.						
Tait, Robert L	Revolutionary pension	22	1	Resolution	95	Rev. Pensions	369	Favorable; bill	462	Passed	Indef. postp'd.	
Talbot, David J	Correction of error in land certificate.	24	1	Petition	57	Public Lands	Jan. 15, 1836	Favorable; bill	1[illegible]5	Passed	Passed, with amendment.	App'd July 2, 1836
Talbot, Edward Allen	Grant of patent	20	1	Senate bill	767	Whole House	....	....	149	Passed	....	App'd May 23, 1828
Talbot, Elisha	Remission of duties on distillery	14	1	Petition	267	Ways and Means	Feb. 24, 1816	Adverse	......	Referred to Committee Whole House.		
Talbott, George W	(See John H. Talbott, heirs of)	27	2	....	368, 651							
Talbot, Jesse	(See John W. Branaugh and J. Talbot.)	19	2	....	226							
Talbott, John Q	Pension	14	1	Petition	41	Pens. & Rev. Clm's.	April 14, 1816	Favorable; bill	171	Passed	Passed, with amendment.	App'd April 30, 1816
Talbott, John H., heirs of.	Indemnity for an unsatisfied land warrant.	27	2	Petition	368	Public Lands	508	Adverse	......	Laid on table.		
Talbot, Richard	Continuation of pension	16	2	Petition	88	Rev. Pensions	Feb. 18, 1821	Adverse	......	Leave to withdraw.		
Talbott, Richard C	Settlement of accounts as a captain in the United States army.	18	1	Petition	195	Military Affairs	Feb. 11, 1824	Adverse	......	Laid on table.		
Talbot, Thomas, *et al.*	Compensation for property taken by Indians.	20	1	Petition	312	Indian Affairs	Feb. 25, 1828	Adverse	......	Laid on table	....	Leave to withdraw.
Talbot, Thomas, *et al.*	Compensation for property taken by Indians.	25	3	Petition	124	Indian Affairs.						
Talbot, Thomas, *et al.*	Compensation for property taken by Indians.	26	1	Pet. & papers	181, 623	Indian Affairs.						
Talbot, Thomas, *et al.*	Compensation for property taken by Indians.	28	1	Report & papers.	694	Indian Affairs	370	Adverse	......	Leave to withdraw.		
Talbot, Thomas, *et al.*	Compensation for property taken by Indians.	30	1	Senate bill	269	Indian Affairs	299	With't amend.	45	Referred to Committee Whole House.		
Talbot, Thomas, *et al.*	Compensation for property taken by Indians.	30	2	Senate bill	336	....	....	....	45	Passed	....	App'd March 3, 1849
Talbut, Thomas S	Fishing bounty on the Ann Louisa.	27	2	Petition	548	Commerce.						
Talcott, General George	Extra compensation for services as chief of the Ordinance department, United States Army.	31	2	House bill	288	Whole House	....	....	465			

List of private claims presented to the House of Representatives of the United States from the 1st to the 31st Congress, inclusive—Continued.

Names of claimants.	Nature or object of the claim.	Congress.	Session.	How brought before the House of Reps.	Page of journal.	To what committee of the House referred.	No. or date of the report.	Nature of the report.	No. of the bill.	How disposed of by the House of Reps.	How disposed of by the Senate.	Date of the act of Congress, and remarks.
Talcott, William, assignee of.	(See Thomas Sanford)	26	1		182							
Talcott, William	Indemnity for French spoliations prior to 1800.	26	1	Memorial	182	Foreign Affairs	343	Favorable; bill	319	Referred to Committee Whole House.		
Taliaferro, John	Compensation as surgeon mate in revolutionary war.	24	2	Memorial	307	Rev. Claims.						
Taliaferro, John, (Va.)	Per diem and mileage in contesting seat in Congress.	29	1	Memorial	872	Elections	June 17, 1846	Favorable; res.		Laid on table.		
Taliaferro, John, (Va.)	Per diem and mileage in contesting seat in Congress.	31	2	Petition	133	Elections.						
Taliaferro, John	(See Lieut. Jonathan Dye, widow of.)	30	1		110							
Taliaferro, Laurence	Payment for rent of house for Indian agency.	28	1	Petition	362	Indian Affairs	365	Adverse		Laid on table.		
Taliaferro, Laurence	Payment for rent of house for Indian agency.	30	1	Memorial	344	Indian Affairs				Discharged; laid on table.		
Taliaferro, Laurence	Payment for rent of house for Indian agency.	31	1	Pet. & papers	906					Leave to withdraw.		
Taliaferro, Nicholas, heirs of.	Commutation of half-pay	23	2	Petition	38	Rev. Claims	Dec. 23, 1834	Adverse		Laid on table.		
Tall, Elijah, *et al*	Compensation for capture of vessel in war of 1812.	14	2	House bill	236				65	Passed	Passed	App'd Feb. 8, 1817
Tallery, John, *et al.*	Compensation for revolutionary services.	10	2	Petition	362	Public Lands				Discharged; referred to select committee.		
Talley, James, widow of.	Revolutionary pension	28	2	Petition	111	Rev. Pensions.						
Tallery, John	Compensation for services rendered and hardships sustained in revolutionary war.	10	2	Petition	363	Public Lands				Disch'd, and to Select.		
Talley, John A., widow of.	Five years' half-pay	28	1	Petition	82	Invalid Pensions	23	Adverse		Laid on table.		
Talley, Mildred	(See James Talley, widow of)	28	2		111							
Talley, Sarah	(See John A. Talley, widow of)	28	1		82							
Tallman, John	Increase of pension	13	1	House bill	56	Whole House	July 20, 1813	With amend.	31	Passed	Passed	App'd Aug. 2, 1813
Tallman, Peleg	Indemnity for French spoliations prior to 1800.	24	2	Memorial	116	Foreign Affairs.						
Tallman, Peleg	Indemnity for French spoliations prior to 1800.	26	1	Memorial	182	Foreign Affairs	343	Favorable; bill	319	Referred to Committee Whole House.		
Tallman, Peleg	Increase of pension	26	2	Petition	55	Invalid Pensions	232	Adverse		Laid on table.		
Talmadge, Benjamin	Liquidation of certain loan office certificates.	4	1	Rep. of Secretary Treasury.	388	Claims	76	Adverse		Laid on table.		
Talmadge, Stephen	Revolutionary pension	24	1	Petition	137	Rev. Pensions	275	Favorable; bill	282	Passed	Passed	App'd June 28, 1835
Talton, Phillis	(See Cuff Wells, former widow of.)	26	1		706							
Tancred, schooner, owners of.	(See Glover Broughton)	29	1		177							
Tan-de-het-se, (an Indian)	Pension	20	2	Res. and papers.	121	Military Pensions	Feb. 13, 1829	By bill	440	Passed.		
Tan-de-het-se, (an Indian)	Pension	21	1	House bill	49	Military Pensions			440			
Tan-de-het-se, (an Indian)	Pension	21	1	Senate bill	340	Military Pensions	Mar. 6, 1830	With amends.	60	Passed		App'd May 30, 1830
Tandy, Willis	Pension	13	3	House bill	740	Whole House	Mar. 1, 1815	With't amend.	303	Passed	Passed	App'd March 3, 1815
Tandy, Willis	Increase of pension	14	1	Petition and docs.	621	Pens. & Rev. Cl'ms.						
Tandy, Willis	Arrears and increase of pension	14	2	Petition	363	Pens. & Rev. Cl'ms.						
Tandy, Willis	Arrears and increase of pension	15	1	Documents	136	Pens. & Rev. Cl'ms.						
Taney, Augustine, and wife	Indemnity for property destroyed in war of 1812.	22	1	Senate bill	975	Claims	June 12, 1832	With't amend.	91	Passed	Passed	App'd July 14, 1832

List of private claims presented to the House of Representatives of the United States from the 1st to the 31st Congress, inclusive—Continued.

Names of claimants.	Nature or object of the claim.	Congress.	Session.	How brought before the House of Reps.	Page of journal.	To what committee of the House referred.	No. or date of the report.	Nature of the report.	No. of the bill.	How disposed of by the House of Reps.	How disposed of by the Senate.	Date of the act of Congress, and remarks.
Taney, Francis L., trustees of.	Payment of a certain commercial claim.	10	1	Petition	216	Claims	April 5, 1808	Favorable; bill	88	Referred to Committee Whole House.		
Taney, Francis L , trustees of.	Payment of a certain commercial claim.	10	1	Senate bill	270	Whole House	April 23, 1808	With amend.	16	Passed	Concurred in.	App'd April 25, 1808
Tankersley, John	Compensation for services and for losses sustained in Indian wars.	18	2	Petition	70	Claims.						
Tankersley, John	Compensation for services and for losses sustained in Indian wars.	19	1	Petition	44	Claims	Feb. 6, 1826	Adverse		Laid on table.		
Tannehill, Adamson	Release from repayment of certain government money.	13	3	Petition	543	Claims.						
Tannehill, Adamson	Release from repayment of certain government money.	14	2	Petition	354	Claims.						
Tannehill, Wilkins	(See Erasmus Chapman and R. H. Boone, assignee of.)	19	1		209							
Tanner, James	Confirmation of title to land	15	1	Petition	312	Priv. Land Claims.						
Tanner, James	Confirmation of title to land	16	1	Petition	71	Priv. Land Claims.						
Tanner, James	Confirmation of title to land	17	1	Petition	55	Public Lands.						
Tanner, James	Confirmation of title to land	18	1	Petition	55	Public Lands.						
Tanner, John and Edward.	Pre-emption right to certain mill sites.	11	3	Petition	442	Public Lands.						
Tanner, John	Release from payment of certain bonds.	16	1	Petition	203	Commerce.						
Tanner, Lemuel	(See Pierre Dufresne, assignee of.)	23	2		442							
Tanner, Samuel T	(See Jona. Holmes, attorney of)	18	2		183							
Tanner, Samuel T	(See Wm. Eldridge, attorney of.)	18	2		183							
Tant, James	(See James S. Douglass, *et al.*)	22	2		105							
Tapman, John, heirs of	Compensation for naval services in revolutionary war.	24	1	Resolution	982	Naval Affairs.						
Tapman, John, heirs of	Compensation for naval services in revolutionary war.	24	2	Petition	85	Naval Affairs	28	Adverse		Laid on table.		
Tapman, John, heirs of	Compensation for naval services in revolutionary war.	25	2	Petition	84	Naval Affairs.						
Tapp, Bayles	Reissue of bounty land warrant	14	1	Resolution	658	Military Affairs.						
Tapp, John	Pension	21	1	Petition	75	Military Pensions.						
Tapp, Mary	(See William Tapp, widow of)	9	2		503							
Tapp, Vincent	Naval pension	11	3	House bill	604	Whole House	Mar. 2, 1811	With amend.	218	Passed	Passed	App'd March 3, 1811
Tapp, William	Compensation for services and supplies furnished in rev. war.	3	1	Petition	66							House refuse to refer.
Tapp, William, widow of	Commutation pay	9	2	Petition	503	Claims.						
Tappan, Amos	(See Mary Bradstreet and Amos Tappan.)	27	2		549							
Tappan, Arthur, and Henry D. Levall.	Restoration of merchandise seized by U. S. revenue officers.	12	2	Petition	610	Ways and Means.						
Tappan, Arthur, and Henry D. Levall.	Restoration of merchandise seized by U. S. revenue officers.	12	2	Senate bill	705	Ways and Means.	Feb. 25, 1813	With't amend.	61	Passed	Passed	App'd March 2, 1813
Tappan, Arthur	Release from forfeiture on certain importations.	13	1	Petition	30	Ways and Means.						
Tappan, Arthur	Release from forfeiture on certain importations.	13	2	Petition	263	Ways and Means.	Mar. 11, 1814	Favorable; bill	163	Rejected.		
Tappan, David	Compensation for time while in captivity, and pay for arms and accoutrements lost at time of capture.	2	1	Petition	498					Referred to Secretary War.		

List of private claims presented to the House of Representatives of the United States from the 1st to the 31st Congress, inclusive—Continued.

Names of claimants.	Nature or object of the claim.	Congress.	Session.	How brought before the House of Reps.	Page of journal.	To what committee of the House referred.	No. or date of the report.	Nature of the report.	No. of the bill.	How disposed of by the House of Reps.	How disposed of by the Senate.	Date of the act of Congress, and remarks.
Tappan, John	That duties paid on imports be refunded.	18	1	Petition	27	Ways and Means	Jan. 15, 1824	Favorable; bill	60	Passed	Passed	App'd May 19, 1824
Tappan, Lewis, and G. Searle.	Release from penalties incurred by the non-importation laws.	12	2	Petition	612	Ways and Means	....	....	......	....	....	See act Feb. 27, 1813
Tappan, Peter	Restoration of pension	17	1	Petition	30	Rev. Pensions	....	....	......	....	....	See act Feb. 4, 1822
Tappan, Samuel	Pension	14	1	Petition	558	Pens. & Rev. Cl'ms.	April 6, 1816	Adverse	......	Laid on table.		
Tarascon, Lewis Amastatius	(See Triol & Co.)	5	2	....	130							
Tarbell, Joseph, by Eliza, widow of.	Provision for support of self and her children.	14	2	Petition	40	Naval Affairs	....	....	......	Discharged; referred to Com. Whole House on S. bill.	....	See act Mar. 3, 1819
Tarbell, Joseph, child of	Balance of naval pension due	25	3	Memorial	360	Naval Affairs.						
Tarbell, Joseph, child of	Balance of naval pension due	26	1	Memorial	179	Naval Affairs.						
Tarbell, William	Invalid pension	11	2	House bill	283	Whole House	April 9, 1810	With amend.	107	Passed	Passed	App'd Apirl 27, 1810
Tarbox & Brown	(See Brown & Tarbox.)	31	1	....	214							
Tarbox, Roswell	(See Solomon Tarbox, representatives of.)	27	2	....	1158							
Tarbox, Samuel	Fishing bounty	17	2	Petition	51	Commerce.						
Tarbox, Solomon, representatives of.	Revolutionary pension	27	2	Petition	1158	Rev. Pensions.						
Tarbox, Solomon, representatives of.	Revolutionary pension	31	1	Petition	582	Rev. Claims.						
Tarbox, Solomon, representatives of.	Revolutionary pension	31	2	Petition	174	Rev. Pensions	42	Adverse	......	Laid on table.		
Tardiveau, Bartholomew, sole heir of, by devisee.	Confirmation of title to land in Illinois.	16	2	Petition	79	Priv. Land Claims.	Jan. 24, 1821	Adverse	......	Rejected.		
Tardiveau, Peter, devisee of.	(See Bartholomew Tardiveau, sole heir of, &c.)	16	2	....	79							
Tarkington, Sylvanus	Invalid pension	29	1	Petition	714	Invalid Pensions	July 25, 1846	Adverse	......	Laid on table.		
Tarlton, Eleanor	(See Jeremiah Tarlton, widow of.)	26	1	....	950							
Tarlton, Jeremiah, widow of.	Revolutionary pension	26	1	Resolution	950	Rev. Pensions.						
Tarn, John, by Susannah, widow of.	Revolutionary pension	31	1	Petition	311	Rev. Pensions	441	Favorable; bill	371	Referred to Committee Whole House.		
Tarn, John, by Susannah, widow of.	Revolutionary pension	31	2	Petition	38	....	....	....	......	Leave to withdraw.		
Tarr, Jonathan, (Mass.)	(See George Gott and others)	23	1	....	239							
Tarrant, Larkin M	Additional pay for provisions furnished United States troops.	21	1	Petition	40	Military Pensions	....	....	......	Disch'd; and to Claims.		
Tarrington, Capt. William.	Compensation for aid extended to American seamen.	25	2	Rep. of Secretary State.	899	Commerce	903	Favorable; bill	797	Referred to Committee Whole House.		
Tarrington, Capt. William.	Compensation for aid extended to American seamen.	25	3	Bill of last sess.	529	Whole House	....	....	797			
Tarver, Hartwell H	Compensation for provisions furnished U. S. troops, Florida war.	26	1	Petition	960	Claims.						
Tarver, Hartwell H	Compensation for provisions furnished U. S. troops, Florida war.	26	2	Petition	148	Claims.						
Tarvin, Elijah and Elisha.	(See William Tarvin, heirs of)	18	1	....	105							
Tarvin, George C., (Ky.).	Compensation for work on government building in Kentucky.	25	2	Petition	88	Claims	Jan. 4, 1838	Adverse	......	Laid on table.		
Tarvin, William, heirs of.	Confirmation of title to land	18	1	Petition	105	Public Lands	....	....	......	Referred to Committee Whole House on bill No. 57.		
Tarvin, William, heirs of.	Confirmation of title to land	18	2	Petition	47	Priv. Land Claims.						

List of private claims presented to the House of Representatives of the United States from the 1st to the 31st Congress, inclusive—Continued.

Names of claimants.	Nature or object of the claim.	Congress.	Session.	How brought before the House of Reps.	Page of journal.	To what committee of the House referred.	No. or date of the report.	Nature of the report.	No. of the bill.	How disposed of by the House of Reps.	How disposed of by the Senate.	Date of the act of Congress, and remarks.
Task, Oxford	Invalid pension	10	2	House bill	499	Whole House	Feb. 23, 1809	With amend.	158	Passed	Passed	App'd March 3, 1809
Tasker, Matthew	Naval pension	27	3	Petition	350	Naval Pension.						
Tasker, Matthew	Naval pension	29	1	Petition	68	Rev. Pensions	728	Adverse		Laid on table.		
Tate, Adam	Pension	15	2	Petition	196	Rev. Pensions	Feb. 11, 1819	Adverse		Laid on table.		
Tate, Charles	(See John McClellan, sureties of)	25	2		169							
Tate, David, (Ala.)	Compensation for supplies furnished United States army.	16	2	Petition	113	Claims.						
Tate, David, (Ala.)	Compensation for supplies furnished United States army.	19	1	Senate bill	474	Claims	Jan. 20, 1826	With't amend.	85	Passed		App'd May 20, 1826
Tate, David	Confirmation of title to land	18	2	Petition	42	Public Lands	Jan. 28, 1825	Favorable; bill	301	Passed	Passed	App'd March 3, 1825
Tate, David, (Ky.)	Compensation for revolutionary services.	22	1	Petition	62	Rev. Claims.						
Tate, David, sen., (Tenn.)	Invalid pension	21	2	Petition	43	Military Pensions.						
Tate, David, (Pa.)	Invalid pension	31	1	Petition	411	Invalid Pensions.						
Tate, Robert L	(See Robert L. Tait)	21	1		275							
Tatem, Henry, by Henry A., heir of.	Compensation for revolutionary services.	27	2	Petition	307	Rev. Claims	978	Adverse		Laid on table.		
Tatem, Thomas, (Va.)	Balance due for timber furnished United States navy.	26	1	Petition	622	Claims	May 25, 1840	Adverse		Laid on table.		
Tatem, Thomas, (Va.)	Balance due for timber furnished United Stated navy.	28	1	Petition	262	Claims	344	Adverse		Laid on table.		
Tatem, William, (Va.)	Indemnity for money lost in United States mail.	24	1	Memorial	481	P. Of. & P. Roads.						
Tatem, William, (Va.)	Indemnity for money lost in United States mail.	25	2	Petition	425	P. Of. & P. Roads.	631	Adverse		Laid on table.		
Tatem, William, (Va.)	Indemnity for money lost in United States mail.	26	1	Petition	342	P. Of. & P. Roads.	April 4, 1840	Adverse		Laid on table.		
Tatham, Benjamin, *et al.*	Extension of patent	29	1	Petition	571	Patents	534	Favorable; bill	356	Referred to Committee Whole House.		
Tatham, Benjamin, *et al.*	Extension of patent	31	1	Petition	644	Patents.						
Tatham, George N., *et al.*	(See Benjamin Tatham, *et al.*)	29	1		571							
Tatham, Henry B.	(See Benjamin Tatham, *et al.*)	29	1		571							
Tatham, William	Compensation for topographical services.	12	2	Memorial	562	Military Affairs				Discharged		Leave to withdraw.
Tatham, William	Compensation for topographical services.	12	2	Petition	615	Claims				Referred to Secretary of War.		
Tatham, William	Compensation for topographical services.	13	1	Rep. of Secretary War.	67					Laid on table.		
Tatham, William	Compensation for topographical services.	13	3	Petition and rep't Sec. of War.	668, 713	Select	Feb. 14, 1845	Favorable; bill	295	Referred to Committee Whole House.		
Tatham, William	Compensation for topographical services.	14	1	Petition and rep't Sec. of War.	209, 311	Military Affairs.						
Tatham, William	Compensation for topographical services.	14	2	Petition	243	Select	Feb. 10, 1816	Adverse		Laid on table.		
Tatlow, Joseph	Compensation for a vessel impressed into service of United States.	1	3	Petition	383					Referred to Secretary of War.		
Tatlow, Joseph	Compensation for a vessel impressed into service of United States.	3	2	Rep. of Secretary War.	284	Claims				Laid on table.		
Tatlow, Joseph	Compensation for a vessel impressed into service of United States.	4	1	Petition and docs.	389	Claims	Dec. 28, 1795	Adverse		Leave to withdraw.		
Tatom, Absalom, executors of.	Confirmation of title to land	13	3	Petition	700	Public Lands.						

List of private claims presented to the House of Representatives of the United States from the 1st to the 31st Congress, inclusive—Continued.

3—57

Names of claimants.	Nature or object of the claim.	Congress.	Session.	How brought before the House of Reps.	Page of journal.	To what committee of the House referred.	No. or date of the report.	Nature of the report.	No. of the bill.	How disposed of by the House of Reps.	How disposed of by the Senate.	Date of the act of Congress, and remarks.
Tatom, Absalom, executors of.	Confirmation of title to land	14	1	Petition	49	Public Lands	Jan. 24, 1816	Report	......	Laid on table.		
Tatom, Absalom, executors of.	Confirmation of title to land	14	2	Petition	60	Priv. Land Claims	Jan. 14, 1817	....	......	Leave to withdraw.		
Tatom, Absalom, executors of.	Confirmation of title to land	15	1	Petition	312	Priv. Land Claims	....	....	......	....	....	See act April 4, 1848.
Tatum, Dorothea	(See Henry Tatum, widow of)	25	1	....	91							
Tatum, Henry	Compensation for revolutionary services.	14	2	Petition and docs.	90, 343	Rev. Claims.						
Tatum, Henry	Compensation for revolutionary services.	15	1	Petition and docs.	31	Pens. & Rev. Cl'ms.						
Tatum, Henry	Compensation for revolutionary services.	15	2	Petition and docs.	126	Pens. & Rev. Cl'ms.	185	Adverse	......	Laid on table.		
Tatum, Lieut. Henry, (Va.)	Commutation of half-pay	22	2	Petition	217	Rev. Claims.						
Tatum, Lieut. Henry, (Va.)	Commutation of half-pay	23	1	Petition	41	Rev. Claims.						
Tatum, Lieut. Henry, (Va.)	Commutation of half-pay	23	2	Petition	56	Rev. Claims.						
Tatum, Henry, widow of.	Revolutionary pension	25	1	Petition	91	....	....	....	......	Laid on table.		
Tatum, Henry, widow of.	Revolutionary pension	25	2	Petition	236	Rev. Pensions	....	....	......	Discharged; laid on table.		
Tatum, Henry, widow of.	Revolutionary pension	26	1	Petition	323	Rev. Pensions	424	Adverse	......	Laid on table.		
Tatum, Nathaniel P.	Full contract price for timber furnished United States navy.	23	1	Petition	437	Claims	May 27, 1834	Favorable; bill	494	Referred to Committee Whole House.		
Tatum, Nathaniel P.	Full contract price for timber furnished United States navy.	24	1	Petition	50	Claims	Dec. 21, 1835	Favorable; bill	17	Passed	Passed	App'd June 23, 1836
Taulbec, Isaac D., representatives of.	Remuneration for a horse lost in Black Hawk war.	30	1	Petition	77	Claims	161	Adverse	......	Laid on table.		
Tausooner, William	(See Wyandott Indians)	27	3	....	259							
Tavenor, Alexander	(See Alexander Torrence, widow of)	28	1	....	72							
Tayloe, Benj. Ogle	(See John Tayloe, executor of.)	22	2	....	206							
Tayloe, Benj. Ogle	Fulfilment of contract for occupancy of building as Gen'l Post Office.	27	2	Petition	246	P. Of. & P. Roads.	Aug. 30, 1842	Favorable	J. R. 21	Referred to Committee Whole House.		
Tayloe, Benj. Ogle	Fulfilment of contract for occupancy of building as Gen'l Post Office.	27	3	Joint resolution.	232	Whole House	Feb. 6, 1843	With amend.	J. R. 21	Passed	Pas'd amended	Laid on table in House.
Tayloe, Benj. Ogle	Fulfilment of contract for occupancy of building as Gen'l Post Office	28	1	Petition	117	Claims.						
Tayloe, Benj. Ogle	Fulfilment of contract for occupancy of building as Gen'l Post Office.	29	1	Petition and docs.	194	Claims	795	Favorable; bill	524	Referred to Committee Whole House.		
Tayloe, Benj. Ogle	Fulfilment of contract for occupancy of building as Gen'l Post Office.	30	1	Petition and docs.	154	Claims	151	Favorable; bill	130	Passed	Passed	App'd Aug. 14, 1848
Tayloe, John, executor of.	Indemnity for loss of vessel under charter of United States.	22	2	Petition	206	Foreign Affairs.						
Taylor, Abigail	(See Gad. Taylor, widow of)	28	1	....	944							
Taylor, Andrew, (N. Y.).	Settlement for services as deputy quartermaster in revolutionary war.	3	2	Memorial & rep't of Sec. War.	226, 284	Claims.						
Taylor, Andrew, (N. Y.).	Settlement for services as deputy quartermaster in revolutionary war.	4	1	Memorial	386	Claims	Dec. 22, 1795	Adverse	......	Leave to withdraw.		
Taylor, Major Andrew, (N. Y.)	Balance of pay and subsistence due him.	7	1	Memorial	160	Claims	Mar. 30, 1802	Adverse	......	Laid on table.		
Taylor, Anne	(See Captain Samuel Taylor, of South Carolina, widow of.)	26	1	....	630							

List of private claims presented to the House of Representatives of the United States from the 1st to the 31st Congress, inclusive—Continued.

Names of claimants.	Nature or object of the claim.	Congress.	Session.	How brought before the House of Reps.	Page of journal.	To what committee of the House referred.	No. or date of the report.	Nature of the report.	No. of the bill.	How disposed of by the House of Reps.	How disposed of by the Senate.	Date of the act of Congress, and remarks.
Taylor, Anson H	Compensation as a despatch rider in 1832.	31	2	Petition	343	Claims.						
Taylor, General Augustine, widow of.	Revolutionary pension	24	2	Petition	45	Rev. Pensions	10	Favorable; bill	768	Referred to Committee Whole House.		
Taylor, General Augustine, widow of.	Revolutionary pension	25	2	Petition	38	Rev. Pensions	161	Favorable; bill	186	Referred to Committee Whole House.		
Taylor, General Augustine, widow of.	Revolutionary pension	25	3	Bill of last sess.	375	Whole House	Jan. 25, 1837	With't amend.	186	Passed	Adverse.	
Taylor, Benjamin R., administrator of.	Compensation as assistant surgeon in Florida war.	27	2	Petition	1049	Claims.						
Taylor, Benjamin R., administrator of.	Compensation as assistant surgeon in Florida war.	27	3	Pet. and papers	101	Claims.						
Taylor, Benoni, *et al*	Land reservation under treaty of Dancing Rabit Creek.	23	1	Petition	523	Indian Affairs.						
Taylor, Betty	Continuation of revolutionary pension.	28	1	Petition	850	Rev. Pensions	....	....	......	....	....	See act June 17, 1844
Taylor, Catharine	Invalid pension	28	1	Resolution	557	Rev. Pensions	....	....	......	....	....	See act June 17, 1844
Taylor, Charles M., sureties of.	Release from liability	20	1	Petition	168	Judiciary	....	....	......	Discharged; laid on table.		
Taylor, Charles M., sureties of.	Release from liability	23	1	Petition	219	Judiciary.						
Taylor, Dr. Charles, heirs of.	Commutation of half-pay	23	2	Petition	128	Rev. Claims.						
Taylor, Dr. Charles, heirs of.	Commutation of half-pay	24	1	Petition	103	Rev. Claims	563	Favorable; bill	555	Referred to Committee Whole House.		
Taylor, Dr. Charles, heirs of.	Commutation of half-pay	25	2	Petition	40	Rev. Claims	137	Favorable; bill	155	Passed	Adverse.	
Taylor, Dr. Charles, heirs of.	Commutation of half-pay	25	3	Petition	84	Rev. Claims	24	Favorable; bill	922	Referred to Committee Whole House.		
Taylor, Dr. Charles, heirs of.	Commutation of half-pay	26	1	Petition	163	Rev. Claims.						
Taylor, Dr. Charles, heirs of.	Commutation of half-pay	26	2	Petition	36	Rev. Claims	181	Adverse.	......	Laid on table.		
Taylor, Dr. Charles, heirs of.	Commutation of half-pay	27	2	Petition	61	Rev. Claims	401	Adverse	......	Laid on table.		
Taylor, Dr. Charles, executor of.	Commutation of half-pay	29	1	Petition	233	Rev. Claims.						
Taylor, Dr. Charles, representatives of.	Commutation of half-pay	31	1	Petition	234	Rev. Claims.						
Taylor, Charles, (Va)	Invalid pension	30	1	Petition	423	Invalid Pensions	634	Adverse	......	Laid on table.		
Taylor, Charles, (Va)	Invalid pension	30	2	Petition	350	....	....	....	......	Leave to withdraw.		
Taylor, Charles, (Ala)	Pre-emption right to land	25	3	Petition	122	Priv. Land Claims.						
Taylor, Cornelius, (Ill)	Pre-emption right to land	15	1	Petition	122	Priv. Land Claims.						
Taylor, Cornelius, (Fla)	Extra compensation for carrying United States mail.	25	2	Petition	110	P. Of. & P. Roads.	992	Favorable; bill	852	Referred to Committee Whole House.		
Taylor, Cornelius, (Fla)	Extra compensation for carrying United States mail.	25	3	Bill of last sess.	432	Whole House	Feb. 1, 1839	With't amend.	852	Passed	Passed	App'd March 3, 1839
Taylor, Creed, *et al*	Release from payment of certain judgment.	29	2	Senate bill	380	P. Of. & P. Roads.	....	....	S. 135			
Taylor, Creed, *et al*	Release from payment of certain judgment.	30	1	Senate bill	683	P. Of. & P. Roads.	606	Favorable	S. 69	Referred to Committee Whole House.		
Taylor, Creed, *et al*	Release from payment of certain judgment.	30	2	Senate bill	319	Whole House	Jan. 26, 1849	With't amend.	S. 69	Passed	....	App'd Feb. 6, 1849

List of private claims presented to the House of Representatives of the United States from the 1st to the 31st Congress, inclusive—Continued.

Names of claimants.	Nature or object of the claim.	Congress.	Session.	How brought before the House of Reps.	Page of journal.	To what committee of the House referred.	No. or date of the report.	Nature of the report.	No. of the bill.	How disposed of by the House of Reps.	How disposed of by the Senate.	Date of the act of Congress, and remarks.
Taylor, Creed	(See Joseph De Hauterive, heirs of.)	31	2	....	270							
Taylor, Daniel	Pension	21	2	Petition	68	Military Pensions	....	....	......	Laid on table.		
Taylor, David, and Issi Fletcher.	Payment for services and reimbursement of expenses in curing a sick soldier of United States army.	14	2	Petition	29	Claims	....	....	......	Discharged; laid on table.		
Taylor, David, (N. Y.)	Indemnity for staves burnt by United States troops.	16	1	Petition	145	Claims	Feb. 4, 1820	Adverse	......	Laid on table.		
Taylor, David, (N. Y.)	Indemnity for staves burnt by United States troops.	17	1	Petition	39	Claims	Dec. 20, 1821	Adverse	......	Laid on table.		
Taylor, David, (N. C.)	Payment of claim against the United States, which has been audited by Treasury Department.	29	2	Memorial	396	Indian Affairs.						
Taylor, David, (Conn.)	Pension	20	2	Petition	31	Military Pensions	....	....	......	Discharged; leave to withdraw.		
Taylor, Edward	Invalid pension	30	1	Petition	440	Invalid Pensions	554	Favorable; bill	454	Referred to Committee Whole House.		
Taylor, Edward	Invalid pension	30	2	Bill of last sess.	318	Whole House	Jan. 26, 1849	With't amend.	454	Passed	With't amend.	
Taylor, Edward	Invalid pension	31	1	Petition	348	Invalid Pensions	385	Adverse	......	Laid on table.		
Taylor, Edmund H.	(See Col Francis Taylor, administrator of.)	30	1	....	664							
Taylor, Elijah	Additional compensation for revolutionary services.	22	1	Petition	77	Rev. Claims	....	....	......	Discharged; laid on table.		
Taylor, Elijah	Additional compensation for revolutionary services.	22	2	Petition	29	Rev. Claims.						
Taylor, Elijah	Additional compensation for revolutionary services.	23	1	Petition	54	Rev. Claims.						
Taylor, Eliphalet	Invalid pension	3	1	Rep. of Secretary War.	350	Claims.						
Taylor, Eliphalet	Invalid pension	4	1	Res. and docs.	373	Claims	Feb. 18, 1796	Favorable; bill	156	Passed	Passed	App'd April 20, 1796
Taylor, Elizabeth	(See Major William Taylor, Ky., widow of.)	21	2	....	209							
Taylor, Elnathan	Invalid pension	6	1	Petition	577	Claims	Feb. 3, 1800	Adverse	......	Rejected.		
Taylor, Elnathan, widow of.	Invalid pension	25	2	Resolution	618	Rev. Claims	....	....	......	Discharged; laid on table.		
Taylor, Ezekiel, heirs of.	Revolutionary pension	29	1	Petition	209	Rev. Pensions.						
Taylor, Ezekiel, heirs of.	Revolutionary pension	29	2	Petition	162	Rev. Pensions.						
Taylor, Francis	Compensation for revolutionary services.	1	2	Petition and rep't Secretary War.	339, 385	....	....	....	......	Laid on table.		
Taylor, Francis	(See Henry Field, representatives of.)	8	1	....	514							
Taylor, Maj. Francis, (Va.)	Depreciation of one years' pay	4	1	Memorial	437	Claims	May 7, 1796	Adverse	......	Leave to withdraw.		
Taylor, Col. Francis, heirs of.	Commutation of five years' full pay instead of half-pay for life.	23	1	Petition	97	Rev. Claims.						
Taylor, Col. Francis, heirs of.	Commutation of five years' full pay instead of half-pay for life.	23	2	Petition	77	Rev. Claims.						
Taylor, Col. Francis, heirs of.	Commutation of five years' full pay instead of half-pay for life.	24	1	Petition	63	Rev. Claims	492	Favorable; bill	494	Referred to Committee Whole House.		
Taylor, Col. Francis, heirs of.	Commutation of five years' full pay instead of half-pay for life.	24	2	House bill	200	Whole House	....	....	494			
Taylor, Col. Francis, heirs of.	Commutation of five years' full pay instead of half-pay for life.	25	2	Petition	40	Rev. Claims	127	Favorable; bill	145	Passed	Discharged.	

List of private claims presented to the House of Representatives of the United States from the 1st to the 31st Congress, inclusive—Continued.

Names of claimants.	Nature or object of the claim.	Congress.	Session.	How brought before the House of Reps.	Page of journal.	To what committee of the House referred.	No. or date of the report.	Nature of the report.	No. of the bill.	How disposed of by the House of Reps.	How disposed of by the Senate.	Date of the act of Congress, and remarks.
Taylor, Col. Francis, heirs of.	Commutation of five years' full pay instead of half pay for life.	25	3	Petition	86	Rev. Claims.						
Taylor, Col. Francis, heirs of.	Commutation of five years' full pay instead of half pay for life.	26	1	Petition	163	Rev. Claims.						
Taylor, Col. Francis, heirs of.	Compensation of five years' full pay instead of half pay for life.	27	2	Petition	61	Rev. Claims	400	Adverse		Laid on table.		
Taylor, Col. Francis, heirs of.	Commutation of five years' full pay instead of half pay for life.	29	1	Memorial	327	Rev. Claims	380	Favorable; bill	288	Referred to Committee Whole House.		
Taylor, Col. Francis, administrator of.	Commutation of five years' full pay instead of half pay for life.	30	1	Petition	664	Rev. Claims.						
Taylor, Col. Francis, administrator of.	Commutation of five years' full pay instead of half-pay for life.	30	2	Petition	174	Rev. Claims.						
Taylor, Col. Francis, administrator of.	Commutation of five years' full pay instead of half-pay for life.	31	1	Petition	233, 661	Rev. Claims.						
Taylor, Frederick	Invalid pension	30	1	Petition	522	Invalid Pensions	587	Adverse		Laid on table.		
Taylor, Gad., widow of	Revolutionary pension	28	1	Petition	944	Rev. Pensions.						
Taylor, Gamaliel, and sureties of.	Release from certain liability as U. States marshal.	30	1	Senate bill	976	Judiciary			S. 232			
Taylor, Gamaliel, and sureties of.	Release from certain liability as U. States marshal.	31	1	Senate bill	870	Judiciary			S. 180			
Taylor, Gamaliel, and sureties of.	Release from certain liability as U. States marshal.	31	2	Senate bill	49	Judiciary	Dec. 12, 1850	With't amend.	S. 180	Passed	Concurred in	App'd Dec. 24, 1850
Taylor, Garland B., *et al*.	(See Garland Burnley, representatives of.)	22	2		142							
Taylor, George, jr.	Increase of compensation as chief clerk in the State Department.	3	1	Petition	32	Select	Mar. 11, 1794	Favorable; res.	69	Passed	Rejected.	
Taylor, George, jr., *et al*.	Increase of compensation as clerk in the various Executive departments.	3	1	Senate bill	180	Whole House	June 4, 1794	With't amend.	S. 17	Passed		App'd June 7, 1794
Taylor, George K.	Compensation as a judge of the circuit court of United States.	7	2	Petition	307	Whole House	Jan. 27, 1803	Adverse		Rejected		Leave to withdraw.
Taylor, George, (Va.)	Indemnity for French spoliations prior to 1800.	18	1	Petition	131	Judiciary				Discharged; laid on table.		
Taylor, George, (Va.)	Indemnity for French spoliations prior to 1800.	20	2	Petition	61	Foreign Affairs	82	Adverse		Laid on table.		
Taylor, George, (Va.)	Indemnity for French spoliations prior to 1800.	22	1	Petition	54	Foreign Affairs.						
Taylor, George, (Va.)	Indemnity for French spoliations prior to 1800.	24	2	Memorial	46	Foreign Affairs.						
Taylor, George, (Va.)	Indemnity for French spoliations prior to 1800.	25	2	Petition	71	Foreign Affairs				Discharged; laid on table.		
Taylor, George, (Va.)	Indemnity for French spoliations prior to 1800.	26	1	Petition	340	Claims.						
Taylor, George, (Va.)	Indemnity for French spoliations prior to 1800.	26	2	Petition	55	Foreign Affairs				Discharged; referred to Com. Whole House.		
Taylor, George, (Va.)	Indemnity for French spoliations prior to 1800.	27	2	Petition	72	Foreign Affairs.						
Taylor, George, (Va.)	Indemnity for French spoliations prior to 1800.	27	3	Petition	61	Foreign Affairs.						
Taylor, George, (Va.)	Indemnity for French spoliations prior to 1800.	28	1	Petition	103	Foreign Affairs.						
Taylor, George, (Va.)	Indemnity for French spoliations prior to 1800.	28	2	Petition	55	Foreign Affairs.						

List of private claims presented to the House of Representatives of the United States from the 1st *to the* 31st *Congress, inclusive*—Continued.

Names of claimants.	Nature or object of the claim.	Congress.	Session.	How brought before the House of Reps.	Page of journal.	To what committee of the House referred.	No. or date of the report.	Nature of the report.	No. of the bill.	How disposed of by the House of Reps.	How disposed of by the Senate.	Date of the act of Congress, and remarks.
Taylor, George, (Va.)	Indemnity for French spoliations prior to 1800.	29	1	Petition	92	Foreign Affairs.						
Taylor, George, (Va.)	Indemnity for French spoliations prior to 1800.	30	1	Petition	118	Foreign Affairs	Jan. 4, 1848	Favorable; bill	21	Referred to Committee Whole House.		
Taylor, George, (Va.)	Indemnity for French spoliations prior to 1800.	31	1	Petition	256	Foreign Affairs	355	Favorable; bill	318	Referred to Committee Whole House.		
Taylor, George, (Va.)	Indemnity for French spoliations prior to 1800.	31	2	Petition	72	Foreign Affairs.						
Taylor, George, (D. C.)	Indemnity for French spoliations prior to 1800.	26	1	Memorial	182	Foreign Affairs	343	Favorable; bill	319	Referred to Committee Whole House.		
Taylor, George, jr., (N. Y.)	Compensation for revolutionary services.	21	1	Petition	70	Military Pensions	April 2, 1830	Adverse		Laid on table.		
Taylor, George and Jesse.	Confirmation of Indian land title	23	1	Petition	158	Public Lands.	Feb. 21, 1834	Favorable; bill	316	Referred to Committee Whole House.		
Taylor, George and Jesse.	Confirmation of Indian land title	24	1	Petition	258, 260	Public Lands.				Discharged; laid on table.		
Taylor, George, (Ga.)	Invalid pension or five years' full pay.	28	2	Petition	272	Invalid Pensions.						
Taylor, George, attorney of.	Compensation as an express rider during Florida war.	29	1	Petition	219	Invalid Pensions	302	Adverse		Laid on table.		
Taylor, George	Compensation for work done on La Pleasance Bay road.	28	1	Petition	239	Claims	131	Favorable; bill	121	Passed	Passed	App'd June 15, 1844
Taylor, George, (Ky.)	Bounty land or pension, services in war of 1812.	30	1	Petition	208	Invalid Pensions	142	Adverse		Laid on table.		
Taylor, Grant	Invalid pension	13	3	Petition	640	Pens. & Rev. Cl'ms.	Feb. 20, 1815	Favorable; bill	303	Passed	Passed	App'd March 3, 1815
Taylor, Griffin	Renewal of military land warrant.	6	2	Petition	765	Select	Feb. 18, 1801	Adverse		Rejected.		
Taylor, Griffin	Renewal of military land warrant.	7	2	Petition	314	Select				Leave to withdraw.		
Taylor, Henry R., & wife.	Indemnity for horse lost in service of United States, in 1812.	23	1	Petition	567	Claims	532	Favorable; bill	538	Referred to Committee Whole House.		
Taylor, Henry R., & others	Indemnity for horse lost in service of United States, in 1812.	24	1	Petition	51	Claims	26	Favorable; bill	26	Passed	Passed	App'd Feb. 9, 1836
Taylor, Huldah	(See Gen. Augustine Taylor, widow of.)	24	2		45							
Taylor, Isaac, & John Harvey.	Remission of duties on merchandise destroyed by fire.	3	2	Petition	267	Select	Dec. 16, 1794	Favorable		Referred to Committee Whole House.		
Taylor, Isaac S.	Permission to change entry of land	28	1	Petition	113	Priv. Land Claims.						
Taylor, Isaac W.	Arrears of pension	25	2	Petition	401	Invalid Pensions				Discharged.		
Taylor, Isaac W.	Arrears of pension	25	3	Petition	89	Invalid Pensions	Jan. 9, 1839	Adverse		Laid on table.		
Taylor, Jacob, (Ky.)	Pension	21	2	Petition	106	Military Pensions.						
Taylor, Jacob, former widow of.	Revolutionary pension	29	2	Petition	301	Rev. Claims.						
Taylor, Jacob, former widow of.	Revolutionary pension	30	1	Petition	188	Rev. Claims	116	Adverse		Laid on table.		
Taylor, James	Compensation for revolutionary services and payment for supplies furnished in revolutionary war.	2	1	Petition	487					Referred to Secretary of war.		
Taylor, James	Compensation for revolutionary services and payment for supplies furnished in revolutionary war.	3	2	Rep. of Secretary of War.	278	Claims	May 2, 1795	Adverse		Laid on table.		
Taylor, James	Compensation for revolutionary services and payment for supplies furnished in revolutionary war.	4	1	Petition and docs.	598	Claims	May 31, 1796	Adverse		Laid on table.		

List of private claims presented to the House of Representatives of the United States from the 1st to the 31st Congress, inclusive—Continued.

Names of claimants.	Nature or object of the claim.	Congress.	Session.	How brought before the House of Reps.	Page of journal.	To what committee of the House referred.	No. or date of the report.	Nature of the report.	No. of the bill.	How disposed of by the House of Reps.	How disposed of by the Senate.	Date of the act of Congress, and remarks.
Taylor, James, (Ky.)	Credit, as quartermaster general, of money which fell into the hands of British, at Detroit.	13	1	Petition	31	Claims.						
Taylor, James, (Ky.)	Settlement of accounts as paymaster and quartermaster general of army in war of 1812.	22	1	Petition	575	Claims.						
		22	2	Senate bill	166	Claims	96	With amend.	S. 35	Passed	Concurred in.	App'd March 2, 1833
Taylor, James, (Ky.)	Further allowance as quartermaster general.	23	1	Senate bill	754	Claims	552	With't amend.	S. 102	Laid on table.		
Taylor, James, (Ky.)	Further allowance as quartermaster general.	23	2	Petition	41	Claims				Discharged; leave to withdraw.		Leave to withdraw rescinded.
Taylor, James, (Ky.)	Further allowance as quartermaster general.	25	2	Petition	87	Claims.						
Taylor, James, (Ky.)	Further allowance as quartermaster general.	26	1	Petition	306	Claims	422	Adverse		Laid on table.		
Taylor, James, (Ohio)	Pension	15	1	Petition	126	Pens. & Rev. Cl'ms.	100	Adverse		Leave to withdraw.		
Taylor, James, (Ohio)	Pension	17	1	Petition	113	Referred to Secretary of War.	Feb. 19, 1822	Report		Leave to withdraw.		
Taylor, James, (Mass.)	Arrears of pension	21	2	Resolution	165	Military Pensions.						
Taylor, James, (Mass.)	Arrears of pension	23	1	Petition	113	Rev. Pensions.						
Taylor, James, (Mass.)	Arrears of pension	23	2	Petition	66	Rev. Pensions	57	Favorable; bill	657	Referred to Committee Whole House.		
Taylor, James, (Mass.)	Arrears of pension	24	1	Petition	137	Rev. Pensions	183	Favorable; bill	188	Passed	Passed	App'd June 28, 1836
Taylor, James, (Mass.)	Arrears of pension	25	3	Petition	81	Invalid Pensions	Jan. 16, 1839	Adverse		Laid on table.		
Taylor, James, (Mass.)	Arrears of pension	26	1	Petition	287	Invalid Pensions	March 5, 1840	Adverse		Laid on table.		
Taylor, James, (Mass.)	Arrears of pension	27	2	Petition	1299					Leave to withdraw.		
Taylor, James, (Mass.)	Arrears of pension	29	1	Petition	578	Rev. Pensions	785	Adverse		Laid on table.		
Taylor, James	(See Joseph Brown)	24	2		78							
Taylor, James, (Mass.)	Compensation for services in custom-house, New Bedford.	28	1	Petition	204	Ways and Means.						
Taylor, James, (Ala.)	(See William Futch, administrator of.)	22	1		417							
Taylor, James	(See William H. Bedford, agent.)	28	1		262							
Taylor, James, (Ga.)	Grant of register to foreign built vessel.	23	1	Petition	301	Commerce	Feb. 26, 1834	Favorable; bill	326	Passed	Passed	App'd May 2, 1834
Taylor, James, of Va., heirs of.	Compensation for revolutionary services.	30	1	Petition	114	Rev. Pensions				Discharged; laid on table.		Leave to withdraw.
Taylor, Jane	(See James Plunkett, heirs of.)	23	1		567							
Taylor, Janet, *et al.*	(See John Paul Jones)	22	1		78							
Taylor, Jaquelin	To refund certain duties	31	2	Petition	37	Commerce.						
Taylor, Jeremiah	Invalid pension	24	2	Resolution	419	Invalid Pensions				Discharged; laid on table.		
Taylor, Jesse, widow of	Revolutionary pension	30	1	Senate bill	976	Rev. Pensions	Aug. 12, 1848	With't amend.	S. 179	Passed		App'd Aug. 14, 1848
Taylor, John, (Mass.)	Compensation for revolutionary services.	2	1	Petition	440					Referred to Secretary of War.		
Taylor, John, (Mass.)	Compensation for revolutionary services.	2	2	Rep. of Secretary War.	649	Whole House.						
Taylor, John, (Mass.)	Compensation for revolutionary services.	3	1	Rep. of Secretary War.	131	Select	May 26, 1794	Favorable; bill ordered.	62	Passed	Passed	App'd June 7, 1794
Taylor, John, (Mass.)	Revolutionary pension	3	2	Rep. of Secretary War.	262	Claims.						
Taylor, John, (Mass.)	Revolutionary pension	4	1	Petition	425	Claims	May 7, 1796	Adverse		Rejected.		
Taylor, John, (Mass.)	Revolutionary pension	15	1	Res. and petition.	229, 257	Pens. & Rev. Cl'ms.						

List of private claims presented to the House of Representatives of the United States from the 1st to the 31st Congress, inclusive—Continued.

Names of claimants.	Nature or object of the claim.	Congress.	Session.	How brought before the House of Reps.	Page of journal.	To what committee of the House referred.	No. or date of the report.	Nature of the report.	No. of the bill.	How disposed of by the House of Reps.	How disposed of by the Senate.	Date of the act of Congress, and remarks.
Taylor, John, (Mass.)	Revolutionary pension	15	2	Petition	43	Pens. & Rev. Cl'ms.						
Taylor, John M	Liquidation of certificate of revolutionary debt.	4	1	Rep. of Secretary Treasury.	388	Claims	74	Adverse	......	Laid on table.		
Taylor, John M	Liquidation of certain bills of credit, New Hampshire issue.	4	1	Rep. of Secretary Treasury.	388	Claims	74	Adverse	......	Laid on table.		
Taylor, John M	Liquidation of certain treasury warrants.	4	1	Memorial	482	Claims.						
Taylor, John M	Liquidation of certain treasury warrants.	5	2	Memorial	192	Claims	Feb. 23, 1798	Adverse	......	Laid on table.		
Taylor, John M	(See John Taylor, of Virginia, heir of.)	22	2	....	67							
Taylor, John	Grant of land as a Canadian refugee.	12	1	House bill	248	Whole House	Mar. 21, 1812	With amend.	85	Passed	Passed	App'd April 23, 1812
Taylor, John	Invalid pension	12	1	House bill	361	Whole House	June 15, 1812	With amend.	138	Passed	Passed	App'd July 5, 1812
Taylor, John	Naval pension	15	1	Petition	91	Naval Affairs	Jan. 8, 1818	Favorable; bill	34	Passed	Postponed.	
Taylor, John Brickwood	(See James Dallas and John N. Taylor, heirs of.)	15	1	....	226							
Taylor, John Brickwood	Payment of a revolutionary loan office certificate.	21	2	Petition	67	Rev. Claims	Feb. 4, 1831	Favorable; bill	598	Referred to Committee Whole House.		
Taylor, John Brickwood	Payment of a revolutionary loan office certificate.	22	1	Senate bill	152	Rev. Claims	Feb. 20, 1832	With't amend.	32	Passed	Passed	App'd July 13, 1832
Taylor, John Noble, heirs of.	(See James Dallas and John N. Taylor, heirs of.)	15	1	....	226							
Taylor, John, (Tenn.)	Revolutionary pension	15	1	Resolution	229	Pens. & Rev. Cl'ms.	....	....	......	....	....	See act Mar. 18, 1818
Taylor, John, (N. H.)	Revolutionary pension	15	1	Petition	257	Pens. & Rev. Cl'ms.						
Taylor, John, (N. H.)	Revolutionary pension	15	2	Petition	43	Pens. & Rev. Cl'ms.						
Taylor, John, (N. H.)	Revolutionary pension	17	1	Petition	30	Pens. & Rev. Cl'ms.	....	....	......	....	....	See act Feb. 4, 1822
Taylor, John, (N. H.)	Arrears of pension	20	2	Petition	78	Military Pensions.						
Taylor, John, (N. H.)	Arrears of pension	21	1	Petition	144	Military Pensions	April 6, 1830	Adverse	......	Laid on table.		
Taylor, John, (N. H.)	Arrears of pension	21	2	Petition	120	Military Pensions.						
Taylor, John, (N. H.)	Arrears of pension	22	1	Resolution	93	Invalid Pensions	231	Favorable; bill	344	Passed	Laid on table.	
Taylor, John, (N. H.)	Arrears of pension	22	2	Petition	39	Invalid Pensions	Dec. 19, 1832	Favorable; bill	226	Passed	Passed	App'd March 2, 1833
Taylor, John, (N. H.)	Arrears of pension	23	1	Petition	45	Invalid Pensions	Mar. 21, 1834	Adverse	......	Laid on table.		
Taylor, John, (N. H.)	Arrears of pension	24	2	Petition	117	Invalid Pensions	....	....	......	Discharged; laid on table.		
Taylor, John, (N. H.)	Arrears of pension	25	2	Petition	587	Rev. Pensions	....	....	......	Discharged; laid on table.		
Taylor, John, (S. C.)	Pension	21	2	Resolution	141	Military Pensions	....	....	......	Disch'd; recommitted.		
Taylor, John, (Ala.,) administrator of.	To cancel sale of land purchased of United States.	21	2	Petition	178	Public Lands	Jan. 20, 1830	By bill	567	Referred to Committee Whole House.		
Taylor, John, (Ala.,) administrator of.	To cancel sale of land purchased of United States.	21	2	Senate bill	245	Public Lands	Feb. 2, 1831	With't amend.	105	Passed	....	App'd Feb. 12, 1831
Taylor, John, (Va.,) heir of.	Commutation of half-pay	22	2	Petition	67	Rev. Claims	22	Favorable; bill	654	Referred to Committee Whole House.		
Taylor, John, (Va.,) heir of.	Commutation of half-pay	23	1	Petition	43	Rev. Claims	90	Favorable; bill	98	Passed	Passed as am'd.	App'd June 30, 1834
Taylor, John, (N. Y.)	Invalid naval pension	23	2	Petition	58	Invalid Pensions	Jan. 15, 1835	Adverse	......	Laid on table.		
Taylor, John W., (N. Y.)	Benefit of acts of Congress granting bounty land to Canadian refugees.	26	1	Petition	701	Priv. Land Claims.	July 21, 1840	Adverse	......	Laid on table.		
Taylor, John W., (N. Y.)	Benefit of acts of Congress granting bounty land to Canadian refugees.	30	1	Memorial	617	Priv. Land Claims.	....	....	......	....	....	See House bill No. 578

List of private claims presented to the House of Representatives of the United States from the 1st to the 31st Congress, inclusive—Continued.

Names of claimants.	Nature or object of the claim.	Congress.	Session.	How brought before the House of Reps.	Page of journal.	To what committee of the House referred.	No. or date of the report.	Nature of the report.	No. of the bill.	How disposed of by the House of Reps.	How disposed of by the Senate.	Date of the act of Congress, and remarks.
Taylor, John B	(See Benjamin R. Taylor, administrator of.)	27	2		1049							
Taylor, John, (Ind.)	Pension	28	1	Petition	432	Rev. Pensions.						
Taylor, John, (Ind.)	Pension	29	1	Petition	258	Rev. Pensions				Discharged; laid on table.		
Taylor, Jonathan, and Jos. M. Street.	Permission to complete payment on certain mineral lands in Illinois.	16	1	Petition	102	Public Lands				Discharged; referred to Secretary Treasury.		
Taylor, Jonathan	(See Taylor, Morrison, and Wilkins, representatives of.)	16	1		325							
Taylor, Col. Jonathan	Compensation for services rendered to suppress Burr insurrection.	20	1	Senate bill	433	Claims	April 4, 1828	With't amend.	S. 89	Passed		App'd May 26, 1828
Taylor, Jonathan, administrator of.	Payment of same amount of money as was allowed Charles Wilkins, executor of, in a similar case.	24	1	Resolution	347	Claims	Mar. 29, 1836	Favorable; bill	513	Referred to Committee Whole House.		
Taylor, Jonathan, administrator of.	Payment of same amount of money as was allowed Charles Wilkins, executor of, in a similar case.	25	2	Petition	37	Claims	23	Favorable; bill	35	Passed	Passed	App'd April 7, 1838
Taylor, Joseph Spencer	Revolutionary pension	3	1	Rep. of Secretary War.	131	Select.						
Taylor, Joseph Spencer	Revolutionary pension	4	1	Petition	406	Claims	Jan. 26, 1796	Adverse		Laid on table.		
Taylor, Joseph, (Pa.)	Compensation for revolutionary services.	4	1	Petition	433	Claims	May 7, 1796	Adverse		Laid on table.		
Taylor, Joseph, (Pa.)	Revolutionary pension	27	2	Documents	218	Invalid Pensions	219	Adverse		Laid on table.		
Taylor, Joseph, (Pa.)	Revolutionary pension	28	2	Petition	199	Invalid Pensions.						
Taylor, Joseph, (Pa.)	Revolutionary pension	29	1	Petition	319	Invalid Pensions.						
Taylor, Joseph, (Pa.)	Revolutionary pension	29	2	Petition	89	Invalid Pensions.						
Taylor, Joseph, (Pa.)	Revolutionary pension	30	1	Resolution	181	Invalid Pensions	629	Favorable; bill	504	Passed	With't amend.	
Taylor, Joseph, (Pa.)	Revolutionary pension	31	1	Petition	898	Invalid Pensions.						
Taylor, Josiah	(See William H. Bedford, agent)	28	1		262							
Taylor, J. R	Increase of compensation as postmaster at Maysville, Illinois.	20	2	Petition	106	P. Of. & P. Roads.						
Taylor, Judith	(See Henry Fields, representatives of.)	8	1		514							
Taylor, Lydia	(See Elnathan Taylor, widow of.)	25	2		618							
Taylor, Lydia, (Ky)	(See William Taylor, of Kentucky, widow of.)	23	1		383							
Taylor, Maria	Confirmation of title to land	31	1	Senate bill	1185	Priv. Land Claims			S. 316			
Taylor, Martin	Grant of military bounty land	20	1	Resolution	314	Military Affairs.						
Taylor, Mary	(See Nathaniel Taylor, heirs and representatives of)	14	2		205							
Taylor, Mary, (Va.)	(See Richard Taylor, of Virginia, heirs of.)	22	2		127							
Taylor, Mary, (Pa.)	(See Matthew Taylor, of Pennsylvania, widow of.)	25	2		405							
Taylor, Mary	(See John Briggs, heirs of)	26	1		360							
Taylor, Matthew, widow of.	Revolutionary pension	25	2	Petition	405	Rev. Pensions	669	Adverse		Referred to Committee Whole House on bill No. 456.		
Taylor, Matthew, widow of.	Revolutionary pension	25	3	House bill	375	Whole House			456			
Taylor & McNeal, *et al*	Compensation for scows used for defence of Baltimore in 1812.	14	1	Petition & report Sec. of War.	284, 364	Claims	April 1, 1816	By bill		Passed	Passed	App'd April 29, 1816

List of private claims presented to the House of Representatives of the United States from the 1st to the 31st Congress, inclusive—Continued.

Names of claimants.	Nature or object of the claim.	Congress.	Session.	How brought before the House of Reps.	Page of journal.	To what committee of the House referred.	No. or date of the report.	Nature of the report.	No. of the bill.	How disposed of by the House of Reps.	How disposed of by the Senate.	Date of the act of Congress, and remarks.
Taylor, Morrison, and Wilkins.	Compensation for improvements made at salt works in Illinois, under lease from United States.	16	1	Petition	325	....	....	....	......	Referred to Secretary Treasury.		
Taylor, Morrison, and Wilkins.	Compensation for improvements made at salt works in Illinois, under lease from United States.	21	1	Petition	122	Claims	133	Favorable; bill	177	Passed	Passed	App'd May 20, 1830
Taylor, Morrison, and Wilkins.	Interest due on treasury drafts	23	2	Petition	49	Claims	53	Favorable; bill	651	Referred to Committee Whole House.		
Taylor, Morrison, and Wilkins.	Interest due on treasury drafts	24	1	Petition	50	Claims	Dec. 21, 1835	By bill	32	Passed	Passed	App'd Feb. 18, 1836
Taylor, Mrs., *et al*	Payment of claims against Ottowa Indians.	29	1	Memorial	160	Indian Affairs	287	Adverse	......	Laid on table.		
Taylor, Najah	(See Richards, Upson, & Co.	11	2	....	173							
Taylor, Nathan	Revolutionary pension	10	1	House bill	232	Whole House	April 19, 1808	With amend.	78	Passed	Passed	App'd April 25, 1808
Taylor, Nathan, widow of.	Arrears of pension	24	2	Resolution	53	Rev. Pensions	....	....	......	Discharged; laid on table.		
Taylor, Nathan, (N. H.).	Grant of revolutionary bounty land.	23	1	Petition	110	Rev. Claims.						
Taylor, Nathaniel	Pre emption right to Chickasaw land.	13	2	Petition	269	....	....	....	......	Referred to Secretary of War.		
Taylor, Nathaniel	Compensation for improvements made on Chickasaw land.	14	1	Petition	75	Select	....	....	......	Discharged	....	Leave to withdraw.
Taylor, Nathaniel, heirs and representatives of.	Indemnity for loss of iron works by fire, through government agent.	14	2	Petition	205	Public Lands.						
Taylor, Nathaniel, heirs and representatives of.	Indemnity for loss of iron works by fire, through government agent	25	2	Resolution	671	Indian Affairs.						
Taylor, Nathaniel, heirs and representatives of.	Indemnity for loss of iron works by fire, through government agent	25	3	Resolution	91	Indian Affairs	92	Adverse	......	Laid on table.		
Taylor, P. W.	(See A. Avery, *et al*)	25	2	....	478							
Taylor, R.	(See John Ross *et al.*, Cherokee agents.)	20	2	....	292							
Taylor, Capt. Reuben, heirs of.	Commutation of half pay	23	1	Petition	110	Rev. Claims.						
Taylor, Reuben, (Pa.)	Increase of pension	28	1	Petition	76	Rev. Pensions	....	....	......	Discharged; laid on table.		
Taylor, Reuben, (Pa.)	Increase of pension	28	2	Petition	59	Rev. Pensions	....	....	......	Discharged; laid on table.		
Taylor, Reuben, (Illinois).	(See Ezekiel Taylor, heirs of)	29	1	....	209							
Taylor, Richard, (Ky.)	Increase of pension	8	2	Memorial	95	Claims	Feb. 13, 1805	Favorable; bill	65	Passed	Passed	App'd March 3, 1805
Taylor, Richard, (Ky.)	Arrears of pension	11	1	Petition	19	Claims.						
Taylor, Richard, (Ky.)	Arrears of pension	11	2	Petition	146	Claims	Jan. 11, 1810	By bill	62	Postponed.		
Taylor, Richard, (Ky.)	Arrears of pension	12	1	Petition	28	Claims.						
Taylor, Richard, (Ky.)	Arrears of pension	20	1	Senate bill	466	Military Pensions	April 4, 1828	With't amend.	S. 127	Passed	....	App'd April 28, 1828
Taylor, sen., Capt. Richard, (Kentucky.)	Compensation for revolutionary services, &c.	11	3	Petition	437	Claims	Dec. 27, 1810	Adverse	......	Laid on table.		
Taylor, sen., Capt. Richard, (Kentucky.)	Compensation for revolutionary services, &c.	12	1	Petition	19	Claims	June 12, 1812	Adverse	......	Laid on table.		
Taylor, sen., Capt. Richard, (Kentucky.)	Compensation for revolutionary services, &c.	13	3	Resolution	509	Pens. & Rev. Cl'ms.						
Taylor, sen., Capt. Richard, (Kentucky.)	Compensation for revolutionary services, &c.	14	2	Petition	31	Pens. & Rev. Cl'ms.						
Taylor, sen., Capt. Richard, heirs of, (Ky.)	Arrears of pension	19	2	Senate bill	348	Military Pensions	Mar. 1, 1827	With't amend	S. 79	Passed	....	App'd March 3, 1827

List of private claims presented to the House of Representatives of the United States from the 1st to the 31st Congress, inclusive—Continued.

Names of claimants.	Nature or object of the claim.	Congress.	Session.	How brought before the House of Reps.	Page of journal.	To what committee of the House referred.	No. or date of the report.	Nature of the report.	No. of the bill.	How disposed of by the House of Reps.	How disposed of by the Senate.	Date of the act of Congress, and remarks.
Taylor, sen., Capt. Richard, heirs of, (Ky.)	Commutation of half-pay	23	1	Petition	158	Rev. Claims.						
Taylor, Richard, (Ky.)	Settlement of accounts as deputy quartermaster general.	20	1	Senate bill	410	Claims	....	....	S. 75			
Taylor, Richard, (Ky.)	Relief against operation of act of Congress, January 25, 1825.	21	1	Resolution	365	Judiciary	Mar. 2, 1830	By bill	313	Passed	Passed	App'd Mar. 31, 1830
Taylor, Richard, of Va., representatives of.	Renewal of lost certificates	22	2	Resolution	127	Rev. Claims.						
Taylor, Com. Richard	Naval invalid pension	14	2	Petition	345	Rev. Claims	77	With't amend.	......	Passed	....	App'd March 1, 1817
Taylor, Robert, (Md.)	(See John Ross, *et al.*)	11	2	....	235							
Taylor, Robert E., and others.	(See Thomas Ritson, representatives of.)	26	1	....	182							
Taylor, Robert, (D. C.)	(See William O'Neal and Robert Taylor.)	14	1	....	33							
Taylor, Robert, (Pa.)	(See Gray & Taylor, and Joseph Tagart.)	26	1	....	327							
Taylor, Robert, (Va.)	(See De Charles Taylor, executor of.)	29	1	....	233							
Taylor, Ruth	(See Samuel Taylor, of New York, widow of.)	26	2	....	50							
Taylor, Sally	(See John Burbank, heir of.)	30	1	....	344							
Taylor, Samuel, (N. J.)	Invalid pension	3	2	Rep. of Secretary War.	350	Claims	Feb. 28, 1795	Favorable; bill	130	Postponed.		
Taylor, Samuel, (N. J.)	Invalid pension	4	1	House bill	470	Whole House	Mar. 18, 1796	With amend.	156	Passed	Passed	App'd April 20, 1796
Taylor, Samuel, (Ark.)	Pre-emption right to land	20	2	Resolution	67	Public Lands.						
Taylor, Samuel, (Ark.)	Pre-emption right to land	21	1	Resolution	213	Public Lands.						
Taylor, Samuel, (Ark.)	Pre emption right to land	21	2	Petition	83	Public Lands	....	....	......	Discharged; laid on table.		
Taylor, Capt. Samuel, (S. C.,) widow of.	Grant of bounty land for revolutionary services.	26	1	Petition	630	Rev. Claims.						
Taylor, Samuel, (N. Y.,) widow of.	Revolutionary pension	26	2	Petition	50	Rev. Claims.						
Taylor, Samuel	To satisfy bounty land warrant	26	1	Petition	703	Public Lands.						
Taylor, Samuel	To satisfy bounty land warrant	27	2	Petition	62	Public Lands.						
Taylor, Samuel	Indemnity for French spoliations prior to 1800.	31	1	Petition	285	Foreign Affairs	355	Favorable; bill	318	Referred to Committee Whole House.		
Taylor, Stephen, *et al.*	Revolutionary pension	26	1	Petition	707	Rev. Pensions.						
Taylor, Susannah	(See Lieut. Wm. Houston, widow of.)	2	1	....	472							
Taylor, Susannah	(See William Houston, former widow of.)	13	1	....	18							
Taylor, Thomas, jr.	Payment for work done in President's grounds and on streets in Washington city.	18	2	Senate bill	278	Dist. of Columbia.	March 1, 1825	With't amend.	38	Passed	Passed	App'd March 3, 1825
Taylor, Thomas W., (Ill.)	Compensation for horse taken for use of United States, Indian war.	24	1	Petition	92	Claims.						
Taylor, Thomas W., (Ill.)	Compensation for horse taken for use of United States, Indian war.	25	3	Petition	122	Claims	275	Favorable; bil	1144	Referred to Committee Whole House.		
Taylor, Thomas W., (Ill.)	Compensation for horse taken for use of United States, Indian war.	26	1	Petition	167	Claims	15	Favorable	34	Passed	....	App'd May 2, 1840
Taylor, Thomas, (Tenn.)	Pension	21	1	Resolution	254	Military Pensions.						
Taylor, Thomas, (Tenn.)	Pension	21	2	Resolution	110	Military Pensions.						
Taylor, Thomas, (Ga.)	Pension	21	2	Resolution	86	Military Pensions.						

List of private claims presented to the House of Representatives of the United States from the 1st to the 31st Congress, inclusive—Continued.

Names of claimants.	Nature or object of the claim.	Congress.	Session.	How brought before the House of Reps.	Page of journal.	To what committee of the House referred.	No. or date of the report.	Nature of the report.	No. of the bill.	How disposed of by the House of Reps.	How disposed of by the Senate.	Date of the act of Congress, and remarks.
Taylor, Thomas, (Ga.)	Pension	22	1	Petition	120	Rev. Pensions	410	Favorable; bill	510	Referred to Committee Whole House.		
Taylor, Thomas, (N. H.)	Invalid pension	23	2	Petition	274	Invalid Pensions.						
Taylor, Thomas	Bounty land for services in war of 1812.	27	2	Petition	720	Invalid Pensions	....	....	......	Discharged; referred to Priv. Land Claims.		
Taylor, Thomas M., and Francis B. Stockton.	Release from payment of money lost by failure of a bank wherein it was deposited.	31	1	Senate bill	1075	Naval Affairs	Aug. 1, 1850	With't amend.	S. 189	Referred to Committee Whole House.		
Taylor, Thompson	Pension	21	1	Resolution	254	Military Pensions	....	....	......	Discharged; laid on table.		
Taylor, Thompson	Pension	21	2	Resolution	110	Military Pensions.						
Taylor, Thornton, heirs of	Compensation for revolutionary services.	22	1	Documents	165	Rev. Claims	June 26, 1832	Favorable; bill	660	Referred to Committee Whole House.		
Taylor, Thornton, heirs of	Commutation of five years' full pay	23	1	Resolution	227	Rev. Claims.						
Taylor, Thornton, heirs of	Commutation of five years' full pay	23	2	Resolution	167	Rev. Claims.						
Taylor, Thornton, heirs of	Commutation of five years' full pay	24	1	Senate bill	899	Claims	June 15, 1835	With't amend.	126	Passed	....	App'd July 2, 1836
Taylor, Thornton, heirs of	Interest on commutation of half-pay.	24	2	Documents	92	Claims.						
Taylor, Thornton, heirs of	Interest on commutation of half-pay.	25	2	Petition	70	Rev. Claims	249	Favorable; bill	290	Postponed.		
Taylor, Thornton, heirs of	Interest on commutation of half pay.	26	1	Petition	164	Rev. Claims.						
Taylor, Thornton, heirs of	Interest on commutation of half pay.	27	2	Petition	61	Rev. Claims	402	Adverse	......	Laid on table.		
Taylor, Thornton, heirs of	Interest on commutation of half-pay.	28	1	Petition	117	Rev. Claims.						
Taylor, Thurston M.	Compensation for services as first lieutenant, United States navy.	31	1	Petition	698	Naval Affairs.						
Taylor, Tilford	To correct error in entry of land	24	2	Petition	269	Public Lands.						
Taylor, Tilford	To correct error in entry of land	25	2	Petition	95	Public Lands	Mar. 20, 1838	Favorable; bill	663	Referred to Committee Whole House.		
Taylor, Tilford	To correct error in entry of land	25	3	Bill of last sess.	376	Whole House	Jan. 25, 1839	With't amend.	663	Passed	Passed	App'd March 2, 1839
Taylor, Vincent	Compensation for provisions taken for use of United States troops.	21	1	Petition	597	Claims	May 11, 1830	Adverse	......	Laid on table.		
Taylor, Vincent	Compensation for provisions taken for use of United States troops.	23	1	Petition	448	Claims	April 4, 1834	Adverse	......	Laid on table.		
Taylor, W., *et al.*	(See James Tilton, *et al.*)	30	1	....	328	....	....	....	118			
Taylor, Walter H	(See William H. Duncan)	24	1	....	670							
Taylor, William	Commutation of full pay in lieu of half-pay for life.	1	2	Memorial	218	Ref'd to Secretary War.	Jan. 28, 1890	Report	......	Laid on table.		
Taylor, William, and Ezekiel Walker.	Remission of forfeiture on cargo in 1811.	15	1	Petition and rep't Sec. Treasury.	24, 47	Ways and Means	Feb. 3, 1818	Adverse	......	Referred to Committee Whole House.		
Taylor, William, and Ezekiel Walker.	Remission of forfeiture on cargo in 1811.	15	2	Rep't of last sess.	35	Whole House	Nov. 24, 1818	Adverse	......	Rejected.		
Taylor, William, (Ky.)	Restoration of pension	17	1	Petition	227	Rev. Pensions	....	....	......	Discharged; referred to Com. Whole House.	....	Leave to withdraw.
Taylor, William, (Ky.)	Restoration of pension	17	2	Petition	31	Rev. Pensions.						
Taylor, William, (Ky.,) widow of.	Five years' half-pay	23	1	Petition	383	Claims	June 4, 1834	Adverse	......	Laid on table.		
Taylor, Major Wm., (Ky.,) widow of.	Commutation of half-pay	21	2	Petition	209	Rev. Claims	....	....	......	Discharged; laid on table.		
Taylor, Major Wm., (Ky.,) heirs-at-law of.	Commutation of half-pay	23	1	Petition	110	Rev. Claims.						

List of private claims presented to the House of Representatives of the United States from the 1st to the 31st Congress, inclusive—Continued.

Names of claimants.	Nature or object of the claim.	Congress.	Session.	How brought before the House of Reps.	Page of journal.	To what committee of the House referred.	No. or date of the report.	Nature of the report.	No. of the bill.	How disposed of by the House of Reps.	How disposed of by the Senate.	Date of the act of Congress, and remarks.
Taylor, William Rufus...	(See Jonathan Taylor, administrator of.)	24	1	....	347							
Taylor, William Rufus...	See Nathaniel Ashby, heirs of) ..	25	3	....	361							
Taylor, William, (La.,) a New Orleans branch pilot.	Permission to locate certain lands.	28	1	Petition	77	Priv. Land Claims.	9	Favorable....	35	Passed with amendm't.	Passed	App'd June 17, 1844
Taylor, Major Wm., (Mo.,) widow of.	Arrears of pension............	28	1	Petition	913	Rev. Pensions.						
Taylor, Major Wm., (Mo.,) widow of.	Arrears of pension............	29	1	Petition	463	Rev. Pensions	669	Adverse	......	Laid on table.		
Taylor, William, trustee of, (Md.)	Indemnity for French spoliations prior to 1800.	26	1	Memorial	182	Foreign Affairs....	343	Favorable; bill	319	Referred to Committee Whole House.		
Taylor, William, *et al*....	Indemnity for losses sustained by burning of the U. States frigate Missouri.	29	1	Memorial	345	Naval Affairs.						
Taylor, Colonel Zachariah.	Allowance for office rent, and for money in lieu of double rations as superintendant of the western military department.	20	1	Resolution	346	Claims	Mar. 12, 1828	Adverse	......	Laid on table.		
Tayon, Charles, (Mo.)...	Confirmation of title to land	15	1	Petition	199	Priv. Land Claims.						
Tayon, Charles, (Mo.)...	Confirmation of title to land	16	1	Petition	71	Priv. Land Claims.						
Mayon, Charles, (Mo.)...	Confirmation of title to land	17	1	Petition	55	Public Lands.						
Tayon, Louis..........	(See Louis Fayon)	16	1	....	36							
Tays, Elizabeth.........	(See Robert Smith, heir of).....	28	2	....	987							
Tazewell, William	Allowance for losses and expenses incurred as secretary of legation in France.	6	1	Petition	624	Select	April 9, 1800	Favorable: bill	257	Passed	Passed	App'd May 7, 1800
Teackle, Littleton Dennis.	(See Maryland, agents for State of.)	19	2	....	240							
Teadwell, Sarah	Provision for future support as widow of revolutionary soldier.	21	1	Petition	448	Rev. Claims	....	....	......	Discharged; laid on table.		
Teakle, Severn, heirs of ..	Commutation of half-pay for life .	23	1	Petition	137	Rev. Claims......	June 11, 1834	Adverse	......	Laid on table.		
Teal, Christopher, heirs & representatives of.	Confirmation of title to land	27	2	Petition	140	Priv. Land Claims.						
Teal, Hiram, & Co......	Indemnity for losses on contract with United States government.	27	3	Petition	456	Claims.						
Teal, Hiram, & Co......	Indemnity for losses on contract with United States government.	28	1	Petition	274	Claims.						
Teal, Hiram, & Co......	Indemnity for losses on contract with United States government.	28	2	Petition	67	Claims.						
Teal, Hiram, & Co......	Indemnity for losses on contract with United States government.	29	1	Petition	116	Claims	841	Adverse	......	Laid on table.		
Teal, Nathaniel.........	(See Thomas Tyner, *et al*).......	24	1	....	497							
Teasdall, Richard, administrator of.	Indemnity for French spoliations prior to 1800.	26	1	Memorial	182	Foreign Affairs....	343	Favorable; bill	319	Referred to Committee Whole House.		
Teas, James F..........	Reimbursement of money paid for mail service.	26	1	Resolution	552	P. Of. & P. Roads.	....	....	......	Discharged; laid on table.		
Teas, Sarah............	(See William Teas, widow of.)...	28	1	....	319							
Teas, William, administrator of.	Commutation of half-pay	22	2	Petition	88	Rev. Claims......	Jan. 15, 1833	Favorable; bill	685	Referred to Committee Whole House.		
Teas, William, administrator of.	Commutation of half pay	23	1	Petition	39	Rev. Claims......	Jan. 2, 1834	Favorable; bill	121	Passed	Passed	App'd June 30, 1834
Teas, William, widow of.	Revolutionary pension.........	28	1	Petition	319	Rev. Pensions.						
Teas, William, widow of.	Revolutionary pension.........	28	2	Petition	184	Rev. Pensions.						
Teas, William, widow of.	Revolutionary pension.........	30	1	Petition	359	Rev. Pensions.						

List of private claims presented to the House of Representatives of the United States from the 1st to the 31st Congress, inclusive—Continued.

Names of claimants.	Nature or object of the claim.	Congress.	Session.	How brought before the House of Reps.	Page of journal.	To what committee of the House referred.	No. or date of the report.	Nature of the report.	No. of the bill.	How disposed of by the House of Reps.	How disposed of by the Senate.	Date of the act of Congress, and remarks.
Teas, William, widow of.	Revolutionary pension	30	2	Petition	408					Leave to withdraw.		
Teas, William, widow of.	Revolutionary pension	31	1	Petition	194	Rev. Pensions.						
Teas, William, widow of.	Revolutionary pension	31	2	Petition	175	Rev. Pensions	51	Adverse		Laid on table.		
Teater, Samuel L.	Indemnity for horse lost in Seminole war, 1818.	23	1	Documents	154	Claims.						
Teater, Samuel L.	Indemnity for horse lost in Seminole war, 1818.	28	1	Petition	262	Claims.						
Tebbs, Faushee, *et al.*	(See John Tebbs, heirs-at-law of.)	22	2		88							
Tebbs, John, heirs-at-law of.	Commutation of half-pay	22	2	Petition	88	Rev. Claims.						
Tebbs, John, heirs-at-law of.	Commutation of half-pay	23	1	Petition	92	Rev. Claims.						
Tebbs, John, heirs at law of.	Commutation of half-pay	23	2	Petition	106	Rev. Claims.						
Tebbs, John, heirs-at-law of.	Commutation of half-pay	24	1	Petition	103	Rev. Claims.						
Tebbs, John, heirs-at-law of.	Commutation of half-pay	25	2	Petition	76	Rev. Claims.						
Tebbs, John, heirs-at-law of.	Commutation of half pay	29	1	Petition	352	Rev. Claims.						
Tebbs, Thomas, heirs of.	Five years' full pay as a surgeon in revolutionary war.	23	1	Petition	110	Rev. Claims.						
Tebbs, Thomas, heirs of.	Five years' full pay as a surgeon in revolutionary war.	23	2	Petition	106	Rev. Claims	Dec. 29, 1834	Adverse		Laid on table.		
Tebbs, Thomas, heirs of.	Five years' full pay as a surgeon in revolutionary war.	24	1	Petition	138	Rev. Claims	Jan. 21, 1836	Adverse		Laid on table.		
Tebbs, Thomas, heirs of.	Five years' full pay as a surgeon in revolutionary war.	24	2	Petition	126	Rev. Claims				Discharged; laid on table.		
Tebbs, Thomas, heirs of.	Five years' full pay as a surgeon in revolutionary war.	25	2	Petition	70	Rev. Claims	Jan. 11, 1838	Adverse		Laid on table.		
Tee, William, *et al.*	Increase of compensation as keeper of light vessels.	22	1	Petition	61	Commerce.						
Tee, William	Invalid pension	30	1	Petition	717	Invalid Pensions	May 18, 1848	Favorable; bill	507	Passed	Referred to Naval Affairs.	
Tee, William	Invalid pension	31	1	Petition	500	Rev. Claims				Discharged, and to Invalid Pensions.		
Teel, John, (Pa)	Compensation for certain services in revolutionary war.	21	1	Petition	57	Rev. Claims	Jan. 29, 1830	Favorable; bill	176	Rejected.		
Teel, John, (Pa)	Compensation for certain services in revolutionary war.	22	1	Petition	35	Rev. Claims	Dec. 30, 1831	Favorable; bill	169	Referred to Committee Whole House.		
Tees, Joseph	(See Tees & Van Hook)	22	2		266							
Tees & Van Hook	Additional compensation for ship timber furnished United States.	22	2	Petition	266	Naval Affairs.						
Tees & Van Hook	Indemnity for losses on contract with Navy Department.	23	1	Petition	459	Naval Affairs				Discharged; laid on table.		
Teft, J. K.	(See F. D. P. De Villiers, administrator of.)	27	2		1064							
Telfair, Catharine	(See Capt. Isaiah Wool, heir of.)	24	1		752							
Telfair, Edward, and John Wereat.	Payment for supplies furnished United States army.	2	2	Petition	683					Referred to Secretary Treasury.		
Telfair, Edward, and John Wereat.	Payment for supplies furnished United States army.	3	1	Petition and rep't Sec. Treasury.	78					Laid on table		Leave to withdraw.

List of private claims presented to the House of Representatives of the United States from the 1st to the 31st Congress, inclusive—Continued.

Names of claimants.	Nature or object of the claim.	Congress.	Session.	How brought before the House of Reps.	Page of journal.	To what committee of the House referred.	No. or date of the report.	Nature of the report.	No. of the bill.	How disposed of by the House of Reps.	How disposed of by the Senate.	Date of the act of Congress, and remarks.
Telfair, Mary M	(See Israel Pearce, heirs of.)	25	3		124							
Teller, Garret, assignee of.	Confirmation of title to land, Indian grant.	18	1	Petition	31	Priv. Land Claims.	Jan. 9, 1824	Adverse		Laid on table.		
Teller, Henry R	Compensation for occupation of and injuries to property by British in revolutionary war.	17	1	Petition	46	Pens. & Rev. Cl'ms.	450	Adverse		Laid on table.		
Teller, Henry R	Compensation for occupation of and injuries to property by British in revolutionary war.	18	2	Petition	127	Pens. & Rev. Cl'ms.						
Teller, Henry R	Compensation for occupation of and injuries to property by British in revolutionary war.	19	1	Petition	153	Rev. Claims.						
Teller, Henry R	(See Garret Teller, assignee of.)	18	1		31							
Teller, Oliver, *et al.*	(See Jacobus De Peyster, administrator of.)	4	1		467							
Teller, Remson	Compensation for services rendered and indemnity for losses sustained in revolutionary war.	25	2	Petition and docs.	391, 699, 721	Rev. Claims.						
Teller, Tobias	Revolutionary pension	22	1	Petition	196	Rev. Pensions				Discharged; laid on table.		
Tellott, Jeremiah, executor of.	Indemnity for French spoliations prior to 1800.	26	1	Memorial	182	Foreign Affairs	343	Favorable; bill	319	Referred to Committee Whole House.		
Temple, Josiah	Invalid pension	10	2	House bill	499	Whole House	Feb. 23, 1809	With amends.	158	Passed	Passed	App'd March 3, 1809
Temple, Tabatha	(See John Tinsley, heirs of.)	30	1		360							
Templeman, John	Payment of revolutionary certificate.	4	1	Rep. of Secretary Treasury.	388	Claims	May 31, 1796	Adverse		Laid on table.		
Templeton, James, (Penn.)	Compensation for revolutionary services.	21	2	Petition	143	Claims	Jan. 21, 1831	Adverse		Laid on table.		
Templeton, James, (Penn.)	Compensation for revolutionary services	22	1	Petition	25	Claims	Jan. 18, 1832	Adverse		Laid on table.		
Templeton, James, (Penn.)	Revolutionary pension	25	2	Petition	180	Rev. Pensions				Discharged; referred to Com. Whole House on bill No. 369.		
Ten Broeck, Abraham	Reimbursement of costs at suit of United States against him.	15	1	Petition	415	Judiciary	April 10, 1818	Adverse		Laid on table.		
Ten Broeck, Adam, widow of.	Revolutionary pension	31	1	Petition	232	Rev. Pensions.						
Ten Broeck, Hannah	(See Adam Ten Broeck, widow of.)	31	1		232							
Ten Broeck, Maria	(See Andrew Hermans, former widow of.)	25	2		116							
Ten Eyck, Anthony	Allowance for outfit as commissioner to Sandwich islands.	30	1	Resolution	320	Foreign Affairs.						
Ten Eyck, Anthony	Allowance for outfit as commissioner to Sandwich islands.	31	1	General appropriation bill.	1034	Whole House	Aug. 27, 1850	With amend't.	334	Passed	Passed, with amendment.	App'd Sept. 30, 1850
Ten Eyck, Conrad	(See John S. Langham, sureties of.)	22	1		473							
Ten Eyck, Conrad	Allowance made at Pottawatomie treaty.	29	2	Documents	149	Indian Affairs				Discharged; laid on table.		
Ten Eyck, Conrad, administrator of.	Compensation for services, &c., as United States marshal for Michigan.	29	2	Memorial	164	Judiciary.						
Ten Eyck, Conrad, administrator of.	Compensation for services, &c., as United States marshal for Michigan.	30	1	Petition	81	Judiciary.						

List of private claims presented to the House of Representatives of the United States from the 1st to the 31st Congress, inclusive—Continued.

Names of claimants.	Nature or object of the claim.	Congress.	Session.	How brought before the House of Reps.	Page of journal.	To what committee of the House referred.	No. or date of the report.	Nature of the report.	No. of the bill.	How disposed of by the House of Reps.	How disposed of by the Senate.	Date of the act of Congress, and remarks.
Ten Eyck, Conrad, legal representatives of.	Compensation for services, &c., as United States marshal for Michigan.	31	1	Petition	520	Judiciary	174	Favorable; bill	185	Referred to Committee Whole House.		
Ten Eyck, Conrad, legal representatives of.	Compensation for services, &c., as United States marshal for Michigan.	31	2	Bill of last sess.	103	Whole House	Jan. 3, 1851	With't amend.	185	Passed	Ref'd to Com. on Judiciary	
Ten Eyck, Henry	Increase of pension	9	2	House bill	608	Whole House	March 2, 1807	With amend.	216	Passed	Passed	App'd March 3, 1807
Ten Eyck, Henry	Invalid pension	10	1	House bill	232	Whole House	April 19, 1808	With amend.	78	Passed	Passed	App'd April 25, 1808
Tenery, William	Compensation for revolutionary services and for bounty land.	18	1	Petition	48	Pens. & Rev. Cl'ms.				Discharged; referred to Secretary War.		
Tennant, Thomas, & Geo. Stiles.	Grant of registry to certain vessels.	15	1	Petition	202	Com. and Manuf.	April 1, 1818	Adverse		Laid on table.		
Tennant, Thomas	(See William Patterson & Sons, *et al.*)	16	1		85							
Tennel, George	Invalid pension	11	2	House bill	283	Whole House	April 9, 1810	With amend.	107	Passed	Passed	App'd April 27, 1810
Tennent, Gilbert, administrator of.	Compensation for services as surgeon in revolutionary war.	2	1	Petition	458					Referred to Secretary War.		
Tennent, Gilbert, administrator of.	Compensation for services as surgeon in revolutionary war.	3	1	Petition and rep't Sec. War.	77					Laid on table.		
Tennery, George F	(See Michael Tennery, heir of.)	9	1		351							
Tennery, George F	(See Major Platt Bayles, heir of.)	9	1		351							
Tennery, Joseph L	(See Wyandott Indians.)	27	3		256		160		776			
Tennery, Michael, heir of.	Indemnity for losses sustained and for services in the revolutionary war.	9	1	Petition	351					Laid on table.		
Tennessee, Gen. Assembly of, for citizens of.	Compensation for services in Seminole war.	17	1	Memorial	26	Select	April 3, 1822	By bill	152	Passed	Passed	App'd May 4, 1822
Tennessee, Gen. Assembly of, for citizens of.	Relief from construction given by the United States accounting officers to the act of May 4, 1822.	18	1	Petition	62	Military Affairs				Discharged; referred to Com. Whole House.		
Tennessee, Gen. Assembly of, for citizens of.	Relief from construction given by the United States accounting officers to the act of May 4, 1822.	18	1	Senate bill	164	Military Affairs	Jan. 21, 1824	With't amend.	11	Passed with amendm't.	Concurred in.	App'd May 26, 1824
Tennessee, militia of	Pay while in service of the United States in 1814.	20	1	Rep. of Secretary War.	237	Military Affairs				Discharged; laid on table.		
Tennessee, inhabitants of State of.	Remission of fine incurred of selling spirituous liquors.	14	1	Petition	563	Ways and Means.						
Tennessee, sundry citizens of.	Relief in relation to occupant lands in the Salt Lick reservation.	24	1	Petition	57	Public Lands	369	Favorable; bill	372	Referred to Committee Whole House.		
Tennessee, sundry citizens of.	Relief in relation to occupant lands in the Salt Lick reservation.	25	2	Petition	43	Priv. Land Claims.	407	Favorable; bill	418	Passed	Passed	App'd March 3, 1839
Tennessee, sundry citizens of.	Extension of right of pre-emption	26	1	Petition	364	Priv. Land Claims.	99	Favorable; bill	95	Passed	Passed	App'd July 20, 1840
Tennessee volunteers	(See John P. Long)	25	2		274							
Tennessee volunteers	(See Richard Warner, *et al.*)	24	2		80							
Tennessee volunteers	(See T. C. H. Miller, *et al.*)	24	2		80							
Tennessee volunteers	(See Archibald Beard, *et al.*)	30	1		239							
Tennessee mounted volunteers.	(See Gillespie, Peake, Vernon, *et al.*)	30	1		448							
Tennessee dragoons	(See Captain John B. Crozier)	28	1		706							
Tennessee, volunteers of.	Compensation for time lost in going to place of rendezvous during Florida war.	24	2	Presid'ts message.	26	Claims	Feb. 8, 1837	Favorable; bill	316	Referred to Committee Whole House.		

List of private claims presented to the House of Representatives of the United States from the 1st to the 31st Congress, inclusive—Continued.

Names of claimants.	Nature or object of the claim.	Congress.	Session.	How brought before the House of Reps.	Page of journal.	To what committee of the House referred.	No. or date of the report.	Nature of the report.	No. of the bill.	How disposed of by the House of Reps.	How disposed of by the Senate.	Date of the act of Congress, and remarks.
Tennessee, volunteers of..	Compensation for time lost in going to place of rendezvous during Florida war.	24	2	Amend'nt to Senate bill.	523	....	....	....	S. 755	Rejected.		
Tennessee, mounted infantry of.	Compens'n for equipping, though not called into service.	25	2	Petition	630	Claims.						
Tennessee, mounted infantry of.	Compens'n for equipping, though not called into service.	25	3	Resolution	270	Claims.						
Tennessee, mounted infantry of.	Compens'n for equipping, though not called into service.	26	1	Resolution	383	Military Affairs.						
Tennessee, volunteers of..	Additional compensation for services and losses.	25	2	Petition	120	Claims.						
Tennessee, volunteers of..	Additional compensation for services and losses.	25	3	Petition	86	Claims.						
Tennessee, volunteers of..	Additional compensation for services and losses.	26	1	Petition	169	Claims.						
Tennessee, volunteers of..	Additional compensation for services and losses.	26	2	Petition	38	Claims.						
Tennessee, volunteers of..	Additional compensation for services and losses.	28	1	Petition	337	Claims.						
Tennessee, volunteers of..	Per diem allowance of pay and forage for horses.	26	1	Petition	940	Claims.						
Tennessee, volunteers....	Compensation for horses lost in Florida war.	25	2	Petition	1208	Claims.						
Tennessee volunteers.....	Compensation for horses lost in Florida war.	26	2	Petition	130	Claims.						
Tennessee, staff of the governor of.	Pay for organizing volunteers in 1836.	25	2	Resolution	979	Claims.						
Tennessee, staff of the governor of.	Pay for organizing volunteers in 1836.	25	3	Resolution	172	Claims.						
Tennessee, staff of the governor of.	Pay for organizing volunteers in 1836.	26	1	Resolution	442	Military Affairs.						
Tennessee, State of......	In relation to horses lost in Mexican war.	30	1	Resolution	448	Military Affairs.						
Tennessee, volunteers of..	Compensation for military services.	31	1	House bill......	956	Military Affairs....	....	....	304			
Tennessee, volunteers of..	Compensation for military services.	31	2	House bill	293	Military Affairs....	32	Favorable; bill	304	Referred to Committee Whole House.		
Tennessee, sundry citizens of the State of.	Confirmation of title to land	24	1	Petition	112	Priv. Land Claims.						
Tennessee and Selma Rail road Company.	Pre-emption to certain tracts of land.	26	2	Senate bill	113	Public Lands.....	Feb. 12, 1841	With amends.	S. 63	Referred to Committee Whole House.		
Tennessee and Selma Railroad Company.	Pre-emption to certain tracts of land.	27	2	Senate bill	114	Public Lands.....	....	....	S. 60			
Tenney, Samuel, widow of.	Revolutionary pension..........	20	2	Memorial	289	Whole House.						
Tenney, Samuel, widow of.	Revolutionary pension..........	21	1	Petition	37	Rev. Claims......	May 4, 1830	Adverse	......	Laid on table.		
Tenney, Samuel, widow of.	Revolutionary pension..........	21	2	Memorial	74	Select.						
Tenney, Samuel, widow of.	Revolutionary pension..........	24	1	Petition	382	Rev. Pensions.....	....	....	......	Discharged; laid on table.		
Tenney, Tabetha	(See Samuel Tenney, widow of.).	20	2	....	289							
Tennille, Francis, heirs of.	Indemnity under Yazoo land act of 1814.	20	2	Petition	101	Judiciary	Jan. 13, 1829	Favorable; bill	365	Referred to Committee Whole House.		
Tennille, Francis, heirs of.	Indemnity under Yazoo land act of 1814.	21	1	Petition	52	Judiciary	Dec. 31, 1829	Favorable; bill	53	Passed	Passed	App'd April 2, 1830
Tennille, Mary B., *et al.* .	(See Francis Tennille, heirs of)..	20	2	....	101							

List of private claims presented to the House of Representatives of the United States from the 1st to the 31st Congress, inclusive—Continued.

Names of claimants.	Nature or object of the claim.	Congress.	Session.	How brought before the House of Reps.	Page of journal.	To what committee of the House referred.	No. or date of the report.	Nature of the report.	No. of the bill.	How disposed of by the House of Reps.	How disposed of by the Senate.	Date of the act of Congress, and remarks.
Tennille, William A., (Ga.)	Relief against judgment in favor of United States.	20	1	Petition	242	Judiciary				Discharged; aid on table.		
Tennille, William A., (Ga.)	Relief against judgment in favor of United States.	20	2	Petition	26	Judiciary				Discharged; laid on table.		
Tennille, William A., (Ga.)	Relief against judgment in favor of United States.	21	1	Petition	100	Judiciary	April 29, 1830	Adverse		Referred to Committee Whole House.		
Tennille, William A., (Ga.)	Relief against judgment in favor of United States.	21	2	Petition & docs	61, 82	Judiciary	Feb. 8, 1831	Adverse		Referred to Committee Whole House.		
Tennille, William A., (Ga.)	Relief against judgment in favor of United States.	22	1	Senate bill	816	Claims	June 6, 1832	With amend.	118	Passed	Concurred in	App'd July 14, 1832
Tennille, William A., (Ga.)	Pension	21	2	Petition	43	Invalid Pensions.						
Tennille, William A., (Ga.)	Pension	22	1	Petition	68	Rev. Pensions	185	Favorable; bill	264	Referred to Committee Whole House.		
Tennille, William A., (Ga.)	Pension	22	2	House bill	92	Whole House	Dec. 23, 1832	With amend.	264	Passed	Passed	App'd Jan. 30, 1833
Tennison, Anthony, widow of.	Revolutionary pension	27	3	Petition	151	Rev. Pensions.						
Tennison, Samuel	Revolutionary pension	21	1	Petition	149	Military Pensions	May 4, 1830	Adverse		Laid on table.		
Tennison, Susannah	(See Anthony Tennison, widow of)	27	3		151							
Tenny, Nathan	Compensation for horse lost in service of United States.	21	1	Petition	264	Claims	Mar. 12, 1830	Adverse		Laid on table.		
Tenure, Leah	(See Michael Tenure, widow of).	26	1		286							
Tenure, Michael, widow of.	Revolutionary pension	26	1	Petition	286	Rev. Pensions	July 21, 1840	By bill	501	Referred to Committee Whole House.		
Tenure, Michael, widow of.	Revolutionary pension	27	2	Petition	517	Rev. Pensions	566	Favorable; bill	362	Ordered to 3d reading.		
Tenure, Michael, widow of.	Revolutionary pension	27	3	Bill of last sess.	87				362	Passed	Indef. postp'd.	
Terre Aux Boeuf, inhabitants of.	Confirmation of title to land	22	1	Petition	64	Priv. Land Claims.	62	Favorable; bill	125	Passed	Passed	App'd June 25, 1832
Terrell, Dorothy, by John Wing	Balance of pension	29	1	Petition	292	Invalid Pensions	156	By bill	159	Passed	Indef. postp'd.	
Terrell, George, *et al*	(See Jasper Strong, *et al.*)	25	2		1209							
Terrell, Harry	Compensation for wagon and team taken for use of army.	3	1	Petition	29					Laid on table.		
Terrell, Harry	Compensation for wagon and team taken for use of army.	3	2	Petition	296	Claims	Mar. 2, 1795	Adverse		Laid on table.		
Terrell, Harry	Compensation for wagon and team taken for use of army.	4	1	Petition	409	Claims	May 31, 1796	Adverse		Laid on table.		
Terrell, Joel	Invalid pension	13	2	House bill	344	Whole House	Mar. 31, 1814	With't amend.	166	Passed	Passed	App'd April 18, 1814
Terry, Enos, (Ohio)	Indemnity for mill dam destroyed by officer of the United States.	15	2	Petition	133	Claims.						
Terry, Enos, (Ohio)	Indemnity for mill dam destroyed by officer of the United States.	17	1	Petition	61	Claims	Feb. 22, 1822	Adverse		Recommitted.		
				Report and docs.	366	Claims	Mar. 27, 1822	Adverse		Referred to Committee Whole House.		
Terry, Enos, (Ohio)	Indemnity for mill-dam destroyed by officer of the United States.	18	1	Petition	75	Claims	Feb. 26, 1823	Adverse.		Referred to Committee Whole House.		
Terry, Enos, (Ohio)	Indemnity for mill-dam destroyed by officer of the United States.	19	1	Petition	94	Claims	Jan. 11, 1826	Adverse		Laid on table.		
Terry, Kibble	(See William H. Bedford, agent.)	28	1		262							
Terry, Nancy	(See John Davis, former widow of.)	26	1		323							
Terry, Obadiah, widow of.	Revolutionary pension	26	1	Petition	950	Rev. Pensions.						
Terry, Sarah	(See Obadiah Terry, widow of).	26	1		950							
Terry, William A.	Invalid pension	21	1	Petition	448	Military Pensions.						
Terry, William A.	Invalid pension	21	2	Petition	67	Military Pensions.						

3—59

List of private claims presented to the House of Representatives of the United States from the 1st to the 31st Congress, inclusive—**Continued.**

Names of claimants.	Nature or object of the claim.	Congress.	Session.	How brought before the House of Reps.	Page of journal.	To what committee of the House referred.	No. or date of the report	Nature of the report.	No. of the bill.	How disposed of by the House of Reps.	How disposed of by the Senate.	Date of the act of Congress, and remarks.
Terry, William A	Invalid pension	22	1	Petition	534	Rev. Pensions				Discharged; laid on table.		
Tervin, Elijah, *et al.*	Confirmation of title to land	14	1	Petition	72	Public Lands.						
Tervin, Richard	Confirmation of title to land	10	2	Petition	391	Public Lands.						
Tervin, Richard	Confirmation of title to land	11	2	Petition	112	Public Lands	Mar. 20, 1810	Favorable res., and bill.	137	Laid on table.		
Tervin, Richard	Confirmation of title to land	11	3	Petition	458	Public Lands	Jan. 7, 1811	By bill	170	Passed	Passed	Vetoed by President.
Tervin, Richard	Confirmation of title to land	11	3	Senate bill	612	Whole House	Mar. 2, 1	Title amended.	68	Passed	Concurred in.	App'd March 3, 1811
Terwilliger, Benjamin T	Revolutionary pension	22	1	Petition	329	Rev. Pensions.						
Terwilliger, Cornelius	Revolutionary pension	22	1	Petition	329	Rev. Pensions.						
Terwilliger, Peter V	Revolutionary pension	22	1	Petition	329	Rev. Pensions.						
Tesson, Louis Honoré	(See Louis Tesson Honoré.)	23	1		397							
Tevebaugh, Jacob, heirs of.	Confirmation of title to land	12	2	House bill	609	Whole House	Jan. 18, 1813	With't amend.	222	Passed	Passed	App'd Feb. 13, 1813
Tevis, Rezin	Increase of pension and bounty land.	29	1	Petition	947	Invalid Pensions.						
Tevis, Rezin	Increase of pension and bounty land.	30	1	Petition	782	Invalid Pensions	808	Adverse		Laid on table.		
Tevis, William	Revolutionary pension	26	1	Petition	1252	Rev. Pensions	714	Adverse		Laid on table.		
Tew, Henry	Invalid pension	21	2	Petition	43	Military Pensions.						
Tew, Henry	Invalid pension	22	1	Petition	51	Rev. Pensions	Dec. 29, 1831	Favorable; bill	166	Passed	Indef. postp'd.	
Tewksbury, Elizabeth	(See James Tewksbury, widow of.)	28	1		724							
Tewksbury, James, widow of.	Compensation for extra service in United States navy.	28	1	Petition	724	Naval Affairs.						
Texas, mounted rangers of.	(See Capt. B. F. Hill, *et al*)	31	1		1012							
Texas, mounted regiment of.	Compensation for military services.	30	1	Joint resolution.	428	Whole House	May 19, 1848	With amend.	J. R. 9	Passed	Passed	Appd June 16, 1848
Texas, State of	Payment for disarming troops	29	2	Gen'l appropriation bill.	163	Whole House	Feb. 5, 1847	With amend.	599	Passed	Passed, with amendment.	App'd March 3, 1847
Texas, State of	Reimbursement for payment made to volunteers in 1848 and 1849.	31	1	House bill	998	Whole House			314			
Texas, volunteers of	Compensation for services in 1845.	29	1	House bill	344	Whole House	Mar. 3, 1846	With amend.	179	Passed	Passed, with amendment.	App'd May 8, 1846
Texas, volunteers of	Compensation for military services	30	1	Joint resolution.	321	Military Affairs			J. R. 9			
Texas, volunteers of	Compensation for services under requisition of Maj. Gen. Brook.	31	2	House bill	117	Whole House	Jan. 29, 1851	With amend.	433	Passed	Passed, with amendment.	App'd Feb. 27, 1851; see act also of March 3, 1851.
Thacher, Henry and Winslow L.	Fishing bounty on schooner Emeline.	22	2	Petition	261	Commerce.						
Thacher, Henry and Winslow L., *et al.*	Fishing bounty on schooner Emeline.	23	1	Petition	235	Commerce	Feb. 4, 1834	Favorable; bill	280	Referred to Committee Whole House.		
Thackara, Juliana	(See Thomas Thackara, widow of.)	15	1		52							
Thackara, Thomas, widow of.	Bounty land for revolutionary services.	15	1	Petition	52	Pens. & Rev. Cl'ms.	96	Adverse		Rejected.		
Thacker, Joel	Pension for services in war of 1812.	28	2	Petition	396	Invalid Pensions.						
Thacker, Joel	Pension for services in war of 1812.	29	1	Petition	425	Invalid Pensions	811	Favorable; bill	536	Referred to Committee Whole House.		
Thacker, Joel	Pension for services in war of 1812.	30	1	Petition	261	Invalid Pensions	370	Favorable; bill	341	Passed	Passed, second session.	App'd March 3, 1849
Thacker, Joel	Pension for services in war of 1812.	31	2	Petition	71	Invalid Pensions.						
Thacker, Reuben	Pension	14	2	Petition	132	Pens. & Rev. Cl'ms.	Jan. 29, 1817	Favorable; bill	91	Passed	Passed	App'd March 3, 1817
Tharp, sen., Robert	Revolutionary pension	28	2	Petition	284	Rev. Pensions.						
Tharp, Wm., attorney of.	Arrears of pay due certain soldiers, and for money advanced for public purposes.	13	2	Petition and rep't Sec. of War.	313,					Laid on table		Leave to withdraw.
Tharp, Wm., attorney of.	Arrears of pay due certain soldiers, and for money advanced for public purposes.	19	1	Senate bill	488	Claims	May 12, 1826	With't amend.	114	Passed		App'd May 22, 1826

List of private claims presented to the House of Representatives of the United States from the 1st to the 31st Congress, inclusive—Continued.

Names of claimants.	Nature or object of the claim.	Congress.	Session.	How brought before the House of Reps.	Page of journal.	To what committee of the House referred.	No. or date of the report.	Nature of the report.	No. of the bill.	How disposed of by the House of Reps.	How disposed of by the Senate.	Date of the act of Congress, and remarks.
Tharp, Wm., attorney of..	Balance due under former act....	19	2	Petition.......	202	Military Affairs.						
Tharp, Wm., attorney of..	Balance due under former act....	20	1	Petition & papers.	201	Claims..........	May 2, 1828	Adverse.....	......	Laid on table.		
Tharp, Wm., attorney of..	Settlement of his accounts as sutler.	21	1	Petition.......	144	Claims..........	April 5, 1830	Adverse.....	......	Recommitted.		
					549	Claims..........	April 19, 1830	Favorable; bill	435	Referred to Committee Whole House.	....	Leave to withdraw certain papers on page 585.
Tharp, Wm., attorney of..	Settlement of his accounts as sutler.	21	2	House bill.....	264	Whole House....	Feb. 4, 1831	With't amend.	435	Passed.		
Tharp, Wm., attorney of..	Settlement of his accounts as sutler.	22	1	Petition.......	26	Claims..........	Dec. 19, 1831	Favorable; bill	24	Passed............	Passed......	App'd Feb. 24, 1832
Tharp, Wm., attorney of..	Revision and further allowance of his accounts.	22	2	Senate bill.....	166	Claims..........	Feb. 15, 1833	With amend..	S. 31	Passed............	Concurred in.	App'd March 2, 1833
Tharp, Wm., attorney of..	Revision and further allowance of his accounts.	23	2	Senate bill.....	265	Claims..........	Feb. 25, 1835	With't amend.	S. 70	Referred to Committee Whole House.		
Tharp, Wm., attorney of..	Authority to institute suit against the United States.	24	1	Senate bill.....	1128	....	....	....	S. 233	Referred to Committee Whole House.		
Tharp, Wm., attorney of..	Payment of claim against the United States as sutler.	24	2	Memorial......	80	Claims..........	23	Favorable; bill	936	Referred to Committee Whole House.		
Tharp, Wm., attorney of..	Payment of claim against the United States as sutler.	25	2	Petition.......	37	Claims..........	63	Favorable; bill	75	Passed............	Passed......	App'd June 7, 1838
Tharp, William, (Missouri)	Confirmation of title to land.....	15	2	Petition.......	110	Priv. Land Claims.	....	....	......	....	....	See act Mar. 3, 1818
Tharp, William, (Ky.)...	Pre-emption right to land.......	23	2	Petition.......	57	Public Lands.....	....	....	......	Discharged; laid on table.		
Thatcher, Amos R.......	Compensation for horse lost in United States service.	17	1	Petition.......	289	Claims.						
Thatcher, Elizabeth H...	(See John Wardrobe, heirs of)..	29	2	....	83							
Thatcher, Eunice, *et al.*..	(See Daniel Starr, heirs of).....	25	3	....	217							
Thatcher, George.......	(See Isaac Bolster)............	4	1	....	472							
Thatcher, James S., administrator of.	Release from am't charged against him on 3d Auditor's book.	28	1	Petition.......	738	Naval Affairs.						
Thatcher, John.........	Increase of pension.............	8	2	Petition.......	90	Whole House.						
Thatcher, Pleasants, heirs of.	Compensation for services in revolutionary war, also for pay and clothing due deceased.	24	1	Petition.......	105	Rev. Claims.....	Mar. 3, 1836	Adverse.....	......	Laid on table......	....	Provided in act June 15, 1844.
Thatcher, Winslow, L., *et al.*	(See Henry and W. L. Thacher).	22	2	....	261							
Thatcher, Stephen.......	Release from payment of a certain account as collector of customs.	18	2	Senate bill.....	284	Ways and Means..	Mar. 1, 1825	With't amend.	47	Passed............	....	App'd March 3, 1825
Thaxter, Joseph........	(See James Rackliff, *et al.*)......	20	1	....	162							
Thaxter, Thomas.......	To refund duties on certain imports.	17	1	Petition.......	117	Commerce.......	April 13, 1822	Adverse.....	......	Laid on table.		
Thayer, Elias Bond.....	(See Col. Wm. Bond, representatives of.)	23	2	....	109							
Thayer, Jerijah.........	Restoration of pension..........	17	1	Petition.......	88	Rev. Pensions.						
Thayer, Jerijah.........	Restoration of pension..........	17	2	Petition.......	119	Whole House.						
Thayer, Jerijah.........	Restoration of pension..........	19	1	Petition.......	150	Military Pensions..	164	Adverse.....	......	Recommitted.		
					507	Military Pensions..	May 3, 1826	Adverse.....	......	Laid on table.		
Thayer, Parmenius......	Pension......................	22	2	Petition.......	320	Invalid Pensions.						
Thayer, Col. S..........	Settlement of his accounts......	23	1	House bill.....	253	Whole House....	June 14, 1834	With't amend	238	Passed............	Passed......	App'd June 27, 1834
Thayer, Simeon........	Invalid pension................	1	3	Petition and rep't of Sec. War.	346, 393	....	....	....	......	Laid on table.		
Thayer, Simeon........	Invalid pension................	2	2	Rep. of Secretary War.	650	Whole House....	Feb. 6, 1793	Favorable; bill	229	Passed............	Passed......	App'd March 2, 1793
Thayer, Stephen, late widow of.	Revolutionary pension..........	26	1	Petition.......	626	Rev. Pensions.						

List of private claims presented to the House of Representatives of the United States from the 1st to the 31st Congress, inclusive—Continued.

Names of claimants.	Nature or object of the claim.	Congress.	Session.	How brought before the House of Reps.	Page of journal.	To what committee of the House referred.	No. or date of the report.	Nature of the report.	No. of the bill.	How disposed of by the House of Reps.	How disposed of by the Senate.	Date of the act of Congress, and remarks.
Thayer, Wm., representatives of.	Relief from operation of a certain law concerning military land scrip.	24	1	Petition	478	Public Lands.						
Thayer, Wm., representatives of.	Relief from operation of a certain law concerning military land scrip.	24	2	Petition	125	Public Lands.						
Thebo, Francis	Land under Spanish grant	22	1	Memorial	263	Priv. Land Claims.	Feb. 17, 1832	Favorable; bill	380	Referred to Committee Whole House.		
Theobold, Francis R.	Remission of fine imposed by collector of New Orleans.	24	1	Petition	101	Commerce	Jan. 12, 1836	Favorable; bill	118	Passed	Passed	App'd June 23, 1836
Theobold, Thomas	(See Dr. Samuel Y. Keene, representatives of.)	23	1		42							
Therese, Marie, representatives of	Confirmation of title to land	17	1	Petition	101	Priv. Land Claims.	Jan. 31, 1822	Favorable	68	Passed	Passed	App'd May 7, 1822
Theus, James	(See Samuel Legare, *et al.*)	4	1		493							
Theus, Simeon, administrator of.	Payment of certain money found due South Carolina.	21	1	Petition	145	Ways and Means.	260	Favorable; bill	317	Referred to Committee Whole House.		
Theus, Simeon, representatives of.	Payment of certain money found due South Carolina.	21	1	Senate bill	615	Whole House	May 24, 1830	With't amend.	121	Passed		App'd May 31, 1830
Theveatt, Archibald	Compensation for a horse lost in United States service.	10	1	Petition	156	Claims.						
Theveatt, Archibald	Compensation for a horse lost in United States service.	10	2	Petition	381	Claims.						
Theveatt, Archibald	Compensation for a horse lost in United States service.	11	2	Petition	121	Claims	Mar. 24, 1810	Adverse		Laid on table.		
Thibault, John B., representatives of.	Authority to locate or enter land	22	1	Petition	125	Priv. Land Claims.	Jan. 10, 1832	Favorable; bill	231	Referred to Committee Whole House.		
Thibault, John B., representatives of.	Authority to locate or enter land	22	2	House bill	92	Whole House	Dec. 22, 1832	With't amend.	231	Passed	Passed	App'd June 28, 1833
Thierer, Jacob	Indemnity for property destroyed by order of Captain Gilpin.	31	1	Petition	731	Claims.						
Thigpine, Captain	Compensation for military services.	26	2	Petition	124	Claims.						
Thigpine, Captain	Compensation for military services.	27	2	Petition	94	Claims.						
Thing, Nathaniel	Pension	21	2	Petition	103	Military Pensions.						
Thing, Nathiniel	Pension	22	1	Petition	122	Rev. Pensions.						
Thirber, Ezra	(See King & Thurber)	21	1		50							
Thistle, Hezekiah L	Compensation for use of patent packsaddle by United States.	24	2	Memorial	215	Military Affairs.						
Thistle, Hezekiah L	Compensation for horse lost in service of United States.	26	1	Petition	622	Claims.						
Thistle, Hezekiah L	Compensation for horse lost in service of United States.	26	2	Petition	107	Claims.						
Thistle, Hezekiah L	Compensation for horse lost in service of United States.	27	2	Petition	738	Claims.						
Thistle, Hezekiah L	Compensation for horse lost in service of United States.	27	2	Senate bill	550	Claims	April 12, 1842	Bill amended.	121	Passed	Concurred in	App'd Aug. 11, 1842
Thistle, Hezekiah L	Settlement of account as timber agent, &c.	29	1	Memorial	753	Naval Affairs.						
Thistle, Hezekiah L	Settlement of account as timber agent, &c.	30	1	Memorial	277	Naval Affairs.						
Thistle, Hezekiah L	Settlement of account as timber agent, &c.	31	1	Papers	1471					Leave to withdraw.		

List of private claims presented to the House of Representatives of the United States from the 1st to the 31st Congress, inclusive—Continued.

Names of claimants.	Nature or object of the claim.	Congress.	Session.	How brought before the House of Reps.	Page of journal.	To what committee of the House referred.	No. or date of the report.	Nature of the report.	No. of the bill.	How disposed of by the House of Reps.	How disposed of by the Senate.	Date of the act of Congress, and remarks.
Thody, Thomas	Compensation for false imprisonment.	26	1	Petition	298	Judiciary.						
Thody, Thomas	Compensation for false imprisonment.	27	2	Petition	357	Judiciary.						
Thody, Thomas	Compensation for false imprisonment.	27	3	Petition	132	Judiciary.						
Thody, Thomas	Compensation for false imprisonment.	29	1	Petition	441	Judiciary	323	Adverse	......	Laid on table.		
Thody, Thomas	Compensation for false imprisonment.	31	1	Petition	541	Judiciary.						
Tholozan, John Eli	Confirmation of title to land	15	1	Petition	226	Priv. Land Claims.						
Tholozan, John Eli	Confirmation of title to land	16	1	Petition	323	Priv. Land Claims.						
Tholozan, John Eli, *et al.*	Confirmation of title to land	23	1	Senate bill	845	Public Lands	Jan. 27, 1834	With amend.	S. 127	Passed	....	App'd June 30, 1834
Thom, George	Reimbursement of expenses while surveying on the United States boundary commission.	31	1	Petition	668	Military Affairs	....	....	......	....	....	Provided for in civil and diplomatic appropriation bill, September 30, 1850.
Thom, A. C., *et al.*, (Ind.)	To correct error in survey of lands.	26	1	Petition	353	Public Lands.						
Thomas, Abishai, attorney	(See Richard Blackledge, executor of.)	3	1	....	68							
Thomas, Alexander	Compensation for services in revolutionary war.	16	2	Petition	57	Pens. & Rev. Cl'ms.						
Thomas, Alexander, heirs of.	Compensation for services in revolutionary war.	24	2	Petition	307	Rev. Pensions.						
Thomas, Alexander, heirs of.	Compensation for services in revolutionary war.	26	1	Petition	282	Rev. Pensions.						
Thomas, Benjamin P., *et al*	(See Philemon Thomas, *et al.*)	18	1	....	105							
Thomas, Caleb, widow of.	Extension of act granting pensions to widows.	27	3	Petition	401	....	....	....	......	Laid on table.		
Thomas, Caleb, widow of.	Revolutionary pension	28	1	Petition	944	Rev. Pensions.						
Thomas, Caleb, widow of.	Revolutionary pension	29	2	Petition	112	Rev. Pensions	41	Adverse	......	Laid on table.		
Thomas, Caleb, widow of.	Revolutionary pension	30	2	Petition	282	Rev. Pensions	Feb. 13, 1849	....	......	Discharged; laid on table.		
Thomas, Charles, representatives of.	Permission to fund certificate of public debt.	5	2	Petition	283	Whole House.						
Thomas, Charles	Payment for work on Mars Hill, Military road.	25	2	Military Acad'my appropri'n bill.	294	Whole House	July 5, 1838	With amends.	412	Passed	Passed	App'd July 7, 1838
Thomas, Major Charles, *et al.*	Settlement of accounts for building fort in Arkansas.	28	1	Army appropriation bill.	196	Whole House	April 15, 1844	With amends.	31	Passed	Passed	App'd June 17, 1844
Thomas, Claiborne	(See James Thomas, *et al.*)	27	3	....	240							
Thomas, Cornelius, widow of.	Pension	29	1	Petition	82	Naval Affairs.						
Thomas, David, (Pa.)	Increase of naval pension	19	2	Petition	32	Naval Affairs	....	....	......	Discharged; laid on table.		
Thomas, David, (Pa.)	Grant of land for military services.	20	2	Petition	61	Naval Affairs	....	....	......	Discharged; laid on table.		
Thomas, David	To refund duties improperly exacted.	29	1	Petition	208	Claims	578	Favorable; bill	396	Passed	Ref'd to Com. on Claims.	
Thomas, David	To refund duties improperly exacted.	29	2	Petition	128	Claims	28	Favorable; bill	607	Referred to Committee Whole House.		
Thomas, David	To refund duties improperly exacted.	30	1	Petition	153	Claims	94	Favorable; bill	76	Passed	Passed 2d sess.	App'd Mar. 3, 1849
Thomas, Ebenezer	(See Eleazer Thomas)	16	1	....	33							

List of private claims presented to the House of Representatives of the United States from the 1st to the 31st Congress, inclusive—Continued.

Names of claimants.	Nature or object of the claim.	Congress.	Session.	How brought before the House of Reps.	Page of journal.	To what committee of the House referred.	No. or date of the report.	Nature of the report.	No. of the bill.	How disposed of by the House of Reps.	How disposed of by the Senate.	Date of the act of Congress, and remarks.
Thomas, Eleazer	Pension	16	1	Petition	33	Rev. Pensions	April 22, 1820	Adverse	......	Laid on table.		
Thomas, Elias	(See Joseph Cox & Elias Thomas)	7	2	....	283							
Thomas, Esther	(See Joseph Thomas, widow of)	25	2	....	664							
Thomas, Evan	Restoration of pension	24	2	Memorial	84	Rev. Pensions.						
Thomas, Evan	Revolutionary pension	25	2	Petition	984	Rev. Pensions	....	....	......	Discharged.		
Thomas, Evan	Revolutionary pension	26	1	Petition	175	Rev. Pensions	....	....	......	Discharged; laid on table.		
Thomas, Frances Ann	(See John L. Thomas, widow of)	22	2	....	346							
Thomas, George C	Invalid pension	31	1	Petition	680	Invalid Pensions	302	Favorable; bill	271	Referred to Committee Whole House.		
Thomas, George C	Invalid pension	31	2	Bill of last sess.	181	Whole House	Jan. 24, 1851	With't amend.	271	Passed	Adverse report	.
Thomas, Gertrude	(See John Thomas, of N. York, widow of.)	28	1	....	114							
Thomas, Gregory, *et al.*	Compensation for damages sustained by collision with United States steamer.	29	1	Memorial	171	Claims	162	Favorable; bill	166	Passed	Passed	App'd Aug. 8, 1846
Thomas, Hannah, & John.	Additional compensation for land sold to the United States.	10	2	Petition	351	Com. and Manuf.						
Thomas, Isaac, and William M. Wilson.	Confirmation of title to land	22	1	Petition	33	Priv. Land Claims.	382	Favorable; bill	474	Referred to Committee Whole House.		
Thomas, Israel, (Ky.)	Invalid pension	27	2	Petition	130	Invalid Pensions	212	Adverse	......	Recommitted.		
Thomas, Israel, (Ky.)	Invalid pension	27	2	....	1002	Invalid Pensions	923	Favorable; bill	535	Ordered to 3d reading.		
Thomas, Israel, (Ky.)	Invalid pension	27	3	Bill of last sess.	89	....	....	....	535	Passed	Passed	App'd March 3, 1843
Thomas, Israel, (Ky.)	Remuneration for losses sustained and disabilities.	28	1	Petition	236	Claims	129	Adverse	......	Laid on table	....	Leave to withdraw.
Thomas, Isaiah, (Mass.)	To cancel bonds for duties on types imported.	2	2	Petition	657	....	....	....	......	Referred to Secretary Treasury.		
Thomas, Isaiah, (Mass.)	To cancel bonds for duties on types imported.	3	2	Petition and rep't Sec. Treasury.	284	Select	Feb. 16, 1795	Adverse	......	Laid on table.		
Thomas, Jacob, heirs-at-law of.	Permission to complete payment for public land forfeited.	23	2	Petition	166	Priv. Land Claims.	....	....	......	Discharged; laid on table.		
Thomas, Jacob, heirs at-law of.	Permission to complete payment for public land forfeited.	24	1	Petition	538	Priv. Land Claims.	....	....	......	Discharged; laid on table.		
Thomas, Jacob, heirs-at-law of.	Permission to complete payment for public land forfeited.	26	2	Petition	98	Priv. Land Claims.	192	Adverse	......	Laid on table.		
Thomas, Jacob, heirs-at-law of.	Permission to complete payment for public land forfeited.	28	1	Petition	434	Priv. Land Claims.	....	....	......	Discharged.		
Thomas, Jacob, heirs-at-law of.	Permission to complete payment for public land forfeited.	28	2	Resolution	94	Priv. Land Claims.	....	....	......	Discharged; laid on table.		
Thomas, James	Settlement of accounts as deputy quartermaster general.	17	2	Petition and docs	95, 136	Claims.						
Thomas, James	Settlement of accounts as deputy quartermaster general.	21	1	Senate bill	552	Claims	May 26, 1830	With't amend.	S. 109	Referred to Committee Whole House.		
Thomas, James	Settlement of accounts as deputy quartermaster general.	21	2	Senate bill	164	Claims	March 2, 1831	With amend.	S. 58	Passed	Concurred in	App'd March 2, 1831
Thomas, James	Equitable settlement of accounts.	22	1	Petition	1109	Whole House.						
Thomas, James	Equitable settlement of accounts.	23	1	Petition	94	Claims.						
Thomas, James	Equitable settlement of accounts.	23	2	Senate bill	244	Judiciary	Feb. 4, 1835	With't amend.	68	Referred to Committee Whole House.		
Thomas, James	Equitable settlement of accounts.	24	1	Senate bill	320	Judiciary	April 12, 1836	With't amend.	60	Passed	....	App'd July 2, 1836
Thomas, James	Indemnity for Indian depredations.	20	2	Resolution	151	Indian Affairs	....	....	......	Disch'd; and to Claims.		
Thomas, James	Indemnity for Indian depredations.	23	1	Petition	79	Indian Affairs	....	....	......	Discharged; laid on table.		

List of private claims presented to the House of Representatives of the United States from the 1st to the 31st Congress, inclusive—Continued.

ames of claimants.	Nature or object of the claim.	Congress.	Session.	How brought before the House of Reps.	Page of journal.	To what committee of the House referred.	No. or date of the report.	Nature of the report.	No. of the bill.	How disposed of by the House of Reps.	How disposed of by the Senate.	Date of the act of Congress, and remarks.
Thomas, James	(See William H. Bedford)	28	1		262							
Rhomas, James, (Ky.)	(See Nicholas Shrader, sureties of)	22	1		442							
Thomas, James, *et al*	Appropriation of land to satisfy bounty-land warrant.	27	3	Petition	240	Rev. Pensions.						
Thomas, James, heir of	Compensation for services in war of 1812.	31	2	Petition	107	Naval Affairs.						
Thomas, Jesse, (Va.)	Payment for hire of horses, wagon, and driver.	8	1	Petition	486	Claims.						
Thomas, Jesse	Continuation of pension	16	2	Petition	240	Rev. Pensions				Discharged; laid on table.		
Thomas, Joel, (Mich)	Confirmation of title to land	21	1	Petition	298	Priv. Land Claims.	May 26, 1830	Adverse		Laid on table.		
Thomas, Joel, (Mich)	Confirmation of title to land	22	1	Petition	125	Priv. Land Claims.	Jan. 10, 1832	Favorable; bill	227	Referred to Committee Whole House.		
Thomas, Joel, (Mich)	Confirmation of title to land	22	2	Bill of last sess.	92	Whole House	Dec. 22, 1832	With't amend.	227	Passed	Passed	App'd Feb. 5, 1833
Thomas, John, (Md.)	Depreciation of pay as surgeon's mate.	3	1	Petition and rep't Sec. of War.	60, 93	Select	April 22, 1794	Report.		Laid on table.		
Thomas, John, (Md.)	Depreciation of pay as surgeon's mate.	12	1	Petition	167	Claims.						
Thomas, John, (Mass)	(See Hannah and John Thomas)	10	2		351							
Thomas, John A., (Conn.)	Exoneration from refunding money of which he was robbed while in service of United States.	14	2	Petition	46	Claims	Dec. 20, 1816	Adverse		Rejected.		
Thomas, John A., (Conn.)	Exoneration from refunding money of which he was robbed while in service of United States.	20	1	Petition	30	Claims	Dec. 21, 1827	Adverse		Laid on table.		
Thomas, Gen. John, (Ky.)	Settlement of accounts as commandant of Kentucky militia.	16	2	Petition	91	Claims	Jan. 15, 1821	Favorable; bill	200	Referred to Committee Whole House.		
Thomas, Gen. John, (Ky.)	Settlement of accounts as commandant of Kentucky militia.	17	1	Petition	238	Claims	Feb. 13, 1822	Favorable; bill	87	Passed	Passed	App'd May 1, 1822
Thomas, John J., (Ky)	Restoration of pension	17	2	Petition	47	Rev. Pensions.						
Thomas, John, & Co., (Ohio.)	Compensation for flour taken for use of United States troops.	17	1	Petition	61	Claims	Feb. 15, 1822	Adverse		Referred to Committee Whole House.		
Thomas, John, & Co., (Ohio.)	Compensation for flour taken for use of United States troops.	18	1	Petition	71	Military Affairs	Jan. 15, 1824	Favorable; bill	59	Passed	Passed	App'd May 17, 1824
Thomas, John, (Md.)	Balance due for work at Washington navy yard; also for use of improvements in ship building.	18	1	Petition	332	Naval Affairs.						
Thomas, John, (Md.)	Compensation for improvements in ship building.	18	2	Petition	116	Naval Affairs				Discharged.		Leave to withdraw.
Thomas, John, (Md.)	Compensation for improvements in ship building.	19	1	Petition	176	Naval Affairs	May 6, 1826	Adverse		Laid on table.		
Thomas, John H., (La)	Confirmation of title to land	19	1	Petition	444	Priv. Land Claims.						
Thomas, John H., (La)	Confirmation of title to land	19	2	Petition	49	Priv. Land Claims.	Jan. 30, 1827	Adverse		Laid on table.		
Thomas, John H., (La)	Confirmation of title to land	20	1	Petition	33	Priv. Land Claims.						
Thomas, John H., (La)	Confirmation of title to land	21	1	Petition	40	Priv. Land Claims.	Mar. 30, 1830	Favorable; bill	397	Referred to Committee Whole House.		
Thomas, John H., (La)	Confirmation of title to land	22	1	Petition	32	Priv. Land Claims.	Dec. 22, 1831	Favorable; bill	82	Passed	Passed	App'd May 19, 1832
Thomas, John	(See Canadian refugees.)											
Thomas, John	(See William Trask, heir of)	26	1		701							
Thomas, John, widow of	Five years' half-pay	19	2	Petition	307	Military Pensions.						
Thomas, John, widow of	Five years' half pay	20	1	Petition	57	Military Pensions.	Feb. 13, 1828	Favorable; bill	164	Passed	Rejected.	
Thomas, John, widow of	Five years' half-pay	21	2	Petition	231	Military Pensions.	Feb. 15, 1831	Favorable; bill	629	Passed	With't amend.	
Thomas, John, widow of	Five years' half-pay	22	1	Petition	68	Invalid Pensions.	Jan. 10, 1832	Favorable; bill	235	Passed	Laid on table.	

List of private claims presented to the House of Representatives of the United States from the 1st to the 31st Congress, inclusive—Continued.

Names of claimants.	Nature or object of the claim.	Congress.	Session.	How brought before the House of Reps.	Page of journal	To what committee of the House referred.	No. or date of the report.	Nature of the report.	No. of the bill.	How disposed of by the House of Reps.	How disposed of by the Senate.	Date of the act of Congress, and remarks.
Thomas, John, widow of..	Five years' half-pay...........	22	2	Petition	53	Invalid Pensions ..	Dec. 19, 1832	Favorable; bill	628	Referred to Committee Whole House.		
Thomas, John, widow of..	Five years' half-pay...........	23	1	Petition	159	Invalid Pensions ..	Jan. 10, 1834	Favorable; bill	175	Passed	Passed	App'd June 30, 1834
Thomas, John L., widow of, (Md.)	Balance of pay and naval pension.	22	2	Petition	346	Naval Affairs.						
Thomas, John L., widow of, (Md.)	Increase of pension	25	2	Petition	594	Naval Affairs......	....	....	......	Discharged; laid on table.		
Thomas, John, heirs of, (Mass.)	Bounty land for revolutionary services.	25	2	Petition	177	Rev. Claims......	336	Adverse		Recommitted.		
					1060	Rev. Claims......	969	Adverse.	......	Laid on table.		
Thomas, Capt. John, (Va.)	Five years' full pay, with interest.	22	1	Petition	66	Rev. Pensions	129	Favorable; bill	200	Referred to Committee Whole House.		
Thomas, Capt. John, (Va.)	Five years' full pay, with interest.	22	2	House bill	66	Whole House.....	Dec. 15, 1832	With't amend.	200	Passed	Passed	App'd March 3, 1833
Thomas, Capt. John, heirs of, (Va.)	Half-pay........................	25	3	Petition	124	Rev. Claims.						
Thomas, Capt. John, heirs of, (Va.)	Half-pay........................	26	1	Petition	164	Rev. Claims.						
Thomas Capt. John, heirs of, (Va.)	Half-pay........................	26	2	Petition	35	Rev. Claims.						
Thomas, Capt. John, heirs of, (Va.)	Half-pay........................	27	2	Petition	89	Rev. Claims......	403	Adverse	......	Laid on table.		
Thomas, Capt. John, heirs of, (Va.)	Half-pay........................	29	1	Memorial	298	Rev. Claims.						
Thomas, Capt. John, heirs of, (Va.)	Half-pay........................	29	2	Petition	135	Rev. Claims.						
Thomas, Capt. John, heirs of, (Va.)	Half-pay........................	31	1	Petition	759	....	....	....	......	Leave to withdraw.		
Thomas, Capt. John, heirs of, (Va.)	Half-pay........................	31	2	Petition	141	Rev. Pensions	60	Adverse	......	Laid on table.		
Thomas, John, heirs of, (Indiana.)	Right of pre-emption...........	26	1	Petition	611	Priv. Land Claims.	336	Favorable; bill	308	Referred to Committee Whole House.		
Thomas, John, widow of, (N. Y.)	Revolutionary pension.........	28	1	Petition	114	Rev. Pensions	....	....	......	Discharged; laid on table.		
Thomas, John, *et al.*, (Mass)	Indemnity for French spoliations prior to 1800.	28	1	Petition	115	Foreign Affairs.						
Thomas, Joseph, widow of.	Revolutionary pension.........	25	2	Petition	664	Rev Pensions.....	....	....	......	Discharged; laid on table.		
Thomas, Joseph S., (N.Y.)	Indemnity for property destroyed in war of 1812.	13	3	Petition	723	Claims	Feb. 18, 1815	Favorable; bill	297	Passed	Passed	App'd March 3, 1815
Thomas, Joseph S., (N.Y.)	Balance due on property destroyed in war of 1812.	24	1	Petition	207	Claims	233	Adverse.	......	Laid on table.		
Thomas, Joseph S., (N.Y.)	Balance due on property destroyed in war of 1812.	23	1	Petition	35	Claims	Dec. 18, 1833	Adverse	......	Laid on table.		
Thomas, Joseph S., (N.Y.)	Balance due on property destroyed in war of 1812.	25	2	Petition	52	Claims	Dec. 28, 1837	Adverse	......	Laid on table.		
Thomas, Joseph S., (N.Y.)	Balance due on property destroyed in war of 1812.	26	2	Petition	80	Claims	33	Adverse	......	Laid on table.		
Thomas, Joseph	Compensation for gun lost in service of United States.	21	2	Resolution	285	Claims.						
Thomas, Judith.........	(See John Thomas, widow of)...	19	2	....	307							
Thomas, Linza	Invalid pension...............	25	3	Resolution	402	Invalid Pensions.						
Thomas, Linza	Invalid pension...............	26	1	Petition	326	Invalid Pensions ..	666	Adverse	......	Laid on table.		
Thomas, Linza	Invalid pension...............	27	2	Petition	841	Invalid Pensions.						

List of private claims presented to the House of Representatives of the United States from the 1st to the 31st Congress, inclusive—Continued.

Names of claimants.	Nature or object of the claim.	Congress.	Session.	How brought before the House of Reps.	Page of journal.	To what committee of the House referred.	No. or date of the report.	Nature of the report.	No. of the bill.	How disposed of by the House of Reps.	How disposed of by the Senate.	Date of the act of Congress, and remarks.
Thomas, L. A., & Thomas Rogers.	Compensation for legal defence of Indians charged with murder.	29	1	Memorial	1054	Claims.						
Thomas, L. A., & Thomas Rogers.	Compensation for legal defence of Indians charged with murder.	29	2	Petition	56	Claims.						
Thomas, L. A., & Thomas Rogers.	Compensation for legal defence of Indians charged with murder.	31	1	Senate bill	1219	Indian Affairs			S. 82			
Thomas, L. A., & Thomas Rogers.	Compensation for legal defence of Indians charged with murder.	31	1	House bill	1012	Whole House		With amends.	331	Passed	Passed	App'd Sept. 30, 1850
Thomas, L. A., & Thomas Rogers.	Compensation for legal defence of Indians charged with murder.	31	2	Senate bill	207	Whole House	Jan. 29, 1851	Adverse	S. 82	Laid on table.		
Thomas, Ludwick	Invalid pension	2	1	Petition	448					Referred to Secretary of War.		
Thomas, Margaret M.	(See Richard Thomas, widow of.)	30	1		344							
Thomas, Capt. Mark, heirs of.	Ten per cent. on unsatisfied bounty land warrant.	27	3	Petition	426	Rev. Claims	253	Adverse		Laid on table.		
Thomas, Martin, (Mo.)	Confirmation of title to land	15	1	Petition	267	Priv. Land Claims.						
Thomas, Martin, (Mo.)	Confirmation of title to land	15	2	Petition	207	Priv. Land Claims.						
Thomas, Martin, (Mo.)	Confirmation of title to land	16	1	Petition	72	Priv. Land Claims.						
Thomas, Martin, (Mo.)	Confirmation of title to land	17	1	Petition	55	Public Lands.						
Thomas, Martin, (Mo.)	Confirmation of title to land	18	1	Petition	55	Public Lands.						
Thomas, Martin	(See Frederick Goets, administrator of.)	18	2	Petition	59							
Thomas, Martin	Extra compensation as superintendent of United States lead mines	25	3	Memorial	462	Claims.						
Thomas, Martin	Extra compensation as superintendent of United States lead mines.	26	1	Memorial	170	Claims.						
Thomas, Martin	Extra compensation as superintendent of United States lead mines.	29	1	Memorial	283	Claims	576	Favorable; bill	394	Referred to Committee Whole House.		
Thomas, Martin	Extra compensation as superintendent of United States lead mines.	30	1	Petition	153	Claims	60	Adverse		Laid on table		Leave to withdraw.
Thomas, Minor, (Ind.)	Permission to locate certain land warrant.	20	1	Res. and docs.	72	Priv. Land Claims.	Jan. 8, 1828	Adverse		Laid on table		Leave to withdraw.
Thomas, Minor, (Ind.)	Permission to locate certain land warrant.	20	2	Res. and docs.	41	Public Lands.	Jan. 7, 1829	Adverse		Laid on table		Leave to withdraw.
Thomas, Nathan'l, (Mass.)	Revolutionary pension	21	2	Petition	188	Rev. Pensions.						
Thomas, Nicholas, jr., (Me.)	Additional compensation for taking Census.	22	1	Petition	672	Judiciary.						
Thomas, Nicholas, heirs of	Pension for revolutionary services.	27	2	Petition	329	Rev. Pensions	784	Adverse		Laid on table.		
Thomas, Nicholas, heirs of	Pension for revolutionary services.	27	3	Petition	73	Rev. Pensions.						
Thomas, Philemon, *et al.*	Confirmation of certain land grants	18	1	Petition	105	Priv. Land Claims.				Discharged; referred to Claims.		Res. to refer to Ways and Means.
Thomas, Philemon, *et al.*	Confirmation of certain land grants	25	2	Petition & docs.	792					Leave to withdraw.		
Thomas, Gen'l Philemon, (La.)	Grand of land for military services	23	1	Senate bill	692	Public Lands.	June 17, 1834	With amend.	92	Passed	Concurred in.	App'd June 30, 1834
Thomas, Philip	Invalid pension	3	1	Rep. of Secretary of War.	131	Select	May 26, 1794	Res. to refer to Sec. War.	J R. 12	Passed	Passed	App'd June 9, 1794
Thomas, Philip	Invalid pension	4	1	Rep. of Secretary of War.	448	Claims.						
Thomas, Philip, (Md.)	Pension for services in war of 1812	15	2	Petition	88	Pens. & Rev. Cl'ms.	176	Adverse		Laid on table.		
Thomas, Phineas	Indemnity for Indian depredations.	28	1	Petition	351	Indian Affairs	486	Adverse		Laid on table.		
Thomas, Pierre	(See E. Marin, *et al.*)	22	1		64							
Thomas, Polly	(See Caleb Thomas, widow of)	27	3		401							

3—60

List of private claims presented to the House of Representatives of the United States from the 1st to the 31st Congress, inclusive—Continued.

Names of claimants.	Nature or object of the claim.	Congress.	Session.	How brought before the House of Reps.	Page of journal.	To what committee of the House referred.	No. or date of the report.	Nature of the report.	No. of the bill.	How disposed of by the House of Reps.	How disposed of by the Senate.	Date of the act of Congress, and remarks.
Thomas, Richard, widow of.	Renewal of pension	30	1	Petition	344	Naval Affairs	444	Favorable; bill	375	Referred to Committee Whole House.		
Thomas, Sally	(See Cornelius Thomas, widow of.)	29	1		82							
Thomas, Samuel A	Permission to redeem forfeited land	14	1	Petition	39	Claims				Discharged		Leave to withdraw.
Thomas, Samuel A	Grant of land and balance due on same remitted.	19	1	Petition	442	Ways and Means	May 4, 1826	Adverse		Referred to Committee Whole House.		
Thomas, Samuel A	Grant of land and balance due on same remitted.	20	1	Petition	276	Ways and Means	Feb. 25, 1828	Adverse		Laid on table.		
Thomas, Seneca, (an Indian.)	Pension	18	1	House bill	106	Whole House	Jan. 19, 1824	With amend.	35	Passed	Passed	App'd May 19, 1824
Thomas, Seneca, (an Indian.)	Arrears of pension	29	1	Petition	203	Invalid Pensions	246	Adverse		Laid on table.		
Thomas, Seneca, (an Indian.)	Arrears of pension	29	2	Petition	69	Invalid Pensions.						
Thomas, Seneca, (an Indian.)	Arrears of pension	31	2	Petition	199	Invalid Pensions.						
Thomas, Solomon	Pension	16	1	Petition	33	Rev. Pensions	April 22, 1820	Adverse		Laid on table.		
Thomas, Stephen	Revolutionary pension	16	1	Petition	95	Rev. Pensions	Jan. 14, 1820	Adverse		Laid on table.		
Thomas, William	Revolutionary pension	2	1	Petition	539					Referred to Secretary War.		
Thomas, William	Revolutionary pension	2	2	Petition	623	Referred to Secretary of War.	Feb. 8, 1893	Report		Laid on table.		
Thomas, William, (Ky.)	Compensation for revolutionary services.	23	2	Petition	257	Rev. Pensions.						
Thomas, William	Compensation for a horse lost in public service.	25	2	Documents	396	Claims				Discharged; laid on table.		
Thomas, William	Compensation for a horse lost in public service.	25	3	Documents	207	Claims	315	Adverse		Laid on table.		
Thomas, William, (N. Y.	Invalid pension	26	1	Petition	288	Invalid Pensions.						
Thomas, William, (Md.)	Invalid pension	27	3	Petition	102, 109	Invalid Pensions.						
Thomas, William, *et al.*	(See Col. Bullitt, heirs of.)	27	3		155							
Thomas, William	(See Capt. John Thomas, heirs of.)	31	2		141							
Thomas, William	(See Louis F. Beeler, *et al.*)	30	1		115		482					
Thomas, William B.	(See James Thomas, heirs of.)	31	2		107							
Thomas, Zachariah	Compensation for services as a spy in revolutionary war.	23	2	Petition	490					Laid on table.		
Thomason, Elisha	Permission to purchase a certain tract of land.	30	1	Petition	137	Priv. Land Claims.	179	Favorable; bill	189	Passed.		
Thomason, Elisha	Permission to purchase a certain tract of land.	30	2	House bill from Senate.	166				189		Passed	App'd Jan. 8, 1849
Thompson, Alex., (N. Y.)	Revolutionary pension	24	1	Petition	406	Rev. Pensions	April 20, 1836	Report		Laid on table.		
Thompson, Alex., (N. Y.)	Revolutionary pension	26	1	Petition	626	Rev. Pensions.						
Thompson, Alex., (N. Y.)	Revolutionary pension	27	2	Petition	239	Rev. Pensions				Leave to withdraw.		
Thompson, Alexander R., widow of.	Compensation for horses lost in Florida war.	25	3	Petition	454	Military Affairs				Discharged; referred to Com. of Claims.		
Thompson, Alexander R., widow of.	Compensation for horses lost in Florida war.	26	1	Petition	170	Claims.						
Thompson, Alexander, R., widow of.	$10,000 as compensation for services of husband and for losses sustained in Florida war.	26	1	Petition	296	Military Affairs.						
Thompson, Alexander, R., widow of.	Annuity in consideration of death of husband.	27	2	Senate bill	1138	Military Affairs	Aug. 20, 1842	With't amend.	S. 242	Passed		App'd Aug. 29, 1842

List of private claims presented to the House of Representatives of the United States from the 1st to the 31st Congress, inclusive—Continued.

Names of claimants.	Nature or object of the claim.	Congress.	Session.	How brought before the House of Reps.	Page of journal.	To what committee of the House referred.	No. or date of the report.	Nature of the report.	No. of the bill.	How disposed of by the House of Reps.	How disposed of by the Senate.	Date of the act of Congress, and remarks.
Thompson, Alexander, R., widow of.	Compensation for services not provided for by act of August 29, 1842.	27	3	Senate bill	495	Whole House		With't amend.	S. 92	Passed		App'd March 3, 1843
Thompson, Alexander, R., widow of.	Settlement of accounts and payment of balance.	28	2	Joint resolution	469				J. R. 18	Passed	Passed	App'd March 1, 1845
Thompson, Alexander, R., widow of.	Benefit of act of July 5, 1838, granting additional rations to officers of army, &c.	27	2	Petition	330	Military Affairs.						
Thompson, Alexander, R., widow of.	Pension	28	1	Petition	528	Military Affairs	511	Favorable; bill	387	Referred to Committee Whole House.		
Thompson, Alexander, R., widow of.	Pension	29	1	Memorial	501	Military Affairs				Discharged; referred to Invalid Pensions.		
Thompson, Alexander, R., widow of.	Pension	30	1	Petition	722	Invalid Pensions	630	Favorable; bill	505	Referred to Committee Whole House.		
Thompson, Alexander, R., widow of.	Pension	31	1	Petition	468	Invalid Pensions	235	Favorable; bill	230	Referred to Committee Whole House.		
Thompson, Amos	Balance due for services as chaplain in revolutionary war.	4	1	Petition	422	Claims	May 7, 1796	Adverse		Rejected.		
Thompson, Amos, (Conn.)	Revolutionary pension	24	2	Petition	133	Rev. Pensions	79	Favorable; bill	824	Referred to Committee Whole House.		
Thompson, Amos, (Conn.)	Revolutionary pension	25	2	Petition	38	Rev. Pensions	156	Favorable; bill	181	Passed	Passed	App'd June 28, 1838
Thompsom, Anderson	(See Charles Whiteby, surety of.)	22	1		733							
Thompson, Andrew	(See William Thompson, administrator of.)	5	3		460							
Thompson, Atchison	Compensation for clothing and supplies furnished an Indian.	1	1	Petition	77					Laid on table.		
Thompson & Bathurst	(See Kantzow & Biel, agents of.)	18	2		136							
Thompson, Benjamin	(See John Blake, *et al.*)	2	1		465							
Thompson, Benj., (Del.)	(See Canadian refugees.)											
Thompson, Benj., (Maine)	Invalid pension	2	2	Rep. of Secretary War.	649					Referred to Committee Whole House.		
Thompson, Benj., (Maine)	Invalid pension	3	1	Rep. of Secretary War.	131	Select	May 26, 1794	Res. to refer to Sec. War.	J. R. 12	Passed	Passed	App'd June 9, 1794
Thompson, Benj., (Maine)	Invalid pension	4	1	Rep. of Secretary War.	445	Claims.						
Thompson, Benj., (N. H.)	Pension	22	1	Resolution	211	Rev. Pensions				Discharged; laid on table.		
Thompson, Benj., (Ohio)	Arrears of pension	22	2	Petition	171	Rev. Pensions				Discharged; laid on table.		
Thompson, Benj., (Ohio)	Arrears of pension	23	1	Petition	46	Rev. Pensions				Discharged; laid on table.		
Thompson, Benj., (Ga.)	Increase of pension	23	2	Petition	39	Rev. Pensions	Dec. 29, 1834	Adverse		Laid on table.		
Thompson, Benj., (Ga.)	Increase of pension	24	1	Resolution	437	Rev. Pensions.						
Thompson, Benjamin, and D. F. Davidson.	Restitution of tonnage duties illegally collected.	30	2	Petition	282	Naval Affairs.						
Thompson, B. J	(See Isaac Crow, assignee of.)	27	2		622							
Thompson, Beriah	Pension	21	2	Petition	110	Rev. Pensions	Dec. 29, 1834	Adverse		Laid on table.		
Thompson, Bethia	(See Josiah Thompson, widow of.)	23	2		165							
Thompson & Boggs	(See Boggs & Thompson.)	26	1		292							
Thompson, Burwell J., (Maine.	Confirmation of title to land	15	1	Petition	226	Priv. Land Claims.						
Thompson, Burwell J., (Maine.)	Confirmation of title to land	16	1	Petition	71	Priv. Land Claims.						

List of private claims presented to the House of Representatives of the United States from the 1st to the 31st Congress, inclusive—**Continued.**

Names of claimants.	Nature or object of the claim.	Congress.	Session.	How brought before the House of Reps.	Page of journal.	To what committee of the House referred.	No. or date of the report.	Nature of the report.	No. of the bill.	How disposed of by the House of Reps.	How disposed of by the Senate.	Date of the act of Congress, and remarks.
Thompson, Burwell J., (Maine.)	Confirmation of title to land	17	1	Petition	55	Public Lands.						
Thompson, Burwell J., (Maine.)	Confirmation of title to land	18	1	Petition	55	Public Lands	.....	.....	.....	.....	.....	See act May 26, 1824
Thompson, Charles C. B., widow of.	Naval pension	22	2	Petition	120	Naval Affairs	123	Favorable; bill	751	Referred to Committee Whole House.		
Thompson, Charles C. B., widow of.	Naval pension	23	1	Petition	74	Naval Affairs	.....	.....	.....	Discharged; laid on table.		
Thompson, Charles C. B., administrator of.	Compensation for certain services rendered government.	23	1	Petition	129	Foreign Affairs	Jan. 16, 1834	Report and bill	S. 164	Discharged; referred to Naval Affairs.		
Thompson, Charles C. B., administrator of.	Compensation for certain services rendered government.	23	2	Petition	116	Foreign Affairs.						
Thompson, Charles C. B., administrator of.	Compensation for certain services rendered government.	24	1	Senate bill	936	Naval Affairs	June 17, 1836	Adverse	.....	Referred to Committee Whole House.		
Thompson, C. S., (Mich.)	Relief on a contract for carrying mail.	31	1	Petition	890	P. Of. & P. Roads.						
Thompson, C. S., (Mich.)	Relief on a contract for carrying mail.	31	2	Petition	327	P. Of. & P. Roads.						
Thompson, David, (Miss.)	Confirmation of title to land	12	1	Petition	26	Public Lands.						
Thompson, David, (Miss.)	Confirmation of title to land	12	2	Petition	663	Public Lands.						
Thompson, David, (Miss.)	Confirmation of title to land	14	2	Petition	285	Priv. Land Claims.						
Thompson, Diantha	(See Wm. Thompson, widow of)	26	1	.....	118							
Thompson & Dickey	Indemnity for French spoliations prior to 1800.	26	1	Memorial	182	Foreign Affairs	343	Favorable; bill	319	Referred to Committee Whole House.		
Thompson, Edward	Depreciation of revolutionary pay	3	1	Petition	60	.....	.....	.....	.....	Referred to Secretary War.		
Thompson, Edward	Depreciation of revolutionary pay	3	2	Petition and rep't Sec. of War.	278	.....	.....	.....	.....	Laid on table.		
Thompson, Edward	Invalid pension	2	1	Petition	477	.....	.....	.....	.....	Referred to Secretary War.		
Thompson, Edward	Invalid pension	3	1	Petition	95	.....	.....	.....	.....	Laid on table.		
Thompson, Edward	Invalid pension	4	1	Petition	556	Claims.						
Thompson, Edward	Invalid pension	4	2	Report	655	Claims	Jan. 23, 1797	Adverse	.....	Rejected.		
Thompson, Edward	Invalid pension	5	2	Petition	90	Claims	.....	.....	.....	Discharged; laid on table.		
Thompson, Edw'd, (Phila.)	(See Haggerty & Austin)	21	2	.....	128							
Thompson, Edw'd, (Phila.)	(See New York, Insurance Companies of.)	22	1	.....	473							
Thompson, E. C. B., *et al.*	Pension	23	2	Petition	102	Naval Affairs	Feb. 25, 1835	Adverse	.....	Laid on table.		
Thompson, Egbert	(See Exploring Expedition)	27	3	.....	149	.....	270	.....	818			
Thompson, Eliza	(See John Smith, of Philadelphia, executrix of.)	26	1	.....	182							
Thompson, Elizabeth	(See Mrs. George Thompson, executrix of.)	15	1	.....	34							
Thompson, Elizabeth	(See John Thompson and wife)	19	1	.....	206							
Thompson, Elizabeth	(See John Thompson, widow of.)	28	1	.....	251							
Thompson, Emma	(See Charles C. B. Thompson, widow of.)	22	2	.....	120							
Thompson, Ezekiel, (Mass)	To be exonerated from refunding money of which he was robbed.	13	3	Petition	715	Ways and Means	.....	.....	.....	Disch'd; and to Claims.		
Thompson, Farley D.	(See Chileon White, sureties of)	27	2	.....	129							
Thompson, Farley D.	(See John S. Napier, surety of.)	29	1	.....	492							

List of private claims presented to the House of Representatives of the United States from the 1st to the 31st Congress, inclusive—Continued.

Names of claimants.	Nature or object of the claim.	Congress.	Session.	How brought before the House of Reps.	Page of journal.	To what committee of the House referred.	No. or date of the report.	Nature of the report.	No. of the bill.	How disposed of by the House of Reps.	How disposed of by the Senate.	Date of the act of Congress, and remarks.
Thompson, Flanders, heirs of.	Permission to enter land in lieu of other land.	31	1	Petition	1003	Priv. Land Claims.						
Thompson, Francis, (N.Y.)	Drawback of duties on cotton	17	1	Petition	416	Commerce.						
Thompson, Francis B., (Ill.)	Compensation for horse lost in Indian war of 1832.	24	1	Petition	670	Claims	661	Adverse	.....	Laid on table.		
Thompson, G. L.	Indemnity against Mexico	27	2	Petition	215	Foreign Affairs.						
Thompson, G. L.	(See John Baldwin, *et al*)	27	2	....	215							
Thompson, Mrs. George, executrix of.	Indemnity for property destroyed in war of 1812.	15	1	Letter of Com'r Claims.	34	Claims.						
Thompson, Mrs. George, executrix of.	Indemnity for property destroyed in war of 1812.	16	1	Report of Com'r Claims.	211	Claims	Feb. 11, 1820	Adverse	.....	Laid on table		
Thompson, Mrs. George, executrix of.	Indemnity for property destroyed in war of 1812.	23	1	Petition	335	Claims	Mar. 7, 1834	Adverse.	.....	Laid on table.		
Thompson, Mrs. George, executrix of.	Indemnity for property destroyed in war of 1812.	28	1	Petition	510	Claims.						
Thompson, Mrs. George, executrix of.	Indemnity for property destroyed in war of 1812.	28	2	Petition	59	Claims	5	Adverse	.....	Laid on table.		
Thompson, George	Permission to purchase land with Continental money.	16	1	Petition	188	Public Lands	Feb. 3, 1820	Adverse	.....	Rejected.		
Thompson, Hannah	(See Joseph Thompson, heir of.)	26	1	....	727							
Thompson, Henry, (Ky.)	Invalid pension	23	1	Petition	436	Invalid Pensions	June 24, 1834	Adverse	.....	Laid on table.		
Thompson, Henry, (Ky)	Invalid pension	23	2	Petition	131	Invalid Pensions	Jan. 6, 1835	Adverse	.....	Laid on table.		
Thompson, Henry, (Ky.)	Invalid pension	24	1	Petition	67	Invalid Pensions	Mar. 3, 1836	Adverse	.....	Laid on table.		
Thompson, Henry, (Ky)	Invalid pension	24	2	Petition	213	Invalid Pensions	Jan. 26, 1837	Adverse	.....	Laid on table.		
Thompson, Henry, (Ky.)	Invalid pension	25	2	Petition	269, 400	Invalid Pensions	....	....	.....	Discharged; laid on table.		
Thompson, Henry, (Ky.)	Invalid pension	29	1	Petition	511	Invalid Pensions.						
Thompson, Horace B	Pension	14	2	Petition	383	Pens. & Rev. Cl'ms.	....	....	.....	Leave to withdraw.		
Thompson, Hugh, administrator of.	Indemnity for French spoliations prior to 1800.	29	2	Memorial	171	Foreign Affairs.						
Thompson, Hugh	(See Thompson & Dickey.)	26	1	....	182	Foreign Affairs.						
Thompson, Ignatius, and Isaiah Dill.	Redemption of bills of credit	24	2	Petition	269	Rev. Claims.						
Thompson, Isaac	Pension and grant of land for revolutionary services.	15	1	Petition	101	Pens. & Rev. Cl'ms.	Feb. 18, 1818	Adverse	.....	Leave to withdraw.		
Thompson, Jacob	Grant of land	22	1	Memorial	388	Public Lands	Mar. 17, 1832	Adverse	.....	Laid on table.		
Thompson, Jacob	Grant of land	22	2	Petition	55	Public Lands	....	....	.....	Discharged; laid on table.		
Thompson, Jacob	Grant of land	23	1	Petition	523	Indian Affairs.						
Thompson, James, (N. Y.)	Drawback of duties on merchandise.	10	1	Petition	114	Com. and Manuf.						
Thompson, James, (N. Y.)	Drawback of duties on merchandise.	10	2	Petition	360	Com. and Manuf.	Feb. 16, 1809	Adverse	.....	Leave to withdraw.		
Thompson, James, (Ohio.)	Further time to make payments of public lands.	11	2	Petition	249	Public Lands.						
Thompson, James, (Ohio.)	Further time to make payments of public lands.	16	2	Petition	249	Public Lands.						
Thompson, James, & Isaac Richardson, (Ohio).	Grant of land	16	2	Petition	249	Public Lands.						
Thompson, Captain James, (Del.) *et al.*	Compensation for services in war of 1812.	18	2	Memorial	187	Military Affairs	....	....	.....	Disch'd; and to Claims		
Thompson, James, (Ohio).	Revolutionary pension	24	1	Petition	670	Rev. Pensions.						
Thompson, James, (Ohio).	Revolutionary pension	24	2	Petition	84	Rev. Pensions	....	....	.....	Discharged; laid on table.		

List of private claims presented to the House of Representatives of the United States from the 1st to the 31st Congress, inclusive—Continued.

Names of claimants.	Nature or object of the claim.	Congress.	Session.	How brought before the House of Reps.	Page of journal.	To what committee of the House referred.	No. or date of the report.	Nature of the report.	No. of the bill.	How disposed of by the House of Reps.	How disposed of by the Senate.	Date of the act of Congress, and remarks.
Thompson, James, (Ohio).	Revolutionary pension	25	2	Petition	182	Rev. Pensions				Discharged; laid on table.		
Thompson, James, (Ohio).	Revolutionary pension	25	3	Petition	173	Rev. Pensions	Jan. 16, 1839	Adverse; verbal.		Laid on table.		
Thompson, James	(See Isaac Lawrence, *et al.*)	14	2		101							
Thompson, James, (S. C.,) widow of.	Relief on account of services of husband to government.	27	3	Petition	336	Rev. Pensions.						
Thompson, J. H., (La.)	Indemnity for injuries to property by United States troops.	30	2	Petition	389, 419	Claims.						
Thompson, J. H., (La.)	Indemnity for injuries to property by United States troops.	31	1	Petition	193	Claims.						
Thompson, Jane	(See Colonel Archibald Laughrey, heirs of.)	29	2		192		30		611			
Thompson, Jeduthan, widow of.	Pension	27	2	Petition	105	Rev. Pensions	784	Adverse		Laid on table.		
Thompson, Jesse, (Md.)	Restoration of revolutionary pension.	18	1	Petition	108	Pens. & Rev. Cl'ms.		Adverse		Discharged; and to Rev. Pensions.		
Thompson, Jesse, (N. Y.).	Revolutionary pension	20	1	Petition	49	Rev. Pensions.						
Thompson, Jesse, (N. Y.).	Revolutionary pension	21	2	Petition	127	Military Pensions.						
Thompson, Jesse, (N. Y.).	Revolutionary pension	22	1	Petition	131	Rev. Pensions.						
Thompson, Job	Pension	22	1	Petition	204	Military Pensions.	Feb. 17, 1829	Adverse		Laid on table.		
Thompson, Joel	Payment for property pressed into service of United States.	25	2	Petition	655	Claims				Discharged.		
Thompson, Joel	Payment for property pressed into service of United States.	26	1	Petition	170	Claims.						
Thompson, John, (Pa.)	Grant of land for revolutionary services.	8	1	Petition	419	Claims	Dec. 26, 1803	Adverse		Rejected.		
Thompson, John, (Pa.)	Grant of land for revolutionary services.	11	2	Petition	173	Public Lands				Discharged		Leave to withdraw.
Thompson, John, (Va.)	Settlement of accounts for revolutionary services.	11	1	Petition	28	Claims.						
Thompson, John, (Va.)	Settlement of accounts for revolutionary services.	11	2	Petition	150	Claims	Jan. 23, 1810	Adverse		Referred to Committee Whole House.		
					276	Whole House	Mar. 9, 1810	Favorable; bill	103	Passed	Rejected.	
Thompson, John, (Va.)	Settlement of accounts for revolutionary services.	11	3	Petition	462	Claims.						
Thompson, John, (Va.)	Settlement of accounts for revolutionary services.	12	1	Petition	13	Claims	Mar. 13, 1812	By bill	87	Passed	Passed	App'd May 8, 1812
Thompson, John, (Va.)	Interest on balance of account under act of May 8, 1812.	12	1	Petition	355	Claims.						
Thompson, John, (Va.)	Interest on balance of account under act of May 8, 1812.	12	2	Petition	556	Claims	Jan. 13, 1813	By bill	228	Referred to Committee Whole House.		
Thompson, John, (Va.)	Interest on balance of account under act of May 8, 1812.	13	1	Petition	15	Claims				Discharged		Leave to withdraw.
Thompson, John, (Va.)	Interest on balance of account under act of May 8, 1812.	13	2	Petition	169	Claims	Dec. 17, 1813	Adverse		Rejected.		
Thompson, John, (Va.)	Interest on balance of account under act of May 8, 1812.	13	2	Petition	314	Pens. & Rev. Cl'ms.				Discharged		Leave to withdraw.
Thompson, John, (Va.)	Interest on balance of account under act of May 8, 1812.	14	1	Petition	532	Pens. & Rev. Cl'ms.				Discharged		Leave to withdraw.
Thompson, John, (Va.)	Interest on balance of account under act of May 8, 1812.	14	2	Petition	70	Pens. & Rev. Cl'ms.	Jan. 13, 1817	By bill	50	Indef. postponed.		
Thompson, John, (Va.)	Interest on balance of account under act of May 8, 1812.	15	1	Petition	26	Pens. & Rev. Cl'ms.	Dec. 19, 1817	By bill	14	Passed	Rejected.	

List of private claims presented to the House of Representatives of the United States from the 1st to the 31st Congress, inclusive—Continued.

Names of claimants.	Nature or object of the claim.	Congress.	Session.	How brought before the House of Reps.	Page of journal.	To what committee of the House referred.	No. or date of the report.	Nature of the report.	No. of the bill.	How disposed of by the House of Reps.	How disposed of by the Senate.	Date of the act of Congress, and remarks.
Thompson, John, (Va.)	Interest on balance of account under act of May 8, 1812.	15	1	Senate bill	216	Whole House	April 10, 1818	With't amend.	S. 17	Passed		App'd Apirl 14, 1818
Thompson, John	Compensation for services in revolutionary war.	2	1	Petition	507					Referred to Secretary War.		
Thompson, John	Compensation for services in revolutionary war.	5	2	Petition	87	Claims	April 17, 1798	Adverse		Laid on table.		
Thompson, John	Compensation for services in revolutionary war.	5	3	Petition	432	Whole House.						
Thompson, John, (Va.)	Invalid pension	13	2	Petition	314	Pens. & Rev. Cl'ms.				Discharged		Leave to withdraw.
Thompson, John, (Va.)	Invalid pension	21	1	Petition	520	Military Pensions	May 3, 1830	Adverse		Laid on table.		
Thompson, John, (Va.)	Invalid pension	22	1	Petition	36	Invalid Pensions				Discharged.		
Thompson, John, (Va.)	Invalid pension	23	1	Petition	112	Invalid Pensions	June 28, 1834	Adverse		Laid on table.		
Thompson, John, (Va.)	Invalid pension	23	2	Petition	391	Invalid Pensions.						
Thompson, John, (Va.)	Invalid pension	24	1	Petition	275	Invalid Pensions				Discharged; laid on table.		
Thompson, John, (Va.)	Invalid pension	24	2	Petition	86	Invalid Pensions	Jan. 19, 1837	Adverse		Laid on table.		
Thompson, John, (Va.)	Invalid pension	25	2	Petition	75	Invalid Pensions				Discharged; laid on table.		
Thompson, John, (Va.)	Invalid pension	26	3	Petition	89	Invalid Pensions				Discharged; laid on table.		
Thompson, John, (Va.)	Invalid pension	26	1	Petition	327	Invalid Pensions.						
Thompson, John, of Virginia, widow of.	Pension for revolutionary services of husband.	28	1	Petition	251	Rev. Pensions				Leave to withdraw.		
Thompson, John, (Va.)	Balance of account for laying brick on fortifications.	13	2	Petition	341	Claims				Discharged		Leave to withdraw.
Thompson, John, (Va.)	Indemnity for losses by breach of contract with United States.	22	1	Petition	78	Claims	Feb. 8, 1832	Favorable, and res. to refer to Com. Warrington.		Referred to Committee on Claims.		
Thompson, John, (Va.)	Indemnity for losses by breach of contract with United States.	22	2	Petition	28	Claims	Dec. 14, 1832	Favorable; bill	617	Referred to Committee Whole House.		
Thompson, John, (Va.)	Indemnity for losses by breach of contract with United States.	23	1	Petition	34	Claims	Dec. 13, 1833	By bill	12	Passed	Passed	App'd April 18, 1834
Thompson, John, (Va.)	Indemnity for losses by breach of contract with United States.	24	1	Documents	49	Claims.						
Thompson, John	(See Robt. Milnor and Jno. Thomson.)	25	2		409							
Thompson, sen., John, (Orleans Territory.)	Compensation for services as land commissioner.	12	1	Petition	248	Claims.						
Thompson, jr., John, (Orleans Territory.)	Compensation for services as clerk to land commissioners.	12	1	Petition	272	Claims	May 5, 1812	Adverse				
Thompson, jr., John, (Orleans Territory.)	Compensation for services as clerk to land commissioners.	12	2	Petition	569					Leave to withdraw.		
Thompson, jr, John, (Orleans Territory.)	Compensation for services as clerk to land commissioners.	13	2	Petition	185	Claims	March 7, 1813	Adverse		Laid on table.		
Thompson, jr., John, (Orleans Territory.)	Compensation for services as clerk to land commissioners.	13	3	Petition	523	Public Lands.						
Thompson, jr., John, widow of, (Orleans Territory.)	Compensation for services as clerk to land commissioners.	22	2	Petition	94	Claims	Jan. 23, 1833	Favorable; bill	708	Referred to Committee Whole House.		
Thompson, jr., John, widow of, (Orleans Territory.)	Compensation for services as clerk to land commissioners.	23	1	Petition	34	Claims	Jan. 7, 1834	Favorable; bill	141	Passed	Passed	App'd June 28, 1834
Thompson, John, and wife.	(See Lieut. Edward Spear, former widow of.)	14	2		46							

List of private claims presented to the House of Representatives of the United States from the 1st to the 31st Congress, inclusive—Continued.

Names of claimants.	Nature or object of the claim.	Congress.	Session.	How brought before the House of Reps.	Page of journal.	To what committee of the House referred.	No. or date of the report.	Nature of the report.	No. of the bill.	How disposed of by the House of Reps.	How disposed of by the Senate.	Date of the act of Congress, and remarks.
Thompson, John, (Maine.)	Pension	21	1	Petition	168	Military Pensions	May 3, 1830	Adverse		Laid on table.		
Thompson, John, (Ohio)	Increase of pension	21	2	Petition	159	Military Pensions.						
Thompson, John, (Ohio)	Increase of pension	22	1	Petition	188	Rev. Pensions				Discharged; laid on table.		
Thompson, John, sureties of.	Refunding money illegally collected from them.	19	1	Petition	78	Claims	9	Favorable; bill	22	Passed	Passed	App'd March 3, 1826
Thompson, John, and wife.	Grant of land patent to William H. Salmon.	19	1	Petition	206	Public Lands	Mar. 1, 1826	Adverse		Laid on table		Leave to withdraw.
Thompson, John, *et al.*, (La.)	Confirmation of title to land	19	1	Papers and docs.	413	Public Lands.						
Thompson, John, *et al.*, (La.)	Confirmation of title to land	19	2	Papers and docs.	50	Priv. Land Claims.	49	Favorable; bill	378	Referred to Committee Whole House.		
Thompson, John, *et al.*, (La.)	Confirmation of title to land	20	1	Papers and docs.	40	Public Lands.						
Thompson, John, *et al.*, (La.)	Confirmation of title to land	20	2	Petition	34	Priv. Land Claims.	Dec. 31, 1828	Adverse		Laid on table.		
Thompson, John, *et al.*, (La.)	Confirmation of title to land	23	1	Petition, &c	638	Public Lands.						
Thompson, John, *et al.*, (La.)	Confirmation of title to land	23	2	Petition, &c	48	Priv. Land Claims.						
Thompson, John, *et al.*, (La.)	Confirmation of title to land	24	1	Petition and docs.	155	Priv. Land Claims.	93	Adverse		Ordered to be printed.		
Thompson, John, (La.)	Grant of bounty land and pension.	20	1	Petition	637	Military Pensions.						
Thompson, John, (Ohio)	(See Andrew Marshall, surety of.)	20	2		106							
Thompson, John W. B	Remuneration for losses in Florida war.	24	2	Petition	266	Claims	Jan. 31, 1837	Adverse		Referred to Invalid Pensions.		
Thompson, John F	Further time to complete payment for lands.	16	2	Petition	35	Priv. Land Claims.						
Thompson, John B	(See Lewis & Clark and companions.)											
Thompson, John W.	Compensation for wagon and team lost in service of United States.	16	2	Petition	66	Claims	Jan. 24, 1821	Adverse		Laid on table.		
Thompson, John W.	Compensation for wagon and team lost in service of United States.	27	2	Petition	534	Claims.						
Thompson, John S.	(See Archibald Beard, *et al.*)	30	1		239		597		478			
Thompson, John P., (Ten.)	Grant of bounty land as assignee of certain soldiers in war of 1812.	18	1	Petition	69	Public Lands	Jan. 20, 1824	Adverse		Laid on table.		
Thompson, John, assignee of, (Tenn.)	Compensation for horse lost in service of United States.	28	1	Petition	262	Claims.						
Thompson, Joseph, heirs of.	Confirmation of title to land	26	1	Senate bill	837	Priv. Land Claims.	June 23, 1840	With't amend.	S. 284	Referred to Committee Whole House.		
Thompson, Joseph, heirs of.	Confirmation of title to land	26	2	Senate bill	176	Priv. Land Claims.			S. 77			
Thompson, Joseph, heirs of.	Confirmation of title to land	27	2	Senate bill	521	Priv. Land Claims.			S. 47			
Thompson, Joseph, heirs of.	Revolutionary pension	26	1	Petition	727	Rev. Pensions.						
Thompson, Joseph, heirs of.	Revolutionary pension	27	2	Petition	97	Rev. Pensions	784	Adverse		Laid on table.		
Thompson, Joseph, heirs of.	Revolutionary pension	27	3	Petition	73	Rev. Pensions	295	Adverse		Laid on table.		
Thompson, Joseph	Compensation for extra mail service	28	1	Petition	941	P. Of. & P. Roads.						
Thompson, Joshua	Revolutionary pension	18	2	Petition	251	Rev. Pensions	Feb. 28, 1825	Adverse		Laid on table.		

List of private claims presented to the House of Representatives of the United States from the 1st to the 31st Congress, inclusive—Continued.

Names of claimants.	Nature or object of the claim.	Congress.	Session.	How brought before the House of Reps.	Page of journal.	To what committee of the House referred.	No. or date of the report.	Nature of the report.	No. of the bill.	How disposed of by the House of Reps.	How disposed of by the Senate.	Date of the act of Congress, and remarks.
Thompson, Joshua	Revolutionary pension	19	1	Petition	88	Select				Discharged; laid on table.		
Thompson, Josiah, widow of.	Five years' revolutionary half pay.	23	2	Resolution	165	Military Affairs				Discharged; laid on table.		
Thompson, Josias, (Va.)	Amount due as superintendent of Cumberland road.	21	2	Petition	160	Claims.						
Thompson, Josias, (Va.)	Amount due as superintendent of Cumberland road.	22	1	Petition	74	Claims.						
Thompson, Josias, (Va.)	Amount due as superintendent of Cumberland road.	22	2	Petition	114	Claims.						
Thompson, Josias, (Va.)	Amount due as superintendent of Cumberland road.	23	1	Petition	55	Claims	June 27, 1834	Favorable; bill	554	Referred to Committee Whole House.		
Thompson, Josias, (Va.)	Amount due as superintendent of Cumberland road.	24	1	Petition	51	Claims	63	Favorable; bill	76	Passed	Laid on table.	
Thompson, Josias, (Va.)	Amount due as superintendent of Cumberland road.	25	2	Petition	73	Claims	663	Favorable; bill	636	Referred to Committee Whole House.		
Thompson, Josias, (Va.)	Amount due as superintendent of Cumberland road.	25	3	Bill of last sess.	380	Whole House	Jan. 25, 1839	With amend.	636	Passed	Adverse report.	
Thompson, Josias, (Va.)	Amount due as superintendent of Cumberland road.	26	1	Petition	168	Claims	23	Favorable; bill	42	Passed	Indef. postp'd.	
Thompson, Josias, (Va.)	Amount due as superintendent of Cumberland road.	27	2	Petition	155	Claims	471	Favorable; bill	321	Passed	Adverse.	
Thompson, Lydalize	(See John Thompson, jr.)	22	2		94							
Thompson, Margaretta	(See Joseph Vidal *et al.*)	12	2		663							
Thompson, Mary	(See James Thompson, of South Carolina, widow of)	27	3		336							
Thompson, Mary E	Revolutionary claim	28	1	Documents	294	Rev. Claims.						
Thompson, Mary E	Revolutionary claim	29	1	Petition	104	Rev. Claims	235	Adverse		Laid on table.		
Thompson, Mary W	(See Alex. R. Thompson, widow of.)	25	3		454							
Thompson, Manlius V	Balance due on contract for pork furnished United States army.	22	1	Letters & papers.	338	Claims	Mar. 6, 1832	Adverse		Laid on table.		
Thompson, Manlius V	(See Milus W. Dickey, executors of.)	28	1		338							
Thompson, Mathew	Invalid pension	29	1	Petition	257	Invalid Pensions	818	Favorable; bill	543	Referred to Committee Whole House.		
Thompson, Nancy	(See Smith Thompson, widow of.)	31	2		132							
Thompson, Nathan, widow of.	Pension	26	1	Documents	936	Rev. Pensions	July 10, 1840	Adverse		Laid on table.		
Thompson, Nathaniel	Revolutionary pension	9	1	Petition	241	Claims	Mar. 28, 1806			Indefinitely postponed.		Leave to withdraw.
Thompson, Nathaniel	Revolutionary pension	14	1	Petition	346	Pens. & Rev. Clm's.	April 11, 1816	Favorable; bill	171	Passed.	Passed	App'd April 30, 1816
Thompson, Nathaniel	Increase of pension	15	1	Petition	23	Pens. & Rev. Cl'ms.				Discharged.		Leave to withdraw.
Thompson, Philip R	(See Dr. Augustine Slaughter, administrator of.)	24	1		104							
Thompson & Prentice	(See John Baldwin, *et al.*)	27	2		215							
Thampson, R. Augustus	(See Nathaniel Denby, sureties of.)	30	2		350							
Thompson, Robert	Revolutionary pension	15	2	Petition	143	Pens. & Rev. Cl'ms.	Jan. 12, 1819	Adverse		Laid on table.		
Thompson, Samuel, (Canada.)	Indemnity for loss of property in war of 1812.	14	2	Petition	71	Select	33	Favorable; bill		Laid on table.		
Thompson, Samuel, (Canada.)	Indemnity for loss of property in war of 1812.	15	1	Petition	28	Select	April 6, 1818	Favorable	182	Rejected.		
Thompson, Samuel, (Canada.)	Indemnity for loss of property in war of 1812.	18	2	Petition	210	Claims.						

List of private claims presented to the House of Representatives of the United States from the 1st to the 31st Congress, inclusive—Continued.

Names of claimants.	Nature or object of the claim.	Congress.	Session.	How brought before the House of Reps.	Page of journal.	To what committee of the House referred.	No. or date of the report.	Nature of the report.	No. of the bill.	How disposed of by the House of Reps.	How disposed of by the Senate.	Date of the act of Congress, and remarks.
Thompson, Samuel, *et al.*, (Mo.)	Confirmation of title to land	15	1	Petition	226	Priv. Land Claims.						
Thompson, Samuel, *et al.*, (Mo.)	Confirmation of title to land ...	16	1	Petition	71	Priv. Land Claims.						
Thompson, Samuel, *et al.*, (Mo.)	Confirmation of title to land	17	1	Petition	55	Public Lands.						
Thompson, Samuel, *et al.*, (Mo.)	Confirmation of title to land	18	1	Peti ion	55	Public Lands....	....	....	.....	....	....	See act May 26, 1824
Thompson, Samuel, (Ohio.)	Payment for blankets furnished in war of 1812.	21	1	Petition	376	Claims.						
Thompson, Samuel, (Ohio.)	Payment for blankets furnished in war of 1812.	21	2	Petition	62	Claims.						
Thompson, Samuel, (Ohio)	Payment for blankets furnished in war of 1812.	22	1	Petition	54	Claims	Feb. 17, 1832	Favorable; bill	382	Referred to Committee Whole House.		
Thompson, Samuel, (Ohio)	Payment for blankets furnished in war of 1812.	23	1	Petition	34	Claims	Dec. 13, 1833	Favorable; bill	2	Passed	Passed	App'd April 15, 1834
Thompson, Samuel, (Me).	(See John McKown, *et al.*)	22	2	....	397							
Thompson, Samuel	Increase of pension..............	14	2	Petition	347	Pens. & Rev. Cl'ms.						
Thompson, Samuel......	Increase of pension	20	2	Petition	59	Military Pensions..	Jan. 13, 1827	Adverse	......	Laid on table.		
Thompson, Samuel, (Mass)	Pension	21	2	Petition	158	Military Pensions.						
Thompson, Samuel, (Mass)	Pension	22	1	Petition	123	Rev. Pensions.						
Thompson, Samuel, widow of.	Revolutionary pension..........	26	1	Petition	706	Rev. Pensions	551	Adverse	......	Laid on table.		
Thompson, Samuel, widow of.)	Revolutionary pension..........	26	2	Petition	35	Rev. Pensions.						
Thompson, Samuel, widow of.)	Revolutionary pension..........	27	2	Petition	59	Rev. Pensions	296	Favorable; bill	264	Passed	Indef. postp'd.	
Thompson, Sarah	(See Wm. Thompson, of Georgia, widow of.)	3	2	....	249							
Thompson, Sarah	(See Lieutenant Edward Spear, former widow of.)	14	2	....	46							
Thompson, Shadrack.....	(See Nathaniel Sample, attorney of.)	23	2	....	77							
Thompson, Shelden, *et al.*	(See Jonas Harrison, sureties of.).	18	1	....	154							
Thompson, Sill	(See Tho's Tupper, assignee, &c.)	22	2	....	142							
Thompson, Sill, & Co ...	(See Tho's Tupper, assignee, &c.)	22	2	....	142							
Thompson, Smith, widow of.	Revolutionary pension.........	31	2	Petition	132	Rev. Pensions	75	Adverse	......	Laid on table.		
Thompson, Thomas	(See Joseph Vidal, *et al.*).......	12	2	....	663							
Thompson, Thomas, (Pa.)	Invalid pension.................	27	2	Documents.....	218	Invalid Pensions.						
Thompson, Thomas, (Pa)	Invalid pension.................	28	2	Petition	199	Invalid Pensions.						
Thompson, Thomas, (Pa.)	Invalid pension.................	29	1	Petition and docs.	319	Invalid Pensions.						
Thompson, Thomas, (Pa.)	Increase of pension	30	1	Resolution	403	Invalid Pensions ..	582	Adverse	......	Laid on table.		
Thompson, Thomas, (Pa.)	Compensation for services in war of 1812.	28	1	Petition	114	Claims	563	Adverse	......	Laid on table.		
Thompson, Thomas, (Pa.)	Balance of pay due for services in war of 1812.	28	2	Petition	307	Claims	99	Adverse	......	Laid on table.		
Thompson, Wm., (Ga.,) widow of.	Pay, &c., due for revolutionary services.	3	2	Petition	249	Claims	Feb. 25, 1795	Adverse	......	Referred to Commitee Whole House.		
Thompson, Wm., (Ga.,) widow of.	Pay, &c., due for revolutionary services.	4	2	Rep. and res....	634	Claims	Jan. 2, 1797	Adverse	......	Laid on table.		
Thompson, William	Compensation for revolutionary services.	4	1	Petition	370	Claims	Jan. 20, 1796	Adverse	......	Rejected.		

List of private claims presented to the House of Representatives of the United States from the 1st to the 31st Congress, inclusive—Continued.

Names of claimants.	Nature or object of the claim.	Congress.	Session.	How brought before the House of Reps.	Page of journal.	To what committee of the House referred.	No. or date of the report.	Nature of the report.	No. of the bill.	How disposed of by the House of Reps.	How disposed of by the Senate.	Date of the act of Congress, and remarks.
Thompson, William, administrator of.	Pay due for revolutionary services.	5	3	Petition	460	Claims	Feb. 7, 1799	Adverse	......	Laid on table.		
Thompson, William T., (N. O.)	Pay for certain supplies furnished United States.	19	1	Petition	131	Claims	Mar. 24, 1826	Adverse	......	Laid on table.		
Thompson, William T., (N. O.)	Pay for certain supplies furnished United States.	19	2	Petition	44	Claims	Dec. 29, 1826	Adverse	......	Laid on table.		
Thompson, William, (Va.)	Settlement of accounts as paymaster.	19	1	Petition	312	Claims	April 14, 1826	Adverse	......	Laid on table.		
Thompson, William, (Va.)	Settlement of accounts as paymaster.	19	2	Petition	78	Claims	Jan. 5, 1827	Favorable; bill	351	Referred to Committee Whole House.		
Thompson, William, (Va.)	Settlement of accounts as paymaster.	20	1	Petition	38	Claims	Dec. 17, 1827	Favorable; bill	6	Passed	Passed	App'd Mar. 10, 1828
Thompson, William R	Compensation for extra mail service.	30	2	Petition	150	P. Of. & P. Roads.						
Thompson, William	Naval invalid pension	17	1	Petition	141	Naval Affairs	Feb. 19, 1822	Favorable; bill	92	Passed	Indef. postp'd.	
Thompson, William	Naval invalid pension	19	1	Resolution	92	Naval Affairs	84	Favorable; bill	115	Passed	Passed	App'd Mar. 20, 1826
Thompson, William	Arrears of pension	19	2	Petition	65	Naval Affairs	Dec. 27, 1826	Adverse	......	Laid on table.		
Thompson, William	Increase of pension	21	2	Pet. and docs.	325	Naval Affairs	86	Favorable; bill	639	Passed	With't amend.	
Thompson, William, widow of.	Pension for services on board United States brig Oneida.	26	2	Petition	118	Invalid Pensions	218	Adverse	......	Laid on table.		
Thompson, Wm., (Ind.)	Revolutionary pension	24	1	Petition	944	Rev. Pensions.						
Thompson, Wm., (Ind.)	Revolutionary pension	24	2	Pet. and docs.	50, 102	Rev. Pensions	Jan. 20, 1837	Adverse	......	Laid on table.		
Thompson, William H., administrator of.	Indemnity for French spoliations prior to 1800.	26	1	Memorial	182	Foreign Affairs	343	Favorable; bill	319	Referred to Committee Whole House.		
Thompson, William	Compensation for horse lost in Florida war.	26	1	House bill	645	Claims	....	....	256			
Thompson, William	Compensation for horse lost in Florida war.	28	1	Petition	278, 975	Claims	85	Adverse	......	Laid on table.		
Thompson & Wright	Land claim	18	1	Resolution	264	Select	121	Favorable	220	Passed	Passed	App'd May 26, 1824
Thomson, James, (Ohio)	Pre-emption right to land	14	1	Petition	249	Public Lands	Mar. 12, 1816	Adverse	......	Laid on table.		
Thomson, John	(See Milnor & Thomson)	25	2	....	409							
Thomson, Samuel, (N. Y.)	Balance due as superintendent of custom-house.	26	1	Petition	701	Claims.						
Thomson, Samuel, (N. Y.)	Balance due as superintendent of custom-house.	26	2	Petition	212	Claims.						
Thomson, Samuel, (N. Y.)	Balance due as superintendent of custom-house.	27	2	Petition	155	Claims	735	Adverse	......	Laid on table.		
Thomure, Joseph	Confirmation of title to land	29	1	Petition	262	Priv. Land Claims.						
Thooft, Barnard	Drawback of duties on exports	18	1	Petition	132	Ways and Means.	Jan. 16, 1824	Favorable; bill	66	Passed	Passed	App'd May 17, 1824
Thorburn, James	Indemnity for French spoliations prior to 1800.	26	1	Memorial	182	Foreign Affairs	343	Favorable; bill	319	Referred to Committee Whole House.		
Thorburn, James, trustee of,	(See Warren Ashley, executor of.)	25	3	....	119							
Thorla, Thomas	Revolutionary pension	20	2	Petition	109	Military Pensions	....	....	......	Discharged; referred to Com. Whole House.		
Thorla, Thomas	Revolutionary pension	21	1	Petition	37	Military Pensions	....	....	......	Discharged; laid on table.		
Thorla, Thomas	Revolutionary pension	22	1	Petition	105	Military Pensions	....	....	......	Discharged; laid on table.		
Thorn, Allen D., surety of.	Release from liability	18	2	Resolution	224	Ways and Means.						

List of private claims presented to the House of Representatives of the United States from the 1st to the 31st Congress, inclusive—Continued.

Names of claimants.	Nature or object of the claim.	Congress.	Session.	How brought before the House of Reps.	Page of journal.	To what committee of the House referred.	No. or date of the report.	Nature of the report.	No. of the bill.	How disposed of by the House of Reps.	How disposed of by the Senate.	Date of the act of Congress, and remarks.
Thorn, Allen D., surety of.	Release from liability	19	1	Memorial & res.	113, 176	Ways and Means				Discharged; laid on table.		
Thorn, Allen D., surety of.	Release from liability	19	2	Memorial, &c.	50	Judiciary				Discharged; laid on table.		
Thorn, Charlotte M. R.	(See Robert L. Thorn, widow of.)	20	2		88							
Thorne, James	(See Elbert Anderson, administrator of.)	21	2		45							
Thorn, Lieut. Jonathan	(See Stephen Decatur, widow of *et al.*)	19	2		98		74		70			
Thorn, Joseph, (Ga.)	Remission of duties on merchandise.	14	2	Petition	28	Ways and Means.						
Thorn, Joseph, (Ga.)	Remission of duties on merchandise.	15	1	Petition	45	Ways and Means	Jan. 14, 1818	Favorable; bill	38	Passed	Rejected.	
Thorn, Joseph, (Ga.)	Remission of duties on merchandise.	16	1	Petition	344	Commerce.						
Thorn, Joseph, (Ga.)	Remission of duties on merchandise.	17	1	Petition	92	Commerce				Discharged; referred to Ways and Means.		
Thorn, Joseph, (Ga.)	Remission of duties on merchandise.	22	1	Petition	80	Commerce	Jan. 10, 1832	Adverse		Laid on table.		
Thorn, Robert L., widow of.	Naval pension	20	2	Petition	88	Naval Affairs	103	Adverse		Laid on table.		
Thorne, William, (N. Y.)	Indemnity for damages to property in revolutionary war.	4	1	Rep. of Secretary War.	388	Claims.						
Thorne, William, (N. Y.)	Indemnity for damages to property in revolutionary war.	5	2	Petition	218	Claims	Mar. 13, 1798	Adverse		Laid on table.		
Thorne, William, (N. Y.)	(See Benjamin Pringle, agent of.)	5	2		218							
Thorn, William, (Canada.)	Grant of land for services as pilot in 1812.	14	2	Petition	81	Public Lands				Discharged; referred to Com. on Claims.		See act of April 20, 1818, chapter 124.
Thorn, William S., widow of.	Commutation of half-pay	26	1	Petition	281	Rev. Claims.						
Thorn, William S., widow of.	Commutation of half-pay	26	2	Petition	77	Rev. Claims.						
Thorn, William S., widow of.	Commutation of half-pay	27	2	Petition	154	Rev. Claims	543	Adverse		Laid on table.		
Thornburg, Geo., (Ohio.)	Compensation for a horse lost in public service.	24	1	Petition	943	Claims	June 18, 1836	Adverse		Laid on table.		
Thornburg, Geo., (Ohio.)	Compensation for a horse lost in public service.	24	2	Petition	309	Claims	Feb. 2, 1837			Referred to 3d Auditor.		
Thorndike, David		25	2		962					Leave to withdraw.		
Thorndike, Elizabeth	(See Henry Thorndike, administratrix of, *et al.*)	12	1		263							
Thorndike, Henry, administratrix of, *et al.*	Indemnity for vessel and cargo seized by Spanish vessel of war.	12	1	Petition and docs.	263, 284					Referred to Secretary State.		
Thorndike, Hezekiah.	Invalid pension	13	1	House bill	56	Whole House	July 20, 1813	With't amend.	31	Passed	Passed	App'd Aug. 2, 1813
Thorndike, Israel, (Mass.)	Drawback of duties on certain goods	10	2	Memorial	521	Com. and Manuf.	Feb. 18, 1809	Adverse		Laid on table.		
Thorndike, Israel, (Mass.)	Drawback of duties on certain goods	13	2	Senate bill	403	Com. and Manuf.	April 13, 1814	With't amend.	S. 53	Indef. postp'd.		
Thorndike, Israel, (Mass.)	Indemnity for loss of vessel and cargo captured by a Russian vessel of war.	19	1	Resolution	113	Foreign Affairs	25	Favorable		Discharged.		
Thorndike, Israel, executors of.	Indemnity for French spoliations prior to 1800.	26	1	Memorial	182	Foreign Affairs	343	Favorable; bill	319	Referred to Committee Whole House.		
Thorndike, Israel, executors of.	Payment of French indemnities	29	2	Memorial	129	Foreign Affairs.						

List of private claims presented to the House of Representatives of the United States from the 1st to the 31st Congress, inclusive—Continued.

Names of claimants.	Nature or object of the claim.	Congress.	Session.	How brought before the House of Reps.	Page of journal.	To what committee of the House referred.	No. or date of the report.	Nature of the report.	No. of the bill.	How disposed of by the House of Reps.	How disposed of by the Senate.	Date of the act of Congress, and remarks.
Thornley, sen., Caleb, *et al.*	Pre-emption right to land	4	1	Petition	388	Select						See act May 18, 1896
Thornley, jr., Caleb	(See Caleb Thornley, sen., *et al.*)	4	1		388							
Thornley, John	(See Calob Thornley, sen., *et al.*)	4	1		388							
Thornley, Samuel	(See Caleb Thornley, sen., *et al.*)	4	1		388							
Thornley, William	(See Caleb Thornley, sen., *et al.*)	4	1		388							
Thornton, Ann	(See John Thornton, widow of)	25	2		198							
Thornton, Arthur W.	Compensation for extra services in United States army.	18	1	Petition	77	Claims.						
Thornton, Arthur W.	Compensation for extra services in United States army.	18	2	Petition	37	Claims	Jan. 6, 1825	Adverse		Laid on table.		
Thornton, Arthur W.	Compensation for extra services in United States army.	19	1	Petition	366	Claims	April 7, 1826	Adverse		Laid on table.		
Thornton, Daniel	(See Canadian refugees)	4	1		614							
Thornton, D. M. F.	Indemnity for stores, &c., in United States ship Erie.	23	1	Petition	160	Naval Affairs				Discharged; laid on table.		
Thornton, D. M. F.	Allowance in settlement of accounts.	28	1	Senate resolution.	942	Naval Affairs			J. R. 7			
Thornton, D. M. F.	Allowance in settlement of accounts.	28	2	Senate resolution.	131	Naval Affairs	Jan. 28, 1845	With't amend.	J. R. 5	Passed	Passed	App'd Feb. 13, 1845
Thornton, Francis A.	(See Presley Thurston, heirs of)	22	1		672							
Thornton, Jane	(See Col. John Thornton, of Virginia, widow of.)	21	1		320							
Thornton, Col. John, of Va., widow of.	Grant of bounty land for revolutionary services.	21	1	Petition	320	Rev. Claims.						
Thornton, Col. John, of Va., widow of.	Grant of bounty land for revolutionary services.	21	2	Petition	44	Rev. Claims	Feb. 2, 1831	Favorable; bill	593	Referred to Committee Whole House.		
Thornton, Col. John, of Va., widow of.	Grant of bounty land for revolutionary services.	22	1	Petition	34	Rev. Claims	Jan. 6, 1832	Favorable; bill	218	Referred to Committee Whole House.		
Thornton, Col. John, of Va., widow of.	Grant of bounty land for revolutionary services.	22	2	Bill of last sess.	67	Whole House	Dec. 15, 1832	With't amend.	218	Passed	Passed	App'd Feb. 9, 1833
Thornton, John, widow of.	Revolutionary pension	25	2	Petition	198	Rev. Pensions				Discharged; laid on table.		
Thornton, Michael	Relief in relation to certain bounty land.	24	1	Petition	112	Priv. Land Claims.	141	Favorable; bill	148	Passed	Indef. postp'd.	
Thornton, Michael	Relief in relation to certain bounty land.	24	2	Senate bill	579				S. 157	Referred to Committee Whole House.		
Thornton, Presley, (Va.)	Pension	5	2	House bill	127	Whole House	Jan. 11, 1798	Bill amended.	38	Passed	Passed	App'd Feb. 2, 1798
Thornton, Presley, (Va.)	Compensation for services rendered, &c., in revolutionary war.	4	2	Petition	660	Claims	Feb. 10, 1797	Adverse		Rejected.		
Thornton, Presley, (Va.)	Liquidation and settlement of accounts.	10	1	Petition	52	Select.						
Thornton, Presley, (Va.)	Liquidation and settlement of accounts.	11	2	Petition	237	Claims.						
Thornton, Presley, (Va.)	Liquidation and settlement of accounts.	11	3	Petition	439	Claims				Leave to withdraw.		
Thornton, Presley, heirs of, (Va.)	Commutation of half-pay	22	1	Petition	672	Rev. Claims	May 14, 1832	Favorable; bill	571	Referred to Committee Whole House.		
Thornton, Presley, heirs of, (Va.)	Commutation of half-pay	23	1	Petition	43	Rev. Claims	Dec. 17, 1833	Favorable; bill	38	Passed	Laid on table.	
Thornton, Presley, heirs of, (Va.)	Commutation of half-pay	23	2	Petition	37	Rev. Claims.						
Thornton, Presley, heirs of, (Va.)	Commutation of half-pay	24	1	Petition	62	Rev. Claims	Jan. 29, 1836	Favorable; bill	257	Referred to Committee Whole House.		
Thornton, Presley, heirs of, (Va.)	Commutation of half-pay	24	2	Bill of last sess.	63	Whole House			257			

List of private claims presented to the House of Representatives of the United States from the 1st to the 31st Congress, inclusive—Continued.

Names of claimants.	Nature or object of the claim.	Congress.	Session.	How brought before the House of Reps.	Page of journal.	To what committee of the House referred.	No. or date of the report.	Nature of the report.	No. of the bill.	How disposed of by the House of Reps.	How disposed of by the Senate.	Date of the act of Congress, and remarks.
Thornton, Presley, heirs of, (Va.)	Commutation of half-pay	25	2	Petition	70	Rev. Claims	242	Favorable; bill	283	Passed.		
Thornton, Presley, heirs of, (Va.)	Commutation of half-pay	25	3	Petition	84	Rev. Claims	35	Favorable; bill	935	Referred to Committee Whole House.		
Thornton, Presley, heirs of, (Va.)	Commutation of half-pay	26	1	Petition	164	Rev. Claims.						
Thornton, Presley, heirs of, (Va.)	Commutation of half-pay	27	2	Petition	61	Rev. Claims	979	Adverse		Laid on table.		
Thornton, Presley, heirs of, (Va.)	Commutation of half-pay	28	1	Petition	117	Rev. Claims	356	Favorable; bill	269	Postponed.		
Thornton, Presley, heirs of, (Va.)	Commutation of half-pay	29	1	Petition	91	Rev. Claims	12	Favorable; bill	25	Referred to Committee Whole House.		
Thornton, Presley, heirs of, (Va.)	Commutation of half-pay	30	1	Petition	109	Rev. Claims	672	Favorable; bill	536	Referred to Committee Whole House.		
Thornton, Presley, heirs of, (Va.)	Commutation of half-pay	30	2	Bill of last sess.	319	Whole House	Jan. 26, 1849	With't amend.	536	Passed.		
Thornton, Presley, heirs of, (Va.)	Commutation of half-pay	31	1	Petition	270	Rev. Claims.						
Thornton, Presley, (Tenn.)	Revolutionary pension	24	1	Petition	670	Rev. Claims				Discharged; laid on table.		
Thornton, Reuben, *et al.*	(See John Winston, heirs of.)	24	2		270							
Thornton, Robert, (Pa.)	(See Stephen Decatur, widow of *et al.*)											
Thornton, Robert, (Pa.)	Compensation for services at Tripoli	20	1	Petition	309	Naval Affairs	Mar. 18, 1828	Adverse.				
Thornton, Wm., (D. C.)	Deficiency of compensation and increase of salary, &c.	12	1	Petition	295	Ways and Means.						
Thornton, Wm., (D. C.)	Increase of compensation	13	1	Petition	61	Ways and Means.						
Thornton, Wm., (D. C.)	Increase of compensation	13	2	Petition	384	Ways and Means.						
Thornton, Wm., (D. C.)	Increase of compensation	13	3	Petition	740	Claims				Discharged; referred to Sec. of State.		
Thornton, Wm., (D. C.)	Increase of compensation	14	1	Petition	84	Ways and Means.						
Thornton, Wm., (D. C.)	Increase of compensation	14	2	Petition	64	Ways and Means	Jan. 25, 1817	Favorable		Refer'd to Select Committee.		
Thornton, Wm., (D. C.)	Increase of compensation	15	1	Petition	411	Ways and Means.						
Thornton, Wm., (D. C.)	Increase of compensation	18	1	Petition	160	Judiciary				Discharged; referred to Ways and Means.		
Thornton, Wm., (D. C.)	Increase of compensation	18	2	Letter	273	Claims.						
Thornton, Wm., (D. C.)	Increase of compensation	19	1	Petition	492	Claims.						
Thornton, Wm., (D. C.)	(See Alexander S. Smoot & Wm. Thornton.)	13	3		561							
Thorowgood, Lemuel, widow of.	(See William Thorowgood, guardian of.)	15	2		61							
Thorowgood, Lemuel, widow of.	Revolutionary pension	25	2	Petition	1209	Rev. Pensions.						
Thorowgood, Lemuel, widow of.	Revolutionary pension	25	3	Petition & docs.	86, 283	Rev. Claims.						
Thorowgood, Lemuel, widow of.	Revolutionary pension	26	1	Petition	167	Rev. Claims				Discharged; referred to Rev. Pensions.		
Thorowgood, Lemuel, widow of.	Revolutionary pension	26	2	Petition	212	Rev. Claims.						
Thorowgood, Lemuel, widow of.	Revolutionary pension	27	2	Petition	309	Rev. Claims				Discharged; laid on table.		

List of private claims presented to the House of Representatives of the United States from the 1st to the 31st Congress, inclusive—Continued.

Names of claimants.	Nature or object of the claim.	Congress.	Session.	How brought before the House of Reps.	Page of journal.	To what committee of the House referred.	No. or date of the report.	Nature of the report.	No. of the bill.	How disposed of by the House of Reps.	How disposed of by the Senate.	Date of the act of Congress, and remarks.
Thorowgood & Smith....	Indemnity for French spoliations prior to 1800.	26	1	Memorial......	182	Foreign Affairs....	343	Favorable; bill	319	Referred to Committee Whole House.		
Thorowgood, Wm., guardian of.	Payment for two loan office certificates.	15	2	Petition	61	Pens. & Rev. Cl'ms.	Dec. 16, 1818	Adverse	......	Laid on table.		
Thorp, Charles, widow of.	Revolutionary pension..........	30	1	Petition	482	Rev. Pensions	374	Adverse	......	Laid on table.		
Thorp, Charles, widow of.	Revolutionary pension..........	30	2	Petition	240	Rev. Pensions	....	....	......	Leave to withdraw.		
Thorp, Elizabeth........	(See Charles Thorp, widow of)..	30	1	....	482							
Thorp, Eliphalet, (Mass.).	Allowance of rations as captain in revolutionary war.	3	1	Petition and rep't Sec. of War.	24, 93	Select.						
Thorpe, Ezra..........	Compensation for revolutionary services.	15	1	Petition	184	Select..........	....	....	......	Discharged.	....	Leave to withdraw.
Thorpe, Issachar, *et al* ...	Payment of an order for clothing furnished United States.	14	2	Petition	191	Claims.						
Thorpe, Issachar, *et al* ...	Payment of an order for clothing furnished United States.	15	1	Petition	85	Claims.						
Thorpe, Issachar, *et al* ...	Payment of an order for clothing furnished United States.	16	1	Petition	328	Claims.						
Thorpe, Issachar, *et al* ...	Payment of an order for clothing furnished United States.	16	2	Petition	71	Claims.						
Thorpe, James..........	(See Issachar Thope, *et al.*).....	14	2	....	191							
Thorpe, John, (Va.).....	Compensation for revolutionary services.	12	1	Petition	236	Claims.						
Thorpe, John B., (N. Y.).	Amount due on account of capture of vessel and cargo in 1812.	20	1	Petition	795	Commerce.						
Thorp, John, (Maine)....	Fishing bounty on schooner Pacific.	25	2	Petition	1026	Commerce	....	....	......	Discharged; laid on table.		
Thorp, John, (Maine)....	Fishing bounty on schooner Pacific.	26	1	Petition and res.	561, 710	Commerce.						
Thorp, John, (Maine)....	Fishing bounty on schooner Pac fic.	27	2	Petition	268	Commerce.						
Thorp, John, (Maine)....	Fishing bounty on schooner Pacific.	29	2	Petition	182	Commerce.						
Thorpe, Thomas	Increase of compensation as superintendent of public buildings.	18	2	Petition	158	Ways and Means.						
Thorp, Thomas E.......	Compensation for horse lost in war with Mexico.	30	1	Petition	305	Claims..........	238	By bill	238	Referred to Committee Whole House.		
Thouron, Nicholas E	Patent for eighty acres of land....	29	2	Memorial......	323	Priv. Land Claims.	75	Favorable; bill	688	Referred to Committee Whole House.		
Thrasher, Josiah	Revolutionary pension..........	24	1	Petition	433	Rev. Pensions	....	....	......	Discharged; laid on table.		
Thrasher, Josiah	Revolutionary pension..........	25	2	Petition	181	Rev. Pensions	....	....	......	Discharged; laid on table.		
Three Brothers, schooner .	(See George Dyer, jr., *et al.*)....	27	3	....	88	....	....	....	391			
Throckmorton, Capt. J...	Balance on contract for transporting United States troops.	27	2	Senate bill	411	Claims..........	598	Adverse	S. 97	Rejected.		
Throckmorton, Capt. J...	Balance on contract for transporting United States troops.	28	2	Senate bill	415	....	....	....	S. 97	Referred to Committee Whole House.		
Throckmorton, Capt. J...	Balance on contract for transporting United States troops.	29	1	Senate bill	972	Claims..........	798	With't amend.	S. 55	Referred to Committee Whole House.		
Throckmorton, Capt. J...	Balance on contract for transporting United States troops.	30	1	Petition	154	Claims..........	38	Favorable; bill	35	Passed	Passed	App'd Aug. 5, 1848
Throop, John...........	(See John Thorp, of Maine).....	25	2	....	1026							
Throop, Josiah	(See Canadian refugees)	4	2	....	614							

List of private claims presented to the House of Representatives of the United States from the 1st to the 31st Congress, inclusive—Continued.

Names of claimants.	Nature or object of the claim.	Congress.	Session.	How brought before the House of Reps.	Page of journal.	To what committee of the House referred.	No. or date of the report.	Nature of the report.	No. of the bill.	How disposed of by the House of Reps.	How disposed of by the Senate.	Date of the act of Congress, and remarks.
Throop, Josiah, (N. Y.)	Grant of land as a Canadian refugee.	10	1	Memorial	59	Select	Dec. 22, 1807	Favorable; bill	21	Referred to Committee Whole House.		
Throop, Josiah, (N. Y.)	Grant of land as a Canadian refugee.	11	2	Memorial	124	Public Lands				Discharged		Leave to withdraw.
Throop, Josiah, heir of, (N. Y.)	Grant of land as a Canadian refugee.	20	2	Petition	40	Rev. Claims	Jan. 12, 1829	Adverse		Laid on table.		
Throop, Josiah, heir of, (N. Y.)	Grant of land as a Canadian refugee.	21	1	Petition	378	Public Lands.						
Throop, William	(See Josiah Throop, heir of)	20	2		40							
Throop, William, (N. Y.)	Compensation for revolutionary services.	19	2	Petition	104	Rev. Claims	Jan. 24, 1827	Adverse		Laid on table		Leave to withdraw.
Throop, William, (N. Y.)	Compensation for revolutionary services.	20	1	Petition	278	Rev. Claims						Leave to withdraw.
Thruston, Algernon S	Further credit in settlement of his accounts.	22	2	Senate bill	441	Ways and Means	Mar. 1, 1823	With't amend.	S. 95	Passed		App'd March 2, 1833
Thruston, Ann	(See Charles M. Thruston, widow of.)	14	2		129							
Thruston, Buckner	(See William Cranch, *et al.*)	11	3		496							
Thruston, Charles M	Revolutionary pension	9	2	House bill	608	Whole House	Mar. 2, 1807	Bill amended	216	Passed	Passed	App'd March 3, 1807
Thurston, Charles M	Arrears of pension	10	1	Petition	90	Claims				Disch'd, and to Select.		
Thruston, Charles M., widow of.	Continuation of pension	14	2	Petition	129	Pens. & Rev. Cl'ms.				Discharged; laid on table.		
Thruston, Charles M., heirs and representatives of.	Commutation of half-pay	22	2	Petition	137	Rev. Claims.						
Thruston, Charles M., heirs and representatives of.	Commutation of half-pay	23	1	Petition	157	Rev. Claims.						
Thruston, Charles M., heirs and representatives of.	Commutation of half-pay	23	2	Petition	147	Rev. Claims.						
Thruston, Charles M., heirs and representatives of.	Commutation of half-pay	24	1	Petition	138	Rev. Claims.						
Thruston, Charles M., heirs and representatives of.	Commutation of half-pay	24	2	Petition	126	Rev. Claims.						
Thruston, Charles M., heirs and representatives of.	Commutation of half-pay	25	2	Petition	70	Rev. Claims				Discharged; laid on table.		
Thruston, Charles M., heirs and representatives of.	Commutation of half-pay	25	3	Petition	85	Rev. Claims				Discharged.		
Thruston, Jason, (Ind.)	Bounty land for revolutionary services.	23	2	Petition	197	Rev. Claims.						
Thuing, Edward, *et al.*	Additional compensation for services as officer in Mexico.	31	1	Petition	408	Military Affairs.						
Thurber, Amos	Revolutionary pension	27	3	Petition	260	Rev. Pensions				Discharged.		Leave to withdraw.
Thurber, Ezra	Indemnity for a house burned occupied by U. S. troops.	11	2	Petition	132	Claims	Dec. 26, 1809	Adverse		Referred to Committee Whole House.		
Thurber, Ezra	(See King & Thurber.)	16	2		285							
Thurber, Ezra	Release from suit on account of property bought of United States agent.	25	2	Petition	112	Judiciary				Discharged; laid on table.		
Thurber, Ezra	Release from suit on account of property bought of United States agent.	26	1	Petition	704	Judiciary.						
Thurber, Ezra	Release from suit on account of property bought of United States agent.	26	2	Petition	106	Priv. Land Claims.						

List of private claims presented to the House of Representatives of the United States from the 1st to the 31st Congress, inclusive—Continued.

Names of claimants.	Nature or object of the claim.	Congress.	Session.	How brought before the House of Reps.	Page of journal.	To what committee of the House referred.	No. or date of the report.	Nature of the report.	No. of the bill.	How disposed of by the House of Reps.	How disposed of by the Senate.	Date of the act of Congress, and remarks.
Thurber, Ezra	Release from suit on account of property bought of United States agent.	27	2	Petition	484	Judiciary.						
Thurgar, George C. C.	(See Smith, Thurgar, & Co.)	29	1		151							
Thurman, Charles	Revolutionary pension	23	1	Petition	577	Rev. Pensions.						
Thurman, John R.	Pension	23	1	Petition	493	Rev. Pensions.						
Thurman, John C.	Correction of error in land entry	23	2	Petition	175	Public Lands				Discharged; laid on table.		
Thurston, Daniel	Revolutionary pension	24	1	Petition	106	Rev. Pensions				Discharged; laid on table.		
Thurston, John, (S. C.)	Pay and rations as chaplain in U. States service.	13	1	Petition	18	Claims.						
Thurston, John, (S. C.)	Pay and rations as chaplain in U. States service	13	2	Petition	189	Claims	Feb. 7, 1814	Adverse		Leave to withdraw.		
Thurston, John, *et al.*	Commutation of revolutionary half-pay.	1	2	Petition	168					Referred to Secretary War.		
Thurston, John, executors of.	Indemnity for French spoliations prior to 1800.	26	1	Memorial	182	Foreign Affairs	343	Favorable	319	Referred to Committee Whole House.		
Thurston, John, heir of	Indemnity for French spoliations prior to 1800.	29	2	Memorial	87	Foreign Affairs.						
Thurston, Richard, *et al.*	Reimbursement of duties paid on imports	18	2	Petition	69	Ways and Means.						
Thweatt, George	Compensation for horse lost in service of United States.	20	1	Petition	440	Claims.						
Thweatt, George	Compensation for horse lost in service of United States.	20	2	Petition	118	Claims.						
Thweatt, George	Compensation for horse last in service of United States.	21	1	Petition	117, 294	Claims.						
Thweatt, Thomas, heirs of.	Commutation of half pay	23	1	Petition	157	Rev. Claims.						
Thweatt, Thomas, heirs of.	Commutation of half-pay	23	2	Petition	120	Rev. Claims.						
Thweatt, Thomas, heirs of.	Commutation of half-pay	24	1	Petition	63	Rev. Claims.						
Thweatt, Thomas, heirs of.	Commutation of half-pay	26	1	Petition	360	Rev. Claims.						
Thweatt, William, executors of.	Commutation of half-pay	23	1	Petition	40	Rev. Claims.						
Thweatt, William, executors of.	Commutation of half-pay	23	2	Petition	101	Rev. Claims.						
Tibbetts, Abner	Revolutionary pension	28	2	Petition	251	Rev. Pensions.						
Tibbetts, John	Restoration of pension	17	1	Petition	92	Rev. Pensions				Discharged; laid on table.		
Tibbetts, Simeon	Revolutionary pension	21	2	Petition	103	Military Pensions.						
Tibbetts, Simeon	Revolutionary pension	22	1	Petition	68	Rev. Pensions	Dec. 29, 1831	Adverse		Laid on table.		
Tibbetts, Solomon	Pension for services as a soldier in war of 1812.	24	1	Petition	188	Invalid Pensions	Feb. 16, 1836	Adverse		Laid on table.		
Tibbs, Joseph	Change of land entry	15	1	Senate bill	245	Public Lands	Feb. 18, 1818	Report and bill	23	Passed	Passed	App'd March 9, 1818
Tice, John	(See Wm. Pennington, assignee of.)	23	2		91							
Tick-o-nees-ka, (Cherokee Indian.)	Compensation for loss of pre-emption right to land.	29	1	Petition	1038	Indian Affairs.						
Tiernan, Luke, executor of	Indemnity for French spoliations prior to 1800.	29	2	Petition	489	Foreign Affairs.						
Tiernan, Luke	(See Wm. Duncan, trustee of.)	26	1		182							
Tiernan, Luke	(See Charles Ghequire, trustee o	26	1		182							

List of private claims presented to the House of Representatives of the United States from the 1st to the 31st Congress, inclusive—**Continued.**

Names of claimants.	Nature or object of the claim.	Congress.	Session.	How brought before the House of Reps.	Page of journal.	To what committee of the House referred.	No. or date of the report.	Nature of the report.	No. of the bill.	How disposed of by the House of Reps.	How disposed of by the Senate.	Date of the act of Congress, and remarks.
Tiers, Cornelius	Compensation for losses on naval contract.	23	2	Petition	344	Claims.						
Tiers, Cornelius	Compensation for losses on naval contract.	24	1	Petition	93	Claims	690	Rep. and res. to refer to Sec. Navy for report.	......	Adopted.		
Tiers, Cornelius	Compensation for losses on naval contract.	25	2	Rep. of Secretary Treasury.	101	Claims	508	Report and bill	506	Referred to Committee Whole House.		
Tiers, Cornelius	Compensation for losses on naval contract.	25	3	Bill of last sess.	379	Whole House	Jan. 25, 1839	With't amend.	506	Passed	Passed, with amendment.	Amend't not concurred in by House.
Tiers, Cornelius	Compensation for losses on naval contract.	26	1	Petition	168	Cliams	21	Report and bill	40	Passed	Passed, with amendment.	App'd July 20, 1840
Tiers, Cornelius	Reconsideration of his claim on naval contract.	27	2	Petition	951	Claims.						
Tiers, Cornelius	Reconsideration of his claim on naval contract.	27	3	Petition	43	Claims.						
Tiers, Cornelius	Reconsideration of his claim on naval contract.	28	1	Petition	567	Claims.						
Tiers, Cornelius	Reconsideration of his claim on naval contract.	29	1	Petition	90	Claims.						
Tiffany, George	Release from payment of $382 as collector of internal tax for New York.	15	2	Petition	196	Ways and Means	Feb. 10, 1819	Adverse	......	Laid on table.		
Tiffany, Hosea	Revolutionary pension	21	2	Petition	61	Military Pensions.						
Tiffany, Hosea	Revolutionary pension	22	1	Petition	120	Rev. Pensions	369	Report and bill	464	Referred to Committee Whole House.		
Tiffany, Joel	Revolutionary pension	22	1	Petition	381	Rev. Pensions	....	....	......	Discharged; laid on table.		
Tiffany, Joel	Revolutionary pension	25	2	Petition	984	Rev. Pensions	....	....	......	Discharged; laid on table.		
Tiffany, Joel	Revolutionary pension	26	1	Petition	727	Rev. Pensions.						
Tiffany, Joel	Revolutionary pension	27	2	Petition	97	Rev. Pensions	101	Report and bill	147	Passed	Indef. postp'd.	
Tiffany, Joel	Revolutionary pension	27	3	Petition	73	Rev. Pensions	....	....	......	Discharged; laid on table.		
Tiffany, Philemon	Revolutionary pension	20	1	Resolution	266	Military Pensions	April 29, 1828	By bill	283	Passed.		
Tiffany, Philemon	Revolutionary pension	20	2	House bill	55	Whole House	Jan. 15, 1829	With amend.	311	Passed	Laid on table.	
Tiffany, Philemon	Revolutionary pension	21	1	Petition	49	Military Pensions	Jan. 15, 1830	By bill	72	Passed	Passed	App'd May 20, 1830
Tiffany, Sylvester	Invalid pension	24	1	Resolution	487	Invalid Pensions	....	....	......	Discharged; laid on table.		
Tiffany, Sylvester	Invalid pension	24	2	Petition	120	Invalid Pensions	88	By bill	831	Referred to Committee Whole House.		
Tiffany, Sylvester	Invalid pension	25	2	Resolution	39	Invalid Pensions	321	By bill	363	Passed	Adverse report.	
Tiffany, Sylvester	Invalid pension	25	3	Petition	188	Invalid Pensions	258	By bill	1129	Referred to Committee Whole House.		
Tiffany, Sylvester	Invalid pension	26	1	Petition	160	Invalid Pensions	202	By bill	214	Passed	Passed	App'd July 20, 1840
Tiffany, Thomas	Revolutionary pension	21	2	Petition	61	Military Pensions.						
Tiffany, Thomas	Revolutionary pension	22	1	Petition	120	Rev. Pensions	369	By bill	464	Referred to Committee Whole House.		
Tiffany, Timothy	Revolutionary pension	22	1	Resolution	499	Rev. Pensions.						
Tifft, Almy	(See Jonathan Maxson, heir of.)	30	1	....	459							
Tifft, Amasa A	Invalid pension	22	2	Petition	345	Invalid Pensions.						
Tifft, Amasa A	Invalid pension	23	1	Petition	44	Invalid Pensions	274	By bill	311	Referred to Committee Whole House.		

List of private claims presented to the House of Representatives of the United States from the 1st to the 31st Congress, inclusive—Continued.

Names of claimants.	Nature or object of the claim.	Congress.	Session.	How brought before the House of Reps.	Page of journal.	To what committee of the House referred.	No. or date of the report.	Nature of the report.	No. of the bill.	How disposed of by the House of Reps.	How disposed of by the Senate.	Date of the act of Congress, and remarks.
Tifft, Amasa A	Invalid pension	23	2	Bill of last sess.	336	Whole House	Feb. 6, 1835	With't amend.	311	Passed	Passed	App'd March 3, 1835
Tifft, Amos	(See Silas Beebe, and others)	20	2		48							
Tilden, Charles	Invalid pension	3	2	Rep. of Secretary War.	350	Claims	Mar. 3, 1795	Discharged and postponed.		Laid on table.		
Tilden, Charles	Invalid pension	4	1	Rep. of Secretary War.	445	Claims.						
Tilden, Horatio	Payment for services as an officer of militia, war of 1812.	23	1	Petition	384	Claims	358	Adverse		Laid on table.		
Tilden, John, widow of	Repeal of limit for presenting claims in act for relief of widows, &c., of persons lost in sloop Wasp.	25	2	Petition	594, 723	Naval Affairs	994	By bill	856	Referred to Committee Whole House.		
Tilden, John, widow of	Repeal of limit for presenting claims in act for relief of widows, &c., of persons lost in sloop Wasp.	25	3	Bill of last sess.	432	Whole House	Feb. 1, 1839	With't amend.	856	Passed	Passed	App'd March 3, 1839
Tilden, John, widow of	Repeal of limit for presenting claims in act for relief of widows, &c., of persons lost in sloop Wasp.	26	1	Petition	626	Naval Affairs.						
Tilford, James	Equitable settlement of claims arising out of war of 1812.	22	1	Petition	63	Claims	308	By bill	388	Referred to Committee Whole House.		
Tilford, James	Equitable settlement of claims arising out of war of 1812.	23	1	Petition	138	Claims	125	By bill	133	Passed	Reported with amendment.	
Tilford, James	Equitable settlement of claims arising out of war of 1812.	24	1	Petition	50	Claims	1	By bill	1	Passed	Passed	App'd Feb. 17, 1836
Tilford, William H	Payment for horse lost in United States service.	25	2	Documents	575	Claims				Discharged.		
Tilghman, Edward, jr	(See Joseph H. Wilson and others)	13	2		172							
Tilghman, Lloyd	Indemnity for damage to his property in war with Mexico.	30	2	Petition	441	Claims.						
Tilghman, Lloyd	Indemnity for damage to his property in war with Mexico.	31	1	Petition	582	Claims.						
Tilghman, William, and others.	Compensation as United States judges under act of 13th February, 1801, notwithstanding the repeal of said act.	7	2	Petition	307	Whole House	Jan. 27, 1803	Res. adverse		Resolution adopted		Leave to withdraw.
Tilghman, William	(See Tench Francis, executor of.)	16	1		197							
Tillard, Wm. S., heirs of.	Value of tobacco destroyed by British at Tracy's Landing, Maryland, in war of 1812.	24	1	Petition	584	Claims.						
Tillard, Wm. S., representatives of.	Value of tobacco destroyed by British at Tracy's Landing, Maryland, in war of 1812.	24	2	Petition	81	Claims	253	Adverse		Laid on table.		
Tillard, Wm. S., representatives of.	Value of tobacco destroyed by British at Tracy's Landing, Maryland, in war of 1812.	27	3	Petition	85	Claims	158	Report and bill.	772	Referred to Committee Whole House.		
Tillard, Wm. S., representatives of.	Value of tobacco destroyed by British at Tracy's Landing, Maryland, in war of 1812.	28	1	Petition	110	Claims	84	Report and bill	101	Referred to Committee Whole House.		
Tillard, Wm. S., representatives of.	Value of tobacco destroyed by British at Tracy's Landing, Maryland, in war of 1812.	29	1	Petition	172	Claims	132	Report and bill	137	Rejected.		
Tillard, Wm. S., representatives of.	Value of tobacco destroyed by British at Tracy's Landing, Maryland, in war of 1812.	30	1	Petition	153	Claims	257	Report and bill	250	Referred to Committee Whole House.		

List of private claims presented to the House of Representatives of the United States from the 1st to the 31st Congress, inclusive—**Continued.**

Names of claimants.	Nature or object of the claim.	Congress.	Session.	How brought before the House of Reps.	Page of journal.	To what committee of the House referred.	No. or date of the report.	Nature of the report.	No. of the bill.	How disposed of by the House of Reps.	How disposed of by the Senate.	Date of the act of Congress, and remarks.
Tillard, Wm. S., representatives of.	Value of tobacco destroyed by British at Tracy's Landing, Maryland, in war of 1812.	31	1	Petition	510	Claims.						
Tillett, James	Invalid pension, war of 1812	31	2	Petition	132, 146	Invalid Pensions.						
Tillett, Samuel	Payment of draft of Wm. Stirmans, for services as teacher of Choctaw Indians.	24	1	Resolution	347	Claims	362	Adverse		Laid on table.		
Tillett, Samuel	Payment of draft of Wm. Stirmans, for services as teacher of Choctaw Indians.	24	2	Resolution	78	Claims.						
Tillett, Samuel	Payment of draft of Wm. Stirmans, for services as teacher of Choctaw Indians.	25	2	Petition	88	Claims	858	Adverse		Laid on table.		
Tilley, Samuel, widow of	Revolutionary pension	25	2	Petition	119	Rev. Pensions				Discharged; laid on table.		
Tillien, Henry	Invalid pension	3	1	Rep. of Secretary War.	131	Select	May 26, 1794	To refer to Secretary, with instructions.	R. 12	Passed	Passed	App'd June 9, 1794
Tillinghast, Samuel	Pension	21	2	Petition	126	Military Pensions.						
Tillinghast, Samuel	Pension	22	1	Petition	80	Rev. Pensions				Discharged; laid on table.		
Tillinghast, Thomas G., administrator of.	Equitable settlement of account of deceased, a lieutenant, and lost in sloop-of-war Wasp.	19	1	Petition	225	Naval Affairs	Mar. 1, 1826	Adverse		Laid on table.		
Tillinghast, Wm. H.	(See Etting, Mickle, and W. H. Tillinghast.)	31	1	————	270							
Tillotson, Isaac	Restoration of pension	17	1	Petition	45	Rev. Pensions				Leave given to withdraw.		
Tillotson, Shubal, and others	Patents for lands in Louisiana on which they reside.	27	1	Petition	100	Public Lands.						
Tilton, Daniel, & Sons	Indemnity for French spoliations prior to 1800.	26	1	Memorial	182	Foreign Affairs	343	Favorable; bill	319	Referred to Committee Whole House.		
Tilton, James	Allowance for postage, forage, servants, &c., as surgeon general, from date of appointment.	13	2	Petition	401	Claims				Discharged.		
Tilton, James, and others	Settlement of accounts as officers of United States navy.	30	1	Senate bill	328	Naval Affairs	Feb. 29, 1848	With't amend.	118	Referred to Committee Whole House.		
Tilton, John	Increase of pension	15	2	House bill	41				203	Passed	Passed	App'd March 3, 1839
Tilton, Judith	Pension for revolutionary services of husband.	28	1	Petition	950	Whole House on bill No. 7.						App'd June 18, 1844
Tilton, Stephen, heirs of	Indemnity for French spoliations prior to 1800.	29	2	Memorial	75	Foreign Affairs	Feb. 9, 1847	By bill	561	Referred to Committee Whole House.		
Tilton, Stephen	Indemnity for French spolia ions prior to 1800.	26	1	Memorial	182	Foreign Affairs	343	Favorable; bil	319	Referred to Committee Whole House.		
Tilton, Sylvester	Invalid pension	3	1	Rep. of Secretary War.	131	Select	May 26, 1794	To refer to Secretary, with instructions.	R. 12	Passed	Passed	App'd June 9, 1794
Tilton, Sylvester	Invalid pension	12	1	House bill	361	Whole House	June 15, 1812	Favorable	138	Passed	Passed	App'd July 5, 1812
Timberlake, Jonh B.	Credit as naval purser for $3,084, advanced to Lieut. John Trippe.	15	2	Senate bill	248	Naval Affairs	Feb. 18, 1819	With't amend.	30	Passed	Passed	App'd March 1, 1819
Timberlake, John B.	Credit for money advanced to the crews of frigates United States and President.	17	1	Petition	145	Naval Affairs				Discharged; leave to withdraw.		

List of private claims presented to the House of Representatives of the United States from the 1st to the 31st Congress, inclusive—Continued.

Names of claimants.	Nature or object of the claim.	Congress.	Session.	How brought before the House of Reps.	Page of journal.	To what committee of the House referred.	No. or date of the report.	Nature of the report.	No. of the bill.	How disposed of by the House of Reps.	How disposed of by the Senate.	Date of the act of Congress, and remarks.
Timberlake, Joseph	Additional compensation as postmaster at Fredericksburg, Virginia.	15	1	Petition	223	P. Of. and P. Roads				Discharged; laid on table.		
Timberlake, Joseph	Additional compensation as postmaster at Fredericksburg, Virginia.	15	2	Petition	66	P. Of. & P. Roads				Discharged; laid on table.		
Timberlake, Joseph	Additional compensation as postmaster at Fredericksburg, Virginia.	16	1	Petition	280	P. Of. & P. Roads	Mar. 3, 1820	Adverse		Laid on table.		
Times, James	Change of land entry	16	1	Petition	252	Public Lands	Feb. 29, 1820	Rep't and res. adverse.		Resolution adopted.		
Timmons, Samuel, widow of.	Pension or bounty land for services of deceased in the war of 1812.	29	1	Petition	872	Invalid Pensions.						
Timony, Daniel	Pay for materials and work on Cumberland road.	23	1	Resolution	589	Claims	455	Adverse		Laid on table		See report No. 449.
Tims, Elizabeth	Compensation for injury sustained by decease of Mr. Blair, member of Congress at her house.	24	2	Memorial	315	Dist. of Columbia				Discharged; laid on table.		
Tiner, Joshua	Compensation for services in Georgia in 1784, during the troubles with the Creek Indians.	21	1	Petition	448	Claims	Mar. 24, 1830	Adverse		Laid on table.		
Tingle, George E	Compensation for services as clerk to executive of Florida.	21	1	Petition	151	Territories	205	Report and bill.	256	Referred to Committee Whole House.		
Tingle, George E	Compensation for services as clerk to executive of Florida.	21	2	Bill of last sess.	265	Whole House	Feb. 4, 1831	With't amend.	256	Passed	Rep'td without amendment.	
Tingle, George E	Compensation for services as clerk to executive of Florida.	22	1	Petition	31	Territories	235	Report and bill.	315	Referred to Committee Whole House.		
Tingle, George E	Compensation for services as clerk to executive of Florida.	22	1	Senate bill	830	Claims	June 7, 1832	With't amend.	38	Passed	Passed	App'd July 13, 1832
Tinkham, Ebenezer	Invalid pension	3	2	Rep. of Secretary War.	350	Claims	March 3, 1795	To discharge & postpone.		Laid on table.		
Tinkham, Ebenezer	Invalid pension	4	1	Rep. of Secretary War.	445	Claims	Feb. 18, 1796	Favorable; bill ordered.	156	Passed	Passed	App'd April 20, 1796
Tinkham, Ebenezer, and others.	Arrearages of pension	5	2	Memorial	117	Whole House.						
Tinkham, Ebenezer	Increase of pension	10	2	House bill	499	Whole House	Feb. 28, 1809	Favorable; bill	158	Passed	Passed	App'd March 3, 1809
Tinkham, Seth	Indemnity for French spoliations prior to 1800.	26	1	Memorial	182	Foreign Affairs	343	Favorable; bill	319	Referred to Committee Whole House.		
Tinsley, John, heir of	Compensation for revolutionary services.	30	1	Petition	360	Rev. Pensions	307	Adverse		Laid on table.		
Tinsley, Jonathan	Invalid pension	10	2	House bill	499	Whole House	Feb. 28, 1808	Favorable	158	Passed	Passed	App'd March 3, 1809
Tipper, William	Pay and interest due for revolutionary services in Col. Dixon's regiment of N. Carolina militia.	8	1	Petition	663	Whole House on bill No. 184.						
Tippett, Cartwright, and others.	Additional compensation as cryer and bailiffs to U. States court.	14	2	Petition	378	Judiciary	Feb. 18, 1817	Rep't and res. adverse.		Resolution adopted.		
Tippett, Edward D	Compensation for certain military services.	25	3	Petition	461	Claims.						
Tippett, Edward D	Compensation for certain military services.	26	1	Petition	170	Claims.						
Tippett, Edward D	Compensation for certain military services.	26	2	Petition	79	Claims.						

List of private claims presented to the House of Representatives of the United States from the 1st to the 31st Congress, inclusive—Continued.

Names of claimants.	Nature or object of the claim.	Congress.	Session.	How brought before the House of Reps.	Page of journal.	To what committee of the House referred.	No. or date of the report.	Nature of the report.	No. of the bill.	How disposed of by the House of Reps.	How disposed of by the Senate.	Date of the act of Congress, and remarks.
Tippett, Stephen	Extension of time to file proof in support of land title.	19	2	Rep. of Secretary Treasury.	50	Priv. Land Claims.	49	Report and bill	378	Referred to Committee Whole House.		
Tippett, Stephen, representatives of.	Authority to locate land in Louisiana.	21	1	Senate bill	452	Priv. Land Claims.	Mar. 24, 1830	With't amend.	85	Referred to Committee Whole House.		
Tippett, Stephen, representatives of.	Authority to locate land in Louisiana.	21	2	Senate bill	387	Priv. Land Claims.	Mar. 2, 1831	With't amend.	158	Passed	Passed	App'd March 2, 1831
Tipton, Abraham, heir of.	Commutation of pay for services as captain in revolutionary army.	23	2	Petition	345	Rev. Claims.						
Tipton, Abraham, heir of.	Commutation of pay for services as captain in revolutionary army.	24	1	Petition	104	Rev. Claims.						
Tipton, Abraham, heir of.	Commutation of pay for services as captain in revolutionary army.	24	2	Petition	216	Rev. Claims.						
Tipton, Abraham, heir of.	Commutation of pay for services as captain in revolutionary army.	25	2	Petition	82	Rev. Claims	618	Adverse	......	Laid on table.		
Tipton, Abraham, heir of.	Commutation of pay for services as captain in revolutionary army.	25	3	Petition	125	Rev. Claims	....	....	......	Discharged.		
Tipton, Abraham, heir of.	Commutation of pay for services as captain in revolutionary army.	26	1	Petition	166	Rev. Claims	....	....	......	Discharged; laid on table.		
Tipton, Abraham, heir of.	Commutation of pay for services as captain in revolutionary army.	26	2	Petition	35	Rev. Claims.						
Tipton, Abraham, heir of.	Commutation of pay for services as captain in revolutionary army.	30	1	Petition	752	Rev. Claims.						
Tipton, Jonathan	Pension for revolutionary services.	29	2	Petition	164	Rev. Pensions.						
Tipton, Jonathan	Pension for revolutionary services.	30	1	Petition	189	Rev. Pensions	448	Adverse	......	Referred to Committee Whole House.		
Tipton, Jonathan	(See James Morrow and Jonathan Tipton.)	26	1	....	352							
Tipton, Luke	Pension for revolutionary services.	21	2	Resolution	102	Military Pensions.						
Tipton, Luke	Pension for revolutionary services.	22	1	Resolution	446	Rev. Pensions.						
Tipton, Luke	Pension for revolutionary services.	30	1	Petition	426	Rev. Pensions.						
Tipton, William, (Tenn.)	Revolutionary pension	20	1	Petition	440	Military Pensions	235	Report and bill	275	Referred to Committee Whole House.		
Tipton, William, (Tenn.)	Revolutionary pension	20	2	Bill of last sess.	285	Whole House	Feb. 13, 1829	With't amend.	275	Passed	Reported with't amendment.	
Tipton, William, (Tenn.)	Revolutionary pension	21	1	Petition	37	Military Pensions	37	Report and bill	50	Passed	Passed	App'd May 28, 1830
Tipton, William, (Mo.)	To enter land occupied by his ferry	22	1	Petition	91	Priv. Land Claims	....	....	......	Discharged; laid on table.		
Tirel, Josiah	Invalid pension	22	2	Resolution	261	Invalid Pensions.						
Tirel, Josiah	Invalid pension	23	1	Petition	72	Invalid Pensions	399	Report and bill	418	Referred to Committee Whole House.		
Tirel, Josiah	Invalid pension	23	2	Bill of last sess.	336	Whole House	Feb. 6, 1835	With't amend.	418	Passed.		
Tirel, Josiah	Invalid pension	28	1	Petition	89	Invalid Pensions.						
Tires, Rezin	Pension—Indian wars	26	1	Petition	624	Rev. Pensions.						
Tisdale, Barney, & others.	Release from judgment against them at suit of United States.	22	1	Petition	868	Judiciary	....	....	......	Discharged; laid on table.		
Tisdale, Elijah	Relief from judgmant against him as collector of internal revenue in Indiana.	8	1	Petition	512	Claims	Jan. 16, 1804	Rep. and resl'n adverse.	......	Resolution adopted.		
Tisdale, Hannah	(See Elijah Shaw, daughter of)	28	1	....	946							
Tisdale, James, administrator of.	Indemnity for French spoliations prior to 1800.	26	1	Memorial	182	Foreign Affairs	343	Favorable; bill	319	Referred to Committee Whole House.		
Tisdell, Cuthbert	Pension	21	2	Resolutions	209	Military Pensions.						

List of private claims presented to the House of Representatives of the United States from the 1st to the 31st Congress, inclusive—Continued.

Names of claimants.	Nature or object of the claim.	Congress.	Session.	How brought before the House of Reps.	Page of journal.	To what committee of the House referred.	No. or date of the report.	Nature of the report.	No. of the bill.	How disposed of by the House of Reps.	How disposed of by the Senate.	Date of the act of Congress, and remarks.
Tise, Frederick	Compensation for property taken in Canada by United States troops.	22	1	Petition	513	Claims	April 16, 1832	Adverse	......	Laid on table.		
Tise, Frederick	Compensation for property taken in Canada by United States troops.	22	2	Petition	74	Claims.						
Tise, Frederick	Compensation for property taken in Canada by United States troops.	23	1	Petition	96	Priv. Land Claims.						
Tison, Albert	Confirmation of title to land in Missouri.	15	1	Petition	350	Priv. Land Claims.	....	....	......	Discharged; laid on table.		
Tison, Albert	Confirmation of title to land in Missouri.	24	1	Petition	257	Public Lands.						
Tison, Albert	Confirmation of title to land in Missouri.	24	2	Petition	98	Priv. Land Claims.						
Tison, Albert, representatives of.	Confirmation of title to land in Missouri.	27	2	Petition	383	Priv. Land Claims.						
Tison, Thomas	Pension	20	1	Petition	428	Military Pensions.						
Titcomb, Benjamin	Compensation for services, &c., in revolutionary war.	2	1	Petition	494	....	....	....	......	Referred to Secretary War.		
Titcomb, Benjamin	Compensation for services, &c., in revolutionary war.	2	2	Petition	616	Select.						
Titcomb, Benjamin	Compensation for services, &c., in revolutionary war.	3	2	Petition	285	Claims.						
Titcomb, Benjamin	Compensation for services, &c., in revolutionary war.	4	1	Petition	375	Claims	Dec. 22, 1795	Adverse	......	Referred to Committee Whole House.		
Titcomb, Benjamin	Compensation for services, &c., in revolutionary war.	4	2	Rep't of last sess.	613	Whole House.						
Titcomb, Jonathan	Compensation for services as brigadier general in Mississippi militia, and as purchasing commissary in revolutionary war.	3	1	Petition	47	....	....	....	......	Referred to Secretary War.		
Titcomb, Jonathan	Compensation for services as brigadier general in Mississippi miiltia, and as purchasing commissary in revolutionary war.	3	2	Rep. of Secretary War.	278	....	....	....	......	Laid on table.		
Titcomb, Jonathan	Compensation for services as brigadier general in Mississippi militia, and as purchasing commissary in revolutionary war.	4	1	Petition & report Sec. of War.	373	Claims.						
Titcomb, Jonathan	Compensation for services as brigadier general in Mississippi militia, and as purchasing commissary in revolutionary war.	4	2	Petition & report Sec. of War.	614	Claims.						
Tittell, Isaac	Compensation for horse lost in Seminole campaign.	23	1	Documents	154	Claims.						
Tittermary, Richard, heirs of.	Indemnity for French spoliations prior to 1800.	31	1	Petition	323	Foreign Affairs	355	Favorable; bill	318	Referred to Committee Whole House.		
Tittermary, Robert, & Son.	Indemnity for French spoliations prior to 1800.	26	1	Memorial	182	Foreign Affairs	343	Favorable; bill	319	Referred to Committee Whole House.		
Titus, George W	Pension for wounds received in war of 1812.	17	2	Petition	35	Pens. & Rev. Cl'ms.	....	....	......	Referred to Secretary War.	....	Sec. of War reported Dec. 19, 1822.
Titus, John, and Elisha Tibbetts, trustees of.	(See New York, United Insurance Company of.)	26	1	....	182							
Titus, Sally Ann	Renewal of a patent	30	1	Petition	263	Patents.						

List of private claims presented to the House of Representatives of the United States from the 1st to the 31st Congress, inclusive—Continued.

Names of claimants.	Nature or object of the claim.	Congress.	Session.	How brought before the House of Reps.	Page of journal.	To what committee of the House referred.	No. or date of the report.	Nature of the report.	No. of the bill.	How disposed of by the House of Reps.	How disposed of by the Senate.	Date of the act of Congress, and remarks.
Titus, Solomon	Revolutionary pension	21	1	Documents	447	Military Pensions				Discharged; laid on table.		
Titus, Solomon, widow of.	Revolutionary pension	25	3	Petition	460	Rev. Pensions				Discharged.		
Titus, Solomon, widow of.	Revolutionary pension	26	1	Petition	175	Rev. Pensions				Discharged; laid on table.		
Titus, Timothy	Leave to redeem farm sold to satisfy United States troops.	16	2	Petition	101	Ways and Means				Discharged; laid on table.		
Titus, Walter, & Co.	Remission of duties under tariff of 1828 on goods ordered prior to passage of said act.	21	2	Petition	96	Ways and Means.						
Titus, Walter, & Co.	Reimbursement of amount of increased duty on certain goods.	22	1	Petition	186	Ways and Means.						
Titus, Walter, & Co.	Reimbursement of amount of increased duty on certain goods.	29	1	Petition	69	Commerce	150	Adverse		Laid on table.		
Tizdale, John	(See William Hoghland, & others, attorney for.)											
Tobey, Daniel	(See Nathaniel Seavey and others)	14	2		278							
Tobey, Lemuel	Pension for revolutionary services.	21	2	Petition	230	Military Pensions.						
Tobey, Lemuel	Pension for revolutionary services.	23	1	Petition	459	Rev. Pensions.						
Tobey, Lemuel	Pension for revolutionary services.	23	2	Petition	66, 303	Rev. Pensions.						
Tobey, Lemuel	Pension for revolutionary services.	24	1	Petition	107	Rev. Pensions				Discharged; laid on table.		
Tobey, Lemuel	Pension for revolutionary services.	24	2	Petition	217	Rev. Pensions				Discharged; laid on table		
Tobey, Lemuel	Pension for revolutionary services.	25	2	Petition	273	Rev. Pensions				Discharged; referred to Com. Whole House.		
Tobey, William	Additional compensation as postmaster at New Bedford, Miss.	4	1	Petition	445	Select						See House bill No. 184
Tobin, Robert	400 acres of land in lieu of a Virginia military warrant.	24	2	Resolution	318	Priv. Land Claims				Discharged; laid on table.		
Tobin, Samuel	Restoration of pension	17	2	Petition	119	Whole House on bill No. 207.						See act March 1, 1823
Todd, Archibald, widow of.	Pension for revolutionary services.	25	3	Petition	673					Laid on table.		
Todd, Archibald, widow of.	Pension for revolutionary services.	26	1	Peti ion	359	Rev. Pensions.						
Todd, Archibald, widow of.	Pension for revolutionary services.	27	2	Petition	153	Rev. Pensions	784	Adverse		Laid on table.		
Todd, Archibald, widow of.	Pension for revolutionary services	28	1	Petition	189	Rev. Pensions				Discharged; laid on table.		
Todd, Bernard, heirs of	Compensation for property destroyed by British, war of 1812.	29	1	Memorial	381	Claims	639	Adverse		Laid on table.		
Todd, Bernard, heirs of	Compensation for property destroyed by British, war of 1812.	29	2	Memorial	67	Claims.						
Todd, Bernard, heirs of	Compensation for property destroyed by British, war of 1812.	30	1	Memorial	108	Claims	255	Report and bill	248	Referred to Committee Whole House.		
Todd, Bernard, heirs of	Compensation for property destroyed by British, war of 1812.	30	2	Bill of last sess.	142	Whole House	Dec. 22, 1848	With't amend.	248	Passed	Reported, without amend't.	
Todd, Bernard, heirs of	Compensation for property destroyed by British, war of 1812.	31	1	Petition	397	Claims	157	Report and bill	175	Referred to Committee Whole House.		
Todd, Bernard, heirs of	Compensation for property destroyed by British, war of 1812.	31	2	Bill of last sess.	103	Whole House	Jan. 3, 1851	With't amend.	175	Passed	Reported, without amend't.	
Todd, Charles	Compensation for wagon and team impressed into service of United States, war of 1812.	13	3	Petition and rep't Sec. Navy.	537	Claims	Feb. 10, 1815	By bill	290	Passed	Postponed.	

List of private claims presented to the House of Representatives of the United States from the 1st to the 31st Congress, inclusive—Continued.

Names of claimants.	Nature or object of the claim.	Congress.	Session.	How brought before the House of Reps.	Page of journal.	To what committee of the House referred.	No. or date of the report.	Nature of the report.	No. of the bill.	How disposed of by the House of Reps.	How disposed of by the Senate.	Date of the act of Congress, and remarks.
Todd, Charles	Compensation for wagon and team impressed into service of United States, war of 1812.	14	1	Petition	284	Claims	Feb. 10, 1816	By bill	......	Passed	Passed	App'd April 27, 1816
Todd, Charles H	To refund duties erroneously paid.	28	1	Petition	104	Ways and Means.						
Todd, Charles H	Contract for mail between Panama and Oregon.	30	1	Petition	722	Naval Affairs	818	Adverse	......	Laid on table.		
Todd, Davis	Indemnity for Indian depredations	24	1	Petition	96	Indian Affairs.						
Todd, Elisha	(See Joseph Boggs and others)	22	2	....	122							
Todd, Elisha	(See Reuben E. Gentry and others)	23	1	....	138							
Todd, Francis, executor of.	Indemnity for French spoliations prior to 1800.	26	1	Memorial	182	Foreign Affairs	343	Favorable; bill	319	Referred to Committee Whole House.		
Todd, Henrietta H	(See James P. Wallace, heirs of).	24	1	....	425							
Todd, Henry	(See Peter and John S. Craig & Co.)	21	1	....	38							
Todd, Isaac	Confirmation of title to land in Mississippi.	12	1	Petition	110	Public Lands.						
Todd, Isaac, and James McGill, assignees of.	Confirmation of title to land in Mississippi.	27	3	Petition	77	Public Lands	6	Report and bill	625	Passed	Passed	App'd March 3, 1843
Todd, Jehiel	Increase of pension	23	2	Petition	101	Rev. Pensions	....	....	......	Discharged; laid on table.		
Todd, John, or Joseph	Pension	12	1	House bill	361	Whole House	June 15, 1812	Favorable	138	Passed	Passed	App'd July 5, 1812 John in the bill, Joseph in the law.
Todd, Joseph	(See Joshua T. Chase, and others.)	20	1	....	29							
Todd, Levi	Half pay for services of deceased as lieutenant in Clarke's Virginia revolutionary regiment.	23	2	Res. and papers.	165, 434	Rev. Claims.						
Todd, Levi	Half-pay for services of deceased as lieutenant in Clarke's Virginia revolutionary regiment.	24	1	Documents	16	Rev. Claims.						
Todd, Levi	Half-pay for services of deceased as lieutenant in Clarke's Virginia revolutionary regiment.	24	2	Petition	119	Claims	202	Adverse	......	Laid on table.		
Todd, Levi	Half-pay for services of deceased as lieutenant in Clarke's Virginia revolutionary regiment.	26	1	Petition	630	Claims	....	....	......	Discharged; laid on table		
Todd, Levi L	(See Nathaniel Ashley, heirs of.)	25	2	....	546							
Todd, Paxton W	Compensation for a horse lost in United States service.	23	2	Petition	275	Claims.						
Todd, Paxton W	Compensation for a horse lost in United States service.	24	1	Petition	508	Claims	April 5, 1836	Adverse	......	Laid on table.		
Todd, Robert M	Indemnity for French spoliations prior to 1800.	26	1	Memorial	182	Foreign Affairs	343	Favorable	319	Referred to Committee Whole House.		
Todd, Samuel P	Commission on bills of exchange negotiated while acting purser of Brazil squadron.	29	1	Memorial	400, 1139	Naval Affairs.						
Todd, Samuel P	Allowance on all funds negotiated by him as special agent for Brazil squadron.	30	1	Petition	263	Naval Affairs	....	....	......	Discharged; laid on table.		
Todd, Samuel P	Allowance on all funds negotiated by him as special agent for Brazil squadron.	31	1	Petition	371	Naval Affairs.						

List of private claims presented to the House of Representatives of the United States from the 1st to the 31st Congress, inclusive—**Continued.**

ames of claimants.	Nature or object of the claim.	Congress.	Session.	How brought before the House of Reps.	Page of journal.	To what committee of the House referred.	No. or date of the report.	Nature of the report.	No. of the bill.	How disposed of by the House of Reps.	How disposed of by the Senate.	Date of the act of Congress, and remarks.
Todd, Thomas	Bounty land for services in war of 1812.	24	1	Resolution	542	Priv. Land Claims.	678	Report and bill.	638	Referred to Committee Whole House.		
Todd, Thomas	Bounty land for services in war of 1812.	24	2	Res. and docs	48	Priv. Land Claims.						
Todd, Thomas	Bounty land for services in war of 1812.	25	2	Resolution	43	Priv. Land Claims.	282	Report and bill.	325	Referred to Committee Whole House.		
Todd, Thomas	Bounty land for services in war of 1812.	25	3	Bill of last sess.	377	Whole House	Jan. 25, 1839	With't amend.	325	Passed	Passed	App'd March 3, 1839
Todd, Thomas W	Indemnity for costs of suit against him as paymaster of Virginia militia, the United States being in debt to him.	16	1	Petition	34	Claims	29	Adverse		Laid on table		Leave to withdraw.
Todd, W. H.	(See Benjamin Deane, agent of.)	23	1		195							
Todd, Yale	Revolutionary pension	2	2	Rep. of Secretary War.	649	Whole House						See act Feb. 28, 1793
Todd, Yale	Revolutionary pension	3	1	Rep. of Secretary War.	131	Select	May 26, 1794	Rep. Sec. War, with instructions.	R. 12	Passed	Passed	App'd June 9, 1794
Todd, ——	(See Store & Todd.)	16	1		212							
To-hon-do-che, *alias* Big Skin, *alias* Faunde Het-sey, a Seneca warrior.	Pension for wounds received in war of 1812.	15	2	Resolution	123	Pens. & Rev. Cl'ms.				Discharged; laid on table.		
To-hon-do-che, *alias* Big Skin, *alias* Faunde Het-sey, a Seneca warrior.	Pension for wounds received in war of 1812.	19	1	Resolution	450	Military Pensions	194	Favorable		Referred to Committee Whole House on bill No. 118.		
To-hon-do-che, *alias* Big Skin, *alias* Faunde Het-sey, a Seneca warrior.	Pension for wounds received in war of 1812.	19	2	House bill	85	Whole House			314			Bill became a law omitting claimant's name
Toland, Henry	Release from liability as surety for John and W. H. Smith.	20	2	Petition	89	Ways and Means				Discharged; laid on table.		
Toland, Henry	Release from liability as surety for John and W. H. Smith.	21	1	Petition	100	Judiciary				Discharged; laid on table.		
Tolar, Robert	Compensation for rifle taken for United States, war of 1812.	18	1	Petition	276	Claims	Feb. 27, 1824	Adverse		Laid on table.		
Tolbert, Silas	(See Ab'm M. Scott and others)	13	3		533							
Tolbort, William D	(See Louisiana, branch pilots at New Orleans.)	28	1		77							
Toledam, R	(See Clark Woodruff, assignee of)	27	2		622							
Tollet, Wesley	Confirmation of title to land in Arkansas.	22	2	Petition	132	Public Lands.						
Tollet, Wesley	Confirmation of title to land in Arkansas.	23	1	Petition	93	Public Lands				Discharged; laid on table.		
Tolly, John and Thomas	(See Joseph Stewart and others)	13	3		751							
Tolman, Thomas	(See Samuel Safford and others)	2	2		706							
Tolrou, Douglass	(See Louis F. Beeler and others)	30	1		115							
Tom, Thomas	Invalid pension	3	1	Rep. of Secretary War.	131	Select	May 26, 1794	Favorable; bill ordered.	62	Passed	Passed	App'd June 7, 1794
Tom, ——	(See Hoyt & Tom)	26	1		182							
Tomb, George	(See Wm. Morrison and others)	28	1		904							
Tomiton, Jasper	Invalid pension	12	1	House bill	361	Whole House	June 15, 1812	Favorable	138	Passed	Passed	App'd July 5, 1812
Tomkins, Charles	(See Arnold Henry Dohrman, agent for legal representatives of.)	14	2		345							
Tomlin, Jasper	Bounty land for revolutionary services.	12	2	Petition	641	Public Lands.						

List of private claims presented to the House of Representatives of the United States from the 1st to the 31st Congress, inclusive—Continued.

Names of claimants.	Nature or object of the claim.	Congress.	Session.	How brought before the House of Reps.	Page of journal.	To what committee of the House referred.	No. or date of the report.	Nature of the report.	No. of the bill.	How disposed of by the House of Reps.	How disposed of by the Senate.	Date of the act of Congress, and remarks.
Tomlinson, David, attorney of.	Indemnity for French spoliations prior to 1800.	26	1	Memorial	182	Foreign Affairs	343	Favorable; bill	319	Referred to Committee Whole House.		
Tomlinson, Harris, heirs of.	Pension for revolutionary services.	27	3	Petition	317	Rev. Pensions	....	....	....	....	....	Leave to withdraw, 2d sess., 28th Cong.
Tomlinson, Henry	Exemption from duties on a distillery he was prevented from using by service in militia.	14	1	Petition	198	Ways and Means	....	....	....	Discharged; laid on table.		
Tomlinson, Jabez	Invalid pension	3	1	Rep. of Secretary War.	131	Select	May 26, 1794	Favorable; bill ordered.	62	Passed	Passed	App'd June 7, 1794
Tomlinson, Jabez and Eliphalet.	(See Ithamar Canfield)	6	1	....	649							
Tomlinson, Lemuel	Revolutionary pension	16	1	Resolution	63	Rev. Pensions	347	Adverse	....	Laid on table.		
Tomlinson, Peter, administrator of.	Indemnity for French spoliations prior to 1800.	26	1	Memorial	182	Foreign Affairs	343	Favorable; bill	319	Referred to Committee Whole House.		
Tomm, Henry	Invalid pension	3	1	Rep. of Secretary War.	131	Select	May 26, 1794	Favorable; bill ordered.	62	Passed	Passed	App'd June 7, 1794
Tompkins, Charles	(See Leighton Wood and others)	3	1	....	88							
Tompkins, Charles, heirs of.	Compensation for revolutionary services.	24	2	Petition	215	Rev. Claims.						
Tompkins, Charles, heirs of.	Compensation for revolutionary services.	25	2	Petition	393	Rev. Claims	....	....	....	Discharged; laid on table.		
Tompkins, Charles, heirs of.	Compensation for revolutionary services.	26	1	Petition	167	Rev. Claims.						
Tompkins, Christop'r, widow of.	Revolutionary pension	26	1	Petition	323	Rev. Pensions.						
Tompkins, Christop'r, widow of.	Revolutionary pension	27	2	Petition	58	Rev. Pensions	575	Report and bill	371	Engrossed.		
Tompkins, Christop'r, widow of.	Revolutionary pension	27	3	Bill of last sess.	87	....	....	....	371	Passed	Rept'd without amendment.	
Tompkins, Christop'r, widow of.	Revolutionary pension	30	1	Petition	679	Rev. Pensions	776	Report and bill	613	Referred to Committee Whole House.		
Tompkins, Christop'r, widow of.	Revolutionary pension	30	2	Bill of last sess.	362	Whole House	Feb. 2, 1839	With't amend.	613	Passed	Refer'd to Rev. Claims.	
Tompkins, Christop'r, widow of.	Revolutionary pension	31	1	Petition	628	Rev. Pensions	297	Report and bill	266	Referred to Committee Whole House.		
Tompkins, Christop'r, widow of.	Revolutionary pension	31	2	Bill of last sess.	182	Whole House	Jan. 24, 1851	With amend.	266	Passed	Refer'd to Pensions.	
Tompkins, Daniel D.	Settlement of account for advances and disbursements during war of 1812.	17	2	Resolution	113	Select	88	Report and bill	284	Passed	Passed	App'd Feb. 21, 1823
Tompkins, Daniel D.	Payment of amount found due under act of February, 1823.	18	1	President's mess.	34	Ways and Means	1	Report and bill	2	Passed	Passed	App'd Dec. 26, 1823
Tompkins, Daniel D.	Additional allowance for advances, &c.	18	1	President's mess.	339	Ways and Means	107	Res. to refer to President.	....	Adopted.		
Tompkins, Daniel D.	Additional allowance for advances, &c.	18	1	President's mess.	467	Ways and Means	April 30, 1824	By bill	215	Passed	Passed	App'd May 26, 1824
Tompkins, Daniel D., heirs of.	Interest on amounts found due deceased by acts of 1823, 1824.	29	1	Petition	234	Judiciary	200	Report and bill	193	Referred to Committee Whole House.		
Tompkins, Daniel D., heirs of.	Interest on amounts found due deceased by acts of 1823, 1824.	29	2	Bill of last sess.	381	Whole House	Feb. 19, 1847	With't amend.	193	Passed	Passed	App'd Feb. 22, 1847
Tompkins, Daniel	(See Edward Devitt, & others)	31	1	....	255							
Tompkins, Gideon	Fishing bounty	16	1	Petition	27	Ways and Means	Dec. 27, 1819	Report and res. adverse.	....	Adopted.		

List of private claims presented to the House of Representatives of the United States from the 1st to the 31st Congress, inclusive—Continued.

Names of claimants.	Nature or object of the claim.	Congress.	Session.	How brought before the House of Reps.	Page of journal.	To what committee of the House referred.	No. or date of the report.	Nature of the report.	No. of the bill.	How disposed of by the House of Reps.	How disposed of by the Senate.	Date of the act of Congress, and remarks.
Tompkins & Murray	Relief from penalties incurred by importing British goods.	12	2	Petition	549	Ways and Means	Nov. 25, 1812	Favorable; bill ordered.	239	Rejected		See act Feb. 27, 1813
Tompkins, Nancy	(See John Place, mother of)	21	2		137							
Tompkins, Robert, representatives of.	Commutation pay for revolutionary services.	3	2	Petition	293	Claims	Mar. 2, 1795	Adverse		Laid on table.		
Tompkins, Robert, representatives of.	Commutation pay for revolutionary services.	4	1	Petition	409					Rejected.		
Tompkins, Samuel	Indemnity for property confiscated in Canada, war of 1812.	14	2	Petition	131	Claims				Discharged.		
Tompkins, Samuel	Indemnity for property confiscated in Canada, war of 1812.	15	1	Petition	261	Claims				Discharged.		
Tompkins, Samuel	(See Canadian volunteers)	4	2		614							
Tongue, Anna	(See John Stewart, heir of)	23	2		157							
Tongue, James	Payment for warehouse burnt by the British in war of 1812.	24	1	Petition	584	Claims.						
Tongue, James	Payment for warehouse burnt by the British in war of 1812.	24	2	Petition	120	Claims	321	Adverse		Laid on table.		
Tongue, James	Payment for warehouse burnt by the British in war of 1812.	25	2	Petition	1086	Claims	1046	Report and bill	880	Referred to Committee Whole House.		
Tongue, James	Payment for warehouse burnt by the British in war of 1812.	25	3	Bill of last sess.	432	Whole House	Feb. 1, 1839	With't amend.	880	Passed	Adverse report.	
Tongue, James	(See William Hodson, administrators of.)											
Tool, Jacob, widow of	Bounty land for services of deceased in war of 1812.	31	1	Petition	1221	Public Lands.						
Toomey, John	Compensation for services as a soldier in revolutionary war.	13	1	Petition	114	Claims				Discharged.		
Toomey, John	Compensation for services as a soldier in revolutionary war.	13	2	Petition	231	Pensions.						
Toorea, Mary	(See William Mc Ghee, heirs of.)	30	1		398							
Toop, John	Compensation for property destroyed by United States troops near Nashville, war of 1812.	16	1	Petition	53	Claims	Jan. 19, 1820	Adverse		Laid on table.		
Toop, John	Compensation for property destroyed by United States troops near Nashville, war of 1812.	18	1	Petition	336	Military Affairs	114	Report and bill	198	Amended and passed.	Passed	App'd May 19, 1824
Topp, John S.	(See William H. Bedford, agent).	28	1		262							
Toppan, Dolly	(See Eliza Ann Young and Dolly Toppan.)	19	1		222							
Toppan, Edward, & others	Drawback of duty on merchandise shipped to New Orleans in 1803	8	2	Memorial	96	Com. and Manuf.	Feb. 5, 1805	By bill	48	Referred to Committee Whole House.		
Toppan, Edward, & others	Drawback of duty on merchandise shipped to New Orleans in 1803	9	1	Memorial	193	Com. and Manuf.	Dec. 16, 1805	Favorable; bill ordered.	79	Passed	Rejected.	
Toppan, Edward, & others	Drawback of duty on merchandise shipped to New Orleans in 1803	9	2	Memorial	519	Com. and Manuf.	Feb. 3, 1807	By bill	192	Referred to Committee Whole House.		
Toppan, Edward, & others	Drawback of duty on merchandise shipped to New Orleans in 1803	10	1	Memorial	162	Com. and Manuf.						
Toppan, Edward	Indemnity for French spoliations prior to 1800.	26	1	Memorial	182	Foreign Affairs	343	Favorable; bill	319	Referred to Committee Whole House.		
Toppan, Edward	(See Josiah Smith, executors of.)	26	1		182							
Toppan, Richard, & Wm. Stanwood, heirs of.	Indemnity for French spoliations prior to 1800.	28	1	Petition	514	Foreign Affairs.						

List of private claims presented to the House of Representatives of the United States from the 1st to the 31st Congress, inclusive—Continued.

Names of claimants.	Nature or object of the claim.	Congress.	Session.	How brought before the House of Reps.	Page of journal.	To what committee of the House referred.	No. or date of the report.	Nature of the report.	No. of the bill.	How disposed of by the House of Reps.	How disposed of by the Senate.	Date of the act of Congress, and remarks.
Toppan, S.	Indemnity for French spoliations prior to 1800.	26	1	Memorial	182	Foreign Affairs	343	Favorable; bill	319	Referred to Committee Whole House.		
Topping, William H.	Additional compensation as secretary to commissioners to examine New York custom-house.	29	1	Petition	283	Claims	372	Adverse		Laid on table		Leave to withdraw.
Torrans, William H.	(See John Mangnall, representatives of.)	5	2		270							
Torrant, A. L. surety of.	Release from liability	24	1	Petition	206	Claims	347	Adverse		Laid on table.		
Torrants, G. W.	Compensation for extra services in Mexican war.	30	2	Petition	430	Military Affairs.						
Torrence, Alexander, widow of.	Pension for revolutionary services.	28	1	Petition	72	Rev. Pensions				Discharged; laid on table.		
Torrence, Alexander, widow of.	Pension for revolutionary services.	30	2	Resolution	657					Leave to withdraw.		
Torrence, Thomas.	Invalid pension	3	1	Rep. of Secretary of War.	131	Select	May 26, 1794	To refer to Sec. with instructions.	R. 12	Passed	Passed	App'd June 9, 1794
Torrence, Thomas	Invalid pension	3	2	Rep. of Secretary of War.	337	Claims	Feb. 28, 1795	Favorable; bill ordered.	130	Passed	Postponed.	
Torrence, Thomas	Invalid pension	4	1	Rep. of Secretary War.	445	Claims	Feb. 18, 1796	Favorable; bill ordered.	156	Passed	Passed	App'd April 20, 1796
Torres, Juan Jose	Confirmation of title to land in Louisiana.	20	1	Petition	40	Priv. Land Claims.	Jan. 11, 1828	Adverse		Laid on table.		
Torrey, Ann	(See Bailey & Torrey)	20	1		67							
Torrey, Domingo	Confirmation of title to land in Pensacola.	23	1	Petition	294	Priv. Land Claims.						
Torrey, Jesse	Compensation for extra exertions and sufferings in revolutionary war.	16	1	Petition	114	Pens. & Rev. Cl'ms.	267	R p't and res. adverse.		Laid on table.		
Torrey, Jesse	Compensation for extra exertions and sufferings in revolutionary war.	16	2	Rep't and resol'n of last session.	154					Resolution adopted.		Leave to withdraw.
Torrey, Jesse	$1,000 for great services, &c., in revolutionary war.	17	1	Petition	285	Whole House on bill No. 91.						
Torrey, Jesse	Revolutionary pension	22	1	Petition	189	Rev. Pensions.						
Torrey, John	Reimbursement of money paid on account of United States for wagonage in revolutionary war.	2	1	Petition	446					Referred to Secretary Treasury.		
Torrey, Joseph, administrator of.	Payment due for revolutionary services.	2	1	Petition and rep't Sec. of War.	445	Whole House	Nov. 8, 1791	Rep. and res. adverse.		Resolution adopted.		
Torrey, Joseph, heirs of	Commutation of pay due as a major in revolutionary army.	23	1	Petition	39	Rev. Claims	133	Report and bill	143	Passed	Passed, with amendment.	App'd June 30, 1834
Torrey, Joseph W	Compensation for services as a lawyer in Territory of Michigan.	21	2	Petition	100	Judiciary	44	Report and bill	574	Referred to Committee Whole House.		
Torrey, Joseph W	Compensation for services as a lawyer in Territory of Michigan.	22	1	Petition	62	Judiciary	49	Report and bill	101	Passed	Passed	App'd May 31, 1832
Torreyre, John	(See Canadian Refugees)	6	2		748							
Torry, George	Indemnity for French spoliations prior to 1800.	26	1	Memorial	182	Foreign Affairs	343	Favorable; bill	319	Referred to Committee Whole House.		
Torry, William T.	Indemnity for French spoliations prior to 1800.	26	1	Memorial	182	Foreign Affairs	343	Favorable; bill	319	Referred to Committee Whole House.		
To'man, Joshua B., father of.	Bounty land due as a Canadian volunteer, war of 1812.	17	1	Petition	314	Priv. Land Claims.				Discharged; laid on table.		See Canadian volunteers.

List of private claims presented to the House of Representatives of the United States from the 1st to the 31st Congress, inclusive—Continued.

Names of claimants.	Nature or object of the claim.	Congress.	Session.	How brought before the House of Reps.	Page of journal.	To what committee of the House referred.	No. or date of the report.	Nature of the report.	No. of the bill.	How disposed of by the House of Reps.	How disposed of by the Senate.	Date of the act of Congress, and remarks.
Totter, Benjamin J	Amount of difference in a naval lieutenant and master's pay for a certain time.	27	2	Petition	48	Naval Affairs	563	Report and bill	358	Bill engrossed.		
Totter, Benjamin J	Amount of difference in a naval lieutenant and master's pay for a certain time.	27	3	Bill of last sess.	87				358	Passed	Passed	App'd March 1, 1843
Totter, George M	(See Exploring Expedition)	27	3		149							
Totter, G., President of	(See New Haven, Rhode Island, Insurance Company of.)	26	1		182							
Totty, Barnet	(See William H. Bedford, agent.)	28	1		262							
Toulmin, John B	Confirmation of title to land in Mobile.	21	2	Senate bill	387	Priv. Land Claims.	March 2, 1831	With't amend.	144	Passed	Passed	App'd March 2, 1831
Toulmin, T. S	Payment for horse lost in war of 1812.	18	1	Petition	160	Claims.						
Toulon, Jacques, *alias* Jas. Grappe.	Confirmation of title to land in Louisiana.	22	2	Petition	41	Priv. Land Claims.						
Tourney, James	Confirmation of title to land in Louisiana.	25	3	Petition	463	Priv. Land Claims.						
Touro, Abraham, executors of.	Indemnity for French spoliations prior to 1800.	26	1	Memorial	182	Foreign Affairs	343	Favorable; bill	319	Referred to Committee Whole House.		
Tousard, Lewis	Commutation of pension for life for revolutionary services.	3	1	Petition	39	Select	Feb. 7, 1794	Favorable; bill ordered.	16	Passed	Passed, with amendment.	App'd Apirl 30, 1794. See appropriation act, June 9, 1794.
Tousard, Lewis	Equitable settlement of his accounts as engineer and inspector general of artillery.	7	1	Petition	178	Select	April 12, 1802	Report and bill	57	Passed wtth amendm't.	Passed	App'd April 21, 1802
Tower, Abraham and Levi.	(See Thomas Leach and others)	8	2		639							
Toutant, Jacques	Confirmation of title to land in Louisiana.	22	1	Petition	64	Priv. Land Claims.	62	Report and bill	125	Passed	Passed	App'd June 25, 1832
Tower, Benjamin	Invalid pension	3	2	Rep. of Secretary War.	337	Claims	March 3, 1795	To postpone		Laid on table.		
Tower, Benjamin	Invalid pension	4	1	Report former	445	Claims	Feb. 18, 1796	Favorable; bill ordered.	156	Passed	Passed	App'd April 20, 1796
Tower, Benjamin	Invalid pension	13	1	House bill	56	Whole House	July 20, 1813	Favorable	31	Passed	Passed	App'd Aug. 2, 1813
Towers, John T	To be placed on similar footing with other printing contractors	31	2	Petition	271	Printing.						
Towle, David	Invalid pension; war of 1812	28	1	Petition	788	Invalid Pensions.						
Towle, David	Invalid pension; war of 1812	28	2	Petition	88	Invalid Pensions.						
Towle, David	Invalid pension; war of 1812	29	1	Petition	199	Invalid Pensions	504	Adverse		Laid on table.		
Towle, David	Invalid pension; war of 1812	30	1	Petition	698	Invalid Pensions	709	Report and bill	554	Referred to Committee Whole House.		
Towle, David	Invalid pension; war of 1812	30	2	Bill of last sess.	319	Whole House	Jan. 26, 1849	With't amend.	554	Passed	Reported, without amend't.	
Towle, David	Invalid pension; war of 1812	31	1	Petition	233	Invalid Pensions.						
Towle, David	Invalid pension; war of 1812	31	2	Petition	443	Invalid Pensions	78	Report and bill	482	Ref'd to Com. W. H.		
Towles, John	The location of a confirmed claim on any public land.	22	1	Petition	33	Public Lands.						
Towles, Oliver	Compensation for revolutionary services and reimbursement of expenses while in captivity.	2	1	Petition	456					Referred to Secretary of War.		
Towles, Oliver	Compensation for revolutionary services and reimbursement of expenses while in captivity.	2	2	Rep. of Secretary War.	710					Laid on table.		

List of private claims presented to the House of Representatives of the United States from the 1st to the 31st Congress, inclusive—Continued.

Names of claimants.	Nature or object of the claim.	Congress.	Session.	How brought before the House of Reps.	Page of journal.	To what committee of the House referred.	No. or date of the report.	Nature of the report.	No. of the bill.	How disposed of by the House of Reps.	How disposed of by the Senate.	Date of the act of Congress, and remarks.
Towles, Oliver, widow of	Compensation for revolutionary services and reimbursement of expenses while in captivity.	18	2	Petition	183	Pens. & Rev. Cl'ms.						
Town, ——	(See Smith & Town)	25	2		113							
Town, Edmund	Pension	21	2	Petition	127	Military Pensions				Discharged; laid on table.		
Town, Elisha	Refunding overpayment on a patent	24	2	Senate bill	162	Claims	Jan. 10, 1837	With't amend.	62	Referred to Committee Whole House.		
Town, Elisha	Refunding overpayment on a patent	25	2	Senate bill	101	Claims	Dec. 22, 1837	With't amend.	6	Referred to Committee Whole House.		
Town, Elisha	Refunding overpayment on a patent	25	3	Senate bill	51	Patents	Jan. 2, 1839	With't amend.	13	Passed	Passed	App'd Feb. 6, 1839
Town, Ithiel	Renewal of patent	23	1	Petition	111	Judiciary.						
Town, Thomas B	(See Timothy Curren, administrator of.)	25	2		655							
Townes, John	Compensation for military services in revolutionary war.	2	2	Petition	689					Referred to Secretary War.		See report Sec. War, March 2, 1793.
Townes, John, heirs of	Commutation pay for revolutionary services.	23	2	Petition	47	Rev. Claims.						
Townes, John, heirs of	Commutation pay for revolutionary services.	24	1	Petition	213	Rev. Claims.						
Townes, John, heirs of	Commutation pay for revolutionary services.	25	2	Petition	81	Rev. Claims	853	Report and bill.	771	Postponed.		
Townes, John, heirs of	Commutation pay for revolutionary services.	26	1	Petition	164	Rev. Claims						See report No. 436.
Townes, John, heirs of	Commutation pay for revolutionary services.	27	2	Petition	61	Rev. Claims	404	Adverse		Laid on table.		
Townes, John, heirs of	Commutation pay for revolutionary services.	28	1	Petition	319	Rev. Claims.						
Townes, John, heirs of	Commutation pay for revolutionary services.	28	2	Petition	89	Rev. Claims.						
Townes, John, heirs of	Commutation pay for revolutionary services.	29	1	Petition	461	Rev. Claims.						
Townes, John, heirs of	Commutation pay for revolutionary services.	29	2	Petition	150	Rev. Claims.						
Townes, John, heirs of	Compensation for revolutionary services.	30	1	Petition	117	Rev. Claims.						
Townes, John, heirs of	Compensation for revolutionary services.	30	2	Petition	224	Rev. Claims.						
Townes, John, heirs of	Commutation pay for revolutionary services.	31	1	Petition	....	Rev. Claims.						
Townley, George	Payment for supplies furnished revolutionary army.	20	2	Petition	177	Rev. Claims				Discharged		Leave to withdraw.
Townley, George	Payment for supplies furnished revolutionary army.	21	1	Petition	38	Rev. Claims				Discharged.		
Townley, George	Payment for supplies furnished revolutionary army.	22	1	Petition	29	Rev. Claims.						
Townley, George	Payment for supplies furnished revolutionary army.	23	1	Petition	89	Rev. Claims.						
Townley, George	Payment for supplies furnished revolutionary army.	23	2	Petition	37	Rev. Claims.						
Townley, George	Payment for supplies furnished revolutionary army.	24	1	Petition	102	Rev. Claims.						

List of private claims presented to the House of Representatives of the United States from the 1st to the 31st Congress, inclusive—Continued.

Names of claimants.	Nature or object of the claim.	Congress.	Session.	How brought before the House of Reps.	Page of journal.	To what committee of the House referred.	No. or date of the report.	Nature of the report.	No. of the bill.	How disposed of by the House of Reps.	How disposed of by the Senate.	Date of the act of Congress, and remarks.
Townley, George	Payment for supplies furnished revolutionary army.	25	2	Petition	178	Rev. Claims	.....	.....	.....	Discharged; laid on table.		
Townley, George	Payment for supplies furnished revolutionary army.	25	3	Petition	85	Rev. Claims	.....	.....	.....	Discharged.		
Townley, George	Payment for supplies furnished revolutionary army.	26	1	Petition	167	Rev. Claims	Mar. 5, 1840	Adverse	.....	Laid on table.		
Townley, George	Payment for supplies furnished revolutionary army.	30	1	Petition	948	Rev. Claims.						
Townley, Thomas F	(See Don Miguel Eslava, heirs of.)	18	1	.....	86							
Townsley, Thos. F., guardian of the children of.	$799 damages on United States commissariat drafts.	23	1	Petition	111	Claims	287	Report and bill	324	Laid on table.		
Townsley, Thos. F., guardian of the children of.	$799 damages on United States commissariat drafts.	24	1	Petition	50	Claims	4	Report and bill	4	Passed	Passed	App'd Feb. 17, 1836
Towns, Thomas	Pension and payment for wagon and team impressed in U. States service, revolutionary war.	21	1	Petition	498	Rev. Claims	.....	.....	.....	Discharged; laid on table.		
Towns, Thomas	Pension and payment for wagon and team impressed in U. States service, revolutionary war.	28	1	Petition	754	Rev. Claims.						
Towns, Thomas	Pension and payment for wagon and team impressed in U. States service, revolutionary war.	29	1	Petition	731	Rev. Claims.						
Townsend, Andrew	Pension	20	2	Petition	204	Military Pensions	.....	.....	.....	Discharged; laid on table.		
Townsend, Bronson, & Co.	(See Rufus Spalding, and other.)	15	2	.....	148							
Townsend, Charles, and Jonas Williams.	Compensation for services as commissioners on claims for property destroyed on Niagara frontier in war of 1812.	15	2	Petition	234	Claims	.....	.....	.....	Discharged; laid on table.		
Townsend, Charles, and Jonas Williams.	Compensation for services as commissioners on claims for property destroyed on Niagara frontier in war of 1812.	16	1	Petition	28	Claims	Dec. 20, 1819	Adverse	.....	Adopted; recommitted.		
							Jan. 13, 1820	Adverse	.....	Laid on table.		
Townsend, Charles, and Jonas Williams.	Compensation for services as commissioners on claims for property destroyed on Niagara frontier in war of 1812.	16	2	Rep. of last sess.	56	Whole House	Jan. 26, 1821	Amended	.....	Rejected.		
Townsend, Charles	Compensation for services as commissioner on claims for property destroyed on Niagara frontier in war of 1812.	17	1	Petition	38	Claims	Jan. 3, 1822	Adverse	.....	Referred to Committee Whole House.		
Townsend, Charles	Compensation for services as commissioner on claims for property destroyed on Niagara frontier in war of 1812.	17	2	Rep. of last sess.	95	Whole House	Jan. 2, 1823	Concurrence in res. of Com. on Claims.				
Townsend, Charles	Compensation for services as commissioner on claims for property destroyed on Niagara frontier in war of 1812.	18	1	Petition	129	Claims	Feb. 2, 1824	Adverse	.....	Referred to Committee Whole House.		
Townsend, Charles	Compensation for services as commissioner on claims for property destroyed on Niagara frontier in war of 1812.	28	2	Petition	141	Claims	64	Adverse	.....	Laid on table.		

List of private claims presented to the House of Representatives of the United States from the 1st to the 31st Congress, inclusive—Continued.

Names of claimants.	Nature or object of the claim.	Congress.	Session.	How brought before the House of Reps.	Page of journal.	To what committee of the House referred.	No. or date of the report.	Nature of the report.	No. of the bill.	How disposed of by the House of Reps.	How disposed of by the Senate.	Date of the act of Congress, and remarks.
Townsend, Daniel Y.	(See Walter Titus, & Co.)	21	2	....	96							
Townsend, Isaiah, & others.	Release from liability as sureties for Gerrit L. Dox.	21	1	Petitions	52, 66	P. Of. & P. Roads.	109	Report & bill	150	Passed	Passed	App'd May 29, 1830
Townsend, Jacob	Compensation for damages to property by United States troops in war of 1812.	22	1	Petition	26	Claims	Feb. 1, 1832	Adverse	......	Laid on table.		
Townsend, Jacob	Compensation for damages to property by United States troops in war of 1812.	22	2	Petition	29	Claims	Jan. 9, 1833	Adverse	......	Laid on table.		
Townsend, Jacob	Compensation for damages to property by United States troops in war of 1812.	23	1	Petition	35	Claims	130	Adverse	......	Laid on table.		
Townsend, John A.	Indemnity for French spoliations prior to 1800.	26	1	Memorial	182	Foreign Affairs	343	Favorable; bill	319	Referred to Committee Whole House.		
Townsend, John K., and others.	Indemnity for French spoliations prior to 1800.	29	2	Memorial	83	Foreign Affairs.						
Townsend, Martin	Invalid pension	31	1	Petition	519	Invalid Pensions						
Townsend, Moses	(See Benjamin Crowninshield, and others.)	22	1	....	186							
Townsend, Moses, executor of.	Indemnity for French spoliations prior to 1800.	29	2	Memorial	135	Foreign Affairs.						
Townsend, Seth	Increase of pension	19	1	Resolution	416	Naval Affairs	April 14, 1826	....	......	Laid on table	....	Leave to withdraw.
Townsend, Sylvanus	Payment of two revolutionary loan office certificates.	11	3	Petition	267	Claims.						
Townsend, Sylvanus	Payment of two revolutionary loan office certificates.	14	2	Resolution	100	Pens. & Rev. Cl'ms.	Feb. 3, 1817	By bill	96	Referred to Committee Whole House on bill No. 1.		
Townsend, Sylvanus	Payment of two revolutionary loan office certificates.	15	1	Resolution	50	Pens. & Rev. Cl'ms.	....	....	......	Discharged	....	Leave to withdraw.
Townsend, Sylvanus	Pension	21	2	Petition	43	Military Pensions.						
Townsend, Sylvanus	Pension	22	1	Petition	67	Rev. Pensions	162	Report & bill.	237	Referred to Committee Whole House.		
Townsend, Sylvanus	Pension	22	2	Bill of last sess.	123	....	....	....	237	Laid on table.		
Townsend, William	Compensation for six anchors taken for United States service.	17	2	Petition and rep't Sec. Navy.	216	Naval Affairs	....	....	......	Leave to withdraw.		
Townsend, William	Compensation for six anchors taken for United States service.	18	1	Petition	135	Naval Affairs	May 20, 1824	Report and bill for 1 anchor.	236	Referred to Committee Whole House.		
Townsend, William	Compensation for six anchors taken for United States service.	18	2	Bill of last sess.	259	Whole House	Feb. 22, 1825	With't amend.	235	Passed	Passed	App'd March 3, 1825
Townsend, William	Compensation for five anchors taken for United States service.	22	1	Petition	292	Naval Affairs.						
Townsend, William	Compensation for five anchors taken for United States service.	22	2	Petition	45	Naval Affairs.						
Townsend, William B.	(See Theodore Dwight and others)	19	1	....	221							
Townshend, M.	Indemnity for French spoliations prior to 1800.	26	1	Memorial	182	Foreign Affairs	343	Favorable; bill	319	Referred to Committee Whole House.		
Towson, Nathan	Additional compensation as pay master general, U. States army.	22	1	Petition	74	Military Affairs	Jan. 6, 1832	By bill	217	Passed	Passed	App'd Mar. 15, 1832
Tozar, John	Compensation for revolutionary services.	2	1	Petition	451	....	....	....	......	Referred to Secretary of War.		
Tozer, John	Compensation for injuries received in revolutionary war.	9	1	Petition	277	Claims	Mar. 28, 1806	Adverse	......	....	....	Leave to withdraw.

List of private claims presented to the House of Representatives of the United States from the 1st to the 31st Congress, inclusive—Continued.

Names of claimants.	Nature or object of the claim.	Congress.	Session.	How brought before the House of Reps.	Page of journal.	To what committee of the House referred.	No. or date of the report.	Nature of the report.	No. of the bill.	How disposed of by the House of Reps.	How disposed of by the Senate.	Date of the act of Congress, and remarks.
Tozer, John	Compensation for injuries received in revolutionary war.	9	2	Petition	474	Claims	Oct. 22, 1806	Adverse				Leave to withdraw.
Tozer, John	Compensation for injuries received in revolutionary war.	10	1	Petition	59	Whole House						See bills No. 100 and 119.
Tozier, William	Pension	22	2	Petition	152	Invalid Pensions	Feb. 15, 1833	Report and bill	738	Referred to Committee Whole House.		
Tozier, William	Pension	23	1	Petition	44	Invalid Pensions	1	Report and bill	1	Passed	Passed	App'd June 25, 1834
Tozier, William	Increase of pension	31	2	Petition	246	Invalid Pensions.						
Trabue, or Trauleue, Chas. C.	Compensation for horse and equipments lost in Seminole war.	23	1	Documents	154	Claims.						
Trabue, or Trauleue, Chas. C.	Compensation for horse and equipments lost in Seminole war.	28	1	Petition	262	Claims.						
Trabue, Daniel	Revolutionary pension	24	1	Petition	260	Rev. Pensions	510	Favorable; bill	507	Passed	Passed	App'd June 28, 1836
Tracy, Alfred, and others	Permission to locate certain land	23	2	Petition	201	Public Lands.						
Tracy, Alfred, and others	Permission to locate certain land	24	1	Petition	114	Public Lands.						
Tracy, Dolly	(See Solomon Tracy, widow of)	30	1		198							
Tracy, Elisha	Compensation for extra services rendered, and to cover losses in discharge of duties.	21	1	Senate bill	442	Claims	354	Adverse	S. 77	Referred to Committee Whole House.		Leave to withdraw.
Tracy, Elisha, administrators of.	Reimbursement of money advanced for use of United States government.	29	1	Petition	519	Claims.						
Tracy, Elisha, representatives of.	Compensation for services as commissary in war of 1812.	30	1	Petition	636	Claims.						
Tracy, Ira, and Joseph Landon.	(See Bateman Fisk, sureties of)	14	2		69							
Tracy, Ira, heirs of	Indemnity for property destroyed by enemy in 1813.	23	1	Resolution	501	Claims.						
Tracy, Levi	Revolutionary pension	22	1	Petition	381	Rev. Pensions	438	Favorable; bill	542	Referred to Committee Whole House.		
Tracy, Nathaniel	Liquidation and settlement of claim against government.	1	2	Petition	274					Referred to Secretary Treasury.		
Tracy, Nathaniel	Liquidation and settlement of claim against government.	2	1	Rep. of Secretary Treasury.	580					Laid on table.		
Tracy, Nathaniel, representatives of.	Payment of two loan office certificates.	24	1	Petition	851	Rev. Claims	799	Favorable; bill	716	Referred to Committee Whole House.		
Tracy, Nathaniel, representatives of.	Payment of two loan office certificates.	25	2	Petition	49	Rev. Claims	120	Favorable; bill	138	Postponed.		
Tracy, Nathaniel, representatives of.	Payment of two loan office certificates.	26	1	Petition	166	Rev. Claims	330	Favorable; bill	302	Referred to Committee Whole House.		
Tracy, Nathaniel, representatives of.	Payment of two loan office certificates.	29	2	Memorial	131	Rev. Claims	76	Minority and majority report and bill.	689	Referred to Committee Whole House.		
Tracy, Nathaniel, representatives of.	Payment of two loan office certificates.	30	1	Petition	136	Rev. Claims	July 19, 1848	Adverse		Laid on table.		
Tracy, Solomon	Revolutionary pension	23	1	Resolution	107	Rev. Pensions				Discharged; laid on table.		
Tracy, Solomon, widow of.	Revolutionary pension	30	1	Petition	198	Rev. Pensions	345	Adverse		Laid on table.		
Tracy, Thomas	Pension	21	1	Petition	353	Invalid Pensions				Discharged; laid on table.		
Tracy, William	Bounty land for services in war of 1812.	30	2	Petition	102	Public Lands.						

List of private claims presented to the House of Representatives of the United States from the 1st to the 31st Congress, inclusive—Continued.

Names of claimants.	Nature or object of the claim.	Congress.	Session.	How brought before the House of Reps.	Page of journal.	To what committee of the House referred.	No. or date of the report.	Nature of the report.	No. of the bill.	How disposed of by the House of Reps.	How disposed of by the Senate.	Date of the act of Congress, and remarks.
Trafton, John	Indemnity against effect of judgment against him by Samuel Bachelder.	22	1	Petition	130	P. Of. & P. Roads.	Jan. 25, 1832	Adverse	......	Laid on table.		
Trafton, John	Indemnity against effect of judgment against him by Samuel Bachelder.	23	1	Petition	153	P. Of. & P. Roads.						
Trafton, John	Indemnity against effect of judgment against him by Samuel Bachelder.	25	2	Petition	110	P. Of. & P. Roads.	659	Adverse	......	Laid on table.		
Trafton, John	Indemnity against effect of judgment against him by Samuel Bachelder.	26	2	Petition	81	Claims	24	Adverse	......	Laid on table.		
Trafton, John	Indemnity against effect of judgment against him by Samuel Bachelder.	27	2	Petition	55	P. Of. & P. Roads.	32	Adverse	......	Laid on table.		
Trafton, John	Indemnity against effect of judgment against him by Samuel Bachelder.	28	1	Petition	132	Claims.						
Trafton, Captain Joshua, heirs and legal representatives of.	Commutation pay	29	1	Memorial	450	Rev. Claims.						
Trafton, Captain Joshua, heirs and legal representatives of.	Commutation pay	29	2	Petition	233	Rev. Claims.						
Trafton, Captain Joshua, heirs and legal representatives of.	Commutation pay	30	1	Petition	635	Rev. Claims.						
Trahan, Gregorie	(See Joseph Green and others.)	2	1	....	581							
Trahand, Jean Marie, heirs of.	Confirmation of title to land	20	2	Petition	41	Priv. Land Claims.						
Trahand, Jean Marie, heirs of.	Confirmation of title to land	21	1	Petition	51	Priv. Land Claims.	89	Favorable; bill	123	Passed	Passed	App'd May 28, 1830
Train, Isaac	Pension	20	2	Petition	49	Rev. Pensions.						
Trainer, Edward	Pension	20	1	Resolution	448	Military Pensions.	....	....	......	Discharged; laid on table.		
Trainer, James, widow of.	Naval pension	14	1	Petition	274	Pens. & Rev. Cl'ms	....	....	......	Discharged; referred to Sec. of War.		
Trainer, Mary	(See James Trainer, widow of.)	14	1	....	274							
Trakem, Amelia & Lethe.	Grant of land under treaty of Dancing Rabbit Creek.	22	1	Resolution	262	Public Lands.						
Tramell, Dennis	Pension	25	2	Senate bill	1155	Rev. Pensions	July 7, 1838	With't amend.	S. 286	Referred to Committee Whole House.		
Tramell, Dennis	Pension	25	3	Petition	130	Rev. Pensions	Jan. 10, 1839	Favorable; bill	1014	Passed	Passed	App'd March 3, 1839
Trapman, Jahucke & Co.	Excess of duties on salt	17	1	Petition	253	Ways and Means	Mar. 6, 1822	Favorable	108	Passed	Passed	App'd May 7, 1822
Transylvania Company	(See Richard Henderson & Co.)	3	2	....	285							
Trask, Primus	(See Primus Hall)	24	2	....	153							
Trask, William, heirs of.	Bounty land for services in war of 1812.	26	1	Petition	701	Priv. Land Claims.	449	Favorable; bill	361	Referred to Committee Whole House.		
Travers, Henry K.	Reward for gallantry	14	1	Petition	249	Naval Affairs	April 11, 181	By bill	......	Passed	Passed	App'd Feb. 8, '17, supplement to act April 29, 1816, in favor of Jos. Stewart, *et al.*
Travers, Jeremiah	Reward for gallantry	14	1	Petition	249	Naval Affairs	April 11, 1816	By bill	......	Passed	Passed	

List of private claims presented to the House of Representatives of the United States from the 1st to the 31st Congress, inclusive—Continued.

Names of claimants.	Nature or object of the claim.	Congress.	Session.	How brought before the House of Reps.	Page of journal.	To what committee of the House referred.	No. or date of the report.	Nature of the report.	No. of the bill.	How disposed of by the House of Reps.	How disposed of by the Senate.	Date of the act of Congress, and remarks.
Travers, John	Relief by special act of Congress as insolvent debtor.	7	1	Petition	153	Select	April 1, 1802	Favorable; bill		Referred to Committee Whole House.		No. of bill not on journal.
Travers, Mathias	Reward for gallantry	14	1	Petition	249	Naval Affairs	April 11, 1816	By bill		Passed	Passed	App'd Feb. 8, '17, supplement to act April 29, 1816, in favor of Jos. Stewart, *et al.*
Traverse, Mathias	Revolutionary pension	21	1	Petition	56	Rev. Pensions	412	Favorable; bill	423	Passed	Passed	App'd June 28, 1836
Travers, Robert Travers, Samuel Travers, Spicer	Reward for gallantry	14	1	Petition	249	Naval Affairs	April 11, 1816	By bill		Passed	Passed	App'd Feb. 8, '17, sup. to act Ap'l 29, '16, in fav'r J. Stewart, *et al.*
Traverse, William	Payment for property taken for use of Georgia volunteers.	25	2	Petition	397	Claims	965	Favorable; bill	837	Referred to Committee Whole House.		
Traverse, William	Payment for property taken for use of Georgia volunteers.	25	3	Bill of last sess.	432	Whole House	Feb. 1, 1839	With't amend.	837	Passed	Passed	App'd March 3, 1839
Traverse, William, heirs of	Indemnity for Indian depredations in Florida.	25	3	Petition	121	Claims	162	Adverse		Laid on table.		
Traverse, William, heirs of	Indemnity for Indian depredations in Florida.	28	1	Petition	133	Claims.						
Traversie, Joseph	Annuity and grant	6	2	Appropriat'n bill.	752	Whole House	Feb. 18, 1801	With amends.	277	Passed	Passed	App'd March 3, 1801
Travis, Joseph	Compensation for property taken for use of United States army.	3	1	Petition	48					Laid on table.		
Travis, Joseph	Compensation for storehouse destroyed in revolutionary war.	15	2	Petition	209	Pens. & Rev. Cl'ms.				Discharged; laid on table.		
Travis, Joseph, widow and heirs of.	Payment of certain certificates issued during revolutionary war.	23	1	Petition	491	Rev. Claims.						
Travis, Joseph	Payment of certain certificates issued during revolutionary war.	28	1	Petition	132	Claims.						
Travis, M. W.	(See Martin S. Aiken, *et al.*)	17	1		359							
Travis, Robert	Revolutionary pension	23	1	Petition	36	Rev. Pensions.						
Travis, Samuel, and others	Usual pay while prisoners in England.	14	1	Petition	392	Naval Affairs	Mar. 20, 1816	Favorable; bill		Passed	Passed	App'd April 27, 1816
Trawbridge, John	(See Noble Benedict, and others)	3	2		299							
Tray, Elijah	Invalid pension	2	2	Rep. of Secretary War.	649	Whole House.						
Tray, Elijah	Invalid pension	3	1	Rep. of Secretary War.	131	Select	May 26, 1794	Res. to refer to Sec. War.	J. R. 12	Passed	Passed	App'd June 9, 1794
Tray, Elijah	Invalid pension	4	1	Rep. of Secretary War.	445	Claims.						
Treadegar Iron Works	(See Virginia, State of)	29	1		576							
Treadwell, Daniel	Invalid pension	10	2	House bill	499	Whole House	Feb. 23, 1809	Bill amended.	158	Passed	Passed	App'd March 3, 1809
Treadwell, Mary	(See Captain William Treadwell, widow of.)	18	1		101							
Treadwell, Moses	Fishing bounty on vessel and cargo.	21	1	Petition	447	Commerce	April 7, 1830	Favorable; bill	410	Referred to Committee Whole House.		
Treadwell, Moses	Fishing bounty on vessel and cargo.	24	1	Petition	479	Commerce	514	Favorable; bill	478	Referred to Committee Whole House.		
Treadwell, Moses	Fishing bounty on vessel and cargo.	25	2	Petition	41	Commerce	Dec. 28, 1837	Adverse		Laid on table.		
Treadwell, Captain Wm., widow of.	Provision to be made for support of.	18	1	Petition	101	Pens. & Rev. Cl'ms.	Jan. 6, 1824	Adverse		Laid on table.		
Treadwell, William, heirs of.	To secure benefit of land warrant.	21	1	Resolution	195	Rev. Claims	150	Favorable; bill	200	Passed	With't amend.	
Treadwell, William, heirs of.	To secure benefit of land warrant.	21	2	Resolution	57	Rev. Claims	57	Favorable; bill	547	Referred to Committee Whole House.		

List of private claims presented to the House of Representatives of the United States from the 1st to the 31st Congress, inclusive—Continued.

Names of claimants.	Nature or object of the claim.	Congress.	Session.	How brought before the House of Reps.	Page of journal.	To what committee of the House referred.	No. or date of the report.	Nature of the report.	No. of the bill.	How disposed of by the House of Reps.	How disposed of by the Senate.	Date of the act of Congress, and remarks.
Treasure, Richard	Indemnity against a fraud	4	1	Petition	450	Claims	May 7, 1796	Adverse.				
Treat, Anna	Relief; son slain in service of United States.	1	2	Petition	158	Ref'd to Secretary War.	Mar. 19, 1790	Report		Laid on table.		
Treat, Charles	Grant of land for services in revolutionary war.	12	1	Petition	22	Public Lands.						
Treat, Charles	Increase of pension and bounty land.	21	1	Petition	120	Rev. Pensions	April 7, 1830	Adverse		Laid on table.		
Tredick, Henry, jr	Indemnity for French spoliations prior to 1800.	26	1	Memorial	182	Foreign Affairs	343	Favorable; bill	319	Referred to Committee Whole House.		
Treat, Samuel	Indemnity for losses sustained by naval contract.	22	1	Petition	378	Naval Affairs.						
Trefoe, Charles & Michael.	(See Philipina Beckley, heirs of.)	11	2		227							
Tregal, Roger	Reward for gallantry	14	1	Petition	249	Naval Affairs	April 11, 1816	By bill		Passed	Passed	Feb. 18, 1817, supplement to act of April 29, 1816, in favor of Jos. Stewart, *et al.*
Tregarie, Louis, assignee of.	Land claim in Louisiana	24	1	Rep. of Secretary Treasury.	362	Priv. Land Claims.						
Treglohan, Philip, representatives of.	Compensation for services as pilot in United States navy.	2	1	Petition	501					Referred to Secretary War.		
Tregg, Samuel	Invalid pension	5	3	Memorial	478	Claims	Mar. 2, 1799	Adverse		Laid on table.		
Tregg, Samuel	Invalid pension	6	1	Petition	605	Claims	April 11, 1800			Leave to withdraw.		
Tregg, Samuel	Invalid pension	6	2	Petition	735	Claims	Dec. 15, 1800	Adverse		Laid on table.		
Trego, Eli, and others	(See John Kirlin, executors of.)	18	2		229							
Tremper, John J	Confirmation of Yazoo land title	21	1	Petition	59	Claims	April 2, 1830	Adverse		Laid on table.		
Trenchard, Edward, widow of.	Naval pension	22	2	Petition	54	Naval Pensions.						
Trenchard, Edward, widow of.	Naval pension	23	1	Petition	74	Naval Pensions.						
Trenchard, Edward, widow of.	Pension from death of husband to June 30, 1834.	23	2	Petition	102	Naval Pensions	Feb. 25, 1835	Adverse		Laid on table.		
Trenchard, Edward, and others.	Restoration of pension	28	1	Petition & mem'l	78, 104	Naval Affairs.				Discharged; referred to Com. Whole House.		
Trenchard, Edward, and others.	Restoration of pension	28	2	Petition	73	Rev. Pensions.						
Trenholm, George A	(See John Fraser and G. A. Trenholm.)	28	1		76							
Trenholm, John H., and Wm. M. Belt, assignee of.	Relief on account of loss by contract for public printing.	31	1	Senate amend'nt to House bill.	1509	Ways and Means			334	Disagreed to.		
Trent, John	Captains half pension	5	2	House bill	127	Whole House	Jan. 11, 1798	With amend.	38	Passed	Passed	App'd Feb. 2, 1798
Trepagnie, Augustine	(See Joseph Green, and others)	2	1		581							
Trepagnie, Prique	(See Joseph Green, and others)	2	1		581							
Tressler, Frederick	Revolutionary pension	28	1	Petition	251	Rev. Pensions.				Discharged; laid on table.		
Trevett, Benjamin, heirs of.	Compensation for naval services	25	2	Petition	574	Naval Affairs				Discharged; laid on table.		
Trevett, Samuel R., and others.	Increase of compensation	16	1	Petition	249	Commerce				Discharged; laid on table.		
Treville, John D	(See John De Treville, heirs of)	23	2		256							
Trevitt, Robert	Arrears of pension	29	2	Petition	53	Invalid Pensions.						
Trevitt, Robert	Arrears of pension	31	1	Petition	582	Invalid Pensions	389	Adverse		Laid on table.		

List of private claims presented to the House of Representatives of the United States from the 1st to the 31st Congress, inclusive—Continued.

Names of claimants.	Nature or object of the claim.	Congress.	Session.	How brought before the House of Reps.	Page of journal.	To what committee of the House referred.	No. or date of the report.	Nature of the report.	No. of the bill.	How disposed of by the House of Reps.	How disposed of by the Senate.	Date of the act of Congress, and remarks.
Trezevant, Peter, for wife.	(See Robert Farquhar, heir of) ..	3	1	....	78							
Trezevant, Peter	Settlement of accounts; vouchers burnt in public office.	18	1	Petition	253	Claims.						
Tribble, Alfred..........	Permission to enter land at certain price.	23	2	Petition	348	Public Lands.						
Tribon, Francis	Invalid pension...............	30	1	Memorial	675	Invalid Pensions ..	704	Favorable; bill	550	Referred to Committee Whole House.		
Tribon, Francis	Invalid pension...............	30	2	Bill of last sess..	319	Whole House	Jan. 26, 1849	With't amend	550	Passed.		
Tribon, Francis	Invalid pension...............	31	1	Petition	417	Invalid Pensions.						
Tribon, Francis	Invalid pension...............	31	2	Petition	443	Invalid Pensions ..	79	Favorable; bill	483	Referred to Committee Whole House.		
Trickel, Emanuel	Confirmation of title to land	18	2	Report of register and receiver of land office.	182, 287	Public Lands.....	....	....	......	Referred to Secretary Treasury.		
Trickel, Emanuel	Confirmation of title to land	19	1	Report of register and receiver of land office.	64	Public Lands.....	33 May 5, 1826	Adverse ...... Favorable; bill	 254	Recommitted. Referred to Committee Whole House.		
Trickel, Emanuel, widow and heirs of.	Confirmation of title to land	27	2	Petition	140	Priv. Land Claims.	280	Favorable; bill	246	Passed.		
Trickel, Emanuel, widow and heirs of.	Confirmation of title to land	27	3	Petition	188	Priv. Land Claims.						
Trigg, Samuel	Invalid pension..............	5	3	Petition	478	Claims..........	March 2, 1799	Adverse	......	Laid on table.		
Trigg, Samuel..........	Invalid pension..............	6	1	Petition	605	Claims	April 11, 1800	Adverse	......	Leave to withdraw.		
Trigg, Samuel..........	Invalid pension..............	6	2	Petition	735	Claims	Dec. 15, 1800	Adverse.......	......	Rejected.		
Trigg, Stephen, heirs of ..	Seven years' half-pay	23	1	Petition	57	Rev. Claims......						
Trigg, Wm., and others ..	(See Stephen Trigg, heirs of) ...	23	1	....	57							
Trigg, Major William....	Compensation for horse and other property lost in public service.	23	1	Petition	47	Claims	Dec. 20, 1833	Adverse.......	......	Laid on table.		
Trigg, Major William....	Compensation for horse and other property lost in public service.	28	1	Petition	335	Claims.						
Trim, Benjamin H.......	Revolutionary pension..........	17	2	Resolution	184	Rev. Pensions	....	....	......	Discharged; aid on table.		
Trim, Benjamin H.......	Revolutionary pension..........	20	2	Petition	82	Rev. Pensions	....	....	......	Discharged; laid on table.		
Trim, Benjamin H.......	Revolutionary pension..........	21	1	Petit'on	49	Rev. Pensions	....	....	......	Discharged; laid on table.		
Trimble, James	Permission to change location of land.	23	1	Petition	382	Public Lands.						
Trimble, John	Increase of pension	27	2	Petition	1050	Invalid Pensions.						
Trimble, John	Increase of pension	29	1	Petition	370	Invalid Pensions..	....	....	......	Discharged; laid on table.		
Trimble, Joseph.........	Invalid pension...............	22	1	Resolution	194	Invalid Pensions ..	292	Favorable; bill	377	Passed	Ref'd to Com. on Pensions.	
Trimble, Joseph.........	Invalid pension...............	23	1	Resolution	82	Invalid Pensions ..	69	Favorable; bill	79	Passed	Passed, with amendment.	App'd June 30, 1834
Triole & Co............	Permission to fund certain loan office certificates.	5	2	Petition	130	Whole House.						
Tripania, Delphine Isabelle.	(See Francis B. De Bellvue, widow of)	28	2	....	56							
Tripe, Thomas..........	Extension of patent right........	16	1	Petition	249	Judiciary	....	....	......	Discharged; laid on table.		
Tripler, Thomas	Discharge from prison at suit of United States.	16	2	Petition	47	Judiciary.						

List of private claims presented to the House of Representatives of the United States from the 1st to the 31st Congress, inclusive—Continued.

Names of claimants.	Nature or object of the claim.	Congress.	Session.	How brought before the House of Reps.	Page of journal.	To what committee of the House referred.	No. or date of the report.	Nature of the report.	No. of the bill.	How disposed of by the House of Reps.	How disposed of by the Senate.	Date of the act of Congress, and remarks.
Triplett, George, heirs of.	Commutation of half-pay	22	2	Petition	118	Rev. Claims.						
Triplett, Hedgeman, (Ky.)	Commutation of half-pay	22	2	Petition	105	Select	Feb. 11, 1833	Favorable; bill	733	Referred to Committee Whole House.		
Triplett, Hedgeman, (Ky.)	Commutation of half-pay	23	1	Petition	158	Rev. Claims.						
Triplett, Peter	Pension	19	1	Resolution	141	Rev. Pensions	164	Adverse.	......	Laid on table.		
Triplett, Peter	Arrears of pension	21	2	Petition	68	Military Pensions.						
Triplett, Peter	Arrears of pension	22	1	Petition	105	Rev. Pensions.						
Triplett, Peter	Arrears of pension	23	1	Petition	97	Rev. Pensions	June 16, 1834	Favorable; bill	368	Referred to Committee Whole House.		
Triplett, Peter	Arrears of pension	23	2	Bill of last sess.	337	Whole House	Feb. 6, 1835	With't amend.	368	Passed	Passed	App'd March 3, 1835
Triplett, Sarah	Revolutionary pension	29	1	Petition	103	Rev. Pensions	617	Adverse	......	Laid on table.		
Triplett, Thomas T.	Compensation for services as commissioner for assessing the improvements made by Creek Indians.	22	2	Resolution	341	Indian Affairs	Feb. 26, 1833	Favorable; bill	755	Referred to Committee Whole House.		
Triplett, Thomas T.	Compensation for services as commissioner for assessing the improvements made by Creek Indians.	23	1	Petition	67	Indian Affairs	Mar. 16, 1834	Favorable; bill	368	Referred to Committee Whole House.		
Triplett, Thomas T.	Compensation for services as commissioner for assessing the improvements made by Creek Indians.	23	2	Resolution	305	Indian Affairs.						
Triplett, Thomas T.	Compensation for services as commissioner for assessing the improvements made by Creek Indians.	24	1	Petition	153	Indian Affairs	587	Favorable; bill	568	Referred to Committee Whole House.		
Triplett, Thomas T.	Compensation for services as commissioner for assessing the improvements made by Creek Indians.	25	2	Resolution	43	Indian Affairs	211	Favorable; bill	247	Referred to Committee Whole House.		
Triplett, Thomas T.	Compensation for services as commissioner for assessing the improvements made by Creek Indians.	25	3	Bill of last sess.	376	Whole House	Jan. 25, 1839	With't amend.	247	Passed	Passed	App'd March 2, 1839
Triplett, sen., Thomas	Commutation of half-pay	22	1	Petition	62	Rev. Claims	96	Favorable; bill	186	Referred to Committee Whole House.		
Triplett, sen., Thomas	Commutation of half-pay	22	2	Bill of last sess.	66	Whole House	Dec. 15, 1832	With't amend.	186	Passed	Passed	App'd March 2, 1833
Triplett, Thomas, heirs of.	Repayment of money erroneously paid another.	24	1	Memorial	870	Rev. Claims.						
Triplett, Thomas, heirs of.	Repayment of money erroneously paid another.	24	2	Memorial	126	Rev. Claims.						
Triplett, Thomas, heirs of.	Repayment of money erroneously paid another.	25	2	Memorial	70	Rev. Claims	563	Favorable; bill	552	Postponed.		
Triplett, Thomas, heirs of.	Repayment of money erroneously paid another.	25	3	House bill	264	Rev. Claims	173	Adverse	552	Laid on table.		
Triplett, Thomas, jr., and H. Daniel.	To adjust and compromise claim in favor of United States.	27	2	Senate bill	1169	Judiciary	Aug. 20, 1842	With't amend.	296	Passed	....	App'd Aug. 29, 1842
Triplett, William	(See Stephen Decatur, widow of, *et al.*)	23	1	....	36	....	45	....	50			
Triplett, William, heirs of.	Commutation pay	23	1	Petition	221	Rev. Claims.						
Triplett, William	Confirmation of title to land	28	2	Petition	172	Public Lands.						

List of private claims presented to the House of Representatives of the United States from the 1st to the 31st Congress, inclusive—Continued.

Names of claimants.	Nature or object of the claim.	Congress.	Session.	How brought before the House of Reps.	Page of journal.	To what committee of the House referred.	No. or date of the report.	Nature of the report.	No. of the bill.	How disposed of by the House of Reps.	How disposed of by the Senate.	Date of the act of Congress, and remarks.
Triplett, William	Confirmation of title to land	29	2	Petition	168	Priv. Land Claims.	57	Favorable; bill	659	Referred to Committee Whole House.		
Triplett, William	Confirmation of title to land	30	1	Petition	239	Priv. Land Claims.	183	Favorable; bill	193	Passed	Passed	App'd Aug. 14, 1848
Tripp, Gilbert T.	Compensation for services as a seaman on board of the United States ships Cayene and Erie.	28	2	Petition	354	Naval Affairs.						
Tripp, George W., & others	Confirmation to a pre-emption purchase.	25	3	Petition	463	Priv. Land Claims.						
Tripp, George W., & others	Confirmation to a pre-emption purchase.	28	1	Petition	159	Public Lands	32	Adverse		Laid on table.		
Tripp, Henry D. and Mary	(See Jacob Doggett, heirs of.)	15	2		28							
Tripp, Lemuel	Fishing bounty	15	1	Petition	242	Com. and Munuf.				Discharged; laid on table.		
Trofton, Elias D., *et al.*	Compensation for services in Rhode Island brigade.	14	2	Petition	283	Priv. Land Claims.						
Trofton, Elias D., *et al.*	Compensation for services in Rhode Island brigade.	23	2	Memorial	67	Select	Feb. 25, 1835	Favorable; bill	769	Referred to Committee Whole House.		
Trofton, Elias D, *et al.*	Compensation for services in Rhode Island brigade.	24	1	Documents	136	Select	337	Favorable; bill	352	Referred to Committee Whole House.		
Trofton, Jotham	Revolutionary pension	24	1	Resolution	666	Rev. Pensions				Discharged; laid on table.		
Troop, John	Remission of forfeiture on vessel and cargo.	14	2	Petition	427	Com. and Manuf.				Discharged; laid on table.		
Troskslawski, Joseph	Compensation for services as surveyor of Greensburg district, Louisiana.	31	1	Petition	511	Public Lands.						
Trotman, William	(See Joshua W. Prout, administrator of.)	18	2		284				S. 41			
Trott, Adolphus G.	For letters patent to issue	18	2	Senate bill	131	Judiciary	Jan. 28, 1825	With't amend.	S. 16	Passed		App'd Feb. 5, 1825
Trott, John, (R. I.)	(See Freeborn Sisson, and others)	14	1		449							
Trotter, George J.	Compensation for carrying United States mail.	27	2	Petition	818	P. Of. & P. Roads.						
Trotter, George J.	Compensation for carrying United States mail.	27	3	Petition	188	P. Of. & P. Roads.				Discharged; laid on table.		
Trotter, Joseph	Money in lieu of land	24	1	Gen. appropriat'n bill.	1012	Whole House	June 27, 1836	With amends.	695	Passed	Passed	App'd July 2, 1836
Trotter, Loudon, daughter of.	Pension	27	2	Petition	936	Rev. Pensions				Discharged; laid on table.		
Trotter, Loudon, daughter of.	Pension	28	1	Petition	609	Rev. Pensions.						
Trotter, William B.	Indemnity on contract for losses in supplying rations to Indians.	24	1	Petition	96	Indian Affairs.						
Trougot, Reynhart	Revolutionary pension	22	1	Petition	865	Rev. Pensions.						
Trougot, Reynhart	Revolutionary pension	22	2	Resolution	57	Rev. Pensions	Jan. 7, 1833	Favorable; bill	664	Referred to Committee Whole House.		
Trougot, Reynhart	Revolutionary pension	26	1	Petition	797	Rev. Pensions.						
Trougot, Reynhart	Revolutionary pension	26	2	Petition	87					Discharged; laid on table.		
Trouillet, Alexis, & others	(See Lewis Baudin, & others)	15	2	Petition	33							
Trouillet, Isabella, assignee of.	Confirmation of title to land in Alabama.	24	2	Petition	83	Priv. Land Claims.				Discharged; laid on table.		
Trouillet, Isabella, assignee of.	Confirmation of title to land in Alabama.	25	2	Petition	180	Priv. Land Claims.						

List of private claims presented to the House of Representatives of the United States from the 1st to the 31st Congress, inclusive—Continued.

Names of claimants.	Nature or object of the claim.	Congress.	Session.	How brought before the House of Reps.	Page of journal.	To what committee of the House referred.	No. or date of the report.	Nature of the report.	No. of the bill.	How disposed of by the House of Reps.	How disposed of by the Senate.	Date of the act of Congress, and remarks.
Trouillet, John, legal representatives of.	Confirmation of title to land	15	1	Petition	212	Priv. Land Claims.	Feb. 18, 1818	By bill	92	Passed	Passed	App'd April 9, 1818
Trouillet, Louis Lefroid, & others.	(See Peter, Trouillet, heirs of)	12	1		60							
Trouillet, Peter, heirs of	Confirmation of title to land	12	1	Petition	60	Public Lands.						
Trouillet, Peter, heirs of	Confirmation of title to land	13	1	Petition	57	Public Lands.						
Trouillet, Peter, heirs of	Confirmation of title to land	15	1	Petition	212	Priv. Land Claims.	Mar. 10, 1818	Favorable; bill	131	Referred to Committee Whole House.		
Trouillet, Peter, heirs of	Confirmation of title to land	15	2	House bill	115	Whole House			131			
Trouillet, Peter, heirs of	Confirmation of title to land	22	1	Petition	594	Priv. Land Claims.						
Trouin, Francis	Revolutionary pension	6	2	Petition	780	Claims	Feb. 10, 1801	Adverse		Laid on table.		
Trousdale, Cincinnatus, & John G. Connelly.	Same pay as is allowed to United States officers for appointments temporarily filled by them in Mexican war.	31	1	Senate bill	998	Military Affairs			S. 13			
Trousdale, Cincinnatus, & John G. Connelly.	Same pay as is allowed to United States officers for appointments temporarily filled by them in Mexican war.	31	2	Senate bill	291	Military Affairs	Feb. 18, 1851	Without amend.	S. 13	Passed		App'd March 3, 1831
Trouster, A. J.	(See David R. Denham, & others)	25	3		121		162					
Trout, Jeremiah	Invalid pens on	27	2	Papers	68	Invalid Pensions	217	Adverse		Laid on table.		
Troutman, Geo., & others.	Compensation for provisions furnished United States army in 1812.	17	1	Petition	100	Claims.						
Trover, John, (Ky.)	Pension	20	2	Petition	31	Rev. Pensions				Discharged; referred to Com. Whole House.		
Trover, John, (Ky.)	Pension	21	1	Petition	47	Military Pensions.						
Trover, John, (Ky.)	Pension	21	2	Petition	68	Military Pensions.						
Trover, John, (Ky.)	Pension	22	1	Petition	113	Rev. Pensions.						
Trow, Bartholomew, heirs of.	Remuneration for revolutionary services.	25	2	Memorial	53	Claims	334	Adverse		Laid on table.		
Trow, Bartholomew, heirs of.	Remuneration for revolutionary services.	25	3	Petition	335	Rev. Claims				Discharged.		
Trow, Bartholomew, heirs of.	Remuneration for revolutionary services.	26	1	Petition	739	Rev. Claims.						
Trow, Bartholomew, heirs of.	Remuneration for revolutionary services.	27	2	Petition	154	Rev. Claims	223	Adverse		Laid on table.		
Trow, Solomon	Revolutionary pension	2	1	Petition	542					Referred to Secretary War.		
Trow, Solomon	Revolutionary pension	2	2	Petition	623					Laid on table.		
Trowbridge, Cynthia	(See Ira Trowbridge, widow of)	25	2		406							
Trowbridge, Ira, widow of.	Pension	25	2	Petition	406	Invalid Pensions				Discharged; laid on table.		
Trowbridge, Isaac	Release from contract to carry U. States mail.	1	2	Petition	158	Postmaster General.	Mar. 17, 1790	Report		Laid on table.		
Trowbridge, James	(See Martin S. Aiken, *et al.*)	17	1		359							
Trowbridge, James	Pension	11	3	House bill	283	Whole House	Mar. 23, 1810	With amend.	107	Passed	Passed	App'd March 3, 1811
Trowbridge, James	Increase of pension	21	2	Petition	127	Military Pensions.						
Trowbridge, James	Increase of pension	22	1	Petition	72	Invalid Pensions	Jan. 10, 1832	Adverse		Laid on table.		
Trowbridge, John, (Ky.)	Invalid pension	25	3	Petition	461	Invalid Pensions.						
Trowbridge, John, (Ky.)	Invalid pension	26	1	Petition	163	Invalid Pensions	278	Adverse		Laid on table.		
Trowbridge, Stephen	Restoration of pension	17	2	Petition	163	Whole House				Leave to withdraw.		
Troxell, Abraham	Pension	19	1	Petition	52	Rev. Pensions	164	Adverse		Laid on table.		
Troxell, David, (Tenn.)	Invalid pension	29	1	Petition	472	Invalid Pensions.						

List of private claims presented to the House of Representatives of the United States from the 1st to the 31st Congress, inclusive—Continued.

Names of claimants.	Nature or object of the claim.	Congress.	Session.	How brought before the House of Reps.	Page of journal.	To what committee of the House referred.	No. or date of the report.	Nature of the report.	No. of the bill.	How disposed of by the House of Reps.	How disposed of by the Senate.	Date of the act of Congress, and remarks.
Troxell, David, (Tenn.)	Invalid pension	30	1	Petition	435	Rev. Pensions	695	Adverse		Laid on table.		
Troxell, David, (Tenn.)	Invalid pension	31	1	Petition	276	Invalid Pensions				Discharged; and to Rev. Pensions.		
Troxell, David, (Tenn.)	Invalid pension	31	2	Petition	431	Rev. Pensions	53	Adverse		Laid on table.		
Truax, Abraham C	Payment of claim	20	1	Senate bill	414	Claims	Mar. 24, 1828	With't amend.	S. 78	Passed		App'd May 24, 1828
Truax, Abraham, widow of	Revolutionary pension	25	2	Resolution	531	Rev. Pensions				Discharged; laid on table.		
Truax, Abraham, widow of	Revolutionary pension	26	1	Petition	175	Rev. Pensions				Discharged; laid on table.		
Truax, Elizabeth	(See Abraham Truax, widow of.)	25	2		531							
Truby, Samuel	Pension	14	1	Petition	41	Pens. & Rev. Cl'ms.		Favorable; bill		Passed	Passed	App'd April 30, 1816
Trudeau, Charles Levalle	Permission to locate land confirmed	14	1	Petition	180	Public Lands	Feb. 2, 1816	Favorable; bill	66	Passed	Passed, with amendment.	App'd April 27, 1816
Trudeau, Charlotte P	Confirmation of title to land in Mississippi.	16	1	Petition	46	Priv. Land Claims.	Jan. 13, 1820	Adverse		Leave to withdraw.		
Trudeau, Rene, and wife	(See Dr. John Watkins, heirs of.)	15	1		280							
Trudeau, Rene	Confirmation of title to land in Louisiana.	24	2	Petition	273	Priv. Land Claims.						
Trudeau, Rene	(See Louis Brazeaux, legal representatives of.)	25	2		418							
True, Samuel	Pension and bounty land warrant.	29	1	Petition	101	Invalid Pensions				Discharged; laid on table.		
Truehart, Daniel, heirs of.	Indemnity for property destroyed by enemy in revolutionary war.	25	2	Petition	546	Rev. Claims				Discharged; laid on table.		
Truehart, Daniel, heirs of.	Indemnity for property destroyed by enemy in revolutionary war.	25	3	Petition	85	Rev. Claims				Discharged.		
Truehart, Daniel, heirs of.	Indemnity for property destroyed by enemy in revolutionary war.	26	1	Petition	166	Rev. Claims.						
Truehart, Daniel, heirs of.	Indemnity for property destroyed by enemy in revolutionary war.	27	2	Petition	62	Rev. Claims	1073	Adverse		Laid on table.		
Trueman, Maj. Alexander, children of.	Compensation for services rendered United States.	2	2	House bill	628	Whole House	Nov. 28, 1792	By bill	199	Passed	Passed	App'd Feb. 27, 1793
Trueman, Maj. Alexander, children of.	Further provisions for	6	1	Petition	535	Claims	Mar. 14, 1800	Favorable; bill	244	Passed	Passed	App'd May 14, 1800
Trueman, Maj. Alexander, children of.	Further provisions for	6	2	Appropriat'n bill.	752	Whole House	Feb. 18, 1801	With amends.	277	Passed	Passed	App'd March 3, 1801
Trueman, John	Revolutionary pension	2	1	Petition	554					Referred to Secretary War.		
Trueman, John	Revolutionary pension	3	2	Rep. of Secretary War.	278					Laid on table.		
Trull, George	To refund excess of duties	29	1	House bill	206	Whole House	Feb. 27, 1846	By bill	54	Passed	Title amended, and passed.	App'd Aug. 8, 1846
Trumble, James	Permission to locate land in lieu of others.	24	1	Petition	112	Priv. Land Claims.	140	Favorable; bill	147	Passed	Indef. postp'd.	
Trumbull, George	(See George Turnbull.)	22	1		116		247					
Trumbull, Gurdon	Balance due superintendent of public works.	23	1	Gen'l appropriation bill.	283	Whole House			283	Passed.	Passed	App'd June 27, 1834
Trumento, Agostino	Drawback on spirits	18	2	Petition	186	Ways and Means.						
Truslow, Benjamin	Revolutionary pension	27	2	Petition	747	Rev. Pensions	962	Favorable; bill	561	Ordered to 3d reading.		
Truslow, Benjamin	Revolutionary pension	27	3	Bill of last sess.	89				561	Passed	Passed	App'd March 3, 1843
Trussel, Moses	Increase of pension	13	1	House bill	56	Whole House	July 20, 1813	With't amend.	31	Passed	Passed	App'd Aug. 2, 1813
Truex, John, by Catherine widow of.	Revolutionary pension	22	1	Petition	143	Rev. Pensions				Discharged; laid on table.		

List of private claims presented to the House of Representatives of the United States from the 1st to the 31st Congress, inclusive—Continued.

Names of claimants.	Nature or object of the claim.	Congress.	Session.	How brought before the House of Reps.	Page of journal.	To what committee of the House referred.	No. or date of the report.	Nature of the report.	No. of the bill.	How disposed of by the House of Reps.	How disposed of by the Senate.	Date of the act of Congress, and remarks.
Truxton, Commodore, estate of.	Indemnity for French spoliations prior to 1800.	26	1	Memorial	182	Foreign Affairs	343	Favorable; bill	319	Referred to Committee Whole House.		
Truxton, Thomas, heirs of.	Prize money for capture of French frigate.	22	2	Petition	105	Naval Affairs	87	Adverse		Laid on table.		
Tryer, Andrew	Restoration of pension	17	1	Petition	37	Rev. Pensions				Disch'd; laid on table.		
Tayon, Edward K	Relief on account of loss of goods by falling of public store-house in Philadelphia.	31	1	Petition	1467	Ways and Means.						
Tryon, Jeremiah	Remuneration for services and sufferings in 1791.	24	2	Petition	311	Invalid Pensions.						
Tryon, Moses	Difference in salvage as per acts of 1799 and 1800 and other relief.	8	1	Petition	409	Claims	Mar. 13, 1804			Postponed.		
Tryon, Moses	Difference in salvage as per acts of 1799 and 1800 and other relief.	8	2	Petition	6	Claims.						
Tryon, Moses	Difference in salvage as per acts of 1799 and 1800 and other relief.	9	1	Petition	199	Claims	April 11, 1806	Report		Indefinitely postponed.		
Tryon, Moses	Difference in salvage as per acts of 1799 and 1800 and other relief.	9	2	Petition	481	Claims.						
Tryon, Moses	Difference in salvage as per acts of 1799 and 1800 and other relief.	12	1	Memorial	92	Claims.						
Tryon, Moses	Difference in salvage as per acts of 1799 and 1800 and other relief.	14	2	Petition	141					Referred to Secretary Navy.		
Tryon, Solomon	Revolutionary pension	24	2	Petition	45	Rev. Pensions	12	Adverse		Laid on table.		
Tryon, William, (N. Y.).	Indemnity for loss of property by the United States troops and for house rent.	18	1	Petition	295	Claims.						
Tryon, William, (N. Y.).	Indemnity for loss of property by the United States troops and for house rent.	19	2	Petition	217	Claims				Discharged.		
Tryon, William, (N. Y.).	Indemnity for loss of property by the United States troops and for house rent.	20	1	Petition	196	Claims	Mar. 24, 1828	Report		Laid on table.		
Tryon, William, (N. Y.).	Indemnity for loss of property by the United States troops and for house rent.	21	1	Petition	472	Claims	April 20, 1830	Adverse		Laid on table.		
Tryon, William, (N. Y.).	Indemnity for loss of property by the United States troops and for house rent.	21	2	Petition	271	Claims				Discharged; referred to Com. of Claims.		
Tryon, William, (N. Y.).	Indemnity for loss of property by the United States troops and for house rent.	22	1	Petition	222	Claims	Jan. 30, 1832	Adverse		Laid on table.		
Tryon, William, (N. Y.).	Indemnity for loss of property by the United States troops and for house rent.	25	2	Resolution	530, 574	Claims	May 11, 1838	Adverse		Laid on table.		
Tryon, William, (N. Y.).	Indemnity for loss of property by the United States troops and for house rent.	25	3	Petition	122	Claims	106	Adverse		Laid on table.		
Tryon, William, (N. Y.).	Indemnity for loss of property by the United States troops and for house rent.	26	1	Petition	702	Claims.						
Tryon, William, (N. Y.).	Indemnity for loss of property by the United States troops and for house rent.	27	2	Petition	55	Claims	26	Adverse		Laid on table.		

List of private claims presented to the House of Representatives of the United States from the 1st to the 31st Congress, inclusive—**Continued.**

Names of claimants.	Nature or object of the claim.	Congress.	Session.	How brought before the House of Reps.	Page of journal.	To what committee of the House referred.	No. or date of the report.	Nature of the report.	No. of the bill.	How disposed of by the House of Reps.	How disposed of by the Senate.	Date of the act of Congress, and remarks.
Tscheffely, Frederick D.	Compensation for extra services as clerk in the General Land Office.	19	2	Petition	26	Claims	11	Adverse	......	Laid on table.		
Tschudy, Catharine	Pre-emption right to land	18	1	House bill	151	Whole House	May 13, 1824	With amend.	65	Passed.	Passed	App'd May 26, 1824
Tubberman, Henry	Not stated on journal	15	1	....	452	....	....	....	......	Leave to withdraw.		
Tubbs, Annanias	Invalid pension	11	2	House bill	483	Whole House	April 9, 1810	With amends.	107	Passed	Passed	App'd April 27, 1810
Tubbs, Ichabod	Revolutionary pension	21	2	Petition	61	Military Pensions.						
Tubbs, Ichabod	Revolutionary pension	22	1	Petition	287	Military Pensions.						
Tubbs, John	Revolutionary pension	23	1	Petition	113	Rev. Pensions	....	....	......	Discharged; laid on table.		
Tubbs, John, heirs of	Revolutionary pension	25	2	Petition	391	Rev. Pensions	....	....	......	Discharged; laid on table.		
Tubbs, Samuel, *et al*	Remuneration for suffering at Wyoming massacre.	25	2	Petition	867	Rev. Claims	863	Adverse	......	Laid on table.		
Tuck, Eady	(See John Tuck, widow of)	30	1	....	137							
Tuck, Edward	Invalid pension	10	2	House bill	499	Whole House	March 2, 1809	With amends.	158	Passed	Passed	App'd March 3, 1809
Tuck, Gideon, *et al.*	Indemnity for French spoliations prior to 1800.	31	1	Petition	407	Commerce.						
Tuck, John, widow of	Revolutionary pension	30	1	Petition	137	Rev. Pensions.						
Tuck, John, widow of	Revolutionary pension	30	2	Petition	121	Rev. Pensions	68	Favorable; bill	768	Referred to Committee Whole House.		
Tuck, John, widow of	Revolutionary pension	31	1	Petition	624	Rev. Pensions	311	Adverse	......	Laid on table.		
Tuck, Richard	Relief; seizure and condemnation of sloop Swift.	11	3	Petition	515	Com. and Manuf.						
Tuck, Samuel B	Compensation for coal furnished government.	26	1	Petition	939	Claims.						
Tuck, Samuel B	Compensation for coal furnished government.	26	2	Petition	80	Claims	105	Adverse	......	Laid on table.		
Tuck, Samuel B	Compensation for coal furnished government.	27	2	Petition	459	Claims	734	Adverse	......	Laid on table.		
Tuck, Samuel B	Compensation for coal furnished government.	27	3	Petition	43	Claims	3	Favorable; bill	621	Passed	Indef. postp'd.	
Tuck, Samuel B	Compensation for coal furnished government.	28	1	Petition	71	Claims	71	Favorable; bill	93	Passed	Passed	Appd June 15, 1844
Tucker, Aaron	Invalid pension	24	2	Petition	71	Invalid Pensions	74	Favorable; bill	820	Referred to Committee Whole House.		
Tucker, Aaron	Invalid pension	25	2	Petition	163	Invalid Pensions	574	Favorable; bill	564	Passed	Passed	App'd July 7, 183
Tucker, Aaron	Arrears of pension	29	1	Petition	65	Invalid Pensions	Jan. 14, 1846	Adverse	.....	Laid on table.		
Tucker, Aaron	Arrears of pension	30	1	Petition	204	Invalid Pensions	196	Favorable; bill	206	Passed	Adverse.	
Tucker, Amy	(See Benj. Lawson, former widow of.)	23	2	....	49							
Tucker, Catharine	(See F. W. Geyer, heir of.)	31	1	....	409	....	355	....	318			
Tucker, Daniel	(See Canadian refugees)	4	2	....	614							
Tucker, Daniel	Compensation for services as deputy quartermaster in revolutionary war.	4	1	Rep. of Secretary Treasury.	388	Claims	74	Adverse	......	Laid on table.		
Tucker, Daniel, administrator of.	Credit for vouchers destroyed by fire.	3	2	Petition	286	Claims	Mar. 2, 1795	Adverse	......	Laid on table.		
Tucker, Daniel, administrator of.	Credit for vouchers destroyed by fire.	4	1	Petition	598	Claims	May 31, 1796	Adverse	......	Laid on table.		
Tucker, David	Revolutionary pension	26	1	Petition	937	Rev. Pensions	714	Adverse	......	Laid on table.		
Tucker, George, heirs of.	Confirmation of title to land	26	2	Senate bill	178	Priv. Land Claims.	Feb. 12, 1841	With't amend.	S. 83	Referred to Committee Whole House.		

List of private claims presented to the House of Representatives of the United States from the 1st to the 31st Congress, inclusive—Continued.

Names of claimants.	Nature or object of the claim.	Congress.	Session.	How brought before the House of Reps.	Page of journal.	To what committee of the House referred.	No. or date of the report.	Nature of the report.	No. of the bill.	How disposed of by the House of Reps.	How disposed of by the Senate.	Date of the act of Congress, and remarks.
Tucker, Gideon	Indemnity for French spoliations prior to 1800.	26	1	Memorial	182	Foreign Affairs	343	Favorable; bill	319	Referred to Committee Whole House.		
Tucker, Gideon	(See Benj. Goodhue, executor of.)	26	1		182							
Tucker, Gideon	(See Thomas Perkins, executor of)	26	1		182							
Tucker, Gideon, *et al.*	Indemnity for French spoliations prior to 1800.	29	2	Memorial	113	Foreign Affairs.						
Tucker, Huldah	(See Zephaniah Tucker, widow of)	25	2		54							
Tucker, James	Bounty land for services in United States army.	13	3	Petition	467	Pens. & Rev. Cl'ms.				Discharged		Leave to withdraw.
Tucker, James, and John Judge.	Compensation for improvement in manufacture of anchors.	22	2	Petition	313	Naval Affairs	Feb. 27, 1833	Report		Referred to Secretary of Navy.		
Tucker, James, and John Judge.	Compensation for improvement in manufacture of anchors.	23	1	Rep. of Secretary Navy.	78	Naval Affairs	428	Favorable; bill	454	Referred to Committee Whole House.		
Tucker, James, and John Judge.	Compensation for improvement in manufacture of anchors.	24	1	Petition	138	Naval Affairs	98	Favorable; bill	113	Passed		App'd July 1, 1836
Tucker, Jesse, widow of.	Revolutionary pension	29	1	Petition & papers.	86	Rev. Pensions	785	Adverse		Laid on table.		
Tucker, Jesse, widow of.	Revolutionary pension	30	1	Petition & papers.	156	Rev. Pensions	538	Adverse		Laid on table.		
Tucker, John	Compensation for services and extra expenses as clerk of Supreme Court of United States.	2	1	Petition	529	Select	Mar. 8, 1792	Favorable		Laid on table.		
Tucker, John	Compensation for services and extra expenses as clerk of Supreme Court of United States.	2	2	Resolution	660	Select	Jan. 2, 1793	Bill ordered	213	Rejected.		
Tucker, John	Restoration of pension	17	2	Petition	92	Whole House.						
Tucker, John	Payment of final settlement certificate.	19	1	Resolution	121	Rev. Claims.						
Tucker, John, (Miss.)	Pre-emption right to land	23	2	Petition	241	Public Lands				Discharged; laid on table.		
Tucker, John, (La.)	Confirmation of title to land	29	2	Memorial	198	Priv. Land Claims.						
Tucker, John, (La.)	Confirmation of title to land	30	1	Memorial	109	Priv. Land Claims.						
Tucker, John, (Ill.)	Authority to locate land warrant	30	1	Petition	323	Public Lands	Feb. 29, 1848	Adverse		Laid on table.		
Tucker, John	Compensation as chaplain to Florida militia.	30	2	Resolution	346	Military Affairs.						
Tucker, Jonathan	Remission of penalty for violation of revenue laws.	27	2	Petition	321	Commerce.						
Tucker, Joseph	Compensation for services in revolutionary war.	1	2	Petition	213	Referred to Secretary of War.	May 25, 1790	Report		Laid on table.		
Tucker, Joseph	Compensation for services in revolutionary war.	2	1	Rep. of Secretary War.	450	Whole House	Nov. 7, 1791	Adverse		Rejected.		
Tucker, Joseph, widow of.	To abate balance due United States from estate of deceased.	9	1	Petition	276	Claims	Feb. 26, 1806	Adverse.		Laid on table.		
Tucker, Joseph	Bounty land for services in revolutionary war.	16	1	Petition	188	Pens. & Rev. Cl'ms.				Discharged; referred to Secretary War.		
Tucker, Joshua, widow of.	Relief; husband died in service of United States.	15	1	Petition	31	Military Affairs				Discharged; laid on table.		
Tucker & Lauries	(See Alex. Dalrymple, agents of).	15	1		84							
Tucker, Mary	(See Joseph Tucker, widow of)	9	1		276							
Tucker, Mary	(See Joshua Tucker, widow of)	15	1		31							
Tucker, Mary	(See William Tucker, widow of).	23	2		141							
Tucker, Nathaniel, heirs of.	Pension	25	2	Petition	272	Rev. Claims	862	Adverse		Laid on table.		
Tucker, Nathaniel, heirs of.	Pension	26	1	Petition	707	Rev. Pensions.						

List of private claims presented to the House of Representatives of the United States from the 1st to the 31st Congress, inclusive—Continued.

Names of claimants.	Nature or object of the claim.	Congress.	Session.	How brought before the House of Reps.	Page of journal.	To what committee of the House referred.	No. or date of the report.	Nature of the report.	No. of the bill.	How disposed of by the House of Reps.	How disposed of by the Senate.	Date of the act of Congress, and remarks.
Tucker, Richard D......	Indemnity for French spoliations prior to 1800.	26	1	Memorial	182	Foreign Affairs ...	343	Favorable; bill	319	Referred to Committee Whole House.		
Tucker, Richard D......	(See Isaac Winslow and R. D. Tucker.)	14	1	....	169							
Tucker, Robert, and wife..	(See Benjamin Lawson, former widow of.)	23	2	....	49							
Tucker, Samuel, (Maine).	Revolutionary pension..........	9	2	Petition	504	Select.						
Tucker, Samuel, (Maine).	Revolutionary pension..........	10	1	Petition	38	Select.						
Tucker, Samuel, (Mass.)..	Compensation for services in navy, revolutionary war.	12	1	Petition	263	Claims.						
Tucker, Samuel, (Mass.)..	Compensation for services in navy, revolutionary war.	13	1	Petition	11	Claims	....	....	......	Discharged.		
Tucker, Samuel, (Mass.)..	Compensation for services in navy, revolutionary war.	13	2	Petition	234	Pens. & Rev. Cl'ms.	92	Adverse; res. to withdraw.	......	Referred to Committee Whole House.		
Tucker, Samuel, (Mass.)..	Compensation for services in navy, revolutionary war.	14	1	Petition	497	Pens. & Rev. Cl'ms.						
Tucker, Samuel, (Mass.)..	Compensation for services in navy, revolutionary war.	14	2	Petition	31	Pens. & Rev. Cl'ms.						
Tucker, Samuel, (Mass.)..	Compensation for services in navy, revolutionary war.	15	1	Petition	38	Pens. & Rev. Cl'ms.	Feb. 5, 1818	Adverse	......	Laid on table.		
Tucker, Samuel, (Mass.)..	Compensation for services in navy, revolutionary war.	16	1	Petition	174	Pens. & Rev. Cl'ms.	281	Adverse	......	Laid on table.		
Tucker, Samuel, (Mass.)..	Compensation for services in navy, revolutionary war.	16	2	Senate bill	202	Naval Affairs.....	Feb. 20, 1821	With't amend.	S. 25	Passed	....	App'd March 2, 1821
Tucker, Thomas William, and Samuel A. Crapo.	(See Francis & Thompson, attorneys of.)	25	2	....	772							
Tucker, William, widow of.	Pre-emption right to land	23	2	Petition	141	Public Lands.....	Feb. 5, 1835	By bill	710	Postponed.		
Tucker, William, widow of.	Pre-emption right to land	24	1	Petition	114	Public Lands.	226	Favorable; bill	236	Referred to Committee Whole House.		
Tucker, William, widow of.	Pre emption right to land	24	2	House bill......	62	Whole House	....	....	236			
Tucker, William, widow of.	Pre-emption right to land	25	2	Petition	42	Public Lands.....	312	Favorable; bill	350	Referred to Committee Whole House.		
Tucker, William, widow of.	Pre-emption right to land	25	3	House bill	377	Whole House.....	....	....	350			
Tucker, William, widow of.	Pre-emption right to land	26	1	Petition	177	Public Lands.....	82	Favorable; bill	74	Postponed.		
Tucker, William, widow of.	Pre-emption right to land	26	2	House bill	164	Whole House.....	Jan. 8, 1841	With't amend.	74	Passed	Passed	App'd Feb. 27, 1841
Tucker, William, widow of.	Extension of time to enter land...	27	3	Senate bill	209	Public Lands.....	Jan. 24, 1843	With't amend.	S. 76	Passed	Passed	App'd Jan. 28, 1843
Tucker, William	(See Clement Hayden, administrator of.)	15	1	....	312							
Tucker, William	Pension for revolutionary services.	30	1	Petition	618	Rev. Pensions	July 19, 1848	....	......	Discharged; laid on table.		
Tucker, Zephaniah, widow of.	Compensation for services of husband in revolutionary war.	25	2	Petition	54	Rev. Pensions	496	Favorable; bill	499	Passed	Adverse.	
Tucker, Zephaniah, widow of.	Compensation for services of husband in revolutionary war.	26	2	Senate bill	334	Whole House	....	....	S. 205			
Tucker, Zephaniah, widow of.	Revolutionary pension..........	27	2	Senate bill	232	Whole House	Feb. 9, 1842	With't amend.	S. 28	Passed	....	App'd Mar. 19, 1842
Tuckerman, jr., Edward, *et al.*	Permission to import merchandise from Great Britain.	10	2	Petition	413	Com. and Manuf.						
Tuckerman, Henry H....	Debenture on goods returned to England.	15	2	Petition	26	Com. and Manuf.						
Tuckerman, Henry H....	Debenture on goods returned to England.	20	1	Petition	31	Com. and Manuf.						

List of private claims presented to the House of Representatives of the United States from the 1st to the 31st Congress, inclusive—Continued.

Names of claimants.	Nature or object of the claim.	Congress.	Session.	How brought before the House of Reps.	Page of journal.	To what committee of the House referred.	No. or date of the report.	Nature of the report.	No. of the bill.	How disposed of by the House of Reps.	How disposed of by the Senate.	Date of the act of Congress, and remarks.
Tuckerman, Henry H.	Debenture on goods returned to England.	20	2	Petition	59	Ways and Means	Jan. 28, 1829	Favorable; bill	397	Referred to Commitee Whole House.		
Tuckerman, Henry H.	Debenture on goods returned to England.	21	1	Petition	39	Com. and Manuf.	Feb. 10, 1830	Favorable; bill	222	Referred to Committee Whole House.		
Tuckerman, Henry H.	Debenture on goods returned to England.	21	2	House bill	264	Whole House	Feb. 4, 1831	With't amend.	222	Passed.		
Tuckerman, Henry H.	Debenture on goods returned to England.	22	1	Petition	24	Ways and Means	Dec. 15, 1831	Favorable; bill	1	Passed	Passed	App'd Jan. 18, 1832
Tuckerman, Stephen	(See Daniel Evans, sureties of)	21	2		382							
Tudor, Delia	(See William Tudor, widow of)	22	2		244							
Tudor, Delia	(See William Tudor, jr., mother of.)	24	2		180							
Tudor, William, widow of.	Commutation of half-pay	22	2	Petition	244	Rev. Claims				Discharged; laid on table.		
Tudor, William, widow of.	Commutation of half-pay	23	1	Petition	47	Rev. Claims	Mar. 12, 1835	Adverse		Laid on table.		
Tudor, jr., William, mother of.	Compensation for services as diplomatic agent to Peru.	24	2	Petition	180	Foreign Affairs	200	Favorable; bill	919	Referred to Committee Whole House.		
Tudor, jr., William, mother of.	Compensation for services as diplomatic agent to Peru.	25	2	Petition	39	Foreign Affairs	264	Favorable; bill	307	Referred to Committee Whole House.		
Tudor, jr., William, mother of.	Compensation for services as diplomatic agent to Peru.	25	3	House bill	377	Whole House	Jan. 25, 1839	With't amend.	307	Passed	Passed	App'd March 3, 1839
Tudor, jr., William, mother of.	Allowance for outfit as diplomatic agent to Peru.	26	1	Petition	714	Foreign Affairs.						
Tuels, Charles, widow of.	Allowance for outfit as diplomatic agent to Peru.	27	2	Petition	69	Rev. Pensions				Discharged; laid on table.		
Tuffs & Clark	Indemnity for losses on certain sugars, &c.	23	1	Petition	145	Ways and Means	199	Favorable; bill	222	Referred to Committee Whole House.		
Tuffs & Clark	Indemnity for losses on certain sugars, &c.	23	2	House bill	82	Whole House	Dec. 24, 1834	With't amend.	222	Passed	Passed	App'd Jan. 27, 1835
Tuillier, Charles	(See John Tuillier, heirs of)	20	2		41							
Tuillier, Francis Isidore	Confirmation of title to land	20	2	Petition	41	Priv. Land Claims.						
Tuillier, Francis Isidore	Confirmation of title to land	21	1	Petition	51	Priv. Land Claims.	77	Favorable; bill	109	Passed	Passed	App'd May 28, 1830
Tuillier, John, heirs of	Confirmation of title to land	20	2	Petition	41	Priv. Land Claims.						
Tuillier, John, heirs of	Confirmation of title to land	21	1	Petition	51	Priv. Land Claims.	86	Favorable; bill	122	Passed	Passed	App'd May 28, 1830
Tuillier, Joseph	(See John Tuillier, heirs of)	20	2		41							
Tuit, John	Revolutionary pension	25	2	Resolution	528	Rev. Pensions				Discharged; laid on table.		
Tukey, Frances	(See Richard Carr, sister of)	27	3		60							
Tuley, William	Confirmation of title to land	15	1	Petition	56	Priv. Land Claims.						
Tumbo, William	(See Stephen Decatur, widow of)	23	1		36		45		50			
Tumey, William	(See William Turney, Va.)	21	2		109							
Tumlinson, James	Pension	20	2	Petition	31	Military Pensions.						
Tumlinson, James	Pension	21	1	Petition	67	Military Pensions.						
Tuneur, James	Pension	22	1	Petition	187	Rev. Pensions	375	Favorable; bill	494	Referred to Committee Whole House.		
Tunnell, Luther	Compensation for services rendered as express rider.	27	2	Petition	1298	Claims.						
Tunno, Adam	Indemnity for French spoliations prior to 1800.	26	1	Memorial	182	Foreign Affairs	343	Favorable; bill	319	Referred to Committee Whole House.		
Tunno, Adam, *et al.*	(See McFarlane & Player, assignee of)	7	2		258							
Tunno & Cox, *et al*	Indemnity for French spoliations prior to 1800.	7	1	Memorial	82	Secretary of State	Feb. 15, 1802	Report		Laid on table.		

List of private claims presented to the House of Representatives of the United States from the 1st to the 31st Congress, inclusive—Continued.

Names of claimants.	Nature or object of the claim.	Congress.	Session.	How brought before the House of Reps.	Page of journal.	To what committee of the House referred.	No. or date of the report.	Nature of the report.	No. of the bill.	How disposed of by the House of Reps.	How disposed of by the Senate.	Date of the act of Congress, and remarks.
Tunno & Cox, *et al*	Indemnity for French spoliations prior to 1800.	26	1	Memorial	182	Foreign Affairs	343	Favorable; bill	319	Referred to Committee Whole House.		
Tunno, Thomas	(See Tunno & Cox, *et al.*)	7	1		82							
Tunsdale, Peyton R	Payment for horse and equipments lost in Seminole war.	23	1	Documents	154	Claims.						
Tupman, John, heirs of	(See John Tapman, heirs of)	24	1		992							
Tupper, Charles C., widow of.	Restoration of pension	28	2	Petition	135	Invalid Pensions.						
Tupper, Emily E	(See Charles C. Tupper, widow of.)	28	2		135							
Tupper, Frank A	Compensation for services as weigher and guager at Savannah, Ga.	28	2	Petition	472	Commerce.						
Tupper, Percia	(See Samuel Tupper, executrix of.)	21	1		189							
Tupper, Peter C., agent of	Payment of a loan office certificate.	14	2	Petition	154	Claims				Discharged; referred to Pens. & Rev. Cl'ms.		
Tupper, Peter C., agent of	Payment of a loan office certificate.	15	1	Petition	27	Pens. & Rev. Cl'ms.						
Tupper, Samuel, executrix of.	Indemnity for barn destroyed by enemy in 1812.	21	1	Papers and docs.	189	Claims	332	Favorable; bill	378	Referred to Committee Whole House.		
Tupper, Samuel, executrix of.	Indemnity for barn destroyed by enemy in 1812.	22	1	Petition	43	Claims	Dec. 19, 1831	By bill	16	Passed	Passed	App'd March 7, 1832
Tupper, Thomas, assignee of.	Payment of certain due bills	22	2	Petition	142	Claims	115	Indefinite		Laid on table.		
Tupper, Thomas, assignee of.	Payment of certain due bills	23	1	Petition	33	Claims	202	Favorable; bill	369	Referred to Committee Whole House.		
Tupper, Thomas, assignee of.	Payment of certain due bills	23	2	Petition and docs.	422	Claims	Feb. 20, 1835	Res. to stay proceedings.		Adopted.		
Tupper, Thomas, assignee of.	Payment of certain due bills	24	1	Petition	50	Claims	Dec. 21, 1835	Favorable; bill	8	Passed	Passed	App'd June 11, 1836
Turberville, Geo. L., heirs of.	Commutation of half-pay	22	2	Petition	46	Rev. Claims.						
Turberville, Geo. L., heirs of.	Commutation of half-pay	23	1	Petition	65	Rev. Claims.						
Turberville, Geo. L., heirs of.	Commutation of half-pay	23	2	Petition	77	Rev. Claims.						
Turberville, Geo. L., heirs of.	Commutation of half-pay	24	1	Petition	103	Rev. Claims	Mar. 3, 1836	Adverse		Laid on table.		
Turk & Henderson	Reimbursement of expenses at Washington while settling accounts.	16	1	Petition	52	Claims	Jan. 7, 1820	Adverse		Laid on table.		
Turk, Hiram K	Reimbursement of amount paid for medical attendance on account of injury received from an Indian.	25	2	Petition	274	Claims	555	Adverse		Laid on table.		
Turley, Stephen	(See Duff Green, attorney)	19	2		134							
Turman, Benjamin, heirs of.	Compensation for property taken for public use.	28	1	Petition	251	Claims	501	Adverse		Laid on table.		
Turnbull, Dr. Andrew, heirs of.	Confirmation of title to land in Florida.	17	1	Petition	110	Priv. Land Claims.						
Turnbull, Dr. Andrew, heirs of.	Confirmation of title to land in Florida.	20	1	Petition	33	Priv. Land Claims.	Dec. 20, 1827	Adverse		Recommitted.		
Turnbull, Dr. Andrew, heirs of.	Confirmation of title to land in Florida.	20	1	Petition	83	Priv. Land Claims.	Jan. 8, 1828	Adverse		Laid on table.		
Turnbull, Dr. Andrew, heirs of.	Confirmation of title to land in Florida.	21	1	Petition	93	Priv. Land Claims.						

List of private claims presented to the House of Representatives of the United States from the 1st to the 31st Congress, inclusive—Continued.

Names of claimants.	Nature or object of the claim.	Congress.	Session.	How brought before the House of Reps.	Page of journal.	To what committee of the House referred.	No. or date of the report.	Nature of the report.	No. of the bill.	How disposed of by the House of Reps.	How disposed of by the Senate.	Date of the act of Congress, and remarks.
Turnbull, Dr. Andrew, heirs of.	Confirmation of title to land in Florida.	24	1	Petition	112	Priv. Land Claims.	Jan. 21 1836	Favorable; bill	199	Referred to Committee Whole House.		
Turnbull, George	Payment for building bridge over Labusha, Mississippi.	22	1	Resolution	116	Claims	247	Adverse.	......	Referred to Committee Whole House.		
Turnbull, James	Relief; wounded at Dartmoor prison	14	1	Petition	33	Naval Affairs.						
Turnbull, John, representatives of.	Confirmation of title to lands in Alabama.	15	1	House bill	387	....	....	....	160	Referred to Committee Whole House.		
Turnbull, Nichol, *et al.*	(See Dr. Andrew Turnbull, heirs of)	17	1	....	110							
Turnbull, Robert	Reservation of half-section of land.	23	2	Petition	348	Public Lands.						
Turnbull, Walter	Permission to locate land	24	1	Petition	425	Priv. Land Claims.	....	....	......	Discharged; laid on table.		
Turnbull, William, *et al.*	Compensation for supplies furnished United States army.	6	1	Petition	571	Claims	May 9, 1800	Adverse	......	Laid on table.		
Turner, Abigail	(See Stephen Turner, widow of).	22	1	....	556							
Turner, Abner W., (Me.)	Pension	21	1	Petition	143	Military Pensions.	April 7, 1830	Adverse	......	Laid on table.		
Turner, Abner W., (Me.)	Pension	21	2	Petition	81	Military Pensions.						
Turner, Abner W., (Me.)	Pension	22	1	Petition	161	Invalid Pensions	April 11, 1832	Adverse	......	Laid on table.		
Turner, Abner W., (Me.)	Pension	26	1	Petition	708	Invalid Pensions.						
Turner, Abner	Title to land at certain price, or right of pre-emption to other land be granted.	23	1	Petition	98	Public Lands	....	....	......	Discharged; laid on table.		
Turner, Abner	Confirmation of title to land	23	1	Petition	98	Public Lands	....	....	......	Discharged, laid on table.		
Turner, Alexander	Revolutionary pension	13	3	Petition	455	Pens. & Rev. Cl'ms.	....	....	......	Discharged; referred to Secretary War.		
Turner, Alexander, widow and children of.	Commutation of half-pay	23	2	Petition	114	Rev. Claims	....	....	......	Discharged; laid on table.		
Turner, Ann	(See John H. Stone, heirs of.)	9	1	....	249							
Turner, Charles William	To refund certain duties paid on vessel at New Orleans.	27	3	Petition	136	Claims.						
Turner, Charles William	To refund certain duties paid on vessel at New Orleans.	28	1	Petition	366	Commerce.						
Turner, Cyrus, heirs-at-law of.	Compensation for losses sustained in furnishing Indians with beef.	29	1	Petition	144	Indian Affairs	557	Favorable; bill	196	Recommitted.		
Turner, Cyrus, heirs-at-law of.	Compensation for losses sustained in furnishing Indians with beef.	29	1	House bill	606	Indian Affairs	April 6, 1846	With't amend.	196	Passed	Passed	App'd Aug. 8, 1846
Turner, Daniel	Indemnity for expense of conveying minister to Curacoa.	22	2	General appropriation bill.	145	Whole House	Jan. 7, 1833	With amend.	669	Passed	Passed	App'd Mar. 2, 1833
Turner, David	Invalid pension	3	1	Petition and rep't Sec. of War.	26	Select	April 22, 1794	Adverse.	......	Laid on table.		
Turner, Edward	Additional compensation as register land office, Mississippi Territory.	10	1	Petition	171	Claims.						
Turner, Edward	Additional compensation as register land office, Mississippi Territory.	10	2	Petition	381	Claims.						
Turner, Edward	Additional compensation as register land office, Mississippi Territory.	11	2	Petition	112	Claims	Dec. 20, 1809	Adverse	......	Laid on table.		
Turner, Elisha, widow of.	Revolutionary pension	25	2	Petition	351	Rev. Pensions	....	....	......	Referred to Committee Whole House on bill No. 456.		
Turner, Elisha, widow of.	Revolutionary pension	26	2	Petition	200	Rev. Pensions.						
Turner, Elisha, widow of.	Revolutionary pension	27	2	Petition	97	Rev. Pensions	784	Adverse	......	Laid on table.		
Turner, Elisha, widow of.	Revolutionary pension	27	3	Petition	73	Rev. Pensions	....	....	......	Discharged; laid on table.		

List of private claims presented to the House of Representatives of the United States from the 1st to the 31st Congress, inclusive—Continued.

Names of claimants.	Nature or object of the claim.	Congress.	Session.	How brought before the House of Reps.	Page of journal.	To what committee of the House referred.	No. or date of the report.	Nature of the report.	No. of the bill.	How disposed of by the House of Reps.	How disposed of by the Senate.	Date of the act of Congress, and remarks.
Turner, E., attorney	(See Philipina Beckley, heirs of.)	11	2		227							
Turner, Enoch	Invalid pension	2	2	Rep. of Secretary War.	649	Whole House.						
Turner, Enoch	Invalid pension	3	1	Rep. of Secretary War.	131	Select	May 27, 1794	Res. to refer to Sec. War.	J.R. 12	Passed	Passed	App'd June 9, 1794
Turner, Enoch	Invalid pension	3	2	Rep. of Secretary War.	337	Claims	Feb. 28, 1795	Favorable.				
Turner, Enoch	Invalid pension	4	1	Rep. of Secretary War.	445	Claims	Feb. 18, 1796	Favorable; bill	156	Passed	Passed	App'd April 20, 1796
Turner, Enoch	Increase of pension	10	2	House bill	499	Whole House	Feb. 23, 1809	Bill amended.	158	Passed	Passed	App'd March 3, 1809
Turner, Enoch	Compensation for horse lost in service of the United States.	16	1	Petition	142	Claims	Jan. 17, 1820	Adverse		Laid on table.		
Turner, Forbes	Pension	21	2	Petition	126	Invalid Pensions.						
Turner, Frances	Pension	22	1	Petition	580	Invalid Pensions				Discharged; laid on table.		Should be Frances Carter, late widow of Jesse Kent.
Turner, George	Compensation for wood, &c., used by United States army in 1791.	5	2	Memorial	81	Claims	Dec. 21, 1797	Adverse.		Leave to withdraw.		
Turner, George	Title in fee simple to certain land.	5	3	Memorial	495	Select	Feb. 27, 1799	By bill	175	Passed	Passed	App'd March 2, 1899
Turner, George	Relief for expenses incurred in attendance on Congress to quiet claim to land.	7	1	Petition	63, 82	Select.						
Turner, George, (Ohio)	Grant of land presented him by Indians.	9	1	Memorial	222	Public Lands	Jan. 2, 1806	Adverse		Laid on table.		
Turner, George, (Ohio)	Confirmation of title to land	21	1	Petition	319	Public Lands				Discharged; laid on table		
Turner, George F	Compensation for a horse lost in Florida war.	26	1	Petition	337	Claims.						
Turner, George F	Compensation for a horse lost in Florida war.	26	2	Petition	135	Claims.						
Turner, Henry E	Land claim	19	2	Petition	27	Public Lands				Discharged.		Leave to withdraw.
Turner, Henry W	Indemnity for losses caused by illegal seizure of vessel.	23	1	Memorial	37	Foreign Affairs.						
Turner, Henry W., heirs of, &c.	Indemnity for losses caused by illegal seizure of vessel.	31	1	Petition	348	Judiciary				Discharged; referred to Foreign Affairs.		
Turner, Henry	Invalid pension	6	1	Petition	564	Claims	Feb. 3, 1800	Adverse		Laid on table.		
Turner, Henry	Invalid pension	14	2	House bill	307	Whole House	Feb. 21, 1817	With amend.	91	Passed	Passed	App'd March 3, 1817
Turner, Jacob, heirs of	Commutation pay	23	1	Resolution	427	Rev. Claims.						
Turner, James	Compensation for horse lost in service of the United States.	15	2	Petition	24	Claims	Nov. 30, 1818	Adverse.		Laid on table.		
Turner, James	Compensation for horse lost in service of the United States.	19	1	Petition	337	Claims	April 10, 1826	Adverse		Laid on table.		
Turner, James	Compensation for horse lost in service of the United States.	20	1	Petition	127	Claims				Discharged; laid on table.		
Turner, James	(See Reuben E. Gentry, *et al.*)	23	1		138							
Turner, James	Revolutionary pension	23	1	Petition	308	Rev. Pensions.						
Turner, Jane	(See Alexander Turner, widow & children of.)	23	2		114							
Turner, Jesse	Confirmation of title to land	30	1	Senate bill	683	Priv. Land Claims		With't amend.	S. 79	Passed		App'd Aug. 14, 1848
Turner, John	Invalid pension	1	3	Petition	388					Referred to Secretary of War.		
Turner, John	Invalid pension	3	2	Rep. of Secretary War.	278	Claims.						

List of private claims presented to the House of Representatives of the United States from the 1st to the 31st Congress, inclusive—Continued.

Names of claimants.	Nature or object of the claim.	Congress.	Session.	How brought before the House of Reps.	Page of journal.	To what committee of the House referred.	No. or date of the report.	Nature of the report.	No. of the bill.	How disposed of by the House of Reps.	How disposed of by the Senate.	Date of the act of Congress, and remarks.
Turner, John	Invalid pension	4	1	Rep. of Secretary War.	373	Claims	Dec. 28, 1795	Adverse	......	Rejected.		
Turner, John	Compensation for revolutionary services, &c.	3	2	Petition	308	Claims.						
Turner, John, (Mass.)	Revolutionary pension	16	1	Petition	45	Rev. Pensions	350	Adverse	......	Discharged; laid on table.		
Turner, John, (Mass.)	Revolutionary pension	24	1	Petition & report.	1165	Rev. Pensions	....	....	......	Discharged; laid on table.		
Turner, John, (Ky.)	Invalid pension	28	2	Petition	353	Invalid Pensions.						
Turner, John, (Ky.)	Invalid pension	29	1	Petition & papers	298, 1203	Invalid Pensions	July 26, 1846	Adverse	......	Laid on table.		
Turner, John L., heirs of.	Arrears of pension	31	1	Petition	768	Rev. Claims	....	....	......	Discharged; referred to Com. on Judiciary.		
Turner, John, (Mo.)	Compensation for two horses stolen by Indians.	25	2	Petition	426	Indian Affairs	....	....	......	Discharged.		
Turner, John, (Mo.)	Compensation for two horses stolen by Indians.	26	1	Petition	181	Indian Affairs	....	....	......	Discharged; referred to Com. on Claims.		
Turner, John T.	Bounty land for military services.	30	1	Petition	664	Rev. Claims.						
Turner, Julius	Pension	13	3	House bill	740	Whole House	Mar. 1, 1815	With't amend.	303	Passed	Passed	App'd March 3, 1815
Turner, Lydia	(See Elisha Turner, widow of.)	25	2	....	351							
Turner, Maltiah	Increase of pension	14	2	Resolution	209	Pens. & Rev. Cl'ms.						
Turner, Moses, (Vt.)	Discharge from imprisonment at suit of United States.	14	1	Petition	138	Select.	Jan. 23, 1816	Favorable; bill	50	Passed	Passed	App'd April 29, 1816
Turner, Moses	Arrears of pension	22	2	Petition	216	Rev. Claims.						
Turner, Moses	Arrears of pension	27	3	Petition	482	Rev. Claims	295	Adverse	......	Laid on table.		
Turner, Peter, widow of.	Pension	20	1	Petition	60	Military Pensions	....	....	......	Discharged; laid on table.		
Turner, Peter, widow of.	Pension	21	1	Petition	49	Military Pensions	....	....	......	Discharged; laid on table.		
Turner, Peter, widow of.	Pension	21	1	Senate bill	340	Military Pensions	Mar. 6, 1830	With amend.	60	Passed	Concurred in.	App'd May 26, 1830
Turner, Philip	Compensation as surgeon general United States army.	10	1	Petition	17	Claims	....	....	......	Discharged; referred to Select Committee.		
Turner, Philip	Compensation as surgeon general United States army.	10	1	Senate bill	219	Whole House	April 14, 1808	With't amend.	S. 12	Passed	....	App'd April 22, 1808
Turner, Philip, heirs of.	Interest on commutation of half-pay.	23	1	Petition	156	Rev. Claims	176	Favorable; bill	195	Passed	With't amend.	
Turner, Philip, heirs of.	Interest on commutation of half pay.	23	2	Petition	105	Rev. Claims.						
Turner, Philip, heirs of.	Interest on commutation of half-pay.	24	1	Petition	102	Rev. Claims	298	Favorable; bill	311	Referred to Committee Whole House.		
Turner, Philip, heirs of.	Interest on commutation of half-pay.	24	2	House bill	200	Whole House	....	....	311			
Turner, Philip, heirs of.	Interest on commutation of half-pay.	25	2	Petition	40	Rev. Claims	105	Favorable; bill	121	Reconsideration pending.		
Turner, Philip, heirs of.	Interest on commutation of half-pay.	26	1	Petition	164	Rev. Claims.						
Turner, Philip, heirs of.	Interest on commutation of half-pay.	27	2	Petition	61	Rev. Claims	405	Adverse	......	Laid on table.		
Turner, Philip, heirs of.	Interest on commutation of half-pay.	31	1	Petition	391	Rev. Claims.						
Turner, Philip	Invalid pension	9	2	Petition	479	Claims	....	....	......	....	Disc'd; ref'd to Select Com.	
Turner, Rachael	(See Peter Turner, widow of.)	20	1	....	60							

List of private claims presented to the House of Representatives of the United States from the 1st to the 31st Congress, inclusive—Continued.

Names of claimants.	Nature or object of the claim.	Congress.	Session.	How brought before the House of Reps.	Page of journal.	To what committee of the House referred.	No. or date of the report.	Nature of the report.	No. of the bill.	How disposed of by the House of Reps.	How disposed of by the Senate.	Date of the act of Congress, and remarks.
Turner, Richard	Pay for rations furnished United States troops.	19	2	Petition	240	Claims	....	....	....	Discharged.		
Turner, Smith	Restoration of pension	17	2	Petition	224	Pens. & Rev. Cl'ms.	....	....	....	Discharged; laid on table.		
Turner, Stephen, widow of	Further relief	22	1	Resolution	499	Claims.						
Turner, Stephen, widow of	Pension	22	1	Petition	556	Invalid Pensions.						
Turner, Susan	(See Samuel Colson, heir of)	29	1	....	199							
Turner, Tarlton, *et al.*	(See Cyrus Turner, heir-at-law of.)	29	1	....	144							
Turner, Thomas, executors of.	Allowance for services rendered in settlement of accounts as commissioners of navy pension fund.	15	1	Petition	279	Naval Affairs	Mar. 24, 1818	By bill	159	Referred to Committee Whole House.		
Turner, Thomas, executors of.	Allowance for services rendered in settlement of accounts as commissioners of navy pension fund.	15	2	House bill	181	Whole House	Jan. 13, 1819	With amend.	159	Passed	Passed	App'd Feb. 27, 1819
Turner, Thomas	Increase of compensation as collector at Georgetown.	25	2	Petition	175	Commerce	....	....	....	Discharged.		
Turner, Captain Thomas	Revolutionary pension	24	1	Resolution	279	Rev. Pensions.						
Turner, Titus J.	Pension	16	1	Petition	59	Rev. Pensions	350	Adverse	....	Laid on table.		
Turner, William D	Money in lieu of bounty land	31	2	Petition	326	Public Lands.						
Turner, William J	Compensation for forage furnished army in Florida war.	30	1	Petition	435	Claims	599	Favorable; bill	480	Referred to Committee Whole House.		
Turney, Aaron	Revolutionary pension	26	1	Petition	171	Rev. Pensions	....	....	....	Discharged; laid on table.		
Turney, Abel, or Abiel	Invalid pension	1	2	Petition	213	Secretary of War	May 24, 1790	Report	....	Laid on table.		
Turney, Abel, or Abiel	Invalid pension	1	3	Rep. of Secretary War.	379	Select	Feb. 26, 1791	Favorable; bill	152	Passed	Passed	App'd Mar. 27, 1792
Turney, Abel, or Abiel	Arrears of pension	16	1	Petition	190	Pens. & Rev. Cl'ms.	292	Adverse	....	Laid on table.		
Turney, Abel, or Abiel	Arrears of pension	17	2	Petition	30	Pens. & Rev. Clm's.	519	Adverse	....	Laid on table.		
Turney, Abel, or Abiel	Arrears of pension	18	1	Petition	97	Pens. & Rev. Cl'ms.	May 4, 1824	Adverse	....	Referred to Committee Whole House.		
Turney, Abel, or Abiel	Arrears of pension	19	1	Petition	250	Invalid Pensions	164	Adverse	....	Laid on table.		
Turney, Asa	Compensation for revolutionary services	15	2	Petition	110	Pens. & Rev. Cl'ms.	183	Adverse	....	Rejected.		
Turney, Clarissa	(See Burr Gilbert, former widow of.)	26	1	....	284							
Turney, David, wife of	(See Clarissa Turney.)											
Turney, Ellen	(See Samuel Squires, former widow of.)	25	3	....	127							
Turney, Ellen	(See James Chapman, former widow of.)	26	1	....	171							
Turney, Ellen	(See Aaron Turney, widow of)	26	1	....	171							
Turney, Toney	Invalid pension	1	2	Petition	174	Secretary of War	May 31, 1790	Report	....	Laid on table.		
Turney, Toney	Invalid pension	2	2	Rep. of Secretary War.	649	Whole House.						
Turney, Toney	Invalid pension	3	1	Rep. of Secretary War.	131	Select	May 26, 1794	Res. to refer to Sec. War.	J. R. 12	Passed	Passed	App'd Jan. 9, 1794
Turney, Toney	Invalid pension	4	1	Rep. of Secretary War.	445	Claims.						
Turney, Toney	Invalid pension	11	2	House bill	283	Whole House	April 8, 1810	With amend.	107	Passed	Passed	App'd April 27, 1810
Turney, William, (Va.)	Pension	20	1	Petition	37	Military Pensions	....	....	....	Discharged; laid on table.		
Turney, William, (Va.)	Pension	21	1	Petition	49	Military Pensions.						
Turney, William, (Va.)	Pension	21	1	Senate bill	340	Whole House	March 6, 1830	With't amend.	S. 60	Passed	....	App'd May 20, 1830

List of private claims presented to the House of Representatives of the United States from the 1st to the 31st Congress, inclusive—**Continued.**

Names of claimants.	Nature or object of the claim.	Congress.	Session.	How brought before the House of Reps.	Page of journal.	To what committee of the House referred.	No. or date of the report.	Nature of the report.	No. of the bill.	How disposed of by the House of Reps.	How disposed of by the Senate.	Date of the act of Congress, and remarks.
Turney, William, (Va.)	To rectify mistake in name	21	2	Senate bill	109	Military Pensions	Dec. 31, 1830	With't amend.	S. 32	Passed		App'd March 2, 1831
Turney, William, (Ohio)	Pension	25	2	Petition	85	Invalid Pensions	347	Adverse		Laid on table.		
Turney, William, (Mo.)	Arrears of pension	28	1	Petition	428	Invalid Pensions	451	Adverse		Laid on table.		
Turney, William, (Mo.)	Arrears of pension	29	1	Petition	226	Invalid Pensions	347	Adverse		Laid on table.		
Turnipseed, Daniel	Indemnity for Indian depredations	28	2	Petition	65	Claims.						
Turnipseed, Daniel	Indemnity for Indian depredations	29	1	Petition	190	Claims	672	Adverse		Laid on table.		
Turnure, Lawrence	Revolutionary pension	21	1	Resolution	431	Military Pensions				Discharged; laid on table.		
Turpin, John, widow of	Naval pension	21	1	Petition	378	Naval Affairs				Discharged; laid on table.		
Turpin, Margaret	(See John Turpin, widow of)	21	1		378							
Turpin, Obadiah	Increase of pension	23	1	Resolution	643	Rev. Pensions.						
Turpin, Obadiah	Increase of pension	24	1	Resolution	57	Rev. Pensions				Discharged; laid on table.		
Turpin, William, (Ky.)	(Not stated)	19	2	Petition	133	Rev. Claims				Discharged; laid on table.		
Turrentine, Samuel	(See John S. West, of N. C.)	11	3		473							
Turrentine, Samuel	Compensation for support of certain prisoners.	14	1	Petition	535	Claims.						
Turrill, Abden, mother of.	Bounty land for military services	15	1	Senate bill	388	Military Pensions	Mar. 31, 1818	With amend't.	S. 40	Passed		App'd April 14, 1818
Turrell, Enoch	Pension	24	2	Petition	572	Invalid Pensions				Discharged; laid on table.		
Turvin, Elijah	Confirmation of title to land	15	1	Petition	56	Priv. Land Claims				Discharged; laid on table.		
Turvin, Richard	Confirmation of title to land	15	1	Petition	56	Priv. Land Claims				Discharged; laid on table.		
Tustian, Thomas	(See Thomas Fustian.)											
Tuthill, Major Barnabas, heirs of.	Seven years' half-pay	24	1	Petition	536	Rev. Claims				Discharged; laid on table.		
Tutt, Ann Mason	(See Charles P. Tutt, widow of.)	26	1		1009							
Tutt, Charles P., widow of.	Compensation for extra service as navy agent.	26	1	Petition	1009	Claims.						
Tutt, Charles P., widow of.	Compensation for extra services as navy agent.	26	2	Petition	80	Claims	241	Adverse		Laid on table.		
Tutt, Frederick	(See William Zoll, *et al.*)	15	2		190		220					
Tutt, Richard, postmaster, (S. C.)	Increase of compensation	20	1	Petition	100	P. Of. and P. Roads				Discharged; laid on table.		
Tuttle, Aaron	Invalid pension	3	1	Rep't of Secretary War.	131	Select	May 31, 1794	Indefinite.				
Tuttle, Aaron	Invalid pension	4	1	Rep. of Secretary War.	445	Claims.						
Tuttle, Aaron	Invalid pension	10	2	House bill	499	Whole House	Feb. 23, 1809	With amend.	158	Passed	Passed	App'd March 3, 1809
Tuttle, Aaron	Increase of pension	14	2	Petition	180	Pens. & Rev. Cl'ms.						
Tuttle & Baker, surviving partner of.	Indemnity for property destroyed by the British.	22	2	Petition	177	Claims.						
Tuttle & Baker, surviving partner of.	Indemnity for property destroyed by the British.	23	1	Petition	89	Claims	234	Adverse		Laid on table.		
Tuttle, Caleb	Revolutionary pension	22	2	Petition	40	Rev. Pensions				Discharged; laid on table.		
Tuttle, Caharine	(See Jonathan Tuttle, widow of.)	25	2		117							
Tuttle, C. C.	(See James Brown, heirs of.)	11	2		240							
Tuttle, Hezekiah	Revolutionary pension	18	1	Petition	155	Pens. & Rev. Cl'ms.	Feb. 25, 1824	Adverse		Laid on table.		
Tuttle, James M.	Permission to correct error in entry of land.	23	2	Petition	141	Pubilc Lands.	Jan. 22, 1835	By bill	670	Passed	Laid on table.	

List of private claims presented to the House of Representatives of the United States from the 1st to the 31st Congress, inclusive—Continued.

Names of claimants.	Nature or object of the claim.	Congress.	Session.	How brought before the House of Reps.	Page of journal.	To what committee of the House referred.	No. or date of the report.	Nature of the report.	No. of the bill.	How disposed of by the House of Reps.	How disposed of by the Senate.	Date of the act of Congress, and remarks.
Tuttle, James M.	Permission to correct error in entry of land.	24	1	Petition	114	Public Lands	Jan. 27, 1836	By bill	238	Passed	Adverse.	
Tuttle, James M.	Permission to correct error in entry of land.	25	2	Petition	42	Public Lands	241	Favorable; bill	281	Referred to Committee Whole House.		
Tuttle, James M.	Permission to correct error in entry of land.	25	3	House bill	376	Whole House			281	Passed	Passed	App'd March 2, 1839
Tuttle, Jehiel	Invalid pension	26	2	Petition	54	Invalid Pensions.						
Tuttle, Jehiel	Invalid pension	27	2	Petition	268	Invalid Pensions	940	Adverse		Laid on table.		
Tuttle, Jehiel	Invalid pension	28	1	Petition	60	Invalid Pensions.						
Tuttle, Jehiel	Invalid pension	29	1	Petition	59	Invalid Pensions				Discharged; laid on table.		
Tuttle, Jehiel	Invalid pension	29	2	Petition	177	Invalid Pensions				Discharged; laid on table.		
Tuttle, John	Invalid pension	31	1	Petition	233	Invalid Pensions.						
Tuttle, Johnson	Compensation for services in revolutionary army.	13	1	Petition	50	Claims				Discharged.		
Tuttle, Johnson	Compensation for services in revolutionary army.	13	2	Petition	287	Pens. & Rev. Cl'ms.						
Tuttle, Jonathan, widow of.	Revolutionary pension	25	2	Petition	117	Rev. Pensions				Discharged; laid on table.		
Tuttle, Joseph, (Vt.)	(See Benjamin Lamb, administrator of.)	20	1		440							
Tuttle, Joseph, (N. Y.)	Revolutionary pension	24	1	Petition	282	Rev. Pensions	410	Favorable; bill	421	Passed	Passed	App'd June 28, 1836
Tuttle, Josiah, administrator of.)	Relief from judgment at suit of United States.	15	2	Petition	294	Ways and Means				Discharged; laid on table.		
Tuttle, Levi	Invalid pension	11	3	House bill	604	Whole House	Mar. 2, 1811	With amend.	218	Passed	Passed	App'd March 3, 1811
Tuttle, Nicholas	Invalid pension	3	1	Petition	103					Referred to Secretary of War.		
Tuttle, Nicholas	Invalid pension	3	2	Rep. of Secretary War.	278	Claims.						
Tuttle, Peter	Pension	21	1	Resolution	255	Military Pensions				Discharged; laid on table.		
Tuttle, Peter	Pension	21	2	Petition	110	Invalid Pensions	Jan. 25, 1831	Adverse		Laid on table.		
Tuttle, Stephen	(See Guy Maxwell, heirs of.)	18	1		131							
Tuttle, Thaddeus	Revolutionary pension	24	1	Petition	56	Rev. Pensions	157	Favorable; bill	166	Passed	Passed	App'd June 28, 1836
Tuttle, Thaddeus, *et al.*	(See William McGill)	15	1		320							
Tuttle, William	Equitable settlement of claim	19	1	Petition	31	Select				Discharged; laid on table.		
Twiggs, David E., *et al*	Indemnity for costs of suits brought against them for acts done in discharge of duty.	22	1	Senate bill	540	Claims	437	With amend.	S. 160	Passed	Concurred in.	App'd July 14, 1832
Twiggs, L., *et al.*	Certain allowances and arrearages.	22	2	Petition	425	Naval Affairs	Feb. 26, 1833	Favorable; bill	756	Referred to Committee Whole House.		
Twiggs, Mrs. Priscilla D.	Relief on account of service and death of her husband and son in war with Mexico.	30	1	Petition	313	Rev. Pensions	438	Adverse		Laid on table.		
Twiggs, Mrs. Priscilla D.	To be allowed a portion of prize-money to which Commodore Decatur was entitled.	30	2	Petition	210	Naval Affairs	102	Recommendi'g Senate bill.	348			
Twiggs, Mrs. Priscilla D.	To be allowed a portion of prize-money to which Commodore Decatur was entitled.	31	1	Petition	434	Naval Affairs.						
Twiney, Toney	(See Toney Turney)	1	2		174							

List of private claims presented to the House of Representatives of the United States from the 1st to the 31st Congress, inclusive—Continued.

Names of claimants.	Nature or object of the claim.	Congress.	Session.	How brought before the House of Reps.	Page of journal.	To what committee of the House referred.	No. or date of the report.	Nature of the report.	No. of the bill.	How disposed of by the House of Reps.	How disposed of by the Senate.	Date of the act of Congress, and remarks.
Twining, Nathaniel	Indemnity for losses and injuries sustained by certain mail contract.	1	2	Memorial	209	Select	May 20, 1790	Favorable; bill	72	Passed	Passed	App'd July 1, 1790
Twist, Martha	(See Stephen Twist, widow of.)	28	2		71							
Twist, Stephen	Pension	19	1	Petition	34	Pens. & Rev. Cl'ms.						
Twist, Stephen	Pension	20	1	Petition	50	Military Pensions				Discharged; laid on table.		
Twist, Stephen	Pension	21	1	Petition	47	Military Pensions	May 12, 1828	Adverse		Laid on table.		
Twist, Stephen	Pension	21	1	Senate bill	340	Military Pensions	Mar. 6, 1830	With amend	60	Passed	Passed	App'd May 20, 1830
Twist, Stephen, widow of.	Remuneration for services of husband, and for services of self as nurse in United States service.	28	2	Petition	71	Claims	29	Adverse		Laid on table.		
Twist, Stephen, widow of.	Remuneration for services of husband and for services of self as nurse in United States service.	29	1	Petition	218	Invalid Pensions				Discharged; laid on table.		
Twitchell, Timothy	(See Joseph Forsyth & T. Twitchell.)	20	1		581							
Twitchell, Timothy	Pay for land containing live oak timber conveyed to United States.	22	1	Petition	33	Claims	241	Favorable; bill	528	Passed	Passed	App'd July 14, 1832
Two Brothers	(See Joseph W. Green)	23	1		617							
Two Brothers, schooner	(See James Williams, executors of)	19	1		492							
Two Brothers, schooner	(See Andrew Blake)	28	1		182							
Two Sons, schooner	(See Charles Gordon)	27	2		319		736		413			
Tycer, Ellis	Pension	24	2	Resolution	146	Rev. Pensions				Discharged; laid on table.		
Tylee, Carlisle D	Interest on money advanced, and indemnity for property destroyed by enemy.	17	1	Petition	183	Claims				Discharged; laid on table.		
Tyler, Andrew F	Invalid pension	27	3	Petition	228	Invalid Pensions.						
Tyler, Andrew F	Invalid pension	28	1	Petition	566	Invalid Pensions.						
Tyler, Andrew F	Invalid pension	29	1	Petition	503	Invalid Pensions	July 25, 1846	Adverse		Laid on table.		
Tyler, Benjamin	Revolutionary pension	17	2	Petition	165	Pens. & Rev. Cl'ms.				Discharged; laid on table.		
Tyler, Daniel	Reimbursement of money advanced for use of government.	21	1	House bill	190	Military Affairs	Jan. 20, 1830	Favorable; bill	136	Passed	Passed	App'd May 29, 1830
Tyler, Daniel	Permission to import iron, &c., free of duty.	24	1	Senate bill	940	Manufactures	June 23, 1836	Adverse	S. 143	Referred to Committee Whole House.		
Tyler, Daniel, widow of.	Revolutionary pension	28	2	Petition	367	Rev. Pensions.						
Tyler, Daniel, widow of.	Revolutionary pension	29	1	Petition	162	Rev. Pensions	527	Adverse		Laid on table.		
Tyler, Dudley	Arrears of revolutionary pay	1	1	Petition	70	Referred to Secretary of War.						
Tyler, Dudley	Arrears of revolutionary pay	1	2	Petition	137	Referred to Secretary of War.	Jan. 15, 1790	Report		Laid on table.		
Tyler, H. B	(See Nathaniel Tyler, heirs of.)	23	1		137		337		365			
Tyler, H. B	(See Richard Smith, executor of.)	23	2		194				S. 2[illegible]			
Tyler, Isaac B	(See Hugh Howell and J. B. Tyler.)	14	2		311							
Tyler, Isaac B., (N. Y.)	Payment for services rendered United States army, and for property destroyed by British.	22	1	Petition	220	Claims	Feb. 6, 1832	Adverse		Recommitted.		
Tyler, James	Pension	25	3	Resolution	116	Rev. Pensions.						
Tyler, James	Pension	26	1	Petition	175	Rev. Pensions.						

List of private claims presented to the House of Representatives of the United States from the 1st to the 31st Congress, inclusive—Continued.

Names of claimants.	Nature or object of the claim.	Congress.	Session.	How brought before the House of Reps.	Page of journal.	To what committee of the House referred.	No. or date of the report.	Nature of the report.	No. of the bill.	How disposed of by the House of Reps.	How disposed of by the Senate.	Date of the act of Congress, and remarks.
Tyler, James	Arrears of pay and bounty land for services in Mexico.	31	1	Petition	719	Claims.						
Tyler, Jeremiah	Renewal of pension	16	2	Petition	240	Rev. Pensions						Leave to withdraw, 1st session, 17th Cong.
Tyler, John	(See Wm. G. Mumford, executor of.)	5	2		264							
Tyler, John S., attorney of.	(See Abiel Wenship's heirs)	26	1		182							
Tyler, John S., attorney of.	(See Josiah Willard)	26	1		182							
Tyler, John	(See Thomas Turner, executors of)	15	1		279							
Tyler, Joseph	Invalid pension	4	2	Rep. of Secretary War.	651	Claims	Feb. 6, 1797	Favorable; bill	224	Passed	Postponed.	
Tyler, Joseph	Invalid pension	5	2	House bill	127	Whole House	Jan. 11, 1798	Amended	38	Passed	Passed	App'd Feb. 2, 1798
Tyler, Joseph	Increase of pension	12	1	House bill	361	Whole House	June 5, 1812	With't amend.	138	Passed	Passed	App'd July 5, 1812
Tyler, Joseph	Restoration of pension	17	2	Petition	25	Rev. Pensions.						
Tyler, Nathaniel, heirs of.	Scrip for bounty land granted by Virginia.	23	1	Petition	137	Judiciary	337	Favorable; bill	365	Referred to Committee Whole House.		
Tyler, Nathaniel, heirs of.	Scrip for bounty land granted by Virginia.	23	2	House bill	163	Whole House	Jan. 3, 1835	With't amend.	365	Passed	Passed, with amendment.	Amendments not acted on by the House.
Tyler, Nathaniel, heirs of.	Scrip for bounty land granted by Virginia.	24	1	Petition	53	Judiciary	73	Favorable; bill	89	Passed	Adverse; laid on table.	
Tyler, Sally	(See Daniel Tyler, widow of)	28	2		367							
Tyler, Simeon	Pension	21	2	Petition	230	Military Pensions.						
Tyler, Thomas, heirs of	Confirmation of title to land	19	1	Petition	134	Priv. Land Claims.						
Tyler, Thomas, heirs of	Conrfimation of title to land	19	2	Petition	99	Priv. Land Claims.						
Tyler, Truman	(See Thomas Turner, executors of)	15	1		279							
Tyler, William	(See Louis F. Beeler, *et al.*)	30	1		115		482					
Tyner, Thomas, *et al.*	Compensa ion for extra work on national road.	24	1	Petition	497	Claims	786	Favorable; bill	711	Referred to Committee Whole House.		
Tyner, Thomas, *et al.*	Compensation for extra work on national road.	25	2	Petition	37	Claims	56	Favorable; bill	68	Passed	Passed	App'd April 20, 1838
Tyree, Francis	Compensation for property taken and destroyed by United States army.	5	2	Petition	291					Laid on table.		
Tyree, Francis	Compensation for property taken and destroyed by United States army.	5	3	Petition	478	Claims	Mar. 2, 1799	Adverse		Leave to withdraw.		
Tyrrell, Asahel	Revolutionary pension	27	3	Petition	259	Rev. Pensions.						
Tyson, James	Right of pre-emption as New Orleans branch pilot.	28	1	Petition	77	Priv. Land Claims.	9	Favorable; bill	35	Passed	Passed	App'd June 17, 1844
Tyson, Jesse	Indemnity for French spoliations prior to 1800.	26	1	Memorial	182	Foreign Affairs	343	Favorable; bill	319	Referred to Committee Whole House.		
Tyson, John S.	(See Jonathan W. Sherburne, administrator of.)	24	1		750							
Tyson, Maria S.	Payment of loan office certificate	11	3	Petition	509	Claims.						
Tyson, Maria S.	Payment of loan office certificate	12	1	Petition	120	Claims.						
Tyson, Maria S.	Payment of loan office certificate	12	2	Petition	686	Claims.						
Tyson, Maria S.	Payment of loan office certificate	13	2	Petition	201	Pens. & Rev. Cl'ms.	38	Adverse		Laid on table.		
Tyson, Maria S.	Payment of loan office certificate	14	1	Petition	421	Pens. & Rev. Cl'ms				Discharged; laid on table.		
Tyson, Maria S.	Payment of loan office certificate	14	2	Petition	205	Pens. & Rev. Cl'ms.	Feb. 3, 1816	By bill	96	Referred to Committee Whole House.		
Tyson, Thomas	(See Louis F. Beeler, *et al.*	30	1		115		482					

List of private claims presented to the House of Representatives of the United States from the 1st to the 31st Congress, inclusive—Continued.

Names of claimants.	Nature or object of the claim.	Congress.	Session.	How brought before the House of Reps.	Page of journal.	To what committee of the House referred.	No. or date of the report.	Nature of the report.	No. of the bill.	How disposed of by the House of Reps.	How disposed of by the Senate.	Date of the act of Congress, and remarks.
Ulmer, Christiana	(See Philip Ulmer, widow of)	14	2		205							
Ulmer, Colonel George	Compensation for services of two companies of volunteers, war of 1812.	13	2	Petition	336	Military Affairs				Referred to Secretary War.		
Ulmer, Colonel George	Payment for time under arrest, to time of acquittal.	13	3	Petition	506	Military Affairs				Referred to Secretary War.		
Ulmer, George	Increase of pension	16	1	Petition	225	Pens. & Rev. Cl'ms.						
Ulmer, Philip	Pension	13	2	Petition	209	Pens. & Rev. Cl'ms.	Mar. 28, 1814	Adverse		Referred to Committee Whole House.		
Ulmer, Philip	Pension	13	3	Petition	485	Pens. & Rev. Cl'ms.						
Ulmer, Philip	Pension	14	1	Petition	64	Pens. & Rev. Cl'ms.		Favorable	171	Passed	Passed	App'd April 29, 1816
Ulmer, Philip, widow of	Continuation of pension	14	2	Petition	205	Pens. & Rev. Cl'ms.	Jan. 29, 1817	Adverse		Rejected.		
Umbrella makers of Philadelphia.	To refund duties on umbrella stretchers.	25	2	Petition	390	Manufactures	697	Favorable	669	Referred to Committee Whole House.		
Umbrella makers of Philadelphia.	To refund duties on umbrella stretchers.	25	3	House bill	380				669	Passed	Passed	App'd March 3, 1839
Underhill, Henry	Pre-emption right to land	26	1	Petition	363	Public Lands				Discharged; laid on table.		
Underhill, Thomas, heirs of.	Compensation for damages sustained by United States troops, revolutionary war.	24	1	Petition	990	Rev. Claims.						
Underhill, Thomas, heirs of.	Compensation for damages sustained by United States troops, revolutionary war.	24	2	Petition	270	Rev. Claims.						
Underhill, Thomas, heirs of.	Compensation for damages sustained by United States troops, revolutionary war.	28	2	Petition	140	Rev. Claims.						
Underhill, Thomas, heirs of.	Compensation for damages sustained by United States troops, revolutionary war.	29	1	Petition	146	Rev. Claims	119	Adverse		Laid on table.		
Underwood, Jehu	Compensation for property destroyed by Indians in Florida.	21	2	Petition	111	Claims	Jan. 21, 1831	Adverse		Laid on table.		
Underwood, John, & others.	Increase of compensation as clerk in office of First Auditor Treasury.	18	2	Petition	158	Ways and Means				Discharged; laid on table.		
Underwood, John, & others.	Increase of compensation as clerk in office of First Auditor Treasury.	24	1	Petition	214	Ways and Means.						
Underwood, John, & others.	Increase of compensation as clerk in office of First Auditor Treasury.	25	2	Petition	51	Claims				Discharged.		
Underwood, John, & others.	Increase of compensation as clerk in office of First Auditor Treasury.	25	3	Petition	86	Claims.						
Underwood, John, & others.	Increase of compensation as clerk in office of First Auditor Treasury.	26	1	Petition	168	Claims	22	Favorable	41	Passed	Indef. postp'd.	
Underwood, John, & others.	Increase of compensation as clerk in office of First Auditor Treasury.	27	2	Petition	55	Claims	60	Favorable	95	Passed	Passed	App'd Aug. 24, 1842
Underwood, John W	Compensation for extra services	30	1	Petition	219	Claims.						
Underwood, John	Indemnity for losses sustained in Florida in 1812.	21	2	Petition	138	Claims.						
Underwood, Lieut. Joseph A., mother of.	Compensation for services rendered, and for loss of son.	27	2	Petition	236	Naval Affairs	757	Favorable	441	Referred to Committee Whole House.		
Underwood, Lieut. Joseph A., mother of.	Compensation for services rendered, and for loss of son.	27	3	House bill	88	Whole House			441	Passed	Indef. postp'd.	
Underwood, Lieut. Joseph A., mother of.	(See Exploring Expedition)	27	3		149							

3—67

List of private claims presented to the House of Representatives of the United States from the 1st to the 31st Congress, inclusive—**Continued.**

Names of claimants.	Nature or object of the claim.	Congress.	Session.	How brought before the House of Reps.	Page of journal.	To what committee of the House referred.	No. or date of the report.	Nature of the report.	No. of the bill.	How disposed of by the House of Reps.	How disposed of by the Senate.	Date of the act of Congress, and remarks.
Underwood, Joshua D., et al	For exchange of land	24	2	Senate bill	553	Priv. Land Claims			S. 137			
Underwood, Phineas	Relief in relation to land twice patented.	18	2	Petition	160	Public Lands.						
Underwood, Phineas	Relief in relation to land twice patented.	19	1	Petition	154	Priv. Land Claims.	73	Favorable	101	Passed	Passed	App'd May 22, 1826
Underwood, Robert	Settlement of certain certificates	4	1	Report of Secretary Treasury	388	Claims	Mar. 31, 1796	Adverse		Laid on table.		
Underwood, Sylvia	(See Lieut. Joseph A. Underwood, mother of.)	27	2		236							
Underwood, Thomas	Payment of prize drawn in United States lottery.	4	2	Petition	703	Claims.						
Underwood, Thomas	Payment for prize drawn in United States lottery.	5	2	Petition	229	Claims	Mar. 19, 1798	Adverse		Laid on table.		
Underwood, William H.	(See Samuel Rockwell, representatives of.)	26	1		623							
Underwood, William, widow of.	Reimbursement of money advanced United States, revolutionary war.	26	2	Petition	48	Rev. Claims	Jan. 4, 1841			Laid on table.		
Underwood, William, widow of.	Reimbursement of money advanced United States, revolutionary war.	27	2	Petition	1209	Rev. Claims	1089	Adverse		Laid on table.		
Union Bank of Georgetown.	Reimbursement of money lost by robbery of Baltimore post office.	25	2	Petition	73	P. Of. and P. Roads.	Jan. 20, 1838			Discharged; laid on table.		
Union Bank of Maryland	For correction of error in award of commissioners in case of schooner Trim.	24	2	Petition	132	Foreign Affairs.						
Union Bank of Florida	Payment of money advanced Territory for defence against Indians.	30	1	Petition	485	Claims	728	Favorable	569	Referred to Committee Whole House.		
Union Bank of Florida	Payment of money advanced Territory for defence against Indians	30	2	House bill	319	Whole House	Jan. 26, 1849	With't amend.	569	Passed	Passed	App'd March 3, 1849
Union Gold Mining Company.	Remission of duties on machinery.	24	1	Petition	94	Ways and Means	Jan. 27, 1836	Favorable	223	Referred to Committee Whole House.		
Union Gold Mining Company.	Remission of duties on machinery.	24	2	House bill	62	Whole House			223			
Union, John	Pension	11	2	House bill	283	Whole House	Mar. 15, 1810	With amends.	107	Passed	Passed	App'd April 27, 1810
Union, schooner	(See Joseph Baker, *et al.*)	27	2		822							
United Brethren, society of.	Confirmation of title to land	2	1	Petition	467	Select.						
United Brethren, society of.	For survey and grant of certain lands	4	1	Petition	408	Select	Feb. 5, 1796	Favorable	147	Passed	Passed	App'd June 1, 1796
United Brethren, society of.	Compensation for depredations on property by United States army.	13	2	Petition	304	Select	76	Adverse		Laid on table.		
United States, owners of ship.	Release of forfeiture	13	1	Senate bill	82	Ways and Means	Jan. 20, 1813	With't amend	S. 20	Passed	Passed	App'd July 29, 1813
United States Bank	(See Williamson Smith, assignee of.)	27	2		514							
United States, creditors of.	For arrears of interest on money loaned.	2	1	Petition	441					Laid on table.		
United States, citizens and owners of ships registered in Philadelphia.	Relief from payment of duties imposed on foreign vessels.	25	1	Petition	395	Com. and Manuf.	Feb. 8, 1796	Favorable; res.		Referred to Committee Whole House.		
United States frigate Philadelphia, officers & others of.	Interference of United States for rescue from slavery of officers and crew.	8	1	Petition	663	Ways and Means	Mar. 21, 1804	Favorable	219	Passed	Passed	App'd Mar. 26, 1804
United States and Mexico, claimants under Convention.	Payment of award under Convention.	27	1	Petition	350					Laid on table		See act Sept. 1, 1841

List of private claims presented to the House of Representatives of the United States from the 1st to the 31st Congress, inclusive—Continued.

Names of claimants.	Nature or object of the claim.	Congress.	Session.	How brought before the House of Reps.	Page of journal.	To what committee of the House referred.	No. or date of the report.	Nature of the report.	No. of the bill.	How disposed of by the House of Reps.	How disposed of by the Senate.	Date of the act of Congress, and remarks.
University of Indiana, trustees of.	Compensation for deficiency in grant of land.	28	1	Petition	83	Public Lands.						
Unkhart, Edward	(See Gustavus W. Dreyer.)	29	1		609							
Unsworth, John, widow of.	Payment of certain prize-money	22	1	Petition	441					Referred to Committee Whole House on bill No 98.		
Unsworth, Mary	(See John Unsworth, widow of)	22	1		441							
Updegraff, Isaac, widow of.	Pension	25	2	Petition	729	Rev. Pensions	807	Favorable	752	Passed.		
Updegraff, Isaac, widow of.	Pension	25	3	Petition	225	Rev. Pensions	178	Favorable	1041	Passed	Passed	App'd March 3, 1839
Updegraff, Mary	(See Isaac Updegraff, widow of)	25	2		729							
Updegraff, Mary, a portion of the heirs of.	To be allowed to receive money unclaimed by one of the heirs.	27	3	Petition	394	Rev. Claims.						
Updike, Daniel	Release from imprisonment as surety on bond to United States.	12	2	Petition	657	Select	Feb. 8, 1813	Favorable	251	Passed	Passed	App'd March 3, 1813
Updike, Daniel E	Payment of certificates of revolutionary debt.	22	2	Petition	216	Rev. Claims.						
Updike, James	Pension	28	2	Petition	140	Rev. Pensions.						
Upp, Jacob	Confirmation of title to land	14	2	Petition	163	Priv. Land Claims.						
Upp, Jacob	Confirmation of title to land	16	1	Petition	89	Priv. Land Claims.	April 1, 1820	Adverse		Laid on table.		
Upper Mississippi land company.	An act providing for the imdemnification of certain land claimants.	13	2	Senate bill	316	Whole House	March 9, 1814	With amend.	37	Passed	Concurred in.	App'd Mar. 31, 1814
Uppinghouse, James, heirs of.	To cancel certain land warrant	31	1	Petition	899	Judiciary	414	Adverse		Laid on table		Leave to withdraw.
Upshaw, Colonel James	For issue of scrip for lost land warrant.	22	2	Resolution	170	Public Lands.						
Upshaw, Captain Thomas, heirs and representatives of.	For interest on half-pay due for revolutionary services.	31	1	Petition	661	Rev. Claims.						
Upson, Gustavus	(See Richards, Upson & Co)	11	2		173							
Upson, Noah	Pension	3	1	Rep. of Secretary War.	175					Laid on table.		
Upson, Noah	Pension	3	2	Rep. of Secretary War.	278	Claims.						
Upson, Noah	Pension	4	1	Resolution	445	Claims.						
Upson, Noah	Pension	4	2	Resolution	614	Claims.						
Upton, Benjamin, & others.	For payment of semi-annual pension certificate.	25	2	Petition	581					Laid on table.		
Upton, Benjamin	Continuation of pension	27	2	Petition	255	Naval Affairs	603	Adverse		Laid on table.		
Upton, Clothworthy	(See Elizabeth H. Fenno)	30	3		477							
Upton, Samuel, *et al.*	Relief from seizure and sale of vessel and cargo.	12	1	Petition	14	Com. and Manuf.						
Upton, Samuel, *et al.*	Relief from seizure and sale of vessel and cargo.	12	1	Petition	94					Referred to Secretary State.		
Urine, Mahitabel	Pension	28	1	Petition	950					Ref'd to Com. W. H.		
Urguhart, John	Compensation for attending United States troops at Fort Mitchell.	23	1	Appropriat'n bill.	178	Whole House	Feb. 15, 1834	With amend.	181	Passed	Passed	App'd June 30, 1834
Urguhart, Thomas & David	Relief for violating revolutionary laws.	10	2	Memorial	470	Com. and Manuf.						
Ursuline, Nuns	Grant of land in city of New Orleans.	12	1	Petition	114	Select	Feb. 26, 1812	Favorable	79	Passed	Passed	App'd April 23, 1812
Use, H. & R., assignee of.	For suspension of action on claim No. 38, of P. A. Lelachaise, *et al.*	26	1	Petition	362					Laid on table.		

List of private claims presented to the House of Representatives of the United States from the 1st to the 31st Congress, inclusive—Continued.

Names of claimants.	Nature or object of the claim.	Congress.	Session.	How brought before the House of Reps.	Page of journal.	To what committee of the House referred.	No. or date of the report.	Nature of the report.	No. of the bill.	How disposed of by the House of Reps.	How disposed of by the Senate.	Date of the act of Congress, and remarks.
Use, H. & R., assignee of.	For suspension of action on claim No. 38, of P. A. Lelachaise, *et al.*	27	2	Petition	99	Priv. Land Claims.	July 27, 1842	Adverse	......	Laid on table.		
Usher, Alice	Pension	27	2	Petition	239	Rev. Pensions	573	Favorable	369	Referred to Committee Whole House.		
Usher, Alice	Pension	27	3	House bill	87	Whole House	......	......	369	Passed	Indef. postp'd.	
Usher, Alice	Pension	28	1	Petition	346	Rev. Pensions	390	Favorable	29½	Passed	Passed	App'd June 17, 1844
Usher, William	To be released from judgment	31	2	Petition	51	Judiciary.						
Usse, Yo-ha-lo, (Indian)	Confirmation of title to land	23	2	Petition	392	Public Lands.						
Usse, Yo-ha lo, (Indian)	Confirmation of title to land	24	1	Documents	212	Indian Affairs	588	Favorable	565	Referred to Committee Whole House.		
Usse, Yo-ha-lo, (Indian)	Confirmation of title to land	25	2	Documents	43	Indian Affairs	Dec. 22, 1837	Favorable	167	Referred to Committee Whole House.		
Usse, Yo-ha-lo, (Indian)	Confirmation of title to land	25	3	House bill	375	Whole House	Dec. 26, 1839	With't amend.	167	Passed	Passed	App'd March 3, 1839
Ustick, William, jr	Remission of duty on Claret wine.	4	2	Petition	634	Com. and Manuf.	397	Adverse	......	Laid on table.		
Utley, Asa	Pension	23	1	Petition	308	Rev. Pensions	......	......	......	Discharged; laid on table.		
Utsey, Captain John, *et al.*	Compensation for military services.	17	2	Petition	65	Military Affairs.						
Utt, Elias	Pension	3	1	Rep. of Secretary War.	131	Select	May 26, 1794	Favorable	62	Passed	Passed	App'd June 7, 1794
Utt, sen., Elias	Increase of pension	16	1	Petition	355	Rev. Pensions.						
Utt, Elias, (Pa.)	Pension	17	1	Resolution	265	Rev. Pensions.						
Utter, John	Pension	3	1	Rep. of Secretary War.	175	Select	......	......	......	Laid on table.		
Utter, John	Pension	3	2	Rep. of Secretary War.	278	Claims.						
Utter, John	Pension	4	1	Rep. of Secretary War.	445	Claims	Feb. 18, 1796	Favorable	156	Passed	Passed	App'd April 20, 1796
Utter, John	Increase of pension	11	2	Petition	283	Whole House	April 10, 1810	Favorable	107	Passed	Passed	App'd April 27, 1810
Utter, Samuel	Pension	19	1	Resolution	266	Military Pensions.	164	Adverse	......	Laid on table.		
Utterback, Benjamin	Pension	20	2	Resolution	92	Military Pensions.						
Vacher, John Francis	Compensation for revolutionary services.	1	2	Petition and rep't Sec. of War.	177, 251	......	......	......	......	Laid on table.		
Vail, Aaron	Exemption from certain foreign tonnage duties.	1	3	Petition	390	......	......	......	......	Referred to Secretary Treasury.		
Vail, Aaron	Exemption from certain foreign tonnage duties.	3	2	Rep. of Secretary Treasury.	284	......	......	......	......	Laid on table.		
Vail, Aaron, widow of	Relief in relation to a claim under a treaty with Spain.	18	2	Petition	75	Foreign Affairs	23	Adverse	......	Laid on table.		
Vail, Aaron, heir of	Settlement of claims as consul at L'Orient.	25	2	Memorial	267	Foreign Affairs	637	Favorable	614	Referred to Committee Whole House.		
Vail, Aaron, heir of	Settlement of claims as consul at L'Orient.	25	3	House bill	380	Whole House	Jan. 25, 1839	With't amend.	614	Passed.		

List of private claims presented to the House of Representatives of the United States from the 1st to the 31st Congress, inclusive—Continued.

Names of claimants.	Nature or object of the claim.	Congress.	Session.	How brought before the House of Reps.	Page of journal.	To what committee of the House referred.	No. or date of the report.	Nature of the report.	No. of the bill.	How disposed of by the House of Reps.	How disposed of by the Senate.	Date of the act of Congress, and remarks.
Vail, Aaron, heir of......	Settlement of claims as consul at L'Orient.	26	1	Petition	182	Foreign Affairs.						
Vail, Aaron, heir of......	Settlement of claims as consul at L'Orient.	26	1	Senate bill	837	Commerce	660	Adverse	S. 285	Laid on table.		
Vail, Aaron, heir of......	Settlement of claims as consul at L'Orient.	26	2	Senate bill	210	Foreign Affairs....	....	....	S. 144			
Vail, Aaron, heir of......	Settlement of claims as consul at L'Orient.	27	2	Senate bill	155	Foreign Affairs....	April 13, 1842	With't amend.	S. 64	Passed	Passed	App'd May 10, 1842
Vail, Eugene A.........	(See heirs of Col. Fleury, & others)	19	2	....	202							
Vail, Samuel	Confirmation of title to land in Louisiana.	22	1	Petition	33	Priv. Land Claims.						
Vail, Samuel	Confirmation of title to land in Louisiana.	22	2	Petition	32	Priv. Land Claims.						
Vail, Samuel	Confirmation of title to land in Louisiana.	23	1	Petition	48	Priv. Land Claims.	216	Favorable....	234	Passed	Passed	App'd June 28, 1834
Valck & Co., (Baltimore).	Reimbursement of excessive duties on wine.	4	1	Memorial	448	Com. and Manuf. .	Mar. 7, 1796	Adverse	......	Rejected	....	Leave to withdraw.
Valck & Co., trustees of..	Indemnity for French spoliations prior to 1800.	26	1	Memorial	182	Foreign Affairs....	343	Favorable; bill	319	Referred to Committee Whole House.		
Valecour, Jean Batt, heirs of.	Confirmation of title to land	12	2	House bill	609	Whole House.....	Jan. 18, 1813	With amend..	222	Passed	Passed	App'd Feb. 13, 1813
Valentine, André........	For the fee of his improved lands.	23	2	Petition	138	Priv. Land Claims.	....	....	......	Discharged; laid on table.		
Valentine, Bernard	Bounty land for revolutionary services.	22	2	Resolution	121	Public Lands.....	48	Favorable....	693	Referred to Committee Whole House.		
Valentine, Jacob	Invalid pension...............	3	1	Rep. of Secretary War.	131	Select	May 26, 1794	Res. to refer to Sec. War.	J. R. 12	Passed	Passed	App'd June 9, 1794
Valentine, Jacob	Invalid pension...............	4	1	Rep. of Secretary War.	445	Claims	Mar. 4, 1796	Res. to refer to Sec. War.	J. R. 16	Passed	Passed	App'd April 17, 1796
Valentine, Jacob	Invalid pension...............	4	1	Petition	458	Claims	May 31, 1796	Adverse	......	Laid on table.		
Valentine, Jacob	Invalid pension...............	4	2	Res. and docs...	614	Claims.						
Valentine, James........	For an adjustment of his account for services in revolutionary war.	9	2	Petition	611	Whole House.						
Valentine, John, and John Curle.	Compensation for services and losses in revolutionary war.	4	2	Petition	660	Claims	Jan. 31, 1797	Adverse	......	Rejected.		
Valentine & McMeehan ..	Compensation for work on Cumberland road.	23	1	Resolution	589	Claims	445	Adverse	......	Laid on table	....	See report No. 449.
Valenzin, David, representatives of.	Indemnity for losses by capture of his vessel by U. States schooner Enterprise.	8	1	Petition	440	Claims	Dec. 12, 1803	Rep. not found.	......	Recommitted.		
							Feb. 1, 1804	Supp'l report .	201	Passed	Passed	App'd Mar. 26, 1804
Valenzin, David, representatives of.	Amount re-appropriated.........	12	1	Naval appropriation bill.	157	Whole House	Feb. 5, 1812	With amends.	59	Passed	Passed	App'd Feb. 24, 1812
Valiant, Wm., mother of..	Pay and bounty land due for military service.	16	1	Petition	334	Public Lands.....	April 11, 1820	Favorable....	135	Referred to Committee Whole House.		
Valiant, Wm., mother of..	Pay and bounty land due for military service.	16	2	Bill of last sess..	73	Whole House	Dec. 14, 1820	With't amend.	135	Passed	Passed	App'd Jan. 17, 1821
Valkenburgh, Bar. J. V...	Payment of sundry revolutionary certificates.	19	2	Senate bill	276	Rev. Claims......	Feb. 13, 1827	With't amend.	69	Passed	Passed	App'd March 3, 1827
Vallé, Charles C.........	(See Francis Vallé, heirs of)	15	2	....	67							
Vallé, Charles F. A......	Confirmation of title to land (old mines) in Missouri.	22	1	Petition	263	Priv. Land Claims.	303	Favorable....	380	Referred to Committee Whole House.		

List of private claims presented to the House of Representatives of the United States from the 1st to the 31st Congress, inclusive—Continued.

Names of claimants.	Nature or object of the claim.	Congress.	Session.	How brought before the House of Reps.	Page of journal.	To what committee of the House referred.	No. or date of the report.	Nature of the report.	No. of the bill.	How disposed of by the House of Reps.	How disposed of by the Senate.	Date of the act of Congress, and remarks.
Vallé, Francis, heirs of...	Confirmation of title to land in Missouri.	15	2	Petition	47, 67	Priv. Land Claims.						
Vallé, Francis, heirs of...	Confirmation of title to land in Missouri.	17	1	Petition	55	Public Lands.						
Vallé, Francis, heirs of...	Confirmation of title to land in Missouri.	18	1	Petition	55	Public Lands.						
Vallé, Francis, heirs of...	Confirmation of title to land in Missouri.	19	1	Petition	133	Public Lands.....	75	Favorable....	104	Passed.		
Vallé, Francis, heirs of...	Confirmation of title to land in Missouri.	19	2	Petition	27	Public Lands.....	4	Favorable....	282	Passed.		
Vallé, Francis, heirs of...	Confirmation of title to land in Missouri.	20	1	Petition	33	Public Lands.....	82	Favorable....	80	Passed	Passed	App'd May 24, 1828
Vallé, Francis, 2d.......	(See Francis Vallé, heirs of)	15	2	....	47							
Vallé, Francis B.	Confirmation of title to land (old mines) in Missouri.	22	1	Petition	263	Priv. Land Claims.	303	Favorable....	380	Referred to Committee Whole House.		
Vallé, François.........	Arrears of pension............	29	1	Petition	572	Invalid Pensions ..	827	Adverse	.....	Laid on table.		
Vallé, Jean Baptiste	(See Francis Vallé, heirs of)	15	2	....	67							
Vallé, Jean B...........	Permission to change location of land.	24	2	Senate bill	578	....	....	....	S. 151			
Vallé, Jean B...........	Permission to change location of land.	25	2	Senate bill	483	Priv. Land Claims.	April 6, 1838	With't amend.	S. 63	Referred to Committee Whole House.		
Vallé, Jean B...........	Permission to change location of land.	25	3	Senate bill	107	Public Lands.....	Jan. 15, 1839	With't amend.	S. 51	Passed	....	App'd Feb. 6, 1839
Vallé, John B.	Confirmation of title to land (old mines) in Missouri.	22	1	Petition	263	Priv. Land Claims.	303	Favorable....	380	Referred to Committee Whole House.		
Vallé, John Baptiste, heirs of.	Confirmation of Spanish land grant	31	1	Petition	299	Priv. Land Claims.	347	Adverse	......	Laid on table.		
Valleau, Charles, wife of, and others.	Compensation for loss of improvements on land.	25	2	Petition	373	Priv. Land Claims.	....	....	......	Discharged; laid on table.		
Vallery, Jean Baptiste....	Confirmation of title to land in Louisiana.	22	1	Petition	336	Priv. Land Claims.	323	Favorable....	406	Referred to Committee Whole House.		
Vallery, Jean Baptiste, heir of.	Confirmation of title to land in Louisiana.	27	2	Senate bill	359	Priv. Land Claims.	Feb. 26, 1842	With amend..	S. 76	Passed	Passed	App'd July 6, 1842
Valnerie, Francis........	(See Joseph Val De Hauterive, heirs of.)	31	2	....	270							
Valverdi, Isabella, attorney of.	Indemnity for losses resulting from invasion of Florida in 1818.	22	1	Petition	472	Foreign Affairs.						
Van Aermar, William....	Pension	19	2	Petition	91	Military Pensions.						
Van Alstine, Abraham...	Redemption of paper money placed in his hands for public use.	1	2	Petition	177	....	....	....	......	Referred to Secretary Treasury.		
Van Alstine, Abraham...	Redemption of paper money placed in his hands for public use.	2	2	Rep. of Secretary Treasury.	625	....	....	....	......	Laid on table.		
Van Alstine, Abraham J..	Compensation for building material for public use.	3	1	Petition	59	....	....	....	......	Referred to Secretary Treasury.		
Van Alstine, Abraham J..	Compensation for building material for public use.	3	2	Rep. of Secretary Treasury.	284	Claims	Mar. 2, 1795	Adverse	......	Laid on table.		
Van Alstine, Abraham J..	Compensation for building material for public use.	4	1	Petition & docs.	598	Claims	May 31, 1796	Adverse	......	Laid on table.		
Van Alstine, Alexander ..	(See Peter Bargy, assignee of.) ..	28	1	....	941	....	525					
Van Anglen, John.......	Pension for revolutionary services.	10	1	Pension bill	232	Whole House	April 19, 1808	With amend..	78	Passed	Passed, with amendment.	App'd April 25, 1808
Van Antwerp, Jeremiah ..	(See Major John Campbell, heirs of.)	21	1	....	295							

List of private claims presented to the House of Representatives of the United States from the 1st to the 31st Congress, inclusive—Continued.

Names of claimants.	Nature or object of the claim.	Congress.	Session.	How brought before the House of Reps.	Page of journal.	To what committee of the House referred.	No. or date of the report.	Nature of the report.	No. of the bill.	How disposed of by the House of Reps.	How disposed of by the Senate.	Date of the act of Congress, and remarks.
Van Antwerp, John	Invalid pension	3	1	Rep. of Secretary War.	131	Select	May 26, 1794	Res. to refer to Sec. War.	J R. 12	Passed	Passed	App'd June 9, 1794
Van Antwerp, John	Invalid pension	4	1	Resolution	445	Claims	May 4, 1796	Res. to refer to Sec. War.	J. R. 16	Passed	Passed	App'd April 17, 1796
Van Antwerp, John	Invalid pension	4	2	Res. and docs	614	Claims.						
Van Antwerpen, John widow of.	Pension for revolutionary services.	25	2	Petition	272	Rev. Pensions				Discharged.		
Van Antwerpen, Rachel	(See John Van Antwerpen, widow of.)											
Van Arnan, William	(See Willett's regiment, officers and men of.)	16	1		85							
Van Artsdalen, Jacob C.	Pension for revolutionary services.	21	2	Resolution	275	Military Pensions.						
Van Artsdalen, Jocob C.	Pension for revolutionary services.	22	1	Resolution	94	Rev. Pensions.						
Vanausdal, Cornelius	Confirmation of pre-emption claim	29	1	Memorial	493	Public Lands.						
Van Benthuysen	(See Wendall & Van Benthuysen)	30	2		415							
Van Bergen, Peter	Pension for revolutionary services.	22	1	Petition	470	Rev. Pensions.						
Van Bibber, Andrew A.	(See administrator of Isaac Garretson.)	24	1		751							
Van Billon, John Henry	Invalid pension	8	2	Petition	142	Claims.						
Van Brunt, Rulif	Indemnity for property destroyed by United States troops.	28	2	Petition	120	Claims				Leave to withdraw.		
Van Brunt, Rulif	Indemnity for property destroyed by United States troops.	29	1	Petition	476	Claims.						
Van Brunt, Rulif	Indemnity for property destroyed by United States troops.	29	2	Petition	69	Claims.						
Van Brunt, Rulif	Indemnity for property destroyed by United States troops.	30	1	Petition	66	Claims.						
Van Brunt, Rulif	Indemnity for property destroyed by United States troops.	30	2	Petition	86	Claims.						
Van Brunt, Rulif	Indemnity for property destroyed by United States troops.	31	1	Petition	234	Military Affairs	6	Adverse		Laid on table.		
Van Burkleo, William	Pension	23	2	Petition	166	Invalid Pensions	71	Adverse		Laid on table.		
Van Buskirk, Jacobus	Compensation for wood furnished, revolutionary war.	4	1	Rep. of Secretary Treasury.	388	Claims	May 31, 1796	Adverse		Laid on table.		
Van Camp, Isaac	Pension	21	2	Petition	43	Miltary Pensions.						
Van Camp, Isaac	Increase of pension	25	2	Petition	180	Rev. Claims.						
Van Camp, Isaac	Increase of pension	25	3	Petition	85	Rev. Claims.						
Van Camp, Isaac	Compensation for revolutionary services and for property lost.	27	2	Petition	749	Rev. Claims	980	Adverse		Laid on table.		
Van Campen, John	Commutation pay	24	1	Petition	137	Rev. Claims	581	Adverse		Laid on table.		
Van Campen, Moses	Pension	21	2	Petition	43	Military Pensions.						
Van Campen, Moses	Commutation pay for revolutionary services.	24	2	Petition	73	Rev. Claims.						
Van Campen, Moses	Commutation pay for revolutionary services.	24	2	Senate bill	251	Rev. Claims	204	Adverse	S. 90	Referred to Committee Whole House.		
Van Campen, Moses	Commutation pay for revolutionary services.	25	2	Senate bill	700	Rev. Claims	937	With't amend.	S. 159	Passed	Passed	App'd June 12, 1838
Van Campen, Moses	Interest on commutation pay	29	1	Petition	494	Rev. Pensions				Laid on table.		
Van Campen, Moses	Interest on commutation pay	29	2	Petition	82	Rev. Claims				Discharged; laid on table.		
Van Campen, Moses	Interest on commutation pay	30	1	Petition	99	Rev. Claims	824	Favorable	641	Referred to Committee Whole House.		
Van Campen, Moses	Interest on commutation pay	31	1	Petition	194	Military Affairs.						

List of private claims presented to the House of Representatives of the United States from the 1st to the 31st Congress, inclusive—Continued.

Names of claimants.	Nature or object of the claim.	Congress.	Session.	How brought before the House of Reps.	Page of journal.	To what committee of the House referred.	No. or date of the report.	Nature of the report.	No. of the bill.	How disposed of by the House of Reps.	How disposed of by the Senate.	Date of the act of Congress, and remarks.
Vance, Jacob, or Jacob L.	Compensation for a horse lost in war of 1812.	15	2	Petition	205	Claims.						
Vance, Jacob, or Jacob L.	Compensation for a horse lost in war of 1812.	25	3	Petition	462	Claims.						
Vance, Jacob, or Jacob L.	Compensation for a horse lost in war of 1812.	26	1	Petition	168	Claims.						
Vance, Jacob, or Jacob L.	Compensation for a horse lost in war of 1812.	26	2	Petition	182	Claims.						
Vance, Jacob, or Jacob L.	Compensation for a horse lost in war of 1812.	27	2	Petition	56	Claims	342	Adverse		Laid on table.		
Vance, Jacob, or Jacob L.	Compensation for a horse lost in war of 1812.	28	2	Petition	276	Cliams	51	Favorable	531	Passed	Rep'd without amendment.	
Vance, Jacob, or Jacob L.	Compensation for a horse lost in war of 1812.	29	1	Petition	207	Claims	193	Favorable	184	Referred to Committee Whole House.		
Vance, Jacob, or Jacob L.	Compensation for a horse lost in war of 1812.	29	2	House bill	71	Whole House	Dec. 18, 1846	With amend.	184	Passed	Passed	App'd March 3, 1847
Vance, Joseph	Compensation for cattle lost by the imprudence of an officer of the government.	16	1	Petition	295	Claims	April 3, 1820	Adverse		Laid on table.		
Vance, Joseph	Compensation for cattle lost by the imprudence of an officer of the government.	17	1	Petition	73	Claims.						
Vance, Joseph	Right to complete the payments due for certain forfeited land.	24	1	Petition	510					Referred to Committee Whole House on bill No. 130.		
Vance, Robert, heirs of	Commutation pay for revolutionary services.	25	2	Petition	575	Rev. Claims.						
Vance, Robert, heirs of	Commutation pay for revolutionary services.	25	3	Petition	125	Rev. Claims.						
Vance, Robert, heirs of	Commutation pay for revolutionary services.	26	1	Petition	360	Rev. Claims	June 23, 1840	Adverse		Laid on table.		
Vance, Robert, heirs of	Commutation pay for revolutionary services.	26	2	Petition	122	Rev. Claims	179	Adverse		Laid on table.		
Vance, Sally	(See mother of Thaddeus Carby.)	17	1		269							
Vance, Samuel	(See Joshua W. Prout, administrator of.)	17	1		380							
Vance, Samuel	Pension for revolutionary services.	22	1	Petition	45	Rev. Pensions.						
Vance, William	Pension	23	1	Petition	113	Rev. Pensions				Discharged; leave to withdraw.		
Van Cleef, John M.	(See Edward B. Dudley and others)	16	1		207							
Van Courtland, Philip, executor of.	Commutation pay for revolutionary services.	29	2	Petition	89	Rev. Claims.						
Vandeford, Benjamin, widow of.	Pension for services in the exploring expedition.	28	1	Petition	203	Naval Affairs.						
Vandeford, Benjamin, widow of.	Pension for services in the exploring expedition.	29	1	Petition	1055	Naval Affairs.						
Vandeford, Benjamin, widow of.	Pension for services in the exploring expedition.	30	1	Petition	408	Naval Affairs	444	Favorable	375	Referred to Committee Whole House.		
Vandeford, Elizabeth	(See Benjamin Vandeford, widow of.)	28	1		203							
Vandenburgh, Bartholomew, widow of.	Pension for revolutionary services.	27	2	Petition	360	Rev. Pensions	574	Favorable	370	Ordered to 3d reading.		

List of private claims presented to the House of Representatives of the United States from the 1st to the 31st Congress, inclusive—Continued.

ames of claimants.	Nature or object of the claim.	Congress.	Session.	How brought before the House of Reps.	Page of journal.	To what committee of the House referred.	No. or date of the report.	Nature of the report.	No. of the bill.	How disposed of by the House of Reps.	How disposed of by the Senate.	Date of the act of Congress, and remarks.
Vandenburgh, Bartholomew, widow of.	Pension for revolutionary services.	27	3	House bill.....	87	....	....	....	370	Passed.		
Vandenburgh, Eve	(See Bartholomew Vandenburgh, widow of.)											
Vandenburgh, James.....	Pension for revolutionary services.	22	1	Resolution	194	Rev. Pensions	375	Favorable....	469	Referred to Committee Whole House.		
Vandenburgh, James.....	Pension for revolutionary services.	23	1	Petition	46	Rev. Pensions.						
Vandenburgh, Wynant W.	Compensation for public services .	29	1	Petition	220	Rev. Claims.						
Vandenburgh, Wynant W.	Compensation for public services .	31	1	Petition	257	Rev. Claims.						
Vanderbilt, Catherine	Pension	26	2	Petition	122	Rev. Pensions	Feb. 12, 1841	Adverse	......	Laid on table.		
Vanderbilt, Cornelius	Compensation for transportation of the mail.	24	2	Petition	37	Claims.						
Vanderbilt, Cornelius	Compensation for transportation of the mail.	25	2	Petition	574	Claims	722	Adverse	......	Laid on table.		
Vanderbilt, John, administrator of.	(See Johnnes E. Lott, and others.)	5	2	....	144							
Vanderburgh, Henry	Compensation for revolutionary services.	10	2	Petition	380	Select.						
Vandercook, Michael S...	Remission of duties on spirits destroyed by fire.	14	1	Petition	399	Ways and Means..	....	....	......	Referred to Committee Whole House.		
Vanderhayden, Jacob	(See Canadian refugees)........	4	2	....	614							
Vanderlyn, John	Additional compensation for portrait of Washington.	23	1	Resolution	855	....	....	....	......	....	....	Paid out of the contingent fund.
Vanderlier, Henry heir of.	Payment of balance due for revolutionary services.	18	2	Petition	135	Pens. & Rev. Cl'ms.	....	....	......	Discharged; leave to withdraw.		
Vanderlier, John........	(See Henry Vanderlier, heir of.) .											
Vanderpool, Abraham B..	Correction of an error in settlement	18	2	Petition	239	Ways and Means.						
Vanderslice, Henry, representatives of.	Compensation for revolutionary services.	25	3	Petition	381	Rev. Claims.						
Vanderslice, Henry, representatives of.	Compensation for revolutionary services.	28	1	Petition	222	Claims.						
Vanderslice, John	(See Henry Vanderslice, representatives of.)											
Vanderslice, Thomas J...	Right of pre-emption as New Orleans branch pilot.	28	1	Petition	77	Priv. Land Claims.	9	Favorable....	35	Passed	Passed	App'd June 17, 1844
Vanderveer, Albert	Pension for revolutionary services.	24	1	Petition	433	Rev. Pensions....	....	....	......	Discharged; laid on table.		
Vanderveer, Albert	Pension for revolutionary services.	24	2	Petition	158	Rev. Pensions.....	118	Adverse	......	Laid on table.		
Vanderveer, John	Compensation for a horse lost in war of 1812.	18	2	Petition	70	Claims.						
Vandervoort, Jacob, heirs of.	Pension for services, war of 1812.	28	1	Petition	683	Naval Affairs.						
Vandervoort, Paul.......	Compensation for revolutionary services.	10	1	Petition	174	Whole House.						
Vandervoort, Paul.......	Compensation for revolutionary services.	10	2	Petition	369	Claims.						
Vandervoort, Paul.......	Payment of a revolutionary certificate.	18	2	Petition	251	Select.						
Vandervoort, Paul.......	Payment of a revolutionary certificate.	29	1	Petition	126	Rev. Claims......	....	....	......	Leave to withdraw.		
Van Drunen, William, and George Wolcott.	Increase of compensation as surveyors of the customs.	14	2	Petition	233	Ways and Means.						

List of private claims presented to the House of Representatives of the United States from the 1st to the 31st Congress, inclusive—**Continued.**

Names of claimants.	Nature or object of the claim.	Congress.	Session.	How brought before the House of Reps.	Page of journal.	To what committee of the House referred.	No. or date of the report.	Nature of the report.	No. of the bill.	How disposed of by the House of Reps.	How disposed of by the Senate.	Date of the act of Congress, and remarks.
Van Drunen, William, and George Wolcott.	Increase of compensation as surveyors of customs.	15	1	Petition	90	Ways and Means.						
Van Drunen, William, and George Wolcott.	Increase of compensation as surveyors of customs.	15	2	Petition	73	Com. and Manuf.						
Van Drunen, William, and George Wolcott.	Increase of compensation as surveyors of customs.	16	1	Petition	29	Commerce.						
Vandeusen, Abraham, widow of.	Pension for revolutionary services.	25	2	Petition	272	Rev. Pensions.						
Vandeusen, Annytie	(See Abraham Vandensen widow of.)											
Van Deventer, Jacobus	(See Johannes E. Lott & others)	5	2		144							
Van Doren, Jacob, widow of.	Revolutionary pension	26	1	Petition	286	Rev. Pensions	424	Adverse		Laid on table.		
Van Doren, Jane	(See Jacob Van Doren, widow of.)											
Van Driesen, Joseph S.	Pension	14	1	Petition	92	Pens. & Rev. Cl'ms.	April 11, 1816	Favorable; bill		Passed	Passed	App'd April 30, 1816
Van Driesen, Joseph S.	Increase of pension	15	1	Petition	168	Pens. & Rev. Cl'ms.						
Van Driesen, Joseph S., guardian of the heir of.	Pension for military services	27	2	Petition	526	Rev. Pensions	784	Adverse		Laid on table.		
Van Driesen, Mary M.	(See Jos. S. Van Driesen, guardian of the heir of.)	14	1		92							
Vandruff, Joshua	Indemnity for Indian depredations.	22	1	Resolution	194	Claims	Mar. 1, 1832	Adverse		Laid on table.		
Vandruff, Joshua	Indemnity for Indian depredations.	24	2	Petition & docs.	395	Military Affairs.						
Vandruff, Joshua	Indemnity for Indian depredations.	26	1	Petition & docs.	623	Claims.						
Van Dyke, Charles	Pension	15	1	Petition and rep't Sec. Navy.	136, 288					Laid on table.		
Van Dyke, Henry, heir of.	Prize money as an officer, United States navy.	27	2	Petition and rep't Sec. Navy.	70, 735	Naval Affairs.						
Van Dyke, Henry, heir of.	Prize money as an officer, United States navy.	29	1	Petition	328	Naval Affairs	361	Adverse		Laid on table.		
Van Dyke, Henry	(See John Van Dyke, heirs of)	30	2		117							
Van Dyke, John	Arrears of pension	24	2	Petition	272	Rev. Pensions				Discharged; laid on table.		
Van Dyke, John	Arrears of pension	25	2	Petition	182	Rev. Pensions				Discharged; laid on table.		
Van Dyke, John, heir of.	Indemnity for property destroyed, revolutionary war.	30	2	Petition	117	Rev. Claims.						
Van Dyke, John, heir of.	Commutation pay for revolutionary services.	31	2	Petition	33	Rev. Claims.						
Van Dyck, Lawrence	(See Jehoiakim Van Valkenburgh)	29	1		85							
Van Eps, Evert	Invalid pension	3	2	Rep. of Secretary War.	278	Claims.						
Van Eps, Evert	Invalid pension	4	1	Rep. of Secretary War.	445	Claims	Mar. 4, 1796	Res. to refer to Sec. War.	J. R. 16	Passed	Passed	App'd April 17, 1796
Van Everen, Cornelia	(See Myndert Van Everen, heirs of.)											
Van Everen, Myndert, heirs of.	Half-pay in lieu of bounty land	17	1	Petition	68	Military Affairs	Feb. 21, 1822	Adverse		Leave to withdraw.		
Van Fleet, Daniel	Pension	25	2	Petition	572	Rev. Pensions				Discharged; laid on table.		
Van Fossen, John	Additional compensation for attendance as a witness.	22	1	Petition	1041	Accounts	July 14, 1832	Favorable		Laid on table.		
Van Fossen, John	Additional compensation for attendance as a witness.	22	2	Petition	45	Accounts.						

List of private claims presented to the House of Representatives of the United States from the 1st to the 31st Congress, inclusive—Continued.

Names of claimants.	Nature or object of the claim.	Congress.	Session.	How brought before the House of Reps.	Page of journal.	To what committee of the House referred.	No. or date of the report.	Nature of the report.	No. of the bill.	How disposed of by the House of Reps.	How disposed of by the Senate.	Date of the act of Congress, and remarks.
Vanfossan, Peter, by John, administrator of.	Compensation for a horse impressed, revolutionary war.	2	1	Petition and rep't Sec. of War.	507, 580	....	....	....	......	Laid on table.		
Van Gaasbeck, Thomas...	Pension for revolutionary services.	21	1	Resolution	248	Military Pensions..	May 2, 1830	Adverse	......	Laid on table.		
Van Gaasbeck, Thomas...	Pension for revolutionary services.	21	2	Resolution	48	Select.						
Vangine, Saracen Boi François.	Grant of land under Quapaw treaty.	19	2	Petition	137	Public Lands.....	60	Favorable....	401	Referred to Committee Whole House.		
Vangorden, James	Bounty land for services, war of 1812.	30	1	Petition	172	Public Lands.....	....	....	......	Discharged; laid on table.		
Van Gover, John........	(See John M. Burt, administrator of.)	24	2	....	315							
Van Grundy, John	Remission of the forfeiture of his land.	21	1	Petition	360	Priv. Land Claims.						
Van Heer, Bartholomew..	Compensation for revolutionary services.	3	1	Memorial	96	Select	May 14, 1794	Adverse	.....	Laid on table.		
Van Hook, William	(See Tees & Van Hook)	22	2	....	266							
Van Horn, Abraham.....	Pension for revolutionary services.	27	2	Petition	869	Rev. Pensions.....	921	Favorable	533	Ordered to 3d reading.		
Van Horn, Abraham.....	Pension for revolutionary services.	27	3	House bill......	89	....	....	....	533	Passed	Indef. postp'd.	
Van Horn, Augustus V., and others.	Indemnity for seizure of their ship by the French government in 1809.	18	1	Memorial	387	Foreign Affairs.						
Van Horne & Clarkson...	Indemnity for French spoliations prior to 1800.	26	1	Memorial	182	Foreign Affairs....	343	Favorable; bill	319	Referred to Committee Whole House.		
Van Horn, Cornelius, and others.	Pension for services in Indian wars.	23	2	Petition	115	Whole House.						
Van Horne, C..........	(Not stated)..................	31	2	Additional docs..	158	Military Affairs.						
Van Horn, Daniel.......	Pension for revolutionary services.	23	1	Resolution	618	Rev. Pensions.						
Van Horn, Garret	Indemnity for French spoliations prior to 1800.	26	1	Memorial	182	Foreign Affairs ...	343	Favorable; bill	319	Referred to Committee Whole House.		
Van Horn, Isaac	Compensation for labor, &c., on Cumberland road.	23	1	Resolution	589	Claims	455	Adverse	......	Laid on table	....	See report No. 449.
Van Horn, James	Indemnity for destruction of mill by the enemy.	15	1	Petition	222	Claims	Feb. 18, 1818	Adverse	......	Rejected.		
Van Horn, James	Indemnity for destruction of mill by the enemy.	26	1	Petition	702	Claims.						
Van Horne, James P.....	(See New York Insurance Company.)	26	1	....	182							
Van Horn, Joseph.......	(See David Zeigler and others)...	8	1	....	460							
Van Horn J., and others..	Indemnity for destruction of regimental library and other property by a flood at Camp Salado.	31	1	Petition	639	Military Affairs.						
Van Horn, Samuel	Pension	22	1	Petition	441	Rev. Pensions.						
Van Horsie, Abraham and Jane.	(See heirs of Jellis, or Tellis, Fonda.)	27	2	....	62							
Van Ingen, Dirk........	Compensation for services as surgeon in revolutionary war.	2	2	Petition	687	....	....	....	......	Laid on table.		
Van Ingen, Dirk, heirs of.	Compensation for services as surgeon in revolutionary war.	24	1	Petition	281	Rev. Claims.						
Van Ingen, Dirk, heirs of.	Compensation for services as surgeon in revolutionary war.	25	2	Petition	985	Rev. Claims......	....	....	......	Discharged; laid on table.		
Van Ingen, Dirk, heirs of.	Compensation for services as surgeon in revolutionary war.	27	2	Petition	47	Rev. Claims......	536	Adverse	......	Laid on table.		
Van Ingen, Dirk, sole heir of.	Arrears of pay due.............	30	2	Petition	76	Rev. Claims.						

List of private claims presented to the House of Representatives of the United States from the 1st to the 31st Congress, inclusive—Continued.

Names of claimants.	Nature or object of the claim.	Congress.	Session.	How brought before the House of Reps.	Page of journal.	To what committee of the House referred.	No. or date of the report	Nature of the report.	No. of the bill.	How disposed of by the House of Reps.	How disposed of by the Senate.	Date of the act of Congress, and remarks.
Van Ingen, Dirk, sole heir of.	Arrears of pay due	31	1	Petition	307	Rev. Claims	419	Adverse	......	Laid on table.		
Van Kirk, John	Pension	21	1	Petition and docs.	36, 318	Military Pensions.						
Van Kirk, John	Pension	21	2	Petition	137	Military Pensions.						
Van Kleeck, Lawrence	Additional compensation as collector of internal revenue.	21	2	Petition	160	Claims	67	Favorable	604	Referred to Committee Whole House.		
Van Kleeck, Lawrence	Additional compensation as collector of internal revenue.	21	1	Petition	42	Claims	Dec. 19, 1831	Favorable	39	Passed	Passed	App'd Feb. 18, 1832
Van Meter, H	(See John Reynolds and H. Van Meter.)	21	1	....	236							
Van Meter, Henry	Pension for services in the war of 1812.	29	1	Memorial	1140	Invalid Pensions.						
Vanmetre, Joseph	(See Bryant R. Young and others)	23	1	....	499							
Vann, Avery	Indemnity for property destroyed by Indians.	20	1	Resolution	409	Claims	April 24, 1828	Adverse	......	Laid on table.		
Vann, David	(See John Ridge and others)	23	1	....	196							
Van Natta, John	Grant of land for revolutionary services.	19	1	Resolution	410	Priv. Land Claims.						
Van Ness, Abner E	Compensation for services as surveyor of public lands.	28	1	Petition	352	Public Lands.						
Van Ness, Abner E	Compensation for services as surveyor of public lands.	28	2	Petition	56	Public Lands	68	Favorable	549	Referred to Committee Whole House.		
Van Ness, Abner E	Compensation for services as surveyor of public lands.	29	1	Petition	121	Claims.						
Van Ness, Abner E	Compensation for services as surveyor of public lands.	30	1	Petition	156	Public Lands.						
Van Ness, Abraham D	(See David Van Ness, heirs of)	30	1	....	887							
Van Ness, Cornelius P	Extra compensation as minister to Spain.	26	2	Documents	131	Foreign Affairs.						
Van Ness, Cornelius P	Extra compensation as minister to Spain.	27	2	Documents	557	Foreign Affairs	919	Adverse	......	Laid on table.		
Van Ness, David, heirs of.	Commutation pay for revolutionary services.	30	1	Petition	887	Rev. Claims.						
Van Ness, Effie	(See Garrett Van Ness, widow of.)	26	1	....	285							
Van Ness, Eugene	(See Nehemiah Brush, executors of.)	29	1	....	465							
Van Ness, Garrett, widow of.	Pension for revolutionary services.	26	1	Petition	285	Rev. Pensions	472	Favorable	386	Referred to Committee Whole House.		
Van Ness, Garrett, widow of.	Pension for revolutionary services.	27	2	Petition	153	Rev. Pensions	121	Favorable	167	Passed	Passed	App'd Aug. 30, 1842
Van Ness, John D	(See David Van Ness, heirs of)	30	1	....	887							
Vannettin, John, and his company of volunteers.	Compensation for services, war of 1812.	24	2	Documents	308	Claims	254	Adverse	......	Laid on table.		
Vannettin, John, and his company of volunteers.	Compensation for services, war of 1812.	25	2	Documents	88	Claims	582	Favorable	566	Referred to Committee Whole House.		
Vannettin, John, and his company of volunteers.	Compensation for services, war of 1812.	25	3	House bill	380	Whole House	Jan. 26, 1839	With't amend.	566	Passed	Passed	App'd March 3, 1839
Van Noorden, Hadrianus.	Indemnity for capture of schooner Betsey by the French, in 1796.	19	2	Petition	84	Ways and Means.						
Van Noorden, Hadrianus.	Indemnity for French spoliations prior to 1800.	26	1	Memorial	182	Foreign Affairs	343	Favorable; bill	319	Referred to Committee Whole House.		
Van Norstrand, Matthew	Pension	23	2	Petition	105	Rev. Pensions.						

List of private claims presented to the House of Representatives of the United States from the 1st to the 31st Congress, inclusive—Continued.

Names of claimants.	Nature or object of the claim.	Congress.	Session.	How brought before the House of Reps.	Page of journal.	To what committee of the House referred.	No. or date of the report.	Nature of the report.	No. of the bill.	How disposed of by the House of Reps.	How disposed of by the Senate.	Date of the act of Congress, and remarks.
Vannoy, Mason	(See sureties of William & George Gould.)	29	1		411							
Van Orden, Andreas	Revolutionary pension	22	1	Petition	56	Rev. Pensions.						
Van Orden, Andreas	(See Henry Van Orden, heirs of.)	24	2		390							
Van Orden, Benjamin	Pension	22	1	Petition	558	Rev. Pensions.						
Van Orden, Henry, heir of	Permission to locate land warrant.	24	2	Memorial	390	Public Lands.						
Van Orden, John, widow of.	Pension for revolutionary services.	26	1	Petition	286	Rev. Pensions.						
Van Orden, Peter	Compensation for revolutionary services.	21	1	Petition	98	Military Pensions	May 4, 1830	Adverse		Laid on table.		
Van Orden, Peter	Compensation for revolutionary services.	22	1	Petition and docs.	515	Rev. Pensions	395	Favorable	494	Referred to Committee Whole House.		
Van Patten, Andries	Compensation for supplies furnished for public use.	10	1	Petition	96	Claims.						
Van Patten, Andries	Compensation for supplies furnished for public use.	10	2	Petition	348	Claims.						
Van Patten, Andries	Compensation for supplies furnished for public use.	11	2	Petition	120	Claims				Discharged.		
Van Patten, Andries	Compensation for supplies furnished for public use.	11	3	Petition	441	Claims.						
Van Patten, Andries	Compensation for supplies furnished for public use.	12	1	Petition	24	Claims	Feb. 19, 1812	Adverse		Laid on table.		
Van Pelt, John, (Ky.)	Further compensation for revolutionary services.	12	1	Petition	165	Claims.						
Van Pelt, John, widow of, (N. Y.)	Pension for revolutionary services.	28	2	Petition	114	Rev. Pensions.						
Van Pelt, Sarah	(See John Van Pelt, widow of.)											
Van Rensselaer, Catharine N.	(See Nicholas N. Bogart, heirs of)	31	1		307							
Van Rensselaer, Henry K., widow of.	Pension for revolutionary services.	25	3	Petition	216	Rev. Pensions				Discharged.		
Van Rensselaer, Henry K., widow of.	Pension for revolutionary services.	26	1	Petition	175	Rev. Pensions	714	Adverse		Laid on table.		
Van Rensselaer, Henry K., widow of.	Pension for revolutionary services.	28	1	Petition	481	Rev. Pensions.						
Van Rensselaer, Henry K., widow of.	Pension for revolutionary services.	29	1	Petition	233	Rev. Pensions	523	Adverse		Laid on table		Leave to withd'w, Dec. 18, 1848.
Van Rensselaer, James	Compensation for revolutionary services.	19	1	Petition	176	Rev. Claims	Feb. 26, 1826	Adverse		Laid on table.		
Van Rensselaer, J. J.	(See William Baker, N. Y.)	22	1		288		480					
Van Rensselaer, Jas., heirs of.	Commutation pay for revolutionary services.	25	2	Petition	391	Rev. Claims.						
Van Rensselaer, Killian, & others.	Compensation for supplies furnished revolutionary army.	3	1	Petition	21					Referred to Secretary Treasury.		
Van Rensselaer, Killian, & others.	Compensation for supplies furnished revolutionary army.	3	2	Rep. of Secretary Treasury.	284	Claims	Mar. 2, 1795	Adverse		Laid on table.		
Van Rensselaer, Killian, & others.	Compensation for supplies furnished revolutionary army.	4	1	Memorial	598	Claims	May 31, 1796	Adverse		Laid on table.		
Van Rensselaer, Killian, & others.	Compensation for supplies furnished revolutionary army.	5	2	Memorial	184	Claims	Feb. 20, 1798	Adverse		Rejected.		
Van Rensselear, Nancy	(See Henry K. Van Rensselear, widow of.)	25	3		216							

List of private claims presented to the House of Representatives of the United States from the 1st to the 31st Congress, inclusive—Continued.

Names of claimants.	Nature or object ot the claim.	Congress.	Session.	How brought before the House of Reps.	Page of journal.	To what committee of the House referred.	No. or date of the report.	Nature of the report.	No. of the bill.	How disposed of by the House of Reps.	How disposed of by the Senate.	Date of the act of Congress, and remarks.
Van Rensselear, Phillip...	(See James Van Rensselear, heirs of.)	25	2	....	391							
Van Rensselear, Col. Solomon.	Pension	15	1	Documents.....	277	Pens. & Rev. Cl'ms.						
Van Rensselear, Col. Solomon.	Pension	15	2	Hsuse bill......	41	....	....	....	203	Passed	Passed	App'd March, 3 1819
Van Rensselear, William..	(See Killian Van Rensselear, and others.)	3	1	....	21							
Van Reswick, Wilfred....	(See Lewis Ratcliff, and others.)..	26	1	....	606							
Van Schaick, Myndert ...	(See John Hone, and others)....	21	2	....	137							
Van Scyoc, Stephen, and others.	Compensation for transportation of military stores.	13	1	Petition	36	Claims	....	....	......	Discharged; referred to Sec. of War.		
Van Sice, John, and others.	Compensation for supplies furnished Indian agents.	3	2	Petition	286	Claims	Dec. 22, 1795	Adverse	......	Leave to withdraw.		
Van Sice, John C.......	Pension for revolutionary services and disabilities.	29	1	Petition	232	Rev. Pensions	616	Adverse	......	Laid on table.		
Van Sickle, David.......	To be restored to pension roll	17	1	Petition	334	....	....	....	......	Referred to Committee Whole House on bill No. 37.		
Van Sickle, David.......	(See Willett's regiment, officers and men of.)	16	1	....	85							
Van Slyck, Cornelius, attorney.	Pension for sundry Indians......	1	3	Petition and rep't Secretary War.	368, 462	....	....	....	......	Laid on table.		
Van Slyck, John........	Pension for services in the war of 1812.	26	1	Petition	797	Invalid Pensions.						
Van Slyck, John........	Pension for services in the war of 1812.	26	2	Petition	77	Invalid Pensions...	60	Adverse	......	Laid on table.		
Van Slyck, John........	Pension for services in the war of 1812.	27	2	Petition	154	Invalid Pensions.						
Van Slyck, John........	Pension for services in the war of 1812.	29	1	Petition	284	Invalid Pensions ..	772	Favorable	512	Referred to Committee Whole House.		
Van Slyck, John........	Pension for services in the war of 1812.	29	2	House bill	212	....	....	....	512	Passed	Passed	App'd March 3, 1847
Van Syckel, Elijah	Remission of duties on sugar destroyed by fire.	17	2	Petition	142	Ways and Means.						
Van Syckel, Elijah	Remission or extension of time for payment of duties on sugar destroyed by fire.	18	1	Petition	213	Ways and Means..	Feb. 17, 1824	Favorable ...	120	Referred to Committee Whole House.		
Van Syckel, Elijah	Extension of the time of payment of duties, &c.	18	1	Senate bill	430	Ways and Means..	April 21, 1824	With't amend.	87	Passed	Passed	App'd May 5, 1824
Van Syckel, Elijah	Remission of duties on sugar.....	20	1	Petition	163	Whole House.						
Van Tassell, Jacob	Indemnity for property destroyed by the enemy in revolutionary war, in consequence of its being in service of U. States troops.	15	1	Petition	265	Pens. & Rev. Cl'ms.						
Van Tassell, Jacob	Indemnity for property destroyed by the enemy in revolutionary war, in consequence of its being in service of U. States troops.	15	2	Petition	51	Pens. & Rev. Cl'ms.	Dec. 4, 1818	Adverse	......	Rejected.		
Van Tassell, Jacob	Indemnity for property destroyed by the enemy in revolutionary war, in consequence of its being in service of U. States troops.	20	2	Petition	204	Rev. Claims.						

List of private claims presented to the House of Representatives of the United States from the 1st to the 31st Congress, inclusive—Continued.

Names of claimants.	Nature or object of the claim.	Congress.	Session.	How brought before the House of Reps.	Page of journal.	To what committee of the House referred.	No. or date of the report.	Nature of the report.	No. of the bill.	How disposed of by the House of Reps.	How disposed of by the Senate.	Date of the act of Congress, and remarks.
Van Tassell, Jacob	Indemnity for property destroyed by the enemy in revolutionary war, in consequence of its being in service of U. States troops.	21	1	Petition	50	Rev. Claims.						
Van Tassell, Jacob	Indemnity for property destroyed by the enemy in revolutionary war, in consequence of its being in service of U. States troops.	22	1	Petition	55	Rev. Claims.						
Van Tassell, Tryon	(See William Baker, N. Y.)	22	1	....	288	....	480					
Vanuxem & Clark	Indemnity for French spoliations prior to 1800.	26	1	Memorial	182	Foreign Affairs	343	Favorable; bill	319	Referred to Committee Whole House.		
Vanuxem, James	Extension of credit on certain duties.	3	1	Memorial	185	Select	May 31, 1794	Favorable	63	Passed	Passed	App'd June 4, 1794
Vanuxem, James	(See Orange Webb, agent of.)	5	3	....	497							
Vanuxem, J., administrator of.	Indemnity for French spoliations prior to 1800.	26	1	Memorial	182	Foreign Affairs	343	Favorable; bill	319	Referred to Committee Whole House.		
Vanuxem, James	Indemnity for French spoliations prior to 1800.	26	1	Memorial	182	Foreign Affairs	343	Favorable; bill	319	Referred to Committee Whole House.		
Vanuxem, James, heirs of.	Indemnity for French spoliations prior to 1800.	28	1	Petition	369	Foreign Affairs.						
Vanuxem, James, heirs of.	Indemnity for French spoliations prior to 1800.	29	2	Memorial	235	Foreign Affairs.						
Vanuxem, James, heirs of.	Indemnity for French spoliations prior to 1800.	31	1	Petition	270	Foreign Affairs	355	General bill	318	Referred to Committee Who'e House.		
Vanuxem & Lambert	(See George Le Roy, agent of.)	1	3	....	372							
Van Valkenburgh, Bar. J.	Bounty land for revolutionary services.	21	1	Petition	49	Rev. Claims	Feb. 8, 1830	Adverse	......	Laid on table.		
Van Valkenburgh, Bar. J.	Bounty land for revolutionary servi es.	21	2	Petition	128	Priv. Land Claims.	Feb. 1, 1831	Adverse	......	Laid on table.		
Van Valkenburg, Jehoiachim, heirs of.	Relief; killed by Indians in revolutionary war.	29	1	Petition	85	Rev. Pensions	237	Adverse	......	Laid on table.		
Van Valkenburg, Jehoiachim, heirs of.	Relief; killed by Indians in revolutionary war.	29	2	Petition	54	Rev. Pensions	84	Adverse	......	Laid on table.		
Van Valkenburg, Jehoiachim, heirs of.	Relief; killed by Indiaps in revolutionary war.	30	1	Petition	576	Rev. Pensions	527	Adverse	......	Laid on table.		
Van Valkenburg, Jehoiachim, heirs of.	Relief; killed by Indians in revolutionary war.	31	1	Petition	270	Rev. Pensions	66	Adverse	......	Laid on table.		
Van Valkenburgh, Lambert L.	Pension	23	2	Resolution	53	Invalid Pensions	67	Favorable	688	Passed.		
Van Valkenburgh, Lambert L.	Pension	24	1	Resolution	353	Invalid Pensions	....	....	......	Discharged; laid on table.		
Van Valkenburgh, Lambert L.	Pension	25	2	Petition	118	Invalid Pensions	....	....	......	Discharged; laid on table.		
Van Valkenburgh, Robert.	Pension	23	1	Petition	190	Invalid Pensions.						
Van Valkenburgh, Robert.	Pension	23	2	Petition	86	Invalid Pensions	Feb. 24, 1834	Adverse	......	Laid on table.		
Van Veighten, Capt. Derick.	Reimbursement of money advanced on public account.	15	1	Petition	161	Claims	Feb. 10, 1818	Adverse	......	Recommitted.		
Van Veighten, Capt. Derick.	Reimbursement of money advanced on public account.	15	2	Petition	33	Claims	Dec. 3, 1818	Adverse	......	Laid on table.		
Van Ville, Raymond	Bounty land for services, war of 1812.	24	1	Petition	664	Public Lands	....	....	......	Discharged; laid on table.		
Van Ville, Raymond	Bounty land for services, war of 1812.	24	2	Petition	390	Public Lands.						

List of private claims presented to the House of Representatives of the United States from the 1st to the 31st Congress, inclusive—Continued.

Names of claimants.	Nature or object of the claim.	Congress.	Session.	How brought before the House of Reps.	Page of journal.	To what committee of the House referred.	No. or date of the report.	Nature of the report.	No. of the bill.	How disposed of by the House of Reps.	How disposed of by the Senate.	Date of the act of Congress, and remarks.
Van Voorhis, Daniel	(See John Pierce, and D. V. V.)	23	1		188							
Van Voorst, Jellis D	Arrears of revolutionary pay	3	2	Petition & report Sec. of War.	286, 323					Laid on table.		
Van Voorst, Jellis D	Arrears of revolutionary pay	4	1	Petition	466	Claims	May 31, 1796	Adverse		Laid on table.		
Van Voorst, John J	Pension for revolutionary services.	22	1	Petition	381	Rev. Pensions	411	Favorable	511	Ref'd to Com. W. H.		
Van Vranken, John J	Pension for revolutionary services.	27	2	Petition	69	Rev. Pensions	May 24, 1842	Adverse		Laid on table.		
Van Wart, Amy	(See Isaac Van Wart, widow of.)	27	2		333							
Van Wart, Benjamin, widow of.	Compensation for revolutionary services.	28	1	Petition	947	Rev. Pensions.						
Van Wart, Ellen	(See Benjamin Van Wart, widow of.)											
Van Wart, Isaac	Annuity	6	2	Appropriat'n bill.	752				277	Passed	Passed	App'd March 3, 1801
Van Wart, Isaac, widow of.	To be placed on the revolutionary pension roll.	27	2	Resolution	333	Rev. Pensions	303	Favorable	272	Passed	Indef. postp'd.	
Van Wart & Richards	(See Richards & Van Wart)	30	2		164							
Vanwey, Henry	Further compensation for revolutionary services.	12	1	Petition	193	Claims	Mar. 2, 1812	Adverse		Rejected.		
Van Wick, Philip G	(See executors of Philip Van Cortland.)	29	2		89							
Van Wickle, Simon, heirs of.	Compensation for revolutionary services.	28	1	Petition	983	Rev. Claims.						
Van Winkell, Abraham	Exchange of public lands purchased.	15	1	Senate bill	245	Public Lands	Feb. 18, 1818	With't amend.	S. 23	Passed	Passed	App'd March 9, 1818
Van Winkle, Jacob M., & John Randall.	Indemnity for goods destroyed in the public stores.	26	2	Petition	196	Commerce.						
Van Woert, Lewis, attorney of.	Compensat'n for revolutionary supplies and disabilities.	2	1	Petition	489							
				Rep. of Secretary Treasury.	580					Laid on table.		
Van Woert, Lewis, attorney of.	Compensat'n for revolutionary supplies and disabilities.	3	2	Petition	299	Claims.						
Van Woert, Lewis, attorney of.	Compensat'n for revolutionary supplies and disabilities.	4	1	Resolution	373	Claims	Dec. 23, 1795	Adverse		Leave to withdraw.		
Van Wyck, John C	(See William Van Wyck, executors of.)	26	1		182		343		319			
Van Wyck, William D., executors of	Indemnity for French spoliations prior to 1800.	26	1	Memorial	182	Foreign Affairs	343	Favorab'e	319	Referred to Committee Whole House.		
Van Zant, George C	Compensation as surveyor of public lands.	25	2	Petition	1047	Claims	960	Favorable		Discharged; referred to Secretary Treasury.		
Van Zant, Peter P	Liquidation of a claim	1	2	Petition	269					Referred to Secretary Treasury.		
Van Zant, Peter P	Liquidation of a claim	3	1	Rep. of Secretary Treasury.	78					Laid on table.		
Van Zant, Peter P	Compensatation for supplies furnished for public use.	5	2	Petition	157	Claims	Mar. 7, 1798	Adverse		Rejected.		
Van Zant & Rockwell	(See Levi Cantrall, attorneys of.)	16	1		250							
Varhine, Avet	Pension for revolutionary services.	21	1	Resolution	244	Military Pensions				Discharged; laid on table.		See bill No. 248, and page 479.
Varian, David D	Compensation for a horse lost in war of 1812.	25	3	Documents	565	Claims.						
Varian, David D., administrator of.	Compensation for a horse lost in war of 1812.	26	1	Petition	170	Claims	July 10, 1840	Adverse		Laid on table.		

List of private claims presented to the House of Representatives of the United States from the 1st to the 31st Congress, inclusive—Continued.

Names of claimants.	Nature or object of the claim.	Congress.	Session.	How brought before the House of Reps.	Page of journal.	To what committee of the House referred.	No. or date of the report.	Nature of the report.	No. of the bill.	How disposed of by the House of Reps.	How disposed of by the Senate.	Date of the act of Congress, and remarks.
Varney, Phineas	Release from imprisonment and discharge of judgment.	11	2	Petition	133	Select	Jan. 31, 1810	Favorable	76	Passed	Rejected.	
Varnum, Isaac, widow of	Pension for services in war of 1812	15	2	Petition	27	Military Affairs.						
Varnum, John	Invalid pension	4	1	Rep. of Secretary War.	445	Claims	Feb. 18, 1796	Favorable; bill ordered.	156	Passed	Passed	App'd April 20, 1796
Varser, Miles	(See William H. Bedford, agent.)	28	1		262							
Vase, Peter T.	Correction of error in distribution of French indemnity.	26	1	Petition	712	Ways and Means.						
Vasques, Antoine, & others representatives of.	Permission to locate floating land claims.	27	3	Petition	240	Priv. Land Claims.	185	Favorable	803	Passed	Reported with't amendment.	
Vasques, Antoine, & others, representatives of.	Permission to locate floating land claims.	28	1	House bill	212	Priv. Land Claims.	213	Favorable	47	Passed.		
Vasques, Baroney	(See Z. M. Pike and companions.)	10	1		189							
Vasques, B. and others	Confirmation of title to land in Missouri.	15	1	Petition	280	Priv. Land Claims.						
Vasse, Ambrose	Payment of an award under British treaty.	15	1	Petition	24	Ways and Means.						
Vasse, Ambrose	Payment of an award under British treaty.	15	2	Petition	26	Ways and Means.	Feb. 3, 1819	Favorable	305	Referred to Committee Whole House.		
Vasse, Ambrose	Payment of an award under British treaty.	16	1	Documents	442	Ways and Means.	April 21, 1820	By bill	140	Passed	Passed	App'd May 15, 1820
Vasse, Ambrose	Interest on claim allowed by act of May 15, 1820.	18	1	Petition	66	Ways and Means.						
Vasse, Ambrose	Interest on claim allowed by act of May 15, 1820.	18	2	Petition	187	Ways and Means.	Feb. 14, 1825	Adverse		Laid on table.		
Vasse, Ambrose	Interest on claim allowed by act of May 15, 1820.	19	1	Petition	152	Ways and Means.						
Vasse, Ambrose	Indemnity for French spoliations prior to 1800.	26	1	Memorial	182	Foreign Affairs	343	Favorable; bill	319	Referred to Committee Whole House.		
Vass, Philip	Confirmation of title to land in Missouri.	14	1	Petition	210	Public Lands	Mar. 12, 1816	Adverse		Laid on table.		
Vass, Vincent	Compensation for revolutionary services.	25	3	Petition	124	Rev. Claims.						
Vass, Vincent	Compensation for revolutionary services.	26	1	Petition	167	Rev. Claims.						
Vass, Vincent	Pension for revolutionary services.	26	1	Petition	918	Rev. Pensions.						
Vass, Vincent	Pension for revolutionary services.	26	2	Petition	35	Rev. Claims	6	Adverse		Laid on table.		
Vass, Vincent	Pension for revolutionary services.	27	2	Petition	73	Rev. Claims	200	Adverse		Laid on table.		
Vattier, Charles	Share of land granted to French emigrants in Ohio.	8	1	Petition	435	Claims				Discharged; leave to withdraw.		
Vattier, or Vittier, Charles.	Share of land granted to French emigrants in Ohio.	8	2	Petition	47	Claims.						
Vattier, Charles	Pension	25	2	Petition	405	Invalid Pensions	681	Favorable	660	Passed	Passed	App'd July 9, 1838
Vattier, Charles	Extension of his pension	26	1	Petition	624	Rev. Pensions	714	Adverse		Laid on table.		
Vaughn, Augustus M., and others.	Increase of compensation as post office clerks.	31	2	Petition	173	P. Of. & P. Roads.						
Vaughn, Benjamin	Arrears of pension	23	1	Petition	46	Rev. Pensions.						
Vaughn, Benjamin	Arrears of pension	24	1	Petition	213	Rev. Pensions	Jan. 29, 1836	Adverse		Laid on table.		
Vaughn, Benjamin	Arrears of pension	25	2	Petition	55	Rev. Pensions	397	Adverse		Laid on table.		
Vaughn, George	Invalid pension	3	1	Petition	55							
				Rep. of Secretary War.	93	Select.						
Vaughn, George	Invalid pension	4	1	Petition	434	Claims	May 7, 1796	Adverse		Leave to withdraw.		

List of private claims presented to the House of Representatives of the United States from the 1st to the 31st Congress, inclusive—Continued.

Names of claimants.	Nature or object of the claim.	Congress.	Session.	How brought before the House of Reps.	Page of journal.	To what committee of the House referred.	No. or date of the report.	Nature of the report.	No. of the bill.	How disposed of by the House of Reps.	How disposed of by the Senate.	Date of the act of Congress, and remarks.
Vaughn, George	Invalid pension	8	2	Petition	23	Claims				Discharged; referred to Com. Whole House.		
Vaughn, George	Invalid pension	11	1	Petition and rep't Sec. of War.	15	Claims				Discharged; leave to withdraw.		
Vaughn, George	Invalid pension	11	2	House bill	283	Whole House	Mar. 24, 1810	With amends.	107	Passed	Passed	App'd April 27, 1810
Vaughn, George	Invalid pension	12	1	Petition	59	Claims	June 12, 1812	Adverse.		Laid on table.		
Vaughn, George	Arrears of pension	13	1	Petition	18	Claims				Discharged.		
Vaughn, George	Increase of pension	14	2	Resolution	186	Pens. & Rev. Cl'ms.						
Vaughan, James B., executor of.	Compensation for brick furnished navy agent.	21	2	Petition	45	Claims.						
Vaughan, James B., executor of.	Compensation for brick furnished navy agent.	23	1	Petition	34	Claims	68	Favorable	13	Passed	Passed	App'd Feb. 5, 1834
Vaughn, John	Pension	3	2	Rep. of Secretary War.	278	Claims	Feb. 28, 1795	Favorable; bill ordered.	130	Passed	Postponed.	
Vaughn, John	Pension	4	1	Rep. of Secretary War.	445	Claims	Feb. 18, 1796	Favorable; bill ordered.	156	Passed	Passed	App'd April 20, 1796
Vaughan, John	Indemnity for loss on bullion at the mint, by error in computing value.	5	2	Petition	252	Claims	May 19, 1798	Favorable; bill ordered.	103	Passed	Rejected.	
Vaughan, John	Indemnity for loss on bullion at the mint, by error in computing value.	5	3	Petition	464	Claims	Feb. 21, 1799	Favorable		Referred to Committee Whole House.		
Vaughan, John	Indemnity for loss on bullion at the mint, by error in computing value.	6	1	Pet. and docs	539	Claims	Jan. 6, 1800	Favorable; bill ordered.	185	Passed	Passed	App'd Feb. 11, 1800
Vaughn, J	Compensation for services in Mexican war.	31	1	Petition	583	Military Affairs.						
Vaughn, Phebe	(See heirs of John Mowry)	29	1		591							
Vaughn, Thomas C	Reimbursement of an overpayment for land.	22	1	Resolution	562	Public Lands.						
Vaughn, Thomas C	Reimbursement of an overpayment for land.	22	2	Resolution	59	Public Lands.						
Vaughn, Violette	Continuation of a pension	28	1	Petition	849	Rev. Pensions.						
Vaughan, Westley	(See Alex'r McCorkle and others.)	24	2		312							
Vaughan, Wm., and others	Prize-money for a capture in late war.	15	1	Petition	394	Naval Affairs				Discharged; laid on table.		
Vaughan, William	Full pay while waiting orders to sail.	24	2	Petition	102	Naval Affairs	309	Adverse		Laid on table.		
Vaughan, William	Full pay while waiting orders to sail.	25	2	Petition	234	Naval Affairs				Discharged; laid on table.		
Vaughan, William	Full pay while waiting orders to sail.	26	1	Petition	702	Claims.						
Vaughan, William	Full pay while waiting orders to sail.	27	2	Petition	103	Claims	25	Adverse		Laid on table.		
Vaughn, William	(See assignees of Thomas Tupper)	22	2		142							
Vaughn, Wm. B	Extensi n of time on a contract	28	1	Petition	621	Naval Affairs.						
Vaughn, Wm. E	(See Augustus M. Vaughn and others.)	31	2		173							
Vaught, Thomas T	Increase of compensation as postmaster.	16	1	Petition	144	P. Of. & P. Roads.	Mar. 3, 1820	Adverse		Laid on table.		
Vauguine, Don Francis	Confirmation of title to land	22	1	House bill	421	Whole House	Feb. 29, 1832	With't amend.	425	Passed	Passed	App'd June 25, 1832
Vauguine, Francis	Confirmation of title to land	22	1	House bill	421	Whole House	Feb. 29, 1832	With't amend.	425	Passed	Passed	App'd June 25, 1832
Vauguine, Stephen	Indemnity for Indian depredations.	21	2	Documents	138	Indian Affairs.						

List of private claims presented to the House of Representatives of the United States from the 1st to the 31st Congress, inclusive—Continued.

Names of claimants.	Nature or object of the claim.	Congress.	Session.	How brought before the House of Reps.	Page of journal.	To what committee of the House referred.	No. or date of the report.	Nature of the report.	No. of the bill.	How disposed of by the House of Reps.	How disposed of by the Senate.	Date of the act of Congress, and remarks.
Vauguine, Stephen	Confirmation of title to land	22	1	House bill	421	Whole House	Feb. 29, 1832	With't amend.	425	Passed	Passed	App'd June 25, 1832
Vause, William, administrator of.	Commutation pay for revolutionary services.	23	1	Petition	97	Rev. Claims.						
Vause, William, administrator of.	Commutation pay for revolutionary services.	24	1	Petition	138	Rev. Claims	429	Favorable	435	Referred to Committee Whole House.		
Vause, William, administrator of.	Commutation pay for revolutionary services.	25	2	Petition	40	Rev. Claims	246	Favorable	287	Passed.		
Vause, William, administrator of.	Commutation pay for revolutionary services.	25	3	Petition	226	Rev. Claims	221	Favorable	1078	Referred to Committee Whole House.		
Vause, William, administrator of.	Commutation pay for revolutionary services.	26	1	Petition	165	Rev. Claims.						
Vause, William, administrator of.	Commutation pay for revolutionary services.	26	2	Petition	35	Rev. Claims.						
Vause, William, administrator of.	Commutation pay for revolutionary services.	27	2	Petition	96	Rev. Claims	544	Adverse	......	Laid on table.		
Vause, William, administrator of.	Commutation pay for revolutionary services.	29	1	Petition	670	Rev. Claims.						
Vavasseur, John	Confirmation of title to land in Louisiana.	22	2	Petition	89	Priv. Land Claims.	18	Favorable	648	Referred to Committee Whole House.		
Vavasseur, John	Confirmation of title to land in Louisiana.	23	1	Petition	93	Priv. Land Claims.	72	Favorable	82	Passed	Passed	App'd June 27, 1834
Vawler, William	Indemnity for Indian depredations.	12	1	Petition	44	Claims	....	....	......	Discharged; leave to withdraw.		
Vawter, E. F., surety of.	Release from liability	18	1	Petition	89	P. Of. & P. Roads.	Feb. 6, 1824	Favorable	103	Passed	Passed	App'd May 17, 1824
Vawters, William, heirs of.	Commutation pay for revolutionary services.	21	1	Documents	359	Rev. Claims	313	Favorable	373	Referred to Committee Whole House.		
Vawters, William, heirs of.	Commutation pay for revolutionary services.	22	1	Petition	29	Rev. Claims	44	Favorable	93	Passed	Passed	App'd May 25, 1832
Vawters, William, heirs of.	Half-pay in lieu of commutation	23	1	Petition	221	Rev. Claims	Jan. 24, 1834	Adverse	......	Laid on table.		
Vawters, William, heirs of.	Half-pay in lieu of commutation	23	2	Petition	95	Rev. Claims	63	Favorable	678	Referred to Committee Whole House.		
Vawters, William, heirs of.	Half-pay in lieu of commutation	24	1	Petition	63	Rev. Claims	Jan. 20, 1836	Adverse	......	Laid on table.		
Vawters, William, heirs of.	Half-pay in lieu of commutation	24	2	Petition	155	Rev. Claims	156	Favorable	883	Referred to Committee Whole House.		
Vawters, William, heirs of.	Half-pay in lieu of commutation	25	2	Petition	40	Rev. Claims	118	Favorable	136	Passed.		
Vawters, William, heirs of.	Half-pay in lieu of commutation	26	1	Petition	167	Rev. Claims.						
Vawters, William, heirs of.	Half-pay in lieu of commutation	27	2	Petition	96	Rev. Claims	1025	Favorable	598	Referred to Committee Whole House.		
Vawters, William, heirs of.	Half-pay in lieu of commutation	29	1	Petition	476	Rev. Claims.						
Vawters, William, heirs of.	Half-pay in lieu of commutation	30	1	Petition and rep't Sec. of War.	978, 1123	....	....	....	......	Laid on table.	....	
Veal, Susan	(See Mary Elliott, and others)	22	2	....	40							Leave to withd'w, 31st Cong., 1st session.
Veaux, J. and L., assignee of.	Patent for certain lands in Wisconsin.	25	2	Senate bill	1012	Priv. Land Claims.	July 2, 1838	Adverse	S. 299	Referred to Committee Whole House.		
Veaux, James, and others.	Patent for certain lands in Wisconsin.	25	2	Senate bill	508	Priv. Land Claims.	782	Adverse	S. 17	Referred to Committee Whole House.		
Veazie, Joseph	Pension for revolutionary services.	24	2	Petition	44	Rev. Pensions	150	Favorable	879	Referred to Committee Whole House.		
Veazie, Joseph	Pension for revolutionary services.	25	2	Petition	38	Rev. Pensions	166	Favorable	191	Passed.		
Veazie, Joseph	Pension for revolutionary services.	26	2	Petition	87	Rev. Pensions						
Veil, Just	(See Lewis A. Petray and Just Veil.)	17	2	....	136							

List of private claims presented to the House of Representatives of the United States from the 1st to the 31st Congress, inclusive—Continued.

Names of claimants.	Nature or object of the claim.	Congress.	Session.	How brought before the House of Reps.	Page of journal.	To what committee of the House referred.	No. or date of the report.	Nature of the report.	No. of the bill.	How disposed of by the House of Reps.	How disposed of by the Senate.	Date of the act of Congress, and remarks.
Veillon, Etienne	Confirmation of title to land in Louisiana.	22	1	House bill	107	Whole House	Mar. 23, 1832	With't amend	125	Passed	Passed	App'd June 25, 1832
Ven, Jacob, widow of	Bounty of $50 due husband	14	1	Petition	64	Claims.						
Ven, Jacob, widow of	Bounty of $50 due husband	14	2	Petition	30	Claims	Dec. 20, 1816	Adverse		Rejected.		
Ven, Rachel	(See Jacob Ven, widow of)	14	1		64							
Venable, Richard R. or K.	Confirmation of title to land in Missouri.	15	2	Petition	110	Priv. Land Claims.						
Venable, Richard R. or K.	Confirmation of title to land in Missouri.	17	1	Petition	55	Public Lands.						
Venable, Richard R. or K.	Confirmation of title to land in Missouri.	17	2	Petition	55	Public Lands.						
Venable, Sarah	(See Peter Woosely or Oosely, heirs of.)	18	1		307				S. 50			
Venus, John	Revolutionary pension	10	1	House bill	232	Whole House	April 19, 1808	With't amend.	78	Passed	Passed	App'd April 25, 1808
Venus, British ship, owners of.	Indemnity for the capture of their vessel by the Peacock.	15	1	Civil appropriat'n bill.	251	Whole House	Mar. 28, 1818	With't amend	90	Passed	Passed	App'd April 9, 1818
Vercher, M.	(See Henry Fredieu and others.)	30	1		976							
Verdier, John Baptist	Payment of three final certificates which have been fraudulently obtained from him.	5	2	Petition	282	Claims	July 13, 1798	Further time		Postponed.		
Verdier, John Baptist	Payment of three final certificates which have been fraudulently obtained from him.	5	3	Petition	430	Claims	March 2, 1799	Further time		Postponed.		
Verdier, John Baptist	Payment of three final certificates which have been fraudulently obtained from him.	6	1	Petition	642	Claims	April 26, 1800	Favorable		Referred to Committee Whole House.		
Verley, Jacob	Revolutionary pension	18	1	Resolution	228	Rev. Pensions	Mar. 19, 1824	Adverse		Laid on table		Leave to withdraw.
Vermeule, Cornelius	Confirmation of title to land	7	1	Senate bill	111	Whole House	Mar. 24, 1802	With't amend.	S. 3	Passed		App'd Mar. 30, 1802
Vermeule, Cornelius	(See Edah Vermeule and others.)	9	1		192							
Vermeule, Edah, and others	Indemnity for property destroyed by United States troops.	9	1	Petition	192	Claims	Jan. 24, 1806	Adverse		Laid on table		Leave to withdraw.
Vermeule, Frederick	(See Edah Vermeule and others.)	9	1		192							
Vermilion, Charles	(See Louis F. Beeler and others.)	30	1		115							
Vermillion, Cornelius	Permission to apply payment on forfeited land to new location.	18	1	Petition	177	Priv. Land Claims.						
Vermillion, Cornelius	Permission to apply payment on forfeited land to new location.	18	2	Petition	122	Priv. Land Claims.	Jan. 11, 1825	Adverse		Laid on table.		
Vermillion, Cornelius	Permission to apply payment on forfeited land to new location.	19	1	Resolution	70	Public Lands				Discharged		Leave to withdraw.
Vermilyea, Napier & Bennett.	(See Napier, Vermilyea & Bennet, *et al.*)	18	1		328				S. 58			
Vermilyea, Thomas	Indemnity for illegal seizure of his ship, the Ganges, by the French in 1798.	15	1	Petition	353					Referred to Secretary of State.		
Vermont, postmaster at Bennington.	Increase of compensation	15	1	Petition	352	P. Of. & P. Roads.						
Vermont, postmaster at Burlington.	Increase of compensation	15	1	Resolution	311	P. Of. & P. Roads.						
Vermont, militia of	Compensation for services at battle of Plattsburg.	24	2	Senate bill	260	Military Affairs	Feb. 14, 1837	With amend.	S. 117	Referred to Committee Whole House.		
Vermont, militia of	Compensation for services at battle of Plattsburg.	25	2	Resolution	107	Military Affairs.						

List of private claims presented to the House of Representatives of the United States from the 1st to the 31st Congress, inclusive—Continued.

Names of claimants.	Nature or object of the claim.	Congress.	Session.	How brought before the House of Reps.	Page of journal.	To what committee of the House referred.	No. or date of the report.	Nature of the report.	No. of the bill.	How disposed of by the House of Reps.	How disposed of by the Senate.	Date of the act of Congress, and remarks.
Vermont, militia of	Compensation for services at battle of Plattsburg.	26	1	Petition	182	Military Affairs.						
Vermont, militia of	Compensation for services at battle of Plattsburg.	30	1	Senate bill	1001	Military Affairs	July 19, 1848	With't amend.	S. 190	Passed	Passed	App'd Aug. 14, 1848
Vermont, militia of	Compensation for services at battle of Plattsburg.	31	1	Petition	471	Military Affairs	198	Favorable; bill	205	Referred to Committee Whole House.		
Vermont, militia and citizens of.	Compensation for services on frontier in 1839.	25	3	House bill	489	Whole House	....	....	1109			
Vermont, militia and citizens of.	Compensation for services on frontier in 1839.	26	1	Petition	182, 711	Military Affairs	July 2, 1840	Favorable	461	Referred to Committee Whole House.		
Vermont, militia and citizens of.	Compensation for services on frontier in 1839.	26	2	Petition	79	Military Affairs	126	Favorable	631	Referred to Committee Whole House.		
Vermont, legislature of	Refunding expenses in defending frontier in 1839.	27	3	Resolution	228	Military Affairs.						
Vermont, legislature of	Refunding expenses in defending frontier in 1839.	31	2	Res. and docs.	239	Military Affairs	23	Favorable	455	Referred to Committee Whole House.		
Vernet, Ann	(See Jesse Brown, daughter of)	30	1	....	92							
Vernet, John	Permission to import goods from Martinico.	12	1	Petition	190	Com. and Manuf.						
Vernon, Elizabeth N	(See Samuel Vernon, executrix of)	26	1	....	182							
Vernon, Samuel, executrix of.	Indemnity for French spoliations prior to 1800.	26	1	Memorial	182	Foreign Affairs	343	Favorable	319	Referred to Commitee Whole House.		
Vernon, Samuel, executrix of.	Indemnity for French spoliations prior to 1800.	29	2	Memorial	161	Foreign Affairs.						
Vernon, William, (Mass.)	Indemnity for French spoliations prior to 1800.	26	1	Memorial	182	Foreign Affairs	343	Favorable	319	Referred to Committee Whole House.		
Vernon, William	(See Charles Bulfinch and others)	26	1	....	202							
Vernon, William	(See Wm. A. Vernon, executor of.)	29	2	....	161							
Vernon, William A., executor of.	Indemnity for French spoliations prior to 1800.	29	2	Memorial	161	Foreign Affairs.						
Vernon, William, & others.	Indemnity for French spoliations prior to 1800.	31	1	Memorial	392	Foreign Affairs	355	Favorable	318	Referred to Committee Whole House.		
Verplanck, Gulian, representatives of.	Indemnity for French spoliations prior to 1800.	26	1	Memorial	182	Foreign Affairs	343	Favorable	319	Referred to Committee Whole House.		
Verplanck, Johnston	(See Theodore Dwight and others)	19	1	....	221							
Verplanck, Johnston	(See Gulian Verplanck, representatives of.)	26	1	....	182							
Verplank, Phillip	Liquidation and settlement of a claim against the United States	1	2	Petition	269	....	....	....	......	Referred to Secretary Treasury.		
Verplank, Phillip	Liquidation and settlement of a claim against the United States.	2	1	Rep. of Secretary Treasury.	580	....	....	....	......	Laid on table.		
Verplast, Nicholas	Invalid pension	25	2	Petition	171	Naval Affairs.	532	Favorable	524	Passed	Passed	App'd July 9, 1838
Verree, George	(See McFarlane & Player, assignee of.)	7	2	....	258							
Very, Isaac	Pension	21	1	Petition	52	Military Affairs.						
Very, Jonathan	Bounty on fishing vessel	6	2	Petition	805	Com. and Manuf.	Feb. 23, 1801	Adverse	......	Rejected.		
Very, Jonathan	Bounty on fishing vessel	8	2	Petition	63	Select.						
Very, Jonathan	Bounty on fishing vessel	9	1	Petition	212	Com. and Manuf.						
Vest, John	Remission of a military fine	4	1	Petition	381	Select	Jan. 25, 1796	Adverse	......	Laid on table.		
Vethake, Eliza Seely	(See Isaac Seely, heir of)	31	1	....	1095							
Via, William	Pension for revolutionary services.	29	1	Petition Documents	86 126	Rev. Pensions. Rev. Pensions.						
Via, William	Pension for revolutionary services.	29	2	Petition	150	Rev. Pensions	21	Adverse	......	Laid on table.		

List of private claims presented to the House of Representatives of the United States from the 1st to the 31st Congress, inclusive—Continued.

Names of claimants.	Nature or object of the claim.	Congress.	Session.	How brought before the House of Reps.	Page of journal.	To what committee of the House referred.	No. or date of the report.	Nature of the report.	No. of the bill.	How disposed of by the House of Reps.	How disposed of by the Senate.	Date of the act of Congress, and remarks.
Via, William	Pension for revolutionary services.	30	1	Petition	155	Rev. Pensions	446	Favorable	377	Passed.		
Viall, Samuel	To be restored to pension roll	17	2	Petition	36	Rev. Pensions.						
Viator, Widow	(See Antonio Segura, and others.)	24	1		907							
Vibbert, Russell	Bounty land for military services	15	2	Petition	66	Military Affairs.						
Vicary, Ben, (colored)	Pension for disabilities, revolutionary war.	8	2	Petition	151	Claims.						
Vicary, J.	Indemnity for French spoliations prior to 1800.	26	1	Memorial	182	Foreign Affairs	343	Favorable; bill	319	Referred to Committee Whole House.		
Vicary, Samuel	Indemnity for French spoliations prior to 1800.	26	1	Memorial	182	Foreign Affairs	343	Favorable; bill	319	Referred to Committee Whole House.		
Vice, John	Pension for revolutionary services.	29	1	Documents	266	Rev. Pensions	522	Adverse		Laid on table.		
Vice, William	Pension for revolutionary services.	28	2	Memorial	73	Rev. Pensions.						
Vick, Hartwell	Change of location, or reimbursement of payment on land.	22	1	Senate bill	129	Public Lands	July 6, 1832	Favorable	27	Passed	Passed	App'd July 14, 1832
Vick, Hartwell	Permission to locate land lost by survey.	22	2	Petition	55	Public Lands.						
Vick, Hartwell, widow and heirs of.	Two sections of land as indemnity for losses in the purchase of tract of land.	23	1	Petition	195	Priv. Land Claims.						
Vick, Hartwell, widow and heirs of.	Two sections of land as indemnity for losses in the purchase of tract of land.	23	2	Petition	242	Priv. Land Claims.	98	Favorable; bill	723	Referred to Committee Whole House.		
Vick, Silvia C.	(See Hartwell Vick, widow and heirs of.)											
Vickery, Benjamin	Pension	10	2	House bill	449	Whole House	Feb. 20, 1809	With amends.	158	Passed	Passed	App'd March 3, 1809
Vickory, Merifield	Increase of pension	26	1	Petition	324	Rev. Pensions				Discharged; laid on table.		
Vickory, William	Pension	20	1	Petition	30	Military Pensions.						
Vickory, William	Pension	20	2	Petition	55	Military Pensions	Feb. 13, 1829	General bill	440	Passed	Laid on table.	
Vickory, William	Pension	21	1	Petition	49	Military Pensions						See bill approved May 20, 1830.
Victor, Felix	Pay and emolument as an officer of revolutionary army.	2	2	Petition	694					Referred to Secretary of War.		
Victor, Felix	Pay and emolument as an officer of revolutionary army.	3	1	Report Secretary of War.	93	Select.						
Victor, John	(See Sarah Victor, administrator of)	30	1		358							
Victor, Sarah, heirs of	Payment of the balance due on pension.	29	1	Memorial	104	Rev. Pensions				Discharged; laid on table.		
Victor, Sarah, heirs of	Payment of the balance due on pension.	30	1	Petition	156	Rev. Pensions	225	Adverse		Laid on table.		
Victor, Sarah, administrator of.	Arrears and increase of pension	30	1	Petition	358	Rev. Pensions				Discharged; laid on table.		
Victor, Theodore, & others	That certain duties may be refunded	25	2	Petition	278	Commerce	688	Adverse		Laid on table.		
Victor, Theodore, & others	Release from two certain custom-house bonds.	31	1	Senate bill	591				S. 46	Passed	Passed	App'd March 6, 1850
Vidal, Jacintha	(See Joseph Vidal and others.)											
Vidal, Joseph, and others	Confirmation of Spanish grant to land in Mississippi.	12	2	Petition	663	Public Lands.						
Vidal, Joseph, and others	Confirmation of Spanish grant to land in Mississippi.	13	2	Petition	174	Public Lands.						
Vidal, Joseph, and others	Confirmation of Spanish grant to land in Mississippi.	13	3	Petition	662	Public Lands.						

List of private claims presented to the House of Representatives of the United States from the 1st to the 31st Congress, inclusive—Continued.

Names of claimants.	Nature or object of the claim.	Congress.	Session.	How brought before the House of Reps.	Page of journal.	To what committee of the House referred.	No. or date of the report.	Nature of the report.	No. of the bill.	How disposed of by the House of Reps.	How disposed of by the Senate.	Date of the act of Congress, and remarks.
Vidal, Joseph, and others	Confirmation of Spanish grant to land in Mississippi.	14	1	Petition	75	Public Lands.						
Vidal, Joseph, and others	Confirmation of Spanish grant to land in Mississippi.	14	2	Petition	41	Priv. Land Claims.						
Vidal, Joseph, and others	Confirmation of Spanish grant to land in Mississippi.	15	1	Petition	173	Priv. Land Claims.						
Vidal, Joseph, and others	Confirmation of Spanish grant to land in Mississippi.	16	2	Petition	60	Priv. Land Claims.						
Vidal, Joseph, and others	Confirmation of Spanish grant to land in Mississippi.	17	1	Petition	34	Priv. Land Claims.						
Vidal, Joseph, and others	Confirmation of Spanish grant to land in Mississippi.	17	2	Petition	27	Priv. Land Claims.	77	Bill for relief of heirs, &c.	363	Passed.		
Vidal, Joseph, and others	Confirmation of Spanish grant to land in Mississippi.	18	1	Petition	28	Priv. Land Claims.	Jan. 2, 1824	Adverse	......	Laid on table.		
Vidal, Joseph, and others	Confirmation of Spanish grant to land in Mississippi.	19	1	Petition	44	Priv. Land Claims.	....	....	......	Discharged; laid on table.		
Viel, Just	(See Louis A. Petray and Just Viel.)											
Vienna, de	(See Marquis de Vienna)	8	1	....	484							
Vienne, J. R.	Compensation for taking census	27	3	Senate bill	115	Claims	Jan. 17, 1843	With't amend.	S. 27	Passed	Passed	App'd Jan. 28, 1843
Vieux, jr., James, and others	Confirmation of title to land in Michigan.	21	1	Petition	68	Priv Land Claims.	Mar. 23, 1830	Adverse	......	Laid on table.		
Vieux, Joseph	Confirmation of title to land in Michigan.	21	1	Petition	68	Priv. Land Claims.	Mar. 23, 1830	Adverse	......	Laid on table.		
Vieux, Paul	Confirmation of title to land in Michigan.	21	1	Petition	68	Priv. Land Claims.	Mar. 23, 1830	Adverse	......	Laid on table.		
Vigo, Col. Francis	Reimbursement of advances to Gen. Clark's Illinois regiment in 1778.	23	1	Petition	135	Rev. Pensions	....	....	......	Discharged; laid on table.		
Vigo, Col. Francis	Reimbursement of advances to Gen. Clark's Illinois regiment in 1778.	23	2	Petition	101, 320	Rev. Claims	122	Adverse	......	Laid on table.		
Vigo, Col. Francis	Reimbursement of advances to Gen. Clark's Illinois regiment in 1778.	24	1	Petition	63	Rev. Claims	317	Favorable	330	Referred to Committee Whole House.		
Vigo, Col. Francis, heirs of.	Reimbursement of advances to Gen. Clark's Illinois regiment in 1778.	25	2	Petition	40	Rev. Claims	118	Favorable	136	Passed	Reported with amendment.	
Vigo, Col. Francis, heirs of.	Reimbursement of advances to Gen. Clark's Illinois regiment in 1778.	25	3	Petition	84	Rev. Claims	Dec. 21, 1838	Favorable	911	Referred to Committee Whole House.		
Vigo, Col. Francis, heirs of.	Reimbursement of advances to Gen. Clark's Illinois regiment in 1778.	26	1	Petition	166	Rev. Claims.						
Vigo, Col. Francis, heirs of.	Reimbursement of advances to Gen. Clark's Illinois regiment in 1778.	26	1	Senate bill	811	Rev. Claims	....	....	S. 21			
Vigo, Col. Francis, heirs of.	Reimbursement of advances to Gen. Clark's Illinois regiment in 1778.	27	2	Petition	93	Rev. Claims	525	Adverse	......	Referred to Committee Whole House.		
Vigo, Col. Francis, heirs of.	Reimbursement of advances to Gen. Clark's Illinois regiment in 1778.	28	1	Petition	72	Rev. Claims.						
Vigo, Col. Francis, heirs of.	Reimbursement of advances to Gen. Clark's Illinois regiment in 1778.	29	1	Petition	106	Rev. Claims	313	Favorable	251	Referred to Committee Whole House.		
Vigo, Col. Francis, heirs of,	Reimbursement of advances to Gen. Clark's Illinois regiment in 1778.	30	1	Petition	69, 130	Rev. Claims	216	Favorable	216	Referred to Committee Whole House.		
Vigo, Col. Francis, heirs of.	Reimbursement of advances to Gen. Clark's Illinois regiment in 1778.	30	2	House bill	368	Whole House	....	With't amend.	216	Passed	Reported with't amendment.	
Vigo, Col. Francis, heirs of.	Reimbursement of advances to Gen. Clark's Illinois regiment in 1778.	31	1	Petition	416, 688, 863	Rev. Claims.						

List of private claims presented to the House of Representatives of the United States from the 1st to the 31st Congress, inclusive—Continued.

Names of claimants.	Nature or object of the claim.	Congress.	Session.	How brought before the House of Reps.	Page of journal.	To what committee of the House referred.	No. or date of the report.	Nature of the report.	No. of the bill.	How disposed of by the House of Reps.	How disposed of by the Senate.	Date of the act of Congress, and remarks.
Vigo, Col. Francis, heirs of.	Reimbursement of advances to Gen. Clark's Illinois regiment in 1778.	31	2	Resolution	236	Claims.						
Vigus, Cyrus	Release from a fraudulent judgment.	29	1	Petition	316	Judiciary.						
Villalobos, Jose A., and others.	Permission to test title to land by suit.	30	1	Senate bill	678	Claims	July 12, 1848	With't amend.	S. 115	Passed with amendm't.	Passed as am'd	App'd July 20, 1848
Villard, Andrew Joseph	Indemnity for property destroyed by the enemy in 1814.	14	1	Petition	239	Claims	Feb. 16, 1816	Adverse		Rejected.		
Villard, Andrew Joseph	Indemnity for property destroyed by the enemy in 1814.	15	1	Petition	38	Claims	25	Adverse.		Laid on table.		
Villars, Antoine, infant son of.	(See Joseph Villers, and others)	15	1		76							
Villars, Joseph, and others.	Confirmation of title to land in Missouri.	15	1	Petition	76	Priv. Land Claims.						
Villars, Joseph, and others.	Confirmation of title to land in Missouri.	16	1	Petition	71	Priv. Land Claims.						
Villars, Joseph, and others.	Confirmation of title to land in Missouri.	17	1	Petition	54	Public Lands.						
Villars, Joseph, and others.	Confirmation of title to land in Missouri.	18	1	Petition	55	Public Lands.						
Villars, Madam, heirs of.	Confirmation of title to land in Missouri.	15	1	Petition	76	Priv. Land Claims.						
Villeré, Jacques	Indemnity for property destroyed by government officer.	14	1	Petition	438	Claims.						
Villeré, Jacques	Indemnity for property destroyed by government officer	14	2	Petition	148	Claims	Feb. 22, 1817	Favorable	154	Passed	Passed	App'd March 3, 1817
Villeré, Jacques, and others	Compensation for slaves taken by the enemy.	14	2	Petition	306					Referred to Secretary of State.		
Villeré, Jacques, and others	Compensation for slaves taken by the enemy.	15	1	Rep. of Secretary State.	46	Claims	Dec. 23, 1817	Adverse		Leave to withdraw.		
Vinal, Lemuel	Indemnity for British captures	23	1	Petition	213	Foreign Affairs.						
Vinal, Lemuel	Indemnity for British captures	28	2	Petition	46	Foreign Affairs.						
Vinall, William	Indemnity from the payment of certain contracts.	9	1	Petition	189	Claims	Dec. 11, 1805	Adverse		Leave to withdraw.		
Vincennes, Elizabeth	(See Reuben E. Gentry, and other.)	25	2		43							See bill No. 248.
Vincennes, inhabitants of	Grants of land for certain military services.	4	1	Petition	522	Whole House.						
Vincennes University	Confirmation of certain land sales.	14	1	Petition	36	Public Lands	Feb. 15, 1816	Favorable; bill		Passed	Passed	App'd April 27, 1816
Vincent, Isaac	Pension	1	3	Petition & report Sec. of War.	370, 393					Laid on table.		
Vincent, Isaac	Pension	11	3	House bill	604	Whole House	March 2, 1811	With amend.	218	Passed	Passed	App'd March 3, 1811
Vincent, Jesse	Indemnity in land for losses by Choctaw treaty.	24	1	Petition	57	Public Lands	208	Favorable	208	Referred to Committee Whole House.		
Vincent, Joseph	Compensation for naval stores in revolutionary war.	20	1	Memorial	64	Rev. Claims	Jan. 15, 1828	Adverse		Laid on table.		
Vincent, Joseph	Compensation for naval stores in revolutionary war.	20	2	Petition	26	Rev. Claims	Jan. 29, 1829	Adverse		Laid on table.		
Vincent, Joseph	Compensation for naval stores in revolutionary war.	21	1	Petition	37	Rev. Claims	Dec. 29, 1839	Adverse		Laid on table.		
Vincent, Thomas	Remission of the forfeiture of a vessel and cargo.	12	2	Petition	553	Ways and Means.				Referred to Committee Whole House.		
Vincent, Thomas	Remission of the forfeiture of a vessel and cargo.	13	1	Petition	36	Ways and Means.						

List of private claims presented to the House of Representatives of the United States from the 1st to the 31st Congress, inclusive—Continued.

3—70

Names of claimants.	Nature or object of the claim.	Congress.	Session.	How brought before the House of Reps.	Page of journal.	To what committee of the House referred.	No. or date of the report.	Nature of the report.	No. of the bill.	How disposed of by the House of Reps.	How disposed of by the Senate.	Date of the act of Congress, and remarks.
Vine, Jean Baptiste	Confirmation of title to land at Green Bay.	20	2	Petition	64	Public Lands	40	Favorable	357	Referred to Committee Whole House.		
Vine, Jean Baptiste	Confirmation of title to land at Green Bay.	21	1	Petition	93	Public Lands.						
Vine, Jean Baptiste	Confirmation of title to land at Green Bay.	22	1	Petition	125	Public Lands	362	Adverse	......	Laid on table.		
Vineyard, Barbara	(See widow of Martin Bowers)	28	1	....	262							
Vineyard, John	Pension for revolutionary services.	22	1	Petition	67	Rev. Pensions	103	Favorable	190	Referred to Committee Whole House.		
Vineyard, John	Pension for revolutionary services.	22	2	House bill	66	Whole House	....	....	190	Laid on table.		
Vineyard, John	(See Walter McCoy and John Vineyard.)	27	2	....	375							
Vineyard, William	Pension	14	1	Petition	32	Pens. & Rev. Cl'ms.	April 11, 1816	By bill	......	Passed	Passed	App'd April 30, 1816
Vinson, Thomas	Pension for revolutionary services.	21	2	Resolution	57	Military Pensions.						
Vinton, John, widow of	To be restored to pension roll	27	2	Petition	320	Rev. Pensions.						
Vinton, John, widow of	To be restored to pension roll	27	3	Petition	365	Rev. Pensions.						
Vinton, John, widow of	Pension	28	1	Petition	839	Whole House.						
Vinton, Lieut. John R.	Pay according to his brevet rank	23	2	Petition	304	Military Affairs	....	....	......	Disch'd; laid on table.		
Vinton, Lieut. John R.	Commencement of pay with date of brevet.	24	1	Petition	504	Military Affairs.						
Vinton, Susannah	(See John Vinton, widow of.)	27	2	....	320							
Vintree, Francis	Bounty land for revolutionary services.	12	1	Petition	315	Claims.						
Vintree, Francis	Bounty land for revolutionary services.	12	2	Petition	551	Public Lands.						
Viol, John	Pay as a gunner in revolutionary navy while prisoner.	15	1	Petition	156	Pens. & Rev. Cl'ms.	Feb. 20, 1818	Adverse	......	Rejected.		
Virago, schooner	(See Thomas Stagg, jr., and others)	7	1	....	27							
Virgil, Asa	Invalid pension	3	2	Rep. of Secretary War.	337	Claims	Feb. 28, 1795	Favorable; bill ordered.	130	Passed	Postponed.	
Virgil, Asa	Invalid pension	4	1	Rep. of Secretary War.	425	Claims	Feb. 18, 1796	Favorable; bill ordered.	156	Passed	Passed	App'd April 20, 1796
Virginia line, revolutionary war, officers and soldiers of.	Confirmation of title to land in Northwest Territory.	1	2	House bill	270	Whole House	Jan. 19, 1790	With amend.	85	Passed	Passed	App'd Aug. 10, 1790
Virginia line, revolutionary war, officers and soldiers of.	Indemnity for depreciation of pay.	10	2	Petition	375, 458	Select.						
Virginia line, revolutionary war, officers and soldiers of.	Indemnity for depreciation of pay.	11	2	Petition	195	Select.						
Virginia line, revolutionary war, officers and soldiers of.	Indemnity for depieciation of pay.	11	3	Petition	460	Select.						
Virginia line, revolutionary war, officers and soldiers of.	Half-pay for life	11	2	Petition	316	Select.						
Virginia line, revolutionary war, officers and soldiers of.	For scrip receivable in payment for lands in lieu of unsatisfied warrants.	21	1	Senate bill	621	Public Lands	May 13, 1830	With't amend	S. 134	Passed with amendm't.	Passed as am'd.	App'd May 30, 1830
Virginia line, revolutionary war, officers and soldiers of.	Explanatory of act May 30, 1830	22	1	Resolution	57	Public Lands	2	Favorable	124	Passed	Passed	App'd May 21, 1832

List of private claims presented to the House of Representatives of the United States from the 1st to the 31st Congress, inclusive—Continued.

Names of claimants.	Nature or object of the claim.	Congress.	Session.	How brought before the House of Reps.	Page of journal.	To what committee of the House referred.	No. or date of the report.	Nature of the report.	No. of the bill.	How disposed of by the House of Reps.	How disposed of by the Senate.	Date of the act of Congress, and remarks.
Virginia militia, 20th brigade.	(See Daniel Gould, and others)	14	1	....	83							
Virginia, merch'ts of Portsmouth.	Indemnity for French spoliations prior to 1800.	7	1	Memorial	162	Select.						
Virginia, inhabit'ts of Norfolk.	Indemnity for French spoliations prior to 1800.	7	1	Memorial	167	Select.						
Virginia, inhabit'ts of Norfolk.	Indemnity for French spolia ions prior to 1800.	14	2	Petition	123	Foreign Relations.						
Virginia, inhabit'ts of Norfolk.	Indemnity for French spoliations prior to 1800.	15	1	Petition	126	Select.						
Virginia, inhabit'ts of Norforlk and Portsmouth.	Indemnity for French spoliations prior to 1800.	22	1	Memorial	261	Foreign Affairs.						
Virginia, inhabit'ts of Norfolk and Portsmouth.	Indemnity for French spoliations prior to 1800.	27	3	Petition	60	Foreign Affairs.						
Virginia, Council of Norfolk.	Compensation for use of town hall by United States.	28	1	Petition	415	Claims.						
Virginia, merchants of Norfolk.	Remission of duties on goods destroyed by fire.	8	1	Petition	646	Com. and Manuf.						
Virginia, merchants of Petersburgh.	Remission of penalty for violation of non-importation act.	12	2	Petition	591	....	....	....	......	Laid on table.		
Virginia, distillers of Berkley county.	Remission of duty on stills	14	2	Petition	337	....	....	....	......	Referred to Committee W. Ho. on bill 72.	....	See act March 3, 1817
Vrginia, distillers of Rockbridge county.	Remission of certain forfeitures	14	2	Petition	284	Ways and Means.						
Virginia, custom-house officers at Norfolk.	Increase of compensation	14	1	Petition	512	Ways and Means.	....	....	......	Discharged; laid on table.		
Virginia, custom-house officers at Tappahannock.	Increase of compensation	17	2	Resolution	58	Commerce.						
Virginia, custom house officers at Folly Landing.	Increase of compensation	19	2	Resolution	160	Commerce.						
Virginia, custom house officers at Hampton.	Increase of compensation	19	2	Resolution	309	Commerce.						
Virginia, custom-house officers at City Point.	Increase of compensation	21	1	Resolution	261	Commerce.						
Virginia, custom-house officers at Petersburgh.	Increase of compensation	27	2	Memorial	93	Commerce.						
Virginia, monum'tal church at Richmond.	Remission of duty on an organ	15	1	Petition	168	Ways and Means.	Jan. 26, 1818	Adverse	......	Laid on table.		
Virginia, churchwardens of Elizabeth city parish.	Payment for a bell destroyed whil in public use.	20	1	Petition	68	Claims.						
Virginia, churchwardens of Elizabeth city parish.	Payment for a bell destroyed while in public use.	20	2	Petition	90	Claims.						
Virginia, churchwardens of Elizabeth city parish.	Payment for a bell destroyed while in public use.	21	1	Petition	56	Claims	14	Favorable	21	Passed	Passed	App'd Feb. 11, 1830
Virginia, church St. James at Wheeling.	Remission of duty on a bell	24	1	Petition	852	Ways and Means.						
Virginia, workmen at armory, Harper's Ferry.	Compensation for repairing public works.	22	2	Petition	165	Military Affairs.						
Virginia, armorers at Harper's Ferry.	Increase of compensation	23	1	Petition	307	Military Affairs.						
Virginia and Ohio, citizens of.	Permission to locate Virginia military continental land warrants in Ohio.	18	2	Memorial	65	Public Lands.						

List of private claims presented to the House of Representatives of the United States from the 1st to the 31st Congress, inclusive—Continued.

Names of claimants.	Nature or object of the claim.	Congress.	Session.	How brought before the House of Reps.	Page of journal.	To what committee of the House referred.	No. or date of the report.	Nature of the report.	No. of the bill.	How disposed of by the House of Reps.	How disposed of by the Senate.	Date of the act of Congress, and remarks.
Virginia, State of........	For interest on money borrowed for use of general government, war of 1812.	18	1	President's mess.	389	Claims.						
Virginia, State of........	For interest on money borrowed for use of general government, war of 1812.	18	2	Resolution	62	Claims	11	Favorable....	252	Passed............	Passed	App'd March 3, 1825
Virginia, commissioner of.	Reimbursement of payments made to the officers of the State line, revolutionary army.	22	1	Petition	64	Select	191	Favorable....	276	Referred to Committee Whole House.		
Virginia, commissioner of.	Reimbursement of payments made to the officers of the State line, revolutionary army.	22	1	Senate bill	430	Whole House.....	July 4, 1832	With amend..	S. 88	Passed with amend't..	Passed as am'd	App'd July 5, 1832
Virginia, commissioner of.	Explanatory of act of July 5, 1832.	22	2	Joint resolution..	223	Whole House.....	....	....	J.R. 16	Passed.		
Virginia, commissioner of.	For an act amendatory of the act of July 5, 1832.	28	1	Memorial	914	Ways and Means..	475	Favorable....	361	Referred to Committee Whole House.		
Virginia, commissioner of.	For an act amendatory of the act of July 5, 1832.	29	1	Memorial	221	Ways and Means..	71	Favorable....	91	Referred to Committee Whole House.		
Virginia, commissioner of.	For an act amendatory of the act of July 5, 1832.	30	1	Petition	277	Claims.						
Virginia, legislature of....	Grant of land to satisfy outstanding revolutionary land warrants.	26	1	Resolution	361	Public Lands	436	Favorable....	280	Ord. to be engrossed..		
Virginia, University of ...	Remission of duties on architectural models.	19	1	Resolution	120	Ways and Means..	Jan. 31, 1826	Favorable....	81	Passed	Passed	App'd May 13, 1826
Virginia, Petersburgh Railroad Company.	Remission of duty on railroad iron.	22	1	Memorial	576	Ways and Means.						
Virginia, Petersburgh Railroad Company.	Remission of duty on a locomotive.	23	1	Petition	244	Ways and Means.						
Virginia, Petersburgh Railroad Company.	Remission of duty on railroad iron.	27	3	Memorial	76	Ways and Means.						
Virginia, Petersburgh Railroad Company.	Remission of duty on railroad iron.	27	3	Senate bill	250	....	....	....	S. 84	Rejected.		
Virginia, City Point Railroad Company.	Remission of duty on spikes	27	2	Petition	311	Ways and Means..	464	Adverse	......	Laid on table.		
Virginia, judge of western district.	Increase of salary..............	27	2	Memorial	7	Judiciary.						
Virginia, judge of western district.	Increase of salary..............	27	3	Petition	44	Judiciary.						
Virginia, judge of western district.	Increase of salary..............	28	1	Petition	193	Judiciary.						
Virginia, judge of western district.	Increase of salary..............	28	2	Petition	164	Judiciary.						
Virginia, judge of western district.	Increase of salary..............	30	2	Petition	192	Judiciary.........	Feb. 1, 1849	Favorable....	751	Referred to Committee Whole House.		
Virginia, Alexandria, citizens of.	Reimbursement to them of amount advanced general government by Virginia to aid in erecting public buildings.	30	1	Petition	714	Dist. of Columbia.						
Virginia, Alexandria and Orange Railroad Company, assignees of the State.	Reimbursement to them of amount advanced general government by Virginia to aid in erecting public buildings.	31	1	Memorial	1427	Claims	494	Favorable....	395	Referred to Committee Whole House.		

List of private claims presented to the House of Representatives of the United States from the 1st to the 31st Congress, inclusive—Continued.

Names of claimants.	Nature or object of the claim.	Congress.	Session.	How brought before the House of Reps.	Page of journal.	To what committee of the House referred.	No. or date of the report.	Nature of the report.	No. of the bill.	How disposed of by the House of Reps.	How disposed of by the Senate.	Date of the act of Congress, and remarks.
Virginia, Alexandria and Orange Railroad Company, assignees of the State.	Reimbursement to them of amount advanced general government by Virginia to aid in erecting public buildings.	31	1	Senate bill	1335	Whole House	....	....	S. 283			
Virginia, Alexandria and Orange Railroad Company, assignees of the State.	Reimbursement to them of amount advanced general government by Virginia to aid in erecting public buildings.	31	2	Senate bill	409	Whole House	....	....	S. 283			
Virginia, Treadegar Iron Works.	Compensation for guns manufactured on contract with Navy Department.	29	1	Petition	576	Claims	March 4, 1846	Adverse	......	Laid on table.		
Virginia, Treadegar Iron Works.	Compensation for guns manufactured on contract with Navy Department.	30	1	Petition	522	Claims.						
Virginia, Woolen Manufacturing Company of Richmond.	Remission of forfeiture for non-fulfilment on contract with War Department.	30	2	Memorial	328	Military Affairs	....	....	......	Discharged; laid on table.		
Virginia, Woolen Manufacturing Company of Richmond.	Remission of forfeiture for non-fulfilment on contract with War Department.	31	1	Memorial	599	Military Affairs	282	Favorable	258	Referred to Committee Whole House.		
Virginia, Woolen Manufacturing Company of Richmond.	Remission of forfeiture for non-fulfilment on contract with War Department.	31	2	Bill of last sess.	181	Whole House	Jan. 24, 1851	With't amend.	258	Passed.		
Virginia, clerks in the post office, Norfolk.	Increase of compensation	31	2	Petition	173	P. Of. & P. Roads.						
Virginia, clerks in the post office, Petersbugh.	Increase of compensation	31	2	Petition	184	P. Of. & P. Roads.						
Virginia, clerks in the post office, Wheeling.	Increase of compensation	31	2	Petition	192, 204	P. Of. & P. Roads.						
Virginia, Zazoo Land Company.	Compensation for land ceded by Georgia to United States.	8	1	Memorial	504	Select	Jan. 7, 1804	Adverse	......	Laid on table.		
Visor, Andrew	Pension	22	1	Petition	574	Rev. Pensions.						
Visor, Andrew	Pension	22	2	Petition	341	Rev. Pensions.						
Visscher, or Fisher, Gerrit, administrator of.	Permission to import property of deceased from Great Britain.	12	1	Petition	269	....	....	....	......	Referred to Committee Whole House on bill No. 46.		
Visscher, Naunning J	(See Gerrit Visscher, or Fisher, administrator of.)	12	1	....	269							
Vixen, United States brig, officers and crew of.	Aid from government to discharge debts incurred in a foreign land.	13	1	Petition	28	Claims	July 19, 1813	Favorable	44	Passed	Passed	App'd Aug. 2, 1813
Vixen, United States brig, officers and crew of.	Prize-money for certain captures	14	1	Petition and rep't Sec. of Navy.	560	Naval Affairs	April 17, 1816	Adverse	......	Laid on table.		
Vliet, Garrett	Compensation for services as surveyor.	25	2	Documents	87	Claims	848	Favorable	764	Referred to Committee Whole House.		
Vliet, Garrett	Compensation for services as surveyor.	25	3	Bill of last sess.	431	Whole House	Feb. 1, 1839	With't amend.	764	Passed	Adverse report.	
Vliet, Garrett	Compensation for services as surveyor.	26	1	Petition	168	Claims	19	Favorable	38	Passed	Indef. postp'd.	
Vliet, Garrett	Compensation for services as surveyor.	26	2	Petition	52	Claims	10	Favorable	548	Referred to Committee Whole House.		
Vliet, Garrett	Compensation for services as surveyor.	27	2	Petition	749	Claims	843	Favorable	486	Ordered to 3d reading.		

List of private claims presented to the House of Representatives of the United States from the 1st to the 31st Congress, inclusive—Continued.

Names of claimants.	Nature or object of the claim.	Congress.	Session.	How brought before the House of Reps.	Page of journal.	To what committee of the House referred.	No. or date of the report.	Nature of the report.	No. of the bill.	How disposed of by the House of Reps.	How disposed of by the Senate.	Date of the act of Congress, and remarks.
Vliet, Garrett	Compensation for services as surveyor.	27	3	Bill of last sess.	89				486	Passed	Passed	App'd March 3, 1843
Vochez, John B.	(See Stephen Zacharie and others.)	3	1		138							
Vogder, Schultz, and Shinnick.	(See Jacob Shinnick and others)	13	3		522							
Voght, John F. H.	(See Charles Ahrenfeldt & Voght.)	30	1		387							
Voight, Henry, U. S. mint.	To be exonerated from liability for bullion stolen by Oliver Hale.	6	1	Petition	614	Claims				Discharged.		
Volant, schooner	(See John Burton and others).	19	1		336							
Volk, George S.	(See Louis F. Beeler and others).	30	1		115		482					
Von Heer, Major B.	(See Canadian refugees.)	4	2		614							
Von Heer, Bartholomew	Invalid pension	6	1	Petition	535	Claims	Jan. 17, 1800	Adverse		Rejected.		
Von Heer, Bartholomew	Invalid pension	7	1	Petition	213					Laid on table.		
Von Kapff & Auspack	Indemnity for French spoliations prior to 1800.	26	1	Memorial	182	Foreign Affairs	343	Favorable	319	Referred to Committee Whole House.		
Von Kapff, B. J.	(See R. C. Boislandry, trustee of.)	26	1		182							
Von Kapff & Brune	Drawback on German playing cards.	19	1	Petition	130	Ways and Means	April 27, 1826	Favorable	236	Passed.		
Von Kapff & Brune	Drawback on German playing cards.	19	2	Petition	60	Ways and Means.						
Von Kapff & Brune	Drawback on German playing cards.	19	2	Senate bill	97	Ways and Means	27	With't amend.	S. 26	Passed	Passed	App'd Feb. 8, 1827
Von Malachowsky, Mauritz	(See M. V. Malachowsky, widow of.)	31	1		640							
Von Pfister, Alexander	(See William Macomb, executors of.)	4	2		686							
Von Quenaudon, D.	Refunding amount advanced for forage in Florida in 1837.	25	3	Petition	206	Claims.						
Von Schmidt, Peter	Compensaion for a model of a dry dock.	28	1	Petition	322, 723	Naval Affairs				Discharged; laid on table.		
Von Schmidt, Peter	Compensation for a model of a dry dock.	29	1	Senate bill	1075	Claims	797	With't amend.	S. 93	Referred to Committee Whole House.		
Von Schmidt, Peter	Compensation for services as translator.	28	1	Senate bill	942	Naval Affairs	May 28, 1844	With't amend.	S. 140	Referred to Committee Whole House.		
Von Schmidt, Peter	Compensation for services as translator.	28	2	Petition	205	Naval Affairs	Jan. 28, 1845	Favorable	556	Passed	Passed	App'd Feb. 20, 1845
Von Schmidt, Peter	For an adjustment of a claim against United States.	28	2	Petition	111	Foreign Affairs.						
Von Weisenfels, Lieutenant Frederick, heirs of.	Bounty land for revolutionary services.	31	1	Petition	371	Rev. Claims.						
Voorhees, Albert	Restoration to pension roll	17	1	Petition	269					Referred to Committee Whole House.		
Voorhees, James J.	Pension	19	2	Petition	31	Military Pensions.						
Voorhees, James J.	Pension	20	1	Petition	365	Military Pensions.						
Voorhees, James J.	Pension	21	1	Petition	49	Military Pensions.						
Voorhees, John	Pension	25	2	Resolution	1026	Rev. Pensions.						
Voorhees, John S.	Revolutionary pension	26	1	Petition	175	Rev. Pensions				Discharged; laid on table.		
Voorhees, J. and P.	Compensation for mail services	27	3	Petition	373	P. Of. & P. Roads.	Feb. 28, 1843	Favorable	J. R. 45	Passed	Passed	App'd March 3, 1843
Voorhees, Luke	Pension	22	2	Petition	93	Invalid Pensions.						
Voorhees, Luke	Pension	23	1	Petition	389	Invalid Pensions	407	Favorable; bill	423	Referred to Committee Whole House.		
Voorhees, Luke	Pension	23	2	Bill of last sess.	336	Whole House	Feb. 6, 1835	With't amend.	423	Passed	Indef. postp'd.	
Voorhees, Luke	Pension	24	1	Petition	98	Invalid Pensions	278	Favorable; bill	285	Passed	Passed	App'd June 28, 1836
Voorhees, Philip F., U. S. navy.	Indemnity for expenses while in command of United States ship John Adams.	23	1	Petition	523	Naval Affairs.						

List of private claims presented to the House of Representatives of the United States from the 1st to the 31st Congress, inclusive—Continued.

Names of claimants.	Nature or object of the claim.	Congress.	Session.	How brought before the House of Reps.	Page of journal.	To what committee of the House referred.	No. or date of the report.	Nature of the report.	No. of the bill.	How disposed of by the House of Reps.	How disposed of by the Senate.	Date of the act of Congress, and remarks.
Voorhees, Philip F., U. S. navy.	Indemnity for expenses while in command of United States ship John Adams.	23	2	Petition	129	Naval Affairs.						
Voorhees, Philip F., U. S. navy.	Indemnity for expenses while in command of United States ship John Adams.	24	1	Petition	139	Naval Affairs	225	Favorable; bill	325	Ord'd to be engrossed.		
Voorhees, Philip F., U. S. navy.	Indemnity for expenses while in command of United States ship John Adams.	24	2	Bill of last sess.	198				325	Passed	Passed	App'd March 3, 1837
Voorhees, Philip F., U. S. navy.	(See Louis Warrington, & others.)	28	1		285							
Vosburgh, Catharine	(See Eliakim Vosburgh, widow of.)											
Vosburg, Eliakim, widow of.	Continuation of pension	27	2	Petition	48	Rev. Pensions	784	Adverse		Laid on table.		
Vose, Edward	Pension	3	1	Rep. of Secretary War.	131	Select	May 26, 1794	Res. to refer to Sec. War.	J.R.12	Passed	Passed	App'd June 9, 1794
Vose, Edward	Pension	3	2	Rep. of Secretary War.	262	Claims	Feb. 28, 1795	Favorable; bill ordered.	130	Passed	Postponed.	
Vose, Edward	Pension	4	1	Rep. of Secretary War.	445	Claims	Feb. 18, 1796	Favorable; bill ordered.	156	Passed	Passed	App'd April 20, 1796
Vose, Miriam	(See Samuel Vose, widow of.)	25	2		52							
Vose, Peter T., & J. Foster	For correction of error in the distribution of French Indemnity.	26	1	Petition	712	Ways and Means.						
Vose, Samuel widow of	For the benefit of the act of July 4, 1836.	25	2	Petition	52	Rev. Pensions	Jan. 25, 1838	By bill	456	Referred to Committee Whole House.		
Vose, William	Arrears of pension	28	1	Petition	116	Invalid Pensions	41	Adverse		Laid on table.		
Vought, Godfrey	Revolutionary pension	24	1	Petition	263	Rev. Pensions	370	Favorable; bill	373	Passed	Passed	App'd June 28, 1836
Vowell, Ebenezer	Compensation for retained rations.	14	1	Petition	462	Claims.						
Vowell, John C	Indemnity for French spoliations prior to 1800.	26	1	Memorial	182	Foreign Affairs	343	Favorable; bill	319	Referred to Committee Whole House.		
Vowell, John C	Indemnity for French spoliations prior to 1800.	31	1	Petition	256	Foreign Affairs	335	Favorable; bill	318	Referred to Committee Whole House.		
Vowell, J. and T	Indemnity for French spoliations prior to 1800.	26	1	Memorial	182	Foreign Affairs	343	Favorable; bill	319	Referred to Committee Whole House.		
Vowell, Thomas and John.	(See James Sanderson, and others.)	14	1		292							
Vowell, Thomas	Indemnity for French spoliations prior to 1800.	24	2	Petition	121	Foreign Affairs.						
Vowell, Thomas, administrator of.	Indemnity for French spoliations prior to 1800.	31	1	Petition	256	Foreign Affairs	355	Favorable; bill	318	Referred to Committee Whole House.		
Vowell, Thomas	(See Cospar Haymen, representatives of.)	26	1		714							
Vowles, Henry	Compensation for use of and damage to a house used by United States troops as a barracks.	2	2	Petition	619					Rejected.		
Vreeland, Daniel, widow of.	Pension for revolutionary services.	27	2	Petition	69	Rev. Pensions	104	Favorable	150	Passed	Passed	App'd July 27, 1842
Vreeland, Jacob, widow of.	Pension for revolutionary services.	25	2	Petition	664	Rev. Pensions.						
Vreeland, Jacob, widow of.	Pension for revolutionary services.	25	3	Petition	216	Rev. Pensions				Discharged; laid on table.		
Vreeland, Jacob, widow of.	Pension for revolutionary services.	26	1	Petition	322	Rev. Pensions	424	Adverse		Laid on table.		
Vreeland, Nicholas	Renewal of loan office certificates.	2	2	Petition	662	Whole House.						
Vreeland, Nicholas, heirs of.	Renewal of loan office certificates.	15	2	Senate bill	280	Pens. & Rev. Cl'ms.	Feb. 25, 1819	With't amend.	S. 47			
Vreeland, Nicholas, heirs of.	Renewal of loan office certificates.	16	1	Senate bill	113	Pens. & Rev. Cl'ms.	Jan. 12, 1820	With't amend.	S. 14	Passed	Passed	App'd April 5, 1820
Vreeland, Peter, widow of.	Pension for revolutionary services.	27	2	Petition	807	Rev. Pensions	July 21, 1842	Adverse		Laid on table.		

List of private claims presented to the House of Representatives of the United States from the 1st to the 31st Congress, inclusive—Continued.

ames of claimants.	Nature or object of the claim.	Congress.	Session.	How brought before the House of Reps.	Page of journal.	To what committee of the House referred.	No. or date of the report.	Nature of the report.	No. of the bill.	How disposed of by the House of Reps.	How disposed of by the Senate.	Date of the act of Congress, and remarks.
Vreeland, Peter, widow of.	Pension for revolutionary services.	27	3	Petition	107	Rev. Pensions	295	Adverse		Laid on table.		
Vrian, Jacques Jean	Confirmation of a certain right of pre-emption.	25	3	Petition	451	Public Lands.						
Vroman, Adam J	Pension	20	2	Petition	262	Military Pensions.						
Vroman, Adam J	Pension	22	1	Resolution	66	Rev. Pensions.						
Vroman, Bartholomew E.	Pension	25	2	Petition	116	Rev. Pensions	579	Adverse		Laid on table.		
Vroman, Jonas E., or Josiah E.	Pension	21	1	Petition	199	Rev. Claims	Feb. 10, 1830	Adverse		Laid on table.		
Vrooman, Jonas E., or Josiah E.	Pension	22	1	Petition	387	Rev. Claims	Mar. 2, 1832	Adverse		Laid on table.		
Vrooman, Josias E	Indemnity for revolutionary services and sufferings.	25	2	Petition	116	Rev. Pensions	578	Adverse		Laid on table.		
Vrooman, Maria and Catharine.	(See heirs of Peter Deitz)	19	2		216							
Vrooman, Peter	Redemption of Continental money.	25	2	Petition	576	Rev. Claims				Discharged; laid on table.		
Vrooman, Peter, (N. Y.).	Arrears of pension	25	2	Petition	404	Rev. Pensions				Discharged; laid on table		
Vrooman, Peter, (N. Y.).	Compensation for provisions furnished, war of 1812.	25	2	Petition	51	Claims	901	Adverse		Laid on table.		
Vrooman, Peter, (N. Y.).	Compensation for provisions furnished, war of 1812.	25	3	Petition	120	Claims	Mar. 2, 1832	Adverse		Laid on table.		
Wabash and Illinois land company.	Confirmation of title to land	11	3	Petition	458	Public Lands	Jan. 11, 1830	Adverse		Laid on table.		
Wacksmith, J. G., executor of.	Indemnity for French spoliations prior to 1800.	26	1	Memorial	182	Foreign Affairs	343	Favorable; bill	319	Referred to Committee Whole House.		
Waddel, George	Pension	27	2	Memorial	808	Invalid Pensions	809	Favorable	464	Ordered to 3d reading.		
Waddel, George	Pension	27	3	House bill	89				464	Passed	Passed	App'd March 3, 1843
Waddel James P., *et al*	(See James Brown, Tenn., heirs of.)	30	1		99							
Waddel, Sarah	(See Robert Waddel, widow of.)	29	1		731							
Waddel, Robert, widow of.	Compensation for services in Indian war.	29	1	Petition	731	Claims.						
Waddel, William C. H	For balance of judgment against heirs as marshal, New York.	23	1	Senate bill	375	Claims	355	With amend.	56	Passed	Passed	App'd June 30, 1834
Wadding, Joshua	(See Thomas L. Ogden, *et al.*)	18	2		109				12			
Waddington, Samuel, heirs of.	For money and land for services in Mexican war.	30	2	Petition	385	Public Lands						Leave to withdraw.
Waddy, William	Compensation for revolutionary services.	4	1	Petition	379	Claims	Jan. 20, 1796	Adverse		Laid on table.		
Wade, Amos, (N. C.)	Refund certain duties under act of May, 1828.	21	1	Petition	68	Ways and Means	Feb. 1, 1831	Adverse		Laid on table.		
Wade, Amos, (N. C.)	Refund certain duties under act of May, 1828.	21	2	Petition	54	Ways and Means				Discharged; laid on table.		

List of private claims presented to the House of Representatives of the United States from the 1st to the 31st Congress, inclusive—Continued.

Names of claimants.	Nature or object of the claim.	Congress.	Session.	How brought before the House of Reps.	Page of journal.	To what committee of the House referred.	No. or date of the report.	Nature of the report.	No. of the bill.	How disposed of by the House of Reps.	How disposed of by the Senate.	Date of the act of Congress, and remarks.
Wade, Amos, (N. C.)	Refund certain duties under act of May, 1828.	22	1	Petition	50	Ways and Means.						
Wade, Amos, (N. C.)	Refund certain duties under act of May, 1828.	23	1	Petition	215	Ways and Means				Discharged; laid on table.		
Wade, Amos, (N. C.)	Refund certain duties under act of May, 1828.	25	2	Petition	281	Ways and Means				Discharged.		
Wade, Amos, (N. C.)	Refund certain duties under act of May, 1828.	26	1	Petition	179	Ways and Means	501	Adverse		Laid on table.		
Wade, Amos, (N. C.)	Refund certain duties under act of May, 1828.	27	3	Petition	102	Ways and Means.						
Wade, Anna, (La.)	Confirmation of title to land	14	2	Petition	192	Priv. Land Claims				Discharged; laid on table.		
Wade, Anna, (La.)	Conrfimation of title to land	15	1	Petition	173	Priv. Land Claims				Dscharged; laid on table.		
Wade, Edward, (Md.)	Revolutionary pension	2	1	Petition	486					Referred to Secretary War.		
Wade, Edward, (Penn.)	Pension	4	1	Petition	447	Claims	Feb. 18, 1796	Favorable	156	Passed	Passed	App'd April 20, 1796
Wade, Edward, by Washington Wade, heir of.	Commutation pay	25	2	Petition	382	Rev. Claims	951	Favorable	826	Passed	Laid on table.	
Wade, Edward, by Washington Wade, heirs of.	Commutation pay	25	3	Petition	84	Rev. Claims	6	Favorable	904	Referred to Committee Whole House.		
Wade, Edward, by Washington Wade, heirs of.	Commutation pay	26	1	Petition	165	Rev. Claims.						
Wade, Edward, by Washington Wade, heirs of.	Commutation pay	31	1	Petition	390	Rev. Claims.						
Wade, Elisha, (Ind.)	Reimbursement for deficiency in land.	18	1	Petition	69	Public Lands	2	Adverse		Laid on table.		
Wade, George	Pension	29	1	Petition	189	Invalid Pensions	809	Favorable	534	Referred to Committee Whole House.		
Wade, Ichabod, and Elizabeth.	(See William Mumford, *et al.*)	19	2		286							
Wade, James F	For loss of horse, Seminole war	23	1	Documents	154	Claims.						
Wade, James F	For loss of horse, Seminole war	28	1	Petition	262	Claims.						
Wade, John T., widow of.	Revolutionary pension	28	1	Petition	1042	Naval Affairs.						
Wade, Jonathan, widow of.	Revolutionary pension	25	3	Petition	110	Rev. Pensions	309	Adverse		Laid on table.		
Wade, Margaret	(See Jonathan Wade, widow of)	25	3		110							
Wade, Margaret	(See John T. Wade, widow of)	28	1		1042							
Wade, Zebulon	Naval pension	11	1	Petition	46	Claims.						
Wade, Zebulon	Naval pension	11	2	Petition	226	Claims	Mar. 20, 1810	Adverse.		Laid on table.		
Wade, Zebulon	Naval pension	13	2	Petition	214	Pens. & Rev. Cl'ms.	April 7, 1814			Discharged		Leave to withdraw.
Wade, Zebulon	Naval pension	19	2	Petition	65	Naval Affairs	Jan. 17, 1827	Adverse		Laid on table.		
Wade, Zebulon	Naval pension	21	1	Petition	58	Naval Affairs	April 20, 1830	Adverse		Laid on table.		
Wade, Zebulon	Naval pension	21	2	Petition	43	Military Pensions.						
Wade, Zebulon	Naval pension	22	1	Petition	206	Invalid Pensions	206	Favorable	288	Passed	Passed	App'd July 14, 1832
Wade, Zebulon	Naval pension	22	2	Resolution	64	Invalid Pensions		Favorable	626	Passed	Rejected.	
Wade, Zebulon	Naval pension	24	2	Petition	41	Naval Affairs	109	Adverse		Laid on table.		
Wade, Zebulon	Naval pension	25	2	Petition	276	Naval Affairs				Discharged; laid on table.		
Wade, Zebulon	Naval pension	25	3	Petition	131	Naval Affairs.						
Wade, Zebulon	Naval pension	26	1	Petition	180	Naval Affairs	545	Adverse		Laid on table.		
Wade, Zebulon	Naval pension	27	3	Petition	91	Naval Affairs				Discharged; laid on table.		

List of private claims presented to the House of Representatives of the United States from the 1st to the 31st Congress, inclusive—Continued.

Names of claimants.	Nature or object of the claim.	Congress.	Session.	How brought before the House of Reps.	Page of journal.	To what committee of the House referred.	No. or date of the report.	Nature of the report.	No. of the bill.	How disposed of by the House of Reps.	How disposed of by the Senate.	Date of the act of Congress, and remarks.
Wadsworth, Charles, widow of.	Refund amount advanced by Purser Wadsworth.	14	2	Petition	143	Secretary of Navy.	Feb. 6, 1817	....	......	Refer'd to Select Committee.		
Wadsworth, Elizabeth	(See Charles Wadsworth, widow of.)	14	2	....	143							
Wadsworth, Col. Jeremiah, executor of.	Payment of lost loan office certificate.	29	1	Petition	430	Ways and Means.						
Wadsworth, Col. Jeremiah, executor of.	Payment of lost loan office certificate.	30	1	Petition	170	Ways and Means.						
Wadsworth, Joseph	Increase of pension	18	1	Petition	234	Pens. & Rev. Cl'ms.	....	....	......	Discharged; laid on table.		
Wadsworth, Gen. Peleg, heirs of.	Commutation pay	29	1	Petition	487	Rev. Claims.						
Wadsworth, Gen. Peleg, heirs of.	Commutation pay	29	2	Petition	233	Rev. Claims.						
Wadsworth, Gen. Peleg, heirs of.	Commutation pay	30	1	Petition	635	Rev. Claims.						
Wadsworth, Wiswell	(See Richard Skinner)	19	1	....	222							
Waesche, Frederick	(See George Repold, administrator of.)	26	1	....	182							
Waff, Thomas	(See Stephen Carpenter, administrator of.)	26	1	....	182							
Waff, Thomas	(See Stephen Carpenter, administrator of.)	21	1	....	171							
Wager, Catharine	(See John Wager, widow of)	16	2	....	97							
Wager, jr., John, widow of.	Indemnity for loss sustained by failure, on part of United States, respecting purchase of property at Harper's Ferry.	16	2	Petition	97	Select	68	Favorable	270	Laid on table.		
Waggaman, George A	(See Clark Woodruff, assignees of)	27	2	....	622							
Waggaman, Emanuel	Pension	3	1	Rep. of Secretary War.	131	Select	May 26, 1794	Jt. res. to refer to Sec. War.	J.R. 12	Passed	Passed	App'd June 9, 1794
Waggoner, Andrew	Pension	10	1	House bill	232	Whole House	April 19, 1808	Favorable	78	Passed	Passed	App'd April 23, 1808
Waggoner, Andrew	Compensation for slave lost in public service.	28	2	Petition	65	Claims	65	Adverse	......	Laid on table.		
Waggoner, Charles, (colored man.)	Pension	14	2	Petition	199	Naval Affairs	....	....	......	Discharged; laid on table.		
Waggoner, Jacob	Correction of land entry	26	1	Petition	366	Priv. Land Claims.						
Waggoner, Jacob	Correction of land entry	30	1	Petition	929	Public Lands.						
Waggoner, John	Pension	21	1	Petition	385	Military Pensions.	Mar. 26, 1830	Favorable	390	Referred to Committee Whole House.		
Waggoner, John	Pension	21	2	House bill	316	....	....	....	390	Passed	Ref'd to Com. on Pensions.	
Waggoner, John	Pension	22	1	Petition	68	Rev. Pensions	....	....	......	Discharged	....	Leave to withdraw.
Waggoner, Peter D.	(See Casper B. Cook, *et al.*)	30	1	....	278							
Waggoner, Capt. Reuben.	Compensation for revolutionary services.	23	2	Resolution	490	Rev. Claims.						
Waggoner, Capt. Reuben.	Compensation for revolutionary services.	24	1	Petition	104	Rev. Claims	236	Adverse	......	Discharged; laid on table.		
Waggoner, Capt. Reuben.	Compensation for revolutionary services.	25	2	Resolution	81	Rev. Claims.						
Wagoner, Henry, (Pa.)	Pension	2	1	Petition	458	....	....	....	......	Laid on table.		
Wagoner, Henry, (Pa.)	Pension	3	2	Petition	307	....	....	....	......	Laid on table.		
Wagoner, Henry, (Va.)	Pension	27	2	Petition	218	Invalid Pensions	420	Adverse	......	Laid on table.		

List of private claims presented to the House of Representatives of the United States from the 1st to the 31st Congress, inclusive—Continued.

Names of claimants.	Nature or object of the claim.	Congress.	Session.	How brought before the House of Reps.	Page of journal.	To what committee of the House referred.	No. or date of the report.	Nature of the report.	No. of the bill.	How disposed of by the House of Reps.	How disposed of by the Senate.	Date of the act of Congress, and remarks.
Wagoner, Henry, (Va.)	Pension	31	1	Petition	755	Invalid Pensions.						
Wagner, John	Compensation for work in Capitol	31	2	Petition	321	Accounts.						
Wagoner, John Peter	Commutation pay	22	1	Petition	143	Rev. Claims	199	Favorable	285	Referred to Committee Whole House.		
Wagoner, John Peter	Commutation pay	22	2	House bill	171				285	Passed	Passed	App'd March 2, 1833
Wagoner, John Peter, widow of.	For amount of the commutation drawn by Thomas Triplett, and not paid over.	26	2	Petition	161	Rev. Claims.						
Wagoner, John Peter, widow of.	For amount of the commutation drawn by Thomas Triplett, and not paid over.	27	2	Petition	96	Rev. Claims	406	Adverse		Laid on table.		
Wagoner, Rebecca	(See John P. Wagoner, widow of.)	26	2		161							
Wagstaff, Samuel	Indemnity for house destroyed by British.	17	1	Petition	361	Claims	Mar. 22, 1822	Adverse				Leave to withdraw.
Wagstaff, Samuel	Indemnity for house destroyed by British.	19	2	Resolution	102	Claims	Jan. 22, 1827	Adverse		Laid on table.		
Wagstaff, Samuel	Indemnity for house destroyed by British.	20	1	Petition	47	Claims				Discharged; laid on table.		
Wagstaff, Samuel, representatives of.	Indemnity for house destroyed by British.	21	1	Petition	499	Claims	392	Favorable	459	Referred to Committee Whole House.		
Wagstaff, Samuel, representatives of.	Indemnity for house destroyed by British.	22	1	Petition	69	Claims	Dec. 19, 1831	Favorable	27	Passed	Passed	App'd March 7, 1832
Waid, Freelove, widow of.	Revolutionary pension	28	2	Petition	470	Rev. Pensions	171	Favorable	641	Referred to Committee Whole House.		
Waid, Freelove, widow of.	Revolutionary pension	29	1	Petition	462	Rev. Pensions.						
Waid, Freelove, widow of.	Revolutionary pension	29	2	Petition	150	Rev. Pensions	25	Adverse		Laid on table.		
Waid, Increase	(See Freelove Waid, widow of.)	28	2		470							
Waid, Lieut. Thomas	For amount rejected in settlement of account.	14	1	Petition	111	Claims				Discharged; laid on table.		
Wailes, Levin	(See William Garrard, *et al.*)	13	1		37							
Wain, John, heir of	Revolutionary pension	27	3	Petition	259	Rev. Pensions	Feb. 25, 1843					Leave to withdraw.
Waine, John, heir of	Revolutionary pension	28	1	Petition	901	Rev. Pensions.						
Wainwright, Henry	Refund certain duties.	24	1	Senate bill	643	Ways and Means	Sept. 30, 1836	With't amend.	105	Passed		App'd July 2, 1836
Wainwright, R. D. *et al.*, officers of Marine corps.	For pay and emoluments stopped prior to 1827.	22	1	Memorial	443	Military Affairs.						
Wainwright, Col. Robert D.	Increase of pension	25	3	Petition	225	Naval Affairs	Jan. 25, 1839	Favorable	1073	Referred to Committee Whole House.		
Wait, Aaron	Drawback on certain goods	6	2	Memorial	788	Manufactures	Feb. 21, 1801	Adverse.		Laid on table.		
Wait, Cyrenus	(See John B. Curd, and C. Wait.)	24	2		146							
Wait, Edward	Indemnity for property destroyed by order of General Macomb, war of 1812.	13	3	Petition	732	Claims	Feb. 15, 1815	Favorable	297	Passed	Passed	App'd Mar 3, 1815
Wait, Horace, *et al.*	Bounty on fishing vessel lost	18	1	Petition	193	Commerce.						
Wait, Horace, *et al.*	Bounty on fishing vessel lost	19	1	Petition	62	Commerce	April 4, 1826	Favorable	205	Passed.		
Wait, Horace, *et al.*	Bounty on fishing vessel lost	19	2	Senate bill	97	Commerce	Mar. 2, 1827	With't amend.	25	Passed		App'd Mar. 3, 1827
Wait, John	Amount of arrears due soldiers	1	2	Petition	148					Laid on table.		
Wait, John, (Maine)	Indemnity for French spoliations prior to 1800.	8	1	Memorial	595	Claims	Mar. 13, 1804			Postponed.		
Wait, Mary	(See Jesse Wood.)	27	3		423							
Wait, Obed, *et al.*	Increase of compensation as Judge	28	1	Petition	78	Judiciary.						
Wait, Roswell	Indemnity for property destroyed by order of General Macomb, war of 1812.	13	3	Petition	732	Claims	Feb. 15, 1815	Favorable	297	Passed	Passed	App'd March 3, 1815

List of private claims presented to the House of Representatives of the United States from the 1st to the 31st Congress, inclusive—Continued.

Names of claimants.	Nature or object of the claim.	Congress.	Session.	How brought before the House of Reps.	Page of journal.	To what committee of the House referred.	No. or date of the report.	Nature of the report.	No. of the bill.	How disposed of by the House of Reps.	How disposed of by the Senate.	Date of the act of Congress, and remarks.
Wait, Roswell	Indemnity for property destroyed by order of General Macomb, war of 1812.	17	1	Petition	274	Claims	....	....	......	Discharged; laid on table.		
Wait, Roswell	Indemnity for property destroyed by order of General Macomb, war of 1812.	17	2	Petition	30	Claims	....	....	......	Discharged	....	Leave to withdraw.
Waite, Stephen, *et al.*	Addition compensation as weigher, &c.	12	2	Petition	643	Ways and Means	....	....	......	Discharged.		
Wait, William, and others	Restoration of pension	22	1	Petition	44	Rev. Pensions	365	Favorable	460	Passed	Postponed.	
Wakefield, Henry or Harry	Compensation for time, suffering, and expenses as a prisoner in Canada, war of 1812.	14	2	Petition	38	Claims.						
Wakefield, Henry or Harry	Compensation for time, suffering, and expenses as a prisoner in Canada, war of 1812.	15	1	Petition	55	Claims	Feb. 24, 1818	Adverse	......	Laid on table.		
Wakefield, Henry or Harry	Compensation for time, suffering, and expenses as a prisoner in Canada, war of 1812.	15	2	Petition	33	Claims	40	Favorable	230	Referred to Committee Whole House.		
Wakefield, Henry or Harry	Compensation for time, suffering, and expenses as a prisoner in Canada, war of 1812.	16	1	Petition	28	Claims	Dec. 22, 1819	Adverse	......	Laid on table.		
Wakefield, Henry or Harry	Compensation for time, suffering, and expenses as a prisoner in Canada, war of 1812.	24	2	Petition	215	Military Affairs.						
Wakefield, Henry or Harry	Compensation for time, suffering, and expenses as a prisoner in Canada, war of 1812.	25	2	Petition	52	Claims	369	Adverse	......	Recommitted.		
Wakefield, Henry or Harry	Compensation for time, suffering, and expenses as a prisoner in Canada, war of 1812.	26	1	Petition	294	Claims.						
Wakefield, Henry or Harry	Compensation for time, suffering, and expenses as a prisoner in Canada, war of 1812.	26	2	Petition	36	Military Affairs.						
Wakefield, Henry or Harry	Compensation for time, suffering, and expenses as a prisoner in Canada, war of 1812.	28	1	Petition	145	Claims.						
Wakefield, Henry or Harry	Compensation for time, suffering, and expenses as a prisoner in Canada, war of 1812.	30	1	Petition	603	Claims.						
Wakelie, John	Increase of pension	11	2	House bill	283	Whole House	Mar. 24, 1810	Favorable	107	Passed	Passed	App'd April 27, 1810
Wakelee, Jonathan, widow of.	Revolutionary pension	25	3	Petition	126	Rev. Pensions	246	Favorable	1117	Referred to Committee Whole House.		
Wakelee, Jonathan, widow of.	Revolutionary pension	26	1	Petition	171	Rev. Pensions	636	Favorable	469	Referred to Committee Whole House.		
Wakelee, Jonathan, widow of.	Revolutionary pension	27	2	Petition	59	Rev. Pensions	96	Favorable	142	Passed	Passed	App'd July 9, 1842
Wakeman, Jabez	Revolutionary pension	16	1	Petition	252	Rev. Pensions	April 6, 1820	Adverse	......	Laid on table.		
Wakeman, Jabez	Revolutionary pension	22	1	Resolution	228	Rev. Pensions	....	....	......	Discharged; laid on table.		
Walback, Lieut. John B.	Compensation for extra services as aid to General Wilkinson.	8	2	Memorial	30	Secretary of War	....	....	......	Laid on table.		
Walback, Lieut. John B.	Compensation for extra services as aid to General Wilkinson.	10	1	Memorial	30	Claims.						

List of private claims presented to the House of Representatives of the United States from the 1st to the 31st Congress, inclusive—Continued.

Names of claimants.	Nature or object of the claim.	Congress.	Session.	How brought before the House of Reps.	Page of journal.	To what committee of the House referred.	No. or date of the report.	Nature of the report.	No. of the bill.	How disposed of by the House of Reps.	How disposed of by the Senate.	Date of the act of Congress, and remarks.
Walbridge, Silas	Pension	21	1	Petition	471	Military Pensions				Discharged; laid on table.		
Walbridge, Silas	Pension	22	2	Petition	382	Rev. Pensions.						
Walcott, Dr. Alexander	Compens tion for services, Indian treaty.	21	1	House bill	326	Whole House	Mar. 16, 1830	With amend.	278	Passed	Passed	App'd April 7, 1830. See bill No. 299.
Walden, Catherine	(See John Walden, widow of)	27	2		524							
Walden, David	Revolutionary pension	24	1	Resolution	286	Rev. Pensions				Discharged; laid on table.		
Walden, Elijah, administratrix and heir of.	Balance due for revolutionary services.	29	1	Petition	523	Rev. Pensions.						
Walden, John, widow of	Revolutionary pension	27	2	Petition	524	Rev. Pensions.						
Walderum, John	For wood furnished army, revolutionary war.	4	1	Rep. of Secretary Treasury.	388	Claims	74	Adverse		Laid on table.		
Waldo, Daniel, & Co.	Liquidation of bills, Massachusetts issue.	4	1	Rep. of Secretary Treasury.	388	Claims	74	Adverse		Laid on table.		
Waldo, Daniel, & Co.	Liquidation of bills, Massachusetts issue.	12	1	Petition	12	Claims.						
Waldo, David	For principal and interest on Continental bills.	29	2	Petition	428	Rev. Claims.						
Waldo, Edward	Pension	3	1	Rep. of Secretary War.	131	Select	May 26, 1794	Res. to refer to Sec. War.	J. R. 12	Passed	Passed	App'd June 9, 1794
Waldo, Edward	Pension	3	2	Rep. of Secretary War.	262	Claims	Feb. 28, 1795	Favorable; bill	130	Passed	Postponed.	
Waldo, Edward	Pension	4	1	Rep. of Secretary War.	447	Claims	Feb. 18, 1796	Favorable; bill	156	Passed	Passed	App'd April 20, 1796
Waldo, E. F. & S. C.	(See Godfrey Wenwood, heirs of)	28	1		89							
Waldo, Hannah	(See Jesse Waldo, widow of)	26	1		706							
Waldo, Jesse, widow of	(See Samuel Thompson)	26	1		706							
Waldo, John J., & Co.	Liquidation of certain bills of credit.	4	1	Rep. of Secretary Treasury.	388	Claims	74	Adverse		Laid on table.		
Waldo, Jonathan	Permission to fund certain bills	4	1	Petition	387	Select				Discharged; referred to Ways and Means.		
Waldo, William T., heir of.	Indemnity for French spoliations prior to 1800.	26	1	Memorial	182	Foreign Affairs	343	Favorable; bill	319	Referred to Committee Whole House.		
Waldoborough, Maine, merchants of.	Relief from certain liabilities on goods imported from Great Britain.	13	1	Petition	52	Ways and Means.						
Waldoborough, Maine, merchants of.	Relief from certain liabilities on goods imported from Great Britain.	13	2	Petition	234	Ways and Means	April 5, 1810					Leave to withdraw.
Waldon, John	Revolutionary pension	20	2	Resolution	72	Military Pensions				Discharged; referred to Com. Whole House.		
Waldron, Charles	Compensat'n for property destroyed by United States army.	24	2	Petition	208	Claims	214	Adverse		Laid on table.		
Waldron, Charles	Compensat'n for property destroyed by United States army.	25	2	Petition	52	Claims				Discharged.		
Waldron, Charles	Compensat'n for property destroyed by United States army.	25	3	Petition	189	Claims.						
Waldron, Charles	Compensat'n for property destroyed by United States army.	26	1	Petition	167	Claims.						
Waldron, Charles	Compensat'n for property destroyed by United States army.	27	2	Petition	154	Claims.						

List of private claims presented to the House of Representatives of the United States from the 1st to the 31st Congress, inclusive—Continued.

Names of claimants.	Nature or object of the claim.	Congress.	Session.	How brought before the House of Reps.	Page of journal.	To what committee of the House referred.	No. or date of the report.	Nature of the report.	No. of the bill.	How disposed of by the House of Reps.	How disposed of by the Senate.	Date of the act of Congress, and remarks.
Waldron, Charles	Compensat'n for property destroyed by United States army.	27	3	Petition	43	Claims	20	Favorable	646	Passed		App'd March 3, 1843
Waldron, Charles	Stores furnished United States army in 1835 and 1836.	27	3	Petition	136	Claims.						
Waldron, Charles	Stores furnished United States army in 1835 and 1836.	28	2	Petition	72	Claims.						
Waldron, Charles	Stores furnished United States army in 1835 and 1836.	30	1	Petition	228	Claims	158	Favorable	162	Referred to Committee Whole House.		
Waldron, Charles	Stores furnished United States army in 1835 and 1836.	30	2	House bill	143				162	Passed	Passed	App'd Jan. 8, 1849
Waldron, Charles	For beef furnished United States army.	31	1	Petition	369	Claims				Discharged; laid on table.		
Waldron, Charles	For beef furnished United States army.	31	2	Petition	83	Claims.						
Waldron, Nathaniel S.	Compensation for services in suppressing Indian hostilities.	25	3	Petition	293	Naval Affairs.						
Waldron, Nathaniel S.	Compensation for services in suppressing Indian hostilities.	26	1	Petition	180	Naval Affairs.						
Waldron, Richard, Ohio.	Pension	31	1	Petition	501	Invalid Pensions.						
Waldron, R. R.	(See Exploring Expedition)	27	3		149							
Waldron, Thos. W.	(See Exploring Expedition)	27	3		149							
Waldworth, Charles	Pension	28	2	Petition	57	Invalid Pensions				Discharged; laid on table.		
Wales, Thomas, heir of D. Holmes, deceased.	(See Henry Bass & Co.)	26	1		182		343		319			
Walker, A. B.	(See Kinchen Carr, administrator of.)	28	2		239							
Walker, Alexander	Pension	24	1	Petition	663	Rev. Pensions	652	Adverse		Laid on table.		
Walker, Andrew	Donation of land for revolutionary services.	9	1	Petition	189	Claims				Discharged; referred to Com. Whole House.		
Walker, Andrew	(See William H. Bedford, agent)	28	1		262							
Walker, Benjamin	(See Baron De Steuben, executors of.)	4	1		545							
Walker, Benjamin	Permission to locate certain lands.	25	2	Petition	373	Public Lands	Mar. 7, 1838	Favorable	632	Referred to Committee Whole House.		
Walker, Benjamin	Permission to locate certain lands.	25	3	House bill	376	Whole House	Jan. 25, 1839	Favorable	632	Passed	Passed	App'd March 3, 1839
Walker, Benjamin	Arrears of pension	26	1	Petition	602	Invalid Pensions.						
Walker, Benjamin	Arrears of pension	26	2	Petition	77	Invalid Pensions	Feb. 12, 1841	Adverse		Laid on table.		
Walker, Carlton, (N. C.)	Increase of compensation for naval service.	9	1	Petition	278	Ways and Means.						
Walker, Carlton, (N. C.)	Increase of compensation for naval service.	9	2	Petition	483	Ways and Means.						
Walker, Caleb	(See William Thompson)	19	2		78				351			
Walker, Catharine	(See Sam'l P. Walker, widow of)	31	1		533							
Walker, Dabney	Compensation for mail service	25	2	Resolution	761	P. Of. & P. Roads.				Discharged.		
Walker, Daniel, heirs of.	Indemnity for French spoliations prior to 1800.	26	1	Memorial	182	Foreign Affairs	343	Favorable; bill	319	Referred to Committee Whole House.		
Walker, David representatives of.	Compensation for services in revolutionary war.	22	1	Resolution	389	Rev. Pensions.						
Walker, David, representatives of.	Compensation for services in revolutionary war.	23	2	Petition	327	Rev. Pensions	Feb. 5, 1835	Adverse		Laid on table.		
Walker, D., by attorney for heirs.	Indemnity for French spoliations prior to 1800.	31	1	Petition	196	Foreign Affairs	355	Favorable	318	Referred to Committee Whole House.		

List of private claims presented to the House of Representatives of the United States from the 1st to the 31st Congress, inclusive—Continued.

Names of claimants.	Nature or object of the claim.	Congress.	Session.	How brought before the House of Reps.	Page of journal.	To what committee of the House referred.	No. or date of the report.	Nature of the report.	No. of the bill.	How disposed of by the House of Reps.	How disposed of by the Senate.	Date of the act of Congress, and remarks.
Walker, Dudley	Compensation for extra services as purser.	24	1	Petition	214	Naval Affairs	411	Favorable	422	Referred to Committee Whole House.		
Walker, Dudley	Compensation for extra services as purser.	25	2	Petition	41	Naval Affairs	259	Favorable	302	Referred to Committee Whole House.		
Walker, Dudley	Compensation for extra services as purser.	25	3	House bill	377				302	Passed	Passed, with amendment.	App'd March 3, 1839
Walker, Dudley	Allowance of certain charges rejected by Fourth Auditor.	29	1	Memorial	890	Naval Affairs.						
Walker, Elias R.	Payment for horse, &c., lost in Seminole war.	23	1	Documents	154	Claims.						
Walker, Elias R.	Payment for horse, &c., lost in Seminole war.	28	1	Petition	262	Claims.						
Walker, Elijah	Donation of lands for wounds received in erecting mills.	25	2	Petition	919	Public Lands				Discharged.		
Walker, Elizabeth, (Cherokee.)	For reservation of lands under treaty of July 8, 1817.	24	1	Petition	537	Indian Affairs.						
Walker, Ezekiel	(See William Taylor and Ezekiel Walker.)	15	1		24							
Walker, Ezekiel	Pension	16	1	Resolution	254	Rev. Pensions				Discharged; laid on table.		
Walker, George, family of.	Extra pay for services in public office.	3	1	Resolution	209	Select	47	Favorable	69	Passed	Rejected.	
Walker, George, and others.	Compensation for services in quartermaster's department, war of 1812.	16	1	Petition	28	Claims	Dec. 27, 1819	Adverse		Laid on table.		
Walker, Lieut. Geo. W.	Compensation for extra services in quartermaster's department.	23	1	Petition	189	Naval Affairs.						
Walker, George H.	Permission to enter certain tracts of land in Michigan.	24	1	Petition	612	Indian Affairs.						
Walker, George H.	Permission to enter certain tracts of land in Michigan.	26	1	Petition	954	Public Lands.						
Walker, George H.	Permission to enter certain tracts of land in Michigan.	27	2	Petition	132	Public Lands	480	Favorable	332	Passed	Passed	App'd April 11, 1842
Walker, Gideon	Pension	3	2	Rep. of Secretary War.	337	Claims.						
Walker, Gideon	(See Wm. H. Bedford, agent.)	28	1		262							
Walker, Gideon	Compensation for services as soldier in United States army in 1792 to 1795.	28	1	Petition	74	Claims	31	Adverse		Laid on table.		
Walker, Gideon	Compensation for services as soldier in United States army in 1792 to 1795.	28	2	Petition	118	Claims.						
Walker, Gideon	Compensation for services as soldier in United States army in 1792 to 1795.	29	1	Petition	148	Claims	477, 647	Adverse		Laid on table.		
Walker, Gideon	Compensation for services as soldier in United States army in 1792 to 1795.	30	1	Petition	207	Claims	252	Favorable	245	Passed	Ref'd to Com. on Claims.	
Walker, Gideon	Compensation for services as soldier in United States army in 1792 to 1795.	31	1	Petition	255	Claims	12	Favorable	14	Passed.		
Walker, Henry	Pension	22	1	Memorial	97	Rev. Pensions.						

List of private claims presented to the House of Representatives of the United States from the 1st to the 31st Congress, inclusive—Continued.

Names of claimants.	Nature or object of the claim.	Congress.	Session.	How brought before the House of Reps.	Page of journal.	To what committee of the House referred.	No. or date of the report.	Nature of the report.	No. of the bill.	How disposed of by the House of Reps.	How disposed of by the Senate.	Date of the act of Congress, and remarks.
Walker, Henry C., and Isaiah.	Permission to change location of land.	27	3	Petition	259	Public Lands	160	Favorable	776	Referred to Committee Whole House.		
Walker, James, Cherokee Indian.	Revolutionary pension	19	1	Petition	35	Rev. Pensions	164	Adverse.		Referred to Committee Whole House.		
Walker, James, Cherokee Indian.	Restoration of pension	21	1	Resolution	65	Military Pensions.						
Walker, James, Cherokee Indian.	Revolutionary pension	22	1	Resolution	44	Rev. Pensions	...	...	...	Discharged; laid on table.		
Walker, James	Commute pension for land	21	1	Petition	100	Public Lands	...	...	...	Discharged; laid on table.		
Walker, James, *et al.*	Compensation for opening a route for United States mail.	24	2	Senate bill	579	Whole House	...	...	200			
Walker, James, and John Kinkle, and others.	Increase of compensation for mail service.	25	2	Senate bill	301	P. Of. & P. Roads.	745	With amend.	S. 20	Referred to Committee Whole House.		
Walker, James, and John Kinkle, and others.	Increase of compensation for mail service.	25	3	Petition	132	P. Of. & P. Roads.	144	Favorable	1012	Referred to Committee Whole House.		
Walker, James, and John Kinkle, and others.	Increase of compensation for mail service.	26	1	Senate bill	227	P. Of. & P. Roads.	...	...	S. 29			
Walker, James, and John Kinkle, and others.	Increase of compensation for mail service.	26	1	Petition	752	P. Of. & P. Roads.	325	Favorable	290	Referred to Committee Whole House.		
Walker, James, and John Kinkle, and others.	Increase of compensation for mail service.	27	2	Petition	217	P. Of. & P. Roads.						
Walker, James, and John Kinkle, and others.	Increase of compensation for mail service.	27	3	Petition	340	P. Of. & P. Roads.	169	Favorable	781	Referred to Committee Whole House.		
Walker, James, and John Kinkle, and others.	Increase of compensation for mail service.	28	1	Petition	76	P. Of. & P. Roads.	537	Favorable	415	Referred to Committee Whole House.		
Walker, James, and John Kinkle, and others.	Increase of compensation for mail service.	28	2	House bill	344	...	...	...	415	Passed	Passed	App'd Feb. 27, 1845
Walker, James, and John Kinkle, and others.	Increase of compensation for mail service.	29	1	Documents	389	P. Of. & P. Roads.						
Walker, Jeremiah, (La.)	Confirmation of title to land	19	2	Petition	65	Priv. Land Claims.	...	...	...	Discharged	...	Leave to withdraw.
Walker, Jeremiah, (La.)	Confirmation of title to land	20	1	Petition	40	Priv. Land Claims.	211	Favorable	241	Referred to Committee Whole House.		
Walker, Jeremiah, (La.)	Confirmation of title to land	20	2	House bill	269	Whole House	Feb. 9, 1829	...	241	Passed	Ref'd to Public Lands.	
Walker, Jeremiah, (La.)	Confirmation of title to land	21	1	Petition	173	Priv. Land Claims.	161	Favorable	205	Passed	Passed	App'd May 29, 1830
Walker, Joel, Wyandot Indian.	Permission to change location of land.	27	3	Petition	259	Public Lands	160	Favorable	776	Referred to Committee Whole House.		
Walker, John W	(See Theodore Dwight, *et al.*)	19	1	...	221							
Walker, John	(See Thomas Rook, *et al.*)	21	1	...	558							
Walker, John W.	(See Robert Coltman, *et al.*)	23	1	...	418							
Walker, John W., surety of.	Release from liability to Post Office Department.	28	2	Petition	235	P. Of. & P. Roads.						
Walker, John	(See Thomas Tyner, *et al.*)	24	1	...	497							
Walker, John	Pension	29	1	Petition	1203	Claims.						
Walker, John	Pension	29	2	Petition	87	Claims.						
Walker, John	Pension	30	1	Petition	405	Claims	398	Adverse	...	Laid on table.		
Walker, John Peter	Confirmation of title to land	21	2	Senate bill	121	Priv. Land Claims.	Feb. 2, 1831	With amend.	40	Passed amended.	Concurred in	App'd March 2, 1831
Walker, John, by Sarah Shatto, heirs of.	Bounty land due her brother	29	1	Petition	592	Priv. Land Claims.						
Walker, John, by Sarah Shatto, heirs of.	Bounty land due her brother	29	2	Petition	92	Priv. Land Claims.						

List of private claims presented to the House of Representatives of the United States from the 1st to the 31st Congress, inclusive—Continued.

ames of claimants.	Nature or object of the claim.	Congress.	Session.	How brought before the House of Reps.	Page of journal.	To what committee of the House referred.	No. or date of the report.	Nature of the report.	No. of the bill.	How disposed of by the House of Reps.	How disposed of by the Senate.	Date of the act of Congress, and remarks.
Walker, John, by Sarah Shatto, heirs of.	Bounty land due her brother	30	2	Petition	204	Priv. Land Claims.						
Walker, John, by Sarah Shatto, heirs of.	Bounty land due her brother	31	1	Petition	362	Priv. Land Claims.						
Walker, John, jr., heir of.	Compensation for loss of two negroes.	24	1	Petition	853	Indian Affairs.						
Walker, John, jr., heir of.	Compensation for loss of two negroes.	25	2	Petition	173	Indian Affairs	333	Adverse	......	Laid on table.		
Walker, J., U. S. army	(See James Tilton, *et al.*)	30	1	......	328							
Walker, John T., (Wyandot Indian.)	Permission to change location of land.	27	3	Petition	259	Public Lands	160	Favorable	776	Referred to Committee Whole House.		
Walker, Jonathan	Released as surety of deputy postmaster, New Jersey.	19	2	Petition	27	P. Of. & P. Roads.	Jan. 2, 1827	......	......	Laid on table.		
Walker, Jonathan, (Mass.)	Relief for losses and injuries on the coast of Mexico, 1836.	25	2	Memorial	50	Foreign Affairs	......	......	......	Discharged.		
Walker, Jonathan, (Mass.)	Relief for losses and injuries on the coast of Mexico, 1836.	26	1	Petition	182	Foreign Affairs	......	......	......	Discharged; laid on table.		
Walker, Jonathan	Relief by refunding a certain fine imposed on him.	29	1	Petition	101, 749	Claims	622	Adverse	......	Laid on table.		
Walker, Joseph, by citizens of Ohio.	Confirmation of title to land	8	2	Petition	106	Select.						
Walker, Joseph	Confirmation of title to land	21	2	Senate bill	121	Priv. Land Claims.	Feb. 2, 1831	With amend.	40	Passed	Concurred in.	App'd March 2, 1831
Walker, Joseph	Confirmation of title to land	28	1	Petition	795	Priv. Land Claims.						
Walker, Joseph, (La.)	Confirmation of title to land	29	2	Petition	180	Priv. Land Claims.						
Walker, Joseph, (La.)	Confirmation of title to land	30	1	Petition	109	Priv. Land Claims.						
Walker, Joseph T., attorney for certain claimants in Florida.	For supplies furnished and for services rendered in Florida war.	29	1	Petition	574	Military Affairs.						
Walker, Joseph T., attorney for certain claimants in Florida.	For supplies furnished and for services rendered in Florida war.	29	2	Petition	172	Military Affairs.						
Walker, Joseph T., attorney for certain claimants in Florida.	For supplies furnished and for services rendered in Florida war.	30	1	Petition	435	Claims.						
Walker, Mansfield	Compensation for revolutionary services	7	2	Petition	379	......	......	......	......	Laid on table.		
Walker, Mansfield	Compensation for revolutionary services.	8	1	Petition	579	Claims.						
Walker, Mansfield	Compensation for revolutionary services.	11	2	Petition	165	Claims.						
Walker, Maria L	(See Dr. John Talve Griffin)	25	2	......	269							
Walker, Martha	(See Thomas Walker, widow of)	1	1	......	27							
Walker, Martin O	Permission to bid for mail contract.	30	2	House bill	125	P. Of. and P. Roads.	Dec. 20, 1848	Favorable	682	Referred to Committee Whole House.		
Walker, Matthew, farmily of.	Extra compensation for public services.	3	1	Resolution	209	Select	47	Favorable	69	Passed	Rejected.	
Walker, Matthew R., (Wyandot Indian.)	Change location of land	27	3	Petition	259	Public Lands	160	Favorable	776	Referred to Committee Whole House.		
Walker, Patrick	Increase of pension	30	1	Senate bill	639	Whole House	April 1, 1848	With't amend.	150	Passed	......	App'd April 8, 1848
Walker, Patrick	Continuation of pension	30	2	Senate bill	237	Whole House	Feb. 3, 1849	With't amend.	386	Passed	......	App'd Feb. 22, 1849
Walker, Peter Celestino, heirs of.	Confirmation of title to land	21	2	Senate bill	121	Priv. Land Claims.	Feb. 2, 1831	With amend.	40	Passed with amendm't.	Concurred in.	App'd March 2, 1831

List of private claims presented to the House of Representatives of the United States from the 1st to the 31st Congress, inclusive—Continued.

Names of claimants.	Nature or object of the claim.	Congress.	Session.	How brought before the House of Reps.	Page of journal.	To what committee of the House referred.	No. or date of the report.	Nature of the report.	No. of the bill.	How disposed of by the House of Reps.	How disposed of by the Senate.	Date of the act of Congress, and remarks.
Walker, Richard L.	For maintenance of United States seamen.	19	1	Resolution	362	Ways and Means	April 26, 1826	Favorable	228	Passed.		
Walker, Richard L.	For maintenance of United States seamen.	19	2	Resolution	96	Ways and Means				Discharged.		
Walker, Robert, (N. Y.)	Revolutionary pension	22	1	Petition	412	Rev. Pensions				Discharged; laid on table.		
Walker, Robert, heirs of	Indemnity for French spoliations prior to 1800.	30	1	Petition	118	Foreign Affairs						See general appropriation bill No. 21.
Walker, Robert, heirs of	Indemnity for French spoliations prior to 1800.	31	1	Petition	425	Foreign Affairs	355	Favorable	318	Referred to Committee Whole House.		
Walker, Samuel, and others	Indemnity for damages on property by United States troops in 1812.	15	1	Petition	90	Claims				Discharged; laid on table.		
Walker, Samuel, and others	Indemnity for damages on property by United States troops in 1812.	15	2	Petition	24	Claims	Nov. 26, 1818	Favorable	204	Referred to Committee Whole House.		
Walker, Samuel, and others	Indemnity for damages on property by United States troops in 1812.	16	1	Petition	136	Claims	Jan. 14, 1820	Adverse		Laid on table.		
Walker, Samuel, and others	Indemnity for damages on property by United States troops in 1812.	16	2	Petition	119	Claims				Discharged; laid on table.		
Walker, Samuel, and others	Indemnity for damages on property by United States troops in 1812.	17	1	Petition	201	Claims	April 5, 1822	Favorable	154	Passed.		
Walker, Samuel, and others	Indemnity for damages on property by United States troops in 1812.	17	2	Petition	83	Ways and Means				Discharged		Leave to withdraw.
Walker, Samuel, and others	Indemnity for damages on property by United States troops in 1812.	17	2	Senate bill	174	Claims	Jan. 31, 1823	With't amend.	27	Passed		App'd March 3, 1823
Walker, Samuel	For rations furnished United States troops, war of 1812.	17	1	Senate bill	374	Claims	Mar. 25, 1822	With't amend.	41	Passed		App'd May 7, 1822
Walker, Samuel	Increase of pension	23	1	Petition	309	Invalid Pensions	Feb. 21, 1834	Adverse		Laid on table.		
Walker, Samuel	(See William McCreery, administrator of.)	26	1		182							
Walker, Samuel	Compensation for injuries received whilst working on public buildings.	27	3	Petition	155	Public Buildings				Discharged; laid on table.		
Walker, Samuel	Compensation for injuries received whilst working on public buildings	28	2	Petition	149	Dist. of Columbia.						
Walker, Samuel	Compensation for injuries received whilst working on public buildings.	29	1	Petition	701	Claims						
Walker, Samuel	Compensation for work done at Norfolk.	30	1	General appropriation bill.	388	Whole House		With amends.	219	Passed	Passed	App'd Aug. 12, 1848
Walker, Samuel	(See Joseph Brown)	24	2		78							
Walker, Samuel D.	Drawback on tobacco	20	2	Petition	49	Referred to Secretary Treasury.						
Walker, Samuel D.	Drawback on tobacco	23	1	Petition	838	Ways and Means	Jan. 14, 1834	Favorable	187	Passed	Passed	App'd June 30, 1834
Walker, Samuel D.	Drawback on tobacco	23	2	Petition	68	Ways and Means	Feb. 3, 1835			Discharged; laid on table.		
Walker, Samuel D.	Drawback on tobacco	24	1	Petition	95	Ways and Means	104	Favorable	119	Rejected.		
Walker, Samuel D.	Drawback on tobacco	24	1	Petition	409	Ways and Means	433	Favorable	447	Referred to Committee Whole House.		
Walker, Samuel D.	Drawback on tobacco	25	2	Petition	42	Ways and Means	Jan. 3, 1838	Favorable	272	Referred to Committee Whole House.		
Walker, Samuel D.	Drawback on tobacco	25	3	House bill	376	Ways and Means	Jan. 26, 1839	Favorable	272	Passed.		
Walker, Samuel D.	Drawback on tobacco	26	1	Petition	178	Judiciary	Feb. 29, 1840	Favorable	24	Passed.		

List of private claims presented to the House of Representatives of the United States from the 1st to the 31st Congress, inclusive—**Continued.**

Names of claimants.	Nature or object of the claim.	Congress.	Session.	How brought before the House of Reps.	Page of journal.	To what committee of the House referred.	No. or date of the report.	Nature of the report.	No. of the bill.	How disposed of by the House of Reps.	How disposed of by the Senate.	Date of the act of Congress, and remarks.
Walker, Samuel D.	Drawback on tobacco	27	2	Petition	55	Ways and Means.						
Walker, Samuel D.	Drawback on tobacco	28	1	Petition	210	Ways and Means	488	Favorable	372	Referred to Committee Whole House.		
Walker, Samuel D.	Drawback on tobacco	29	1	Petition	116	Ways and Means	Jan. 8, 1846	Favorable	52	Passed	Passed	App'd Aug. 8, 1846
Walker, Capt. Samuel H.	For the purchase of certain rifles, guns, &c.	29	2	Memorial	172	Military Affairs.						
Walker, Samuel P.	Indemnity for French spoliations prior to 1800.	31	1	Petition	533	Foreign Affairs	355	Favorable	318	Referred to Committee Whole House.		
Walker, Tandy	Relief for disabilities incurred whilst acting as spy in the Creek war.	15	2	Petition	40	Select	Jan. 6, 1819	Favorable	26	Laid on table.		
Walker, Tandy	Relief for disabilities incurred whilst acting as spy in the Creek war.	16	1	Petition, &c.	53	Pens. & Rev. Cl'ms.				Discharged; laid on table.		
Walker, Tandy	Pension	17	2	Petition	31	Pens. & Rev. Cl'ms.	Dec. 16, 1822	Favorable	195	Passed.		
Walker, Tandy	Pension	18	2	Petition	84	Pens. & Rev. Cl'ms.						
Walker, Tandy	Pension	19	1	Petition	108	Military Pensions	164	Adverse.		Laid on table.		
Walker, Tandy	Pension	20	1	Petition	163	Military Pensions	171	Favorable	202	Referred to Committee Whole House.		
Walker, Tandy	Pension	20	2	House bill	198	Whole House	Jan. 23, 1829		202	Passed.		
Walker, Tandy	Pension	25	2	Petition	89	Invalid Pensions	278	Favorable	321	Passed	Passed	App'd July 7, 1838
Walker, Tandy	Compensation for services and property lost in Seminole war.	25	2	Documents	89	Claims.						
Walker, Thigh, (Indian)	(See John Walker, jr.)	25	2		173							
Walker, Thomas, widow of	Relief as a Canadian refugee	1	1	Petition	27	Select				Referred to Secretary of Treasury.		
Walker, Thomas, widow of	Relief as a Canadian refugee	3	2	Rep. of Secretary Treasury.	284					Laid on table.		
Walker, Thomas, widow of	Relief as a Canadian refugee	6	1	Rep. of Secretary Treasury.	603	Select	May 9, 1800			Laid on table.		
Walker, Thomas, widow of	Relief as a Canadian refugee	6	2	House bill	768	Whole House	Jan. 26, 1801	Favorable	280	Passed	Passed	App'd Feb. 18, 1801
Walker, Thomas A.	(See James Smith, *et al.*)	26	1		1147							
Walker, Timothy, & others	Compensat'n for property destroyed at Charlestown, Mass., in 1775.	24	1	Memorial	404	Claims	582			Laid on table.		
Walker, William M.	(See John H. Piatt)	17	1		387							
Walker, William, (Pa.)	Increase of pension	19	1	Petition	108	Military Pensions						Leave to withdraw.
Walker, William, (Tenn.)	Revolutionary pension	20	1	Resolution	317	Military Pensions	Dec. 12, 1828	Favorable	311	Passed.		
Walker, William, (Tenn.)	Revolutionary pension	21	1	Petition	49	Military Pensions	Jan. 5, 1830	General bill	72	Passed	Passed	App'd May 29, 1830, name omitted in act.
Walker, William, (Tenn.)	Revolutionary pension	22	1	Resolution	569	Rev. Pensions				Discharged; laid on table.		
Walker, William	(See J. E. Groce, agent of.)	22	1		173							
Walker, William, executor of.	Indemnity for property destroyed by the British.	22	1	Petition	512	Claims	April 6, 1832	Adverse		Laid on table.		
Walker, William	Confirmation of title to land	20	1	Resolution	28	Public Lands	42	Favorable	34	Passed	Passed	App'd April 22, 1828
Walker, William, (Tenn.)	Release from balance due United States	22	2	Resolution	90	P. Of. and P. Roads.						
Walker, William, (Ala.)	Correct error in land title	23	1	Petition	50	Public Lands	Jan. 2, 1834	Favorable	124	Passed.		
Walker, William, (Ala.)	Correct error in land title	23	2	Resolution	128	Public Lands	Dec. 30, 1835	Favorable	596	Referred to Committee Whole House.		
Walker, William, (Ala.)	Correct error in land title	24	1	Petition	114	Public Lands	189	Favorable	196	Passed.		
Walker, William, (Ala.)	Correct error in land title	24	2	Petition	47	Public Lands	17	Favorable	774	Referred to Committee Whole House.		
Walker, William, (Ala.)	Correct error in land title	25	2	Resolution	87	Public Lands	95	Favorable	112	Passed	Passed	Appd June 28, 1838

Names of claimants.	Nature or object of the claim.	Congress.	Session.	How brought before the House of Reps.	Page of journal.	To what committee of the House referred.	No. or date of the report.	Nature of the report.	No. of the bill.	How disposed of by the House of Reps.	How disposed of by the Senate.	Date of the act of Congress, and remarks.
Walker, William, (N. Y.)	Pension	24	2	Resolution	79	Rev. Pensions				Discharged; laid on table.		
Walker, William, (N. Y.)	Pension	25	2	Resolution	161	Rev. Pensions.						
Walker, William	Increase of pension	25	2	Petition	1007	Invalid Pensions				Discharged.		
Walker, William	Increase of pension	26	1	Petition	306	Invalid Pensions	263	Adverse		Laid on table.		
Walker, Wm.	Increase of compensation	25	2	Petition	277	P. Of. & P. Roads.	632	Adverse		Laid on table.		
Walker, William, *et al.*	Change location of land	27	3	Petition	259	Public Lands	160	Favorable	776	Referred to Committee Whole House.		
Walker, Wiseman, administrator of.	Indemnity for property destroyed by Indians.	20	2	Resolution	103	Ways and Means				Discharged; laid on table.		
Walker, Wiseman, administrator of.	Indemnity for property destroyed by Indians.	21	2	Resolution	112	Claims	Dec. 29, 1830	Adverse		Laid on table.		
Walker, Wiseman, administrator of.	Indemnity for property destroyed by Indians.	22	1	Petition	25	Claims	Dec. 28, 1831	Adverse		Laid on table.		
Walker, Wiseman, administrator of.	Indemnity for property destroyed by Indians.	24	1	Petition	96	Indian Affairs.						
Walker, Wiseman, administrator of.	Indemnity for property destroyed by Indians.	24	2	Petition	160	Indian Affairs.						
Walker, W. M.	(See Exploring Expedition)	27	3		149							
Walker, Zachariah	Compensation for saving public records.	29	1	Petition	380	Claims	735	Adverse		Laid on table.		
Walkington, George	Release from imprisonment	13	2	Petition	309	Select	77	Favorable	153	Passed	Passed	App'd Mar. 31, 1814
Walklee, Thomas	Pension	20	1	Resolution	131	Military Pensions	Feb. 23, 1828	Adverse		Laid on table.		
Walklee, Thomas	Pension	20	2	Petition	229	Military Pensions				Discharged; laid on table.		
Walklee, Thomas	Pension	21	1	Petition	260	Military Pensions				Discharged; laid on table.		
Wall, Ann	(See Daniel Wall, widow of)	21	2		209							
Wall, Benjamin, sureties of.	Relief from a certain judgment	13	2	Petition	209	Ways and Means	58	Favorable	184	Passed	Passed	App'd April 18, 1814
Wall, Burges	Pension	28	1	Petition	103	Invalid Pensions	42	Adverse		Laid on table.		
Wall, Daniel, widow of	Compensation for revolutionary services.	21	2	Petition	209	Rev. Claims.						
Wall, Gilbert	(See Richard and Gilbert Wall)	19	1		225							
Wall, John	Bounty land for revolutionary services.	15	2	Petition	103	Pens. & Rev. Cl'ms.	Dec. 18, 1818	Adverse		Laid on table.		
Walls, John, (Ohio)	Compensation for loss of horse in late war.	17	1	Petition	151	Claims				Discharged; laid on table.		
Wall, John, heirs of	Permission to locate land	29	1	Petition	690	Priv. Land Claims.	698	Favorable	472	Referred to Committee Whole House.		
Wall, John, heirs of	Permission to locate land	30	1	Petition	109	Priv. Land Claims.	Mar. 9, 1848			Discharged		Leave to withdraw.
Wall, John, heirs of	Permission to locate land	30	1	Senate bill	976	Priv. Land Claims.			176			
Wall, John, heirs of	Permission to locate land	30	2	Senate bill	119	Whole House	Mar. 3, 1849	With amend.	176	Passed with amendm't.		
Wall, Noah, (Ark.)	Confirmation of title to land	22	1	House bill	421	Public Lands	Feb. 28, 1832	Favorable	425	Passed	Passed	App'd June 25, 1832
Wall, Richard and Gilbert.	For prize-money under Com. J. P. Jones's capture.	19	1	Petition	225	Naval Affairs				Discharged; laid on table.		
Wall, Richard and Gilbert.	For prize-money under Com. J. P. Jones's capture.	21	2	Petition	222	Naval Affairs				Discharged		Leave to withdraw.
Wall, Richard and Gilbert.	For prize-money under Com. J. P. Jones's capture.	23	1	Petition	71	Rev. Claims.						
Wall, Richard and Gilbert.	For prize-money under Com. J. P. Jones's capture.	24	1	Petition	104	Rev. Claims	823	Adverse		Laid on table.		

List of private claims presented to the House of Representatives of the United States from the 1st to the 31st Congress, inclusive—**Continued.**

Names of claimants.	Nature or object of the claim.	Congress.	Session.	How brought before the House of Reps.	Page of journal.	To what committee of the House referred.	No. or date of the report.	Nature of the report.	No. of the bill.	How disposed of by the House of Reps.	How disposed of by the Senate.	Date of the act of Congress, and remarks.
Wall, Richard, (S. C.)	Compensation for revolutionary services	20	1	Petition	31	Rev. Claims	251	Adverse		Laid on table.		
Wall, Richard, (S. C.)	Compensation for revolutionary services.	20	2	Petition	27	Rev. Claims	Jan. 22, 1829	Adverse		Laid on table.		
Wall, Richard, (S. C.)	Compensation for revolutionary services.	21	1	Petition	38	Rev. Claims	111	Adverse		Referred to Committee Whole House.		
Wall, Richard, (S. C.)	Compensation for revolutionary services.	22	1	Petition	46	Rev. Claims	288	Favorable	372	Referred to Committee Whole House.		
Wall, Richard, (S. C.)	Compensation for revolutionary services.	24	2	Petition	270	Rev. Claims.						
Wall, Samuel	Compensation for revolutionary services.	2	1	Petition	475	Secretary of War	Jan. 31, 1792			Laid on table.		
Wall, Samuel	Payment for loss of horse in war of 1812.	12	2	Petition	691	Claims.						
Wall, Samuel, and Patrick Doyle.	For prize-money, war with Tripoli.	25	2	Memorial	172	Naval Affairs				Discharged.		
Wall, Thomas, *alias* Thos. Golland, a Choctaw Indian.	For land under Dancing Rabbit Creek treaty.	22	1	Resolution	711	Indian Affairs.						
Wall, Thomas, *et al.*	To be placed on equal footing as to pay with laborers on public grounds.	31	1	Petition	1082	Dist. of Columbia.						
Wall, William	Compensation for a horse lost in Seminole war.	23	1	Documents	154	Claims.						
Wall, William, agent of	Compensation for a horse lost in Seminole war.	28	1	Petition	262	Claims.						
Wallace, Capt. Adam, heirs of.	Bounty land for revolutionary services.	23	1	Petition	243	Rev. Claims.						
Wallace, Alexander	Pension	29	2	Petition	54	Rev. Pensions.						
Wallace, Alexander	Pension	30	1	Petition	114	Rev. Pensions	22	Adverse		Laid on table.		
Wallace, Cadwalader, *et al.*	Permission to change Virginia military for other lands.	25	3	Petition	135	Public Lands.						
Wallace, Cadwalader, *et al.*	Permission to change Virginia military for other lands.	26	1	Petition	333	Public Lands	509	Favorable	408	Referred to Committee Whole House.		
Wallace, Cadwalader, *et al.*	Permission to change Virginia military for other lands.	27	2	Petition	62	Public Lands	189	Adverse		Laid on table.		
Wallace, Cadwalader, *et al.*	Permission to change Virginia military for other lands.	27	3	Petition	112	Public Lands	175	Adverse		Laid on table.		
Wallace, Cadwalader, *et al.*	Permission to change Virginia military for other lands.	29	2	Petition	199	Public Lands.						
Wallace, Cadwalader, *et al.*	Permission to change Virginia military for other lands.	30	2	Senate bill	264	Public Lands	118	With't amend.	44	Referred to Committee Whole House.		
Wallace, Cesar	Confirmation of title to land	19	1	Report of register Land Office.	64	Public Lands	33	Adverse		Recommitted.		
Wallace, Cesar	Confirmation of title to land	19	1	Report of register Land Office.	516	Public Lands	May 5, 1826	Favorable	254	Laid on table.		
Wallace, Cesar	Confirmation of title to land	26	1	Petition	365	Priv. Land Claims.						
Wallace, Cornelius	Pension	24	1	Petition	663	Rev. Pensions	Jan. 7, 1836	Adverse		Laid on table.		
Wallace, Cornelius	Pension	24	2	Petition	512	Rev. Pensions				Discharged; laid on table.		
Wallace, Cornelius	Pension	25	2	Petition	55	Rev. Pensions				Discharged.		

List of private claims presented to the House of Representatives of the United States from the 1st to the 31st Congress, inclusive—Continued.

Names of claimants.	Nature or object of the claim.	Congress.	Session.	How brought before the House of Reps.	Page of journal.	To what committee of the House referred.	No. or date of the report.	Nature of the report.	No. of the bill.	How disposed of by the House of Reps.	How disposed of by the Senate.	Date of the act of Congress, and remarks.
Wallace, Cornelius	Pension	25	3	Petition	88	Rev. Pensions	....	....	......	Discharged.		
Wallace, David, sen., representatives of.	Indemnity for French spoliations prior to 1800.	26	1	Memorial	182	Foreign Affairs	343	Favorable; bill	319	Referred to Committee Whole House.		
Wallace, Ebenezer	Pension	3	2	Rep. of Secretary War.	337	Claims.						
Wallace, Frances	(See John Wallace, widow of.)	31	1	....	898							
Wallace, Hugh	Pension	4	1	Petition	411	Claims	May 31, 1796	Adverse	......	Laid on table.		
Wallace, Jacob	Confirmation of title to land in Louisiana.	27	2	Senate bill	359	Priv. Land Claims.	Feb. 26, 1842	With amend.	S. 76	Passed	Concurred in	App'd July 6, 1842
Wallace, Jacob	Pension	24	1	Petition	433	Rev. Pensions	432	Favorable	444	Passed	Passed	App'd June 28, 1836
Wallace, James	Confirmation of title to land in Louisiana.	18	2	Report of register and receiver of land office.	64	Public Lands	33	Adverse	......	Recommitted.		
Wallace, James	Confirmation of title to land in Louisiana.	19	1	Report of register and receiver of land office.	516	Public Lands	May 5, 1826	Favorable	254	Laid on table.		
Wallace, James P., heirs of.	Indemnity for Mexican spoliations on brandy in 1825.	24	1	Petition	425	Foreign Affairs	....	....	......	Discharged; laid on table.		
Wallace, Jesse	Permission to correct land entry	18	1	Petition	288	Public Lands.						
Wallace, John, (Maine)	Pension	24	1	Resolution	666	Rev. Pensions	....	....	......	Discharged; laid on table.		
Wallace, Lieut. John, heirs of.	Compensation for revolutionary services.	29	2	Petition	86	Rev. Pensions	....	....	......	Discharged; laid on table.		
Wallace, John, widow of	Pension	31	1	Petition	898	Rev. Pensions	364	Adverse	......	Laid on table.		
Wallace, John S	Pension	24	1	Petition	433	Rev. Pensions	652	Adverse	......	Laid on table.		
Wallace, John	(See Thomas Tyner)	24	1	....	497							
Wallace, Joseph	(See Jeremiah D. Hayden, sureties of.)	21	2	....	573							
Wallace, Moses, widow of.	Relief; loss of husband, revolutionary war.	4	1	Petition	427	Claims	May 31, 1796	Adverse	......	Laid on table.		
Wallace, Col. Robert	Payment for loss of horses, war of 1812.	25	2	Resolution	103	Claims	1035	Adverse	......	Laid on table.		
Wallace, Col. Robert	Payment for loss of horses, war of 1812.	25	3	Documents	120	Claims.						
Wallace, Col. Robert	Payment for loss of horses, war of 1812.	26	1	Petition	170	Claims.						
Wallace, Col. Robert	Payment for loss of horses, and compensation for services in war of 1812.	29	1	Petition	119	Claims	823	Favorable	548	Referred to Committee Whole House.		
Wallace, Col. Robert	Payment for loss of horses, and compensation for services in war of 1812.	30	1	Petition	154	Claims	166	Favorable	166	Passed.		
Wallace, Col. Robert	Payment for loss of horses, and compensation for services in war of 1812.	30	2	House bill	152	Whole House	Dec. 27, 1848	With't amend.	166	Passed	Passed	App'd Jan. 8, 1849
Wallace, Sarah	(See Moses Wallace, widow of)	4	1	....	427							
Wallace, Thomas, heirs of.	Compensation for revolutionary services.	22	1	Documents	265	Rev. Claims	325	Favorable	408	Referred to Committee Whole House.		
Wallace, Thomas, heirs of.	Compensation for revolutionary services.	23	1	Petition	43	Rev. Claims.	57	Favorable	67	Passed	Passed	App'd June 30, 1834
Wallace, Thomas	Additional grant of land	26	1	Memorial	610	Priv. Land Claims.						

List of private claims presented to the House of Representatives of the United States from the 1st to the 31st Congress, inclusive—Continued.

Names of claimants.	Nature or object of the claim.	Congress.	Session.	How brought before the House of Reps.	Page of journal.	To what committee of the House referred.	No. or date of the report.	Nature of the report.	No. of the bill.	How disposed of by the House of Reps.	How disposed of by the Senate.	Date of the act of Congress, and remarks.
Wallace, Weymouth	Pension	2	2	Rep. of Secretary War.	649	Whole House.						
Wallace, Weymouth	Pension	3	1	Rep. of Secretary War.	131	Select	May 26, 1794	Favorable	J. R. 12	Passed	Passed	App'd June 9, 1794
Wallace, Weymouth	Pension	4	1	Resol'n and rep't Sec. of War.	373	Claims	Feb. 18, 1796	Favorable	156	Passed	Passed	App'd April 20, 1796
Wallace, William	Pension	10	1	House bill	232	Whole House	Mar. 17, 1808	Favorable	78	Passed	Passed	App'd April 25, 1808
Wallace, William	Increase of pension	10	1	House bill	232	Whole House	April 17, 1808	Favorable	78	Passed	Passed	App'd April 25, 1808
Wallace, William, *et al.*	(See Joseph Clay, administrators of.)	15	1		165							
Wallace, William B.	For benefit of act of May, 1826	22	1	Petition	135	Rev. Claims.						
Wallace, Lieut. Wm., heirs of.	Commutation pay	25	2	Petition	177	Rev. Claims	330	Adverse		Laid on table.		
Wallace, Lieut. Wm., heirs of.	Commutation pay	27	2	Petition	607	Rev. Claims	April 21, 1842	Adverse		Laid on table.		
Wallace, William, (Maine)	Pension	26	1	Resolution	561	Rev. Pensions	423	Adverse		Laid on table.		
Wallace, William, (Maine)	Pension	26	1	Petition	707	Rev. Pensions	424	Adverse		Laid on table.		
Wallace, William, (Ill.)	Pension	30	1	Petition	628, 1142	Invalid Pensions				Discharged; laid on table.		
Wallace, William P., and J. R. McFadon.	To refund certain duties	31	1	Petition	425	Military Affairs	121	Favorable	135	Referred to Committee Whole House.		
Wallas, John.	Indemnity for French spoliations prior to 1800.	26	1	Memorial	182	Foreign Affairs	343	Favorable; bill	319	Referred to Committee Whole House.		
Wallis, Alexander	(See Alexander Wallace.)	29	2		54							
Wallis, George	(See Missouri and Indiana militia)	24	1		810							
Wallis, George	Indemnity for cattle destroyed by Indians.	27	3	Documents	168	Indian Affairs.						
Wallis, George	Indemnity for cattle destroyed by Indians.	28	1	Petition	132	Indian Affairs	150	Favorable	138	Passed	Passed	App'd June 15, 1844
Wallis, Joseph, *et al.*	(See Jeremiah D. Hayden, sureties of.)	22	1		943							
Wallis, Matthew S	(See Wm. H. Bedford, agent.)	28	1		262							
Waller, David	Pension	25	2	Senate bill	1155				291	Referred to Committee Whole House.		
Waller, David	Pension	25	3	Senate bill	653				33	Referred to Committee Whole House.		
Waller, David	Pension	26	1	Senate bill	802	Rev. Pensions	May 25, 1840	With't amend.	35	Referred to Committee Whole House.		
Waller, David	Pension	26	2	Senate bill	113	Rev. Pensions	Feb. 12, 1841	With't amend.	3	Referred to Committee Whole House.		
Waller, David	Pension	27	2	Senate bill	108	Whole House	Mar. 12, 1842	With't amend.	8	Passed		App'd Mar. 19, 1842
Waller, Elias, *alias* Wallen Elias.	Additional compensation for repairing government house at St. Augustine.	23	2	Petition	256	Claims.						
Waller, Elias, *alias* Wallen Elias.	Additional compensation for repairing government house at St. Augustine.	24	1	Petition	50	Claims	234	Adverse		Laid on table.		
Waller, Elias, *alias* Wallen Elias.	Additional compensation for repairing government house at St. Augustine.	24	2	Petition	308	Claims	304	Adverse		Laid on table.		
Waller, Elias, *alias* Wallen Elias.	Additional compensation for repairing government house at St. Augustine.	25	2	Petition	275	Claims				Discharged.		

List of private claims presented to the House of Representatives of the United States from the 1st to the 31st Congress, inclusive—Continued.

Names of claimants.	Nature or object of the claim.	Congress.	Session.	How brought before the House of Reps.	Page of journal.	To what committee of the House referred.	No. or date of the report.	Nature of the report.	No. of the bill.	How disposed of by the House of Reps.	How disposed of by the Senate.	Date of the act of Congress, and remarks.
Waller, Elias, *alias* Wallen Elias.	Additional compensation for repairing government house at St. Augustine.	25	3	Petition	87	Claims	223	Adverse	......	Laid on table.		
Waller, Elias, *alias* Wallen Elias.	Additional compensation for repairing government house at St. Augustine.	29	1	Petition	772	Claims.						
Waller, Hampton, (Va.) .	Pension	21	1	Resolution	212	Military Pensions..	May 7, 1830	Adverse	......	Laid on table.		
Waller, Henry, (N. Y.)..	Indemnity for house occupied by United States troops and destroyed by British.	15	1	Petition	283	Claims	Mar. 13, 1818	Adverse	......	Laid on table.		
Waller, Henry, (N. Y.)..	Indemnity for house occupied by United States troops and destroyed by British.	22	1	Petition	188	Claims	Feb. 24, 1832	Adverse	......	Laid on table.		
Waller, Henry, (N. Y.)..	Indemnity for house occupied by United States troops and destroyed by British.	22	1	Senate bill	844	Claims	July 5, 1832	With amend..	141	Passed with amendm't	....	App'd July 14, 1832
Waller, Henry, (N. Y.)..	Indemnity for house occupied by United States troops and destroyed by British.	22	2	Senate bill	277	Claims	Mar. 2, 1833	Adverse	65	Rejected.		
Waller, Henry, (N. Y.)..	Indemnity for house occupied by United States troops and destroyed by British.	23	1	Senate bill	654	Claims	553	With't amend.	66	Rejected.		
Waller, Henry, (N. Y.)..	Indemnity for house occupied by United States troops and destroyed by British.	24	1	Petition	284	Claims.						
Waller, Henry, (N. Y.)..	Indemnity for house occupied by United States troops and destroyed by British.	25	3	Petition	121	Claims.						
Waller, Jane	Reimbursement for money paid for land previously patented, and for damages.	25	2	Senate bill	1155	Public Lands.....	July 6, 1838	With amend..	28	Referred to Committee Whole House.		
Waller, Jane	Reimbursement for money paid for land previously patented, and for damages.	26	1	Senate bill	802	Public Lands.....	July 17, 1840	With't amend.	82	Referred to Committee Whole House.		
Waller, jr., Joseph, and others.	Confirmation of title to land	15	1	Petition	157	Priv Land Claims.						
Waller, R. P..........	(See Thomas Griffin, executor of)	26	1	....	167	....	446					
Waller, Walter	Pension	22	1	Resolution	560	Invalid Pensions ..	....	....	......	Discharged; laid on table.		
Waller, Walter	Pension	22	2	Petition	171	Invalid Pensions ..	Feb. 25, 1833	Favorable	748	Referred to Committee Whole House.		
Waller, Walter	Pension	23	1	Petition	44	Invalid Pensions ..	1	Favorable	1	Passed with amendm't	Rejected.	
Waller, William	Correct error in land entry.......	19	1	Resolution	241	Public Lands.						
Waller, William	Correct error in land entry.......	26	2	Petition	49	Priv. Land Claims.	40	Favorable	568	Referred to Committee Whole House.		
Waller, William	Correct error in land entry.......	27	2	Petition	661	Priv Land Claims.	755	Favorable	436	Passed	Passed	App'd July 27, 1842
Waller, William, attorney	(See Jared E. Groce)..........	21	1	....	413	....	328					
Waller, William G......	Relief for injuries received in United States service.	27	2	Memorial	783	Invalid Pensions ..	817	Adverse	......	Laid on table.		
Walley & Foster.......	Debenture on pepper exported....	15	2	Petition	26	Com. and Manuf..	....	....	......	Discharged; laid on table.		
Walley & Foster.......	Debenture on pepper exported....	17	1	Senate bill	374	Ways and Means..	74	Adverse	49	Laid on table.		
Walley & Foster.......	Debenture on pepper exported....	17	2	Senate bill	67	Ways and Means..	55	Adverse	8	Laid on table.		

List of private claims presented to the House of Representatives of the United States from the 1st to the 31st Congress, inclusive—Continued.

Names of claimants.	Nature or object of the claim.	Congress.	Session.	How brought before the House of Reps.	Page of journal.	To what committee of the House referred.	No. or date of the report.	Nature of the report.	No. of the bill.	How disposed of by the House of Reps.	How disposed of by the Senate.	Date of the act of Congress, and remarks.
Walley & Foster	Debenture on pepper exported	18	1	Petition	74	Ways and Means.						
Walley & Foster	Debenture on pepper exported	18	2	Petition	312	Ref'd to Secretary Treasury.						
Walley & Foster	Debenture on pepper exported	19	1	Petition	221	Ways and Means	85	Favorable	120	Passed	Passed, with amendment.	App'd May 20, 1826
Walley, Thomas	For payment of certain bills of credit.	1	3	Memorial	376	...	...	...	...	Laid on table.		
Walley, T., administrator of.	Indemnity for French spoliations prior to 1800.	26	1	Memorial	182	Foreign Affairs	343	Favorable; bill	319	Referred to Committee Whole House.		
Walley, Thomas, administrator of.	Indemnity for French spoliations prior to 1800.	22	1	Petition	186	Foreign Affairs.						
Walley, S. H	(See T. Walley)	26	1	...	182							
Wallier, John	(See William H. Bedford, agent.)	28	1	...	262							
Walling, Catherine	(See Thos. Walling, widow of.)	28	1	...	1042							
Walling, Joseph	Restoration of pension	24	2	Resolution	222	Rev. Pensions	Feb. 23, 1837	...	...	Laid on table.		
Walling, Thomas, widow of.	Re-enactment of navy pension laws	28	1	Petition	1042	Naval Affairs.						
Wallingford, Samuel late widow of.	Commutation pay	3	2	Petition	274	Claims	Mar. 2, 1795	Adverse	...	Laid on table.		
Wallingford, Samuel, late widow of.	Commutation pay	4	1	Petition	373	Cliams	May 31, 1796	Adverse	...	Laid on table.		
Wallingford, Samuel, late widow of.	Commutation pay	4	2	Petition	696	Claims	Feb. 16, 1797	Adverse.	...	Laid on table.		
Wallis, George	(See George Wallace)	4	2	Petition	696	Claims.						
Wallis, Joseph	(See Joseph Wallace)											
Wallis, Matthew S.	(See Matthew Wallace.)											
Walmsley, Jonathan	(See Daniel Gould, *et al.*)	14	1	...	83							
Waln, Robert, administrator of.	Indemnity for French spoliations prior to 1800.	26	1	Memorial	182	Foreign Affairs	343	Favorable; bill	319	Referred to Committee Whole House.		
Waln, R. assignee of	Indemnity for French spoliations prior to 1800.	26	1	Memorial	182	Foreign Affairs	343	Favorable; bill	319	Referred to Committee Whole House.		
Waln, S. Morris, & Co	Remission of duties on wine destroyed by fire.	23	1	Petition	214	Ways and Means	Feb. 4, 1834	Favorable	276	Referred to Committee Whole House.		
Waln, S. Morris, & Co	Remission of duties on wine destroyed by fire.	23	2	House bill	300	Whole House	Feb. 6, 1835	Favorable	276	Passed.		
Waln, S. Morris, & Co	Remission of duties on wine destroyed by fire.	24	1	Petition	53	Ways and Means	642	Favorable	134	Referred to Committee Whole House.		
Waln, S. Morris, & Co	Remission of duties on wine destroyed by fire.	24	2	House bill	342	Ways and Means	Feb. 4, 1837	Favorable	134	Referred to Committee Whole House.		
Waln, S. Morris, & Co	Remission of duties on wine destroyed by fire.	25	2	Petition	42	Ways and Means	1014	Adverse	...	Laid on table.		
Waln, S. Morris, & Co	Remission of duties on wine destroyed by fire.	27	2	Petition	153	Ways and Means	997	Favorable	577	Referred to Committee Whole House.		
Waln, S. Morris, & Co	Remission of duties on wine destroyed by fire.	27	3	House bill	91	Whole House	Dec. 23, 1842	Favorable	577	Passed.		
Waln, S. Morris, & Co	Remission of duties on wine destroyed by fire.	28	1	Petition	159	Ways and Means.						
Waln, S. Morris, & Co	Remission of duties on wine destroyed by fire.	30	1	Petition	116	Claims	41	Favorable	38	Passed.		
Waln, S. Morris, & Co	Remission of duties on wine destroyed by fire.	31	1	Petition	323	Commerce	331	Favorable	289	Referred to Committee Whole House.		
Waln, S. Morris, & Co	Remission of duties on window glass broken.	24	1	Petition	604	Ways and Means	642	Favorable	617	Referred to Committee Whole House.		

List of private claims presented to the House of Representatives of the United States from the 1st to the 31st Congress, inclusive—Continued.

Names of claimants.	Nature or object of the claim.	Congress.	Session.	How brought before the House of Reps.	Page of journal.	To what committee of the House referred.	No. or date of the report.	Nature of the report.	No. of the bill.	How disposed of by the House of Reps.	How disposed of by the Senate.	Date of the act of Congress, and remarks.
Wain, S. Morris, & Co.	Remission of duties on window glass broken.	25	2	Petition	42	Ways and Means	1015	Adverse	......	Laid on table.		
Walriss, or Watriss, Henry.	Relief on certain contracts for iron suspended by government.	26	1	Petition	294	Claims.						
Walriss, or Watriss, Henry.	Relief on certain contracts for iron suspended by government.	27	2	Petition	381	Claims.						
Walsh, Charles S., administrator of.	For services as chargé des affaires to Spain.	25	2	Memorial	172	Foreign Affairs	639	Favorable	616	Referred to Committee Whole House.		
Walsh, Charles S., administrator of.	For services as chargé des affaires to Spain.	25	3	House bill	380	Whole House	Jan. 25, 1839	Favorable	616	Passed	Passed	App'd March 2, 1839
Walsh, David	Compensation for work done on Cumberland road.	23	1	Resolution	589	Claims	455	Adverse	......	......	......	See report No. 449.
Walsh, John	Pension	10	2	House bill	499	Whole House	Feb. 20, 1809	Favorable	158	Passed	Passed	App'd March 3, 1809
Walsh, Nicholas	(See Nicholas Welsh)	15	2	......	23							
Walsh, Ralph	Compensation as inspector at New York.	2	2	Petition	678	......	......	......	......	Laid on table.		
Walsh, Robert M.	For services as acting chargé des affaires to Mexico.	31	1	Petition	816	Foreign Affairs.						
Walsh, Robert M.	For services as acting chargé des affaires to Mexico.	31	2	Petition	446	Foreign Affairs	106	Adverse	......	......	......	Provided for in bill No. 461; approved Mar. 3, 1851.
Walsh, Thomas	For benefit of act of 2d March, 1821.	17	1	Petition	61	Whole House	......	......	......	Discharged; laid on table.		
Walsworth, Charles	Pension	29	1	Petition	161	Invalid Pensions	499	Adverse	......	Laid on table.		
Walsworth, Charles	Pension	30	1	Petition	389	......	......	......	......	......	......	Leave to withdraw.
Walter, Aaron, (N. Y.)	Indemnity for property captured by enemy in 1812.	22	1	Petition	899	Claims.						
Walter, Conrad	(See Conrad Watts)	25	2	......	54							
Walter, George	Compensation for revolutionary services.	29	1	Petition	310	Rev. Claims.						
Walter, George	Invalid pension	10	1	House bill	232	Whole House	Mar. 17, 1808	Favorable	78	Passed	Passed	App'd April 25, 1808
Walter, Jacob F	To refund money paid as patent fee.	24	1	Petition	49	Claims	84	Favorable	99	Passed	Passed	App'd June 23, 1836
Walter, John	Pension	4	2	Petition	677	Claims	Feb. 9, 1797	Adverse	......	Laid on table.		
Walter, John	Pension	17	2	Petition	47	Pens. & Rev. Cl'ms.	Dec. 20, 182[illegible]	Adverse	......	......	......	Leave to withdraw.
Walter, Joseph H	Indemnity for injury to his plantation by improvement of Cape Fear river.	25	3	Petition	462	Claims	Feb. 25, 1839	Favorable; res.	......	Referred to Secretary War.		
Walter, Joseph H	Indemnity for injury to his plantation by improvement of Cape Fear river.	26	1	Rep. of Secretary War.	336	Claims.						
Walter, Joseph H	Indemnity for injury to his plantation by improvement of Cape Fear river.	27	3	Petition	193	Claims.						
Walter, Leonard	Compensation for revolutionary services.	2	1	Petition	44	Secretary of War.						
Walter, Leonard	Compensation for revolutionary services.	2	2	Rep. of Secretary War.	735	......	......	......	......	Laid on table.		
Walter, Lynde, and W.	Indemnity for French spoliations prior to 1800.	26	1	Memorial	182	Foreign Affairs	343	Favorable; bill	319	Referred to Committee Whole House.		
Walter, Martin, widow of	Pension	30	1	Petition	1152	Rev. Pensions.						
Walter, Michael, heir of.	Compensation for revolutionary services.	31	1	Petition	383	Rev. Claims.						

List of private claims presented to the House of Representatives of the United States from the 1st to the 31st Congress, inclusive—Continued.

Names of claimants.	Nature or object of the claim.	Congress.	Session.	How brought before the House of Reps.	Page of journal.	To what committee of the House referred.	No. or date of the report.	Nature of the report.	No. of the bill.	How disposed of by the House of Reps.	How disposed of by the Senate.	Date of the act of Congress, and remarks.
Walter, Phebe	(See Martin Walter, widow of.)	30	1		1152							
Walterhouse, John	Compensation for property destroyed by British in 1813.	15	2	Petition	148	Claims.						
Walterhouse & Helmes	(See Elijah Hathaway)	15	2		148							
Walthall, William T	Compensation for services on board of ship St. Louis.	29	1	Petition	219	Naval Affairs	765	Favorable	504	Referred to Committee Whole House.		
Walthall, William T	Compensation for services on board of ship St. Louis.	29	2	House bill	212	Whole House	Jan. 22, 1847	Favorable	504	Passed	Passed	App'd March 3, 1847
Walthers, Sarah	Confirmation of title to land	22	2	Petition	96	Priv. Land Claims.	Dec. 29, 1832	Adverse		Laid on table.		
Walthour, Andrew, executors of.	Payment for negro slave taken by Indians.	22	1	Petition	31	Indian Affairs.						
Walthour, Andrew, executors of.	Payment for negro slave taken by Indians.	23	1	Petition	50	Indian Affairs.						
Walton, Anna	Extension of pension	30	1	Petition	230	Rev. Pensions	Jan. 25, 1848	Adverse		Laid on table.		
Walton, George W	Payment for loss of stage and horses by Indians.	26	1	Petition	621	Claims.						
Walton, George W	Payment for loss of stage and horses by Indians.	26	2	Petition	135	Claims	108	Adverse		Laid on table.		
Walton, George W	Payment for loss of stage and horses by Indians.	27	2	Petition	94	Claims	772	Adverse		Laid on table.		
Walton, Henry	Compensation for damages and property taken in revolutionary war.	2	1	Rep. of Secretary Treasury.	580					Laid on table.		
Walton, Jonathan, & Co.	Indemnity for losses on treasury notes.	21	1	Petition	523	Ways and Means	383	Favorable	446	Referred to Committee Whole House.		
Walton, Jonathan, & Co.	Indemnity for losses on treasury notes.	22	1	Petition	471	Ways and Means	394	Favorable	493	Referred to Committee Whole House.		
Walton, Jonathan, & Co.	Indemnity for losses on treasury notes.	23	1	Petition	56	Ways and Means	Jan. 15, 1834	Favorable	200	Passed	Passed	App'd June 30, 1834
Walton, Jacob, devisees of.	Compensation for damages done to property by United States army.	2	1	Petition	495	Secretary Treasury.	April 17, 1792			Laid on table.		
Walton, James	Pre-emption right to land	20	2	Petition	34	Public Lands.				Discharged; laid on table.		
Walton, James	Pre-emption right to land	21	1	Petition	100	Public Lands				Discharged; laid on table.		
Walton, John B	Payment for property destroyed by Indians.	29	1	Memorial	151	Claims.						
Walton, John	Pension	13	2	Petition	250	Pens. & Rev. Cl'ms.				Referred to Secretary War.		
Walton, Josiah	Pension	3	2	Rep. of Secretary War.	337	Claims	Feb. 28, 1795	Favorable; bill	130	Passed.		
Walton, Josiah	Pension	4	1	Rep. of Secretary War.	447	Claims	Feb. 18, 1796	Favorable; bill	156	Passed	Passed	App'd April 20, 1796
Walton, Martin, administrator of.	For loss of horse sold by United States officer in Florida.	25	2	Documents	396	Claims				Discharged.		
Walton, Samuel	Indemnity for French spoliations prior to 1800.	26	1	Memorial	182	Foreign Affairs	343	Favorable; bill	319	Referred to Committee Whole House.		
Walton, William P	(See John Graves, *et al.*)	27	2		620							
Walton, William, (Ala.)	Confirmation of title to land	27	2	Petition	143	Priv. Land Claims.	Jan. 7, 1833	Adverse		Laid on table		Leave to withdraw.
Walworth, Hiram	(See Martin J. Aiken.)	17	1		359							
Wamsly, James	Restoration of pension	29	1	Resolution	1069	Rev. Pensions.						
Wamsly, Capt. Jonathan	(See Daniel Gould, *et al.*)	14	1		83							

List of private claims presented to the House of Representatives of the United States from the 1st to the 31st Congress, inclusive—Continued.

Names of claimants.	Nature or object of the claim.	Congress.	Session.	How brought before the House of Reps.	Page of journal.	To what committee of the House referred.	No. or date of the report	Nature of the report.	No. of the bill.	How disposed of by the House of Reps.	How disposed of by the Senate.	Date of the act of Congress, and remarks.
Wamsley, Capt. Jonathan.	Reimbursement of expenses and supplies, &c., of troops, war of 1812.	18	1	Petition	75	Claims	Jan. 16, 1824	Adverse	......	Laid on table.		
Wamsley, Capt. Jonathan.	Reimbursement of expenses and supplies, &c., of troops, war of 1812.	21	1	Petition	235	Claims	Mar. 10, 1830	Adverse	......	Laid on table.		
Wamsley, Capt. Jonathan.	Reimbursement of expenses and supplies, &c., of troops, war of 1812.	22	1	Petition	133	Claims	Jan. 16, 1832	Adverse	......	Laid on table.		
Wamsley, William, *et al.*, officers and soldiers of Virginia line.	To be allowed and paid 300 acres land and £60 bounty under resolution of Virginia, Oct., 1780.	23	1	Petition	41	Rev. Claims.						
Wandall, Oliver	Liquidation of bills of credit	4	1	Rep. Sec. Treas.	388	Claims	74	Adverse	......	Laid on table.		
Wandell, David	Compensation for revolutionary services.	13	2	Petition	258	Pens. & Rev. Cl'ms.	....	....	......	Discharged; referred to Secretary War.		
Wann, Edward	Pension	20	1	Petition	478	Military Pensions	April 5, 1828	Adverse	......	Laid on table.		
Wankee, Wm., and James Stewart.	Bounty land for services in Mexico	31	1	Petition	349	Public Lands.						
Wanton, Edward	(See F. M. Arredondo, *et al.*)	19	1	....	252							
Wanton, Edward M., administrator of.	Compensation for goods and merchandise destroyed by United States troops in Florida.	28	1	Petition	802	Claims.						
Wanton, Edward M., administrator of.	Compensation for goods and merchandise destroyed by United States troops in Florida.	28	2	Petition	71	Claims.						
Wanton, James M., administrator of.	Payment for destruction of property in Florida by citizens by order of United States officer.	28	1	Petition	862	Claims.						
Wanton, James M. administrator of.	Payment for destruction of property in Florida by citizens by order of United States officer.	28	2	Petition	71	Claims.						
Wanton, James M. administrator of.	Payment for destruction of property in Florida by citizens by order of United States officer.	29	1	Petition	474	Military Affairs	556	Favorable	380	Referred to Committee Whole House.		
Wapler, Lieut. Samuel	Commutation pay	23	1	Petition	158	Rev. Claims.						
Wapler, Lieut. Samuel, heirs of.	Commutation pay	31	1	Petition	712	Rev. Claims	415	....	......	Laid on table.		
Warburgh, Frederick J.	Patent for improvement in lamps and manufacturing candles.	17	1	Petition	293	Judiciary	Mar. 13, 1822	Favorable; bill	121	Passed	Passed	App'd May 7, 1822
Ward, Abner, (N. H.)	Pension	19	2	Petition	59	Military Pensions	....	....	......	Discharged.		
Ward, Allen	Renewal of patent	24	1	Petition	806	Patents.						
Ward, Andrew	(See William H. Bedford, agent)	28	1	....	262							
Ward, Benjamin, (Ohio)	Pension	21	1	Petition	372	Military Pensions.						
Ward, Benjamin, (Ohio)	Pension	22	2	Petition	120	Rev. Pensions	....	....	......	Discharged; laid on table.		
Ward, Burrell	(See William H. Bedford, agent)	28	1	....	262							
Ward, Charles, widow of.	Continuation of pension	28	1	Petition	72	Rev. Pensions	....	....	......	Discharged; laid on table.		
Ward, Charles, widow of.	Continuation of pension	29	1	Petition	658	Rev. Pensions.						
Ward, Charles, widow of.	Continuation of pension	29	2	Petition	172	Rev. Pensions.						
Ward, Charles, widow of.	Continuation of pension	30	1	Petition	355	Rev. Pensions.						
Ward, Charles, widow of.	Continuation of pension	30	2	Petition	121	Rev. Pensions	67	Favorable	767	Referred to Committee Whole House.		

List of private claims presented to the House of Representatives of the United States from the 1st to the 31st Congress, inclusive—Continued.

Names of claimants.	Nature or object of the claim.	Congress.	Session.	How brought before the House of Reps.	Page of journal.	To what committee of the House referred.	No. or date of the report.	Nature of the report.	No. of the bill.	How disposed of by the House of Reps.	How disposed of by the Senate.	Date of the act of Congress, and remarks.
Ward, Christopher	Pension	20	2	Resolution	76	Military Pensions				Discharged; referred to Com. Whole House.		
Ward, Christopher	Pension	21	1	Petition	49	Military Pensions	Jan. 5, 1830	Favorable	72	Passed	Passed	App'd May 20, 1830
Ward, Daniel	(See George Wheeler and C. Morison.)	21	2		255							
Ward, Deborah	(See John Ward, widow of)	22	1		412							
Ward, Elizabeth	(See James Ward, widow of)	28	1		717							
Ward, Frances Ann	Relief in consequence of loss of husband in United States service.	14	1	Petition	111	Claims				Discharged; laid on table.		Leave to withdraw.
Ward, George Curwen	Relief from duty on stills	5	1	Petition	37					Laid on table.		
Ward, George Curwen	Relief from duty on stills	5	2	Petition	82	Ways and Means.						
Ward, George R	To be released from surety on bond of Berryman & Ebbetts.	29	2	Memorial	308	Commerce.						
Ward, George R	To be released from surety on bond of Berryman & Ebbetts.	30	1	Petition	110	Judiciary	368	Favorable	335	Referred to Committee Whole House.		
Ward, George R	To be released from surety on bond of Berryman & Ebbetts.	30	2	House bill	656	Whole House			335			
Ward, George R	To be released from surety on bond of Berryman & Ebbetts.	31	1	Petition	534	Judiciary.						
Ward, George R	To be released from surety on bond of Berryman & Ebbetts.	31	2	Petition	36	Judiciary	46	Favorable	41	Referred to Committee Whole House.		
Ward, Hannah	Pension for services of husband	28	1	Petition	950	Whole House.						
Ward, Harriet	Pension	29	1	Senate bill	1075	Naval Affairs	July 24, 1846	With't amend.	147	Passed		App'd Aug. 6, 1846
Ward, Henry S	(See Nehemiah Hubbard, administrator of.	29	1		352							
Ward, Ichabod	Payment of certificate for interest issued in revolutionary war.	21	1	Petition	320	Rev. Claims	320	Favorable	375	Referred to Committee Whole House.		
Ward, Ichabod	Payment of certificate for interest issued in revolutionary war.	22	1	Petition	29	Rev. Claims	Dec. 23, 1831	Favorable	109	Passed	Passed	App'd June 15, 1832
Ward, Isaac H	Pension	20	2	Petition	99	Military Pensions	Feb. 16, 1829	Adverse		Laid on table.		
Ward, James	(See W. Thweatt, executors of)	23	1		40							
Ward, James	Permission to locate land warrant	25	3	Resolution	191	Public Lands.						
Ward, Jesse	(See William H. Bedford, agent)	28	1		262							
Ward, James, widow of	Pension	28	1	Petition	717	Rev. Pensions.						
Ward, Jasper, *et al.*	Indemnity for Spanish spoliation, and imprisonment of officers and crew of the Saratoga.	14	1	Petition	295	Claims	March 8, 1816	Adverse				Leave to withdraw.
Ward, John, acting partner of Ward & Co.	Renewal of final settlement certificate.	4	2	Petition	677	Claims.						
Ward, John, acting partner of Ward & Co.	Renewal of final settlement certificate.	5	2	Petition	232	Claims.						
Ward, John, *et al.*	Confirmation of title to land	9	1	Petition	242	Public Lands	Jan. 24, 1806	Not found		Referred to Committee Whole House.		
Ward, John	Pension	13	3	House bill	740	Whole House	Mar. 1, 1815	Favorable	303	Passed	Passed	App'd March 3, 1815
Ward, John, & Co.	Indemnity for loss on sales of six per cent. stock by United States treasurer	28	1	Petition	105	Ways and Means	507	Adverse		Laid on table.		
Ward, John B	Compensation for revolutionary services.	3	1	Petition	131	Select.						
Ward, John J., widow of.	Compensation for services rendered at Fortress Monroe.	19	1	Petition	442	Claims				Discharged; laid on table.		
Ward, John W., (Ala.)	Indemnity for loss sustained in building district court-house.	19	1	Petition	83	Commerce	Mar. 17, 1826	Adverse		Laid on table.		

List of private claims presented to the House of Representatives of the United States from the 1st to the 31st Congress, inclusive—Continued.

Names of claimants.	Nature or object of the claim.	Congress.	Session.	How brought before the House of Reps.	Page of journal.	To what committee of the House referred.	No. or date of the report.	Nature of the report.	No. of the bill.	How disposed of by the House of Reps.	How disposed of by the Senate.	Date of the act of Congress, and remarks.
Ward, John W., (Ala.)	Indemnity for loss sustained in building district court house.	20	1	Petition	298							Leave to withdraw.
Ward, John W	Pension for revolutionary services of father.	29	1	Petition	713	Rev. Pensions	606	Adverse		Laid on table.		
Ward, John, widow of	Pension	22	1	Petition	412	Rev. Pensions				Discharged; laid on table.		
Ward, John, widow of	Pension	24	1	Petition	406	Rev. Pensions				Discharged; laid on table.		
Ward, John	Compensation for work done on Cumberland road.	23	1	Res. and papers.	589	Claims	455	Adverse				See report No. 449.
Ward, Jonathan, *et al.*	(See Stephen Ward, heirs of)	[illegible]	2		102							
Ward, Joseph	Payment of certain bills of credit.	1	3	Memorial	376					Laid on table.		
Ward, Joseph	Payment of certain bills of credit.	4	1	Rep. of Secretary Treasur	388	Claims	74	Adverse		Laid on table.		
Ward, Joseph	Payment of certain bills of credit.	5	2	Memorial	202	Claims	Mar. 12, 1798	Adverse		Laid on table.		
Ward, Joseph, *et al.*	Payment of certain bills of credit.	7	1	Petition	42	Sec. of Treasury	Jan. 28, 1802	Report by Sec. Treasury.		Referred to Committee Whole House.		
Ward, Joseph, *et al.*	Payment of certain bills of credit.	7	2	Petition	248	Claims	Dec. 17, 1802	Adverse		Laid on table.		
Ward, Joseph, *et al.*	Payment of certain bills of credit.	10	1	Petition	92	Sec. of Treasury	Jan. 6, 1808	Report by Sec. Treasury.		Laid on table.		
Ward, Joseph, *et al.*	Payment of certain bills of credit.	12	1	Petition	164	Claims.						
Ward, Joseph D., (N. C.)	Additional compensation for services in Clerk's office, House of Representatives.	28	1	Petition	988	Claims.						
Ward, Joseph D., (N. C.)	Additional compensation for services in Clerk's office, House of Representatives.	30	2	Petition	269	Accounts	107	Adverse		Laid on table.		
Ward, Joseph Dodson	Pension	30	1	Petition	877	Invalid Pensions	713	Favorable	558	Referred to Committee Whole House.		
Ward, Joseph Dodson	Pension	30	2	House bill	319	Whole House	Jan. 26, 1849	Favorable	558	Passed	Passed, with amendment.	
Ward, Joseph Dodson	Increase of pension	31	1	Petition	223	Invalid Pensions	55	Favorable	85	Referred to Committee Whole House.		
Ward, Joseph Dodson	Increase of pension	31	2	House bill	154	Whole House	Jan. 18, 1851		85	Passed	Passed, with amendment	App'd March 3, 1851
Ward, Joseph or Lindsay	Compensation for removal of and provisions furnished Pottowatomie Indians	28	1	Petition	927	Claims	529	Favorable	407	Referred to Committee Whole House.		
Ward, Joseph or Lindsay	Compensation for removal of and provisions furnished Pottowatomie Indians.	28	2	House bill	344				407	Passed.		
Ward, Joseph or Lindsay	Compensation for removal of and provisions furnished Pottowatomie Indians.	29	1	Petition	114	Indian Affairs	318	Favorable	256	Referred to Committee Whole House.		
Ward, Joseph or Lindsay	Compensation for removal of and provisions furnished Pottowatomie Indians.	29	2	House bill	71	Indian Affairs	Dec. 18, 1846	Favorable	256	Referred to Committee Whole House.		
Ward, Joseph or Lindsay	Compensation for removal of and provisions furnished Pottowatomie Indians.	30	1	Petition	66	Indian Affairs	73	Favorable	56	Passed	Passed	App'd Feb. 15, 1848
Ward, Josiah	Pension	3	2	Rep. of Secretary War.	350	Claims.						
Ward, Kerley	Increase of pension	11	2	House bill	283	Whole House	Mar. 24, 1810	Favorable	107	Passed	Passed	App'd April 27, 1810

List of private claims presented to the House of Representatives of the United States from the 1st to the 31st Congress, inclusive—Continued.

Names of claimants.	Nature or object of the claim.	Congress.	Session.	How brought before the House of Reps.	Page of journal.	To what committee of the House referred.	No. or date of the report.	Nature of the report.	No. of the bill.	How disposed of by the House of Reps.	How disposed of by the Senate.	Date of the act of Congress, and remarks.
Ward, Mary	(See Charles Ward, widow of)	28	1		72							
Ward, Mary C.	(See John Ward, widow of)	19	1		442							
Ward, Michael, *et al.*	Compensation for services and imprisonment of witnesses attending United States court.	19	1	Petition & resl'n.	284	Judiciary	87	Favorable	121	Passed	Passed	App'd May 20, 1826
Ward, Nahum	Payment of loan office certificates.	19	1	Petition	88	Rev. Claims	101	Adverse		Laid on table		Leave to withdraw.
Ward, Nahum	For services during revolutionary war.	19	2	Petition	133	Rev. Claims				Discharged.		
Ward, Nehemiah	Pension	22	2	Petition	63	Invalid Pensions	Feb. 15 1833	Favorable	738	Referred to Committee Whole House.		
Ward, Nehemiah	Pension	23	1	Petition	44	Invalid Pensions	1	Favorable	1	Passed	Passed as am'd.	App'd June 25, 1834
Ward, Reese B.	Correction of land entry	26	2	Petition	49	Public Lands	123	Favorable	628	Referred to Committee Whole House.		
Ward, Reese B.	Correction of land entry	27	2	Senate bill	1126	Public Lands	July 27, 1842	Without amend.	299	Passed		App'd Aug. 11, 1842
Ward, Richard	For government aid for using his patent for torpedo shot.	20	2	Petition	32	Naval Affairs				Discharged		Leave to withdraw.
Ward, Richard	For government aid for using his patent for torpedo shot.	21	2	Petition	56	Naval Affairs.						
Ward, Richard	For government aid for using his patent for torpedo shot.	22	1	Petition	222	Naval Affairs				Discharged.		
Ward, Richard, *et al.*	(See Jacob Barker, assignee of)	18	2		223							
Ward, Robert G.	To be released from payment of certain costs at suit of United States.	27	2	Petition	223	Judiciary.						
Ward, Robert G.	To be released from payment of certain costs at suit of United States.	28	1	Petition	59	Judiciary	147	Favorable	135	Passed.		
Ward, Robert G., & others	To be released from a judgment against them as surety of Wm. Ward.	29	1	Petition	320	P. Of. & P. Roads.						
Ward, Robert G., & other	To be released from a judgment against them as surety of Wm. Ward.	30	1	Petition	1163	P. Of. & P. Roads.						
Ward, Robert G., & others	To be released from a judgment against them as surety of Wm. Ward.	30	2	Petition	270	P. Of. & P. Roads.	Feb. 28, 1849			Discharged; laid on table.		
Ward, Robert G., & others	To be released from a judgment against them as surety of Wm. Ward.	31	1	Petition	259	Judiciary.						
Ward, Robert G., & others	To be released from a judgment against them as surety of Wm. Ward.	31	2	Petition	36	Judiciary	66	Favorable	J.R. 41	Referred to Committee Whole House.		
Ward, Robert J.	(See Matthews Flournoy and R. J. Ward.)	21	1		236							
Ward, Samuel	Payment for lost certificate	5	2	Memorial	202	Claims	Feb. 26, 1798	Adverse				Leave to withdraw.
Ward, Samuel, (N. Y.)	(See Abraham Whipple)	15	1		388							
Ward, Samuel	(See Walter S. Chandler)	18	1		210							
Ward, Sarah	(See John Ward, widow of)	22	1		412							
Ward, Stephen, heirs of	Indemnity for property destroyed by British.	15	2	Petition	102	Pens. & Rev. Cl'ms.	Dec. 30, 1818	Adverse				Leave to withdraw.
Ward, Stephen, heirs of	Indemnity for property destroyed by British.	16	1	Petition	76	Pens. & Rev. Cl'ms.	Jan. 4, 1820	Adverse		Laid on table.		

List of private claims presented to the House of Representatives of the United States from the 1st to the 31st Congress, inclusive—Continued.

Names of claimants.	Nature or object of the claim.	Congress.	Session.	How brought before the House of Reps.	Page of journal.	To what committee of the House referred.	No. or date of the report.	Nature of the report.	No. of the bill.	How disposed of by the House of Reps.	How disposed of by the Senate.	Date of the act of Congress, and remarks.
Ward, Stephen, heirs of	Indemnity for property destroyed by British.	22	1	Petition	333	Rev. Claims.						
Ward, Stephen, heirs of	Indemnity for property destroyed by British	22	2	Petition	53	Rev. Claims.						
Ward, Stephen, heirs of	Indemnity for property destroyed by British.	23	1	Petition	65	Rev. Claims	73	Adverse		Laid on table.		
Ward, Stephen, heirs of	Indemnity for property destroyed by British.	23	2	Petition		Rev. Claims						Omitted on journal.
Ward, Stephen, heirs of	Indemnity for property destroyed by British.	24	1	Petition	62	Rev. Claims.						
Ward, Stephen, heirs of	Indemnity for property destroyed by British.	24	2	Petition	42	Rev. Claims.						
Ward, Stephen, heirs of	Indemnity for property destroyed by British.	27	2	Petition	105	Rev. Claims.						
Ward & Smith	Payment for advances made in 1847 for use of Navy Department.	30	1	Senate bill	1157	Claims	Aug. 14, 1848	Amended	309	Passed amended	Passed	App'd Aug. 14, 1848
Ward, Thomas, (N. Y.)	Pension	3	2	Rep. of Secretary War.	337	Claims.						
Ward, Thomas, (N. Y.)	Pension	5	2	House bill	127	Claims	Feb. 6, 1797	Favorable	38	Passed	Passed	App'd Feb. 2, 1798
Ward, Thomas, (Penn)	Pension	20	1	Petition	417	Military Pensions				Discharged; laid on table.		
Ward, Thomas, (Penn)	Arrears of pension	23	1	Petition	46	Rev. Pensions				Discharged; laid on table.		
Ward, Thomas and Henry	Remission of certain duties	16	2	Petition	205	Ways and Means				Discharged; laid on table.		
Ward, Thomas and Henry	(See Elnathan Atwater, *et al*)	12	1		50							
Ward, William, *et al.*	(See John Ward, children of.)	9	1		212							
Ward, William, (N. Y.)	Pension	21	1	Petition	36	Military Pensions				Discharged; laid on table.		
Ward, William, (West Point.)	Pension	21	1	Petition	197	Military Pensions	April 2, 1830	Adverse		Dischraged; laid on table.		
Ward, William, (N. Y.)	Compensation for revolutionary services	21	1	Petition	37	Rev. Claims	Dec. 29, 1829	Adverse		Laid on table.		
Ward, William, (N. Y.)	Compensation for revolutionary services.	21	2	Petition	45	Rev. Claims				Discharged; laid on table.		
Ward, Zebulon, (Indiana.)	Pension	20	2	Resolution	91	Military Pensions				Discharged; laid on table.		
Wardell, Henry	Bounty on fishing schooner	23	1	Petition	212	Commerce.						
Wardell, Sarah	(See Samuel Brown, heir of.)	31	2		74							
Warden, Ichabod	Increase of pension	26	1	Petition	286	Rev. Pensions	424	Adverse		Laid on table.		
Warden, Sarah	(See William Warden, widow of.)	28	1		741							
Warden, William	Pension	24	1	Petition	507	Invalid Pensions	721	Favorable	669	Passed	Passed	App'd June 28, 1836
Warden, William	Refund money stolen by Indians	26	1	Petition	353	Indian Affairs				Disch'd; and to Claims.		
Warden, William, widow of.	Pension	28	1	Petition	744	Rev. Pensions.						
Warden, William, *et al.*	Payment for property destroyed by Indians.	26	1	Petition	961	Claims.						
Warder & Bros., attorney and trustee of Fry & Spalding.	(See Fry & Spalding.)	17	1		124							
Wardrobe, John, attorney of.	Indemnity for French spoliations prior to 1800.	26	1	Memorial	182	Foreign Affairs	343	Favorable; bill	319	Referred to Committee Whole House.		

List of private claims presented to the House of Representatives of the United States from the 1st to the 31st Congress, inclusive—Continued.

Names of claimants.	Nature or object of the claim.	Congress.	Session.	How brought before the House of Reps.	Page of journal.	To what committee of the House referred.	No. or date of the report.	Nature of the report.	No. of the bill.	How disposed of by the House of Reps.	How disposed of by the Senate.	Date of the act of Congress, and remarks.
Wardrobe, John, heirs of.	Indemnity for French spoliations prior to 1800.	29	2	Petition	83	Foreign Affairs.						
Wardrobe, John, heirs of	Indemnity for French spoliations prior to 1800.	31	1	Petition	197	Foreign Affairs	355	Favorable; bill	318	Referred to Committee Whole House.		
Wardwell, Allen	Pension	24	2	Petition	271	Rev. Pensions				Discharged; laid on table.		
Wardwell, Allen	Pension	25	2	Petition	587	Rev. Pensions.						
Wardwell, Allen	Pension	25	3	Petition	126	Rev. Pensions.						
Wardwell, Allen	Pension	26	1	Petition	173	Rev. Pensions.						
Wardwell, Allen	Pension	27	2	Petition	59	Rev. Pensions				Laid on table.		
Wardwell, Leonard	Pension	26	1	Petition	1001	Invalid Pensions	674	Adverse		Laid on table.		
Wardwell, Leonard	Pension	27	2	Petition	154	Invalid Pensions	420	Adverse		Laid on table.		
Wardwell, Leonard	Pension	29	1	Petition	228	Invalid Pensions				Discharged; laid on table.		
Wardwell, Leonard	Pension	30	1	Petition	1072							Leave to withdraw.
Wardwell, Nathan (Mass.)	Pension	22	1	Resolution	261	Rev. Pensions.						
Wardsworth, George, widow of.	Permission to resume the purchase of certain lands.	24	1	Petition	113	Public Lands.						
Wardsworth, Laura	(See George Wardsworth, widow of.)	24	1		113							
Ware, Asa	Increase of pension	9	1	Petition	189	Claims	Mar. 28, 1806			Indefinitely postponed.		Leave to withdraw.
Ware, Asa	Increase of pension	9	2	House bill	618	Whole House	Feb. 28, 1807	Favorable	216	Passed	Passed	App'd March 3, 1807
Ware, Catherine	Re-enactment of navy pens on law.	22	1	Petition	857	Pens. & Rev. Cl'ms.						
Ware, Charlotte	(See Samuel Ware, widow of)	21	2		160							
Wares, Charlotte	(See John Ware, widow of.)	22	1		187							
Ware, Elias	Pension	14	2	Petition	267	Pens. & Rev. Cl'ms.	Jan. 29, 1817	Favorable	91	Passed	Passed	App'd March 3, 1817
Ware, Elias	Restoration of pension	17	2	Petition	233	Rev. Pensions				Discharged		Leave to withdraw.
Ware, Elias	Restoration of pension	22	1	Resolution	817	Rev. Pensions				Discharged; laid on table.		
Ware, Elias	Arrears of pension	24	2	Petition	316	Invalid Pensions	Jan. 21, 1837	Favorable	864	Referred to Committee Whole House.		
Ware, Elias	Arrears of pension	25	2	Petition	55	Rev. Pensions	Jan. 12, 1838	Adverse		Laid on table.		
Ware, Lieut. Francis, representatives of.	Commutation pay	29	1	Petition	120	Rev. Claims	390	Favorable	289	Referred to Committee Whole House.		
Ware, Lieut. Francis, representatives of.	Commutation pay	30	1	Petition	145	Rev. Claims	176	Favorable	186	Passed.		
Ware, Lieut. Francis, representatives of.	Commutation pay	31	1	Petition	628	Rev. Claims.						
Ware, James, (N. Y.)	Pension	14	2	Petition	38	Naval Affairs	Jan. 20, 1817	Adverse		Laid on table.		
Ware, James, (Miss.)	Pension	22	1	Petition	72	Rev. Pensions.						
Ware, James, (seaman)	Remuneration for property stolen at Tripoli.	24	1	Petition	273	Naval Affairs.						
Ware, James, (seaman)	Remuneration for property stolen at Tripoli.	24	2	Petition	85	Naval Affairs	27	Adverse		Laid on table.		
Ware, James, (seaman)	Remuneration for property stolen at Tripoli.	25	2	Petition	723	Naval Affairs				Discharged; laid on table.		
Ware, James, (Penn.)	Pension	27	2	Petition	224	Naval Affairs	597	Adverse		Laid on table.		
Ware, Jeremiah	(See Jeremiah Weare)	21	2		126							
Wares, John, widow of	Renewal of pension	22	1	Petition	187	Naval Affairs.						
Ware, Jonathan	Compensation for military services.	21	2	Petition	73	Claims	Jan. 3, 1831	Adverse		Laid on table.		
Ware, Joseph	Increase of pension	10	1	House bill	232	Whole House	Mar. 17, 1808	Favorable	78	Passed	Passed	App'd April 25, 1808
Ware, Nathaniel A.	Confirmation of title to land	22	1	Senate bill	806	Public Lands	June 8, 1832	With't amend.	101	Passed		App'd July 13, 1832

List of private claims presented to the House of Representatives of the United States from the 1st to the 31st Congress, inclusive—Continued.

Names of claimants.	Nature or object of the claim.	Congress.	Session.	How brought before the House of Reps.	Page of journal.	To what committee of the House referred.	No. or date of the report.	Nature of the report.	No. of the bill.	How disposed of by the House of Reps.	How disposed of by the Senate.	Date of the act of Congress, and remarks.
Ware, Phineas	Renewal of a lost certificate	2	1	Petition	447					Referred to Secretary Treasury.		
Ware, Robert, attorney	(See Willis Wilson, heirs of.)	23	2		376							
Ware, Samuel, (N. Y.,) widow of.	Renewal of pension	21	2	Petition	106	Naval Affairs.						
Ware, Samuel, (N. Y.,) widow of.	Pension	28	1	Petition	103	Invalid Pensions.						
Ware, William	(See William Weare)	3	1		131							
Waresch, Jacob	Bounty land and extra pay for services in Mexico.	30	2	Petition	123	Rev. Pensions	69	Adverse		Laid on table.		
Warfield, George F	Indemnity for spoliation by rulers of the Island of St. Domingo.	16	1	Petition	85	Secretary of State						
Warfield, George F., and others.	Indemnity for French spoliations prior to 1800.	29	2	Memorial	113	Foreign Affairs.						
Warfield, George F., and others.	Indemnity for French spoliations prior to 1800.	31	1	Petition	196	Foreign Affairs	355	Favorable	318	Referred to Committee Whole House.		
Warfield, Samuel	Payment for arms and equipments taken for use of army.	28	1	Petition	106	Rev. Claims.						
Warfield, Wm. H	Indemnity for French spoliations prior to 1800.	31	1	Petition	196	Foreign Affairs	355	Favorable	318	Referred to Committee Whole House.		
Warfington, Richard	(See Lewis Clark and others.)	7	2		284							
Warfington, Richard	(See Alexander Willard.)	9	2		470							
Warington, James	(See Joseph Blachford.)	2	2		615							
Waring, John, and Noble Young.	Compensation for medical services at public hospital.	23	1	Petition	498	Dist. of Columbia.						
Waring, Joseph H	Compensation for services as clerk in Treasury Department.	27	2	Petition	140	Claims.						
Waring, Joseph H	Compensation for services as clerk in Treasury Department.	27	3	Petition	43	Claims	23	Adverse		Laid on table.		
Waring, William	For payment of certain drafts given by United States agent.	22	2	Petition	142	Claims	115	Adverse		Laid on table.		
Waring, William	For payment of certain drafts given by United States agent.	23	1	Petition	33	Claims	202	Favorable	369	Referred to Committee Whole House.		
Waring, William	For payment of certain drafts given by United States agent.	24	1	Petition	50	Claims	8	Favorable	8	Referred to Committee Whole House.		
Warman, James	Compensation for horse impressed into United States service.	29	1	Petition	690	Claims	778	Adverse.		Laid on table.		
Warman, Capt. Thomas	(See William L. Ross.)	30	1		674							
Warne, Willet	Release from judgment against him as surety on revenue bond.	13	1	Petition	18	Ways and Means	July 24, 1813	Favorable	51	Passed	Passed	App'd Aug. 2, 1813
Warner, Betsy	(See Ichabod Warner, widow of.)	26	1		938							
Warner, Betsy, widow of Nathan Thompson.	(See Nathan Thompson.)	26	1		936							
Warner, Betsy	(See Zelotus Warner, widow of.)	25	2		272							
Warner, Elizabeth	(See Zelotus Warner)	13	2		179							
Warner, Daniel	Bounty land for military services	24	1	Resolution	341	Priv. Land Claims	399	Favorable	404	Referred to Committee Whole House.		
Warner, Daniel	Bounty land for military services	25	2	Resolution	43	Priv. Land Claims.	142	Favorable	163	Referred to Committee Whole House.		
Warner, Daniel	Bounty land for military services	25	3	House bill	375				163	Passed	Passed	App'd March 3, 1839
Warner, Ebenezer	Payment for work done on light-houses Lake Superior.	30	2	Petition	210	Commerce		General appropriation bill.	692	Passed	Passed	App'd March 3, 1849

3—74

List of private claims presented to the House of Representatives of the United States from the 1st to the 31st Congress, inclusive—**Continued.**

Names of claimants.	Nature or object of the claim.	Congress.	Session.	How brought before the House of Reps.	Page of journal.	To what committee of the House referred.	No. or date of the report.	Nature of the report.	No. of the bill.	How disposed of by the House of Reps.	How disposed of by the Senate.	Date of the act of Congress, and remarks.
Warner, George	Restoration of pension	25	2	Petition	586	Rev. Pensions				Discharged; laid on table.		
Warner, Hepzibah	(See John Warner, widow of)	28	1		645							
Warner, Ichabod, widow of.	Pension	26	1	Petition	938	Invalid Pensions.						
Warner, Jacob, widow of.	Pension	22	2	Petition	118	Rev. Claims				Discharged; laid on table.		
Warner, Jason	(See Wm. Ferguson, administrator of.)	20	2		262							
Warner, John	Pension	22	1	Petition	35	Rev. Pensions.						
Warner, John, widow of.	Pension	28	1	Petition	645	Rev. Pensions.						
Warner, Martin, (Conn.).	For fishing bounty	14	2	Petition	284	Com. and Manuf.				Discharged; laid on table.		
Warner, Martin, (Conn.).	For fishing bounty	15	1	Senate bill	239	Com. and Manuf.	Mar. 30, 1818	With't amend.	21	Passed		App'd April 4, 1818
Warner, Mary	(See Robert Greer, heirs of)	23	1		243							
Warner, Mears	Payment for horse and equipage	23	1	Documents	154	Claims.						
Warner, Mears, (per Wm. H. Bedford.)	Payment for horse and equipage	28	1	Petition	262	Claims.						
Warner, Nicholas	Restoration of pension	25	2	Petition	586	Rev. Pensions				Discharged; laid on table.		
Warner, Peter, (Indiana)	Permission to purchase certain land.	24	2	Senate bill	246	Priv. Land Claims.	Feb. 2, 1837	With't amend.	14	Referred to Committee Whole House.		
Warner, Peter, (Indiana).	Permission to purchase certain land.	25	2	Senate bill	130	Priv. Land Claims.	Jan. 5, 1838	With't amend.	8	Referred to Committee Whole House.		
Warner, Peter, (Indiana).	Permission to purchase certain land.	25	3	Senate bill	547	Priv. Land Claims.	Feb. 16, 1839	With't amend	137	Referred to Committee Whole House.		
Warner, Peter, (Indiana).	Permission to purchase certain land.	26	1	Senate bill	799	Priv. Land Claims.	July 10, 1840	With't amend.	153	Passed		App'd July 20, 1840
Warner, Richard, & others, officers of Tennessee volunteer.	Compensation for losses sustained by reason of being discharged prior to expiration of time.	24	2	Petition	80	Claims	Feb. 8, 1837	General bill	916	Referred to Committee Whole House.		
Warner, Samuel	Pension	2	2	Rep. of Secretary War.	649	Whole House.						
Warner, Samuel	Pension	3	1	Rep. of Secretary War.	131	Select	May 26, 1794	Refer'd to Secretary War.	J. R. 12	Passed	Passed	App'd June 9, 1794
Warner, Samuel	Pension	4	1	Rep. of Secretary War.	445	Claims	Feb. 18, 1796	Favorable	156	Passed	Passed	App'd April 20, 1796
Warner, Samuel A.	(See William H. Bedford, agent).	28	1		262							
Warner, Samuel	Pension	24	1	Senate bill	811	Naval Affairs	May 17, 1836	With't amend.	242	Referred to Committee Whole House.		
Warner, Sarah	(See Jacob Warner, widow of)	22	2		118							
Warner, Seth, heirs of	Compensation for revolutionary services.	30	1	Petition	962	Rev. Claims.						
Warner, Susannah	(See Wm. Read, widow of.)	28	1		405							
Warner, Thomas	Pension	26	1	Petition	284	Rev. Pensions.						
Warner, Thomas	Pension	26	2	Petition	35	Rev. Pensions.						
Warner, Thomas	Pension	27	2	Petition	59	Rev. Pensions	784	Adverse		Laid on table.		
Warner, William	(See Joseph Falconer)	20	2		43							
Warner, Zelotus, widow of.	Pension	13	2	Petition	179	Pensions						Leave to withdraw.
Warner, Zelotus, widow of.	Pension	25	2	Petition	272	Invalid Pensions				Discharged.		
Warner, Zelotus, widow of.	Pension	25	3	Petition	29	Invalid Pensions	Jan. 16, 1839	Adverse		Laid on table.		
Warnock, John P	Compensation for mail service	30	2	Petition	409	P. Of. & P. Roads.				Disch'd; laid on table.		
Warnock, John P	Increase of compensation for mail service.	31	1	Petition	484	P. Of. & P. Roads.						Leave to withdraw.

List of private claims presented to the House of Representatives of the United States from the 1st to the 31st Congress, inclusive—Continued.

Names of claimants.	Nature or object of the claim.	Congress.	Session.	How brought before the House of Reps.	Page of journal.	To what committee of the House referred.	No. or date of the report.	Nature of the report.	No. of the bill.	How disposed of by the House of Reps.	How disposed of by the Senate.	Date of the act of Congress, and remarks.
Warpole, George A.	(See Indians, Wyandot)	27	3		295							
Warrell, Doct. Edward	Compensation for medical attendance in Florida.	26	1	Memorial	331	Military Affairs.						
Warrell, Robert	Pension	14	2	House bill	307	Pens. & Rev. Cl'ms.	Jan. 29, 1817	Favorable	91	Passed	Passed	App'd March 3, 1817
Warren, Abiah	(See Ebenezer T. Warren, widow of.)	22	1		455							
Warren, Ashley, and Jas. Thornburn.	Claiming their portion of an item of $75,179 27, in the claim of R. W. Meade, &c.	26	1	Petition	350	Foreign Affairs.						
Warren, Benjamin	Compensation for losses sustained, and injuries received, during revolutionary war.	1	2	Petition	178					Laid on table.		
Warren, Benjamin	Compensation for losses sustained, and injuries received, during revolutionary war.	2	1	Petition	442	Referred to Secretary of War.	Feb. 8, 1793			Laid on table.		
Warren, Benjamin	Compensation for losses sustained, and injuries received, during revolutionary war.	2	2	Rep. of Secretary War.	696					Laid on table.		
Warren, Daniel H.	Pension	28	2	Petition	117	Invalid Pensions	76	Favorable	560	Passed.		
Warren, Daniel H.	Pension	29	1	Petition	209	Invalid Pensions	210	Favorable	204	Passed	Passed	App'd Aug. 8, 1846
Warren, Daniel H.	Increase of pension	29	2	Petition	162	Invalid Pensions.						
Warren, Daniel H.	Increase of pension	30	1	Petition	175	Invalid Pensions	288	Favorable	284	Passed.		
Warren, David, (Vt.)	Increase of pension	15	1	Resolution	100	Pens. & Rev. Cl'ms.	April 1, 1818	Favorable	172	Passed	Indef. postp'd.	
Warren, David, (Vt.)	Increase of pension	22	1	Petition	383	Invalid Pensions	Mar. 9, 1832	Adverse		Laid on table.		
Warren, Ebenezer T., widow of.	Reimbursem't of money erroneously paid into the United States Treasury.	22	1	Senate bill	455	Ways and Means	Jan. 8, 1832	With amend.	66	Passed		App'd July 14, 1832
Warren, Franklin	(See E. L. Phelps, administrator of.)	19	1		252							
Warren, Henry, collector, Plymouth.	To refund fishing bounty paid by him into United States Treasury.	10	2	Petition	511	Com. and Manuf.	Feb. 10, 1809	Favorable	162	Referred to Committee Whole House.		
Warren, Henry, collector, Plymouth.	To refund fishing bounty paid by him into United States Treasury.	11	1	Petition	17	Com. and Manuf.						
Warren, Henry, collector.	Indemnity for damages recovered and paid into U. S. Treasury.	16	1	Petition	76	Ways and Means	April 18, 1820	Adverse				Leave to withdraw.
Warren, Henry, collector.	Indemnity for damages recovered and paid into U. S. Treasury.	16	2	Petition	177	Ways and Means				Discharged; laid on table.		
Warren, Henry, collector, Missouri.	Additional compensation as collector of customs, Missouri.	12	1	Petition	61	Ways and Means	Dec. 30, 1811	Favorable	34	Referred to Committee Whole House.		
Warren, Henry, (Mass.)	(See James Warren)	14	1		300							
Warren, Hugh	Pension	28	1	Resolution	557	Rev. Pensions.						
Warren Insurance Company, R. I.	Indemnity for French spoliations prior to 1800.	26	1	Memorial	182	Foreign Affairs	343	Favorable; bill	319	Referred to Committee Whole House.		
Warren Insurance Company, R. I.	Indemnity for French spoliations prior to 1800.	31	1	Petition	307	Foreign Affairs	355	Favorable; bill	318	Referred to Commitee Whole House.		
Warren, Gen. James	For settlement of his claims	1	2	Petition	188	Referred to Secretary Treasury.	April 17, 1790			Referred to Committee Whole House.		
Warren, James	For bounty and increase of pension as an officer in U. States navy.	12	2	Petition	584	Claims				Laid on table.		
Warren, James	Compensation for services as officer in United States navy, revolutionary war.	15	1	Petition	55	Naval Affairs				Discharged		Leave to withdraw.

List of private claims presented to the House of Representatives of the United States from the 1st to the 31st Congress, inclusive—**Continued.**

Names of claimants.	Nature or object of the claim.	Congress.	Session.	How brought before the House of Reps.	Page of journal.	To what committee of the House referred.	No. or date of the report.	Nature of the report.	No. of the bill.	How disposed of by the House of Reps.	How disposed of by the Senate.	Date of the act of Congress, and remarks.
Warren, Lieut James....	For proportion of certain prize-money.	14	1	Petition	200	Pens. & Rev. Cl'ms.	....	....	.....	Discharged; laid on table.		
Warren, Lieut James....	For proportion of certain prize-money.	15	2	Petition	116	Naval Affairs	Feb. 26, 1819	Adverse	.....	Laid on table.		
Warren, Lieut James....	For proportion of certain prize-money.	16	2	Petition	200	Naval Affairs	Feb. 20, 1821	Adverse.	.....	Laid on table.		
Warren, James, (N Y.)..	Pension	14	1	Resolution	158	Pens. & Rev. Cl'ms.	....	....	.....	Discharged.	....	Leave to withdraw.
Warren, John, (Tenn.)..	Pension	20	2	Petition	39	Military Pensions..	Feb. 16, 1829	Adverse	.....	Laid on table.		
Warren, John, (Tenn.)..	Pension	21	1	Petition	123	Military Pensions..	April 6, 1830	Adverse ...	.....	Laid on table.		
Warren, John	Benefit of act of May, 1828	21	2	Resolution	71	Claims.						
Warren, John B........	Refund certain money expended for government.	29	1	Memorial	510	Claims.						
Warren, Gen. Joseph, heir of.	Commutation pay	26	1	Memorial	280	Rev. Claims.						
Warren, Gen. Joseph, heir of.	Commutation pay	27	2	Memorial	96	Rev. Claims......	745	Favorable; bill	435	Ordered to 3d reading.		
Warren, Gen. Joseph, hei of.	Commutation pay	27	3	Bill of last sess..	88	....	....	....	435	Passed.		
Warren, Gen. Joseph, heir of.	Commutation pay	28	1	Petition	62	Rev. Claims.						
Warren, Gen. Joseph, heir of.	Commutation pay	28	2	Petition	144	Rev. Claims.						
Warren, Gen. Joseph, heir of.	Commutation pay	29	1	Petition	177	Rev. Claims......	166	Favorable; bill	175	Referred to Committee Whole House.		
Warren, Gen. Joseph, heir of.	Commutation pay	29	2	Bill of last sess.	71	Whole House.....	July 24, 1846	With't amend.	175	Passed	Passed	App'd March 3, 1847
Warren, Lyman M., and Truman A.	(See Leon L. St. German)......	20	1	....	28							
Warren, Samuel........	Commutation pay	24	2	Senate bill	180	Rev. Claims......	286	Favorable	82	Referred to Committee Whole House.		
Warren, Samuel	Commutation pay	25	2	Senate bill	147	Rev. Claims......	Jan. 17, 1838	Favorable	90	Passed	....	App'd June 12, 1838
Warren, Thomas........	Pension...................	14	1	Petition	71	Pens. & Rev. Cl'ms.	....	....	.....	Discharged; laid on table.		
Warren, Uriah, (N Y)..	Pension	14	2	Petition	79	Pens. & Rev. Cl'ms.	Jan. 29, 1817	Favorable	91	Passed	Passed, with amendment	App'd March, 3 1817
Warren, Uriah, (N. Y.)..	Arrears of pension...........	25	2	Petition	663	Invalid Pensions ..	....	....	.....	Discharged; laid on table.		
Warren, Uriah, (N. Y.)..	Arrears of pension...........	26	1	Petition	163	Invalid Pensions ..	555	Adverse	.....	Laid on table.		
Warren, Uriah, (N. Y)..	Arrears of pension	27	3	Petition	152	Invalid Pensions.						
Warren, Uriah, (N. Y.)..	Arrears of pension...........	28	1	Petition	513	Invalid Pensions.						
Warren, William	Pension	2	2	Rep. of Secretary War.	649	Whole House.						
Warren, William	Pension	3	1	Rep. of Secretary War.	131	Select..........	May 26, 1794	Jt. res. to refer to Sec. War.	J.R.12	Passed	Passed	App'd June 9, 1794
Warren, William	Pension	3	2	Rep. of Secretary War.	262	Claims.						
Warren, William	Pension	4	1	Report Secretary of War.	445	Claims	Feb. 18, 1796	Favorable	156	Passed	Passed	App'd April 20, 1796
Warren, William	Increase of pension...........	12	1	House bill......	361	Whole House.....	June 15, 1812	Favorable	136	Passed	Passed	App'd July 5, 1812
Warren, William	Arrears of pension...........	15	1	Petition	35	Pens. & Rev. Cl'ms.	April 1, 1818	Favorable	172	Passed	Indef. postp'd.	
Warren, William, (Ohio.)	Payment for a horse lost in United States service.	19	2	Resolution	94	Claims	....	....	.....	Discharged.		

List of private claims presented to the House of Representatives of the United States from the 1st to the 31st Congress, inclusive—Continued.

Names of claimants.	Nature or object of the claim.	Congress.	Session.	How brought before the House of Reps.	Page of journal.	To what committee of the House referred.	No. or date of the report.	Nature of the report.	No. of the bill.	How disposed of by the House of Reps.	How disposed of by the Senate.	Date of the act of Congress, and remarks.
Warren, William, (Ohio.)	Payment for a horse lost in United States service.	20	1	Resolution	66	Claims	Jan. 2, 1828	Adverse		Laid on table.		
Warren, William, (Ohio.)	Payment for a horse lost in United States service.	21	2	Resolution	98	Claims.						
Warren, William	Pension	22	2	Petition	217	Invalid Pensions.						
Warren, William	Pension	23	1	House bill	86	Whole House	Jan. 2, 1834	Favorable	42	Passed	Passed	App'd June 30, 1834
Warren, Wyncoop	Payment for loss of baggage in United States service.	24	1	Petition	94	Claims				Discharged; laid on table.		
Warrington, James	(See Joseph Blanchford)	2	2		615							
Warrington, Lewis, *et al.*	For their proportion of the prize Epervier.	28	1	Memorial	285	Naval Affairs	240	Adverse		Laid on table.		
Warrington, Lewis, *et al.*	For their proportion of the prize Epervier.	30	1	Petition	513	Naval Affairs	April 26, 1848	Favorable	435	Referred to Committee Whole House.		
Warrington, Lewis, *et al.*	For their proportion of the prize Epervier.	31	1	Petition	682	Naval Affairs	202	Favorable	210	Referred to Committee Whole House.		
Warrington, Lewis, *et al.*	For their proportion of the prize Epervier.	31	1	Senate bill	1280				121	Referred to Committee Whole House.		
Warrington, Lewis, *et al.*	For their proportion of the prize Epervier.	31	2	Senate bill	438	Whole House			121			
Warrington, William	Bounty land for revolutionary services.	27	2	Petition	833	Rev. Claims	870	Adverse		Laid on table.		
Warrior, armed brig	(See Noah Brown and others)	15	1		183							
Warson, James	Pension	11	2	House bill	283	Whole House	Mar. 24, 1810	Favorable	107	Passed	Passed	App'd April 27, 1810
Wartsbough, John	(See Benjamin Woodworth, assignee of)	19	1		407							
Wash, John, executor of	Pension	30	2	Petition	385	Rev. Pensions.						
Wash, Robert	For relief as holder of certificate issued for land injured by earthquake.	21	2	Senate bill	185	Public Lands	March 2, 1831	With amend.	711	Passed with amendm't.		App'd March 2, 1831
Washbaugh, David, and Jacob Deckert.	To be released as surety of John Maclay.	19	2	Petition	217	Ways and Means				Discharged.		
Washbaugh, David, and Jacob Deckert.	To be released as surety of John Maclay.	20	1	Petition	31	Judiciary	Dec. 24, 1827	Adverse		Laid on table.		
Washam, Jeremiah, (Ala.)	Restoration of right to certain lands.	21	1	Petition	111	Priv. Land Claims				Discharged; laid on table.		
Washam, Jeremiah, (Ala.)	Restoration of right to certain lands.	22	1	Petition	908	Priv. Land Claims				Discharged; laid on table.		
Washburn, Abiel	Pension	28	2	Petition	206	Invalid Pensions.						
Washburn, Eliab	Pension	22	1	Resolution	450	Rev. Pensions.						
Washburn, Eleanore	(See Daniel Rankin, former widow of.)	31	1		542							
Washburn, Hannah	(See Salmon Washburn, widow of.)	25	2		230							
Washburn, Isaiah, (N. Y.)	Pension	17	2	Petition	69	Rev. Pensions				Discharged		Leave to withdraw.
Washburn, Isaiah, (N. Y.)	Pension	18	1	Petition	193	Rev. Pensions.						
Washburn, Isaiah, (N. Y.)	Pension	22	1	Petition	130	Rev. Pensions				Discharged; laid on table.		
Washburn, James, and John Alexander.	Relief from penalties incurred by violation of importation laws.	13	1	Petition	37	Com. and Manuf.						
Washburn, James, and John Alexander.	Relief from penalties incurred by violation of importation laws.	13	2	Petition	266	Com. and Manuf.	Mar. 25, 1814					Leave to withdraw.
Washburn, Lewis	Pension	31	1	Petition	983	Invalid Pensions.						
Washburn, Luther	Bounty land for revolutionary services.	28	1	Petition	216	Rev. Claims.						

List of private claims presented to the House of Representatives of the United States from the 1st to the 31st Congress, inclusive—Continued.

Names of claimants.	Nature or object of the claim.	Congress.	Session.	How brought before the House of Reps.	Page of journal.	To what committee of the House referred.	No. or date of the report.	Nature of the report.	No. of the bill.	How disposed of by the House of Reps.	How disposed of by the Senate.	Date of the act of Congress, and remarks.
Washburn, Samuel	To be allowed forage, &c	16	2	Petition	40	Claims	Feb. 7, 182[illegible]	Adverse	......	Laid on table.		
Washburn, Samuel, and Geo. W. Cochran.	Pre emption right to certain lands in Ohio.	25	3	Petition	135	Public Lands.						
Washburn, Samuel	Pre-emption right, &c	27	1	Petition	100	Public Lands.						
Washburn, Salmon, widow of.	Pension for revolutionary services.	25	2	Petition	23[illegible]	Rev. Pensions	......	......	......	Discharged; laid on table.		
Washburn, Sarah	Continuation of pension	28	1	Petition	850	Rev. Pensions.						
Washburn, Bushrod, and Law Lewis, and others.	Confirmation of title to land	9	1	Petition	320	Public Lands	......	......	......	Laid on table.		
Washburn, Bushrod, and Law Lewis, and others.	Confirmation of title to land	9	2	Petition	502	Public Lands.						
Washington city, corporation and inhabitants of.	For settlement of claim against government.	24	1	Petition	66	Dist. of Columbia.						
Washington and Eastern Branch Bridge Co.	(See District of Columbia.)	13	3	......	455							
Washington, Henry	For damages in consequence of abrogation of contract.	30	1	Senate bill	684	Public Lands	April 15, 1848	With amend.	106	Referred to Committee Whole House.		
Washington, Henry	For damages in consequence of abrogation of contract.	30	2	Senate bill	319	......	......	......	106	Passed with amendm'.	Concurred in.	App'd Feb. 1, 1849
Washington, James G.	(See William H. Bedford, agent.)	28	1	......	262							
Washington, John	Compensation for services against Indians in 1790.	28	2	Petition	346	Rev. Claims.						
Washington, Lund, sen.	Compensation for services of son as clerk, War Department.	26	1	Petition	622	Claims.						
Washington, Lund, sen.	Compensation for services of son as clerk, War Department.	27	2	Petition	56	Claims	241	Adverse	......	Laid on table.		
Washington, Lund, sen.	Compensation for services of son as clerk, War Department.	27	3	Petition	43	Claims	143	Adverse	......	Laid on table.		
Washington, Lund, sen.	Compensation for services of son as clerk, War Department.	28	1	Petition	417	Claims	382	Favorable	280	Passed	Passed	App'd June 19, 1844
Washington, Margaret, and Maria McPherson *et al.*	(See William McPherson.)	23	1	......	306							
Washington pilot boat	(See Gregory Thomas, *et al.*)	29	1	......	171							
Washington, Peter G.	Compensation as acting Treasurer United States.	31	1	Petition	194	Judiciary.						
Washington, Peter G.	Compensation as acting Treasurer United States.	31	2	Petition	447	Judiciary	71	Favorable	481	Referred to Committee Whole House.		
Washington, Thomas, executor of.	For interest in certain Yazoo lands	10	1	Petition	166	Whole House.						
Washington, William	Pension	3	1	Rep. of Secretary War.	131	Select	May 26, 1794	J't. res. to refer to Sec. War.	J. R. 12	Passed	Passed	App'd June 9, 1794
Washington, Wm. H.	Compensation for house destroyed by order of U. States officer.	13	3	Petition	462	Claims	35	Favorable	243	Passed	Passed	App'd March 1, 1815
Wasley, Benjamin F.	(See Benjamin F. Wesley.)	25	2									
Wasp, sloop of war, representatives of officers and crew.	Extra pay and prize money.)	14	1	Senate bill	500	Naval Affairs	Mar. 25, 1816	With amend.	52	Passed	Concurred in.	App'd April 20, 1816
Wass, Wilmot	Fishing bounty	18	2	Petition	208	Commerce.						
Wass, Wilmot	Fishing bounty	19	1	Petition	247	Commerce	......	......	......	Discharged; laid on table.		
Was-sa-gro, (Indian)	For allowance of claim to a reservation under Choctaw treaty.	28	2	Petition	118	Indian Affairs.						
Wasson, G. J	(See J. E. Ball and G. J. Wasson)	30	1	......	379							

List of private claims presented to the House of Representatives of the United States from the 1st to the 31st Congress, inclusive—Continued.

Names of claimants.	Nature or object of the claim.	Congress.	Session.	How brought before the House of Reps.	Page of journal.	To what committee of the House referred.	No. or date of the report.	Nature of the report.	No. of the bill.	How disposed of by the House of Reps.	How disposed of by the Senate.	Date of the act of Congress, and remarks.
Wasson, Joseph	Pension	4	2	Rep. of Secretary War.	651	Claims	Feb. 6, 1797	Favorable	224	Passed.		
Wasson, Joseph	Pension	5	2	House bill	127	Whole House	Jan. 11, 1798	Favorable	38	Passed	Passed	App'd Feb. 2, 1798
Wasson, Robert	Pension	21	1	Resolution	270	Military Pensions	Mar. 30, 1830	General bill	248	Passed.		
Wasson, Thomas	Indemnity for Indian depredations.	24	2	Petition	210	Indian Affairs.						
Wasson, Thomas	(See Reuben E. Gentry and others)	25	2									
Wate, Major Jason	Commutation pay	2	1	Petition	457	Secretary of War.						
Wate, Major Jason	Commutation pay	2	2	Rep't of Secretary War.	696					Laid on table.		
Water, John S	(See Sarah M. Charlton, *et al.*)	26	2		329							
Waterhouse, John, and Michael Helmes.	Indemnity for property destroyed by British.	15	2	Petition	148	Claims				Discharged; laid on table.		
Waterhouse, Nathaniel	Pension	25	3	Petition	674					Laid on table.		
Waterman, Dr. Asher, heir of.	Commutation pay	24	1	Petition	105	Rev. Claims.						
Waterman, Benjamin	Reimbursement of money paid for transportation of mail.	22	1	Petition	710	P. Of. & P. Roads.						
Waterman, Benjamin	Reimbursement of money paid for transportation of mail.	23	1	Petition	218	P. Of. & P. Roads.	324	Adverse		Laid on table.		
Waterman, Benjamin	Reimbursement of money paid for transportation of mail.	24	1	Petition	474	P. Of. & P. Roads.						
Waterman, Benjamin	Reimbursement of money paid for transportation of mail.	26	2	Petition	130	P. Of. & P. Roads.						
Waterman, Charles, (Ohio)	Pension	21	1	Petition	523	Military Pensions				Discharged; laid on table.		
Waterman, Charles, (Ohio)	Pension	21	2	Petition	120	Military Pensions.						
Waterman, Charles, (Ohio)	Pension	22	1	Petition	35	Rev. Pensions.						
Waterman, David and Erastus.	(See Abraham Packard and others)	22	1		514							
Waterman, Esther	(See William Waterman, widow of.)	25	2		53							
Waterman, Flavius	Reimbursement of money	19	1	Petition	226	Public Lands				Discharged; laid on table.		
Waterman, Henry	Patent for certain improvements	28	2	Petition	149	Patents.						
Waterman, John, heirs of.	Commutation pay	23	2	Petition	165	Rev. Pensions.						
Waterman, John, heirs of.	Commutation pay	24	1	Petition	205	Rev. Pensions	508	Adverse		Laid on table.		
Waterman, Luther, heirs of.	Commutation pay	23	2	Petition	165	Rev. Pensions.						
Waterman, Luther, heirs of.	Commutation pay	24	1	Petition	205	Rev. Pensions	508	Adverse		Laid on table.		
Waterman, Silas	Pension	27	3	Petition	61	Rev. Pensions	34	Adverse.		Laid on table.		
Waterman, Silas	Pension	28	2	Petition	207	Invalid Pensions.						
Waterman, Silas	Pension	29	1	Petition	93	Invalid Pensions	153	Favorable	156	Passed.		
Waterman, Silas	Pension	29	2	Petition	69	Invalid Pensions	73	Favorable	683	Referred to Committee Whole House.		
Waterman, Silas	Pension	30	1	Petition	104	Invalid Pensions	85	Favorable	72	Passed	Passed	App'd June 26, 1848
Waterman, Silas	Increase of pension	31	1	Petition	510	Invalid Pensions.						
Waterman, William, (Vt.)	Pension	4	1	Rep. of Secretary War.	445	Claims	Feb. 18, 1796	Favorable	156	Passed	Passed	App'd April 20, 1796
Waterman, William, widow of.	Pension	25	2	Petition	53	Rev. Pensions	Jan. 25, 1838	Favorable	456	Referred to Committee Whole House.		
Waters, Abigail	Pre emption right to land	24	1	Petition	257	Public Lands.						
Waters, Asa H	Pension	28	1	Petition	872	Rev. Pensions				Discharged; laid on table.		

List of private claims presented to the House of Representatives of the United States from the 1st to the 31st Congress, inclusive—**Continued.**

Names of claimants.	Nature or object of the claim.	Congress.	Session.	How brought before the House of Reps.	Page of journal.	To what committee of the House referred.	No. or date of the report.	Nature of the report.	No. of the bill.	How disposed of by the House of Reps.	How disposed of by the Senate.	Date of the act of Congress, and remarks.
Waters, Daniel	Compensation for revolutionary services.	3	1	Petition	17					Referred to Secretary War.		
Waters, Daniel	Compensation for revolutionary services.	3	1	Rep. of Secretary War.	111	Select	April 22, 1794			Laid on table.		
Waters, Elizebeth	(See Cap. Richard Waters, widow of.)	23	1		436							
Waters, George W., and M. W. Bateman.	For grant of land	22	1	Petition	264	Public Lands				Discharged; laid on table.		
Waters, John	Pension	17	1	Petition	37	Rev. Pensions				Discharged; laid on table.		
Waters, John, heirs of	Bounty land for revolutionary services.	24	1	Petition	536	Rev. Claims	June 15, 1836	Adverse		Laid on table.		
Waters, John, heirs of	Bounty land for revolutionary services.	24	2	Petition	40	Rev. Claims	203	Adverse		Laid on table.		
Waters, John, heirs of	Bounty land for revolutionary services.	25	2	Petition	70	Rev. Claims	367	Adverse		Laid on table.		
Waters, Joseph G.	See Moses Townsend)	29	2		135							
Waters, Philemon, by W. B. Waters, his son.	For lands to which he was entitled for services in army.	13	2	Petition	316	Claims.						
Waters, Philip	Pension	21	1	Petition	213	Military Pensions				Discharged; laid on table.		
Waters, Captain Richard, widow of.	Pension	23	1	Petition	436	Rev. Pensions				Discharged; laid on table.		
Waters, Talman J., (N. Y.)	(See A. D. Duff, surety of.)	17	1		310							
Waters, Thomas	(See William Thompson, assignee of)	19	1		312							
Waters, Wilkes B.	(See Philemon Waters, son of)	13	2		316							
Wathon, A., and others	Relief for the Ohio and Mississippi mail line company.	31	2	Petition	32	P. Of. & P. Roads.						
Watkins, Abigail	(See Seth Watkins, widow of)	29	1		168							
Watkins, Alfred L	Pre emption right to land	24	1	Petition	65	Public Lands.						
Watkins, Alfred L	Pre emption right to land	24	2	Petition	89	Public Lands.						
Watkins, Alfred L	Pre-emption right to land	25	2	Petition	374	Public Lands				Discharged; laid on table.		
Watkins, Charles F., (La.)	Confirmation of title to land	22	1	Petition	336	Priv Land Claims				Discharged; laid on table.		
Watkins, Eleanor B.	(See Gassaway Watkins, widow of)	28	2		346							
Watkins, Gassaway, (Md.)	Renewal of military land warrant.	4	2	Petition	631	Claims.						
Watkins, Gassaway, (Md.)	Renewal of military land warrant.	5	2	Petition	229	Claims	100	Adverse.				
Watkins, Gassaway, (Md.)	Compensation for revolutionary services.	10	1	Rep. of Secretary War.	193		Mar. 3, 1808	Rep't of Sec'ry War.		Laid on table.		
Watkins, Gassaway, (Md.)	Continuation of pension	16	2	Petition	225	Rev. Pensions	Feb. 15, 1821	Adverse				Leave to withdraw.
Watkins, Gassaway, widow of.	Pension	28	2	Petition	346	Rev. Pensions.						
Watkins, Gassaway, widow of.	Payment of lost certificate	29	1	Petition	682	Claims	646	Favorable	429	Referred to Committee Whole House.		
Watkins, Gassaway, widow of.	Payment of lost certificate	29	2	House bill	210	Claims	Jan. 22, 1847	Favorable	429	Passed.		
Watkins, Gassaway, widow of.	Payment of lost certificate	30	1	Petition	154	Claims	484	Favorable	402	Passed.		
Watkins, Hannah	(See Robert Watkins, heirs of widow of.)	29	1		340							
Watkins, Jesse	(See Reuben E. Gentry, & others)	24	1		294							

List of private claims presented to the House of Representatives of the United States from the 1st to the 31st Congress, inclusive—Continued.

Names of claimants.	Nature or object of the claim.	Congress.	Session.	How brought before the House of Reps.	Page of journal.	To what committee of the House referred.	No. or date of the report.	Nature of the report.	No. of the bill.	How disposed of by the House of Reps.	How disposed of by the Senate.	Date of the act of Congress, and remarks.
Watkins, Doc. John, heirs of.	Confirmation of title to land	15	1	Petition	85, 280	Public Lands				Discharged; laid on table.		
Watkins, Doc. John, heirs of.	Confirmation of title to land	16	1	Petition	36	Public Lands				Discharged; laid on table.		
Watkins, Doc. John, heirs of.	Confirmation of title to land	17	1	Petition	54	Public Lands				Discharged; laid on table.		
Watkins, Doc. John, heirs of.	Confirmation of title to land	18	1	Petition	55	Public Lands	Jan. 16, 1824	General bill	65	Passed	Passed	App'd May 26, 1824
Watkins, John	For bounty land	30	1	Petition	146	Military Affairs	Aug. 10, 1848					Leave to withdraw.
Watkins, Leonard, widow of.	Pension	20	1	Petition	310	Military Pensions	May 13, 1828	Adverse		Laid on table.		
Watkins, Mary	(See Leonard Watkins, widow of)	20	1		310							
Watkins, Richard	Remuneration for loss on contract for grading Cumberland road.	23	2	Petition	391	Claims.						
Watkins, Richard	Remuneration for loss on contract for grading Cumberland road.	24	1	Petition	206	Claims	363	Adverse		Laid on table.		
Watkins, Richard	Payment for loss of horse, war of 1812.	25	3	Petition	461	Claims.						
Watkins, Richard	Payment for loss of horse, war of 1812.	26	1	Petition	170	Claims.						
Watkins, Robert, heirs of.	Commutation pay	22	2	Petition	90	Rev. Claims.						
Watkins, Robert, heirs of.	Commutation pay	24	1	Resolution	1082	Rev. Claims.						
Watkins, Robert, heirs of.	Commutation pay	25	2	Petition	516	Rev. Claims.						
Watkins, Robert, heirs of.	Commutation pay	25	3	Petition	283	Rev. Claims.						
Watkins, Robert, heirs of.	Commutation pay	26	1	Petition	167	Rev. Claims.						
Watkins, Robert, heirs of, widow of.	Arrears of pension	29	1	Memorial	340	Rev. Pensions.						
Watkins, Robert, heirs of, widow of.	Arrears of pension	29	2	Petition	150	Rev. Pensions	10	Adverse.		Laid on table.		
Watkins, Seth	Pension	21	1	Petition	411	Military Pensions	April 29, 1830	Adverse		Laid on table.		
Watkins, Seth, widow of.	Pension	29	1	Petition	168	Rev. Pensions	650	Adverse		Laid on table.		
Watkins, William	Compensation for loss of horse, Florida war.	26	2	Petition	60	Claims.						
Watkinson, David, & Co., merchants, Conn.	Refund duties paid on iron	23	1	Petition	47	Ways and Means	222	Favorable	244	Referred to Committee Whole House.		
Watkinson, David, & Co., merchants, Conn.	Refund duties paid on iron	23	2	House bill	299	Whole House	Jan. 31, 1835	Favorable	244			
Watkinson, David, & Co., merchants, Conn.	Refund duties paid on iron	24	1	Petition	95	Ways and Means.						
Watkinson, David, & Co., merchants, Conn.	Refund duties paid on iron	26	1	Petition	297	Ways and Means	709	Adverse		Laid on table.		
Watkinson, David, & Co., merchants, Conn.	Refund duties paid on iron	27	2	Petition	55	Ways and Means	872	Favorable	498	Referred to Committee Whole House.		
Watkinson, David, & Co., merchants, Conn.	Refund duties paid on iron	27	3	House bill	90	Whole House	Dec. 23, 1842	Favorable	498	Passed	Passed	App'd March 3, 1843
Watlington, Francis	Compensation for keeping Florida light-ship, and as inspector.	25	2	Petition	579	Commerce				Discharged.		
Watlington, Francis	Compensation for keeping Florida light-ship, and as inspector.	25	3	Petition	92	Commerce	167	Adverse		Laid on table.		
Watriss, Henry, (N. Y.).	Indemnity for suspension of contract for iron, &c.	26	1	Petition	294	Claims.						
Watrous, Richard	Pension	2	2	Rep. of Sec. War.	649	Whole House	Jan. 3, 1793	Favorable	214	Passed.		

3—75

List of private claims presented to the House of Representatives of the United States from the 1st to the 31st Congress, inclusive—**Continued.**

Names of claimants.	Nature or object of the claim.	Congress.	Session.	How brought before the House of Reps.	Page of journal.	To what committee of the House referred.	No. or date of the report.	Nature of the report.	No. of the bill.	How disposed of by the House of Reps.	How disposed of by the Senate.	Date of the act of Congress, and remarks.
Watrous, Richard	Pension	3	1	Rep. of Secretary War.	131	Select	May 26, 1794	Favorable	J. R. 12	Passed	Passed	App'd June 9, 1794
Watrous, Richard	Pension	4	1	Resolution & rep.	445	Claims	Feb. 18, 1796	Favorable	156	Passed	Passed	App'd April 20, 1796
Watson, Abner	Pension	29	1	Petition	86	Rev. Pensions	430	Adverse		Laid on table.		
Watson, Abraham	Compensation for revolutionary services.	2	1	Petition	440	Secretary of War.						
Watson, Abraham	Compensation for revolutionary services.	2	2	Rep. of Secretary War.	704					Laid on table.		
Watson, Abraham	Compensation for revolutionary services.	5	2	Rep. of Secretary War.	118	Claims	July 13, 1798			Discharged.		
Watson, Abraham	Compensation for revolutionary services.	5	3	Petition	430	Claims	May 2, 1799	Adverse		Laid on table.		
Watson, Abraham	Compensation for revolutionary services.	6	2	Petition	732	Claims	Jan. 9, 1801	Adverse.		Laid on table.		
Watson, Alexander, administrator of, (N. Y.)	Payment for property destroyed by British.	23	1	Petition	35	Claims.						
Watson, Alex., (Florida.)	Payment for property destroyed by Indians.	25	2	Petition	397	Claims	1001	Adverse		Laid on table.		
Watson, Alex., (Florida.)	Payment for property destroyed by Indians.	25	3	Petition	87	Claims.						
Watson, Alex., (Florida.)	Payment for property destroyed by Indians.	26	1	Petition and res.	397, 624	Claims	694	Adverse		Laid on table.		
Watson, Alex., (Florida.)	Payment for property destroyed by Indians.	26	1	Memorial	1009	Claims.						
Watson, Alex., (Florida.)	Payment for property destroyed by Indians.	26	2	Petition	125	Claims.						
Watson, Alex., (Florida.)	Payment for property destroyed by Indians	27	2	Petition and res.	85, 428	Claims	July 29, 1842	Favorable	S. 293	Referred to Committee Whole House.		
Watson, Alex., (Florida.)	Payment for property destroyed by Indians.	30	2	Petition	193	Claims	135	Adverse		Laid on table.		
Watson, Amariah	To perfect purchase to quantity of land	14	1	Petition	239	Public Lands	March 1, 1816	Adverse		Laid on table.		
Watson, Ann	(See Timothy Watson, widow of.)	24	1		641							
Watson, Augustus	Compensation for a horse lost in public service.	12	1	Petition	174	Claims.						
Watson, Benjamin M., administrator of.	Indemnity for French spoliations prior to 1800.	26	1	Memorial	182	Foreign Affairs	343	Favorable; bill	319	Referred to Committee Whole House.		
Watson, Benjamin	Pension	24	2	Petition	41	Invalid Pensions	Dec. 23, 1835	Adverse		Laid on table.		
Watson, Benjamin	Pension	25	2	Petition	118	Invalid Pensions				Discharged; laid on table.		
Watson, Benjamin	Pension	27	3	Petition	96	Invalid Pensions	Jan. 19, 1842	Adverse		Laid on table.		
Watson, Benjamin	Pension	30	1	Petition	886	Invalid Pensions.	Aug. 8, 1848			Discharged; laid on table.		
Watson, C. C. and J., and others, (Philadelphia.)	Remission of certain duties	16	1	Petition	212	Ways and Means.						
Watson, Chabot, & Co.	Compensation for coal, &c., furnished United States vessels.	31	1	Petition	536	Claims	153	Favorable	171	Referred to Committee Whole House.		
Watson, Chabot, & Co.	Compensation for coal, &c., furnished United States vessels.	31	2	House bill	103	Whole House	Jan. 3, 1851	Adverse	171			
Watson, Daniel	Pension.	27	3	Petition	72	Invalid Pensions.						
Watson, Ebenezer	Patent for altering bank notes	16	1	Petition	23	Judiciary				Disch'd; laid on table.		
Watson, Enoch	Confirmation of title to land	25	2	Documents	193	Public Lands				Discharged.		
Watson, Hugh A., (Ala.)	To correct error in entry of land	20	1	Petition	458	Public Lands				Discharged.		

List of private claims presented to the House of Representatives of the United States from the 1st to the 31st Congress, inclusive—Continued.

Names of claimants.	Nature or object of the claim.	Congress.	Session.	How brought before the House of Reps.	Page of journal.	To what committee of the House referred.	No. or date of the report.	Nature of the report.	No. of the bill.	How disposed of by the House of Reps.	How disposed of by the Senate.	Date of the act of Congress, and remarks.
Watson & Halloway	(See Halloway & Watson)	19	2		154							
Watson, James, (Pa.)	Indemnity for lost certificate and sum of money lost by fire.	2	1	Petition	483					Referred to Secretary Treasury.		
Watson, James, (Pa.)	Indemnity for lost certificate and sum of money lost by fire.	3	2	Rep. of Secretary Treasury.	284					Laid on table.		
Watson, James, widow of.	Indemnity for French spoliations prior to 1800.	20	1	Petition	40	Foreign Affairs	1			Laid on table.		
Watson, James, heirs of.	Payment for horse stolen by Indians.	25	2	Petition	426	Indian Affairs				Discharged.		
Watson, James, heirs of.	Payment for horse stolen by Indians.	26	1	Petition	721	Indian Affairs.						
Watson, James, administrator of.	Release from liability as surety on certain bonds.	25	2	Petition	544	Naval Affairs.						
Watson, James B., assignee of P. G. Hambaugh.	Payment for property destroyed by Indians.	29	1	Petition	415	Claims	278	Adverse.		Laid on table.		
Watson, James C	To refund money paid for the purchase of slaves to the late Creek regiment of warriors captured from Seminoles in 1838, and sale prevented by Gen. Arbuckle.	26	1	Petition	335	Claims.						
Watson, James C	To refund money paid for the purchase of slaves to the late Creek regiment of warriors captured from Seminoles in 1838, and sale prevented by Gen. Arbuckle.	26	2	Petition	52	Claims.						
Watson, James C	To refund money paid for the purchase of slaves to the late Creek regiment of warriors captured from Seminoles in 1838, and sale prevented by Gen. Arbuckle.	27	2	Petition	94	Indian Affairs	558	Favorable	351	Referred to Committee Whole House.		
Watson, James C	To refund money paid for the purchase of slaves to the late Creek regiment of warriors captured from Seminoles in 1838, and sale prevented by Gen. Arbuckle.	28	1	Petition	131	Claims	132	Favorable	122	Referred to Committee Whole House.		
Watson, James C	To refund money paid for the purchase of slaves to the late Creek regiment of warriors captured from Seminoles in 1838, and sale prevented by Gen. Arbuckle.	28	2	House bill	345				122	Discharged.		
Watson, James C., heirs of.	To refund money paid for the purchase of slaves to the late Creek regiment of warriors captured from Seminoles in 1838, and sale prevented by Gen. Arbuckle.	29	1	Petition	67	Claims	535	Favorable	357	Referred to Committee Whole House.		
Watson, James C., heirs of.	To refund money paid for the purchase of slaves to the late Creek regiment of warriors capture from Seminoles in 1838, and sale prevented by Gen. Arbuckle.	30	1	Petition	69	Claims	724	Favorable	567	Referred to Committee Whole House.		
Watson, James C., heirs of.	To refund money paid for the purchase of slaves to the late Creek regiment of warriors capture from Seminoles in 1838, and sale prevented by Gen. Arbuckle.	30	2	Petition	519							Leave to withdraw.

List of private claims presented to the House of Representatives of the United States from the 1st to the 31st Congress, inclusive—**Continued.**

Names of claimants.	Nature or object of the claim.	Congress.	Session.	How brought before the House of Reps.	Page of journal.	To what committee of the House referred.	No. or date of the report.	Nature of the report.	No. of the bill.	How disposed of by the House of Reps.	How disposed of by the Senate.	Date of the act of Congress, and remarks.
Watson, James C., administratrix of.	To refund money paid for the purchase of slaves to the late Creek regiment of warriors captured from Seminoles in 1838, and sale prevented by Gen. Arbuckle.	31	1	Petition	284	Claims	102	Favorable	119	Referred to Committee Whole House.		
Watson, Jemima	(See Wm. Watson, widow of)	24	2		397							
Watson, John, (Conn.)	Pension	1	2	Petition	170	Secretary of War	Mar. 17, 1790			Laid on table.		
Watson, John, (Conn.)	Pension	2	2	Rep. of Secretary War.	649	Whole House	Jan. 3, 1793	Favorable	214	Passed.		
Watson, John, (Conn.)	Pension	3	1	Rep. of Secretary War.	131	Select	May 26, 1794	Referred to Sec. War.	J R. 12	Passed	Passed	App'd June 9, 1794
Watson, John, heirs of	Confirmation of title to land	15	2	Petition	40	Priv. Land Claims.						
Watson, John, heirs of	Confirmation of title to land	21	1	Petition	131	Priv. Land Claims.						
Watson, John	Permission to change location of land.	19	1	Petition	58	Public Lands	54	Favorable	77	Passed	Passed	App'd May 22, 1826
Watson, John	(See Charles Josslyn, sureties of).	21	1		133							
Watson, John	Payment for loss of horse, war of 1812.	20	1	Resolution	43	Claims	33	Adverse		Laid on table.		
Watson, John	Payment for loss of horse, war of 1812.	20	2	Rep't of last sess.	81	Claims	27	Favorable	343	Referred to Committee Whole House.		
Watson, John	Payment for loss of horse, war of 1812.	21	1	Rep't of last sess.	44	Claims	3	Favorable	3	Passed.	Passed	App'd Feb. 11, 1830
Watson, John, (Conn.)	Indemnity for damages done by British to ship built for United States.	21	1	Petition	200, 447	Naval Affairs						Leave to withdraw.
Watson, John, (Conn.)	Indemnity for damages done by British to ship built for United States.	21	1	Petition	447	Naval Affairs				Discharged; laid on table.		
Watson, John, (Conn.)	Indemnity for damages done by British to ship built for United States.	21	2	Petition	209	Naval Affairs	112	Adverse		Laid on table.		
Watson, John, (Conn.)	Indemnity for damages done by British to ship built for United States.	22	1	Petition	222	Claims	Mar. 9, 1832			Laid on table.		
Watson, John, (Conn.)	Indemnity for damages done by British to ship built for United States.	22	2	Petition	168	Commerce.						
Watson, John, (Conn.)	Indemnity for damages done by British to ship built for United States.	24	1	Petition	534	Claims	632	Adverse		Laid on table.		
Watson, John, (Conn.)	Indemnity for damages done by British to ship built for United States.	25	3	Petition	569	Naval Affairs.						
Watson, John, (Conn.)	Indemnity for damages done by British to ship built for United States.	26	1	Petition	303	Naval Affairs.						
Watson, John L	(See George Taylor, attorney of).	29	1		219							
Watson, Joseph	Compensation for selling lands in Michigan, and as aid to governor, &c., &c.	13	3	Petition	487	Claims	Mar. 2, 1815					Leave to withdraw.
Watson, Joseph, (Ohio)	Compensation for services as secretary to Indian department, Northwestern Territory, &c.	22	1	Senate bill	540	Claims			74	Referred to Committee Whole House.		

List of private claims presented to the House of Representatives of the United States from the 1st to the 31st Congress, inclusive—Continued.

Names of claimants.	Nature or object of the claim.	Congress.	Session.	How brought before the House of Reps.	Page of journal.	To what committee of the House referred.	No. or date of the report.	Nature of the report.	No. of the bill.	How disposed of by the House of Reps.	How disposed of by the Senate.	Date of the act of Congress, and remarks.
Watson, Joseph, heirs of, (Ohio.)	Compensation for services as secretary to Indian department, Northwestern Territory, &c.	29	2	Senate bill	381	Indian Affairs	Feb. 20, 1847	With't amend.	145	Referred to Committee Whole House.		
Watson, Joseph, representatives of, (Ohio.)	Compensation for services as secretary to Indian department, Northwestern Territory, &c.	31	1	Senate bill	191	.....	.....	.....	100	Referred to Committee Whole House.		
Watson, Joseph	Pension	26	1	Petition	602	Invalid Pensions.						
Watson, Joseph	Pension	27	2	Petition	515	Invalid Pensions	581	Favorable	377	Referred to Committee Whole House.		
Watson, Joseph	Pension	27	3	House bill	96	Whole House	Dec. 23, 1842	Favorable	377	Passed.		
Watson, Joseph	Pension	28	1	Petition	79	Invalid Pensions	97	Favorable	113	Passed.		
Watson, Joseph	Pension	28	2	Petition	112	Invalid Pensions	93	Favorable	578	Passed.		
Watson, Joseph	Pension	29	1	Petition	93	Invalid Pensions	54	Favorable	43	Passed	Passed	App'd July 15, 1846
Watson, Joseph J	Arrears and increase of pension	30	1	Petition	459	Invalid Pensions	585	Adverse	.....	Laid on table.		
Watson, Josiah	Increase of compensation as postmaster.	14	2	Petition	384	P. Of. & P. Roads	.....	.....	.....	Discharged; laid on table.		
Watson, Lucy	(See John Rowe)	25	2	.....	271							
Watson, Marston, administrator of.	Indemnity for French spoliations prior to 1800.	26	1	Memorial	182	Foreign Affairs	343	Favorable; bill	319	Referred to Committee Whole House.		
Watson & Paul, surviving partner of.	Indemnity for French spoliations prior to 1800.	26	1	Memorial	182	Foreign Affairs	343	Favorable; bill	319	Referred to Committee Whole House.		
Watson, Samuel, and Geo Hoppas.	Renewal of lost certificates	21	1	Petition	202	Priv. Land Claims.	231	Favorable	288	Passed.		
Watson, Samuel S	Pre-emption right to certain lands.	24	2	Petition	389	Public Lands.						
Watson, Samuel S	Pre-emption right to certain lands.	25	2	Petition	951	Public Lands.						
Watson, Samuel S	Pre-emption right to certain lands.	25	3	Petition	182	Public Lands	97	Adverse	.....	Laid on table.		
Watson, Samuel	Pension	28	1	Petition	89	Rev. Pensions	.....	.....	.....	Discharged; laid on table.		
Watson, Thos., and others.	Compensation for locating military land warrants.	31	1	Petition	216	Public Lands.						
Watson, Timothy, widow of.	Compensation for revolutionary services and death of husband.	24	1	Memorial	641	Rev. Pensions	.....	.....	.....	Discharged; laid on table.		
Watson, Timothy, widow of.	Compensation for revolutionary services and death of husband.	25	3	Petition	368	Rev. Pensions	Feb. 16, 1839	Favorable	1149	Referred to Committee Whole House.		
Watson, Timothy, widow of.	Compensation for revolutionary services and death of husband.	26	1	Petition	172, 175	Rev. Pensions	.....	.....	.....	Discharged; laid on table.		
Watson, Timothy, widow of.	Compensation for revolutionary services and death of husband.	28	1	Petition	839	Whole House.						
Watson, Westgate	(See William Holloway and others)	19	2	.....	105							
Watson, William, heirs of.	Confirmation of title to land	21	1	Petition	131	Priv. Land Claims	.....	.....	.....	Discharged; laid on table.		
Watson, William, (N. Y.,) widow of.	(See Israel Honeywell, representatives of.)	24	2	.....	397							
Watson, William R	Increase of commission on duties collected.	28	1	Petition	1020	Commerce.						
Watson, Zachariah	Pension	22	1	Petition	36	Rev. Pensions.						
Watters, George	Increase of pension	10	1	House bill	232	Whole House	April 19, 1808	Favorable	78	Passed	Passed	App'd April 25, 1808
Watters, Joseph, administrator of.	Payment of depreciated loan office certificate.	6	1	Petition	622	Claims	Mar. 31, 1800	Adverse	.....	Laid on table.		
Waterston, David A	Compensation as clerk in office of surveyor general, Louisiana.	30	1	Senate bill	975	Claims	July 1, 1848	With't amend.	172	Passed	.....	App'd Aug. 14, 1848
Waterston, David A	For amendment of above act	31	1	Senate bill	1142	Claims	Sept. 16, 1850	With't amend.	287	Passed	.....	App'd Sept. 20, 1850

List of private claims presented to the House of Representatives of the United States from the 1st to the 31st Congress, inclusive—Continued.

Names of claimants.	Nature or object of the claim.	Congress.	Session.	How brought before the House of Reps.	Page of journal.	To what committee of the House referred.	No. or date of the report.	Nature of the report.	No. of the bill.	How disposed of by the House of Reps.	How disposed of by the Senate.	Date of the act of Congress, and remarks.
Waterson, George	Compensation for statements of imprisonment for debt in District Columbia.	24	2	Resolution	279	Ways and Means						Provided for in general bill No. 776, civil and diplomatic.
Waterson, G., and N. Van sant.	For subscription to their statistical table.	20	1	House bill	170	Library	Jan. 14, 1828	Favorable	76	Passed	Passed	App'd April 3, 1825
Waterson. G., and N. Vansant.	To purchase, &c., additional copies of statistical table.	22	2	House bill	123	Whole House	Jan. 3, 1833	Favorable	421	Passed	Passed	App'd Feb. 19, 1833
Wattles, Cynthia	(See Daniel Wattles, widow of.)	27	2		1227							
Wattles, Daniel, widow of	Pension	27	2	Petition	1227	Rev. Pensions.						
Wattles, Nathaniel, president of Marine Insurance Company.	(See Virginia, Alexandria, Marine Insurance Company.)	29	2		87							
Wattles, Nathaniel, president of Marine Insurance Company, of Alexandria.	Indemnity for French spoliations prior to 1800.	26	1	Memorial	182	Foreign Affairs	343	Favorable; bil	319	Referred to Committee Whole House.		
Wattles, Simon D., representatives of.	Compensation for loss of son and brother, being their only support.	15	1	Petition	217	Military Affairs	Mar. 20, 1818	Adverse				Leave to withdraw.
Watts, Alexander	Bounty land for military services	18	1	Petition	97	Public Lands	Jan. 20, 1824	Adverse		Laid on table.		
Watts, Alexander	Pension	19	1	Petition	78	Military Pensions	Feb. 23, 1826	Favorable	118	Passed.		
Watts, Alexander	Pension	19	2	House bill	85	Whole House	Dec. 22, 1826	Favorable	314	Passed	Passed	App'd March 3, 1827
Watts, Archibald	Payment of three loan office certificates.	22	1	Petition	62	Rev. Pensions	165	Favorable	239	Referred to Committee Whole House.		
Watts, Archibald	Payment of three loan office certificates.	22	2	House bill	92		Dec. 22, 1832		239	Passed	Passed	App'd Feb. 27, 1833
Watts, Catherine	(See John Watts, widow of.)	16	1		88							
Watts, Conrad	Pension	23	2	Petition	101	Rev. Pensions				Discharged; laid on table.		
Watts, Conrad	Pension	24	1	Petition	137	Rev. Pensions				Discharged; laid on table.		
Watts, Conrad	Pension	25	2	Petition	54	Rev. Pensions	Mar. 23, 1838	Adverse		Laid on table.		
Watts, Conrad	Pension	25	3	Petition	128	Rev. Pensions				Discharged.		
Watts, Conrad	Pension	26	1	Petition	307	Rev. Pensions	490	Adverse		Laid on table.		
Watts, Conrad	Pension	27	2	Petition	59	Rev. Pensions	784	Adverse.		Laid on table.		
Watts. Charles, (Ind.)	Pension	26	1	Petition	324	Rev. Pensions				Discharged; laid on table.		
Watts, Edward, mother of.	Pension in consideration of death of her son.	25	2	Petition	275	Naval Affairs	March 6, 1838	Adverse		Laid on table.		
Watts, Edward, mother of.	Pension in consideration of death of her son.	26	1	Petition	713	Naval Affairs.						
Watts, Eleanor B.	Pension	25	2	Petition	312	Rev. Pensions				Discharged; laid on table.		
Watts, George, executors of, &c.	Relief in case of register of ship Nancy.	7	2	Memorial	321	Com. and Manuf.						
Watts, George, executors of, &c.	Relief in case of register of ship Nancy.	8	1	Memorial	546	Com. and Manuf.	Mar. 1, 1804	Rep. not found.		Postponed.		
Watts, George, executors of, &c.	Relief in case of register of ship Nancy.	9	1	Petition	312	Com. and Munuf.						
Watts, George, administrator of.	Remission of tonnage	9	2	Petition	554	Com. and Manuf.						
Watts, John, widow of	Grant of land for revolutionary services.	16	1	Petition	88	Pens. & Rev. Cl'ms.	Jan. 5, 1820	Adverse.				
Watts, John H., (Ala.)	(See John Wilson.)	21	1		60							
Watts, Julian	(See General Henry Miller.)	31	1		445							
Watts, Olive Rindge	(See Edward Watts, mother of.)	25	2		275							

List of private claims presented to the House of Representatives of the United States from the 1st to the 31st Congress, inclusive—Continued.

Names of claimants.	Nature or object of the claim.	Congress.	Session.	How brought before the House of Reps.	Page of journal.	To what committee of the House referred.	No. or date of the report.	Nature of the report.	No. of the bill.	How disposed of by the House of Reps.	How disposed of by the Senate.	Date of the act of Congress, and remarks.
Watts, Robert, *et al.*	(See William Alexander, Earl of Stirling.)	23	1		306							
Watts, Samuel	Drawback on duties	5	2	Petition	257	Com. and Manuf.						
Watts, Samuel	Drawback on duties	5	3	Petition	467	Com. and Manuf.	Jan. 28, 1799	Favorable	148½	Passed	Passed	App'd Feb. 19, 1799
Watts, Williams, widow and heirs of.	Commutation pay	27	3	Petition	210	Rev. Claims	252	Adverse		Laid on table.		
Watts, Col., officers and soldiers of Pennsylvania Flying Camp.	For pay from time of capture until their release.	2	1	Petition	507					Referred to Secretary of War.		
Waugh, James, representatives of.	For script on military land warrant.	28	1	Petition	621	Public Lands.						
Waugh, Lorenzo	(See James Waugh, representative of.)	28	1		621							
Waugh, Samuel	(See Elijah Sandford, and others.)	19	1		82							
Waugh, Thaddeus	Pension	10	2	House bill	499	Whole House	Feb. 20, 1809	Favorable	59 or 158	Passed	Passed	See act March 3, 1809
Way & Gideon	Aid in publishing and perfecting journals.	18	1	Petition	61	Library	Feb. 25, 1824	Adverse		Laid on table.		
Way, Henry	(See William Thompson)	19	2									
Way, Isaac	Pension	21	1	Petition	362	Military Pensions	April 29, 1830	Adverse.		Laid on table.		
Way, Isaac	Pension	21	2	Petition	231	Military Pensions.						
Way, Captain Joseph	Compensation for military services.	7	1	Petition	201					Referred to Secretary of War.		
Way, Layman	Compensation for loss of sight in transporting soldiers, &c.	14	1	Petition	208	Pens. & Rev. Cl'ms.	April 11, 1816	Favorable	171	Laid on table.		
Way, Layman	Compensation for loss of sight in transporting soldiers, &c.	14	2	Petition	363	Pens. & Rev. Cl'ms.				Discharged; laid on table.		
Way, Ralph	Pension	15	2	Petition	300	Rev. Pensions				Discharged; laid on table.		
Wayland, Abraham, *et al.*	Pre-emption right to land	26	1	Petition	961	Priv. Land Claims.						
Wayland, James	Pension	2	2	Rep. of Secretary of War.	649	Whole House	Jan. 3, 1793	Favorable	214	Passed.		
Wayland, James	Pension	3	1	Rep. of Secretary of War.	131	Select	May 26, 1794	Favorable	J. R. 12	Passed	Passed	App'd June 9, 1794
Wayland, James	Pension	4	2	House bill	283	Whole House	Mar. 24, 1810	Favorable	107	Passed	Passed	App'd April 27, 1810
Wayland, John G., administrator of	Compension for horse impressed into revolutionary service.	3	2	Petition	34[illegible]	Claims.						
Wayman, John, administrator of.	Payment for horse lost in revolutionary war.	3	2	Petition	343	Claims.						
Wayman, John, administrator of.	Payment for horse lost in revolutionary war.	4	1	Petition								Leave to withdraw.
Wayman, John, administrator of.	Payment for horse lost in revolutionary war.	4	1	Res. and rep't	373	Claims	Jan. 6, 1796	Adverse.				Leave to withdraw.
Wayne, General Anthony, heirs of.	Credit for money disbursed, and compensation for revolutionary services.	11	3	Senate bill	480	Whole House	Jan. 14, 1811	With't amend	41	Passed	Passed	App'd Jan. 21, 1811
Wayne, General Anthony, heirs of.	Credit for money disbursed, and compensation for revolutionary services.	11	2	House bill	487	Whole House	Jan. 17, 1811	General appropriation bill.	177	Passed	Passed	App'd Feb. 20, 1811
Weakley, Prudence	(See Thomas Weakly, widow of)	30	1		342							
Weakley, Thomas, widow of.	Benefit of act allowing half-pay and pension to widow.	30	1	Petition	342	Rev. Pensions	347	Adverse		Laid on table.		
Weare, Jonathan	Restoration of pension	21	2	Petition	126	Military Pensions.						

List of private claims presented to the House of Representatives of the United States from the 1st to the 31st Congress, inclusive—Continued.

Names of claimants.	Nature or object of the claim.	Congress.	Session.	How brought before the House of Reps.	Page of journal.	To what committee of the House referred.	No. or date of the report.	Nature of the report.	No. of the bill.	How disposed of by the House of Reps.	How disposed of by the Senate.	Date of the act of Congress, and remarks.
Weare, Jonathan	Restoration of pension	22	1	Petition	68	Rev. Pensions	365	Favorable	460	Passed.		
Weare, William	Pension	3	1	Rep. of Secretary War.	131	Select	May 26, 1794	Referred to Sec of War, with instructions.	J.R. 12	Passed	Passed	App'd June 9, 1794
Wealch, Thomas, heirs of.	Arrears of pay and bounty land	27	2	Petition	524	Rev. Pensions	784	Adverse		Laid on table.		
Weatherlee, Isaac	Pension	21	2	Resolution	58	Military Pensions.						
Weatherley, Joseph, (Pa.)	Compensation for taking reports of aliens and granting licenses, &c.	18	1	Petition	197	Claims.						
Weatherley, Joseph, (Pa.)	Compensation for taking reports of aliens and granting licenses, &c.	18	2	Petition	30	Claims	Feb. 2, 1825	Adverse		Laid on table.		
Weatherley, Thomas M.	Pension	20	2	Resolution	152	Military Pensions				Discharged; laid on table.		
Weathered, Francis M.	Payment for horse lost in United States service.	21	1	Petition	360	Claims	Mar. 12, 1830	Adverse		Laid on table.		
Weatherford, John, (Ala.)	Confirmation of title to land	18	2	Petition	42	Public Lands	Jan. 28, 1825	Favorable	301	Passed	Passed	App'd March 3, 1825
Weatherhead, Amaziah	Pension	14	2	Petition	283	Priv. Land Claims.						
Weatherhead, Amaziah	Pension	23	2	Petition	67	Select	Feb. 25, 1835	Favorable	767	Referred to Committee Whole House.		
Weatherhead, Amaziah	Pension	24	1	Documents	136	Select	337	Favorable	352	Referred to Committee Whole House.		
Weatherhead, John or Joseph, (Mass.)	Increase of compensation as master armorer.	19	2	Petition	189	Military Affairs				Discharged.		
Weatherhead, John or Joseph, (Mass.)	Increase of compensation as master armorer.	20	1	Petition	57	Military Affairs				Discharged; laid on table.		
Weatherhead, John or Joseph, (Mass.)	Increase of compensation as master armorer.	23	1	Petition	307	Military Affairs				Discharged; laid on table.		
Weatherhead, Robert	Permission to enter land	22	1	Petition	107	Priv. Land Claims.	276	Favorable	355	Referred to Committee Whole House.		
Weathers, Sarah	(See Thomas H. Boyle, daughter of.)	15	1		13							
Weathers, Thomas	Compensation for loss of wagon and horses.	13	3	Petition	466	Claims	Nov. 14, 1814	Favorable	228	Passed.		
Weathers, Thomes	Compensation for loss of wagon and horses.	14	1	Petition	54	Claims				Discharged; laid on table.		
Weaver, Casper W	(See Casper W. Weaver)	26	1		836							
Weaver, Christian	Pension	17	1	Petition	469	Rev. Pensions						Leave to withdraw.
Weaver, Christian	Pension	17	2	Petition	52	Rev. Pensions				Discharged; laid on table.		Leave to withdraw.
Weaver, David	Pension	1	2	Rep. of Secretary War.	250	Select	July 16, 1790	Favorable	88	Passed	Passed	App'd Aug. 11, 1790
Weaver, David	Increase of pension	11	2	House bill	283	Whole House	Mar. 24, 1810	Favorable	107	Passed	Passed	App'd April 27, 1810
Weaver, Geo. M., heirs of.	Pension	29	1	Petition	646	Rev. Pensions.						
Weaver, George M., *et al.*	(See George M. Weaver, heirs of.)	29	1		648							
Weaver, Jacob	Pension	23	1	Petition	379	Rev. Pensions	364	Favorable	391	Referred to Committee Whole House.		
Weaver, Jacob	Pension	23	2	House bill	337	Whole House	Feb. 6, 1835	Favorable	391	Passed.		
Weaver, Jacob	Pension	24	1	Petition	57	Rev. Pensions	59	Favorable	73	Passed	Passed	App'd May 14, 1836
Weaver, John	Compensation for wagon and team pressed into U. States service.	2	1	Petition	547					Referred to Secretary War.		
Weaver, John	Compensation for wagon and team pressed into U. States service.	2	2	Rep of Secretary War.	696					Laid on table.		
Weaver, John	Confirmation of title to land	15	1	Petition	50	Priv. Land Claims.				Discharged; laid on table.		

List of private claims presented to the House of Representatives of the United States from the 1st to the 31st Congress, inclusive—Continued.

Names of claimants.	Nature or object of the claim.	Congress.	Session.	How brought before the House of Reps.	Page of journal.	To what committee of the House referred.	No. or date of the report.	Nature of the report.	No. of the bill.	How disposed of by the House of Reps.	How disposed of by the Senate.	Date of the act of Congress, and remarks.
Weaver, John	Confirmation of title to land	17	1	Petition	5[illegible]	Public Lands				Discharged; laid on table.		
Weaver, John	Confirmation of title to land	18	1	Petition	55	Public Lands	Jan. 16, 1824	General bill	65	Passed with amendm't.	Passed	App'd May 26, 1824
Weaver, John	Pension	22	2	Resolution	182	Invalid Pensions				Discharged; laid on table.		
Weaver, John	Pension	23	1	Resolution	92	Invalid Pensions	Dec. 24, 1833	Adverse.		Laid on table.		
Weaver, John	Pension	24	1	Petition	613	Invalid Pensions	733	Favorable	677	Passed.		
Weaver, John	Pension	25	2	House bill	142	Invalid Pensions	190	Favorable	216	Passed.		
Weaver, John	Pension	25	3	House bill	449	Whole House	Feb. 4, 1839	Favorable	1094	Referred to Committee Whole House.		
Weaver, John	Pension	26	1	Petition	161	Invalid Pensions	353	Favorable	332	Referred to Committee Whole House.		
Weaver, John A., heirs of	Pension	26	1	Petition	705	Rev. Pensions.						
Weaver, John	(See John A. Weaver, heirs of)	26	1		705							
Weaver, Rebecca L., *et al.*	(See Captain Aquilla Stinchcomb, heir of.)	31	1		1141							
Weaver, Samuel	Pension	17	1	Petition	387	Rev. Pensions.						
Weaver, Thomas, sureties of, *et al.*	Extension of time to entitle them to drawback on railroad iron	27	3	Petition	207	Judiciary	Jan. 25, 1843	Favorable	725	Passed	Passed	App'd March 3, 1843
Weaver, William A.	Arrears of pension	23	2	Petition	41	Naval Affairs.						
Weaver, William A.	Arrears of pension	24	1	Petition	99	Naval Affairs.						
Weaver, William A.	Compensation for services in Census office.	28	1	Petition	84	Claims.						
Webb, Amos	Confirmation of title to land	22	1	Petition	133	Public Lands	Jan. 13, 1832	Adverse		Laid on table.		
Webb, Amos, and F. Mulford.	(See Stephen Fobb, heirs of)	24	1		211							
Webb, Azariah	Compensation for services rendered and provisions furnished revolutionary army.	19	1	Petition	423	Rev. Claims				Discharged; laid on table.		
Webb, Azariah	Compensation for services rendered and provisions furnished revolutionary army.	19	2	Petition	133	Rev. Claims	Feb. 13, 1827	Adverse		Laid on table.		
Webb, Azariah	Compensation for military services.	21	1	Petition	615	Rev. Claims				Discharged; laid on table.		
Webb, Azariah	Compensation for military services.	21	2	Petition	189	Rev. Claims.						
Webb, Azariah	Compensation for military services.	22	1	Petition	62	Rev. Claims.						
Webb, Benjamin	Pension	25	1	Petition	69					Laid on table.		
Webb, Benjamin	(See Wm. H. Bedford)	28	1		262							
Webb, Charles	Pension	2	2	Rep. of Secretary War.	649	Whole House	Jan. 3, 1793	Favorable	214	Passed.		
Webb, Charles M.	Payment for horse lost in United States service.	14	1	Petition	300	Claims	March 1, 1816	Adverse.		Laid on table.		
Webb, Col. Charles, heirs of.	For arrears of pay	24	1	Petition	140	Invalid Pensions.						
Webb, Col. Charles, heirs of.	For arrears of pay	24	2	Petition	267	Rev. Pensions				Discharged; laid on table.		
Webb, Col. Charles, heirs of.	For arrears of pay	25	2	Petition	585	Rev. Pensions				Discharged; laid on table.		
Webb, Col. Charles, heirs of.	For arrears of pay	26	1	Resolution	938	Invalid Pensions.						
Webb, Constant	Increase of pension	10	2	House bill	499	Whole House	Feb. 20, 1809	Favorable	158	Passed	Passed	App'd March 3, 1809
Webb, Cornelius	Pension	25	2	Petition	271	Rev. Pensions				Discharged; laid on table.		

List of private claims presented to the House of Representatives of the United States from the 1st to the 31st Congress, inclusive—Continued.

Names of claimants.	Nature or object of the claim.	Congress.	Session.	How brought before the House of Reps.	Page of journal.	To what committee of the House referred.	No. or date of the report.	Nature of the report.	No. of the bill.	How disposed of by the House of Reps.	How disposed of by the Senate.	Date of the act of Congress, and remarks.
Webb, Cornelius	Pension	26	2	Resolution	117	Rev. Pensions.						
Webb, Daniel, and James Comstock.	Grant of lands in lieu of lands entered by them.	25	2	Petition	983	Public Lands	....	....	......	Discharged; laid on table.		
Webb, Eli	Compensation for constructing railroad.	23	2	Petition	235	Claims.						
Webb, Eli	Compensation for constructing railroad.	24	1	Petition	282	Claims	339	Adverse	......	Laid on table.		
Webb, Eliza	(See Orange Webb, widow of)	15	1	....	223							
Webb, George	Additional compensation for services, and to be reimbursed for certain moneys lost.	1	3	Petition	388	....	....	Ref'd to Sec. Treasury.				
Webb, George	Additional compensation for services, and to be reimbursed for certain moneys lost.	2	1	Rep. of Secretary Treasury.	471	Select	Jan. 4, 1792	Favorable	158	Referred to Committee Whole House.		
Webb, George, representatives of.	Liquidation and settlement of accounts.	13	1	Petition	89	Pens. & Rev. Cl'ms.						
Webb, George, representatives of.	Liquidation and settlement of accounts.	13	3	Petition	666	Rev. Claims.						
Webb, George, representatives of.	Liquidation and settlement of accounts.	14	1	Petition	346	Pens. & Rev. Cl'ms.						
Webb, George, representatives of.	Liquidation and settlement of accounts.	14	2	Petition	90	Pens. & Rev. Cl'ms.						
Webb, George	Restoration of pension	17	1	Petition	45	Rev. Pensions	....	....	......	Discharged; laid on table.		
Webb, George	(See William H. Bedford)	28	1	....	262							
Webb, Isaac, (Ky.)	Benefit of act for relief of surviving revolutionary officers.	22	1	Petition	289	Rev. Claims	Feb. 21, 1832	Adverse	......	Laid on table.		
Webb, Isaac	(See Charles Webb, heirs of)	24	1	....	140							
Webb, Isaiah	(See William H. Bedford)	28	1	....	262							
Webb, John	Compensation for property destroyed by enemy.	2	2	Petition	686	....	....	....	......	Laid on table.		
Webb, John B., *et al*	(See Joseph Webb, heirs of)	26	2	....	60							
Webb, John C	Payment for lands bought of Creeks and sold by United States.	25	2	Memorial	919	Public Lands	....	....	......	Discharged.		
Webb, John C	Payment for lands bought of Creeks and sold by United States.	26	1	Petition	178	Public Lands.						
Webb, Joseph, jr	Pension	22	2	Petition	63	Invalid Pensions	Feb. 15, 1833	Favorable	738	Referred to Committee Whole House.		
Webb, Joseph, jr	Pension	23	1	Petition	44	Invalid Pensions	1	Favorable	1	Passed	Passed	App'd June 25, 1834
Webb, Joseph, heirs of	Indemnity for property destroyed by British.	26	2	Petition	60	Claims.						
Webb, Joseph, heirs of	Indemnity for property destroyed by British.	27	2	Petition	509	Claims.						
Webb, Joseph, heirs of	Indemnity for property destroyed by British.	27	3	Petition	139	Claims	205	Adverse	......	Laid on table.		
Webb, Joseph, heirs of	Indemnity for property destroyed by British.	28	1	Petition	346	Claims	243	Adverse	......	Laid on table.		
Webb, Joseph, (Maine)	Increase of pension	31	1	Petition	257	Invalid Pensions.						
Webb, Josiah H	Compensation for wounds received by Indians whilst mail carrier.	9	1	Petition	309	Claims.						
Webb, Josiah H	Compensation for wounds received by Indians whilst mail carrier.	11	2	Petition	115	Select	Dec. 18, 1809	Favorable	38	Referred to Committee Whole House.		

List of private claims presented to the House of Representatives of the United States from the 1st to the 31st Congress, inclusive—Continued.

Names of claimants.	Nature or object of the claim.	Congress.	Session.	How brought before the House of Reps.	Page of journal.	To what committee of the House referred.	No. or date of the report.	Nature of the report.	No. of the bill.	How disposed of by the House of Reps.	How disposed of by the Senate.	Date of the act of Congress, and remarks.
Webb, Josiah H	Compensation for wounds received by Indians whilst mail carrier.	11	3	Petition	465	Select.						
Webb, Josiah H	Compensation for wounds received by Indians whilst mail carrier.	12	1	Petition	23	Select	Nov. 22, 1811	Favorable	9	Passed	Passed	App'd Dec. 12, 1811
Webb, Josiah H	Increase of pension	21	1	Petition	38	P. Of. & P. Roads.	183	Favorable	225	Referred to Committee Whole House.		
Webb, Josiah H	Increase of pension	21	2	House bill	264	Whole House	Feb. 4, 1831	Favorable	225	Rejected.		
Webb, Josiah H	Increase of pension	22	1	Petition	27	P. Of. & P. Roads	77	Favorable	153	Passed.		
Webb, Josiah H	Grant of annuity	27	2	House bill	274	Whole House	Jan. 25, 1842	Favorable	74	Passed	Passed	App'd May 18, 1842
Webb, Josiah H	Grant of annuity	27	3	House bill	53	Whole House	Dec. 14, 1842	Favorable	615	Passed	Passed	App'd Dec. 24, 1842
Webb, Josiah H	Grant of annuity	27	3	House bill	394	Whole House	Feb. 17, 1843	Favorable	804	Passed	Passed	App'd March 3, 1843
Webb, Captain Lewis	Commutation pay	24	1	Resolution	545	Rev. Claims.						
Webb, Captain Lewis	Commutation pay	24	2			Rev. Claims.						
Webb, Captain Lewis	Commutation pay	25	2	Petition	542	Claims				Discharged; laid on table.		
Webb, Captain Lewis	Commutation pay	25	3	Resolution	275	Rev. Claims				Discbaged.		
Webb, Captain Lewis	Commutation pay	26	1	Petition	167	Rev. Claims.						
Webb, Mary	Compensation for services and death of husband in revolutionary war.	9	2	Petition	549	Claims	Mar. 3, 1807			Laid on table.		
Webb, Moses	Restoration of pension	17	1	Petition	285							Leave to withdraw.
Webb, Orange, for James Vaeuxen.	Relief in consequence of the condemnation of sugars among the wreck of the Gratitude.	5	3	Petition	497					Laid on table.		
Webb, Orange	Permission to import goods ordered prior to proclamation in 1800.	12	1	Petition	265	Whole House						See bill No. 46.
Webb, Orange, widow of.	Renewal of patent	15	1		223	Judiciary	Mar. 13, 1818	Adverse				Leave to withdraw.
Webb, Robert, *et al.*, heirs	(See Pleasant Thatcher)	24	1	Petition	105							
Webb, Thomas, (N. Y.).	Release from judgment	21	1	Petition	295	Judiciary	Feb. 18, 1830	Adverse		Laid on table.		
Webb, William, and Conyers White.	Settlement of claim for cattle sold to and for use of revolutionary army.	1	3	Petition	359					Referred to Secretary War.		
Webb, William, and Conyers White.	Settlement of claim for cattle sold to and for use of revolutionary army.	2	1	Rep. of Secretary War	580					Laid on table.		
Webb, William, and Conyers White.	Settlement of claim for cattle sold to and for use of revolutionary army.	4	1	Petition	438	Claims	May 7, 1796	Adverse				Leave to withdraw.
Webb, William, and Conyers White.	Settlement of claim for cattle sold to and for use of revolutionary army.	5	3	Petition	464	Claims	Mar. 8, 1802	Adverse.		Laid on table.		
Webb, William, and Conyers White.	Settlement of claim for cattle sold to and for use of revolutionary army.	7	1	Petition	90	Claims.						
Webb, William, and Conyers White.	Settlement of claim for cattle sold to and for use of revolutionary army.	11	2	Petition	118	Claims.						
Webb, William, and Conyers White.	Settlement of claim for cattle sold to and for usa of revolutionary army.	12	2	Petition	574	Claims.						
Webb, William, and Conyers White.	Settlement of claim for cattle sold to and for use of revolutionary army.	23	2	Petition	38	Rev. Claims.						

List of private claims presented to the House of Representatives of the United States from the 1st to the 31st Congress, inclusive—Continued.

Names of claimants.	Nature or object of the claim.	Congress.	Session.	How brought before the House of Reps.	Page of journal.	To what committee of the House referred.	No. or date of the report	Nature of the report.	No. of the bill.	How disposed of by the House of Reps.	How disposed of by the Senate.	Date of the act of Congress, and remarks.
Webb, William, and Conyers White.	Settlement of claim for cattle sold to and for use of revolutionary army.	24	1	Petition	64	Claims.						
Webb, William, and Conyers White.	Settlement of claim for cattle sold to and for use of revolutionary army.	24	2	Petition	39	Rev. Claims.						
Webb, William, and Conyers White.	Settlement of claim for cattle sold to and for use of revolutionary army.	25	2	Petition	72	Rev. Claims.						
Webb, William, and Conyers White.	Settlement of claim for cattle sold to and for use of revolutionary army.	25	3	Petition	226	Rev. Claims				Discharged; laid on table.		
Webb, William, and Conyers White.	Settlement of claim for cattle sold to and for use of revolutionary army.	26	1	Petition	167	Rev. Claims				Discharged; laid on table.		
Webber, Benjamin	Arrears of pension	25	2	Petition	403	Rev. Pensions				Discharged; laid on table.		
Webber, Benjamin	Arrears of pension	26	1	Petition	175	Rev. Pensions				Discharged; laid on table.		
Webber, Christiana	(See John Webber, widow of.)	31	1		595							
Webber, John	Pension	19	1	Petition	128	Military Pensions	164	Adverse		Laid on table.		
Webber, John, widow of.	Pension and bounty land	31	1	Petition	595	Rev. Pensions	442	Favorable	372	Referred to Committee Whole House.		
Webber John, (D. C.)	Increase of pension	21	2	Petition	218	Military Pensions.						
Webber, John	Additional compensation for taking census.	22	1	Petition	42	Claims	435	Favorable	535	Referred to Committee Whole House.		
Webber, John	Additional compensation for taking census.	23	1	Petition	34	Claims	10	Favorable	10	Passed	Passed	App'd May 10, 1834
Webber, John A.	Compensation as military storekeeper.	29	1	Petition	474	Military Affairs				Discharged; laid on table.		
Webber, Seth, and others.	Reimbursement of money paid on copper improperly charged.	15	2	Petition	186	Com. and Manuf.	Mar. 1, 1819	Favorable	302	Passed	Passed	App'd March 3, 1819
Webber, Stephen	Pension	22	1	Petition	122	Rev. Pensions	Dec. 29, 1831	Adverse		Laid on table.		
Webber, William	Confirmation of title to land	22	1	House bill	421	Public Lands	Feb. 28, 1832	Favorable	425	Passed	Passed	App'd June 25, 1832
Webhorn, Benjamin, *et al.*	(See Wm. L. Hupper, *et al.*)	14	2		39							
Webler, John, widow of.	Pension and bounty land for services in Mexican war.	31	1	Petition	595	Rev. Pensions	442	Favorable	372	Referred to Committee Whole House.		
Webster, Charles	(See John Needham, *et al.*)	15	1		136							
Webster, David, *et al.*	Pre emption right to land	26	1	Petition	1004	Public Lands.						
Webster, Elizabeth	Extension of pension	28	1	Petition	839	Whole House.						
Webster, Hannah	Pension	28	2	Petition	135	Rev. Claims.						
Webster, Hiram B., (N. O.)	Authority to enter certain lands	28	1	Petition	77	Priv. Land Claims.	9	Favorable	35	Passed	Passed	App'd June 1, 1844
Webster, Humphrey	Pension	14	1	Petition	63	Pens. & Rev. Cl'm.	April 11, 1816	Favorable	171	Passed	Passed	App'd April 30, 1816
Webster, Humphrey	Increase of pension	14	2	Petition	45	Pens. & Rev. Cl'ms.	Jan. 29, 1817	Favorable	91	Referred to Committee Whole House.		
Webster, Humphrey	Increase of pension	15	1	Petition	63	Pens. & Rev. Cl'ms.				Discharged; laid on table.		
Webster, Isaac	Pension	2	2	Rep. of Secretary War.	649	Whole House	Jan. 3, 1793	Favorable	214	Passed		See act Feb. 28, 1793
Webster, Isaac	Pension	3	1	Rep. of Secretary War.	131	Select	May 26, 1794	Refer'd to Secretary War.	J. R. 12	Passed	Passed	App'd June 9, 1794
Webster, Isaac	Pension	4	2	Res. and docs.	614	Claims	Feb. 6, 1797	Favorable	224	Passed.		
Webster, Isaac	Pension	5	2	House bill	147	Whole House	Jan. 11, 1798	Favorable	38	Passed	Passed	App'd Feb. 2, 1798

List of private claims presented to the House of Representatives of the United States from the 1st to the 31st Congress, inclusive—Continued.

Names of claimants.	Nature or object of the claim.	Congress.	Session.	How brought before the House of Reps.	Page of journal.	To what committee of the House referred.	No. or date of the report.	Nature of the report.	No. of the bill.	How disposed of by the House of Reps.	How disposed of by the Senate.	Date of the act of Congress, and remarks.
Webster, John A.	Indemnity for horses killed in service during war of 1812.	14	1	Petition	317	Claims				Discharged; laid on table.		
Webster, John A., representatives of.	Indemnity for property lost while sailing master in U. S. navy.	19	1	Senate bill	300	Claims	138	With't amend.	48	Passed	Passed	App'd May 20, 1826
Webster, John	Pension	23	1	Senate bill	501	Naval Affairs	April 18, 1834	With amend.	28	Passed	Passed	App'd June 30, 1834
Webster, John	For settlement of accounts, &c.	13	3	Petition	521	Claims	Dec. 28, 1814	Favorable	248	Passed	Passed	App'd Feb. 13, 1815
Webster, John, collector.	To be allowed his portion of certain fines.	15	1	Petition	237	Ways and Means.				Discharged; laid on table.		
Webster, John, collector.	To be allowed his portion of certain fines.	16	1	Petition	198	Select	89	Favorable	136	Referred to Committee Whole House.		
Webster, John, collector.	To be allowed his portion of certain fines.	16	2	House bill	176				136	Passed	Passed	App'd Mar. 3, 1821
Webster, John, collector.	For settlement of accounts as collector.	15	2	Petition	78	Select	112	Favorable	295	Passed.		
Webster, John, collector.	For settlement of accounts as collector.	16	1	Petition	198	Select.						
Webster, John	For balance due as collector	20	2	Petition	203	Ways and Means.				Discharged; laid on table.		
Webster, John	For balance due as collector	21	1	Petition	358	Claims				Discharged; laid on table.		
Webster, John B.	Restoration of pension	17	1	Petition	124	Rev. Pensions				Discharged; laid on table.		
Webster, John, surety of.	Release from liability	25	2	Petition	279	Judiciary				Discharged; laid on table.		
Webster, John, surety of.	Release from liability	25	3	Petition	120	Claims	57	Adverse		Laid on table.		
Webster, John, surety of.	Release from liability	26	1	Petition	339	Claims.						
Webster, John, surety of.	Release from liability	27	2	Petition	154	Claims	493	Adverse.		Laid on table.		
Webster, Capt. Lucian B.	Commission as assistant quartermaster.	29	1	Petition	65	Military Affairs	23	Adverse		Laid on table.		
Webster, Mary	(See Peter Webster, widow of.)	19	1		250							
Webster, Noah	Permission to import dictionary free of duty.	18	2	Petition	80	Ways and Means.	Jan. 10, 1825	Favorable	263	Passed	Passed	App'd March 3, 1825
Webster, Noah	Extension of patent for spelling book.	21	1	Petition	39	Judiciary				Discharged; laid on table.		
Webster, Peter, widow of.	Pension	19	1	Petition	250	Military Pensions.	164	Adverse.		Laid on table.		
Webster, Sally	Pension	26	1	Petition	303	Naval Affairs.						
Webster, Thomas	Pension	14	1	Petition	136	Pens. & Rev. Cl'ms.	Mar. 23, 1816					Leave to withdraw.
Webster, Thomas	Pension	15	1	Petition	83	Pens. & Rev. Cl'ms.				Discharged; laid on table.		
Wedderburn, William	(See Alexander Scott, and others, assignee of)	9	1		192							
Weddington, William L.	Confirmation of title to land	25	2	Documents	281	Priv. Land Claims.	Jan. 20, 1838	Adverse		Laid on table.		
Weed, Alexander	Pension	31	2	Petition	67	Invalid Pensions.						
Weed, Benjamin	Pension	21	2	Petition	208	Military Pensions.						
Weed, Benjamin	Pension	22	1	Petition	163	Rev. Pensions.				Discharged; laid on table.		
Weed, Calvin	(See Hannah Weed)	13	2		172							
Weed, Maj. Elijah J., widow of.	Pension	25	3	House bill	244	Whole House			525			
Weed, Maj. Elijah J., administrator of.	Equitable settlement of accounts.	28	2	Petition	299	Claims	155	Favorable	627	Referred to Committee Whole House.		
Weed, Maj. Elijah J., administrator of.	Equitable settlement of accounts.	29	1	Petition	124	Claims	29	Favorable	35	Passed.		

List of private claims presented to the House of Representatives of the United States from the 1st to the 31st Congress, inclusive—Continued.

Names of claimants.	Nature or object of the claim.	Congress.	Session.	How brought before the House of Reps.	Page of journal.	To what committee of the House referred.	No. or date of the report.	Nature of the report.	No. of the bill.	How disposed of by the House of Reps.	How disposed of by the Senate.	Date of the act of Congress, and remarks.
Weed, Maj. Elijah J., administrator of.	Equitable settlement of accounts	30	1	Petition	153	Claims	56	Favorable	41	Laid on table.		
Weed, Maj. Elijah J., administrator of.	Equitable settlement of accounts	30	2	Petition	118	Claims						Leave to withdraw.
Weed, Elnathan	Pension	22	1	Petition	36	Rev. Pensions	112	Favorable	193	Referred to Committee Whole House.		
Weed, Elnathan	Pension	22	2	House bill	66	Whole House			193			
Weed, Hannah	Relief in consequence of death of son at Queenstown.	13	2	Petition	172	Claims	Feb. 7, 1814			Referred to Committee Whole House.		
Weed, Hannah	Relief in consequence of death of son at Queenstown.	13	3	Petition	485	Claims				Discharged.		
Weed, Hannah	Relief in consequence of death of son at Queenstown.	14	1	Petition	83	Claims				Discharged; laid on table.		
Weed, Hannah	Relief in consequence of death of son at Queenstown.	15	1	Petition	168	Claims	Feb. 11, 1818	Adverse		Laid on table.		
Weed, Reuben	Payment for corn and oats furnished United States army.	2	1	Petition	441					Referred to Secretary of Treasury.		
Weed, Reuben	Payment for corn and oats furnished United States army.	3	2	Rep. of Secretary Treasury.	284					Laid on table.		
Weed, Seth	Pension	10	1	House bill	232	Whole House	Mar. 17, 1808	Favorable	78	Passed	Passed	App'd April 25, 1808
Weed, Seth	Increase of pension	15	2	Petition	215	Pens. & Rev. Cl'ms.				Discharged; laid on table.		
Weed, Seth	Increase of pension	16	1	Petition	137					Referred to Secretary War.		
Weed, Seth	Increase of pension	16	2	Rep't of Secretary War.	36					Referred to Committee Whole House.		
Weed, Smith, &c., executors of.	(See John Stafford)	21	1		104							
Weeden, Peleg, (R. I.)	Pension	21	2	Petition	159	Military Pensions.						
Weeden, Peleg, (R. I.)	Pension	22	1	Petition	80	Rev. Pensions	411	Favorable	511	Referred to Committee Whole House.		
Weeden, William	For a grant of land in lieu of land sold by State of Arkansas.	22	1	Petition	33	Public Lands	Mar. 6, 1832	Favorable	448	Referred to Committee Whole House.		
Weeden, William	For a grant of land in lieu of land sold by State of Arkansas.	23	1	Petition	75	Public Lands	Jan. 7, 1834	Favorable	137	Passed	Passed	App'd June 28, 1834
Weeden, Dr. Frederick	Compensation for services as surgeon, and furnishing medicines.	26	1	Petition	338	Claims.						
Weeden, Dr. Frederick	Compensation for services as surgeon, and furnishing medicines.	26	2	Petition	124	Claims	106	Adverse		Laid on table.		
Weeden, Dr. Frederick	Compensation for services as surgeon, and furnishing medicines.	27	1	Petition	312							Leave to withdraw.
Weeden, Dr. Frederick	Compensation for five barrels of pork furnished volunteers.	26	1	Petition	339	Claims.						
Weeden, John, executor of.	Pension	26	1	Petition	283	Rev. Pensions	490	Adverse		Laid on table.		
Weeden, John, executor of.	Pension	27	2	Petition	58	Rev. Pensions	784	Adverse.		Laid on table		
Weeks, David P.	Increase of pension	25	3	Petition	570	Invalid Pensions.						
Weeks, George	Relief in relation to lot No. 61, public lands on Rouse's point, New York.	25	2	Petition	274	Claims	516	Adverse		Laid on table.		
Weeks, Gilbert	Compensation for use of vessel in transporting articles for use of army.	18	1	Petition	85	Pens. & Rev. Cl'ms.	Feb. 23, 1824	Adverse		Laid on table.		

List of private claims presented to the House of Representatives of the United States from the 1st *to the* 31st *Congress, inclusive*—Continued.

Names of claimants.	Nature or object of the claim.	Congress.	Session.	How brought before the House of Reps.	Page of journal.	To what committee of the House referred.	No. or date of the report.	Nature of the report.	No. of the bill.	How disposed of by the House of Reps.	How disposed of by the Senate.	Date of the act of Congress, and remarks.
Weeks, Gilbert	Compensation for use of vessel in transporting articles for use of army.	21	1	Petition	57	Pens. & Rev. Cl'ms.				Discharged; laid on table.		
Weeks, James	Payment for vessel and cargo scuttled by order of committee of safety.	2	1	Petition	456					Rejected.		
Weeks, James	Payment for vessel and cargo scuttled by order of committee of safety.	2	2	Petition	634					Rejected.		
Weeks, Jedediah	Restoration of pension	17	2	Petition	224					Referred to Secretary of War.		
Weeks, John	Arrears of pay for military services.	30	2	Petition	263	Claims.						
Weeks, Joseph P.	Remission of certain penalties	11	2	Petition	313	Com. and Manuf.	Mar. 30, 1810	Favorable	85	Passed	Passed	App'd May 1, 1810
Weeks, Phebe	(See Thomas Weeks, widow of.)	25	2		729							
Weeks, Philip, and wife.	(See Robert Durkee, heirs of)	11	1		60							
Weeks, Samuel	Increase of pension	24	2	Petition	125	Rev. Pensions	100	Adverse		Laid on table.		
Weeks, Sarah C.	Allowance of two years' pension	28	1	Petition	950							
Weeks, Thomas, widow of.	Pension	25	2	Petition	729	Rev. Pensions	791	Favorable	740	Passed.		
Weeks, Thomas, widow of.	Pension	26	1	Petition	172	Rev. Pensions.						
Weeks, William	Release from payment of money as paymaster, U. States vouchers lost.	4	1	Petition	370	Claims	Jan. 15, 1796	Adverse				Leave to withdraw.
Weems, Henry	Pension	12	1	House bill	361	Whole House.	June 8, 1812	Favorable	138	Passed	Passed	App'd July 5, 1812
Weems, John, widow of.	Compensation for services, &c., raising cannon of Barney's flotilla.	31	1	Petition	1251	Claims.						
Weems, John, widow of.	Compensation for services, &c., raising cannon of Barney's flotilla.	31	2	Documents	365	Claims.						
Weems, Rachel	(See John Weems, widow of)	31	1		1251							
Weems, Stephen H.	Compensation for services as consul at Guatemala.	31	1	Petition	1034	Ways and Means.	Jan. 19, 1850	Gen. appropr'n bill.	334	Passed	Passed	App'd Sept. 30, 1850
Weidman, Mary	(See Philip Weidman, widow of)	27	2		85							
Weidman, Philip, widow of	Relief for suffering and loss by Indians in Florida.	27	2	Memorial	85	Claims	771	Adverse		Laid on table.		
Weidner, Michael	Pension	29	1	Petition	280	Rev. Pensions.						
Weidner, Michael	Pension	29	2		54	Rev. Pensions.						
Weightman, assistant surgeon.	Payment for professional services.	25	3	Documents	205	Claims.						
Weightman, assistant surgeon.	Payment for professional services.	26	1	Petition & docs.	170	Claims.						
Weightman, assistant surgeon.	Payment for professional services.	26	2	Petition	135	Claims.						
Weiland, F. Y.	Donation of land in lieu of losses by Choctaw treaty.	24	1	Petition	57	Public Lands	208	Favorable	208	Referred to Committee Whole House.		
Weire, Alice	(See Samuel Kenny, late widow of.)	2	1		463							
Weir, David	Donation of land	31	1	Petition	700	Priv. Land Claims.						
Weir, Robert	Compensation for historical painting.	24	2	House bill	128	Ways and Means.	Dec. 27, 1836	General bill	776	Passed	Passed	App'd March 3, 1837
Weir, Samuel, *et al.*	Pre-emption right to land purchased from Indians.	3	2	Memorial	332	Select	Feb. 24, 1795			Laid on table.		

List of private claims presented to the House of Representatives of the United States from the 1st to the 31st Congress, inclusive—Continued.

Names of claimants.	Nature or object of the claim.	Congress.	Session.	How brought before the House of Reps.	Page of journal.	To what committee of the House referred.	No. or date of the report.	Nature of the report.	No. of the bill.	How disposed of by the House of Reps.	How disposed of by the Senate.	Date of the act of Congress, and remarks.
Weismen, Charles	Indemnity for French spoliations prior to 1800.	26	1	Memorial	182	Foreign Affairs	343	Favorable; bill	319	Referred to Committee Whole House.		
Weiss, Henry	Pension	3	1	Rep't of Secretary War.	131	Select	May 26, 1794	Res. to refer to Sec. War.	J. R. 12	Passed	Passed	App'd June 9, 1794
Weissenfels, Chas. Fred'k	Reimbursements of money expended during revolutionary war.	3	1	Petition	76					Referred to Secretary War.		
Weissenfels, Chas. Fred'k	Reimbursements of money expended during revolutionary war.	3	1	Rep. of Secretary War.	93	Select.						
Weissenfels, Chas. Fred'k.	Reimbursements of money expended during revolutionary war.	3	1	Report of Select Committee.	127					Laid on table.		
Weissenfels, Chas. Fred'k.	Increase of compensation as late collector of customs, New York	2	2	Memorial	628					Referred to Secretary Treasury.		
Weissenfels, Chas. Fred'k.	Increase of compensation as late collector of customs, New York.	3	2	Rep. of Secretary Treasury.	234	Select	Jan. 26, 1795	Favorable	75	Passed	Passed	App'd Feb. 14, 1795
Weissenfels, Colonel F. H., heir of.	Compensation for sacrifices of her ancestor in revolutionary war.	25	3	Memorial	81	Rev. Claims				Discharged; laid on table.		
Weissenfels, Colonel F. H., heir of	Compensation for sacrifices of her ancestor in revolutionary war.	26	1	Petition	166	Rev. Claims	614	Adverse		Laid on table.		
Weissenfels, Colonel F. H., heir of.	Compensation for sacrifices of her ancestor in revolutionary war.	27	2	Petition	227	Rev. Claims	1072	Adverse		Laid on table.		
Weist, Henry	Compensation for mail service	9	1	Petition	307					Referred to Postmaster General.		
Weist, Henry	Compensation for mail service	9	1	Rep't of Postmaster General.	313	Claims	Mar. 12, 1806	Adverse		Laid on table.		
Weist, Henry	Compensation for mail service	12	2	Petition	689					Referred to Postmaster General.		
Weist, Henry	Compensation for mail service	14	2	Petition	314							
Weist, Henry	Compensation for mail service	22	2	Petition	218	P. Of. & P. Roads.						
Weitzel, Elizabeth	(See John Weitzel, widow of.)	25	2		658							
Weitzel, George	Settlement of claim	2	2	Petition	674					Referred to Secretary Treasury.		
Weitzel, George	Settlement of claim	3	2	Report of Secretary Treasury	281					Laid on table.		
Weitzel, John, widow of.	Payment for provisions and arms furnished.	25	2	Petition	658	Rev. Claims				Discharged; laid on table.		
Welch, Dr. Andrew	Payment for medical attendance in Florida.	25	3	Documents	205	Claims.						
Welch, Dr. Andrew	Payment for medical attendance in Florida.	26	1	Petition	170	Claims.						
Welch, Dr. Andrew	Payment for medical attendance in Florida.	26	2	Petition	135	Claims.						
Welch, David	Compensation for revolutionary services.	2	1	Petition	455					Referred to Secretary of War.		
Welch, David	Pension	3	1	Rep. of Secretary War.	131	Select	May 26, 1794	Favorable	J. R. 12	Passed	Passed	App'd June 9, 1794
Welch, David	Pension	4	1	Res. and report	415	Claims	Feb. 18, 1796	Favorable	156	Passed	Passed	App'd April 20, 1796
Welch, David	Pension	27	3	Senate bill	551	Whole House			104	Passed.		App'd March 3, 1843
Welch, John, heirs of	Pension	24	2	Petition	90	Rev. Pensions				Discharged; laid on table.		
Welch, John, *et al.*, (Cherokees)	Restoration of lands	29	1	Memorial	1124	Indian Affairs.						
Welch, Oliver	Permission to change entry of land.	24	1	Documents	261	Priv. Land Claims.	Feb. 5, 1836	Favorable	295	Referred to Committee Whole House.		
Welch, Oliver	Permission to change entry of land.	24	2	House bill	200	Whole House			295			

List of private claims presented to the House of Representatives of the United States from the 1st to the 31st Congress, inclusive—Continued.

3—77

Names of claimants.	Nature or object of the claim.	Congress.	Session.	How brought before the House of Reps.	Page of journal.	To what committee of the House referred.	No. or date of the report.	Nature of the report.	No. of the bill.	How disposed of by the House of Reps.	How disposed of by the Senate.	Date of the act of Congress, and remarks.
Welch, Oliver	Permission to change entry of land	25	2	Documents	43	Priv. Land Claims.	144	Favorable	165	Referred to Committee Whole House.		
Welch, Oliver	Permission to change entry of land	25	3	House bill	375	Whole House	Jan. 25, 1839	Favorable	165	Passed.		
Welch, Oliver	Permission to change entry of land	26	1	Petition	179	Priv. Land Claims.	94	Favorable	90	Passed	Passed	App'd July 20, 1840
Weld, Edward	Permission to fund lost certificate	9	2	Petition	509	Ways and Means	Jan. 21, 1807	Favorable	543			
Weld, Edward	Permission to fund lost certificate	10	1	Petition	14	Ways and Means	Nov. 23, 1807	Favorable	38	Passed	Passed	App'd Mar. 11, 1808
Weld, Hannah, *et al.*	(See Richard Toppan, heirs of, and others.)	28	1		514							
Weld, Moses	Pension	20	1	Petition	45	Military Pensions	Dec. 12, 1828	Favorable	311	Passed.		
Weld, Moses	Restoration of pension	21	1	Petition	48	Military Pensions	Jan. 5, 1830	Favorable	72	Passed	Passed	App'd May 30, 1830
Welden, Catharine	(See John Welden, widow of.)	27	2		524							
Welden, John, widow of	(See John Walden, widow of.)	27	2		524							
Welden, Ira	Pension	21	1	Petition	471	Military Pensions				Discharged; laid on table.		
Wellborn, jr., Isaac, and William.	Confirmation of title to land	23	1	Petition	656	Public Lands.						
Wellborn, jr., Isaac, and William.	Confirmation of title to land	23	2	Petition	40	Public Lands	10	Favorable	583			
Wellborn, jr., Isaac, and William.	Confirmation of title to land	24	1	Petition	155	Public Lands	227	Favorable	239	Referred to Committee Whole House.		
Wellborn, jr., Isaac, and William.	Confirmation of title to land	24	2	House bill	62	Whole House	Dec. 16, 1836	Favorable	239	Referred to Committee Whole House.		
Wellborn, jr., Isaac, and William, (Ala.)	Confirmation of title to land	25	2	Petition	87	Petition	91	Favorable	108	Passed	Passed	App'd April 6, 1838
Welborn, Lewis	Pension	27	2	Petition	219	Invalid Pensions	784	Adverse		Laid on table.		
Welborn, William	Compensation for transporting baggage during war of 1812.	20	2	Resolution	56	Claims	Jan. 5, 1829	Adverse		Laid on table.		
Weller, Frederick	Restoration of pension	28	1	Petition	72	Rev. Pensions.						
Weller, Frederick	Increase of pension	30	2	Petition	385	Rev. Pensions.						
Weller, Samuel	Payment for materials furnished at Platsburg, New York.	27	3	Petition	220	Claims	130	Favorable	749	Passed	Passed	App'd March 3, 1843
Wellington, Samuel	Pension	20	2	Petition	43	Military Pensions	Jan. 21, 1829	Adverse		Laid on table.		
Wellington, Samuel	Increase of pension	21	1	Petition	168	Military Pensions	April 6, 1830	Adverse		Laid on table.		
Wellman, jr., Jacob	Pension	3	2	Rep. of Secretary War.	337	Claims	Feb. 28, 1795	Favorable	130	Laid on table.		
Wellman, jr., Jacob	Pension	4	1	Rep. of Secretary War.	145	Claims	Feb. 18, 1796	Favorable	156	Passed	Passed	App'd April 20, 1796
Wellman, Mercy	(See Aquilla Cleaveland, widow of.)	25	3		127							
Wellman, Timothy	(See Denton Hall and Nathan)	10	1		173							
Wellman, Timothy, *et al.*	(See Francis Lewis Taney, trustee of.)	10	1		254							
Wells, Amasa	Pension	22	1	Petition	593	Rev. Pensions				Discharged; laid on table.		
Wells, Amos	Compensation as a secret agent, United States army.	23	1	Petition	191	Claims.						
Wells, Amos	Compensation as a secret agent, United States army.	31	2	Petition	123	Claims.						
Wells, Arnold	For settlement of accounts	4	1	Rep. of Secretary Treasury.	388	Claims	74	Adverse		Laid on table.		
Wells, Arnold	For settlement of accounts	4	1	Rep. of Secretary Treasury.	388	Claims	74	Adverse		Laid on table.		
Wells, Asa	Remuneration for expenses incurred in forcing revenue laws.	14	1	Petition	459	Claims				Discharged; laid on table.		

List of private claims presented to the House of Representatives of the United States from the 1st to the 31st Congress, inclusive—**Continued.**

Names of claimants.	Nature or object of the claim.	Congress.	Session.	How brought before the House of Reps.	Page of journal.	To what committee of the House referred.	No. or date of the report.	Nature of the report.	No. of the bill.	How disposed of by the House of Reps.	How disposed of by the Senate.	Date of the act of Congress, and remarks.
Wells, Asa	Remuneration for expenses incurred in forcing revenue laws.	14	2	Petition	79	Claims	Feb. 13, 1817	Favorable	136	Passed	Passed	App'd March 3, 1817
Wells, Bayze	Pension	3	1	Rep. of Secretary War.	131	Select	May 26, 1794	Favorable	J. R. 12	Passed	Passed	App'd June 9, 1794
Wells, Bayze	Pension	9	1	Petition	209	Claims	Mar. 28, 1806					Leave to withdraw.
Wells, Bayze, heir of	Pension	26	1	Petition	706	Rev. Pensions.						
Wells, Bazaleel	Remuneration of money paid in settlement of accounts of land under act for relief of purchasers.	18	1	Petition	95	Public Lands	Jan. 27, 1824	Favorable	87	Passed	Passed	App'd May 18, 1824
Wells, Benjamin, collector at Somerset, Ohio.	For his share of fines for violation of revenue laws; which have been remitted by government.	15	1	Petition	237	Ways and Means				Discharged; laid on table.		
Wells, Benjamin, collector at Somerset, Ohio.	For his share of fines for violation of revenue laws; which have been remitted by government.	16	1	Petition	170	Select	Mar. 20, 1820	Adverse.		Laid on table.		
Wells, Benjamin, collector at Somerset, Ohio.	For his share of fines for violation of revenue laws; which have been remitted by government.	17	1	Petition	133	Judiciary.						
Wells, Benjamin, collector at Somerset, Ohio.	For his share of fines for violation of revenue laws; which have been remitted by government.	17	2	Petition	47	Judiciary.						
Wells, Benjamin, collector at Somerset, Ohio.	For his share of fines for violation of revenue laws; which have been remitted by government.	18	1	Petition	132	Ways and Means	Feb. 16, 1824					Leave to withdraw.
Wells, Benjamin, collector at Somerset, Ohio.	For his share of fines for violation of revenue laws; which have been remitted by government.	18	2	Petition	136	Ways and Means.						
Wells, Benjamin, collector at Somerset, Ohio.	For his share of fines for violation of revenue laws; which have been remitted by government.	19	1	Resolution	61	Judiciary	184	Adverse		Laid on table.		
Wells, Benjamin, collector at Somerset, Ohio.	For his share of fines for violation of revenue laws; which have been remitted by government.	21	1	Petition	144	Claims				Discharged; laid on table.		
Wells, Benjamin, collector at Somerset, Ohio.	For his share of fines for violation of revenue laws; which have been remitted by government.	22	2	Petition	189	Claims	Jan. 30, 1832	Adverse		Laid on table.		
Wells, Benjamin, collector at Somerset, Ohio.	Compensation for losses, &c., sustained, in person and property, in discharge of duties as collector of internal revenue.	5	2	Petition	82	Claims	May 2, 1798	Deferred.				
Wells, Benjamin, collector at Somerset, Ohio.	Compensation for losses, &c., sustained, in person and property, in discharge of duties as collector of internal revenue.	6	1	Petition	610	Claims	April 21, 1800	Deferred.				
Wells, Benjamin, collector at Somerset, Ohio.	Compensation for losses, &c., sustained, in person and property, in discharge of duties as collector of internal revenue.	7	2	Petition	258	Claims	Feb. 1, 1803	Deferred.				
Wells, Benjamin, collector at Somerset, Ohio.	Compensation for losses, &c., sustained, in person and property, in discharge of duties as collector of internal revenue.	8	1	Petition	446	Claims	Nov. 30, 1803	Favorable	144	Referred to Committee Whole House.		

List of private claims presented to the House of Representatives of the United States from the 1st to the 31st Congress, inclusive—Continued.

Names of claimants.	Nature or object of the claim.	Congress.	Session.	How brought before the House of Reps.	Page of journal.	To what committee of the House referred.	No. or date of the report.	Nature of the report.	No. of the bill.	How disposed of by the House of Reps.	How disposed of by the Senate.	Date of the act of Congress, and remarks.
Wells, Benjamin, & others.	For settlement of accounts as collector of revenue.	13	3	Petition	521	Claims	Dec. 28, 1814	Favorable	248	Passed	Passed, with amendment.	App'd Feb. 13, 1815
Wells, Benjamin	For settlement of accounts by comptroller on principles of equity.	15	2	Petition	78	Select	112	Favorable	295	Passed.		
Wells, Benjamin	For settlement of accounts by comptroller on principles of equity.	18	2	Petition	91	Judiciary				Referred to Secretary Treasury.		
Wells, Benjamin	For settlement of accounts by comptroller on principles of equity.	20	2	Petition	264	Judiciary				Discharged; laid on table.		
Wells, Benjamin	For interest on settlement of his accounts at the Treasury Department.	19	1	Resolution	465	Claims				Discharged; laid on table.		
Wells, Benjamin	For interest on settlement of his accounts at the Treasury Department.	20	2	Petition	176	Claims	Feb. 4, 1829	Adverse		Laid on table.		
Wells, Benjamin	To be paid balance due him as collector of revenue.	20	2	Petition	203	Ways and Means				Discharged; laid on table.		
Wells, Benjamin	To be paid balance due him as collector of revenue.	21	1	Petition	358	Clamis				Discharged; laid on table.		
Wells, Benjamin	To refund the amount of cost paid by him on several suits.	19	1	Resolution	326	Ways and Means	184	Favorable	246	Passed.		
Wells, Benjamin	To refund the amount of cost paid by him on several suits.	19	2	Resolution	58	Ways and Means	Feb. 17, 1827	Adverse		Laid on table.		
Wells, Benjamin	To refund the amount of cost paid by him on several suits.	20	1	Resolution	175	Claims	Feb. 8, 1828	Adverse		Laid on table.		
Wells, Benjamin	To refund the amount of cost paid by him on several suits.	20	2	Petition	60	Ways and Means	Dec. 17, 1828	Adverse		Laid on table.		
Wells, Benjamin	Compensation for services rendered, and for reimbursement of money expended while in office of commissary department during revolutionary war.	21	1	Petition	116	Rev. Claims	241	Favorable	297	Passed	Passed	App'd May 29, 1830
Wells, Benjamin	Compensation for services as forage master, revolutionary war.	15	1	Petition	378	Pens. & Rev. Cl'ms.	Mar. 30, 1829	Adverse		Laid on table.		
Wells, Benjamin	Compensation for services as forage master, revolutionary war.	15	2	Petition	146					Referred to Secretary War.		
Wells, Benjamin	Compensation for services as forage master, revolutionary war.	20	2	Petition	79	Rev. Claims	Jan. 29, 1829	Adverse		Laid on table.		
Wells, Benjamin	Increase of pension	22	2	Petition	345	Invalid Pensions.						
Wells, Benjamin	(See John Wells)	15	1		237							
Wells, Cornelius	Increase of pension	21	2	Petition	212	Military Pensions.						
Wells, Cornelius	Increase of pension	22	1	Petition	192	Rev. Pensions				Discharged; laid on table.		
Wells, Cornelius	Increase of pension	27	3	Petition	283	Rev. Pensions.						
Wells, Cornelius	Increase of pension	28	1	Petition	262	Rev. Pensions.						
Wells, Cuff, former widow of.	Pension	26	1	Petition	706	Rev. Pensions.						
Wells, Cuff, former widow of.	Pension	26	2	Petition	274	Rev. Pensions	132	Favorable; bill	640	Referred to Committee Whole House.		
Wells, Cuff, former widow of.	Pension	27	2	Petition	59	Rev. Pensions	289	Favorable; bill	257	Passed	Passed	App'd Aug. 27, 1842
Wells, Captain	(See Mississppi cavalry)	15	1		287							
Wells, Dorothy, (La.)	Confirmation of title to land	20	1	Petition	166	Public Lands	Feb. 7, 1828	Adverse		Laid on table.		
Wells, Dorothy, (La.)	Confirmation of title to land	20	2	Petition	50	Public Lands	Dec. 31, 1828	Adverse		Laid on table.		

List of private claims presented to the House of Representatives of the United States from the 1st to the 31st Congress, inclusive—Continued.

Names of claimants.	Nature or object of the claim.	Congress.	Session.	How brought before the House of Reps.	Page of journal.	To what committee of the House referred.	No. or date of the report.	Nature of the report.	No. of the bill.	How disposed of by the House of Reps.	How disposed of by the Senate.	Date of the act of Congress, and remarks.
Wells, Dorothy, (La.)	Confirmation of title to land	21	1	Petition	51	Public Lands	95	Favorable	252	Referred to Committee Whole House.		
Wells, Dorothy, (La.)	Confirmation of title to land	21	2	House bill	265	Whole House	Feb. 4, 1831	Favorable	252	Passed.		
Wells, Dorothy, (La.)	Confirmation of title to land	22	1	Petition	32	Public Lands	60	Favorable	120	Passed	Passed	App'd June 25, 1832
Wells, Eleanor	(See Eleanor Wills)	20	1		46							
Wells, Elisha, (N. Y.)	Pension	22	2	Petition	176	Invalid Pensions.						
Wells, Elizabeth	(See Horace Wells, widow of)	31	2		134							
Wells, Lt George R.	Indemnity for damages recovered against him for arresting persons by order of government.	15	1	Petition	132	Claims	Mar. 27, 1818	Favorable	52	Passed	Passed	App'd April 20, 1818
Wells, Henry	(See Samuel Brown, *et al.*)	4	1		370							
Wells, Henry	Pension	26	1	Petition	388	Invalid Pensions	530	Favorable	426	Referred to Committee Whole House.		
Wells, Henry	Pension	27	2	Petition	60	Invalid Pensions	146	Favorable	193	Passed	Passed	App'd July 27, 1842
Wells, Horace, widow of.	Compensation for the benefit of discovery by husband of exhilerating gas.	31	2	Petition	134	Patents.						
Wells, Isaac	Pension	25	2	Petition	629	Rev. Pensions				Discharged; laid on table.		
Wells, James H.	(See Charles Sigourney and J. H. Wells.)	12	2		564							
Wells, James, (Ohio)	Pension	21	1	Petition	168	Military Pensions	April 6, 1830	Adverse		Laid on table.		
Wells, John Kent	Relief as Canadian refugee	9	2	Petition	530					Laid on table.		
Wells, John Kent	Relief as Canadian refugee	11	3	Petition	447					Referred to Secretary of War.		
Wells, John & Benjamin	Drawback on certain goods	15	2	Petition	77	Com. and Manuf				Discharged; laid on table.		
Wells, John & Benjamin	Drawback on certain goods	20	2	Petition	113	Ways and Means				Discharged; laid on table.		
Wells, John & Benjamin	Drawback on certain goods	22	1	Petition	142	Ways and Means				Discharged; laid on table.		
Wells, John, (N. Y.)	Compensat'n for property destroyed by order of General McComb, 1812.	13	3	Petition	723	Claims	Feb. 15, 1815	Favorable	297	Passed	Passed	App'd March 3, 1815
Wells, John, collector of Westmoreland county, Pennsylvania.	For settlement of accounts as collector of internal revenue, &c.	13	3	Petition	521	Claims	Dec. 28, 1814	Favorable	248	Passed	Passed, with amendments.	App'd Feb. 13, 1815
Wells, John, collector of Westmoreland county, Pennsylvania.	For settlement of accounts as collector of internal revenue, &c.	15	1	Petition	237	Select				Discharged; laid on table.		
Wells, John, collector of Westmoreland county, Pennsylvania.	For settlement of accounts as collector of internal revenue, &c.	15	2	Petition	55	Select	49	Favorable	240	Referred to Committee Whole House.		
Wells, John, collector of Westmoreland county, Pennsylvania.	For settlement of accounts as collector of internal revenue, &c.	16	1	Petition	148	Select	71	Favorable	90	Referred to Committee Whole House.		
Wells, John, collector of Westmoreland county, Pennsylvania.	For settlement of accounts as collector of internal revenue, &c.	17	1	Petition	99	Ways and Means	Jan. 18, 1822	Adverse		Laid on table.		
Wells, John, collector of Westmoreland county, Pennsylvania.	For settlement of accounts as collector of internal revenue, &c.	17	2	Petition	71	Ways and Means	Jan. 17, 1823	Adverse		Laid on table.		

List of private claims presented to the House of Representatives of the United States from the 1st to the 31st Congress, inclusive—Continued.

Names of claimants.	Nature or object of the claim.	Congress.	Session.	How brought before the House of Reps.	Page of journal.	To what committee of the House referred.	No. or date of the report.	Nature of the report.	No. of the bill.	How disposed of by the House of Reps.	How disposed of by the Senate.	Date of the act of Congress, and remarks.
Wells, John, collector of Westmoreland county, Pennsylvania.	For settlement of accounts as collector of internal revenue, &c.	19	1	Petition	245	Ways and Means				Laid on table.		
Wells, John, collector of Westmoreland county, Pennsylvania.	For settlement of accounts as collector of internal revenue, &c.	20	1	Petition	195	Claims	Feb. 6, 1828	Adverse		Laid on table.		
Wells, John, collector of Westmoreland county, Pennsylvania.	For settlement of accounts as collector of internal revenue, &c.	20	2	Petition	113	Claims	Jan. 15, 1829	Adverse		Laid on table.		
Wells, John, collector of Westmoreland county, Pennsylvania.	For settlement of accounts as collector of internal revenue, &c.	21	1	Petition	83	Claims	30	Adverse		Laid on table.		
Wells, John, (Pa.)	Pension	21	1	Petition	523	Military Pensions	May 1, 1830	Adverse		Laid on table.		
Wells, John	Correct error in land entry	22	1	Petition	121	Priv. Land Claims.						
Wells, John	Pension	25	2	Petition	605	Naval Affairs				Discharged; laid on table.		
Wells, John, executor of	Payment for canteens furnished army.	23	1	Petition	639	Rev. Claims.						
Wells, John, and others	Indemnity for French spoliations prior to 1800.	27	2	Petition	46	Foreign Affairs.						
Wells, Joseph	Payment for property taken and used by United States troops, war of 1812.	17	1	Petition	256	Claims				Discharged; laid on table.		
Wells, Joseph	Payment for property taken and used by United States troops, war of 1812.	21	1	Petition	135	Claims	Jan. 6, 1830	Adverse		Laid on table.		
Wells, Capt. Jos., (N. Y.)	Compensation for services rendered and money advanced in United States service.	21	1	Petition	377	Military Affairs				Discharged; laid on table.		
Wells, Lemuel	Permission to import goods ordered prior to proclamation of 1810.	12	1	Petition	134	Whole House	Jan. 7, 1812	Favorable	46	Referred to Committee Whole House.		
Wells, Lemuel, heirs of	Bounty land for military services	29	1	Memorial	807	Priv. Land Claims.						
Wells, Lemuel, heirs of	Bounty land for military services	31	1	Petition	711	Priv. Land Claims.	July 25, 1850	Favorable	362	Referred to Committee Whole House.		
Wells, Levi, executors of	Confirmation of title to land	14	2	Petition	148	Public Lands	60	Favorable		Ref'd to Com. W. H.		
Wells, Mary	Compensation or support for loss of son Daniel, killed at Baltimore.	16	1	Petition	174	Military Affairs	Feb. 18, 1820	Adverse		Laid on table.		
Wells, Mary	Compensation or support for loss of son Daniel, killed at Baltimore.	17	2	Petition	208	Pens. & Rev. Cl'ms.				Discharged		Leave to withdraw.
Wells, Mary	Compensation or support for loss of son Daniel, killed at Baltimore.	27	2	Petition	879	Militia.						
Wells, Mary	Compensation or support for loss of son Daniel, killed at Baltimore.	27	3	Petition	441	Militia.						
Wells, Mary	(See William Wells)	13	2		197, 214							
Wells & Miller, (Balt.)	Indemnity for French spoliations prior to 1800.	31	1	Petition	840	Foreign Affairs	335	Favorable	318	Referred to Committee Whole House.		
Wells, Paoli	Pension	25	3	Petition	127	Rev. Pensions	Jan. 16, 1839	Adverse		Laid on table.		

List of private claims presented to the House of Representatives of the United States from the 1st to the 31st Congress, inclusive—Continued.

Names of claimants.	Nature or object of the claim.	Congress.	Session.	How brought before the House of Reps.	Page of journal.	To what committee of the House referred.	No. or date of the report.	Nature of the report.	No. of the bill.	How disposed of by the House of Reps.	How disposed of by the Senate.	Date of the act of Congress, and remarks.
Wells, Peter	Pension	24	1	Petition	670	Rev. Pensions				Discharged; laid on table.		
Wells, Reno	Indemnity for Indian depredations.	22	1	Petition	194	Claims	Mar. 1, 1832	Adverse		Laid on table.		
Wells, Riuwah, jr.	Indemnity for loss of property in Black Hawk war.	30	1	Memorial, &c.	147, 148	Claims	48	Adverse		Laid on table.		
Wells, Richard, and others	Payment for bills of credit heretofore issued by Congress.	1	2	Petition	165	Select	Mar. 20, 1790			Laid on table.		
Wells, Richard, sen.	(See Captain Edward Dyer, representative of.)	28	2		104							
Wells, Samuel	Pension	11	3	House bill	604	Claims	Mar. 1, 1811	Favorable	218	Passed	Passed	App'd March 3, 1811
Wells, Samuel	Increase of pension	12	1	Petition	41	Claims	June 12, 1812	Adverse		Laid on table.		
Wells, Simeon	Restoration of pension	17	2	Petition	40	Rev. Pensions				Discharged		Leave to withdraw.
Wells & Spring	Indemnity in consequence of protest of government draft.	31	1	Petition	434	Naval Affairs.						
Wells, Silas	Bounty land for military services.	26	1	Petition	947	Public Lands.	627	Adverse		Laid on table.		
Wells, Stephen	Pension	4	1	House bill	470	Whole House	Feb. 18, 1796	Favorable	156	Passed	Passed	App'd April 20, 1796
Wells, Col. Thomas	(See Henry O'Kelly, assignee of)	2	2		697							
Wells, Thomas	Compensation for revolutionary services	4	1	Petition	379	Claims.						
Wells, Thomas	Compensation for revolutionary services.	4	2	Petition	614	Claims	Feb. 21, 1797	Report		Laid on table.		
Wells, Thomas	Compensation for revolutionary services.	5	2	Petition	89	Claims.						
Wells, Thomas C.	Compensation for extra services as keeper of Potomac bridge.	28	2	Petition	367	Dist. of Columbia.	79			Discharged.		
Wells, Thomas C.	Compensation for extra services as keeper of Potomac bridge.	29	1	Petition	331	Public Buildings & Grounds.						
Wells, Thomas C.	Compensation for extra services as keeper of Potomac bridge.	31	1	Petition	589	Dist. of Columbia.	272	Favorable	253	Laid on table.		
Wells, Thomas H.	Permission to enter land	28	2	Petition	299	Public Lands.						
Wells, Titus	(See Ebenezer Stocker, administrator of.)	26	1		182							
Wells, Titus	(See Abraham Tours, administrator of.)	26	1		182							
Wells, William	Pre emption right to land	10	1	Senate bill	199	Public Lands	March 9, 1808	With't amend.	9	Passed with amendm't	Concurred in	App'd Mar. 18, 1808
Wells, William	Compensation for agent and interpreter.	12	1	Petition	59	Claims.						
Wells, William, widow of	Compensation for corn taken by Gen. Harrison.	13	2	Petition	197, 214	Claims	Jan. 12, 1814	Favorable	84	Passed.		
Wells, William, widow of	Compensation for corn taken by Gen. Harrison.	14	2	Petition	235	Claims	Feb. 12, 1817	Favorable	130	Referred to Committee Whole House.		
Wells, William	Indemnity for loss of steamer Caroline destroyed by British authorities in 1837.	27	2	Petition	326	Foreign Affairs.						
Wells, William Waine, jr.	Indemnity for land granted to him by Miami Indians	22	1	Senate bill	795	Indian Affairs	Jan. 1, 1832	With't amend.	99	Passed		App'd July 14, 1332
Welsh, Ann	(See Captain John Walsh, widow of.)	2	2		631							
Welsh, Henry	Increase of pension	25	2	Petition	404	Rev. Pensions				Discharged; laid on table.		
Welsh, James	Settlement of accounts for revolutionary services.	2	2	Petition	652					Laid on table.		
Welsh, James	Pension	19	2	Resolution	52	Military Pensions.	Jan. 26, 1827	Adverse		Laid on table.		

List of private claims presented to the House of Representatives of the United States from the 1st to the 31st Congress, inclusive—Continued.

Names of claimants.	Nature or object of the claim.	Congress.	Session.	How brought before the House of Reps.	Page of journal.	To what committee of the House referred.	No. or date of the report.	Nature of the report.	No. of the bill.	How disposed of by the House of Reps.	How disposed of by the Senate.	Date of the act of Congress, and remarks.
Welsh, James	Pension	20	2	Resolution	187	Military Pensions				Discharged; laid on table.		
Welsh, J.	Indemnity for French spoliations prior to 1800.	26	1	Memorial	182	Foreign Affairs	343	Favorable; bill	319	Referred to Committee Whole House.		
Welsh, John, heirs of	Pension	27	2	Petition	1030	Rev. Pensions				Discharged; laid on table.		
Welsh, Captain John, widow of.	Compensation for loss of husband killed by Indians.	2	2	Petition	631					Laid on table.		
Welsh, Captain John, widow of.	Compensation for loss of husband killed by Indians.	4	2	Petition	630	Claims.						
Welsh, Captain John, widow of.	Compensation for loss of husband killed by Indians.	5	2	Petition	97	Whole House.						
Welsh, Captain John, widow of.	Compensation for loss of husband killed by Indians.	10	1	Petition	101	Whole House.						
Welsh, Captain John, widow of.	Commutation pay	2	2	Petition	631					Laid on table.		
Welsh, Captain John, widow of.	Commutation pay	3	2	Petition	288	Claims				Laid on table.		
Welsh, Captain John, widow of.	Commutation pay	4	1	Resolution	373	Claims.						
Welsh, Captain John, widow of.	Commutation pay	4	2	Documents	614	Claims	Feb. 7, 1897	Adverse		Laid on table.		
Welsh, Captain John, widow of.	Commutation pay	5	2	Petition	108	Whole House	Dec. 19, 1797	Adverse		Laid on table.		
Welsh, Captain John, widow of.	Commutation pay	14	2	Petition	59	Pens. & Rev. Cl'ms.	19	Adverse.		Laid on table.		
Welsh, Jonas	Permission to import coaco ordered prior to proclamation.	12	1	Petition	276	Com. and Manuf.						
Welsh, Captain Nathaniel, heirs of.	Bounty land for revolutionary services.	22	2	Petition	32	Public Lands.						
Welsh, Captain Nathaniel, heirs of.	Bounty land for revolutionary services.	23	1	Petition	48	Public Lands	560	Adverse		Laid on table.		
Welsh, Nicholas	Increase of pension	14	2	Petition	376	Pens. & Rev. Cl'ms.	Jan. 29, 1817	Favorable	91	Passed	Passed	App'd March 3, 1817
Welsh, Nicholas	Increase of pension	15	2	Petition	20	Pens. & Rev. Cl'ms.	Feb. 5, 1819	Favorable	308	Referred to Committee Whole House.		
Welsh, Nicholas	Increase of pension	17	1	Petition	78	Pens. & Rev. C'm.						
Welsh, Nicholas	Increase of pension	17	2	Petition	31	Pens. & Rev. Cl'ms.	Dec. 16, 1822	Favorable	195	Referred to Committee Whole House.		
Welsh, Robert P.	Indemnity for property lost by the blowing up of ship Fulton.	25	2	Petition	544	Naval Affairs				Discharged.		
Welsh, Robert P.	Indemnity for property lost by the blowing up of ship Fulton.	26	1	Petition	180	Naval Affairs.						
Welsh, Thomas N.	(See Churchill Gibbs, administrator of.)	30	1		165							
Welsh, William, heirs of.	Pension	27	2	Memorial	1030	Rev. Pensions				Discharged; laid on table.		
Welton, Jonah	Pension	24	1	Petition	853	Rev. Pensions.						
Welty, Abraham	Change location of land	13	2	Petition	259	Public Lands				Discharged.		
Wendall, Joseph H.	Settlement of accounts as late paymaster United States army.	22	2	Petition	91	Claims	33	Adverse		Laid on table.		
Wendall, Jacob	Bounty on fishing vessel	15	1	Senate bill	388	Com. and Manuf.	May 27, 1818	General bill	41	Passed	Passed	App'd April 4, 1818
Wendell, Henry R	Arrears of pension	28	2	Petition	353	Invalid Pensions.						
Wendell, Henry R	Arrears of pension	29	1	Petition	203	Invalid Pensions.						

List of private claims presented to the House of Representatives of the United States from the 1st to the 31st Congress, inclusive—Continued.

Names of claimants.	Nature or object of the claim.	Congress.	Session.	How brought before the House of Reps.	Page of journal.	To what committee of the House referred.	No. or date of the report.	Nature of the report.	No. of the bill.	How disposed of by the House of Reps.	How disposed of by the Senate.	Date of the act of Congress, and remarks.
Wendell, Henry R	Arrears of pension	30	1	Petition	55	Invalid Pensions				Discharged; laid on table.		
Wendell, Henry R	Arrears of pension	30	2	Petition	136	Invalid Pensions.						
Wendell, Jane	Confirmation of title to land	20	1	Resolution	28	Public Lands	42	Favorable	34	Passed	Passed	App'd April 22, 1828
Wendell, Capt. John H	For benefit of act of 15th May, 1828.	20	2	Petition	205	Rev. Claims	Feb. 5, 1829	Adverse		Laid on table.		
Wendell, Capt. John H	For benefit of act of 15th May, 1828.	21	1	Petition	104	Military Pensions	119	Favorable	160	Passed	Passed	App'd May 28, 1830
Wendell, Capt. John H	For benefit of act of 15th May, 1828.	21	2	Petition	54	Rev. Claims	24	Favorable	543	Referred to Committee Whole House.		
Wendell, Capt. John H	For benefit of act of 15th May, 1828.	22	1	Petition	44	Rev. Claims	57	Favorable	108	Passed	Passed	App'd July 4, 1832
Wendell, Capt. John H., heirs of.	Commutation pay	24	1	Petition	63	Rev. Claims	394	Adverse		Laid on table.		
Wendell & Van Benthuysen.	Extra compensation as public printers.	30	2	Petition	415	Printing.						
Wendell & Van Benthuysen.	Extra compensation as public printers.	31	2	Petition	283	Printing.						
Wendell, William	Bounty land for military services	31	1	Petition	720	Public Lands.						
Wendeman, Philip	Compensation for Indian depredations.	25	3	Petition	121	Claims	162	Adverse		Laid on table.		
Wendt, Frederick	Pension	17	1	Petition	155	Rev. Pensions				Discharged; laid on table.		
Wenman, Richard	Compensation as crier of district court.	18	2	Petition	186	Judiciary.						
Wenman, Richard	Compensation as crier of district court.	20	1	Petition	46	Judiciary				Dischraged; laid on table.		
Wentling, George	Pension	28	1	Petition	318	Rev. Pensions	323	Favorable	231	Passed.		
Wentling, George	Pension	28	2	Petition	55	Rev. Pensions	49	Favorable	525	Passed.		
Wentling, George	Pension	29	1	Senate bill	605	Rev. Pensions	April 6, 1846	With't amend.	117	Passed		App'd May 13, 1846
Winteringer, Nathan	(See Nathan Winteringer)	23	1		525							
Wentworth, Amos	Pension	25	3	Petition	223	Rev. Pensions				Discharged.		
Wentworth, Amos, widow of.	Pension	26	1	Petition	175	Rev. Pensions	714	Adverse		Laid on table.		
Wentworth, Lydia	(See Amos Wentworth, widow of)	25	3		223							
Wentworth, Polly	Pension	27	3	Petition	59	Invalid Pensions.						
Wentwood, Eliza, *et al.*	(See Godfrey Wentwood, heirs of)	18	1		453							
Wentwood, Godfrey	Indemnity for property destroyed by British.	6	1	Petition	634	Select.						
Wentwood, Godfrey, heirs of.	Pension for revolutionary services.	18	1	Petition	453	Pens. & Rev. Cl'ms.						Leave to withdraw.
Wentwood, Godfrey, heirs of.	Pension for revolutionary services.	25	3	Petition	495	Rev. Claims				Discharged.		
Wentwood, Godfrey, heirs of.	Pension for revolutionary services.	26	1	Petition	165	Rev. Claims.						
Wentwood, Godfrey, heirs of.	Pension for revolutionary services.	26	2	Petition	76	Rev. Claims	169	Adverse		Laid on table.		
Wentwood, Godfrey, heirs of.	Pension for revolutionary services.	28	1	Petition	89	Rev. Claims.						
Wentwood, Godfrey, heirs of.	Pension for revolutionary services.	28	2	Petition	45	Rev. Claims.						
Wentwood, Godfrey, heirs of.	Pension for revolutionary services.	29	1	Petition	91	Rev. Claims	26	Adverse		Laid on table.		

List of private claims presented to the House of Representatives of the United States from the 1st to the 31st Congress, inclusive—Continued.

Names of claimants.	Nature or object of the claim.	Congress.	Session.	How brought before the House of Reps.	Page of journal.	To what committee of the House referred.	No. or date of the report.	Nature of the report.	No. of the bill.	How disposed of by the House of Reps.	How disposed of by the Senate.	Date of the act of Congress, and remarks.
3—78 Wentwood, Godfrey, heirs of.	Pension for revolutionary services.	30	1	Petition	103	Rev. Claims.						
Wentwood, Godfrey, heirs of.	Pension for revolutionary services.	31	1	Petition	628	Rev. Claims.						
Wentwood, Sally C	(See Godfrey Wentwood, heirs of)	18	1		453							
Wentz, George W., and others.	(See Abraham Nanna)	18	1		291							
Wentz, Hannah	(See Abraham Nanna)	12	1		11							
Wereat, John	Allowance of depreciation of money advanced to army.	2	1	Petition	578					Referred to Secretary Treasury.		
Wereat, John	Allowance of depreciation of money advanced to army.	2	2	Rep. of Secretary Treasury.	626					Laid on table.		
Wereat, John	For supplies furnished United States army.	2	2	Petition	683					Referred to Secretary Treasury.		
Wereat, John	For supplies furnished United States army.	3	1	Rep. of Secretary Treasury.	78							Leave to withdraw.
Werey, Catherine	(See Michael Werey, heirs of.)	27	2		524							
Werey, Elizabeth	(See Michael Werey, heirs of.)	27	2		524							
Werey, Michael, heirs of	Bounty land	27	2	Petition	524	Rev. Pensions	784	Adverse		Laid on table.		
Werner, Christopher	Repayment of money improperly paid into the treasury.	24	1	Memorial	924	Claims	758	Favorable	692	Referred to Committee Whole House.		
Werner, Christopher	Repayment of money improperly paid into the treasury.	25	2	Memorial	37	Claims	54	Favorable	66	Passed.		
Werner, Christopher	Repayment of money improperly paid into the treasury.	26	1	Petition	168	Claims	Feb. 29, 1840			Referred to Patents.		
Werner, William	Bounty land and other compensation for services in exploring expedition.	9	1	President's mess.	284					Laid on table.		
Werner, William	Bounty land and other compensation for services in exploring expedition.	9	2	President's mess.	470							
Werner, William	Bounty land and other compensation for services in exploring expedition.	9	2	President's mess.	507	Select	Jan. 23, 1807	Favorable	183	Passed	Passed	App'd March 3, 1807
Wernwag, Lewis	Extension of patent	14	1	Petition	179	Select				Discharged; laid on table.		
Wernwag, Lewis	Extension of patent	14	2	Petition	213	Select				Discharged; laid on table.		
Wernwag, Lewis	Extension of patent	18	2	Petition	91	Judiciary				Discharged		Leave to withdraw.
Wernwag, Lewis	Extension of patent	20	1	Petition	280	Judiciary				Discharged; laid on table.		
Wernwag, Lewis	Extension of patent	21	1	Petition	50	Judiciary				Discharged; laid on table.		
Wernwag, Lewis, & Co	Compensation for work done on Cumberland road.	24	1	Resolution	207	Claims.						
Wernway, Lewis, & Co	Compensation for work done on Cumberland road.	24	2	Petition	209	Claims.						
Wert *alias* West, William H.	(See Wm. H. West.)	25	2		397		836					
Wesche, John H., of the firm of Wesche & Co.	Indemnity for losses under contract annulled by government for supplies for Mexican army.	30	2	Petition	138	Claims.						

List of private claims presented to the House of Representatives of the United States from the 1st to the 31st Congress, inclusive—Continued.

Names of claimants.	Nature or object of the claim.	Congress.	Session.	How brought before the House of Reps.	Page of journal.	To what committee of the House referred.	No. or date of the report.	Nature of the report.	No. of the bill.	How disposed of by the House of Reps.	How disposed of by the Senate.	Date of the act of Congress, and remarks.
Wesche, John H., of the firm of Wesche & Co.	Indemnity for losses under contract annulled by government for supplies for Mexican army.	31	1	Petition	509	Foreign Affairs.						
Wesley, Benjamin F.	Pension	24	2	Petition	48	Invalid Pensions	49	Favorable	796	Referred to Committee Whole House.		
Wesley, Benjamin F.	Pension	25	2	Petition	39	Invalid Pensions	427	Favorable	434	Passed.		
Wesley, Benjamin F.	Pension	25	3	Petition	163	Invalid Pensions	148	Favorable	1017	Passed.		
Wesley, Benjamin F.	Pension	26	1	Petition	162	Invalid Pensions	273	Adverse		Laid on table.		
Wesley, Benjamin F.	Pension	28	1	Petition	583	Invalid Pensions.						
Wesley, Benjamin F.	Pension	28	2	Petition	187	Invalid Pensions.						
Wesley, Benjamin F.	Pension	31	1	Petition	193	Invalid Pensions	49	Favorable	79	Referred to Committee Whole House.		
Wesley, Benjamin F.	Pension	31	2	House bill	75	Invalid Pensions	Dec. 20, 1850	Favorable	79	Laid on table.		
Wesson, James	Compensation for revolutionary services.	2	1	Petition	475					Referred to Secretary of War.		
West, Alva, widow of	Pension	25	2	Petition	116	Rev. Pensions.						
West, Amos	Pension	25	3	Petition	216	Rev. Pensions				Discharged; laid on table.		
West, Ann B.	(See Charles West, widow of)	8	2		87							
West, Ann, by son	(See Jackson West, widow of)	24	2		44							
West, Ann	(See Hugh West, widow of)	16	2		78							
West, Benajah	Pension	22	1	Petition	187	Rev. Pensions				Discharged; laid on table.		
West, Benjamin	Pension	16	2	Resolution	31	Rev. Pensions	Feb. 15, 1821	Adverse				Leave to withdraw.
West, Benjamin	Pension	19	2	Petition	215	Military Pensions				Discharged.		
West, Benjamin, heirs of.	Asking government to purchase father's library.	19	2	Petition	38	Library	Feb. 24, 1827	Adverse		Laid on table.		
West, Charles, widow of.	Patent for bounty land	8	2	Petition	87	Claims.						
West, Charles, widow of.	Patent for bounty land	9	1	Petition	193	Priv. Land Claims.				Laid on table.		
West, Charles, widow of.	Patent for bounty land	9	2	Petition	646							Leave to withdraw.
West, Charles, (Md.)	Pension	20	2	Petition	288	Military Pensions				Discharged; laid on table.		
West, Eli	Pension	29	1	Petition	101	Invalid Pensions	433	Adverse		Laid on table.		
West, Emanuel J.	Pre-emption right to land	18	1	Petition	315	Public Lands				Discharged; laid on table.		
West, Feleciana	Reimbursement of duties on railroad iron.	30	1	House bill	793	Ways and Means			477	Referred to Committee Whole House.		
West, Feleciana	Reimbursement of duties on railroad iron.	31	1	House bill	1315	Whole House			261			
West, Gardner, widow of.	Arrears of pay for military services	30	2	Petition	360	Invalid Pensions	Feb. 13, 1849	Adverse		Laid on table.		
West, Gardner, widow of.	Arrears of pay for military services	31	1	Petition	417	Invalid Pensions	105	Favorable	122	Passed	Passed	App'd Sept. 16, 1850
West, George	Pension	29	1	Petition	591	Invalid Pensions	814	Favorable	539	Referred to Committee Whole House.		
West, Hezekiah	Compensation for revolutionary services.	16	1	Petition	126	Pens. & Rev. Cl'ms.	Feb. 21, 1820	Adverse		Laid on table.		
West, Hezekiah	Compensation for revolutionary services.	20	2	Resolution	166	Rev. Claims	Jan. 22, 1829	Adverse		Laid on table.		
West, Hezekiah	Compensation for revolutionary services.	21	1	Petition	67	Military Pensions	April 2, 1830	Adverse		Laid on table.		
West, Hugh	Additional compensation as surveyor of the port of Alexandria.	8	1	Memorial	574	Ways and Means.						
West, Hugh	Additional compensation as surveyor of the port of Alexandria.	9	1	Petition	242	Ways and Means.						

List of private claims presented to the House of Representatives of the United States from the 1st to the 31st Congress, inclusive—Continued.

Names of claimants.	Nature or object of the claim.	Congress.	Session.	How brought before the House of Reps.	Page of journal.	To what committee of the House referred.	No. or date of the report.	Nature of the report.	No. of the bill.	How disposed of by the House of Reps.	How disposed of by the Senate.	Date of the act of Congress, and remarks.
West, Hugh	Additional compensation as surveyor of the port of Alexandria.	9	2	Resolution	482	Ways and Means.						
West, Hugh, widow of	For proportion of certain vessels condemned.	16	2	Petition	78	Judiciary				Discharged; laid on table.		
West, Isaac	Pension	22	1	Petition	44	Rev. Pensions	371	Favorable	466	Passed.		
West, Jackson, widow of	Pension	24	2	Petition	44	Rev. Pensions	125	Favorable	805	Referred to Committee Whole House.		
West, Jackson, widow of	Pension	25	2	Petition	38	Rev. Pensions	163	Favorable	188	Passed	Passed	App'd June 28, 1838
West, John, heirs of	Compensation for services rendered and for clothing furnished during revolutionary war.	16	1	Petition	126	Pens. & Rev. Cl'ms.	Feb. 21, 1820	Adverse		Laid on table.		
West, John, heirs of	Compensation for services rendered and for clothing furnished during revolutionary war.	20	2	Resolution	166	Pens. & Rev. Cl'ms.	Jan. 22, 1829	Adverse		Laid on table.		
West, John, heirs of	Compensation for services rendered and for clothing furnished during revolutionary war.	21	1	Petition	67	Military Pensions	April 2, 1830	Adverse		Laid on table.		
West, John, heirs of	Compensation for services rendered and for clothing furnished during revolutionary war.	23	2	Petition	489	Rev. Pensions.						
West, John, heirs of	Compensation for services rendered and for clothing furnished during revolutionary war.	24	1	Petition	157	Rev. Claims				Discharged; laid on table.		
West, John S., late marshal of North Carolina.	Repayment of certain moneys erroneously paid into treasury.	11	3	Petition	472	Claims.						
West, John S., late marshal of North Carolina.	Repayment of certain moneys erroneously paid into treasury.	12	1	Petition	12	Claims	May 6, 1812	Favorable	83	Referred to Committee Whole House.		
West, John S., late marshal of North Carolina.	Repayment of certain moneys erroneously paid into treasury.	12	2	Petition	553	Claims.						
West, Joseph	For balance due as deputy paymaster general in revolutionary war.	3	1	Petition	68					Laid on table.		
West, Joseph, (Md.)	Pension	22	1	Petition	412	Rev. Claims.	June 26, 1832	Adverse		Laid on table.		
West, Joseph, (Md.)	Pension	24	1	Resolution	1035	Rev. Pensions.						
West, Joseph, (Md.)	Pension	24	2	Petition	84	Rev. Pensions				Discharged; laid on table.		
West, Joseph, (Md.)	Pension	25	2	Resolution	973	Rev. Pensions				Discharged; laid on table.		
West, Joseph, (Md.)	Pension	26	1	Petition	175	Rev. Pensions	490	Adverse		Discharged; laid on table.		
West, Judith	Indemnity for French spoliations prior to 1800.	26	1	Memorial	182	Foreign Affairs	343	Favorable; bill	319	Referred to Committee Whole House.		
West, Nathaniel, *et al.*	Drawback of duties	4	1	Memorial	383	Com. and Manuf.						
West, Nathaniel	Relief from penalties	13	2	Petition	314	Ways and Means	Mar. 29, 1814			Laid on table		Leave to withdraw.
West, Nathaniel	Indemnity for French spoliations prior to 1800.	26	1	Memorial	182	Foreign Affairs	343	Favorable; bill	319	Referred to Committee Whole House.		
West, Oliver, & Co.	(See Cook, Anthony, Mahon, *et al.*)	30	1		826							
West, Rebecca	Compensation for property destroyed by British.	15	2	Petition	148	Claims				Discharged; laid on table.		
West, Sarah	(See Gardner West, widow of)	30	2		360							
West, Capt. Thomas, heirs of.	Commutation pay	23	1	Petition	376	Rev. Claims.						
West, Capt. Thomas, heirs of.	Commutation pay	25	2	Petition	575	Rev. Claims				Discharged; laid on table		

List of private claims presented to the House of Representatives of the United States from the 1st to the 31st Congress, inclusive—Continued.

Names of claimants.	Nature or object of the claim.	Congress.	Session.	How brought before the House of Reps.	Page of journal.	To what committee of the House referred.	No. or date of the report.	Nature of the report.	No. of the bill.	How disposed of by the House of Reps.	How disposed of by the Senate.	Date of the act of Congress, and remarks.
West, Thomas	Pension	24	2	Petition	217	Rev. Pensions	179	Favorable	900	Referred to Committee Whole House.		
West, Thomas	Pension	25	2	Petition	38	Rev. Pensions	179	Favorable	204	Passed	Passed	App'd June 28, 1838
West, William W	(See Daniel C. Clark, assignees of)	25	2		397							
Westbrook, Andrew	Payment for property destroyed by British.	16	1	Petition	47	Select	May 11, 1820	Adverse				Leave to withdraw.
Westbrook, Andrew	Payment for property destroyed by British.	18	2	Petition	186	Claims.						
Westbrook, Andrew	Payment for property destroyed by British.	19	1	Petition	270	Claims	April 14, 1826	Adverse		Laid on table.		
Westbrook, Andrew	Payment for property destroyed by British.	19	2	Petition	30	Priv. Land Claims.	58	Favorable	397	Referred to Committee Whole House.		
Westbrook, Andrew	Payment for property destroyed by British.	20	1	Petition	33	Priv. Land Claims.	20	Favorable	16	Passed	Passed	App'd May 23, 1823
Westbrook, Andrew	Compensation for land taken by United States.	21	1	Petition	71	Military Affairs	Jan. 25, 1830	Adverse		Laid on table.		
Westbrook, Andrew	Compensation for land taken by United States.	22	1	Petition	226	Military Affairs	Feb. 13, 1832	Adverse		Laid on table.		
Westbrook, Andrew	Payment for material furnished and labor performed for United States.	22	1	Resolution	735	Claims.						
Westbrook, Frederick	For settlement of his accounts	17	2	Petition	30	Claims	Dec. 20, 1822	Adverse		Laid on table.		
Westbrook, Jonathan	Pension	21	2	Petition	48	Military Pensions.						
Westbrook, Jonathan	Pension	22	1	Petition	105	Rev. Pensions.						
Westbrook, Jonathan	Pension	22	1	Petition	164	Rev. Pensions.						
Westbrook, Samuel	Compensation for revolutionary services.	21	2	Petition	44	Rev. Claims.						
Westchester, ship, (N. Y.)	For new register	27	3	Senate bill	76	Whole House		With't amend.	23	Passed		App'd Dec. 23, 1842
Westcott, Caleb	Indemnity for destruction of property, revolutionary war.	4	1	Petition	467	Claims	May 31, 1796	Adverse		Laid on table.		
Westcott, Major John	Payment for money expended at Sackett's Harbor.	29	1	Petition	648	Claims.						
Westcott, Captain Joseph	Relief in consequence of dropping public money into the sea.	13	2	Petition	184	Claims	Feb. 28, 1814			Laid on table.		
Westcott, Captain Joseph	Relief in consequence of dropping public money into the sea.	14	2	Petition	95	Claims	Jan. 13, 1817	Adverse		Laid on table.		
Westcott, Joseph	Arrears of pension, &c	25	2	Petition	198	Claims	Jan. 30, 1838	Adverse		Referred to Claims.		
Westcott, Joseph	Pension	14	1	Petition	283	Pens. & Rev. Cl'ms.	April 11, 1816	Favorable	171	Passed	Passed	App'd April 30, 1816
Westcott, Joseph, (N. Y.)	Increase of pension	14	2	Petition	237	Pens. & Rev. Cl'ms.	Jan. 29, 1807	Favorable	91	Passed.		
Westcott, Joseph, (N. Y.)	Increase of pension	15	1	Petition	23	Pens. & Rev. Cl'ms.						
Westcott, Joseph, (N. Y.)	Increase of pension	15	2	House bill	41	Pens. & Rev. Cl'ms.	Nov. 26, 1818	Favorable	203	Passed	Passed	App'd March 3, 181
Westervelt, James	(See Matthew Du Bois)	12	1		141							
Westfall, Capt. Abraham, widow of.	Increase of pension	26	1	Petition	630	Rev. Pensions.						
Westfall, Capt. Abraham, widow of.	Increase of pension	26	2	Petition	195	Rev. Pensions.						
Westfall, Capt. Abraham, widow of.	Increase of pension	27	2	Petition	62	Rev. Pensions	784	Adverse		Laid on table.		
Westfall, Alfred	Payment for horse lost in Indian war.	25	2	Senate bill	1249	Claims	1062	With't amend.	201	Referred to Committee Whole House.		
Westfall, Charles W	(See Frederick Goetz)	16	1		274							
Westfall, Dinah	(See Capt. Ab'm Westfall, widow of.)	26	1		630							

List of private claims presented to the House of Representatives of the United States from the 1st *to the* 31st *Congress, inclusive*—Continued.

Names of claimants.	Nature or object of the claim.	Congress.	Session.	How brought before the House of Reps.	Page of journal.	To what committee of the House referred.	No. or date of the report.	Nature of the report.	No. of the bill.	How disposed of by the House of Reps.	How disposed of by the Senate.	Date of the act of Congress, and remarks.
Westfall, Nicholas F.	Compensation for revolutionary services.	1	3	Petition	380					Referred to Secretary of State.		
Westfall, Nicholas F.	Compensation for revolutionary services.	2	1	Petition	446	Select.						
Westfall, Nicholas F.	Compensation for revolutionary services.	2	1	House bill	463	Whole House	Nov. 29, 1791	Favorable	152, 159	Passed	Passed	App'd Mar. 27, 1792
Westfall, N. E.	Pension	14	1	Petition	323	Pens. & Rev. Cl'ms.	April 11, 1816	Favorable	171	Laid on table.		
Westlake, Josiah	Increase of pension	22	1	Resolution	499	Invalid Pensions				Discharged; laid on table.		
Westlake, Josiah	Increase of pension	22	2	Resolution	35	Invalid Pensions				Discharged; laid on table.		
Westlake, Josiah	Increase of pension	23	1	Petition	54	Invalid Pensions	286	Favorable	322	Referred to Committee Whole House.		
Westlake, Josiah	Increase of pension	23	2	House bill	336	Invalid Pensions	Feb. 6, 1835	Favorable	322	Passed.		
Westlake, Josiah	Increase of pension	24	1	Petition	275	Invalid Pensions	407	Favorable	417	Passed.		
Westlake, Josiah	Increase of pension	25	2	Resolution	38	Invalid Pensions	189	Favorable	215	Passed.		
Westlake, Josiah	Increase of pension	25	3	Petition	189	Invalid Pensions	140	Favorable	1007	Passed.		
Westlake, Josiah	Increase of pension	26	1	Petition	327	Invalid Pensions						
Westlake, Josiah	Increase of pension	26	2	Petition	55	Invalid Pensions	157	Favorable	669	Referred to Committee Whole House.		
Westlake, Josiah	Increase of pension	27	2	Petition	154	Invalid Pensions	924	Favorable	536	Referred to Committee Whole House.		
Westlake, Josiah	Increase of pension	27	3	House bill	89	Whole House	Dec. 23, 1842	Favorable	536	Passed.		
Westner, George	Permission to change location of land.	14	1	Petition	36	Public Lands	Jan. 4, 1816	Favorable		Passed	Passed	App'd Feb. 6, 1816
Westphal, Carl W.	(See Frederick Goetz)	16	1		274							
Weston, Cyrus	Pension	29	1	Petition	679	Invalid Pensions				Discharged; laid on table.		
Weston, Ezra, *et al.*	Fishing bounty	8	2	Petition	63	Select.						
Weston, Ezra, *et al.*	Fishing bounty	9	1	Petition	242	Com. and Manuf.						
Weston, Ezra, *et al.*	Fishing bounty	11	2	Petition	108	Com. and Manuf.						
Weston, Ezra, *et al.*	Indemnity for loss of vessel burnt by French in 1812.	12	1	Petition	199	Select				Referred to Secretary of State.		
Weston, Hannah	(See Josiah Weston, widow of)	29	1		219							
Weston, Josiah, widow of.	Pension	29	1	Petition	219	Rev. Pensions.						
Weston, Josiah, widow of.	Pension	30	1	Petition	359	Rev. Pensions	535	Adverse		Laid on table.		
Weston, Josiah, widow of.	Pension	31	1	Petition	439	Rev. Pensions	255	Adverse		Laid on table.		
Weston, Levi	Pension	25	2	Petition	181	Rev. Pensions				Discharged; laid on table.		
Westwood, John S., executor of.	Additional compensation as late inspector and surveyor.	26	1	Petition	622	Claims	429	Adverse		Laid on table.		
Wetherell, James	(See James Witherell)	25	2		197							
Wetherell, Joseph	(Not stated)	18	1	Petition	585							Leave to withdraw.
Wetmore, Alphonso	For settlement of accounts at Treasury Department.	23	1	Petition	47	Claims	223	Adverse		Laid on table		
Wetmore, Alphonso	Arrears of pension	28	1	Petition	273	Invalid Pensions	192	Adverse		Laid on table.		
Wetmore, Alphonso, surety of.	Release from liability	26	1	Petition	297	Judiciary				Discharged; laid on table.		
Wetmore, Alphonso, surety of.	Release from liability	26	2	Petition	78	Judiciary.						
Wetmore, Alphonso, surety of.	Release from liability	27	2	Petition	297	Judiciary	856	Adverse		Laid on table.		

List of private claims presented to the House of Representatives of the United States from the 1st to the 31st Congress, inclusive—Continued.

Names of claimants.	Nature or object of the claim.	Congress.	Session.	How brought before the House of Reps.	Page of journal.	To what committee of the House referred.	No. or date of the report.	Nature of the report.	No. of the bill.	How disposed of by the House of Reps.	How disposed of by the Senate.	Date of the act of Congress, and remarks.
Wetmore, Alphonso, surety of.	Release from liability	28	1	Petition	685	Judiciary.						
Wetmore, Chancey	(See Elisha Hubbard, administrator of.)	29	1		189							
Wetmore, Hezekiah	Compensation, &c., for services rendered as deputy paymaster general, revolutionary war.	3	1	Petition	103					Referred to Secretary Treasury.		
Wetmore, Hezekiah	Compensation, &c., for services rendered as deputy paymaster general, revolutionary war.	3	2	Rep. of Secretary Treasury.	284					Laid on table.		
Wetmore, Hezekiah, widow of.	Commutation and other pay	15	2	Petition	190	Pens. & Rev. Cl'ms.				Discharged; laid on table.		
Wetmore, Sarah	(See Hezekiah Wetmore, widow of.	15	2		190							
Wetmore, Wm. S., and James Hamilton.	For adjustment and payment of certain bonds.	31	1	Senate bill	520	Judiciary.						
Wetzel, William Y	(See A. L. Wills and W. Y. Wetyal.)	22	1		390							
Wever, Casper W	Compensation for superintending the improvements on Pennsylvania avenue.	26	1	Senate bill	836	Dist. of Columbia.	May 26, 1840	With't amend.	256	Referred to Committee Whole House.		
Wever, Casper W	Compensation for superintending the improvements on Pennsylvania avenue.	26	2	Senate bill	256	Whole House	Feb. 11, 1841	With't amend.	168			
Wever, Casper W	Compensation for superintending the improvements on Pennsylvania avenue.	26	2	Petition	133	Dist. of Columbia.	Feb. 12, 1841	With't amend.	616	Referred to Committee Whole House.		
Wever, Casper W	Compensation for superintending the improvements on Pennsylvania avenue.	27	2	Petition	64	Dist. of Columbia.	Jan. 1, 1842	With't amend.	471	Referred to Committee Whole House.		
Wever, Casper W	Compensation for superintending the improvements on Pennsylvania avenue.	27	3	House bill	89	Whole House	Dec. 23, 1843	With't amend.	471	Passed	Passed	App'd Feb. 15, 1843
Weyandt, Lieut. Jacob	Compensation for revolutionary services.	2	1		459					Laid on table.		
Weyandt, Paul	(See Lieut. Jacob Weyandt.)	2	1	Petition	459							
Weyman, Joseph L., surety of.	Release from liability	20	1	Petition	39	Judiciary				Discharged		Leave to withdraw.
Weyman, Joseph L., surety of.	Extension of time to pay judgment	20	2	Petition	227	Commerce	Feb. 11, 1829	Favorable		Referred to Secretary of Treasury.		
Weyman, Joseph L., surety of.	Extension of time to pay judgment	20	2	Senate bill	353	Commerce	Mar. 2, 1829	Favorable	90	Laid on table.		
Weyman, Joseph L., surety of.	Extension of time to pay judgment	21	1	Petition	75	Commerce.				Discharged; laid on table.		
Weymouth, Dean	Pension	14	2	Petition	376	Pens. & Rev. Cl'ms.				Discharged; laid on table.		
Weymouth, Dean	Pension	15	1	Petition	89	Pens. & Rev. Cl'ms.	Feb. 5, 1819	Favorable	308	Referred to Committee Whole House.		
Weymouth, Dean	Pension	15	2	Petition	23	Pens. & Rev. Cl'ms.						
Weymouth, Dean	Pension	16	1	Petition	106	Pens. & Rev. Cl'ms.						
Weymouth, Dean	Pension	18	1	Senate bill	309	Pens. & Rev. Cl'ms.	Mar. 24, 1824	Favorable	46	Passed	Passed	App'd May 21, 1824
Weymouth, Dean	Compensation as private N. York volunteers.	18	1	Petition	387	Military Affairs	111	Favorable	192	Passed	Passed	App'd May 19, 1824
Weymouth, Ichabod	Pension	31	1	Petition	406	Invalid Pensions	378	Favorable	326	Ref'd to Com. W. H.		

List of private claims presented to the House of Representatives of the United States from the 1st to the 31st Congress, inclusive—Continued.

Names of claimants.	Nature or object of the claim.	Congress.	Session.	How brought before the House of Reps.	Page of journal.	To what committee of the House referred.	No. or date of the report.	Nature of the report.	No. of the bill.	How disposed of by the House of Reps.	How disposed of by the Senate.	Date of the act of Congress, and remarks.
Weymouth, William W.	Remission of certain penalties	11	2	Petition	228	Com. and Manuf.	Feb. 21, 1810	Favorable	85	Passed	Passed	App'd May 1, 1810
Whaley, Caleb J.	Pension and indemnity for losses sustained in war of 1812.	15	1	Petition	165	Pens. & Rev. Cl'ms.	April 1, 1818	Favorable	172	Passed.		
Whaley, Capt. James	For settlement of accounts	18	1	Resolution	152	Claims	Feb. 26, 1824	Adverse	......	Laid on table.		
Whaley, Capt. James	Compensation for services, &c., war of 1812.	19	1	Resolution	76	Claims	......	......	......	Discharged; laid on table.		
Whaley, Capt. James	Arrears of pension	29	1	Petition	319	Invalid Pensions	......	......	......	Discharged; laid on table.		
Whaley, Jonathan	Pension	4	1	Rep. of Secretary War.	445	Claims	Feb. 15, 1796	Favorable	156	Passed	Passed	App'd April 20, 1796
Whaley, Matthew, widow of.	Pension	26	1	Petition	706	Rev. Pensions.						
Whaley, Matthew, widow of.	Pension	26	2	Petition	35	Rev. Pensions.	Feb. 12, 1841	Favorable	652	Referred to Committee Whole House.		
Whaley, Oliver	(See Samuel Whaley)	26	1	......	284							
Whaley, Samuel, widow of.	Pension	26	1	Petition	284	Rev. Pensions	490	Adverse	......	Laid on table.		
Whall, Robert	Pension	20	2	Petition	262	Military Pensions	Dec. 11, 1828	Favorable	311	Laid on table.		
Whall, Robert	Pension	21	1	Petition	30	Military Pensions	Dec. 12, 1830	Favorable	72	Passed	Passed	App'd May 20, 1830; name omitted in bill.
Whann, Adam	Increase of compensation as postmaster at Elkton.	30	1	Petition	571	P. Of. & P. Roads.	Mar. 28, 1848	......	......	Discharged; laid on table.		
Wharry, John	Compensation as surveyor of public lands.	25	2	Petition	1047	Claims	960	Favorable	......	Referred to Secretary Treasury.		
Wharry, John	To be released from judgment	27	2	Memorial	749	Judiciary	848	Favorable	491	Referred to Committee Whole House.		
Wharry, John	To be released from judgment	27	3	House bill	89	Whole House	Dec. 23, 1842	Favorable	491	Passed	Passed	App'd March 1, 1843
Wharton, Samuel	Compensation for taking census of North Carolina.	17	2	Petition	22	Claims	54	Favorable	233	Referred to Committee Whole House.		
Wharton, Samuel	Compensation for taking census of North Carolina.	18	1	Petition	33	Claims	Dec. 11, 1842	Favorable	32	Passed	Passed	App'd Feb. 4, 1824
Wharton, Thomas F.	To refund certain tonnage duties	12	1	Petition	49	Com. and Manuf.	......	......	......	......	......	Leave to withdraw.
Wharton, Dr. Wm. D.	Compensation for professional services.	25	2	Documents	205	Claims.						
Wharton, Dr. Wm. D.	Compensation for professional services.	26	1	Documents	170	Claims.						
Wharton, Dr. Wm. D.	Compensation for professional services.	26	2	Petition	135	Claims.						
Whayland, James	Pension	1	2	Petition	174	Secretary of War.	May 31, 1809	Report	......	Laid on table.		
Wheat, Eli, *et al.*	Remission of penalty as sureties of James W. Carter.	26	1	Petition	1187	P. Of. & P. Roads.						
Wheat, Eli, *et al.*	Remission of penalty as sureties of James W. Carter.	26	2	Petition	90	Judiciary.						
Wheat, Eli, *et al.*	Remission of penalty as sureties of James W. Carter.	27	2	Petition	63	Judiciary	447	Favorable	301	Passed	Passed	App'd Aug. 11, 1842
Wheatley, Catharine	(See Samuel Wheatley, widow of.)	27	2	......	1158							
Wheatly, Samuel, widow of.	Pension	27	2	Petition	1158	Rev. Pensions	1004	Adverse.	......	Laid on table.		
Wheatly, Thomas	Payment for horse lost in United States service.	20	1	Resolution	175	Claims	Feb. 18, 1828	Adverse	......	Laid on table.		
Wheatly, Thomas	Payment for horse lost in United States service.	20	2	Resolution	50	Claims	15	Favorable	334	Referred to Committee Whole House.		
Wheatly, Thomas	Payment for horse lost in United States service.	21	1	Petition	205	Claims	Feb. 24, 1830	Favorable	281	Passed	Passed	App'd May 28, 1830

List of private claims presented to the House of Representatives of the United States from the 1st to the 31st Congress, inclusive—Continued.

Names of claimants.	Nature or object of the claim.	Congress.	Session.	How brought before the House of Reps.	Page of journal.	To what committee of the House referred.	No. or date of the report.	Nature of the report.	No. of the bill.	How disposed of by the House of Reps.	How disposed of by the Senate.	Date of the act of Congress, and remarks.
Wheatly, William	Compensation for services as clerk to penitentiary, District of Columbia.	26	1	Petition	605	Dist. of Columbia.				Discharged; laid on table.		
Wheatly, William	Compensation for services as clerk to penitentiary, District of Columbia.	26	2	Petition	80	Dist. of Columbia.						
Wheatly, William	Compensation for services as clerk to penitentiary, District of Columbia.	27	2	Petition	64	Dist. of Columbia.	197	Adverse		Laid on table.		
Wheatly, William	Compensation for services as clerk to penitentiary, District of Columbia.	27	3	Petition	344	Dist. of Columbia.						
Wheatly, William	Compensation for services as clerk to penitentiary, District of Columbia.	28	1	Petition	263	Dist. of Columbia.				Discharged; laid on table.		
Wheatly, William	Compensation for services as clerk to penitentiary, District of Columbia.	28	2	Petition	214	Dist. of Columbia.				Discharged; laid on table.		
Wheaton, Henry	For outfit as chargé de affairs to Prussia.	24	1	Petition	142	Foreign Affairs	213	Favorable	217	Referred to Committee Whole House.		
Wheaton, Joseph	Reimbursement of amount of judgment against him.	1	3	Petition	354					Referred to Secretary Treasury.		
Wheaton, Joseph	Compensation as sergeant at-arms of House of Representatives.	5	2	Memorial	212	Ways and Means	Mar. 19, 1798	Adverse		Laid on table.		
Wheaton, Joseph	Compensation for revolutionary services.	11	3	Petition	553	Claims.						
Wheaton, Joseph	To be paid an amount of award in in his favor by United States court.	12	1	Petition	38	Claims						Leave to withdraw.
Wheaton, Joseph	To be paid an amount of award in in his favor by United States court.	14	1	Petition	111	Claims	Jan. 22, 1816	Favorable		Passed	Passed	App'd April 26, 1816
Wheaton, Joseph, wife and agent of.	Paym'nt for whisky furnished Navy Department.	13	2	Petition	322	Claims	88	Adverse				Leave to withdraw.
Wheaton, Joseph, wife and agent of.	Paym'nt for whisky furnished Navy Department.	14	2	Petition	71	Claims						Leave to withdraw.
Wheaton, Joseph, wife and agent of.	Paym'nt for whisky furnished Navy Department.	15	1	Petition	55	Claims				Discharged; laid on table.		
Wheaton, Joseph	Settlement of accounts as deputy quartermaster general.	15	2	Petition	24	Military Pensions	Dec. 2, 1818	Favorable	211	Passed	Passed	App'd March 3, 1819
Wheaton, Joseph	Relief; the act of last session having failed to produce settlement	16	1	Petition	38	Claims	Jan. 6, 1820	Adverse		Referred to Attorney General.		
Wheaton, Joseph	Relief; the act of last session having failed to produce settlement-	16	2	Petition	35	Claims	15	Adverse		Laid on table.		
Wheaton, Joseph	Relief; the act of last session having failed to produce settlement.	18	1	Petition	43	Military Affairs	Jan. 26, 1824	Adverse		Laid on table.		
Wheaton, Joseph	Compensation for time lost in setling accounts.	17	1	Petition	38	Military Affairs	Dec. 19, 1821	Adverse		Laid on table.		
Wheaton, Joseph	Compensation for time lost in setling accounts.	17	2	Petition	43	Military Affairs	43	Adverse		Laid on table.		
Wheaton, Joseph	To be paid amount allowed by accounting officer of United States for certain expenses.	17	1	Petition	184	Claims				Discharged; laid on table.		

List of private claims presented to the House of Representatives of the United States from the 1st to the 31st Congress, inclusive—Continued.

Names of claimants.	Nature or object of the claim.	Congress.	Session.	How brought before the House of Reps.	Page of journal.	To what committee of the House referred.	No. or date of the report.	Nature of the report.	No. of the bill.	How disposed of by the House of Reps.	How disposed of by the Senate.	Date of the act of Congress, and remarks.
Wheaton, Joseph	To be paid amount allowed by accounting officer of United States for certain expenses.	18	1	Petition	52	Claims	Jan. 12, 1824	Favorable	52	Passed	Passed	App'd May 18, 1824
Wheaton, Joseph, (D. C.)	Compensation for services rendered and horses lost in United States service.	19	1	Petition	152	Military Affairs				Discharged		Leave to withdraw.
Wheaton, Joseph, (D. C.)	Compensation for services rendered and horses lost in United States service.	19	2	Petition, &c	116	Military Affairs	Feb. 12, 1827	Adverse		Discharged		Leave to withdraw.
Wheaton, Josephus	(See John McGilbry, *et al.*)	22	1		264							
Wheeden, Madison	To be allowed six months pay withheld by Fourth Auditor.	27	2	Memorial	669	Claims.						
Wheeden, Madison	To be allowed six months pay withheld by Fourth Auditor.	27	3	Memorial	155	Claims.						
Wheeden, Madison	To be allowed six months pay withheld by Fourth Auditor.	28	1	Memorial	325	Naval Affairs				Discharged; laid on table.		
Whedden, Samuel	Pension	25	3		677	Rev. Pensions				Discharged		Leave to withdraw.
Wheeland, Michael, heir of.	Continuation of pension	22	1	Petition	671	Rev. Pensions				Discharged; laid on table.		
Wheeland, William	Payment for losses sustained by attendance as witness, U. States court.	6	1	Petition	693	Claims				Discharged.		
Wheeler, Catherine	Pension for revolutionary services of her husband.	1	2	Petition	167	Secretary of War	June 28, 1790			Laid on table.		
Wheeler, Artemus	That his right to patent rifle be purchased by government.	17	1	Petition	323	Military Affairs				Discharged; referred to Secretary War.		
Wheeler, Asa	(See James H. Elford, administrator of.)	23	2		274							
Wheeler, Benjamin	Pension	17	1	Petition	150	Rev. Pensions				Discharged; laid on table.		
Wheeler, Benjamin	Indemnity for French spoliations prior to 1800.	26	1	Memorial	182	Foreign Affairs	343	Favorable; bill	319	Referred to Committee Whole House.		
Wheeler, Beriah, (Vt.)	Pension	21	1	Petition	75	Military Pensions				Discharged; laid on table.		
Wheeler, Daniel, & Simon Cock, by attorney.	For extension of patent	15	1	Petition	261	Com. and Manuf.						
Wheeler, Ebenezer	Pension	21	2	Petition	80	Military Pensions.						
Wheeler, Ebenezer	Pension	22	1	Petition	67	Rev. Pensions				Discharged; laid on table.		
Wheeler, Ezra	Restoration of pension	24	1	Resolution	951	Rev. Pensions				Discharged; laid on table.		
Wheeler, George, *et al.*	(See George Ficklin and Daniel Ward.)	22	1		132							
Wheeler, Jesse	Compensation for revolutionary services of son.	24	1	Resolution	49	Claims	Jan. 6, 1836	Adverse		Laid on table.		
Wheeler, Jonathan	Compensation as clerk to assistant commissary, and for destruction of building by enemy.	2	2	Petition	683					Referred to Secretary Treasury.		
Wheeler, Jonathan	Compensation as clerk to assistant commissary, and for destruction of building by enemy.	3	2	Rep. of Secretary Treasury.	284					Laid on table.		

List of private claims presented to the House of Representatives of the United States from the 1st to the 31st Congress, inclusive—Continued.

Names of claimants.	Nature or object of the claim.	Congress.	Session.	How brought before the House of Reps.	Page of journal.	To what committee of the House referred.	No. or date of the report.	Nature of the report.	No. of the bill.	How disposed of by the House of Reps.	How disposed of by the Senate.	Date of the act of Congress, and remarks.
Wheeler, Jonathan	Compensation as clerk to assistant commissary, and for destruction of building by enemy.	4	1	Rep. of Secretary Treasury.	470	Claims	May 31, 1796	Adverse	......	Laid on table.		
Wheeler, Jonathan	Compensation as clerk to assistant commissary, and for destruction of building by enemy.	4	2	Res. and docs.	614	Claims.						
Wheeler, Joseph	(See Israel Pearce, heirs of)	27	2									
Wheeler, Joshua	Pension	18	2	Petition	54	Pens. & Rev. Cl'ms.						
Wheeler, Joshua	Pension	19	1	Resolution	200	Military Pensions	Feb. 23, 1826	Favorable	118	Passed.		
Wheeler, Joshua	Pension	19	2	House bill	85	Whole House	Dec. 22, 1826	Favorable	314	Passed	Passed	App'd March 3, 1827
Wheeler, Joshua	Increase of pension	24	1	Petition	51	Invalid Pensions.						
Wheeler, Richard, heirs of.	Bounty land for revolutionary services.	24	1	Petition	534	Rev. Claims	716	Adverse	......	Laid on table.		
Wheeler, Salsbury	Increase of pension, &c	30	1	Petition	414	Rev. Pensions	......	......	......	Discharged; laid on table.		
Wheeler, Samuel	(See Dana, Wheeler, & Bartlett)	12	2	......	696							
Wheeler, Samuel, (Boston)	Reimbursement of excess of duties	21	2	Petition	110	Ways and Means.						
Wheeler, Sylvester	Pension	14	2	Resolution	73	Pens. & Rev. Cl'ms.	......	......	......	Discharged; laid on table.		
Wheeler, Wm., (N. H.)	Restoration of pension	17	1	Petition	128	Rev. Pensions	......	......	......	Discharged; laid on table.		
Wheeler, Wm., (N. Y.)	Pension	22	1	Petition	381	Rev. Pensions	......	......	......	Discharged; laid on table.		
Wheeler, Zenas, (Mass.)	Compensation for revolutionary services.	19	2	Petition	25	Rev. Claims	......	......	......	Discharged.		
Wheeler, Zenas, (Mass.)	Compensation for revolutionary services.	20	1	Petition	45	Rev. Claims	Dec. 24, 1827	Adverse	......	Laid on table.		
Wheeler, Zenas, (Mass.)	Compensation for revolutionary services.	22	1	Petition	44	Rev. Claims	Dec. 29, 1831	Adverse	......	Laid on table.		
Wheelock, Lieut. Abel	For settlement of accounts	16	2	Petition	164	Claims	Jan. 31, 1821	Adverse	......	Laid on table.		
Wheelock, Sill	Reimbursement of excess duties	30	1	Senate bill	957	Commerce	Jan. 26, 1848	With't amend.	142	Passed	......	App'd Aug 14, 1848
Wheelock, Jotham	Exchange of scrip for land warrant	25	3	Senate bill	162	Rev. Claims.						
Wheelwright, Abraham	(See Joseph Knight, administrator of.)	26	1	......	182							
Wheelwright, Capt. Dan'l, heir of.	Half-pay for revolutionary services.	28	2	Petition	239	Rev. Claims.						
Wheelwright, Capt. Dan'l, heir of.	Half-pay for revolutionary services.	29	1	Petition	202	Rev. Claims.						
Wheelwright, Ebenezer	Fishing bounty	26	1	Petition	289	Commerce	315	Favorable	278	Referred to Committee Whole House.		
Wheelwright, Ebenezer	Fishing bounty	28	1	Petition	110	Commerce	62	Favorable	87	Passed.		
Wheelwright, Ebenezer	Fishing bounty	28	2	Petition	82	Commerce.						
Wheelwright, Ebenezer	Fishing bounty	29	1	Petition	106	Commerce	92	Favorable	111	Passed.		
Wheelwright, Ebenezer	Fishing bounty	30	1	Petition	157	Commerce.						
Wheelwright, Ebenezer	Fishing bounty	30	2	Petition	203	Commerce.						
Wheelwright, Ebenezer	Fishing bounty	31	1	Petition	235	Commerce.						
Wheelwright, Ebenezer, executor of.	(See Wm. Coombs, and others)	26	1	......	182							
Wheelwright, Ebenezer	Indemnity for French spoliations prior to 1800.	27	3	Resolutions	291	Foreign Affairs	......	General bill	57	Referred to Committee Whole House.		
Wheeper, David	(See Capt. Zebulon M. Pike)	10	1	......	189							
Whelpley, Ebenezer, (N. Y.)	Pension	21	2	Petition	208	Military Pensions.						

List of private claims presented to the House of Representatives of the United States from the 1st to the 31st Congress, inclusive—Continued.

Names of claimants.	Nature or object of the claim.	Congress.	Session.	How brought before the House of Reps.	Page of journal.	To what committee of the House referred.	No. or date of the report.	Nature of the report.	No. of the bill.	How disposed of by the House of Reps.	How disposed of by the Senate.	Date of the act of Congress, and remarks.
Whelpley, Ebenezer, (N. Y.)	Pension	22	1	Petition	255	Rev. Pensions				Discharged; laid on table.		
Wherrey, Maccay	Confirmation of title to land	15	1	Petition	312	Priv. Land Claims.						
Wherrey, Maccay	Confirmation of title to land	16	1	Petition	71	Priv. Land Claims.						
Wherrey, Maccay	Confirmation of title to land	17	1	Petition	54	Public Lands.						
Wherrey, Maccay	Confirmation of title to land	18	1	Petition	55	Public Lands	Jan. 16, 1824	General bill	65	Passed	Passed	App'd May 26, 1824
Whetstone, Simon	Pre-emption right to land	25	3	Petition	135	Public Lands.						
Whetstone, Simon	Pre-emption right to land	26	2	Petition	50	Public Lands.						
Whicher, William	Pension	30	1	Petition	823	Invalid Pensions	703	Favorable	549	Referred to Committee Whole House.		
Whicher, William	Pension	30	2	House bill	319	Whole House	Jan. 26, 1849	Favorable	549	Passed.		
Whicher, William	Pension	31	1	Petition	396	Invalid Pensions	93	Favorable	115	Passed	Passed	App'd Sep. 28, 1850
Whidden, James	Pension	25	2	Resolution	464	Rev. Pensions				Discharged; laid on table.		
Whidden, James	Pension	26	1	Petition	307	Rev. Pensions.						
Whidden, Samuel	(See Samuel Whedden.)	25	3		677							
Whileber, John	Pension	3	1	Rep. of Secretary War.	131	Select	May 26, 1794	Favorable	J. R. 12	Passed	Passed	App'd June 9, 1794
Whiley & Taylor	To refund excess of duties	29	1	House bill	206	Whole House	Feb. 27, 1846	With't amend.	54	Passed	Title amended and passed.	App'd Aug. 8, 1846
Whinrey, Thomas	Pension	31	2	Petition	192	Invalid Pensions.						
Whippey, Zebulon	Compensation for military services	13	2	Petition	297	Claims	73	Adverse				Leave to withdraw.
Whipple, Abraham	Commutation pay, &c	1	3	Petition	392					Referred to Secretary War.		
Whipple, Abraham	Commutation pay, &c	2	2	Rep. of Secretary War.	696					Laid on table.		
Whipple, Abraham	Commutation pay, &c	7	2	Petition	303	Claims	Feb. 26, 1803	Further time.		Postponed.		
Whipple, Abraham	Commutation pay, &c	10	2	Petition	369	Select.						
Whipple, Abraham	Compensation for losses and injuries received.	11	2	Petition	147	Select.	May 27, 1810	Favorable	118	Referred to Committee Whole House.		
Whipple, Abraham	Compensation for losses and injuries received.	11	3	Petition	454	Claims.						
Whipple, Abraham	Compensation for losses and injuries received	12	1	Petition	12	Select.	Nov. 13, 1811	Favorable	3	Passed	Passed	Appd Dec. 12, 1811
Whipple, Abraham	Increase of pension	21	2	Report and bill	325	Naval Affairs	86	Favorable	639	Passed.		
Whipple, Abraham	(See Samuel Ward.)	15	1		388							
Whipple, John	Indemnity for property destroyed by British.	15	2	Petition	237	Claims				Discharged; laid on table.		
Whipple, John	Indemnity for property destroyed by British.	17	1	Petition	60	Claims	Jan. 18, 1822	Adverse		Laid on table.		
Whipple, John	Indemnity for property destroyed by British.	18	1	Petition	75	Claims	Dec. 22, 1823	Adverse		Laid on table.		
Whipple, John, heir of	Payment for services rendered and losses sustained revolutionary war	25	3	Petition	457	Rev. Claims.						
Whipple, John, heir of	Payment for services rendered and losses sustained revolutionary war	26	1	Petition	167	Rev. Claims				Discharged.		
Whipple, Joseph	Increase of compensation as collector.	2	1	Petition	521					Referred to Secretary Treasury.		
Whipple, Joseph	Increase of compensation as collector.	2	2	Rep. of Secretary Treasury.	626	Claims				Laid on table.		
Whipple, Rufus	Pension	16	1	Petition	122	Rev. Pensions	April 22, 1820	Adverse.		Laid on table.		
Whistler, Major John	To be credited with $300 lost	15	1	Petition	190	Claims	77	Adverse		Laid on table.		
Whiston, Harrison	(See Harrison Wihtson)	28	2		59							

List of private claims presented to the House of Representatives of the United States from the 1st to the 31st Congress, inclusive—Continued.

Names of claimants.	Nature or object of the claim.	Congress.	Session.	How brought before the House of Reps.	Page of journal.	To what committee of the House referred.	No. or date of the report.	Nature of the report.	No. of the bill.	How disposed of by the House of Reps.	How disposed of by the Senate.	Date of the act of Congress, and remarks.
Whit, William	Compensation for damage by United States troops.	13	3	House bill	602	Whole House	Dec. 19, 1814	Favorable	242	Passed	Passed	App'd Jan. 27, 1815
Whitaker, Elizabeth	Indemnity for property destroyed by British.	15	1	Petition	426	Claims				Discharged; laid on table.		
Whitaker, Elizabeth	Indemnity for property destroyed by British.	16	1	Petition	35	Claims	Jan. 3, 1820	Adverse		Laid on table.		
Whitaker, Elizabeth	Indemnity for property destroyed by British.	17	1	Petition	119	Claims				Discharged; laid on table.		
Whitaker, Elizabeth	Indemnity for property destroyed by British.	19	1	Petition	151	Claims	Jan. 19, 1826	Adverse		Laid on table.		
Whitaker, Elizabeth, (Pa.)	Restoration of pension	20	1	Petition	224	Naval Affairs	March 7, 1828	Adverse		Laid on table.		
Whitaker, Elizabeth, (Pa.)	Restoration of pension	20	2	Petition	52	Naval Affairs	103	Adverse		Laid on table.		
Whitaker, Ephraim, (New York.)	Pension	20	1	Petition	196	Rev. Claims	Jan. 30, 1828	Adverse				Leave to withdraw.
Whitaker, Ephraim, (New York.)	Pension	21	1	Petition	156	Military Pensions	117	Favorable	157	Passed	Passed	App'd May 29, 1830
Whitaker, Ephraim, (New York.)	Arrears of pension	22	1	Petition	66	Rev. Pensions	29	Favorable	73	Passed	Passed	App'd July 3, 1832
Whitaker, Ephraim	Commutation pay	21	2	Petition	54	Rev. Claims	25	Favorable	544	Referred to Committee Whole House.		
Whitaker, Ephraim	Commutation pay	22	2	Petition	167	Rev. Claims	28	Favorable	673	Referred to Committee Whole House.		
Whitaker, Ephraim	Commutation pay	23	1	Petition	70	Rev. Claims	63	Favorable	73	Passed	Passed	App'd June 30, 1834
Whitaker, Ephraim	Commutation pay	25	2	Petition	722	Rev. Claims				Discharged; laid on table.		
Whitaker, James	(Not stated)	20	1	Res. and petition.	174	Claims				Discharged; laid on table.		
Whitaker, James, *et al*	Confirmation of title to land	21	1	Petition	173	Judiciary	Jan. 29, 1830	Favorable	180	Passed.		
Whitaker, Nathaniel	For pro rata of slave vessel condemned and sold.	6	1	Petition	555					Referred to Secretary Treasury.		
Whitaker, Nell or Neal	Pension	22	1	Resolution	176	Rev. Pensions	381	Favorable	472	Passed	Indef. postp'd.	
Whitaker, Wm. W	(See James Wilson, *et al.*)	18	2		69							
Whitaker, Wm. W., surety of.	(See Amos Ewards)	18	2		69							
Whitcher, William	(See William Whicher)	30	1		823							
Whitcomb, Asahel	Pension	25	2	Petition	117	Invalid Pensions				Discharged.		
Whitcomb, Asahel	Pension	26	1	Petition	163	Invalid Pensions				Discharged; laid on table.		
Whitcomb, Francis	Pension	3	2	Rep. of Secretary War.	337	Claims	Feb. 28, 1795	Favorable	130	Passed.		
Whitcomb, Francis	Pension	4	1	Rep. of Secretary War.	445	Claims	Feb. 18, 1796	Favorable	156	Passed	Passed	App'd April 20, 1796
Whitcomb, Rasselas, *et al.*	Compensation as surveyor of public lands.	25	2	Petition	1047	Claims	960			Discharged; referred to Sec. Treasury.		
White, Alexander A	Confirmation of title to land	16	1	Petition	280	Priv. Land Claims				Discharged; laid on table.		
White, Captain Alexander, heirs of.	Commutation pay	23	1	Petition	41	Rev. Claims.						
White, Captain Alexander, heirs of.	Commutation pay	23	2	Petition	84	Rev. Claims.						
White, Captain Alexander, heirs of.	Commutation pay	24	1	Petition	205	Rev. Claims	456	Adverse		Laid on table.		

List of private claims presented to the House of Representatives of the United States from the 1st to the 31st Congress, inclusive—**Continued.**

ames of claimants.	Nature or object of the claim.	Congress.	Session.	How brought before the House of Reps.	Page of journal.	To what committee of the House referred.	No. or date of the report.	Nature of the report.	No. of the bill.	How disposed of by the House of Reps.	How disposed of by the Senate.	Date of the act of Congress, and remarks.
White, Captain Alexander, heirs of.	Commutation pay	29	1	Petition	'423	Rev. Claims				Discharged; laid on table.		
White, Alfred	Release from judgment	29	2	Senate bill	380	P. Of. & P. Roads.			S. 129			
White, Alfred	Release from judgment	30	1	Senate bill	957	P. Of. & P. Roads.	July 19, 1848	With't amend.	S. 167	Passed		App'd July 25, 1848
White, Andrew	Increase of pension	16	1	Petition	117	Pens. & Rev. Cl'ms.				Discharged; laid on table.		
White, Anna	(See Gordon White, widow of)	29	1		670							
White, Anthony	(See William H. Bedford, agent)	28	1		262							
White, Anthony	Payment for lost certificate	26	1	Petition	165	Pens. & Rev. Cl'ms.						
White, Anthony W	Reimbursement for money advanced United States for support of 1st dragoons.	1	2	Memor'l & report Sec. of War.	172, 255	Select.						
White, Anthony W	Reimbursement for money advanced United States for support of 1st dragoons.	2	1	Petition	563	Select	April 18, 1792	Favorable	182	Passed.		
White, Anthony W., widow of.	Reimbursement for money advanced United States for support of 1st dragoons.	23	1	Petition	54	Rev. Claims.						
White, Anthony W., widow of.	Reimbursement for money advanced United States for support of 1st dragoons.	23	2	Petition	38	Rev. Claims	49	Favorable	640	Referred to Committee Whole House.		
White, Anthony W., widow of.	Reimbursement for money advanced United States for support of 1st drogoons.	24	1	Petition	63	Rev. Claims	145	Favorable	152	Referred to Committee Whole House.		
White, Anthony W., widow of.	Reimbursement for money advanced United States for support of 1st dragoons.	24	2	House bill	62	Whole House	Feb. 1, 1837	With't amend.	152			
White, Anthony W., widow of.	Reimbursement for money advanced United States for support of 1st dragoons.	25	2	Petition	40	Rev. Claims	315	Favorable	356	Passed	Passed	App'd July 7, 1838
White, Asa and Jabez	Release from mail contract	25	2	Senate bill	745	Judiciary	May 24, 1838	With't amend.	165	Referred to Committee Whole House.		
White, Asa and Jabez	Release from mail contract	25	3	Senate bill	477	Judiciary	286	With't amend.	107	Referred to Committee Whole House.		
White, Asa and Jabez	Release from mail contract	26	1	Petition	300	P. Of. & P. Roads.						
White, Asa and Jabez	Release from mail contract	26	2	Petition	57	P. Of. & P. Roads.						
White, Asa and Jabez	Release from mail contract	27	2	Petition	57	P. Of. & P. Roads.	Feb. 12, 1842	Favorable	203	Passed	Passed	App'd July 27, 1842
White, Bartholomew	Indemnity for cost of suit for being engaged in the Burr conspiracy	12	1	Petition	274					Leave to withdraw		Not referred.
White, Bartholomew, widow of.	Pension, &c.	14	2	Petition	163	Claims				Discharged; laid on table.		
White, Benjamin, widow of.	Remission of duties, &c.	16	1	Petition	191	Commerce				Discharged; laid on table.		
White, Benjamin, (N. Y.)	Release from judgment	17	1	Petition	64	P. Of. & P. Roads.	Feb. 11, 1822	Favorable	83	Passed.		
White, Benjamin	Bounty land for military services	29	2	Petition	58	Priv. Land Claims.						
White, Benjamin	Bounty land for military services	30	1	Petition	183	Public Lands	125	Favorable	116	Passed	Passed	App'd Aug. 5, 1848
White, Benjamin	Pension	2[illegible]	1	Resolution	499	Invalid Pensions	April 11, 1832	Adverse		Laid on table.		
White, Bennet and Jas. B.	(See Captain William Davenport)	29	1		1103							
White, Bridget	(See James White, widow of)	6	1		619							
White, Buckminster, widow of.	Pension	27	3	Petition	365	Rev. Pensions.						

List of private claims presented to the House of Representatives of the United States from the 1st to the 31st Congress, inclusive—Continued.

Names of claimants.	Nature or object of the claim.	Congress.	Session.	How brought before the House of Reps.	Page of journal.	To what committee of the House referred.	No. or date of the report.	Nature of the report.	No. of the bill.	How disposed of by the House of Reps.	How disposed of by the Senate.	Date of the act of Congress, and remarks.
White, Buckminster, widow of.	Pension	28	1	Petition	839	Whole House.						
White, Buckminster, widow of.	Pension	30	1	Petition	229	Rev. Pensions	Jan. 25, 1848	Adverse		Laid on table.		
White, Caleb	Pension	21	1	Petition	99	Military Pensions				Discharged; laid on table.		
White, Campbell P.	Remission of duties	13	3	Petition	674	Ways and Means				Discharged.		
White, Campbell P.	Remission of duties	14	1	Petition	355	Ways and Means				Discharged; laid on table.		
White, Charles	Remission of certain penalties	4	2	Petition	613	Com. and Manuf.	Dec. 27, 1797	Adverse		Laid on table.		
White, Charles	Remission of certain penalties	5	2	Petition	260	Com. and Manuf.						
White, Charles	Remission of certain penalties	5	3	Petition	467	Com. and Manuf.	March 2, 1799			Discharged.		
White, Chileon, surety of.	Release from liability	27	2	Petition	129	P. Of. & P. Roads.						
White, Chileon, surety of.	Release from liability	27	3	Petition	155	P. Of. & P. Roads.	97	Adverse		Laid on table.		
White, Chileon, surety of.	Release from liability	28	1	Petition	106	P. Of. & P. Roads.	Feb. 15, 1844	Adverse		Laid on table.		
White, Chileon, surety of.	Release from liability	29	1	Petition	103	P. Of. & P. Roads.				Laid on table.		
White, Chileon, surety of.	Release from liability	30	1	Petition	299	P. Of. & P. Roads.	314	Adverse		Laid on table.		
White, Chileon, surety of.	Release from liability	30	2	Petition	387	P. Of. & P. Roads.				Leave to withdraw.		
White, Congers	(See William C. Webb and C White.)	1	3		359							
White, C. J.	(See Joseph White, heirs of.)	26	1		182							
White, Daniel G., widow of.	Pension	23	2	Petition	303	Invalid Pensions.						
White, Daniel G., widow of.	Pension	27	3	Petition	301	Rev. Pensions.						
White, Col. David	Pension	20	2	Memorial	312	Military Pensions				Discharged; laid on table.		
White, David L.	Compensation as collector of customs.	22	1	Petition	536	Commerce.						
White, David L.	Compensation as collector of customs.	25	2	Petition	320	Commerce	Jan. 27, 1838	Adverse		Laid on table.		
White, David, & R. Brown	(See Brown & White)	28	1		744							
White, David	Compensation for revolutionary services.	25	2	Documents	393	Rev. Claims				Discharged; laid on table.		
White, E. A.	(See M. A. Price & E. A. White)	27	2		383							
White, Elijah, *et al.*	Compensat'n for property destroyed by Indians.	29	1	Senate bill	1016	Whole House	July 13, 1846	With't amend.	43			
White, Elijah, *et al.*	Compensat'n for property destroyed by Indians.	29	2	Senate bill	240	Whole House	Feb. 9, 1847	With't amend.	72	Passed		App'd March, 3 1847
White, Elijah	Extra compensation as Indian agent	29	1	Senate bill	1041	Indian Affairs	Jan. 24, 1846	Favorable	71	Passed		App'd Aug. 10, 1846
White, Elijah	Increase of compensation as Indian agent.	29	2	Petition	375	Indian Affairs.						
White, Elizabeth	(See Nathaniel Tucker)	25	2		272							
White, Elizabeth	(See Capt. Wm. Davenport)	26	1		961							
White, Fielding F.	Reimbursement of money paid for apprehending mail robbers.	21	1	Documents	205	P. Of. & P. Roads.	140	Favorable; bill	188	Passed	Passed	App'd May 29, 1830
White, Fortune C.	Pension	16	1	Petition	80					Referred to Secretary of War		
White, Frederick, (N. Y.)	For payment of certain due bills given by assistant quartermaster.	16	2	Petition	216	Claims.						
White, Frederick, (N. Y.)	For payment of certain due bills given by assistant quartermaster.	17	1	Petition	60	Claims	69	Adverse		Laid on table.		

List of private claims presented to the House of Representatives of the United States from the 1st *to the* 31st *Congress, inclusive*—Continued.

Names of claimants.	Nature or object of the claim.	Congress.	Session.	How brought before the House of Reps.	Page of journal.	To what committee of the House referred.	No. or date of the report.	Nature of the report.	No. of the bill.	How disposed of by the House of Reps.	How disposed of by the Senate.	Date of the act of Congress, and remarks.
White, Frederick, (N. Y.)	For payment of certain due bills given by assistant quartermaster.	18	2	Petition	37	Claims	Jan. 3, 1825	Adverse	......	Laid on table.		
White, Frederick, heirs of	Compensation for use and occupation of land for military purposes.	24	1	Petition	405	Claims	689	Adverse	......	Laid on table.		
White, Frederick, heirs of	Compensation for use and occupation of land for military purposes	24	2	Petition	145	Claims	Jan. 24, 1837	Adverse	......	Laid on table.		
White, Frederick, heirs of	Compensation for use and occupation of land for military purposes.	25	2	Petition	234	Claims	May 17, 1838	Adverse	......	Laid on table.		
White, Frederick, (N. Y.)	(See Thomas Tupper, assignee.)											
White, George G.	Pension	22	1	Petition	509	Rev. Pensions	....	....	......	Discharged; laid on table.		
White, George	Pension	24	1	Petition	52	Invalid Pensions	723	Favorable; bill	671	Passed	Passed	App'd June 28, 1836
White, Gilman	Indemnity for French spoliations prior to 1800.	26	1	Memorial	182	Foreign Affairs	343	Favorable; bill	343	Referred to Committee Whole House.		
White, Gilman	(See Thomas Brown, executor of)	26	1	....	182							
White, Gilman, heirs of	(See Thomas B. White)	29	2	....	101							
White, Gordon, widow of.	Pension	29	1	Petition	670	Rev. Pensions	826	Adverse	......	Laid on table.		
White, Haffield	Indemnity for Continental money taken by British.	3	1	Petition	22	....	....	....	......	Referred to Secretary War.		
White, Haffield	Indemnity for Continental money taken by British.	3	2	Rep. of Secretary War.	250	Claims	Feb. 25, 1795	Adverse	......	Laid on table.		
White, Haffield	Indemnity for Continental money taken by British.	14	1	Petition	112	Rev. Claims	Feb. 13, 1816	Adverse	......	Laid on table.		
White, Hannah A., *et al.*	(See Jabez Brown, N. Y.)	28	1	....	284							
White, Hannah A.	Pension	31	2	Petition	100	Invalid Pensions.						
White, Henry, heirs of	Permission to locate land	27	2	Petition	330	Military Affairs.						
White, Henry, heirs of	Permission to locate land	30	1	Petition	525	Public Lands	....	....	......	Discharged; laid on table.		
White, Hugh Lawson	Compensation for military services.	3	2	Petition	320	....	....	....	......	Referred to Secretary War.		
White, Hugh Lawson	Compensation for military services.	4	1	Rep. of Secretary War.	627	Select	Jan. 17, 1797	Favorable	......	Referred to Committee Whole House.		
White, Hugh, and Richard Martin.	Payment for timber furnished navy.	5	1	Petition	673	....	....	....	......	Referred to Secretary of Treasury.		
White, Hugh, and Richard Martin.	Payment for timber furnished navy.	6	2	Rep. of Secretary Treasury.	807	Whole House.						
White, Hugh, and Richard Martin.	Payment for timber furnished navy.	7	1	Petition	19	Claims	Dec. 30, 1801	Adverse	......	Laid on table.		
White, Hulda	(See Thomas White, widow of)	23	1	....	304							
White, Isaac, heirs, &c.	(See Capt. Tarpley White)	23	1	....	158							
White, Jabez	(See Asa White)	25	2	....	745							
White, Capt. Jacob	Pension	24	2	Petition	246	Rev. Pensions.						
White, Capt. Jacob	Pension	25	2	Resolution	186	Rev. Pensions.						
White, Capt. Jacob	Pension	25	3	Petition	348	Rev. Pensions	307	Adverse	......	Laid on table.		
White, Capt. Jacob	Pension	27	3	Petition	134	Rev. Pensions	22	Favorable	648	Passed	Passed	App'd Feb. 27, 1843
White, Jacob, (Ky.)	Pension	27	3	Petition	137	Rev. Pensions.						
White, Jacob, administrator of.	Compensation for revolutionary services.	3	2	Petition	261	Claims.						
White, Jacob, administrator of.	Compensation for revolutionary services.	4	1	Petition	373	Claims.						
White, James, administrator of.	Reimbursement for losses on Continental money.	6	1	Petition	619	Claims	Mar. 19, 1800	Adverse	......	Laid on table.		

List of private claims presented to the House of Representatives of the United States from the 1st to the 31st Congress, inclusive—Continued.

Names of claimants.	Nature or object of the claim.	Congress.	Session.	How brought before the House of Reps.	Page of journal.	To what committee of the House referred.	No. or date of the report.	Nature of the report.	No. of the bill.	How disposed of by the House of Reps.	How disposed of by the Senate.	Date of the act of Congress, and remarks.
White, Capt. James, heirs of.	Reimbursement of money advanced during revolutionary war.	24	1	Petition	105	Rev. Claims.						
White, James B., *et al*.	(See Captain William Davenport, heirs of.)	29	1		1103							
White, James	Increase of pension	14	1	House bill	622	Whole House	April 11, 1816	Favorable	171	Passed	Passed	App'd April 30, 1816
White, James	Grant of land for revolutionary services.	18	2	Petition	232	Pens. & Rev. Cl'ms.						
White, James	Additional pay for erecting public buildings.	25	2	Petition	426	Indian Affairs				Discharged; laid on table.		
White, James	Additional pay for erecting public buildings.	25	3	Petition	188	Indian Affairs	199	Adverse		Laid on table.		
White, James	(See Tarl on Ellege)	25	2		1209							
White, James M., *et al*.	(See John T. Smith, heirs of.)	29	1		311							
White, Joel W., and E. Pomeroy.	Compensation for carrying United States mail.	23	1	Petition	379	P. Of. & P. Roads.	Mar. 20, 1834	Adverse		Laid on table.		
White, Joel W., and E. Pomeroy.	Compensation for carrying United States mail.	24	1	Petition	411	P. Of. & P. Roads.						
White, Joel W., and E. Pomeroy.	Compensation for carrying United States mail.	24	2	Petition	271	P. Of. & P. Roads.						
White, Col. John, widow of.	Liquidation and settlement of accounts, &c.	1	1	Petition	88					Referred to Secretary Treasury.		
White, John	Compensation as commissioner to settle account between United States and Pennsylvania, Delaware, and Maryland.	1	1	Petition	73	Select.						
White, John, administrator of.	Settlement of claim against United States.	1	2	Petition	271					Laid on table.		
White, John	Compensation for services on board frigate Trumbull.	3	2	Petition	261	Claims.						
White, John	Compensation for services on board frigate Trumbull.	4	1	Petition	373	Claims.						
White, John, (Phila.)	Extra pay as collector of customs.	4	1	Petition	478	Claims	May 31, 1796			Laid on table.		
White, John, (Phila.)	Extra pay as collector of customs.	4	2	Petition	657	Claims.						
White, John P	Release from surety bond	11	2	Petition	169	Com. and Manuf.	April 7, 1810	Report		Referred to Committee Whole House.		
White, John	(See Joseph Clark, and others)	13	2		305							
White, John	Arrears of pension	18	1	Petition	314	Rev. Pensions	Mar. 31, 1824	Adverse		Laid on table.		
White, John	Payment for work done on Cumberland road.	23	1	Resolution	589	Claims	455	Adverse		Laid on table		See report No. 449.
White, John	Payment of cost, &c., sustained at suit of United States.	24	1	Petition	48	Claims	161	Adverse		Laid on table.		
White, John	Payment of cost, &c., sustained at suit of United States.	29	1	Petition	146	Claims	224	Adverse		Laid on table.		
White, John, Major, heirs of.	Bounty land and half-pay	29	2	Petition	69	Rev. Pensions.						
White, John, Major, heirs of.	Bounty land and half-pay	30	1	Petition	110	Rev. Pensions.						
White, John, Major, heirs of.	Bounty land and half-pay	30	2	Petition	392	Rev. Claims	53	Favorable	757	Referred to Committee Whole House.		
White, John, Major, heirs of.	Pension	31	1	Petition	257	Rev. Claims.						
White, Major John, heirs of.	Pension	31	2	Petition	226							Leave to withdraw

List of private claims presented to the House of Representatives of the United States from the 1st to the 31st Congress, inclusive—Continued.

Names of claimants.	Nature or object of the claim.	Congress.	Session.	How brought before the House of Reps.	Page of journal.	To what committee of the House referred.	No. or date of the report.	Nature of the report.	No. of the bill.	How disposed of by the House of Reps.	How disposed of by the Senate.	Date of the act of Congress, and remarks.
White, Lieut. John, heirs of.	Commutation pay	23	1	Petition	158	Rev. Claims.						
White, Lieut. John, heirs of.	Commutation pay	23	2	Petition	120	Rev. Claims.						
White, Lieut. John, heirs of.	Commutation pay	24	1	Petition	63	Rev. Claims	165	Adverse		Laid on table.		
White, Lieut. John, heirs of.	Commutation pay	25	2	Petition			247	Adverse		Laid on table.		
White, Lieut. John, heirs of.	Commutation pay	25	3	Petition			7	Adverse		Laid on table.		
White, John, Major, heirs of.	Commutation pay	28	1	Petition	300	Rev. Claims.						
White, Jonah	Pre-emption right to land	23	2	Resolution	243	Public Lands	79	Favorable	696	Postponed.		
White, Jonathan, assignee of.	Renewal of certain land warrants lost.	14	1	Petition	35	Public Lands	Jan. 11, 1816	Favorable		Passed	Passed	App'd Feb. 6, 1816
White, Jonathan, widow of.	Arrears of pension	16	2	Petition	78	Rev. Pensions	Feb. 15, 1821	Adverse				Leave to withdraw.
White, Joseph	Indemnity for vessel and cargo captured by British.	3	1	Petition	19					Referred to Secretary Treasury.		
White, Joseph	For the reward of $500 allowed by resolution for the apprehension of James Bowers.	3	1	Petition	120	Select	Mar. 22, 1794			Referred to Secretary of War.		
White, Joseph, widow of.	For the reward of $500 allowed by resolution for the apprehension of James Bowers.	4	2	Petition	612	Claims.						
White, Joseph, widow of.	For the reward of $500 allowed by resolution for the apprehension of James Bowers.	5	2	Petition	318	Claims	May 29, 1798	Adverse		Laid on table.		
White, Joseph, widow of.	For the reward of $500 allowed by resolution for the apprehension of James Bowers.	18	1	Petition	59	Pens. & Rev. Cl'ms.	Dec. 23, 1823	Adverse		Laid on table.		
White, Joseph, widow of.	For the reward of $500 allowed by resolution for the apprehension of James Bowers.	31	1	Petition	598	Judiciary	169	Adverse		Discharged.		
White, Joseph, jr.	Drawback on goods	10	1	Petition	17	Com. and Manuf.						
White, Joseph	Pension	10	2	House bill	499	Whole House	Feb. 20, 1809	Favorable	158	Passed	Passed	App'd March 3, 1809
White, Joseph	Reimbursement of money advanced to recruit sailors.	13	2	Petition	302	Claims	Mar. 23, 1814	Adverse		Laid on table.		
White, Joseph, F., (N. Y.)	Reimbursement of money loaned to government.	17	1	Petition	51	Claims	28	Adverse.				
White, Joseph H.	(See Lewis & Clark.)	9	2	Res and docs	507	Select	Jan. 23, 1807	Favorable	183	Passed	Passed	App'd March 3, 1807
White, Joseph M.	Compensation for legal services	18	1	Resolution	420	Ways and Means	May 6, 1824	Favorable	221	Passed	Passed	App'd May 26, 1824
White, Joseph R.	(See Augustus Willett, heirs of.)	26	2		77							
White, Joseph, representatives of.	(See William Fetyplace.)	23	2		59							
White, Joseph, heirs of	Indemnity for French spoliations prior to 1800.	26	1	Memorial	182	Foreign Affairs	343	Favorable; bill	319	Referred to Committee Whole House.		
White, Joseph, heir of	Indemnity for French spoliations prior to 1800.	29	2	Memorial	228	Foreign Affairs.						
White, Joseph, heir of	Indemnity for French spoliations prior to 1800.	26	1	Memorial	182	Foreign Affairs	343	Favorable; bill	319	Referred to Committee Whole House.		
White, Joshua	(See William H. Bedford, agent.)	28	1		262							

List of private claims presented to the House of Representatives of the United States from the 1st to the 31st Congress, inclusive—Continued.

Names of claimants.	Nature or object of the claim.	Congress.	Session.	How brought before the House of Reps.	Page of journal.	To what committee of the House referred.	No. or date of the report.	Nature of the report.	No. of the bill.	How disposed of by the House of Reps.	How disposed of by the Senate.	Date of the act of Congress, and remarks.
White, Joshua, executors of.	Release from payment of certain duties.	16	1	Petition	218	Ways and Means				Discharged; laid on table.		
White, Joshua, executors of.	Release from payment of certain duties.	16	1	Senate bill	353	Ways and Means	April 6, 1820	With amend.	57	Passed with amendm't.	Concurred in.	App'd April 11, 1820
White & Ketchim, mail contractors.	Relief from the effects of an order from Postmaster General.	27	3	Petition	153	P. Of. and P. Roads.						
White, Lemuel	Pension	25	2	Senate bill	994	Rev. Pensions	July 2, 1838	With't amend.	232	Referred to Committee Whole House.		
White, Lemuel	Pension	26	1	Senate bill	640	Rev. Pensions	April 4, 1840	With't amend.	15	Referred to Committee Whole House.		
White, Lemuel	Pension	26	2	Senate bill	113	Rev. Pensions	Feb. 12, 1841	With't amend.	1	Passed		App'd March 3, 1841
White, Levi, (Mass.)	Restoration of pension	17	1	Petition	77	Rev. Pensions				Discharged; laid on table.		
White, Levi, (Mass.)	Restoration of pension	19	2	Petition	215	Rev. Pensions				Discharged; laid on table.		
White, Lewis, representatives of.	Permission to change location of land.	20	1	Petition	485	Public Lands.						
White, Lucy	(See Joseph White, widow of)	4	2		612							
White, Luke	Compensation for revolutionary services.	3	2	Petition	309	Claims.						
White, Luke	Compensation for revolutionary services.	4	1	Resolution	373	Claims	Jan. 4, 1796	Adverse				Leave to withdraw.
White, Luke, (N. Y.)	Pension	22	1	Resolution	140	Military Pensions.						
White, Luke, (N. Y.)	Pension	23	1	Petition	128	Rev. Pensions	Jan. 9, 1824	Adverse		Laid on table.		
White, Margaret	(See Anthony W. White, widow of.)	23	1		54							
White, Martha	(See Daniel G. White, widow of).	27	3		301							
White, Mary	(See Jonathan White, widow of).	16	2		78							
White, Mary and Sarah	(See Benjamin White, widow and daughter of.)	16	1		191							
White, Mary	Continuation of pension	28	1	Petition	850	Rev. Pensions.						
White, Mary	(See Bartholomew White)	14	2		163							
White, Mathew B.	Increase of pension	15	1	Petition	23	Pens. & Rev. Cl'ms.				Discharged; laid on table.		
White, Michael	Pension	31	1	Petition	257	Invalid Pensions	393	Adverse		Laid on table.		
White, Moses	Settlement of claim for additional compensation for revolutionary services.	2	1	Petition	491					Referred to Secretary Treasury.		
White, Moses	Settlement of claim for additional compensation for revolutionary services.	3	2	Rep. of Secretary Treasury.	312					Laid on table.		
White, Moses	Settlement of claim for additional compensation for revolutionary services.	4	1	Petition	441	Claims	May 31, 1796	Adverse		Laid on table.		
White, Moses	Settlement of claim for additional compensation for revolutionary services.	5	2	Petition	386	Claims	July 13, 1798	Indefinite		Discharged.		
White, Moses	Settlement of claim for additional compensation for revolutionary services.	5	3	Petition	420	Claims	Feb. 4, 1799	Favorable		Referred to Committee Whole House.		
White, Moses	Settlement of claim for additional compensation for revolutionary services.	6	1	Petition	602	Claims	Feb. 24, 1800	Adverse		Laid on table.		

List of private claims presented to the House of Representatives of the United States from the 1st to the 31st Congress, inclusive—Continued.

Names of claimants.	Nature or object of the claim.	Congress.	Session.	How brought before the House of Reps.	Page of journal.	To what committee of the House referred.	No. or date of the report.	Nature of the report.	No. of the bill.	How disposed of by the House of Reps.	How disposed of by the Senate.	Date of the act of Congress, and remarks.
White, Moses	Settlement of claim for additional compensation for revolutionary services.	7	2	Petition	291		Jan. 27, 1803	Favorable	93	Passed	Passed	App'd March 2, 1803
White, Moses, heirs of	Arrears of pension	30	1	Senate bill	976	Invalid Pensions	July 19, 1848	With't amend.	175	Passed		App'd July 25, 1848
White, Moses, and Charlotte Hazen.	(See Moses Hazen, executor of)	8	1		582							
White, Nancy, assignee of.	Pension	17	1	Petition	78	Claims						Leave to withdraw.
White, Nathaniel, widow of	Increase of pension	29	1	Petition	348	Rev. Pensions	358	Adverse		Laid on table.		
White, N. A.	Bounty land for military services	30	1	Petition	147	Military Affairs						Leave to withdraw.
White, Nelly	Pension	28	1	Resolution	557	Rev. Claims.						
White, Orin	Compensation for laying out a road	22	1	Petition	264	Public Lands	341	Adverse		Laid on table.		
White, O. B	(See Cook, Anthony, Mahon, and others.)	30	1		826							
White, Peter	Pension	17	1	Petition	26	Rev. Pensions				Discharged; laid on table.		
White, P. M	(See George Reinholdt, administrator of.)	26	1		182		343		319			
White, Philip	Pension	2	2	Rep. of Secretary War.	649	Whole House	Jan. 3, 1793	Favorable	214	Passed		App'd Feb. 28, 1793
White, Philip	Pension	3	1	Rep. of Secretary War.	131	Select	May 26, 1794	Favorable	12	Passed	Passed	App'd June 9, 1794
White & Price	(See Price & White.)	27	2		383							
White, Ransom	Compensation for pilot boat pressed in United States service.	28	2	Petition	355	Claims.						
White, Ransom	Compensation for pilot boat pressed in United States service.	29	1	Petition	533	Claims.						
White, Ransom	Compensation for pilot boat pressed in United States service.	31	1	Petition	1179	Rev. Claims.						
White, Rebecca	(See Nathaniel White, widow of.)	29	1		348							
White, Richard H	Compensation for procuring witnesses at suit of United States.	25	2	Petition	924	Judiciary				Discharged; laid on table.		
White, Richard	Extra compensation as assistant messenger to Auditor.	29	1	Petition	149	P. Of. & P. Roads.						
White, Richard	Extra compensation as assistant messenger to Auditor.	29	2	Petition	161	P. Of. & P. Roads.						
White, Richard	Increase of compensation	31	2	Petition	252	P. Of. and P. Roads.						
White, Robert	Increase of pension	14	1	Senate bill	252	Pens. & Rev. Cl'ms.	Jan. 30, 1816	With amend.		Passed		App'd Feb. 22, 1816
White, Robert, (Vermont.)	Increase of pension	23	1	Petition	45	Invalid Pensions	Dec. 20, 1833	Adverse		Laid on table.		
White, Robert, representatives of.	Commutation pay	22	2	Petition	165	Rev. Claims.						
White, Robert, representatives of.	Commutation pay	24	1	Senate bill	932	Rev. Claims	June 28, 1836	Adverse	139	Laid on table.		
White, Robert, representatives of.	Commutation pay	25	2	Petition	198	Rev. Claims.						
White, Robert, heirs of	Payment of pension withheld	25	2	Senate bill	763	Rev. Claims	915	With amend.	179	Laid on table.		
White, Robert, (Ohio)	Increase of pension	26	1	Petition	286	Invalid Pensions				Discharged; laid on table.		
White, Robert, (Ohio)	Increase of pension	27	2	Petition	97	Invalid Pensions	954	Adverse		Laid on table.		
White, Robert, (Ohio)	Increase of pension	27	3	Petition	72	Invalid Pensions.						
White, Robert, (Ohio)	Increase of pension	31	2	Petition	95	Invalid Pensions.						
White, Samuel B	Increase of pension	10	2	House bill	499	Whole House	Feb. 20, 1809	Favorable	158	Passed	Passed	App'd March 3, 1809
White, Samuel B., widow of.	Pension	22	1	Petition	287	Rev. Claims				Discharged; laid on table.		

List of private claims presented to the House of Representatives of the United States from the 1st to the 31st Congress, inclusive—Continued.

Names of claimants.	Nature or object of the claim.	Congress.	Session.	How brought before the House of Reps.	Page of journal.	To what committee of the House referred.	No. or date of the report.	Nature of the report.	No. of the bill.	How disposed of by the House of Reps.	How disposed of by the Senate.	Date of the act of Congress, and remarks.
White, Samuel	Pension	12	1	Petition	36	Claims	June 12, 1812	Adverse	......	Laid on table.		
White, Samuel	Pension	13	1	Petition	44	Claims	June 29, 1813	General bill	31	Passed	Passed	App'd March 2, 1813
White, Samuel	Pension	13	3	House bill	740	Whole House	May 1, 1815	Favorable	303	Passed	Passed	App'd March 3, 1815
White, Samuel	Compensation for revolutionary services.	15	1	Petition	217	Pens. & Rev. Cl'ms.	Feb. 13, 1818	Adverse	......	Laid on table.		
White, Captain Samuel	Reimbursement of certain expenses	15	2	Petition	144	Claims	....	....	......	Discharged; laid on table.		
White, Captain Samuel	Reimbursement of certain expenses	16	1	Petition	199	Claims	Feb. 7, 1830	Adverse	......	Laid on table.		
White, Captain Samuel	Reimbursement of certain expenses.	17	2	Petition	82	Claims	Jan. 29, 1823	Adverse	......	Laid on table.		
White, Captain Samuel	Reimbursement of certain expenses.	17	2	Petition	83	Ways and Means	Jan. 8, 1823	Adverse	......	Laid on table.		
White, Captain Samuel	Reimbursement of certain duties.	18	1	Senate bill	328	Ways and Means	Mar. 22, 1824	With't amend.	56	Passed	Passed	App'd May 26, 1824
White, Samuel	Restoration of pension	20	1	Resolution	370	Military Pensions	....	....	......	Discharged; laid on table.		
White, Samuel	Restoration of pension	24	1	Senate bill	811	Rev. Pensions	Jan. 3, 1836	Adverse	199	Referred to Committee Whole House.		
White, Samuel	Restoration of pension	24	2	Senate bill	579	Whole House	....	....	181			
White, Samuel	Restoration of pension	26	1	Senate bill	799	Rev. Pensions	....	....	S. 19			
White, Sarah	(See Thomas White, widow of.)	27	2	....	375							
White, Sarah	(See Samuel B. White, widow of.)	22	1	....	287							
White, Seth, (Mass.)	Pension	21	1	Petition	143	Military Pensions	April 2, 1830	Adverse	......	Laid on table.		
White, Stanley	Repayment of money paid for land	28	1	Petition	508	Public Lands	446	Favorable	183	Ref'd to Com. W H.		
White, Stanley	Repayment of money paid for land	28	2	House bill	343	Whole House	Feb. 7, 1845	Favorable	183	Passed	Passed	App'd March 3, 1845
White, Stephen, executor of.	Indemnity for French spoliations prior to 1800.	26	1	Memorial	182	Foreign Affairs	343	Favorable; bill	319	Referred to Committee Whole House.		
White, Stephen, (Tenn).	Compensation for property lost in war of 1812.	23	1	Resolution	513	Claims.						
White, Stephen, agent of.	(See Alert, owners of.)	26	1	....	182							
White, Stephen	(See William Fettyplace.)	23	2	....	259							
White, Solomon	(See Dexter Hungerford)	27	2	....	381							
White, Capt. Tarpley, heirs of.	Commutation pay	23	1	Petition	158	Rev. Claims.						
White, Capt. Tarpley, heirs of.	Commutation pay	23	2	Petition	120	Rev. Claims.						
White, Capt. Tarpley, heirs of.	Commutation pay	24	1	Petition	63	Rev. Claims	165	Favorable	171	Referred to Committee Whole House.		
White, Capt. Tarpley, heirs of.	Commutation pay	24	2	House bill	62	Whole House	Dec. 16, 1836	Favorable	171	Referred to Committee Whole House.		
White, Capt. Tarpley, heirs of.	Commutation pay	25	2	Petition	72	Rev. Claims	247	Favorable	288	Passed.		
White, Capt. Tarpley, heirs of.	Commutation pay	25	3	Petition	85	Rev. Claims	5	Favorable	903	Referred to Committee Whole House.		
White, Capt. Tarpley, heirs of.	Commutation pay	26	1	Petition	165	Rev. Claims	617	Adverse	......	Laid on table.		
White, Capt. Tarpley, heirs of.	Commutation pay	27	2	Petition	61	Rev. Claims	547	Adverse	......	Laid on table.		
White, Capt. Tarpley, heirs of.	Commutation pay	28	1	Petition	300	Rev. Claims.						
White, Capt. Tarpley, heirs of.	Commutation pay	28	2	Petition	185	Rev. Claims.						
White, Thomas, sen.	Additional compensation for revolutionary services.	16	2	Petition	132	Pens. & Rev. Cl'ms.	Jan. 17, 1821	Adverse	......	Laid on table.		
White, Thomas, sen.	Additional compensation for revolutionary services.	17	1	Petition	276	Pens. & Rev. Cl'ms.	Mar. 8, 1822	Adverse	......	Laid on table.		

List of private claims presented to the House of Representatives of the United States from the 1st to the 31st Congress, inclusive—Continued.

Names of claimants.	Nature or object of the claim.	Congress.	Session.	How brought before the House of Reps.	Page of journal.	To what committee of the House referred.	No. or date of the report.	Nature of the report.	No. of the bill.	How disposed of by the House of Reps.	How disposed of by the Senate.	Date of the act of Congress, and remarks.
White, Thomas, widow of.	Reimbursement of certain moneys of which he was robbed.	23	1	Petition	304	Claims	353	Adverse	......	Laid on table.		
White, Thomas, widow of.	Pension	27	2	Petition	375	Rev. Pensions	571	Favorable	367	Ordered to 3d reading.		
White, Thomas, widow of.	Pension	27	3	House bill	87	....	....	....	367	Passed.		
White, Thomas, widow of.	Pension	30	1	Petition	493	Rev. Pensions	518	Favorable	446	Referred to Committee Whole House.	....	Leave to withdraw.
White, Thomas, widow of.	Pension	30	2	House bill	318	Whole House	Jan. 26, 1846	Favorable	446	Passed.		
White, Thomas B.	Indemnity for French spoliations prior to 1800.	29	2	Petition	101	Foreign Affairs.						
White, Thompson	Pre emption right to land	12	1	Petition	98	Public Lands.						
White, Thompson	Pre-emption right to land	12	2	Petition	663	Public Lands.						
White, Vassel, (Mass.)	Pension	9	1	Petition	196	Claims	Mar. 28, 1806					
White, Vassel, (Mass.)	Pension	14	2	Resolution	87	Pens. & Rev. Cl'ms	....	....	......	Discharged; laid on table.		
White, Vassel, (Mass.)	Pension	18	1	Petition	65	Pens. & Rev. Cl'ms.	Jan. 2, 1824	Adverse	......	Laid on table.		
White, Vassel, (Mass.)	Pension	19	1	Resolution	76	Military Pensions.	164	Adverse	......	Laid on table.		
White, Vassel, (Mass.)	Pension	19	2	House bill	85	Military Pensions.	Dec. 22, 1826	Favorable	314	Passed	Passed	App'd March 3, 1827
White & Wheat	(See Wheat & White)	26	1	....	1187							
White, William	Pension	1	2	Rep. of Secretary War.	250	Select	July 16, 1790	Favorable	88	Passed	Passed	App'd Aug. 11, 1790
White, William, heirs of	Commutation pay	1	3	Rep. of Secretary War.	373	Whole House.						
White, Capt. William	Payment of claim f r revolutionary services.	2	1	House bill	463	Whole House	Nov. 29, 1791	Favorable	152. 159	Passed	Passed	App'd Mar. 27 1792
White, William	Reduction of duties on wine	5	1	Petition	67	....	....	....	......	Laid on table.		
White, William	Reduction of duties on wine	5	2	Petition	92	Ways and Means.	Jan. 2, 1798	Adverse	......	Discharged.		
White, William	Reduction of duties on wine	6	1	Petition	578	Ways and Means.	May 10, 1800	....	......	Discharged.		
White, William, (Ky.)	Compensation for damages by United States troops.	9	2	Petition	555	Claims	....	....	......	Discharged; laid on table.		
White, William, (Ky.)	Compensation for damages by United States troops.	10	1	Petition	177	Claims	Feb. 25, 1808	Favorable; res.				
White, William, (Ky.)	Compensation for damages by United States troops.	10	2	Petition	350	Claims	Nov. 18, 1808	Favorable	106	Passed.		
White, William, (Ky.)	Compensation for damages by United States troops.	11	2	Petition	127	Claims	Dec. 26, 1809	Favorable	51	Referred to Committee Whole House.		
White, William, (Ky.)	Compensation for damages by United States troops.	13	3	Petition	455	Claims	15	Favorable	242	Passed	Passed	App'd Jan. 28, 1815
White, William	Pension	21	1	Petition	353	Military Pensions.						
White, William, heirs of, *et al.*	Bounty land for revolutionary services.	21	1	Petition	618	Priv. Land Claims.	....	....	......	Discharged; laid on table.		
White, William, heirs of, *et al.*	Bounty land for revolutionary services.	21	2	Petition	161	Priv. Land Claims.						
White, William	Payment of certain drafts given by assistant quartermaster general.	22	2	Petition	142	Claims	115	Adverse	......	Laid on table.		
White, William	Payment of certain drafts given by assistant quartermaster general.	23	1	Petition	33	Claims	202	Adverse	369	Referred to Committee Whole House.		
White, William	Payment of certain drafts given by assistant quartermaster general.	24	1	Petition	50	Claims	8	Favorable	8	Referred to Committee Whole House.		
White, William, (Va.)	Increase of pension	23	1	Petition	216	Invalid Pensions	Mar. 21, 1834	Adverse	......	Laid on table.		
White, William, (Va.)	Increase of pension	23	2	Petition	86	Invalid Pensions	Jan. 12, 1835	Adverse	......	Laid on table.		
White, William, (Va.)	Increase of pension	24	1	Petition	98	Invalid Pensions	Jan. 14, 1836	Adverse	......	Laid on table.		
White, William, (Va.)	Increase of pension	24	2	Petition	86	Invalid Pensions	Dec. 30, 1836	Adverse	......	Laid on table.		

List of private claims presented to the House of Representatives of the United States from the 1st to the 31st Congress, inclusive—Continued.

Names of claimants.	Nature or object of the claim.	Congress.	Session.	How brought before the House of Reps.	Page of journal.	To what committee of the House referred.	No. or date of the report.	Nature of the report.	No. of the bill.	How disposed of by the House of Reps.	How disposed of by the Senate.	Date of the act of Congress, and remarks.
White, William, (Va.)	Increase of pension	25	2	Petition	401	Invalid Pensions				Discharged; laid on table.		
White, William, (Va.)	Increase of pension	28	1	Petition	236	Invalid Pensions				Discharged.		
White, William, (Mo.)	Pension	25	2	Petition	401	Invalid Pensions				Discharged.		
White, William, (Mo.)	Pension	25	3	Petition	89	Invalid Pensions	Jan. 9, 1839	Adverse		Laid on table.		
White, William, widow of.	Pension	30	1	Petition	113	Rev. Pensions	136	Favorable	125	R. f'd to Com W. H.		
White, William, widow of	Pension	30	2	House bill	143	Whole House	Dec. 22, 1848	Favorable	125	Passed	Passed	App'd Feb. 8, 1849
White, Wright	Remission of duties on goods	4	1	Petition	370	Whole House	88	Adverse				Leave to withdraw.
White, ——, Col., heirs of.	Arrears of pension	23	1	Petition	570	Invalid Pensions.						
White, Zelpha	(See William White, widow of.)	30	1		113							
Whiteby, Chas., surety of.	Release from liability	22	1	Petition	733	Judiciary.						
Whitecar, Joseph, (N. Y.)	Pension	19	1	Petition	364	Military Pensions	164	Adverse		Laid on table.		
Whitecar, Joseph, (N. Y.)	Pension	19	2	Petition	322							Leave to withdraw.
White-eyes, Geo. Morgan	Additional compensation to reimburse Secretary of War for advances made.	1	2	House bill	294	Whole House		General bill	100	Passed	Passed	App'd Aug. 12, 1790
Whitefield, William	Pension	20	2	Petition	204	Military Pensions				Discharged; laid on table.		
Whiteford, Michael	Compensation for military services.	28	1	Petition	743	Claims.						
Whitehead, Armstead	Increase of pension	14	2	Documents	267	Pens. & Rev. Cl'ms.	Jan. 29, 1817	Adverse		Laid on table.		
Whitehead, Armstead	Increase of pension	15	1	Documents	136					Referred to Secretary of War.		
Whitehead, John	Renewal of patent	23	1	Petition	221	Select	Feb. 11, 1834	Adverse		Laid on table.		
Whitehead, John	(See John W. Simonton and others)	26	1		304							
Whitehead, N. C	(Not stated)	29	1	Petition	635	Naval Affairs	April 6, 1846			Discharged; laid on table.		
Whitehead, N. C	Indemnity for French spoliations prior to 1800.	26	1	Memorial	182	Foreign Affairs	343	Favorable; bill	319	Referred to Committee Whole House.		
Whitehead, Swepson	Payment for timber furnished United States navy.	22	1	Petition	266	Claims	Feb. 7, 1832	Resolution		Referred to Secretary of Navy.		
Whitehead, Swepson, administrator of.	(See Warren Ashley, executor of.)	25	3		119							
Whitehead, William	Relief, having settled on land not subject to entry.	12	1	Petition	60	Public Lands.						
Whitehead, William	Relief, having settled on land not subject to entry.	12	2	Petition	663	Public Lands.						
Whitehead, William, *et al.*	Refund certain duties	16	2	Senate bill	300	Whole House			56			
Whitehead, William, *et al.*	Refund certain duties	17	1	Petition	99	Ways and Means	Feb. 2, 1822	Favorable	73	Laid on table.		
Whitehead, William, *et al.*	Refund certain duties	17	2	House bill	77	Whole House			73			
Whitehead, William, *et al.*	Refund certain duties	18	1	Petition	27	Ways and Means	Jan. 15, 1824	Favorable	60	Passed	Passed	App'd May 19, 1824
Whitehead, Col. Wm. A.	To be allowed the amount of rejected items in his account.	24	2	Documents	266	Commerce.						
Whitehead, Col. Wm. A.	To be allowed the amount of rejected items in his account.	25	2	Documents	413	Commerce				Discharged; laid on table.		
Whitehead, Col. Wm. A.	To be allowed the amount of rejected items in his account.	25	3	Petition	92	Commerce	100	Favorable	974	Referred to Committee Whole House.		
Whitehead, William A.	For money paid for chartering boat.	25	2	Petition	176	Claims	May 17, 1838	Favorable	974	Passed	Passed	App'd July 7, 1838
Whitehead, Wm. A.	For a credit on his account as collector.	25	3	Petition	205	Claims.						
Whitehead, Wm. A.	For a credit on his account as collector.	26	1	Petition	167	Claims				Discharged; laid on table.		
Whitehead, Wm. A.	For a credit on his account as collector.	26	1	Senate bill	189	Claims	April 4, 1840	With't amend.	2	Referred to Committee Whole House.		

List of private claims presented to the House of Representatives of the United States from the 1st to the 31st Congress, inclusive—Continued.

Names of claimants.	Nature or object of the claim.	Congress.	Session.	How brought before the House of Reps.	Page of journal.	To what committee of the House referred.	No. or date of the report.	Nature of the report.	No. of the bill.	How disposed of by the House of Reps.	How disposed of by the Senate.	Date of the act of Congress, and remarks.
Whitehead, Wm. A.	For a credit on his account as collector.	27	2	Petition	76	Claims	28	Adverse		Laid on table.		
Whitehill, Stewart H.	For a loan of money	16	1	Petition	174	Ways and Means				Discharged; laid on table.		
Whitehorn, Jno. G., *et al.*	Remission of duties	14	1	Petition	449	Com. and Manuf.				Discharged; laid on table.		
Whitehorn, Jno. G., *et al.*	Remission of duties	14	2	Petition	284	Select.						
Whitehorn, Jno. G., *et al.*	Remission of duties	19	2	Petition	187	Ways and Means.						
Whitehorn, Jno. G., *et al*	Remission of duties	23	1	Petition	215	Ways and Means.						
Whitehorn, Jno. G., *et al.*	Remission of duties	23	2	Petition	57	Ways and Means.						
Whitehorn, Jno. G., *et al.*	Remission of duties	24	1	Petition	143	Ways and Means.						
Whitehorn, Jno. G., *et al.*	Remission of duties	24	1	Petition	280	Ways and Means.						
Whitehorn, Jno. G., *et al.*	Remission of duties	24	2	Petition	213	Ways and Means	256	Adverse		Laid on table.		
Whitehorn, John	Pension	10	1	House bill	232	Whole House	Mar. 17, 1808	Favorable	78	Passed		App'd April 25, 1808
Whitehorn, Sally	(See Thos. Whitehorn, widow of)	25	2		547							
Whitehorn, Samuel	Pension	21	2	Petition	126	Military Pensions.						
Whitehorn, Samuel	Pension	22	1	Petition	83	Rev. Pensions.						
Whitehorn, Thomas, widow of.	Pension	25	2	Petition	547	Rev. Pensions				Discharged; laid on table.		
Whitehouse, Joseph	Compensation for services rendered in exploring expedition.	9	1	Presidt's message.	284					Laid on table.		
Whitehouse, Joseph	Compensation for services rendered in exploring expedition.	9	2	Presid'ts message.	470	Select	Dec. 22, 1806	Report		Referred to Committee Whole House.		
Whitehouse, Joseph	Compensation for services rendered in exploring expedition.			Resolution	507	Select	Jan. 23, 1807	Favorable	183	Passed	Passed	App'd March 3, 1807
Whiteley, David R.	Pension	24	2	Petition	212	Invalid Pensions	Feb. 2, 1837	Adverse		Laid on table.		
Whiteley, David R.	Pension	25	2	Petition	119	Invalid Pensions				Discharged; laid on table.		
Whiteley, David R.	Pension	25	3	Petition	90	Invalid Pensions				Discharged; laid on table.		
Whiteley, David R.	Pension	26	1	Petition	161	Invalid Pensions.						
Whiteman, Elizabeth	(See John Whiteman, widow of).	27	2		524							
Whiteman, Isaac, heirs of.	Indemnity for Indian depredations.	28	1	Petition	351	Indian Affairs	486	Adverse		Discharged; laid on table.		
Whiteman, John, widow of	Pension	27	2	Petition	524	Rev. Pensions	1105	Favorable	613	Referred to Committee Whole House.		
Whiteman, John, widow of	Pension	27	3	Petition	91	Whole House	Dec. 23, 1842	Favorable	613	Passed		
Whitemore, Elizabeth, *et al.*	(See Jonathan Whitemore, heirs of.)	23	2		197							
Whitemore, Jonathan, heirs of.	Compensation for revolutionary services.	23	2	Petition	197	Rev. Claims.						
Whitemore, Jonathan, heirs of.	Compensation for revolutionary services.	27	2	Petition	376	Rev. Claims	662	Adverse		Laid on table.		
Whitemore, Mary, *et al.*	(See Jonathan Whitemore, heirs of.)	23	2		197							
Whiteside, David	Confirmation of title to land	15	1	Petition	60	Public Lands				Discharged; laid on table.		
Whitesides, David	Settlement of claim for mail service.	24	1	Petition	602	Claims	April 15, 1836	Adverse.				
Whitesides, James A., *et al.*	Permission to correct error in land entry.	29	1	Petition	88	Public Lands	136	Favorable	142	Passed	Passed	App'd Aug. 8, 1846
Whitesides, Joel, *et al*	Refund money overpaid to United States.	25	2	Petition	548	Public Lands				Discharged.		

List of private claims presented to the House of Representatives of the United States from the 1st to the 31st Congress, inclusive—Continued.

Names of claimants.	Nature or object of the claim.	Congress.	Session.	How brought before the House of Reps.	Page of journal.	To what committee of the House referred.	No. or date of the report.	Nature of the report.	No. of the bill.	How disposed of by the House of Reps.	How disposed of by the Senate.	Date of the act of Congress, and remarks.
Whitesides, Joel, *et al*	Refund money overpaid to United States.	25	3	Petition	93	Claims.						
Whitesides, Joel, *et al*	Refund money overpaid to United States.	26	1	Petition	803	Public Lands	....	....	....	Discharged; laid on table.		
Whitesides, Joel, *et al*	Refund money overpaid to United States.	28	1	Petition	852	Public Lands.						
Whitesides, Joel, *et al*	Refund money overpaid to United States.	28	2	Petition	70	Public Lands.						
Whitesides, Mary	(See Peter Whitesides, widow of)	29	2	....	128							
Whitesides, Peter, widow of.	Indemnity for French spoliations prior to 1800.	26	1	Memorial	182	Foreign Affairs	343	Favorable	318	Referred to Committee Whole House.		
Whitesides, Peter, widow of.	Indemnity for French spoliations prior to 1800.	29	2	Memorial	128	Foreign Affairs.						
Whitesides, Peter, widow of.	Indemnity for French spoliations prior to 1800.	31	1	Petition	1239	Judiciary	355	Favorable; bill	318	Referred to Committee Whole House.		
Whitesides, Sarah, *et al.*	(See Caleb Dobbins, *et al.*)	14	2	....	391							
Whitesides, Thomas	Settlement of accounts	19	2	Petition	159	Claims	....	....	....	Discharged.		
Whitesides, Captain William B.	Compensation for services as spy	21	2	Petition	114	Claims	Jan. 7, 1831	Adverse	....	Laid on table.		
Whitesides, Captain William B.	Compensation for services as spy	22	1	Petition	226	Claims.						
Whitesides, Captain William B., heirs of.	Compensation for services as spy	24	1	Petition	851	Claims.						
Whitesides, Captain William B., heirs of.	Compensation for services as spy	24	2	Petition	160	Claims.						
Whitfield, Wm. L., *et al.*	For restoration of a certain amount improperly paid into treasury.	15	1	Petition	356	Ways and Means	....	....	....	Discharged; laid on table.		
Whitfield, Wm. L., *et al.*	For restoration of a certain amount improperly paid into treasury.	15	2	Petition	183	Ways and Means	Jan. 14, 1819	Adverse	....	Laid on table.		
Whitfield, William	Compensation for distributing stock among Indians.	29	1	Petition	316	Ways and Means.						
Whitford, Thomas	Pension	21	2	Petition	159	Military Pensions.						
Whiting, Amos, *et al*	(See Nathaniel Sawyer, *et al.*)	14	1	....	153							
Whiting, Daniel	Payment of a certain due bill given by assistant quartermaster general.	17	1	Petition	46	Claims	69	Adverse	....	Laid on table.		
Whiting, Ebenezer, widow of.	Pension	30	1	Petition	874	Rev. Pensions	Aug. 12, 1848	....	....	....	....	Leave to withdraw
Whiting, Elizabeth	(See Ebenezer Whiting, widow of)	30	1	Petition	874							
Whiting, Francis B., *et al.*	(See Henry White, heirs of)	29	2	....	223							
Whiting, Henry S., executors of.	Release as surety of Windsor Maynard.	18	2	Petition	158	Ways and Means.						
Whiting, Henry S., executors of.	Release as surety of Windsor Maynard.	19	1	Petition	177	Judiciary	....	....	....	....	....	Leave to withdraw
Whiting, Henry	Arrears of pension	21	1	Petition	499	Military Pensions	May 4, 1830	Adverse	....	Laid on table.		
Whiting, Henry, heirs of	Compensation for revolutionary services.	29	2	Petition	223	Rev. Claims.						
Whiting, Henry, heirs of	Compensation for revolutionary services.	30	1	Petition	575	Rev. Claims.						
Whiting, Henry, heirs of	Compensation for revolutionary services.	31	1	Petition	472	Rev. Claims.						
Whiting, Captain John	Compensation for military services.	13	2	Petition	196	Claims	Jan. 19, 1814	Adverse.	....	....	....	Leave to withdraw
Whiting, Captain John	Compensation for military services.	15	1	Petition	202	Military Affairs	Mar. 14, 1818	Adverse	....	Laid on table.		

List of private claims presented to the House of Representatives of the United States from the 1st to the 31st Congress, inclusive—Continued.

Names of claimants.	Nature or object of the claim.	Congress.	Session.	How brought before the House of Reps.	Page of journal.	To what committee of the House referred.	No. or date of the report.	Nature of the report.	No. of the bill.	How disposed of by the House of Reps.	How disposed of by the Senate.	Date of the act of Congress, and remarks.
Whiting, Joshua, attorney of.	Compensation for revolutionary services.	3	2	Petition	249	Claims	Feb. 25, 1795	Adverse	......	Laid on table.		
Whiting, Joshua, attorney of.	Compensation for revolutionary services.	5	2	Petition	89	Claims	Mar. 19, 1798	Adverse	......	Laid on table.		
Whiting, Josiah	Pension	22	1	Petition	710	Rev. Pensions.						
Whiting, Captain Lewis, heirs of.	Compensation for revolutionary services.	25	2	Petition	390	Rev. Claims	....	....	......	Discharged; laid on table.		
Whiting, Captain Lewis, heirs of.	Compensation for revolutionary services.	25	3	Petition	85	Rev. Claims	....	....	......	Discharged.		
Whiting, Captain Lewis, heirs of.	Compensation for revolutionary services.	26	1	Petition	164	Rev. Claims	611	Adverse	......	Discharged; laid on table.		
Whiting, Captain Lewis, heirs of.	Compensation for revolutionary services.	27	3	Petition	45	Rev. Claims	254	Adverse	......	Discharged; laid on table.		
Whiting, Captain Lewis, heirs of.	Compensation for revolutionary services.	28	1	Petition	101	Rev. Claims.						
Whiting, Captain Lewis, heirs of.	Compensation for revolutionary services.	28	2	Petition	104	Rev. Claims.						
Whiting, Captain Lewis, heirs of.	Compensation for revolutionary services.	29	1	Petition	172	Rev. Claims	644	Adverse	......	Laid on table.		
Whiting, Louisa	(See Maj. Tobias Whiting, widow of.)	28	1	....	252							
Whiting, Samuel	Pension	2	2	Rep. of Secretary War.	649	Whole House	Jan. 3, 1793	Favorable	214	Passed.		
Whiting, Samuel	Pension	3	1	Rep. of Secretary War.	131	Select	May 26, 1794	Favorable	J.R. 12	Passed	Passed	App'd June 9, 1794
Whiting, Samuel	Pension	3	2	Rep. of Secretary War.	262	Claims.						
Whiting, Samuel	Compensation for apprehending postmaster.	10	1	Petition	54	....	....	....	......	Referred to Postmaster General.		
Whiting, Samuel	Compensation for apprehending postmaster.	10	1	Rep't of Postmaster General.	119	Select	Feb. 3, 1808	Favorable	54	Passed	Passed	App'd Feb. 25, 1808
Whiting & Thatcher	(See Thatcher & Whiting)	29	1	....	160							
Whiting, Maj. Tobias, widow of.	Pension	28	1	Petition	252	Invalid Pensions	....	....	.....	Discharged; laid on table.		
Whiting, Maj. Tobias, widow of.	Pension	29	1	Petition	209	Invalid Pensions	July 13, 1846	....	.....	Discharged	....	Leave to withdraw.
Whittet, Robert	Pension	24	1	Petition	407	Invalid Pensions	....	....	.....	Discharged; laid on table.		
Whittet, Robert	Pension	25	2	Petition	57	Invalid Pensions	299	Favorable	339	Passed.		
Whittet, Robert	Pension	25	3	Petition	90	Invalid Pensions	78	Favorable	956	Passed.		
Whittet, Robert	Pension	26	1	Petition	162	Invalid Pensions	205	Favorable	217	Passed.		
Whittet, Robert	Pension	26	2	Petition	77	Invalid Pensions	59	Adverse	......	Laid on table.		
Whittet, Robert	Pension	27	2	Petition	60	Invalid Pensions	258	Adverse	......	Laid on table.		
Whittet, Robert	Pension	28	2	Petition	578	Invalid Pensions.						
Whittet, Robert	Pension	29	1	Petition	1203	Invalid Pensions.						
Whittet, Robert	Pension	30	1	Petition	485	Invalid Pensions	550	Favorable	450	Referred to Committee Whole House.		
Whittet, Robert	Pension	30	2	Petition	318	Whole House	Jan. 26, 1849	With amend.	450	Passed.		
Whitlock, Alice	(See T. Picket, widow of.)	23	2	....	128							
Whitlock, Ambrose	Refund certain moneys of which he was robbed as paymaster.	15	2	Petition	228	Claims	....	....	......	Discharged; laid on table.		
Whitlock, Ambrose	Refund certain moneys of which he was robbed as paymaster.	16	1	Petition	52	Claims	30	Adverse	......	Laid on table.		

List of private claims presented to the House of Representatives of the United States from the 1st to the 31st Congress, inclusive—Continued.

Names of claimants.	Nature or object of the claim.	Congress.	Session.	How brought before the House of Reps.	Page of journal.	To what committee of the House referred.	No. or date of the report.	Nature of the report.	No. of the bill.	How disposed of by the House of Reps.	How disposed of by the Senate.	Date of the act of Congress, and remarks.
Whitlock, Ambrose	Compensation for services as pay master.	15	2	Petition	228	Military Affairs				Discharged; laid on table.		
Whitlock, Ambrose	Compensation for services as pay master.	16	1	Petition	52	Claims.						
Whitlock, Ephraim	Permission to locate certain land warrants.	4	1	Petition	387	Select.						
Whitlock, Ephraim D., lieutenant in Navy.	For full pay and rations	23	1	Petition	189	Naval Affairs.						
Whitlock, John	Pension	5	2	Petition	184	Claims	April 17, 1798	Adverse		Laid on table.		
Whitlock, John	Pension	5	3	Petition	432	Whole House.						
Whitlock, William	Settlement of accounts	2	1	Petition	439					Referred to Secretary Treasury.		
Whitlock, William	Settlement of accounts	3	2	Rep. of Secretary Treasury.	284							
Whitlock, William	Settlement of accounts	4	1	Documents	452	Claims	May 31, 1797	Adverse		Referred to Secretary of Treasury.		
Whitlock, William	Settlement of accounts	4	2	Documents	614	Claims.						
Whitlow, Charles	Permission to import seed, &c., free of duty.	12	1	Petition	45	Com. and Manuf.						
Whitman, George	Permission to import iron free of duty.	24	1	Senate bill	365	Manufactures	March 3, 1836	Adverse	62	Referred to Committee Whole House.		
Whitman, George	Permission to import iron free of duty.	24	2	Petition	213	Ways and Means				Discharged; laid on table.		
Whitman, George	Permission to import iron free of duty.	24	2	Senate bill	260	Manufactures	Jan. 26, 1837	Adverse	111	Laid on table.		
Whitman, George	Permission to import iron free of duty.	25	2	Petition	255	Ways and Means.						
Whitman, George	Permission to import iron free of duty.	25	2	Senate bill	1276	Whole House	July 7, 1838	With amend.	147	Passed	Concurred in.	App'd July 7, 1838
Whitman, George	For settlement of accounts	27	2	Joint resolution.	461	P. Of. & P. Roads.	April 1, 1842	Favorable	6	Passed	Passed	App'd April 14, 1842
Whitman, George	(See Vance Johnson.)	29	1		423							
Whitman, John, (Mass.).	Pension	24	2	Petition	121	Rev. Pensions	Jan. 7, 1837	Adverse		Laid on table.		
Whitman, John, (Mass.).	Pension	25	2	Petition	350	Rev. Pensions.						
Whitman, John, (Mass.).	Pension	26	1	Petition	1[illegible]5	Rev. Pensions				Discharged; laid on table.		
Whitman, Lieut. Wm. O.	Compensation for loss of clothing on vessel wrecked.	31	1	Petition	857	Claims.						
Whitmarsh, Charles, *et al.*	For fishing bounty	25	3	Petition	103	Commerce	189	Adverse		Laid on table.		
Whitmarsh, Micah, widow of.	Pension	27	3	Petition	58	Rev. Pensions				Laid on table.		
Whitmarsh, Micah, widow of.	Pension	27	3	Petition	573	Rev. Pensions.						
Whitmarsh, Micah, widow of.	Commutation pay and interest	30	1	Petition	239	Rev. Pensions	831	Adverse		Laid on table.		
Whitmarsh, Micah, widow of.	Commutation pay and interest	30	2	Petition	236	Rev. Pensions						Leave to withdraw.
Whitmore, Amy	(See Wm. Whitmore, widow of.)	11	1		60							
Whitmore, Andrew, widow of.	Pension	26	1	Resolution	562	Rev. Pensions.						
Whitmore, Ebenezer	Indemnity for French spoliations prior to 1800.	26	1	Memorial	182	Foreign Affairs	343	Favorable; bill	319	Referred to Committee Whole House.		
Whitmore, Enoch	Restoration of pension	17	1	Petition	137	Rev. Pensions				Discharged; laid on table.		

List of private claims presented to the House of Representatives of the United States from the 1st to the 31st Congress, inclusive—Continued.

Names of claimants.	Nature or object of the claim.	Congress.	Session.	How brought before the House of Reps.	Page of journal.	To what committee of the House referred.	No. or date of the report.	Nature of the report.	No. of the bill.	How disposed of by the House of Reps.	How disposed of by the Senate.	Date of the act of Congress, and remarks.
Whitmore, Enoch	Restoration of pension	19	1	Petition	290	Military Pensions	164	Adverse	......	Laid on table.		
Whitmore, Gordon	Indemnity for French spoliations prior to 1800.	26	1	Memorial	182	Foreign Affairs	343	Favorable; bill	319	Referred to Committee Whole House.		
Whitmore, John	Pension	30	1	Petition	147	Invalid Pensions	355	Adverse	......	Laid on table.		
Whitmore, Joseph	Increase of pension	11	3	House bill	604	Clamis	Mar. 1, 1811	Favorable	218	Passed	Passed	App'd March 3, 1811
Whitmore, Lucy	(See Andrew Whitmore, widow of.)	26	1	....	562							
Whitmore, William, widow of.	Pension	11	1	Petition	60	Claims.						
Whitmore, William, widow of.	Pension	27	1	Petition	101	Rev. Pensions.						
Whitner, Benj. T., *et al.*	Confirmation of title to land	24	1	Petition	751	Public Lands.						
Whitney, Abel	To be released from payment of money lost.	4	1	Petition	396	Claims	Mar. 3, 1796	Adverse	......	Laid on table.		
Whitney, Abel	Increase of compensation as collector of revenue.	5	2	Petition	100	....	....	....	......	Referred to Secretary Treasury.		
Whitney, Abel	Increase of compensation as collector of revenue.	5	2	Rep. of Secretary Treasury.	100	....	April 18, 1795	....	......	Laid on table.		
Whitney, Elisha Dana	(See Frederick Dawson, *et al.*)	30	1	....	617							
Whitney, Daniel	For patents, surveys, &c., of certain lands.	23	1	Petition	450	Priv Land Claims.	396	Favorable	415	Referred to Committee Whole House.		
Whitney, Daniel	For patents, surveys, &c., of certain lands.	24	1	Petition	50	Priv. Land Claims.	182	Favorable	172	Referred to Committee Whole House.		
Whitney, Daniel	For patents, surveys, &c., of certain lands.	24	2	House bill	203	Whole House	....	....	172			
Whitney, Daniel	For patents, surveys, &c., of certain lands.	25	2	Senate bill	508	Priv. Land Claims.	782	Adverse	17	Referred to Committee Whole House.		
Whitney, Daniel	(See Lieut. Burdine, assignee of.)	23	1	....	567							
Whitney, Ebenezer	Restoration of pension	20	1	Resolution	88	Military Pensions	Feb. 13, 1828	Favorable	166	Passed.		
Whitney, Ebenezer	Restoration of pension	20	2	House bill	55	Whole House	Dec. 12, 1825	Favorable	311	Passed.		
Whitney, Ebenezer	Restoration of pension	21	1	Petition	75	Military Pensions	Jan. 5, 1830	Favorable	72	Passed	Passed	App'd May 20, 1830
Whitney, Ebenezer	Restoration of pension	21	2	Resolution	42	Military Pensions.						
Whitney, Eli, heirs of	Renewal of patent	12	1	Petition	295	Select	May 7, 1812	Favorable	126	Referred to Committee Whole House.		
Whitney, Eli, heirs of	Compensation for invention of cotton gin.	30	1	Petition	322	Select.						
Whitney, Franklin	Remuneration for expenses incurred in sustaining application for patent.	27	2	Petition	1049	Patents.						
Whitney, Franklin	Remuneration for expenses incurred in sustaining application for patent.	29	1	Petition	120	Patents.						
Whitney, Henry	Compensation for extra services as clerk on board of frigate	23	1	Petition	66	Naval Affairs	181	Favorable	199	Passed	Passed	App'd June 30, 1834
Whitney, John, (Mass.)	Indemnity as refugee	7	2	Petition	321	Claims	Feb. 26, 1803	Report	......	Laid on table.		
Whitney, John, (Mass.)	Indemnity as refugee	8	1	Petition	621	Claims.						
Whitney, John, (Mass.)	Indemnity as refugee	9	1	Petition	227	Select.						
Whitney, John, (Mass.)	Indemnity as refugee	10	1	Petition	40	Select.						
Whitney, John, *et al*	Relief from penalties for infraction of embargo act.	13	2	Petition	311	Select	87	Favorable	169	Passed	Passed	App'd April 18, 1814
Whitney, John H.	(See John Skinner & Sons)	26	1	....	714							
Whitney, John H.	(See John Skinner, administrator of.)	26	1	....	182							

List of private claims presented to the House of Representatives of the United States from the 1st to the 31st Congress, inclusive—Continued.

Names of claimants.	Nature or object of the claim.	Congress.	Session.	How brought before the House of Reps.	Page of journal.	To what committee of the House referred.	No. or date of the report.	Nature of the report.	No. of the bill.	How disposed of by the House of Reps.	How disposed of by the Senate.	Date of the act of Congress, and remarks.
Whitney, Joshua, agent of.	Compensation for revolutionary services.	4	2	Petition	627	Claims	Feb. 21, 1797	Report		Referred to Committee Whole House.		
Whitney, Joshua, agent of.	Compensation for revolutionary services.	5	2	Report	89	Whole House.						
Whitney, Joshua, agent of.	Compensation for revolutionary services.	6	1	Petition	535	Claims	Mar. 27, 1800	Report		Referred to Committee Whole House.		
Whitney, Joshua, (N. Y.,) *et al.*	(See Guy Maxwell, heirs of)	18	1		131							
Whitney, Josiah, attorney.	(See Phineas Miller, heirs of)	9	1		239							
Whitney, Michael	(See William Leech, executor of)	29	2		129							
Whitney, Nathan	Pension	22	1	Petition	45	Rev. Claims				Discharged; laid on table.		
Whitney, Phineas, jr	(See Peter Howe, *et al.*)	13	3		677					Discharged; laid on table.		
Whitney, Phineas	Pension	24	1	Petition	98	Invalid Pensions	June 22, 1836	Adverse		Laid on table.		
Whitney, Phineas	Pension	25	2	Petition	118	Invalid Pensions				Discharged.		
Whitney, R. P	Compensation for horse lost in military service.	30	1	Petition	146	Claims	429	Adverse		Laid on table.		
Whitney, Sarah	Continuation of pension	28	1	Petition	850	Rev. Pensions.						
Whitney, Seth	Pension	24	1	Petition	662	Rev. Pensions	783	Favorable	705	Referred to Committee Whole House.		
Whitney, Seth	Pension	25	2	Petition	38	Rev. Pensions	266	Favorable	309	Passed	Passed	App'd June 28, 1838
Whitney, William	Bounty land	25	2	Petition	577	Military Affairs				Discharged.		
Whitsel, Jacob, (Va.)	(See Jacob Whitzel)	4	1		379							
Whitsett, James	Pension	23	1	Petition	72	Invalid Pensions	Jan. 7, 1834	Favorable	154	Passed.		
Whitsett, James	Pension	24	1	Petition	98	Invalid Pensions	Jan. 15, 1836	Favorable	161	Passed.	Passed	App'd June 28, 1836
Whitsett, John	Confirmation of title to land	23	2	Petition	391	Public Lands	Feb. 27, 1835	Favorable	770	Referred to Committee Whole House.		
Whitsett, John	Confirmation of title to land	24	1	Petition	154	Public Lands	366	Favorable	369	Referred to Committee Whole House.		
Whitsett, John	Confirmation of title to land	25	2	Petition	42	Public Lands	206	Favorable	241	Referred to Committee Whole House.		
Whitsett, John	Confirmation of title to land	25	3	House bill	376	Whole House	Jan. 25, 1838	Favorable	241	Passed	Passed	App'd March 2, 1839
Whitsett, John, heirs of	For benefit of act of 2d March, 1829, to enter land at minimum price.	29	1	Petition	353	Public Lands	311	Favorable	249	Referred to Committee Whole House.		
Whitsett, John, heirs of	For benefit of act of 2d March, 1829, to enter land at minimum price.	29	2	House bill	61	Public Lands	Dec. 18, 1846	Favorable	249	Passed.		
Whitsett, John, heirs of	For benefit of act of 2d March, 1829, to enter land at minimum price.	30	1	Petition	607	Public Lands	May 16, 1848	Favorable	489	Passed.		
Whitsett, John	Increase of pension	27	2	Petition	1050	Invalid Pensions.						
Whitsett, William, sureties of.	Release from liability	17	2	Petition	228	Claims.						
Whitson, Harrison	Compensation for provisions and forage.	28	2	Petition	59	Claims	43	Favorable	517	Passed.		
Whitson, Harrison	Compensation for provisions and forage.	29	1	Petition	424	Claims	787	Favorable	517	Passed.		
Whitson, Harrison	Compensation for provisions and forage.	29	2	House bill	212	Whole House	Jan. 22, 1847	Favorable	517	Passed	Passed	App'd March 3, 1847
Whittaker, Ephraim	(See Ephraim Whitaker.)											
Whittal, Jacob	(See Martin Brunner,)	24	1		913							

List of private claims presented to the House of Representatives of the United States from the 1st to the 31st Congress, inclusive—Continued.

Names of claimants.	Nature or object of the claim.	Congress.	Session.	How brought before the House of Reps.	Page of journal.	To what committee of the House referred.	No. or date of the report.	Nature of the report.	No. of the bill.	How disposed of by the House of Reps.	How disposed of by the Senate.	Date of the act of Congress, and remarks.
Whittel, Robert	(See Robert Whittle.)	24	1		407							
Whittemore, Amos and William.	For extension of patent	10	2	Petition	504	Select	Feb. 27, 1809	Favorable	168	Passed	Passed	App'd March 3, 1809
Whittemore, Ebenezer, and others.	(See William Kittridge.)	2	1		521							
Whittemore, Nathaniel	Restoration of pension	17	1	Petition	77	Rev. Pensions				Discharged; laid on table.		
Whittemore, Nathaniel	Restoration of pension	20	1	Petition	45	Military Pensions	April 23, 1828	Adverse		Laid on table.		
Whitten, Easton	Correct error in land entry	22	1	Petition	33	Public Lands.						
Whitten, Easton	Correct error in land entry	23	1	Petition	638	Public Lands.						
Whitten, George	Pension	27	3	Petition	60	Invalid Pensions	218	Favorable	814	Referred to Committee Whole House.		
Whitten, George	Pension	28	1	Senate bill	942	Invalid Pensions	June 7, 1844	With't amend.	95	Referred to Committee Whole House.		
Whitten, George	Pension	28	2	Senate bill	178	Invalid Pensions	Jan. 7, 1845	With't amend.	54	Passed	Passed	App'd Feb. 13, 1845
Whitten, George W	Pension	30	2	Petition	476	Invalid Pensions				Discharged; laid on table.		
Whitten, Joseph	Payment of certificate of debt	16	1	Petition	217	Pens. & Rev. Cl'ms.	Mar. 6, 1820	Adverse		Laid on table.		
Whitten, Judeth	(See James Hibbert, former widow of.)	25	2		1120							
Whittenburg, Samuel and William.	(See Archibald Beard, *et al.*)	30	1		239							
Whitticar, Simon C	Reimbursement of money paid as surety.	20	2	Petition	116	Ways and Means				Discharged; laid on table.		
Whittical, Simon C	Reimbursement of money paid as surety.	21	1	Petition	63							Leave to withdraw.
Whittical, Simon C	Reimbursement of money paid as surety.	21	1	Senate bill	352	Ways and Means	Mar. 12, 1830	Fvorable	61	Referred to Committee Whole House.		
Whittical, Simon C	Reimbursement of money paid as surety.	21	2	Senate bill	79	Ways and Means	14	Favorable	3	Passed	Passed	App'd March 2, 1831
Whittle, Conway, heirs of.	Indemnity for French spoliations prior to 1800.	26	1	Memorial	182	Foreign Affairs	343	Favorable	319	Referred to Committee Whole House.		
Whittle, Conway, administrator of.	Indemnity for French spoliations prior to 1800.	29	2	Memorial	224	Foreign Affairs.						
Whittle, Fortesque, surviving partner.	For correction of error under late treaty with France.	25	2	Senate bill	675	Ways and Means	Mar. 30, 1838	With't amend	283	Passed		App'd April 4, 1838
Whittle, George	Pension	26	1	Resolution	562	Invalid Pensions	663	Adverse		Laid on table.		
Whittle, John G	(See Exploring Expedition)	27	3		149							
Whittlesey, Daniel	Increase of compensation as keeper of light-house.	25	2	Petition	46	Commerce				Discharged.		
Whittlesey, Daniel	Increase of compensation as keeper of light-house.	26	1	Petition	177	Commerce	388	Adverse		Laid on table.		
Whittlesey, Elisha, *et al.*	For grant of land	14	2	Petition	280	Roads and Canals				Discharged; laid on table.		
Whittlesey, Samuel, sureties of.	To cancel bond given by him as paymaster, New York militia.	15	1	Petition	47	Ways and Means	26	Favorable	24	Rejected.		
Whittlesey, Samuel, sureties of.	To cancel bond given by him as paymaster, New York militia.	16	1	Petition	190	Ways and Means	Mar. 27, 1820	Adverse.		Laid on table.		
Whittlesey, Samuel, sureties of.	To cancel bond given by him as paymaster, New York militia.	16	2	Petition and rep't.	28	Ways and Means	Nov. 27, 1820	Favorable	154	Passed	Passed, with amendment.	App'd July 11, 1821
Whittlesey, Samuel, sureties of.	Release from payment of interest on judgment.	18	1	Petition	177	Ways and Means	Feb. 23, 1824	Adverse		Laid on table.		

List of private claims presented to the House of Representatives of the United States from the 1st to the 31st Congress, inclusive—Continued.

Names of claimants.	Nature or object of the claim.	Congress.	Session.	How brought before the House of Reps.	Page of journal.	To what committee of the House referred.	No. or date of the report.	Nature of the report.	No. of the bill.	How disposed of by the House of Reps.	How disposed of by the Senate.	Date of the act of Congress, and remarks.
Whittlet, Robert	Pension	24	1	Petition	407	Invalid Pensions				Discharged; laid on table.		
Whittlet, Robert	Pension	25	3	Petition	90	Invalid Pensions	Jan. 2, 1839	Favorable	956	Passed.		
Whittlet, Robert	Pension	30	2	House bill	318	Whole House	Jan. 26, 1849	Favorable	450	Passed.		
Whitzal, Jacob	Confirmation of title to land	4	1	Petition	379	Select.						
Whitzal, Jacob	Compensation for military services	14	2	Petition	164	Pens. & Rev. Cl'ms.	Jan. 20, 1817	Adverse				Leave to withdraw.
Whitzal, Jacob	Compensation for services against Indians.	8	1	Petition	502	Claims.						
Whitzal, Jacob	Compensation for services against Indians.	8	2	Petition	89	Claims.						
Whitzal, Jacob	Compensation for services against Indians.	9	1	Petition	188	Claims.						
Whitzal, Jacob, heir of	Compensation for services against Indians.	14	2	Petition	164	Pens. & Rev. Cl'ms.	Jan. 20, 1817	Adverse				Leave to withdraw.
Wick, Hannah Jane	(See John Wick, widow of)	29	1		541							
Wick, John, widow of	Pension	29	1	Petition	541	Rev. Pensions.						
Wick, John, widow of	Pension	29	2	Report	150	Rev. Pensions.	24	Adverse		Laid on table.		
Wicks, Daniel, representatives of.	For payment of certain certificate	22	1	Petition	260	Rev. Claims	Mar. 2, 1832	Favorable	440	Passed.		
Wickes, Thomas	Compensation for revolutionary services.	1	2	Petition	193					Referred to Secretary of Treasury.		
Wickes, Thomas	Compensation for revolutionary services.	2	2	Report of Secretary Treasury	626					Laid on table.		
Wickersham, William	For deficiency in land	21	1	Petition	122	Public Lands				Discharged; laid on table.		
Wickersham, William	For deficiency in land	21	2	Petition	192	Public Lands				Discharged; laid on table.		
Wickersham, William	For deficiency in land	22	1	Petition	79	Public Lands	Jan. 3, 1832	Adverse		Discharged; laid on table.		
Wickersham, William	For deficiency in land	22	2	Petition	143	Public Lands				Discharged; laid on table.		
Wickham, William	Indemnity for property destroyed by enemy.	18	1	Petition	585							Leave to withdraw.
Wickham, William	Indemnity for property destroyed by enemy.	23	2	Petition	60	Claims.						
Wickham, William	Indemnity for property destroyed by enemy.	24	1	Petition	207	Claims.						
Wickham, William	Indemnity for property destroyed by enemy.	24	2	Petition	81	Claims	38	Adverse		Laid on table.		
Wickham, William	Indemnity for property destroyed by enemy.	25	2	Petition	398	Claims	May 17, 1838	Adverse		Laid on table.		
Wickham, William	Indemnity for property destroyed by enemy.	29	2	Petition and docs.	135, 149	Claims.						
Wickham, William	Indemnity for property destroyed by enemy.	30	1	Petition and docs.	480	Claims				Discharged; laid on table.		
Wickham, William	For right to certain fishery	25	2	Petition	113	Commerce	308	Favorable	345	Referred to Committee Whole House.		
Wickham, William	For right to certain fishery	26	1	Petition	176	Commerce	32	Favorable	51	Passed	Passed	App'd May 8, 1840
Wickham, ——	(See Orson Crane, sureties of)	25	2		51							
Widger, Joseph, widow of	Continuation of pension	25	2	Petition	113	Naval Affairs				Discharged; laid on table.		
Widger, Joseph, widow of	Continuation of pension	26	1	Petition	303	Naval Affairs.						
Widger, Rebecca	(See Joseph Widger, widow of)	25	2		113							

List of private claims presented to the House of Representatives of the United States from the 1st to the 31st Congress, inclusive—Continued.

Names of claimants.	Nature or object of the claim.	Congress.	Session.	How brought before the House of Reps.	Page of journal.	To what committee of the House referred.	No. or date of the report.	Nature of the report.	No. of the bill.	How disposed of by the House of Reps.	How disposed of by the Senate.	Date of the act of Congress, and remarks.
Widrig, Conrad	Pension	24	2	Resolution	222	Rev. Pensions	211	Favorable	927	Referred to Committee Whole House.		
Widrig, Conrad	Pension	25	2	Resolution	38	Rev. Pensions	169	Favorable	194	Passed.		
Widrig, Conrad	Pension	25	3	Petition	226	Rev. Pensions	184	Favorable	1043	Passed.		
Widrig, Conrad	Pension	26	1	Petition	172	Rev. Pensions	147	Favorable	157	Passed	Indef. postp'd.	
Widrig, Conrad	Pension	26	2	Petition	34	Rev. Pensions	Feb. 20, 1841	Adverse		Laid on table.		
Widrig, Conrad	Pension	27	2	Petition	59	Rev. Pensions	784	Adverse		Laid on table.		
Widrig, Conrad	Pension	28	1	Petition	84	Rev. Pensions				Discharged; laid on table.		
Wiggins, B. B.	Remuneration for losses sustained at suit of United States.	30	1	Petition	891	Claims.						
Wiggins, Eleanor	(See Wm. Wiggins, widow of)	26	1		830							
Wiggins, Elizabeth	(See Thos. Wiggins, widow of)	22	1		113							
Wiggins, Job, heirs of	Confirmation of title to land	22	1	Petition	1088	Priv. Land Claims.						
Wiggins, Richard C.	(See Daniel Jones, *et al.*)	9	1		324							
Wiggins, Thomas	For patent of his land	21	1	Senate bill	558	Public Lands	May 4, 1830	With't amend.	115	Referred to Committee Whole House.		
Wiggins, Thomas, widow of.	Arrears of pension	22	1	Petition	113	Rev. Claims	Jan. 11, 1832	Adverse		Laid on table.		
Wiggins, William, widow of.	Pension	26	1	Petition	830	Rev. Pensions				Discharged; laid on table.		
Wiggins, William, widow of.	Pension	27	3	Petition	401	Rev. Pensions.						
Wiggington, Polly	(See Gabriel Jones, child of)	26	1		323							
Wigham, Robert, widow of	Pension	22	2	Petition	266	Rev. Pensions				Discharged; laid on table.		
Wigham, Robert, widow of	Pension	23	1	Petition	490	Rev. Pensions				Discharged		Leave to withdraw.
Wigham, Prudence	(See Robert Wigham, widow of.)	22	2		266							
Wight, A. G. S.	For compromise of a certain judgment at suit of United States.	26	1	Senate bill	216	P. Of. & P. Roads.	Mar. 4, 1840	With amend.	77	Passed		App'd May 27, 1840
Wigh'man, George	Relief, &c., as prisoner, revolutionary war.	21	1	Petition	472	Rev. Claims				Discharged; laid on table.		
Wightman, Hannah	(See John Hart, widow of.)	28	2		140							
Wigle, John	Correct error in land entry	24	1	Petition	671	Public Lands	719	Favorable	667	Referred to Committee Whole House.		
Wigle, John	Correct error in land entry	25	2	Petition	42	Public Lands				Discharged.		
Wigle, John	Correct error in land entry	26	1	Petition	178	Public Lands.						
Wilber, Joseph	Pension	23	2	Petition	210	Invalid Pensions	Feb. 24, 1835	Adverse		Laid on table.		
Wilcox, Barbara	Pre-emption right to land	23	1	Petition	442	Priv. Land Claims.	April 17, 1834	Adverse		Laid on table.		
Wilcox, Benjamin, (R. I.)	Pension	20	2	Petition	262	Military Pensions	Feb. 17, 1829	Adverse		Laid on table.		
Wilcox, Charles	(See Wm. H. Bedford)	28	1		262							
Wilcox, David	Pension	19	1	Resolution	320	Military Pensions				Discharged; laid on table.		
Wilcox, David	Pension	21	1	Petition	356	Military Pensions				Discharged; laid on table.		
Wilcox, Dinah	Continuation of pension	28	1	Petition	850	Rev. Pensions.						
Wilcox, Ebenezer	Payment for horse lost and hay furnished during war of 1812.	24	1	Petition	91	Claims	481	Report		Referred to 3d Auditor Treasury.		
Wilcox, Ezra	Pension	4	1	Rep. of Secretary of War.	445	Claims	Feb. 18, 1796	Favorable	156	Passed	Passed	App'd April 20, 1796
Wilcox, James	(See Wm. H. Bedford.)	28	1		262							
Wilcox, James C	Donation of land in leiu of losses by Choctaw Indians.	24	1	Petition	57	Public Lands	208	Favorable	208	Referred to Committee Whole House.		

List of private claims presented to the House of Representatives of the United States from the 1st to the 31st Congress, inclusive—Continued.

Names of claimants.	Nature or object of the claim.	Congress.	Session.	How brought before the House of Reps.	Page of journal.	To what committee of the House referred.	No. or date of the report.	Nature of the report.	No. of the bill.	How disposed of by the House of Reps.	How disposed of by the Senate.	Date of the act of Congress, and remarks.
Wilcox, James, (N. J.)	Restoration of pension	17	2	Petition	24	Rev. Pensions				Discharged		Leave to withdraw.
Wilcox, James, (N. J.)	Restoration of pension	20	1	Petition	37	Military Pensions				Discharged; laid on table.		
Wilcox, James, (N. J.)	Restoration of pension	21	1	Petition	149	Military Pensions	April 27, 1830	Adverse		Laid on table.		
Wilcox, James, (N. J.)	Restoration of pension	21	2	Petition	68	Military Pensions.						
Wilcox, James, (N. J.)	Restoration of pension	22	1	Petition	524	Rev. Pensions				Discharged; laid on table.		
Wilcox, James, (N. J.)	Restoration of pension	25	2	Petition	180	Rev. Pensions				Discharged; laid on table.		
Wilcox, James	(See Josiah Savage, *et al.*)	18	1		27							
Wilcox, Joel	Pension	2	2	Rep. of Secretary War.	649	Whole House	Jan. 3, 1793	Favorable	214	Passed.		
Wilcox, Joel	Pension	3	1	Rep. of Secretary War.	131	Select	May 26, 1794	Favorable	J.R. 12	Passed	Passed	App'd June 9, 1794
Wilcox, Joseph	Increase of compensation as marshal D. C.	10	1	Petition	248	Select.						
Wilcox, Joseph	Increase of compensation as marshal D. C.	10	2	Petition	362	Select.						
Wilcox, Col. Jos., mother and guardian of.	For land in consideration of military services in Canada.	15	1	Petition	85	Public Lands.						
Wilcox, Col. Jos., mother and guardian of.	For land in consideration of military services in Canada.	21	1	Petition	147	Priv. Land Claims	Feb. 15, 1830	Adverse		Laid on table.		
Wilcox, Joseph, heirs of	For carrying G. A. Hughes, bearer of despatches from France, to United States.	17	2	Senate bill	174	Foreign Affairs	Feb. 3, 1823	With't amend.	28	Passed		App'd March 3, 1823
Wilcox, Joseph, (N. Y.)	Pension	20	2	Petition	203	Military Pensions				Discharged; laid on table.		
Wilcox, J. H. G.	Compensation for occupation of a house by United States troops in 1812.	26	1	Petition	339	Claims.						
Wilcox, J. H. G.	Compensation for occupation of a house by United States troops in 1812.	27	2	Petition	792	Claims.						
Wilcox, J. H. G.	Compensation for occupation of a house by United States troops in 1812.	27	3	Petition	175	Claims.						
Wilcox, Lemuel	(See John McIntire, *et al.*)	16	1		186							
Wilcox, Martin, sureties of	To be released from a certain judgment.	26	1	Petition	297	Judiciary	July 21, 1840	Favorable	510	Referred to Committee Whole House.		
Wilcox, Martin, sureties of	To be released from a certain judgment.	27	3	Petition	402	Judiciary	197	Favorable	805	Referred to Committee Whole House.		
Wilcox, Martin, sureties of	To be released from a certain judgment.	29	1	Petition	209	Judiciary	230	Adverse		Laid on table.		
Wilcox, Norris	Compensation for services rendered as marshal of Connecticut.	22	2	Resolution	331	Judiciary.						
Wilcox, Norris	Compensation for services rendered as marshal of Connecticut.	24	1	Resolution	407	Judiciary.						
Wilcox, Phineas	Pension	3	2	Rep't of Secretary War.	350	Claims.						
Wilcox, Richard H.	Renewal of register for ship	15	1	Petition	242	Com. and Manuf.	April 2, 1818	Adverse.		Laid on table.		
Wilcox, Stephen	Pension	19	1	Petition	77	Military Pensions	164	Adverse		Laid on table.		
Wilcox, Stephen	Pension	20	1	Petition	223	Military Pensions	April 29, 1828	Favorable	283	Passed.		

List of private claims presented to the House of Representatives of the United States from the 1st to the 31st Congress, inclusive—Continued.

Names of claimants.	Nature or object of the claim.	Congress.	Session.	How brought before the House of Reps.	Page of journal.	To what committee of the House referred.	No. or date of the report.	Nature of the report.	No. of the bill.	How disposed of by the House of Reps.	How disposed of by the Senate.	Date of the act of Congress, and remarks.
Wilcox, Stephen	Pension	20	2	House bill	55	Military Pensions	Dec. 12, 1828	Favorable	311	Referred to Committee Whole House.		
Wilcox, Stephen	Pension	21	1	Petition	49	Military Pensions	Jan. 5, 1830	Favorable	72	Passed	Passed	App'd May 20, 1830
Wilcox, Thomas	Compensation for a horse lost in 1807.	10	1	Petition	180	Claims.						
Wilcox, Thomas	Compensation for a horse lost in 1807.	11	2	Petition	121	Claims	Mar. 24, 1810	Report	......	Laid on table.		
Wilcox, Wm. and Joseph, (N. Y.) sureties.	Release from judgment as sureties of Martin Wilcox.	26	1	Petition	297	Judiciary	July 21, 1840	Favorable	510	Referred to Committee Whole House.		
Wilcox, Wm. and Joseph, (N. Y.) sureties.	Release from judgment as sureties of Martin Wilcox.	27	3	House bill	402	Judiciary	197	Favorable	805	Referred to Committee Whole House.		
Wilcox, Wm. and Joseph, (N. Y.) sureties of.	Release from judgment as sureties of Martin Wilcox.	29	1	Petition	209	Judiciary	230	Adverse	......	Laid on table.		
Wilcox, Wm., and Trueman Heminway (N. Y.)	For discontinuance of suit against them by United States.	26	1	Petition	1515	Judiciary.						
Wilcox, Wm., and Trueman Heminway (N. Y.)	For discontinuance of suit against them by United States.	26	2	Petition	135	Judiciary.						
Wilcox, Wm., and Trueman Heminway (N. Y.)	For discontinuance of suit against them by United States.	27	2	Petition	247	Judiciary.						
Wilcox, Wm., and Trueman Heminway (N. Y.)	For discontinuance of suit against them by Unit d States.	27	3	Petition	309	Judiciary.						
Witcoxen, Thomas H.	To refund $50 paid on execution in favor of United States.	19	1	Resolution	326	Ways and Means	....	....	......	Discharged; laid on table.		
Witcoxen, Thomas H.	To refund $50 paid on execution in favor of United States.	20	1	Petition	245	Ways and Means	....	....	......	Discharged; laid on table.		
Wild, Abigail, widow of	(See Ebenezer Wild, widow of).	25	2	....	913							
Wild, Daniel	Indemnity for French spoliations prior to 1800.	26	1	Memorial	182	Foreign Affairs	343	Favorable; bill	319	Referred to Committee Whole House.		
Wild, Ebenezer, widow of.	Pension	25	2	Petition	913	Rev. Pensions.						
Wildcat, U. S. schooner, representatives of officers and crew of.	(See Mordecai Boothe, *et al.*)	21	1	....	447							
Wilde, James, by Richard H. Wilde.	For settlement of his accounts as paymaster United States army.	15	2	Senate bill	87	Claims	Dec. 30, 1818	With't amend.	6	Referred to Committee Whole House.		
Wilde, James, by Richard H. Wilde.	For settlement of his accounts as paymaster United States army.	17	2	Petition	64	Claims	Jan. 13, 1823	Favorable	228	Referred to Committee Whole House.		
Wilde, Richard H.	To concel certain bonds given to export Africans.	20	1	Petition	59	Judiciary	76	Favorable	17	Referred to Committee Whole House.		
Wilde, Richard H., by R Campbell & G. B. Cummings.	Reimbursement of moneys expended in the purchase of certain Africans.	20	1	Petition	279	Whole House	April 26, 1828	Favorable	17	Referred to Committee Whole House.		
Wilde, Richard H., by R Campbell & G. B. Cummings.	Reimbursement of moneys expended in the purchase of certain Africans.	20	1	Senate bill	123	Judiciary	April 26, 1828	With amend.	35	Passed	Concurred in.	App'd May 2, 1828
Wilde, Lieutenant Richard, daughter of.	Pension	23	1	Senate bill	649	Invalid Pensions	Jan. 23, 1834	With't amend.	61	Rejected.		
Wilde, Lieutenant Richard, daughter of.	Pension	24	1	Senate bill	602	Invalid Pensions	Jan. 7, 1836	With't amend.	94	Passed	....	App'd June 15, 1836
Wilde, Lieutenant Richard, representatives of.	Interest on amount allowed by act of June 15, 1836.	25	3	Petition	124	Rev. Claims	....	....	......	Discharged.		
Wilde, Lieutenant Richard, representatives of.	Interest on amount allowed by act of June 15, 1836.	27	2	Petition	154	Rev. Claims	357	Adverse	......	Laid on table.		

List of private claims presented to the House of Representatives of the United States from the 1st to the 31st Congress, inclusive—Continued.

Names of claimants.	Nature or object of the claim.	Congress.	Session.	How brought before the House of Reps.	Page of journal.	To what committee of the House referred.	No. or date of the report.	Nature of the report.	No. of the bill.	How disposed of by the House of Reps.	How disposed of by the Senate.	Date of the act of Congress, and remarks.
Wilde, Lieutenant Richard, representatives of.	Interest on amount allowed by act of June 15, 1836.	27	3	Senate bill	250	Judiciary	Feb. 9, 1843	With't amend.	70	Laid on table.		
Wilde, Lieutenant Richard, representatives of.	Interest on amount allowed by act of June 15, 1836.	28	2	Petition	206	Claims.						
Wilder, Ephraim, widow of.	Pension	30	2	Petition	92	Invalid Pensions	37	Adverse	......	Laid on table.		
Wilder, James	(See John McCarroll.)	23	1	....	113							
Wilder, Joshua	Indemnity for property confiscated in Canada.	14	2	Petition	112	Claims	Jan. 27, 1817	Adverse	......	....	....	Leave to withdraw.
Wilder, Joshua	Pension	24	1	Documents	691	Rev. Pensions	....	....	......	Discharged; laid on table.		
Wilder, Oshea, (N. Y.)	Permission to purchase lands at minimum price.	21	1	Petition	298	Agriculture	....	....	......	Discharged; laid on table.		
Wilder, Shubail	Pension	20	2	Resolution	75	Military Pensions.						
Wilder, Shubail	Pension	21	2	Petition	158	Military Pensions.						
Wilder, Shubail	Pension	22	1	Petition	123	Rev. Pensions	June 16, 1832	Adverse	......	Laid on table.		
Wilder, Tabitha	(See Ephraim Wilder, widow of)	30	2	....	92							
Wilderman, Jacob	Compensat'n for services as mounted ranger in 1813.	20	2	Petition	102	Claims	41	Favorable	362	Referred to Committee Whole House.		
Wilderman, Jacob	Compensat'n for services as mounted ranger in 1812.	21	1	Petition	93	Claims	41	Favorable	55	Passed	Passed	App'd May 20, 1830
Wildes, Ann, & Eliza M. Kidwell, heirs of.	(See Claudius Besse)	29	2	....	163							
Wile, Conrad, administrator of.	(See Isaac Melchier, representatives of.)	16	1	....	39							
Wiles, Isaac, (Ohio.)	Pension	23	1	Petition	639	Invalid Pensions	....	....	......	Discharged; laid on table.		
Wiles, Isaac, (Ohio.)	Pension	24	1	Petition	99	Invalid Pensions	....	....	......	Discharged; laid on table.		
Wiley, Lieut. Aldrich, heirs of.	For balance standing to his credit on the books of War Department.	23	1	Petition	418	Rev. Claims.						
Wiley, Lieut. Aldrich, heirs of.	For balance standing to his credit on the books of War Department.	23	2	Petition	113	Rev. Claims.						
Wiley, David, widow of.	Compensation as surveyor for U. States.	12	2	Petition	598	Claims	Feb. 6, 1813	Favorable	254	Passed	Passed	App'd March 3, 1813
Wiley, Jacob	Pension	26	1	Petition	325	Rev. Pensions	551	Adverse	......	Laid on table.		
Wiley, John	Reimbursement of money advanced United States, revolutionary war.	1	2	Petition	197	....	....	....	......	Referred to Secretary War.		
Wiley, John F	Pension	23	1	House bill	427	Invalid Pensions	361	Favorable	388	Referred to Committee Whole House.		
Wiley, John F	Pension	23	2	Petition	436	Whole House	....	Favorable	388	Passed.		
Wiley, John F	Pension	24	1	Petition	201	Invalid Pensions	260	Favorable	269	Passed	Indef. postp'd.	
Wiley, John F	Pension	24	2	Petition	86	Invalid Pensions	....	....	......	Discharged; laid on table.		
Wiley, John F	Pension	25	2	Petition	71	Invalid Pensions	228	Favorable	266	Passed.		
Wiley, John F	Pension	25	3	Petition	89	Invalid Pensions	96	Favorable	972	Passed.		
Wiley, John F	Pension	26	1	Petition	162	Invalid Pensions	....	....	......	Discharged; laid on table.		
Wiley, John F	Pension	26	2	Petition	36	Invalid Pensions.						
Wiley, John F	Pension	27	2	Petition	60	Invalid Pensions	804	Favorable	461	Laid on table.		
Wiley, John F	Pension	27	3	Petition	89	Whole House	Dec. 23, 1842	Favorable	461	Passed	Passed	App'd March 3, 1843

List of private claims presented to the House of Representatives of the United States from the 1st to the 31st Congress, inclusive—Continued.

Names of claimants.	Nature or object of the claim.	Congress.	Session.	How brought before the House of Reps.	Page of journal.	To what committee of the House referred.	No. or date of the report.	Nature of the report.	No. of the bill.	How disposed of by the House of Reps.	How disposed of by the Senate.	Date of the act of Congress, and remarks.
Wiley, John, and Jefferson Grea.	Payment for improvements made by them on land sold by United States to others.	24	1	Petition	114	Public Lands	301	Favorable	315	Referred to Committee Whole House.		
Wiley, John, and Jefferson Grea.	Payment for improvements made by them on land sold by United States to others.	24	2	House bill	200	Whole House	....	Favorable	315	Referred to Committee Whole House.		
Wiley, John, and Jefferson Grea.	Payment for improvements made by them on land sold by United States to others.	25	2	Petition	42	Public Lands	205	Favorable	240	Referred to Committee Whole House.		
Wiley, John, and Jefferson Grea.	Payment for improvements made by them on land sold by United States to others.	25	3	House bill	376	Whole House	Jan. 25, 1839	Favorable	240	Passed	Passed	App'd March 2, 1839
Wiley, John M.	Compensation for horse lost in Florida.	26	1	Petition	336	Claims.						
Wiley, John M.	Compensation for horse lost in Florida.	26	2	Petition	52	Claims.						
Wiley, Joseph, *et al.*	For a grant of land in lieu of land by United States to an Indian.	27	2	Petition	379	Priv. Land Claims.						
Wiley, Matthew	Pension	25	2	Petition	71	Rev. Pensions	642	Favorable	618	Passed.		
Wiley, Matthew	Pension	25	3	Petition	188	Rev. Pensions	122	Favorable	989	Passed.		
Wiley, Matthew	Pension	26	1	Petition	172	Rev. Pensions	157	Favorable	167	Passed	Indef. postp'd.	
Wiley or Willey, Seth	Pension	25	3	Petition	128	Invalid Pensions.						
Wiley or Willey, Seth	Pension	26	1	Petition	163	Invalid Pensions	645	Favorable	478	Referred to Committee Whole House.		
Wiley, Susannah	(See David Wiley, widow of)	12	2	....	598							
Wiley, Tabitha	Pension	14	1	Petition	41	Rev. Pensions	....	....	......	Disch'd; laid on table.		
Wiley or Willey, Wm. D	Compensation for horse lost in Florida.	26	1	Petition	336	Claims.						
Wiley, William	For distribution of prize-money, frigate Philadelphia.	19	2	House bill	98	Naval Affairs	74	Favorable	70	Referred to Committee Whole House.		
Wiley, William	For distribution of prize-money, frigate Philadelphia.	21	1	House bill	137	Naval Affairs	Jan. 7, 1830	Favorable	82	Laid on table.		
Wiley, William	For distribution of prize-money, frigate Philadelphia.	22	1	Papers	29	Naval Affairs	Dec. 23, 1831	Favorable	98	Referred to Committee Whole House.		
Wiley, William	For distribution of prize-money, frigate Philadelphia.	23	1	House bill	101	Naval Affairs	45	Favorable	50	Referred to Committee Whole House.		
Wilgus, Samuel, heirs of	Grant of land for revolutionary services	24	1	Petition	853	Public Lands.						
Wilgus, William	Pension	23	2	Petition	191	Invalid Pensions	384	Favorable	403	Referred to Committee Whole House.		
Wilgus, William	Pension	23	2	House bill	336	Whole House	Feb. 6, 1835	Favorable	403	Passed	Passed	App'd March 3, 1835
Wilhemi, John P.	Permission to import slaves from West Indies.	14	1	Petition	435	Com. and Manuf.	....	....	......	Discharged; laid on table.		
Wilhied, Frederick, (Md.)	Pension	20	1	Petition	242	Military Pensions	April 29, 1828	Favorable	283	Passed.		
Wilhied, Frederick, (Md.)	Pension	20	2	House bill	55	Whole House	Dec. 12, 1828	Favorable	311	Passed.		
Wilhied, Frederick, (Md.)	Pension	21	1	Petition	49	Military Pensions	....	....	......	Discharged; laid on table.		
Wilhied, Frederick, (Md.)	Pension	22	1	Resolution	89	Rev. Pensions	....	....	......	Discharged; laid on table.		
Wilhied, Frederick, (Md.)	Pension	24	1	Resolution	274	Rev. Pensions	440	Favorable	453	Passed	Indef. postp'd.	
Wilhied, Frederick, (Md.)	Pension	25	2	Resolution	38	Rev. Pensions	176	Favorable	201	Passed.		
Wilhied, Frederick, (Md.)	Pension	25	3	Resolution	126	Rev. Pensions	....	....	......	Discharged; laid on table.		

List of private claims presented to the House of Representatives of the United States from the 1st to the 31st Congress, inclusive—Continued.

Names of claimants.	Nature or object of the claim.	Congress.	Session.	How brought before the House of Reps.	Page of journal.	To what committee of the House referred.	No. or date of the report.	Nature of the report.	No. of the bill.	How disposed of by the House of Reps.	How disposed of by the Senate.	Date of the act of Congress, and remarks.
Wilhoet, Enoch, (Ill.)	Correction of error in land entry	22	2	Senate bill	277	Public Lands	Feb. 11, 1832	With't amend.	68	Passed	....	App'd Feb. 19, 1833
Wilkes, Charles J.	Payment for instruments brought from South Sea expedition.	21	1	Petition	39	Naval Affairs	305	Favorable	360	Passed	Passed	App'd May 5, 1830
Wilkes, Charles J.	Compensation for purchasing and superintending the making of instruments.	22	1	Petition	99	Naval Affairs	Dec. 23, 1831	Favorable	91	Passed	Passed	App'd July 11, 1832
Wilkes, Charles, *et al.*	Compensation for losses sustained in consequence of the wreck of United States ship Peacock.	28	1	Petition	515	Naval Affairs	427	....	......	Discharged.		
Wilkes, Charles	(See Exploring Expedition)	27	3	....	149							
Wilkins, Asa, (Vt.)	Pension	20	1	Petition	124	Rev. Pensions	April 29, 1828	Favorable	283	Passed.		
Wilkins, Asa, (Vt.)	Pension	20	2	House bill	55	Whole House	Dec. 12, 1828	Favorable	311	Passed.		
Wilkins, Asa, (Vt.)	Pension	21	1	Petition	49	Military Pensions	Jan. 5, 1830	Favorable	72	Passed	Passed	App'd May 20, 1830
Wilkins, Charles	For balance due for supplies furnished United States troops.	18	1	Petition	32	Claims	96	Adverse	......	Laid on table.		
Wilkins, Charles	For balance due for supplies furnished United States troops.	18	2	Petition	174	Claims.						
Wilkins, Charles, execut'rs of.	(See Taylor, Morrison, & Wilkins.)	21	1	....	122							
Wilkins, Henry, and wife	(See Daniel Grabill, late widow of)	19	1	....	366							
Wilkins, James	(See John E. Hunt, *et al.*)	27	2	....	334							
Wilkins, James C., *et al.*	Permission to correct land entry	21	2	Petition	47	Priv. Land Claims.						
Wilkins, James W.	Compensation for services as purser.	31	1	Petition	191	Naval Affairs	234	Favorable	229	Referred to Committee Whole House.		
Wilkins, John, jr.	Correction of error in land entry, &c.	6	1	Petition	583	Select.						
Wilkins, Jno., jr., late quartermaster general U. S. A., administrator of.	For a settlement of his accounts by proper officers.	16	1	Petition	198	Select.						
Wilkins, Jno., jr., late quartermaster general U. S. A., administrator of.	For a settlement of his accounts by proper officers.	20	1	Senate bill	414	Claims	May 1, 1828	With't amend.	81	Referred to Committee Whole House.		
Wilkins, Jno., jr., late quartermaster general U. S. A., administrator of.	For a settlement of his accounts by proper officers.	20	2	Petition	49	Claims	3	Favorable	313	Referred to Committee Whole House.		
Wilkins, Jno., jr., late quartermaster general U. S. A., administrator of.	For a settlement of his accounts by proper officers.	21	1	Petition	35	Claims	1	Favorable	1	Passed	Passed	App'd Mar. 18, 1823
Wilkins, John	Permission of certain fines and forfeitures.	15	1	Petition	323	Ways and Means	....	....	......	Discharged; laid on table.		
Wilkins, Jonathan	Pension	10	1	House bill	232	Whole House	April 19, 1808	Favorable	78	Passed	Passed	App'd April 25, 1808
Wilkins, Littlejohn	Compensation for horse and equipments lost in Florida war.	26	1	Resolution	1023	Military Affairs.						
Wilkins, Littlejohn	Compensation for horse and equipments lost in Florida war.	26	2	Petition	79	Military Affairs	93	Favorable	599	Referred to Committee Whole House.		
Wilkins, Robert B.	Pension	3	2	Rep. of Secretary War.	337	Claims	Feb. 28, 1795	Favorable	130	Passed	Indef. postp'd	
Wilkins, Robert B.	Pension	4	1	Rep. of Secretary War.	445	Claims	Feb. 18, 1796	Favorable	156	Passed	Passed	App'd April 20, 1796
Wilkins, Robert B.	Pension	5	2	Memorial	157	Claims	Mar. 14, 1798	Adverse	......	Laid on table.		
Wilkins, Robert B.	Increase of pension	9	1	Petition	309	Claims	Mar. 28, 1806	....	......	....	....	Leave to withdraw.
Wilkins, Robert B.	Increase of pension	12	1	House bill	361	Whole House	June 15, 1812	Favorable	138	Passed	Passed	App'd July 5, 1812

List of private claims presented to the House of Representatives of the United States from the 1st to the 31st Congress, inclusive—Continued.

Names of claimants.	Nature or object of the claim.	Congress.	Session.	How brought before the House of Reps.	Page of journal.	To what committee of the House referred.	No. or date of the report	Nature of the report.	No. of the bill.	How disposed of by the House of Reps.	How disposed of by the Senate.	Date of the act of Congress, and remarks.
Wilkins, Robert B.	Increase of pension	15	1	Petition	178	Pens. & Rev. Cl'ms.	....	....	......	Discharged.		
Wilkins, Robert, (Va.)	Extension of time to locate land warrant.	17	2	Petition	40	Public Lands	Dec. 7, 1822	General bill	196	Laid on table.		
Wilkins, Ross	Increase of compensation as judge.	22	2	Petition	314	Territories.						
Wilkins, Ross	Increase of compensation as judge.	23	1	Petition	93	Territories.						
Wilkins, William	Compensation for revolutionary services.	4	1	Petition	425	Claims	May 7, 1796	Adverse	......	....	....	Leave to withdraw.
Wilkins, Willis, (Tenn.)	To change location of land	31	1	Petition	976	Public Lands.						
Wilkinson, Ann	(See T. J. Wilkinson, widow of.)	27	2	....	227							
Wilkinson, Asel	Compensation as pilot on board of Com. Perry's fleet, war of 1812.	23	1	Petition	34	Claims	65	Favorable	75	Passed	Passed	App'd June 28, 1834
Wilkinson, Asel	Pension	31	1	Petition	236	Naval Affairs	233	Favorable	228	Referred to Committee Whole House.		
Wilkinson, Asel	Pension	31	2	House bill	181	Whole House	Jan. 24, 1851	Favorable	228	Passed.		
Wilkinson, Celestine T.	(See Gen. James Wilkinson, widow of.)	19	2	....	59							
Wilkinson, Charles	Compensation for disabilities incurred in United States service.	25	2	Petition	278	Commerce	....	....	......	Discharged.		
Wilkinson, David, (N. Y.)	Compensation for his invention, called the guage lathe, used by United States.	30	1	Petition	287	Patents.						
Wilkinson, David, (N. Y.)	Compensation for his invention, called the guage lathe, used by United States.	30	1	Senate bill	976	Patents	July 25, 1848	With't amend.	187	Passed	....	App'd Aug. 14, 1848
Wilkinson, David & James	(See John Wilkinson, widow of.)	24	2	....	208							
Wilkinson, Emilie	(See Francis Valle, heirs of)	19	1	....	134							
Wilkinson, Major General James.	Compensation, &c., for fuel furnished and transporting baggage.	12	1	Senate bill	398	Whole House	June 26, 1812	With amend.	42	Passed	Concurred in	App'd July 1, 1812
Wilkinson, Major General James.	Indemnity for judgment, interest, and costs obtained by Gen. Adair, for false imprisonment.	15	2	Petition	220	Claims	....	....	......	Discharged; laid on table.		
Wilkinson, Major General James.	Indemnity for judgment, interest, and costs obtained by Gen. Adair, for false imprisonment.	16	1	Petition	216	Select	77	Favorable	103	Passed	Passed	App'd May 11, 1820
Wilkinson, Gen. James, widow of.	Pension	19	2	Petition	59	Military Pensions	....	....	......	Discharged.		
Wilkinson, Lieut. James B.	(See Zebulon M. Pike and companions.)	10	1	....	189							
Wilkinson, James	Payment of claim of damages against Ottowa Indians.	27	2	House bill	334	Claims	51	Favorable	86	Passed.		
Wilkinson, James	Payment of claim of damages against Ottowa Indians.	27	3	Petition	12	Claims	12	Favorable	633	Passed	Passed	App'd March 1, 1843
Wilkinson, Jefferson	Compensation for work at Cape Henry light-house.	28	2	Petition	36	Commerce.						
Wilkinson, Jesse, late commandant.	Indemnity for damages decreed for acts done under orders from Navy Department.	20	1	Petition	168	Naval Affairs	192	Favorable	220	Passed.		
Wilkinson, Jesse, late commandant.	Indemnity for damages decreed for acts done under orders from Navy Department.	20	1	Senate bill	466	Whole House	April 1, 1828	With't amend.	104	Passed	....	App'd May 24, 1828
Wilkinson, John	Pension	22	2	Petition	345	Rev. Pensions.						

List of private claims presented to the House of Representatives of the United States from the 1st to the 31st Congress, inclusive—Continued.

Names of claimants.	Nature or object of the claim.	Congress.	Session.	How brought before the House of Reps.	Page of journal.	To what committee of the House referred.	No. or date of the report.	Nature of the report.	No. of the bill.	How disposed of by the House of Reps.	How disposed of by the Senate.	Date of the act of Congress, and remarks.
Wilkinson, John	Pension	24	1	Petition	57	Rev. Pensions				Discharged; laid on table.		
Wilkinson, John, heirs of.	Compensat'n for property destroyed by British.	24	2	Petition	208	Claims	Feb. 24, 1837	Adverse		Laid on table.		
Wilkinson, John, heirs of.	Compensat'n for property destroyed by British.	25	2	Petition	88	Claims.				Discharged.		
Wilkinson, John, heirs of.	Compensat'n for property destroyed by British.	25	3	Petition	86	Claims	40	Favorable	937	Referred to Committee Whole House.		
Wilkinson, John, heirs of.	Compensat'n for property destroyed by British	26	1	Petition	168	Claims	14	Favorable	33	Passed	Indef postp'd.	
Wilkinson, John, heirs of.	Compensat'n for property destroyed by British.	26	2	Petition	101	Claims	15	Favorable	553	Referred to Committee Whole House.		
Wilkinson, John, heirs of	Compensat'n for property destroyed by British.	27	2	Petition	94	Claims	3	Favorable	42	Recommitted.		
Wilkinson, John, heirs of	Compensat'n for property destroyed by British.	27	3	Petition	73	Claims	75	Favorable	704	Passed	Indef. postp'd.	
Wilkinson, John, heirs of	Compensat'n for property destroyed by British.	28	1	Petition	110	Claims.						
Wilkinson, John, heirs of	Compensat'n for property destroyed by British.	29	1	Petition	274	Claims	321	Adverse.		Laid on table.		
Wilkinson, John G.	Compensation for services as pension agent.	31	1	Petition	313	Naval Affairs	43	Favorable	73	Referred to Committee Whole House.		
Wilkinson, John G.	Compensation for services as pension agent.	31	2	House bill	75	Whole House	Dec. 20, 1851	Favorable	73	Laid on table.		
Wilkinson, Joseph, (Ky.).	Release from confinement for money as collector of customs.	10	2	Petition	484	Select.						
Wilkinson, Joseph, (Ky.).	Release from confinement for money as collector of customs.	11	1	Petition	37	Select	June 19, 1809	Favorable	27	Passed	Passed	App'd June 28, 1809
Wilkinson, Joseph, commandant.	Pension	17	1	Petition	45	Rev. Pensions	Jan. 2, 1822	Adverse		Laid on table.		
Wilkinson, Joseph, commandant.	Compensation for revolutionary services.	25	2	Petition	54	Rev. Pensions				Discharged; laid on table.		
Wilkinson, Joseph, commandant.	Compensation for revolutionary services.	26	1	Petition	175	Rev. Pensions	714	Adverse		Laid on table.		
Wilkinson, Mary	Pension	28	2	Petition	346	Whole House.						
Wilkinson, Mott	Increase of pension	28	1	Petition	706	Rev. Pensions				Discharged; laid on table.		
Wilkinson, Mott	Increase of pension	28	2	Petition	184	Rev. Pensions.						
Wilkinson, Mott	Increase of pension	29	1	Petition	257	Rev. Pensions	519	Adverse		Laid on table.		
Wilkinson, Mott	Increase of pension	29	2	Petition	82	Rev. Pensions.						
Wilkinson, Mott	Increase of pension	30	1	Resolution	542	Rev. Pensions.						
Wilkinson, Mott	Increase of pension	31	1	Petition	668	Rev. Pensions	351	Adverse		Laid on table.		
Wilkinson, Reuben, representatives of.	Compensat'n for property destroyed by Indians.	21	1	House bill	463	Whole House	Mar. 26, 1830	Favorable; bill	392	Referred to Committee Whole House.		
Wilkinson, Reuben, representatives of.	Compensat'n for property destroyed by Indians.	22	1	Resolution	183	Ways and Means	243	Favorable; bill	331	Referred to Committee Whole House.		
Wilkinson, Samuel	Compensation for revolutionary services.	4	1	Petition	379	Claims.						
Wilkinson, Samuel	Compensation for revolutionary services.	4	2	Resolution, &c.	614	Claims	Jan. 4, 1997	Adverse.		Laid on table.		
Wilkinson, Samuel	Restoration of pension	17	1	Petition	269	Whole House				Discharged; laid on table.		

List of private claims presented to the House of Representatives of the United States from the 1st to the 31st Congress, inclusive—Continued.

Names of claimants.	Nature or object of the claim.	Congress.	Session.	How brought before the House of Reps.	Page of journal.	To what committee of the House referred.	No. or date of the report.	Nature of the report.	No. of the bill.	How disposed of by the House of Reps.	How disposed of by the Senate.	Date of the act of Congress, and remarks.
Wilkinson, T. J., widow of.	To refund money improperly held by General Land Office.	27	2	Petition	227	Claims.						
Wilkinson, Walter	(See Francis Valle, heirs of)	15	2		67							
Wilkinson, William	Pension	14	2	Petition	283	Pens. & Rev. Cl'ms.						
Wilkinson, William	Pension	23	2	Petition	67	Select	Feb. 25, 1835	Favorable; bill	769	Referred to Committee Whole House.		
Wilkinson, William	Pension	24	1	Petition	136	Select	337	Favorable; bill	352	Referred to Committee Whole House.		
Wilkinson, William	Additional compensation for revolutionary services.	25	2	Petition	1029	Rev. Pensions				Discharged; laid on table.		
Wilkinson, Young	Compensation for revolutionary services.	15	1	Petition	89	Pens. & Rev. Cl'ms.				Discharged; laid on table.		
Willard, Alexander	Compensation for services in exploring expedition.	9	1	President's mess.	284					Laid on table.		
Willard, Alexander	Compensation for services in exploring expedition	9	2	President's mess.	470	Select	Dec. 22, 1806	Report		Referred to Committee Whole House.		
Willard, Alexander	Compensation for services in exploring expedition.	9	2	Resolution	507	Select	Jan. 23, 1807	Favorable; bill	183	Passed	Passed	App'd March, 3 1807
Willard, Aurilla	(See George Willard, widow of).	25	2		90							
Willard, Burrows	Compensation as surveyor of public lands	25	2	Petition	1047	Claims	960	Favorable; res.		Referred to Secretary Treasury.		
Willard, George C., heirs and representatives of.	Permission to enter lands at minimum price.	24	1	Petition	435	Public Lands	533	Favorable; bill	527	Referred to Committee Whole House.		
Willard, George C., heirs and representatives of.	Permission to enter lands at minimum price.	25	2	Petition	42	Public Lands	203	Favorable; bill	236	Referred to Committee Whole House.		
Willard, George, widow of	Permission to enter lands at minimum price.	25	2	Petition	90	Public Lands				Discharged.		
Willard, George, widow of	Permission to enter lands at minimum price.	25	3	House bill	375	Whole House	Jan. 25, 1839	Favorable; bill	236	Passed.		
Willard, George, widow of	Permission to enter lands at minimum price.	26	1	Petition	178	Public Lands.						
Willard, Humphrey, or Henry, (N. Y.)	Bounty land for revolutionary services.	25	3	Petition	449	Priv. Land Claims.						
Willard, Humphrey, or Henry, (N. Y.)	Bounty land for revolutionary services.	26	1	Petition	281	Rev. Claims.						
Willard, Humphrey, or Henry, (N. Y.)	Bounty land for revolutionary services.	26	2	Petition	35	Rev. Claims	185	Adverse		Laid on table.		
Willard, John, (N. Y.)	(See T. P. Baldwin, surety of)	19	2		37							
Willard, Jonathan, (N. H.)	Pension	3	2	Rep. of Secretary of War	350	Claims.						
Willard, Jonathan, (N. H.)	Pension	4	1	Resl'n and report	445	Claims	Feb. 18, 1796	Favorable; bill	156	Passed	Passed	App'd April 20, 1796
Willard, Jonathan, (N. H.)	Increase of pension	9	2	House bill	608	Whole House	Feb. 24, 1807	Favorable; bill	216	Passed	Passed	App'd May 3, 1807
Willard, Jonathan, (N. H.)	Increase of pension	13	2	House bill	377	Whole House	Mar. 31, 1814	Favorable; bill	166	Passed	Passed	App'd April 18, 1814
Willard, Josiah, attorney of.	Indemnity for French spoliations prior to 1800.	26	1	Memorial	182	Foreign Affairs	431	Favorable; bill	319	Referred to Committee Whole House.		
Willard, Samuel	Pension	13	1	Petition	22	Claims				Discharged.		
Willard, Samuel	Pension	14	1	Petition	301	Pens. & Rev. Cl'ms.				Discharged.		
Willard, William, (Conn.)	Additional compensation as surveyor of customs	20	1	Petition	163	Commerce				Discharged; laid on table.		
Willard, Orilla	(See George C. Willard, widow of)	21	1		435							
Willbank, James	Compensation for professional services at Philadelphia navy yard.	23	2	Petition	237	Naval Affairs	99	Favorable	724	Referred to Committee Whole House.		

List of private claims presented to the House of Representatives of the United States from the 1st to the 31st Congress, inclusive—Continued.

Names of claimants.	Nature or object of the claim.	Congress.	Session.	How brought before the House of Reps.	Page of journal.	To what committee of the House referred.	No. or date of the report.	Nature of the report.	No. of the bill.	How disposed of by the House of Reps.	How disposed of by the Senate.	Date of the act of Congress, and remarks.
Willborn, Curtis	Confirmation of title to land	15	1	Petition	312	Priv. Land Claims.				Discharged; laid on table.		
Willborn, Curtis	Confirmation of title to land	16	1	Petition	71	Priv. Land Claims.				Discharged; laid on table.		
Willborn, Curtis	Confirmation of title to land	17	1	Petition	54	Public Lands				Discharged; laid on table.		
Willborn, Curtis	Confirmation of title to land	18	1	Petition	55	Public Lands	Jan. 16, 1824	Favorable	65	Passed	Passed	App'd May 26, 1824
Willborn, James	Confirmation of title to land	15	1	Petition	312	Priv. Land Claims.				Discharged; laid on table.		
Willborn, James	Confirmation of title to land	16	1	Petition	72	Priv. Land Claims.				Discharged; laid on table.		
Willborn, James	Confirmation of title to land	17	1	Petition	54	Public Lands				Discharged; laid on table.		
Willborn, James	Confirmation of title to land	18	1	Petition	55	Public Lands	Jan. 16, 1824	Favorable	65	Passed	Passed	App'd May 26, 1824
Willett, Augustin, representatives of.	Compensation for revolutionary services, and reimbursement of money expended, &c.	25	2	Petition	200	Rev. Claims				Discharged; laid on table.		
Willett, Augustin, representatives of.	Compensation for revolutionary services, and reimbursement of money expended, &c.	26	1	Petition	361	Rev. Claims.						
Willett, Augustin, representatives of.	Compensation for revolutionary services, and reimbursement of money expended, &c.	26	2	Petition	77	Rev. Claims	Feb. 12, 1841	Adverse		Laid on table.		
Willett, Augustin, representatives of.	Compensation for revolutionary services, and reimbursement of money expended, &c.	27	2	Petition	62	Rev. Claims	1088	Adverse		Laid on table.		
Willett, Augustin, representatives of.	Compensation for revolutionary services, and reimbursement of money expended, &c.	28	1	Petition	84, 117	Rev. Claims.						
Willett, Augustin, representatives of.	Compensation for revolutionary services, and reimbursement of money expended, &c.	28	2	Petition	252	Rev. Claims.						
Willett, Augustin, representatives of.	Compensation for revolutionary services, and reimbursement of money expended, &c.	29	1	Petition	439	Rev. Claims.						
Willett, Augustin, representatives of.	Compensation for revolutionary services, and reimbursement of money expended, &c.	30	1	Petition	435	Rev. Claims.						
Willets, Dudley	Release from contract to pay for land.	27	3	Petition	103, 316	Public Lands.						
Willet, Edward, (Ky.)	Payment of interest on certain bills of exchange.	22	1	Petition	575	Claims.						
Willet, Edward, (Ky.)	Payment of interest on certain bills of exchange.	22	2	Petition	74	Claims	19	Favorable	650	Referred to Committee Whole House.		
Willet, Edward, (Ky.)	Payment of interest on certain bills of exchange.	23	1	Petition	34	Claims	16	Favorable	16	Passed	Passed	App'd Feb. 5, 1834
Willett, Edward, executors of.	Repeal of proviso in the act of 5th February, 1834.	24	2	Petition	395	Claims.						
Willett, Edward, executors of.	Repeal of proviso in the act of 5th February, 1834.	25	2	Petition	273	Claims	Feb. 6, 1838	Adverse		Laid on table.		
Willet, Gilbert	Pension	16	1	Petition	252	Rev. Pensions	April 6, 1820	Adverse		Laid on table.		
Willet, Henry S.	Increase of compensation as clerk in navy yard, New York.	25	2	Petition	398	Naval Affairs				Discharged; laid on table.		

List of private claims presented to the House of Representatives of the United States from the 1st to the 31st Congress, inclusive—Continued.

Names of claimants.	Nature or object of the claim.	Congress.	Session.	How brought before the House of Reps.	Page of journal.	To what committee of the House referred	No. or date of the report.	Nature of the report.	No. of the bill.	How disposed of by the House of Reps.	How disposed of by the Senate.	Date of the act of Congress, and remarks.
Willet, Henry S.	Increase of compensation as clerk in navy yard, New York.	28	2	Petition	188	Naval Affairs.						
Willett, Joseph R.	(See Augustin Willett, heirs of)	25	2		200							
Willet's regiment, officers and men of.	Benefit of act of 18th March, 1818.	16	1	Petition	85	Rev. Pensions	Jan. 14, 1820	Adverse		Laid on table.		
Willet, Levi, by Thomas	Confirmation of title to land	20	1	Resolution	28	Public Lands	42	Favorable	34	Passed	Passed	App'd April 22, 1828
Willet, Marinus, *et al*	(See New York city, collector of the port of New York.)	26	2		783							
Willet, Marinus, (N. Y.)	Compensation for revolutionary services	20	1	Petition	110	Rev. Claims	Jan. 18, 1828	Adverse		Laid on table.		Leave to withdraw.
Willey, Seth	(See Seth Wiley.)	25	3		128							
Willets, Peter N.	Increase of pension	31	1	Petition	257	Invalid Pensions						
Williams, Abigail	(See Heil Williams, widow of.)	30	1		786							
Williams, Absolem	For exchange of land	20	1	Petition	246	Public Lands				Discharged; laid on table.		
Williams, Alexander	Balance due for revolutionary services.	11	1	Petition	55	Claims.						
Williams, Alexander	Bounty in land and money for revolutionary services.	21	2	Resolution	96	Rev. Claims				Discharged; laid on table.		
Williams & Alden	(See Alden & Williams.)	31	1		727							
Williams, Alice	(See J. C. Williams, widow of)	27	2		320							
Williams, Amos A.	Arrears of pension	23	1	Petition	216	Invalid Pensions	Mar. 23, 1834	Adverse		Laid on table.		
Williams, Amy, daughter of Amos Stanton.	(See Amos Stanton.)	25	2		586							
Williams, Asa, (Mass.)	Restoration of pension	17	1	Petition	186	Whole House				Discharged; laid on table.		
Williams, Batholomew, (N. York.)	Pension	22	1	Resolution	250	Rev. Pensions				Discharged; laid on table.		
Williams, Benjamin	Compensation for revolutionary services.	11	2	Petition	249	Claims	Mar. 24, 1810	Adverse		Laid on table.		
Williams, Benjamin	Compensation for revolutionary services.	15	2	Petition	163	Pens. & Rev. Cl'ms.	Feb. 11, 1819	Adverse		Laid on table.		
Williams, Benjamin	Increase of pension	24	2	Petition	103	Invalid Pensions	Jan. 7, 1837	Adverse		Laid on table.		
Williams, Benjamin, widow of.	(See John Swaggart and Mary Williams.)	18	1		101							
Williams, Benoni	Pension	23	1	Petition	53	Rev. Pensions				Discharged; laid on table.		
Williams, Benoni	Pension	25	3	Petition	673					Laid on table.		
Williams, Beverly	Pension	14	1	House bill	622	Pens. & Rev. Cl'ms.	April 11, 1816	Favorable	171	Passed	Passed	App'd April 30, 1816
Williams, Capt. Beverly	Increase of pension	27	2	Petition	1158	Invalid Pensions.						
Williams, Caleb, and Stephen W. Hunt.	Remission of duties on certain goods	25	2	Petition	923	Commerce.	1020	Adverse		Laid on table.		
Williams, Caleb, and Stephen W. Hunt.	Remission of duties on certain goods.	2	3	Petition	121	Commerce.	169	Adverse		Laid on table		Leave to withdraw
Williams & Carey, assignees of.	For proceeds of sale of schooner Friendship.	9	2	Petition	607					Laid on table.		
Williams & Carroll	Released from payment of half duties on distillery.	13	3	Petition	666	Ways and Means.				Discharged.		
Williams, Catharine	(See John Williams, widow of)	26	1		627							
Williams, Catharine	(See John Williams, widow of)	2[illegible]	2		67							
Williams, Charity	(See Captain Theodore Williams widow of.)	18	1		42							
Williams, Charles	Compensation for wagon and horses lost in United States service.	14	2	Petition	355	Claims	Feb. 13, 1817	Favorable; bil	135	Passed	Passed	App'd March 3, 1817

List of private claims presented to the House of Representatives of the United States from the 1st to the 31st Congress, inclusive—Continued.

Names of claimants.	Nature or object of the claim.	Congress.	Session.	How brought before the House of Reps.	Page of journal.	To what committee of the House referred.	No. or date of the report.	Nature of the report.	No. of the bill.	How disposed of by the House of Reps.	How disposed of by the Senate.	Date of the act of Congress, and remarks.
Williams, Charles, widow of.	Relief, in consequence of the death of husband in United States service	9	2	Petition	503	Claims.						
Williams, Cornelius	Pension	14	1	Petition	318	Pens. & Rev. Cl'ms.		Favorable; bill	171	Passed	Passed	App'd April 30, 1816
Williams, Capt. Cornelius, heirs of.	Pension	28	1	Petition	786	Rev. Pensions.						
Williams, Cumberland D., administrator of.	Indemnity for French spoliations prior to 1800.	26	1	Memorial	182	Foreign Affairs	343	Favorable; bill	319	Referred to Committee Whole House.		
Williams, Daniel, representatives of.	For two years' full pay in lieu of commutation half-pay.	24	1	Petition	753	Rev. Claims.						
Williams, Daniel, representatives of.	For two years' full pay in lieu of commutation half-pay.	24	2	Petition	92	Rev. Claims.						
Williams, Daniel, representatives of.	For two years' full pay in lieu of commutation half pay.	25	2	Petition	49	Rev. Claims	717	Favorable; bill	686	Passed	Passed	App'd July 7, 1838
Williams, David	Renewal of land warrant	31	1	Petition	1284	Public Lands.						
Williams, David, one of the captors of Andre.	Annuity or compensation for services.	6	2	House bill	752	Ways and Means	Jan. 5, 1801	Favorable; bill	277	Passed	Passed	App'd March 3, 1801
Williams, David, one of the captors of Andre.	Increase of pension	21	1	Petition	356	Military Pensions	April 27, 1830	Adverse		Laid on table.		
Williams, David, one of the captors of Andre.	Increase of pension	22	2	Resolution	48	Military Pensions				Discharged; laid on table.		
Williams, David, widow of.	Increase of pension	25	3	Resolution	289	Rev. Pensions				Discharged.		
Williams, David, widow of.	Increase of pension	26	1	Petition	281	Rev. Pensions	551	Adverse		Laid on table.		
Williams, David, widow of.	Increase of pension	27	3	Petition	101	Rev. Pensions	136	Favorable	761	Passed	Passed	App'd March 3, 1843
Williams, David F	(See David F. Williamson)	29	1		176							
Williams, Edwin	Asking Congress to purchase his works.	30	2	Petition	534	Library.						
Williams, E. H	(See H. W. Crouch, administrator of)	25	2		629							
Williams, E., agent of	Indemnity for French spoliations prior to 1800.	26	1	Memorial	182	Foreign Affairs	343	Favorable; bill	319	Referred to Committee Whole House.		
Williams, Eleazer	Indemnity for expenditures as Indian agent.	24	2	House bill	100	Ways and Means	Dec. 21, 1836	Favorable; bill	757	Passed	Passed	App'd March 3, 1837
Williams, Eleazer and Thomas.	Grant of land as compensation for losses and military services.	20	2	Petition	229	Priv. Land Claims				Discharged; laid on table.		
Williams, Eli	Grant of land as compensation for expenses in supplying northwestern army.	5	2	Petition	207	Select	Jan. 23, 1798	Favorable	117	Passed	Passed	App'd July 16, 179
Williams, Elisha O	Additional compensation as inspector of tobacco in Georgetown.	7	1	Petition	176	Select.						
Williams, Eliza S	(See Isaac Williams, widow of)	23	1		450							
Williams, Elizabeth	(See Daniel Kidder, widow of.)	25	2		53							
Williams, Elizabeth	(See Charles Williams, widow of.)	9	2		503							
Williams, Elizabeth	(See Thomas Wilson, widow of.)	21	1		262							
Williams, Ezekiel	Compensation as postmaster	5	2	Petition	95	P. Of. & P. Roads.						
Williams, Ezekiel	Compensation as postmaster	5	3	Petition	425	P. Of. & P. Roads				Referred to Postmaster General.		
Williams, Ezekiel	(See Cornelius Williams, heirs of.)	28	1		786							
Williams, Ezekiel	Remission of duties	14	2	Petition	69	Ways and Means	Jan. 25, 1817	Favorable	72	Referred to Committee Whole House.		
Williams, jr., Ezekiel	(See William Hildrup, administrator of.)	8	1		544							
Williams, Flavel	(See Martin S. Aikin, *et al.*)	17	1		359							

List of private claims presented to the House of Representatives of the United States from the 1st to the 31st Congress, inclusive—Continued.

Names of claimants.	Nature or object of the claim.	Congress.	Session.	How brought before the House of Reps.	Page of journal.	To what committee of the House referred.	No. or date of the report.	Nature of the report.	No. of the bill.	How disposed of by the House of Reps.	How disposed of by the Senate.	Date of the act of Congress, and remarks.
Williams, Frederick	Drawback on French wines	16	2	Petition	199	Commerce				Discharged; laid on table.		
Williams, Frederick	(See Isaac Crow, assignee of.)	27	2		140, 622							
Williams, George	(See Henry Williams, *et al.*)	30	2		237							
Williams, George, (Ohio.)	Compensation for lands of his ancestor which has enured to the government.	26	1	Petition	947	Priv. Land Claims.	June 30, 1840	Adverse		Laid on table.		
Williams, George, administrator of.	Indemnity for French spoliations prior to 1800.	26	1	Memorial	182	Foreign Affairs	343	Favorable; bill	319	Referred to Committee Whole House.		
Williams, George	(See Alden & Williams)	31	1		433							
Williams, Gilbert, widow of.	Pension	27	2	Petition	748	Rev. Pensions	784	Adverse		Laid on table.		
Williams, Gilbert, widow of.	Pension	27	3	Petition	73	Rev. Pensions.						
Williams, Gilbert, widow of.	Pension	28	1	Resolution	313, 318	Rev. Pensions.						
Williams, Heil, widow of.	Arrears of pension	30	1	Petition	786	Rev. Pensions				Discharged; laid on table		
Williams, Henry, *et al.*	Indemnity for loss of schooner Ticonic.	30	2	Senate bill	237	Claims	Feb. 21, 1849	With't amend.	211	Passed		App'd March 3, 1849
Williams, Henry, (Ky.)	Indemnity for horses impressed into United States service.	14	2	Petition	101	Claims.				Discharged; laid on table.		
Williams, Henry, (Ky.)	Indemnity for horses impressed into United States service.	15	1	Petition	130	Claims	63	Adverse				Leave to withdraw.
Williams, Henry, (Ky.)	Indemnity for horses impressed into United States service.	21	1	Petition	170	Claims	198	Favorable	149	Passed	Passed	App'd May 28, 1830
Williams, Henry H	Indemnity for injuries to property by United States army.	2	1	Petition	521					Referred to Secretary Treasury.		
Williams, Henry H.	For payment of certain drafts accepted by Postmaster General.	27	2	Petition	540	Judiciary	953	Adverse		Laid on table.		
Williams, Henry H.	For payment of certain drafts accepted by Postmaster General.	28	2	Petition	208	P. Of. & P. Roads.						
Williams, Henry H.	For payment of certain drafts accepted by Postmaster General.	29	1	Petition	436	P. Of. & P. Roads						
Williams, Hezekiah	Indemnity for damages by reason of Cumberland road crossing mill-dam.	25	3	Rep. of Secretary War.	368	Claims.						
Williams, Hezekiah	Indemnity for damages by reason of Cumberland road crossing mill dam.	26	1	Petition	170	Claims.						
Williams, Horatio A.	Release from the payment of a certain judgment.	22	1	Petition	868	Judiciary				Discharged; laid on table.		
Williams, Isaac	For a settlement of his accounts, &c.	9	1	Petition	321					Referred to Secretary of State.		
Williams, Isaac	Confirmation of title to land	15	1	Petition	367	Priv. Land Claims.						
Williams, Isaac	Confirmation of title to land	16	1	Petition	71	Priv. Land Claims.						
Williams, Isaac	Confirmation of title to land	17	1	Petition	54	Public Land						
Williams, Isaac	Confirmation of title to land	18	1	Petition	55	Public Lands	Jan. 16, 1824	Favorable	65	Passed	Passed	App'd May 26, 1824
Williams, Isaac, widow of	To re-enter land, &c.	23	1	Petition	450	Priv. Land Claims.	395	Favorable	414	Referred to Committee Whole House.		
Williams, Isaac, widow of	Permission to complete payment for land.	24	1	Petition	208	Priv. Land Claims.	291	Favorable	296	Referred to Committee Whole House.		

List of private claims presented to the House of Representatives of the United States from the 1st to the 31st Congress, inclusive—Continued.

Names of claimants	Nature or object of the claim.	Congress.	Session.	How brought before the House of Reps.	Page of journal.	To what committee of the House referred.	No. or date of the report.	Nature of the report.	No. of the bill.	How disposed of by the House of Reps.	How disposed of by the Senate.	Date of the act of Congress, and remarks.
Williams, Isaac	To re-enter land	24	2	House bill	200	Whole House	Jan. 13, 1837	Favorable	296	Passed	Passed	App'd March 3, 1837
Williams, Isaac, (postmaster.)	Released from the payment of a certain judgment and costs.	7	2	Petition	251	Claims.						
Williams, Isaac, (postmaster.)	Released from the payment of a certain judgment and costs.	18	1	Petition	253	P. Of. & P. Roads				Discharged		Leave to withdraw.
Williams, Isaac	(See James Whitaker, *et al.*)	21	1		173							
Williams, Jacob	Increase of pension	13	1	House bill	56	Whole House	July 20, 1813	Favorable	31	Passed	Passed	App'd Aug. 2, 1813
Williams, Jacob, widow of	Pension	25	3	Petition	216	Rev. Pensions				Discharged; laid on table.		
Williams, Jacob, widow of	Pension	26	1	Petition	173	Rev. Pensions	347	Favorable	326	Referred to Committee Whole House.		
Williams, Jacob, widow of	Pension	27	2	Petition	1189	Rev. Pensions	1003	Favorable	582	Referred to Committee Whole House.		
Williams, Jacob, widow of	Pension	27	3	House bill	91	Whole House	Dec. 23, 1812	Favorable	582	Passed	Passed	App'd March 1, 1843
Williams, Jacob, widow of	Pension—explanatory of act of 1st March, 1843.	28	1	Senate joint res.	948	Rev. Pensions	May 21, 1844	With't amend.	19	Passed		App'd May 31, 1844
Williams, James	(See J. Williams & John H. King)	25	2		668							
Williams, James	Compensation for revolutionary services.	13	2	Petition	174	Pensions	64	Adverse		Laid on table.		
Williams, James	Compensation for loss of a horse in United States service.	11	1	Petition	41	Claims.						
Williams, James	Compensation for loss of a horse in United States service.	13	2	Petition	202	Claims	Jan. 19, 1814	Adverse		Laid on table.		
Williams, James B.	Authority to enter land	28	1	Petition	77	Public Lands	9	Favorable	35	Passed	Passed	App'd June 17, 1844
Williams, James	(See John Gooding and Jas. Williams.	15	1		480							
Williams, James, executors of.	Indemnity for loss of schooner Two Brothers and cargo.	19	1	Petition	492	Foreign Affairs				Discharged; laid on table.		
Williams, James, executors of.	Indemnity for loss of schooner Two Brothers and cargo	19	2	Petition	229	Foreign Affairs				Discharged; laid on table.		
Williams, James, executors of	Indemnity for loss of slaves carried off by British.	20	1	Petition	166	Foreign Affairs	Jan. 26, 1828	Adverse		Laid on table.		
Williams, James, executors of	Indemnity for loss of slaves carried off by British.	20	2	Petition	101	Foreign Affairs	Jan. 24, 1829	Adverse		Laid on table.		
Williams, James, administrator of.	Indemnity for loss of slaves carried off by British.	23	1	Petition	213	Foreign Affairs.						
Williams, James, administrator of.	Indemnity for loss of slaves carried off by British.	23	2	Petition	157	Foreign Affairs.						
Williams, James, administrator of.	Indemnity for loss of slaves carried off by British.	24	1	Petition	115	Foreign Affairs	235	Adverse		Laid on table.		
Williams, James, administrator of.	Indemnity for loss of slaves carried off by British.	24	2	Petition	209	Foreign Affairs.						
Williams, James, administrator of.	Indemnity for loss of slaves carried off by British.	25	2	Petition	71	Foreign Affairs	503	Adverse		Laid on table.		
Williams, James, administrator of.	Indemnity for loss of slaves carried off by British.	27	2	Petition	633	Foreign Affairs	948	Adverse		Rejected.		
Williams, James	Pension	21	2	Petition	82	Rev. Claims.						
Williams, James	Pension	22	1	Petition	35	Rev. Pensions				Discharged; laid on table.		
Williams, James A	To correct error in land entry	4	2	Petition	47	Public Lands	14	Favorable	771	Referred to Committee Whole House.		
Williams, James A	To correct error in land entry	25	1	Petition	87	Public Lands	97	Favorable	114	Passed	Passed	App'd June 28, 1838

List of private claims presented to the House of Representatives of the United States from the 1st to the 31st Congress, inclusive—Continued.

Names of claimants.	Nature or object of the claim.	Congress.	Session.	How brought before the House of Reps.	Page of journal.	To what committee of the House referred.	No. or date of the report.	Nature of the report.	No. of the bill.	How disposed of by the House of Reps.	How disposed of by the Senate.	Date of the act of Congress, and remarks.
Williams, James, (Mass.).	For reward and compensation in defending action of damages by a deserter.	26	1	Petition	293	Claims.						
Williams, James, (Mass.).	For reward and compensation in defending action of damages by a deserter.	27	2	Petition	56	Claims	33	Adverse	......	Laid on table.		
Williams, James, (Mass.).	For reward and compensation in defending action of damages by a deserter.	28	2	Petition	206	Claims.						
Williams, James	(See Henry Ashton, surety of.) ..	27	2	....	106							
Williams, James, heirs of.	Indemnity for French spoliations prior to 1800.	31	1	Petition	271	Foreign Affairs....	335	Favorable....	318	Referred to Committee Whole House.		
Williams, James W., widow of.	For mileage as a member of Congress.	27	3	Resolution	134	Accounts.						
Williams, J. C., widow of.	Restoration of pension	27	2	Petition	320	Rev. Pensions.						
Williams, Jeremiah......	Pension	22	1	Petition	120	Rev. Pensions	....	....	......	Discharged; laid on table.		
Williams, John	(See Stephen Decatur, heirs of.) ..	23	1	....	36							
Williams, John R.......	Indemnity for loss of property on board the Caladonia.	13	1	Petition	22	Claims	....	....	......	Discharged		
Williams, John R.......	Indemnity for loss of property on board the Caladonia.	13	2	Petition	185	Claims	Feb. 27, 1814	Adverse......	......	Laid on table.		
Williams, John R.......	Compensation for property pillaged from him by American soldiers	15	1	Petition	286	Claims	Mar. 13, 1818	Adverse	......	Laid on table.		
Williams, John R.......	Remission of interest on purchase money due for land.	13	1	Petition	22	Public Lands.....	....	....	......	Discharged.		
Williams, John R.......	Remission of interest on purchase money due for land.	13	2	Petition	375	Public Lands.....	April 5, 1814	Favorable	181	Referred to Committee Whole House.		
Williams, John R.......	Remission of interest on purchase money due for land.	13	3	Petition	22	Public Lands.						
Williams, John R.......	Permission to reconvey land to United States, and cancel bonds.	13	2	Petition	266	Public Lands.....	....	....	......	Discharged.		
Williams, John R.......	Indemnity for use and occupation of property by United States troops, &c.	21	2	Petition	212	Claims.						
Williams, John R.......	Indemnity for use and occupation of property by United States troops, &c.	24	2	Petition	309	Claims	219	Adverse	......	Laid on table.		
Williams, John R.......	Indemnity for use and occupation of property by United States troops, &c.	28	1	Petition	717	Claims.						
Williams, John R.......	Indemnity for use and occupation of property by United States troops, &c.	28	2	Petition	71	Claims	102	Favorable	584	Referred to Committee Whole House.		
Williams, John R.......	Indemnity for use and occupation of property by United States troops, &c.	29	1	Petition	58	Claims	191	Favorable	182	Passed	Passed	App'd Aug. 8, 1846
Williams, John R.......	For a credit of amount of debt and interest due United States on his lands, in lieu of damages allowed by act of August 8, 1846.	29	2	House bill......	62	Claims	Dec. 23, 1846	Favorable	574	Referred to Committee Whole House.		

List of private claims presented to the House of Representatives of the United States from the 1st to the 31st Congress, inclusive—Continued.

Names of claimants.	Nature or object of the claim.	Congress.	Session.	How brought before the House of Reps.	Page of journal.	To what committee of the House referred.	No. or date of the report.	Nature of the report.	No. of the bill.	How disposed of by the House of Reps.	How disposed of by the Senate.	Date of the act of Congress, and remarks.
Williams, John R.	For a credit of amount of debt and interest due United States on his lands, in lieu of damages allowed by act of August 8, 1846.	29	2	Senate bill	381	Claims	Feb. 26, 1847	With't amend.	25	Laid on table.		
Williams, John R.	For a credit of amount of debt and interest due United States on his lands, in lieu of damages allowed by act of August 8, 1846.	30	1	Petition	68, 235	Claims	5	Adverse		Laid on table.		
Williams, John R.	Confirmation of title to land	27	3	Senate bill	495	Public Lands	Mar. 2, 1843	With't amend	102	Passed		App'd March 3, 1843
Williams, John R., and James May.	Confirmation of title to land	20	1	Resolution	28	Public Lands	42	Favorable	34	Passed	Passed	App'd April 17, 1828
Williams, John	Increase of pension	2	1	Petition	522					Laid on table.		
Williams, John	(See Timothy and John Williams.)	7	1		97							
Williams, John	For bounty land	24	1	Petition	409	Public Lands.						
Williams, John	For bounty land	24	2	Petition	939	Claims.						
Williams, John	Indemnity for French spoliations prior to 1800.	25	2	Petition	71	Foreign Affairs				Discharged.		
Williams, John and Mary	Indemnity for French spoliations prior to 1800.	26	1	Petition	939	Claims.						
Williams, John, (N. J.)	Pension	12	1	Petition	233	Claims	June 8, 1812	Favorable	138	Passed	Passed	App'd July 5, 1812
Williams, John	Confirmation of title to land	3	2	Petition	267	Select.						
Williams, John	Confirmation of title to land	4	1	Petition	381	Select				Discharged; referred to Com. Whole House.		
Williams, John D., *et al.*	Remission of forfeiture of schooner Cayo.	13	2	Petition	177	Ways and Means.						
Williams, John B.	Pension	13	2	Petition	368	Invalid Pensions				Discharged		Leave to withdraw.
Williams, John B.	Pension	14	1	Resolution	158	Pens. & Rev. Cl'ms		Favorable	171	Passed	Passed	App'd April 30, 1816
Williams, John P.	(See John Dodge, heirs of)	18	1		343							
Williams, John	(See Sewell, Williams, & Sewell)	19	1		291							
Williams, John, widow of	Continuation of pension	19	1	Petition	93	Military Pensions	164	Adverse		Laid on table.		
Williams, John C.	(See Barham, F. and F., representatives of.)	20	1		448							
Williams, John L., (Pa.)	Payment for land relinquished to the United States.	22	1	Petition	23	Claims	241	Favorable	328	Passed	Passed	App'd July 14, 1832
Williams, John & Horatio	To be released from payment of judgment in favor of U. States.	22	1	Petition	868	Judiciary				Discharged; laid on table.		
Williams, John S.	Compensation for work done, and materials furnished, on Cumberland road.	23	1	Res. and papers	589	Claims	455	Adverse				See report No. 449
Williams, John, heir of	Bounty land for revolutionary services.	26	1	Petition	359	Rev. Claims.						
Williams, John, heir of	Pension	26	1	Resolution	950	Rev. Pensions.						
Williams, John, heir of	Indemnity for French spoliations prior to 1800.	26	1	Memorial	182	Foreign Affairs	343	Favorable; bill	319	Referred to Committee Whole House.		
Williams, John, widow of	Indemnity for French spoliations prior to 1800.	29	2	Memorial	67	Foreign Affairs.						
Williams, John, widow of	Pension	26	1	Petition	627	Naval Affairs	July 21, 1840	Favorable	523	Referred to Committee Whole House.		
Williams, Capt. Jno., sister of.	Pension	31	1	Petition	337	Rev. Claims	127	Adverse		Laid on table		Leave to withdraw.
Williams, Jonas, and Chas. Townsend.	Compensation as commissioners to take testimony in relation to claims.	15	2	Petition	234	Claims.						

List of private claims presented to the House of Representatives of the United States from the 1st to the 31st Congress, inclusive—Continued.

Names of claimants.	Nature or object of the claim.	Congress.	Session.	How brought before the House of Reps.	Page of journal.	To what committee of the House referred.	No. or date of the report.	Nature of the report.	No. of the bill.	How disposed of by the House of Reps.	How disposed of by the Senate.	Date of the act of Congress, and remarks.
Williams, Jonas, and Chas. Townsend.	Compensation as commissioners to take testimony in relation to claims.	16	1	Petition	28	Judiciary	Dec. 20, 1819	Adverse......	......	Laid on table.		
Williams, Jonas, and Chas. Townsend.	Compensation as commissioners to take testimony in relation t claims.	16	2	Petition	56	Whole House	Jan. 26, 1821	Adverse......	......	Laid on table.		
Williams, Jonathan.....	To be released from payment of money expended for use of Military Academy.	11	2	Petition	167	Claims	....	....	......	Referred to Secretary War.		
Williams, Jonathan.....	To be released from payment of money expended for use of Military Academy.	11	2	Rep. of Secretary War.	256	Whole House.						
Williams, Jonathan.....	To be released from payment of money expended for use of Mil tary Acad-my	11	3	Petition	454	Claims.						
Williams, Jonathan......	To be released from payment of money exp nded for use of Mili tary Academy.	12	1	Petition	20	Claims	Jan. 24, 1812	Favorable; bill	53	Passed	Postponed.	
Williams, Joseph........	(See James Williams, executor of)	19	1	....	492							
Williams, Joseph, attorney of.	Indemnity for French spoliations prior to 1800.	26	1	Memorial	182	Foreign Affairs....	343	Favorable; bill	319	Referred to Committee Whole House.		
Williams, Joseph, administrator of.	Indemnity for French spoliation prior to 1800.	26	1	Memorial	182	Fo eign Affairs....	343	Favorable; bill	319	Referred to Committee Whole House.		
Williams, Joseph........	Restoration of pension..........	17	1	Petition	37	Rev. Pensions	....	....	......	Discharged; laid on table.		
Williams, Joseph........	(See Josiah Savage, *et al.*)......	18	1	....	27							
Williams, Joseph........	Restoration of pension..........	29	1	....	232	Rev. Pensions.						
Williams, Joseph, jr.....	Pension	30	2	Petition	203	Invalid Pensions ..	....	....	......	Discharged; laid on table.		
Williams, Joseph, jr.....	Pension	31	1	Petition	226	Invalid Pensions ..	Feb. 5, 1851	....	......	....	....	Leave to withdraw
Williams, Joseph P.....	Confirmation of title to land	31	1	Senate bill	979	....	....	....	40	Passed	....	App'd July 29, 1850
Williams, Joshua	Pension	21	1	Petition	294	Military Pensions..	May 4, 1830	Adverse	......	Laid on table.		
Williams, Josiah or Isaiah.	Bounty land for revolutionary services.	30	1	Petition	647	Rev. Pensions	....	....	......	Discharged; laid on table.		
Williams, J., and John H. King.	Indemnity for loss on contract with Post Office Department.	25	2	Petition	668	P. Of. & P. Roads.	....	....	......	Discharged.		
Williams, J., and John H. King.	Indemnity for loss on contract with Post Office Departm nt.	25	3	Petition	132	P. Of. & P. Roads.						
Williams, J., and John H. King.	Indemnity for loss on contract with Post Office department.	26	1	Petition	183	P. Of. & P. Roads.						
Williams, Laban........	Pension	25	3	Petition	564	Invalid Pensions.						
Williams, Laban........	Pension	26	1	Petition	163	Invalid Pensions ..	255	Adverse	......	Laid on table.		
Williams, Lancelot......	Pension	29	1	Petition	673	Invalid Pensions ..	July 25, 1846	Adverse	......	Laid on table.		
Williams, Lanry........	Indemnity for damages sustained during mission under Cherokee treaty.	29	1	Memorial	256	Indian Affairs.....	....	....	......	....	....	Leave to withdraw.
Williams, Lanry........	Indemnity for damages sustained during mission under Cherokee treaty.	30	1	Memorial	369	Indian Affairs.....	644	Favorable....	510	Referred to Committee Whole House.		
Williams, Lanry........	Indemnity for damages sustained during mission under Cherokee treaty.	30	2	House bill......	318	Whole House.....	Jan. 26, 1849	Favorable....	510	Passed	Passed	App'd March 3, 1849

List of private claims presented to the House of Representatives of the United States from the 1st to the 31st Congress, inclusive—Continued.

Names of claimants.	Nature or object of the claim.	Congress.	Session.	How brought before the House of Reps.	Page of journal.	To what committee of the House referred.	No. or date of the report.	Nature of the report.	No. of the bill.	How disposed of by the House of Reps.	How disposed of by the Senate.	Date of the act of Congress, and remarks.
Williams, Lemuel, (Miss.)	Compensation for superintending erection of custom-house.	28	1	Petition	61	Commerce				Discharged; laid on table.		
Williams, Lemuel, (Miss.)	Compensation for superintending erection of custom house.	29	1	Petition	258	Commerce	172	Adverse		Laid on table.		
Williams, Lemuel, (Miss.)	Compensation for superintending erection of custom-house.	31	1	Petition	392	Commerce.						
Williams, Linus	Indemnity for losses in war with Great Britain.	31	1	Petition	231	Claims.						
Williams, Margaret	(See Richard Fortune.)	25	2		771							
Williams, Margaret	(See Capt. John Williams, sister of.)	31	1		337							
Williams, Mary	Indemnity for property destroyed by Indians.	27	2	Petition	75	Claims.						
Williams, Mary	(See Jacob Williams, widow of.)	25	3		216							
Williams, Mary Ann	(See Thomas Williams, Indian, widow of.)	31	1		257							
Williams, Mary Ann, and others.	(See John Rose)	21	1		784							
Williams, Mary, *et al.*	(See Thomas Williams, administrator of.)	20	1		198							
Williams, Mary	(See William Williams)	25	3		135							
Williams, Mary	(See Peter Williams, widow of.)	25	2		547							
Williams, Matthew	Pension	14	1	House bill	622	Pens. & Rev. Cl'ms.	April 11, 1816	Favorable	171	Passed	Passed	App'd April 30, 1816
Williams, Michael	Pension	24	2	Petition	212	Invalid Pensions				Discharged; laid on table.		
Williams, Michael	(See Stephen Decatur, heirs of)	23	1		36							
Williams, Captain Nathan, heirs of.	Commutation pay, and remuneration for property lost.	25	2	Petition	47	Rev. Claims				Discharged; laid on table.		
Williams, Captain Nathan, heirs of.	Commutation pay, and remuneration for property lost.	26	1	Petition	165	Rev. Claims.						
Williams, Captain Nathan, heirs of.	Commutation pay, and remuneration for property lost.	26	2	Petition	35	Rev. Claims	174	Adverse		Laid on table.		
Williams, Captain Nathan, heirs of.	Commutation pay, and remuneration for property lost.	27	2	Petition	62	Rev. Claims	41	Adverse		Laid on table.		
Williams, Captain Nathan, heirs of.	Commutation pay, and remuneration for property lost.	29	1	Petition	424	Rev. Claims.						
Williams, Nath'l, (N. C.)	Release from imprisonment at suit of United States.	14	2	Petition	24	Select	Dec. 11, 1816	Favorable	1	Passed	Passed	App'd Jan. 2, 1817
Williams, N. F	(See Joseph Williams)	26	1		182							
Williams, Nancy	(See David Williams, captor of Major Andre.)	25	3		289							
Williams, N. F., attorney of.	Indemnity for French spoliations prior to 1800.	26	1	Memorial	182	Foreign Affairs	343	Favorable; bill	319	Referred to Committee Whole House.		
Williams, O., & Co.	(See Ottowa Indians)	29	1		160							
Williams, Peter	Permission to change location of land.	21	2	Petition	46	Priv. Land Claims.	Jan. 5, 1831	Adverse		Laid on table.		
Williams, Peter, widow of	Pension	25	2	Petition	547	Rev. Pensions				Discharged; laid on table.		
Williams, Prince, (colored man.)	Pension for injuries received at U. States capitol.	12	1	Petition	107	Select.						
Williams, Rachel	(See John Williams, widow of.)	19	1		93							
Williams, Rebecca	(See Joseph Falconer, executor of)	20	2		43							
Williams, Recamah	Pension	17	1	Petition	30	Pens. & Rev. Cl'ms.	Dec. 18, 1821	Adverse		Laid on table.		

List of private claims presented to the House of Representatives of the United States from the 1st to the 31st Congress, inclusive—Continued.

3—84

Names of claimants.	Nature or object of the claim.	Congress.	Session.	How brought before the House of Reps.	Page of journal.	To what committee of the House referred.	No. or date of the report.	Nature of the report.	No. of the bill.	How disposed of by the House of Reps.	How disposed of by the Senate.	Date of the act of Congress, and remarks.
Williams, Robert	Compensation for revolutionary services.	1	2	Petition	213	....	....	....	....	Referred to Secretary War.		
Williams, Robert	Compensation for revolutionary services.	2	1	Rep. of Secretary War.	450	Whole House	Nov. 7, 1891	Adverse	....	Laid on table.		
Williams, Robert	Compensation for services as teamster during revolutionary war.	3	1	Petition	60	....	....	....	....	Referred to Secretary of War.		
Williams, Robert	Compensation for services as teamster during revolutionary war.	3	2	Rep of Secretary War.	278	....	....	....	....	Laid on table.		
Williams, Robert, (Ohio)	For correction of error in survey of land.	17	1	Petition	93	Public Lands	43	Adverse	....	Laid on table.		
Williams, jr., Robert	(See John Michael, representatives of.)	18	1	....	111							
Williams, Robert, & Thos Blake.	Compensation for extra services in the pay and clothier's department, revolutionary army.	22	2	Petition	40	Rev. Claims.						
Williams, Robert, assignee of.	Payment for forage furnished United States troops in Florida.	27	2	Petition	515	Claims.						
Williams, Robert, assignee of.	Payment for forage furnished United States troops in Florida.	..	..	....	58	Claims	15	Favorable	638	Passed	Passed	App'd March 1, 1843
Williams, Samuel	Compensation for revolutionary services.	20	1	Petition	78	Rev. Claims	....	....	....	Discharged; laid on table.		
Williams, Samuel	(See John W. Medcalf, *et al.*)	25	2	....	1052							
Williams, Samuel	Pension	28	1	Resolution	557	Rev. Pensions.						
Williams, S Hill	Indemnity for property destroyed in Florida war.	25	3	Petition	121	Claims	162	Adverse	....	Laid on table.		
Williams, Samuel H., assignee of.	Indemnity for damages and for use of property, Florida war.	29	2	Memorial	146	Claims.						
Williams, schooner	(See Abner Lowell, *et al.*)	27	2	....	318							
Williams & Sewell	(See Stewart Williams & Co.)	19	1	....	291							
Williams, Serod	Claim for short mileage	26	2	Letter	221	Whole House	....	....	....	Laid on table.		
Williams, Sherod	Claim for short mileage	27	2	Letter	127	Mileage	876	Adverse	....	Laid on table.		
Williams, Staples, and Williams.	To cancel certain bonds for duties.	30	2	Petition	241	Commerce.						
Williams, Staples, and Williams.	To cancel certain bonds for duties.	31	1	Petition	201	Commerce	79	Favorable	95	Passed.		
Williams, Stephen	Compensation for services as teamster during revolutionary war.	3	1	Petition	60	....	....	....	....	Referred to Secretary War.		
Williams, Stephen	Compensation for services as teamster during revolutionary war.	[illegible]	2	Rep. of Secretary War.	278	....	....	....	....	Laid on table.		
Williams, Tabitha	(See Gilbert Williams, widow of)	27	2	....	748							
William, Tall, (Indian chief,) widow of.	Compensation for revolutionary services.	2	1	Petition	33[illegible]	Rev. Pensions.						
Williams, Thaddeus	Compensation for wounds received in Indian war.	[illegible]	1	Petition	475	....	....	....	....	Referred to Secretary of War.		
Williams, Thaddeus	Compensation for wounds received in Indian war.	[illegible]	1	Rep. of Secretary War.	131	Select	May 26, 1794	Favorable	J. R. 12	Passed	Passed	App'd June 9, 1794
Williams, Thaddeus	Compensation for wounds received in Indian war.	[illegible]	2	Rep. of Secretary War.	262	Claims.						
Williams, Thaddeus	Compensation for wounds received in Indian war.	4	1	Resolution, &c.	445	Claims	Feb. 18, 1796	Favorable	156	Passed	Passed	App'd April 20, 1796
Williams, Capt. Theodore, widow of.	Compensation for revolutionary services.	18	1	Petition	42	Pens. & Rev. Cl'ms.	Dec. 19, 1823	Adverse	....	Laid on table.		

List of private claims presented to the House of Representatives of the United States from the 1st to the 31st Congress, inclusive—Continued.

Names of claimants.	Nature or object of the claim.	Congress.	Session.	How brought before the House of Reps.	Page of journal.	To what committee of the House referred.	No. or date of the report.	Nature of the report.	No. of the bill.	How disposed of by the House of Reps.	How disposed of by the Senate.	Date of the act of Congress, and remarks.
Williams, Thomas and Jos. Carey, assignees of.	For proceeds of sale of schooners Friendship and Congo.	9	2	Petition	607					Laid on table.		
Williams, Thomas	Compensation for revolutionary services.	2	1	Petition	475					Referred to Secretary War.		
Williams, Thomas	Pension	13	3	House bill	740	Whole House	Mar. 1, 1815	Favorable	303	Passed	Passed	App'd March 3, 1815
Williams, Thos., (Indian,)	Indemnity for loss of property for leaving Canada and joining Americans.	14	1	Petition	157					Referred to Secretary of War.		
Williams, Thos., (Indian.)	Indemnity for loss of property for leaving Canada and joining Americans.	15	1	Rep. of Secretary War.	325					Laid on table.		
Williams, Thomas, (Pa.)	Grant of land for revolutionary services.	17	1	Petition	46	Priv. Land Claims				Discharged; laid on table.		
Williams, Thomas, (Pa.)	Grant of land for revolutionary services.	17	2	Petition	122	Priv. Land Claims.	Jan. 17, 1823	Favorable	236	Laid on table.		
Williams, Thomas, (Pa.)	Grant of land for revolutionary services.	18	1	House bill	180	Priv. Land Claims.	Feb. 13, 1824	Favorable	114	Passed	Passed	App'd May 18, 1824
Williams, Thomas S		18	2		316							
Williams, Thos., (Indian,) widow of.	Pension	31	1	Petition	257	Indian Affairs.						Leave to withdraw.
Williams, Thos., (Indian,) widow of.	Pension	31	2	Petition	107	Indian Affairs	89	Favorable	487	Referred to Committee Whole House.		
Williams, Thomas, administrator of.	Compensation for slaves carried off by British.	20	1	Petition	198	Judiciary				Discharged; laid on table.		
Williams, Thomas, widow of.	For work done for United States	21	1	Petition	262	Claims	188	Favorable	230	Passed	Passed	App'd May 29, 1830
Williams, Thomas, and John R.	Confirmation of title to land	20	1	Resolution	28	Public Lands	42	Favorable	34	Passed	Passed	App'd April 22, 1828
Williams, Thomas	Compensation for services and loss of horse in war of 1812.	22	2	Petition	74	Claims	23	Adverse		Laid on table.		
Williams, Thomas H	(See John Jennings, heirs of.)	24	1		138							
Williams, Thomas	Pension	28	1	Petition	857	Rev. Pensions.						
Williams, Thomas A.	(See James Graham and others)	29	1		1162							
Williams, Timothy, and John.	Indemnity for French spoliations prior to 1800.	7	1	Petition	97					Referred to Secretary of State.		
Williams, Timothy	Payment of certificate of revolutionary debt.	4	1	Rep. of Secretary Treasury.	388	Claims	74	Adverse		Laid on table.		
Williams, Wm. C., attorney of.	(See Williams & Carey, assignees of.)	9	2		607							
Williams, William	Pension	14	2	Petition	406	Pens. & Rev. Cl'ms.				Discharged; laid on table.		
Williams, William	Pension	15	1	Petition	311							Leave to withdraw.
Williams, Wm. T., (Ga.)	Payment for soldiers' certificates	15	2	Petition	144	Military Affairs				Discharged; laid on table.		
Williams, Wm. T., (Ga.)	Payment for soldiers' certificates	10	2	Petition	89	Claims				Discharged		Leave to withdraw
Williams, William, *et al.*	(See George Brown, sureties of)	21	1		132							
Williams, William	Indemnity for Indian depredations.	22	1	Petition	384	Claims	Mar. 12, 1832	Adverse		Laid on table.		
Williams, William	(See Benj. Oden, assignee of)	22	2		186							
Williams, William H	Indemnity for destruction of house.	25	2	Petition	398	Claims	June 12, 1838	Adverse		Laid on table.		
Williams, William H	Indemnity for destruction of house.	25	3	Petition	87	Claims	56	Adverse		Laid on table.		
Williams, William H	Indemnity for destruction of house	25	3	Petition	121	Claims	162	Adverse		Laid on table.		
Williams, sen., Wm., heirs of.	Permission to change location of land.	25	3	Petition	135	Public Lands	276	Favorable	1145	Referred to Committee Whole House.		

List of private claims presented to the House of Representatives of the United States from the 1st to the 31st Congress, inclusive—Continued.

Names of claimants.	Nature or object of the claim.	Congress.	Session.	How brought before the House of Reps.	Page of journal.	To what committee of the House referred.	No. or date of the report.	Nature of the report.	No. of the bill.	How disposed of by the House of Reps.	How disposed of by the Senate.	Date of the act of Congress, and remarks.
Williams, sen., Wm., heirs of.	Permission to change location of land.	26	1	Petition	178	Public Lands	81	Favorable	73	Passed	Passed	App'd July 20, 1840
Williams, Wm., (N. C.)	Pension	27	2	Petition	374	Rev. Pensions	784	Adverse		Laid on table.		
Williams, Williams S.	(See Indians, Kansas)	19	1									
Williams, Willis L., and others.	(See Jaques Clamorgan)	29	1		311							
Williamson, Alexander	Payment of pension lost in mail	25	2	Petition	405	Rev. Pensions				Discharged; laid on table.		
Williamson, Alexander	Payment of pension lost in mail	25	3	Petition	403	Rev. Pensions	Feb. 16, 1839	Adverse		Laid on table.		
Williamson, Chas., administrator of.	Patent for land for which deceased held certificate of purchase.	23	1	Petition	211	Priv. Land Claims.	270	Favorable	307	Referred to Committee Whole House.		
Williamson, Chas., administrator of.	Patent for land for which deceased held certificate of purchase.	24	1	Petition	65	Priv. Land Claims.	72	Favorable	88	Passed.		
Williamson, Chas., administrator of.	Patent for land for which deceased held certificate of purchase.	25	2	Resolution	109	Priv. Land Claims.	Dec. 22, 1837	Favorable	159	Referred to Committee Whole House.		
Williamson, Chas., administrator of.	Patent for land for which deceased held certificate of purchase.	25	3	House bill	375	Whole House	Jan. 25, 1839	Favorable	159	Passed	Passed	App'd March 3, 1839
Williamson, David	(See Zachariah Coopman, trustee of.)	26	1		182							
Williamson, David	(See Robert Patton & Co.)	8	2		127							
Williamson, David	(See William B. Magruder & Co., trustees of.)	26	1		182							
Williamson, David Foster.	Pre-emption right to land	29	1	Petition	176	Public Lands.						
Williamson, David Foster.	Pre-emption right to land	29	1	Petition	178	Public Lands.						
Williamson, David Foster.	Pre-emption right to land	29	1	Senate bill	232	Public Lands	250	With't amend.	36	Passed		App'd April 27, 1846
Williamson, Elizabeth	(See Joseph Johnson, former widow of.)	30	1		358							
Williamson, Fred'ck, *et al.*	Pension	14	1	Petition	59	Pens. & Rev. Cl'ms.				Discharged; laid on table.		
Williamson, Fred'ck, *et al.*	Pension	15	1	Petition	107	Naval Affairs				Discharged; referred to Secretary Navy.		
Williamson, George, *et al.*	That the proceeds of sale of vessel, deposited in the treasury of Massachusetts, be transferred to United States Treasury.	2	2	Petition	626					Referred to Secretary of Treasury.		
Williamson, Geo. B., late P. M.	To be released from the payment of certain money destroyed by fire.	27	3	Petition	323	P. Of. & P. Roads.						
Williamson, Henry	Pre-emption right to certain lands.	25	2	Petition	548	Public Lands				Discharged.		
Williamson, Henry	Pre-emption right to certain lands.	26	1	Petition	178	Public Lands.						
Williamson & Jamison	(See Jamison & Williamson)	25	2		480							
Williamson, James, widow of.	Pension	26	1	Petition	323	Rev. Pensions.						
Williamson, James, widow of.	Pension	26	2	Petition	122	Rev. Pensions.						
Williamson, James, widow of.	Pension	29	1	Petition	257	Rev. Pensions	826	Adverse		Laid on table.		
Williamson, John, attorney of.	Indemnity for French spoliations prior to 1800.	26	1	Memorial	182	Foreign Affairs	343	Favorable; bill	319	Referred to Committee Whole House.		
Williamson, John L., *et al.*, grantees.	(See William Bryan)	28	2		531							
Williamson, John G.	(See Exploring Expedition)	27	3		149							
Williamson, John P., *et al.*	(See Benjamin Wall, sureties of)	13	2	Petition	209	Ways and Means	53	Favorable	184	Passed	Passed	App'd April 18, 1814

List of private claims presented to the House of Representatives of the United States from the 1st to the 31st Congress, inclusive—**Continued.**

Names of claimants.	Nature or object of the claim.	Congress.	Session.	How brought before the House of Reps.	Page of journal.	To what committee of the House referred.	No. or date of the report.	Nature of the report.	No. of the bill.	How disposed of by the House of Reps.	How disposed of by the Senate.	Date of the act of Congress, and remarks.
Williamson, Littleton	Pension	20	2	Petition	204	Military Pensions				Discharged; laid on table.		
Williamson, Littleton, heirs of.	(See Capt. Raines Cook, heirs of)	24	2		91							
Williamson, Milecent	(See William T. Talbott)	15	2		172							
Williamson, Nancy	(See Jas. Williamson, widow of)	26	1		323							
Williamson, Patton, *et al.*	(See Samuel Meeker)	21	1		99							
Williamson, Robert, *et al.*	Compensation for vessel impressed into United States service and captured by enemy.	14	2	Petition	398	Claims				Discharged		Leave to withdraw.
Williamson, Wm., (Ohio.)	Pre-emption right to certain lands	17	2	Petition	209	Public Lands				Discharged		Leave to withdraw.
Williamson, Wm., (N. Y.)	Pension	20	2	Petition	175	Military Pensions				Discharged; laid on table.		
Williamson, Wm., (N. Y.)	Pension	21	1	House bill	130	Whole House	Jan. 5, 1830	Favorable	72	Passed	Passed	App'd May 20, 1830
Williamson, Wm., (Miss.)	Correct error in land entry	22	1	Petition	33	Public Lands	Jan. 3, 1832	Favorable	179	Passed	Passed	App'd Mar. 15, 1832
Willing & Curwen, surviving partner of.	Payment of certain drawback lost by failure to take export oath in time.	27	2	Petition	72	Commerce.						
Willing & Curwen, surviving partner of.	Payment of certain drawback lost by failure to take export oath in time.	28	1	Petition	136	Commerce	489	Favorable	373	Referred to Committee Whole House.		
Willing & Curwen, surviving partner of.	Payment of certain drawback lost by failure to take export oath in time.	28	2	House bill	343	Whole House	Feb. 7, 1845	Favorable	373	Passed.		
Willing & Curwen, surviving partner of.	Payment of certain drawback lost by failure to take export oath in time.	29	1	Petition	302	Commerce	570	Favorable	388	Passed	Indef. postp'd.	
Willing & Francis	Indemnity for French spoliations prior to 1800.	26	1	Memorial	182	Foreign Affairs	343	Favorable; bill	319	Referred to Committee Whole House.		
Willing, Richard and Thos. M.	(See Willing & Francis.)	26	1		182							
Willing, Richard	(See Thomas Lloyd Moore, administrator of.)	26	1		182							
Willington, Samuel	Pension	4	1	Rep. of Secretary War	445	Claims	Feb. 18, 1796	Favorable	156	Passed	Passed	App'd April 20, 1796
						Rev. Claims.						
Willington, Samuel	Increase of pension	16	1	Petition	245	Pens. & Rev. Cl'ms.						
Willington, Samuel	Increase of pension	16	2	Petition	109	Pens. & Rev. Cl'ms.						
Willink, John Abraham	Drawback on sugar	19	1	Petition	335	Ways and Means	185	Favorable	243	Passed		
Willink, John Abraham	Drawback on sugar	19	2	Senate bill	81	Ways and Means	Dec. 27, 1826	With't amend.	14	Passed	Passed	App'd March 2, 1827
Willis, Alexander	Pension	29	2	Petition	54	Rev. Pensions.						
Willis, Anthony G., heirs of.	Compensation for wagon and team impressed into U. S. service.	31	2	Petition	78	Military Affairs	24	Favorable	468	Referred to Committee Whole House.		
Willis, Benjamin	Bounty land	27	2	Petition	534	Priv. Land Claims.						
Wilis, Bird C., surety	(See Joseph Pettipool.)	17	1		488							
Willis, Elijah H., (N. C.)	Compensation for services as temporary inspector of customs.	30	1	Petition	278	Commerce	Feb. 8, 1848	Favorable	172	Passed	Passed	App'd Aug. 5, 1848
Willis, Elijah H., (N. C.)	Relief on account of illegal exactions of customs.	31	1	Petition	519	Claims.						
Willis, George	Compensation for loss of pilot boat.	25	2	Petition	410	Commerce				Discharged.		
Willis, George	Compensation for loss of pilot boat.	25	4	Petition	349	Commerce	240	Favorable	1102	Referred to Committee Whole House.		
Willis, George	Compensation for loss of pilot boat.	26	1	Petition	176	Commerce	34	Favorable	54	Passed	Passed	App'd May 2, 1840
Willis, George	Pension	6	1	Petition	569	Claims	Feb. 3, 1800	Adverse.				

List of private claims presented to the House of Representatives of the United States from the 1st to the 31st Congress, inclusive—Continued.

Names of claimants.	Nature or object of the claim.	Congress.	Session.	How brought before the House of Reps.	Page of journal.	To what committee of the House referred.	No. or date of the report.	Nature of the report.	No. of the bill.	How disposed of by the House of Reps.	How disposed of by the Senate.	Date of the act of Congress, and remarks.
Willis, Henry, representatives of.	Confirmation of title to land	13	3	Petition	497	Public Lands				Discharged.		
Willis, Henry, representatives of.	Confirmation of title to land	14	1	Petition	61	Public Lands.						
Willis, Henry, representatives of.	Confirmation of title to land	14	2	Petition	50	Priv. Land Claims.						
Willis, Henry, representatives of.	Confirmation of title to land	15	1	Petition	190	Priv. Land Claims.						
Willis, Henry, representatives of.	Confirmation of title to land	15	2	Petition	194	Priv. Land Claims.	94	Adverse		Laid on table.		
Willis, Henry, representatives of.	Confirmation of title to land	16	1	Petition	211	Priv. Land Claims.	68	Favorable	73	Passed	Passed	App'd May 8, 1820
Willis, Henry, representatives of.	To amend act of 8th May, 1820, so as to except certain town lots.	16	2	Petition	35	Priv. Land Claims.	Nov. 28, 1820	Favorable	157	Passed	Passed	App'd Dec. 29, 1820
Willis, Henry, widow of	Damages by refusal of land officer to allow location of land warrant.	17	1	Petition	289	Public Lands				Discharged; laid on table.		
Willis, James	Compensation for arrears of pay and clothing furnished in revolutionary war.	2	2	Petition	615					Referred to Secretary War.		
Willis, Jesse	Permission to correct error in land entry.	18	2	Petition	137	Priv. Land Claims.						
Willis, Jesse H	(See James Mennie, assignee of.)	24	1		751							
Willis, Jesse H	Permission to locate land	26	1	Petition	954	Public Lands.						
Willis, Jesse H	Permission to locate land	27	1	Petition	101	Public Lands.						
Willis, Jesse H	Permission to locate land	27	2	Petition	1373	Priv. Land Claims.	1106	Adverse		Laid on table.		
Willis, Joseph, (Mass.)	Restoration of pension	17	1	Petition	180	Whole House				Discharged; laid on table.		
Willis, Lewis B	For balance due him as late paymaster United States army.	19	2	Petition	190	Claims	Feb. 2, 1827	Adverse		Laid on table.		
Willis, Lewis B	For balance due him as late pay master United States army.	20	1	Petition	31	Claims	9	Adverse		Laid on table.		
Willis, Lewis B	For balance due him as late paymaster United States army.	28	1	Petition	78	Claims	2	Adverse		Laid on table.		
Willis, Lewis B	For balance due him as late paymaster United States army.	30	1	Petition	414	Claims.						
Willis, Lewis B	Compensation for services as surveyor.	24	1	Petition	156	Commerce	435	Favorable	445	Referred to Committee Whole House.		
Willis, Lewis B	Compensation for services as surveyor.	25	2	Petition	41	Commerce	201	Favorable	233	Referred to Committee Whole House.		
Willis, Lewis B	Compensation for services as surveyor.	25	3	House bill	375	Whole House	Jan. 25, 1839	Favorable	233	Passed	Passed	App'd March 3, 1839
Willis, Robert	Bounty due for mail services	16	1	Resolution	318	Military Affairs	April 4, 1820	Resolution		Laid on table.		
Willis, William	Arrears of pension	21	2	Petition	68	Military Pensions.						
Willis, William	Arrears of pension	27	2	Petition	884	Rev. Pensions	916	Favorable; bill	530	Passed	Passed	App'd Aug. 29, 1842
Williston, Consider, children of.	Commutation pay	31	2	Petition	87	Rev. Claims.						
Willmarth, Daniel, (Mich.)	Pre-emption right to land	22	2	Petition	314	Public Lands.						
Willmarth, Daniel, (Mich.)	Pre-emption right to land	23	1	Petition	449	Public Lands.						
Willmarth, Ephraim	Pension	2	2	Rep. of Secretary War.	649	Whole House.						
Willmarth, Ephraim	Pension	3	1	Rep. of Secretary War.	131	Select	May 26, 1794	Favorable	J.R. 12	Passed	Passed	App'd June 9, 1794

List of private claims presented to the House of Representatives of the United States from the 1st to the 31st Congress, inclusive—Continued.

Names of claimants.	Nature or object of the claim.	Congress.	Session.	How brought before the House of Reps.	Page of journal.	To what committee of the House referred.	No. or date of the report.	Nature of the report.	No. of the bill.	How disposed of by the House of Reps.	How disposed of by the Senate.	Date of the act of Congress, and remarks.
Willmarth, Ephraim	Pension	5	2	House bill	127	Whole House	Jan. 11, 1798	Favorable	38	Passed	Passed	App'd Feb. 2, 1798
Willock, James	Arrears of pension	24	2	Petition	216	Rev. Pensions.						
Willock, Thomas	Indemnity for French spoliations prior to 1800.	26	1	Memorial	182	Foreign Affairs	343	Favorable; bill	319	Referred to Committee Whole House.		
Willock, Thomas	Release from penalty for the illegal use of the register of schooner Addy.	3	2	Petition	248	Select				Laid on table.		
Wiloby, John	Reward for gallantry	14	1	Petition	249	Naval Affairs	April 11, 1816	Favorable		Passed	Passed	App'd Feb. 8, 1817
Willoughby, Edlyne	Pension	21	1	Resolution	229	Military Pensions	Feb. 15, 1830	Favorable	248	Passed	Indef. postp'd.	
Willoughby, Joseph	(See Abigail Barnum, *et al.*)	8	1		446							
Willis, Conrad	Compensation for improvements made at United States salt licks, Illinois.	16	2	Petition	188	Claims				Discharged; laid on table.		
Willis, Conrad, widow of.	Continuation of pension	18	1	Petition	61	Rev. Pensions	Jan. 12, 1824	Adverse		Laid on table.		
Willis, Elizabeth	(See Conrad Willis, widow of)	18	1		61							
Wills, Eleanor	(See Michael Reed)	20	1		46							
Wills, Eleanor	(See Luke Wills, widow of)	22	1	Petition	545							
Wills, Enoch	Pension	9	1	Petition	241	Claims	Mar. 28, 1806			Indefinitely postponed.		Leave to withdraw.
Wills, James B	Payment for wood delivered at Fort Leavenworth.	25	2	Petition	398	Claims	840	Adverse		Laid on table.		
Wills, James B	Payment for wood delivered at Fort Leavenworth.	25	3	Petition	122	Claims	163	Adverse		Laid on table.		
Wills, John	Indemnity for French spoliations prior to 1800.	26	1	Memorial	182	Foreign Affairs	343	Favorable; bill	319	Referred to Committee Whole House.		
Wills, Josiah	(See Williams, Staples & Williams.)	30	2		241							
Wills, Luke, widow of	Renewal of pension	22	1	Petition	545	Naval Affairs				Discharged; laid on table.		
Wills, Luke, widow of	Renewal of pension	24	2	Petition	399	Naval Affairs.						
Wills, Luke, widow of	Renewal of pension	29	1	Petition	690	Rev. Pensions.						
Wills, Luke, widow of	Renewal of pension	29	2	Report	150	Rev. Pensions	22	Adverse		Laid on table.		
Wills, Nathaniel H	Pension	30	2	Petition	126	Invalid Pensions.						
Wills, Nathaniel H	Pension	31	1	Petition	1154	Invalid Pensions.						
Wills, Nelson, (Va.)	(See Peter Winfray, surety of)	22	1		266							
Wills, Samuel	Pension	11	3	House bill	604	Claims	March 1, 1811	Favorable	218	Passed	Passed	App'd March 3, 1811
Wills, Stephen	(See Stephen Wells)	4	1		445							
Wills, Thomas C	Increase of compensation as keeper of Potomac bridge.	31	1	Petition	589	Dist. of Columbia	April 23, 1850	Favorable	253	Laid on table.		
Willspaugh, Cornelius	Compensation for work on public roads.	28	1	Petition	239	Claims	131	Favorable	121	Passed	Passed	App'd June 15, 1844
Willson & Brothers	Remission of duty on goods destroyed by fire.	31	1	Petition	1499	Commerce.						
Wilmarth, Ephraim	(See Ephrain Willmarth)	2	2		649							
Wilmington and Raleigh Railroad Company.	Permission to pay duty on railroad iron by carrying United States mail.	31	1	Petition	588	P. Of. & P. Roads	April 9, 1850	Favorable	217	Passed	Passed	App'd April 19, 1850
Wilmot, John, *et al*	Refund certain duties paid on coffee	11	2	Petition	350	Com. and Munuf.						
Wilmot, John, *et al*	Refund certain duties paid on coffee	12	1	Petition	138	Claims				Discharged.		
Wilmot, John, *et al*	Refund certain duties paid on coffee	13	1	Petition	44	Claims.						
Wilmot, John	Refund certain duties paid on goods	14	2	Petition	296	Ways and Means				Discharged; laid on table.		
Wilmot, John	Refund certain duties paid on goods	15	1	Petition	64	Ways and Means	92	Favorable	82	Referred to Committee Whole House.		

List of private claims presented to the House of Representatives of the United States from the 1st to the 31st Congress, inclusive—Continued.

Names of claimants.	Nature or object of the claim.	Congress.	Session.	How brought before the House of Reps.	Page of journal.	To what committee of the House referred.	No. or date of the report.	Nature of the report.	No. of the bill.	How disposed of by the House of Reps.	How disposed of by the Senate.	Date of the act of Congress, and remarks.
Wilmot, John	Refund certain duties paid on goods	16	1	Petition	24	Ways and Means	58	Adverse	.....	Laid on table.		
Wilmot, John	Refund certain duties paid on goods	16	1	Petition	213	Ways and Means	Feb. 18, 1824	Favorable	125	Passed	Passed	App'd May 18, 1824
Wilmot, John	Indemnity for spoliation by Henry Christophe, the ruler of the Island of St. Domingo.	16	1	Petition	85	Foreign Affairs	....	....	.....	Discharged; referred to Sec. of State.		
Wilmott, Robert, (Ky.)	Commutation pay	21	1	Petition	523	Rev. Claims	Mar. 8, 1832	Favorable	454	Laid on table.		
Wilmott, Robert, (Ky.)	Commutation pay	21	2	Petition	209	Rev. Claims	....	....	.....	Laid on table.		
Wilmot, Robert, (Ky.)	Commutation pay	22	1	Petition	387	Rev. Claims	355	Favorable	454	Referred to Committee Whole House.		
Wilmott, Robert, (Ky.)	Commutation pay	23	1	Petition	80	Rev. Claims	62	Favorable	72	Passed	Passed	App'd June 30, 1834
Wilmott, Robert, (Ky.)	Interest on commutation pay	24	1	Petition	152	Rev. Claims.						
Wilmott, Robert, (Ky.)	Interest on commutation pay	25	2	Petition	546	Rev. Claims	Mar. 20, 1838	Favorable	664	Postponed.		
Wilmott, Robert, (Ky.)	Interest on commutation pay	26	1	Petition	167	Rev. Claims.						
Wilmott, Robert, executors of, (Ky.)	Interest on commutation pay	28	2	Petition	56	Rev. Claims	....	....	.....	Discharged	....	Leave to withdraw.
Wilmott, Robert, executors of, (Ky.)	Interest on commutation pay	29	1	Petition	292	Rev. Claims.						
Wilmott, Robert, executors of, (Ky.)	Interest on commutation pay	31	1	Petition	648	Rev. Claims.						
Wilmouth, George	(See Exploring Expedition)	27	3	Petition	149							
Wilson, Aaron, jr	Pension	28	2	....	470	Invalid Pensions	....	....	.....	Discharged; laid on table.		
Wilson, Abiel, lieutenant.	Indemnity for property lost in Canada.	15	1	Petition	60	Claims	....	....	.....	Discharged; laid on table.		
Wilson, Abiel, lieutenant.	Indemnity for property lost in Canada.	16	1	Petition	71	Priv. Land Claims	....	....	.....	Discharged; laid on table.		
Wilson, Albah, *et al.*	(See Wm. H. Hines, sureties of)	29	1	....	460							
Wilson, Alexander, (Va.)	Indemnity for French spoliations prior to 1800.	26	1	Memorial	182	Foreign Affairs	343	Favorable; bill	319	Referred to Committee Whole House.		
Wilson, Alexander	Confirmation of title to land	12	2	House bill	609	Whole House	Jan. 18, 1813	Favorable	222	Passed	Passed	App'd Feb. 13, 1813
Wilson, Alexander, executors of.	Copy right of book on Natural History of Birds.	18	2	Petition	118	Judiciary.						
Wilson, Amy	(See Valentine Wilson, widow of)	23	2	....	234							
Wilson, Andrew	Increase of pension	29	1	Petition	806	Invalid Pensions	829	Adverse	.....	Laid on table.		
Wilson, Andrew	Pension	2	1	Petition	507	....	....	....	.....	Laid on table.		
Wilson, Andrew, jr.	(See Elnathan Atwater)	12	1	....	88							
Wilson, Andrew	Payment for horse lost in United States service.	17	1	Petition	93	Claims.						
Wilson, Andrew	Fishing bounty	20	2	Petition	141	Commerce	Jan. 19, 1829	Favorable	379	Referred to Committee Whole House.		
Wilson, Andrew	Fishing bounty	21	1	Petition	82	Commerce	Dec. 29, 1829	Favorable	38	Passed	Passed	App'd April 7, 1830
Wilson, Andrew	Pension	21	2	Petition	52	Military Pensions.						
Wilson, Ann	(See Lieut. James Wilson, widow of.)	11	2	....	244							
Wilson, Arthur	Pension	29	1	Petition	487	Invalid Pensions.						
Wilson, Arthur	Pension	30	1	Petition	233	Invalid Pensions	452	Favorable	382	Passed.		
Wilson & Brother	(See Willson & Brother)	31	1	....	1499							
Wilson, Bryce	(Not stated)	26	1	....	819	Public Lands	Dec. 24, 1840	....	.....	Discharged.		
Wilson, Catherine	(See James Wilson, widow of.)	27	2	....	70							
Wilson, Charles, family of.	For extra pay as clerk in public office in Philadelphia.	3	1	Resolution	209	Select	47	Favorable	69	Passed	Rejected.	
Wilson, Charles	Pension	30	1	Petition	838	Invalid Pensions	....	....	.....	Discharged; laid on table.		

List of private claims presented to the House of Representatives of the United States from the 1st to the 31st Congress, inclusive—Continued.

Names of claimants.	Nature or object of the claim.	Congress.	Session.	How brought before the House of Reps.	Page of journal.	To what committee of the House referred.	No. or date of the report.	Nature of the report.	No. of the bill.	How disposed of by the House of Reps.	How disposed of by the Senate.	Date of the act of Congress, and remarks.
Wilson, Charles	Pension	30	2	Petition	239	Invalid Pensions	Jan. 17, 1849	Favorable	724	Passed	Passed	App'd Feb. 1, 1849
Wilson, Clark, assignee of.	Renewal of patent	28	2	Memorial	135	Patents				Discharged; laid on table.		
Wilson, Cornelius	(See William Peden, or Pedre.)	26	1		340							
Wilson, Cornelius	Compensation for services rendered in removing Cherokee Indians.	27	2	Petition	94	Claims	1017	Favorable	590	Referred to Committee Whole House.		
Wilson, Cornelius	Compensation for services rendered in removing Cherokee Indians.	27	3	House bill	91	Whole House	Dec. 23, 1842	Favorable	590	Passed	Passed	App'd Jan. 20, 1843
Wilson, Daniel	Increase of pension	25	3	Petition	218	Invalid Pensions				Discharged; laid on table.		
Wilson, Daniel	Increase of pension	29	2	Petition	53	Invalid Pensions				Discharged; laid on table.		
Wilson, Daniel	Increase of pension	30	1	Petition	78	Invalid Pensions.						
Wilson, Daniel	Increase of pension	30	2	Petition	271	Invalid Pensions	84	Favorable	780	Passed	Passed	App'd March 3, 1849
Wilson, Daniel	Reward of gallantry	14	1	Petition	249	Naval Affairs	April 11, 1816	Favorable		Passed	Passed	App'd Feb. 8, 1817
Wilson, David	(See John Ross, *et al.*)	11	2		235							
Wilson, David	Pension	24	1	Petition	354	Invalid Pensions				Discharged; laid on table.		
Wilson, David	Pension	25	2	Petition	118	Invalid Pensions	226	Favorable	264	Passed.		
Wilson, David	Pension	26	1	Petition	162	Invalid Pensions	212	Favorable	224	Passed	Indef. postp'd.	
Wilson, David	Pension	27	3	Petition	346	Invalid Pensions.						
Wilson, David	Pension	28	1	Petition	622	Invalid Pensions.						
Wilson, David, heir of	Indemnity for French spoliations prior to 1800.	26	1	Memorial	182	Foreign Affairs	343	Favorable; bill	319	Referred to Committee Whole House.		
Wilson, David, heir of	Indemnity for French spoliations prior to 1800.	31	1	Petition	416	Foreign Affairs	355	Favorable	318	Referred to Committee Whole House.		
Wilson, Major Ebenezer, (N. Y.)	Pension	23	1	Petition	570	Invalid Pensions				Discharged; laid on table.		
Wilson, Edward	To change location of land	14	1	Senate bill	441	Public Lands	Mar. 5, 1816	With amend.	41	Passed	Concurred in	App'd April 20, 1816
Wilson, Eleanor	(See Philip Wilson)	11	3		501							
Wilson, Eleanor	Remission of balance due by he on land purchased of United States.	14	2	Petition	406	Public Lands				Discharged; laid on table.		
Wilson, E. K.	(See Robert C. Scott, *et al.*)	23	1		93							
Wilson, Eli	Confirmation of title to land	31	1	Petition	487	Judiciary.						
Wilson, Eli	Confirmation of title to land	31	2	Petition	165	Judiciary	Jan. 21, 1851			Discharged; laid on table.		
Wilson, Elizabeth J. and Ann C.	(See James Wilson, representatives of.)	23	1		380							
Wilson, Elizabeth	(See Thomas Wilson, widow of.)	28	1		351							
Wilson, Elizabeth	Pension	28	1	Petition	840	Rev. Pensions.						
Wilson, George	For settlement of accounts against United States.	19	2	Senate bill	175	Claims	61	Adverse	53 B.	Referred to Committee Whole House.		
Wilson & Hallett, (Mobile)	Reimbursement of duties paid on salt.	20	1	Petition	557	Ways and Means.						
Wilson & Hallett, (Mobile)	Reimbursement of duties paid on salt.	20	2	Petition	49	Ways and Means	Dec. 21, 1838	Favorable	351	Referred to Committee Whole House.		
Wilson & Hallett, (Mobile)	Reimbursement of duties paid on salt.	21	1	Petition	111	Ways and Means				Discharged; laid on table.		
Wilson, George, (Penn.)	Relief as purchaser of land, the original certificate being lost.	20	2	Senate bill	349	Claims	Mar. 2, 1829	With amend.	79	Passed	Passed	App'd March 2, 1829
Wilson, George, representatives of.	For land and other emoluments due deceased for revolutionary services.	7	2	Remonstrance	303	Claims.						

List of private claims presented to the House of Representatives of the United States from the 1st to the 31st Congress, inclusive—Continued.

Names of claimants.	Nature or object of the claim.	Congress.	Session.	How brought before the House of Reps.	Page of journal.	To what committee of the House referred.	No. or date of the report.	Nature of the report.	No. of the bill.	How disposed of by the House of Reps.	How disposed of by the Senate.	Date of the act of Congress, and remarks.
Wilson, Henry	Restoration of pension	17	2	Petition	163	Whole House.						
Wilson, Henry C.	(See Wm. Drayton, heirs of)	20	1		225							
Wilson, Captain Henry	Compensation for brevet rank	21	1	Memorial	276	Military Affairs				Discharged; laid on table.		
Wilson, Major Henry	Confirmation of title to land	24	2	Petition	391	Priv. Land Claims.						
Wilson, Major Henry	Confirmation of title to land	25	3	Resolution	267	Priv. Land Claims.						
Wilson, Major Henry	Confirmation of title to land	25	3	Senate bill	372	Priv. Land Claims.	Feb. 6, 1839	With't amend	S. 169	Passed		App'd Feb. 12, 1839
Wilson, Henry	For exchange of land	26	1	Senate bill	837	Priv. Land Claims.	June 23, 1840	With't amend.	S. 308	Referred to Committee Whole House.		
Wilson, Henry	Pension	26	2	Senate bill	229				S. 134	Referred to Committee Whole House.		
Wilson, Henry, (La.)	Permission to change land entry	26	1	Petition	366	Priv. Land Claims.	333	Favorable	305	Referred to Committee Whole House.		
Wilson, Isaac	Pension	23	2	Petition	303	Invalid Pensions.						
Wilson, James	Confirmation of title to land	1	2	Memorial	179					Referred to Secretary Treasury.		
Wilson, James	Confirmation of title to land	2	1	Memorial	472	Select	April 3, 1792			Laid on table.		
Wilson, James, jr.	Relief for breach of revenue laws.	10	1	Petition	40	Com. and Manuf.						
Wilson, James, jr.	Relief for breach of revenue laws.	10	2	Petition	515	Com. and Manuf.	Feb. 16, 1809					Leave to withdraw.
Wilson, James	Pre-emption right to land	14	1	Petition	121	Public Lands	Mar. 13, 1816	Adverse		Laid on table.		
Wilson, James	For distribution of prize money	19	2	House bill	98	Naval Affairs	74	Favorable	70	Referred to Committee Whole House.		
Wilson, James	For distribution of prize money	21	1	House bill	137	Naval Affairs	Jan. 7, 1830	Favorable	82	Laid on table.		
Wilson, James	For distribution of prize money	22	1	House bill	29	Naval Affairs	Dec. 23, 1831	Favorable	98	Referred to Committee Whole House.		
Wilson, James	For distribution of prize money	23	1	House bill	101	Naval Affairs	45	Favorable	50	Referred to Committee Whole House.		
Wilson, Lieutenant James, widow of.	Arrears of pay for revolutionary services.	11	2	Petition	244	Claims.						
Wilson, Lieutenant, James widow of.	Arrears of pay for revolutionary services.	15	1	Petition	44	Pens. & Rev. Cl'ms.				Discharged; laid on table.		
Wilson, James	Pension	17	2	Petition	165	Pens. & Rev. Cl'ms.						
Wilson, James	Pension	18	1	Petition	135	Pens. & Rev. Cl'ms.		Favorable	35	Passed	Passed	App'd May 19, 1824
Wilson, James	Increase of compensation as deputy postmaster.	20	2	Resolution	152	P. Of. & P. Roads				Discharged; laid on table.		
Wilson, James, (Ala.)	Confirmation of title to land	21	1	Petition	413	Priv. Land Claims.				Discharged; laid on table.		
Wilson, James, (Vt.)	Pension	22	1	Petition	381	Rev. Pensions.						
Wilson, James, (Ark.)	Damages sustained on United States protested draft.	22	2	Resolution	286	Judiciary.						
Wilson, James, (Ark.)	Damages sustained on United States protested draft.	24	1	Petition	53	Judiciary				Discharged; laid on table.		
Wilson, James, *et al.*	(See Amos Edwards, sureties of.)	18	2		69							
Wilson, James, heirs of	To be released from lien by United States on lot of ground in Alexandria, Virginia.	23	1	Petition	380	Dist. of Columbia.						
Wilson, James, heirs of	To be released from lien by United States on lot of ground in Alexandria, Virginia.	23	2	Petition	237	Judiciary	Feb. 2, 1835	Fvorable	759	Passed.		
Wilson, James, heirs of	To be released from lien by United States on lot of ground in Alexandria, Virginia.	24	1	Petition	212	Judiciary	Mar. 3, 1836	Favorable	411	Referred to Committee Whole House.		

List of private claims presented to the House of Representatives of the United States from the 1st to the 31st Congress, inclusive—Continued.

Names of claimants.	Nature or object of the claim.	Congress.	Session.	How brought before the House of Reps.	Page of journal.	To what committee of the House referred.	No. or date of the report.	Nature of the report.	No. of the bill.	How disposed of by the House of Reps.	How disposed of by the Senate.	Date of the act of Congress, and remarks.
Wilson, James, heirs of	To be released from lien by United States on lot of ground in Alexandria, Virginia.	25	2	Petition	41	Judiciary	Jan. 9, 1828	Favorable	352	Referred to Committee Whole House.		
Wilson, James, heirs of	To be released from lien by United States on lot of ground in Alexandria, Virginia.	25	3	House bill	377	Whole House	Jan. 25, 1839	Favorable	352	Passed	Passed	App'd March 2, 1839
Wilson, James	Pension	27	3	Petition	152	Invalid Pensions	166	Adverse		Laid on table.		
Wilson, James	Pension	28	2	Petition	470	Invalid Pensions				Discharged; laid on table.		
Wilson, James, (D. C.)	Increase of compensation as gate-keeper at Capitol.	27	3	Petition	366	Public Buildings & Grounds.						
Wilson, James, (D. C.)	Increase of compensation as gate-keeper at Capitol.	28	1	Petition	136	Accounts.						
Wilson, James	(See William Morrison, *et al*)	28	1		904							
Wilson, James, heirs of	Indemnity for French spoliations prior to 1800.	29	2	Petition	87	Foreign Affairs.						
Wilson, James, *et al.*	Refund duties paid on certain goods.	30	1	Petition	207	Commerce	321	Favorable	294	Referred to Committee Whole House.		
Wilson, James, widow of	Pension	27	2	Petition	70	Rev. Pensions	295	Favorable	263	Passed	Indef. postp'd.	
Wilson, James, widow of	Pension	27	3	Petition	43	Rev. Pensions	18	Favorable	640	Passed.		
Wilson, James, widow of	Pension	30	1	Petition	264	Rev. Pensions	Aug. 8, 1838			Discharged; laid on table.		
Wilson, Capt. James, heir of.	Compensation for revolutionary services.	29	1	Petition	524	Rev. Claims.						
Wilson, James Armstrong, heirs of.	One years' pay and interest for revolutionary services.	29	1	Petition	218	Rev. Claims.						
Wilson, James Armstrong, heirs of.	Pension	29	2	Petition	162	Rev. Pensions.						
Wilson, James C	Increase of compensation as clerk in office of chief engineer.	30	1	Petition	218	Military Affairs.						
Wilson, James C	Increase of compensation as clerk in office of chief engineer.	30	2	Petition	127	Ways and Means.						
Wilson, James C	Increase of compensation as clerk in office of chief engineer.	31	1	Petition	284	Military Affairs.						
Wilson, James C	Increase of compensation as clerk in office of chief engineer.	31	2	Petition	37	Ways and Means.						
Wilson, Janet, and Susan, Rawlings.	Permission to locate land warrant.	24	1	Petition	152	Rev. Claims.						
Wilson, Jesse, (Ky.)	For grant of land in lieu of Spanish grant.	18	1	Petition	71	Priv. Land Claims.	Jan. 6, 1824	Adverse		Laid on table.		
Wilson, John	Pension	1	2	Petition	206	Secretary of War.	May 24, 1790			Laid on table.		
Wilson, John	Pension	3	2	Rep't of Secretary War.	337	Claims	Feb. 28, 1795	Favorable	130	Passed	Postponed.	
Wilson, John	Compensation for supplies furnished to army, and injuries received during revolutionary war.	2	1	Petition	468	Secretary Treasury.	April 17, 1792			Laid on table.		
Wilson, John	Pension	2	1	Petition	493					Referred to Secretary of War.		
Wilson, John, (Vt.)	Pension	4	1	Rep. of Secretary War.	445	Claims	Feb. 18, 1796	Favorable	156	Passed	Passed	App'd April 20, 1796
Wilson, John A., (Penn.)	Permission to redeem property sold by United States for taxes.	17	1	Petition	276	Ways and Means.				Discharged.		
Wilson, John A., (Tenn.)	Increase of compensation as deputy postmaster.	18	1	Petition	295	P. Of. & P. Roads.						

List of private claims presented to the House of Representatives of the United States from the 1st to the 31st Congress, inclusive—Continued.

Names of claimants.	Nature or object of the claim.	Congress.	Session.	How brought before the House of Reps.	Page of journal.	To what committee of the House referred.	No. or date of the report.	Nature of the report.	No. of the bill.	How disposed of by the House of Reps.	How disposed of by the Senate.	Date of the act of Congress, and remarks.
Wilson, John A., (Tenn.)	Increase of compensation as deputy postmaster.	19	2	Petition	187	P. Of. & P. Roads				Discharged.		
Wilson, John A., (Tenn.)	Released from prison on judgment in favor of United States.	18	1	Petition	345	Judiciary				Discharged; referred to Sec. Treasury.		
Wilson, John, administrator of.	Permission to make last payment on lands forfeited	21	1	Petition	60	Public Lands	13	Favorable	18	Passed	Passed	App'd May 28, 1830
Wilson, John, heirs of	For certain public lands for revolutionary services.	27	1	Petition	100	Public Lands.						
Wilson, John, heirs of	For certain public lands for revolutionary services.	27	2	Petition	62	Public Lands.						
Wilson, Lieut. John, (Ky.) heirs of.	Commutation pay	21	1	Petition	199	Rev. Claims	333	Favorable	394	Referred to Committee Whole House.		
Wilson, Lieut. John, (Ky.) heirs of.	Commutation pay	22	1	Petition	29	Rev. Claims	183	Favorable	260	Referred to Committee Whole House.		
Wilson, Lieut. John, (Ky.) heirs of.	Commutation pay	22	2	House bill	92	Whole House	Dec. 28, 1832	Favorable	260	Passed	Passed	App'd Feb. 27, 1832
Wilson, Lieut. John, (Ky.) heirs of.	Commutation pay	24	1	Resolution	675	Whole House	July 1, 1836	Adverse		Laid on table.		
Wilson, Lieut. John, (Ky.) heirs of.	Commutation pay	24	2	Petition	106	Rev. Claims				Discharged; laid on table.		
Wilson, jr., John	Arrears of pension	21	1	Petition	318	Military Pensions				Discharged; laid on table.		
Wilson, John, (Mass.)	Pension	13	2	Petition	169	Pensions	Mar. 28, 1814	Favorable	166	Referred to Committee Whole House.		
Wilson, John C., (Tenn.)	Release from liability as surety of John Parker, deputy postmaster.	22	1	Petition	558	Judiciary				Discharged; laid on table.		
Wilson, John, (Mo.)	To correct error in land entry	23	1	Petition	448	Public Lands	April 17, 1834	Favorable	433	Passed	Passed	App'd June 30, 1834
Wilson, John, (Ark.)	Permission to change location of land.	24	1	Petition	207	Priv. Land Claims.						
Wilson, John	Compensation for services as inspector general of Missouri militia, Indian war.	24	1	Petition	430	Claims	703	Favorable	656	Referred to Committee Whole House.		
Wilson, John	Compensation for services as inspector general of Missouri militia, Indian war.	25	2	Petition	37	Claims	52	Favorable	61	Passed	Passed	App'd April 20, 1838
Wilson, John	(See Gilbert Dench, heirs of)	24	2		303							
Wilson, John	(See Zebulon M. Pike and companions.)	10	1		189							
Wilson, John, (N. Y.)	Pension	23	2	Petition	39	Rev. Pensions.						
Wilson, John, (N. Y.)	Pension	26	2	Petition	84	Invalid Pensions.						
Wilson, John, (N. Y.)	Pension	27	2	Petition	618	Invalid Pensions.						
Wilson, John, (N. Y.)	Pension	30	1	Petition	440	Invalid Pensions	549	Favorable	449	Referred to Committee Whole House.		
Wilson, John, (N. Y.)	Pension	30	2	House bill	318	Whole House	Jan. 26, 1849	Favorable	449	Passed.		
Wilson, John, (N. Y.)	Pension	31	1	Petition	537	Invalid Pensions.						
Wilson, John, attorney of.	Indemnity for French spoliations prior to 1800.	26	1	Memorial	182	Foreign Affairs	343	Favorable	319	Referred to Committee Whole House.		
Wilson, John, (Ind.)	Compensation for horse lost in United States service.	26	1	Resolution	439, 940	Claims	686	Adverse		Laid on table.		
Wilson, John, (Ind.)	Compensation for horse lost in United States service.	26	2	Petition	52	Claims.						
Wilson, John	Indemnity for French spoliations prior to 1800.	26	1	Memorial	182	Foreign Affairs	343	Favorable	319	Referred to Committee Whole House.		

List of private claims presented to the House of Representatives of the United States from the 1st to the 31st Congress, inclusive—Continued.

Names of claimants.	Nature or object of the claim.	Congress.	Session.	How brought before the House of Reps.	Page of journal.	To what committee of the House referred.	No. or date of the report	Nature of the report.	No. of the bill.	How disposed of by the House of Reps.	How disposed of by the Senate.	Date of the act of Congress, and remarks.
Wilson, John S.	Remueration for lands purchased of United States to which government had no title.	25	3	Petition	267	Priv. Land Claims.						
Wilson, John S.	Remueration for lands purchased of United States to which government had no title.	26	1	Petition	179	Priv. Land Claims.	June 19, 1840	Favorable	457	Referred to Committee Whole House.		
Wilson, John S., (Ala.)	Pre-emption right to land	26	1	Senate bill	803	Public Lands	Apr l 24, 1840	With't amend.	133	Referred to Committee Whole House.		
Wilson, John P.	(See Willis Wilson, executors of)	23	1		306							
Wilson, Joseph, collector.	That certain payments made to fishing vessels be placed to his credit.	10	2	Memorial	414	Com. and Manuf.	Feb. 10, 1809	Favorable	162	Referred to Committee Whole House.		
Wilson, Joseph, collector.	That certain payments made to fishing vessels be placed to his credit.	11	1	Memorial	17	Com. and Manuf.						
Wilson, Joseph	Pre emption right to land	11	2	Petition	116	Public Lands	Mar. 17, 1810	Favorable	137	Laid on table.		
Wilson, Joseph	Pre-emption right to land	11	3	Petition	475	Public Lands	Jan. 7, 1811	Favorable	170	Passed	Passed	Vetoed by President.
Wilson, Joseph	Pre-emption right to land	11	3	Senate bill	612	Whole House	Mar. 2, 1811	With amend.	68	Passed	Concurred in	App'd March 3, 1811
Wilson, Joseph H., & others	Reimbursement of a certain sum of money loaned to American consul at Cadiz.	13	2	Petition	172	Claims				Discharged.		
Wilson, Joseph	Payment for a horse shot by a United States soldier, war of 1812.	14	1	Petition	291	Claims	Mar. 8, 1816	Favorable; bill	115	Passed	Passed	App'd April 26, 1816
Wilson, Joseph	To be released from imprisonment at suit of United States.	16	2	Petition	131	Judiciary.						
Wilson, Joseph, (D. C.)	Pension	20	1	Petition	440	Military Pensions	April 29, 1828	Favorable	283	Passed.		
Wilson, Joseph, (D. C.)	Pension	20	2	House bill	55	Whole House	Dec. 12, 1828	Favorable	311	Passed.		
Wilson, Joseph, (D. C.)	Pension	21	1	Petition	49	Military Pensions	Jan. 5, 1830	Favorable; bill	72	Passed	Passed	App'd May 20, 1830
Wilson, Joseph, (Ohio)	Pension	24	2	Petition	80	Claims	20	Adverse		Laid on table.		
Wilson, Joseph, (Ohio)	Pension	24	2	Petition	122	Rev. Pensions				Discharged; laid on table.		
Wilson, Joseph, (Chio)	Pension	25	3	Petition	173	Rev. Pensions				Discharged.		
Wilson, Joseph, purser	Compensation for loss sustained by reason of supervision of the Phenix Bank of Charleston, &c.	29	1	Memorial	218	Naval Affairs.						
Wilson, Joseph, purser	Compensation for loss sustained by reason of supervision of the Phenix Bank of Charleston, &c.	29	2	Memorial	141	Naval Affairs						Leave to withdraw.
Wilson, Joseph, purser	Compensation for loss sustained by reason of supervision of the Phenix Bank of Charleston, &c.	29	2	Senate bill	306	Naval Affairs	Feb. 16, 1847	With't amend.	5	Referred to Committee Whole House.		
Wilson, Joseph, purser	Compensation for loss sustained by reason of supervision of the Phenix Bank of Charleston, &c.	30	1	Senate bill	203	Naval Affairs			2	Passed		App'd June 13, 1848
Wilson, Joseph, representatives of.	Compensation for revolutionary services.	29	1	Memorial	327	Rev. Pensions.						
Wilson, Louis D.	(See William Ross, assignee of)	26	1		182							
Wilson, Matthew	(See Isaac Smith and others)	13	3		666							
Wilson, Mary	(See Mary Nail)	23	1		45							
Wilson, Mary	(See Thomas Wilson, widow of.)	28	1		605							
Wilson, Margaret	(See Benj. Marshall, widow of)	24	1		138							
Wilson, Nancy	(See Capt. Wm. Wilson)	26	1		328							

Names of claimants.	Nature or object of the claim.	Congress.	Session.	How brought before the House of Reps.	Page of journal.	To what committee of the House referred.	No. or date of the report.	Nature of the report.	No. of the bill.	How disposed of by the House of Reps.	How disposed of by the Senate.	Date of the act of Congress, and remarks.
Wilson, Dr. Nathaniel	Pension	15	2	Resolution	248	Pens. & Rev. Cl'ms.				Discharged; laid on table.		
Wilson, Peggy	(See Wm. Wilson, Indian, widow of.)	21	1		264							
Wilson, Peter	Pension	28	1	Petition	366	Rev. Pensions	329	Favorable	237	Passed.		
Wilson, Peter	Pension	28	2	Petition	113	Rev. Pensions	141	Favorable	622	Referred to Committee Whole House.		
Wilson, Peter	(See John Vanderbilt)	5	2		144							
Wilson, Philip	Indemnity for British spoliation	4	2	Petition	696					Laid on table.		
Wilson, Philip	Indemnity for British spoliation	5	2	Petition	264					Laid on table.		
Wilson, sen., Philip, of Philadelphia.	Compensation for property taken and used by United States army in 1778.	6	2	Petition	732	Claims	Dec. 2, 1800	Adverse		Laid on table.		
Wilson, sen., Philip, of Philadelphia.	Compensation for property taken and used by United States army in 1778.	7	1	Petition	17	Claims	Dec. 28, 1801	Adverse		Laid on table.		
Wilson, sen., Philip, of Philadelphia.	Compensation for property taken and used by United States army in 1778.	8	1	Petition	435	Claims	Nov. 18, 1803	Adverse		Laid on table.		
Wilson, sen., Philip, of Philadelphia.	Compensation for property taken and used by United States army in 1778.	9	1	Petition	206	Claims.						
Wilson, sen., Philip, of Philadelphia.	Compensation for property taken and used by United States army in 1778.	10	1	Petition	28	Select.						
Wilson, sen., Philip, of Philadelphia.	Compensation for property taken and used by United States army in 1778.	10	2	Petition	378	Select.						
Wilson, sen., Philip, of Philadelphia.	Compensation for property taken and used by United States army in 1778.	11	1	Petition	42	Claims.						
Wilson, sen., Philip, of Philadelphia.	Compensation for property taken and used by United States army in 1778.	11	2	Petition	168	Com. and Manuf.						
Wilson, sen., Philip, of Philadelphia.	Compensation for property taken and used by United States army in 1778.	11	3	Petition	438	Claims	Jan. 9, 1811	Adverse		Laid on table.		
Wilson, sen., Philip, of Philadelphia, widow of.	Compensation for property taken and used by United States army in 1778.	11	3	Petition	501					Laid on table.		
Wilson, sen., Philip, of Philadelphia, widow of.	Compensation for property taken and used by United States army in 1778.	23	1	Petition	71	Rev. Claims.						
Wilson, sen., Philip, of Philadelphia, widow of.	Compensation for property taken and used by United States army in 1778.	23	2	Petition	106	Rev. Claims.						
Wilson, sen., Philip, of Philadelphia, widow of.	Compensation for property taken and used by United States army in 1778.	24	1	Petition	103	Rev. Claims.						
Wilson, sen., Philip, of Philadelphia, widow of.	Compensation for property taken and used by United States army in 1778.	25	2	Petition	111	Rev. Claims.				Discharged; laid on table.		

List of private claims presented to the House of Representatives of the United States from the 1st to the 31st Congress, inclusive—Continued.

Names of claimants.	Nature or object of the claim.	Congress.	Session.	How brought before the House of Reps.	Page of journal.	To what committee of the House referred.	No. or date of the report.	Nature of the report.	No. of the bill.	How disposed of by the House of Reps.	How disposed of by the Senate.	Date of the act of Congress, and remarks.
Wilson, Richard, (D. C.)	Release from confinement	7	2	Petition	245	Select	Dec. 20, 1802			Referred to Committee Whole House.		
Wilson, Richard, (D. C.)	Balance of compensation for revolutionary services.	8	1	Petition	500	Claims				Referred to Committee Whole House.		
Wilson, Richard, (Md.)	Payment of money advanced and services rendered during revolutionary war.	11	3	Petition	441	Claims	Feb. 1, 1811	Adverse		Laid on table.		
Wilson, Robert, (engineer)	Pension	5	2	House bill	137	Whole House	Jan. 11, 1798	Favorable	38	Passed	Passed	App'd Feb. 2, 1798
Wilson, Robert M., (Ohio)	Increase of pension	21	1	Petition	36	Military Pensions				Discharged; laid on table.		
Wilson, Robert, (S. C.)	Pension	21	1	Resolution	254	Military Pensions	May 3, 1830	Favorable	454	Referred to Committee Whole House.		
Wilson, Robert, (S. C.)	Pension	21	2	House bill	318	Whole House	Feb. 16, 1831	Favorable	454	Passed.		
Wilson, Robert, (S. C.)	Pension	22	1	Petition	435	Rev. Pensions.						
Wilson, Robert, (S. C.)	Increase of pension	31	1	Resolution	493	Rev. Pensions	443	Favorable	373	Referred to Committee Whole House.		
Wilson, R. J. T	Indemnity for French spoliations prior to 1800.	29	2	Petition	87	Foreign Affairs.						
Wilson, Samuel, (Ohio)	Pension	20	2	Petition	204	Military Pensions				Discharged; laid on table.		
Wilson Samuel	(See William H. Bedford)	28	1		262							
Wilson, Simon W., (Del.)	For settlement of claim against the United States.	1	2	Petition	272					Referred to Secretary Treasury.		
Wilson, Simon W., (Del.)	For settlement of claim against the United States.	2	2	Rep. of Secretary Treasury.	604					Laid on table.		
Wilson, Stebbins	Compensation for military services.	3	1	Petition	18					Referred to Secretary War.		
Wilson, Thomas	Release from imprisonment	11	2	Petition	163	Select				Discharged		Leave to withdraw.
Wilson, Thomas, (Penn.)	Additional compensation for rations furnished United States army.	12	1	Petition	110	Claims	228	Favorable	67	Passed	Passed	App'd April 8, 1812
Wilson, Thomas, (Penn.)	Additional compensation for rations furnished United States army.	13	2	Petition	181	Claims	Feb. 25, 1814	Favorable	140	Passed	Passed	App'd Mar. 38, 1814
Wilson, Thomas, (Penn.)	Additional compensation for rations furnished United States army.	15	1	Petition	273	Military Affairs				Discharged; laid on table.		
Wilson, Thomas, (Penn.)	Additional compensation for rations furnished United States army.	15	2	House bill	295	Military Affairs	Feb. 20, 1819	Favorable	326	Passed	Passed	App'd March 3, 1819
Wilson, Thomas, (Penn.)	Compensation as quartermaster United States during war of 1812.	17	1	Petition	68	Claims						Leave to withdraw.
Wilson, Thomas, (Va.)	Pension	22	2	Petition	397	Invalid Pensions.						
Wilson, Thomas, (Va.)	Pension	25	3	Petition	218	Invalid Pensions	291	Favorable	1155	Referred to Committee Whole House.		
Wilson, Thomas, (Va.)	Pension	26	1	Petition	168	Invalid Pensions	190	Favorable	202	Passed	Indef. postp'd.	
Wilson, Thomas, (Va.)	Pension	26	2	Petition	77	Invalid Pensions	48	Favorable	577	Referred to Committee Whole House.		
Wilson, Thomas, widow of	Pension	28	1	Petition	605	Rev. Pensions	340	Adverse		Laid on table.		
Wilson, Thomas, widow of	Pension	31	2	Petition	265							Leave to withdraw.
Wilson, T. C	Compensation for services on coast survey.	27	3	Petition	206	Naval Affairs.						
Wilson, Thomas, (Ind.,) widow of.	Pension	28	1	Petition	351	Rev. Pensions.						
Wilson, Thomas J	Compensation for services as commissioners appointed to treat with Indians.	31	1	Petition	231	Claims.						

List of private claims presented to the House of Representatives of the United States from the 1st to the 31st Congress, inclusive—Continued.

Names of claimants.	Nature or object of the claim.	Congress.	Session.	How brought before the House of Reps.	Page of journal.	To what committee of the House referred.	No. or date of the report.	Nature of the report.	No. of the bill.	How disposed of by the House of Reps.	How disposed of by the Senate.	Date of the act of Congress, and remarks.
Wilson, Uriah	Pension	30	1	Petition	657	Rev. Pensions.						
Wilson, Uriah	Pension	30	2	Petition	123	Rev. Pensions	120	Adverse		Laid on table.		
Wilson, Uriah	Pension	31	1	Petition	232	Rev. Pensions	263	Adverse		Laid on table.		
Wilson, Valentine, widow of.	Arrears of pension	23	2	Resolution	234	Rev. Pensions.						
Wilson, Valentine, widow of.	Arrears of pension	24	1	Petition	57	Rev. Pensions	58	Favorable	72	Passed	Passed	App'd May 14, 1836
Wilson, William, *et al.*	Relief in consequence of the capture and condemnation of the brig Jesse and cargo at Charleston, South Carolina.	7	2	Petition	291					Referred to Secretary of State.		
Wilson, William, *et al.*	Relief in consequence of the capture and condemnation of the brig Jesse and cargo at Charleston, South Carolina.	7	2	Rep. of Secretary State.	335	Claims	Feb. 15, 1803	Adverse				Leave to withdraw.
Wilson, William, *et al.*	Relief in consequence of the capture and condemnation of the brig Jesse and cargo at Charleston, South Carolina.	9	1	Petition	315	Com. and Manuf.						
Wilson, William, *et al.*	Relief in consequence of the capture and condemnation of the brig Jesse and cargo at Charleston, South Carolina.	10	1	Petition	27	Com. and Manuf.						
Wilson, William, *et al.*, (Cherokee Indians.)	Permission to sell land secured to them by treaty.	17	2	Petition	96	Public Lands	72	Adverse		Laid on table.		
Wilson, William, widow of.	Permission to sell land secured by treaty.	21	1	Petition	264	Public Lands				Discharged; laid on table.		
Wilson, William	(See Louis F. Beeler)	30	1		115							
Wilson, William	Compensation for revolutionary services.	13	3	Petition	519	Pens. & Rev. Cl'ms.	Dec. 9, 1814					Leave to withdraw.
Wilson, William	Pension	14	2	Resolution	209	Pens. & Rev. Cl'ms.	Jan. 29, 1817	Favorable	91	Passed	Passed	App'd March 3, 1817
Wilson, William H	Confirmation of title to land	22	1	Petition	336	Priv. Land Claims.	382	Favorable	474	Referred to Committee Whole House.		
Wilson, William	Pension	22	1	Petition	441	Rev. Pensions				Discharged; laid on table.		
Wilson, William	Pension	24	1	Resolution	922	Rev. Pensions				Discharged; laid on table.		
Wilson, William	Pension	25	2	Petition	405	Rev. Pensions				Discharged; laid on table.		
Wilson, William	Remuneration for loss of money remitted by United States mail.	27	2	Petition	1066	P. Of. & P. Roads.						
Wilson, William	Remuneration for loss of money remitted by United States mail.	27	3	Petition	44	P. Of. and P. Roads.						
Wilson, William	Remuneration for loss of money remitted by United States mail.	29	1	Memorial	303	Claims	221	Adverse		Laid on table.		
Wilson, Captain William, widow of.	Pension	26	1	Petition	323	Rev. Pensions	456	Favorable	370	Referred to Committee Whole House.		
Wilson, Captain William, widow of.	Pension	27	2	Petition	329	Rev. Pensions.						
Wilson, Captain William, widow of.	Pension	27	3	Petition	107	Rev. Pensions	66	Favorable	703	Passed	Passed	App'd Mar. 3, 1843
Wilson, Captain William, widow of.	Increase of pension	28	1	Petition	85	Rev. Pensions	449	Favorable	347	Passed.		

List of private claims presented to the House of Representatives of the United States from the 1st to the 31st Congress, inclusive—Continued.

Names of claimants.	Nature or object of the claim.	Congress.	Session.	How brought before the House of Reps.	Page of journal.	To what committee of the House referred.	No. or date of the report.	Nature of the report.	No. of the bill.	How disposed of by the House of Reps.	How disposed of by the Senate.	Date of the act of Congress, and remarks.
Wilson, William, trustee of.	Indemnity for French spoliations prior to 1800.	26	1	Memorial	182	Foreign Affairs	343	Favorable	319	Referred to Committee Whole House.		
Wilson, William, administrator of.	Indemnity for French spoliations prior to 1800.	27	2	Petition	72	Foreign Affairs.						
Wilson, William, administrator of.	Indemnity for French spoliations prior to 1800.	30	1	Petition	118	Foreign Affairs	Jan. 4, 1848	Favorable	21	Referred to Committee Whole House.		
Wilson, Wm. H., (Va.)	Pension	26	1	Petition	336	Invalid Pensions	646	Favorable	479	Referred to Committee Whole House.		
Wilson, Wm. H., (Va.)	Pension	27	2	Petition	98	Invalid Pensions.						
Wilson, Wm. H., (Va.)	Pension	28	1	Petition	333	Invalid Pensions.						
Wilson, Wm. H., (Va.)	Pension	29	1	Petition	440	Invalid Pensions	500	Adverse	......	Laid on table.		
Wilson, Wm. H., (Va.)	Pension	30	1	Petition	339	Invalid Pensions	551	Favorable	451	Ref'd to Com W. H.		
Wilson, Wm. H., (Va.)	Pension	30	2	House bill	648	Whole House	Mar. 3, 1849	Favorable	451	Passed	Passed	App'd March 3, 1849
Wilson, W. T., *et al.*	Reimbursement for loss of money in transmission of United States mail.	31	2	Petition	266	P. Of. & P. Roads.						
Wilson, William, & Sons.	Reimbursement of certain duties	24	1	Petition	95	Ways and Means.						
Wilson, William, & Sons	Reimbursement of certain duties	25	2	Petition	72	Ways and Means	....	....	......	Discharged.		
Wilson, Capt. Willis, (Va.)	Commutation pay	9	1	Petition	228	Claims	Feb. 20, 1806	....	......	Referred to Committee Whole House.		
Wilson, Capt. Willis, (Va.)	Commutation pay	15	1	Petition	242	Pens. & Rev. Cl'ms.	Feb. 24, 1818	Adverse	......	Laid on table.		
Wilson, Capt. Willis, (Va.) heirs of.	For half pay under act of July 5, 1832, paid to fraudulent claimant.	23	1	Petition	243	Rev. Claims.						
Wilson, Capt. Willis, (Va.) heirs of.	For half pay under act of July 5, 1832, paid to fraudulent claimant.	23	2	Petition	376	Rev. Claims.						
Wilson, Capt. Willis, (Va.) heirs of.	For half pay under act of July 5, 1832, paid to fraudulent claimant	24	1	Petition	103	Rev. Claims	March 3, 1836	Adverse	......	Laid on table.		
Wilt, Jacob	Pension	27	3	Petition	236	Rev. Pensions	263	Adverse	......	Laid on table.		
Wiltbank, James	Payment for professional services at Philadelphia navy yard.	23	2	Petition	237	Naval Affairs	99	Favorable	724	Referred to Committee Whole House.		
Wiltbank, James	Payment for professional services at Philadelphia navy yard.	24	1	Petition	99	Naval Affairs	78	Favorable	94	Passed	....	App'd June 23, 1836
Wiltner, Col. Ludowick	Continuation of half-pay for life for revolutionary services.	23	1	Petition	40	Rev. Claims.						
Wiltner, Col. Ludowick	Continuation of half-pay for life for revolutionary services.	23	2	Petition	76	Rev. Claims	....	....	......	Discharged	....	Leave to withdraw.
Wilton, Harry	Compensation for wagon and horse lost in United States service.	23	2	Petition	68	Claims.						
Wilton, Harry	Compensation for wagon and horse lost in United States service.	24	1	Petition	213	Claims	Feb. 14, 1837	Resolution	......	Referred to 3d Auditor.		
Wilton, Henry	(See Exploring Expedition)	27	3									
Wiltsie, Martin	(See Jacobus De Peyster)	4	1	....	467							
Winans, Abraham, widow of	Pension	30	1	Petition	460	Rev. Pensions	....	....	......	Discharged	....	Leave to withdraw.
Winans, Eliza	(See Stephen Johnson, heirs of)	29	1									
Winans, Capt. John, heirs of.	Commutation pay	28	2	Petition	169	Rev. Pensions.						
Winans, Capt. John, heirs of.	Commutation pay	30	2	Resolution	664	....	....	....	......	....	....	Leave to withdraw
Winans, Martha	(See Abraham Winans, widow of)	30	1	....	460							
Winans, Silas, former widow of.	Pension	29	1	Petition	510	Rev. Pensions	770	Favorable	509	Referred to Committee Whole House.		

List of private claims presented to the House of Representatives of the United States from the 1st to the 31st Congress, inclusive—Continued.

Names of claimants.	Nature or object of the claim.	Congress.	Session.	How brought before the House of Reps.	Page of journal.	To what committee of the House referred.	No. or date of the report.	Nature of the report.	No. of the bill.	How disposed of by the House of Reps.	How disposed of by the Senate.	Date of the act of Congress, and remarks.
Winans, Silas, former widow of.	Pension	29	2	House bill	57	Whole House	Jan. 22, 1847	Favorable	509	Passed	Passed	App'd March 3, 1847
Winants, Josiah	Compensation for house destroyed in 1814.	16	1	Petition	181	Claims	Feb. 18, 1820	Adverse		Laid on table.		
Winch, Joshua	Arrears of pension	23	2	Petition	164	Rev. Pensions				Discharged; laid on table.		
Winch, Joshua	Arrears of pension	24	1	Petition	127	Rev. Pensions	134	Adverse		Laid on table.		
Winchel, Benjamin, attorney of.	Grant of land for military services.	12	1	Petition	25	Public Lands	Jan. 10, 1812	Adverse		Laid on table.		
Winchester, David, President of the Baltimore Insurance Company.	Indemnity for French spoliations prior to 1800.	26	1	Memorial	182	Foreign Affairs	343	Favorable; bill	319	Referred to Committee Whole House.		
Winchester, Jabez	Pension	21	1	Petition	596	Military Affairs.						
Winchester, Jabez	Pension	21	2	Petition	127	Military Affairs.						
Winchester, Jabez	Pension	22	1	Petition	67	Rev. Pensions	105	Favorable	190	Referred to Committee Whole House.		
Winchester, Jabez	Pension	22	2	House bill	66	Whole House			190	Laid on table.		
Winchester, James	Compensation for expenses incurred in furnishing Indians.	9	1	Petition	193	Clamis	Feb. 28, 1806			Referred to Committee Whole House.		
Winchester, Silas	Pension	19	1	Petition	310	Military Pensions	164	Adverse		Laid on table.		
Winchester, Silas	Arrears of pension	22	1	Petition	188	Rev. Pensions				Discharged; laid on table.		
Winchester, Silas	Arrears of pension	24	1	Petition	56	Rev. Pensions	April 12, 1836	Adverse		Laid on table.		
Winchester, Silas	Arrears of pension	24	2	Petition	117	Rev. Pensions.						
Winchester, Silas	Arrears of pension	31	2	Petition	100	Rev. Pensions.						
Wind, Frederick	Confirmation of title to land	17	2	Petition	259							Leave to withdraw.
Wind, Judge, *et al.*	(See Indians, Cherokee, old settlers.)	30	2		416							
Windell, John, agent	(See Jean Baptiste Dumon.)	5	2		157							
Windle, Joseph H.	For certain credits on account as paymaster, U. S. army.	21	1	Petition	448	Claims	April 22, 1830	Adverse		Laid on table.		
Windham, Sarah	(See Joshua Lamb.)	25	2		1029							
Windmuller, Solomon	For benefit of insolvent act	24	2	Petition	125	Judiciary.						
Windsor, Richard	Compensation for services rendered in exploring expediton.	9	1	President's mess.	284					Laid on table.		
Windsor, Richard	Compensation for services rendered in exploring expedition.	9	1	President's mess.	470	Select	Dec. 22, 1806	Report		Referred to Committee Whole House.		
Windsor, Richard	Compensation for services rendered in exploring expedition.	9	2	Resolution	507	Select	Jan. 23, 1807	Favorable	183	Passed	Passed	App'd March 3, 1807
Winecore, John B.	Pension	25	2	Petition	400	Invalid Pensions				Discharged; laid on table.		
Winecore, John B.	Pension	26	1	Petition	182	Military Affairs.						
Winey, Jacob, *et al*	To be allowed the amount of depreciation pay.	1	3	Petition	376	Select				Discharged; referred to Secretary Treasury.		
Wincy, Jacob, *et al*	To be allowed the amount of depreciation pay.	2	2	Rep. of Secretary Treasury.	625					Laid on table.		
Winfield, David, (N. Y.)	Pension	22	1	Petition	329	Rev. Pensions.						
Winfray, Peter, sureties of.	To refund money paid United States	22	1	Petition	266	Judiciary				Discharged; laid on table.		
Winfray, Valentine	Payment for horses lost in United States service.	16	1	Petition	209	Claims				Discharged; laid on table.		
Wing, John, *et al.*	(See Dorothy Terrell.)	29	1		292							

3—86

List of private claims presented to the House of Representatives of the United States from the 1st to the 31st Congress, inclusive—Continued.

Names of claimants.	Nature or object of the claim.	Congress.	Session.	How brought before the House of Reps.	Page of journal.	To what committee of the House referred.	No. or date of the report.	Nature of the report.	No. of the bill.	How disposed of by the House of Reps.	How disposed of by the Senate.	Date of the act of Congress, and remarks.
Wing, Moses	Increase of pension	9	2	House bill	618	Whole House	Feb. 24, 1807	Favorable	216	Passed	Passed	App'd March 3, 1807
Wing, Moses	Increase of pension	16	1	Petition	176	Pens. & Rev. Cl'ms.				Discharged; laid on table.		
Wing, Sands	(See Gilbert Howland)	12	1		196							
Wing, Warner	For grant of land	22	1	Petition	294	Public Lands.						
Wing, Warner	Compensation for services as secretary of board of commissioners, Michigan.	19	1	House bill	264	Public Lands	77	Favorable	105	Passed.		
Wing, Warner	Compensation for services as secretary of board of commissioners, Michigan.	19	2	Resolution	29	Public Lands	2	Favorable	280	Passed	Passed	App'd Dec. 29, 1826
Wingard, James C.	Pension	14	2	Petition	70	Pens. & Rev. Cl'ms.				Discharged; laid on table.		
Wingard, James C.	Increase of pension	15	1	Petition	297	Pens. & Rev. Cl'ms.	April 1, 1818	Favorable	172	Passed	Indef. postp'd.	
Wingard, James C.	Increase of pension	15	2	House bill	41	Pens. & Rev. Cl'ms.	Nov. 26, 1818	Favorable	203	Passed	Passed	App'd March 3, 1819
Wingard, John B.	Compensation for services in office of First Comptroller.	29	1	Memorial	151	Claims	731	Adverse		Laid on table.		
Wingate, Francis, (N. H.)	Indemnity for loss sustained on contract with United States.	22	1	Petition	188	Claims	Feb. 6, 1832	Adverse		Laid on table.		
Wingate, Isaac, *et al.*	(See Hedgeman Triplett)	22	2		105							
Wingate, Jeremiah, heirs of.	Confirmation of title to land	30	1	Petition	740	Priv. Land Claims.						
Wingate, Jonathan	Pension	30	1	Petition	636	Rev. Pensions.						
Wingfield, William	Pension	23	1	Petition	308	Invalid Pensions	Mar. 4, 1834	Adverse		Laid on table.		
Wingfield, William	Pension	23	2	Petition	166	Invalid Pensions				Discharged; laid on table.		
Wingfield, William	Pension	24	1	Petition	426	Invalid Pensions				Discharged; laid on table.		
Wingfield, William	Pension	25	2	Petition	407	Invalid Pensions				Discharged; laid on table.		
Wingfield, William	Pension	25	3	Petition	89	Invalid Pensions	Jan. 22, 1839	Adverse		Laid on table.		
Wingfield, William	Pension	27	2	Petition	219	Invalid Pensions	431	Adverse		Laid on table.		
Winkle, Frederick F.	Pension	25	2	Petition	920	Invalid Pensions				Discharged; laid on table.		
Winkle, Frederick F.	Pension	26	1	Petition	163	Invalid Pensions				Discharged; laid on table.		
Winlock, Joseph, (Ky.)	For settlement of claim	19	2	Petition	65	Whole House				Discharged.		
Winn, John	Indemnity for cargo of schooner Joseph, plundered by Spain.	25	2	Petition	635	Foreign Affairs	873	Adverse		Laid on table.		
Winn, John W.	(See Charles Floyd, heirs of)	14	1		43							
Winn, John L.	(See John Stafford)	21	1		104							
Winn, John, heirs of	Renewal of a land warrant	26	1	Petition	797	Priv. Land Claims.	515	Favorable	416	Referred to Committee Whole House.		
Winn, John, heirs of	Arrears of pension	26	1	Petition	962	Rev. Pensions.						
Winn, Joseph	Indemnity for French spoliations prior to 1800.	26	1	Memorial	182	Foreign Affairs	343	Favorable; bill	319	Referred to Committee Whole House.		
Winn, Rebecca, widow of.	(See Timothy Winn)	28	1		262							
Winn, Richard	In relation to land claim	24	1	Papers	839	Priv. Land Claims.				Discharged; laid on table.		
Winn, Timothy, agent	(See Joshua Whiting)	4	2		627							
Winn, Timothy, executor of.	For extra compensation as purser.	26	2	Petition	80	Claims.						

List of private claims presented to the House of Representatives of the United States from the 1st to the 31st Congress, inclusive—Continued.

Names of claimants.	Nature or object of the claim.	Congress.	Session.	How brought before the House of Reps.	Page of journal.	To what committee of the House referred.	No. or date of the report.	Nature of the report.	No. of the bill.	How disposed of by the House of Reps.	How disposed of by the Senate.	Date of the act of Congress, and remarks.
Winn, Timothy, executor of.	For extra compensation as purser.	27	2	Petition	549	Claims.						
Winn, Timothy, widow of.	For extra services as purser	28	1	Petition	262	Claims				Discharged		Leave to withdraw.
Winn, Timothy, widow of.	For extra services as purser	31	1	Petition	277	Naval Affairs	290	Favorable	264	Referred to Committee Whole House.		
Winne, William, (N. Y.).	Pension	21	1	Petition	498	Military Pensions				Discharged; laid on table.		
Winner, James, *et al.*	Additional compensation for arms furnished United States.	19	1	Petition	36, 98	Claims	61	Favorable	85	Passed	Passed	App'd May 20, 1826
Winner, Joseph	Increase of compensation as collector and inspector.	9	1	Petition	234	Ways and Means.						
Winner, Joseph	Indemnity for expenses incurred at suit of United States.	16	1	Petition	496					Laid on table.		
Winney, Jeremiah H.	Increase of pension	24	2	Petition	311	Invalid Pensions.						
Winney, Jeremiah H.	Increase of pension	25	2	Petition	269	Invalid Pensions				Discharged; laid on table.		
Winney, Jeremiah H.	Increase of pension	26	1	Petition	162	Invalid Pensions	256	Adverse		Laid on table.		
Winsh, Jacob	Pre-emption right	18	1	House bill	151	Whole House	May 13, 1824	With amend.	65	Passed	Passed	App'd May 26, 1824
Winship, Abiel, heirs of	Indemnity for French spoliations prior to 1800.	26	1	Memorial	182	Foreign Affairs	343	Favorable; bill	319	Referred to Committee Whole House.		
Winship, Ebenezer	Reimbursement for supplies furnished in revolutionary war.	2	1	Petition	526					Referred to Secretary Treasury.		
Winslett, John, .)	Payment for wagon and horses taken to remove Indians.	22	2	Documents	125	Indian Affairs	Feb. 6, 1833	Favorable; bill	727	Referred to Committee Whole House.		
Winslett, John, (Ark.)	Payment for wagon and horses taken to remove Indians.	23	1	Petition	67	Indian Affairs	Dec. 30, 1833	Favorable; bill	100	Passed	Passed	App'd June 28, 1834
Winslow, Beverly, *et al.*	Compensation for advances made and supplies furnished United States troops.	2	1	Petition	461					Referred to Secretary Treasury.		
Winslow, Beverly, *et al.*	Compensation for advances made and supplies furnished United States troops.	3	2	Rep. of Secretary Treasury.	284					Laid on table.		
Winslow, Beverly, *et al.*	Compensation for advances made and supplies furnished United troops.	4	1	Rep. of Secretary Treasury.	383	Claims	Jan. 26, 1796					Leave to withdraw.
Winslow, Daniel	Relief under contract to furnish beef to United States.	31	2	Petition	180	Naval Affairs.						
Winslow, Edward	(See George Adams and others)	26	1		712							
Winslow, Frederick, *et al.*	Indemnity for French spoliations prior to 1800.	31	1	Petition	633	Foreign Affairs	355	Favorable; bill	318	Referred to Committee Whole House.		
Winslow, George A.	Compensation for revolutionary services.	25	3	Petition	462	Claims.						
Winslow, George A.	Compensation for revolutionary services.	26	1	Petition	168	Claims	678	Adverse		Laid on table.		
Winslow, George A.	Compensation for revolutionary services.	26	2	Petition	81	Claims.						
Winslow, George A.	Compensation for revolutionary services.	27	2	Petition	55	Claims.						
Winslow, George A.	Compensation for revolutionary services.	27	3	Petition	139	Claims	42	Favorable; bill	667	Passed	Passed	App'd March 3, 1843
Winslow, Isaac, *et al.*	Remission of duties on spirits	14	1	Petition	169	Ways and Means				Discharged; laid on table.		

List of private claims presented to the House of Representatives of the United States from the 1st to the 31st Congress, inclusive—Continued.

Names of claimants.	Nature or object of the claim.	Congress.	Session.	How brought before the House of Reps.	Page of journal.	To what committee of the House referred.	No. or date of the report.	Nature of the report.	No. of the bill.	How disposed of by the House of Reps.	How disposed of by the Senate.	Date of the act of Congress, and remarks.
Winslow, Isaac	Indemnity for French spoliations prior to 1800.	26	1	Memorial	182	Foreign Affairs	343	Favorable; bill	319	Referred to Committee Whole House.		
Winslow, Isaac, & Sons	To refund certain duties	28	1	Petition	102	Claims.						
Winslow, Isaac, & Sons	To refund certain duties	29	2	Petition	147	Claims		General bill				App'd Aug. 10, 1846
Winslow, Isaac, and Thos. S.	Indemnity for loss of gin by fire	26	1	Petition	292	Commerce	308	Favorable	270	Referred to Committee Whole House.		
Winslow, Isaac, and Thos. S.	Indemnity for loss of gin by fire	27	2	Petition	57	Commerce	901	Favorable	522	Referred to Committee Whole House.		
Winslow, Isaac, and Thos.	Indemnity for loss of gin by fire	27	3	House bill	89	Whole House	Dec. 23, 1842	Favorable	522	Passed	Passed	App'd Jan. 20, 1843
Winslow, Jared	Pension	25	2	Petition	722	Invalid Pensions	878	Favorable	783	Passed.		
Winslow, Jared	Pension	25	3	Petition	90	Invalid Pensions	80	Favorable	958	Passed.		
Winslow, Jared	Pension	26	1	Petition	162	Invalid Pensions	185	Favorable	197	Passed		App'd July 20, 1840
Winslow, Lieut. J. A.	Compensation for extra military services.	28	1	Petition	449	Naval Affairs.						
Winslow, Nathan	Fishing bounty	4	2	Petition	615					Referred to Secretary of Treasury.		
Winslow, Oliver	Pension	16	2	Petition	176	Rev. Pensions	Feb. 15, 1822	Adverse				Leave to withdraw.
Winslow, Samuel T.	Pension	24	1	Petition	51	Invalid Pensions	July 1, 1836	Adverse		Laid on table.		
Winslow, Samuel T.	Pension	24	2	Petition	42	Invalid Pensions	71	Adverse		Laid on table.		
Winslow, Samuel T.	Pension	25	2	Petition	663	Invalid Pensions				Discharged; laid on table.		
Winslow, Samuel T.	Pension	25	3	Petition	349	Invalid Pensions.						
Winslow, Samuel T.	Pension	26	1	Petition	359	Invalid Pensions	July 21, 1840	Favorable	521	Referred to Committee Whole House.		
Winslow, Samuel T.	Pension	27	2	Petition	91	Invalid Pensions	260	Adverse		Laid on table.		
Winslow, Samuel T.	Pension	28	1	Petition	568	Invalid Pensions.						
Winslow, Samuel T.	Pension	28	2	Petition	87	Invalid Pensions.						
Winslow, Samuel T.	Pension	29	1	Petition	436	Invalid Pensions	561	Adverse		Laid on table.		
Winslow, Samuel T.	Pension	30	1	Petition	508	Invalid Pensions				Discharged; laid on table.		
Winslow, Samuel T.	Pension	31	1	Petition	214	Invalid Pensions	70	Adverse		Laid on table		Leave to withdraw.
Winslow, Thomas S.	(See Isaac and T. S. Winslow)	26	1		292							
Winslow, Thomas S.	For register of barque Cornwallis.	31	1	Petition	756	Commerce	May 16, 1850	Favorable	288	Passed	Passed	App'd May 23, 1850
Winsor, Christopher, widow of.	Pension	26	1	Resolution	950	Rev. Pensions.						
Winsor, Martin	(See Nathan Winsor, jr., *et al.*)	17	1		255							
Winsor, jr., Nathan, *et al.*	Fishing bounty	17	1	Petition	255	Commerce				Discharged; laid on table.		
Winsor, jr., Nathan, *et al.*	Fishing bounty	17	2	Petition	26	Commerce				Discharged		Leave to withdraw.
Winsor, jr., Nathan, *et al.*	Fishing bounty	18	1	Petition	30	Commerce.						
Winsor, Prudence	(See Christopher Winsor, widow of.)	26	1		950							
Winstead, Francis	Compensation for revolutionary services.	19	2	Petition	265	Claims				Discharged.		
Winston, Isaac	Pension	22	1	Petition	66	Rev. Pensions				Discharged; laid on table.		
Winston, John T., and Anthony.	To be allowed to enter certain land in lieu of former purchase.	19	1	Petition	53	Public Lands	Dec. 23, 1825	Adverse		Laid on table.		
Winston, Capt. John, heirs of.	Commutation of half-pay	22	1	Petition	470	Rev. Claims	407	Favorable	507	Referred to Committee Whole House.		
Winston, Capt. John, heirs of.	Commutation of half-pay	23	1	Petition	39	Rev. Claims.						

List of private claims presented to the House of Representatives of the United States from the 1st to the 31st Congress, inclusive—Continued.

Names of claimants.	Nature or object of the claim.	Congress.	Session.	How brought before the House of Reps.	Page of journal.	To what committee of the House referred.	No. or date of the report.	Nature of the report.	No. of the bill.	How disposed of by the House of Reps.	How disposed of by the Senate.	Date of the act of Congress, and remarks.
Winston, Capt. John, heirs of.	Commutation of half-pay	23	2	Petition	77	....	118	Favorable	752	Referred to Committee Whole House.		
Winston, Capt. John, heirs of.	Commutation of half-pay	24	1	Petition	103	Rev. Claims	153	Favorable	162	Referred to Committee Whole House.		
Winston, Capt. John, heirs of.	Commutation of half-pay	24	2	Petition	270	Rev. Claims.						
Winston, Capt. John, heirs of.	Commutation of half-pay	24	2	House bill	62	Whole House	Dec. 16, 1836	Favorable	162	Referred to Committee Whole House.		
Winston, Capt. John, heirs of.	Commutation of half-pay	25	2	Petition	40	Rev. Claims	195	Favorable	221	Passed.		
Winston, Capt. John, heirs of.	Commutation of half pay	25	3	Petition	85	Rev. Claims.						
Winston, Capt. John, heirs of.	Commutation of half-pay	26	1	Petition	163	Rev. Claims	604	Adverse	......	Discharged.		
Winston, Capt. John, heirs of.	Commutation of half-pay	27	2	Petition	62	Rev. Claims	686	Adverse	......	Laid on table.		
Winston, Capt. John, heirs of.	Commutation of half-pay	27	3	Petition	70	Rev. Claims	222	Adverse	......	Laid on table.		
Winston, Capt. John, heirs of.	Commutation of half-pay	29	1	Petition	310	Rev. Claims.						
Winston, Thos. B., (Miss.)	Relief as notary public	29	2	Joint resolution	430	Judiciary	Feb. 26, 1847	Favorable	J. R. 60	Referred to Committee Whole House.		
Winston, William B., heirs of.	Compensation for revolutionary services.	24	1	Resolution	990	Rev. Pensions.						
Winston, William B., heirs of.	Compensation for revolutionary services.	25	2	Resolution	1048	Rev. Pensions	....	....	......	Discharged; laid on table.		
Winston, William B., heirs of.	Compensation for revolutionary services.	26	1	Petition	173	Rev. Pensions	115	Favorable	125	Referred to Committee Whole House.		
Winston, William B., heirs of.	Compensation for revolutionary services.	26	2	House bill	194	Whole House	Jan. 16, 1841	Favorable	125	Passed.		
Winter, Elisha	Compensation for expenses in prosecuting robbers.	8	2	Petition	55	Claims	Jan. 24, 1805	....	......	....	....	Leave to withdraw.
Winter, Elisha J	Compensation for horses and harness taken for use of United States.	13	1	Senate bill	46	Claims	....	....	......	....	....	Leave to withdraw.
Winter, Elisha J	Compensation for horses and harness taken for use of United States.	13	1	Petition	107	Claims	July 19, 1813	With amend.	25	Passed	Concurred in.	App'd July 26, 1813
Winter, Elisha, (N. O.)	Confirmation of title to land	11	2	Petition	182	Public Lands	Feb. 5, 1810	....	......	....	....	Leave to withdraw.
Winter, Elisha, (N. O.)	Confirmation of title to land	12	1	Petition	219	Public Lands	Mar. 20, 1812	Favorable	90	Referred to Committee Whole House.		
Winter, Elisha, (N. O.)	Confirmation of title to land	12	2	Petition	567	Public Lands.						
Winter, Elisha, (N. O.,) representative of.	Confirmation of title to land	14	1	Petition	100	Public Lands	63	Favorable	118	Laid on table.		
Winter, Elisha, (N. O.,) representative of.	Confirmation of title to land	14	2	Petition	60	Priv. Land Claims.	51	Favorable	57	Referred to Committee Whole House.		
Winter, Elisha, (N. O.,) representative of.	Confirmation of title to land	15	1	Petition	25	Priv. Land Claims.	7, 20, 36	Favorable	20 83	Referred to Committee Whole House.		
Winter, Elisha, (N. O.,) representative of.	Confirmation of title to land	16	1	Senate bill	511	Priv. Land Claims.	....	....	75	Laid on table.		
Winter, Elisha, representatives of.	Confirmation of title to land in Arkansas.	19	2	Memorial	159	Priv. Land Claims.	....	....	......	Discharged; laid on table.		

List of private claims presented to the House of Representatives of the United States from the 1st to the 31st Congress, inclusive—Continued.

Names of claimants.	Nature or object of the claim.	Congress.	Session.	How brought before the House of Reps.	Page of journal.	To what committee of the House referred.	No. or date of the report.	Nature of the report.	No. of the bill.	How disposed of by the House of Reps.	How disposed of by the Senate.	Date of the act of Congress, and remarks.
Winter, Elisha, and sons, representatives of.	Confirmation of title to land in Arkansas.	20	1	Resolution	166	Priv. Land Claims.						
Winter, Elisha, and sons, representatives of.	Confirmation of title to land in Arkansas.	21	1	Senate bill	158	Priv. Land Claims.	April 6, 1830	With amend.	21	Referred to Committee Whole House.		
Winter, Elisha, *et al.*	Authority to try title to land in Arkansas.	20	1	Resolution	413	Public Lands.						
Winter, Elisha, heirs of	Confirmation of title to land	22	1	Memorial, &c.	75	Priv. Land Claims.	405	Favorable	503	Referred to Commitee Whole House.		
Winter, Elisha, heirs of	Confirmation of title to land	22	2	House bill	92	Whole House	Dec. 28, 1832	Favorable	503	Laid on table.		
Winter, Elisha, heirs of	Confirmation of title to land	23	1	Petition	196	Priv. Land Claims.	303	Favorable	338	Laid on table.		
Winter, Elisha, heirs of	Confirmation of title to land	24	1	Senate bill	320	Priv. Land Claims.	554	With amend.	1	Referred to Committee Whole House.		
Winter, Elisha, heirs of	Confirmation of title to land	24	2	Senate bill	527	Whole House.	Feb. 25, 1837	With amend.	49	Referred to Committee Whole House.		
Winter, Elisha, heirs of	Confirmation of title to land	25	2	Senate bill	332	Priv. Land Claims.	Feb. 7, 1838	With amend.	84	Referred to Committee Whole House.		
Winter, Elisha, heirs of	Confirmation of title to land	25	3	Resolution	173	Priv Land Claims.						
Winter, Gabriel	(See E. Winter, representatives of.)	19	2		159							
Winter, Gabriel	(See Don Carlos De Villemont)	22	1		95							
Winter, Jacob, (N. Y.)	Pension	22	1	Petition	509	Invalid Pensions.						
Winter, Jacob, (N. Y.)	Pension	23	1	Petition	617	Invalid Pensions				Discharged		Leave to withdraw
Winter, Jacob, (N. Y.)	Arrears of pension	27	2	Petition	526	Invalid Pensions	819	Adverse		Laid on table.		
Winter, James, (La.)	Confirmation of title to land	20	1	Petition	51	Priv. Land Claims.	Jan. 11, 1828	Adverse		Laid on table.		
Winter, John, attorney of.	(See Jacob Beck, *et al.*)	3	2		332							
Winter, John, attorney of.	(See Thomas Price, *et al.*)	3	1		132							
Winter, Joseph	Drawback on merchandise	14	1	Petition	386	Com. and Manuf.	April 12, 1816	Adverse		Ref'd to Com. W H.		
Winter, Joseph	Drawback on merchandise	14	2	Petition	101	Com. and Manuf.	Dec. 31, 1816	Favorable	36	Passed	Passed	App'd March 3, 1817
Winter, Juvenil	Pension	22	1	Resolution	82	Rev. Pensions	395	Favorable	494	Referred to Committee Whole House.		
Winter, Nathan	Restoration of pension	17	1	Petition	118	Rev. Pensions				Discharged; laid on table.		
Winter, Samuel	Compensation for horse, &c., lost in Seminole war.	23	1	Petition	368	Rev. Claims.						
Winter, Samuel	Compensation for horse, &c., lost in Seminole war.	23	1	Petition	154	Claims.						
Winter, Timothy	Pension	5	2	Petition	164	Claims	Feb. 27, 1798	Adverse		Laid on table.		
Winter, William, heirs of.	Confirmation of title to land	14	1	Petition	100	Public Lands	63	Favorable	118	Laid on table.		
Winter, William, heirs of.	Confirmation of title to land	15	1	Petition	25	Priv. Land Claims.	7, 20, and 36	Favorable	83	Referred to Committee Whole House.		
Winter, William, heirs of.	Confirmation of title to land	16	1	Senate bill	511				75	Disch'd; laid on table.		
Winteringer, Nathan	Compensation for boat and cargo impressed into U. States service.	18	1	Petition	195	Military Affairs.				Discharged		Leave to withdraw
Winteringer, Nathan	Compensation for boat and cargo impressed into U. States service.	23	1	Petition	525	Military Affairs.						
Winteringer, Nathan	Compensation for boat and cargo impressed into U. States service.	23	2	Petition	77	Military Affairs.						
Winteringer, Nathan	Compensation for boat and cargo impressed into U. States service.	24	1	Petition	152	Claims	417	Adverse		Laid on table.		
Winteringer, Nathan	Compensation for boat and cargo impressed into U. States service.	26	1	Petition	961	Claims.						
Winteringer, Nathan	Compensation for boat and cargo impressed into U. States service.	31	1	Petition	510	Claims	497	Adverse		Laid on table.		

List of private claims presented to the House of Representatives of the United States from the 1st to the 31st Congress, inclusive—Continued.

Names of claimants.	Nature or object of the claim.	Congress.	Session.	How brought before the House of Reps.	Page of journal.	To what committee of the House referred.	No. or date of the report.	Nature of the report.	No. of the bill.	How disposed of by the House of Reps.	How disposed of by the Senate.	Date of the act of Congress, and remarks.
Winthrop, Joseph	(See Henry Sayward, sureties of.)	11	3	....	505							
Winthrop, Sargeant	Renewal of land warrant	14	1	Petition	356	Public Lands	....	....	......	Discharged; laid on table.		
Winthrop, Thomas L., and others.	Indemnity for land relinquished to United States.	25	2	Senate bill	785	Judiciary	956	With amend.	208	Referred to Committee Whole House.		
Winton, John	Payment for lands granted by United States to an Indian.	19	2	Petition	37	Public Lands	17	Favorable	317	Referred to Committee Whole House.		
Winton, John	Payment for lands granted by United States to an Indian.	20	1	Petition	59	Public Lands	66	Favorable	63	Passed	Passed	App'd May 24, 1828
Wirble, Henry, (Ky.)	Grant of land for revolutionary services.	20	2	Petition	33	Rev. Claims	Dec. 18, 1828	Adverse	......	Laid on table.		
Wire, Jacob, (Maine.)	Patent for certain lands under Spanish grant.	22	1	Petition	263	Public Lands	Feb. 17, 1832	Favorable	380	Referred to Committee Whole House.		
Wirgman, Charles	Refund certain duties	11	3	Petition	496	Com. and Manuf	Feb. 9, 1811	Favorable	203	Referred to Committee Whole House.		
Wirgman, Charles	Refund certain duties	12	1	Petition	11	Com. and Manuf	Nov. 13, 1811	Favorable	2	Referred to Committee Whole House.		
Wirgman, Charles	Refund certain duties	14	2	Petition	330	Ways and Means.						
Wirgman, Charles	Refund certain duties	15	1	Petition	59	Ways and Means	Jan. 20, 1818	Favorable	46	Passed	Passed	App'd April 20, 1818
Wirt, John T., widow of.	Compensation for two horses taken by General Wilkinson, war of 1812.	18	1	Petition	345	Claims	April 3, 1824	Adverse	......	Laid on table.		
Wirt, John T., widow of.	Compensation for two horses taken by General Wilkinson, war of 1812.	30	1	Petition	491	Claims	418	Adverse	......	Laid on table.		
Wirt, John T., widow of	Compensation for two horses taken by General Wilkinson, war of 1812.	31	2	Petition	145	Claims.						
Wirt, John T.	For settlement of accounts as assistant quartermaster general.	14	1	Petition	48	Secretary of War	Feb. 28, 1816	Favorable	......	Passed	Passed	App'd April 2, 1816
Wirt, Sarah	(See John T. Wirt, widow of.)	18	1	....	345							
Wirtz, William	Compensation as assistant commissary.	2	1	Petition	471	....	....	....	......	Referred to Secretary of War.		
Wirtz, William	Compensation as assistant commissary.	2	2	Petition	663	....	....	....	......	Referred to Secretary of War.		
Wirtz, William	Compensation as assistant commissary.	3	1	Report Secretary of War.	78	....	....	....	......	Laid on table.		
Wiscassett, Maine, merchants of.	Relief from liability for goods imported.	13	1	Petition	52	Ways and Means.						
Wiscassett, Maine, merchants of.	Relief from liability for goods imported.	13	2	Petition	234	Ways and Means	....	....	......	....	....	Leave to withdraw.
Wisconsin Territory, legislature of.	For appropriation to pay the expenses of the session of legislature.	28	1	Petition	238	Territories	155	Favorable	144	Passed.		
Wisconsin Territory, legislature of.	For appropriation to pay the expenses of the session of legislature.	28	2	Petition	140	Territories	119	Favorable	602	Referred to Committee Whole House.		
Wisconsin, citizens of	Compensation for losses sustained in consequence of their removal from public lands.	26	2	Petition	131	Public Lands.						
Wisconsin, citizens of	Compensation for losses sustained in consequence of their removal from public lands.	27	2	Petition	764	Public Lands.						

List of private claims presented to the House of Representatives of the United States from the 1st to the 31st Congress, inclusive—Continued.

Names of claimants.	Nature or object of the claim.	Congress.	Session.	How brought before the House of Reps.	Page of journal.	To what committee of the House referred.	No. or date of the report.	Nature of the report.	No. of the bill.	How disposed of by the House of Reps.	How disposed of by the Senate.	Date of the act of Congress, and remarks.
Wisconsin, citizens of Iowa county.	Compensat'n for property destroyed by Indians.	27	3	Petition	365	Claims.						
Wisconsin, citizens, of, in behalf of.	(See Laman Gibbs)	31	2		360							
Wisdom, Francis	Payment for musket captured by British.	23	1	Petition	246	Claims	Jan. 26, 1834	Adverse		Laid on table.		
Wise, Christian	Compensation for revolutionary services.	29	1	Petition	149	Rev. Claims				Discharged; laid on table.		
Wise, Enoch G.	Compensation for loss of horses in United States service.	24	1	Petition	430	Claims	793	Adverse		Laid on table.		
Wise, George S.	For settlement of accounts as purser for articles purchased by order of commander.	13	3	Petition	659	Claims	Feb. 1, 1815	Favorable	278	Laid on table.		
Wise, George S.	For settlement of accounts as purser for articles purchased by order of commander.	14	1	Petition	48	Claims	Jan. 3, 1816	Favorable	40	Passed	Postponed.	
Wise, George S.	For settlement of accounts as purser for articles purchased by order of commander.	18	2	Petition	185	Naval Affairs	66	Favorable	330	Passed	Indef. postp'd.	
Wise, George S.	For settlement of accounts as purser for articles purchased by order of commander.	19	1	Petition	62	Naval Affairs	4	Favorable	8	Passed.		
Wise, Hannah	(See Captain James Hubbard)	24	2		177							
Wise, Henry	Pension	18	2	Petition	117	Pens. & Rev. Cl'ms.				Discharged; laid on table.		
Wise, Henry A., & others	Compensation for mail service	31	1	Petition	1184	P. Of. & P. Roads.						
Wise, Jane	Restoration of pension	27	2	Petition	320	Rev. Pensions.						
Wise, John, Samuel and William.	Payment of a sum deducted from mail contract.	29	1	Petition	1073	P. Of. & P. Roads.						
Wise, Lydia	Continuation of pension	28	1	Petition	850	Rev. Pensions.						
Wise, Mary	Restoration of pension	27	2	Petition	320	Rev. Pensions.						
Wise, Michael, (Me.)	Indemnity for French spoliations prior to 1800.	26	1	Memorial	182	Foreign Affairs	343	Favorable; bill	319	Referred to Committee Whole House.		
Wise, Major Samuel, heirs of.	Commutation pay	2	1	Rep. of Secretary War.	459	Select	Nov. 25, 1791	Favorable; bill	159	Passed	Passed	App'd Mar. 27, 1792
Wiseman, Abraham	Authority to withdraw entry of land, and transfer money to other lands.	15	1	Senate bill	245	Public Lands	Feb. 19, 1818	With't amend.	23	Passed		App'd March 9, 1818
Wiseman, Bigbie & Co.	(See Begbie, Wiseman & Co.)	30	2		76							
Wiseman, Caleb, (Va.)	Pension	20	1	Petition	124	Military Pensions	April 29, 1828	Favorable	283	Passed.		
Wiseman, Caleb, (Va.)	Pension	20	2	House bill	55	Whole House	Dec. 12, 1828	Favorable	311	Passed	Laid on table.	
Wiseman, Caleb, (Va.)	Pension	21	1	Petition	49	Military Pensions	Jan. 5, 1830	Favorable	72	Passed	Passed	App'd May 20, 1830
Wiseman, Lt. Noah, heir and widow of.	Half pay pension	26	1	Petition	296	Military Affairs.						
Wiseman, Lt. Noah, heir and widow of.	Half-pay pension	27	2	Petition	1023	Military Affairs.						
Wiseman, Lt. Noah, heir and widow of.	Half-pay pension	27	3	Petition	101	Military Affairs	Jan. 14, 1843	Adverse		Laid on table.		
Wiseman, Lt. Noah, heir and widow of.	Half-pay pension	30	1	Petition	458	Rev. Pensions.						
Wiseman, Lt. Noah, heir and widow of.	Half-pay pension	30	2	Petition	116	Rev. Pensions	74	Adverse		Laid on table.		
Wiseman, Lt. Noah, heir and widow of.	Half-pay pension	31	1	Petition	524	Rev. Pensions				Discharged; aid on table.		

List of private claims presented to the House of Representatives of the United States from the 1st to the 31st Congress, inclusive—Continued.

Names of claimants.	Nature or object of the claim.	Congress.	Session.	How brought before the House of Reps.	Page of journal.	To what committee of the House referred.	No. or date of the report.	Nature of the report.	No. of the bill.	How disposed of by the House of Reps.	How disposed of by the Senate.	Date of the act of Congress, and remarks.
3—87 Wiser, Peter	For bounty land and other compensation for services in exploring expedition.	9	1	President's mess.	284					Laid on table.		
Wiser, Peter	For bounty land and other compensation for services in exploring expedition.	9	2	President's mess.	470	Select	Dec. 22, 1806	Not found		Referred to Committee Whole House.		
Wiser, Peter	For bounty land and other compensation for services in exploring expedition.	9	2	Resolution	507	Select	Jan. 23, 1807	Favorable	183	Passed	Passed	App'd March 3, 1807
Wish, L. J. A., widow of	Pension	23	1	Petition	36	Naval Affairs.						
Wish, Mary	(See L. J. A. Wish, widow of)	23	1		36							
Wishart, Capt. Thomas	For settlement of his accounts	2	1	Petition	465					Referred to Secretary War.		
Wishart, Capt. Thomas	For settlement of his accounts	2	2	Rep. of Secretary War.	671	Select	Jan. 25, 1793	Favorable	224	Passed	Passed	App'd Feb. 21, 1793
Wishart, Thomas, heirs of	Commutation pay	22	1	Petition	575	Claims	509	Favorable	569	Passed.		
Wishart, Thomas, heirs of	Commutation pay	23	1	Petition	575	Claims	19	Favorable	917	Referred to Committee Whole House.		
Wishart, Thomas, heirs of	Commutation pay	23	2	Petition	38	Claims.						
Wishart, Thomas, heirs of	Commutation pay	24	1	Petition	62	Claims.						
Wishart, Thomas, heirs of	Commutation pay	24	2	Petition	40	Claims.						
Wishart, Thomas, heirs of	Commutation pay	25	2	Petition	70	Claims	584	Favorable	569	Passed.		
Wishart, Thomas, heirs of	Commutation pay	25	3	Petition	84	Claims	19	Favorable	917	Referred to Committee Whole House.		
Wishart, Thomas, heirs of	Commutation pay	26	1	Petition	164	Claims.						
Wishart, Thomas, heirs of	Commutation pay	26	2	Petition	35	Claims.						
Wishart, Thomas, heirs of	Commutation pay	27	2	Petition	61	Claims	981	Adverse		Laid on table.		
Wishart, Thomas, heirs of	Commutation pay	29	1	Petition	266	Claims	141	Favorable	144	Referred to Committee Whole House.		
Wishart, Thomas, heirs of	Commutation pay	29	2	House bill	307	Whole House	Feb. 6, 1847	Favorable	144	Rejected.		
Wishart, Thomas, heirs of	Commutation pay	30	1	Petition	145	Rev. Claims.						
Wishart, Thomas, heirs of	Commutation pay	30	2	Petition	420	Rev. Claims.						
Wishart, Thomas, heirs of	Commutation pay	31	1	Petition	270	Rev. Claims	182	Favorable	192	Referred to Committee Whole House.		
Wisler, Michael	Pension	3	1	Petition	103					Referred to Secretary War.		
Wisler, Michael	Pension	3	2	Rep. of Secretary War.	278					Laid on table.		
Wislizenus, Adolphus	Compensation for services rendered and medicines furnished during war with Mexico.	30	1	Petition	170	Claims	404	Favorable	354	Referred to Committee Whole House.		
Wislizenus, Adolphus	Compensation for services rendered and medicines furnished during war with Mexico.	30	2	House bill	605	Whole House	Mar. 2, 1849	Favorable	354	Passed	Passed	App'd March 3, 1849
Wisner, Jacob	Pension	21	1	Resolution	433	Military Pensions				Discharged; laid on table.		
Wisner, Jacob	Pension	22	2	Resolution	65	Military Pensions.						
Wisner, Jacob	Arrears of pension	24	1	Resolution	964	Rev. Pensions.						
Witbeck, Volkert	Indemnity for property destroyed by flood whilst keeper of the light-house.	23	1	Petition	155	Claims	Feb. 7, 1834	Adverse		Laid on table.		
Witham, Thomas	Indemnity for French spoliations prior to 1800.	26	1	Memorial	182	Foreign Affairs	343	Favorable; bill	319	Referred to Committee Whole House.		

List of private claims presented to the House of Representatives of the United States from the 1st to the 31st Congress, inclusive—Continued.

Names of claimants.	Nature or object of the claim.	Congress.	Session.	How brought before the House of Reps.	Page of journal.	To what committee of the House referred.	No. or date of the report.	Nature of the report.	No. of the bill.	How disposed of by the House of Reps.	How disposed of by the Senate.	Date of the act of Congress, and remarks.
Witherall, Horace	Pension	27	2	House bill	1171	Invalid Pensions	946	Favorable; bill	550	Referred to Committee Whole House.		
Witherall, Horace	Pension	27	3	House bill	89	Whole House	Dec. 23, 1842	Favorable; bill	550	Passed	Passed	App'd March 3, 1843
Witherall, James	Compensation for revolutionary services.	24	1	Petition	152	Rev. Claims	395	Favorable	402	Referred to Committee Whole House.		
Witherall, James	Compensation for revolutionary services.	24	2	Senate bill	579				177	Referred to Committee Whole House.		
Witherall, James	Compensation for revolutionary services.	25	2	Petition	40	Rev. Claims	124	Favorable; bill	142	Referred to Committee Whole House.		
Witherall, James	Compensation for revolutionary services.	25	2	Senate bill	197	Whole House	Jan. 3, 1838	With amend.	36	Passed	Concurred in	App'd May 25, 1838
Witherall, James, (Mich.)	Confirmation of title to land	20	1	Resolution	28	Public Lands	42	Favorable; bil	34	Passed	Passed	App'd April 22, 1828
Witherall, Lot	Pension	21	1	Resolution	207	Military Pensions				Discharged; laid on table.		
Witherlee & Jarvis	Remission of certain duties	16	1	Senate bill	108	Ways and Means	Jan. 14, 1820	Favorable; bill	13	Passed with amendm't.	Concurred in.	App'd April 11, 1820
Withers, James	Commutation pay	22	1	Petition	51	Rev. Pensions.						
Withers, James	Commutation pay	22	2	Petition	40	Rev. Claims	Feb. 6, 1838	Adverse		Laid on table.		
Withers, James	Commutation pay	25	2	Senate bill	197	Rev. Claims	Jan. 26, 1838	With amend.	36	Passed	Concurred in.	App'd May 25, 1838
Withers, Michael	Extension of patent	20	1	Petition	225	Judiciary				Discharged; laid on table.		
Withers, Thomas C	Payment for wagon and horses lost in United States service.	15	2	Petition	258	Claims				Discharged; laid on table.		
Withers, Thomas C	Payment for wagon and horses lost in United States service.	16	1	Petition	78	Claims	Dec. 27, 1819	Adverse		Laid on table.		
Withers, Thomas C	Payment for wagon and horses lost in United States service.	16	1	Petition	148	Claims	Mar. 21, 1820	Favorable; bill	111	Passed	Passed	App'd May 8, 1820
Withers, Thomas C	For amendment of the act approved May 8, 1820.	18	2	Resolution	64	Claims.						
Withers, Thomas C	For amendment of the act approved May 8, 1820.	19	1	Resolution	136	Claims	45	Favorable; bill	61	Passed.		
Withers, Thomas C	For amendment of the act approved May 8, 1820.	19	2	Resolution	51	Claims	55	Favorable; bill	393	Passed	Passed	App'd March 2, 1827
Withers, William R	Permission to return bounty land and receive money in lieu.	16	1	Petition	343	Pens. & Rev. Cl'ms.				Discharged; laid on table.		
Withers, William R	Compensation for revolutionary ser vices.	20	1	Petition	39	Rev. Claims	Jan. 11, 1828	Adverse		Laid on table.		
Withers, William R	Compensation for revolutionary services.	20	2	Petition	70	Military Pensions				Discharged; laid on table.		
Withers, William R	Compensation for revolutionary ser vices.	21	1	Petition	98	Rev. Claims				Discharged; laid on table.		
Withers, William R	Compensation for revolutionary services.	21	2	Petition	82	Rev. Claims				Discharged; laid on table.		
Withers, William R	Compensation for revolutionary services.	22	1	Petition	106	Rev. Claims.						
Witherspoon, David, assignee.	For the pension heretofore allowed by the State of South Carolina.	7	2	Petition	321					Referred to Committee Whole House on bill No 177.		See act March 3, 1804
Witherspoon, Thomas	Increase of compensation as clerk to circuit court.	16	1	Petition	199	Judiciary	Mar. 13, 1818	Adverse				Leave to withdraw.
Witherspoon, Thomas, assignee of.	Indemnity for French spoliations prior to 1800.	26	1	Memorial	182	Foreign Affairs	343	Favorable; bill	319	Referred to Committee Whole House.		
Withington, Ebenezer	Pension	21	2	Petition	43	Military Pensions				Discharged; laid on table.		

List of private claims presented to the House of Representatives of the United States from the 1st to the 31st Congress, inclusive—Continued.

Names of claimants.	Nature or object of the claim.	Congress.	Session.	How brought before the House of Reps.	Page of journal.	To what committee of the House referred.	No. or date of the report.	Nature of the report.	No. of the bill.	How disposed of by the House of Reps.	How disposed of by the Senate.	Date of the act of Congress, and remarks.
Withington, Ebenezer	Pension	22	1	Resolution	93	Rev. Pensions				Discharged; laid on table.		
Withington, Samuel	Pension	20	1	Petition	365	Military Pensions	Feb. 13, 1828	Favorable	166	Passed.		
Withington, Samuel	Pension	21	1	House bill	130	Whole House	Jan. 5, 1830	Favorable	72	Passed	Passed	App'd May 20, 1830
Withington, Samuel, widow of.	Compensation for revolutionary services.	20	1	Petition	51	Rev. Claims	Jan. 11, 1828	Adverse		Laid on table.		
Withington, Samuel, widow of.	Compensation for revolutionary services.	20	2	Petition	50	Whole House	Dec. 12, 1828	Favorable	311	Passed.		
Withington, Unice	(See Samuel Withington, widow of.)	20	1		51							
Withrow, David	Pension	31	1	Petition	1269	Rev. Pensions.						
Withrow, David	Pension	31	2	Petition	431	Rev. Pensions	58	Adverse		Laid on table.		
Withrow, Samuel	Confirmation of title to land	30	2	Petition	91	Public Lands	115	Favorable	793	Referred to Committee Whole House.		
Withrow, Thomas	Compensation for loss sustained as mail contractor.	29	1	Petition	514	P. Of. & P. Roads				Discharged; laid on table.		
Witlee, Daniel T.	For money advanced for Red river raft.	29	2	Army appropria'n bill.	150	Whole House	Feb. 23, 1847	With amend.	597	Passed	Passed	App'd March 2, 1847
Witner, Peter	Renewal of loan office certificate	4	1	Petition	467	Claims.						
Witner, Peter	Renewal of loan office certificate	4	2	Petition	614	Claims	Feb. 1, 1797	Adverse		Laid on table.		
Witt, Daniel	Pension	29	1	Petition	279	Invalid Pensions	844	Adverse		Laid on table.		
Witter, Daniel S.	Indemnity for Indian depredations	22	1	Petition	512	Claims	April 6, 1832	Adverse		Laid on table.		
Witter, Josiah	Pension	2	1	Petition	479					Referred to Secretary War.		
Witter, Josiah	Pension	2	2	Rep. of Secretary War.	649	Whole House	Jan. 3, 1793	Favorable; bill	214	Passed	Passed	App'd Feb. 28, 1793
Witter, Josiah	Arrears of pension	3	1	Rep. of Secretary War.	75	Select	Mar. 5, 1794	Favorable		Referred to Secretary War.		
Witter, Josiah	Pension	3	2	Rep. of Secretary of War.	262	Claims.						
Witter, Josiah	Arears of pension	4	1	Petition	441	Claims	May 31, 1796	Adverse		Laid on table.		
Witter, Josiah	Reimbursement for expenses incurred whilst prisoner, revolutionary war.	3	1	Petition	185					Referred to Secretary War.		
Wittig, Henry, administrator of.	Remission of duties on stills	14	1	Petition	392	Ways and Means	Mar. 6, 1816	Adverse		Referred to Committee Whole House.		See act of April 19, 1816.
Witz, John	Pension	17	1	Petition	227	Rev. Claims				Discharged; laid on table.		
Witz, John	Pension	17	2	Petition	228	Rev. Claims				Laid on table.		
Witz, John	Pension	18	1	Petition	134	Rev. Claims	Feb. 23, 1824	Adverse		Laid on table.		
Wizent, William L.	Pre-emption right to land	30	2	Senate bill	564	Whole House	Mar. 3, 1849	With't amend.	277	Passed	Passed	App'd March 3, 1849
Wizick, Valentine	Compensation for mail services	1	3	Petition	383					Referred to Secretary War.		
Wizick, Valentine	Compensation for mail services	3	2	Rep. of Secretary War.	278					Laid on table.		
Wizlizenus, Adolphus	(See Adolphus Wislizinus.)	30	1		170							
Woart, William	Indemnity for French spoliations prior to 1800.	26	1	Memorial	182	Foreign Affairs	343	Favorable; bill	319	Referred to Committee Whole House.		
Wockley, Stephen, attorney of.	Compensation for mail services	5	2	Petition	302	Claims	May 18, 1798	Adverse		Laid on table.		
Wockley, Stephen, attorney of.	Compensation for mail services	6	2	Petition	741							Leave to withdraw.
Wogan, J.	Confirmation of title to land	22	1	Petition	64	Priv Land Claims.	62	Favorable	125	Passed	Passed	App'd June 25, 1832

List of private claims presented to the House of Representatives of the United States from the 1st to the 31st Congress, inclusive—**Continued.**

Names of claimants.	Nature or object of the claim.	Congress.	Session.	How brought before the House of Reps.	Page of journal.	To what committee of the House referred.	No. or date of the report.	Nature of the report.	No. of the bill.	How disposed of by the House of Reps.	How disposed of by the Senate.	Date of the act of Congress, and remarks.
Wolcott, Alexander	Increase of compensation as collector of customs.	14	2	Petition	255	Ways and Means	Feb. 7, 1817	Favorable	112	Referred to Committee Whole House.		
Wolcott, Benijah	Grant of land for services against Indians.	15	1	Petition	184	Public Lands	....	....	......	Discharged; laid on table.		
Wolcott, Benijah, (Ohio.)	Compensat'n for property destroyed in late war.	20	1	Petition	366	Claims	202	Adverse	......	Laid on table.		
Wolcott, George	Increase of compensation as surveyor of customs.	14	2	Petition	233	Ways and Means.						
Wolcott, George	Increase of compensation as surveyor of customs.	15	1	Petition	90	Ways and Means	....	....	......	Discharged; laid on table		
Wolcott, George	Increase of compensation as surveyor of customs.	15	2	Petition	73	Com. and Manuf.						
Wolcott, George	Increase of compensation as surveyor of customs.	16	1	Petition	29	Com. and Manuf.	....	....	......	Discharged; laid on table.		
Wolcott, Giles	Compensation for services rendered and money expended as an officer of revolutionary war.	5	2	Petition	102	Claims	Mar. 15, 1798	Adverse	......	Laid on table.		
Wolcott, Giles	Compensation for services rendered and money expended as an officer of revolutionary war.	13	2	Petition	266	Pens. & Rev. Cl'ms	....	....	......	....	....	Leave to withdraw.
Wolcott, James, widow of.	Remuneration for lands sold by United States, granted to widow by her half brother, an Indian.	19	1	Petition	74	Indian Affairs	26	Favorable	40	Passed	Passed	App'd May 18, 1826
Wolcott, Mary	(See James Wolcott, widow of)	19	1	....	74							
Wolcott, Oliver	Continuation of pay as judge of circuit court.	7	2	Petition	307	Whole House	Jan. 27, 1803	Adverse	......	....	....	Leave to withdraw.
Woleber, Abraham, (N.Y.)	Increase of pension	8	2	Petition	109	Whole House.						
Woleber, Abraham, widow of.	Pension	26	2	Petition	50	Rev. Pensions.						
Woleber, Dorothy	(See Abraham Woleber, widow of.)	26	2	....	50							
Woleber, Peter	Pension	3	1	Rep. of Secretary War.	131	Select	May 26, 1794	Favorable	J. R. 12	Passed	Passed	App'd June 9, 1794
Wolever, John	Pension	21	2	Petition	87	Military Pensions.						
Wolfe, Christiana	Compensation for revolutionary services.	1	2	Petition	222	....	....	....	......	Referred to Secretary of War.		
Wolfe, Christiana	Compensation for revolutionary services.	1	2	Rep. of Secretary War.	250	Select	July 16, 1790	Favorable	88	Passed	Passed	App'd Aug. 11, 1790
Wolf, Frederick	Pension	21	1	Resolution	228	Military Pensions	April 6, 1830	Adverse	......	Laid on table.		
Wolf, Frederick	Pension	22	2	Petition	176	Rev. Pensions	....	....	......	Discharged; laid on table.		
Wolf, Frederick	Pension	23	1	Petition	69	Rev. Pensions.						
Wolf, Frederick	Pension	24	1	Resolution	406	Rev. Pensions.						
Wolf, Jacob	Pension	21	2	Resolution	261	Military Pensions.						
Wolf, John, widow of	Pension	26	1	Petition	625	Rev. Pensions	469	Favorable	383	Referred to Committee Whole House.		
Wolf, John, widow of	Pension	27	2	Petition	59	Rev. Pensions	116	Favorable	162	Passed	Indef. postp'd.	
Wolf, Mary	(See John Wolf, widow of)	26	1	....	625							
Wolfender, John	Pension	27	3	Petition	341	Naval Affairs	Feb. 16, 1843	Favorable	794	Passed	Passed	App'd March 3, 1843
Wolfley, Lewis A., heirs of.	Pension	30	1	Petition	1052	Invalid Pensions	804	Favorable	625	Referred to Committee Whole House.		
Wolfley, Lewis A., heirs of.	Pension	30	2	House bill	267	Whole House	Jan. 17, 1949	....	......	Stricken from calendar.	....	Leave to withdraw.
Wolfolk, Austin	Confirmation of title to land	28	1	Petition	76	Priv. Land Claims.						

List of private claims presented to the House of Representatives of the United States from the 1st to the 31st Congress, inclusive—**Continued.**

Names of claimants.	Nature or object of the claim.	Congress.	Session.	How brought before the House of Reps.	Page of journal.	To what committee of the House referred.	No. or date of the report.	Nature of the report.	No. of the bill.	How disposed of by the House of Reps.	How disposed of by the Senate.	Date of the act of Congress, and remarks.
Wolfolk, Austin	Confirmation of title to land	29	1	Petition	824	Priv. Land Claims.						
Wolfskill, Joseph	(See Reuben E. Gentry and others)	24	1		294							
Wolfskill, William	Indemnity for property taken by Indians.	20	1	Petition	312	Indian Affairs	Feb. 25, 1828	Adverse		Laid on table		Leave to withdraw.
Wolfskill, William	Indemnity for property taken by Indians.	25	3	Petition	124	Indian Affairs.						
Wolfskill, William	Indemnity for property taken by Indians.	30	2	Petition				General appropriation bill.	692	Passed	Passed	App'd March 3, 1849
Wolm, Shem	(See Shem Wulm.)	21	1		213							
Wolverton, Hiram	(See Peter Bargy, jr., *et al.*)	21	1		364							
Wolverton, Stephen	Additional compensation as keeper of light-house.	24	1	Petition	506	Commerce.						
Wolverton, Stephen	Additional compensation as keeper of light-house.	24	2	Petition	82	Commerce.						
Wolverton, Stephen	Additional compensation as keeper of light-house.	25	2	Petition	84	Commerce	Jan. 4, 1830	Adverse		Laid on table.		
Worm, Edward	Pension	20	1	Petition	278	Military Pensions				Discharged; laid on table.		
Worm, Edward	Pension	20	2	Petition	178	Military Pensions				Discharged; laid on table.		
Worm, Edward	Pension	21	1	Petition	84	Military Pensions				Discharged; laid on table.		Leave to withdraw.
Wood, Abel	Pension	9	2	House bill	618	Whole House	Feb. 28, 1807	Favorable	216	Passed	Passed	App'd March 3, 1807
Wood, jr., Abel	(See Orchard Cook, *et al.*)	4	2		727							
Wood, Abiel	For certain offsetts in a suit now pending against him.	23	1	Petition	79	Judiciary	486	Favorable; bill	495	Referred to Committee Whole House.		
Wood, Abiel, administrator of.	For certain offsetts in a suit now pending against him.	24	1	Petition	53	Judiciary	311	Adverse		Laid on table.		
Wood, Abiel	(See sureties of Joseph Hurd.)											
Wood, Abiel, (Maine.)	Indemnity for French spoliations prior to 1800.	26	1	Memorial	182	Foreign Affairs	343	Favorable; bill	319	Referred to Committee Whole House.		
Wood, Abigail	(See Luke Purkins.)	25	2		405							
Wood, Abner	Indemnity for French spoliations prior to 1800.	26	1	Memorial	182	Foreign Affairs	343	Favorable; bill	319	Referred to Committee Whole House.		
Wood, Abner	Pension	22	1	Petition	219	Rev. Pensions				Discharged; laid on table.		
Wood, Absolem, heirs of.	Arrears of pension	24	1	Petition	477	Rev. Pensions.						
Wood, Adam	Patent of land bought of United States.	23	1	Petition	385	Priv. Land Claims.						
Wood, Amos	Pension	21	2	Petition	208	Military Pensions.						
Wood, Amos	Pension	22	1	Petition	35	Rev. Pensions				Discharged; laid on table.		
Woods, Andrew	Pre-emption right to land	4	1	Petition	388	Select.						
Woods, Auke	Compensation for services as pension agent.	27	2	Petition	312	Rev. Pensions	784	Adverse		Laid on table.		
Wood, Ann	(See Eli Wood, widow of.)	18	1		173							
Wood, Ann	(See Thomas Wood, widow of.)	25	2		118							
Wood, Benjamin	Pension	25	2	Petition	268	Invalid Pensions				Discharged.		
Wood, Benjamin	Pension	25	3	Petition	87	Invalid Pensions	Feb. 6, 1839	Adverse		Laid on table.		
Wood, Benjamin	Pension	27	2	Petition	386	Invalid Pensions	629	Adverse		Laid on table.		
Wood, Benjamin T., and wife.	Compensation for damages	27	3	Petition	141	Claims	16	Adverse		Laid on table.		

List of private claims presented to the House of Representatives of the United States from the 1st to the 31st Congress, inclusive—Continued.

Names of claimants.	Nature or object of the claim.	Congress.	Session.	How brought before the House of Reps.	Page of journal.	To what committee of the House referred.	No. or date of the report.	Nature of the report.	No. of the bill.	How disposed of by the House of Reps.	How disposed of by the Senate.	Date of the act of Congress, and remarks.
Wood, Benjamin F., and wife.	Compensation for damages	28	2	Petition	70	Claims	416	Adverse		Laid on table.		
Wood, Capt. Caleb, representatives of.	Pension	15	1	Petition	142	Pens. & Rev. Cl'ms.						
Wood, Cary M.	Indemnity for property illegally sold for taxes.	9	1	Petition	247	Claims	Jan. 28, 1806	Adverse				Leave to withdraw.
Wood, Catharine	(See George Wood, widow of)	27	2		612							
Wood, Charles	(See Mathews, Wood, & Hall)	24	2		119							
Wood, Charles, (N. Y.)	Pension	26	1	Resolution	284	Rev. Pensions.						
Wood, Charles, heirs of	Bounty land	27	2	Petition	886	Public Lands.						
Wood, Earl	Pension	25	2	Petition	56	Invalid Pensions				Discharged; laid on table.		
Wood, Captain Edward, heirs of.	Commutation pay	12	1	Petition	146	Claims.						
Wood, Captain Edward, heirs of.	Commutation pay	14	2	Petition	123	Pens. & Rev. Cl'ms.				Discharged; laid on table.		
Wood, Captain Edward, heirs of.	Commutation pay	15	1	Petition	246	Pens. & Rev. Cl'ms.	April 3, 1818	Adverse				Leave to withdraw.
Wood, Captain Edward, heirs of.	Commutation pay	15	2	Petition	125	Pens. & Rev. Cl'ms.	Jan. 4, 1819	Adverse		Laid on table.		
Wood, Captain Edward, heirs of.	Commutation pay	16	1	Petition	312	Pens. & Rev. Cl'ms.	Mar. 24, 1820	Adverse		Laid on table.		
Wood, Captain Edward, heirs of.	Commutation pay	16	2	Petition	83	Whole House.						
Wood, Captain Edward, heirs of.	Commutation pay	17	1	Petition	141	Pens. & Rev. Cl'ms.	29	Adverse		Laid on table.		
Wood, Captain Edward, heirs of.	Commutation pay	17	2	Resolution	41	Pens. & Rev. Cl'ms	46	Adverse		Laid on table.		
Wood, Captain Edward, heirs of.	Commutation pay	18	1	Petition	52	Pens. & Rev. Cl'ms.				Discharged; laid on table.		
Wood, Captain Edward, heirs of.	Commutation pay	19	1	Petition	182	Rev. Claims.						
Wood, Captain Edward, heirs of.	Commutation pay	19	2	Petition	158	Rev. Claims	53	Adverse		Laid on table.		
Wood, Captain Edward, heirs of.	Commutation pay	20	1	Petition	32	Rev. Claims	98	Adverse		Laid on table.		
Wood, Captain Edward, heirs of.	Commutation pay	24	1	Petition	432	Rev. Claims.						
Wood, Captain Edward, heirs of.	Commutation pay	24	2	Petition	91	Rev. Claims	97	Adverse		Laid on table.		
Wood, Edward, & Co.	Payment for provisions, United States steamer.	30	1	Petition	1157	Claims.						
Wood, Edward, & Co.	Payment for provisions, United States steamer.	31	1	Petition	677	Claims.						
Wood, Edmund W.	Pension	19	1	Resolution	509	Military Pensions	May 5, 1826	Adverse		Laid on table.		
Wood, Edmund W.	Pension	19	2	House bill	85	Whole House	Dec. 22, 1826	Favorable	314	Passed	Passed	App'd March 3, 1827
Wood, Eli	Pension	16	2	Petition	34	Rev. Pensions	Feb. 15, 1821	Adverse				Leave to withdraw.
Wood, Eli	Pension	17	1	Petition	133	Rev. Pensions				Discharged; laid on table.		
Wood, Eli	Pension	17	2	Petition	163	Whole House				Discharged		Leave to withdraw.
Wood, Eli, widow of.	Pension	18	1	Petition	173	Rev. Pensions	Mar. 24, 1824	Adverse		Laid on table.		
Woods, Elijah	Confirmation of title to land	3	2	Petition	285	Whole House.						
Woods, Elijah	Confirmation of title to land	4	1	Petition	379	Select.						

List of private claims presented to the House of Representatives of the United States from the 1st to the 31st Congress, inclusive—Continued.

Names of claimants.	Nature or object of the claim.	Congress.	Session.	How brought before the House of Reps.	Page of journal.	To what committee of the House referred.	No. or date of the report.	Nature of the report.	No. of the bill.	How disposed of by the House of Reps.	How disposed of by the Senate.	Date of the act of Congress, and remarks.
Wood, Enos	Pension	21	2	Petition	85	Military Pensions.						
Wood, Ephraim	Pension	22	1	Petition	472	Invalid Pensions				Discharged; laid on table.		
Woods, Fleming P.	Pay for a gun given up to United States.	20	1	Petition	366	Claims	Mar. 24, 1828	Adverse		Laid on table.		
Wood, Fleming, and Egbert Harris.	Indemnity for property seized by United States officers for alleged violation on Indian lands.	28	2	Petition	117	Indian Affairs	120	Adverse		Laid on table.		
Wood, Fleming, and Egbert Harris.	Indemnity for property seized by United States officers for alleged violation on Indian laws.	31	1	Petition	385	Indian Affairs.						
Wood, Fleming, and Egbert Harris.	Indemnity for property seized by United States officers for alleged violation on Indian lands.	31	2	Petition	445	Indian Affairs	88	Adverse		Laid on table.		
Wood, F	(See D. W. Haley, *et al.*)	26	1		605							
Wood, Francis, *et al.*	Indemnity for Indian depredations.	24	1	Petition	426	Indian Affairs.						
Wood, Francis, *et al.*	Indemnity for Indian depredations.	24	2	Petition	93	Indian Affairs				Discharged; laid on table.		
Wood, Francis, *et al.*	Indemnity for Indian depredations.	25	2	Petition	97	Indian Affairs				Discharged.		
Wood, Gabriel	Indemnity for French spoliations prior to 1800.	26	1	Memorial	182	Foreign Affairs	343	Favorable	319	Referred to Committee Whole House.		
Wood, George	Compensation for revolutionary services.	23	1	Petition	96	Rev. Claims.						
Wood, George	Compensation for revolutionary services.	24	2	Petition	394	Claims	247	Favorable		Discharged; referred to Third Auditor.		
Wood, George, widow of.	Continuation of pension	27	2	Petition	612	Rev. Pensions.						
Wood, Hugh, widow of.	Pension	29	1	Petition	766	Rev. Pensions	826	Adverse		Laid on table.		
Wood, Hugh, widow of.	Pension	29	2	Petition	92	Rev. Pensions.						
Wood, Hugh, widow of.	Pension	30	1	Petition	460	Rev. Pensions				Discharged; laid on table.		
Wood, Hugh, widow of.	Pension	30	2	Petition	116	Rev. Pensions	Jan. 17, 1849	Adverse		Laid on table.		
Wood, Hugh, widow of.	Pension	31	1	Petition	298	Rev. Pensions	21	Adverse		Laid on table.		
Wood, Ichabod	Pension	21	2	Petition	120	Military Pensions.						
Wood, Ichabod	Pension	22	1	Petition	67	Rev. Pensions	367	Favorable	462	Passed	Indef. postp'd.	
Wood, Ira A.	(See Martin S. Aikin)	17	1		359							
Wood, James, (Ohio)	Bounty land for revolutionary services.	22	1	Petition	143	Rev. Claims	Jan. 20, 1832	Adverse		Laid on table.		
Wood, James	To be released from payment of judgment at suit of United States.	29	1	Petition	327	Claims	353	Adverse		Laid on table.		
Wood, James	(See Reuben E. Gentry, *et al.*)	28	2		515							
Wood, Maj. James, widow of.	Pension	30	1	Petition	560	Invalid Pensions	625	Favorable	500	Passed.		
Wood, James, (Tenn.)	Relief from loss of military land warrant.	31	1	Petition	584	Priv. Land Claims.	208	Adverse		Laid on table.		
Wood, Jesse, (N. Y.)	Compensation for military services.	22	1	Petition	49	Claims.						
Wood, Jesse, heirs of	Payment of loan office certificates.	25	3	Petition	223	Rev. Pensions				Discharged.		
Wood, Jesse, heirs of	Payment of loan office certificates.	27	2	Petition	1157	Rev. Pensions	1056	Adverse		Laid on table.		
Wood, Jesse, former widow of.	Payment of loan office certificates.	27	3	Documents	423	Claims.						
Wood, Jethro, heirs of	For extension of patent	30	1	Senate bill	328	Patents	398	Adverse	108	Laid on table.		
Wood, Job	Pension	17	2	Petition	56	Pens. & Rev. Cl'ms.	Jan. 31, 1823	Adverse		Laid on table.		
Wood, Job	Pension	22	1	Petition	383	Invalid Pensions	434	Favorable	533	Referred to Committee Whole House.		

List of private claims presented to the House of Representatives of the United States from the 1st to the 31st Congress, inclusive—**Continued.**

Names of claimants.	Nature or object of the claim.	Congress.	Session.	How brought before the House of Reps.	Page of journal.	To what committee of the House referred.	No. or date of the report.	Nature of the report.	No. of the bill.	How disposed of by the House of Reps.	How disposed of by the Senate.	Date of the act of Congress, and remarks.
Wood, Job	Pension	23	1	Petition	241	Invalid Pensions	232	Favorable	258	Referred to Committee Whole House.		
Wood, Job	Pension	23	2	House bill	299	Whole House	Jan. 31, 1835	Favorable	258	Passed	Indef. postp'd.	
Wood, Job	Pension	24	1	Petition	98	Invalid Pensions	244	Favorable	251	Passed	Indef. postp'd.	
Wood, Job	Pension	25	3	Petition	128	Invalid Pensions				Discharged; laid on table.		
Wood, Job	Pension	26	1	House bill	510	Invalid Pensions	171	Favorable	182	Passed	Indef. postp'd.	
Wood, Job	Pension	27	2	Documents	68	Invalid Pensions	261	Adverse		Laid on table.		
Wood, Job	Pension	27	3	Petition	151	Invalid Pensions	141	Adverse		Laid on table.		
Wood, John	Compensation for revolutionary services.	1	2	Petition	221					Referred to Secretary of Treasury.		
Wood, John	Pension	3	2	Rep. of Secretary Treasury.	284					Laid on table.		
Wood, John	Pension	4	1	Rep. of Secretary Treasury.	532	Claims.						
Wood, John	Pension	4	2	Resolution, &c.	614	Claims	Jan. 10, 1797	Adverse		Laid on table.		
Wood, John	Revolutionary pension	11	2	House bill	283	Whole House	Mar. 24, 1810	Favorable	107	Passed	Passed	App'd April 27, 1810
Wood, John, representatives of.	Settlement of claim for supplies to commissioner, Indian affairs.	5	3	Petition	429	Claims.						
Wood, John	Compensation for services rendered and money advanced as captain militia, New York.	8	1	Petition	443	Claims	Dec. 6, 1803	Report		Referred to Committee Whole House.		
Wood, John	Pension	16	2	Petition	34	Rev. Pensions	Feb. 15, 1821	Adverse				Leave to withdraw.
Wood, Capt. John, (Cherokee Indian.)	Confirmation of title to land	17	2	Petition	83	Public Lands	Feb. 12, 1823	Adverse		Laid on table.		
Wood, Capt. John, (Cherokee Indian.)	Confirmation of title to land	21	1	Petition	60	Public Lands	82	Favorable	117	Passed	Passed	App'd May 28, 1830
Woods, John, (Ky.)	Pension	20	2	Resolution	314	Military Pensions				Discharged; laid on table.		
Woods, John, (Ky.)	Pension	21	2	Petition	43	Military Pensions.						
Wood, John, (Mass.)	Pension	21	2	Petition	208	Military Pensions.						
Wood, John, (Mass.)	Pension	22	1	Petition	35	Rev. Pensions				Discharged; laid on table.		
Wood, John, (Mass.)	Pension	24	1	Petition	282	Rev. Pensions				Discharged; laid on table.		
Wood, John, (Ark.)	Pre-emption right to land	24	1	Petition	58	Public Lands.						
Wood, John, (Maine)	Pension	24	1	Petition	473	Invalid Pensions				Discharged; laid on table.		
Woods, John, (Ky.)	Pension	26	1	Resolution	563	Invalid Pensions.						
Wood, John, widow of	Pension	28	1	Petition	346	Rev. Pensions				Discharged; laid on table.		
Wood, Joseph, (Ohio)	Compensation for services rendered as receiver of public moneys in land office.	18	1	Senate bill	149	Public Lands	Jan. 16, 1824	With amend.	10	Passed		App'd May 4, 1824
Wood, Joseph	Pension	25	2	Resolution	618	Rev. Pensions				Discharged; laid on table.		
Wood, Joseph	Pension	26	1	Petition	175	Rev. Pensions				Discharged; laid on table.		
Wood, Josiah	Compensation for supplies furnished United States army.	5	2	Petition	149	Claims	Feb. 6, 1798	Adverse		Laid on table.		
Wood, Leigton, *et al.*	Increase of compensation as clerks in Treasury Department, Philadelphia.	3	1	Petition	88	Select	47	Favorable	69	Passed	Rejected.	

List of private claims presented to the House of Representatives of the United States from the 1st *to the* 31st *Congress, inclusive*—Continued.

3—88

Names of claimants.	Nature or object of the claim.	Congress.	Session.	How brought before the House of Reps.	Page of journal.	To what committee of the House referred.	No. or date of the report.	Nature of the report.	No. of the bill.	How disposed of by the House of Reps.	How disposed of by the Senate.	Date of the act of Congress, and remarks.
Wood, Mary	(See Hugh Wood, widow of)	29	1		766							
Wood, Margaret	(See John Wood, widow of.)	28	1		346							
Wood, Matthew	Pension	18	2	Petition	232	Rev. Pensions	Feb. 23, 1825	Adverse		Laid on table.		
Wood, Mercy	(See Reuben Wood, widow of)	27	2		320							
Wood, Nathan	Pension	2	1	Petition	509					Laid on table.		
Wood, Nathan B.	Compensation as commissary of army.	20	2	Petition	28	Claims	7	Favorable	318	Referred to Committee Whole House.		
Wood, Nathan B.	Compensation as commissary of army.	20	2	Senate bill	294				36	Referred to Committee Whole House.		
Wood, Nathan B.	Compensation as commissary of army.	21	1	Petition	35	Claims	2	Favorable	2	Passed	Passed	App'd Jan. 30, 1830
Wood, Nicholas	Restoration of pension	17	1	Petition	67	Rev. Pensions				Discharged; laid on table.		
Wood, Reuben, widow of.	Restoration of pension	27	2	Petition	320	Rev. Pensions.						
Wood, Reuben, widow of.	Restoration of pension	27	3	Petition	365	Rev. Pensions.						
Wood, Reuben, widow of.	Restoration of pension	28	1	Petition	839	Whole House.						
Wood, Reuben, widow of.	Restoration of pension	30	1	Petition	229	Rev. Pensions	Jan. 25, 1843	Adverse		Laid on table.		
Wood, Sarah	(See Wm. Wood, widow of)	19	1		93							
Wood, Sarah	(See Maj. James Wood, widow of)	30	1		560							
Wood, Silas M.	Arrears of pension	27	2	Petition	239	Invalid Pensions	411	Adverse		Laid on table.		
Wood, Sylvanus, (Mass.)	Pension	20	2	Petition	31	Military Pensions	Feb. 13, 1829	Favorable	440	Passed.		
Wood, Sylvanus, (Mass.)	Pension	21	1	Petition	67	Military Pensions	Jan. 5, 1830	Favorable	72	Passed	Passed	App'd May 20, 1830
Wood, Sylvanus, (Mass.)	Increase of pension	25	3	Petition	97	Rev. Pensions	Jan. 16, 1839	Adverse		Laid on table.		
Wood, Theodore, assignee of.	Confirmation of title to land	15	2	Petition	117	Military Affairs	67	Favorable	260	Referred to Committee Whole House.		
Wood, Theodore, assignee of.	Confirmation of title to land	16	1	Petition	408	Military Affairs	April 14, 1820					Leave to withdraw.
Wood, Thomas, heirs of.	Compensation for revolutionary services.	24	2	Petition	44	Rev. Pensions				Discharged; laid on table.		
Wood, Thomas, widow of	Pension	25	2	Petition	1118	Rev. Pensions				Discharged; laid on table.		
Wood, William	Increase of pension	10	2	House bill	499	Whole House	Feb. 20, 1809	Favorable	158	Passed	Passed	App'd March 3, 1809
Wood, William, widow of	Pension	19	1	Petition	93	Military Pensions	164	Adverse		Laid on table.		
Wood, William, (Ohio)	Pension	21	2	Petition	209	Military Pensions.						
Wood, William W.	To be allowed the pay, &c., as assistant surgeon, U. S. navy.	22	1	Petition	259	Naval Affairs.						
Wood, William, heirs of.	For the issue of certificates of Virginia land warrants.	25	2	Petition	178	Priv. Land Claims.	557	Favorable	546	Referred to Committee Whole House.		
Wood, William, heirs of.	For the issue of certificates of Virginia land warrants.	26	1	Petition	178	Priv. Land Claims.				Discharged; laid on table.		
Wood, ———	(See Smith & Wood)	26	1		182							
Wood, William, *et al.*	Indemnity for loss sustained in Mexican war.	31	1	Petition	324	Claims.						
Wood, and others	(See McKnight, Brent & Wood.)	30	1		236							
Woodall, Abraham	Permission to enter land in lieu of section entered by mistake.	23	2	Petition	392	Public Lands.						
Woodall, Abraham	Permission to enter land in lieu of section entered by mistake.	24	1	Petition	114	Public Lands.	190	Favorable	196	Passed.		
Woodall, Abraham	Permission to enter land in lieu of section entered by mistake.	24	2	Petition	47	Public Lands	13	Favorable	770	Referred to Committee Whole House.		
Woodall, Abraham	Permission to enter land in lieu of section entered by mistake.	25	2	Petition	87	Public Lands	93	Favorable	115	Passed	Passed	App'd June 28, 1838
Woodberry, Jacob T.	(See John Pickett and others.)	29	1		331							

List of private claims presented to the House of Representatives of the United States from the 1st to the 31st Congress, inclusive—Continued.

Names of claimants.	Nature or object of the claim.	Congress.	Session.	How brought before the House of Reps.	Page of journal.	To what committee of the House referred.	No. or date of the report.	Nature of the report.	No. of the bill.	How disposed of by the House of Reps.	How disposed of by the Senate.	Date of the act of Congress, and remarks.
Woodbridge, Dudley	Confirmation of title to land	3	2	Petition	291	Select	Feb. 17, 1795	Adverse		Laid on table.		
Woodbridge, James A	Confirmation of title to land	27	2	Petition	681	Priv. Land Claims.						
Woodbridge, James A	Confirmation of title to land	27	3	Petition	45	Priv. Land Claims.						
Woodbridge, John E	Compensation for services as paymaster, Ohio militia.	24	1	Petition	534	Claims	592	Adverse		Laid on table.		
Woodbridge, William	Compensation for extra services as secretary of Michigan Territory.	21	1	Petition	379	Judiciary	April 12, 1830	Adverse		Laid on table.		
Woodbridge, William	Compensation for extra services as secretary of Michigan Territory.	22	1	Petition	676	Indian Affairs.						
Woodbridge & Snow	Indemnity for French spoliations prior to 1800.	26	1	Memorial	182	Foreign Affairs	343	Favorable; bill	319	Referred to Committee Whole House.		
Woodbridge, Wm., agent.	(See Michael Rivard.)	20	1		28							
Woodbridge, William, assignee.	(See James May.)	20	1		28							
Woodbridge, William, and H. Chapman.	Compensation for adjusting claim to lots in Detroit.	22	1	Petition	514	Public Lands.						
Woodbridge, William, and H. Chapman.	Compensation for adjusting claim to lots in Detroit.	22	2	Petition	42	Judiciary				Discharged; laid on table.		
Woodbridge, William, and H. Chapman.	Compensation for adjusting claim to lots in Detroit.	23	1	Senate bill	845	Judiciary	Jan. 27, 1834	Adverse	S. 124	Laid on table.		
Woodbridge, William, and H. Chapman.	Compensation for adjusting claim to lots in Detroit.	23	2	Petition	59	Territories.						
Woodbridge, William, and H. Chapman.	Compensation for adjusting claim to lots in Detroit.	30	1	Senate bill	913	Judiciary	June 17, 1848	With't amend.	S. 146	Referred to Committee Whole House.		
Woodbridge, William, and H. Chapman.	Compensation for adjusting claim to lots in Detroit.	30	2	Senate bill	161	Whole House			146			
Woodbridge, William, and H. Chapman.	Compensation for adjusting claim to lots in Detroit.	31	1	Petition	216	Judiciary	176	Favorable	189	Referred to Committee Whole House.		
Woodbridge, William, and H. Chapman.	Compensation for adjusting claim to lots in Detroit.	31	2	House bill	103	Whole House	Jan. 3, 1851	Favorable	189	Passed.		
Woodbrige, William	Confirmation of title to land	20	1	Resolution	28	Public Lands	42	Favorable	34	Passed	Passed	App'd April 22, 1828
Woodburn, Dorrance B	Remission of duties on distillery	14	1	Petition	512	Ways and Means				Discharged; laid on table.		
Woodburn, Dorrance B	Remission of duties on distillery	14	2	Petition	81	Ways and Means				Discharged; laid on table.		
Woodburn, Moses	Pension	21	1	Petition	128	Military Pensions				Discharged; laid on table.		
Woodbury, H., attorney of	Indemnity for French spoliations prior to 1800.	31	1	Petition	407	Commerce	355	Favorable	318	Referred to Committee Whole House.		
Woodbury, James	Arrears of pension	25	2	Petition	1120	Naval Affairs.						
Woodbury, James, heir of.	Arrears of pension	28	1	Petition	912	Naval Affairs.						
Woodbury, jr., John	(See Theodore Stanwood.)	21	2		54							
Woodbury, Mary, a half-breed Indian.	For payment of money stipulated under treaty.	31	1	Petition	312	Indian Affairs.						
Woodbury, Mary, a half breed Indian.	For payment of money stipulated under treaty.	31	2	Petition	207	Indian Affairs	19	Favorable	451	Referred to Committee Whole House.		
Woodbury, Samuel, administrator of.	Indemnity for French spoliations prior to 1800.	29	2	Petition	87	Foreign Affairs.						
Woodbury, Will W	(See William Cutter, *et al*)	24	1		127							
Woodcock, Sam'l, (Conn.)	Bounty land for revolutionary services.	20	1	Petition	166	Priv. Land Claims.	Feb. 12, 1828	Adverse		Laid on table.		
Woodcock, Sam'l, (Conn.)	Bounty land for revolutionary services.	21	1	Petition	68	Military Pensions				Discharged; laid on table.		

List of private claims presented to the House of Representatives of the United States from the 1st to the 31st Congress, inclusive—Continued.

Names of claimants.	Nature or object of the claim.	Congress.	Session.	How brought before the House of Reps.	Page of journal.	To what committee of the House referred.	No. or date of the report.	Nature of the report.	No. of the bill.	How disposed of by the House of Reps.	How disposed of by the Senate.	Date of the act of Congress, and remarks.
Woodcock, Sam'l, (Conn.)	Bounty land for revolutionary services.	21	2	Petition	88	Military Pensions.						
Woodcock, Sam'l, (Conn.)	Bounty land for revolutionary services.	22	1	Petition	56	Priv. Land Claims.	Jan. 25, 1832	Adverse	......	Laid on table.		
Woodcock, William	Compensation for revolutionary services.	23	1	Petition	157	Rev. Claims.						
Wooden, John	Pension	22	1	Resolution	434	Rev. Claims.						
Wooden, John	Pension	23	1	Resolution	202	Rev. Claims.						
Woodfin, Hannah	(See Thomas R. Woodfin, widow of.)	23	1	....	140							
Woodfin, Thomas, R. widow of.	For fishing bounty	23	1	Petition	140	Commerce	Jan. 14, 1834	Favorable	193	Passed	Passed	App'd June 30, 1834
Woodfolk, Joseph	Payment for bill of exchange for provisions furnished United States army.	18	1	Petition	253	Claims	Mar. 5, 1824	Adverse	......	Laid on table.		
Woodford, Daniel	(See Daniel Woolfolk.)	28	1	....	84							
Woodford, Gen. William, heir of.	Grant of land for revolutionary services.	23	2	Petition	47	Rev. Claims	Dec. 15, 1831	Adverse	......	Laid on table.		
Woodford, Gen William, heir of.	For offset of Continental money against indebtedness.	24	2	Petition	39	Rev. Claims.						
Woodland, Charles	Reward for gallantry	14	1	Petition	249	Naval Affairs	April 11, 1816	Favorable	......	Passed	Passed	App'd Feb. 8, 1817
Woodland, Richard	Indemnity for vessel burnt by Barney's flotilla.	17	1	Petition	73	Claims	Jan. 18, 1822	Adverse	......	Laid on table.		
Woodliff, Elizabeth, representatives of.	(See Francis Eppes.)	26	1	....	164							
Woodliff, Martha	(See Francis Eppes.)	25	2	....	49							
Woodman, Benjamin	To be released from judgment at suit of United States.	19	1	Petition	310	Judiciary	....	....	......	Discharged	....	Leave to withdraw.
Woodman, Benjamin	Pension	21	2	Petition	158	Military Pensions.						
Woodman, Benjamin	Pension	22	1	Petition	46	Invalid Pensions	Jan. 11, 1832	Adverse	......	Laid on table.		
Woodman, Benjamin	Pension	23	1	Petition	44	Invalid Pensions.						
Woodman, Caleb M.	For restoration of land sold for direct tax.	15	1	Petition	132	Ways and Means	....	....	......	Discharged; laid on table.		
Woodman, Jeremiah	Restoration of pension	22	2	Petition	93	Invalid Pensions	....	....	......	Discharged; laid on table.		
Woodman, John	Compensation as assistant commissary, revolutionary war.	2	1	Petition	520	....	....	....	......	Referred to Secretary War.		
Woodman, Joshua	Pension	16	1	Petition	225	Pens. & Rev. Cl'ms.	....	....	......	Discharged; laid on table.		
Woodman, Samuel	Pension	15	2	Petition	65	Rev. Pensions	Dec. 11, 1808	Adverse	......	Laid on table.		
Woodman, Joseph	Increase of pension	10	2	House bill	499	Whole House	Feb. 20, 1809	Favorable	158	Passed	Passed	App'd March 3, 1809
Woodrow, Simeon	Pension	21	1	Petition	291	Military Pensions	April 6, 1830	Adverse	......	Laid on table.		
Woodrow, Simeon	Pension	21	2	Petition	103	Military Pensions.						
Woodrow, Simeon	Pension	22	1	Petition	35	Rev. Pensions	Dec. 22, 1831	Adverse	......	Laid on table.		
Woodruff, Archibald	Indemnity for vessel and cargo destroyed by French in 1813.	24	1	Petition	202	Foreign Affairs	....	....	......	Discharged; laid on table.		
Woodruff, Clark	Patent for cert in lands, &c.	27	2	Senate bill	409	Public Lands	Mar. 2, 1842	With amend.	110	Passed	Concurred in.	App'd May 10, 1842
Woodruff, Clark	For act explanatory of act of 10th May, 1842.	27	2	Senate bill	1169	Whole House	July 27, 1842	With't amend.	277	Passed	Passed	App'd Aug. 4, 1842
Woodruff, Clark, assignee of.	Indemnity for losses by reason of refusal of proper officer to issue patent for land.	27	2	Petition	622	Priv. Land Claims.	....	....	......	....	....	Leave to withdraw.

List of private claims presented to the House of Representatives of the United States from the 1st *to the* 31st *Congress, inclusive*—**Continued.**

Names of claimants.	Nature or object of the claim.	Congress.	Session.	How brought before the House of Reps.	Page of journal.	To what committee of the House referred.	No. or date of the report.	Nature of the report.	No. of the bill.	How disposed of by the House of Reps.	How disposed of by the Senate.	Date of the act of Congress, and remarks.
Woodruff, Clark, assignee of.	Indemnity for losses by reason of refusal of proper officer to issue patent for land.	27	3	Petition	45	Priv. Land Claims.						
Woodruff, Elias, *et al*	(See Allen Smith)	24	1		91							
Woodruff, Elisha	Pension	31	1	Petition	1073	Invalid Pensions.						
Woodruff, Gedor	Pension	21	1	Petition	143	Military Pensions				Discharged; laid on table.		
Woodruff, Gedor	Restoration of pension	22	1	Petition	35	Rev. Pensions	412	Favorable	512	Referred to Committee Whole House.		
Woodruff, John	Compensation for revolutionary services.	22	1	Petition	44	Rev. Claims.						
Woodruff, Joseph	Indemnity for Indian depredations.	25	3	Petition	121	Claims	162	Adverse		Laid on table.		
Woodruff, Major	Indemnity for Indian depredations.	29	1	Petition	75	Claims.						
Woodruff, William	Pension	2	2	Rep. of Secretary War.	649	Whole House.						
Woodruff, William	Pension	3	1	Rep. of Secretary War.	131	Select	May 26, 1794	Favorable	J. R. 12	Passed	Passed	App'd June 9, 1794
Woodruff, William	Pension	11	3	House bill	604	Claims	Mar. 1, 1811	Favorable	218	Passed	Passed	App'd March 3, 1810
Woodruff, William R.	Permission to correct error in land entry.	24	1	Petition	708	Public Lands.						
Woodruff, Wyatt	(See William H. Bedford, agent).	28	1		262							
Woodrum, Samuel	Compensation for services, &c., rendered during war of 1812.	20	2	Petition	327	Naval Affairs				Discharged; laid on table.		
Woodrup & Sims	Indemnity for French spoliations prior to 1800.	26	1	Memorial	182	Foreign Affairs	343	Favorable; bill	319	Referred to Committee Whole House.		
Woodside, James D.	(See John Woodside, administrator of.)	22	2		29							
Woodside, John, administrator of.	Commutation pay	22	2	Petition	29	Rev. Claims.						
Woodside, John, administrator of.	Commutation pay	23	1	Petition	41	Rev. Claims.						
Woodside, John, administrator of.	Commutation pay	23	2	Petition	113	Rev. Claims.						
Woodside, John, administrator of.	Commutation pay	24	1	Petition	664	Rev. Claims	857	Adverse		Laid on table.		
Woodside, John, administrator of.	Commutation pay	24	2	Petition	92	Rev. Claims.						
Woodsides, John, senr	For extra compensation for services in Treasury Department, Philadelphia.	3	1	Petition	88	Select	47	Adverse		Laid on table.		
Woodsides, John, jr	For extra compensation for services in Treasury Department, Philadelphia.	3	1	Petition	88	Select	47	Adverse		Laid on table.		
Woodsides, John	(See James L. Cathcart)	12	1		361							
Woodside, William	Pension	21	1	Resolution	255	Military Pensions				Discharged; laid on table.		
Woodside, William	Pension	21	2	Resolution	49	Military Pensions.						
Woodson, Sam'l H., (Ky.)	(See Joseph Crockett, surety of).	18	2		223							
Woodson, Tarleton, executor of.	Compensation for revolutionary services.	1	3	Petition	380					Referred to Secretary War.		
Woodson, Tarleton, executor of.	Compensation for revolutionary services.	18	1	Petition	215	Pens. & Rev. Cl'ms.	April 29, 1824	Adverse		Laid on table.		

List of private claims presented to the House of Representatives of the United States from the 1st to the 31st Congress, inclusive—**Continued.**

Names of claimants.	Nature or object of the claim.	Congress.	Session.	How brought before the House of Reps.	Page of journal.	To what committee of the House referred.	No. or date of the report.	Nature of the report.	No. of the bill.	How disposed of by the House of Reps.	How disposed of by the Senate.	Date of the act of Congress, and remarks.
Woodson, Tarleton, executor of.	Compensation for revolutionary services.	23	1	Petition	439	Rev. Claims.						
Woodson, Tarleton, executor of.	Compensation for revolutionary services.	23	2	Petition	289	Rev. Claims.						
Woodson, Tarleton, executor of.	Compensation for revolutionary services.	24	1	Petition	104	Rev. Claims	546	Favorable	536	Referred to Committee Whole House.		
Woodson, Tarleton, executor of.	Compensation for revolutionary services.	25	2	Petition	40	Rev. Claims	136	Favorable	154	Passed.		
Woodson, Tarleton, executor of.	Compensation for revolutionary services.	25	3	Petition	85	Rev. Claims	22	Favorable	920	Passed	Passed	App'd March 3, 1839
Woodson, Tarleton, executor of.	Commutation pay	10	1	Petition	104	Whole House.						
Woodson, Tarleton, executor of.	Commutation pay	10	2	Petition	495	Claims.						
Woodson, Tarleton, executor of.	Commutation pay	13	2	Petition	242	Pens. & Rev. Cl'ms.	92	Adverse	......	Laid on table.		
Woodson, Tarleton, executor of.	Commutation pay	16	2	Resolution	173	....	....	....	......	....	....	Leave to withdraw
Woodson, Tarleton, executor of.	Commutation pay	25	2	Petition	177	Rev. Claims	562	Favorable	551	Passed.		
Woodson, Tarleton, executor of.	Commutation pay	25	3	Petition	85	Rev. Claims	21 & 22	Favorable	919, 920	Passed.		
Woodson, Tarleton, executor of.	Commutation pay	26	1	Petition	166	Rev. Claims.						
Woodson, Tarleton, executor of.	Commutation pay	26	2	Petition	106	Rev. Claims	173	Adverse	......	Laid on table.		
Woodson, Tarleton, executor of.	Commutation pay	27	2	Petition	96	Rev. Claims	546	Adverse	......	Laid on table.		
Woodson, Tarleton, executor of.	Commutation pay	27	3	Petition	44	Rev. Claims	256	Adverse	......	Laid on table.		
Woodson, Tarleton, executor of.	Commutation pay	28	1	Petition	190	Rev. Claims.						
Woodson, Tarleton, executor of.	Commutation pay	28	2	Petition	73	Rev. Claims.						
Woodson, Tarleton, executor of.	Commutation pay	29	1	Petition	68	Rev. Claims	316	Favorable	253	Referred to Committee Whole House.		
Woodson, Tarleton, executor of.	Commutation pay	29	2	House bill	382	Whole House	Feb. 19, 1847	Favorable	253	Laid on table.		
Woodson, Tarleton, executor of.	Commutation pay	30	1	Petition	69	Rev. Claims.						
Woodward, Daniel	Pension	24	2	Petition	207	Rev. Pensions	....	....	......	Discharged; laid on table.		
Woodward, Elizabeth	(See Seth Woodward, widow of).	27	2	....	533							
Woodward, Henry	Release from payment of surety bond.	11	2	Petition	169	Com. and Manuf.						
Woodward, Josiah	Relief on account of seizure of ship and sale of cargo.	31	2	Petition	88	Claims.						
Woodward, John	Payment of £34 14 0, with interest, for revolutionary services.	24	1	Resolution	540	Rev. Claims	519	Adverse	......	Laid on table.		
Woodward, John	For payment of note executed by H. Huntingdon, for revolutionary services.	26	1	Pension	939	Claims.						

List of private claims presented to the House of Representatives of the United States from the 1st to the 31st Congress, inclusive—Continued.

Names of claimants.	Nature or object of the claim.	Congress.	Session.	How brought before the House of Reps.	Page of journal.	To what committee of the House referred.	No. or date of the report.	Nature of the report.	No. of the bill.	How disposed of by the House of Reps.	How disposed of by the Senate.	Date of the act of Congress, and remarks.
Woodward, John	For payment of note executed by H. Huntingdon, for revolutionary services.	27	2	Petition	55	Rev. Claims	355	Adverse	......	Laid on table.		
Woodward, John	Reward for gallantry	13	3	House bill	685	Whole House	Jan. 13, 1815	Favorable	259	Passed.		
Woodward, John	Reward for gallantry	14	1	House bill	249	Whole House	April 11, 1816	Favorable	......	Passed	Passed	App'd April 29, 1816
Woodward, John, widow of.	Pension	27	2	Petition	59	Rev. Pensions	103	Favorable	149	Passed	Indef. postp'd.	
Woodward, Jonas	(See Lieut. Timothy Morseman)	27	2	....	69							
Woodward, Joshua	Pension	31	1	Petition	647	Rev. Claims	309	Adverse	......	Laid on table.		
Woodward, Nimrod	Indemnity for damages sustained by use of farm by United States troops.	15	1	Petition	38	Claims	....	....	......	Discharged; referred to Secretary War.		
Woodward, Pompey	Pension	22	1	Petition	631	Invalid Pensions	....	....	......	Discharged; laid on table.		
Woodward, Samuel	(See Daniel Spring)	23	1	....	186							
Woodward, Sarah	(See John Woodward, widow of)	27	2	....	59							
Woodward, Sarah	Extension of pension	26	2	Petition	51	Rev. Pensions	Feb. 12, 1840	Favorable	652	Referred to Committee Whole House.		
Woodward, Seth, widow of.	Continuation of pension	27	2	Petition	611	Rev. Pensions	784	Adverse	......	Laid on table.		
Woodward, William, *et al.*	To refund certain money deposited in Patent Office.	24	1	Petition	92	Claims	62	Favorable	75	Passed	Passed	App'd June 14, 1836
Woodward, William	Compensation for mail service	30	1	Petition	819	Claims	755	Adverse	......	Laid on table.		
Woodworth, Azel	Pension	3	1	Rep. of Secretary War.	131	Select	May 26, 1794	Favorable	J. R. 12	Passed	Passed	App'd June 9, 1794
Woodworth, Azel	Pension	4	1	Rep. of Secretary War.	445	Claims	Feb. 15, 1796	Favorable	159	Passed	Passed	App'd April 20, 1796
Woodworth, Azel	Increase of pension	12	1	House bill	361	Whole House	June 15, 1812	Favorable	138	Passed	Passed	App'd July 5, 1812
Woodworth, Artema	Confirmation of title to land	24	1	Petition	853	Priv. Land Claims.						
Woodworth, Benjamin	(See George Daffin, assignee of)	18	1	....	432							
Woodworth, Benjamin	(See Thomas M. Peck, assignee of)	19	1	....	407							
Woodworth, Benjamin	(See Joseph Pickell, assignee of)	19	1	....	407							
Woodworth, Jonathan	Compensation for revolutionary services.	13	2	Petition	172	Pensions	....	....	......	Discharged	....	Leave to withdraw.
Woodworth, Jonathan, heirs of.	Compensation for revolutionary services.	15	2	Petition	266	Rev. Pensions	....	....	......	Discharged; laid on table.		
Woodworth, Jonathan, heirs of.	Compensation for revolutionary services.	16	1	Petition	445	Rev. Pensions	April 22, 1820	Adverse	......	Laid on table.		
Woodworth, Josiah	Pension	22	1	Resolution	176	Rev. Pensions.						
Woodworth, Nathaniel	For grant of land	15	1	Petition	44	Public Lands	Dec. 29, 1817	Adverse	......	Laid on table.		
Woodworth, Robert P	For patent for certain land	24	2	Petition	268	Public Lands.						
Woodworth, Robert	For difference of pay between assistant and past assistant surgeon	27	2	Petition	343, 869	Claims	768	Adverse	......	Laid on table.		
Woodworth, Rosswell	Pension	9	1	Petition	306	Claims.						
Woodworth, Rosswell	Increase of pension	10	1	House bill	232	Whole House	April 19, 1808	Favorable	78	Passed	Passed	App'd April 25, 1808
Woodworth, Roswell, (New York.)	Pension	16	1	Petition	325	Pens. & Rev. Cl'ms.	....	....	......	Discharged; laid on table.		
Woodworth, Roswell, (New York.)	Pension	17	1	Petition	305	Pens. & Rev. Cl'ms.	57	Adverse	......	Laid on table.		
Woodworth, Roswell, (New York.)	Pension	18	1	Petition	330	Pens. & Rev. Cl'ms.	April 22, 1824	Adverse	......	Laid on table.		
Woodworth, Roswell, (New York.)	Pension	18	2	Petition	159	Pens. & Rev. Cl'ms.	....	....	......	Discharged; laid on table.		

List of private claims presented to the House of Representatives of the United States from the 1st to the 31st Congress, inclusive—Continued.

Names of claimants.	Nature or object of the claim.	Congress.	Session.	How brought before the House of Reps.	Page of journal.	To what committee of the House referred.	No. or date of the report.	Nature of the report.	No. of the bill.	How disposed of by the House of Reps.	How disposed of by the Senate.	Date of the act of Congress, and remarks.
Woodworth, Roswell, (New York.)	Pension	21	2	Petition	336	Military Pensions.						
Woodworth, Roswell, (New York.)	Pension	23	1	Petition	655	Invalid Pensions.						
Woodworth, Roswell, (New York.)	Pension	28	2	Petition	60	Rev. Pensions				Discharged; laid on table.		
Woodworth, William, administrators of.	Extension of patent	31	1	Petition	338	Patents	150	Favorable	168	Referred to Committee Whole House.		
Woodworth, Zeba	Pension	11	2	House bill	283	Whole House	Mar. 24, 1810	Favorable	107	Passed	Passed	App'd April 27, 1810
Woody, James	Bounty land	15	2	Petition	40	Military Affairs				Discharged; laid on table.		
Wool, Capt. Isaiah, or Josiah, heirs of.	Bounty land and other compensation for revolutionary services.	24	1	Petition	752	Rev. Claims.						
Wool, Capt. Isaiah, or Josiah, heirs of.	Bounty land and other compensation for revolutionary services.	24	2	Petition	158	Rev. Claims	Feb. 2, 1837	Adverse		Laid on table.		
Wool, Capt. Isaiah, or Josiah, heirs of.	Bounty land and other compensation for revolutionary services.	25	2	Petition	658	Rev. Claims	974	Adverse		Laid on table.		
Wool, Capt. Isaiah, or Josiah, heirs of.	Bounty land and other compensation for revolutionary services.	26	1	Petition	282	Rev. Claims.						
Wool, Capt. Isaiah, or Josiah, heirs of.	Bounty land and other compensation for revolutionary services.	26	2	Petition	214	Rev. Claims.						
Wool, Capt. Isaiah, or Josiah, heirs of.	Bounty land and other compensation for revolutionary services.	27	2	Petition	826	Rev. Claims	861	Adverse		Laid on table.		
Wool, Gen. John E	Allowance for back rations	24	1	Petition	96	Military Affairs	132	Favorable	143	Referred to Committee Whole House.		
Wool, Gen. John E	Allowance for back rations	24	2	House bill	198	Whole House.			143			
Wool, Gen. John E	Allowance for back rations	25	2	Petition	41	Military Affairs	378	Favorable	402	Referred to Committee Whole House.		
Wool, Gen. John E	Allowance for back rations	25	3	House bill	378	Whole House	Jan. 25, 1839	Favorable	402	Laid on table.		
Wool, Gen. John E	Allowance for back rations	26	1	Petition	182	Military Affairs	April 4, 1840	Favorable	312	Referred to Committee Whole House.		
Wool, John S	To legalize certain purchases made under Cherokee treaty.	24	2	House bill	197	Indian Affairs	Jan. 13, 1837	Favorable	840	Passed	Passed	App'd Feb. 9, 1837
Woolen, Thomas	Reward for gallantry	14	1	Petition	249	Naval Affairs	April 11, 1816	Favorable		Passed	Passed	App'd Feb. 8, 1817
Woolley, Col. A. R	Equitable settlement of accounts	23	1	Senate bill	654	Military Affairs	May 29, 1834	With amend.	172	Passed	Concurred in	App'd June 30, 1834
Wooley, Jonathan	Increase of pension	12	1	House bill	361	Whole House	June 15, 1812	Favorable	138	Passed	Passed	App'd July 5, 1812
Woolery, Jacob	Permission to change entry of land	16	2	Petition	141	Public Lands	Jan. 18, 1821	Adverse		Laid on table.		
Woolfolk, Austin	(See Austin Wolfolk)	28	1		76							
Woolford, Daniel	Pension	28	1	Petition	84	Invalid Pensions	234	Adverse		Laid on table.		
Woolsey, Ellen	(See Lieut. Wm. G. Woolsey)	29	1		152							
Woolsey, Daniel	Pension	25	2	Petition	587	Rev. Pensions				Discharged; laid on table.		
Woolsey, Daniel	Pension	26	1	Petition	175	Rev. Pensions				Discharged; laid on table.		
Woolsey, ——	(See Coit, Woolsey, & Howland.)	26	1		182							
Woolsey, G. M	Indemnity for French spoliations prior to 1800.	26	1	Memorial	182	Foreign Affairs	343	Favorable; bill	319	Referred to Committee Whole House.		
Woolsey, George	Permission to change entry of land	24	2	Petition	599	Public Lands	Mar. 30, 1836	Favorable	526	Passed	Passed	App'd July 2, 1836
Woolsey, Henry L	Compensation for services rendered at light house.	27	2	Communication	374	Commerce				Discharged		Leave to withdraw.
Woolsey, Melancthon L	Indemnity for property destroyed by United States troops, war of 1812.	15	2	Petition	40	Military Affairs	Jan. 7, 1819	Adverse		Discharged; laid on table.		

List of private claims presented to the House of Representatives of the United States from the 1st to the 31st Congress, inclusive—Continued.

ames of claimants.	Nature or object of the claim.	Congress.	Session.	How brought before the House of Reps.	Page of journal.	To what committee of the House referred.	No. or date of the report.	Nature of the report.	No. of the bill.	How disposed of by the House of Reps.	How disposed of by the Senate.	Date of the act of Congress, and remarks.
Woolsey, Melancthon T..	Permission to transfer pay, &c., as captain to settle debt due Bank of Utica, New York.	22	1	Petition	220	Naval Affairs.						
Woolsey, Melanchton T..	Permission to transfer pay, &c., as captain to settle debt due Bank of Utica, New York.	22	2	Petition	96	Judiciary.........	....	....	......	....	....	See Senate bill 137.
Woolsey, Melanchton T..	For further settlement of accounts.	24	1	Senate bill	804	Whole House.....	Jan. 27, 1836	With't amend.	137	Passed	....	App'd May 14, 1836
Woolsey, Melanchton T..	To be exhonerated from certain claims held by United States.	24	1	Petition	99	Naval Affairs.....	217	Favorable	224	Referred to Committee Whole House.		
Woolsey, Melanchton T..	To be exhonerated from eertain claims held by United States.	24	1	House bill	1060	Claims..........	791	Favorable	713	Referred to Committee Whole House.		
Woolsey, Melanchton T..	To be exhonerated from certain clams held by United States.	25	2	House bill	37	Claims	57	Favorable....	69	Passed	Passed	App'd April 20, 1838
Woolsey, Lieut. William G., widow of.	Continuation of pension	29	1	Petition	152	Naval Affairs.	147	Favorable....	151	Referred to Committee Whole House.		
Woolsey, Lieut. William G., widow of.	Continuation of pension	29	2	Petition	169	Naval Affairs.						
Woolstrandorf, John.....	(See Stephen Decatur, heirs of.)..	23	1	....	36							
Woolsey, Peter, representatives of.	For bounty land, arrears of pay and pension.	18	1	Senate bill	307	Military Affairs....	May 17, 1824	With amend..	50	Laid on table.		
Woolsey, Peter, representatives of.	For bounty land, arrears of pay and pension.	19	1	Senate bill	466	Priv. Land Claims.	April 29, 1826	With't amend.	69	Passed	....	App'd May 20, 1826
Wooster, Charles W.....	(See Jasper Ward, *et al.*).......	24	1	....	295							
Wooster, General David, widow of.	Interest on pension granted......	1	2	Petition	182	....	....	....	......	Referred to Secretary of Treasury.		
Wooster, General David, widow of.	Interest on pension granted......	2	1	Rep. of Secretary Treasury.	580	....	....	....	......	Laid on table.		
Wooster, General David, widow of.	For half pay..................	6	1	Petition	629	Claims	April 28, 1800	....	......	Discharged.		
Wooster, General David, widow of.	For half-pay..................	25	2	Petition	576	Rev. Claims......	....	....	......	Discharged; laid on table.		
Wooster, Mary	(See General David Wooster, widow of.)	1	2	Petition	182							
Wooster, Capt. Thomas..	Commutation pay	25	2	Petition	576	Rev. Claims......	....	....	......	Discharged; laid on table.		
Wooten, John..........	Pension	4	2	Petition	666	Claims	Feb. 5, 1797	....	......	....	....	Referred to 5th section of act Mar. 23, 1792
Wooten, Lemuel........	Payment for wagon and team lost in military service of the United States.	16	1	Petition	285	Claims	April 3, 1820	Adverse	......	Laid on table	....	Leave to withdraw
Wooten, Lemuel........	Payment for wagon and team lost in military service of the United States.	17	1	Petition	100	Claims	....	Adverse	......	Laid on table.		
Wooten, Lemuel........	Payment for wagon and team lost in military service of the United States.	18	1	Petition	214	Claims	Mar. 27, 1822	Adverse	......	Laid on table.		
Wooten, Lemuel........	Payment for wagon and team lost in military service of the United States.	18	2	Report	120	Claims	31	Favorable....	284	Passed	Passed	App'd March 3, 1825
Wooten, William	Compensation for wagon and team lost, and for slave killed in Creek war.	24	2	Petition	103	Claims.						

List of private claims presented to the House of Representatives of the United States from the 1st to the 31st Congress, inclusive—Continued.

Names of claimants.	Nature or object of the claim.	Congress.	Session.	How brought before the House of Reps.	Page of journal.	To what committee of the House referred.	No. or date of the report.	Nature of the report.	No. of the bill.	How disposed of by the House of Reps.	How disposed of by the Senate.	Date of the act of Congress, and remarks.
Wooten, William	Compensation for wagon and team lost, and for slave killed in Creek war.	25	2	Petition	255	Claims	Feb. 2, 1838	Adverse	......	Laid on table.		
Wooten, William	Compensation for wagon and team lost, and for slave killed in Creek war.	26	1	Petition	338	Claims.						
Wordehoo, Antoine	Grant of patent for tract of land	29	1	Petition	578	Public Lands.						
Worden, John L.	Compensation for services in higher grade in United States navy.	29	1	Petition	201	Naval Affairs	475	Favorable	330	Referred to Committee Whole House.		
Worden, Joseph, (N. Y.)	Pension	22	1	Petition	509	Rev. Pensions	....	....	......	Discharged; laid on table.		
Worden, William	Arrears of pension	25	2	Petition	267	Invalid Pensions.						
Wordsworth, Capt. Ichabod, heirs of.	Pension	25	2	Petition	116	Rev. Pensions	580	Adverse	......	Laid on table.		
Worfington, Richard	For grant of land for services in exploring expedition.	9	1	President's mess.	284	....	....	....	......	Laid on table.		
Worfington, Richard	For grant of land for services in exploring expedition.	9	2	President's mess.	470	Select	Jan. 23, 1807	Favor'ble; general bill.	183	Passed	Passed	App'd March 3, 1807
Work, John	Compensation for provisions furnished militia in United States service.	15	1	Petition	130	Military Affairs	Jan. 26, 1818	Favorable	56	Passed	Passed	App'd April 20 1818
Work, John	For three months' extra pay as assistant surveyor.	31	1	Petition	501	Military Affairs.						
Work, William	Compensation for services in commissary department.	19	1	Resolution	275	Military Pensions	164	Adverse	......	Laid on table.		
Workman, John L	Pension	23	1	House bill	86	Whole House	Jan. 3, 1834	Favorable	42	Passed	Passed	App'd June 30, 1834
Worle, John	Arrears of pension	30	2	Petition	224	Invalid Pensions	....	....	......	Discharged; laid on table.		
Worley, Caleb	Pension	3	1	Petition	61	....	April 22, 1794	....	......	Laid on table.		
Worley, Caleb	Pension	3	2	Resolution	250	Claims	Feb. 25, 1795	Adverse	......	Laid on table.		
Worley, Caleb	Pension	4	1	Resolution	373	Claims.						
Worley, Caleb	Pension	4	2	Resolution	614	Claims	Jan. 17, 1797	Adverse	......	....	....	Leave to withdraw.
Worley, George	Payment for Yazoo lands	22	1	Petition	417	Public Lands	March 6, 1832	Adverse	......	Laid on table.		
Worley, James	(See Barnet Eichelberger)	3	1	....	107							
Wormley, Hugh W	Arrears and increase of pension	26	2	Petition	54	Invalid Pensions	152	Favorable	663	Referred to Committee Whole House.		
Wormley, Hugh W	Arrears and increase of pension	27	2	Petition	68	Invalid Pensions	145	Favorable	192	Passed	Indef. postp'd.	
Wormley, Hugh W	Arrears and increase of pension	27	3	Petition	107	Invalid Pensions	72	Adverse	......	Laid on table.		
Wormley, Hugh W	Arrears and increase of pension	28	1	Petition	107	Invalid Pensions	53	Adverse	67	Passed.		
Wormley, Hugh W	Arrears and increase of pension	31	1	Petition	375	Invalid Pensions	478	Adverse	375	Referred to Committee Whole House.		
Wormstead, Joseph W	Fishing bounty	23	1	Petition	140	Commerce	Jan. 10, 1834	Favorable	180	Passed.		
Wormstead, Joseph W	Fishing bounty	23	2	Petition	56	Commerce.						
Wormstead, Joseph W	Fishing bounty	24	1	Petition	5[illegible]	Commerce	47	Favorable	59	Passed	Passed	App'd May 14, 1836
Worrell, Dr. Edward	Compensation as assistant surgeon	26	1	Petition	331	Military Affairs.						
Worrell, Gen. Isaac, former widow of.	Commission on money disbursed in war of 1812.	21	1	Petition	34	Claims	Dec. 30, 1829	Adverse	......	Laid on table.		
Worrell, Gen. Isaac, former widow of.	Commission on money disbursed in war of 1812.	23	2	Petition	37	Claims.						
Worrell, Gen. Isaac, former widow of.	Commission on money disbursed in war of 1812.	24	1	Petition	207	Claims	Jan. 26, 1836	Adverse	......	Laid on table.		

List of private claims presented to the House of Representatives of the United States from the 1st to the 31st Congress, inclusive—Continued.

Names of claimants.	Nature or object of the claim.	Congress.	Session.	How brought before the House of Reps.	Page of journal.	To what committee of the House referred.	No. or date of the report.	Nature of the report.	No. of the bill.	How disposed of by the House of Reps.	How disposed of by the Senate.	Date of the act of Congress, and remarks.
Worrell, Gen. Isaac, former widow of.	Commission on money disbursed in war of 1812.	25	2	Petition	275	Claims	May 15, 1838	Adverse		Laid on table.		
Worrell, Gen. Isaac, former widow and heirs of.	Pension	25	2	Petition	115	Rev. Pensions				Discharged; laid on table.		
Worrell, Jonathan	Pension	18	1	Petition	75	Rev. Pensions	Jan. 9, 1824	Adverse		Laid on table.		
Worrell, Jonathan	Pension	19	1	Petition	129	Military Pensions	164	Adverse		Laid on table.		
Worrell, Robert	Pension	14	2	Resolution	209	Pens. & Rev. Cl'ms.				Discharged; laid on table.		
Worrell, Stephen	Pension	23	2	Petition	328	Invalid Pensions.						
Worsham, Alexander	To be released from judgment and costs at suit against him for enlistment of a minor.	15	1	Petition	21	Claims	21	Adverse		Laid on table.		
Worsham, Alexander	To be released from judgment and costs at suit against him for enlistment of a minor.	16	1	Petition	42	Claims	20	Adverse		Laid on table.		
Worth, Lieut. Algeron, widow of.	Pension	28	1	Petition	718	Naval Affairs.						
Worth, Gorham A.	(See Samuel Edmonds)	24	2		400							
Worth, Gorham A.	(See Samuel Edmonds)	27	3									
Worth, Margaret L.	(See Gen. Wm. Worth)	31	1		706							
Worth, Margaret	(See Lieut. Algeron Worth)	28	1		718							
Worth, Susan	Pension	31	1	Petition	193	Invalid Pensions	10	Adverse		Laid on table.		
Worth, Wm. J.	(See J. Stafford, executors of)	23	1		192							
Worth, Gen. William, widow of.	Pension	31	1	Senate bill	706	Rev. Pensions	484	Adverse	128	Referred to Committee Whole House.		
Worth, Gen. William, widow of.	Pension	31	2	Senate bill	405	Rev. Pensions	Aug. 1, 1850	Favorable	128	Referred to Committee Whole House.		
Worthen, Judith	Arrears of pension	29	1	Petition	59	Rev. Pensions	356	Adverse		Laid on table.		
Worthen, Judith	Arrears of pension	31	1	Senate bill	1035	Rev. Claims	July 25, 1850	With't amend.	50	Referred to Committee Whole House.		
Worther, Robert	Pre-emption right to land	26	1	Petition	609	Priv. Land Claims.						
Worthington, Gad, collector of tax.	Credit for public moneys stolen	15	1	Petition	44	Ways and Means	Jan. 19, 1818	Favorable	45	Passed.		
Worthington, Gad, collector of tax.	Credit for public moneys stolen	15	2	Petition	26	Ways and Means	Nov. 27, 1818	Favorable	206	Referred to Committee Whole House.		
Worthington, Gad, collector of tax.	Credit for public moneys stolen	16	1	Petition	27	Ways and Means	Dec. 13, 1819	Favorable	2	Rejected.		
Worthington, Gad, collector of tax.	Credit for public moneys stolen	17	1	Petition	38	Ways and Means	Jan. 2, 1822	Favorable	17	Passed	Passed	App'd April 17, 1822
Worthington, Samuel	Permission to enter certain lands or to have money refunded.	28	1	Petition	257	Public Lands	68	Adverse		Laid on table.		
Worthington, Samuel	Permission to enter certain lands or to have money refunded.	29	1	Petition	494	Claims	779	Adverse		Laid on table.		
Worthington, Tho's, widow and executors of.	To be released as surety of Samuel Finley, receiver in land office.	20	1	Petition	484	Judiciary				Discharged; laid on table.		
Worthington, Eho's, widow and executors of.	To be released as surety of Samuel Finley, receiver in land office.	21	2	Petition	83	Judiciary	21	Favorable	536	Referred to Committee Whole House.		
Worthington, Tho's, widow and executors of.	To be released as surety of Samuel Finley, receiver in land office.	21	2	Senate bill	381	Whole House	Mar. 2, 1831	With amend.	115	Rejected.		
Worthington, Tho's, widow and executors of.	To be released as surety of Samuel Finley, receiver in land office.	22	1	Petition	144	Judiciary	181	With amend.	256	Referred to Committee Whole House.		
Worthington, Tho's, widow and executors of.	To be released as surety of Samuel Finley, receiver in land office.	22	2	House bill	92	Whole House	Dec. 28, 1832	With amend.	256	Referred to Committee Whole House.		

List of private claims presented to the House of Representatives of the United States from the 1st to the 31st Congress, inclusive—Continued.

Names of claimants.	Nature or object of the claim.	Congress.	Session.	How brought before the House of Reps.	Page of journal.	To what committee of the House referred.	No. or date of the report.	Nature of the report.	No. of the bill.	How disposed of by the House of Reps.	How disposed of by the Senate.	Date of the act of Congress, and remarks.
Worthington, William	Increase of pension	9	2	House bill	618	Whole House	Feb. 24, 1807	Favorable	216	Passed	Passed	App'd March 3, 1807
Wortliarn, James F	(See Wm. H. Bedford.)	28	1		262							
Wren, Solomon	For proportion of prize money for capture and destruction of Philadelphia frigate.	19	2	House bill	98	Naval Affairs	74	Favorable	70	Referred to Committee Whole House.		
Wren, Solomon	For proportion of prize money for capture and destruction of Philadelphia frigate.	20	1	Petition	278	Naval Affairs	201	Adverse		Laid on table.		
Wren, Solomon	For proportion of prize money for capture and destruction of Philadelphia frigate.	20	2	Petition	32	Naval Affairs	37	Adverse		Laid on table.		
Wren, Solomon	For proportion of prize money for capture and destruction of Philadelphia frigate.	21	1	House bill	137	Naval Affairs	Jan. 7, 1830	Favorable	82	Referred to Committee Whole House.		
Wren, Solomon	For proportion of prize money for capture and destruction of Philadelphia frigate.	22	1	Petition	29	Naval Affairs	Dec. 23, 1831	Favorable	98	Referred to Committee Whole House.		
Wren, Solomon	For proportion of prize money for capture and destruction of Philadelphia frigate.	23	1	House bill	101	Naval Affairs	45	Favorable	50	Referred to Committee Whole House.		
Wren, Woodson	Confirmation of title to land	17	1	Petition	361	Public Lands				Discharged; laid on table.		
Wren, Woodson	Confirmation of title to land	17	2	Petition	27	Priv. Land Claims.	51	Favorable	204	Passed	Passed	App'd March 3, 1823
Wren, Woodson	Confirmation of title to land	18	1	Resolution	128	Priv. Land Claims.						
Wren, Woodson	Confirmation of title to land	21	1	Senate bill	615	Priv. Land Claims.	May 11, 1830	With't amend.	117	Referred to Committee Whole House.		
Wren, Woodson	Confirmation of title to land	21	2	Senate bill	186	Priv. Land Claims.	Feb. 1, 1831	With't amend.	62	Passed	Passed	App'd March 3, 1831
Wren, Woodson	Permission to locate lands under act of 3d March, 1819.	22	1	Petition	65	Priv. Land Claims.				Discharged; laid on table.		
Wren, Woodson	Permission to locate lands under act of 3d March, 1819.	22	2	Petition	54	Public Lands				Discharged; laid on table.		
Wren, Woodson	Permission to locate lands under act of 3d March, 1819.	23	1	Petition	138	Priv. Land Claims.	273	Adverse		Discharged; laid on table.		
Wren, Woodson	Permission to locate lands under act of 3d March, 1819.	23	2	Petition	242	Priv. Land Claims.				Discharged; laid on table.		
Wren, Woodson	Confirmation of title to land	28	1	Petition	301	Priv. Land Claims.	207	Favorable	162	Passed	Passed	App'd June 15, 1844
Wright, Aaron M., sureties of.	Release from payment of judgment.	21	1	Petition	69	Judiciary.						
Wright, Abraham	Renewal of land warrant	25	2	Petition	59	Priv. Land Claims.				Discharged.		
Wright, Abraham	Renewal of land warrant	25	3	Petition	91	Priv. Land Claims.	Jan. 22, 1839	Favorable	J.R. 39	Passed	Passed	App'd March 2, 1839
Wright, Amos C	Compensation for services as assistant surgeon.	25	2	Petition	574	Claims	May 15, 1838	Indefinite		Referred to 3d Auditor.		
Wright, Andrew	Additional compensation for services rendered in Treasury Department.	4	1	Petition	486	Claims.						
Wright, Andrew	Additional compensation for services rendered in Treasury Department.	4	2	Petition	614	Claims.						
Wright, Andrew, widow of.	Pension	29	1	Petition	86	Rev. Pensions	826	Adverse		Laid on table.		
Wright, Andrew, widow of.	Pension	30	1	Petition	156	Rev. Pensions	303	Adverse		Laid on table.		
Wright, Ann O	(See Ann Byrd)	29	1		104							
Wright, Anthony, executor of.	Payment for wagon and team impressed into U. States service.	17	1	Petition	195	Pens. & Rev. Cl'ms.	Feb. 15, 1822	Adverse		Laid on table.		

List of private claims presented to the House of Representatives of the United States from the 1st to the 31st Congress, inclusive—Continued.

Names of claimants.	Nature or object of the claim.	Congress.	Session.	How brought before the House of Reps.	Page of journal.	To what committee of the House referred.	No. or date of the report.	Nature of the report.	No. of the bill.	How disposed of by the House of Reps.	How disposed of by the Senate.	Date of the act of Congress, and remarks.
Wright, Anthony W	Payment of lost loan office certificate.	26	1	Petition	753	Rev. Claims	330	Favorable	302	Referred to Committee Whole House.		
Wright, Benjamin	Compensation for loss sustained on Continental money.	25	2	Petition	1177	Rev. Claims				Discharged.		
Wright, Benjamin	Compensation for loss sustained on Continental money.	25	3	Petition	125	Rev. Claims.						
Wright, Benjamin	Compensation for loss sustained on Continental money.	26	1	Petition	167	Rev. Claims.						
Wright, Beriah	Pension	25	2	Resolution	108	Invalid Pensions				Discharged; laid on table.		
Wright, Beriah	Pension	26	2	Resolution	88	Invalid Pensions	76	Favorable	591	Referred to Committee Whole House.		
Wright, Beriah	Pension	27	2	Petition	459	Invalid Pensions	613	Adverse		Laid on table.		
Wright, Beriah	Pension	29	1	Petition	261	Invalid Pensions	508	Adverse		Laid on table.		
Wright, Beriah	Pension	30	1	Petition	339	Invalid Pensions	454	Favorable	384	Passed.		
Wright & Brothers	To refund excess of duties paid on umbrellas.	25	2	Petition	393	Commerce	697	Favorable	669	Referred to Committee Whole House.		
Wright, Christopher	(See James Rackliff, *et al.*)	20	1		162							
Wright, David	Compensation for services rendered as gunsmith, revolutionary war.	27	2	Petition	525	Rev. Claims	666	Adverse		Laid on table.		
Wright, Dorcas	(See Timothy Page)	25	2		347							
Wright, Edward S.	To be released from liability on a certain bond.	26	1	Petition	697	Judiciary.						
Wright, Elizabeth	(See Jonathan Wright, heirs of).	21	2		62							
Wright, Elizabeth	(See William Wright, widow of.)	30	1		332							
Wright, Ephraim	Pension	17	1	Petition	50	Rev. Pensions				Discharged.		
Wright, Francis	Remission of certain duties	4	1	Petition	381	Com. and Manuf.						
Wright, Francis, heirs of.	Renewal of land warrant	18	2	Petition	60	Public Lands	Feb. 24, 1835	Favorable	355	Passed	Passed	App'd March 3, 1825
Wright, George	Compensation for use of his invention for making percussion caps.	31	1	Petition	392	Military Affairs	197	Favorable	204	Referred to Committee Whole House.		
Wright, Henry	Compensation for property taken by United States officers.	16	1	Petition	474	Claims				Discharged; laid on table.		
Wright, Henry	(See William Bunce, administrator of.)	28	2		214							
Wright, Henry Allen	Indemnity for French spoliations prior to 1800.	31	1	Petition	486	Commerce	355	Favorable	318	Referred to Committee Whole House.		
Wright, Isra	Pension	28	1	Petition	211	Invalid Pensions	178	Adverse		Laid on table.		
Wright, Isaac, (Mass.)	Pension	19	1	Petition	250	Military Affairs	164	Adverse		Laid on table.		
Wright, Isaac H.	Permission to change land entry	28	2	Petition	258	Public Lands.						
Wright, Israel	Pension	24	1	Petition	433	Rev. Pensions				Discharged; laid on table.		
Wright, James	Pension	3	1	Petition	103					Referred to Secretary War.		
Wright, James, jr.	Pension	26	1	Petition	326	Invalid Pensions	474	Favorable	388	Referred to Committee Whole House.		
Wright, James, jr.	Pension	30	2	Petition	337	Invalid Pensions				Discharged; laid on table.		
Wright, James	Pension	31	1	Petition	276	Invalid Pensions.						
Wright, Maj. James, heirs of.	Commutation pay	29	1	Petition	638	Rev. Claims.						
Wright, Jeremiah	Pension	26	1	Petition	707	Invalid Pensions.						
Wright, Jeremiah	Pension	26	2	Petition	36	Invalid Pensions	223	Adverse		Laid on table.		
Wright, Jeremiah	Pension	27	2	Petition	428	Invalid Pensions	675	Adverse		Laid on table.		

List of private claims presented to the House of Representatives of the United States from the 1st to the 31st Congress, inclusive—Continued.

Names of claimants.	Nature or object of the claim.	Congress.	Session.	How brought before the House of Reps.	Page of journal.	To what committee of the House referred.	No. or date of the report.	Nature of the report.	No. of the bill.	How disposed of by the House of Reps.	How disposed of by the Senate.	Date of the act of Congress, and remarks.
Wright, Jeremiah	Pension	27	3	Petition	285	Invalid Pensions.						
Wright, Jeremiah	Pension	28	1	Petition	803	Invalid Pensions.						
Wright, Joel, (Va.)	Release from judgment at suit of United States, as surety of Le Roy Jourdon.	22	1	Petition	74	Judiciary	95	Favorable	185	Referred to Committee Whole House.		
Wright, Joel, (Va.)	Release from judgment at suit of United States, as surety of Le Roy Jourdon.	22	2	House bill	66	Whole House	Dec. 15, 1832	Favorable	185	Passed.		
Wright, Joel, (Va.)	Release from judgment at suit of United States, as surety of Le Roy Jourdon.	23	1	Petition	38	Judiciary	51	Favorable	59	Passed.		
Wright, Joel, (Va.)	Release from judgment at suit of United States, as surety of Le Roy Jourdon.	23	2	Petition	57	Judiciary.						
Wright, Joel, (Va.)	Release from judgment at suit of United States, as surety of Le Roy Jourdon.	24	1	Petition	106	Judiciary				Discharged; laid on table.		
Wright, John, (Pa.)	Pension	3	1	Rep. of Secretary War.	131	Select	May 26, 1794	Favorable	J.R. 12	Passed	Passed	App'd June 9, 1794
Wright, John, (Pa.)	Pension	3	2	Rep. of Secretary War.	337	Claims	Feb. 28, 1795	Favorable	130	Passed	Indef. postp'd.	
Wright, John, (Pa.)	Pension	4	1	Res. and report.	445	Claims	Feb. 18, 1796	Favorable	156	Passed	Passed	App'd April 20, 1796
Wright, John, (Pa.)	Increase of pension	15	1	House bill	405	Whole House	April 1, 1818	Favorable	172	Passed	Indef. postp'd.	
Wright, John G., administrator of.	Grant of land for revolutionary services.	11	3	Petition	463	Public Lands.						
Wright, John	Compensation for horse lost in United States service.	17	2	Petition	187	Claims				Discharged.		
Wright, John, (Va.)	Restoration of pension	17	1	Petition	142	Whole House.						
Wright, John E., (N. Y.)	Pension	25	2	Petition	268	Invalid Pensions				Discharged		Leave to withdraw.
Wright, John E., (N. Y.)	Pension	25	3	Petition	90	Invalid Pensions	290	Favorable	1154	Referred to Committee Whole House.		
Wright, John E., (N. Y.)	Pension	26	1	Petition	162	Invalid Pensions	189	Favorable	201	Passed.		
Wright, John E., (N. Y.)	Pension	26	2	Petition	36	Invalid Pensions	89	Favorable	594	Referred to Committee Whole House.		
Wright, John E., (N. Y.)	Pension	27	2	Petition	154	Invalid Pensions	312	Favorable	281	Passed	Indef. postp'd.	
Wright, John E., (N. Y.)	Pension	28	1	Petition	885	Invalid Pensions.						
Wright, John E., (N. Y.)	Pension	28	2	Petition	140	Invalid Pensions	75	Favorable	559	Passed	Passed	App'd March 3, 1845
Wright, John, (Ohio.)	Increase of pension	25	3	Petition	215	Rev. Pensions				Discharged; laid on table.		
Wright, Jonathan A. C., (Boston.)	Restoration of goods seized by revenue officers.	12	2	Petition	615	Ways and Means.						
Wright, Jordan, A.	Release from judgment at suit of United States.	22	1	Petition	868	Judiciary				Discharged; laid on table.		
Wright, Joseph, administrator of.	Compensation for modeling a likeness and cutting dies under resolution of Congress.	3	2		261			General bill				App'd Jan. 2, 1795
Wright, Joseph, (Pa.)	Pension	31	1	Petition	323	Invalid Pensions.						
Wright, Joseph, (Pa.)	Pension	31	2	Petition	162	Invalid Pensions						Leave to withdraw.
Wright, Jotham, widow & heirs of.	Continuation of pension	21	2	Petition	62	Military Pensions.						
Wright, Jotham, widow & heirs of.	Compensation for revolutionary services.	27	3	Petition	207	Rev. Pensions.						

List of private claims presented to the House of Representatives of the United States from the 1st to the 31st Congress, inclusive—Continued.

Names of claimants.	Nature or object of the claim.	Congress.	Session.	How brought before the House of Reps.	Page of journal.	To what committee of the House referred.	No. or date of the report.	Nature of the report.	No. of the bill.	How disposed of by the House of Reps.	How disposed of by the Senate.	Date of the act of Congress, and remarks.
Wright, Jotham, widow & heirs of.	For issue of certain land warrants.	31	1	Petition	1184	Public Lands.						
Wright, ——	(See Thomas & Wright)	18	1		364							
Wright, Lucy	(See Andrew Wright, widow of).	29	1		86							
Wright, Mary	Continuation of pension	28	1	Petition	850	Rev. Pensions.						
Wright, Maurice	Permission to enter land at minimum price.	25	3	Petition	134	Public Lands	118	Adverse		Laid on table.		
Wright, Maurice	Permission to enter land at minimum price.	26	1	Petition	611	Public Lands	628	Adverse		Laid on table.		
Wright, Moses, (Ky.)	Pension	26	1	Petition	547	Invalid Pensions.						
Wright, Moses, (Ky.)	Pension	28	1	Petition	452	Invalid Pensions.						
Wright, Moses, (Ky.)	Pension	28	2	Petition	209	Invalid Pensions.						
Wright, Moses, (Ky.)	Pension	29	1	Petition	319	Invalid Pensions	845	Adverse		Laid on table.		
Wright, Moses, (Ky.)	Pension	31	2	Petition	118	Invalid Pensions.						
Wright, ——	(See Crocker, Hichborn & Wright)	26	1		182							
Wright, Nahum	Pension	3	2	Rep. of Secretary War.	337	Claims	Feb. 28, 1795	Favorable	130	Passed	Indef. postp'd.	
Wright, Nahum	Pension	4	1	Rep. of Secretary War.	445	Claims	Feb. 18, 1796	Favorable	156	Passed	Passed	App'd April 20, 1796
Wright, Oakley H	Pension	28	2	Petition	414	Rev. Pensions.						
Wright, Oakley H	Pension	29	1	Documents	970	Invalid Pensions.						
Wright, Reuben	Compensation for property destroyed in Indian war.	24	1	Documents	206	Claims.						
Wright, Richard	Arrears of pay for revolutionary services.	11	2	Petition	282	Claims	Mar. 20, 1810	Adverse		Laid on table.		
Wright, Robert	(See Elias B. Caldwell, heirs of).	28	1		583							
Wright, Robert	To refund fine imposed by Post Office Department.	28	1	Petition	583	P. Of. & P. Roads.						
Wright, Samuel T., widow of.	Pension	24	2	Petition	213	Rev. Pensions.						
Wright, Samuel T., widow of.	Pension	26	1	Petition	172	Rev. Pensions.						
Wright, Simon	For exchange of land	24	1	Petition	113	Public Lands	Jan. 28, 1836	Adverse		Laid on table.		
Wright, Thomas T.	Indemnity for Indian depredations.	28	2	Petition	84	Claims	149	Adverse		Laid on table.		
Wright, Wm. H. D. C.	Compensation for diplomatic services.	21	1	House bill	326	Foreign Affairs	Feb. 22, 1830	Favorable	275	Passed	Passed	App'd May 29, 1830
Wright, William, representatives of.	Renewal of lost certificate	4	1	Petition	503	Claims	Feb. 7, 1797	Report		Postponed.		
Wright, William, representatives of.	Renewal of lost certificate	5	2	Petition	232	Claims.						
Wright, William, representatives of.	Renewal of lost certificate	6	1	Petition	607	Claims	April 22, 1800	Adverse		Laid on table.		
Wright, William, representatives of.	Renewal of lost certificate	6	2	Resolution	731	Claims	Jan. 26, 1801	Adverse		Laid on table.		
Wright, William, representatives of.	Renewal of lost certificate	11	2	Petition	313	Claims.						
Wright, William, representatives of.	Renewal of lost certificate	24	2	Petition	95	Rev. Claims.						
Wright, William, representatives of.	Renewal of lost certificate	25	2	Petition	72	Rev. Claims	248	Favorable	289	Referred to Committee Whole House.		
Wright, William, representatives of.	Renewal of lost certificate	26	1	Petition	164	Rev. Claims	330	Favorable	302	Referred to Committee Whole House.		

List of private claims presented to the House of Representatives of the United States from the 1st to the 31st Congress, inclusive—Continued.

Names of claimants.	Nature or object of the claim.	Congress.	Session.	How brought before the House of Reps.	Page of journal.	To what committee of the House referred.	No. or date of the report.	Nature of the report.	No. of the bill.	How disposed of by the House of Reps.	How disposed of by the Senate.	Date of the act of Congress, and remarks.
Wright, William, representatives of.	Renewal of lost certificate	27	2	Petition	96	Rev. Claims	1082	Adverse		Laid on table.		
Wright, William, widow of.	Pension	30	1	Res. and petition.	332 358	Rev. Pensions	388	Adverse		Laid on table.		
Wright, William, widow of.	Pension	31	1	Res. and petition.	830	Rev. Pensions	313	Adverse		Laid on table.		
Wright, William	Relief in the case of his lands destroyed, &c.	16	1	Petition	123	Public Lands	Jan. 13, 1820	Adverse		Laid on table.		
Wright, William H	For deficiency in appropriation to pay balance due to him.	23	1	House bill	474	Whole House	April 3, 1834	Favorable	404	Passed	Passed	App'd June 30, 1834
Wrighter, Jacob	Increase of pension	14	1	Senate bill	252	Pens. & Rev. Cl'ms.	Jan. 30, 1816	With amend.		Passed	Passed	App'd Feb. 22, 1816
Wrinkle, Abraham	Confirmation of title to land	23	1	Petition	76	Priv. Land Claims.	106	Favorable	114	Passed.		
Wroe, Absalom	Pension	24	1	Petition	585	Rev. Pensions				Discharged.		
Wroe, Absalom	Pension	24	2	Petition	217	Rev. Pensions				Discharged; laid on table.		
Wulm, Shem, (Ohio)	Pension	20	1	Petition	310	Military Pensions	Mar. 28, 1828	Adverse		Laid on table.		
Wulm, Shem, (Ohio)	Pension	21	1	Resolution	213	Military Pensions				Discharged; laid on table.		
Wulm, Shem, (Ohio)	Pension	22	1	Petition	103	Invalid Pensions				Discharged; laid on table.		
Wunder, George, (Phila.)	Pension	20	1	Petition	64	Military Pensions	Feb. 13, 1828	Favorable	166	Passed.		
Wunder, George, (Phila.)	Pension	21	1	Petition	49	Military Pensions	Jan. 5, 1830	Favorable	72	Passed	Passed	App'd May 20, 1830
Wyandott Indians	(See Indians, Wyandotts)	9	2		492							
Wyatt, Benjamin, (Maine)	Indemnity for French spoliations prior to 1800.	26	1	Memorial	182	Foreign Affairs	343	Favorable; bill	319	Referred to Committee Whole House.		
Wyatt, Hannah	(See John Price)	27	3		132							
Wyatt, Martha	(See Pittiman Wyatt, widow of.)	10	1		29							
Wyatt, Pittiman	Pension	3	1	Rep. of Secretary War.	131	Select	May 26, 1794	Favorable	62	Passed	Passed	App'd June 7, 1794
Wyatt, Pittiman, widow of	Continuation of pension	10	1	Petition	29	Claims.						
Wyatt, Spery	Increase of pension	23	2	Petition	303	Rev. Pensions				Discharged; laid on table.		
Wyatt, Spery	Increase of pension	24	1	Petition	107	Rev. Pensions	178	Adverse		Laid on table.		
Wyatt, Thomas	Pension and bounty land	16	1	Petition	355	Pens. & Rev. Cl'ms.				Discharged; laid on table.		
Wyatt, Thomas	Pension	12	1	House bill	361	Whole House	June 15, 1812	Favorable	138	Passed	Passed	App'd July 5, 1812
Wyatt, William	Increase of pension	16	1	Petition	88	Pens. & Rev. Cl'ms.				Discharged.		
Wyatt, William	Compensation for expenses in getting government draft cashed.	26	1	Petition	621	Claims.						
Wycoff, Isaac	Settlement of certificate of debt	4	1	Rep. of Secretary Treasury.	388	Claims	74	Adverse		Laid on table.		
Wyckoff, Alice	(See Cornelius Wickoff, widow of.)	25	2		403							
Wyckoff, Cornelius, widow of.	Continuation of pension	25	2	Petition	403	Rev. Pensions				Discharged.		
Wickoff, Jacob V. D	Compensation for hardware furnished New York custom house.	28	1	Petition	788	Claims.						
Wickoff, Jacob V. D	Compensation for hardware furnished New York custom-house.	28	2	Petition	381	Claims.						
Wickoff, John W	Pension	25	3	Petition	460	Invalid Pensions.						
Wickoff, John W	Pension	26	1	Petition	163	Invalid Pensions	251	Adverse		Laid on table.		
Wigant, John C	Pension	1	1	Petition	369	Secretary of War.						
Wyley, Robert	Pension	2	2	Rep. of Secretary of War.	649	Whole House	Jan. 3, 1793	Favorable	214	Passed.		

List of private claims presented to the House of Representatives of the United States from the 1st to the 31st Congress, inclusive—Continued.

Names of claimants.	Nature or object of the claim.	Congress.	Session.	How brought before the House of Reps.	Page of journal.	To what committee of the House referred.	No. or date of the report.	Nature of the report.	No. of the bill.	How disposed of by the House of Reps.	How disposed of by the Senate.	Date of the act of Congress, and remarks.
Wyley, Robert	Pension	3	1	Rep. of Secretary War.	131	Select	May 26, 1794	Favorable	J. R. 12	Passed	Passed	App'd June 9, 1794
Wyllys, Thomas	Pension	21	2	Petition	40	Military Pensions.						
Wyllys, Thomas	Pension	22	1	Petition	35	Rev. Pensions	....	....	......	Discharged; laid on table.		
Wyman, Benjamin	Compensation for services in connexion with treaty with Spain.	18	2	Resolution	56	Ways and Means	Feb. 25, 1825	Favorable	358	Passed.		
Wyman, James	Pension	24	2	Petition	41	Naval Affairs	110	Adverse	......	Laid on table.		
Wyman, James	Pension	25	2	Petition	198	Invalid Pensions	927	Favorable	812	Passed.		
Wyman, James	Pension	26	1	Petition	162	Invalid Pensions.						
Wyman, James	Pension	28	1	Petition	143	Invalid Pensions.						
Wyman, James	Pension	29	1	Petition	149	Invalid Pensions	51	Favorable	40	Passed	Passed	App'd July 15, 1846
Wyman, John	Increase of pension	25	2	Petition	399	Invalid Pensions	....	....	......	Discharged; laid on table.		
Wyman, Seth	Pension	4	1	Rep. of Secretary War.	445	Claims	Feb. 18, 1796	Favorable	156	Passed	Passed	App'd April 20, 1796
Wyman, Seth	Increase of pension	9	2	House bill	608	Whole House	Feb. 24, 1807	Favorable	216	Passed	Passed	App'd March 3, 1807
Wyman, William	Payment of amount due for recruiting men, &c.	8	1	Petition	419	Claims	Nov. 23, 1803	Adverse	......	Discharged	....	Leave to withdraw.
Wyman, William	Pension	24	1	Petition	666	Rev. Pensions	....	....	......	Discharged; laid on table.		
Wyncopp, Cornelius	Compensation for revolutionary services.	1	2	Petition	177	....	....	....	......	Referred to Secretary of War.		
Wyncopp, Cornelius	Compensation for revolutionary services.	1	2	Rep. of Secretary War.	177	....	April 23, 1790	....	......	Laid on table.		
Wyncopp, Cornelius, heirs of.	Payment of loan office certificate	29	1	Petition	1139	Ways and Means.						
Wyncopp, Jacobus	Compensation for losses sustained, revolutionary war.	1	2	Petition	193	....	....	....	......	Referred to Secretary War.		
Wyncopp, Jacobus	Compensation for losses sustained, revolutionary war.	1	2	Rep. of Secretary War.	193	....	....	....	......	Laid on table.		
Wynne, Daniel	(See John Smith.)	29	1									
Wynne, John	For depreciation of revolutionary pay.	3	1	Petition	62	Select	Mar. 24, 1794	Adverse	......	Laid on table.		
Wyne, William	Confirmation of title to land	27	2	Senate bill	1126	Public Lands	July 29, 1842	With't amend.	258	Passed	....	App'd Aug. 11, 1842
Wynn, William	Confirmation of title to land	28	1	Senate bill	985	Public Lands	....	....	102			
Wynn, William	Pre-emption right to enter land	30	1	Senate bill	976	Public Lands	Aug. 8, 1848	With't amend.	195	Laid on table.		
Wyoming, sufferers, heirs of.	Remuneration for losses sustained	25	2	Petition	177	Rev. Claims	1032	Adverse	......	Laid on table.		
Wyoming sufferers, heirs of.	Remuneration for losses sustained	26	1	Resolution	553, 630	Rev. Claims.						
Wyrick, Philip	Invalid pension	22	1	Resolution	327	Invalid Pensions	Feb. 29, 1832	Adverse	......	Laid on table.		
Wyrick, Philip	Invalid pension	28	1	Petition	1069	Invalid Pensions.						

List of private claims presented to the House of Representatives of the United States from the 1st to the 31st Congress, inclusive—Continued

Names of claimants.	Nature or object of the claim.	Congress.	Session.	How brought before the House of Reps.	Page of journal.	To what committee of the House referred.	No. or date of the report.	Nature of the report.	No. of the bill.	How disposed of by the House of Reps.	How disposed of by the Senate.	Date of the act of Congress, and remarks.
Yahn, Henry	(See administrator of John Young.)	18	2		229							
Yahn, Philip	(See executors of John Kerlin)	19	1		131							
Yale, James	Bounty land for services, war of 1812.	29	1	Petition	123	Military Affairs.						
Yale College, president, &c.	Remission of duties on philosophical apparatus.	1	2	Petition	148					Referred to Secretary Treasury.		
Yale College, president, &c.	Remission of duties on philosophical apparatus.	2	1	Rep. of Secretary Treasury.	580					Laid on table.		
Yancey, Charles	Pension	23	1	Petition	96	Invalid Pensions	Feb. 10, 1834	Adverse		Laid on table.		
Yancey, Charles	Pension	23	2	Petition	95	Invalid Pensions				Discharged; laid on table.		
Yancey, Leighton, heirs of.	Commutation pay for revolutionary services.	24	1	Petition	274	Rev. Claims.						
Yancey, Leighton, heirs of.	Commutation pay for revolutionary services.	24	2	Petition	39	Rev. Claims	Dec. 26, 1836	Adverse		Laid on table.		
Yancey, Leighton, heirs of.	Commutation pay for revolutionary services.	25	2	Petition	72	Rev. Claims	366	Adverse		Laid on table.		
Yancey, Leighton, heirs of.	Commutation pay for revolutionary services.	26	1	Petition	164	Rev. Claims	234	Adverse		Laid on table.		
Yancey, Leighton, heirs of.	Commutation pay for revolutionary services.	27	2	Petition	61	Rev. Claims	548	Adverse		Laid on table.		
Yandez, Peter	(See Peter Yendes)	18	1		176							
Yantes, John	Permission to enter certain lands in Missouri.	23	1	Petition	113	Public Lands	Jan. 9, 1834	Favorable	170	Passed	Passed	App'd June 18, 1834
Yard, James	Drawback of duty on exported wines.	6	1	Petition	562	Commerce	Feb. 3, 1800	Favorable	191	Passed	Passed	App'd Feb. 27, 1800
Yard, James, assignee of, (Pa.)	Indemnity for French spoliations prior to 1800.	26	1	Memorial	182	Foreign Affairs	343	Favorable	319	Referred to Committee Whole House.		
Yard, Shandy, (free col'd.)	Indemnity for losses, &c., while captive at Tripoli.	7	2	Petition	382					Laid on table.		
Yard, Shandy, (free col'd.)	Indemnity for losses, &c., while captive at Tripoli.	8	1	Petition	440	Claims	Nov. 16, 1803	Adverse		Rejected.		
Yarnall, Abner H., widow of.	Naval pension	29	2	Memorial	180	Naval Affairs.						
Yarnall, Ann T.	(See Abner H. Yarnall.)	29	2		180							
Yarnall, John J., executors of.	Equitable settlement of his accounts	14	2	Senate bill	460	Whole House	Feb. 24, 1817	With't amend.		Passed	Passed	App'd March 1, 1817
Yarnall, Peter, and Samuel Mitchell.	Release from the penalty of a bond for the fulfilment of a contract.	21	1	Petition	262	Claims	May 11, 1830	Adverse		Referred to Committee Whole House.		
Yarnall, Peter, and Samuel Mitchell.	Release from the penalty of a bond for the fulfilment of a contract.	22	1	Petition	34	Claims	252	Adverse		Referred to Committee Whole House.		
Yarnall, Peter, and Samuel Mitchell.	Release from the penalty of a bond for the fulfilment of a contract.	24	1	Petition	271	Judiciary.						
Yarnall, Peter, and Samuel Mitchell.	Release from the penalty of a bond for the fulfilment of a contract.	24	2	Petition	145	Select	236	Favorable	940	Referred to Committee Whole House.		
Yarnall, Peter, and Samuel Mitchell.	Release from the penalty of a bond for the fulfilment of a contract.	25	2	Petition	102	Select	230	Favorable	268	Referred to Committee Whole House.		

List of private claims presented to the House of Representatives of the United States from the 1st to the 31st Congress, inclusive—**Continued.**

Names of claimants.	Nature or object of the claim.	Congress.	Session.	How brought before the House of Reps.	Page of journal.	To what committee of the House referred.	No. or date of the report.	Nature of the report.	No. of the bill.	How disposed of by the House of Reps.	How disposed of by the Senate.	Date of the act of Congress, and remarks.
Yarnall, Peter, and Samuel Mitchell.	Release from the penalty of a bond for the fulfilment of a contract.	25	3	House bill	376	Whole House	....	....	268			
Yarnall, Peter, and Samuel Mitchell.	Release from the penalty of a bond for the fulfilment of a contract.	26	1	Resolution	596	Select	492	Report and bill.	393	Referred to Committee Whole House.		
Yarnall, Peter, and Samuel Mitchell.	Release from the penalty of a bond for the fulfilment of a contract.	27	2	Petition	90	Claims.						
Yarnall, Peter, and Samuel Mitchell.	Release from the penalty of a bond for the fulfilment of a contract.	27	3	Petition	43	Claims	50	Adverse	......	Laid on table.		
Yarnall, Peter, and Samuel Mitchell.	Release from the penalty of a bond for the fulfilment of a contract.	28	1	Petition	610	Claims.						
Yarrington, Anna	(See widow of Jonathan Park)	26	1	....	706							
Yates, Allen	Confirmation of title to a reservation of land.	24	1	Petition	96	Indian Affairs.						
Yates, Allen, widow of	Confirmation of title to a reservation of land.	25	2	Petition	43	Indian Affairs	146	Favorable	168	Referred to Committee Whole House.		
Yates, Allen, widow of	Confirmation of title to a reservation of land.	25	3	House bill	375	Whole House	....	Favorable	168	Passed	Passed	App'd March 3, 1839
Yates, Milley	(See Allen Yates, widow of)	24	1	....	96							
Yates, Lieut. Bartholomew, representatives of.	Emolument due the representatives of deceased officers.	6	1	Petition	624	Claims	May 24, 1800	....	......	Leave to withdraw.		
Yates, Lieut. Bartholomew, administrator of.	Compensation for revolutionary services.	16	1	Petition	211	Claims	Feb. 18, 1820	Adverse	......	Rejected		
Yates, or Yeates, Charles, executor of.	Payment of sundry loan office certificates.	20	1	Senate amendm't to House bill.	846	....	....	....	62	Passed with amendm't.	Passed as am'd.	App'd May 26, 1828
Yates, or Yeates, Charles, executor of.	Interest on payment authorized by act of May 26, 1828.	21	1	Petition	523	Rev. Claims	April 16, 1830	Favorable	426	Passed	Passed	App'd May 29, 1830
Yates, Dr. George, representatives of.	Commutation pay as a revolutionary surgeon.	22	2	Resolution	57	Rev. Claims.						
Yates, Dr. George, representatives of.	Commutation pay as a revolutionary surgeon.	23	1	Petition	70	Rev. Claims.						
Yates, Dr. George, representatives of.	Commutation pay as a revolutionary surgeon.	23	2	Resolution	106	Rev. Claims.						
Yates, Dr. George, representatives of.	Commutation pay as a revolutionary surgeon.	24	1	Resolution	144	Rev. Claims.						
Yates, Dr. George, representatives of.	Commutation pay as a revolutionary surgeon.	24	2	Petition	39	Rev. Claims.						
Yates, Dr. George, representatives of.	Commutation pay as a revolutionary surgeon.	25	2	Petition	72	Rev. Claims	854	Favorable	772	Referred to Committee Whole House.		
Yates, Dr. George, representatives of.	Commutation pay as a revolutionary surgeon.	25	3	House bill	431	Whole House	....	....	772			
Yates, Dr. George, representatives of.	Commutation pay as a revolutionary surgeon.	26	1	Petition	166	Rev. Claims	714	Adverse	......	Laid on table.		
Yates, Dr. George, representatives of.	Compensation for services as surgeon's mate.	27	3	Resolution	138	Rev. Claims	257	Adverse	......	Laid on table.		
Yates, Lieut. George J., widow of.	Pension for revolutionary services.	26	1	Petition	707	Rev. Pensions	490	Adverse	......	Laid on table.		
Yates, Lieut. George J., widow of.	Pension for revolutionary services.	27	2	Petition	48	Rev. Pensions	784	Adverse	......	Laid on table.		

List of private claims presented to the House of Representatives of the United States from the 1st to the 31st Congress, inclusive—Continued.

Names of claimants.	Nature or object of the claim.	Congress.	Session.	How brought before the House of Reps.	Page of journal.	To what committee of the House referred.	No. or date of the report.	Nature of the report.	No. of the bill.	How disposed of by the House of Reps.	How disposed of by the Senate.	Date of the act of Congress, and remarks.
Yates, Lieut. George J., widow of.	Pension for revolutionary services.	27	3	Petition	145	Rev. Pensions	295	Adverse	......	Laid on table.		
Yates, John	Pension	19	1	Petition	34	Pens. & Rev. Cl'ms.	164	Adverse	......	Laid on table.		
Yates, Captain John, representatives of.	Compensation for revolutionary supplies.	30	1	Petition	559	Rev. Claims.						
Yates, John Van Ness	(See sureties of Solomon Sonthwick.)	21	1	....	66							
Yates, Matthew	(See widow of Stephen Decatur, and others.)	20	1	....	295	....	201	....	S. 50			
Yates, Millry	(See Allen Yates, widow of.)	25	2	....	43							
Yates, Nancy	(See Lieut. George J. Yates, widow of.)	26	1	....	707							
Yates, Robert	(See representatives of Bartholomew Yates.)	6	1	....	624							
Yates, Sarah	(See representatives of Capt. John Yates.)	30	1	....	559							
Yates, Samuel	Release from a judgment in favor of United States.	15	1	Petition	231	Ways and Means.						
Yates, William	Invalid pension	3	1	Rep. of Secretary War	131	Select	May 26, 1794	Res. to refer to Sec. War.	J. R. 12	Passed	Passed	App'd June 9, 1794
Yates, William, heirs of	Compensation for revolutionary services.	30	1	Petition	1013	Rev. Pensions.						
Yates, William, heirs of	Compensation for revolutionary services.	31	1	Petition	595	Rev. Pensions	452	Adverse	......	Laid on table.		
Yaw, Joseph	(See Thomas Marsh and J. Yaw).	18	1	....	115							
Yaw, Joseph, widow of	Indemnity for property sold on a judgment against deceased as surety for T. Marsh.	21	1	Petition	39	Ways and Means	....	....	......	Discharged; laid on table.		
Yaw, Sarah	(See Joseph Yaw, widow of)	21	1	....	39							
Yawn, Henry	(See Samuel Smith)	18	2	....	229							
Yeager, Henry, daughter of	Pension for revolutionary services.	26	1	Petition	937	Rev. Pensions.						
Yearhouse, George	Arrears of revolutionary pay	3	1	Petition	60	....	....	....	......	Referred to Secretary War.		
Yearhouse, George	Arrears of revolutionary pay	3	2	Rep. of Secretary War.	278	Claims	....	....	......	Laid on table.		
Yearhouse, George	Arrears of revolutionary pay	5	2	Petition	127	Claims	March 5, 1798	Adverse	......	Laid on table.		
Yearty, Jacob	Indemnity for property destroyed by Indians.	30	1	Petition	522	Claims	397	Adverse	......	Laid on table.		
Yeaton, Charles	Pension for privateer service	21	1	Senate bill	452	Naval Affairs	April 29, 1830	With't amend.	86	Referred to Committee Whole House.		
Yeaton, Hopely	Compensation for services and reimbursement of expenses as superintendent of building revenue cutter.	4	1	Petition and rep't Sec. Treasury.	441, 472	Whole House	April 11, 1796	Favorable; bill ordered.	167	Passed	Passed	App'd May 6, 1796
Yeaton, Hopely	Pension for revolutionary naval services.	11	3	Petition	441	Claims	....	....	......	Leave to withdraw.		
Yeck, Charles	(See Louis F. Beeler and others).	30	1	....	115	....	482					
Yell, Archibald, administrator of.	Per diem and mileage as member of Congress.	30	1	Resolution	966	Accounts.						
Yellott, Jeremiah, heirs of.	Indemnity for French spoliations prior to 1800.	29	2	Memorial	83	Foreign Affairs.						
Yendell, Samuel	Compensation for revolutionary services.	29	1	Petition	939	Rev. Pensions.						

List of private claims presented to the House of Representatives of the United States from the 1st to the 31st Congress, inclusive—Continued.

Names of claimants.	Nature or object of the claim.	Congress.	Session.	How brought before the House of Reps.	Page of journal.	To what committee of the House referred.	No. or date of the report.	Nature of the report.	No. of the bill.	How disposed of by the House of Reps.	How disposed of by the Senate.	Date of the act of Congress, and remarks.
Yendes, Peter	Compensation for horse lost in war of 1812.	18	1	Petition	176	Claims	Mar. 12, 1824	Favorable	156	Passed.		
Yendes, Peter	Compensation for horse lost in war of 1812.	18	2	Petition	130	Claims	Jan. 21, 1825	Favorable	287	Passed	Passed	App'd March 3, 1825
Yeogar, Peter	Compensation for a horse lost in the war of 1812.	18	2	Petition	46	Claims	Jan. 3, 1825	Adverse	......	Laid on table.		
Yeoman, Joshua	Pension for revolutionary services.	15	2	Petition	222	Pens. & Rev. Cl'ms.						
Yeoman, Joshua	Pension for revolutionary services.	16	1	Petition	291	Rev. Pensions	April 22, 1820	Adverse	......	Laid on table.		
Yeoman, Joshua	Pension for revolutionary services.	19	2	Petition	64	Military Pensions.						
Yeoman, Joshua	Pension for revolutionary services.	20	1	Petition	278	Military Pensions.						
Yeoman, Joshua	Pension for revolutionary services.	21	1	Petition	36	Military Pensions.						
Yeomans, John, widow of	Benefit of the relief of surviving revolutionary officer.	21	1	Petition	74	Rev. Claims	154	Favorable	196	Passed	Passed	App'd May 29, 1830
Yeomans, Martin	(See John Yeomans, widow of)	21	1	....	74							
Yerby, Elizabeth	(See Joseph White, heir of)	26	1	....	182							
Yerby, Elizabeth, heirs of.	Indemnity for French spoliations prior to 1800.	31	1	Petition	425	Foreign Affairs	355	General bill	318	Referred to Committee Whole House.		
Yerby, William W.	Confirmation of title to a quarter section of land.	29	2	Memorial	109	Public Lands.						
Yerby, William W., and others.	(See heirs of Elizabeth Yerby)	31	1	....	425							
Yerger, Capt. John, heirs of.	Indemnity for French spoliations prior to 1800.	31	1	Petition	450	Foreign Affairs	355	General bill	318	Referred to Committee Whole House.		
Yerks, John	Pension for revolutionary services.	22	1	Petition	219	Rev. Pensions.						
Yielding, Richard	Exchange of military bounty land	19	1	Petition	94	Public Lands	54	Favorable	77	Passed	Passed	App'd May 22, 1826; leave to withdraw.
Yoast, Francis	Exchange of an erroneous entry of land.	28	1	Petition	532	Public Lands	Mar. 29, 1844	Favorable	286	Passed.		
Yoast, Francis	Exchange of an erroneous entry of land.	29	1	Petition	463	Public Lands.						
Yoast, Francis	Exchange of an erroneous entry of land.	31	1	Petition	325	Public Lands.						
Yoder, Jacob, and William Hamilton.	Confirmation of title to land in Indiana.	12	1	Petition	22	Public Lands.						
Yoder, Jacob, and William Hamilton.	Confirmation of title to land in Indiana.	12	2	Petition	549	Public Lands.						
Yoder, Jacob, and William Hamilton.	Confirmation of title to land in Indiana.	13	2	Petition	170	Public Lands	Mar. 29, 1814	Adverse	......	Leave to withdraw.		
Yoder, Jacob, and William Hamilton.	Confirmation of title to land in Indiana.	14	2	Petition	91	Priv. Land Claims.						
Yo-ho-lo, Usse	(See Usse Yo-ho-lo.)	24	1	....	212							
Yonge, William P.	Reimbursement of illegal tonnage duties.	17	2	Petition	166	Ways and Means.						
Yonge, William P.	Reimbursement of illegal tonnage duties.	18	1	Petition	526	Ways and Means.						
Yonge, William P.	Reimbursement of illegal tonnage duties.	18	2	Petition	178	Ways and Means	Jan. 28, 1825	Favorable	299	Passed	Passed	App'd March 3, 1825
Yonge, William P.	Damage of cotton used for military purposes.	30	1	Petition	137	Claims	600	Favorable	481	Referred to Committee Whole House.		
Yonge, William P.	Damage of cotton used for military purposes.	30	2	Bill of last sess.	318	Whole House	Jan. 26, 1849	With't amend.	481	Passed	Passed	App'd March 3, 1849
Yool, William, heirs of	Pension	28	1	Petition	434	Naval Affairs.						
Yool, William, heirs of	Pension	29	1	Petition	139	Naval Affairs.						

List of private claims presented to the House of Representatives of the United States from the 1st to the 31st Congress, inclusive—Continued.

Names of claimants.	Nature or object of the claim.	Congress.	Session.	How brought before the House of Reps.	Page of journal.	To what committee of the House referred.	No. or date of the report.	Nature of the report.	No. of the bill.	How disposed of by the House of Reps.	How disposed of by the Senate.	Date of the act of Congress, and remarks.
Yool, William, heirs of	Pension	29	2	Petition	149	Naval Affairs.						
York, Abigail	Pension under act of 1838	26	1	Resolution	561	Rev. Pensions.						
York, Abigail	(See widow of Nathaniel Randal)	26	1		707							
York, A. A	(See Senate bill, No. 118)	30	1		328							
York, A. A	(See Senate bill, No. 81)	30	2		319							
York, Charles	(See sureties of Silas Holmes)	26	2		249							
York, Edward	(See representatives of Edward Ogden and E. Y.)	27	2		829							
York, Jabez	Pension	31	1	Petition	595	Invalid Pensions.						
York, John	Release from imprisonment on a judgment in favor of U. States.	8	2	Petition	93	Select	Jan. 25, 1805	Favorable	43	Passed	Passed	App'd March 2, 1805
York, Joseph	Arrears of pension	23	1	Petition	569	Rev. Pensions.						
York, Joseph, widow of	Compensat'n for property destroyed by the enemy in war of 1812.	26	1	Petition	294	Claims.						
York, Joseph, widow of	Compensat'n for property destroyed by the enemy in war of 1812.	26	2	Petition	38	Claims	Jan. 16, 1841	Adverse		Laid on table.		
York, Joshua	Arrears of pension	23	2	Petition	198	Rev. Pensions				Discharged; laid on table.		
York, Joshua	Arrears of pension	24	1	Petition	108	Rev. Pensions				Discharged; laid on table.		
York, Lavinia	(See Joseph York, widow of.)	26	1		294							
Yorke, Samuel	Invalid pension	3	1	Petition and rep't Secretary War.	77, 93	Select.						
York, Sawnee, representatives of.	Arrears of pension	24	2	Petition	73	Rev. Pensions	62	Favorable	812	Referred to Committee Whole House.		
York, Sawnee, representatives of.	Arrears of pension	25	2	Petition	40	Rev. Claims	173	Favorable	198	Passed	Passed	App'd July 9, 1838
York, Stephen	Indemnity for property lost in Canada, war of 1812.	28	2	Petition	283	Claims.						
York, Stephen	Indemnity for property lost in Canada, war of 1812.	29	2	Petition	49	Claims.						
York, Stephen	Indemnity for property lost in Canada, war of 1812.	31	1	Petition	269	Claims.						
York, William	Pension for revolutionary services.	24	1	Petition	157	Rev. Pensions	Jan. 19, 1836	Favorable	180	Passed	Indef. postp'd.	
York, William	Pension for revolutionary services.	24	2	Petition	84	Rev. Pensions	11	Favorable	769	Referred to Committee Whole House.		
York, William	Pension for revolutionary services.	25	2	Petition	38	Rev. Pensions	160	Favorable	185	Passed	Adverse report.	
York, William	Pension for revolutionary services.	26	1	Petition	172	Rev. Pensions	158	Favorable	168	Passed.		
York, William R	Increase of pension	28	1	Petition	443	Rev. Pensions				Discharged; laid on table.		
Youce, ———	(See Bast & Youce)	20	2		52							
Youman, James	Pension for naval services	21	1	Petition	447	Naval Affairs.						
Yaumans, Jonas	Pension	22	1	Petition	164	Rev. Pensions	397	Favorable	496	Referred to Committee Whole House.		
Youmans, Jonathan	Pension for revolutionary services.	26	1	Petition	286	Rev. Pensions.						
Young, Abby	(See heirs of Daniel Mills)	27	2		62							
Young, Abner	Bounty land for services, war of 1812.	15	1	Petition	184	Public Lands.						
Young, Alexander, representatives of.	Reimbursement of overpaid duties on merchandise.	17	1	Petition	248	Ways and Means				Discharged; laid on table		
Young, Alexander, representatives of.	Reimbursement of overpaid duties on merchandise.	17	2	Petition	163	Commerce				Discharged; laid on table.		
Young, Alexander, representatives of.	Reimbursement of overpaid duties on merchandise.	18	1	Petition	133	Commerce				Discharged; leave to withdraw.		

List of private claims presented to the House of Representatives of the United States from the 1st to the 31st Congress, inclusive—Continued.

Names of claimants.	Nature or object of the claim.	Congress.	Session.	How brought before the House of Reps.	Page of journal.	To what committee of the House referred.	No. or date of the report.	Nature of the report.	No. of the bill.	How disposed of by the House of Reps.	How disposed of by the Senate.	Date of the act of Congress, and remarks.
Young, Alexander, representatives of.	Reimbursement of overpaid duties on merchandise.	18	2	Petition	47	Commerce.						
Young, Alexander, representatives of.	Reimbursement of overpaid duties on merchandise.	19	1	Petition	38	Commerce	May 23, 1826	Favorable	250	Passed.		
Young, Alexander, representatives of.	Reimbursement of overpaid duties on merchandise.	19	2	Petition	45	Commerce	Dec. 18, 1826	Favorable	296	Passed	Passed	App'd March 2, 1827
Young, Andrew, and Jas. Bennett.	Compensation for arms lost in public service.	18	1	Petition and docs.	214	Military Affairs.						
Young, Anne	(See representat's of John Durkee.)	12	1		183							
Young, Benjamin	(See Joseph Bryan, and others.)	27	2		1395							
Young, Bryant R., and others.	Sale of certain unsurveyed lands	23	1	Petition	499	Public Lands.						
Young, Bryant R., and others.	Sale of certain unsurveyed lands	23	2	Petition	77	Public Lands				Discharged; laid on table.		
Young, Catherine	Pension in consideration of the death of her son on board ship Peacock.	14	2	Petition	199	Naval Affairs.						
Young, Catherine	Pension in consideration of the death of her son on board ship Peacock.	15	1	Petition	32	Naval Affairs	Dec. 22, 1817	Adverse		Rejected.		
Young, Catherine	Pension in consideration of the death of her son on board ship Peacock.	18	1	Petition	176	Naval Affairs	Feb. 2, 1824	Adverse		Laid on table.		
Young, Charles	Pension	24	1	Resolution	923	Invalid Pensions				Discharged; laid on table.		
Young, Charles	Pension	28	1	Petition	211	Invalid Pensions	271	Adverse		Laid on table.		
Young, Edward L	Additional compensation for surveying coast of North Carolina.	19	1	Petition	225	Naval Affairs	Feb. 20, 1826	Adverse		Laid on table.		
Young, Edward L	Pension for injuries received in naval service.	24	1	Petition	796	Naval Affairs.						
Young, Edward L	Pension for injuries received in naval service.	24	2	Petition	121	Naval Affairs	108	Adverse		Laid on table.		
Young, Edward L	Pension for injuries received in naval service.	30	1	Petition	218	Naval Affairs.						
Young, Edward L	Pension for injuries received in naval service.	30	2	Petition	127	Naval Affairs.						
Young, Edward L	Naval invalid pension	31	1	Petition	743	Invalid Pensions.						
Young, Eliza Ann, and Dolly Toppan.	Bounty on a fishing vessel	19	1	Petition	222	Commerce.						
Young, Elizabeth	Indemnity for revolutionary losses and injuries.	1	2	Petition	163					Laid on table.		
Young, Elizabeth	Compensation due her husband for taking census of Cherokees in Arkansas.	26	1	Resolution	435	Indian Affairs.						
Young, Garver, & Co	(See James S. Evans & Co.)	26	1		620							
Young, George	Compensation for revolutionary services.	10	1	Petition	87	Claims				Referred to Committee Whole House.		
Young, George M	Compensation for work on a dredging machine.	27	3	Petition	236	Claims.						
Young, Harrison	(See Joseph Bryan and others)	27	2		1395							
Young, Ignatius F	Reimbursement of costs in a suit with United States.	20	2	Petition	89	Ways and Means	Jan. 7, 1829	Adverse		Laid on table.		
Young, James H	(See William H. Bedford, agent.)	28	1		262							

List of private claims presented to the House of Representatives of the United States from the 1st to the 31st Congress, inclusive—Continued.

Names of claimants.	Nature or object of the claim.	Congress.	Session.	How brought before the House of Reps.	Page of journal.	To what committee of the House referred.	No. or date of the report	Nature of the report.	No. of the bill.	How disposed of by the House of Reps.	How disposed of by the Senate.	Date of the act of Congress, and remarks.
Young, James, (N. Y.)	Pension for revolutionary services.	17	1	Petition	165	Rev. Pensions.						
Young, James, (N. Y.)	Pension for revolutionary services.	17	2	Petition	117	Pens. & Rev. Cl'ms.				Discharged; leave to withdraw.		
Young, James, (Maine)	Indemnity for French spoliations prior to 1800.	26	1	Memorial	182	Foreign Affairs	343	Favorable; bill	319	Referred to Committee Whole House.		
Young, James, (Virginia)	Indemnity for French spoliations prior to 1800.	26	1	Memorial	182	Foreign Affairs	343	Favorable; bill	319	Referred to Committee Whole House.		
Young, James, (La.)	Confirmation of a land claim	20	2	Petition	41	Priv. Land Claims.	Jan. 5, 1829	Adverse		Laid on table.		
Young, James, (La.)	Confirmation of a land claim	27	3	Petition	52	Priv. Land Claims.	58	Favorable	691	Passed	Passed	App'd March 3, 1843
Young, James, widow of	Relief, in consideration of naval services.	25	2	Petition	723	Naval Affairs				Laid on table.		
Young, James, widow of	Relief, in consideration of naval services.	25	3	Petition	225	Naval Affairs.						
Young, James, widow of	Relief, in consideration of naval services.	26	1	Petition	180	Naval Affairs.						
Young, James, of Washington, D. C.	Permission to purchase a lot of public ground.	23	1	Petition	187	Dist. of Columbia.	416	Favorable	437	Referred to Committee Whole House.		
Young, James, of Washington, D. C.	Permission to purchase a lot of public ground.	23	2	House bill	162	Whole House		Favorable	437	Passed	Passed	App'd March 3, 1835
Young, James	Compensation for property lost in war of 1812.	25	2	Resolution	1149	Claims.						
Young, James	Compensation for property lost in war of 1812.	25	3	Petition	188	Claims	297	Adverse		Laid on table.		
Young, James, heirs of	Indemnity for French spoliations prior to 1800.	31	1	Petition	743	Foreign Affairs	355	General bill	318	Referred to Committee Whole House.		
Young, Jesse	Increase of pension	13	3	Petition	562	Pens. & Rev. Cl'ms.	Feb. 20, 1815	Favorable	303	Passed	Passed	App'd March 3, 1815
Young, Jesse	Increase of pension	30	1		78, 104, 112, 200	Invalid Pensions	84	Favorable	71	Ref'd to Com. W. H.		
Young, Jesse	Increase of pension	30	2	House bill	466				71	Passed	Passed	App'd Feb. 22, 1849
Young, John, of Mass.	Pension for revolutionary services.	14	1	Petition	170	Pens. & Rev. Cl'ms.						
Young, John, of Mass.	Pension for revolutionary services.	14	1	Senate bill	252	Pens. & Rev. Cl'ms.	Feb. 14, 1816	With amends.		Passed with amendm't	Passed as am'd.	App'd Feb. 22, 1816
Young, John, of Penn., administrators of.	Additional compensation for arms furnished.	18	2	Petition	228	Claims.						
Young, John, of Penn., administrators of.	Additional compensation for arms furnished.	19	1	Petition	322	Claims.						
Young, John, of Penn., administrators of.	Additional compensation for arms furnished.	19	2	Petition	64	Claims.						
Young, John, of Tenn.	Compensation for a horse lost in war of 1812.	19	1	Petition	248	Claims	Mar. 17, 1826	Adverse		Laid on table.		
Young, John, of Mass.	Increase of pension	23	1	Petition	45	Invalid Pensions	Jan. 14, 1834	Adverse		Laid on table.		
Young, Rev. John	Pension for revolutionary services.	23	1	Resolution	250	Rev. Pensions				Discharged; laid on table.		
Young, Rev. John	Pension for revolutionary services.	24	2	Petition	50	Rev. Pensions				Discharged; laid on table.		
Young, John, (Ky.)	Pension for revolutionary services.	23	1	Petition	308	Rev. Pensions.						
Young, John, (Ky.)	Pension for revolutionary services.	26	1	Petition	433	Rev. Pensions.						
Young, John, (Ky.)	Pension for revolutionary services.	28	1	Petition	141	Rev. Pensions.						
Young, John, (Ky.)	Pension for revolutionary services.	28	2	Petition	83	Rev. Pensions.						
Young, John, (Ky.)	Pension for revolutionary services.	30	1	Petition	115	Rev. Pensions	211	Adverse		Laid on table.		
Young, John, (Ky.)	Pension for revolutionary services.	30	2	Petition	446	Rev. Pensions				Leave to withdraw.		
Young, John, (Md.)	(Ses Buchanan & Young.)	26	1		182							

List of private claims presented to the House of Representatives of the United States from the 1st to the 31st Congress, inclusive—Continued.

ames of claimants.	Nature or object of the claim.	Congress.	Session.	How brought before the House of Reps.	Page of journal.	To what committee of the House referred.	No. or date of the report.	Nature of the report.	No. of the bill.	How disposed of by the House of Reps.	How disposed of by the Senate.	Date of the act of Congress, and remarks.
Young, John J.	Arrears of pension	23	2	Petition	67	Naval Affairs				Laid on table.		
Young, John J.	Indemnity for wounds and disabilities U. S. navy.	24	1	Memorial	61	Naval Affairs.						
Young, John J.	Indemnity for wounds and disabilities U. S. navy.	24	2	Memorial	158	Naval Affairs.						
Young, John J.	Naval pension	28	2	Memorial	103	Naval Affairs.						
Young, John J.	Naval pension	30	1	Memorial	494	Naval Affairs	335	Favorable	313	Referred to Committee Whole House.		
Young, John J.	Naval pension	30	2	House bill	143	Whole House	Dec. 22, 1849	Favorable	313	Passed	Passed	App'd March 3, 1849
Young, Jonathan, jr	Invalid pension	5	2	Petition	247	Claims	514	Adverse		Laid on table.		
Young, Jonathan M	Arrears of pension	30	1	Petition	666	Invalid Pensions				Discharged; laid on table.		
Young, Joseph, (N. C.)	Bounty land for services in war of 1812.	16	1	Petition	39	Priv. Land Claims.	Dec. 30, 1819	Adverse		Leave to withdraw.		
Young, Joseph, (N. C.)	Bounty land for services in war of 1812.	17	1	Petition	142	Public Lands.						
Young, Joseph, representatives of.	Compensation for property taken for public use.	25	2	Petition	40	Rev. Claims	128	Report and bill	146	Postponed.		
Young, Joseph, representatives of.	Compensation for property taken for pub'ic use.	26	1	Memorial	163	Rev. Claims.						
Young, Joseph, representatives of.	Compensation for property taken for public use.	27	2	Petition	105	Rev. Claims	1074	Adverse		Laid on table.		
Youngs, Joseph, heirs of	Indemnity for property destroyed, revolutionary war.	15	2	Petition	102	Claims				Leave to withdraw.		
Youngs, Joseph, heirs of	Indemnity for property destroyed, revolutionary war.	17	1	Petition	387	Pens. & Rev. Cl'ms.	Mar. 29, 1822	Adverse		Laid on table.		
Youngs, Joseph, representatives of.	Indemnity for property destroyed, revolutionary war.	19	1	Resolution	298	Rev. Claims	154	Adverse		Laid on table.		
Youngs, Joseph, representatives of.	Indemnity for property destroyed, revolutionary war.	23	2	Petition	37	Rev. Claims	68	Favorable	689	Referred to Committee Whole House.		
Youngs, Joseph, representatives of.	Indemnity for property destroyed, revolutionary war.	24	1	Petition	62	Rev. Claims	272	Favorable	279	Referred to Committee Whole House.		
Youngs, Joseph, representatives of.	Indemnity for property destroyed, revolutionary war.	27	3	Petition	44	Rev. Claims	260	Adverse		Laid on table.		
Young, Joseph, (Mass.,) executors of.	Indemnity for French spoliations prior to 1800.	26	1	Memorial	182	Foreign Affairs	343	Favorable; bill	319	Referred to Committee Whole House.		
Young, Joseph, (Md.,) executors of.	Indemnity for French spoliations prior to 1800.	26	1	Memorial	182	Foreign Affairs	343	Favorable; bill	319	Referred to Committee Whole House.		
Young, Joseph	Reimbursem't of payment as surety for J. Garretson.	19	2	Petition	187	P. Of. & P. Roads.						
Young, Joseph	Reimbursem't of payment as surety for J. Garretson.	20	1	Petition	126	P. Of. & P. Roads.	113	Favorable	126	Laid on table.		
Young, Joseph	Reimbursem't of payment as surety for J. Garretson.	21	1	Petition	146	P. Of. & P. Roads.	164	Favorable	201	Rejected.		
Young, Joseph, representatives of.	Reimbursem't of payment as surety for J. Garretson.	24	2	House bill	200	Whole House	Jan. 13, 1837	With't amend.	279	Passed	Indef. postp'd.	
Young, Joseph	(See representatives of John Pratt)	27	2		99							
Young, Joseph H	Confirmation of land claim	26	1	Petition	365	Priv. Land Claims.						
Young, Judith H.	(See widow of Robert Young)	22	1		260							
Young, King, (Indian)	Pension for military service and disability.	14	1	Resolution	240	Pens. & Rev. Cl'ms.	Feb. 15, 1816	Favorable		Passed	Passed	App'd April 26, 1816
Young, Leonard	Invalid pension	1	2	Petition and rep't Sec. of War.	185, 199					Laid on table.		

List of private claims presented to the House of Representatives of the United States from the 1st to the 31st Congress, inclusive—Continued.

Names of claimants.	Nature or object of the claim.	Congress.	Session.	How brought before the House of Reps.	Page of journal.	To what committee of the House referred.	No. or date of the report.	Nature of the report.	No. of the bill.	How disposed of by the House of Reps.	How disposed of by the Senate.	Date of the act of Congress, and remarks.
Young, Llewellin	Compensation for revolutionary services.	18	2	Petition	278					Laid on table.		
Young, Llewellin	Compensation for revolutionary services.	19	1	Petition	68	Select.						
Young, Llewellin	Compensation for revolutionary services.	20	1	Petition	196	Select				Discharged.		
				Resolution	270	Military Pensions				Discharged; laid on table.		
Young, Martha R	(See James Young, widow of)	25	2		723							
Young, Mary	(See heir of William Leggett)	31	2		326							
Young, Moses	Compensation for revolutionary services and losses.	1	2	Petition	160					Laid on table.		
Young, Moses	Balance due him as secretary of legation.	2	1	Petition	521	Select	April 11, 1792	Favorable		Laid on table.		
Young, Moses	Balance due him as secretary of legation.	2	2	Memorial	628	Whole House				Rejected.		
Young, Moses	Compensation for services as secretary to Franklin, &c.	2	2	Memorial	636					Referred to Secretary Treasury.		
Young, Moses	Additional compensation for services as secretary and consul.	8	1	Petition	649					Laid on table.		
Young, Moses	Additional compensation for services as secretary and consul.	8	1	Senate bill	686	Claims	Mar. 26, 1804	With't amend.	S. 34	Passed	Passed	App'd Mar. 26, 1804
Young, Moses	Settlement of claim for services as secretary, &c.	8	2	Petition	66	Claims.						
Young, Moses	Settlement of claim for services as secretary, &c.	9	1	Petition	207	Claims.						
Young, Moses	Settlement of claim for services as secretary, &c.	9	2	Petition	498	Claims.						
Young, Moses	Settlement of claim for services as secretary, &c.	10	1	Petition	83	Select.						
Young, Moses	Settlement of claim for services as secretary, &c.	11	2	Petition	115	Claims	Mar. 14, 1810	Favorable	102	Passed	Passed	App'd April 25, 1810
Young, Nimrod	Reimbursement of expenses of his son who died of disease contracted in the public service.	14	2	Petition	34	Military Affairs	Feb. 21, 1817	Adverse		Laid on table.		
Young, Dr. Noble	(See Dr. John Warring and Noble Young.)	23	1		498							
Young, Philip	Pension for revolutionary services.	22	1	Petition	470	Rev. Pensions.						
Young, Ralph	Increase of pension	28	2	Petition	366	Rev. Pensions.						
Young, Ralph	Increase of pension	29	1	Petition	86	Rev. Pensions	Feb. 25, 1846	Adverse		Laid on table.		
Young, Reuben, and Ann, administrator of.	Revolutionary pension due said Reuben.	28	1	Petition	707	Rev. Pensions.						
Young, Reuben, and Ann, administrator of.	Revolutionary pension due said Reuben.	28	2	Petition	58	Rev. Claims.						
Young, Richard	Arrears of a forfeiture due him	19	1	Petition	31	Ways and Means	Dec. 21, 1825	Adverse		Rejected.		
Young, Rob't, (Alexandria)	(See James Sanderson and others.)	14	1		292							
Young, Robert	(See William H. Bedford, agent.)	28	1		262							
Young, Robert, (Pa.)	Bounty land for revolutionary services.	15	1	Petition	55	Pens. & Rev. Cl'ms.						
Young, Robert, (N. J.)	Pension for revolutionary services.	21	1	Petition	36	Military Pensions	May 21, 1830	Favorable	478	Referred to Committee Whole House.		
Young, Robert, (N. J.)	Pension for revolutionary services.	22	2	Petition	40	Rev. Pensions				Discharged; laid on table.		

List of private claims presented to the House of Representatives of the United States from the 1st to the 31st Congress, inclusive—Continued.

Names of claimants.	Nature or object of the claim.	Congress.	Session.	How brought before the House of Reps.	Page of journal.	To what committee of the House referred.	No. or date of the report.	Nature of the report.	No. of the bill.	How disposed of by the House of Reps.	How disposed of by the Senate.	Date of the act of Congress, and remarks.
Young, Robert, widow of.	Pension for revolutionary services.	26	1	Petition	324	Rev. Pensions.						
Young, Robert, widow of.	Compensation for revolutionary services.	2[illegible]	1	Petition	260	Rev. Claims	Feb. 9, 1832	Adverse	......	Laid on table.		
Young, Robert, (Ky.)	Commutation pay for revolutionary services.	22	2	Resolution	273	Rev. Claims.						
Young, Robert, (Ky.)	Commutation pay for revolutionary services.	23	2	Petition	197	Rev. Claims.						
Young, Gen. Robert, representatives of.	Compensation for tobacco destroyed by the enemy in 1814.	31	1	Petition	668	Claims.						
Young, Rufus	Invalid pension	22	1	Petition	189	Invalid Pensions	Feb. 9, 1832	Adverse	......	Laid on table.		
Young, Samuel, (Pa.)	Pension for revolutionary services	17	1	Petition	60	Rev. Pensions.						
Young, Samuel, (Pa.)	Pension for revolutionary services.	18	1	Petition	65	Rev. Pensions	Jan. 12, 1824	Adverse	......	Laid on table.		
Young, Samuel, (Pa.)	Pension for revolutionary services.	19	1	Petition	20	Military Pensions	164	Adverse	......	Laid on table.		
Young, Samuel, (N. Y.)	Pension for revolutionary services.	20	1	Petition	58	Rev. Claims	Feb. 22, 1828	Adverse	......	Laid on table.		
Young, Samuel, (N. Y.)	Pension for revolutionary services.	2[illegible]	1	Petition	523	Military Pensions	314	Favorable	397	Passed	Indef. postp'd.	
Young, Samuel, (N. Y.)	Pension for revolutionary services.	22	1	Petition	105	Rev. Pensions.						
Young, Samuel, (N. Y.)	Pension for revolutionary services.	22	2	Petition	53	Rev. Claims.						
Young, Samuel, (N. Y.)	Pension for revolutionary services.	23	1	Petition	89	Rev. Claims.						
Young, Samuel, (N. C.)	Additional compensation for transportation of the mail.	20	1	Petition	457	P. Of. & P. Roads	April 28, 1828	Adverse	......	Laid on table.		
Young, Samuel, (Maine)	Invalid pension	24	1	Petition	98	Invalid Pensions	June 22, 1836	Adverse	......	Laid on table.		
Young, Samuel, assignee of.	Arrears of pay for revolutionary services.	3	1	Petition and rep't Sec. of War.	31, 93	Select	April 22, 1794	Adverse	......	Laid on table.		
Young, Samuel C	Confirmation of title to land	11	2	Petition	112	Public Lands	Mar. 17, 1810	Adverse	......	Referred to Committee Whole House.		
Young, Samuel C	Confirmation of title to land	11	3	Petition	457	Public Lands.						
Young, Sarah	Pension	22	1	Petition	163	Rev. Pensions.						
Young, Stephen	Pension for revolutionary services.	21	2	Resolution	165	Military Pensions.						
Young, William, and other.	Increase of compensation as inspector of customs.	4	2	Petition	678	Com. and Manuf.						
Young, William	(See Thomas Farrer and William Young.)	13	3	....	497							
Young, William	Increase of pension	14	2	Petition	327	Pens. & Rev. Cl'ms.						
Young, William	(See heirs of Joseph Cross)	22	1	....	435							
Young, William, (Ky.)	Compensation for services and property lost in revolutionary war.	18	2	Petition	41	Pens. & Rev. Cl'ms.	Dec. 20, 1824	Adverse	......	Laid on table.		
Young, William, (Ky.)	Compensation for services and property lost in revolutionary war.	19	1	Petition	46	Rev. Claims.						
Young, William, (Ky.)	Compensation for services and property lost in revolutionary war.	19	2	Petition	32	Rev. Claims	20	Adverse	......	Laid on table.		
Young, William, (Ky.)	Pension for revolutionary pension.	20	2	Resolution	187	Military Pensions	....	....	......	Discharged; laid on table.		
Young, William, heir of.	Pension	27	3	Petition	260	Rev. Pensions	....	....	......	Discharged; leave to withdraw.		
Young, William, heirs of.	Reimbursement of expenses incurred on public account.	22	1	Petition	227	Indian Affairs	389	Favorable	481	Referred to Committee Whole House.		
Young, William, heirs of.	Reimbursement of expenses incurred on public account.	23	1	Petition	114	Indian Affairs	Jan. 16, 1834	Adverse	......	Laid on table.		
Young, William, heirs of.	Reimbursement of expenses incurred on public account.	24	1	Petition	426	Indian Affairs	....	....	......	Discharged; laid on table.		
Young, William, heirs of.	Reimbursement of expenses incurred on public account.	25	2	Petition	542	Claims	709	Adverse	......	Laid on table.		

List of private claims presented to the House of Representatives of the United States from the 1st to the 31st Congress, inclusive—Continued.

Names of claimants.	Nature or object of the claim.	Congress.	Session.	How brought before the House of Reps.	Page of journal.	To what committee of the House referred.	No. or date of the report.	Nature of the report.	No. of the bill.	How disposed of by the House of Reps.	How disposed of by the Senate.	Date of the act of Congress, and remarks.
Young, William, (Pa.)	(See Jones & Clark, executor of,)	26	1	....	182							
Young, Uri, and others	Bounty land	31	1	Petition	893	Rev. Pensions	322	Adverse	.....	Laid on table.		
Younger, Joshua	Pension for revolutionary services.	14	2	Petition	141	Pens. & Rev. Cl'ms.						
Younglove, Isaiah, brother of.	Compensation for revolutionary services.	27	3	Petition	132	Rev. Claims	258	Adverse	.....	Laid on table.		
Younglove, John	Invalid pension	1	2	House bill	271	....	....	....	88	Passed	Passed	App'd Aug. 11, 1790
Younglove, Samuel	(See brother of Isaiah Younglove.)	27	3	....	132							
Zachari, Stephen	Remission of tonnage duty on an unregistered vessel.	2	1	Petition	453	Select	Nov. 18, 1791	Favorable	.....	Laid on table.		
Zacharie, Stephen, & others	Drawback on exported wine	3	1	Petition	138	....	....	....	.....	Laid on table.		
Zacharia, James W., & Co.	Compensation for goods destroyed at New Orleans.	25	2	Documents	514	Ways and Means.						
Zacharie, Stephen, heirs of	Indemnity for French spoliations prior to 1800.	30	1	Petition	117	Foreign Affairs	Jan. 4, 1848	General bill	21	Referred to Committee Whole House.		
Zachary, James W.	Release from a judgment in favor of United States.	22	1	Senate bill	205	Judiciary	Jan. 24, 1832	With't amend.	S. 51	Passed	Passed	App'd July 13, 1832
Zane, Ebenezer	Permission to locate certain land	4	1	Senate bill	526	Select	May 7, 1796	With't amend	S. 42	Passed with amendm't.	Passed	App'd May 17, 1796
Zane, Isaac	Confirmation of title to land purchased of Wyandott Indians.	6	1	Memorial	581	Select	Feb. 21, 1800	Favorable	213	Referred to Committee Whole House.		
Zane, Isaac	Confirmation of title to land purchased of Wyandott Indians.	7	1	Memorial	34	Select	Jan. 22, 1802	Favorable	14	Recommitted.		
				Amended bill	135	Whole House	Mar. 27, 1802	With't amend.	35	Passed	Passed	App'd April 2, 1802
Zantzinger, Rich'd A., widow of.	Pension for revolutionary services.	28	2	Senate bill	249	Military Affairs	Feb. 25, 1845	With't amend.	S. 59	Laid on table.		
Zantzinger, William P.	Indemnity for depreciat'n on Treasury notes.	20	2	Petition	230	Naval Affairs	Feb. 17, 1829	Favorable	448	Referred to Committee Whole House.		
Zantzinger, William P.	Indemnity for depreciat'n on Treasury notes.	22	2	Petition	109	Claims	78	Favorable	720	Passed	Passed	App'd Feb. 19, 1833
Zantzinger, William P.	Certain allowances in settlement of accounts, and indemnity for certain losses.	22	2	Petition	152	Naval Affairs	46	Favorable	690	Referred to Committee Whole House.		
Zantzinger, William P.	Certain allowances in settlement of accounts, and indemnity for certain losses.	23	1	Petition	190	Naval Affairs	189	Favorable	209	Referred to Committee Whole House.		
Zantzinger, William P.	Certain allowances in settlement of accounts, and indemnity for certain losses.	23	2	House bill	82	Whole House	Dec. 15, 1834	With't amend.	209	Passed	Passed	App'd Jan. 27, 1835
Zantzinger, William P.	Arrears of pay as purser United States navy.	23	2	Petition	436	Naval Affairs.						
Zantzinger, William P.	Arrears of pay as purser United States navy.	21	1	Petition	99	Naval Affairs	781	Adverse	.....	Laid on table.		

List of private claims presented to the House of Representatives of the United States from the 1st to the 31st Congress, inclusive—Continued.

Names of claimants.	Nature or object of the claim.	Congress.	Session.	How brought before the House of Reps.	Page of journal.	To what committee of the House referred.	No. or date of the report.	Nature of the report.	No. of the bill.	How disposed of by the House of Reps.	How disposed of by the Senate.	Date of the act of Congress, and remarks.
Zantzinger, William P.	Arrears of pay as purser United St tes navy.	27	2	Petition	247	Claims	1037	Adverse		Laid on table.		
Zantzinger, William P.	Credit for pursers stores thrown overboard.	28	1	Petition	440	Claims	313	Favorable	R. 17	Passed	Passed	Appd June 15, 1844
Zantzinger, William P.	Further indemnity for stores thrown overboard.	28	2	Memorial	82	Claims	4	Favorable	453	Referred to Committee Whole House.		
Zantzinger, William P.	Further indemnity for stores thrown overboard.	29	1	Memorial	303	Claims	435	Favorable	303	Referred to Committee Whole House.		
Zantzinger, William P.	Further indemnity for stores thrown overboard.	30	1	Memorial	116	Claims	250	Favorable	243	Referred to Committee Whole House.		
Zantzinger, William P.	Further indemnity for stores thrown overboard.	31	1	Petition	501	Naval Affairs.						
Zantzinger, Capt. J. P.	Pay and rations as flag captain of Brazil station.	30	1	Petition	414	Naval Affairs.						
Zapp, John	Compensation for revolutionary services.	2	2	Petition	540					Laid on table.		
Zaurdi, Joseph E.	(See agent for the estate of Anthony Pachece.)	26	1		337							
Zeabold, John, mother of	Allowance under act of April 20, 1816.	18	1	Petition	175	Naval Affairs	Mar. 29, 1824	Favorable	177	Passed	Passed	App'd April 22, 1824
Zeiber, Philip	(See executors of George Shulz.)	2	1		459							
Zeigler, David, and others.	Right of pre-emption to a mill site in behalf of John Vanhorn.	8	1	Petition	460	Select	Jan. 20, 1804	Adverse		Referred to Committee Whole House.		
Zeilman, Anthony	Bounty land for services in war of 1812.	25	2	Petition	577	Military Affairs				Discharged.		
Zevely, Hezekiah	Pension for naval services	26	1	Memorial	713	Naval Affairs.						
Zimmerman, George	(See administrator of John Young)	18	2		228							
Zimmerman, Jacob	Pension for revolutionary services.	17	1	Petition	220	Pens. & Rev. Cl'ms.	Mar. 8, 1822	Favorable		Referred to Committee Whole House on bill No 91.		
Zimmerman, Jacob	Pension for revolutionary services.	17	2	Petition	31	Pens. & Rev. Cl'ms.				Leave to withdraw.		
Zimmerman, Jacob	Pension for revolutionory services	18	1	Petition	47					Referred to Committee Whole House on bill No. 35.		
Zimmerman, Jocob	Pension for revolutionary services.	18	2	Petition	30	Pens. & Rev. Cl'ms.						
Zimmerman, Jacob	Pension for revolutionary services.	19	1	Petition	53	Military Pensions	May 5, 1826	Favorable		Referred to Committee Whole House.		
Zimmerman, Jacob	Pension for revolutionary services.	19	2	Petition	49	Military Pensions.						
Zimmerman, Jacob	Pension for revolutionary services.	20	1	Petition	124	Military Pensions	April 29, 1828	By bill	283	Passed.		
Zimmerman, Jacob	Pension for revolutionary services.	20	2	House bill	55	Whole House	Jan. 15, 1829	With amends.	311	Passed	Laid on table.	
Zimmerman, Jacob	Pension for revolutionary services.	21	1	Petition	49	Military Pensions	Jan. 5, 1836	By bill	72	Passed	Passed	Bill became a law omitting petitioners name.
Zimmerman, Jacob	Pension for military services and disabilities.	30	2	Petition	359	Invalid Pensions	Feb. 13, 1849	Favorable	772	Passed.		
Zimmerman, Jacob	Pension for military services and disabilities.	31	1	Petition	391	Invalid Pensions	92	Favorable	114	Passed	Passed, with amendment.	App'd July 29, 1850
Zimmerman, John Henry	Arrears of pay for military services and compensation for horse lost in public service.	5	2	Petition	210	Claims	Mar. 9, 1798	Adverse		Laid on table.		
Zimmerman, John, widow of.	Pension	24	2	Petition	44	Rev. Pensions.				Discharged; laid on table.		
Zimmerman, Matthias	Pension	20	2	Petition	31	Military Pensions	Dec. 30, 1828	Adverse		Laid on table.		

List of private claims presented to the House of Representatives of the United States from the 1st to the 31st Congress, inclusive—Continued.

Names of claimants.	Nature or object of the claim.	Congress.	Session.	How brought before the House of Reps.	Page of journal.	To what committee of the House referred.	No. or date of the report.	Nature of the report.	No. of the bill.	How disposed of by the House of Reps.	How disposed of by the Senate.	Date of the act of Congress, and remarks.
Zink, J. H. or S. H.	Compensation for subsistence furnished volunteers.	30	1	Petition	345	Claims	352	Adverse	......	Laid on table.		
Zock, Francis	Compensation for a horse lost in the public service.	16	1	Petition	140	Claims	Jan. 22, 1820	Adverse	......	Laid on table.		
Zock, Francis	Compensation for a horse lost in the public service.	18	1	Petition	114	Claims	103	Adverse	......	Referred to Committee Whole House.		
Zock, Francis	Compensation for a horse lost in the public service.	19	1	Petition	73	Claims	Jan. 25, 1826	Adverse	......	Laid on table.		
Zock, Francis	Compensation for a horse lost in the public service.	19	2	Petition	35	Claims	Dec. 18, 1826	Adverse	......	Referred to Committee Whole House.		
Zock, Francis	Compensation for a horse lost in the public service.	20	1	Petition	58	Claims	Jan. 11, 1828	Adverse	......	Laid on table.		
Zock, Francis	Compensation for a horse lost in the public service.	20	2	Petition	32	Claims.						
Zock, Francis	Compensation for a horse lost in the public service.	21	1	Petition	83	Claims	Jan. 18, 1830	Adverse	......	Laid on table.		
Zock, Francis, representatives of.	Compensation for a horse lost in the public service.	29	1	Petition	178	Claims	336	Adverse	......	Laid on table.		
Zoll, Jacob	Pension for revolutionary services.	25	2	Memorial	579	Rev. Pensions.						
Zoll, Jacob	Pension for revolutionary services.	25	3	Documents	675	....	....	....	......	Laid on table.		
Zoll, William, and others.	For the benefit of the act of March 18, 1818.	15	2	Petition	190	Rev. Pensions	Jan. 21, 1819	Adverse	......	Rejected.		
Zook, Catharine	(See heirs of Andrew Snyder)	29	1	....	731							